T0400990

2019

Harris

New Jersey

Manufacturers Directory

Exclusive Provider of
Dun & Bradstreet Library Solutions

Published December 2019 next update December 2020

Publisher

Mergent Inc.
444 Madison Ave
New York, NY 10022

©Mergent Inc All Rights Reserved
2019 Mergent Business Press
ISSN 1080-2614
ISBN 978-1-64141-216-2

MERGENT
BUSINESS PRESS
by FTSE Russell

TABLE OF CONTENTS

SUMMARY OF CONTENTS

Number of Companies 12,124
Number of Decision Makers 26,030
Minimum Number of Employees 4

EXPLANATORY NOTES

How to Cross-Reference in This Directory

Sequential Entry Numbers. Each establishment in the Geographic Section is numbered sequentially (G-0000). The number assigned to each establishment is referred to as its "entry number." To make cross-referencing easier, each listing in the Geographic, SIC, Alphabetic and Product Sections includes the establishment's entry number. To facilitate locating an entry in the Geographic Section, the entry numbers for the first listing on the left page and the last listing on the right page are printed at the top of the page next to the city name.

Source Suggestions Welcome

Although all known sources were used to compile this directory, it is possible that companies were inadvertently omitted. Your assistance in calling attention to such omissions would be greatly appreciated. A special form on the facing page will help you in the reporting process.

Analysis

Every effort has been made to contact all firms to verify their information. The one exception to this rule is the annual sales figure, which is considered by many companies to be confidential information. Therefore, estimated sales have been calculated by multiplying the nationwide average sales per employee for the firm's major SIC/NAICS code by the firm's number of employees. Nationwide averages for sales per employee by SIC/NAICS codes are provided by the U.S. Department of Commerce and are updated annually. All sales—sales (est)—have been estimated by this method. The exceptions are parent companies (PA), division headquarters (DH) and headquarter locations (HQ) which may include an actual corporate sales figure—sales (corporate-wide) if available.

Types of Companies

Descriptive and statistical data are included for companies in the entire state. These comprise manufacturers, machine shops, fabricators, assemblers and printers. Also identified are corporate offices in the state.

Employment Data

The employment figure shown in the Geographic Section includes male and female employees and embraces all levels of the company: administrative, clerical, sales and maintenance. This figure is for the facility listed and does not include other plants or offices. It should be recognized that these figures represent an approximate year-round average. These employment figures are broken into codes A through G and used in the Product and SIC Sections to further help you in qualifying a company. Be sure to check the footnotes on the bottom of pages for the code breakdowns.

Standard Industrial Classification (SIC)

The Standard Industrial Classification (SIC) system used in this directory was developed by the federal government for use in classifying establishments by the type of activity they are engaged in. The SIC classifications used in this directory are from the 1987 edition published by the U.S. Government's Office of Management and Budget. The SIC system separates all activities into broad industrial divisions (e.g., manufacturing, mining, retail trade). It further subdivides each division. The range of manufacturing industry classes extends from two-digit codes (major industry group) to four-digit codes (product).

For example:

Industry Breakdown	Code	Industry, Product, etc.
*Major industry group	20	Food and kindred products
Industry group	203	Canned and frozen foods
*Industry	2033	Fruits and vegetables, etc.

*Classifications used in this directory

Only two-digit and four-digit codes are used in this directory.

Arrangement

1. The **Geographic Section** contains complete in-depth corporate data. This section is sorted by cities listed in alphabetical order and companies listed alphabetically within each city. A County/City Index for referencing cities within counties precedes this section.

IMPORTANT NOTICE: It is a violation of both federal and state law to transmit an unsolicited advertisement to a facsimile machine. Any user of this product that violates such laws may be subject to civil and criminal penalties, which may exceed $500 for each transmission of an unsolicited facsimile. Mergent Inc. provides fax numbers for lawful purposes only and expressly forbids the use of these numbers in any unlawful manner.

2. The **Standard Industrial Classification (SIC) Section** lists companies under approximately 500 four-digit SIC codes. An alphabetical and a numerical index precedes this section. A company can be listed under several codes. The codes are in numerical order with companies listed alphabetically under each code.

3. The **Alphabetic Section** lists all companies with their full physical or mailing addresses and telephone number.

4. The **Product Section** lists companies under unique Harris categories. An index preceding this section lists all product categories in alphabetical order. Companies can be listed under several categories.

USER'S GUIDE TO LISTINGS

GEOGRAPHIC SECTION

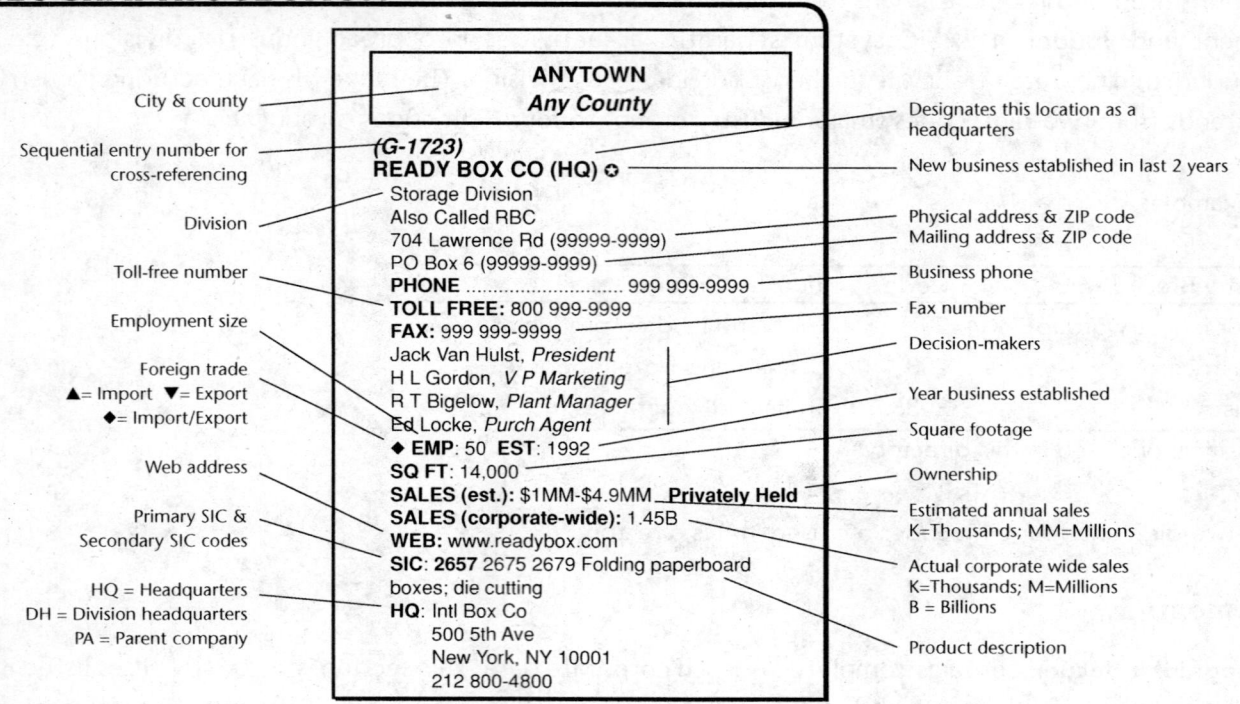

City & county

Sequential entry number for cross-referencing

Division

Toll-free number

Employment size

Foreign trade
▲= Import ▼= Export
◆= Import/Export

Web address

Primary SIC & Secondary SIC codes

HQ = Headquarters
DH = Division headquarters
PA = Parent company

ANYTOWN
Any County

(G-1723)
READY BOX CO (HQ) ✪
Storage Division
Also Called RBC
704 Lawrence Rd (99999-9999)
PO Box 6 (99999-9999)
PHONE 999 999-9999
TOLL FREE: 800 999-9999
FAX: 999 999-9999
Jack Van Hulst, *President*
H L Gordon, *V P Marketing*
R T Bigelow, *Plant Manager*
Ed Locke, *Purch Agent*
◆ **EMP:** 50 **EST:** 1992
SQ FT: 14,000
SALES (est.): $1MM-$4.9MM __Privately Held__
SALES (corporate-wide): 1.45B
WEB: www.readybox.com
SIC: 2657 2675 2679 Folding paperboard boxes; die cutting
HQ: Intl Box Co
500 5th Ave
New York, NY 10001
212 800-4800

Designates this location as a headquarters

New business established in last 2 years

Physical address & ZIP code
Mailing address & ZIP code

Business phone

Fax number

Decision-makers

Year business established

Square footage

Ownership

Estimated annual sales
K=Thousands; MM=Millions

Actual corporate wide sales
K=Thousands; M=Millions
B = Billions

Product description

SIC SECTION

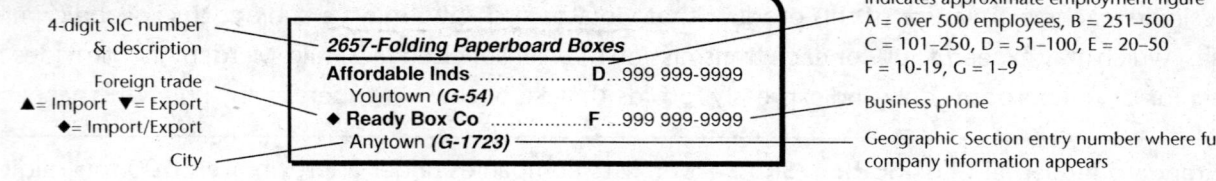

4-digit SIC number & description

Foreign trade
▲= Import ▼= Export
◆= Import/Export

City

2657-Folding Paperboard Boxes
Affordable Inds .... D...999 999-9999
Yourtown *(G-54)*
◆ **Ready Box Co** ....F....999 999-9999
Anytown *(G-1723)*

Indicates approximate employment figure
A = over 500 employees, B = 251–500
C = 101–250, D = 51–100, E = 20–50
F = 10-19, G = 1–9

Business phone

Geographic Section entry number where full company information appears

ALPHABETIC SECTION

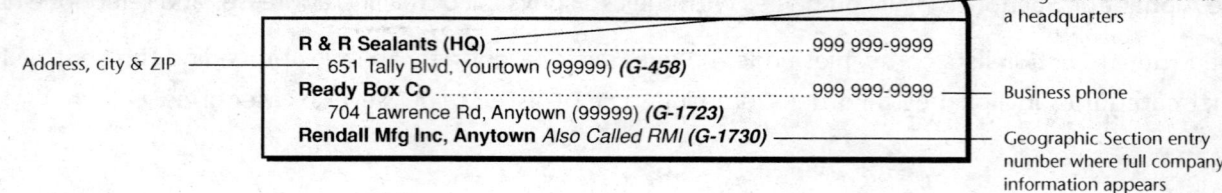

Address, city & ZIP

R & R Sealants (HQ) 999 999-9999
651 Tally Blvd, Yourtown (99999) *(G-458)*
Ready Box Co 999 999-9999
704 Lawrence Rd, Anytown (99999) *(G-1723)*
Rendall Mfg Inc, Anytown *Also Called RMI (G-1730)*

Designates this location as a headquarters

Business phone

Geographic Section entry number where full company information appears

PRODUCT SECTION

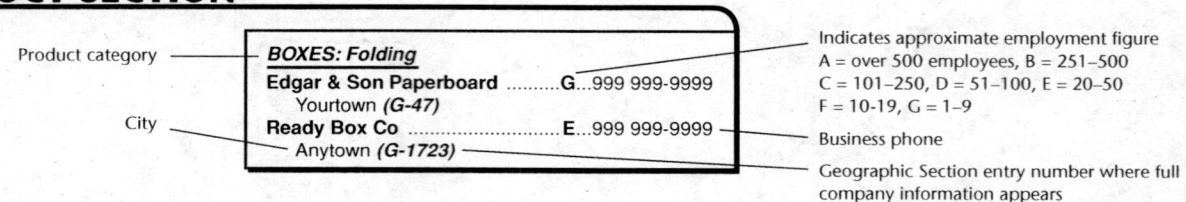

Product category

City

BOXES: Folding
Edgar & Son Paperboard ....G...999 999-9999
Yourtown *(G-47)*
Ready Box Co ....E...999 999-9999
Anytown *(G-1723)*

Indicates approximate employment figure
A = over 500 employees, B = 251–500
C = 101–250, D = 51–100, E = 20–50
F = 10-19, G = 1–9

Business phone

Geographic Section entry number where full company information appears

GEOGRAPHIC SECTION
Companies sorted by city in alphabetical order
In-depth company data listed

STANDARD INDUSTRIAL CLASSIFICATIONS
Alphabetical index of classifcation descriptions
Numerical index of classifcation descriptions
Companies sorted by SIC product groupings

ALPHABETIC SECTION
Company listings in alphabetical order

PRODUCT INDEX
Product categories listed in alphabetical order

PRODUCT SECTION
Companies sorted by product and manufacturing service classifications

GEOGRAPHIC

SIC

ALPHABETIC

PRDT INDEX

PRODUCT

New Jersey
County Map

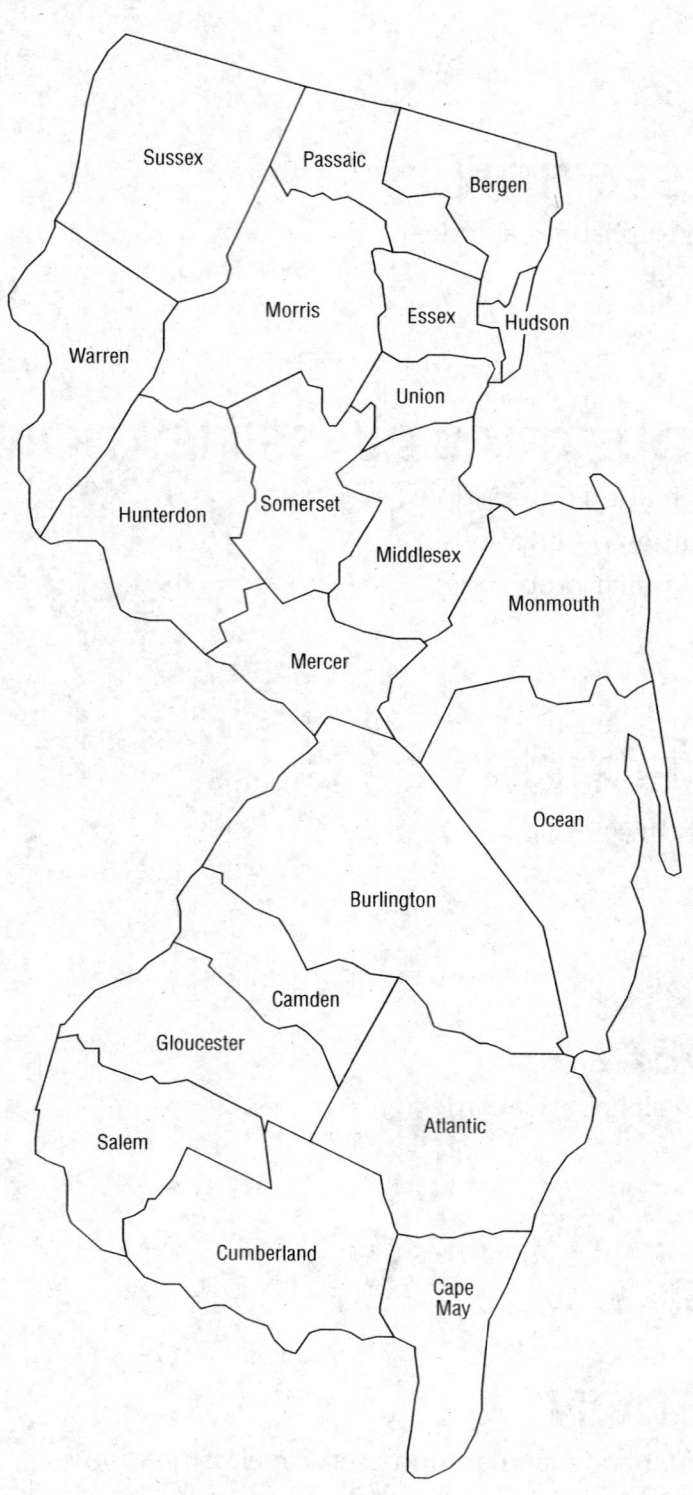

COUNTY/CITY CROSS-REFERENCE INDEX

Atlantic

City	ENTRY #
Absecon	(G-1)
Atlantic City	(G-88)
Brigantine	(G-911)
Buena	(G-939)
Cologne	(G-1773)
Dorothy	(G-2071)
Egg Harbor City	(G-2651)
Egg Harbor Township (G-2673)	
Egg Harbor Twp	(G-2703)
Elwood	(G-2860)
Galloway	(G-3719)
Hammonton	(G-4124)
Landisville	(G-5205)
Linwood	(G-5448)
Margate City	(G-5890)
Mays Landing	(G-5992)
Northfield	(G-7509)
Pleasantville	(G-8805)
Pomona	(G-8849)
Richland	(G-9249)
Somers Point	(G-9936)
Ventnor City	(G-11152)

Bergen

City	ENTRY #
Allendale	(G-5)
Bergenfield	(G-369)
Bogota	(G-533)
Carlstadt	(G-1117)
Cliffside Park	(G-1536)
Closter	(G-1751)
Cresskill	(G-1941)
Demarest	(G-2024)
Dumont	(G-2111)
East Rutherford	(G-2268)
Edgewater	(G-2432)
Elmwood Park	(G-2807)
Emerson	(G-2861)
Englewood	(G-2871)
Englewood Cliffs	(G-2956)
Fair Lawn	(G-3080)
Fairview	(G-3356)
Fort Lee	(G-3544)
Franklin Lakes	(G-3611)
Garfield	(G-3723)
Glen Rock	(G-3826)
Hackensack	(G-3874)
Harrington Park	(G-4161)
Hasbrouck Heights	(G-4181)
Hillsdale	(G-4364)
Ho Ho Kus	(G-4439)
Leonia	(G-5287)
Little Ferry	(G-5474)
Lodi	(G-5550)
Lyndhurst	(G-5639)
Mahwah	(G-5710)
Maywood	(G-6001)
Midland Park	(G-6168)
Montvale	(G-6394)
Moonachie	(G-6450)
New Milford	(G-6989)
North Arlington	(G-7366)
Northvale	(G-7513)
Norwood	(G-7557)
Oakland	(G-7614)
Old Tappan	(G-7731)
Oradell	(G-7741)
Palisades Park	(G-7767)
Paramus	(G-7787)
Park Ridge	(G-7846)
Ramsey	(G-9133)
Ridgefield	(G-9250)
Ridgefield Park	(G-9298)
Ridgewood	(G-9321)
River Edge	(G-9359)
River Vale	(G-9365)
Rochelle Park	(G-9420)
Rockleigh	(G-9515)
Rutherford	(G-9613)
Saddle Brook	(G-9636)
Saddle River	(G-9690)
South Hackensack	(G-10145)
Teaneck	(G-10621)
Tenafly	(G-10658)
Teterboro	(G-10670)
Twp Washinton	(G-11017)
Upper Saddle River	(G-11134)
Waldwick	(G-11297)
Wallington	(G-11380)
Westwood	(G-11824)
Wood Ridge	(G-12000)
Woodcliff Lake	(G-12045)
Wyckoff	(G-12101)

Burlington

City	ENTRY #
Beverly	(G-445)
Birmingham	(G-455)
Bordentown	(G-573)
Burlington	(G-945)
Burlington Township	(G-995)
Chesterfield	(G-1436)
Cinnaminson	(G-1439)
Columbus	(G-1798)
Cookstown	(G-1803)
Crosswicks	(G-1949)
Delanco	(G-2002)
Delran	(G-2008)
Eastampton	(G-2371)
Florence	(G-3473)
Hainesport	(G-4067)
Jobstown	(G-4835)
Lumberton	(G-5621)
Maple Shade	(G-5858)
Marlton	(G-5919)
Medford	(G-6019)
Medford Lakes	(G-6037)
Moorestown	(G-6500)
Mount Holly	(G-6723)
Mount Laurel	(G-6736)
New Gretna	(G-6988)
Palmyra	(G-7781)
Pemberton	(G-8357)
Rancocas	(G-9159)
Riverside	(G-9389)
Riverton	(G-9405)
Roebling	(G-9526)
Shamong	(G-9855)
Southampton	(G-10359)
Tabernacle	(G-10618)
Vincentown	(G-11182)
Westampton	(G-11783)
Willingboro	(G-11988)
Wrightstown	(G-12099)

Camden

City	ENTRY #
Atco	(G-86)
Audubon	(G-111)
Barrington	(G-166)
Bellmawr	(G-327)
Berlin	(G-414)
Blackwood	(G-458)
Brooklawn	(G-913)
Camden	(G-1038)
Cherry Hill	(G-1332)
Chesilhurst	(G-1428)
Clementon	(G-1531)
Collingswood	(G-1766)
Delair	(G-1999)
Erial	(G-3011)
Gibbsboro	(G-3794)
Glendora	(G-3837)
Gloucester City	(G-3840)
Haddon Heights	(G-4043)
Haddon Township	(G-4051)
Haddonfield	(G-4053)
Laurel Springs	(G-5207)
Lindenwold	(G-5443)
Magnolia	(G-5707)
Mount Ephraim	(G-6720)
Oaklyn	(G-7650)
Pennsauken	(G-8380)
Pine Hill	(G-8621)
Runnemede	(G-9604)
Sicklerville	(G-9906)
Somerdale	(G-9929)
Stratford	(G-10505)
Turnersville	(G-11016)
Voorhees	(G-11279)
Waterford Works	(G-11462)
West Berlin	(G-11577)

Cape May

City	ENTRY #
Avalon	(G-116)
Cape May	(G-1091)
Cape May Court House (G-1106)	
Dennisville	(G-2027)
Marmora	(G-5958)
Ocean City	(G-7688)
Ocean View	(G-7701)
Rio Grande	(G-9355)
Sea Isle City	(G-9748)
Stone Harbor	(G-10503)
Tuckahoe	(G-11012)
Villas	(G-11178)
West Cape May	(G-11683)
Wildwood	(G-11941)
Wildwood Crest	(G-11948)
Woodbine	(G-12008)

Cumberland

City	ENTRY #
Bridgeton	(G-749)
Cedarville	(G-1317)
Dividing Creek	(G-2069)
Dorchester	(G-2070)
Leesburg	(G-5286)
Mauricetown	(G-5991)
Millville	(G-6221)
Newport	(G-7333)
Port Elizabeth	(G-8877)
Port Norris	(G-8885)
Rosenhayn	(G-9594)
Vineland	(G-11183)

Essex

City	ENTRY #
Belleville	(G-288)
Bloomfield	(G-488)
Caldwell	(G-1020)
Cedar Grove	(G-1266)
East Orange	(G-2251)
Essex Fells	(G-3012)
Fairfield	(G-3132)
Glen Ridge	(G-3825)
Irvington	(G-4553)
Livingston	(G-5501)
Maplewood	(G-5873)
Millburn	(G-6195)
Montclair	(G-6356)
Newark	(G-7026)
Nutley	(G-7578)
Orange	(G-7749)
Roseland	(G-9530)
Short Hills	(G-9863)
South Orange	(G-10192)
Verona	(G-11164)
West Caldwell	(G-11635)
West Orange	(G-11757)

Gloucester

City	ENTRY #
Bridgeport	(G-734)
Clarksboro	(G-1518)
Clayton	(G-1523)
Deptford	(G-2063)
Franklinville	(G-3636)
Gibbstown	(G-3798)
Glassboro	(G-3806)
Grenloch	(G-3869)
Logan Township	(G-5584)
Malaga	(G-5788)
Mantua	(G-5851)
Mickleton	(G-6086)
Mount Royal	(G-6816)
Mullica Hill	(G-6854)
Newfield	(G-7320)
Paulsboro	(G-8327)
Pitman	(G-8743)
Sewell	(G-9833)
Swedesboro	(G-10570)
Thorofare	(G-10698)
Wenonah	(G-11572)
West Deptford	(G-11689)
Westville	(G-11809)
Williamstown	(G-11949)
Woodbury	(G-12025)
Woodbury Heights	(G-12040)
Woolwich Township	(G-12097)

Hudson

City	ENTRY #
Bayonne	(G-201)
Guttenberg	(G-3870)
Harrison	(G-4163)
Hoboken	(G-4442)
Jersey City	(G-4678)
Kearny	(G-4839)
North Bergen	(G-7379)
Secaucus	(G-9750)
Union City	(G-11104)
Weehawken	(G-11567)
West New York	(G-11735)

Hunterdon

City	ENTRY #
Annandale	(G-53)
Asbury	(G-57)
Bloomsbury	(G-532)
Califon	(G-1031)
Clinton	(G-1745)
Flemington	(G-3425)
Frenchtown	(G-3708)
Glen Gardner	(G-3821)
Hampton	(G-4146)
High Bridge	(G-4280)
Lambertville	(G-5186)
Lebanon	(G-5249)
Milford	(G-6192)
Oldwick	(G-7738)
Pittstown	(G-8751)
Ringoes	(G-9334)
Rosemont	(G-9592)
Stockton	(G-10501)
Three Bridges	(G-10704)
Whitehouse	(G-11915)
Whitehouse Station	(G-11919)

Mercer

City	ENTRY #
East Windsor	(G-2332)
Ewing	(G-3013)
Hamilton	(G-4100)
Hightstown	(G-4293)
Hopewell	(G-4526)
Lawrence Township	(G-5214)
Lawrenceville	(G-5221)
Pennington	(G-8359)
Princeton	(G-8897)
Princeton Junction	(G-9047)
Robbinsville	(G-9406)
Titusville	(G-10735)
Trenton	(G-10885)
West Windsor	(G-11782)
Windsor	(G-11995)

Middlesex

City	ENTRY #
Avenel	(G-117)
Carteret	(G-1245)
Colonia	(G-1774)
Cranbury	(G-1806)
Dayton	(G-1950)
Dunellen	(G-2119)
East Brunswick	(G-2124)
East Windsor	(G-2365)
Edison	(G-2442)
Fords	(G-3529)
Green Brook	(G-3859)
Highland Park	(G-4286)
Hopelawn	(G-4525)
Iselin	(G-4590)
Jamesburg	(G-4671)
Keasbey	(G-4908)
Kendall Park	(G-4917)
Laurence Harbor	(G-5210)
Metuchen	(G-6045)
Middlesex	(G-6089)
Milltown	(G-6214)
Monmouth Junction	(G-6276)
Monroe	(G-6321)
Monroe Township	(G-6325)

	ENTRY #		ENTRY #		ENTRY #		ENTRY #		ENTRY #
New Brunswick	(G-6908)	Oakhurst	(G-7607)	Randolph	(G-9169)	Ringwood	(G-9343)	Hopatcong	(G-4517)
North Brunswick	(G-7447)	Ocean	(G-7651)	Riverdale	(G-9369)	Totowa	(G-10807)	Lafayette	(G-5024)
Old Bridge	(G-7710)	Ocean Grove	(G-7699)	Rockaway	(G-9433)	Wanaque	(G-11391)	Montague	(G-6354)
Parlin	(G-7861)	Oceanport	(G-7705)	Roxbury Township	(G-9599)	Wayne	(G-11463)	Newton	(G-7335)
Perth Amboy	(G-8509)	Perrineville	(G-8507)	Stirling	(G-10489)	West Milford	(G-11724)	Ogdensburg	(G-7708)
Piscataway	(G-8623)	Port Monmouth	(G-8879)	Succasunna	(G-10508)	Woodland Park	(G-12068)	Sandyston	(G-9699)
Plainsboro	(G-8780)	Red Bank	(G-9219)	Towaco	(G-10864)			Sparta	(G-10375)
Port Reading	(G-8890)	Roosevelt	(G-9527)	Wharton	(G-11850)	**Salem**		Stanhope	(G-10476)
Sayreville	(G-9700)	Rumson	(G-9601)	Whippany	(G-11875)	Carneys Point	(G-1241)	Stockholm	(G-10500)
Sewaren	(G-9831)	Sea Girt	(G-9744)			Deepwater	(G-1998)	Sussex	(G-10556)
South Amboy	(G-10129)	Shrewsbury	(G-9880)	**Ocean**		Elmer	(G-2792)	Tranquility	(G-10884)
South Plainfield	(G-10204)	Spring Lake	(G-10420)	Barnegat	(G-154)	Monroeville	(G-6351)	Vernon	(G-11156)
South River	(G-10348)	Tennent	(G-10668)	Barnegat Light	(G-164)	Norma	(G-7365)		
Spotswood	(G-10414)	Tinton Falls	(G-10705)	Bay Head	(G-200)	Pedricktown	(G-8346)	**Union**	
Woodbridge	(G-12011)	Union Beach	(G-11101)	Bayville	(G-238)	Penns Grove	(G-8377)	Berkeley Heights	(G-387)
		Wall	(G-11314)	Beach Haven	(G-255)	Pennsville	(G-8500)	Clark	(G-1495)
Monmouth		Wall Township	(G-11315)	Beachwood	(G-257)	Pilesgrove	(G-8580)	Cranford	(G-1897)
Allenhurst	(G-21)	West Long Branch	(G-11719)	Brick	(G-710)	Pittsgrove	(G-8750)	Elizabeth	(G-2704)
Allentown	(G-23)			Forked River	(G-3535)	Salem	(G-9692)	Elizabethport	(G-2787)
Allenwood	(G-32)	**Morris**		Island Heights	(G-4637)	Woodstown	(G-12094)	Fanwood	(G-3372)
Asbury Park	(G-71)	Boonton	(G-536)	Jackson	(G-4638)			Garwood	(G-3779)
Atlantic Highlands	(G-104)	Brookside	(G-916)	Lakehurst	(G-5039)	**Somerset**		Hillside	(G-4372)
Belford	(G-281)	Budd Lake	(G-917)	Lakewood	(G-5041)	Basking Ridge	(G-175)	Kenilworth	(G-4920)
Belmar	(G-346)	Butler	(G-996)	Lavallette	(G-5212)	Bedminster	(G-258)	Linden	(G-5315)
Bradley Beach	(G-610)	Cedar Knolls	(G-1296)	Long Beach Township		Belle Mead	(G-286)	Mountainside	(G-6831)
Brielle	(G-906)	Chatham	(G-1318)	(G-5591)		Bernardsville	(G-435)	Murray Hill	(G-6860)
Clarksburg	(G-1520)	Chester	(G-1429)	Ltl Egg Hbr	(G-5613)	Bound Brook	(G-600)	New Providence	(G-6993)
Cliffwood	(G-1546)	Denville	(G-2028)	Manahawkin	(G-5790)	Branchburg	(G-611)	North Plainfield	(G-7505)
Colts Neck	(G-1776)	Dover	(G-2073)	Manchester	(G-5845)	Bridgewater	(G-781)	Plainfield	(G-8756)
Cream Ridge	(G-1931)	East Hanover	(G-2192)	Mantoloking	(G-5850)	Far Hills	(G-3374)	Rahway	(G-9075)
Creamridge	(G-1940)	Flanders	(G-3398)	New Egypt	(G-6983)	Franklin Park	(G-3633)	Roselle	(G-9546)
Deal	(G-1997)	Florham Park	(G-3480)	Pine Beach	(G-8582)	Gladstone	(G-3804)	Roselle Park	(G-9577)
Eatontown	(G-2373)	Gillette	(G-3801)	Point Pleasant Beach		Hillsborough	(G-4299)	Scotch Plains	(G-9728)
Englishtown	(G-2999)	Green Village	(G-3868)	(G-8823)		Kingston	(G-5007)	Springfield	(G-10425)
Fair Haven	(G-3078)	Kenvil	(G-4992)	Point Pleasant Boro	(G-8835)	Liberty Corner	(G-5295)	Summit	(G-10520)
Farmingdale	(G-3376)	Kinnelon	(G-5014)	Ship Bottom	(G-9862)	Manville	(G-5854)	Union	(G-11018)
Freehold	(G-3642)	Lake Hiawatha	(G-5034)	Surf City	(G-10554)	Martinsville	(G-5961)	Vauxhall	(G-11151)
Hazlet	(G-4253)	Lake Hopatcong	(G-5035)	Toms River	(G-10737)	Neshanic Station	(G-6904)	Westfield	(G-11793)
Highlands	(G-4291)	Landing	(G-5199)	Waretown	(G-11392)	Peapack	(G-8342)		
Holmdel	(G-4491)	Ledgewood	(G-5276)	West Creek	(G-11684)	Pluckemin	(G-8822)	**Warren**	
Howell	(G-4530)	Lincoln Park	(G-5297)	Whiting	(G-11937)	Raritan	(G-9208)	Alpha	(G-35)
Keansburg	(G-4838)	Long Valley	(G-5607)			Rocky Hill	(G-9525)	Belvidere	(G-357)
Keyport	(G-4997)	Madison	(G-5685)	**Passaic**		Skillman	(G-9918)	Blairstown	(G-484)
Lincroft	(G-5310)	Mendham	(G-6038)	Bloomingdale	(G-525)	Somerset	(G-9941)	Buttzville	(G-1016)
Little Silver	(G-5499)	Millington	(G-6207)	Clifton	(G-1550)	Somerville	(G-10099)	Columbia	(G-1791)
Long Branch	(G-5593)	Mine Hill	(G-6272)	Haledon	(G-4081)	South Bound Brook	(G-10143)	Great Meadows	(G-3853)
Manalapan	(G-5799)	Montville	(G-6437)	Haskell	(G-4194)	Warren	(G-11395)	Hackettstown	(G-3993)
Manasquan	(G-5827)	Morris Plains	(G-6601)	Hawthorne	(G-4204)	Watchung	(G-11455)	Hardwick	(G-4160)
Marlboro	(G-5892)	Morristown	(G-6630)	Hewitt	(G-4273)			Hope	(G-4524)
Matawan	(G-5966)	Mount Arlington	(G-6710)	Little Falls	(G-5451)	**Sussex**		Johnsonburg	(G-4837)
Middletown	(G-6159)	Mountain Lakes	(G-6819)	Newfoundland	(G-7329)	Andover	(G-44)	Oxford	(G-7766)
Millstone Township	(G-6209)	Netcong	(G-6907)	North Haledon	(G-7494)	Augusta	(G-115)	Phillipsburg	(G-8540)
Millstone Twp	(G-6213)	Parsippany	(G-7870)	Oak Ridge	(G-7599)	Branchville	(G-701)	Port Murray	(G-8880)
Morganville	(G-6579)	Pequannock	(G-8503)	Passaic	(G-8047)	Byram Township	(G-1017)	Stewartsville	(G-10482)
Neptune	(G-6861)	Pine Brook	(G-8583)	Paterson	(G-8118)	Franklin	(G-3597)	Washington	(G-11437)
North Middletown	(G-7502)	Pompton Plains	(G-8856)	Pompton Lakes	(G-8850)	Hamburg	(G-4087)		
				Prospect Park	(G-9072)	Highland Lakes	(G-4285)		

GEOGRAPHIC SECTION

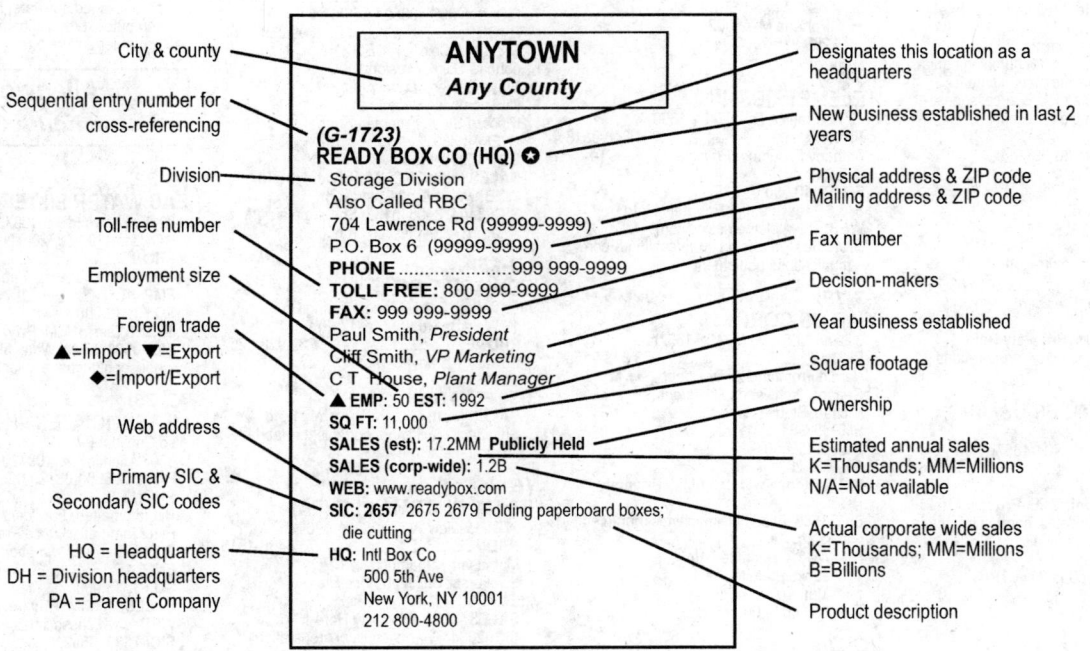

City & county

Sequential entry number for cross-referencing

Division

Toll-free number

Employment size

Foreign trade
▲=Import ▼=Export
◆=Import/Export

Web address

Primary SIC & Secondary SIC codes

HQ = Headquarters
DH = Division headquarters
PA = Parent Company

ANYTOWN
Any County

(G-1723)
READY BOX CO (HQ) ✪
Storage Division
Also Called RBC
704 Lawrence Rd (99999-9999)
P.O. Box 6 (99999-9999)
PHONE 999 999-9999
TOLL FREE: 800 999-9999
FAX: 999 999-9999
Paul Smith, *President*
Cliff Smith, *VP Marketing*
C T House, *Plant Manager*
▲ **EMP:** 50 **EST:** 1992
SQ FT: 11,000
SALES (est): 17.2MM **Publicly Held**
SALES (corp-wide): 1.2B
WEB: www.readybox.com
SIC: 2657 2675 2679 Folding paperboard boxes; die cutting
HQ: Intl Box Co
500 5th Ave
New York, NY 10001
212 800-4800

Designates this location as a headquarters

New business established in last 2 years

Physical address & ZIP code
Mailing address & ZIP code

Fax number

Decision-makers

Year business established

Square footage

Ownership

Estimated annual sales
K=Thousands; MM=Millions
N/A=Not available

Actual corporate wide sales
K=Thousands; MM=Millions
B=Billions

Product description

See footnotes for symbols and codes identification.
- This section is in alphabetical order by city.
- Companies are sorted alphabetically under their respective cities.
- To locate cities within a county refer to the County/City Cross Reference Index.

IMPORTANT NOTICE: It is a violation of both federal and state law to transmit an unsolicited advertisement to a facsimile machine. Any user of this product that violates such laws may be subject to civil and criminal penalties which may exceed $500 for each transmission of an unsolicited facsimile. Harris InfoSource provides fax numbers for lawful purposes only and expressly forbids the use of these numbers in any unlawful manner.

Absecon
Atlantic County

(G-1)
ABSECON ELECTRIC MOTOR WORKS
500 White Horse Pike (08201-2429)
PHONE 609 641-1523
Dennis Pruchnicki, *President*
Joseph Pruchnicki, *Corp Secy*
EMP: 4
SQ FT: 2,000
SALES (est): 330K **Privately Held**
WEB: www.femyers.com
SIC: 7694 5999 Electric motor repair; motors, electric

(G-2)
DIAMOND SCOOTERS INC
Also Called: Mobility123
645 S Mill Rd Ste 1 (08201-4802)
PHONE 609 646-0003
Denise M Penn, *President*
EMP: 7
SALES: 1.5MM **Privately Held**
SIC: 1541 1521 3534 3448 Renovation, remodeling & repairs: industrial buildings; general remodeling, single-family houses; elevators & moving stairways; ramps: prefabricated metal

(G-3)
MACO APPLIANCE PARTS & SUP CO
1101 N New Rd (08201-9303)
PHONE 609 272-8222
Rich Comunale, *Principal*

EMP: 8
SALES (est): 710K **Privately Held**
SIC: 5063 3585 Electrical supplies; heating & air conditioning combination units

(G-4)
SHOP-RITE SUPERMARKETS INC
Also Called: Shop Rite 633
616 White Horse Pike (08201-2302)
PHONE 609 646-2448
Ricky Wilkes, *Branch Mgr*
EMP: 149
SALES (corp-wide): 890MM **Privately Held**
SIC: 5411 5912 2051 Supermarkets, chain; drug stores & proprietary stores; bread, cake & related products
HQ: Shop Rite Supermarkets, Inc.
5000 Riverside Dr
Keasbey NJ 08832
908 527-3300

Allendale
Bergen County

(G-5)
ACUITIVE TECHNOLOGIES INC
50 Commerce Dr (07401-1623)
PHONE 973 617-7175
Alex Khowaylo, *CEO*
Jim Malayter, *Principal*
Mike McCarthy, *Principal*
Dave Washburn, *CFO*
EMP: 11
SQ FT: 8,800
SALES (est): 821.9K **Privately Held**
SIC: 3842 Surgical appliances & supplies

(G-6)
CATALENT CTS LLC
75 Commerce Dr (07401-1600)
PHONE 201 785-0275
Vincent Santamaria, *Branch Mgr*
EMP: 110 **Publicly Held**
SIC: 2834 Pharmaceutical preparations
HQ: Catalent Cts, Llc
10245 Hickman Mills Dr
Kansas City MO 64137

(G-7)
DATAPROBE INC (PA)
1 Pearl Ct B (07401-1658)
PHONE 201 934-9944
David Weiss, *President*
Sy Weiss, *Chairman*
James Kalymnios, *Vice Pres*
Douglas Osowiecky, *Vice Pres*
Geraldine Weiss, *Treasurer*
▲ **EMP:** 27
SQ FT: 20,000
SALES (est): 3MM **Privately Held**
WEB: www.dataprobe.com
SIC: 3661 Telephone & telegraph apparatus

(G-8)
EDGEWELL PERSONAL CARE LLC
75 Commerce Dr (07401-1600)
P.O. Box 701 (07401-0701)
PHONE 201 785-8000
Steve Randolph, *Engineer*
Adebimpe Bimp Ogunade, *Human Resources*
EMP: 147
SALES (corp-wide): 2.3B **Publicly Held**
WEB: www.playtexproductsinc.com
SIC: 2844 Toilet preparations

HQ: Edgewell Personal Care, Llc
1350 Timberlake Mano
Chesterfield MO 63017
314 594-1900

(G-9)
HEIGHTS JEWELERS LLC
11 Ceely Ct (07401-2101)
PHONE 201 825-2381
Marc Appelbaum,
EMP: 11
SQ FT: 2,000
SALES: 1.2MM **Privately Held**
SIC: 5094 3911 Jewelry; jewelry apparel

(G-10)
KINGCHEM LIFE SCIENCE LLC (PA)
5 Pearl Ct (07401-1656)
PHONE 201 825-9988
Fumin Wang, *President*
George Liu, *General Mgr*
Min Lu, *General Mgr*
Yongcan Wang, *General Mgr*
Zhongli Xu, *General Mgr*
EMP: 13
SALES (est): 7MM **Privately Held**
SIC: 2833 Medicinal chemicals

(G-11)
LEISTRITZ ADVANCED TECH CORP (HQ)
Also Called: Leistritz Pump
165 Chestnut St Ste 1 (07401-2230)
PHONE 201 934-8262
Jeffrey De Daul, *President*
Joseph Latronica, *Engineer*
Tim Lebo, *Engineer*
Chris Rogers, *Engineer*
Declan Candela, *Project Engr*

▲ **EMP:** 27
SQ FT: 24,000
SALES (est): 23.1MM
SALES (corp-wide): 358.4MM **Privately Held**
WEB: www.leistritz.com
SIC: 5084 3561 Pumps & pumping equipment; hydraulic systems equipment & supplies; machine tools & accessories; pumps & pumping equipment
PA: Leistritz Ag
　　Markgrafenstr. 36-39
　　Nurnberg　90459
　　911 430-60

(G-12)
MEDICON INC
17 Beechwood Rd (07401-1801)
PHONE..........................201 669-7456
Robert Marsanico, *President*
EMP: 4
SALES (est): 309K **Privately Held**
SIC: 2834 Pharmaceutical preparations

(G-13)
PRATT INDUSTRIES USA INC
Also Called: Pratt Displays
3 Pearl Ct Unit 3f (07401-1657)
PHONE..........................201 934-1900
EMP: 66
SALES (corp-wide): 2.5B **Privately Held**
SIC: 2653 Display items, corrugated: made from purchased materials
PA: Pratt Industries, Inc.
　　1800 Sarasot Bus Pkwy Ne C
　　Conyers GA 30013
　　770 918-5678

(G-14)
PROMOTION IN MOTION INC (PA)
Also Called: Promotion In Motion Companies
25 Commerce Dr (07401-1617)
P.O. Box 8 (07401-0008)
PHONE..........................201 962-8530
Michael Rosenberg, *President*
Kevin Walsh, *President*
Keith Von Zup, *Vice Pres*
Robert Purcell, *CFO*
◆ **EMP:** 55
SQ FT: 45,000
SALES (est): 146.5MM **Privately Held**
WEB: www.promotioninmotion.com
SIC: 2064 5441 5145 2066 Candy & other confectionery products; candy, nut & confectionery stores; confectionery; chocolate & cocoa products

(G-15)
SSAM SPORTS INC (PA)
Also Called: Putterwheel
234 Macintyre Ln (07401-1441)
PHONE..........................917 553-0596
Sang Kim, *President*
▲ **EMP:** 4 EST: 2011
SALES (est): 447.4K **Privately Held**
SIC: 7999 7372 7389 Sports instruction, schools & camps; application computer software;

(G-16)
SSAM SPORTS INC
Also Called: 4 D Motion
2 Myrtle Ave Unit 599 (07401-7040)
P.O. Box 599 (07401-0599)
PHONE..........................917 553-0596
Sang Kim, *President*
EMP: 5
SALES (corp-wide): 447.4K **Privately Held**
SIC: 7999 7372 Sports instruction, schools & camps; application computer software
PA: Ssam Sports, Inc.
　　234 Macintyre Ln
　　Allendale NJ 07401
　　917 553-0596

(G-17)
STRYKER CORPORATION
Stryker Spine
2 Pearl Ct (07401-1611)
PHONE..........................201 760-8000
Spencer Stiles, *Branch Mgr*
EMP: 60

SALES (corp-wide): 13.6B **Publicly Held**
SIC: 3841 Surgical & medical instruments
PA: Stryker Corporation
　　2825 Airview Blvd
　　Portage MI 49002
　　269 385-2600

(G-18)
TELEMETRICS INC
75 Commerce Dr (07401-1600)
PHONE..........................201 848-9818
Anthony E Cuomo, *Principal*
▲ **EMP:** 40
SQ FT: 10,000
SALES (est): 9MM **Privately Held**
WEB: www.telemetricsinc.com
SIC: 3663 Television broadcasting & communications equipment

(G-19)
WAB US CORP
3 Pearl Ct Ste E (07401-1657)
PHONE..........................973 873-9155
Harald Frommherz, *President*
Genard Kschwendt, *President*
Michael Stebler, *Vice Pres*
EMP: 9 EST: 2017
SQ FT: 22,000
SALES: 200K
SALES (corp-wide): 3.6MM **Privately Held**
SIC: 3569 Assembly machines, non-metalworking
HQ: Willy A. Bachofen Ag
　　Junkermattstrasse 11
　　Muttenz BL 4132
　　616 867-100

(G-20)
WORDMASTERS
213 E Allendale Ave (07401-2016)
PHONE..........................201 327-4201
Nancy McGrath, *Owner*
Lisa Kennedy, *Exec Dir*
EMP: 6
SALES: 400K **Privately Held**
WEB: www.wordmasterschallenge.com
SIC: 2731 Books: publishing only

Allenhurst
Monmouth County

(G-21)
CRAVINGS
Also Called: Cravings Gourmet Desserts
310 Main St (07711-1038)
PHONE..........................732 531-7122
Jan Walker, *Owner*
EMP: 10
SQ FT: 1,100
SALES: 500K **Privately Held**
SIC: 5812 2051 Eating places; bakery: wholesale or wholesale/retail combined

(G-22)
KOADINGS INC
Also Called: Polymite
540 N Edgemere Dr (07711-1348)
P.O. Box 481 (07711-0481)
PHONE..........................732 517-0784
Mark Midneck, *President*
EMP: 5 EST: 1996
SALES: 600K **Privately Held**
SIC: 2952 Roofing materials

Allentown
Monmouth County

(G-23)
AGNO PHARMA
5 Wingate Ct (08501-1936)
PHONE..........................609 223-0638
James Chen, *Owner*
Raymond Dagnino, *Director*
EMP: 4 EST: 2007
SALES (est): 293.7K **Privately Held**
SIC: 2834 Pharmaceutical preparations

(G-24)
ALLENTOWN INC (PA)
165 Route 526 (08501-2017)
P.O. Box 698 (08501-0698)
PHONE..........................609 259-7951
Michael A Coiro Sr, *CEO*
John M Coiro, *President*
Steve Benigni, *District Mgr*
Jill Thompson, *Vice Pres*
Richard Stout, *Foreman/Supr*
◆ **EMP:** 330
SQ FT: 220,000
SALES (est): 75.2MM **Privately Held**
WEB: www.allentowninc.com
SIC: 3444 3496 5162 Sheet metalwork; cages, wire; plastics products

(G-25)
EDWARD T BRADY
Also Called: Brady Manufacturing Co
12 Waldron Rd (08501-1718)
PHONE..........................732 928-0257
Edward T Brady, *Owner*
EMP: 7
SQ FT: 24,000
SALES (est): 500.4K **Privately Held**
SIC: 3448 Buildings, portable: prefabricated metal

(G-26)
ESJAY PHARMA LLC (PA)
27 Ridgeview Way (08501-1964)
PHONE..........................732 438-1816
Muthusamy Shanmugan, *CEO*
Sivakumar Chinniah, *Vice Pres*
EMP: 11
SALES: 3MM **Privately Held**
SIC: 2834 Pharmaceutical preparations

(G-27)
HEAVENLY HAVENS CREAMERY LLC
33 S Main St (08501-1615)
PHONE..........................609 259-6600
Joy Havens, *Mng Member*
EMP: 5
SALES (est): 87.3K **Privately Held**
SIC: 2656 2024 Frozen food & ice cream containers; dairy based frozen desserts

(G-28)
NOTIE CORP
177 Route 526 (08501-2017)
PHONE..........................609 259-3477
Dave E Weatherholtz, *Ch of Bd*
Elaine Weatherholtz, *Vice Pres*
Michael Weatherholtz, *Treasurer*
EMP: 5
SQ FT: 7,200
SALES (est): 400K **Privately Held**
SIC: 2448 Pallets, wood

(G-29)
PRECAST SYSTEMS INC
57 Sharon Station Rd (08501-1902)
PHONE..........................609 208-0569
Bruce Post, *President*
EMP: 25 EST: 1981
SQ FT: 2,000
SALES (est): 4.7MM **Privately Held**
SIC: 3272 Concrete products, precast

(G-30)
RIEPHOFF SAW MILL INC
763 Route 524 (08501-2005)
PHONE..........................609 259-7265
John S Falconio, *President*
Eva Riephoff, *Corp Secy*
EMP: 19
SQ FT: 8,000
SALES: 5MM **Privately Held**
SIC: 2421 2448 Lumber: rough, sawed or planed; wood pallets & skids

(G-31)
SCIMAR TECHNOLOGIES LLC
32 Cliffwood Dr (08501-2041)
PHONE..........................609 208-1796
Michael Conroy,
Donna Conroy,
EMP: 4

SALES (est): 144.5K **Privately Held**
SIC: 7371 7372 7389 Computer software systems analysis & design, custom; prepackaged software; business oriented computer software; home entertainment computer software;

Allenwood
Monmouth County

(G-32)
EAC WATER FILTERS INC
2215 Allenwood Rd (08720)
P.O. Box 119 (08720-0119)
PHONE..........................888 524-8088
Joseph Whelan, *President*
EMP: 10
SQ FT: 10,000
SALES (est): 1MM **Privately Held**
SIC: 3589 5722 Water filters & softeners, household type; appliance parts

(G-33)
I F ASSOCIATES INC
Also Called: I F A
3303 Atlantic Ave (08720-7014)
P.O. Box 680 (08720-0680)
PHONE..........................732 223-2900
Pat Iammatteo, *President*
Ester Iammatteo, *Vice Pres*
Brandy Borden, *Manager*
EMP: 15
SQ FT: 15,000
SALES: 4.1MM **Privately Held**
WEB: www.ifassociatesinc.com
SIC: 7389 3552 Design, commercial & industrial; ; fiber & yarn preparation machinery & equipment

(G-34)
SEALED UNIT PARTS CO INC
Also Called: Supco
2230 Landmark Pl (08720-7038)
P.O. Box 21 (08720-0021)
PHONE..........................732 223-1201
Anthony Mancuso, *Ch of Bd*
Chris Mancuso, *Chairman*
Joe Whelan, *Corp Secy*
Laurie Vasilantone, *Opers Staff*
Kim Nathaniel, *Purch Agent*
◆ **EMP:** 141
SALES (est): 33.6MM **Privately Held**
WEB: www.supco.com
SIC: 3585 3625 Parts for heating, cooling & refrigerating equipment; relays, for electronic use

Alpha
Warren County

(G-35)
ALPHA LEHIGH TOOL & MCH CO INC
41 Industrial Rd (08865-4080)
PHONE..........................908 454-6481
William L Green, *President*
Charles Spitale, *Prdtn Mgr*
Teri Green, *Human Res Dir*
Terry Suiter, *Officer*
EMP: 38 EST: 1956
SQ FT: 33,000
SALES (est): 7.2MM **Privately Held**
WEB: www.alphalehigh.com
SIC: 3599 Machine shop, jobbing & repair

(G-36)
AUTOMATIC TRANSFER INC
2 Industrial Rd (08865-4081)
PHONE..........................908 213-2830
Al Lacosta, *President*
▲ **EMP:** 4
SQ FT: 3,500
SALES (est): 290K **Privately Held**
SIC: 3861 Toners, prepared photographic (not made in chemical plants)

(G-37)
GLEN MAGNETICS INC
1165 3rd Ave (08865-4799)
PHONE..........................908 454-3717
John Di Sarro, *President*

Cabot Thomas, *Vice Pres*
Gwendolyn Di Sarro, *Treasurer*
EMP: 35
SQ FT: 53,000
SALES: 2.2MM **Privately Held**
WEB: www.glenmagnetics.com
SIC: 3612 5065 Power transformers, electric; electronic parts & equipment

(G-38)
HUNTERDON TRANSFORMER CO INC (PA)
75 Industrial Rd (08865-4080)
PHONE..............................908 454-2400
Mark Brock, *President*
Morris Bock, *President*
Donald Gordon, *Chairman*
Peter Droelle, *Treasurer*
Richard McCabe, *VP Sales*
▲ **EMP:** 75 **EST:** 1957
SQ FT: 42,000
SALES (est): 14.2MM **Privately Held**
WEB: www.hunterdontransformer.com
SIC: 3612 Power transformers, electric

(G-39)
LINDE NORTH AMERICA INC
Also Called: Linde Elec & Specialty Gasses
80 Industrial Rd (08865-4083)
PHONE..............................908 454-7455
Fred Hicks, *Safety Mgr*
Ron Robinson, *Safety Mgr*
John Ballard, *Manager*
EMP: 100
SALES (corp-wide): 1.4B **Privately Held**
SIC: 2813 Oxygen, compressed or liquefied
HQ: Messer North America, Inc.
 200 Somerset Corporate Bl
 Bridgewater NJ 08807
 908 464-8100

(G-40)
POWER POOL PLUS INC
7 Edge Rd (08865-9721)
PHONE..............................908 454-1124
Dudley Hulse, *President*
◆ **EMP:** 6
SALES (est): 2MM **Privately Held**
WEB: www.powerpoolplus.com
SIC: 4213 5063 7359 7629 Refrigerated products transport; generators; equipment rental & leasing; generator repair; electric motor & generator parts

(G-41)
SAFE MAN LLC
801 Vulcanite Ave (08865-4780)
PHONE..............................800 320-2589
Richard N Its, *President*
EMP: 6
SALES (est): 565.8K **Privately Held**
SIC: 3499 Fabricated metal products

(G-42)
SHERIDAN PRINTING COMPANY INC
Also Called: Sheridan Communications
1425 3rd Ave (08865-4605)
PHONE..............................908 454-0700
James Sheridan, *CEO*
Wayne L Pesaresi, *President*
Elizabeth F Pesaresi, *Treasurer*
Erinn Pesaresi, *VP Sales*
EMP: 40 **EST:** 1956
SQ FT: 40,000
SALES (est): 4.8MM **Privately Held**
WEB: www.sheridanprinting.com
SIC: 2741 Technical papers: publishing & printing

(G-43)
TORELCO INC
55 Industrial Rd (08865-4080)
PHONE..............................908 387-0814
Matt Peterson, *President*
EMP: 15 **EST:** 2007
SALES (est): 3.5MM **Privately Held**
SIC: 3677 Electronic coils, transformers & other inductors

Andover
Sussex County

(G-44)
BARRIER ENTERPRISES INC
175 Stanhope Sparta Rd (07821-4905)
PHONE..............................973 770-3983
Thomas Stiffen, *CEO*
EMP: 7
SQ FT: 4,000
SALES (est): 564K **Privately Held**
SIC: 3713 Truck bodies & parts

(G-45)
BERK GOLD STAMPING CORPORATION (PA)
196 Pequest Rd (07821-2020)
PHONE..............................973 786-6052
Ronald E Stagnari, *President*
EMP: 50
SQ FT: 60,000
SALES (est): 4.4MM **Privately Held**
WEB: www.berkgoldstamping.com
SIC: 3999 2789 Gold stamping, except books; bookbinding & related work

(G-46)
G R BOWLER INC
511 Maxim Dr (07821-2927)
PHONE..............................973 525-7172
Gary Bowler, *President*
EMP: 4
SALES (est): 282.3K **Privately Held**
SIC: 3829 Measuring & controlling devices

(G-47)
JA-BAR SILICONE CORP
252 Brighton Rd (07821-5032)
P.O. Box 1249 (07821-1249)
PHONE..............................973 786-5000
Gilbert Jacobs, *President*
Richard Latham, *General Mgr*
Myrtle G Jacobs, *Corp Secy*
Robert J Lisofski, *Exec VP*
Mark Derr, *Vice Pres*
EMP: 83 **EST:** 1965
SQ FT: 24,000
SALES (est): 13.6MM **Privately Held**
WEB: www.jabar.com
SIC: 3053 Gaskets, packing & sealing devices

(G-48)
KEURIG DR PEPPER INC
562 Ervey Rd (07821-5625)
PHONE..............................908 684-4400
EMP: 93 **Publicly Held**
SIC: 2086 Soft drinks: packaged in cans, bottles, etc.
PA: Keurig Dr Pepper Inc.
 53 South Ave
 Burlington MA 01803

(G-49)
MMTC INC
5 Stonypoint Rd (07821-5810)
PHONE..............................609 520-9699
Fred Sterzer, *President*
EMP: 6
SALES (est): 764K **Privately Held**
SIC: 3825 Microwave test equipment

(G-50)
NEW JERSEY FENCE & GUARDRAIL
Also Called: Crest Wood Fence
32 Main St (07821-4515)
PHONE..............................973 786-5400
James E Hofmann, *President*
EMP: 15
SQ FT: 1,000
SALES (est): 1.9MM **Privately Held**
SIC: 2411 Rails, fence: round or split

(G-51)
SUTHERLAND PACKAGING INC
254 Brighton Rd (07821-5032)
P.O. Box 1429 (07821-1429)
PHONE..............................973 786-5141
Tom Sutherland, *President*
Daniel Sutherland, *Vice Pres*
Elizabeth Sutherland, *Treasurer*

Louise Chattaway, *Personnel*
Paul Rachanow, *Accounts Mgr*
EMP: 60
SQ FT: 100,000
SALES (est): 16.9MM **Privately Held**
WEB: www.sudsbox.com
SIC: 2653 Boxes, corrugated: made from purchased materials

(G-52)
V E N INC
Also Called: N V E Pharmaceuticals
15 Whitehall Rd (07821-2115)
PHONE..............................973 786-7862
Robert Occhifinto, *President*
Mike Williams, *Plant Mgr*
Keith Woods, *Facilities Mgr*
Steve Taylor, *Traffic Mgr*
Jenna Gately, *Purchasing*
▲ **EMP:** 220 **EST:** 1982
SQ FT: 250,000
SALES (est): 51.1MM **Privately Held**
WEB: www.stacker2.com
SIC: 2023 2086 Dietary supplements, dairy & non-dairy based; carbonated soft drinks, bottled & canned

---

Annandale
Hunterdon County

(G-53)
BALLANTINE LABORATORIES INC
312 Old Allerton Rd (08801-3214)
PHONE..............................908 713-7742
G Dean McAdoo, *Ch of Bd*
Russell D McAdoo, *President*
Greg McAdoo, *Vice Pres*
Keitha McAdoo, *Admin Sec*
EMP: 7
SQ FT: 6,000
SALES (est): 2.8MM **Privately Held**
WEB: www.ballantinelabs.com
SIC: 3825 8734 3829 Test equipment for electronic & electrical circuits; measuring instruments & meters, electric; testing laboratories; measuring & controlling devices

(G-54)
INGERSOLL-RAND COMPANY
1467 Route 31 S (08801-3118)
P.O. Box 970 (08801-0970)
PHONE..............................908 238-7000
Joe Jones, *Branch Mgr*
Patti Tironi, *Director*
EMP: 150 **Privately Held**
WEB: www.ingersoll-rand.com
SIC: 5085 5072 3546 8742 Industrial supplies; hardware; power-driven handtools; marketing consulting services
HQ: Ingersoll-Rand Company
 800 Beaty St Ste B
 Davidson NC 28036
 704 655-4000

(G-55)
SUROMA LTD LIABILITY COMPANY
Also Called: Badge Company of New Jersey
223 Hamden Rd (08801-3366)
PHONE..............................908 735-7700
Robert Marlow, *General Mgr*
EMP: 5
SALES (est): 328.3K **Privately Held**
WEB: www.badgeconj.com
SIC: 3999 5999 Badges, metal: policemen, firemen, etc.; police supply stores

(G-56)
ZETA PRODUCTS INC
18 Westgate Dr (08801-1647)
PHONE..............................908 688-0440
Michael Naso, *President*
Angelo Marzullo, *Sales Staff*
▲ **EMP:** 38 **EST:** 1977
SQ FT: 20,000
SALES (est): 5.6MM **Privately Held**
WEB: www.zetaproducts.com
SIC: 3861 5044 Microfilm equipment: cameras, projectors, readers, etc.; microfilm equipment

---

Asbury
Hunterdon County

(G-57)
ALLGRIND PLASTICS INC
6 Vliet Farm Rd (08802-1171)
P.O. Box 363, Bloomsbury (08804-0363)
PHONE..............................908 479-4400
William C Willoughby, *President*
Tammy Hillyer, *Purchasing*
Doug Slack, *Data Proc Staff*
Regina Willoughby, *Admin Sec*
EMP: 12
SQ FT: 43,550
SALES (est): 2.5MM **Privately Held**
WEB: www.allgrind.com
SIC: 3089 Injection molding of plastics; plastic processing

(G-58)
AMEX TOOL CO
4 Fox Hill Ln (08802-1176)
PHONE..............................908 735-5176
Hubert Stria, *President*
Ronald Stria, *Vice Pres*
EMP: 10
SQ FT: 7,000
SALES: 800K **Privately Held**
SIC: 3599 Machine shop, jobbing & repair

(G-59)
ANTHRACITE INDUSTRIES INC (HQ)
405 Old Main St (08802-1220)
P.O. Box 144 (08802-0144)
PHONE..............................908 537-2155
Marvin Riddle III, *CEO*
Stephen A Riddle, *CEO*
Carol A Kalmar, *President*
Lue Fish, *Vice Pres*
▼ **EMP:** 4
SQ FT: 2,700
SALES (est): 5.5MM
SALES (corp-wide): 126.7MM **Privately Held**
SIC: 3295 Minerals, ground or otherwise treated
PA: Asbury Carbons, Inc.
 405 Old Main St
 Asbury NJ 08802
 908 537-2155

(G-60)
ASBURY CARBONS INC (PA)
405 Old Main St (08802-1220)
PHONE..............................908 537-2155
Stephen A Riddle, *CEO*
H Marvin Riddle III, *Ch of Bd*
Carol A Kalmar, *President*
Sue Rish, *Vice Pres*
William T Meglaughlin Jr, *CFO*
◆ **EMP:** 2
SQ FT: 6,000
SALES (est): 126.7MM **Privately Held**
SIC: 1499 3295 1241 5051 Graphite mining: graphite, natural: ground, pulverized, refined or blended; coal mining services; metals service centers & offices; pencil lead: black, indelible or colored: artists'; erasers: rubber or rubber & abrasive combined

(G-61)
ASBURY GRAPHITE MILLS INC (HQ)
405 Old Main St (08802-1220)
P.O. Box 144 (08802-0144)
PHONE..............................908 537-2155
Steven A Riddle, *CEO*
Lewis Fish, *Vice Pres*
Jason Billins, *Plant Mgr*
Susan Rish, *CFO*
Derek Guidry, *Manager*
◆ **EMP:** 35 **EST:** 1895
SQ FT: 100,000
SALES (est): 28MM
SALES (corp-wide): 126.7MM **Privately Held**
WEB: www.asbury.com
SIC: 3295 Minerals, ground or treated

PA: Asbury Carbons, Inc.
405 Old Main St
Asbury NJ 08802
908 537-2155

(G-62)
ASBURY GRAPHITE MILLS INC
156 Asbury West Portal Rd (08802-1128)
PHONE...........................908 537-2157
Gary Zeigler, *Branch Mgr*
EMP: 52
SALES (corp-wide): 126.7MM **Privately Held**
WEB: www.asbury.com
SIC: 3295 Minerals, ground or treated
HQ: The Asbury Graphite Mills Inc
405 Old Main St
Asbury NJ 08802
908 537-2155

(G-63)
ASBURY LOUISIANA INC (HQ)
405 Old Main St (08802-1220)
P.O. Box 144 (08802-0144)
PHONE...........................908 537-2155
Stephen A Riddle, *CEO*
H Marvin Riddle III, *Ch of Bd*
Carol Kalmar, *President*
Lewis S Fish, *Vice Pres*
Gary Ziegler, *Vice Pres*
▲ **EMP:** 50
SQ FT: 10,000
SALES (est): 45.2MM
SALES (corp-wide): 126.7MM **Privately Held**
SIC: 3624 Carbon & graphite products
PA: Asbury Carbons, Inc.
405 Old Main St
Asbury NJ 08802
908 537-2155

(G-64)
HART CONSTRUCTION SERVICE
466 Mine Rd (08802-1106)
PHONE...........................908 537-2060
Ronald Hart, *Owner*
EMP: 6
SALES (est): 320K **Privately Held**
SIC: 3531 1521 Plows: construction, exca-
vating & grading; single-family housing
construction

(G-65)
JERSEY CIDER WORKS LLC
360 County Road 579 (08802-1231)
PHONE...........................908 940-4115
EMP: 6
SALES (est): 400.3K
SALES (corp-wide): 250K **Privately Held**
SIC: 2084 Wines
PA: Jersey Cider Works, Llc
42 Erwin Park Rd
Montclair NJ 07042
917 604-0067

(G-66)
JOHNTHAN LEASING CORP
Also Called: Don Schreiber Co
630 Fox Farm Rd (08802-1102)
PHONE...........................908 226-3434
Eugene R Kistler, *President*
Saul Siegel, *General Mgr*
Nathan Connell, *Manager*
Alene Reed, *Shareholder*
Barry Reed, *Shareholder*
EMP: 30
SALES (est): 2.2MM **Privately Held**
WEB: www.donschreiber.com
SIC: 2782 Looseleaf binders & devices

(G-67)
MASON DISPLAY INNOVATIONS INC
Also Called: M D I
1 Deer Hill Rd (08802-1312)
PHONE...........................609 860-0675
EMP: 14
SQ FT: 70,000
SALES (est): 1.1MM **Privately Held**
SIC: 7389 3993 Business Services

(G-68)
PACIFIC COAST SYSTEMS LLC
4 Fox Hill Ln (08802-1176)
PHONE...........................908 735-9955
Diana Schaeffer,

Ron Stria,
EMP: 5
SALES (est): 565.4K **Privately Held**
SIC: 3728 Aircraft training equipment

(G-69)
REED PRESENTATIONS INC (PA)
Also Called: R P I
630 Fox Farm Rd (08802-1102)
PHONE...........................908 832-0007
Barry A Reed, *CEO*
Alene Reed, *Treasurer*
Nathan Connell, *Manager*
Sandra D'Emilio, *Director*
EMP: 19
SALES (est): 3.3MM **Privately Held**
SIC: 2782 Library binders, looseleaf

(G-70)
VITAL SIGNS MEDCL LEGL CONSLTN
10 Magnolia Ln (08802-1184)
P.O. Box 157 (08802-0157)
PHONE...........................908 537-7857
William Kaminski, *Principal*
EMP: 11 **EST:** 2001
SALES (est): 1MM **Privately Held**
SIC: 3993 Signs & advertising specialties

Asbury Park
Monmouth County

(G-71)
ASBURY AWNG MFG & INSTALLATION
Also Called: Monmouth and Ocean County Awng
508 Main St (07712-6916)
PHONE...........................732 775-4881
Chris Zatorski, *President*
EMP: 8
SALES (est): 1MM **Privately Held**
SIC: 3444 1799 Awnings, sheet metal;
awning installation

(G-72)
CARLTON COKE MET FNISHINGS LLC
1004 1st Ave (07712-5820)
PHONE...........................732 774-2210
Robert P Micele, *Principal*
EMP: 5
SALES (est): 411.3K **Privately Held**
SIC: 3471 Plating of metals or formed
products

(G-73)
COASTER INC
Also Called: Coaster, The
1011 Main St Ste B (07712-5963)
PHONE...........................732 775-3010
Ellen Carroll, *President*
Thomas Carroll, *Principal*
Joseph Garrett, *Accounts Exec*
EMP: 10
SALES (est): 500K **Privately Held**
WEB: www.thecoaster.net
SIC: 2711 Newspapers, publishing & print-
ing

(G-74)
DARK CITY BREWERY LLC
1001 Main St (07712-5922)
PHONE...........................917 273-4995
John Palmieri, *Mng Member*
Kevin Sherpe, *Mng Member*
EMP: 8
SALES (est): 235.3K **Privately Held**
SIC: 2082 Beer (alcoholic beverage)

(G-75)
DAYTON GREY CORP
1008 1st Ave (07712-5820)
PHONE...........................732 869-0060
Dan France, *President*
Leven Stein, *Vice Pres*
EMP: 11
SQ FT: 8,000

SALES: 1MM **Privately Held**
WEB: www.daytongrey.com
SIC: 3559 Metal finishing equipment for
plating, etc.

(G-76)
F L FELDMAN ASSOCIATES
811 Memorial Dr (07712-5829)
PHONE...........................732 776-8544
Frank L Feldman, *President*
EMP: 10
SQ FT: 8,000
SALES (est): 800K **Privately Held**
WEB: www.customwoodworking.info
SIC: 2431 2434 Woodwork, interior & or-
namental; wood kitchen cabinets

(G-77)
GENE MIGNOLA INC
704 Cookman Ave (07712-7008)
PHONE...........................732 775-9291
Gene Mignola, *President*
EMP: 4
SQ FT: 2,000
SALES: 170K **Privately Held**
SIC: 2211 Basket weave fabrics, cotton

(G-78)
KNOCK OUT GRAPHICS INC
522 Cookman Ave Ste 3n (07712-7140)
PHONE...........................732 774-3331
Margaret Brunette, *President*
Kyle Lepree, *Vice Pres*
EMP: 14
SQ FT: 800
SALES (est): 1.8MM **Privately Held**
SIC: 2752 Commercial printing, litho-
graphic

(G-79)
LIGHTHOUSE EXPRESS INC
809 Memorial Dr (07712-5829)
PHONE...........................732 776-9555
Isaac Abadi, *President*
EMP: 7 **EST:** 1995
SALES: 800K **Privately Held**
WEB: www.lighthouseexpress.com
SIC: 3499 3961 Giftware, brass goods;
costume jewelry

(G-80)
MCLAIN STUDIOS INC
Also Called: Mc Lain Screen Printing
1203 Main St (07712-5940)
P.O. Box 147 (07712-0147)
PHONE...........................732 775-0271
James W Mc Lain, *President*
EMP: 4 **EST:** 1945
SQ FT: 2,000
SALES (est): 406.7K **Privately Held**
WEB: www.mclainstudios.com
SIC: 2396 3993 Screen printing on fabric
articles; signs & advertising specialties

(G-81)
PORT A (PA)
911 Kingsley St (07712-6216)
PHONE...........................732 776-6511
EMP: 12 **EST:** 2011
SALES (est): 1.8MM **Privately Held**
SIC: 3421 Table & food cutlery, including
butchers'

(G-82)
STREAMSERVE INC (HQ)
100 Tormee Dr (07712-7502)
PHONE...........................781 863-1510
Dennis Ladd, *President*
Paul Mc Feeters, *CFO*
Ulf Kasshag, *Treasurer*
G Ndor Rentsch, *Director*
Tina Santos, *Admin Sec*
EMP: 28
SALES (est): 23.2MM
SALES (corp-wide): 2.2B **Privately Held**
WEB: www.streamserve.com
SIC: 7372 Prepackaged software
PA: Open Text Corporation
275 Frank Tompa Dr
Waterloo ON N2L 0
519 888-7111

(G-83)
SUPER CHROME INC
1004 1st Ave (07712-5820)
PHONE...........................732 774-2210

Robert Micele, *Principal*
EMP: 5
SALES (est): 261.7K **Privately Held**
SIC: 3471 Anodizing (plating) of metals or
formed products

(G-84)
TERRISS CONSOLIDATED INDS
807 Summerfield Ave (07712-6970)
P.O. Box 110 (07712-0110)
PHONE...........................732 988-0909
Judith L Bodnovich, *CEO*
Stephen Bodnovich, *Vice Pres*
Marc J Epstein, *Vice Pres*
Joan Goldberg, *Vice Pres*
Edward Della Zanna, *Sales Mgr*
▼ **EMP:** 9 **EST:** 1895
SQ FT: 30,000
SALES (est): 2.8MM **Privately Held**
WEB: www.terriss.com
SIC: 3556 Beverage machinery

(G-85)
UNIVERSAL FILTERS INC
1207 Main St Ste A (07712-5964)
PHONE...........................732 774-8555
Jerrold D Kolton, *President*
David Tafara, *Vice Pres*
▲ **EMP:** 20
SALES (est): 3.4MM **Privately Held**
WEB: www.universalfilters.com
SIC: 3569 Filters, general line: industrial

Atco
Camden County

(G-86)
FORGET ME NOT CHOCOLATES BY NA
121 Lakeside Dr (08004-3036)
PHONE...........................856 753-8916
H Cadet, *Principal*
EMP: 5
SALES (est): 310.2K **Privately Held**
WEB: www.forgetmenotchocolates.com
SIC: 2066 Chocolate

(G-87)
PRE-FAB STRUCTURES INC (PA)
907 Wedgewood Way (08004-1336)
PHONE...........................856 768-4257
Leslie W Johnson, *President*
Terri Johnson, *Vice Pres*
EMP: 5
SALES (est): 592.8K **Privately Held**
WEB: www.pre-fabstructures.com
SIC: 3448 Prefabricated metal buildings

Atlantic City
Atlantic County

(G-88)
A C DISPLAY STUDIOS INC
2715 Arctic Ave (08401-3840)
P.O. Box 1174, Brigantine (08203-7174)
PHONE...........................609 345-0814
Fax: 609 345-2715
EMP: 6
SQ FT: 6,000
SALES (est): 611.5K **Privately Held**
SIC: 3993 Mfg Signs/Advertising Special-
ties

(G-89)
DONNA KARAN INTERNATIONAL INC
1931 Atlantic Ave (08401-6705)
PHONE...........................609 345-3402
EMP: 8
SALES (corp-wide): 3B **Publicly Held**
SIC: 2335 Women's, juniors' & misses'
dresses
HQ: Donna Karan International Inc.
240 W 40th St
New York NY 10018
212 789-1500

▲ = Import ▼=Export
◆ =Import/Export

(G-90)
FRALINGERS INC (PA)
Also Called: Fralinger's Org Salt Wtr Taffy
1325 Boardwalk Ste 1 (08401-7287)
PHONE..............................609 345-2177
Frank Glaser, *President*
EMP: 37 EST: 1885
SQ FT: 800
SALES (est): 3.9MM **Privately Held**
WEB: www.fralingers.com
SIC: 2066 5145 5441 2064 Chocolate & cocoa products; confectionery; confectionery; candy & other confectionery products

(G-91)
FRALINGERS INC
1519 Boardwalk (08401-7012)
PHONE..............................609 345-2177
Frank Glaser, *Manager*
EMP: 9
SALES (corp-wide): 3.9MM **Privately Held**
WEB: www.fralingers.com
SIC: 2064 Candy & other confectionery products
PA: Fralingers Inc
   1325 Boardwalk Ste 1
   Atlantic City NJ 08401
   609 345-2177

(G-92)
GANTER DISTILLERS LIABILIT
807 Baltic Ave (08401-5230)
PHONE..............................609 344-7867
EMP: 5
SALES (est): 332.9K **Privately Held**
SIC: 2085 Distilled & blended liquors

(G-93)
HANDS ON WHEELS
509 Atlantic Ave (08401-7601)
PHONE..............................609 892-4693
Peace Toleito, *Principal*
EMP: 4
SALES (est): 235K **Privately Held**
SIC: 3312 Wheels

(G-94)
HEADQUARTERS PUB LLC
Also Called: Tun Tavern Brewery & Rest
2 Convention Blvd (08401-4137)
PHONE..............................609 347-2579
Montgomery Dahm, *Managing Prtnr*
Diane Tharp, *Manager*
Tom Scannapieco,
EMP: 50 EST: 1998
SQ FT: 7,600
SALES (est): 7.6MM **Privately Held**
WEB: www.tuntavern.com
SIC: 2082 5921 Beer (alcoholic beverage); beer (packaged)

(G-95)
JAMES CANDY COMPANY (PA)
Also Called: Bayard's Chocolate House
1519 Boardwalk (08401-7012)
PHONE..............................609 344-1519
Frank J Glaser, *President*
Maureen Glaser, *Vice Pres*
▲ EMP: 50
SQ FT: 40,000
SALES: 6MM **Privately Held**
WEB: www.seashoretaffy.com
SIC: 5441 5145 2064 Confectionery; candy & other confectionery products

(G-96)
LINDA SPOLITINO
Also Called: Seagull Stain Glass
1917 Kuehnle Ave (08401-1703)
PHONE..............................609 345-3126
Linda Spolitino, *Owner*
Linda Spilitino, *Partner*
EMP: 7
SQ FT: 2,000
SALES: 225K **Privately Held**
SIC: 3231 Stained glass: made from purchased glass

(G-97)
LOCKHEED MARTIN CORPORATION
Lockheed Martin A Traffic MGT
Aasl Bldg 316 (08405-0001)
PHONE..............................609 485-7601
Dan Francis, *General Mgr*
EMP: 1018 **Publicly Held**
WEB: www.lockheedmartin.com
SIC: 3812 Search & navigation equipment
PA: Lockheed Martin Corporation
   6801 Rockledge Dr
   Bethesda MD 20817

(G-98)
MOTORS AND DRIVES INC
Also Called: Park Electric Motor Co
1413 Marmora Ave (08401-2338)
PHONE..............................609 344-8058
Gene Moir Jr, *Manager*
Charlie Bogdany, *Manager*
Paul Hamadyk, *Manager*
EMP: 4
SALES (corp-wide): 1.5MM **Privately Held**
WEB: www.motorsanddrives.com
SIC: 5999 7694 Motors, electric; electric motor repair
PA: Motors And Drives, Inc
   5 Asbury Ave
   Freehold NJ 07728
   732 462-7683

(G-99)
MYRIAMS DREAM BOOK BINDERY
1102 Atlantic Ave (08401-4803)
PHONE..............................609 345-5555
Adrienna Epstein, *Principal*
Emma Todd, *Principal*
EMP: 4
SALES: 6K **Privately Held**
SIC: 2789 Bookbinding & related work

(G-100)
OFFSHORE ENTERPRISES INC
433 N Maryland Ave (08401-2533)
P.O. Box 477, Brigantine (08203-0477)
PHONE..............................609 345-9099
Jonathan Weiss, *President*
EMP: 4
SALES (est): 230K **Privately Held**
SIC: 3949 Fishing equipment

(G-101)
PVH CORP
Also Called: Van Heusen
32 N Michigan Ave (08401-4117)
PHONE..............................609 344-6273
EMP: 9
SALES (corp-wide): 9.6B **Publicly Held**
SIC: 2321 Men's & boys' dress shirts
PA: Pvh Corp.
   200 Madison Ave Bsmt 1
   New York NY 10016
   212 381-3500

(G-102)
RAPHEL MARKETING INC
118 S Newton Pl (08401-5615)
PHONE..............................609 348-6646
Neil Raphel, *President*
Neil Raphel, *President*
Ruth Raphel, *President*
Murray Raphel, *Vice Pres*
EMP: 7
SQ FT: 2,000
SALES (est): 630K **Privately Held**
SIC: 8742 2741 Marketing consulting services; miscellaneous publishing

(G-103)
SWAROVSKI NORTH AMERICA LTD
2801 Pacific Ave (08401-6347)
PHONE..............................609 344-1323
Leslie Adam, *Branch Mgr*
EMP: 4
SALES (corp-wide): 4.7B **Privately Held**
SIC: 3961 Costume jewelry
HQ: Swarovski North America Limited
   1 Kenney Dr
   Cranston RI 02920
   401 463-6400

(G-104)
BRICK-WALL CORP (PA)
25 1st Ave Ste 200 (07716-1285)
PHONE..............................732 787-0226
Lawrance Hesse, *President*
Larry Mulcahy, *CFO*
EMP: 29
SALES (est): 3.6MM **Privately Held**
SIC: 2951 5032 Asphalt paving mixtures & blocks; gravel; sand, construction

(G-105)
CARTON BREWING COMPANY LLC
6 E Washington Ave (07716-1230)
PHONE..............................732 654-2337
Chris Wecht, *Opers Staff*
Doug Edwards, *Marketing Staff*
La Carton IV,
▲ EMP: 6
SALES (est): 750.5K **Privately Held**
SIC: 2082 5921 Beer (alcoholic beverage); beer (packaged)

(G-106)
FOOD CIRCUS SUPER MARKETS INC
Also Called: Store 266
9 East Ave 36 (07716)
P.O. Box 133 (07716-0133)
PHONE..............................732 291-4079
Joe Grande, *Controller*
Lou Vaccaro, *Branch Mgr*
EMP: 100
SALES (corp-wide): 146.4MM **Privately Held**
WEB: www.foodcircus.com
SIC: 5411 5992 5812 2051 Supermarkets, chain; florists; eating places; bread, cake & related products
PA: Food Circus Super Markets, Inc.
   853 State Route 35
   Middletown NJ 07748
   732 671-2220

(G-107)
IWS LICENSE CORP
29 4th Ave (07716-1208)
PHONE..............................732 872-0014
EMP: 15
SALES (est): 1MM **Privately Held**
SIC: 2741 Misc Publishing

(G-108)
JERSEY PRINTING ASSOCIATES INC
153 1st Ave Ste 1 (07716-1292)
P.O. Box 355 (07716-0355)
PHONE..............................732 872-9654
Gregory J Heh, *President*
Charlie McCullagh, *Vice Pres*
Patricia Pfleger, *Admin Sec*
EMP: 45 EST: 1981
SQ FT: 36,000
SALES (est): 5.6MM **Privately Held**
WEB: www.jerseyprinting.com
SIC: 2752 2789 5112 Commercial printing, offset; bookbinding & related work; social stationery & greeting cards

(G-109)
JULIAN BAIT COMPANY INC
Also Called: Julian Enterprises
990 State Route 36 (07716-2024)
PHONE..............................732 291-0050
Joseph Julian, *President*
Alexandra Julian, *Treasurer*
Josephine Julian, *Admin Sec*
EMP: 6 EST: 1964
SQ FT: 1,000
SALES (est): 460.7K **Privately Held**
SIC: 5091 3949 Fishing equipment & supplies; fishing equipment

(G-110)
PREMIER GRAPHICS INC
165 1st Ave C (07716-1265)
PHONE..............................732 872-9933
Sal Madalone, *President*

Toni Madalone, *Vice Pres*
EMP: 20
SQ FT: 10,000
SALES (est): 2.9MM **Privately Held**
WEB: www.premiergraphics.com
SIC: 2752 Commercial printing, offset

(G-111)
AMERICAN MLLWRIGHT RIGGING LLC
119 Washington Ter (08106-1625)
PHONE..............................856 457-9574
William Marley, *President*
EMP: 20
SALES: 5MM **Privately Held**
SIC: 1796 3441 Machine moving & rigging; fabricated structural metal

(G-112)
CORBI PRINTING CO INC
Also Called: Municipal Record Service
106 W Atlantic Ave (08106-1439)
PHONE..............................856 547-2444
Thomas G Corbi, *President*
Mary Corbi, *Vice Pres*
EMP: 8
SQ FT: 3,600
SALES (est): 1.2MM **Privately Held**
SIC: 2752 Commercial printing, offset

(G-113)
MODERN METRIC MACHINE COMPANY
101 W Nicholson Rd (08106-1411)
PHONE..............................856 547-4044
Paul Volkwine, *President*
Rose Ann Volkwine, *Corp Secy*
EMP: 6 EST: 1977
SQ FT: 4,000
SALES: 750K **Privately Held**
SIC: 3599 Machine shop, jobbing & repair

(G-114)
SIKA CORPORATION
Also Called: Sika Liquid Plasics Division
251 S White Horse Pike (08106-1306)
PHONE..............................856 298-2313
Sam Girgenti, *Director*
EMP: 20
SALES (corp-wide): 7.1B **Privately Held**
SIC: 2821 Plastics materials & resins
HQ: Sika Corporation
   201 Polito Ave
   Lyndhurst NJ 07071
   201 933-8800

(G-115)
CLOGIC LLC
Also Called: Clogic Defense
4 Sunset Ln (07822-2100)
PHONE..............................973 934-5223
Diana-Lynn Herbst, *Branch Mgr*
EMP: 7
SALES (est): 705.3K
SALES (corp-wide): 2.3MM **Privately Held**
SIC: 3795 Tanks & tank components
PA: Clogic, Llc
   800 Hawks Nest Ct
   Ponte Vedra Beach FL 32082
   860 324-2227

(G-116)
SEVEN MILE PUBG & CREATIVE
355 24th St (08202-1816)
P.O. Box 134 (08202-0134)
PHONE..............................609 967-7707
Monica Coskey, *Mng Member*
David Coskey, *Officer*

EMP: 10 **EST:** 2006
SALES: 800K **Privately Held**
SIC: 2741 Miscellaneous publishing

Avenel
Middlesex County

(G-117)
A&M INDUSTRIAL INC
Also Called: A&M Petro Marine Division
22b Cragwood Rd (07001-2234)
PHONE....................................908 862-1800
Chris Pichalski, *Finance Mgr*
John Smickenbecker, *Branch Mgr*
EMP: 10
SALES (corp-wide): 43.5MM **Privately
Held**
WEB: www.am-ind.com
SIC: 3498 Pipe fittings, fabricated from
purchased pipe
PA: A&M Industrial, Inc.
37 W Cherry St
Rahway NJ 07065
732 574-1111

(G-118)
ABLE FAB CO
18 Mileed Way (07001-2403)
PHONE....................................732 396-0600
William Demott, *President*
EMP: 36 **EST:** 1976
SQ FT: 12,000
SALES (est): 4MM **Privately Held**
WEB: www.archerday.com
SIC: 3443 3444 3441 1711 Plate work for
the metalworking trade; pipe, sheet metal;
fabricated structural metal; plumbing,
heating, air-conditioning contractors

(G-119)
ACCELY INC
381 Blair Rd (07001-2201)
PHONE....................................609 598-1882
Nilesh Shah, *CEO*
Alvi Gandhi, *President*
Jake Wessel, *Exec VP*
Nikhil Mane, *Consultant*
Sam Vaddi, *Director*
EMP: 10
SALES: 3.3MM
SALES (corp-wide): 977.1K **Privately
Held**
SIC: 7372 Application computer software
PA: Accely Pte. Ltd.
3 Dunkirk Avenue
Singapore
910 141-08

(G-120)
ARCHER DAY INC
18 Mileed Way (07001-2403)
PHONE....................................732 396-0600
William Demott, *President*
EMP: 50
SQ FT: 7,000
SALES (est): 10.8MM **Privately Held**
SIC: 3312 1731 3441 Plate, steel; electri-
cal work; fabricated structural metal

(G-121)
**ARTISTIC DOORS AND
WINDOWS INC**
10 S Inman Ave (07001-1508)
PHONE....................................732 726-9400
Rick Autovino Enrico, *CEO*
John Autovino, *Vice Pres*
Gaetano Cichy, *Vice Pres*
Guy Cichy, *Vice Pres*
Jason Adamshick, *Project Mgr*
◆ **EMP:** 22
SQ FT: 32,000
SALES (est): 5.2MM **Privately Held**
SIC: 2431 Doors & door parts & trim,
wood; windows & window parts & trim,
wood

(G-122)
AVIONIC INSTRUMENTS LLC
1414 Randolph Ave (07001-2402)
P.O. Box 498 (07001-0498)
PHONE....................................732 388-3500
Carol Soltz, *Vice Pres*
Doris Ulloa, *Prdtn Mgr*

Dan Scardelli, *Materials Mgr*
Stephen Gross, *Opers Staff*
Tim Duhamel, *QC Mgr*
EMP: 200
SQ FT: 35,000
SALES (est): 50.5MM
SALES (corp-wide): 3.8B **Publicly Held**
WEB: www.avionicinstruments.com
SIC: 3629 Inverters, nonrotating: electrical;
power conversion units, a.c. to d.c.: static-
electric
HQ: Transdigm, Inc.
4223 Monticello Blvd
Cleveland OH 44121

(G-123)
BARBEITOS INC
6 Pocahont Pl (07001-1516)
PHONE....................................732 726-9543
Martha Amarante, *President*
EMP: 4
SALES (est): 211.5K **Privately Held**
SIC: 2051 Cakes, pies & pastries

(G-124)
CARAVAN INC
160 Essex Ave E (07001-2045)
P.O. Box 427 (07001-0427)
PHONE....................................732 590-0210
Michael Caracappa, *President*
Patricia Caracappa, *Treasurer*
▲ **EMP:** 16
SQ FT: 5,600
SALES (est): 4.2MM **Privately Held**
SIC: 3537 Trucks: freight, baggage, etc.:
industrial, except mining

(G-125)
D L PRINTING CO INC
283 Prospect Ave (07001-1156)
PHONE....................................732 750-1917
Dave Lospinoso, *President*
Stacie Lospinoso, *Treasurer*
EMP: 5
SQ FT: 2,000
SALES (est): 714K **Privately Held**
WEB: www.dlprinting.net
SIC: 2752 Commercial printing, offset

(G-126)
ESSEX COATINGS LLC
135 Essex Ave E (07001-2019)
PHONE....................................732 855-9400
Ejlat Feuer,
▲ **EMP:** 10
SQ FT: 2,000
SALES (est): 1.9MM **Privately Held**
SIC: 2435 Hardwood plywood, prefinished

(G-127)
FLAVORS OF ORIGIN INC (PA)
Also Called: Flavor Materials International
10 Engelhard Ave (07001)
PHONE....................................732 499-9700
Paul Ahn, *President*
Deepak Arora, *Vice Pres*
Cinthia Maldonado, *Opers Mgr*
Bryan Warren, *Safety Mgr*
Arlene White, *Accounts Mgr*
◆ **EMP:** 20
SQ FT: 40,000
SALES (est): 16.9MM **Privately Held**
WEB: www.flavormaterials.com
SIC: 5149 2899 2087 Flavourings & fra-
grances; essential oils; flavoring extracts
& syrups

(G-128)
FUEL ONE INC
869 Us Highway 1 (07001-1357)
PHONE....................................732 726-9500
EMP: 4
SALES (est): 305K **Privately Held**
SIC: 2869 Fuels

(G-129)
**G R IMPEX LTD LIABILITY CO
(PA)**
Also Called: Falcon Papers & Plastics
2 Terminal Way Bldg A (07001)
PHONE....................................301 873-5333
Laura Santiago, *Accountant*
Gautam Bhatia, *Mng Member*
Sam Bhatia,
◆ **EMP:** 11
SQ FT: 20,000

SALES (est): 17.3MM **Privately Held**
WEB: www.falconpapers.com
SIC: 5111 2621 Printing & writing paper;
packaging paper

(G-130)
**GENTEK BUILDING PRODUCTS
INC**
11 Cragwood Rd (07001-2202)
PHONE....................................732 381-0900
Kerry Higgs, *Manager*
EMP: 33 **Privately Held**
WEB: www.gentekinc.com
SIC: 3355 Aluminum rolling & drawing
HQ: Gentek Building Products, Inc.
3773 State Rd
Cuyahoga Falls OH 44223

(G-131)
**INTERBAHM INTERNATIONAL
INC**
10 Engelhard Ave (07001)
PHONE....................................732 499-9700
Paul Ahn, *President*
Mario Natale, *Accountant*
EMP: 45
SALES (est): 4.6MM **Privately Held**
SIC: 2087 2899 5149 Flavoring extracts &
syrups; essential oils; flavourings & fra-
grances

(G-132)
JOY SNACKS LLC
365 Blair Rd Ste A (07001-2231)
PHONE....................................732 272-0707
AVI Weinstein, *Vice Pres*
Mendy Cinner, *Director*
EMP: 15 **EST:** 2016
SQ FT: 22,000
SALES (est): 2MM **Privately Held**
SIC: 2064 Granola & muesli, bars & clus-
ters; nuts, candy covered

(G-133)
K R ELECTRONICS INC
91 Avenel St (07001-1749)
PHONE....................................732 636-1900
Charles Kiall, *President*
EMP: 13
SQ FT: 10,000
SALES (est): 2.2MM **Privately Held**
WEB: www.krfilters.com
SIC: 3679 Microwave components; elec-
tronic circuits

(G-134)
KEURIG DR PEPPER INC
433 Blair Rd (07001-2215)
PHONE....................................732 388-5545
Robert Hofmann, *Branch Mgr*
EMP: 100 **Publicly Held**
SIC: 2086 Soft drinks: packaged in cans,
bottles, etc.
PA: Keurig Dr Pepper Inc.
53 South Ave
Burlington MA 01803

(G-135)
MAGIC PRINTING CORP
386 Avenel St (07001-1146)
PHONE....................................732 726-0620
Steven Glassman, *President*
EMP: 14
SQ FT: 3,000
SALES: 1.4MM **Privately Held**
SIC: 2759 5099 Thermography; invitation
& stationery printing & engraving; rubber
stamps

(G-136)
**MICROCAST TECHNOLOGIES
CORP**
17 Mileed Way (07001-2403)
PHONE....................................732 943-7356
EMP: 6 **Privately Held**
SIC: 3369 White metal castings (lead, tin,
antimony), except die
PA: Microcast Technologies Corp.
1611 W Elizabeth Ave
Linden NJ 07036

(G-137)
MIZCO INTERNATIONAL INC
Also Called: Cellular Innovations
80 Essex Ave E (07001-2020)
PHONE....................................732 912-2000
Albert Mizrahi, *President*
David Strumeier, *Exec VP*
Tom Buske, *Vice Pres*
Sam Mizarahi, *Vice Pres*
Isaac Mizrahi, *Vice Pres*
▲ **EMP:** 100
SALES (est): 46.9MM **Privately Held**
WEB: www.mizco.com
SIC: 5043 3629 3663 3661 Photographic
cameras, projectors, equipment & sup-
plies; battery chargers, rectifying or non-
rotating; mobile communication
equipment; telephone cords, jacks,
adapters, etc.; batteries, rechargeable

(G-138)
**MULTI-PLASTICS EXTRUSIONS
INC**
30 Production Way (07001-1628)
PHONE....................................732 388-2300
Raul Soto, *Prdtn Mgr*
Gordon Sutherland, *Safety Mgr*
Bruce Gandarillas, *Human Res Mgr*
Ed McDonald, *Chief Mktg Ofcr*
Geovanny Langlois, *Analyst*
EMP: 17
SALES (corp-wide): 198MM **Privately
Held**
SIC: 2821 Plastics materials & resins
HQ: Multi-Plastics Extrusions, Inc.
600 Dietrich Ave
Hazleton PA 18201
570 455-2021

(G-139)
NATIONAL FENCE SYSTEMS INC
Also Called: Nfs
1033 Rte One Avenel (07001)
PHONE....................................732 636-5600
Anthony Martinez, *President*
Dennis Grady, *CFO*
Linda Martinez, *Admin Sec*
▼ **EMP:** 85
SQ FT: 14,500
SALES (est): 17MM **Privately Held**
WEB: www.nationalfencesystems.com
SIC: 1799 5211 2499 Fence construction;
fencing; fencing, wood

(G-140)
**PILOT CHEMICAL COMPANY
OHIO**
267 Homestead Ave (07001-2006)
PHONE....................................732 634-6613
Tom Peterson, *Manager*
EMP: 15
SQ FT: 20,000
SALES (corp-wide): 110.9MM **Privately
Held**
SIC: 2841 2869 Detergents, synthetic or-
ganic or inorganic alkaline; industrial or-
ganic chemicals
PA: Pilot Chemical Company Of Ohio
9075 Cntre Pnte Dr Ste 40
West Chester OH 45069
513 326-0600

(G-141)
PQ CORPORATION
2 Paddock St (07001)
PHONE....................................732 750-9040
Merrill Colmery, *Opers-Prdtn-Mfg*
Christine Salaiz, *Buyer*
Kelly Obrien, *Sales Staff*
Lou Henderson, *Manager*
Ken Clark, *Technical Staff*
EMP: 24
SQ FT: 80,000
SALES (corp-wide): 1.6B **Publicly Held**
WEB: www.pqcorp.com
SIC: 2819 2842 Industrial inorganic chem-
icals; specialty cleaning, polishes & sani-
tation goods
HQ: Pq Corporation
300 Lindenwood Dr
Malvern PA 19355
610 651-4200

(G-142)
**PREMIER DIE CASTING
COMPANY**
1177 Rahway Ave (07001-2196)
PHONE...................................732 634-3000
Leonard Cordaro, *President*
▲ EMP: 60 EST: 1945
SQ FT: 82,500
SALES (est): 14.2MM **Privately Held**
WEB: www.diecasting.com
SIC: 3599 Machine shop, jobbing & repair

(G-143)
PROCTER & GAMBLE MFG CO
100 Essex Ave E (07001-2020)
PHONE...................................732 602-4500
Kathleen Rasmussen, *Foreman/Supr*
Allan Pimentel, *Engineer*
Sandy Moshier, *Branch Mgr*
EMP: 100
SALES (corp-wide): 67.6B **Publicly Held**
SIC: 2841 2079 2099 2844 Detergents;
synthetic organic or inorganic alkaline;
shortening & other solid edible fats;
peanut butter; toilet preparations; cake
mixes, prepared: from purchased flour
HQ: The Procter & Gamble Manufacturing
Company
1 Procter And Gamble Plz
Cincinnati OH 45202
513 983-1100

(G-144)
R L PLASTICS INC
20 Production Way (07001-1628)
PHONE...................................732 340-1100
Melvin Laufer, *President*
Hindy Laufer, *Controller*
▲ EMP: 5 EST: 1949
SQ FT: 14,000
SALES (est): 508.5K **Privately Held**
WEB: www.rlplastics.net
SIC: 2392 5131 5023 Tablecloths: made
from purchased materials; yard goods,
woven; linens, table

(G-145)
**SAVINO DEL BENE USA INC
(HQ)**
34 Engelhard Ave (07001-2217)
PHONE...................................347 960-5568
Andrea Fanti, *Ch of Bd*
Silvano Brandani, *President*
Massimiliano Brandani, *Vice Pres*
Fred Sheinblum, *CFO*
Filippo Occaso, *Admin Sec*
◆ EMP: 55
SQ FT: 10,000
SALES (est): 514.2MM
SALES (corp-wide): 485.8MM **Privately
Held**
WEB: www.bos.sdbusa.com
SIC: 3799 4731 All terrain vehicles (ATV);
freight forwarding
PA: Trasporti Internazionali Agenzia Marit-
tima Savino Del Bene Spa
Via Del Botteghino 24/26
Scandicci FI 50018
055 521-91

(G-146)
**SNAPPLE DISTRIBUTORS INC
(HQ)**
Also Called: Dpsg
433 Blair Rd Ste 1 (07001-2215)
PHONE...................................732 815-2800
Joseph Poli, *President*
Robert Hofmann, *Vice Pres*
Igor Katsman, *Vice Pres*
▲ EMP: 29
SQ FT: 150,000
SALES (est): 8.4MM **Publicly Held**
SIC: 2086 Soft drinks: packaged in cans,
bottles, etc.

(G-147)
**STEELSTRAN INDUSTRIES INC
(PA)**
Also Called: A. L. Don Co.
35 Mileed Way (07001-2403)
P.O. Box 30 (07001-0030)
PHONE...................................732 574-0700
Peter Gronbeck, *CEO*
Susan Gronbeck, *President*
Arthur Jeronimo, *COO*

Thomas Burns, *Vice Pres*
▲ EMP: 21
SQ FT: 33,000
SALES (est): 16.6MM **Privately Held**
SIC: 5082 2298 3732 5085 Ladders;
ropes & fiber cables; boat building & repairing; industrial supplies; metals service
centers & offices; transportation equipment & supplies

(G-148)
SYNERGEM INC
2323 Randolph Ave Ste 2 (07001-2412)
PHONE...................................732 692-6308
Amy P Silverman, *President*
Thomas Demayer, *Chairman*
Lisa Cancilla, *Production*
Peggy Downey, *Finance Mgr*
Michelle Orr, *Accounts Mgr*
▲ EMP: 20
SQ FT: 17,700
SALES (est): 4.2MM **Privately Held**
WEB: www.synergem.com
SIC: 3695 Magnetic & optical recording
media

(G-149)
TATARA GROUP INC
Also Called: Nu Steel
381 Blair Rd (07001-2201)
PHONE...................................732 231-6031
Rahul Katyal, *President*
Paresh Mehta, *Vice Pres*
▲ EMP: 6
SALES (est): 592.3K **Privately Held**
SIC: 5719 5211 4225 2392 Kitchenware;
bathroom fixtures, equipment & supplies;
general warehousing & storage; wash-
cloths & bath mitts: made from purchased
materials

(G-150)
THERMO-GRAPHICS INC
386 Avenel St (07001-1146)
PHONE...................................908 486-0100
Seth Batzar, *President*
Arlene Batzar, *Vice Pres*
▲ EMP: 6
SQ FT: 4,500
SALES: 540K **Privately Held**
WEB: www.thermographics.com
SIC: 2752 Commercial printing, offset

(G-151)
TRS INC
Also Called: Trs Containers
301 Essex Ave E (07001-2054)
P.O. Box 188 (07001-0188)
PHONE...................................732 636-3300
Ted S Sobel, *President*
Rena Sneed, *Marketing Staff*
◆ EMP: 23
SQ FT: 1,800
SALES (est): 4.4MM **Privately Held**
WEB: www.trscontainer.com
SIC: 5999 5085 3443 Packaging materi-
als: boxes, padding, etc.; commercial
containers; industrial vessels, tanks &
containers

(G-152)
TSI NOMENCLATURE INC
1400 Rahway Ave (07001-2226)
P.O. Box 390 (07001-0390)
PHONE...................................732 340-0646
Shawn Scott, *President*
EMP: 5
SQ FT: 10,000
SALES (est): 818K **Privately Held**
SIC: 3613 Panelboards & distribution
boards, electric

(G-153)
USA TEALIGHT INC
4 Cragwood Rd (07001-2203)
PHONE...................................732 943-2408
Michael Zohar, *President*
Neal Bochner, *COO*
◆ EMP: 15
SALES (est): 6.3MM **Privately Held**
SIC: 3999 Candles

Barnegat
Ocean County

(G-154)
AHE MANUFACTURING INC
127 S Main St (08005-2312)
PHONE...................................609 660-8000
John Whitaker, *Principal*
▲ EMP: 15
SALES (est): 451.1K **Privately Held**
SIC: 3534 Elevators & moving stairways

(G-155)
AIRBRUSH ACTION INC
79 S Main St Ste 1 (08005-2315)
PHONE...................................732 223-7878
▲ EMP: 7
SQ FT: 2,800
SALES (est): 1.1MM **Privately Held**
SIC: 2721 Periodicals-Publishing/Printing

(G-156)
CASUAL CLASSICS INC
11 Dori Ln (08005-2110)
PHONE...................................916 294-9880
John D Homsy, *President*
▲ EMP: 5
SALES (est): 411.6K **Privately Held**
SIC: 2519 7389 Lawn & garden furniture,
except wood & metal; design services

(G-157)
CEDGE INDUSTRIES INC
Also Called: Edgeco
237 Rahway Rd (08005-2606)
PHONE...................................201 641-3222
C James Esposito, *President*
Rena Esposito, *Vice Pres*
EMP: 18
SALES (est): 2.4MM **Privately Held**
WEB: www.edgecoamerica.com
SIC: 3841 Surgical & medical instruments

(G-158)
DOT GRAPHIX INC
79 S Main St Ste 13 (08005-2316)
PHONE...................................609 994-3416
Joe Lopes, *President*
EMP: 10
SALES (est): 520K **Privately Held**
SIC: 2759 Screen printing

(G-159)
**EASTERN CONCRETE
MATERIALS INC**
201 Route 539 (08005-1030)
P.O. Box 1327, Euless TX (76039-1327)
PHONE...................................609 698-2800
Tracy Davies, *Branch Mgr*
EMP: 9
SALES (corp-wide): 1.5B **Publicly Held**
SIC: 3273 Ready-mixed concrete
HQ: Eastern Concrete Materials, Inc.
250 Pehle Ave Ste 503
Saddle Brook NJ 07663
201 797-7979

(G-160)
M G S
309 Route 72 (08005-1035)
PHONE...................................609 698-7000
EMP: 4 EST: 2010
SALES (est): 180K **Privately Held**
SIC: 1321 Natural Gas Liquids Production

(G-161)
SGH INC
Also Called: Southern Ocean Mar Sportswear
79 S Main St Ste 2 (08005-2315)
PHONE...................................609 698-8868
Fax: 609 698-5700
EMP: 7
SQ FT: 2,100
SALES (est): 550K **Privately Held**
SIC: 2395 Custom Embroidery Silkscreen-
ing & Promitonal Products

(G-162)
STAFFORD PARK SOLAR 1 LLC
500 Barnegat Blvd N (08005-2233)
PHONE...................................:609 607-9500
Greg Walters, *Partner*
Edward Walters,

EMP: 4
SALES (est): 469.4K **Privately Held**
SIC: 3433 Heating equipment, except elec-
tric

(G-163)
**THOMAS CLARK FIBERGLASS
LLC**
145 Old Halfway Rd (08005-1024)
PHONE...................................609 492-9257
EMP: 4
SALES (est): 395.9K **Privately Held**
SIC: 2221 3229 Manmade Broadwoven
Fabric Mill Mfg Pressed/Blown Glass

Barnegat Light
Ocean County

(G-164)
CAPTAIN JOHN INC
16 E 12th St (08006-1412)
PHONE...................................609 494-2094
Marion O Larson, *CEO*
Keith Larson, *Manager*
EMP: 10
SALES (est): 598.6K **Privately Held**
SIC: 3949 Fishing tackle, general

(G-165)
CYCLASE DYNAMICS INC
16 E 27th St (08006-1522)
P.O. Box 339 (08006-0339)
PHONE...................................973 420-3259
Stephen F Vatner MD, *Principal*
Patricio Abarzua, *Vice Pres*
EMP: 6
SALES: 200K **Privately Held**
SIC: 2834 Pharmaceutical preparations

Barrington
Camden County

(G-166)
ANCHOR OPTICAL CO
101 E Gloucester Pike (08007-1331)
PHONE...................................856 546-1965
Alan Kreutzer, *Manager*
EMP: 200
SQ FT: 1,500
SALES (est): 7.7MM **Privately Held**
WEB: www.anchoroptics.com
SIC: 3827 Magnifying instruments, optical

(G-167)
ANDREW P MC HUGH INC
Also Called: Art Press Printing
124 Clements Bridge Rd # 2 (08007-1834)
PHONE...................................856 547-8953
Robert Mc Hugh, *President*
Roberta Mc Hugh, *Corp Secy*
Janet Mc Hugh, *Vice Pres*
EMP: 6 EST: 1956
SQ FT: 4,000
SALES: 400K **Privately Held**
SIC: 2752 Commercial printing, offset; lith-
ographing on metal

(G-168)
BERG EAST IMPORTS INC
Also Called: Berg Furniture USA
120 E Gloucester Pike (08007-1330)
PHONE...................................908 354-5252
Aharon Lieber, *President*
Almot Liber, *President*
Gideon Adler, *Treasurer*
Larry Newman, *Accounts Mgr*
▲ EMP: 76
SQ FT: 144,000
SALES (est): 7.3MM **Privately Held**
SIC: 2511 5021 Juvenile furniture: wood;
juvenile furniture

(G-169)
COOPER BURIAL VAULTS CO
621 Atlantic Ave (08007-1108)
PHONE...................................856 547-8405
Paul Cooper, *President*
Joanne Cooper, *Treasurer*
EMP: 9 EST: 1977
SQ FT: 12,000

GEOGRAPHIC

SALES (est): 1.5MM **Privately Held**
SIC: 3272 Burial vaults, concrete or pre-cast terrazzo

(G-170)
COOPER-WILBERT VAULT CO INC (PA)
621 Atlantic Ave (08007-1108)
PHONE.................................856 547-8405
Paul E Cooper, *President*
Joanne D Cooper, *Corp Secy*
Florence Cooper, *Admin Sec*
EMP: 20
SQ FT: 12,000
SALES (est): 4.5MM **Privately Held**
SIC: 3272 Burial vaults, concrete or pre-cast terrazzo

(G-171)
DERMATOLOGICAL SOC OF NJ INC
208 White Horse Pike (08007-1322)
PHONE.................................856 546-5600
Trsr Kerri Hollis, *Principal*
EMP: 4
SALES: 83.4K **Privately Held**
SIC: 2834 Dermatologicals

(G-172)
EDMUND OPTICS INC (PA)
Also Called: Edmund Scientific Co
101 E Gloucester Pike (08007-1331)
PHONE.................................856 547-3488
Robert Edmund, *CEO*
Paula Bao, *Prdtn Mgr*
Jim Bride, *Buyer*
Shunying Husted, *Buyer*
Laurie A Lund, *Buyer*
◆ **EMP:** 220 **EST:** 1942
SQ FT: 96,000
SALES (est): 144.4MM **Privately Held**
WEB: www.edsci.com
SIC: 3211 5961 Flat glass; catalog sales

(G-173)
INTERNATIONAL PAPER COMPANY
100 E Gloucester Pike (08007-1330)
PHONE.................................856 546-7000
Andy Fescoe, *Manager*
EMP: 185
SALES (corp-wide): 23.3B **Publicly Held**
WEB: www.internationalpaper.com
SIC: 2621 Paper mills
PA: International Paper Company
6400 Poplar Ave
Memphis TN 38197
901 419-9000

(G-174)
ISCO
1 Commerce Dr Bldg 3 (08007-1515)
PHONE.................................856 672-9182
Aaron Snethen, *Manager*
EMP: 4
SALES (est): 449.6K **Privately Held**
SIC: 2448 Wood pallets & skids

Basking Ridge
Somerset County

(G-175)
ARLA FOODS INGREDIENTS N AMER
106 Allen Rd Ste 401 (07920-3851)
PHONE.................................908 604-8551
Jasan Jensen, *President*
EMP: 10
SQ FT: 1,000
SALES (est): 1MM
SALES (corp-wide): 11.9B **Privately Held**
SIC: 2023 5149 Dried & powdered milk & milk products; concentrated whey; milk, canned or dried
HQ: Arla Foods Ingredients Group P/S
Sonderhoj 10-12
Viby 8260
961 377-73

(G-176)
BDIPLUS INC
26 Liberty Ridge Rd (07920-2972)
PHONE.................................347 597-2539
Ravi Arasan, *Principal*
EMP: 5
SALES (est): 275.2K **Privately Held**
SIC: 7372 Prepackaged software

(G-177)
CALADRIUS BIOSCIENCES INC (PA)
110 Allen Rd Ste 2 (07920-4500)
PHONE.................................908 842-0100
Gregory B Brown, *Ch of Bd*
David J Mazzo, *President*
Todd C Girolamo, *Senior VP*
Joseph Talamo, *CFO*
Douglas Losordo, *Chief Mktg Ofcr*
EMP: 22
SQ FT: 11,600
SALES (est): 2.6MM **Publicly Held**
WEB: www.cornichegroup.com
SIC: 2834 8731 Pharmaceutical preparations; biological research

(G-178)
CAMBRIDGE INDUSTRIES GROUP
4 Raritan Pl (07920-4227)
PHONE.................................917 669-7337
Hong Bi, *Sales Dir*
Iris Wong, *Officer*
EMP: 4 **EST:** 2017
SALES (est): 317.7K **Privately Held**
SIC: 3674 Semiconductors & related devices

(G-179)
CELGENE CORPORATION
106 Allen Rd (07920-3851)
PHONE.................................908 673-9000
Joseph Macowski, *Buyer*
Sol J Barer, *Branch Mgr*
Julie Mathew, *Manager*
Helen Liu, *Prgrmr*
Suzette Dowling, *Director*
EMP: 5
SALES (corp-wide): 15.2B **Publicly Held**
SIC: 2834 Pharmaceutical preparations
PA: Celgene Corporation
86 Morris Ave
Summit NJ 07901
908 673-9000

(G-180)
DAIICHI SANKYO INC
Also Called: Sankyo U S A
211 Mount Airy Rd (07920-2311)
PHONE.................................908 992-6400
Glenn Gormley, *President*
EMP: 15 **Privately Held**
WEB: www.benicar.com
SIC: 2834 Pharmaceutical preparations
HQ: Daiichi Sankyo, Inc.
211 Mount Airy Rd
Basking Ridge NJ 07920
908 992-6400

(G-181)
DEVCO CORPORATION
131 Morristown Rd Bldg B (07920-1654)
PHONE.................................201 337-1600
Bill E Durnan Jr, *Principal*
Dondi Rust, *Research*
Mackay Lindsay, *Financial Analy*
Samantha Dluoik, *Accounts Exec*
Julia Ballou, *Pub Rel Staff*
EMP: 7 **EST:** 1963
SALES (est): 1.6MM **Privately Held**
SIC: 3569 Lubrication equipment, industrial

(G-182)
ELECTROCORE INC
150 Allen Rd Ste 201 (07920-2977)
PHONE.................................973 290-0097
Daniel S Goldberger, *CEO*
Carrie S Cox, *Ch of Bd*
Eric J Liebler, *Senior VP*
Frank Amato, *Vice Pres*
Dan Duhart, *Vice Pres*
EMP: 64
SALES: 992.9K **Privately Held**
SIC: 3845 Electromedical equipment

(G-183)
FOUNDATION FOR EMBRYONIC
Also Called: FAEEC
140 Allen Rd (07920-2976)
PHONE.................................973 656-2847
Richard Scott, *President*
David Sharpell, *Controller*
Rebekah Zimmerman, *Director*
EMP: 4 **EST:** 2013
SQ FT: 1,500
SALES (est): 9.6MM **Privately Held**
SIC: 2835 In vitro diagnostics

(G-184)
FROZEN FALLS LLC
413 King Gorge Rd Ste 202 (07920)
PHONE.................................908 350-3939
EMP: 4
SALES (est): 278.2K **Privately Held**
SIC: 2026 Yogurt

(G-185)
GRONIGER USA LLC
180 Mount Airy Rd (07920-2065)
PHONE.................................704 588-3873
Horst Groninger, *President*
EMP: 4 **EST:** 2004
SALES (est): 240.6K **Privately Held**
SIC: 3565 Packaging machinery

(G-186)
INVENTIV HEALTH CLINICAL LLC (DH)
131 Morristown Rd (07920-1654)
PHONE.................................973 348-1000
EMP: 5 **EST:** 2010
SALES (est): 671.2K **Privately Held**
SIC: 2834 Mfg Pharmaceutical Preparations
HQ: Inventiv Health, Inc.
1 Van De Graaff Dr
Burlington MA 02210
800 416-0555

(G-187)
LEXICON PHARMACEUTICALS INC
110 Allen Rd Ste 3 (07920-4500)
P.O. Box 132167, The Woodlands TX (77393-2167)
PHONE.................................609 466-5500
Suman Wason, *Vice Pres*
Tim Bingham, *Manager*
EMP: 12 **Publicly Held**
WEB: www.lexgen.com
SIC: 2834 Pharmaceutical preparations
PA: Lexicon Pharmaceuticals, Inc.
8800 Technology Forest Pl
The Woodlands TX 77381

(G-188)
M/C COMMUNICATIONS LLC
Also Called: Physician's Weekly
180 Mount Airy Rd Ste 205 (07920-2064)
PHONE.................................908 766-0402
Clay Romweber, *Branch Mgr*
EMP: 15
SALES (corp-wide): 9.6MM **Privately Held**
SIC: 2741 Art copy & poster publishing
PA: M/C Communications, Llc
180 Mount Airy Rd Ste 102
Basking Ridge NJ 07920
908 766-0402

(G-189)
MATHESON TRI-GAS INC (DH)
150 Allen Rd Ste 302 (07920-2977)
PHONE.................................908 991-9200
Scott Kallman, *Ch of Bd*
Mike Sinicropi, *President*
Keith Spencer, *General Mgr*
Paul Strange, *General Mgr*
Steve Foster, *Exec VP*
◆ **EMP:** 70
SQ FT: 50,000
SALES: 1.8B **Privately Held**
WEB: www.matheson-trigas.com
SIC: 2813 5084 Industrial gases; nitrogen; oxygen, compressed or liquefied; argon; welding machinery & equipment; safety equipment

(G-190)
MATHESON TRI-GAS INC
Also Called: Matheson Gas Products
150 Allen Rd Ste 301 (07920-2977)
PHONE.................................908 991-9200
Rita Peters, *Purch Mgr*
Chad Williams, *Sales Staff*
Joseph Barnett, *Branch Mgr*
Grant Boice, *Software Dev*
EMP: 30
SQ FT: 14,355 **Privately Held**
WEB: www.matheson-trigas.com
SIC: 2813 5084 Industrial gases; welding machinery & equipment
HQ: Matheson Tri-Gas, Inc.
150 Allen Rd Ste 302
Basking Ridge NJ 07920
908 991-9200

(G-191)
MICROSEMI STOR SOLUTIONS INC
180 Mount Airy Rd (07920-2065)
PHONE.................................908 953-9400
Cheri Russell, *Branch Mgr*
EMP: 5
SALES (corp-wide): 5.3B **Publicly Held**
SIC: 3674 Modules, solid state
HQ: Microsemi Storage Solutions, Inc.
1380 Bordeaux Dr
Sunnyvale CA 94089
408 239-8000

(G-192)
MILLINGTON QUARRY INC
135 Stonehouse Rd (07920-2630)
P.O. Box 367, Millington (07946-0367)
PHONE.................................908 542-0055
Gary A Mahan, *President*
EMP: 100
SQ FT: 3,000
SALES (est): 5.6MM **Privately Held**
SIC: 1429 Trap rock, crushed & broken-quarrying

(G-193)
NOGPO INC
4 Patriot Hill Dr (07920-4214)
PHONE.................................908 642-3545
Ashok Muttin, *CEO*
Rakesh Hate, *Shareholder*
Hot Marlin, *Shareholder*
Dan Stark, *Shareholder*
EMP: 10 **EST:** 2013
SALES (est): 547.4K **Privately Held**
SIC: 7372 Business oriented computer software

(G-194)
ONCODE-MED INC
11 Georgetown Ct (07920-4243)
PHONE.................................908 998-3647
Rongshan LI, *President*
EMP: 6
SALES (est): 227.2K **Privately Held**
SIC: 8071 3841 7389 Pathological laboratory; hypodermic needles & syringes;

(G-195)
PHYSICIANS WEEKLY LLC (HQ)
180 Mount Airy Rd Ste 205 (07920-2064)
PHONE.................................908 766-0421
Ezra Ernst, *President*
Rachel Ciufo, *COO*
Kelly Matthews, *Opers Staff*
Janine Anthes, *Manager*
Amy Johnson, *Manager*
EMP: 9
SALES: 5MM
SALES (corp-wide): 9.6MM **Privately Held**
SIC: 2741 Art copy & poster publishing
PA: M/C Communications, Llc
180 Mount Airy Rd Ste 102
Basking Ridge NJ 07920
908 766-0402

(G-196)
REGADO BIOSCIENCES INC
106 Allen Rd Ste 401 (07920-3851)
PHONE.................................908 580-2109
EMP: 7
SALES (est): 602.7K **Privately Held**
SIC: 2834 Mfg Pharmaceutical Preparations

(G-197)
SIBI DISTRIBUTORS
1370 Meiners Dr (07920-3540)
PHONE....................................908 658-4448
Joseph Jibis, *Principal*
EMP: 4
SALES (est): 189.4K **Privately Held**
SIC: 2051 Bread, cake & related products

(G-198)
SQUIRE CORRUGATED CONT CORP
110 Allen Rd Ste 3 (07920-4500)
PHONE....................................908 862-9111
James Beneroff, *President*
Elliot Beneroff, *Corp Secy*
Richard Beneroff, *Corp Secy*
Juliana Kearney, *Manager*
Tina Wright, *Manager*
EMP: 95
SQ FT: 30,000
SALES (est): 20.2MM **Privately Held**
WEB: www.squirebox.com
SIC: 2653 Boxes, corrugated: made from purchased materials

(G-199)
TORRENT PHARMA INC (DH)
150 Allen Rd Ste 102 (07920-3856)
PHONE....................................269 544-2299
Sanjay Gupta, *CEO*
Kamesh Venugopal, *President*
Dawn Chitty, *Vice Pres*
Amit Shah, *Vice Pres*
Chip McCorkle, *Director*
EMP: 30
SQ FT: 2,000
SALES (est): 98.8MM **Privately Held**
WEB: www.torrentpharma.com
SIC: 2834 Pharmaceutical preparations
HQ: Torrent Pharmaceuticals Limited
Torrent House, Off Ashram Road,
Ahmedabad GJ 38000
792 659-9000

Bay Head
Ocean County

(G-200)
SHORE BET PAINTING AND CNSTR
102 Osborne Ave (08742-4619)
P.O. Box 235 (08742-0235)
PHONE....................................732 996-3455
Jeff Belleth, *Owner*
EMP: 4
SALES (est): 385.9K **Privately Held**
SIC: 3479 Painting, coating & hot dipping

Bayonne
Hudson County

(G-201)
AL RICHRDS HOMEMADE CHOCOLATES
851 Broadway (07002-3018)
PHONE....................................201 436-0915
Alfred Stancampiano, *President*
Richard Stancampiano, *Treasurer*
EMP: 10
SQ FT: 6,000
SALES (est): 847K **Privately Held**
WEB: www.alrichardschocolates.com
SIC: 2064 Chocolate candy, except solid chocolate; licorice candy

(G-202)
AP&G CO INC
Also Called: Catchmaster
75 E 2nd St (07002-4255)
PHONE....................................718 492-3648
Steven Frisch, *Ch of Bd*
Ilona Frisch, *President*
Rick McDonald, *COO*
Jonathan Frisch, *Vice Pres*
Irv Burger, *Controller*
◆ EMP: 80

SALES (est): 28.9MM **Privately Held**
WEB: www.catchmaster.com
SIC: 2879 Pesticides, agricultural or household

(G-203)
AUBREY DAVID INC
260 Broadway Ste 1 (07002-2583)
PHONE....................................201 653-2200
Jennifer Arago, *President*
Vj Curtis, *Admin Dir*
▲ EMP: 20 EST: 1995
SALES (est): 2.4MM **Privately Held**
WEB: www.aubreydavid.com
SIC: 3911 5944 Jewelry, precious metal; jewelry stores

(G-204)
BASHA USA LLC
390 Broadway (07002-3624)
PHONE....................................201 339-9770
Akram Dadros, *President*
EMP: 6
SALES (est): 779K **Privately Held**
SIC: 3556 Smokers, food processing equipment

(G-205)
BAYONNE COMMUNITY NEWS
447 Broadway (07002-3623)
PHONE....................................201 437-2460
Lusha Malato, *President*
EMP: 22
SQ FT: 1,600
SALES (est): 991.2K **Privately Held**
SIC: 2711 Newspapers: publishing only, not printed on site

(G-206)
BAYONNE DRYDOCK & REPAIR CORP
Also Called: Bdd
100 Military Ocean Trml (07002)
PHONE....................................201 823-9295
Micheal Cranston, *President*
Kevin Sullivan, *General Mgr*
Mike Dimesa, *Superintendent*
Melanie Lopez, *Purchasing*
Eddie Jordan, *Human Resources*
▲ EMP: 20 EST: 1997
SALES (est): 6.7MM **Privately Held**
WEB: www.bayonnedrydock.com
SIC: 3731 4491 Shipbuilding & repairing; marine cargo handling

(G-207)
BOOKAZINE CO INC (PA)
75 Hook Rd (07002-5006)
PHONE....................................201 339-7777
Robert Kallman, *CEO*
Irwin Kallman, *Ch of Bd*
Richard Kallman, *Vice Pres*
Larry Usdin, *CFO*
Harold Axelrod, *Controller*
◆ EMP: 86
SQ FT: 125,000
SALES (est): 458.3MM **Privately Held**
SIC: 5192 2741 Books; catalogs: publishing only, not printed on site

(G-208)
CEJON INC
53 Hook Rd (07002-5061)
PHONE....................................201 437-8780
▲ EMP: 23
SQ FT: 11,000
SALES (est): 1.6MM **Publicly Held**
SIC: 3111 5137 Leather Tanning/Finishing Whol Women's/Child's Clothing
PA: Steven Madden, Ltd.
5216 Barnett Ave
Long Island City NY 11104

(G-209)
CLARK STEK-O CORP
148 E 5th St (07002-4252)
PHONE....................................201 437-0770
Jim Norton, *President*
Robert Bergfield, *Vice Pres*
Charles Lee Jr, *Treasurer*
EMP: 100 EST: 1898
SQ FT: 100,000
SALES (est): 8.5MM **Privately Held**
SIC: 2891 Adhesives & sealants

(G-210)
CLAYTON BLOCK COMPANY LLC (HQ)
440 Hook Rd (07002-5026)
PHONE....................................201 339-8585
William Clayton Jr,
Daniel Clayton,
Douglas Clayton,
EMP: 35 EST: 1919
SQ FT: 35,000
SALES (est): 7.2MM
SALES (corp-wide): 31.8MM **Privately Held**
SIC: 3271 3272 Concrete block & brick; concrete products, precast
PA: Clayton Block Company, Inc.
1355 Campus Pkwy Ste 200
Wall Township NJ 07753
888 763-8665

(G-211)
CNS CONFECTIONERY PRODUCTS LLC
33 Hook Rd (07002-5006)
PHONE....................................201 823-1400
Eva Deutsch, *President*
Mirim Gross, *Principal*
Carol Ranier, *Finance Mgr*
▲ EMP: 12
SQ FT: 45,000
SALES (est): 2.4MM **Privately Held**
SIC: 2064 2068 5149 5145 Fruit & fruit peel confections; salted & roasted nuts & seeds; nuts: dried, dehydrated, salted or roasted; seeds: dried, dehydrated, salted or roasted; milk, canned or dried; nuts, salted or roasted; bakery equipment & supplies

(G-212)
CONTROL INDUSTRIES INC (PA)
Also Called: Control Demolition
197 E 22nd St Ste 4 (07002-5062)
PHONE....................................201 437-3826
Donna Bubnis, *President*
Robert Bubnis, *Vice Pres*
EMP: 2
SALES (est): 1.2MM **Privately Held**
SIC: 1794 1442 1795 Excavation work; construction sand & gravel; concrete breaking for streets & highways; demolition, buildings & other structures; dismantling steel oil tanks

(G-213)
DEE & L LLC
67 Lefante Dr (07002-5024)
P.O. Box 3431 (07002-0288)
PHONE....................................201 858-0138
Morris Helfgott, *COO*
David Herzog, *Mng Member*
▼ EMP: 15
SQ FT: 25,000
SALES (est): 3.1MM **Privately Held**
SIC: 2035 Mayonnaise

(G-214)
DUNBAR SALES COMPANY INC
Also Called: Steven's Dunbar Companies
39 Avenue C Ste 1 (07002-5403)
P.O. Box 8 (07002-0008)
PHONE....................................201 437-6500
William Rubenstein, *President*
EMP: 7
SALES: 3MM **Privately Held**
SIC: 2851 Paints & allied products

(G-215)
EUROPEAN AMRCN FOODS GROUP INC (PA)
Also Called: Euro American Foods Group
698 Kennedy Blvd (07002-2767)
PHONE....................................201 436-6106
Antonio R Fasolino, *President*
Joseph T Gianasio, *CFO*
▲ EMP: 24
SQ FT: 50,000
SALES (est): 33.1MM **Privately Held**
SIC: 2099 2079 2033 Pasta, uncooked: packaged with other ingredients; edible oil products, except corn oil; seasonings; tomato: packaged in cans, jars, etc.; tomato products: packaged in cans, jars, etc.

(G-216)
FLORTEK CORPORATION
39 W 55th St (07002-4112)
PHONE....................................201 436-7700
Warren S Harris, *President*
EMP: 25
SQ FT: 40,000
SALES (est): 7.3MM **Privately Held**
SIC: 2752 2782 Cards, lithographed; looseleaf binders & devices

(G-217)
FLUITEC INTERNATIONAL LLC
179 W 5th St (07002-1102)
PHONE....................................201 946-4584
Frank Magnotti, *CEO*
Andre Annicq, *Chairman*
Simon Bard, *Vice Pres*
April Pannell, *Controller*
Darin Carfaro, *Regl Sales Mgr*
EMP: 4
SALES (est): 1.1MM **Privately Held**
WEB: www.fluitec.com
SIC: 3829 5084 Physical property testing equipment; industrial machinery & equipment

(G-218)
GEL SPICE CO INC (PA)
48 Hook Rd (07002-5007)
P.O. Box 285 (07002-0285)
PHONE....................................201 339-0700
Andre Engel, *President*
John Castrataro, *Senior VP*
Steve Thomas, *Senior VP*
Sherman Engel, *Vice Pres*
Joe Mandel, *Vice Pres*
◆ EMP: 275
SQ FT: 184,000
SALES (est): 74.5MM **Privately Held**
WEB: www.gel-spice.com
SIC: 2099 5149 Spices, including grinding; spices & seasonings

(G-219)
GEL SPICE CO LLC
48 Hook Rd (07002-5007)
P.O. Box 285 (07002-0285)
PHONE....................................201 339-0700
Gershon Engel, *Senior VP*
EMP: 250
SQ FT: 150,000
SALES (est): 130MM **Privately Held**
SIC: 2099 Seasonings & spices

(G-220)
GORDON TERMINAL SERVICE CO PA
Also Called: Gordon Terminal Service Co. NJ
2 Hook Rd (07002-5007)
P.O. Box 143 (07002-0143)
PHONE....................................201 437-8300
Thomas Gordon, *Branch Mgr*
Jim Zago, *Manager*
EMP: 100
SALES (corp-wide): 33.9MM **Privately Held**
WEB: www.gtscofnj.com
SIC: 4225 7389 2992 General warehousing; packaging & labeling services; lubricating oils & greases
PA: Gordon Terminal Service Co. Of Pa.
1000 Ella St
Mckees Rocks PA 15136
412 331-9410

(G-221)
GP WINE WORKS LLC
Also Called: Gotham Project
82 E 3rd St (07002-4294)
PHONE....................................201 997-6055
Bruce Schneider,
Charles Bieler,
EMP: 4 EST: 2012
SALES (est): 258.7K **Privately Held**
SIC: 2084 Wines

(G-222)
HENRY RAC HOLDING CORP
Also Called: Henry Repeating Arms Company
59 E 1st St (07002-4256)
PHONE....................................201 858-4400
Anthony Imperato, *President*
▲ EMP: 85
SQ FT: 31,000

SALES (est): 13.6MM **Privately Held**
WEB: www.henryrepeating.com
SIC: 5941 3484 Firearms; rifles or rifle
   parts, 30 mm. & below

(G-223)
HUDSON AWNING CO INC
Also Called: Hudson Awning & Sign Co
27 Cottage St (07002-4334)
PHONE..............................201 339-7171
   Edward Burak, *President*
   Lynda Burak, *Vice Pres*
EMP: 30 **EST:** 1881
SQ FT: 6,000
SALES (est): 3.3MM **Privately Held**
WEB: www.hudsonawning.com
SIC: 2394 3444 Canopies, fabric: made
   from purchased materials; awnings, sheet
   metal

(G-224)
IN-LINE SHTMTL FABRICATORS
85 E 21st St (07002-4533)
PHONE..............................201 339-8121
   Miguel Gutierrez, *President*
   Dorthy Gutierrez, *Vice Pres*
   Matt Dorans, *Treasurer*
   Robert Dorans, *Admin Sec*
EMP: 7
SQ FT: 4,000
SALES (est): 599.4K **Privately Held**
SIC: 1711 1761 3444 Warm air heating &
   air conditioning contractor; ventilation &
   duct work contractor; sheet metalwork;
   sheet metalwork

(G-225)
JERHEL PLASTICS INC
63 Hook Rd (07002-5004)
PHONE..............................201 436-6662
   Leonard Mecca, *President*
   Peggy Mecca, *Treasurer*
   Helen Mecca, *Admin Sec*
◆ **EMP:** 8
SQ FT: 10,000
SALES (est): 2MM **Privately Held**
WEB: www.jerhel.net
SIC: 3089 Plastic containers, except foam

(G-226)
KENRICH PETROCHEMICALS
INC (PA)
570 Broadway (07002-4280)
P.O. Box 32 (07002-0032)
PHONE..............................201 823-9000
   Salvatore J Monte, *President*
   Eric Monte, *President*
   Charles A Lucania, *Vice Pres*
   Erika G Monte, *Vice Pres*
   Michelle Monte, *Vice Pres*
▲ **EMP:** 30 **EST:** 1945
SQ FT: 67,700
SALES (est): 2.6MM **Privately Held**
SIC: 2869 Plasticizers, organic: cyclic &
   acyclic

(G-227)
LAFARGE NORTH AMERICA INC
6 Commerce St (07002-5019)
P.O. Box 273 (07002-0273)
PHONE..............................201 437-2575
   Cliff Stripling, *Branch Mgr*
EMP: 6
SALES (corp-wide): 27.6B **Privately Held**
WEB: www.lafargenorthamerica.com
SIC: 3241 Cement, hydraulic
HQ: Lafarge North America Inc.
   8700 W Bryn Mawr Ave
   Chicago IL 60631
   773 372-1000

(G-228)
M & RS MILLER AUTO GEAR &
PRT
Also Called: Miller Auto Parts
699 Kennedy Blvd (07002-2713)
PHONE..............................201 339-2270
   Mario Protocollo, *President*
   Rosalea Protocollo, *Vice Pres*
EMP: 11
SQ FT: 8,500
SALES (est): 1MM **Privately Held**
SIC: 5013 5531 3599 Automotive sup-
   plies & parts; automotive supplies; auto-
   motive accessories; automotive parts;
   machine shop, jobbing & repair

(G-229)
MURALO COMPANY INC (PA)
Also Called: Elder & Jenks Co Div
148 E 5th St (07002-4252)
PHONE..............................201 437-0770
   James S Norton, *President*
   Edward Norton III, *Vice Pres*
   Shashi Patel, *Vice Pres*
   Peter Seaborg, *Vice Pres*
   Chuck Lee Jr, *CFO*
◆ **EMP:** 180 **EST:** 1924
SQ FT: 350,000
SALES (est): 34.7MM **Privately Held**
WEB: www.muralo.com
SIC: 2851 Paints & allied products

(G-230)
P D Q PLASTICS INC
7 Hook Rd (07002-5006)
P.O. Box 1001 (07002-1001)
PHONE..............................201 823-0270
   Barry Nathans, *President*
EMP: 20 **EST:** 1969
SQ FT: 50,000
SALES (est): 3.5MM **Privately Held**
WEB: www.pdqplastics.com
SIC: 3089 Pallets, plastic

(G-231)
PRIMETIME TRADING CORP
148 E 5th St (07002-4252)
PHONE..............................646 580-8223
   Moses Steinberg, *CEO*
▲ **EMP:** 22
SQ FT: 15,000
SALES: 4.5MM **Privately Held**
SIC: 3944 5023 Games, toys & children's
   vehicles; kitchenware

(G-232)
PRINCE CHIKOVANI INC
Also Called: Prince-Chikovani
363 Avenue A Fl 1 (07002-1329)
PHONE..............................347 622-2789
   David Kavleli, *President*
   Malkhaz Ramishvili, *Vice Pres*
EMP: 5 **EST:** 2014
SQ FT: 2,000
SALES (est): 233.6K **Privately Held**
SIC: 2099 Food preparations

(G-233)
ROYAL WINE CORPORATION
(PA)
Also Called: Baron Herzog
63 Lefante Dr (07002-5024)
PHONE..............................718 384-2400
   David Herzog, *Ch of Bd*
   ARI Cinner, *General Mgr*
   Nathan Herzog, *Exec VP*
   Mordechai Herzog, *Senior VP*
   Phillip Herzog, *Senior VP*
◆ **EMP:** 110 **EST:** 1948
SQ FT: 184,000
SALES (est): 44MM **Privately Held**
SIC: 2084 5182 Wines; wine; liquor

(G-234)
ROYAL WINE CORPORATION
Also Called: Hks Marketing
63 Lefante Dr (07002-5024)
PHONE..............................201 535-9006
   David Herzog, *Branch Mgr*
EMP: 110
SALES (corp-wide): 44MM **Privately Held**
SIC: 2084 5182 Wines; wine; liquor
PA: Royal Wine Corporation
   63 Lefante Dr
   Bayonne NJ 07002
   718 384-2400

(G-235)
STEVEN INDUSTRIES INC
39 Avenue C Ste 1 (07002-5403)
P.O. Box 8 (07002-0008)
PHONE..............................201 437-6500
   Stephen Rubenstein, *President*
   William Rubenstein, *Vice Pres*
EMP: 25
SQ FT: 200,000
SALES (est): 3.5MM **Privately Held**
WEB: www.rubensteinprop.com
SIC: 5198 2891 2851 Paints; adhesives;
   paints & allied products

(G-236)
UNITED MEDICAL PC (PA)
988 Broadway (07002-4036)
PHONE..............................201 339-6111
   Arnold M Alday, *Principal*
   Randa M Hamadeh, *Principal*
   Marwa Hazzah, *Principal*
   Mark A Hoffman, *Principal*
EMP: 12 **EST:** 1996
SALES (est): 4.3MM **Privately Held**
SIC: 3841 8011 Diagnostic apparatus,
   medical; internal medicine practitioners;
   cardiologist & cardio-vascular specialist

(G-237)
XSTATIC PRO INC
Proxcases
55 Hook Rd 46 (07002-5006)
PHONE..............................718 237-2299
   Gabriel Menashe, *Branch Mgr*
EMP: 13
SALES (corp-wide): 1.3MM **Privately
Held**
SIC: 3161 Musical instrument cases
PA: Xstatic Pro, Inc.
   55 Hook Rd 46
   Bayonne NJ 07002
   718 237-2299

┌─────────────────────────────┐
│   **Bayville**   │
│   *Ocean County*   │
└─────────────────────────────┘

(G-238)
ACE-CRETE PRODUCTS INC
Also Called: New Jersey Polverizing
250 Hickory Ln (08721-2115)
PHONE..............................732 269-1400
   Nick Grippaldi, *Manager*
EMP: 12
SALES (corp-wide): 1.3MM **Privately
Held**
SIC: 3273 Ready-mixed concrete
PA: Ace-Crete Products Inc
   4 Rita St
   Syosset NY 11791
   516 921-9595

(G-239)
AMERICAN CUSTOM
FABRICATORS
Also Called: A C F
215 Hickory Ln Ste A (08721-2114)
PHONE..............................732 237-0037
   Robert Schinder, *President*
   Jacqueline Schinder, *Admin Sec*
EMP: 8
SQ FT: 3,500
SALES (est): 1.2MM **Privately Held**
WEB: www.acfmarine.com
SIC: 3355 Rails, rolled & drawn, aluminum

(G-240)
ATLANTIC COASTAL WELDING
INC
16 Butler Blvd (08721-3002)
PHONE..............................732 269-1088
   John Gallo, *President*
   John J Gallo, *President*
EMP: 10
SQ FT: 6,000
SALES (est): 1.4MM **Privately Held**
SIC: 3599 3444 Machine shop, jobbing &
   repair; sheet metalwork

(G-241)
B AND G MUSIC LLC
2 Teal Pl (08721-1620)
PHONE..............................732 779-4555
   Rebecca Barbera,
   Gerard McKittrick,
EMP: 5
SALES: 20K **Privately Held**
SIC: 3651 Music distribution apparatus

(G-242)
CC PACKAGING LLC (PA)
93 Storm Jib Ct (08721-1417)
P.O. Box 170 (08721-0170)
PHONE..............................732 213-9008
   George Cannan Jr, *Exec VP*
   Caroline Costante, *Vice Pres*
   Steven Zaccaro, *Plant Mgr*
◆ **EMP:** 8 **EST:** 2008

SALES (est): 940.6K **Privately Held**
SIC: 2899 Chemical preparations

(G-243)
E-TEC MARINE PRODUCTS INC
245 Hickory Ln (08721-2253)
PHONE..............................732 269-0442
   Allen Thomas, *Manager*
EMP: 5
SALES (corp-wide): 4.2MM **Privately
Held**
WEB: www.etecmarine.com
SIC: 3354 Aluminum extruded products
PA: E-Tec Marine Products, Inc.
   7555 Garden Rd Ste B
   West Palm Beach FL
   561 848-8351

(G-244)
EMPIRE BLENDED PRODUCTS
INC
Also Called: Empire Blended Distributors
250 Hickory Ln (08721-2115)
PHONE..............................732 269-4949
   Jay Gornitzky, *President*
   Martin Tanzer, *Vice Pres*
   Rick Dufresne, *Sales Staff*
▼ **EMP:** 25
SQ FT: 70,000
SALES (est): 9.6MM **Privately Held**
WEB: www.empireblended.com
SIC: 3272 Concrete products, precast

(G-245)
GREENER CORP (PA)
4 Helmly St (08721-2188)
PHONE..............................732 341-3880
   Theodore M Wojtech, *President*
   Matthew D Wojtech, *Vice Pres*
   Susan Tyler, *Opers Staff*
   Bruce Cowper, *Technology*
   Jason Dwulet, *Technical Staff*
EMP: 30 **EST:** 1964
SQ FT: 10,000
SALES (est): 4.5MM **Privately Held**
WEB: www.greenercorp.com
SIC: 3565 Packaging machinery

(G-246)
HENRIQUES YACHTS WORKS
198 Hilton Ave (08721-2136)
PHONE..............................732 269-1180
   Natalia Henriquescosta, *President*
   Natalia Henriques-Costa, *President*
   Maria Henriques-Demers, *Vice Pres*
EMP: 6
SQ FT: 28,000
SALES (est): 1.3MM **Privately Held**
WEB: www.integritymarine.com
SIC: 3732 Boats, fiberglass: building & re-
   pairing

(G-247)
MACHINERY ELECTRICS
904 Main St (08721-2231)
PHONE..............................732 536-0600
   Joseph D'Arpa, *Owner*
EMP: 5
SQ FT: 2,000
SALES: 300K **Privately Held**
WEB: www.machineryelectrics.com
SIC: 3613 5084 Control panels, electric;
   industrial machinery & equipment

(G-248)
MOSSE BEVERAGE INDUSTRIES
LLC
15 Osprey Ln (08721-2061)
PHONE..............................732 977-5558
   Viktoria Peraze, *Mng Member*
EMP: 6
SQ FT: 2,200
SALES: 136K **Privately Held**
SIC: 2086 Fruit drinks (less than 100%
   juice): packaged in cans, etc.

(G-249)
NEW JERSEY PULVERIZING CO
INC
Also Called: Ace Crete Product
250 Hickory Ln (08721-2115)
PHONE..............................732 269-1400
   Nick Grippaldi, *Manager*
EMP: 14

SALES (corp-wide): 2.8MM **Privately Held**
SIC: **1442** 3273 1446 Common sand mining; ready-mixed concrete; industrial sand
PA: New Jersey Pulverizing Co Inc
4 Rita St
Syosset NY 11791
516 921-9595

(G-250)
PLASTASONICS INC
235 Hickory Ln Ste B (08721-2254)
PHONE...........................732 998-8361
Fred Lietz, *President*
Gary Kuskin, *Vice Pres*
Debbie Kuskin, *Treasurer*
Betty Lietz, *Admin Sec*
EMP: 14
SQ FT: 3,500
SALES: 2.5MM **Privately Held**
SIC: **3089** Molding primary plastic; injection molding of plastics

(G-251)
TOWER SYSTEMS INC
Also Called: Atlantic Towers
235 Hickory Ln (08721-2254)
P.O. Box D (08721-0289)
PHONE...........................732 237-8800
Steve Tull, *President*
Shelley Golden, *Vice Pres*
▼ **EMP:** 4
SALES (est): 813.1K **Privately Held**
WEB: www.atlantictowers.com
SIC: **3339** Primary nonferrous metals

(G-252)
TREK INC
43 Cranmer Rd (08721-1713)
P.O. Box 275 (08721-0275)
PHONE...........................732 269-6300
John J Dynarski, *President*
Joyce Dynarski, *Admin Sec*
▲ **EMP:** 5
SALES (est): 724.6K **Privately Held**
WEB: www.treklabel.com
SIC: **2672** 8742 Labels (unprinted), gummed: made from purchased materials; management consulting services

(G-253)
WHEELS MOTOR SPORTS INC
13 Penny Ln (08721-1253)
PHONE...........................732 606-9208
Thomas Cleary Sr, *President*
EMP: 7
SALES: 4.1MM **Privately Held**
WEB: www.wheelsmotorsports.com
SIC: **3751** Motorcycles, bicycles & parts

(G-254)
ZONE TWO INC
245 Hickory Ln Ste 2 (08721-2253)
PHONE...........................732 237-0766
Rick Gettis, *President*
EMP: 12
SQ FT: 10,000
SALES: 700K **Privately Held**
SIC: **2759** 2396 Screen printing; automotive & apparel trimmings

---

Beach Haven
Ocean County

(G-255)
CRUST AND CRUMB BAKERY
800 N Bay Ave Ste 9 (08008-2008)
PHONE...........................609 492-4966
Lou Richards, *Owner*
Anne Richards, *Owner*
EMP: 4
SALES (est): 140K **Privately Held**
SIC: **2051** Bakery: wholesale or wholesale/retail combined

(G-256)
MOD HATTER
1103 N Bay Ave (08008-2110)
PHONE...........................609 492-0999
Vina Berman, *Owner*
EMP: 5
SALES (est): 506.8K **Privately Held**
SIC: **2353** Hats & caps

Beachwood
Ocean County

(G-257)
AUTOMATED TAPPING SYSTEMS INC
1110 Beach Ave (08722-2202)
P.O. Box 1033, Brick (08723-0106)
PHONE...........................732 899-2282
William R Pfister, *President*
Craig Wood, *Plant Supt*
EMP: 12
SQ FT: 1,800
SALES: 1.1MM **Privately Held**
WEB: www.automatedtappingsystems.com
SIC: **3545** 3541 Machine tool attachments & accessories; taps, machine tool; machine tools, metal cutting type

---

Bedminster
Somerset County

(G-258)
AERIE PHARMACEUTICALS INC
550 Hills Dr Ste 310 (07921-1537)
PHONE...........................908 470-4320
Kyle Vick, *Associate*
EMP: 54 **Publicly Held**
SIC: **2834** Pharmaceutical preparations
PA: Aerie Pharmaceuticals, Inc.
4301 Emperor Blvd Ste 400
Durham NC 27703

(G-259)
ALLERGAN INC
1 Crossroads Dr (07921-2688)
PHONE...........................908 306-0374
EMP: 51 **Privately Held**
SIC: **2834** Drugs acting on the central nervous system & sense organs
HQ: Allergan, Inc.
5 Giralda Farms
Madison NJ 07940
862 261-7000

(G-260)
AMARIN CORPORATION PLC
1430 Us Highway 206 # 100 (07921-4602)
PHONE...........................908 719-1315
Declan Doogan, *Principal*
Joseph T Kennedy, *Exec VP*
Craig B Granowitz, *Chief Mktg Ofcr*
Gwen Fisher, *VP Corp Comm*
Steven Ketchum, *Officer*
EMP: 29
SALES: 3.9MM **Privately Held**
SIC: **2834** Pharmaceutical preparations

(G-261)
AQUARIUS BIOTECHNOLOGIES INC
1545 Rte 206 S Ste 302 (07921)
PHONE...........................908 443-1860
Jerome Jabbour JD, *Exec VP*
George Bobotas PHD, *Exec VP*
Addel Fawzy PHD, *Exec VP*
Gary Gaglione, *CFO*
EMP: 5
SALES (est): 74.8K
SALES (corp-wide): 119.7K **Publicly Held**
SIC: **2834** Pharmaceutical preparations
PA: Matinas Biopharma Holdings, Inc.
1545 Route 206 Ste 302
Bedminster NJ 07921
908 443-1860

(G-262)
COMPUTER COMPANY NORTH AMERICA
356 Wren Ln (07921-1930)
PHONE...........................909 265-3390
Wendell Wilson, *Owner*
EMP: 12
SALES (est): 805.3K **Privately Held**
SIC: **5045** 3575 Computer peripheral equipment; computer terminals, monitors & components

(G-263)
EKR THERAPEUTICS INCORPORATED
1545 Us Highway 206 # 300 (07921-2560)
PHONE...........................877 435-2524
John E Bailye, *CEO*
Bill McKee, *COO*
Susan C Bacso, *VP Opers*
EMP: 102
SQ FT: 9,000
SALES (est): 9.8MM
SALES (corp-wide): 24.7K **Privately Held**
WEB: www.ekrtx.com
SIC: **2834** Druggists' preparations (pharmaceuticals)
HQ: Chiesi Usa, Inc.
175 Regency Woods Pl # 600
Cary NC 27518
919 678-6611

(G-264)
ETHICON INC
135 Us Highway 202 206 # 4 (07921-2608)
PHONE...........................908 306-0327
Darrell Chilton, *Branch Mgr*
EMP: 225
SALES (corp-wide): 81.5B **Publicly Held**
WEB: www.ethiconinc.com
SIC: **3842** Ligatures, medical
HQ: Ethicon Inc.
Us Route 22
Somerville NJ 08876
732 524-0400

(G-265)
ETHICON INC
Also Called: Ethicon Endo-Surgery
135 Us Highway 202 206 # 4 (07921-2608)
P.O. Box 16509, New Brunswick (08901)
PHONE...........................908 218-0707
Clifford Holland, *Branch Mgr*
EMP: 225
SALES (corp-wide): 81.5B **Publicly Held**
SIC: **3842** Ligatures, medical
HQ: Ethicon Inc.
Us Route 22
Somerville NJ 08876
732 524-0400

(G-266)
INO THERAPEUTICS LLC (DH)
1425 Us Route 206 (07921)
P.O. Box 9001, Hampton (08827-9001)
PHONE...........................908 238-6600
Eric Goodman, *Project Engr*
Elizabeth Larkin, *CFO*
Matthew Bennett, *Marketing Mgr*
Ravi Iyer, *Director*
Daniel Tasse,
◆ **EMP:** 63
SALES (est): 35MM **Privately Held**
SIC: **5122** 2834 Pharmaceuticals; pharmaceutical preparations
HQ: Therakos, Inc.
1425 Us Route 206
Bedminster NJ 07921
800 828-6316

(G-267)
KYOWA KIRIN INC
135 Rte 202 206 Ste 6 (07921)
PHONE...........................908 234-1096
Tom Stratford, *CEO*
Leonard Paolillo, *President*
Len Paolillo, *Vice Pres*
Allan Watson, *CFO*
Dawn Bazydlo, *Accounting Mgr*
EMP: 65 **EST:** 1998
SALES: 30MM **Privately Held**
SIC: **2834** Pharmaceutical preparations
HQ: Kyowa Kirin International Plc
Unit 16 Galabank Business Park
Galashiels TD1 1
189 666-4000

(G-268)
MALLINCKRODT ARD INC
Also Called: Mallinckrodt Pharmaceuticals
1425 Us Highway 206 (07921-2653)
PHONE...........................510 400-0700
Don M Bailey, *President*
EMP: 7 **Privately Held**
SIC: **2834** Pharmaceutical preparations

HQ: Mallinckrodt Ard Llc
1425 Us Highway 206
Bedminster NJ 07921
908 238-6600

(G-269)
MALLINCKRODT ARD LLC (HQ)
1425 Us Highway 206 (07921-2653)
PHONE...........................908 238-6600
Don M Bailey, *President*
David J Medeiros, *Exec VP*
Michael H Mulroy, *Exec VP*
Steven C Halladay, *Senior VP*
Eric J Liebler, *Senior VP*
EMP: 12
SALES (est): 82.7MM **Privately Held**
WEB: www.questcor.com
SIC: **2834** Pharmaceutical preparations

(G-270)
MALLINCKRODT HOSPITAL PDTS INC
1425 Us Route 206 (07921)
PHONE...........................908 238-6600
EMP: 4 **Privately Held**
SIC: **2834** Pharmaceutical preparations
HQ: Mallinckrodt Hospital Products Inc.
1425 Us Route 206
Bedminster NJ 07921
314 654-2000

(G-271)
MALLINCKRODT HOSPITAL PDTS INC (HQ)
1425 Us Route 206 (07921)
PHONE...........................314 654-2000
Kathleen A Schaefer, *President*
John E Einwalter, *Treasurer*
▲ **EMP:** 32
SALES (est): 42.1MM **Privately Held**
WEB: www.cadencepharm.com
SIC: **2834** Pharmaceutical preparations

(G-272)
MATINAS BIOPHARMA INC
1545 Route 206 Ste 302 (07921)
PHONE...........................908 443-1860
Addel Fawzy PHD, *Exec VP*
Jerome Jabbour JD, *Exec VP*
Gary Gaglione, *CFO*
Richard Samas, *Accountant*
Douglas Kling, *Executive*
EMP: 10
SQ FT: 5,500
SALES (est): 119.7K **Publicly Held**
SIC: **2833** Fish liver oils: refined or concentrated for medicinal use
PA: Matinas Biopharma Holdings, Inc.
1545 Route 206 Ste 302
Bedminster NJ 07921
908 443-1860

(G-273)
MATINAS BIOPHARMA HOLDINGS INC (PA)
1545 Route 206 Ste 302 (07921)
PHONE...........................908 443-1860
Herbert Conrad, *Ch of Bd*
Jerome D Jabbour, *President*
Abdel A Fawzy, *Exec VP*
Douglas F Kling, *Senior VP*
Raphael J Mannino, *Senior VP*
EMP: 10
SQ FT: 5,900
SALES: 119.7K **Publicly Held**
SIC: **2834** Pharmaceutical preparations

(G-274)
MENTOR GRAPHICS CORPORATION
550 Hills Dr Ste 100 (07921-1537)
PHONE...........................908 604-0800
Bill Dunham, *Engineer*
EMP: 125
SALES (corp-wide): 95B **Privately Held**
WEB: www.mentor.com
SIC: **7372** Business oriented computer software
HQ: Mentor Graphics Corporation
8005 Sw Boeckman Rd
Wilsonville OR 97070
503 685-7000

GEOGRAPHIC

(G-275)
NAUTILUS NEUROSCIENCES INC
135 Rte 202 (07921)
PHONE..................................908 437-1320
William Maichle, *CEO*
James L Fares, *CEO*
Peter A Lankau, *Ch of Bd*
Eric Liebler, *President*
Neil Milano, *CFO*
EMP: 5
SALES (est): 874.4K **Privately Held**
SIC: 2834 Pharmaceutical preparations

(G-276)
PHILIP MORRIS USA INC
2 Crossroads Dr Ste 200b (07921-1565)
PHONE..................................908 781-6400
Fran Telegotis, *Manager*
EMP: 11
SALES (corp-wide): 25.3B **Publicly Held**
WEB: www.philipmorrisusa.com
SIC: 2111 Cigarettes
HQ: Philip Morris Usa Inc.
　　6601 W Brd St
　　Richmond VA 23230
　　804 274-2000

(G-277)
QRX PHARMA INCORPORATED
1430 Us Highway 206 # 230 (07921-4602)
PHONE..................................908 506-2900
Michael Schroeder, *Principal*
EMP: 13
SALES (est): 1.9MM **Privately Held**
SIC: 2834 Pharmaceutical preparations
PA: Qrxpharma Limited
　　L11 Se 1 100 Walker St
　　North Sydney NSW

(G-278)
SILOA INC
2493c Lamington Rd (07921-2619)
PHONE..................................908 234-9040
Mark Bellard, *President*
Joseph Walsh, *Director*
▲ EMP: 4
SALES (est): 220K **Privately Held**
WEB: www.siloa.com
SIC: 2844 Toilet preparations

(G-279)
TAP PHARMACEUTICAL PRODUCTS
500 Hills Dr Ste 125 (07921-1538)
PHONE..................................908 470-9700
EMP: 4
SALES (corp-wide): 16.6B **Privately Held**
SIC: 2834 Mfg Pharmaceutical Preparations
HQ: Tap Pharmaceutical Products Inc.
　　675 N Field Dr
　　Lake Forest IL 60045
　　847 582-2000

(G-280)
TOF ENERGY CORPORATION
90 Washington Valley Rd (07921-2118)
PHONE..................................908 691-2422
Jyde Adelakun, *COO*
◆ EMP: 64
SQ FT: 265
SALES (est): 2MM **Privately Held**
SIC: 1381 1389 1711 3825 Drilling oil & gas wells; pumping of oil & gas wells; solar energy contractor; electrical energy measuring equipment; anthracite mining services, contract basis

---
Belford
Monmouth County

(G-281)
BESEECH LTD LIABILITY COMPANY
259 East Rd (07718-1608)
PHONE..................................908 461-7888
William Acevedo,
EMP: 5
SALES (est): 149.4K **Privately Held**
SIC: 7372 7389 Application computer software;

(G-282)
FRANK J ZECHMAN
Also Called: Zeeks Tees
515 Highway 36 (07718-1523)
PHONE..................................732 495-0077
EMP: 9
SQ FT: 1,200
SALES: 800K **Privately Held**
SIC: 2759 Commercial Printing

(G-283)
KERRY WILKENS INC
Also Called: Jean's Canvas Products
780 State Route 36 (07718-1421)
PHONE..................................732 787-0070
Kerry Wilkens, *President*
▼ EMP: 8
SQ FT: 1,600
SALES (est): 1MM **Privately Held**
WEB: www.jeanscanvas.com
SIC: 2394 Liners & covers, fabric: made from purchased materials

(G-284)
UNIVERSITY PUBLICATIONS INC
562 Morley Ct (07718-1156)
PHONE..................................212 268-4222
EMP: 5
SALES (est): 370K **Privately Held**
SIC: 2759 Commercial Printing

(G-285)
ZEEKS TEES
515 State Route 36 (07718-1523)
PHONE..................................732 291-2700
Frank J Zechman, *Owner*
EMP: 10
SALES: 750K **Privately Held**
WEB: www.zeekstees.com
SIC: 2759 Screen printing

Belle Mead
Somerset County

(G-286)
FOUNDATION SOFTWARE INC
58 Livingston Dr (08502-4624)
PHONE..................................908 359-0588
Srecko Lazanja, *President*
EMP: 4
SALES: 500K **Privately Held**
WEB: www.pengi.com
SIC: 7372 Business oriented computer software

(G-287)
SANHERB BIOTECH INC
4 Mccullough Close (08502-4323)
P.O. Box 6111, Hillsborough (08844-6111)
PHONE..................................347 946-5896
Albert Tang, *Ch of Bd*
Sophie Xiao, *President*
Fan Zhou, *President*
Amy Wang, *Sales Mgr*
EMP: 11
SALES (est): 1.4MM **Privately Held**
SIC: 2833 Drugs & herbs: grading, grinding & milling

Belleville
Essex County

(G-288)
ABBOTT ARTKIVES LLC
Also Called: Abbott Screen Printing
187 Branch Brook Dr (07109-3607)
PHONE..................................201 232-9477
Steven Bornemann,
EMP: 5 EST: 1936
SALES: 325K **Privately Held**
WEB: www.abbott-artkives.com
SIC: 2759 Screen printing

(G-289)
AERO PRODUCTS CO INC
21 N 8th St (07109-1117)
PHONE..................................973 759-0959
David Bucci, *President*
Diane Bucci, *Admin Sec*

▲ EMP: 12 EST: 1932
SQ FT: 10,000
SALES (est): 1.7MM **Privately Held**
SIC: 3599 Machine shop, jobbing & repair

(G-290)
AEROCON INC
Also Called: Subsidariry of Vac-U-Max
69 William St (07109-3040)
PHONE..................................800 405-2376
Stevens P Pendleton, *President*
EMP: 80
SQ FT: 40,000
SALES (est): 6.5MM **Privately Held**
WEB: www.aerocon.net
SIC: 3535 Conveyors & conveying equipment

(G-291)
BLOOMFIELD IRON CO INC
Also Called: Railing Designs Unlimited
21 Florence Ave (07109-1107)
P.O. Box 246, Mountain Lakes (07046-0246)
PHONE..................................973 748-7040
EMP: 6 EST: 1950
SQ FT: 4,800
SALES (est): 450K **Privately Held**
SIC: 3312 3462 Mfg Structural Steel

(G-292)
BRUSSO HARDWARE LLC
67-69 Greylock Ave (07109)
PHONE..................................212 337-8510
Richard Bing, *Mng Member*
EMP: 10
SALES (est): 1.4MM **Privately Held**
SIC: 5072 3599 Hardware; machine & other job shop work

(G-293)
COMMUNIQUE INC
Also Called: Precision Specialties
120 Greylock Ave (07109-3324)
PHONE..................................973 751-7588
Rich Pfuhler, *President*
Lorrie Howell, *Associate Dir*
Eva Pfuhler, *Admin Sec*
EMP: 7
SQ FT: 3,400
SALES (est): 870K **Privately Held**
SIC: 3965 5085 Fasteners; industrial supplies

(G-294)
EASTERN MOLDING CO INC
597 Main St (07109-3494)
PHONE..................................973 759-0220
Peter De Nicholas, *President*
EMP: 8 EST: 1947
SQ FT: 15,000
SALES (est): 1.3MM **Privately Held**
SIC: 3069 3061 3053 Molded rubber products; mechanical rubber goods; gaskets, packing & sealing devices

(G-295)
EMPRO PRODUCTS CO INC
47 Montgomery St (07109-1305)
PHONE..................................973 302-4351
Darshan Mehta, *President*
Mehta Kalpi, *Controller*
▲ EMP: 8
SQ FT: 10,000
SALES (est): 1MM **Privately Held**
SIC: 3993 Sigris, not made in custom sign painting shops

(G-296)
FOAM RUBBER FABRICATORS INC
740 Washington Ave (07109-2897)
PHONE..................................973 751-1445
Irving Lerner, *President*
EMP: 22
SQ FT: 30,000
SALES (est): 5.5MM **Privately Held**
SIC: 5199 2821 Foam rubber; plastics materials & resins

(G-297)
J F I PRINTING
357 Cortlandt St (07109-5222)
PHONE..................................973 759-3444
Joe Iannone, *President*
EMP: 5

SALES: 400K **Privately Held**
SIC: 2759 Commercial printing

(G-298)
KHAN ZESHAN
Also Called: Xenon-Vr
55 Salter Pl (07109-1164)
PHONE..................................973 619-4736
Zeshan Khan, *Owner*
EMP: 7
SALES (est): 269K **Privately Held**
SIC: 3851 3841 Ophthalmic goods; lenses, ophthalmic; intraocular lenses; ophthalmic instruments & apparatus; optometers

(G-299)
MAGNETIC TICKET & LABEL CORP
151 Cortlandt St (07109-3130)
PHONE..................................973 759-6500
Michael Hale, *Vice Pres*
Yahya Kashani, *Plant Mgr*
EMP: 30
SALES (corp-wide): 121MM **Privately Held**
SIC: 2679 2771 Labels, paper: made from purchased material; greeting cards
HQ: Magnetic Ticket & Label Corporation
　　8719 Diplomacy Row
　　Dallas TX 75247
　　214 634-8600

(G-300)
MENU SOLUTIONS INC
233 Cortlandt St (07109-3126)
PHONE..................................718 575-5160
Irwin Joel Borracas, *CEO*
◆ EMP: 75 EST: 1996
SALES (est): 3.2MM **Privately Held**
WEB: www.menucovers.biz
SIC: 2752 Commercial printing, lithographic

(G-301)
MILLER & SON
24 Belleville Ave (07109-3035)
PHONE..................................973 759-6445
Elizabeth Miller, *President*
Ed Milller, *Vice Pres*
George A Miller, *Plant Mgr*
EMP: 8 EST: 1913
SQ FT: 20,000
SALES: 1.5MM **Privately Held**
SIC: 3471 Electroplating of metals or formed products

(G-302)
MK WOOD INC
681 Main St (07109-3461)
PHONE..................................973 450-5110
Mourad Khalil, *Principal*
▲ EMP: 4 EST: 2011
SALES (est): 758.3K **Privately Held**
SIC: 5031 2434 Kitchen cabinets; wood kitchen cabinets

(G-303)
MONA SLIDE FASTENERS INC (PA)
Also Called: Mona Belts
233 Cortlandt St (07109-3126)
PHONE..................................718 325-7700
Joel Barrocas, *President*
Mona Barrocas, *Vice Pres*
▲ EMP: 50 EST: 1944
SQ FT: 30,000
SALES (est): 13.1MM **Privately Held**
SIC: 3965 Buttons & parts

(G-304)
OCEAN FOAM FABRICATORS LLC
740 Washington Ave (07109-2820)
PHONE..................................973 745-1445
Andrew Berkowitz,
EMP: 20
SALES: 5MM **Privately Held**
SIC: 3086 Plastics foam products

(G-305)
ORTHODOX BAKING CO INC
555 Cortlandt St (07109-3329)
PHONE..................................973 844-9393
Josheph Oberlander, *President*

EMP: 20
SALES (est): 2.8MM **Privately Held**
SIC: 2051 Bread, cake & related products

(G-306)
PACKAGEMAN
331 Main St (07109-5200)
PHONE.....................201 898-1922
Yashar Novruz, *Administration*
EMP: 4
SALES (est): 146.1K **Privately Held**
SIC: 2631 Container, packaging & boxboard

(G-307)
PETRONIO SHOE PRODUCTS CORP
Also Called: Master Shoe Products
305 Cortlandt St (07109-3292)
PHONE.....................973 751-7579
Donald Rinaldi, *President*
▲ EMP: 10 EST: 1926
SQ FT: 20,000
SALES (est): 1.5MM **Privately Held**
WEB: www.instantshoeshine.com
SIC: 2891 Adhesives; cement, except linoleum & tile

(G-308)
PRESSURE CONTROLS INC
406 Cortlandt St (07109-3204)
PHONE.....................973 751-5002
Paul Emmarco, *President*
Paul L Emmarco, *Vice Pres*
Tommy Santin, *Vice Pres*
Paul Lind, *Manager*
EMP: 9 EST: 1966
SQ FT: 10,000
SALES (est): 890K **Privately Held**
SIC: 3823 3643 3625 Pressure measurement instruments, industrial; current-carrying wiring devices; relays & industrial controls

(G-309)
PULSONICS INC
69 William St (07109-3040)
PHONE.....................800 999-6785
Stevens P Pendleton, *President*
Charlotte Pendleton, *Corp Secy*
Henry Kadel, *Vice Pres*
EMP: 10
SQ FT: 23,000
SALES (est): 300K **Privately Held**
WEB: www.pulsonics.com
SIC: 3569 3535 3443 Assembly machines, non-metalworking; conveyors & conveying equipment; fabricated plate work (boiler shop)

(G-310)
RED DIAMOND CO - ATHC LETERING
Also Called: National Sports Sales
368 Cortlandt St (07109-3204)
PHONE.....................973 759-2005
Michael Tartaglia, *Owner*
Marc S Tartaglia Jr, *Vice Pres*
EMP: 6 EST: 1946
SQ FT: 7,500
SALES (est): 685.1K **Privately Held**
SIC: 2759 7389 2396 2395 Screen printing; embroidering of advertising on shirts, etc.; automotive & apparel trimmings; pleating & stitching

(G-311)
RIVERSIDE GRAPHICS INC
243 Cortlandt St (07109-3126)
PHONE.....................201 876-9000
Paul Caprio, *President*
EMP: 12 EST: 2003
SALES (est): 1.7MM **Privately Held**
SIC: 2759 7331 7319 Stationery: printing; mailing service; distribution of advertising material or sample services

(G-312)
ROBERT FREEMAN
Also Called: N E A Products Co
320 Washington Ave (07109-3249)
PHONE.....................973 751-0082
Robert Freeman, *Principal*
EMP: 6
SQ FT: 7,000

SALES: 600K **Privately Held**
SIC: 3465 7389 Automotive stampings; packaging & labeling services

(G-313)
ROBERT STEWART INC (PA)
120 Little St (07109-3238)
PHONE.....................973 751-5151
Fax: 973 751-2383
▲ EMP: 3 EST: 1919
SALES (est): 4.6MM **Privately Held**
SIC: 2323 Mfg Men's/Boy's Neckwear

(G-314)
SALEM MANUFACTURING CORP
115 Roosevelt Ave (07109-3403)
PHONE.....................973 751-6331
Jerome Lipiec, *President*
Urairat Lipiec, *Treasurer*
Richard Lipiec, *Shareholder*
EMP: 10
SQ FT: 6,000
SALES: 720K **Privately Held**
SIC: 3451 Screw machine products

(G-315)
SPENCER INDUSTRIES INC (PA)
80 Holmes St (07109-3185)
P.O. Box 128 (07109-0128)
PHONE.....................973 751-2200
Martin J Lawrence, *President*
Nicole Lawrence, *Project Mgr*
Denise Glendenning, *Opers Staff*
▲ EMP: 22 EST: 1963
SQ FT: 22,000
SALES (est): 4.8MM **Privately Held**
WEB: www.spencerindinc.com
SIC: 3679 Electronic circuits

(G-316)
TERMINAL PRINTING CO
85 Washington Ave (07109-2928)
P.O. Box 30, Hoboken (07030-0030)
PHONE.....................201 659-5924
John Bado III, *Owner*
Virginia Bado, *Corp Secy*
EMP: 4
SALES (est): 300.2K **Privately Held**
SIC: 2759 Commercial printing

(G-317)
TRI-CHEM INC
681 Main St Ste 24 (07109-3471)
PHONE.....................973 751-9200
Andrew D Mc Knight, *Ch of Bd*
Patricia McKnight, *President*
Richard Y Keegan, *Treasurer*
EMP: 10
SQ FT: 12,000
SALES (est): 1.1MM **Privately Held**
SIC: 2397 5092 Schiffli machine embroideries; hobby goods; arts & crafts equipment & supplies

(G-318)
UNIPACK INC
Also Called: UNIPACK,INC.
681 Main St Ste 27 (07109-3471)
PHONE.....................973 450-9880
Jitu Patel, *Branch Mgr*
EMP: 15
SALES (corp-wide): 7.3MM **Privately Held**
WEB: www.unipackinc.com
SIC: 2834 Pharmaceutical preparations
PA: Unipack, Inc.
3253 Old Frankstown Rd
Pittsburgh PA 15239
724 733-7381

(G-319)
VAC-U-MAX (PA)
Also Called: Aerocon
69 William St (07109-3040)
PHONE.....................973 759-4600
Stevens P Pendleton, *President*
Rose Brosius, *Vice Pres*
Mitchell Katz, *Vice Pres*
Doan Pendleton, *Vice Pres*
Mark McGuire, *Purch Mgr*
◆ EMP: 50
SQ FT: 27,000

SALES (est): 18.4MM **Privately Held**
WEB: www.vac-u-max.com
SIC: 3494 3563 3535 Valves & pipe fittings; air & gas compressors; pneumatic tube conveyor systems

(G-320)
VAC-U-MAX
69 William St (07109-3040)
PHONE.....................973 759-4600
EMP: 15
SALES (corp-wide): 18.4MM **Privately Held**
WEB: www.vac-u-max.com
SIC: 3589 Vacuum cleaners & sweepers, electric: industrial
PA: Vac-U-Max
69 William St
Belleville NJ 07109
973 759-4600

(G-321)
VERNW PRINTING COMPANY
Also Called: Verna Printing
85 Washington Ave (07109-2928)
PHONE.....................973 751-6462
John A Vernacchia, *Owner*
EMP: 5 EST: 1979
SQ FT: 1,000
SALES: 165K **Privately Held**
SIC: 2759 2752 Letterpress printing; commercial printing, offset

(G-322)
VICTORY TOOL & MFG CO
231 Valley St 233 (07109-3285)
PHONE.....................973 759-8733
Victor Maccagnan, *President*
Lucille Maccagnan, *Corp Secy*
EMP: 8 EST: 1973
SQ FT: 4,000
SALES (est): 857.4K **Privately Held**
SIC: 3544 Special dies & tools

(G-323)
VMC DIE CUTTING CORP
357 Cortlandt St (07109-5222)
PHONE.....................973 450-4655
Victor Reczynski, *Owner*
EMP: 11
SALES (est): 1.5MM **Privately Held**
SIC: 3544 2675 Special dies & tools; die-cut paper & board

(G-324)
WHEAL-GRACE CORP
300 Ralph St (07109-3381)
P.O. Box 67 (07109-0067)
PHONE.....................973 450-8100
Nancy Salvini, *President*
Scott Nagle, *Vice Pres*
Tracy Lockett, *Plant Mgr*
John Lesiak, *Prdtn Mgr*
Beth Salvini, *Treasurer*
EMP: 35
SALES (est): 8.5MM **Privately Held**
WEB: www.wheal-grace.com
SIC: 2732 2754 Book printing; commercial printing, gravure

(G-325)
WILLIAM R TATZ INDUSTRIES
Also Called: Charcole Products
11 Railroad Pl (07109-3413)
PHONE.....................973 751-0720
William Tatz, *CEO*
Joseph Tatz, *President*
Richard Tatz, *Treasurer*
EMP: 7
SQ FT: 13,000
SALES (est): 410K **Privately Held**
SIC: 2064 2045 2865 Candy & other confectionery products; cake mixes, prepared: from purchased flour; food dyes or colors, synthetic

(G-326)
WOODPECKERS INC
Also Called: Woodpeckers
323 Cortlandt St (07109-3201)
PHONE.....................973 751-4744
Petros Karantonis, *President*
◆ EMP: 12
SQ FT: 60,000

SALES (est): 1.9MM **Privately Held**
WEB: www.woodpeckers-furniture.com
SIC: 2511 Wood household furniture

Bellmawr
Camden County

(G-327)
AMOROSOS BAKING CO
151 Benigno Blvd (08031-2515)
P.O. Box 1145 (08099-5145)
PHONE.....................215 471-4740
Leonard Amoroso Jr, *President*
Daniel Amoroso Jr, *Vice Pres*
▼ EMP: 300 EST: 1922
SQ FT: 80,000
SALES (est): 69.5MM **Privately Held**
WEB: www.amorosobaking.com
SIC: 2051 Bakery: wholesale or wholesale/retail combined

(G-328)
BOXWORKS INC
1100 Market St (08031-2810)
P.O. Box 108, Gloucester City (08030-0108)
PHONE.....................856 456-9030
Ted White, *President*
EMP: 7
SALES (est): 1.1MM **Privately Held**
WEB: www.boxworks.com
SIC: 2653 2441 2449 Corrugated & solid fiber boxes; nailed wood boxes & shook; rectangular boxes & crates, wood

(G-329)
BRENNAN PENROD CONTRACTORS LLC
420 Benigno Blvd Unit B (08031-2519)
PHONE.....................856 933-1100
George Fields, *Webmaster*
Bob Penrod,
Craig Brennan,
EMP: 18
SALES (est): 748.2K **Privately Held**
SIC: 1721 3443 Painting & paper hanging; liners/lining

(G-330)
DORAZIO FOODS INC
Also Called: D'Orazio Frozen Foods
960 Creek Rd (08031-1672)
PHONE.....................856 931-1900
Anthony Dorazio, *President*
Terri D'Orazio-Bank, *Vice Pres*
Frank D Orazio, *Vice Pres*
Kevin Keoghan, *Inv Control Mgr*
EMP: 75
SQ FT: 25,000
SALES (est): 9.6MM **Privately Held**
WEB: www.dorazio.com
SIC: 2099 Food preparations

(G-331)
EASY ANALYTIC SOFTWARE INC
101 Haag Ave (08031-2506)
P.O. Box 1217 (08099-5217)
PHONE.....................856 931-5780
Christine Ditullio, *Controller*
Robert Katz, *Branch Mgr*
EMP: 4
SALES (est): 224.3K **Privately Held**
SIC: 7372 Application computer software
PA: Easy Analytic Software Inc
7359 196th St
Flushing NY 11366

(G-332)
FAMILY SCREEN PRINTING INC
124 Harding Ave Ste 124 # 124 (08031-2412)
PHONE.....................856 933-2780
Robert Armstrong, *President*
EMP: 15
SALES (est): 1.4MM **Privately Held**
WEB: www.familyscreenprinting.com
SIC: 2282 2396 2395 Embroidery yarn: twisting, winding or spooling; automotive & apparel trimmings; pleating & stitching

(G-333)
GREEN HORSE MEDIA LLC
Also Called: Evergreen Printing Company
101 Haag Ave (08031-2506)
P.O. Box 786 (08099-0786)
PHONE..................................856 933-0222
John Dreisbach, *Vice Pres*
Melissa Smith, *Vice Pres*
Christine Burt, *Controller*
Darrin Forchic, *Sales Staff*
Jim Lamb, *Sales Staff*
▲ **EMP:** 130 **EST:** 1955
SQ FT: 90,000
SALES: 22MM **Privately Held**
WEB: www.egpp.com
SIC: 2752 Commercial printing, offset

(G-334)
HIT PROMO LLC
Also Called: Admints & Zagabor
440 Benigno Blvd Unit D (08031-2521)
PHONE..................................800 237-6305
Arthur W Schmidt III, *CEO*
Christopher John Schmidt, *President*
James Przybyszewski, *Regional Mgr*
Ashley Quarella, *Train & Dev Mgr*
Laura Giordano, *Sales Associate*
▲ **EMP:** 110
SALES: 17MM
SALES (corp-wide): 220.2MM **Privately Held**
SIC: 2759 8743 Promotional printing; promotion service
PA: Hit Promotional Products, Inc.
7150 Bryan Dairy Rd
Largo FL 33777
727 541-5561

(G-335)
INTERNATIONAL PAPER COMPANY
370 Benigno Blvd (08031-2512)
PHONE..................................856 931-8000
Andy Fescoe, *Manager*
EMP: 137
SALES (corp-wide): 23.3B **Publicly Held**
WEB: www.internationalpaper.com
SIC: 2621 Paper mills
PA: International Paper Company
6400 Poplar Ave
Memphis TN 38197
901 419-9000

(G-336)
J & J SNACK FOODS CORP
361 Benigno Blvd Ste A (08031-2501)
PHONE..................................856 933-3597
Brenda Usdin, *Controller*
Bill Mullen, *Manager*
EMP: 150
SALES (corp-wide): 1B **Publicly Held**
WEB: www.jjsnack.com
SIC: 2052 2099 2051 2053 Pretzels; cookies; food preparations; bread, cake & related products; frozen bakery products, except bread
PA: J & J Snack Foods Corp.
6000 Central Hwy
Pennsauken NJ 08109
856 665-9533

(G-337)
M PARKER AUTOWORKS INC
Also Called: Factory Fit
150 Heller Pl 17w (08031-2503)
PHONE..................................856 933-0801
Michael P Manning, *President*
Frank Colonna, *Vice Pres*
EMP: 21
SALES (est): 3.6MM **Privately Held**
WEB: www.factoryfit.com
SIC: 3357 3694 Automotive wire & cable, except ignition sets: nonferrous; engine electrical equipment

(G-338)
MAGGIO PRINTING LLC
Also Called: Maggio Fine
171 Heller Pl (08031-2503)
PHONE..................................856 931-7805
Rick Rossano, *Sales Staff*
Charles Maggio Jr,
EMP: 48
SALES (est): 598.3K **Privately Held**
SIC: 2759 Business forms: printing

(G-339)
MERCER RUBBER COMPANY
Also Called: Mercer Gasket and Shim
110 Benigno Blvd (08031-2540)
PHONE..................................856 931-5000
Gloria Taraborelli, *Ch of Bd*
Peter Taraborelli Jr, *President*
Dean Taraborelli, *Vice Pres*
▲ **EMP:** 25 **EST:** 1939
SQ FT: 480,000
SALES: 4.5MM **Privately Held**
WEB: www.mercergasket.com
SIC: 3053 5085 Gaskets, packing & sealing devices; gaskets & seals

(G-340)
NATIONAL AUTO DETAILING NETWRK
111 Harding Ave (08031-2413)
PHONE..................................856 931-5529
Peter Moran, *President*
Steven Isreal, *COO*
EMP: 25
SQ FT: 3,500
SALES (est): 1MM **Privately Held**
SIC: 7542 2842 5169 Washing & polishing, automotive; polishing preparations & related products; chemicals & allied products

(G-341)
PIROLLI PRINTING CO INC
860 W Browning Rd (08031-1724)
PHONE..................................856 933-1285
Kathleen Pirolli, *Ch of Bd*
Eugene Pirolli, *President*
Mark Pirolli, *Treasurer*
Matthew J Pirolli, *Admin Sec*
EMP: 18
SQ FT: 5,000
SALES (est): 3.2MM **Privately Held**
WEB: www.pirolliprinting.com
SIC: 2752 Commercial printing, offset

(G-342)
SEALION METAL FABRICATORS INC
776 Creek Rd (08031-2424)
PHONE..................................856 933-3914
Louis D'Orazio, *President*
Michael J Natale, *Corp Secy*
Michael Natale, *CFO*
EMP: 14 **EST:** 1957
SQ FT: 15,000
SALES: 2.5MM **Privately Held**
SIC: 3799 Trailers & trailer equipment; boat trailers

(G-343)
SEVIROLI FOODS INC
960 Creek Rd (08031-1672)
PHONE..................................856 931-1900
Terry Bank, *Manager*
EMP: 5
SALES (est): 393.8K
SALES (corp-wide): 78.1MM **Privately Held**
SIC: 2038 Frozen specialties
PA: Seviroli Foods, Inc.
385 Oak St
Garden City NY 11530
516 222-6220

(G-344)
TBT GROUP INC
191 Heller Pl (08031-2503)
PHONE..................................856 753-4500
Daniel Declemnet, *CEO*
Eric M Weiss, *President*
EMP: 8
SQ FT: 1,700
SALES (est): 1.3MM **Privately Held**
SIC: 3675 8711 Electronic capacitors; engineering services

(G-345)
W B MASON CO INC
151 Heller Pl (08031-2503)
PHONE..................................888 926-2766
EMP: 61
SALES (corp-wide): 773MM **Privately Held**
SIC: 5943 5712 2752 Office forms & supplies; office furniture; commercial printing, lithographic

PA: W. B. Mason Co., Inc.
59 Center St
Brockton MA 02301
781 794-8800

Belmar
Monmouth County

(G-346)
A PS INLET MARINA LLC
610 5th Ave (07719-2114)
PHONE..................................732 681-3303
Erika Gerzsenyi,
Robert Gerzsenyi,
Zoltan Gerzsenyi,
EMP: 5
SQ FT: 1,000
SALES (est): 644.4K **Privately Held**
WEB: www.apsinletmarina.com
SIC: 3732 4493 5551 5541 Boat building & repairing; boat yards, storage & incidental repair; sails & equipment; marine service station

(G-347)
CONSTANTIA BLYTHEWOOD LLC
1111 N Point Blvd (07719)
PHONE..................................732 974-4100
EMP: 57
SALES (corp-wide): 2.6MM **Privately Held**
SIC: 3497 Metal foil & leaf
HQ: Constantia Blythewood, Llc
1111 Northpoint Blvd
Blythewood SC 29016
803 404-6581

(G-348)
DEITZ CO INC
1750 Hwy 34 (07719)
P.O. Box 1108, Wall (07719-1108)
PHONE..................................732 295-8212
Steven Deitz, *President*
Stephen J Deitz Jr, *President*
Charles E Deitz, *Vice Pres*
Charles Dietz, *Vice Pres*
EMP: 12
SQ FT: 12,000
SALES (est): 1.9MM **Privately Held**
WEB: www.deitzco.com
SIC: 3565 3559 Packaging machinery; pharmaceutical machinery

(G-349)
GEMCRAFT INC
1921 State Route 71 (07719-3247)
PHONE..................................732 449-8944
John Shenin, *President*
EMP: 4
SALES (est): 300K **Privately Held**
SIC: 2434 Wood kitchen cabinets

(G-350)
HYCHEM CORPORATION
611 Main St Ste B-2 (07719-5103)
PHONE..................................732 280-8803
Henry Yard, *President*
▲ **EMP:** 4 **EST:** 2001
SQ FT: 1,200
SALES (est): 400K **Privately Held**
WEB: www.hychemcorp.com
SIC: 2899 5169 Chemical preparations; chemicals & allied products

(G-351)
NJR CLEAN ENERGY VENTURES CORP (HQ)
1415 Wyckoff Rd (07719)
PHONE..................................732 938-1000
Warren Downes, *CEO*
Rhonda M Figueroa, *Director*
Valori Mark, *Director*
EMP: 450
SALES (est): 436.4K
SALES (corp-wide): 2.9B **Publicly Held**
SIC: 1311 Natural gas production
PA: New Jersey Resources Corp
1415 Wyckoff Rd
Wall Township NJ 07727
732 938-1000

(G-352)
OCTOPUS YACHTS LTD LBLTY CO
2400 Belmar Blvd Ste C-1 (07719-4098)
PHONE..................................732 698-8550
Aaron Held,
EMP: 10
SALES (est): 1.7MM **Privately Held**
SIC: 3669 Sirens, electric: vehicle, marine, industrial & air raid

(G-353)
RKE ATHELTIC LETTERING
1901 State Route 71 1c (07719-3277)
PHONE..................................732 280-1111
Gregory Kapalko, *Owner*
EMP: 7
SALES (est): 977.3K **Privately Held**
SIC: 3949 Sporting & athletic goods

(G-354)
SONETRONICS INC (PA)
1718 H St (07719-3140)
P.O. Box L (07719-0430)
PHONE..................................732 681-5016
Gary Kuskin, *Ch of Bd*
Debi Kuskin, *Vice Pres*
▲ **EMP:** 80 **EST:** 1961
SQ FT: 19,500
SALES (est): 11.8MM **Privately Held**
WEB: www.sonetronics.com
SIC: 3661 3089 Communication headgear, telephone; injection molding of plastics

(G-355)
SURFS UP CANDLE & CHARM
Also Called: Surf's Up Candle
1703 Main St 3 (07719-5212)
PHONE..................................848 404-9559
Michelle Fontanez, *Mng Member*
EMP: 5
SALES (est): 646.7K **Privately Held**
SIC: 5999 3999 Candle shops; candles

(G-356)
WATONKA PRINTING INC
Also Called: Instant Business Cards
1608 State Route 71 (07719-2802)
PHONE..................................732 974-8878
William Reinhard Jr, *President*
EMP: 7
SQ FT: 2,500
SALES (est): 504.5K **Privately Held**
SIC: 2759 2752 2761 2677 Thermography; commercial printing, lithographic; manifold business forms; envelopes

---

Belvidere
Warren County

(G-357)
ARTISAN MODEL MOLD
Also Called: A M M
275 Buckhorn Dr (07823-2708)
PHONE..................................908 453-3524
Ronald Stanwick, *Owner*
EMP: 5
SALES: 160K **Privately Held**
SIC: 3999 Models, general, except toy

(G-358)
CONVEYER INSTALLERS AMERICA
5 Tamarack Rd (07823-2521)
PHONE..................................908 453-4729
Allen Orchard, *Owner*
EMP: 4
SALES: 400K **Privately Held**
SIC: 3535 Belt conveyor systems, general industrial use

(G-359)
COUNTY OF WARREN
Also Called: Road Dept
519 S 185 County Rd (07823)
PHONE..................................908 475-7975
Frederick Miller, *Principal*
EMP: 65 **Privately Held**
WEB: www.co.warren.nj.us
SIC: 3531 Construction machinery

PA: County Of Warren
165 County Road 519 Ste 1
Belvidere NJ 07823
908 475-6500

(G-360)
DSM NUTRITIONAL PRODUCTS LLC
206 Macks Island Dr (07823-1199)
PHONE..................................908 475-7093
Christolph Goppelsrober, *Principal*
EMP: 152
SALES (corp-wide): 10.6B **Privately Held**
SIC: 2836 2834 Biological products, except diagnostic; veterinary biological products; vitamin, nutrient & hematinic preparations for human use
HQ: Dsm Nutritional Products, Llc
45 Waterview Blvd
Parsippany NJ 07054
800 526-0189

(G-361)
DSM NUTRITIONAL PRODUCTS LLC
253 260 Macks Island Dr (07823)
PHONE..................................908 475-0150
Michael J Adams, *Opers-Prdtn-Mfg*
EMP: 450
SALES (corp-wide): 10.6B **Privately Held**
WEB: www.nutraaccess.com
SIC: 2834 Pharmaceutical preparations
HQ: Dsm Nutritional Products, Llc
45 Waterview Blvd
Parsippany NJ 07054
800 526-0189

(G-362)
DSM NUTRITIONAL PRODUCTS LLC
200 Roche Dr (07823-2100)
PHONE..................................908 475-5300
Michael Adams, *Branch Mgr*
EMP: 152
SALES (corp-wide): 10.6B **Privately Held**
SIC: 2834 Pharmaceutical preparations
HQ: Dsm Nutritional Products, Llc
45 Waterview Blvd
Parsippany NJ 07054
800 526-0189

(G-363)
DSM NUTRITIONAL PRODUCTS LLC
218 Roche Dr (07823-2100)
PHONE..................................908 475-5300
Dr Christolph Goppelsrober, *Branch Mgr*
EMP: 240
SALES (corp-wide): 10.6B **Privately Held**
WEB: www.nutraaccess.com
SIC: 2834 Pharmaceutical preparations
HQ: Dsm Nutritional Products, Llc
45 Waterview Blvd
Parsippany NJ 07054
800 526-0189

(G-364)
GREAT NORTHERN COMMERCIAL SVCS
401 Greenwich St (07823-1406)
PHONE..................................908 475-8855
Anna Quinn, *President*
Dennis Quinn, *Principal*
EMP: 7
SQ FT: 8,000
SALES: 750K **Privately Held**
WEB: www.greatnortherngraphics.com
SIC: 2752 Commercial printing, lithographic

(G-365)
PV DEROCHE LLC
Also Called: Deroche Canvas
283 County Route 519 (07823)
P.O. Box 443 (07823-0443)
PHONE..................................908 475-2266
James Van Stone, *CEO*
Daniel Deroche, *President*
EMP: 34
SQ FT: 20,000
SALES (est): 1.3MM **Privately Held**
SIC: 2394 Convertible tops, canvas or boat: from purchased materials

(G-366)
S J SCREW COMPANY INC
Also Called: S Johnson & Son
Front & Hardwick St (07823)
P.O. Box 66 (07823-0066)
PHONE..................................908 475-2155
Sven G Johnson, *President*
Erik H Johnson, *Vice Pres*
EMP: 40 EST: 1933
SQ FT: 35,000
SALES (est): 7.3MM **Privately Held**
SIC: 3451 Screw machine products

(G-367)
T M INDUSTRIES INC
2013 Brookfield Glen Dr (07823-2855)
PHONE..................................908 730-7674
Gerda A Tietje, *President*
EMP: 8
SQ FT: 1,500
SALES (est): 1MM **Privately Held**
SIC: 3569 Lubrication equipment, industrial

(G-368)
WESTERN ELECTRONICS DIST
300 5th St (07823-1802)
PHONE..................................908 475-3303
Joe Hyziak, *Vice Pres*
EMP: 5
SALES (est): 447.3K **Privately Held**
SIC: 3679 Electronic circuits

Bergenfield
Bergen County

(G-369)
AIM COMPUTER ASSOCIATES INC
19 Dover Ct (07621-3902)
PHONE..................................201 489-3100
David Hendlish, *President*
EMP: 8
SQ FT: 1,200
SALES (est): 540K **Privately Held**
WEB: www.aimcomputer.com
SIC: 7374 7372 Data entry service; business oriented computer software

(G-370)
AMERICAN FORECLOSURES INC
15 W Main St Apt 1 (07621-2131)
P.O. Box 601, Oradell (07649-0601)
PHONE..................................201 501-0200
Craig Laube, *President*
Cynthia Ehrlich, *Vice Pres*
EMP: 12
SALES (est): 950K **Privately Held**
WEB: www.americanforeclosures.com
SIC: 2721 6531 Periodicals: publishing only; real estate agents & managers

(G-371)
ASTI CORP
Also Called: Asti Magnetics
45 W Broad St (07621-2866)
PHONE..................................201 501-8900
Henry Akiya, *President*
Sal Rutigliano, *Vice Pres*
Paul Rutigliano, *Treasurer*
▲ EMP: 14
SQ FT: 10,000
SALES: 9MM **Privately Held**
WEB: www.astimag.com
SIC: 3679 Recording & playback heads, magnetic

(G-372)
BANICKI SHEET METAL INC
44 Garden St (07621-2744)
PHONE..................................201 385-5938
EMP: 7
SALES (est): 640K **Privately Held**
SIC: 1711 3585 3444 Plumbing/Heat/Ac Contr Mfg Refrig/Heat Equip Mfg Sheet Metalwork

(G-373)
BERGEN MARZIPAN & CHOCOLATE
205 S Washington Ave (07621-2918)
PHONE..................................201 385-8343

Serpin Adanan, *President*
Gunter Schott, *Finance Other*
▲ EMP: 4
SALES (est): 250K **Privately Held**
SIC: 2066 2064 Chocolate & cocoa products; marzipan (candy)

(G-374)
CNR PRODUCTS CO
74 Portland Ave (07621-2307)
PHONE..................................201 384-7003
Peter Rebsch, *Owner*
EMP: 5
SQ FT: 3,000
SALES (est): 324.6K **Privately Held**
WEB: www.cnrproducts.com
SIC: 3993 Signs, not made in custom sign painting shops

(G-375)
GLOBAL EXPRESS FREIGHT INC
136 W Central Ave (07621-1208)
PHONE..................................201 376-6613
Alfonso Rivera, *President*
EMP: 4 EST: 2014
SQ FT: 1,000
SALES: 500K **Privately Held**
SIC: 3537 Trucks: freight, baggage, etc.: industrial, except mining

(G-376)
HARLEY TOOL & MACHINE INC
24 Mcdermott Pl (07621-3706)
PHONE..................................201 244-8899
John Robert Harley, *President*
EMP: 4 EST: 1925
SALES: 400K **Privately Held**
SIC: 3599 5051 Machine shop, jobbing & repair; aluminum bars, rods, ingots, sheets, pipes, plates, etc.

(G-377)
HITRONS SOLUTIONS INC
88 Portland Ave Ste M (07621-2364)
PHONE..................................201 244-0300
EMP: 10
SQ FT: 2,000
SALES: 2.1MM **Privately Held**
SIC: 3261 Whol Plumbing Equipment/Supplies Mfg Plumbing Fixture Fittings

(G-378)
HITRONS SOLUTIONS INC
88 Portland Ave Ste M (07621-2364)
PHONE..................................201 244-0300
Steve Chung, *President*
Thomas Masters, *Managing Dir*
David Kim, *Vice Pres*
Eun Joung Chung, *CFO*
David Cho, *Accounts Exec*
▲ EMP: 10
SALES (est): 4MM **Privately Held**
SIC: 3261 8748 Bidets, vitreous china; business consulting

(G-379)
MAGIC METAL WORKS INC
40 W Englewood Ave (07621-3714)
PHONE..................................201 384-8457
George Dabaghian, *President*
Vic Dabaghian, *Corp Secy*
Jacques Dabaghian, *Vice Pres*
EMP: 6
SQ FT: 6,400
SALES (est): 510K **Privately Held**
SIC: 3469 Electronic enclosures, stamped or pressed metal

(G-380)
N B C ENGRAVING CO INC
160 Woodbine St (07621-3521)
P.O. Box 1036, Hackensack (07602-1036)
PHONE..................................201 387-8011
Camillo Scagliotti, *President*
John Scagliotti, *Vice Pres*
EMP: 6
SQ FT: 1,000
SALES: 350K **Privately Held**
WEB: www.nbcengraving.com
SIC: 3555 Plates, metal: engravers'

(G-381)
NEW JERSEY EYE CENTER INC
1 N Washington Ave (07621-2125)
PHONE..................................201 384-7333

Joseph Dello Russo, *Principal*
Frank Parisi, *Med Doctor*
EMP: 14
SALES (est): 2.3MM **Privately Held**
SIC: 3851 Eyes, glass & plastic

(G-382)
PEACOCK PRODUCTS INC
48 Woodbine St (07621-3520)
P.O. Box 127 (07621-0127)
PHONE..................................201 385-5585
Craig Langslet, *President*
Eric Langslet, *President*
▲ EMP: 16
SQ FT: 8,000
SALES (est): 2.4MM **Privately Held**
SIC: 2759 Commercial printing

(G-383)
ROY D SMITH INC
20 Foster St (07621-4302)
P.O. Box 537 (07621-0537)
PHONE..................................201 384-4163
Eric Zymet, *President*
EMP: 5
SQ FT: 1,600
SALES (est): 370K **Privately Held**
SIC: 2752 Commercial printing, lithographic

(G-384)
SAP-SEAL PRODUCTS INC
52 Woodbine St Ste 2 (07621-3525)
PHONE..................................201 385-5553
Earnie Ness, *President*
Mark Knutzen, *Marketing Staff*
EMP: 5 EST: 1998
SALES (est): 28.9K **Privately Held**
WEB: www.sapseal.com
SIC: 3261 2891 Bolt caps, vitreous china or earthenware; adhesives & sealants

(G-385)
TECHNOLOGY DYNAMICS INC (PA)
100 School St Ste 1 (07621-2900)
PHONE..................................201 385-0500
Aron Levy, *President*
Daniel J Cavalli, *Vice Pres*
Dwight Dixon, *Vice Pres*
Daniel Ellenback, *Vice Pres*
Rajendra Dhiman, *Engineer*
▲ EMP: 58 EST: 1976
SQ FT: 30,000
SALES (est): 34.4MM **Privately Held**
WEB: www.theallpower.com
SIC: 5063 3679 3613 Electrical apparatus & equipment; static power supply converters for electronic applications; power switching equipment

(G-386)
TECHNOLOGY DYNAMICS INC
Nova Electric
100 School St (07621-2900)
PHONE..................................201 385-0500
Aron Levy, *President*
Carol Dawkins, *Sales Mgr*
Howard Schrier, *Executive*
EMP: 100
SALES (corp-wide): 34.4MM **Privately Held**
WEB: www.theallpower.com
SIC: 3621 3679 Frequency converters (electric generators); inverters, rotating: electrical; power supplies, all types: static
PA: Technology Dynamics, Inc.
100 School St Ste 1
Bergenfield NJ 07621
201 385-0500

Berkeley Heights
Union County

(G-387)
ALIGN PHARMACEUTICALS LLC
200 Connell Dr Ste 1500 (07922-2811)
PHONE..................................908 834-0960
Greg Preston, *VP Mktg*
Robert Sosnowski,
▲ EMP: 5

SALES (est): 106.4K **Publicly Held**
WEB: www.cyclacel.com
SIC: 2834 Pharmaceutical preparations
PA: Cyclacel Pharmaceuticals, Inc.
　　200 Connell Dr Ste 1500
　　Berkeley Heights NJ 07922

(G-388)
AMAS PHARMACEUTICALS LLC
100 Connell Dr Ste 2300 (07922-2741)
PHONE..............................908 883-1129
John Sachariah, *Mng Member*
Mary Sachariah, *Mng Member*
EMP: 35
SALES (est): 5.9MM **Privately Held**
SIC: 2834 Pharmaceutical preparations

(G-389)
AT&T TECHNOLOGIES INC
1 Oak Way (07922-2732)
PHONE..............................201 771-2000
Morris Tanenbaum, *Ch of Bd*
Thomas R Thomsen, *President*
William J Warwick, *President*
E Wayne Weeks Jr, *President*
Michael A Brunner, *Exec VP*
▼ **EMP:** 97200 **EST:** 1869
SQ FT: 433,000
SALES: 11.4B
SALES (corp-wide): 170.7B **Publicly Held**
SIC: 3661 3357 3351 3679 Switching equipment, telephone; carrier equipment, telephone or telegraph; fiber optics communications equipment; fiber optic cable (insulated); wire, copper & copper alloy; power supplies, all types: static; wiring boards; nautical instruments; sonar systems & equipment
HQ: At&T Corp.
　　1 At&T Way
　　Bedminster NJ 07921
　　800 403-3302

(G-390)
BOEING COMPANY
400 Connell Dr Ste 6200 (07922-2810)
PHONE..............................908 464-6959
Matthew M Hoff, *Branch Mgr*
EMP: 4518
SALES (corp-wide): 101.1B **Publicly Held**
SIC: 3721 Aircraft
PA: The Boeing Company
　　100 N Riverside Plz
　　Chicago IL 60606
　　312 544-2000

(G-391)
BRIAN LENHART INTERACTIVE LLC
2 Ridge Dr E (07922-2112)
PHONE..............................610 737-5314
Brian Lenhart, *Owner*
EMP: 5
SALES (est): 297.9K **Privately Held**
SIC: 2241 Apparel webbing

(G-392)
CELGENE CORPORATION
300 Connell Dr Ste 6000 (07922-2372)
PHONE..............................908 464-8101
Courtney Barry, *Opers Dir*
Monica Cantonetti, *Opers Dir*
Tanesha Duncan, *Opers Dir*
Patricia Tramontana, *Opers Dir*
Lisa Serme, *Opers Staff*
EMP: 15
SALES (corp-wide): 15.2B **Publicly Held**
SIC: 2834 Pharmaceutical preparations
PA: Celgene Corporation
　　86 Morris Ave
　　Summit NJ 07901
　　908 673-9000

(G-393)
CELGENE CORPORATION
400 Connell Dr Ste 4000 (07922-2797)
PHONE..............................908 967-1432
Robert J Hugin, *Principal*
Michael Sturniolo, *Director*
Piyali Chowdhury, *Associate Dir*
EMP: 12
SALES (corp-wide): 15.2B **Publicly Held**
SIC: 2834 Pharmaceutical preparations

PA: Celgene Corporation
　　86 Morris Ave
　　Summit NJ 07901
　　908 673-9000

(G-394)
CHEMTRADE SOLUTIONS LLC
Also Called: General Chemical
235 Snyder Ave (07922-1140)
PHONE..............................908 464-1500
Jerry Kirwan, *Plant Mgr*
Robert Braddock, *Branch Mgr*
Mark Rerek, *Director*
EMP: 15
SALES (corp-wide): 1.2B **Privately Held**
SIC: 2819 Aluminum compounds
HQ: Chemtrade Solutions Llc
　　90 E Halsey Rd Ste 301
　　Parsippany NJ 07054

(G-395)
CONNELL MINING PRODUCTS LLC
Also Called: Celco
200 Connell Dr (07922-2805)
PHONE..............................908 673-3700
Donna Maas, *President*
Howard Jaffe, *Vice Pres*
Paul King, *Vice Pres*
Richard Ringler, *VP Opers*
Michael Gilbert, *Purch Mgr*
◆ **EMP:** 100
SALES (est): 12.1MM
SALES (corp-wide): 418.3MM **Privately Held**
SIC: 1081 Metal mining services
PA: The Connell Company
　　200 Connell Dr Ste 4100
　　Berkeley Heights NJ 07922
　　908 673-3700

(G-396)
CORMEDIX INC (PA)
400 Connell Dr Ste 5000 (07922-2809)
PHONE..............................908 517-9500
Khoso Baluch, *CEO*
Myron Kaplan, *Ch of Bd*
Jack Armstrong, *Exec VP*
Liz Masson, *Exec VP*
Phoebe Mounts, *Exec VP*
EMP: 9
SALES: 429.8K **Publicly Held**
SIC: 2834 Drugs acting on the central nervous system & sense organs

(G-397)
CYCLACEL PHARMACEUTICALS INC (PA)
200 Connell Dr Ste 1500 (07922-2811)
PHONE..............................908 517-7330
David U'Prichard, *Ch of Bd*
Christopher S Henney, *Vice Ch Bd*
Spiro Rombotis, *President*
Paul McBarron, *COO*
David Chiao, *Vice Pres*
EMP: 16
SALES: 150K **Publicly Held**
WEB: www.cyclacel.com
SIC: 2834 Pharmaceutical preparations

(G-398)
E G L COMPANY INC
Also Called: E G L
100 Industrial Rd (07922-1523)
PHONE..............................908 508-1111
Harold R Cortese Jr, *President*
Doug Cortese, *General Mgr*
◆ **EMP:** 110 **EST:** 1931
SQ FT: 80,000
SALES (est): 20MM **Privately Held**
WEB: www.egl-neon.com
SIC: 3641 3229 5169 Electrodes, cold cathode fluorescent lamp; tubing, glass; industrial gases

(G-399)
GO WADDLE INC
23 Baldwin Dr (07922-1744)
PHONE..............................301 452-5084
Suma Reddy, *Principal*
Vishal Reddy, *Principal*
EMP: 4
SALES (est): 170K **Privately Held**
SIC: 2741

(G-400)
HP ENTERPRISE
Also Called: Hpfs
200 Connell Dr Ste 5000 (07922-2816)
PHONE..............................908 898-4728
Al Smith, *President*
Pam Miodus, *Sales Staff*
Thomas Schaefer, *Marketing Staff*
Barbara Hunt, *Admin Asst*
EMP: 15
SALES (est): 4.2MM **Privately Held**
SIC: 7372 Prepackaged software

(G-401)
INCOM (AMERICA) INC
330 Snyder Ave (07922-1505)
PHONE..............................908 464-3366
Ahmed G Singer, *President*
Wendell Tomimbang, *Vice Pres*
EMP: 5
SQ FT: 32,000
SALES (est): 433.9K **Privately Held**
WEB: www.incom-america.com
SIC: 3694 Harness wiring sets, internal combustion engines

(G-402)
J K OFFICE MACHINE INC
33 Debbie Pl (07922-1705)
PHONE..............................908 273-8811
James Martin, *President*
Neal Pauline, *Vice Pres*
EMP: 5 **EST:** 1969
SQ FT: 2,500
SALES: 625K **Privately Held**
SIC: 3579 7629 Mailing, letter handling & addressing machines; business machine repair, electric

(G-403)
J MICHAELS JEWELERS INC
370 Springfield Ave (07922-1107)
PHONE..............................908 771-9800
Michael Bernardo, *President*
Michael Bernado, *President*
EMP: 4
SQ FT: 1,200
SALES (est): 487.6K **Privately Held**
SIC: 5944 3915 5094 Jewelry, precious stones & precious metals; lapidary work & diamond cutting & polishing; jewelry; diamonds (gems)

(G-404)
KARL NEUWEILER INC
Also Called: Neuweiler, K H
23 Russo Pl (07922-1606)
PHONE..............................908 464-6532
Daniel Neuweiler, *President*
Ann Neuweiler, *Vice Pres*
EMP: 9 **EST:** 1953
SQ FT: 6,000
SALES: 1.5MM **Privately Held**
WEB: www.neuweiler.com
SIC: 3451 Screw machine products

(G-405)
KNOTTS COMPANY INC
350 Snyder Ave (07922-1500)
P.O. Box 611 (07922-0611)
PHONE..............................908 464-4800
Richard L Howe, *President*
Mark Howe, *VP Sls/Mktg*
George Mehaffey, *Treasurer*
Stephen Harrold, *Sales Staff*
Carol Kulevich, *Marketing Staff*
EMP: 36
SQ FT: 14,000
SALES (est): 12.2MM **Privately Held**
WEB: www.knottsco.com
SIC: 3535 5085 Unit handling conveying systems; industrial supplies

(G-406)
LAUDERDALE MILLWORK INC
77 Industrial Rd (07922-1539)
PHONE..............................908 508-9550
John Lauderdale, *President*
EMP: 10
SALES (est): 1.1MM **Privately Held**
SIC: 2431 Millwork

(G-407)
LUMITRON CORP
Also Called: Lumitron Arospc Ltg Components
35 Russo Pl (07922-1622)
P.O. Box 394 (07922-0394)
PHONE..............................908 508-9100
Gil Chassie, *President*
Karen Chassie, *Vice Pres*
Jerry Rosario, *Mfg Staff*
Amy Tefft, *Sales Associate*
EMP: 10 **EST:** 1970
SQ FT: 1,500
SALES (est): 1.8MM **Privately Held**
WEB: www.lumitroncorp.com
SIC: 3641 Lamps, incandescent filament, electric

(G-408)
MAINSTREAM FLUID & AIR LLC (PA)
47 Russo Pl (07922-1606)
PHONE..............................908 931-1010
Derrick Markham, *Mng Member*
James Markham,
EMP: 14
SQ FT: 25,000
SALES: 6MM **Privately Held**
SIC: 3585 Air conditioning equipment, complete; heating & air conditioning combination units; air conditioning condensers & condensing units

(G-409)
PDS BIOTECHNOLOGY CORPORATION (PA)
300 Connell Dr Ste 4000 (07922-2817)
PHONE..............................800 208-3343
Frank Bedu-Addo, *President*
Andrew Saik, *CFO*
Lauren Wood, *Chief Mktg Ofcr*
Bill Roscoe, *Manager*
Cheryl Askew, *Associate Dir*
EMP: 10 **EST:** 2009
SQ FT: 20,410
SALES (est): 1.2MM **Publicly Held**
SIC: 2834 8731 Pharmaceutical preparations; biological research

(G-410)
PERCO INC
620 Springfield Ave (07922-1055)
P.O. Box 23 (07922-0023)
PHONE..............................908 464-3000
Jim Dinaio, *President*
Annemarie Dinaio, *Shareholder*
EMP: 10
SQ FT: 6,500
SALES: 1.2MM **Privately Held**
SIC: 2759 Commercial printing

(G-411)
SCIENTIFIC MODELS INC
Also Called: Micro-Mark
340 Snyder Ave (07922-1595)
PHONE..............................908 464-7070
Sandra Frisoli, *Director*
▲ **EMP:** 22 **EST:** 1946
SQ FT: 16,000
SALES (est): 6.2MM **Privately Held**
WEB: www.scientificmodels.com
SIC: 5092 3999 Hobby supplies; models, except toy

(G-412)
SHELL PACKAGING CORPORATION (PA)
Also Called: Flexcon Container
200 Connell Dr Ste 1200 (07922-2822)
PHONE..............................908 871-7000
Ken Beckerman, *President*
Stephen M Beckerman, *President*
Jim Flynn, *Vice Pres*
Edythe Benisrael, *Accounting Mgr*
Jason Grasso, *Sales Staff*
▲ **EMP:** 49
SQ FT: 6,000
SALES (est): 14MM **Privately Held**
WEB: www.flexcontainer.com
SIC: 2631 3086 3443 Packaging board; packaging & shipping materials, foamed plastic; fabricated plate work (boiler shop)

(G-413)
TWILL INC
22 Russo Pl (07922-1606)
PHONE..................................908 665-1700
George Robert Twill, *President*
Peter Twill, *Vice Pres*
EMP: 15 **EST:** 1947
SQ FT: 17,800
SALES: 2.2MM **Privately Held**
WEB: www.twill.com
SIC: 2752 Commercial printing, offset

Berlin
Camden County

(G-414)
ARIES FILTERWORKS INC
117 Jackson Rd (08009-9160)
PHONE..................................856 626-1550
Michael C Gottlieb, *President*
Jeffery H Gottlieb, *Vice Pres*
Lawrence Gottlieb, *Vice Pres*
Lynne Gottlieb, *Vice Pres*
April Megaw, *Purch Agent*
EMP: 43 **EST:** 2010
SALES (est): 1.9MM **Privately Held**
SIC: 3589 Water filters & softeners, household type; water purification equipment, household type

(G-415)
BELTOR MANUFACTURING CORP
50 Union Ave Ste 12 (08009)
PHONE..................................856 768-5570
Derek Torok, *President*
EMP: 5 **EST:** 1945
SQ FT: 2,100
SALES: 660K **Privately Held**
SIC: 2391 3841 Curtains, window: made from purchased materials; surgical & medical instruments

(G-416)
BOCCELLA PRECAST LLC
324 New Brooklyn Rd (08009-9506)
P.O. Box 32 (08009-0032)
PHONE..................................856 767-3861
Joseph Boccella, *Mng Member*
▲ **EMP:** 10
SALES (est): 4MM **Privately Held**
SIC: 3272 Concrete products, precast

(G-417)
BRIDGESTATE FOUNDRY CORP
175 Jackson Rd (08009-2608)
PHONE..................................856 767-0400
Ed Ciel, *President*
EMP: 4 **EST:** 1962
SQ FT: 2,000
SALES (est): 1.3MM
SALES (corp-wide): 11.9MM **Privately Held**
WEB: www.campbellfoundry.com
SIC: 3321 Gray iron castings; manhole covers, metal
PA: Campbell Foundry Company
800 Bergen St
Harrison NJ 07029
973 483-5480

(G-418)
BRINGHURST BROS INC
Also Called: Bringhurst Meats
38 W Taunton Rd (08009-9702)
PHONE..................................856 767-0110
Ralph A Bringhurst Jr, *President*
Jeff Bringhurst, *Corp Secy*
EMP: 22 **EST:** 1934
SQ FT: 12,000
SALES (est): 1.5MM **Privately Held**
WEB: www.bringhurstmeats.com
SIC: 5421 2011 5812 5147 Meat markets, including freezer provisioners; pork products from pork slaughtered on site; meat by-products from meat slaughtered on site; caterers; meats & meat products; animal & marine fats & oils; sausages & other prepared meats

(G-419)
BUILDERS FIRSTSOURCE INC
210 Williamstown Rd (08009-9730)
PHONE..................................856 767-3153
Manish Kharbanda, *Branch Mgr*
EMP: 20
SALES (corp-wide): 7.7B **Publicly Held**
WEB: www.hopelumber.com
SIC: 2449 Containers, plywood & veneer wood
PA: Builders Firstsource, Inc.
2001 Bryan St Ste 1600
Dallas TX 75201
214 880-3500

(G-420)
CLASSIC GRAPHIC INC
Also Called: Minuteman Press
35 W White Horse Pike (08009-1273)
PHONE..................................856 753-0055
Kevin J Humphrey, *President*
Karen Humphrey, *Treasurer*
EMP: 5
SQ FT: 1,600
SALES (est): 903.6K **Privately Held**
SIC: 2752 Commercial printing, lithographic

(G-421)
COMPUTA-BASE-MACHINING INC
411 N Grove St (08009-9704)
P.O. Box 340 (08009-0340)
PHONE..................................856 767-9517
Agustin Rosado, *President*
Suchi Srinivasan, *Vice Pres*
Bart Sichel, *Chief Mktg Ofcr*
Sherri Schachter, *Manager*
EMP: 17 **EST:** 1981
SQ FT: 22,000
SALES (est): 3.4MM **Privately Held**
WEB: www.computabase.com
SIC: 3599 Machine shop, jobbing & repair

(G-422)
HANSON & ZOLLINGER INC
Also Called: Alliance Contract Mfg
117 Jackson Rd (08009-9160)
PHONE..................................856 626-3440
Robert Zollinger, *President*
Michael Hanson, *Vice Pres*
▲ **EMP:** 12
SALES: 3MM **Privately Held**
SIC: 3537 3231 Tables, lift: hydraulic; medical & laboratory glassware: made from purchased glass

(G-423)
J B & SONS CONCRETE PRODUCTS (PA)
358 New Brooklyn Rd (08009-9513)
P.O. Box 35, Sicklerville (08081-0035)
PHONE..................................856 767-4140
Joe Boccella, *President*
◆ **EMP:** 11
SALES (est): 1.1MM **Privately Held**
SIC: 3272 5211 Concrete products, precast; masonry materials & supplies

(G-424)
JOHNS MANVILLE CORPORATION
437 N Grove St (08009-9704)
P.O. Box 130 (08009-0130)
PHONE..................................856 768-7000
Jason Rogers, *Production*
Andrew Reid, *Electrical Engi*
Samuel A Jones Jr, *Persnl Mgr*
Eddie Harp, *Marketing Mgr*
Roger Stahl, *Manager*
EMP: 250
SALES (corp-wide): 225.3B **Publicly Held**
WEB: www.jm.com
SIC: 3296 Mineral wool
HQ: Johns Manville Corporation
717 17th St Ste 800
Denver CO 80202
303 978-2000

(G-425)
KESKES PRINTING LLC
5 W Taunton Ave (08009-1441)
P.O. Box 205 (08009-0205)
PHONE..................................856 767-4733
Joseph C Keskes, *Owner*
Jean Keskes, *Mng Member*
Joseph Keskes, *Mng Member*
EMP: 5 **EST:** 1972
SQ FT: 2,250
SALES: 300K **Privately Held**
WEB: www.keskes.com
SIC: 2752 2759 Commercial printing, offset; letterpress printing

(G-426)
LCN PARTNERS INC
Also Called: Lcn Solutions
115 Cross Keys Rd (08009-9477)
PHONE..................................215 755-1000
Joseph Robbins, *President*
EMP: 18
SALES (est): 346.5K **Privately Held**
SIC: 4899 1731 3661 3663 Data communication services; voice, data & video wiring contractor; fiber optics communications equipment; antennas, transmitting & communications; antennas, radar or communications

(G-427)
MOUNTAIN PRINTING COMPANY INC
27 N Atlantic Ave (08009-1694)
P.O. Box 608 (08009-0608)
PHONE..................................856 767-7600
Rose Marie De Pasquale, *President*
Millie Clerkin, *Office Mgr*
▲ **EMP:** 33 **EST:** 1962
SQ FT: 23,000
SALES (est): 7.8MM **Privately Held**
WEB: www.mountainprinting.com
SIC: 2752 Commercial printing, offset

(G-428)
PETERS LABORATORIES
1 Hillside Ln (08009-1703)
PHONE..................................856 767-4144
Peter Serubo, *President*
Susan Zatkins, *Vice Pres*
EMP: 12
SALES (est): 502.8K **Privately Held**
SIC: 3999 Manufacturing industries

(G-429)
SAR INDUSTRIAL FINISHING INC
104 N Route 73 (08009-9636)
PHONE..................................609 567-2772
Ralph Mauro, *President*
EMP: 15
SALES (est): 1.6MM **Privately Held**
SIC: 3471 Finishing, metals or formed products

(G-430)
T J ECKARDT ASSOCIATES INC
Also Called: Honeywell Authorized Dealer
230 Williamstown Rd (08009-9730)
P.O. Box 570, Sicklerville (08081-0570)
PHONE..................................856 767-4111
Thomas J Eckardt, *President*
Bernadette Eckardt, *Treasurer*
Harry Eckardt, *Marketing Staff*
Stacy Ammons, *Admin Asst*
EMP: 15
SQ FT: 5,000
SALES (est): 3.2MM **Privately Held**
WEB: www.tjeckardt.com
SIC: 1711 3444 Warm air heating & air conditioning contractor; ducts, sheet metal

(G-431)
UFP BERLIN LLC
Also Called: Universal Forest Products
159 Jackson Rd (08009-2608)
PHONE..................................856 767-0596
Maury Mejia, *Director*
David Goldman,
EMP: 150 **EST:** 2010
SALES: 22.2MM
SALES (corp-wide): 4.4B **Publicly Held**
SIC: 2421 5031 Building & structural materials, wood; building materials, exterior; building materials, interior
PA: Universal Forest Products, Inc.
2801 E Beltline Ave Ne
Grand Rapids MI 49525
616 364-6161

(G-432)
UNITED ASPHALT COMPANY
237 N Grove St (08009-9662)
P.O. Box 291, Cedar Brook (08018-0291)
PHONE..................................856 753-9811
Mark Umosella Sr, *President*
Tim McLain, *General Mgr*
James Umosella, *Purch Mgr*
▲ **EMP:** 26 **EST:** 1963
SQ FT: 20,000
SALES: 13MM **Privately Held**
SIC: 2952 Roofing materials; roofing felts, cements or coatings

(G-433)
WEILER & SONS LLC
Also Called: W & S Steel Products
170 Jackson Rd (08009-2607)
PHONE..................................856 767-8842
Michael P Weiler, *Mng Member*
Michael Weiler, *Mng Member*
EMP: 4
SQ FT: 2,500
SALES (est): 537.5K **Privately Held**
SIC: 3479 Chasing on metals

(G-434)
WINSLOW RENTAL & SUPPLY INC
204 Williamstown Rd (08009-9730)
P.O. Box 517 (08009-0517)
PHONE..................................856 767-5554
Tom Dixon Sr, *President*
Charlotte Dixon, *Vice Pres*
EMP: 7
SQ FT: 4,000
SALES (est): 3.1MM **Privately Held**
WEB: www.winslowrental.com
SIC: 5082 7353 7359 3546 General construction machinery & equipment; heavy construction equipment rental; stores & yards equipment rental; saws & sawing equipment

Bernardsville
Somerset County

(G-435)
BERNARDSVILLE NEWS
17 Morristown Rd (07924)
PHONE..................................908 766-3900
Pete Conover, *Principal*
EMP: 4 **EST:** 2001
SALES (est): 218.3K **Privately Held**
SIC: 2711 Newspapers

(G-436)
CLASSIC SILKS COM I
131 Roundtop Rd (07924-2106)
PHONE..................................908 204-0940
Ganesh Prasad, *Principal*
EMP: 4
SALES (est): 182.8K **Privately Held**
SIC: 2299 Textile goods

(G-437)
CONTINENTAL CUP COMPANY LLC
90 Boulderwood Dr (07924-1402)
PHONE..................................602 803-4666
Rick Timone, *President*
EMP: 4
SALES (est): 252.9K **Privately Held**
SIC: 2656 Paper cups, plates, dishes & utensils

(G-438)
GREENBROOK STAIRS INC
14 Dayton St (07924-2535)
P.O. Box 126, Basking Ridge (07920-0126)
PHONE..................................908 221-9145
Keith Fitting, *President*
Calvin Foots, *Vice Pres*
EMP: 7
SQ FT: 3,500
SALES (est): 1.3MM **Privately Held**
WEB: www.greenbrookstairs.com
SIC: 2431 Staircases & stairs, wood

GEOGRAPHIC

(G-439)
MEADOWBROOK INVENTIONS INC
260 Mine Brook Rd (07924-2117)
P.O. Box 960 (07924-0960)
PHONE..............................908 766-0606
Harold Sutton, *President*
Roberta Ruschmann, *Principal*
Zbigniew Swiderski, *Plant Mgr*
Joe Colleran, *Executive*
Sarah Snyder, *Executive Asst*
◆ EMP: 30 EST: 1948
SQ FT: 40,000
SALES (est): 6MM Privately Held
WEB: www.meadowbrookglitter.com
SIC: 3952 Artists' materials, except pencils & leads

(G-440)
OTEX SPECIALTY NARROW FABRICS (PA)
4 Essex Ave Ste 403 (07924-2265)
PHONE..............................908 879-3636
Denise A Offray, *President*
Timothy Offray, *Business Mgr*
▲ EMP: 9
SALES (est): 36.4MM Privately Held
SIC: 2241 Narrow fabric mills

(G-441)
PARKER PUBLICATIONS INC
Also Called: Caldwell Progress
17 Morristown Rd 19 (07924-2312)
P.O. Box 687 (07924-0687)
PHONE..............................908 766-3900
Steven W Parker, *President*
Cort Parker, *Principal*
Liz Parker, *Principal*
Nancy Parker, *Principal*
EMP: 50
SQ FT: 5,000
SALES (est): 3.7MM Privately Held
WEB: www.parkerexpressions.com
SIC: 2711 Newspapers, publishing & printing

(G-442)
PRETTY UGLY LLC
20 Olcott Sq (07924-2317)
PHONE..............................908 620-0931
Drew Matilsky,
▲ EMP: 17 EST: 2011
SALES (est): 2.2MM Privately Held
SIC: 3942 5092 Dolls & stuffed toys; dolls

(G-443)
R & B PRINTING INC
Also Called: Bernardsville Print Center
19-21 Mine Brook Rd Fl 1 (07924-2492)
PHONE..............................908 766-4073
Richard Steinberg, *President*
Beth Steinberg, *Vice Pres*
EMP: 9
SQ FT: 2,500
SALES (est): 1.8MM Privately Held
SIC: 2752 7334 2789 2396 Commercial printing, offset; photocopying & duplicating services; bookbinding & related work; automotive & apparel trimmings

(G-444)
SWCE INC (PA)
Also Called: Swce Group, The
360 Mount Harmony Rd (07924-1415)
PHONE..............................908 766-5695
Terrence K Schroeder, *President*
EMP: 20
SALES (est): 2.8MM Privately Held
SIC: 7372 8243 Prepackaged software; data processing schools

Beverly
Burlington County

(G-445)
AE LITHO OFFSET PRINTERS INC
Also Called: Aelitho Group
450 Broad St (08010-1546)
P.O. Box 9000 (08010-9000)
PHONE..............................609 239-0700
Jeff Bozzi, *CEO*

EMP: 69
SQ FT: 50,000
SALES: 12MM
SALES (corp-wide): 20MM Privately Held
WEB: www.aelitho.com
SIC: 2752 Lithographing on metal; commercial printing, offset
PA: Intellicor Llc
330 Eden Rd
Lancaster PA 17601
717 291-3100

(G-446)
ALCOP ADHESIVE LABEL CO
826 Perkins Ln (08010-1619)
P.O. Box 398 (08010-0398)
PHONE..............................609 871-4400
Wilmer Webster III, *President*
Wilmer P Webster III, *President*
Brook Webster, *Vice Pres*
John Webster, *Vice Pres*
EMP: 9
SQ FT: 16,000
SALES (est): 3.7MM Privately Held
SIC: 2759 Labels & seals: printing

(G-447)
ASPEN MANUFACTURING CO INC
Also Called: Aspen Appliance Parts
703 Van Rossum Ave Unit 5 (08010-1739)
PHONE..............................609 871-6400
▲ EMP: 7 EST: 1998
SQ FT: 4,500
SALES (est): 540K Privately Held
SIC: 3469 Mfg Metal Stampings

(G-448)
CAMPBELL CONVERTING CORP
703 Van Rossum Ave Unit 2 (08010-1739)
PHONE..............................609 835-2720
Claude Campbell, *President*
Gavin Campbell, *Vice Pres*
John Campbell, *Vice Pres*
EMP: 8
SQ FT: 14,000
SALES (est): 847K Privately Held
SIC: 7389 2759 Printers' services: folding, collating; business forms: printing

(G-449)
COLORCRAFT SIGN CO
400 Magnolia St (08010-1526)
PHONE..............................609 386-1115
Stephenson J Molnar, *Owner*
Linda Molnar, *Co-Owner*
EMP: 11
SQ FT: 5,000
SALES: 300K Privately Held
WEB: www.colorcraftsign.com
SIC: 3993 2759 2399 5999 Signs, not made in custom sign painting shops; screen printing; emblems, badges & insignia; trophies & plaques; badges

(G-450)
DISTINCTIVE WDWRK BY ROB HOFFM
703 Van Rossum Ave Unit 1 (08010-1739)
PHONE..............................609 877-8122
Rob Hoffman, *Owner*
EMP: 6
SALES (est): 360K Privately Held
SIC: 2499 Decorative wood & woodwork

(G-451)
FYTH LABS INC
Also Called: Lm PC Products
455 Warren St E (08010-1432)
PHONE..............................856 313-7362
Chad Martin, *President*
EMP: 6
SALES (est): 600.1K Privately Held
WEB: www.fliinvent.com
SIC: 8711 3577 Consulting engineer; electrical or electronic engineering; computer peripheral equipment

(G-452)
INTERSTATE WELDING & MFG CO
1510 Village Ct (08010-2021)
PHONE..............................800 676-4666
Joseph Marcello Russomanno, *President*

Florence Russomanno, *Admin Sec*
EMP: 15
SQ FT: 7,000
SALES (est): 3.8MM Privately Held
WEB: www.iwminc.com
SIC: 1711 3312 3325 8711 Mechanical contractor; structural shapes & pilings, steel; alloy steel castings, except investment; consulting engineer

(G-453)
PIONEER RAILING INC
401 Railroad Ave (08010)
PHONE..............................609 387-0981
EMP: 6 EST: 1946
SALES (est): 720.8K Privately Held
SIC: 3446 Mfg Custom Ornamental Iron & Metal Work

(G-454)
SMARTPLAY INTERNATIONAL INC
1550 Bridgeboro Rd (08010-2216)
PHONE..............................609 880-1860
David Michaud, *President*
Thomas C Markert, *Exec VP*
Zachary Luneau, *Project Mgr*
Russell Wells, *Project Mgr*
Wayne Ryba, *Foreman/Supr*
▲ EMP: 30
SQ FT: 15,000
SALES: 5.7MM Privately Held
WEB: www.smartplay.com
SIC: 3999 Coin-operated amusement machines

Birmingham
Burlington County

(G-455)
CABINET TRONICS INC
100 Birmingham Rd (08011)
P.O. Box 198 (08011-0198)
PHONE..............................609 267-2625
Michael Lockwood, *President*
Lori Lockwood, *Vice Pres*
EMP: 15
SQ FT: 12,000
SALES (est): 2.2MM Privately Held
WEB: www.cabinettronics.com
SIC: 2431 Millwork

(G-456)
CGM US INC (PA)
Also Called: Photon Technology Intl
300 Birmingham Rd (08011)
PHONE..............................609 894-4420
Charles G Marianik, *Ch of Bd*
Ronald Kovach, *Exec VP*
Joseph Marshaleck, *Vice Pres*
EMP: 20
SQ FT: 9,600
SALES (est): 5.6MM Privately Held
WEB: www.pti-nj.com
SIC: 3827 3845 Optical instruments & lenses; laser systems & equipment, medical

(G-457)
LANXESS SYBRON CHEMICALS INC (DH)
200 Birmingham Rd (08011)
P.O. Box 66 (08011-0066)
PHONE..............................609 893-1100
Markus Linke, *President*
◆ EMP: 199
SQ FT: 200,000
SALES (est): 104.3MM
SALES (corp-wide): 8.2B Privately Held
WEB: www.ion-exchange.com
SIC: 2899 3589 2843 Water treating compounds; water filters & softeners, household type; textile processing assistants
HQ: Lanxess Corporation
111 Ridc Park West Dr
Pittsburgh PA 15275
800 526-9377

Blackwood
Camden County

(G-458)
A & J CARPETS INC
Also Called: A&J Flooring Outlet
4461 Route 42 (08012-1711)
PHONE..............................856 227-1753
James Depaino, *President*
Andrew Depaino, *Vice Pres*
EMP: 5
SQ FT: 15,000
SALES (est): 1MM Privately Held
SIC: 5713 2273 2434 Carpets; carpets & rugs; wood kitchen cabinets

(G-459)
AROSE INC (PA)
1001 Lower Landing Rd # 412 (08012-3119)
PHONE..............................856 481-4351
Kemp Cook, *President*
Frank Beierschmitt, *Vice Pres*
EMP: 37
SQ FT: 2,500
SALES (est): 3.4MM Privately Held
WEB: www.aroseinc.com
SIC: 1731 5065 5063 3357 Telephone & telephone equipment installation; communication equipment; wire & cable; communication wire; telephone equipment & systems

(G-460)
AVERSAS ITALIAN BAKERY INC
801 Route 168 (08012-1472)
PHONE..............................856 227-8005
Ralph Aversa, *President*
Catherine Aversa, *Treasurer*
EMP: 22
SQ FT: 10,000
SALES (est): 6.4MM Privately Held
WEB: www.aversasbakery.com
SIC: 5149 5461 2051 Bakery products; bakeries; bread, cake & related products

(G-461)
BRADBURY BURIAL VAULT CO INC
Also Called: Delaware Valley Vault
761 Lower Landing Rd (08012-5132)
PHONE..............................856 227-2555
Lawrence A Kenney Sr, *Ch of Bd*
Lawrence A Kenney Jr, *President*
William Kenney, *Vice Pres*
▲ EMP: 20 EST: 1940
SQ FT: 17,000
SALES (est): 3.3MM Privately Held
SIC: 3272 Burial vaults, concrete or precast terrazzo

(G-462)
CAESARS PASTA LLC
1001 Lower Landing Rd (08012-3124)
PHONE..............................856 227-2585
Stephen Leins, *Plant Mgr*
▲ EMP: 40
SQ FT: 24,000
SALES (est): 8.5MM Privately Held
SIC: 2038 Frozen specialties

(G-463)
DELAWARE VALLEY VAULT CO INC
761 Lower Landing Rd (08012-5132)
PHONE..............................856 227-2555
Lawrence A Kenney Jr, *President*
William T Kenney, *Vice Pres*
EMP: 8
SALES (est): 763.8K Privately Held
SIC: 3272 5087 Burial vaults, concrete or precast terrazzo; concrete burial vaults & boxes

(G-464)
DUNE GRASS PUBLISHING LLC
39 Indiana Ave (08012-3819)
PHONE..............................609 774-6562
EMP: 5 EST: 2013
SALES (est): 201.6K Privately Held
SIC: 2741 Miscellaneous publishing

(G-465)
E C D VENTURES INC
Also Called: Qwik Pack & Ship
3501 Route 42 Ste 130 (08012-1780)
PHONE.....................856 875-1100
Eric Dettrey, *President*
EMP: 4
SALES (est): 362.1K **Privately Held**
WEB: www.qwikpackusa.com
SIC: 7389 5113 4822 4731 Mailbox
rental & related service; corrugated &
solid fiber boxes; facsimile transmission
services; agents, shipping; moving serv-
ices; invitation & stationery printing & en-
graving

(G-466)
GCE MARKET INC (PA)
1001 Lower Landing Rd # 307
(08012-3120)
PHONE.....................856 401-8900
Jaydeep Patel, *President*
Rina Patel, *CFO*
Lawrance Kuo, *Sales Staff*
Raj Mushiana, *Manager*
Ajay Kulkarni, *Info Tech Mgr*
▲ EMP: 6 EST: 2000
SALES (est): 1.2MM **Privately Held**
WEB: www.gcemarket.com
SIC: 3674 Semiconductors & related de-
vices

(G-467)
GLASSBLOWERSCOM LLC (PA)
234 Bells Lake Rd (08012-1640)
P.O. Box 8089 (08012-8089)
PHONE.....................856 232-7898
Thomas J Cachaza,
EMP: 4
SALES (est): 675.6K **Privately Held**
WEB: www.glassblowers.com
SIC: 3229 Pressed & blown glass

(G-468)
GRAPHIC IMPRESSIONS PRTG CO
4391 Route 42 (08012-1710)
PHONE.....................856 728-2266
Joseph Rocca, *Partner*
Daniel Rocca, *Principal*
EMP: 5
SALES (est): 725.9K **Privately Held**
SIC: 2752 Commercial printing, offset

(G-469)
I SEE OPTICAL LABORATORIES (PA)
44 W Church St (08012-3965)
PHONE.....................856 227-9300
Michael Pak, *President*
EMP: 13
SQ FT: 3,000
SALES (est): 1.3MM **Privately Held**
WEB: www.eyeglasslenses.com
SIC: 3851 Lens grinding, except prescrip-
tion: ophthalmic

(G-470)
J L ERECTORS INC
835 Camden Ave (08012-4659)
PHONE.....................856 232-9400
Joel Lyons, *President*
James Lyons, *Corp Secy*
EMP: 25
SALES (est): 6.5MM **Privately Held**
WEB: www.jlerectors.com
SIC: 3272 Precast terrazo or concrete
products

(G-471)
JOHNSON ASSOCIATES SYSTEMS INC
900 Route 168 Ste F4 (08012-3209)
PHONE.....................856 228-2175
Hosea Johnson, *President*
EMP: 10
SQ FT: 3,000
SALES: 2MM **Privately Held**
WEB: www.jasystemsinc.com
SIC: 7374 3842 Data processing service;
prosthetic appliances

(G-472)
JOHNSON CONTROLS INC
1001 Lower Landing Rd # 409
(08012-3119)
PHONE.....................856 245-9977
Barry Safranek, *Manager*
EMP: 26 **Privately Held**
SIC: 2531 Seats, automobile
HQ: Johnson Controls, Inc.
5757 N Green Bay Ave
Milwaukee WI 53209
414 524-1200

(G-473)
JONTOL UNLIMITED LLC (PA)
1134 S Black Horse Pike (08012-2703)
PHONE.....................858 652-1113
Gregory Tolver, *Marketing Staff*
James Jones, *Mng Member*
Kenneth Robertson, *Mng Member*
EMP: 7
SALES (est): 1.6MM **Privately Held**
SIC: 1542 3711 5045 5049 Commercial
& office building, new construction; commercial & office buildings, renovation &
repair; military motor vehicle assembly;
computers, peripherals & software; law
enforcement equipment & supplies; industrial supplies; safety equipment & supplies

(G-474)
KARCHER NORTH AMERICA INC
500 University Ct (08012-3230)
PHONE.....................856 228-1800
Elliot Younessian, *CEO*
EMP: 12
SALES (corp-wide): 2.8B **Privately Held**
SIC: 3589 Commercial cleaning equip-
ment; dirt sweeping units, industrial; vac-
uum cleaners & sweepers, electric:
industrial
HQ: Karcher North America, Inc.
4555 Airport Way Fl 4
Denver CO 80239
303 762-1800

(G-475)
MJG TECHNOLOGIES INCORPORATED
832 Camden Ave (08012-4660)
P.O. Box 314, Pitman (08071-0314)
PHONE.....................856 228-6118
Jeff Genzel, *Vice Pres*
▼ EMP: 7
SALES: 250K **Privately Held**
WEB: www.electricmatch.com
SIC: 2892 Squibbs, electric

(G-476)
OMNIPLANAR INC
Also Called: Honeywell Scanning & Mobility
90 Coles Rd (08012-4683)
PHONE.....................800 782-4263
Eric Batterman, *President*
Garrett K Russell, *General Mgr*
Donald Chandler, *Vice Pres*
EMP: 4
SQ FT: 2,500
SALES (est): 341.4K
SALES (corp-wide): 41.8B **Publicly Held**
WEB: www.omniplanar.com
SIC: 3577 Magnetic ink & optical scanning
devices
HQ: Metrologic Instruments, Inc.
534 Fellowship Rd
Mount Laurel NJ 08054
856 228-8100

(G-477)
PINTO PRINTING
12 Sycamore Dr (08012-3147)
PHONE.....................856 232-2550
Cathy Pinto, *Principal*
EMP: 4
SALES (est): 299.5K **Privately Held**
SIC: 2752 Commercial printing, litho-
graphic

(G-478)
PORTABLE DEFENSE LLC
54 Gravers Ln (08012-5201)
PHONE.....................856 228-3010
Michael P Mosiondz, *Principal*

EMP: 4
SALES (est): 202.8K **Privately Held**
SIC: 3812 Defense systems & equipment

(G-479)
RESIDEX LLC
1001 Lower Landing Rd # 412
(08012-3119)
PHONE.....................856 232-0880
Peter Bonsted, *Manager*
EMP: 6
SALES (corp-wide): 3.1B **Privately Held**
WEB: www.residex.com
SIC: 2879 Insecticides & pesticides
HQ: Residex, Llc
29380 Beck Rd
Wixom MI 48393

(G-480)
REVEL NAIL LLC
90 Coles Rd (08012-4683)
PHONE.....................855 738-3501
Phon Malone,
Reed Sutton,
EMP: 31
SALES (est): 1.5MM **Privately Held**
SIC: 2844 Manicure preparations

(G-481)
STEWART BUSINESS FORMS INC
138 Frankford Ave (08012-3723)
P.O. Box 715, Voorhees (08043-0715)
PHONE.....................856 768-2011
Gail Stewart, *President*
James Stewart, *Vice Pres*
EMP: 10
SQ FT: 8,000
SALES (est): 1.6MM **Privately Held**
SIC: 2759 5112 2761 Business forms:
printing; business forms; manifold busi-
ness forms

(G-482)
US VISION INC (HQ)
Also Called: J C Penney Optical
1 Harmon Dr (08012-5103)
PHONE.....................856 228-1000
Mark Robinski, *Regional Mgr*
Thomas Spaulding, *District Mgr*
Sean Keegan, *Prdtn Mgr*
Brian Seay, *Inv Control Mgr*
Becky Henszey, *Buyer*
▲ EMP: 412
SQ FT: 20,000
SALES (est): 625.9MM
SALES (corp-wide): 793.8MM **Privately
Held**
WEB: www.usvision.com
SIC: 3827 5995 Optical instruments &
lenses; eyeglasses, prescription
PA: Refac Optical Group
1 Harmon Dr
Blackwood NJ 08012
856 228-1000

(G-483)
VORTEX SUPPLY LLC
1001 Lower Landing Rd # 205
(08012-3124)
PHONE.....................856 352-6681
Adam Huesser, *Mng Member*
EMP: 6 EST: 2015
SALES (est): 280.6K **Privately Held**
SIC: 3471 Polishing, metals or formed
products

Blairstown
Warren County

(G-484)
ALEXANDER JAMES CORP
845 State Route 94 (07825-4102)
PHONE.....................908 362-9266
Francesca Fazzolari, *President*
Alex Davidson, *Corp Secy*
David Robinson, *Vice Pres*
Carol Gamsby, *Sales Staff*
▲ EMP: 100 EST: 1976
SQ FT: 21,000

SALES (est): 15.5MM **Privately Held**
WEB: www.james-alexander.com
SIC: 7389 3842 Packaging & labeling
services; surgical appliances & supplies

(G-485)
HEALTHCARE CART
71 Auble Rd (07825-3011)
PHONE.....................201 406-4797
Chris Sunda, *Owner*
EMP: 5 EST: 2011
SALES: 1MM **Privately Held**
SIC: 3841 Surgical & medical instruments

(G-486)
INDUSTRIAL METAL INC
169 Cedar Lake Rd (07825-9610)
PHONE.....................908 362-0084
Dan Ohern, *President*
▲ EMP: 9
SQ FT: 8,640
SALES (est): 1.5MM **Privately Held**
WEB: www.industrialmetal.com
SIC: 3441 Fabricated structural metal

(G-487)
PICTURE WINDOW SOFTWARE LLC
47 Cook Rd (07825-9792)
P.O. Box 649 (07825-0649)
PHONE.....................908 362-4000
Clay Greene, *President*
EMP: 4 EST: 1995
SALES (est): 731.5K **Privately Held**
WEB: www.pwin.com
SIC: 7372 Prepackaged software

Bloomfield
Essex County

(G-488)
A PLUS INSTALLS LLC
Also Called: A Plus Installation
29 27 Curtis St Fl 1 Flr 1 (07003)
PHONE.....................201 255-4412
Olya Shumilova, *President*
EMP: 5
SALES (est): 438.6K **Privately Held**
SIC: 5719 2591 5963 Venetian blinds;
vertical blinds; window shades; drapes &
curtains, house-to-house

(G-489)
ACKK STUDIOS LLC
411 E Passaic Ave (07003-5312)
PHONE.....................973 876-1327
Brian Allanson,
EMP: 7 EST: 2012
SALES (est): 202.8K **Privately Held**
SIC: 7372 Prepackaged software

(G-490)
ALLOY SOFTWARE INC
400 Broadacres Dr Ste 100 (07003-3175)
PHONE.....................973 661-9700
Vladimir Vinogradskiy, *President*
EMP: 10
SALES (est): 1MM **Privately Held**
SIC: 7371 7372 Software programming
applications; business oriented computer
software

(G-491)
BANKS BROS CORPORATION (PA)
24 Federal Plz (07003-5636)
PHONE.....................973 680-4488
Stanley Banks, *President*
Lawrence Banks, *President*
EMP: 65
SQ FT: 40,000
SALES (est): 21.4MM **Privately Held**
WEB: www.banksbroscorp.com
SIC: 3053 3069 3714 Gasket materials;
sheeting, rubber or rubberized fabric;
motor vehicle parts & accessories

(G-492)
BUDGET PRINT CENTER
332 Broad St (07003-2728)
PHONE.....................973 743-0073
Thomas C Destefano, *Owner*
EMP: 8

SQ FT: 1,100
SALES (est): 570K **Privately Held**
SIC: 2752 7389 7334 2791 Commercial printing, offset; printing broker; photocopying & duplicating services; typesetting; bookbinding & related work; automotive & apparel trimmings

(G-493)
C M FURNACES INC
103 Dewey St (07003-4298)
PHONE......................................973 338-6500
David Neill, *President*
Jim Neill, *Vice Pres*
Terri Monaco, *Purch Mgr*
John Daiuto, *Engineer*
Ramon Morales, *Engineer*
◆ EMP: 30
SQ FT: 25,000
SALES (est): 9.3MM **Privately Held**
WEB: www.cmfurnaces.com
SIC: 3567 Heating units & devices, industrial: electric

(G-494)
CAMBRIDGE BAGELS INC
Also Called: Cambridge Bagel Factory
648 Bloomfield Ave (07003-2511)
PHONE......................................973 743-5683
Jim Best, *President*
EMP: 15
SQ FT: 2,000
SALES (est): 633.3K **Privately Held**
SIC: 5461 2051 Bagels; bagels, fresh or frozen

(G-495)
CAW LLC
248 Montgomery St (07003-4930)
PHONE......................................973 429-7004
Oscar Costa, *Mng Member*
Maria Costa,
EMP: 16
SQ FT: 11,000
SALES (est): 1.7MM **Privately Held**
SIC: 2431 Millwork

(G-496)
COLES AND BLENMAN NETWORK LLC
117 Orange St (07003-4703)
PHONE......................................973 432-7041
Frank Blenman, *CEO*
EMP: 5
SALES (est): 110.8K **Privately Held**
SIC: 7371 7372 Computer software development & applications; application computer software

(G-497)
COMPLETE OPTICAL LABORATORY
Also Called: Ecca
1255 Broad St Ste 202 (07003-3061)
PHONE......................................973 338-8886
Dwayne Carter, *President*
EMP: 15
SQ FT: 5,000
SALES (est): 2MM **Privately Held**
SIC: 5049 8042 5995 3851 Optical goods; offices & clinics of optometrists; optical goods stores; ophthalmic goods

(G-498)
COSRICH GROUP INC (DH)
51 La France Ave 55 (07003-5681)
PHONE......................................866 771-7473
Laura Hite, *President*
▲ EMP: 22
SQ FT: 200,000
SALES (est): 4.6MM
SALES (corp-wide): 2.5B **Privately Held**
WEB: www.cosrich.com
SIC: 2844 Cosmetic preparations
HQ: Pmc, Inc.
    12243 Branford St
    Sun Valley CA 91352
    818 896-1101

(G-499)
COSTA CUSTOM CABINETS INC
Also Called: Costa's Cabinets
248 Montgomery St (07003-4930)
PHONE......................................973 429-7004
Oscar Costa, *President*
Manny Forlenza, *Accountant*

EMP: 13
SQ FT: 12,000
SALES (est): 1.6MM **Privately Held**
SIC: 2541 1751 Cabinets, except refrigerated: show, display, etc.: wood; cabinet building & installation

(G-500)
CSG SYSTEMS INC
1455 Broad St Ste 110 (07003-3039)
PHONE......................................973 337-4400
Cynthia Jenkins, *Info Tech Mgr*
EMP: 26 **Publicly Held**
SIC: 2752 Commercial printing, lithographic
HQ: Csg Systems, Inc.
    18020 Burt St
    Elkhorn NE 68022

(G-501)
GLOBAL STRATEGY INSTITUTE A
55 Park Ave Unit 35 (07003-2663)
P.O. Box 1868, Montclair (07042-7868)
PHONE......................................973 615-7447
John Floropoulos, *President*
EMP: 5
SALES (est): 222.7K **Privately Held**
SIC: 2721 7812 8733 Trade journals: publishing only, not printed on site; educational motion picture production, television; noncommercial social research organization; economic research, noncommercial

(G-502)
HADDAD BROS INC
118 John F Kennedy Dr N (07003-3372)
PHONE......................................718 377-5505
John Isseco, *Branch Mgr*
EMP: 50
SALES (corp-wide): 6.4MM **Privately Held**
WEB: www.haddadbros.com
SIC: 2361 2369 2335 Girls' & children's dresses, blouses & shirts; girls' & children's outerwear; women's, juniors' & misses' dresses
PA: Haddad Bros. Inc.
    28 W 36th St Rm 1026
    New York NY 10018
    212 563-2117

(G-503)
J T MURDOCH SHOES
Also Called: Murdoch, J T Shoes
623 Bloomfield Ave (07003-2502)
P.O. Box 505 (07003-0505)
PHONE......................................973 748-6484
Mary Murdoch, *President*
EMP: 10 EST: 1949
SQ FT: 1,600
SALES: 1MM **Privately Held**
SIC: 5661 2252 Children's shoes; men's shoes; women's shoes; shoes, orthopedic; socks

(G-504)
JANET SHOPS INC
550 Bloomfield Ave (07003-3302)
PHONE......................................973 748-4992
Robert Bluestone, *President*
EMP: 10
SQ FT: 10,000
SALES (est): 780K **Privately Held**
SIC: 5621 2326 Ready-to-wear apparel, women's; medical & hospital uniforms, men's

(G-505)
L3HARRIS TECHNOLOGIES INC
Also Called: Exelis Geospatial Systems
1515 Broad St (07003-3002)
PHONE......................................585 269-6600
William Gattle, *President*
David Melcher, *President*
Christopher D Young,
EMP: 163
SALES (corp-wide): 6.8B **Publicly Held**
SIC: 3812 Search & navigation equipment
PA: L3harris Technologies, Inc.
    1025 W Nasa Blvd
    Melbourne FL 32919
    321 727-9100

(G-506)
LOUIS A NELSON INC
224 Glenwood Ave (07003-2416)
PHONE......................................973 743-7404
David Sibilia, *President*
Stephen Cariani, *Exec VP*
EMP: 12 EST: 1947
SQ FT: 6,000
SALES: 1.5MM **Privately Held**
SIC: 2821 Molding compounds, plastics

(G-507)
LS RUBBER INDUSTRIES INC (HQ)
24 Federal Plz (07003-5636)
PHONE......................................973 680-4488
Andrew Banks, *President*
Lawrence Banks, *President*
Anjum Qureshi, *General Mgr*
Stanley F Banks, *Corp Secy*
EMP: 10
SQ FT: 35,000
SALES: 1MM
SALES (corp-wide): 21.4MM **Privately Held**
SIC: 3069 3714 3053 Foam rubber; motor vehicle parts & accessories; gaskets, packing & sealing devices
PA: Banks Bros Corporation
    24 Federal Plz
    Bloomfield NJ 07003
    973 680-4488

(G-508)
LUMMUS OVERSEAS CORPORATION
Lummus Heat Transf Systems Div
1515 Broad St (07003-3002)
PHONE......................................973 893-3000
Mohammed Tolba, *President*
Michael Blaney, *General Mgr*
Catherine Bensulock, *Principal*
Arthur Carlotti, *Principal*
Kaye Bell-Reiter, *Human Res Dir*
EMP: 40
SALES (corp-wide): 153.1MM **Privately Held**
SIC: 3511 3625 Turbines & turbine generator sets; relays & industrial controls
PA: Lummus Overseas Corporation
    1515 Broad St
    Bloomfield NJ 07003
    973 893-1515

(G-509)
LUMMUS TECHNOLOGY VENTURES LLC
1515 Broad St Ste A110 (07003-3054)
PHONE......................................973 893-1515
Patrick K Mullen, *CEO*
Kirsten B David, *Exec VP*
Michael S Taff, *CFO*
EMP: 7 EST: 1992
SALES (est): 172.6K **Privately Held**
SIC: 8711 4731 3441 1531 Engineering services; freight transportation arrangement; fabricated structural metal; ; general management consultant

(G-510)
MID-STATE ENTERPRISES INC
Also Called: Latex Products Division
49 Ackerman St (07003-4253)
P.O. Box 25, Hawthorne (07507-0025)
PHONE......................................973 427-6040
David C Humphreys, *President*
Sandra Humphreys, *Admin Sec*
EMP: 10
SALES (est): 1.3MM **Privately Held**
SIC: 3061 Oil & gas field machinery rubber goods (mechanical)

(G-511)
MINOR RUBBER CO INC (PA)
Also Called: M R
49 Ackerman St (07003-4299)
PHONE......................................973 338-6800
David C Humphreys, *President*
Tom Fitzhenry, *Vice Pres*
Sandra Humphreys, *Vice Pres*
Sandy Humphreys, *Vice Pres*
Theresa Trumpore, *Treasurer*
EMP: 50 EST: 1914
SQ FT: 30,000

SALES (est): 6.9MM **Privately Held**
WEB: www.minorrubber.com
SIC: 3061 3052 Appliance rubber goods (mechanical); rubber & plastics hose & beltings

(G-512)
NOSHPEAK LLC
38 Patton Dr (07003-5224)
PHONE......................................978 631-7662
Lingeswaran Kandasamy,
Kalaivani Rasalingam,
EMP: 15
SALES (est): 305.2K **Privately Held**
SIC: 7372 7389 Application computer software;

(G-513)
NTE ELECTRONICS INC
44 Farrand St (07003-2516)
PHONE......................................973 748-5089
Andrew Licari, *President*
▲ EMP: 72
SALES (est): 7.5MM
SALES (corp-wide): 14.6MM **Privately Held**
WEB: www.nteinc.com
SIC: 3674 3675 3676 Semiconductors & related devices; electronic capacitors; electronic resistors
PA: Solid State, Incorporated
    46 Farrand St
    Bloomfield NJ 07003
    973 429-8700

(G-514)
OBJECTIF LUNE LLC (DH)
300 Broadacres Dr Ste 410 (07003-3153)
PHONE......................................973 780-0100
Didier Gombert, *CEO*
Ton Van Schaick, *CFO*
Martin Dallaire,
Bertrand Guignat,
Jean Nault,
EMP: 15
SALES (est): 5.1MM
SALES (corp-wide): 183.7K **Privately Held**
WEB: www.empoweryourprinter.com
SIC: 7372 Prepackaged software
HQ: Objectif Lune Inc
    2030 Boul Pie-Ix Bureau 500
    Montreal QC H1V 2
    514 875-5863

(G-515)
OBJECTIF LUNE LLC
300 Broadacres Dr Ste 410 (07003-3153)
PHONE......................................203 878-7206
EMP: 5
SALES (corp-wide): 183.7K **Privately Held**
WEB: www.empoweryourprinter.com
SIC: 7372 Prepackaged software
HQ: Objectif Lune Llc
    300 Broadacres Dr Ste 410
    Bloomfield NJ 07003
    973 780-0100

(G-516)
RADIX M I S
Also Called: Radix Computer Carrers
50 Hazelwood Rd (07003-5112)
PHONE......................................973 707-2121
Buddy Simpson, *President*
Michael Hart, *Finance Other*
EMP: 3
SQ FT: 1,500
SALES: 2MM **Privately Held**
WEB: www.radixjobs.com
SIC: 7379 7372 Computer related consulting services; prepackaged software

(G-517)
ROMBIOLO LLC
168 Broughton Ave (07003-4006)
PHONE......................................973 680-0405
Natalia Sierpes, *Principal*
EMP: 8
SALES (est): 610.2K **Privately Held**
SIC: 2051 Bread, cake & related products

(G-518)
STANLAR ENTERPRISES INC
24 Federal Plz (07003-5636)
PHONE......................................973 680-4488

Stanley F Banks, *President*
Lawrence Banks, *Vice Pres*
EMP: 24
SQ FT: 35,000
SALES (est): 2.2MM
SALES (corp-wide): 21.4MM **Privately Held**
SIC: 2392 Mattress pads
PA: Banks Bros Corporation
24 Federal Plz
Bloomfield NJ 07003
973 680-4488

(G-519)
STOBBS PRINTING CO INC
18 Washington St (07003-3412)
P.O. Box 91 (07003-0091)
PHONE...................................973 748-4441
Gayle Tungstead, *President*
EMP: 5 **EST:** 1931
SQ FT: 10,000
SALES (est): 250K **Privately Held**
SIC: 2752 Commercial printing, offset

(G-520)
SURROUND TECHNOLOGIES LLC (PA)
650 Bloomfield Ave # 102 (07003-2512)
PHONE...................................973 743-1277
Lee Paul,
EMP: 8
SALES: 750K **Privately Held**
WEB: www.surroundtech.com
SIC: 7372 Prepackaged software

(G-521)
ULTIMATE HAIR WORLD LTD LBLTY
Also Called: Tnss Enterprises
16 Molter Pl (07003-4706)
PHONE...................................973 622-6900
Natasha James, *Mng Member*
EMP: 10
SALES (est): 277.9K **Privately Held**
SIC: 3999 Doll wigs (hair)

(G-522)
WORRALL COMMUNITY NEWSPAPERS
Also Called: Independent Press, The
266 Liberty St (07003-2673)
P.O. Box 110 (07003-0110)
PHONE...................................973 743-4040
Bill Van Sant, *Editor*
Steve Proctor, *Regional Mgr*
EMP: 5
SALES (corp-wide): 6.6MM **Privately Held**
WEB: www.localsource.com
SIC: 2711 Newspapers: publishing only, not printed on site
PA: Worrall Community Newspapers Inc
1291 Stuyvesant Ave
Union NJ
908 686-7700

(G-523)
ZALLER STUDIOS INC
265 Watsessing Ave (07003-5726)
PHONE...................................973 743-5175
Gabriel Pereira, *President*
John Szalkowski, *General Mgr*
All Pereira, *Vice Pres*
Jack Pereira, *Vice Pres*
Dave Takacs, *Vice Pres*
EMP: 5
SQ FT: 30,000
SALES (est): 1.1MM **Privately Held**
SIC: 7336 3577 Silk screen design; graphic displays, except graphic terminals

(G-524)
ZWIER CORP
Also Called: Universal Company
497 Bloomfield Ave (07003-3304)
P.O. Box 4193, Clifton (07012-8193)
PHONE...................................973 748-4009
Michael Zwier, *President*
Joan Bertoli, *Vice Pres*
EMP: 4
SALES: 750K **Privately Held**
SIC: 2759 2791 2752 Screen printing; typesetting; commercial printing, lithographic

---

Bloomingdale
Passaic County

(G-525)
AKADEMA INC
Also Called: Academy of Proplayers
46 Star Lake Rd Ste B (07403-1244)
PHONE...................................973 304-1470
Joe Gilligan Jr, *CEO*
Lawrence Gilligan, *President*
Kris Totten, *Vice Pres*
Ryan Monaghan, *Warehouse Mgr*
Christopher Riecken, *Manager*
▲ **EMP:** 23
SQ FT: 25,000
SALES (est): 3.3MM **Privately Held**
WEB: www.akademapro.com
SIC: 3949 5941 5091 Baseball equipment & supplies, general; baseball equipment; athletic goods

(G-526)
CENTRAL SHIPPEE INC
Also Called: Allied Felt Group Div
46 Star Lake Rd (07403-1244)
P.O. Box 135 (07403-0135)
PHONE...................................973 838-1100
Donald A Hubner, *Ch of Bd*
Eric Hubner, *President*
Cornelius E Hubner Sr, *Vice Pres*
▲ **EMP:** 29
SQ FT: 17,000
SALES (est): 4.9MM **Privately Held**
WEB: www.centralshippee.com
SIC: 5199 2511 5023 Felt; wood household furniture; linens, table

(G-527)
ELECTRONIC POWER DESIGNS INC
Also Called: Epd
132 Union Ave (07403-1817)
PHONE...................................973 838-7055
Greg Brown, *President*
Sheila Brown, *Treasurer*
Elaine Barone, *Director*
EMP: 17
SQ FT: 7,500
SALES: 2.5MM **Privately Held**
SIC: 3613 3625 Panelboards & distribution boards, electric; control equipment, electric

(G-528)
ENERGY BEAMS INC
185 Hamburg Tpke (07403-1141)
PHONE...................................973 291-6555
John Richard, *CEO*
Tom Richard, *President*
EMP: 15 **EST:** 1966
SQ FT: 8,000
SALES (est): 3.2MM **Privately Held**
WEB: www.energybeams.com
SIC: 3589 3567 3563 3561 Commercial cleaning equipment; industrial furnaces & ovens; air & gas compressors; pumps & pumping equipment; machine tool accessories; metal heat treating

(G-529)
GERVENS ENTERPRISES INC
122 Hamburg Tpke Ste D (07403-1201)
PHONE...................................973 838-1600
William G Gervens, *President*
Glen M Schumacher, *Vice Pres*
Stacey G Poplawski, *Treasurer*
Deborah G Schumacher, *Treasurer*
EMP: 11
SQ FT: 3,500
SALES: 1.5MM **Privately Held**
SIC: 3446 1796 Railings, bannisters, guards, etc.: made from metal pipe; gates, ornamental metal; fire escapes, metal; machinery installation

(G-530)
SIGN ON INC
4 Maple Lake Rd (07403-1908)
PHONE...................................201 384-7714
Manohar G Massand, *President*
Kiran Massand, *Vice Pres*
EMP: 4

SALES: 250K **Privately Held**
SIC: 3993 2791 Electric signs; typesetting

(G-531)
VIBRATION MUNTINGS CONTRLS INC (PA)
Also Called: Korfund Dynamics
113 Main St (07403-1673)
PHONE...................................800 569-8423
John Wilson Jr, *CEO*
John P Giuliano, *President*
James J Nizzo, *Managing Dir*
Tom Steele, *Exec VP*
Amal Marzouq, *Engineer*
▲ **EMP:** 100 **EST:** 2005
SQ FT: 70,000
SALES: 35MM **Privately Held**
WEB: www.vmc-kdc.com
SIC: 3069 3496 Hard rubber & molded rubber products; miscellaneous fabricated wire products

---

Bloomsbury
Hunterdon County

(G-532)
WARREN PALLET COMPANY INC
601 County Road 627 (08804-3426)
PHONE...................................908 995-7172
Donald Tigar Sr, *President*
Lisa Tigar, *Manager*
Donald Tigar Jr, *Admin Sec*
EMP: 19
SQ FT: 4,800
SALES: 1.2MM **Privately Held**
SIC: 7699 2448 Pallet repair; pallets, wood

Bogota
Bergen County

(G-533)
JESCO IRON CRAFTS INC
Also Called: Jescraft
201 W Fort Lee Rd (07603-1207)
PHONE...................................201 488-4545
Michael Brown, *President*
Cory Mahady, *Opers Mgr*
EMP: 15 **EST:** 1946
SQ FT: 15,000
SALES (est): 2MM **Privately Held**
SIC: 3423 3444 Hand & edge tools; sheet metalwork

(G-534)
ORGANIZE IT-ALL INC (PA)
Also Called: O I A
24 River Rd Ste 201 (07603-1522)
PHONE...................................201 488-0808
James Lee, *President*
Michael Chiang, *Vice Pres*
Richard Eng, *Vice Pres*
Elise Fiorentelli, *Vice Pres*
Pauline MA, *Financial Exec*
◆ **EMP:** 48
SALES (est): 6.6MM **Privately Held**
SIC: 2599 3639 7699 Factory furniture & fixtures; major kitchen appliances, except refrigerators & stoves; household appliance repair services

(G-535)
OUTWATER PLSTCS/INDUSTRIES INC (PA)
Also Called: Outwater Plastics Industries
24 River Rd Ste 108 (07603-1535)
P.O. Box 500 (07603-0500)
PHONE...................................201 498-8750
Peter Kessler, *President*
David Norburg, *Managing Dir*
Susan Molnar, *Treasurer*
Cheryl McGee, *Admin Sec*
◆ **EMP:** 86
SQ FT: 160,000
SALES (est): 28.7MM **Privately Held**
WEB: www.outwater.com
SIC: 5072 2599 Hardware; bar furniture

Boonton
Morris County

(G-536)
ADRON INC
94 Fanny Rd (07005-1048)
P.O. Box 270 (07005-0270)
PHONE...................................973 334-1600
Louis J Amaducci, *President*
Robert L Amaducci, *Vice Pres*
Diane Rutter, *Purchasing*
Kathleen M Dunne, *Admin Sec*
EMP: 30
SQ FT: 20,000
SALES (est): 5.8MM **Privately Held**
WEB: www.adron.com
SIC: 2869 2844 2087 Industrial organic chemicals; toilet preparations; flavoring extracts & syrups

(G-537)
AEROPANEL CORPORATION
661 Myrtle Ave (07005-1916)
PHONE...................................973 335-9636
Jack Miller, *Vice Pres*
Sue Abate, *Sales Mgr*
EMP: 59
SALES (corp-wide): 6.5MM **Privately Held**
WEB: www.aeropanel.com
SIC: 3613 3812 3769 5088 Panel & distribution boards & other related apparatus; search & navigation equipment; guided missile & space vehicle parts & auxiliary equipment; aircraft equipment & supplies
PA: Aeropanel Corporation
2200 Post Oak Blvd
Houston TX 77056
713 552-0979

(G-538)
AIR TECHNOLOGY INC
429 Rockaway Valley Rd # 1100 (07005-8103)
P.O. Box 625 (07005-0625)
PHONE...................................973 334-4980
EMP: 4
SALES (corp-wide): 1.7MM **Privately Held**
SIC: 3312 Stainless steel
PA: Air Technology Inc
31 Glenbourne Dr
Boonton NJ 07005
973 334-3375

(G-539)
ALBAPALANT USA INC
5 Cheryl Ln (07005-9005)
PHONE...................................201 831-9200
EMP: 4
SALES (est): 240.7K **Privately Held**
SIC: 3567 Industrial furnaces & ovens

(G-540)
ALPHA TECH SERVICES
121 Hawkins Pl Ste 197 (07005-1127)
PHONE...................................973 283-2011
John Stevens, *President*
EMP: 8
SALES (est): 1MM **Privately Held**
SIC: 3577 Bar code (magnetic ink) printers

(G-541)
AMERICAN INTERNATIONAL CONT
Also Called: Ai Container
3 Mars Ct Ste 4 (07005-9308)
PHONE...................................973 917-3331
Dan Bourneuf, *President*
◆ **EMP:** 10 **EST:** 2010
SQ FT: 9,000
SALES: 4MM **Privately Held**
SIC: 3559 2656 Pharmaceutical machinery; frozen food & ice cream containers

(G-542)
AMERICAN MDLAR PWR SLTIONS INC
Also Called: Amps
429 Rockaway Valley Rd (07005-8101)
P.O. Box 604 (07005-0604)
PHONE...................................973 588-4026

Greg Lowndes, *President*
Daryl Killian, *Prdtn Mgr*
Andrea Marrone, *Treasurer*
Elizabeth Frawley, *Executive Asst*
EMP: 6
SALES (est): 1.6MM **Privately Held**
SIC: 3621 Generating apparatus & parts, electrical

(G-543)
ANGLERS SELECT LLC
Also Called: Eco Pro Tungsten
311 Mechanic St (07005-1830)
PHONE........................973 396-2959
Frank Wagenhosser, *Mng Member*
EMP: 8
SALES (est): 505.8K **Privately Held**
SIC: 3949 Fishing equipment

(G-544)
BIO-CHEM FLUIDICS INC
Also Called: Bio-Chem Valve
85 Fulton St Unit 12 (07005-1912)
PHONE........................973 263-3001
Tim O Sullivan, *President*
Bill Heinzmann, *Vice Pres*
Mark Nielsen, *Vice Pres*
Stephen Powell, *Vice Pres*
Joe Turiello, *Vice Pres*
▲ **EMP:** 60
SQ FT: 8,000
SALES (est): 17MM
SALES (corp-wide): 1.5B **Privately Held**
WEB: www.biochemvalve.com
SIC: 3491 Solenoid valves
HQ: Halma Holdings Inc.
11500 Northlake Dr # 306
Cincinnati OH 45249
513 772-5501

(G-545)
CARBONE AMERICA SCP DIVISION
400 Myrtle Ave 1 (07005-1839)
PHONE........................973 334-0700
Kenneth Pohing, *Principal*
EMP: 4
SALES (est): 323.2K **Privately Held**
SIC: 3999 Manufacturing industries

(G-546)
COMMUNICATION DEVICES INC (PA)
Also Called: CDI
85 Fulton St Unit 2 (07005-1912)
PHONE........................973 334-1980
Tadhg Kelly, *President*
Wade Clark, *President*
Robert Kelly, *Vice Pres*
◆ **EMP:** 15
SALES (est): 4.1MM **Privately Held**
WEB: www.commdevices.com
SIC: 3663 3825 Multiplex equipment; test equipment for electronic & electric measurement; network analyzers

(G-547)
CREATIVE CABINET DESIGNS INC
301 Main St (07005-1739)
PHONE........................973 402-5886
Manuel Silva, *President*
Maria Silva, *Vice Pres*
EMP: 10
SQ FT: 3,200
SALES (est): 190K **Privately Held**
SIC: 5712 2511 5031 1751 Cabinet work, custom; kitchen & dining room furniture; kitchen cabinets; cabinet & finish carpentry

(G-548)
DACO LIMITED PARTNERSHIP (PA)
Also Called: Dauphin North America
100 Fulton St (07005-1910)
PHONE........................973 263-1100
Nick Bayvel, *CEO*
Gary Chin, *President*
Roger Vasseur, *Regional Mgr*
Ben Payne, *Opers Mgr*
Carol Washor, *Manager*
▲ **EMP:** 70
SQ FT: 68,000

SALES (est): 27.9MM **Privately Held**
SIC: 5021 5049 2522 Chairs; scientific instruments; chairs, office: padded or plain, except wood

(G-549)
DAVIS SIGN SYSTEMS INC
65 Harrison St (07005-2033)
PHONE........................973 394-9909
Elaine Davis, *President*
EMP: 4
SQ FT: 7,000
SALES (est): 250K **Privately Held**
WEB: www.davissignsystems.com
SIC: 3993 Signs & advertising specialties

(G-550)
ELECTROMAGNETIC TECH INDS INC
50 Intervale Rd Ste 11 (07005-1060)
PHONE........................973 394-1719
John Howard, *President*
Chuck Fung, *President*
Thomas Economou, *COO*
▼ **EMP:** 65
SQ FT: 12,000
SALES: 25MM **Privately Held**
WEB: www.etiworld.com
SIC: 3679 3812 3663 Microwave components; antennas, radar or communications; antennas, transmitting & communications

(G-551)
ENTERIS BIOPHARMA INC
83 Fulton St (07005-1909)
PHONE........................973 453-3518
Joel Tune, *CEO*
Brian Zietsman, *President*
Paul Shields, *COO*
EMP: 1
SALES (est): 10.3MM **Publicly Held**
SIC: 2834 Pharmaceutical preparations
HQ: Swk Holdings Corporation
14755 Preston Rd Ste 105
Dallas TX 75254
972 687-7250

(G-552)
ESCADAUS INC
2 Wood Glen Way (07005-9738)
PHONE........................973 335-8888
Henry Kuo, *President*
EMP: 5
SQ FT: 3,500
SALES (est): 43.6K **Privately Held**
SIC: 3264 3499 Magnets, permanent: ceramic or ferrite; magnets, permanent: metallic

(G-553)
EVH LLC
Also Called: Audrey Hepburn Collection
6 Mars Ct Unit F5 (07005-9309)
PHONE........................973 257-0076
Edward Katz, *Mng Member*
EMP: 10
SQ FT: 28,000
SALES (est): 647.9K **Privately Held**
SIC: 2329 Men's & boys' sportswear & athletic clothing

(G-554)
FLOTTEC LLC (PA)
5 Hillcrest Rd (07005-9441)
PHONE........................973 588-4717
Frank Cappuccitti,
◆ **EMP:** 5
SALES (est): 1MM **Privately Held**
WEB: www.flottec.com
SIC: 2879 Trace elements (agricultural chemicals)

(G-555)
GP JAGER INC
328 W Main St (07005-1148)
P.O. Box 50 (07005-0050)
PHONE........................973 750-1180
Gregory Jager, *President*
Zuzanna Stolc, *Administration*
EMP: 4 EST: 2015
SALES (est): 657.8K **Privately Held**
SIC: 3589 Water treatment equipment, industrial; sewage treatment equipment

(G-556)
ICON ORTHOPEDIC CONCEPTS LLC
Also Called: Edge Orthopedics
6 Mars Ct Ste 3 (07005-9309)
PHONE........................973 794-6810
Steven Bridgio, *President*
Anna Kroll, *COO*
EMP: 5 EST: 2012
SQ FT: 3,180
SALES (est): 415.5K **Privately Held**
SIC: 3842 Orthopedic appliances
PA: Plasmology4, Inc.
8502 E Princess Dr # 210
Scottsdale AZ 85255

(G-557)
INSTOCK WIRELESS COMPONENTS
50 Intervale Rd Ste 1 (07005-1060)
PHONE........................973 335-6550
Michael Davo, *CEO*
▲ **EMP:** 10
SALES: 1.8MM **Privately Held**
SIC: 4812 3661 Cellular telephone services; carrier equipment, telephone or telegraph

(G-558)
JANKE & COMPANY INC
Also Called: Electronic Brazing Co Div
283 Myrtle Ave (07005-1753)
PHONE........................973 334-4477
Edward K Malavarca, *President*
EMP: 5
SALES (est): 707.7K **Privately Held**
SIC: 3825 Electrical power measuring equipment

(G-559)
JOHANSON MANUFACTURING CORP
301 Rockaway Valley Rd (07005-9192)
PHONE........................973 658-1051
Nancy Johanson, *CEO*
Rocco Melchione, *President*
Walter Hutton, *Exec VP*
Jon Krawczyk, *Branch Mgr*
EMP: 200 EST: 1945
SQ FT: 35,000
SALES (est): 31.8MM **Privately Held**
SIC: 3679 Electronic circuits

(G-560)
MARLO MANUFACTURING CO INC
301 Division St (07005-1826)
PHONE........................973 423-0226
Salvatore Pirruccio, *CEO*
Sal Pirruccio, *CEO*
Corrado Tommasi, *CFO*
EMP: 39
SQ FT: 35,000
SALES (est): 10.2MM **Privately Held**
WEB: www.marlomfg.com
SIC: 3599 Tubing, flexible metallic

(G-561)
MERCHANDISING DISPLAY CORP
Also Called: Mdc
14 Deer Trl (07005-9024)
PHONE........................973 299-8400
Arthur W Linz, *President*
EMP: 4 EST: 1964
SQ FT: 3,500
SALES (est): 340K **Privately Held**
SIC: 3993 Signs & advertising specialties

(G-562)
MERSEN USA PTT CORP (DH)
400 Myrtle Ave (07005-1839)
PHONE........................973 334-0700
Marc Sharlecois, *President*
Claudio Clemente, *Vice Pres*
Gary Pavlosky, *Treasurer*
Jeff Hewitt, *Admin Sec*
◆ **EMP:** 125
SQ FT: 250,000
SALES (est): 238MM
SALES (corp-wide): 2MM **Privately Held**
SIC: 3624 Brushes & brush stock contacts, electric

HQ: Mersen Usa Holding Corp.
400 Myrtle Ave
Boonton NJ 07005
973 334-0700

(G-563)
METRO PRTG & PROMOTIONS LLC
311 Mechanic St 2 (07005-1830)
PHONE........................973 316-1600
Scott Santucci, *President*
EMP: 15
SQ FT: 10,000
SALES (est): 2.1MM **Privately Held**
SIC: 2752 Commercial printing, lithographic

(G-564)
PIPELINE EQP RESOURCES CO LLC
Also Called: Perc
9 Mars Ct Ste 4 (07005-9310)
PHONE........................888 232-7372
Robert Engdahl, *Mng Member*
EMP: 8
SALES (est): 2.5MM **Privately Held**
SIC: 1321 3449 Natural gas liquids; miscellaneous metalwork

(G-565)
R&D MICROWAVES LLC
301 Rockaway Valley Rd # 3 (07005-9192)
PHONE........................908 212-1696
Ken Jackson, *Purchasing*
Stephanie Turzilli, *Purchasing*
Marek Antkowiak,
EMP: 20
SALES: 4MM **Privately Held**
WEB: www.rdmicrowaves.com
SIC: 3663 Radio & TV communications equipment

(G-566)
ROYAL PALLET INC
771 Knoll Rd (07005-9633)
PHONE........................973 299-0445
Dennis G Whipple, *Principal*
EMP: 4
SALES (est): 397.6K **Privately Held**
SIC: 2448 Pallets, wood & wood with metal

(G-567)
S W I INTERNATIONAL INC
Also Called: Super Wash
487 Division St (07005-1828)
PHONE........................973 334-2525
Edward Smith, *President*
EMP: 4
SALES (est): 190K **Privately Held**
SIC: 2841 Detergents, synthetic organic or inorganic alkaline

(G-568)
SCULPTURED STONE INC
501b Division St (07005)
PHONE........................973 557-1482
Jerome Matisik, *President*
EMP: 12
SALES (est): 270K **Privately Held**
SIC: 3281 Cut stone & stone products

(G-569)
SYTHEON LTD
315 Wootton St Ste N (07005-1900)
PHONE........................973 988-1075
Ratan K Chaudhuri, *President*
Francois Marchio, *COO*
◆ **EMP:** 4
SALES (est): 226K **Privately Held**
SIC: 2833 Organic medicinal chemicals: bulk, uncompounded

(G-570)
TECHNICAL ADVANTAGE INC (PA)
Also Called: Advantage Engineering Group
34 Farber Hill Rd (07005-9223)
PHONE........................973 402-5500
Stewart Klepesch, *President*
Bruce Hirschorn, *Vice Pres*
Deborah Hirschhorn, *Shareholder*
EMP: 5
SQ FT: 11,000

SALES (est): 754K **Privately Held**
WEB: www.aeg-corp.com
SIC: 3571 7389 Electronic computers; design, commercial & industrial

(G-571)
TELEMARK CNC LLC
429 Rockaway Valley Rd (07005-8101)
PHONE................................973 794-4857
William Hovey,
EMP: 5
SALES: 990K **Privately Held**
SIC: 3451 Screw machine products

(G-572)
VALLEY PLASTIC MOLDING CO
Also Called: Boonton Plastic Molding Co
30 Plane St Ste 4 (07005-1758)
P.O. Box 30 (07005-0030)
PHONE................................973 334-2100
Pat Berhman, *Owner*
Mike Berhman, *Co-Owner*
EMP: 10 EST: 1916
SQ FT: 10,000
SALES: 1MM **Privately Held**
SIC: 3089 6512 Molding primary plastic; commercial & industrial building operation

Bordentown
Burlington County

(G-573)
A D J GROUP LLC
12 Trainor Cir (08505-4277)
PHONE................................609 743-2099
Art D Angelo,
EMP: 4
SALES: 350K **Privately Held**
SIC: 3549 Marking machines, metalworking

(G-574)
ADVANCED TECHNICAL SUPPORT INC
Also Called: A T S Rheosystems
231 Crosswicks Rd (08505-2602)
PHONE................................609 298-2522
Steven M Colo, *President*
Kaj Hedman, *Principal*
Peter Kw Herh, *Principal*
Nick Roye, *Principal*
August J Colo, *CFO*
EMP: 100
SQ FT: 30,000
SALES (est): 13.7MM **Privately Held**
SIC: 3826 Analytical instruments

(G-575)
AONE TOUCH INC
35 E Burlington St (08505-1763)
PHONE................................732 261-6841
George Sara, *CEO*
EMP: 6
SALES: 800K **Privately Held**
SIC: 7374 5044 5045 7372 Computer processing services; calculating machines; calcvlators, electronic; accounting machines using machine readable programs; prepackaged software

(G-576)
ATS MECHANICAL INC
Also Called: Honeywell Authorized Dealer
74 Crosswicks St (08505-1768)
PHONE................................609 298-2323
Andrew Steward, *President*
EMP: 7
SALES (est): 947.8K **Privately Held**
SIC: 3585 Air conditioning equipment, complete

(G-577)
BAI BRANDS LLC
201 Elizabeth St (08505-1402)
PHONE................................609 586-0500
EMP: 7 **Publicly Held**
SIC: 2086 Soft drinks: packaged in cans, bottles, etc.
HQ: Bai Brands Llc
1800 E State St
Trenton NJ 08609

(G-578)
CARPENTER & PATERSON INC
2 Altran Ct Ste 2 # 2 (08505-9630)
PHONE................................609 227-2750
Bob Cieslikowski, *Branch Mgr*
Tom Armour, *Manager*
EMP: 30
SALES (corp-wide): 32.3MM **Privately Held**
WEB: www.carpenterpaterson.com
SIC: 8742 3432 Transportation consultant; plumbing fixture fittings & trim
PA: Carpenter & Paterson, Inc.
434 Latigue Rd
Westwego LA 70094
504 431-7722

(G-579)
CCBCC OPERATIONS LLC
948 Farnsworth Ave (08505-2106)
PHONE................................609 324-7424
Ron Wilson, *President*
EMP: 75
SALES (corp-wide): 4.6B **Publicly Held**
SIC: 2086 Soft drinks: packaged in cans, bottles, etc.
HQ: Ccbcc Operations, Llc
4100 Coca Cola Plz
Charlotte NC 28211
704 364-8728

(G-580)
ELEISON PHARMACEUTICALS INC
311 Farnsworth Ave Ste 1 (08505-1796)
PHONE................................215 416-7620
Edwin J Thomas, *CEO*
EMP: 5
SALES: 950K **Privately Held**
SIC: 2833 Medicinals & botanicals

(G-581)
FAUBEL PHARMA SERVICES
3 3rd St Ste 102 (08505-1370)
PHONE................................908 730-7563
▲ EMP: 4
SALES (est): 285.8K **Privately Held**
SIC: 2834 Pharmaceutical preparations

(G-582)
GRAHAM PACKAGING COMPANY LP
201 Elizabeth St (08505-1402)
PHONE................................717 849-8500
Jeff Owens, *Plant Mgr*
Stephen Kearney, *Admin Mgr*
EMP: 28
SALES (corp-wide): 1MM **Privately Held**
WEB: www.grahampackaging.com
SIC: 3089 Plastic containers, except foam
HQ: Graham Packaging Company, L.P.
700 Indian Springs Dr # 100
Lancaster PA 17601
717 849-8500

(G-583)
HOMETOWN OFFICE SUPS & PRTG CO
Also Called: Hometown Office Sups & Prtg Co
192 Us Highway 130 (08505-2253)
PHONE................................609 298-9020
Earl Hall, *President*
Rosemary Pezzano, *Broker*
EMP: 5
SALES (est): 530K **Privately Held**
SIC: 5943 2752 Office forms & supplies; offset & photolithographic printing

(G-584)
IN-PHASE TECHNOLOGIES INC
401 Bordentown Hedding Rd (08505-4747)
PHONE................................609 298-9555
Edward J Macmullen, *President*
Howard Salvesen, *Vice Pres*
Cindy Desimone, *Sr Software Eng*
Jessica Rinderer, *Admin Asst*
EMP: 27
SQ FT: 20,000
SALES (est): 7.4MM **Privately Held**
WEB: www.in-phasetech.com
SIC: 3663 Microwave communication equipment

(G-585)
M W TRAILER REPAIR INC
400 Rising Sun Rd (08505-4709)
PHONE................................609 298-1113
Michael Welsh, *President*
EMP: 10
SQ FT: 8,000
SALES: 1.6MM **Privately Held**
WEB: www.mwtrailer.com
SIC: 3715 5012 5013 5511 Truck trailers; trailers for trucks, new & used; trailer parts & accessories; trucks, tractors & trailers: new & used

(G-586)
MEGATRAN INDUSTRIES (PA)
Also Called: Nwl Transformers
312 Rising Sun Rd (08505-9626)
PHONE................................609 227-4300
James P Seitz, *President*
David Seitz, *Exec VP*
Robert Guenther, *Vice Pres*
Lottie Randow, *Vice Pres*
Bryan Pike, *Engineer*
▲ EMP: 60
SQ FT: 130,000
SALES (est): 45MM **Privately Held**
WEB: www.nwl.com
SIC: 3675 3612 3822 3625 Electronic capacitors; power transformers, electric; auto controls regulating residntl & coml environmt & applncs; relays & industrial controls

(G-587)
MELTON SALES & SERVICE
Also Called: Melton Industries
1723 Burlington (08505)
PHONE................................609 699-4800
Lori Mlynarski, *Purch Mgr*
Christopher Robles, *Manager*
Chris Robles, *Executive*
Nadine Melton, *Admin Sec*
EMP: 25 **Privately Held**
WEB: www.meltonindustries.com
SIC: 3812 3519 Defense systems & equipment; diesel engine rebuilding
PA: Melton Sales & Service
13 Petticoat Bridge Rd
Columbus NJ 08022

(G-588)
MERSHON CONCRETE LLC
5251 Us Highway 130 (08505-4401)
P.O. Box 254 (08505-0254)
PHONE................................609 298-2150
Randolph E Mershon Jr, *President*
John Molesworth, *Corp Secy*
Pat Greeber, *Vice Pres*
EMP: 40 EST: 1952
SQ FT: 30,000
SALES (est): 8.7MM **Privately Held**
SIC: 3272 3273 3446 Tanks, concrete; steps, prefabricated concrete; ready-mixed concrete; architectural metalwork

(G-589)
MICRODYSIS INC
Also Called: DOING BUSINESS AS
1200 Florence Columbus Rd # 21 (08505-4200)
PHONE................................609 642-1184
Joseph Z Huang, *President*
EMP: 5
SQ FT: 300
SALES (est): 304.1K **Privately Held**
WEB: www.microdysis.com
SIC: 3825 3826 3569 Analog-digital converters, electronic instrumentation type; analytical instruments; liquid automation machinery & equipment

(G-590)
NATIONAL DIVERSIFIED SALES INC
Also Called: Nds
401 Bordentown Hedding Rd (08505-4747)
PHONE................................559 562-9888
EMP: 6
SALES (corp-wide): 1.2B **Privately Held**
SIC: 3089 5083 Plastic containers, except foam; farm equipment parts & supplies
HQ: National Diversified Sales, Inc.
21300 Victory Blvd # 215
Woodland Hills CA 91367
559 562-9888

(G-591)
NWL INC (HQ)
Also Called: Nwl Capacitors
312 Rising Sun Rd (08505-9626)
PHONE................................609 298-7300
David Seitz, *President*
Bob Guenther, *Vice Pres*
Robert W Seitz, *Vice Pres*
Tony Sufler, *Vice Pres*
Erin Carroll, *Buyer*
◆ EMP: 180
SQ FT: 130,000
SALES: 37.5MM
SALES (corp-wide): 45MM **Privately Held**
SIC: 3612 3679 Power transformers, electric; power supplies, all types: static
PA: Megatran Industries
312 Rising Sun Rd
Bordentown NJ 08505
609 227-4300

(G-592)
PACOR INC (PA)
333 Rising Sun Rd (08505-9611)
PHONE................................609 324-1100
Ronald A Latini, *President*
William Wheatley, *Vice Pres*
Becky Dillon, *Controller*
▲ EMP: 50 EST: 1921
SQ FT: 55,000
SALES (est): 35MM **Privately Held**
WEB: www.pacorinc.com
SIC: 5033 3086 3296 Insulation materials; insulation or cushioning material, foamed plastic; mineral wool

(G-593)
PRINCE SPORTS INC
Also Called: Ektelon, Viking Athletics
334 Rising Sun Rd (08505)
PHONE................................609 291-5800
Gordon Boggis, *CEO*
Alistair Thorburn, *Principal*
Richard E Margin, *Vice Pres*
▲ EMP: 80
SQ FT: 35,000
SALES (est): 8.1MM **Privately Held**
WEB: www.princesports.com
SIC: 3949 Rackets & frames: tennis, badminton, squash, lacrosse, etc; tennis equipment & supplies
PA: Nautic Partners, Llc
100 Westminster St # 1220
Providence RI 02903

(G-594)
RBDEL INC
Also Called: UPS Store 5952
272 Dunns Mill Rd (08505-4748)
PHONE................................609 324-0040
Richard De Luca, *Principal*
EMP: 5
SALES (est): 408.2K **Privately Held**
SIC: 2542 Postal lock boxes, mail racks & related products

(G-595)
STEPAN COMPANY
Also Called: Fieldsboro Plant
4th St Fieldsboro (08505)
PHONE................................609 298-1222
Gary Traverso, *Opers-Prdtn-Mfg*
EMP: 75
SALES (corp-wide): 1.9B **Publicly Held**
WEB: www.stepan.com
SIC: 2869 2843 2842 Industrial organic chemicals; surface active agents; specialty cleaning, polishes & sanitation goods
PA: Stepan Company
22 W Frontage Rd
Northfield IL 60093
847 446-7500

(G-596)
TOMMYS PALLET YARD LLC
2499 Old York Rd (08505-4460)
PHONE................................609 424-3996
EMP: 4
SALES (est): 501.6K **Privately Held**
SIC: 2448 Pallets, wood

G E O G R A P H I C

(G-597)
TOWN FORD INC
860 Us Highway 206 (08505-1505)
PHONE.................................609 298-4990
Randy Johnson, *President*
EMP: 55
SQ FT: 15,000
SALES (est): 12.2MM **Privately Held**
SIC: 5511 7538 7532 7515 Automobiles, new & used; general automotive repair shops; top & body repair & paint shops; passenger car leasing; passenger car rental; motor vehicle parts & accessories

(G-598)
VANCO USA LLC
1170 Florence Columbus Rd (08505-4293)
PHONE.................................609 499-4141
Carl Massaro, *Mng Member*
EMP: 65
SQ FT: 100,000
SALES (est): 4.6MM **Privately Held**
SIC: 3715 Semitrailers for truck tractors

(G-599)
VANCO USA LLC (DE)
1170 Florence Columbus Rd (08505-4293)
PHONE.................................609 499-4141
Carl Massaro,
EMP: 140
SQ FT: 100,000
SALES (est): 18.2MM **Privately Held**
SIC: 3715 3537 Truck trailers; industrial trucks & tractors

Bound Brook
Somerset County

(G-600)
ANJU CLINPLUS LLC
1661 Route 22 West (08805-1258)
PHONE.................................732 764-6969
EMP: 15 EST: 2017
SALES (est): 406.2K
SALES (corp-wide): 28.2MM **Privately Held**
SIC: 7372 Prepackaged software
PA: Anju Software, Inc.
    4500 S Lkshore Dr Ste 620
    Tempe AZ 85282
    630 246-2527

(G-601)
CYALUME SPECIALTY PRODUCTS INC
Also Called: Jfc Technologies
100 W Main St Ste A10 (08805-1972)
PHONE.................................732 469-7760
James G Schleck, *President*
Zivi Nedivi, *Principal*
Hemant Desai, *Vice Pres*
Dina Kisver, *Vice Pres*
▲ EMP: 50
SQ FT: 40,000
SALES (est): 2.1MM
SALES (corp-wide): 41.2MM **Publicly Held**
WEB: www.jfctechnologies.com
SIC: 2833 2834 8731 Medicinals & botanicals; druggists' preparations (pharmaceuticals); commercial physical research
HQ: Cyalume Technologies Holdings, Inc.
    910 Se 17th St Ste 300
    Fort Lauderdale FL 33316

(G-602)
IMPERIAL METAL PRODUCTS INC
8 W Chimney Rock Rd (08805)
PHONE.................................908 647-8181
EMP: 5
SQ FT: 3,000
SALES (est): 885.7K **Privately Held**
SIC: 3441 Manufactures Facricated Metal

(G-603)
MARX NJ GROUP LLC
Also Called: Halo Mark
14 Easy St Ste 14e4 (08805-1168)
PHONE.................................732 901-3880
Joseph Marx,
Donald Marx,
Thomas Marx,

EMP: 30 EST: 2016
SALES: 8MM **Privately Held**
SIC: 3444 Sheet metalwork

(G-604)
POLYMER MOLDED PRODUCTS
10 Easy St (08805-1147)
PHONE.................................732 907-1990
Urena Ayala, *Principal*
EMP: 6
SALES (est): 643.2K **Privately Held**
SIC: 3089 Injection molded finished plastic products

(G-605)
ROYAL CABINET COMPANY INC
15 Easy St (08805-1168)
PHONE.................................908 203-8000
Paul Y McDonald, *President*
EMP: 30 EST: 1963
SQ FT: 21,000
SALES (est): 4.2MM **Privately Held**
WEB: www.royalcabinet.com
SIC: 1799 2434 5712 Kitchen & bathroom remodeling; wood kitchen cabinets; customized furniture & cabinets

(G-606)
SR INTERNATIONAL ROCK INC
7 Easy St Ste E (08805-1147)
PHONE.................................908 864-4700
Raj Raju, *President*
▲ EMP: 13
SQ FT: 16,000
SALES: 300K **Privately Held**
SIC: 5032 3281 Granite building stone; marble, building: cut & shaped

(G-607)
STAR PROMOTIONS INC
Also Called: Graphic Concepts
11 Maiden Ln (08805-2023)
PHONE.................................732 356-5959
Gerald Truppelli, *President*
Jerry Truppelli, *Owner*
EMP: 14
SQ FT: 8,000
SALES (est): 2.2MM **Privately Held**
SIC: 2752 2791 2789 Photo-offset printing; typesetting; bookbinding & related work

(G-608)
STAVOLA CONSTRUCTION MTLS INC
Also Called: Stavola Contracting
810 Thompson Ave (08805-1124)
P.O. Box 482, Red Bank (07701-0482)
PHONE.................................732 356-5700
Juan Berrios, *Plant Mgr*
James M Stavola, *Manager*
Jim Bean, *Info Tech Mgr*
EMP: 47
SALES (corp-wide): 9.3MM **Privately Held**
WEB: www.stavola.com
SIC: 3281 5032 2951 Stone, quarrying & processing of own stone products; stone, crushed or broken; asphalt paving mixtures & blocks
PA: Stavola Construction Materials, Inc.
    175 Drift Rd
    Tinton Falls NJ 07724
    732 542-2328

(G-609)
STEPS TO LITERACY LLC
4 Easy St (08805-1147)
P.O. Box 6737, Bridgewater (08807-0737)
PHONE.................................732 560-8363
Elaine Thompson,
Bill Thompson,
EMP: 20
SQ FT: 20,000
SALES (est): 3.7MM **Privately Held**
SIC: 8748 3999 Business consulting; education aids, devices & supplies

---

Bradley Beach
Monmouth County

(G-610)
EA PILOT SUPPLY
603 Fletcher Lake Ave (07720-1317)
PHONE.................................201 934-8449
Spencer Ryan, *Owner*
EMP: 6
SALES (est): 330K **Privately Held**
SIC: 5999 3669 Electronic parts & equipment; smoke detectors

Branchburg
Somerset County

(G-611)
ADVANCED INDUSTRIAL CONTROLS
Also Called: Aic
10 County Line Rd Ste 30 (08876-6009)
PHONE.................................908 725-7575
Doug Morrison, *President*
EMP: 6
SQ FT: 4,200
SALES (est): 630K **Privately Held**
SIC: 3625 8711 Relays & industrial controls; electrical or electronic engineering

(G-612)
AIR LIQUIDE ADVANCED MATERIALS
197 Meister Ave Bldg A (08876-6022)
PHONE.................................908 231-9060
Paul C Burlingame, *Branch Mgr*
EMP: 10
SALES (corp-wide): 125.9MM **Privately Held**
SIC: 5169 8733 2813 Industrial gases; noncommercial research organizations; industrial gases
HQ: Air Liquide Advanced Materials Inc.
    9811 Katy Fwy Ste 100
    Houston TX 77024
    713 624-8000

(G-613)
ALLOY WELDING CO
6 Culnen Dr Ste A (08876-5463)
PHONE.................................908 218-1551
Marilyn Scharffenberger, *CEO*
Leonard F Scharffenberger, *President*
Len Scharffenberge, *Export Mgr*
EMP: 11 EST: 1946
SQ FT: 27,000
SALES: 4.2MM **Privately Held**
WEB: www.alloyweldingco.com
SIC: 3441 Fabricated structural metal

(G-614)
ALOE SCIENCE INC
Also Called: Aloe Creme Laboratories Div
160 Meister Ave Ste 20 (08876-3474)
PHONE.................................908 231-8888
Douglas Siegel, *President*
EMP: 20
SALES (est): 2.1MM **Privately Held**
SIC: 2844 Suntan lotions & oils; face creams or lotions

(G-615)
ALTIMA INNOVATIONS INC
211 Evans Way (08876-3766)
PHONE.................................732 474-1500
Fayez Azeez, *Treasurer*
Mohan Devineni, *Director*
EMP: 4 EST: 2014
SALES (est): 208.5K **Privately Held**
SIC: 2834 Pharmaceutical preparations

(G-616)
AMERICAN LEISTRITZ EXTRUDER
169 Meister Ave (08876-3464)
PHONE.................................908 685-2333
Carlos Pellegrini, *Sales Staff*
Sarah Scovens, *Marketing Staff*
Bill Novak, *Manager*
EMP: 19

SALES (est): 3.5MM
SALES (corp-wide): 358.4MM **Privately Held**
WEB: www.alec-usa.com
SIC: 3559 Synthetic filament extruding machines
PA: Leistritz Ag
    Markgrafenstr. 36-39
    Nurnberg 90459
    911 430-60

(G-617)
AMERICAN SPRAYTECH LLC
205 Meister Ave (08876-6032)
PHONE.................................908 725-6060
Allen S Lalwani, *Principal*
Robert Flaherty, *Opers Mgr*
Robert Swiatecki, *Opers Staff*
George Abraham, *Production*
Emery Williams, *Production*
EMP: 35
SQ FT: 24,000
SALES (est): 7.4MM **Privately Held**
WEB: www.americanspraytech.com
SIC: 7389 2844 2813 Packaging & labeling services; toilet preparations; aerosols

(G-618)
AMNEAL PHARMACEUTICALS LLC
65 Readington Rd Bldg B (08876-3557)
PHONE.................................908 409-6823
Chirag Patel, *CEO*
EMP: 8
SALES (corp-wide): 1.6B **Publicly Held**
SIC: 2834 Pharmaceutical preparations
HQ: Amneal Pharmaceuticals Llc
    400 Crossing Blvd Fl 3
    Bridgewater NJ 08807

(G-619)
AMNEAL PHARMACEUTICALS LLC
131 Chambers Brook Rd (08876-3587)
PHONE.................................908 231-1911
Todd Branning, *CFO*
Bryan Reasons, *CFO*
EMP: 32
SALES (corp-wide): 1.6B **Publicly Held**
SIC: 2834 5122 Pharmaceutical preparations; pharmaceuticals
HQ: Amneal Pharmaceuticals Llc
    400 Crossing Blvd Fl 3
    Bridgewater NJ 08807

(G-620)
ARGYLE INDUSTRIES INC
160 Meister Ave Ste 12 (08876-3474)
P.O. Box 390, Whitehouse (08888-0390)
PHONE.................................908 725-8800
James Kane, *President*
Carrie Troyan, *Accounting Mgr*
▲ EMP: 12
SQ FT: 3,000
SALES (est): 6.9MM **Privately Held**
WEB: www.argyleindustries.com
SIC: 5051 3599 3444 Aluminum bars, rods, ingots, sheets, pipes, plates, etc.; machine shop, jobbing & repair; sheet metalwork

(G-621)
ARNA MARKETING GROUP INC
60 Readington Rd (08876-3540)
PHONE.................................908 625-7395
Mette Brusdal, *President*
Kathy Campos, *Human Res Mgr*
EMP: 67
SQ FT: 10,000
SALES (est): 11.6MM **Privately Held**
SIC: 7331 2678 7389 2752 Direct mail advertising services; writing paper & envelopes: made from purchased materials; presorted mail service; commercial printing, lithographic; promotional printing, lithographic

(G-622)
ARNA MARKETING INC
60 Readington Rd (08876-3540)
P.O. Box 5102, North Branch (08876-1309)
PHONE.................................908 231-1100
Steven Hegna, *President*
Linda Guerrera, *Vice Pres*
Norman Hegna, *Vice Pres*
Lawrence R Noll, *Vice Pres*

Jim Mohney, *Mfg Dir*
EMP: 40 **EST:** 1952
SQ FT: 25,000
SALES (est): 14.8MM **Privately Held**
WEB: www.aepcompany.com
SIC: 5112 5961 2754 Envelopes; stationery; mail order house, order taking office only; commercial printing, gravure

(G-623)
ASA HYDRAULIK OF AMERICA INC
160 Meister Ave Ste 20a (08876-3499)
PHONE..................908 541-1500
Thomas Euler-Rolle, *President*
James Matthews, *Vice Pres*
▲ **EMP:** 7
SQ FT: 5,000
SALES (est): 2.7MM **Privately Held**
WEB: www.asahyd.com
SIC: 5084 3443 Hydraulic systems equipment & supplies; heat exchangers: coolers (after, inter), condensers, etc.

(G-624)
AZ-EM USA BRANCHBURG NJ
70 Meister Ave (08876-3440)
PHONE..................908 429-0020
John Whybrow, *Chairman*
◆ **EMP:** 7
SALES (est): 905.3K **Privately Held**
SIC: 3679 Electronic circuits

(G-625)
BETTER SLEEP INC
100 Readington Rd (08876-3414)
PHONE..................908 464-2200
Fax: 908 393-0126
▲ **EMP:** 17 **EST:** 1951
SALES (est): 3.7MM **Privately Held**
SIC: 3496 2392 Mfg Misc Fabricated Wire Products Mfg Household Furnishings

(G-626)
BIOSEARCH MEDICAL PRODUCTS INC
35 Industrial Pkwy (08876-6005)
PHONE..................908 252-0595
Martin C Dyck, *President*
Robert Lee, *CFO*
Robert J Moravsik, *Admin Sec*
EMP: 70
SQ FT: 35,000
SALES (est): 3.8MM
SALES (corp-wide): 6MM **Publicly Held**
WEB: www.biosearch.com
SIC: 3841 Surgical & medical instruments
PA: Hydromer, Inc.
35 Indtl Pkwy
Branchburg NJ 08876
908 526-2828

(G-627)
BYRAM LABORATORIES INC (PA)
Also Called: Byram Labs
1 Columbia Rd (08876-3518)
PHONE..................908 252-0852
Monte Prince, *CEO*
Bill Kirk, *Exec VP*
Alex Thompson, *Vice Pres*
Kevin Jezorek, *Mfg Staff*
William Kirk, *VP Sales*
EMP: 30 **EST:** 1910
SQ FT: 16,000
SALES (est): 8.5MM **Privately Held**
WEB: www.byramlabs.com
SIC: 3825 7629 Measuring instruments & meters, electric; electrical measuring instrument repair & calibration

(G-628)
CIMQUEST INC
3434 Rte 22 Ste 130 (08876-6011)
PHONE..................732 699-0400
Robert Hassold, *CEO*
Susan Chilone, *Mktg Dir*
Theresa Martino, *Manager*
EMP: 55
SALES (est): 1.2MM **Privately Held**
SIC: 7373 3999 7374 Computer-aided design (CAD) systems service; barber & beauty shop equipment; data processing & preparation

(G-629)
CLORDISYS SOLUTIONS INC
50 Tannery Rd Ste 1 (08876-6034)
P.O. Box 549, Lebanon (08833-0549)
PHONE..................908 236-4100
Jennifer Czarneski, *President*
Brian Campanale, *Engineer*
Pierre Pais, *Engineer*
Daniel Paznek, *Engineer*
Bill Soest, *Technical Staff*
▲ **EMP:** 25
SALES (est): 5MM **Privately Held**
WEB: www.clordisys.com
SIC: 3841 3559 Surgical & medical instruments; pharmaceutical machinery

(G-630)
COESIA HEALTH & BEAUTY INC (PA)
335 Chambers Brook Rd (08876-7213)
PHONE..................908 707-8008
Goran Adolfsson, *President*
▲ **EMP:** 16 **EST:** 2013
SALES (est): 15.1MM **Privately Held**
SIC: 3535 3599 Bucket type conveyor systems; custom machinery

(G-631)
COLORON PLASTICS CORPORATION
169 Meister Ave (08876-3464)
PHONE..................908 685-1210
Kenneth Kirchner, *President*
EMP: 24
SQ FT: 16,000
SALES (est): 5.3MM **Privately Held**
SIC: 2865 Dyes & pigments

(G-632)
COVER CO INC
19 Readington Rd (08876-3520)
PHONE..................908 707-9797
Frank Patel, *President*
▲ **EMP:** 25
SQ FT: 25,000
SALES (est): 2.5MM **Privately Held**
WEB: www.pegasus-products.com
SIC: 3999 3949 Hot tub & spa covers; sporting & athletic goods

(G-633)
CROWN GLASS CO INC
990 Evergreen Dr (08876-3898)
PHONE..................908 642-1764
Erin Adams, *Partner*
Chris Coletti, *Office Mgr*
EMP: 4
SQ FT: 9,000
SALES: 800K **Privately Held**
SIC: 3231 Products of purchased glass

(G-634)
CUSTOM MOLDERS CORP
Also Called: Cmg Plastics
160 Meister Ave Ste 1 (08876-3474)
PHONE..................908 218-7997
Joseph Caro, *President*
EMP: 65
SALES (est): 78.8K **Privately Held**
WEB: www.custommolders.com
SIC: 3089 Injection molding of plastics

(G-635)
CUSTOM MOLDERS GROUP LLC (PA)
Also Called: Cmg
160 Meister Ave Ste 1 (08876-3474)
PHONE..................908 218-7997
Joseph Caro, *Mng Member*
Glen Loh,
EMP: 5
SALES (est): 1.8MM **Privately Held**
SIC: 2821 Molding compounds, plastics

(G-636)
CUTTING BOARD COMPANY
2 Dreahook Rd (08876-3729)
PHONE..................908 725-0187
Theresa Pizzelanti, *Manager*
EMP: 5
SALES (corp-wide): 550K **Privately Held**
SIC: 3613 Distribution cutouts

PA: The Cutting Board Company
291 Route 22 E Bldg 6
Lebanon NJ 08833
908 725-0187

(G-637)
ELI LILLYBRANCHBURG
33 Imclone Dr (08876-3903)
PHONE..................908 541-8000
EMP: 6
SALES (est): 768.3K **Privately Held**
SIC: 2834 Pharmaceutical preparations

(G-638)
EMD PERFORMANCE MATERIALS CORP
70 Meister Ave (08876-3440)
PHONE..................908 429-3500
EMP: 450
SALES (corp-wide): 16.9B **Publicly Held**
SIC: 2899 3825 Oils & essential oils; integrated circuit testers
HQ: Emd Performance Materials Corp.
1200 Intrepid Ave Ste 3
Philadelphia PA 19112
888 367-3275

(G-639)
FALCON SAFETY PRODUCTS INC (HQ)
25 Imclone Dr (08876-3998)
P.O. Box 1299, Somerville (08876-1299)
PHONE..................908 707-4900
Phil Lapin, *CEO*
Greg Mas, *Exec VP*
Bob Schmalzigan, *Controller*
Rashid Moore, *Admin Asst*
▲ **EMP:** 70
SQ FT: 55,000
SALES (est): 56.5MM
SALES (corp-wide): 57.8MM **Privately Held**
WEB: www.falconsafety.com
SIC: 3563 Spraying & dusting equipment
PA: The Parker Acquisition Group Inc
25 Imclone Dr
Branchburg NJ 08876
908 707-4900

(G-640)
FEMENELLA & ASSOCIATES INC
10 County Line Rd Ste 24 (08876-6009)
PHONE..................908 722-6526
Arthur Femenella, *President*
Nancy Femenella, *Corp Secy*
Patrick Baldoni, *Vice Pres*
Karen Gilbert, *Office Mgr*
Allison Unger, *Manager*
EMP: 8
SQ FT: 1,000
SALES: 5.9MM **Privately Held**
SIC: 3231 Stained glass: made from purchased glass

(G-641)
FLEXLINK SYSTEMS INC
Also Called: Hapa
335 Chambers Brook Rd (08876-7213)
PHONE..................973 983-2700
Jeff Roth, *Accounting Mgr*
EMP: 23 **Privately Held**
SIC: 3535 Conveyors & conveying equipment
HQ: Flexlink Systems, Inc.
6580 Snowdrift Rd Ste 200
Allentown PA 18106
610 973-8200

(G-642)
FLEXLINK SYSTEMS INC
Also Called: Gottscho Printing Systems
335 Chambers Brook Rd (08876-7213)
PHONE..................908 947-2140
EMP: 5 **Privately Held**
SIC: 3535 Conveyors & conveying equipment
HQ: Flexlink Systems, Inc.
6580 Snowdrift Rd Ste 200
Allentown PA 18106
610 973-8200

(G-643)
G M STAINLESS INC (PA)
41 Imclone Dr (08876-3903)
PHONE..................908 575-1834
Walter W Gauer, *President*

Carol Gauer, *Corp Secy*
EMP: 14
SQ FT: 20,000
SALES (est): 2.1MM **Privately Held**
WEB: www.gmstainless.com
SIC: 3312 5051 Bar, rod & wire products; bars, metal

(G-644)
GEOLYTICS INC
3322 Us Highway 22 # 806 (08876-3476)
P.O. Box 5336, North Branch (08876-1303)
PHONE..................908 707-1505
Natasha Vasilev, *President*
EMP: 6
SALES (est): 485.7K **Privately Held**
WEB: www.geolytics.com
SIC: 8732 2741 Market analysis or research; maps: publishing & printing

(G-645)
HAHNS WOODWORKING
181 Meister Ave (08876-3464)
PHONE..................908 722-2742
Scott Hahn, *President*
EMP: 12
SQ FT: 20,000
SALES (est): 3.6MM **Privately Held**
WEB: www.hahnswoodworking.com
SIC: 2431 Doors, wood; garage doors, overhead: wood

(G-646)
HYDROMER INC (PA)
35 Indtl Pkwy (08876)
PHONE..................908 526-2828
Peter M Von Dyck, *CEO*
Manfred F Dyck, *Ch of Bd*
Martin C Dyck, *Exec VP*
Joseph A Ehrhard Jr, *Exec VP*
John Konar, *Vice Pres*
◆ **EMP:** 36
SQ FT: 35,000
SALES: 6MM **Publicly Held**
WEB: www.hydromer.com
SIC: 8731 2261 Biotechnical research, commercial; medical research, commercial; chemical coating or treating of cotton broadwoven fabrics

(G-647)
IMCLONE SYSTEMS LLC
33 Imclone Dr (08876-3903)
PHONE..................908 218-0147
Joe Toronoski, *Principal*
Kim Consolino, *Supervisor*
Hari Mohan, *Network Enginr*
John M D, *Bd of Directors*
Marcelene Kent, *Administration*
EMP: 75
SALES (corp-wide): 24.5B **Publicly Held**
WEB: www.imclone.com
SIC: 8731 2836 2834 Biotechnical research, commercial; biological products, except diagnostic; pharmaceutical preparations
HQ: Imclone Systems Llc
440 Us Highway 22
Bridgewater NJ 08807
908 541-8000

(G-648)
IMCLONE SYSTEMS LLC
50 Imclone Dr (08876-3904)
PHONE..................908 541-8100
Jennifer Clark, *Engineer*
Domenick Pardo, *Engineer*
Evelyn Haley, *Branch Mgr*
Zhengang Wang, *Analyst*
EMP: 5
SALES (corp-wide): 24.5B **Publicly Held**
WEB: www.imclone.com
SIC: 2834 Pharmaceutical preparations
HQ: Imclone Systems Llc
440 Us Highway 22
Bridgewater NJ 08807
908 541-8000

(G-649)
INIVEN LLC
5 Columbia Rd (08876-3518)
PHONE..................908 722-3770
Marc Benou, *President*
EMP: 7 **EST:** 2015

SALES (est): 492.6K **Privately Held**
SIC: 3661 3663 Fiber optics communications equipment; telemetering equipment, electronic

(G-650)
JOHNSON & JOHNSON
6 Greenwood Ct (08876-3604)
PHONE..................................732 524-0400
Gabe Jacinto, *Research*
Brian Gaida, *Engineer*
Dimpy Gupta, *Senior Engr*
Paula Cabra, *Finance*
Candice Debencik, *Sales Staff*
EMP: 80
SALES (corp-wide): 81.5B **Publicly Held**
SIC: 2676 Feminine hygiene paper products
PA: Johnson & Johnson
　　1 Johnson And Johnson Plz
　　New Brunswick NJ 08933
　　732 524-0400

(G-651)
KATADIN INC
53 Dreahook Rd (08876-3728)
PHONE..................................908 526-0166
James Brogan, *President*
Elaine Brogan, *Vice Pres*
EMP: 4 EST: 2001
SALES (est): 260.7K **Privately Held**
SIC: 2431 Interior & ornamental woodwork & trim

(G-652)
KINEDYNE LLC (HQ)
3040 Us Highway 22 # 150 (08876-3594)
PHONE..................................908 231-1800
Daniel C Schlotterback, *President*
Stephen Tucker, *Plant Mgr*
Jason Lueck, *Engineer*
Roger Perlstein, *VP Sls/Mktg*
Tobey Rumack, *VP Finance*
◆ EMP: 12
SALES (est): 52.8MM **Privately Held**
WEB: www.kinedyne.com
SIC: 3714 Motor vehicle parts & accessories

(G-653)
KRONOS SAASHR INC
Also Called: Saas.com
3040 Rte 22 (08876-3594)
PHONE..................................978 250-9800
Robert Delponte, *President*
Mark Julien, *CFO*
Mike Messier, *Consultant*
Alyce Moore, *Admin Sec*
EMP: 40
SALES (est): 4.1MM
SALES (corp-wide): 1.1B **Privately Held**
SIC: 7372 Prepackaged software
HQ: Kronos Incorporated
　　900 Chelmsford St # 312
　　Lowell MA 01851
　　978 250-9800

(G-654)
LABERN MACHINE PRODUCTS LLC
Also Called: Labern Realty
3388 Us Highway 22 (08876-3500)
PHONE..................................908 722-1970
Lawrence Remaly Jr, *Mng Member*
EMP: 8
SQ FT: 22,000
SALES (est): 726K **Privately Held**
SIC: 3451 Screw machine products

(G-655)
LIFECELL CORPORATION
220 Evans Way Ste 3 (08876-3880)
PHONE..................................908 947-1100
Doris Admin, *Branch Mgr*
EMP: 5 **Privately Held**
SIC: 2834 Pharmaceutical preparations
HQ: Lifecell Corporation
　　1 Millennium Way
　　Branchburg NJ 08876
　　908 947-1100

(G-656)
LIFECELL CORPORATION (DH)
1 Millennium Way (08876-3876)
PHONE..................................908 947-1100
Lisa Colleran, *President*

John Sowell, *Manager*
▲ EMP: 196
SQ FT: 120,000
SALES: 428MM **Privately Held**
WEB: www.lifecell.com
SIC: 2834 Pharmaceutical preparations
HQ: Allergan, Inc.
　　5 Giralda Farms
　　Madison NJ 07940
　　862 261-7000

(G-657)
LUCIANO PACKAGING TECH INC
29 County Line Rd (08876-3417)
PHONE..................................908 722-3222
Lawrence Luciano, *President*
Howard Leary, *Vice Pres*
Donald Rowe, *Vice Pres*
Nancy Smith, *Manager*
EMP: 7
SQ FT: 10,000
SALES (est): 1.6MM **Privately Held**
WEB: www.lucianopackaging.com
SIC: 1796 3565 8742 Machinery installation; packaging machinery; industry specialist consultants

(G-658)
LYLE/CARLSTROM ASSOCIATES INC
131 Chambers Brook Rd (08876-3587)
P.O. Box 9, Far Hills (07931-0009)
PHONE..................................908 526-2270
EMP: 25
SQ FT: 23,000
SALES (est): 2.7MM **Privately Held**
SIC: 2541 2542 Mfg Wood Glass Metal And Acrylic Fixtures

(G-659)
MERCK SHARP & DOHME CORP
203 River Rd (08876-3672)
PHONE..................................908 685-3892
Donald Thompson, *Branch Mgr*
EMP: 9
SALES (corp-wide): 42.2B **Publicly Held**
SIC: 2834 Pharmaceutical preparations
HQ: Merck Sharp & Dohme Corp.
　　2000 Galloping Hill Rd
　　Kenilworth NJ 07033
　　908 740-4000

(G-660)
NEXT MEDICAL PRODUCTS LLC
45 Columbia Rd (08876-3518)
P.O. Box 5148, North Branch (08876-1302)
PHONE..................................908 722-4549
Dick Smith, *Sales Staff*
John Buday, *Director*
Sergio Peguero, *Director*
Julia Jacobson,
EMP: 11
SALES: 990K **Privately Held**
SIC: 3841 Surgical & medical instruments

(G-661)
NJRLS ENTERPRISES INC
Also Called: R L S Enterprises
3380 Us Highway 22 3a (08876-4000)
PHONE..................................732 846-6010
Richard L Stecklow, *President*
▲ EMP: 12
SQ FT: 10,000
SALES: 3MM **Privately Held**
SIC: 3565 Packaging machinery

(G-662)
NORDEN INC (DH)
Also Called: Norden Packaging
230 Industrial Pkwy Ste A (08876-3580)
PHONE..................................908 252-9483
Geron Adolffon, *President*
Fedrick Nilsson, *President*
Fredrik Nilsson, *Sales Mgr*
EMP: 2
SQ FT: 28,000
SALES (est): 5.1MM **Privately Held**
WEB: www.norden.com
SIC: 3565 Packaging machinery
HQ: Norden Machinery Ab
　　Sodra Vagen 30
　　Kalmar 392 4
　　480 447-700

(G-663)
ONGUARD FENCE SYSTEMS LTD
18 Culnen Dr (08876-5400)
PHONE..................................908 429-5522
EMP: 30
SQ FT: 27,000
SALES (est): 5MM **Privately Held**
SIC: 3089 Mfg Plastic Products
HQ: Crystal Window & Door Systems, Ltd.
　　3110 Whitestone Expy
　　Flushing NY 11354
　　718 961-7300

(G-664)
PARADISE BARXON CORP
Also Called: Symtech Enterprise Intl
185 Industrial Pkwy Ste H (08876-3484)
PHONE..................................908 707-9141
Yeong Lim, *President*
Yatinkumar Patel, *Admin Sec*
EMP: 4
SQ FT: 3,000
SALES (est): 68.1K **Privately Held**
WEB: www.pbcus.com
SIC: 3577 Decoders, computer peripheral equipment; bar code (magnetic ink) printers; optical scanning devices

(G-665)
PARKER ACQUISITION GROUP INC (PA)
25 Imclone Dr (08876-3903)
P.O. Box 1299, Somerville (08876-1299)
PHONE..................................908 707-4900
Philip M Lapin, *President*
Howard Jacobs, *Director*
David Lowenstein, *Director*
EMP: 1
SQ FT: 55,000
SALES (est): 57.8MM **Privately Held**
SIC: 3861 Photographic equipment & supplies

(G-666)
PEGASUS PRODUCTS INC
19 Readington Rd (08876-3568)
PHONE..................................908 707-1122
Frank Patel, *President*
Roshan Patel, *Cust Mgr*
EMP: 40 EST: 1982
SQ FT: 49,900
SALES (est): 6.8MM **Privately Held**
SIC: 3081 Unsupported plastics film & sheet

(G-667)
PHOENIX CHEMICAL INC
151 Industrial Pkwy (08876-3451)
PHONE..................................908 707-0232
John Imperante, *President*
Carol Horn, *Research*
John Gray, *Regl Sales Mgr*
Phyllis Sica, *Admin Sec*
▲ EMP: 13
SALES (est): 4MM **Privately Held**
WEB: www.phoenix-chem.com
SIC: 2869 Amines, acids, salts, esters

(G-668)
PLASTI FOAM
Also Called: Structural Foam Plastics
68 County Line Rd (08876-3467)
PHONE..................................908 722-5254
Auto Delbro, *Partner*
John Rosania, *Partner*
William S Rosania, *Partner*
EMP: 80
SQ FT: 89,000
SALES (est): 6.4MM **Privately Held**
WEB: www.plastifoam.com
SIC: 3089 Injection molding of plastics

(G-669)
POLYCEL STRUCTURAL FOAM INC
60 Readington Rd (08876-3540)
PHONE..................................908 722-5254
Kurt Joeger, *Principal*
Otto D Prado, *Principal*
EMP: 90
SQ FT: 60,000
SALES (est): 19.4K **Privately Held**
SIC: 3089 Injection molding of plastics; pallets, plastic

(G-670)
POLYCEL STRUCTURAL FOAM INC
68 County Line Rd (08876-3467)
PHONE..................................908 722-5254
Kurt Joerger, *CEO*
Ayman Sawaged, *President*
▲ EMP: 29
SALES: 10.5MM **Privately Held**
WEB: www.polycel.com
SIC: 3089 Injection molding of plastics; pallets, plastic

(G-671)
PRECISION GRAPHICS INC
21 County Line Rd (08876-3417)
PHONE..................................908 707-8880
Robert T Weissman, *President*
David Weisman, *Vice Pres*
Mary Pantano, *Office Admin*
▲ EMP: 58
SQ FT: 25,000
SALES (est): 16.5MM **Privately Held**
SIC: 3672 7389 Circuit boards, television & radio printed; design, commercial & industrial

(G-672)
PRO-PACK CORP
160 Meister Ave Ste 18 (08876-3474)
PHONE..................................908 725-5000
Gary Glassman, *President*
EMP: 8
SQ FT: 2,500
SALES (est): 1.2MM **Privately Held**
SIC: 3953 5199 7311 Signs & advertising specialties; advertising specialties; advertising agencies; advertising consultant

(G-673)
PURE TECH INTERNATIONAL INC
3040 Us Highway 22 # 130 (08876-3594)
PHONE..................................908 722-4968
EMP: 9
SALES (corp-wide): 1.1B **Privately Held**
SIC: 3052 Garden hose, plastic
HQ: Pure Tech International, Inc.
　　201 Industrial Pkwy
　　Branchburg NJ 08876

(G-674)
PURE TECH INTERNATIONAL INC (HQ)
201 Industrial Pkwy (08876-3449)
PHONE..................................908 722-4800
Kenneth Baker, *President*
▲ EMP: 1
SQ FT: 9,900
SALES (est): 35.6MM
SALES (corp-wide): 1.1B **Privately Held**
SIC: 3052 3082 2821 3089 Garden hose, plastic; tubes, unsupported plastic; thermoplastic materials; vinyl resins; polyvinyl chlorice resins (PVC); injection molding of plastics; recycling, waste materials
PA: Tekni-Plex, Inc.
　　460 E Swedesford Rd # 3000
　　Wayne PA 19087
　　484 690-1520

(G-675)
RATHGIBSON NORTH BRANCH LLC
100 Aspen Hill Rd (08876-3563)
PHONE..................................908 253-3260
Mike Schwartz, *Mng Member*
Jeff Nelb,
▲ EMP: 180 EST: 2010
SQ FT: 250,000
SALES (est): 173.4MM
SALES (corp-wide): 225.3B **Publicly Held**
SIC: 3317 Tubing, mechanical or hypodermic sizes: cold drawn stainless
HQ: Rathgibson Holding Co Llc
　　2505 Foster Ave
　　Janesville WI 53545

(G-676)
REBTEX INC
40 Industrial Pkwy (08876-6027)
PHONE..................................908 722-3549
Robert P Brandell, *President*
Thomas G Brandell, *Vice Pres*

Michele Senatore, *Admin Sec*
EMP: 110
SQ FT: 108,000
SALES (est): 18.8MM **Privately Held**
WEB: www.rebtex.com
SIC: 2258 2261 Dyeing & finishing lace goods & warp knit fabric; dyeing cotton broadwoven fabrics

(G-677)
RED RAY MANUFACTURING
10 County Line Rd Ste 3 (08876-6008)
PHONE....................908 722-0040
Bannos Thomas, *President*
EMP: 4 EST: 2013
SALES (est): 270K **Privately Held**
SIC: 3999 Manufacturing industries

(G-678)
ROCHE DIAGNOSTICS CORPORATION
1080 Us Highway 202 S (08876-3771)
PHONE....................908 253-0707
Piyathida Katapituk, *Manager*
Mikhail Golbin, *Technology*
Stephanie Berdejo, *Technician*
EMP: 18
SALES (corp-wide): 57.2B **Privately Held**
SIC: 2834 Pharmaceutical preparations
HQ: Roche Diagnostics Corporation
9115 Hague Rd
Indianapolis IN 46256
800 428-5076

(G-679)
SANDER MECHANICAL SERVICE INC
Also Called: Honeywell Authorized Dealer
55 Columbia Rd (08876-3518)
PHONE....................732 560-0600
Robert J Bittel, *President*
Maureen Dibenedetto, *Accounts Exec*
EMP: 40 EST: 1965
SALES (est): 11.9MM **Privately Held**
WEB: www.sanmec.com
SIC: 1711 3585 Mechanical contractor; heating & air conditioning combination units

(G-680)
SAVOURY SYSTEMS INTL LLC
Also Called: Ssi
230 Industrial Pkwy Ste C (08876-3580)
PHONE....................908 526-2524
Donald L Hawks III, *President*
Richard Nikola, *COO*
William Gambrell, *Vice Pres*
Alex Carillo, *Opers Staff*
Gaetan Sourceau, *CFO*
EMP: 25
SALES (est): 809.2K
SALES (corp-wide): 19.2MM **Privately Held**
SIC: 2087 Flavoring extracts & syrups
HQ: Brookside Flavors & Ingredients Llc
201 Tresser Blvd Ste 320
Stamford CT 06901
203 595-4520

(G-681)
SCHERING-PLOUGH CORP
3070 Us Highway 22 (08876-3548)
PHONE....................908 595-3638
Keith Holland, *Principal*
EMP: 9 EST: 2010
SALES (est): 978.1K **Privately Held**
SIC: 2834 Pharmaceutical preparations

(G-682)
SCHUTZ CONTAINER SYSTEMS INC (DH)
200 Aspen Hill Rd (08876-3564)
P.O. Box 5950, North Branch (08876-5950)
PHONE....................908 429-1637
Frederick Wenzel, *President*
Dan Dengler, *Engineer*
Dennis Wagoner, *Engineer*
Ian Miller, *Financial Exec*
Nipa Patel, *Financial Analy*
▲ **EMP:** 75
SQ FT: 76,000
SALES (est): 176.4MM
SALES (corp-wide): 2B **Privately Held**
SIC: 2655 Fiber cans, drums & containers

(G-683)
SCHUTZ CORP (HQ)
200 Aspen Hill Rd (08876-3564)
P.O. Box 5950, North Branch (08876-5950)
PHONE....................908 526-6161
Udo Schutz, *Ch of Bd*
Peter Schafer, *President*
Joseph Allen, *Purch Mgr*
Norman Burke, *CFO*
Jur Juergen Huebbe, *Treasurer*
◆ **EMP:** 90
SQ FT: 76,000
SALES (est): 176.4MM
SALES (corp-wide): 2B **Privately Held**
SIC: 2655 Fiber cans, drums & similar products
PA: Schutz-Werke Gmbh & Co. Kg
Schutzstr. 12
Selters (Westerwald) 56242
262 677-0

(G-684)
SPECIFIED TECHNOLOGIES INC
Also Called: STI
210 Evans Way (08876-3767)
PHONE....................908 526-8000
Charbel H Tagher, *President*
Chua Kiang, *Regional Mgr*
Mike Pergola, *Regional Mgr*
Gabe Dimarino, *Senior VP*
Daniel Cianfaglione, *Engineer*
◆ **EMP:** 150
SQ FT: 35,000
SALES (est): 52.6MM **Privately Held**
WEB: www.stifirestop.com
SIC: 3569 Firefighting apparatus & related equipment

(G-685)
SUPERIOR TOOL & MFG CO
42 Columbia Rd Ste 2 (08876-3582)
PHONE....................908 526-9011
Edward Braunig, *President*
EMP: 8 EST: 1959
SQ FT: 11,000
SALES (est): 1.2MM **Privately Held**
WEB: www.superiortoolonline.com
SIC: 3599 Machine shop, jobbing & repair

(G-686)
SYMRISE INC
180 Industrial Pkwy (08876-3452)
PHONE....................908 429-6824
Fredrick Thor, *Branch Mgr*
EMP: 75
SALES (corp-wide): 3.6B **Privately Held**
SIC: 2869 Perfume materials, synthetic
HQ: Symrise Inc.
300 North St
Teterboro NJ 07608
201 288-3200

(G-687)
TAYLOR FORGE STAINLESS INC
22 Readington Rd (08876-3521)
P.O. Box 610, Somerville (08876-0610)
PHONE....................908 722-1313
Jim Takacs, *Vice Pres*
Kim Kanopka, *Vice Pres*
Jainna Santos, *Purch Agent*
Vanda Esty, *Purchasing*
Stanley Grant, *QA Dir*
EMP: 100
SQ FT: 80,000
SALES (est): 22.1MM **Privately Held**
SIC: 3494 5085 Pipe fittings; valves & fittings

(G-688)
TEE-RIFIC GOLF CENTER
3091 Us Highway 22 (08876-3528)
PHONE....................908 253-9300
EMP: 10
SALES (est): 891.3K **Privately Held**
SIC: 3949 Mfg Sporting/Athletic Goods

(G-689)
TOP SAFETY PRODUCTS COMPANY
Also Called: Calgonate
160 Meister Ave Ste 16 (08876-3474)
PHONE....................908 707-8680
Gerald P Kutsop, *President*
Ken Kallish, *General Mgr*

Joe Kutsop, *Sr Consultant*
EMP: 14
SQ FT: 10,000
SALES (est): 2MM **Privately Held**
SIC: 3842 First aid, snake bite & burn kits

(G-690)
TRIAD TOOL & DIE CO
9 Commerce St (08876-6039)
PHONE....................908 534-1784
Eric P Wichelhaus, *President*
Margaret Hurley, *Corp Secy*
Rosann Daluesio, *Admin Sec*
EMP: 60 EST: 1933
SQ FT: 11,000
SALES (est): 4.8MM **Privately Held**
WEB: www.triadtool.com
SIC: 3599 Machine shop, jobbing & repair

(G-691)
TRIMLINE MEDICAL PRODUCTS CORP
34 Columbia Rd (08876-3519)
P.O. Box 220, Skaneateles Falls NY (13153-0220)
PHONE....................908 429-0590
Richard Jacobson, *President*
Paul Vonderheyden, *Vice Pres*
Tara S Crane, *Accounting Mgr*
▲ **EMP:** 152
SQ FT: 30,000
SALES (est): 8.6MM
SALES (corp-wide): 2.7B **Publicly Held**
WEB: www.trimlinemed.com
SIC: 3841 Blood pressure apparatus
HQ: Welch Allyn Inc
4341 State Street Rd
Skaneateles Falls NY 13153
315 685-4100

(G-692)
ULTIMATE TRINING MUNITIONS INC (PA)
55 Readington Rd (08876-3542)
PHONE....................908 725-9000
Maxine Nordmeyer, *President*
Tony Lambraia, *Vice Pres*
Steve Cassidy, *Project Engr*
Jessica Michalak, *Manager*
Martin Peverley, *Info Tech Mgr*
◆ **EMP:** 32
SALES (est): 5.8MM **Privately Held**
SIC: 5941 3949 Ammunition; shooting equipment & supplies, general

(G-693)
VIS USA LLC
210 Meister Ave (08876-6046)
PHONE....................908 575-0606
Rene Morf, *MIS Mgr*
Rene Morph,
▲ **EMP:** 11
SQ FT: 20,000
SALES (est): 920K **Privately Held**
SIC: 3496 Conveyor belts

(G-694)
VIVA INTERNATIONAL INC
Also Called: Viva International Group
3140 Rte 22 (08876-3548)
P.O. Box 1275, Somerville (08876-1275)
PHONE....................908 595-6200
Fabrizio Gamberini, *President*
EMP: 300
SALES (est): 25.7MM
SALES (corp-wide): 242.1K **Privately Held**
SIC: 3851 Eyeglasses, lenses & frames
HQ: Marcolin U.S.A. Eyewear Corp.
3140 Rte 22
Branchburg NJ 08876
908 595-6200

(G-695)
WOLOCK & LOTT TRANSMISSION EQP
25 Chambers Brook Rd (08876-3552)
P.O. Box 5323, North Branch (08876-1303)
PHONE....................908 218-9292
Richard W Palmer, *President*
J Robert Layman, *Corp Secy*
EMP: 19 EST: 1963
SQ FT: 16,000

SALES (est): 6.4MM **Privately Held**
WEB: www.wolocklott.com
SIC: 5063 3612 Transformers & transmission equipment; transmission & distribution voltage regulators

(G-696)
WORLD WIDE METRIC INC (PA)
37 Readington Rd (08876-3542)
P.O. Box 5267, North Branch (08876-1303)
PHONE....................732 247-2300
George Contos, *CEO*
Theo Contos, *President*
Gary Contos, *Admin Sec*
▲ **EMP:** 15
SQ FT: 40,000
SALES (est): 18MM **Privately Held**
WEB: www.worldwidemetric.com
SIC: 5088 3494 Marine supplies; valves & pipe fittings

(G-697)
ZAHK SALES INC
1405 Boxwood Dr (08876-3674)
PHONE....................516 633-9179
Husein Kermalli, *President*
EMP: 4
SALES (est): 330K **Privately Held**
SIC: 2821 Plastics materials & resins

(G-698)
ZEUS INDUSTRIAL PRODUCTS INC
134 Chubb Way (08876-3935)
P.O. Box 298, Raritan (08869-0298)
PHONE....................908 292-6500
Roger Jones, *Director*
EMP: 200
SALES (corp-wide): 255.3MM **Privately Held**
WEB: www.zeusinc.com
SIC: 3082 Tubes, unsupported plastic
PA: Zeus Industrial Products, Inc.
620 Magnolia St
Orangeburg SC 29115
803 531-2174

(G-699)
ZEUS SCIENTIFIC INC
200 Evans Way (08876-3767)
P.O. Box 38, Raritan (08869-0038)
PHONE....................908 526-3744
Scott Tourville, *CEO*
John Tourville, *COO*
▲ **EMP:** 85 EST: 1976
SQ FT: 22,000
SALES (est): 12.5MM **Privately Held**
WEB: www.zeussci.com
SIC: 3841 Diagnostic apparatus, medical

(G-700)
ZZYZX LLC
Also Called: Iniven
5 Columbia Rd (08876-3518)
PHONE....................908 722-3770
Marc Benou, *President*
EMP: 7 EST: 2015
SALES (est): 380.6K **Privately Held**
SIC: 3661 3663 Fiber optics communications equipment; telemetering equipment, electronic

---

Branchville
Sussex County

(G-701)
ADVANCE PROCESS SYSTEMS LIM
130 Gunn Rd (07826-4167)
PHONE....................201 400-9190
Thomas Todaro, *Manager*
Mark Tarby, *Manager*
EMP: 9
SALES (est): 557.8K **Privately Held**
SIC: 8748 3559 3324 3356 Systems analysis & engineering consulting services; systems engineering consultant, ex. computer or professional; semiconductor manufacturing machinery; aerospace investment castings, ferrous; titanium & titanium alloy: rolling, drawing or extruding

(G-702)
ALECTO SYSTEMS LLC
130 Gunn Rd (07826-4167)
P.O. Box 2976, North Canton OH (44720-0976)
PHONE..........................973 875-6721
Thomas J Todaro,
EMP: 9
SQ FT: 1,200
SALES (est): 916.4K **Privately Held**
SIC: 3677 8711 Inductors, electronic; engineering services

(G-703)
BEHRINGER FLUID SYSTEMS INC
17 Ridge Rd (07826-4363)
PHONE..........................973 948-0226
Shawn Fantry, *Principal*
EMP: 5
SALES (est): 497.5K **Privately Held**
SIC: 3677 Electronic coils, transformers & other inductors

(G-704)
BRANCHVILLE BAGELS INC
332 Us Highway 206 N (07826-5086)
P.O. Box 296 (07826-0296)
PHONE..........................973 948-7077
Ricardo Rodregus, *Partner*
Ramon Rogriguez, *Partner*
EMP: 4
SALES (est): 467.2K **Privately Held**
SIC: 5411 5461 2051 Delicatessens; bagels; bagels, fresh or frozen

(G-705)
CONCRETE STONE & TILE CORP (PA)
Also Called: C S T Pavers
17 Ridge Rd (07826-4366)
P.O. Box 2191 (07826-2191)
PHONE..........................973 948-7193
Ronald Krueger, *President*
Carey Krueger, *Vice Pres*
Mariusz Rudy, *Plant Mgr*
Steve Baird, *Sales Mgr*
Eric Bischof, *Sales Mgr*
▲ EMP: 50
SQ FT: 25,000
SALES (est): 9.4MM **Privately Held**
WEB: www.cstpavers.com
SIC: 3272 Paving materials, prefabricated concrete

(G-706)
CUSTOM METERING COMPANY INC
36 Mattison Ave (07826-4354)
P.O. Box 696, Sparta (07871-0696)
PHONE..........................973 946-4195
Robert Ehling, *President*
EMP: 2
SALES: 1MM **Privately Held**
SIC: 3825 Meters: electric, pocket, portable, panelboard, etc.

(G-707)
GEORGES WINE AND SPIRITS GALLE
7 Main St (07826-5526)
PHONE..........................973 948-9950
George Delgado, *President*
EMP: 4
SALES (est): 635.6K **Privately Held**
SIC: 5921 5411 5812 2026 Wine; wine & beer; grocery stores, independent; caterers: farmers' cheese; fresh fruits & vegetables

(G-708)
HB TECHNIK USA LTD LBLTY PRTNR
Also Called: Hb-Technik-Usa LLC
99 George Hill Rd (07826-4311)
PHONE..........................973 875-8688
Sharon Peham,
▲ EMP: 4
SALES (est): 78.9K **Privately Held**
SIC: 2499 Bakers' equipment, wood

(G-709)
PAVESTONE LLC
183 Ridge Rd (07826)
PHONE..........................973 948-7193
David Jones, *Principal*
EMP: 48 **Privately Held**
SIC: 3241 Cement, hydraulic
HQ: Pavestone, Llc
5 Concourse Pkwy Ste 1900
Atlanta GA 30328
404 926-3167

Brick
Ocean County

(G-710)
AMERICAN RAIL COMPANY INC
1133 Industrial Pkwy B (08724-2582)
P.O. Box 790 (08723-0790)
PHONE..........................732 785-1110
Charles Montanye Jr, *President*
EMP: 15 EST: 1998
SALES (est): 1.9MM **Privately Held**
WEB: www.americanrail.com
SIC: 3743 Railroad locomotives & parts, electric or nonelectric

(G-711)
ANCHOR CONCRETE PRODUCTS INC
975 Burnt Tavern Rd (08724-2003)
PHONE..........................732 458-9440
Fax: 732 458-1086
EMP: 70
SALES (corp-wide): 23.5B **Privately Held**
SIC: 3271 5032 Mfg Of Masonry Blocks And Concrete Slabs
HQ: Anchor Concrete Products, Inc
331 Newman Springs Rd # 236
Red Bank NJ 07701
732 292-2648

(G-712)
CHARLES F KILIAN
Also Called: Essential Machining
682 Rolling Hills Ct (08724-1177)
PHONE..........................732 458-3554
Charles Killian, *Owner*
Charles Kilian, *Owner*
EMP: 4 EST: 1966
SQ FT: 5,500
SALES (est): 190K **Privately Held**
SIC: 3599 3541 Machine shop, jobbing & repair; machine tools, metal cutting type

(G-713)
CNO CORPORATION
Also Called: Floors At Home
611 Yellowbrick Rd (08724-3335)
P.O. Box 936, Point Pleasant Boro (08742-0936)
PHONE..........................732 785-5799
Tom Ciano, *Owner*
EMP: 4
SALES (est): 78.9K **Privately Held**
SIC: 2273 Carpets & rugs

(G-714)
CORIM INTERNATIONAL COFFEE IMP (PA)
Also Called: Corim Industries
1112 Industrial Pkwy (08724-2508)
PHONE..........................800 942-4201
Sam Teren, *CEO*
Rame Teren, *President*
Natan Teren, *Treasurer*
▲ EMP: 78
SALES (est): 22.8MM **Privately Held**
WEB: www.corimindustries.com
SIC: 2095 Roasted coffee

(G-715)
CREATIVE DESSERTS
42 Capri Dr (08723-7633)
PHONE..........................732 477-0808
Michael Daskalovitz, *President*
EMP: 4
SQ FT: 100
SALES (est): 421.5K **Privately Held**
WEB: www.creativedesserts.com
SIC: 2051 Bakery: wholesale or wholesale/retail combined

(G-716)
EAST COAST STORAGE EQP CO INC (PA)
Also Called: Ecseco
620 Burtis St (08723-5559)
PHONE..........................732 451-1316
Audra J Parisis, *President*
John Geddes, *Sales Staff*
Sidney Smith, *Manager*
Javier Ramirez, *Director*
Paul Parisi, *Business Dir*
EMP: 20
SQ FT: 15,000
SALES (est): 2.9MM **Privately Held**
WEB:
www.eastcoaststorageequipment.com
SIC: 2542 2541 8711 5084 Racks, merchandise display or storage: except wood; garment racks, wood; structural engineering; conveyor systems; steel building construction; structural steel erection

(G-717)
EASTERN REGIONAL WATERWAY
2316 2nd Ave (08723)
PHONE..........................732 684-0409
John Okinsky,
EMP: 10 EST: 2014
SALES (est): 642.9K **Privately Held**
SIC: 3489 Ordnance & accessories

(G-718)
FRITH GROUP (PA)
445 Brick Blvd Ste 103 (08723-6036)
PHONE..........................732 281-8343
EMP: 4 EST: 2009
SALES (est): 646.1K **Privately Held**
SIC: 7372 Application computer software

(G-719)
GANGI GRAPHICS INC
1669 Route 88 (08724-3050)
PHONE..........................732 840-8680
John Gangi, *President*
Michael Gangi, *Vice Pres*
Paul Gangi, *CFO*
EMP: 7
SALES: 750K **Privately Held**
WEB: www.gangigraphics.com
SIC: 7336 2752 2791 Graphic arts & related design; commercial printing, offset; typesetting

(G-720)
H & R WELDING LLC
307 Drum Point Rd (08723-6831)
PHONE..........................732 920-4881
Robert Hager, *Partner*
Jason Hager, *Partner*
Justin Hager, *Partner*
EMP: 8
SQ FT: 2,000
SALES (est): 1.6MM **Privately Held**
SIC: 3325 Steel foundries

(G-721)
J A M I ENTERPRISE INC
Also Called: J E I
1129 Industrial Pkwy A (08724-2589)
PHONE..........................732 714-6811
Michael Herman, *President*
Jamie Herman, *Vice Pres*
EMP: 4
SALES: 500K **Privately Held**
SIC: 3679 Electronic circuits

(G-722)
J C ORTHOPEDIC INC (PA)
1680 Route 88 (08724-3051)
PHONE..........................732 458-7900
Frank Digironomo, *President*
▲ EMP: 6
SALES (est): 511.7K **Privately Held**
SIC: 3842 5999 Orthopedic appliances; orthopedic & prosthesis applications

(G-723)
JERSEY SHORE PUBLICATIONS
Also Called: Jersey Shore Vacation Magazine
749 Bay Ave (08724-4809)
PHONE..........................732 892-1276
George Valente, *Owner*
EMP: 8

SALES (est): 46.3K **Privately Held**
WEB: www.jerseyshorevacation.com
SIC: 2741 Guides: publishing & printing

(G-724)
JOSANTOS CNSTR & DEV LLC
13 Riverview Dr (08723-5752)
PHONE..........................732 202-7389
Joe Santos,
EMP: 6 EST: 2008
SALES (est): 611.9K **Privately Held**
SIC: 3271 1521 Blocks, concrete: landscape or retaining wall; single-family housing construction; patio & deck construction & repair; new construction, single-family houses

(G-725)
MARINER SALES AND POWER INC (PA)
Also Called: Marine East
834 Mantoloking Rd (08723-5239)
PHONE..........................732 477-7484
David M Thompson, *President*
Barb Thompson, *Vice Pres*
EMP: 8
SQ FT: 7,000
SALES (est): 2MM **Privately Held**
WEB: www.marineeast.com
SIC: 3429 Marine hardware

(G-726)
MARKETING ADMINISTRATION ASSOC
Also Called: Milltex Manufacturing
1101 Industrial Pkwy (08724-2507)
PHONE..........................732 840-3021
Martin Metzger, *President*
EMP: 5
SQ FT: 3,600
SALES (est): 650K **Privately Held**
SIC: 5023 2392 Decorative home furnishings & supplies; blankets, comforters & beddings

(G-727)
MASSAGE CHAIR INC
1692 Route 88 Ste 1 (08724-3014)
PHONE..........................732 201-7777
Nicholas Fahmie, *President*
EMP: 4
SALES (est): 125.1K **Privately Held**
SIC: 3999 Manufacturing industries

(G-728)
PARAMOUNT PRODUCTS CO INC
1104 Industrial Pkwy (08724-2508)
PHONE..........................732 458-9200
Harold C Vogel Jr, *President*
EMP: 14 EST: 1946
SQ FT: 2,500
SALES (est): 1.4MM **Privately Held**
SIC: 3469 Stamping metal for the trade

(G-729)
PLASTIC BY ALL LLC
1127 Industrial Pkwy B (08724-2588)
PHONE..........................732 785-5900
Wayne Marz, *President*
EMP: 4
SALES (est): 484.9K **Privately Held**
SIC: 2295 Resin or plastic coated fabrics

(G-730)
RUSSO SEAMLESS GUTTER LLC
45 Cherie Dr (08724-8120)
PHONE..........................732 836-0151
Salvator Russo,
EMP: 4
SALES: 87K **Privately Held**
SIC: 3089 Gutters (glass fiber reinforced), fiberglass or plastic

(G-731)
SEA HABOR MARINE INC
310 Firehouse Rd (08723-6880)
PHONE..........................732 477-8577
Frank Cannella, *President*
EMP: 4
SALES (est): 405.1K **Privately Held**
SIC: 3441 Fabricated structural metal for ships

(G-732)
SPADONE ALFA SELF LBRCTED PDTS
Also Called: Spadone Bearings
532 Vincent Dr (08723-4016)
PHONE..................................203 972-8848
John Novak, *Principal*
EMP: 16
SALES: 950K **Privately Held**
SIC: 3568 Power transmission equipment

(G-733)
TERRESTRIAL IMAGING LLC
375 Herbertsville Rd (08724-1636)
PHONE..................................800 359-0530
Christopher Lopresti,
Mike Lopresti,
EMP: 6 **EST:** 2015
SALES (est): 550.2K **Privately Held**
SIC: 3728 Aircraft parts & equipment

Bridgeport
Gloucester County

(G-734)
AMERICAN DAWN INC
520 Pdricktown Rd Ste B (08014)
PHONE..................................856 467-9211
Leslie Sutton, *Principal*
EMP: 9
SALES (corp-wide): 27.9MM **Privately Held**
SIC: 2299 5023 5131 2393 Linen fabrics; linens & towels; textiles, woven; cushions, except spring & carpet: purchased materials; pillows, bed: made from purchased materials
PA: American Dawn, Inc.
401 W Artesia Blvd
Compton CA 90220
310 223-2000

(G-735)
CHELTEN HOUSE PRODUCTS INC (PA)
607 Heron Dr (08014)
P.O. Box 434 (08014-0434)
PHONE..................................856 467-1600
Steven Dabrow, *President*
Jason Dabrow, *COO*
Kenneth Pawloski, *CFO*
▼ **EMP:** 110 **EST:** 1965
SQ FT: 138,000
SALES (est): 26.2MM **Privately Held**
WEB: www.cheltenhouse.com
SIC: 2035 Dressings, salad: raw & cooked (except dry mixes); seasonings & sauces, except tomato & dry

(G-736)
EMERSON AUTOMATION SOLUTIONS
4 Killdeer Ct Ste 200 (08014)
PHONE..................................856 542-5252
Steve Oestereicher, *General Mgr*
EMP: 15
SALES (corp-wide): 17.4B **Publicly Held**
SIC: 3491 7699 Industrial valves; valve repair, industrial
HQ: Emerson Automation Solutions Final Control Us Lp
19200 Northwest Fwy
Jersey Village TX 77065

(G-737)
FEDERAL PRETZEL BAKING CO (PA)
300 Eagle Ct (08014)
PHONE..................................215 467-0505
Florence Sciambi, *Trustee*
EMP: 20
SQ FT: 3,700
SALES: 1.2MM **Privately Held**
SIC: 2052 Pretzels

(G-738)
FERRO CORPORATION
170 Route 130 S (08014)
P.O. Box 309 (08014-0309)
PHONE..................................856 467-3000
Steve Wood, *Branch Mgr*
EMP: 135

SALES (corp-wide): 1.6B **Publicly Held**
WEB: www.ferro.com
SIC: 2865 2899 Cyclic crudes & intermediates; chemical preparations
PA: Ferro Corporation
6060 Parkland Blvd # 250
Mayfield Heights OH 44124
216 875-5600

(G-739)
FLOWSERVE CORPORATION
401 Heron Dr (08014)
P.O. Box 563 (08014-0563)
PHONE..................................856 241-7800
Dave Siek, *Manager*
EMP: 60
SALES (corp-wide): 3.8B **Publicly Held**
SIC: 3561 Industrial pumps & parts
PA: Flowserve Corporation
5215 N Oconnor Blvd Connor
Irving TX 75039
972 443-6500

(G-740)
J & J SNACK FOODS CORP
Also Called: Uptown Bakeries
300 Eagle Ct (08014)
PHONE..................................856 467-9552
Tom Hunter, *Principal*
EMP: 129
SALES (corp-wide): 1.1B **Publicly Held**
WEB: www.jjsnack.com
SIC: 2053 2087 2086 2024 Frozen bakery products, except bread; syrups, drink; mineral water, carbonated: packaged in cans, bottles, etc.; ices, flavored (frozen dessert); cookies; bread, cake & related products
PA: J & J Snack Foods Corp.
6000 Central Hwy
Pennsauken NJ 08109
856 665-9533

(G-741)
MODINE MANUFACTURING COMPANY
244 High Hills Rd (08014)
P.O. Box 370 (08014-0370)
PHONE..................................856 467-9710
EMP: 6
SALES (corp-wide): 1.3B **Publicly Held**
SIC: 3443 ,5013 Whol Automotive Radiators
PA: Modine Manufacturing Company Inc
1500 Dekoven Ave
Racine WI 53403
262 636-1200

(G-742)
OMEGA ENGINEERING INC
Also Called: Omega Process Controls
1 Omega Cir (08014)
P.O. Box 336 (08014-0336)
PHONE..................................856 467-4200
William Keating, *Branch Mgr*
EMP: 200
SALES (corp-wide): 2B **Privately Held**
WEB: www.omega.com
SIC: 3625 3823 Relays & industrial controls; pH instruments, industrial process type
HQ: Omega Engineering, Inc.
800 Connecticut Ave 5n01
Norwalk CT 06854
203 359-1660

(G-743)
POLYMER ADDITIVES INC
Also Called: Valtris Specialty Chemicals
170 Us Route 130 S (08014)
P.O. Box 309 (08014-0309)
PHONE..................................856 467-8247
EMP: 17 **Privately Held**
SIC: 5169 2899 Chemicals & allied products; chemical preparations; fire retardant chemicals
HQ: Polymer Additives, Inc.
7500 E Pleasant Valley Rd
Independence OH 44131
216 875-7200

(G-744)
SEW-EURODRIVE INC
200 High Hill Rd (08014)
P.O. Box 481 (08014-0481)
PHONE..................................856 467-2277

Michael Zlockie, *Opers Staff*
Bernadette Jones, *Administration*
EMP: 40
SALES (corp-wide): 3.4B **Privately Held**
WEB: www.seweurodrive.com
SIC: 3566 5063 Drives, high speed industrial, except hydrostatic; power transmission equipment, electric
HQ: Sew-Eurodrive, Inc.
1295 Old Spartanburg Hwy
Lyman SC 29365
864 439-7537

(G-745)
SEW-EURODRIVE INC
2107 High Hill Rd (08014)
PHONE..................................856 467-2277
Michael Zlockie, *Branch Mgr*
Jurgen Blickle, *Director*
EMP: 57
SALES (corp-wide): 3.4B **Privately Held**
WEB: www.seweurodrive.com
SIC: 3566 Speed changers, drives & gears
HQ: Sew-Eurodrive, Inc.
1295 Old Spartanburg Hwy
Lyman SC 29365
864 439-7537

(G-746)
STATE TECHNOLOGY INC
610 Pedricktown Rd (08014)
P.O. Box 266 (08014-0266)
PHONE..................................856 467-8009
John Dozier, *President*
EMP: 6
SQ FT: 4,000
SALES: 800K **Privately Held**
WEB: www.stiservice.com
SIC: 8734 3841 7699 5047 Calibration & certification; diagnostic apparatus, medical; professional instrument repair services; electro-medical equipment

(G-747)
SULZER PUMP SERVICES (US) INC
Also Called: Sulzer Bingham Pumps
621 Heron Dr (08014)
P.O. Box 487 (08014-0487)
PHONE..................................856 542-5046
Ginny Johnston, *Branch Mgr*
EMP: 16
SQ FT: 15,000
SALES (corp-wide): 3.3B **Privately Held**
WEB: www.sulzerpumps.com
SIC: 7692 Welding repair
HQ: Sulzer Pump Services (Us) Inc.
101 Old Underwood Rd G
La Porte TX 77571
281 417-7110

(G-748)
XYLEM DEWATERING SOLUTIONS INC (HQ)
84 Floodgate Rd (08014-1001)
P.O. Box 191 (08014-0191)
PHONE..................................856 467-3636
Colin Sobil, *President*
Grant Salstrom, *President*
Kenneth Albaugh, *Regional Mgr*
Alan Mawby, *Senior Buyer*
James Gu, *Engineer*
◆ **EMP:** 225 **EST:** 1976
SQ FT: 51,000
SALES: 330MM **Publicly Held**
WEB: www.godwinpumps.com
SIC: 7353 3561 5084 Heavy construction equipment rental; pumps & pumping equipment; pumps & pumping equipment

---

Bridgeton
Cumberland County

(G-749)
ADAMS BILL PRINTING & GRAPHICS
Also Called: Adams Printing
300 Ramah Rd (08302-6948)
PHONE..................................856 455-7177
William G Adams II, *Owner*
Mary Adams, *Co-Owner*
EMP: 7
SQ FT: 2,000

SALES: 500K **Privately Held**
SIC: 2752 Commercial printing, offset

(G-750)
AFFORDABLE LEAD SOLUTIONS LLC
26 Blew Valley Ln (08302-6870)
PHONE..................................856 207-1348
Sam Thompson, *Mng Member*
EMP: 6
SALES: 180K **Privately Held**
SIC: 2851 Paint removers

(G-751)
ARDAGH GLASS INC
Also Called: Verallia North America
443 S East Ave (08302-3461)
PHONE..................................508 478-2500
John Yankovitch, *Manager*
EMP: 230
SALES (corp-wide): 242.1K **Privately Held**
WEB: www.sgcontainers.com
SIC: 3221 Glass containers
HQ: Ardagh Glass Inc.
10194 Crosspoint Blvd
Indianapolis IN 46256

(G-752)
BORTON ENTERPRISES
178 Woodruff Rd (08302-5941)
PHONE..................................856 453-9221
Corrine Borton, *President*
EMP: 10
SALES (est): 402.6K **Privately Held**
SIC: 2711 Newspapers, publishing & printing

(G-753)
BRAMBILA JORGE STUCCO & STONE
148 S Giles St (08302-2432)
PHONE..................................856 451-2039
Jorge Brambila, *Owner*
EMP: 4
SALES (est): 199.1K **Privately Held**
SIC: 3299 Stucco

(G-754)
BUONA VITA INC
1 S Industrial Blvd (08302-3401)
PHONE..................................856 453-7972
Paul Infranco, *President*
Molly Ketcham, *HR Admin*
EMP: 80
SALES (est): 32MM **Privately Held**
WEB: www.buonavitainc.com
SIC: 2099 Food preparations

(G-755)
BURDOL INC
Also Called: Print Signs and Designs
1791 S Burlington Rd (08302-4303)
PHONE..................................856 453-0336
Susan Lucas, *President*
Aaron Crispin, *Vice Pres*
EMP: 8
SQ FT: 4,200
SALES (est): 1.3MM **Privately Held**
SIC: 2752 2759 Commercial printing, offset; letterpress printing

(G-756)
COVIA HOLDINGS CORPORATION
1660 S Burlington Rd (08302-4338)
P.O. Box 1024 (08302-0713)
PHONE..................................856 451-6400
William P Light, *Manager*
EMP: 22
SALES (corp-wide): 142.6MM **Publicly Held**
WEB: www.unimin.com
SIC: 1446 Industrial sand
HQ: Covia Holdings Corporation
3 Summit Park Dr Ste 700
Independence OH 44131
440 214-3284

(G-757)
CUMBERLAND DAIRY INC
80 Edward Ave (08302-1230)
P.O. Box 308, Rosenhayn (08352-0308)
PHONE..................................856 451-1300
Carmine Catalana, *President*

Frank Catalana, *Vice Pres*
EMP: 45
SALES (corp-wide): 19.8MM **Privately Held**
SIC: 2026 2024 Milk processing (pasteurizing, homogenizing, bottling); yogurt; ice cream & frozen desserts
PA: Cumberland Dairy, Inc.
899 Landis Ave
Rosenhayn NJ 08352
800 257-8484

(G-758)
FRANK BURTON & SONS INC
333 W Broad St (08302-1401)
PHONE..................................856 455-1202
Robert J Burton, *President*
William Burton, *Vice Pres*
Thomas Burton, *Treasurer*
Donald F Burton Jr, *Admin Sec*
EMP: 9 **EST:** 1933
SALES (est): 1.3MM **Privately Held**
WEB: www.frankburtons.com
SIC: 5074 2434 1711 Plumbing & hydronic heating supplies; vanities, bathroom: wood; plumbing contractors

(G-759)
INNOVATION FOODS LLC
71 Bridgeton Ave (08302-1218)
PHONE..................................856 455-2209
Rachel Catalana, *President*
John Cowan, *CFO*
▲ **EMP:** 14
SQ FT: 40,000
SALES (est): 8K
SALES (corp-wide): 19.8MM **Privately Held**
SIC: 3411 Food & beverage containers
PA: Cumberland Dairy, Inc.
899 Landis Ave
Rosenhayn NJ 08352
800 257-8484

(G-760)
JAMES KINKADE
Also Called: Cumberland & Salem Guide
9 Oak Dr (08302-4524)
P.O. Box 735 (08302-0448)
PHONE..................................856 451-1177
James Kinkade, *President*
EMP: 16
SALES (est): 697.1K **Privately Held**
SIC: 2711 Newspapers

(G-761)
JAYNES SIGNWORK
143 Pcks Crnr Cohansey Rd (08302-5519)
PHONE..................................856 362-0503
Jayne Cuff, *Principal*
EMP: 4
SALES (est): 258.2K **Privately Held**
SIC: 3993 Signs & advertising specialties

(G-762)
LASSONDE PAPPAS AND CO INC
1019 Parsonage Rd (08302-4229)
PHONE..................................856 455-1001
EMP: 30
SALES (corp-wide): 402MM **Privately Held**
SIC: 2033 Fruit juices: packaged in cans, jars, etc.; fruits: packaged in cans, jars, etc.
HQ: Lassonde Pappas And Company, Inc.
1 Collins Dr Ste 200
Carneys Point NJ 08069
856 455-1000

(G-763)
LEONE INDUSTRIES INC
443 S East Ave (08302-3498)
PHONE..................................856 455-2000
Peter Leone, *President*
David J Leone, *Vice Pres*
◆ **EMP:** 350
SQ FT: 255,000
SALES (est): 34.9MM
SALES (corp-wide): 242.1K **Privately Held**
WEB: www.leoneglass.com
SIC: 3221 Glass containers
PA: Ard Holdings
Rue Charles Martel 56
Luxembourg

(G-764)
MARTIN CORPORATION
171 N Pearl St (08302-1929)
P.O. Box 479 (08302-0373)
PHONE..................................856 451-0900
Will Martin, *President*
Judith S Martin, *Vice Pres*
EMP: 19 **EST:** 1948
SQ FT: 90,000
SALES (est): 2.8MM **Privately Held**
SIC: 2261 2262 Dyeing cotton broadwoven fabrics; dyeing: manmade fiber & silk broadwoven fabrics

(G-765)
MKS INC
Also Called: Emerging Technologies
7 N Industrial Blvd (08302-3420)
PHONE..................................856 451-5545
Ken Brattlie, *President*
Lauren A Brattlie, *Treasurer*
Samuel Brattlie, *Shareholder*
James Peery, *Shareholder*
Paula Peery, *Shareholder*
EMP: 30
SQ FT: 9,000
SALES (est): 5.2MM **Privately Held**
WEB: www.quantaflex.com
SIC: 3646 3641 Commercial indusl & institutional electric lighting fixtures; electric lamps

(G-766)
NATIONAL REFRIGERANTS INC
661 Kenyon Ave (08302-4842)
PHONE..................................856 455-4555
John McDevit, *Plant Mgr*
EMP: 50
SALES (corp-wide): 91.1MM **Privately Held**
WEB: www.refrigerants.com
SIC: 3822 Air conditioning & refrigeration controls
PA: National Refrigerants, Inc.
11401 Roosevelt Blvd
Philadelphia PA 19154
215 698-6620

(G-767)
PALMETTO ADHESIVES COMPANY
1785 S Burlington Rd (08302-4303)
PHONE..................................856 451-0400
Tom Wilson, *Branch Mgr*
EMP: 12 **Privately Held**
SIC: 2891 Adhesives
PA: Palmetto Adhesives Company
112 Guess St
Greenville SC 29605

(G-768)
PERDUE FARMS INC
73 Silver Lake Rd (08302-6022)
PHONE..................................609 298-4100
Reggie Byrd, *Plant Mgr*
Efrem Andrews, *Human Res Mgr*
Jennifer Cannon, *Marketing Staff*
George Wilson, *Surgery Dir*
EMP: 4
SALES (corp-wide): 5.9B **Privately Held**
SIC: 2015 Poultry slaughtering & processing
PA: Perdue Farms Inc.
31149 Old Ocean City Rd
Salisbury MD 21804
410 543-3000

(G-769)
PERK & PANTRY
97 Trench Rd Ste 4 (08302-5706)
PHONE..................................856 451-4333
EMP: 4
SALES (est): 310K **Privately Held**
SIC: 5411 2051 2499 5812 Ret Groceries

(G-770)
POOR BOY PALLET LLC
45 Finley Rd (08302-6078)
PHONE..................................856 451-3771
Gary Macklin, *Mng Member*
Dennis Macklin,
EMP: 25
SALES (est): 3.6MM **Privately Held**
SIC: 2448 Pallets, wood

(G-771)
RUTGERS FOOD INNOVATION CENTER
450 E Broad St (08302-2849)
PHONE..................................856 459-1900
Sharese Porter, *Manager*
Michael Dubois, *Director*
Donna Schaffner, *Director*
EMP: 16
SALES (est): 2.2MM **Privately Held**
SIC: 2035 Dressings, salad: raw & cooked (except dry mixes)

(G-772)
SEABROOK BROTHERS & SONS INC
85 Finley Rd (08302-6078)
P.O. Box 5103 (08302-5103)
PHONE..................................856 455-8080
Charles F Seabrook II, *Vice Ch Bd*
James M Seabrook Jr, *President*
Andrew Carpenter, *COO*
William Seabrook, *Vice Pres*
Patricia Mosley, *Purch Mgr*
▲ **EMP:** 200 **EST:** 1978
SQ FT: 350,000
SALES: 100.8MM **Privately Held**
WEB: www.seabrookfarms.com
SIC: 2037 Vegetables, quick frozen & cold pack, excl. potato products

(G-773)
SOUTH JERSEY WATER COND SVC
760 Shiloh Pike (08302-1460)
PHONE..................................856 451-0620
D David Wilson Sr, *President*
EMP: 27 **EST:** 1967
SQ FT: 9,000
SALES (est): 2.3MM **Privately Held**
SIC: 7389 5999 0782 3589 Water softener service; product sterilization service; water purification equipment; lawn services; swimming pool filter & water conditioning systems

(G-774)
TERRIGNOS BAKERY
632 N Pearl St (08302-1299)
PHONE..................................856 451-6368
Mario Terrigno Sr, *President*
EMP: 32 **EST:** 1963
SQ FT: 5,000
SALES (est): 1.5MM **Privately Held**
SIC: 5461 2051 Bakeries; bread, cake & related products

(G-775)
THOMAS COBB & SONS
146 Cobbs Mill Rd (08302-5543)
PHONE..................................856 451-0671
William A Cobb, *Partner*
William Rex Cobb, *Partner*
William Cobb, *Opers Staff*
EMP: 7
SQ FT: 30,000
SALES: 201K **Privately Held**
SIC: 2421 Sawmills & planing mills, general

(G-776)
ULTRA CLEAN TECHNOLOGIES CORP
1274 Highway 77 (08302-5986)
PHONE..................................856 451-2176
Bruce Riley, *CEO*
▲ **EMP:** 30
SALES: 10MM **Privately Held**
WEB: www.ultracleantechnologies.com
SIC: 3677 Filtration devices, electronic

(G-777)
W W MANUFACTURING CO INC
60 Rosenhayn Ave (08302-1217)
PHONE..................................856 451-5700
Peater Lesche, *President*
Ingrid Hawk, *Treasurer*
EMP: 11 **EST:** 1964
SQ FT: 8,000
SALES: 1.2MM **Privately Held**
WEB: www.wwmfg.com
SIC: 3524 3441 7692 Lawn & garden equipment; fabricated structural metal; welding repair

(G-778)
WEBERS CANDY STORE
111 Old Cohansey Rd (08302-5673)
PHONE..................................856 455-8277
William Weber IV, *Owner*
EMP: 7 **EST:** 1888
SQ FT: 3,000
SALES (est): 210K **Privately Held**
SIC: 2064 5441 5145 Candy & other confectionery products; candy; confectionery; confectionery

(G-779)
WHIBCO INC (PA)
Also Called: Penn Rillton Div, The
87 E Commerce St (08302-2601)
PHONE..................................856 455-9200
Jane B Sorgren, *Ch of Bd*
Wade R Sjogren, *President*
Walter R Sjogren Jr, *Vice Pres*
EMP: 15
SQ FT: 12,000
SALES (est): 18.3MM **Privately Held**
WEB: www.whibco.com
SIC: 1442 5051 1446 Construction sand mining: foundry products; foundry sand mining

(G-780)
WWF OPERATING COMPANY
Also Called: Whitewave Foods
70 Rosenhayn Ave (08302-1237)
PHONE..................................856 459-3890
Richard Purdy, *General Mgr*
EMP: 16
SALES (corp-wide): 762.4MM **Privately Held**
SIC: 2026 Milk processing (pasteurizing, homogenizing, bottling)
HQ: Wwf Operating Company
12002 Airport Way
Broomfield CO 80021
214 303-3400

Bridgewater
Somerset County

(G-781)
3D BIOTEK LLC
1031 Us 206 Ste 202 (08807)
PHONE..................................908 801-6138
Weing Lau, *COO*
James W Fay, *Exec VP*
Faribourz Payvandi, *Vice Pres*
Qing Liu,
▲ **EMP:** 5
SQ FT: 1,000
SALES (est): 706.9K **Privately Held**
SIC: 3821 Laboratory apparatus & furniture

(G-782)
AFL TELECOMMUNICATIONS INC
745 Us Highway 202/206 (08807-1758)
PHONE..................................908 707-9500
Ashish Vengsarkar, *CEO*
Frank W Smith, *COO*
Harry Agront, *Purch Mgr*
Ronen Simovitch, *VP Engrg*
Naresh Patel, *Technical Mgr*
EMP: 30
SQ FT: 15,000
SALES (est): 10.5MM **Privately Held**
SIC: 3357 Fiber optic cable (insulated)
HQ: America Fujikura Ltd
170 Ridgeview Cir
Duncan SC 29334
800 235-3423

(G-783)
ALEMBIC PHARMACEUTICALS INC (DH)
750 Us Highway 202 # 100 (08807-5530)
PHONE..................................908 393-9604
Craig Salmon, *President*
Alexander Villanueva, *Vice Pres*
Cecilia Carfora, *CFO*
Armando Kellum, *VP Sales*
Sapneel Patel, *Office Mgr*
EMP: 3
SQ FT: 3,300

SALES (est): 1.8MM
SALES (corp-wide): 498.7MM **Privately
Held**
SIC: 2834 Tablets, pharmaceutical; pow-
ders, pharmaceutical
HQ: Alembic Global Holding Sa
    Rue Fritz-Courvoisier 40
    La Chaux-De-Fonds NE 2300
    329 679-595

(G-784)
ALPHARMA US INC
400 Crossing Blvd Ste 701 (08807-2863)
PHONE..................................201 228-5090
Michael J Locke, *President*
▲ EMP: 22
SALES (est): 5MM **Privately Held**
SIC: 2834 Pharmaceutical preparations

(G-785)
AMARIN PHARMA INC
440 Route 22 (08807-2477)
PHONE..................................908 719-1315
Joseph S Zakrzewski, *Ch of Bd*
John Thero, *President*
Joseph T Kennedy, *Exec VP*
Paul Huff, *Senior VP*
Steve Ketchum, *Senior VP*
EMP: 60
SALES (est): 25.4MM **Privately Held**
SIC: 2834 Pharmaceutical preparations
PA: Amarin Corporation Plc
    2 Pembroke House
    Dublin

(G-786)
AMNEAL PHARMACEUTICALS INC
400 Crossing Blvd Fl 3 (08807-2863)
PHONE..................................908 409-6822
EMP: 1249
SALES (corp-wide): 1.6B **Publicly Held**
SIC: 2834 3999 Druggists' preparations
(pharmaceuticals); atomizers, toiletry
PA: Amneal Pharmaceuticals, Inc.
    400 Crossing Blvd Fl 3
    Bridgewater NJ 08807
    908 947-3120

(G-787)
AMNEAL PHARMACEUTICALS INC (PA)
400 Crossing Blvd Fl 3 (08807-2863)
PHONE..................................908 947-3120
Paul Meister, *Ch of Bd*
Chirag Patel, *Co-CEO*
Chintu Patel, *Co-CEO*
Andrew Boyer, *Exec VP*
Patrick Roche, *Vice Pres*
EMP: 12
SALES: 1.6B **Publicly Held**
SIC: 2834 Pharmaceutical preparations

(G-788)
AMNEAL PHARMACEUTICALS LLC (HQ)
400 Crossing Blvd Fl 3 (08807-2863)
PHONE..................................908 947-3120
Andrew S Boyer, *Exec VP*
Scott Hunter, *Vice Pres*
Eddy Cruz, *Senior Buyer*
Todd Branning, *CFO*
Jenna Pappas, *HR Admin*
▲ EMP: 50
SALES: 1B
SALES (corp-wide): 1.6B **Publicly Held**
SIC: 2834 3999 Druggists' preparations
(pharmaceuticals); atomizers, toiletry
PA: Amneal Pharmaceuticals, Inc.
    400 Crossing Blvd Fl 3
    Bridgewater NJ 08807
    908 947-3120

(G-789)
AMNEAL-AGILA LLC
400 Crossing Blvd Fl 3 (08807-2863)
PHONE..................................908 947-3120
Todd Branning, *CFO*
EMP: 10 EST: 2012
SQ FT: 40,000
SALES: 2MM
SALES (corp-wide): 1.6B **Publicly Held**
SIC: 2834 Pharmaceutical preparations

HQ: Amneal Pharmaceuticals Llc
    400 Crossing Blvd Fl 3
    Bridgewater NJ 08807

(G-790)
APPLEGATE FARMS LLC
750 Rte 202 Ste 300 (08807-5530)
PHONE..................................908 725-2768
Stephen McDonnell, *CEO*
Eric Miller, *Senior VP*
Gina Asoudegan, *Vice Pres*
Kerry Collins, *Vice Pres*
Diane Kull, *Vice Pres*
▲ EMP: 106
SALES (est): 35.7MM
SALES (corp-wide): 9.5B **Publicly Held**
SIC: 2011 2013 Meat by-products from
meat slaughtered on site; sausages &
other prepared meats
PA: Hormel Foods Corporation
    1 Hormel Pl
    Austin MN 55912
    507 437-5611

(G-791)
ARCADIA CONSMR HEALTHCARE INC
Also Called: Kramer Consumer Healthcare
440 Us Highway 22 Ste 210 (08807-2477)
PHONE..................................800 824-4894
Rick Kornhauser, *CEO*
Piero Velarde, *Finance Dir*
▲ EMP: 12
SQ FT: 1,200
SALES (est): 3.2MM **Privately Held**
WEB: www.kramerlabs.com
SIC: 2834 2879 5122 Cough medicines;
fungicides; herbicides; drugs & drug pro-
prietaries

(G-792)
ARGONAUTUS LLC
867 Country Club Rd (08807-1140)
PHONE..................................908 393-4379
Luba Krpenko, *General Mgr*
EMP: 5
SALES: 500K **Privately Held**
SIC: 3634 Coffee makers, electric: house-
hold

(G-793)
ARIBA INC
1160 Us Highway 22 # 110 (08807-2931)
PHONE..................................908 333-3400
Melissa Rado, *Manager*
EMP: 43
SALES (corp-wide): 28.2B **Privately Held**
WEB: www.ariba.com
SIC: 7372 Business oriented computer
software
HQ: Ariba, Inc.
    3420 Hillview Ave Bldg 3
    Palo Alto CA 94304

(G-794)
ASHLAND LLC
1005 Route 202/206 (08807-1275)
PHONE..................................908 243-3500
EMP: 5
SALES (corp-wide): 3.7B **Publicly Held**
SIC: 2851 2821 2911 7549 Paints & allied products; plastics materials & resins;
polyesters; ester gum; heavy distillates;
oils, lubricating; trailer maintenance;
water treating compounds
HQ: Ashland Llc
    50 E Rivercenter Blvd # 1600
    Covington KY 41011
    859 815-3333

(G-795)
ASHLAND SPCALTY INGREDIENTS GP
1005 Route 202/206 (08807-1275)
PHONE..................................908 243-3500
EMP: 146
SALES (corp-wide): 3.7B **Publicly Held**
SIC: 2869 Industrial organic chemicals
HQ: Ashland Specialty Ingredients G.P.
    5200 Laser Pkwy
    Dublin OH 43017
    302 594-5000

(G-796)
AVAIL INC (PA)
Also Called: Service Apex
564a Union Ave (08807-3146)
PHONE..................................732 560-2222
Ken Griggs Sr, *President*
Ken Griggs Jr, *Vice Pres*
EMP: 6
SQ FT: 1,200
SALES (est): 929.6K **Privately Held**
WEB: www.serviceapex.com
SIC: 2211 2759 Shirting fabrics, cotton;
advertising literature: printing

(G-797)
AVANTOR PERFORMANCE MTLS LLC
1013 Route 202/206 (08807-1275)
PHONE..................................610 573-2759
EMP: 6
SALES (corp-wide): 1.4B **Publicly Held**
SIC: 2819 Industrial inorganic chemicals
HQ: Avantor Performance Materials, Llc
    100 W Matsonford Rd
    Radnor PA 19087
    610 573-2600

(G-798)
AVENTIS INC
55 Corporate Dr (08807-1265)
PHONE..................................800 981-2491
Joseph Palladino, *President*
Susan Esposito, *Vice Pres*
Gregory Irace, *Vice Pres*
Lorri Agnew-Smith, *Project Mgr*
Margaret Fitzgerald, *Project Mgr*
▲ EMP: 1358
SALES (est): 179.6MM **Privately Held**
SIC: 2834 Vitamin, nutrient & hematinic
preparations for human use
PA: Sanofi
    54 Rue La Boetie
    Paris 8e Arrondissement 75008

(G-799)
AVENTIS PHRMCTICALS FOUNDATION
55 Corporate Dr (08807-1265)
P.O. Box 6912 (08807-0912)
PHONE..................................908 981-5000
G Belle, *Principal*
EMP: 19
SALES: 0 **Privately Held**
SIC: 2834 Pharmaceutical preparations

(G-800)
BAUSCH & LOMB INCORPORATED (DH)
400 Somerset Corp Blvd (08807-2867)
P.O. Box 25169, Lehigh Valley PA (18002-
5169)
PHONE..................................585 338-6000
Fred Hassan, *Ch of Bd*
Matt Sleeman, *Business Mgr*
Alan H Farnsworth, *Exec VP*
Robert D Bailey, *Vice Pres*
Yolande Barnard, *Vice Pres*
◆ EMP: 400
SALES (est): 2.5B
SALES (corp-wide): 8.3B **Privately Held**
WEB: www.bausch.com
SIC: 3851 2834 3841 Ophthalmic goods;
contact lenses; magnifiers (readers &
simple magnifiers); pharmaceutical prepa-
rations; solutions, pharmaceutical; drug-
gists' preparations (pharmaceuticals);
vitamin preparations; ophthalmic instru-
ments & apparatus
HQ: Bausch & Lomb Holdings Incorporated
    450 Lexington Ave
    New York NY 10017
    585 338-6000

(G-801)
BAUSCH & LOMB INCORPORATED
400 Somerset Corp Blvd (08807-2867)
PHONE..................................908 927-1400
John Lafave, *Vice Pres*
Pepi Bruno, *Plant Mgr*
John Darcy, *Project Mgr*
Robin Kneeshaw, *Opers Staff*
Kearsten Hanley, *Mfg Staff*
EMP: 330

SALES (corp-wide): 8.3B **Privately Held**
SIC: 3851 Ophthalmic goods
HQ: Bausch & Lomb Incorporated
    400 Somerset Corp Blvd
    Bridgewater NJ 08807
    585 338-6000

(G-802)
BAUSCH HEALTH AMERICAS INC (HQ)
Also Called: Valeant Pharmaceuticals Intl
400 Somerset Corp Blvd (08807-2867)
PHONE..................................908 927-1400
J Michael Pearson, *CEO*
G Mason Morfit, *President*
Margaret Mulligan, *Exec VP*
Robert Chai Onn, *Exec VP*
Robert Rosiello, *Exec VP*
▲ EMP: 355 EST: 1994
SQ FT: 110,000
SALES (est): 3B
SALES (corp-wide): 8.3B **Privately Held**
WEB: www.icnpharm.com
SIC: 2834 Pharmaceutical preparations
PA: Bausch Health Companies Inc
    2150 Boul Saint-Elzear O
    Sainte-Rose QC H7L 4
    514 744-6792

(G-803)
BAUSCH HEALTH US LLC (DH)
400 Somerset Corp Blvd (08807-2867)
P.O. Box 25169, Lehigh Valley PA (18002-
5169)
PHONE..................................908 927-1400
Richard K Masterson, *President*
Rajiv De Silva, *COO*
Brian Stolz, *Exec VP*
Peter Blott, *CFO*
Phillip W Loberg, *CFO*
EMP: 28
SALES (est): 47.7MM
SALES (corp-wide): 8.3B **Privately Held**
SIC: 2834 Pharmaceutical preparations
HQ: Bausch Health Americas, Inc.
    400 Somerset Corp Blvd
    Bridgewater NJ 08807
    908 927-1400

(G-804)
BAUSCH HEALTH US LLC
700 Rte 202 206n (08807-2552)
PHONE..................................908 927-1400
Randy Holmberg, *Engineer*
Brett Freeman, *Sales Staff*
Noel Keller, *Sales Staff*
Sarah Balcewicz, *Manager*
Gemma Pimentel, *Manager*
EMP: 4
SALES (corp-wide): 8.3B **Privately Held**
SIC: 2834 Pharmaceutical preparations
HQ: Bausch Health Us, Llc
    400 Somerset Corp Blvd
    Bridgewater NJ 08807

(G-805)
BIOVAIL DISTRIBUTION COMPANY
700 Us Highway 202/206 (08807-1704)
PHONE..................................908 927-1400
William Wells, *Principal*
EMP: 4
SALES (est): 243.4K **Privately Held**
SIC: 2834 Pharmaceutical preparations

(G-806)
BRADDOCK HEAT TREATING COMPANY
123 Chimney Rock Rd (08807-3126)
PHONE..................................732 356-2906
Steven R Braddock, *CEO*
William K Braddock, *President*
EMP: 46
SQ FT: 20,000
SALES (est): 10.9MM
SALES (corp-wide): 19.2MM **Privately
Held**
SIC: 3398 Metal heat treating
HQ: Braddock Metallurgical, Inc.
    14600 Duval Pl W
    Jacksonville FL 32218
    386 267-0955

GEOGRAPHIC

(G-807)
BRISTOL-MYERS SQUIBB COMPANY
685 Us Highway 202/206 (08807-1750)
PHONE...................................908 218-3700
John Mamone, *Branch Mgr*
EMP: 500
SALES (corp-wide): 22.5B **Publicly Held**
WEB: www.bms.com
SIC: 2834 Pharmaceutical preparations
PA: Bristol-Myers Squibb Company
430 E 29th St Fl 14
New York NY 10016
212 546-4000

(G-808)
BROTHER INTERNATIONAL CORP (HQ)
200 Crossing Blvd Fl 1 (08807-2861)
PHONE....................................908 704-1700
Kazufumi Ikeda, *President*
◆ EMP: 340
SQ FT: 93,000
SALES: 1.7B **Privately Held**
WEB: www.brothersupport.com
SIC: 5044 3579 3559 5084 Office equipment; typing & word processing machines; typewriters & parts; word processing equipment; sewing machines & hat & zipper making machinery; sewing machines & attachments, industrial; sewing machines, industrial; sewing machines, household; electric; electronic parts & equipment; facsimile equipment

(G-809)
BTA PHARMACEUTICALS INC
700 Us Highway 202/206 (08807-1704)
PHONE....................................908 927-1400
Tanya Carro, *Vice Pres*
EMP: 44
SALES: 950K **Privately Held**
SIC: 2834 Pharmaceutical preparations

(G-810)
C TECHNOLOGIES INC
Also Called: Ctechnologiesinc.com
685 Us Highway 202/206 # 102 (08807-1750)
PHONE....................................908 707-1009
Craig Harrison, *President*
Samantha Duffy, *Buyer*
Mary Vernieri, *Finance*
Anna Santos, *Manager*
EMP: 40
SALES (est): 7.7MM **Privately Held**
WEB: www.ctechnologiesinc.com
SIC: 3229 Fiber optics strands

(G-811)
CHAPTER ENTERPRISES INC
Also Called: New Jersey Line X
8w Chimney Rock Rd (08807)
PHONE....................................732 560-8500
Michael Terlizzi, *President*
EMP: 6
SQ FT: 4,000
SALES (est): 1.1MM **Privately Held**
SIC: 5531 3479 Automobile & truck equipment & parts; coating of metals & formed products

(G-812)
CMS TECHNOLOGY INC
10 Finderne Ave Ste A (08807-3365)
PHONE....................................512 913-1898
John Meccia, *CEO*
Robert Buchs, *Controller*
EMP: 12
SALES: 917.1K **Privately Held**
SIC: 2819 Industrial inorganic chemicals

(G-813)
CONVATEC INC (HQ)
Also Called: Convatec Healthcare A, S.A.R.
1160 Rte 22 Ste 201 (08807-2931)
PHONE....................................908 231-2179
Paul Moraviec, *CEO*
Dave Johnson, *President*
Gino Henry, *Business Mgr*
Adrienne McNally, *Senior VP*
Fiona Adam, *Vice Pres*
▲ EMP: 274

SALES (est): 2.4B
SALES (corp-wide): 1.8B **Privately Held**
WEB: www.convatec.com
SIC: 3841 Surgical & medical instruments

(G-814)
COUNTY OF SOMERSET
Also Called: Recycling
40 Polhemus Ln (08807-3391)
PHONE....................................732 469-3363
William Saller, *Superintendent*
EMP: 150 **Privately Held**
WEB: www.rce.rutgers.edu
SIC: 4953 9111 3341 3231 Refuse collection & disposal services; county supervisors' & executives' offices; secondary nonferrous metals; products of purchased glass; pulp mills
PA: County Of Somerset
20 Grove St
Somerville NJ 08876
908 231-7000

(G-815)
CSM WORLDWIDE INC (PA)
36 S Adamsville Rd 7 (08807-3212)
PHONE....................................908 233-2882
Atul Shah, *CEO*
Michael S Torstrup, *President*
Michael Carousso, *Project Engr*
James McKee, *Finance Mgr*
▲ EMP: 20 EST: 1897
SALES (est): 6.1MM **Privately Held**
WEB: www.csmworldwide.com
SIC: 3564 Air purification equipment

(G-816)
D R KENYON & SON INC
400 Us Highway 22 (08807-2463)
PHONE....................................908 722-0001
Loren W Jones, *President*
EMP: 10
SQ FT: 45,000
SALES: 2MM **Privately Held**
SIC: 3552 Finishing machinery, textile

(G-817)
DENBY USA LIMITED
1065 Rte 22 Ste 3b (08807-2949)
PHONE....................................800 374-6479
Susan Beers, *Principal*
Dave Hinrichsen, *Network Mgr*
EMP: 7 EST: 2015
SALES (est): 197.8K **Privately Held**
SIC: 2499 Tiles, cork

(G-818)
DEWY MEADOW FARMS INC (PA)
Also Called: Dewy Meadow Foods, Inc.
1018 Rector Rd (08807-1318)
PHONE....................................908 218-5655
Randolph Krogoll, *President*
EMP: 15
SALES (est): 1.3MM **Privately Held**
SIC: 2038 Frozen specialties

(G-819)
ENALTEC LABS INC
991 Route 22 Ste 200 (08807-2957)
PHONE....................................908 864-8000
Vikas Yadav, *Principal*
Sumit Gupta, *Principal*
Susheel Koul, *Principal*
Anand Shah, *Principal*
EMP: 4
SALES (est): 156.7K
SALES (corp-wide): 20.8MM **Privately Held**
SIC: 2834 Pharmaceutical preparations; antihistamine preparations; diuretics
PA: Enaltec Labs Private Limited
1706, 17th Floor, Kesar Solitaire, Plot No. 5
Navi Mumbai MH 40070
226 750-7000

(G-820)
ETHICON INC
Also Called: Ethicon Endo - Surgery
520 Us Highway 22 Ste 1 (08807-2410)
P.O. Box 6999 (08807-0999)
PHONE....................................908 253-6464
Eugene T Reilly Jr, *President*
EMP: 24

SALES (corp-wide): 81.5B **Publicly Held**
WEB: www.ethiconinc.com
SIC: 3842 Surgical appliances & supplies
HQ: Ethicon Inc.
Us Route 22
Somerville NJ 08876
732 524-0400

(G-821)
EVAPCO-BLCT DRY COOLING INC
685 Route 202/206 Ste 300 (08807-1775)
PHONE....................................908 379-2665
William G Bartley, *CEO*
William Wurtz, *President*
Andrew Smith, *Business Mgr*
Danny Xiao, *Exec VP*
Toby Athron, *Vice Pres*
▲ EMP: 25
SQ FT: 6,000
SALES (est): 8.1MM
SALES (corp-wide): 382.7MM **Privately Held**
SIC: 3629 Condensers, for motors or generators
PA: Evapco, Inc.
5151 Allendale Ln
Taneytown MD 21787
410 756-2600

(G-822)
EXCERPTA MEDICA INC (DH)
Also Called: Instrctnal Cmpt Based Training
685 Us Highway 202/206 (08807-1750)
PHONE....................................908 547-2100
Eric Engstrof, *CEO*
Ronald H Schlosser, *President*
Louis J Andreozzi, *Vice Pres*
Robert Issler, *Treasurer*
Ronald Van Olffen, *Program Mgr*
EMP: 65
SQ FT: 25,000
SALES (est): 19.2MM
SALES (corp-wide): 9.6B **Privately Held**
SIC: 7389 2721 2731 2741 Convention & show services; trade journals: publishing only, not printed on site; pamphlets: publishing only, not printed on site; newsletter publishing
HQ: Relx Inc.
230 Park Ave Ste 700
New York NY 10169
212 309-8100

(G-823)
EYETECH INC
700 Us Highway 202/206 (08807-1704)
PHONE....................................646 454-1779
Steven Bettis, *President*
EMP: 13
SALES (est): 1.3MM
SALES (corp-wide): 8.3B **Privately Held**
SIC: 2834 Pharmaceutical preparations
PA: Bausch Health Companies Inc
2150 Boul Saint-Elzear O
Sainte-Rose QC H7L 4
514 744-6792

(G-824)
EZ-DUMPSTER LLC
829 Madison Ave (08807-1199)
PHONE....................................908 752-2787
Robert Noble, *Principal*
EMP: 4
SALES (est): 119K **Privately Held**
SIC: 2673 Bags: plastic, laminated & coated

(G-825)
GARRETT MOORE
Also Called: Officeclocks.com
1048 Hoffman Rd (08807-2121)
PHONE....................................908 231-9231
Garrett Moore, *Owner*
EMP: 4
SQ FT: 2,200
SALES: 300K **Privately Held**
SIC: 3873 7631 5944 Clocks, assembly of; clock repair; clock & watch stores

(G-826)
GEARS IV LLC
11 Jeffrey Ln (08807-1405)
PHONE....................................201 401-3035
Michael Schwertfeger, *Principal*
EMP: 4

SALES (est): 279.9K **Privately Held**
SIC: 3566 Gears, power transmission, except automotive

(G-827)
GENERON BIOMED INC
1200 Us Highway 22 # 2000 (08807-2943)
PHONE....................................908 203-4701
Xianfeng Cheng, *Ch of Bd*
Jagan Kalaimani, *Principal*
EMP: 5
SALES (est): 229.7K **Privately Held**
SIC: 2834 Pharmaceutical preparations

(G-828)
HAMAMATSU CORPORATION (DH)
360 Foothill Rd (08807-2932)
P.O. Box 6910 (08807-0910)
PHONE....................................908 231-0960
Craig Walling, *President*
Bill Moore, *Business Mgr*
Eric Atanda, *Vice Pres*
Thomas Baker, *Vice Pres*
Mary Boyle, *Vice Pres*
▲ EMP: 90
SQ FT: 74,431
SALES (est): 57.3MM **Privately Held**
WEB: www.hps-industrial.com
SIC: 3671 5065 3674 3641 Photomultiplier tubes; electronic tubes: receiving & transmitting or industrial; electronic parts; semiconductors & related devices; electric lamps
HQ: Photonics Management Corp.
360 Foothill Rd
Bridgewater NJ 08807
908 231-0960

(G-829)
HAMAMATSU CORPORATION
Hamamatsu Photonic Systems
360 Foothill Rd (08807-2932)
PHONE....................................908 526-0941
Akira Hiruma, *Branch Mgr*
EMP: 20 **Privately Held**
WEB: www.hps-industrial.com
SIC: 3825 3641 Instruments to measure electricity; electric lamps
HQ: Hamamatsu Corporation
360 Foothill Rd
Bridgewater NJ 08807
908 231-0960

(G-830)
HENKEL US OPERATIONS CORP
10 Finderne Ave Ste B (08807-3365)
PHONE....................................908 685-7000
Yuhong Hu, *Technical Mgr*
Cristina Dejesus, *Research*
Terry Maher, *Research*
Matthew Bankaitis, *Engineer*
Matthew Gustin, *Accounts Mgr*
EMP: 50
SALES (corp-wide): 22.7B **Privately Held**
SIC: 2891 Adhesives; sealants
HQ: Henkel Us Operations Corporation
1 Henkel Way
Rocky Hill CT 06067
860 571-5100

(G-831)
HUE BOX LLC
9 Sally Ct (08807-5600)
PHONE....................................908 904-9501
Ziang Jiao,
EMP: 8
SALES (est): 95.9K **Privately Held**
SIC: 5812 7372 Eating places; application computer software

(G-832)
IMAGINE COMMUNICATIONS CORP
Also Called: Harris Broadcast
1160 Us Highway 22 (08807-2931)
PHONE....................................201 469-6740
P Harris Morris, *CEO*
Ryan Reigner, *Engineer*
Russell Johnson, *Branch Mgr*
EMP: 31
SALES (corp-wide): 3.8B **Privately Held**
SIC: 3663 Radio broadcasting & communications equipment; television broadcasting & communications equipment

HQ: Imagine Communications Corp.
3001 Dallas Pkwy Ste 300
Frisco TX 75034
469 803-4900

(G-833)
IMCLONE SYSTEMS LLC (HQ)
Also Called: Lilly
440 Us Highway 22 (08807-2477)
PHONE...................908 541-8000
John H Johnson, *CEO*
Christine Bonacci, *Assistant VP*
Howard Smulewitz, *Assistant VP*
Joseph Stoneback, *Mfg Staff*
Yanxia LI, *Research*
◆ EMP: 180
SQ FT: 45,000
SALES (est): 242.7MM
SALES (corp-wide): 24.5B Publicly Held
WEB: www.imclone.com
SIC: 2836 2834 Biological products, except diagnostic; pharmaceutical preparations
PA: Eli Lilly And Company
Lilly Corporate Ctr
Indianapolis IN 46285
317 276-2000

(G-834)
IMPAX LABORATORIES LLC
Also Called: Impax Labs
100 Somerset Corp Blvd # 3000
(08807-2859)
PHONE...................732 595-4600
EMP: 11
SALES (corp-wide): 1.6B Publicly Held
SIC: 2834 Pharmaceutical preparations
HQ: Impax Laboratories, Llc
30831 Huntwood Ave
Hayward CA 94544
510 240-6000

(G-835)
INDUSTRONIC INC
1170 Us Highway 22 # 108 (08807-2933)
PHONE...................908 393-5960
Wolfgang Stallmeyer, *President*
Axel Breidenbruch, *Vice Pres*
EMP: 4
SALES (est): 363.6K
SALES (corp-wide): 42.5MM Privately Held
WEB: www.industronic.com
SIC: 3629 3669 5065 5999 Electronic generation equipment; intercommunication systems, electric; communication equipment; communication equipment
PA: Industronic, Industrie-Electronic Gmbh & Co Kg
Carl-Jacob-Kolb-Weg 1
Wertheim 97877
934 287-10

(G-836)
INGREDION INCORPORATED
Also Called: Corn Products International
10 Finderne Ave Ste A (08807-3365)
PHONE...................908 685-5000
Matthew Seilus, *Project Mgr*
Dustin Morris, *Production*
Esteban Rocha, *Engineer*
Erhan Yildiz, *Engineer*
Oreolu Fadahunsi, *Sales Staff*
EMP: 71
SALES (corp-wide): 5.8B Publicly Held
SIC: 2046 Wet corn milling
PA: Ingredion Incorporated
5 Westbrook Corporate Ctr # 500
Westchester IL 60154
708 551-2600

(G-837)
INSMED INCORPORATED (PA)
10 Finderne Ave Bldg 10 # 10
(08807-3365)
PHONE...................908 977-9900
William H Lewis, *Ch of Bd*
David Green, *Research*
Mosha Deng, *Manager*
Rahul Bhatia, *Director*
Vincent Cerio, *Director*
EMP: 171
SQ FT: 117,022

SALES: 9.8MM Publicly Held
WEB: www.insmed.com
SIC: 2834 Pharmaceutical preparations; drugs acting on the respiratory system

(G-838)
J C W INC
Also Called: Natural Green
795 E Main St (08807-3338)
PHONE...................732 560-8061
Clifford Woody, *President*
Jean Woody, *Corp Secy*
EMP: 20
SQ FT: 1,500
SALES (est): 4.8MM Privately Held
WEB: www.naturalgreen.com
SIC: 3562 0782 Casters; lawn & garden services

(G-839)
JUNIPER NETWORKS INC
200 Somerset Corp Blvd (08807-2862)
PHONE...................908 947-4436
Vince Molinaro, *Exec VP*
Chaitanya Kadiyala, *Manager*
EMP: 72 Publicly Held
WEB: www.juniper.net
SIC: 7373 7372 Computer integrated systems design; prepackaged software
PA: Juniper Networks, Inc.
1133 Innovation Way
Sunnyvale CA 94089

(G-840)
LAVITSKY COMPUTER LABORATORIES
865 Sherwood Rd (08807-1320)
PHONE...................908 725-6206
Eric Lavitsky, *President*
EMP: 6
SQ FT: 3,000
SALES (est): 1MM Privately Held
WEB: www.lavitsky.com
SIC: 3571 7378 7371 Electronic computers; computer maintenance & repair; computer software development

(G-841)
LEGEND MACHINE & GRINDING
36 S Adamsville Rd (08807-3212)
PHONE...................908 685-1100
Eric Butler, *Principal*
EMP: 12
SALES (est): 980K Privately Held
SIC: 3599 Grinding castings for the trade

(G-842)
LIFECELL CORPORATION
95 Corporate Dr (08807-1265)
PHONE...................908 947-1100
Joseph F Woody, *Branch Mgr*
EMP: 16 Privately Held
SIC: 2834 Pharmaceutical preparations
HQ: Lifecell Corporation
1 Millennium Way
Branchburg NJ 08876
908 947-1100

(G-843)
LIGNO TECH USA INC
Also Called: Lignotech U S A
721 Us Highway 202 (08807-2510)
PHONE...................908 429-6660
Ray Douglas, *Vice Pres*
EMP: 7 EST: 1954
SALES (est): 1MM Privately Held
WEB: www.ltus.com
SIC: 2819 2869 Industrial inorganic chemicals; industrial organic chemicals

(G-844)
LINDE GAS NORTH AMERICA LLC (DH)
200 Somerset Corp Blvd # 7000
(08807-2882)
PHONE...................908 508-3000
Wolfgang Reitzle, *CEO*
Patrick F Murphy, *President*
Mark D Weller, *Chairman*
Philippe D Brunet, *Vice Pres*
Mike Walsh,
◆ EMP: 750
SQ FT: 215,000
SALES (est): 1.2B Privately Held
SIC: 2813 Oxygen, compressed or liquefied; nitrogen; argon; hydrogen

HQ: Linde Ag
Klosterhofstr. 1
Munchen 80331
893 575-701

(G-845)
LINDE GAS USA LLC (DH)
200 Somset Corp B 7000 (08807)
P.O. Box 94737, Cleveland OH (44101-4737)
PHONE...................908 464-8100
Patrick Murphy, *President*
Mark Weller, *Exec VP*
John Brull, *Senior VP*
Glen Radomski, *Mfg Staff*
Jonathan Hoy, *Treasurer*
◆ EMP: 95 EST: 1917
SQ FT: 20,000
SALES (est): 170.2MM
SALES (corp-wide): 1.4B Privately Held
SIC: 2813 5084 Oxygen, compressed or liquefied; welding machinery & equipment
HQ: Messer Industries Gmbh
Messer-Platz 1
Bad Soden Am Taunus 65812
619 677-600

(G-846)
LM MATRIX SOLUTIONS LLC
991 Us Highway 22 Ste 200 (08807-2957)
PHONE...................908 756-7952
Leon M McBride,
EMP: 5
SALES: 250K Privately Held
WEB: www.lmmatrixsolutionsllc.com
SIC: 7372 7378 7379 Operating systems computer software; computer maintenance & repair; computer related maintenance services; computer related consulting services; computer hardware requirements analysis

(G-847)
MATRIXX INITIATIVES INC (PA)
Also Called: Zicam
1 Grand Blvd (08807)
P.O. Box 28486, Scottsdale AZ (85255-0158)
PHONE...................877 942-2626
Marc L Rovner, *CEO*
Sam Kamdar, *COO*
Raj Shah, *Finance Dir*
Ken Becker, *Manager*
EMP: 25
SQ FT: 23,000
SALES (est): 4.8MM Privately Held
SIC: 2834 Drugs acting on the respiratory system

(G-848)
MEDICIS PHARMACEUTICAL CORP (HQ)
700 Us Highway 202/206 (08807-1704)
PHONE...................866 246-8245
Jonah Shacknai, *CEO*
Jason D Hanson, *COO*
Vincent Ippolito, *Exec VP*
Seth Rodner, *Exec VP*
Mitchell Wortzman PHD, *Exec VP*
◆ EMP: 16
SQ FT: 13,000
SALES (est): 73.6MM
SALES (corp-wide): 8.3B Privately Held
WEB: www.medicis.com
SIC: 2834 Dermatologicals
PA: Bausch Health Companies Inc
2150 Boul Saint-Elzear O
Sainte-Rose QC H7L 4
514 744-6792

(G-849)
MESSER LLC (DH)
Also Called: Messer North America
200 Somerset Corp Blvd # 7000
(08807-2882)
PHONE...................908 464-8100
Jens Luehring, *President*
David McDaniel, *Plant Mgr*
Phillip Dersham, *Production*
Marlana Whitley, *Production*
Pj Scala, *Buyer*
◆ EMP: 200
SQ FT: 215,000

SALES (est): 1.4B
SALES (corp-wide): 1.4B Privately Held
WEB: www.linde.com
SIC: 2813 3569 3561 3823 Oxygen, compressed or liquefied; nitrogen; argon; hydrogen; gas separators (machinery); pumps & pumping equipment; industrial flow & liquid measuring instruments
HQ: Messer North America, Inc.
200 Somerset Corporate Bl
Bridgewater NJ 08807
908 464-8100

(G-850)
MESSER LLC
Linde Electronics
200 Somerset Corp Blvd (08807-2862)
PHONE...................512 330-0153
Patrick Murphy, *Manager*
EMP: 400
SALES (corp-wide): 1.4B Privately Held
SIC: 2813 Oxygen, compressed or liquefied
HQ: Messer Llc
200 Somerset Corp Blvd # 7000
Bridgewater NJ 08807
908 464-8100

(G-851)
MESSER NORTH AMERICA INC (DH)
200 Somerset Corporate Bl (08807-2862)
PHONE...................908 464-8100
Jens Luehring, *President*
Robert White, *General Mgr*
Sebastian Elizagaray, *Business Mgr*
Duncan Young, *Business Mgr*
Cristina Jackson, *Vice Pres*
◆ EMP: 277
SQ FT: 215,000
SALES (est): 1.5B
SALES (corp-wide): 1.4B Privately Held
WEB: www.bocsureflow.com
SIC: 2813 3569 3559 3561 Industrial gases; oxygen, compressed or liquefied; nitrogen; argon; gas producers, generators & other gas related equipment; cryogenic machinery, industrial; pumps & pumping equipment; turbines & turbine generator sets; flow instruments, industrial process type
HQ: Messer Group Gmbh
Messer-Platz 1
Bad Soden Am Taunus 65812
619 677-600

(G-852)
MICROSOFT CORPORATION
400 Commons Way Ste 279 (08807-2821)
PHONE...................908 809-7320
Eric Schroeder, *Program Mgr*
EMP: 35
SALES (corp-wide): 125.8B Publicly Held
SIC: 7372 Prepackaged software
PA: Microsoft Corporation
1 Microsoft Way
Redmond WA 98052
425 882-8080

(G-853)
MOUNTAIN LLC
400 Crossing Blvd Fl 5 (08807-2863)
PHONE...................908 409-6823
Starr Diethorn,
Robert Stewart,
EMP: 5
SALES (est): 229.7K
SALES (corp-wide): 1.6B Publicly Held
SIC: 2834 3999 Druggists' preparations (pharmaceuticals); atomizers, toiletry
HQ: Amneal Pharmaceuticals Llc
400 Crossing Blvd Fl 3
Bridgewater NJ 08807

(G-854)
NATIONAL STRCH CHEM HOLDG CORP (HQ)
10 Finderne Ave (08807-3365)
PHONE...................908 685-5000
Ned W Bandler, *President*
Herbert J Baumgarten, *Vice Pres*
Tony Delio, *Vice Pres*
Rebecca Wulfsohn, *Engineer*
Rachel Foley, *Accountant*
▼ EMP: 900

SQ FT: 550,000
SALES (est): 321.8MM
SALES (corp-wide): 5.8B **Publicly Held**
SIC: **2891** 2046 2869 Adhesives &
sealants; wet corn milling; industrial or-
ganic chemicals; vinyl acetate
PA: Ingredion Incorporated
5 Westbrook Corporate Ctr # 500
Westchester IL 60154
708 551-2600

(G-855)
NATL ADHESIES DIV OF HENKE
10 Finderne Ave (08807-3365)
PHONE..............................908 685-7000
Brian Henke, *Principal*
▲ EMP: 4
SALES (est): 243.1K **Privately Held**
SIC: **2891** Adhesives

(G-856)
NESTLE HEALTHCARE NTRTN
INC (HQ)
Also Called: Nestle Health Science
1007 Us Highway 202/206 (08807-1275)
P.O. Box 697, Florham Park (07932-0697)
PHONE..............................800 422-2752
Greg Behar, *CEO*
◆ EMP: 140 **EST:** 1951
SALES (est): 630MM
SALES (corp-wide): 92B **Privately Held**
SIC: **2032** Canned specialties
PA: Nestle S.A.
Avenue Nestle 55
Vevey VD 1800
219 242-111

(G-857)
NITTA CASINGS INC
141 Southside Ave (08807-3256)
PHONE..............................800 526-3970
Rodney Moore, *President*
Roseann Salerno, *Vice Pres*
Bruce Zacharias, *Vice Pres*
Gregg Possiel, *Maint Spvr*
Jeff Holmes, *Inv Control Mgr*
▼ EMP: 165 **EST:** 1969
SQ FT: 120,000
SALES (est): 26.1MM **Privately Held**
WEB: www.nittacasings.com
SIC: **2013** 5149 Sausage casings, natural;
sausage casings
PA: Nitta Gelatin Inc.
2-22, Futamata
Yao OSK 581-0

(G-858)
NJS ASSOCIATES COMPANY
1170 Route 22 Ste 209 (08807-2928)
PHONE..............................973 960-8688
EMP: 5
SALES (est): 99K **Privately Held**
SIC: **2834** 5912 Pharmaceutical prepara-
tions; drug stores

(G-859)
ONPHARMA INC
400 Somerset Corporate Bl (08807-2867)
PHONE..............................408 335-6850
Matt Stepovich, *President*
Michael Parsons, *Vice Pres*
EMP: 6
SALES (est): 797.8K
SALES (corp-wide): 8.3B **Privately Held**
SIC: **2834** Pharmaceutical preparations
HQ: Orapharma, Inc.
700 Route 202/206
Bridgewater NJ 08807
908 927-1400

(G-860)
ORACLE CORPORATION
400 Crossing Blvd Fl 6 (08807-2863)
PHONE..............................908 547-6200
Joydip Chakraborty, *Senior Engr*
Al Domingo, *Manager*
Jack Coyne, *Technology*
Theresa Ho, *Technical Staff*
Balaji Nagalamadaka, *Technical Staff*
EMP: 191
SALES (corp-wide): 39.5B **Publicly Held**
WEB: www.oracle.com
SIC: **7372** Business oriented computer
software

PA: Oracle Corporation
500 Oracle Pkwy
Redwood City CA 94065
650 506-7000

(G-861)
ORTHO BIOTECH PRODUCTS
LP
430 Route 22 (08807-2463)
P.O. Box 6908 (08807-0908)
PHONE..............................908 541-4000
Carol Webb, *Executive*
EMP: 66
SALES (est): 10.1MM
SALES (corp-wide): 81.5B **Publicly Held**
WEB: www.jnj.com
SIC: **2834** Pharmaceutical preparations
PA: Johnson & Johnson
1 Johnson And Johnson Plz
New Brunswick NJ 08933
732 524-0400

(G-862)
OSMOTICA PHARMACEUTICAL
CORP
400 Crossing Blvd (08807-2863)
PHONE..............................908 809-1300
Brian Markison, *CEO*
Praveen Tyle, *President*
Dennis Hall, *Vice Pres*
Samer Kaba, *Vice Pres*
Tak Lee, *Vice Pres*
▲ EMP: 198
SQ FT: 90,000
SALES (est): 1.8MM **Privately Held**
SIC: **2834** Pharmaceutical preparations
PA: Osmotica Holdings Corp Limited
City House, Floor 3, 6 Karaiskaki
Limassol

(G-863)
OSMOTICA PHARMACEUTICALS
PLC (PA)
400 Crossing Blvd (08807-2863)
PHONE..............................908 809-1300
Brian Markison, *CEO*
James Schaub, *President*
Andrew Einhorn, *CFO*
Christopher Klein, *Admin Sec*
EMP: 9
SQ FT: 25,000
SALES (est): 263.7MM **Publicly Held**
SIC: **2834** Pharmaceutical preparations

(G-864)
PFIZER INC
400 Crossing Blvd Fl 7 (08807-2863)
PHONE..............................212 733-2323
Yingqun Wang, *Engrg Dir*
Keith Colmey, *Engineer*
Graci Russ, *Manager*
Tony Decicco, *Director*
Jennifer Holahan, *Director*
EMP: 146
SALES (corp-wide): 53.6B **Publicly Held**
WEB: www.pfizer.com
SIC: **2834** 2833 Pharmaceutical prepara-
tions; medicinals & botanicals
PA: Pfizer Inc.
235 E 42nd St
New York NY 10017
212 733-2323

(G-865)
PHARMING HEALTHCARE INC
685 Us Highway 202/206 (08807-1775)
PHONE..............................908 524-0888
Robin Wright, *CEO*
Anne-Marie De Groot, *Admin Sec*
EMP: 45
SALES: 90MM
SALES (corp-wide): 105.6MM **Privately**
Held
SIC: **2834** 2836 3841 Proprietary drug
products; biological products, except di-
agnostic; surgical & medical instruments
PA: Pharming Group N.V.
Darwinweg 24
Leiden 2333
715 247-400

(G-866)
PHOTONICS MANAGEMENT
CORP (HQ)
360 Foothill Rd (08807-2920)
P.O. Box 6910 (08807-0910)
PHONE..............................908 231-0960
Teruo Hiruma, *President*
Akira Hiruma, *Vice Pres*
Connie Lazarus, *Sales Mgr*
Sanjay Gidvani, *Sales Engr*
Alison Perrine, *Marketing Staff*
EMP: 3
SQ FT: 30,000
SALES (est): 70.4MM **Privately Held**
SIC: **5065** 3825 5047 8732 Electronic
tubes: receiving & transmitting or indus-
trial; measuring instruments & meters,
electric; medical equipment & supplies;
research services, except laboratory

(G-867)
PIPING SOLUTIONS INC
81 Chimney Rock Rd Ste 4 (08807-3179)
PHONE..............................732 537-1009
Ernest E Stone III, *President*
Steve Labondra, *Vice Pres*
EMP: 6
SQ FT: 6,000
SALES (est): 1.2MM **Privately Held**
SIC: **3498** Fabricated pipe & fittings

(G-868)
PRESTIGE MILLWORK LLC
27e Kearney St Ste B (08807)
PHONE..............................908 526-5100
Daniel Bugasch, *Mng Member*
▲ EMP: 27
SQ FT: 50,000
SALES: 6.7MM **Privately Held**
SIC: **2431** Millwork

(G-869)
PRIME REBAR LLC
36 Adamsville Rd (08807-3110)
PHONE..............................908 707-1234
Blima Schwartz,
EMP: 30
SALES (est): 6.4MM **Privately Held**
SIC: **3441** Fabricated structural metal

(G-870)
PRYSMIAN CBLES SYSTEMS
USA LLC
111 Chimney Rock Rd (08807-3126)
PHONE..............................732 469-5902
Draka Cableteq, *Manager*
EMP: 12 **Privately Held**
SIC: **3357** Building wire & cable, nonfer-
rous
HQ: Prysmian Cables And Systems, Usa,
Llc
4 Tesseneer Dr
Highland Heights KY 41076
859 572-8000

(G-871)
PVH CORP
Also Called: Van Heusen
1001 Frontier Rd Ste 100 (08807-2902)
P.O. Box 6968 (08807-0968)
PHONE..............................908 685-0050
Jason Evanchik, *Vice Pres*
Dana Rappe, *Vice Pres*
Matt M Skinner, *Vice Pres*
Julie Barton, *Compensation Mg*
Michael Zaccaro, *Manager*
EMP: 8
SALES (corp-wide): 9.6B **Publicly Held**
WEB: www.pvh.com
SIC: **5611** 2321 Men's & boys' clothing
stores; men's & boys' furnishings
PA: Pvh Corp.
200 Madison Ave Bsmt 1
New York NY 10016
212 381-3500

(G-872)
PVH CORP
Also Called: Van Heusen
1001 Frontier Rd Ste 100 (08807-2902)
PHONE..............................908 685-0050
April Delaney, *Manager*
EMP: 4

SALES (corp-wide): 9.6B **Publicly Held**
WEB: www.pvh.com
SIC: **2321** Men's & boys' dress shirts
PA: Pvh Corp.
200 Madison Ave Bsmt 1
New York NY 10016
212 381-3500

(G-873)
PVH CORP
Also Called: Van Heusen
1001 Frontier Rd 100 (08807-2902)
PHONE..............................908 685-0148
Christine Grosse, *Manager*
EMP: 6
SALES (corp-wide): 9.6B **Publicly Held**
WEB: www.pvh.com
SIC: **2321** Men's & boys' dress shirts
PA: Pvh Corp.
200 Madison Ave Bsmt 1
New York NY 10016
212 381-3500

(G-874)
QUALCOMM INCORPORATED
500 Smrst Corp Blvd Fl 4 (08807-2856)
PHONE..............................908 443-8000
John Batey, *Vice Pres*
Rod Dir, *Vice Pres*
James B Hettesheimer, *Senior Buyer*
Mazhar Alidina, *Manager*
Sanjay Bapat, *Engineer*
EMP: 79
SALES (corp-wide): 22.7B **Publicly Held**
WEB: www.qualcomm.com
SIC: **3663** Radio & TV communications
equipment
PA: Qualcomm Incorporated
5775 Morehouse Dr
San Diego CA 92121
858 587-1121

(G-875)
RENESAS ELECTRONICS AMER
INC
Also Called: Intersil Design Center
440 Us Highway 22 Ste 100 (08807-2477)
PHONE..............................908 685-6000
Phil Farmer, *Principal*
Donald Preslar, *Principal*
Greg Williams, *Principal*
Paul Sferrazza, *Manager*
EMP: 35 **Privately Held**
WEB: www.intersil.com
SIC: **3674** Semiconductors & related de-
vices
HQ: Renesas Electronics America Inc.
1001 Murphy Ranch Rd
Milpitas CA 95035
408 432-8888

(G-876)
RF360 TECHNOLOGIES INC
500 Somerset Corp Blvd (08807-2856)
PHONE..............................848 999-3582
James Wilson, *President*
Akash Palkhiwala, *Treasurer*
John Delmastro, *Admin Sec*
EMP: 42 **EST:** 2016
SALES (est): 113.5K
SALES (corp-wide): 22.7B **Publicly Held**
SIC: **3425** Saw blades & handsaws
HQ: Rf360 Holdings Singapore Pte. Ltd.
166 Kallang Way
Singapore
684 578-88

(G-877)
ROUTE 22 FUEL LLC
1240 Us Highway 22 (08807-2978)
PHONE..............................908 526-5270
Milkhi Ram, *Manager*
EMP: 7
SALES (est): 797.4K **Privately Held**
SIC: **2869** Fuels

(G-878)
S & W PRECISION TOOL CORP
3 Holly Ct (08807-2559)
PHONE..............................908 526-6097
Joseph Wielgus, *President*
Carol Wielgus, *Treasurer*
EMP: 12
SQ FT: 10,000
SALES (est): 930K **Privately Held**
SIC: **3469** Metal stampings

▲ = Import ▼=Export
◆ =Import/Export

(G-879)
SALIX PHARMACEUTICALS LTD (DH)
400 Somerset Corp Blvd (08807-2867)
PHONE..............................866 246-8245
Joseph Papa, *President*
Steve Tenery, *Regl Sales Mgr*
Peggy Vanderman, *Regl Sales Mgr*
Joe Barraco, *Sales Staff*
Amy Bartholomew, *Sales Staff*
▲ EMP: 89
SQ FT: 215,000
SALES (est): 191.4MM
SALES (corp-wide): 8.3B **Privately Held**
WEB: www.salix.com
SIC: 2834 Drugs acting on the gastroin-
testinal or genitourinary system
HQ: Bausch Health Americas, Inc.
400 Somerset Corp Blvd
Bridgewater NJ 08807
908 927-1400

(G-880)
SANOFI US SERVICES INC (HQ)
55 Corporate Dr (08807-1265)
PHONE..............................336 407-4994
Christopher A Viehbacher, *CEO*
Gerald P Belle, *President*
Kevin Buckle, *President*
Mark Kwiatek, *President*
Margaret Sparks, *President*
▲ EMP: 1500
SQ FT: 500,000
SALES (est): 6.3B **Privately Held**
WEB: www.aventispharma-us.com
SIC: 2834 Drugs acting on the cardiovas-
cular system, except diagnostic

(G-881)
SANOFI US SERVICES INC
55 Corporate Dr (08807-1265)
PHONE..............................336 407-4994
EMP: 7 **Privately Held**
WEB: www.aventispharma-us.com
SIC: 2834 Pharmaceutical preparations
HQ: Sanofi Us Services Inc.
55 Corporate Dr
Bridgewater NJ 08807
336 407-4994

(G-882)
SANOFI US SERVICES INC
200 Cronjing Blvd Fl 2 Flr 2 (08807)
PHONE..............................908 231-4000
Jeremy Bond, *Counsel*
Barbara Fanelli, *Vice Pres*
Jamie Brantner, *Purch Agent*
Otmane Boussif, *Research*
Douglas Wells, *Research*
EMP: 23 **Privately Held**
WEB: www.aventispharma-us.com
SIC: 2834 Pharmaceutical preparations
HQ: Sanofi Us Services Inc.
55 Corporate Dr
Bridgewater NJ 08807
336 407-4994

(G-883)
SANOFI US SERVICES INC
Also Called: Sanofi Avntis Phrmctcals Group
1041 Rte 202/206 (08807-1291)
P.O. Box 6800 (08807-0800)
PHONE..............................908 231-4000
Timothy Salmon, *Counsel*
Abdelhak Oualim, *Project Dir*
Mark Hem, *Branch Mgr*
Harvey Lieberman, *Manager*
Alan Harvey, *Consultant*
EMP: 10 **Privately Held**
WEB: www.aventispharma-us.com
SIC: 8731 2834 Biological research; phar-
maceutical preparations
HQ: Sanofi Us Services Inc.
55 Corporate Dr
Bridgewater NJ 08807
336 407-4994

(G-884)
SANOFI-AVENTIS US LLC (DH)
Also Called: Winthrop
55 Corporate Dr (08807-1265)
PHONE..............................908 981-5000
Joseph Palladino, *President*
Margaret Sparks, *Counsel*
Gregory Irace, *Senior VP*
Jim Caro, *Vice Pres*

Paul Deutsch, *Vice Pres*
▲ EMP: 80
SALES (est): 277.7MM **Privately Held**
SIC: 2834 Pharmaceutical preparations

(G-885)
SANOFI-SYNTHELABO INC
55 Corporate Dr (08807-1265)
PHONE..............................908 231-2000
EMP: 567 **Privately Held**
WEB: www.sanofi-synthelabous.com
SIC: 8731 2834 Chemical laboratory, ex-
cept testing; pharmaceutical preparations
HQ: Sanofi-Synthelabo Inc.
55 Corporate Dr
Bridgewater NJ 08807

(G-886)
SANOFI-SYNTHELABO INC (HQ)
55 Corporate Dr (08807-1265)
P.O. Box 5925 (08807-5925)
PHONE..............................908 981-5000
George Doherty, *President*
Jack Dean, *Senior VP*
Varavani Docs, *Vice Pres*
Brandi Robinson, *Vice Pres*
Tracee Joseph, *Buyer*
◆ EMP: 305
SALES (est): 2.2B **Privately Held**
WEB: www.sanofi-synthelabous.com
SIC: 2834 Pharmaceutical preparations

(G-887)
SAVIENT PHARMACEUTICALS INC (HQ)
400 Crossing Blvd Fl 3 (08807-2863)
PHONE..............................732 418-9300
Louis Ferrari, *President*
Richard Crowley, *COO*
Philip K Yachmetz, *Senior VP*
John P Hamill, *CFO*
Kenneth M Bahrt, *Chief Mktg Ofcr*
EMP: 17
SQ FT: 48,469
SALES (est): 1.6MM
SALES (corp-wide): 2MM **Privately Held**
WEB: www.savientpharma.com
SIC: 2833 Medicinals & botanicals

(G-888)
SCL
7 Emmons Ct (08807-4700)
PHONE..............................908 391-9882
Durga RAO, *CEO*
Chris RAO, *Owner*
EMP: 23 EST: 1988
SALES (est): 1.1MM **Privately Held**
WEB: www.scl.co.uk
SIC: 3672 Printed circuit boards

(G-889)
SHORT LOAD CONCRETE LLC
81 Chimney Rock Rd Ste 1 (08807-3179)
PHONE..............................732 469-4420
Dave Wellema, *President*
EMP: 4 EST: 2016
SALES (est): 110.5K **Privately Held**
SIC: 3273 Ready-mixed concrete

(G-890)
SMS ELECTRIC MOTOR CAR LLC
18 Totten Dr (08807-2367)
PHONE..............................215 428-2502
Martin Karo,
Thomas Del Franco,
◆ EMP: 17
SQ FT: 30,000
SALES (est): 980K **Privately Held**
SIC: 7694 Electric motor repair

(G-891)
SOLARIS PHARMA CORPORATION
1031 Rte 202/206 200 (08807-1275)
PHONE..............................908 864-0404
Srinivasan Raghavan, *President*
EMP: 5
SALES (est): 689.5K **Privately Held**
SIC: 2834 Pharmaceutical preparations

(G-892)
SPX COOLING TECHNOLOGIES INC
1200 Us Highway 22 Ste 14 (08807-2943)
PHONE..............................908 450-8027
Dorothy Sakele, *Branch Mgr*
EMP: 20
SALES (corp-wide): 1.5B **Publicly Held**
WEB: www.cts.spx.com
SIC: 3443 Cooling towers, metal plate
HQ: Spx Cooling Technologies, Inc.
7401 W 129th St
Overland Park KS 66213
913 664-7400

(G-893)
SPX DRY COOLING USA LLC
1200 Rte 22 Ste 1 (08807-2943)
PHONE..............................908 450-8027
Andreas Coumnas, *President*
EMP: 20 EST: 2016
SALES: 0
SALES (corp-wide): 172.9MM **Privately Held**
SIC: 3585 Air conditioning units, complete:
domestic or industrial
PA: Paharpur Cooling Towers Limited
8/1/B,Paharpur House,
Kolkata WB 70002
334 013-3000

(G-894)
SS EQUIPMENT HOLDINGS LLC
Also Called: X Hockey Pro Shops
1425 Frontier Rd (08807-2903)
PHONE..............................732 627-0006
Matthew Setola, *President*
EMP: 20 EST: 2015
SQ FT: 5,000
SALES: 2MM **Privately Held**
SIC: 5941 3949 Hockey equipment, ex-
cept skates; hockey equipment & sup-
plies, general

(G-895)
SWAROVSKI NORTH AMERICA LTD
400 Commons Way (08807-2800)
PHONE..............................908 253-7057
Tara Kepp, *Branch Mgr*
EMP: 4
SALES (corp-wide): 4.7B **Privately Held**
SIC: 3423 Jewelers' hand tools
HQ: Swarovski North America Limited
1 Kenney Dr
Cranston RI 02920
401 463-6400

(G-896)
TALON7 LLC
991 Us Highway 22 Ste 200 (08807-2957)
PHONE..............................908 595-2121
Chris Whiteley, *Principal*
EMP: 13 EST: 2014
SALES (est): 2.6MM **Privately Held**
SIC: 3699 Security control equipment &
systems

(G-897)
TRI-MET INDUSTRIES INC
36 Adamsville Rd (08807-3110)
PHONE..............................908 231-0004
EMP: 6
SALES (est): 150.3K **Privately Held**
SIC: 3999 Atomizers, toiletry

(G-898)
TRIGEN LABORATORIES LLC
400 Crossing Blvd (08807-2863)
PHONE..............................732 721-0070
Dave Purdy, *President*
JD Schaub, *COO*
Kevin Hudy, *Vice Pres*
Doug Subers, *CFO*
Steve Squashic, *Treasurer*
▲ EMP: 3317
SALES (est): 120.4MM
SALES (corp-wide): 862MM **Privately Held**
SIC: 2834 Pharmaceutical preparations
PA: Avista Capital Holdings, L.P.
65 E 55th St Fl 18
New York NY 10022
212 593-6900

(G-899)
UNIONMED TECH INC
1031 Us Highway 202/206 # 101
(08807-1275)
PHONE..............................917 714-3418
Ming Fang, *CEO*
Yong Jing, *COO*
EMP: 5
SALES (est): 245.5K **Privately Held**
SIC: 3841 Surgical lasers

(G-900)
UP UNITED LLC
495 N Bridge St (08807-7500)
PHONE..............................718 383-5700
Kenneth Farina, *Principal*
EMP: 50
SALES (est): 2MM **Privately Held**
SIC: 3081 Plastic film & sheet

(G-901)
V CUSTOM MILLWORK INC
1480 Us Highway 22 (08807-2909)
PHONE..............................732 469-9600
Susan Schumer, *President*
EMP: 15
SQ FT: 30,000
SALES (est): 1.6MM **Privately Held**
SIC: 2431 5031 Millwork; millwork

(G-902)
VALERITAS HOLDINGS INC
750 Route 202 Ste 600 (08807-2597)
PHONE..............................908 927-9920
Peter J Devlin, *Ch of Bd*
John E Timberlake, *President*
Geoffrey Jenkins, *Exec VP*
Erick J Lucera, *Vice Pres*
Mark Conley, *Treasurer*
EMP: 82
SQ FT: 9,700
SALES: 26.4MM **Privately Held**
SIC: 2834 Pharmaceutical preparations

(G-903)
VERTICAL PHARMACEUTICALS LLC
400 Crossing Blvd (08807-2863)
PHONE..............................732 721-0070
Steven Squashic, *CEO*
Maryanne Zebrowski, *General Mgr*
Bill Kellens, *District Mgr*
Adam Huntenburg, *Accountant*
Chris Theer, *Accountant*
▲ EMP: 55
SQ FT: 5,000
SALES (est): 21.4MM
SALES (corp-wide): 45MM **Privately Held**
SIC: 2834 Pharmaceutical preparations
HQ: Vertical/Trigen Holdings, Llc
400 Crossing Blvd
Bridgewater NJ 08807
732 721-0070

(G-904)
VERTICAL/TRIGEN HOLDINGS LLC (HQ)
Also Called: Osmotica
400 Crossing Blvd (08807-2863)
PHONE..............................732 721-0070
Brian Markison, *CEO*
EMP: 11
SALES (est): 21.4MM
SALES (corp-wide): 45MM **Privately Held**
SIC: 2834 Pharmaceutical preparations
PA: Osmotica Pharmaceutical Us Llc
895 Sawyer Rd
Marietta GA 30062
770 509-4500

(G-905)
ZOETIS PRODUCTS LLC
440 Rte 22 (08807-2477)
P.O. Box 1399 (08807)
PHONE..............................973 660-5000
EMP: 13
SALES (corp-wide): 5.8B **Publicly Held**
WEB: www.alpharma.com
SIC: 2834 Pharmaceutical preparations
HQ: Zoetis Products Llc
100 Campus Dr Ste 3
Florham Park NJ 07932
973 660-5000

Brielle
Monmouth County

(G-906)
COOKMAN CREAMERY LLC
1 Mariners Bnd (08730-1251)
PHONE....................................732 361-5215
Norah Marler, *Principal*
EMP: 5
SALES (est): 199.8K **Privately Held**
SIC: 2021 Creamery butter

(G-907)
MONMOUTH MARINE ENGINES INC
536 Union Ln (08730-1421)
P.O. Box 85 (08730-0085)
PHONE....................................732 528-9290
Paul Mika, *President*
EMP: 13
SQ FT: 3,000
SALES (est): 4.2MM **Privately Held**
WEB: www.monmouthmarineengines.com
SIC: 5084 5551 7699 3731 Engines, gasoline; marine supplies; marine engine repair; barges, building & repairing; fireboats, building & repairing; fishing vessels, large: building & repairing

(G-908)
NEWMAN ORNAMENTAL IRON WORKS
207 Union Ave (08730-1815)
PHONE....................................732 223-9042
Richard Newman, *CEO*
EMP: 12
SQ FT: 4,000
SALES (est): 2.2MM **Privately Held**
WEB: www.newmanironworks.com
SIC: 3446 Architectural metalwork

(G-909)
TOMS RIVER PRINTING CORP
Also Called: Action Instant Printing Center
11 S Tamarack Dr (08730-1245)
PHONE....................................732 240-2033
Birte Hofmann, *President*
Robert Hofmann, *Treasurer*
EMP: 4
SQ FT: 14,000
SALES (est): 433.2K **Privately Held**
SIC: 2752 7334 Commercial printing, offset; photocopying & duplicating services

(G-910)
VALUE ADDED VICE SOLUTIONS LLC
1111 Shore Dr (08730-1127)
PHONE....................................201 400-3247
EMP: 5 EST: 2010
SALES (est): 472K **Privately Held**
SIC: 4813 3679 Voice telephone communications; voice controls

Brigantine
Atlantic County

(G-911)
BAR LAN INC
Also Called: Kwik Kopy Printing
327 Gull Cv (08203-3637)
PHONE....................................856 596-2330
Paul Barbera, *President*
Joe Nolan, *Corp Secy*
EMP: 4
SQ FT: 1,400
SALES (est): 300K **Privately Held**
SIC: 2752 2791 2789 Commercial printing, offset; typesetting; bookbinding & related work

(G-912)
PRIMAL SURF
3106 Revere Blvd (08203-1050)
PHONE....................................609 264-1999
Michael Laielli, *Principal*
EMP: 4

SALES (est): 664.4K **Privately Held**
WEB: www.primalsurf.com
SIC: 5091 3949 Surfing equipment & supplies; surfboards

Brooklawn
Camden County

(G-913)
AMERAL INTERNATIONAL INC
7 Railroad Ln (08030-2619)
PHONE....................................856 456-9000
Louis Grieco, *President*
◆ EMP: 16
SQ FT: 11,000
SALES (est): 3.3MM **Privately Held**
WEB: www.ameral.com
SIC: 3679 Harness assemblies for electronic use: wire or cable

(G-914)
C & L MACHINING COMPANY INC
110 S New Broadway (08030-2554)
P.O. Box 167, Gloucester City (08030-0167)
PHONE....................................856 456-1932
George Cohen, *President*
James C Lewis, *Vice Pres*
EMP: 5
SQ FT: 5,000
SALES (est): 650K **Privately Held**
SIC: 3561 3562 Industrial pumps & parts; ball bearings & parts

(G-915)
ROLFERRYS SPECIALTIES INC
601 New Broadway (08030-2625)
PHONE....................................856 456-2999
Francis Ferry, *President*
EMP: 7
SQ FT: 2,400
SALES (est): 881.7K **Privately Held**
SIC: 2261 5947 5999 2759 Screen printing of cotton broadwoven fabrics; gifts & novelties; trophies & plaques; screen printing

Brookside
Morris County

(G-916)
ANVIMA TECHNOLOGIES LLC
Also Called: R& D Consulting
68 Woodland Rd (07926)
PHONE....................................973 531-7077
Nelson Pinilla, *Principal*
Victoria Pinilla, *VP Mktg*
EMP: 4
SALES (est): 296.4K **Privately Held**
SIC: 7371 8999 8733 3823 Computer software systems analysis & design, custom; search & rescue service; scientific research agency; industrial instrmnts msrmnt display/control process variable; structural engineering

Budd Lake
Morris County

(G-917)
AGILENT TECHNOLOGIES INC
Also Called: Keysight Technologies
550 Clark Dr Ste 2 (07828-4317)
PHONE....................................973 448-7129
Tim Buntin, *Manager*
EMP: 22
SALES (corp-wide): 4.9B **Publicly Held**
WEB: www.agilent.com
SIC: 3825 Instruments to measure electricity
PA: Agilent Technologies, Inc.
5301 Stevens Creek Blvd
Santa Clara CA 95051
408 345-8886

(G-918)
AMERICAN SENSOR TECH INC (HQ)
450 Clark Dr Ste 4 (07828-4312)
PHONE....................................973 448-1901
Richard E Tasker, *President*
Michael P Eldredge, *Exec VP*
Bernadette Scarola, *Human Res Mgr*
◆ EMP: 75
SQ FT: 33,000
SALES (est): 12.9MM
SALES (corp-wide): 13.9B **Privately Held**
WEB: www.astsensors.com
SIC: 3829 Pressure transducers
PA: Te Connectivity Ltd.
Rheinstrasse 20
Schaffhausen SH 8200
526 336-677

(G-919)
BASF CORPORATION
Also Called: BASF Engineering Plastics
450 Clark Dr Ste 3 (07828-4312)
PHONE....................................973 426-5429
Lynn Griffin, *Administration*
EMP: 33
SALES (corp-wide): 71.7B **Privately Held**
WEB: www.basf.com
SIC: 2869 Industrial organic chemicals
HQ: Basf Corporation
100 Park Ave
Florham Park NJ 07932
973 245-6000

(G-920)
CHARABOT & CO INC
400 International Dr (07828-4306)
PHONE....................................201 812-2762
Marc Thelott, *President*
Diane Niven, *Vice Pres*
▲ EMP: 10 EST: 1996
SQ FT: 38,000
SALES (est): 1.9MM
SALES (corp-wide): 281.4MM **Privately Held**
WEB: www.charabot.com
SIC: 2844 5149 Concentrates, perfume; flavourings & fragrances
HQ: Soc Charabot Sa
10 Avenue Yves Emmanuel Baudoin
Grasse 06130
492 420-835

(G-921)
DSRV INC
330 Waterloo Valley Rd # 2 (07828-1395)
PHONE....................................973 631-1200
Jean-Claude Piel, *CEO*
▲ EMP: 12
SQ FT: 10,900
SALES (est): 2MM **Privately Held**
SIC: 2835 In vitro diagnostics

(G-922)
ESG LLC
21 Tall Oaks Ln (07828-2539)
PHONE....................................973 347-2969
Vincent Loconte, *Manager*
EMP: 10
SQ FT: 18,000
SALES (est): 1.5MM **Privately Held**
SIC: 3579 Addressing machines, plates & plate embossers

(G-923)
FRATELLI BERETTA USA INC
750 Clark Dr (07828-4314)
PHONE....................................201 438-0723
Simone Bocchini, *President*
Mike Romano, *Prdtn Mgr*
Giovanni Annoni, *CFO*
◆ EMP: 96
SQ FT: 178,000
SALES (est): 20MM
SALES (corp-wide): 425MM **Privately Held**
WEB: www.fratelliberettausa.com
SIC: 2013 Sausages & related products, from purchased meat
PA: Salumificio Fratelli Beretta Spa
Via Fratelli Bandiera 12
Trezzo Sull'adda MI 20056
029 098-51

(G-924)
GIVAUDAN FRAGRANCES CORP
300 Waterloo Valley Rd (07828-1384)
PHONE....................................973 448-6500
Patricia Brennan, *Purchasing*
Linda Gelpi, *Human Res Mgr*
Joseph Ciccone, *Manager*
Patricia Hopkins, *Manager*
William Drake, *Info Tech Dir*
EMP: 200
SALES (corp-wide): 5.5B **Privately Held**
SIC: 2844 2869 Cosmetic preparations; perfume materials, synthetic
HQ: Givaudan Fragrances Corporation
1199 Edison Dr Ste 1-2
Cincinnati OH 45216
513 948-3428

(G-925)
L3 TECHNOLOGIES INC
Also Called: Space and Navigation
450 Clark Dr Ste 1 (07828-4312)
PHONE....................................973 446-4000
Paul Wengen, *Principal*
Rhoel Velasquez, *Controller*
Mark Meisner, *Software Engr*
Thomas Fabrizio, *Director*
EMP: 300
SALES (corp-wide): 6.8B **Publicly Held**
SIC: 3812 Defense systems & equipment
HQ: L3 Technologies, Inc.
600 3rd Ave Fl 34
New York NY 10016
212 697-1111

(G-926)
LUCAS WORLD INC
100 International Dr (07828-1383)
P.O. Box 840551, Houston TX (77284-0551)
PHONE....................................832 293-3770
Jose Maria Guerra, *President*
Juan Salinas, *Vice Pres*
EMP: 7
SALES (est): 12.8MM
SALES (corp-wide): 34.2B **Privately Held**
SIC: 2064 Lollipops & other hard candy
HQ: Matre, Inc.
6885 Elm St
Mc Lean VA 22101

(G-927)
M + 4 INC
Also Called: Classic Coves
98 Crease Rd (07828-1002)
PHONE....................................973 527-3262
Robert A Maute, *President*
EMP: 5
SALES (est): 308.3K **Privately Held**
WEB: www.classiccoves.com
SIC: 3645 3646 Residential lighting fixtures; commercial indusl & institutional electric lighting fixtures

(G-928)
MACRO SENSORS
450 Clark Dr Ste 4 (07828-4312)
PHONE....................................856 662-8000
John Magdziak, *Manager*
EMP: 13 EST: 2015
SALES (est): 2.3MM **Privately Held**
SIC: 3829 Measuring & controlling devices

(G-929)
MARS INCORPORATED
Also Called: Information Services Intl
100 International Dr (07828-1383)
PHONE....................................973 691-3500
Joe Hennessy, *Manager*
EMP: 10
SALES (corp-wide): 34.2B **Privately Held**
SIC: 2047 2024 2066 Cat food; ice cream, packaged: molded, on sticks, etc.; chocolate candy, solid
PA: Mars, Incorporated
6885 Elm St Ste 1
Mc Lean VA 22101
703 821-4900

(G-930)
MICROELETTRICA-USA LLC
300 International Dr # 2 (07828-4305)
PHONE....................................973 598-0806
Alex Marton, *General Mgr*
Ryan Feeney, *Engineer*
Susan Richards, *Finance*

Vanessa Giordano, *Office Mgr*
▲ EMP: 20
SALES (est): 5.4MM
SALES (corp-wide): 711.6K **Privately Held**
SIC: 3999 3564 Railroad models, except toy; blowers & fans
HQ: Knorr-Bremse Services Gmbh
Moosacher Str. 80
Munchen 80809
893 547-0

(G-931)
NEW VIEW MEDIA
Also Called: Weekly News, The
1 Old Wolfe Rd Ste 203 (07828-3213)
PHONE..................................973 691-3002
Mary Lalama, *Partner*
Alan Goldsher, *Partner*
EMP: 25
SALES (est): 62K **Privately Held**
SIC: 2711 Newspapers: publishing only, not printed on site

(G-932)
ROBERTET INC (HQ)
400 International Dr (07828-4306)
PHONE..................................201 405-1000
Peter N Lombardo, *President*
Kent Swan, *President*
Philippe Maubert, *Chairman*
▲ EMP: 35 EST: 1979
SQ FT: 25,000
SALES (est): 18.8MM
SALES (corp-wide): 281.4MM **Privately Held**
WEB: www.robertet.fr
SIC: 5149 2844 2087 Flavourings & fragrances; toilet preparations; flavoring extracts & syrups
PA: Robertet Sa
37 Avenue Sidi Brahim
Grasse 06130
493 098-181

(G-933)
ROBERTET FRAGRANCES INC (HQ)
400 International Dr (07828-4306)
P.O. Box 650, Oakland (07436-0650)
PHONE..................................201 405-1000
Christophe Maubert, *President*
Peter Lombardo, *COO*
Joseph Lattarulo, *Senior VP*
Stephen Dente, *Vice Pres*
Garyy Johnsen, *Vice Pres*
▲ EMP: 50
SQ FT: 35,000
SALES (est): 20.7MM
SALES (corp-wide): 281.4MM **Privately Held**
SIC: 2844 Perfumes & colognes
PA: Robertet Sa
37 Avenue Sidi Brahim
Grasse 06130
493 098-181

(G-934)
RUDOLPH TECHNOLOGIES INC
550 Clark Dr Ste 1 (07828-4317)
P.O. Box 860 (07828-0860)
PHONE..................................973 347-3891
Elvino M Da Silveira, *Vice Pres*
Todd Curtin, *Buyer*
Bill Favier, *Engineer*
Tim Gleamza, *Engineer*
Jon Lien, *Engineer*
EMP: 65
SALES (corp-wide): 273.7MM **Publicly Held**
WEB: www.rudolphtech.com
SIC: 3829 Measuring & controlling devices
PA: Rudolph Technologies, Inc.
16 Jonspin Rd
Wilmington MA 01887
978 253-6200

(G-935)
SAN MAREL DESIGNS INC
Also Called: Mariell
98 Us Highway 46 Ste 10 (07828-1818)
PHONE..................................973 426-9554
Nan Derasmi, *President*
EMP: 8
SQ FT: 3,300

SALES (est): 978.7K **Privately Held**
SIC: 3961 Costume jewelry, ex. precious metal & semiprecious stones

(G-936)
SAXTON FALLS SAND & GRAVEL CO
Waterloo Valley Rd (07828)
P.O. Box 576, Stanhope (07874-0576)
PHONE..................................908 852-0121
Richard P Schindelar, *President*
EMP: 25 EST: 1960
SQ FT: 1,000
SALES (est): 3.7MM **Privately Held**
SIC: 1442 5191 Construction sand mining; gravel mining; soil, potting & planting

(G-937)
SKC POWERTECH INC
850 Clark Dr Ste 2 (07828-4313)
PHONE..................................973 347-7000
Chul Chai, *President*
▲ EMP: 11
SALES (est): 4.8MM **Privately Held**
SIC: 3691 Batteries, rechargeable

(G-938)
TRONEX INTERNATIONAL INC (PA)
300 International Dr (07828-4305)
P.O. Box 95000, Philadelphia PA (19195-0001)
PHONE..................................973 335-2888
Donald L Chu, *President*
Danny Qiu, *Manager*
Steve Rummel, *Manager*
Gustavo Lopez, *Info Tech Mgr*
▲ EMP: 50
SALES (est): 14.4MM **Privately Held**
WEB: www.tronexcompany.com
SIC: 3842 5047 Surgical appliances & supplies; medical & hospital equipment

---

Buena
Atlantic County

(G-939)
CPB INC
Also Called: Trade Images
701 S Harding Hwy (08310-9732)
PHONE..................................856 697-2700
David Bird, *President*
EMP: 22
SQ FT: 37,000
SALES (est): 1.7MM **Privately Held**
WEB: www.cpb.com
SIC: 7389 2541 2434 Trade show arrangement; cabinets, except refrigerated: show, display, etc.: wood; wood kitchen cabinets

(G-940)
IMMUNOGENETICS INC
Lincoln Ave & Wheat Rd (08310)
PHONE..................................856 697-1441
Earl Lewis, *Ch of Bd*
Paul Woitach, *President*
John Ambrose, *President*
EMP: 56
SQ FT: 40,000
SALES (est): 3MM
SALES (corp-wide): 65.8MM **Publicly Held**
WEB: www.askigi.com
SIC: 3999 Pet supplies
PA: Teligent, Inc.
105 Lincoln Ave
Buena NJ 08310
856 697-1441

(G-941)
S P INDUSTRIES INC
Also Called: Hotpack
1002 Harding Hwy (08310-1528)
PHONE..................................215 672-7800
Ronald E Dimaria, *Principal*
EMP: 75
SQ FT: 71,000
SALES (corp-wide): 1.5B **Privately Held**
WEB: www.virtis.com
SIC: 3821 Incubators, laboratory

HQ: S P Industries, Inc.
935 Mearns Rd
Warminster PA 18974
215 672-7800

(G-942)
TELIGENT INC (PA)
105 Lincoln Ave (08310)
P.O. Box 687 (08310-0687)
PHONE..................................856 697-1441
James C Gale, *Ch of Bd*
Jason Grenfell-Gardner, *President*
Damian Finio, *CFO*
Carole Ben-Maimon, *Director*
Bhaskar Chaudhuri, *Director*
EMP: 183
SQ FT: 33,000
SALES: 65.8MM **Publicly Held**
WEB: www.askigi.com
SIC: 2834 Dermatologicals

(G-943)
TELIGENT INC
711 S Harding Hwy (08310)
PHONE..................................856 697-1441
Carlene Lloyd, *CFO*
EMP: 15
SALES (corp-wide): 65.8MM **Publicly Held**
WEB: www.askigi.com
SIC: 2836 2834 Biological products, except diagnostic; pharmaceutical preparations
PA: Teligent, Inc.
105 Lincoln Ave
Buena NJ 08310
856 697-1441

(G-944)
TRITON ASSOCIATED INDUSTRIES
N Brewster Rd (08310)
P.O. Box 627 (08310-0627)
PHONE..................................856 697-3050
Leonard G Vanderweel, *President*
Linda M Vanderweel, *Corp Secy*
Wayne T Edwards, *Exec VP*
EMP: 50
SQ FT: 28,000
SALES (est): 4MM **Privately Held**
SIC: 3229 3231 Pressed & blown glass; scientific & technical glassware: from purchased glass

---

Burlington
Burlington County

(G-945)
A SMITH & SON INC
300 W Broad St (08016-1412)
PHONE..................................609 747-0800
John R Smith, *President*
EMP: 8
SQ FT: 4,600
SALES (est): 1.3MM **Privately Held**
SIC: 3479 Etching & engraving

(G-946)
ACTON MOBILE INDUSTRIES INC
2013 Route 130 N (08016-9729)
PHONE..................................610 485-5100
Carl Bennett, *Principal*
EMP: 8
SALES (est): 1MM **Privately Held**
SIC: 2451 Mobile homes

(G-947)
AMERICAN CASEIN COMPANY (PA)
Also Called: Amoco
109 Elbow Ln (08016-4123)
PHONE..................................609 387-2988
Adam Cabot, *CEO*
Roger Hare Jr, *Controller*
Sandra Fine, *Hum Res Coord*
▲ EMP: 50 EST: 1956
SQ FT: 30,000
SALES (est): 10.9MM **Privately Held**
WEB: www.americancasein.com
SIC: 2023 2891 Dried milk preparations; adhesives & sealants

(G-948)
AMERICAN CUSTOM DRYING CO
Also Called: A C D
109 Elbow Ln (08016-4123)
PHONE..................................609 387-3933
Adam Cabot, *CEO*
▲ EMP: 42 EST: 1969
SQ FT: 38,000
SALES (est): 8.3MM **Privately Held**
WEB: www.americancustomdrying.com
SIC: 2023 2099 Dry, condensed, evaporated dairy products; food preparations

(G-949)
AMYS OMELETTE HSE BURLINGTON (PA)
637 High St (08016-2736)
PHONE..................................609 386-4800
Ted Kopsaftis, *Principal*
EMP: 15
SALES (est): 727.9K **Privately Held**
SIC: 5812 2064 2038 Diner; breakfast bars; breakfasts, frozen & packaged

(G-950)
ANIMALS ETC INC
210 Mitchell Ave (08016)
P.O. Box 606 (08016-0606)
PHONE..................................609 386-8442
Kathleen P Lance, *President*
▲ EMP: 4
SALES (est): 412.8K **Privately Held**
SIC: 5999 3999 Pets; pet supplies

(G-951)
B4INC INC
Also Called: Yesco Sign & Lighting
1208 Columbus Rd Ste F (08016-3439)
PHONE..................................609 747-9600
Brianna Persichetti, *Principal*
EMP: 10
SALES (est): 1MM **Privately Held**
SIC: 3993 Signs & advertising specialties

(G-952)
BARTLETT PRINTING & GRAPHIC
4495 Route 130 S (08016-2247)
PHONE..................................609 386-1525
Clifford Lewis, *CEO*
Cynthia Lewis, *President*
EMP: 6
SQ FT: 6,000
SALES: 200K **Privately Held**
WEB: www.bartlettprinting.com
SIC: 2752 2791 Commercial printing, offset; lithographing on metal; typesetting

(G-953)
BARTON & COONEY LLC (PA)
300 Richards Run (08016-2120)
PHONE..................................609 747-9300
Steve Angel, *Opers Staff*
Joseph Walker, *Prgrmr*
Scott Miller, *Software Dev*
Paul Kusiak, *Director*
Patrick Doyle,
EMP: 53
SQ FT: 85,000
SALES (est): 11.7MM **Privately Held**
WEB: www.bartoncooney.com
SIC: 7331 2752 Mailing service; commercial printing, offset

(G-954)
BE & K PLASTICS LLC
340 E Broad St (08016-1850)
PHONE..................................609 386-3200
Boris Pismichenko,
EMP: 14
SALES (est): 2MM **Privately Held**
SIC: 3089 Injection molding of plastics

(G-955)
BURLINGTON PRESS CORPORATION
328 High St Ste C (08016-4421)
PHONE..................................609 387-0030
Richard Lewis,
EMP: 10
SQ FT: 3,000
SALES (est): 1.7MM **Privately Held**
WEB: www.burlingtonprint.com
SIC: 2752 Commercial printing, offset

(G-956)
CELLUNET MANUFACTURING COMPNAY
Also Called: Joseph Titone & Sons'
460 Veterans Dr (08016-1259)
PHONE..................................609 386-3361
John Titone, *CEO*
◆ **EMP:** 12
SQ FT: 15,000
SALES (est): 1.1MM **Privately Held**
SIC: 3999 Hair & hair-based products

(G-957)
CEMENTEX PRODUCTS INC
Also Called: Cementex Insulated Tools
650 Jacksonville Rd (08016-3333)
P.O. Box 1428 (08016-7028)
PHONE..................................609 387-1040
Steve Russo, *President*
▲ **EMP:** 34
SQ FT: 20,000
SALES (est): 12.2MM **Privately Held**
WEB: www.cementexusa.com
SIC: 3423 Hand & edge tools

(G-958)
CENTRAL SAFETY EQUIPMENT CO (PA)
Also Called: Centryco
300 W Broad St (08016-1412)
P.O. Box 250 (08016-0250)
PHONE..................................609 386-6448
Mary T Gordon, *President*
Jack Jurechko, *Vice Pres*
▲ **EMP:** 29 **EST:** 1946
SQ FT: 30,000
SALES (est): 5.9MM **Privately Held**
WEB: www.centryco.com
SIC: 2395 Permanent pleating & pressing, for the trade

(G-959)
CNG PUBLISHING COMPANY
43 Manchester Way (08016-4300)
PHONE..................................973 768-0978
Catherine Gore, *President*
Mary Gore, *Vice Pres*
EMP: 5
SALES (est): 230.6K **Privately Held**
SIC: 2731 Book publishing

(G-960)
COAST RUBBER AND GASKET INC
1208 Columbus Rd Ste G (08016-3439)
PHONE..................................609 747-0110
Vito Massa, *President*
Frank J Valenziano, *Vice Pres*
Philip Valenziano, *Treasurer*
EMP: 6
SQ FT: 2,500
SALES (est): 630K **Privately Held**
SIC: 3053 5085 Gaskets, all materials; rubber goods, mechanical

(G-961)
COLGATE-PALMOLIVE COMPANY
400 Elbow Ln (08016-4130)
PHONE..................................609 239-6001
Owen James, *Branch Mgr*
EMP: 25
SALES (corp-wide): 15.5B **Publicly Held**
WEB: www.colgate.com
SIC: 2844 Toothpastes or powders, dentifrices
PA: Colgate-Palmolive Company
　300 Park Ave Fl 3
　New York NY 10022
　212 310-2000

(G-962)
DELAWARE VALLEY SIGN CORP (PA)
Also Called: Dvs Industries
112 Connecticut Dr (08016-4104)
PHONE..................................609 386-0100
George M Kennedy, *President*
John Bennett, *Vice Pres*
EMP: 95
SALES (est): 7.4MM **Privately Held**
SIC: 1799 3993 3444 Sign installation & maintenance; signs & advertising specialties; sheet metalwork

(G-963)
DELTA PAPER CORPORATION
122 Kissel Rd (08016-4172)
PHONE..................................856 532-0333
Bill Bregman, *CEO*
EMP: 50
SQ FT: 48,000
SALES (est): 15.7MM **Privately Held**
WEB: www.deltapaper.com
SIC: 2671 2621 Paper coated or laminated for packaging; newsprint paper

(G-964)
DUBLIN MANAGEMENT ASSOC OF NJ
Also Called: Lynch Industries
321 High St (08016-4411)
PHONE..................................609 387-1600
Michael A Carrozza, *President*
Brian Gozdan, *President*
Thomas J Gorman, *Principal*
Gregory Hammell, *Vice Pres*
Eric Miller, *Vice Pres*
▲ **EMP:** 120
SALES (est): 13.6MM **Privately Held**
WEB: www.lynchexhibits.com
SIC: 3993 7389 7319 Displays & cutouts, window & lobby; exhibit construction by industrial contractors; display advertising service

(G-965)
DYNATEC SYSTEMS INC (PA)
360 Connecticut Dr (08016-4108)
PHONE..................................609 387-0330
Thomas Doherty, *President*
Judy Doherty, *Treasurer*
William Fisher, *Admin Sec*
▲ **EMP:** 12
SQ FT: 4,500
SALES (est): 5.9MM **Privately Held**
WEB: www.dynatecsystems.com
SIC: 3826 1629 3589 5074 Environmental testing equipment; waste water & sewage treatment plant construction; water treatment equipment, industrial; water purification equipment

(G-966)
F S BRAINARD & CO
Also Called: West Electronics
5 Terri Ln Ste 15 (08016-4906)
P.O. Box 366 (08016-0366)
PHONE..................................609 387-4300
Bradford Brainard Jr, *President*
EMP: 10 **EST:** 1930
SQ FT: 10,000
SALES (est): 2.1MM **Privately Held**
WEB: www.meter-master.com
SIC: 3823 Industrial instrmnts msrmnt display/control process variable

(G-967)
FISHER CANVAS PRODUCTS INC
415 Saint Mary St (08016-1825)
PHONE..................................609 239-2733
Frederick H Fisher, *President*
EMP: 5
SQ FT: 12,000
SALES (est): 430K **Privately Held**
WEB: www.boatcanvas.net
SIC: 5551 5091 2394 Marine supplies & equipment; boat accessories & parts; canvas boat seats

(G-968)
FISHER SERVICE CO
120 Kissel Rd (08016-4172)
PHONE..................................609 386-5000
Matthew Doyle, *Principal*
EMP: 6
SALES (est): 820.1K **Privately Held**
SIC: 3491 Industrial valves

(G-969)
FRANKLIN ELECTRONIC PUBLS INC (PA)
3 Terri Ln Ste 6 (08016-4903)
P.O. Box 535, Princeton Junction (08550-0535)
PHONE..................................609 386-2500
Barry J Lipsky, *President*
Toshihide Hokari, *COO*
Frank A Musto, *CFO*

Debbie Callsen, *Accountant*
Thomas Ponsel, *Manager*
◆ **EMP:** 77
SQ FT: 5,000
SALES: 12MM **Privately Held**
WEB: www.franklin.com
SIC: 2741 5065 3695 3571 Technical manuals: publishing only, not printed on site; electronic parts & equipment; computer software tape & disks: blank, rigid & floppy; electronic computers; book publishing

(G-970)
GARELICK FARMS LLC
Cumberland Blvd Rr 130 (08016)
PHONE..................................609 499-2600
Ron Loffredo, *Principal*
EMP: 110 **Publicly Held**
WEB: www.overthemoonmilk.com
SIC: 2026 2033 Milk processing (pasteurizing, homogenizing, bottling); canned fruits & specialties
HQ: Garelick Farms, Llc
　1199 W Central St Ste 1
　Franklin MA 02038
　508 528-9000

(G-971)
GARLEY INC
46 Tall Timber Ln (08016-9758)
PHONE..................................215 788-5756
Eugene Whitley, *President*
EMP: 4 **EST:** 1950
SQ FT: 10,000
SALES: 360K **Privately Held**
WEB: www.garleyinc.com
SIC: 2541 Counters or counter display cases, wood; table or counter tops, plastic laminated

(G-972)
GENERATION BRANDS
6 Campus Dr (08016-2280)
PHONE..................................856 764-0500
Kevin M Fagan, *President*
Charlotte Brumbaugh, *Payroll Mgr*
Paul Cordero, *Supervisor*
▲ **EMP:** 4
SALES (est): 86.9K **Privately Held**
SIC: 3645 Residential lighting fixtures

(G-973)
INSTRMENT VLVE SVCS BURLINGTON
120 Kissel Rd (08016-4172)
PHONE..................................609 386-5000
Glenn Scott, *Principal*
EMP: 5
SALES (est): 320K **Privately Held**
SIC: 3491 Industrial valves

(G-974)
INTERNATIONAL PRODUCTS CORP (PA)
201 Connecticut Dr (08016-4105)
PHONE..................................609 386-8770
Charles Granito Sr, *President*
Kathy Wyrofsky, *Vice Pres*
Jennifer Sun, *Research*
Laurie Rossman, *Admin Asst*
EMP: 15 **EST:** 1919
SALES (est): 2MM **Privately Held**
WEB: www.ipcol.com
SIC: 2992 2842 Lubricating oils & greases; specialty cleaning, polishes & sanitation goods

(G-975)
INTERPLAST INC
100 Connecticut Dr (08016-4104)
P.O. Box 1328 (08016-0928)
PHONE..................................609 386-4990
Allen Langman, *President*
Jared Langman, *General Mgr*
A Benjamin Naimoli, *Vice Pres*
▲ **EMP:** 15
SQ FT: 26,000
SALES (est): 4MM **Privately Held**
WEB: www.interplastinc.com
SIC: 2821 Plastics materials & resins

(G-976)
JEMS PHARMA LLC
301 High St (08016-4411)
PHONE..................................609 386-0141

Richard Kozlowski, *President*
URS Janssen, *General Mgr*
EMP: 4 **EST:** 2013
SALES (est): 279.6K **Privately Held**
SIC: 2834 Pharmaceutical preparations

(G-977)
KLEIN DISTRIBUTORS INC
Also Called: Agway
600 E Route 130 (08016-1846)
PHONE..................................732 446-7632
Michael Klein, *Branch Mgr*
EMP: 6
SALES (corp-wide): 2.3MM **Privately Held**
SIC: 5261 3999 5999 Nurseries & garden centers; pet supplies; pet food
PA: Klein Distributors Inc
　600 N Rte 130
　Burlington NJ 08016
　609 386-0500

(G-978)
MAG SIGNS
1208 Columbus Rd Ste F (08016-3439)
PHONE..................................609 747-9600
Rob Persichetti, *Owner*
EMP: 12
SQ FT: 10,000
SALES: 1.8MM **Privately Held**
WEB: www.effectivesignworks.com
SIC: 3993 Electric signs

(G-979)
MERCHANT & EVANS INC (PA)
Also Called: Zip Rib
308 Connecticut Dr (08016-4108)
PHONE..................................609 387-3033
James Buck, *Ch of Bd*
Steven J Buck, *President*
Lisa Purden, *Treasurer*
◆ **EMP:** 44
SQ FT: 45,000
SALES (est): 7.6MM **Privately Held**
WEB: www.ziprib.com
SIC: 3446 5051 Architectural metalwork; metals service centers & offices

(G-980)
MODERN STORE EQUIPMENT
2045 Route 130 N (08016-9729)
PHONE..................................609 241-7438
David F Dunigan, *President*
John Hamon, *Superintendent*
Sara Casimates, *COO*
Layne Brown, *Cust Mgr*
Lisa Dunigan, *Admin Sec*
EMP: 13
SALES (est): 3.1MM **Privately Held**
SIC: 5021 5078 2542 Shelving; refrigerators, commercial (reach-in & walk-in); pallet racks: except wood

(G-981)
PENN METAL FINISHING CO INC
700 Jacksonville Rd (08016-3342)
PHONE..................................609 387-3400
Louis F Willa Jr, *President*
Charlotte Willa, *Vice Pres*
EMP: 9 **EST:** 1966
SQ FT: 26,000
SALES (est): 1.1MM **Privately Held**
WEB: www.pennmetal.net
SIC: 3479 2851 Coating of metals & formed products; paints & allied products

(G-982)
PIXELL CREATIVE GROUP LLC
Also Called: Gary Ell Photography
302 Wood St (08016-4408)
PHONE..................................609 410-3024
Gary Ell, *Owner*
EMP: 5
SALES (est): 170K **Privately Held**
SIC: 7335 3669 Commercial photography; visual communication systems

(G-983)
RIMTEC MANUFACTURING CORP
1702 Beverly Rd (08016-1010)
PHONE..................................609 387-0011
Minoru Oba, *President*
Steve Landin, *Business Mgr*
Ray Johnson Jr, *Prdtn Mgr*
Ray Johnston Jr, *Safety Mgr*

Andy Loyer, *Maint Spvr*
◆ **EMP:** 97
SQ FT: 51,000
SALES (est): 38.1MM **Privately Held**
WEB: www.rimtec.com
SIC: 2821 Polyvinyl chloride resins (PVC)
HQ: Riken Americas Corporation
   342 Riken Ct
   Hopkinsville KY 42240
   270 874-4131

(G-984)
SAMSENG TISSUE CO
122 Kissel Rd Ste C (08016-4225)
PHONE..................................609 479-3997
Ana Chu, *CEO*
Ana Chiu, *CEO*
Sebastian Choi, *Vice Pres*
▲ **EMP:** 13
SALES (est): 443.2K **Privately Held**
SIC: 2676 Towels, napkins & tissue paper
   products

(G-985)
SOUTH JERSEY CIRCUITS
340 E Broad St Unit 1c (08016-1850)
PHONE..................................609 479-3994
Diane Beharry, *Principal*
EMP: 5
SALES (est): 290.3K **Privately Held**
SIC: 3672 Printed circuit boards

(G-986)
STULZ-SICKLES STEEL
COMPANY (PA)
2 Campus Dr (08016-2280)
PHONE..................................609 531-2172
Rob Ogilvie, *CEO*
Mike Morgan, *Vice Pres*
Michael Harlan, *CFO*
Ron Colla, *Sales Mgr*
Kevin Kolacki, *Manager*
◆ **EMP:** 20 **EST:** 1916
SQ FT: 32,000
SALES (est): 14.9MM **Privately Held**
WEB: www.stulzsicklessteel.com
SIC: 5051 3548 Steel; electrodes, electric
   welding

(G-987)
THERMO FISHER SCIENTIFIC
INC
19 London Rd (08016-2972)
PHONE..................................609 239-3185
Anthony Miles-Sales Rep, *Principal*
EMP: 14
SALES (corp-wide): 24.3B **Publicly Held**
WEB: www.thermo.com
SIC: 3826 Analytical instruments
PA: Thermo Fisher Scientific Inc.
   168 3rd Ave
   Waltham MA 02451
   781 622-1000

(G-988)
TUCKER INTERNATIONAL LLC
460 Veterans Dr B (08016-1259)
PHONE..................................856 216-1333
Michael J Goldman, *President*
▲ **EMP:** 11
SALES (est): 1.7MM **Privately Held**
WEB: www.tuckertoys.com
SIC: 3944 Games, toys & children's vehi-
   cles

(G-989)
TUSCAN/LEHIGH DAIRIES INC
(HQ)
Also Called: Lehigh Valley Dairy Farms
117 Cumberland Blvd (08016-9722)
PHONE..................................570 385-1884
Rachel Gonzalez, *President*
Gregg Tanner, *Vice Pres*
Timothy A Smith, *Treasurer*
EMP: 82
SQ FT: 15,000
SALES (est): 39.5MM **Publicly Held**
SIC: 2026 2086 Milk processing (pasteur-
   izing, homogenizing, bottling); fruit drinks
   (less than 100% juice): packaged in cans,
   etc.

(G-990)
UNITED HOSPITAL SUPPLY
CORP
4422 Route 130 S (08016-2291)
P.O. Box 1238 (08016-0838)
PHONE..................................609 387-7580
Matthew Lyons, *President*
Jonathan Lyons, *Vice Pres*
Adam Lyons, *Treasurer*
Mark Lyons, *Admin Sec*
▼ **EMP:** 110 **EST:** 1968
SQ FT: 77,000
SALES (est): 25MM **Privately Held**
WEB: www.lab-design.com
SIC: 3499 3821 Safes & vaults, metal; lab-
   oratory furniture

(G-991)
UNITED STATES PIPE FNDRY
LLC
Also Called: Pressure Pipe Division
1101 E Pearl St Ste 1 (08016-1999)
PHONE..................................609 387-6000
Richard Janicki, *Enginr/R&D Mgr*
EMP: 120
SALES (corp-wide): 1.4B **Publicly Held**
SIC: 3321 Gray & ductile iron foundries
HQ: United States Pipe And Foundry Com-
   pany Llc
   2 Chase Corporate Dr # 200
   Hoover AL 35244
   205 263-8540

(G-992)
WEBB PRESS
340 E Broad St (08016-1850)
PHONE..................................609 386-0100
Bob Albasi, *Owner*
EMP: 5
SALES (est): 362.9K **Privately Held**
SIC: 2761 Manifold business forms

(G-993)
WEST ELECTRONICS INC
5 Terri Ln (08016-4906)
P.O. Box 366 (08016-0366)
PHONE..................................609 387-4300
Joseph Bernardo, *Ch of Bd*
EMP: 15
SQ FT: 5,000
SALES (est): 1.5MM **Privately Held**
SIC: 3679 Power supplies, all types: static

(G-994)
ZACS INTERNATIONAL LLC
2107 Route 130 N Unit 2 (08016-9747)
PHONE..................................609 368-3482
Benedetto Catarinicchia, *Principal*
Tricia Hutman, *Director*
EMP: 5
SALES (est): 215.4K **Privately Held**
SIC: 8712 2521 Architectural services;
   wood office furniture

Burlington Township
Burlington County

(G-995)
ALVA-TECH INC
1208 Columbus Rd Ste G (08016-3439)
PHONE..................................609 747-1133
Philip P Valenziano, *President*
Frank P Valenziano, *Vice Pres*
Kathleen Turner, *Treasurer*
▲ **EMP:** 10
SQ FT: 9,000
SALES (est): 2.2MM **Privately Held**
WEB: www.alva-tech.com
SIC: 3089 2891 Injection molding of plas-
   tics; adhesives & sealants

Butler
Morris County

(G-996)
BIOS INTERNATIONAL CORP
10 Park Pl Ste 3 (07405-1371)
PHONE..................................973 492-8400
Harvey Padden, *President*
Scott Calvert, *Vice Pres*

EMP: 22
SALES (est): 3.7MM **Privately Held**
SIC: 3826 3564 Environmental testing
   equipment; blowers & fans

(G-997)
BUTLER PRTG & LAMINATING
INC
250 Hamburg Tpke (07405-1526)
P.O. Box 836 (07405-0836)
PHONE..................................973 838-8550
Jim Berezny, *President*
◆ **EMP:** 125
SQ FT: 110,000
SALES (est): 28.3MM **Privately Held**
WEB: www.butlerprinting.com
SIC: 2759 3089 2295 Imprinting; laminat-
   ing of plastic; laminating of fabrics

(G-998)
COMPUTER CONTROL CORP
10 Park Pl Ste 1 (07405-1371)
PHONE..................................973 492-8265
Harvey Padden, *President*
Scott Calvert, *Vice Pres*
EMP: 14
SQ FT: 13,000
SALES (est): 2MM **Privately Held**
WEB: www.biosint.com
SIC: 3625 3672 Control equipment, elec-
   tric; printed circuit boards

(G-999)
DELTA SALES COMPANY INC
Also Called: Airoyal Division
1355 State Rt 23 (07405-1726)
PHONE..................................973 838-0371
Robert Infante, *President*
EMP: 10
SQ FT: 1,500
SALES (est): 1MM **Privately Held**
WEB: www.airoyal.com
SIC: 3561 Cylinders, pump

(G-1000)
FORCE INDUSTRIES LLC
32 Boonton Ave 1 (07405-1346)
PHONE..................................973 332-1532
Jamie Marie Tacinelli, *Principal*
EMP: 4
SALES (est): 159.3K **Privately Held**
SIC: 3999 Manufacturing industries

(G-1001)
GOFFCO INDUSTRIES LLC
10 Park Pl Ste 300 (07405-1310)
PHONE..................................973 492-0150
Leslie Gough Jr, *President*
Leslie R Gough Jr, *Principal*
EMP: 7
SALES (est): 740K **Privately Held**
WEB: www.goffco.com
SIC: 2752 Commercial printing, offset

(G-1002)
HAPPY CHEF INC
22 Park Pl Ste 2 (07405-1380)
PHONE..................................973 492-2525
James R Nadler, *President*
Joseph H Nadler, *Chairman*
Howard Curtin, *VP Sales*
Vanessa Petway, *Manager*
Deedee Kanhai, *Info Tech Mgr*
▼ **EMP:** 45
SQ FT: 30,000
SALES (est): 14.3MM **Privately Held**
WEB: www.happychefuniforms.com
SIC: 5136 5137 5023 2326 Uniforms,
   men's & boys'; uniforms, women's & chil-
   dren's; linens, table; towels; service ap-
   parel (baker, barber, lab, etc.), washable:
   men's; uniforms, except athletic:
   women's, misses' & juniors'; women's &
   misses' outerwear

(G-1003)
HIGH POINT BREWING CO INC
Also Called: High Point Wheat Beer Company
22 Park Pl (07405-1377)
PHONE..................................973 838-7400
Greg Zaccardi, *President*
Norm Rost, *Vice Pres*
▲ **EMP:** 4
SQ FT: 3,000
SALES (est): 450.4K **Privately Held**
SIC: 2082 Beer (alcoholic beverage)

(G-1004)
HSH ASSOC FINANCIAL
PUBLISHERS
1200 State Rt 23 (07405-2036)
PHONE..................................973 838-3330
EMP: 7
SALES (est): 87.2K **Privately Held**
SIC: 5812 2721 Eating Place Periodicals-
   Publishing/Printing

(G-1005)
INTEGRATED PACKAGING INDS
INC (PA)
45 Carey Ave Ste 210 (07405-1475)
PHONE..................................973 839-0500
Keith Traub, *President*
David Golden, *Vice Pres*
Stephanie Adler, *Project Mgr*
Dina Thum, *Mktg Dir*
Amy Sova, *Office Mgr*
EMP: 20
SQ FT: 20,000
SALES (est): 6.2MM **Privately Held**
WEB: www.integratedpackaging.net
SIC: 7336 3086 4783 Package design;
   packaging & shipping materials, foamed
   plastic; packing & crating

(G-1006)
JIGSAW PUBLISHING LLC
Also Called: Umbrella Publishing
8 Hemlock Ct (07405-1124)
PHONE..................................973 838-4838
▲ **EMP:** 1
SALES (est): 3MM **Privately Held**
SIC: 2741 Misc Publishing

(G-1007)
M S PLASTICS AND PACKG CO
10 Park Pl Ste 100 (07405-1300)
PHONE..................................973 492-2400
Al Saraisky, *President*
Ellen Saraisky, *Vice Pres*
Frank Trent, *Sales Staff*
Joyce Debenedetto, *Office Admin*
EMP: 19 **EST:** 1965
SQ FT: 7,500
SALES (est): 3.7MM **Privately Held**
WEB: www.msplastics.com
SIC: 5199 2673 Packaging materials;
   bags: plastic, laminated & coated

(G-1008)
MESA LABORATORIES INC
10 Park Pl (07405-1371)
PHONE..................................973 492-8400
Brian Roberts, *Director*
EMP: 33
SALES (corp-wide): 103.1MM **Publicly
Held**
SIC: 3823 Industrial instrmnts msrmnt dis-
   play/control process variable
PA: Mesa Laboratories, Inc.
   12100 W 6th Ave
   Lakewood CO 80228
   303 987-8000

(G-1009)
MESA LABORATORIES- BGI INC
10 Park Pl (07405-1371)
PHONE..................................973 492-8400
John Sullivan, *President*
EMP: 30
SALES (est): 1.7MM **Privately Held**
SIC: 3826 Analytical instruments

(G-1010)
MY WAY PRINTS INC
Also Called: PIP Printing
1376 State Rt 23 Ste E (07405-1742)
PHONE..................................973 492-1212
Myron Friedman, *President*
Gary Friedman, *Vice Pres*
EMP: 5
SQ FT: 2,900
SALES: 600K **Privately Held**
SIC: 2752 7389 Commercial printing, off-
   set; design services

(G-1011)
PEERLESS CONCRETE
PRODUCTS CO
246 Main St (07405-1025)
PHONE..................................973 838-3060
Clara Monaco, *President*

Philip Monaco, *Corp Secy*
Paul Monaco Jr, *Vice Pres*
EMP: 35
SQ FT: 10,000
SALES (est): 5MM **Privately Held**
WEB: www.peerlessconcrete.com
SIC: 3272 Septic tanks, concrete; tanks, concrete

(G-1012)
PRECISION FORMS INC
97 Decker Rd (07405-1561)
PHONE..............................973 838-3800
William J Sulski, *President*
Sandra L Sulski, *Corp Secy*
Sandra Sulski, *Vice Pres*
Steve Wikfors, *Foreman/Supr*
Wanda Mejia, *Opers Staff*
EMP: 26 **EST:** 1955
SQ FT: 13,000
SALES (est): 4MM **Privately Held**
WEB: www.precisionformsinc.com
SIC: 3599 Amusement park equipment; machine shop, jobbing & repair

(G-1013)
ROBERT F GAISER INC
292 Main St (07405-1025)
P.O. Box 807 (07405-0807)
PHONE..............................973 838-9254
Mildred Gaiser, *President*
Kurt Gaiser, *Vice Pres*
Stephen Gaiser, *Treasurer*
Lisa Dore, *Admin Sec*
▲ **EMP:** 12 **EST:** 1940
SQ FT: 7,200
SALES (est): 1.3MM **Privately Held**
WEB: www.beauveste.com
SIC: 2389 Clergymen's vestments

(G-1014)
RS MICROWAVE CO INC
22 Park Pl (07405-1377)
P.O. Box 273 (07405-0273)
PHONE..............................973 492-1207
Richard V Snyder, *President*
EMP: 48
SQ FT: 31,000
SALES (est): 8.1MM **Privately Held**
WEB: www.rsmicro.com
SIC: 3679 Microwave components

(G-1015)
STANTON PRECISION PRODUCTS LLC
10 Park Pl Bldg 4 (07405-1371)
PHONE..............................973 838-6951
Charles Stanton,
Sean Stanton,
William Stanton,
EMP: 6
SALES (est): 707.8K **Privately Held**
SIC: 3599 Machine shop, jobbing & repair

Buttzville
Warren County

(G-1016)
CRAMER PLATING INC
4 Hoyt Ln (07829)
PHONE..............................908 453-2887
Jean Cramer, *President*
EMP: 25 **EST:** 1958
SQ FT: 10,000
SALES (est): 2.2MM **Privately Held**
SIC: 3471 Plating of metals or formed products

Byram Township
Sussex County

(G-1017)
CARTRIDGE ACTUATED DEVICES
40 Old Indian Spring Rd (07821-3920)
PHONE..............................973 347-2281
Terry Cavalier, *Principal*
Ed Soohoo, *Administration*
EMP: 24

SALES (corp-wide): 351.7MM **Privately Held**
WEB: www.cartactdev.com
SIC: 2892 3489 5169 Detonators, high explosives; fuse powder; ordnance & accessories; explosives
HQ: Cartridge Actuated Devices, Inc
51 Dwight Pl
Fairfield NJ 07004
973 575-8760

(G-1018)
KANOMAX USA INC
219 Us Highway 206 (07821)
P.O. Box 372, Andover (07821-0372)
PHONE..............................973 786-6386
Minoro Kano, *President*
Debra Garrison, *Accountant*
Koji Miyasaka, *Marketing Mgr*
Bob Casale, *Marketing Staff*
▲ **EMP:** 8
SQ FT: 10,000
SALES: 2.5MM **Privately Held**
SIC: 3829 Geophysical & meteorological testing equipment

(G-1019)
TIN SIGH STOP
5 Meteor Trl (07821-3614)
PHONE..............................973 691-2712
James Odonohue, *Principal*
EMP: 4
SALES (est): 236.4K **Privately Held**
SIC: 3356 Tin

Caldwell
Essex County

(G-1020)
AL AND JOHN INC
Also Called: Glen Rock Ham
147 Clinton Rd (07006-6601)
PHONE..............................973 742-4990
Alexander Oldja, *President*
Michael Landech, *CFO*
◆ **EMP:** 300 **EST:** 1976
SQ FT: 65,000
SALES (est): 60.5MM **Privately Held**
SIC: 2013 Ham, boiled: from purchased meat

(G-1021)
CROSSFIRE PUBLICATIONS
551 Bloomfield Ave C14 (07006-7502)
PHONE..............................516 352-9087
Gregory Russo, *Owner*
EMP: 4
SALES (est): 188.1K **Privately Held**
WEB: www.crossfirepublications.com
SIC: 2741 Miscellaneous publishing

(G-1022)
DEVON TRADING CORP
5 Fairfield Rd (07006-4732)
PHONE..............................973 812-9190
Fran Orzech, *President*
Susan Orzech, *Treasurer*
Andrew Leichter, *Admin Sec*
▲ **EMP:** 20
SQ FT: 20,000
SALES (est): 4MM **Privately Held**
SIC: 5049 3911 Religious supplies; rosaries or other small religious articles, precious metal

(G-1023)
EME ELECTRICAL CONTRACTORS
35 Roseland Ave (07006-5901)
PHONE..............................973 228-6608
C Edward Bierals, *President*
EMP: 4
SALES (est): 370K **Privately Held**
SIC: 1731 1711 7692 General electrical contractor; plumbing contractors; warm air heating & air conditioning contractor; welding repair

(G-1024)
ESSEX PRODUCTS INTERNATIONAL
Also Called: Epi
494 Mountain Ave (07006-4571)
PHONE..............................973 226-2424
Kevin Schumacher, *President*
EMP: 26 **EST:** 2000
SQ FT: 1,200
SALES (est): 2.2MM **Privately Held**
WEB: www.epi-inc.net
SIC: 8711 3699 3567 Engineering services; electrical equipment & supplies; industrial furnaces & ovens

(G-1025)
GELOTTI CONFECTIONS LLC
194 Bloomfield Ave (07006-5327)
PHONE..............................973 403-9968
Russell Bleeker, *Principal*
EMP: 8
SALES (est): 489.1K **Privately Held**
SIC: 2024 Ice cream & frozen desserts

(G-1026)
LARSON-JUHL US LLC
165 Clinton Rd (07006-6605)
PHONE..............................973 439-1801
Tom McCarthy, *Branch Mgr*
EMP: 31
SALES (corp-wide): 225.3B **Publicly Held**
SIC: 2499 Picture frame molding, finished
HQ: Larson-Juhl Us Llc
3900 Steve Reynolds Blvd
Norcross GA 30093
770 279-5200

(G-1027)
MINUTEMAN PRESS
359 Bloomfield Ave (07006-5118)
PHONE..............................973 403-0146
Anthony Olivri, *Principal*
EMP: 4 **EST:** 2011
SALES (est): 254.1K **Privately Held**
SIC: 2752 Commercial printing, lithographic

(G-1028)
PROVOST SQUARE ASSOCIATES INC
6 Provost Sq (07006-5130)
PHONE..............................973 403-8755
Barbara Mamchur, *President*
EMP: 10
SALES (est): 1.1MM **Privately Held**
SIC: 3911 Rings, finger: precious metal

(G-1029)
RECORDER NEWSPAPER
6 Brookside Ave (07006-5604)
PHONE..............................973 226-4000
EMP: 4
SALES (est): 212.8K **Privately Held**
SIC: 2711 Newspapers-Publishing/Printing

(G-1030)
SELDOM SEEN DESIGNS LLC (PA)
9 Summit Dr (07006-4591)
PHONE..............................973 535-8805
Len Braunstein, *Mng Member*
▲ **EMP:** 5
SALES (est): 727.3K **Privately Held**
SIC: 2273 5023 Carpets & rugs; rugs

Califon
Hunterdon County

(G-1031)
BRITTINGHAM SFTWR DESIGN INC
Also Called: Bsdi
440 Hwy 513 (07830)
P.O. Box 357 (07830-0357)
PHONE..............................908 832-2691
Mark Brittingham, *President*
Pamela Brittingham, *Vice Pres*
EMP: 9

SALES: 300K **Privately Held**
WEB: www.bsdiweb.com
SIC: 7372 Application computer software; business oriented computer software

(G-1032)
NEWSPAPER MEDIA GROUP LLC
Also Called: Hudson Reporter
19 Winchester Dr (07830-3507)
PHONE..............................201 798-7800
EMP: 40
SALES (corp-wide): 6.7MM **Privately Held**
SIC: 2711 Commercial printing & newspaper publishing combined
PA: Newspaper Media Group Llc
2 Executive Campus # 400
Cherry Hill NJ 08002
856 779-3800

(G-1033)
POWER BAG AND FILM LLC
189 W Valley Brook Rd (07830-3530)
P.O. Box 534 (07830-0534)
PHONE..............................908 832-6648
Trevor Power, *Mng Member*
EMP: 6
SQ FT: 100,000
SALES (est): 1.6MM **Privately Held**
WEB: www.powerbagandfilm.com
SIC: 2673 Plastic bags: made from purchased materials

(G-1034)
RAWCO LLC
Also Called: Rawco Precision Manufacturing
452 County Road 513 (07830-4030)
PHONE..............................908 832-7700
Jeffery W Riley,
Lori Riley,
EMP: 8
SALES: 800K **Privately Held**
SIC: 3599 Machine shop, jobbing & repair

(G-1035)
TOLTEC PRODUCTS LLC
68 Beavers Rd (07830-3203)
PHONE..............................908 832-2131
Arnold Shapack,
Becky Shapack,
Michael Shapack,
Nancy Shapack,
Sarah Shapack,
EMP: 5
SALES (est): 1.2MM **Privately Held**
WEB: www.toltecproducts.com
SIC: 2542 Fixtures, store: except wood

(G-1036)
TRANSTAR TRUCK BODY & WLDG CO
514 County Road 513 (07830-4019)
P.O. Box 226 (07830-0226)
PHONE..............................908 832-2688
Dominick Tranquilli, *President*
EMP: 7
SQ FT: 10,000
SALES (est): 1.2MM **Privately Held**
SIC: 3713 7532 Truck bodies (motor vehicles); body shop, trucks

(G-1037)
WEISSCO POWER LTD LIABILITY CO
516 County Road 513 (07830-4019)
P.O. Box 223 (07830-0223)
PHONE..............................908 832-2173
Stacy Weiss,
Eric Weiss,
EMP: 9
SQ FT: 7,500
SALES (est): 1.1MM **Privately Held**
SIC: 7378 3629 Computer maintenance & repair; electronic generation equipment

Camden
Camden County

(G-1038)
A & A SOFT PRETZEL COMPANY
1100 N 32nd St (08105-4224)
PHONE..............................856 338-0208

Nick Panara, *Partner*
Albert Panara Sr, *Partner*
Albert Panara Jr, *Partner*
Linda S Panara, *Partner*
EMP: 7
SQ FT: 9,100
SALES (est): 430K **Privately Held**
SIC: 2052 5145 Pretzels; pretzels

(G-1039)
**AMERICAN WATER - PRIDESA
LLC (PA)**
1 Water St (08102-1658)
PHONE..............................856 435-7711
Eric Sabolsice,
▲ **EMP:** 6
SALES (est): 971.5K **Privately Held**
SIC: 2899 Desalter kits, sea water

(G-1040)
**ART METALCRAFT PLATING CO
INC**
Also Called: A-1 Fasteners
529 S 2nd St (08103-3307)
PHONE..............................215 923-6625
Cesare Dolente, *President*
EMP: 12 **EST:** 1940
SQ FT: 45,000
SALES (est): 1.4MM **Privately Held**
WEB: www.artmetalcraft.com
SIC: 3471 Plating of metals or formed
products; polishing, metals or formed
products

(G-1041)
**BERNARD MILLER
FABRICATORS**
1135 Mount Ephraim Ave (08103-2721)
PHONE..............................856 541-9499
Bernie Miller Sr, *Owner*
EMP: 7
SQ FT: 1,800
SALES: 750K **Privately Held**
SIC: 2434 2541 2517 2511 Wood kitchen
cabinets; counter & sink tops; wood tele-
vision & radio cabinets; wood household
furniture

(G-1042)
BRIGHT LIGHTS USA INC
9th & Liberty (08104)
PHONE..............................856 546-5656
Daniel Farber, *Manager*
EMP: 40
SALES (corp-wide): 10MM **Privately
Held**
WEB: www.brightlightsusa.com
SIC: 3724 4226 Aircraft engines & engine
parts; special warehousing & storage
PA: Bright Lights Usa, Inc.
11000 Midlantic Dr
Mount Laurel NJ 08054
856 546-5656

(G-1043)
**CAMDEN IRON & METAL INC
(DH)**
1500 S 6th St (08104-1402)
PHONE..............................856 365-7500
Joseph Balzano, *CEO*
Kristen Campbell, *Controller*
Stephen D'Ottavi, *Human Resources*
Christina Bunting, *Office Mgr*
Joe Cirillo, *Manager*
EMP: 15
SALES (est): 4.2MM
SALES (corp-wide): 4.3B **Privately Held**
SIC: 3312 Blast furnaces & steel mills

(G-1044)
**CAMDEN IRON & METAL LLC
(DH)**
Also Called: EMR
201 N Front St (08102-1661)
PHONE..............................856 969-7065
Joseph Valzano, *President*
Jeff Omlley, *Treasurer*
◆ **EMP:** 100
SQ FT: 10,000
SALES (est): 61.8MM
SALES (corp-wide): 4.3B **Privately Held**
WEB: www.camdeniron.com
SIC: 3312 4953 5093 Blast furnaces &
steel mills; refuse systems; metal scrap &
waste materials

(G-1045)
CAMDEN TOOL INC
129 York St (08102-2799)
P.O. Box 653 (08101-0653)
PHONE..............................856 966-6800
Tony Devlin, *President*
Dennis J Devlin, *Corp Secy*
EMP: 23 **EST:** 1952
SQ FT: 7,600
SALES (est): 5.9MM **Privately Held**
WEB: www.camdentool.com
SIC: 5084 3545 3541 Metalworking tools
(such as drills, taps, dies, files); reamers;
tools & accessories for machine tools;
machine tools, metal cutting type

(G-1046)
**CAMPBELL COMPANY OF
CANADA**
1 Campbell Pl (08103-1701)
P.O. Box 95008 (08101-5008)
PHONE..............................856 342-4800
EMP: 6
SALES (est): 592.2K
SALES (corp-wide): 8.1B **Publicly Held**
SIC: 2032 2033 Soups, except seafood:
packaged in cans, jars, etc.; fruit juices:
packaged in cans, jars, etc.
PA: Campbell Soup Company
1 Campbell Pl
Camden NJ 08103
856 342-4800

(G-1047)
**CAMPBELL SOUP COMPANY
(PA)**
1 Campbell Pl (08103-1799)
PHONE..............................856 342-4800
Keith R McLoughlin, *CEO*
Brian Skerlong, *Business Mgr*
Luca Mignini, *COO*
Carlos Barroso, *Senior VP*
Adam G Ciongoli, *Senior VP*
EMP: 1200
SALES: 8.1B **Publicly Held**
WEB: www.campbellsoups.com
SIC: 2038 2033 2052 2051 Frozen spe-
cialties; dinners, frozen & packaged;
breakfasts, frozen & packaged; lunches,
frozen & packaged; canned fruits & spe-
cialties; chili sauce, tomato: packaged in
cans, jars, etc.; cookies & crackers;
bread, cake & related products; potato
chips & similar snacks; soups & broths:
canned, jarred, etc.

(G-1048)
CAMPBELL SOUP COMPANY
827 Memorial Ave Bldg 80 (08103)
PHONE..............................856 342-4759
EMP: 6
SALES (corp-wide): 8.1B **Publicly Held**
SIC: 5461 2038 2033 2052 Bakeries;
frozen specialties; canned fruits & specialties; cookies & crackers; bread, cake
& related products; potato chips & similar
snacks
PA: Campbell Soup Company
1 Campbell Pl
Camden NJ 08103
856 342-4800

(G-1049)
**CAMPBELL SOUP SUPPLY CO
LLC (HQ)**
Also Called: Campbell-Soup Company
1 Campbell Pl (08103-1799)
PHONE..............................856 342-4800
Bill Oshea,
EMP: 6
SALES (est): 2.1MM
SALES (corp-wide): 8.1B **Publicly Held**
WEB: www.campbellsoups.com
SIC: 5461 2013 Bakeries; sausages &
other prepared meats
PA: Campbell Soup Company
1 Campbell Pl
Camden NJ 08103
856 342-4800

(G-1050)
CATHOLIC STAR HERALD
15 N 7th St (08102-1104)
PHONE..............................856 583-6142
Carl Peters, *Director*

EMP: 9
SALES: 1.1MM **Privately Held**
WEB: www.saintraymonds.cape-
mayschools.com
SIC: 2711 2752 Newspapers: publishing
only, not printed on site; commercial printing, lithographic

(G-1051)
CENTRAL METALS INC
1054 S 2nd St (08103-3243)
PHONE..............................215 462-7464
Joseph G Giangiullio, *President*
Tabitha Collins, *General Mgr*
Joe Jacovelli, *Vice Pres*
Suzanne Mastroeni, *Controller*
Renee Guarino, *Accountant*
EMP: 70
SQ FT: 70,000
SALES (est): 17.4MM **Privately Held**
WEB: www.centralmetals.com
SIC: 3441 Building components, structural
steel

(G-1052)
CHANNEL LOGISTICS LLC
Also Called: Space-Eyes
121 Market St Ste 2 (08102-2409)
PHONE..............................856 614-5441
Jatin S Bains, *Mng Member*
Brent Baker, *Info Tech Mgr*
EMP: 15
SQ FT: 2,500
SALES (est): 1.2MM **Privately Held**
WEB: www.channellogistics.com
SIC: 7372 7371 Prepackaged software;
software programming applications

(G-1053)
COMARCO PRODUCTS INC
Also Called: Comarco Quality Pork Products
501 Jackson St (08104-1409)
PHONE..............................856 342-7557
Thomas Hoversen, *President*
Chris Cook, *Vice Pres*
Eric Hoversen, *Vice Pres*
John Barrett, *Opers Staff*
Kelly Hoversen, *Engineer*
EMP: 80
SQ FT: 42,000
SALES (est): 5.2MM **Privately Held**
WEB: www.comarco.com
SIC: 5812 2011 Eating places; meat pack-
ing plants

(G-1054)
**CONTEMPRARY GRPHICS
BNDERY INC**
1200 Ferry Ave (08104-1810)
PHONE..............................856 663-7277
Tim Moreton, *President*
Bob Powell, *President*
Ivette Ayala-Jennings, *Accounting Mgr*
Debra Hupp, *Human Res Dir*
Lori Borden, *Executive*
EMP: 200
SQ FT: 115,000
SALES (est): 54.2MM **Privately Held**
WEB: www.contemporarygraphics.com
SIC: 2657 2752 Folding paperboard
boxes; commercial printing, offset

(G-1055)
CRESCENT BOTTLING CO INC
1001 N 25th St (08105-3825)
PHONE..............................856 964-2268
William Holscher, *President*
EMP: 5 **EST:** 1896
SQ FT: 4,000
SALES (est): 748.8K **Privately Held**
SIC: 5921 2086 Hard liquor; bottled &
canned soft drinks

(G-1056)
CSC BRANDS LP
1 Campbell Pl (08103-1701)
PHONE..............................800 257-8443
Timothy B Hassett, *President*
EMP: 10
SALES (est): 1.2MM
SALES (corp-wide): 8.1B **Publicly Held**
SIC: 2032 Canned specialties
PA: Campbell Soup Company
1 Campbell Pl
Camden NJ 08103
856 342-4800

(G-1057)
D K TRADING INC
Also Called: State Metal Trading
941 S 2nd St (08103-3208)
PHONE..............................856 225-1130
Yale Dorfman, *President*
▲ **EMP:** 7
SALES (est): 704.9K
SALES (corp-wide): 27.4MM **Privately
Held**
WEB: www.statemetalindustries.com
SIC: 3499 Aerosol valves, metal
PA: State Metal Industries, Inc.
941 S 2nd St
Camden NJ 08103
856 964-1510

(G-1058)
**DIOCESE OF CAMDEN NEW
JERSEY (PA)**
Also Called: Diocesan Media Center, The
631 Market St (08102-1103)
PHONE..............................856 756-7900
Joseph Pozusa, *Chancellor*
Rev Nicholas A Dimarzio, *Bishop*
Nicholas Dimarzio, *Bishop*
Bartholomew J Eustace, *Bishop*
George H Guilfoyle, *Bishop*
EMP: 1260 **EST:** 1937
SQ FT: 5,000
SALES (est): 67.5MM **Privately Held**
WEB: www.saintraymonds.cape-
mayschools.com
SIC: 8661 2711 Catholic Church; newspa-
pers: publishing only, not printed on site

(G-1059)
**DYNAMIC BLENDING COMPANY
INC**
1475 S 6th St (08104-1105)
PHONE..............................856 541-6626
Terrence Riley, *CEO*
Julian E West, *President*
Terrance J O Reilly, *Vice Pres*
EMP: 10
SQ FT: 15,000
SALES (est): 1.6MM **Privately Held**
SIC: 2841 Soap: granulated, liquid, cake,
flaked or chip; detergents, synthetic or-
ganic or inorganic alkaline

(G-1060)
ELMCO TWO INC
1045 Cambridge Ave (08105-3930)
P.O. Box 561, Pennsauken (08110-0561)
PHONE..............................856 365-2244
Bernard Kofoet, *President*
EMP: 8 **EST:** 1962
SALES (est): 1MM **Privately Held**
SIC: 3444 7692 Sheet metal specialties,
not stamped; welding repair

(G-1061)
EMDUR METAL PRODUCTS INC
Also Called: Emdur Art Products
1115 Mount Vernon St (08103-2782)
P.O. Box 421, Cherry Hill (08003-0421)
PHONE..............................856 541-1100
Jerome Emdur, *President*
EMP: 10 **EST:** 1952
SQ FT: 32,000
SALES: 300K **Privately Held**
SIC: 3999 3873 Plaques, picture, lami-
nated; clocks, assembly of

(G-1062)
F & R PALLETS INC
Also Called: J & R Pallets
201 Erie St (08102-2619)
PHONE..............................856 964-8516
Ronald Abate, *President*
Frances Abate, *Vice Pres*
Namsoo Suk, *CTO*
Chad Pindar, *Planning*
EMP: 30
SQ FT: 6,200
SALES (est): 2.6MM **Privately Held**
SIC: 2448 7699 Pallets, wood; pallet re-
pair

(G-1063)
FAST DOORS LLC
1661 Davis St (08103-3004)
PHONE..............................856 966-3278
Albert David Pooner,

EMP: 5
SALES (est): 489.3K **Privately Held**
SIC: **3442** Metal doors

(G-1064)
FBM GALAXY INC
Also Called: Specialty Products & Insul Co
2201 Mount Ephraim Ave (08104-3232)
PHONE..................................856 966-1105
Doug Magill, *Branch Mgr*
EMP: 25
SALES (corp-wide): 2B **Publicly Held**
WEB: www.spi-co.com
SIC: **5033 3296** Insulation materials; glass wool
HQ: Fbm Galaxy, Inc.
1650 Manheim Pike Ste 202
Lancaster PA 17601
717 569-3900

(G-1065)
FW WINTER INC
550 Delaware Ave (08102-2100)
PHONE..................................856 963-7490
Friedrich W Winter, *President*
Daniel Martelli, *Plant Mgr*
Tony Mologne, *Sales Mgr*
Dr Deepak Madan, *Director*
Ginny Walsh, *Administration*
▲ EMP: 25
SQ FT: 60,000
SALES (est): 6.8MM **Privately Held**
WEB: www.fwwinter.com
SIC: **3399 5051** Powder, metal; metals service centers & offices

(G-1066)
GEORGIA-PACIFIC LLC
1101 S Front St (08103-3200)
PHONE..................................856 966-7600
Mike Kauth, *Manager*
EMP: 100
SALES (corp-wide): 40.7B **Privately Held**
WEB: www.gp.com
SIC: **3275 3299 3531** Gypsum products; stucco; construction machinery
HQ: Georgia-Pacific Llc
133 Peachtree St Nw
Atlanta GA 30303
404 652-4000

(G-1067)
HOARDERS EXPRESS LLC
529 Market St (08102-1216)
PHONE..................................856 963-8471
Ronald Ford Jr,
EMP: 75
SALES (est): 4MM **Privately Held**
SIC: **3579** Sorters, filing (office)

(G-1068)
HOLTEC GOVERNMENT SERVICES LLC
1 Holtec Blvd (08104-2413)
PHONE..................................856 291-0600
Kalyan Niyogi, *President*
Joy Russell, *Vice Pres*
Martha Singh, *Treasurer*
EMP: 4
SALES (est): 275.7K
SALES (corp-wide): 1.3B **Privately Held**
SIC: **3273 3536 4013** Ready-mixed concrete; cranes, industrial plant; belt line railroads
PA: Holtec International
1001 N Us Highway 1
Jupiter FL 33477
561 745-7772

(G-1069)
HOLTEC INTERNATIONAL
1 Holtec Blvd (08104-2413)
PHONE..................................856 797-0900
Robert Galvin, *CFO*
EMP: 400
SALES (corp-wide): 1.3B **Privately Held**
SIC: **2819 8711** Nuclear fuel scrap, reprocessing; engineering services
PA: Holtec International
1001 N Us Highway 1
Jupiter FL 33477
561 745-7772

(G-1070)
INDUSTRIAL HYDRAULICS & RUBBER
458 Atlantic Ave (08104-1016)
PHONE..................................856 966-2600
Michael Donaghue,
EMP: 9
SALES (est): 904.2K **Privately Held**
SIC: **1799 3492** Hydraulic equipment, installation & service; hose & tube couplings, hydraulic/pneumatic

(G-1071)
JAYMAR PRECISION INC
1169 Cooper St (08102-1011)
PHONE..................................856 365-8779
Chuck Vanaltvorst, *President*
EMP: 6
SQ FT: 6,525
SALES (est): 735.8K **Privately Held**
SIC: **3599** Machine shop, jobbing & repair

(G-1072)
JOSEPH OAT HOLDINGS INC
2500 S Broadway (08104-2409)
PHONE..................................856 541-2900
Martin Kaplan, *CEO*
Michael Holtz, *President*
Ron Kaplan, *President*
Robert Sax, *President*
Jay Murphy, *Vice Pres*
◆ EMP: 68 EST: 1788
SQ FT: 130,000
SALES (est): 15.5MM **Privately Held**
WEB: www.josephoat.com
SIC: **3443 3441 3412** Fabricated plate work (boiler shop); plate work for the nuclear industry; tanks, standard or custom fabricated; metal plate; boiler & boiler shop work; fabricated structural metal; barrels, shipping: metal; drums, shipping: metal

(G-1073)
KAPLAN & ZUBRIN (PA)
Also Called: K & Z Pickle Co
Second Kaighns Ave (08103)
P.O. Box 1006 (08101-1006)
PHONE..................................856 964-1083
Ronald Kaplan, *President*
Richard Kaplan, *Corp Secy*
EMP: 20 EST: 1940
SQ FT: 25,000
SALES (est): 2.4MM **Privately Held**
WEB: www.kaplanzubrinpickles.com
SIC: **2035** Pickles, sauces & salad dressings

(G-1074)
L3 TECHNOLOGIES INC
Communication Systems - E Div
1 Federal St (08103-1088)
PHONE..................................856 338-3000
Mark Simon, *President*
Val Snyder, *Division Pres*
Roslyn Hardwick, *Empl Rel Dir*
Steven Kipp, *Manager*
Julio Martinez, *Manager*
EMP: 800
SALES (corp-wide): 6.8B **Publicly Held**
SIC: **3663** Radio & TV communications equipment
HQ: L3 Technologies, Inc.
600 3rd Ave Fl 34
New York NY 10016
212 697-1111

(G-1075)
MAFCO WORLDWIDE CORPORATION (DH)
Also Called: Mafco Magnasweet
300 Jefferson St (08104-2113)
PHONE..................................856 964-8840
Steven Taub, *President*
Peter Vora, *Senior VP*
Lee Collison, *Vice Pres*
Leon Gorgol, *Vice Pres*
Tom Cotton, *Purchasing*
◆ EMP: 108
SQ FT: 390,000
SALES (est): 40.5MM **Privately Held**
WEB: www.mafcolicorice.com
SIC: **2064** Licorice candy

HQ: Flavors Holdings Inc.
35 E 62nd St
New York NY 10065
212 572-8677

(G-1076)
MAFCO WORLDWIDE LLC
300 Jefferson St (08104-2113)
PHONE..................................856 964-8840
EMP: 16
SALES (est): 2.5MM **Privately Held**
SIC: **2834** Pharmaceutical preparations

(G-1077)
MAGNETIC METALS CORPORATION (DH)
1900 Hayes Ave (08105-3656)
P.O. Box 3320, Cherry Hill (08034-0314)
PHONE..................................856 964-7842
Henry Rowan Jr, *Ch of Bd*
Frank Raneiro, *Owner*
Mark Nguyen, *Buyer*
Eunice Rodriguez, *Buyer*
Karen Coffaro, *Technology*
▲ EMP: 140 EST: 1942
SQ FT: 180,000
SALES (est): 43.9MM
SALES (corp-wide): 1B **Privately Held**
WEB: www.magmet.com
SIC: **3542** Magnetic forming machines
HQ: Indel, Inc.
10 Indel Ave
Rancocas NJ 08073
609 267-9000

(G-1078)
NEW JERSEY RIVET CO LLC
1785 Haddon Ave (08103-3096)
PHONE..................................856 963-2237
Dan Brown, *Plant Mgr*
Dennis Van Name, *Mng Member*
Michael Van Name, *Mng Member*
◆ EMP: 15 EST: 1938
SQ FT: 27,000
SALES (est): 3.1MM **Privately Held**
WEB: www.njrivet.com
SIC: **3452** Rivets, metal

(G-1079)
NEWMAN GLASS WORKS INC
1515 Haddon Ave (08103-3196)
P.O. Box 18, Lafayette Hill PA (19444-0018)
PHONE..................................215 925-3565
Herb Shore, *President*
Barry Shore, *Vice Pres*
David Shore, *Treasurer*
EMP: 14 EST: 1932
SQ FT: 15,200
SALES (est): 2.1MM **Privately Held**
WEB: www.newmanglass.com
SIC: **1793 5231 3231** Glass & glazing work; glass; products of purchased glass

(G-1080)
NOVELTY HAIR GOODS CO
1138 S Broadway 40 (08103-2206)
PHONE..................................856 963-5876
EMP: 6 EST: 1926
SQ FT: 50,000
SALES (est): 45.2K **Privately Held**
SIC: **3999** Mfg Misc Products

(G-1081)
NUTSCO INC
1115 S 2nd St (08103-3232)
PHONE..................................856 966-6400
Francesco Assis, *CEO*
Patricio Assis, *Vice Pres*
▲ EMP: 12
SQ FT: 48,000
SALES (est): 3.1MM **Privately Held**
WEB: www.nutsco.com
SIC: **2068** Nuts: dried, dehydrated, salted or roasted

(G-1082)
PATRICK J KELLY DRUMS INC
1810 River Ave (08105-3630)
PHONE..................................856 963-1795
Patrick Kelly, *Shareholder*
EMP: 8
SALES (corp-wide): 13.5MM **Privately Held**
SIC: **3412** Metal barrels, drums & pails

PA: Patrick J. Kelly Drums, Inc.
6226 Pidcock Creek Rd
New Hope PA 18938
215 598-0666

(G-1083)
PLASTICS CONSULTING & MFG CO
Also Called: P C M
1435 Ferry Ave (08104)
PHONE..................................800 222-0317
Steven Schwartz, *President*
Russell G Shallcross, *Vice Pres*
Nina Wiggins, *Facilities Mgr*
Melissa Schwartz, *Shareholder*
▲ EMP: 25
SQ FT: 49,000
SALES (est): 3.9MM **Privately Held**
WEB: www.pcmc.com
SIC: **3479** Coating of metals with plastic or resins

(G-1084)
R F PRODUCTS INC (PA)
1500 Davis St (08103-3013)
PHONE..................................856 365-5500
Robert M Minke, *President*
Carmine Abbondante, *General Mgr*
Rosanne P Minke, *Corp Secy*
Rosanne Minke, *Vice Pres*
William E Smith, *Vice Pres*
EMP: 40
SQ FT: 90,000
SALES (est): 5.4MM **Privately Held**
WEB: www.rfproductsinc.com
SIC: **3663** Radio & TV communications equipment

(G-1085)
RECORDED PUBLICATIONS LABS
Also Called: Rpl
1100 E State St (08105-3538)
PHONE..................................856 963-3000
John S Oliano, *Ch of Bd*
Ronald J Oliano, *President*
Lisa Oliano, *Admin Sec*
EMP: 20
SQ FT: 27,000
SALES (est): 1.4MM **Privately Held**
SIC: **7819 7812 3652** Video tape or disk reproduction; motion picture & video production; pre-recorded records & tapes

(G-1086)
SCIENCE PUMP CORPORATION
1431 Ferry Ave (08104-1307)
PHONE..................................856 963-7700
Steven Schwartz, *President*
Russell G Fhallcross, *Vice Pres*
EMP: 20
SQ FT: 2,000
SALES (est): 2.8MM **Privately Held**
WEB: www.pcmco.com
SIC: **3829 3559 3564 3561** Measuring & controlling devices; ozone machines; blowers & fans; pumps & pumping equipment

(G-1087)
SELL ALL PROPERTIES LLC
301 Market St Ste 1 (08102-1528)
PHONE..................................856 963-8800
Eugene Alford,
Norma Sellers,
EMP: 10
SQ FT: 1,400
SALES (est): 905.8K **Privately Held**
SIC: **6531 3088** Selling agent, real estate; plastics plumbing fixtures

(G-1088)
STATE METAL INDUSTRIES INC (PA)
941 S 2nd St (08103-3292)
PHONE..................................856 964-1510
Andrew Gorgol, *President*
Yale Dorfman, *Senior VP*
Michael Dorfman, *Vice Pres*
Richard Kuhl, *Vice Pres*
Jim Marmion, *CFO*
▲ EMP: 94 EST: 1948
SQ FT: 15,000

SALES (est): 27.4MM **Privately Held**
WEB: www.statemetalindustries.com
SIC: 3341 Secondary nonferrous metals

(G-1089)
UNITED STATES COLD STORAGE INC (HQ)
2 Aquarium Dr Ste 400 (08103-1000)
PHONE....................................856 354-8181
David M Harlan, *CEO*
Randy Dorrell, *General Mgr*
Daniel Goodhard, *General Mgr*
Tim Herm, *General Mgr*
Michael Irvin, *General Mgr*
◆ EMP: 304 EST: 1899
SQ FT: 7,800
SALES (est): 590.6MM
SALES (corp-wide): 13.5B **Privately Held**
WEB: www.uscold.com
SIC: 2097 4222 Block ice; warehousing, cold storage or refrigerated
PA: John Swire & Sons Limited
      Swire House
      London
      207 834-7717

(G-1090)
WILLIAM DULING
Also Called: General Metal & Glass Co
613 Kaighn Ave 15 (08103-2308)
PHONE....................................856 365-6323
William Duling, *Owner*
EMP: 6 EST: 1950
SQ FT: 4,000
SALES (est): 401.6K **Privately Held**
SIC: 1793 3231 Glass & glazing work; products of purchased glass

Cape May
Cape May County

(G-1091)
ACME MARKETS INC
Lafayette & Ocean Sts (08204)
PHONE....................................609 884-7217
Michael Davis, *Manager*
EMP: 25
SALES (corp-wide): 60.5B **Privately Held**
WEB: www.acmemarkets.com
SIC: 5411 2051 Supermarkets, chain; bread, cake & related products
HQ: Acme Markets, Inc.
      75 Valley Stream Pkwy # 100
      Malvern PA 19355
      610 889-4000

(G-1092)
CAPE MAY BREWING LTD LBLTY CO
Also Called: Cape May Brewing Company
1288 Hornet Rd (08204)
PHONE....................................609 849-9933
EMP: 11
SALES (est): 1.6MM
SALES (corp-wide): 4.7MM **Privately Held**
SIC: 2082 Beer (alcoholic beverage)
PA: Cape May Brewing Limited Liability Company
      409 Breakwater Rd
      Cape May NJ 08204
      609 849-9933

(G-1093)
CAPE MAY BREWING LTD LBLTY CO (PA)
Also Called: Cape May Brewing Company
409 Breakwater Rd (08204-4537)
PHONE....................................609 849-9933
Edward Belski, *President*
EMP: 26
SALES (est): 4.7MM **Privately Held**
SIC: 2082 Beer (alcoholic beverage)

(G-1094)
CAPE PUBLISHING INC
513 Washington St Fl 2 (08204-1427)
P.O. Box 2383 (08204-7383)
PHONE....................................609 898-4500
Bernar Haas, *CEO*
Kathleen Hayes, *Accounts Exec*
EMP: 5

SALES (est): 345.5K **Privately Held**
SIC: 2741 Miscellaneous publishing

(G-1095)
COHANSEY COVE
705 Jonathan Hoffman Rd (08204-4308)
PHONE....................................609 884-7726
Karen Keirsey, *Principal*
EMP: 4 EST: 2011
SALES (est): 291.7K **Privately Held**
SIC: 2741 Miscellaneous publishing

(G-1096)
COLD SPRING ICE INC
Also Called: Lobster House
906 Schellenger St (08204-1775)
P.O. Box 497 (08204-0497)
PHONE....................................609 884-3405
Keith Laudeman, *President*
Clara Burkhardt, *Manager*
EMP: 5
SALES (est): 330K **Privately Held**
SIC: 2097 Manufactured ice

(G-1097)
DOUBLE DIAMOND TECHNOLOGIES
705 Route 9 (08204-4611)
P.O. Box 303, Ocean View (08230-0303)
PHONE....................................609 624-1414
David P Catanoso, *President*
EMP: 6
SALES (est): 460K **Privately Held**
WEB: www.doublediamondtech.com
SIC: 3695 Computer software tape & disks: blank, rigid & floppy

(G-1098)
FISHERMENS ENERGY NJ LLC
985 Ocean Dr (08204-1855)
PHONE....................................609 286-9650
Chris Wissemann, *CEO*
Daniel Cohen, *Mng Member*
EMP: 13
SALES (est): 2MM **Privately Held**
SIC: 3621 Windmills, electric generating

(G-1099)
GLOBE ENGINEERING CORP
1213 Delaware Ave (08204-2606)
PHONE....................................609 898-0349
Albert Kuintzle, *President*
EMP: 5 EST: 1962
SQ FT: 6,600
SALES (est): 468.5K **Privately Held**
SIC: 3444 3599 Sheet metal specialties, not stamped; machine shop, jobbing & repair

(G-1100)
MARK I INDUSTRIES INC
910 Shunpike Rd (08204-4333)
PHONE....................................609 884-0051
Robert Bartle, *President*
EMP: 10
SQ FT: 1,000
SALES (est): 670K **Privately Held**
SIC: 3324 Steel investment foundries

(G-1101)
SAMPLE MEDIA INC
Also Called: Cape May Star & Wave
600 Park Blvd Ste 5 (08204-1265)
PHONE....................................609 884-2021
Jennifer Kopp, *Principal*
EMP: 5
SALES (est): 439.2K
SALES (corp-wide): 3.9MM **Privately Held**
SIC: 2711 Newspapers
PA: Sample Media, Inc
      112 E 8th St
      Ocean City NJ 08226
      609 399-5411

(G-1102)
SEA HARVEST INC
985 Ocean Dr (08204-1855)
PHONE....................................609 884-3000
Daniel Cohen, *President*
Barry Cohen, *Corp Secy*
Maxi Cohen, *Vice Pres*
EMP: 25
SQ FT: 750

SALES (est): 1.8MM **Privately Held**
SIC: 4499 2091 Boat cleaning; canned & cured fish & seafoods

(G-1103)
TMU INC
Also Called: Tooling & Mfg Unlimited
910 Shunpike Rd Ste A (08204-4334)
PHONE....................................609 884-7656
Robert Bartle, *President*
EMP: 16 EST: 1964
SQ FT: 12,000
SALES (est): 2.4MM **Privately Held**
WEB: www.tmuinc.com
SIC: 3469 3556 3549 Machine parts, stamped or pressed metal; food products machinery; metalworking machinery

(G-1104)
W J R B INC
Also Called: Cape May Winery & Vineyard
711 Town Bank Rd (08204-4410)
PHONE....................................609 884-1169
Arthur Craig Jr, *President*
EMP: 7
SALES (est): 942.6K **Privately Held**
WEB: www.wjrb.com
SIC: 2084 5921 Wines; wine

(G-1105)
WILLOW CREEK WINERY INC
160 Stevens St 168 (08204-1092)
PHONE....................................609 770-8782
Barbara Wilde, *President*
EMP: 4
SALES (est): 437.2K **Privately Held**
SIC: 2084 Wines

Cape May Court House
Cape May County

(G-1106)
ANNE ALANNA INC
41 Pierces Point Rd (08210-2518)
PHONE....................................609 465-3787
Ed Obropta, *Owner*
EMP: 5 EST: 2001
SALES (est): 654.5K **Privately Held**
WEB: www.alannaanne.com
SIC: 2261 Screen printing of cotton broad-woven fabrics

(G-1107)
BILLY D DUMPSTER SERVICE LLC
1 Kimbles Beach Rd (08210-2077)
PHONE....................................609 465-5990
William Drury, *Principal*
EMP: 8
SALES (est): 833.1K **Privately Held**
SIC: 3443 Dumpsters, garbage

(G-1108)
CANVAS CREATIONS
14 Swainton Goshen Rd (08210-1457)
PHONE....................................609 465-8428
Clinton R Clement Jr, *Partner*
Scott Beck, *Partner*
▲ EMP: 4
SQ FT: 1,200
SALES (est): 300K **Privately Held**
SIC: 2394 Canvas boat seats; convertible tops, canvas or boat: from purchased materials; sails: made from purchased materials

(G-1109)
CHOCOLATE FACE CUPCAKE
1963 Route 9 N (08210-1158)
PHONE....................................609 624-2253
EMP: 4
SALES (est): 255.6K **Privately Held**
SIC: 2051 Bread, cake & related products

(G-1110)
COMMERCIAL WATER SPORTS INC
28 Clermont Dr (08210-1157)
PHONE....................................609 624-3404
Rob Guarini, *CEO*
▼ EMP: 5
SALES (est): 735.4K **Privately Held**
SIC: 3732 Boat building & repairing

(G-1111)
INTER REP ASSOCIATES INC (PA)
131 Kimbles Beach Rd (08210-2079)
PHONE....................................609 465-0077
Robert Leafey, *President*
EMP: 8
SALES (est): 1.8MM **Privately Held**
SIC: 5084 3559 7389 Industrial machine parts; glass making machinery: blowing, molding, forming, etc.;

(G-1112)
LICENSEE SERVICES INC
502 S Main St (08210-2350)
P.O. Box 716 (08210-0716)
PHONE....................................609 465-2003
Fred Spiewak, *President*
Ed Paone, *Vice Pres*
Cecil Bryan, *Purchasing*
Sue Lawrik, *Pub Rel Mgr*
EMP: 15
SQ FT: 400,000
SALES (est): 2MM **Privately Held**
SIC: 2759 Screen printing

(G-1113)
NATALI VINEYARDS LLC
221 Route 47 N (08210-1328)
PHONE....................................609 465-0075
Alfred Natali, *Mng Member*
EMP: 6
SALES (est): 467K **Privately Held**
SIC: 2084 5921 Wines; wine

(G-1114)
SIGNARAMA
Also Called: Sign-A-Rama
315 S Main St (08210-2359)
PHONE....................................609 465-9400
EMP: 5 EST: 2017
SALES (est): 63.7K **Privately Held**
SIC: 3993 Signs & advertising specialties

(G-1115)
THOMAS INSTRUMENTATION INC
118 Kings Hwy (08210-1233)
PHONE....................................609 624-7777
Thomas Gluyes, *President*
Cassandra Gluyas, *President*
EMP: 10
SALES (corp-wide): 1.8MM **Privately Held**
WEB: www.tiweb.net
SIC: 3577 7371 Computer peripheral equipment; custom computer programming services
PA: Thomas Instrumentation Inc.
      133 Landing Rd
      Cape May Court House NJ 08210
      609 624-2630

(G-1116)
THOMAS INSTRUMENTATION INC (PA)
133 Landing Rd (08210-1113)
PHONE....................................609 624-2630
Cassandra Gluyas, *CEO*
Thomas W Gluyas, *President*
Jan Gluyas, *CFO*
Angie Irizzary, *Sales Staff*
Jeff Niccoli, *Marketing Mgr*
EMP: 14
SALES (est): 1.8MM **Privately Held**
WEB: www.tiweb.net
SIC: 8711 7371 3825 3679 Electrical or electronic engineering; custom computer programming services; analog-digital converters, electronic instrumentation type; electronic circuits; harness assemblies for electronic use: wire or cable; printed circuit boards

Carlstadt
Bergen County

(G-1117)
A & S PACKAGING & DISPLAY
120 Kero Rd (07072-2601)
PHONE....................................201 531-1900
Roy Andersen, *President*

Joanne Andersen, *Admin Sec*
EMP: 10
SQ FT: 26,000
SALES (est): 1.6MM **Privately Held**
WEB: www.aspkg.com
SIC: 3086 Packaging & shipping materials, foamed plastic

(G-1118)
ADVANCED POLYMER INC
400 Paterson Plank Rd (07072-2306)
PHONE...................................201 964-3000
Kuni Nakamura, *President*
Elizabeth Cogollo, *Opers Mgr*
Carlo Serpe, *Warehouse Mgr*
Filip Kuzmanovski, *Engineer*
Greg Nelson, *Natl Sales Mgr*
▲ **EMP:** 17
SALES (est): 6.3MM **Privately Held**
WEB: www.advpolymer.com
SIC: 2899 5169 Acid resist for etching; polyurethane products

(G-1119)
AGFA CORPORATION
580 Gotham Pkwy (07072-2405)
PHONE...................................201 440-0111
Bob Caplan, *Principal*
Debbie Linksey, *Administration*
EMP: 50
SALES (corp-wide): 494.6MM **Privately Held**
SIC: 2752 3861 Photo-offset printing; photographic equipment & supplies
HQ: Agfa Corporation
611 River Dr Ste 305
Elmwood Park NJ 07407
800 540-2432

(G-1120)
AGFA CORPORATION
580 Gotham Pkwy (07072-2405)
PHONE...................................201 288-4101
Fax: 201 288-3943
EMP: 20
SALES (corp-wide): 633.6MM **Privately Held**
SIC: 2752 Mfg Photo Offset Printing
HQ: Agfa Corporation
10 S Academy St
Greenville SC 07407
800 526-5441

(G-1121)
ALLFASTENERS USA LLC
480 Meadow Ln (07072-3006)
PHONE...................................201 783-8836
Vern Macgregor, *Branch Mgr*
EMP: 21 **Privately Held**
SIC: 3429 Builders' hardware
HQ: Allfasteners Usa, Llc
959 Lake Rd
Medina OH 44256
440 232-6060

(G-1122)
ALLIED ENVELOPE CO INC (PA)
Also Called: Allied Printing Resources
33 Commerce Rd (07072-2504)
PHONE...................................201 440-2000
Robert James Royer, *President*
Christopher Royer, *Admin Sec*
▲ **EMP:** 50
SQ FT: 58,000
SALES (est): 12MM **Privately Held**
SIC: 5112 2752 Envelopes; commercial printing, lithographic

(G-1123)
AMERICAN CONSOLIDATION INC
500 Washington Ave (07072-2900)
PHONE...................................201 438-4351
Steve Sachs, *CEO*
Dominick Rizzitano, *President*
Bernard Geik, *Chairman*
Danny Ho, *Opers Mgr*
Jim Casson, *Manager*
◆ **EMP:** 90
SQ FT: 200,000
SALES (est): 10.3MM **Privately Held**
WEB: www.americanconsolidation.com
SIC: 3999 Atomizers, toiletry

(G-1124)
ARCY MANUFACTURING CO INC
575 Industrial Rd (07072-1611)
PHONE...................................201 635-1910
Bob Mattesky, *President*
Jackie Nieves, *Manager*
▼ **EMP:** 11
SQ FT: 12,000
SALES (est): 1.9MM **Privately Held**
SIC: 3053 Gaskets, all materials; packing, metallic; packing, rubber; gaskets & sealing devices

(G-1125)
ARDE INC (DH)
Also Called: Arde Barinco or Arde
875 Washington Ave (07072-3001)
PHONE...................................201 784-9880
Warren Boley, *President*
Jim Maser, *Principal*
Linda Dozier, *Info Tech Mgr*
John Brueckl, *Administration*
EMP: 57 **EST:** 1951
SQ FT: 40,000
SALES: 25.7MM
SALES (corp-wide): 1.9B **Publicly Held**
WEB: www.ardeinc.com
SIC: 3443 Tanks, standard or custom fabricated: metal plate
HQ: Inc Aerojet Rocketdyne Of De
8900 De Soto Ave
Canoga Park CA 91304
818 586-1000

(G-1126)
ARDE INC
875 Washington Ave (07072-3001)
PHONE...................................201 784-9880
EMP: 60
SALES (corp-wide): 1.9B **Publicly Held**
SIC: 3369 Machinery castings, nonferrous: ex. alum., copper, die, etc.
HQ: Arde Inc.
875 Washington Ave
Carlstadt NJ 07072
201 784-9880

(G-1127)
ATLANTIC COOLG TECH & SVCS LLC
Also Called: Atlantank
80 Kero Rd (07072-2604)
PHONE...................................201 939-0900
Kenny Wood, *Opers Mgr*
Jacob Wood, *Purch Mgr*
Steve Cilento, *Engineer*
Mark S Alberti, *Mng Member*
Katherine Cabrera, *Technology*
▲ **EMP:** 30
SQ FT: 16,000
SALES: 5.8MM **Privately Held**
WEB: www.atlanticcooling.com
SIC: 2499 Cooling towers, wood or wood & sheet metal combination

(G-1128)
BETA INDUSTRIES CORP
Also Called: Beta Tech
707 Commercial Ave (07072-2602)
PHONE...................................201 939-2400
Arnold Serchuk, *President*
Stuart Serchuck, *VP Sls/Mktg*
Sandra Titsch, *Controller*
Sandy Tish, *Manager*
Stuart Serchuk, *Director*
EMP: 9
SQ FT: 40,000
SALES: 2MM **Privately Held**
SIC: 3861 3826 3442 Photographic equipment & supplies; analytical instruments; metal doors, sash & trim

(G-1129)
BETA PLASTICS
120 Amor Ave (07072-2103)
P.O. Box 808, Lyndhurst (07071-0808)
PHONE...................................201 933-1400
Alfred Teo, *President*
Stanley Band, *Vice Pres*
Brian Stevenson, *Manager*
Annie Teo, *Admin Sec*
EMP: 200
SQ FT: 110,000

SALES (est): 31.1MM **Privately Held**
WEB: www.betaplastics.com
SIC: 2673 Plastic bags: made from purchased materials
PA: Alpha Industries Management, Inc.
800 Page Ave
Lyndhurst NJ 07071

(G-1130)
BM USA INCORPORATED (HQ)
Also Called: Madison Shoe Company
75 Triangle Blvd (07072-2702)
PHONE...................................800 624-5499
James Mullaney, *President*
Mark Koonin, *Admin Sec*
Randy Routh, *Admin Sec*
▲ **EMP:** 23
SALES: 35MM
SALES (corp-wide): 193.4K **Privately Held**
SIC: 3143 Men's footwear, except athletic

(G-1131)
BRAVO PRINT & MAIL INC
491a Washington Ave (07072-2813)
PHONE...................................201 806-3750
Patrick Conway, *CEO*
Jim Petrillo, *President*
Timothy Donovan, *Principal*
James Petrillo, *Principal*
EMP: 8
SQ FT: 7,500
SALES (est): 1.3MM **Privately Held**
SIC: 2752 Commercial printing, offset

(G-1132)
BROOKAIRE COMPANY LLC
329 Veterans Blvd (07072-2708)
PHONE...................................973 473-7527
John Mornan,
EMP: 14
SQ FT: 15,750
SALES: 4MM **Privately Held**
SIC: 3564 Filters, air: furnaces, air conditioning equipment, etc.

(G-1133)
BURGER MAKER INC (PA)
Also Called: Schweid & Sons
666 16th St (07072-1922)
PHONE...................................201 939-4747
David Schweid, *President*
Jamie Schweid, *Vice Pres*
Donovan Ford, *Opers Staff*
Porsche Henry, *QC Mgr*
Karen Tiseo, *Accountant*
▲ **EMP:** 30
SALES (est): 10.7MM **Privately Held**
SIC: 2011 Beef products from beef slaughtered on site

(G-1134)
C AND R PRINTING CORPORATION
400 Gotham Pkwy Ste 4 (07072-2401)
PHONE...................................201 528-8912
EMP: 10
SQ FT: 30,000
SALES (est): 1.3MM **Privately Held**
SIC: 7331 2759 Direct Mail Advertising Services Commercial Printing

(G-1135)
C T A MANUFACTURING CORP
263 Veterans Blvd (07072-2708)
PHONE...................................201 896-1000
Jack Dreyfus, *Ch of Bd*
Michael Borghard, *President*
Fernande Dreyfus, *Corp Secy*
Donna Reiff, *Director*
▲ **EMP:** 25 **EST:** 1978
SQ FT: 15,000
SALES (est): 15MM **Privately Held**
WEB: www.ctatools.com
SIC: 3714 3423 Motor vehicle parts & accessories; mechanics' hand tools
PA: Dreyco Inc
263 Veterans Blvd
Carlstadt NJ 07072
201 896-9000

(G-1136)
CARNEGIE DELI PRODUCTS INC
605 Washington Ave (07072-2901)
PHONE...................................201 507-5557
Sarri Harper, *Mktg Dir*

Richard O'Donell, *Director*
EMP: 70
SQ FT: 25,000
SALES (est): 9.6MM
SALES (corp-wide): 5.8MM **Privately Held**
WEB: www.carnegiedeli.com
SIC: 2011 2051 Meat packing plants; bread, cake & related products
PA: Carnegie Successors Inc
854 7th Ave Frnt
New York NY 10019
212 757-2245

(G-1137)
CAUDALIE USA INC
30 Commerce Rd (07072-2503)
PHONE...................................201 939-4969
Mathilde Thomas, *Principal*
EMP: 5 **EST:** 2012
SALES (est): 403.5K **Privately Held**
SIC: 2449 Shipping cases, wood: wirebound

(G-1138)
CIC LETTER SERVICE INC
111 Commerce Rd (07072-2510)
PHONE...................................201 896-1900
Donald Gundry, *President*
Michael Mackey, *Vice Pres*
Kevin Mackey, *CFO*
Raymond Janicki, *Admin Sec*
EMP: 60
SALES (est): 2.9MM **Privately Held**
SIC: 7331 2752 Mailing service; commercial printing, lithographic

(G-1139)
CIRCLE VISUAL INC
Also Called: Circle Fabrics
340 13th St (07072-1918)
PHONE...................................212 719-5153
Oscar Balloveras, *President*
◆ **EMP:** 20 **EST:** 1958
SQ FT: 5,000
SALES (est): 5.8MM **Privately Held**
SIC: 5131 5023 2396 Piece goods & other fabrics; linens, table; decorative home furnishings & supplies; ribbons & bows, cut & sewed

(G-1140)
CITROIL ENTERPRISES INC
Also Called: Citroil Aromatic
444 Washington Ave (07072-2806)
PHONE...................................201 933-8405
Vivian R Glueck, *President*
Henry Rosenberg, *Exec VP*
Andy Blum, *Vice Pres*
Brian Coady, *Vice Pres*
Reid Rhodes, *CFO*
◆ **EMP:** 10 **EST:** 1963
SQ FT: 22,000
SALES (est): 1.5MM **Privately Held**
WEB: www.citroil.com
SIC: 2087 Concentrates, drink

(G-1141)
CITROMAX FLAVORS INC
444 Washington Ave (07072-2806)
PHONE...................................201 933-8405
Vivian Glueck, *President*
Murilo Basso, *General Mgr*
Lucas Fornaciari, *General Mgr*
Jacob Glueck, *Principal*
◆ **EMP:** 9
SALES (est): 1MM **Privately Held**
SIC: 2087 Beverage bases, concentrates, syrups, powders & mixes

(G-1142)
CITROMAX USA INC
444 Washington Ave (07072-2806)
PHONE...................................201 933-8405
Vivian Glueck, *President*
Michele Distefano, *Purch Mgr*
Steve Swaby, *Manager*
EMP: 30 **EST:** 2012
SALES (est): 639.5K **Privately Held**
SIC: 2087 Flavoring extracts & syrups

(G-1143)
CITY THEATRICAL INC (PA)
475 Barell Ave (07072-2809)
PHONE...................................201 549-1160
Gary Fails, *CEO*

Andras Joo, *Project Mgr*
Domenic Fulvio, *Mfg Staff*
Matteo Vigni, *Engineer*
Alex Garcia, *Human Resources*
▲ **EMP:** 35
SQ FT: 40,000
SALES (est): 13.8MM **Privately Held**
WEB: www.citytheatrical.com
SIC: 5719 3648 Lighting fixtures; lighting
equipment

(G-1144)
CMYK PRINTING INC
651 Garden St (07072-1609)
PHONE..................................201 458-1300
Charles Ambrogio, *CEO*
Robert Ryan, *President*
EMP: 10
SQ FT: 10,000
SALES: 2.5MM **Privately Held**
SIC: 2752 Commercial printing, offset

(G-1145)
COORDINATED METALS INC
626 16th St (07072-1929)
PHONE..................................201 460-7280
Frank Grippi, *Ch of Bd*
Paul Santo, *Vice Pres*
John Darby, *Project Mgr*
William Delvalle, *Project Mgr*
Eric Luz, *Project Mgr*
▲ **EMP:** 67
SQ FT: 35,754
SALES: 20.8MM **Privately Held**
WEB: www.cmi-metals.com
SIC: 1799 3441 Ornamental metal work;
building components, structural steel

(G-1146)
COSMETIC COATINGS INC
219 Broad St (07072-1903)
P.O. Box 95 (07072-0095)
PHONE..................................201 438-7150
Richard Gottesman, *President*
Robert Fishman, *Admin Sec*
EMP: 20
SALES (est): 3.9MM **Privately Held**
SIC: 2844 Cosmetic preparations

(G-1147)
CREATIVE LAMINATING INC
179 Commerce Rd (07072-2501)
PHONE..................................201 939-1999
Chris Wise, *President*
▲ **EMP:** 20 **EST:** 1978
SQ FT: 35,000
SALES (est): 2.7MM **Privately Held**
SIC: 7389 3554 Laminating service; docu-
ment embossing; die cutting & stamping
machinery, paper converting

(G-1148)
CRYSTAL WORLD INC
283 Veterans Blvd (07072-2708)
PHONE..................................201 488-0909
Ryuju Nakai, *President*
Kikuko Klawitter, *Corp Secy*
▲ **EMP:** 25
SQ FT: 14,600
SALES (est): 2.6MM
SALES (corp-wide): 598.4MM **Privately
Held**
WEB: www.crystalworld.com
SIC: 3229 Glass furnishings & accessories
HQ: True World Holdings Llc
24 Link Dr Unit D
Rockleigh NJ 07647
201 750-0024

(G-1149)
DELTA PROCUREMENT INC
Also Called: US Gov Turamco
400 Gotham Pkwy (07072-2400)
PHONE..................................201 623-9353
Mustafa Avci, *President*
◆ **EMP:** 5
SQ FT: 65,000
SALES: 2.5MM **Privately Held**
SIC: 5932 2899 3429 Building materials,
secondhand; chemical preparations; ma-
rine hardware

(G-1150)
DESIGN DISPLAY GROUP INC (PA)
105 Amor Ave (07072-2102)
PHONE..................................201 438-6000
Andrew Freedman, *President*
Bart Manion, *General Mgr*
Carmine D'Agosto, *Exec VP*
Jonathon Loew, *Exec VP*
Joel Cuevas, *Project Mgr*
▲ **EMP:** 113
SQ FT: 125,000
SALES (est): 18.9MM **Privately Held**
WEB: www.designdisplaygroup.com
SIC: 3089 3993 2541 Injection molded
finished plastic products; injection mold-
ing of plastics; displays & cutouts, window
& lobby; display fixtures, wood

(G-1151)
DESIGNER SIGN SYSTEMS LLC
Also Called: Barbieri, Anthony J
50 Broad St (07072-2006)
PHONE..................................212 939-5577
Judith Barbieri, *President*
Anthony Barbieri, *Vice Pres*
Monica Rincon, *Project Mgr*
Kathy Rodriguez, *Project Mgr*
Rick Tarrant, *Project Mgr*
EMP: 12
SQ FT: 10,000
SALES (est): 2.2MM **Privately Held**
SIC: 3993 Signs, not made in custom sign
painting shops

(G-1152)
DOHRMAN PRINTING CO INC
445 Industrial Rd (07072-1615)
PHONE..................................201 933-0346
Ken Bell, *President*
Lisa Bell, *Vice Pres*
EMP: 7
SALES (est): 621.3K **Privately Held**
WEB: www.dohrmanprinting.com
SIC: 2752 Commercial printing, offset

(G-1153)
DOOR STOP LLC
Also Called: Doorstop
109 Kero Rd (07072-2601)
PHONE..................................718 599-5112
Mike Keller, *Mng Member*
Michael Sklar,
EMP: 10
SALES (est): 1MM **Privately Held**
SIC: 2431 5046 Doors, wood; partitions

(G-1154)
DREYCO INC (PA)
263 Veterans Blvd (07072-2708)
PHONE..................................201 896-9000
Jack Dreyfus, *Ch of Bd*
Michael Borghard, *Exec VP*
Karen Dreyfus Borghard, *Vice Pres*
▼ **EMP:** 10 **EST:** 1950
SQ FT: 10,000
SALES (est): 15MM **Privately Held**
WEB: www.dreycoinc.com
SIC: 5013 5072 5085 3423 Automotive
supplies & parts; hand tools; industrial
supplies; hand & edge tools

(G-1155)
ECCE PANIS INC
447 Gotham Pkwy (07072-2409)
PHONE..................................877 706-0510
EMP: 4
SALES (est): 150K **Privately Held**
SIC: 2051 Mfg Bread/Related Products

(G-1156)
FERRUM INDUSTRIES INC
735 Commercial Ave (07072-2602)
PHONE..................................201 935-1220
Lawrence Wolfin, *President*
Richard Wolfin, *Vice Pres*
EMP: 15
SQ FT: 8,500
SALES (est): 1MM **Privately Held**
SIC: 3451 Screw machine products

(G-1157)
FLAVORS OF ORIGIN INC
Also Called: Flavor Materials International
700 Gotham Pkwy (07072-2402)
PHONE..................................201 460-8306
Ian Gorinsten, *Branch Mgr*
EMP: 4
SALES (est): 215.9K
SALES (corp-wide): 16.9MM **Privately
Held**
WEB: www.flavormaterials.com
SIC: 2087 Extracts, flavoring
PA: Flavors Of Origin Inc.
10 Engelhard Ave
Avenel NJ 07001
732 499-9700

(G-1158)
FLEX PRODUCTS LLC
640 Dell Rd Ste 1 (07072-2202)
PHONE..................................201 440-1570
Bradford Philip,
Ed Friedhoff,
EMP: 75
SQ FT: 65,000
SALES (est): 10.6MM
SALES (corp-wide): 111MM **Privately
Held**
WEB: www.flex-products.com
SIC: 3083 3089 Laminated plastics plate
& sheet; plastic containers, except foam;
plastic hardware & building products
PA: Sinclair & Rush, Inc.
111 Manufacturers Dr
Arnold MO 63010
636 282-6800

(G-1159)
GLOBE PACKAGING CO INC
Also Called: Globe Casing Co
368 Paterson Plank Rd (07072-2306)
PHONE..................................201 896-1144
Isreal Bank, *President*
David Knoebel, *Vice Pres*
Adam Stein, *Marketing Staff*
Batia Bank, *Admin Sec*
◆ **EMP:** 9
SQ FT: 4,000
SALES (est): 1.8MM **Privately Held**
WEB: www.globecasing.com
SIC: 3089 Food casings, plastic

(G-1160)
GRAND LIFE INC
40 Broad St (07072-2006)
PHONE..................................201 556-8975
Suk Kan OH, *CEO*
Steve Yi, *Exec VP*
Jason Pak, *CFO*
EMP: 9 **EST:** 2015
SQ FT: 4,000
SALES: 14MM **Privately Held**
SIC: 2515 Mattresses & bedsprings

(G-1161)
GROBET FILE COMPANY AMER LLC (PA)
Also Called: Grobet USA
750 Washington Ave (07072-3088)
PHONE..................................201 939-6700
Randy Diamond, *Warehouse Mgr*
Tami McCrickard, *Purch Mgr*
Aslam Abbsi, *Buyer*
Lori Fischer, *CFO*
Laurie Fisher, *CFO*
EMP: 55
SALES (est): 10.6MM **Privately Held**
SIC: 3423 3545 3519 Cutting dies, except
metal cutting; cutting tools for machine
tools; parts & accessories, internal com-
bustion engines

(G-1162)
H & H GRAPHIC PRINTING INC
400 Gotham Pkwy Ste 1 (07072-2401)
PHONE..................................201 369-9700
Steven Braunstein, *Owner*
EMP: 4
SALES (est): 344.5K **Privately Held**
SIC: 2759 Commercial printing

(G-1163)
HACKENSACK STEEL CORP
645 Industrial Rd (07072-1611)
PHONE..................................201 935-0090
Anthony Fasciano, *President*

EMP: 20 **EST:** 1963
SQ FT: 8,000
SALES (est): 8.9MM **Privately Held**
SIC: 3441 Fabricated structural metal

(G-1164)
HARTIN PAINT & FILLER CORP
219 Broad St (07072-1903)
P.O. Box 116 (07072-0116)
PHONE..................................201 438-3300
Richard Gottesman, *President*
Robert Fishman, *Vice Pres*
EMP: 25 **EST:** 1940
SQ FT: 25,000
SALES (est): 4.3MM **Privately Held**
SIC: 2851 Lacquers, varnishes, enamels &
other coatings

(G-1165)
HEINZELMAN HEAT TREATING LLC
790 Washington Ave (07072-3008)
PHONE..................................201 933-4800
Nick Bugliarello-Wondrich, *Principal*
Nick Bugliarello - Wondrich,
EMP: 25 **EST:** 1915
SQ FT: 30,000
SALES (est): 2.1MM **Privately Held**
SIC: 3398 Metal heat treating

(G-1166)
HOUGHTON CHEMICAL CORPORATION
30 Amor Ave (07072-2103)
PHONE..................................201 460-8071
Chuck McCarte, *Plant Mgr*
Stephen Olson, *Traffic Mgr*
Walter Engel, *Branch Mgr*
EMP: 16
SQ FT: 60,635
SALES (corp-wide): 14.9MM **Privately
Held**
WEB: www.houghton.com
SIC: 5169 2899 2842 Organic chemicals,
synthetic; chemical preparations; an-
tifreeze compounds; specialty cleaning,
polishes & sanitation goods
PA: Houghton Chemical Corporation
52 Cambridge St
Allston MA 02134
617 254-1010

(G-1167)
IMPACT DISPLAYS INC
310 13th St (07072-1918)
PHONE..................................201 804-6262
Gill Horowitz, *Co-President*
Brian Mullins, *Co-President*
Nick Smith, *Project Mgr*
Jon Martins, *Prdtn Mgr*
Jared Hershkin, *Sales Staff*
◆ **EMP:** 32
SQ FT: 11,000
SALES (est): 5.1MM **Privately Held**
SIC: 3993 Signs & advertising specialties

(G-1168)
INNERSPACE TECHNOLOGY INC
728 Garden St (07072-1625)
PHONE..................................201 933-1600
James E Blockburger, *President*
Harold K Fletcher, *President*
EMP: 5
SQ FT: 20,000
SALES: 1MM
SALES (corp-wide): 12.1MM **Publicly
Held**
WEB: www.innerspacetechnology.com
SIC: 3812 7371 3829 Sonar systems &
equipment; computer software develop-
ment; measuring & controlling devices
PA: Tel-Instrument Electronics Corp.
1 Branca Rd
East Rutherford NJ 07073
201 933-1600

(G-1169)
ISOCOLOR INC
631 Central Ave (07072-1538)
PHONE..................................201 935-4494
Henri V Debar, *President*
Christian Voignier, *Vice Pres*
EMP: 6
SQ FT: 150

SALES (est): 520K Privately Held
WEB: www.isocolor.com
SIC: 3826 Analytical instruments

(G-1170)
JINPAN INTERNATIONAL USA LTD
Also Called: Jing
390 Veterans Blvd (07072-2704)
PHONE......................201 460-8778
▲ EMP: 5
SALES (est): 1.1MM Privately Held
SIC: 3677 Mfg Electronic Coils/Transformers

(G-1171)
JST POWER EQUIPMENT INC
390 Veterans Blvd (07072-2704)
PHONE......................201 460-8778
LI Zhiyuan, Ch of Bd
Ling Xiangsheng, Vice Ch Bd
Mark Du, CFO
Jing Yuqing, Admin Sec
▲ EMP: 4
SQ FT: 130
SALES (est): 58.5K Privately Held
WEB: www.jstusa.net
SIC: 3677 Coil windings, electronic

(G-1172)
KANAR INC
1 Kero Rd (07072-2604)
PHONE......................201 933-2800
Mehmet Kanar, Managing Prtnr
EMP: 10
SALES: 430.5K Privately Held
SIC: 5122 3999 Cosmetics, perfumes &
hair products; barber & beauty shop
equipment

(G-1173)
KATZS DELICATESSEN MFG
100 Industrial Rd (07072-1614)
PHONE......................212 254-2246
Peter Carter,
Jake Dell,
James Jorgeson,
EMP: 20
SQ FT: 30,000
SALES (est): 725.5K Privately Held
SIC: 2011 Meat packing plants

(G-1174)
KEURIG DR PEPPER INC
600 Commercial Ave (07072-2607)
PHONE......................201 933-0070
Dan Denisoff, Manager
EMP: 100 Publicly Held
WEB: www.yoo-hoo.com
SIC: 2086 Soft drinks: packaged in cans,
bottles, etc.
PA: Keurig Dr Pepper Inc.
53 South Ave
Burlington MA 01803

(G-1175)
KISSLER & CO INC
770 Central Blvd (07072-3009)
PHONE......................201 896-9600
Jerry Kissler, President
Barry Kissler, Vice Pres
Jeff Stokem, Warehouse Mgr
Doug Tanner, Purch Mgr
Sean Kaplan, Natl Sales Mgr
◆ EMP: 20
SALES (est): 4.6MM Privately Held
WEB: www.kissler.com
SIC: 7629 5084 3432 Tool repair, electric;
industrial machinery & equipment; plumbing fixture fittings & trim

(G-1176)
KNICKERBOCKER BED COMPANY
770 Commercial Ave (07072-2602)
P.O. Box 55, Little Ferry (07643-0055)
PHONE......................201 933-3100
Milton Polevey, President
▼ EMP: 20
SALES (est): 3.2MM Privately Held
WEB: www.bedbridge.com
SIC: 2514 Frames for box springs or bedsprings: metal

(G-1177)
KOHL & MADDEN PRTG INK CORP (DH)
651 Garden St (07072-1609)
PHONE......................201 935-8666
Brad Bergey, President
Eugene Standora, Treasurer
EMP: 22 EST: 1905
SQ FT: 7,500
SALES (est): 24.9MM Privately Held
SIC: 2893 3565 3555 Printing ink; packaging machinery; printing trades machinery
HQ: Sun Chemical Corporation
35 Waterview Blvd Ste 100
Parsippany NJ 07054
973 404-6000

(G-1178)
KP EXCAVATION LLC
570 Commerce Blvd Unit B (07072-3013)
PHONE......................201 933-4200
Kimberly Pembroke, President
EMP: 30
SALES (est): 1MM Privately Held
SIC: 1081 Metal mining services

(G-1179)
KROHN TECHNICAL PRODUCTS INC
Also Called: Krohn Industries
303 Veterans Blvd (07072-2708)
P.O. Box 98 (07072-0098)
PHONE......................201 933-9696
John Krohn, President
EMP: 18
SALES (est): 1.8MM
SALES (corp-wide): 4.1MM Privately Held
WEB: www.krohnindustries.com
SIC: 2899 3999 Plating compounds; barber & beauty shop equipment
PA: Krohn Industries Incorporated
303 Veterans Blvd
Carlstadt NJ
201 933-9696

(G-1180)
LACKA SAFE CORP
400 Meadow Ln (07072-3006)
PHONE......................201 896-9200
Faruk Lacka, President
Frank Lacka, Vice Pres
Jaime Torrejon, Marketing Staff
Pranvera Lacka, Manager
EMP: 10
SALES (est): 1.5MM Privately Held
SIC: 5999 3499 Safety supplies & equipment; locks, safe & vault: metal

(G-1181)
LATTA GRAPHICS INC
Also Called: Yes Press
651 Garden St (07072-1609)
P.O. Box 31, Little Ferry (07643-0031)
PHONE......................201 440-4040
Eileen Latta, President
Mark Ehrmann, Manager
EMP: 30
SQ FT: 12,000
SALES (est): 6.2MM Privately Held
WEB: www.yespress.com
SIC: 2789 2759 2752 Bookbinding & related work; commercial printing; commercial printing, offset

(G-1182)
LODOR OFFSET CORPORATION
Also Called: Victoria Offset
111 Amor Ave (07072-2102)
PHONE......................201 935-7100
Donald Samuels, President
Gary Samuels, Principal
Lester Samuels, Vice Pres
EMP: 10
SALES (est): 1.4MM Privately Held
SIC: 2621 2893 2952 2899 Printing
paper; printing ink; asphalt felts & coatings; chemical preparations

(G-1183)
LV ADHESIVE INC
341 Michele Pl (07072-2304)
PHONE......................201 507-0080
Linda Owen, President

Steve Owen, Vice Pres
EMP: 50 EST: 1977
SQ FT: 22,000
SALES (est): 9.9MM Privately Held
WEB: www.lvadhesive.com
SIC: 2672 2671 Adhesive papers, labels
or tapes: from purchased material; plastic
film, coated or laminated for packaging

(G-1184)
MANHATTAN DOOR CORP
109 Kero Rd (07072-2601)
PHONE......................718 963-1111
Martin Sklar, Ch of Bd
Friment Sklar, Vice Pres
Vadim Shelomyanov, Info Tech Dir
EMP: 80 EST: 1962
SQ FT: 33,000
SALES (est): 14.3MM Privately Held
SIC: 2431 Doors, wood

(G-1185)
MAR-KAL PRODUCTS CORP
145 Commerce Rd (07072-2501)
PHONE......................973 783-7155
Hans F Schmid, President
Nancy Schmid, Treasurer
EMP: 45 EST: 1963
SQ FT: 30,000
SALES (est): 2.2MM Privately Held
WEB: www.markalproducts.com
SIC: 3999 2396 Decalcomania work, except on china & glass; automotive & apparel trimmings

(G-1186)
MASTER PRINTING INC
445 Industrial Rd (07072-1615)
PHONE......................201 842-9100
John Aresta, President
Ralph Castellano, Prdtn Mgr
Joseph Aresta Jr, Admin Sec
EMP: 20
SQ FT: 25,000
SALES (est): 3.4MM Privately Held
WEB: www.masterprintinginc.com
SIC: 2752 Commercial printing, offset

(G-1187)
METRO SELIGER INDUSTRIES INC
330 Washington Ave (07072-2806)
PHONE......................201 438-4530
Anthony Aveni, President
Richard Skolnik, Sales Staff
EMP: 160
SQ FT: 125,000
SALES (est): 6.7MM Privately Held
SIC: 7331 7374 2752 Direct mail advertising services; calculating service (computer); commercial printing, lithographic;
promotional printing, lithographic

(G-1188)
MODERN SHOWCASE INC
610 Commercial Ave (07072-2602)
PHONE......................201 935-2929
John Kang, President
▲ EMP: 10
SALES (est): 1.3MM Privately Held
WEB: www.modernshowcase.com
SIC: 2542 Office & store showcases & display fixtures

(G-1189)
NATALE MACHINE & TOOL CO INC
Also Called: Circle D Light
339 13th St (07072-1917)
PHONE......................201 933-5500
Dominick Natale, President
Karen Natale Conway, Vice Pres
Lynn Natale, Treasurer
▲ EMP: 11 EST: 1947
SQ FT: 15,000
SALES (est): 1.8MM Privately Held
WEB: www.circle-d.com
SIC: 3648 Floodlights

(G-1190)
NES ENTERPRISES INC
513 Washington Ave (07072-2802)
P.O. Box 1377, Springfield (07081-5377)
PHONE......................201 964-1400
Sheldon Salkovitch, CEO
EMP: 9

SQ FT: 6,000
SALES: 960K Privately Held
SIC: 2353 2396 Hats, caps & millinery;
screen printing on fabric articles

(G-1191)
NEW TOP INC
Also Called: Daniel & Ellissa
40 Broad St (07072-2006)
PHONE......................201 438-3990
Bam Le Cho, President
◆ EMP: 40
SQ FT: 50,000
SALES (est): 4.4MM Privately Held
SIC: 2321 5136 Men's & boys' furnishings;
men's & boys' clothing

(G-1192)
NORTHERN ARCHITECTURAL SYSTEMS
599 Gotham Pkwy (07072-2403)
PHONE......................201 943-6400
Robert Pecorella, President
EMP: 27
SALES (corp-wide): 24.7MM Privately Held
SIC: 3442 Metal doors, sash & trim
PA: Northern Architectural Systems, Inc.
111 Central Ave
Teterboro NJ 07608
201 943-6400

(G-1193)
OUTPUT SERVICES GROUP INC
Also Called: OSG Billing Services
775 Washington Ave (07072-3002)
PHONE......................201 871-1100
Albert Abbatiello, Manager
EMP: 9
SALES (corp-wide): 48.5MM Privately Held
SIC: 2759 Commercial printing
HQ: Output Services Group, Inc.
100 Challenger Rd Ste 303
Ridgefield Park NJ 07660

(G-1194)
OXBERRY LLC
427 9th St (07072-1212)
PHONE......................201 935-3000
Alfred I Thumim,
Anna Ferraro,
EMP: 8
SQ FT: 28,000
SALES (est): 974.9K Privately Held
WEB: www.oxberry.com
SIC: 3641 3577 3861 Electric lamps;
computer peripheral equipment; cameras
& related equipment

(G-1195)
PAN TECHNOLOGY INC
117 Moonachie Ave (07072-2507)
PHONE......................201 438-7878
Bob Rossomando, President
Gary Spero, Vice Pres
James Difino, Plant Mgr
Deborah Rossomando, Purch Mgr
Brian Villardi, QC Mgr
▲ EMP: 46 EST: 1949
SQ FT: 60,000
SALES: 14MM Privately Held
WEB: www.pantechnology.com
SIC: 2893 Printing ink

(G-1196)
PANTONE LLC
590 Commerce Blvd (07072-3098)
PHONE......................201 935-5500
Ondrej Kruk, President
William D Apostol, Vice Pres
Billy Chien, Vice Pres
Lisa Herbert, Vice Pres
Terence Lam, Vice Pres
▲ EMP: 140 EST: 1977
SQ FT: 80,000
SALES (est): 25.3MM
SALES (corp-wide): 19.8B Publicly Held
WEB: www.Pantone.com
SIC: 2754 Commercial printing, gravure
HQ: X-Rite, Incorporated
4300 44th St Se
Grand Rapids MI 49512
616 803-2100

56   2019 Harris New Jersey
Manufacturers Directory   ▲ = Import ▼=Export
◆ =Import/Export

(G-1197)
PARAGON IRON INC
550 Industrial Rd Ste 3 (07072-1630)
PHONE...........................201 528-7307
John Danubio, *President*
Antoinette Naggio, *Office Mgr*
EMP: 16
SQ FT: 5,520
SALES (est): 837.1K **Privately Held**
SIC: 3449 Bars, concrete reinforcing: fabricated steel

(G-1198)
PEEQ IMAGING
480 Gotham Pkwy (07072-2410)
PHONE...........................212 490-3850
Michael Laraia, *Vice Pres*
EMP: 75 EST: 2017
SALES (est): 7.1MM **Privately Held**
SIC: 2752 Promotional printing, lithographic

(G-1199)
PERTECH PRINTING INKS INC
Also Called: Pertech Corp K & E Printing
140 Grand St (07072-2105)
PHONE...........................908 354-1700
Roger Tusche, *President*
Peter Reissig, *Vice Pres*
▲ EMP: 31
SQ FT: 18,000
SALES (est): 5.2MM **Privately Held**
WEB: www.pertechinks.com
SIC: 3952 Ink, drawing: black & colored

(G-1200)
PETERSON STEEL RULE DIE CORP
35 Broad St (07072-2006)
PHONE...........................201 935-6180
Leonard Esposito, *President*
Neal Esposito, *Vice Pres*
Susan Esposito Jacob, *Admin Sec*
EMP: 13 EST: 1963
SQ FT: 13,000
SALES (est): 2.1MM **Privately Held**
SIC: 3544 Special dies & tools

(G-1201)
PHILIP HOLZER AND ASSOC LLC
350 Michele Pl (07072-2304)
PHONE...........................212 691-9500
Stuart Holzer, *Mng Member*
Eric Bernstein,
David Nicholas,
James Nicholas,
Gerry Ritterman,
EMP: 40
SALES (est): 3.6MM **Privately Held**
WEB: www.tanaseybert.com
SIC: 2752 2791 2789 Commercial printing, lithographic; typesetting; bookbinding & related work

(G-1202)
PLASTIC REEL CORP OF AMERICA (PA)
Also Called: PRC of America
40 Triangle Blvd (07072-2701)
PHONE...........................201 933-5100
Ben Zuk, *President*
Pat Baccarella, *Vice Pres*
Robert Basili, *Vice Pres*
John Durkin, *Vice Pres*
▲ EMP: 20
SALES (est): 2.6MM **Privately Held**
WEB: www.prcofamerica.com
SIC: 3089 5043 3572 Plastic containers, except foam; cases, plastic; injection molding of plastics; motion picture cameras, equipment & supplies; computer storage devices

(G-1203)
POLYAIR INTER PACK INC
Polyair Packaging Division
495 Meadow Ln (07072-3006)
PHONE...........................201 804-1725
Joseph Hickey, *Plant Mgr*
Chris Franch, *Branch Mgr*
Lisa Seeley, *Admin Asst*
EMP: 72

SALES (corp-wide): 1B **Privately Held**
WEB: www.polyair.com
SIC: 5199 2671 Packaging materials; packaging paper & plastics film, coated & laminated
HQ: Polyair Canada Limited
330 Humberline Dr
Etobicoke ON M9W 1
416 679-6600

(G-1204)
POLYAIR INTER PACK INC
495 Meadow Ln (07072-3006)
PHONE...........................201 804-1700
EMP: 100
SALES (est): 8.9MM **Privately Held**
SIC: 2394 Liners & covers, fabric: made from purchased materials

(G-1205)
POTTERS INDUSTRIES LLC
600 Industrial Rd (07072-1619)
PHONE...........................201 507-4169
Timothy Scribner, *Engineer*
Andy Gray, *Branch Mgr*
Deniece N Dyall, *Technology*
EMP: 28
SALES (corp-wide): 1.6B **Publicly Held**
WEB: www.flexolite.com
SIC: 3231 Reflector glass beads, for highway signs or reflectors
HQ: Potters Industries, Llc
300 Lindenwood Dr
Malvern PA 19355
610 651-4700

(G-1206)
PRECISION METAL MACHINING INC
Also Called: P M M I
800 Central Blvd Ste C (07072-3016)
PHONE...........................201 843-7427
Pat Funicelli, *President*
Ann Funicelli, *Treasurer*
EMP: 28 EST: 1959
SQ FT: 35,000
SALES (est): 5.8MM **Privately Held**
WEB: www.gopmmi.com
SIC: 3599 Machine shop, jobbing & repair

(G-1207)
PREMIUM COLOR GROUP LLC
Also Called: Premium Clor Graphics Handpack
651 Garden St (07072-1609)
PHONE...........................973 472-7007
Frank Malanga, *Plant Mgr*
Debbie Feliciano, *Production*
Greg Zoccoli, *Sales Staff*
Andy Griffin,
Mark Fitzgerald,
EMP: 40
SALES (est): 7MM **Privately Held**
SIC: 2759 Commercial printing

(G-1208)
PRINT PEEL
341 Michele Pl (07072-2304)
PHONE...........................201 507-0080
Steve Owen, *Vice Pres*
EMP: 50
SALES (est): 2.3MM **Privately Held**
SIC: 2752 Commercial printing, lithographic

(G-1209)
PROSPECT TRANSPORTATION INC (PA)
630 Industrial Rd (07072-1619)
PHONE...........................201 933-9999
Melissa Eichholz, *President*
Izabela Flot, *Principal*
Charles W Eichholz, *COO*
Jackie Cotton, *VP Sales*
Jack McNamara, *VP Mktg*
EMP: 100 EST: 1986
SQ FT: 26,000
SALES (est): 21.1MM **Privately Held**
WEB: www.prospect-trans.com
SIC: 4212 2869 3443 Petroleum haulage, local; fuels; fuel tanks (oil, gas, etc.): metal plate

(G-1210)
REGGIANI LIGHTING USA INC
372 Starke Rd (07072-2108)
PHONE...........................201 372-1717
John Savoretti, *President*
Matteo Reggiani, *Vice Pres*
Kathyrn Reid, *Sales Staff*
Andrew Scamporino, *Mktg Dir*
Marie Imperiale, *Clerk*
▲ EMP: 10
SQ FT: 25,000
SALES (est): 2.4MM
SALES (corp-wide): 22.9K **Privately Held**
SIC: 3646 5063 Commercial indusl & institutional electric lighting fixtures; lighting fixtures, commercial & industrial
HQ: Reggiani Spa Illuminazione
Viale Monza 16
Sovico MB 20845
039 207-11

(G-1211)
SAFIRE SILK INC
Also Called: Silver Silk
135 Grand St (07072-2106)
PHONE...........................201 636-4061
Paul Kim, *Ch of Bd*
▲ EMP: 7
SQ FT: 4,000
SALES (est): 1.1MM **Privately Held**
SIC: 2329 Men's & boys' sportswear & athletic clothing

(G-1212)
SAPUTO CHEESE USA INC
Advantage International Foods
861 Washington Ave (07072-3001)
PHONE...........................201 508-6400
David Rowan, *Branch Mgr*
EMP: 50
SALES (corp-wide): 3.7B **Privately Held**
SIC: 2022 Cheese spreads, dips, pastes & other cheese products
HQ: Saputo Cheese Usa Inc.
1 Overlook Pt Ste 300
Lincolnshire IL 60069

(G-1213)
SAWITZ STUDIOS INC
Also Called: Sawitz Store Fixture
130 Grand St (07072-2105)
PHONE...........................201 842-9444
Dan Sawitz, *President*
June Sawitz, *Corp Secy*
EMP: 32
SQ FT: 38,000
SALES (est): 5.4MM **Privately Held**
WEB: www.sawitzstorefixture.com
SIC: 2541 2511 Store fixtures, wood; wood household furniture

(G-1214)
SCREEN REPRODUCTIONS CO INC
Also Called: Photo Screen of N J
850 Washington Ave (07072-3014)
PHONE...........................201 935-0830
Larry Weissenberg, *President*
EMP: 30 EST: 1956
SQ FT: 23,000
SALES (est): 4.3MM **Privately Held**
WEB: www.screenreproduction.com
SIC: 2621 Wallpaper (hanging paper)

(G-1215)
SECURITY HOLDINGS LLC (PA)
Also Called: Pioneer Industries
111 Kero Rd (07072-2601)
PHONE...........................201 457-0286
Mitchell Dorf, *Mng Member*
Leinis Santa Maria, *Executive Asst*
Jeffrey Haversat,
Robert Haversat,
EMP: 96
SALES (est): 17MM **Privately Held**
SIC: 3442 Metal doors

(G-1216)
SHREE JI PRINTING CORPORATION
55 Veterans Blvd (07072-2713)
PHONE...........................201 842-9500
Dilid Patel, *President*
EMP: 30
SQ FT: 22,000

(G-1217)
SINCLAIR AND RUSH INC
640 Dell Rd (07072-2202)
PHONE...........................862 262-8189
EMP: 8
SALES (est): 845K **Privately Held**
SIC: 3089 Molding primary plastic; plastic processing

(G-1218)
SNAPPLE BEVERAGE CORP
600 Commercial Ave (07072-2607)
PHONE...........................201 933-0070
Bill Pedoto, *Plant Mgr*
EMP: 75 **Publicly Held**
SIC: 2086 Bottled & canned soft drinks
HQ: Snapple Beverage Corp
900 King St
Rye Brook NY 10573

(G-1219)
SNS ORIENTAL RUGS LLC
455 Barell Ave (07072-2809)
PHONE...........................201 355-8786
Sahigh Kashi, *Mng Member*
▲ EMP: 5
SALES (est): 719.8K **Privately Held**
SIC: 5023 2273 Rugs; carpets & rugs

(G-1220)
SPECIALITY PHARMA MFG LLC
609 Industrial Rd (07072-1611)
PHONE...........................201 675-3411
James Geraghty, *Mng Member*
EMP: 5
SALES (est): 292.2K **Privately Held**
SIC: 2834 Pharmaceutical preparations

(G-1221)
STANBEE COMPANY INC (PA)
70 Broad St (07072-2006)
P.O. Box 436 (07072-0436)
PHONE...........................201 933-9666
Michael Berkson, *President*
▲ EMP: 30
SQ FT: 52,000
SALES (est): 6.6MM **Privately Held**
WEB: www.stanbee.com
SIC: 2211 Shoe fabrics

(G-1222)
SUN CHEMICAL CORPORATION
631 Central Ave (07072-1599)
PHONE...........................201 933-4500
Mason Clarke, *Opers Mgr*
Steve Pokolic, *Production*
Barry Duffy, *Technical Mgr*
Alexander Chudolij, *Research*
Maurizio Franzoso, *Engineer*
EMP: 180 **Privately Held**
WEB: www.sunchemical.com
SIC: 2893 Printing ink
HQ: Sun Chemical Corporation
35 Waterview Blvd Ste 100
Parsippany NJ 07054
973 404-6000

(G-1223)
SUN CHEMICAL CORPORATION
U S Ink
651 Garden St (07072-1609)
PHONE...........................201 935-8666
Steven Cornwell, *Plant Mgr*
Frank Costagliola, *Purch Mgr*
Ron Himawan, *Engineer*
Stephanie Porter, *Human Res Dir*
Michael Dodd, *Manager*
EMP: 13 **Privately Held**
WEB: www.sunchemical.com
SIC: 2893 Printing ink
HQ: Sun Chemical Corporation
35 Waterview Blvd Ste 100
Parsippany NJ 07054
973 404-6000

(G-1224)
SUN NOODLE NEW JERSEY LLC
40 Kero Rd (07072-2604)
PHONE...........................201 530-1100
Shawn Kim, *Manager*
Ken Uki, *Manager*

GEOGRAPHIC

▲ **EMP:** 8
SALES (est): 1.3MM **Privately Held**
SIC: 2098 Noodles (e.g. egg, plain & water), dry

(G-1225)
TABCO TECHNOLOGIES LLC (PA)
400 Gotham Pkwy (07072-2400)
PHONE..............................201 438-0422
Alp Ojalvo, *Opers Staff*
Turgay Pektas, *Mng Member*
◆ **EMP:** 6
SQ FT: 11,000
SALES: 5MM **Privately Held**
WEB: www.tabcotech.com
SIC: 5051 3714 5013 Aluminum bars, rods, ingots, sheets, pipes, plates, etc.; motor vehicle parts & accessories; automotive supplies

(G-1226)
TEC CAST INC (PA)
440 Meadow Ln (07072-3006)
P.O. Box 6596 (07072-0596)
PHONE..............................201 935-3885
Robert Morehardt, *President*
Lynn Biss, *CFO*
EMP: 44
SQ FT: 150,000
SALES: 7.5MM **Privately Held**
SIC: 3365 3544 Aerospace castings, aluminum; industrial molds

(G-1227)
TEXTOL SYSTEMS INC
735 Commercial Ave (07072-2602)
PHONE..............................201 935-1220
Lawrence Wolfin, *President*
Richard Wolfin, *Vice Pres*
▲ **EMP:** 24
SQ FT: 9,000
SALES (est): 4.5MM **Privately Held**
WEB: www.textol.com
SIC: 2241 3625 Trimmings, textile; actuators, industrial

(G-1228)
THIRD RIVER MANUFACTURING LLC
503 Washington Ave (07072-2802)
PHONE..............................201 935-2795
Ameet Shreemal,
EMP: 8
SALES (est): 1.1MM **Privately Held**
SIC: 3599 Machine shop, jobbing & repair

(G-1229)
THUMANN INCORPORATED (PA)
Also Called: Thumanns
670 Dell Rd Ste 1 (07072-2292)
PHONE..............................201 935-3636
Robert S Burke, *President*
Robert Burke Jr, *Vice Pres*
EMP: 205 **EST:** 1949
SQ FT: 130,000
SALES: 81.1MM **Privately Held**
WEB: www.thumanns.com
SIC: 2013 Sausages from purchased meat

(G-1230)
TOYO INK AMERICA LLC
350 Starke Rd Ste 400 (07072-2113)
PHONE..............................201 804-0620
EMP: 16 **Privately Held**
SIC: 2893 Printing ink
HQ: Toyo Ink America, Llc
1225 N Michael Dr
Wood Dale IL 60191
630 930-5100

(G-1231)
TRANSGLOBE USA INC
175 Broad St (07072-2002)
PHONE..............................973 465-1998
John L Zhang, *President*
▲ **EMP:** 5
SALES (est): 310K **Privately Held**
SIC: 3161 Luggage

(G-1232)
TRICO WEB LLC
75 Broad St (07072-2006)
PHONE..............................201 438-3860

Donald Juiliano, *COO*
EMP: 6 **EST:** 2010
SALES (est): 784.2K **Privately Held**
SIC: 2759 Commercial printing

(G-1233)
TUNNEL BARREL & DRUM CO INC
329 Veterans Blvd (07072-2708)
PHONE..............................201 933-1444
Anthony Urcioli, *President*
Joseph Binder, *Corp Secy*
Yolanda Urcioli, *Vice Pres*
▲ **EMP:** 27 **EST:** 1903
SQ FT: 27,500
SALES (est): 9.5MM **Privately Held**
SIC: 5085 2655 Drums, new or reconditioned; drums, fiber: made from purchased material

(G-1234)
UNIMAC GRAPHICS LLC
350 Michele Pl (07072-2304)
PHONE..............................201 372-1000
Gregory C Matonti, *President*
James Sandham, *CFO*
▲ **EMP:** 250
SALES: 62.6MM
SALES (corp-wide): 124.2MM **Privately Held**
WEB: www.unimacgraphics.com
SIC: 2759 Commercial printing
PA: Union Graphics Inc
350 Michele Pl
Carlstadt NJ 07072
201 372-1000

(G-1235)
VERNON DISPLAY GRAPHICS INC
Also Called: Seri-Arts
145 Commerce Rd (07072-2501)
PHONE..............................201 935-7117
Andrew Gabriel, *General Mgr*
Todd Smith, *Vice Pres*
EMP: 50
SALES (est): 8.3MM
SALES (corp-wide): 65MM **Privately Held**
WEB: www.vernoncompany.com
SIC: 2759 Screen printing
PA: The Vernon Company
604 W 4th St N
Newton IA 50208
641 792-9000

(G-1236)
VISION TEN INC
180 Broad St (07072-1906)
PHONE..............................201 935-3000
Dr Alfred I Thumim, *President*
Tiffany Bolen, *Vice Pres*
EMP: 10
SQ FT: 54,232
SALES (est): 840K **Privately Held**
SIC: 3844 3699 X-ray apparatus & tubes; electrical equipment & supplies

(G-1237)
WATER-JEL HOLDING COMPANY
50 Brd St (07072)
PHONE..............................201 507-8300
James Hartnett, *CEO*
Joe Dacorta, *Vice Pres*
Jim Geraghty, *Vice Pres*
Paul Slot, *Vice Pres*
John McAndris Jr, *CFO*
▲ **EMP:** 70
SALES (est): 9.2MM **Privately Held**
WEB: www.waterjel.com
SIC: 3842 First aid, snake bite & burn kits

(G-1238)
WATER-JEL TECHNOLOGIES LLC
50 Broad St (07072-2006)
PHONE..............................201 438-1598
James Hartnett, *President*
Mark Lait, *Managing Dir*
Paul Slot, *COO*
Scott Stevenson, *Buyer*
Robert Zega, *QC Mgr*
▲ **EMP:** 70
SQ FT: 145,000

SALES (est): 18.2MM **Privately Held**
SIC: 3842 First aid, snake bite & burn kits

(G-1239)
WEIR WELDING COMPANY INC (PA)
316 12th St (07072-1919)
P.O. Box 311 (07072-0311)
PHONE..............................201 939-2284
Charles J Weir, *President*
Chris Little, *VP Admin*
Thomas Weir, *Vice Pres*
Michael Diffley, *Project Mgr*
Paul Emeigh, *Project Mgr*
EMP: 25
SQ FT: 100,000
SALES (est): 16MM **Privately Held**
SIC: 3441 Fabricated structural metal

(G-1240)
WISDOM USA INC
175 Broad St (07072-2002)
PHONE..............................201 933-1998
◆ **EMP:** 10
SQ FT: 58,000
SALES (est): 2.2MM **Privately Held**
SIC: 5099 3161 Luggage; luggage

Carneys Point
Salem County

(G-1241)
BAHADIR USA LLC
431 S Pnnsville Auburn Rd (08069)
PHONE..............................856 517-3080
Ismail Kilic, *President*
EMP: 6
SQ FT: 17,000
SALES (est): 650.4K **Privately Held**
SIC: 3841 Diagnostic apparatus, medical; medical instruments & equipment, blood & bone work

(G-1242)
LASSONDE PAPPAS AND CO INC (DH)
1 Collins Dr Ste 200 (08069-3640)
PHONE..............................856 455-1000
Mark A McNeil, *CEO*
Scott Langley, *Vice Pres*
Melissa Lackey, *Project Mgr*
Sean Jackson, *Opers Mgr*
Stephanie Shafer, *Materials Mgr*
◆ **EMP:** 85
SQ FT: 600,000
SALES (est): 364.5MM
SALES (corp-wide): 402MM **Privately Held**
WEB: www.clementpappas.com
SIC: 2033 Fruit juices: packaged in cans, jars, etc.; fruits: packaged in cans, jars, etc.
HQ: Pappas Lassonde Holdings, Inc.
1 Collins Dr Ste 200
Carneys Point NJ 08069
856 455-1000

(G-1243)
PAPPAS LASSONDE HOLDINGS INC (DH)
1 Collins Dr Ste 200 (08069-3640)
PHONE..............................856 455-1000
Mark A McNeil, *CEO*
Jean Pattuso, *Chairman*
EMP: 6
SALES (est): 364.5MM
SALES (corp-wide): 402MM **Privately Held**
SIC: 2033 6719 Fruit juices: packaged in cans, jars, etc.; fruits: packaged in cans, jars, etc.; investment holding companies, except banks
HQ: Industries Lassonde Inc
755 Rue Principale
Rougemont QC J0L 1
450 469-4926

(G-1244)
TOWNSHIP OF CARNEYS POINT
Also Called: Carneys Point Fire Company Aux
Walker Ave & D St (08069)
PHONE..............................856 299-4973

Dolores Wolfer, *President*
EMP: 14 **Privately Held**
SIC: 9224 3569 ; firefighting apparatus & related equipment
PA: Township Of Carneys Point
303 Harding Hwy
Carneys Point NJ 08069
856 299-0070

Carteret
Middlesex County

(G-1245)
ANGELS BAKERY USA LLC
110 Raskulinecz Rd (07008-1000)
PHONE..............................718 389-1400
Joseph Angel, *President*
Jen McCollum Roberts, *Vice Pres*
EMP: 30
SALES (est): 6MM **Privately Held**
SIC: 2051 Bakery: wholesale or wholesale/retail combined

(G-1246)
ARCHITCTURAL METAL FABRICATORS
66 Grant Ave (07008-2720)
PHONE..............................718 765-0722
Gam Kagan, *Principal*
EMP: 4 **EST:** 2011
SALES (est): 549.8K **Privately Held**
SIC: 3446 Architectural metalwork

(G-1247)
ARCHITECTURAL METALS INC
Also Called: Architctral Metals Fabricaters
66 Grant Ave (07008-2720)
PHONE..............................718 765-0722
Gam Kagan, *President*
EMP: 7
SQ FT: 4,000
SALES (est): 1.1MM **Privately Held**
SIC: 3441 Fabricated structural metal

(G-1248)
ARDAGH GLASS INC
50 Bryla St (07008-1111)
PHONE..............................732 969-0827
Frank Conway, *Manager*
EMP: 500
SALES (corp-wide): 242.1K **Privately Held**
WEB: www.sgcontainers.com
SIC: 3221 Glass containers
HQ: Ardagh Glass Inc.
10194 Crosspoint Blvd
Indianapolis IN 46256

(G-1249)
BASF CATALYSTS LLC
700 Blair Rd (07008-1221)
PHONE..............................732 205-5000
Scott Elliott, *Opers Staff*
Larry Drummond, *Manager*
EMP: 139
SALES (corp-wide): 71.7B **Privately Held**
SIC: 2819 Industrial inorganic chemicals
HQ: Basf Catalysts Llc
33 Wood Ave S
Iselin NJ 08830
732 205-5000

(G-1250)
BERJE INCORPORATED (PA)
700 Blair Rd (07008-1221)
PHONE..............................973 748-8980
Kim Bleimann, *CEO*
Dave Herbst, *President*
Carol Dowles, *Business Mgr*
Barry Dowles, *Exec VP*
Nehla A Murad, *Senior VP*
◆ **EMP:** 100 **EST:** 1950
SQ FT: 235,000
SALES (est): 106MM **Privately Held**
WEB: www.berje.com
SIC: 5169 2869 Aromatic chemicals; perfumes, flavorings & food additives

(G-1251)
BRUKER OST LLC
600 Milik St (07008-1115)
PHONE..............................732 541-1300
Jeff Parrell, *President*

Joseph Ingato, *Controller*
EMP: 140
SALES (est): 1.4MM
SALES (corp-wide): 1.9B **Publicly Held**
SIC: 3357 Nonferrous wiredrawing & insulating
HQ: Bruker Energy & Supercon Technologies, Inc.
15 Fortune Dr
Billerica MA 01821

(G-1252)
EVERFLOW SUPPLIES INC (PA)
100 Middlesex Ave (07008-3499)
PHONE....................908 436-1100
Lazar Templer, *President*
David Templer, *Exec VP*
Mark Shaingarten, *Senior Buyer*
Abraham Sharaby, *Finance Dir*
Robert Gemal, *Regl Sales Mgr*
▲ **EMP:** 25
SALES (est): 11.3MM **Privately Held**
SIC: 5074 3494 Plumbing fittings & supplies; plumbing & heating valves

(G-1253)
FMC CORPORATION
500 Roosevelt Ave (07008-3504)
PHONE....................732 541-3000
Jerry Sibley, *Branch Mgr*
EMP: 61
SALES (corp-wide): 4.7B **Publicly Held**
SIC: 2812 Soda ash, sodium carbonate (anhydrous)
PA: Fmc Corporation
2929 Walnut St
Philadelphia PA 19104
215 299-6000

(G-1254)
FOLGORE MOBIL WELDING INC
Also Called: F M W Piping Contractors
526 Roosevelt Ave (07008-3017)
P.O. Box 190 (07008-0190)
PHONE....................732 541-2974
Joseph Folgore, *President*
Chuck Jablon, *VP Opers*
Karen Dorsey, *Project Mgr*
Julie Hyer, *Project Mgr*
Meoi Plummer, *Project Mgr*
EMP: 42
SQ FT: 8,000
SALES (est): 10MM **Privately Held**
SIC: 7692 Welding repair

(G-1255)
FUJIPOLY AMERICA CORPORATION
900 Milik St (07008-1117)
P.O. Box 119 (07008-0119)
PHONE....................732 969-0100
Frank Hobler, *President*
Deborah Mullen, *Purch Mgr*
Lino Santis, *QC Mgr*
Richard Potts, *Controller*
James Hopkins, *Sales Mgr*
▲ **EMP:** 32
SQ FT: 24,600
SALES (est): 14MM **Privately Held**
WEB: www.fujipoly.com
SIC: 3678 Electronic connectors
HQ: Fuji Polymer Industries Co.,Ltd.
1-3-18, Nishiki, Naka-Ku
Nagoya AIC 460-0

(G-1256)
GREEN GLOBE USA LLC
21 Louis St (07008-2104)
PHONE....................201 577-4468
Upendra Sabat,
EMP: 7
SALES (est): 239.8K **Privately Held**
SIC: 1629 1711 3999 8742 Dam construction; solar energy contractor; manufacturing industries; management consulting services

(G-1257)
INTERTEK USA INC
Also Called: Intertek Caleb Brett
1000 Port Carteret Dr C (07008-3527)
PHONE....................732 969-5200
Preston Smith, *Branch Mgr*
Roy Pike, *Manager*
Celia Vanpelt, *Manager*
EMP: 38

SQ FT: 2,500
SALES (est): 3.6B **Privately Held**
WEB: www.itscb.com
SIC: 2911 Petroleum refining
HQ: Intertek Usa Inc.
200 Westlke Prk Blvd 40
Houston TX 77079
713 543-3600

(G-1258)
KEURIG DR PEPPER INC
1200 Milik St (07008-1119)
PHONE....................732 969-1600
Laura Tzanavaris, *President*
EMP: 14 **Publicly Held**
SIC: 2086 Soft drinks: packaged in cans, bottles, etc.; carbonated beverages, non-alcoholic: bottled & canned; iced tea & fruit drinks, bottled & canned; mineral water, carbonated: packaged in cans, bottles, etc.
PA: Keurig Dr Pepper Inc.
53 South Ave
Burlington MA 01803

(G-1259)
LM FOODS LLC
Also Called: Aquamar
100 Raskulinecz Rd (07008-1000)
PHONE....................732 855-9500
Mark Olivito, *CEO*
Jinha Choi, *General Mgr*
Woody Asuncion, *Vice Pres*
Eok Jeon, *Plant Mgr*
Yong Lee, *Electrical Engi*
▲ **EMP:** 61
SQ FT: 72,000
SALES (est): 13.4MM **Privately Held**
WEB: www.lmfoods.com
SIC: 2092 Seafoods, fresh: prepared

(G-1260)
NEW YORK POPULAR INC
Also Called: Popularity Products
400 Federal Blvd (07008-1006)
PHONE....................718 499-2020
Benjamin Tebele, *CEO*
Albert Tebele, *Ch of Bd*
Edward Tebele, *Admin Sec*
▲ **EMP:** 100
SQ FT: 50,000
SALES (est): 18.1MM **Privately Held**
WEB: www.popularityproducts.com
SIC: 2389 5136 5137 Men's miscellaneous accessories; men's & boys' clothing; women's & children's clothing

(G-1261)
NOURHAN TRADING GROUP INC
62 Minue St (07008-1105)
PHONE....................732 381-8110
Mike Ahmed,
▲ **EMP:** 4
SALES (est): 606.4K **Privately Held**
SIC: 2011 Canned meats (except baby food), meat slaughtered on site

(G-1262)
NU-WORLD CORPORATION (HQ)
Also Called: Nu World
300 Milik St (07008-1113)
PHONE....................732 541-6300
Jonathan Rosenbaum, *CEO*
Stuart Dolleck, *President*
Christine Scillieri, *Vice Pres*
Hugo Barzola, *Engineer*
Stuart Mont, *CFO*
▲ **EMP:** 232
SQ FT: 131,000
SALES (est): 92.9MM **Privately Held**
WEB: www.nwcos.com
SIC: 2844 Cosmetic preparations

(G-1263)
OXFORD INSTRS HOLDINGS INC (DH)
600 Milik St (07008-1199)
P.O. Box 429 (07008-0429)
PHONE....................732 541-1300
Martin Lamaison, *President*
Maarten Kramer, *President*
Peter Williams, *Chairman*
Andrew Mackintosh, *COO*
Dan Gambogi, *Project Mgr*
◆ **EMP:** 44

SQ FT: 100,000
SALES (est): 32.6MM
SALES (corp-wide): 429.1MM **Privately Held**
SIC: 3264 5047 Magnets, permanent: ceramic or ferrite; medical equipment & supplies

(G-1264)
PERIMETER SOLUTIONS LP
500 Roosevelt Ave (07008-3504)
PHONE....................732 541-3000
Joseph Keber, *Purchasing*
Renea Medling, *Accounting Mgr*
Thomas C Falk, *Branch Mgr*
Carol Leone, *Manager*
Pascal Medina, *Manager*
EMP: 108 **Privately Held**
SIC: 2819 Phosphates, except fertilizers: defluorinated & ammoniated
HQ: Perimeter Solutions Lp
8000 Maryland Ave Ste 350
Saint Louis MO 63105
314 983-7500

(G-1265)
Q-EXIMTRADE INC (PA)
1336 Roosevelt Ave (07008-1302)
P.O. Box 60 (07008-0060)
PHONE....................732 366-4667
Emilio Quisumbing, *President*
▲ **EMP:** 5
SQ FT: 4,000
SALES (est): 680.6K **Privately Held**
WEB: www.qeximtrade.com
SIC: 3961 Costume jewelry

Cedar Grove
Essex County

(G-1266)
AIRDYE SOLUTIONS LLC (PA)
21 Glen Rock Rd (07009-1645)
PHONE....................540 433-9101
Evan Smith, *CEO*
Jesse Leskanic, *CTO*
EMP: 23
SALES (est): 12.1MM **Privately Held**
SIC: 2899 Ink or writing fluids

(G-1267)
APTIMIZED LLC
579 Pompton Ave Ste 104 (07009-1754)
PHONE....................203 733-2868
William Mills, *President*
EMP: 4
SQ FT: 500
SALES (est): 253.5K **Privately Held**
SIC: 7372 Application computer software

(G-1268)
AQUA PRODUCTS INC (DH)
25 Rutgers Ave (07009-1443)
PHONE....................973 857-2700
Giora Erlich, *President*
Kathleen A McClarnon, *Corp Secy*
Mark Raile, *Exec VP*
Joseph Porat, *Vice Pres*
Silvana Salazar, *Production*
▲ **EMP:** 165
SQ FT: 9,700
SALES (est): 36.3MM
SALES (corp-wide): 265K **Privately Held**
SIC: 3589 Swimming pool filter & water conditioning systems
HQ: Foridra Srl
S.S. Adriatica 16 17/A
Castelfidardo AN 60022
071 721-1048

(G-1269)
BELLEVILLE WIRE CLOTH CO INC (PA)
18 Rutgers Ave (07009-1444)
PHONE....................973 239-0074
James E Crowley, *President*
Jim Crowely, *Vice Pres*
Kenneth Crowley, *Vice Pres*
Augusto Gujansky, *Research*
Dan Steele, *Sales Staff*
▲ **EMP:** 43 **EST:** 1919
SQ FT: 20,000

SALES (est): 6.6MM **Privately Held**
WEB: www.bwire.com
SIC: 3496 Miscellaneous fabricated wire products

(G-1270)
BLOOMFIELD LIFE INC
632 Pompton Ave (07009-1736)
PHONE....................973 233-5001
Malcolm A Borg, *CEO*
EMP: 10
SALES (est): 349.5K
SALES (corp-wide): 156.2MM **Privately Held**
SIC: 2711 Newspapers
HQ: North Jersey Media Group Inc.
150 River St
Hackensack NJ 07601
201 646-4000

(G-1271)
CARGILLE-SACHER LABS INC (PA)
Also Called: Cargille Laboratories
55 Commerce Rd (07009-1289)
PHONE....................973 239-6633
John J Cargille, *President*
William J Sacher, *Vice Pres*
Dora Sanders, *Shareholder*
Robin David Sanders, *Shareholder*
Catherine Cargille Sacher, *Admin Sec*
▲ **EMP:** 22 **EST:** 1924
SQ FT: 16,000
SALES: 3.5MM **Privately Held**
WEB: www.cargille.com
SIC: 3826 Nephelometers, except meteorological

(G-1272)
CONTRACT FILLING INC
10 Cliffside Dr (07009-1227)
PHONE....................973 433-0053
William Lizzi, *President*
Geoff Handel, *COO*
▲ **EMP:** 200
SQ FT: 9,500
SALES (est): 30.3MM **Privately Held**
SIC: 2844 Toilet preparations

(G-1273)
CORRIGAN CENTER FOR INTEGRATIV
67 Haller Dr (07009-1704)
PHONE....................973 239-0700
Dr Lynn Corrigan, *President*
EMP: 5
SALES (est): 114.1K **Privately Held**
SIC: 8093 8322 2834 Weight loss clinic, with medical staff; general counseling services; thyroid preparations

(G-1274)
DIGITAL DESIGN INC
67 Sand Park Rd (07009-1281)
PHONE....................973 857-9500
Edward J Gerri, *President*
Louis Di Cianni, *Vice Pres*
Sam Rankins, *Opers Mgr*
EMP: 30
SQ FT: 25,000
SALES (est): 4.9MM **Privately Held**
WEB: www.genesisinkjet.com
SIC: 8711 3555 3953 Designing: ship, boat, machine & product; printing trades machinery; marking devices

(G-1275)
DMS INC
218 Little Falls Rd 7-8 (07009-1277)
PHONE....................973 928-3040
Gail Stuit, *President*
◆ **EMP:** 9 **EST:** 1993
SALES (est): 1.1MM **Privately Held**
SIC: 2295 Resin or plastic coated fabrics

(G-1276)
DOMINO PRINTING
Control Print Division
67 Sand Park Rd (07009-1243)
PHONE....................973 857-0900
Richard L Pellegrini, *Principal*
R Coventry, *Opers Mgr*
W Niven, *Technical Mgr*
T Milot, *Internal Med*
EMP: 58 **Privately Held**
WEB: www.domino-printing.com

SIC: 3555 Printing trades machinery
HQ: Domino Uk Limited
    Domino House
    Cambridge CAMBS CB23

(G-1277)
ELNIK SYSTEMS LLC
107 Commerce Rd (07009-1207)
PHONE..................................973 239-6066
Clause Joens, *CEO*
Claus Joens, *CEO*
Yelena Sukonik, *Engineer*
Inge Joens,
Frank Leonard,
▲ EMP: 35
SQ FT: 18,000
SALES (est): 6.6MM **Privately Held**
SIC: 3567 Vacuum furnaces & ovens

(G-1278)
**FAIRFIELD GOURMET FOOD
CORP (PA)**
Also Called: Cookie Cupboard
11 Cliffside Dr (07009-1234)
PHONE..................................973 575-4365
ARI Margulies, *CEO*
Harris Beber, *Vice Pres*
Howard Freundlich, *Vice Pres*
Victor Ostreicher, *Vice Pres*
Dawn Fallon, *Regl Sales Mgr*
◆ EMP: 95
SALES: 148.2MM **Privately Held**
WEB: www.davidscookies.com
SIC: 2052 5461 Cookies; cookies

(G-1279)
INFOR METAL & TOOLING MFG
16 Commerce Rd (07009-1206)
PHONE..................................973 571-9520
Charles Insel, *President*
George J Insel, *Vice Pres*
Trudy Insel, *Admin Sec*
▼ EMP: 10
SQ FT: 20,000
SALES (est): 1.6MM **Privately Held**
SIC: 3544 3469 Special dies & tools; machine parts, stamped or pressed metal

(G-1280)
KLABIN FRAGRANCES INC
71 Village Park Rd (07009-1212)
PHONE..................................973 857-3600
Saul Klabin, *President*
Justin Klabin, *Vice Pres*
EMP: 12
SQ FT: 13,600
SALES (est): 3.3MM **Privately Held**
WEB: www.klabin-usa.com
SIC: 2844 Perfumes & colognes

(G-1281)
MAT LOGO CENTRAL LLC
Also Called: Logomatcentral.com
216 Little Falls Rd (07009-1276)
PHONE..................................973 433-0311
Michael Becker,
EMP: 4
SQ FT: 2,500
SALES (est): 788.5K **Privately Held**
SIC: 3069 Rubber floor coverings, mats & wallcoverings; mats or matting, rubber; flooring, rubber: tile or sheet

(G-1282)
METAL CUTTING CORPORATION
Also Called: Mc
89 Commerce Rd (07009-1205)
PHONE..................................973 239-1100
Jordan Jablons, *President*
Joshua Jablons, *Exec VP*
Barbara Osborne, *QC Mgr*
Bob Mekita, *Engineer*
Victor Trzuskot, *Engineer*
▲ EMP: 60
SQ FT: 52,000
SALES (est): 11.6MM **Privately Held**
WEB: www.metalcutoff.com
SIC: 3679 5051 3469 Electronic circuits; metals service centers & offices; machine parts, stamped or pressed metal

(G-1283)
MONITEUR DEVICES INC
36 Commerce Rd (07009-1206)
PHONE..................................973 857-1600
John Unoski, *Vice Pres*

Gene Bohensky, *Vice Pres*
Robert Unoski, *Vice Pres*
Chris Carter, *Sales Mgr*
Greg Stockwell, *Sales Staff*
▲ EMP: 11
SQ FT: 10,000
SALES (est): 2MM **Privately Held**
WEB: www.moniteurdevices.com
SIC: 3669 Intercommunication systems, electric

(G-1284)
**MW JENKINS SONS
INCORPORATED**
Also Called: Jenkins Brush Comp
444 Pompton Ave (07009-1813)
P.O. Box 303 (07009-0303)
PHONE..................................973 239-5150
Craig Sigler, *President*
Eric W Eucker, *Vice Pres*
EMP: 12 EST: 1877
SQ FT: 10,000
SALES (est): 1.8MM **Privately Held**
WEB: www.jenkinsbrush.com
SIC: 3991 Brushes, household or industrial

(G-1285)
OASIS ENTERTAINMENT GROUP
17 Frederick Ct (07009-1340)
P.O. Box 3073, Clifton (07012-0373)
PHONE..................................973 256-7077
Linda Brooks, *Manager*
EMP: 5
SALES (est): 307.1K **Privately Held**
SIC: 2741 Music books: publishing only, not printed on site

(G-1286)
OMNIA INDUSTRIES INC
5 Cliffside Dr (07009-1278)
P.O. Box 330 (07009-0330)
PHONE..................................973 239-7272
Alberto Comini, *President*
Denyse Comini Becker, *Vice Pres*
Alexander Comini, *Vice Pres*
Fred Marzullo, *Vice Pres*
George Bardi, *Controller*
▲ EMP: 40
SQ FT: 24,000
SALES (est): 6.4MM **Privately Held**
WEB: www.omniaindustries.com
SIC: 3446 5039 Architectural metalwork; architectural metalwork

(G-1287)
PLAST-O-MATIC VALVES INC
1384 Pompton Ave Ste 1 (07009-1095)
PHONE..................................973 256-3000
Judith Delorernzo, *Ch of Bd*
Tim Delorenzo, *President*
Anthony Buda, *Mfg Mgr*
Angela Powell, *Purchasing*
Larri Ann Searles, *Purchasing*
▲ EMP: 74 EST: 1967
SQ FT: 52,000
SALES (est): 17.8MM **Privately Held**
WEB: www.plastomatic.com
SIC: 3491 5085 3083 3082 Industrial valves; industrial supplies; laminated plastics plate & sheet; unsupported plastics profile shapes

(G-1288)
**PRECISION MFG GROUP LLC
(DH)**
Also Called: Servometer
501 Little Falls Rd (07009-1239)
PHONE..................................973 785-4630
Anatole Penchuk, *CEO*
Glenn Weinrich, *COO*
Robert Collins, *Engineer*
Edgar Usman, *Engineer*
Gerard O'Donovan, *CFO*
EMP: 75 EST: 2014
SQ FT: 26,000
SALES: 17MM
SALES (corp-wide): 185.9MM **Privately Held**
WEB: www.servometer.com
SIC: 3599 3498 3643 Bellows, industrial: metal; couplings, pipe: fabricated from purchased pipe; contacts, electrical
HQ: Matthew Warren, Inc.
    9501 Tech Blvd Ste 401
    Rosemont IL 60018
    847 349-5760

(G-1289)
PRINTWRAP CORPORATION
95 Sand Park Rd (07009-1270)
PHONE..................................973 239-1144
Richard Neiman, *President*
Roger Neiman, *Vice Pres*
Andrew Neiman, *Admin Sec*
EMP: 17
SQ FT: 20,000
SALES (est): 3.1MM **Privately Held**
WEB: www.printwrap.com
SIC: 2752 2621 5111 Wrappers, lithographed; paper mills; printing paper

(G-1290)
**RANDCASTLE EXTRUSION
SYSTEMS**
220 Little Falls Rd # 6 (07009-1254)
PHONE..................................973 239-1150
Keith Luker, *President*
EMP: 6
SQ FT: 3,000
SALES: 720K **Privately Held**
SIC: 3821 8734 Laboratory apparatus, except heating & measuring; product testing laboratories

(G-1291)
REPROMATIC PRINTING INC
Also Called: Proforma
216 Little Falls Rd # 3 (07009-1276)
PHONE..................................973 239-7610
Paul Molinari, *President*
Alyce Molinari, *Vice Pres*
Joan Molinari, *Admin Sec*
EMP: 4
SQ FT: 2,500
SALES: 700K **Privately Held**
WEB: www.repromatic.com
SIC: 2752 Commercial printing, offset

(G-1292)
SAMA PLASTICS CORP
20 Sand Park Rd (07009-1210)
PHONE..................................973 239-7200
Mark Wolsberg, *President*
▼ EMP: 35
SQ FT: 3,600
SALES (est): 8.6MM **Privately Held**
SIC: 3089 3993 Plastic processing; displays & cutouts, window & lobby

(G-1293)
TEX GUL INC
874 Pompton Ave Ste A2 (07009-1213)
PHONE..................................973 857-3200
Akram Choudhry, *President*
▲ EMP: 9
SQ FT: 2,500
SALES (est): 1.1MM **Privately Held**
SIC: 2211 Broadwoven fabric mills, cotton

(G-1294)
TRANSPORT PRODUCTS INC
20 Village Park Rd (07009-1247)
PHONE..................................973 857-6090
Debbie Petrosino, *President*
Fred Biancone, *Vice Pres*
Lauren Vitkovsky, *Purch Mgr*
Lou Saggese, *Purchasing*
EMP: 8
SQ FT: 8,000
SALES (est): 973.5K **Privately Held**
SIC: 3069 5085 Molded rubber products; gaskets; springs

(G-1295)
**UNITED SPPORT SLTONS - LMT
INC (PA)**
134 Sand Park Rd (07009-1240)
PHONE..................................973 857-2298
Anatoly Lesenskyj, *President*
Sanjay Parimi, *COO*
Frank Melchiorre, *Purchasing*
Patrick Lang, *CFO*
EMP: 2
SQ FT: 330,000
SALES: 9B **Privately Held**
SIC: 3469 Metal stampings

Cedar Knolls
Morris County

(G-1296)
ADVANTICE HEALTH LLC
7 E Frederick Pl Ste 100 (07927-1815)
PHONE..................................973 946-7550
Steve Cagle, *President*
James Barton, *CFO*
Amy Scarlatella, *Marketing Staff*
Jill Rivera, *Manager*
EMP: 11
SQ FT: 3,000
SALES (est): 4.8MM **Privately Held**
WEB: www.alterna.net
SIC: 2834 Pharmaceutical preparations

(G-1297)
**AFA POLYTEK NORTH AMERICA
INC**
240 Cedar Knolls Rd # 201 (07927-1621)
PHONE..................................862 260-9450
Ariel Bretch, *CEO*
Marion Figur, *President*
◆ EMP: 15 EST: 2008
SALES (est): 3MM
SALES (corp-wide): 120.4MM **Privately Held**
SIC: 3523 Sprayers & spraying machines, agricultural
PA: Afa Dispensing Group B.V.
    Grasbeemd 1
    Helmond 5705
    492 502-600

(G-1298)
AMLOID CORPORATION
7 Ridgecale Ave Ste 1a (07927-1120)
PHONE..................................973 328-0654
Michael Albarelli Jr, *President*
Joseph D Albarelli, *Vice Pres*
Michael Albarelli III, *Vice Pres*
Eric Kiel. *Vice Pres*
Daniel McMahon, *Vice Pres*
▲ EMP: 10 EST: 1916
SQ FT: 9,000
SALES (est): 16.1MM **Privately Held**
SIC: 3944 Games, toys & children's vehicles

(G-1299)
APPLIED NUTRITION CORP
10 Saddle Rd (07927-1901)
PHONE..................................973 734-0023
Richard Finkel, *President*
EMP: 26
SQ FT: 14,000
SALES (est): 2.4MM **Privately Held**
WEB: www.medicalfood.com
SIC: 5499 2099 Health foods; food preparations

(G-1300)
CARGILLE-SACHER LABS INC
4 E Frecerick Pl (07927-1801)
PHONE..................................973 267-8888
John J Cargille, *President*
EMP: 16
SALES (corp-wide): 3.5MM **Privately Held**
WEB: www.cargille.com
SIC: 3499 Tablets, bronze or other metal
PA: Cargille-Sacher Laboratories Inc.
    55 Commerce Rd
    Cedar Grove NJ 07009
    973 239-6633

(G-1301)
CELGENE CORPORATION
45 Horsehill Rd Ste 107 (07927-2009)
PHONE..................................908 673-9000
Shan Shao, *Research*
Robert Haviri, *Branch Mgr*
Michael Taranto, *Manager*
Keith Usiskin, *Exec Dir*
Suttner Lisa, *Director*
EMP: 800
SALES (corp-wide): 15.2B **Publicly Held**
SIC: 2834 Pharmaceutical preparations
PA: Celgene Corporation
    86 Morris Ave
    Summit NJ 07901
    903 673-9000

(G-1302)
COMMERCIAL BUSINESS FORMS INC
Also Called: Print Cbf
240 Cedar Knolls Rd # 203 (07927-1621)
PHONE..................................973 682-9000
Michael H Gordon, *President*
Steve Stringas, *Accounts Mgr*
Fran Van Ness, *Accounts Mgr*
Bob Carroll, *Sales Staff*
Veronica Zulauf, *Sales Staff*
EMP: 8
SALES (est): 1.1MM **Privately Held**
WEB: www.printcbf.com
SIC: 2759 Advertising literature: printing

(G-1303)
EDGEWELL PERSONAL CARE LLC
240 Cedar Knolls Rd (07927-1621)
PHONE..................................973 753-3000
Mario Soussou, *Branch Mgr*
Benjamin Emmett, *Manager*
EMP: 5
SALES (corp-wide): 2.3B **Publicly Held**
SIC: 2844 Shaving preparations; lotions, shaving; suntan lotions & oils; hair preparations, including shampoos
HQ: Edgewell Personal Care, Llc
1350 Timberlake Mano
Chesterfield MO 63017
314 594-1900

(G-1304)
EMPLOYMENT HORIZONS INC
10 Ridgedale Ave (07927-1104)
PHONE..................................973 538-8822
Robert Johnston, *CFO*
Matthew Putts, *Exec Dir*
Jacqueline Burns, *Director*
EMP: 300
SQ FT: 17,500
SALES: 11.1MM **Privately Held**
SIC: 8331 2671 Vocational rehabilitation agency; packaging paper & plastics film, coated & laminated

(G-1305)
FOSTER AND COMPANY INC (PA)
Also Called: Chem Power Mfg Div
15 Wing Dr (07927-1019)
PHONE..................................973 267-4100
Richard Foster, *Ch of Bd*
Robert Foster, *Corp Secy*
Ken Foster, *Exec Dir*
EMP: 30
SQ FT: 27,000
SALES (est): 13.7MM **Privately Held**
WEB: www.fostercomfg.com
SIC: 5085 2819 Industrial supplies; chemicals, high purity: refined from technical grade

(G-1306)
HAKAKIAN BEHZAD
52 Horsehill Rd (07927-2004)
PHONE..................................973 267-2506
EMP: 35
SALES (est): 1.3MM **Privately Held**
SIC: 2273 Mfg Carpets/Rugs

(G-1307)
KINLY INC
2 Ridgedale Ave Ste 100 (07927-1108)
PHONE..................................973 585-3000
James De Poortere, *CEO*
Don Sommer, *Vice Pres*
Bill Twomey, *Vice Pres*
Thomas Volk, *Vice Pres*
Michael Mulcahy, *Sales Staff*
EMP: 20
SALES (est): 15.1MM
SALES (corp-wide): 242.1K **Privately Held**
SIC: 3669 5043 Visual communication systems; photographic equipment & supplies
HQ: Kinly Ltd
6 Fleming Road Kirkton Campus
Livingston EH54

(G-1308)
LINDEN GROUP CORPORATION
2b Wing Dr (07927-1020)
PHONE..................................973 983-8809
Ken Chen, *President*
Chris Chen, *Vice Pres*
James Chen, *Vice Pres*
Bob Colaizzo, *QC Mgr*
Mark Uchino, *Sales Staff*
▲ EMP: 18
SQ FT: 14,000
SALES (est): 2.4MM **Privately Held**
WEB: www.tlgc.com
SIC: 7379 7373 3575 Computer related consulting services; systems software development services; systems integration services; computer system selling services; computer-aided system services; computer terminals, monitors & components

(G-1309)
MARK LITHOGRAPHY INC
Also Called: Mark Lithographers
4 Saddle Rd (07927-1901)
P.O. Box 362 (07927-0362)
PHONE..................................973 538-5557
Charles Tumminello, *President*
Stephen Tumminello, *Admin Sec*
EMP: 40 EST: 1961
SQ FT: 17,000
SALES (est): 4.6MM **Privately Held**
WEB: www.marklitho.com
SIC: 2752 Commercial printing, offset

(G-1310)
MORRIS COUNTY DUPLICATING
8 Farview Ave (07927-1527)
PHONE..................................973 993-8484
Ernest D'Angelo, *President*
◆ EMP: 80
SQ FT: 25,000
SALES (est): 9.5MM **Privately Held**
WEB: www.mcdonline.com
SIC: 2752 Commercial printing, offset

(G-1311)
MYOS RENS TECHNOLOGY INC
45 Horsehill Rd Ste 106 (07927-2009)
PHONE..................................973 509-0444
Joseph Mannello, *CEO*
Robert J Hariri, *Ch of Bd*
Neerav Padliya, *Vice Pres*
Joe Dipietro, *Controller*
▲ EMP: 9
SQ FT: 5,225
SALES: 360K **Privately Held**
SIC: 2834 Pharmaceutical preparations

(G-1312)
NIAGARA CONSERVATION CORP
45 Horsehill Rd Ste 105 (07927-2009)
PHONE..................................973 829-0800
William Cutler, *President*
Kevin Wilham, *Vice Pres*
Matt Voorhees, *Manager*
EMP: 14
SALES (corp-wide): 15.8MM **Privately Held**
WEB: www.niagaraconservation.com
SIC: 3822 Auto controls regulating residntl & coml environmt & applncs
PA: Niagara Conservation Corp.
1200 Lkeside Pkwy Ste 450
Flower Mound TX 75028
682 292-0018

(G-1313)
OLI SYSTEMS INC
240 Cedar Knolls Rd # 301 (07927-1621)
PHONE..................................973 539-4996
Marshall Rafal, *President*
Arjun Ramesh, *Engineer*
Prodip Kundu, *Senior Engr*
EMP: 20
SQ FT: 4,000
SALES (est): 4MM **Privately Held**
WEB: www.olisystems.com
SIC: 7372 8731 Business oriented computer software; biotechnical research, commercial

(G-1314)
TRUKMANNS INC
Also Called: Trukmann's Reprographics
4 Wing Dr (07927-1020)
PHONE..................................973 538-7718
Paul Korman, *President*
Ernest Minotti, *Principal*
Will Korman, *Vice Pres*
Erick Mendez, *Prdtn Mgr*
Matt Korman, *Sales Staff*
EMP: 25
SQ FT: 37,000
SALES (est): 4.9MM **Privately Held**
WEB: www.trukmanns-orders.com
SIC: 2759 2752 3993 Screen printing; commercial printing, lithographic; signs & advertising specialties

(G-1315)
UNIQUE SYSTEMS INC
4 Saddle Rd (07927-1901)
PHONE..................................973 455-0440
Olof A Eriksen, *President*
Elaine Eriksen, *Vice Pres*
Kenneth Eriksen, *Vice Pres*
Robert Harris, *Engineer*
David Bond, *Project Leader*
▲ EMP: 12 EST: 1973
SQ FT: 15,000
SALES (est): 3MM **Privately Held**
WEB: www.uniquesystems.com
SIC: 3589 Commercial cleaning equipment

(G-1316)
WINERY PAK LLC
3 Wing Dr Ste 101 (07927-1010)
PHONE..................................800 434-4599
Larry Chasin, *Principal*
EMP: 6
SALES (est): 340.9K **Privately Held**
SIC: 2084 Wines

Cedarville
Cumberland County

(G-1317)
OWENS PLASTIC PRODUCTS INC
393 Main St (08311-2542)
P.O. Box 118 (08311-0118)
PHONE..................................856 447-3500
Gloria Owens, *President*
Christopher Owens, *Opers Staff*
Adrienne Debourgion Owens, *Treasurer*
EMP: 7
SQ FT: 15,000
SALES (est): 874.5K **Privately Held**
WEB: www.owensplasticproducts.com
SIC: 3089 3083 Injection molded finished plastic products; laminated plastics plate & sheet

---

Chatham
Morris County

(G-1318)
AMARYLLIS INC (PA)
418 River Rd (07928-1272)
P.O. Box 208 (07928-0208)
PHONE..................................973 635-0500
Ling Chang, *President*
Jan Chang, *Vice Pres*
▲ EMP: 6
SALES: 1.5MM **Privately Held**
SIC: 3999 2771 Novelties, bric-a-brac & hobby kits; greeting cards

(G-1319)
BURLING INSTRUMENTS INC
16 River Rd (07928-1916)
P.O. Box 298 (07928-0298)
PHONE..................................973 665-0601
Harry Bentas, *President*
Roger Nation, *Vice Pres*
Michael Wetterer, *Vice Pres*
EMP: 11
SQ FT: 11,240

SALES (est): 1.1MM **Privately Held**
WEB: www.burlinginstruments.com
SIC: 3822 3823 Auto controls regulating residntl & coml environmt & applncs; temperature instruments: industrial process type

(G-1320)
CHATHAM LAWN MOWLER
Also Called: Chatham Lawnmower Service
14 Commerce St (07928-2703)
PHONE..................................973 635-8855
Scott Sampson, *Owner*
EMP: 4
SQ FT: 3,600
SALES (est): 409.7K **Privately Held**
SIC: 5261 7699 5063 3546 Lawnmowers & tractors; lawn mower repair shop; generators; saws & sawing equipment

(G-1321)
INNOVATION IN MEDTECH LLC
5 Rolling Hill Dr (07928-1609)
P.O. Box 326, Fairfield CT (06824-0326)
PHONE..................................888 202-5939
David Cassak, *Managing Prtnr*
Stephen Levin, *Managing Prtnr*
EMP: 9
SALES (est): 549.5K **Privately Held**
SIC: 2721 Magazines: publishing & printing

(G-1322)
INVESSENCE INC
1 Main St Ste 202 (07928-2426)
PHONE..................................201 977-1955
Jigar Vyas, *CEO*
Christopher Lengle, *Officer*
EMP: 5
SALES (est): 156K **Privately Held**
SIC: 7372 7389 Business oriented computer software; financial services

(G-1323)
ISP CHEMICALS LLC
Also Called: Isp Sutton Laboratories
116 Summit Ave (07928-2727)
P.O. Box 837 (07928-0837)
PHONE..................................973 635-1551
John Cavan, *Branch Mgr*
EMP: 50 **Privately Held**
WEB: www.ispcorp.com
SIC: 2869 2844 Amines, acids, salts, esters; toilet preparations
HQ: Isp Chemicals Llc
455 N Main St
Calvert City KY 42029
270 395-4165

(G-1324)
JUVENTIO LLC
466 Southern Blvd Ste 2 (07928-1462)
PHONE..................................973 908-8097
Thomas Ford, *CEO*
Michael Graziano, *CFO*
Mike Graziano, *CFO*
EMP: 5
SQ FT: 2,000
SALES (est): 905.8K **Privately Held**
SIC: 2834 Pharmaceutical preparations

(G-1325)
KILLIAN GRAPHICS
142 Southern Blvd (07928-1324)
P.O. Box 91 (07928-0091)
PHONE..................................973 635-5844
Ron Killian, *Owner*
EMP: 5
SALES: 90K **Privately Held**
SIC: 7311 2752 Advertising agencies; promotional printing, lithographic

(G-1326)
LIFE LINERS INC (PA)
6 Essex Rd (07928-2056)
PHONE..................................973 635-9234
Stephen Asthalter, *President*
EMP: 2
SQ FT: 5,000
SALES (est): 1.3MM **Privately Held**
SIC: 2262 3569 Fire resistance finishing: manmade & silk broadwoven; firefighting apparatus & related equipment

(G-1327)
MINDWISE MEDIA LLC
26 Floral St (07928-1660)
PHONE....................................973 701-0685
Scott Pendergrast,
EMP: 5
SQ FT: 500
SALES (est): 390K **Privately Held**
WEB: www.mindwise.com
SIC: 4813 2721 ; periodicals

(G-1328)
NATIONAL HOME PLANNING SERVICE
Also Called: Chirgotis, Wm G
79 Thornley Dr (07928-1361)
PHONE....................................973 376-3200
William G Chirgotis, *President*
Lawrence Tranquilli, *Vice Pres*
Wilma Tranquilli, *Admin Sec*
EMP: 4
SQ FT: 3,000
SALES (est): 230K **Privately Held**
WEB: www.nationalhome.com
SIC: 2741 8712 Miscellaneous publishing;
architectural services

(G-1329)
NATIONAL MANUFACTURING CO INC
12 River Rd (07928-1989)
PHONE....................................973 635-8846
Robert Staudinger, *President*
Reggie Zhou, *President*
Peter Colby, *General Mgr*
Kristina Sterni, *General Mgr*
David Carnell, *Business Mgr*
▲ **EMP:** 150 **EST:** 1944
SQ FT: 50,000
SALES (est): 31.8MM **Privately Held**
WEB: www.natlmfg.com
SIC: 3469 Stamping metal for the trade

(G-1330)
THEWAL INC
Also Called: Chatham Print & Design
12 Center St (07928-2521)
PHONE....................................973 635-1880
Susan Kessel, *President*
Walter Francis III, *Prdtn Mgr*
Ellen Schreiber, *Bookkeeper*
Thelma Francis, *Services*
Debbie Kostibos, *Services*
EMP: 10
SQ FT: 4,500
SALES (est): 1.5MM **Privately Held**
WEB: www.chatmm.com
SIC: 2752 2791 Commercial print-
ing, offset; typesetting; bookbinding & re-
lated work

(G-1331)
UNIKEN INC
466 Southern Blvd Ste 2 (07928-1462)
PHONE....................................917 324-0399
Bimal Gandhi, *CEO*
Robert Levine, *COO*
Ajay Dubey, *Adv Board Mem*
Levine Robert, *Vice Pres*
Vivek Bhiwapurkar, *Project Mgr*
EMP: 5 **EST:** 2013
SALES (est): 156K **Privately Held**
SIC: 7372 Business oriented computer
software

Cherry Hill
Camden County

(G-1332)
ADLERS PHARMACY LTC INC
100 Dobbs Ln Ste 205 (08034-1436)
PHONE....................................856 685-7440
Mark Adler, *President*
Mark Price, *Pharmacist*
EMP: 20 **EST:** 2001
SQ FT: 8,000
SALES: 16MM **Privately Held**
SIC: 2834 Proprietary drug products

(G-1333)
AGA FOODSERVICE INC (PA)
110 Woodcrest Rd (08003-3648)
PHONE....................................856 428-4200

Iain Whyte, *President*
◆ **EMP:** 78
SQ FT: 220,000
SALES (est): 11.9MM **Privately Held**
WEB: www.agafoodservice.com
SIC: 3556 Food products machinery

(G-1334)
AGOURA HILLS GROUP
4 Executive Campus # 104 (08002-4105)
PHONE....................................818 888-0400
EMP: 4
SALES (corp-wide): 439.3K **Privately Held**
SIC: 3995 Casket linings
HQ: Agoura Hills Group
4 Executive Campus # 104
Cherry Hill NJ 08002

(G-1335)
AGOURA HILLS GROUP (DH)
Also Called: Ilg
4 Executive Campus # 104 (08002-4105)
P.O. Box 686, Woodland Hills CA (91365-0686)
PHONE....................................818 888-0400
Timothy Clark, *President*
Ling Zito, *Vice Pres*
Cindy Michaels, *CFO*
▲ **EMP:** 50
SQ FT: 18,000
SALES (est): 7.2MM
SALES (corp-wide): 439.3K **Privately Held**
WEB: www.ilgweb.com
SIC: 3955 3861 Print cartridges for laser &
other computer printers; photographic
equipment & supplies
HQ: Turbon Ag
Ruhrdeich 10
Hattingen 45525
232 450-40

(G-1336)
AIR DISTRIBUTION SYSTEMS INC
Also Called: ADS
1000 Astoria Blvd (08003-2311)
PHONE....................................856 874-1100
Charles Doyle, *President*
John F Dickson, *Vice Pres*
EMP: 75
SQ FT: 35,000
SALES (est): 17.4MM **Privately Held**
WEB: www.adsduct.com
SIC: 3444 1711 Ducts, sheet metal;
plumbing, heating, air-conditioning con-
tractors

(G-1337)
AIRGAS USA LLC
1910 Old Cuthbert Rd (08034-1416)
PHONE....................................609 685-4241
Joseph Anastasi, *Branch Mgr*
EMP: 19
SALES (corp-wide): 125.9MM **Privately Held**
SIC: 5169 5084 5085 2813 Industrial
gases; gases, compressed & liquefied;
carbon dioxide; dry ice; welding machinery & equipment; safety equipment; welding supplies; industrial gases; carbon
dioxide; nitrous oxide; dry ice, carbon
dioxide (solid); industrial inorganic chemicals; calcium carbide
HQ: Airgas Usa, Llc
259 N Radnor Chester Rd
Radnor PA 19087
610 687-5253

(G-1338)
ALADDIN INSTRUMENTS CORP
22 Cherrywood Ct (08003-1900)
PHONE....................................774 326-4919
EMP: 5
SALES (est): 564.2K **Privately Held**
SIC: 3823 Industrial instrmnts msrmnt dis-
play/control process variable

(G-1339)
ALPHAGRAPHICS
2050 Springdale Rd # 700 (08003-2045)
PHONE....................................856 761-8000
Art Coley, *CEO*
Rudy Baron, *President*
Janet Oneal, *Project Mgr*

Tommy E Auger, *CFO*
Leah Baron, *Admin Sec*
EMP: 12
SALES (est): 2.6MM **Privately Held**
SIC: 2752 7336 Commercial printing, litho-
graphic; graphic arts & related design

(G-1340)
AURORA INFORMATION SYSTEMS
1873 Marlton Pike E # 220 (08003-2034)
PHONE....................................856 596-4180
Jerry Cully, *President*
John Sooy, *Vice Pres*
EMP: 8
SQ FT: 1,100
SALES (est): 869.1K **Privately Held**
WEB: www.foodpro.com
SIC: 7373 7372 Systems software devel-
opment services; prepackaged software

(G-1341)
AUTOMATED OFFICE INC
Also Called: DMC Soft
9 Executive Campus (08002-4502)
PHONE....................................888 362-7638
Bruce Bergeron, *President*
Al Giacomucci, *Director*
EMP: 5
SQ FT: 600
SALES (est): 550K **Privately Held**
SIC: 5734 7372 7379 Software, business
& non-game; prepackaged software; com-
puter related consulting services

(G-1342)
BAXTER HEALTHCARE CORPORATION
2 Esterbrook Ln (08003-4002)
PHONE....................................856 489-2104
Ed Deluise, *Opers Staff*
Thomas McDevitt, *Mfg Staff*
Clifford Powell Jr, *QC Mgr*
Erick Guevara, *Engineer*
Anura Perera, *Engineer*
EMP: 66
SALES (corp-wide): 11.1B **Publicly Held**
SIC: 3841 Surgical & medical instruments
HQ: Baxter Healthcare Corporation
1 Baxter Pkwy
Deerfield IL 60015
224 948-2000

(G-1343)
BEST DRAPERIES INC
Also Called: Best Drapery & Blind Mfg Co
1 Kresson Rd (08034-3206)
PHONE....................................856 429-5453
James Logan, *President*
EMP: 5
SQ FT: 1,800
SALES (est): 450K **Privately Held**
SIC: 2591 Shade, curtain & drapery hard-
ware; window blinds

(G-1344)
BEST DRAPERY INC
Also Called: Best Drapery and Design
1 Crescent Way (08002-4201)
PHONE....................................856 429-2242
James Logan, *President*
EMP: 7
SQ FT: 1,800
SALES: 700K **Privately Held**
WEB: www.ebestdesign.com
SIC: 2591 Shade, curtain & drapery hard-
ware; window blinds

(G-1345)
BESTWORK INDS FOR THE BLIND
1940 Olney Ave 200 (08003-2016)
PHONE....................................856 424-2510
Belinda Moore, *President*
Mary Heyse, *Info Tech Mgr*
EMP: 70
SALES: 3.1MM **Privately Held**
SIC: 8331 2326 2339 Sheltered work-
shop; skill training center; work experi-
ence center; men's & boys' work clothing;
women's & misses' outerwear

(G-1346)
BIRDS EYE FOODS INC (DH)
121 Woodcrest Rd (08003-3620)
PHONE....................................585 383-1850
Neil Harrison, *President*
David Hogbert, *President*
Robert G Montgomery, *Senior VP*
Carl W Caughran, *Vice Pres*
Chris Puma, *CFO*
◆ **EMP:** 250
SALES (est): 368.9MM
SALES (corp-wide): 9.5B **Publicly Held**
WEB: www.agrilinkfoods.com
SIC: 2096 2052 2038 2035 Potato chips
& other potato-based snacks; cookies &
crackers; whipped topping, frozen; pick-
les, sauces & salad dressings; vegeta-
bles, quick frozen & cold pack, excl.
potato products

(G-1347)
BITTNER INDUSTRIES INC
Also Called: Minuteman Press
2060 Springdale Rd # 700 (08003-2099)
PHONE....................................856 817-8400
Frank Bittner, *President*
Cherie L Bittner, *Treasurer*
EMP: 8
SQ FT: 5,000
SALES (est): 1.2MM **Privately Held**
SIC: 2752 Commercial printing, litho-
graphic

(G-1348)
BPS WORLDWIDE INC
1860 Greentree Rd (08003-2031)
PHONE....................................856 874-0822
Robert Malmud, *Principal*
Cynthia Maiorano, *Vice Pres*
Gary Shull, *Vice Pres*
EMP: 45
SQ FT: 40,000
SALES: 10MM **Privately Held**
SIC: 3578 Automatic teller machines (ATM)

(G-1349)
BREAD & BAGELS
1600 Church Rd (08002-1203)
PHONE....................................856 667-2333
Heechul Bang, *Owner*
EMP: 10
SQ FT: 2,500
SALES (est): 520K **Privately Held**
SIC: 2051 Breads, rolls & buns; bagels,
fresh or frozen

(G-1350)
BUSINESS DEV SOLUTIONS INC
311 Hadleigh Dr (08003-1979)
PHONE....................................856 433-8005
Robert Bloom, *President*
EMP: 7
SALES (est): 610K **Privately Held**
WEB: www.bdsdatabase.com
SIC: 8742 7372 Management information
systems consultant; prepackaged soft-
ware

(G-1351)
C JACKSON ASSOCIATES INC
Also Called: AlphaGraphics
2050 Springdale Rd # 700 (08003-4021)
PHONE....................................856 761-8000
Charles Jackson, *President*
Frances Jackson, *Vice Pres*
Gary Jackson, *Treasurer*
David Jackson, *Admin Sec*
EMP: 20
SQ FT: 18,000
SALES (est): 260.5K **Privately Held**
SIC: 2752 7331 2789 Commercial print-
ing, lithographic; mailing service; book-
binding & related work

(G-1352)
CDK INDUSTRIES LLC
Also Called: Whips International
900 Haddonfield Rd Ste 6 (08002-2749)
P.O. Box 444 (08003-0444)
PHONE....................................856 488-5456
James Walford, *Mng Member*
EMP: 3
SQ FT: 2,400
SALES: 1.5MM **Privately Held**
SIC: 3949 2395 Sporting & athletic goods;
embroidery & art needlework

(G-1353)
CLARITY IMAGING SOLUTIONS INC
4 Executive Campus # 104 (08002-4105)
PHONE...................................866 684-2212
Simon McCouaig, *President*
Steven Injaian, *Vice Pres*
EMP: 8
SALES (est): 1MM **Privately Held**
SIC: 3955 Print cartridges for laser & other computer printers

(G-1354)
CROCES PASTA PODUCTS
Also Called: Croce & Longo Associates
811 Marlton Pike W (08002-3528)
PHONE...................................856 795-6000
Joseph Croce, *President*
EMP: 5
SALES: 350K **Privately Held**
SIC: 2099 Pasta, uncooked: packaged with other ingredients

(G-1355)
DAMAN INTERNATIONAL INC
Also Called: Caps Padel
105 Rye Rd (08003-1308)
PHONE...................................917 945-9708
Karishma Vohra, *President*
▲ **EMP:** 2
SQ FT: 400
SALES: 1MM **Privately Held**
SIC: 2329 Riding clothes:, men's, youths' & boys'

(G-1356)
DETERMINE INC
200 Lake Dr E (08002-1171)
PHONE...................................800 608-0809
Michael Brodsky, *Ch of Bd*
Alan Howe, *Vice Ch Bd*
Patrick Stakenas, *President*
Alison Farber, *Business Mgr*
David M Cravens, *Vice Pres*
EMP: 48
SQ FT: 8,795
SALES: 28.1MM
SALES (corp-wide): 90MM **Publicly Held**
WEB: www.selectica.com
SIC: 7372 7373 Prepackaged software; computer integrated systems design
PA: Corcentric, Inc.
200 Lake Dr E Ste 200 # 200
Cherry Hill NJ 08002
800 608-0809

(G-1357)
DPI COPIES PRTG & GRAPHICS INC
2070 Marlton Pike E Ste 3 (08003-1281)
PHONE...................................856 874-1355
Michael Jones, *President*
EMP: 15
SQ FT: 5,000
SALES (est): 2.4MM **Privately Held**
WEB: www.dpicherryhill.com
SIC: 2752 Commercial printing, offset

(G-1358)
EDWARDS CREATIVE PRODUCTS INC
Also Called: Ecp
910 Beechwood Ave (08002-3497)
PHONE...................................856 665-3200
Edward Cohen, *Ch of Bd*
Charles Cohen, *President*
Leona Cohen, *Admin Sec*
EMP: 15 **EST:** 1953
SQ FT: 9,000
SALES (est): 798.6K **Privately Held**
WEB: www.edwardscreative.com
SIC: 2842 3089 3634 Stain removers; novelties, plastic; electric housewares & fans

(G-1359)
ELITE SURF SNOW SKATEBOARD SP
259 Marlton Pike E (08034-2406)
PHONE...................................856 427-7873
EMP: 4 **EST:** 2007
SALES (est): 160K **Privately Held**
SIC: 3949 Mfg Sporting/Athletic Goods

(G-1360)
EUROPEAN COFFEE CLASSICS INC
Also Called: Melita USA
1401 Berlin Rd Ste A (08034-1402)
PHONE...................................856 428-7202
▲ **EMP:** 20
SQ FT: 104,000
SALES (est): 6MM
SALES (corp-wide): 1.8B **Privately Held**
SIC: 2095 Roasted coffee
HQ: Melitta North America, Inc.
13925 58th St N
Clearwater FL 33760
727 535-2111

(G-1361)
FEDEX OFFICE & PRINT SVCS INC
1160 Route 70 E (08034-2131)
PHONE...................................856 427-0099
EMP: 20
SALES (corp-wide): 69.6B **Publicly Held**
WEB: www.kinkos.com
SIC: 7334 7312 3993 2791 Photocopying & duplicating services; outdoor advertising services; signs & advertising specialties; typesetting; bookbinding & related work; coated & laminated paper
HQ: Fedex Office And Print Services, Inc.
7900 Legacy Dr
Plano TX 75024
800 463-3339

(G-1362)
FISCHLERS DAWNPOINT
212 Walt Whitman Blvd (08003-3521)
PHONE...................................856 428-2092
EMP: 4 **EST:** 2005
SALES (est): 160K **Privately Held**
SIC: 2759 Commercial Printing

(G-1363)
FRIDAY MORNING QUARTERBACK
1930 Marlton Pike E F36 (08003-4102)
PHONE...................................856 424-6873
Kal Rudman, *President*
Lucille Rudman, *Admin Sec*
EMP: 40 **EST:** 1972
SQ FT: 4,400
SALES (est): 2.7MM **Privately Held**
WEB: www.fmqb.com
SIC: 2741 2721 Miscellaneous publishing; periodicals

(G-1364)
FRONTEND GRAPHICS INC
1951 Old Cuthbert Rd # 414 (08034-1411)
PHONE...................................856 547-1600
Elizabeth A Maul, *President*
Karen Ryan, *Vice Pres*
Jonathan Raduns, *Sales Staff*
EMP: 8
SQ FT: 2,500
SALES (est): 1.2MM **Privately Held**
WEB: www.frontendgraphics.com
SIC: 2759 7336 4212 Screen printing; graphic arts & related design; mail carriers, contract

(G-1365)
G H KRAUSS MANUFACTURING CO
1209 Route 38 (08002-2851)
PHONE...................................856 662-0815
Gordon H Krauss, *Owner*
EMP: 4
SQ FT: 2,000
SALES (est): 190K **Privately Held**
SIC: 3643 7389 Current-carrying wiring devices; packaging & labeling services

(G-1366)
GANNETT STLLITE INFO NTWRK LLC
Courier Post
301 Cuthbert Blvd (08002-2905)
P.O. Box 5300 (08034-0430)
PHONE...................................856 663-6000
Dan Martin, *President*
EMP: 88

SALES (corp-wide): 2.9B **Publicly Held**
WEB: www.usatoday.com
SIC: 2711 Newspapers
HQ: Gannett Satellite Information Network, Llc
7950 Jones Branch Dr
Mc Lean VA 22102
703 854-6000

(G-1367)
GAW ASSOCIATES INC
Also Called: Gaw Technology
670 Deer Rd Bldg A (08034-1438)
PHONE...................................856 608-1428
Kathleen Gaw-Betz, *President*
Chuck Gaw, *Vice Pres*
EMP: 10
SQ FT: 8,000
SALES (est): 4.8MM **Privately Held**
WEB: www.gawtechnology.com
SIC: 3444 2522 5021 3572 Metal housings, enclosures, casings & other containers; office furniture, except wood; office & public building furniture; computer storage devices

(G-1368)
GLAXOSMITHKLINE LLC
24 Cohasset Ln (08003-1964)
PHONE...................................609 472-8175
EMP: 27
SALES (corp-wide): 39.5B **Privately Held**
SIC: 2834 Pharmaceutical preparations
HQ: Glaxosmithkline Llc
5 Crescent Dr
Philadelphia PA 19112
215 751-4000

(G-1369)
GRAN ALL MRBLE TILE IMPRTS INC (PA)
932 Marlton Pike W (08002-3509)
PHONE...................................856 354-4747
George Siampos, *President*
Foti Tsakiris, *Vice Pres*
▲ **EMP:** 3 **EST:** 1995
SQ FT: 5,500
SALES (est): 2.1MM **Privately Held**
WEB: www.allmarblegranite.com
SIC: 3281 5211 5722 Granite, cut & shaped; tile, ceramic; kitchens, complete (sinks, cabinets, etc.)

(G-1370)
HALDOR USA INC
100 Springdale Rd 83-206 (08003-3300)
PHONE...................................856 254-2345
Ilan Kadosh Tamari, *Principal*
Morr Avissara, *COO*
Ram I Alt, *Senior VP*
Ram Alt, *Vice Pres*
Pete Koste, *Vice Pres*
EMP: 30
SALES (est): 2.7MM **Privately Held**
SIC: 3841 Surgical instruments & apparatus

(G-1371)
HARSCO CORPORATION
1960 Old Cuthbert Rd # 100 (08034-1456)
PHONE...................................856 779-7795
EMP: 20
SALES (corp-wide): 1.7B **Publicly Held**
SIC: 7359 7353 5082 3443 Equipment rental & leasing; heavy construction equipment rental; construction & mining machinery; scaffolding; fuel tanks (oil, gas, etc.): metal plate; cryogenic tanks, for liquids & gases; cylinders, pressure: metal plate; heat exchangers: coolers (after, inter), condensers, etc.; evaporative condensers, heat transfer equipment; railroad maintenance & repair services
PA: Harsco Corporation
350 Poplar Church Rd
Camp Hill PA 17011
717 763-7064

(G-1372)
HIKMA PHARMACEUTICALS USA INC
Also Called: Injectable Mfg Fcilty
2 Esterbrook Ln (08003-4002)
PHONE...................................856 424-3700
Brian Frost, *General Mgr*
Clifford H Powell, *Manager*

John Schiller, *Manager*
Jamie Fagan, *IT/INT Sup*
Julie Hill, *Exec Dir*
EMP: 200
SQ FT: 372,000
SALES (corp-wide): 2B **Privately Held**
SIC: 2834 Pharmaceutical preparations
HQ: Hikma Pharmaceuticals Usa Inc.
246 Industrial Way W # 7
Eatontown NJ 07724
732 542-1191

(G-1373)
ICUP INC
1152 Marlkress Rd Ste 200 (08003-2314)
PHONE...................................856 751-2045
Steven Trachtenberg, *CEO*
Erica McKeen, *Buyer*
Preeya Patel, *Accountant*
Ryan Conard, *Sales Staff*
Brandon Bouchard, *Manager*
▲ **EMP:** 30
SQ FT: 100,000
SALES (est): 6.2MM **Privately Held**
WEB: www.icupinc.com
SIC: 3089 2679 3229 3231 Novelties, plastic; gift wrap & novelties, paper; pressed & blown glass; products of purchased glass; novelties & specialties, metal

(G-1374)
ILKEM MARBLE AND GRANITE INC
Also Called: Ilkem Marble & Granite
2010 Springdale Rd # 300 (08003-2056)
PHONE...................................856 433-8714
Fatih Karaca, *Vice Pres*
EMP: 6
SALES (est): 1MM **Privately Held**
SIC: 3281 5032 Marble, building: cut & shaped; granite building stone

(G-1375)
IMAGINE AUDIO LLC
304 Haddonfield Rd (08002-2204)
PHONE...................................856 488-1466
Mark Balver,
Shira Balver,
EMP: 5
SQ FT: 3,000
SALES (est): 820.4K **Privately Held**
SIC: 2517 Home entertainment unit cabinets, wood

(G-1376)
IMPORTANT PAPERS INC
Also Called: Important Papers & Printing
12 Downing St (08003-1519)
PHONE...................................856 751-4544
Ruth Barnett, *President*
EMP: 5
SQ FT: 5,000
SALES (est): 710.8K **Privately Held**
SIC: 2759 5943 5112 5941 Commercial printing; stationery stores; business forms; camping equipment

(G-1377)
INDUSTRIAL STL & FASTENER CORP
167 Old Blmont Ave Fl 2 Flr 2 (08034)
P.O. Box 2470 (08034-0202)
PHONE...................................610 667-2220
Stephen Gelman, *President*
Alan Gelman, *Vice Pres*
EMP: 2
SQ FT: 5,000
SALES (est): 5.8MM **Privately Held**
SIC: 5051 5072 1081 Steel; hardware; metal mining services

(G-1378)
JBAT INC
Also Called: Cherry Hill Precision Co
28 Coles Ave (08002-1224)
PHONE...................................856 667-7307
John Schallenhammer, *President*
Andrew Schallenhammer, *Vice Pres*
Theresa Schallenhammer, *Treasurer*
EMP: 22 **EST:** 1967
SQ FT: 7,200
SALES (est): 3.9MM **Privately Held**
WEB: www.cherryhillprecision.com
SIC: 3599 Machine shop, jobbing & repair

(G-1379)
K R B PRINTING FOR BUSINESS
1165 Marlkress Rd Ste G (08003-2330)
PHONE...................................856 751-5200
Robert Barbera, *Partner*
Kurt Barbera, *Partner*
Sherre Knable, *Cust Mgr*
EMP: 15
SQ FT: 1,800
SALES: 1.7MM **Privately Held**
SIC: 2752 Commercial printing, offset

(G-1380)
KEYSTONE EUROPE LLC
616 Hollywood Ave (08002-2821)
PHONE...................................856 663-4700
Steve Tidwell, *Principal*
Jill Fox, *Controller*
EMP: 5 **EST:** 2012
SALES (est): 336.5K
SALES (corp-wide): 118.4MM **Privately Held**
SIC: 5047 3843 2844 Dental equipment & supplies; dental equipment & supplies; toilet preparations
PA: Mycone Dental Supply Co., Inc.
480 S Democrat Rd
Gibbstown NJ 08027
856 663-4700

(G-1381)
KYOCERA INTERNATIONAL INC
1515 Burnt Mill Rd (08003-3637)
PHONE...................................856 691-7000
Robert Barron, *Branch Mgr*
EMP: 80 **Publicly Held**
SIC: 3674 Photovoltaic devices, solid state
HQ: Kyocera International, Inc.
8611 Balboa Ave
San Diego CA 92123
858 492-1456

(G-1382)
LAP MARKETING MGT SVCS INC
104 Old Carriage Rd (08034-3330)
PHONE...................................609 654-9266
EMP: 10
SALES (est): 694.7K **Privately Held**
SIC: 3661 Mfg Telephone/Telegraph Apparatus

(G-1383)
LIBERTY CNSTR & INV GROUP
Also Called: US Led Installation Group
1878 Marlton Pike E Ste 7 (08003-2090)
PHONE...................................267 784-7931
Shawn Nan, *President*
EMP: 5
SALES (est): 216.8K **Privately Held**
SIC: 3674 Light emitting diodes

(G-1384)
LOCKHEED MARTIN CORPORATION
Also Called: Lockheed Martin Adv
3 Executive Campus # 600 (08002-4160)
P.O. Box 61511, King of Prussia PA
(19406-0911)
PHONE...................................856 792-9811
Janet Russell, *Engineer*
Krystle Cipolla, *Finance*
Wendell G Rakosky, *Human Res Dir*
Kathleen Spivey, *Branch Mgr*
EMP: 245 **Publicly Held**
WEB: www.lockheedmartin.com
SIC: 3812 Search & navigation equipment
PA: Lockheed Martin Corporation
6801 Rockledge Dr
Bethesda MD 20817

(G-1385)
LRP AND P GRAPHICS
Also Called: Lrp and Profit
1165 Marlkress Rd Ste M (08003-2330)
P.O. Box 1536 (08034-0069)
PHONE...................................856 424-0158
EMP: 20
SALES (est): 1.9MM **Privately Held**
SIC: 2754 Gravure Commercial Printing

(G-1386)
MAARKY THERMAL SYSTEMS INC
1415 Marlton Pike E # 604 (08034-2210)
PHONE...................................856 470-1504

Ranga Nadig, *President*
Michael Phipps, *Vice Pres*
Michael Arico, *Engineer*
Madhura Nadig, *Accounts Mgr*
EMP: 8 **EST:** 2011
SALES (est): 2.5MM **Privately Held**
WEB: www.maarky.com
SIC: 3443 Condensers, steam; heat exchangers, condensers & components

(G-1387)
MAC COSMETICS INC
2000 Route 38 Ste 200 (08002-2100)
PHONE...................................856 661-9024
Nicole Maze, *Manager*
Melissa Gibson, *Exec Dir*
EMP: 15 **Publicly Held**
WEB: www.danreadcosmetics.com
SIC: 2844 Shampoos, rinses, conditioners: hair
HQ: M.A.C. Cosmetics Inc.
130 Prince St Fl 5
New York NY 10012
212 965-6300

(G-1388)
MANNING PUBLICATION CO
1233 Heartwood Dr (08003-2739)
PHONE...................................856 375-2597
Marjan Bace, *Partner*
Lee Fitzpatrick, *Partner*
▲ **EMP:** 12
SQ FT: 2,000
SALES (est): 940K **Privately Held**
SIC: 2731 Books: publishing only

(G-1389)
MARLTON PIKE PRECISION LLC
728 Beechwood Ave (08002-2805)
P.O. Box 334, Marlton (08053-0334)
PHONE...................................856 665-1900
Tony Sala, *President*
EMP: 15 **EST:** 1948
SQ FT: 10,000
SALES: 950K **Privately Held**
SIC: 3599 Machine shop, jobbing & repair

(G-1390)
MASTERPIECE KITCHENS INC
2060 Springdale Rd # 800 (08003-4028)
PHONE...................................609 518-7887
John Nyman, *President*
EMP: 3
SQ FT: 1,400
SALES: 2MM **Privately Held**
WEB: www.masterpiecekitchens.net
SIC: 2434 Wood kitchen cabinets

(G-1391)
MD INTERNATIONAL INC
Also Called: Opalsoft Consulting
383 Kings Hwy N Ste B1 (08034-1014)
PHONE...................................856 779-7633
Dennis Panchal, *President*
EMP: 6 **EST:** 1986
SQ FT: 1,500
SALES (est): 309K **Privately Held**
WEB: www.opalsoftconsult.com
SIC: 7379 3695 Computer related consulting services; computer software tape & disks: blank, rigid & floppy

(G-1392)
MEDIABRIDGE PRODUCTS LLC
1951 Old Cuthbert Rd (08034-1411)
PHONE...................................856 216-8222
Robert Vezirian, *President*
Jarrod Coburn, *Manager*
EMP: 37 **EST:** 2007
SQ FT: 14,000
SALES (est): 25.5MM **Privately Held**
SIC: 3663 Cable television equipment

(G-1393)
MELITTA USA INC
1401 Berlin Rd Ste A (08034-1402)
PHONE...................................856 428-7202
Martin Miller, *Manager*
EMP: 50
SALES (corp-wide): 1.8B **Privately Held**
WEB: www.melitta.com
SIC: 2095 Coffee roasting (except by wholesale grocers)

HQ: Melitta Usa, Inc.
13925 58th St N
Clearwater FL 33760
727 535-2111

(G-1394)
METAL DYNAMIX LLC
670 Deer Rd Ste 201 (08034-1438)
PHONE...................................856 235-4559
Charles Gaw,
EMP: 9
SALES (est): 1.6MM **Privately Held**
WEB: www.metaldynamix.com
SIC: 3444 Sheet metalwork

(G-1395)
MINNITI J HAIR REPLACEMENT INC
Also Called: Joseph Mnniti Hair Replacement
905 Marlton Pike W (08002-3529)
PHONE...................................856 427-9600
Joseph Minniti, *President*
EMP: 6
SALES (est): 602.3K **Privately Held**
SIC: 3999 Hair & hair-based products

(G-1396)
MPLAYER ENTERTAINMENT LLC
329 Greenleigh Ct (08002-2307)
PHONE...................................302 229-3034
Kevin Pineda, *Mng Member*
Kyle Davidson,
EMP: 6 **EST:** 2016
SALES (est): 135.3K **Privately Held**
SIC: 7372 7389 Application computer software;

(G-1397)
NAVISTAR INC
535 Route 38 Ste 300 (08002-2972)
PHONE...................................856 486-2300
EMP: 70
SALES (corp-wide): 10.2B **Publicly Held**
SIC: 3711 Motor vehicles & car bodies
HQ: Navistar, Inc.
2701 Navistar Dr
Lisle IL 60532
331 332-5000

(G-1398)
NEW SKYSONIC SURVEILLANCE
7905 Browning Rd Ste 200 (08002)
PHONE...................................856 317-0600
Leo Lui, *President*
Janice Xu,
EMP: 4
SALES (est): 436.8K **Privately Held**
SIC: 7382 3699 6211 Security systems services; security devices; security control equipment & systems; distributors, security

(G-1399)
NEWSPAPER MEDIA GROUP LLC (PA)
2 Executive Campus # 400 (08002-4102)
PHONE...................................856 779-3800
Angela Smith, *Principal*
EMP: 26
SALES (est): 6.7MM **Privately Held**
SIC: 2711 Newspapers, publishing & printing

(G-1400)
NORTHEAST MEDICAL SYSTEMS CORP
901 Beechwood Ave (08002-3405)
PHONE...................................856 910-8111
Joseph Conte, *President*
David Oberg, *Vice Pres*
EMP: 7
SALES: 1.7MM **Privately Held**
WEB: www.northeastmedicalsystems.com
SIC: 3841 3845 Diagnostic apparatus, medical; electromedical equipment

(G-1401)
NUCLEAR DIAGNOSTIC PRODUCTS OF
Also Called: Cherry Hill Pharmacy
2 Keystone Ave Ste 200 (08003-1629)
PHONE...................................856 489-5733

Rodney Prosser, *President*
Dennis Lucas, *Mng Member*
Jennifer Pasquarosa, *Manager*
EMP: 11
SALES (est): 1.1MM **Privately Held**
SIC: 2834 Pharmaceutical preparations

(G-1402)
NUMERICAL CONTROL PROGRAM SVC
917 Northwood Ave (08002-3415)
PHONE...................................856 665-8737
EMP: 7 **EST:** 1966
SQ FT: 9,500
SALES (est): 52.4K **Privately Held**
SIC: 3599 Machine Shop Jobbing

(G-1403)
OPEN SOLUTIONS INC
2091 Springdale Rd Ste 7 (08003-4005)
PHONE...................................856 424-0150
Tim Lenhoff, *Senior VP*
EMP: 24
SALES (est): 3.3MM **Privately Held**
SIC: 7372 Business oriented computer software

(G-1404)
PAD AND PUBL ASSEMBLY CORP
Also Called: Lrp and P Graphics
1165 Marlkress Rd Ste M (08003-2330)
P.O. Box 1536 (08034-0069)
PHONE...................................856 424-0158
Joan Buehler, *President*
Carl Buehler, *Vice Pres*
Gwyn Andrews, *Administration*
EMP: 25
SQ FT: 6,600
SALES (est): 4.1MM **Privately Held**
WEB: www.padandpub.com
SIC: 2754 2791 2789 2752 Commercial printing, gravure; typesetting; bookbinding & related work; commercial printing, lithographic

(G-1405)
PANPAC LLC
1971 Old Cuthbert Rd (08034-1417)
PHONE...................................856 376-3576
Rahul Kaushik,
◆ **EMP:** 15
SQ FT: 25,000
SALES (est): 3.7MM **Privately Held**
SIC: 3555 Printing trades machinery

(G-1406)
PEAK FINANCE HOLDINGS LLC (DH)
121 Woodcrest Rd (08003-3620)
PHONE...................................856 969-7100
Mark Foley, *Purchasing*
EMP: 1
SALES (est): 2.4B
SALES (corp-wide): 9.5B **Publicly Held**
SIC: 2092 2099 2045 2038 Prepared fish or other seafood cakes & sticks; pancake syrup, blended & mixed; cake flour: from purchased flour; bread & bread type roll mixes: from purchased flour; pancake mixes, prepared: from purchased flour; breakfasts, frozen & packaged
HQ: Pinnacle Foods Inc.
399 Jefferson Rd
Parsippany NJ 07054
973 541-6620

(G-1407)
PENNANT INGREDIENTS INC
1941 Old Cuthbert Rd (08034-1417)
PHONE...................................856 428-4300
EMP: 7
SALES (corp-wide): 30.1MM **Privately Held**
SIC: 2099 Food preparations
HQ: Pennant Ingredients, Inc.
64 Chester St
Rochester NY 14611
585 235-8160

(G-1408)
PHILADELPHIA INQUIRER
53 Haddonfield Rd Ste 300 (08002-4809)
PHONE...................................856 779-3840
Kurt Heine, *Principal*

▲ = Import ▼=Export
◆ =Import/Export

Jason Di Ridolfo, *Executive*
EMP: 6
SALES (est): 344.5K **Privately Held**
SIC: 2711 Newspapers, publishing & printing

(G-1409)
PINNACLE FOODS GROUP LLC
121 Woodcrest Rd (08003-3620)
PHONE.............................856 969-7100
Robert Gamgort, *CEO*
Michelle Rothermich, *Vice Pres*
Amy Skalny, *Vice Pres*
Christopher Straub, *Vice Pres*
Jack Kroeger, *Chief Mktg Ofcr*
EMP: 129
SALES (corp-wide): 9.5B **Publicly Held**
SIC: 2038 Frozen specialties
HQ: Pinnacle Foods Group Llc
399 Jefferson Rd
Parsippany NJ 07054

(G-1410)
POLYSYSTEMS INC
2 Executive Campus # 320 (08002-4102)
PHONE.............................312 332-5670
Graham Bartholomae, *Engineer*
Louis Frano, *Engineer*
Tom Nace, *Accountant*
Patrick Chase, *Manager*
Marianne Clifford, *Manager*
EMP: 8
SALES (corp-wide): 8.3MM **Privately Held**
WEB: www.polysystems.com
SIC: 7372 Application computer software
PA: Polysystems, Inc.
225 W Washington St # 2300
Chicago IL 60606
312 332-2114

(G-1411)
PRESSWORKS
Also Called: Ipp/Pressworks
1879 Old Cuthbert Rd # 28 (08034-1433)
PHONE.............................856 427-9001
Diane Reilly, *Partner*
Dennis Reilly, *Partner*
▲ EMP: 5
SALES: 350K **Privately Held**
SIC: 2759 Promotional printing

(G-1412)
RANDELLS CSTM FNITURE KITCHENS
1864 Marlton Pike E (08003-2029)
PHONE.............................856 216-9400
Randell Wyville, *Owner*
EMP: 12
SALES (est): 970.2K **Privately Held**
SIC: 2499 Decorative wood & woodwork

(G-1413)
RBS INTRNTONAL DIRECT MKTG LLC (PA)
2 Executive Campus # 200 (08002-4102)
PHONE.............................856 663-2500
EMP: 5
SALES (est): 3.7MM **Privately Held**
SIC: 7372 8743 Prepackaged software; public relations services

(G-1414)
SERENE HOUSE USA INC
Also Called: Michael
1814 Marlton Pike E # 350 (08003-2057)
PHONE.............................609 980-1214
Bo Jeansson, *President*
EMP: 5
SALES: 9MM **Privately Held**
SIC: 2899 5169 Oils & essential oils; essential oils

(G-1415)
SMS BUILDING SYSTEMS LTD LBLTY
5 N Olney Ave Ste 100a (08003-1622)
PHONE.............................856 520-8769
Steven Lulias, *Partner*
William Kanupke, *Partner*
EMP: 10

SALES: 1MM **Privately Held**
SIC: 7382 1731 3646 Confinement surveillance systems maintenance & monitoring; voice, data & video wiring contractor; commercial indusl & institutional electric lighting fixtures

(G-1416)
SPRINGDALE FARM MARKET INC
1638 Springdale Rd (08003-2738)
PHONE.............................856 424-8674
Maryann Jarvis, *President*
John Ebert, *Vice Pres*
Tom Jarvis, *Vice Pres*
Mary Ebert, *Admin Sec*
EMP: 35
SQ FT: 45,000
SALES (est): 1.2MM **Privately Held**
SIC: 0161 5812 5992 5947 Corn farm, sweet; tomato farm; eating places; florists; gift, novelty & souvenir shop; fruit & vegetable markets; bread, cake & related products

(G-1417)
SUN NEON SIGN AND ELECTRIC CO
4 Saddle Ln (08002-1528)
PHONE.............................856 667-6977
Stuart Rosner, *Owner*
EMP: 7 EST: 1947
SALES (est): 570K **Privately Held**
SIC: 1731 1799 3993 General electrical contractor; sign installation & maintenance; neon signs

(G-1418)
SURGICAL LSER SFETY CUNCIL INC
405 Hialeah Dr (08002-2036)
PHONE.............................216 272-0805
Allen Seftel, *President*
Stephen Nakada, *Vice Pres*
Mandeep Singh, *Treasurer*
Linda Groce, *Manager*
Richard Pearl, *Consultant*
EMP: 7
SALES (est): 262.6K **Privately Held**
SIC: 3845 3842 Laser systems & equipment, medical; personal safety equipment

(G-1419)
SWAROVSKI NORTH AMERICA LTD
2000 Route 38 (08002-2100)
PHONE.............................856 662-5453
Dana Cooley, *President*
EMP: 7
SALES (corp-wide): 4.7B **Privately Held**
SIC: 3961 Costume jewelry
HQ: Swarovski North America Limited
1 Kenney Dr
Cranston RI 02920
401 463-6400

(G-1420)
T3I GROUP LLC
Phillips Decision Pt Resources
1111 Marlkress Rd Ste 101 (08003-2334)
PHONE.............................856 424-1100
Edyta Krzton, *Research*
Terry White, *Program Dir*
EMP: 40 **Privately Held**
WEB: www.telecomweb.com
SIC: 2741 2721 8732 7379 Miscellaneous publishing; periodicals: publishing & printing; market analysis or research; computer related consulting services
PA: T3i Group Llc
747 3rd Ave
New York NY 10017

(G-1421)
TAPESTRY INC
2000 Route 38 Ste 1720 (08002-2178)
PHONE.............................856 488-2220
Marleen Grassia, *Branch Mgr*
EMP: 15
SALES (corp-wide): 6B **Publicly Held**
WEB: www.coach.com
SIC: 3171 Handbags, women's

PA: Tapestry, Inc.
10 Hudson Yards
New York NY 10001
212 594-1850

(G-1422)
TASTY CAKE SOUTH JERSEY
1871 Old Cuthbert Rd B (08034-1415)
PHONE.............................856 428-8414
John Zagiel, *Executive*
EMP: 4
SALES (est): 194K **Privately Held**
SIC: 2051 Bakery: wholesale or wholesale/retail combined

(G-1423)
TOTAL TECHNOLOGY INC
950 Kings Hwy N Ste 105 (08034-1518)
PHONE.............................856 617-0502
Maria C McCabe, *President*
Nicole Hamilton, *Finance*
EMP: 24
SQ FT: 750
SALES (est): 4.8MM **Privately Held**
WEB: www.totaltechnologyinc.net
SIC: 8711 3577 Engineering services; data conversion equipment, media-to-media: computer

(G-1424)
TURBON INTERNATIONAL INC (DH)
Also Called: Turbon USA
4 Executive Campus # 104 (08002-4105)
PHONE.............................800 282-6650
Aldo Deluca, *CEO*
Dean Edwards, *President*
Steven Injaian, *Admin Sec*
◆ EMP: 2
SQ FT: 130,000
SALES (est): 24MM
SALES (corp-wide): 439.3K **Privately Held**
SIC: 3955 Print cartridges for laser & other computer printers
HQ: Turbon Ag
Ruhrdeich 10
Hattingen 45525
232 450-40

(G-1425)
TURBON INTERNATIONAL INC
Turbon Group, The
4 Executive Campus # 104 (08002-4105)
PHONE.............................413 386-6739
Al Deluca, *CEO*
Jennifer Benedict, *Accountant*
Cassie Gruber, *Director*
EMP: 19
SALES (corp-wide): 439.3K **Privately Held**
SIC: 3955 Print cartridges for laser & other computer printers
HQ: Turbon International Inc
4 Executive Campus # 104
Cherry Hill NJ 08002
800 282-6650

(G-1426)
VIRID BIOSCIENCES LIMITED
Also Called: Viridbio Solutions
246 Sandringham Rd (08003-1550)
PHONE.............................732 410-9573
Vishal Soni, *Mng Member*
EMP: 10
SALES: 500K **Privately Held**
SIC: 5047 7371 8731 8742 Diagnostic equipment, medical; custom computer programming services; biological research; business consultant; in vitro diagnostics

(G-1427)
WILLINGS NUTRACEUTICAL CORP
1936 Olney Ave Ste A (08003-2016)
PHONE.............................856 424-9088
Yan Wang, *President*
EMP: 14
SALES (est): 1.3MM **Privately Held**
SIC: 3086 3089 2023 4225 Packaging & shipping materials, foamed plastic; blister or bubble formed packaging, plastic; dietary supplements, dairy & non-dairy based; general warehousing & storage

(G-1428)
WHIMSY DIDDLES LLC
59 Briarhill Dr (08089-1234)
PHONE.............................609 560-1323
Peter D Connet, *Principal*
EMP: 4 EST: 2007
SALES (est): 387.2K **Privately Held**
SIC: 3499 Novelties & giftware, including trophies

(G-1429)
AB COASTER LLC
Also Called: ABS Company, The
360 State Route 24 Ste 4 (07930-2925)
P.O. Box 9 (07930-0009)
PHONE.............................908 879-2713
Silvia Milaschewski, *Cust Mgr*
Michael Ritter, *Accounts Exec*
Cindy Ramos, *Mktg Dir*
Kim Healey, *Info Tech Mgr*
Sean Gagnon,
EMP: 10
SALES (est): 1.5MM **Privately Held**
SIC: 8742 3949 Marketing consulting services; sporting & athletic goods

(G-1430)
ABACUS ELECTRIC & PLUMBING
95 W Main St Ste 252 (07930-2487)
PHONE.............................908 269-8057
Ken Ryan,
EMP: 4
SALES (est): 250.8K **Privately Held**
SIC: 3699 1711 Electrical equipment & supplies; plumbing, heating, air-conditioning contractors

(G-1431)
BRANDED SCREEN PRINTING
45 Warren St Ste A (07930-3609)
P.O. Box 687 (07930-0687)
PHONE.............................908 879-7411
Chris Smith, *Owner*
EMP: 4
SALES (est): 382.8K **Privately Held**
SIC: 2759 Screen printing

(G-1432)
COMEX SYSTEMS INC
101 Pleasant Hill Rd (07930-2140)
P.O. Box 142, Placida FL (33946-0142)
PHONE.............................800 543-6959
Doug Pryblowski, *President*
EMP: 5
SQ FT: 2,400
SALES (est): 529.4K **Privately Held**
WEB: www.comexsystems.com
SIC: 2731 Books: publishing only

(G-1433)
DOUGLAS MAYBURY ASSOC
385 State Route 24 Ste 3e (07930-2910)
PHONE.............................908 879-5878
Kevin Maybury, *Owner*
EMP: 4
SALES (est): 260K **Privately Held**
SIC: 2752 Business forms, lithographed

(G-1434)
HURRICANE HUTCH
190 Lamerson Rd (07930-2425)
PHONE.............................908 256-5912
Kenneth Hoffman, *Principal*
EMP: 4
SALES: 950K **Privately Held**
SIC: 3499 Fabricated metal products

(G-1435)
THOMAS PUBLISHING COMPANY LLC
Also Called: Thomas Register
95 W Main St Ste 8 (07930-2487)
PHONE.............................973 543-4994

Robert Probst, *Manager*
EMP: 25
SALES (corp-wide): 185.1MM **Privately Held**
WEB: www.inboundlogistics.com
SIC: 2741 2721 7374 Directories: publishing only, not printed on site; trade journals: publishing only, not printed on site; data processing service
PA: Thomas Publishing Company Llc
    5 Penn Plz Fl 8
    New York NY 10001
    212 695-0500

Chesterfield
Burlington County

(G-1436)
BELLA ACQUA INC
Also Called: Acqua Bella Mfg and Supply
214 Sykesville Rd Ste 1a (08515-2419)
PHONE..........................609 324-9024
Scott Crosbie, *President*
EMP: 10
SALES: 2MM **Privately Held**
WEB: www.acquabella.net
SIC: 3624 Carbon specialties for electrical use

(G-1437)
SOMERSET CPITL MARK TR MGT INC
1 Donlonton Cir (08515-9786)
PHONE..........................848 228-0842
Isaac Inyang, *President*
EMP: 10
SALES (est): 784.5K **Privately Held**
SIC: 3612 Transmission & distribution voltage regulators

(G-1438)
TOWNSEND MACHINE INC
246 Sykesville Rd (08515-2407)
PHONE..........................609 723-2603
Barclay A Townsend, *President*
Barclay Townsend, *President*
Lorraine Townsend, *Corp Secy*
Cindy Von Smith, *Office Mgr*
EMP: 40
SQ FT: 24,000
SALES (est): 5.9MM **Privately Held**
WEB: www.gotownsend.com
SIC: 3599 Machine shop, jobbing & repair

Cinnaminson
Burlington County

(G-1439)
ACTEGA NORTH AMERICA INC
1450 Taylors Ln (08077-2512)
PHONE..........................856 829-6300
Steven Kramer, *Principal*
EMP: 13
SALES (corp-wide): 501.4K **Privately Held**
SIC: 2851 Paints & allied products
HQ: Actega North America, Inc.
    950 S Chester Ave Ste B2
    Delran NJ 08075
    856 829-6300

(G-1440)
AIRGAS USA LLC
600 Union Landing Rd (08077-2002)
PHONE..........................856 829-7878
Jill Morrison, *Manager*
EMP: 22
SALES (corp-wide): 125.9MM **Privately Held**
SIC: 5169 5084 5085 2813 Industrial gases; gases, compressed & liquefied; carbon dioxide; dry ice; welding machinery & equipment; safety equipment; welding supplies; industrial gases; carbon dioxide; nitrous oxide; dry ice, carbon dioxide (solid); industrial inorganic chemicals; calcium carbide
HQ: Airgas Usa, Llc
    259 N Radnor Chester Rd
    Radnor PA 19087
    610 687-5253

(G-1441)
AQUA PRODUCTS INC
2703 River Rd (08077-1627)
P.O. Box 231, Riverton (08077-0231)
PHONE..........................856 829-8444
Samuel J Jones Sr, *President*
▼ **EMP:** 25
SALES (est): 4.4MM **Privately Held**
SIC: 2842 Cleaning or polishing preparations

(G-1442)
ARMADILLO AUTOMATION INC
Also Called: Onyx Valve
835 Industrial Hwy Ste 4 (08077-1929)
PHONE..........................856 829-2888
David Gardellin, *CEO*
▲ **EMP:** 40
SQ FT: 12,500
SALES (est): 9.4MM **Privately Held**
WEB: www.onyxvalve.com
SIC: 3823 3491 Industrial process control instruments; industrial valves

(G-1443)
BABCOCK & WILCOX COMPANY
1000 Taylors Ln Ste 4 (08077-2026)
PHONE..........................609 261-2424
Paul Kain, *Branch Mgr*
EMP: 7
SALES (corp-wide): 1B **Publicly Held**
SIC: 3511 Steam turbines
HQ: The Babcock & Wilcox Company
    20 S Van Buren Ave
    Barberton OH 44203
    330 753-4511

(G-1444)
BOSSEN ARCHITECTURAL MILLWORK
1818 Bannard St (08077-1808)
P.O. Box 133, Riverton (08077-0133)
PHONE..........................856 786-1100
Joseph H Bossen, *President*
Joseph Bossen, *Executive*
EMP: 14
SQ FT: 23,000
SALES (est): 3.1MM **Privately Held**
SIC: 5211 5031 2541 Millwork & lumber; kitchen cabinets; display fixtures, wood

(G-1445)
CAPITAL LABEL AND AFFIXING CO
1100 Taylors Ln Ste 5 (08077-2586)
P.O. Box 2366 (08077-5366)
PHONE..........................856 786-1700
EMP: 2
SQ FT: 15,000
SALES (est): 1.2MM **Privately Held**
SIC: 2672 Mfg Coated/Laminated Paper

(G-1446)
CLOTHES HORSE INTERNATIONAL
2200 Wallace Blvd Ste A (08077-2578)
PHONE..........................856 829-8460
Katrina Coldren, *President*
EMP: 12
SQ FT: 3,000
SALES: 1.1MM **Privately Held**
WEB: www.theclotheshorse.com
SIC: 2399 Horse blankets

(G-1447)
COMPUFAB SALES INC
2303 Garry Rd Ste 1 (08077-2560)
PHONE..........................856 786-0175
Otto Steiner, *President*
EMP: 4
SALES (est): 452.9K **Privately Held**
SIC: 3674 Semiconductors & related devices

(G-1448)
DEB MAINTENANCE INC
1000 Union Landing Rd (08077-2502)
P.O. Box 13, Riverton (08077-0013)
PHONE..........................856 786-0440
Kenneth Williams, *President*
Deborah Hess, *Corp Secy*
EMP: 30
SQ FT: 35,000

SALES (est): 5.2MM **Privately Held**
SIC: 3443 Tanks, lined: metal plate; vessels, process or storage (from boiler shops): metal plate

(G-1449)
DEJANA TRCK UTILITY EQP CO LLC
Also Called: Dejana Trck Grter Philadelphia
2502 Route 130 N (08077-3019)
PHONE..........................856 303-1315
Sal Silvestri, *Branch Mgr*
EMP: 24 **Publicly Held**
WEB: www.dejana.com
SIC: 3711 Truck & tractor truck assembly
HQ: Dejana Truck & Utility Equipment Company, Llc
    490 Pulaski Rd
    Kings Park NY 11754
    631 544-9000

(G-1450)
DELVA TOOL & MACHINE CORP (PA)
1603 Industrial Hwy (08077-2503)
PHONE..........................856 786-8700
Stephan Voellinger, *President*
Charles Magro, *Engineer*
EMP: 76 **EST:** 1962
SQ FT: 20,000
SALES (est): 27.5MM **Privately Held**
WEB: www.delvatool.com
SIC: 3599 Machine shop, jobbing & repair

(G-1451)
DELVA TOOL & MACHINE CORP
1911 Rowland St (08077-1923)
P.O. Box 2249 (08077-5249)
PHONE..........................856 829-0109
Jim Valentine, *Opers Staff*
Stephan J Voellinger, *Branch Mgr*
EMP: 53
SALES (corp-wide): 27.5MM **Privately Held**
SIC: 3599 Machine shop, jobbing & repair
PA: Delva Tool & Machine Corp
    1603 Industrial Hwy
    Cinnaminson NJ 08077
    856 786-8700

(G-1452)
DETREX CORPORATION
Also Called: Solvent & Envmtl Svcs Div
835 Industrial Hwy Ste 1 (08077-1929)
PHONE..........................856 786-8686
Una Bauso, *Branch Mgr*
EMP: 6 **Privately Held**
WEB: www.detrex.com
SIC: 3589 Commercial cleaning equipment
HQ: Detrex Corporation
    1000 Belt Line Ave
    Cleveland OH 44109
    216 749-2605

(G-1453)
DU-MOR BLADE CO INC
1002 Union Landing Rd (08077-2502)
PHONE..........................856 829-9384
Harry C Morris, *President*
Margaret Morris, *Corp Secy*
Chris Morris, *Vice Pres*
Elaine Morris, *VP Sales*
▲ **EMP:** 20
SQ FT: 9,000
SALES (est): 3.2MM **Privately Held**
WEB: www.dumorblade.com
SIC: 3421 Knife blades & blanks

(G-1454)
DYNAMIC MACHINING INC
1920 Bannard St (08077-1901)
PHONE..........................856 273-9830
Harold Budman, *President*
Ginny Zimmer, *Info Tech Mgr*
EMP: 19
SQ FT: 14,600
SALES (est): 5MM **Privately Held**
SIC: 3599 Machine shop, jobbing & repair

(G-1455)
EDKER INDUSTRIES INC
1401 Union Landing Rd (08077-2558)
PHONE..........................856 786-1971
Edward C Kerbaugh Jr, *President*
Tom Kerbaugh, *President*
Virginia Kerbaugh, *Admin Sec*

EMP: 45 **EST:** 1967
SQ FT: 12,000
SALES (est): 7.9MM **Privately Held**
SIC: 3444 Sheet metal specialties, not stamped

(G-1456)
ENSER CORPORATION (PA)
1902 Taylors Ln (08077-2580)
PHONE..........................856 829-5522
Marco Arnone, *President*
Eric Venskytis, *Shareholder*
Michael Wahner, *Shareholder*
EMP: 70
SQ FT: 30,000
SALES (est): 9.6MM **Privately Held**
WEB: www.enser.com
SIC: 8711 7373 3554 7361 Mechanical engineering; computer-aided design (CAD) systems service; fourdrinier machines, paper manufacturing; labor contractors (employment agency)

(G-1457)
FOUNDATION MONITORING
Also Called: Fmw Drilling
515 Wellfleet Rd (08077-4426)
PHONE..........................856 829-0410
John L Snyder, *President*
Theresa A Snyder, *Vice Pres*
EMP: 4
SALES (est): 411K **Privately Held**
SIC: 1381 8748 Service well drilling; environmental consultant

(G-1458)
G N J INC (PA)
Also Called: Dunkin' Donuts
N Riderton Rd Rr 130 (08077)
PHONE..........................856 786-1127
Shailesh Doshi, *President*
Kal Shah, *Vice Pres*
EMP: 19
SALES (est): 1.7MM **Privately Held**
SIC: 5461 2051 Doughnuts; doughnuts, except frozen

(G-1459)
GAB ELECTRONIC SERVICES LLC
1703 Industrial Hwy Ste 8 (08077-2582)
PHONE..........................856 786-0108
Donald Bogle, *President*
EMP: 25 **EST:** 1976
SQ FT: 6,000
SALES: 2MM **Privately Held**
WEB: www.rhrtechnologies.com
SIC: 3672 Printed circuit boards

(G-1460)
GRIFFIN SIGNS INC
484 N Randolph Ave (08077)
PHONE..........................856 786-8517
Michele Angerame, *President*
Robert Perry, *Vice Pres*
EMP: 45
SQ FT: 25,000
SALES (est): 9MM **Privately Held**
WEB: www.griffinsigns.com
SIC: 1799 3993 8748 Sign installation & maintenance; fence construction; signs, not made in custom sign painting shops; traffic consultant

(G-1461)
H-E TOOL & MFG CO INC
800 Industrial Hwy Unit A (08077-1949)
PHONE..........................856 303-8787
Pauline Hamin, *President*
David D'Antonio, *COO*
EMP: 35
SQ FT: 43,000
SALES: 4.3MM
SALES (corp-wide): 113MM **Privately Held**
WEB: www.h-etool.com
SIC: 3544 Special dies & tools
PA: Sea Box, Inc.
    1 Sea Box Dr
    Cinnaminson NJ 08077
    856 303-1101

▲ = Import ▼=Export
◆ =Import/Export

(G-1462)
HAROLD F FISHER & SONS INC
Also Called: Fisher, Harold & Sons
875 Industrial Hwy Ste 8 (08077-1944)
PHONE..............................800 624-2868
Frank Fisher, *President*
Barbara Fisher, *Vice Pres*
EMP: 5
SALES (est): 670.4K **Privately Held**
SIC: 2394 Canvas covers & drop cloths;
tarpaulins, fabric: made from purchased
materials

(G-1463)
HENRY OLSEN MACHINE
Also Called: Olsen, H Machine
2504 Route 73 (08077-4113)
PHONE..............................856 662-2121
Henry Olsen, *Owner*
David Olsen, *Co-Owner*
EMP: 5
SQ FT: 1,900
SALES (est): 366.7K **Privately Held**
SIC: 3599 Machine shop, jobbing & repair

(G-1464)
HOEGANAES CORPORATION (DH)
1001 Taylors Ln (08077-2034)
PHONE..............................856 303-0366
Bob Kuhle, *General Mgr*
Kalathur Narasimhan, *Vice Pres*
Joel Feit, *Vice Pres*
Fran Hanejko, *Vice Pres*
Thomas Lewandowski, *Vice Pres*
◆ EMP: 277
SQ FT: 504,000
SALES: 176MM
SALES (corp-wide): 11B **Privately Held**
WEB: www.hoeganaes.com
SIC: 3312 3399 Blast furnaces & steel
mills; metal powders, pastes & flakes

(G-1465)
INTEGRTED LAMINATE SYSTEMS INC
1301 Industrial Hwy (08077-2552)
PHONE..............................856 786-6500
Chris Sparacio, *President*
Kim Staryeu, *Project Mgr*
Don Reckeweg, *Purchasing*
Joanne Butler, *Manager*
EMP: 54
SALES (est): 9.4MM **Privately Held**
SIC: 3843 Cabinets, dental

(G-1466)
INVENTORS SHOP LLC
800 Industrial Hwy Unit A (08077-1949)
PHONE..............................856 303-8787
Harry Keeny, *General Mgr*
Jack Grace, *Purchasing*
Gina Tobin, *Sales Associate*
Jim Brennan, *Mng Member*
Craig Marty, *Manager*
EMP: 24
SALES (est): 2.4MM **Privately Held**
SIC: 8999 3544 Actuarial consultant; spe-
cial dies & tools

(G-1467)
J A W PRODUCTS INC
835 Industrial Hwy # 125 (08077-1929)
P.O. Box 2593 (08077-4993)
PHONE..............................856 829-3210
Earl Weightman, *President*
Elenore Weightman, *Vice Pres*
EMP: 12
SQ FT: 3,300
SALES (est): 1.8MM **Privately Held**
WEB: www.jawproducts.com
SIC: 3843 5047 3599 Dental equipment &
supplies; dental equipment & supplies;
machine shop, jobbing & repair

(G-1468)
KOBOLAK & SON INC
1818 Bannard St (08077-1808)
PHONE..............................856 829-6106
Erno Kobolak, *President*
EMP: 8
SALES (est): 893.5K **Privately Held**
SIC: 2434 Wood kitchen cabinets

(G-1469)
KT MT CORP (PA)
Also Called: Aall American Fasteners
2303 Garry Rd Unit 12 (08077-2560)
PHONE..............................877 791-4426
Kimberly A Tenenbaum, *President*
Mark D Tenenbaum, *Vice Pres*
Michael Spillane, *Executive*
EMP: 18 EST: 1998
SQ FT: 10,000
SALES: 3.5MM **Privately Held**
WEB: www.aallamericanfasteners.com
SIC: 5085 3452 Fasteners, industrial:
nuts, bolts, screws, etc.; bolts, nuts, rivets
& washers

(G-1470)
LYNN MECHANICAL CONTRACTORS
1810 Rowland St (08077-1852)
PHONE..............................856 829-1717
Raymond W Lynn Sr, *President*
Clare Lynn, *Corp Secy*
Raymond W Lynn Jr, *Vice Pres*
EMP: 13 EST: 1946
SQ FT: 14,000
SALES: 1.4MM **Privately Held**
SIC: 3535 3444 Conveyors & conveying
equipment; sheet metal specialties, not
stamped

(G-1471)
MARY BRIDGET ENTERPRISES
2305 Garry Rd Ste B (08077-2596)
PHONE..............................609 267-4830
Jim Daly, *Owner*
EMP: 20
SALES (est): 1.8MM **Privately Held**
SIC: 2759 2395 Screen printing; embroi-
dery & art needlework

(G-1472)
MATESON CHEMICAL CORPORATION
510 Whitmore St (08077-1626)
PHONE..............................215 423-3200
Joseph Cammarasana, *President*
James Mateson, *Treasurer*
Christopher Mateson, *Admin Sec*
EMP: 9 EST: 1953
SQ FT: 10,000
SALES (est): 2.3MM **Privately Held**
WEB: www.matesonchemical.com
SIC: 2819 Industrial inorganic chemicals

(G-1473)
MICRO-TEK CORPORATION
1600 Taylors Ln (08077-2520)
P.O. Box 2134 (08077-5134)
PHONE..............................856 829-3855
Brian W Gordon, *President*
▲ EMP: 3
SALES (est): 1.6MM **Privately Held**
SIC: 3357 8711 Nonferrous wiredrawing &
insulating; consulting engineer

(G-1474)
MIDLANTIC COLOR GRAPHICS LLC
2303 Garry Rd Ste 9 (08077-2560)
P.O. Box 2388 (08077-5388)
PHONE..............................856 786-3113
Henry Chou, *Technology*
Thomas Gain,
Michael Gain,
Mike Gain,
EMP: 4
SALES (est): 531.8K **Privately Held**
WEB: www.midlanticonline.com
SIC: 2759 Screen printing

(G-1475)
MONTGOMERY INVESTMENT TECH (PA)
700 Route 130 N Ste 105 (08077-3346)
PHONE..............................610 688-8111
George Montgomery, *President*
Greg Vermeychuk, *Research*
EMP: 9
SQ FT: 1,000
SALES (est): 1.5MM **Privately Held**
WEB: www.wallstreetnet.com
SIC: 7372 Business oriented computer
software

(G-1476)
NATIONAL CASEIN NEW JERSEY INC
401 Marthas Ln (08077-1551)
P.O. Box 226, Riverton (08077-0226)
PHONE..............................856 829-1880
Trever Williams, *Manager*
David Lowery, *Director*
EMP: 30
SALES (corp-wide): 4.8MM **Privately Held**
SIC: 3089 2891 Molding primary plastic;
adhesives
PA: National Casein Of New Jersey, Incor-
porated
601 W 80th St
Chicago IL 60620
773 846-7300

(G-1477)
O & S RESEARCH INC
1912 Bannard St (08077-1901)
P.O. Box 221, Riverton (08077-0221)
PHONE..............................856 829-2800
Anderson Mc Cabe, *President*
Arthur Kania, *Corp Secy*
Warren Thielz, *Mfg Spvr*
Fred Fogleman, *QA Dir*
Lorraine Domask, *Controller*
▲ EMP: 35
SQ FT: 29,000
SALES (est): 6.8MM
SALES (corp-wide): 6.3MM **Publicly Held**
WEB: www.osresearch.com
SIC: 3827 Lenses, optical: all types except
ophthalmic; prisms, optical
PA: Opt-Sciences Corporation
1912 Bannard St
Cinnaminson NJ 08077
856 829-2800

(G-1478)
OPT-SCIENCES CORPORATION (PA)
1912 Bannard St (08077-1901)
P.O. Box 221, Riverton (08077-0221)
PHONE..............................856 829-2800
Anderson L McCabe, *President*
Arthur J Kania, *Admin Sec*
EMP: 46
SQ FT: 5,000
SALES (est): 6.3MM **Publicly Held**
WEB: www.optsciences.com
SIC: 3827 Optical instruments & apparatus

(G-1479)
PECHTERS SOUTHERN NJ LLC
Also Called: Psnj
2 Surrey Ln (08077)
P.O. Box 2069 (08077-5069)
PHONE..............................856 786-8000
James Fisher, *General Mgr*
EMP: 7
SALES: 950K **Privately Held**
SIC: 2051 Bread, cake & related products

(G-1480)
PEDRICK TOOL & MACHINE CO
1515 River Rd (08077-1516)
P.O. Box 190, Riverton (08077-0190)
PHONE..............................856 829-8900
Ralph M S Scott, *President*
EMP: 3
SQ FT: 12,500
SALES: 1MM **Privately Held**
WEB: www.pedrick.com
SIC: 3599 Machine shop, jobbing & repair

(G-1481)
PHARMAKON CORP
2200 Wallace Blvd Ste C (08077-2578)
P.O. Box 2174 (08077-5174)
PHONE..............................856 829-3161
William H Shaffer Sr, *President*
Bruce Shaffer, *Vice Pres*
EMP: 15
SQ FT: 5,000
SALES (est): 1.4MM **Privately Held**
SIC: 3999 Advertising display products

(G-1482)
PHOENIX RESINS INC
Also Called: Mas Epoxies
602 Union Landing Rd (08077-2002)
P.O. Box 2310 (08077-5310)
PHONE..............................888 627-3769
James B Currell Jr, *CEO*
Tony Delima, *President*
Maryann Mc Farland, *Corp Secy*
EMP: 10
SQ FT: 2,300
SALES: 500K **Privately Held**
WEB: www.masepoxies.com
SIC: 2821 Epoxy resins

(G-1483)
SAMUEL ELLIOTT INC
Also Called: Apollo Graphics NJ
1818 Bannard St (08077-1808)
P.O. Box 81, Palmyra (08065-0081)
PHONE..............................856 773-6000
Mary Bossen, *President*
John Bossen, *General Mgr*
Sam Bossen, *Treasurer*
EMP: 20
SALES (est): 1.8MM **Privately Held**
WEB: www.samuelelliott.com
SIC: 2759 Commercial printing

(G-1484)
SHELBY MECHANICAL INC
1009 Broad St (08077-1543)
PHONE..............................856 665-4540
Stephen Zemaitatis Jr, *President*
Joe Amendola, *Division Mgr*
Dan McFadden, *Superintendent*
Michael Mulligan, *Exec VP*
Wayne Hoffmann, *Vice Pres*
EMP: 50
SQ FT: 25,000
SALES (est): 24.4MM
SALES (corp-wide): 21.7MM **Privately Held**
SIC: 1711 1389 1629 Boiler maintenance
contractor; construction, repair & disman-
tling services; oil refinery construction;
power plant construction
HQ: Riggs Distler & Company, Inc.
4 Esterbrook Ln
Cherry Hill NJ 08003
856 433-6000

(G-1485)
SITARAS TOASTERS EQUIPMENT LLC
602 Union Landing Rd (08077-2002)
PHONE..............................732 910-2678
Nicki Mpogiatzis,
EMP: 7 EST: 2014
SALES (est): 624.8K **Privately Held**
SIC: 3589 Commercial cooking & food-
warming equipment

(G-1486)
SOURCE DIRECT INC
Also Called: Source Direct Plastics Div
2200 Garry Rd Ste 3 (08077-2595)
PHONE..............................856 768-7445
Sundeep Thakrar, *President*
Bob Thakrar, *Vice Pres*
▲ EMP: 15
SQ FT: 50,000
SALES: 10MM **Privately Held**
WEB: www.sourcedirectinc.com
SIC: 2673 Plastic bags: made from pur-
chased materials

(G-1487)
T-M VACUUM PRODUCTS INC (PA)
630 S Warrington Ave (08077-1898)
P.O. Box 2248 (08077-5248)
PHONE..............................856 829-2000
Fred T Stuffer, *President*
Ken Chew, *Engineer*
Ed Urbanski, *Engineer*
Roland Johnson, *Admin Sec*
▼ EMP: 35 EST: 1965
SQ FT: 25,000
SALES (est): 5MM **Privately Held**
WEB: www.tmvacuum.com
SIC: 3567 Vacuum furnaces & ovens

(G-1488)
T-M VACUUM PRODUCTS INC
630 S Warrington Ave (08077-1898)
P.O. Box 2248 (08077-5248)
PHONE..............................856 829-2000
EMP: 10
SALES (corp-wide): 5MM Privately Held
WEB: www.tmvacuum.com
SIC: 3599 Machine shop, jobbing & repair
PA: T-M Vacuum Products, Inc.
630 S Warrington Ave
Cinnaminson NJ 08077
856 829-2000

(G-1489)
TGZ ACQUISITION COMPANY LLC
Also Called: Jace Systems
855 Industrial Hwy Ste 4 (08077-1933)
PHONE..............................856 669-6600
Tom Zieser, Mng Member
Wayne Maurer, Manager
EMP: 16
SALES (est): 3.3MM Privately Held
SIC: 7352 3842 Medical equipment rental; orthopedic appliances

(G-1490)
THEPOSITIVE PRESS
2020 Bannard St (08077-1902)
PHONE..............................856 266-8765
EMP: 4
SALES (est): 107.5K Privately Held
SIC: 2741 Misc Publishing

(G-1491)
TOMKEN PLATING
625 Pear St (08077-1915)
P.O. Box 2323 (08077-5323)
PHONE..............................856 829-0607
Thomas H Kennedy, President
Eric Kennedy, Vice Pres
Gertrude M Kennedy, Treasurer
EMP: 8
SQ FT: 11,000
SALES (est): 1.2MM Privately Held
SIC: 3471 Plating of metals or formed products

(G-1492)
TRANSAXLE LLC (PA)
2501 Route 73 (08077-4114)
P.O. Box 2306 (08077-5306)
PHONE..............................856 665-4445
Bill Clark, General Mgr
Anne Monaco, Buyer
Matt Goebel, QC Mgr
David Gordan, Controller
David Gorden, Controller
▲ EMP: 210 EST: 1979
SALES (est): 80.9MM Privately Held
SIC: 5013 3714 Truck parts & accessories; differentials & parts, motor vehicle

(G-1493)
TRI-DIM FILTER CORPORATION
Also Called: Tri Dim Filter
1306 Sylvania Ave (08077-2715)
PHONE..............................856 786-2447
EMP: 4
SALES (corp-wide): 4.5B Privately Held
SIC: 3564 Filters, air: furnaces, air conditioning equipment, etc.
HQ: Tri-Dim Filter Corporation
93 Industrial Dr
Louisa VA 23093
540 967-2600

(G-1494)
UNITEX INTERNATIONAL INC
2702 Cindel Dr Ste 3 (08077-2035)
PHONE..............................856 786-5000
▲ EMP: 4
SALES (est): 621.5K Privately Held
SIC: 2869 Mfg Industrial Organic Chemicals

Clark
Union County

(G-1495)
BOULEVARD LUNCH SERVICE INC
251 Willow Way (07066-2835)
PHONE..............................732 381-5772
Henry F Forfa, President
Phyllis Forfa, Corp Secy
EMP: 15
SQ FT: 4,000
SALES (est): 1.3MM Privately Held
SIC: 2099 Ready-to-eat meals, salads & sandwiches

(G-1496)
CONTEMPORARY CABLING COMPANY
90 Brookside Ter (07066-2862)
PHONE..............................732 382-5064
John Ross, President
Gina Ross, Vice Pres
EMP: 5
SALES (est): 500K Privately Held
WEB: www.contemporarycable.com
SIC: 1731 2298 Fiber optic cable installation; cable, fiber

(G-1497)
FALCON GRAPHICS INC
Also Called: Falcon Printing
70 Westfield Ave (07066-3225)
PHONE..............................908 232-1991
Anthony Archambault, President
Nicholas Archambault, Treasurer
Michael Archambault, Director
EMP: 7
SQ FT: 4,500
SALES: 1MM Privately Held
SIC: 2752 7336 Commercial printing, offset; graphic arts & related design

(G-1498)
J J ORLY INC
67 Walnut Ave Ste 307 (07066-1687)
P.O. Box 945 (07066-0945)
PHONE..............................908 276-9212
William Herbert, President
EMP: 15
SALES (est): 2.2MM Privately Held
WEB: www.jjorly.com
SIC: 3469 Stamping metal for the trade

(G-1499)
JAY-BEE OIL & GAS INC (PA)
Also Called: Jay Bee Oil & Gas Company
60 Walnut Ave Ste 190 (07066-1647)
PHONE..............................908 686-1493
Randy Broda, President
Deborah B Morgan, Vice Pres
Shane Dowell, Office Mgr
Brian Paugh, Manager
EMP: 75 EST: 1989
SALES (est): 51.8MM Privately Held
SIC: 1381 Directional drilling oil & gas wells

(G-1500)
KARNAK CORPORATION (PA)
330 Central Ave (07066-1199)
PHONE..............................732 388-0300
Sarah J Jelin, President
Mike Brehm, COO
Chris Salazar, COO
John McDermott, Vice Pres
Fred Mansfield, VP Opers
▲ EMP: 65 EST: 1933
SQ FT: 65,000
SALES (est): 18.5MM Privately Held
WEB: www.karnakcorp.com
SIC: 2952 Roofing materials; roof cement: asphalt, fibrous or plastic

(G-1501)
KARNAK MIDWEST LLC (HQ)
330 Central Ave (07066-1199)
PHONE..............................732 388-0300
Robert Andrews, CFO
Sarah Jane Jelin,
James D Hannah,
EMP: 5

SALES (est): 2.3MM
SALES (corp-wide): 18.5MM Privately Held
SIC: 2952 Roofing materials
PA: Karnak Corporation
330 Central Ave
Clark NJ 07066
732 388-0300

(G-1502)
KERRY FLAVOR SYSTEMS US LLC
Also Called: Kerry Ingredients & Flavours
160 Terminal Ave (07066-1319)
PHONE..............................513 771-4682
EMP: 250 Privately Held
SIC: 2087 Mfg Flavor Extracts/Syrup
PA: Kerry Flavor Systems Us, Llc
10261 Chester Rd
Cincinnati OH 45215

(G-1503)
KERRY INC
222 Terminal Ave (07066-1317)
PHONE..............................845 584-3081
EMP: 6 Privately Held
SIC: 2099 Food preparations
HQ: Kerry Inc.
3400 Millington Rd
Beloit WI 53511
608 363-1200

(G-1504)
LOREAL USA INC
30 Terminal Ave (07066-1322)
PHONE..............................732 499-6617
Vinayak Srinivasan, Assistant VP
Surabhi Singh, Research
Jim Murphy, Branch Mgr
Deborah Orak, Manager
Vimal Gusani, Network Analyst
EMP: 150
SALES (corp-wide): 4.4B Privately Held
WEB: www.lorealparisusa.com
SIC: 2844 Hair preparations, including shampoos; cosmetic preparations; perfumes & colognes
HQ: L'oreal Usa, Inc.
10 Hudson Yards
New York NY 10001
212 818-1500

(G-1505)
LOREAL USA INC
100 Terminal Ave (07066-1319)
PHONE..............................212 818-1500
Ken Fischer, Principal
Lauren Dininno, Vice Pres
Emily Espinosa, Vice Pres
Amy Freedman, Vice Pres
Kristan Maurer, Vice Pres
EMP: 100
SALES (corp-wide): 4.4B Privately Held
WEB: www.lorealparisusa.com
SIC: 2844 5122 Hair preparations, including shampoos; drugs, proprietaries & sundries
HQ: L'oreal Usa, Inc.
10 Hudson Yards
New York NY 10001
212 818-1500

(G-1506)
LOREAL USA INC
159 Terminal Ave (07066-1320)
PHONE..............................732 499-6690
Frederic Cervantes, Vice Pres
Camilla Wang, Manager
EMP: 100
SALES (corp-wide): 4.4B Privately Held
WEB: www.lorealparisusa.com
SIC: 2844 8731 Hair preparations, including shampoos; cosmetic preparations; perfumes & colognes; commercial physical research
HQ: L'oreal Usa, Inc.
10 Hudson Yards
New York NY 10001
212 818-1500

(G-1507)
LOREAL USA INC
175 Terminal Ave (07066-1320)
PHONE..............................732 499-2809
L Attal, President
J Donoso, Manager

EMP: 7
SALES (corp-wide): 4.4B Privately Held
WEB: www.lorealparisusa.com
SIC: 2844 Toilet preparations
HQ: L'oreal Usa, Inc.
10 Hudson Yards
New York NY 10001
212 818-1500

(G-1508)
MASTERTASTE INC (DH)
Also Called: Kerry Ingredients and Flavours
160 Terminal Ave (07066-1319)
PHONE..............................732 882-0202
Gerry Behan, President
Mike Gransee, CFO
William Coole, Admin Sec
◆ EMP: 101
SALES (est): 84MM Privately Held
WEB: www.mastertaste.com
SIC: 2087 Flavoring extracts & syrups
HQ: Kerry Inc.
3400 Millington Rd
Beloit WI 53511
608 363-1200

(G-1509)
NB VENTURES INC (PA)
Also Called: Gep
100 Walnut Ave Ste 304 (07066-1247)
PHONE..............................732 382-6565
Subhash Makhija, CEO
Jagadish Turimella, COO
Stephen Bucalo, Vice Pres
Patrick Callahan, Vice Pres
Tunir Chatterjee, Vice Pres
EMP: 250
SQ FT: 17,776
SALES (est): 145MM Privately Held
WEB: www.globaleprocure.com
SIC: 8742 5045 7372 7371 Business consultant; computer software; application computer software; business oriented computer software; computer software development & applications

(G-1510)
NU-PLAN BUSINESS SYSTEMS INC
64 Washington St (07066-3223)
PHONE..............................732 231-6944
Howard R Rinn, President
EMP: 4 EST: 1973
SQ FT: 6,000
SALES (est): 361.9K Privately Held
WEB: www.nu-plan.com
SIC: 5112 2752 Stationery & office supplies; offset & photolithographic printing

(G-1511)
OFFICE NEEDS INC
1120 Raritan Rd Ste 2 (07066-1349)
P.O. Box 5804 (07066-5804)
PHONE..............................732 381-7770
Sharon Katcher, President
Gary Katcher, Vice Pres
EMP: 9
SQ FT: 2,500
SALES (est): 1.2MM Privately Held
SIC: 5112 2759 5021 Office supplies; letterpress printing; office furniture

(G-1512)
PHILLIP BALDEROSE
Also Called: Budget Instant Printing
70 Westfield Ave (07066-3225)
PHONE..............................732 574-1330
Phillip Balderose, Owner
EMP: 4
SQ FT: 1,100
SALES (est): 318.4K Privately Held
SIC: 2752 Photo-offset printing

(G-1513)
PLATINUM PLATING SPECIALISTS
11 Blake Dr (07066-1646)
PHONE..............................732 221-2575
EMP: 5
SALES (est): 260.6K Privately Held
SIC: 3471 Plating of metals or formed products

2019 Harris New Jersey
Manufacturers Directory
▲ = Import ▼=Export
◆ =Import/Export

(G-1514)
RAILPACE CO INC
257 Oak Ridge Rd (07066-2761)
PHONE...................................732 388-4984
Dennis Connell, *Partner*
EMP: 4
SALES (est): 180K **Privately Held**
SIC: 2731 Book publishing

(G-1515)
SHANGHAI OPTICS INC (PA)
17 Brant Ave Ste 6 (07066-1548)
P.O. Box 846, Old Bridge (08857-0846)
PHONE...................................732 321-6915
Qiao He, *President*
Johnny Lee, *Vice Pres*
Cheryl Balosie, *Sales Staff*
EMP: 10
SALES (est): 950.8K **Privately Held**
WEB: www.shanghai-optics.com
SIC: 3827 Optical instruments & apparatus

(G-1516)
TANTER INC
Also Called: Horizon Printing
151 Westfield Ave Ste 3 (07066-2415)
PHONE...................................732 382-3555
Walter Swierc, *President*
Stanley Swierc, *Vice Pres*
EMP: 5
SQ FT: 2,500
SALES (est): 470K **Privately Held**
SIC: 2752 2791 2789 Commercial printing, offset; typesetting; bookbinding & related work

(G-1517)
THAL PRECISION INDUSTRIES LLC
33 Terminal Ave (07066-1321)
P.O. Box 281, Lincroft (07738-0281)
PHONE...................................732 381-6106
Thomas Nagler, *President*
Paul Thal, *General Mgr*
James Thal, *Consultant*
EMP: 9 EST: 1980
SALES (est): 1.3MM **Privately Held**
WEB: www.thalprecision.com
SIC: 3544 Forms (molds), for foundry & plastics working machinery

Clarksboro
Gloucester County

(G-1518)
DEWALT MANUFACTURING CO INC
88 W Cohawkin Rd (08020-1100)
PHONE...................................856 423-1207
Roger Dewalt, *President*
EMP: 4 EST: 1960
SQ FT: 5,000
SALES (est): 484K **Privately Held**
SIC: 3599 Machine shop, jobbing & repair

(G-1519)
EXCEL HYDRAULICS LLC
152 Berkley Rd (08020-1156)
P.O. Box 260, Mount Royal (08061-0260)
PHONE...................................856 241-1145
Chad Graham, *COO*
Bob Chew, *Sales Mgr*
Dana Harrington, *Manager*
Robert Chew,
EMP: 32
SQ FT: 3,000
SALES (est): 6MM **Privately Held**
WEB: www.excelhydraulics.com
SIC: 7699 3593 Hydraulic equipment repair; fluid power actuators, hydraulic or pneumatic

Clarksburg
Monmouth County

(G-1520)
FORESIGHT ENVIROPROBE INC
19 Trenton Lakewood Rd (08510-1118)
P.O. Box 6385, Freehold (07728-6385)
PHONE...................................609 259-1244
Tom McChesney, *President*
Ralph Mufgrave, *Vice Pres*
EMP: 6
SALES (est): 900K **Privately Held**
SIC: 1382 Geological exploration, oil & gas field

(G-1521)
HYBRID-TEK LLC
9 Trenton Lakewood Rd # 2 (08510-1114)
PHONE...................................609 259-3355
John Lee, *Mng Member*
Brian Hammond, *Manager*
EMP: 10
SQ FT: 2,000
SALES (est): 1.5MM **Privately Held**
WEB: www.hybrid-tek.com
SIC: 3674 Hybrid integrated circuits

(G-1522)
MILLSTONE DQ INC
Also Called: Dairy Queen
40 Trenton Lakewood Rd (08510-1110)
PHONE...................................609 259-6733
Sanj Kanwar, *President*
EMP: 9
SALES (est): 510K **Privately Held**
SIC: 5812 2052 Ice cream stands or dairy bars; cones, ice cream

Clayton
Gloucester County

(G-1523)
ALERIS ROLLED PRODUCTS INC
Also Called: Clayton Rolling Mill
838 N Delsea Dr (08312-1004)
PHONE...................................856 881-3600
EMP: 115 **Privately Held**
SIC: 3341 Aluminum smelting & refining (secondary)
HQ: Aleris Rolled Products, Inc.
25825 Science Park Dr # 400
Beachwood OH 44122
216 910-3400

(G-1524)
AURA BADGE CO
264 W Clayton Ave (08312-1818)
P.O. Box 655 (08312-0655)
PHONE...................................856 881-9026
Philip Barbaro, *President*
Robert Barbaro, *Vice Pres*
▲ EMP: 60 EST: 1952
SQ FT: 40,000
SALES: 4.6MM **Privately Held**
WEB: www.aurabadge.com
SIC: 3999 3993 Identification badges & insignia; advertising novelties

(G-1525)
HUNGERFORD & TERRY INC (PA)
Also Called: H & T
226 N Atlantic Ave (08312-1335)
P.O. Box 650 (08312-0650)
PHONE...................................856 881-3200
Thomas Carrocino, *President*
Harold Aronovitch, *Vice Pres*
Kenneth M Sayell, *Vice Pres*
Nick Sangillo, *Sales Associate*
▼ EMP: 50
SQ FT: 85,000
SALES (est): 25.1MM **Privately Held**
WEB: www.hungerfordterry.com
SIC: 1499 3589 Greensand mining; water treatment equipment, industrial

(G-1526)
INVERSAND COMPANY INC (HQ)
226 N Atlantic Ave (08312-1335)
PHONE...................................856 881-2345
Alan A Davis, *President*
Kenneth Sayell, *VP Sales*
▲ EMP: 10 EST: 1929
SQ FT: 1,000
SALES (est): 3MM
SALES (corp-wide): 25.1MM **Privately Held**
WEB: www.inversand.com
SIC: 5169 1446 Industrial chemicals; filtration sand mining

PA: Hungerford & Terry, Inc.
226 N Atlantic Ave
Clayton NJ 08312
856 881-3200

(G-1527)
MARLYN SHEET METAL INC
606 N Delsea Dr (08312-1220)
PHONE...................................856 863-6900
Lynn Brandt, *President*
Julius Brandt, *President*
EMP: 15
SQ FT: 7,000
SALES (est): 3.2MM **Privately Held**
SIC: 3444 Sheet metalwork

(G-1528)
REVERE INDUSTRIES LLC (PA)
Also Called: Revere Packaging
838 N Delsea Dr (08312-1004)
PHONE...................................856 881-3600
David Charles, *President*
David Korus, *Vice Pres*
Ron Lapointe, *Vice Pres*
John Wherry, *Vice Pres*
Gary Stone, *VP Opers*
◆ EMP: 110
SQ FT: 275,000
SALES (est): 53MM **Privately Held**
WEB: www.revereindustries.com
SIC: 3497 3089 Foil containers for bakery goods & frozen foods; food casings, plastic

(G-1529)
SHOREWAY INDUSTRY
260 W Clayton Ave (08312-1818)
PHONE...................................856 307-2020
Kimberly Critchfield, *Partner*
Joann Critchfield, *Partner*
EMP: 4
SQ FT: 5,300
SALES (est): 380K **Privately Held**
SIC: 3561 Industrial pumps & parts

(G-1530)
WILLIAM CROMLEY
Also Called: K & C Fundraising
101 S Delsea Dr (08312-1913)
PHONE...................................856 881-6019
EMP: 4
SQ FT: 2,000
SALES (est): 170K **Privately Held**
SIC: 2395 Pleating/Stitching Services

Clementon
Camden County

(G-1531)
BIMBO BAKERIES USA INC
1340 Blckwood Clemtons Rd (08021-5610)
PHONE...................................856 435-0500
Grace Batten, *Manager*
EMP: 80 **Privately Held**
WEB: www.englishmuffin.com
SIC: 2051 Bread, cake & related products
HQ: Bimbo Bakeries Usa, Inc
255 Business Center Dr # 200
Horsham PA 19044
215 347-5500

(G-1532)
ELECTRONICS BOUTIQUE AMER INC
1468 Blckwood Clmenton Rd (08021-5778)
PHONE...................................856 435-3900
Anthony Le Vecchia, *Manager*
EMP: 6
SALES (corp-wide): 8.2B **Publicly Held**
SIC: 3944 Games, toys & children's vehicles
HQ: Electronics Boutique Of America Inc.
625 Westport Pkwy
Grapevine TX 76051
817 424-2000

(G-1533)
GIAMBRIS QUALITY SWEETS INC
Also Called: Giambri's Candy
26 Brand Ave (08021-4211)
PHONE...................................856 783-1099
David Giambri, *President*

EMP: 6
SQ FT: 6,000
SALES (est): 300K **Privately Held**
WEB: www.giambriscandy.com
SIC: 5441 2064 5961 Candy; candy & other confectionery products; food, mail order

(G-1534)
ROBERT WYNN
36 Windmill Dr (08021-5821)
PHONE...................................856 435-6398
Robert Wynn, *Principal*
EMP: 5
SALES (est): 31K **Privately Held**
SIC: 3679 Recording heads, speech & musical equipment

(G-1535)
ROYER GRAPHICS INC
101 Lincoln Dr (08021-2820)
PHONE...................................856 344-7935
Anthony J Cannuli, *President*
Toni Stouhr, *Admin Sec*
EMP: 7
SQ FT: 7,000
SALES (est): 440K **Privately Held**
SIC: 2752 7336 Commercial printing, offset; commercial art & illustration

Cliffside Park
Bergen County

(G-1536)
B B SUPPLY CORP
421 Nelson Ave (07010-1819)
PHONE...................................201 313-9021
Slobodan Ristovic, *Branch Mgr*
EMP: 13
SALES (corp-wide): 2MM **Privately Held**
SIC: 3545 Cutting tools for machine tools
PA: B B Supply Corp
40 Arnot St Unit 14
Lodi NJ 07644
201 313-9021

(G-1537)
DAMORE JEWELERS
731 Anderson Ave (07010-2189)
PHONE...................................201 945-0530
Barbara Zaccone, *President*
John D'Amore, *President*
Katherine D'Amore, *Corp Secy*
Eleni Ingenito, *Buyer*
Mike Duch, *Sales Mgr*
▲ EMP: 10 EST: 1946
SQ FT: 5,000
SALES (est): 1.5MM **Privately Held**
WEB: www.damorejewelers.com
SIC: 5944 7631 3911 Jewelry, precious stones & precious metals; jewelry repair services; jewelry, precious metal

(G-1538)
EDUCLOUD INC
Also Called: Mathcloud
206 Grant Ave (07010-2502)
PHONE...................................201 944-0445
Penni Ross, *Editor*
Jae Choi, *CFO*
EMP: 20
SQ FT: 20,000
SALES (est): 1.3MM **Privately Held**
SIC: 7372 Educational computer software

(G-1539)
GLASSCARE INC
666 Anderson Ave (07010-1921)
P.O. Box 7 (07010-0007)
PHONE...................................201 943-1122
Mel Neulander, *President*
Michael Slepakoff, *General Mgr*
EMP: 15
SQ FT: 12,000
SALES (est): 2.5MM **Privately Held**
WEB: www.glasscare.com
SIC: 2591 3993 7549 1799 Drapery hardware & blinds & shades; signs & advertising specialties; glass tinting, automotive; glass tinting, architectural or automotive; glass & glazing work

GEOGRAPHIC

(G-1540)
INTERSTATE ARCHITECTURAL & IR
243 Laird Ave (07010-1206)
PHONE..................201 941-0393
Richard Papp, *President*
Steve Heaps, *Treasurer*
EMP: 8
SQ FT: 3,300
SALES (est): 490K **Privately Held**
WEB: www.iai.50megs.com
SIC: 3446 Architectural metalwork

(G-1541)
MAIN FUEL LLC
73 Palisade Ave (07010-1014)
PHONE..................201 941-2707
EMP: 4
SALES (est): 198.9K **Privately Held**
SIC: 2869 Mfg Industrial Organic Chemicals

(G-1542)
NELLSAM GROUP INC
36 Washington Ave Fl 1 (07010-3025)
PHONE..................201 951-9459
Nelly Reyes, *Principal*
EMP: 4 EST: 2015
SALES (est): 338.4K **Privately Held**
SIC: 2844 Toilet preparations

(G-1543)
NORTH BERGEN MARBLE & GRANITE
217 Palisade Ave (07010-1226)
PHONE..................201 945-9988
Demetrios Markopoulous, *President*
Jim Markopolous, *Manager*
EMP: 4
SALES (est): 420K **Privately Held**
SIC: 2542 5032 Carrier cases & tables, mail; except wood; marble building stone

(G-1544)
SOUTH AMERICAN IMPORTS CORP
7 Cecelia Ave (07010-2705)
PHONE..................201 941-2020
EMP: 7
SALES (est): 538.9K **Privately Held**
SIC: 2022 Mfg Cheese

(G-1545)
UNCLE JIMMYS CHEESECAKES
420 Palisade Ave (07010-2824)
PHONE..................201 248-1820
EMP: 4
SALES (est): 396.7K **Privately Held**
SIC: 2591 Window blinds

Cliffwood
Monmouth County

(G-1546)
ELKEM INC
443 County Rd (07721-1168)
PHONE..................732 566-1700
Thomas W Kent, *President*
EMP: 8 EST: 1969
SQ FT: 10,000
SALES (est): 1MM **Privately Held**
WEB: www.elkem-inc.net
SIC: 3471 Electroplating of metals or formed products

(G-1547)
SPRIALSEAL INC
Also Called: Spiralseal
284 Cliffwood Ave (07721-1128)
PHONE..................732 738-6113
Gabor Szep, *President*
Dean Georgatos, *Vice Pres*
▲ EMP: 7
SQ FT: 5,000
SALES (est): 500K **Privately Held**
SIC: 7699 3053 Precision instrument repair; gaskets, packing & sealing devices

(G-1548)
V P I INDUSTRIES INC
77 Cliffwood Ave Ste 3b (07721-1087)
PHONE..................732 583-6895

Harry Weisfeld, *President*
Sheila Weisfeld, *Corp Secy*
EMP: 7
SQ FT: 3,700
SALES (est): 1.2MM **Privately Held**
WEB: www.vpiindustries.com
SIC: 3651 5731 Audio electronic systems; radio, television & electronic stores

(G-1549)
VESTAL PUBLISHING CO INC
Also Called: Vestal Printing
280 Cliffwood Ave Ste A (07721-1196)
PHONE..................732 583-3232
Robert M Rybnicky, *President*
Jeff Schiller, *Vice Chairman*
EMP: 7
SQ FT: 3,750
SALES (est): 913.3K **Privately Held**
SIC: 2752 Commercial printing, offset

Clifton
Passaic County

(G-1550)
21ST CENTURY FINISHING INC
40 Webro Rd (07012-1426)
PHONE..................201 797-0212
George Olmo, *CEO*
Karen Demaio, *President*
Rich Pometti, *Manager*
EMP: 23
SQ FT: 40,000
SALES (est): 4.4MM **Privately Held**
WEB: www.21finishing.com
SIC: 3544 Paper cutting dies

(G-1551)
A J P SCIENTIFIC INC
Also Called: ENG SCIENTIFIC
82 Industrial St E (07012-1708)
P.O. Box 1589 (07015-1589)
PHONE..................973 472-7200
Henry Eng, *President*
Mary Eng, *Admin Sec*
EMP: 7
SQ FT: 10,000
SALES: 977.1K **Privately Held**
WEB: www.engscientific.com
SIC: 2385 2899 2836 Waterproof outerwear; chemical preparations; biological products, except diagnostic

(G-1552)
A TO Z PRINTING & PROMOTION
1455 Main Ave Ste 2 (07011-2127)
PHONE..................973 916-9995
Eyad Asmar, *Principal*
EMP: 7
SALES (est): 764K **Privately Held**
SIC: 2752 Commercial printing, offset

(G-1553)
ACCESSREC LLC
55 Park Slope (07011)
PHONE..................973 955-0514
Seb Ragon, *Vice Pres*
▲ EMP: 4
SALES (est): 210K **Privately Held**
SIC: 3082 Unsupported plastics profile shapes

(G-1554)
ACCURATE PLASTIC PRINTERS LLC
30 Colfax Ave (07013-2059)
PHONE..................973 591-0180
Carlos Agudelo, *Mng Member*
Jakie Agudelo,
▲ EMP: 20
SQ FT: 10,000
SALES (est): 3.2MM **Privately Held**
WEB: www.accuplastic.com
SIC: 2752 Commercial printing, lithographic

(G-1555)
ACME & DORF DOOR CORP
490 Getty Ave 500 (07011-2152)
PHONE..................973 772-6774
Leonard Dorf, *President*
Nancy Dorf, *Corp Secy*
EMP: 6

SQ FT: 5,000
SALES (est): 570K **Privately Held**
SIC: 3442 Metal doors; window & door frames

(G-1556)
ACME INTERNATIONAL INC
2a Monhegan St (07013-2008)
P.O. Box 661 (07012-0661)
PHONE..................973 594-4866
Aftad Ahmed, *President*
Naila Ahmed, *Vice Pres*
Eli Ahmed, *Admin Sec*
◆ EMP: 3
SALES: 2.5MM **Privately Held**
SIC: 3841 Surgical instruments & apparatus

(G-1557)
ADVANCED ORTHMOLECULAR RES INC
Also Called: Advanced Orthmolecular RES LLC
30-38 Industrial St W (07012)
PHONE..................317 292-9013
Su Kania, *President*
Vincent Purita, *Manager*
Todd Frankovic, *Director*
EMP: 7
SALES: 1.5MM
SALES (corp-wide): 66.3MM **Privately Held**
SIC: 2023 5499 Dietary supplements, dairy & non-dairy based; health foods
PA: Advanced Orthomolecular Research Inc
3900 12 St Ne
Calgary AB T2E 8
403 250-9997

(G-1558)
AERO MANUFACTURING CO
310 Allwood Rd (07012-1786)
P.O. Box 1250 (07012-0750)
PHONE..................973 473-5300
Wayne Phillips, *Principal*
Jimmy Hilton, *Plant Mgr*
Nancy Ortiz, *Admin Sec*
▲ EMP: 73 EST: 1946
SQ FT: 150,000
SALES (est): 17.5MM **Privately Held**
WEB: www.aeromfg.com
SIC: 3589 3431 Commercial cooking & foodwarming equipment; metal sanitary ware

(G-1559)
AFFIL ENDOSCOPY SERVICES CL
925 Clifton Ave Ste 100 (07013-2724)
PHONE..................201 842-0020
Donna Benevenga, *Principal*
Joseph Roth, *Med Doctor*
EMP: 8
SALES (est): 1.2MM **Privately Held**
SIC: 3845 Endoscopic equipment, electromedical

(G-1560)
AIRFILTRONIX CORP (HQ)
154 Huron Ave (07013-2949)
PHONE..................973 779-5577
Ronald R Feller, *President*
Christopher Proffitt, *Admin Sec*
EMP: 5
SQ FT: 5,500
SALES: 425K
SALES (corp-wide): 2.8MM **Privately Held**
WEB: www.airfiltronix.com
SIC: 3821 3444 Laboratory equipment: fume hoods, distillation racks, etc.; sheet metalwork
PA: Micro-Tek Laboratories Inc
154 Huron Ave
Clifton NJ 07013
973 779-5577

(G-1561)
ALORIS TOOL TECHNOLOGY CO INC
407 Getty Ave (07011-2121)
P.O. Box 1529 (07015-1529)
PHONE..................973 772-1201
Rich Roslowski, *President*

Gregory Brajkovic, *Vice Pres*
EMP: 30 EST: 1946
SQ FT: 30,000
SALES (est): 4.4MM **Privately Held**
WEB: www.aloris.com
SIC: 3545 Tool holders; tools & accessories for machine tools

(G-1562)
ALPHA PROCESSING CO INC
210 Delawanna Ave (07014-1550)
P.O. Box 936 (07014-0936)
PHONE..................973 777-1737
Richard Jenny, *President*
▲ EMP: 45 EST: 1940
SQ FT: 20,000
SALES: 4.3MM **Privately Held**
SIC: 3479 Coating of metals & formed products

(G-1563)
AMERICAN MARKING SYSTEMS INC (PA)
Also Called: Paterson Stamp Works
1015 Paulison Ave (07015-3610)
P.O. Box 1677 (07015-1677)
PHONE..................973 478-5600
John A Collins III, *Ch of Bd*
John Shaughnessy, *Benefits Mgr*
EMP: 25 EST: 1888
SQ FT: 10,000
SALES (est): 10.3MM **Privately Held**
WEB: www.ams-stamps.com
SIC: 3953 Embossing seals & hand stamps

(G-1564)
AMERICAN STAMP MFG CO
Also Called: American/Krengel Stamp Mfg Co
1015 Paulison Ave (07011-3610)
PHONE..................212 227-1877
Randy Botc, *President*
EMP: 14
SQ FT: 7,000
SALES: 800K **Privately Held**
SIC: 3953 Embossing seals & hand stamps

(G-1565)
AMERIVATOR SYSTEMS CORPORATION
220 Scoles Ave (07012-1126)
PHONE..................973 471-1200
Daniel Sedrak, *President*
Nabila Sedrak, *Vice Pres*
▲ EMP: 6 EST: 1999
SALES: 2MM **Privately Held**
SIC: 3534 Elevators & equipment

(G-1566)
ATLANTIC CASTING & ENGINEERING
Also Called: Atlantic C&E
810 Bloomfield Ave (07012-1199)
P.O. Box 4016 (07012-0416)
PHONE..................973 779-2450
James Binns, *CEO*
Brian Jmcgrady, *President*
Brian McGrady, *President*
Dan Lenino, *Vice Pres*
Gregory Rohrbacker, *Vice Pres*
▲ EMP: 160 EST: 1937
SQ FT: 40,000
SALES: 20MM **Privately Held**
WEB: www.atlantic-ce.com
SIC: 3599 3365 Machine & other job shop work; aerospace castings, aluminum

(G-1567)
ATLAS INDUSTRIAL MFG CO (PA)
81 Somerset Pl (07012-1197)
PHONE..................973 779-3970
Frank De Lorenzo, *President*
Tom Ciampi, *Plant Mgr*
Hasu Darji, *Engineer*
Ramsey Mahadeen, *Treasurer*
Frank J De Lorenzo Jr, *Admin Sec*
▲ EMP: 38 EST: 1922
SQ FT: 41,000
SALES (est): 6.3MM **Privately Held**
SIC: 3443 Heat exchangers, plate type

(G-1568)
AUTOMATED FLEXIBLE CONVEYORS
55 Walman Ave (07011-3416)
PHONE....................................973 340-1695
Kevin Devaney, *President*
Grace Faria, *Vice Pres*
EMP: 15
SQ FT: 12,000
SALES: 1.8MM **Privately Held**
WEB: www.afcsolutions.com
SIC: 3535 3564 Conveyors & conveying
   equipment; blowers & fans

(G-1569)
AVON PRODUCTS INC
1166 Broad St (07013-3343)
PHONE....................................973 779-5590
EMP: 4
SALES (corp-wide): 10.7B **Publicly Held**
SIC: 2844 Mfg Cosmetics Fragrances
PA: Avon Products, Inc.
   777 3rd Ave Fl 31
   New York NY 10017
   212 282-5000

(G-1570)
B & B IRON WORKS
1 Broad St (07013-1000)
PHONE....................................862 238-7203
Mauro Belgiovine, *President*
Anthony Belgiovine, *Project Engr*
Diane Belgiovine, *Admin Sec*
EMP: 30
SQ FT: 10,000
SALES (est): 7.9MM **Privately Held**
SIC: 3441 Fabricated structural metal

(G-1571)
BARANTEC INC
777 Passaic Ave Ste 345 (07012-1878)
PHONE....................................973 779-8774
Diane Bersen, *Vice Pres*
Talia Israel, *Mfg Staff*
Helene Stewart, *Manager*
Ted Bielitz, *Info Tech Mgr*
EMP: 10
SQ FT: 2,100
SALES: 2.5MM
SALES (corp-wide): 19.7MM **Privately
   Held**
WEB: www.barantec.com
SIC: 3678 5065 Electronic connectors;
   electronic parts & equipment
HQ: Baran Advanced Technologies (1986)
   Ltd
   8 Omarim
   Omer 84965
   732 511-020

(G-1572)
BAY STATE MILLING COMPANY
404 Getty Ave (07011)
PHONE....................................973 772-3400
Don Galati, *Plant Mgr*
Peter Carmony, *Manager*
EMP: 65
SALES (corp-wide): 154.8MM **Privately
   Held**
WEB: www.bsm.com
SIC: 2041 Wheat mill feed
PA: Bay State Milling Company
   100 Congress St Ste 2
   Quincy MA 02169
   617 328-4423

(G-1573)
BENJAMIN MOORE & CO
203 Kuller Rd (07011-2857)
PHONE....................................973 569-5000
Raymond Elustondo, *Manager*
EMP: 70
SALES (corp-wide): 225.3B **Publicly
   Held**
WEB: www.benjaminmoore.com
SIC: 5231 2851 Paint; paints: oil or alkyd
   vehicle or water thinned
HQ: Benjamin Moore & Co.
   101 Paragon Dr
   Montvale NJ 07645
   201 573-9600

(G-1574)
BETTER TEAM USA CORPORATION
95b Industrial St E (07012-1707)
PHONE....................................973 365-0947
Horacio Dibattista, *President*
Jensen Dibattista, *Manager*
EMP: 30
SALES (est): 3.9MM **Privately Held**
SIC: 2389 Men's miscellaneous acces-
   sories

(G-1575)
BIWAL MANUFACTURING CO INC
48 Industrial St W (07012-1712)
PHONE....................................973 778-0105
Joseph Mrocka, *President*
EMP: 30
SQ FT: 12,000
SALES (est): 4.7MM **Privately Held**
SIC: 3599 Machine shop, jobbing & repair

(G-1576)
BLUE DOME INC
Also Called: Blue Dome Press
335 Clifton Ave (07011-2618)
PHONE....................................646 415-9331
Ahmet Idil, *Vice Pres*
Katharine Branning, *Vice Pres*
EMP: 5
SALES (est): 331.4K **Privately Held**
SIC: 2731 Books: publishing only

(G-1577)
BRANDMUSCLE INC
200 Clifton Blvd Ste 6 (07011-3652)
PHONE....................................973 685-0022
EMP: 7
SALES (corp-wide): 2.3B **Privately Held**
SIC: 2754 Commercial printing, gravure
HQ: Brandmuscle, Inc.
   1100 Superior Ave E # 500
   Cleveland OH 44114
   216 464-4342

(G-1578)
BREURE SHEET METAL CO INC
Also Called: Bruere Heating & AC
46 Walman Ave (07011-3411)
PHONE....................................973 772-6423
Matthew Breure Jr, *President*
Josephine Breure, *Admin Sec*
EMP: 6
SQ FT: 3,000
SALES (est): 630.6K **Privately Held**
SIC: 1711 3444 Heating & air conditioning
   contractors; sheet metalwork

(G-1579)
BUONAVENTURA BAG AND CASES LLC
Also Called: Burkley Case
95 Main Ave Ste 1 (07014-1749)
PHONE....................................212 960-3442
Serkan Demiray,
EMP: 5
SALES (est): 364.5K **Privately Held**
SIC: 3111 Handbag leather

(G-1580)
CARAUSTAR CLIFTON PRIMARY PACK
43 Samworth Rd (07012-1714)
PHONE....................................973 472-4900
Carl Oberg, *President*
Ed Goddard, *Vice Pres*
James Walden, *Admin Sec*
EMP: 250
SQ FT: 57,000
SALES (est): 27.2MM
SALES (corp-wide): 3.8B **Publicly Held**
WEB: www.caraustar.com
SIC: 2679 Paperboard products, converted
HQ: Caraustar Industries, Inc.
   5000 Austell Powder Sprin
   Austell GA 30106
   770 948-3101

(G-1581)
CGW NEWS LLC
107 Mount Prospect Ave (07013-1919)
PHONE....................................973 473-3972
Christine Witmyer, *Principal*
EMP: 4

SALES (est): 139.2K **Privately Held**
SIC: 2711 Newspapers

(G-1582)
CHALLENGE PRINTING CO INC (PA)
Also Called: Challenge Printing Company The
2 Bridewell Pl (07014-1726)
PHONE....................................973 471-4700
Theodore Sasso, *President*
Qing Li, *Manager*
Michael Smith, *Manager*
Kevin Donohue, *Supervisor*
Asock Avadhani, *Technology*
▲ EMP: 203
SQ FT: 55,000
SALES (est): 48.7MM **Privately Held**
WEB: www.challprint.com
SIC: 2752 2754 Commercial printing, off-
   set; labels: gravure printing; circulars:
   gravure printing

(G-1583)
CHICAGO PNEUMATIC TOOL (DH)
Also Called: Titan
222 Getty Ave (07011-1870)
PHONE....................................973 928-5222
John J Staudinger, *CEO*
Attila Mozsolits, *CFO*
▲ EMP: 16
SQ FT: 10,000
SALES (est): 2.2MM
SALES (corp-wide): 4.2B **Privately Held**
WEB: www.titanti.com
SIC: 3452 3423 Bolts, nuts, rivets & wash-
   ers; wrenches, hand tools
HQ: Epiroc Usa Llc
   8001 Arista Pl Unit 400
   Broomfield CO 80021
   844 437-4762

(G-1584)
CLIFTON METAL PRODUCTS CO INC
41 Clifton Blvd (07011-3893)
PHONE....................................973 777-6100
David Denboer, *President*
Deiter Kemmerich, *Treasurer*
Dorothy Grimes, *Manager*
EMP: 17
SQ FT: 20,000
SALES (est): 3.5MM **Privately Held**
WEB: www.cliftonmetal.com
SIC: 3444 Sheet metal specialties, not
   stamped

(G-1585)
COINING MFG
35 Monhegan St Ste 4 (07013-2000)
PHONE....................................973 253-0500
Edward J Farley, *Principal*
EMP: 8 EST: 2015
SALES (est): 143.1K **Privately Held**
SIC: 3469 Stamping metal for the trade

(G-1586)
COMODO GROUP INC (PA)
1255 Broad St (07013-3398)
PHONE....................................888 266-6361
Melih Abdulhayoglu, *CEO*
Steve Subar, *President*
John Siverd, *Partner*
Joe Smith, *Business Mgr*
Jon Land, *Exec VP*
EMP: 88
SALES (est): 28.9MM **Privately Held**
WEB: www.comodo.com
SIC: 3663 4813 ;

(G-1587)
COMUS INTERNATIONAL INC (PA)
454 Allwood Rd (07012-1706)
PHONE....................................973 777-6900
Robert P Romano, *President*
Joseph Perez, *Vice Pres*
John Rollo, *Vice Pres*
Joseph Romano, *Vice Pres*
Maurice Baenen, *Engineer*
▲ EMP: 125
SQ FT: 40,000

SALES (est): 29.5MM **Privately Held**
WEB: www.comus-intl.com
SIC: 3613 3625 Switches, electric power
   except snap, push button, etc.; relays,
   electric power

(G-1588)
CONTINENTAL FOOD & BEV INC
Also Called: Inca Kola
495 River Rd (07014-1520)
PHONE....................................973 815-1600
Elizabeth Berman, *President*
Randall Berman, *COO*
◆ EMP: 15
SQ FT: 23,000
SALES: 14MM **Privately Held**
SIC: 2086 5149 Soft drinks: packaged in
   cans, bottles, etc.; soft drinks

(G-1589)
CONVEYORS BY NORTH AMERICAN
156 Huron Ave (07013-2949)
PHONE....................................973 777-6600
Gloria Kolodziej, *President*
Joseph Kolodziej Jr, *Vice Pres*
Josephine Malitsch, *Admin Sec*
EMP: 9
SQ FT: 18,000
SALES: 650K **Privately Held**
SIC: 3535 Conveyors & conveying equip-
   ment

(G-1590)
COPACK INTERNATIONAL INC
23 Carol St (07014-1420)
P.O. Box 496, Carlstadt (07072-0496)
PHONE....................................973 405-5151
Peter J Gould, *President*
EMP: 20
SQ FT: 61,000
SALES (est): 1.4MM **Privately Held**
SIC: 7389 3565 Packaging & labeling
   services; packaging machinery

(G-1591)
CORBO JEWELERS INC
Also Called: Corbo Jewelers of Styertowne
1055 Bloomfield Ave (07012-2198)
PHONE....................................973 777-1635
Michael Corbo, *Manager*
Stephen Corbo, *Manager*
EMP: 10
SALES (corp-wide): 8.5MM **Privately
   Held**
WEB: www.corbojewelers.com
SIC: 3915 5944 7631 Jewel cutting,
   drilling, polishing, recutting or setting; jew-
   elry, precious stones & precious metals;
   watch repair
PA: Corbo Jewelers, Inc.
   58 Park Ave
   Rutherford NJ 07070
   201 438-3855

(G-1592)
CROSS COUNTRY BOX CO INC
474 Getty Ave (07011-2149)
PHONE....................................973 673-8349
Dan Goldman, *President*
Irene Goldman, *Treasurer*
EMP: 11
SQ FT: 3,700
SALES: 700K **Privately Held**
WEB: www.crosscountrybox.com
SIC: 2652 Boxes, newsboard, metal
   edged: made from purchased materials

(G-1593)
CRYSTEX COMPOSITES LLC
125 Clifton Blvd (07011-3806)
PHONE....................................973 779-8866
George L Flores, *CEO*
Delvis Flores, *VP Opers*
Charles Clement,
Gary Rosenblum,
EMP: 33
SQ FT: 100,000
SALES (est): 5.4MM **Privately Held**
WEB: www.crystexcomposites.com
SIC: 3299 Ceramic fiber

(G-1594)
CURTAIN CARE PLUS INC
17 Industrial St W (07012-1711)
PHONE....................................800 845-6155

Jimmy Kazanjian, *Principal*
Mason Kirsch, *Principal*
Yosenny Martinez, *Accounts Exec*
EMP: 5
SALES (est): 397.3K **Privately Held**
SIC: 5714 2259 Curtains; curtains, knit

(G-1595)
CUSTOM BOOK BINDERY INC
9 Sheridan Ave (07011-2731)
PHONE.............................973 815-1400
Lance Belostock, *President*
EMP: 12
SQ FT: 6,000
SALES: 900K **Privately Held**
WEB: www.custombookbindery.com
SIC: 2752 2759 Commercial printing, off-
set; bookbinding & related work

(G-1596)
DATA DELAY DEVICES (PA)
3 Mount Prospect Ave (07013-1915)
PHONE.............................973 202-3268
Annibale Lupi, *President*
Lydia Lupi, *Exec VP*
EMP: 23 **EST:** 1964
SQ FT: 24,000
SALES (est): 3.2MM **Privately Held**
WEB: www.datadelay.com
SIC: 3679 3674 3672 Electronic circuits;
delay lines; semiconductors & related de-
vices; printed circuit boards

(G-1597)
DELGEN PRESS INC
250 Delawanna Ave (07014-1337)
PHONE.............................973 472-2266
Fax: 973 667-1855
EMP: 5
SQ FT: 3,500
SALES: 700K **Privately Held**
SIC: 2752 2759 Lithographic Commercial
Printing Commercial Printing

(G-1598)
DIKEMAN LAMINATING CORPORATION
181 Sargeant Ave (07013-1993)
PHONE.............................973 473-5696
Thomas R Snyder, *President*
Jeffery Snyder, *Vice Pres*
Jean Snyder, *Admin Sec*
▲ **EMP:** 32 **EST:** 1949
SQ FT: 20,000
SALES (est): 6.8MM **Privately Held**
SIC: 2672 3083 Coated & laminated
paper; plastic finished products, lami-
nated

(G-1599)
DIOCESE OF PATERSON
Also Called: Beacon, The
597 Valley Rd (07013-2237)
P.O. Box 1887 (07015-1887)
PHONE.............................973 279-8845
Richard Sokerka, *President*
Victor Winkler, *Principal*
EMP: 15
SQ FT: 5,000
SALES (est): 957.8K **Privately Held**
SIC: 2711 Newspapers: publishing only,
not printed on site

(G-1600)
DISPOSABLE HYGIENE LLC (PA)
Also Called: Anthem
60 Page Rd (07012-1452)
PHONE.............................973 779-1982
Michael Kaminski, *Vice Pres*
Amy Sidradzki, *Vice Pres*
David Espinoza, *Warehouse Mgr*
Rajesh Prakash, *Mng Member*
◆ **EMP:** 127
SALES (est): 49.1MM **Privately Held**
SIC: 2844 Cosmetic preparations

(G-1601)
DIVERSIFIED FAB PDTS LTD LBLTY
158 River Rd (07014-1571)
PHONE.............................973 773-3189
Michael Fessak, *Mng Member*
EMP: 4
SALES (est): 343.8K **Privately Held**
SIC: 3444 Sheet metal specialties, not
stamped

(G-1602)
DOMEL INC
3 Grunwald St (07013-2118)
PHONE.............................973 614-1800
Melvin Cohen, *President*
John Cozza, *Vice Pres*
John Morse, *Vice Pres*
EMP: 35
SQ FT: 35,000
SALES (est): 6.5MM **Privately Held**
WEB: www.domelinc.com
SIC: 3355 Structural shapes, rolled, alu-
minum

(G-1603)
DOMINION COLOUR CORP USA
881 Allwood Rd Ste 2 (07012-1900)
PHONE.............................973 279-9591
Ken Tsujiuchi, *Manager*
▲ **EMP:** 10
SALES (est): 1.2MM **Privately Held**
WEB: www.dominioncolour.com
SIC: 2865 Color pigments, organic
HQ: Dominion Colour Corporation
515 Consumers Rd Unit 700
North York ON M2J 4
416 791-4200

(G-1604)
DRITAC FLOORING PRODUCTS LLC
60 Webro Rd (07012-1426)
PHONE.............................973 614-9000
Yale E Block, *Branch Mgr*
EMP: 13
SALES (corp-wide): 33.9MM **Privately Held**
WEB: www.basicadhesives.com
SIC: 2891 Adhesives
PA: Dritac Flooring Products Llc
60 Webro Rd
Clifton NJ 07012
973 614-9000

(G-1605)
DRITAC FLOORING PRODUCTS LLC (PA)
60 Webro Rd (07012-1426)
PHONE.............................973 614-9000
Steve Lontchar, *President*
Stan Pawigon, *CFO*
Drena Dixon, *Finance Mgr*
David Clarkson, *Sales Staff*
John Lio, *Marketing Staff*
◆ **EMP:** 60
SQ FT: 40,000
SALES (est): 33.9MM **Privately Held**
WEB: www.basicadhesives.com
SIC: 2891 Adhesives & sealants

(G-1606)
DYE INTO PRINT INC
167 Fornelius Ave (07013-1845)
PHONE.............................973 772-8019
Mathew Letterman, *President*
EMP: 62
SQ FT: 60,000
SALES (est): 5.8MM **Privately Held**
WEB: www.dyeintoprint.com
SIC: 2269 2759 2262 Dyeing: raw stock
yarn & narrow fabrics; commercial print-
ing; finishing plants, manmade fiber & silk
fabrics

(G-1607)
DYNAMETRIC TOOL INC
27 Somerset Pl (07012-1123)
PHONE.............................973 471-8009
Francis Csapo, *President*
EMP: 4 **EST:** 1977
SQ FT: 6,000
SALES: 200K **Privately Held**
SIC: 3599 Machine shop, jobbing & repair

(G-1608)
DYNAMIC PRINTING & GRAPHICS
250 Delawanna Ave (07014-1337)
PHONE.............................973 473-7177
Lou Mascola, *President*
Paul Janacek, *Vice Pres*
Greg Tolve, *Vice Pres*
EMP: 12
SQ FT: 7,500

SALES (est): 1.7MM **Privately Held**
WEB: www.dynamic-inc.com
SIC: 7336 2752 Graphic arts & related de-
sign; commercial printing, offset

(G-1609)
E & M BINDERY INC
11 Peekay Dr (07014-1544)
PHONE.............................973 777-9300
Mark Berkowitz, *CEO*
Gary Markovits, *President*
Steve Schechtman, *Vice Pres*
Lorraine Mann, *Controller*
EMP: 120 **EST:** 1962
SQ FT: 50,000
SALES (est): 18MM **Privately Held**
WEB: www.embindery.com
SIC: 2789 Binding only: books, pamphlets,
magazines, etc.

(G-1610)
ECSI INTERNATIONAL INC (HQ)
Also Called: E C S I
790 Bloomfield Ave Ste C1 (07012-1181)
P.O. Box 677 (07012-0677)
PHONE.............................973 574-8555
Arthur Birch, *Ch of Bd*
Connie Steeper, *Business Mgr*
Tom Isdanavich, *Vice Pres*
Robert Oliver, *Vice Pres*
Ronald Thomas, *Vice Pres*
EMP: 15
SQ FT: 12,500
SALES: 5.9MM
SALES (corp-wide): 981.7K **Publicly Held**
WEB: www.anti-terrorism.com
SIC: 3699 Security control equipment &
systems
PA: Electronic Control Security Inc.
790 Bloomfield Ave Ste C1
Clifton NJ 07012
973 574-8555

(G-1611)
EDWARD W HIEMER & CO
141 Wabash Ave (07011-1651)
PHONE.............................973 772-5081
Judith Van Wie, *President*
Gerhard Hiemer, *Admin Sec*
EMP: 12 **EST:** 1929
SQ FT: 6,800
SALES: 970.8K **Privately Held**
SIC: 3231 Stained glass: made from pur-
chased glass

(G-1612)
ELECTRO LIFT INC
204 Sargeant Ave (07013-1932)
PHONE.............................973 471-0204
David Erenstoft, *President*
Allan Rayot, *Engineer*
Alice Devereaux, *CFO*
Steve Pilione, *Mktg Dir*
Dolores Erenstoft, *Admin Sec*
EMP: 26 **EST:** 1932
SQ FT: 6,000
SALES (est): 8MM **Privately Held**
WEB: www.electrolift.com
SIC: 3536 Hoists

(G-1613)
ELECTRONIC CONTROL SEC INC (PA)
790 Bloomfield Ave Ste C1 (07012-1142)
PHONE.............................973 574-8555
Arthur Barchenko, *President*
Edward Snow, *COO*
Edward V Badolato, *Adv Board Mem*
Juda S Engelmayer, *Adv Board Mem*
Thomas Isdanavich, *Vice Pres*
EMP: 15
SQ FT: 12,200
SALES: 981.7K **Publicly Held**
SIC: 3699 Security control equipment &
systems

(G-1614)
ELECTRONIC MFG SVCS INC
48 Industrial St W (07012-1712)
PHONE.............................973 916-1001
Farra Diamond, *CEO*
EMP: 16

SALES (est): 817.7K **Privately Held**
SIC: 3679 Microwave components; loads,
electronic; harness assemblies for electronic use: wire or cable

(G-1615)
ELEKTROMEK INC
60 Webro Rd (07012-1426)
PHONE.............................973 614-9000
EMP: 18
SQ FT: 17,000
SALES (est): 2.5MM **Privately Held**
SIC: 2891 Mfg Adhesives/Sealants

(G-1616)
ERIKA-RECORD LLC
37 Atlantic Way (07012-1141)
PHONE.............................973 614-8500
Carl Rinaldi, *Manager*
Max Oehler,
Fritz Beindorf,
◆ **EMP:** 9
SQ FT: 5,500
SALES (est): 2.2MM **Privately Held**
WEB: www.erikarecord.com
SIC: 3556 Bakery machinery

(G-1617)
EXCELLENT PRTG & GRAPHICS LLC
333 Hazel St (07011-2812)
PHONE.............................973 773-6661
Fawzi A Abuyasser, *Opers Spvr*
Mutasem Abdelghani, *Mng Member*
Alexandra Zeidan, *Manager*
EMP: 10
SQ FT: 20,000
SALES: 1MM **Privately Held**
WEB: www.excellent-printing.com
SIC: 2752 Commercial printing, offset

(G-1618)
EXELIS INC/NORTHROP
77 River Rd (07014-2000)
PHONE.............................973 284-4212
Northrop Grumman Systems Corp, *Partner*
Paul Quattrone, *Manager*
Karen Gelormine, *Administration*
EMP: 10
SALES (est): 603.4K **Privately Held**
SIC: 3728 Aircraft parts & equipment

(G-1619)
FASTENATION INC
120 Brighton Rd Ste 2 (07012-1666)
PHONE.............................973 591-1277
David Petak, *President*
Jayne Petak, *Vice Pres*
EMP: 20
SQ FT: 18,000
SALES (est): 4.8MM **Privately Held**
WEB: www.fastenation.com
SIC: 3965 Fasteners

(G-1620)
FIDELITY INDUSTRIES INC
Also Called: Warehouse
750 Bloomfield Ave Ste 1 (07012-1257)
PHONE.............................973 777-2592
Mordecai Rivkin, *President*
EMP: 45
SALES (corp-wide): 18.9MM **Privately Held**
WEB: www.fidelitywall.com
SIC: 3069 Wallcoverings, rubber
PA: Fidelity Industries Inc
559 Rte 23
Wayne NJ 07470
973 696-9120

(G-1621)
FIT FABRICATION LLC
310 Colfax Ave (07013-1794)
PHONE.............................973 685-7344
EMP: 8
SALES (est): 1MM **Privately Held**
SIC: 3999 Manufacturing industries

(G-1622)
FRENCH TEXTILE CO INC
835 Bloomfield Ave Ste 1 (07012-1147)
PHONE.............................973 471-5000
Roy Aibel, *CEO*
EMP: 10

SALES (est): 982.5K **Privately Held**
SIC: 2298 2396 Nets, rope; veils & veiling:
bridal, funeral, etc.

(G-1623)
FUCHS AUDIO TECH LTD LBLTY CO
407 Getty Ave (07011-2121)
PHONE......................................973 772-4420
Andrew Fuchs,
Annette Fuchs,
Annette J Fuchs,
▲ EMP: 10 EST: 2003
SQ FT: 5,000
SALES (est): 850K **Privately Held**
SIC: 3651 Amplifiers: radio, public address
or musical instrument

(G-1624)
GENUA & MULLIGAN PRINTING
Also Called: Minuteman Press
1 Trenton Ave (07011-1807)
PHONE......................................973 894-1500
Joe Mulligan, *President*
Joe Genua, *Partner*
Lynda Day, *Project Mgr*
EMP: 21
SQ FT: 4,000
SALES (est): 3.2MM **Privately Held**
WEB: www.minutemanpress.org
SIC: 2752 Commercial printing, litho-
graphic

(G-1625)
GLEN MILLS INC
220 Delawanna Ave (07014-1550)
PHONE......................................973 777-0777
Peter H Kendall, *President*
Anita Ahrens, *Treasurer*
Douglas Ahrens, *Sales Executive*
Stanley Goldberg, *Exec Dir*
▲ EMP: 10
SQ FT: 12,000
SALES: 3.7MM **Privately Held**
WEB: www.glenmills.com
SIC: 3821 Laboratory apparatus & furniture

(G-1626)
GLOBE INDUSTRIES CORP
48 Industrial St W (07012-1712)
PHONE......................................973 992-8990
Anthony Melillo, *President*
Mark Melillo, *Corp Secy*
▲ EMP: 10 EST: 1962
SQ FT: 11,200
SALES (est): 920K **Privately Held**
SIC: 3544 3599 Special dies, tools, jigs &
fixtures; custom machinery

(G-1627)
GLUE FOLD INC
40 Webro Rd (07012-1426)
PHONE......................................973 575-8400
Isabelle Garcia, *General Mgr*
Paul Delalla, *General Mgr*
EMP: 80
SALES (est): 7MM **Privately Held**
SIC: 2621 Envelope paper
PA: Perfect Finishing Inc.
40 Webro Rd
Clifton NJ 07012

(G-1628)
GMPC PRINTING
1 Trenton Ave (07011-1807)
PHONE......................................973 546-6060
Mike Finucane, *Treasurer*
Jim Cox, *Accountant*
Ruben Velazquez, *Accounts Exec*
Bill Reda, *Director*
Michael Finucane, *Officer*
EMP: 8
SALES (est): 823.5K **Privately Held**
SIC: 2752 Commercial printing, offset

(G-1629)
GRAPHIC EXPRESS MENU CO INC
200 Clifton Blvd Ste 6 (07011-3652)
PHONE......................................973 685-0022
Kathy Heflin, *Exec VP*
Chris Hesburgh, *Exec VP*
Evelyn Nugent, *Exec VP*
Adam Meier, *CFO*
EMP: 25
SQ FT: 27,000

SALES (est): 4.5MM **Privately Held**
WEB: www.graphicexpressmenu.com
SIC: 3083 2672 Laminated plastic sheets;
coated & laminated paper

(G-1630)
GROSS PRINTING ASSOCIATES INC
180 Brighton Rd (07012-1451)
PHONE......................................718 832-1110
Abraham Lebowitz, *President*
Samson Gross, *Vice Pres*
EMP: 16
SQ FT: 13,000
SALES (est): 3.2MM **Privately Held**
SIC: 2752 Commercial printing, litho-
graphic

(G-1631)
H POWER CORP
1373 Broad St (07013-4200)
PHONE......................................973 249-5444
H Gibbard, *Principal*
EMP: 4
SALES (est): 292K **Privately Held**
SIC: 3621 Motors & generators

(G-1632)
HANDI-HUT INC
3 Grunwald St (07013-2118)
PHONE......................................973 614-1800
Melvin Cohen, *President*
Richard T Cohen, *Corp Secy*
John Morse, *Vice Pres*
EMP: 30
SQ FT: 30,000
SALES (est): 5.5MM **Privately Held**
WEB: www.handi-hut.com
SIC: 3448 3449 3444 3442 Buildings,
portable: prefabricated metal; miscella-
neous metalwork; sheet metalwork; metal
doors, sash & trim

(G-1633)
HEMPEL (USA) INC
127 Kingsland Ave (07014-2034)
PHONE......................................201 939-2801
Joel Benetti, *Opers-Prdtn-Mfg*
EMP: 5
SALES (corp-wide): 1.9MM **Privately
Held**
WEB: www.us.hempel.com
SIC: 2851 Marine paints
HQ: Hempel (Usa), Inc.
600 Conroe Park North Dr
Conroe TX 77303
936 523-6000

(G-1634)
HICUBE COATING LLC
200 Circle Ave (07011-2870)
P.O. Box 828 (07015-0828)
PHONE......................................973 883-7404
Jonathan Hirsh,
Lisa Giannotti, *Admin Asst*
▲ EMP: 4
SALES (est): 480K **Privately Held**
SIC: 2655 Ammunition cans or tubes,
board laminated with metal foil

(G-1635)
HIGH VISION CORPORATION
211 River Rd (07014-1518)
PHONE......................................862 238-7636
Kimi Weing, *Owner*
▲ EMP: 4
SALES (est): 398.7K
SALES (corp-wide): 41.1MM **Privately
Held**
SIC: 3827 Optical instruments & lenses
PA: Shanghai Dong Da I&E Co., Ltd.
Room 110c, Floor 11, Jia Hua Finance
Building, No.133, Tiantong
Shanghai 20008
216 317-3056

(G-1636)
HOWARD PACKAGING CORP
86 Cobble St (07013-2224)
P.O. Box 3609, Wayne (07474-3609)
PHONE......................................973 904-0022
Howard Jacobs, *President*
EMP: 6

SALES (est): 794.3K **Privately Held**
WEB: www.freezaframe.com
SIC: 3861 Photographic equipment & sup-
plies

(G-1637)
HUDSON COSMETIC MFG CORP
Also Called: Paramount Cosmetics
93 Entin Rd Ste 4 (07014-1500)
PHONE......................................973 472-2323
Sanford Salzman, *President*
Dana Graham, *Plant Mgr*
Ken Schweizer, *Plant Engr*
EMP: 65
SQ FT: 40,000
SALES (est): 11.3MM **Privately Held**
WEB: www.paramountcosmetics.net
SIC: 2844 Cosmetic preparations

(G-1638)
ICELANDIRECT INC (PA)
127 Kingsland Ave Ste 101 (07014-2034)
PHONE......................................800 763-4690
Mark H Stenberg, *CEO*
Brandon Miller, *President*
Christina Carlini, *Exec VP*
Andrea Patino, *Vice Pres*
Bruce Huff, *Prdtn Mgr*
▲ EMP: 15
SQ FT: 14,000
SALES (est): 13.9MM **Privately Held**
SIC: 5122 2023 Vitamins & minerals; di-
etary supplements, dairy & non-dairy
based

(G-1639)
INFRONT MEDICAL LLC
1033 Us Highway 46 A202 (07013-2473)
PHONE......................................888 515-2532
John Kuczynski, *Principal*
EMP: 6 EST: 2013
SQ FT: 1,200
SALES: 50K **Privately Held**
SIC: 3842 Implants, surgical

(G-1640)
INGRASSELINO PRODUCTS LLC
63 Dewey St (07013-1139)
PHONE......................................800 960-1316
Peter J Ingrasselino, *Mng Member*
EMP: 5
SALES: 250K **Privately Held**
SIC: 2033 2035 5141 Canned fruits &
specialties; seasonings & sauces, except
tomato & dry; food brokers

(G-1641)
INNOVATIVE COSMTC CONCEPTS LLC
Also Called: Llc, Incoco Products
61 Kuller Rd (07011-3475)
PHONE......................................973 225-0264
FA Park, *President*
▲ EMP: 75
SALES (est): 16.9MM **Privately Held**
WEB: www.innovativecosmetics.net
SIC: 2844 Cosmetic preparations

(G-1642)
INTERNATIONAL DELIGHTS LLC
Also Called: Exquisities
230 Brighton Rd (07012-1414)
PHONE......................................973 928-5431
Spiro Sayegh,
Nicolas Sayegh,
▲ EMP: 130
SQ FT: 30,000
SALES (est): 29.7MM **Privately Held**
SIC: 2051 Bread, cake & related products

(G-1643)
INTERNATIONAL PAPER COMPANY
261 River Rd (07014-1551)
PHONE......................................973 405-2400
Jeffrey Gross, *Accounts Mgr*
Margaret Nepola, *Sales Staff*
EMP: 8
SALES (corp-wide): 23.3B **Publicly Held**
SIC: 2621 Paper mills

PA: International Paper Company
6400 Poplar Ave
Memphis TN 38197
901 419-9000

(G-1644)
ITT CORPORATION
Also Called: ITT Defense Electronics & Svcs
100 Kingsland Rd (07014-1919)
PHONE......................................973 284-0123
R Tucci, *Manager*
EMP: 58
SALES (corp-wide): 2.7B **Publicly Held**
WEB: www.ittind.com
SIC: 3625 Control equipment, electric
HQ: Itt Llc
1133 Westchester Ave N-100
White Plains NY 10604
914 641-2000

(G-1645)
J&E BUSINESS SERVICES LLC
Also Called: Pinnacle Grphic Communications
1 Trenton Ave (07011-1807)
PHONE......................................973 984-8444
Jeffrey P Green,
EMP: 6
SALES (est): 550.1K **Privately Held**
SIC: 7389 3993 2759 7334 Packaging &
labeling services; signs & advertising specialties; commercial printing; photocopying & duplicating services; advertising
specialties

(G-1646)
JASSMINE CORP
489 Getty Ave (07011-2168)
PHONE......................................848 565-0515
Younes Seddiki, *CEO*
EMP: 6 EST: 1997
SQ FT: 10,000
SALES: 1.2MM **Privately Held**
SIC: 2052 Cookies

(G-1647)
JIMMYS COOKIES LLC
125 Entin Rd (07014-1424)
PHONE......................................973 779-8500
Howard Hirsch, *CEO*
Michael Pisani, *President*
Deborah Kinzley, *CFO*
EMP: 130
SQ FT: 90,000
SALES (est): 20.9MM **Privately Held**
SIC: 2052 2045 Cookies; doughs, frozen
or refrigerated: from purchased flour

(G-1648)
K M MEDIA GROUP LLC
Also Called: Peachtree Kay
220 Entin Rd (07014-1423)
PHONE......................................973 330-3000
Steve Tumminello, *Vice Pres*
Fred Golden, *VP Bus Dvlpt*
Rick Levy, *Director*
Richard Kirschenbaum,
Mike Costello,
EMP: 89
SQ FT: 50,000
SALES: 18.5MM **Privately Held**
SIC: 2759 Commercial printing

(G-1649)
KAY PRINTING & ENVELOPE CO INC
Also Called: Rga Graphics
220 Entin Rd (07014-1423)
PHONE......................................973 330-3000
Richard Kirschenbaum, *President*
Mike Costello, *Vice Pres*
Manny Rosa, *Plant Mgr*
Eileen Ringen, *Prdtn Mgr*
Emil Mirsik, *Production*
EMP: 50 EST: 1974
SQ FT: 50,000
SALES (est): 9.5MM **Privately Held**
WEB: www.kayprinting.com
SIC: 2752 Commercial printing, offset

(G-1650)
L3HARRIS TECHNOLOGIES INC
Also Called: Harris Corporation
77 River Rd (07014-2000)
PHONE......................................973 284-0123
Chris Bernhardt, *Branch Mgr*

EMP: 136
SALES (corp-wide): 6.8B **Publicly Held**
SIC: 3812 Search & navigation equipment
PA: L3harris Technologies, Inc.
　　1025 W Nasa Blvd
　　Melbourne FL 32919
　　321 727-9100

(G-1651)
L3HARRIS TECHNOLOGIES INC
77 River Rd (07014-2000)
PHONE..................................973 284-0123
Timothy Ringler, *Manager*
EMP: 26
SALES (corp-wide): 6.8B **Publicly Held**
WEB: www.ittind.com
SIC: 3625 Control equipment, electric
PA: L3harris Technologies, Inc.
　　1025 W Nasa Blvd
　　Melbourne FL 32919
　　321 727-9100

(G-1652)
L3HARRIS TECHNOLOGIES INC
Also Called: Harris Corporation
77 River Rd (07014-2000)
PHONE..................................973 284-0123
Mark Chubik, *Branch Mgr*
EMP: 148
SALES (corp-wide): 6.8B **Publicly Held**
SIC: 3812 Navigational systems & instruments
PA: L3harris Technologies, Inc.
　　1025 W Nasa Blvd
　　Melbourne FL 32919
　　321 727-9100

(G-1653)
LAMART CORP
37 Chestnut St (07011-2805)
PHONE..................................973 772-6262
EMP: 10 EST: 2010
SALES (est): 3.1MM **Privately Held**
SIC: 3089 Plastics products

(G-1654)
LAMART CORPORATION (PA)
16 Richmond St (07011-2899)
P.O. Box 1648 (07015-1648)
PHONE..................................973 772-6262
Steven B Hirsh, *President*
Alan Hirsh, *Vice Pres*
Mark Rubin, *Controller*
Ovier Guzman, *Manager*
◆ EMP: 140
SQ FT: 40,000
SALES (est): 93.3MM **Privately Held**
WEB: www.lamartcorp.com
SIC: 2672 Tape, pressure sensitive: made from purchased materials; adhesive backed films, foams & foils; adhesive papers, labels or tapes: from purchased material; metallic covered paper: made from purchased materials

(G-1655)
LAMART CORPORATION
162 Circle Ave (07011-2810)
PHONE..................................973 772-6262
James Landrum, *Branch Mgr*
EMP: 6
SALES (corp-wide): 93.3MM **Privately Held**
SIC: 3089 Plastic processing
PA: Lamart Corporation
　　16 Richmond St
　　Clifton NJ 07011
　　973 772-6262

(G-1656)
LEGACY VULCAN LLC
208 Piaget Ave (07011-2255)
PHONE..................................973 253-8828
Voitek Roszkowski, *Principal*
EMP: 26 **Publicly Held**
WEB: www.vulcanmaterials.com
SIC: 1422 Crushed & broken limestone
HQ: Legacy Vulcan, Llc
　　1200 Urban Center Dr
　　Vestavia AL 35242
　　205 298-3000

(G-1657)
LEGEND STONE PRODUCTS
185 River Rd (07014-1518)
PHONE..................................973 473-7088

Emin Aydin, *Owner*
▲ EMP: 6
SALES (est): 619.8K **Privately Held**
SIC: 3423 Stonecutters' hand tools

(G-1658)
LEXINGTON GRAPHICS CORP
161 Elmwood Dr (07013-1129)
PHONE..................................973 345-2493
Henry H Brandhorst, *President*
EMP: 5
SALES (est): 463.2K **Privately Held**
SIC: 2752 7336 Commercial printing, offset; graphic arts & related design

(G-1659)
LIGHT INC
Also Called: Ant Stores
345 Clifton Ave (07011-2618)
PHONE..................................973 777-2704
Mustafa Ozcan, *President*
Huseyin Senturk, *Vice Pres*
Ahmet Idil, *Treasurer*
▲ EMP: 9 EST: 2001
SQ FT: 5,000
SALES (est): 1MM **Privately Held**
SIC: 2741 5942 8748 Miscellaneous publishing; book stores; business consulting

(G-1660)
LMP PRINTING CORP
Also Called: Minuteman Press
1 Trenton Ave (07011-1807)
PHONE..................................973 428-1987
Mike Finucane, *President*
Patricia Finucane, *Treasurer*
EMP: 4
SALES (est): 433.1K **Privately Held**
SIC: 2752 Commercial printing, lithographic

(G-1661)
LUBRIZOL GLOBAL MANAGEMENT
1 Industrial St W (07012-1711)
PHONE..................................973 471-1300
Stephen K Scher, *CEO*
Roger Williams, *Warehouse Mgr*
Carlos Garcia, *Maintence Staff*
EMP: 15
SALES (corp-wide): 225.3B **Publicly Held**
WEB: www.pharma.noveoninc.com
SIC: 2899 Chemical preparations
HQ: Lubrizol Global Management, Inc
　　9911 Brecksville Rd
　　Brecksville OH 44141
　　216 447-5000

(G-1662)
LUKACH INTERIORS INC
208 River Rd (07014-1519)
PHONE..................................973 777-1499
Mike Lukach, *President*
EMP: 10
SQ FT: 10,000
SALES: 1.2MM **Privately Held**
SIC: 2431 5712 Woodwork, interior & ornamental; customized furniture & cabinets

(G-1663)
MAGNUSON PRODUCTS
6 Chelsea Rd (07012-1667)
PHONE..................................973 472-9292
Albert Reisch Jr, *President*
Pamela Reisch, *Treasurer*
EMP: 12
SQ FT: 23,000
SALES (est): 958.3K
SALES (corp-wide): 9.9MM **Privately Held**
SIC: 2842 2841 Cleaning or polishing preparations; soap & other detergents
PA: E. M. Sergeant Pulp And Chemical Co., Inc.
　　6 Chelsea Rd
　　Clifton NJ 07012
　　973 472-9111

(G-1664)
MASOULEH CORP (PA)
Also Called: Citgo
301 River Rd (07014-1549)
PHONE..................................973 470-8900
Faramarz Ebrahimi, *President*
Fred Ebrahimi, *Vice Pres*

EMP: 25
SQ FT: 2,000
SALES (est): 4.4MM **Privately Held**
SIC: 5541 1382 Filling stations, gasoline; oil & gas exploration services

(G-1665)
MASTERS INTERIORS INC
1500 Main Ave Ste 23 (07011-2124)
PHONE..................................973 253-0784
Kevin Costello, *President*
EMP: 35
SALES (est): 1.7MM **Privately Held**
SIC: 7389 2512 Interior design services; upholstered household furniture

(G-1666)
MAX GURTMAN & SONS INC
622 Lexington Ave (07011-1229)
P.O. Box 1849 (07015-1849)
PHONE..................................973 478-7000
Franklin Gurtman, *President*
EMP: 5 EST: 1934
SQ FT: 10,000
SALES (est): 430K **Privately Held**
SIC: 3444 3441 Sheet metalwork; fabricated structural metal

(G-1667)
MELTOM MANUFACTURING INC
22 Franklin Ave (07011-2214)
PHONE..................................973 546-0058
Joseph Chudzik, *President*
EMP: 5
SQ FT: 3,600
SALES: 158.1K **Privately Held**
SIC: 3451 Screw machine products

(G-1668)
METROPOLITAN FOODS INC (PA)
Also Called: Driscoll Foods
174 Delawanna Ave (07014-1550)
PHONE..................................973 672-9400
Tim Driscoll, *President*
Joe Vione, *Area Mgr*
Casey Stangle, *Business Mgr*
Martin Rapport, *Vice Pres*
Vito Scardigno, *VP Prdtn*
▲ EMP: 153
SQ FT: 220,000
SALES (est): 404.9MM **Privately Held**
WEB: www.driscollfoods.com
SIC: 5142 5149 2099 5141 Packaged frozen goods; dried or canned foods; food preparations; food brokers

(G-1669)
MICRO-TEK LABORATORIES INC (PA)
Also Called: Physitemp Instruments
154 Huron Ave (07013-2949)
PHONE..................................973 779-5577
Ronald R Feller, *President*
Christopher Proffitt, *Admin Sec*
EMP: 7
SQ FT: 5,500
SALES (est): 2.8MM **Privately Held**
WEB: www.physitemp.com
SIC: 3823 3821 3829 3822 Temperature instruments: industrial process type; laboratory equipment: fume hoods, distillation racks, etc.; measuring & controlling devices; auto controls regulating residntl & coml environmt & applncs; semiconductors & related devices

(G-1670)
MODERN FUEL INC
158 Colfax Ave (07013-1857)
PHONE..................................973 471-1501
EMP: 5 EST: 2010
SALES (est): 251.5K **Privately Held**
SIC: 2869 Fuels

(G-1671)
MPHASE TECHNOLOGIES INC (PA)
777 Passaic Ave Ste 385 (07012-1874)
PHONE..................................973 256-3737
Anshu Bhatnagar, *CEO*
Ronald A Durando, *President*
Gustave T Dotoli, *COO*
Christopher Cutchen, *CFO*
EMP: 15

SALES: 2.5MM **Publicly Held**
WEB: www.mphasetech.com
SIC: 3699 3691 3663 Electrical equipment & supplies; storage batteries; radio & TV communications equipment; satellites, communications

(G-1672)
NALUCO INC
Also Called: American Flyer
23 Carol St (07014-1420)
PHONE..................................800 601-8198
Joseph Liang, *President*
Grace Liang, *Vice Pres*
EMP: 87
SQ FT: 80,000
SALES (est): 7.6MM **Privately Held**
WEB: www.americanflyer.com
SIC: 5099 3161 Luggage; luggage; clothing & apparel carrying cases; suitcases; attache cases

(G-1673)
NB BOOKBINDING INC
356 Getty Ave Bldg 2 (07011)
PHONE..................................973 247-1200
Nicolas Bassil, *President*
Christine Bassil, *Vice Pres*
Pitiya Bassil, *Manager*
▲ EMP: 8
SQ FT: 20,000
SALES: 550K **Privately Held**
SIC: 2789 Binding only: books, pamphlets, magazines, etc.

(G-1674)
NES JEWELRY INC
43 Samworth Rd (07012-1714)
PHONE..................................646 213-4094
Yosi Arish, *COO*
EMP: 70 **Privately Held**
SIC: 3961 Costume jewelry
PA: Nes Jewelry, Inc.
　　10 W 33rd St Rm 803
　　New York NY 10001

(G-1675)
NEW JERSEY WIRE CLOTH CO INC
55 Park Slope (07011)
PHONE..................................973 340-0101
John Rafanello, *President*
EMP: 8
SALES (est): 396.6K **Privately Held**
SIC: 3496 Miscellaneous fabricated wire products

(G-1676)
NEW LINE PRTG & TECH SOLUTIONS
790 Bloomfield Ave Ste 3 (07012-1142)
PHONE..................................973 405-6133
John Luciano, *President*
Barry Clark, *Sales Staff*
Elena Manzi, *Mktg Dir*
Danielle Treboski, *Administration*
EMP: 7
SQ FT: 750
SALES (est): 881.8K **Privately Held**
SIC: 2759 5045 Business forms: printing; computer software

(G-1677)
NEWARK WIRE CLOTH COMPANY
160 Fornelius Ave (07013-1844)
PHONE..................................973 778-4478
Richard W Campbell, *President*
James L Campbell, *Vice Pres*
Robert D Lucki, *Vice Pres*
▲ EMP: 28 EST: 1911
SQ FT: 30,000
SALES (est): 6.5MM **Privately Held**
WEB: www.newarkwire.com
SIC: 3496 Fabrics, woven wire

(G-1678)
NIJAMA CORPORATION
Also Called: Empanada King
132 Getty Ave (07011-1840)
P.O. Box 213, Little Ferry (07643-0213)
PHONE..................................973 272-3223
Marino Roa, *President*
EMP: 5 EST: 2002

SALES (est): 289.6K **Privately Held**
SIC: 2045 Doughs, frozen or refrigerated:
from purchased flour

(G-1679)
NPS PUBLIC FURNITURE CORP
Also Called: National Public Seating
149 Entin Rd (07014-1424)
PHONE...................................973 594-1100
Barry Stauber, *Co-CEO*
Benjamin Grunwald, *Co-CEO*
Leo Drel, *Regl Sales Mgr*
Devora Mandelbaum, *Admin Sec*
◆ EMP: 93 EST: 1997
SALES (est): 44MM **Privately Held**
WEB: www.nationalpublicseating.com
SIC: 5021 2514 Chairs; chairs, household:
metal

(G-1680)
OKLAHOMA SOUND CORP (PA)
Also Called: O S C
149 Entin Rd (07014-1424)
PHONE...................................800 261-4112
Benjamin Grunwald, *CEO*
Barry Stauber, *President*
Devora Mandelbaum, *Admin Sec*
▲ EMP: 50 EST: 1982
SQ FT: 18,000
SALES (est): 8.6MM **Privately Held**
WEB: www.oklahomasound.com
SIC: 3651 Public address systems

(G-1681)
ORORA VISUAL LLC
1155 Bloomfield Ave (07012-2308)
PHONE...................................973 916-2804
EMP: 7
SALES (est): 937.9K **Privately Held**
SIC: 2752 Advertising posters, litho-
graphed

(G-1682)
**PALLMANN PULVERIZERS CO
INC**
Also Called: Pallmann Industries
820 Bloomfield Ave (07012-1116)
PHONE...................................973 471-1450
Hartmut Pallmann, *President*
Ingo Pallmann, *Shareholder*
EMP: 30 EST: 1959
SQ FT: 30,000
SALES (est): 6.6MM **Privately Held**
WEB: www.pallmannpulverizers.com
SIC: 3532 5084 Pulverizers (stationary),
stone; grinders, stone: stationary; pulver-
izing machinery & equipment; crushing
machinery & equipment

(G-1683)
PAPILLON RIBBON & BOW INC
35 Monhegan St (07013-2000)
PHONE...................................973 928-6128
CHI-Yin Wong, *President*
Igual Pua, *President*
Jimmy Cheung, *Vice Pres*
▲ EMP: 25
SQ FT: 12,000
SALES (est): 5.8MM **Privately Held**
WEB: www.papillonribbon.com
SIC: 5131 2396 Ribbons; ribbons & bows,
cut & sewed

(G-1684)
PARAMOUNT COSMETICS INC
93 Entin Rd Ste 4 (07014-1500)
PHONE...................................973 472-2323
Sandy Salzman, *President*
Steven E Schifrien, *Vice Pres*
Dana Graham, *Plant Mgr*
Cathy Chmielewski, *Opers Staff*
Ken Schweizer, *Plant Engr*
▲ EMP: 90
SQ FT: 120,000
SALES (est): 19.9MM **Privately Held**
WEB: www.paramanet.com
SIC: 2844 Cosmetic preparations

(G-1685)
**PASSAIC METAL & BLDG SUPS
CO (PA)**
Also Called: Siding Depot
5 Central Ave Ste 1 (07011-2399)
P.O. Box 1849 (07015-1849)
PHONE...................................973 546-9000
Franklin S Gurtman, *President*

Michael Gurtman, *Vice Pres*
Pete Jimenez, *Sales Staff*
Rey Pampco, *Sales Staff*
Andrew Wohr, *Sales Staff*
EMP: 100 EST: 1913
SALES (est): 106.3MM **Privately Held**
WEB: www.pampco.com
SIC: 5033 5031 5051 5075 Roofing &
siding materials; doors & windows; doors;
windows; sheets, metal; air conditioning &
ventilation equipment & supplies; sheet
metalwork; mineral wool

(G-1686)
PAVEXPRESS
499 River Rd (07014-1520)
PHONE...................................201 330-8300
Kenneth F Pavlik, *Principal*
EMP: 7
SALES (est): 652.9K **Privately Held**
SIC: 2741 Miscellaneous publishing

(G-1687)
PDM LITHO INC
220 Entin Rd (07014-1423)
PHONE...................................718 301-1740
Jeffrey M Alpert, *President*
Aaron Craig, *Chairman*
Joel Sachs, *Chairman*
Bob Sussman, *Vice Pres*
Bart Sussman, *Admin Sec*
EMP: 25
SQ FT: 18,000
SALES (est): 4MM **Privately Held**
WEB: www.pdmlitho.com
SIC: 2752 Commercial printing, litho-
graphic

(G-1688)
PENETONE CORPORATION (PA)
Also Called: West Penetone
125 Kingsland Ave Ste 205 (07014-2032)
PHONE...................................201 567-3000
Elwood W Phares II, *CEO*
Wayne Dory, *Division Mgr*
Michael Bradford, *Vice Pres*
Bruce Muretta, *Vice Pres*
Michael Nelson, *Vice Pres*
EMP: 25
SALES (est): 25.3MM **Privately Held**
WEB: www.protectivecream.com
SIC: 2842 2992 Cleaning or polishing
preparations; degreasing solvent; lubricat-
ing oils & greases

(G-1689)
PEREG GOURMET SPICES LTD
Also Called: Pereg Gourmet Natural Foods
25 Styertowne Rd (07012-1713)
PHONE...................................718 261-6767
Ilan Eshed, *President*
▲ EMP: 9
SQ FT: 5,000
SALES (est): 1.6MM **Privately Held**
SIC: 2099 5149 Seasonings & spices;
spices & seasonings; specialty food items

(G-1690)
PHILIPS ELEC N AMER CORP
Gemini Industries
215 Entin Rd (07014-1424)
PHONE...................................973 471-9450
Michael O'Neal, *Manager*
EMP: 100
SALES (corp-wide): 20.8B **Privately Held**
WEB: www.usa.philips.com
SIC: 3663 5064 5065 Antennas, transmit-
ting & communications; electrical enter-
tainment equipment; video cassette
recorders & accessories; radio & televi-
sion equipment & parts; communication
equipment; telephone & telegraphic
equipment
HQ: Philips North America Llc
3000 Minuteman Rd Ms1203
Andover MA 01810
978 659-3000

(G-1691)
PICTURE KNITS INC
489 Getty Ave (07011-2168)
PHONE...................................973 340-3131
Rory McNamara, *President*
Leon Benitez, *President*
Eduardo Benitez, *Vice Pres*
Mirna Benitez, *Admin Sec*

EMP: 32
SQ FT: 31,500
SALES (est): 3MM **Privately Held**
SIC: 2211 2221 Broadwoven fabric mills,
cotton; broadwoven fabric mills, man-
made

(G-1692)
**PILKINGTON NORTH AMERICA
INC**
125 Kingsland Ave (07014-2032)
PHONE...................................973 470-5703
EMP: 192 **Privately Held**
SIC: 3211 Flat glass
HQ: Pilkington North America, Inc.
811 Madison Ave Fl 3
Toledo OH 43604
419 247-3731

(G-1693)
PJM SOFTWARE INC
33 Mayer Dr (07012-1651)
P.O. Box 10732, New Brunswick (08906-
0732)
PHONE...................................973 330-0405
Peter Moore, *President*
James Krick, *Vice Pres*
EMP: 4
SALES (est): 50K **Privately Held**
WEB: pjmsoftware.com
SIC: 7372 Prepackaged software

(G-1694)
PMJE WELDING LLC
310 Colfax Ave Unit A (07013-1794)
PHONE...................................973 685-7344
EMP: 6
SALES (est): 107.3K **Privately Held**
SIC: 7692 Welding repair

(G-1695)
POLYMER TECHNOLOGIES INC
10 Clifton Blvd Ste 3 (07011-3802)
PHONE...................................973 778-9100
Neal Goldenberg, *President*
J Melvin Goldenberg, *Vice Pres*
▲ EMP: 84
SQ FT: 33,000
SALES (est): 16.7MM **Privately Held**
WEB: www.polymertek.com
SIC: 2821 Plastics materials & resins

(G-1696)
POLYTECH DESIGNS INC
26 W 1st St (07011-2103)
PHONE...................................973 340-1390
Zaki Shasha, *President*
Zak Shasha, *Engineer*
▲ EMP: 11
SQ FT: 6,000
SALES (est): 1.6MM **Privately Held**
WEB: www.polytechdesign.com
SIC: 3052 3429 Transmission belting, rub-
ber; pulleys metal

(G-1697)
**PRECISE CMPNENTS TL
DESIGN INC**
10 Clifton Blvd Unit A4 (07011-3802)
PHONE...................................973 928-2928
Harry Benedikt, *President*
Lee Kim Benedikt, *Vice Pres*
EMP: 8
SQ FT: 6,400
SALES (est): 800K **Privately Held**
SIC: 3841 3842 Surgical & medical instru-
ments; surgical appliances & supplies

(G-1698)
PRECISION SAW & TOOL CORP
56 Colfax Ave (07013-1944)
PHONE...................................973 773-7302
James Montesano, *President*
Janet Montesano, *Treasurer*
EMP: 11
SQ FT: 3,000
SALES (est): 1.1MM **Privately Held**
WEB: www.precisionsaw.com
SIC: 7699 5251 3546 Knife, saw & tool
sharpening & repair; tools; saws & sawing
equipment

(G-1699)
PRINCE BLACK DISTILLERY INC
Also Called: Black Prince
691 Clifton Ave (07011-4203)
P.O. Box 1999 (07015-1999)
PHONE...................................212 695-6187
Robert Guttag, *President*
▲ EMP: 29 EST: 1934
SQ FT: 120,000
SALES (est): 5.4MM **Privately Held**
WEB: www.blackprincedistillery.com
SIC: 2085 Distilled & blended liquors

(G-1700)
**PRINT FACTORY LTD LIABILITY
CO**
Also Called: Print Factory Nyc
730 Clifton Ave (07013-1862)
PHONE...................................973 866-5230
Ramsey Contreras,
EMP: 5
SQ FT: 900
SALES (est): 360.4K **Privately Held**
SIC: 2752 7336 Business form & card
printing, lithographic; commercial art &
graphic design

(G-1701)
PULSAR MICROWAVE CORP
48 Industrial St W (07012-1712)
PHONE...................................973 779-6262
Charlie Bobroski, *President*
Michael Chilimintris, *President*
William Eickhoff, *Chiropractor*
EMP: 25
SQ FT: 4,000
SALES (est): 8.6MM **Privately Held**
WEB: www.pulsarmicrowave.com
SIC: 5065 3825 Radio parts & acces-
sories; radio frequency measuring equip-
ment

(G-1702)
Q10 PRODUCTS LLC
Also Called: Creative Organization
1 Entin Rd Ste 7a (07014-1574)
P.O. Box 475, Tenafly (07670-0475)
PHONE...................................201 567-9299
Alfred Silber,
▲ EMP: 12
SALES (est): 1.5MM **Privately Held**
SIC: 5023 3999 Home furnishings; pet
supplies

(G-1703)
QUALITY INDUSTRIES INC
204 Getty Ave (07011-1804)
PHONE...................................973 478-4425
Jerry K Ponikowski, *President*
EMP: 12
SQ FT: 8,000
SALES: 1.1MM **Privately Held**
WEB: www.4qii.com
SIC: 3599 Machine shop, jobbing & repair

(G-1704)
QUALITY STAYS LLC (PA)
10 Underwood Pl Ste 2 (07013-2219)
PHONE...................................800 868-8195
▲ EMP: 5
SALES (est): 511.7K **Privately Held**
SIC: 3965 Fasteners, buttons, needles &
pins

(G-1705)
**RANCO PRECISION SHEET
METAL**
40 Colorado St (07014)
P.O. Box 1101 (07014-1101)
PHONE...................................973 472-8808
John Karpi, *President*
EMP: 9 EST: 1959
SQ FT: 5,000
SALES (est): 1.3MM **Privately Held**
SIC: 3444 Sheet metal specialties, not
stamped

(G-1706)
**RECYCLED PPRBD INC
CLIFTON**
1 Ackerman Ave (07011-1501)
PHONE...................................201 768-7468
Fax: 973 546-1349
EMP: 23
SQ FT: 200,000

SALES (est): 4.7MM **Privately Held**
SIC: 2675 Mfg Die-Cut Paper/Paperboard

(G-1707)
REGISTER LITHOGRAPHERS LTD
1155 Bloomfield Ave (07012-2308)
PHONE..............................973 916-2804
Joseph Fishman, *President*
Eugene Markowitz, *Vice Pres*
Joseph Goldbrenner, *Treasurer*
EMP: 54
SQ FT: 40,000
SALES (est): 43.7MM **Privately Held**
SIC: 2752 Commercial printing, offset

(G-1708)
SABER ASSOCIATES
1111 Paulison Ave (07011-3600)
PHONE..............................973 777-3800
Dean Emmolo, *Partner*
EMP: 40
SALES (est): 3.6MM **Privately Held**
WEB: www.saberassociates.com
SIC: 3567 Industrial furnaces & ovens

(G-1709)
SAFAS CORPORATION (PA)
2 Ackerman Ave (07011-1502)
PHONE..............................973 772-5252
Akbar Ghahary, *Ch of Bd*
Fateme Ghahary, *President*
Azam Alexander, *Corp Secy*
Bill Palowski, *Controller*
▲ EMP: 30
SQ FT: 85,000
SALES (est): 8.9MM **Privately Held**
WEB: www.safascorp.com
SIC: 2821 Plastics materials & resins

(G-1710)
SANDY ALEXANDER INC (PA)
Also Called: Modern Graphic Arts
200 Entin Rd (07014-1494)
PHONE..............................973 470-8100
Michael Graff, *CEO*
Louis Scharfstein, *President*
Eric Reinitz, *General Mgr*
Steven Babat, *COO*
Neal Alexander, *Exec VP*
▼ EMP: 180
SQ FT: 134,000
SALES (est): 90.2MM **Privately Held**
WEB: www.sandyinc.com
SIC: 2752 Commercial printing, offset

(G-1711)
SCHER CHEMICALS INC
Industrial West (07012)
PHONE..............................973 471-1300
Stephen K Scher, *President*
Judith Donner, *Vice Pres*
EMP: 2780 EST: 1932
SQ FT: 50,000
SALES (est): 184.1MM
SALES (corp-wide): 225.3B **Publicly Held**
WEB: www.pharma.noveoninc.com
SIC: 2869 Fatty acid esters, aminos, etc.
HQ: Lubrizol Global Management, Inc
9911 Brecksville Rd
Brecksville OH 44141
216 447-5000

(G-1712)
SCIENTIFIC ALLOYS CORP
5 Troast Ct (07011-2131)
PHONE..............................973 478-8323
Wayne R Connelly, *President*
Phil Jacobs, *Vice Pres*
William Pian, *Vice Pres*
EMP: 14
SQ FT: 27,500
SALES (est): 1.5MM **Privately Held**
WEB: www.bgaspheres.com
SIC: 3443 3399 Fabricated plate work
(boiler shop); metal powders, pastes &
flakes

(G-1713)
SEMELS EMBROIDERY INC
1078 Route 46 (07013-2420)
PHONE..............................973 473-6868
Charlotte Semel, *President*
Dolly Semel, *Vice Pres*
EMP: 13 EST: 1937

SQ FT: 6,000
SALES: 2MM **Privately Held**
SIC: 2395 7389 2759 2396 Embroidery
products, except schiffli machine; printers'
services: folding, collating; commercial
printing; automotive & apparel trimmings

(G-1714)
SEMI CONDUCTOR MANUFACTURING
Also Called: Semiconductor Manufacturing
5 Troast Ct (07011-2131)
PHONE..............................973 478-2880
Wayne R Connelly, *President*
William Pian, *Corp Secy*
EMP: 43
SQ FT: 12,500
SALES (est): 6.3MM **Privately Held**
WEB:
www.semiconductormanufacturing.com
SIC: 3674 1793 3341 Microcircuits, inte-
grated (semiconductor); glass & glazing
work; secondary nonferrous metals

(G-1715)
SHERMAN PRINTING CO INC
161 Elmwood Dr (07013-1129)
P.O. Box 2304 (07015-2304)
PHONE..............................973 345-2493
Dan Gillan, *President*
Doris Gillan, *Treasurer*
EMP: 4
SALES (est): 320K **Privately Held**
SIC: 2752 2759 Commercial printing, off-
set; letterpress printing

(G-1716)
SHINDO INTERNATIONAL INC
200 Entin Rd (07014-1423)
PHONE..............................973 470-8100
Hisako Shindo, *President*
James Lundquist, *Treasurer*
EMP: 35
SQ FT: 5,000
SALES (est): 3.2MM **Privately Held**
SIC: 2752 7336 Color lithography; com-
mercial art & graphic design
PA: Flexceed Co., Ltd.
6707-1, To
Naka IBR 311-0

(G-1717)
SHOWTECH INC
40 Entin Rd (07014-1542)
PHONE..............................973 249-6336
Daniel Zazzali, *President*
George P Zazzali, *Vice Pres*
EMP: 8
SALES: 1MM **Privately Held**
SIC: 2541 Cabinets, except refrigerated:
show, display, etc.: wood

(G-1718)
SIGN A RAMA
Also Called: Sign-A-Rama
681 Van Houten Ave (07013-2130)
PHONE..............................973 471-5558
Steven Budd, *President*
EMP: 4
SALES: 230K **Privately Held**
SIC: 3993 Signs & advertising specialties

(G-1719)
SIGNS OF 2000
421 Broad St (07013-1407)
PHONE..............................973 253-1333
Ray Salem, *Owner*
Eva N Cecli, *Manager*
EMP: 10
SALES (est): 889.7K **Privately Held**
SIC: 3993 Electric signs

(G-1720)
SILK CITY SNACKS LLC
200 Clifton Blvd (07011-3652)
PHONE..............................973 928-3161
Jim Burns, *CEO*
James Burn III, *President*
James Brown, *Exec VP*
John Tannachion,
▲ EMP: 25 EST: 2010
SALES (est): 4.3MM **Privately Held**
SIC: 2052 Cookies & crackers

(G-1721)
SITE DRAINER LLC
18 Sebago St (07013-1924)
PHONE..............................862 225-9940
Antonio Perez, *President*
EMP: 6
SQ FT: 4,500
SALES (est): 74.9K **Privately Held**
SIC: 3589 Sewage & water treatment
equipment

(G-1722)
SOMETHING DIFFERENT LINEN INC
167 Fornelius Ave (07013-1845)
PHONE..............................973 272-0601
Mitchell Smith, *President*
Melvin Atlas, *Vice Pres*
Araceib Baez, *Vice Pres*
Lina Bonilla, *Vice Pres*
◆ EMP: 125
SALES (est): 15.1MM **Privately Held**
WEB: www.tablecloths.net
SIC: 2299 Linen fabrics

(G-1723)
SPARK WIRE PRODUCTS CO INC
158 River Rd (07014-1571)
PHONE..............................973 773-6945
Paul Fessak, *President*
EMP: 7 EST: 1956
SQ FT: 7,000
SALES (est): 700K **Privately Held**
SIC: 2542 Racks, merchandise display or
storage: except wood; stands, merchan-
dise display: except wood

(G-1724)
STAINLESS METAL SOURCE INTL
Also Called: SMS International
207 Piaget Ave (07011-2235)
PHONE..............................973 977-2200
Chanoch Shiloh, *President*
Das Meneon, *Vice Pres*
▲ EMP: 7
SQ FT: 6,500
SALES (est): 2MM **Privately Held**
SIC: 5051 3312 Steel; stainless steel

(G-1725)
STARLIGHT ONE CORP
10 Van Orden Pl (07011-2922)
PHONE..............................862 684-0561
Mousa Kariti, *President*
Mohammed Kariti, *Vice Pres*
EMP: 2
SQ FT: 120
SALES: 1.2MM **Privately Held**
SIC: 2392 Blankets, comforters & beddings

(G-1726)
SUNCO & FRENCHIE LTD LBLTY CO
489 Getty Ave Door2 (07011-2168)
PHONE..............................973 478-1011
▲ EMP: 4 EST: 2011
SALES (est): 359.6K **Privately Held**
SIC: 5149 2082 Specialty food items; malt
beverage products

(G-1727)
SUSSEX HUMUS & SUPPLY INC
29 Kenyon St (07013-1729)
PHONE..............................973 779-8812
Joseph De Santis, *President*
Laurel Ann De Santis, *Corp Secy*
Glenn De Santis, *Vice Pres*
EMP: 4 EST: 1975
SALES (est): 359.3K **Privately Held**
SIC: 1499 Peat mining & processing

(G-1728)
SWEPCO TUBE LLC
1 Clifton Blvd (07011-3899)
P.O. Box 1899 (07015-1899)
PHONE..............................973 778-3000
Ken Schultz,
Steve Oberhelman,
EMP: 145 EST: 1939
SQ FT: 330,000
SALES (est): 67MM **Privately Held**
WEB: www.swepcotube.com
SIC: 3356 Nonferrous rolling & drawing

(G-1729)
TANZOLA PRINTING INC
Also Called: Sir Speedy
270 Colfax Ave (07013-1700)
PHONE..............................973 779-0858
Joe Tanzola, *President*
Ellen Tanzola, *Corp Secy*
EMP: 4 EST: 1980
SQ FT: 1,500
SALES (est): 240K **Privately Held**
SIC: 2752 7334 2789 Commercial print-
ing, offset; photocopying & duplicating
services; bookbinding & related work

(G-1730)
TAPTASK LLC
83 Rolling Hills Rd (07013-4117)
P.O. Box Msc 128449, Atlanta GA (30322-
0001)
PHONE..............................201 294-2371
Ekrem Kurucan,
Talha Koc,
Sinan Sahin,
EMP: 4
SALES (est): 98.3K **Privately Held**
SIC: 7372 Business oriented computer
software; application computer software

(G-1731)
TBC COLOR IMAGING INC
Also Called: Tbc Digital
200 Entin Rd (07014-1423)
PHONE..............................973 470-8100
Michael Graff, *President*
Steven Borbat, *COO*
Kevin St Germaine, *CFO*
Jack Schero, *Executive*
EMP: 26 EST: 1991
SALES (est): 2.5MM **Privately Held**
WEB: www.tbccolor.com
SIC: 2759 Commercial printing

(G-1732)
TIN PANDA INC
875 Blocmfield Ave (07012-1118)
PHONE..............................973 916-0707
Edwin Daz, *Principal*
EMP: 5
SALES (est): 580.6K **Privately Held**
SIC: 3356 Tin

(G-1733)
UNITED MEDICAL PC
535 Lexington Ave (07011-1923)
PHONE..............................201 456-0222
Byong Park, *Branch Mgr*
EMP: 5
SALES (corp-wide): 4.3MM **Privately
Held**
SIC: 3841 Diagnostic apparatus, medical
PA: United Medical P.C.
988 Broadway
Bayonne NJ 07002
201 339-6111

(G-1734)
VAN NESS PLASTIC MOLDING CO
400 Brighton Rd (07012-1013)
PHONE..............................973 778-9500
William Van Ness, *President*
◆ EMP: 200
SQ FT: 170,000
SALES (est): 51.1MM **Privately Held**
WEB: www.vannessplastic.com
SIC: 3089 Molding primary plastic

(G-1735)
VIP INDUSTRIES INC
90 Brighton Rd (07012-1606)
PHONE..............................973 472-7500
John Sonatore, *President*
Michael Yannibelli, *VP Opers*
Natalia Sanchez, *Opers Staff*
Eric Sonatore, *VP Finance*
▲ EMP: 50
SQ FT: 24,000
SALES (est): 7.7MM **Privately Held**
WEB: www.vipindustriesinc.com
SIC: 3679 Harness assemblies for elec-
tronic use: wire or cable

76   2019 Harris New Jersey
Manufacturers Directory   ▲ = Import ▼=Export
◆ =Import/Export

(G-1736)
VO-TOYS INC (PA)
Also Called: V I P
179 Entin Rd (07014-1424)
PHONE..................................973 482-8915
Arthur Hirschberg, *President*
Gary Hirschberg, *Corp Secy*
▲ EMP: 44
SALES (est): 34.8MM **Privately Held**
WEB: www.vo-toys.com
SIC: 5199 3999 Pets & pet supplies; pet
supplies

(G-1737)
WAGNER RACK INC
2 Broad St (07013-1098)
PHONE..................................973 278-6966
Ron Wagner, *President*
Wendy Prior, *Treasurer*
EMP: 25
SQ FT: 14,500
SALES (est): 4.6MM **Privately Held**
WEB: www.wagnerrack.com
SIC: 2541 Counters or counter display
cases, wood

(G-1738)
WALDEN LANG IN-PAK SERVICE
474 Getty Ave 2 (07011-2149)
PHONE..................................973 595-5250
Brian Billes, *President*
Jack Pires, *Corp Secy*
Greg A Regina, *Vice Pres*
EMP: 30 EST: 1992
SQ FT: 20,000
SALES (est): 2.4MM **Privately Held**
SIC: 2782 Sample books

(G-1739)
WESTROCK CP LLC
1401 Broad St Ste 1 (07013-4237)
PHONE..................................973 594-6000
Michael Smurfit, *CEO*
EMP: 25
SALES (corp-wide): 16.2B **Publicly Held**
WEB: www.smurfit-stone.com
SIC: 2631 Paperboard mills
HQ: Westrock Cp, Llc
1000 Abernathy Rd
Atlanta GA 30328

(G-1740)
WRAP-ADE MACHINE CO INC
Also Called: Wrapade
180 Brighton Rd Ste B (07012-1451)
PHONE..................................973 773-6150
Robert B Mc Closky, *President*
EMP: 12 EST: 1932
SQ FT: 6,000
SALES (est): 1.2MM **Privately Held**
WEB: www.standuppouch.com
SIC: 3565 5084 Packaging machinery; in-
dustrial machinery & equipment

(G-1741)
X-L PLASTICS INC
Also Called: Champion Plastics Div
220 Clifton Blvd (07011-3695)
PHONE..................................973 777-9400
Melvin Fischman, *President*
Arnold Fischman, *Vice Pres*
Zalmen Waldman, *Purch Agent*
John Callahan, *Sales Mgr*
Lesia Glodava, *Manager*
▲ EMP: 140
SQ FT: 135,000
SALES (est): 44.5MM **Privately Held**
WEB: www.xlplastics.com
SIC: 2673 3082 Plastic bags: made from
purchased materials; tubes, unsupported
plastic

(G-1742)
XPET LLC
179 Entin Rd (07014-1424)
P.O. Box 1294 (07012-0794)
PHONE..................................973 272-7502
Gary S Hirschberg, *Principal*
Stella Luna, *Manager*
▲ EMP: 22
SALES (est): 1.6MM **Privately Held**
SIC: 3999 Pet supplies

(G-1743)
ZENIA PHARMA LLC
575 Grove St Unit F1 (07013-3178)
PHONE..................................973 246-9718
Aurelije Zovko, *Principal*
EMP: 5 EST: 2007
SALES (est): 479.2K **Privately Held**
SIC: 2834 Pharmaceutical preparations

(G-1744)
ZIGGY SNACK FOODS LLC
200 Clifton Blvd Ste 1 (07011-3652)
PHONE..................................917 662-6038
Joel Draber, *Mng Member*
Leonid Rofin,
Zigman Sigmond Smitler,
EMP: 30
SQ FT: 20,400
SALES (est): 2.8MM **Privately Held**
SIC: 5963 2096 Snacks, direct sales; pop-
corn, already popped (except candy cov-
ered)

Clinton
Hunterdon County

(G-1745)
GREENROCK RECYCLING LLC
3 Frontage Rd (08809)
PHONE..................................908 713-0008
Brian Plushanski, *Owner*
EMP: 6
SALES (est): 147.1K **Privately Held**
SIC: 3271 Concrete block & brick

(G-1746)
**GULBRANDSEN
TECHNOLOGIES INC (PA)**
Also Called: Gulbrandsen Chemicals
2 Main St (08809-1328)
P.O. Box 5523 (08809-5523)
PHONE..................................908 735-5458
Donald Gulbrandsen, *CEO*
Peder L Gulbrandsen, *President*
Fredrika Gulbrandsen, *Vice Pres*
Thomas Madsen, *Opers Mgr*
Satish Patel, *Senior Engr*
▼ EMP: 40
SQ FT: 2,000
SALES (est): 19.4MM **Privately Held**
SIC: 2899 Chemical preparations

(G-1747)
MED-CON TECH LTD LBLTY CO
24 E Main St Unit 5033 (08809-7006)
PHONE..................................888 654-0856
Anthony Londino, *CEO*
EMP: 4
SALES (est): 147K **Privately Held**
SIC: 2759 Schedule, ticket & tag printing &
engraving

(G-1748)
PHILLIPS COMPANIES INC (PA)
7 Frontage Rd (08809-1293)
PHONE..................................973 483-4124
▼ EMP: 100
SALES (est): 11MM **Privately Held**
SIC: 3273 3271 Mfg Ready-Mixed Con-
crete Mfg Concrete Block/Brick

(G-1749)
SIERRA VIDEO SYSTEMS
6 State Route 173 (08809-1269)
P.O. Box 2462, Grass Valley CA (95945-
2462)
PHONE..................................530 478-1000
Adel Ghanem, *President*
David Bright, *Vice Pres*
▲ EMP: 44
SQ FT: 28,500
SALES (est): 6.4MM **Privately Held**
WEB: www.sierravideo.com
SIC: 3651 Household audio & video equip-
ment

(G-1750)
SUNFLOWER SEED
38 Old Highway 22 (08809-1305)
PHONE..................................908 735-3822
Edith Stern, *Owner*
EMP: 4

SALES (est): 348.3K **Privately Held**
SIC: 2833 Vitamins, natural or synthetic:
bulk, uncompounded

Closter
Bergen County

(G-1751)
ATLAS WOODWORKING INC
15 Naugle St (07624-1206)
PHONE..................................201 784-1949
Kenneth J Ewald, *President*
Shirl Ewald, *Vice Pres*
EMP: 9
SQ FT: 5,000
SALES: 2MM **Privately Held**
SIC: 3553 Cabinet makers' machinery

(G-1752)
CARTIHEAL INC
3 Reuten Dr (07624-2123)
PHONE..................................917 703-6992
Nir Altschuler, *CEO*
EMP: 6
SALES (est): 337.7K **Privately Held**
SIC: 3827 Optical instruments & lenses

(G-1753)
EN TECH CORP
91 Ruckman Rd Ste 1 (07624-2118)
PHONE..................................201 784-1034
Eugene Camali, *Branch Mgr*
EMP: 15
SALES (corp-wide): 7.8MM **Privately
Held**
SIC: 3321 Sewer pipe, cast iron
PA: En Tech Corp
91 Ruckman Rd
Closter NJ 07624
718 389-2058

(G-1754)
EN TECH CORP (PA)
Also Called: Manhattan Gunite
91 Ruckman Rd (07624-2117)
PHONE..................................718 389-2058
Eugene Camali, *President*
EMP: 17
SQ FT: 8,000
SALES (est): 7.8MM **Privately Held**
SIC: 3321 Sewer pipe, cast iron

(G-1755)
FLAVOR DEVELOPMENT CORP
10 Reuten Dr (07624-2115)
PHONE..................................201 784-8188
Joe Staffieri, *President*
Kathy Shubert, *Purchasing*
Lynn McQuade, *Bookkeeper*
Andrew Marquez, *Technician*
EMP: 10
SALES (est): 1.7MM **Privately Held**
WEB: www.flavordev.com
SIC: 2869 Perfumes, flavorings & food ad-
ditives

(G-1756)
H RITANI LLC
101 Carlson Ct (07624-1336)
PHONE..................................888 974-8264
Harout Aghjayan,
Ani Aghjayan,
▲ EMP: 20
SALES (est): 2.5MM **Privately Held**
WEB: www.ritani.com
SIC: 3911 Jewelry, precious metal

(G-1757)
HOME ORGANIZATION LLC
570 Piermont Rd Ste 136 (07624-3100)
PHONE..................................201 351-2121
Aviad Stark, *Mng Member*
EMP: 11
SQ FT: 400
SALES (est): 1.6MM **Privately Held**
SIC: 3089 4813 Organizers for closets,
drawers, etc.: plastic;

(G-1758)
**INTECH POWERCORE
CORPORATION**
250 Herbert Ave (07624-1333)
PHONE..................................201 767-8066

George Bartosch, *President*
EMP: 8 EST: 2012
SQ FT: 3,800
SALES (est): 773.2K **Privately Held**
SIC: 3569 3537 Lubricating equipment; ta-
bles, lift: hydraulic

(G-1759)
J A MACHINE & TOOL CO INC
84 Herbert Ave (07624-1313)
PHONE..................................201 767-1308
Andrew Petrinic, *President*
Jimmy Petrinic, *Corp Secy*
EMP: 11
SQ FT: 100,000
SALES (est): 1.7MM **Privately Held**
SIC: 3545 3728 Precision tools, machin-
ists'; aircraft parts & equipment

(G-1760)
**LUXURY AND TRASH LTD LBLTY
CO**
Also Called: L & T
1 Closter Cmns 258 (07624-3113)
P.O. Box 939, Alpine (07620-0939)
PHONE..................................201 315-4018
Maureen D Ben Sadigh,
Maureen Ben Sadigh,
EMP: 5
SQ FT: 1,000
SALES: 5MM **Privately Held**
SIC: 2331 2326 Women's & misses'
blouses & shirts; men's & boys' work
clothing

(G-1761)
MORRISON PRESS INC
10 Mckinley St Ste 3 (07624-2727)
PHONE..................................201 488-4848
EMP: 10 EST: 1920
SQ FT: 3,000
SALES (est): 1.6MM **Privately Held**
SIC: 2752 Lithographic Commercial Print-
ing

(G-1762)
**RETROGRAPHICS PUBLISHING
INC**
3 Reuten Dr (07624-2123)
PHONE..................................201 501-0505
Norman Lavine, *President*
Eric Caren, *Vice Pres*
EMP: 4
SALES (est): 497.1K **Privately Held**
SIC: 2621 5199 Catalog, magazine &
newsprint papers; gifts & novelties

(G-1763)
VENTURE STATIONERS INC
570 Piermont Rd Ste A17 (07624-3100)
PHONE..................................212 288-7235
Jamel Ezra, *President*
Effy Barmoshe, *COO*
Joseph Sheena, *Vice Pres*
Benjamin Ezra, *Admin Sec*
EMP: 27
SQ FT: 27,000
SALES (est): 2.8MM **Privately Held**
SIC: 5943 5948 3999 Office forms & sup-
plies; luggage & leather goods stores;
fruits, artificial & preserved

(G-1764)
VINTAGE PRINT GALLERY
3 Reuten Dr (07624-2123)
PHONE..................................201 501-0505
Norman Lavine, *Principal*
▲ EMP: 10
SALES (est): 844.7K **Privately Held**
SIC: 2752 Commercial printing, offset

(G-1765)
**WORLDWIDE SOLAR MFG
LLC ✪**
39 Walker Ave (07624-2832)
PHONE..................................201 297-1177
Shefali Desai,
EMP: 4 EST: 2018
SALES (est): 133.3K **Privately Held**
SIC: 5074 3674 Heating equipment & pan-
els, solar; solar cells

G
E
O
G
R
A
P
H
I
C

Collingswood
Camden County

(G-1766)
AINSWORTH MEDIA
Also Called: Retrospect The For Local News
732 Haddon Ave (08108-3712)
P.O. Box 296 (08108-0296)
PHONE...................856 854-1400
Brett Ainsworth, *Owner*
EMP: 6 **EST:** 1970
SQ FT: 4,500
SALES (est): 468.9K **Privately Held**
SIC: 2711 Newspapers, publishing & printing

(G-1767)
GADREN MACHINE CO INC (PA)
Also Called: Gade Float Valves
590 N Atl Ave Apt 305 (08108)
P.O. Box 117, Mount Ephraim (08059-0117)
PHONE...................856 456-4329
George Gadren, *President*
George S Gadren Sr, *President*
Gary S Gadren, *Vice Pres*
George S Gadren Jr, *Vice Pres*
Francis J Gadren, *VP Sales*
▲ **EMP:** 19 **EST:** 1937
SALES (est): 1.9MM **Privately Held**
WEB: www.gadrenmachine.com
SIC: 3492 3451 3494 3491 Fluid power valves & hose fittings; screw machine products; valves & pipe fittings; industrial valves

(G-1768)
GLAXOSMITHKLINE LLC
505 S Vineyard Blvd (08108-1321)
PHONE...................856 952-6023
Elizabeth Moeller, *Principal*
EMP: 26
SALES (corp-wide): 39.5B **Privately Held**
SIC: 2834 Pharmaceutical preparations
HQ: Glaxosmithkline Llc
5 Crescent Dr
Philadelphia PA 19112
215 751-4000

(G-1769)
JUBILI BEAD & YARN SHOPPE
713 Haddon Ave (08108-3711)
PHONE...................856 858-7844
Judy Weinstien, *Owner*
EMP: 6
SALES (est): 538.8K **Privately Held**
WEB: www.jubilibeadsandyarns.com
SIC: 2299 5947 5999 Yarns, specialty & novelty; gift shop; miscellaneous retail stores

(G-1770)
MCMUNN ASSOCIATES
900 Haddon Ave Ste 302 (08108-2127)
PHONE...................856 858-3440
Larry McMunn, *President*
Deborah Stephens, *Vice Pres*
Anna Demarco, *Production*
EMP: 25
SALES (est): 2.2MM **Privately Held**
SIC: 2721 Statistical reports (periodicals): publishing & printing

(G-1771)
SEVERINO PASTA MFG CO INC
110 Haddon Ave (08108-2087)
PHONE...................856 854-3716
Peter Severino, *President*
Louis Severino, *Vice Pres*
Joseph Severino, *Opers Staff*
Angelica Diodato, *Mktg Dir*
Leah Feriozzi, *Executive Asst*
EMP: 22
SQ FT: 7,000
SALES (est): 7.7MM **Privately Held**
SIC: 5149 5499 2098 2038 Pasta & rice; health & dietetic food stores; macaroni & spaghetti; frozen specialties

(G-1772)
TECHSETTERS INC
900 Haddon Ave Ste 300 (08108-2112)
PHONE...................856 240-7905

John Rogosich, *President*
Patricia Anton, *President*
Mildred Jaggard, *Vice Pres*
EMP: 20
SALES (est): 1.9MM **Privately Held**
WEB: www.techsetters.com
SIC: 2731 7336 2791 Books: publishing & printing; commercial art & graphic design; typesetting

Cologne
Atlantic County

(G-1773)
ABSECON MILLS INC
901 W Aloe St (08213)
PHONE...................609 965-5373
Randolph S Taylor, *President*
Douglass A Taylor, *COO*
David Adair, *Exec VP*
▲ **EMP:** 125 **EST:** 1978
SQ FT: 150,000
SALES (est): 20.4MM **Privately Held**
WEB: www.absecon.com
SIC: 2211 2221 Upholstery fabrics, cotton; broadwoven fabric mills, manmade

Colonia
Middlesex County

(G-1774)
AM CRUZ INTERNATIONAL LLC
13 New York Ave (07067-1741)
PHONE...................732 340-0066
Lou Cordeiro,
EMP: 5 **EST:** 1970
SQ FT: 800
SALES (est): 560K **Privately Held**
SIC: 3559 Refinery, chemical processing & similar machinery

(G-1775)
SIGN ENGINEERS INC
13 New York Ave (07067-1741)
PHONE...................732 382-4224
Jitendra Royal, *President*
Matha Royal, *Admin Sec*
EMP: 5
SALES (est): 360K **Privately Held**
SIC: 3993 Signs & advertising specialties

Colts Neck
Monmouth County

(G-1776)
A KESSLER KREATION INC
31 Continental Ct (07722-1408)
PHONE...................732 431-2468
EMP: 4 **EST:** 2007
SALES (est): 358.2K **Privately Held**
SIC: 3499 5199 Novelties & giftware, including trophies; gifts & novelties

(G-1777)
CAMTEC INDUSTRIES INC
28 Saddle Ridge Rd (07722-1035)
PHONE...................732 332-9800
Anthony Mauro, *Owner*
Carol Mauro, *Principal*
EMP: 15
SALES (est): 1.7MM **Privately Held**
WEB: www.camtecindustries.com
SIC: 3449 3089 Miscellaneous metalwork; plastic hardware & building products

(G-1778)
COINING MANUFACTURING LLC
11 Lafayette Ky (07722-1774)
P.O. Box 142 (07722-0142)
PHONE...................973 253-0500
Courtney Chronley, *General Mgr*
EMP: 40 **EST:** 2014
SALES (est): 6MM **Privately Held**
SIC: 3469 Stamping metal for the trade

(G-1779)
COLT MEDIA INC
Also Called: Clover Hill Coffee Co
4 Wedgewood Ave (07722-1137)
PHONE...................732 946-3276
George Schneider, *President*
EMP: 4
SALES: 500K **Privately Held**
SIC: 2731 Books: publishing only

(G-1780)
D&S FISHERIES LLC
6 Birch Ln (07722-2018)
PHONE...................914 438-3197
Michael Sarapochillo, *President*
Michael Lawrence Sarapochillo, *President*
Lawrence Sarapochillo, *Vice Pres*
EMP: 4
SALES (est): 292.4K **Privately Held**
SIC: 3732 Fishing boats: lobster, crab, oyster, etc.: small

(G-1781)
DR TIELMANN INC
Also Called: Fibercontrol
4 Hialeah Dr (07722-1215)
P.O. Box 198, Holmdel (07733-0198)
PHONE...................732 332-1860
D R Tielmann, *President*
Debora Evankow, *Director*
EMP: 5
SQ FT: 3,000
SALES (est): 685.6K **Privately Held**
WEB: www.fibercontrol.com
SIC: 3661 Telegraph & related apparatus

(G-1782)
FERRO INDUSTRIES INCORPORATED
14 Evergreen Ln (07722-1276)
PHONE...................732 246-3200
Fax: 732 246-7417
EMP: 45
SQ FT: 110,000
SALES (est): 6.1MM **Privately Held**
SIC: 3651 Mfg Home Audio/Video Equipment

(G-1783)
FOLIO ART GLASS INC
73 State Route 34 S (07722)
PHONE...................732 431-0044
Barbara Folio, *President*
Raymond Folio, *Vice Pres*
EMP: 5
SQ FT: 3,000
SALES: 500K **Privately Held**
WEB: www.theforgeonline.com
SIC: 3231 3229 5719 Stained glass: made from purchased glass; glass furnishings & accessories; glassware

(G-1784)
GRECO INDUSTRIES LLC
7 Colts Gait Ln (07722-1468)
P.O. Box 547 (07722-0547)
PHONE...................732 919-6200
Camille M Greco, *Principal*
EMP: 9
SALES (est): 1.4MM **Privately Held**
SIC: 3089 Garbage containers, plastic

(G-1785)
HERITAGE PUBLISHING
440 State Route 34 Ste 2 (07722-2525)
PHONE...................732 747-7770
EMP: 4
SALES (est): 320.5K **Privately Held**
SIC: 2741 Miscellaneous publishing

(G-1786)
PMM INC
11 Lafayette Ky (07722-1774)
P.O. Box 142 (07722-0142)
PHONE...................908 692-1465
Ed Fairful, *CEO*
▲ **EMP:** 30
SALES: 5MM **Privately Held**
SIC: 3412 Metal barrels, drums & pails

(G-1787)
R R J CO INC
13 Provincial Pl (07722-1152)
PHONE...................732 544-1514
Ronald H Holford Jr, *President*

Jeffrey E Holford, *Vice Pres*
Dave Osbourne, *Vice Pres*
▲ **EMP:** 35
SQ FT: 12,000
SALES (est): 3.7MM **Privately Held**
WEB: www.rrjco.com
SIC: 3672 Printed circuit boards

(G-1788)
SQUASH BEEF LLC
12 Downing Hill Ln (07722-1415)
PHONE...................917 577-8723
Anthony Frassetti, *President*
EMP: 5
SALES: 500K **Privately Held**
SIC: 2741

(G-1789)
TRI G MANUFACTURING LLC
Also Called: Tri-G Manufacturing
8 Iroquois Ct (07722-1821)
PHONE...................732 460-1881
Justin J Sallusto,
EMP: 10
SALES (est): 603.3K **Privately Held**
SIC: 2399 Horse & pet accessories, textile

(G-1790)
WESTROCK CP LLC
21 Millpond Ln (07722-1563)
PHONE...................732 866-1890
EMP: 88
SALES (corp-wide): 16.2B **Publicly Held**
WEB: www.smurfit-stone.com
SIC: 2631 Paperboard mills
HQ: Westrock Cp, Llc
1000 Abernathy Rd
Atlanta GA 30328

Columbia
Warren County

(G-1791)
10-31 INCORPORATED
Also Called: ART DISPLAY ESSENTIALS
2 W Crisman Rd (07832-2709)
PHONE...................908 496-4946
William Stender, *President*
Chris Midkiff, *Marketing Mgr*
Lynne Stender, *Manager*
▲ **EMP:** 23
SQ FT: 18,000
SALES (est): 5.1MM **Privately Held**
WEB: www.10-31.com
SIC: 2541 2434 2511 5961 Cabinets, except refrigerated: show, display, etc.: wood; wood kitchen cabinets; wood household furniture; catalog & mail-order houses

(G-1792)
BROOK HOLLOW WINERY LLC
594 State Hwy 94 (07832)
PHONE...................908 496-8200
Paul Ritter,
EMP: 5
SALES (est): 417.7K **Privately Held**
SIC: 2084 Wines

(G-1793)
GENERAL STAMPING CO INC
Also Called: GSC
309 Sr 94 (07832)
PHONE...................973 627-9500
Robert P Dato, *President*
Damon Dato, *Exec VP*
Lauren Glory, *Accountant*
EMP: 13
SQ FT: 15,000
SALES (est): 3.8MM **Privately Held**
SIC: 3469 Stamping metal for the trade

(G-1794)
IMPERIAL MACHINE & TOOL CO (HQ)
8 W Crisman Rd (07832-2709)
PHONE...................908 496-8100
George H Joest, *CEO*
Christian M Joest, *President*
Tom Golembeski, *CFO*
Chriatina G Joest, *VP Sales*
Samantha Joest Peterson, *Manager*
▼ **EMP:** 12

SQ FT: 30,000
SALES (est): 4.1MM
SALES (corp-wide): 1.5B **Publicly Held**
SIC: 3825 3599 Instruments to measure
electricity; custom machinery
PA: Kaiser Aluminum Corporation
27422 Portola Pkwy # 350
Foothill Ranch CA 92610
949 614-1740

(G-1795)
INTERTEST INC (PA)
303 State Route 94 Ste 1 (07832-2841)
PHONE..................................908 496-8008
Bill Habermann, *President*
Stephen Hamilton, *Sales Staff*
EMP: 30
SQ FT: 10,000
SALES (est): 11.2MM **Privately Held**
SIC: 5084 5046 3861 Industrial machin-
ery & equipment; commercial equipment;
cameras & related equipment

(G-1796)
ORATON CUSTOM PRODUCTS
407 State Route 94 (07832-2528)
PHONE..................................908 235-9424
EMP: 4
SALES (est): 400.1K **Privately Held**
SIC: 3953 Marking devices

(G-1797)
RICKLYN CO INC
43 Centerville Rd (07832-2201)
PHONE..................................908 689-6770
Kevin Nook, *CEO*
Suzanne Nook, *Admin Sec*
EMP: 6 EST: 1963
SALES (est): 851.9K **Privately Held**
SIC: 7692 3444 Welding repair; sheet
metalwork

Columbus
Burlington County

(G-1798)
**CORONIS BUILDING SYSTEMS
INC**
92 Columbus Jobstown Rd (08022-1327)
PHONE..................................609 261-2200
Emanuel A Coronis Jr, *President*
Magdalene Coronis, *Corp Secy*
▼ **EMP:** 20
SQ FT: 17,000
SALES (est): 4.4MM **Privately Held**
WEB: www.trussframe.com
SIC: 3441 Building components, structural
steel

(G-1799)
CUPCAKE CELEBRATIONS
107 Paddock Dr (08022-9726)
PHONE..................................973 885-0826
EMP: 4
SALES (est): 158.9K **Privately Held**
SIC: 2051 Bread, cake & related products

(G-1800)
DRAZTIC DESIGNS LLC
Also Called: Tri Tech Telecom
205 Petticoat Bridge Rd (08022-1406)
PHONE..................................609 678-4200
David Camp, *Mng Member*
EMP: 50
SQ FT: 1,200
SALES (est): 1.7MM **Privately Held**
SIC: 3663 Radio & TV communications
equipment

(G-1801)
**K2 MILLWORK LTD LIABILITY
CO**
Also Called: K 2 Mill Work
2180 Hedding Rd (08022-2069)
PHONE..................................609 379-6411
Michael W Kocubinski, *Principal*
EMP: 4
SALES (est): 199.5K **Privately Held**
SIC: 2431 Millwork

(G-1802)
MELTON SALES & SERVICE (PA)
Also Called: Melton Industries
13 Petticoat Bridge Rd (08022-1401)
PHONE..................................609 699-4800
John F Melton, *Ch of Bd*
Floyd Melton, *Parts Mgr*
Amber Herbert, *Accounting Mgr*
Ken Fairchilds, *Director*
Patti Puma, *Admin Asst*
EMP: 40
SQ FT: 70,000
SALES (est): 10MM **Privately Held**
SIC: 3812 3519 Defense systems &
equipment; diesel engine rebuilding

Cookstown
Burlington County

(G-1803)
DRYTECH INC
54 Wrghtstown Cokstown Rd (08511-1020)
P.O. Box 128 (08511-0128)
PHONE..................................609 758-1794
Tony Jones, *Principal*
▲ **EMP:** 25
SQ FT: 6,000
SALES (est): 8MM **Privately Held**
SIC: 3585 3769 3728 5084 Refrigeration
& heating equipment; guided missile &
space vehicle parts & auxiliary equip-
ment; aircraft parts & equipment; food in-
dustry machinery

(G-1804)
**EXPORT MANAGEMENT
CONSULTANTS**
Also Called: EMC Aviation
54 Wrghtstown Cokstown Rd (08511-1020)
P.O. Box 249 (08511-0249)
PHONE..................................609 758-1166
Anthony Jones, *President*
EMP: 25
SQ FT: 16,500
SALES (est): 1.8MM **Privately Held**
WEB: www.drytechinc.com
SIC: 3728 Aircraft assemblies, subassem-
blies & parts

(G-1805)
RALPH CLAYTON & SONS LLC
Also Called: Clayton Concrete
58 Goldman Dr (08511-1022)
PHONE..................................800 662-3044
William Gangel, *Manager*
EMP: 25
SALES (corp-wide): 106.4MM **Privately
Held**
WEB: www.claytonco.com
SIC: 3273 Ready-mixed concrete
PA: Ralph Clayton & Sons L.L.C.
1355 Campus Pkwy
Wall Township NJ 07753
732 363-1995

Cranbury
Middlesex County

(G-1806)
ABJ LLC (PA)
Also Called: Abj Drone Services
2661 Us Highway 130 (08512-3300)
PHONE..................................888 225-1931
VIP Jain, *Mng Member*
EMP: 9 EST: 2017
SALES (est): 1.8MM **Privately Held**
SIC: 3721 Motorized aircraft

(G-1807)
AKORN INC
5 Cedarbrook Dr Ste 7 (08512-3606)
PHONE..................................609 662-9100
Saeed Khan, *Branch Mgr*
EMP: 32
SALES (corp-wide): 694MM **Publicly
Held**
SIC: 2834 Pharmaceutical preparations

PA: Akorn, Inc.
1925 W Field Ct Ste 300
Lake Forest IL 60045
847 279-6100

(G-1808)
**AMERINDIA TECHNOLOGIES
INC**
101 Interchange Plz # 201 (08512-3716)
PHONE..................................609 664-2224
Arun Mehta, *President*
Neena Mehta, *Vice Pres*
Rajesh Mittal, *Vice Pres*
Pranshi Gupta, *Finance Dir*
Aabha Sharma, *Technology*
EMP: 35
SQ FT: 3,000
SALES (est): 2.4MM **Privately Held**
WEB: www.amerindia.net
SIC: 1731 7371 7372 7373 Safety & se-
curity specialization; computer software
systems analysis & design, custom; com-
puter software development & applica-
tions; application computer software;
systems software development services

(G-1809)
**AMICUS THERAPEUTICS INC
(PA)**
1 Cedarbrook Dr (08512-3618)
PHONE..................................609 662-2000
John F Crowley, *Ch of Bd*
Evan Katz, *General Mgr*
Kurt J W Andrews, *Senior VP*
Simon Jordan, *Senior VP*
Jill Weimer, *Senior VP*
EMP: 157
SQ FT: 90,000
SALES (est): 91.2MM **Publicly Held**
SIC: 2834 Pharmaceutical preparations

(G-1810)
**AMICUS THERAPEUTICS US
INC**
1 Cedarbrook Dr (08512-3618)
PHONE..................................609 662-2000
Bradley Campbell, *President*
Daphne Quimi, *Treasurer*
Ellen Rosenberg, *Officer*
EMP: 4
SQ FT: 90,000
SALES (est): 523.5K
SALES (corp-wide): 91.2MM **Publicly
Held**
SIC: 2834 Pharmaceutical preparations
PA: Amicus Therapeutics, Inc.
1 Cedarbrook Dr
Cranbury NJ 08512
609 662-2000

(G-1811)
ANKUR INTERNATIONAL INC
Also Called: Marble and Granite Design Ctr
1206 Cranbury S River Rd (08512)
PHONE..................................609 409-6009
Binod Toshniwal, *President*
Anita Tushinal, *Principal*
Anita Toshniwal, *Finance*
◆ **EMP:** 12
SQ FT: 45,000
SALES (est): 3.7MM **Privately Held**
WEB: www.ankurinc.com
SIC: 5032 1411 Granite building stone;
marble building stone; dimension stone

(G-1812)
ANTRONIX INC (PA)
440 Forsgate Dr (08512-3518)
PHONE..................................609 860-0160
Daniel Tang, *President*
Neil Tang, *Vice Pres*
Suphie Tang, *Vice Pres*
Michael Wu, *Chief Engr*
Christine Chen, *Human Res Mgr*
▲ **EMP:** 30
SQ FT: 36,500
SALES (est): 135.1MM **Privately Held**
WEB: www.antronix.net
SIC: 3663 5063 Cable television equip-
ment; electrical apparatus & equipment

(G-1813)
AUROBINDO PHARMA USA INC
102 Melrich Rd (08512-3520)
PHONE..................................609 409-6774

Robert Cunard, *CEO*
G Prasad, *Vice Pres*
Ramprasad Reddy, *Admin Sec*
EMP: 5
SALES (corp-wide): 1.6B **Privately Held**
SIC: 2834 Pharmaceutical preparations
HQ: Aurobindo Pharma U.S.A., Inc.
279 Prnctn Hightstown Rd
East Windsor NJ 08520
732 839-9400

(G-1814)
BERRY GLOBAL INC
4 Aurora Dr Ste 403 (08512-3262)
PHONE..................................609 395-4199
EMP: 127 **Publicly Held**
WEB: www.6sens.com
SIC: 3089 3081 Plastic containers, except
foam; cups, plastic, except foam; bottle
caps, molded plastic; caps, plastic; un-
supported plastics film & sheet
HQ: Berry Global, Inc.
101 Oakley St
Evansville IN 47710
812 424-2904

(G-1815)
BRACCO RESEARCH USA INC
4c Cedarbrook Dr (08512-3612)
PHONE..................................609 514-2517
Michael F Tweedle, *President*
EMP: 46
SQ FT: 30,000
SALES (est): 8.6MM **Privately Held**
WEB: www.bru.bracco.com
SIC: 2834 Pharmaceutical preparations
HQ: Bracco U.S.A. Inc.
259 Prospect Plains Rd
Monroe Township NJ 08831
609 514-2200

(G-1816)
BROWN AND PERKINS INC
1193 Cranbury S River Rd (08512)
P.O. Box 412 (08512-0412)
PHONE..................................609 655-1150
Edward T Comly II, *President*
John C Comly, *Vice Pres*
William F Comly, *Treasurer*
Dave Vactor, *Sales Staff*
▲ **EMP:** 18
SQ FT: 28,800
SALES (est): 5MM **Privately Held**
SIC: 3496 Slings, lifting: made from pur-
chased wire

(G-1817)
**BRUNNQUELL IRON WORKS
INC**
2557 Us Highway 130 Ste 3 (08512-3509)
PHONE..................................609 409-6101
David G Brunnquell, *President*
Gerard J Brunnquell, *Treasurer*
Mary Bellach, *Controller*
EMP: 35 EST: 1925
SALES (est): 5.6MM **Privately Held**
WEB: www.brunnquelironworks.com
SIC: 3441 Fabricated structural metal

(G-1818)
CABLETENNA CORP
Also Called: Antronics
440 Forsgate Dr (08512-3518)
PHONE..................................609 395-9400
Daniel Tang, *President*
Suphie Tang, *Vice Pres*
EMP: 9
SQ FT: 24,000
SALES (est): 880K **Privately Held**
SIC: 3663 5063 Cable television equip-
ment; electrical apparatus & equipment

(G-1819)
CABOKI LLC
3 Corporate Dr (08512-3642)
PHONE..................................609 642-2108
Linda Caboki, *Principal*
▲ **EMP:** 4 EST: 2012
SALES (est): 240K **Privately Held**
SIC: 2844 Hair preparations, including
shampoos

(G-1820)
CARACO PHARMACEUTICAL LABS
270 Prospect Plains Rd (08512-3605)
PHONE..............................609 819-8200
Jay Patel, *Human Resources*
Jitendra Doshi, *Exec Dir*
EMP: 7
SALES (est): 506.5K **Privately Held**
SIC: 2834 Pharmaceutical preparations

(G-1821)
CHRISTIAN DIOR PERFUMES LLC
Also Called: L V M H Perfumes & Cosmetics
283 Prospect Plains Rd A (08512-3717)
PHONE..............................609 409-3628
Brent Strouse, *Director*
EMP: 8
SALES (corp-wide): 361.7MM **Privately Held**
WEB: www.saniflo.com
SIC: 2844 Perfumes, natural or synthetic; cosmetic preparations
HQ: Christian Dior Perfumes Llc
19 E 57th St
New York NY 10022
212 931-2200

(G-1822)
CHURCH & DWIGHT CO INC
326 Cranbury Half Acre Rd (08512-5010)
PHONE..............................609 655-6101
Tom Bennis, *Branch Mgr*
EMP: 14
SALES (corp-wide): 4.1B **Publicly Held**
WEB: www.churchdwight.com
SIC: 2812 Sodium bicarbonate
PA: Church & Dwight Co., Inc.
500 Charles Ewing Blvd
Ewing NJ 08628
609 806-1200

(G-1823)
CISPHARMA INC
1212 Cranbury S River Rd (08512)
PHONE..............................609 235-9807
Mukesh Desai, *President*
Ravi Annamaneni, *Chairman*
Peddanna Gumudavelli, *Vice Pres*
Srini Paruchuri, *Vice Pres*
Hasmukh Patel, *Vice Pres*
▲ EMP: 13
SALES (est): 5.2MM **Privately Held**
SIC: 2834 Pharmaceutical preparations

(G-1824)
CLAYTON MANUFACTURING COMPANY
Also Called: Clayton Industries
10 S River Rd Ste 6 (08512-3615)
PHONE..............................609 409-9400
Alan Ulbrecht, *Sales Staff*
Richard Slynn, *Manager*
EMP: 13
SALES (corp-wide): 109.8MM **Privately Held**
WEB: www.claytonindustries.com
SIC: 3569 Generators: steam, liquid oxygen or nitrogen
PA: Clayton Manufacturing Company
17477 Hurley St
City Of Industry CA 91744
626 443-9381

(G-1825)
CMIC CMO USA CORPORATION
Cedar Brook Corporate Ctr (08512)
PHONE..............................609 395-9700
Kunihide Ichikawa, *President*
Gary Wada, *Vice Pres*
Sunil Jeevandoss, *Prdtn Mgr*
Mahogany Mingo, *Production*
Pramila Agrawal, *QC Mgr*
EMP: 41
SALES (est): 17.2MM **Privately Held**
SIC: 2834 8731 Pharmaceutical preparations; biotechnical research, commercial
HQ: Cmic Co., Ltd.
1-1-1, Shibaura
Minato-Ku TKY 105-0

(G-1826)
COMM PORT TECHNOLOGIES INC
1 Corporate Dr Ste F (08512-3635)
PHONE..............................732 738-8780
Manny Patel, *President*
Channi Shah, *Vice Pres*
Carlos Mira, *Sales Staff*
▲ EMP: 2
SQ FT: 10,000
SALES: 4MM **Privately Held**
WEB: www.comm-port.com
SIC: 1731 3663 5731 Fiber optic cable installation; radio & TV communications equipment; video cameras, recorders & accessories

(G-1827)
CONSOLIDATED CONT HOLDINGS LLC
Also Called: Consoldate Cntiner Holdings NJ
4 Pleasant Hill Rd (08512-3637)
PHONE..............................609 655-0855
EMP: 70
SALES (corp-wide): 1.6B **Privately Held**
SIC: 3089 Plastic containers, except foam
PA: Consolidated Container Holdings Llc
2500 Windy Ridge Pkwy Se
Atlanta GA 30339
678 742-4600

(G-1828)
COOPER LIGHTING LLC
1 Broadway Rd (08512-5423)
PHONE..............................609 395-4277
Gary Gredell, *Principal*
EMP: 100 **Privately Held**
WEB: www.corelite.com
SIC: 3645 3646 Residential lighting fixtures; commercial indusl & institutional electric lighting fixtures
HQ: Cooper Lighting, Llc
1121 Highway 74 S
Peachtree City GA 30269
770 486-4800

(G-1829)
DATO COMPANY INC (PA)
Also Called: Sir Speedy
8 Plainsboro Rd (08512-3233)
PHONE..............................732 225-2272
Robert Chido, *President*
Jean Chido, *Office Mgr*
▲ EMP: 7
SQ FT: 2,000
SALES (est): 1.4MM **Privately Held**
SIC: 2752 Commercial printing, lithographic

(G-1830)
DOW JONES & COMPANY INC
4300 N Rt 1 & Ridge Rd (08512)
PHONE..............................609 520-4000
Brendan Intindola, *Editor*
Bart Ziegler, *Editor*
Qubilah Goodson, *Counsel*
Molly Evans, *Vice Pres*
Henry Osei, *Maint Spvr*
EMP: 15
SALES (corp-wide): 10B **Publicly Held**
SIC: 2711 Newspapers, publishing & printing
HQ: Dow Jones & Company, Inc.
1211 Avenue Of The Americ
New York NY 10036
609 627-2999

(G-1831)
E-BEAM SERVICES INC
118 Melrich Rd (08512-3595)
PHONE..............................513 933-0031
Peter Tuzzolo, *Manager*
EMP: 30
SALES (corp-wide): 5MM **Privately Held**
WEB: www.e-beamservices.com
SIC: 7389 3699 2821 Product sterilization service; electrical equipment & supplies; plastics materials & resins
PA: E-Beam Services, Inc.
270 Duffy Ave Ste H
Hicksville NY 11801
516 622-1422

(G-1832)
ENDO PHRMACEUTICALS VALERA INC
8 Clarke Dr (08512-3617)
PHONE..............................609 235-3230
James C Gale, *Ch of Bd*
David Holveck, *President*
Petr F Kuzma, *Vice Pres*
Jeremy D Middleton, *Vice Pres*
Andrew T Drechsler, *CFO*
EMP: 14
SQ FT: 21,274
SALES (est): 3.1MM **Privately Held**
SIC: 2834 Pharmaceutical preparations; drugs affecting neoplasms & endrocrine systems; drugs acting on the gastrointestinal or genitourinary system
HQ: Endo Pharmaceuticals, Inc.
1400 Atwater Dr
Malvern PA 19355
484 216-0000

(G-1833)
EXEMPLIFY BIOPHARMA INC
3000 Eastpark Blvd (08512-3532)
PHONE..............................732 500-3208
Yadan Chen, *President*
EMP: 1
SALES (est): 1.3MM **Privately Held**
SIC: 2834 Pharmaceutical preparations

(G-1834)
FBM BAKING MACHINES INC
1 Corporate Dr Ste D (08512-3635)
PHONE..............................609 860-0577
Frank Signorile, *President*
▲ EMP: 7
SQ FT: 15,000
SALES: 3MM **Privately Held**
WEB: www.fbmbakingmachines.com
SIC: 3556 Food products machinery

(G-1835)
GIVAUDAN FLAVORS CORPORATION
6 Santa Fe Way (08512-3288)
PHONE..............................973 463-8192
Gilles Andrier, *CEO*
Louie Damico, *President*
Maurizio Volpi, *President*
Anne Tayac, *Principal*
Tom Hallam, *CFO*
EMP: 6 EST: 2017
SALES (est): 850.7K **Privately Held**
SIC: 2869 Flavors or flavoring materials, synthetic

(G-1836)
GIVAUDAN FLAVORS CORPORATION
Spicetec Flavors & Seasonings
6 Santa Fe Way (08512-3288)
PHONE..............................609 409-6200
Joanna Holmes, *Branch Mgr*
EMP: 80
SALES (corp-wide): 5.5B **Privately Held**
WEB: www.conagra.com
SIC: 2087 Flavoring extracts & syrups
HQ: Givaudan Flavors Corporation
1199 Edison Dr
Cincinnati OH 45216
513 948-8000

(G-1837)
GROWTECH LLC
2 Corporate Dr Ste E (08512-3604)
PHONE..............................732 993-8683
Alex Zaleski, *Principal*
EMP: 75
SALES (est): 2MM **Privately Held**
SIC: 2064 Candy & other confectionery products

(G-1838)
HALSTED CORPORATION
Also Called: Halsted Bag
51 Commerce Dr Ste 3 (08512-3531)
PHONE..............................201 333-0670
Michael Murphy, *President*
Henry Jaszewski, *Treasurer*
Robert Zdanowicz, *Controller*
Justin Murphy, *VP Sales*
Patrick Thompson, *Sales Staff*
◆ EMP: 40 EST: 1876
SQ FT: 40,000
SALES (est): 6.1MM **Privately Held**
WEB: www.halstedbag.com
SIC: 2299 2393 2673 Burlap, jute; canvas bags; plastic bags: made from purchased materials

(G-1839)
ILLINOIS TOOL WORKS INC
Also Called: I T W Covid
32 Commerce Dr Ste 1 (08512-3529)
PHONE..............................609 395-5600
Nick Martino, *Branch Mgr*
EMP: 50
SALES (corp-wide): 14.7B **Publicly Held**
SIC: 2821 2759 Plastics materials & resins; commercial printing
PA: Illinois Tool Works Inc.
155 Harlem Ave
Glenview IL 60025
847 724-7500

(G-1840)
INNOPHOS INC
259 Prospect Plains Rd A (08512-3706)
PHONE..............................973 587-8735
EMP: 5
SALES (corp-wide): 801.8MM **Publicly Held**
SIC: 2819 2874 Industrial inorganic chemicals; phosphates
HQ: Innophos, Inc.
259 Prospect Plains Rd A
Cranbury NJ 08512
609 495-2495

(G-1841)
INNOPHOS LLC (HQ)
Also Called: Novel Ingredient Services, LLC
259 Prospect Plains Rd A (08512-3706)
PHONE..............................609 495-2495
Sharon Peek, *Vice Pres*
Lily Ruan, *Vice Pres*
Philip Genchi, *Research*
Malchus Kharatishvili, *Research*
Cindy G annotti, *Asst Controller*
◆ EMP: 6
SQ FT: 40,000
SALES (est): 6.8MM
SALES (corp-wide): 801.8MM **Publicly Held**
WEB: www.novelingredient.com
SIC: 2819 Industrial inorganic chemicals
PA: Innophos Holdings, Inc.
259 Prospect Plains Rd A
Cranbury NJ 08512
609 495-2495

(G-1842)
INNOPHOS HOLDINGS INC (PA)
259 Prospect Plains Rd A (08512-3706)
PHONE..............................609 495-2495
Kim Ann Mink, *Ch of Bd*
Dennis Dean, *Vice Chairman*
Valerie Coyne, *Business Mgr*
Michael Lestino, *Counsel*
Amy Hartzell, *Senior VP*
EMP: 89
SALES: 801.8MM **Publicly Held**
SIC: 2874 2819 5169 Phosphatic fertilizers; industrial inorganic chemicals; chemicals & allied products

(G-1843)
INNOPHOS INC (DH)
259 Prospect Plains Rd A (08512-3706)
PHONE..............................609 495-2495
Randolph Gress, *President*
Ricardo Suarez, *COO*
Louis Calvarin PHD, *Vice Pres*
William Farran, *Vice Pres*
Amy Hartzell, *Vice Pres*
◆ EMP: 700
SALES (est): 365.1MM
SALES (corp-wide): 801.8MM **Publicly Held**
WEB: www.innophos.com
SIC: 2819 Industrial inorganic chemicals
HQ: Innophos Investments Ii, Inc.
259 Prospect Plains Rd
Cranbury NJ 08512
609 495-2495

(G-1844)
INNOPHOS INVESTMENTS II INC (DH)
259 Prospect Plains Rd (08512-3706)
PHONE..................................609 495-2495
Randolph Gress, *Ch of Bd*
Iris Alvarado, *Vice Pres*
Charles Brodheim, *Vice Pres*
Bruce Brown, *Vice Pres*
William Farran, *Vice Pres*
EMP: 6 EST: 2012
SALES (est): 365.1MM
SALES (corp-wide): 801.8MM **Publicly Held**
SIC: 2874 2819 Phosphates; industrial inorganic chemicals
HQ: Innophos Investments Holdings, Inc.
259 Prospect Plains Rd
Cranbury NJ 08512
609 495-2495

(G-1845)
INNOPHOS INVSTMNTS HLDINGS INC (HQ)
259 Prospect Plains Rd (08512-3706)
PHONE..................................609 495-2495
Randy Gress, *President*
William Farran, *Vice Pres*
Wilma Harris, *Vice Pres*
Richard Heyse, *CFO*
Mark Feuerbach, *Treasurer*
EMP: 2
SALES (est): 481.9MM
SALES (corp-wide): 801.8MM **Publicly Held**
SIC: 2874 2819 Phosphatic fertilizers; industrial inorganic chemicals
PA: Innophos Holdings, Inc.
259 Prospect Plains Rd A
Cranbury NJ 08512
609 495-2495

(G-1846)
IRIS ID SYSTEMS INC
8 Clarke Dr Ste 1 (08512-3617)
PHONE..................................609 819-4747
Charles Koo, *President*
Dan Westadt, *Controller*
Thomas Dewinter, *Manager*
▲ EMP: 23
SALES (est): 3.9MM **Privately Held**
SIC: 3861 Photographic equipment & supplies

(G-1847)
JAKTOOL LLC
Also Called: Jevek Solutions
259 Prospect Plains Rd (08512-3706)
PHONE..................................609 664-2451
Jeffrey Kinsberg, *President*
Cristy Richards, *Vice Pres*
EMP: 10
SQ FT: 10,100
SALES: 1MM **Privately Held**
SIC: 3841 8711 Surgical & medical instruments; engineering services

(G-1848)
JLI MARKETING & PRINTING CORP
6 Corporate Dr Ste 1 (08512-3616)
PHONE..................................732 828-8877
Charles J Jendrejeski, *President*
Peter Lengyel, *Vice Pres*
EMP: 13
SQ FT: 15,000
SALES (est): 1.8MM **Privately Held**
WEB: www.jlisigns.com
SIC: 2752 Commercial printing, offset

(G-1849)
KEELEY AEROSPACE LTD
2559 Us Highway 130 (08512-3509)
PHONE..................................951 582-2113
Sungtaick Lee, *CEO*
Brian Keeley, *Vice Pres*
EMP: 22
SQ FT: 22,300
SALES (est): 2.6MM **Privately Held**
WEB: www.kaltd.com
SIC: 3728 7389 Aircraft body & wing assemblies & parts; design services

HQ: Hanwha International Llc
300 Frank W Burr Blvd
Teaneck NJ 07666
201 347-3000

(G-1850)
KLUS PHARMA INC
Also Called: Kelun Pharmaceutical
8 Clarke Dr Ste 4 (08512-3617)
PHONE..................................609 662-1913
EMP: 13
SALES (est): 1.9MM **Privately Held**
SIC: 2834 5122 Druggists' preparations (pharmaceuticals); pharmaceuticals

(G-1851)
KOS PHARMACEUTICALS INC (HQ)
1 Cedarbrook Dr (08512-3618)
PHONE..................................609 495-0500
Adrian Adams, *CEO*
▲ EMP: 20
SALES (est): 51.8MM
SALES (corp-wide): 32.7B **Publicly Held**
WEB: www.kospharm.com
SIC: 2834 Pharmaceutical preparations
PA: Abbvie Inc.
1 N Waukegan Rd
North Chicago IL 60064
847 932-7900

(G-1852)
KRONOS WORLDWIDE INC
5 Cedarbrook Dr Ste 2 (08512-3606)
PHONE..................................609 860-6200
Dr Larry Wigdor, *CEO*
Gregory Swalwell, *Exec VP*
Bob Berthke, *Opers Staff*
Joseph Maas, *Human Res Mgr*
Paulraj Selvanayagam, *Prgrmr*
EMP: 35
SQ FT: 20,000
SALES (corp-wide): 2.3B **Publicly Held**
SIC: 2816 2899 Titanium dioxide, anatase or rutile (pigments); chemical preparations
HQ: Kronos Worldwide, Inc.
5430 Lbj Fwy Ste 1700
Dallas TX 75240
972 233-1700

(G-1853)
KT AMERICA CORP
Also Called: Avanti
2650 Us Highway 130 Ste I (08512-3327)
PHONE..................................609 655-5333
Rajiv Toprani, *President*
Ashok Mehta, *Vice Pres*
Jineet Lilani, *Engineer*
Ritu Gandhi, *Manager*
Raju Nankani, *Associate*
◆ EMP: 10
SQ FT: 3,000
SALES (est): 2.4MM **Privately Held**
WEB: www.ktamer.com
SIC: 2221 2393 Polypropylene broadwoven fabrics; textile bags

(G-1854)
LAMITECH INC (DH)
322 Half Acre Rd (08512-3254)
PHONE..................................609 860-8037
Joseph Artiga, *President*
◆ EMP: 34
SQ FT: 120,000
SALES (est): 120.8MM **Privately Held**
SIC: 5113 2631 Paperboard & products; coated paperboard
HQ: Matrix Packaging Of Florida Inc
1001 Brickell Bay Dr
Miami FL 33131
305 358-9696

(G-1855)
LEARNING LINKS-USA INC
26 Haypress Rd (08512-3401)
P.O. Box 326 (08512-0326)
PHONE..................................516 437-9071
Russell Wagner, *President*
Lynda Bradley, *Vice Pres*
EMP: 4
SQ FT: 30,000
SALES (est): 417K **Privately Held**
SIC: 2731 Books: publishing only

(G-1856)
LEGACY CONVERTING INC (PA)
3 Security Dr Ste 301 (08512-3263)
PHONE..................................609 642-7020
Darren Slosberg, *CEO*
Jason Slosberg MD, *President*
Terry Girifalco, *President*
David Morales, *Vice Pres*
Sirena Carnevale, *Opers Mgr*
▲ EMP: 33
SQ FT: 70,000
SALES (est): 6.6MM **Privately Held**
WEB: www.legacyconverting.com
SIC: 2679 Paper products, converted

(G-1857)
LENG-DOR USA INC (DH)
11 Commerce Dr (08512-3503)
PHONE..................................732 254-4300
Apolo Ruz Martinez, *Assistant VP*
Ricardo Mendoza, *Director*
▲ EMP: 11
SALES (est): 2.9MM
SALES (corp-wide): 1.1MM **Privately Held**
WEB: www.lengdor.com
SIC: 2099 Food preparations
HQ: Leng D'or Sa
Calle Industria (Pg Ind Conde Sert) 21
Castellbisbal 08755
937 724-280

(G-1858)
LOREAL USA INC
35 Broadway Rd (08512-5411)
PHONE..................................609 860-7500
Elyssa Dunleavy, *Assistant VP*
George Blizzard, *Vice Pres*
Kathy Oldak, *Transportation*
John Bihuniak, *Manager*
Badam Srikanth, *Manager*
EMP: 700
SALES (corp-wide): 4.4B **Privately Held**
WEB: www.lorealparisusa.com
SIC: 2844 5122 Hair preparations, including shampoos; cosmetic preparations; perfumes & colognes; drugs, proprietaries & sundries
HQ: L'oreal Usa, Inc.
10 Hudson Yards
New York NY 10001
212 818-1500

(G-1859)
LOVING PETS CORPORATION
110 Melrich Rd Ste 1 (08512-3524)
PHONE..................................609 655-3700
Eric Abbey, *President*
Shane Layton, *Vice Pres*
▲ EMP: 45
SALES: 30MM **Privately Held**
SIC: 5199 3999 Pet supplies; pet supplies

(G-1860)
LUMIKO USA INC
Also Called: Heliolite
47 Commerce Dr 3 (08512-3503)
PHONE..................................609 409-6900
Mike Lee, *President*
▲ EMP: 5 EST: 1989
SQ FT: 43,000
SALES (est): 541.6K **Privately Held**
SIC: 3229 5063 5013 Bulbs for electric lights; electrical apparatus & equipment; motor vehicle supplies & new parts

(G-1861)
MAGNIFICA INC
5 Cedarbrook Dr (08512-3606)
PHONE..................................323 202-0386
James Lee, *CEO*
▲ EMP: 3
SALES (est): 5.8MM **Privately Held**
SIC: 2834 5122 Pharmaceutical preparations; pharmaceuticals

(G-1862)
MAIN TAPE COMPANY INC (PA)
1 Capital Dr Ste 101 (08512-3264)
PHONE..................................609 395-1704
Joseph Musanti, *President*
Joseph Vanore, *Treasurer*
◆ EMP: 160
SQ FT: 150,000

SALES (est): 44.6MM **Privately Held**
WEB: www.maintape.com
SIC: 2672 Tape, pressure sensitive: made from purchased materials

(G-1863)
MARMON INDUSTRIAL LLC
101 Interchange Plz # 106 (08512-3716)
PHONE..................................609 655-4287
Rick Hooper, *Manager*
EMP: 12
SALES (corp-wide): 225.3B **Publicly Held**
SIC: 3743 Railway motor cars
HQ: Marmon Industrial Llc
181 W Madison St Fl 26
Chicago IL 60602
312 372-9500

(G-1864)
MIDSTATE FILIGREE SYSTEMS INC
22 Brick Yard Rd (08512-5002)
P.O. Box 435 (08512-0435)
PHONE..................................609 448-8700
Harry Wise, *President*
Gene McDermott, *Exec VP*
Renee Reilly, *Vice Pres*
▲ EMP: 65
SQ FT: 80,000
SALES (est): 11.2MM **Privately Held**
SIC: 3272 Slabs, crossing: concrete

(G-1865)
NORLAND PRODUCTS INC
2540 Us Highway 130 # 100 (08512-3519)
PHONE..................................609 395-1966
Tim Norland, *President*
Carroll Foreman, *COO*
Richard Norland, *Vice Pres*
Daniel Beerbohm, *Project Engr*
Neal Wagman, *Sales Mgr*
EMP: 20 EST: 1960
SQ FT: 15,000
SALES (est): 5.7MM **Privately Held**
WEB: www.norlandprod.com
SIC: 2891 3827 2899 Adhesives; optical instruments & lenses; gelatin: edible, technical, photographic or pharmaceutical

(G-1866)
ORORA PACKAGING SOLUTIONS
Also Called: Landsberg New Jersey Div 1088
1 Capital Dr Ste 102 (08512-3264)
PHONE..................................609 249-5200
Anthony Panzica, *VP Sales*
Stephen Williams, *Branch Mgr*
EMP: 35 **Privately Held**
SIC: 5113 2653 Paper & products, wrapping or coarse; boxes, corrugated: made from purchased materials
HQ: Orora Packaging Solutions
6600 Valley View St
Buena Park CA 90620
714 562-6000

(G-1867)
OUTLOOK THERAPEUTICS INC
7 Clarke Dr (08512-3627)
PHONE..................................609 619-3990
Randy H Thurman, *Ch of Bd*
Lawrence A Kenyon, *President*
Terry Dagnon, *COO*
Jennifer M Kissner, *Senior VP*
Elizabeth Yamashita, *Vice Pres*
EMP: 56
SQ FT: 66,000
SALES: 3MM **Privately Held**
SIC: 2834 Pharmaceutical preparations

(G-1868)
PALATIN TECHNOLOGIES INC
4b Cedarbrook Dr (08512-3641)
PHONE..................................609 495-2200
John K A Prendergast, *Ch of Bd*
Carl Spana, *President*
Stephen T Wills, *COO*
EMP: 19
SQ FT: 10,000
SALES: 60.3MM **Privately Held**
WEB: www.palatin.com
SIC: 2834 Pharmaceutical preparations

G
E
O
G
R
A
P
H
I
C

(G-1869)
PAPA JOHNS NEW JERSEY
Also Called: Pj Food Service
1267 S River Rd Ste 400 (08512-3632)
PHONE....................................609 395-0045
Al Watson, *Manager*
◆ EMP: 75 EST: 2009
SALES (est): 11MM
SALES (corp-wide): 1.5B **Publicly Held**
SIC: 2099 Pizza, refrigerated: except
frozen
HQ: Pj Food Service, Inc.
2002 Papa Johns Blvd
Louisville KY 40299

(G-1870)
PAULAUR CORPORATION
105 Melrich Rd (08512-3589)
PHONE....................................609 395-8844
Vincent Toscano, *President*
Paulette Toscano, *Owner*
Clifford S Rodkey, *Vice Pres*
Michael Toscano, *Vice Pres*
Andrew Toscano, *VP Mfg*
▲ EMP: 100
SQ FT: 144,000
SALES (est): 21.1MM **Privately Held**
WEB: www.paulaur.com
SIC: 2099 5411 Food preparations; gro-
cery stores

(G-1871)
PEARSON EDUCATION INC
258 Prospect Plains Rd (08512-3605)
PHONE....................................609 395-6000
Dave Romagnoli, *Branch Mgr*
EMP: 27
SALES (corp-wide): 5.3B **Privately Held**
WEB: www.phgenit.com
SIC: 2731 Book publishing
HQ: Pearson Education, Inc.
221 River St
Hoboken NJ 07030
201 236-7000

(G-1872)
PLANT FOOD COMPANY INC
38 Hightstwn Crnbry Sta (08512-5099)
P.O. Box 351 (08512-0351)
PHONE....................................609 448-0935
Theodore Platz, *President*
William Lubas, *Treasurer*
▼ EMP: 20
SQ FT: 10,000
SALES (est): 6.1MM **Privately Held**
WEB: www.plantfoodco.com
SIC: 2873 2899 3523 Plant foods, mixed:
from plants making nitrog. fertilizers;
chemical preparations; fertilizing machin-
ery, farm

(G-1873)
PMV PHARMACEUTICALS INC
8 Clarke Dr Ste 3 (08512-3617)
PHONE....................................650 241-2822
David H Mack PHD, *CEO*
Winston Kung, *COO*
Deepika Jalota, *Senior VP*
Salim Yazji, *Chief Mktg Ofcr*
EMP: 7 EST: 2015
SALES (est): 508K **Privately Held**
SIC: 2834 Solutions, pharmaceutical

(G-1874)
**PRINCETON
CHROMATOGRAPHY INC**
1206 S River Rd Ste 1 (08512-3701)
PHONE....................................609 860-1803
Linda Caldwell, *President*
Walton Caldwell III, *Vice Pres*
EMP: 9
SQ FT: 4,000
SALES (est): 1.2MM **Privately Held**
WEB: www.pci-hplc.com
SIC: 3826 Liquid chromatographic instru-
ments

(G-1875)
PRINCETON LIGHTWAVE INC
2555 Route 130 Ste 1 (08512-3527)
PHONE....................................609 495-2600
Mark Itzler, *CEO*
Sabbir Rangwala, *President*
Alfred Mottola, *Marketing Staff*
EMP: 34
SQ FT: 20,000

SALES (est): 8.1MM
SALES (corp-wide): 22.8MM **Privately
Held**
WEB: www.princetonlightwave.com
SIC: 3699 3674 Laser systems & equip-
ment; semiconductors & related devices
PA: Argo Ai, Llc
2545 Railroad St Ste 400
Pittsburgh PA 15222
412 709-6992

(G-1876)
**RAFAEL PHARMACEUTICALS
INC (PA)**
1 Duncan Dr (08512-3643)
PHONE....................................609 409-7050
Sanjeev Luther, *CEO*
Mona M Wahba, *Senior VP*
Paul Bingham, *Vice Pres*
Jehan Rowlands, *Vice Pres*
Mike Stelmah, *VP Mfg*
EMP: 25
SQ FT: 10,000
SALES (est): 5.7MM **Privately Held**
WEB: www.cornerstonepharma.com
SIC: 2834 Solutions, pharmaceutical

(G-1877)
RAHWAY STEEL DRUM CO INC
26 Brick Yard Rd (08512-5002)
PHONE....................................732 382-0113
Anthony Foglia, *President*
Mildred Foglia, *Corp Secy*
Michael Foglia, *Vice Pres*
EMP: 27
SQ FT: 6,000
SALES (est): 8.1MM **Privately Held**
WEB: www.rahwaysteeldrum.com
SIC: 3412 5085 Metal barrels, drums &
pails; drums, new or reconditioned

(G-1878)
RASI LABORATORIES INC
Also Called: Rasi Labs
320 Half Acre Rd (08512-3254)
PHONE....................................732 873-8500
Ramakrishna Gogineni, *President*
Surendra Vallabhaneni, *Vice Pres*
Suneetha Gogineni, *CFO*
▲ EMP: 70
SQ FT: 180,000
SALES: 24MM **Privately Held**
WEB: www.rasilaboratories.com
SIC: 2834 Vitamin preparations

(G-1879)
ROBOTUNITS INC
8 Corporate Dr Ste 1 (08512-3630)
PHONE....................................732 438-0500
Juergen Roth, *President*
▲ EMP: 6
SQ FT: 7,355
SALES: 750K
SALES (corp-wide): 4.4MM **Privately
Held**
WEB: www.robotunits.com
SIC: 5084 3535 8742 Conveyor systems;
conveyors & conveying equipment; au-
tomation & robotics consultant
HQ: Robotunits Gmbh
Dr. Walter Zumtobel StraBe 2
Dornbirn 6850
557 222-0002

(G-1880)
SCHOLASTIC BOOK FAIRS INC
2540 Us Highway 130 # 105 (08512-3519)
PHONE....................................609 578-4142
Loretta Daddone, *Branch Mgr*
EMP: 6
SALES (corp-wide): 1.6B **Publicly Held**
WEB: www.scholasticbookfairs.com
SIC: 2741 Miscellaneous publishing
HQ: Scholastic Book Fairs, Inc.
1080 Greenwood Blvd
Lake Mary FL 32746
407 829-7300

(G-1881)
SETARAM INC (DH)
2555 Us Highway 130 Ste 2 (08512-3527)
PHONE....................................908 262-7060
Sylvain Calzaroni, *CEO*
Fabrice Bancel, *Export Mgr*
George Levites, *Technical Mgr*
Link Brown, *Sales Staff*

Reena Rahi, *Manager*
EMP: 5
SQ FT: 4,700
SALES: 3MM
SALES (corp-wide): 83.5K **Privately Held**
WEB: www.setaram.com
SIC: 3826 Instruments measuring thermal
properties; differential thermal analysis in-
struments; thermal analysis instruments,
laboratory type; thermogravimetric ana-
lyzers
HQ: Kep Technologies High Tech Products
Setaram Setaram Instrumentation Kep
En
Caluire-Et-Cuire 69300
472 102-525

(G-1882)
SHAW INDUSTRIES INC
1267 S River Rd Ste 100 (08512-3639)
PHONE....................................609 655-8300
Vance Bell, *Manager*
EMP: 350
SALES (corp-wide): 225.3B **Publicly
Held**
SIC: 2273 Carpets & rugs
HQ: Shaw Industries, Inc.
616 E Walnut Ave
Dalton GA 30721

(G-1883)
SOLVAY USA INC
Cn 1120 (08512)
PHONE....................................609 860-4000
EMP: 79
SALES (corp-wide): 12.8MM **Privately
Held**
WEB: www.food.us.rhodia.com
SIC: 2819 Industrial inorganic chemicals
HQ: Solvay Usa Inc.
504 Carnegie Ctr
Princeton NJ 08540
609 860-4000

(G-1884)
**SUN PHARMACEUTICAL INDS
INC**
1 Commerce Dr (08512-3503)
PHONE....................................609 495-2800
Jitendra Doshi, *CEO*
EMP: 50
SALES (corp-wide): 1.3B **Privately Held**
SIC: 2834 Pharmaceutical preparations
HQ: Sun Pharmaceutical Industries, Inc.
270 Prospect Plains Rd
Cranbury NJ 08512
609 495-2800

(G-1885)
**SUN PHARMACEUTICAL INDS
INC (HQ)**
270 Prospect Plains Rd (08512-3605)
PHONE....................................609 495-2800
Subramanian Kalyanasundaram, *CEO*
Prashant Sagare, *General Mgr*
Gilbert Travasso, *General Mgr*
Arshad Jamil, *Counsel*
Robert Kurkiewicz, *Senior VP*
▲ EMP: 400
SQ FT: 82,000
SALES (est): 509.1MM
SALES (corp-wide): 1.3B **Privately Held**
SIC: 2834 Pharmaceutical preparations
PA: Sun Pharmaceutical Industries Limited
Sun House, Plot No. 201 B/1, Western
Express Highway,
Mumbai MH 40006
224 324-4324

(G-1886)
**TARO PHARMACEUTICALS USA
INC**
1 Commerce Dr (08512-3503)
PHONE....................................609 655-9002
Joel Sokol, *Director*
EMP: 30
SALES (corp-wide): 250.2MM **Privately
Held**
WEB: www.taropharma.net
SIC: 5122 2834 Pharmaceuticals; phar-
maceutical preparations
HQ: Taro Pharmaceuticals U.S.A., Inc.
3 Skyline Dr Ste 120
Hawthorne NY 10532
914 345-9000

(G-1887)
TRIARCO INDUSTRIES LLC
259 Prospect Plains Rd A (08512-3706)
PHONE....................................973 942-5100
Randy Gress, *CEO*
Jean Marie Mainente, *Senior VP*
Hermanus Kieftenbeld, *CFO*
EMP: 6
SALES (est): 133.4K
SALES (corp-wide): 801.8MM **Publicly
Held**
SIC: 2834 Vitamin, nutrient & hematinic
preparations for human use
PA: Innophos Holdings, Inc.
259 Prospect Plains Rd A
Cranbury NJ 08512
609 495-2495

(G-1888)
TRUMPF INC
2601 Route 130 (08512-5421)
PHONE....................................609 925-8200
Mark Gottdiener, *Engineer*
Stefan Heinemann, *Engineer*
Mark Klawinsky, *Engineer*
Gary Sheridan, *Regl Sales Mgr*
Lukas Baechler, *Sales Staff*
EMP: 24
SALES (corp-wide): 4.2B **Privately Held**
WEB: www.us.trumpf.com
SIC: 3542 Sheet metalworking machines
HQ: Trumpf, Inc.
111 Hyde Rd
Farmington CT 06032
860 255-6000

(G-1889)
TRUMPF PHOTONICS INC
2601 Us Highway 130 (08512-5421)
PHONE....................................609 925-8200
Peter Hoecklin, *President*
Burke Doar, *Senior VP*
Bjoern Dymke, *Vice Pres*
Peter Hafner, *Vice Pres*
James Rogowski, *Vice Pres*
▲ EMP: 140
SALES (est): 34.9MM
SALES (corp-wide): 4.2B **Privately Held**
SIC: 3542 Sheet metalworking machines
HQ: Trumpf, Inc.
111 Hyde Rd
Farmington CT 06032
860 255-6000

(G-1890)
TULEX PHARMACEUTICALS INC
5 Cedarbrook Dr (08512-3606)
PHONE....................................609 619-3098
James Lee, *CEO*
▲ EMP: 15
SALES (est): 1MM **Privately Held**
SIC: 2834 Pharmaceutical preparations

(G-1891)
**UTRECHT MANUFACTURING
CORP (DH)**
Also Called: Utrecht Art Supply
6 Corp Dr Ste 1 (08512)
PHONE....................................609 409-8001
Michael Ippolito, *CEO*
◆ EMP: 85
SQ FT: 54,000
SALES (est): 63.5MM
SALES (corp-wide): 177.2MM **Privately
Held**
WEB: www.utrecht.com
SIC: 3952 5999 5961 Artists' materials,
except pencils & leads; artists' equipment;
drafting materials; artists' supplies & ma-
terials: drafting equipment & supplies; arts
& crafts equipment & supplies, mail order
HQ: Dick Blick Company
1849 Green Bay Rd Ste 310
Highland Park IL 60035
847 681-6800

(G-1892)
WEST PATTERN WORKS INC
124 S Main St (08512-3145)
PHONE....................................609 443-6241
Doug Trendell, *President*
John Kwiatkowski, *Corp Secy*
William Davis, *Vice Pres*
EMP: 13
SQ FT: 11,000

▲ = Import ▼=Export
◆ =Import/Export

SALES: 1.5MM **Privately Held**
WEB: www.westpatternworks.com
SIC: 3543 3544 Foundry cores; industrial molds

(G-1893)
WORLD AND MAIN LLC (DH)
324a Half Acre Rd (08512-3254)
PHONE..............................609 860-9990
Lauren Vankirk, *Sales Staff*
Bryan Yeazel, *Mng Member*
Cara Allard, *Director*
Maria Arhontoulis, *Director*
EMP: 225
SALES (est): 49MM
SALES (corp-wide): 1.8MM **Privately Held**
SIC: 1711 3429 Plumbing contractors; builders' hardware
HQ: Nova Capital Management Limited
Octagon Point Suite 301
London EC2V
207 901-1760

(G-1894)
YINLINK INTERNATIONAL INC
2 Corporate Dr Ste A (08512-3604)
PHONE..............................973 818-4664
Pengfei Yin, *CEO*
EMP: 200
SALES: 50MM **Privately Held**
SIC: 2833 2023 Vitamins, natural or synthetic: bulk, uncompounded; dietary supplements, dairy & non-dairy based

(G-1895)
YOUR PRINTER V20 LTD
Also Called: AlphaGraphics
6 Corporate Dr Ste 1 (08512-3616)
PHONE..............................609 771-4000
David Kovacs, *President*
Mike Russo, *Principal*
Ellis Galimidi, *Vice Pres*
Charlie Jendrejeski, *Vice Pres*
Ken Seibel, *Vice Pres*
EMP: 32
SALES: 12MM **Privately Held**
SIC: 2752 7331 Commercial printing, offset; mailing service

(G-1896)
YUNTA USA INC
2553 Us Highway 130 Ste 3 (08512-3522)
PHONE..............................614 835-6588
Nick Xu, *President*
EMP: 1
SQ FT: 5,000
SALES: 20MM **Privately Held**
SIC: 5199 2035 5999 3423 General merchandise, non-durable; vegetables, pickled; binoculars & telescopes; screw drivers, pliers, chisels, etc. (hand tools)

Cranford
Union County

(G-1897)
ACTIVUS SOLUTIONS LLC
217 Bloomingdale Ave (07016-2563)
PHONE..............................973 713-0696
EMP: 10 EST: 2017
SALES (est): 636.5K **Privately Held**
SIC: 2834 Mfg Pharmaceutical Preparations

(G-1898)
AKRIMAX PHARMACEUTICALS LLC
11 Commerce Dr Ste 103 (07016-3513)
PHONE..............................908 372-0506
Donald C Olsen, *President*
Joseph Krivulka, *Chairman*
Leonard Mazur, *Chairman*
Ted Hoag, *District Mgr*
Mitchell Arnold, *Vice Pres*
▼ EMP: 75
SQ FT: 12,000
SALES: 85MM **Privately Held**
SIC: 2834 Pharmaceutical preparations

(G-1899)
ALL-STATE INTERNATIONAL INC (PA)
Also Called: All-State Legal
1 Commerce Dr (07016-3508)
PHONE..............................908 272-0800
Robert Busch, *CEO*
Doug Tyler, *Opers Mgr*
Joe Fuzak, *CFO*
Mark Scocco, *Info Tech Mgr*
Denise Graham, *Technical Staff*
▲ EMP: 190
SQ FT: 154,000
SALES (est): 31.5MM **Privately Held**
SIC: 2761 2754 2759 3953 Continuous forms, office & business; business forms: gravure printing; stationery: gravure printing; seals: gravure printing; financial note & certificate printing & engraving; embossing seals, corporate & official

(G-1900)
AMICI IMPORTS INC
335 Centennial Ave Unit 7 (07016-6108)
PHONE..............................908 272-8300
Jeffrey Desantis, *CEO*
Charles Cashin, *Senior VP*
▲ EMP: 12
SALES (est): 1.1MM **Privately Held**
SIC: 5713 2273 Rugs; carpets & rugs

(G-1901)
BAB PRINTING JAN SERVICE (PA)
Also Called: Weaver Associates Printing
945 Lincoln Ave E (07016-3155)
PHONE..............................908 272-6224
John Weaver, *President*
Harrison L Weaver, *President*
EMP: 8
SQ FT: 6,000
SALES (est): 1.2MM **Privately Held**
SIC: 2752 Commercial printing, offset

(G-1902)
BADGER BLADES LLC
216 North Ave E Ste 2 (07016-2473)
P.O. Box 269, Green Mountain Falls CO (80819-0269)
PHONE..............................908 325-6587
A Sundiland, *General Mgr*
Ashton Sundiland, *General Mgr*
Jonathan Lin, *Opers Mgr*
EMP: 7
SALES (est): 444.5K **Privately Held**
SIC: 3441 Building components, structural steel

(G-1903)
BERRY BUSINESS PROCEDURE CO
Also Called: Berry Business Forms
6 Park St (07016-3439)
P.O. Box 845 (07016-0845)
PHONE..............................908 272-6464
David Cheek, *President*
Patricia Cheek, *Corp Secy*
EMP: 6 EST: 1956
SQ FT: 5,000
SALES (est): 630K **Privately Held**
WEB: www.berryprinting.com
SIC: 2752 5112 Commercial printing, offset; letters, circular or form: lithographed; business forms

(G-1904)
CITIUS PHARMACEUTICALS INC (PA)
11 Commerce Dr Ste 100 (07016-3513)
PHONE..............................978 938-0338
Leonard Mazur, *Ch of Bd*
Myron Holubiak, *President*
Mazur Leonard, *Business Mgr*
Andrew Scott, *Vice Pres*
Jaime Bartushak, *CFO*
EMP: 7
SALES (est): 1.1MM **Publicly Held**
SIC: 2834 Pharmaceutical preparations

(G-1905)
COLTWELL INDUSTRIES INC
55 Winans Ave (07016-3144)
PHONE..............................908 276-7600
George J Bengivenga, *Vice Pres*
Anthony J Bengivenga, *Vice Pres*

Anthony Bengivenga, *Vice Pres*
Alissa Robbins, *Regl Sales Mgr*
▲ EMP: 10
SQ FT: 23,000
SALES (est): 2MM **Privately Held**
WEB: www.coltwell.com
SIC: 3354 Aluminum extruded products

(G-1906)
CONSTRUCTION SPECIALTIES INC
APC Daylighter
49 Meeker Ave (07016-3163)
PHONE..............................908 272-2771
Christopher Donohue, *Regl Sales Mgr*
Ronald Dadd, *Branch Mgr*
Talon Baez, *Manager*
Arthur La Pointe, *Manager*
EMP: 50
SALES (corp-wide): 379MM **Privately Held**
WEB: www.c-sgroup.com
SIC: 5031 3356 3354 Skylights, all materials; nonferrous rolling & drawing; aluminum extruded products
PA: Construction Specialties Inc.
3 Werner Way Ste 100
Lebanon NJ 08833
908 236-0800

(G-1907)
DURST CORPORATION INC (PA)
Also Called: Jaclo Industries
129 Dermody St (07016-3217)
PHONE..............................800 852-3906
Dana Egert, *President*
◆ EMP: 25 EST: 1911
SQ FT: 50,000
SALES (est): 13MM **Privately Held**
WEB: www.durstcorp.com
SIC: 5074 3432 3494 Plumbing fittings & supplies; lawn hose nozzles & sprinklers; valves & pipe fittings

(G-1908)
E F BRITTEN & CO INC
22 South Ave W (07016-2695)
P.O. Box 246 (07016-0246)
PHONE..............................908 276-4800
Richard Stokes, *President*
Margaret M Turner, *Vice Pres*
Emily Petix, *Admin Sec*
▲ EMP: 14
SQ FT: 27,500
SALES: 1.2MM **Privately Held**
WEB: www.efbritten.com
SIC: 3443 3398 Cylinders, pressure: metal plate; brazing (hardening) of metal

(G-1909)
ENZON PHARMACEUTICALS INC (PA)
20 Commerce Dr Ste 135 (07016-3614)
PHONE..............................732 980-4500
Andrew Rackear, *CEO*
Jonathan Christodoro, *Ch of Bd*
Richard L Feinstein, *CFO*
▲ EMP: 3
SQ FT: 500
SALES: 6.9MM **Publicly Held**
WEB: www.enzon.com
SIC: 2834 6794 Pharmaceutical preparations; franchises, selling or licensing

(G-1910)
FEDERAL PLASTICS CORPORATION
570 South Ave E Bldg F1 (07016-3250)
PHONE..............................908 272-5800
Peter T Triano Jr, *President*
Michael Triano, *Vice Pres*
Peter N Triano Sr, *Shareholder*
▲ EMP: 32
SQ FT: 86,000
SALES (est): 7.3MM **Privately Held**
WEB: www.federalplastics.com
SIC: 3087 5162 3083 2821 Custom compound purchased resins; plastics resins; laminated plastics plate & sheet; plastics materials & resins

(G-1911)
GLITTEREX CORP
7 Commerce Dr (07016-3507)
PHONE..............................908 272-9121

Edward Chumura, *President*
Rene Getler, *Corp Secy*
Frank Eulie, *Vice Pres*
◆ EMP: 65 EST: 1963
SQ FT: 20,000
SALES (est): 9.9MM **Privately Held**
WEB: www.glitterex.com
SIC: 3081 3497 Plastic film & sheet; metal foil & leaf

(G-1912)
GORTON HEATING CORP
546 South Ave E (07016-3208)
PHONE..............................908 276-1323
Linda Mast, *President*
Marie Klinefelter, *President*
Linda K Mast, *Admin Sec*
EMP: 6 EST: 1887
SQ FT: 3,000
SALES (est): 700K **Privately Held**
WEB: www.gorton-valves.com
SIC: 3494 Valves & pipe fittings

(G-1913)
HHH MACHINE CO
20 Quine St (07016-3130)
PHONE..............................908 276-1220
Howard Hull, *President*
Kenneth Hull, *Vice Pres*
EMP: 9 EST: 1965
SQ FT: 5,000
SALES (est): 1.2MM **Privately Held**
WEB: www.hhhmachine.com
SIC: 3599 3561 Machine shop, jobbing & repair; pumps & pumping equipment

(G-1914)
KITCHEN AND MORE INC
542 South Ave E (07016-3208)
PHONE..............................908 272-3388
Joosub Park, *Owner*
EMP: 13
SALES (est): 2.3MM **Privately Held**
SIC: 2434 Wood kitchen cabinets

(G-1915)
MADAN PLASTICS INC
370 North Ave E (07016-2435)
P.O. Box 487 (07016-0487)
PHONE..............................908 276-8484
Steven Skoler, *President*
Michael Madan, *General Mgr*
Alexander Friend, *Vice Pres*
Paul Bauer, *MIS Staff*
EMP: 100 EST: 1956
SQ FT: 52,000
SALES (est): 1.9MM **Privately Held**
WEB: www.madanplastics.com
SIC: 3089 3471 Thermoformed finished plastic products; electroplating of metals or formed products; finishing, metals or formed products

(G-1916)
MAINSTREAM LLC
230 Cristiani St (07016-3214)
P.O. Box 353 (07016-0353)
PHONE..............................908 931-1010
Derrick Markham,
James Markham,
Rick Markham,
EMP: 4
SALES (est): 320K **Privately Held**
WEB: www.customahu.com
SIC: 3594 Motors: hydraulic, fluid power or air

(G-1917)
METROPOLITAN COMPACTORS SVC
21 Quine St (07016-3130)
PHONE..............................908 653-0168
Michael J Walker, *President*
EMP: 8
SQ FT: 10,000
SALES (est): 488.2K **Privately Held**
SIC: 3589 Garbage disposers & compactors, commercial

(G-1918)
NATIONAL CHRISTMAS PDTS INC
Also Called: National Tree Company
2 Commerce Dr (07016-3509)
PHONE..............................908 709-4141
Joseph Puleo, *President*

Richard Puleo, *Vice Pres*
Salvatore Puleo Jr, *Vice Pres*
◆ **EMP:** 30
SQ FT: 50,000
SALES (est): 4.7MM **Privately Held**
SIC: 3999 Christmas trees, artificial; Christmas tree ornaments, except electrical & glass

(G-1919)
NORTHROP GRUMMAN SYSTEMS CORP
Also Called: Sperry Marine Division
12 Park St (07016-3439)
PHONE.............................908 276-6677
Bonnie Herrington, *Branch Mgr*
EMP: 4 **Publicly Held**
WEB: www.sperry.ngc.com
SIC: 3812 Search & navigation equipment
HQ: Northrop Grumman Systems Corporation
　2980 Fairview Park Dr
　Falls Church VA 22042
　703 280-2900

(G-1920)
ORIENT CORPORATION OF AMERICA (HQ)
Also Called: Manufacturing Chem Dyestuff
6 Commerce Dr Ste 301 (07016-3515)
PHONE.............................908 298-0990
Akihiro Takahashi, *President*
Masatoshi Matsuura, *Exec VP*
Senta Okada, *Treasurer*
Robert Galligan, *Sales Staff*
Mike Williston, *Sales Staff*
▲ **EMP:** 5
SQ FT: 2,000
SALES (est): 4.2MM **Privately Held**
WEB: www.orient-usa.com
SIC: 2865 Dyes & pigments

(G-1921)
PARKER-HANNIFIN CORPORATION
Chomerics Division
135 Bryant Ave (07016-3212)
PHONE.............................908 458-8101
David Hill, *Branch Mgr*
EMP: 56
SALES (corp-wide): 14.3B **Publicly Held**
WEB: www.parker.com
SIC: 3496 Miscellaneous fabricated wire products
PA: Parker-Hannifin Corporation
　6035 Parkland Blvd
　Cleveland OH 44124
　216 896-3000

(G-1922)
PETRO PACKAGING CO INC
16 Quine St (07016-3130)
P.O. Box 546 (07016-0546)
PHONE.............................908 272-4054
Rick Petrozziello, *President*
John Petrozziello, *Vice Pres*
EMP: 45 EST: 1970
SQ FT: 20,000
SALES (est): 12.8MM **Privately Held**
WEB: www.petropackaging.com
SIC: 2821 3081 Plastics materials & resins; packing materials, plastic sheet

(G-1923)
PHARMACEUTIC LITHO LABEL INC (PA)
450 North Ave E (07016-2476)
PHONE.............................336 785-4000
Keith Dovel, *President*
Howard Auerbach, *Chairman*
Len Dillon, *Admin Sec*
▲ **EMP:** 120 EST: 1928
SQ FT: 45,000
SALES (est): 14.6MM **Privately Held**
WEB: www.plymouthprinting.com
SIC: 2752 2759 Commercial printing, lithographic; letterpress printing

(G-1924)
RADNET INC
Also Called: Cranford Diagnostic Imaging
25 S Union Ave (07016-2843)
PHONE.............................908 709-1323
Drew M Netter, *Manager*
EMP: 15 **Publicly Held**

WEB: www.mrii.com
SIC: 8071 3699 Medical laboratories; electrical equipment & supplies
PA: Radnet, Inc.
　1510 Cotner Ave
　Los Angeles CA 90025

(G-1925)
RADNET INC
25 S Union Ave (07016-2843)
PHONE.............................908 709-1323
EMP: 15 **Publicly Held**
SIC: 3845 Electromedical equipment
PA: Radnet, Inc.
　1510 Cotner Ave
　Los Angeles CA 90025

(G-1926)
ROUSES PT PHARMACEUTICALS LLC
11 Commerce Dr Ste 101 (07016-3513)
PHONE.............................239 390-1495
Robert Sanzen, *Mng Member*
EMP: 6
SALES (est): 2.1MM **Privately Held**
SIC: 2834 Dermatologicals

(G-1927)
STAIRWORKS INC
335 Centennial Ave Unit 8 (07016-6108)
PHONE.............................908 276-2829
Mark Freemen, *President*
EMP: 4
SALES: 240K **Privately Held**
SIC: 2431 Staircases & stairs, wood

(G-1928)
TOFUTTI BRANDS INC
50 Jackson Dr (07016-3504)
PHONE.............................908 272-2400
David Mintz, *Ch of Bd*
Steven Kass, *CFO*
▼ **EMP:** 8
SQ FT: 6,200
SALES: 13MM **Privately Held**
WEB: www.tofutti.com
SIC: 2024 2099 Tofu desserts, frozen; tofu, except frozen desserts

(G-1929)
TOTALCAT GROUP INC (HQ)
135 Dermody St (07016-3217)
PHONE.............................908 497-9610
Carlos E Aguero, *President*
EMP: 3 EST: 2006
SALES (est): 3.3MM
SALES (corp-wide): 110.2MM **Privately Held**
SIC: 2819 Catalysts, chemical
PA: Metalico, Inc.
　135 Dermody St
　Cranford NJ 07016
　908 497-9610

(G-1930)
US BLADE MFG CO INC
90 Myrtle St (07016-3236)
PHONE.............................908 272-2898
Anthony J Calenda, *President*
Pat Cosgrove, *Principal*
▲ **EMP:** 50
SQ FT: 100,000
SALES (est): 9.4MM **Privately Held**
WEB: www.usblade.com
SIC: 3421 Knife blades & blanks

Cream Ridge
Monmouth County

(G-1931)
CENTRAL ART & ENGINEERING INC
500 Goldman Dr (08514-2529)
P.O. Box 289 (08514-0289)
PHONE.............................609 758-5922
John Makkay Jr, *President*
EMP: 8 EST: 1970
SQ FT: 1,000
SALES (est): 665.5K **Privately Held**
SIC: 3999 Models, general, except toy

(G-1932)
CENTRAL ART & ENGINERING INC
Also Called: Impact Visal Systems
500 Goldman Dr (08514-2529)
P.O. Box 289 (08514-0289)
PHONE.............................609 758-5922
John Makkay, *President*
▼ **EMP:** 9
SQ FT: 17,000
SALES: 895K **Privately Held**
SIC: 3993 Signs, not made in custom sign painting shops

(G-1933)
CREAM RIDGE WINERY
145 Route 539 (08514-1520)
P.O. Box 98 (08514-0098)
PHONE.............................609 259-9797
R Thomas Amabile, *President*
Tim Schlitzer, *General Mgr*
Jackie Schlitzer, *Property Mgr*
Aileen Amabile, *Manager*
EMP: 8
SALES (est): 1.3MM **Privately Held**
WEB: www.creamridgewinery.com
SIC: 5921 5947 2084 Wine; gift shop; wines

(G-1934)
DENEKA PRINTING SYSTEMS INC (PA)
100c Goldman Dr (08514-2530)
PHONE.............................609 752-0964
P Kenneth Deneka, *President*
EMP: 4
SQ FT: 3,000
SALES (est): 653.9K **Privately Held**
WEB: www.denekaprintingsystems.com
SIC: 3555 Printing trades machinery

(G-1935)
GARDEN STATE FABRICATORS
575 Monmouth Rd (08514-2506)
P.O. Box 156, Adelphia (07710-0156)
PHONE.............................732 928-5006
Michael Jaeger, *Owner*
EMP: 5
SQ FT: 6,000
SALES: 400K **Privately Held**
SIC: 3089 Cases, plastic

(G-1936)
HENRY JACKSON RACING ENGINES
787 Monmouth Rd (08514-2401)
PHONE.............................609 758-7476
Henry A Jackson, *President*
Henry Jackson, *President*
EMP: 5
SQ FT: 5,000
SALES: 300K **Privately Held**
SIC: 3519 Internal combustion engines

(G-1937)
INNOVATIVE PRESSURE CLG LLC
10 Arnytown Hrnerstown Rd (08514-1805)
PHONE.............................609 738-3100
Barbara Vanhandel,
EMP: 8
SALES: 180K **Privately Held**
SIC: 3589 High pressure cleaning equipment

(G-1938)
NATIONAL ELECTRIC WIRE CO INC
100 Goldman Dr (08514-2530)
PHONE.............................609 758-3600
Steven Herr, *President*
▲ **EMP:** 36
SQ FT: 18,000
SALES: 7.1MM **Privately Held**
SIC: 3351 Copper rolling & drawing

(G-1939)
RAKO MACHINE PRODUCTS INC
845 Monmouth Rd (08514-2311)
PHONE.............................609 758-1200
John Vandertuyn, *President*
EMP: 7
SQ FT: 2,500

SALES (est): 570K **Privately Held**
SIC: 3599 Machine shop, jobbing & repair

Creamridge
Monmouth County

(G-1940)
BRAYCO INC
951 County Hwy 537 (08514)
PHONE.............................609 758-5235
Randy Bray, *President*
Jody Bray, *Vice Pres*
Lydia Mancini, *Treasurer*
EMP: 15
SQ FT: 4,000
SALES (est): 3.2MM **Privately Held**
WEB: www.brayco.net
SIC: 3441 Fabricated structural metal

Cresskill
Bergen County

(G-1941)
ALTUS PCB LLC
45 Legion Dr (07626-2143)
PHONE.............................877 442-5887
Zohar Shinar, *Mng Member*
▲ **EMP:** 10
SALES (est): 1.5MM **Privately Held**
SIC: 3672 Printed circuit boards

(G-1942)
HELEN MORLEY LLC
35 Buckingham Rd (07626-1630)
PHONE.............................201 348-6459
Helen Morley, *Mng Member*
EMP: 34
SQ FT: 4,000
SALES (est): 2.5MM **Privately Held**
SIC: 2339 Aprons, except rubber or plastic: women's, misses', juniors'

(G-1943)
INNOVATIVE DESIGN INC
80 Broadway (07626-2164)
PHONE.............................201 227-2555
Vivian Siegel, *President*
Andrew Siegel, *President*
▲ **EMP:** 9 EST: 1998
SALES (est): 860.5K **Privately Held**
SIC: 2395 Embroidery & art needlework

(G-1944)
SILVER PALATE KITCHENS INC
211 Knickerbocker Rd (07626-1830)
P.O. Box 512 (07626-0512)
PHONE.............................201 568-0110
Peter Harris, *President*
◆ **EMP:** 21 EST: 1977
SALES (est): 6MM **Privately Held**
WEB: www.silverpalate.com
SIC: 2099 2035 2043 2098 Vinegar; seasonings & sauces, except tomato & dry; dressings, salad: raw & cooked (except dry mixes); mustard, prepared (wet); pickled fruits & vegetables; oats, rolled: prepared as cereal breakfast food; macaroni products (e.g. alphabets, rings & shells), dry; gourmet food stores

(G-1945)
SUN COAST PRECISION INSTRUMENT
80 Broadway Fl 1 (07626-2164)
PHONE.............................646 852-2331
Richard Chitos, *President*
EMP: 4
SALES (est): 291K **Privately Held**
SIC: 3829 Measuring & controlling devices

(G-1946)
VASCULAR THERAPIES INC
105 Union Ave (07626-2129)
PHONE.............................201 266-8310
Rosanne Terraciano, *Vice Pres*
EMP: 5
SQ FT: 3,894
SALES (est): 229.7K **Privately Held**
SIC: 2834 Drugs acting on the cardiovascular system, except diagnostic

(G-1947)
VASCULAR THERAPIES LLC
105 Union Ave Ste 2 (07626-2129)
PHONE..................................201 266-8310
John McDermott, *CEO*
Samuel Liang, *Mng Member*
Rosanne Terraciano,
EMP: 5
SALES (est): 1.1MM **Privately Held**
SIC: 3841 Surgical & medical instruments

(G-1948)
WILLRICH PRECISION INSTR CO
80 Broadway Ste 105 (07626-2153)
PHONE..................................866 945-5742
George Chitos, *CEO*
Richard D Chitos, *President*
EMP: 7
SQ FT: 3,000
SALES (est): 4MM **Privately Held**
WEB: www.willrich.com
SIC: 3829 Measuring & controlling devices

Crosswicks
Burlington County

(G-1949)
BLUE LINE PLANNING INC
153 Crsswcks Chstrfeld Rd (08515-9609)
P.O. Box 319 (08515-0319)
PHONE..................................609 577-0100
EMP: 4
SALES (est): 189K **Privately Held**
SIC: 7372 Prepackaged software

Dayton
Middlesex County

(G-1950)
(GT) GLOBAL TECH INC
Also Called: Research Dev & Manufacture
32 Marc Dr (08810-1388)
PHONE..................................732 447-7083
EMP: 10 EST: 1997
SALES (est): 446.2K **Privately Held**
SIC: 3999 Manufacturing industries

(G-1951)
ARCHTECH ELECTRONICS CORP
117 Docks Corner Rd Ste A (08810-2529)
PHONE..................................732 355-1288
Paul Foung, *CEO*
Kirk Lee, *President*
Peggy Foung, *Chairman*
James Yeager, *Buyer*
Peggy Hu, *CFO*
▲ EMP: 39
SQ FT: 20,000
SALES: 7MM **Privately Held**
SIC: 3643 5063 5045 Current-carrying
wiring devices; electrical apparatus &
equipment; computer peripheral equip-
ment

(G-1952)
AUROBINDO PHARMA USA INC
Aurohealth
6 Wheeling Rd (08810-1526)
PHONE..................................732 839-9402
John Segura, *Branch Mgr*
EMP: 6
SALES (corp-wide): 1.6B **Privately Held**
SIC: 2834 Pharmaceutical preparations
HQ: Aurobindo Pharma U.S.A., Inc.
279 Prnctn Hightstown Rd
East Windsor NJ 08520
732 839-9400

(G-1953)
AUROBINDO PHARMA USA INC
2400 Us Highway 130 (08810-1519)
PHONE..................................732 839-9400
Anthony Donato, *Vice Pres*
Theresa Perniciaro, *Vice Pres*
Gangadharrao Gorla, *Manager*
Mahesh K Pinnamaneni, *CIO*
Vijay Kondakkagari, *Info Tech Mgr*
EMP: 5

SALES (corp-wide): 1.6B **Privately Held**
SIC: 2834 Pharmaceutical preparations
HQ: Aurobindo Pharma U.S.A., Inc.
279 Prnctn Hightstown Rd
East Windsor NJ 08520
732 839-9400

(G-1954)
AUROLIFE PHARMA LLC
6 Wheeling Rd (08810-1526)
PHONE..................................732 839-9746
Swaminathan Sambamurty, *Branch Mgr*
EMP: 20
SALES (corp-wide): 1.6B **Privately Held**
SIC: 2834 Pharmaceutical preparations
HQ: Aurolife Pharma Llc
2400 Us Highway 130
Dayton NJ 08810

(G-1955)
AUROLIFE PHARMA LLC (DH)
2400 Us Highway 130 (08810-1519)
PHONE..................................732 839-4377
Swaminathan Sambamurty, *CFO*
▲ EMP: 152
SQ FT: 100,000
SALES (est): 178MM
SALES (corp-wide): 1.6B **Privately Held**
WEB: www.aurobindousa.com
SIC: 2834 Pharmaceutical preparations
HQ: Aurobindo Pharma U.S.A., Inc.
279 Prnctn Hightstown Rd
East Windsor NJ 08520
732 839-9400

(G-1956)
BWAY CORPORATION
7 Wheeling Rd (08810-1526)
PHONE..................................732 997-4100
Arthur Smith, *Branch Mgr*
Larry Smith, *Maintence Staff*
EMP: 129
SALES (corp-wide): 1.1B **Privately Held**
SIC: 3411 Metal cans
HQ: Bway Corporation
375 Northridge Rd Ste 600
Atlanta GA 30350

(G-1957)
CARY COMPOUNDS LLC
5 Nicholas Ct (08810-1558)
PHONE..................................732 274-2626
Abier Baynur, *Purch Mgr*
Dino STA Ana, *Buyer*
Cheryl Dorry, *Buyer*
Brad Wright, *QC Mgr*
Kenneth B Cary Jr,
◆ EMP: 20
SQ FT: 67,000
SALES (est): 14.2MM **Privately Held**
WEB: www.carycompounds.com
SIC: 2821 Plastics materials & resins

(G-1958)
CELL DISTRIBUTORS INC (PA)
319 Ridge Rd (08810-1532)
PHONE..................................718 473-0162
Schneur Lang, *President*
Chaim Langsam, *Vice Pres*
Yosef Langsam, *CFO*
EMP: 40 EST: 2008
SQ FT: 28,000
SALES: 35MM **Privately Held**
SIC: 2621 Stationery, envelope & tablet pa-
pers

(G-1959)
CENTRAL MILLS INC
Also Called: Imagine Screen Printing
473 Ridge Rd (08810-1323)
PHONE..................................732 329-2009
Mark Fischeein, *Branch Mgr*
EMP: 5
SALES (corp-wide): 79.1MM **Privately Held**
SIC: 2329 2759 Men's & boys' sportswear
& athletic clothing; screen printing
PA: Central Mills, Inc.
473 Ridge Rd
Dayton NJ 08810
732 329-2009

(G-1960)
CENTRAL MILLS INC (PA)
Also Called: Freeze
473 Ridge Rd (08810-1323)
PHONE..................................732 329-2009
Charles Tebele, *Ch of Bd*
Solomon Shalam, *President*
Maurice Shalam, *Admin Sec*
▲ EMP: 300
SQ FT: 10,000
SALES (est): 91.3MM **Privately Held**
SIC: 2329 2339 2369 2322 Athletic
(warmup, sweat & jogging) suits: men's &
boys'; sportswear, women's; girls' & chil-
dren's outerwear; men's & boys' under-
wear & nightwear; women's & children's
nightwear; men's & boys' furnishings

(G-1961)
FLEETSOURCE LLC
Also Called: A G S
2382 Us Highway 130 (08810-1519)
PHONE..................................732 566-4970
Kenneth Dorward,
Harry Dorward,
▲ EMP: 35
SQ FT: 20,000
SALES (est): 3.7MM **Privately Held**
WEB: www.fltsource.com
SIC: 7513 7538 7359 3714 Truck rental
& leasing, no drivers; general truck repair;
equipment rental & leasing; motor vehicle
parts & accessories; engine electrical
equipment

(G-1962)
FLINT GROUP US LLC
Also Called: Flint Group North America
6 Corn Rd (08810-1527)
PHONE..................................732 329-4627
Dennis Noreen, *Branch Mgr*
EMP: 9
SQ FT: 30,000
SALES (corp-wide): 177.9K **Privately Held**
WEB: www.flintink.com
SIC: 2893 Printing ink
HQ: Flint Group Us Llc
17177 N Laurel Park Dr # 300
Livonia MI 48152
734 781-4600

(G-1963)
FOLICA INC (PA)
Also Called: Folica.com
11 Corn Rd Ste B (08810-1527)
PHONE..................................609 860-8430
Carl Gish, *President*
Sylvia Zori, *General Mgr*
Puneet Agrawal, *CFO*
Shuo C Huang, *Shareholder*
▲ EMP: 50
SQ FT: 30,000
SALES (est): 12.4MM **Privately Held**
WEB: www.folica.com
SIC: 3999 Hair, dressing of, for the trade

(G-1964)
FRENCHTOASTCOM LLC
Also Called: French Toast
321 Herrod Blvd (08810-1564)
PHONE..................................732 438-5500
Michael Arking, *President*
EMP: 10
SQ FT: 600,000
SALES (est): 2.6MM **Privately Held**
SIC: 5137 2369 Sportswear, women's &
children's; girls' & children's outerwear
PA: Lollytogs, Ltd.
100 W 33rd St Ste 1012
New York NY 10001
212 502-6000

(G-1965)
G-III APPAREL GROUP LTD
Black Rivet Mens
308 Herrod Blvd (08810-1563)
PHONE..................................732 438-0209
EMP: 100
SALES (corp-wide): 3B **Publicly Held**
WEB: www.g-iii.com
SIC: 2386 5632 Garments, leather; pants,
leather; women's accessory & specialty
stores

PA: G-Iii Apparel Group, Ltd.
512 7th Ave Fl 35
New York NY 10018
212 403-0500

(G-1966)
G-III LEATHER FASHIONS INC
308 Herrod Blvd (08810-1563)
PHONE..................................212 403-0500
EMP: 100
SALES (corp-wide): 3B **Publicly Held**
SIC: 7323 3172 2386 Credit reporting
services; personal leather goods; leather
& sheep-lined clothing
HQ: G-Iii Leather Fashions, Inc.
512 Fashion Ave Fl 35
New York NY 10018
212 403-0500

(G-1967)
GRAPHCORR LLC
4 Corn Rd (08810-1527)
PHONE..................................732 355-0088
Louis Federico, *General Mgr*
Nicholas Dottino, *Senior VP*
EMP: 16
SQ FT: 50,630
SALES (est): 2.7MM
SALES (corp-wide): 16.2B **Publicly Held**
WEB: www.southerncontainer.com
SIC: 2653 Corrugated boxes, partitions,
display items, sheets & pad
HQ: Westrock - Southern Container, Llc
1000 Abernathy Rd Ste 125
Atlanta GA 30328
770 448-2193

(G-1968)
GUARDIAN DRUG COMPANY INC
2 Charles Ct (08810-1508)
PHONE..................................609 860-2600
Arvind B Dhruv, *President*
▲ EMP: 90
SQ FT: 136,000
SALES (est): 31.8MM **Privately Held**
WEB: www.guardiandrug.com
SIC: 2834 Drugs acting on the gastroin-
testinal or genitourinary system; antacids

(G-1969)
IMAGINE SCREEN PRTG & PROD LLC
473 Ridge Rd (08810-1323)
PHONE..................................732 329-2009
EMP: 200
SQ FT: 25,000
SALES (est): 7MM **Privately Held**
SIC: 2752 Commercial printing, litho-
graphic

(G-1970)
IMPACT UNLIMITED INC (PA)
Also Called: Impact Xm
250 Ridge Rd (08810-1502)
P.O. Box 558 (08810-0558)
PHONE..................................732 274-2000
Jared Pollacco, *President*
Sandie Stransky, *Exec VP*
Joseph Haggerty, *CFO*
Ronald Jordan, *Accounts Mgr*
Jason Nolan, *Manager*
▲ EMP: 150
SQ FT: 10,000
SALES: 60MM **Privately Held**
WEB: www.impactunlimited.com
SIC: 2541 Store & office display cases &
fixtures

(G-1971)
INTER PARFUMS INC
60 Stults Rd (08810-1522)
PHONE..................................609 860-1967
Alex Canavan, *Manager*
EMP: 50
SALES (corp-wide): 675.5MM **Publicly Held**
WEB: www.interparfumsinc.com
SIC: 2844 Toilet preparations
PA: Inter Parfums, Inc.
551 5th Ave
New York NY 10176
212 983-2640

(G-1972)
INTERNTNAL FLVORS FRGRNCES INC
Also Called: I F F
150 Docks Corner Rd (08810-1565)
P.O. Box 439 (08810-0439)
PHONE..................................732 329-4600
Saumya Dwivedi, *Research*
Allan Coulson, *Branch Mgr*
Jay Gerbino, *Manager*
Matthew Petrone, *Technology*
Stephen Donaldson, *Technical Staff*
EMP: 55
SALES (corp-wide): 3.9B **Publicly Held**
WEB: www.iff.com
SIC: 2087 Extracts, flavoring
PA: International Flavors & Fragrances Inc.
521 W 57th St
New York NY 10019
212 765-5500

(G-1973)
JESE APPAREL LLC (PA)
Also Called: Silverwear
8 Nicholas Ct B (08810-1559)
PHONE..................................732 969-3200
Jay Weitzman, *Mng Member*
Edward Baranoff,
Steven Shalom,
Elias Zakay,
▲ EMP: 17
SQ FT: 5,700
SALES (est): 7.1MM **Privately Held**
SIC: 5137 2389 5139 Women's & children's sportswear & swimsuits; sportswear, women's & children's; apparel for handicapped; footwear

(G-1974)
KATE SPADE & COMPANY
Also Called: Liz Claiborne
120 Herrod Blvd Ste 8 (08810-1528)
P.O. Box 935 (08810-0935)
PHONE..................................609 395-3109
Fax: 609 395-3138
EMP: 20
SALES (corp-wide): 1.2B **Publicly Held**
SIC: 2335 Mfg Women's/Misses' Dresses
PA: Kate Spade & Company
2 Park Ave Rm 8r
New York NY 10016
212 354-4900

(G-1975)
KEYSTONE DYEING AND FINISHING (PA)
10 Pine Hill Ct (08810-1631)
PHONE..................................718 482-7780
Louis Silverman, *President*
Allen Jenkins, *Treasurer*
▲ EMP: 3
SQ FT: 3,000
SALES: 2.3MM **Privately Held**
SIC: 2258 2262 2261 Dyeing & finishing lace goods & warp knit fabric; dyeing: manmade fiber & silk broadwoven fabrics; dyeing cotton broadwoven fabrics

(G-1976)
L & L WELDING CONTRACTORS
3 Wheeling Rd (08810-1526)
PHONE..................................609 395-1600
Frank Lagattuta, *President*
Thomas Lagattuta, *Shareholder*
EMP: 10 EST: 1947
SQ FT: 7,000
SALES (est): 2.2MM **Privately Held**
SIC: 3443 Weldments

(G-1977)
LINDE GAS NORTH AMERICA LLC
Also Called: Lifegas
174 Ridge Rd Ste A (08810)
PHONE..................................732 438-9977
Willie Beale, *Branch Mgr*
EMP: 19 **Privately Held**
SIC: 2813 Nitrogen; oxygen, compressed or liquefied
HQ: Linde Gas North America Llc
200 Somerset Corp Blvd # 7000
Bridgewater NJ 08807

(G-1978)
LOLLYTOGS LTD
Also Called: Lt Apparel Group
321 Herrod Blvd (08810-1564)
PHONE..................................732 438-5500
Kris Showman, *Vice Pres*
Mary Adams, *Regl Sales Mgr*
Morris Sutton, *Branch Mgr*
EMP: 14
SALES (corp-wide): 2.6MM **Privately Held**
SIC: 5137 2369 2361 1541 Women's & children's clothing; girls' & children's outerwear; girls' & children's dresses, blouses & shirts; industrial buildings & warehouses
PA: Lollytogs, Ltd.
100 W 33rd St Ste 1012
New York NY 10001
212 502-6000

(G-1979)
LOLLYTOGS LTD
Also Called: French Toast
321 Herrod Blvd (08810-1564)
P.O. Box 1001 (08810-1001)
PHONE..................................732 438-5500
EMP: 100
SQ FT: 600,000
SALES (corp-wide): 2.2MM **Privately Held**
SIC: 2369 5137 Mfg Girl/Youth Outerwear Whol Women's/Child's Clothing
PA: Lollytogs, Ltd.
100 W 33rd St Ste 1012
New York NY 10001
212 502-6000

(G-1980)
MINCING TRADING CORPORATION
Also Called: Mincing Overseas Spice Company
10 Tower Rd (08810-1571)
PHONE..................................732 355-9944
Manoj K Ruparelia, *President*
Joann Conway, *Engineer*
Harshad K Ruparelia, *Treasurer*
Kaushik Jobanbutra, *Controller*
Mala Hari, *Accountant*
▲ EMP: 29 EST: 1927
SQ FT: 50,000
SALES (est): 6.7MM
SALES (corp-wide): 3.6MM **Privately Held**
WEB: www.mincing.com
SIC: 2099 5149 Seasonings & spices; spices, including grinding; spices & seasonings
PA: Mincing International Inc.
10 Tower Rd
Dayton NJ 08810
732 355-9944

(G-1981)
NETWORK ACCESS SYSTEMS INCORPR
19 Issac Dr (08810-1314)
PHONE..................................732 355-9770
Bruce Lin, *President*
Roy Jao, *Corp Secy*
Suo Jao, *Vice Pres*
EMP: 9
SQ FT: 6,000
SALES (est): 760K **Privately Held**
WEB: www.naspc.com
SIC: 3695 Computer software tape & disks: blank, rigid & floppy

(G-1982)
NORTHWIND ENTERPRISES INC
Also Called: Impact Xm
250 Ridge Rd (08810-1502)
PHONE..................................732 274-2000
Jared Pollacco, *President*
Joseph Haggerty, *Corp Secy*
EMP: 40
SQ FT: 206,000

SALES (est): 22MM
SALES (corp-wide): 60MM **Privately Held**
WEB: www.atlanticexhibits.com
SIC: 3993 5046 7319 7336 Signs & advertising specialties; display equipment, except refrigerated; display advertising service; commercial art & graphic design; advertising, promotional & trade show services; trade show arrangement
PA: Impact Unlimited, Inc.
250 Ridge Rd
Dayton NJ 08810
732 274-2000

(G-1983)
PHARMEDIUM SERVICES LLC
36 Stults Rd (08810-1540)
PHONE..................................847 457-2362
William R Spaulding, *CEO*
EMP: 44
SALES (corp-wide): 167.9B **Publicly Held**
SIC: 2834 Pharmaceutical preparations
HQ: Pharmedium Services, Llc
150 N Field Dr Ste 350
Lake Forest IL 60045
800 523-7749

(G-1984)
PIRAMAL GLASS - USA INC (HQ)
329 Herrod Blvd (08810-1564)
PHONE..................................856 293-6400
Niraj Tipre, *CEO*
David Ardire, *Vice Pres*
Jatin Arora, *Accounts Exec*
Pinakin Shah, *Sales Executive*
Dominique Adams, *Manager*
▲ EMP: 35
SALES (est): 251.4MM
SALES (corp-wide): 193.6MM **Privately Held**
SIC: 3221 Glass containers
PA: Piramal Glass Private Limited
Peninsula Corporate Park
Mumbai MH 40001
223 046-6901

(G-1985)
RAM PRODUCTS INC
182 Ridge Rd Ste D (08810-1594)
PHONE..................................732 651-5500
Richard L Wiesen, *President*
▲ EMP: 9
SQ FT: 4,000
SALES (est): 1.3MM **Privately Held**
WEB: www.1010files.com
SIC: 3545 Drill bits, metalworking

(G-1986)
RHODIUM SOFTWARE INC
10 Scotto Pl (08810-1393)
PHONE..................................848 248-2906
Kandan Kanakaraj, *President*
Rajan Rajarathinam, *Chairman*
EMP: 6
SALES (est): 460K **Privately Held**
WEB: www.rhodiumsoftware.com
SIC: 7372 Prepackaged software

(G-1987)
RICHMOND INDUSTRIES INC
1 Chris Ct (08810-1536)
PHONE..................................732 355-1616
Keith Digrazio, *President*
Jennifer Williams, *Vice Pres*
EMP: 32 EST: 1959
SQ FT: 40,000
SALES (est): 8MM **Privately Held**
WEB: www.richmond-industries.com
SIC: 3366 Copper foundries

(G-1988)
SLT FOODS INC
Also Called: Slt Imports
303 Ridge Rd (08810-1580)
PHONE..................................732 661-1030
Sandip Patel, *President*
Dinesh Jani, *Finance*
Sejal Patel, *Manager*
◆ EMP: 18
SQ FT: 75,400
SALES: 38.6MM **Privately Held**
SIC: 5149 2045 Pasta & rice; prepared flour mixes & doughs

(G-1989)
SONOCO PRODUCTS COMPANY
5 Stults Rd (08810-1541)
PHONE..................................609 655-0300
Jon Greenwalk, *Manager*
EMP: 70
SALES (corp-wide): 5.3B **Publicly Held**
WEB: www.sonoco.com
SIC: 2655 3411 Cans, composite: foil-fiber & other: from purchased fiber; metal cans
PA: Sonoco Products Company
1 N 2nd St
Hartsville SC 29550
843 383-7000

(G-1990)
SUNSHINE BOUQUET COMPANY (PA)
3 Chris Ct Ste A (08810-1543)
P.O. Box 892 (08810-0892)
PHONE..................................732 274-2900
John Simko, *President*
Andrew Johnston, *CFO*
▲ EMP: 150
SQ FT: 65,000
SALES: 208MM **Privately Held**
WEB: www.sunshinebouquet.com
SIC: 5193 3999 Flowers, fresh; flowers, artificial & preserved

(G-1991)
SWISS MADISON LLC
19 Stults Rd (08810-1541)
PHONE..................................434 623-4766
Mendel Gricman, *Mng Member*
Samuel Greisman,
EMP: 19
SQ FT: 2,000
SALES (est): 500K **Privately Held**
SIC: 2499 Seats, toilet

(G-1992)
TIN MAN SNACKS LLC
351 Herrod Blvd (08810-1564)
PHONE..................................732 329-9100
Joe Glusak, *President*
Charles Fern,
Vincent Mastria,
EMP: 30
SALES (est): 5.4MM **Privately Held**
SIC: 2099 Food preparations

(G-1993)
TOTAL RELIANCE LLC
11b Corn Rd (08810-1527)
PHONE..................................732 640-5079
Brian Kirst, *Co-Owner*
Adam Napoli, *Co-Owner*
EMP: 18
SQ FT: 64,000
SALES (est): 1.5MM **Privately Held**
SIC: 7331 4731 7372 Direct mail advertising services; freight transportation arrangement; prepackaged software

(G-1994)
WESTROCK RKT COMPANY
1 Corn Rd (08810-1527)
P.O. Box 440 (08810-0440)
PHONE..................................732 274-2500
Todd Crowell, *Branch Mgr*
EMP: 100
SQ FT: 100,000
SALES (corp-wide): 16.2B **Publicly Held**
WEB: www.rocktenn.com
SIC: 2653 Boxes, corrugated: made from purchased materials
HQ: Westrock Rkt, Llc
1000 Abernathy Rd Ste 125
Atlanta GA 30328
770 448-2193

(G-1995)
WHOLE YEAR TRADING CO INC
117 Docks Corner Rd Ste B (08810-2529)
PHONE..................................732 238-1196
Jane Han, *President*
Charles Hou, *Vice Pres*
▲ EMP: 4
SQ FT: 5,000
SALES: 150K **Privately Held**
SIC: 3089 Planters, plastic

(G-1996)
WOOD TEXTURES
251 Herrod Blvd (08810-1539)
PHONE................................732 230-5005
Thomas Wu, *Principal*
▲ EMP: 9
SALES (est): 1.4MM **Privately Held**
SIC: 2599 Factory furniture & fixtures

Deal
Monmouth County

(G-1997)
AMBO CONSULTING LLC
Also Called: Smart Gear Toys
82 Norwood Ave Ste 2 (07723-1375)
PHONE................................732 663-0000
Sam Cohen, *CEO*
Jason Cohen, *President*
▲ EMP: 3
SQ FT: 2,500
SALES (est): 2.4MM **Privately Held**
SIC: 5092 3944 Toys & games; games, toys & children's vehicles

Deepwater
Salem County

(G-1998)
CHEMOURS COMPANY
Bldg 603 Rr 130 (08023)
PHONE................................856 540-3398
John Moriarty, *Manager*
EMP: 7
SALES (corp-wide): 6.6B **Publicly Held**
WEB: www.dupont.com
SIC: 2992 Lubricating oils & greases
PA: The Chemours Company
1007 Market St
Wilmington DE 19898
302 773-1000

Delair
Camden County

(G-1999)
ALUMINUM SHAPES LLC
9000 River Rd (08110-3296)
PHONE................................888 488-7427
Johnson Shao, *CEO*
EMP: 302
SALES (est): 38MM **Privately Held**
SIC: 3365 3354 Aluminum foundries; aluminum extruded products

(G-2000)
AUDIO AND VIDEO LABS INC
Also Called: Oasis CD Manufacturing
7905 N Crescent Blvd (08110-1402)
PHONE................................856 661-5772
Micah Solomon, *Principal*
Bob Wilson, *Vice Pres*
EMP: 20 **Privately Held**
WEB: www.oasiscd.com
SIC: 3652 Compact laser discs, prerecorded
HQ: Audio And Video Labs, Inc.
9600 Ne Cascades Pkwy # 180
Portland OR 97220
800 289-6923

(G-2001)
SHAPES/ARCH HOLDINGS LLC (PA)
Also Called: Arch America
9000 River Rd (08110-3204)
PHONE................................856 662-5500
Thomas Riddle, *CEO*
Mark Klitsch, *Production*
▲ EMP: 375
SQ FT: 1,500,000
SALES (est): 150.3MM **Privately Held**
SIC: 3354 3365 Aluminum extruded products; aluminum foundries

Delanco
Burlington County

(G-2002)
AMERICAN STRIP STEEL INC
901 Coopertown Rd (08075-5205)
PHONE................................856 461-8300
Leroy Scheckler, *President*
Krystine Lee, *Office Mgr*
EMP: 4
SALES (corp-wide): 107.9MM **Privately Held**
SIC: 5051 3441 3316 Steel; fabricated structural metal; cold finishing of steel shapes
HQ: American Strip Steel Inc.
400 Metuchen Rd
South Plainfield NJ 07080
800 526-1216

(G-2003)
ATCO PALLET COMPANY
1000 Creek Rd (08075-5214)
P.O. Box 5115 (08075-0515)
PHONE................................856 461-8141
David Hajduk, *President*
EMP: 25
SQ FT: 15,000
SALES (est): 4.2MM **Privately Held**
SIC: 2448 Pallets, wood

(G-2004)
COLD HEADED FASTENERS INC
401 Creek Rd Ste D (08075-5243)
P.O. Box 5488, Riverside (08075-5488)
PHONE................................856 461-3244
Charles C Massey, *President*
EMP: 6
SQ FT: 12,000
SALES (est): 1.1MM **Privately Held**
WEB: www.coldheadedfasteners.com
SIC: 3452 3499 5085 Screws, metal; welding tips, heat resistant: metal; fasteners, industrial: nuts, bolts, screws, etc.

(G-2005)
COSTUME GALLERY INC
700 Creek Rd (08075-5212)
PHONE................................609 386-6601
Ellen Ferreira, *CEO*
Rick Ferreira, *President*
Diane Wallace, *Manager*
▲ EMP: 3
SALES (est): 5MM **Privately Held**
SIC: 2389 Uniforms & vestments; costumes

(G-2006)
MEDLAUREL INC
Also Called: Laurel Manufacturers
620 Cooper St (08075-4670)
P.O. Box 5306, Riverside (08075-0378)
PHONE................................856 461-6600
Daniel Iosc, *President*
Ted Gorczynski, *Vice Pres*
Tricia Meyer, *Vice Pres*
Tricia Sell, *Vice Pres*
▲ EMP: 36
SQ FT: 50,000
SALES (est): 7.4MM **Privately Held**
WEB: www.laurelmfg.com
SIC: 2541 3469 3993 3444 Wood partitions & fixtures; machine parts, stamped or pressed metal; signs & advertising specialties; sheet metalwork

(G-2007)
STYLEX INC
740 Coopertown Rd (08075-5252)
P.O. Box 5038 (08075-0438)
PHONE................................856 461-5600
John Golden, *President*
Aleksander Calkowski, *Engineer*
Joe Kowalonek, *CFO*
Bruce Golden, *Treasurer*
Kim Fisher, *Credit Mgr*
◆ EMP: 185 EST: 1950
SQ FT: 140,000
SALES (est): 35.6MM **Privately Held**
WEB: www.stylexseating.com
SIC: 2522 Chairs, office: padded or plain, except wood

Delran
Burlington County

(G-2008)
ACTEGA NORTH AMERICA INC (DH)
950 S Chester Ave Ste B2 (08075-1271)
PHONE................................856 829-6300
Mark Westwell, *President*
Lee Andrews, *VP Sls/Mktg*
Brian Long, *CFO*
◆ EMP: 250
SALES (est): 92.1MM
SALES (corp-wide): 501.4K **Privately Held**
WEB: www.actega.com/kelstar
SIC: 2851 2952 Paints & allied products; coating compounds, tar
HQ: Actega Gmbh
Abelstr. 43
Wesel 46483
281 670-8

(G-2009)
BILLOWS ELECTRIC SUPPLY CO INC (PA)
1813 Underwood Blvd (08075-1232)
PHONE................................856 751-2200
Jeffrey Billow, *President*
Bob White, *COO*
Mitch Billows, *Vice Pres*
David Lowenstein, *Vice Pres*
Christopher McCammitt, *Project Mgr*
EMP: 130
SALES (est): 265.2MM **Privately Held**
SIC: 5063 3679 3621 3643 Electrical supplies; lighting fixtures; electronic circuits; motors & generators; current-carrying wiring devices; noncurrent-carrying wiring services

(G-2010)
BIOCLIMATIC AIR SYSTEMS LLC
600 Delran Pkwy Ste D (08075-1255)
PHONE................................856 764-4300
Stephen Zitin,
EMP: 22
SQ FT: 20,000
SALES (est): 4.5MM
SALES (corp-wide): 10.2MM **Privately Held**
WEB: www.bioclimatic.com
SIC: 3564 Air purification equipment
PA: Bioclimatic Inc
600 Delran Pkwy Ste D
Delran NJ 08075
856 764-4300

(G-2011)
BIOCLIMATIC INC (PA)
600 Delran Pkwy Ste D (08075-1255)
PHONE................................856 764-4300
Stephen Zitin, *President*
Michelle Bottino, *Vice Pres*
EMP: 30
SQ FT: 10,000
SALES (est): 10.2MM **Privately Held**
SIC: 3564 Air purification equipment

(G-2012)
C R BARD INC
Dabol Division
1822 Underwood Blvd (08075-1233)
PHONE................................856 461-0946
Alan Grumbling, *Plt & Fclts Mgr*
EMP: 9
SQ FT: 15,640
SALES (corp-wide): 15.9B **Publicly Held**
WEB: www.crbard.com
SIC: 3841 Surgical & medical instruments
HQ: C. R. Bard, Inc.
1 Becton Dr
Franklin Lakes NJ 07417
908 277-8000

(G-2013)
CARNEGIE PHARMACEUTICALS LLC
600 Delran Pkwy Ste C (08075-1255)
PHONE................................732 783-7013
Rakesh Grover, *CEO*

EMP: 25 EST: 2015
SALES (est): 1MM **Privately Held**
SIC: 2834 Pharmaceutical preparations

(G-2014)
CHERUBINI YACHTS LTD LBLTY CO
51 Norman Ave (08075-1009)
PHONE................................856 764-5319
David Cherubini,
EMP: 9
SALES (est): 138.1K **Privately Held**
WEB: www.cherubiniyachts.com
SIC: 3732 Yachts, building & repairing

(G-2015)
DOMTAR
2900 Cindel Dr (08075)
PHONE................................201 942-2077
EMP: 6
SALES (est): 670.3K **Privately Held**
SIC: 3089 Plastics products

(G-2016)
DORALEX INC
403 Saint Mihiel Dr (08075-3030)
P.O. Box 265, Riverside (08075-0285)
PHONE................................856 764-0694
Fax: 856 764-7402
EMP: 6
SQ FT: 2,000
SALES (est): 510K **Privately Held**
SIC: 8731 3679 Research And Development Of Electronic Components And Mfrs Electronic Components

(G-2017)
LAUDA-BRINKMANN LP
1819 Underwood Blvd Ste 2 (08075-1246)
PHONE................................856 764-7300
Richard Jezykowski, *CEO*
Susan Colfer, *Opers Mgr*
Jeff Wilson, *Sales Dir*
Mike Andress, *Sales Mgr*
Jillian Kennedy, *Sales Mgr*
▲ EMP: 12
SALES (est): 2.7MM **Privately Held**
SIC: 3585 Parts for heating, cooling & refrigerating equipment

(G-2018)
LAUDA-BRINKMANN MANAGEMENT INC
1819 Underwood Blvd Ste 2 (08075-1246)
PHONE................................856 764-7300
Richard Jezykowski, *CEO*
EMP: 12
SALES (est): 1.3MM
SALES (corp-wide): 92.1MM **Privately Held**
SIC: 3585 Parts for heating, cooling & refrigerating equipment
PA: Lauda Dr. R. Wobser Gmbh & Co. Kg
Pfarrstr. 41-43
Lauda-Konigshofen 97922
934 350-30

(G-2019)
PITNEY BOWES INC
1835 Underwood Blvd Ste 1 (08075-1249)
PHONE................................856 764-2240
Rcihard Potero, *Manager*
EMP: 200
SALES (corp-wide): 3.5B **Publicly Held**
SIC: 3579 7359 Postage meters; business machine & electronic equipment rental services
PA: Pitney Bowes Inc.
3001 Summer St Ste 3
Stamford CT 06905
203 356-5000

(G-2020)
SIMON & SCHUSTER INC
100 Front St (08075-1181)
P.O. Box 500, Riverside (08075-7500)
PHONE................................856 461-6500
David Schaesfer, *Vice Pres*
Dave Schaeffer, *Vice Pres*
Pat Kelman, *Plant Mgr*
Charlie Schlag, *Supervisor*
EMP: 350
SALES (corp-wide): 27.7B **Publicly Held**
SIC: 2741 Miscellaneous publishing

HQ: Simon & Schuster, Inc.
1230 Ave Of The Americas
New York NY 10020
212 698-7000

(G-2021)
SPL HOLDINGS LLC
Also Called: H.N. Lucas & Son
211 Carriage Ln (08075-1237)
PHONE.....................................856 764-2400
Pamela S Lloyd,
Stephen H Lloyd,
EMP: 12
SQ FT: 6,700
SALES (est): 1.4MM **Privately Held**
SIC: 3599 Machine shop, jobbing & repair

(G-2022)
WOYSHNER SERVICE COMPANY INC
Also Called: Wsc International
813 Edgewood Ave (08075-1207)
PHONE.....................................856 461-9196
EMP: 4
SALES: 1MM **Privately Held**
SIC: 3568 Mfg Power Transmission Equipment

(G-2023)
ZANOTTI TRANSBLOCK USA CORP
1810 Underwood Blvd Ste 1 (08075-1254)
PHONE.....................................917 584-9357
John Boschetti, *President*
EMP: 2 **EST:** 2014
SQ FT: 15,000
SALES: 3MM **Privately Held**
SIC: 3585 Refrigeration & heating equipment

Demarest
Bergen County

(G-2024)
BLU-J2 LLC
Also Called: Strap-Its
91 Alpine Ct (07627-2318)
PHONE.....................................201 750-1407
Julie Slavitt, *Mng Member*
Judy Simon,
EMP: 4
SALES (est): 329.7K **Privately Held**
SIC: 2389 Apparel for handicapped

(G-2025)
COINING TECHNOLOGIES INC
35 Monhegan St (07627)
PHONE.....................................866 897-2304
Martin G Rosansky, *President*
Jake Allen, *Business Mgr*
Dennis Decker, *Vice Pres*
Donna Parker, *Vice Pres*
Raymond Reboli, *Vice Pres*
▲ **EMP:** 70
SQ FT: 52,000
SALES (est): 12.9MM **Privately Held**
SIC: 3469 Stamping metal for the trade

(G-2026)
US FRONTLINE NEWS INC
139 Anderson Ave (07627-1301)
PHONE.....................................646 284-6233
Ryu Fujiwara, *President*
EMP: 30
SALES (est): 4MM **Privately Held**
WEB: www.usfl.com
SIC: 2721 Magazines: publishing only, not printed on site

Dennisville
Cape May County

(G-2027)
BLUEWATER INDUSTRIES INC
Also Called: Bluewater Wldg & Fabrication
1089 Rt 47 (08214)
PHONE.....................................609 427-1012
Ed Myland, *President*
EMP: 15
SQ FT: 10,000

SALES: 1.3MM **Privately Held**
WEB: www.bluewaterwelding.com
SIC: 7692 Welding repair

Denville
Morris County

(G-2028)
ACUSTRIP COMPANY INC (PA)
124 E Main St Apt 109b (07834-2169)
PHONE.....................................973 299-8237
Ron Schornstein, *Principal*
Joni Aragona, *Admin Mgr*
EMP: 16
SALES (est): 2.3MM **Privately Held**
SIC: 3826 Liquid testing apparatus

(G-2029)
ALLURE PET PDTS LTD LBLTY CO
Also Called: Huggle Hounds
321 Palmer Rd (07834)
PHONE.....................................973 339-9655
Julie Kruss, *Partner*
Robert Slynn, *Partner*
▲ **EMP:** 11
SALES (est): 373.7K **Privately Held**
SIC: 3942 Dolls & stuffed toys

(G-2030)
ANDIS INC
Also Called: Citizen of Morris County, The
124 E Main St (07834-2100)
P.O. Box 7 (07834-0007)
PHONE.....................................973 627-0400
Fax: 973 627-0403
EMP: 6
SQ FT: 2,000
SALES (est): 290K **Privately Held**
SIC: 2711 Newspapers-Publishing/Printing

(G-2031)
ANTHONY & SONS BAKERY ITLN BKY
20 Luger Rd (07834-2639)
PHONE.....................................973 625-2323
Anthony Dattolo, *President*
Joseph Dattolo, *Principal*
Richard Martinez, *COO*
Baldo Dattolo, *Vice Pres*
Robert Tobia, *Vice Pres*
▲ **EMP:** 98 **EST:** 1984
SQ FT: 30,000
SALES (est): 26.6MM **Privately Held**
WEB: www.anthonyandsonsbakery.com
SIC: 2051 5149 Bakery: wholesale or wholesale/retail combined; groceries & related products

(G-2032)
COMPONENTS CORPORATION
6 Kinsey Pl (07834-2692)
PHONE.....................................866 426-6726
Byron Minter, *President*
Monica Minter, *Corp Secy*
Christopher Minter, *Vice Pres*
William Gordon, *VP Mfg*
Sherry Vanderhoof, *Prdtn Mgr*
EMP: 17 **EST:** 1943
SQ FT: 12,000
SALES (est): 2.6MM **Privately Held**
WEB: www.componentscorp.com
SIC: 3678 Electronic connectors

(G-2033)
CUSTOM DECORATORS SERVICE
415 E Main St Ste 3 (07834-2557)
PHONE.....................................973 625-0516
Walter Kunzel, *Owner*
EMP: 6 **EST:** 1970
SALES (est): 489K **Privately Held**
SIC: 5023 2512 Draperies; upholstered household furniture

(G-2034)
DENVILLE DIAGNOSTICS IMAGING
Also Called: Denville Diagnostic Imaging
161 E Main St Ste 101 (07834-2647)
PHONE.....................................973 586-1212
Michael Dwyre, *CEO*

Peter Barba, *CFO*
EMP: 21
SQ FT: 1,000
SALES (est): 4.1MM **Privately Held**
SIC: 3826 Magnetic resonance imaging apparatus

(G-2035)
DIAGENODE INC
400 Morris Ave Ste 101 (07834-1362)
PHONE.....................................862 209-4680
Didier Allaer, *CEO*
Ignacio Mazon, *General Mgr*
Rosemarie Koster, *Finance Mgr*
Chrystle Richardson, *Accountant*
Tracy Faustermann, *Accounts Mgr*
▲ **EMP:** 7
SQ FT: 3,000
SALES (est): 1.7MM **Privately Held**
SIC: 3821 Laboratory apparatus & furniture

(G-2036)
EAGLE COMMUNICATIONS INC
2902 Vantage Ct (07834-3452)
PHONE.....................................973 366-6181
Angelo Salvatore, *President*
EMP: 4 **EST:** 2000
SALES: 400K **Privately Held**
SIC: 3661 Telephone station equipment & parts, wire

(G-2037)
FGH SYSTEMS INC
10 Prospect Pl (07834-2632)
PHONE.....................................973 625-8114
Frank G Hohmann, *President*
Eric Hohmann, *Corp Secy*
▲ **EMP:** 17
SQ FT: 12,000
SALES (est): 3MM **Privately Held**
WEB: www.fghsystems.com
SIC: 3599 Machine shop, jobbing & repair

(G-2038)
GENERAL RELIANCE CORPORATION
88 Ford Rd Ste 20 (07834-1357)
PHONE.....................................973 361-1400
George Michelin, *CEO*
Sheldon Masser, *President*
Doreen Cornelius, *COO*
Chris Schmidt, *Vice Pres*
Rick Souther, *Prdtn Mgr*
EMP: 44 **EST:** 1960
SQ FT: 22,000
SALES (est): 9.5MM **Privately Held**
WEB: www.generalreliance.com
SIC: 3679 Harness assemblies for electronic use: wire or cable; electronic circuits

(G-2039)
GERARDI PRESS INC
3 Luger Rd Ste 3 # 3 (07834-2638)
P.O. Box 545 (07834-0545)
PHONE.....................................973 627-2600
Keith Gerardi, *President*
Valerie Bradley, *Accounting Mgr*
Gus Metz, *Admin Sec*
EMP: 8
SQ FT: 18,800
SALES: 1.2MM **Privately Held**
WEB: www.gerardipress.com
SIC: 2752 Commercial printing, offset

(G-2040)
INTEGRATED PACKG SYSTEMS INC
Also Called: Ips
3 Luger Rd Ste 5 (07834-2638)
PHONE.....................................973 664-0020
Robert W Fields, *President*
Michael T McNeila, *Exec VP*
Janice Mastropaolo, *Manager*
▲ **EMP:** 8
SQ FT: 18,000
SALES (est): 2.1MM **Privately Held**
WEB: www.ipsnj.com
SIC: 3569 5084 Liquid automation machinery & equipment; packaging machinery & equipment

(G-2041)
J & R CUSTOM WOODWORKING INC
449 E Main St (07834-2515)
PHONE.....................................973 625-4114
Joel Kriegsfeld, *President*
Rhea Kriegsfeld, *Admin Sec*
EMP: 5 **EST:** 1971
SQ FT: 2,100
SALES (est): 518.2K **Privately Held**
SIC: 2434 Wood kitchen cabinets

(G-2042)
JUSTICE LABORATORY SOFTWARE
Also Called: PC Science Training Center
1 Indian Rd Ste 2 (07834-2000)
P.O. Box 1227 (07834-8227)
PHONE.....................................973 586-8551
George Schriner, *President*
EMP: 8 **EST:** 1999
SALES (est): 682.7K **Privately Held**
WEB: www.justiceinnovations.com
SIC: 7372 Prepackaged software

(G-2043)
KUDAS INDUSTRIES INC
6 Dorchester Dr (07834-3809)
PHONE.....................................412 751-0260
Todd G Kudas, *Principal*
EMP: 10
SALES (est): 1MM **Privately Held**
SIC: 3999 Manufacturing industries

(G-2044)
LB ELECTRIC CO - NORTH LLC
12 Knoll Top Ct (07834-3623)
PHONE.....................................973 366-2188
Leon Baptiste, *Branch Mgr*
EMP: 8
SALES (corp-wide): 10.4MM **Privately Held**
SIC: 4911 3699 1731 Electric services; electrical equipment & supplies; electrical work
PA: Lb Electric Co. - North, Llc
50 Commerce Rd
Cedar Grove NJ 07009
973 571-2200

(G-2045)
MECA ELECTRONICS INC
459 E Main St (07834-2515)
PHONE.....................................973 625-0661
William Davo, *President*
Thomas Hickey, *Vice Pres*
Joseph Scarano, *QC Mgr*
Yolanda Ruiz, *Sales Associate*
David Yatcilla, *Manager*
EMP: 51 **EST:** 1961
SQ FT: 8,000
SALES (est): 4.6MM **Privately Held**
WEB: www.e-meca.com
SIC: 3679 Microwave components

(G-2046)
MEMORY INTERNATIONAL CORP
25 Redwood Rd (07834-3502)
PHONE.....................................973 586-2653
Don Chuan, *President*
EMP: 12
SALES (est): 1MM **Privately Held**
SIC: 3674 Semiconductors & related devices

(G-2047)
METALIS USA INC
88 Ford Rd (07834-1378)
P.O. Box 1115 (07834-8115)
PHONE.....................................973 625-3500
James Cote, *President*
Michael Mullen, *Vice Pres*
▲ **EMP:** 18 **EST:** 1978
SQ FT: 35,000
SALES (est): 5.2MM **Privately Held**
WEB: www.co-planar.com
SIC: 3469 Stamping metal for the trade

(G-2048)
MINARDI BAKING CO INC
20 Luger Rd (07834-2639)
PHONE.....................................973 742-1107
Thomas Minardi, *President*
Joseph Minardi, *Corp Secy*

John C Minardi, *Vice Pres*
EMP: 45 EST: 1922
SQ FT: 7,000
SALES (est): 4.5MM **Privately Held**
SIC: 5149 5461 2051 Bakery products;
bakeries; bread, cake & related products

(G-2049)
PLANITROI INC (PA)
Also Called: Plan It Roi
100-10 Ford Rd Ste 10 (07834)
PHONE..................................973 664-0700
Paul Baum, *CEO*
Andrew Bauer, *CFO*
▲ EMP: 65
SQ FT: 55,000
SALES (est): 21.1MM **Privately Held**
WEB: www.planitroi.com
SIC: 7373 8742 3571 Computer system
selling services; management consulting
services; electronic computers

(G-2050)
QUALSERV IMPORTS INC
Also Called: Pata Pal
3125 State Route 10 (07834-3493)
PHONE..................................973 620-9234
David Quincey, *President*
▲ EMP: 3
SQ FT: 1,000
SALES (est): 2.4MM **Privately Held**
SIC: 5199 2631 Gifts & novelties; pets &
pet supplies; container, packaging &
boxboard

(G-2051)
REDMOND BCMS INC
103 Pocono Rd (07834-2948)
PHONE..................................973 664-2000
Georgia Redmond, *President*
EMP: 70 EST: 1952
SQ FT: 40,000
SALES (est): 8.3MM **Privately Held**
WEB: www.redmondbcms.com
SIC: 2752 2791 2789 2759 Newspapers,
lithographed only; typesetting; bookbind-
ing & related work; commercial printing

(G-2052)
REVELATION GALLERY INC
Also Called: Revelation Art Gallery
22 Broadway (07834-2704)
PHONE..................................973 627-6558
Josh Cramer, *President*
EMP: 4
SALES (est): 295.2K **Privately Held**
SIC: 5999 2499 8999 Art dealers; picture
& mirror frames, wood; art restoration

(G-2053)
RHEIN MEDICAL INC (HQ)
Also Called: Rhein Manufacturing
4 Stewart Ct (07834-1028)
PHONE..................................727 209-2244
John A Bee, *President*
Carl E Wortham, *Vice Pres*
EMP: 18
SQ FT: 30,000
SALES (est): 4.2MM
SALES (corp-wide): 25MM **Privately
Held**
WEB: www.rheinmedical.com
SIC: 3841 5047 Surgical instruments &
apparatus; surgical equipment & supplies
PA: Katena Products, Inc.
6 Campus Dr Ste 310
Parsippany NJ 07054
973 989-1600

(G-2054)
RICONPHARMA LLC (HQ)
100 Ford Rd Ste 9 (07834-1396)
PHONE..................................973 627-4685
Billa Praveen Reddy, *Vice Pres*
Satya Valiveti, *Vice Pres*
Akash Arabole, *Project Mgr*
Donna Brunner, *Bookkeeper*
Raj Devalapalli, *Mng Member*
EMP: 34
SQ FT: 10,000
SALES (est): 5.5MM **Privately Held**
WEB: www.riconpharma.com
SIC: 2834 Pharmaceutical preparations

(G-2055)
ROLO SYSTEMS
Also Called: Denville Dairy
34a Broadway (07834-2704)
PHONE..................................973 627-4214
Jack Fine, *President*
Lois Fine, *Vice Pres*
EMP: 22
SQ FT: 900
SALES (est): 3.1MM **Privately Held**
WEB: www.denvilleprobarbers.com
SIC: 2024 5812 Ice cream & frozen
desserts; ice cream stands or dairy bars

(G-2056)
RUDOLPH INSTRUMENTS INC
Also Called: Digipol Technologies
400 Morris Ave Ste 120 (07834-1362)
PHONE..................................973 227-0139
Kumar Utukuri, *President*
EMP: 5 EST: 1948
SQ FT: 6,000
SALES: 500K **Privately Held**
WEB: www.rudolphinst.com
SIC: 3826 Analytical instruments

(G-2057)
**SENSOR MEDICAL
TECHNOLOGY LLC**
4 Stewart Ct (07834-1028)
PHONE..................................425 358-7381
Gregory L Heacock, *CEO*
Louise Culham, *Exec VP*
EMP: 5 EST: 2012
SALES (est): 629.9K **Privately Held**
SIC: 3851 3841 5048 Lens coating, oph-
thalmic; lenses, ophthalmic; ophthalmic
instruments & apparatus; ophthalmic
goods

(G-2058)
SPECIAL OPTICS INC
3 Stewart Ct (07834-1038)
PHONE..................................973 366-7289
Robert Bradford, *Ch of Bd*
David J Manzi, *President*
Bob Stewart, *Plant Mgr*
Alice Harding, *Production*
Steven Morales, *Sales Mgr*
EMP: 18 EST: 1969
SQ FT: 25,000
SALES (est): 3.6MM **Privately Held**
WEB: www.specialoptics.com
SIC: 3851 Ophthalmic goods

(G-2059)
**SPECIALTY PHARMASOURCE
LLC**
400 Morris Ave Ste 121 (07834-1362)
PHONE..................................973 784-4965
S Valiveti, *Mng Member*
EMP: 15 EST: 2016
SALES (est): 678.1K **Privately Held**
SIC: 8731 3821 5047 Chemical labora-
tory, except testing; clinical laboratory in-
struments, except medical & dental;
medical & hospital equipment

(G-2060)
**TRI-POWER CONSULTING SVCS
LLC**
2 Richwood Pl (07834-2615)
PHONE..................................973 227-7100
Richard Modes, *Project Mgr*
Anthony L Rosa, *Engineer*
Kyle Hobin, *Design Engr*
Steve Woodward, *CFO*
Anthony La Rosa,
EMP: 30
SALES (est): 13.8MM **Privately Held**
WEB: www.tripower.net
SIC: 5085 3549 Industrial supplies; mark-
ing machines; metalworking

(G-2061)
TX TECHNOLOGY LLC
Also Called: Chatlos Systems
100 Ford Rd Ste 18 (07834-1396)
PHONE..................................973 442-7500
Barry Borodkin, *President*
Don Black, *General Mgr*
Mike Wertz, *Manager*
▲ EMP: 120
SQ FT: 12,000

SALES (est): 19.9MM **Privately Held**
WEB: www.txtechnology.com
SIC: 3823 Pressure measurement instru-
ments, industrial

(G-2062)
YANKEE TOOL INC
17 Edgewater Dr (07834-1811)
PHONE..................................973 664-0878
John Pierce, *President*
Linda Pierce, *Vice Pres*
EMP: 10
SQ FT: 6,000
SALES: 200K **Privately Held**
SIC: 2844 Manicure preparations

Deptford
Gloucester County

(G-2063)
DEPTFORD PLATING CO INC
Dein Ave Rr 41 (08096)
P.O. Box 5056 (08096-0056)
PHONE..................................856 227-1144
Theodore H Smolenski, *President*
Henrietta Smolenski, *Corp Secy*
EMP: 7 EST: 1966
SQ FT: 8,000
SALES: 300K **Privately Held**
SIC: 3471 Electroplating of metals or
formed products

(G-2064)
**INTERNATIONAL ROLLFORMS
INC (PA)**
Also Called: Garment Bar
8 International Ave (08096)
P.O. Box 5426 (08096-0426)
PHONE..................................856 228-7100
Jack Vosbikian, *President*
Thomas Vosbikian, *Owner*
Mark Wellner, *Vice Pres*
EMP: 30
SQ FT: 64,500
SALES (est): 22.3MM **Privately Held**
WEB: www.intl-rollforms.com
SIC: 3356 3469 Nonferrous rolling & draw-
ing; stamping metal for the trade

(G-2065)
PIN POINT CONTAINER CORP
669 Tanyard Rd (08096-6229)
PHONE..................................856 848-2115
Bruce Baelz, *President*
Phyliss Baelz, *Vice Pres*
EMP: 6
SQ FT: 5,000
SALES (est): 1.3MM **Privately Held**
SIC: 2653 3544 Boxes, corrugated: made
from purchased materials; dies, steel rule

(G-2066)
SOUTH JERSEY METAL INC
1651 Hurffville Rd (08096)
P.O. Box 5148 (08096-0148)
PHONE..................................856 228-0642
Joseph Wagner III, *President*
Sue Wagner, *Treasurer*
EMP: 25 EST: 1945
SQ FT: 17,500
SALES (est): 3.3MM **Privately Held**
WEB: www.southjerseymetal.com
SIC: 2514 3444 Metal kitchen & dining
room furniture; sheet metalwork

(G-2067)
**SWAROVSKI NORTH AMERICA
LTD**
1750 Deptford Center Rd (08096-5222)
PHONE..................................856 686-1805
Lorie Summers, *Branch Mgr*
EMP: 4
SALES (corp-wide): 4.7B **Privately Held**
SIC: 3961 Costume jewelry
HQ: Swarovski North America Limited
1 Kenney Dr
Cranston RI 02920
401 463-6400

(G-2068)
**WORK ZONE CONTRACTORS
LLC**
664 Oak Ave (08096-4560)
PHONE..................................856 845-8201
Kathleen M Santanello, *Principal*
EMP: 9
SALES (est): 1.4MM **Privately Held**
SIC: 3669 Signaling apparatus, electric

Dividing Creek
Cumberland County

(G-2069)
**COVIA HOLDINGS
CORPORATION**
1100 Whitehead Rd (08315)
P.O. Box 145, Millville (08332-0145)
PHONE..................................856 785-2700
Waverly Hale, *Branch Mgr*
EMP: 29
SALES (corp-wide): 142.6MM **Publicly
Held**
WEB: www.unimin.com
SIC: 1446 Industrial sand
HQ: Covia Holdings Corporation
3 Summit Park Dr Ste 700
Independence OH 44131
440 214-3284

Dorchester
Cumberland County

(G-2070)
DORCHESTER SHIPYARD INC
13 Front St (08316)
P.O. Box 600 (08316-0600)
PHONE..................................856 785-8040
John Kelleher, *President*
EMP: 16
SALES (est): 3.7MM **Privately Held**
SIC: 3731 Shipbuilding & repairing

Dorothy
Atlantic County

(G-2071)
HAPPLE PRINTING
81 Cape May Ave (08317-9740)
P.O. Box 36 (08317-0036)
PHONE..................................609 476-0100
Ken Happle, *Owner*
EMP: 6
SALES (est): 135.1K **Privately Held**
SIC: 2752 Commercial printing, offset

(G-2072)
VIKING MOLD & TOOL CORP
64 Tuckahoe Rd (08317-9702)
PHONE..................................609 476-9333
James C Sullivan Jr, *President*
James C Sullivan Sr, *Vice Pres*
EMP: 9
SQ FT: 5,700
SALES (est): 1.2MM **Privately Held**
SIC: 3544 Forms (molds), for foundry &
plastics working machinery

Dover
Morris County

(G-2073)
**ALCOA POWER GENERATING
INC**
Also Called: Howmet Corporation-Dover Cast
9 Roy St (07801-4308)
PHONE..................................973 361-0300
James B Johnson, *General Mgr*
EMP: 7
SALES (corp-wide): 13.4B **Publicly Held**
SIC: 3324 Steel investment foundries
HQ: Alcoa Power Generating Inc.
201 Isabella St Ste 500
Pittsburgh PA 15212
412 553-4545

(G-2074)
AMSCOT STRUCTURAL PDTS CORP
241 E Blackwell St (07801-4140)
PHONE....................973 989-8800
Scott Roman, *President*
EMP: 20
SQ FT: 17,000
SALES (est): 4.8MM **Privately Held**
WEB: www.amscotnj.com
SIC: 3568 Bearings, bushings & blocks

(G-2075)
BLANC INDUSTRIES INC (PA)
88 King St Ste 1 (07801-3655)
PHONE....................973 537-0090
Didier Blanc, *President*
▲ EMP: 45
SQ FT: 46,500
SALES (est): 12.3MM **Privately Held**
WEB: www.blancind.com
SIC: 3993 Signs & advertising specialties

(G-2076)
BLUEBIRD AUTO RENTL SYSTEMS LP (PA)
200 Mineral Springs Rd (07801-1636)
PHONE....................973 989-2423
Angela M Margolit, *Partner*
Phil Jones, *Partner*
Francine Dunn, *Manager*
Jeff Swysh, *Manager*
Dave Zadrozny, *Software Dev*
EMP: 34
SQ FT: 5,400
SALES (est): 4.9MM **Privately Held**
WEB: www.bluebird-technologies.com
SIC: 5734 7372 7371 Software, business
& non-game; business oriented computer
software; computer software systems
analysis & design, custom

(G-2077)
BRINKER INDUSTRIES
Also Called: Brinker Displays
88 King St Ste 1 (07801-3655)
PHONE....................973 678-1200
Didier Blanc, *President*
▲ EMP: 35
SQ FT: 120,000
SALES (est): 4.1MM **Privately Held**
WEB: www.brinkerdisplays.com
SIC: 3993 Displays & cutouts, window &
lobby

(G-2078)
COCOCARE PRODUCTS INC
85 Franklin Rd Ste 3a (07801-5632)
P.O. Box 311 (07802-0311)
PHONE....................973 989-8880
Gerald Jay Dubin, *President*
Jane P Dubin, *Admin Sec*
EMP: 30 EST: 1969
SALES (est): 5.7MM **Privately Held**
WEB: www.cococare.com
SIC: 2844 Cosmetic preparations; shampoos, rinses, conditioners: hair

(G-2079)
CRYSTAL DELTRONIC INDUSTRIES (PA)
Also Called: Isowave Division
60 Harding Ave (07801-4710)
PHONE....................973 328-6898
Stuart Samuelson, *President*
Deborah Samuelson, *Corp Secy*
Juanita Washington, *Executive*
EMP: 23
SQ FT: 18,000
SALES (est): 2MM **Privately Held**
WEB: www.deltroniccrystal.com
SIC: 3674 3679 Optical isolators; electronic crystals

(G-2080)
CRYSTAL DELTRONIC INDUSTRIES
Also Called: Isowave Division
60 Harding Ave (07801-4710)
PHONE....................973 328-7000
Stewart Samuelson, *President*
EMP: 12

SALES (corp-wide): 2MM **Privately Held**
WEB: www.deltroniccrystal.com
SIC: 3674 7361 Optical isolators; employment agencies
PA: Crystal Deltronic Industries Inc
60 Harding Ave
Dover NJ 07801
973 328-6898

(G-2081)
DABURN WIRE & CABLE CORP (PA)
Also Called: Daburn Electronics & Cable
44 Richboynton Rd (07801-2650)
PHONE....................973 328-3200
Jim Flaherty, *General Mgr*
Edward A Flaherty, *Principal*
▲ EMP: 9
SALES (est): 1.8MM **Privately Held**
SIC: 3357 5063 3699 Nonferrous wire-drawing & insulating; electronic wire &
cable; electrical equipment & supplies

(G-2082)
DANA POLY CORP
85 Harrison St Dover (07801)
PHONE....................800 474-1020
Mendy Rosner, *President*
Marvin Rosner, *Vice Pres*
Nick Harkavy, *VP Sales*
Ian Turk, *Accounts Exec*
Sol Yudkowsky, *Accounts Exec*
EMP: 40
SQ FT: 65,000
SALES: 20MM **Privately Held**
WEB: www.minibagusa.com
SIC: 2673 Plastic bags: made from purchased materials

(G-2083)
ENVIRNMNTAL DSIGN GRPHIC ENTPS
Also Called: Dmr Sign Systems
215 State Route 10 (07869-2413)
PHONE....................973 361-1829
Andrew K Tunkel, *President*
EMP: 5
SQ FT: 4,400
SALES: 250K **Privately Held**
WEB: www.dmrsign.com
SIC: 2759 7336 Screen printing; graphic
arts & related design

(G-2084)
FRAMECO INC
158 W Clinton St Ste B (07801-3410)
PHONE....................973 989-1424
EMP: 25
SQ FT: 35,000
SALES (est): 202.7K **Privately Held**
SIC: 2499 Mfr Wooden Picture Frames

(G-2085)
H & W TOOL CO INC (PA)
22 Lee Ave (07801-4333)
PHONE....................973 366-0131
Richard Winstead, *President*
Phyllis Winstead, *Corp Secy*
EMP: 17
SQ FT: 5,400
SALES (est): 4.9MM **Privately Held**
WEB: www.hwtool.com
SIC: 3544 3542 3841 3769 Industrial
molds; machine tools, metal forming type;
surgical & medical instruments; guided
missile & space vehicle parts & auxiliary
equipment; machine tool accessories

(G-2086)
HIGHLAND PRODUCTS INC
River St (07801)
PHONE....................973 366-0156
Barrett Sangster, *President*
EMP: 4 EST: 1957
SQ FT: 3,500
SALES: 100K **Privately Held**
SIC: 3089 Plastic processing

(G-2087)
HOWMET CASTINGS & SERVICES INC
Alcoa Howmet, Dover
9 Roy St (07801-4308)
PHONE....................973 361-0300
Alexander Alford, *Manager*

EMP: 900
SALES (corp-wide): 14B **Publicly Held**
SIC: 3324 3369 Commercial investment
castings, ferrous; nonferrous foundries
HQ: Howmet Castings & Services, Inc.
1616 Harvard Ave
Newburgh Heights OH 44105
216 641-4400

(G-2088)
HOWMET CASTINGS & SERVICES INC
Also Called: Alcoa Howmet, Dover
9 Roy St (07801-4308)
PHONE....................973 361-0300
EMP: 400
SALES (corp-wide): 14B **Publicly Held**
SIC: 3324 Commercial investment castings, ferrous
HQ: Howmet Castings & Services, Inc.
1616 Harvard Ave
Newburgh Heights OH 44105
216 641-4400

(G-2089)
HOWMET CASTINGS & SERVICES INC
Also Called: Alcoa Hwmet Dver Alloy Oprtons
10 Roy St (07801-4325)
PHONE....................973 361-2310
Alexander Alford, *Manager*
EMP: 331
SALES (corp-wide): 14B **Publicly Held**
SIC: 3324 Commercial investment castings, ferrous
HQ: Howmet Castings & Services, Inc.
1616 Harvard Ave
Newburgh Heights OH 44105
216 641-4400

(G-2090)
INSTANT PRINTING OF DOVER INC
241 E Blackwell St (07801-4140)
PHONE....................973 366-6855
Anna Medore, *President*
Peter Medore, *Vice Pres*
EMP: 7 EST: 1968
SQ FT: 5,000
SALES (est): 976.2K **Privately Held**
SIC: 2752 7334 2791 2789 Commercial
printing, offset; photocopying & duplicating services; typesetting; bookbinding &
related work; commercial printing

(G-2091)
JAN PACKAGING INC
100 Harrison St (07801-4750)
P.O. Box 448 (07802-0448)
PHONE....................973 361-7200
Edward Malavarca, *CEO*
Karl R Malavarca, *President*
Katherine Caristia, *COO*
Roger Sorhagen, *Vice Pres*
Colleen Barry, *Opers Mgr*
EMP: 70 EST: 1952
SQ FT: 250,000
SALES (est): 21.4MM **Privately Held**
SIC: 4783 4225 2449 Packing goods for
shipping; crating goods for shipping; general warehousing & storage; wood containers

(G-2092)
JDV EQUIPMENT CORP
1 Princeton Ave Ste 2 (07801-2557)
PHONE....................973 366-6556
Robert T Abbott, *President*
Sean King, *Vice Pres*
Joe Barringer, *Sales Mgr*
Ryan Kelly, *Sales Engr*
▲ EMP: 6
SQ FT: 3,000
SALES (est): 1.4MM **Privately Held**
SIC: 3589 5084 Water treatment equipment, industrial; industrial machinery &
equipment

(G-2093)
JERSEY SHEET METAL & MACHINE
90 E Dickerson St (07801-4633)
P.O. Box 428 (07802-0428)
PHONE....................973 366-8628
Richard T Hammond Jr, *President*

Garret Hammond, *Admin Sec*
EMP: 20
SQ FT: 15,000
SALES (est): 3.8MM **Privately Held**
SIC: 3444 Sheet metal specialties, not
stamped

(G-2094)
LINK BIO INC
69 King St Ste 2 (07801-2800)
PHONE....................973 625-1333
Massimo Calafiore, *President*
Daniel Wizorek, *Finance*
Maria Gisondi, *Manager*
▲ EMP: 9
SALES (est): 1.4MM
• SALES (corp-wide): 198.9MM **Privately
Held**
SIC: 3842 Implants, surgical
HQ: Deru Gmbh
Oststr. 4-10
Norderstedt 22844
405 544-5880

(G-2095)
LINKSPINE INC
69 King St Ste 2 (07801-2800)
PHONE....................973 625-1333
Aaron Snyder, *Project Engr*
Dennis Farrell, *VP Mktg*
EMP: 4
SALES (est): 435.8K **Privately Held**
SIC: 3841 Surgical & medical instruments

(G-2096)
MEDICA
53 Richboynton Rd (07801-2649)
PHONE....................760 634-5440
Jarka Bartl, *President*
Simona Bartl, *Vice Pres*
Malkcom Vero, *Sales Dir*
EMP: 9
SALES (est): 1.3MM **Privately Held**
WEB: www.medica-dme.com
SIC: 2835 In vitro diagnostics

(G-2097)
MINITEC CORPORATION
158 W Clinton St Ste V (07801-3410)
PHONE....................973 989-1426
Scott Mindlin, *President*
Herb Mindlin, *Corp Secy*
Lou Mason, *Vice Pres*
EMP: 7 EST: 1963
SQ FT: 5,000
SALES: 696K **Privately Held**
SIC: 3469 Metal stampings

(G-2098)
MOTION CONTROL TECH INC
158 W Clinton St Ste Ff (07801-3410)
PHONE....................973 361-2226
Frank Heidinger, *President*
Bernie Heidinger, *Vice Pres*
▲ EMP: 15
SQ FT: 4,000
SALES: 2MM **Privately Held**
WEB: www.mct-inc.net
SIC: 2298 Cable, fiber

(G-2099)
MPT RACING INC
Also Called: Mpt Industries
85 Franklin Rd Ste 6b (07801-5632)
PHONE....................973 989-9220
Michael Trueba Jr, *President*
EMP: 7
SQ FT: 6,500
SALES (est): 1MM **Privately Held**
WEB: www.mptindustries.com
SIC: 3714 Motor vehicle parts & accessories

(G-2100)
NEPTUNE PRODUCTS INC
353 E Blackwell St (07801-4302)
P.O. Box 829 (07802-0829)
PHONE....................973 366-8200
Richard H Schroeder, *President*
Peggy Sinnott, *Admin Sec*
EMP: 10 EST: 1948
SQ FT: 4,500
SALES (est): 1.8MM **Privately Held**
SIC: 3594 Fluid power pumps

▲ = Import ▼=Export
◆ =Import/Export

GEOGRAPHIC

(G-2101)
NEW STANDARD PRINTING CORP
118 Lincoln Ave (07801-2816)
P.O. Box 276, Blairstown (07825-0276)
PHONE.....................973 366-0006
Michael Wetzel, *President*
EMP: 8
SQ FT: 1,500
SALES (est): 1.1MM Privately Held
SIC: 2752 Commercial printing, offset

(G-2102)
NORTHWEST INSTRUMENT INC
69 King St (07801-2800)
PHONE.....................973 347-6830
Bo Xing, *President*
Aili Liu, *Vice Pres*
David Xing, *Manager*
▲ EMP: 15
SALES (est): 1.2MM Privately Held
SIC: 3829 Surveying & drafting equipment

(G-2103)
PATCHWORKS CO INC
18 N Salem St (07801-4119)
PHONE.....................973 627-2002
Charles Barber, *President*
Greg Barber, *Vice Pres*
Chris Brauchle, *Vice Pres*
EMP: 5
SALES (est): 510K Privately Held
WEB: www.thepatchworks.com
SIC: 2395 2759 2399 Emblems, embroidered; promotional printing; emblems, badges & insignia

(G-2104)
RIDGE PRECISION PRODUCTS INC
288 Us Highway 46 Ste D (07801-2081)
PHONE.....................973 361-3508
Mark J Leone, *President*
Victoria Ponte, *Admin Sec*
EMP: 9
SQ FT: 12,000
SALES (est): 1.4MM Privately Held
SIC: 3599 Machine shop, jobbing & repair

(G-2105)
SCIMEDX CORPORATION
53 Richboynton Rd (07801-2649)
PHONE.....................800 221-5598
Thomas Britten, *Ch of Bd*
Maria Focht, *Supervisor*
Maria Soledad Focht, *Supervisor*
◆ EMP: 25
SQ FT: 10,000
SALES (est): 5.4MM Privately Held
WEB: www.scimedx.com
SIC: 3841 5049 Diagnostic apparatus, medical; laboratory equipment, except medical or dental

(G-2106)
SERVICE METAL FABRICATING INC
Also Called: Precision Shape Solutions
243 E Blackwell St (07801-4140)
PHONE.....................973 989-7199
Corey Akers, *Manager*
EMP: 5
SALES (corp-wide): 16MM Privately Held
WEB: www.servicemetal.com
SIC: 3444 Sheet metalwork
PA: Service Metal Fabricating Inc
10 Stickle Ave
Rockaway NJ 07866
973 625-8882

(G-2107)
TECHNICAL GLASS PRODUCTS INC
243 E Blackwell St (07801-4140)
PHONE.....................973 989-5500
Joseph Murray, *President*
Al Lorenzo, *Corp Secy*
EMP: 5
SQ FT: 3,000
SALES (est): 427K Privately Held
WEB: www.technicalglassinc.com
SIC: 3229 Scientific glassware

(G-2108)
TERRA DESIGNS INC (PA)
241 E Blackwell St Rear (07801-4140)
PHONE.....................973 328-1135
Anna Salibello, *President*
Chris Salibello, *Vice Pres*
Salvatore Salibello, *Treasurer*
▼ EMP: 15
SQ FT: 10,000
SALES (est): 1.3MM Privately Held
SIC: 3253 1743 Ceramic wall & floor tile; tile installation, ceramic

(G-2109)
TOTAL TECH MEDICAL LLC
289 Munt Hope Ave Apt J14 (07801)
PHONE.....................973 980-6458
Joseph Scafa,
EMP: 9
SALES (est): 478.4K Privately Held
SIC: 5047 3845 3841 Instruments, surgical & medical; diagnostic equipment, medical; ultrasonic scanning devices, medical; laser systems & equipment, medical; diagnostic apparatus, medical

(G-2110)
WIRE DISPLAYS INC
88 King St Ste 1 (07801-3655)
PHONE.....................973 537-0090
Didier Blanc, *Ch of Bd*
EMP: 12
SQ FT: 5,100
SALES (est): 2.2MM
SALES (corp-wide): 12.3MM Privately Held
WEB: www.wiredisplaysinc.com
SIC: 3496 Miscellaneous fabricated wire products
PA: Blanc Industries Inc.
88 King St Ste 1
Dover NJ 07801
973 537-0090

Dumont
Bergen County

(G-2111)
BAUER SPORT SHOP
48 Dumont Ave (07628-3015)
PHONE.....................201 384-6522
Mike Hegel,
Alan Bergman,
EMP: 4
SQ FT: 1,000
SALES (est): 230.4K Privately Held
SIC: 5941 2395 Sporting goods & bicycle shops; embroidery products, except schiffli machine

(G-2112)
CRICKET ENTERPRISES
60 Hillcrest Dr (07628-2007)
PHONE.....................201 387-7978
Neil Klein, *Owner*
Judith Klein, *Principal*
EMP: 7
SALES (est): 280K Privately Held
SIC: 3669 Emergency alarms

(G-2113)
HOJIBLANCA USA INC
175 Washington Ave Ste 18 (07628-2936)
PHONE.....................201 384-3007
Enrique Escudero, *CEO*
▲ EMP: 7
SALES (est): 729.6K Privately Held
SIC: 2079 2084 2099 Olive oil; wines; vinegar

(G-2114)
KEYSTONE PRINTING INC
21c E Madison Ave (07628-2415)
PHONE.....................201 387-7252
Michael C Worner, *Principal*
EMP: 7 EST: 1975
SQ FT: 4,400
SALES (est): 1MM Privately Held
WEB: www.keystoneprintingnj.com
SIC: 2752 Commercial printing, offset

(G-2115)
KLM MECHANICAL CONTRACTORS
109 W Shore Ave (07628-2332)
PHONE.....................201 385-6965
Kenneth Loehr, *President*
Keith Loehr, *Principal*
Gary Loehr, *Vice Pres*
EMP: 13 EST: 1967
SQ FT: 15,000
SALES (est): 1.7MM Privately Held
SIC: 1711 1761 3564 3444 Mechanical contractor; sheet metalwork; blowers & fans; sheet metalwork

(G-2116)
KODAY PRESS INC
69 Armour Pl (07628)
PHONE.....................201 387-0001
Eugene Koblentz, *President*
EMP: 12 EST: 1932
SQ FT: 16,000
SALES (est): 1.1MM Privately Held
SIC: 2759 Promotional printing

(G-2117)
PTL SHEET METAL INC
70 Davies Ave (07628-2505)
PHONE.....................201 501-8700
Candice Mac William, *President*
EMP: 4
SQ FT: 6,000
SALES (est): 638.3K Privately Held
SIC: 3444 1711 Ducts, sheet metal; ventilation & duct work contractor

(G-2118)
WASTE NOT COMPUTERS & SUPPLIES
94 Washington Ave (07628-3026)
PHONE.....................201 384-4444
Peter J Farrell, *President*
EMP: 6
SQ FT: 1,500
SALES (est): 720K Privately Held
WEB: www.wastenotcomputers.com
SIC: 5112 3955 Computer & photocopying supplies; ribbons, inked: typewriter, adding machine, register, etc.

Dunellen
Middlesex County

(G-2119)
AVENEL PALLET CO INC
1800 S 2nd St (08812)
P.O. Box 276 (08812-0276)
PHONE.....................732 752-0500
Vincent Colonna Jr, *President*
EMP: 10
SQ FT: 9,000
SALES (est): 1.5MM Privately Held
SIC: 5031 2448 Pallets, wood; wood pallets & skids

(G-2120)
BEST VALUE RUGS & CARPETS INC
215 Rt 22 E (08812)
PHONE.....................732 752-3528
Daljit Chadha, *President*
EMP: 5
SQ FT: 2,000
SALES (est): 1.5MM Privately Held
SIC: 5712 5713 5021 2499 Furniture stores; carpets; rugs; furniture; tiles, cork; tile, ceramic

(G-2121)
BLACHER CANVAS PRODUCTS INC
604 Bound Brook Rd (08812-1006)
PHONE.....................732 968-3666
George Rodoussakis, *President*
Irene Rodoussakis, *Vice Pres*
EMP: 7 EST: 1947
SQ FT: 6,000
SALES (est): 775K Privately Held
SIC: 2394 Awnings, fabric: made from purchased materials

(G-2122)
PEDESTAL PALLET INC
777 N Avenue Ext (08812-1019)
P.O. Box 450 (08812-0450)
PHONE.....................732 968-7488
John Ruotolo, *Principal*
EMP: 8
SALES (est): 1.3MM Privately Held
SIC: 2448 Pallets, wood; pallets, wood & wood with metal

(G-2123)
PFIZER INC
43 Spruce Hollow Rd (08812-1836)
PHONE.....................908 251-5685
Nora Tsivgas, *Branch Mgr*
EMP: 225
SALES (corp-wide): 53.6B Publicly Held
SIC: 2834 Pharmaceutical preparations
PA: Pfizer Inc.
235 E 42nd St
New York NY 10017
212 733-2323

East Brunswick
Middlesex County

(G-2124)
ALL SEASONS DOOR & WINDOW INC (PA)
28 Edgeboro Rd (08816-1635)
PHONE.....................732 238-7100
King T Yu, *President*
Suger Yu, *General Mgr*
Steven Yu, *Vice Pres*
Yee Chih, *Manager*
Jeff Chou, *Manager*
▲ EMP: 40
SQ FT: 35,000
SALES (est): 5.4MM Privately Held
SIC: 2431 Doors & door parts & trim, wood; windows & window parts & trim, wood

(G-2125)
ALLU GROUP INC
25 Kimberly Rd Ste A (08816-2038)
PHONE.....................201 288-2236
Mardi Ohanessian, *President*
◆ EMP: 14
SQ FT: 10,000
SALES (est): 5.4MM
SALES (corp-wide): 35.4MM Privately Held
WEB: www.ideachip.com
SIC: 3621 Commutators, electric motor
PA: Allu Group Oy
Jokimaentie 1
Pennala 16320
388 214-0

(G-2126)
AM WOOD INC
18 Kennedy Blvd (08816-1248)
PHONE.....................732 246-1506
Tatiana Elperin, *Manager*
EMP: 10
SALES (corp-wide): 1.3MM Privately Held
SIC: 2431 1752 Moldings, wood: unfinished & prefinished; wood floor installation & refinishing
PA: Am Wood Inc
2901 Nostrand Ave
Brooklyn NY
718 765-1200

(G-2127)
AMERIGEN PHARMACEUTICALS LTD (PA)
197 State Route 18 (08816-1440)
PHONE.....................732 993-9826
John Kratochwil, *Principal*
Al Delia, *Principal*
Tamara Elder, *Director*
EMP: 12
SALES (est): 1.5MM Privately Held
SIC: 2834 Pharmaceutical preparations

(G-2128)
BANDEMAR NETWORKS LLC
3 New Dover Rd (08816-2746)
PHONE.....................732 991-5112

Cesar Bandera, *CEO*
Allan Stevens, *Partner*
Mark Capuano, *Manager*
EMP: 4
SALES: 100K **Privately Held**
SIC: 7371 7372 4813 7812 Computer
software systems analysis & design, custom; computer software development &
applications; educational computer software; telephone/video communications;
motion picture & video production

(G-2129)
BIMBO BAKERIES USA INC
Also Called: Maier's Sunbeam Bakery
5 Alvin Ct (08816-2001)
PHONE....................................732 390-7715
Cris Siddeno, *Manager*
EMP: 60 **Privately Held**
SIC: 2051 Bakery: wholesale or whole-
sale/retail combined
HQ: Bimbo Bakeries Usa, Inc
255 Business Center Dr # 200
Horsham PA 19044
215 347-5500

(G-2130)
BIOTECH SUPPORT GROUP LLC
29 Hershey Rd (08816-2634)
PHONE....................................732 613-1967
Swapan Roy, *Mng Member*
EMP: 5
SALES: 100K **Privately Held**
SIC: 2869 Laboratory chemicals, organic

(G-2131)
CERAMSOURCE INC
26 Kennedy Blvd Ste B (08816-1260)
P.O. Box 6026 (08816-6026)
PHONE....................................732 257-5002
Yong Gong Wang, *Principal*
Warren Elton, *Regl Sales Mgr*
Anthony Venutolo, *Director*
▲ EMP: 16
SALES: 1.9MM **Privately Held**
SIC: 3299 Ceramic fiber

(G-2132)
CHIC LLC
Also Called: Leon Levin
200 State Route 18 Ste 1 (08816-1466)
PHONE....................................732 354-0035
Charles Godfrey, *President*
▲ EMP: 8
SQ FT: 2,500
SALES: 6.1MM
SALES (corp-wide): 119.2K **Privately
Held**
WEB: www.chic.com
SIC: 5137 2337 2339 2331 Blouses;
skirts; skirts, separate: women's, misses'
& juniors'; jackets & vests, except fur &
leather: women's; slacks: women's,
misses & juniors'; shorts (outerwear):
women's, misses' & juniors'; culottes:
women's, misses' & juniors'; T-shirts &
tops, women's: made from purchased
materials
PA: Knitastiks, Inc.
450 Park Ave Ste 2100
New York NY 10022
212 354-7770

(G-2133)
COILHOSE PNEUMATICS INC
Acme Quality Products
19 Kimberly Rd (08816-2010)
PHONE....................................732 432-7177
Gregory Samman, *Principal*
EMP: 20
SALES (corp-wide): 60.7MM **Privately
Held**
WEB: www.coilhose.com
SIC: 3569 3011 Filters; tire & inner tube
materials & related products
PA: Coilhose Pneumatics, Inc.
19 Kimberly Rd
East Brunswick NJ 08816
732 390-8480

(G-2134)
DODSON GLOBAL INC
27 Cotters Ln (08816-2002)
PHONE....................................732 238-7001
Allen Goodrich, *Principal*
▲ EMP: 7 EST: 2007

SALES (est): 875.7K **Privately Held**
SIC: 3317 Steel pipe & tubes

(G-2135)
DRAKE CORP
110 Tices Ln (08816-2048)
PHONE....................................732 254-1530
Ralph Drake, *President*
Louie Filipe, *General Mgr*
Tom Hohl, *COO*
Diego Discacciati, *Vice Pres*
Alida Maiola, *Vice Pres*
◆ EMP: 8
SALES (est): 1.7MM **Privately Held**
WEB: www.plastifin.com
SIC: 7361 2392 Employment agencies;
chair covers & pads: made from pur-
chased materials

(G-2136)
DRIFIRE LLC
28 Kennedy Blvd Ste 300 (08816-1255)
PHONE....................................866 266-4035
Darryl Schimeck, *CEO*
Bob Pastene, *Vice Pres*
Scott Willis, *Vice Pres*
Patrick Gainer, *CFO*
EMP: 30
SALES (est): 6.7MM **Privately Held**
SIC: 2321 Men's & boys' furnishings

(G-2137)
E R SQUIBB & SONS LLC (HQ)
25 Kennedy Blvd (08816-1259)
PHONE....................................732 246-3195
R Radcliffe, *Principal*
EMP: 7
SALES (est): 53.6MM
SALES (corp-wide): 22.5B **Publicly Held**
WEB: www.bms.com
SIC: 2834 Pharmaceutical preparations
PA: Bristol-Myers Squibb Company
430 E 29th St Fl 14
New York NY 10016
212 546-4000

(G-2138)
**EAST BRUNSWICK SEWERAGE
AUTH**
25 Harts Ln (08816-2034)
PHONE....................................732 257-8313
Fax: 732 257-0605
EMP: 16
SQ FT: 2,000
SALES (est): 2.5MM **Privately Held**
SIC: 3589 Mfg Service Industry Machinery

(G-2139)
ELBEE LITHO INC
292 Dunhams Corner Rd (08816-2624)
PHONE....................................732 698-7738
Barry Zaslavsky, *President*
EMP: 4
SQ FT: 5,000
SALES (est): 280K **Privately Held**
SIC: 2752 7389 Commercial printing, off-
set; printing broker

(G-2140)
ELITE PACKAGING CORP
40 Cotters Ln Ste E (08816-2043)
PHONE....................................732 651-9955
Mario Magali, *President*
Victor Martinez, *Supervisor*
▲ EMP: 18
SQ FT: 50,000
SALES (est): 3.8MM **Privately Held**
SIC: 3565 Packaging machinery

(G-2141)
**ELKEM SILICONES USA CORP
(DH)**
2 Tower Center Blvd # 1601 (08816-1100)
PHONE....................................732 227-2060
J Christopher York, *President*
Bertrand Mollet, *Treasurer*
◆ EMP: 25
SALES (est): 38MM
SALES (corp-wide): 64.2B **Privately Held**
WEB: www.bluestarsilicones.com
SIC: 2819 Industrial inorganic chemicals
HQ: Elkem Asa
Drammensveien 169
Oslo 0277
224 501-00

(G-2142)
EMC CORPORATION
Businessedge Solutions
1 Tower Center Blvd Fl 23 (08816-1145)
PHONE....................................732 549-8500
Shail Jain, *Manager*
Savio Dcruz, *Sr Consultant*
EMP: 730
SALES (corp-wide): 90.6B **Publicly Held**
WEB: www.emc.com
SIC: 3572 Computer storage devices
HQ: Emc Corporation
176 South St
Hopkinton MA 01748
508 435-1000

(G-2143)
EMPIRE SPECIALTY FOODS INC
6 Brookdale Rd (08816-4219)
PHONE....................................646 773-2630
Yildiray Hamzacebi, *Principal*
▲ EMP: 4 EST: 2011
SALES (est): 284.9K **Privately Held**
SIC: 2099 Food preparations

(G-2144)
ESAW INDUSTRIES INC
5 Litchfield Rd (08816-5036)
PHONE....................................732 613-1400
Eddy Chow, *President*
Susan Chow, *Vice Pres*
EMP: 6
SQ FT: 20,000
SALES (est): 570K **Privately Held**
SIC: 3571 Electronic computers

(G-2145)
EUCLID CHEMICAL COMPANY
77 Milltown Rd Ste B7 (08816-2302)
PHONE....................................732 390-9770
Bill Falland, *Vice Pres*
EMP: 10
SALES (corp-wide): 5.5B **Publicly Held**
WEB: www.epoxychemicals.com
SIC: 2899 Chemical preparations
HQ: The Euclid Chemical Company
19218 Redwood Rd
Cleveland OH 44110
800 321-7628

(G-2146)
FOUR BROS VENTURES INC
15 Timothy Ln (08816-4562)
PHONE....................................732 890-9469
Eurya Chauhan, *Co-Owner*
EMP: 4
SALES (est): 137.9K **Privately Held**
SIC: 7372 Prepackaged software

(G-2147)
FU WEI INC
Also Called: Fu WEI International
40 Cotters Ln Bldg B (08816-2043)
PHONE....................................732 937-8388
Jason Nichols, *CEO*
Yugin LI, *President*
▲ EMP: 7
SQ FT: 100,000
SALES: 5MM **Privately Held**
SIC: 2759 8743 2521 Commercial print-
ing; promotion service; benches, office:
wood

(G-2148)
**HERITAGE PHARMA HOLDINGS
INC (HQ)**
Also Called: Avet Phrmcuticals Holdings Inc
1 Tower Center Blvd # 1700 (08816-1145)
PHONE....................................732 429-1000
William S Marth, *President*
Arshad Jamil, *Research*
Nimish Patel, *Manager*
Samir Vij, *Manager*
Jessica Glickman, *Analyst*
EMP: 1
SALES (est): 41.6MM **Privately Held**
SIC: 2834 Pharmaceutical preparations

(G-2149)
HERITAGE PHARMA LABS INC
Also Called: Avet Pharmaceuticals Labs Inc.
8 Elkins Rd (08816-2005)
PHONE....................................732 238-7880
David Aronson, *Manager*
EMP: 10 **Privately Held**

SIC: 2834 Pharmaceutical preparations
HQ: Heritage Pharma Labs Inc.
21 Cotters Ln Ste B
East Brunswick NJ 08816
732 238-7880

(G-2150)
**HERITAGE PHARMA LABS INC
(DH)**
Also Called: Avet Pharmaceuticals Labs Inc.
21 Cotters Ln Ste B (08816-2050)
PHONE....................................732 238-7880
Jeffery Glazer, *CEO*
Sonal Mehta, *Research*
Jayanti Shah, *Plant Engr*
▲ EMP: 120
SALES (est): 31.1MM **Privately Held**
WEB: www.emcureusa.com
SIC: 2834 8731 Pharmaceutical prepara-
tions; commercial physical research
HQ: Heritage Pharma Holdings, Inc.
1 Tower Center Blvd # 1700
East Brunswick NJ 08816
732 429-1000

(G-2151)
**HERITAGE PHARMACEUTICALS
INC (DH)**
Also Called: Avet Pharmaceuticals Inc.
1 Tower Center Blvd # 1700 (08816-1145)
PHONE....................................732 429-1000
Fakrul Sayeed MD, *CEO*
John W Denman, *President*
Scott Delaney, *President*
Mike Schmidt, *Vice Pres*
Lew Soars, *Vice Pres*
▲ EMP: 33
SALES (est): 10.5MM **Privately Held**
WEB: www.heritagepharma.com
SIC: 2834 Pharmaceutical preparations
HQ: Heritage Pharma Holdings, Inc.
1 Tower Center Blvd # 1700
East Brunswick NJ 08816
732 429-1000

(G-2152)
INTERSOURCE USA INC
25 Kimberly Rd Ste A (08816-2038)
P.O. Box 6026 (08816-6026)
PHONE....................................732 257-5002
Edwin Wang, *President*
Hong Jiang, *Vice Pres*
Zane Reed, *Sales Associate*
▲ EMP: 10
SQ FT: 5,000
SALES (est): 1.1MM **Privately Held**
WEB: www.intersourceusa.com
SIC: 3299 5085 Ceramic fiber; industrial
supplies

(G-2153)
J S PALUCH CO INC
6 Alvin Ct Ste 1 (08816-2001)
PHONE....................................732 238-2412
David Hoser, *General Mgr*
EMP: 25
SALES (corp-wide): 87.6MM **Privately
Held**
WEB: www.jspaluch.com
SIC: 2731 2741 Pamphlets: publishing
only, not printed on site; miscellaneous
publishing
PA: J. S. Paluch Co., Inc.
3708 River Rd Ste 400
Franklin Park IL 60131
847 678-9300

(G-2154)
LENS DEPOT INC
40c Cotters Ln Ste D (08816-2037)
PHONE....................................732 993-9766
▲ EMP: 14
SQ FT: 5,000
SALES (est): 2.4MM **Privately Held**
SIC: 5048 3851 Whol Ophthalmic Goods
Mfg Ophthalmic Goods

(G-2155)
MAUSER USA LLC (DH)
35 Cotters Ln Ste C (08816-2032)
PHONE....................................732 353-7100
Hans-Peter Schaefer, *CEO*
Siegfried Weber, *Vice Pres*
Tony Deacons, *Plant Mgr*
Evan Dorries, *Sales Staff*
Mark Inman, *Sales Staff*

◆ **EMP: 25**
SALES (est): 554.1MM
SALES (corp-wide): 1.1B **Privately Held**
WEB: www.mausergroup.com
SIC: 3412 2655 Barrels, shipping: metal;
fiber cans, drums & containers
HQ: Mauser Holding International Gmbh
Schildgesstr. 71-163
Bruhl 50321
223 278-1000

(G-2156)
MCI SERVICE PARTS
Also Called: Motor Sport Industry
35 Cotters Ln (08816-2032)
PHONE..............................732 967-9081
Ken Rosenblum, *Opers Mgr*
Todd Brightlow, *Manager*
EMP: 7
SALES (est): 735.3K **Privately Held**
SIC: 2099 Popcorn, packaged: except already popped

(G-2157)
MON-ECO INDUSTRIES INC
Also Called: MEI
5 Joanna Ct Ste G (08816-2285)
PHONE..............................732 257-7942
Sergio Buzzerio, *President*
EMP: 17
SQ FT: 25,000
SALES (est): 3.9MM **Privately Held**
SIC: 2891 Adhesives

(G-2158)
MRC GLOBAL (US) INC
28 Kennedy Blvd Ste 100 (08816-1255)
PHONE..............................732 225-4005
EMP: 11
SALES (corp-wide): 4.5B **Publicly Held**
SIC: 1311 Crude Petroleum/Natural Gas
Production
HQ: Mrc Global (Us) Inc.
1301 Mckinney St Ste 2300
Houston TX 77010
877 294-7574

(G-2159)
NEWCO VALVES LLC
Also Called: Newmans
19a Cotters Ln (08816-2002)
PHONE..............................732 257-0300
Charlie Neter, *Branch Mgr*
EMP: 27 **Publicly Held**
WEB: www.newcovalves.com
SIC: 5085 3494 Industrial supplies; valves
& pipe fittings
HQ: Newco Valves, Llc
13127 Trinity Dr
Stafford TX 77477
281 325-0041

(G-2160)
NORTHEAST CHEMICALS INC (PA)
2 Tower Center Blvd (08816-1100)
P.O. Box 188, Milltown (08850-0188)
PHONE..............................508 634-6900
Jimmy W Hsu, *President*
Joe Busch, *Vice Pres*
Fred Borelli, *Shareholder*
▲ **EMP:** 22
SQ FT: 12,000
SALES (est): 32.2MM **Privately Held**
SIC: 2869 2819 5169 Industrial organic
chemicals; industrial inorganic chemicals;
industrial chemicals

(G-2161)
NORTHEAST CHEMICALS INC (PA)
2 Tower Center Blvd Fl 12 (08816-1100)
P.O. Box 188, Milltown (08850-0188)
PHONE..............................732 227-0100
Fred Borelli, *CEO*
Jimmy W Hsu, *President*
Joseph Busch, *Vice Pres*
Frank Russo, *CFO*
EMP: 28
SQ FT: 270,000
SALES: 32.2MM **Privately Held**
SIC: 2869 2819 5169 Industrial organic
chemicals; industrial inorganic chemicals;
industrial chemicals

(G-2162)
NORTHEAST CHEMICALS INC
7 Elkins Rd (08816-2006)
PHONE..............................732 673-6966
Jay Hsu, *Branch Mgr*
EMP: 12
SALES (corp-wide): 32.2MM **Privately Held**
SIC: 2869 2819 Industrial organic chemicals; industrial inorganic chemicals
PA: Northeast Chemicals, Inc.
2 Tower Center Blvd Fl 12
East Brunswick NJ 08816
732 227-0100

(G-2163)
PEPSI
Also Called: Pepsico
5 Lexington Ave (08816-5033)
PHONE..............................732 238-1598
Anne Hlinka, *Project Mgr*
William Warren, *Marketing Staff*
John Ledva, *Director*
EMP: 5
SALES (est): 242.2K **Privately Held**
SIC: 2086 Carbonated soft drinks, bottled
& canned

(G-2164)
PERL PIGMENTS LLC
400 Cotters Ln (08816)
P.O. Box 1223, Teaneck (07666-1223)
PHONE..............................201 836-1212
Allen Perl,
EMP: 6
SALES (est): 650K **Privately Held**
SIC: 3339 Zinc smelting (primary), including zinc residue

(G-2165)
PINNACLE MATERIALS INC (PA)
39 Edgeboro Rd (08816-1636)
P.O. Box 680, Monmouth Junction (08852-0680)
PHONE..............................732 254-7676
Christine Yakman, *President*
Christine Yackman, *Corp Secy*
David Boussmrski, *Project Mgr*
Toni Lynn Bronson, *Finance Mgr*
EMP: 41 EST: 1996
SQ FT: 20,000
SALES (est): 3.9MM **Privately Held**
WEB: www.pinnaclematerials.com
SIC: 1442 Construction sand & gravel

(G-2166)
POLYORGANIC TECHNOLIGIES CORP
26 Kennedy Blvd Ste C (08816-1260)
PHONE..............................609 288-8233
Charles F Bruno, *CEO*
Jay Bruno, *Partner*
Wayne J Nathan, *VP Sales*
▼ **EMP:** 6
SALES (est): 1.5MM **Privately Held**
SIC: 5169 2873 Organic chemicals, synthetic; fertilizers: natural (organic), except compost

(G-2167)
PREM-KHICHI ENTERPRISES INC
Also Called: Metalgraphics
9 Colburn Rd (08816-1102)
PHONE..............................973 242-0300
Peter Permar, *President*
EMP: 14
SQ FT: 20,000
SALES: 850K **Privately Held**
SIC: 3471 2851 Finishing, metals or
formed products; paints & allied products

(G-2168)
PRIME CODING SERVICES LLC
58 Frost Ave (08816-4509)
PHONE..............................732 254-3036
Flor Bajar, *Owner*
Sue Sahlin, *Technology*
Nick Addeo, *Director*
EMP: 8
SALES (est): 659.5K **Privately Held**
SIC: 2833 Codeine & derivatives

(G-2169)
PROHASKA & CO INC
34 Allwood Rd (08816-1349)
PHONE..............................732 238-3420
Bernie Prohaska, *President*
Yvonne Prohaska, *Treasurer*
EMP: 7
SQ FT: 1,000
SALES (est): 1MM **Privately Held**
WEB: www.prohaskaadvertising.com
SIC: 2752 7311 Commercial printing, lithographic; advertising agencies

(G-2170)
R H A AUDIO COMMUNICATIONS
Also Called: R H A Audio Communications
725 State Route 18 (08816-4933)
PHONE..............................732 257-9180
Robert Bielicki, *President*
EMP: 4 EST: 1971
SQ FT: 1,000
SALES: 600K **Privately Held**
SIC: 3663 Radio & TV communications
equipment

(G-2171)
RACEWAY PETROLEUM INC
114 Ryders Ln (08816-1336)
PHONE..............................732 729-7350
EMP: 7 **Privately Held**
SIC: 3644 Raceways
PA: Raceway Petroleum Inc
1411 Stelton Rd
Piscataway NJ 08854

(G-2172)
RACEWAY PETROLEUM INC
523 State Route 18 (08816-3044)
PHONE..............................732 613-4404
Pardeep Anand, *Manager*
Sandeep Prashar, *Supervisor*
EMP: 42 **Privately Held**
SIC: 5411 3644 Convenience stores, independent; raceways
PA: Raceway Petroleum Inc
1411 Stelton Rd
Piscataway NJ 08854

(G-2173)
RARITAN PHRMCTCALS INCOPORATED
8 Joanna Ct (08816-2108)
PHONE..............................732 238-1685
Vin Nayak, *President*
Sultan Reshamwala, *Vice Pres*
▲ **EMP:** 200
SQ FT: 260,000
SALES (est): 75.4MM **Privately Held**
WEB: www.raritanpharm.com
SIC: 2834 Druggists' preparations (pharmaceuticals)

(G-2174)
RP PRODUCTS LLC
Also Called: Wallscape
646 State Route 18 (08816-3722)
PHONE..............................732 254-4222
Ron Papaleo, *CFO*
Paul Dimaggio,
▲ **EMP:** 5
SALES (est): 491.5K **Privately Held**
SIC: 3069 Rubber floor coverings, mats &
wallcoverings

(G-2175)
SCREENED IMAGES INC
7 Joanna Ct Ste H (08816-2284)
PHONE..............................732 651-8181
Fred Moskiwitz, *President*
Stuart Weisenfeld, *Vice Pres*
EMP: 30
SQ FT: 35,000
SALES (est): 3MM
SALES (corp-wide): 1.1B **Publicly Held**
SIC: 2261 2262 2396 Screen printing of
cotton broadwoven fabrics; screen printing: manmade fiber & silk broadwoven
fabrics; automotive & apparel trimmings
HQ: Edge Inc Corporate
1440 Broadway Fl 22
New York NY 10018
212 279-7200

(G-2176)
SHOWTIME EXPRESS
5 Lexington Ave (08816-5033)
PHONE..............................732 238-2701
EMP: 4 EST: 2012
SALES (est): 330K **Privately Held**
SIC: 3537 Mfg Industrial Trucks/Tractors

(G-2177)
SIMPLY AMAZING LLC
233 State Route 18 Ste 22 (08816-1903)
PHONE..............................732 249-4151
Jane Jablons, *Branch Mgr*
EMP: 16
SALES (corp-wide): 48.6MM **Privately Held**
SIC: 3643 Outlets, electric: convenience
PA: Simply Amazing Llc
200 Performance Dr
Mahwah NJ 07495
201 529-3700

(G-2178)
SPICE CHAIN CORPORATION
35 Kimberly Rd (08816-2010)
PHONE..............................800 584-0422
EMP: 90 **Privately Held**
SIC: 2099 Food preparations
PA: Spice Chain Corporation
9 Elkins Rd
East Brunswick NJ 08816

(G-2179)
SPORTS IMPACT INC
52 Yorktown Rd (08816-3325)
PHONE..............................732 257-1451
Marc Groman, *Manager*
EMP: 5
SALES (corp-wide): 559K **Privately Held**
SIC: 2721 Magazines: publishing only, not
printed on site
PA: Sports Impact Inc
25 Winston Ln
Garrison NY 10524
914 232-8890

(G-2180)
STAR PHARMA INC
42 Devon Dr (08816-5331)
PHONE..............................718 466-1790
Krishna Chaluvadi, *CEO*
EMP: 6
SALES (est): 682.4K **Privately Held**
SIC: 2834 Pharmaceutical preparations

(G-2181)
STRIDES PHARMA INC
2 Tower Center Blvd # 1102 (08816-1100)
PHONE..............................609 773-5000
EMP: 5
SALES (corp-wide): 216.9MM **Privately Held**
SIC: 2834 Pharmaceutical preparations
HQ: Strides Pharma, Inc.
2 Tower Center Blvd # 1102
East Brunswick NJ 08816
609 773-5000

(G-2182)
STRIVE PHARMACEUTICALS INC (PA)
19 Lexington Ave (08816-5034)
PHONE..............................609 269-2001
Priyank Pandya, *Director*
EMP: 6
SALES (est): 10MM **Privately Held**
SIC: 2834 5122 Pharmaceutical preparations; pharmaceuticals

(G-2183)
SUPREME MANUFACTURING CO INC
5 Connerty Ct (08816-1633)
PHONE..............................732 254-0087
Clifford Krause, *President*
◆ **EMP:** 46
SQ FT: 19,000
SALES (est): 7.4MM **Privately Held**
WEB: www.supreme-mfg.com
SIC: 2086 Soft drinks: packaged in cans,
bottles, etc.

GEOGRAPHIC

(G-2184)
SUZIE MAC SPECIALTIES INC
3 Joanna Ct Ste C (08816-2283)
PHONE................................732 238-3500
Suzanne Macdougall, *President*
EMP: 20
SQ FT: 25,000
SALES (est): 1.6MM **Privately Held**
WEB: www.suziemac.com
SIC: 2752 7311 2396 Decals, litho-
graphed; advertising posters, litho-
graphed; calendars, lithographed;
advertising consultant; automotive & ap-
parel trimmings

(G-2185)
SV PHARMA INC
9 Autumn Ln (08816-5500)
PHONE................................732 651-1336
Purnachandra R Akkineni, *Principal*
EMP: 5 EST: 2010
SALES (est): 602.5K **Privately Held**
SIC: 2834 Pharmaceutical preparations

(G-2186)
TECKCHEK (PA)
77 Milltown Rd Ste C4 (08816-2302)
PHONE................................919 497-0136
William Mundell, *Principal*
Stephen Hutton, *Business Mgr*
EMP: 7
SALES (est): 1.9MM **Privately Held**
SIC: 2741 Miscellaneous publishing

(G-2187)
**TRIANGLE HOME FASHIONS
LLC**
Also Called: Lush Decor
120 Tices Ln (08816-2052)
PHONE................................732 355-9800
Jenny Zhu, *President*
Jared Cohen, *COO*
Allen Darwin, *Vice Pres*
Jeffrey Swartz, *Vice Pres*
▲ EMP: 7
SALES: 1.1MM **Privately Held**
SIC: 2392 5023 Sheets, fabric: made from
purchased materials; sheets, textile

(G-2188)
VAHL INC
34 Kennedy Blvd Ste 2 (08816-1261)
PHONE................................732 249-4042
Henry G Dieken, *President*
EMP: 48 EST: 1938
SQ FT: 42,000
SALES (est): 10.4MM **Privately Held**
SIC: 3728 Aircraft body assemblies &
parts; aircraft assemblies, subassemblies
& parts

(G-2189)
VANGUARD CONTAINER CORP
35 Cotters Ln Ste 1 (08816-2032)
PHONE................................732 651-9717
Edward Gunn, *President*
EMP: 40
SQ FT: 85,000
SALES (est): 4.6MM
SALES (corp-wide): 1.1B **Privately Held**
SIC: 3089 Plastic containers, except foam
HQ: Mauser-Werke Gmbh
Schildgesstr. 71-163
Bruhl 50321
223 278-1000

(G-2190)
VENDING TRUCKS INC
5 Litchfield Rd (08816-5036)
PHONE................................732 969-5400
Howard Seasonwein, *President*
Lambert Belandres, *Accounts Mgr*
Dean Neuman, *Accounts Mgr*
EMP: 25
SQ FT: 5,000
SALES (est): 5.5MM **Privately Held**
WEB: www.vendingtrucks.com
SIC: 8742 3711 Marketing consulting serv-
ices; automobile assembly, including spe-
cialty automobiles

(G-2191)
**VITAMIN RETAILER MAGAZINE
INC**
431 Cranbury Rd Ste C (08816-3698)
PHONE................................732 432-9600
Daniel McSweeney, *President*
Bryan Zak, *Production*
Megan Conway, *Adv Mgr*
Barry Young, *Advt Staff*
Gary Pfaff, *Manager*
EMP: 9
SALES (est): 1MM **Privately Held**
WEB: www.vitaminretailer.com
SIC: 2721 Magazines: publishing only, not
printed on site

East Hanover
Morris County

(G-2192)
201 FOOD PACKING INC
Also Called: Tree-Ripe Products
7 Great Meadow Ln (07936)
PHONE................................973 463-0777
Joel Fishman, *President*
▼ EMP: 15 EST: 1977
SQ FT: 12,000
SALES (est): 1.7MM **Privately Held**
SIC: 2087 Cocktail mixes, nonalcoholic

(G-2193)
**ALLIANCE TECHNOLOGIES
GROUP**
57 Eagle Rock Ave (07936-3169)
PHONE................................973 664-1151
Phil De Palma, *CEO*
Peter De Palma Jr, *President*
EMP: 6
SQ FT: 6,000
SALES: 1MM **Privately Held**
WEB: www.alliancetechnologies.biz
SIC: 3625 Relays & industrial controls

(G-2194)
ANUCO INC
911 Charles Dr Unit 3 (07936)
PHONE................................973 887-9465
Bob Nugent, *President*
Marion Nugent, *Corp Secy*
EMP: 10
SQ FT: 4,000
SALES (est): 1.3MM **Privately Held**
SIC: 2752 Commercial printing, offset

(G-2195)
**BAVELLE TECH SLTIONS LTD
LBLTY**
100 Eagle Rock Ave # 301 (07936-3149)
PHONE................................973 992-8086
Ester Rechter, *Office Mgr*
Oren David, *Mng Member*
EMP: 10
SALES (est): 209.9K **Privately Held**
SIC: 8748 7371 7372 7373 Systems en-
gineering consultant, ex. computer or pro-
fessional; custom computer programming
services; custom computer programming
services; application computer software;
systems engineering, computer related

(G-2196)
C & S TOOL CO
304 Ridgedale Ave (07936-2397)
PHONE................................973 887-6865
Robert Sadowski, *President*
John Sadowski, *Vice Pres*
EMP: 10
SQ FT: 3,300
SALES (est): 1MM **Privately Held**
WEB: www.cstool.com
SIC: 3599 3544 Machine shop, jobbing &
repair; special dies, tools, jigs & fixtures

(G-2197)
**CADBURY ADAMS USA LLC
(HQ)**
100 Deforest Ave (07936-2813)
PHONE................................973 503-2000
Matthew Shattock,
Trevor Bond,
Jim Cali,
Daniel Chung,

Bruce N Futterer,
▲ EMP: 32
SALES (est): 91.7MM **Publicly Held**
WEB: www.cadburyadams.com
SIC: 2064 2844 Candy & other confec-
tionery products; mouthwashes

(G-2198)
CALCULAGRAPH CO (PA)
Also Called: Control Products
280 Ridgedale Ave (07936-2302)
PHONE................................973 887-9400
Clifford W Moodie, *President*
William C Moodie Jr, *Chairman*
Peter Gagliardi, *Project Mgr*
Richard Glasson, *Chief Engr*
Nick Desalvia, *Engineer*
EMP: 59 EST: 1871
SQ FT: 30,000
SALES (est): 9.9MM **Privately Held**
WEB: www.cpi-nj.com
SIC: 3643 3822 Current-carrying wiring
devices; auto controls regulating residntl
& coml environmt & applncs

(G-2199)
CALCULAGRAPH CO
T/A Control Products
272 Ridgedale Ave 280 (07936-2393)
PHONE................................973 887-9400
Cliff Moodie, *Manager*
EMP: 50
SALES (corp-wide): 9.9MM **Privately
Held**
WEB: www.cpi-nj.com
SIC: 3643 Electric switches
PA: Calculagraph Co (Inc)
280 Ridgedale Ave
East Hanover NJ 07936
973 887-9400

(G-2200)
COHERENT INC
Also Called: Coherent Advnced Crystal Group
31 Farinella Dr (07936-2001)
PHONE................................973 240-6851
Dominic Loiacono, *General Mgr*
Daniel Rubbo, *Opers Staff*
Michael Kolesnikov, *Engineer*
Maryellen Wilson, *Director*
EMP: 68
SALES (corp-wide): 1.7B **Publicly Held**
SIC: 3679 3827 Electronic crystals; optical
instruments & lenses
PA: Coherent, Inc.
5100 Patrick Henry Dr
Santa Clara CA 95054
408 764-4000

(G-2201)
**COMPRELLI EQUIPMENT AND
SVC**
Also Called: Ces Fence
9 Brace Dr (07936-3023)
PHONE................................973 428-8687
Jeff Compralli, *President*
EMP: 8
SALES (est): 1.1MM **Privately Held**
SIC: 2499 Fencing, docks & other outdoor
wood structural products

(G-2202)
COMVERGE GIANTS INC (DH)
120 Eagle Rock Ave # 190 (07936-3158)
PHONE................................973 884-5970
Robert Chiste, *CEO*
Tom V Denoer, *Senior VP*
Leonardo Matute, *Engineer*
David Ford, *Human Res Mgr*
Todd St John, *Info Tech Mgr*
EMP: 1
SALES (est): 2.4MM
SALES (corp-wide): 2.3B **Publicly Held**
SIC: 3822 Hardware for environmental reg-
ulators

(G-2203)
CONTROL PRODUCTS INC
272 Ridgedale Ave 280 (07936-2304)
PHONE................................973 887-5000
Clifford W Moodie, *President*
William C Moodie Jr, *Chairman*
Angelo Digirolamo, *Controller*
Mary E Moodie, *Admin Sec*
EMP: 60
SQ FT: 30,000

SALES (est): 4.9MM
SALES (corp-wide): 9.9MM **Privately
Held**
WEB: www.controlproducts.com
SIC: 3829 Measuring & controlling devices
PA: Calculagraph Co (Inc)
280 Ridgedale Ave
East Hanover NJ 07936
973 887-9400

(G-2204)
**CRAFTSMEN PHOTO
LITHOGRAPHERS**
38 Beach St (07936-3505)
PHONE................................973 316-5791
Samuel J Newick, *President*
Ross P Newick, *Corp Secy*
Warren Newick, *Vice Pres*
EMP: 20 EST: 1947
SQ FT: 12,000
SALES (est): 2.4MM **Privately Held**
SIC: 2752 2791 2789 Commercial print-
ing, offset; photolithographic printing;
typesetting; bookbinding & related work

(G-2205)
DOS INDUSTRIAL SALES LLC
7d Great Meadow Ln (07936-1721)
PHONE................................973 887-7800
Justin Kuhn, *Director*
EMP: 4
SALES (est): 317.6K **Privately Held**
SIC: 3613 3444 Power connectors, elec-
tric; forming machine work, sheet metal

(G-2206)
**DRISCOLL LABEL COMPANY
INC**
19 West St (07936-2822)
PHONE................................973 585-7291
John Raguso Jr, *President*
EMP: 18 EST: 1971
SQ FT: 16,000
SALES (est): 1.8MM **Privately Held**
WEB: www.driscolllabel.com
SIC: 2759 Labels & seals: printing

(G-2207)
EDWARD BROWN
Also Called: Ebco Tool
8 Great Meadow Ln B (07936)
PHONE................................973 887-5255
Edward Brown, *Owner*
EMP: 4 EST: 1957
SQ FT: 3,600
SALES (est): 365.7K **Privately Held**
SIC: 3523 Barn, silo, poultry, dairy & live-
stock machinery

(G-2208)
**ELANA TILE CONTRACTORS
INC**
8 Merry Ln Ste B (07936-3938)
PHONE................................973 386-0991
Jeremia Padula, *President*
▲ EMP: 6
SQ FT: 5,600
SALES (est): 420K **Privately Held**
SIC: 1743 3281 Marble installation, inte-
rior; tile installation, ceramic; cut stone &
stone products

(G-2209)
FASTSIGNS
50 State Route 10 Ste 2 (07936-1015)
PHONE................................973 887-6700
Linda C Specht,
Scott S Specht,
EMP: 8
SQ FT: 2,000
SALES (est): 970.6K **Privately Held**
SIC: 3993 Signs & advertising specialties

(G-2210)
**FOUGERA PHARMACEUTICALS
INC**
Also Called: Pharmaderm
1 Health Plz (07936-1016)
PHONE................................973 514-4241
Qin Ren, *Vice Pres*
Cristian Pardo, *Sales Staff*
Brian Markison, *Branch Mgr*
EMP: 40

SALES (corp-wide): 51.9B **Privately Held**
WEB: www.altanapharma-us.com
SIC: 2834 Druggists' preparations (pharmaceuticals)
HQ: Fougera Pharmaceuticals Inc.
   60 Baylis Rd
   Melville NY 11747
   631 454-7677

(G-2211)
GENERAL METAL MANUFACTURING CO
Also Called: G M Fence Co
170 State Route 10 (07936-2107)
PHONE................................973 386-1818
Lee Rothfeld, *President*
▲ EMP: 20 EST: 1925
SQ FT: 27,000
SALES (est): 2.9MM **Privately Held**
WEB: www.gmfence.com
SIC: 2499 5031 3496 5039 Fencing, wood; fencing, wood; fencing, made from purchased wire; wire fence, gates & accessories

(G-2212)
GIVAUDAN FLAVORS CORPORATION
245 Merry Ln (07936-3900)
P.O. Box 560 (07936-0560)
PHONE................................973 386-9800
Joseph Fabbri, *Plant Mgr*
Thomas Kirsch, *Research*
Tracey Mara, *Human Resources*
Ron Gregory, *Info Tech Dir*
EMP: 185
SALES (corp-wide): 5.5B **Privately Held**
SIC: 2869 2087 Perfumes, flavorings & food additives; extracts, flavoring
HQ: Givaudan Flavors Corporation
   1199 Edison Dr
   Cincinnati OH 45216
   513 948-8000

(G-2213)
GIVAUDAN FRAGRANCES CORP
Also Called: Givaudan Flavors
245 Merry Ln (07936-3900)
PHONE................................973 386-9800
Dennis Mirda, *Manager*
Eileen Moyer, *Director*
Mark Rainey, *Director*
EMP: 200
SALES (corp-wide): 5.5B **Privately Held**
SIC: 2087 Flavoring extracts & syrups
HQ: Givaudan Fragrances Corporation
   1199 Edison Dr Ste 1-2
   Cincinnati OH 45216
   513 948-3428

(G-2214)
GIVAUDAN FRAGRANCES CORP
Also Called: Givaudan East
717 Ridgedale Ave (07936-3163)
PHONE................................973 576-9500
Abenaa Brew, *Research*
Sanjeev Bawa, *Business Anlyst*
Ezgi Todurge, *Marketing Staff*
John Vernieri, *Branch Mgr*
EMP: 138
SALES (corp-wide): 5.5B **Privately Held**
SIC: 2869 Industrial organic chemicals
HQ: Givaudan Fragrances Corporation
   1199 Edison Dr Ste 1-2
   Cincinnati OH 45216
   513 948-3428

(G-2215)
GIVAUDAN FRAGRANCES CORP
717 Ridgedale Ave (07936-3163)
PHONE................................973 560-1939
Jun Dizon, *Project Mgr*
Lisa Dahl, *Planning*
EMP: 138
SALES (corp-wide): 5.5B **Privately Held**
SIC: 2869 Perfume materials, synthetic
HQ: Givaudan Fragrances Corporation
   1199 Edison Dr Ste 1-2
   Cincinnati OH 45216
   513 948-3428

(G-2216)
GOLD STAR DISTRIBUTION LLC
Also Called: Goldstar Performance Products
120 Eagle Rock Ave # 326 (07936-3175)
PHONE................................973 882-5300

Steven Hankin,
EMP: 13
SQ FT: 1,200
SALES: 2MM **Privately Held**
SIC: 2023 Dietary supplements, dairy & non-dairy based

(G-2217)
INNOPHOS LLC
43 West St (07936-2822)
PHONE................................973 808-5900
Mindee Green,
EMP: 7
SALES (corp-wide): 801.8MM **Publicly Held**
SIC: 5149 2087 Health foods; flavoring extracts & syrups
HQ: Innophos, Llc
   259 Prospect Plains Rd A
   Cranbury NJ 08512
   609 495-2495

(G-2218)
IPSCO APOLLO PUNCH & DIE CORP
10 Great Meadow Ln (07936)
P.O. Box 252 (07936-0252)
PHONE................................973 884-0900
Claire Tulino, *President*
Robert Gaito, *Vice Pres*
EMP: 7
SQ FT: 20,000
SALES: 300K **Privately Held**
SIC: 3544 Punches, forming & stamping

(G-2219)
ITG BRANDS LLC
50 Williams Pkwy Ste B (07936-2110)
PHONE................................973 386-9087
Vincent Addona, *Branch Mgr*
EMP: 6
SALES (corp-wide): 38.9B **Privately Held**
SIC: 2121 Cigars
HQ: Itg Brands, Llc
   714 Green Valley Rd
   Greensboro NC 27408
   336 335-7000

(G-2220)
JETTRON PRODUCTS INC
56 State Route 10 (07936-1006)
P.O. Box 337 (07936-0337)
PHONE................................973 887-0571
Edward C Balzarotti, *President*
Lola R Balzarotti, *Corp Secy*
Ruth Mack, *Systems Dir*
Edward Balzarotti, *Info Tech Mgr*
EMP: 30 EST: 1959
SQ FT: 12,500
SALES (est): 2.6MM **Privately Held**
SIC: 3498 3679 Tube fabricating (contract bending & shaping); electronic circuits

(G-2221)
LANXESS SOLUTIONS US INC
Anderol Division
215 Merry Ln (07936-3900)
PHONE................................973 887-7411
Ernest Marcel, *Branch Mgr*
EMP: 150
SALES (corp-wide): 8.2B **Privately Held**
WEB: www.cromptoncorp.com
SIC: 2869 2992 Hydraulic fluids, synthetic base; lubricating oils & greases; oils & greases, blending & compounding
HQ: Lanxess Solutions Us Inc.
   2 Armstrong Rd Ste 101
   Shelton CT 06484
   203 573-2000

(G-2222)
MONDELEZ INTERNATIONAL INC
200 Deforest Ave (07936-2833)
PHONE................................973 503-2000
Scott Thomas, *Research*
Miguel Llanos, *Project Engr*
Christopher Wenda, *Sales Staff*
EMP: 25 **Publicly Held**
SIC: 2022 Imitation cheese
PA: Mondelez International, Inc.
   3 Parkway North Blvd # 300
   Deerfield IL 60015

(G-2223)
MOTIF INDUSTRIES INC
299 Ridgedale Ave Ste 5 (07936-2307)
PHONE................................973 575-1800
Eyal Elkayam, *President*
▲ EMP: 15
SQ FT: 10,000
SALES (est): 3.9MM **Privately Held**
WEB: www.motif-industries.com
SIC: 3851 3543 Eyeglasses, lenses & frames; industrial patterns

(G-2224)
NABISCO ROYAL ARGENTINA INC (HQ)
200 Deforest Ave (07936-2891)
P.O. Box 1944 (07936-1944)
PHONE................................973 503-2000
Beth Culligan, *President*
EMP: 7
SALES (est): 2.3MM **Publicly Held**
SIC: 2052 Biscuits, dry

(G-2225)
NEW ADVENTURES LLC
6 Deforest Ave Ste 7 (07936-2831)
PHONE................................973 884-8887
Beth Reiling, *Partner*
Joseph Reiling, *Partner*
▲ EMP: 5
SALES (est): 480K **Privately Held**
SIC: 3942 Dolls & stuffed toys

(G-2226)
NOVARTIS CORPORATION (DH)
1 S Ridgedale Ave (07936-3142)
PHONE................................212 307-1122
Christi Shaw, *Ch of Bd*
Stephanie Brown, *Vice Pres*
Thomas Fellers, *Vice Pres*
Denise Globe, *Vice Pres*
Caroline Adams, *Opers Staff*
◆ EMP: 30 EST: 1903
SALES (est): 49.4B
SALES (corp-wide): 51.9B **Privately Held**
WEB: www.novartis.com
SIC: 2879 2032 2865 2834 Agricultural chemicals; canned specialties; cyclic crudes & intermediates; drugs acting on the cardiovascular system, except diagnostic
HQ: Novartis International Ag
   Lichtstrasse 35
   Basel BS 4056
   613 241-111

(G-2227)
NOVARTIS CORPORATION
Also Called: Novartis Pharmaceuticals
1 Health Plz (07936-1016)
PHONE................................862 778-8300
Gabriel Galvan, *General Mgr*
Frederica Detakacsy, *Regional Mgr*
Leslie Fields, *Project Mgr*
Jack Saari, *Maint Spvr*
Ursula Knauf, *Opers Staff*
EMP: 56
SALES (corp-wide): 51.9B **Privately Held**
WEB: www.novartis.com
SIC: 2834 Pharmaceutical preparations
HQ: Novartis Corporation
   1 S Ridgedale Ave
   East Hanover NJ 07936
   212 307-1122

(G-2228)
NOVARTIS CORPORATION
59 State Route 10 (07936-1080)
PHONE................................973 503-7488
Joe Stein, *Manager*
Rajeev Hegde, *Info Tech Mgr*
Maryann Sauter, *Admin Asst*
EMP: 500
SALES (corp-wide): 51.9B **Privately Held**
WEB: www.novartis.com
SIC: 2834 Druggists' preparations (pharmaceuticals)
HQ: Novartis Corporation
   1 S Ridgedale Ave
   East Hanover NJ 07936
   212 307-1122

(G-2229)
NOVARTIS PHARMACEUTICALS CORP (DH)
Also Called: NPS
1 Health Plz (07936-1016)
P.O. Box 6656, Saint Louis MO (63125-0656)
PHONE................................862 778-8300
Marie-France Tschudin, *President*
Andre Wyss, *President*
Gerlinde Wussler, *Regional Mgr*
Alex Gorsky, *COO*
Robert Heinrich, *Vice Pres*
◆ EMP: 4600 EST: 1968
SALES: 49.4B
SALES (corp-wide): 51.9B **Privately Held**
WEB: www.pharma.us.novartis.com
SIC: 2834 Pharmaceutical preparations
HQ: Novartis Corporation
   1 S Ridgedale Ave
   East Hanover NJ 07936
   212 307-1122

(G-2230)
NOVARTIS PHARMACEUTICALS CORP
1 Health Plz (07936-1016)
PHONE................................862 778-8300
EMP: 6
SALES (corp-wide): 51.9B **Privately Held**
SIC: 3826 2834 Analytical instruments; pharmaceutical preparations
HQ: Novartis Pharmaceuticals Corporation
   1 Health Plz
   East Hanover NJ 07936
   862 778-8300

(G-2231)
NOVARTIS PHARMACEUTICALS CORP
1 S Ridgedale Ave (07936-3142)
PHONE................................862 778-8300
Paul Costa, *Principal*
Julie Kane, *Vice Pres*
David Eardley, *Opers Staff*
Daniel Rush, *Marketing Staff*
Athanasia Zarkadas, *Manager*
EMP: 9
SALES (corp-wide): 51.9B **Privately Held**
SIC: 2834 Pharmaceutical preparations
HQ: Novartis Pharmaceuticals Corporation
   1 Health Plz
   East Hanover NJ 07936
   862 778-8300

(G-2232)
NOVEL INGRDENT INV HLDINGS INC
72 Deforest Ave (07936-2811)
PHONE................................973 808-5900
EMP: 13
SALES (est): 51.9K
SALES (corp-wide): 801.8MM **Publicly Held**
SIC: 2833 Vitamins, natural or synthetic: bulk, uncompounded
PA: Innophos Holdings, Inc.
   259 Prospect Plains Rd A
   Cranbury NJ 08512
   609 495-2495

(G-2233)
NOVEL INGREDIENT HOLDINGS INC
72 Deforest Ave (07936-2811)
PHONE................................973 808-5900
EMP: 13
SALES (est): 38.3K
SALES (corp-wide): 801.8MM **Publicly Held**
SIC: 2833 Vitamins, natural or synthetic: bulk, uncompounded
PA: Innophos Holdings, Inc.
   259 Prospect Plains Rd A
   Cranbury NJ 08512
   609 495-2495

(G-2234)
PEGASUS GROUP PUBLISHING INC
188 State Route 10 Fl 2 (07936-2107)
PHONE................................973 884-9100
Bruce Warren, *President*
EMP: 12

SQ FT: 2,000
SALES (est): 900K **Privately Held**
SIC: 2731 Books: publishing & printing

(G-2235)
QUEST INTL FLAVORS FRAGRANCES
717 Ridgedale Ave (07936-3163)
PHONE........................973 576-9500
Damas Thoman, *President*
Ravi Waran, *Director*
◆ **EMP:** 450
SALES (est): 54.7MM
SALES (corp-wide): 5.5B **Privately Held**
SIC: 2844 5122 Toilet preparations; perfumes
HQ: Givaudan Fragrances Corporation
1199 Edison Dr Ste 1-2
Cincinnati OH 45216
513 948-3428

(G-2236)
RONED PRINTING & REPRODUCTION
6 Deforest Ave Ste 2 (07936-2831)
PHONE........................973 386-1848
Ron Russo, *President*
EMP: 5
SQ FT: 5,000
SALES (est): 450K **Privately Held**
WEB: www.roned.com
SIC: 2752 Commercial printing, offset

(G-2237)
SANDOZ INC
1 Health Plz (07936-1016)
PHONE........................862 778-8300
Christian Danis, *Vice Pres*
Oliver Esman, *Vice Pres*
Anthony Maffia, *Vice Pres*
Louis Schmukler, *Opers Mgr*
Martin Grubhofer, *Purchasing*
EMP: 528
SALES (corp-wide): 51.9B **Privately Held**
SIC: 2834 5122 Pharmaceutical preparations; drugs, proprietaries & sundries
HQ: Sandoz Inc.
100 College Rd W
Princeton NJ 08540
609 627-8500

(G-2238)
SEQIRUS INC
1 Health Plz Ste 310 (07936-1016)
PHONE........................919 577-5000
EMP: 5 **Privately Held**
SIC: 2836 Vaccines & other immunizing products
HQ: Seqirus Inc.
475 Green Oaks Pkwy
Holly Springs NC 27540
919 577-5000

(G-2239)
SIGNAL CRAFTERS TECH INC
57 Eagle Rock Ave (07936-3169)
PHONE........................973 781-0880
Al Vnencak, *President*
EMP: 5 **EST:** 1979
SQ FT: 6,000
SALES (est): 1MM **Privately Held**
WEB: www.signalcrafters.com
SIC: 3699 3825 Electronic training devices; test equipment for electronic & electrical circuits

(G-2240)
STATE ELECTRONICS PARTS CORP
36 State Route 10 Ste 6 (07936-1075)
P.O. Box 436 (07936-0436)
PHONE........................973 887-2550
Thomas Sutcliffe, *President*
Tom Russin, *Finance Mgr*
Dave Reed, *Sales Executive*
▼ **EMP:** 20 **EST:** 1956
SQ FT: 10,000
SALES (est): 3.7MM **Privately Held**
WEB: www.state-elec.com
SIC: 3676 5065 Electronic resistors; electronic parts

(G-2241)
THERMO X-PRESS PRINTING LLC
12d Great Meadow Ln (07936-1705)
PHONE........................973 585-6505
Stephen Stringas, *President*
EMP: 7 **EST:** 2010
SALES (est): 543.6K **Privately Held**
SIC: 5111 2752 Printing & writing paper; commercial printing, lithographic

(G-2242)
TITANIUM INDUSTRIES INC
64 State Route 10 (07936-1006)
PHONE........................973 428-1900
Bob Reilly, *Principal*
EMP: 7
SALES (est): 640.1K **Privately Held**
SIC: 3356 Titanium

(G-2243)
TRIM BRUSH COMPANY INC
22 Littell Rd Bldg 1 (07936-1002)
PHONE........................973 887-2525
Bruce M Carton, *President*
Diane M Carton, *Corp Secy*
EMP: 6
SQ FT: 15,000
SALES (est): 840K **Privately Held**
SIC: 5087 2842 Cleaning & maintenance equipment & supplies; cleaning or polishing preparations

(G-2244)
UNDERCOVER CHOCOLATE CO LLC
50 Williams Pkwy Ste B2 (07936-2110)
PHONE........................973 668-5000
EMP: 5
SALES (est): 286.1K **Privately Held**
SIC: 2066 Chocolate

(G-2245)
VISCOT MEDICAL LLC (PA)
32 West St (07936-2822)
P.O. Box 351 (07936-0351)
PHONE........................973 887-9273
Gary J Pieringer, *President*
Ann Pieringer, *Vice Pres*
◆ **EMP:** 35 **EST:** 1974
SQ FT: 10,000
SALES (est): 7.3MM **Privately Held**
SIC: 3841 3843 Surgical & medical instruments; dental equipment & supplies

(G-2246)
WEISS-AUG CO INC (PA)
220 Merry Ln (07936-3921)
PHONE........................973 887-7600
Dieter Weissenrieder, *President*
Brad Bennis, *Business Mgr*
Dan Lindsay, *Business Mgr*
Nick Poreman, *Business Mgr*
Pablo Villarreal, *Business Mgr*
▲ **EMP:** 164
SQ FT: 97,000
SALES (est): 36.6MM **Privately Held**
WEB: www.weiss-aug.com
SIC: 3089 3469 Injection molding of plastics; stamping metal for the trade

(G-2247)
WIN-TECH PRECISION PRODUCTS
5a Littell Rd (07936-1027)
PHONE........................973 887-8727
Rashmika Patel, *President*
▲ **EMP:** 4
SQ FT: 2,000
SALES (est): 606.5K **Privately Held**
SIC: 3599 Machine shop, jobbing & repair

(G-2248)
YARDE METALS INC
603 Murray Rd (07936-2201)
PHONE........................973 463-1166
Bryan Doherty, *Manager*
EMP: 27
SALES (corp-wide): 11.5B **Publicly Held**
WEB: www.yarde.com
SIC: 3312 3353 Stainless steel; foil, aluminum

HQ: Yarde Metals, Inc.
350 S Grand Ave Ste 5100
Los Angeles CA 90071
860 406-6061

(G-2249)
ZINAS SALADS INC
11 Great Meadow Ln (07936-1703)
PHONE........................973 428-0660
Zina Shaknovich, *President*
Ruth Sigman, *Treasurer*
William Horstman, *Admin Sec*
EMP: 22
SQ FT: 8,000
SALES (est): 4MM **Privately Held**
SIC: 2099 Salads, fresh or refrigerated

(G-2250)
ZYMET INC
7 Great Meadow Ln (07936)
PHONE........................973 428-5245
Karl I Loh, *President*
Sam Ringel, *Vice Pres*
Keith Lamb, *Research*
Edward Ibe, *Technical Staff*
Jay Parton, *Admin Sec*
EMP: 10
SQ FT: 8,000
SALES (est): 1.8MM **Privately Held**
SIC: 2891 Adhesives

East Orange
Essex County

(G-2251)
CROSS COUNTER INC (PA)
200 Freeway Dr E (07018-3809)
PHONE........................973 677-0600
Nancy Canavan, *Principal*
EMP: 4
SALES (est): 1.2MM **Privately Held**
SIC: 3131 Counters

(G-2252)
I K CONSTRUCTION INC
174 Evergreen Pl 805 (07018-2001)
P.O. Box 944, South Orange (07079-0944)
PHONE........................908 925-5200
Ian Katwaroo, *President*
EMP: 20
SQ FT: 2,188
SALES (est): 4.4MM **Privately Held**
SIC: 3441 Fabricated structural metal

(G-2253)
JORGENSEN CARR LTD
45 Glenwood Pl (07017-3013)
PHONE........................201 792-2278
Michael Jorgensen, *President*
Kenneth Carr, *Partner*
EMP: 5
SALES: 700K **Privately Held**
SIC: 1751 2499 Cabinet building & installation; decorative wood & woodwork

(G-2254)
JUST US BOOKS INC
356 Glenwood Ave Ste 7a (07017-3010)
PHONE........................973 672-7701
Wade Hudson, *President*
Cheryl Willis Hudson, *Vice Pres*
▲ **EMP:** 4
SQ FT: 600
SALES: 2MM **Privately Held**
WEB: www.cherylwhudson.com
SIC: 2731 Books: publishing only

(G-2255)
KMBA FASHIONS INC
272 Elmwood Ave Bldg 3 (07018-1802)
PHONE........................973 789-1652
William Cotton Jr, *President*
Andre Wilson, *Vice Pres*
Craig Jones, *Treasurer*
Ronald Parker, *Admin Sec*
EMP: 6
SALES: 25K **Privately Held**
WEB: www.kmbafashions.com
SIC: 2329 2339 Men's & boys' sportswear & athletic clothing; athletic clothing: women's, misses' & juniors'

(G-2256)
NEWARK AUTO TOP CO INC
Also Called: Newark Auto Products
23 Centerway (07017-5354)
P.O. Box 4365 (07019-4365)
PHONE........................973 677-9935
Benjamin Hershkowitz, *Ch of Bd*
EMP: 10 **EST:** 1907
SQ FT: 30,000
SALES (est): 1.5MM **Privately Held**
SIC: 2273 5013 2396 3714 Automobile floor coverings, except rubber or plastic; automotive trim; automotive trimmings, fabric; motor vehicle parts & accessories; synthetic rubber

(G-2257)
PARAMOUNT BAKERIES INC
18-28 Springdale Ave (07019)
PHONE........................973 482-6638
Fernando Frazao, *Manager*
EMP: 4
SALES (corp-wide): 10.8MM **Privately Held**
SIC: 2051 Bread, cake & related products
PA: Paramount Bakeries Inc.
61 Davenport Ave
Newark NJ 07107
973 482-6638

(G-2258)
PARAMOUNT WIRE CO INC
2-8 Central Ave (07018-3912)
PHONE........................973 672-0500
Charles B Coates, *President*
Robert Coates, *Corp Secy*
Marilyn Bergman, *Vice Pres*
▲ **EMP:** 35 **EST:** 1929
SQ FT: 1,000
SALES (est): 2.9MM **Privately Held**
SIC: 3357 Nonferrous wiredrawing & insulating

(G-2259)
PELCO PACKAGING CORPORATION
545 N Arlington Ave Ste 7 (07017-4005)
P.O. Box 196, Stirling (07980-0196)
PHONE........................973 675-4994
Arthur J Brinker, *President*
▲ **EMP:** 15 **EST:** 1949
SQ FT: 20,000
SALES (est): 1.3MM
SALES (corp-wide): 3.2MM **Privately Held**
WEB: www.pelcopackaging.com
SIC: 3089 Plastic containers, except foam
PA: Engineered Plastic Products, Inc.
269 Mercer St
Stirling NJ 07980
908 647-3500

(G-2260)
PRINTING DELITE INC
279 To 281 Sanford St (07018)
PHONE........................973 676-3033
Phillipe Gomez, *President*
EMP: 6
SQ FT: 2,800
SALES (est): 822K **Privately Held**
SIC: 2752 2791 Commercial printing, offset; typesetting

(G-2261)
QUALLIS BRANDS LLC
211 Glenwood Ave (07017-2009)
PHONE........................862 252-0664
Calvin Quallis,
EMP: 5
SALES (est): 323K **Privately Held**
SIC: 3999 7389 Barber & beauty shop equipment

(G-2262)
SCI-BORE INC
364 Glenwood Ave Ste 8c (07017-3006)
PHONE........................973 414-9001
Fax: 973 414-9003
EMP: 7
SQ FT: 2,000
SALES: 602.1K **Privately Held**
SIC: 3677 Mfg Machine Parts

(G-2263)
SHEARMAN CABINETS
195 N Munn Ave (07017-4206)
PHONE.....................................973 677-0071
Thomas Shearman, *Owner*
Mark Shearman, *Co-Owner*
EMP: 8
SALES (est): 702.4K **Privately Held**
SIC: 2434 Wood kitchen cabinets

(G-2264)
TAYLOR WINDOWS INC
Also Called: Taylor Window Factory
61 Central Ave (07018-3908)
PHONE.....................................973 672-3000
Pat Di Gravina, *President*
EMP: 10
SQ FT: 20,000
SALES (est): 880K **Privately Held**
SIC: 3442 Storm doors or windows, metal

(G-2265)
**TECHNICAL AIDS TO
INDEPENDENCE**
219 S 18th St Unit 2 (07018-3902)
PHONE.....................................973 674-1082
Allan Fenton, *President*
Elfreida Fenton, *Corp Secy*
John Fenton, *Vice Pres*
EMP: 11
SQ FT: 80,000
SALES (est): 1.7MM **Privately Held**
WEB: www.techaids.com
SIC: 3672 Printed circuit boards

(G-2266)
**TOKEN TORCH LTD LIABILITY
CO**
3 Hudson Ave (07018-2309)
PHONE.....................................973 629-1805
Bertha Tyson,
Joshua Tyson,
EMP: 11 EST: 2007
SALES (est): 650K **Privately Held**
SIC: 2741 Miscellaneous publishing

(G-2267)
WATER ON TIME BOTTLED
59 N 14th St (07017-5112)
PHONE.....................................862 252-9798
EMP: 5 EST: 2015
SALES (est): 179.2K **Privately Held**
SIC: 2086 Water, pasteurized: packaged in
cans, bottles, etc.

East Rutherford
Bergen County

(G-2268)
A & S FROZEN INC
Also Called: Caravan Products
96 E Union Ave (07073-2125)
PHONE.....................................201 672-0510
John Stone, *President*
EMP: 50
SALES (est): 6.4MM **Privately Held**
SIC: 2041 2053 Doughs, frozen or refrig-
erated; frozen bakery products, except
bread

(G-2269)
ALPINE GROUP INC (PA)
1 Meadowlands Plz Ste 800 (07073-2152)
PHONE.....................................201 549-4400
Steven S Elbaum, *Ch of Bd*
K Mitchell Posner, *Exec VP*
Stewart H Wahrsager, *Senior VP*
Dana Sidur, *Vice Pres*
Corey Teague, *Vice Pres*
EMP: 410
SQ FT: 5,900
SALES (est): 45.5MM **Privately Held**
SIC: 2821 3496 Plastics materials &
resins; cable, uninsulated wire: made
from purchased wire

(G-2270)
AMBER ROAD INC (HQ)
1 Meadowlands Plz # 1500 (07073-2151)
PHONE.....................................201 935-8588
James W Preuninger, *CEO*
Barry M V Williams, *Ch of Bd*

Kae-Por Chang, *Managing Dir*
Albert C Cooke III, *Senior VP*
Brad Hoffman, *Vice Pres*
EMP: 143
SQ FT: 11,000
SALES: 85.1MM
SALES (corp-wide): 148.5MM **Privately
Held**
WEB: www.managementdynamics.com
SIC: 7372 Business oriented computer
software
PA: E2open, Llc
9600 Great Hills Trl 300e
Austin TX 78759
866 432-6736

(G-2271)
APPETIZERS MADE EASY INC
Also Called: Joseph Epstein Food Entps
25 Branca Rd Ste B (07073-2169)
PHONE.....................................201 531-1212
Matt Brown, *President*
Karen Wolf, *Vice Pres*
Lewis Ochs, *CFO*
EMP: 25
SQ FT: 5,500
SALES (est): 7.9MM **Privately Held**
WEB: www.horsdoeuvresunlimited.com
SIC: 2038 Frozen specialties

(G-2272)
**ART MOLD & TOOL
CORPORATION**
742 Paterson Ave (07073-1028)
PHONE.....................................201 935-3377
Ted Ura, *President*
Mark Ura, *Admin Sec*
EMP: 9
SQ FT: 6,500
SALES (est): 680K **Privately Held**
WEB: www.artmarkmold.com
SIC: 3544 Industrial molds

(G-2273)
ARTHUR A KAPLAN CO INC
Also Called: Galaxy of Graphics
30 Murray Hill Pkwy # 300 (07073-2181)
PHONE.....................................201 806-2100
Arthur A Kaplan, *CEO*
Reid Alan Fader, *President*
Ellen Fader, *Corp Secy*
EMP: 30 EST: 1956
SQ FT: 30,000
SALES (est): 2.5MM **Privately Held**
SIC: 2741 2621 Art copy: publishing only,
not printed on site; poster & art papers

(G-2274)
ATEKSIS USA CORP (HQ)
1 Meadowlands Plz Ste 200 (07073-2152)
PHONE.....................................646 508-9074
Mehmet Kis, *President*
Emhra Gurpinar, *Vice Pres*
EMP: 4
SALES: 933K
SALES (corp-wide): 2.7MM **Privately
Held**
SIC: 3674 Integrated circuits, semiconduc-
tor networks, etc.
PA: Ateksis Profesyonel Ses Ve Goruntu
Sistemleri Sanayi Ve Ticaret Limited
Sirketi
Bayraktar Bulvari, No:34 Serifali Ma-
hallesi
Istanbul (Anatolia) 34775
216 425-9966

(G-2275)
BEACUT ABRASIVES CORP
788 Paterson Ave (07073-1030)
PHONE.....................................973 249-1420
Vladimir Smilovic, *President*
▲ EMP: 11
SQ FT: 6,000
SALES (est): 3.4MM **Privately Held**
WEB: www.beacutabrasives.com
SIC: 5085 3291 Abrasives; abrasive prod-
ucts

(G-2276)
**BERGEN INTERNATIONAL LLC
(PA)**
196 Paterson Ave Ste 202 (07073-1841)
PHONE.....................................201 299-4499
Dick Leahy, *CEO*
Dennis Keane, *President*

Richard Long, *CFO*
Ashley Barfield, *Admin Asst*
EMP: 7 EST: 1998
SALES (est): 4.6MM **Privately Held**
WEB: www.bergeninternational.com
SIC: 2899 Foam charge mixtures

(G-2277)
BIG APPLE JEWELRY MFG
62 Railroad Ave (07073-2008)
PHONE.....................................201 531-1600
Albert Sirazi, *President*
EMP: 7
SQ FT: 1,500
SALES (est): 979.5K **Privately Held**
SIC: 3911 Jewelry, precious metal

(G-2278)
BLOOMFIELD DRAPERY CO INC
948 Paterson Ave Ste A (07073-1062)
PHONE.....................................973 777-3566
Steven Gold, *President*
Madeline Gold, *Vice Pres*
EMP: 11 EST: 1934
SQ FT: 5,000
SALES (est): 1.4MM **Privately Held**
SIC: 2391 Curtains, window: made from
purchased materials; draperies, plastic &
textile: from purchased materials

(G-2279)
BRABANTIA USA INC
20 Murray Hill Pkwy # 260 (07073-2182)
PHONE.....................................201 933-3192
Nicole Gnudi, *Managing Dir*
Huub Der Kinderen, *Project Mgr*
Thijs Cremers, *Business Anlyst*
Judith Paulussen, *Marketing Staff*
Bart Van Elderen, *Manager*
▲ EMP: 10
SALES (est): 1.4MM
SALES (corp-wide): 126.7MM **Privately
Held**
SIC: 3634 Housewares, excluding cooking
appliances & utensils
HQ: Bis International Holding B.V.
De Haak 14
Valkenswaard 5555
402 282-222

(G-2280)
BYLADA FOODS LLC
1 Branca Rd (07073-2121)
PHONE.....................................201 933-7474
EMP: 11
SALES (corp-wide): 9.4MM **Privately
Held**
SIC: 2099 Food preparations
PA: Bylada Foods Llc
140 W Commercial Ave
Moonachie NJ 07074
201 933-7474

(G-2281)
C Q CORPORATION
480 Paterson Ave (07073-1281)
PHONE.....................................201 935-8488
EMP: 15 EST: 1975
SQ FT: 65,000
SALES (est): 2MM **Privately Held**
SIC: 2396 7336 3953 Mfg Auto/Apparel
Trimming Commercial Art/Graphic Design
Mfg Marking Devices

(G-2282)
CAMBREX CORPORATION (PA)
1 Meadowlands Plz # 1510 (07073-2214)
PHONE.....................................201 804-3000
Shlomo Yanai, *Ch of Bd*
Steven M Klosk, *President*
Bruno Biscaro, *President*
Simon Edwards, *President*
Joe Nettleton, *President*
EMP: 122
SALES: 532MM **Publicly Held**
WEB: www.cambrex.com
SIC: 2834 Pharmaceutical preparations;
drugs acting on the respiratory system;
drugs acting on the gastrointestinal or
genitourinary system; drugs acting on the
central nervous system & sense organs

(G-2283)
CAPITOL FOAM PRODUCTS INC
75 E Union Ave (07073-2127)
P.O. Box 7564 (07073-7564)
PHONE.....................................201 933-5277
Bart A Krupp, *President*
Isodoro Lerea, *Vice Pres*
Mike Pazar, *Plant Engr*
Paulette Nedrow, *Controller*
Fred Krupp, *Shareholder*
EMP: 45 EST: 1966
SQ FT: 90,000
SALES (est): 8MM **Privately Held**
WEB: www.capitolfoamproducts.com
SIC: 3086 Plastics foam products

(G-2284)
CARAVAN INGREDIENTS INC
96 E Union Ave (07073-2125)
PHONE.....................................201 672-0510
EMP: 32
SALES (corp-wide): 1B **Privately Held**
SIC: 2099 Food preparations
HQ: Caravan Ingredients Inc.
8250 Flint St
Lenexa KS 66214
913 890-5500

(G-2285)
DAWN BIBLE STUDENTS ASSN
Also Called: Gleeson Agency
199 Railroad Ave (07073-1915)
PHONE.....................................201 438-6421
Kenneth Fernets, *Manager*
EMP: 6 EST: 1932
SQ FT: 15,000
SALES: 357.6K **Privately Held**
SIC: 2731 7922 Pamphlets: publishing &
printing; books: publishing & printing;
radio producers; television program, in-
cluding commercial producers

(G-2286)
ENER-G RUDOX INC
180 E Union Ave (07073-2124)
P.O. Box 467, Carlstadt (07072-0467)
PHONE.....................................201 438-0111
Alan Barlow, *CEO*
Ryan Goodman, *President*
David Suarez, *Vice Pres*
Angela Cont, *Project Mgr*
Salvador Ulloa, *Engineer*
▲ EMP: 39
SALES (est): 11MM **Privately Held**
SIC: 3585 Heating & air conditioning com-
bination units; heating equipment, com-
plete
HQ: Ener-G Cogen International Limited
Millstream Maidenhead Road
Windsor BERKS

(G-2287)
**EVOQUA WATER
TECHNOLOGIES LLC**
20 Murray Hill Pkwy # 140 (07073-2182)
PHONE.....................................201 531-9338
Mark Cardaci, *Principal*
Mevlut Colak, *Engineer*
EMP: 12
SALES (corp-wide): 1.3B **Publicly Held**
SIC: 3589 8731 Water filters & softeners,
household type; commercial physical re-
search
HQ: Evoqua Water Technologies Llc
210 6th Ave Ste 3300
Pittsburgh PA 15222
724 772-0044

(G-2288)
**FEDEX OFFICE & PRINT SVCS
INC**
120 Route 17 (07073-2104)
PHONE.....................................201 672-0508
EMP: 7
SALES (corp-wide): 69.6B **Publicly Held**
WEB: www.kinkos.com
SIC: 2759 7334 Commercial printing; pho-
tocopying & duplicating services
HQ: Fedex Office And Print Services, Inc.
7900 Legacy Dr
Plano TX 75024
800 463-3339

(G-2289)
FLORAL GLASS INDUSTRIES INC
99 Murray Hill Pkwy # 10 (07073-2205)
PHONE.....................................201 939-4600
Charles Kaplanek Jr, *President*
Paul Bieber, *Exec VP*
Stanley Lane, *CFO*
EMP: 26
SQ FT: 40,000
SALES (est): 4.1MM **Privately Held**
SIC: 5039 3211 5023 Glass construction materials; flat glass; home furnishings

(G-2290)
FXI INC
Also Called: Foamex
13 Manor Rd (07073-2119)
PHONE.....................................201 933-8540
Jim Darcy, *Manager*
EMP: 65 **Privately Held**
SIC: 3086 Packaging & shipping materials, foamed plastic
HQ: Fxi, Inc.
1400 N Providence Rd # 2000
Media PA 19063

(G-2291)
HELIDEX LLC
Also Called: Helidex Offshore
186 Paterson Ave Ste 303 (07073-1837)
PHONE.....................................201 636-2546
Chawki Benteftifa, *President*
Sid Benteftifa, *General Mgr*
Charles Becht,
◆ EMP: 6
SQ FT: 2,500
SALES (est): 1.2MM **Privately Held**
SIC: 3334 3449 8711 3441 Primary aluminum; landing mats, aircraft: metal; engineering services; fabricated structural metal

(G-2292)
HUDSON GROUP (HG) INC (HQ)
1 Meadowlands Plz (07073-2150)
PHONE.....................................201 939-5050
Joseph Didomizio, *President*
Brian Berkner, *President*
Alan Kessler, *President*
Joseph Landolfi, *President*
Anita Booe, *Partner*
▲ EMP: 277
SQ FT: 20,000
SALES (est): 1.5B
SALES (corp-wide): 8.7B **Privately Held**
SIC: 2731 Book publishing
PA: Dufry Ag
Brunngasslein 12
Basel BS 4052
612 664-444

(G-2293)
KANSAI SPECIAL AMERCN MCH CORP
Also Called: Kansai Special USA
1 Madison St Ste F11 (07073-1605)
PHONE.....................................973 470-8321
Chester Hadyka, *Manager*
▲ EMP: 4
SALES (est): 476K **Privately Held**
SIC: 3559 Sewing machines & attachments, industrial
PA: Morimoto Mfg.Co.,Ltd.
1-4-17, Suna
Shijonawate OSK 575-0

(G-2294)
KLEIN USA INC
1 Madison St Ste F (07073-1605)
PHONE.....................................973 246-8181
Tim Mayhew, *Sales Staff*
Jesse Sevol, *Manager*
▲ EMP: 12
SALES (est): 1.5MM
SALES (corp-wide): 723.3K **Privately Held**
SIC: 3231 Doors, glass: made from purchased glass
HQ: Klein Iberica Sau
Poligono Industrial Can Cuias (Cr N-150 Km 1), Edif. Klein
Montcada I Reixac 08110
935 751-010

(G-2295)
LINK COLOR NA INC
23c Poplar St (07073-1208)
PHONE.....................................201 438-8222
Opher Hakem, *Owner*
▲ EMP: 6
SALES (est): 280K **Privately Held**
WEB: www.linkcolorna.com
SIC: 2754 Color printing, gravure

(G-2296)
LINOLEUM SALES COMPANY INC
135 Park Ave (07073-1819)
PHONE.....................................201 438-1844
Jeffrey Davidson, *President*
Gregory Davidson, *Vice Pres*
EMP: 4
SQ FT: 2,000
SALES: 500K **Privately Held**
SIC: 3069 Flooring, rubber: tile or sheet; balls, rubber; bath sprays, rubber

(G-2297)
LO GATTO BOOKBINDING
390 Paterson Ave (07073-1339)
P.O. Box 7483 (07073-7483)
PHONE.....................................201 438-4344
Medo Lo Gatto, *President*
Michael Lo Gatto, *Treasurer*
Elisa Lo Gatto, *Admin Sec*
EMP: 6 EST: 1967
SQ FT: 4,000
SALES (est): 747.1K **Privately Held**
WEB: www.mtvncontractor.com
SIC: 2789 Binding only: books, pamphlets, magazines, etc.; gold stamping on books

(G-2298)
LUMISCOPE CO INC
33 Whelan Rd (07073-2122)
PHONE.....................................678 291-3207
Allen J Beeber, *Ch of Bd*
Marc Bernstein, *President*
▲ EMP: 60
SQ FT: 35,000
SALES (est): 8.7MM **Privately Held**
WEB: www.lumiscope.net
SIC: 3841 5047 3842 3829 Surgical & medical instruments; surgical equipment & supplies; electro-medical equipment; diagnostic equipment, medical; surgical appliances & supplies; measuring & controlling devices

(G-2299)
MAMAMANCINIS HOLDINGS INC (PA)
25 Branca Rd (07073-2161)
PHONE.....................................201 532-1212
Carl Wolf, *Ch of Bd*
Matthew Brown, *President*
Allan Sabatier, *Vice Pres*
Lawrence Morgenstein, *CFO*
EMP: 3
SQ FT: 24,213
SALES: 28.5MM **Publicly Held**
SIC: 2011 2015 2035 2013 Meat packing plants; beef products from beef slaughtered on site; sausages from meat slaughtered on site; turkey, processed: frozen; seasonings & sauces, except tomato & dry; frozen meats from purchased meat

(G-2300)
MARIJON DYEING & FINISHING CO
219 Murray Hill Pkwy (07073-2114)
PHONE.....................................201 933-9770
Frank J Mummolo, *President*
John Grimaldi, *CFO*
Kim Blanco, *Human Res Dir*
EMP: 184 EST: 1954
SQ FT: 100,000
SALES (est): 10.2MM **Privately Held**
SIC: 2262 Finishing plants, manmade fiber & silk fabrics

(G-2301)
MCGONEGAL MANUFACTURING CO
Also Called: Themac
405 Railroad Ave (07073-1747)
P.O. Box 444 (07073-0444)
PHONE.....................................201 438-2313
Joseph Cremona, *President*
Fran Lundy, *Admin Sec*
EMP: 5
SQ FT: 5,500
SALES: 300K **Privately Held**
SIC: 3541 Grinding machines, metalworking

(G-2302)
METROPOLITAN MANUFACTURING INC
450 Murray Hill Pkwy (07073-2145)
PHONE.....................................201 933-8111
Anthony Terrigno, *President*
Sara Salguero, *Officer*
▲ EMP: 60
SQ FT: 40,000
SALES (est): 4.8MM **Privately Held**
SIC: 2331 2335 2337 2339 Women's & misses' blouses & shirts; women's, juniors' & misses' dresses; women's & misses' suits & coats; women's & misses' outerwear

(G-2303)
MG DECOR LLC
100 Schindler Ct Apt 308 (07073-2185)
PHONE.....................................201 923-5493
Madz Gill, *Mng Member*
Ajeeth Sharma,
▲ EMP: 11 EST: 2015
SALES (est): 722.8K **Privately Held**
SIC: 3229 Christmas tree ornaments, from glass produced on-site

(G-2304)
MIL-COMM PRODUCTS COMPANY INC
2 Carlton Ave Ste C (07073-1646)
PHONE.....................................201 935-8561
Frances J Furlong, *Ch of Bd*
R Gordon Furlong, *President*
Wendy Servilio, *Business Mgr*
John Scheld, *CTO*
EMP: 10
SQ FT: 22,000
SALES (est): 1.6MM **Privately Held**
WEB: www.mil-comm.com
SIC: 2992 Lubricating oils

(G-2305)
MUSHROOM WISDOM INC
1 Madison St Ste F6 (07073-1605)
PHONE.....................................973 470-0010
Masaki Shirota, *President*
Meagan McLaughlin, *Accountant*
John Lopez, *Sales Mgr*
Martin Agurto, *Manager*
▲ EMP: 11
SQ FT: 5,000
SALES (est): 1.8MM **Privately Held**
WEB: www.maitake.com
SIC: 2099 2032 Food preparations; canned specialties

(G-2306)
NATURAL WIRELESS LLC
23a Poplar St (07073-1208)
PHONE.....................................201 438-2865
Dror Shuchman, *Mng Member*
Ralph Hayon,
▲ EMP: 42
SQ FT: 4,000
SALES (est): 10.7MM **Privately Held**
SIC: 3663 Radio & TV communications equipment

(G-2307)
ORACLE AMERICA INC
1 Meadowlands Plz Ste 700 (07073-2153)
PHONE.....................................609 750-0640
EMP: 58
SALES (corp-wide): 39.8B **Publicly Held**
SIC: 7372 Prepackaged Software Services
HQ: Oracle America, Inc.
500 Oracle Pkwy
Redwood City CA 94065
650 506-7000

(G-2308)
ORACLE CORPORATION
1 Meadowlands Plz # 1400 (07073-2150)
PHONE.....................................201 842-7000
Harshivl Shah, *Sales Staff*
Aj Andrews, *Branch Mgr*
Fong Hui, *Technical Staff*
Eleanor Wenzke, *Technical Staff*
EMP: 302
SALES (corp-wide): 39.5B **Publicly Held**
SIC: 7372 Business oriented computer software
PA: Oracle Corporation
500 Oracle Pkwy
Redwood City CA 94065
650 506-7000

(G-2309)
PANTHERA DENTAL INC
1 Meadowlands Plz Ste 200 (07073-2152)
PHONE.....................................201 340-2766
Gabriel Robichaud, *CEO*
Bernard Robichaud, *Vice Pres*
David Solomon, *VP Sales*
EMP: 9
SALES (est): 402.3K **Privately Held**
SIC: 3843 Dental equipment & supplies

(G-2310)
PMC INC
Also Called: General Foam
13 Manor Rd (07073-2119)
PHONE.....................................201 933-8540
James Darcy, *Manager*
EMP: 273
SQ FT: 200,000
SALES (corp-wide): 2.5B **Privately Held**
SIC: 3086 Plastics foam products
HQ: Pmc, Inc.
12243 Branford St
Sun Valley CA 91352
818 896-1101

(G-2311)
PRESTIGE LABORATORIES INC
100 Oak St (07073-1220)
PHONE.....................................973 772-8922
Gerald Bieber, *President*
▲ EMP: 25
SQ FT: 31,000
SALES (est): 5.9MM **Privately Held**
SIC: 5169 2842 Industrial chemicals; specialty cleaning, polishes & sanitation goods

(G-2312)
PRIMA-TEC ELECTRONICS CORP
316 Main St (07073-1752)
P.O. Box 436 (07073-0436)
PHONE.....................................201 947-4052
Thomas Butler, *President*
Maria Pisano, *Admin Sec*
EMP: 3
SALES: 1MM
SALES (corp-wide): 1MM **Privately Held**
SIC: 3679 Electronic circuits
HQ: F-T-B International Corp.
26 Broadway Ste 9m1
New York NY 10004
212 514-5400

(G-2313)
PURITY LABS
1 Maple St (07073-1221)
PHONE.....................................201 372-0236
Allison Crispino, *Principal*
EMP: 5
SALES (est): 611.7K **Privately Held**
SIC: 3491 Water works valves

(G-2314)
ROBERT COLANERI
Also Called: Colaneri Brothers
236 Park Ave 238 (07073-1919)
PHONE.....................................201 939-4405
Robert Colaneri, *Owner*
EMP: 4 EST: 1949
SQ FT: 4,500
SALES (est): 200K **Privately Held**
SIC: 3524 7699 Lawn & garden mowers & accessories; plows (garden tractor equipment); lawn mower repair shop

▲ = Import ▼ =Export
◆ =Import/Export

(G-2315)
ROYCE ASSOCIATES A LTD PARTNR (PA)
35 Carlton Ave (07073-1613)
PHONE..................................201 438-5200
A J Royce IV, *Partner*
Harry Anand, *Partner*
Albert Royce III, *Partner*
Wylie Royce, *Partner*
Greg Gipson, *Plant Mgr*
▲ EMP: 55 EST: 1929
SQ FT: 48,000
SALES (est): 19.7MM **Privately Held**
SIC: 2869 3089 2842 2851 Industrial organic chemicals; plastic processing; polishing preparations & related products; varnishes; chemical preparations

(G-2316)
ROYCE INTERNATIONAL CORP
35 Carlton Ave (07073-1613)
PHONE..................................201 438-5200
A Jay Royce III, *President*
EMP: 5
SALES (est): 395.3K **Privately Held**
SIC: 2869 Industrial organic chemicals

(G-2317)
RUSH INDEX TABS INC
Also Called: Rush Printing and Binding Svcs
60 Willow St (07073-1210)
PHONE..................................800 914-3036
Jay Cohen, *President*
Scott Cohen, *President*
EMP: 65
SQ FT: 53,000
SALES (est): 6.8MM **Privately Held**
WEB: www.trustrush.com
SIC: 2675 Index cards, die-cut: made from purchased materials

(G-2318)
SAMAD BROTHERS INC
419 Murray Hill Pkwy (07073-2107)
PHONE..................................201 372-0909
David Samad, *President*
Malcolm Samad, *Treasurer*
▲ EMP: 12
SQ FT: 20,000
SALES (est): 2.9MM **Privately Held**
SIC: 5023 2273 Rugs; carpets & rugs

(G-2319)
STAR-GLO INDUSTRIES LLC (PA)
2 Carlton Ave (07073-1646)
PHONE..................................201 939-6162
Jeong Cho, *General Mgr*
Dennis Azzolina, *Vice Pres*
Edward Peterhoff, *Vice Pres*
Gene Thomas, *Vice Pres*
Dave Oddo, *Purch Mgr*
▲ EMP: 122
SQ FT: 170,000
SALES (est): 18.1MM **Privately Held**
WEB: www.starglo.com
SIC: 3069 3599 Molded rubber products; machine shop, jobbing & repair

(G-2320)
STEAMIST INC
25 E Union Ave Ste 1 (07073-2254)
PHONE..................................201 933-0700
Jeffrey P Noll, *President*
▲ EMP: 40 EST: 1943
SQ FT: 33,000
SALES (est): 10.6MM
SALES (corp-wide): 360.7MM **Privately Held**
WEB: www.steamist.com
SIC: 3569 Generators: steam, liquid oxygen or nitrogen
PA: R.A.F. Industries, Inc.
    165 Township Line Rd # 2100
    Jenkintown PA 19046
    215 572-0738

(G-2321)
STONE SURFACES INC
890 Paterson Plank Rd (07073-2130)
PHONE..................................201 935-8803
Michael Sakosits, *President*
Felice Cappuccia, *Vice Pres*
▲ EMP: 57
SQ FT: 11,000

SALES (est): 6MM **Privately Held**
SIC: 1411 1429 Granite dimension stone; marble, crushed & broken-quarrying

(G-2322)
SUN CHEMICAL CORPORATION
Also Called: U S Ink Division
390 Central Ave (07073-1216)
PHONE..................................201 438-4831
Mike Wehner, *Sales Mgr*
Julie Dye, *Sales Staff*
Bill Griffen, *Manager*
EMP: 20 **Privately Held**
WEB: www.sunchemical.com
SIC: 2893 2899 Printing ink; chemical preparations
HQ: Sun Chemical Corporation
    35 Waterview Blvd Ste 100
    Parsippany NJ 07054
    973 404-6000

(G-2323)
TECHNO CITY INC
1 Meadowlands Plz Ste 200 (07073-2152)
PHONE..................................862 414-3282
Israfil Demir, *Principal*
EMP: 5
SALES (est): 226.9K **Privately Held**
SIC: 3571 Electronic computers

(G-2324)
TECHNTIME BUS SLTONS LTD LBLTY
Also Called: Pro Academy
1 Madison St Ste B4 (07073-1605)
PHONE..................................973 246-8153
Haciee Dinc, *Controller*
Fatih Ormanoglu, *Sr Ntwrk Engine*
Erdem Cosgun,
▲ EMP: 10
SQ FT: 600
SALES (est): 4MM **Privately Held**
SIC: 3699 7373 5734 5021 Security control equipment & systems; computer integrated systems design; modems, monitors, terminals & disk drives: computers; office furniture; school desks

(G-2325)
TEL-INSTRUMENT ELEC CORP (PA)
Also Called: TIC
1 Branca Rd (07073-2121)
PHONE..................................201 933-1600
Robert H Walker, *Ch of Bd*
Jeffrey C O'Hara, *President*
EMP: 41
SQ FT: 27,000
SALES: 12.1MM **Publicly Held**
WEB: www.telinst.com
SIC: 3674 3829 Semiconductors & related devices; aircraft & motor vehicle measurement equipment

(G-2326)
TODD SHELTON LLC
450 Murray Hill Pkwy C2 (07073-2225)
PHONE..................................844 626-6355
Todd Shelton,
▲ EMP: 6
SQ FT: 5,000
SALES (est): 419.2K **Privately Held**
SIC: 2326 5611 Men's & boys' work clothing; men's & boys' clothing stores

(G-2327)
TRANS WORLD MARKETING CORP (PA)
360 Murray Hill Pkwy (07073-2190)
PHONE..................................201 935-5565
William V Carafello, *President*
James Cavaluzzi, *Chairman*
Gerald Molitor, *Exec VP*
▲ EMP: 101 EST: 1966
SQ FT: 140,000
SALES (est): 17.1MM **Privately Held**
WEB: www.transworldmarketing.com
SIC: 3993 Signs & advertising specialties

(G-2328)
UNITED GUTTER SUPPLY INC
Also Called: Eagle Gutter Supply
1 Maple St Ste 1 # 1 (07073-1232)
PHONE..................................201 933-6316
Richard Wille, *President*

EMP: 25
SQ FT: 28,000
SALES (est): 3.4MM **Privately Held**
SIC: 3444 Gutters, sheet metal

(G-2329)
VERICO TECHNOLOGY LLC
405 Murray Hill Pkwy (07073-2136)
PHONE..................................201 842-0222
EMP: 152
SALES (corp-wide): 132.7MM **Privately Held**
SIC: 3555 Mfg Printing Trades Machinery
HQ: Verico Technology Llc
    230 Shaker Rd
    Enfield CT 06082
    800 492-7286

(G-2330)
WOODWARD JOGGER AERATORS INC (PA)
45 Carlton Ave (07073-1613)
PHONE..................................201 933-6800
Joseph Giorgio, *President*
▲ EMP: 18
SALES (est): 3MM **Privately Held**
SIC: 3554 Paper industries machinery

(G-2331)
ZENITH PRECISION INC
536 Paterson Ave (07073-1282)
PHONE..................................201 933-8640
Matteo De Gennaro, *President*
John Antico, *Vice Pres*
Andrew D Gennaro, *Vice Pres*
EMP: 10 EST: 1966
SQ FT: 5,000
SALES (est): 870K **Privately Held**
SIC: 3545 3769 Precision tools, machinists'; guided missile & space vehicle parts & auxiliary equipment

---

East Windsor
Mercer County

(G-2332)
ABBOTT POINT OF CARE INC
104 Windsor Center Dr (08520-1423)
PHONE..................................609 371-8923
Feth Hunter, *Manager*
EMP: 120
SALES (corp-wide): 30.5B **Publicly Held**
SIC: 3841 Diagnostic apparatus, medical
HQ: Abbott Point Of Care Inc.
    400 College Rd E
    Princeton NJ 08540
    609 454-9000

(G-2333)
ACCELRX LABS LLC
55 Lake Dr (08520-5320)
PHONE..................................609 301-6446
Doug Van Pelt, *Mng Member*
EMP: 4
SQ FT: 30,000
SALES (est): 311.1K **Privately Held**
SIC: 2834 Pharmaceutical preparations

(G-2334)
ADVENTURE INDUSTRIES LLC (PA)
59 Lake Dr (08520-5320)
PHONE..................................609 426-1777
Michael Koretsky,
Frank Koretsky,
EMP: 5
SQ FT: 10,000
SALES: 1MM **Privately Held**
WEB: www.adventureindustries.com
SIC: 3199 5099 Novelties, leather; novelties, durable

(G-2335)
APRECIA PHARMACEUTICALS CO
89 Twin Rivers Dr (08520-5212)
PHONE..................................215 359-3300
Kyle Smith, *Project Mgr*
Bridget Johnson, *Opers Staff*
Ratilal Patel, *QC Dir*
Pat Zafarino, *Branch Mgr*
Jaedeok Yoo, *CTO*
EMP: 50

SALES (corp-wide): 19MM **Privately Held**
SIC: 2834 Pharmaceutical preparations
HQ: Aprecia Pharmaceuticals, Llc
    10901 Kenwood Rd
    Blue Ash OH 45242
    513 864-4107

(G-2336)
ARCA INDUSTRIAL INC
31 Dennison Dr (08520-5307)
PHONE..................................732 339-0450
Jerry Huang, *President*
◆ EMP: 6
SQ FT: 3,000
SALES (est): 1.6MM **Privately Held**
SIC: 3441 3315 Fabricated structural metal; cable, steel: insulated or armored

(G-2337)
AUREX LABS LTD LBLTY CO
10 Lake Dr (08520-5321)
PHONE..................................609 308-2304
Sree Ranga Aravapalli, *Mng Member*
EMP: 12 EST: 2014
SALES: 2.3MM **Privately Held**
SIC: 2834 Pharmaceutical preparations

(G-2338)
AURO PACKAGING LLC
203 Windsor Center Dr (08520-1410)
PHONE..................................732 839-9408
Swami S Iyer, *Principal*
EMP: 20
SQ FT: 45,350
SALES (est): 1.1MM
SALES (corp-wide): 1.6B **Privately Held**
SIC: 2834 Pharmaceutical preparations
HQ: Aurobindo Pharma U.S.A., Inc.
    279 Prnctn Hightstown Rd
    East Windsor NJ 08520
    732 839-9400

(G-2339)
AUROBINDO PHARMA USA INC
279 Prnctn Hightstown Rd (08520-1401)
PHONE..................................732 839-9400
Julie Faria, *Project Mgr*
Pushpendra Singh, *Asst Mgr*
Paul McMahon, *Director*
EMP: 4
SALES (corp-wide): 1.6B **Privately Held**
SIC: 2834 Pharmaceutical preparations
HQ: Aurobindo Pharma U.S.A., Inc.
    279 Prnctn Hightstown Rd
    East Windsor NJ 08520
    732 839-9400

(G-2340)
AUROBINDO PHARMA USA INC (HQ)
279 Prnctn Hightstown Rd (08520-1401)
PHONE..................................732 839-9400
Robert G Cunard, *CEO*
Kaushik Bhansali, *Purchasing*
Kiran Nagabandhi, *Controller*
▲ EMP: 40
SQ FT: 45,000
SALES: 854.4MM
SALES (corp-wide): 1.6B **Privately Held**
WEB: www.aurobindousa.com
SIC: 2834 Pharmaceutical preparations
PA: Aurobindo Pharma Limited
    Water Mark Building,Plot No.11,Survey No. 9,
    Hyderabad TS 50008
    406 672-5000

(G-2341)
AUROBINDO PHARMA USA LLC
279 Prnceton Highstown Rd (08520-1401)
PHONE..................................732 839-9400
Robert Cunard, *CEO*
EMP: 30
SALES (est): 1.6MM
SALES (corp-wide): 1.6B **Privately Held**
SIC: 2834 Pharmaceutical preparations
HQ: Aurobindo Pharma U.S.A., Inc.
    279 Prnctn Hightstown Rd
    East Windsor NJ 08520
    732 839-9400

(G-2342)
AUROLIFE PHARMA LLC
Unit Iii 203 Windsor (08520)
PHONE..................................732 839-9408

Gangadhar Gorla, *VP Finance*
EMP: 5
SALES (corp-wide): 1.6B **Privately Held**
SIC: 2834 Pharmaceutical preparations
HQ: Aurolife Pharma Llc
　　2400 Us Highway 130
　　Dayton NJ 08810

(G-2343)
AUROMEDICS PHARMA LLC
279 Prncton Hightstown Rd (08520-1401)
PHONE..................................732 823-4122
EMP: 10
SALES (est): 676.7K **Privately Held**
SIC: 2834 Mfg Pharmaceutical Preparations

(G-2344)
AUROMEDICS PHARMA LLC
279 Prncton Hightstown Rd (08520-1401)
PHONE..................................732 839-9400
Mark Fedele, *President*
Vincent Andolina, *Vice Pres*
▲ EMP: 40
SALES: 855.2MM
SALES (corp-wide): 1.6B **Privately Held**
SIC: 2834 Pharmaceutical preparations
PA: Aurobindo Pharma Limited
　　Water Mark Building,Plot No.11,Survey
　　No. 9,
　　Hyderabad TS 50008
　　406 672-5000

(G-2345)
AVYAKTA IT SERVICES LLC
37 Sussex Ln (08520-5111)
PHONE..................................609 790-7517
Sirisha Panchagnula, *Principal*
EMP: 10
SALES (est): 439.2K **Privately Held**
SIC: 7371 7372 8331 7389 Computer
　　software development & applications;
　　computer software systems analysis &
　　design, custom; application computer
　　software; job training & vocational rehabil-
　　itation services;

(G-2346)
BIOFARMA US LLC
55 Lake Dr (08520-5320)
PHONE..................................609 301-6446
Joann Culmone, *Principal*
Luigi Cogolo,
EMP: 10
SALES (est): 1.1MM **Privately Held**
SIC: 2023 Dietary supplements, dairy &
　　non-dairy based

(G-2347)
CONAIR CORPORATION
Also Called: Scunci Division
150 Milford Rd (08520-6124)
PHONE..................................239 673-2125
Gary McWhorter, *Opers Mgr*
Vanessa Vazquez, *Prdtn Mgr*
Luis Estrada, *Engineer*
Scott Pace, *Natl Sales Mgr*
Alyssa Lucas, *Manager*
EMP: 65
SALES (corp-wide): 2B **Privately Held**
WEB: www.conair.com
SIC: 3634 Electric housewares & fans
PA: Conair Corporation
　　1 Cummings Point Rd
　　Stamford CT 06902
　　203 351-9000

(G-2348)
CONAIR CORPORATION
Also Called: Cuisinarts Division
150 Milford Rd (08520-6124)
PHONE..................................609 426-1300
Sam Rajkovich, *Vice Pres*
Duane Hein, *Engineer*
Andres Almanza, *Finance Dir*
Roxanne Sarmiento, *Sales Staff*
Alyssa Lucas, *Manager*
EMP: 250
SALES (corp-wide): 2B **Privately Held**
WEB: www.conair.com
SIC: 3634 2844 3999 3661 Dryers, elec-
　　tric: hand & face; toilet preparations; bar-
　　ber & beauty shop equipment; telephone
　　& telegraph apparatus

PA: Conair Corporation
　　1 Cummings Point Rd
　　Stamford CT 06902
　　203 351-9000

(G-2349)
DAVLYN INDUSTRIES INC
366 Prncton Hightstown Rd (08520-1411)
PHONE..................................609 655-5974
Tamaki Shimamoto, *President*
▲ EMP: 200
SQ FT: 150,000
SALES (est): 43.4MM **Privately Held**
WEB: www.davlyn-ind.com
SIC: 2844 5122 Cosmetic preparations;
　　cosmetics, perfumes & hair products
HQ: Shiseido Americas Corporation
　　900 3rd Ave Fl 15
　　New York NY 10022
　　212 805-2300

(G-2350)
ESJAY PHARMA LLC
70 Lake Dr (08520-5321)
PHONE..................................609 469-5920
Muthusamy Shanmugam, *President*
EMP: 4
SALES (corp-wide): 3MM **Privately Held**
SIC: 2834 Pharmaceutical preparations
PA: Esjay Pharma Llc
　　27 Ridgeview Way
　　Allentown NJ 08501
　　732 438-1816

(G-2351)
FORDOZ PHARMA CORP
69 Prnceton Hightstown Rd (08520-1900)
PHONE..................................609 469-5949
Xin He, *CEO*
EMP: 13
SQ FT: 5,000
SALES (est): 787K **Privately Held**
SIC: 2834 Solutions, pharmaceutical

(G-2352)
HOVIONE LLC
40 Lake Dr (08520-5321)
PHONE..................................609 918-2600
Kristine Senft, *Vice Pres*
Peter Villax, *Vice Pres*
David Storey, *Project Mgr*
Ana Vilela, *Project Mgr*
Ashima Phukan, *Buyer*
▲ EMP: 51
SQ FT: 23,000
SALES (est): 17.1MM
SALES (corp-wide): 221.8MM **Privately Held**
WEB: www.hovione.com
SIC: 2834 Druggists' preparations (phar-
　　maceuticals)
HQ: Hovione FarmaciEncia, S.A.
　　Quinta SAo Pedro
　　Loures 2674-
　　219 829-000

(G-2353)
INFINLIGHT PRODUCTS INC (PA)
859130 N 126e (08520)
PHONE..................................888 665-7708
Sonora Chiu, *President*
Alex Yeng, *Vice Pres*
EMP: 5
SALES (est): 585.1K **Privately Held**
SIC: 3645 Residential lighting fixtures

(G-2354)
MCGRAW-HILL GLBL EDCTN HLDNGS
104 Windsor Center Dr (08520-1423)
PHONE..................................609 371-8301
David Weidinger, *Principal*
Kate Ishchanka, *Finance Mgr*
Tom Greitz, *Director*
Stephen Wroblewski, *Director*
EMP: 53
SALES (corp-wide): 908MM **Privately Held**
SIC: 2731 Textbooks: publishing & printing
PA: Mcgraw-Hill Global Education Holdings, Llc
　　2 Penn Plz Fl 20
　　New York NY 10121
　　800 338-3987

(G-2355)
MUSE MONTHLY LLC
192 Dorchester Dr (08520-1122)
PHONE..................................609 443-3509
Christina Blok, *Principal*
EMP: 4
SALES (est): 124.4K **Privately Held**
SIC: 2711 Newspapers

(G-2356)
NOVITIUM PHARMA LLC
70 Lake Dr (08520-5321)
PHONE..................................609 469-5920
Chad Gassert, *CEO*
Thorappadi Vijayaraj, *Vice Pres*
EMP: 8
SQ FT: 36,000
SALES (est): 602.3K **Privately Held**
SIC: 2834 Proprietary drug products

(G-2357)
ORGANICA AROMATICS CORP
20 Lake D (08520)
PHONE..................................609 443-3333
Muhammed Majeed, *Chairman*
EMP: 5
SALES: 397.9K **Privately Held**
SIC: 2099 Seasonings & spices

(G-2358)
ROOF DECK INC
Also Called: Rdi
80 Twin Rivers Dr (08520-5213)
P.O. Box 295, Hightstown (08520-0295)
PHONE..................................609 448-6666
Mary Lou Jaroschak, *President*
EMP: 15
SQ FT: 22,000
SALES: 0 **Privately Held**
WEB: www.roofdeckinc.com
SIC: 3444 Roof deck, sheet metal

(G-2359)
SABINSA CORPORATION (PA)
20 Lake Dr (08520-5321)
PHONE..................................732 777-1111
Jayasankar Nair, *CEO*
Muhammed Majeed, *Ch of Bd*
Kalyanam Nagabhushankm, *President*
Alexander Husarenko, *General Mgr*
Brittney Brunson, *Purch Mgr*
▲ EMP: 27
SQ FT: 38,000
SALES (est): 10.3MM **Privately Held**
WEB: www.sabinsa.com
SIC: 2834 Pharmaceutical preparations

(G-2360)
SHISEIDO AMERICA INC (DH)
366 Prncton Hightstown Rd (08520-1411)
PHONE..................................609 371-5800
Tamaki Shimamoto, *President*
▲ EMP: 168
SQ FT: 216,000
SALES (est): 175.4MM **Privately Held**
SIC: 5122 2844 Cosmetics; cosmetic
　　preparations
HQ: Shiseido Americas Corporation
　　900 3rd Ave Fl 15
　　New York NY 10022
　　212 805-2300

(G-2361)
SHISEIDO AMERICAS CORPORATION
Also Called: Shiseido Amrcas Innovation Ctr
366 Prncton Hightstown Rd (08520-1411)
PHONE..................................609 371-5800
Shyama Dasai, *Branch Mgr*
Ernie Fuente, *Business Dir*
EMP: 9 **Privately Held**
WEB: www.davlyn-ind.com
SIC: 2844 Cosmetic preparations
HQ: Shiseido Americas Corporation
　　900 3rd Ave Fl 15
　　New York NY 10022
　　212 805-2300

(G-2362)
THERMO SYSTEMS LLC
84 Twin Rivers Dr (08520-5213)
PHONE..................................609 371-3300
Zack Arencibia, *Engineer*
David J Musto,
Gregory Smith,

EMP: 52
SQ FT: 16,000
SALES (est): 18.5MM **Privately Held**
WEB: www.thermosystems.com
SIC: 3822 7373 Auto controls regulating
　　residntl & coml environmt & applncs; sys-
　　tems integration services

(G-2363)
TUNNEL NETWORKS INC
53 Winchester Dr (08520-2608)
PHONE..................................609 414-9799
Byron Stokes, *President*
EMP: 8
SQ FT: 2,000
SALES: 195K **Privately Held**
SIC: 7372 Business oriented computer
　　software

(G-2364)
WINDSOR LABS LLC
55 Lake Dr (08520-5320)
PHONE..................................609 301-6446
Bruce Bassett, *Manager*
Krystal Cole, *Manager*
EMP: 7
SALES (est): 119.8K **Privately Held**
SIC: 2834 Pharmaceutical preparations

┌─────────────────────────┐
│   **East Windsor**   │
│   *Middlesex County*   │
└─────────────────────────┘

(G-2365)
BRILLIANT LIGHT POWER INC
493 Old Trenton Rd (08512-5601)
PHONE..................................609 490-0427
EMP: 30 EST: 1991
SALES (est): 1.7MM **Privately Held**
SIC: 5085 8731 3568 Power transmission
　　equipment & apparatus; energy research;
　　chain, power transmission

(G-2366)
CARNEGIE SURGICAL LLC (PA)
151 One Mile Rd (08512-2536)
PHONE..................................866 782-7144
Sami Ahmad, *Marketing Mgr*
Ahmad Nawaz,
▲ EMP: 8 EST: 2008
SALES (est): 1.1MM **Privately Held**
SIC: 3841 Surgical & medical instruments

(G-2367)
ELEMENTIS CHROMIUM INC (HQ)
469 Old Trenton Rd (08512-5601)
PHONE..................................609 443-2000
Dennis Valentino, *President*
Jackie Lee, *Buyer*
Mark Metyi, *Research*
Alvin Saathoff, *Plant Engr*
Timothy Stupak, *Credit Staff*
EMP: 130
SALES (est): 28.3MM
SALES (corp-wide): 822.2MM **Privately Held**
SIC: 2819 Industrial inorganic chemicals
PA: Elementis Plc
　　Caroline House
　　London WC1V
　　207 067-2999

(G-2368)
ELEMENTIS GLOBAL LLC (HQ)
Also Called: Elementis Specialities
469 Old Trenton Rd (08512-5601)
PHONE..................................609 443-2000
Dennis Valentino, *President*
Greg McClatchy, *President*
Gary Castellino, *Vice Pres*
Ling Dawes, *Vice Pres*
Richard Demarchi, *Vice Pres*
◆ EMP: 200
SQ FT: 77,000
SALES (est): 161.8MM
SALES (corp-wide): 822.2MM **Privately Held**
SIC: 2899 Vegetable oils, vulcanized or
　　sulfurized
PA: Elementis Plc
　　Caroline House
　　London WC1V
　　207 067-2999

(G-2369)
ELEMENTIS SPECIALTIES INC (HQ)
469 Old Trenton Rd (08512-5601)
PHONE..................................609 443-2000
Neil Carr, *President*
Eric Post, *General Mgr*
Marie Yeager, *General Mgr*
William J French, *COO*
Tony Depaola, *Vice Pres*
◆ EMP: 145
SQ FT: 70,000
SALES (est): 212.5MM
SALES (corp-wide): 822.2MM **Privately Held**
WEB: www.elementis-specialties.com
SIC: 2851 8731 2899 2865 Paints & paint additives; commercial physical research; chemical preparations; cyclic crudes & intermediates; inorganic pigments
PA: Elementis Plc
Caroline House
London WC1V
207 067-2999

(G-2370)
ELEMENTIS SPECIALTIES INC
469 Old Trenton Rd (08512-5601)
PHONE..................................201 432-0800
Howard Bird, *Vice Pres*
Wayne Arndt, *Engineer*
EMP: 19
SALES (corp-wide): 822.2MM **Privately Held**
SIC: 2851 2816 Paints & allied products; inorganic pigments
HQ: Elementis Specialties, Inc.
469 Old Trenton Rd
East Windsor NJ 08512
609 443-2000

Eastampton
Burlington County

(G-2371)
ASLEGACY SPIRITS LLC
8 Adam Ct (08060-4701)
PHONE..................................609 784-8383
Dasine Asberry, *Mng Member*
EMP: 4
SALES (est): 172.3K **Privately Held**
SIC: 5182 2085 2084 Liquor; neutral spirits; vodka (alcoholic beverage); neutral spirits, fruit

(G-2372)
GROWMARK FS LLC
2545 Route 206 (08060-5421)
PHONE..................................609 267-7054
EMP: 18
SALES (corp-wide): 7.2B **Privately Held**
SIC: 2875 2873 2874 5191 Fertilizers, mixing only; nitrogenous fertilizers; nitrogen solutions (fertilizer); phosphatic fertilizers; pesticides; seeds: field, garden & flower
HQ: Growmark Fs, Llc
308 Ne Front St
Milford DE 19963
302 422-3002

Eatontown
Monmouth County

(G-2373)
ABOUDI PRINTING LLC
132 Lewis St Ste B (07724-3925)
PHONE..................................732 542-2929
EMP: 4
SALES (est): 362.1K **Privately Held**
SIC: 2752 Commercial printing, lithographic

(G-2374)
ALGEN DESIGN SERVICES INC
40 Industrial Way E (07724-3317)
P.O. Box 188, Colts Neck (07722-0188)
PHONE..................................732 389-3630
Edwin Thomas, *President*

Alex Thomas, *Vice Pres*
Genevive Thomas, *Vice Pres*
EMP: 50
SQ FT: 48,000
SALES (est): 7.3MM **Privately Held**
WEB: www.algendesign.com
SIC: 3679 Electronic loads & power supplies

(G-2375)
ALKALINE CORPORATION
Also Called: Allersearch Labs
38 Industrial Way E Ste 2 (07724-3320)
PHONE..................................732 531-7830
Isidore Bale, *President*
EMP: 9
SALES (est): 1.4MM **Privately Held**
SIC: 2844 3842 Face creams or lotions; suntan lotions & oils; colognes; sterilizers, hospital & surgical

(G-2376)
AMEDIA NETWORKS INC
Also Called: (A DEVELOPMENT STAGE COMPANY)
541 Industrial Way W B (07724-4242)
PHONE..................................732 440-1992
Frank Galuppo, *President*
James D Gardner, *CFO*
John R Colton, *CTO*
Stuart J Waldman, *Internal Med*
William F Lenahan,
EMP: 18 EST: 1994
SALES (est): 3.1MM **Privately Held**
WEB: www.ttrtech.com
SIC: 3577 Computer peripheral equipment

(G-2377)
AMERICAN OIL & SUPPLY CO
Also Called: A O S
22 Meridian Rd Ste 6 (07724-2278)
PHONE..................................732 389-5514
Stanley J Ziemski, *Ch of Bd*
EMP: 11
SQ FT: 25,000
SALES (est): 960K **Privately Held**
WEB: www.americanoilsupply.com
SIC: 2992 Lubricating oils & greases

(G-2378)
AOS THERMAL COMPOUNDS LLC
22 Meridian Rd Ste 6 (07724-2278)
PHONE..................................732 389-5514
John Ziemski, *General Mgr*
Vijay Patel, *COO*
Jennifer Decker, *Marketing Mgr*
Steve Ottaviano, *Manager*
Victor Papanu, *Officer*
EMP: 14
SQ FT: 5,000
SALES (est): 3.6MM **Privately Held**
WEB: www.aosco.com
SIC: 2891 Adhesives, paste

(G-2379)
BAL-EDGE CORPORATION
Also Called: Brim Technologies
151 Industrial Way E (07724-3322)
PHONE..................................973 895-8826
Edward Sullivan, *President*
EMP: 4
SALES: 862.8K **Privately Held**
SIC: 2869 Laboratory chemicals, organic

(G-2380)
BIOTECH ATLANTIC INC
6 Industrial Way W Ste E1 (07724-4265)
PHONE..................................732 389-4789
Fax: 732 389-3837
▲ EMP: 10
SQ FT: 2,400
SALES (est): 740K **Privately Held**
SIC: 2835 Mfg Diagnostic Devices

(G-2381)
BRECOFLEX CO LLC
222 Industrial Way W (07724-2206)
PHONE..................................732 460-9500
Bernd Fuellemann, *President*
Bob Beveridge, *Mfg Mgr*
Michaela Schilling, *Purchasing*
Michael Langston, *Engineer*
Tom Runko, *Engineer*
▲ EMP: 75
SQ FT: 59,800

SALES (est): 15.8MM **Privately Held**
SIC: 3052 Plastic belting

(G-2382)
BURPEE MEDSYSTEMS LLC
15 Christopher Way (07724-3325)
PHONE..................................732 544-8900
Janet Burpee, *CEO*
Steve Burpee, *President*
George Burpee, *COO*
Donna Haag, *Vice Pres*
Christopher Wilczynski, *VP Opers*
EMP: 6
SQ FT: 2,500
SALES (est): 1.9MM **Privately Held**
WEB: www.burpeetech.com
SIC: 3841 3842 Surgical & medical instruments; surgical appliances & supplies
PA: Seisa Medical, Inc.
9005 Montana Ave
El Paso TX 79925

(G-2383)
CAREGILITY CORPORATION
81 Corbett Way (07724-2264)
PHONE..................................732 413-6000
Ron Gaboury, *CEO*
EMP: 30
SALES (est): 1MM
SALES (corp-wide): 131.2MM **Privately Held**
SIC: 3669 3651 Visual communication systems; recording machines, except dictation & telephone answering
PA: Ytc Holdings, Inc.
81 Corbett Way
Eatontown NJ 07724
732 413-6000

(G-2384)
COBHAM NEW JERSEY INC
Also Called: Aeroflex Ctrl Components Inc
40 Industrial Way E (07724-3317)
PHONE..................................732 460-0212
Jill Kale, *CEO*
John Ekis, *General Mgr*
▲ EMP: 86
SQ FT: 46,000
SALES: 15MM
SALES (corp-wide): 2.3B **Privately Held**
WEB: www.aeroflex-kdi.com
SIC: 5065 3679 Electronic parts & equipment; microwave components
HQ: Cobham Microelectronic Solutions Inc.
310 Dino Dr
Ann Arbor MI 48103

(G-2385)
COMFORT RVOLUTION HOLDINGS LLC
442 Highway 35 Fl 1 (07724-2252)
P.O. Box 1290 (07724-5290)
PHONE..................................732 272-9111
Michael Fux, *CEO*
Thomas Bruno, *CFO*
Dan Lufkin,
◆ EMP: 15
SALES (est): 5.1MM **Privately Held**
SIC: 2515 Box springs, assembled

(G-2386)
CONCORDE SPECIALTY GASES INC
36 Eaton Rd (07724-2254)
PHONE..................................732 544-9899
Gregory Harquail, *President*
Robert Casper, *Chairman*
Teri Sciamarelli, *Director*
Carla Dinen, *Admin Asst*
◆ EMP: 26 EST: 1994
SQ FT: 25,000
SALES (est): 6.9MM **Privately Held**
WEB: www.concordegas.com
SIC: 2813 Industrial gases

(G-2387)
DANIEL C HERRING CO INC
Also Called: D C Herring Co
20 Meridian Rd Ste 6 (07724-2270)
PHONE..................................732 530-6557
Daniel A Herring, *President*
Joyce Herring, *Vice Pres*
Tom Pedrazzo, *Vice Pres*
EMP: 10
SQ FT: 8,000

SALES (est): 3MM **Privately Held**
WEB: www.dancingdjs.com
SIC: 3052 Rubber & plastics hose & beltings

(G-2388)
DIAMOND SG INTL LTD LBLTY CO
20 Meridian Rd Ste 9 (07724-2270)
PHONE..................................732 861-9850
Hongvan Quan,
EMP: 6
SQ FT: 4,600
SALES: 1MM **Privately Held**
SIC: 3087 Custom compound purchased resins

(G-2389)
EAST COAST DISTRIBUTORS INC
Also Called: Pdec
1 Industrial Way E (07724-2255)
PHONE..................................732 223-5995
Joseph Sodano, *President*
EMP: 15
SQ FT: 16,500
SALES (est): 7MM **Privately Held**
SIC: 5045 2754 Computers, peripherals & software; business forms: gravure printing

(G-2390)
ELECTRONIC CONCEPTS INC (HQ)
526 Industrial Way W (07724-2212)
P.O. Box 1278 (07724-5278)
PHONE..................................732 542-7880
Bernard Lavene, *Ch of Bd*
Philip Lepore, *Treasurer*
▲ EMP: 123
SQ FT: 64,000
SALES (est): 19.4MM
SALES (corp-wide): 19.4MM **Privately Held**
WEB: www.ecicaps.com
SIC: 3675 Electronic capacitors
PA: Energy Storage Corp.
526 Industrial Way W
Eatontown NJ 07724
732 542-7880

(G-2391)
ELLIS/KUHNKE CONTROLS INC
Also Called: Ellis Controls
132 Lewis St Ste A2 (07724-3925)
PHONE..................................732 291-3334
G Corson Ellis Jr, *Ch of Bd*
Howard Boyce, *President*
Frances M Ruane, *Treasurer*
Sandeep Gandhi, *Controller*
EMP: 5 EST: 1969
SQ FT: 5,000
SALES: 2MM **Privately Held**
WEB: www.ekci.com
SIC: 3824 Controls, revolution & timing instruments; counters, revolution; gauges for computing pressure temperature corrections

(G-2392)
ENERGY STORAGE CORP (PA)
526 Industrial Way W (07724-2212)
P.O. Box 1278 (07724-5278)
PHONE..................................732 542-7880
Bernard Lavene, *President*
Philip Lepore, *Treasurer*
Len Bondar, *Manager*
Suellen Anton, *Admin Sec*
EMP: 90
SQ FT: 64,000
SALES (est): 19.4MM **Privately Held**
SIC: 3861 3675 Film, sensitized motion picture, X-ray, still camera, etc.; electronic capacitors

(G-2393)
GLAMOROUS GLO
42 Carolyn Ct (07724-1364)
PHONE..................................732 361-3235
Jason Macfarland, *Owner*
EMP: 4 EST: 2012
SALES (est): 323.5K **Privately Held**
SIC: 2869 Tanning agents, synthetic organic

(G-2394)
GRAPE BGINNINGS HANDSON WINERY
151 Industrial Way E B (07724-3322)
PHONE................................732 380-7356
EMP: 4
SALES (est): 343.7K **Privately Held**
SIC: 2084 Wines

(G-2395)
GWF ASSOCIATES LLC
1 Sheila Dr Ste 8 (07724-2658)
PHONE................................732 933-8780
Sean Feehan, *Vice Pres*
Kelly McCann, *Accounts Mgr*
George Feehan,
EMP: 20
SQ FT: 2,500
SALES (est): 2MM **Privately Held**
SIC: 7372 Educational computer software

(G-2396)
HAMPTON FORGE LTD (PA)
446 Highway 35 Ste 3 (07724-4290)
PHONE................................732 389-5507
Messod Felix Amar, *President*
Susan Amar, *Treasurer*
Suso Balanza, *Treasurer*
Steve Cohen, *Credit Mgr*
Annerys Hernandez, *Sales Staff*
◆ EMP: 32
SQ FT: 3,000
SALES (est): 4.9MM **Privately Held**
WEB: www.hamptonforge.com
SIC: 3914 Cutlery, stainless steel

(G-2397)
HIGH ENERGY GROUP LTD LBLTY CO
331 Newman Spg Rd (07724)
PHONE................................732 741-9099
Elaine Coffey,
▲ EMP: 7
SQ FT: 3,500
SALES: 950K **Privately Held**
SIC: 3612 3648 3645 5063 Distribution
transformers, electric; lighting equipment;
street lighting fixtures; residential lighting
fixtures; power wire & cable; miscella-
neous fabricated wire products

(G-2398)
HIKMA INJECTABLES USA INC
Also Called: West-Ward Injectables, Inc.
200 Industrial Way W (07724-2206)
PHONE................................732 542-1191
George J Muench, *Treasurer*
EMP: 5
SALES (est): 99K
SALES (corp-wide): 2B **Privately Held**
SIC: 2834 Pharmaceutical preparations
HQ: Eurohealth (U.S.A.), Inc
401 Industrial Way W
Eatontown NJ 07724

(G-2399)
HIKMA PHARMACEUTICALS USA INC (DH)
Also Called: Fka West-Ward Pharmaceuticals
246 Industrial Way W # 7 (07724-4241)
PHONE................................732 542-1191
Michael Raya, *CEO*
Brian Hoffmann, *President*
Claire Johnson, *Business Mgr*
Daniel Motto, *Exec VP*
Kristy Ronco, *Exec VP*
◆ EMP: 277 EST: 1946
SQ FT: 30,000
SALES (est): 171.8MM
SALES (corp-wide): 2B **Privately Held**
WEB: www.west-ward.com
SIC: 2834 Pharmaceutical preparations

(G-2400)
HIKMA PHARMACEUTICALS USA INC
Also Called: Oral Manufacturing
465 Industrial Way W (07724-2209)
PHONE................................732 542-1191
EMP: 10
SALES (corp-wide): 2B **Privately Held**
SIC: 2834 Pharmaceutical preparations

(G-2401)
IACOBUCCI USA INC
151 Industrial Way E A2 (07724-3322)
PHONE................................732 935-6633
Emilio Iacobucci, *President*
Lucio Iacobucci, *Vice Pres*
EMP: 5 EST: 1996
SALES (est): 49.2K
SALES (corp-wide): 595.3K **Privately Held**
WEB: www.iacobuccigroup.com
SIC: 3161 Luggage
HQ: Iacobucci Hf Aerospace Spa
Strada Sc Asi 1/S 16-18
Ferentino FR 03013
077 539-251

(G-2402)
IMMUNOSTICS INC
38 Industrial Way E Ste 5 (07724-3320)
PHONE................................732 918-0770
Kenn Kupits, *CEO*
EMP: 5
SALES (est): 133.6K **Privately Held**
SIC: 3841 Diagnostic apparatus, medical
PA: Boditech Med Inc.
43 Geodudanji 1-Gil, Dongnae-Myeon
Chuncheon 24398

(G-2403)
IMMUNOSTICS COMPANY INC
38 Industrial Way E Ste 1 (07724-3334)
PHONE................................732 918-0770
Kenn Kupits, *President*
Vincent Lastella, *Vice Pres*
▲ EMP: 45
SQ FT: 18,000
SALES (est): 7.9MM **Privately Held**
WEB: www.immunostics.com
SIC: 3841 Diagnostic apparatus, medical

(G-2404)
INNOVATIVE POWER SOLUTIONS LLC
Also Called: Ips
373 South St (07724-1863)
PHONE................................732 544-1075
Eli Liebermann,
Santiago Lagunas,
Bill Schatzow,
▲ EMP: 35 EST: 1999
SQ FT: 10,000
SALES (est): 9.8MM **Privately Held**
WEB: www.ips-llc.com
SIC: 3621 Motors & generators

(G-2405)
INTERNATIONAL DATA GROUP INC
6 Windsor Dr (07724-2140)
PHONE................................732 460-9404
Susane Hann, *Branch Mgr*
EMP: 10
SALES (corp-wide): 1.6B **Privately Held**
WEB: www.workscape.net
SIC: 2721 Trade journals: publishing only,
not printed on site
PA: International Data Group, Inc.
1 Exeter Plz Fl 15
Boston MA 02116
508 875-5000

(G-2406)
K K S CRITERION CHOCOLATES
125 Lewis St (07724-3454)
PHONE................................732 542-7847
George Karagias, *President*
EMP: 40 EST: 1929
SQ FT: 4,000
SALES (est): 2.2MM **Privately Held**
WEB: www.criterionchocolates.com
SIC: 5441 2066 Candy; chocolate & cocoa
products

(G-2407)
KESSLER-ELLIS PRODUCTS CO (PA)
Also Called: Ket
10 Industrial Way E Ste 6 (07724-3390)
PHONE................................732 935-1320
G Corson Ellis III, *Ch of Bd*
Louis Fligor, *Engineer*
John Gruskos, *Sales Staff*
Stan Kurc, *Sales Staff*
Phil Marsh, *Info Tech Dir*
▲ EMP: 60
SQ FT: 31,000
SALES (est): 12.4MM **Privately Held**
WEB: www.kep.com
SIC: 3824 3823 Controls, revolution & tim-
ing instruments; counter type registers;
flow instruments, industrial process type

(G-2408)
LAIRD & COMPANY (PA)
1 Laird Rd (07724-9724)
PHONE................................732 542-0312
Larrie W Laird, *President*
John E Laird III, *Exec VP*
Susan Herrmann, *Sales Staff*
Vince Capitolo, *Manager*
Earle Drake, *Manager*
◆ EMP: 40
SQ FT: 155,000
SALES (est): 43.7MM **Privately Held**
WEB: www.lairdandcompany.com
SIC: 2084 5182 Brandy; brandy & brandy
spirits

(G-2409)
MANZI PRINTING
132 Lewis St Ste B2 (07724-3926)
PHONE................................732 542-1927
Mike Manzi, *Owner*
EMP: 4
SALES (est): 97.5K **Privately Held**
SIC: 2752 Commercial printing, offset

(G-2410)
MECHANICAL INGENUITY CORP
28 Eaton Rd Ste 3 (07724-2274)
PHONE................................732 842-8889
Peter Manning, *CEO*
Howard Beckerman, *Vice Pres*
◆ EMP: 20
SALES (est): 3.6MM **Privately Held**
WEB: www.mechanicalingenuity.com
SIC: 3679 Electronic circuits

(G-2411)
MOTION SYSTEMS CORP
600 Industrial Way W (07724-2214)
PHONE................................732 389-1600
William Wolf, *President*
▼ EMP: 73
SQ FT: 100,000
SALES (est): 17.7MM **Privately Held**
WEB: www.Motionsystems.com
SIC: 3593 Fluid power cylinders & actua-
tors

(G-2412)
NATIONAL PRTECTIVE SYSTEMS INC
1 Meridian Rd (07724-2242)
PHONE................................732 922-3609
Douglas D'Agata, *CEO*
EMP: 14
SALES (est): 1.9MM **Privately Held**
SIC: 3812 7382 Search & detection sys-
tems & instruments; security systems
services

(G-2413)
OSTEOTECH INC
51 James Way (07724-2289)
PHONE................................732 544-5942
EMP: 20 **Privately Held**
SIC: 3841 Surgical & medical instruments
HQ: Osteotech, Inc.
51 James Way
Eatontown NJ 07724
732 542-2800

(G-2414)
OSTEOTECH INC (DH)
51 James Way (07724-2289)
PHONE................................732 542-2800
Sam Owusu-Akyaw, *President*
Robert M Wynalek, *President*
Robert W Honneffer, *Exec VP*
Mark H Burroughs, *CFO*
EMP: 115
SQ FT: 38,400
SALES (est): 71.3MM **Privately Held**
SIC: 3841 Surgical & medical instruments

HQ: Medtronic, Inc.
710 Medtronic Pkwy
Minneapolis MN 55432
763 514-4000

(G-2415)
OSTEOTECH INC
201 Industrial Way W (07724-2288)
PHONE................................732 542-2800
Lisa Melveney, *Opers Mgr*
Jennifer Walsh, *Opers Staff*
Laurie Dunham, *Buyer*
Rudy Duke, *Engineer*
Linda Pedersen, *Engineer*
EMP: 15 **Privately Held**
SIC: 3841 Surgical & medical instruments
HQ: Osteotech, Inc.
51 James Way
Eatontown NJ 07724
732 542-2800

(G-2416)
PAW BIOSCIENCE PRODUCTS LLC
38 Industrial Way E Ste 5 (07724-3320)
PHONE................................732 460-0088
Benjamin Willemstyn, *President*
▼ EMP: 3
SQ FT: 5,000
SALES (est): 1.8MM
SALES (corp-wide): 1.4B **Publicly Held**
WEB: www.pawbioscience.com
SIC: 5047 5122 2834 Medical equipment
& supplies; biologicals & allied products;
pharmaceutical preparations
HQ: Vwr Corporation
Radnor Corp Ctr 1 200
Radnor PA 19087
610 386-1700

(G-2417)
PROTEC SECURE CARD LTD LBLTY
Also Called: PSC
80 Corbett Way (07724-2263)
PHONE................................732 542-0700
Mark Goldberg, *COO*
Vincent F Serpico, *CFO*
Juan Mejia, *Mng Member*
Yogan Ponnusamy, *Director*
▲ EMP: 25
SQ FT: 13,000
SALES (est): 2.9MM **Privately Held**
SIC: 3089 Identification cards, plastic

(G-2418)
QUADRAMED CORPORATION
23 Christopher Way # 303 (07724-3335)
PHONE................................732 751-0400
Steven McCoy, *Branch Mgr*
EMP: 30
SALES (corp-wide): 3B **Privately Held**
WEB: www.quadramed.com
SIC: 7372 7322 8742 Business oriented
computer software; collection agency, ex-
cept real estate; hospital & health serv-
ices consultant
HQ: Quadramed Corporation
2300 Corp Park Dr Ste 400
Herndon VA 20171
703 709-2300

(G-2419)
QUINTUM TECHNOLOGIES INC (DH)
71 James Way (07724-2272)
PHONE................................732 460-9000
Cheng T Chen, *CEO*
Kurt Baumann, *President*
Rajiv Bhatia, *Vice Pres*
Chuck Rutledge, *VP Mktg*
Tim Thornton, *CTO*
▲ EMP: 54 EST: 1998
SQ FT: 15,000
SALES (est): 4.9MM
SALES (corp-wide): 595.3MM **Publicly Held**
WEB: www.quintumtechnologies.com
SIC: 3651 Telephone & telegraph appara-
tus
HQ: Network Equipment Technologies, Inc.
4 Technology Park Dr
Westford MA 01886
510 713-7300

(G-2420)
SHORE PRINTED CIRCUITS INC
3 Meridian Rd (07724-2242)
PHONE..................................732 380-0590
Charles F Rose, *President*
Steve Pierce, *General Mgr*
David Rose, *Vice Pres*
Glenn Stillwagon, *QC Mgr*
▲ EMP: 27
SQ FT: 2,500
SALES (est): 6.3MM **Privately Held**
WEB: www.shore-pc.com
SIC: 3672 Circuit boards, television & radio printed

(G-2421)
SPARTON AYDIN LLC
Also Called: Kep Marine
10 Industrial Way E (07724-3332)
PHONE..................................732 935-1320
Anthony Zuccarelli, *Principal*
EMP: 10
SALES (corp-wide): 374.9MM **Privately Held**
WEB: www.kep.com
SIC: 3629 Electronic generation equipment
HQ: Sparton Aydin, Llc
1 Riga Ln
Birdsboro PA 19508
610 404-7400

(G-2422)
SUBCOM LLC (DH)
250 Industrial Way W (07724-2206)
PHONE..................................732 578-7000
David Coughlan, *CEO*
Thomas M Lynch, *CFO*
Christina Jeffrey, *Bd of Directors*
Maryann Brereton, *Admin Sec*
▲ EMP: 311
SALES (est): 265.8MM
SALES (corp-wide): 41MM **Privately Held**
SIC: 7373 5063 8999 1731 Computer systems analysis & design; insulators, electrical; communication services; communications specialization; telephone & telegraph apparatus
HQ: Crown Subsea Communications Holding, Inc.
875 3rd Ave
New York NY 10022
212 891-2100

(G-2423)
T O NAJARIAN ASSOCIATES
1 Industrial Way W Ste D5 (07724-4207)
PHONE..................................732 389-0220
Tavit Najarian, *President*
Paul McRae, *Managing Dir*
Joel Ritner, *Engineer*
Cindy Maynard, *Human Res Dir*
Catherine Lane, *VP Mktg*
EMP: 60
SQ FT: 9,958
SALES (est): 10MM **Privately Held**
WEB: www.najarian.com
SIC: 8711 3535 4499 8713 Consulting engineer; robotic conveyors; marine salvaging & surveying services; surveying services

(G-2424)
TE CONNECTIVITY CORPORATION
250 Industrial Way W (07724-2206)
PHONE..................................610 893-9800
EMP: 309
SALES (corp-wide): 13.9B **Privately Held**
SIC: 3678 Electronic connectors
HQ: Te Connectivity Corporation
1050 Westlakes Dr
Berwyn PA 19312
610 893-9800

(G-2425)
TECH GIANT LLC
556 Industrial Way W (07724-4236)
PHONE..................................888 800-7745
Stuart Husney, *President*
Jason Betesh, *Vice Pres*
EMP: 3
SQ FT: 100,000
SALES: 1MM **Privately Held**
SIC: 3651 Speaker systems

(G-2426)
THOMAS SMOCK WOODWORKING
Also Called: Smock, Thomas Woodworking
306 Broad St (07724-1602)
PHONE..................................732 542-9167
Thomas Smock, *Owner*
EMP: 5
SQ FT: 10,000
SALES (est): 372K **Privately Held**
SIC: 2439 Trusses, wooden roof

(G-2427)
UNITED SOUND ARTS INC
Also Called: Kimbo Educational
1 Industrial Way W D-E (07724-2255)
P.O. Box 477, Long Branch (07740-0477)
PHONE..................................732 229-4949
James Kimble, *President*
EMP: 13 EST: 1954
SQ FT: 4,000
SALES (est): 2.8MM **Privately Held**
WEB: www.kimboed.com
SIC: 3652 Pre-recorded records & tapes

(G-2428)
VENARUM MEDICAL LLC
20 Meridian Rd Ste 9 (07724-2270)
PHONE..................................732 996-8513
Janet Burpee, *Mng Member*
EMP: 10
SALES (est): 89.2K **Privately Held**
SIC: 3841 8731 Catheters; biotechnical research, commercial

(G-2429)
VICTORY INTERNATIONAL USA LLC
40 Christopher Way (07724-3327)
PHONE..................................732 417-5900
Anil K Monga, *CEO*
Sean Monga, *Vice Pres*
Michael Zemble, *CFO*
April Conway, *Human Res Mgr*
◆ EMP: 15
SQ FT: 60,000
SALES: 40MM **Privately Held**
SIC: 5999 2844 Perfumes & colognes; perfumes & colognes

(G-2430)
YORK TELECOM CORPORATION (HQ)
Also Called: Yorktel
81 Corbett Way (07724-2264)
PHONE..................................732 413-6000
Ron Gaboury, *CEO*
York Wang, *Ch of Bd*
Jim Anderson, *President*
James Deblasio, *Exec VP*
David Anstee, *Senior VP*
◆ EMP: 90
SQ FT: 35,000
SALES (est): 130.2MM
SALES (corp-wide): 131.2MM **Privately Held**
SIC: 3669 3651 Visual communication systems; recording machines, except dictation & telephone answering
PA: Ytc Holdings, Inc.
81 Corbett Way
Eatontown NJ 07724
732 413-6000

(G-2431)
YTC HOLDINGS INC (PA)
81 Corbett Way (07724-2264)
PHONE..................................732 413-6000
Ronald Gaboury, *President*
EMP: 2
SALES (est): 131.2MM **Privately Held**
SIC: 3669 3651 Visual communication systems; recording machines, except dictation & telephone answering

---

Edgewater
Bergen County

(G-2432)
ADORAGE INC
1055 River Rd Apt Th10 (07020-1382)
PHONE..................................201 886-7000

EMP: 4
SALES: 360K **Privately Held**
SIC: 2844 Mfg Toilet Preparations

(G-2433)
ANNA J CHUNG LTD
5 Park St (07020-1407)
PHONE..................................917 575-8100
Daniel Cho, *President*
Anna Chung, *Vice Pres*
EMP: 12
SALES: 2MM **Privately Held**
SIC: 3911 5944 Jewelry, precious metal; jewelry, precious stones & precious metals

(G-2434)
BONDI DIGITAL PUBLISHING LLC
33 Hilliard Ave (07020-1209)
PHONE..................................212 405-1655
Murat Aktar, *Mng Member*
David Anthony, *Mng Member*
Carey Taylor, *Mng Member*
EMP: 5
SALES (est): 481.4K **Privately Held**
SIC: 2721 Magazines: publishing & printing

(G-2435)
C S HOT STAMPING
20 Edgewater Pl (07020-1206)
PHONE..................................201 840-4004
Carmen Marino, *Owner*
EMP: 6
SALES (est): 407.3K **Privately Held**
SIC: 2396 Printing & embossing on plastics fabric articles

(G-2436)
COFFEE ASSOCIATES INC (PA)
178 Old River Rd (07020-1699)
P.O. Box 240 (07020-0240)
PHONE..................................201 945-1060
Willian D Callas, *Principal*
▼ EMP: 35 EST: 1970
SQ FT: 25,000
SALES (est): 14.3MM **Privately Held**
WEB: www.themised.com
SIC: 5149 7389 2095 Coffee, green or roasted; coffee service; roasted coffee

(G-2437)
ECHO THERAPEUTICS INC (PA)
1809 Hudson Park (07020-1575)
PHONE..................................732 201-4189
Alan W Schoenbart, *CEO*
Alan Schoenbart, *CFO*
EMP: 17
SQ FT: 2,800
SALES (est): 476.8K **Publicly Held**
WEB: www.sontra.com
SIC: 3845 Electromedical apparatus

(G-2438)
FRACTAL SOLUTIONS CORP
725 River Rd Unit 32135 (07020-1171)
PHONE..................................201 608-6828
EMP: 4
SALES (est): 217.3K **Privately Held**
SIC: 2834 Intravenous solutions

(G-2439)
GUESS INC
39 The Promenade Bldg 300 (07020-2126)
PHONE..................................201 941-3683
EMP: 25
SALES (corp-wide): 2.5B **Publicly Held**
SIC: 2325 Mfg Men's/Boy's Trousers
PA: Guess , Inc.
1444 S Alameda St
Los Angeles CA 90021
213 765-3100

(G-2440)
METROLPOLIS MASTERING LP
Also Called: Sterling Sound
33 Hilliard Ave (07020-1209)
PHONE..................................212 604-9433
Murat Aktar, *Partner*
EMP: 28 EST: 1998
SALES (est): 206K **Privately Held**
WEB: www.sterling-sound.com
SIC: 3652 8999 Master records or tapes, preparation of; music arranging & composing

(G-2441)
TEXTRON INC
143 River Rd (07020-1002)
PHONE..................................201 945-1500
EMP: 30
SALES (corp-wide): 12.1B **Publicly Held**
SIC: 2076 Processes Linseed Oils
PA: Textron Inc.
40 Westminster St
Providence RI 02903
401 421-2800

Edison
Middlesex County

(G-2442)
3I INFOTECH FINANCIAL SOFTWARE (DH)
450 Rritan Ctr Pkwy Ste B (08837)
PHONE..................................732 710-4444
Kumar Ganesan, *CEO*
EMP: 4
SALES (est): 3.1MM **Privately Held**
SIC: 7372 Business oriented computer software

(G-2443)
3I INFOTECH INC
450 Rritan Ctr Pkwy Ste B (08837)
PHONE..................................732 710-4444
EMP: 5 **Privately Held**
SIC: 7372 Business oriented computer software
HQ: 3i Infotech Inc
450 Rritan Ctr Pkwy Ste B
Edison NJ 08837

(G-2444)
AAK USA INC (HQ)
499 Thornall St Ste 5 (08837-2267)
PHONE..................................973 344-1300
Johan Westman, *President*
Mark Becker, *Vice Pres*
Fredrik Nilsson, *Vice Pres*
Hakan Svensson, *Vice Pres*
Dennis Tagarelli, *Vice Pres*
◆ EMP: 95
SALES (est): 75.7MM
SALES (corp-wide): 3B **Privately Held**
WEB: www.aak.com
SIC: 2079 Edible oil products, except corn oil
PA: Aak Ab (Publ)
Skrivaregatan 9
Malmo 215 3
406 278-300

(G-2445)
ABBOTT LABORATORIES
18 Mayfield Ave (08837-3821)
PHONE..................................732 346-6649
EMP: 5
SALES (est): 567.6K **Privately Held**
SIC: 2834 Mfg Pharmaceutical Preparations

(G-2446)
ACME DRAPEMASTER AMERICA INC
125 Clearview Rd (08837-3733)
PHONE..................................732 512-0613
Gregory Fromkin, *President*
Daniel McCarren, *Vice Pres*
Marnie McCarren, *Vice Pres*
▲ EMP: 8
SQ FT: 7,000
SALES (est): 1.5MM **Privately Held**
WEB: www.acmedrapemaster.com
SIC: 2591 Drapery hardware & blinds & shades

(G-2447)
ACTAVIS LLC
47 Brunswick Ave (08817-2576)
PHONE..................................732 947-5300
Ashesh Dave, *Branch Mgr*
Don Risi, *Exec Dir*
EMP: 85 **Privately Held**
SIC: 5122 2834 Pharmaceuticals; pharmaceutical preparations

HQ: Actavis Llc
5 Giralda Farms
Madison NJ 07940
862 261-7000

(G-2448)
AEROGROUP RETAIL HOLDINGS INC
Also Called: Dmg
207 Meadow Rd Ste A (08817-6033)
PHONE...................................732 819-9843
Jules Schneider, *Manager*
EMP: 55
SALES (corp-wide): 50.9MM **Privately Held**
SIC: 3069　Boot or shoe products, rubber; soles, boot or shoe: rubber, composition or fiber
PA: Aerogroup Retail Holdings Inc
201 Meadow Rd
Edison NJ 08817
732 985-6900

(G-2449)
AFLAG PHARMACEUTICALS LLC
163 Jefferson Blvd (08817-3538)
PHONE...................................732 609-4139
Yujin Bi, *Principal*
EMP: 4
SALES (est): 212.2K　**Privately Held**
SIC: 2834　Pharmaceutical preparations

(G-2450)
AFP TRANSFORMERS CORPORATION
970 New Durham Rd (08817-2214)
PHONE...................................732 248-0305
Gregory S Vongas, *President*
Anthony J Miceli, *CFO*
EMP: 95
SQ FT: 55,000
SALES: 8MM
SALES (corp-wide): 45.9MM　**Privately Held**
WEB: www.afp-transformers.com
SIC: 3612 3677　Transformers, except electric; electronic coils, transformers & other inductors
PA: United Capital Corp.
9 Park Pl
Great Neck NY 11021
516 466-6464

(G-2451)
ALCAMI NEW JERSEY CORPORATION
Also Called: Analytical Testing
165 Fieldcrest Ave (08837-3633)
PHONE...................................732 346-5100
Stephan Kutzer, *CEO*
Scott Warner, *Vice Pres*
Adam Lauber, *CFO*
Tim Morgan, *Asst Treas*
Burton Ely, *Asst Sec*
EMP: 100
SALES: 12.2MM
SALES (corp-wide): 225MM　**Privately Held**
SIC: 8071 2834　Testing laboratories; pharmaceutical preparations
HQ: Alcami Corporation
2320 Scientific Park Dr
Wilmington NC 28405
910 254-7000

(G-2452)
AMERCHOL CORPORATION (DH)
136 Talmadge Rd (08817-2812)
PHONE...................................732 248-6000
Thomas J Malafronte, *President*
Alan Fowler, *Manager*
Pat Mayer, *Manager*
◆ **EMP:** 110
SQ FT: 100,000
SALES (est): 10MM
SALES (corp-wide): 61.1B　**Publicly Held**
SIC: 2841 2869 2046 2844　Soap & other detergents; fatty acid esters, aminos, etc.; glucose; suntan lotions & oils; chemical preparations
HQ: Union Carbide Corporation
1254 Enclave Pkwy
Houston TX 77077
281 966-2727

(G-2453)
AMERICAN BINDERY DEPOT INC
191 Talmadge Rd (08817-2848)
PHONE...................................732 287-2370
Tony Cuccinello, *Co-President*
Christopher Scarano, *Co-President*
EMP: 150
SQ FT: 65,000
SALES: 8MM　**Privately Held**
SIC: 2789 2675　Paper cutting; die-cut paper & board

(G-2454)
AMERICAN PIPE BENDERS & FABRIC
191 Vineyard Rd Ste 5 (08817-4751)
PHONE...................................732 287-1122
Andrew Martingano Jr, *President*
Susan Martingano, *Vice Pres*
EMP: 7 **EST:** 1944
SQ FT: 10,000
SALES (est): 911.8K　**Privately Held**
SIC: 3599　Machine shop, jobbing & repair

(G-2455)
AMERICAN TRANSPARENT PLASTIC
180 National Rd (08817-2811)
P.O. Box 556 (08818-0556)
PHONE...................................732 287-3000
Emanuel Parnes, *President*
Herschel Parnes, *Corp Secy*
EMP: 40 **EST:** 1959
SQ FT: 118,000
SALES (est): 6.2MM　**Privately Held**
SIC: 3081 2673　Polyethylene film; bags: plastic, laminated & coated

(G-2456)
AMETEK INC
Also Called: Ametek CTS
52 Mayfield Ave (08837-3821)
PHONE...................................732 417-0501
EMP: 5
SALES (corp-wide): 4.8B　**Publicly Held**
SIC: 3621　Motors & generators
PA: Ametek, Inc.
1100 Cassatt Rd
Berwyn PA 19312
610 647-2121

(G-2457)
ANTRON TECHNOLOGIES INC
40 Brunswick Ave Ste 104 (08817-2589)
PHONE...................................732 205-0415
Sing-Chang Hung, *President*
Berkuei Hung, *Corp Secy*
EMP: 5
SALES (est): 3MM　**Privately Held**
WEB: www.antron.com
SIC: 5045 3577　Computer peripheral equipment; computer peripheral equipment

(G-2458)
APCO EXTRUDERS INC
180 National Rd (08817-2811)
P.O. Box 556 (08818-0556)
PHONE...................................732 287-3000
Manny Parnes, *President*
David Viera, *Vice Pres*
EMP: 42
SALES (est): 9.7MM　**Privately Held**
SIC: 2673　Bags: plastic, laminated & coated

(G-2459)
ARCHON VITAMIN LLC (PA)
3775 Park Ave Unit 1 (08820-2566)
PHONE...................................732 537-1220
▲ **EMP:** 62
SQ FT: 45,000
SALES (est): 18.2MM　**Privately Held**
WEB: www.archonvitamin.com
SIC: 2834　Vitamin preparations

(G-2460)
ARCHON VITAMIN LLC
3775 Park Ave Unit 1 (08820-2566)
PHONE...................................973 371-1700
EMP: 6
SALES (est): 963.7K　**Privately Held**
SIC: 2834　Vitamin preparations

PA: Archon Vitamin, Llc
3775 Park Ave Unit 1
Edison NJ 08820

(G-2461)
AROMIENS INC
98 Mayfield Ave (08837-3821)
PHONE...................................732 225-8689
Shizhong Wang, *Principal*
▲ **EMP:** 5
SALES (est): 678.9K　**Privately Held**
SIC: 2869　Industrial organic chemicals

(G-2462)
ASI COMPUTER TECHNOLOGIES INC
131 Fieldcrest Ave (08837-3622)
PHONE...................................732 343-7100
Rita Chang, *Branch Mgr*
EMP: 11
SALES (corp-wide): 468.9MM　**Privately Held**
SIC: 5734 5045 3571　Computer & software stores; computers, peripherals & software; electronic computers
PA: Asi Computer Technologies Inc
48289 Fremont Blvd
Fremont CA 94538
510 226-8000

(G-2463)
ATLAS AUTO TRIM INC
81 Us Highway 1 (08817-5059)
PHONE...................................732 985-6800
Sanford Dubin, *President*
EMP: 5
SQ FT: 3,000
SALES (est): 420K　**Privately Held**
WEB: www.atlasautotrim.com
SIC: 7532 2399　Interior repair services; upholstery & trim shop, automotive; seat covers, automobile

(G-2464)
AUSTARPHARMA LLC
18 Mayfield Ave (08837-3821)
PHONE...................................732 225-2930
Rong Liu, *CEO*
Dillon Gao, *Vice Pres*
Hongchun Qiu, *Vice Pres*
David Thang, *Vice Pres*
Jason LI, *Opers Staff*
◆ **EMP:** 80
SQ FT: 40,000
SALES (est): 20.7MM　**Privately Held**
SIC: 2834　Adrenal pharmaceutical preparations; tablets, pharmaceutical

(G-2465)
BASF CORPORATION
175 Raritan Center Pkwy (08837-3650)
PHONE...................................973 245-6000
Russ Jacobs, *General Mgr*
EMP: 40
SALES (corp-wide): 71.7B　**Privately Held**
SIC: 2869　Industrial organic chemicals
HQ: Basf Corporation
100 Park Ave
Florham Park NJ 07932
973 245-6000

(G-2466)
BAXTER HEALTHCARE CORPORATION
100 Raritan Center Pkwy # 120 (08837-3615)
PHONE...................................732 225-4700
Joe Seklecki, *Manager*
EMP: 200
SALES (corp-wide): 11.1B　**Publicly Held**
SIC: 2835　Blood derivative diagnostic agents
HQ: Baxter Healthcare Corporation
1 Baxter Pkwy
Deerfield IL 60015
224 948-2000

(G-2467)
BENNETT CABINETS
1251 Us Highway 1 (08837-3197)
PHONE...................................732 548-1616
Michael Bennett, *President*
EMP: 5 **EST:** 1962
SQ FT: 5,000
SALES: 650K　**Privately Held**
SIC: 2434　Wood kitchen cabinets

(G-2468)
BENTLEY LABORATORIES LLC (PA)
111 Fieldcrest Ave (08837-3622)
PHONE...................................732 512-0200
Brian Fitzpatrick, *CEO*
Greg Torchiana, *President*
John Kovacevich, *Exec VP*
Kathy Fitzpatrick, *Vice Pres*
Ann Marie Hansen, *Vice Pres*
▲ **EMP:** 200 **EST:** 1998
SQ FT: 115,000
SALES (est): 66.1MM　**Privately Held**
WEB: www.bentleylaboratories.com
SIC: 2844　Cosmetic preparations

(G-2469)
BIG RED PIN LLC
28 May St Apt 1 (08837-3587)
PHONE...................................732 993-9765
Dino Cicala, *CEO*
EMP: 5
SALES (est): 371.7K　**Privately Held**
SIC: 2752　Commercial printing, lithographic

(G-2470)
BIO-NATURE LABS LTD LBLTY CO
195 Campus Dr (08837-3937)
PHONE...................................732 738-5550
Michael Kruel, *President*
Lily Krue, *Vice Pres*
▼ **EMP:** 50
SQ FT: 35,000
SALES: 1.2MM　**Privately Held**
SIC: 2844 5999　Toilet preparations; cosmetics

(G-2471)
BUCKHEAD MEAT COMPANY
Also Called: Buckhead Beef N E
220 Raritan Center Pkwy (08837-3611)
PHONE...................................732 661-4900
Nella Marabutto, *Human Res Dir*
Glenn Ermoian, *Branch Mgr*
EMP: 105
SQ FT: 50,000
SALES (corp-wide): 60.1B　**Publicly Held**
WEB: www.buckheadbeef.com
SIC: 2013 2048 2011　Sausages & other prepared meats; slaughtering of nonfood animals; lard from carcasses slaughtered on site
HQ: Buckhead Meat Company
4500 Wickersham Dr
College Park GA 30337
404 355-4400

(G-2472)
C SYSTEMS LLC
510 Thornall St Ste 310 (08837-2207)
PHONE...................................732 338-9347
Roger Abram, *Project Mgr*
Larry Kelly, *Project Mgr*
John Nicoletta, *Project Mgr*
CJ Vicarel, *Project Mgr*
Heather Austen, *Opers Staff*
EMP: 12
SALES (est): 1.2MM　**Privately Held**
WEB: www.csystemsllc.net
SIC: 7372　Business oriented computer software

(G-2473)
CAPTIVATE INTERNATIONALLLC
28 May St Apt 1 (08837-3587)
PHONE...................................732 734-0403
Maria Cicala,
EMP: 4
SALES: 20K　**Privately Held**
SIC: 2741　Miscellaneous publishing

(G-2474)
CAPUTO INTERNATIONAL INC
112 Northfield Ave (08837-3805)
PHONE...................................732 225-5777
Joseph Caputo, *President*
Paul Caputo, *Vice Pres*
Vincent Caputo, *Vice Pres*
Samantha Caputo, *Accounts Mgr*
▲ **EMP:** 6
SQ FT: 9,000
SALES (est): 769.9K　**Privately Held**
SIC: 3281　Granite, cut & shaped

(G-2475)
CHACKO JOHN
Also Called: J S Manufacturing
21 Remington Dr (08820-3626)
PHONE.................................732 494-1088
John Chacko, *Owner*
EMP: 4
SALES (est): 540K **Privately Held**
SIC: 3599 Custom machinery

(G-2476)
CHARLES KERR ENTERPRISES INC
Also Called: Mariners Annual
1090 King Georges Post Rd # 802
(08837-3701)
PHONE.................................732 738-6500
Chris Kerr, *President*
EMP: 6
SQ FT: 1,500
SALES (est): 480K **Privately Held**
SIC: 2741 Miscellaneous publishing

(G-2477)
CINCO STAR LLC
2 Karnell Ct (08820-2947)
PHONE.................................732 744-1617
Vinod Zaveri,
Usha Zaveri,
EMP: 5
SQ FT: 1,000
SALES: 1.5MM **Privately Held**
SIC: 3911 Jewelry, precious metal

(G-2478)
CLAYTON BLOCK COMPANY INC
1025 Route 1 (08837-2904)
P.O. Box 3015, Lakewood (08701-9015)
PHONE.................................732 549-1234
Mike Ulikowsky, *Manager*
EMP: 25
SALES (corp-wide): 31.8MM **Privately Held**
WEB: www.claytononline.com
SIC: 5211 3271 3273 Concrete & cinder block; concrete block & brick; ready-mixed concrete
PA: Clayton Block Company, Inc.
1355 Campus Pkwy Ste 200
Wall Township NJ 07753
888 763-8665

(G-2479)
CLEAN BBQ INC
47 Langstaff Ave (08817-3312)
PHONE.................................732 299-8877
Kyung Rhee, *President*
EMP: 5
SQ FT: 15,000
SALES: 2MM **Privately Held**
SIC: 3631 Barbecues, grills & braziers (outdoor cooking)

(G-2480)
COLONIAL WIRE & CABLE CO INC
85 National Rd (08817-2808)
PHONE.................................732 287-1557
Jake Salidino, *Manager*
EMP: 5
SALES (corp-wide): 11.3MM **Privately Held**
WEB: www.colonialwire.com
SIC: 3357 Nonferrous wiredrawing & insulating
PA: Colonial Wire & Cable Co.,Jnc.
40 Engineers Rd
Hauppauge NY 11788
631 234-8500

(G-2481)
COMMUNICATIONS SUPPLY CORP
104 Sunfield Ave (08837-3845)
PHONE.................................732 346-1864
Andy Fallon, *Financial Exec*
Gary Cargulia, *Sales Associate*
Bill Dalton, *Manager*
EMP: 33 **Publicly Held**
WEB: www.gocsc.com
SIC: 4899 3357 Data communication services; building wire & cable, nonferrous

HQ: Communications Supply Corp
200 E Lies Rd
Carol Stream IL 60188
630 221-6400

(G-2482)
COMPREHENSIVE HEALTHCARE SYSTM
2025 Lincoln Hwy (08817-3350)
PHONE.................................732 362-2000
Hassan Mohaideen, *Principal*
Mariam Mohaideen, *Vice Pres*
Satish Kurian, *CFO*
EMP: 100
SQ FT: 2,500
SALES (est): 102.2K **Privately Held**
SIC: 7371 7372 8742 Computer software development; business oriented computer software; management information systems consultant

(G-2483)
CONTI-ROBERT AND CO JV
2045 Lincoln Hwy (08817-3334)
PHONE.................................732 520-5000
William Picken, *Managing Dir*
Lisa Rigatti, *Admin Asst*
EMP: 99
SALES (est): 1MM **Privately Held**
SIC: 1389 Lease tanks, oil field: erecting, cleaning & repairing

(G-2484)
COSPACK AMERICA CORP
3856 Park Ave (08820-2508)
PHONE.................................732 548-5858
▲ EMP: 20
SALES (est): 3MM **Privately Held**
WEB: www.cospackamerica.com
SIC: 3443 Metal parts

(G-2485)
CRANIAL TECHNOLOGIES INC
2163 Oak Tree Rd (08820-1083)
PHONE.................................908 754-0572
EMP: 6 **Privately Held**
SIC: 3842 Orthopedic appliances
PA: Cranial Technologies, Inc.
1395 W Auto Dr
Tempe AZ 85284

(G-2486)
CRODA INC (DH)
300 Columbus Cir Ste A (08837-3907)
PHONE.................................732 417-0800
Sandra Breene, *President*
David Shannon, *Senior VP*
◆ EMP: 75
SQ FT: 36,400
SALES (est): 57.5MM
SALES (corp-wide): 1.7B **Privately Held**
WEB: www.crodausa.com
SIC: 2899 Chemical preparations

(G-2487)
CRODA INVESTMENTS INC (HQ)
300 Columbus Cir Ste A (08837-3907)
PHONE.................................732 417-0800
EMP: 9
SALES (est): 47.6MM
SALES (corp-wide): 1.7B **Privately Held**
SIC: 2899 Chemical preparations
PA: Croda International Public Limited Company
Cowick Hall
Goole N HUMBS DN14
140 586-0551

(G-2488)
CRYOPAK VERIFICATION TECH INC (PA)
551 Raritan Center Pkwy (08837-3918)
PHONE.................................732 346-9200
Carlene Spencer, *Controller*
David Joffe, *Sales Staff*
Ken Fioretti, *Info Tech Dir*
EMP: 14
SALES (est): 3.7MM **Privately Held**
SIC: 5047 3053 Medical equipment & supplies; packing materials

(G-2489)
CURRAN-PFEIFF CORP
Liddle Ave (08837)
P.O. Box 527, Metuchen (08840-0527)
PHONE.................................732 225-0555
George C Pfeiff Sr, *President*
Sang Huifang, *Admin Sec*
EMP: 12 EST: 1924
SQ FT: 30,000
SALES: 310K **Privately Held**
WEB: www.curranpfeiffcorp.com
SIC: 3264 3567 3297 Insulators, electrical: porcelain; industrial furnaces & ovens; nonclay refractories

(G-2490)
CYGATE SFTWR & CONSULTING LLC
Also Called: Sterling System
22 Meridian Rd Unit 9 (08820-2848)
PHONE.................................732 452-1881
Nilesh Dasondi, *President*
Sejal Dasondi, *Vice Pres*
EMP: 5
SQ FT: 5,000
SALES (est): 602.9K **Privately Held**
WEB: www.cygatesoftware.com
SIC: 7372 7379 Prepackaged software; computer related consulting services

(G-2491)
DENTALWORX LAB LTD LBLTY CO
1000 New Durham Rd (08817-2368)
PHONE.................................732 981-9096
Wayne Wong,
EMP: 6
SALES (est): 586.7K **Privately Held**
SIC: 3843 Dental equipment & supplies

(G-2492)
DOLLFUS MIEG COMPANY INC
Also Called: DMC
86 Northfield Ave (08837-3807)
PHONE.................................732 662-1005
Jacques Boubal, *CEO*
◆ EMP: 125
SQ FT: 55,000
SALES (est): 31.2MM
SALES (corp-wide): 1MM **Privately Held**
SIC: 5199 2231 2259 Yarns; apparel & outerwear broadwoven fabrics; convertors, knit goods
HQ: Dmc
13 Rue De Pfastatt
Mulhouse 68200
800 140-270

(G-2493)
DRANETZ TECHNOLOGIES INC (HQ)
1000 New Durham Rd (08817-2368)
P.O. Box 4019 (08818-4019)
PHONE.................................732 248-4358
Robert Hart, *President*
EMP: 68 EST: 1962
SQ FT: 60,000
SALES (est): 12.7MM **Privately Held**
WEB: www.dranetz-bmi.com
SIC: 3825 3829 3823 3699 Test equipment for electronic & electric measurement; measuring & controlling devices; industrial instrmnts msrmnt display/control process variable; electrical equipment & supplies

(G-2494)
DSE HEALTHCARE SOLUTIONS LLC
105 Fieldcrest Ave 502a (08837-3628)
P.O. Box 6321 (08818-6321)
PHONE.................................732 417-1870
Moaiz F Daya, *President*
Robert Stites, *Chairman*
Scott R Emerson, *Exec VP*
William Everett, *Vice Pres*
Ralph Durham, *Purchasing*
▲ EMP: 6
SQ FT: 3,000
SALES (est): 1.4MM **Privately Held**
WEB: www.dsehealth.com
SIC: 2834 Vitamin, nutrient & hematinic preparations for human use

(G-2495)
DSO FLUID HANDLING CO INC
Also Called: Dso Sanitary Supply
300 Mcgaw Dr Ste 2 (08837-3708)
PHONE.................................732 225-9100
Darrin Oppenheim, *Mng Member*
▲ EMP: 20
SQ FT: 20,000
SALES (est): 3.8MM
SALES (corp-wide): 4.5B **Privately Held**
SIC: 3312 3069 Stainless steel; hard rubber & molded rubber products
HQ: Alfa Laval U.S. Holding Inc.
5400 Intl Trade Dr
Richmond VA 23231

(G-2496)
E CHABOT LTD
Also Called: Chabot Jewelry
195 Carter Dr Ste 2 (08817-2068)
PHONE.................................212 575-1026
Ezra Shabot, *President*
Bob Shabot, *Treasurer*
◆ EMP: 50
SALES (est): 11.2MM **Privately Held**
WEB: www.echabot.com
SIC: 5094 3911 Jewelry; jewelry apparel

(G-2497)
EASY AERIAL INC
198 Pear Blossom Dr (08837)
PHONE.................................646 639-4410
Ido Gur, *CEO*
Ivan Stamatovski, *Chief Engr*
Daniel Sirkis,
EMP: 5 EST: 2017
SALES (est): 222.4K **Privately Held**
SIC: 3721 Aircraft

(G-2498)
ECOM GROUP INC (PA)
Also Called: Ecomelectronics
3775 Park Ave Unit 3 (08820-2566)
PHONE.................................718 504-7355
Alan Cohen, *President*
Abraham Cohen, *Vice Pres*
Ezra Cohen, *Admin Sec*
▲ EMP: 20
SQ FT: 42,000
SALES (est): 22.5MM **Privately Held**
SIC: 5731 3261 Consumer electronic equipment; vitreous plumbing fixtures

(G-2499)
EDGE ORTHOTICS INC
209 Pierson Ave (08837-3139)
PHONE.................................732 549-3343
James C Bauman, *President*
Donna Erikson, *Manager*
EMP: 5
SQ FT: 2,500
SALES (est): 617.3K **Privately Held**
SIC: 3842 Limbs, artificial

(G-2500)
EDISON FINISHING
191 Vineyard Rd Ste 3 (08817-4751)
PHONE.................................732 287-6660
John Autovino, *President*
EMP: 6
SQ FT: 10,000
SALES: 1MM **Privately Held**
WEB: www.edisonfinishing.com
SIC: 2499 Decorative wood & woodwork

(G-2501)
EDISON OPHTHALMOLOGY ASSOC LLC
2177 Oak Tree Rd Ste 203t (08820-1082)
PHONE.................................908 822-0070
John C Park, *Mng Member*
EMP: 10
SALES (est): 1.2MM **Privately Held**
SIC: 3851 Lenses, ophthalmic

(G-2502)
ENERGY OPTIONS INC
3 Ethel Rd Ste 300 (08817-2855)
PHONE.................................732 512-9100
Bradley Freeman, *President*
Robert Romandetto, *Manager*
EMP: 30
SQ FT: 10,000

SALES (est): 3.4MM
SALES (corp-wide): 55MM **Privately Held**
SIC: 3822 Air flow controllers, air condition-ing & refrigeration; building services moni-toring controls, automatic
PA: Albireo Energy, Llc
3 Ethel Rd Ste 300
Edison NJ 08817
732 512-9100

(G-2503)
ENTERIX INC
Also Called: Clincial Genomics
236 Fernwood Ave (08837-3839)
PHONE..................................732 429-1899
Lawrence Latointe, *President*
Robert Dachille, *Vice Pres*
Richard J Sands, *CFO*
▲ **EMP:** 25 EST: 1999
SQ FT: 14,000
SALES: 7MM **Privately Held**
WEB: www.enterix.com
SIC: 3845 8733 Ultrasonic scanning de-vices, medical; medical research
PA: Clinical Genomics Pty Ltd
2 Eden Park Dr
Macquarie Park NSW 2113

(G-2504)
ENVIRO PAK INC
125 National Rd (08817-2810)
PHONE..................................732 248-1600
Edward Fitzpatrick, *President*
Joseph Otterbine, *Corp Secy*
EMP: 25
SQ FT: 25,000
SALES (est): 5.1MM **Privately Held**
WEB: www.enviropakdrums.com
SIC: 3443 Containers, shipping (bombs, etc.): metal plate

(G-2505)
EOS ENERGY STORAGE LLC
214 Fernwood Ave Bldg B (08837-3839)
PHONE..................................732 225-8400
Joe Mastrangelo, *CEO*
Edgar Soto, *Opers Staff*
Mack Treece, *CFO*
Jim Morgenson, *VP Sales*
Tyler Kiss, *Accounts Mgr*
EMP: 25
SALES (est): 6.9MM **Privately Held**
SIC: 8731 3699 Energy research; electri-cal equipment & supplies

(G-2506)
ERCO LIGHTING INC (PA)
160 Rrtan Ctr Pkwy Ste 10 (08837)
PHONE..................................732 225-8856
Mark Sieber, *President*
▲ **EMP:** 19
SQ FT: 7,000
SALES (est): 3.8MM **Privately Held**
SIC: 3648 Lighting equipment

(G-2507)
ESSENTRA PLASTICS LLC
95 Campus Dr (08837-3910)
PHONE..................................518 437-5138
James Nixon, *Mng Member*
EMP: 7
SALES (corp-wide): 1.3B **Privately Held**
SIC: 2891 Adhesives & sealants
HQ: Essentra Plastics Llc
3123 Station Rd
Erie PA 16510

(G-2508)
EXCELLENCE IN BAKING INC
Also Called: La Bonbonniere
2062 State Route 27 (08817-3330)
PHONE..................................732 287-1313
Bryan Pansari, *CEO*
EMP: 4 EST: 2010
SALES (est): 294K **Privately Held**
SIC: 2051 Bread, cake & related products

(G-2509)
F & S AWNING AND BLIND CO INC
Also Called: F&S Awning & Sign
13 Coral St (08837-3242)
PHONE..................................732 738-4110
Robert Trotte, *President*
Carol Trotte, *Vice Pres*

EMP: 7
SQ FT: 850
SALES (est): 720K **Privately Held**
SIC: 1799 3993 5131 Awning installation; electric signs; flags & banners

(G-2510)
FABRICTEX LLC
278 Raritan Center Pkwy (08837-3610)
PHONE..................................732 225-3990
Ernest Grinacoff,
◆ **EMP:** 7
SALES (est): 1MM **Privately Held**
SIC: 2297 Nonwoven fabrics

(G-2511)
FERRO CORPORATION
54 Kellogg Ct (08817-2509)
PHONE..................................732 287-4925
Thomas Loschiazo, *Branch Mgr*
EMP: 50
SALES (corp-wide): 1.6B **Publicly Held**
WEB: www.ferro.com
SIC: 2865 2851 2816 Color lakes or ton-ers; color pigments, organic; lacquers, varnishes, enamels & other coatings; in-organic pigments
PA: Ferro Corporation
6060 Parkland Blvd # 250
Mayfield Heights OH 44124
216 875-5600

(G-2512)
FINE MINERALS INTL INC
11 Progress St (08820-1102)
PHONE..................................732 318-6760
Daniel Trinchillo, *President*
▲ **EMP:** 5
SALES (est): 573.4K **Privately Held**
SIC: 3295 Minerals, ground or treated

(G-2513)
FORMER CIRCUIT INC
5 Sutton Pl (08817-2223)
P.O. Box 2162 (08818-2162)
PHONE..................................732 549-0056
Joseph Lipson, *President*
Ronald Lipson, *Vice Pres*
Eva Lipson, *Treasurer*
▲ **EMP:** 8
SQ FT: 5,000
SALES (est): 1.9MM **Privately Held**
WEB: www.luminairelighting.com
SIC: 3646 Commercial indusl & institu-tional electric lighting fixtures

(G-2514)
FOTO FANTASY
2850 Woodbridge Ave (08837-3616)
PHONE..................................732 548-8446
EMP: 4
SALES (est): 240K **Privately Held**
SIC: 7929 2759 Entertainer/Entertainment Group Commercial Printing

(G-2515)
FUJI ELECTRIC CORP AMERICA (HQ)
50 Northfield Ave (08837-3807)
PHONE..................................732 560-9410
Philip Charatz, *CEO*
David Schrader, *Business Mgr*
Sumio Akimatsu, *Vice Pres*
Motoyuki Arai, *Vice Pres*
Koji Yasuda, *Vice Pres*
◆ **EMP:** 54
SQ FT: 4,916
SALES (est): 63.1MM **Privately Held**
WEB: www.fujielectric.com
SIC: 5063 3999 3678 Flashlights; bleach-ing & dyeing of sponges; electronic con-nectors

(G-2516)
FUJIFILM NORTH AMERICA CORP
1100 King Georges Post Rd (08837-3731)
PHONE..................................732 857-3000
Jiro Tsukahara, *Division Mgr*
Masaharu Fukumoto, *Managing Dir*
Larry Taulbee, *District Mgr*
Brian Hammock, *Vice Pres*
Jo Nunn, *Vice Pres*
EMP: 500 **Privately Held**

SIC: 7384 4226 3861 3695 Photofinish laboratories; special warehousing & stor-age; photographic equipment & supplies; magnetic & optical recording media
HQ: Fujifilm North America Corporation
200 Summit Lake Dr Fl 2
Valhalla NY 10595
914 789-8100

(G-2517)
GALAXY METAL PRODUCTS LLC
2960 Woodbridge Ave (08837-3406)
PHONE..................................908 668-5200
Joe Makara, *Principal*
Mike Ceceri, *Sales Mgr*
Rich Frobosilo, *Sales Staff*
Darcie Kuchta, *Planning*
EMP: 45
SQ FT: 35,000
SALES (est): 7.8MM **Privately Held**
SIC: 3442 Metal doors, sash & trim

(G-2518)
GAMKA SALES CO INC
983 New Durham Rd (08817-2253)
PHONE..................................732 248-1400
Weiss, *President*
Ronald Weiss, *Vice Pres*
EMP: 20
SQ FT: 56,000
SALES (est): 6.8MM **Privately Held**
WEB: www.gamka.com
SIC: 7699 7359 7353 7629 Industrial ma-chinery & equipment repair; construction equipment repair; equipment rental & leasing; tool rental; lawn & garden equip-ment rental; rental store, general; earth moving equipment, rental or leasing; gen-erator repair; concrete curing & hardening compounds; engine repair

(G-2519)
GARDEN STATE RECYCL EDISON LLC
355 Meadow Rd (08837-4101)
PHONE..................................732 393-0200
Bill Grove,
Michael Reali,
EMP: 13
SALES (est): 1MM **Privately Held**
WEB: www.gardenstaterecycling.com
SIC: 2611 Pulp manufactured from waste or recycled paper

(G-2520)
GARRATT-CALLAHAN COMPANY
306 Talmadge Rd (08817-2300)
PHONE..................................732 287-2200
Janet Robinson, *Branch Mgr*
EMP: 5
SALES (corp-wide): 69.4MM **Privately Held**
WEB: www.g-c.com
SIC: 2899 Water treating compounds
PA: Garratt-Callahan Company
50 Ingold Rd
Burlingame CA 94010
650 697-5811

(G-2521)
GLOBAL POWER TECHNOLOGY INC (PA)
Also Called: GMC-I New Wrld Btiligungs GMBH
1000 New Durham Rd (08817-2368)
P.O. Box 4019 (08818-4019)
PHONE..................................732 287-3680
Joseph I Gonzalez Rivas, *President*
Robert Hart, *Vice Pres*
Tony Laino, *Facilities Mgr*
Robert Rodgers, *Opers Staff*
Thurman Bridgers, *Engineer*
EMP: 63
SQ FT: 40,000
SALES (est): 19.3MM **Privately Held**
WEB: www.powerqualityseminars.com
SIC: 8711 7371 3825 3823 Engineering services; custom computer programming services; test equipment for electronic & electric measurement; power measuring equipment, electrical; industrial instrmnts msrmnt display/control process variable

(G-2522)
GRAYBAR ELECTRIC COMPANY INC
105 Feldcrest Ave Ste 207 (08837)
PHONE..................................973 404-5555
Don Felter, *Business Mgr*
Scott Kennedy, *Branch Mgr*
EMP: 89
SALES (corp-wide): 7.2B **Privately Held**
WEB: www.graybar.com
SIC: 4783 3645 Packing goods for ship-ping; residential lighting fixtures
PA: Graybar Electric Company, Inc.
34 N Meramec Ave
Saint Louis MO 63105
314 573-9200

(G-2523)
GREYCELL LABS INC
190 State Route 27 # 102 (08820-3538)
PHONE..................................732 444-0123
Jyoti Patel, *President*
Michael Reynolds, *Sales Executive*
Swati Shah, *Manager*
Amy Patel, *Recruiter*
EMP: 20
SALES (est): 1.6MM **Privately Held**
SIC: 7372 7371 Business oriented com-puter software; custom computer pro-gramming services

(G-2524)
HAN HEAN U S A CORP
3856 Park Ave (08820-2508)
PHONE..................................732 494-3256
Pei Y Hou, *Manager*
▲ **EMP:** 7
SALES (est): 659.5K
SALES (corp-wide): 697.8K **Privately Held**
SIC: 3999 Manufacturing industries
PA: Harhean Precision Industrial Co., Ltd.
2f, 124, Tung Ta Rd., Sec. 4,
Hsinchu City 30057
353 627-21

(G-2525)
HANES COMPANIES - NJ LLC
104 Sunfield Ave (08837-3845)
PHONE..................................201 729-9100
Elizabeth Whelan, *Opers Mgr*
Jim Curia, *Manager*
Tom Corrao,
▲ **EMP:** 16
SALES (est): 2.1MM
SALES (corp-wide): 4.2B **Publicly Held**
WEB: www.leggett.com
SIC: 2261 Dyeing cotton broadwoven fab-rics
PA: Leggett & Platt, Incorporated
1 Leggett Rd
Carthage MO 64836
417 358-8131

(G-2526)
HANGER CENTRAL LLC
12 Parkway Pl (08837-3718)
PHONE..................................732 750-1161
Jack Mosseri, *President*
EMP: 6
SQ FT: 3,000
SALES: 200K **Privately Held**
SIC: 3429 Hangers, wall hardware

(G-2527)
HANSSEM
50 Idlewild Rd (08817-4170)
PHONE..................................732 425-7695
Joo Lee, *General Mgr*
EMP: 4
SALES (est): 452.9K **Privately Held**
SIC: 2434 Wood kitchen cabinets

(G-2528)
HB FULLER COMPANY
Also Called: Adhesves Sealants Coatings Div
59 Brunswick Ave (08817-2512)
PHONE..................................732 287-8330
Nate Ranford, *Opers-Prdtn-Mfg*
EMP: 30
SALES (corp-wide): 3B **Publicly Held**
WEB: www.hbfuller.com
SIC: 2891 Adhesives

▲ = Import ▼=Export
◆ =Import/Export

PA: H.B. Fuller Company
1200 Willow Lake Blvd
Saint Paul MN 55110
651 236-5900

(G-2529)
HEPION PHARMACEUTICALS INC (PA)
399 Thornall St Ste 1 (08837-2238)
PHONE..................................732 902-4000
Gary S Jacob, *Ch of Bd*
Robert Foster, *Acting CEO*
Theresa Matkovits, *Exec VP*
John Cavan, *CFO*
Stephen Kilmer, *Investment Ofcr*
EMP: 21 **EST:** 2013
SQ FT: 4,000
SALES (est): 3.1MM **Publicly Held**
SIC: 2834 Pharmaceutical preparations

(G-2530)
HERCULES LLC
20 Lee St (08817-6404)
PHONE..................................732 777-4697
Nidia Lujanhercules, *Branch Mgr*
EMP: 9
SALES (corp-wide): 3.7B **Publicly Held**
SIC: 2891 Adhesives
HQ: Hercules Llc
500 Hercules Rd
Wilmington DE 19808
302 594-5000

(G-2531)
HOWMAN ASSOCIATES INC
Also Called: Howman Controls
12 Garden St (08817-4218)
PHONE..................................732 985-7474
Howard Rood, *President*
EMP: 6
SQ FT: 2,200
SALES (est): 1.3MM **Privately Held**
WEB: www.howman.com
SIC: 3625 Industrial controls: push button, selector switches, pilot

(G-2532)
HUBER INTERNATIONAL CORP
499 Thornall St Ste 8 (08837-2267)
PHONE..................................732 549-8600
Mike Marberry, *President*
Mike Lapradd, *Safety Mgr*
Scott Griles, *Maint Spvr*
John Villareal, *Opers Staff*
Matt Corley, *Purch Mgr*
EMP: 5
SALES (est): 277.5K **Privately Held**
SIC: 3443 Industrial vessels, tanks & containers

(G-2533)
IMPORTERS SERVICE CORP
Also Called: ISC
65 Brunswick Ave (08817-2512)
PHONE..................................732 248-1946
Eric Berliner, *President*
Patricia Berliner, *Admin Sec*
◆ **EMP:** 40 **EST:** 1939
SQ FT: 113,000
SALES (est): 11.3MM **Privately Held**
WEB: www.iscgums.com
SIC: 2861 Gum & wood chemicals

(G-2534)
INNOVATIVE COSMTC CONCEPTS LLC (PA)
Also Called: Innovative Design
399 Thornall St Ste 26 (08837-2243)
PHONE..................................212 391-8110
Robert Murello, *Mng Member*
Michael Murello,
▲ **EMP:** 10
SQ FT: 3,500
SALES (est): 1.3MM **Privately Held**
SIC: 2844 Cosmetic preparations

(G-2535)
ISOMETRIC MICRO FINISH COATING
477 Plainfield Rd (08820-2630)
PHONE..................................732 306-6339
Roy Leo, *Owner*
EMP: 4
SQ FT: 5,000

SALES (est): 220K **Privately Held**
SIC: 3479 Painting, coating & hot dipping

(G-2536)
J G MACHINE WORKS INC
2147 State Route 27 Ste D (08817-3365)
PHONE..................................732 203-2077
John Croddick, *President*
EMP: 9 **EST:** 1953
SQ FT: 10,200
SALES (est): 1MM **Privately Held**
SIC: 3535 3565 Conveyors & conveying equipment; packaging machinery

(G-2537)
J S PALUCH CO INC
510 Thornall St Ste 140 (08837-2230)
PHONE..................................732 516-1900
Robert J Bober, *Branch Mgr*
EMP: 12
SALES (corp-wide): 87.6MM **Privately Held**
SIC: 2731 2721 7371 2741 Book publishing; periodicals; custom computer programming services; miscellaneous publishing
PA: J. S. Paluch Co., Inc.
3708 River Rd Ste 400
Franklin Park IL 60131
847 678-9300

(G-2538)
JAPAN STEEL WORKS AMERICA INC (HQ)
Also Called: J S W
379 Thornall St Ste 5 (08837-2226)
PHONE..................................212 490-2630
Akitoshi Tamura, *President*
▲ **EMP:** 5
SQ FT: 1,700
SALES (est): 7.2MM **Privately Held**
SIC: 5084 3291 Plastic products machinery; abrasive metal & steel products

(G-2539)
JFK SUPPLIES INC
85 Lexington Ave (08817-2937)
PHONE..................................732 985-7800
Fred Schachter, *President*
David Schachter, *COO*
EMP: 10
SALES (est): 1.2MM **Privately Held**
SIC: 5943 5999 5113 3679 Office forms & supplies; medical apparatus & supplies; shipping supplies; electronic loads & power supplies; household appliance stores; beddings & linens

(G-2540)
JM HUBER CORPORATION (PA)
499 Thornall St Ste 8 (08837-2267)
PHONE..................................732 603-3630
Mike Marberry, *Ch of Bd*
William B Goodspeed, *President*
Andrew Trott, *President*
Jeremy Cowper, *Business Mgr*
Mike Moriarty, *Business Mgr*
◆ **EMP:** 86 **EST:** 1883
SQ FT: 200,000
SALES (est): 861.3MM **Privately Held**
WEB: www.huber.com
SIC: 0811 1311 1455 2493 Timber tracts; crude petroleum production; kaolin mining; strandboard, oriented; industrial inorganic chemicals

(G-2541)
JOHN WILEY & SONS INC
41 Saw Mill Pond Rd (08817-6025)
PHONE..................................732 302-2265
John Wiley, *Manager*
EMP: 80
SALES (corp-wide): 1.8B **Publicly Held**
SIC: 2731 Textbooks: publishing only, not printed on site
PA: John Wiley & Sons, Inc.
111 River St Ste 2000
Hoboken NJ 07030
201 748-6000

(G-2542)
JOHNS MANVILLE CORPORATION
Liddle Ave (08837)
PHONE..................................732 225-9190
Raymond Bruno, *Branch Mgr*

EMP: 45
SALES (corp-wide): 225.3B **Publicly Held**
WEB: www.jm.com
SIC: 2493 3086 Insulation & roofing material, reconstituted wood; insulation or cushioning material, foamed plastic
HQ: Johns Manville Corporation
717 17th St Ste 800
Denver CO 80202
303 978-2000

(G-2543)
JOHNSON CONTROLS INC
264 Fernwood Ave (08837-3839)
PHONE..................................732 225-6700
Rick Thomas, *Branch Mgr*
EMP: 55 **Privately Held**
SIC: 8711 5084 1731 7629 Electrical or electronic engineering; controlling instruments & accessories; electronic controls installation; electronic equipment repair; auto controls regulating residntl & coml environmt & applncs
HQ: Johnson Controls, Inc.
5757 N Green Bay Ave
Milwaukee WI 53209
414 524-1200

(G-2544)
KABAB & CURRY EXPRESS
4 Brunswick Ave (08817-2500)
PHONE..................................732 416-6560
Shabbir Shiliwal, *Owner*
EMP: 4
SALES (est): 286.5K **Privately Held**
SIC: 2741 Miscellaneous publishing

(G-2545)
KAIZEN TECHNOLOGIES INC (PA)
1 State Route 27 Ste 10 (08820-3962)
PHONE..................................732 452-9555
Ashok Krisnaswany, *President*
Sunitha Ashwin, *Business Mgr*
Vijay Patil, *Vice Pres*
Vikram Kumar, *Opers Staff*
Ashok Poddar, *Sales Staff*
EMP: 35
SQ FT: 4,000
SALES (est): 19.8MM **Privately Held**
SIC: 7372 Prepackaged software

(G-2546)
KUMAR & KUMAR INC
57 Denise Dr (08820-4603)
PHONE..................................732 322-0435
Ashish Sood, *President*
▲ **EMP:** 5
SALES (est): 200K **Privately Held**
SIC: 3462 Iron & steel forgings

(G-2547)
KWALITY FOODS LTD LIABILITY CO
1734 Oak Tree Rd (08820-2855)
PHONE..................................732 906-1941
Dr Kanti Parekh,
Anand Parekh,
Jyoti Parekh,
EMP: 5
SALES (est): 290K **Privately Held**
SIC: 2024 Ice cream & frozen desserts

(G-2548)
L A DREYFUS CO
3775 Park Ave (08820-2566)
PHONE..................................732 549-1600
Charlean B Gmunder, *President*
William Wrigley, *Chairman*
John Foster, *Vice Pres*
Richard Krema, *Vice Pres*
James Kyle, *Treasurer*
▲ **EMP:** 170 **EST:** 1909
SQ FT: 500,000
SALES (est): 17.7MM
SALES (corp-wide): 34.2B **Privately Held**
WEB: www.wrigley.com
SIC: 2067 Chewing gum base
HQ: Wm. Wrigley Jr. Company
930 W Evergreen Ave
Chicago IL 60642
312 280-4710

(G-2549)
LEATHER WORKS NJ LTD LBLTY CO
55 Parsonage Rd Ste 2100a (08837-2480)
PHONE..................................732 452-1100
Deep Bhatia, *Principal*
▲ **EMP:** 6
SALES (est): 238.6K **Privately Held**
SIC: 2329 5199 Men's & boys' leather, wool & down-filled outerwear; leather, leather goods & furs

(G-2550)
LEGGETT & PLATT INCORPORATED
Also Called: Leggett & Platt 2502
521 Sunfield Ave (08837)
PHONE..................................732 225-2440
EMP: 92
SQ FT: 83,000
SALES (corp-wide): 3.7B **Publicly Held**
SIC: 2515 Mfg Mattresses/Bedsprings
PA: Leggett & Platt, Incorporated
1 Leggett Rd
Carthage MO 64836
417 358-8131

(G-2551)
LION SALES CORP
125 Jackson Ave Ste 5 (08837-3147)
PHONE..................................732 417-9363
Robert Stella, *President*
EMP: 6
SALES (est): 68.5K **Privately Held**
SIC: 2389 Men's miscellaneous accessories

(G-2552)
LOCKHEED MARTIN CORPORATION
2890 Woodbridge Ave Ste 3 (08837-3659)
PHONE..................................732 321-4200
Richard Grazioli, *Manager*
EMP: 20 **Publicly Held**
WEB: www.lockheedmartin.com
SIC: 3674 8711 Semiconductors & related devices; engineering services
PA: Lockheed Martin Corporation
6801 Rockledge Dr
Bethesda MD 20817

(G-2553)
LOOK OF LOVE WIGS INC (PA)
1795b State Route 27 (08817-3483)
PHONE..................................908 687-9502
Robert A Anzivino, *President*
Ingrid Anzivino, *Vice Pres*
▲ **EMP:** 17 **EST:** 1968
SALES (est): 1.2MM **Privately Held**
WEB: www.lookoflove.com
SIC: 3999 5699 Wigs, including doll wigs, toupees or wiglets; wigs, toupees & wiglets

(G-2554)
LUX NATURALS LLC
9 Coral St (08837-3242)
PHONE..................................848 229-2950
Angeline Yellovich, *Mng Member*
Justine Savkob, *Mng Member*
EMP: 8
SALES (est): 758.3K **Privately Held**
SIC: 2844 5122 3999 5199 Toilet preparations; toiletries; candles; candles; general merchandise, mail order

(G-2555)
LVMH FRAGRANCE BRANDS US LLC
208 Fernwood Ave (08837-3839)
PHONE..................................212 931-2668
EMP: 8
SALES (corp-wide): 361.7MM **Privately Held**
WEB: www.parfumsgivenchy.com
SIC: 5122 2844 Perfumes; toilet preparations
HQ: Lvmh Fragrance Brands Us Llc
80 State St
Albany NY 12207
212 931-2600

(G-2556)
LYONDELL CHEMICAL COMPANY
340 Meadow Rd (08837-4102)
PHONE...................................732 985-6262
Amy Bullock, *Buyer*
John Miano, *QC Mgr*
Tim Pennington, *Engineer*
Noel Stewart, *Human Res Dir*
Catherine Koenig, *Branch Mgr*
EMP: 13
SALES (corp-wide): 39.1B **Privately Held**
SIC: 2869 Industrial organic chemicals
HQ: Lyondell Chemical Company
　　1221 Mckinney St Ste 300
　　Houston TX 77010
　　713 309-7200

(G-2557)
MACHINE TECH
3125 Woodbridge Ave Ste 4 (08837-3259)
PHONE...................................732 738-6810
Gordon Scala, *President*
EMP: 12 EST: 2007
SALES (est): 1.7MM **Privately Held**
SIC: 3599 Machine shop, jobbing & repair

(G-2558)
MAMROUT PAPER GROUP CORP
55 Talmadge Rd (08817-3338)
PHONE...................................718 510-5484
Simon Mamrout, *Owner*
EMP: 6
SALES (est): 1.5MM **Privately Held**
SIC: 5113 3089 Industrial & personal service paper; air mattresses, plastic

(G-2559)
MAVERICK INDUSTRIES INC
Also Called: Maverick Housewares
94 Mayfield Ave (08837-3821)
PHONE...................................732 417-9666
Edward H Mackin, *Ch of Bd*
▲ EMP: 11
SQ FT: 9,000
SALES (est): 2.6MM **Privately Held**
WEB: www.maverickhousewares.com
SIC: 3634 5719 Electric household cooking appliances; housewares

(G-2560)
MAXZONE VEHICLE LIGHTING CORP
24 Kilmer Rd (08817-2422)
PHONE...................................732 393-9600
Brook Yang, *Branch Mgr*
EMP: 11
SALES (corp-wide): 524.2MM **Privately Held**
SIC: 3714 Motor vehicle parts & accessories
HQ: Maxzone Vehicle Lighting Corp.
　　15889 Slover Ave Unit A
　　Fontana CA 92337
　　909 822-3288

(G-2561)
MEESHAA INC
Also Called: Diamond Essence
18 Tingley Ln (08820-1463)
PHONE...................................908 279-7985
Monali Shah, *President*
EMP: 6
SALES (est): 380K **Privately Held**
SIC: 3961 Jewelry apparel, non-precious metals

(G-2562)
MENASHA PACKAGING COMPANY LLC
112 Truman Dr (08817-2425)
PHONE...................................732 985-0800
Don Garda, *COO*
Grace Cheung, *Manager*
Michael Samples, *Manager*
Lee Schiedermayer, *Director*
EMP: 146
SALES (corp-wide): 1.7B **Privately Held**
SIC: 2653 Boxes, corrugated: made from purchased materials
HQ: Menasha Packaging Company, Llc
　　1645 Bergstrom Rd
　　Neenah WI 54956
　　920 751-1000

(G-2563)
METAL TEXTILES CORPORATION (HQ)
970 New Durham Rd (08817-2214)
PHONE...................................732 287-0800
Gregory S Vongas, *President*
George Walsh, *Opers Mgr*
Timothy W Miller, *Controller*
Joseph Hodonsky, *VP Sales*
Eric Dimartino, *Marketing Mgr*
▲ EMP: 72
SQ FT: 53,000
SALES: 30MM
SALES (corp-wide): 45.9MM **Privately Held**
WEB: www.metexcorp.com
SIC: 3496 Mesh, made from purchased wire
PA: United Capital Corp.
　　9 Park Pl
　　Great Neck NY 11021
　　516 466-6464

(G-2564)
METAL TEXTILES CORPORATION
Spectrum U V
206 Talmadge Rd (08817-2824)
PHONE...................................800 843-1215
Robert Obusek, *Branch Mgr*
Chuck Petersen, *Executive*
EMP: 37
SALES (corp-wide): 45.9MM **Privately Held**
SIC: 3641 Electric lamps & parts for specialized applications
HQ: Metal Textiles Corporation
　　970 New Durham Rd
　　Edison NJ 08817
　　732 287-0800

(G-2565)
MICRO INNOVATIONS CORP
1090 King Georges Post Rd (08837-3701)
P.O. Box 290399, Brooklyn NY (11229-0399)
PHONE...................................732 346-9333
Eddie Mizrahi, *CEO*
Jesse H Grindeland, *President*
Jerry Pasternak, *Vice Pres*
Bruno Ayanian, *CFO*
Daniel Shabat, *Shareholder*
EMP: 84
SQ FT: 70,000
SALES (est): 11.5MM **Privately Held**
WEB: www.microinv.com
SIC: 3577 5065 Computer peripheral equipment; modems, computer

(G-2566)
MIDDLESEX WATER COMPANY
100 Fairview Ave (08817-2440)
PHONE...................................732 579-0290
Richard Risoldi, *Manager*
Richard M Risoldi, *Manager*
EMP: 147
SALES (corp-wide): 138MM **Publicly Held**
WEB: www.middlesexwater.com
SIC: 3589 4941 Water treatment equipment, industrial; water supply
PA: Middlesex Water Company
　　485c Route 1 S Ste 400
　　Iselin NJ 08830
　　732 634-1500

(G-2567)
MIROAD RUBBER USA LLC
182 Whitman Ave (08817-4724)
PHONE...................................480 280-2543
Eric Yu, *Sales Associate*
Anthony Fue,
EMP: 5
SQ FT: 20,000
SALES (est): 500K **Privately Held**
SIC: 3069 Hard rubber products

(G-2568)
MISSRY ASSOCIATES INC
Also Called: Misco Toys
250 Carter Dr Ste 3 (08817-2069)
PHONE...................................732 752-7500
Morris Missry, *President*
Ezra Missry, *Vice Pres*
◆ EMP: 150

SQ FT: 500,000
SALES (est): 22.2MM **Privately Held**
WEB: www.miscohomeandgarden.com
SIC: 5193 2874 Artificial flowers; phosphatic fertilizers

(G-2569)
MOMENTUM USA INC (PA)
Also Called: Autopartsource
120 Fieldcrest Ave (08837-3656)
PHONE...................................844 300-1553
John Amalfe, *CEO*
Mark Stewart, *Finance Dir*
Dave Carter, *Director*
EMP: 10
SALES (est): 16.2MM **Privately Held**
SIC: 5075 3714 Air filters; brake drums, motor vehicle

(G-2570)
MRS MAZZULAS FOOD PRODUCTS
240 Carter Dr (08817-2097)
PHONE...................................732 248-0555
Christopher Lotito, *President*
Michael Gallina, *General Mgr*
John Leszczak, *COO*
Rosario Picone, *Manager*
▲ EMP: 5
SQ FT: 17,000
SALES: 1.5MM **Privately Held**
WEB: www.mazzula.com
SIC: 2032 2034 Italian foods: packaged in cans, jars, etc.; dehydrated fruits, vegetables, soups

(G-2571)
NEILMAX INDUSTRIES INC
15a Progress St (08820-1278)
PHONE...................................908 756-8800
Neil Max, *President*
▲ EMP: 5
SALES (est): 841.5K **Privately Held**
SIC: 3999 Barber & beauty shop equipment

(G-2572)
NETCOM SYSTEMS INC (PA)
200 Metroplex Dr (08817-2601)
PHONE...................................732 393-6100
Niten Ved, *President*
EMP: 25
SALES (est): 3.4MM **Privately Held**
WEB: www.netcom-sys.com
SIC: 7372 8742 7371 Application computer software; management information systems consultant; computer software development

(G-2573)
NEWARK WIRE WORKS INC
1059 King Georges Rd 10 # 103 (08837)
PHONE...................................732 661-2001
Joann Spellman, *President*
Joanne Spellman, *Admin Sec*
EMP: 40 EST: 1910
SQ FT: 22,000
SALES: 2.4MM **Privately Held**
WEB: www.newarkwireworks.com
SIC: 3496 Miscellaneous fabricated wire products

(G-2574)
NIGHTHAWK INTERACTIVE LLC
1090 King Georges Post Rd # 402 (08837-3701)
PHONE...................................732 243-9922
Joseph Sutton, *Mng Member*
EMP: 4 EST: 2014
SALES (est): 173.6K **Privately Held**
SIC: 2741 Miscellaneous publishing

(G-2575)
NJ ADVANCE MEDIA LLC
2015 State Route 27 # 300 (08817-3392)
PHONE...................................732 902-4300
Matt Kramer, *President*
Lamar Graham, *Vice Pres*
Linda Thompson, *Marketing Mgr*
Jeff Horn, *Manager*
Jay Petrie, *Director*
EMP: 90
SALES (corp-wide): 13.3MM **Privately Held**
SIC: 2711 Newspapers, publishing & printing

PA: Nj Advance Media Llc
　　485 Route 1 S Ste 3
　　Iselin NJ 08830
　　732 902-4300

(G-2576)
NLYTE SOFTWARE AMERICAS LTD (DH)
275 Raritan Center Pkwy (08837-3613)
PHONE...................................650 561-8200
Rob Bearden, *Ch of Bd*
Doug Sabella, *President*
Fred Dirla, *COO*
Mark Harris, *Vice Pres*
Robert Neave, *Vice Pres*
EMP: 130
SALES (est): 21.7MM **Privately Held**
SIC: 7372 Prepackaged software
HQ: Nlyte Software Americas Limited
　　26 Osiers Road
　　London SW18
　　208 877-7200

(G-2577)
NLYTE SOFTWARE INC
275 Raritan Center Pkwy (08837-3613)
PHONE...................................732 395-6920
Doug Sabella, *CEO*
Owen Nisbett, *CFO*
EMP: 30
SQ FT: 10,000
SALES (est): 4.8MM **Privately Held**
SIC: 7372 Prepackaged software
HQ: Nlyte Software Americas Limited
　　275 Raritan Center Pkwy
　　Edison NJ 08837

(G-2578)
NORTHEAST FOODS INC
Also Called: Automatic Roll
1 Gourmet Ln Ste 1 # 1 (08837-2902)
PHONE...................................732 549-2243
John Lyons, *Branch Mgr*
Rose Grajewski, *Manager*
EMP: 80
SALES (corp-wide): 335.5MM **Privately Held**
SIC: 2051 Bakery: wholesale or wholesale/retail combined
PA: Northeast Foods, Inc.
　　601 S Caroline St
　　Baltimore MD 21231
　　410 276-7254

(G-2579)
NOURYON SURFACE CHEMISTRY
Also Called: Akzo Chemicals
340 Meadow Rd (08837-4102)
PHONE...................................732 985-6262
Steve O Brien, *Branch Mgr*
EMP: 100
SQ FT: 5,000
SALES (corp-wide): 1.4B **Privately Held**
WEB: www.akzo-nobel.com
SIC: 2833 2899 2821 2819 Medicinals & botanicals; chemical preparations; plastics materials & resins; industrial inorganic chemicals
HQ: Nouryon Surface Chemistry
　　525 W Van Buren St # 1600
　　Chicago IL 60607
　　312 544-7000

(G-2580)
NOVA DISTRIBUTORS LLC
184 Whitman Ave (08817-4724)
PHONE...................................908 222-1010
Hemant Sanghvi, *Mng Member*
▲ EMP: 17
SQ FT: 20,000
SALES: 6MM **Privately Held**
SIC: 2673 2899 3999 5199 Food storage & trash bags (plastic); plastic bags: made from purchased materials; lighter fluid; cigarette lighters, except precious metal; general merchandise, non-durable; candy & other confectionery products; candy bars, including chocolate covered bars

(G-2581)
NOVEMBAL USA INC
3 Greek Ln (08817-2508)
PHONE...................................732 947-3030
John Fimelliti, *Production*
▲ EMP: 22

SALES (est): 5.7MM
SALES (corp-wide): 5.8MM **Privately Held**
SIC: 3089 Injection molding of plastics
HQ: Tetra Pak Closures France Sas
   Route De Nantes
   Chateaubriant 44110
   240 558-200

(G-2582)
NU-WORLD CORPORATION
340 Mill Rd (08817-6026)
PHONE....................................732 541-6300
Susan Pace, *General Mgr*
EMP: 7 **Privately Held**
SIC: 2844 Cosmetic preparations
HQ: Nu-World Corporation
   300 Milik St
   Carteret NJ 07008
   732 541-6300

(G-2583)
OFFICEMATE INTERNATIONAL CORP (PA)
90 Newfeld Ave Rritan Ctr Raritan Ctr (08837)
P.O. Box 6680 (08818-6680)
PHONE....................................732 225-7422
Shwu-Min Chen, *President*
Jeffrey H Bittens, *Principal*
Peter Chen, *Exec VP*
Martin Yang, *Senior VP*
Edward Chuang, *Project Engr*
▲ EMP: 88
SQ FT: 140,000
SALES (est): 14MM **Privately Held**
WEB: www.officemate.com
SIC: 2678 5112 Stationery: made from
   purchased materials; stationery & office
   supplies

(G-2584)
ORACLE AMERICA INC
399 Thornall St Ste 39 (08837-2265)
PHONE....................................732 623-4821
Raju Prattigodupu, *Manager*
Deepak Sahoo, *Consultant*
EMP: 58
SALES (corp-wide): 39.5B **Publicly Held**
SIC: 7372 Prepackaged software
HQ: Oracle America, Inc.
   500 Oracle Pkwy
   Redwood City CA 94065
   650 506-7000

(G-2585)
OSI LASER DIODE INC
4 Olsen Ave (08820-2419)
PHONE....................................732 549-9001
Deepak Chopra, *President*
EMP: 39
SQ FT: 25,000
SALES (est): 6.8MM
SALES (corp-wide): 1.1B **Publicly Held**
SIC: 3663 Radio & TV communications
   equipment
PA: Osi Systems, Inc.
   12525 Chadron Ave
   Hawthorne CA 90250
   310 978-0516

(G-2586)
PARIO GROUP LLC
70 Stephenville Pkwy (08820-2609)
PHONE....................................732 906-2302
Sumeer Toteja,
EMP: 4
SQ FT: 500
SALES: 100K **Privately Held**
SIC: 7372 Application computer software

(G-2587)
PARTNERS IN VISION INC
1090 King Georges Post Rd # 103
(08837-3702)
PHONE....................................888 748-1112
Judd Sky, *President*
Nina Bouzanis, *Regional Mgr*
Angelo Benfante, *Vice Pres*
Michael Zuk, *Human Res Mgr*
EMP: 3 EST: 1999
SALES: 23.2MM **Privately Held**
SIC: 5995 3229 Opticians; optical glass

(G-2588)
PATEL METAL PLATING INC
6 Emerson St (08820-1642)
PHONE....................................732 574-1770
EMP: 6
SALES: 1MM **Privately Held**
SIC: 3471 Plating/Polishing Service

(G-2589)
PICTURE IT INC
Also Called: Picture It Awards
1703 State Route 27 Ste 2 (08817-3497)
PHONE....................................732 819-0420
Roy Taetzsch, *President*
EMP: 6
SALES (est): 350K **Privately Held**
WEB: www.picawards.com
SIC: 3914 5999 Trophies, plated (all met-
   als); trophies & plaques

(G-2590)
PLANTFUSION
Also Called: Reliant Vitamins
3775 Park Ave (08820-2566)
PHONE....................................732 537-1220
Phil Dijeant, *Owner*
EMP: 4 EST: 2014
SALES (est): 196.1K **Privately Held**
SIC: 2834 Vitamin preparations

(G-2591)
PRINCETON TECH GROUP INTL CORP
182 Whitman Ave (08817-4724)
PHONE....................................732 328-9308
Tony Fue, *President*
EMP: 4
SQ FT: 1,000
SALES: 500K **Privately Held**
SIC: 3621 Motors & generators

(G-2592)
PROGRESS DISPLAYS INC
39 Progress St (08820-1102)
PHONE....................................908 757-6650
Roger L Robinson, *President*
EMP: 4
SALES (est): 263.4K **Privately Held**
SIC: 7313 3993 Printed media advertising
   representatives; signs & advertising spe-
   cialties

(G-2593)
PROGRESS WOODWORK
225 Pierson Ave (08837-3139)
PHONE....................................732 906-8680
EMP: 4
SALES (est): 403.7K **Privately Held**
SIC: 2431 Millwork

(G-2594)
RAND DIVERSIFIED COMPANIES LLC
112 Truman Dr (08817-2425)
PHONE....................................732 985-0800
Don Garda, *COO*
David Kauffman,
Stuart Sklovsky,
John Wuensch,
EMP: 399
SALES (est): 15.2MM **Privately Held**
SIC: 3993 Signs & advertising specialties

(G-2595)
RCF USA INC
110 Talmadge Rd (08817-2812)
PHONE....................................732 902-6100
Roni Nevo, *President*
Tarik Solangi, *Engineer*
▲ EMP: 8 EST: 2002
SQ FT: 2,500
SALES (est): 5.8MM **Privately Held**
SIC: 3651 Speaker monitors
HQ: Rcf Spa
   Via Ettore Majorana 1
   Reggio Emilia RE 42124
   052 227-4411

(G-2596)
RELIANCE VITAMIN LLC
3775 Park Ave Unit 1 (08820-2566)
PHONE....................................732 537-1220
Terrell Vigeant, *President*
Phillip Vigeant, *Vice Pres*
Linda Naselli, *CFO*

Scott Semel, *Accounting Mgr*
Charlie Baccaro, *Manager*
EMP: 212
SALES (est): 20.9MM **Privately Held**
WEB: www.reliancevitamin.com
SIC: 2834 5122 Vitamin preparations; vita-
   mins & minerals

(G-2597)
REUTHER ENGINEERING
154 Silver Lake Ave (08817-5261)
PHONE....................................973 485-5800
Ken Rys, *President*
Douglas Yago, *Opers Staff*
Bob Cromer, *Manager*
Susan Smith, *Info Tech Mgr*
EMP: 18 EST: 1949
SQ FT: 8,500
SALES (est): 2.8MM **Privately Held**
WEB: www.reutherengineering.com
SIC: 3599 7692 Machine shop, jobbing &
   repair; welding repair

(G-2598)
REVLON INC
2147 State Route 27 Fl 3 (08817-3365)
PHONE....................................732 287-1400
Erica Tafaro, *Manager*
Jun Zhang, *Software Dev*
Ann Pfeffer, *Director*
Orane Blake, *Director*
Raymond Schleckser, *Director*
EMP: 50 **Publicly Held**
WEB: www.revlon.com
SIC: 3421 5122 5199 5999 Clippers, fin-
   gernail & toenail; scissors, hand; cosmet-
   ics, perfumes & hair products; toilet
   preparations; wigs; toiletries, cosmetics &
   perfumes; hair preparations, including
   shampoos
PA: Revlon, Inc.
   1 New York Plz Fl 49
   New York NY 10004

(G-2599)
REVLON CONSUMER PRODUCTS CORP
2121 State Route 27 (08817-3329)
PHONE....................................732 287-1400
Mike Helman, *Vice Pres*
Lynn Lesser, *Branch Mgr*
EMP: 100 **Publicly Held**
SIC: 2844 Cosmetic preparations
HQ: Revlon Consumer Products Corpora-
   tion
   1 New York Plz
   New York NY 10004

(G-2600)
ROMA MOULDING INC
115 Northfield Ave (08837-3856)
PHONE....................................732 346-0999
Barry Zimmerman, *Manager*
EMP: 10
SALES (corp-wide): 28.8MM **Privately Held**
SIC: 2499 5023 Picture frame molding,
   finished; frames & framing, picture & mir-
   ror
PA: Roma Moulding Inc
   360 Hanlan Rd
   Woodbridge ON L4L 3
   905 850-1500

(G-2601)
RX TRADE ZONE INC
22 Meridian Rd Unit 15 (08820-2848)
PHONE....................................833 933-6600
Narendar Reddy Yasa, *President*
EMP: 5
SALES: 500K **Privately Held**
SIC: 7371 7372 Computer software devel-
   opment & applications; application com-
   puter software

(G-2602)
S & S SOCIUS INC
Also Called: S & S Manufacturing
115 Fieldcrest Ave (08837-3622)
PHONE....................................732 698-2400
Steven Silverman, *President*
Mitchell Silverman, *Admin Sec*
EMP: 45
SQ FT: 30,000

SALES (est): 7.7MM **Privately Held**
WEB: www.handrails.com
SIC: 3446 Railings, prefabricated metal

(G-2603)
SAAD COLLECTION INC
160 Rrtan Ctr Pkwy Unit 5 (08837)
PHONE....................................732 763-4015
Mohammad Younus, *Branch Mgr*
EMP: 8 **Privately Held**
SIC: 2321 2331 Men's & boys' furnishings;
   women's & misses' blouses & shirts
PA: Saad Collection Inc.
   1165 Broadway Ste 305
   New York NY 10001

(G-2604)
SANKET CORPORATION
15 Wood Acres Dr (08820-2303)
PHONE....................................732 287-0201
Daksha Shah, *CEO*
Ketan Shah, *Vice Pres*
▲ EMP: 12
SALES: 300K **Privately Held**
SIC: 2032 Ethnic foods: canned, jarred,
   etc.

(G-2605)
SELECT ENTERPRISES INC
71 Executive Ave (08817-6017)
P.O. Box 1353 (08818-1353)
PHONE....................................732 287-8622
Tom Lordi, *President*
Robert Hoffman, *Vice Pres*
EMP: 6
SALES (est): 570K **Privately Held**
WEB: www.selecttp.com
SIC: 2448 4212 Pallets, wood; local truck-
   ing, without storage

(G-2606)
SHAHNAWAZ FOOD LLC
19 Ten Eyck Pl (08820-3206)
PHONE....................................908 413-4206
Feroz Khan, *CEO*
EMP: 10
SALES (est): 609.7K **Privately Held**
SIC: 2013 Sausages & other prepared
   meats

(G-2607)
SHANGHAI FREEMEN AMERICAS LLC (HQ)
2035 Route 27 Ste 3005 (08817-3353)
PHONE....................................732 981-1288
Oyang LI, *CEO*
Andrew Falocco, *Marketing Staff*
◆ EMP: 20
SALES (est): 3MM
SALES (corp-wide): 46.8MM **Privately Held**
SIC: 2833 Vitamins, natural or synthetic:
   bulk, uncompounded
PA: Shanghai Freemen Lifescience Co.,
   Ltd.
   No.19 Building, 2500 Lane,Xiupu
   Rd.,Pudong New Area
   Shanghai 20131
   216 118-3110

(G-2608)
SHEKIA GROUP LLC
Also Called: Tsg Cabinets
1130 King Georges Post Rd (08837-3731)
PHONE....................................732 372-7668
Christina Jade, *Mng Member*
▲ EMP: 50
SQ FT: 300,000
SALES (est): 5.8MM **Privately Held**
SIC: 2434 5031 Wood kitchen cabinets;
   kitchen cabinets

(G-2609)
SILGAN CONTAINERS MFG CORP
135 National Rd (08817-2810)
PHONE....................................732 287-0300
Bryce Bedford, *Plant Mgr*
Rob Paprota, *QC Mgr*
EMP: 100
SALES (corp-wide): 4.4B **Publicly Held**
WEB: www.silgancontainers.com
SIC: 3411 Metal cans

GEOGRAPHIC

HQ: Silgan Containers Manufacturing Corporation
21600 Oxnard St Ste 1600
Woodland Hills CA 91367

(G-2610)
SIMPLE HOME AUTOMATION INC
32 Brunswick Ave (08817-2578)
PHONE......................877 405-2397
Elie Chemtob, *CEO*
Marco Chemtob, *CFO*
◆ EMP: 200 EST: 2015
SALES (est): 6.4MM **Privately Held**
SIC: 3491 Automatic regulating & control valves

(G-2611)
SINO MONTHLY NEW JERSEY INC
Also Called: Sino Monthly Jersey
18 Sheppard Pl (08817-3134)
PHONE......................732 650-0688
Chung Liu, *President*
Ivy Lee, *Editor*
EMP: 10
SQ FT: 1,000
SALES (est): 982.8K **Privately Held**
WEB: www.sino-monthly.com
SIC: 2721 Magazines: publishing & printing

(G-2612)
SJD DIRECT MIDWEST LLC
112 Truman Dr (08817-2425)
PHONE......................732 985-8405
EMP: 244
SALES (corp-wide): 28.6MM **Privately Held**
SIC: 3565 Packing & wrapping machinery
PA: Sjd Direct Midwest, Llc
21 Gtewy Cmrc Ctr Dr W
Edwardsville IL 62025
618 931-2151

(G-2613)
SJD DIRECT MIDWEST LLC
3 Ethel Rd Ste 301 (08817-2855)
PHONE......................732 287-2525
EMP: 102
SALES (corp-wide): 38.5MM **Privately Held**
SIC: 3565 Mfg Packaging Machinery
PA: Sjd Direct Midwest, Llc
21 Gtewy Cmrc Ctr Dr W
Edwardsville IL 62025
618 931-2151

(G-2614)
SMALL QUANTITIES NJ INC
66 Ethel Rd (08817-2249)
P.O. Box 4167, Metuchen (08840-4167)
PHONE......................732 248-9009
Harry Mathis, *President*
Michael Mathis, *Vice Pres*
Tom Schindel, *Sales Staff*
EMP: 57 EST: 1958
SQ FT: 22,000
SALES (est): 11.1MM **Privately Held**
SIC: 3469 Stamping metal for the trade

(G-2615)
SOCK DRAWER AND MORE LLC
Also Called: Foozys
95 Mayfield Ave (08837-3820)
P.O. Box 204, Marlboro (07746-0204)
PHONE......................888 637-3399
Darrell Klansky,
EMP: 1
SALES (est): 1MM **Privately Held**
SIC: 2252 Socks

(G-2616)
SOLGEN PHARMACEUTICALS INC
1514 Edison Glen Ter (08837-2940)
PHONE......................732 983-6025
Arpit Patel, *President*
EMP: 20
SALES (est): 1.2MM **Privately Held**
SIC: 2834 Pharmaceutical preparations

(G-2617)
SPECIALTY KRAFT CONVERTERS LLC
150 Fieldcrest Ave (08837-3657)
PHONE......................732 225-2080
EMP: 4
SALES (est): 109.8K **Privately Held**
SIC: 2679 Paperboard products, converted

(G-2618)
SPOTLESS VENETIAN BLIND SERVIC
Also Called: Spotless Shade
1217 Us Highway 1 (08837-3114)
PHONE......................732 548-1711
Scott Fitzgerald, *President*
EMP: 4 EST: 1961
SQ FT: 2,500
SALES (est): 370K **Privately Held**
SIC: 2591 7699 Venetian blinds; window shades; venetian blind repair shop

(G-2619)
ST MARTIN CABINETRY INC
100 Newfield Ave Ste B (08837-3849)
PHONE......................732 902-6020
EMP: 4 EST: 2016
SALES (est): 173.9K **Privately Held**
SIC: 2434 Wood kitchen cabinets

(G-2620)
STELFAST INC
104 Sunfield Ave (08837-3845)
PHONE......................440 879-0077
Allison Pearlstein, *Sales Staff*
EMP: 23
SALES (corp-wide): 158MM **Privately Held**
SIC: 3449 Miscellaneous metalwork
HQ: Stelfast Llc
22979 Stelfast Pkwy
Strongsville OH 44149
440 879-0077

(G-2621)
STRIKEFORCE TECHNOLOGIES INC
1090 King Georges Post Rd (08837-3701)
PHONE......................732 661-9641
Mark L Kay, *Ch of Bd*
George Waller, *Exec VP*
Philip E Blocker, *CFO*
George Stout Jr, *Controller*
Ramarao Pemmaraju, *CTO*
EMP: 8
SALES: 233.8K **Privately Held**
SIC: 7372 Prepackaged software

(G-2622)
SUITE K VALUE ADDED SVCS LLC
31 Executive Ave Ste A (08817-6035)
PHONE......................732 590-0647
Kathleen C Molyneaux, *Branch Mgr*
EMP: 10 **Privately Held**
SIC: 2844 Cosmetic preparations
PA: Suite K Value Added Services Llc
31 Executive Ave Ste A
Edison NJ 08817

(G-2623)
SUITE K VALUE ADDED SVCS LLC
Also Called: Suite-K
31 Executive Ave Ste A (08817-6035)
PHONE......................609 655-6890
Alexandra De Markoff, *Principal*
EMP: 18 **Privately Held**
SIC: 2844 Cosmetic preparations
PA: Suite K Value Added Services Llc
31 Executive Ave Ste A
Edison NJ 08817

(G-2624)
SUITE K VALUE ADDED SVCS LLC (PA)
Also Called: Suite-K
31 Executive Ave Ste A (08817-6035)
PHONE......................609 655-6890
Kathleen Molyneaux, *President*
Kathleen C Molyneaux,
Joseph Pereira, *Administration*
Waiming Chan,
▲ EMP: 72

SQ FT: 156,211
SALES (est): 20.7MM **Privately Held**
SIC: 2844 Cosmetic preparations

(G-2625)
SUNLIGHT AEROSPACE INC
2045 State Route 27 1w (08817-3334)
PHONE......................732 362-7501
Michael Cyrus, *President*
Allan Bruce, *Vice Pres*
EMP: 12
SALES (est): 540.8K **Privately Held**
SIC: 3674 Semiconductors & related devices

(G-2626)
SUPER STUD BUILDING PDTS INC
2960 Woodbridge Ave (08837-3406)
PHONE......................732 662-6200
Raymond Frobosilo, *President*
Annette Frobosilo, *Corp Secy*
Anthony Benavides, *Engineer*
Gregory Burgoyne, *Credit Mgr*
Mark Brunciak, *Accountant*
▲ EMP: 100
SQ FT: 100,000
SALES (est): 32.5MM **Privately Held**
WEB: www.buysuperstud.com
SIC: 3444 Studs & joists, sheet metal

(G-2627)
SWAROVSKI NORTH AMERICA LTD
55 Parsonage Rd Unit 333 (08837-2497)
PHONE......................732 632-1856
EMP: 7
SALES (corp-wide): 4.7B **Privately Held**
SIC: 3961 Costume jewelry
HQ: Swarovski North America Limited
1 Kenney Dr
Cranston RI 02920
401 463-6400

(G-2628)
SWEET SOLUTIONS INC
117 Fieldcrest Ave (08837-3622)
PHONE......................732 512-0777
Nick Chao, *President*
▲ EMP: 8
SQ FT: 15,000
SALES (est): 1MM **Privately Held**
SIC: 2869 Sweeteners, synthetic

(G-2629)
SWISSRAY INTERNATIONAL INC (DH)
1090 King Georges Rd 1203 (08837)
PHONE......................800 903-5543
Gilbert Wai, *CEO*
Jack Lee, *Officer*
EMP: 15
SQ FT: 2,500
SALES: 1.6MM
SALES (corp-wide): 10.4MM **Privately Held**
WEB: www.swissray.com
SIC: 3844 X-ray generators
HQ: Swissray Medical Ag
Turbistrasse 25-27
Hochdorf LU 6280
419 141-212

(G-2630)
T C P RELIABLE MANUFACTURING
Also Called: Tcp/Reliable
551 Raritan Center Pkwy (08837-3918)
PHONE......................732 346-9200
Maurice Barakat, *President*
Anthony Spina, *Treasurer*
▲ EMP: 45
SQ FT: 63,000
SALES (est): 7.1MM
SALES (corp-wide): 33.9MM **Privately Held**
WEB: www.tcpreliable.com
SIC: 3086 Plastics foam products
PA: Tcp Reliable Inc.
551 Raritan Center Pkwy
Edison NJ 08837
848 229-2466

(G-2631)
TAYLOR PRODUCTS INC
255 Raritan Center Pkwy (08837-3613)
P.O. Box 6748 (08818-6748)
PHONE......................732 225-4620
Wayne Schwacke, *Principal*
Jason Rossi, *District Mgr*
Richard P Guerra, *Vice Pres*
Mike Ryder, *Manager*
Patricia Gaynor, *Director*
▲ EMP: 42
SQ FT: 16,000
SALES (est): 19.2MM **Privately Held**
SIC: 5046 7699 2024 Restaurant equipment & supplies; restaurant equipment repair; ices, flavored (frozen dessert)

(G-2632)
TCP RELIABLE INC (PA)
551 Raritan Center Pkwy (08837-3918)
PHONE......................848 229-2466
Maurice Barakat, *CEO*
Michael Davila, *Plant Mgr*
Rafael Forero, *QC Mgr*
Anthony Alleva, *Engineer*
Anthony Spina, *CFO*
▲ EMP: 5
SQ FT: 62,000
SALES (est): 33.9MM **Privately Held**
WEB: www.tcpreliable.com
SIC: 3086 3825 Packaging & shipping materials, foamed plastic; instruments to measure electricity

(G-2633)
TONYS AUTO ENTP LTD LBLTY CO
98 Loring Ave (08817-4322)
PHONE......................203 223-5776
Anthony F Filippone, *Mng Member*
EMP: 4
SALES (est): 309.7K **Privately Held**
SIC: 4212 3465 Local trucking, without storage; body parts, automobile: stamped metal

(G-2634)
TSG LLC
1130 King Georges Post Rd (08837-3731)
PHONE......................732 372-7668
EMP: 8
SALES (est): 832.4K **Privately Held**
SIC: 2434 Wood kitchen cabinets

(G-2635)
TUMI HOLDINGS INC (DH)
499 Thornall St Ste 10 (08837-2267)
PHONE......................908 756-4400
Kyle Gendreau, *CEO*
Peter L Gray, *Exec VP*
Michael J Mardy, *CFO*
Pranay Pattlola, *Software Engr*
Durga Kella, *Sr Software Eng*
EMP: 51
SQ FT: 47,905
SALES: 547.6MM
SALES (corp-wide): 177.9K **Privately Held**
SIC: 3161 3172 5948 Traveling bags; clothing & apparel carrying cases; satchels; card cases; wallets; luggage & leather goods stores
HQ: Samsonite International S.A.
25/F The Gateway Harbour City Twr 2
Tsim Sha Tsui KLN
242 226-11

(G-2636)
UNITED NATURAL TRADING CO
Also Called: Woodstock Farms
96 Executive Ave (08817-6016)
PHONE......................732 650-9905
Daniel V Atwood, *President*
▲ EMP: 100
SQ FT: 100,000
SALES (est): 13.6MM **Publicly Held**
WEB: www.unfi.com
SIC: 2099 5149 Food preparations; dried or canned foods
PA: United Natural Foods, Inc.
313 Iron Horse Way
Providence RI 02908

(G-2637)
VASWANI INC (PA)
75 Carter Dr Ste 1 (08817-2067)
PHONE....................................877 376-4425
Vinay Vaswani, *CEO*
Ishwar Vaswani, *President*
◆ EMP: 52
SALES (est): 27MM **Privately Held**
WEB: www.vaswani.com
SIC: 2499 Picture & mirror frames, wood

(G-2638)
VASWANI INC
75 Carter Dr Ste 1 (08817-2067)
PHONE....................................877 376-4425
EMP: 10
SALES (corp-wide): 33.4MM **Privately
Held**
SIC: 2521 4226 4783 Mfg Wood Office
Furniture Special Warehouse/Storage
Packing/Crating Service
PA: Vaswani Inc.
75 Carter Dr Ste 1
Edison NJ 08817
877 376-4425

(G-2639)
VERMONT CABLEWORKS INC
31 National Rd (08817-2808)
P.O. Box 71, Windsor VT (05089-0071)
PHONE....................................802 674-6555
Richard Sincerbeaux, *President*
Winthrop Townsend, *Admin Sec*
EMP: 7
SQ FT: 6,000
SALES (est): 1.1MM **Privately Held**
SIC: 3643 Current-carrying wiring devices

(G-2640)
VERTIV CORPORATION
3a Fernwood Ave (08837-3800)
PHONE....................................732 225-3741
Bob Jones, *Branch Mgr*
EMP: 32
SALES (corp-wide): 3.1B **Privately Held**
SIC: 3823 7378 Industrial instrmnts
msrmnt display/control process variable;
computer maintenance & repair
HQ: Vertiv Corporation
1050 Dearborn Dr
Columbus OH 43085
614 888-0246

(G-2641)
VICMARR AUDIO INC
9 Kilmer Ct (08817-2428)
PHONE....................................732 289-9111
Richard Cohen, *Ch of Bd*
Victor Cohen, *President*
Mal Cohen, *Vice Pres*
Ron Cohen, *Admin Sec*
◆ EMP: 20
SQ FT: 50,000
SALES: 6.7MM **Privately Held**
SIC: 3699 Electrical equipment & supplies

(G-2642)
VIKING MARINE PRODUCTS INC
Also Called: Viking Fender Company
977 New Durham Rd (08817-2253)
PHONE....................................732 826-4552
Kurt Grimsgaard, *President*
Guy Grimsgaard, *Vice Pres*
▼ EMP: 9
SALES (est): 1.2MM **Privately Held**
SIC: 3429 Marine hardware

(G-2643)
W C OMNI INCORPORATED
Also Called: Omni Wall Coverings
166 National Rd (08817-2811)
PHONE....................................732 248-0999
Gary Tumminello, *President*
Nino Pasqua, *Vice Pres*
▲ EMP: 20
SQ FT: 33,000
SALES (est): 6.4MM **Privately Held**
WEB: www.omniwcinc.com
SIC: 2295 Laminating of fabrics

(G-2644)
W R GRACE & CO-CONN
340 Meadow Rd (08837-4102)
PHONE....................................732 777-4877
EMP: 162

SALES (corp-wide): 1.9B **Publicly Held**
WEB: www.grace.com
SIC: 2819 Catalysts, chemical
HQ: W. R. Grace & Co.-Conn.
7500 Grace Dr
Columbia MD 21044
410 531-4000

(G-2645)
WAKEFERN FOOD CORP
Also Called: Wakefern Personnel
Old Post Rd Rr 1 (08837)
P.O. Box 7812 (08818-7812)
PHONE....................................732 819-0140
Dawn Hudacko, *Buyer*
John Gawryluk, *Research*
John Medina, *Engineer*
Nicholas REO, *Engineer*
Robert Matyas, *Accountant*
EMP: 300
SALES (corp-wide): 890MM **Privately
Held**
SIC: 5149 4213 2026 5411 Groceries &
related products; contract haulers; milk
processing (pasteurizing, homogenizing,
bottling); supermarkets, chain
PA: Wakefern Food Corp.
5000 Riverside Dr
Keasbey NJ 08832
908 527-3300

(G-2646)
WEATHERBEETA USA INC
201 Mill Rd (08837-3801)
PHONE....................................732 287-1182
Darren Nann, *President*
Elaine Dunn, *Opers Staff*
Paul Pels, *Treasurer*
Chris Corn, *Sales Staff*
Jack Levy, *Business Dir*
◆ EMP: 24
SQ FT: 99,000
SALES (est): 8MM **Privately Held**
WEB: www.weatherbeetausa.com
SIC: 5023 2399 Blankets; horse & pet ac-
cessories, textile; horse blankets
HQ: Weatherbeeta Pty Ltd
8 Moncrief Rd
Nunawading VIC 3131

(G-2647)
**WORLDWIDE WHL FLR CVG INC
(PA)**
1055 Us Highway 1 (08837-2904)
PHONE....................................732 906-1400
Alan Braunstein, *President*
Barbara Braunstein, *Corp Secy*
Darren Braunstein, *COO*
Susan Segovia, *Cust Mgr*
Marty Schlesinger, *Director*
▲ EMP: 45
SQ FT: 40,000
SALES (est): 23.7MM **Privately Held**
WEB: www.worldwidefloors.com
SIC: 5713 5023 2273 2591 Carpets; floor
tile; wood flooring; carpets & rugs; win-
dow blinds

(G-2648)
YIPIN FOOD PRODUCTS INC
Also Called: Yi Pin Food Prods
29 Mack Dr (08817-2807)
PHONE....................................718 788-3059
Chiwan Cheung, *CEO*
Siu Hang Lai, *Vice Pres*
Kevin Zhang, *Manager*
Ping Chan, *Admin Sec*
▲ EMP: 12
SQ FT: 15,000
SALES (est): 1.8MM **Privately Held**
SIC: 2035 5149 Seasonings & sauces, ex-
cept tomato & dry; soy sauce; season-
ings, sauces & extracts

(G-2649)
**YORK INTERNATIONAL
CORPORATION**
160 Rritan Ctr Pkwy Ste 6 (08837)
PHONE....................................732 346-0606
Tony Natale, *Branch Mgr*
EMP: 13 **Privately Held**
SIC: 3585 Refrigeration & heating equip-
ment

HQ: York International Corporation
631 S Richland Ave
York PA 17403
717 771-7890

(G-2650)
ZINK HOLDINGS LLC (PA)
114 Tived Ln E (08837-3076)
PHONE....................................781 761-5400
Akiva Klein, *CFO*
Chaim Piekarski,
EMP: 50 EST: 2015
SALES: 10MM **Privately Held**
SIC: 3861 Photographic film, plate & paper
holders

Egg Harbor City
Atlantic County

(G-2651)
ACCENT FENCE INC
1450 Bremen Ave (08215-2820)
P.O. Box 656 (08215-0656)
PHONE....................................609 965-6400
Greg Carnesale, *President*
EMP: 35
SQ FT: 400
SALES (est): 7.5MM **Privately Held**
SIC: 3496 1799 Miscellaneous fabricated
wire products; fence construction

(G-2652)
ATLANTIC INDUS WD PDTS LLC
411 S London Ave (08215-3014)
P.O. Box 1234, Hammonton (08037-5234)
PHONE....................................609 965-4555
Michael Perrone,
Peter Scaffidi,
EMP: 5
SALES: 500K **Privately Held**
SIC: 2448 Pallets, wood

(G-2653)
**BARRETTE OUTDOOR LIVING
INC**
545 Tilton Rd Ste 100 (08215-5136)
PHONE....................................609 965-5450
EMP: 15
SALES (corp-wide): 1.5MM **Privately
Held**
SIC: 3315 Fence gates posts & fittings;
steel
HQ: Barrette Outdoor Living, Inc.
7830 Freeway Cir
Middleburg Heights OH 44130
440 891-0790

(G-2654)
**BUSINESS CARDS TOMORROW
INC**
Also Called: BCT
129 Cincinnati Ave (08215-1998)
PHONE....................................609 965-0808
Brian D'Agostino, *President*
Madeline D'Agostino, *Corp Secy*
EMP: 10 EST: 1980
SQ FT: 2,700
SALES (est): 1.3MM **Privately Held**
WEB: www.bctsouthjersey.com
SIC: 2752 Commercial printing, litho-
graphic

(G-2655)
C HARRY MAREAN PRINTING
1717 Philadelphia Ave (08215-1627)
P.O. Box 294 (08215-0294)
PHONE....................................609 965-4708
C Harry Marean, *Partner*
Lee M Marean, *Partner*
EMP: 5
SQ FT: 2,800
SALES: 75K **Privately Held**
SIC: 2752 2759 Lithographing on metal;
letterpress printing

(G-2656)
**COSTA MAR CNVAS
ENCLOSURES LLC**
1324 Moss Mill Rd (08215-3130)
PHONE....................................609 965-1538
Donna Costa, *CEO*
Chris Costa, *President*
EMP: 46

SQ FT: 2,000
SALES: 6MM **Privately Held**
WEB: www.costamarinecanvas.com
SIC: 7641 3732 2394 Reupholstery; boat
building & repairing; canvas & related
products

(G-2657)
DEMAIO INC
543 Columbia Rd (08215-4131)
PHONE....................................609 965-4094
George V Demaio, *President*
Michele L Demaio, *Vice Pres*
EMP: 20
SQ FT: 3,000
SALES: 2.9MM **Privately Held**
WEB: www.demaios.com
SIC: 4959 1081 8748 Environmental
cleanup services; draining or pumping of
metal mines; systems analysis & engi-
neering consulting services

(G-2658)
DOUGLASS INDUSTRIES INC
Also Called: Douglass Weave Appeal
412 Boston Ave (08215-2603)
P.O. Box 701 (08215-0701)
PHONE....................................609 804-6040
F Naomi Taylor, *CEO*
Howard Taylor, *Principal*
Douglass A Taylor, *COO*
Randolph S Taylor, *Treasurer*
▼ EMP: 33 EST: 1954
SQ FT: 50,000
SALES (est): 19.9MM **Privately Held**
WEB: www.dougind.com
SIC: 5131 2299 Upholstery fabrics,
woven; batting, wadding, padding & fill-
ings

(G-2659)
**EGG HARBOR ROPE
PRODUCTS INC**
5105 White Horse Pike (08215-4016)
P.O. Box 294 (08215-0294)
PHONE....................................609 965-2435
C Harry Marean, *President*
Fred Good, *Treasurer*
EMP: 4 EST: 1963
SQ FT: 5,600
SALES (est): 240K **Privately Held**
SIC: 2298 Rope, except asbestos & wire

(G-2660)
EH YACHTS LLC
Also Called: Egg Harbor Boats
801 Philadelphia Ave (08215-1609)
P.O. Box 702 (08215-0702)
PHONE....................................609 965-2300
Ira Trocki, *Mng Member*
EMP: 84
SALES (est): 14.8MM **Privately Held**
WEB: www.ehyachts.com
SIC: 3732 Yachts, building & repairing

(G-2661)
JERSEY CAPE YACHTS INC
2143 River Rd (08215-4745)
PHONE....................................609 965-8650
Wayne Puglise, *President*
Mark Gnatz, *Prdtn Mgr*
Justin Wighton, *Engineer*
EMP: 52
SQ FT: 90,000
SALES (est): 8.7MM **Privately Held**
SIC: 3732 Boat building & repairing

(G-2662)
JOHN H ABBOTT INC
4 Mullica Way (08215-4226)
PHONE....................................609 561-0303
Sophie Abbott, *President*
Howard Abbott, *Corp Secy*
EMP: 6
SALES (est): 600.7K **Privately Held**
WEB: www.johnhabbott.com
SIC: 2421 Siding (dressed lumber)

(G-2663)
LAUREATE PRESS
1336 W Central Ave (08215-1798)
P.O. Box 343 (08215-0343)
PHONE....................................609 646-1545
Janet Rotellini, *President*
Henry Sartorio, *Admin Sec*
EMP: 6 EST: 1928

GEOGRAPHIC

SQ FT: 3,872
SALES (est): 869.1K **Privately Held**
SIC: 2752 Photo-offset printing

(G-2664)
MARINE ACQUISITION INC
Also Called: Egg Harbor Yacht-Div
801 Philadelphia Ave (08215-1609)
P.O. Box 702 (08215-0702)
PHONE......................................609 965-2300
Rick Trapp, *Ch of Bd*
William C Robinson, *President*
Doug Finney, *Vice Pres*
Joan Sgorbati, *Treasurer*
EMP: 100
SQ FT: 65,480
SALES (est): 12.6MM **Privately Held**
SIC: 3732 5551 Boat building & repairing;
boat dealers

(G-2665)
NEW JRSEY SFOOD MKTG GROUP LLC
143 Leektown Rd (08215-4809)
PHONE......................................609 296-7026
George W Mathis,
EMP: 5
SALES (est): 304.4K **Privately Held**
SIC: 2092 Fresh or frozen packaged fish

(G-2666)
RENAULT WINERY INC
Also Called: Renault Winery Restaurant
72 N Bremen Ave (08215-3195)
PHONE......................................609 965-2111
Joseph P Milza Sr, *President*
Joseph Milza, *Owner*
Damon Scalasro, *Vice Pres*
Richard Buxton, *VP Sales*
Marilyn Nogue, *Administration*
▲ EMP: 50 EST: 1864
SQ FT: 52,000
SALES (est): 4MM **Privately Held**
WEB: www.renaultwinery.com
SIC: 5812 7299 2084 Restaurant, family:
independent; banquet hall facilities; wine
cellars, bonded; engaged in blending
wines

(G-2667)
SCHAIRER BROTHERS
254 S Bremen Ave (08215-3101)
PHONE......................................609 965-0996
Paul Schairer, *Partner*
Anthony Schairer, *Partner*
EMP: 6 EST: 1936
SALES (est): 666.2K **Privately Held**
SIC: 2421 Sawmills & planing mills, general

(G-2668)
TASTE ITALY MANUFACTURING LLC
1301 Bremen Ave (08215-2860)
P.O. Box 1146, Mullica Hill (08062-1146)
PHONE......................................856 223-0707
Patrick Micheletti, *Vice Pres*
Luigi Illiano, *Mng Member*
EMP: 5
SALES (est): 875.8K **Privately Held**
SIC: 2099 Pizza, refrigerated: except
frozen

(G-2669)
TF YACHTS LLC
801 Philadelphia Ave (08215-1609)
PHONE......................................609 965-2300
Robert Weidhaas, *President*
EMP: 23
SALES (est): 1MM **Privately Held**
SIC: 3732 Yachts, building & repairing

(G-2670)
TIME LOG INDUSTRIES INC
312 N Leipzig Ave (08215-3308)
PHONE......................................609 965-5017
Frank Tomasello, *President*
Melissa Tomasello, *Vice Pres*
EMP: 5
SQ FT: 1,500
SALES: 200K **Privately Held**
SIC: 3953 Time stamps, hand: rubber or
metal

(G-2671)
VIKING YACHT COMPANY
2713 Green Bank Rd (08215-4635)
PHONE......................................609 296-6000
EMP: 177
SALES (corp-wide): 280MM **Privately Held**
SIC: 3732 Yachts, building & repairing
PA: Viking Yacht Company
On The Bass Riv Rr 9
New Gretna NJ 08224
609 296-6000

(G-2672)
WELDING & RADIATOR SUPPLY CO
1144 W White Horse Pike (08215-3136)
P.O. Box 609, Allenwood (08720-0609)
PHONE......................................609 965-0433
EMP: 5 EST: 1947
SQ FT: 2,500
SALES: 200K **Privately Held**
SIC: 5172 5984 5084 7692 Whol Petroleum Products Ret Liquefied Petroleum
Gas Whol Industrial Equipment Welding
Services

Egg Harbor Township
Atlantic County

(G-2673)
A E STONE INC (PA)
1435 Doughty Rd (08234-2229)
PHONE......................................609 641-2781
Thomas Ritter, *President*
Tom Collard, *Vice Pres*
Steven C Kurtz, *Vice Pres*
Ross Williamson, *Vice Pres*
Marty Quintiliana, *Project Mgr*
EMP: 40 EST: 1955
SQ FT: 6,600
SALES (est): 11.7MM **Privately Held**
WEB: www.aestone.com
SIC: 2951 1611 1429 Asphalt & asphaltic
paving mixtures (not from refineries);
highway & street paving contractor; igneous rock, crushed & broken-quarrying

(G-2674)
ABSECON ISLAND BEVERAGE CO
6754 Washington Ave B (08234-3807)
PHONE......................................609 653-8123
Matt Helm, *President*
EMP: 4
SQ FT: 7,000
SALES: 1.5MM **Privately Held**
SIC: 3556 Beverage machinery

(G-2675)
ADVANTAGE FIBERGLASS INC
4 Prospect Ave (08234-8519)
PHONE......................................609 926-4606
Thomas Kampert, *President*
EMP: 4
SALES (est): 270.9K **Privately Held**
SIC: 3296 Fiberglass insulation

(G-2676)
ANTHONY EXCAVATING & DEM
22 English Ln (08234-7034)
PHONE......................................609 926-8804
Steven R Anthony, *President*
Laurie Anthony, *Admin Sec*
EMP: 1
SALES: 1MM **Privately Held**
SIC: 1629 1795 2499 Dredging contractor; land clearing contractor; wrecking &
demolition work; mulch, wood & bark

(G-2677)
AST CONSTRUCTION INC
5 Canale Dr (08234-5131)
PHONE......................................609 277-7101
Ted Gendron, *President*
Dan Gendron, *Controller*
EMP: 50
SQ FT: 2,000
SALES (est): 12.3MM **Privately Held**
WEB: www.astconstruction.com
SIC: 3795 Tanks & tank components

(G-2678)
ATLANTIC MASONRY SUPPLY INC
6422 Black Horse Pike (08234-5542)
PHONE......................................609 909-9292
Deborah Tower, *President*
Darlene Tower, *Vice Pres*
EMP: 10
SALES (est): 1.3MM **Privately Held**
WEB: www.atlanticmasonrynj.com
SIC: 3273 Ready-mixed concrete

(G-2679)
BALLY TECHNOLOGIES INC
Also Called: Bally Gaming
3133 Fire Rd (08234-9601)
PHONE......................................609 641-7711
Stan Kozlowski, *Branch Mgr*
Victoria Simon, *Manager*
Jon Rickert, *Data Proc Exec*
EMP: 12
SALES (corp-wide): 3.3B **Publicly Held**
WEB: www.ballygaming.com
SIC: 3944 Games, toys & children's vehicles
HQ: Bally Technologies, Inc.
6650 El Camino Rd
Las Vegas NV 89118
702 897-2284

(G-2680)
BATTISTINI FOODS
20 Brandywine Ct (08234-4882)
PHONE......................................609 476-2184
Timothy Datig, *Owner*
EMP: 7
SQ FT: 5,000
SALES: 900K **Privately Held**
SIC: 2038 Ethnic foods, frozen

(G-2681)
CANADA DRY DSTRG WILMINGTON DE
11 Canale Dr (08234-5132)
P.O. Box 706, Pleasantville (08232-0706)
PHONE......................................609 645-7070
Joe Szarzynski, *Manager*
EMP: 25
SALES (corp-wide): 5.9MM **Privately Held**
WEB: www.cddelval.com
SIC: 2086 Bottled & canned soft drinks
PA: Canada Dry Distributing Co Of Wilmington, De
650 Ships Landing Way
New Castle DE 19720
302 322-1856

(G-2682)
CAPE ATLANTIC SOFTWARE LLC
6523 Mill Rd (08234-9655)
PHONE......................................609 442-1331
Gaey Schaefer,
EMP: 6
SALES (est): 340K **Privately Held**
SIC: 7372 Prepackaged software

(G-2683)
ENROUTE COMPUTER SOLUTIONS INC (PA)
Also Called: E C S
2511 Fire Rd Ste A4 (08234-5618)
PHONE......................................609 569-9255
Anthony Curatolo, *President*
John Rodolico, *Business Mgr*
Charles Wiemer, *COO*
Mark Pushman, *Vice Pres*
Christine Cusack, *Engineer*
EMP: 46
SQ FT: 11,000
SALES: 47.5MM **Privately Held**
WEB: www.enroute-computer.com
SIC: 7371 3721 8734 Computer software
development & applications; research &
development on aircraft by the manufacturer; testing laboratories

(G-2684)
INNOVATIVE CUTNG CONCEPTS LLC
203 Cates Rd (08234-5286)
PHONE......................................609 484-9960
Mike Isley,

Ronald Simmoni,
Martin Sokolski,
EMP: 8
SALES (est): 825.9K **Privately Held**
SIC: 3281 1499 Cut stone & stone products; gem stones (natural) mining

(G-2685)
INTERACTIVE ADVISORY SOFTWARE
3393 Bargaintown Rd # 200 (08234-5955)
PHONE......................................770 951-2929
Stephen Hartney, *Project Mgr*
Nathan Berk, *Mng Member*
Linda Grace, *Director*
EMP: 38
SQ FT: 10,000
SALES (est): 5MM
SALES (corp-wide): 11.7MM **Privately Held**
SIC: 7372 Application computer software
PA: Optima Technologies Inc
1110 Northchase Pkwy Se # 250
Marietta GA 30067
800 821-7355

(G-2686)
JOMAR CORP
115 E Parkway Dr (08234-5112)
P.O. Box 1020, Pleasantville (08232-6020)
PHONE......................................609 646-8000
Carlos R Castro, *President*
Kevin Adams, *Plant Mgr*
Matt Jefferson, *Engineer*
James Chukinas, *Controller*
Ron Gabriele, *Sales Staff*
▲ EMP: 34 EST: 1968
SQ FT: 40,000
SALES: 5MM
SALES (corp-wide): 1B **Privately Held**
WEB: www.jomarcorp.com
SIC: 3559 Plastics working machinery
HQ: Indel, Inc.
10 Indel Ave
Rancocas NJ 08073
609 267-9000

(G-2687)
LEAK DETECTION ASSOCIATES INC
6638 Delilah Rd (08234-5659)
PHONE......................................609 415-2290
Darrell R Morrow, *CEO*
Jeffrey Morrow-Lucas, *COO*
Leslie D Morrow, *Vice Pres*
EMP: 9
SQ FT: 16,000
SALES (est): 1.3MM
SALES (corp-wide): 1.2MM **Privately Held**
SIC: 3829 Measuring & controlling devices
PA: Clj Holdings, Llc
204 W Atlantic Blvd
Ocean City NJ

(G-2688)
LNS INC
Also Called: L N S Industries
24 Buckingham Dr (08234-7253)
PHONE......................................609 927-6656
Lisa Fasola, *President*
Nicholas Fasola, *Vice Pres*
EMP: 12 EST: 2000
SALES: 20K **Privately Held**
SIC: 3089 Injection molded finished plastic
products

(G-2689)
M & W FRANKLIN LLC
Also Called: Eastern Sign Company
3011 Ocean Heights Ave B (08234-7748)
PHONE......................................609 927-0885
Mike Franklin,
Wendy Franklin,
EMP: 5
SQ FT: 1,500
SALES (est): 602.9K **Privately Held**
WEB: www.easternsignco.com
SIC: 3993 Signs & advertising specialties

(G-2690)
MID ATLANTIC GRAPHIX INC
Also Called: Signal Graphics
2558 Tilton Rd (08234-1833)
PHONE......................................609 569-9990
Kathryn Gunnels, *President*

John R Gunnels, *Vice Pres*
John Gunnels, *Vice Pres*
EMP: 8
SQ FT: 5,000
SALES (est): 1.3MM **Privately Held**
SIC: 2752 Commercial printing, offset

(G-2691)
NEXT LEVEL FABRICATION LLC
205 Zion Rd (08234-6963)
PHONE..............................609 703-0682
Frank Bonanata, *Mng Member*
EMP: 5
SALES: 106K **Privately Held**
SIC: 3441 Fabricated structural metal

(G-2692)
PENN-JERSEY BLDG MTLS CO INC (PA)
2819 Fire Rd (08234-4071)
PHONE..............................609 641-6994
Eileen L Johnston, *President*
Pat Phillips, *Plant Mgr*
Timothy Karaso, *Opers Mgr*
Mike Miles, *Opers Mgr*
EMP: 7
SALES (est): 13.3MM **Privately Held**
WEB: www.penn-jersey.net
SIC: 3273 Ready-mixed concrete

(G-2693)
POST TO POST LLC
2545 Fire Rd Ste 1 (08234-5667)
PHONE..............................609 646-9300
Richard Sonsini, *Principal*
Rick Sonsini, *Sales Staff*
EMP: 7 **EST:** 2003
SALES (est): 1MM **Privately Held**
SIC: 3446 Railings, bannisters, guards, etc.: made from metal pipe

(G-2694)
RALPH CLAYTON & SONS LLC
103 Chestnut Ave (08234-5147)
PHONE..............................609 383-1818
Damian Haaf, *Manager*
EMP: 20
SALES (corp-wide): 106.4MM **Privately Held**
WEB: www.claytonco.com
SIC: 3273 Ready-mixed concrete
PA: Ralph Clayton & Sons L.L.C.
1355 Campus Pkwy
Wall Township NJ 07753
732 363-1995

(G-2695)
RSL LLC (PA)
3092 English Creek Ave (08234-5245)
PHONE..............................609 484-1600
Bernd Lewkowitz, *Ch of Bd*
Ron Lewkowitz, *President*
Kevin Kavanagh, *Vice Pres*
Sharon Oran, *Shareholder*
▲ **EMP:** 75 **EST:** 1964
SQ FT: 300,000
SALES (est): 24.5MM **Privately Held**
SIC: 2431 3442 Door frames, wood; sash, door or window: metal

(G-2696)
RSL LLC
3049 Fernwood Ave (08234-5235)
PHONE..............................609 645-9777
Charles Nixon, *Manager*
EMP: 31
SALES (corp-wide): 24.5MM **Privately Held**
SIC: 2431 3429 Door frames, wood; manufactured hardware (general)
PA: Rsl Llc
3092 English Creek Ave
Egg Harbor Township NJ 08234
609 484-1600

(G-2697)
SF LUTZ LLC
Also Called: Bon-Ton Instant Blnds Intriors
3143 Fire Rd Ste F (08234-9640)
P.O. Box 534, Longport (08403-0534)
PHONE..............................609 646-9490
Frederic M Lutz,
EMP: 4
SALES: 400K **Privately Held**
SIC: 2591 Drapery hardware & blinds & shades

(G-2698)
TASTY BAKING COMPANY
Also Called: Tasty Bake Distributing Center
203 Cates Rd (08234-5286)
PHONE..............................609 641-8588
Sean Flynn, *Manager*
EMP: 6
SALES (corp-wide): 3.9B **Publicly Held**
WEB: www.tastykake.com
SIC: 2051 Bakery: wholesale or wholesale/retail combined
HQ: Tasty Baking Company
4300 S 26th St
Philadelphia PA 19112
215 221-8500

(G-2699)
TUCKAHOE SAND & GRAVEL CO INC
2819 Fire Rd (08234-4071)
PHONE..............................609 861-2082
James E Johnston Jr, *President*
EMP: 35 **EST:** 1952
SALES (est): 7.4MM **Privately Held**
WEB: www.tuckahoesand-gravel.com
SIC: 1442 Gravel & pebble mining; gravel mining

(G-2700)
VERIZON COMMUNICATIONS INC
2546 Fire Rd (08234-5651)
PHONE..............................609 646-9939
Bill Beloff, *Manager*
EMP: 100
SALES (corp-wide): 130.8B **Publicly Held**
WEB: www.verizon.com
SIC: 4813 4812 2741 7373 Local telephone communications; voice telephone communications; data telephone communications; cellular telephone services; directories, telephone: publishing only, not printed on site; computer integrated systems design; direct mail advertising services; electrical work
PA: Verizon Communications Inc.
1095 Ave Of The Americas
New York NY 10036
212 395-1000

(G-2701)
W B MASON CO INC
350 Commerce Dr (08234-9589)
PHONE..............................888 926-2766
EMP: 41
SALES (corp-wide): 773MM **Privately Held**
SIC: 5943 5712 2752 Office forms & supplies; office furniture; commercial printing, lithographic
PA: W. B. Mason Co., Inc.
59 Center St
Brockton MA 02301
781 794-8800

(G-2702)
WINSOME DIGITAL INC
Also Called: Gotham Group, The
202 W Parkway Dr (08234-5107)
PHONE..............................609 645-2211
Qiang Wang, *President*
Pete Suchanoff, *Purchasing*
Sarah Bodtmann, *Sales Staff*
Steven Thibaudeau, *Business Anlyst*
Julie Meschko, *Executive*
▲ **EMP:** 16
SALES (est): 3MM **Privately Held**
WEB: www.gothamgroup.com
SIC: 2759 Commercial printing

Egg Harbor Twp
Atlantic County

(G-2703)
TUCKAHOE BREWING COMPANY LLC
3092 English Creek Ave (08234-5245)
PHONE..............................609 645-2739
Stuart Stromfeld, *Mng Member*
Tim Hanna,
Chris Konicki,
James McAfee,

Matt McDevitt,
EMP: 15
SQ FT: 1,000
SALES (est): 589.4K **Privately Held**
SIC: 2082 Beer (alcoholic beverage)

Elizabeth
Union County

(G-2704)
A 1 FENCING INC
166 7th St (07201-2831)
PHONE..............................908 527-1066
Ray Camajo, *Owner*
EMP: 12 **EST:** 1960
SQ FT: 3,000
SALES (est): 1.1MM **Privately Held**
WEB: www.a1fencing.com
SIC: 1799 7692 Fence construction; welding repair

(G-2705)
A&B HEATING & COOLING
107 Trumbull St (07206-2165)
PHONE..............................908 289-2231
Allmon Banks, *Owner*
EMP: 4
SALES (est): 178.1K **Privately Held**
SIC: 3444 Sheet metalwork

(G-2706)
ACTAVIS ELIZABETH LLC (DH)
Also Called: Actavis US
200 Elmora Ave (07202-1106)
PHONE..............................908 527-9100
Sigurbar Olafsson, *President*
Paul M Bisaro, *Principal*
Vivek Bachhawat, *Vice Pres*
Joe Koziol, *Facilities Mgr*
Grace Lepping, *Purch Mgr*
▲ **EMP:** 300
SQ FT: 245,000
SALES (est): 216.1MM **Privately Held**
SIC: 2834 Druggists' preparations (pharmaceuticals)
HQ: Actavis Llc
5 Giralda Farms
Madison NJ 07940
862 261-7000

(G-2707)
ADCO SIGNS OF NJ INC
57 Westfield Ave (07208-3662)
PHONE..............................908 965-2112
Clara Molski, *President*
EMP: 30
SQ FT: 20,000
SALES (est): 3.9MM **Privately Held**
SIC: 3993 3953 Signs, not made in custom sign painting shops; marking devices

(G-2708)
AIR CLEAN CO INC
1135 Chestnut St (07201-1049)
PHONE..............................908 355-1515
Alex Drucker, *President*
EMP: 5
SQ FT: 6,000
SALES (est): 500K **Privately Held**
SIC: 3564 Air purification equipment; air cleaning systems

(G-2709)
ALPHA WIRE CORPORATION (PA)
Also Called: Alphawire
711 Lidgerwood Ave (07202-3115)
PHONE..............................908 925-8000
Philip R Cowen, *Ch of Bd*
Mike Dugar, *President*
Marc Tousignant, *Regional Mgr*
Tim Yontek, *District Mgr*
Mark Vanderwoude, *COO*
EMP: 175
SQ FT: 320,000
SALES (est): 225.8MM **Privately Held**
SIC: 5063 3082 3357 Wire & cable; tubes, unsupported plastic; shipboard cable, nonferrous

(G-2710)
AMERICAN BABY HEADWEAR CO INC (PA)
1000 Jefferson Ave (07201-1394)
PHONE..............................908 558-0017
Joseph Templer, *President*
Julius Templer, *Vice Pres*
Laser Templer, *Vice Pres*
EMP: 80
SQ FT: 35,000
SALES (est): 4.6MM **Privately Held**
SIC: 2369 2381 2353 Headwear: girls', children's & infants'; fabric dress & work gloves; hats, caps & millinery

(G-2711)
AMERICAN CHEMICAL & COATING CO
410 Division St (07201-1962)
PHONE..............................908 353-2260
Qamar V Zaman, *President*
EMP: 4
SQ FT: 7,000
SALES (est): 547.8K **Privately Held**
SIC: 2865 2851 2891 Dyes, synthetic organic; lacquer: bases, dopes, thinner; adhesives

(G-2712)
ATI TRADING INC
765 York St (07201-2035)
PHONE..............................718 888-7918
EMP: 17
SALES (est): 3.4MM **Privately Held**
SIC: 3823 Computer interface equipment for industrial process control

(G-2713)
ATTITUDES IN DRESSING INC (PA)
Also Called: Body Wrappers
107 Trumbull St Bldg B8 (07206-2165)
PHONE..............................908 354-7218
Marie West, *President*
Michael Rubin, *Corp Secy*
Nicholas Karant, *Vice Pres*
Michael Lee, *Sales Mgr*
Trudy Christ, *Mktg Dir*
▲ **EMP:** 320
SQ FT: 185,000
SALES (est): 55.8MM **Privately Held**
SIC: 2339 2369 5137 Athletic clothing: women's, misses' & juniors'; leotards: women's, misses' & juniors'; girls' & children's outerwear; women's & children's clothing

(G-2714)
BELDEN INC
Also Called: Alpha Wire
711 Lidgerwood Ave (07202-3115)
PHONE..............................908 925-8000
Christine Birkner, *Principal*
EMP: 14
SALES (corp-wide): 2.5B **Publicly Held**
WEB: www.belden.com
SIC: 3351 5063 3498 3496 Copper rolling & drawing; electrical apparatus & equipment; fabricated pipe & fittings; miscellaneous fabricated wire products; sheet metalwork
PA: Belden Inc.
1 N Brentwood Blvd Fl 15
Saint Louis MO 63105
314 854-8000

(G-2715)
BELL ARTE INC
Also Called: Bell'arte
10 W Mravlag Pl (07201-2515)
P.O. Box 8912 (07201-0812)
PHONE..............................908 355-1199
Giuseppe Chillemi, *President*
Frank Arena, *Vice Pres*
EMP: 17
SQ FT: 15,000
SALES: 1.7MM **Privately Held**
WEB: www.artebellagallery.com
SIC: 2431 Interior & ornamental woodwork & trim; exterior & ornamental woodwork & trim

GEOGRAPHIC

(G-2716)
BERRY GLOBAL INC
100 Dowd Ave (07206-2130)
PHONE...................................908 353-3850
Scott Christ, *Plant Mgr*
Tahir Khan, *Controller*
Raymond Panek, *Manager*
Frances Villaman, *Manager*
EMP: 120 Publicly Held
WEB: www.6sens.com
SIC: 3089 3081 Bottle caps, molded plastic; unsupported plastics film & sheet
HQ: Berry Global, Inc.
101 Oakley St
Evansville IN 47710
812 424-2904

(G-2717)
BERRY GLOBAL INC
322 3rd St (07206-2007)
PHONE...................................718 205-3115
EMP: 127 Publicly Held
SIC: 3089 Bottle caps, molded plastic
HQ: Berry Global, Inc.
101 Oakley St
Evansville IN 47710
812 424-2904

(G-2718)
BURLINGTON COAT FACTORY
651 Kapkowski Rd Ste 30 (07201-4928)
PHONE...................................908 994-9562
Roberto Manresa, *Manager*
EMP: 68
SALES (corp-wide): 6.6B Publicly Held
SIC: 5137 5136 2311 Women's & children's clothing; men's & boys' clothing; coats, overcoats & vests
HQ: Burlington Coat Factory Warehouse Corporation
1830 N Route 130
Burlington NJ 08016
609 387-7800

(G-2719)
CARGILL INCORPORATED
132 Corbin St (07201-2910)
PHONE...................................908 820-9800
Alfred Rieger, *Branch Mgr*
EMP: 4
SALES (corp-wide): 114.7B Privately Held
SIC: 2087 Flavoring extracts & syrups
PA: Cargill, Incorporated
15407 Mcginty Rd W
Wayzata MN 55391
952 742-7575

(G-2720)
CHECK-IT ELECTRONICS CORP
560 Trumbull St (07206-1409)
PHONE...................................973 520-8435
Richard E Bettle, *President*
George T Van Brunt, *Corp Secy*
EMP: 20
SALES (est): 1.7MM Privately Held
WEB: www.check-it-electronics.com
SIC: 3823 3822 3812 Industrial instrmnts msrmnt display/control process variable; auto controls regulating residntl & coml environmt & applncs; search & navigation equipment

(G-2721)
COCKPIT USA INC
725 New Point Rd (07201-2861)
PHONE...................................212 575-1616
Nicole Grab, *Sales Staff*
Jeffrey Clyman, *Branch Mgr*
Steve Lehmann, *Manager*
EMP: 10
SALES (corp-wide): 10.5MM Privately Held
SIC: 2386 5136 5611 5961 Coats & jackets, leather & sheep-lined; sportswear, men's & boys'; clothing, sportswear, men's & boys'; clothing, mail order (except women's)
PA: Cockpit Usa, Inc.
15 W 39th St Fl 12
New York NY 10018
212 575-1616

(G-2722)
CONSOLIDATED CONTAINER CO LP
Also Called: Contech
28-36 Slater Dr (07206)
PHONE...................................908 289-5862
Dan Citus, *Manager*
EMP: 70
SALES (corp-wide): 14B Publicly Held
SIC: 3089 Plastic containers, except foam
HQ: Consolidated Container Company Lp
2500 Windy Ridge Pkwy Se # 1400
Atlanta GA 30339
678 742-4600

(G-2723)
COUNTRY CLUB PRODUCTS INC
706 Trumbull St (07201-2837)
PHONE...................................908 352-5400
Isaac Mandalaoui, *CEO*
Sol Mandalaoui, *President*
EMP: 7
SQ FT: 5,000
SALES: 15MM Privately Held
SIC: 2211 Pillowcases

(G-2724)
CRINCOLI WOODWORK CO INC
160 Spring St (07201-2660)
PHONE...................................908 352-9332
Peter Crincoli, *President*
EMP: 11
SQ FT: 17,000
SALES (est): 1.5MM Privately Held
WEB: www.crincoliwoodwork.com
SIC: 1521 1542 2431 5712 General remodeling, single-family houses; commercial & office buildings, renovation & repair; woodwork, interior & ornamental; custom made furniture, except cabinets; cabinet work, custom

(G-2725)
DAVES SALAD HOUSE INC
577 Pennsylvania Ave (07201-1101)
PHONE...................................908 965-0773
David Miles, *President*
Michelle Miles, *Vice Pres*
EMP: 6
SQ FT: 1,500
SALES (est): 400K Privately Held
SIC: 2099 Salads, fresh or refrigerated

(G-2726)
DEARBORN A BELDEN CDT COMPANY (HQ)
Also Called: Kerrigan Lewis Wire/Cdt
711 Lidgerwood Ave (07202-3115)
PHONE...................................908 925-8000
Scott Blackwood, *CEO*
Robert Canny, *President*
Ray Grabowski, *Vice Pres*
▲ EMP: 100
SQ FT: 110,000
SALES (est): 9.5MM
SALES (corp-wide): 2.5B Publicly Held
WEB: www.dearborn-cdt.com
SIC: 3643 3699 3694 3496 Current-carrying wiring devices; electrical equipment & supplies; engine electrical equipment; miscellaneous fabricated wire products; nonferrous wiredrawing & insulating; steel wire & related products
PA: Belden Inc.
1 N Brentwood Blvd Fl 15
Saint Louis MO 63105
314 854-8000

(G-2727)
DEB EL FOOD PRODUCTS LLC
2 Papetti Plz (07206-1421)
PHONE...................................908 409-0010
Juan Castillo, *Branch Mgr*
EMP: 60 Privately Held
SIC: 2015 Egg processing
PA: Deb El Food Products Llc
520 Broad St Fl 6
Newark NJ 07102

(G-2728)
DEXMED INC
433 N Broad St Fl 1 (07208-3398)
PHONE...................................732 831-0507
Joseph Stern, *CEO*
Rochel Leah Stern, *Principal*

Toby Schleisinger, *Principal*
EMP: 5
SALES (est): 423.8K Privately Held
WEB: www.dexmed.com
SIC: 5047 3842 3841 Medical equipment & supplies; cotton, including cotton balls: sterile & non-sterile; surgical & medical instruments

(G-2729)
DEXMED LLC
433 N Broad St Fl 1 (07208-3398)
PHONE...................................732 831-0507
Joseph Stern,
Toby Schleslinger,
Rochel Leah Stern,
EMP: 5
SQ FT: 1,500
SALES (est): 264K Privately Held
SIC: 3841 5047 Surgical & medical instruments; instruments, surgical & medical

(G-2730)
DUBON CORP
1356 Stanley Ter (07208-2613)
PHONE...................................212 812-2171
Egmaldo Bonilla, *President*
Lucas Bonilla, *Vice Pres*
EMP: 8
SALES (est): 386.7K Privately Held
SIC: 2013 Sausages & other prepared meats

(G-2731)
DURO BAG MANUFACTURING COMPANY
750 Dowd Ave (07201-2108)
PHONE...................................908 351-2400
Karl Kalkbrenner, *Manager*
EMP: 200
SALES (corp-wide): 2.9B Privately Held
SIC: 2673 Bags: plastic, laminated & coated
HQ: Duro Bag Manufacturing Company
7600 Empire Dr
Florence KY 41042
859 371-2150

(G-2732)
ELEGANT HEADWEAR CO INC (PA)
Also Called: ABG Accessories
1000 Jefferson Ave (07201-1394)
PHONE...................................908 558-1200
Joseph Templer, *President*
Abraham Ausch, *Vice Pres*
Sarah Gerard, *Vice Pres*
John Guevara, *Design Engr*
Jenn Debari, *Sales Staff*
▲ EMP: 150
SQ FT: 250,000
SALES (est): 34.3MM Privately Held
WEB: www.elegantheadwear.com
SIC: 2253 Hats & headwear, knit

(G-2733)
EVOQUA WATER TECHNOLOGIES LLC
624 Evans St (07201-2009)
PHONE...................................908 353-7400
Andrew Lees, *Manager*
EMP: 12
SALES (corp-wide): 1.3B Publicly Held
SIC: 2819 Charcoal (carbon), activated
HQ: Evoqua Water Technologies Llc
210 6th Ave Ste 3300
Pittsburgh PA 15222
724 772-0044

(G-2734)
FAULDING HOLDINGS INC
200 Elmora Ave (07202-1106)
PHONE...................................908 527-9100
Mark Stier, *CFO*
Jatin Shah, *Director*
EMP: 250
SQ FT: 300,000
SALES (est): 24.4MM Publicly Held
SIC: 2834 Druggists' preparations (pharmaceuticals)
HQ: Mayne Pharma International Pty Ltd
1538 Main North Rd
Salisbury South SA 5106

(G-2735)
FEDERAL LORCO PETROLEUM LLC
Also Called: Federal Petroleum
450 S Front St (07202-3009)
PHONE...................................908 352-0542
John Lionetti,
Frank Lo Bello Jr,
EMP: 70
SALES (est): 6.7MM Privately Held
WEB: www.federalpetroleum.com
SIC: 4491 4953 2992 Marine terminals; refuse systems; lubricating oils & greases

(G-2736)
FINE LINEN INC
107 Trumbull St (07206-2165)
PHONE...................................908 469-3634
Isaac Braun, *President*
EMP: 10
SALES: 383.3K Privately Held
SIC: 2392 Household furnishings

(G-2737)
FREEPORT MINERALS CORPORATION
Also Called: Phelps Dodge
48 94 Bayway Ave (07202)
PHONE...................................908 351-3200
William Spellman, *Branch Mgr*
EMP: 86
SQ FT: 200,000
SALES (corp-wide): 18.6B Publicly Held
WEB: www.phelpsdodge.com
SIC: 3351 Copper rolling & drawing
HQ: Freeport Minerals Corporation
333 N Central Ave
Phoenix AZ 85004
602 366-8100

(G-2738)
FREEPORT-MCMORAN INC
48-94 Bayway Ave (07202)
PHONE...................................908 558-4361
EMP: 5
SALES (corp-wide): 18.6B Publicly Held
SIC: 1041 1044 1021 Gold ores; silver ores; copper ores
PA: Freeport-Mcmoran Inc.
333 N Central Ave
Phoenix AZ 85004
602 366-8100

(G-2739)
FUEL BIO HOLDINGS LTD LBLTY CO
534 S Front St (07202-3009)
PHONE...................................908 344-6875
Patrick Doyle,
EMP: 4
SALES (est): 413.8K Privately Held
WEB: www.fuelbio.com
SIC: 2911 Diesel fuels

(G-2740)
FULL CIRCLE MFG GROUP
534 S Front St (07202-3009)
PHONE...................................908 353-8933
Joseph Ioia, *President*
EMP: 10
SALES (est): 1.7MM Privately Held
SIC: 2899 Antifreeze compounds

(G-2741)
GARYLIN TOGS
Also Called: Body Wrappers
107 Trumbull St (07206-2165)
PHONE...................................908 354-7218
Michael Rubin, *President*
Robert Rubin, *Principal*
Eleanor Rubin, *Admin Sec*
EMP: 90 EST: 1955
SQ FT: 50,000
SALES (est): 9.2MM Privately Held
WEB: www.bodywrappers.com
SIC: 2339 2369 Women's & misses' athletic clothing & sportswear; girls' & children's outerwear

(G-2742)
GENERAL FILM PRODUCTS INC
107 Trumbull St Ste 302 (07206-2172)
PHONE...................................908 351-0454
Richard Eisner, *President*
Louis Antonacci, *President*

EMP: 50
SQ FT: 40,000
SALES (est): 9.2MM
SALES (corp-wide): 67.8MM **Privately Held**
SIC: 2673 Plastic & pliofilm bags
PA: Poly-Pak Industries, Inc
125 Spagnoli Rd
Melville NY 11747
800 969-1933

(G-2743)
GIBBONS COMPANY LTD
614 Progress St (07201-2057)
PHONE....................................441 294-5047
▲ EMP: 27
SALES (est): 2.1MM **Privately Held**
SIC: 5311 3161 Department stores; clothing & apparel carrying cases

(G-2744)
GRAY OVERHEAD DOOR CO
439 3rd Ave (07206-1034)
PHONE....................................908 355-3889
Grayton Acosta, President
Benazir Acosta, Corp Secy
EMP: 10
SQ FT: 10,000
SALES (est): 1.2MM **Privately Held**
SIC: 3442 1751 Garage doors, overhead: metal; garage door, installation or erection

(G-2745)
HAYWARD INDUSTRIAL PRODUCTS (HQ)
Also Called: Hayward Plastic Products Div
620 Division St (07201-2004)
P.O. Box 18 (07207-0018)
PHONE....................................908 351-5400
Robert Davis, CEO
Oscar Davis, CEO
Dave Rudiger, Manager
◆ EMP: 250
SALES (est): 71.3MM
SALES (corp-wide): 541.5MM **Privately Held**
SIC: 3089 3492 3491 3494 Plastic hardware & building products; control valves, fluid power: hydraulic & pneumatic; pressure valves & regulators, industrial; line strainers, for use in piping systems; sporting & athletic goods; blowers & fans
PA: Hayward Industries, Inc.
620 Division St
Elizabeth NJ 07201
908 351-5400

(G-2746)
HAYWARD INDUSTRIES INC (PA)
Also Called: Haywood Pool Products
620 Division St (07201-2004)
PHONE....................................908 351-5400
Oscar Davis, Ch of Bd
Kevin P Holleran, President
David Macnair, Vice Pres
Kevin Potucek, Vice Pres
Donna Smith, Vice Pres
◆ EMP: 350 EST: 1925
SQ FT: 30,000
SALES (est): 541.5MM **Privately Held**
WEB: www.haywardnet.com
SIC: 3589 3561 3423 3494 Swimming pool filter & water conditioning systems; pumps & pumping equipment; leaf skimmers or swimming pool rakes; valves & pipe fittings; filters & strainers, pipeline; plastic hardware & building products

(G-2747)
HAYWARD INDUSTRIES INC
628 Henry St Bldg 6 (07201-2016)
PHONE....................................908 351-0899
Reuven Har-Even, Vice Pres
EMP: 5
SALES (corp-wide): 541.5MM **Privately Held**
SIC: 3589 Swimming pool filter & water conditioning systems
PA: Hayward Industries, Inc.
620 Division St
Elizabeth NJ 07201
908 351-5400

(G-2748)
HAYWARD POOL PRODUCTS INC
Also Called: Hayward Flow Control
620 Division St (07201-2004)
PHONE....................................908 351-5400
Oscar Davis, Ch of Bd
Don Smith, Vice Pres
Frank Crippen, Mfg Mgr
Ray Wrixon, Traffic Mgr
Dianne Barbosa, Senior Buyer
◆ EMP: 900 EST: 1980
SQ FT: 20,000
SALES (est): 5.8MM
SALES (corp-wide): 541.5MM **Privately Held**
SIC: 5091 3569 Swimming pools, equipment & supplies; heaters, swimming pool: electric
PA: Hayward Industries, Inc.
620 Division St
Elizabeth NJ 07201
908 351-5400

(G-2749)
IMPERIAL WELD RING CORP INC
80 Front St 88 (07206-1755)
P.O. Box 6646 (07206-6646)
PHONE....................................908 354-0011
Calvin Sierra, President
Alicia Borrero, Office Mgr
EMP: 20 EST: 1959
SQ FT: 12,000
SALES (est): 1.9MM **Privately Held**
SIC: 3429 3498 3494 Metal fasteners; fabricated pipe & fittings; valves & pipe fittings

(G-2750)
INNOVATIVE CONCEPTS DESIGN LLC
Also Called: Gemini Sound
107 Trumbull St Ste 203 (07206-2170)
PHONE....................................732 346-0061
Artie Cabasso, CEO
EMP: 10 EST: 2014
SQ FT: 100,000
SALES (est): 2.3MM **Privately Held**
SIC: 3651 Audio electronic systems

(G-2751)
INTERNATIONAL COCONUT CORP
225 W Grand St (07202-1205)
P.O. Box 3326 (07207-3326)
PHONE....................................908 289-1555
Arthur Kesselhaut, President
Richard Kesselhaut, Vice Pres
▲ EMP: 15 EST: 1978
SQ FT: 15,000
SALES (est): 2.4MM **Privately Held**
WEB: www.internationalcoconut.com
SIC: 2099 Coconut, desiccated & shredded

(G-2752)
JASPER FASHION LTD LBLTY CO
336 Murray St (07202-1723)
PHONE....................................917 561-4533
Moheuddin Ahmed, President
▲ EMP: 10 EST: 2008
SALES (est): 825.7K **Privately Held**
SIC: 5137 2361 Women's & children's clothing: dresses: girls', children's & infants'

(G-2753)
LEGGS HNS BLI PLYTX FCTRY OUTL
651 Kapkowski Rd Ste 1008 (07201-4931)
PHONE....................................908 289-7262
Lasaunja Pretlow, Manager
EMP: 5
SALES (est): 366.4K **Privately Held**
SIC: 2211 Underwear fabrics, cotton

(G-2754)
LITHUANIAN BAKERY T J INC
131 Inslee Pl (07206-2010)
PHONE....................................908 354-0970
John Backiel, President
Janina Backiel, Vice Pres

EMP: 14 EST: 1968
SQ FT: 5,000
SALES (est): 1.7MM **Privately Held**
SIC: 2051 Breads, rolls & buns

(G-2755)
MARINE OIL SERVICE INC
450 S Front St (07202-3009)
PHONE....................................908 282-6440
Joseph Olivieri, Manager
Chico Reyes, Maintence Staff
EMP: 9
SALES (corp-wide): 29.3MM **Privately Held**
WEB: www.marineoilservice.com
SIC: 2992 Lubricating oils
PA: Marine Oil Service, Inc.
201 E City Hall Ave
Norfolk VA 23510
757 543-1446

(G-2756)
MASTERCRAFT ELECTROPLATING
801 Magnolia Ave Ste 4 (07201-1900)
PHONE....................................908 354-4404
Pat Obrien, Principal
EMP: 5
SQ FT: 5,500
SALES (est): 420K **Privately Held**
SIC: 3559 Automotive related machinery

(G-2757)
MASTERCRAFT METAL FINISHING
801 Magnolia Ave (07201-1900)
PHONE....................................908 354-4404
EMP: 5 EST: 2016
SALES (est): 291.2K **Privately Held**
SIC: 3471 Plating/Polishing Service

(G-2758)
METROFUSER LLC (PA)
475 Division St Bldg 1 (07201-2000)
PHONE....................................908 245-2100
Eric Katz, CFO
Marissa Rodriuez, Administration
EMP: 65
SQ FT: 10,000
SALES (est): 14MM **Privately Held**
WEB: www.metrofuser.com
SIC: 3575 Computer terminals

(G-2759)
MIRAGE WHOLESALE GROUP LLC
107 Trumbull St Unit A44 (07206-2165)
PHONE....................................718 757-6590
AVI Jajati, Mng Member
EMP: 6
SALES (est): 236.5K **Privately Held**
SIC: 3161 Traveling bags

(G-2760)
NINE WEST HOLDINGS INC
Also Called: Kasper
651 Kapkowski Rd Ste 2032 (07201-4919)
PHONE....................................908 354-8895
EMP: 8
SALES (corp-wide): 2.2B **Privately Held**
SIC: 2337 Mfg Women's/Misses' Suits/Coats
HQ: Nine West Holdings, Inc.
180 Rittenhouse Cir
Bristol PA 10018
215 785-4000

(G-2761)
NORTH EASTERN PALLET EXCHANGE
725 Spring St Ste 2 (07201-2045)
PHONE....................................908 289-0018
Toll Free:....................................888 -
EMP: 50 EST: 1996
SQ FT: 15,000
SALES (est): 4.7MM **Privately Held**
SIC: 2448 Mfg Pallets

(G-2762)
NORTHEAST BINDERY INC
419 Trumbull St (07206-2114)
PHONE....................................908 436-3737
Bel Ramlochan, President
Jay Ramraj, Vice Pres
EMP: 16

SALES: 1.7MM **Privately Held**
SIC: 2789 Binding only: books, pamphlets, magazines, etc.

(G-2763)
NYP CORP (FRMR NY-PTERS CORP) (PA)
805 E Grand St (07201-2721)
PHONE....................................908 351-6550
Gerald La Belle, President
Jerry Labelle, Vice Pres
Don Ament, Facilities Mgr
Katie Coffey, Purch Mgr
Brad Carl, Sales Staff
▲ EMP: 100 EST: 1945
SQ FT: 60,000
SALES (est): 16.8MM **Privately Held**
WEB: www.nyp-corp.com
SIC: 2393 5199 2221 Textile bags; burlap; broadwoven fabric mills, manmade

(G-2764)
OBARE SERVICES LTD LBLTY CO
593 Meadow St (07201-2364)
P.O. Box 2437 (07207-2437)
PHONE....................................908 456-1887
Dan Obare, CEO
EMP: 4
SQ FT: 1,000
SALES (est): 242.1K **Privately Held**
SIC: 2541 Store & office display cases & fixtures

(G-2765)
ON DEMAND MACHINERY
Also Called: American Graphix
150 Broadway (07206-1856)
P.O. Box 240, Elizabethport (07206-0240)
PHONE....................................908 351-7137
John Jacobson, Owner
Mark Williamson, Prdtn Mgr
EMP: 12
SALES (est): 1.9MM **Privately Held**
WEB: www.odmachinery.com
SIC: 3555 Bookbinding machinery

(G-2766)
PABST ENTERPRISES EQUIPMENT CO
676 Pennsylvania Ave (07201-1214)
PHONE....................................908 353-2880
Robert D Verkouille, CEO
David E Bechtold, President
Jody Sackett, Corp Secy
EMP: 20 EST: 1934
SQ FT: 35,000
SALES (est): 2.1MM **Privately Held**
SIC: 3441 3599 3444 7692 Fabricated structural metal; machine shop, jobbing & repair; sheet metalwork; welding repair

(G-2767)
PAO BA AVO LLC
545 Edgar Rd (07202-3301)
PHONE....................................908 962-9090
Fernando Santos, Manager
EMP: 4
SALES (est): 172.5K **Privately Held**
SIC: 2051 Cakes, bakery: except frozen

(G-2768)
PEACH BOUTIQUE LLC (PA)
1139 E Jersey St Ste 319 (07201-2429)
PHONE....................................908 351-0739
Roslyn Rearden, Mng Member
EMP: 4
SALES: 250K **Privately Held**
WEB: www.peachboutique.com
SIC: 5621 3999 2395 2384 Boutiques; embroidery kits; embroidery & art needlework; robes & dressing gowns; clergymen's vestments

(G-2769)
PEGASUS HOME FASHIONS INC
107 Trumbull St G1s13 (07206-2165)
P.O. Box 9030 (07201-0930)
PHONE....................................908 965-1919
Carmine Spinella, COO
◆ EMP: 160
SALES (est): 21.3MM **Privately Held**
WEB: www.pegasushomefashions.com
SIC: 2392 Cushions & pillows

(G-2770)
PRIDE PRODUCTS MFG LLC
5 Slater Dr (07206-2151)
PHONE..................................908 353-1900
Joseph Yuan, *Principal*
EMP: 12
SALES (est): 387.8K **Privately Held**
SIC: 3944 Games, toys & children's vehicles

(G-2771)
PVH CORP
Also Called: Van Heusen
651 Kapkowski Rd Ste 1416 (07201-4934)
PHONE..................................908 685-0050
Philip Gallina, *Manager*
EMP: 7
SALES (corp-wide): 9.6B **Publicly Held**
WEB: www.pvh.com
SIC: 2321 Men's & boys' furnishings
PA: Pvh Corp.
200 Madison Ave Bsmt 1
New York NY 10016
212 381-3500

(G-2772)
**QUALITY SWISS SCREW
MACHINE CO**
849 4th Ave (07202-3853)
PHONE..................................908 289-4334
Juan Monserrate, *Branch Mgr*
EMP: 4
SALES (corp-wide): 2.1MM **Privately
Held**
WEB: www.qualityswiss.com
SIC: 3469 Machine parts, stamped or
pressed metal
PA: Quality Swiss Screw Machine Co Inc
960 Mountain Ave
Mountainside NJ
908 654-1881

(G-2773)
RAPSOCO INC
648 Newark Ave (07208-3539)
PHONE..................................908 977-7321
Richard Atuahene, *CEO*
EMP: 4
SALES: 500K **Privately Held**
SIC: 3999 Manufacturing industries

(G-2774)
RENAE TELECOM LLC
745 Thomas St (07202-2743)
PHONE..................................908 362-8112
Raymond C Meyers, *
EMP: 99
SALES (est): 9MM **Privately Held**
SIC: 3663 Radio & TV communications
equipment

(G-2775)
ROYAL PRIME INC (PA)
1027 Newark Ave Ste 1 (07208-3592)
PHONE..................................908 354-7600
Andrew Inelli, *President*
◆ **EMP:** 14 **EST:** 1978
SQ FT: 85,000
SALES (est): 3.4MM **Privately Held**
SIC: 3442 Window & door frames

(G-2776)
**SMITHFIELD PACKAGED MEATS
CORP**
Also Called: 814 Americas
814 2nd Ave (07202-3804)
PHONE..................................908 354-2674
Michael Patraceolla, *General Mgr*
Michael Patracuolla, *General Mgr*
EMP: 30 **Privately Held**
SIC: 2011 Meat packing plants
HQ: Smithfield Packaged Meats Corp.
805 E Kemper Rd
Cincinnati OH 45246
513 782-3800

(G-2777)
STARPHIL INC
107 Trumbull St R12 (07206-2165)
PHONE..................................908 353-8943
EMP: 5
SQ FT: 12,000
SALES: 500K **Privately Held**
SIC: 2511 Mfg Wood Household Furniture

(G-2778)
SUPERFLEX LTD
400 S 2nd St (07206-1558)
PHONE..................................718 768-1400
Shimon Elbaz, *Ch of Bd*
Yigal Elbaz, *President*
▲ **EMP:** 50
SQ FT: 60,000
SALES (est): 20.7MM **Privately Held**
WEB: www.superflex.com
SIC: 3644 3052 Electric conduits & fittings; plastic hose

(G-2779)
SUPERIOR LIGHTING INC
1245 Virginia St (07208-3068)
PHONE..................................908 759-0199
Abraham Knopfler, *CEO*
Chaya Knoppler, *President*
▲ **EMP:** 10
SQ FT: 8,000
SALES: 3.4MM **Privately Held**
SIC: 3646 3645 Commercial indusl & institutional electric lighting fixtures; residential lighting fixtures

(G-2780)
**SUPERIOR POWDER COATING
INC (PA)**
Also Called: Spct
600 Progress St (07201-2018)
PHONE..................................908 351-8707
Peter G Markey, *President*
Charles D Briggs, *Vice Pres*
Susan Santiago, *Corp Comm Staff*
▲ **EMP:** 111
SQ FT: 112,000
SALES (est): 17.5MM **Privately Held**
WEB: www.superiorpowder.com
SIC: 3479 Varnishing of metal products

(G-2781)
SWISSRAY AMERICA INC
Also Called: Swissray Medical Systems
1180 Mclester St Ste 2 (07201-2931)
PHONE..................................908 353-0971
Ueli Laupper, *CEO*
Michael J Baker, *CEO*
Rudy Laupper, *Chairman*
▲ **EMP:** 34 **EST:** 1997
SALES (est): 1.2MM
SALES (corp-wide): 10.4MM **Privately
Held**
SIC: 3844 X-ray apparatus & tubes
HQ: Swissray International, Inc.
1090 King Georges Rd 1203
Edison NJ 08837

(G-2782)
TOTAL INSTALLATIONS
Also Called: Total Remodeling
941 Olive St (07201-1922)
PHONE..................................908 943-3211
Javier Barrera, *Owner*
EMP: 4
SALES: 80K **Privately Held**
SIC: 3442 Metal doors, sash & trim

(G-2783)
TWO LITTLE GUYS CO
Also Called: Two Little Guys Lemonade Co
107 Trumbull St Ste 102 (07206-2171)
P.O. Box 43255, Montclair (07043-0255)
PHONE..................................973 744-7502
Steve Prato, *President*
EMP: 8
SALES (est): 650.7K **Privately Held**
SIC: 2086 Bottled & canned soft drinks

(G-2784)
**UNIVERSAL VALVE COMPANY
INC**
478 Schiller St (07206-2183)
PHONE..................................908 351-0606
Martin Pettesch, *Principal*
Mike Farinha, *Prdtn Mgr*
▲ **EMP:** 15
SALES (est): 3.7MM **Privately Held**
WEB: www.universalvalve.com
SIC: 3492 3321 Fluid power valves &
hose fittings; manhole covers, metal

(G-2785)
VF OUTDOOR LLC
Also Called: Tbl Licencing
651 Kapkowski Rd Ste 2034 (07201-4935)
PHONE..................................908 352-5390
EMP: 4
SALES (corp-wide): 13.8B **Publicly Held**
SIC: 3143 Men's footwear, except athletic
HQ: Vf Outdoor, Llc
2701 Harbor Bay Pkwy
Alameda CA 94502
510 618-3500

(G-2786)
WILD FLAVORS INC
Also Called: Wild Juice US
132 Corbin St Bldg 1200 (07201-2910)
PHONE..................................908 820-9800
EMP: 11
SALES (corp-wide): 64.3B **Publicly Held**
SIC: 2087 Flavoring extracts & syrups
HQ: Wild Flavors, Inc.
1261 Pacific Ave
Erlanger KY 41018

Elizabethport
Union County

(G-2787)
EDDIE DOMANI INC
20 Butler St (07206-1527)
PHONE..................................908 469-8863
Eddie Domani, *President*
▲ **EMP:** 4
SALES (corp-wide): 5.9MM **Privately
Held**
SIC: 2325 Slacks, dress: men's, youths' &
boys'
PA: Eddie Domani, Inc.
1431 Broadway Fl 4
New York NY 10018
212 840-5551

(G-2788)
GENESIS LIGHTING MFG INC
107 Trumbull St Ste 104 (07206-2171)
PHONE..................................908 352-6720
Jay Gindoff, *President*
▲ **EMP:** 5
SQ FT: 85,000
SALES (est): 5MM **Privately Held**
SIC: 3646 Commercial indusl & institutional electric lighting fixtures

(G-2789)
IMPACT DESIGN INC
248 3rd St (07206-2052)
PHONE..................................908 289-2900
Martin Templer, *President*
▲ **EMP:** 25
SQ FT: 15,000
SALES (est): 1.5MM **Privately Held**
SIC: 5137 2353 Women's & children's
clothing; hats, caps & millinery

(G-2790)
**PAPETTIS HYGRADE EGG PDTS
INC (DH)**
Also Called: Michael Foods
1 Papetti Plz (07206-1421)
PHONE..................................908 282-7900
Arthur Papetti, *President*
Stephen Papetti, *Exec VP*
Alfred Papetti, *Vice Pres*
Anthony Papetti, *Vice Pres*
Melissa Kriszten, *Production*
▼ **EMP:** 550
SQ FT: 75,000
SALES (est): 136.1MM **Publicly Held**
SIC: 2015 Egg processing; eggs,
processed: desiccated (dried); eggs,
processed: frozen; eggs, processed: dehydrated
HQ: M.G. Waldbaum Company
301 Carlson Pkwy Ste 400
Minnetonka MN 55305
952 258-4000

(G-2791)
PETS FIRST INC
248 3rd St (07206-2052)
PHONE..................................908 289-2900
Martin Templer, *Principal*

▲ **EMP:** 45
SALES (est): 211.7K **Privately Held**
SIC: 2389 Apparel for handicapped

Elmer
Salem County

(G-2792)
A CHEERFUL GIVER INC
300 Front St (08318-2143)
PHONE..................................856 358-4438
Tony Gross, *President*
▲ **EMP:** 10
SQ FT: 15,000
SALES (est): 1.7MM **Privately Held**
WEB: www.acheerfulgiver.com
SIC: 2099 5945 5999 5947 Sauces:
gravy, dressing & dip mixes; arts & crafts
supplies; candle shops; gift shop; candles

(G-2793)
AKS PHARMA INC
201 Front St (08318-2141)
PHONE..................................856 521-0710
EMP: 4
SALES (est): 251.5K **Privately Held**
SIC: 2834 Pharmaceutical preparations

(G-2794)
ARCHER PLASTICS INC
Also Called: Archer Seating Clearing House
1510 Jesse Bridge Rd (08318-4563)
PHONE..................................856 692-0242
Ruth Archer, *President*
Steve Archer, *Vice Pres*
EMP: 5
SALES: 700K **Privately Held**
WEB: www.msequip.com
SIC: 2531 Stadium seating

(G-2795)
**COLE BROTHERS MARBLE &
GRANITE**
892 Parvin Mill Rd (08318-4005)
PHONE..................................856 455-7989
Ruth Cole, *President*
Ben Cole, *Vice Pres*
Benjamin Cole, *Vice Pres*
EMP: 6
SQ FT: 8,000
SALES (est): 774.3K **Privately Held**
WEB: www.colebrothersgranite.com
SIC: 3281 1752 Marble, building: cut &
shaped; granite, cut & shaped; carpet laying; ceramic floor tile installation; linoleum
installation; vinyl floor tile & sheet installation

(G-2796)
ELMER TIMES CO INC
21 State St (08318-2145)
PHONE..................................856 358-6171
Mark Foster, *President*
Preston Foster III, *President*
Pamela S Brunner, *Corp Secy*
EMP: 5
SQ FT: 3,000
SALES (est): 276.3K **Privately Held**
SIC: 2711 Newspapers: publishing only,
not printed on site

(G-2797)
FAVS CORP
Also Called: Enviro Safe Wtr Trtmnt Systems
331 Husted Station Rd (08318-3804)
PHONE..................................856 358-1515
Anthony Favorito, *President*
EMP: 6
SALES (est): 1.2MM **Privately Held**
SIC: 5074 5999 3589 1711 Water purification equipment; water purification
equipment; sewage & water treatment
equipment; plumbing, heating, air-conditioning contractors

(G-2798)
**GOLF COAST POLYMER
SERVICES**
107 Madison Rd (08318-2013)
PHONE..................................856 498-3434
David Bryant, *President*
Gerald Bryant, *Vice Pres*
EMP: 7

SALES (est): 974.5K **Privately Held**
SIC: **3479** Coating of metals with plastic or
resins

(G-2799)
J SPINELLI & SONS INC
Also Called: J Spinelli & Sons Excavating
615 Gershal Ave (08318-4216)
PHONE...................................856 691-3133
Joseph Spinelli III, *President*
Dino Spinelli, *President*
EMP: 50
SALES (est): 7.3MM **Privately Held**
SIC: **4212** 2041 7549 Dump truck
haulage; doughs, frozen or refrigerated;
towing services

(G-2800)
MANUTECH INC
29 State St (08318-2145)
P.O. Box 758 (08318-0758)
PHONE...................................856 358-6136
Ed Deinarowicz, *CEO*
EMP: 4
SQ FT: 6,000
SALES (est): 302.5K **Privately Held**
SIC: **3469** Machine parts, stamped or
pressed metal

(G-2801)
PERFECT SHAPES INC
Also Called: Things 2 B
110 Salem St (08318-2271)
PHONE...................................856 783-3844
Colin Broecker, *President*
EMP: 4
SQ FT: 44,000
SALES: 1MM **Privately Held**
SIC: **5032** 3299 Stucco; stucco

(G-2802)
RICHARD SHAFER
Also Called: Shafer Brothers Trailers
38 Martin Ave (08318-4400)
PHONE 856 358-3483
Richard Shafer, *Owner*
EMP: 4 EST: 1967
SQ FT: 2,400
SALES: 500K **Privately Held**
SIC: **3715** 7539 Trailer bodies; trailer re-
pair

(G-2803)
S J QUARRY MATERIALS INC
615 Gershal Ave (08318-4216)
PHONE...................................856 691-3133
Joseph Spinelli III, *President*
Dino Spinelli, *Assistant VP*
EMP: 55
SALES (est): 5.5MM **Privately Held**
SIC: **1411** Dimension stone

(G-2804)
SIGN SPEC INC
602 Centerton Rd (08318-3918)
PHONE...................................856 663-2292
Charles Jacques, *Vice Pres*
Michael A Pagliuso, *Vice Pres*
EMP: 55
SQ FT: 43,000
SALES (est): 4.5MM **Privately Held**
WEB: www.signspec.com
SIC: **3993** Electric signs

(G-2805)
UNITED RESIN INC
321 Willow Grove Rd (08318-2046)
PHONE...................................856 358-2574
Albert O'Brien, *President*
EMP: 12
SQ FT: 22,000
SALES (est): 885.7K **Privately Held**
WEB: www.unitedresincorp.com
SIC: **2821** Acrylic resins

(G-2806)
VANGUARD PRINTING
531 Garden Rd (08318-3933)
PHONE...................................856 358-2665
Charles Panek, *President*
EMP: 4
SALES (est): 240K **Privately Held**
SIC: **2752** Commercial printing, offset

Elmwood Park
Bergen County

(G-2807)
ADAGIO TEAS INC (PA)
170 Kipp Ave (07407-1123)
PHONE...................................973 253-7400
Michael Cramer, *CEO*
Nicholas Lin, *Engineer*
◆ EMP: 5
SALES (est): 2.6MM **Privately Held**
WEB: www.adagio.com
SIC: **5149** 5499 5719 2095 Tea; tea;
kitchenware; coffee extracts

(G-2808)
AGFA CORPORATION (HQ)
Also Called: AGFA Graphics
611 River Dr Ste 305 (07407-1338)
P.O. Box 471500, Tulsa OK (74147-1500)
PHONE...................................800 540-2432
Gunther Mertenes, *President*
Michael Patrick, *President*
Steve White, *President*
Christina Nota, *Purch Mgr*
David Robison, *Engineer*
▲ EMP: 400
SALES (est): 7.3MM
SALES (corp-wide): 494.6MM **Privately
Held**
WEB: www.agfa.com
SIC: **3861** Photographic equipment & sup-
plies
PA: Agfa-Gevaert
Septestraat 27
Mortsel 2640
344 421-11

(G-2809)
AGFA CORPORATION
611 River Dr Ste 305 (07407-1338)
PHONE...................................201 440-0111
EMP: 50
SALES (corp-wide): 494.6MM **Privately
Held**
SIC: **3861** Photographic equipment & sup-
plies
HQ: Agfa Corporation
611 River Dr Ste 305
Elmwood Park NJ 07407
800 540-2432

(G-2810)
AGFA FINANCE CORP
Also Called: AGFA Corporation, Elmwood
Park
611 River Dr (07407-1325)
PHONE...................................201 796-0058
▲ EMP: 107
SALES (est): 6MM
SALES (corp-wide): 494.6MM **Privately
Held**
SIC: **3861** Photographic equipment & sup-
plies
HQ: Agfa Corporation
611 River Dr Ste 305
Elmwood Park NJ 07407
800 540-2432

(G-2811)
**B&F AND SON MASONRY
COMPANY**
Also Called: B & F Mason Contractors
10 North St (07407-2246)
P.O. Box 187 (07407-0187)
PHONE...................................201 791-7630
Gino Fasolo, *President*
EMP: 45
SALES (est): 5.4MM **Privately Held**
SIC: **3271** 1741 1771 Blocks, concrete:
acoustical; masonry & other stonework;
concrete work

(G-2812)
BLACK & DECKER (US) INC
Also Called: Dewalt Industrial Tools
213 Us Highway 46 (07407-1902)
PHONE...................................201 475-3524
Dan Calabresse, *Principal*
EMP: 6
SALES (corp-wide): 13.9B **Publicly Held**
WEB: www.dewalt.com
SIC: **3546** Power-driven handtools

HQ: Black & Decker (U.S.) Inc.
1000 Stanley Dr
New Britain CT 06053
860 225-5111

(G-2813)
C & S FENCING INC
75 Midland Ave 77 (07407-2414)
PHONE...................................201 797-5440
Ciro Spinella, *President*
Antonino Spinella, *Vice Pres*
Graciela Locancore, *Treasurer*
EMP: 30
SQ FT: 8,400
SALES: 3.4MM **Privately Held**
SIC: **1799** 3446 Fence construction;
fences, gates, posts & flagpoles

(G-2814)
CARIB CHEMICAL CO INC
Also Called: Carib International
103 Main Ave (07407-3203)
PHONE...................................201 791-6700
Michael Granatell, *President*
EMP: 13
SALES (corp-wide): 1.5MM **Privately
Held**
SIC: **2865** Dyes & pigments
PA: Carib Chemical Co Inc
125 Main Ave
Elmwood Park NJ 07407
201 791-6700

(G-2815)
CARIB CHEMICAL CO INC (PA)
Also Called: Grant Industries
125 Main Ave (07407-3203)
PHONE...................................201 791-6700
Michael Granatell, *President*
▲ EMP: 13
SQ FT: 1,000
SALES (est): 1.5MM **Privately Held**
SIC: **2865** 5169 Dyes & pigments;
dyestuffs

(G-2816)
COLEX IMAGING INC
55-57 Bushes Ln (07407)
PHONE...................................201 414-5575
EMP: 4
SALES (est): 458.2K **Privately Held**
SIC: **3861** Printing equipment, photo-
graphic

(G-2817)
COMPUTER SOURCES
37 Leliarts Ln (07407-3201)
PHONE...................................201 791-9443
Igor Kholostoy, *President*
EMP: 2
SQ FT: 800
SALES: 3MM **Privately Held**
SIC: **7373** 7372 Value-added resellers,
computer systems; application computer
software; educational computer software;
operating systems computer software;
publishers' computer software

(G-2818)
**CORBAN ENERGY GROUP
CORP**
418 Falmouth Ave (07407-3305)
PHONE...................................201 509-8555
Daniel Chung, *Principal*
Howard Adams, *Principal*
Connie Lee, *Principal*
Joon Park, *Principal*
John Schlosberg, *Principal*
▲ EMP: 13 EST: 2012
SQ FT: 20,000
SALES: 150MM **Privately Held**
SIC: **1623** 3443 5085 Natural gas com-
pressor station construction; cryogenic
tanks, for liquids & gases; tanks, pressur-
ized

(G-2819)
CUMMINS - ALLISON CORP
Also Called: Cummins-Allison
495 Boulevard Ste 6 (07407-2041)
PHONE...................................201 791-2394
Ralph Nabors, *Manager*
EMP: 6

SALES (corp-wide): 390.1MM **Privately
Held**
WEB: www.gsb.com
SIC: **5044** 7629 3519 Office equipment;
business machine repair, electric; internal
combustion engines
PA: Cummins-Allison Corp
852 Feehanville Dr
Mount Prospect IL 60056
800 786-5528

(G-2820)
CUSTOM CHEMICALS CORP
30 Paul Kohner Pl (07407-2621)
PHONE...................................201 791-5100
Robert C Vielee, *President*
EMP: 600
SQ FT: 105,000
SALES (est): 47.1MM **Privately Held**
SIC: **2893** 2851 2816 Printing ink; lac-
quers, varnishes, enamels & other coat-
ings; inorganic pigments

(G-2821)
DOR-WIN MANUFACTURING CO
109 Midland Ave (07407-2441)
PHONE...................................201 796-4300
Marco Cangialosi, *President*
Rosalba Scaravilli, *Corp Secy*
Sarah Calderone, *Vice Pres*
EMP: 50 EST: 1962
SQ FT: 75,000
SALES (est): 5MM **Privately Held**
WEB: www.dor-winmfg.com
SIC: **3089** 3442 2431 Doors, folding:
plastic or plastic coated fabric; window
frames & sash, plastic; storm doors or
windows, metal; millwork

(G-2822)
DORWIN MANUFACTURING CO
109 Midland Ave (07407-2441)
PHONE...................................201 796-4300
Marco Cangialosi, *President*
Sara Caldiron, *General Mgr*
Roslba Scaravilli, *General Mgr*
EMP: 48
SALES (est): 3.5MM **Privately Held**
SIC: **3442** Metal doors

(G-2823)
**DR PREGERS SENSIBLE FOODS
INC**
9 Boumar Pl (07407-2615)
PHONE...................................201 703-1300
Larry Praeger, *CEO*
Eric Somberg, *Ch of Bd*
Adam Somberg, *President*
Jeff Cohen, *COO*
David Cantor, *Vice Pres*
▲ EMP: 100 EST: 1978
SQ FT: 60,000
SALES (est): 30.9MM **Privately Held**
SIC: **2038** Frozen specialties

(G-2824)
ELMWOOD PRESS INC
85 Main Ave (07407-3203)
PHONE...................................201 794-6273
Gene Murphy, *President*
Al Cowie, *Treasurer*
EMP: 13
SQ FT: 5,000
SALES (est): 1.6MM **Privately Held**
SIC: **2752** Commercial printing, offset

(G-2825)
EMDEON CORPORATION
Also Called: Medical Manager
669 River Dr Ste 240 (07407-1361)
PHONE...................................201 703-3400
EMP: 2258
SQ FT: 14,000
SALES (est): 92.1MM **Privately Held**
SIC: **7373** 3089 Computer Systems De-
sign Mfg Plastic Products

(G-2826)
G & H SOHO INC
413 Market St (07407-2605)
PHONE...................................201 216-9400
James Harris, *President*
Robert Tinkham, *General Mgr*
Gerald F Burstein, *Vice Pres*
Anna Kucharek, *Bookkeeper*
▲ EMP: 15

GEOGRAPHIC

SQ FT: 9,500
SALES (est): 2.3MM **Privately Held**
WEB: www.ghsoho.com
SIC: 2732 Book printing

(G-2827)
GF SUPPLIES LLC (PA)
Also Called: Sigo Signs
319 E 54th St (07407-2712)
PHONE...............................336 539-1666
Jacob Gluck,
Joel Freund,
EMP: 5
SQ FT: 10,000
SALES (est): 2MM **Privately Held**
SIC: 3993 5099 Signs & advertising specialties; signs, except electric

(G-2828)
GRANT INDUSTRIES INC
103 Main Ave (07407-3203)
PHONE...............................201 791-8700
Steven Grant, *Principal*
EMP: 100
SALES (corp-wide): 29.4MM **Privately Held**
SIC: 2834 Pharmaceutical preparations
PA: Grant Industries, Inc.
125 Main Ave
Elmwood Park NJ 07407
201 791-6700

(G-2829)
GRANT INDUSTRIES INC (PA)
125 Main Ave (07407-3203)
PHONE...............................201 791-6700
Steven Grant, *CEO*
Michael Granatell, *President*
David Granatell, *Vice Pres*
Joseph Granatell, *Vice Pres*
Paul Granatell, *Vice Pres*
◆ EMP: 56
SQ FT: 40,000
SALES (est): 29.4MM **Privately Held**
SIC: 2834 Pharmaceutical preparations

(G-2830)
GRANT INDUSTRIES INC
125 Main Ave (07407-3203)
PHONE...............................201 791-6700
EMP: 10
SALES (corp-wide): 29.4MM **Privately Held**
SIC: 2834 Pharmaceutical preparations
PA: Grant Industries, Inc.
125 Main Ave
Elmwood Park NJ 07407
201 791-6700

(G-2831)
INDUSTRIE BITOSSI INC (DH)
Also Called: Italian Tile Decor
410 Market St (07407-2607)
PHONE...............................201 796-0722
Rittoriano Bittosi, *President*
Giacomo Bandino, *CFO*
▲ EMP: 38
SQ FT: 10,000
SALES (est): 2MM **Privately Held**
SIC: 3253 Mosaic tile, glazed & unglazed: ceramic
HQ: Industrie Bitossi Spa
Via Pietramarina 53
Vinci FI 50059
057 170-9535

(G-2832)
INTERNTNAL GLOBL SOLUTIONS INC
Also Called: Green Life America
130 Kipp Ave (07407-1011)
PHONE...............................201 791-1500
Kozo Okada, *Owner*
▲ EMP: 4
SALES (est): 280K **Privately Held**
SIC: 3949 Sporting & athletic goods

(G-2833)
JOHN WM MACY CHEESESTICKS INC
Also Called: John Wm. Macy's Cheesesticks
80 Kipp Ave (07407-1011)
PHONE...............................201 791-8036
John W Macy, *President*
Tim Macy, *Vice Pres*
Angela Praclongo, *QC Mgr*

Joy Macy, *Admin Sec*
▲ EMP: 60
SQ FT: 45,000
SALES (est): 11.2MM **Privately Held**
WEB: www.cheesesticks.com
SIC: 2052 Cookies & crackers

(G-2834)
KEYENCE CORPORATION AMERICA (HQ)
669 River Dr Ste 403 (07407-1361)
PHONE...............................201 930-0100
Tiffany Stallworth, *General Mgr*
Bob Hosler, *COO*
Greg Glover, *Project Mgr*
Ron Maul, *Project Mgr*
Mike Bailey, *Engineer*
▲ EMP: 50
SQ FT: 15,000
SALES (est): 180.3MM **Privately Held**
SIC: 3825 5084 3674 Instruments to measure electricity; measuring & testing equipment, electrical; semiconductors & related devices

(G-2835)
KREISLER INDUSTRIAL CORP (HQ)
180 Van Riper Ave (07407-2622)
PHONE...............................201 289-5554
Edward A Stern, *Ch of Bd*
Michael D Stern, *President*
EMP: 91 EST: 1956
SQ FT: 1,000
SALES (est): 24.1MM
SALES (corp-wide): 40.9MM **Privately Held**
SIC: 3728 Aircraft parts & equipment
PA: Kreisler Manufacturing Corp
180 Van Riper Ave
Elmwood Park NJ 07407
201 791-0700

(G-2836)
KREISLER MANUFACTURING CORP (PA)
Also Called: Kreisler Industrial
180 Van Riper Ave (07407-2610)
PHONE...............................201 791-0700
Michael D Stern, *President*
Edward A Stern, *President*
EMP: 9 EST: 1968
SQ FT: 52,000
SALES (est): 40.9MM **Privately Held**
WEB: www.kreisler-ind.com
SIC: 3728 3724 Aircraft body assemblies & parts; turbines, aircraft type

(G-2837)
LACOA INC
21 Wallace St (07407-2612)
P.O. Box 839 (07407-0839)
PHONE...............................973 754-1000
Hector Baralt, *President*
Marilyn Van Vink, *Manager*
▲ EMP: 9
SALES (est): 1.7MM **Privately Held**
SIC: 2672 2261 2796 2759 Coated & laminated paper; embossing cotton broadwoven fabrics; platemaking services; commercial printing

(G-2838)
LOCAL CONCRETE SUP & EQP CORP
Also Called: Nyc Concrete Materials
475 Market St Ste 3fl (07407-3100)
PHONE...............................201 797-7979
Tino Lemanna, *President*
EMP: 7
SQ FT: 1,435
SALES (est): 501K **Privately Held**
SIC: 3241 Masonry cement

(G-2839)
MARCAL MANUFACTURING LLC (DH)
Also Called: Soundview Paper Company
1 Market St (07407-1401)
PHONE...............................201 796-4000
Fred Smagorinsky, *Mng Member*
M J Jolda,
◆ EMP: 13
SQ FT: 10,000

SALES (est): 282.3MM
SALES (corp-wide): 2.9B **Privately Held**
SIC: 2676 Towels, paper: made from purchased paper
HQ: Soundview Paper Mills Llc
1 Sound Shore Dr Ste 203
Greenwich CT 06830
201 796-4000

(G-2840)
MARCAL PAPER MILLS LLC
1 Market St (07407-1493)
PHONE...............................800 631-8451
Fred Smagorinsky,
EMP: 800
SALES (est): 194.4MM
SALES (corp-wide): 2.9B **Privately Held**
SIC: 2676 Sanitary paper products
HQ: Soundview Paper Mills Llc
1 Sound Shore Dr Ste 203
Greenwich CT 06830
201 796-4000

(G-2841)
MEDICRAFT INC
50 Bushes Ln (07407-3204)
PHONE...............................201 421-3055
Francis Phillips, *President*
EMP: 16 **Privately Held**
SIC: 3841 3354 Surgical & medical instruments; aluminum extruded products
PA: Medicraft, Inc.
7 Paul Kohner Pl
Elmwood Park NJ 07407

(G-2842)
MEDICRAFT INC (PA)
7 Paul Kohner Pl (07407-2614)
PHONE...............................201 797-8820
Francis Phillips, *President*
Michael Phillips, *President*
Mike Phillips, *Vice Pres*
Ian Tnocman, *Engineer*
John Craft, *Systems Dir*
EMP: 19
SQ FT: 4,000
SALES (est): 4.1MM **Privately Held**
WEB: www.medicraftinc.com
SIC: 3841 3354 Diagnostic apparatus, medical; aluminum extruded products

(G-2843)
MINIATURE FOLDING INC
14 Wenzel St (07407-2601)
PHONE...............................201 773-6477
Christopher Taliercio, *President*
EMP: 10
SALES (est): 1.4MM **Privately Held**
WEB: www.miniaturefolding.com
SIC: 2789 Trade binding services

(G-2844)
NAN BREAD DISTRIBUTION
41 Leliarts Ln (07407-3201)
PHONE...............................201 475-9311
Alaa Moustafa, *Owner*
EMP: 4
SALES (est): 212.7K **Privately Held**
SIC: 2051 Bread, cake & related products

(G-2845)
O E M MANUFACTURERS LTD INC
65 Leliarts Ln (07407-3201)
PHONE...............................201 475-8585
Westley Zion, *President*
Stephanie McFarlane, *Vice Pres*
EMP: 8
SQ FT: 5,000
SALES (est): 674.8K **Privately Held**
SIC: 3451 Screw machine products

(G-2846)
PAIGE COMPANY CONTAINERS INC (PA)
1 Paul Kohner Pl (07407-2614)
PHONE...............................201 461-7800
Allan Levine, *President*
Jonathan Chazin, *Corp Secy*
Michael Levine, *Vice Pres*
▼ EMP: 25
SQ FT: 10,000
SALES (est): 5.2MM **Privately Held**
WEB: www.paigecompany.com
SIC: 2653 Boxes, corrugated: made from purchased materials

(G-2847)
PATH SILICONES INC (PA)
21 Wallace St (07407-2612)
P.O. Box 430 (07407-0430)
PHONE...............................201 796-0833
Robert Baldanzi, *CEO*
Ted A Baldanzi, *Admin Sec*
▲ EMP: 10
SQ FT: 30,000
SALES (est): 1.2MM **Privately Held**
SIC: 3339 5169 Silicon refining (primary, over 99% pure); silicon lubricants

(G-2848)
PENN COLOR INC
30 Kohner Dr (07407-2614)
PHONE...............................201 791-5100
Bob Vielee, *General Mgr*
EMP: 175
SALES (corp-wide): 174.4MM **Privately Held**
SIC: 2865 Color pigments, organic
PA: Penn Color, Inc.
400 Old Dublin Pike
Doylestown PA 18901
215 345-6550

(G-2849)
PHILLIPS PRECISION INC
Also Called: Phillips Precision Medicraft
7 Paul Kohner Pl (07407-2614)
PHONE...............................201 797-8820
Michael Phillips, *President*
John Phillips, *President*
Francis Phillips, *Principal*
Mike Gaiella, *Production*
Ralph Ferrara, *Engineer*
EMP: 120
SQ FT: 40,000
SALES (est): 26.9MM **Privately Held**
WEB: www.phillipsprecision.com
SIC: 3841 Medical instruments & equipment, blood & bone work

(G-2850)
PHYTOCEUTICALS INC
37 Midland Ave Ste 1 (07407-2506)
PHONE...............................201 791-2255
Mostafa Omar, *President*
Amira Omar, *Vice Pres*
Iris Wong, *Marketing Staff*
▲ EMP: 4
SQ FT: 2,000
SALES (est): 700K **Privately Held**
WEB: www.phytoc-usa.com
SIC: 5122 2834 Pharmaceuticals; dermatologicals

(G-2851)
POTTI-BAGS INC
120 Ackerman Ave (07407-1605)
PHONE...............................201 796-5555
H Scott Price, *President*
EMP: 5
SALES (est): 714.2K **Privately Held**
SIC: 5113 2673 Bags, paper & disposable plastic; plastic bags: made from purchased materials

(G-2852)
RAMSEY GRAPHICS AND PRINTING
262 Market St Ste 1 (07407-2048)
PHONE...............................201 300-2912
David Ramsey, *President*
EMP: 6
SALES (est): 495.6K **Privately Held**
SIC: 7336 2759 Graphic arts & related design; commercial printing

(G-2853)
RECYCLE-TECH CORP
418 Falmouth Ave (07407-3305)
PHONE...............................201 475-5000
Daniel Chung, *President*
Howard Adams, *General Mgr*
John Kim, *General Mgr*
Joon Park, *Marketing Mgr*
◆ EMP: 10
SALES (est): 4MM **Privately Held**
WEB: www.recycletech.net
SIC: 5093 3559 Plastics scrap; recycling machinery

(G-2854)
RELIABLE ENVELOPE AND GRAPHICS
85 Main Ave (07407-3203)
PHONE..................................201 794-7756
Eugene Murphy, *President*
Al Cowie, *Treasurer*
EMP: 35
SQ FT: 26,000
SALES (est): 5.2MM **Privately Held**
WEB: www.reliableenvelope.com
SIC: 2759 2752 Envelopes: printing; commercial printing, lithographic

(G-2855)
SEALED AIR HOLDINGS
200 Riverfront Blvd # 301 (07407-1038)
PHONE..................................201 791-7600
Warren Kudman, *Principal*
EMP: 5
SALES (est): 482.5K
SALES (corp-wide): 4.7B **Publicly Held**
SIC: 3089 2621 5162 Cases, plastic; paper mills; plastics products
PA: Sealed Air Corporation
2415 Cascade Pointe Blvd
Charlotte NC 28208
980 221-3235

(G-2856)
SOUNDVIEW PAPER HOLDINGS LLC (HQ)
1 Market St (07407-1401)
PHONE..................................201 796-4000
Rob Baron, *President*
▲ **EMP:** 925
SALES (est): 476.8MM
SALES (corp-wide): 2.9B **Privately Held**
SIC: 2656 2676 Sanitary food containers; straws, drinking: made from purchased material; towels, paper: made from purchased paper
PA: Atlas Holdings, Llc
100 Northfield St
Greenwich CT 06830
203 622-9138

(G-2857)
STRAVAL MACHINE CO INC
20 Bushes Ln (07407-3204)
PHONE..................................973 340-9955
Ed Simin, *President*
Maria Nienajadlo, *General Mgr*
Ed S Simin, *Purch Mgr*
Wilson Diaz, *Project Engr*
Zaneta Spoljarik, *Administration*
EMP: 25
SALES (est): 1.2MM **Privately Held**
SIC: 3592 3599 Valves; machine shop, jobbing & repair

(G-2858)
TUFF MFG CO INC
4 Midland Ave (07407-3115)
PHONE..................................201 796-5319
Howard Klein, *President*
EMP: 4
SQ FT: 600
SALES (est): 330K **Privately Held**
SIC: 3531 Construction machinery

(G-2859)
UNIQUE EMBROIDERY INC
64 Bushes Ln (07407-3204)
PHONE..................................201 943-9191
Robby Moutran, *President*
Sonia Besenia, *Corp Secy*
EMP: 11
SQ FT: 2,500
SALES (est): 822.5K **Privately Held**
WEB: www.uniqueembroidery.com
SIC: 2395 Embroidery & art needlework

Elwood
Atlantic County

(G-2860)
SPECIALTY RUBBER INC
4500 White Horse Pike (08217)
P.O. Box 483 (08217-0483)
PHONE..................................609 704-2555
Richard Orosz, *President*
Kevin Orosz, *Vice Pres*

EMP: 5
SQ FT: 2,000
SALES (est): 1.3MM **Privately Held**
WEB: www.specialtyrubber.com
SIC: 5085 3053 Rubber goods, mechanical: gaskets, all materials

---

Emerson
Bergen County

(G-2861)
ACCURATE DIAMOND TOOL CORP
1 Palisade Ave (07630-1880)
PHONE..................................201 265-8868
Daniel Michael, *President*
Muriam Michael, *Corp Secy*
Scott Miller, *Office Mgr*
EMP: 29
SQ FT: 25,000
SALES (est): 5.2MM **Privately Held**
WEB: www.accuratediamondtool.com
SIC: 3545 Diamond cutting tools for turning, boring, burnishing, etc.

(G-2862)
AESYS INC
27 Bland St (07630-1153)
PHONE..................................201 871-3223
Guiseppe Biava, *President*
Colin McGregor, *Principal*
Daniele Gafforelli, *Project Mgr*
Mae Bogdansky, *Finance*
▲ **EMP:** 7
SALES (est): 1MM **Privately Held**
SIC: 3993 Electric signs

(G-2863)
ARTEMIS OPTICS AND COATINGS
Also Called: Arrow Thin Films
9 Ackerman Ave (07630-1801)
PHONE..................................201 847-0887
Jon Herringer, *President*
EMP: 5
SALES (est): 420K **Privately Held**
SIC: 3827 Optical instruments & lenses

(G-2864)
INTERNATIONAL TECH LASERS (PA)
Also Called: Itl
70 Kinderkamack Rd Ste 7 (07630-1812)
PHONE..................................201 262-4580
Isaac Goldlust, *President*
EMP: 2
SQ FT: 1,500
SALES (est): 3.7MM **Privately Held**
SIC: 3949 Hunting equipment

(G-2865)
JAMOL LABORATORIES INC
13 Ackerman Ave (07630-1801)
P.O. Box 313 (07630-0313)
PHONE..................................201 262-6363
Emil Scott Lucia, *President*
EMP: 6
SQ FT: 2,500
SALES (est): 880.1K **Privately Held**
SIC: 2834 Vitamin preparations; iodine, tincture of

(G-2866)
KITTYHAWK DIGITAL LLC
35 Linwood Ave (07630-1851)
PHONE..................................269 767-8399
Richard Narvadez,
EMP: 5
SALES (est): 278.1K **Privately Held**
SIC: 7371 7372 7373 Computer software development; computer systems analysis & design, custom; computer software writing services; educational computer software; systems software development services

(G-2867)
ONT SUTTER
17c Palisade Ave (07630-1821)
PHONE..................................201 265-0262
Ralph Ocker, *President*
Milleis Sutter, *Owner*
EMP: 4 **EST:** 1964

SQ FT: 6,800
SALES (est): 401.4K **Privately Held**
SIC: 2789 Binding only: books, pamphlets, magazines, etc.

(G-2868)
RAYS REPRODUCTION INC
39 Bland St (07630-1153)
PHONE..................................201 666-5650
Raymond Stuart, *President*
Heather Gugger, *Vice Pres*
Irene Stuart, *Vice Pres*
EMP: 9 **EST:** 1978
SQ FT: 3,300
SALES (est): 1.6MM **Privately Held**
WEB: www.raysreproductions.com
SIC: 2752 7336 Commercial printing, offset; commercial art & graphic design

(G-2869)
TOLIN DESIGN INC
16 Bland St (07630-1154)
PHONE..................................201 261-4455
Tony Suarez, *President*
EMP: 5
SALES (est): 750K **Privately Held**
WEB: www.tolindesign.com
SIC: 3728 Aircraft parts & equipment

(G-2870)
WEATHERCRAFT MANUFACTURING CO
13 Emerson Plz E (07630-1823)
PHONE..................................201 262-0055
Salvatore Gebbia, *President*
EMP: 15
SALES (est): 1.9MM **Privately Held**
SIC: 3444 3442 Awnings, sheet metal; metal doors

Englewood
Bergen County

(G-2871)
3LAB INC
37 Smith St (07631-4607)
PHONE..................................201 227-4742
David C Chung, *President*
▲ **EMP:** 10
SALES (est): 1.3MM **Privately Held**
WEB: www.3lab.com
SIC: 2844 Face creams or lotions

(G-2872)
A P M HEXSEAL CORPORATION
44 Honeck St (07631-4134)
PHONE..................................201 569-5700
David Morse, *President*
EMP: 30
SQ FT: 22,000
SALES (est): 6.7MM **Privately Held**
SIC: 3679 3648 Hermetic seals for electronic equipment; lighting equipment

(G-2873)
ACCURATE PRSCSION FSTENER CORP
20 Honeck St (07631-4134)
P.O. Box 5239 (07631-5239)
PHONE..................................201 567-9700
Michael Jacobs, *President*
Elissa Jacobs, *Vice Pres*
Bruce Hendricksen, *Sales Mgr*
EMP: 30
SQ FT: 21,000
SALES (est): 11.7MM **Privately Held**
WEB: www.accurateprecision.com
SIC: 5085 3452 Fasteners, industrial: nuts, bolts, screws, etc.; washers

(G-2874)
ACME GEAR CO INC
130 W Forest Ave (07631-4526)
PHONE..................................201 568-2245
Joseph Gelles, *President*
Rob Faro, *Controller*
Michelle Gelles, *Sales Mgr*
▲ **EMP:** 60 **EST:** 1929
SQ FT: 45,000
SALES (est): 16.7MM **Privately Held**
WEB: www.acmegear.com
SIC: 3566 Speed changers, drives & gears

(G-2875)
AMD FINE LINENS LLC
Also Called: Bellino
471 S Dean St (07631-4920)
PHONE..................................201 568-5255
Arnaldo Miccoli,
▲ **EMP:** 7
SALES (est): 4MM **Privately Held**
SIC: 2299 Linen fabrics

(G-2876)
AMERSHOE CORP
456 Nordhoff Pl (07631-4808)
PHONE..................................201 569-7300
Josh Nathel, *General Mgr*
Neal Liber, *Principal*
Rod Sunga, *Purch Dir*
Dan Nathel, *Info Tech Mgr*
EMP: 5 **EST:** 2014
SALES (est): 135K **Privately Held**
SIC: 3965 Fasteners

(G-2877)
ARTISTIC TYPOGRAPHY CORP
161 Coolidge Ave (07631-4523)
PHONE..................................845 783-1990
Paul Weinstein, *Branch Mgr*
EMP: 9
SALES (corp-wide): 2.2MM **Privately Held**
WEB: www.tagimage.com
SIC: 2759 Commercial printing
PA: Artistic Typography Corp.
151 W 30th St Fl 8
New York NY 10001
212 463-8880

(G-2878)
ARTUS CORP
201 S Dean St (07631-4179)
P.O. Box 511 (07631-0511)
PHONE..................................201 568-1000
Edwin Katzenstein, *President*
Margaret Levi, *Vice Pres*
Raphael Levi, *Treasurer*
EMP: 41 **EST:** 1941
SQ FT: 22,000
SALES (est): 7.3MM **Privately Held**
WEB: www.artuscorp.com
SIC: 3089 3444 Plastic hardware & building products; washers, plastic; sheet metalwork

(G-2879)
AUDIO DYNAMIX INC
170 Coolidge Ave (07631-4522)
PHONE..................................201 567-5488
Esmat Gayed, *President*
Richard Gayed, *Prdtn Mgr*
EMP: 10
SQ FT: 9,000
SALES (est): 1.6MM **Privately Held**
SIC: 3577 7336 Disk & diskette equipment, except drives; package design

(G-2880)
BANILIVY RUG CORP
15 S Dean St (07631-3511)
PHONE..................................212 684-3629
Moussa Banilivy, *President*
Mike Banilivy, *Vice Pres*
▲ **EMP:** 5
SQ FT: 8,000
SALES (est): 3MM **Privately Held**
SIC: 5023 2273 Rugs; carpets & rugs

(G-2881)
BEN-AHARON & SON INC
Also Called: Nyc Rugs
15 Smith St (07631-4607)
PHONE..................................201 541-2388
Ofer B Aharon, *President*
Elya B Aharon, *Vice Pres*
▲ **EMP:** 8
SQ FT: 5,000
SALES (est): 1MM **Privately Held**
SIC: 2273 Carpets, hand & machine made

(G-2882)
BIODYNAMICS LLC (HQ)
84 Honeck St (07631-4133)
PHONE..................................201 227-9255
Jane A Grinch, *President*
James D Ralph, *Vice Pres*
Paul S Starr, *Vice Pres*
Patrick J Darcy, *CFO*

EMP: 7
SALES (est): 1.1MM **Privately Held**
SIC: 3841 8011 Inhalation therapy equipment; orthopedic physician

(G-2883)
BIOSTAT INC
14 N Dean St (07631-2807)
PHONE.............................201 541-5688
Michael Borenstein, *Director*
Shirley Rudolph, *Executive*
EMP: 5
SALES (est): 541.9K **Privately Held**
WEB: www.biostat.com
SIC: 7372 Prepackaged software

(G-2884)
BLITZ SAFE OF AMERICA INC
33 Honeck St (07631-4125)
PHONE.............................201 569-5000
Ira Marlowe, *President*
Melanie Kerr, *Manager*
◆ **EMP:** 17
SQ FT: 4,500
SALES (est): 3.1MM **Privately Held**
WEB: www.blitzsafe.com
SIC: 3663 3669 Radio broadcasting & communications equipment; emergency alarms

(G-2885)
BOUTIQUE USA CORP
1 William St (07631-3588)
PHONE.............................917 476-0472
Jonathan Morgan, *Exec Dir*
EMP: 4
SALES (est): 154.1K **Privately Held**
SIC: 3639 Household appliances

(G-2886)
BRITE CONCEPTS INC
90 W Palisade Ave (07631-2642)
PHONE.............................201 270-8544
David Siegel, *President*
EMP: 5
SALES (est): 500K **Privately Held**
SIC: 8732 2759 Market analysis or research; advertising literature: printing

(G-2887)
BURGESS STEEL HOLDING LLC
200 W Forest Ave (07631-4526)
P.O. Box 5629 (07631-5629)
PHONE.............................201 871-3500
EMP: 3
SALES: 38.1MM **Privately Held**
SIC: 3441 1791 Building components, structural steel; structural steel erection

(G-2888)
BUSHWICK METALS LLC
Also Called: Koons Steel
25 Rockwood Pl (07631-4957)
PHONE.............................610 495-9100
Frank Koons Jr, *CEO*
Frank Koons III, *President*
Rick Perlen, *President*
Norman E Gottschalk Jr, *Vice Pres*
Mike Pannella, *Vice Pres*
EMP: 217
SALES (est): 3.5MM
SALES (corp-wide): 225.3B **Publicly Held**
WEB: www.koonssteel.com
SIC: 3444 5051 3441 Sheet metalwork; steel; fabricated structural metal
HQ: Bushwick Metals Llc
1000 Bridgeport Ave # 208
Shelton CT 06484
888 399-4070

(G-2889)
C & C METAL PRODUCTS CORP (PA)
Also Called: Knobware
456 Nordhoff Pl (07631-4877)
PHONE.............................201 569-7300
Gerald Nathel, *President*
Mitchell Chalfin, *Vice Pres*
Michael Nathel, *Vice Pres*
Willy Clark, *Buyer*
Matthew Nathel, *Treasurer*
▲ **EMP:** 100 **EST:** 1914
SQ FT: 149,000

SALES (est): 7.1MM **Privately Held**
WEB: www.ccmetal.com
SIC: 3965 3544 3961 Fasteners; die sets for metal stamping (presses); jewelry apparel, non-precious metals

(G-2890)
CANAC KITCHENS OF NJ INC
99 N Dean St (07631-2806)
PHONE.............................201 567-9585
Linda Reiter, *President*
Jeff Chinman, *Vice Pres*
EMP: 12
SALES: 2.4MM **Privately Held**
WEB: www.canackitchensnj.com
SIC: 2499 Kitchen, bathroom & household ware: wood

(G-2891)
CANTONE PRESS INC
161 Coolidge Ave (07631-4523)
PHONE.............................201 569-3435
Frank W Cantone Jr, *President*
Lynda McErlean, *Technology*
EMP: 40
SQ FT: 11,000
SALES (est): 7.1MM **Privately Held**
SIC: 2752 Commercial printing, offset

(G-2892)
CENTRAL ADMXTURE PHRM SVCS INC
Also Called: C A P S
160 W Forest Ave (07631-4526)
PHONE.............................201 541-0080
Daniel Buchner, *Branch Mgr*
Charles Mason, *Pharmacist*
Greshka Collazo, *Program Mgr*
John Brandon, *Director*
Bill Jones, *Director*
EMP: 50
SALES (corp-wide): 2.6MM **Privately Held**
WEB: www.capspharmacy.com
SIC: 2834 5122 Pharmaceutical preparations; pharmaceuticals
HQ: Central Admixture Pharmacy Services, Inc.
2525 Mcgaw Ave
Irvine CA 92614

(G-2893)
CLYDE OTIS MUSIC GROUP
Also Called: Iza and Vanessa Music
494 N Woodland St (07631-2028)
P.O. Box 325 (07631-0325)
PHONE.............................845 425-8198
Clyde Otis, *Owner*
EMP: 5
SALES (est): 220K **Privately Held**
WEB: www.tcomg.com
SIC: 2741 Music, sheet: publishing only, not printed on site

(G-2894)
CONKUR PRINTING CO INC
161 Coolidge Ave (07631-4523)
PHONE.............................212 541-5980
Walter Pflumm, *President*
Patricia Pflumm, *Vice Pres*
EMP: 22
SQ FT: 20,000
SALES (est): 2.6MM **Privately Held**
WEB: www.proprintsolutions.com
SIC: 2752 Commercial printing, offset

(G-2895)
D & I PRINTING CO INC
23 Chestnut St (07631-2412)
PHONE.............................201 871-3620
Gus Dovi, *President*
Diane Alessi, *Corp Secy*
EMP: 14
SQ FT: 10,000
SALES: 1.1MM **Privately Held**
SIC: 2752 2789 Commercial printing, offset; bookbinding & related work

(G-2896)
DELL AQUILA BAKING COMPANY
308 W Hudson Ave (07631-1406)
PHONE.............................201 886-0613
Laura Aguilar, *Principal*
EMP: 8

SALES (est): 640.8K **Privately Held**
SIC: 2051 Bread, cake & related products

(G-2897)
DELTA LAMBSKIN PRODUCTS INC
595 Ridge Rd (07631-5119)
PHONE.............................201 871-9233
Millie Dimitriou, *President*
◆ **EMP:** 20
SQ FT: 50,000
SALES (est): 1.9MM **Privately Held**
SIC: 3991 Paint rollers

(G-2898)
DISYS COMMERCE INC
100 W Forest Ave Ste H (07631-4033)
PHONE.............................201 567-0457
Sangwoo Han, *Administration*
EMP: 6
SALES (est): 87K **Privately Held**
SIC: 3111 Accessory products, leather
PA: Ise Commerce Co., Ltd.
Saman Bldg.
Seoul 06078

(G-2899)
EAST COAST DIAMOND TL PDTS INC
1 W Forest Ave Ste 1i (07631-4038)
PHONE.............................212 686-1034
Sheldon Pfefer, *Principal*
EMP: 5
SALES (est): 406K **Privately Held**
SIC: 3291 Abrasive products

(G-2900)
EDUCHAT INC
17 Lane Dr (07631-3734)
PHONE.............................201 871-8649
Ross Kopelman, *CEO*
EMP: 5
SALES (est): 117.2K **Privately Held**
SIC: 7372 Business oriented computer software

(G-2901)
ENGLEWOOD LAB LLC (PA)
88 W Sheffield Ave (07631-4809)
PHONE.............................201 567-2267
David Chung, *CEO*
John H Kim, *COO*
Ken Saavedra, *Project Mgr*
Jay Jim, *Warehouse Mgr*
Frank Dittrick, *Purch Mgr*
▲ **EMP:** 140
SQ FT: 30,000
SALES (est): 44.1MM **Privately Held**
WEB: www.englewoodlab.com
SIC: 2844 Toilet preparations

(G-2902)
ENOR CORPORATION
Also Called: Progard
246 S Dean St (07631-4139)
PHONE.............................201 750-1680
Steven Udwin, *CEO*
David Tarica, *President*
Merle T Udwin, *Corp Secy*
Justin Tarica, *Natl Sales Mgr*
◆ **EMP:** 225 **EST:** 1958
SQ FT: 40,000
SALES (est): 33.6MM **Privately Held**
SIC: 3089 Plastic processing; injection molding of plastics

(G-2903)
EUROPROJECTS INTL INC (PA)
Also Called: Adotta America
500 Nordhoff Pl Ste 5 (07631-4800)
PHONE.............................201 408-5215
Luigi Zannier, *President*
Mila Piazzo, *Asst Controller*
▲ **EMP:** 9
SALES: 13MM **Privately Held**
SIC: 3211 1751 Structural glass; window & door (prefabricated) installation

(G-2904)
EZCOM SOFTWARE INC
25 Rockwood Pl Ste 420 (07631-4971)
PHONE.............................201 731-1800
Carol Weidner, *CEO*
Lynn Wood, *Project Mgr*
Dorie Stahler, *QA Dir*

Felice Levine, *Prgrmr*
EMP: 28
SALES: 4.4MM **Privately Held**
WEB: www.ezcomsoftware.com
SIC: 7372 Business oriented computer software

(G-2905)
FIRMA FOODS USA CORPORATION
25 Rockwood Pl Ste 220 (07631-4959)
PHONE.............................201 794-1181
Claudia Vitelli, *Vice Pres*
▲ **EMP:** 5
SQ FT: 3,000
SALES (est): 266.3K **Privately Held**
SIC: 2099 Pasta, uncooked: packaged with other ingredients

(G-2906)
FORBO SIEGLING LLC
130 Coolidge Ave (07631-4522)
PHONE.............................201 567-6100
Ron Sup no, *Branch Mgr*
EMP: 13
SALES (corp-wide): 13.3B **Privately Held**
SIC: 3052 Rubber & plastics hose & beltings
HQ: Forbo Siegling, Llc
12201 Vanstory Dr
Huntersville NC 28078
704 948-0800

(G-2907)
FRENCH COLOR FRAGRANCE CO INC (PA)
488 Grand Ave (07631-4950)
PHONE.............................201 567-6883
Peter A French, *President*
Angie Dorrity, *Admin Asst*
◆ **EMP:** 25
SQ FT: 8,500
SALES (est): 3.5MM **Privately Held**
WEB: www.frenchcolor.com
SIC: 2865 2844 2816 Dye (cyclic) intermediates; perfumes & colognes; inorganic pigments

(G-2908)
G & A PAVERS LLC
2123 Sterling Blvd (07631-4827)
PHONE.............................201 562-5947
EMP: 4 **EST:** 2010
SALES (est): 267.7K **Privately Held**
SIC: 3531 Pavers

(G-2909)
GEMINI CUT GLASS COMPANY INC
4 E Forest Ave (07631-4137)
PHONE.............................201 568-7722
Eric Zelwiam, *President*
▲ **EMP:** 7 **EST:** 1942
SQ FT: 6,000
SALES (est): 1.1MM **Privately Held**
SIC: 5719 5063 3645 Lighting, lamps & accessories; lighting fixtures; lighting fixtures; chandeliers, residential

(G-2910)
GLENWOOD LLC
Also Called: Glenwood-Palisades
111 Cedar Ln (07631-4803)
P.O. Box 5419 (07631-5419)
PHONE.............................201 569-0050
Judith Gacita, *Controller*
Suzanne Israel, *Consultant*
Christopher Fuhrmann,
Brian Fuhrmann,
David Fuhrmann,
▲ **EMP:** 194
SQ FT: 54,000
SALES (est): 25.4MM **Privately Held**
WEB: www.glenwood-llc.com
SIC: 2834 Pharmaceutical preparations

(G-2911)
HEINRICH BAUER PUBLISHING LP
270 Sylvan Ave Ste 100 (07632-2523)
PHONE.............................201 569-6699
Hubert Boehle, *President*
EMP: 19

SALES (est): 696.9K
SALES (corp-wide): 2.7B **Privately Held**
SIC: 2721 Magazines: publishing only, not printed on site
HQ: Heinrich Bauer Verlag Beteiligungs Gmbh
270 Sylvan Ave Ste 100
Englewood Cliffs NJ 07632
201 569-0006

(G-2912)
HOYT CORPORATION
520 S Dean St (07631-4952)
PHONE.....................................201 894-0707
Michael Bradford, *President*
Ted Hoyt, *COO*
EMP: 43 **EST:** 1961
SQ FT: 30,000
SALES (est): 13.3MM **Privately Held**
WEB: www.hoyt-corp.com
SIC: 3313 3351 3612 3613 Electrometal-lurgical products; extruded shapes, copper & copper alloy; voltage regulators, transmission & distribution; switchgear & switchgear accessories

(G-2913)
INFOSEAL LLC
Also Called: A Division NJ Bus Forms
55 W Sheffield Ave (07631-4804)
PHONE.....................................201 569-4500
Chad Trent, *General Mgr*
Pamela Yost, *Human Resources*
David Harnett,
Ian Ashton,
Andrew Harnett,
◆ **EMP:** 79
SALES (est): 10.3MM **Privately Held**
WEB: www.infoseal.com
SIC: 2761 Manifold business forms

(G-2914)
INTEGRATED DENTAL SYSTEMS LLC
Also Called: IDS
145 Cedar Ln Ste 205 (07631-4821)
PHONE.....................................201 676-2457
Carey Lyons, *CEO*
David Singh, *COO*
EMP: 21
SALES (est): 3.7MM **Privately Held**
SIC: 3843 Dental equipment & supplies

(G-2915)
JAD BAGELS LLC
52 E Palisade Ave (07631-2902)
PHONE.....................................201 567-4500
Mark Urich, *Owner*
EMP: 4
SALES (est): 315.9K **Privately Held**
SIC: 2051 Bagels, fresh or frozen

(G-2916)
KINZEE INDUSTRIES INC
80 Brayton St (07631-3116)
PHONE.....................................201 408-4301
Jeffrey Solomon, *President*
EMP: 18 **EST:** 1946
SQ FT: 117,000
SALES (est): 1.6MM **Privately Held**
SIC: 5031 2434 Kitchen cabinets; building materials, interior; vanities, bathroom: wood

(G-2917)
LBD CORP
Also Called: Cassies Restaurant
18 S Dean St (07631-3515)
PHONE.....................................201 541-6760
Larry Drucker, *President*
EMP: 30
SALES (est): 2.3MM **Privately Held**
SIC: 2599 Food wagons, restaurant

(G-2918)
LEO PRAGER INC
2322 Sterling Blvd (07631-4829)
PHONE.....................................201 266-8888
Peter Schoenfeld, *Ch of Bd*
EMP: 5
SALES (est): 506.5K **Privately Held**
SIC: 2542 Racks, merchandise display or storage: except wood

(G-2919)
LIZ FIELDS LLC
41 Smith St (07631-4607)
PHONE.....................................201 408-5640
Lizette Brodsky,
▲ **EMP:** 6 **EST:** 2009
SALES (est): 538.2K **Privately Held**
SIC: 2335 Wedding gowns & dresses

(G-2920)
LORENZO FOOD GROUP INC
Also Called: Lorenzo & Sons Provisions
196 Coolidge Ave (07631-4522)
PHONE.....................................201 868-9088
Joseph G Lorenzo, *President*
John G Lorenzo, *Vice Pres*
John Lorenzo, *Vice Pres*
Dave Black, *Sales Associate*
Natasha Salvador, *Supervisor*
EMP: 50
SQ FT: 20,000
SALES (est): 12MM **Privately Held**
SIC: 5147 2099 Meats, fresh; ready-to-eat meals, salads & sandwiches

(G-2921)
MARATHON ENTERPRISES INC (PA)
Also Called: Sabrett Hot Dog
9 Smith St (07631-4607)
PHONE.....................................201 935-3330
Boyd G Adelman, *President*
Mark Rosen, *Vice Pres*
Nikki Rosen, *Vice Pres*
Philip Venturini, *Vice Pres*
Vicki Venturini, *Vice Pres*
▲ **EMP:** 15
SQ FT: 4,500
SALES (est): 20.7MM **Privately Held**
WEB: www.sabrett.com
SIC: 2013 Frankfurters from purchased meat

(G-2922)
MARLOW CANDY & NUT CO INC
65 Honeck St (07631-4125)
PHONE.....................................201 569-7606
Eric Lowenthal, *President*
EMP: 25
SQ FT: 18,000
SALES (est): 8.7MM **Privately Held**
WEB: www.marlowcandy.net
SIC: 5145 2064 Candy; nuts, salted or roasted; candy & other confectionery products

(G-2923)
MATISSE CHOCOLATIER INC (PA)
260 Grand Ave Ste 6 (07631-4360)
PHONE.....................................201 568-2288
Lucille Skroce, *President*
Valdo Skroce, *Vice Pres*
EMP: 4
SQ FT: 700
SALES (est): 445.2K **Privately Held**
SIC: 2066 5441 5947 Chocolate; candy; gifts & novelties

(G-2924)
MERCURY FLOOR MACHINES INC
110 S Van Brunt St (07631-3438)
PHONE.....................................201 568-4606
Bill Allen, *President*
Marcos De La O', *CFO*
▲ **EMP:** 20 **EST:** 1958
SQ FT: 8,000
SALES (est): 2.6MM **Privately Held**
WEB: www.mercuryfloormachines.com
SIC: 3291 3589 Abrasive products; floor washing & polishing machines, commercial

(G-2925)
MICROSURFACES INC
1 W Forest Ave Ste 2b (07631-4038)
PHONE.....................................201 408-5596
Athena Guo, *President*
EMP: 6
SQ FT: 1,518
SALES (est): 500K **Privately Held**
WEB: www.memsurface.com
SIC: 3479 Coating of metals with silicon

(G-2926)
MIDDLE EAST MARKETING GROUP (PA)
Also Called: Mem Group
266 S Dean St (07631-4139)
PHONE.....................................201 503-0150
Henri Dimidjian, *President*
Sabrina Kalfayan, *Vice Pres*
Alex Kalfayan, *Admin Sec*
▼ **EMP:** 7 **EST:** 1974
SQ FT: 50,000
SALES (est): 1.7MM **Privately Held**
SIC: 3999 Bric-a-brac

(G-2927)
MUSIC TRADES CORP
Also Called: Music Trades Magazine
80 West St Ste 200 (07631-2743)
P.O. Box 432 (07631-0432)
PHONE.....................................201 871-1965
Brian Majeski, *President*
Paul Majeski, *Vice Pres*
EMP: 6
SQ FT: 1,000
SALES (est): 628.6K **Privately Held**
WEB: www.musictrades.com
SIC: 2721 5736 Magazines: publishing only, not printed on site; musical instrument stores

(G-2928)
NINE WEST HOLDINGS INC
Also Called: Kasper
33 E Palisade Ave (07631-2901)
PHONE.....................................201 541-7004
EMP: 8
SALES (corp-wide): 2.2B **Privately Held**
SIC: 2337 Mfg Women's/Misses Suits/Coats
PA: Nine West Holdings, Inc.
1411 Broadway Fl 15
New York NY 10018
212 642-3860

(G-2929)
PALISADES DENTAL LLC
Also Called: Impact Air 45
111 Cedar Ln (07631-4803)
P.O. Box 5419 (07631-5419)
PHONE.....................................201 569-0050
John Gruen,
EMP: 12
SALES (est): 1.7MM **Privately Held**
WEB: www.palisadesdental-llc.com
SIC: 3843 Drills, dental

(G-2930)
PANDA PLATES INC
Also Called: Yumble
266 Audubon Rd (07631-4311)
PHONE.....................................917 848-8777
Hillel David Parker, *Administration*
EMP: 20
SALES (corp-wide): 1.7MM **Privately Held**
SIC: 2099 Ready-to-eat meals, salads & sandwiches
PA: Panda Plates Inc.
1450 Broadway Fl 40
New York NY 10018
888 997-6623

(G-2931)
PDQ PRINT & COPY INC
Also Called: P D Q Digital
161 Coolidge Ave (07631-4523)
PHONE.....................................201 569-2288
Kelly Rozansky, *President*
Tim Rozansky, *Principal*
EMP: 12
SQ FT: 4,500
SALES (est): 1.4MM **Privately Held**
WEB: www.pdqdigital.com
SIC: 2752 Commercial printing, offset

(G-2932)
PLATON INTERIORS
180 S Van Brunt St (07631-3438)
PHONE.....................................201 567-5533
Fax: 201 567-3335
▲ **EMP:** 8
SALES (est): 620K **Privately Held**
SIC: 2434 Architectural And Furniture Mfg

(G-2933)
PRINT SOLUTIONS LLC
320 S Dean St (07631-4138)
PHONE.....................................201 567-9622
John Vartanian, *Mng Member*
Paul Vartanian,
EMP: 14
SQ FT: 7,000
SALES (est): 1.1MM **Privately Held**
SIC: 2759 Commercial printing

(G-2934)
PROGRESSIVE OFFSET INC
161 Coolidge Ave (07631-4523)
PHONE.....................................201 569-3900
Frank W Cantone Jr, *President*
Miesha Dimeglio, *Creative Dir*
EMP: 30
SQ FT: 20,000
SALES (est): 7.3MM **Privately Held**
WEB: www.prooffset.com
SIC: 2752 Commercial printing, offset

(G-2935)
PROVENCE LLC
Also Called: Balthazar Bakery
214 S Dean St (07631-4139)
PHONE.....................................201 503-9717
Joe Henry, *Plant Mgr*
Yagil Sela, *Opers Staff*
Paula Oland, *Mng Member*
Leydy Valdes, *Relations*
EMP: 120
SQ FT: 14,000
SALES (est): 18.2MM **Privately Held**
SIC: 2051 Bakery: wholesale or wholesale/retail combined

(G-2936)
R YATES CONSUMER PRD LLC
204 Green St (07631-3818)
PHONE.....................................201 569-1030
Russell Yates, *Owner*
EMP: 4
SALES (est): 220K **Privately Held**
SIC: 3843 Dental equipment & supplies

(G-2937)
RENAISSANCE HOUSE
465 Westview Ave (07631-5106)
PHONE.....................................201 408-4048
Sam Laredo, *President*
Raquel Laredo, *Vice Pres*
▲ **EMP:** 3
SALES: 1.2MM **Privately Held**
SIC: 2731 Book publishing

(G-2938)
SABRIMAX CORP
Also Called: Details
50 E Palisade Ave Ste 413 (07631-2943)
PHONE.....................................201 871-0808
Jeffrey M Plitt, *President*
▲ **EMP:** 13
SQ FT: 6,000
SALES: 1MM **Privately Held**
WEB: www.k-poster.com
SIC: 2759 3993 Screen printing; signs & advertising specialties

(G-2939)
SELWAY PARTNERS LLC (PA)
74 Grand Ave B (07631-3506)
PHONE.....................................201 712-7974
Yaron Eitan, *Mng Member*
Winston Churchill,
EMP: 10
SQ FT: 5,000
SALES (est): 11.1MM
SALES (corp-wide): 11.4MM **Privately Held**
SIC: 3663 Television closed circuit equipment

(G-2940)
SHERMAN NAT INC (HQ)
10 Sterling Blvd Ste 302 (07631-4835)
PHONE.....................................201 735-9000
Shannon Leistra, *General Mgr*
Brendon B Scott, *CFO*
◆ **EMP:** 40
SQ FT: 7,000

SALES (est): 28.2MM
SALES (corp-wide): 25.3B **Publicly Held**
WEB: www.natsherman.com
SIC: 5194 5993 5947 2111 Cigarettes;
cigarette store; novelties; cigarettes; ci-
gars
PA: Altria Group, Inc.
6601 W Broad St
Richmond VA 23230
804 274-2200

(G-2941)
SHERMANS 1400 BRDWAY N Y C
LTD
10 Sterling Blvd (07631-4834)
PHONE.....................201 735-9000
Shannon Leistra, *General Mgr*
Brendon Scott, *CFO*
EMP: 60
SALES (est): 2.1MM
SALES (corp-wide): 25.3B **Publicly Held**
SIC: 2111 Cigarettes
PA: Altria Group, Inc.
6601 W Broad St
Richmond VA 23230
804 274-2200

(G-2942)
SNIDERMAN JOHN
Also Called: Allied Embroidery
133 E Palisade Ave Apt H (07631-2249)
PHONE.....................201 569-5482
John Sniderman, *Owner*
EMP: 16
SALES (est): 590K **Privately Held**
SIC: 2395 2396 Embroidery products, ex-
cept schiffli machine; automotive & ap-
parel trimmings

(G-2943)
SOUTH EAST INSTRUMENTS
LLC
111 Cedar Ln (07631-4803)
P.O. Box 5657 (07631-5657)
PHONE.....................201 569-0050
Judith Gacita,
Maureen McGovern,
EMP: 8
SQ FT: 5,000
SALES (est): 429.8K **Privately Held**
SIC: 3843 Ultrasonic dental equipment

(G-2944)
STARFUELS INC
285 Grand Ave (07631-4369)
PHONE.....................201 685-0400
Sara Storey, *Controller*
EMP: 6
SALES (corp-wide): 1MM **Privately Held**
SIC: 1241 2911 3339 Coal mining serv-
ices; oils, fuel; precious metals
HQ: Starfuels, Inc.
50 Main St
White Plains NY 10606
914 289-4800

(G-2945)
STRUCTURED HEALTHCARE
MGT INC
Also Called: Shm
456 Nordhoff Pl (07631-4808)
PHONE.....................201 569-3290
Maurice Reifman, *President*
EMP: 28
SQ FT: 4,200
SALES (est): 2.1MM **Privately Held**
WEB: www.shminc.com
SIC: 7372 7371 Prepackaged software;
custom computer programming services

(G-2946)
TANGENT GRAPHICS INC
23 Chestnut St (07631-2412)
PHONE.....................201 488-2840
Daniel Canner, *President*
John Wehle, *Treasurer*
EMP: 8
SQ FT: 9,200
SALES (est): 1.3MM **Privately Held**
SIC: 2752 2796 2791 Commercial print-
ing, offset; platemaking services; typeset-
ting

(G-2947)
TIME SYSTEMS INTERNATIONAL
CO
142 S Van Brunt St (07631-3438)
PHONE.....................201 871-1200
Samuel Gleich, *President*
Augie Caruso, *VP Sales*
EMP: 30 EST: 1961
SQ FT: 9,600
SALES (est): 4.8MM **Privately Held**
WEB: www.timesystemsint.com
SIC: 5044 3579 Office equipment; time
clocks & time recording devices

(G-2948)
TRUSS ENGINEERING
120 Charlotte Pl Ste 206 (07632-2607)
PHONE.....................201 871-4800
William F Loftus, *Principal*
EMP: 4
SALES (est): 33.2K **Privately Held**
SIC: 2439 Trusses, wooden roof

(G-2949)
UMBRELLA & CHAIRS LLC
Also Called: Schmutzerland
8 Old Quarry Rd (07631-5123)
PHONE.....................973 284-1240
Donald Berkowitz,
Bonnie Berish,
David Rubin,
EMP: 4
SALES (est): 204.6K **Privately Held**
SIC: 3961 7389 Costume jewelry;

(G-2950)
UNITY GRAPHICS & ENGRAVING
CO
Also Called: Unity Engraving Company
210 S Van Brunt St (07631-4012)
P.O. Box 88 (07631-0088)
PHONE.....................201 541-5462
Jerry Mandel, *President*
Mike Sysyn, *Sales Staff*
Unityart-Stev Pilewski, *Art Dir*
EMP: 50 EST: 1930
SQ FT: 20,000
SALES (est): 7.1MM **Privately Held**
SIC: 2752 2796 Commercial printing, litho-
graphic; platemaking services

(G-2951)
UNITY STEEL RULE DIE CO
210 S Van Brunt St (07631-4012)
PHONE.....................201 569-6400
Jerry Mandel, *Owner*
EMP: 40
SALES (est): 4.3MM **Privately Held**
SIC: 3312 3544 Tool & die steel; special
dies, tools, jigs & fixtures

(G-2952)
VICTOR SECURITIES INC
285 Grand Ave Bldg No3 (07631-4369)
PHONE.....................646 481-4835
Kevin Bakhler, *Principal*
EMP: 7
SALES (est): 751.9K **Privately Held**
SIC: 2621 Parchment, securites & bank
note papers

(G-2953)
WESTBURY PRESS INC
1 W Forest Ave (07631-4038)
PHONE.....................201 894-0444
Sanford Zenker, *President*
Al Zenker, *Corp Secy*
EMP: 60 EST: 1954
SQ FT: 40,000
SALES (est): 5.8MM **Privately Held**
WEB: www.westburypress.com
SIC: 2752 2789 Commercial printing, off-
set; bookbinding & related work

(G-2954)
WOHNERS (PA)
29 Bergen St (07631-2907)
PHONE.....................201 568-7307
Robert Vadas Wohner, *General Mgr*
John Wohner, *Vice Pres*
Robert Wohner Jr, *Vice Pres*
▲ EMP: 6
SQ FT: 4,000

SALES (est): 937.2K **Privately Held**
WEB: www.wohners.com
SIC: 5211 2431 Millwork & lumber; mill-
work

(G-2955)
YORK STREET CATERERS INC
196 Coolidge Ave (07631-4522)
PHONE.....................201 868-9088
John Lorenzo, *President*
Joseph Lorenzo, *Vice Pres*
EMP: 250
SALES (est): 45MM **Privately Held**
WEB: www.lorenzofoodgroup.com
SIC: 5812 2011 Caterers; cured meats
from meat slaughtered on site

Englewood Cliffs
Bergen County

(G-2956)
ACE BOX LANDAU CO INC
Also Called: Ace Box Co
600 E Palisade Ave Ste 21 (07632-1826)
P.O. Box 556, Tenafly (07670-0556)
PHONE.....................201 871-4776
Leonard Landau, *President*
EMP: 8 EST: 1950
SALES (est): 2MM **Privately Held**
SIC: 5113 2673 2653 3842 Corrugated &
solid fiber boxes; bags, paper & dispos-
able plastic; plastic & pliofilm bags;
boxes, corrugated: made from purchased
materials; adhesive tape & plasters, med-
icated or non-medicated

(G-2957)
AMATI INTERNATIONAL LLC
560 Sylvan Ave 2053 (07632-3165)
PHONE.....................201 569-1000
David Yarin,
Robert Leopold,
Naoko T Yarin,
Peter Yarin,
▲ EMP: 26
SALES (est): 3MM **Privately Held**
WEB: www.amatiintl.com
SIC: 3645 3646 3641 Residential lighting
fixtures; commercial indusl & institutional
electric lighting fixtures; electric lamps

(G-2958)
AMERICA TECHMA INC
385 Sylvan Ave Ste 28 (07632-2722)
PHONE.....................201 894-5887
Chris S Yu, *CEO*
▲ EMP: 7
SQ FT: 1,200
SALES (est): 4.1MM **Privately Held**
SIC: 5047 5063 3841 Medical & hospital
equipment; electrical apparatus & equip-
ment; surgical & medical instruments

(G-2959)
BARNET PRODUCTS LLC
920 Sylvan Ave Ste 210 (07632-3301)
PHONE.....................201 346-4620
Steve Kosann, *President*
▲ EMP: 15
SQ FT: 5,000
SALES (est): 4.4MM **Privately Held**
WEB: www.barnetproducts.com
SIC: 2869 Fatty acid esters, aminos, etc.

(G-2960)
BAUER PUBLISHING COMPANY
LP (DH)
Also Called: First For Women Magazine
270 Sylvan Ave Ste 210 (07632-2523)
PHONE.....................201 569-6699
Hubert Boehle, *Partner*
Heinz Bauer, *Partner*
Richard Buchert, *Partner*
Henning Lauer, *Partner*
Richard Teehan, *Partner*
▲ EMP: 8
SQ FT: 27,000
SALES (est): 85.3MM
SALES (corp-wide): 2.7B **Privately Held**
WEB: www.bauerpublishing.com
SIC: 2721 Magazines: publishing only, not
printed on site

(G-2961)
BIOALERT TECHNOLOGIES LLC
114 Hollywood Ave (07632-2135)
PHONE.....................551 655-2939
Marc Rosenberg,
EMP: 5
SALES (est): 54.1K **Privately Held**
SIC: 7389 2835 ; microbiology & virology
diagnostic products

(G-2962)
CASTLE INDUSTRIES INC
120 Sylvan Ave Ste 3 (07632-2501)
PHONE.....................201 585-8400
Arthur Schloss, *President*
▲ EMP: 20
SQ FT: 2,500
SALES (est): 2.3MM **Privately Held**
SIC: 3699 Electronic training devices

(G-2963)
COMPETECH SMRTCARD
SLTIONS INC
Also Called: CSS
440 Sylvan Ave Ste 250 (07632-2700)
PHONE.....................201 256-4184
Gregory Thornton, *CEO*
Laura Pace, *Treasurer*
Martin Vaughn, *Exec Dir*
EMP: 9
SQ FT: 2,500
SALES (est): 465.8K **Privately Held**
SIC: 3089 3999 Identification cards, plas-
tic; identification badges & insignia; but-
tons: Red Cross, union, identification

(G-2964)
CONOPCO INC
940 Sylvan Ave (07632-3301)
PHONE.....................201 894-7760
EMP: 5
SALES (corp-wide): 58.3B **Privately Held**
SIC: 2035 Pickles, sauces & salad dress-
ings
HQ: Coropco, Inc.
700 Sylvan Ave
Englewood Cliffs NJ 07632
201 894-7760

(G-2965)
CONOPCO INC
Also Called: Good Humor/Breyers
800 Sylvan Ave (07632-3201)
PHONE.....................920 499-2509
Eric Walsh, *President*
Harold Vastag, *President*
EMP: 240
SALES (corp-wide): 58.3B **Privately Held**
SIC: 2024 Ice cream, packaged: molded,
on sticks, etc.; ices, flavored (frozen
dessert)
HQ: Conopco, Inc.
700 Sylvan Ave
Englewood Cliffs NJ 07632
201 894-7760

(G-2966)
CUSTOM GASKET MFG LLC
640 E Palisade Ave # 201 (07632-1824)
PHONE.....................201 331-6363
Eric Helf, *CEO*
EMP: 12
SALES (est): 556.3K **Privately Held**
SIC: 3053 5085 Gaskets & sealing de-
vices; gaskets & seals

(G-2967)
DOOSAN HEAVY INDS AMER
LLC
140 Sylvan Ave (07632-2514)
PHONE.....................201 944-4554
EMP: 4
SALES (est): 590.5K **Privately Held**
SIC: 3999 Barber & beauty shop equip-
ment

(G-2968)
EMPIRE
TELECOMMUNICATIONS INC
239 Fairview Ave (07632-2036)
PHONE.....................201 569-3339
Sidney Kaplan, *President*
EMP: 11 EST: 1978
SQ FT: 5,000

SALES (est): 1.2MM **Privately Held**
SIC: 3679 Electronic circuits

(G-2969)
ENERGY CHEM AMERICA INC
920 Sylvan Ave (07632-3301)
PHONE..............................201 816-2307
Steven Park, *President*
▲ EMP: 60
SALES (est): 4.4MM **Privately Held**
SIC: 2869 Industrial organic chemicals

(G-2970)
ET BROWNE DRUG CO INC (PA)
Also Called: Palmer's Cocoa Butter Formula
440 Sylvan Ave (07632-2727)
PHONE..............................201 894-9020
Arnold Hayward Neis, *Ch of Bd*
Robert Neis, *President*
◆ EMP: 60
SQ FT: 15,000
SALES (est): 80.3MM **Privately Held**
WEB: www.etbrowne.com
SIC: 2844 Cosmetic preparations; face
creams or lotions; toilet preparations

(G-2971)
FYI MARKETING INC
Also Called: Ciao Milano
22 Laurie Dr (07632-2222)
PHONE..............................646 546-5226
Timothy Delton, *CEO*
EMP: 5
SALES (est): 107.9K **Privately Held**
SIC: 2339 2337 Down-filled coats, jackets
& vests: women's & misses'; women's &
misses' capes & jackets

(G-2972)
GALAXY LED INC
600 Sylvan Ave Ste 106 (07632-3151)
PHONE..............................201 541-5461
Jae Hong Choi, *President*
▲ EMP: 4
SALES: 500K **Privately Held**
SIC: 3648 Lighting equipment

(G-2973)
HEINRICH BAUER VERLAG (HQ)
Also Called: Woman's World Magazine
270 Sylvan Ave Ste 100 (07632-2521)
PHONE..............................201 569-0006
Hubert Boehle, *President*
Richard Teehan, *Corp Secy*
Sebastian Raatz, *Exec VP*
Richard Buchert, *Senior VP*
Dennis Cohen, *Senior VP*
EMP: 22
SQ FT: 7,000
SALES (est): 40.4MM
SALES (corp-wide): 2.7B **Privately Held**
SIC: 2721 Magazines: publishing only, not
printed on site
PA: Heinrich Bauer Verlag Kg
Burchardstr. 11
Hamburg 20095
403 019-0

(G-2974)
HIOSSEN INC (HQ)
Also Called: Osstem
270 Sylvan Ave Ste 1130 (07632-2523)
PHONE..............................888 678-0001
Kyoo OK Choi, *CEO*
Peter Lee, *General Mgr*
Robert Lee, *Treasurer*
Seung W Song, *Treasurer*
Seungmin Bae, *Finance Dir*
▲ EMP: 15
SQ FT: 10,000
SALES (est): 46.4MM **Privately Held**
SIC: 3843 Dental equipment

(G-2975)
HITECHONE INC
440 Sylvan Ave Ste 2508 (07632-2727)
PHONE..............................201 500-8864
Richard Kimsen, *President*
Park Kyu Tae, *Principal*
▲ EMP: 7
SALES (est): 702K **Privately Held**
SIC: 3621 7373 3571 Generators for stor-
age battery chargers; systems engineer-
ing, computer related; electronic
computers

(G-2976)
INFINITY SOURCING SERVICES LLC
560 Sylvan Ave Ste 3155 (07632-3106)
PHONE..............................212 868-2900
Ray Kim, *Mng Member*
EMP: 8
SALES: 22MM **Privately Held**
SIC: 2335 Women's, juniors' & misses'
dresses

(G-2977)
INSTITUTATIONAL EDGE LLC
120 Van Nostrand Ave # 201 (07632-1555)
PHONE..............................201 944-5447
EMP: 6
SQ FT: 900
SALES (est): 490K **Privately Held**
SIC: 2621 Security Broker

(G-2978)
INTELLECT NEUROSCIENCES INC
550 Sylvan Ave Ste 101 (07632-3115)
PHONE..............................201 608-5101
Elliot M Maza, *Ch of Bd*
EMP: 1
SQ FT: 900
SALES: 1.2MM **Privately Held**
SIC: 2834 Druggists' preparations (phar-
maceuticals)

(G-2979)
KAIROS ENTERPRISES LLC
210 Sylvan Ave Ste 22 (07632-2503)
PHONE..............................201 731-3181
Jae Y Kim, *Mng Member*
EMP: 10
SALES: 4.5MM **Privately Held**
SIC: 2282 2821 8742 Manmade & syn-
thetic fiber yarns: twisting, winding, etc.;
plastics materials & resins; marketing
consulting services

(G-2980)
KIKUICHI NEW YORK INC
560 Sylvan Ave Ste 3110 (07632-3131)
PHONE..............................201 567-8388
Ikuyo Yanagisawa, *President*
EMP: 8
SALES (est): 860K **Privately Held**
SIC: 3421 Knives: butchers', hunting,
pocket, etc.

(G-2981)
LG ELCTRNICS MBILECOMM USA INC (DH)
Also Called: Lg Infocomm U.S.A.
1000 Sylvan Ave (07632-3302)
PHONE..............................201 816-2000
Wayne Park, *CEO*
Kyung Joo Hwang, *President*
M Ehtisham Rabbani, *Vice Pres*
Jae Dong Han, *Treasurer*
Demetra Kavadeles, *Pub Rel Staff*
▲ EMP: 100
SQ FT: 67,500
SALES (est): 136.9MM **Privately Held**
SIC: 5065 3663 Mobile telephone equip-
ment; radio & TV communications equip-
ment
HQ: Lg Electronics U.S.A., Inc.
1000 Sylvan Ave
Englewood Cliffs NJ 07632
201 816-2000

(G-2982)
LG ELECTRONICS USA INC (HQ)
Also Called: Lg Group Aic
1000 Sylvan Ave (07632-3318)
PHONE..............................201 816-2000
William Cho, *President*
Eunji Jung, *President*
Eugene Yoo, *General Mgr*
Cassius Titus, *Counsel*
Jong Choi, *Vice Pres*
◆ EMP: 500
SQ FT: 57,000
SALES (est): 9.8B **Privately Held**
WEB: www.lge.com
SIC: 3651 5064 Household audio & video
equipment; electrical appliances, major

(G-2983)
LIMOSYS LLC
550 Sylvan Ave Ste 100 (07632-3115)
PHONE..............................212 222-4433
Omer Haberman, *Opers Mgr*
Rohit Gulia, *Web Dvlpr*
Alexey Chikin, *Software Engr*
Eric Eastman, *Software Dev*
Issac Yehuda,
EMP: 32
SQ FT: 4,000
SALES: 5.5MM **Privately Held**
SIC: 7371 7372 Computer software devel-
opment & applications; business oriented
computer software

(G-2984)
LITTLE FOX INC
720 E Palisade Ave # 104 (07632-3054)
PHONE..............................609 919-9691
Kyung Sook Sung, *Administration*
EMP: 4
SALES (est): 207.8K **Privately Held**
SIC: 2741 Guides: publishing & printing

(G-2985)
OSEM USA INC
333 Sylvan Ave Ste 302 (07632-2733)
PHONE..............................201 871-4433
Gad Propper, *Ch of Bd*
Izzet Ozdogan, *President*
Ron Wise, *Vice Pres*
Kobi Afek, *Marketing Staff*
Emily Jobson, *Manager*
▲ EMP: 8
SALES (est): 1.3MM
SALES (corp-wide): 92B **Privately Held**
WEB: www.osemusa.com
SIC: 2034 Soup mixes
HQ: Osem Investments Ltd.
2 Rimon
Shoham 60829
372 050-50

(G-2986)
PAUL WINSTON FINE JEWELRY GROU (PA)
Also Called: True Romance
619 E Palisade Ave Ste 1 (07632-1834)
PHONE..............................800 232-2728
Isaac Gad, *CEO*
Benjamin Yekutiel, *President*
Xavier Bretillion, *Vice Pres*
Ahuva Nazarian, *Vice Pres*
James Van Nostrand, *Assoc Prof*
▼ EMP: 15
SALES (est): 2.5MM **Privately Held**
SIC: 3911 Jewelry, precious metal

(G-2987)
PCS REVENUE CTRL SYSTEMS INC
560 Sylvan Ave Ste 2050 (07632-3174)
PHONE..............................201 568-8300
Abe Halpern, *President*
David Yaniv, *General Mgr*
Judi Dugan, *Project Mgr*
Tony Diers, *Opers Mgr*
Dov Abramson, *Opers Staff*
▲ EMP: 48
SQ FT: 11,000
SALES (est): 9.8MM **Privately Held**
WEB: www.pcsrcs.com
SIC: 3577 3571 5045 Computer periph-
eral equipment; electronic computers;
computer software

(G-2988)
PRIMACY ENGINEERING INC (PA)
560 Sylvan Ave Ste 1212 (07632-3163)
PHONE..............................201 731-3272
Jaewan Lee, *President*
Albert OH, *Vice Pres*
John Devlin, *Director*
John Salak,
Sun Young Han, *Executive Asst*
EMP: 15
SQ FT: 1,500
SALES (est): 4.1MM **Privately Held**
SIC: 3613 8711 3621 3812 Switchgear &
switchboard apparatus; engineering serv-
ices; motors & generators; search & navi-
gation equipment

(G-2989)
REMO SECURITY DOORS LLC
560 Sylvan Ave Ste 2048 (07632-3165)
PHONE..............................213 983-1010
Omer Barnes,
EMP: 4
SALES (est): 152.5K **Privately Held**
SIC: 3442 Metal doors, sash & trim

(G-2990)
TALENTI GELATO LLC (HQ)
800 Sylvan Ave (07632-3201)
PHONE..............................800 298-4020
Steve Gill, *Mng Member*
EMP: 31
SALES (est): 21.6MM
SALES (corp-wide): 58.3B **Privately Held**
SIC: 2024 Ice cream, bulk
PA: Unilever Plc
Unilever House
London EC4Y
207 822-5252

(G-2991)
TELLAS LTD
600 Sylvan Ave Ste 4 (07632-3120)
PHONE..............................201 399-8888
Richard Helfenbein, *President*
EMP: 21 **Privately Held**
SIC: 2326 2339 Men's & boys' work cloth-
ing; women's & misses' athletic clothing &
sportswear
HQ: Tellas Ltd.
95 Madison Ave
New York NY 10016
212 213-1709

(G-2992)
TOPIFRAM LABORATORIES INC
440 Sylvan Ave Ste 100 (07632-2711)
P.O. Box 1613 (07632-0613)
PHONE..............................201 894-9020
Robert Neis, *President*
Arnold Neis, *Chairman*
Charmane Halas, *Controller*
EMP: 50
SALES (est): 3.3MM
SALES (corp-wide): 80.3MM **Privately
Held**
WEB: www.etbrowne.com
SIC: 2834 8731 2844 Dermatologicals;
commercial physical research; toilet
preparations
PA: E.T. Browne Drug Co., Inc.
440 Sylvan Ave
Englewood Cliffs NJ 07632
201 894-9020

(G-2993)
TRILOGY PUBLICATIONS LLC
560 Sylvan Ave Ste 1240 (07632-3171)
PHONE..............................201 816-1211
Lenore Clark, *Office Mgr*
Rose Reichman,
EMP: 6
SALES (est): 351.4K **Privately Held**
SIC: 2731 Book publishing

(G-2994)
TRIMTEX COMPANY INC
Also Called: St Louis Trimming Div
325 Sylvan Ave Ste 102 (07632-2753)
PHONE..............................201 945-2151
William C Henderson, *President*
Howard Mann, *Chairman*
EMP: 100
SQ FT: 300,000
SALES (est): 3.8MM **Privately Held**
WEB: www.trimtex.com
SIC: 2241 2257 2211 Trimmings, textile;
braids, textile; weft knit fabric mills; broad-
woven fabric mills, cotton

(G-2995)
UNILEVER UNITED STATES INC (HQ)
Also Called: Unilever Hpc-USA
700 Sylvan Ave (07632-3113)
P.O. Box 210253, Dallas TX (75211-0253)
PHONE..............................201 735-9661
Michael B Polk, *President*
John Bird, *Senior VP*
Julio Del Cioppo, *Mktg Dir*
Laura Klauberg, *Marketing Staff*
Peter M Mendelson,
◆ EMP: 1180 EST: 1977

SALES (est): 4.3B
SALES (corp-wide): 58.3B **Privately Held**
WEB: www.unilever.com
SIC: 2086 2024 2038 2844 Bottled & canned soft drinks; ice cream & frozen desserts; frozen specialties; toilet preparations; detergents, synthetic organic or inorganic alkaline; dressings, salad: raw & cooked (except dry mixes)
PA: Unilever N.V.
　　Weena 455
　　Rotterdam
　　102 174-000

(G-2996)
UNILEVER UNITED STATES INC
800 Sylvan Ave (07632-3201)
PHONE................................800 298-5018
Michell Largmann, *Branch Mgr*
EMP: 6
SALES (corp-wide): 58.3B **Privately Held**
SIC: 2035 Pickles, sauces & salad dressings
HQ: Unilever United States, Inc.
　　700 Sylvan Ave
　　Englewood Cliffs NJ 07632
　　201 735-9661

(G-2997)
VITEX LLC
210 Sylvan Ave Ste 25 (07632-2503)
PHONE................................201 296-0145
Michael Ko,
EMP: 7
SALES: 8MM **Privately Held**
WEB: www.vitextech.com
SIC: 5065 3661 Communication equipment; fiber optics communications equipment

(G-2998)
ZENITH ELECTRONICS CORPORATION
1000 Sylvan Ave Fl 1 (07632-3302)
PHONE................................201 816-2071
Tj Lee, *CEO*
EMP: 40 **Privately Held**
WEB: www.zenith.com
SIC: 3651 Household audio & video equipment
HQ: Zenith Electronics Corporation
　　2000 Millbrook Dr
　　Lincolnshire IL 60069
　　847 941-8000

Englishtown
Monmouth County

(G-2999)
ACORN INDUSTRY INC
Also Called: Raason Cabinetry
6 Hoffer Ct (07726-8414)
PHONE................................732 536-6256
David Langner, *President*
EMP: 11
SALES: 1.5MM **Privately Held**
SIC: 2599 Cabinets, factory

(G-3000)
CHEVEUX COSMETICS CORPORATION
30 Park Ave (07726-1607)
P.O. Box 449 (07726-0449)
PHONE................................732 446-7516
Mabel Richardson, *President*
Sharon Griffith, *Corp Secy*
Bill Covey Jr, *Vice Pres*
EMP: 60
SQ FT: 35,000
SALES (est): 6.6MM **Privately Held**
SIC: 2844 Hair preparations, including shampoos

(G-3001)
DAVID BRADLEY CHOCOLATIER INC
520 Us Highway 9 (07726-8264)
PHONE................................732 536-7719
Bradley David, *Branch Mgr*
EMP: 22

SALES (corp-wide): 2.2MM **Privately Held**
SIC: 2066 2064 Chocolate & cocoa products; candy & other confectionery products
PA: David Bradley Chocolatier Inc.
　　92 N Main St Bldg 19
　　Windsor NJ 08561
　　609 443-4747

(G-3002)
GOLDEN TREASURE IMPORTS INC
Also Called: Alisa
522 Us Highway 9 (07726-8241)
PHONE................................732 723-1830
Lisa Morgan, *President*
Alfred Morgan, *Marketing Staff*
EMP: 4
SQ FT: 600
SALES: 641K **Privately Held**
SIC: 5094 3961 Diamonds (gems); costume jewelry

(G-3003)
GREATER MEDIA NEWSPAPERS (DH)
198 Us Highway 9 Ste 100 (07726-3073)
PHONE................................732 358-5200
Peter Smyth, *President*
John Zielinski, *Principal*
Linda Hecht, *Accounts Exec*
Gary D Albertson, *Advt Staff*
Gary Albertson, *Advt Staff*
EMP: 22 EST: 1888
SQ FT: 6,500
SALES (est): 45.5MM
SALES (corp-wide): 257.4MM **Publicly Held**
WEB: www.gmnews.com
SIC: 2711 Newspapers: publishing only, not printed on site; newspapers, publishing & printing
HQ: Greater Media, Inc.
　　3033 Riviera Dr Ste 200
　　Naples FL 34103
　　239 263-5000

(G-3004)
HAIR SYSTEMS INC
30 Park Ave (07726-1607)
P.O. Box 449 (07726-0449)
PHONE................................732 446-2202
Marjorie M Covey, *Chairman*
William E Covey Jr, *COO*
Sunny Shah, *Plant Mgr*
Niaz Khan, *Prdtn Mgr*
Nancy Lastra, *Purchasing*
▲ **EMP:** 70
SQ FT: 55,000
SALES (est): 18MM **Privately Held**
WEB: www.hairsystemsinc.com
SIC: 2844 3565 Bleaches, hair; packing & wrapping machinery

(G-3005)
J NELSON PRESS INC
362 Us Highway 9 Unit 120 (07726-9226)
PHONE................................732 747-0330
Scott Thompsen, *President*
EMP: 5 EST: 1933
SALES (est): 561K **Privately Held**
WEB: www.nelsonpress.net
SIC: 3555 Printing presses

(G-3006)
KUMAR BROS USA LLC (PA)
74 Oxford Ct (07726-1571)
PHONE................................732 266-3091
Siddharth Khattar,
▲ **EMP:** 6
SQ FT: 500
SALES (est): 787.5K **Privately Held**
SIC: 3714 Motor vehicle parts & accessories

(G-3007)
PACKET MEDIA LLC (PA)
198 Us Highway 9 Ste 100 (07726-3073)
P.O. Box 350, Princeton (08542-0350)
PHONE................................856 779-3800
James B Kilgore, *President*
EMP: 3
SALES (est): 41.7MM **Privately Held**
SIC: 2711 3993 Newspapers; signs & advertising specialties

(G-3008)
QUADRANGLE PRODUCTS INC
28 Harrison Ave Unit D (07726-1579)
PHONE................................732 792-1234
Michael Levine, *President*
Gayle Stamer, *Marketing Mgr*
Stephanie Lopresti, *Manager*
▲ **EMP:** 10
SQ FT: 5,000
SALES: 1.2MM **Privately Held**
WEB: www.quadrangleproducts.com
SIC: 3679 5045 Harness assemblies for electronic use: wire or cable; computer peripheral equipment

(G-3009)
STAVOLA CONTRACTING CO INC
120 Old Bergen Mill Rd (07726)
PHONE................................732 935-0156
Joe Stavola, *Manager*
EMP: 4
SALES (corp-wide): 29.9MM **Privately Held**
SIC: 2951 Concrete, bituminous
PA: Stavola Contracting Co Inc
　　175 Drift Rd
　　Tinton Falls NJ 07724
　　732 542-2328

(G-3010)
UNION HILL CORP
29 Park Ave (07726-1622)
PHONE................................732 786-9422
Mike Conforth, *CEO*
▲ **EMP:** 5
SALES (est): 624.3K **Privately Held**
SIC: 2399 Horse & pet accessories, textile

Erial
Camden County

(G-3011)
ERIAL CONCRETE INC
965 Hickstown Rd (08081-1090)
P.O. Box 309, Blackwood (08012-0309)
PHONE................................856 784-8884
Steve Rowanowski, *President*
Emma Rowanowski, *Admin Sec*
EMP: 15
SQ FT: 3,000
SALES (est): 2.8MM **Privately Held**
SIC: 3273 Ready-mixed concrete

Essex Fells
Essex County

(G-3012)
WINSTAR WINDOWS LLC
217 Roseland Ave (07021-1111)
PHONE................................973 403-0574
Gene Kelly, *Mng Member*
EMP: 7
SALES (est): 625.9K **Privately Held**
SIC: 3442 Window & door frames

Ewing
Mercer County

(G-3013)
AFRICA WORLD PRESS
541 W Ingham Ave Ste B (08638-5001)
P.O. Box 1892, Trenton (08607-1892)
PHONE................................609 695-3200
Kassahun Checole, *President*
Senait Kassahun, *Administration*
EMP: 6
SQ FT: 15,000
SALES: 743.7K **Privately Held**
SIC: 2731 Books: publishing only

(G-3014)
ALTARE PUBLISHING INC
100 Campus Town Cir # 103 (08638-1962)
PHONE................................727 237-1330
Ryan Kowalski, *President*
EMP: 6

SALES (est): 621.3K **Privately Held**
SIC: 2741 Miscellaneous publishing

(G-3015)
ANTARES PHARMA INC (PA)
100 Princeton S Ste 300 (08628)
PHONE................................609 359-3020
Leonard S Jacob, *Ch of Bd*
Robert F Apple, *President*
James Tursi, *Exec VP*
Bruce Freundlich, *Vice Pres*
Dan Kelsey, *Vice Pres*
EMP: 111
SQ FT: 13,700
SALES: 63.5MM **Publicly Held**
WEB: www.antarespharma.com
SIC: 2834 3841 Pharmaceutical preparations; surgical & medical instruments

(G-3016)
ARCTIC PRODUCTS CO INC
Also Called: Arctic Ice Cream Co
22 Arctic Pkwy (08638-3041)
PHONE................................609 393-4264
Thomas G Green, *President*
EMP: 12 EST: 1931
SQ FT: 6,000
SALES (est): 1MM **Privately Held**
WEB: www.arcticicecreamco.com
SIC: 2024 Ice cream, bulk

(G-3017)
CAPITAL STEEL SERVICE LLC
82 Stokes Ave (08638-3726)
PHONE................................609 882-6983
Robert Hickman, *President*
▲ **EMP:** 22
SALES: 6MM **Privately Held**
WEB: www.capitalsteel.org
SIC: 5051 3441 Steel; fabricated structural metal

(G-3018)
CAPITOL BINDERY INC
312 Stokes Ave (08638-3732)
PHONE................................609 883-5971
Robert Gugger, *President*
Marilyn Gugger, *Vice Pres*
EMP: 4
SQ FT: 5,000
SALES (est): 385.7K **Privately Held**
WEB: www.capitolbindery.com
SIC: 2789 Binding only: books, pamphlets, magazines, etc.

(G-3019)
CELATOR PHARMACEUTICALS INC (HQ)
200 Princeton S (08628)
PHONE................................609 243-0123
Bruce C Cozadd, *President*
Karen Smith, *Vice Pres*
Matthew P Young, *Treasurer*
Suzanne S Hooper, *Admin Sec*
EMP: 25
SQ FT: 4,785
SALES (est): 2.4MM **Privately Held**
SIC: 2834 Pharmaceutical preparations

(G-3020)
CHESSCO INDUSTRIES INC
Process Research Products
1013 Whitehead Road Ext (08638-2418)
PHONE................................609 882-0400
Anthony Broomer, *Vice Pres*
Seiji Inaoka, *Info Tech Dir*
Phyllis Joan, *Network Mgr*
EMP: 20
SALES (corp-wide): 8.5MM **Privately Held**
WEB: www.processresearch.com
SIC: 2819 3291 Industrial inorganic chemicals; abrasive products
PA: Chessco Industries, Inc.
　　1330 Post Rd E Ste 2
　　Westport CT 06880
　　203 255-2804

(G-3021)
CHURCH & DWIGHT CO INC (PA)
500 Charles Ewing Blvd (08628-3448)
PHONE................................609 806-1200
Matthew T Farrell, *President*
Britta Bomhard, *Exec VP*
Patrick D De Maynadier, *Exec VP*

Carlos Linares, *Exec VP*
Rick Spann, *Exec VP*
EMP: 350
SQ FT: 250,000
SALES: 4.1B **Publicly Held**
WEB: www.churchdwight.com
SIC: 2841 2812 2842 2844 Detergents, synthetic organic or inorganic alkaline; sodium bicarbonate; bleaches, household: dry or liquid; fabric softeners; deodorants, nonpersonal; toothpastes or powders, dentifrices; ammonium compounds, except fertilizers

(G-3022)
CMF LTD INC
599 W Ingham Ave (08638-5001)
P.O. Box 5989, Trenton (08638-0989)
PHONE..................................609 695-3600
Gerald P Donahue, *President*
Michael Donahue, *Vice Pres*
Keith Schultz, *Vice Pres*
EMP: 45
SQ FT: 56,000
SALES (est): 5.6MM **Privately Held**
WEB: www.cmflimited.com
SIC: 3429 Metal fasteners

(G-3023)
CREST ULTRASONICS CORP (HQ)
18 Graphics Dr (08628-1546)
P.O. Box 7266, Trenton (08628-0266)
PHONE..................................609 883-4000
J Michael Goodson, *CEO*
Sami Awad, *President*
John Scheidell, *Regional Mgr*
Mitchelle Vitarelli, *CFO*
Tom Lipski, *CTO*
▲ **EMP:** 7
SQ FT: 55,000
SALES (est): 27.4MM
SALES (corp-wide): 54.6MM **Privately Held**
WEB: www.crest-ultrasonics.com
SIC: 3699 Electrical equipment & supplies
PA: Crestek, Inc.
18 Graphics Dr
Ewing NJ 08628
609 883-4000

(G-3024)
CRESTEK INC (PA)
18 Graphics Dr (08628-1546)
PHONE..................................609 883-4000
J Michael Goodson, *CEO*
▲ **EMP:** 20
SQ FT: 50,000
SALES (est): 54.6MM **Privately Held**
WEB: www.crestek.com
SIC: 3699 3841 3679 Cleaning equipment, ultrasonic, except medical & dental; ultrasonic medical cleaning equipment; power supplies, all types: static

(G-3025)
CUSTOM BLENDS INC
18 Graphics Dr (08628-1546)
PHONE..................................215 934-7080
Harvey Levitt, *President*
Julia Levitt, *Corp Secy*
EMP: 5 **EST:** 1889
SALES: 1MM **Privately Held**
SIC: 2085 3589 2899 Distilled & blended liquors; water treatment equipment, industrial; water treating compounds

(G-3026)
DAVIS HYUNDAI
Also Called: Davis Hyundai & Mitsubishi
1655 N Olden Avenue Ext (08638-3205)
PHONE..................................609 883-3500
Ron Derouin, *Principal*
Miguel Ortiz, *Sales Mgr*
EMP: 18
SALES (est): 5.3MM **Privately Held**
SIC: 5511 3519 Automobiles, new & used; parts & accessories, internal combustion engines

(G-3027)
DISCOVERY SEMICONDUCTORS INC
119 Silvia St (08628-3200)
PHONE..................................609 434-1311
Abhay Joshi, *President*

Sharon V Joshi, *Vice Pres*
Aaron Berry, *Sales Engr*
Rohan Shirodkar, *Webmaster*
EMP: 25
SQ FT: 10,000
SALES: 3.8MM **Privately Held**
WEB: www.discoverysemi.com
SIC: 3674 Semiconductors & related devices

(G-3028)
EASTERN PODIATRY LABS INC
1702 5th St (08638-3039)
PHONE..................................609 882-4444
Thomas Mc Guigan, *President*
EMP: 4
SQ FT: 3,000
SALES (est): 477.1K **Privately Held**
SIC: 3842 Orthopedic appliances

(G-3029)
ESQUIRE BUSINESS FORMS
Also Called: Esquire Graphics & Bus Forms
1668 N Olden Avenue Ext (08638-3209)
PHONE..................................609 883-1155
Roger Melick, *Owner*
EMP: 4
SQ FT: 3,100
SALES (est): 700K **Privately Held**
SIC: 2752 Commercial printing, offset

(G-3030)
EWING RECOVERY CORP
Also Called: Century Metals
1565 6th St (08638-3001)
PHONE..................................609 883-0318
Betty Wallace, *President*
Ronald Mc Closkey, *Vice Pres*
Brian Mc Closkey, *Treasurer*
James Wallace, *Admin Sec*
EMP: 6
SALES (est): 564.5K **Privately Held**
WEB: www.centurymetalsco.com
SIC: 3339 Precious metals

(G-3031)
FMC CORPORATION
Also Called: F M C Research and Dev Div
801-701 Princeton S (08628)
PHONE..................................609 963-6200
Shaaban Elnaggar, *President*
Richard Police, *Branch Mgr*
Upender Garlapati, *Programmer Anys*
Luanne McGovern, *Director*
EMP: 120
SQ FT: 10,000
SALES (corp-wide): 4.7B **Publicly Held**
WEB: www.fmc.com
SIC: 2869 Industrial organic chemicals
PA: Fmc Corporation
2929 Walnut St
Philadelphia PA 19104
215 299-6000

(G-3032)
HARRISON MACHINE AND TOOL INC
21 Lexington Ave (08618-2301)
PHONE..................................609 883-0800
Steven Harrison, *President*
Marie Harrison, *Admin Sec*
EMP: 4
SQ FT: 4,000
SALES (est): 440K **Privately Held**
WEB: www.harrisonmachine.com
SIC: 3599 Machine shop, jobbing & repair

(G-3033)
HEIGHTS USA INC
1445 Lower Ferry Rd (08618-1424)
PHONE..................................609 530-1300
Leigh Jezorek, *President*
Tim Philburn, *COO*
Sheri Petrone, *Human Res Dir*
Julie Mc Clain, *Mktg Dir*
▲ **EMP:** 24
SQ FT: 38,000
SALES (est): 4MM
SALES (corp-wide): 5MM **Privately Held**
WEB: www.heights-usa.com
SIC: 3861 Photographic equipment & supplies
HQ: Heights (U.K.) Limited
Wainstalls Mill
Halifax
142 224-0914

(G-3034)
HERMITAGE PRESS OF NEW JERSEY (PA)
1595 5th St (08638-3099)
PHONE..................................609 882-3600
Mary L Stoeckle, *Ch of Bd*
Michael Stoeckle, *President*
Michael W Stoeckle, *President*
Thomas Stoeckle, *CFO*
Thomas J Stoeckle Jr, *Treasurer*
EMP: 57
SQ FT: 10,000
SALES (est): 8.9MM **Privately Held**
SIC: 2752 7331 Commercial printing, offset; mailing service

(G-3035)
HESS CORPORATION
601 Jack Stephan Way (08628-3019)
PHONE..................................609 882-8477
EMP: 4
SALES (corp-wide): 6.4B **Publicly Held**
SIC: 1382 Oil & gas exploration services
PA: Hess Corporation
1185 Ave Of The Amer
New York NY 10036
212 997-8500

(G-3036)
HOMASOTE COMPANY
932 Lower Ferry Rd (08628-3298)
P.O. Box 7240, Trenton (08628-0240)
PHONE..................................609 883-3300
Warren L Flicker, *President*
Pete Tindall, *VP Opers*
Ronald Fasano, *CFO*
Richard Magnan, *Info Tech Mgr*
Jennifer Birtkovich, *Admin Sec*
EMP: 107 **EST:** 1909
SQ FT: 537,000
SALES: 20MM **Privately Held**
WEB: www.homasote.com
SIC: 2493 2671 Insulation board, cellular fiber; paper coated or laminated for packaging

(G-3037)
HPH PRODUCTS INC
182 Carlton Ave (08618-1402)
PHONE..................................609 883-0052
Jim Deiner, *President*
EMP: 5
SALES: 950K **Privately Held**
SIC: 3643 Current-carrying wiring devices

(G-3038)
JOHN PATRICK PUBLISHING LLC
Also Called: Jppc
1707 4th St (08638-3032)
P.O. Box 5469, Trenton (08638-0469)
PHONE..................................609 883-2700
Wendy Gilleo, *Principal*
Carol Schmerbeck, *Opers Mgr*
Celeste Gama, *Sales Mgr*
Patricia Graham, *Sales Staff*
Tracey Rauh, *Sales Staff*
EMP: 52
SQ FT: 13,000
SALES (est): 6.4MM **Privately Held**
WEB: www.jppc.net
SIC: 2741 2759 Envelopes: printing; newsletter publishing

(G-3039)
JOSEPH NATICCHIA
Also Called: Naticchia's Custom Woodworking
1597 5th St (08638-3034)
PHONE..................................609 882-7709
Joseph Naticchia, *Owner*
EMP: 12
SQ FT: 1,500
SALES (est): 600K **Privately Held**
SIC: 2431 Millwork

(G-3040)
KINETICS INDUSTRIES INC
Also Called: Kinetics Control Systems
140 Stokes Ave (08638-3796)
PHONE..................................609 883-9700
Ronald H Secrest, *President*
Kenneth Morris, *Vice Pres*
Keith Secrest, *Vice Pres*
EMP: 29 **EST:** 1939

SQ FT: 20,000
SALES (est): 8.4MM **Privately Held**
WEB: www.kinetics-industries.com
SIC: 3679 5063 Rectifiers, electronic; electrical apparatus & equipment

(G-3041)
KNITE INC
18 W Piper Ave Ste 201 (08628-1307)
PHONE..................................609 258-9550
Art Suckewer, *President*
David Boyer, *Director*
EMP: 4
SALES (est): 250K **Privately Held**
WEB: www.knite.com
SIC: 3694 Ignition apparatus, internal combustion engines

(G-3042)
KNUDSEN PRECISION MFG
113 Walters Ave (08638-1829)
PHONE..................................609 538-1100
Don Hoven, *President*
Janet Hoven, *Exec VP*
EMP: 12
SQ FT: 7,500
SALES (est): 1.2MM **Privately Held**
SIC: 3599 Machine shop, jobbing & repair

(G-3043)
KRAFTWORK CUSTOM DESIGN
182 Homecrest Ave (08638-3634)
PHONE..................................609 883-8444
Fax: 609 882-3424
EMP: 15
SALES (est): 740K **Privately Held**
SIC: 2759 Commercial Printing

(G-3044)
M K WOODWORKING INC
Also Called: Majer Design
1476 Prospect St (08638-4802)
PHONE..................................609 771-1350
George Majer, *President*
Roland Majer, *Vice Pres*
EMP: 5
SQ FT: 4,000
SALES: 700K **Privately Held**
SIC: 2431 2434 Millwork; wood kitchen cabinets

(G-3045)
MERCK & CO INC
100 Sam Weinroth Rd (08638-1303)
PHONE..................................609 771-8790
Nadine Fetsko, *Principal*
Alexander Ginzburg, *Administration*
EMP: 9
SALES (est): 1.5MM **Privately Held**
SIC: 2834 Pharmaceutical preparations

(G-3046)
MICRODOSE THERAPEUTX INC
Also Called: Microdose Defense Products
7 Graphics Dr (08628-1547)
PHONE..................................732 355-2100
Anand Gumaste, *CEO*
Scott Fleming, *President*
F Scott Fleming, *Senior VP*
Dave Byron, *Vice Pres*
Michael Martin, *Vice Pres*
EMP: 49 **EST:** 1989
SQ FT: 16,000
SALES (est): 6.6MM **Privately Held**
WEB: www.mdtx.com
SIC: 3841 Inhalation therapy equipment

(G-3047)
NANOPV CORPORATION (PA)
Also Called: Nanopv Technology
122 Mountainview Rd (08560-1202)
PHONE..................................609 851-3666
Anna Selvan John, *President*
▲ **EMP:** 12
SQ FT: 40,000
SALES (est): 9.4MM **Privately Held**
WEB: www.nano-pv.com
SIC: 3674 Solar cells

(G-3048)
NAVINTA LLC
1499 Lower Ferry Rd (08618-1414)
PHONE..................................609 883-1135
Mahendra Patel, *Mng Member*
Benjamin Selvaraj, *Manager*
Nikki Kendrick, *Director*

Jay Patel,
▲ **EMP:** 10
SALES (est): 2.7MM **Privately Held**
WEB: www.navinta.com
SIC: 2833 Drugs & herbs: grading, grinding & milling

(G-3049)
NEUROTRON MEDICAL INC
800 Silvia St (08628-3239)
P.O. Box 6480, Trenton (08648-0480)
PHONE.................................609 896-3444
Jack Guldalian, *President*
EMP: 4
SALES (est): 290K **Privately Held**
WEB: www.neumedinc.com
SIC: 3845 Electromedical apparatus

(G-3050)
PFIZER INC
1001 Jack Stephan Way (08628-3015)
PHONE.................................609 434-4920
Brian Clark, *Manager*
EMP: 50
SALES (corp-wide): 53.6B **Publicly Held**
WEB: www.pfizer.com
SIC: 2834 Pharmaceutical preparations
PA: Pfizer Inc.
235 E 42nd St
New York NY 10017
212 733-2323

(G-3051)
PFLAUMER BROTHERS INC (PA)
1008 Whitehead Road Ext (08638-2406)
P.O. Box 309, Norristown PA (19404-0309)
PHONE.................................609 883-4610
Harley McNair, *President*
Craig McNair, *Vice Pres*
Lorraine McNair, *Vice Pres*
Diann Rupprecht, *Treasurer*
Darlene Francis, *Controller*
▲ **EMP:** 6 **EST:** 1934
SQ FT: 6,000
SALES (est): 4.6MM **Privately Held**
WEB: www.pflaumer.com
SIC: 2843 2992 8742 Surface active agents; lubricating oils & greases; industry specialist consultants

(G-3052)
PIERCE-ROBERTS RUBBER COMPANY
1450 Heath Ave (08638-3832)
P.O. Box 5007, Trenton (08638-0007)
PHONE.................................609 394-5245
Christopher Weber, *Vice Pres*
EMP: 18 **EST:** 1911
SQ FT: 65,000
SALES (est): 4.2MM **Privately Held**
WEB: www.pierceroberts.com
SIC: 2822 3069 3061 Synthetic rubber; molded rubber products; mechanical rubber goods

(G-3053)
POWTEK POWDER COATING INC
233 Dickinson St (08638-3450)
PHONE.................................609 394-1144
Fred Martucci, *President*
EMP: 6
SALES (est): 520.2K **Privately Held**
SIC: 3479 Painting, coating & hot dipping

(G-3054)
PRECISION DEVICES INC
20 Lexington Ave Ste 3 (08618-2323)
PHONE.................................609 882-2230
Mark Hoover, *Principal*
EMP: 4
SALES (est): 313.8K **Privately Held**
SIC: 5063 7694 Electrical supplies; electric motor repair

(G-3055)
PURDUE PHARMA LP
100 Prnctn S Corpt Ctr # 250 (08628-3459)
PHONE.................................203 588-8000
Franz Azuolas, *Branch Mgr*
EMP: 5 **Privately Held**
SIC: 2834 Pharmaceutical preparations

PA: Purdue Pharma L.P.
201 Tresser Blvd Fl 1
Stamford CT 06901

(G-3056)
PYROMETER LLC
Also Called: Pyrometer Instrument Company
70 Weber Ave (08638-3763)
PHONE.................................609 443-5522
Stefan Steigerwald, *Principal*
James Schlauch, *Principal*
EMP: 4
SALES (est): 404.1K **Privately Held**
SIC: 3823 Industrial instrmnts msrmnt display/control process variable

(G-3057)
QUANTEM CORP
1457 Lower Ferry Rd Ste 1 (08618-1493)
PHONE.................................609 883-9191
Christopher Bromberg, *Ch of Bd*
John Brienza, *Senior VP*
EMP: 25
SQ FT: 15,000
SALES (est): 4.3MM **Privately Held**
SIC: 3825 Measuring instruments & meters, electric

(G-3058)
RBC BEARINGS INCORPORATED
Also Called: Rbc Bearings-Houston
400 Sullivan Way Ste 1 (08628-3438)
PHONE.................................843 332-2691
Mark Suring, *Branch Mgr*
EMP: 15
SALES (corp-wide): 702.5MM **Publicly Held**
SIC: 3562 Ball & roller bearings
PA: Rbc Bearings Incorporated
102 Willenbrock Rd
Oxford CT 06478
203 267-7001

(G-3059)
RED SEA PRESS INC
Also Called: Africa World Red Sea Press
541 W Ingham Ave Ste B (08638-5001)
PHONE.................................609 695-3200
Kassahun Checole, *President*
EMP: 5
SQ FT: 15,000
SALES (est): 625.8K **Privately Held**
SIC: 2731 Books: publishing only

(G-3060)
REES SCIENTIFIC CORPORATION
1007 Whitehead Road Ext # 1 (08638-2428)
PHONE.................................609 530-1055
Dr Rees Thomas, *President*
William Harrington, *Regional Mgr*
Stephen Hartmann, *Regional Mgr*
Anthony McCormack, *Regional Mgr*
Alex Rivera, *Project Mgr*
▲ **EMP:** 104
SQ FT: 26,000
SALES (est): 24MM **Privately Held**
WEB: www.reesscientific.com
SIC: 3822 3823 Auto controls regulating residntl & coml environmt & applncs; industrial instrmnts msrmnt display/control process variable

(G-3061)
RIEGEL CMMUNICATIONS GROUP INC
1 Graphics Dr (08628-1547)
PHONE.................................609 771-0555
Lou Vassallo, *President*
Jim Esca, *CFO*
▼ **EMP:** 23
SALES (est): 5.4MM **Privately Held**
SIC: 2759 Letterpress printing

(G-3062)
RIEGEL HOLDING COMPANY INC
Also Called: Riegel Printing Company
1 Graphics Dr (08628-1547)
P.O. Box 7430, Trenton (08628-0430)
PHONE.................................609 771-0361
Kathleen Adkins, *President*
Susan Heath, *Exec VP*

Kevin Brown, *Vice Pres*
Zuzana Heath, *Vice Pres*
Jim Reilly, *Vice Pres*
EMP: 53
SQ FT: 42,000
SALES (est): 16MM **Privately Held**
WEB: www.riegelprintinginc.com
SIC: 2752 Commercial printing, offset

(G-3063)
RIVER HORSE BREWERY CO INC
2 Graphics Dr (08628-1546)
PHONE.................................609 883-0890
Chris Walsh, *CEO*
Jack Bryan, *President*
Andrea Whaley, *Office Mgr*
EMP: 10
SQ FT: 10,000
SALES (est): 1.5MM **Privately Held**
SIC: 2082 Beer (alcoholic beverage)

(G-3064)
S L ENTERPRISES INC (PA)
Also Called: Fixturecraft
1603 N Olden Ave (08638-3205)
PHONE.................................908 272-8145
William P Mooney, *President*
Michael Rossetti, *Vice Pres*
EMP: 4
SQ FT: 2,000
SALES (est): 3.6MM **Privately Held**
WEB: www.fixturecraft.com
SIC: 4225 7389 2541 2542 General warehousing; coupon redemption service; store & office display cases & fixtures; partitions & fixtures, except wood

(G-3065)
SHRIJI POLYMERS LLC
1 Graphics Dr (08628-1547)
PHONE.................................609 906-2355
Rajesh Nogaja, *Vice Pres*
EMP: 35
SALES (est): 93.7K
SALES (corp-wide): 35.2MM **Privately Held**
SIC: 3085 Plastics bottles
PA: Shriji Polymers (India) Limited
Plot No. 8, 9 & 15-D, Industrial Area
Ujjain MP 25240
734 252-4071

(G-3066)
SPECIALTY MEASURES
15 Dawes Ave (08638-4609)
PHONE.................................609 882-6071
EMP: 4
SALES (est): 408.9K **Privately Held**
SIC: 3449 7692 Custom roll formed products; automotive welding

(G-3067)
SUPERIOR INTL SRGICAL SUPS LLC
46 Oak Ln (08618-4002)
PHONE.................................609 695-6591
▲ **EMP:** 10
SALES (est): 1.4MM **Privately Held**
SIC: 3842 Mfg Surgical Appliances/Supplies

(G-3068)
SURFACE TECHNOLOGY INC
Also Called: STI
1405 Lower Ferry Rd (08618-1414)
PHONE.................................609 259-0099
Michael D Feldstein, *President*
Barry McCoy, *Sales Staff*
▲ **EMP:** 15 **EST:** 1973
SQ FT: 20,000
SALES (est): 2.7MM **Privately Held**
WEB: www.diamondcoating.com
SIC: 8734 2869 Testing laboratories; industrial organic chemicals

(G-3069)
TEDCO INC
Also Called: Minuteman Press
35 Scotch Rd (08628-2512)
PHONE.................................609 883-0799
Ted Blumenthal, *President*
EMP: 7
SQ FT: 5,000

SALES: 850K **Privately Held**
SIC: 2752 2791 2789 Commercial printing, lithographic; typesetting; bookbinding & related work

(G-3070)
TRENTON CORRUGATED PRODUCTS
17 Shelton Ave (08618)
PHONE.................................609 695-0808
Anthony Pecoraro, *President*
Brad Pecoraro, *Vice Pres*
Gail Pecoraro, *Treasurer*
M Helen Pecoraro, *Admin Sec*
EMP: 50
SQ FT: 150,000
SALES (est): 9.8MM **Privately Held**
WEB: www.trentoncorrugated.com
SIC: 2653 Boxes, corrugated: made from purchased materials; boxes, solid fiber: made from purchased materials

(G-3071)
TRENTYPO INC
304 Stokes Ave (08638-3732)
PHONE.................................609 883-5971
Fax: 609 883-2428
EMP: 15 **EST:** 1960
SQ FT: 6,000
SALES (est): 1MM **Privately Held**
SIC: 2791 2752 2759 Typesetting Services Lithographic Commercial Printing Commercial Printing

(G-3072)
TUSA PRODUCTS INC
1515 Parkway Ave (08628-2730)
PHONE.................................609 448-8333
Matthew Chow, *Principal*
EMP: 8
SQ FT: 40,000
SALES (est): 601.8K **Privately Held**
SIC: 3651 3369 3625 Home entertainment equipment, electronic; machinery castings, nonferrous: ex. alum., copper, die, etc.; switches, electronic applications

(G-3073)
UNIVERSAL DISPLAY CORPORATION (PA)
375 Phillips Blvd Ste 1 (08618-1455)
PHONE.................................609 671-0980
Sherwin I Seligsohn, *Ch of Bd*
Steven V Abramson, *President*
Sidney Rosenblatt, *Exec VP*
Julia J Brown, *Senior VP*
Janice M Dufour, *Vice Pres*
EMP: 104
SALES: 247.4MM **Publicly Held**
WEB: www.universaldisplay.com
SIC: 3674 Light emitting diodes

(G-3074)
UNIVERSAL MEDICAL INC
275 Phillips Blvd (08618-1452)
PHONE.................................800 606-5511
EMP: 19
SQ FT: 1,200
SALES: 300.5K **Privately Held**
SIC: 3845 Mfg Electromedical Equipment

(G-3075)
UNLIMITED PRINT PRODUCTS INC
Also Called: Unlimited Silk Screen Products
41 Lexington Ave (08628-2320)
PHONE.................................609 882-0653
Timothy Mangee, *President*
Karen Yerkes, *Corp Secy*
EMP: 10 **EST:** 1981
SQ FT: 3,600
SALES (est): 1.2MM **Privately Held**
SIC: 2759 7389 Screen printing; embroidering of advertising on shirts, etc.

(G-3076)
VEHICLE TECHNOLOGIES INC
Also Called: Vetex
17 Decou Ave (08628-2908)
PHONE.................................609 406-9626
Nicholas Fenelli, *President*
Mary Fenelli, *Vice Pres*
EMP: 4

SALES (est): 380K **Privately Held**
SIC: 3537 Lift trucks, industrial: fork, plat-form, straddle, etc.

(G-3077)
W GERRIETS INTERNATIONAL INC
130 Winterwood Ave (08638-1836)
PHONE.................................609 771-8111
Hannes Gerriets, *President*
Kalle Verweyen, *Managing Dir*
Bernd Baumeisteer, *Vice Pres*
Benjamin Holland, *Sales Executive*
Claudia Baldenhofer, *Technology*
▲ EMP: 14
SALES (est): 2.2MM **Privately Held**
WEB: www.gi-info.com
SIC: 5049 5045 2391 Theatrical equip-ment & supplies; computers, peripherals & software; curtains & draperies

Fair Haven
Monmouth County

(G-3078)
ART FLAG CO INC
Also Called: Artflag
890 River Rd (07704-3348)
PHONE.................................212 334-1890
George Weiner, *President*
Carmen Weiner, *Vice Pres*
EMP: 18 EST: 1929
SQ FT: 5,000
SALES: 1MM **Privately Held**
SIC: 2399 2396 Flags, fabric; banners, made from fabric; screen printing on fab-ric articles

(G-3079)
DADDY DONKEY LABS LLC
115 Park Rd (07704-3136)
PHONE.................................646 461-4677
EMP: 6
SALES (est): 211K **Privately Held**
SIC: 7372 Prepackaged Software Services

Fair Lawn
Bergen County

(G-3080)
A ZEREGAS SONS INC (PA)
Also Called: Zerega Pasta
20-1 Broadway (07410)
PHONE.................................201 797-1400
John B Vermylen, *President*
Paul A Vermylen, *Chairman*
Mark E Vermylen, *Vice Pres*
Robert A Vermylen, *Vice Pres*
Nicholas Pugliese, *Treasurer*
◆ EMP: 170 EST: 1848
SALES (est): 69.6MM **Privately Held**
WEB: www.zerega.com
SIC: 2098 Macaroni products (e.g. alpha-bets, rings & shells), dry; noodles (e.g. egg, plain & water), dry

(G-3081)
ABG LAB LLC
20-21 Wagaraw Rd Bldg 31b (07410-1322)
PHONE.................................973 559-5663
Dr Elina Tester, *President*
Louis Rinaldi, *COO*
EMP: 5
SALES (est): 337.4K **Privately Held**
SIC: 2834 2844 Pharmaceutical prepara-tions; toilet preparations

(G-3082)
ADVANCED PROTECTIVE PRODUCTS
17-10 River Rd Ste 4c (07410-1250)
PHONE.................................201 794-2000
Thomas Heiss, *President*
Charlotte Heiss, *Treasurer*
▼ EMP: 11
SQ FT: 4,500
SALES (est): 2.5MM **Privately Held**
WEB: www.rust007.com
SIC: 2851 Paints & allied products

(G-3083)
AMERICAN FITTINGS CORP (PA)
Also Called: Amfico
17-10 Willow St (07410-2057)
PHONE.................................201 664-0027
Henry Fischbein, *President*
Allen Fischbein, *Vice Pres*
Dan Fischbein, *Vice Pres*
Robert Fischbein, *Vice Pres*
Rachell Fischbein, *VP Opers*
EMP: 9
SQ FT: 5,000
SALES (est): 2.3MM **Privately Held**
WEB: www.americanfittingscorp.com
SIC: 5063 3644 Conduits & raceways; noncurrent-carrying wiring services

(G-3084)
AMERICAN GRAPHIC SYSTEMS INC
39-26 Broadway (07410-5401)
PHONE.................................201 796-0666
Stanley Schechter, *President*
Steven C Schechter, *Vice Pres*
Diane Schechter, *Treasurer*
Sandra Schechter, *Admin Sec*
EMP: 4
SQ FT: 9,600
SALES (est): 607.5K **Privately Held**
SIC: 2752 7389 3993 2791 Commercial printing, offset; sign painting & lettering shop; signs & advertising specialties; typesetting; bookbinding & related work; commercial printing

(G-3085)
ARTICULIGHT INC
15-06 Morlot Ave (07410-2115)
PHONE.................................201 796-2690
Israel Simchi, *President*
Pamela Simchi, *Vice Pres*
EMP: 6
SALES (est): 1.4MM **Privately Held**
WEB: www.articulight.com
SIC: 5063 3646 Lighting fixtures; orna-mental lighting fixtures, commercial

(G-3086)
ASSOCIATED FABRICS CORPORATION
Also Called: A F C
15-01 Pollitt Dr Ste 7 (07410-2769)
PHONE.................................201 300-6053
Martin Marckowrtz, *President*
Bruce Nocera, *Vice Pres*
Samuel Samson, *Vice Pres*
▲ EMP: 5 EST: 1928
SQ FT: 6,000
SALES (est): 1.5MM **Privately Held**
WEB: www.afcnewyork.com
SIC: 5131 2396 Piece goods & other fab-rics; textiles, woven; knit fabrics; furniture trimmings, fabric

(G-3087)
AUTOREMIND INC
14-25 Plaza Rd Ste N35 (07410-3547)
P.O. Box 105 (07410-0105)
PHONE.................................800 277-1299
Bo Nielsen, *CEO*
Yoav Amiri, *Vice Pres*
EMP: 5
SALES (est): 533.5K **Privately Held**
SIC: 3679 Electronic switches

(G-3088)
AVERY DENNISON CORPORATION
16-00 Pollitt Dr Ste 3 (07410-2765)
PHONE.................................201 956-6100
Susan Guerin, *Branch Mgr*
EMP: 4
SALES (corp-wide): 7.1B **Publicly Held**
SIC: 2672 Coated & laminated paper
PA: Avery Dennison Corporation
207 N Goode Ave
Glendale CA 91203
626 304-2000

(G-3089)
B-TEA BEVERAGE LLC
12-17 River Rd (07410-1490)
PHONE.................................201 512-8400
Michael Tseytin,
Felix Belferman,

Leon Bitelman,
EMP: 20
SQ FT: 1,600
SALES: 1MM **Privately Held**
SIC: 5149 2086 Tea; tea, iced: packaged in cans, bottles, etc.

(G-3090)
BEILIS DEVELOPMENT LLC
20-21 Wagaraw Rd Bldg 31b (07410-1322)
PHONE.................................862 203-3650
Maddy Rubenstein, *CEO*
Natty Rubenstien, *Mng Member*
Eugene Beilis,
▲ EMP: 10
SQ FT: 3,500
SALES: 6MM **Privately Held**
SIC: 2844 Cosmetic preparations

(G-3091)
BEST OF FARMS LLC
12-17 River Rd (07410-1490)
PHONE.................................201 512-8400
Felix Belferman, *Mng Member*
EMP: 5
SALES: 1MM **Privately Held**
SIC: 2024 Dairy based frozen desserts

(G-3092)
CALMAC MANUFACTURING CORP
3-00 Banta Pl (07410-3011)
PHONE.................................201 797-1511
Mark M Maccracken, *Chairman*
Brian Silvetti, *Vice Pres*
Dorothy Sullivan, *Treasurer*
Theresa Zambrano, *Admin Sec*
EMP: 50
SQ FT: 79,100
SALES (est): 11.3MM **Privately Held**
WEB: www.calmac.com
SIC: 3585 Refrigeration equipment, com-plete

(G-3093)
CATALOGUE PUBLISHERS INC
20-10 Maple Ave 35f-2 (07410-1591)
PHONE.................................973 423-3600
Gary Hegger, *President*
EMP: 11
SALES (est): 1.4MM **Privately Held**
WEB: www.cataloguepublishers.com
SIC: 2741 Catalogs: publishing only, not printed on site

(G-3094)
CREATIVE INNOVATIONS INC
Also Called: Metropolitan Cabinet Works
20-21 Wagaraw Rd Bldg 31b (07410-1322)
PHONE.................................973 636-9060
Joseph Batavia, *President*
Anita L Batavia, *Managing Dir*
EMP: 10
SQ FT: 13,500
SALES: 1MM **Privately Held**
SIC: 1751 2522 1799 Cabinet building & installation; office furniture, except wood; counter top installation

(G-3095)
DE ZAIO PRODUCTIONS INC
Also Called: Center Stage Productions
20-10 Maple Ave Bldg 31c (07410-1591)
PHONE.................................973 423-5000
Michael Dezaio, *President*
Jim McGrath, *Exec VP*
▲ EMP: 65
SQ FT: 56,095
SALES (est): 8.1MM **Privately Held**
SIC: 7389 3949 3942 Decoration service for special events; playground equipment; dolls & stuffed toys

(G-3096)
DESSAU INTERNATIONAL
Also Called: Dessau Company
15-01 Pollitt Dr Ste 10 (07410-2769)
PHONE.................................201 791-2005
Richard Dessau, *President*
◆ EMP: 20
SQ FT: 15,000
SALES: 4.5MM **Privately Held**
WEB: www.dessaudiamond.com
SIC: 3545 Cutting tools for machine tools

(G-3097)
DTROVISION LLC
Also Called: Purelink
22-10 States Rte 208 (07410)
PHONE.................................201 488-3232
Minsoo Park, *President*
Howard Schilling, *Sales Dir*
Jake Kim, *Manager*
Young CTS, *Associate*
EMP: 25
SQ FT: 9,000
SALES: 4.1MM **Privately Held**
WEB: www.dtrovision.com
SIC: 3651 Audio electronic systems

(G-3098)
EDGEWATER MANUFACTURING CO INC (PA)
17-10 Willow St (07410-2057)
PHONE.................................201 664-0022
Allen Fischbein, *President*
Dan Fischbein, *Vice Pres*
Rachell Fischbein, *Vice Pres*
▲ EMP: 37
SQ FT: 4,500
SALES (est): 7.9MM **Privately Held**
SIC: 3599 Machine shop, jobbing & repair

(G-3099)
EXCALIBUR BAGEL BKY EQUIP INC
4-1 Banta Pl (07410)
PHONE.................................201 797-2788
Richard Zinn, *President*
Erich Zinn, *Corp Secy*
Shelly Kuo, *Vice Pres*
▲ EMP: 20
SQ FT: 10,000
SALES (est): 3.4MM **Privately Held**
WEB: www.excalibur-equipment.com
SIC: 3556 Food products machinery

(G-3100)
FIRETRAINER SYMTRON
17-01 Pollitt Dr (07410-2801)
PHONE.................................201 794-0200
John J Henning, *Principal*
EMP: 7
SALES (est): 584.2K **Privately Held**
SIC: 3052 Rubber & plastics hose & belt-ings

(G-3101)
FISHER SCIENTIFIC CHEMICAL DIV
1 Reagent Ln (07410-2885)
PHONE.................................609 633-1422
▲ EMP: 25
SALES (est): 6.1MM **Privately Held**
SIC: 3826 Analytical instruments

(G-3102)
FISHER SCIENTIFIC COMPANY LLC
Fisher Fair Lawn
1 Reagent Ln (07410-2885)
PHONE.................................201 796-7100
Joe Baiunco, *Vice Pres*
Fred Vonrein, *Branch Mgr*
EMP: 260
SALES (corp-wide): 24.3B **Publicly Held**
WEB: www.fishersci.com
SIC: 2833 8748 2899 Medicinals & botan-icals; business consulting; chemical preparations
HQ: Fisher Scientific Company Llc
300 Industry Dr
Pittsburgh PA 15275
724 517-1500

(G-3103)
HENRY BROS ELECTRONICS INC (HQ)
17-01 Pollitt Dr Ste 5 (07410-2808)
PHONE.................................201 794-6500
James Henry, *CEO*
Ben Goodwin, *President*
Jim Henry, *President*
Fred Thomas, *Exec VP*
Jim Cotter, *Senior VP*
EMP: 58
SQ FT: 31,801

SALES (est): 39MM **Publicly Held**
SIC: 7373 3699 Computer integrated systems design; electrical equipment & supplies

(G-3104)
HISPANIC OUTLOOK-12 MAG INC
42-32 Debruin Dr (07410-5914)
P.O. Box 68, Paramus (07653-0068)
PHONE..................................201 587-8800
Jose Lopez ISA, *President*
Nicole Lopez ISA, *Vice Pres*
EMP: 7 EST: 2015
SALES (est): 489.6K **Privately Held**
SIC: 2731 Book publishing

(G-3105)
INDUSTRIAL CONSULTING MKTG INC
Also Called: ICM
20-21 Wagaraw Rd Bldg 39 (07410-1322)
PHONE..................................973 427-2474
▲ EMP: 23 EST: 1996
SQ FT: 40,000
SALES (est): 3.8MM **Privately Held**
SIC: 3281 Stone Fabrication Services

(G-3106)
INDUSTRIAL CONSULTING MKTG INC
Also Called: Industrial Consulting & MGT
20-21 Wagaraw Rd Bldg 38 (07410-1322)
PHONE..................................877 405-5200
Alsonso Bertoni, *President*
EMP: 23
SQ FT: 40,000
SALES (est): 547.6K **Privately Held**
SIC: 3281 Cut stone & stone products

(G-3107)
J M M R INC
Also Called: Arthroglide
25-9 Broadway (07410)
PHONE..................................201 612-5104
Joseph Molino, *President*
Michael Rebarber, *Exec VP*
EMP: 4
SALES (est): 264.1K **Privately Held**
WEB: www.jmmr.org
SIC: 8731 3842 Commercial physical research; prosthetic appliances

(G-3108)
JDV PRODUCTS INC
22-01 Raphael St (07410-3043)
PHONE..................................201 794-6467
Eva Dvorak, *President*
▲ EMP: 17
SQ FT: 16,000
SALES (est): 5.3MM **Privately Held**
WEB: www.jdvproducts.com
SIC: 5072 3423 3545 3546 Hand tools; hand & edge tools; machine tool accessories; power-driven handtools; engineering services

(G-3109)
KUIKEN BROTHERS COMPANY (PA)
6-02 Fair Lawn Ave (07410-1219)
P.O. Box 1040 (07410-8040)
PHONE..................................201 796-2082
Douglas Kuiken, *President*
Kenneth H Kuiken, *Vice Pres*
Matthew D Kuiken, *Vice Pres*
Nicholas M Kuiken, *Vice Pres*
Robert E Kuiken, *Vice Pres*
EMP: 38
SQ FT: 60,000
SALES: 156MM **Privately Held**
SIC: 5211 5031 3272 Millwork & lumber; building materials, exterior; building materials, interior; concrete stuctural support & building material

(G-3110)
MADE SOLUTIONS LLC
18-01 River Rd (07410-1257)
PHONE..................................201 254-3693
Jenna Saccurato,
EMP: 4
SQ FT: 6,000

(G-3111)
MONDELEZ GLOBAL LLC
Also Called: Nabisco
22-11 State Rt 208 (07410-2608)
PHONE..................................201 794-4000
Calvin Reed, *Manager*
EMP: 850 **Publicly Held**
WEB: www.kraftfoods.com
SIC: 2052 2051 8731 Biscuits, dry; bakery: wholesale or wholesale/retail combined; commercial physical research
HQ: Mondelez Global Llc
3 N Pkwy Ste 300
Deerfield IL 60015
847 943-4000

(G-3112)
MONDELEZ GLOBAL LLC
Also Called: Nabisco
21-05 Route 208 (07410-2601)
PHONE..................................201 794-4080
John Ferri, *Manager*
EMP: 1000 **Publicly Held**
WEB: www.kraftfoods.com
SIC: 4212 4225 2052 Local trucking, without storage; general warehousing; cookies & crackers
HQ: Mondelez Global Llc
3 N Pkwy Ste 300
Deerfield IL 60015
847 943-4000

(G-3113)
MY MAGIC
0 Plaza Rd (07410)
PHONE..................................201 703-1171
Meir Yeid, *Owner*
EMP: 5 EST: 1979
SALES (est): 226.1K **Privately Held**
SIC: 3999 Magic equipment, supplies & props

(G-3114)
NITKA GRAPHICS INC
13-63 Henrietta Ct (07410-5801)
PHONE..................................201 797-3000
Hy Nitka, *President*
EMP: 10
SQ FT: 6,000
SALES (est): 1.6MM **Privately Held**
WEB: www.nitkainc.com
SIC: 2752 Commercial printing, offset

(G-3115)
PRIVATE LABEL PRODUCTS INC
20-21 Wagaraw Rd Bldg 34 (07410-1322)
PHONE..................................201 773-4230
David Naor, *President*
▲ EMP: 20
SALES (est): 2.4MM **Privately Held**
WEB: www.foodoodler.com
SIC: 3953 Marking devices

(G-3116)
RANGECRAFT MANUFACTURING INC
4-40 Banta Pl (07410-3059)
PHONE..................................201 791-0440
Ramona Panus, *President*
EMP: 10
SQ FT: 5,500
SALES (est): 2MM **Privately Held**
SIC: 3444 Hoods, range: sheet metal

(G-3117)
RINKO ORTHOPEDIC APPLIANCES
25-09 Broadway Ste 1 (07410-3898)
PHONE..................................201 796-3121
Stephen Rinko, *President*
Terri Wassel, *Office Mgr*
EMP: 9 EST: 1955
SQ FT: 3,250
SALES (est): 1.4MM **Privately Held**
WEB: www.rinko.com
SIC: 3842 Orthopedic appliances; prosthetic appliances

(G-3118)
ROBERT MAIN SONS INC
20-21 Wagaraw Rd (07410-1324)
P.O. Box 159, Wyckoff (07481-0159)
PHONE..................................201 447-3700
Robert Main Jr, *President*
Zachary Main, *Principal*
Susan Main, *Corp Secy*
Timothy Den Bleyker, *Vice Pres*
William Main, *Vice Pres*
EMP: 40 EST: 1955
SQ FT: 29,000
SALES (est): 6.7MM
SALES (corp-wide): 35.5MM **Privately Held**
WEB: www.ramsco-inc.com
SIC: 3496 Miscellaneous fabricated wire products
PA: Main, Robert A & Sons Holding Company Inc
555 Goffle Rd
Wyckoff NJ 07481
201 447-3700

(G-3119)
ROBERT WEIDENER
Also Called: Weidener Construction
9 12th St (07410)
PHONE..................................201 703-5700
Robert Weidener, *President*
EMP: 7
SALES (est): 1.8MM **Privately Held**
SIC: 1389 Construction, repair & dismantling services

(G-3120)
SANDVIK INC (DH)
Also Called: Sandvik & Coromant
17-02 Nevins Rd (07410-2886)
P.O. Box 428 (07410-0428)
PHONE..................................201 794-5000
Rick Askin, *President*
Michel Obolensky, *General Mgr*
Ester Codina, *Managing Dir*
Lars Blomberg, *Vice Pres*
Ulf Johansson, *Vice Pres*
◆ EMP: 250 EST: 1919
SQ FT: 168,000
SALES (est): 866.1MM
SALES (corp-wide): 11.1B **Privately Held**
SIC: 3316 3317 3356 3315 Strip steel, cold-rolled: from purchased hot-rolled; wire, flat, cold-rolled strip: not made in hot-rolled mills; tubes, seamless steel; zirconium & zirconium alloy: rolling, drawing or extruding; titanium & titanium alloy: rolling, drawing or extruding; wire products, ferrous/iron: made in wiredrawing plants; machine tool accessories: bits, oil & gas field tools: rock; drilling tools for gas, oil or water wells
HQ: Sandvik Finance B.V.
's-Gravelandseweg 401
Schiedam
102 080-208

(G-3121)
SANDVIK INC
Also Called: Sandvik Coromant
17-2 Nevins Rd (07410)
PHONE..................................281 275-4800
Ray Benson, *Plant Mgr*
Virginia Varela-Eyre, *Marketing Mgr*
EMP: 129
SQ FT: 50,790
SALES (corp-wide): 11.1B **Privately Held**
SIC: 5084 5251 3545 Industrial machinery & equipment; tools; machine tool accessories
HQ: Sandvik, Inc.
17-02 Nevins Rd
Fair Lawn NJ 07410
201 794-5000

(G-3122)
STEPPIN OUT MAGAZINE
21-07 Maple Ave (07410-1524)
P.O. Box 626, Allendale (07401-0626)
PHONE..................................201 703-0911
EMP: 5
SALES (est): 291.9K **Privately Held**
SIC: 2721 Periodicals-Publishing/Printing

(G-3123)
STINGRAY SPORT PDTS LTD LBLTY
20-10 Maple Ave Bldg 35e (07410-1591)
PHONE..................................201 300-6482
Brad Lieberman,
EMP: 4
SQ FT: 2.000
SALES (est): 245.9K **Privately Held**
SIC: 3949 Winter sports equipment; water sports equipment; protective sporting equipment

(G-3124)
SYLVAN CHEMICAL CORPORATION
7 Prescott Pl (07410-4916)
PHONE..................................201 934-4224
Eugene Darvin, *President*
M W Edelstein, *Vice Pres*
Garrett Darvin, *Admin Sec*
EMP: 22
SQ FT: 3,500
SALES (est): 3MM **Privately Held**
WEB: www.sylvanchemical.com
SIC: 2899 5169 Chemical preparations; chemicals & allied products

(G-3125)
T G TYPE-O-GRAPHICS INC
19-03 Maple Ave Ste 3 (07410-1553)
PHONE..................................973 253-3333
Ruth Valdez, *President*
John F Valdez, *Vice Pres*
EMP: 5
SQ FT: 2,600
SALES: 1.2MM **Privately Held**
SIC: 2752 Commercial printing, offset

(G-3126)
TANIS CONCRETE
17-68 River Rd (07410-1206)
PHONE..................................201 796-1556
Charles Tanis, *President*
Mark Tanis, *President*
Jesus Martinez, *VP Bus Dvlpt*
Evelyn Tanis, *Treasurer*
Lou Terletsky, *Sales Mgr*
EMP: 35
SQ FT: 15,000
SALES (est): 6.4MM **Privately Held**
SIC: 3241 3273 8711 1771 Cement, hydraulic; ready-mixed concrete; construction & civil engineering; concrete work

(G-3127)
TARGET COATINGS INC
17-12 River Rd (07410-1206)
P.O. Box 1582, Rutherford (07070-0582)
PHONE..................................800 752-9922
Jeff Weiss, *President*
▼ EMP: 5
SQ FT: 10,000
SALES (est): 618K **Privately Held**
WEB: www.targetcoatings.com
SIC: 5198 2851 Paints; paints & allied products

(G-3128)
WAREHOUSE SOLUTIONS INC
3-29 27th St Fl 4 (07410-3817)
PHONE..................................201 880-1110
Hannah Lebovich, *Manager*
EMP: 14
SALES (corp-wide): 4.2MM **Privately Held**
SIC: 2541 5046 7373 6794 Cabinets, lockers & shelving; shelving, commercial & industrial; computer-aided design (CAD) systems service; patent buying, licensing, leasing
PA: Warehouse Solutions Inc.
365 W Passaic St Ste 235
Rochelle Park NJ 07662
201 880-1110

(G-3129)
WAYSIDE FENCE COMPANY INC
38-06 Broadway (07410-5400)
PHONE..................................201 791-7979
John Weglarz, *President*
EMP: 22
SQ FT: 5,000

SALES: 2.2MM **Privately Held**
WEB: www.waysidefenceco.com
SIC: 5211 5039 3446 Fencing; wire
fence, gates & accessories; partitions &
supports/studs, including accoustical systems

(G-3130)
ZIMMER BIOMET
Also Called: Biomet Fair Lawn, L.P.
20-01 Pollitt Dr (07410-2823)
PHONE.................................201 797-7300
Rolf Klime, *Principal*
▲ **EMP:** 150
SALES (est): 2.8MM
SALES (corp-wide): 7.9B **Publicly Held**
WEB: www.biomet.com
SIC: 3842 Surgical appliances & supplies
HQ: Biomet, Inc.
345 E Main St
Warsaw IN 46580
574 267-6639

(G-3131)
ZOLUU LLC
0-74 Saddle River Rd (07410-5509)
PHONE.................................862 686-1774
Mark Trujillo, *Mng Member*
EMP: 5
SALES: 1.5MM **Privately Held**
SIC: 7372 7389 Business oriented com-
puter software;

Fairfield
Essex County

(G-3132)
224 GRAPHICS INC
Also Called: Allied Wide
1275 Bloomfield Ave (07004-2708)
PHONE.................................973 433-9224
Carl Maul, *President*
Tom Vetter, *Treasurer*
Eric H Anderson, *Admin Sec*
EMP: 14
SQ FT: 20,000
SALES: 1MM **Privately Held**
SIC: 2759 7336 Poster & decal printing &
engraving; commercial art & graphic de-
sign

(G-3133)
**ACCURATE SCREW MACHINE
CORP**
Also Called: A S M
10 Audrey Pl (07004-3402)
PHONE.................................973 276-0379
Paul Stupinski, *Vice Pres*
James Callaghan, *Vice Pres*
Greg Corsi, *Safety Mgr*
Pete Fuentes, *Mfg Staff*
Peter Kaczor, *QC Mgr*
EMP: 60
SQ FT: 16,000
SALES (est): 14.1MM
SALES (corp-wide): 185.9MM **Privately
Held**
WEB: www.accuratescrew.com
SIC: 3451 3999 Screw machine products;
atomizers, toiletry
HQ: Matthew Warren, Inc.
9501 Tech Blvd Ste 401
Rosemont IL 60018
847 349-5760

(G-3134)
ADEMCO INC
Also Called: ADI Global Distribution
14 Madison Rd Unit A (07004-2331)
PHONE.................................973 808-8233
Joe Woitkowski, *Manager*
EMP: 7
SALES (corp-wide): 4.8B **Publicly Held**
WEB: www.adilink.com
SIC: 5063 3669 Electrical apparatus &
equipment; emergency alarms
HQ: Ademco Inc.
1985 Douglas Dr N
Golden Valley MN 55422
800 468-1502

(G-3135)
ADHERENCE SOLUTIONS LLC
75 Lane Rd Ste 404 (07004-1000)
PHONE.................................800 521-2269
Dann Ferara, *CEO*
EMP: 4
SALES (est): 214.7K **Privately Held**
SIC: 8748 7372 Business consulting; busi-
ness oriented computer software

(G-3136)
AIR POWER INC
25 Commerce Rd Ste N (07004-1620)
P.O. Box 1449, West Caldwell (07007-
1449)
PHONE.................................973 882-5418
Hugh Rooney Jr, *President*
Victor Giambattista, *Vice Pres*
EMP: 35
SQ FT: 13,000
SALES: 5.3MM **Privately Held**
SIC: 3444 1711 Ducts, sheet metal; refrig-
eration contractor

(G-3137)
ALISON CONTROL INC
35 Daniel Rd W (07004-2558)
PHONE.................................973 575-7100
Gene Benzenberg, *President*
EMP: 20
SQ FT: 13,500
SALES (est): 4.1MM **Privately Held**
WEB: www.alisoncontrol.com
SIC: 3829 Fire detector systems, non-elec-
tric

(G-3138)
**ALL MTALS FRGE GROUP LTD
LBLTY (PA)**
75 Lane Rd Ste 303 (07004-1061)
PHONE.................................973 276-5000
Elizabeth Rochette, *Accounting Mgr*
Lewis A Weiss, *Mng Member*
◆ **EMP:** 25
SALES (est): 4.8MM **Privately Held**
SIC: 3462 Iron & steel forgings

(G-3139)
**ALLIED PRINTING-GRAPHICS
INC**
4 Madison Rd (07004-2309)
PHONE.................................973 227-0520
Dominick Pascarella, *President*
Ralph Magliocchetti, *Shareholder*
EMP: 5
SALES (est): 1.3MM **Privately Held**
WEB: www.printallied.com
SIC: 2752 Commercial printing, offset

(G-3140)
AM-MAC INCORPORATED
311 Route 46 W Ste C (07004-2419)
PHONE.................................973 575-7567
Judith Spritzer, *President*
John M Spritzer, *Vice Pres*
▲ **EMP:** 10
SQ FT: 12,000
SALES (est): 5.1MM **Privately Held**
WEB: www.am-mac.com
SIC: 3556 5046 5084 Food products ma-
chinery; commercial cooking & food serv-
ice equipment; food industry machinery

(G-3141)
AMARK WIRE LLC
18 Passaic Ave Unit 6 (07004-3834)
PHONE.................................973 882-7818
Joseph Whittaker,
Trac Dam,
Mario Salerno,
George Whittaker,
EMP: 5 EST: 2011
SQ FT: 5,000
SALES (est): 483.8K **Privately Held**
SIC: 3315 Steel wire & related products

(G-3142)
**AMERICAN NATIONAL RED
CROSS**
209 Fairfield Rd (07004-2420)
PHONE.................................973 797-3300
Jocelyn Gilman, *Exec Dir*
EMP: 39

SALES (corp-wide): 2.6B **Privately Held**
WEB: www.redcross.org
SIC: 3999 Buttons: Red Cross, union,
identification
PA: The American National Red Cross
430 17th St Nw
Washington DC 20006
202 737-8300

(G-3143)
**ANDERSON & VREELAND INC
(PA)**
8 Evans St (07004-2200)
P.O. Box 1246, Caldwell (07007-1246)
PHONE.................................973 227-2270
Howard Vreeland Jr, *Ch of Bd*
Darin Lyon, *President*
Lonnie Grieser, *Principal*
Sean Sawa, *Regional Mgr*
Drew Elisius, *Senior VP*
◆ **EMP:** 25 EST: 1978
SALES (est): 74MM **Privately Held**
WEB: www.andersonvreeland.com
SIC: 5084 3555 Printing trades machinery,
equipment & supplies; printing plates

(G-3144)
API INC
10 Industrial Rd (07004-3018)
PHONE.................................973 227-9335
Irwan Rusli, *Principal*
Ruo Xu, *Principal*
EMP: 15 EST: 2001
SALES (est): 2.6MM **Privately Held**
SIC: 2834 Pharmaceutical preparations

(G-3145)
**ARLINGTON PRCSION
CMPNENTS LLC**
Also Called: Arlington Machine & Tool Co
90 New Dutch Ln (07004-2515)
PHONE.................................973 276-1377
John J Staudinger, *President*
▲ **EMP:** 50
SQ FT: 56,000
SALES (est): 389.8K
SALES (corp-wide): 13.9MM **Privately
Held**
SIC: 3728 Aircraft body assemblies & parts
HQ: Whi Global, Llc
13914 E Admiral Pl
Tulsa OK 74116
918 933-6500

(G-3146)
ARTHUR SCHUMAN INC (PA)
Also Called: Schuman Cheese
40 New Dutch Ln (07004-2514)
PHONE.................................973 227-0030
Neal Schuman, *CEO*
Patrick O'Callaghan, *Vice Pres*
Glenn Carrara, *Opers Staff*
Larry Schaefer, *CFO*
Allison Schuman, *Regl Sales Mgr*
◆ **EMP:** 85
SQ FT: 90,000
SALES (est): 181.1MM **Privately Held**
WEB: www.arthurschuman.com
SIC: 2022 Cheese, natural & processed

(G-3147)
ASHA44 LLC
175 Us Highway 46 Unit A (07004-2327)
PHONE.................................201 306-3600
Lester Samuels, *Managing Dir*
Andrea C Samuels, *Managing Dir*
◆ **EMP:** 25
SQ FT: 60,000
SALES: 10MM **Privately Held**
SIC: 2752 2269 Commercial printing, off-
set; printing of narrow fabrics

(G-3148)
ASPE INC
9 Spielman Rd (07004-3403)
P.O. Box 10363 (07004-6363)
PHONE.................................973 808-1155
Rudolph Sachs, *CEO*
Khanh Dim, *Office Mgr*
EMP: 20
SALES: 2.1MM **Privately Held**
WEB: www.aspeusa.com
SIC: 3679 3469 3053 Hermetic seals for
electronic equipment; metal stampings;
gaskets, packing & sealing devices

(G-3149)
AW MACHINERY LLC
7 Just Rd (07004-3407)
PHONE.................................973 882-3223
Rudy Fernandez, *Sales Staff*
Nestor E Gener,
Arthur K Watson,
▼ **EMP:** 11
SQ FT: 9,000
SALES (est): 1.9MM **Privately Held**
WEB: www.awmachinery.com
SIC: 3357 3496 Fiber optic cable (insu-
lated); miscellaneous fabricated wire
products; cable, uninsulated wire: made
from purchased wire

(G-3150)
**BABCOCK & WILCOX POWR
GENERATN**
277 Fairfield Rd Ste 331a (07004-1942)
PHONE.................................973 227-7008
Steve Dutkiewicz, *Branch Mgr*
Ann Shuster, *Clerk*
EMP: 14
SALES (corp-wide): 1B **Publicly Held**
SIC: 3511 Steam turbines
HQ: The Babcock & Wilcox Company
20 S Van Buren Ave
Barberton OH 44203
330 753-4511

(G-3151)
**BAR-LO CARBON PRODUCTS
INC**
31 Daniel Rd (07004-2520)
P.O. Box 10031 (07004-6031)
PHONE.................................973 227-2717
Barry M Flowers, *President*
Lois S Flowers, *Admin Sec*
▲ **EMP:** 26
SQ FT: 25,000
SALES (est): 5.1MM **Privately Held**
WEB: www.barlocarbon.com
SIC: 3545 Precision tools, machinists'

(G-3152)
BART FOODS GROUP LLC
1275 Bloomfield Ave (07004-2708)
PHONE.................................973 650-8837
Gary Bartholomew, *Mng Member*
EMP: 4
SQ FT: 300
SALES (est): 484.7K **Privately Held**
SIC: 5142 2037 Frozen fish, meat & poul-
try; frozen fruits & vegetables

(G-3153)
BELLWOOD AEROMATICS INC
4 Spielman Rd (07004-3404)
PHONE.................................201 670-4617
Eric Beldner, *President*
Adam Beldner, *Vice Pres*
EMP: 4
SALES: 1MM **Privately Held**
WEB: www.belwoodaromatics.com
SIC: 2844 Toilet preparations

(G-3154)
BENCO INC
Also Called: Benco Products New York
10 Madison Rd Ste E (07004-2325)
P.O. Box 866, Pine Brook (07058-0866)
PHONE.................................973 575-4440
Karen Pyonin, *CEO*
Paul Pyonin, *President*
Chris Carey, *Partner*
Mike Day, *Vice Pres*
Kevin Enriquez, *Project Mgr*
EMP: 17
SQ FT: 9,200
SALES: 2MM **Privately Held**
SIC: 1796 3444 5039 5211 Installing
building equipment; sheet metalwork; pre-
fabricated buildings; prefabricated build-
ings; partitions & fixtures, except wood;
vitreous plumbing fixtures

(G-3155)
**BERGEN CABLE TECHNOLOGY
LLC (PA)**
343 Kaplan Dr (07004-2510)
PHONE.................................973 276-9596
Terry Boboige, *President*
Ken Vandervelde, *Plant Mgr*
Debbie Hillman, *Purch Agent*

GEOGRAPHIC

Surendra Patel, *QC Dir*
Ronda Capilli, *Controller*
▲ EMP: 25
SQ FT: 15,000
SALES (est): 4.4MM **Privately Held**
WEB: www.bergencable.com
SIC: 3542 3315 Crimping machinery, metal; cable, steel: insulated or armored

(G-3156)
BERGIO INTERNATIONAL INC (PA)
12 Daniel Rd (07004-2536)
PHONE..................................973 227-3230
Berge Abajian, *Ch of Bd*
EMP: 6
SQ FT: 1,730
SALES: 608.7K **Publicly Held**
SIC: 3911 Jewelry mountings & trimmings

(G-3157)
BEVERAGE WORKS NJ INC
10 Dwight Pl (07004-3414)
PHONE..................................973 439-5700
Erich Becker, *Manager*
EMP: 19 **Privately Held**
SIC: 2086 Bottled & canned soft drinks
PA: The Beverage Works Ny Inc
    1800 State Route 34 # 203
    Wall Township NJ 07719

(G-3158)
BILT RITE TOOL & DIE CO INC
29 Montesano Rd (07004-3387)
PHONE..................................973 227-2882
Dennis George, *President*
EMP: 8 EST: 1956
SQ FT: 4,000
SALES: 2MM **Privately Held**
SIC: 3312 3469 Tool & die steel & alloys; metal stampings

(G-3159)
BONO USA INC
19 Gardner Rd Ste E (07004-2204)
PHONE..................................973 978-7361
Salvatore Russotiesi, *President*
Salvatore Bono, *General Mgr*
▲ EMP: 3
SALES: 5MM **Privately Held**
SIC: 2032 Italian foods: packaged in cans, jars, etc.

(G-3160)
C & M SHADE CORP
53 Dwight Pl (07004-3311)
PHONE..................................201 807-1200
Allen Francus, *President*
Ken Niepokoy, *COO*
William D Apostol, *Vice Pres*
Billy Chien, *Vice Pres*
Brian Rooney, *Info Tech Dir*
EMP: 32
SQ FT: 21,000
SALES (est): 3.8MM **Privately Held**
SIC: 2591 Window shades

(G-3161)
C & S MACHINE INC
22 Commerce Rd Ste Q (07004-1604)
PHONE..................................973 882-1097
Ronald J Woods, *President*
EMP: 15
SQ FT: 12,500
SALES (est): 1.5MM **Privately Held**
SIC: 7699 3552 Industrial equipment services; textile machinery

(G-3162)
CALIZ - MALKO LLC
66 Clinton Rd (07004-2910)
PHONE..................................973 207-5200
Cris Caliz, *CEO*
Alla Malko,
EMP: 4
SQ FT: 5,000
SALES: 200K **Privately Held**
SIC: 2052 Cookies

(G-3163)
CANFIELD PROPERTY GROUP INC
Also Called: Canfield Clinic Systems
253 Passaic Ave Ste 1 (07004-2524)
PHONE..................................973 276-0300

Douglas Canfield, *President*
Joan Newton, *Vice Pres*
Lisa Cramer, *Project Mgr*
Bill Halas, *CFO*
Scott Vansickle, *Info Tech Mgr*
▲ EMP: 15
SALES (est): 2.2MM **Privately Held**
SIC: 3841 Surgical & medical instruments

(G-3164)
CARECAM INTERNATIONAL INC
10 Plog Rd (07004-3302)
PHONE..................................973 227-0720
Haren Gupta MD, *CEO*
Ravinder Jain PHD, *President*
EMP: 20
SQ FT: 8,500
SALES (est): 1.8MM **Privately Held**
SIC: 3089 Blister or bubble formed packaging, plastic

(G-3165)
CARET CORPORATION (PA)
180 Passaic Ave Ste 3 (07004-3513)
PHONE..................................973 423-6098
Ivonne Ruggles, *President*
EMP: 12
SALES (est): 1.4MM **Privately Held**
SIC: 2844 Toilet preparations

(G-3166)
CARTRIDGE ACTUATED DEVICES (HQ)
Also Called: C A D
51 Dwight Pl (07004-3311)
PHONE..................................973 575-8760
James Yake, *Ch of Bd*
Jim Yeats, *President*
Rachel Catapano, *Sales Staff*
John Grant, *Exec Dir*
Dawn Zinn, *Receptionist*
EMP: 30 EST: 1962
SALES (est): 8.1MM
SALES (corp-wide): 351.7MM **Privately Held**
WEB: www.cartactdev.com
SIC: 2892 Explosives
PA: The Fike Corporation
    704 Sw 10th St
    Blue Springs MO 64015
    816 229-3405

(G-3167)
CHICAGO PNEUMATIC TOOL
90 New Dutch Ln (07004-2515)
PHONE..................................973 276-1377
John J Staudinger, *Manager*
EMP: 7
SALES (corp-wide): 4.2B **Privately Held**
SIC: 3451 Screw machine products
HQ: Chicago Pneumatic Tool
    222 Getty Ave
    Clifton NJ 07011
    973 928-5222

(G-3168)
CK MANUFACTURING INC
8 Gardner Rd (07004-2206)
PHONE..................................973 808-3500
Brian W Kaltner, *President*
Daniel Dall'ava, *Chairman*
Richard Cafaro, *Vice Pres*
Ruth Stern, *Admin Sec*
▲ EMP: 20 EST: 1953
SQ FT: 5,000
SALES (est): 2.5MM **Privately Held**
SIC: 3544 Industrial molds

(G-3169)
CLAREMONT DISTILLED SPIRITS
25 Commerce Rd (07004-1619)
PHONE..................................973 227-7027
EMP: 10
SALES (est): 1.2MM **Privately Held**
SIC: 2085 Distilled & blended liquors

(G-3170)
CNI CERAMIC NOZZLES INC
23 Commerce Rd Ste L (07004-1609)
PHONE..................................973 276-1535
Stephen Ziegler, *President*
Thomas Calandrillo, *Vice Pres*
EMP: 8 EST: 1964
SQ FT: 5,000

SALES (est): 710K **Privately Held**
SIC: 3548 Welding & cutting apparatus & accessories

(G-3171)
COLUMBIA PRESS INC
12 Industrial Rd (07004-3018)
P.O. Box 10723 (07004-6723)
PHONE..................................973 575-6535
Charles Puleo, *President*
Alan Puleo, *Vice Pres*
EMP: 32 EST: 1977
SALES (est): 4MM **Privately Held**
SIC: 2752 Commercial printing, offset

(G-3172)
COMMAND NUTRITIONALS LLC
10 Washington Ave Ste 1 (07004-3840)
PHONE..................................973 227-8210
Aakash Dadhania, *Plant Supt*
Rosa Figueiredo, *Office Mgr*
Dave Martocci, *Manager*
Scott Biedron,
▲ EMP: 40 EST: 1972
SQ FT: 55,000
SALES (est): 10.2MM **Privately Held**
WEB: www.commandnutritionals.com
SIC: 2834 Vitamin, nutrient & hematinic preparations for human use

(G-3173)
CONSTANT SERVICES INC
Also Called: Csi
17 Commerce Rd Ste 2 (07004-1662)
PHONE..................................973 227-2990
Vincent Pepe, *President*
Anthony Pepe, *Vice Pres*
Dominick Pepe, *Admin Sec*
EMP: 35
SQ FT: 39,000
SALES (est): 4.5MM **Privately Held**
SIC: 2754 Commercial printing, gravure

(G-3174)
CONTINUITY LOGIC LLC
55 Lane Rd Ste 303 (07004-1015)
PHONE..................................866 321-5079
Tejas Katwala,
Peter Christensen,
EMP: 59
SALES: 7.6MM **Privately Held**
SIC: 7372 Application computer software

(G-3175)
CONTROL & POWER SYSTEMS INC
Also Called: Dmz Industries
17 Spielman Rd (07004-3409)
PHONE..................................973 439-0500
Dov Shevich, *President*
David Lyon, *Vice Pres*
Adam Shea, *Purchasing*
Rafal Skrzypczak, *Engineer*
Kristina Astman, *Technology*
▲ EMP: 34
SQ FT: 14,584
SALES (est): 10.4MM **Privately Held**
WEB: www.c-p-s.com
SIC: 3625 Electric controls & control accessories, industrial

(G-3176)
CONTROL INSTRUMENTS CORP
25 Law Dr (07004-3206)
PHONE..................................973 575-9114
Christopher Schaeffer, *President*
Matthew Schaeffer, *Chairman*
James M Schaeffer, *Vice Pres*
John Schaeffer, *Vice Pres*
Pravin Patel, *Engineer*
EMP: 31
SQ FT: 24,000
SALES (est): 7.7MM **Privately Held**
WEB: www.controlinstruments.com
SIC: 3823 On-stream gas/liquid analysis instruments, industrial

(G-3177)
CUSTOM LABELS INC
345 Kaplan Dr (07004-2510)
PHONE..................................973 473-1934
Abraham Rubin, *President*
EMP: 4
SQ FT: 7,100

SALES (est): 380K **Privately Held**
WEB: www.cpp-flexo.com
SIC: 2759 Labels & seals: printing

(G-3178)
DATASCOPE CORP (DH)
Also Called: Maquet
15 Law Dr (07004-3206)
PHONE..................................973 244-6100
Donald R Lemma, *Vice Pres*
Mark Rappaport, *Vice Pres*
S Arieh Zak, *Vice Pres*
Gary Schwarz, *Research*
Shrenik Daftary, *Engineer*
◆ EMP: 200 EST: 1964
SQ FT: 75,000
SALES (est): 117.5MM
SALES (corp-wide): 6.1B **Privately Held**
WEB: www.datascope.com
SIC: 3845 Electrotherapeutic apparatus; electromedical apparatus
HQ: Getinge Ab
    Lindholmspiren 7a
    Goteborg 417 5
    103 350-000

(G-3179)
DAUM INC (DH)
368 Passaic Ave Ste 300 (07004-2008)
PHONE..................................862 210-8522
Henri Dequatrebarbes, *CEO*
Thierry Collot, *Exec VP*
▲ EMP: 4
SALES (est): 86.1K **Privately Held**
WEB: www.daumusa.com
SIC: 3229 Pressed & blown glass
HQ: Daum
    22 Rue De La Tremoille
    Paris 8e Arrondissement 75008
    155 343-110

(G-3180)
DAVEN INDUSTRIES INC
55 Dwight Pl (07004-3311)
PHONE..................................973 808-8848
Lou Lever, *President*
Phillip Stahl, *Vice Pres*
EMP: 20 EST: 1976
SQ FT: 26,000
SALES (est): 2.9MM **Privately Held**
WEB: www.davenindustries.com
SIC: 3599 3568 3545 Custom machinery; power transmission equipment; machine tool accessories

(G-3181)
DECKHOUSE COMMUNICATIONS INC
1275 Bloomfield Ave Ste 7 (07004-2736)
PHONE..................................201 961-5564
Neslihan Akpinar, *Ch of Bd*
Yasemin Akpinar, *President*
Adnan Akpinar, *COO*
EMP: 6
SQ FT: 1,500
SALES (est): 3.5MM **Privately Held**
SIC: 3663 Satellites, communications

(G-3182)
DEE JAY PRINTING INC
16 Passaic Ave Unit 3 (07004-3835)
PHONE..................................973 227-7787
Jeff Jaffe, *President*
EMP: 8
SQ FT: 5,000
SALES: 900K **Privately Held**
SIC: 2752 Commercial printing, offset

(G-3183)
DELTA CIRCUITS INC
26 Spielman Rd (07004-3412)
PHONE..................................973 575-3000
Pravin Bhuva, *President*
Dimple Bhuva, *Vice Pres*
▲ EMP: 26
SQ FT: 30,000
SALES (est): 4.6MM **Privately Held**
WEB: www.deltacircuits-nj.com
SIC: 3672 Printed circuit boards

(G-3184)
DENTISTRY TODAY INC
100 Passaic Ave Ste 220 (07004-3508)
PHONE..................................973 882-4700
Paul Radcliffe, *President*
John Lannon, *President*

Damon C Adams, *Principal*
Richard Gawel, *Editor*
James F Radcliffe, *Vice Pres*
EMP: 20
SQ FT: 3,700
SALES (est): 3.2MM **Privately Held**
WEB: www.dentistrytoday.net
SIC: 2721 Trade journals: publishing only, not printed on site

(G-3185)
DESIGN OF TOMORROW INC
Also Called: Educational & Lab Systems
24 Sherwood Ln (07004-3602)
PHONE.................................973 227-1000
David Roitburg, *President*
Alex Gizersky, *Vice Pres*
Leon Roitburg, *Treasurer*
▲ **EMP:** 15
SQ FT: 12,000
SALES (est): 4MM **Privately Held**
SIC: 2431 8734 3553 Millwork; testing laboratories; scarfing machines, woodworking

(G-3186)
DM GRAPHIC CENTER LLC
26 Commerce Rd Ste L (07004-1606)
PHONE.................................973 882-8990
Jeannette Matin,
Kaweh K Matin,
EMP: 10
SQ FT: 5,000
SALES (est): 1.5MM **Privately Held**
WEB: www.dmgraphiccenter.com
SIC: 7389 7336 2789 Printers' services: folding, collating; graphic arts & related design; binding only: books, pamphlets, magazines, etc.

(G-3187)
DREW & ROGERS INC (PA)
30 Plymouth St Ste 2 (07004-1622)
PHONE.................................973 575-6210
Thomas M Rogers, *President*
Eugene Aleshevich, *Vice Pres*
Michael Cecala, *Vice Pres*
Greg McDermott, *Vice Pres*
Michael Monteleone, *Vice Pres*
▲ **EMP:** 31 **EST:** 1944
SQ FT: 30,000
SALES (est): 17.4MM **Privately Held**
WEB: www.drew-rogers.com
SIC: 5112 5199 7336 2761 Business forms; advertising specialties; commercial art & graphic design; manifold business forms

(G-3188)
DRIVE-MASTER CO INC
37 Daniel Rd (07004-2521)
PHONE.................................973 808-9709
Peter B Ruprecht Sr, *President*
Christina Knapik, *Vice Pres*
Peter B Ruprecht Jr, *Vice Pres*
Adrienne Ruprecht, *CFO*
Shelby Wells, *Sales Staff*
EMP: 14
SQ FT: 20,185
SALES (est): 3.7MM **Privately Held**
WEB: www.drive-master.com
SIC: 7532 5511 3711 Top & body repair & paint shops; automobiles, new & used; motor vehicles & car bodies

(G-3189)
EDSTON MANUFACTURING COMPANY
125 Clinton Rd Unit 2 (07004-2929)
PHONE.................................908 647-0116
Paul Zuzock, *President*
Emily B Weston, *President*
Jonathan P Weston, *Vice Pres*
Charles F Weston, *Admin Sec*
EMP: 6 **EST:** 1947
SQ FT: 4,900
SALES: 646.2K **Privately Held**
SIC: 3451 3542 Screw machine products; thread rolling machines

(G-3190)
ELMI MACHINE TOOL CORP
15 Spielman Rd 2 (07004-3403)
P.O. Box 1112, Caldwell (07007-1112)
PHONE.................................973 882-1277
Victor Vitencz, *President*

Christine Armitage, *Administration*
EMP: 5 **EST:** 1966
SQ FT: 1,700
SALES: 900K **Privately Held**
WEB: www.elmimachine.com
SIC: 3599 Machine shop, jobbing & repair

(G-3191)
EMSE CORP
Also Called: Emseco
10 Plog Rd (07004-3302)
PHONE.................................973 227-9221
K Alex Rothenberg, *President*
Larry Savastano, *Vice Pres*
Gary Kroeger, *Treasurer*
◆ **EMP:** 13
SQ FT: 8,500
SALES (est): 2.3MM **Privately Held**
WEB: www.emse.com
SIC: 3821 3841 3563 Vacuum pumps, laboratory; surgical & medical instruments; air & gas compressors

(G-3192)
ESSEX WEST GRAPHICS INC (PA)
305 Fairfield Ave (07004-3831)
PHONE.................................973 227-2400
Donald Alldian, *President*
Thomas Guth, *Exec VP*
EMP: 55
SQ FT: 16,700
SALES (est): 5.3MM **Privately Held**
WEB: www.westessexgraphics.com
SIC: 2796 Platemaking services

(G-3193)
EVS BROADCAST EQUIPMENT INC (HQ)
9 Law Dr Ste 4 (07004-3233)
PHONE.................................973 575-7811
Gregory Macchia, *Senior VP*
Johan Vounckx, *Senior VP*
Rod Carrelus, *Finance Mgr*
Anne-Sophie Dupont, *Human Res Mgr*
Angela Chambers, *Executive*
EMP: 25 **EST:** 2007
SALES (est): 2.9MM **Privately Held**
SIC: 3663 Studio equipment, radio & television broadcasting

(G-3194)
EVS BROADCAST EQUIPMENT INC
Also Called: Evs
700 Route 46 E Ste 300 (07004-1532)
PHONE.................................973 575-7811
Frederic Garroy, *General Mgr*
Olivier Heurteaux, *Senior VP*
Quentin Grutman, *Vice Pres*
James Stellpflug, *Vice Pres*
Brandon Gassett, *Technical Staff*
EMP: 15 **Privately Held**
WEB: www.evs-global.com
SIC: 3577 Disk & diskette equipment, except drives
HQ: E.V.S. Broadcast Equipment, Inc.
9 Law Dr Ste 4
Fairfield NJ 07004
973 575-7811

(G-3195)
EXCALIBUR MIRETTI GROUP LLC
285 Eldridge Rd (07004-2508)
PHONE.................................973 808-8399
Roberto Santilli, *Engineer*
Angelo Miretti,
▲ **EMP:** 15
SALES (est): 8.9MM **Privately Held**
WEB: www.exequipment.com
SIC: 5084 3537 Trucks, industrial; forklift trucks

(G-3196)
EXCELLENT BAKERY EQUIPMENT CO
19 Spielman Rd (07004-3409)
P.O. Box 512, Cedar Knolls (07927-0512)
PHONE.................................973 244-1664
Karin M Seruga, *President*
▲ **EMP:** 20
SQ FT: 30,000

SALES (est): 3.5MM **Privately Held**
WEB: www.excellent-bagels.com
SIC: 3556 Food products machinery

(G-3197)
EXPRESS PRINTING SERVICES INC
26 Commerce Rd Ste L (07004-1606)
PHONE.................................973 585-7355
Val Digiacinto, *Owner*
EMP: 4
SALES (est): 122.8K **Privately Held**
SIC: 2752 Commercial printing, lithographic

(G-3198)
EXTREME DIGITAL GRAPHICS INC
7 Kingsbridge Rd Ste 1 (07004-2141)
PHONE.................................973 227-5599
Pat Basile, *President*
Lynn Basile, *Vice Pres*
Berry Basile, *Accounts Exec*
EMP: 10
SALES (est): 1.3MM **Privately Held**
SIC: 2752 Commercial printing, lithographic

(G-3199)
FAIRFIELD LAUNDRY MCHY CORP
5 Montesano Rd Ste 1 (07004-3309)
PHONE.................................973 575-4330
Raymond Hall, *President*
Patrick Niland Sr, *Vice Pres*
EMP: 25
SQ FT: 12,000
SALES (est): 4.2MM **Privately Held**
WEB: www.flmcorp.com
SIC: 3582 Commercial laundry equipment

(G-3200)
FAIRFIELD METAL LTD LBLTY CO
9 Audrey Pl (07004-3401)
PHONE.................................973 276-8440
Arkadiuxz Baginksi, *Mng Member*
EMP: 12
SALES (est): 2.1MM **Privately Held**
SIC: 3444 Siding, sheet metal

(G-3201)
FINN & EMMA LLC
Also Called: Finn Emma
1275 Bloomfield Ave Ste 5 (07004-2736)
PHONE.................................973 227-7770
Maya Heenan, *Accounts Mgr*
Anna Schwengle, *Mng Member*
▲ **EMP:** 5
SALES (est): 406.4K **Privately Held**
SIC: 2329 2261 5651 Athletic (warmup, sweat & jogging) suits: men's & boys'; calendering of cotton fabrics; unisex clothing stores

(G-3202)
FLM GRAPHICS CORPORATION (PA)
123 Lehigh Dr (07004-3010)
PHONE.................................973 575-9450
Frank Misischia, *Ch of Bd*
Tony Gagliardi, *Exec VP*
Vincent Gagliardi, *Exec VP*
Mike Monk, *Vice Pres*
Alan Poidomani, *Production*
EMP: 60 **EST:** 1972
SQ FT: 44,000
SALES (est): 18.8MM **Privately Held**
SIC: 2752 7374 Commercial printing, offset; computer graphics service

(G-3203)
FLOR LIFT OF N J INC
Also Called: Florlift of NJ
19 Gardner Rd Ste M (07004-2204)
PHONE.................................973 429-2200
Casper Vivona, *President*
Louisa Vivona, *Vice Pres*
EMP: 20
SQ FT: 12,000
SALES (est): 328.4K **Privately Held**
SIC: 3534 3535 Elevators & equipment; conveyors & conveying equipment

(G-3204)
FLOWSERVE CORPORATION
142 Clinton Rd (07004-2914)
PHONE.................................973 227-4565
Amy Hartman, *Controller*
EMP: 55
SALES (corp-wide): 3.8B **Publicly Held**
SIC: 3561 Industrial pumps & parts
PA: Flowserve Corporation
5215 N Oconnor Blvd Connor
Irving TX 75039
972 443-6500

(G-3205)
FORDHAM INC
20 Gloria Ln (07004-3306)
PHONE.................................973 575-7840
Thomas R Buckley, *CEO*
James Lombard, *President*
Karen Morgan, *Vice Pres*
EMP: 40
SQ FT: 15,000
SALES (est): 2.6MM **Privately Held**
WEB: www.fordhamjackets.com
SIC: 5999 2759 2339 2337 Banners, flags, decals & posters; commercial printing; women's & misses' outerwear; women's & misses' suits & coats; men's & boys' suits & coats
PA: Redi-Direct Marketing, Inc.
107 Little Falls Rd
Fairfield NJ 07004

(G-3206)
FOREMOST MACHINE BUILDERS INC
23 Spielman Rd (07004-3488)
P.O. Box 10155 (07004-6155)
PHONE.................................973 227-0700
Marlene C Heydenreich, *President*
Clifford J Weinpel, *Exec VP*
Clifford Weinpel, *Vice Pres*
Tim Downing, *Engineer*
Dave Revette, *Electrical Engi*
▲ **EMP:** 51 **EST:** 1947
SQ FT: 48,000
SALES (est): 12.8MM **Privately Held**
WEB: www.foremostmachine.com
SIC: 3559 3535 3532 Plastics working machinery; conveyors & conveying equipment; crushing, pulverizing & screening equipment

(G-3207)
FRAMEWARE INC
Also Called: Profiles of Frameware
8 Audrey Pl (07004-3402)
PHONE.................................800 582-5608
Dean De Luccia, *President*
Carmen Luccia, *VP Opers*
Francklin Ermeus, *Purchasing*
Jim Stemper, *Sales Staff*
◆ **EMP:** 18
SALES (est): 4.3MM **Privately Held**
WEB: www.framewareinc.com
SIC: 3469 2499 3354 7389 Metal stampings; picture frame molding, finished; shapes, extruded aluminum;

(G-3208)
FRIMPEKS INC
30 Sherwood Ln Ste 6 (07004-3603)
PHONE.................................201 266-0116
Sonay Karamanci, *President*
◆ **EMP:** 11
SALES (est): 2.7MM
SALES (corp-wide): 99.6MM **Privately Held**
SIC: 2891 Adhesives
PA: Frimpeks Kimya Ve Etiket Sanayi Ticaret Anonim Sirketi
Polaris Plaza, 54..57 Ahi Evran Caddesi
Istanbul (Europe) 34460
212 867-1000

(G-3209)
FUJITSU GENERAL AMERICA INC
353 Rte 46 W (07004-2415)
PHONE.................................973 575-0380
Tedd Rozylowicz, *President*
Roy Kuczera, *Senior VP*
Cameron S Brown, *Engineer*
Susumu Ohkawara, *CFO*

Cathy Miller, *Accountant*
◆ EMP: 51 EST: 1995
SQ FT: 25,000
SALES (est): 162.4MM **Privately Held**
WEB: www.fujitsugeneral.com
SIC: 3585 Heating & air conditioning combination units
PA: Fujitsu General Limited
　　3-3-17, Suenaga, Takatsu-Ku
　　Kawasaki KNG 213-0

(G-3210)
G P R COMPANY INC
8 Spielman Rd (07004-3404)
PHONE..........................973 227-6160
George H Verhoest, *President*
Richard Verhoest, *Corp Secy*
Paul R Verhoest, *Vice Pres*
Vicky Huynh, *Office Mgr*
EMP: 47
SQ FT: 25,000
SALES: 8.5MM **Privately Held**
WEB: www.gprco.com
SIC: 3599 Machine shop, jobbing & repair

(G-3211)
GALLERIA ENTERPRISES INC
26 Commerce Rd Ste I (07004-1606)
PHONE..........................646 416-6683
Joe Simeone, *President*
Davis Lin, *Vice Pres*
Anthony Margulis, *Vice Pres*
▲ EMP: 5
SQ FT: 3,400
SALES (est): 2.5MM **Privately Held**
SIC: 3999 Umbrellas, canes & parts

(G-3212)
GARFIELD INDUSTRIES INC
62 Clinton Rd Ste 1 (07004-6216)
P.O. Box 839, Caldwell (07007-0839)
PHONE..........................973 575-3322
Deborah Gladstone, *President*
Steven Gelvan, *Vice Pres*
▲ EMP: 32 EST: 1949
SQ FT: 33,000
SALES: 4.3MM **Privately Held**
WEB: www.garfieldindustries.com
SIC: 3291 Buffing or polishing wheels, abrasive or nonabrasive

(G-3213)
GASFLO PRODUCTS INC
19 Industrial Rd (07004-3017)
PHONE..........................973 276-9011
David Panetta, *CEO*
Bill Wagner, *Vice Pres*
Timothy Galvin, *Treasurer*
Jason Johansen, *Manager*
Greg Ruesch, *Technical Staff*
EMP: 37
SQ FT: 16,000
SALES (est): 10.3MM **Privately Held**
WEB: www.gasflo.com
SIC: 3494 3491 Valves & pipe fittings; industrial valves

(G-3214)
GIBRALTAR LABORATORIES INC (HQ)
122 Fairfield Rd (07004-2405)
PHONE..........................973 227-6882
Daniel L Prince, *President*
Jozef Mastej, *VP Opers*
Shiri Hechter, *QA Dir*
Chuck Weibel, *Manager*
Derek Prince, *Director*
EMP: 50
SQ FT: 40,000
SALES: 8.9MM
SALES (corp-wide): 723.7MM **Privately Held**
WEB: www.gibraltarlabsinc.com
SIC: 3841 8734 Diagnostic apparatus, medical; testing laboratories
PA: Sotera Health Llc
　　9100 S Hills Blvd Ste 300
　　Broadview Heights OH 44147
　　440 262-1410

(G-3215)
GLOBAL PRTNERS IN SHELDING INC
Also Called: Gps Specialty Doors
5 Just Rd (07004-3407)
PHONE..........................973 574-9077

Mark Holder, *President*
Taylor Brady, *Project Mgr*
Don Hener, *Engineer*
Will Brown, *Project Engr*
◆ EMP: 33
SQ FT: 17,000
SALES: 7MM **Privately Held**
WEB: www.gps-door.com
SIC: 3353 Aluminum sheet, plate & foil

(G-3216)
GMS LITHO CORP
16 Passaic Ave Unit 3 (07004-3835)
PHONE..........................973 575-9400
Gregory Enright, *President*
EMP: 5
SALES (est): 866.1K **Privately Held**
SIC: 2752 Commercial printing, offset

(G-3217)
GRANULATION TECHNOLOGY INC
12 Industrial Rd (07004-3018)
PHONE..........................973 276-0740
Ashok Niganaye, *President*
EMP: 15
SQ FT: 11,000
SALES (est): 1.9MM **Privately Held**
SIC: 2834 Pharmaceutical preparations

(G-3218)
GRAPH TECH SALES & SERVICE
6 Farmstead Ln (07004-1229)
PHONE..........................201 218-1749
Walter Petronczak, *Principal*
EMP: 13 EST: 2009
SALES (est): 1.9MM **Privately Held**
SIC: 2752 Commercial printing, lithographic

(G-3219)
H & T TOOL CO INC
19 Gardner Rd Ste C (07004-2204)
PHONE..........................973 227-4858
Thomas Schall, *President*
Raymond Mundrick, *Vice Pres*
EMP: 10
SQ FT: 10,000
SALES (est): 1.3MM **Privately Held**
SIC: 3469 Stamping metal for the trade

(G-3220)
H S FOLEX SCHLEUSSNER INC
Also Called: Folex Imaging
24 Just Rd (07004-3413)
PHONE..........................973 575-7626
Adrian Miles, *President*
Allison Dean, *Opers Mgr*
Joey Feliciano, *Manager*
John Ludwig, *Manager*
Jamie Brantner, *Administration*
EMP: 5
SQ FT: 20,000
SALES (est): 42.2K
SALES (corp-wide): 157.9K **Privately Held**
WEB: www.folex-usa.com
SIC: 3081 5113 2621 Film base, cellulose acetate or nitrocellulose plastic; industrial & personal service paper; paper mills
HQ: Celfa Ag
　　Bahnhofstrasse 92
　　Seewen SZ 6423
　　418 197-111

(G-3221)
HANOVIA SPECIALTY LIGHTING LLC
Also Called: Hanovia Colight
6 Evans St (07004-2210)
PHONE..........................973 651-5510
Liming Du, *Mng Member*
Jeffrey Andrews,
▲ EMP: 10
SQ FT: 53,000
SALES (est): 1.8MM **Privately Held**
WEB: www.hanovia-uv.com
SIC: 3641 Ultraviolet lamps

(G-3222)
HARVARD PRINTING GROUP
175 Us Highway 46 (07004-2327)
PHONE..........................973 672-0800
Richard Bitetti, *President*

EMP: 60 EST: 1946
SQ FT: 133,000
SALES (est): 5.9MM **Privately Held**
WEB: www.harvardpress.com
SIC: 2752 Commercial printing, offset

(G-3223)
HBS ELECTRONICS INC
1275 Bloomfield Ave # 17 (07004-2735)
PHONE..........................973 439-1147
Hans Bisesar, *President*
Rocky Bisesar, *Vice Pres*
EMP: 4
SALES (est): 400K **Privately Held**
WEB: www.hbselectronics.com
SIC: 3612 Specialty transformers

(G-3224)
HEAT-TIMER CORPORATION (PA)
20 New Dutch Ln (07004-2513)
PHONE..........................973 575-4004
Michael Pitonyak, *CEO*
Vincent Clerico, *VP Sales*
▲ EMP: 50
SQ FT: 39,000
SALES (est): 14.3MM **Privately Held**
WEB: www.heat-timer.com
SIC: 3822 3669 3491 3625 Electric heat controls; smoke detectors; valves, automatic control; relays & industrial controls; heating equipment, except electric

(G-3225)
HEAT-TIMER CORPORATION
Also Called: Heat-Timer Service
20 New Dutch Ln (07004-2513)
PHONE..........................212 481-2020
John Winston, *Manager*
Winston John, *Manager*
EMP: 30
SALES (est): 4.2MM
SALES (corp-wide): 14.3MM **Privately Held**
WEB: www.heat-timer.com
SIC: 3824 1711 7623 Controls, revolution & timing instruments; heating & air conditioning contractors; refrigeration service & repair
PA: Heat-Timer Corporation
　　20 New Dutch Ln
　　Fairfield NJ 07004
　　973 575-4004

(G-3226)
HEISLER MACHINE & TOOL CO
Also Called: Heisler Industries
224 Passaic Ave (07004-3581)
PHONE..........................973 227-6300
Richard A Heisler, *President*
Ron Heisler, *Vice Pres*
Ronald A Heisler, *Vice Pres*
Jerry Piemonte, *Prdtn Mgr*
Lindsay Gorsky, *Purch Mgr*
◆ EMP: 40 EST: 1920
SQ FT: 24,000
SALES (est): 11.9MM **Privately Held**
WEB: www.heislerind.com
SIC: 3565 Carton packing machines

(G-3227)
HERMA US INC
39 Plymouth St Unit 300 (07004-1643)
PHONE..........................973 521-7254
Peter Goff, *President*
EMP: 6
SALES (est): 352.6K **Privately Held**
SIC: 3565 Labeling machines, industrial

(G-3228)
HILL PHARMA INC
6 Madison Rd (07004-2309)
PHONE..........................973 521-7400
Charles Dong, *President*
Cynthia Cancel, *Admin Asst*
▲ EMP: 12
SALES (est): 1.7MM
SALES (corp-wide): 23.3MM **Privately Held**
SIC: 2834 Druggists' preparations (pharmaceuticals)
PA: Hill Pharmaceutical Co., Ltd.
　　Fenghuangyuan Development Zone
　　Yongzhou 42500
　　746 822-7890

(G-3229)
HOBART SALES AND SERVICE INC
Also Called: Hobart Feg Service Center
4 Gloria Ln (07004-3306)
PHONE..........................973 227-9265
Gordon De Block, *Branch Mgr*
Joe Devito, *Branch Mgr*
Cathy Stampone, *Office Spvr*
EMP: 50
SALES (corp-wide): 14.7B **Publicly Held**
WEB: www.hobartcorp.com
SIC: 3589 Dishwashing machines, commercial; cooking equipment, commercial; commercial cooking & foodwarming equipment
HQ: Hobart Sales And Service, Inc.
　　701 S Ridge Ave
　　Troy OH 45373
　　937 332-3000

(G-3230)
HT STAMPING CO LLC
19 Gardner Rd Ste C (07004-2204)
PHONE..........................973 227-4858
Thomas Schall, *Mng Member*
EMP: 9
SQ FT: 14,000
SALES (est): 567K **Privately Held**
SIC: 3469 Metal stampings

(G-3231)
HUDSON INDUSTRIES CORPORATION (HQ)
Also Called: Milligan & Higgins Div
271 Us Highway 46 F207 (07004-2448)
PHONE..........................973 402-0100
Arnold Palmer, *Ch of Bd*
Lee Kornbluh, *Corp Secy*
Barry Karpf, *Vice Pres*
▲ EMP: 4 EST: 1935
SQ FT: 1,500
SALES (est): 4.5MM **Privately Held**
WEB: www.milligan1868.com
SIC: 2891 2899 Glue; gelatin: edible, technical, photographic or pharmaceutical

(G-3232)
HUNTER MANUFACTURING SVCS INC
19 Just Rd (07004-3407)
PHONE..........................973 287-6701
Ken Hunter, *Director*
EMP: 18
SALES (est): 2.7MM **Privately Held**
SIC: 3599 Machine shop, jobbing & repair

(G-3233)
HYCRETE INC
14 Spielman Rd (07004-3404)
PHONE..........................201 386-8110
Jason Guerack, *CEO*
Richard Guinn, *CEO*
Brian Cchen, *Accountant*
Nelson Macalintal, *Director*
Travis Lesser, *Technician*
▼ EMP: 35
SALES (est): 7.1MM **Privately Held**
SIC: 3271 Concrete block & brick

(G-3234)
IMPERIAL DAX CO INC
Also Called: Dax Haircare
120 New Dutch Ln (07004-2598)
P.O. Box 10002 (07004-6002)
PHONE..........................973 227-6105
David Joy, *President*
▼ EMP: 25
SQ FT: 41,000
SALES (est): 4.8MM **Privately Held**
WEB: www.imperialdax.com
SIC: 2844 Cosmetic preparations; hair preparations, including shampoos

(G-3235)
INDEPENDENT MACHINE COMPANY
Also Called: Independent Converting Eqp
20 Industrial Rd (07004-3018)
PHONE..........................973 882-0060
Jack Santa Lucia, *President*
Bruce Butler, *Vice Pres*
Andrew Lenkiewicz, *Mfg Mgr*
Aleks Pinskiy, *Engineer*
EMP: 20 EST: 1968

SQ FT: 34,000
SALES (est): 4.9MM **Privately Held**
SIC: 3599 Machine shop, jobbing & repair

(G-3236)
INDUSTRIAL BRUSH CO INC
Also Called: Indusco
105 Clinton Rd Ste 1 (07004-2988)
PHONE...................................800 241-9860
Tim Enchelmaier, *President*
David Enchelmaier, *Vice Pres*
▲ EMP: 22
SQ FT: 44,000
SALES (est): 4.1MM **Privately Held**
WEB: www.indbrush.com
SIC: 3991 3545 Brooms & brushes; precision tools, machinists'

(G-3237)
INDUSTRIAL FILTERS COMPANY
9 Industrial Rd (07004-3043)
PHONE...................................973 575-0533
Steven Donker, *President*
Steve Donker, *President*
Marilyn Donker, *Treasurer*
Carol Centanni, *Mktg Dir*
EMP: 7
SQ FT: 12,600
SALES (est): 1.5MM **Privately Held**
WEB: www.indfilco.com
SIC: 3569 Filters, general line: industrial; filters

(G-3238)
INDUSTRIAL LBELING SYSTEMS INC
Also Called: Ilsi
50 Kulick Rd (07004-3308)
PHONE...................................973 808-8188
Yimin Shiuey, *President*
Brad Mack, *CFO*
Wai K Tsang, *Director*
EMP: 23
SQ FT: 25,000
SALES (est): 5.7MM **Privately Held**
SIC: 2759 Labels & seals: printing

(G-3239)
INFINITE CLASSIC INC
30 Sherwood Ln Ste 8 (07004-3603)
PHONE...................................973 227-2790
Baek H Kim, *Ch of Bd*
▲ EMP: 6
SALES (est): 392.3K **Privately Held**
SIC: 3961 Costume jewelry

(G-3240)
INTERNATIONAL CORD SETS INC
Also Called: I C S
6 Spielman Rd (07004-3404)
PHONE...................................973 227-2118
Dieter Baars, *President*
Ralph Mezza, *Vice Pres*
▲ EMP: 16
SQ FT: 12,500
SALES (est): 2MM **Privately Held**
SIC: 3699 Electrical equipment & supplies

(G-3241)
INTERNATIONAL TOOL AND MFG
30 Sherwood Ln Ste 10 (07004-3603)
PHONE...................................973 227-6767
Susan Brock, *President*
Thomas Brock, *Vice Pres*
Ryan Brock, *Treasurer*
EMP: 9
SQ FT: 4,500
SALES (est): 1.2MM **Privately Held**
SIC: 3599 3545 Machine shop, jobbing & repair; precision tools, machinists'

(G-3242)
IVY-DRY INC
299b Fairfield Ave (07004-3863)
P.O. Box 596, Caldwell (07007-0596)
PHONE...................................973 575-1992
Stephen Heydt, *President*
Harry Reicherz, *Vice Pres*
EMP: 8
SQ FT: 10,100
SALES (est): 1.8MM **Privately Held**
SIC: 5122 2833 Medicinals & botanicals; medicinals & botanicals

(G-3243)
JASON INDUSTRIAL INC (HQ)
340 Kaplan Dr (07004-2567)
P.O. Box 10004 (07004-6004)
PHONE...................................973 227-4904
Philip Cohenca, *CEO*
Emilia Cohenca, *Ch of Bd*
Glen Taylor, *Warehouse Mgr*
Jean De Maurienne, *Mfg Staff*
Diane Fobert, *Controller*
◆ EMP: 45 EST: 1965
SQ FT: 30,000
SALES (est): 151.8MM **Privately Held**
WEB: www.jasonindustrial.com
SIC: 5084 3052 Textile machinery & equipment; rubber & plastics hose & beltings

(G-3244)
JERSEY BORING & DRLG CO INC
36 Pier Ln W (07004-2505)
PHONE...................................973 242-3800
Shelley Lach, *President*
EMP: 35
SQ FT: 2,500
SALES (est): 5MM **Privately Held**
WEB: www.jerseyboring.com
SIC: 1481 Test boring for nonmetallic minerals

(G-3245)
JMC DESIGN & GRAPHICS INC
144 Fairfield Rd (07004-2407)
PHONE...................................973 276-9033
Joseph M Caniano, *President*
EMP: 5 EST: 1997
SQ FT: 10,000
SALES (est): 1.3MM **Privately Held**
SIC: 2752 Commercial printing, offset

(G-3246)
JOHN N FEHLINGER CO INC
16 Passaic Ave Unit 8 (07004-3835)
PHONE...................................973 633-0699
John Fehlinger, *Owner*
EMP: 6
SALES (est): 930K **Privately Held**
SIC: 3559 Sewing machines & attachments, industrial

(G-3247)
JRC WEB ACCESSORIES
46 Passaic Ave (07004-3522)
PHONE...................................973 625-3888
Ralph Ryan, *President*
Todd Ryan, *General Mgr*
▲ EMP: 11 EST: 1976
SQ FT: 20,000
SALES (est): 2MM **Privately Held**
SIC: 2655 Cores, fiber: made from purchased material

(G-3248)
KATHY JEANNE INC
7 Industrial Rd (07004-3017)
PHONE...................................973 575-9898
Jeanne Gerish, *President*
Jay M Gerish, *Vice Pres*
▲ EMP: 15
SQ FT: 11,500
SALES (est): 2MM **Privately Held**
WEB: www.kathyjeanneinc.com
SIC: 2353 5137 Hats & caps; hats, trimmed: women's, misses' & children's; hats: women's, children's & infants'

(G-3249)
KEYPOINT INTELLIGENCE LLC (HQ)
Also Called: Buyers Laboratory, LLC
80 Little Falls Rd (07004-2135)
PHONE...................................973 797-2100
Michael Danziger, *CEO*
Mark Lerch, *COO*
Eric Zimmerman, *Director*
EMP: 37
SQ FT: 26,000
SALES (est): 7.6MM **Privately Held**
WEB: www.buyerslab.com
SIC: 2721 Statistical reports (periodicals): publishing only

(G-3250)
KIDS OF AMERICA CORP
103 Route 46 W (07004-3235)
P.O. Box 411, Pine Brook (07058-0411)
PHONE...................................973 808-8242
Stephen Chan, *President*
Peter Joseph, *Senior VP*
Jenny Chan, *Exec Dir*
▲ EMP: 26
SQ FT: 3,000
SALES (est): 3MM **Privately Held**
WEB: www.kidsofamericacorp.com
SIC: 5092 3942 Toys & hobby goods & supplies; dolls & stuffed toys

(G-3251)
KINECT AUTO PARTS CORPORATION
75 Lane Rd Ste 201 (07004-1000)
PHONE...................................862 702-8252
Adam Wang, *President*
EMP: 3 EST: 2015
SALES (est): 6MM **Privately Held**
SIC: 3089 Automotive parts, plastic

(G-3252)
KITCHEN TABLE BAKERS INC
100 Passaic Ave Ste 155 (07004-3563)
PHONE...................................516 931-5113
EMP: 25
SALES (est): 2MM **Privately Held**
SIC: 2052 Mfg Cookies/Crackers

(G-3253)
KTB FOODS INC (HQ)
Also Called: Ktb Acquisition Sub Inc
100 Passaic Ave Ste 155 (07004-3563)
PHONE...................................973 240-0200
Aldo Zuppichini, *CEO*
EMP: 6
SALES (est): 878.5K
SALES (corp-wide): 1MM **Privately Held**
SIC: 2096 Potato chips & similar snacks
PA: That's How We Roll Llc
214 Glenridge Ave
Montclair NJ 07042
973 240-0200

(G-3254)
L&M ARCHITECTURAL GRAPHICS INC
Also Called: L&M Signs
20 Montesano Rd (07004-3310)
PHONE...................................973 575-7665
Justin Lorenzo, *President*
Paul Lorenzo, *Vice Pres*
Peter Lorenzo, *Vice Pres*
Thomas Vitale, *Accounts Exec*
Joseph Mayer, *Sr Project Mgr*
◆ EMP: 16
SQ FT: 10,000
SALES (est): 2.5MM **Privately Held**
WEB: www.lmsigns.com
SIC: 2221 3993 7336 Wall covering fabrics, manmade fiber & silk; signs & advertising specialties; commercial art & graphic design

(G-3255)
LA COUR INC (PA)
36 Kulick Rd (07004-3308)
PHONE...................................973 227-3300
Paul M Lacour, *President*
Tom Ruggieri, *General Mgr*
Matthew Scozzari, *Sales Staff*
EMP: 30
SQ FT: 35,000
SALES (est): 3.4MM **Privately Held**
WEB: www.lacourinc.com
SIC: 2521 2522 5021 5712 Wood office furniture; office furniture, except wood; office furniture; office furniture

(G-3256)
LAB EXPRESS INC
Also Called: Lab Express International
10 Madison Rd Ste A (07004-2325)
PHONE...................................973 227-1700
David Mazzarell, *President*
▲ EMP: 10
SQ FT: 10,000
SALES (est): 2.7MM **Privately Held**
WEB: www.labexpress.com
SIC: 2834 5169 Pharmaceutical preparations; chemicals & allied products

(G-3257)
LABEL GRAPHICS MFG INC
Also Called: Label Graphics II
315 Fairfield Rd (07004-1930)
PHONE...................................973 276-1555
Ali Kahn, *General Mgr*
Edgar Cruz, *Mfg Mgr*
EMP: 9
SALES (corp-wide): 8.4MM **Privately Held**
WEB: www.labelgraphicsmfg.com
SIC: 2672 Labels (unprinted), gummed: made from purchased materials
PA: Label Graphics Manufacturing, Inc.
175 Paterson Ave
Little Falls NJ 07424
973 890-5665

(G-3258)
LB BOOK BINDERY LLC
19 Gardner Rd Ste 1 (07004-2204)
PHONE...................................973 244-0442
Ralph Lozito, *Mng Member*
Frank Lozito,
Michael Lozito,
Sandy Lozito,
▲ EMP: 15
SALES (est): 1MM **Privately Held**
SIC: 2789 Binding only: books, pamphlets, magazines, etc.

(G-3259)
LEADING PHARMA LLC (PA)
3 Oak Rd (07004-2903)
PHONE...................................201 746-9160
Ronald F Gold, *CEO*
Rasik M Gondalia, *President*
Richard Monica, *Treasurer*
EMP: 50
SQ FT: 30,000
SALES: 10.6MM **Privately Held**
SIC: 2834 Pharmaceutical preparations

(G-3260)
LEGRAND AV INC
Also Called: Middle Atlantic Products
300 Fairfield Rd (07004-1932)
PHONE...................................973 839-1011
EMP: 339
SALES (corp-wide): 21.2MM **Privately Held**
SIC: 3444 Casings, sheet metal
HQ: Legrand Av Inc.
6436 City West Pkwy
Eden Prairie MN 55344
866 977-3901

(G-3261)
LEVINE PACKAGING SUPPLY CORP
400 Us Highway 46 (07004-1906)
PHONE...................................973 575-3456
Sanford I Levine, *President*
Neal Levine, *Vice Pres*
Larry Levine, *Treasurer*
Edith Levine, *Admin Sec*
EMP: 30
SQ FT: 40,000
SALES (est): 6.2MM **Privately Held**
SIC: 2653 Boxes, corrugated: made from purchased materials; pallets, solid fiber: made from purchased materials

(G-3262)
LIBERTY SPORT INC
107 Fairfield Rd (07004-2546)
PHONE...................................973 882-0986
Anthony M Di Chiara, *Ch of Bd*
Carmine Di Chiara, *Vice Pres*
Franco Tommasino, *CFO*
Jill Fine, *Regl Sales Mgr*
Alexandra Narrea, *Sales Staff*
▲ EMP: 35 EST: 1938
SQ FT: 60,000
SALES (est): 7.2MM **Privately Held**
WEB: www.libertyoptical.com
SIC: 3851 5048 Frames & parts, eyeglass & spectacle; frames, ophthalmic

(G-3263)
LINK COMPUTER GRAPHICS INC
Also Called: Link Instruments
17a Daniel Rd (07004-2527)
PHONE...................................973 808-8990

Hung-WEI Yeh, *President*
Ken Wong, *Vice Pres*
Todd Schreibman, *Treasurer*
EMP: 9
SQ FT: 4,000
SALES (est): 1.6MM **Privately Held**
WEB: www.linkins.com
SIC: 3577 5045 5065 3825 Computer peripheral equipment; computers, peripherals & software; electronic parts & equipment; instruments to measure electricity

(G-3264)
LION VISUAL LTD LIABILITY CO
Also Called: Texas Canvas
1275 Bloomfield Ave 54b (07004-2708)
PHONE......................973 278-3802
Samantha Dixon, *Manager*
Leonel Navarro,
EMP: 4
SQ FT: 8,400
SALES (est): 202.3K **Privately Held**
SIC: 2394 Awnings, fabric: made from purchased materials

(G-3265)
LIZARD LABEL CO (PA)
Also Called: Intergrated Scales Systems
20 Kulick Rd Ste A (07004-3308)
PHONE......................973 808-3322
Joseph Winter, *President*
John Winter, *Vice Pres*
▲ **EMP:** 10
SQ FT: 8,800
SALES (est): 946.2K **Privately Held**
WEB: www.lizardlabel.com
SIC: 2759 Labels & seals: printing

(G-3266)
LYNRED USA INC
Also Called: Electrophysics
373 Us Highway 46 (07004-2442)
PHONE......................973 882-0211
Bob Demarco, *President*
Frank J Vallese, *President*
Philippe Bensussan, *Chairman*
Roy Braz, *Vice Pres*
Girish Nadkarni, *Vice Pres*
EMP: 35
SQ FT: 10,000
SALES (est): 7.7MM **Privately Held**
WEB: www.electrophysics.com
SIC: 3826 Analytical instruments

(G-3267)
MEDIMTRIKS PHARMACEUTICALS INC
383 Us Highway 46 (07004-2473)
PHONE......................973 882-7512
Bradley Glassman, *CEO*
Alan Goldstein, *Exec VP*
David Addis, *Vice Pres*
Brent Lenczycki, *CFO*
Tom Perez, *Controller*
EMP: 38
SQ FT: 11,000
SALES (est): 12.1MM **Privately Held**
SIC: 5122 2834 Pharmaceuticals; dermatologicals; ointments

(G-3268)
MENNEKES ELECTRONICS INC
277 Fairfield Rd Ste 111 (07004-1931)
PHONE......................973 882-8333
Walter Mennekes, *President*
Paul Di Antonio, *Corp Secy*
Thomas Bodnar, *Vice Pres*
Paul Diantonio, *VP Sales*
Kevin Wammes, *Sales Staff*
▲ **EMP:** 25
SQ FT: 24,000
SALES (est): 12.6MM **Privately Held**
SIC: 5063 3679 Wiring devices; safety switches; electronic switches

(G-3269)
MERCURY LIGHTING PDTS CO INC
20 Audrey Pl (07004-3416)
PHONE......................973 244-9444
John Fedinec, *President*
Scott Fleischer, *Exec VP*
Jorge Correa, *Prdtn Mgr*
Manny Garrido, *Purch Agent*
Carissa Cokeley, *Sales Staff*
▲ **EMP:** 110 **EST:** 1946

SQ FT: 100,000
SALES (est): 27.8MM **Privately Held**
WEB: www.mercltg.com
SIC: 3646 Commercial indusl & institutional electric lighting fixtures

(G-3270)
MICHELE MADDALENA
Also Called: GM Construction
1275 Bloomfield Ave (07004-2708)
PHONE......................973 244-0033
Eugene M Maddalena, *Principal*
Michael Maddalena, *Vice Pres*
EMP: 7
SALES (est): 570.3K **Privately Held**
SIC: 3993 3648 1799 Signs & advertising specialties; lighting equipment; sign installation & maintenance

(G-3271)
MIDDLE ATLANTIC PRODUCTS INC
300 Fairfield Rd (07004-1932)
PHONE......................973 839-1011
Michael L Baker, *President*
Mike Vega, *General Mgr*
Robert Julian, *Vice Pres*
Bill Poling, *Vice Pres*
Timothy Troast, *Project Mgr*
◆ **EMP:** 320
SQ FT: 250,000
SALES (est): 64.8MM
SALES (corp-wide): 21.2MM **Privately Held**
WEB: www.middleatlantic.com
SIC: 3444 Casings, sheet metal
HQ: Legrand Holding, Inc.
60 Woodlawn St
West Hartford CT 06110
860 233-6251

(G-3272)
MODERN DRUMMER PUBLICATIONS
271 Us Highway 46 H212 (07004-2458)
PHONE......................973 239-4140
Isabel Spagnardi, *President*
EMP: 15 **EST:** 1976
SQ FT: 3,000
SALES (est): 1.9MM **Privately Held**
WEB: www.moderndrummer.com
SIC: 2721 2731 Magazines: publishing only, not printed on site; books: publishing only

(G-3273)
MORGAN ADVANCED CERAMICS INC
26 Madison Rd (07004-2309)
PHONE......................973 808-1621
Michael Benson, *General Mgr*
Shannon Mullins, *Vice Pres*
Chris Hart, *Purch Mgr*
Burnside Libby, *Human Res Mgr*
John Stang, *Branch Mgr*
EMP: 50
SALES (corp-wide): 1.3B **Privately Held**
WEB: www.morganelectroceramics.com
SIC: 2899 3251 3644 3297 Fluxes: brazing, soldering, galvanizing & welding; brick & structural clay tile; noncurrent-carrying wiring services; nonclay refractories; porcelain electrical supplies
HQ: Morgan Advanced Ceramics, Inc
2425 Whipple Rd
Hayward CA 94544

(G-3274)
MW INDUSTRIES INC
Also Called: Accurate Screw Machine
10 Audrey Pl (07004-3402)
PHONE......................973 244-9200
EMP: 100
SALES (corp-wide): 185.9MM **Privately Held**
SIC: 3451 Screw machine products
HQ: Mw Industries, Inc.
9501 Tech Blvd Ste 401
Rosemont IL 60018
847 349-5760

(G-3275)
NATIONAL PRECISION TOOL CO
24 Sherwood Ln (07004-3602)
PHONE......................973 227-5005

Leon Roitburg, *President*
Henry Solorzano, *Mfg Staff*
EMP: 21
SALES (est): 3.7MM **Privately Held**
SIC: 3599 Machine & other job shop work; machine shop, jobbing & repair

(G-3276)
NEMA FOOD DISTRIBUTION INC
18 Commerce Rd Ste D (07004-1603)
PHONE......................973 256-4415
Beyhan Nakiboglu, *President*
Galip Kiyakli, *Vice Pres*
▲ **EMP:** 6
SQ FT: 10,000
SALES (est): 1.3MM **Privately Held**
SIC: 2053 2032 2015 5142 Frozen bakery products, except bread; ethnic foods: canned, jarred, etc.; luncheon meat, poultry; meat, frozen: packaged; bakery products, frozen

(G-3277)
NEW AGE METAL FABG CO INC
Also Called: Namf
26 Daniel Rd W (07004-2522)
PHONE......................973 227-9107
Mario Costa, *President*
Margaret Goble, *Office Mgr*
EMP: 70
SQ FT: 40,000
SALES (est): 19.6MM **Privately Held**
SIC: 3444 Sheet metal specialties, not stamped

(G-3278)
NEW JERSEY BUSINESS MAGAZINE
310 Passaic Ave Ste 201 (07004-2523)
PHONE......................973 882-5004
Philip Kirschner, *President*
EMP: 8
SALES (est): 643K
SALES (corp-wide): 9.2MM **Privately Held**
SIC: 2721 Magazines: publishing & printing
PA: New Jersey Business & Industry Association
10 W Lafayette St
Trenton NJ 08608
609 393-7707

(G-3279)
NEXTRON MEDICAL TECH INC
Also Called: Nextron Infusion Services
45 Kulick Rd (07004-3307)
PHONE......................973 575-0614
Eric Nemeth, *CEO*
Silvio Eruzzi, *Ch of Bd*
Loriann Rubino-Chang, *Principal*
Simone Cimino, *CFO*
▲ **EMP:** 95
SALES (est): 8.6MM
SALES (corp-wide): 2B **Privately Held**
SIC: 2834 3845 Intravenous solutions; pacemaker, cardiac
HQ: Amerita, Inc.
7307 S Revere Pkwy # 200
Centennial CO 80112

(G-3280)
NIKO TRADE LTD-USA INC
271 Us Highway 46 D107 (07004-2440)
PHONE......................973 575-4353
Jacob Katz, *President*
EMP: 3
SQ FT: 3,000
SALES: 2MM **Privately Held**
WEB: www.niko-nikcole.com
SIC: 3545 Cutting tools for machine tools

(G-3281)
NJ COPY CENTER LLC
10 Madison Rd Ste C (07004-2325)
PHONE......................973 788-1600
Bradley Gimbel,
EMP: 4
SALES (est): 414.9K **Privately Held**
SIC: 2732 Book printing

(G-3282)
NOMADIC NORTH AMERICA LLC
46 Just Rd (07004-3413)
PHONE......................703 866-9200
Jim Laganke, *Branch Mgr*

EMP: 4
SALES (corp-wide): 25.8MM **Privately Held**
SIC: 3993 Signs & advertising specialties
HQ: Nomadic North America Llc
10505 Furnace Rd Ste 108
Lorton VA 22079
703 866-9200

(G-3283)
NOUVEAUTES INC
70 Clinton Rd Ste 1 (07004-2928)
P.O. Box 1198, Caldwell (07007-1198)
PHONE......................973 882-8850
David W Little, *President*
Jack Simon, *Vice Pres*
EMP: 15
SQ FT: 6,000
SALES (est): 2.1MM **Privately Held**
WEB: www.nouveautesusa.com
SIC: 2066 5199 Chocolate; gifts & novelties

(G-3284)
OMP TECHNOLOGIES INC
24 Commerce Rd Ste H (07004-1665)
PHONE......................973 808-8500
Yufeng Hsiao, *President*
Kanhan Hsiao, *Officer*
EMP: 15
SQ FT: 4,500
SALES (est): 1.8MM **Privately Held**
WEB: www.omptech.com
SIC: 3599 Machine shop, jobbing & repair

(G-3285)
OTIS ELEVATOR INTL INC
105 Fairfield Rd (07004-2546)
PHONE......................973 575-7030
Chris Dlugolecki, *Branch Mgr*
EMP: 125
SALES (corp-wide): 66.5B **Publicly Held**
WEB: www.otis.com
SIC: 3534 1796 7699 5084 Elevators & equipment; elevator installation & conversion; elevators: inspection, service & repair; elevators
HQ: Otis Elevator Company
1 Carrier Pl
Farmington CT 06032
860 674-3000

(G-3286)
OUTFRONT MEDIA LLC
185 Us Highway 46 (07004-2321)
PHONE......................973 575-6900
George Gross, *Manager*
Junella Avjean, *Manager*
Lancey Baskett, *Manager*
Donald Peters, *Manager*
Marta Abbatemarco, *Director*
EMP: 100
SALES (corp-wide): 1.6B **Publicly Held**
SIC: 7312 3993 2759 Outdoor advertising services; signs & advertising specialties; commercial printing
HQ: Outfront Media Llc
405 Lexington Ave Fl 14
New York NY 10174
212 297-6400

(G-3287)
PACE PACKAGING LLC
3 Sperry Rd (07004-2004)
PHONE......................973 227-1040
Mark W Anderson, *President*
Bernie Kroeper, *Controller*
Dave Rosequist, *Sales Staff*
◆ **EMP:** 55
SQ FT: 30,000
SALES (est): 12.8MM
SALES (corp-wide): 585.6MM **Privately Held**
WEB: www.pacepkg.com
SIC: 3565 Packaging machinery
PA: Pro Mach, Inc.
50 E Rivercntr Blvd 180
Covington KY 41011
513 831-8778

(G-3288)
PAR TROY SHEET METAL & AC LLC
122 Clinton Rd (07004-2921)
PHONE......................973 227-1150
Lino Rocha, *Owner*

EMP: 6
SQ FT: 4,800
SALES (est): 732.7K **Privately Held**
SIC: 3444 3446 Ducts, sheet metal; architectural metalwork

(G-3289)
PARAVISTA INC
Also Called: Paravista Imaging and Printing
123 Lehigh Dr (07004-3010)
PHONE..........................732 752-1222
Michael Spallucci, *President*
James Connell, *Vice Pres*
Mark Spallucci, *Vice Pres*
▲ EMP: 27
SQ FT: 30,000
SALES (est): 4.4MM **Privately Held**
WEB: www.paravistainc.com
SIC: 2752 Commercial printing, offset; advertising posters, lithographed

(G-3290)
PARKER LABS
286 Eldridge Rd (07004-2509)
PHONE..........................973 276-9500
Kevin Mc Dermott, *Engineer*
EMP: 4
SALES (est): 202.2K **Privately Held**
SIC: 2834 5122 Pharmaceutical preparations; pharmaceuticals

(G-3291)
PHARMATECH INTERNATIONAL INC
Also Called: Mironova Labs
21 Just Rd (07004-3407)
PHONE..........................973 244-0393
Miroslav Trampota, *President*
EMP: 15
SQ FT: 26,000
SALES (est): 4.1MM **Privately Held**
WEB: www.pharmatech.org
SIC: 5122 2834 Pharmaceuticals; pharmaceutical preparations

(G-3292)
POOF-ALEX HOLDINGS LLC
Also Called: Alex Brands
40 Lane Rd (07004-1012)
PHONE..........................734 454-9552
John Belniak,
EMP: 5
SALES (corp-wide): 11.7MM **Privately Held**
SIC: 3944 Blocks, toy
PA: Poof-Alex Holdings, Llc
10 Glenville St Ste 1
Greenwich CT 06831
203 930-7711

(G-3293)
PPI/TIME ZERO INC (HQ)
11 Madison Rd (07004-2308)
PHONE..........................973 278-6500
Dana Pittman, *President*
Joe Litavis, *Exec VP*
Michael J Shelor, *Exec VP*
Art Russo, *Opers Staff*
Trudy Ganguzza, *Senior Buyer*
EMP: 145
SQ FT: 100,000
SALES (est): 47.2MM
SALES (corp-wide): 69.1MM **Privately Held**
WEB: www.ppi-timezero.com
SIC: 3672 Printed circuit boards
PA: Virtex Enterprises, Lp
12234 N Interstate 35
Austin TX 78753
512 835-6772

(G-3294)
PRINCE STERILIZATION SVCS LLC
122 Fairfield Rd (07004-2405)
PHONE..........................973 227-6882
Daniel Prince, *Mng Member*
▼ EMP: 25
SALES: 10MM **Privately Held**
SIC: 2834 Pharmaceutical preparations

(G-3295)
PRINT COMMUNICATIONS GROUP INC
Also Called: P C G
175 Us Highway 46 Unit A (07004-2327)
PHONE..........................973 882-9444
James Purcaro, *CEO*
Michael D Alessandro, *COO*
Gene Palecco, *Chief Mktg Ofcr*
EMP: 60
SQ FT: 35,000
SALES (est): 7.7MM **Privately Held**
WEB: www.pcgnj.com
SIC: 2759 Thermography

(G-3296)
PROTECH POWDER COATINGS INC (PA)
Also Called: Protech Oxyplast
21 Audrey Pl (07004-3415)
PHONE..........................973 276-1292
David Ades, *President*
Peter Froess, *Plant Mgr*
Robinya Roberts, *Human Res Mgr*
◆ EMP: 86
SQ FT: 42,000
SALES (est): 19.9MM **Privately Held**
WEB: www.protechpowder.com
SIC: 2851 Lacquers, varnishes, enamels & other coatings

(G-3297)
RAINBOW CLOSETS INC (PA)
Also Called: California Closet Co
4 Gardner Rd Ste 5 (07004-2211)
PHONE..........................973 882-3800
Ruth Ginsberg, *President*
Martin Ginsberg, *Vice Pres*
Rochelle Topper, *Asst Sec*
EMP: 52
SQ FT: 6,400
SALES (est): 6.8MM **Privately Held**
SIC: 1799 2511 Closet organizers, installation & design; wardrobes, household; wood

(G-3298)
RECTICO INC
12 Gloria Ln Ste 1 (07004-3315)
PHONE..........................973 575-0009
Scott Sandler, *President*
Fulton W Sandler, *President*
EMP: 16
SQ FT: 14,000
SALES: 1MM **Privately Held**
WEB: www.rectico.com
SIC: 7389 2653 Packaging & labeling services; corrugated boxes, partitions, display items, sheets & pad

(G-3299)
REDI-DATA INC (PA)
5 Audrey Pl (07004-3401)
PHONE..........................973 227-4380
Dori Bruno, *General Mgr*
EMP: 14 EST: 1991
SALES (est): 29.9MM **Privately Held**
SIC: 7375 7372 Data base information retrieval; prepackaged software

(G-3300)
REDI-DIRECT MARKETING INC (PA)
107 Little Falls Rd (07004-2105)
PHONE..........................973 808-4500
James Weaver, *President*
Thomas R Buckley, *CFO*
▲ EMP: 350
SQ FT: 15,000
SALES (est): 45.9MM **Privately Held**
WEB: www.redidata.com
SIC: 7319 7331 7389 7375 Sample distribution; direct mail advertising services; telemarketing services; data base information retrieval; prepackaged software

(G-3301)
RESEARCH AND PVD MATERIALS
373 Us Highway 46 Bldg E (07004-2442)
PHONE..........................973 575-4245
Irene Wasnick, *President*
Melvin Hollander, *Vice Pres*
EMP: 6
SQ FT: 6,000

SALES (est): 653.5K **Privately Held**
SIC: 3499 Tablets, bronze or other metal

(G-3302)
ROBERTET FRAGRANCES INC
30 Stewart Pl (07004-1631)
PHONE..........................973 575-4550
Joseph Rainone, *Branch Mgr*
EMP: 30
SALES (corp-wide): 281.4MM **Privately Held**
SIC: 2844 Perfumes & colognes
HQ: Robertet Fragrances Inc.
400 International Dr
Budd Lake NJ 07828
201 405-1000

(G-3303)
ROBINSON TECH INTL CORP
Also Called: Rti
310 Fairfield Rd (07004-1932)
PHONE..........................973 287-6458
Mark Lin, *President*
Gary Xu, *Vice Pres*
▲ EMP: 9
SQ FT: 26,000
SALES (est): 1.3MM **Privately Held**
SIC: 3291 3312 3399 Abrasive products; fence posts, iron & steel; metal fasteners

(G-3304)
RSI COMPANY
Also Called: Rsi-Fairfield Division
333 Us Highway 46 (07004-2427)
PHONE..........................973 227-7800
Mike Thailer, *Manager*
EMP: 4
SALES (corp-wide): 3.2MM **Privately Held**
WEB: www.rsicomp.com
SIC: 7629 7694 Generator repair; electric motor repair
PA: Rsi Company
24050 Commerce Park # 200
Beachwood OH 44122
216 360-9800

(G-3305)
RUBBER & SILICONE PRODUCTS CO
17 Montesano Rd (07004-3309)
P.O. Box 1215, Caldwell (07007-1215)
PHONE..........................973 227-2300
Jeffery Dylla, *President*
John Cox, *Vice Pres*
Deborah Dylla, *Admin Sec*
▲ EMP: 20
SQ FT: 12,500
SALES (est): 3MM **Privately Held**
SIC: 3069 Molded rubber products

(G-3306)
SAFEGUARD COINBOX INC
101 Clinton Rd (07004-2912)
P.O. Box 1266, Caldwell (07007-1266)
PHONE..........................973 575-0040
Susan Macina, *President*
EMP: 15
SALES (est): 966.3K
SALES (corp-wide): 1.9MM **Privately Held**
WEB: www.safeguardcoinbox.com
SIC: 3469 Boxes: tool, lunch, mail, etc.: stamped metal
PA: Bloomfield Manufacturing Co Inc
29 Crosby Ln
Oakland NJ 07436
973 575-8900

(G-3307)
SAPPHIRE FLVORS FRAGRANCES LLC
6 Commerce Rd (07004-1602)
PHONE..........................973 200-8849
Paul Braccia,
EMP: 10
SQ FT: 35,000
SALES: 1.2MM **Privately Held**
SIC: 2087 Concentrates, flavoring (except drink)

(G-3308)
SCHULKE INC
30 Two Bridges Rd Ste 225 (07004-1515)
PHONE..........................973 521-7163
Matthew Daulby, *Sales Mgr*

Linda Sedlewicz, *Branch Mgr*
EMP: 4
SALES (corp-wide): 125.9MM **Privately Held**
SIC: 2842 Disinfectants, household or industrial plant
HQ: Schulke & Mayr Gmbh
Robert-Koch-Str. 2
Norderstedt 22851
405 210-00

(G-3309)
SCREEN PLAY INC
1275 Bloomfield Ave Ste 5 (07004-2736)
PHONE..........................973 227-9014
Stephen Wacker, *President*
James Hill, *Vice Pres*
EMP: 6
SALES: 400K **Privately Held**
WEB: www.screenplay.com
SIC: 2759 Screen printing

(G-3310)
SENSOR SCIENTIFIC INC (PA)
6 Kingsbridge Rd Ste 4 (07004-2100)
PHONE..........................973 227-7790
G Robert Brinley, *President*
Russ Bolton PHD, *Vice Pres*
◆ EMP: 20
SQ FT: 8,000
SALES (est): 2MM **Privately Held**
WEB: www.sensorsci.com
SIC: 3829 Thermometers & temperature sensors

(G-3311)
SGS USTESTING COMPANY (DH)
291 Fairfield Ave (07004-3833)
PHONE..........................973 575-5252
Christian Jilch, *Ch of Bd*
Nancy Rivera, *Managing Dir*
Francisco Rocca, *Vice Pres*
Mark Connors, *Treasurer*
EMP: 10
SALES (est): 9.7MM
SALES (corp-wide): 6.7B **Privately Held**
SIC: 8732 8734 8071 8731 Commercial nonphysical research; hazardous waste testing; forensic laboratory; soil analysis; product testing laboratory, safety or performance; testing laboratories; biotechnical research, commercial; environmental research; physical property testing equipment
HQ: Sgs North America Inc.
201 Route 17
Rutherford NJ 07070
201 508-3000

(G-3312)
SOLBERN LLC
8 Kulick Rd (07004-3308)
PHONE..........................973 227-3030
Gil Foulon, *Mng Member*
EMP: 37
SQ FT: 23,000
SALES (est): 11.2MM
SALES (corp-wide): 6.8B **Publicly Held**
WEB: www.solbern.com
SIC: 5084 3556 Food product manufacturing machinery; food products machinery
HQ: Markel Ventures, Inc.
4521 Highwoods Pkwy
Glen Allen VA 23060

(G-3313)
SPARKS BELTING COMPANY INC
5 Spielman Rd (07004-3480)
PHONE..........................973 227-4100
David Engelhard, *Regional Mgr*
EMP: 8
SALES (corp-wide): 548MM **Privately Held**
SIC: 3535 Conveyors & conveying equipment
HQ: Sparks Belting Company, Inc.
3800 Stahl Dr Se
Grand Rapids MI 49546

(G-3314)
STANDARD PRTG & MAIL SVCS INC
30 Plymouth St A (07004-1622)
P.O. Box 11021 (07004-7021)
PHONE..........................973 790-3333

Kevin Walsh, *President*
EMP: 14
SALES (est): 2.5MM **Privately Held**
WEB: www.standprint.com
SIC: 2752 7331 2791 2789 Photo-offset printing; mailing service; typesetting; bookbinding & related work

(G-3315)
STAR LITHO INC
175 Us Highway 46 Unit C (07004-2327)
PHONE.....................................973 641-1603
Anthony Aquila Jr, *President*
Anthony Aquila III, *Vice Pres*
Anne Aquila, *Admin Sec*
EMP: 8
SQ FT: 10,000
SALES: 1MM **Privately Held**
SIC: 2752 Commercial printing, offset

(G-3316)
STONE SYSTEMS NEW JERSEY LLC
5 Washington Ave (07004-3812)
PHONE.....................................973 778-5525
Thomas Landers, *Manager*
EMP: 13
SALES (est): 1.6MM **Privately Held**
SIC: 3281 Granite, cut & shaped

(G-3317)
STONE TRUSS SYSTEMS INC (PA)
23 Commerce Rd Ste O (07004-1609)
PHONE.....................................973 882-7377
Francisco Tauriello, *President*
Anthony Tauriello, *Chairman*
Khiamuddin Mohammad, *Project Mgr*
Joanne Di Benedetto, *Controller*
Dina M Tauriello, *Admin Sec*
▲ **EMP:** 25
SQ FT: 4,200
SALES (est): 4.8MM **Privately Held**
WEB: www.stonetrusssystems.com
SIC: 1741 3281 Stone masonry; granite, cut & shaped

(G-3318)
STONEWORK DSIGN CONSULTING INC (PA)
25 Pier Ln W (07004-2504)
PHONE.....................................973 575-0835
Anthony Abdy, *President*
EMP: 40 **EST:** 1998
SALES: 15MM **Privately Held**
SIC: 3253 1743 Ceramic wall & floor tile; terrazzo, tile, marble, mosaic work; tile installation, ceramic

(G-3319)
SUN DIAL & PANEL CORPORATION
Also Called: Sun Display Systems
2 Daniel Rd Ste 102 (07004-2516)
PHONE.....................................973 226-4334
Fax: 973 808-6759
EMP: 23
SQ FT: 10,000
SALES: 2.9MM **Privately Held**
SIC: 3812 Mfg Search/Navigation Equipment

(G-3320)
SUN DISPLAY SYSTEMS LLC
2 Daniel Rd (07004-2516)
PHONE.....................................973 226-4334
Andrea Jandoli, *Purchasing*
Liam Rafferty, *Engineer*
John Chamalian, *Director*
Roger Lokker,
EMP: 35
SQ FT: 12,500
SALES: 4.5MM **Privately Held**
SIC: 3647 Vehicular lighting equipment

(G-3321)
SYNCOM PHARMACEUTICALS INC (PA)
125 Clinton Rd Unit 5 (07004-2929)
P.O. Box 11320 (07004-7320)
PHONE.....................................973 787-2405
James W De Coursin, *President*
Fred Mc Ilreath, *Vice Pres*
Mahendra Shah, *CFO*
▼ **EMP:** 25

SALES (est): 14.2MM **Privately Held**
WEB: www.syncom.net
SIC: 2023 Dietary supplements, dairy & non-dairy based

(G-3322)
TADBIK NJ INC
17 Madison Rd (07004-2308)
PHONE.....................................973 882-9595
Leslie Gurland, *President*
Aryeh Silbert, *Chairman*
◆ **EMP:** 34
SQ FT: 14,400
SALES: 5.6MM
SALES (corp-wide): 183.6MM **Privately Held**
WEB: www.logotech-inc.com
SIC: 2754 Labels: gravure printing
PA: Tadbik Ltd.
4 Boltimor
Petah Tikva 49510
392 780-00

(G-3323)
TALLY DISPLAY CORP
19 Gardner Rd Ste A (07004-2204)
PHONE.....................................973 777-7760
Steve Rose, *President*
Sheldon Hoffman, *Vice Pres*
EMP: 9
SALES (est): 894.1K **Privately Held**
WEB: www.tallydisplay.com
SIC: 3993 Signs & advertising specialties

(G-3324)
TECHNOGYM USA CORP (DH)
700 Us Highway 46 (07004-1591)
PHONE.....................................800 804-0952
Claudio Bellini, *President*
Andrea Severi, *Treasurer*
Patricia Philipp, *Train & Dev Mgr*
Dana Musoiu, *Sales Mgr*
Jay Megna, *Sales Staff*
◆ **EMP:** 12
SQ FT: 6,000
SALES (est): 4.7MM **Privately Held**
WEB: www.technogym.com
SIC: 3949 Exercise equipment
HQ: Technogym Spa
Via Calcinaro 2861
Cesena FC 47521
054 765-0650

(G-3325)
TEVA PHARMACEUTICALS USA INC
8 Gloria Ln Ste 10 (07004-3306)
PHONE.....................................973 575-2775
Robert Tarra, *Manager*
EMP: 102
SALES (corp-wide): 5B **Privately Held**
WEB: www.lemmon.com
SIC: 2834 Pharmaceutical preparations
HQ: Teva Pharmaceuticals Usa, Inc.
1090 Horsham Rd
North Wales PA 19454
215 591-3000

(G-3326)
TEXAS CANVAS CO INC (PA)
Also Called: Awnings By Texas Canvas
1275 Bloomfield Ave 54b (07004-2708)
PHONE.....................................973 278-3802
EMP: 4
SALES (est): 913.3K **Privately Held**
SIC: 2394 Mfg Canvas/Related Products

(G-3327)
THIN STONE SYSTEMS LLC
23 Commerce Rd Ste O (07004-1609)
PHONE.....................................973 882-7377
Frank Tauriello,
▲ **EMP:** 8
SALES (est): 368.3K
SALES (corp-wide): 4.8MM **Privately Held**
WEB: www.stonetrusssystems.com
SIC: 1741 3281 Masonry & other stonework; cut stone & stone products
PA: Stone Truss Systems, Inc.
23 Commerce Rd Ste O
Fairfield NJ 07004
973 882-7377

(G-3328)
TILTON RACK & BASKET CO
66 Passaic Ave (07004-3522)
PHONE.....................................973 226-6010
Joseph Tilton, *President*
EMP: 25 **EST:** 1963
SQ FT: 15,000
SALES (est): 6MM **Privately Held**
WEB: www.tiltonrackandbasket.com
SIC: 3559 Electroplating machinery & equipment

(G-3329)
TITANIUM FABRICATION CORP (HQ)
Also Called: AIAC
110 Lehigh Dr (07004-3013)
PHONE.....................................973 227-5300
Brent Willey, *President*
Dan Williams, *Vice Pres*
◆ **EMP:** 60
SQ FT: 50,000
SALES (est): 33.1MM
SALES (corp-wide): 1B **Privately Held**
WEB: www.tifab.com
SIC: 3443 Heat exchangers: coolers (after, inter), condensers, etc.
PA: American Industrial Acquisition Corporation
1 Harbor Point Rd # 1700
Stamford CT 06902
203 952-9212

(G-3330)
TORPAC INC (PA)
Also Called: Torpac Capsules
333 Us Highway 46 (07004-2427)
PHONE.....................................973 244-1125
Raj Tahil, *President*
James Bondulich, *Opers Mgr*
▲ **EMP:** 25
SQ FT: 6,000
SALES (est): 2.6MM **Privately Held**
WEB: www.torpac.com
SIC: 2899 Gelatin capsules

(G-3331)
TQ3 NORTH AMERICA INC (PA)
23 Commerce Rd Ste I (07004-1609)
PHONE.....................................973 882-7900
Aidan Bradley, *President*
▲ **EMP:** 6
SQ FT: 3,500
SALES (est): 4MM **Privately Held**
SIC: 2851 Paints, waterproof

(G-3332)
TREMONT PRINTING CO
72 Deer Park Rd (07004-1431)
PHONE.....................................973 227-0742
Daniel Cerami, *Owner*
EMP: 4
SALES: 170K **Privately Held**
SIC: 2759 2752 Commercial printing; commercial printing, lithographic

(G-3333)
TRIM AND TASSELS LLC
Also Called: Graduation Outlet
333 Us Highway 46 B (07004-2427)
PHONE.....................................973 808-1566
Pradeep Jalan,
Rashmi Jalan,
Ritu Jalan,
▲ **EMP:** 4
SALES (est): 458K **Privately Held**
SIC: 2431 5023 7389 Window trim, wood; decorative home furnishings & supplies;

(G-3334)
UNICORN GROUP INC
23 Daniel Rd (07004-2527)
PHONE.....................................973 360-5904
James S Devine, *Branch Mgr*
EMP: 76
SALES (corp-wide): 19.1MM **Privately Held**
WEB: www.open4.com
SIC: 7372 7379 Business oriented computer software; computer related consulting services
PA: The Unicorn Group Inc
25b Hanover Rd
Florham Park NJ 07932
973 360-0688

(G-3335)
UNIFOIL CORPORATION
12 Danie Rd (07004-2536)
PHONE.....................................973 244-9900
Joseph Funicelli, *President*
Robert Glaspey, *Vice Pres*
Alejandro Angel, *Plant Supt*
Michael Abate, *Accountant*
Robert Gallino, *Info Tech Dir*
▲ **EMP:** 62 **EST:** 1971
SQ FT: 135,000
SALES (est): 27MM **Privately Held**
WEB: www.unifoil.com
SIC: 2672 Metallic covered paper: made from purchased materials

(G-3336)
UNITED STATES BOX CORP
Also Called: U S Box
14 Madison Rd Ste E (07004-2326)
PHONE.....................................973 481-2000
Alan S Kossoff, *President*
Chris Beli, *General Mgr*
Evan Don Kossoff, *Vice Pres*
Tom Kossoff, *Vice Pres*
Karen Piccone, *Human Res Mgr*
▼ **EMP:** 35 **EST:** 1948
SQ FT: 50,000
SALES: 3.5MM **Privately Held**
WEB: www.usbox.com
SIC: 2631 2652 3089 5113 Folding boxboard; setup paperboard boxes; boxes, plastic; industrial & personal service paper

(G-3337)
V & L MACHINE AND TOOL CO INC
Also Called: Www.vandlmachinetool.com
30 Sherwood Ln Ste 11 (07004-3603)
PHONE.....................................973 439-7216
Michael Sollitto, *President*
George Vecchiet, *Vice Pres*
James Kirch, *Treasurer*
EMP: 6
SQ FT: 7,400
SALES (est): 912.5K **Privately Held**
SIC: 3599 Machine shop, jobbing & repair

(G-3338)
VCOM INTL MULTI-MEDIA CORP (PA)
Also Called: Comprehensive Connectivity Com
80 Little Falls Rd (07004-2135)
P.O. Box 10005 (07004-6005)
PHONE.....................................201 814-0405
Sheldon Goldstein, *President*
Randall Cole, *Vice Pres*
Madelyn Picone, *Vice Pres*
Charlie Mena, *Purchasing*
Ezra Hiller, *Sls & Mktg Exec*
◆ **EMP:** 93 **EST:** 1965
SQ FT: 45,000
SALES (est): 27.1MM **Privately Held**
WEB: www.vcomimc.com
SIC: 3651 5999 5065 Electronic kits for home assembly: radio, TV, phonograph; communication equipment; communication equipment

(G-3339)
VCOM INTL MULTI-MEDIA CORP
Also Called: Alltec Stores
80 Little Falls Rd (07004-2135)
P.O. Box 10005 (07004-6005)
PHONE.....................................201 296-0600
Sheldon Goldstein, *President*
William Kurtzer, *General Mgr*
EMP: 85
SALES (corp-wide): 27.1MM **Privately Held**
SIC: 5999 3651 5065 Alarm & safety equipment stores; household audio & video equipment; electronic parts & equipment
PA: Vcom International Multi-Media Corp.
80 Little Falls Rd
Fairfield NJ 07004
201 814-0405

(G-3340)
VECTOR FOILTEC LLC
55 Lane Rd Ste 110 (07004-1018)
PHONE.....................................862 702-8909

Stefan Lehnert, *Mng Member*
▲ EMP: 4
SALES (est): 938.4K **Privately Held**
WEB: www.foiltecna.com
SIC: 2952 1761 Roofing materials; roofing contractor

(G-3341)
VELA DIAGNOSTICS USA INC
353c Rte 46 W Ste 250 (07004)
PHONE..................................973 852-3740
Tine Normann, *President*
Thomas Keller, *General Mgr*
Gary Raff, *Controller*
EMP: 9
SALES (est): 1.1MM
SALES (corp-wide): 4.9MM **Privately Held**
SIC: 3841 Diagnostic apparatus, medical
PA: Vela Diagnostics Holding Pte. Ltd.
50 Science Park Road
Singapore 11740
667 260-60

(G-3342)
VERTICAN TECHNOLOGIES INC
55 Lane Rd Ste 210 (07004-1015)
PHONE..................................800 435-7257
Stevan H Goldman, *CEO*
Isaac Goldman, *COO*
John Currey, *Vice Pres*
Shailesh Mehrotra, *Vice Pres*
Denise Burgos, *Administration*
EMP: 6 EST: 1981
SALES (est): 168.2K **Privately Held**
SIC: 7372 Prepackaged software

(G-3343)
VICINITY MEDIA GROUP INC
165 Passaic Ave (07004-3521)
PHONE..................................973 276-1688
David Black, *Principal*
Pauline Dunberg, *Marketing Staff*
Michael Reidy, *Art Dir*
EMP: 12 EST: 2012
SALES (est): 729.3K **Privately Held**
SIC: 2711 Newspapers, publishing & printing

(G-3344)
VICINITY PUBLICATIONS INC
Also Called: Suburban Essex Magazine
165 Passaic Ave Ste 107 (07004-3592)
PHONE..................................973 276-1688
David Black, *President*
Cathy Black, *Publisher*
EMP: 9 EST: 1992
SQ FT: 2,000
SALES (est): 960K **Privately Held**
WEB: www.vpmagazines.com
SIC: 2721 Magazines: publishing only, not printed on site

(G-3345)
VITAQUEST INTERNATIONAL LLC
100 Lehigh Dr (07004-3013)
PHONE..................................973 787-9900
Mark Stanisci, *Exec VP*
EMP: 18 **Privately Held**
SIC: 2834 Vitamin preparations
PA: Vitaquest International, Llc
8 Henderson Dr
West Caldwell NJ 07006

(G-3346)
VITAQUEST INTERNATIONAL LLC
Also Called: Windmill Health Products
21 Dwight Pl (07004-3303)
PHONE..................................973 575-9200
Howard Munk, *Branch Mgr*
EMP: 10 **Privately Held**
WEB: www.gardenstatenutritionals.com
SIC: 2834 5122 5149 8742 Vitamin preparations; vitamins & minerals; health foods; marketing consulting services
PA: Vitaquest International, Llc
8 Henderson Dr
West Caldwell NJ 07006

(G-3347)
VIVREAU ADVANCED WATER SYSTEMS
14 Madison Rd Ste 30 (07004-2326)
PHONE..................................212 502-3749
Andrew Hamilton, *Principal*
EMP: 14
SALES (est): 1.4MM **Privately Held**
SIC: 3221 3589 5963 Bottles for packing, bottling & canning: glass; water purification equipment, household type; bottled water delivery

(G-3348)
VOLTIS LLC
55 Dwight Pl Unit A (07004-3311)
PHONE..................................607 349-9411
Byron James, *Mng Member*
Patrick Cupo,
EMP: 6
SALES: 950K **Privately Held**
SIC: 3612 Power & distribution transformers

(G-3349)
W R CHESNUT ENGINEERING INC
2 Industrial Rd 101 (07004-3018)
PHONE..................................973 227-6995
Richard Chesnut, *President*
Norma Chesnut, *Corp Secy*
Albert Mirra, *Purch Agent*
EMP: 19
SQ FT: 16,000
SALES (est): 4.5MM **Privately Held**
WEB: www.chesnuteng.com
SIC: 3555 Printing trades machinery

(G-3350)
W T WINTER ASSOCIATES INC
Also Called: Winter Scale & Equipment
20a Kulick Rd (07004-3308)
PHONE..................................888 808-3611
William T Winter Jr., *President*
Jonathon S Winter, *Vice Pres*
Joseph W Winter, *Treasurer*
Laura C Winter, *Admin Sec*
EMP: 25
SQ FT: 8,600
SALES (est): 4.5MM **Privately Held**
WEB: www.wtwinter.com
SIC: 7629 5064 5084 5046 Electrical repair shops; electrical appliances, television & radio; industrial machinery & equipment; commercial equipment; scales & balances, except laboratory

(G-3351)
WAVELINE INCORPORATED
160 Passaic Ave (07004-3596)
P.O. Box 718, Caldwell (07007-0718)
PHONE..................................973 226-9100
James A Mc Gregor, *President*
Fred Henningsen, *Engineer*
Daniel Scimeca, *Engineer*
Timothy Alexander, *Manager*
Fred Bennington, *Security Dir*
▼ EMP: 35 EST: 1946
SQ FT: 32,000
SALES (est): 7MM **Privately Held**
WEB: www.wavelineinc.com
SIC: 3825 3679 Microwave test equipment; microwave components

(G-3352)
WEST ESSEX GRAPHICS INC
305 Fairfield Ave (07004-3831)
PHONE..................................973 227-2400
Thomas Guth, *Owner*
EMP: 30
SALES (corp-wide): 5.3MM **Privately Held**
WEB: www.westessexgraphics.com
SIC: 3861 Plates, photographic (sensitized)
PA: Essex West Graphics Inc
305 Fairfield Ave
Fairfield NJ 07004
973 227-2400

(G-3353)
WHITEHOUSE PRTG & LABELING LLC
50 Kulick Rd (07004-3308)
PHONE..................................973 521-7648

Yimin Shiuey, *Principal*
David P Matto, *Principal*
Allison Lavallato,
Alyssa Newton,
Patrick Newton,
EMP: 8
SALES: 1MM **Privately Held**
SIC: 2759 Commercial printing

(G-3354)
WM H BREWSTER JR INCORPORATED
Also Called: Wm.h. Brewster Jr
16 Kulick Rd (07004-3308)
PHONE..................................973 227-1050
Salvatore Freda Jr, *CEO*
EMP: 9 EST: 1919
SQ FT: 7,500
SALES (est): 1.7MM **Privately Held**
WEB: www.brewster-washers.com
SIC: 3499 3452 Shims, metal; bolts, nuts, rivets & washers; washers, metal

(G-3355)
WRAPADE PACKAGING SYSTEMS LLC
15 Gardner Rd Ste 200 (07004-2207)
PHONE..................................973 787-1788
William Beattie, *President*
Laurene Beattie,
▲ EMP: 18
SQ FT: 15,000
SALES (est): 5.3MM **Privately Held**
WEB: www.wrapade.com
SIC: 3565 Packaging machinery

Fairview
Bergen County

(G-3356)
ARAMANI INC
369 Henry St (07022-1910)
PHONE..................................201 945-1160
ARA Milkonean, *President*
EMP: 4
SQ FT: 1,112
SALES (est): 360K **Privately Held**
SIC: 2732 Books: printing & binding

(G-3357)
BERTOLOTTI LLC
54 Industrial Ave (07022-1605)
PHONE..................................201 941-3116
John Camisa, *President*
Ronald Camisa, *Vice Pres*
Albert Camisa, *Treasurer*
EMP: 10
SALES (est): 1.2MM **Privately Held**
WEB: www.bertolottidesserts.com
SIC: 2024 5812 Ice cream, bulk; spumoni; ice cream stands or dairy bars

(G-3358)
CLIFFSIDE BODY CORPORATION
130 Broad Ave (07022-1502)
P.O. Box 206 (07022-0206)
PHONE..................................201 945-3970
Edward Greenwald, *President*
Robert Greenwald, *Vice Pres*
Warren Greenwald, *Treasurer*
Guy Bradford, *Marketing Staff*
EMP: 32 EST: 1919
SQ FT: 28,000
SALES: 9.9MM **Privately Held**
WEB: www.cliffsidebody.com
SIC: 7532 3711 5012 5013 Body shop, trucks; truck & tractor truck assembly; truck bodies; truck parts & accessories; truck & bus bodies

(G-3359)
CUTLER BROS BOX & LUMBER CO (PA)
711 W Prospect Ave (07022-1523)
P.O. Box 217 (07022-0217)
PHONE..................................201 943-2535
Gregory Cutler, *President*
Adam Cutler, *Vice Pres*
Jed Cutler, *Vice Pres*
Carolyn Sands, *Treasurer*
EMP: 30 EST: 1875

SQ FT: 20,000
SALES (est): 5.9MM **Privately Held**
WEB: www.cutlerpallets.com
SIC: 2448 2441 3412 2449 Pallets, wood; skids, wood; boxes, wood; metal barrels, drums & pails; wood containers

(G-3360)
EURO MECHANICAL INC
16 Industrial Ave (07022-1605)
PHONE..................................201 313-8050
Ante Pestic, *President*
Francis Franklin, *CFO*
Jenifer Kalaw, *Accountant*
Sancho Varghese, *Accountant*
John Hardcastle, *Manager*
EMP: 12
SALES (est): 2.4MM **Privately Held**
WEB: www.euromechanical.com
SIC: 3498 Pipe fittings, fabricated from purchased pipe

(G-3361)
JOHN M SNIDERMAN INC (PA)
405 Henry St (07022-1911)
P.O. Box 278 (07022-0278)
PHONE..................................201 450-4291
Anita Sniderman, *President*
EMP: 9
SQ FT: 10,800
SALES: 2MM **Privately Held**
WEB: www.johnmsniderman.com
SIC: 2397 5131 Schiffli machine embroideries; piece goods & notions

(G-3362)
KRAUSES HOMEMADE CANDY INC
461 Fairview Ave 465 (07022-1836)
PHONE..................................201 943-4790
Nicole Cinquegrana, *President*
EMP: 10
SQ FT: 3,000
SALES (est): 1.2MM **Privately Held**
SIC: 2064 5441 Candy & other confectionery products; candy

(G-3363)
MARKO ENGRAVING & ART CORP
439 Fairview Ave (07022-1857)
PHONE..................................201 945-6555
EMP: 13
SALES (corp-wide): 1.2MM **Privately Held**
SIC: 3555 2796 Mfg Printing Trades Machinery Platemaking Services
PA: Marko Engraving & Art Corp
19 Baldwin Ave
Weehawken NJ 07086
201 864-6500

(G-3364)
NIKKO CERAMICS INC (HQ)
815 Fairview Ave Ste 9 (07022-1571)
PHONE..................................201 840-5200
Kenji Anzai, *President*
Akiko Mitani, *Chairman*
Kaz Suzuki, *Vice Pres*
▲ EMP: 11
SQ FT: 32,000
SALES: 2MM **Privately Held**
SIC: 5023 5199 3262 China; glassware; gifts & novelties; vitreous china table & kitchenware

(G-3365)
O BERK COMPANY LLC
Aql Decorating
215 Bergen Blvd (07022-1358)
PHONE..................................201 941-1610
Fax: 201 941-5079
EMP: 26
SALES (corp-wide): 53.3MM **Privately Held**
SIC: 2759 Commercial Printing
PA: The O Berk Company L L C
3 Milltown Ct
Union NJ 07083
908 810-2267

(G-3366)
PARK PLUS INC
83 Broad Ave (07022-1501)
PHONE..................................201 917-5778
Ron Astrup, *CEO*

▲ EMP: 45
SALES (est): 546.9K
SALES (corp-wide): 623.2MM **Privately Held**
SIC: 7521 3441 Parking garage; building components, structural steel
PA: Towne Park, Llc
555 E North Ln Ste 5020
Conshohocken PA 19428
410 267-6111

(G-3367)
PCS CRANE SERVICES INC
83 Broad Ave (07022-1501)
PHONE..................................201 366-4250
Robert Williams, *President*
EMP: 10
SQ FT: 60,000
SALES: 2MM **Privately Held**
SIC: 3536 Cranes, industrial plant
PA: Pro Crane Services (Pty) Ltd
53-55 Rigger Road Rtan
Johannesburg GP 1619
113 945-550

(G-3368)
PRIME FUR & LEATHER INC
Also Called: New York Fur
29 Industrial Ave 31 (07022-1605)
PHONE..................................201 941-9600
Brian S Han, *President*
▲ EMP: 15 EST: 1997
SQ FT: 8,000
SALES (est): 1.8MM **Privately Held**
SIC: 2386 Garments, leather; leather & sheep-lined garments

(G-3369)
TANKLEFF INC
Also Called: Iweiss
815 Fairview Ave Ste 10 (07022-1571)
PHONE..................................201 402-6500
David Rosenberg, *CEO*
Jennifer Tankleff, *Vice Pres*
▲ EMP: 36
SQ FT: 18,000
SALES (est): 6.1MM **Privately Held**
WEB: www.iweiss.com
SIC: 2391 Curtains, window: made from purchased materials; draperies, plastic & textile: from purchased materials

(G-3370)
THEBERGE CABINETS INC
202 Broad Ave (07022-1046)
PHONE..................................201 941-1141
Nikola Picinic, *President*
Grace Picinic, *Vice Pres*
David Scarr, *Human Res Dir*
EMP: 8 EST: 1970
SQ FT: 2,000
SALES (est): 1.1MM **Privately Held**
SIC: 2434 Wood kitchen cabinets

(G-3371)
TONE EMBROIDERY CORP
Also Called: Touch of Lace
333 Bergen Blvd (07022-1213)
PHONE..................................201 943-1082
Haim Sasson, *President*
Gabriel Sasson, *Vice Pres*
Henriette Sasson, *Admin Sec*
▲ EMP: 36
SQ FT: 50,000
SALES (est): 7.2MM **Privately Held**
WEB: www.touchoflace.com
SIC: 5131 5949 2397 2395 Lace fabrics; sewing, needlework & piece goods; schiffli machine embroideries; pleating & stitching

Fanwood
Union County

(G-3372)
EAGLEVISION USA LLC
150 North Ave (07023-1209)
PHONE..................................908 322-1892
Nicholaos S Galakis, *Mng Member*
▼ EMP: 6
SALES (est): 231.1K **Privately Held**
SIC: 1459 Clays, except kaolin & ball

(G-3373)
REBUTH METAL SERVICES (PA)
130 Farley Ave (07023-1005)
PHONE..................................908 889-6400
Michael J Rebuth, *President*
Ralph W Rebuth, *Corp Secy*
EMP: 10 EST: 1958
SQ FT: 23,000
SALES (est): 1.9MM **Privately Held**
SIC: 5051 3544 3469 Steel; special dies & tools; stamping metal for the trade

Far Hills
Somerset County

(G-3374)
EDGEMONT PHARMACEUTICALS LLC
92 Roxiticus Rd (07931-2222)
PHONE..................................908 375-8039
Douglas Saltel, *Executive*
EMP: 4
SALES (est): 314.6K **Privately Held**
SIC: 2834 Vitamin, nutrient & hematinic preparations for human use

(G-3375)
ENGRAVED IMAGES LTD
Demunn Pl Rr 202 (07931)
P.O. Box 966 (07931-0966)
PHONE..................................908 234-0323
Heidi P Gammon, *President*
Heide Gammon, *President*
Heide Pfluger, *President*
EMP: 6
SALES (est): 317.9K **Privately Held**
SIC: 5947 2759 Gift shop; invitation & stationery printing & engraving

Farmingdale
Monmouth County

(G-3376)
ALLTEST INSTRUMENTS INC
500 Central Ave (07727-3790)
PHONE..................................732 919-3339
Nathan Nelson, *Principal*
Jeremy Nelson, *Principal*
Brian Consoli, *Manager*
▲ EMP: 17
SQ FT: 18,000
SALES (est): 6.9MM **Privately Held**
SIC: 3825 Instruments to measure electricity

(G-3377)
ANS NUTRITION INC
700 Central Ave (07727-3787)
PHONE..................................212 235-5205
Solomon Brander, *Principal*
EMP: 28
SALES (est): 6.5MM **Privately Held**
SIC: 2834 Vitamin preparations

(G-3378)
BELFER
10 Ruckle Ave (07727-3691)
PHONE..................................732 493-2666
Judi Handel, *Principal*
Debra Grimm, *Accounts Mgr*
EMP: 5
SALES (est): 739.7K **Privately Held**
SIC: 3646 Commercial indusl & institutional electric lighting fixtures

(G-3379)
CENTRAL METAL FABRICATORS INC
300 Central Ave (07727-3789)
PHONE..................................732 938-6900
Frank Crisafulli, *President*
Michael Hopkins, *COO*
Bonnie Alexander, *Manager*
Margaret Crisafulli, *Admin Sec*
EMP: 19
SQ FT: 10,000

SALES: 2.1MM **Privately Held**
WEB: www.central-metal.com
SIC: 3443 3444 Tanks, standard or custom fabricated: metal plate; sheet metalwork

(G-3380)
COLWOOD ELECTRONICS INC
44 Main St (07707-1325)
PHONE..................................732 938-5556
Richard Colaguori, *President*
Steven Colaguori, *Corp Secy*
Donna Colaguori, *Vice Pres*
▲ EMP: 9
SQ FT: 3,500
SALES (est): 1.2MM **Privately Held**
WEB: www.woodburning.com
SIC: 3544 3546 Special dies, tools, jigs & fixtures; power-driven handtools

(G-3381)
COMPOUNDERS INC
15 Marl Rd (07727-1413)
P.O. Box 413 (07727-0413)
PHONE..................................732 938-5007
Harold K Saunders, *President*
EMP: 4
SQ FT: 10,000
SALES (est): 729K **Privately Held**
SIC: 2891 Adhesives

(G-3382)
CROWN ENGINEERING CORP
550 Sqnkum Yellowbrook Rd (07727-3744)
P.O. Box 846 (07727-0846)
PHONE..................................800 631-2153
Michael J Palmer, *President*
Jackie Palmer, *Treasurer*
Steven Pereira, *Marketing Mgr*
Ken Mercure, *Manager*
▲ EMP: 25
SQ FT: 22,500
SALES (est): 5.1MM **Privately Held**
WEB: www.crownengineering.com
SIC: 3443 Fabricated plate work (boiler shop)

(G-3383)
D&E NUTRACEUTICALS INC
700 Central Ave (07727-3787)
PHONE..................................212 235-5200
Sam Zeldes, *President*
Gary Chasser, *COO*
Dariusz Michalski, *Prdtn Mgr*
Nate Plotnick, *Accounts Mgr*
Josh Lieberman, *Sales Executive*
EMP: 20
SALES (est): 4.5MM **Privately Held**
SIC: 2834 5122 Pharmaceutical preparations; pharmaceuticals

(G-3384)
DOERRE FENCE CO LLC
392 Adelphia Rd (07727-3529)
PHONE..................................732 751-9700
Chris Doerre, *Mng Member*
Christine Bosse, *Mng Member*
EMP: 10
SQ FT: 3,000
SALES (est): 901.5K **Privately Held**
SIC: 2499 5211 1799 Fencing, wood; fencing; fence construction

(G-3385)
ENVIRONMENTAL TECHNICAL DRLG
Also Called: Environmental Technical Drlg
408 Cranberry Rd (07727-3511)
PHONE..................................732 938-3222
Michael Ryan Jr, *President*
Ann C Ryan, *Vice Pres*
EMP: 7
SALES: 425K **Privately Held**
SIC: 1799 1389 Core drilling & cutting; bailing, cleaning, swabbing & treating of wells

(G-3386)
HANRAHAN TOOL CO INC
Also Called: Howell Precision Tool Co
415 Cranberry Rd (07727-3512)
PHONE..................................732 919-7300
David W Hanrahan Jr, *President*
Elizabeth Hanrahan, *Vice Pres*
EMP: 7
SQ FT: 4,300

SALES (est): 949.1K **Privately Held**
WEB: www.howellprecision.com
SIC: 3599 3544 Machine shop, jobbing & repair; industrial molds

(G-3387)
LIGHTING WORLD INC
Also Called: Belfer Lighting Manufacturing
10 Ruckle Ave (07727-3691)
P.O. Box 2079, Asbury Park (07712-2079)
PHONE..................................732 919-1224
Bruce Belfer, *President*
Norman Armbrust, *President*
Evelyn Maldonado, *Vice Pres*
Elaine Belfer, *Treasurer*
◆ EMP: 48
SQ FT: 22,000
SALES (est): 6.5MM **Privately Held**
WEB: www.belfer.com
SIC: 3646 3645 Commercial indusl & institutional electric lighting fixtures; residential lighting fixtures

(G-3388)
MARINE CONT EQP CRTFCTION CORP
160 Sqnkum Yellowbrook Rd (07727-3736)
PHONE..................................732 938-6622
Kenneth Allen, *President*
Jennifer Allen, *Vice Pres*
Joyce M Allen, *Treasurer*
EMP: 6 EST: 1967
SQ FT: 5,000
SALES (est): 540K **Privately Held**
SIC: 3829 Physical property testing equipment

(G-3389)
PATTY-O-MATIC INC
183 County Rte 547 (07727)
P.O. Box 404 (07727-0404)
PHONE..................................732 938-2757
Bernard Miles, *President*
June Miles, *Treasurer*
EMP: 12 EST: 1968
SQ FT: 10,000
SALES (est): 2.6MM **Privately Held**
WEB: www.pattyomatic.com
SIC: 3556 7389 Meat processing machinery; personal service agents, brokers & bureaus

(G-3390)
PEKAY INDUSTRIES INC
452 Sqnkum Yellowbrook Rd (07727-3775)
P.O. Box 559 (07727-0559)
PHONE..................................732 938-2722
Peter Kcwalenko Jr, *President*
EMP: 10
SQ FT: 5,000
SALES: 1MM **Privately Held**
SIC: 3674 3643 3429 3296 Solid state electrcnic devices; current-carrying wiring devices; manufactured hardware (general); mineral wool; porcelain electrical supplies

(G-3391)
ROSANO ASPHALT LLC
Asbury Rd Ste 360 (07727)
PHONE..................................732 620-8400
Frank Rosano, *Manager*
EMP: 8
SALES (est): 850K **Privately Held**
SIC: 2951 Road materials, bituminous (not from refineries)

(G-3392)
SPINNINGDESIGNS INC
5106 Rte 34 (07727)
PHONE..................................732 775-7050
Eileen Herman, *President*
Robert Derosa, *Vice Pres*
Michelle Duffy, *Engineer*
EMP: 12
SQ FT: 11,000
SALES: 1.4MM **Privately Held**
SIC: 3993 Signs & advertising specialties

(G-3393)
STEVE GREEN ENTERPRISES
Also Called: Stephan L Green Trailers
74 Sqankum Yellowbrook Rd (07727-3734)
PHONE..................................732 938-5572
Stephan L Green, *President*
Stephan Green, *Owner*

2019 Harris New Jersey
Manufacturers Directory
▲ = Import ▼=Export
◆ =Import/Export

EMP: 14
SQ FT: 50,000
SALES (est): 3.1MM **Privately Held**
SIC: 3523 3799 7549 Trailers & wagons, farm; trailers & trailer equipment; trailer maintenance

(G-3394)
TEA ELLE WOODWORKS
53 Main St (07727-1326)
PHONE..................................732 938-9660
Todd Gleason, *Owner*
EMP: 4
SALES (est): 404.8K **Privately Held**
SIC: 2431 Millwork

(G-3395)
WELD TECH FAB
282 Lemon Rd (07727-3538)
PHONE..................................732 919-2185
Dave Hanick, *Owner*
EMP: 4
SALES: 20K **Privately Held**
SIC: 7692 Welding repair

(G-3396)
WM LEIBER INC
190 Georgia Tavern Rd (07727-3549)
PHONE..................................732 938-2080
William Leiber, *Principal*
EMP: 4
SALES (est): 288.4K **Privately Held**
SIC: 2448 Wood pallets & skids

(G-3397)
YATES SIGN CO INC
Also Called: Allied Enviornmental Signage
69 Megill Rd (07727-3678)
PHONE..................................732 578-1818
Kevin R White, *President*
Michael McClellan, *President*
Kevin White, *Export Mgr*
Kim Rasmussen, *Office Mgr*
EMP: 25 EST: 1923
SQ FT: 17,500
SALES (est): 3.9MM **Privately Held**
WEB: www.yatessignco.com
SIC: 3993 Electric signs

Flanders
Morris County

(G-3398)
AFFINITY CHEMICAL WOODBINE LLC
82 Crenshaw Dr (07836-4725)
PHONE..................................973 873-4070
EMP: 11
SALES (est): 3.5MM **Privately Held**
SIC: 2819 Industrial inorganic chemicals

(G-3399)
ALT SHIFT CREATIVE LLC
15 Mountain Ave (07836-9130)
PHONE..................................609 619-0009
Paul Reidinger,
EMP: 7
SALES: 900K **Privately Held**
SIC: 7372 Application computer software

(G-3400)
ANALYTICAL SALES AND SVCS INC
179 Rte 206 (07836-9262)
PHONE..................................973 616-0700
David A Isom, *President*
Rosanne Isom, *Vice Pres*
Joseph Metelski, *Production*
David Wolford, *Technical Staff*
◆ EMP: 10
SQ FT: 14,500
SALES: 4.7MM **Privately Held**
WEB: www.analytical-sales.com
SIC: 3826 8732 Chromatographic equipment, laboratory type; research services, except laboratory

(G-3401)
ARIAS MOUNTAIN-COFFEE LLC
42 Bartley Rd (07836)
PHONE..................................973 927-9595
Jorge Henao, *Mng Member*
EMP: 10

SALES (corp-wide): 2MM **Privately Held**
SIC: 2095 Roasted coffee
PA: Arias Mountain-Coffee Llc
311 W Main St Ste 2
Rockaway NJ 07866
973 927-9595

(G-3402)
BON VENTURE SERVICES LLC
34 Ironia Rd (07836-9111)
P.O. Box 850 (07836-0850)
PHONE..................................973 584-5699
Mike Garde, *Ch of Bd*
Tom Garde, *President*
Stuart Frazier, *Vice Pres*
Marybeth Piazza, *Vice Pres*
Mary Beth Piazza, *Human Res Mgr*
EMP: 60
SQ FT: 10,000
SALES (est): 9.2MM **Privately Held**
WEB: www.bonventure.net
SIC: 2731 Pamphlets: publishing & printing

(G-3403)
COUGHLAN PRODUCTS LLC
37 Ironia Rd Ste 5 (07836-4422)
PHONE..................................973 845-6440
Mark Ford, *Mng Member*
EMP: 8
SALES (est): 242K **Privately Held**
SIC: 2844 Toilet preparations

(G-3404)
DANI LEATHER USA INC
37 Ironia Rd Ste 2 (07836-4422)
PHONE..................................973 598-0890
Silvano Fumei, *Principal*
▲ EMP: 6
SQ FT: 15,000
SALES (est): 1.1MM
SALES (corp-wide): 212.9K **Privately Held**
SIC: 3111 Leather tanning & finishing
HQ: Dani Spa
Via Concia 186
Arzignano VI 36071
044 445-4111

(G-3405)
DELTA COOLING TOWERS INC (PA)
185 Us Highway 206 (07836-9238)
PHONE..................................973 586-2201
John C Flaherty, *President*
▼ EMP: 41
SALES (est): 11.8MM **Privately Held**
WEB: www.deltacooling.com
SIC: 3443 3589 Cooling towers, metal plate; water treatment equipment, industrial

(G-3406)
DPC CIRRUS
62 Flanders Bartley Rd (07836-4715)
PHONE..................................973 927-2828
Douglas Olson, *Principal*
Ricardo Gonzalez, *Electrical Engi*
EMP: 14
SALES (est): 2.2MM **Privately Held**
SIC: 2835 In vitro & in vivo diagnostic substances

(G-3407)
ELECTRONIC MEASURING DEVICES
Also Called: E M D
15 Mill Rd (07836-9611)
PHONE..................................973 691-4755
Frank Allia, *CEO*
Klaus Ulbrich, *COO*
▲ EMP: 10
SQ FT: 2,600
SALES (est): 1.2MM **Privately Held**
WEB: www.emdsceptre.com
SIC: 3823 8748 Industrial process measurement equipment; business consulting

(G-3408)
ENERGY TRACKING LLC
16 Southwind Dr (07836-9734)
PHONE..................................973 448-8660
Keith Mistry, *Mng Member*
Raji Mistry,
EMP: 8

SALES: 300K **Privately Held**
SIC: 3825 7371 7389 Electrical energy measuring equipment; computer software development;

(G-3409)
ENERGY TRACKING INC
16 Southwind Dr (07836-9734)
PHONE..................................973 448-8660
Keith Mistry, *President*
Jay Mistry, *Vice Pres*
EMP: 5
SQ FT: 3,500
SALES: 200K **Privately Held**
SIC: 3825 Instruments to measure electricity

(G-3410)
FIRST PRIORITY GLOBAL LTD (PA)
160 Gold Mine Rd (07836-9284)
PHONE..................................973 347-4321
Alex N Cherepakhov,
EMP: 15
SALES (est): 7.3MM **Privately Held**
SIC: 3711 Ambulances (motor vehicles), assembly of

(G-3411)
G E INSPECTION TECHNOLOGIES LP
199 Us Highway 206 (07836-4501)
PHONE..................................973 448-0077
Bruce Pellegrino, *Branch Mgr*
EMP: 89 **Privately Held**
SIC: 3829 3844 Ultrasonic testing equipment; radiographic X-ray apparatus & tubes
HQ: G E Inspection Technologies, Lp
721 Visions Dr
Skaneateles NY 13152
315 554-2000

(G-3412)
HAAS LASER TECHNOLOGIES INC (PA)
37 Ironia Rd (07836-4422)
PHONE..................................973 598-1150
Gilbert Haas, *President*
Ann Haas, *Vice Pres*
Ronald Steinhart, *Engineer*
Stephen Roe, *Design Engr*
◆ EMP: 16
SQ FT: 34,600
SALES (est): 2.2MM **Privately Held**
WEB: www.haaslti.com
SIC: 3699 Laser systems & equipment

(G-3413)
INSTANT IMPRINTS
286 Us Highway 206 119b (07836-9582)
PHONE..................................973 252-9500
EMP: 4
SALES (est): 190K **Privately Held**
SIC: 2752 Lithographic Commercial Printing

(G-3414)
JOHNSTON LETTER CO INC
209 Pleasant Hill Rd (07836-9179)
PHONE..................................973 482-7535
James Johnston, *President*
EMP: 4 EST: 1921
SQ FT: 10,000
SALES (est): 194.8K **Privately Held**
SIC: 7338 7331 2791 2789 Letter writing service; direct mail advertising services; typesetting; bookbinding & related work; commercial printing, lithographic

(G-3415)
NAFS PAINTS INC
5 Laurel Dr Unit 4 (07836-4701)
PHONE..................................973 927-0729
James Nafus Jr, *President*
EMP: 6
SALES (est): 575.1K **Privately Held**
SIC: 3949 Hockey equipment & supplies, general

(G-3416)
NORTH JERSEY SPECIALISTS INC
Also Called: N J S
5 Laurel Dr Unit 6 (07836-4701)
PHONE..................................973 927-1616
Richard A Lettorale, *President*
EMP: 5 EST: 1976
SQ FT: 2,500
SALES (est): 838.5K **Privately Held**
WEB: www.northjerseyspecialists.net
SIC: 2851 Epoxy coatings

(G-3417)
ROBERT H HOOVER & SONS INC
Also Called: Transfer Truck & Equipment
149 Gold Mine Rd (07836-9138)
P.O. Box 719 (07836-0719)
PHONE..................................973 347-4210
Robert C Hoover, *Manager*
EMP: 7
SALES (corp-wide): 8.8MM **Privately Held**
WEB: www.hoovertruckcenters.com
SIC: 5511 7538 5531 3492 Trucks, tractors & trailers: new & used; truck engine repair, except industrial; truck equipment & parts; hose & tube fittings & assemblies, hydraulic/pneumatic
PA: Robert H Hoover & Sons Inc
1784 Route 9
Toms River NJ 08755
732 341-2128

(G-3418)
SHIVA SOFTWARE GROUP INC
2 Fennimore Ct (07836-9660)
PHONE..................................973 691-5475
EMP: 35
SALES: 4MM **Privately Held**
SIC: 7372 Prepackaged Software Services

(G-3419)
SIEMENS MEDICAL
Also Called: Dpc Instrument Systems
62 Flanders Bartley Rd (07836-4715)
PHONE..................................973 927-2828
Douglas R Olson, *President*
Jim Guille, *Vice Pres*
David Herzog, *Vice Pres*
Brenda Lynch, *Buyer*
Vickie Barzano, *Engineer*
▲ EMP: 2100
SQ FT: 89,000
SALES (est): 171.9MM
SALES (corp-wide): 95B **Privately Held**
WEB: www.dpconline.com
SIC: 3826 Analytical instruments
HQ: Siemens Healthcare Diagnostics Inc.
511 Benedict Ave
Tarrytown NY 10591
914 631-8000

(G-3420)
SPECIAL TECHNICAL SERVICES
11 Carlton Rd (07836-4409)
PHONE..................................609 259-2626
Ronald Dunster, *President*
Alan Dunster, *Vice Pres*
Allan Dunster, *Research*
Myrtle Dunster, *Treasurer*
EMP: 6 EST: 1966
SQ FT: 6,300
SALES (est): 490K **Privately Held**
SIC: 3625 Relays & industrial controls

(G-3421)
TARGA INDUSTRIES INC
Also Called: Cherokee Rubber Company
5 Laurel Dr Unit 13 (07836-4701)
P.O. Box 339, Chester (07930-0339)
PHONE..................................973 584-3733
Gilbert Stroming II, *President*
Jacquelyn M Stroming, *Vice Pres*
EMP: 10
SQ FT: 4,000
SALES (est): 2MM **Privately Held**
SIC: 3052 Rubber & plastics hose & beltings

(G-3422)
TECHNICAL COATINGS CO (DH)
Also Called: Benjamin Moore
360 Us Highway 206 (07836-9577)
P.O. Box 4000 (07836-4000)
PHONE..............................973 927-8600
Robert J Hodgson, *President*
Dennis Recca, *Engineer*
Joseph Mattos, *Manager*
Walaa Mohamed, *Manager*
James Tantsits, *Manager*
EMP: 20 EST: 1847
SQ FT: 3,200
SALES (est): 35.2MM
SALES (corp-wide): 225.3B **Publicly Held**
SIC: 2851 Lacquers, varnishes, enamels & other coatings; paints & paint additives; varnishes
HQ: Benjamin Moore & Co.
101 Paragon Dr
Montvale NJ 07645
201 573-9600

(G-3423)
TRI-STATE QUIKRETE
150 Gold Mine Rd (07836-9171)
PHONE..............................973 347-4569
Jeffrey R Nanfeldt, *Partner*
Tony Miceli, *Plant Mgr*
Anthony Casavecchia, *Cust Mgr*
EMP: 50
SALES (est): 7.4MM **Privately Held**
SIC: 3272 Dry mixture concrete

(G-3424)
TRIUMPH PLASTICS LLC
99 Bartley Flanders Rd (07836-9642)
PHONE..............................973 584-5500
EMP: 6
SALES (est): 682.1K **Privately Held**
SIC: 3089 Kits, plastic

Flanders
Hunterdon County

(G-3425)
39 IDEA FACTORY ROW LLC
39 Bonetown Rd (08822-4000)
PHONE..............................908 244-8631
David Sturgess,
Simon Kanaan,
EMP: 2
SALES: 5MM **Privately Held**
SIC: 2329 2339 7371 5499 Men's & boys' sportswear & athletic clothing; women's & misses' outerwear; computer software development & applications; vitamin food stores;

(G-3426)
3M COMPANY
500 Rte 202 (08822-6031)
PHONE..............................908 788-4000
Debbie Katz, *Engineer*
David Marston, *Branch Mgr*
EMP: 200
SALES (corp-wide): 32.7B **Publicly Held**
WEB: www.mmm.com
SIC: 5047 3841 Medical equipment & supplies; surgical & medical instruments
PA: 3m Company
3m Center
Saint Paul MN 55144
651 733-1110

(G-3427)
ABILITY2WORK A NJ NNPRFIT CORP
42 State Route 12 (08822-1540)
P.O. Box 368, Whitehouse (08888-0368)
PHONE..............................908 782-3458
Karen Monroy, *CEO*
EMP: 10
SALES (est): 672.7K **Privately Held**
SIC: 2051 Cakes, bakery: except frozen

(G-3428)
ACTIVE LEARNING ASSOCIATES
Also Called: Children's Tecnology Review
126 Main St (08822-1652)
PHONE..............................908 284-0404
Warren Buckleiter, *President*
Ellen Wolock, *Vice Pres*
Megan Billitti, *Office Mgr*
Chris Grabowich, *Manager*
Matthew Dimatteo, *Director*
EMP: 5
SQ FT: 1,000
SALES (est): 266.2K **Privately Held**
WEB: www.littleclickers.com
SIC: 2759 Publication printing

(G-3429)
AMBRO MANUFACTURING INC
Also Called: Special T S Screen Prtg & EMB
6 Kings Ct (08822-6004)
PHONE..............................908 806-8337
Robert Amato, *President*
Linda Amato, *Principal*
Ryan Amato, *Vice Pres*
Sergio Rodriguez, *Sales Staff*
EMP: 12
SQ FT: 5,000
SALES (est): 880K **Privately Held**
SIC: 2396 2395 Screen printing on fabric articles; embroidery & art needlework

(G-3430)
ANTI HYDRO INTERNATIONAL INC
45 River Rd Ste 200 (08822-6026)
P.O. Box 2467 (08822-2467)
PHONE..............................908 284-9000
Pankaj Desai, *CEO*
Piyush Patel, *President*
Suresh Patel, *Vice Pres*
Anil Choksi, *Maintence Staff*
▼ EMP: 10
SQ FT: 30,000
SALES (est): 1.9MM **Privately Held**
WEB: www.anti-hydro.com
SIC: 2821 3241 1799 Epoxy resins; cement, hydraulic; waterproofing

(G-3431)
ARNO THERAPEUTICS INC
200 Route 31 Ste 104 (08822-5812)
P.O. Box 571, Kingston (08528-0571)
PHONE..............................862 703-7170
Arie S Belldegrun, *Ch of Bd*
Joseph Bisaha, *Vice Pres*
Alexander Zukiwski, *Chief Mktg Ofcr*
David M Tanen, *Admin Sec*
EMP: 4
SQ FT: 4,168
SALES (est): 780.5K **Privately Held**
SIC: 2834 Druggists' preparations (pharmaceuticals)

(G-3432)
BAGEL CLUB
20 Commerce St Ste 5 (08822-7700)
PHONE..............................908 806-6022
Jeff Stern, *President*
EMP: 16
SALES (est): 575K **Privately Held**
SIC: 5812 2051 5411 Delicatessen (eating places); bagels, fresh or frozen; delicatessens

(G-3433)
CELLULAR SCIENCES INC
84 Park Ave (08822-1172)
PHONE..............................908 237-1561
Allan Martin, *President*
EMP: 5
SALES (est): 446.5K **Privately Held**
WEB: www.cellularsciences.com
SIC: 2834 Pharmaceutical preparations

(G-3434)
CORNERSTONE PRINTS IMAGING LLC
Also Called: Cornerstone Imaging
179 State Route 31 Ste 8 (08822-5743)
PHONE..............................908 782-7966
Arthur Clark, *Owner*
Carol Clark, *Manager*
EMP: 5
SQ FT: 2,300
SALES (est): 350K **Privately Held**
WEB: www.cornerstone-print.com
SIC: 2752 2791 2789 Commercial printing, lithographic; typesetting; bookbinding & related work

(G-3435)
CRETER VAULT CORP (PA)
417 Route 202 (08822-6021)
PHONE..............................908 782-7771
Richard E Creter, *President*
Camille Creter, *Corp Secy*
EMP: 48 EST: 1918
SQ FT: 35,000
SALES (est): 9.6MM **Privately Held**
WEB: www.beachsaver.com
SIC: 3272 Burial vaults, concrete or precast terrazzo

(G-3436)
DAKA MANUFACTURING LLC
19 Floral Rd (08822-3321)
PHONE..............................908 782-0360
Shelly Sobel,
Martin Sobel,
EMP: 5
SALES: 100K **Privately Held**
SIC: 3423 Hand & edge tools

(G-3437)
DIGITAL ARTS IMAGING LLC
105 State Route 31 Ste 10 (08822-5745)
PHONE..............................908 237-4646
Robert Vernon, *President*
EMP: 12
SQ FT: 7,500
SALES (est): 1.6MM **Privately Held**
SIC: 7336 3993 Graphic arts & related design; signs & advertising specialties

(G-3438)
DMS LABORATORIES INC
2 Darts Mill Rd (08822-7090)
PHONE..............................908 782-3353
Nicholas A Gallo III, *President*
Denise G Darmanian, *Admin Sec*
EMP: 6
SQ FT: 2,000
SALES: 1MM
SALES (corp-wide): 1.3MM **Privately Held**
WEB: www.rapidvet.com
SIC: 5047 2835 Veterinarians' equipment & supplies; veterinary diagnostic substances
PA: Fed Corporate Services Ag
C/O Bmo Treuhand Ag
Neuhausen Am Rheinfall SH 8212
526 755-922

(G-3439)
ENERGY BATTERY
1200 County Road 523 (08822-7097)
PHONE..............................908 751-5918
▲ EMP: 5
SALES (est): 657.5K **Privately Held**
SIC: 3691 Storage batteries

(G-3440)
ENERGY BATTERY GROUP INC
1200 County Road 523 (08822-7097)
PHONE..............................404 255-7529
Rick Hallock, *President*
EMP: 5
SALES (corp-wide): 170.1MM **Privately Held**
SIC: 3621 5063 Storage battery chargers, motor & engine generator type; storage batteries, industrial
PA: Energy Battery Group, Inc.
1800 Roswell Rd Ste 2200
Marietta GA 30062
888 823-0954

(G-3441)
FLEMINGTON ALUMININUM & BRASS
24 Junction Rd (08822-5721)
PHONE..............................908 782-6333
James Kozicki, *President*
Lynne Kozicki, *Vice Pres*
Jim Kozicki, *Sales Executive*
EMP: 6 EST: 1940
SQ FT: 12,000
SALES: 954.7K **Privately Held**
WEB: www.fabonline.net
SIC: 3364 Brass & bronze die-castings

(G-3442)
FLEMINGTON BITUMINOUS CORP
356 State Route 31 (08822-5741)
PHONE..............................908 782-2722
Richard D Mannon, *President*
Hilda Mannon, *Treasurer*
EMP: 10 EST: 1960
SQ FT: 1,200
SALES (est): 1.5MM **Privately Held**
SIC: 2951 Road materials, bituminous (not from refineries)

(G-3443)
FLEMINGTON PRECAST & SUP LLC
18 Allen St (08822-1120)
PHONE..............................908 782-3246
Garrett Hoffman, *Prdtn Mgr*
Frank Palka, *Sales Staff*
Jeffrey W Hoffman,
EMP: 12 EST: 1951
SQ FT: 4,000
SALES: 1.2MM **Privately Held**
SIC: 5084 3272 Pumps & pumping equipment; septic tanks, concrete; burial vaults, concrete or precast terrazzo; concrete products, precast

(G-3444)
FLUID DYNAMICS INC
18 Commerce St Ste 1819 (08822-7708)
P.O. Box 7, Rosemont (08556-0007)
PHONE..............................908 200-5823
Rita Rounds, *President*
Phil Rounds, *Director*
EMP: 4
SQ FT: 3,000
SALES (est): 451K **Privately Held**
WEB: www.fluiddynamics.com
SIC: 3821 Laboratory apparatus & furniture

(G-3445)
GEM VAULT INC
23 Turntable Jct (08822-1541)
P.O. Box 997 (08822-0997)
PHONE..............................908 788-1770
William Brewer, *President*
Bill Brewer, *President*
EMP: 5
SQ FT: 1,500
SALES: 480K **Privately Held**
SIC: 5944 3911 Jewelry, precious stones & precious metals; jewelry, precious metal

(G-3446)
GENERAL PALLET LLC
97 River Rd (08822-5732)
P.O. Box 1000, Readington (08870-1000)
PHONE..............................732 549-1000
Toll Free:..............................888 -
Donald W Baldwin,
EMP: 7 EST: 1966
SALES (est): 730K **Privately Held**
WEB: www.generalpallet.com
SIC: 2448 Pallets, wood

(G-3447)
HEALIOS INC
56 Main St Ste 1d (08822-1474)
P.O. Box 713 (08822-0713)
PHONE..............................908 731-5061
Dupont Guilhem, *Principal*
EMP: 7
SALES (est): 336.5K
SALES (corp-wide): 486.7K **Privately Held**
SIC: 2879 Agricultural chemicals
PA: Healios Gmbh
Sevogelstrasse 32
Basel BS
613 112-009

(G-3448)
HITRAN CORPORATION
362 Highway 31 (08822-5741)
PHONE..............................908 782-5525
John Hindle Jr, *Ch of Bd*
John C Hindle III, *President*
James S Hindle, *Vice Pres*
William Hindle, *Treasurer*
▲ EMP: 150 EST: 1944
SALES (est): 60.2MM **Privately Held**
WEB: www.hitrancorp.com
SIC: 3612 Power transformers, electric

▲ = Import ▼=Export
◆ =Import/Export

(G-3449)
HUNTERDON COUNTY
DEMOCRAT INC (PA)
Also Called: Hunterdon Observer
200 State Route 31 # 202 (08822-5727)
P.O. Box 32 (08822-0032)
PHONE..................................908 782-4747
Catherine T Langley, *President*
EMP: 90 **EST:** 1825
SQ FT: 25,000
SALES (est): 5.2MM **Privately Held**
WEB: www.hcdems.com
SIC: 2711 Commercial printing & newspaper publishing combined

(G-3450)
JEM PRINTING INC
Also Called: Printech
35 Main St (08822-1486)
PHONE..................................908 782-9986
Joseph E Mastrull, *President*
Robert Celentano, *Accounts Exec*
Moukarram Bitar, *Graphic Designe*
Valerie Lezan,
EMP: 5
SQ FT: 1,200
SALES (est): 135.2K **Privately Held**
WEB: www.prin-tech.com
SIC: 2741 2791 2752 Miscellaneous publishing; typesetting; commercial printing, offset

(G-3451)
JERSEY SHORE COSMETICS
LLC
23 Pleasant View Way (08822-4617)
PHONE..................................908 500-9954
Jacquelyn Quattro,
EMP: 10
SQ FT: 2,500
SALES (est): 1.1MM **Privately Held**
SIC: 2844 Face creams or lotions

(G-3452)
JOHANNA FOODS INC (PA)
20 Johanna Farms Rd (08822)
P.O. Box 272 (08822-0272)
PHONE..................................908 788-2200
Robert A Facchina, *President*
Chris Cornwall, *Vice Pres*
▲ **EMP:** 277 **EST:** 1944
SQ FT: 500,000
SALES (est): 178.1MM **Privately Held**
WEB: www.johannafoods.com
SIC: 2033 2026 Fruit juices: packaged in cans, jars, etc.; fruit juices: fresh; yogurt

(G-3453)
KERRY INC
Also Called: Kerry Ingredients
26 Minneakoning Rd (08822-5725)
PHONE..................................908 237-1595
Simon G Statter, *Branch Mgr*
EMP: 60 **Privately Held**
SIC: 2087 Flavoring extracts & syrups
HQ: Kerry Inc.
3400 Millington Rd
Beloit WI 53511
608 363-1200

(G-3454)
KUHL CORP
39 Kuhl Rd (08822-6801)
P.O. Box 26 (08822-0026)
PHONE..................................908 782-5696
Henry Y Kuhl, *President*
Jeffrey Kuhl, *Vice Pres*
Kevin Kuhl, *Vice Pres*
Paul R Kuhl Jr, *CFO*
◆ **EMP:** 62
SQ FT: 60,000
SALES (est): 18.8MM **Privately Held**
SIC: 3556 Poultry processing machinery

(G-3455)
MEL CHEMICALS INC (DH)
Also Called: M E I
500 Brbrtown Pt Breeze Rd (08822-4702)
PHONE..................................908 782-5800
Alan Foster, *Ch of Bd*
Pat Jones, *Business Mgr*
Oliver Butler, *Purch Agent*
Janet Raphagen, *Treasurer*
Kathleen Snook, *Treasurer*
▲ **EMP:** 103 **EST:** 1951

SQ FT: 135,000
SALES (est): 51.8MM
SALES (corp-wide): 487.9MM **Privately Held**
WEB: www.meichem.com
SIC: 5169 3295 2819 3339 Chemicals & allied products; minerals, ground or otherwise treated; industrial inorganic chemicals; primary nonferrous metals; chemical preparations
HQ: Luxfer Group Limited
Lumns Lane
Manchester M27 8
161 300-0600

(G-3456)
METRO OPTICS LLC
38 Winding Way (08822-7039)
P.O. Box 275, Whitehouse Station (08889-0275)
PHONE..................................908 413-0004
Nick T Cloutier, *Manager*
Nick Clothier,
EMP: 15
SQ FT: 20,000
SALES: 1.9MM **Privately Held**
SIC: 3229 Fiber optics strands

(G-3457)
MIDLANTIC SHUTTER &
MILWORK
108 Church St (08822-1645)
PHONE..................................908 806-3400
Paul Cucco, *Owner*
EMP: 7 **EST:** 2000
SALES (est): 896K **Privately Held**
SIC: 2431 Millwork

(G-3458)
ON SITE MANUFACTURING INC
1042 County Road 523 (08822-7034)
P.O. Box 250, Austin IN (47102)
PHONE..................................812 794-6040
Irvin L French, *President*
EMP: 9
SALES (est): 1.6MM **Privately Held**
SIC: 3585 Refrigeration & heating equipment

(G-3459)
PLATINUM DESIGNS LLC
93 Rake Rd (08822-5631)
P.O. Box 232 (08822-0232)
PHONE..................................908 782-4010
Robin Cairl, *Finance*
Ian G Cairl,
EMP: 8
SALES: 1.5MM **Privately Held**
SIC: 2434 Wood kitchen cabinets

(G-3460)
POWERCOMM SOLUTIONS LLC
15 Minneakoning Rd # 311 (08822-5749)
PHONE..................................908 806-7025
Leila Gabel, *Office Mgr*
Raymond Fella,
EMP: 5
SALES (est): 570K **Privately Held**
SIC: 3825 Instruments to measure electricity

(G-3461)
PRECISION DEALER SERVICES
INC
4 Ryerson Rd (08822-7004)
P.O. Box 74, Whitehouse Station (08889-0074)
PHONE..................................908 237-1100
Mark Berry, *President*
EMP: 25
SALES (est): 2.3MM **Privately Held**
SIC: 8742 2541 4731 2431 Materials mgmt. (purchasing, handling, inventory) consultant; cabinets, lockers & shelving; freight transportation arrangement; millwork; fluid meters & counting devices

(G-3462)
PRETTY JEWELRY CO
80 Main St 82 (08822-1482)
PHONE..................................908 806-3377
Mario Marcel, *Owner*
EMP: 4
SALES (est): 103K **Privately Held**
SIC: 7631 3911 Jewelry repair services; jewelry, precious metal

(G-3463)
PRINT SHOPPE INC
15 Minneakoning Rd # 305 (08822-5749)
PHONE..................................908 782-9213
Denise Hayes, *President*
John Crain, *Project Mgr*
Dan Thrush, *Consultant*
EMP: 9
SQ FT: 5,000
SALES (est): 1.4MM **Privately Held**
WEB: www.printshoppe.com
SIC: 2752 Commercial printing, offset

(G-3464)
PRINTCO
Also Called: Prentco
12 Minneakoning Rd 103b (08822-5810)
PHONE..................................908 687-9518
Ron Steinberg, *Owner*
EMP: 4
SALES (est): 408.1K **Privately Held**
SIC: 3544 Special dies & tools

(G-3465)
PVH CORP
Also Called: Van Heusen
41 Liberty Vlg (08822-1561)
PHONE..................................908 788-5880
Catherine Perkins, *Manager*
EMP: 10
SALES (corp-wide): 9.6B **Publicly Held**
WEB: www.pvh.com
SIC: 2321 5621 Men's & boys' dress shirts; sport shirts, men's & boys': from purchased materials; ready-to-wear apparel, women's
PA: Pvh Corp.
200 Madison Ave Bsmt 1
New York NY 10016
212 381-3500

(G-3466)
SERVICE TECH
109 Rake Factory Rd (08822-5626)
PHONE..................................908 788-0072
Todd De Vito, *Owner*
EMP: 4
SALES (est): 490.5K **Privately Held**
SIC: 3357 Appliance fixture wire, nonferrous

(G-3467)
SIMPLEX AMERICAS LLC
20 Bartles Corner Rd (08822-5716)
PHONE..................................908 237-9099
Jeremy Cantilina, *Controller*
Chuck Autrey, *Manager*
Jackie Cometta, *Senior Mgr*
Donald Vogler,
▲ **EMP:** 4
SALES (est): 907.5K **Privately Held**
SIC: 3731 Shipbuilding & repairing

(G-3468)
SKUNKTOWN DISTILLERY LLC
12 Minneakoning Rd 110b (08822-5810)
PHONE..................................908 824-7754
EMP: 4 **EST:** 2017
SALES (est): 149.3K **Privately Held**
SIC: 2085 Distilled & blended liquors

(G-3469)
SOMERVILLE ACQUISITIONS CO
INC (PA)
45 River Rd Ste 300 (08822-6026)
PHONE..................................908 782-9500
Piyush J Patel, *President*
Milton Rosen, *Vice Pres*
Richard Rosen, *Vice Pres*
◆ **EMP:** 175
SALES (est): 28MM **Privately Held**
SIC: 2819 Aluminum compounds

(G-3470)
TECHNIMOLD INC
112 Pine Bank Rd (08822-7165)
PHONE..................................908 232-8331
William Mc Namara, *President*
Carole Mc Namara, *Corp Secy*
EMP: 18
SQ FT: 8,200
SALES (est): 2.2MM **Privately Held**
WEB: www.technimold.com
SIC: 3089 Injection molding of plastics

(G-3471)
THRYV INC
27 Minneakoning Rd # 204 (08822-5761)
PHONE..................................908 237-0956
Ellen Green, *Branch Mgr*
EMP: 15
SALES (corp-wide): 1.8B **Privately Held**
WEB: www.rhdonnelley.com
SIC: 2741 Directories: publishing only, not printed on site
PA: Thryv, Inc.
2200 W Airfield Dr
Dfw Airport TX 75261
972 453-7000

(G-3472)
TITANIUM TECHNICAL
SERVICES
21 New York Ave (08822-1437)
PHONE..................................908 323-9899
Justin Moss, *Principal*
EMP: 5 **EST:** 2016
SALES (est): 133K **Privately Held**
SIC: 3356 Titanium

Florence
Burlington County

(G-3473)
BOYDS PHARMACY INC
Also Called: Good Neighbor Pharmacy
306 Broad St (08518-1912)
P.O. Box 1 (08518-0001)
PHONE..................................609 499-0100
Lardner C Boyd III, *President*
EMP: 12
SALES (est): 2.1MM **Privately Held**
WEB: www.boydspharmacy.com
SIC: 2834 5912 Medicines, capsuled or ampuled; drug stores

(G-3474)
DC FABRICATORS INC
801 W Front St (08518-1121)
PHONE..................................609 499-3000
John Frieling, *Ch of Bd*
Michael Salerno, *Shareholder*
EMP: 135
SQ FT: 1,000
SALES (est): 62MM **Privately Held**
WEB: www.dcfab.com
SIC: 3443 Condensers, steam

(G-3475)
ENDURANCE NET INC
763 B Railroad Ave (08518)
P.O. Box 127, Roebling (08554-0127)
PHONE..................................609 499-3450
Joseph R Scarperia, *President*
▲ **EMP:** 12
SQ FT: 40,000
SALES (est): 1.6MM **Privately Held**
WEB: www.endurancenetinc.com
SIC: 2258 3949 Net & netting products; netting, knit; sporting & athletic goods

(G-3476)
MIDWAY MACHINE PRODUCT
CORP
763a Railroad Ave (08518)
P.O. Box 129 (08518-0129)
PHONE..................................609 499-4377
William Green, *President*
EMP: 9
SQ FT: 6,500
SALES (est): 992.8K **Privately Held**
SIC: 3599 Machine shop, jobbing & repair

(G-3477)
READY PAC PRODUCE INC
Also Called: Ready-Pac Club Chef
700 Railroad Ave (08518)
P.O. Box 6 (08518-0006)
PHONE..................................609 499-1900
Tom Hunter, *Manager*
EMP: 73
SALES (corp-wide): 2.6MM **Privately Held**
WEB: www.readypacproduce.com
SIC: 5148 2099 Fresh fruits & vegetables; salads, fresh or refrigerated

HQ: Ready Pac Produce, Inc.
4401 Foxdale St
Irwindale CA 91706
800 800-4088

(G-3478)
TEX-NET INC
763 Railroad Ave B (08518)
P.O. Box 92 (08518-0092)
PHONE...............................609 499-9111
John Scarperia, *President*
Joseph Scarperia, *Vice Pres*
EMP: 20
SQ FT: 18,000
SALES (est): 2.4MM **Privately Held**
WEB: www.powercage.com
SIC: 2221 5941 Textile mills, broadwoven:
silk & manmade, also glass; golf goods &
equipment

(G-3479)
**TOTAL CONTROL OTHOTICS
LAB**
14 W Front St (08518-1319)
PHONE...............................609 499-2200
Dominick Ciccone, *President*
EMP: 7
SALES (est): 919.2K **Privately Held**
SIC: 3842 Orthopedic appliances

Florham Park
Morris County

(G-3480)
ARMAC INC (PA)
Also Called: Armac Associates
71 Passaic Ave (07932-3040)
PHONE...............................973 457-0002
Herbert J Etzold, *President*
Tara Dailey, *Vice Pres*
Keri Rutkowski, *Executive*
EMP: 10
SQ FT: 2,000
SALES (est): 2.4MM **Privately Held**
SIC: 3842 Splints, pneumatic & wood

(G-3481)
ASCO LP (HQ)
160 Park Ave (07932-1049)
PHONE...............................800 972-2726
Manish Bhandari, *Partner*
Jim Jarosik, *Engineer*
Greg Volz, *Engineer*
Chris Walsh, *Human Res Mgr*
John Matro, *Sales Staff*
◆ **EMP:** 313
SALES (est): 311.7MM
SALES (corp-wide): 17.4B **Publicly Held**
SIC: 3491 Industrial valves
PA: Emerson Electric Co.
8000 West Florissant Ave
Saint Louis MO 63136
314 553-2000

(G-3482)
ASCO INVESTMENT CORP
50-60 Hanover Rd (07932-1503)
PHONE...............................973 966-2000
Jean-Pierre Yaouanc, *President*
Albert Giarrusso, *Senior Buyer*
Eamon Rowan, *VP Finance*
Shawn Burke, *Natl Sales Mgr*
Kent Fowler, *Sales Dir*
▲ **EMP:** 107
SQ FT: 13,000
SALES (est): 16.3MM **Privately Held**
SIC: 3491 Industrial valves

(G-3483)
**ASCO POWER SERVICES INC
(DH)**
160 Park Ave (07932-1049)
PHONE...............................973 966-2000
Armand J Visioli, *President*
Jack Petro, *Vice Pres*
EMP: 10
SALES (est): 12.8MM
SALES (corp-wide): 177.9K **Privately
Held**
WEB: www.redhat3.com
SIC: 3643 Electric switches

HQ: Schneider Electric Usa, Inc.
201 Wshington St Ste 2700
Boston MA 02108
978 975-9600

(G-3484)
**ASCO POWER TECHNOLOGIES
LP (DH)**
160 Park Ave (07932-1049)
PHONE...............................973 966-2000
Michael Quinn, *President*
◆ **EMP:** 300
SQ FT: 126,000
SALES (est): 976.2MM
SALES (corp-wide): 177.9K **Privately
Held**
SIC: 3699 Electrical equipment & supplies
HQ: Schneider Electric Usa, Inc.
201 Wshington St Ste 2700
Boston MA 02108
978 975-9600

(G-3485)
**AUTOMATIC SWITCH COMPANY
(DH)**
50-60 Hanover Rd (07932-1591)
PHONE...............................973 966-2000
Jean-Pierre Yaouanc, *President*
Gregory C Schreiber, *President*
Ed Amaducci, *Manager*
▲ **EMP:** 1200 **EST:** 1906
SQ FT: 220,000
SALES (est): 329MM
SALES (corp-wide): 17.4B **Publicly Held**
WEB: www.ascoval.com
SIC: 3491 3625 3677 3674 Solenoid
valves; control equipment, electric; elec-
tronic coils, transformers & other induc-
tors; semiconductors & related devices;
switchgear & switchboard apparatus; fluid
power valves & hose fittings
HQ: Emerson Electric (U.S.) Holding Cor-
poration
850 Library Ave Ste 204c
Saint Louis MO 63136
314 553-2000

(G-3486)
AUTOMATIC SWITCH COMPANY
Also Called: Asco Power Technology
50 Hanover Rd (07932-1419)
PHONE...............................209 941-4111
John Kovach, *Engineer*
Phil Tibbits, *Branch Mgr*
Chris Myers, *Manager*
EMP: 601
SALES (corp-wide): 17.4B **Publicly Held**
SIC: 3491 Solenoid valves
HQ: Automatic Switch Company
50-60 Hanover Rd
Florham Park NJ 07932
973 966-2000

(G-3487)
**BANDING CENTERS OF
AMERICA**
83 Hanover Rd Ste 160 (07932-1518)
PHONE...............................973 805-9977
EMP: 4
SALES (est): 470K **Privately Held**
SIC: 3842 Mfg Surgical Appliances/Sup-
plies

(G-3488)
**BASF AMERICAS
CORPORATION (DH)**
100 Park Ave (07932-1049)
PHONE...............................973 245-6000
Wayne Smith, *President*
Cecelia Mc Cloud, *Office Mgr*
◆ **EMP:** 11
SALES (est): 6.4MM
SALES (corp-wide): 71.7B **Privately Held**
WEB: www.basf.com
SIC: 2869 Industrial organic chemicals
HQ: Basf Corporation
100 Park Ave
Florham Park NJ 07932
973 245-6000

(G-3489)
BASF CALIFORNIA INC (DH)
100 Campus Dr (07932-1020)
PHONE...............................973 245-6000
◆ **EMP:** 4

SALES (est): 1.3MM
SALES (corp-wide): 71.7B **Privately Held**
SIC: 2869 Industrial organic chemicals
HQ: Basf Catalysts Llc
33 Wood Ave S
Iselin NJ 08830
732 205-5000

(G-3490)
**BASF CATALYSTS HOLDG
CHINA LLC (DH)**
100 Campus Dr (07932-1020)
PHONE...............................973 245-6000
EMP: 5
SALES (est): 1.8MM
SALES (corp-wide): 71.7B **Privately Held**
SIC: 2869 Industrial organic chemicals
HQ: Basf Corporation
100 Park Ave
Florham Park NJ 07932
973 245-6000

(G-3491)
BASF CORPORATION (HQ)
100 Park Ave (07932-1089)
P.O. Box 685 (07932-0685)
PHONE...............................973 245-6000
Wayne T Smith, *CEO*
Peter Eckes, *President*
Kenneth Lane, *President*
Teressa Szelest, *President*
Georg Grossmann, *Principal*
◆ **EMP:** 277 **EST:** 1873
SQ FT: 325,000
SALES (est): 7.7B
SALES (corp-wide): 71.7B **Privately Held**
WEB: www.basf.com
SIC: 2869 2819 2899 2843 Industrial or-
ganic chemicals; industrial inorganic
chemicals; antifreeze compounds; sur-
face active agents; pharmaceutical prepa-
rations; vitamin preparations; agricultural
chemicals
PA: Basf Se
Carl-Bosch-Str. 38
Ludwigshafen Am Rhein 67056
621 600-

(G-3492)
BASF PLANT SCIENCE LP
Also Called: Performance Chemicals
100 Park Ave (07932-1049)
PHONE...............................973 245-3238
Wayne T Smith, *CEO*
EMP: 4
SALES (est): 523.3K **Privately Held**
SIC: 2879 2911 Pesticides, agricultural or
household; petroleum refining

(G-3493)
BASFIN CORPORATION (HQ)
100 Park Ave (07932-1049)
PHONE...............................973 245-6000
Peter Oakley, *President*
Gilbert Barrios, *President*
Frank A Bozich, *President*
Corey Chapek, *President*
Martin Brudermller, *Principal*
◆ **EMP:** 1000
SALES (est): 2.6B
SALES (corp-wide): 71.7B **Privately Held**
SIC: 2869 2819 2899 2843 Industrial or-
ganic chemicals; industrial inorganic
chemicals; antifreeze compounds; sur-
face active agents; agricultural chemicals;
pharmaceutical preparations
PA: Basf Se
Carl-Bosch-Str. 38
Ludwigshafen Am Rhein 67056
621 600-

(G-3494)
**BOOMERANG SYSTEMS INC
(PA)**
30a Vreeland Rd (07932-1904)
PHONE...............................973 538-1194
James V Gelly, *CEO*
James Gelly, *CEO*
Mark R Patterson, *Ch of Bd*
Christopher Mulvihill, *President*
George Gelly, *COO*
EMP: 39 **EST:** 1979
SQ FT: 7,350

SALES (est): 5.4MM **Privately Held**
SIC: 3549 3535 7521 Assembly machines, including robotic; robotic conveyors; automobile storage garage

(G-3495)
CAPINTEC INC (DH)
7 Vreeland Rd Ste 101 (07932-1511)
PHONE...............................201 825-9500
Baris Kalyoncu, *Vice Pres*
David Najjar, *Vice Pres*
Earle Mulrane, *Engineer*
Ralph J Monaco, *CFO*
Michael Flynn, *Controller*
▲ **EMP:** 23
SQ FT: 41,000
SALES (est): 12.2MM
SALES (corp-wide): 2.1B **Privately Held**
SIC: 3829 3823 3845 5045 Nuclear radi-
ation & testing apparatus; temperature in-
struments: industrial process type; patient
monitoring apparatus; computer periph-
eral equipment; surgical appliances &
supplies; surgical & medical instruments
HQ: Eczacibasi Monrol Nukleer Urunler
Sarayi Ve Ticaret Anonim Sirketi
Teknoparki, Tubitak Mahallesi
Kocaeli 41400
262 648-0200

(G-3496)
**CELLECTAR BIOSCIENCES INC
(PA)**
100 Campus Dr Ste 207 (07932-1020)
PHONE...............................608 441-8120
Douglas J Swirsky, *Ch of Bd*
James V Caruso, *President*
Charles T Bernhardt, *CFO*
EMP: 7
SQ FT: 4,000
SALES (est): 3.2MM **Publicly Held**
WEB: www.novelos.com
SIC: 2834 Pharmaceutical preparations

(G-3497)
COMVERGE GIANTS INC
25a Vreeland Rd Ste 300 (07932-1933)
PHONE...............................973 884-5970
John Bunyan, *Branch Mgr*
John N Bunyan, *Branch Mgr*
EMP: 6
SALES (corp-wide): 2.3B **Publicly Held**
SIC: 3822 Hardware for environmental reg-
ulators
HQ: Comverge Giants, Inc.
120 Eagle Rock Ave # 190
East Hanover NJ 07936

(G-3498)
**CREATIONS BY SHERRY LYNN
LLC**
90 Park Ave Ste 414 (07932-1068)
PHONE...............................800 742-3448
Andrew Greenberger,
Sherry Greenberger,
EMP: 4
SALES (est): 50K **Privately Held**
SIC: 3911 Jewelry apparel

(G-3499)
**CUSTOM WORKFLOW
SOLUTIONS LLC (PA)**
Also Called: Cws Software
17 Broadway Fl 2 (07932-2603)
PHONE...............................917 647-9222
Eric Guba, *Vice Pres*
Milton Melamed, *Mng Member*
EMP: 19
SALES (est): 2.1MM **Privately Held**
SIC: 7372 Prepackaged software

(G-3500)
DATAMOTION INC (PA)
200 Park Ave Ste 302 (07932-1040)
PHONE...............................973 455-1245
Bob Bales, *CEO*
Mahesh Muchhala, *Ch of Bd*
Bob Janacek, *Exec VP*
EMP: 28 **EST:** 1999
SALES (est): 7.8MM **Privately Held**
WEB: www.datamotion.com
SIC: 7373 7374 7379 7372 Systems inte-
gration services; data verification service;
; business oriented computer software

(G-3501)
DRS LEONARDO INC
Also Called: Drs Srvillance Support Systems
200 Campus Dr Ste 410 (07932-1007)
PHONE...........................973 898-1500
Michael Hlavaty, *President*
John Riggs, *President*
Richard Danforth, *Principal*
Brian Cardinal, *Vice Pres*
Jeffrey Cutre, *Vice Pres*
EMP: 38
SALES (corp-wide): 9.2B **Privately Held**
SIC: 3812 Search & navigation equipment
HQ: Leonardo Drs, Inc.
    2345 Crystal Dr Ste 1000
    Arlington VA 22202
    703 416-8000

(G-3502)
**EAGLE WORK CLOTHES INC
(PA)**
20 Quail Run (07932-1755)
P.O. Box 388, Union (07083-0388)
PHONE...........................908 964-8888
Charles J Fruchter, *President*
Dennis Fruchter, *Vice Pres*
◆ **EMP:** 37 **EST:** 1946
SQ FT: 35,000
SALES (est): 3.2MM **Privately Held**
WEB: www.eaglewc.com
SIC: 2326 5136 2337 Work garments, ex-
    cept raincoats: waterproof; work uniforms;
    uniforms, men's & boys'; uniforms, except
    athletic: women's, misses' & juniors'

(G-3503)
EXELTIS USA INC (DH)
180 Park Ave Ste 101 (07932-1054)
PHONE...........................973 324-0200
Maria Carell, *President*
Everett Felper, *President*
John Giordano, *Exec VP*
Esmeralda Baxter, *Sales Staff*
David Defelice, *Sales Staff*
▲ **EMP:** 63 **EST:** 1971
SALES (est): 11.7MM
SALES (corp-wide): 5.7MM **Privately
Held**
WEB: www.everettlabs.com
SIC: 2834 5122 Pharmaceutical prepara-
    tions; drugs & drug proprietaries
HQ: Chemo Iberica Sa
    Calle Dulcinea, S/N
    Alcala De Henares 28805
    913 021-560

(G-3504)
**EXELTIS USA DERMATOLOGY
LLC**
180 Park Ave Ste 101 (07932-1054)
PHONE...........................973 805-4060
Maria Carell, *President*
Manuel Barro, *Director*
Ignacio Ponce, *Director*
Sandra Martin Moran, *Admin Sec*
Eduardo Fernandez, *Asst Sec*
EMP: 50 **EST:** 2012
SALES (est): 5.8MM
SALES (corp-wide): 5.7MM **Privately
Held**
SIC: 2834 Pharmaceutical preparations
HQ: Exeltis Usa, Inc.
    180 Park Ave Ste 101
    Florham Park NJ 07932
    973 324-0200

(G-3505)
EZOSE SCIENCES INC
300 Campus Dr Ste 300 (07932-1039)
PHONE...........................862 926-1950
Kiyoshi Nagata, *CEO*
Scott A Siegel, *COO*
Hidehisa Asada, *Vice Pres*
▲ **EMP:** 17
SQ FT: 12,000
SALES (est): 2.7MM **Privately Held**
SIC: 3826 Amino acid analyzers

(G-3506)
FTI INC
Also Called: Tetra Lubricants
8 Vreeland Rd (07932-1501)
PHONE...........................973 443-0004
W B Smith, *CEO*
◆ **EMP:** 4

SQ FT: 20,000
SALES (est): 923.2K **Privately Held**
SIC: 2992 2851 2952 Lubricating oils &
    greases; paints & paint additives; coating
    compounds, tar
PA: Troy Corporation
    8 Vreeland Rd
    Florham Park NJ 07932

(G-3507)
GENERAL DYNAMICS MISSION
7 9 Vreeland Rd (07932)
PHONE...........................973 261-1409
Christopher Marzilli, *President*
Elizabeth Mazea, *Branch Mgr*
Robert Heltzman, *Technician*
EMP: 198
SALES (corp-wide): 36.1B **Publicly Held**
SIC: 3669 3812 Transportation signaling
    devices; search & navigation equipment
HQ: General Dynamics Mission Systems,
    Inc.
    12450 Fair Lakes Cir # 200
    Fairfax VA 22033
    703 263-2800

(G-3508)
**GERBER PRODUCTS COMPANY
(DH)**
Also Called: Nestle Infant Nutrition
12 Vreeland Rd Fl 2 (07932-1521)
PHONE...........................973 593-7500
Kurt T Schmidt, *President*
Kevin L Goldberg, *Vice Pres*
Craig Thompson, *Vice Pres*
Don W Gosline, *Treasurer*
Linda J Brodie, *Asst Treas*
◆ **EMP:** 212 **EST:** 1867
SALES (est): 618.6MM
SALES (corp-wide): 92B **Privately Held**
WEB: www.gerber.com
SIC: 2023 2043 2037 2052 Baby formu-
    las; cereal breakfast foods; fruit juices;
    cookies & crackers; pasteurized & mineral
    waters, bottled & canned; canned & cured
    fish & seafoods
HQ: Nestle Holdings, Inc.
    1812 N Moore St
    Arlington VA 22209
    703 682-4600

(G-3509)
HELLER INDUSTRIES INC (PA)
4 Vreeland Rd Ste 1 (07932-1593)
PHONE...........................973 377-6800
David Heller, *President*
Marc Peo, *President*
David Gross, *Vice Pres*
Hemang Patel, *Facilities Mgr*
Phil Martin, *Opers Staff*
▲ **EMP:** 60
SQ FT: 50,000
SALES (est): 21.5MM **Privately Held**
WEB: www.hellerindustries.com
SIC: 3569 Assembly machines, non-metal-
    working

(G-3510)
HISAMITSU PHRM CO INC
100 Campus Dr Ste 117 (07932-1006)
PHONE...........................973 765-0122
Keniehi Suruta, *President*
EMP: 13
SALES (est): 1.3MM **Privately Held**
SIC: 2834 8731 Pharmaceutical prepara-
    tions; medical research, commercial

(G-3511)
HR ACUITY LLC
25a Vreeland Rd Ste 101 (07932-1903)
PHONE...........................888 598-0161
Deborah Muller, *CEO*
Charlie Holbech, *COO*
Beth Prunier, *Senior VP*
Dushyant Zutshi, *Vice Pres*
EMP: 12
SALES (est): 1.3MM **Privately Held**
SIC: 8742 7372 Human resource consult-
    ing services; business oriented computer
    software

(G-3512)
**HUTCHISON MEDIPHARMA (US)
INC**
25a Vreeland Rd Ste 304 (07932-1921)
PHONE...........................973 567-3254

EMP: 4
SALES (est): 289.9K **Privately Held**
SIC: 2834 Pharmaceutical preparations

(G-3513)
INSPIRE WORKS INC
24 Midwood Dr (07932-1811)
PHONE...........................908 730-7447
James Tagliareni, *President*
James Taglarini, *Principal*
EMP: 12
SALES (est): 833.4K **Privately Held**
WEB: www.inspireworksinc.com
SIC: 7372 Prepackaged software

(G-3514)
LAPP CABLE WORKS INC
29 Hanover Rd (07932-1408)
PHONE...........................973 660-9632
Roland Keller, *President*
Andreas Lapp, *Chairman*
Marc Mackin, *Corp Secy*
Keith Myrick, *COO*
Suman Kundu, *Engineer*
▲ **EMP:** 24
SQ FT: 25,000
SALES (est): 6.6MM
SALES (corp-wide): 355.8K **Privately
Held**
SIC: 3357 Nonferrous wiredrawing & insu-
    lating
HQ: Lapp Holding Na Inc.
    29 Hanover Rd
    Florham Park NJ 07932

(G-3515)
LAPP HOLDING NA INC (HQ)
29 Hanover Rd (07932-1408)
PHONE...........................973 660-9700
Marc Mackin, *President*
Christian Abambari, *Engineer*
Maureen Hedden, *Human Resources*
Martin Tepe, *Manager*
Rick Fiorey, *Supervisor*
▲ **EMP:** 26
SALES (est): 123.2MM
SALES (corp-wide): 355.8K **Privately
Held**
SIC: 3355 Aluminum wire & cable
PA: Lapp Beteiligungs-Kg
    Oskar-Lapp-Str. 2
    Stuttgart
    711 783-801

(G-3516)
LAPP USA INC
29 Hanover Rd (07932-1408)
PHONE...........................973 660-9700
Andreas Lapp, *President*
Tracey Timmons, *Business Mgr*
Patti Piotrowski, *Warehouse Mgr*
Anayanci Hinojosa, *Purch Mgr*
Brian Bookamer, *Engineer*
EMP: 4
SALES (est): 249.3K **Privately Held**
SIC: 3643 Power line cable

(G-3517)
LAPP USA LLC
29 Hanover Rd (07932-1408)
PHONE...........................973 660-9700
Andreas Lapp, *President*
Marc K Mackin, *COO*
Rob Conway, *Exec VP*
George Dann, *Vice Pres*
Michael Judge, *Purch Mgr*
◆ **EMP:** 132
SALES (est): 99.4MM
SALES (corp-wide): 355.8K **Privately
Held**
SIC: 5063 3678 Control & signal wire &
    cable, including coaxial; electronic con-
    nectors
HQ: Lapp Holding Na Inc.
    29 Hanover Rd
    Florham Park NJ 07932

(G-3518)
OLON USA INC
100 Campus Dr Ste 105 (07932-1006)
PHONE...........................973 577-6038
Aldo Donati, *President*
Francesco Saletta, *Vice Pres*
EMP: 15 **EST:** 2012

SALES (est): 808.1K **Privately Held**
SIC: 2899 Gelatin: edible, technical, photo-
    graphic or pharmaceutical
HQ: Olon Spa
    Strada Provinciale Rivoltana 6/7
    Rodano MI 20090
    029 523-1

(G-3519)
PIEMONTE & LIEBHAUSER LLC
25b Vreeland Rd Ste 104 (07932-1925)
PHONE...........................973 937-6200
Robin Kerrs, *Principal*
EMP: 14
SALES (est): 1.7MM **Privately Held**
SIC: 2024 Ice cream & frozen desserts

(G-3520)
**PRECISION ROLL PRODUCTS
INC**
306 Columbia Tpke (07932-1217)
PHONE...........................973 822-9100
Fax: 973 822-9100
▲ **EMP:** 10 **EST:** 2009
SALES (est): 1MM **Privately Held**
SIC: 3356 Nonferrous Rolling/Drawing

(G-3521)
PROFOTO US INC
220 Park Ave Ste 120 (07932-1047)
PHONE...........................973 822-1300
Mark Rezzonico, *President*
Ron Eglentowicz, *Principal*
▲ **EMP:** 14
SQ FT: 6,500
SALES (est): 2.4MM **Privately Held**
SIC: 3861 Photographic equipment & sup-
    plies
HQ: Profoto Ab
    Landsvagen 57
    Sundbyberg 172 6
    844 753-00

(G-3522)
**REGENUS CTR CORE
THERAPIES LLC**
17 Hanover Rd (07932-1411)
P.O. Box 1878, Livingston (07039-1878)
PHONE...........................862 295-1620
Jason Sonners,
Allen Mollenhauer,
EMP: 4
SALES (est): 44.1K **Privately Held**
SIC: 8049 7372 Physical therapist; appli-
    cation computer software

(G-3523)
TRISYS INC
215 Ridgedale Ave Ste 2 (07932-1355)
P.O. Box 484 (07932-0484)
PHONE...........................973 360-2300
Mark Karpilovsky, *President*
Gromov Dmitry, *Vice Pres*
Michelle Karpilovsky, *Marketing Mgr*
Christina Laraia, *Info Tech Mgr*
George Tsintsadze, *Software Dev*
EMP: 5
SQ FT: 4,600
SALES: 2.1MM **Privately Held**
WEB: www.born2e.com
SIC: 7372 Publishers' computer software

(G-3524)
TROY CORPORATION (PA)
8 Vreeland Rd (07932-1501)
P.O. Box 434 (07932-0434)
PHONE...........................973 443-4200
Daryl D Smith, *President*
David Koehl, *Business Mgr*
Ismael Colon, *Vice Pres*
David E Faherty, *Vice Pres*
Alexander M Gerardo, *Vice Pres*
◆ **EMP:** 98
SQ FT: 75,000
SALES (est): 221.2MM **Privately Held**
SIC: 2869 Industrial organic chemicals

(G-3525)
UNICORN GROUP INC (PA)
25b Hanover Rd (07932-1442)
PHONE...........................973 360-0688
Frank Diassi, *Chairman*
EMP: 167
SQ FT: 12,000

SALES (est): 19.1MM **Privately Held**
WEB: www.open4.com
SIC: 7379 7372 Computer related consulting services; business oriented computer software

(G-3526)
WASHINGTON STAMP EXCHANGE INC
Also Called: Art Craft
2 Vreeland Rd (07932-1501)
P.O. Box 311 (07932-0311)
PHONE..................................973 966-0001
Michael August, *President*
Tim Devany, *Corp Secy*
Robin Devany, *Admin Sec*
EMP: 13 EST: 1930
SQ FT: 35,000
SALES (est): 2.4MM **Privately Held**
WEB: www.washpress.com
SIC: 2677 2789 3083 2752 Envelopes; binding & repair of books, magazines & pamphlets; laminated plastic sheets; commercial printing, lithographic

(G-3527)
WORLD WIDE PACKAGING LLC (PA)
Also Called: Wwp
15 Vreeland Rd Ste 4 (07932-1506)
PHONE..................................973 805-6500
Barry A Freda, *CEO*
Barbara Zengewald, *Sales Staff*
▲ EMP: 40
SQ FT: 20,000
SALES (est): 9.8MM **Privately Held**
SIC: 2844 Cosmetic preparations

(G-3528)
ZOETIS PRODUCTS LLC (HQ)
100 Campus Dr Ste 3 (07932-1006)
PHONE..................................973 660-5000
David R Jackson, *Vice Pres*
Adrian Del Valle, *Technical Mgr*
Matthew Farrell,
Juan Ramon Alaix,
Joseph Del Buono,
◆ EMP: 200
SALES (est): 366.9MM
SALES (corp-wide): 5.8B **Publicly Held**
WEB: www.alpharma.com
SIC: 2834 2833 Pharmaceutical preparations; medicinals & botanicals
PA: Zoetis Inc.
10 Sylvan Way Ste 105
Parsippany NJ 07054
973 822-7000

Fords
Middlesex County

(G-3529)
ALLIED PHARMA INC
20 Corrielle St (08863-1909)
PHONE..................................732 738-3295
Mayur Doshi, *President*
Venky Sreedhar, *Consultant*
EMP: 7
SALES: 5.2MM **Privately Held**
SIC: 2834 Pharmaceutical preparations

(G-3530)
BAI LAR INTERIOR SERVICES INC
554 New Brunswick Ave (08863-2195)
PHONE..................................732 738-0350
James E Quinn, *President*
Patrick M Quinn, *Vice Pres*
Denise Sims, *Admin Sec*
EMP: 5
SQ FT: 3,000
SALES: 1MM **Privately Held**
SIC: 2211 5131 7389 Draperies & drapery fabrics, cotton; millinery supplies; interior designer

(G-3531)
CLAUSEN COMPANY INC
1055 King George Rd (08863)
P.O. Box 140 (08863-0140)
PHONE..................................732 738-1165
Donald J Peck, *Ch of Bd*
EMP: 15 EST: 1957

SQ FT: 12,800
SALES (est): 3.3MM **Privately Held**
WEB: www.clausencompany.com
SIC: 2851 2821 Paints & allied products; plastics materials & resins

(G-3532)
JOHNNYS SERVICE CENTER
53 Lawrence St (08863-2019)
PHONE..................................732 738-0569
Gary English, *Owner*
Karen Klemm, *Admin Sec*
EMP: 5
SQ FT: 3,000
SALES (est): 429.6K **Privately Held**
SIC: 7694 7539 Motor repair services; automotive repair shops

(G-3533)
LANXESS SOLUTIONS US INC
Hatco Division
1020 King George Post Rd (08863-2329)
PHONE..................................732 738-1000
Micheal Raab, *Branch Mgr*
EMP: 165
SALES (corp-wide): 8.2B **Privately Held**
WEB: www.cromptoncorp.com
SIC: 2869 2992 Plasticizers, organic; cyclic & acyclic; lubricating oils & greases
HQ: Lanxess Solutions Us Inc.
2 Armstrong Rd Ste 101
Shelton CT 06484
203 573-2000

(G-3534)
ZACK PAINTING CO INC
900 King George Rd (08863-2140)
P.O. Box 120 (08863-0120)
PHONE..................................732 738-7900
David Zack, *President*
EMP: 50 EST: 1923
SQ FT: 15,000
SALES (est): 7.1MM **Privately Held**
WEB: www.zackpainting.com
SIC: 1721 1799 3081 Commercial painting; spraying contractor, non-agricultural; floor or wall covering, unsupported plastic

Forked River
Ocean County

(G-3535)
ADE INC
719 Old Shore Rd (08731-5905)
P.O. Box 538, Lanoka Harbor (08734-0538)
PHONE..................................609 693-6050
Earnie Cretola, *President*
Ernie Tretola, *President*
EMP: 10
SALES (est): 2.6MM **Privately Held**
SIC: 3585 Heating & air conditioning combination units

(G-3536)
BRICK-WALL CORP
Also Called: CJS Hesse
2215 Lacey Rd (08731-5810)
PHONE..................................609 693-6223
Charles Stout, *Manager*
EMP: 20
SALES (est): 2.4MM
SALES (corp-wide): 3.6MM **Privately Held**
SIC: 1611 2951 Highway & street paving contractor; asphalt paving mixtures & blocks
PA: Brick-Wall Corp.
25 1st Ave Ste 200
Atlantic Highlands NJ 07716
732 787-0226

(G-3537)
CLAYTON BLOCK COMPANY INC
2011 Lacey Rd (08731-5806)
PHONE..................................609 693-9600
Ron Mc Millan, *Manager*
EMP: 13

SALES (corp-wide): 31.8MM **Privately Held**
WEB: www.claytononline.com
SIC: 3271 Blocks, concrete or cinder: standard
PA: Clayton Block Company, Inc.
1355 Campus Pkwy Ste 200
Wall Township NJ 07753
888 763-8665

(G-3538)
CORBCO INC
40 Canterbury Dr (08731-5644)
PHONE..................................609 549-6299
EMP: 5
SQ FT: 4,700
SALES: 300K **Privately Held**
SIC: 3081 Manufactures And Packages Products

(G-3539)
CUSTOM AUTO RADIATOR INC
Also Called: C A R
441 S Main St (08731-4647)
PHONE..................................609 242-9700
Charles Monjoy, *President*
Sylvia Monjoy, *Admin Sec*
EMP: 11
SQ FT: 5,000
SALES (est): 1.5MM **Privately Held**
SIC: 3714 5531 Radiators & radiator shells & cores, motor vehicle; automotive parts

(G-3540)
IACOVELLI STAIRS INCORPORATED
707 Challenger Way (08731-5915)
PHONE..................................609 693-3476
Joseph Iacovelli, *President*
EMP: 13
SQ FT: 2,000
SALES: 2MM **Privately Held**
SIC: 2431 Staircases & stairs, wood; stair railings, wood

(G-3541)
ISLAND BEACH DISTILLERY
713 Old Shore Rd (08731-5901)
PHONE..................................609 242-5054
EMP: 4
SALES (est): 284.1K **Privately Held**
SIC: 2085 Distilled & blended liquors

(G-3542)
PIONEER CONCRETE CORP
Also Called: Central Concrete Aggregates
2011 Lacey Rd (08731-5806)
PHONE..................................609 693-6151
Nelson K Walling, *President*
Gary O Walling, *Vice Pres*
EMP: 20 EST: 1986
SALES: 1.9MM **Privately Held**
SIC: 1442 Construction sand mining

(G-3543)
PLASTICS FOR CHEMICALS INC (PA)
710 Old Shore Rd (08731-5900)
PHONE..................................609 242-9100
John T Donovan, *President*
John Donavan, *Partner*
Edward T Norman, *Vice Pres*
EMP: 9
SQ FT: 2,500
SALES (est): 1.8MM **Privately Held**
WEB: www.plastkemiforetagen.se
SIC: 2821 Plastics materials & resins

Fort Lee
Bergen County

(G-3544)
ACTAVIS ELIZABETH LLC
Actavis US
1 Executive Dr (07024-3309)
PHONE..................................908 527-9100
Lee Dress, *Branch Mgr*
EMP: 140 **Privately Held**
SIC: 2834 Druggists' preparations (pharmaceuticals)

HQ: Actavis Elizabeth Llc
200 Elmora Ave
Elizabeth NJ 07202
908 527-9100

(G-3545)
AEON ENGINEERING LLC
442 Main St Ste 5 (07024-2830)
PHONE..................................518 253-7681
Kim James Kyung-Hwan, *Administration*
EMP: 5
SALES (est): 131.8K **Privately Held**
SIC: 3679 8711 Electronic circuits; engineering services

(G-3546)
ANATOLIAN NATURALS INC
1 Bridge Plz N Ste 275 (07024-7586)
PHONE..................................201 893-0142
Volkan Sonmez, *Vice Pres*
EMP: 4
SALES (est): 367.1K **Privately Held**
SIC: 2844 Cosmetic preparations

(G-3547)
AQUALINK LLC
Also Called: Japanese-American Society NJ
304 Main St Ste 2 (07024-4715)
PHONE..................................201 849-9771
Mina Yoshigaki,
Miki Nagano, *Administration*
EMP: 15
SALES: 67K **Privately Held**
WEB: www.jasofnj.org
SIC: 8699 3999 Literary, film or cultural club; artificial flower arrangements

(G-3548)
BAETA CORP
Also Called: (A DEVELOPMENTAL STAGE COMPANY)
1 Bridge Plz N Ste 2 (07024-7586)
PHONE..................................201 471-0988
Leonid Pushkantser, *CEO*
Alexander Gak MD, *Ch of Bd*
Jeff Burkland, *CFO*
Lee Smith, *Chief Mktg Ofcr*
Eugene Gribov, *CTO*
EMP: 6
SALES (est): 410K **Privately Held**
SIC: 3841 Surgical & medical instruments

(G-3549)
BETERRIFIC   CORP (PA)
900 Palisade Ave Apt 1d (07024-4136)
PHONE..................................201 735-7711
Michael Artsis, *CEO*
David M Milch, *Ch of Bd*
EMP: 4
SALES (est): 444.1K **Privately Held**
SIC: 7819 2741 Visual effects production;

(G-3550)
BINEX LINE CORP
2 Executive Dr Ste 755 (07024-3302)
PHONE..................................201 662-7600
Mimi Ji, *Manager*
EMP: 13 **Privately Held**
SIC: 3999 Barber & beauty shop equipment
PA: Binex Line Corp.
19515 S Vermont Ave
Torrance CA 90502

(G-3551)
BLACK SEA FISHERIES
306 Whiteman St Apt 6 (07024-5627)
PHONE..................................973 553-1580
EMP: 4 EST: 2011
SALES (est): 304.1K **Privately Held**
SIC: 2092 Fresh or frozen packaged fish

(G-3552)
CHOCMOD USA INC
2200 Fletcher Ave Ste 3 (07024-5005)
PHONE..................................201 585-8730
Stephen Picard, *President*
Bernard Destombes, *Purchasing*
Christophe Mareau, *Info Tech Mgr*
▲ EMP: 20
SQ FT: 3,500
SALES (est): 2.3MM
SALES (corp-wide): 177.9K **Privately Held**
SIC: 2066 Chocolate & cocoa products

G E O G R A P H I C

HQ: Chocmod
1 Avenue De Flandre
Roncq 59223
320 289-280

(G-3553)
DAICEL CHEMTECH INC
1 Parker Plz (07024-2920)
PHONE................................201 461-4466
Kaguo Asada, *President*
EMP: 6
SALES (est): 593.9K **Privately Held**
SIC: 3585 Air conditioning units, complete: domestic or industrial
PA: Daicel Corporation
3-1, Ofukacho, Kita-Ku
Osaka OSK 530-0

(G-3554)
DAINIPPON SUMITOMO PHARMA AMER (DH)
1 Bridge Plz N Ste 510 (07024-7102)
PHONE................................201 592-2050
▲ EMP: 20
SALES (est): 690.7MM
SALES (corp-wide): 20.5B **Privately Held**
SIC: 2834 Mfg Pharmaceutical Preparations
HQ: Sumitomo Dainippon Pharma Co., Ltd.
2-6-8, Doshomachi, Chuo-Ku
Osaka OSK 541-0
662 035-321

(G-3555)
DIAMOND UNIVERSE LLC
2460 Lemoine Ave Ste 302 (07024-6210)
PHONE................................201 592-9500
Sneha Kheskwani, *Mng Member*
Tony Kheskwani,
▲ EMP: 10
SQ FT: 1,700
SALES (est): 1.1MM **Privately Held**
SIC: 3915 5094 Jewelers' castings; jewelry

(G-3556)
E W WILLIAMS PUBLICATIONS (HQ)
2125 Center Ave Ste 305 (07024-5874)
PHONE................................201 592-7007
Andrew Williams, *President*
Ew Williams, *Founder*
EMP: 16
SALES (est): 1.8MM
SALES (corp-wide): 42.3MM **Privately Held**
WEB: www.williamspublications.com
SIC: 2721 Magazines: publishing only, not printed on site
PA: Pioneer Associates, Inc.
2125 Center Ave Ste 305
Fort Lee NJ 07024
201 592-7007

(G-3557)
EVEREAST TRADING INC
2125 Center Ave Ste 401 (07024-5874)
PHONE................................201 944-6484
Bum Suk Shim, *President*
◆ EMP: 1
SALES: 2MM **Privately Held**
SIC: 2024 2086 Ice cream & frozen desserts; bottled & canned soft drinks

(G-3558)
FINE WEAR U S A
22 E Columbia Ave (07024)
PHONE................................201 313-3777
Ben Huh, *CEO*
EMP: 4
SALES (est): 400K **Privately Held**
SIC: 2389 7219 Uniforms & vestments; laundry, except power & coin-operated

(G-3559)
FRANKLIN MINT LLC
Also Called: Franklin Mint Trading
400 Kelby St Ste 15 (07024-2938)
PHONE................................800 843-6468
Robert H Book, *CEO*
Scott Book, *President*
◆ EMP: 42 EST: 1964

SALES (est): 4.4MM **Privately Held**
WEB: www.franklinmint.com
SIC: 3942 3911 3999 2731 Dolls, except stuffed toy animals; bracelets, precious metal; necklaces, precious metal; pins (jewelry), precious metal; models, general, except toy; books: publishing & printing; figures: pottery, china, earthenware & stoneware

(G-3560)
HERBORIUM GROUP INC (PA)
1 Bridge Plz N Ste 275 (07024-7586)
PHONE................................201 849-4431
Dr Agnes P Olszewski, *CEO*
EMP: 1
SALES (est): 2.9MM **Publicly Held**
SIC: 2833 5122 Medicinals & botanicals; medicinals & botanicals

(G-3561)
HILLER SEPARATION PROCESS LLC
2125 Center Ave Ste 507 (07024-5874)
PHONE................................512 556-5707
Stefan Coppe, *General Mgr*
Stefan Koppe, *General Mgr*
Tracey Langely,
Sheilah Pickel,
▲ EMP: 6
SALES (est): 1MM **Privately Held**
SIC: 3443 Separators, industrial process: metal plate

(G-3562)
HRP CAPITAL INC (PA)
173 Bridge Plz N (07024-7575)
PHONE................................201 242-4938
A Alberto Lugo, *Principal*
EMP: 2 EST: 2008
SALES (est): 12.4MM **Privately Held**
SIC: 2834 Pharmaceutical preparations

(G-3563)
HUB PRINT & COPY CENTER LLC
Also Called: Hub, The
2037 Lemoine Ave (07024-5704)
PHONE................................201 585-7887
Gerard Tonner, *President*
Donna Tonner, *Vice Pres*
EMP: 4
SQ FT: 1,600
SALES (est): 359.3K **Privately Held**
WEB: www.hubprint.com
SIC: 2752 7334 2791 2789 Commercial printing, offset; photocopying & duplicating services; typesetting; bookbinding & related work; agents, shipping; packing goods for shipping

(G-3564)
INTERNTNAL DIGITAL SYSTEMS INC
Also Called: IDS
400 Kelby St Ste 6 (07024-2938)
PHONE................................201 983-7700
Anthony Han, *CEO*
Jung Ye Han, *President*
EMP: 18
SALES (est): 1.5MM **Privately Held**
SIC: 7379 7371 7372 7373 Computer related consulting services; custom computer programming services; custom computer programming services; business oriented computer software; office computer automation systems integration; systems engineering consultant, ex. computer or professional

(G-3565)
J-TECH CREATIONS INC
1 Bridge Plz N Ste 275 (07024-7586)
PHONE................................201 944-2968
Masaki Yamaguchi, *President*
EMP: 5 EST: 2013
SALES: 440K **Privately Held**
SIC: 7372 Application computer software; business oriented computer software; home entertainment computer software

(G-3566)
K & S DRUG & SURGICAL INC
Also Called: Junction Drugs
266 Columbia Ave (07024-4125)
PHONE................................201 886-9191
Khoren Nalbandian, *President*
Seta Nalbandian, *Treasurer*
EMP: 4
SQ FT: 1,000
SALES (est): 850K **Privately Held**
SIC: 5912 3842 5921 Drug stores; surgical appliances & supplies; liquor stores

(G-3567)
KEDRION BIOPHARMA INC (DH)
400 Kelby St Ste 11 (07024-2938)
PHONE................................201 242-8900
Paolo Marcucci, *President*
Michele Barcia, *QC Mgr*
Robert Alpern, *Project Engr*
Peer Hansen, *CFO*
Patricia Look, *Manager*
EMP: 100
SQ FT: 10,078
SALES (est): 284.8MM
SALES (corp-wide): 137.3K **Privately Held**
SIC: 2836 Plasmas
HQ: Kedrion Spa
Localita' Ai Conti
Barga LU 55051
058 376-7100

(G-3568)
LINK2CONSULT INC
1 Bridge Plz N Ste 275 (07024-7586)
PHONE................................888 522-0902
Peter McCree, *President*
Maria Jijon, *Admin Mgr*
EMP: 10
SQ FT: 500
SALES (est): 1.3MM **Privately Held**
WEB: www.link2consult.com
SIC: 7372 Prepackaged software

(G-3569)
LLC DUNN MEADOW
Also Called: Dunn Meadow Pharmacy
1555 Center Ave Ste 1 (07024-4612)
PHONE................................201 297-4603
Craig Cohen, *Owner*
EMP: 10 EST: 2014
SALES (est): 950.9K **Privately Held**
SIC: 2834 Pharmaceutical preparations

(G-3570)
MAXENTRIC TECHNOLOGIES LLC (PA)
2071 Lemoine Ave Ste 302 (07024-6007)
PHONE................................201 242-9800
Houman Ghajari, *Managing Dir*
Phil Dorante, *Vice Pres*
Per Johansson, *Vice Pres*
Bardia Ghajari, *Design Engr*
Nilsson Plymoth, *Corp Comm Staff*
EMP: 25
SALES (est): 6.1MM **Privately Held**
WEB: www.maxentric.com
SIC: 1623 3663 7379 Transmitting tower (telecommunication) construction; satellites, communications;

(G-3571)
MEMOMIND PHARMA INC
2125 Center Ave (07024-5859)
PHONE................................201 302-9020
EMP: 4
SALES (est): 255.6K **Privately Held**
SIC: 2834 Pharmaceutical preparations

(G-3572)
METALLIA USA LLC
2200 Fletcher Ave Ste 7 (07024-5005)
PHONE................................212 536-8002
Avy Buchen,
Morris Weinstein,
◆ EMP: 9
SALES (est): 2.3MM
SALES (corp-wide): 245.8MM **Privately Held**
SIC: 3315 Steel wire & related products
PA: Hartree Partners, Lp
1185 Avenue Of The Americ
New York NY 10036
212 536-8915

(G-3573)
MICROTELECOM LTD LIABILITY CO (PA)
1 Bridge Plz N Ste 275 (07024-7586)
PHONE................................866 676-5679
Yonathan Shechter,
EMP: 3
SQ FT: 2,000
SALES: 2MM **Privately Held**
SIC: 7371 7373 7372 Computer software development; computer systems analysis & design; prepackaged software

(G-3574)
MTEIXEIRA SOAPSTONE VA LLC
1100 Palisade Ave (07024-6328)
PHONE................................201 757-8608
EMP: 4
SALES (est): 223.7K **Privately Held**
SIC: 1499 Soapstone mining

(G-3575)
N J W MAGAZINE
Also Called: Advantage Publications
177 Main St Ste 232 (07024-6936)
PHONE................................201 886-2185
Louise Hafesh, *President*
Joseph Hafesh, *Vice Pres*
▼ EMP: 11
SALES (est): 750K **Privately Held**
SIC: 2721 Periodicals

(G-3576)
NADRI INC
2 Executive Dr Ste 500 (07024-3307)
PHONE................................201 585-0088
Young Tae Choi, *President*
Yool Lee, *Accountant*
▲ EMP: 35
SALES (est): 774.7K **Privately Held**
SIC: 3911 Jewelry, precious metal

(G-3577)
NANA CREATIONS INC
329 Lincoln Ave (07024-6106)
PHONE................................201 263-1112
EMP: 14
SQ FT: 10,000
SALES: 787K **Privately Held**
SIC: 2337 Mfgs Ladies Coats

(G-3578)
NATAL LAMP & SHADE CORP
Also Called: Natalie Lamp & Shade
5 Horizon Rd Apt 2601 (07024-6646)
PHONE................................201 224-7844
George Reisman, *President*
EMP: 50 EST: 1935
SQ FT: 90,000
SALES (est): 3.2MM **Privately Held**
SIC: 3641 5023 3999 Lamps, incandescent filament, electric; lamps: floor, boudoir, desk; shades, lamp or candle

(G-3579)
OBJECUTIVE INC
2125 Center Ave Ste 411 (07024-5812)
PHONE................................201 242-1522
Constantinos Kelleas, *CEO*
Christoper Leeming, *President*
Robert Arvanitis, *Vice Pres*
Ariana Franciscovic, *Marketing Staff*
Anthony King, *CTO*
EMP: 13 EST: 1998
SQ FT: 5,000
SALES (est): 1.8MM **Privately Held**
WEB: www.objecutive.com
SIC: 7372 Business oriented computer software

(G-3580)
OLIVOS USA INC (DH)
1 Bridge Plz N Ste 275 (07024-7586)
PHONE................................201 893-0142
Selcuk Atalay, *CEO*
▲ EMP: 5
SQ FT: 10,000
SALES (est): 31.3MM
SALES (corp-wide): 7.6MM **Privately Held**
WEB: www.olivosusa.com
SIC: 2079 Olive oil

HQ: Olivos Gida Yag Tarim Sanayi Ithalat
　Ihracat Ve Ticaret Anonim Sirketi
　1. Organize Sanayi Bolgesi, No:9
　Ticaret Ve Sanayi Odasi Bulvar
　Manisa 45400
　236 332-5032

(G-3581)
PIONEER ASSOCIATES INC (PA)
2125 Center Ave Ste 305 (07024-5874)
PHONE..................................201 592-7007
Andrew Williams, *President*
EMP: 40 **EST:** 1934
SQ FT: 3,000
SALES (est): 42.3MM **Privately Held**
WEB: www.idhonline.com
SIC: 1623 2721 Electric power line con-
　struction; trade journals: publishing only,
　not printed on site

(G-3582)
**PIONEER POWER SOLUTIONS
INC (PA)**
400 Kelby St Ste 12 (07024-2938)
PHONE..................................212 867-0700
Nathan J Mazurek, *Ch of Bd*
Thomas Klink, *CFO*
Mark Malinosky, *Controller*
Vincent Visconti, *Sales Staff*
EMP: 60
SQ FT: 2,700
SALES: 106.3MM **Publicly Held**
SIC: 3612 Control transformers

(G-3583)
QUICK FROZEN FOODS INTL
2125 Center Ave Ste 305 (07024-5874)
PHONE..................................201 592-7007
Andrew Williams, *President*
▲ **EMP:** 30
SALES (est): 1.1MM **Privately Held**
SIC: 2721 Magazines: publishing only, not
　printed on site

(G-3584)
RUICHEM USA INC
2050 Center Ave Ste 365 (07024-4936)
PHONE..................................978 992-1811
Yinyan Tang, *CEO*
Rebecca Yen, *Office Mgr*
EMP: 5
SALES (est): 99K **Privately Held**
SIC: 2816 Titanium dioxide, anatase or ru-
　tile (pigments)

(G-3585)
SA RICHARDS INC
1600 Parker Ave Apt 23a (07024-7007)
PHONE..................................201 947-3850
Richard Aquino, *President*
EMP: 4
SALES: 800K **Privately Held**
SIC: 2653 Boxes, solid fiber: made from
　purchased materials

(G-3586)
SADELCO INC
96 Linwood Plz (07024-3701)
PHONE..................................201 569-3323
Les Kaplan, *President*
Gail Kaplan, *Admin Sec*
▲ **EMP:** 70 **EST:** 1960
SQ FT: 13,500
SALES (est): 10.1MM **Privately Held**
WEB: www.sadelco.com
SIC: 3825 Test equipment for electronic &
　electrical circuits

(G-3587)
SHERMAN GROUP HOLDINGS
2200 Fletcher Ave Office (07024-5005)
PHONE..................................201 735-9000
Brendon Scott, *CFO*
EMP: 5
SALES (est): 468.6K **Privately Held**
SIC: 2111 Cigarettes

(G-3588)
SIKLU INC (HQ)
2037 Lemoine Ave (07024-5704)
PHONE..................................201 267-9597
Itzik Ben-Bassat, *CEO*
Izik Kirshenbaum, *President*
Ilan Moshe, *General Mgr*
Dganit Nevo, *Opers Staff*
Craig Burgess, *Sales Dir*

EMP: 15
SALES (est): 1.1MM
SALES (corp-wide): 12MM **Privately
Held**
SIC: 3663 Radio broadcasting & communi-
　cations equipment
PA: Siklu Communication Ltd
　43 Hasivim
　Petah Tikva 49595
　392 140-15

(G-3589)
**STAMM INTERNATIONAL CORP
(PA)**
1530 Palisade Ave Ste Phd (07024-5471)
P.O. Box 1929 (07024-8429)
PHONE..................................201 947-1700
Marilyn Skony Stamm, *President*
Maria Vilardi, *Controller*
EMP: 3
SQ FT: 1,000
SALES (est): 64.4MM **Privately Held**
WEB: www.stamminternational.com
SIC: 6719 3585 3564 3433 Investment
　holding companies, except banks; refrig-
　eration & heating equipment; blowers &
　fans; heating equipment, except electric

(G-3590)
**SUNOVION PHARMACEUTICALS
INC**
1 Bridge Plz N Ste 510 (07024-7102)
PHONE..................................201 592-2050
Lisa Haase, *Facilities Mgr*
Rica Minatoya, *Financial Analy*
Hiroshi Nomura, *Branch Mgr*
Alkesh Amin, *Manager*
Carolyn Masone, *Manager*
EMP: 85 **Privately Held**
SIC: 2834 Pharmaceutical preparations
HQ: Sunovion Pharmaceuticals Inc.
　84 Waterford Dr
　Marlborough MA 01752
　508 481-6700

(G-3591)
TYPECOM LLC (PA)
1275 15th St Apt 19a (07024-1936)
P.O. Box 1163 (07024-1163)
PHONE..................................201 969-1901
Richard Barnett, *Mng Member*
Cathy Coda,
EMP: 5
SQ FT: 1,200
SALES (est): 702.6K **Privately Held**
SIC: 2759 7311 Commercial printing; ad-
　vertising agencies

(G-3592)
**US CHINA ALLIED PRODUCTS
INC**
Also Called: Uscap
555 North Ave Apt 12h (07024-2414)
PHONE..................................201 461-9886
▲ **EMP:** 6 **EST:** 1995
SQ FT: 1,000
SALES (est): 480K **Privately Held**
SIC: 3841 Mfg Surgical/Medical Instru-
　ments

(G-3593)
VATECH AMERICA INC
2200 Fletcher Ave 705a (07024-5084)
PHONE..................................201 210-5028
Jai Hoon Kim, *President*
▲ **EMP:** 33
SALES (est): 5.7MM **Privately Held**
SIC: 8021 3844 Dental clinics & offices;
　radiographic X-ray apparatus & tubes
PA: Value Added Technology Co., Ltd.
　13 Samsung 1-Ro 2-Gil
　Hwaseong 18449

(G-3594)
VIVA CHEMICAL CORPORATION
1512 Palisade Ave Apt 5m (07024-5310)
PHONE..................................201 461-5281
Veniamin Nilva, *President*
Constantine Lutsenko, *Vice Pres*
EMP: 8
SQ FT: 2,000
SALES (est): 838.6K **Privately Held**
SIC: 2869 Industrial organic chemicals

(G-3595)
**WORLD CLASS MARKETING
CORP (DH)**
Also Called: A A World Class Corp
2147 Hudson Ter (07024-7729)
PHONE..................................201 313-0022
Coleman Schneider, *CEO*
Benjamin Amoruso, *President*
EMP: 40
SQ FT: 24,000
SALES (est): 9.5MM
SALES (corp-wide): 46.4MM **Privately
Held**
WEB: www.aaworld.com
SIC: 2395 3911 2258 2281 Emblems,
　embroidered; jewelry, precious metal;
　lace & lace products; yarn spinning mills
HQ: Carolace Industries, Inc.
　325 Sylvan Ave Ste 102
　Englewood Cliffs NJ 07632
　201 945-2151

(G-3596)
WYSSMONT COMPANY INC
1470 Bergen Blvd (07024-2197)
PHONE..................................201 947-4600
Joseph Bevacqua, *CEO*
Jayne Kraljic, *Technology*
▲ **EMP:** 24
SQ FT: 6,000
SALES (est): 2.5MM **Privately Held**
WEB: www.wyssmont.com
SIC: 3567 3559 3556 Driers & redriers,
　industrial process; chemical machinery &
　equipment; cutting, chopping, grinding,
　mixing & similar machinery

Franklin
Sussex County

(G-3597)
**ADVANCED IMAGING ASSOC
LLC (PA)**
190 Munsonhurst Rd Ste 1 (07416-1810)
PHONE..................................973 823-8999
Clifford Barker MD, *Principal*
EMP: 6
SALES (est): 657.2K **Privately Held**
WEB: www.advancedimagingassoc.com
SIC: 3826 Magnetic resonance imaging
　apparatus

(G-3598)
**AMERICAN PRVATE LABEL
PDTS LLC**
24b Munsonhurst Rd (07416-1819)
P.O. Box 1025, Goshen NY (10924-8025)
PHONE..................................845 733-8151
Robert Kozic, *COO*
EMP: 4
SALES (est): 208.5K **Privately Held**
SIC: 2844 Depilatories (cosmetic)

(G-3599)
**AURORA RESEARCH COMPANY
INC**
200 Munsonhurst Rd # 201 (07416-1813)
PHONE..................................973 827-8055
Donna Barbetta, *President*
Richard Barbetta, *Vice Pres*
EMP: 5
SQ FT: 3,000
SALES (est): 608K **Privately Held**
WEB: www.auroraresearchgroup.com
SIC: 3572 7373 Tape storage units, com-
　puter; systems software development
　services

(G-3600)
B & C MACHINE CO INC
22 Lasinski Rd Ste I (07416)
P.O. Box 321, Sussex (07461-0321)
PHONE..................................973 823-1120
Robert Van Dyke, *President*
EMP: 5
SQ FT: 4,000
SALES: 800K **Privately Held**
SIC: 3599 Machine shop, jobbing & repair

(G-3601)
**CLINICAL IMAGE RETRIEVAL
SYSTE**
Also Called: Cir Systems
12 Cork Hill Rd Ste 2 (07416-1302)
P.O. Box 6081, Parsippany (07054-7081)
PHONE..................................888 482-2362
Douglas D Haas Jr, *Owner*
Karen Toepper, *Treasurer*
EMP: 6
SQ FT: 1,000
SALES (est): 906.4K **Privately Held**
SIC: 3841 Diagnostic apparatus, medical

(G-3602)
DOUBLE TWENTIES INC
Also Called: Franklin Precast Tanks
20 Park Dr (07416-9758)
PHONE..................................973 827-7563
Alex Kovach, *President*
Wendy Kovach, *Vice Pres*
EMP: 10
SQ FT: 2,500
SALES (est): 1.7MM **Privately Held**
SIC: 3272 Septic tanks, concrete

(G-3603)
FUTURREX INC
24 Munsonhurst Rd Ste F (07416-1803)
P.O. Box 823, Denville (07834-0823)
PHONE..................................973 209-1563
Zbigniew Sobczak, *President*
David Kryscio, *Research*
Andrew Parker, *Engineer*
Krzysztof Konopka, *Manager*
Kerri Leto, *Director*
▲ **EMP:** 19
SALES (est): 5.1MM **Privately Held**
SIC: 2819 Industrial inorganic chemicals

(G-3604)
GORDON BRUSH MFG CO INC
15 Park Dr (07416-9758)
PHONE..................................973 827-4600
EMP: 8
SALES (corp-wide): 15.1MM **Privately
Held**
SIC: 3991 Brooms & brushes
PA: Gordon Brush Mfg. Co., Inc.
　3737 Capitol Ave
　City Of Industry CA 90601
　323 724-7777

(G-3605)
MJS PRECISION INC
12 Cork Hill Rd Ste 3 (07416-1302)
PHONE..................................973 209-1300
Michael Sanclementi, *President*
EMP: 4
SQ FT: 3,000
SALES (est): 531.7K **Privately Held**
SIC: 3599 Machine shop, jobbing & repair

(G-3606)
NEWTON SCREEN PRINTING CO
Also Called: Newton Screenprinting
75 Main St (07416-1422)
PHONE..................................973 827-0486
Paula Lavorgna, *President*
Frank Newton Jr, *Corp Secy*
EMP: 8
SQ FT: 7,000
SALES (est): 780K **Privately Held**
WEB: www.newtonscreen.com
SIC: 2759 5199 Screen printing; advertis-
　ing specialties

(G-3607)
**NUMERITOOL MANUFACTURING
CORP**
58 Woodland Rd (07416-1315)
PHONE..................................973 827-7714
Curtis Allen, *President*
EMP: 5
SQ FT: 2,500
SALES (est): 2.5MM **Privately Held**
SIC: 3566 Drives, high speed industrial,
　except hydrostatic

(G-3608)
NUTRI SPORT PHARMACAL INC
200 N Church Rd (07416-1211)
PHONE..................................973 827-9287
Vince Paternoster, *President*
William D Bernared, *Vice Pres*

▲ = Import ▼=Export
◆ =Import/Export

Mario Ebanietti, *Shareholder*
▲ **EMP:** 15 **EST:** 1997
SALES (est): 1.7MM **Privately Held**
WEB: www.e-nutrisport.com
SIC: 2023 2834 Dietary supplements,
dairy & non-dairy based; vitamin, nutrient
& hematinic preparations for human use

(G-3609)
TECHNOLOGY GENERAL
CORPORATION (PA)
Also Called: Clawson Machine Division
12 Cork Hill Rd (07416-1304)
PHONE....................................973 827-8209
Charles J Fletcher, *President*
Helen S Fletcher, *Treasurer*
EMP: 10
SQ FT: 34,100
SALES (est): 2.1MM **Publicly Held**
WEB: www.eclipsesystem.com
SIC: 3634 3999 Ice crushers, electric;
dock equipment & supplies, industrial

(G-3610)
UNITED SILICA PRODUCTS INC
3 Park Dr (07416-9758)
PHONE....................................973 209-8854
Lynn Marie Kane, *President*
John Boccuzzo, *General Mgr*
James Campbell, *Vice Pres*
Jim Campbell, *Vice Pres*
Lisa Burke, *Purchasing*
▲ **EMP:** 18
SQ FT: 7,500
SALES (est): 2.1MM **Privately Held**
WEB: www.unitedsilica.com
SIC: 3229 Industrial-use glassware

Franklin Lakes
Bergen County

(G-3611)
BARD DEVICES INC (DH)
1 Becton Dr (07417-1815)
PHONE....................................908 277-8000
Timothy Ring, *CEO*
William Longfield, *Chairman*
Todd Schermerhorn, *Vice Pres*
Jeremy Pinsly, *Manager*
Greg Bentley, *Info Tech Dir*
▲ **EMP:** 28
SALES (est): 16.1MM
SALES (corp-wide): 15.9B **Publicly Held**
SIC: 3841 Surgical & medical instruments
HQ: C. R. Bard, Inc.
1 Becton Dr
Franklin Lakes NJ 07417
908 277-8000

(G-3612)
BARD INTERNATIONAL INC
(DH)
Also Called: Bard Asia Pacific Division
1 Becton Dr (07417-1815)
PHONE....................................908 277-8000
William Longfield, *President*
Mike Flores, *General Mgr*
Donald Maddi, *Vice Pres*
Charles Grom, *Controller*
Frank Lupisella, *Controller*
EMP: 64
SALES (est): 14.8MM
SALES (corp-wide): 15.9B **Publicly Held**
WEB: www.bardinternational.com
SIC: 5047 3842 Medical equipment & sup-
plies; surgical appliances & supplies
HQ: C. R. Bard, Inc.
1 Becton Dr
Franklin Lakes NJ 07417
908 277-8000

(G-3613)
BAXTER CORPORATION (PA)
511 Commerce St (07417-1309)
P.O. Box 645 (07417-0645)
PHONE....................................201 337-1212
George Bowen, *President*
Michael Kelley, *Treasurer*
Terry Greenwald, *Info Tech Dir*
EMP: 80
SQ FT: 10,000

SALES (est): 12.3MM **Privately Held**
SIC: 3552 5085 5084 7373 Jacquard
loom parts & attachments; twine; textile
machinery & equipment; computer systems analysis & design

(G-3614)
BD BISCNCES SYSTEMS
RGENTS INC (PA)
1 Becton Dr (07417-1815)
PHONE....................................201 847-6800
Fax: 201 847-4442
EMP: 9
SALES (est): 1.2MM **Privately Held**
SIC: 2819 Mfg Industrial Inorganic Chemi-
cals

(G-3615)
BD VENTURES LLC
1 Becton Dr (07417-1815)
PHONE....................................201 847-6800
Steve Barbato, *CEO*
Mimi Salmon, *Partner*
Emma Frankum, *Principal*
Keith Swajger, *Opers Staff*
Sandra Leister, *Engineer*
EMP: 20
SALES (est): 5.7MM
SALES (corp-wide): 15.9B **Publicly Held**
PA: Becton, Dickinson And Company
1 Becton Dr
Franklin Lakes NJ 07417
201 847-6800

(G-3616)
BECTON DICKINSON AND
COMPANY (PA)
Also Called: B D
1 Becton Dr (07417-1880)
PHONE....................................201 847-6800
Vincent A Forlenza, *Ch of Bd*
Patrick K Kaltenbach, *President*
James Lim, *President*
Alberto Mas, *President*
Thomas E Polen, *President*
◆ **EMP:** 1500 **EST:** 1897
SALES: 15.9B **Publicly Held**
SIC: 3841 3842 3829 3826 Hypodermic
needles & syringes; IV transfusion appa-
ratus; catheters; surgical knife blades &
handles; gloves, safety; surgical appli-
ances & supplies; elastic hosiery, orthopedic (support); thermometers &
temperature sensors; analytical instruments; blood testing apparatus; hemoglo-
binometers; laboratory apparatus &
furniture; pipettes, hemocytometer

(G-3617)
C R BARD INC (HQ)
1 Becton Dr (07417-1815)
PHONE....................................908 277-8000
Timothy M Ring, *CEO*
Jim C Beasley, *President*
Douglas Church, *President*
Timothy P Collins, *President*
John P Groetelaars, *President*
▲ **EMP:** 210 **EST:** 1907
SALES: 3.7B
SALES (corp-wide): 15.9B **Publicly Held**
WEB: www.crbard.com
SIC: 3841 3845 3842 Surgical & medical
instruments; blood transfusion equipment;
surgical instruments & apparatus; elec-
tromedical equipment; electrocardio-
graphs; surgical support systems:
heart-lung machine, exc. iron lung; patient
monitoring apparatus; surgical appliances
& supplies; surgical appliances & supplies; bandages & dressings; implants,
surgical
PA: Becton, Dickinson And Company
1 Becton Dr
Franklin Lakes NJ 07417
201 847-6800

(G-3618)
COLUMBIA INDUSTRIES INC
(PA)
567 Commerce St (07417-1309)
PHONE....................................201 337-7332
Richard Pearson, *Ch of Bd*
Mary Ann Pearson, *Corp Secy*
▲ **EMP:** 8
SQ FT: 30,000

SALES (est): 18.9MM **Privately Held**
SIC: 3713 Truck bodies (motor vehicles)

(G-3619)
DIFCO LABORATORIES INC (HQ)
1 Becton Dr (07417-1815)
PHONE....................................410 316-4113
Michael Meehan, *Vice Pres*
EMP: 5
SQ FT: 46,680
SALES (est): 12.5MM
SALES (corp-wide): 15.9B **Publicly Held**
SIC: 5122 3841 2834 3823 Biologicals &
allied products; surgical & medical instru-
ments; pharmaceutical preparations; in-
dustrial instrmnts msrmnt display/control
process variable; laboratory apparatus &
furniture; culture media
PA: Becton, Dickinson And Company
1 Becton Dr
Franklin Lakes NJ 07417
201 847-6800

(G-3620)
DIRECT COMPUTER
RESOURCES INC (PA)
120 Birch Rd (07417-2718)
PHONE....................................201 848-0018
George Lang, *Ch of Bd*
Joseph J Buonomo, *President*
William Vitiello, *Vice Pres*
EMP: 25
SQ FT: 2,500
SALES (est): 3.9MM **Privately Held**
WEB: www.datavantage.com
SIC: 7372 Prepackaged software

(G-3621)
DOUGHERTY FOUNDATION
PRODUCTS
851 Meadow Ln (07417-1112)
P.O. Box 688 (07417-0688)
PHONE....................................201 337-5748
John Dougherty, *President*
Barbara Dougherty, *Vice Pres*
EMP: 5
SALES (est): 568.6K **Privately Held**
SIC: 3531 Construction machinery

(G-3622)
DOVER TOOL CONNECTICUT
LLC (PA)
620 Franklin Lake Rd (07417-2205)
PHONE....................................203 367-6376
Michael F James, *Mng Member*
EMP: 18
SQ FT: 12,000
SALES (est): 2.4MM **Privately Held**
WEB: www.dovertool.com
SIC: 3724 Aircraft engines & engine parts

(G-3623)
FLEET EQUIPMENT
CORPORATION (PA)
Also Called: FEC
567 Commerce St (07417-1309)
PHONE....................................201 337-3294
Richard Pearson, *Ch of Bd*
Scott Pearson, *Vice Pres*
Mary Ann Pearson, *Treasurer*
Rick Pearson, *CTO*
EMP: 15 **EST:** 1965
SQ FT: 30,000
SALES (est): 6MM **Privately Held**
SIC: 5012 3713 3563 Truck bodies; truck
& bus bodies; air & gas compressors

(G-3624)
GLEN ROCK STAIR CORP
551 Commerce St (07417-1309)
PHONE....................................201 337-9595
James Veenstra, *President*
Nick Veenstra, *President*
Alan Jeltema, *Vice Pres*
Lyn Veenstra, *Treasurer*
Kathy Jeltema, *Admin Sec*
EMP: 35
SQ FT: 15,000
SALES (est): 3.3MM **Privately Held**
SIC: 1751 2431 Finish & trim carpentry;
millwork

(G-3625)
GOLDEN RULE CREATIONS INC
250 Terrace Rd (07417-1621)
P.O. Box 123 (07417-0123)
PHONE....................................201 337-4050
Eric Shicker, *President*
EMP: 4
SALES (est): 173.9K **Privately Held**
WEB: www.goldenrulepatriot.com
SIC: 2395 Emblems, embroidered

(G-3626)
KA-LOR CUBICLE AND SUP CO
INC
483 Bowers Ln (07417-1907)
PHONE....................................201 891-8077
Dennis Brett, *President*
Adelle Brett, *Vice Pres*
EMP: 7
SQ FT: 2,500
SALES (est): 934.8K **Privately Held**
SIC: 3429 Manufactured hardware (gen-
eral)

(G-3627)
M R C MILLWORK & TRIM INC
319 Hobar Ct (07417-2018)
PHONE....................................201 954-2176
Marc McKeon, *President*
EMP: 4
SQ FT: 4,400
SALES (est): 494.2K **Privately Held**
SIC: 2431 Millwork

(G-3628)
MECHTRONICS CORPORATION
939 Huron Rd (07417-2210)
PHONE....................................845 231-1400
Richard J Fellinger, *Ch of Bd*
Anthony Squitieri, *President*
▲ **EMP:** 40 **EST:** 1944
SQ FT: 20,000
SALES (est): 22.8MM **Privately Held**
WEB: www.mech-tronics.com
SIC: 3993 Displays, paint process

(G-3629)
NUTECH CORP
Also Called: Nu Tech
322 Freemans Ln (07417-1012)
PHONE....................................908 707-2097
Nagi Awad, *President*
Jacob Hauser, *Vice Pres*
EMP: 8
SQ FT: 1,800
SALES (est): 829.6K **Privately Held**
SIC: 2843 2899 Textile processing assis-
tants; chemical preparations

(G-3630)
RIPE LIFE WINES LLC
253 Indian Trail Dr (07417-1014)
PHONE....................................201 560-3233
Mary McAuley,
EMP: 6 **EST:** 2012
SALES (est): 246.3K **Privately Held**
SIC: 2084 Wines

(G-3631)
ROMAR MACHINE & TOOL
COMPANY
521 Commerce St (07417-1309)
PHONE....................................201 337-7111
Robert Thum, *President*
Maria Thum, *Treasurer*
EMP: 20
SQ FT: 5,600
SALES (est): 3MM **Privately Held**
WEB: www.romarmachine.com
SIC: 3599 3544 Machine shop, jobbing &
repair; special dies, tools, jigs & fixtures

(G-3632)
VOZEH EQUIPMENT CORP
Also Called: S C T
509 Commerce St Ste 1 (07417-1314)
PHONE....................................201 337-3729
Gregory Vozeh, *CEO*
Christopher Vozeh, *VP Sales*
Karen Vozeh, *Admin Sec*
EMP: 50
SQ FT: 9,000
SALES (est): 11.2MM **Privately Held**
SIC: 3841 5072 Surgical & medical instru-
ments; hand tools

Franklin Park
Somerset County

(G-3633)
CONFECTIONATELY YOURS LLC
3391 State Route 27 # 121 (08823-1360)
PHONE..................................732 821-6863
Mary Gondek, *Owner*
EMP: 20
SQ FT: 2,800
SALES (est): 645.4K **Privately Held**
SIC: 5812 2024 Ice cream stands or dairy
bars; ice cream, bulk

(G-3634)
CRESCENT UNIFORMS LLC
33 Hasbrouck Dr (08823-1825)
PHONE..................................732 398-1866
Asma Usmani, *Mng Member*
Uzma Khan, *Director*
EMP: 10
SALES: 225K **Privately Held**
SIC: 2299 Batting, wadding, padding & fill-
ings

(G-3635)
**M D LABORATORY SUPPLIES
INC**
4 Minebrook Ln (08823-1784)
PHONE..................................732 322-0773
Harsha J Shah, *President*
Jadinkumar C Shah, *Vice Pres*
EMP: 4
SALES: 1.5MM **Privately Held**
SIC: 3229 3826 7389 Glassware, indus-
trial; analytical instruments;

Franklinville
Gloucester County

(G-3636)
**CORE 3 BREWERY LTD LBLTY
CO**
3171 Coles Mill Rd (08322-3012)
PHONE..................................856 562-0386
Alexsandros Skriapas, *Principal*
EMP: 4
SALES (est): 106K **Privately Held**
SIC: 2082 Malt beverages

(G-3637)
**EASTERN MACHINING
CORPORATION**
1197 Fries Mill Rd (08322-2619)
PHONE..................................856 694-3303
Joe Davis, *President*
EMP: 5
SQ FT: 10,000
SALES: 440K **Privately Held**
WEB: www.em-corp.com
SIC: 3599 3451 3541 Machine shop, job-
bing & repair; screw machine products;
machine tools, metal cutting type

(G-3638)
SPARK HOLLAND INC
Also Called: Ichrom Solutions
118 Karenlynn Dr (08322-3800)
PHONE..................................609 799-7250
Debra Crutchfield, *CEO*
John Crutchfield, *President*
Key Contacts Crutchfield, *General Mgr*
Gert Schuurman, *Sales Engr*
Tjipke Beer, *Manager*
EMP: 6
SALES: 1.8MM **Privately Held**
WEB: www.ichrom.com
SIC: 3821 3826 Laboratory equipment:
fume hoods, distillation racks, etc.; analyt-
ical instruments; liquid testing apparatus;
liquid chromatographic instruments; envi-
ronmental testing equipment

(G-3639)
SPECTRUM DESIGN LLC
1106 Grant Ave (08322-3107)
P.O. Box 438 (08322-0438)
PHONE..................................856 694-1870
Steve Monteleone, *Mng Member*
Brenda Monteleone,

EMP: 4
SQ FT: 700
SALES (est): 668.1K **Privately Held**
WEB: www.designedbyspectrum.com
SIC: 7389 3599 Design, commercial & in-
dustrial; custom machinery

(G-3640)
STAR BINDERY INC
963 Lincoln Ave (08322-2704)
PHONE..................................609 519-5732
David Moskowitz, *President*
Annette Moskowitz, *Corp Secy*
EMP: 35
SQ FT: 18,000
SALES: 3MM **Privately Held**
SIC: 2782 Receipt, invoice & memoran-
dum books

(G-3641)
**UNI-TECH DRILLING COMPANY
INC**
61 Grays Ferry Rd (08322-3692)
P.O. Box 407 (08322-0407)
PHONE..................................856 694-4200
Gerald Freck, *President*
David Conover, *Treasurer*
Rita Lawrence, *Controller*
Marlene Mueller, *Admin Sec*
EMP: 25
SQ FT: 10,000
SALES (est): 5.1MM **Privately Held**
WEB: www.unitechdrilling.com
SIC: 1781 1799 5084 1381 Water well
servicing; boring for building construction;
pumps & pumping equipment; drilling
water intake wells

Freehold
Monmouth County

(G-3642)
**ACCESS NORTHERN SECURITY
INC (PA)**
Also Called: Access Controls International
303 W Main St Ste 4 (07728-2522)
PHONE..................................732 462-2500
Paul Grossman, *CEO*
Bill Borowik, *Senior VP*
Paul Kelly, *Vice Pres*
David Steinmetz, *Vice Pres*
EMP: 12
SQ FT: 4,500
SALES (est): 2.8MM **Privately Held**
WEB: www.acisecurity.com
SIC: 3822 1731 Auto controls regulating
residntl & coml environmt & applncs; ac-
cess control systems specialization

(G-3643)
**ADVANTAGE MOLDING
PRODUCTS**
865 Hwy 33 (07728-8475)
PHONE..................................732 303-8667
EMP: 4 EST: 2017
SALES (est): 339.2K **Privately Held**
SIC: 3089 Molding primary plastic

(G-3644)
AGINOVA INC (PA)
3 Chambry Ct (07728-9064)
PHONE..................................732 804-3272
Ashok Sabata, *CEO*
Chris Plummer, *CFO*
Bikash Sabata, *Admin Sec*
EMP: 8
SQ FT: 1,100
SALES (est): 1MM **Privately Held**
WEB: www.aginova.com
SIC: 3822 7371 Thermostats & other envi-
ronmental sensors; computer software
development & applications

(G-3645)
ALERE INC
500 Halls Mill Rd (07728-8811)
PHONE..................................732 620-4244
Margaret Martin, *Vice Pres*
Pooja S Pathak, *Vice Pres*
Eileen L Harvat, *Opers Staff*
Susie Duarte, *Accounts Exec*
John Yonkin, *Manager*
EMP: 375

SALES (corp-wide): 30.5B **Publicly Held**
SIC: 2835 2834 In vivo diagnostics; vitamin, nutrient & hematinic preparations for
human use
HQ: Alere Inc.
51 Sawyer Rd Ste 200
Waltham MA 02453
781 647-3900

(G-3646)
ALERE INC
Also Called: Alere Distribution
569 Halls Mill Rd (07728-8812)
PHONE..................................732 358-5921
EMP: 375
SALES (corp-wide): 30.5B **Publicly Held**
SIC: 2835 In vitro & in vivo diagnostic sub-
stances
HQ: Alere Inc.
51 Sawyer Rd Ste 200
Waltham MA 02453
781 647-3900

(G-3647)
APPLIED IMAGE INC
800 Business Park Dr (07728-9393)
PHONE..................................732 410-2444
Cynthia Snanosky, *President*
Allen Shanosky, *Vice Pres*
Gioia Consoli, *Project Mgr*
▲ EMP: 34
SQ FT: 25,000
SALES (est): 5.5MM **Privately Held**
SIC: 7336 2759 Commercial art & graphic
design; commercial printing

(G-3648)
ART OF SHAVING - FL LLC
3710 Us Highway 9 (07728-4801)
PHONE..................................732 410-2520
EMP: 6
SALES (corp-wide): 67.6B **Publicly Held**
SIC: 5999 2844 3421 5122 Hair care
products; toilet preparations; razor blades
& razors; razor blades
HQ: The Art Of Shaving - Fl Llc
6100 Blue Lagoon Dr # 150
Miami FL 33126

(G-3649)
**ARTHUR GORDON ASSOCIATES
INC**
6 Paragon Way Ste 109 (07728-5925)
PHONE..................................732 431-3361
EMP: 11
SALES (corp-wide): 5MM **Privately Held**
SIC: 2521 Chairs, office: padded, uphol-
stered or plain: wood
PA: Arthur Gordon Associates, Inc.
6 Paragon Way Ste 109
Freehold NJ 07728
212 481-1530

(G-3650)
**AVALON GLOBOCARE CORP
(PA)**
4400 Route 9 S Ste 3100 (07728-4210)
PHONE..................................732 780-4400
Wenzhao Lu, *Ch of Bd*
David Jin, *President*
Meng LI, *COO*
Luisa Ingargiola, *CFO*
Yancen Lu, *Bd of Directors*
EMP: 6
SALES: 1.5MM **Publicly Held**
SIC: 8742 2835 5122 Management con-
sulting services; in vitro & in vivo diagnos-
tic substances; in vitro diagnostics;
biotherapeutics

(G-3651)
AWNING DESIGN INC
1014 Nj 33 Business (07728)
PHONE..................................908 462-1131
Walt Magovern, *Principal*
Steve Prudenti, *Principal*
EMP: 4
SQ FT: 3,000
SALES (est): 15.2K **Privately Held**
SIC: 2394 Awnings, fabric: made from pur-
chased materials

(G-3652)
BARTELL MORRISON (USA) LLC
200 Commerce Ave (07728-9379)
PHONE..................................732 566-5400

Jeff Durgin, *President*
▲ EMP: 19
SALES (est): 3.8MM **Privately Held**
SIC: 3443 Mixers, for hot metal

(G-3653)
BENTON BINDERY INC
43 Sycamore Ave (07728-2916)
PHONE..................................732 431-9064
Phil Engel, *President*
EMP: 10
SALES (est): 1.1MM **Privately Held**
SIC: 2789 Binding only: books, pamphlets,
magazines, etc.

(G-3654)
**BREWERS APPRENTICE THE
INC**
865 State Route 33 Ste 4 (07728-8475)
PHONE..................................732 863-9411
Barbara Hamara, *President*
Jo Ellen Bianchi, *Vice Pres*
Penny Vandooren, *Treasurer*
EMP: 4
SALES: 120K **Privately Held**
WEB: www.brewapp.com
SIC: 2082 Malt beverages

(G-3655)
CAMPUS COORDINATES LLC
1711 Ginesi Dr Ste 1 (07728-8592)
PHONE..................................732 866-6060
Kevin Drake, *Owner*
Roy Piper, *Sales Associate*
EMP: 7
SQ FT: 3,400
SALES: 1MM **Privately Held**
SIC: 2759 Screen printing

(G-3656)
CENTRAL TECHNOLOGY INC
Also Called: Laser Save
843 State Route 33 Ste 11 (07728-8493)
P.O. Box 294, Marlboro (07746-0294)
PHONE..................................732 431-3339
Alan D Yoss, *President*
Howard D Topal, *President*
Judith L Topal, *Vice Pres*
Kay Yoss, *Vice Pres*
Andrew Topal, *Sales Staff*
EMP: 16
SQ FT: 8,500
SALES (est): 1.8MM **Privately Held**
WEB: www.lasersave.com
SIC: 7378 5045 5112 3861 Computer pe-
ripheral equipment repair & maintenance;
computers; computer & photocopying
supplies; photographic equipment & sup-
plies

(G-3657)
**CHARTWELL PROMOTIONS LTD
INC**
1 Chartwell Ct (07728-8115)
PHONE..................................732 780-6900
Vincent Rinaldi, *President*
EMP: 4
SALES: 1MM **Privately Held**
SIC: 2261 2262 5136 Screen printing of
cotton broadwoven fabrics; screen print-
ing: manmade fiber & silk broadwoven
fabrics; sportswear, men's & boys'

(G-3658)
**CLAYTON BLOCK COMPANY
INC**
225 Throckmorton St (07728-8298)
PHONE..................................732 462-1860
Ron Smith, *Manager*
EMP: 7
SALES (corp-wide): 31.8MM **Privately
Held**
WEB: www.claytononline.com
SIC: 3271 Blocks, concrete or cinder: stan-
dard
PA: Clayton Block Company, Inc.
1355 Campus Pkwy Ste 200
Wall Township NJ 07753
883 763-8665

(G-3659)
CRITERION SOFTWARE LLC
205 Us Highway 9 30 (07728-8561)
PHONE..................................908 754-1166
Shashi Alagarasan, *Opers Staff*

Anusha Alagarasan, *Director*
Natasha Alagarasan, *Director*
Andy Somisetty, *Business Dir*
Alag Arasan,
EMP: 17
SQ FT: 500
SALES (est): 887K **Privately Held**
WEB: www.criterion-software.com
SIC: 7376 7372 Computer facilities management; prepackaged software

(G-3660)
CUSTOM BUSINESS SOFTWARE LLC
Also Called: Twisted Networking
87 Broad St (07728-1943)
P.O. Box 6930 (07728-6930)
PHONE................................732 534-9557
David Mound,
EMP: 9
SALES: 250K **Privately Held**
WEB: www.custombs.com
SIC: 7372 Application computer software

(G-3661)
DR TECHNOLOGY INC
73 South St (07728-2317)
PHONE................................732 780-4664
Doris Schwartz, *Ch of Bd*
EMP: 5
SQ FT: 2,500
SALES (est): 670K **Privately Held**
WEB: www.drtechnologyinc.com
SIC: 3564 3443 Air purification equipment; heat exchangers, condensers & components

(G-3662)
ELCO GLASS INDUSTRIES CO INC
16 Tree Line Dr (07728-9287)
PHONE................................732 363-6550
Eli Bavarsky, *President*
Zippi Bavarsky, *CFO*
EMP: 50
SQ FT: 40,000
SALES: 3.8MM **Privately Held**
SIC: 3211 Window glass, clear & colored

(G-3663)
ELITE LANDSCAPING & PAVERS
3102 Kapalua Ct (07728-5915)
P.O. Box 6752 (07728-6752)
PHONE................................732 252-6152
Richard A Castaldi Jr, *President*
EMP: 1
SALES: 2.8MM **Privately Held**
SIC: 3531 Pavers

(G-3664)
ENSYNC INTRCTIVE SOLUTIONS INC
83 South St Ste 202 (07728-2491)
PHONE................................732 542-4001
Claude Jones, *President*
EMP: 5
SQ FT: 2,600
SALES: 300.4K **Privately Held**
SIC: 8711 3663 7379 7376 Consulting engineer; radio & TV communications equipment; computer related maintenance services; computer facilities management; custom computer programming services; computer integrated systems design

(G-3665)
FALCON PRINTING & GRAPHICS
339 W Main St (07728-2517)
PHONE................................732 462-6862
William E Britland, *President*
Greg Pfremmer, *Vice Pres*
EMP: 6
SQ FT: 1,500
SALES (est): 697.3K **Privately Held**
WEB: www.falconprint.com
SIC: 2752 Commercial printing, offset

(G-3666)
FREEHOLD PNTIAC BICK GMC TRCKS
Also Called: Freehold Buick
4404 Us Highway 9 (07728-8311)
PHONE................................732 462-7093
Robert Thugut, *President*

Nick Guarino, *General Mgr*
EMP: 58
SQ FT: 18,000
SALES (est): 12.7MM **Privately Held**
SIC: 5511 7532 7515 7538 Automobiles, new & used; body shop, automotive; passenger car leasing; general automotive repair shops; motor vehicle parts & accessories

(G-3667)
GENEXOSOME TECHNOLOGIES INC
4400 Route 9 N (07728-1383)
PHONE................................646 762-4517
David Jin, *CEO*
Meng LI, *COO*
Luisa Ingargiola, *CFO*
EMP: 19
SALES (est): 182.2K
SALES (corp-wide): 1.5MM **Publicly Held**
SIC: 7372 Prepackaged software
PA: Avalon Globocare Corp.
4400 Route 9 S Ste 3100
Freehold NJ 07728
732 780-4400

(G-3668)
HOBBY PUBLICATIONS INC
Also Called: Picture Framing Magazine
83 South St Ste 307 (07728-2492)
PHONE................................732 536-5160
David Gherman, *President*
Tammy Keck, *Publisher*
Patrick Sarver, *Editor*
Tracey Murch, *Finance Mgr*
Debbie Fintz, *Accountant*
▲ EMP: 35
SQ FT: 4,800
SALES (est): 4.5MM **Privately Held**
WEB: www.hobbypub.com
SIC: 2721 Magazines: publishing only, not printed on site

(G-3669)
ICEBERG COFFEE LLC
865 Rte 33 Ste 4 (07728-8475)
PHONE................................908 675-6972
Jeff Burkard,
Joe Burkard,
EMP: 4 EST: 2015
SALES (est): 127.4K **Privately Held**
SIC: 2086 Bottled & canned soft drinks

(G-3670)
IT SURPLUS LIQUIDATORS
179 South St Ste 1 (07728-2647)
PHONE................................732 308-1935
Igor Gleyzer, *Principal*
EMP: 4
SALES (est): 490.2K **Privately Held**
SIC: 3679 Antennas, receiving

(G-3671)
IVC INDUSTRIES INC
Also Called: Inverness Med Ntrtionals Group
500 Halls Mill Rd (07728-8811)
PHONE................................732 308-3000
Craig Walters, *General Mgr*
John Dettra, *Senior VP*
Jesus Febus, *Senior VP*
Mike Richtmyer, *Vice Pres*
Tim Walker, *Plant Mgr*
EMP: 422
SQ FT: 290,000
SALES (est): 48.6K
SALES (corp-wide): 30.5B **Publicly Held**
WEB: www.invernessmedical.com
SIC: 2834 2833 5499 5961 Vitamin, nutrient & hematinic preparations for human use; vitamins, natural or synthetic: bulk, uncompounded; vitamin food stores; catalog & mail-order houses
HQ: Alere Inc.
51 Sawyer Rd Ste 200
Waltham MA 02453
781 647-3900

(G-3672)
JANICO INC
88 Industrial Ct (07728-8898)
PHONE................................732 370-2223
Saul Siegman, *President*
◆ EMP: 10

SALES (est): 1.7MM **Privately Held**
SIC: 2392 3589 3089 Mops, floor & dust; janitors' carts; garbage containers, plastic

(G-3673)
JDM ENGINEERING INC
60 Jerseyville Ave (07728-2369)
PHONE................................732 780-0770
James P D'Amore, *President*
EMP: 5
SALES (est): 742.1K **Privately Held**
WEB: www.teamjdm.com
SIC: 3462 Automotive & internal combustion engine forgings

(G-3674)
KOLE DESIGN LLC
35 Cedar Ct (07728-1589)
P.O. Box 6095 (07728-6095)
PHONE................................732 409-0211
Lawrence Kolodny,
Terry Kolodny,
EMP: 9
SALES: 800K **Privately Held**
SIC: 3911 Jewelry, precious metal

(G-3675)
LECTRO PRODUCTS INC
22 Francis Mills Rd (07728-7944)
PHONE................................732 462-2463
Wolfgang Storch, *President*
Alfred Pound, *Treasurer*
Ann Pound, *Admin Sec*
EMP: 6 EST: 1958
SQ FT: 12,000
SALES (est): 688.2K **Privately Held**
SIC: 3444 Sheet metal specialties, not stamped

(G-3676)
LIGHTFIELD AMMUNITION CORP
912 State Route 33 (07728-8439)
P.O. Box 162, Adelphia (07710-0162)
PHONE................................732 462-9200
Peter J Saker Jr, *Owner*
Lou Saker, *Co-Owner*
▲ EMP: 8
SALES (est): 2.5MM **Privately Held**
SIC: 3482 3483 Small arms ammunition; ammunition, except for small arms

(G-3677)
LIGHTFIELD LLR CORPORATION
912 State Route 33 (07728-8439)
P.O. Box 162, Adelphia (07710-0162)
PHONE................................732 462-9200
Peter J Saker Jr, *President*
Louis J Saker, *Corp Secy*
EMP: 4
SALES (est): 270K **Privately Held**
SIC: 3842 Surgical appliances & supplies

(G-3678)
LYMPHA PRESS USA
265 Willow Brook Rd # 4 (07728-2875)
PHONE................................732 792-9677
Charlie Berhang, *Principal*
▲ EMP: 9
SALES (est): 647.9K **Privately Held**
SIC: 2741 Miscellaneous publishing

(G-3679)
MIKE DOLLY SCREEN PRINTING
17 Elm St (07728-2203)
PHONE................................732 294-8979
Mike Dolly, *President*
EMP: 12 EST: 1993
SQ FT: 14,000
SALES: 2.5MM **Privately Held**
SIC: 2759 Screen printing

(G-3680)
MONMOUTH BIOPRODUCTS LLC
918 State Route 33 Ste 3 (07728-8438)
PHONE................................732 863-0300
Sean Duddy,
EMP: 5
SQ FT: 4,500
SALES (est): 842K **Privately Held**
SIC: 2836 Bacteriological media

(G-3681)
MOTORS AND DRIVES INC (PA)
Also Called: Best Electric Motor Co
5 Asbury Ave (07728-8111)
PHONE................................732 462-7683
Gene Moir Jr, *Vice Pres*
EMP: 5
SQ FT: 3,000
SALES (est): 1.5MM **Privately Held**
WEB: www.motorsanddrives.com
SIC: 7694 Electric motor repair

(G-3682)
NESTLE USA INC
Also Called: Nestle Beverage Division
61 Jerseyville Ave (07728-2328)
PHONE................................732 462-1300
Chris Hearn, *Plant Mgr*
Jean-Marc Garnier, *Branch Mgr*
EMP: 200
SALES (corp-wide): 92B **Privately Held**
WEB: www.nestleusa.com
SIC: 2095 2099 Roasted coffee; food preparations
HQ: Nestle Usa, Inc.
1812 N Moore St Ste 118
Rosslyn VA 22209
818 549-6000

(G-3683)
NOMAD LCROSSE DISTRS LTD LBLTY
62 Jackson St Ste 2 (07728-2475)
PHONE................................732 431-2255
Sean Obrien,
Scott Littman,
▲ EMP: 5
SQ FT: 8,000
SALES (est): 429.4K **Privately Held**
SIC: 3949 Sporting & athletic goods

(G-3684)
OLD MONMOUTH PEANUT BRITTLE CO
Also Called: Old Monmouth Candy Co
627 Park Ave (07728-2351)
PHONE................................732 462-1311
Harold Gunther, *President*
Susan Gunther, *Vice Pres*
David Gunther, *Manager*
EMP: 5 EST: 1939
SQ FT: 22,000
SALES (est): 517.6K **Privately Held**
WEB: www.oldmonmouthcandies.com
SIC: 2064 5441 Candy & other confectionery products; confectionery

(G-3685)
ONE SOURCE SOLUTIONS LLC
3 Industrial Ct Ste 3 # 3 (07728-9553)
PHONE................................732 536-0578
Tim O Hanley,
John Ford,
EMP: 10
SQ FT: 1,700
SALES (est): 1.3MM **Privately Held**
WEB: www.onesourcesolution.com
SIC: 7372 Business oriented computer software

(G-3686)
OXFORD LAMP INC
Also Called: Oxford Lighting Co
17 Bannard St Ste 30 (07728-1686)
PHONE................................732 462-3755
Sy Janowsky, *President*
Carol Janowsky, *Vice Pres*
EMP: 12
SALES (est): 1.6MM **Privately Held**
SIC: 3641 Electric lamp (bulb) parts

(G-3687)
PLANET POPCORN LLC
Freehold Mall (07728)
PHONE................................732 294-8680
EMP: 8
SQ FT: 200
SALES: 150K **Privately Held**
SIC: 2096 Mfg Potato Chips/Snacks

(G-3688)
POLY SOURCE ENTERPRISES LLC
17 Duchess Ct (07728-7758)
PHONE................................732 580-5409

Robert Macdougall,
EMP: 4
SALES (est): 187.2K **Privately Held**
SIC: 3089 Extruded finished plastic products

(G-3689)
POSTAGE BIN
31 E Main St Ste 4 (07728-2286)
PHONE................................732 333-0915
Marc G Cooper, *Principal*
EMP: 8
SALES (est): 864.6K **Privately Held**
SIC: 3444 Mail (post office) collection or storage boxes, sheet metal

(G-3690)
PRECISION FILAMENTS INC
17 Bannard St Ste 30 (07728-1686)
PHONE................................732 462-3755
Robert McLean, *President*
EMP: 7 **EST:** 1955
SQ FT: 12,500
SALES (est): 590K **Privately Held**
SIC: 3641 Electric lamps & parts for generalized applications; filaments, for electric lamps

(G-3691)
PREMIER MARBLE AND GRAN 2 INC
Also Called: Pg Marble
200 Commerce Ave Ste 200 # 200 (07728-9379)
PHONE................................732 294-7891
Umit Kellegoz, *President*
Ayhan Sahin, *Vice Pres*
EMP: 4
SQ FT: 12,000
SALES (est): 492.3K **Privately Held**
SIC: 3281 Marble, building: cut & shaped; granite, cut & shaped

(G-3692)
PRESTONE PRODUCTS CORPORATION
Also Called: Honeywell
Halls Mill Rd (07728)
PHONE................................732 431-8200
Felix Kon, *Branch Mgr*
EMP: 25
SALES (corp-wide): 3.2MM **Privately Held**
WEB: www.honeywell.com
SIC: 5045 2899 Computers; chemical preparations
HQ: Prestone Products Corporation
6250 N River Rd Ste 6000
Rosemont IL 60018

(G-3693)
PRESTONE PRODUCTS CORPORATION
Also Called: Kik Custom Products
250 Halls Mill Rd (07728-8832)
PHONE................................732 577-7800
Thomas Hines, *Manager*
Tom Hines, *Manager*
EMP: 40
SQ FT: 5,000
SALES (corp-wide): 3.2MM **Privately Held**
WEB: www.honeywell.com
SIC: 2899 Antifreeze compounds
HQ: Prestone Products Corporation
6250 N River Rd Ste 6000
Rosemont IL 60018

(G-3694)
PRINCETON SEPARATIONS INC
100 Commerce Ave (07728-9380)
P.O. Box 296, Adelphia (07710-0296)
PHONE................................732 431-3338
Paul Nix, *President*
Stuart Levinson, *President*
Kiran Desai, *Mfg Dir*
Regina Hatton, *Finance Mgr*
Wilma Crescente, *Manager*
EMP: 20
SQ FT: 12,000
SALES (est): 4.1MM **Privately Held**
WEB: www.prinsep.com
SIC: 3826 Blood testing apparatus

(G-3695)
QCOM INC
4400 Route 9 S Ste 1000 (07728-1383)
PHONE................................732 772-0990
Daniel Wang, *Ch of Bd*
John Sun, *President*
EMP: 30
SALES: 2MM **Privately Held**
SIC: 7372 Business oriented computer software

(G-3696)
QUIET TONE INC
12 Vine St (07728-1620)
PHONE................................732 431-2826
David Loendorf, *President*
Mike Hardy, *Teacher*
Karen Friberg, *Education*
EMP: 5
SALES (est): 330K **Privately Held**
SIC: 3161 Luggage

(G-3697)
RALPH CLAYTON & SONS LLC
Also Called: Clayton Block
64 Institute St (07728-2344)
P.O. Box 5033 (07728-5033)
PHONE................................732 462-1552
Wayne Tart, *Manager*
EMP: 25
SALES (corp-wide): 106.4MM **Privately Held**
WEB: www.claytonco.com
SIC: 3273 Ready-mixed concrete
PA: Ralph Clayton & Sons L.L.C.
1355 Campus Pkwy
Wall Township NJ 07753
732 363-1995

(G-3698)
RAPTOR RESOURCES HOLDINGS INC (PA)
41 Howe Ln (07728-3336)
PHONE................................732 252-5146
Stan Baron, *President*
Craig Gimbel, *Vice Pres*
EMP: 6
SALES (est): 787.5K **Publicly Held**
SIC: 3843 Dental equipment & supplies

(G-3699)
SCHER FABRICS INC
18 Duncan Way (07728-4350)
PHONE................................212 382-2266
▲ **EMP:** 17 **EST:** 1923
SQ FT: 12,000
SALES: 2MM **Privately Held**
SIC: 5131 2396 Whol Piece Goods/Notions Mfg Auto/Apparel Trimming

(G-3700)
SHORE POINT DISTRG CO INC
100 Shore Point Dr (07728-8568)
PHONE................................732 308-3334
James Annarella, *President*
Chip Thompson, *Regional Mgr*
Joanne Augustine, *Inv Control Mgr*
John Macrae, *CFO*
William Gutierrez, *Controller*
▲ **EMP:** 120
SQ FT: 100,000
SALES (est): 21.8MM **Privately Held**
WEB: www.njcoors.com
SIC: 2082 Beer (alcoholic beverage)

(G-3701)
TAG MINERALS INC
41 Howe Ln (07728-3336)
PHONE................................732 252-5146
Al Pietrangelo, *President*
EMP: 4
SALES (est): 175.7K **Publicly Held**
SIC: 1481 Mine exploration, nonmetallic minerals
PA: Raptor Resources Holdings Inc.
41 Howe Ln
Freehold NJ 07728

(G-3702)
US PROPACK INC
341 Fairfield Rd (07728-7829)
P.O. Box 298, Adelphia (07710-0298)
PHONE................................732 294-4500
Stephen Miller, *President*
Mary Jane Esposito, *Manager*

▲ **EMP:** 6
SQ FT: 12,500
SALES (est): 1.1MM **Privately Held**
WEB: www.uspropack.com
SIC: 3086 3993 5199 Packaging & shipping materials, foamed plastic; signs & advertising specialties; packaging materials

(G-3703)
VIDEONET COMM GROUP LLC
7 Seaman Rd (07728-8583)
PHONE................................732 863-5310
Dave Sellick, *Owner*
EMP: 12
SALES (est): 1MM **Privately Held**
WEB: www.bigbandnet.com
SIC: 3663 Digital encoders

(G-3704)
W & E BAUM BRONZE TABLET CORP
Also Called: Baum, W & E
89 Bannard St (07728-1607)
PHONE................................732 866-1881
Richard Baum, *President*
Maurice Zagha, *Vice Pres*
Anna Paczedlik, *Bookkeeper*
EMP: 23 **EST:** 1920
SQ FT: 15,000
SALES (est): 4.9MM **Privately Held**
WEB: www.webaum.com
SIC: 3364 3479 Brass & bronze die-castings; etching & engraving

(G-3705)
WINGOLD EMBROIDERY LLC
5 Monarch Ln (07728-8577)
PHONE................................732 845-9802
EMP: 3
SQ FT: 5,500
SALES: 1.5MM **Privately Held**
SIC: 2241 Mfg Lace & Embroidery

(G-3706)
WOODHUT LLC
210 Jerseyville Ave (07728-2329)
PHONE................................732 414-6440
Merrill Hassell,
EMP: 10
SQ FT: 700
SALES: 1.6MM **Privately Held**
SIC: 2435 Hardwood veneer & plywood

(G-3707)
WYNNPHARM INC
86 W Main St (07728-2134)
PHONE................................732 409-1005
John Barone, *President*
Mariella Scardino, *Vice Pres*
Pietro Barone, *Opers Mgr*
Dori Rachunok, *Opers Mgr*
Deedra Lobosco, *Cust Mgr*
EMP: 7
SALES (est): 4.5MM **Privately Held**
SIC: 2834 Pharmaceutical preparations

Frenchtown
Hunterdon County

(G-3708)
ARCHITECTURAL WDWKG ASSOC
4 7th St (08825-1146)
PHONE................................908 996-7866
John Gehman, *Partner*
Matthias Ritzmann, *Partner*
Patrick Hagerty, *Opers Mgr*
EMP: 7
SQ FT: 12,000
SALES (est): 550K **Privately Held**
SIC: 2431 2499 Woodwork, interior & ornamental; decorative wood & woodwork

(G-3709)
BLUE FISH CLOTHING INC
62 Trenton Ave Frnt Frnt (08825-1256)
PHONE................................908 996-3720
Jennifer Barclay, *Co-COB*
EMP: 155
SQ FT: 18,000

SALES (est): 17.8MM **Privately Held**
SIC: 2339 2369 5621 Women's & misses' outerwear; girls' & children's outerwear; women's clothing stores

(G-3710)
CARAUSTAR INDUSTRIES INC
Also Called: Frenchtown Partition Plant
869 State Route 12 (08825-4223)
PHONE................................908 782-0505
Alan Sochats, *Manager*
EMP: 50
SALES (corp-wide): 3.8B **Publicly Held**
WEB: www.caraustar.com
SIC: 2655 Fiber cans, drums & similar products
HQ: Caraustar Industries, Inc.
5000 Austell Powder Sprin
Austell GA 30106
770 948-3101

(G-3711)
CERBACO LTD
809 Harrison St (08825-1122)
PHONE................................908 996-1333
Alan Flash, *President*
Keith McClean, *Vice Pres*
Michelle Flash, *Treasurer*
EMP: 35
SQ FT: 10,000
SALES (est): 1.9MM **Privately Held**
WEB: www.cerbaco.com
SIC: 3599 3548 3496 Machine shop, jobbing & repair; welding apparatus; miscellaneous fabricated wire products

(G-3712)
F & R GRINDING INC
138 County Road 513 (08825-3732)
PHONE................................908 996-0440
Ronald Nicolato, *President*
Peter Nicolato, *Vice Pres*
EMP: 15
SQ FT: 5,000
SALES (est): 2.4MM **Privately Held**
SIC: 3545 3452 Machine tool accessories; bolts, nuts, rivets & washers

(G-3713)
HUNTERDON COUNTY DEMOCRAT INC
Also Called: Delaware Valley News
207 Harrison St (08825-1110)
PHONE................................908 996-4047
Betty Crouse, *Branch Mgr*
EMP: 4
SALES (corp-wide): 5.2MM **Privately Held**
WEB: www.hcdems.com
SIC: 2711 Newspapers, publishing & printing
PA: Hunterdon County Democrat Inc
200 State Route 31 # 202
Flemington NJ 08822
908 782-4747

(G-3714)
INSTRUMENT SCIENCES & TECH
1131 State Route 12 (08825-4160)
PHONE................................908 996-9920
Thomas Mitchell, *President*
James Sheridan, *Corp Secy*
EMP: 70
SQ FT: 10,000
SALES: 7.4MM **Privately Held**
WEB: www.instrumentsciencesandtechnologies.com
SIC: 3829 Geophysical & meteorological testing equipment

(G-3715)
LONGVIEW COFFEE CO NJ INC
Also Called: Longview Coffee Company
843 State Route 12 B10 (08825-4233)
P.O. Box 538, Stockton (08559-0538)
PHONE................................908 788-4186
Andrew Esserman, *President*
Margaret Esserman, *Vice Pres*
EMP: 25
SQ FT: 10,000
SALES: 5.5MM **Privately Held**
SIC: 2099 2095 Tea blending; roasted coffee

(G-3716)
MV LABORATORIES INC (PA)
843 State Route 12 B17 (08825-4234)
PHONE.................................908 788-6906
Warren Miller, *President*
Phillip Blacher, *Vice Pres*
EMP: 5
SQ FT: 6,000
SALES (est): 688.3K **Privately Held**
WEB: www.mvlaboratories.com
SIC: 3399 Metal powders, pastes & flakes

(G-3717)
ROCKWOOD CORPORATION
Also Called: Speedwell Targets
869a State Route 12 (08825-4223)
PHONE.................................908 355-8600
Michael Panos, *President*
EMP: 8
SQ FT: 12,000
SALES: 5MM **Privately Held**
WEB: www.speedwelltargets.com
SIC: 5941 2741 Sporting goods & bicycle
shops; miscellaneous publishing

(G-3718)
ZERO SURGE INC
889 State Route 12 Ste 2 (08825-4223)
PHONE.................................908 996-7700
James Minadeo, *President*
Brian Warner, *Engineer*
Deborah Peru, *Admin Sec*
◆ EMP: 11
SQ FT: 4,000
SALES (est): 1.9MM **Privately Held**
WEB: www.zerosurge.com
SIC: 3612 Voltage regulators, transmission
& distribution

Galloway
Atlantic County

(G-3719)
**ALLEGRO PRINTING
CORPORATION**
Also Called: Express Press
408 S 4th Ave (08205-9501)
PHONE.................................609 641-7060
Richard H Lamkin, *President*
Ruth Lamkin, *Corp Secy*
David Lore, *Vice Pres*
EMP: 5
SQ FT: 1,500
SALES (est): 554.6K **Privately Held**
WEB: www.expresspressnj.com
SIC: 2789 2752 Bookbinding & related
work; commercial printing, lithographic

(G-3720)
B T PARTNERS INC
3 N New York Rd Ste 23 (08205-3037)
PHONE.................................609 652-6511
Robert Koch, *President*
EMP: 4
SALES (est): 317.3K **Privately Held**
SIC: 2392 Placemats, plastic or textile

(G-3721)
**CASINO PLAYER PUBLISHING
LLC**
333 E Jimmie Leeds Rd # 7 (08205-4123)
PHONE.................................609 404-0600
Glenn Fine, *Mng Member*
Adam Fine,
EMP: 32
SQ FT: 6,100
SALES (est): 3.9MM **Privately Held**
WEB: www.casinocenter.com
SIC: 2721 Magazines: publishing only, not
printed on site

(G-3722)
**GREATER ATL CY GOLF ASSN
LLC**
Also Called: Seaview Golf Resort
401 S New York Rd (08205-9753)
PHONE.................................609 652-1800
Brian Rashley, *Principal*
EMP: 13
SALES (est): 1.2MM **Privately Held**
SIC: 3949 Golf equipment

Garfield
Bergen County

(G-3723)
ABCO TOOL & MACHINE CORP
2 Elm St (07026-3804)
PHONE.................................973 772-8160
Dominick Riccelli, *President*
EMP: 9 EST: 1944
SQ FT: 3,500
SALES (est): 946.7K **Privately Held**
SIC: 3599 Machine shop, jobbing & repair

(G-3724)
ACE FINE ART INC
141 Lanza Ave Bldg 3d (07026-3533)
PHONE.................................201 960-4447
Dong H Jo, *Owner*
▲ EMP: 2
SALES: 1MM **Privately Held**
SIC: 3231 Stained glass: made from pur-
chased glass

(G-3725)
**ACON WATCH CROWN
COMPANY**
260 Division Ave (07026-2521)
P.O. Box 800 (07026-0800)
PHONE.................................973 546-8585
Arnold Cohen, *Owner*
▲ EMP: 11 EST: 1935
SQ FT: 4,000
SALES: 550K **Privately Held**
SIC: 3873 3423 Watches & parts, except
crystals & jewels; jewelers' hand tools

(G-3726)
**ALGAR/DISPLAY CONNECTION
CORP**
70 Outwater Ln Ste 4 (07026-3854)
PHONE.................................201 438-1000
Richard Urso, *President*
Deian Urso, *Vice Pres*
Barbara Urso, *Treasurer*
▲ EMP: 70
SALES (est): 16.2MM **Privately Held**
WEB: www.displayconnection.com
SIC: 2653 Display items, solid fiber: made
from purchased materials

(G-3727)
**ALGENE MARKING EQUIPMENT
CO**
232 Palisade Ave (07026-2998)
P.O. Box 410 (07026-0410)
PHONE.................................973 478-9041
Gary Mann, *President*
Milton Mann, *Vice Pres*
EMP: 5 EST: 1946
SQ FT: 5,000
SALES: 1MM **Privately Held**
SIC: 3555 3952 3544 Printing trades ma-
chinery; ink, drawing: black & colored;
special dies & tools

(G-3728)
**ANATECH MICROWAVE
COMPANY INC**
70 Outwater Ln Ste 3 (07026-3854)
PHONE.................................973 772-7369
Sam Benzacar, *President*
EMP: 5
SALES: 950K **Privately Held**
SIC: 3663 Radio & TV communications
equipment

(G-3729)
**ARTIC ICE MANUFACTURING
CO**
158 Semel Ave (07026-3743)
PHONE.................................973 772-7000
John Minechetti, *President*
Steven Lengel, *Co-Owner*
Gerri Minichetti, *Manager*
Rose Marie Minichetti, *Admin Sec*
EMP: 5
SQ FT: 5,000
SALES (est): 598.8K **Privately Held**
WEB: www.articiceco.com
SIC: 2097 5169 Block ice; ice cubes; dry
ice

(G-3730)
ARTISTIC RAILINGS INC (PA)
500 River Dr (07026-3220)
PHONE.................................973 772-8540
Thomas Zuzik Sr, *President*
Elaine Zuzik, *Vice Pres*
Paul Zuzik, *Vice Pres*
Thomas Zuzik Jr, *Vice Pres*
EMP: 7
SQ FT: 7,600
SALES (est): 964.3K **Privately Held**
WEB: www.artisticrail.com
SIC: 3446 Railings, bannisters, guards,
etc.: made from metal pipe

(G-3731)
BAR-MAID CORPORATION
362 Midland Ave Ste 2 (07026-1736)
PHONE.................................973 478-7070
George Steele, *President*
▲ EMP: 150
SQ FT: 2,000
SALES (est): 5.8MM **Privately Held**
WEB: www.bar-maid.com
SIC: 5078 5044 3632 Refrigeration equip-
ment & supplies; vaults & safes; house-
hold refrigerators & freezers

(G-3732)
BELMONT WHL FENCE MFG INC
112 Monroe St (07026-2913)
PHONE.................................973 472-5121
Aldo Sibeni, *President*
Lucille Marino Harvey, *Vice Pres*
Maria Elena Ponterio, *Treasurer*
EMP: 25
SQ FT: 18,000
SALES (est): 4.8MM **Privately Held**
SIC: 3315 3496 Chain link fencing; miscel-
laneous fabricated wire products

(G-3733)
BRIMAR INDUSTRIES INC
Also Called: Safetysign.com
64 Outwater Ln (07026-3845)
PHONE.................................973 340-7889
Brian D Costello, *President*
Kevin McColl, *Accounts Exec*
Randy Smith, *Sales Staff*
Jason Hodulik, *Chief Mktg Ofcr*
Douglas Auchter, *Manager*
EMP: 50
SQ FT: 90,000
SALES (est): 9.6MM **Privately Held**
WEB: www.brimar-online.com
SIC: 2759 Labels & seals: printing

(G-3734)
CALORIC COLOR CO INC
176 Saddle River Rd A (07026)
PHONE.................................973 471-4748
June Anton, *President*
Connie Sink, *Vice Pres*
Linda Craner, *Admin Sec*
EMP: 10 EST: 1963
SQ FT: 7,800
SALES (est): 1.8MM **Privately Held**
SIC: 2899 3081 Ink or writing fluids; plas-
tic film & sheet

(G-3735)
**CLEAR PLUS WINDSHIELD
WIPERS**
Also Called: Advantage Asia
100 Outwater Ln (07026-2647)
PHONE.................................973 546-8800
Rej Chawla, *Owner*
▲ EMP: 10
SQ FT: 10,000
SALES (est): 720K **Privately Held**
WEB: www.clearplus.com
SIC: 3714 Windshield frames, motor vehi-
cle

(G-3736)
COSMETIC CONCEPTS INC
20 Chestnut St (07026-2820)
PHONE.................................973 546-1234
Atul Desai, *President*
▲ EMP: 150
SQ FT: 25,000
SALES (est): 20.7MM **Privately Held**
SIC: 2844 Cosmetic preparations

(G-3737)
DAS INSTALLATIONS INC
176 Saddle River Rd D (07026)
PHONE.................................973 473-6858
Louis Skvarca, *President*
EMP: 11
SALES: 800K **Privately Held**
SIC: 3535 5084 Conveyors & conveying
equipment; conveyor systems

(G-3738)
**DENTAL MODELS & DESIGNS
INC**
Also Called: Dental Designs
20 Passaic St Ste 3 (07026-3151)
PHONE.................................973 472-8009
David Lauchheimer, *President*
Sheryl Lauchheimer, *Treasurer*
EMP: 4
SQ FT: 1,500
SALES (est): 478.1K **Privately Held**
WEB: www.dentalmodelsanddesigns.com
SIC: 3843 Teeth, artificial (not made in
dental laboratories)

(G-3739)
**DIRECT SALES AND SERVICES
INC**
Also Called: Aunt Gussies Cookies Crackers
141 Lanza Ave Bldg 8 (07026-3533)
PHONE.................................973 340-4480
Marilyn Caine, *CEO*
David Caine, *Ch of Bd*
EMP: 25
SQ FT: 15,000
SALES (est): 5.3MM **Privately Held**
WEB: www.auntgussies.com
SIC: 2052 Cookies & crackers

(G-3740)
E C ELECTROPLATING INC
125 Clark St (07026-1799)
PHONE.................................973 340-0227
Mary Pettit, *Ch of Bd*
James E Calderio, *President*
Anthony Calderio, *Vice Pres*
Theresa Cusmano, *Admin Sec*
EMP: 25
SQ FT: 28,000
SALES (est): 2.9MM **Privately Held**
SIC: 3471 3312 Electroplating of metals or
formed products; blast furnaces & steel
mills

(G-3741)
ECLIPSE MANUFACTURING LLC
438 Lanza Ave (07026-2004)
PHONE.................................973 340-9939
Ziggy Nieradka, *President*
EMP: 4
SQ FT: 4,000
SALES (est): 600K **Privately Held**
SIC: 3469 Machine parts, stamped or
pressed metal

(G-3742)
FLUID COATING SYSTEMS INC
13 Barthold St (07026-2708)
PHONE.................................973 767-1028
Janusz Styga, *President*
EMP: 5
SQ FT: 3,600
SALES: 760K **Privately Held**
SIC: 3999 5033 Sprays, artificial & pre-
served; insulation materials

(G-3743)
FLUID FILTRATION CORP
102 Van Winkle Ave (07026-2940)
PHONE.................................973 253-7070
Farzad Alborzi, *President*
EMP: 10
SQ FT: 5,000
SALES (est): 1.7MM **Privately Held**
WEB: www.fluidfiltr.com
SIC: 3599 Gasoline filters, internal com-
bustion engine, except auto; oil filters, in-
ternal combustion engine, except
automotive

(G-3744)
FRAGALES BAKERY INC
6874 Gaston Ave (07026)
PHONE.................................973 546-0327
Andrew Fragale, *President*

GEOGRAPHIC

EMP: 15
SQ FT: 7,500
SALES (est): 1.7MM **Privately Held**
SIC: 2051 Bread, all types (white, wheat, rye, etc): fresh or frozen

(G-3745)
GEMINI PLASTIC FILMS CORP
535 Midland Ave (07026-1658)
P.O. Box 360 (07026-0360)
PHONE..................................973 340-0700
Andrew Del Presto, *President*
Richard Hulbert, *Vice Pres*
EMP: 40 EST: 1971
SQ FT: 31,000
SALES (est): 7.9MM **Privately Held**
SIC: 2673 3081 Bags: plastic, laminated & coated; polyethylene film

(G-3746)
GENEVIEVES INC
Also Called: Genevieves Home Made Candy Sp
174 Ray St (07026-3670)
PHONE..................................973 772-8816
David Dzwilewski, *President*
Anne Dzwilewski, *Admin Sec*
EMP: 12 EST: 1944
SQ FT: 3,000
SALES (est): 1.6MM **Privately Held**
WEB: www.genevieves.com
SIC: 2066 2064 5961 5441 Chocolate candy, solid; chocolate candy, except solid chocolate; food, mail order; candy; confectionery; gift shop; greeting cards

(G-3747)
IMPRESSIONS SIGNS AND PRTG INC
396 Midland Ave Ste 2 (07026-1627)
PHONE..................................973 653-3058
Daniel Cabrera, *President*
Liza Bernard, *Admin Asst*
EMP: 5
SALES (est): 262.7K **Privately Held**
SIC: 3993 Signs & advertising specialties

(G-3748)
INTERNATIONAL CRYSTAL LABS (PA)
Also Called: Lens Savers Division
11 Erie St Ste 2 (07026-2302)
PHONE..................................973 478-8944
Robert D Herpst, *Ch of Bd*
Theresa Herpst, *President*
Irene Ascuitto, *Vice Pres*
Vladimir Yakimovich, *Vice Pres*
Steven Hanst, *Executive*
◆ EMP: 25 EST: 1962
SQ FT: 9,500
SALES (est): 3.8MM **Privately Held**
WEB: www.lenssavers.com
SIC: 3826 Analytical instruments

(G-3749)
J GENNARO TRUCKING
13 Garfield Pl (07026-1901)
P.O. Box 215, Lodi (07644-0215)
PHONE..................................973 773-0805
Angelo Annuzzi, *President*
Dominick Annuzzi, *Treasurer*
Delores Annuzzi, *Admin Sec*
EMP: 15
SQ FT: 3,500
SALES (est): 1.6MM **Privately Held**
SIC: 4959 1794 1442 Snowplowing; excavation & grading, building construction; construction sand & gravel

(G-3750)
KOHOUTS BAKERY
75 Jewell St Fl 1 (07026-3749)
PHONE..................................973 772-7270
Charles Kohout Jr, *Owner*
EMP: 4
SQ FT: 1,000
SALES (est): 750K **Privately Held**
SIC: 2051 5461 5411 Bakery: wholesale or wholesale/retail combined; bread; grocery stores, independent; delicatessens

(G-3751)
NORTH AMERICAN ILLUMINATION
Also Called: American Lighting
79 Commerce St Ste 2 (07026-1853)
PHONE..................................973 478-4700
Alfred Binder, *President*
Geoffrey Binder, *Vice Pres*
Paul Binder, *Treasurer*
▲ EMP: 18 EST: 1961
SQ FT: 14,000
SALES (est): 3.3MM **Privately Held**
SIC: 3646 Commercial indusl & institutional electric lighting fixtures

(G-3752)
PALMER ELECTRONICS INC
Also Called: Palmer Industries Div
156 Belmont Ave (07026-2395)
PHONE..................................973 772-5900
Victor R Palmeri, *President*
Olga Palmeri, *Admin Sec*
▲ EMP: 16
SQ FT: 8,000
SALES (est): 700K **Privately Held**
WEB: www.palmer-electronics.com
SIC: 3829 3569 3823 Temperature sensors, except industrial process & aircraft; assembly machines, non-metalworking; industrial instrmnts msrmnt display/control process variable

(G-3753)
PAN GRAPHICS INC
45 Hartmann Ave (07026-2299)
PHONE..................................973 478-2100
EMP: 65 EST: 1962
SALES (est): 4.3MM **Privately Held**
SIC: 2796 Engraves Rotary Screens And Copper Rollers

(G-3754)
PAVAN & KIEVIT ENTERPRISES
Also Called: Uehling Instrument Company
113 Dewitt St Ste 210 (07026-2755)
PHONE..................................973 546-4615
Richard Pavan Jr, *President*
John Kievit, *Vice Pres*
EMP: 25
SQ FT: 6,200
SALES (est): 3.9MM **Privately Held**
WEB: www.uehling.com
SIC: 3823 5084 Industrial instrmnts msrmnt display/control process variable; industrial machinery & equipment

(G-3755)
PENTA GLASS INDUSTRIES INC
71 Hepworth Pl (07026-1817)
PHONE..................................973 478-2110
Jim Huddleston, *President*
EMP: 8
SQ FT: 3,200
SALES (est): 940K **Privately Held**
SIC: 1793 3231 Glass & glazing work; products of purchased glass; mirrored glass; glass sheet, bent: made from purchased glass

(G-3756)
PERSONLZED EXPRSSONS BY AUDREY
63 Harrison Ave (07026-1501)
PHONE..................................973 478-5115
Audrey Singer, *President*
Craig Singer, *Vice Pres*
Irwin Singer, *Vice Pres*
▲ EMP: 11
SQ FT: 4,000
SALES (est): 900K **Privately Held**
WEB: www.personalizedexpressionsbyaudrey.com
SIC: 3231 Art glass: made from purchased glass

(G-3757)
POLO MACHINE INC (PA)
223 Banta Ave (07026-3632)
P.O. Box 403 (07026-0403)
PHONE..................................973 340-9984
John Pszpnizzny, *President*
EMP: 4
SALES (est): 370K **Privately Held**
SIC: 3599 Machine shop, jobbing & repair

(G-3758)
PRIMEX COLOR COMPOUNDING (DH)
Also Called: O'Neil Color Compounding Corp
61 River Dr (07026-3145)
PHONE..................................800 282-7933
Mark Bruner, *President*
Philip Dechard, *Vice Pres*
Robert Hillyer, *Opers Mgr*
Linda Dojer, *Purchasing*
Greg Cooper, *Engineer*
EMP: 50 EST: 1955
SALES (est): 30.1MM
SALES (corp-wide): 1.7B **Privately Held**
WEB: www.oneilcolor.com
SIC: 2865 Dyes & pigments
HQ: Primex Plastics Corporation
    1235 N F St
    Richmond IN 47374
    765 966-7774

(G-3759)
PRIMEX PLASTICS CORPORATION
65 River Dr (07026-3196)
PHONE..................................973 470-8000
Cecibel Quinones, *Human Res Mgr*
Aaron Putnam, *Branch Mgr*
Fernando Barboto, *Manager*
EMP: 110
SALES (corp-wide): 1.7B **Privately Held**
WEB: www.primexplastics.com
SIC: 3081 Plastic film & sheet
HQ: Primex Plastics Corporation
    1235 N F St
    Richmond IN 47374
    765 966-7774

(G-3760)
PRODO-PAK CORP
130 Monroe St (07026-1826)
PHONE..................................973 772-4500
EMP: 4
SALES (est): 435.1K **Privately Held**
SIC: 3565 Packaging machinery

(G-3761)
PRODO-PAK CORPORATION
77 Commerce St (07026-1811)
P.O. Box 363 (07026-0363)
PHONE..................................973 777-7770
John Mueller, *President*
Ralph Isler, *Business Mgr*
Marlon Burgos, *Project Engr*
▲ EMP: 20
SQ FT: 20,000
SALES (est): 5.7MM **Privately Held**
WEB: www.prodo-pak.com
SIC: 3565 Packaging machinery

(G-3762)
PRODUCT IDENTIFICATION CO INC
141 Lanza Ave Bldg 19 (07026-3530)
PHONE..................................973 227-7770
Les Weinstock, *President*
Jeff Weinstock, *General Mgr*
Arlene Weinstock, *Corp Secy*
Richard Carlisle, *Plant Mgr*
EMP: 17 EST: 1964
SQ FT: 2,700
SALES (est): 72.1K **Privately Held**
SIC: 2752 2759 Decals, lithographed; labels & seals: printing

(G-3763)
RICKS CLEANOUTS INC
654 River Dr (07026-3822)
PHONE..................................973 340-7454
Rifat Ferhatovic, *President*
EMP: 30
SALES (est): 5.7MM **Privately Held**
WEB: www.rickscleanouts.com
SIC: 2851 Removers & cleaners

(G-3764)
ROYAL SLIDE SALES CO INC (PA)
42 Hepworth Pl (07026-3039)
PHONE..................................973 777-1177
Abraham Levine, *Vice Pres*
▲ EMP: 8 EST: 1947
SQ FT: 40,000

SALES (est): 1.8MM **Privately Held**
SIC: 3965 5131 5199 Zipper; zippers; bags, baskets & cases

(G-3765)
ROYAL ZIPPER MANUFG COMPANY
Also Called: Royal Slide Sales
42 Hepworth Pl (07026-3039)
PHONE..................................973 777-1177
Abraham Levine, *Vice Pres*
Lewis Neuman, *Vice Pres*
EMP: 13
SQ FT: 30,000
SALES (est): 895.7K
SALES (corp-wide): 1.8MM **Privately Held**
SIC: 3965 Zipper
PA: Royal Slide Sales Co Inc
    42 Hepworth Pl
    Garfield NJ 07026
    973 777-1177

(G-3766)
RPL SUPPLIES INC
Also Called: R P L
141 Lanza Ave Bldg 3a (07026-3533)
PHONE..................................973 767-0880
Larry Milazzo, *President*
Henry Fishman, *Vice Pres*
Ashley Van Wingerden, *Sales Staff*
Ken Baitala, *Technology*
◆ EMP: 18
SQ FT: 17,000
SALES (est): 3MM **Privately Held**
WEB: www.rplsupplies.com
SIC: 3861 5699 5947 Photographic equipment & supplies; customized clothing & apparel; novelties

(G-3767)
SHARP IMPRESSIONS INC
163 Belmont Ave Ste 1 (07026-2336)
PHONE..................................201 573-4943
Thomas G Difiore, *President*
Arlene J Difiore, *Treasurer*
EMP: 4
SQ FT: 3,000
SALES (est): 200K **Privately Held**
SIC: 2759 Invitation & stationery printing & engraving

(G-3768)
SIGNS OF SECURITY INC
64 Outwater Ln Ste 2 (07026-3845)
P.O. Box 468 (07026-0468)
PHONE..................................973 340-8404
Stephanie Gunning, *President*
Gianni Gallorini, *Manager*
EMP: 30
SALES (est): 1.9MM **Privately Held**
WEB: www.signsofsecurity.com
SIC: 3993 2752 Signs & advertising specialties; commercial printing, lithographic

(G-3769)
STAR DYNAMIC CORP
100 Outwater Ln (07026-2647)
PHONE..................................732 257-7488
Michelle Schwartzman, *CEO*
David A'ster, *Vice Pres*
Hung Anqui, *Controller*
EMP: 60 EST: 1975
SQ FT: 25,000
SALES (est): 8.9MM **Privately Held**
WEB: www.stardynamic.com
SIC: 3661 Telephone & telegraph apparatus

(G-3770)
STEFAN ENTERPRISES INC
141 Lanza Ave Bldg 16e (07026-3533)
PHONE..................................973 253-6005
Stefan Missbrenner, *President*
Walter Beck, *Vice Pres*
▲ EMP: 20
SALES (est): 3.2MM **Privately Held**
WEB: www.stefanenterprises.com
SIC: 2262 2396 Printing: manmade fiber & silk broadwoven fabrics; automotive & apparel trimmings

(G-3771)
SUMATIC CO INC
102 Dewitt St (07026-2712)
P.O. Box 435 (07026-0435)
PHONE....................................973 772-1288
Michael Sunier, *President*
Thierry Sunier, *Vice Pres*
EMP: 5
SQ FT: 3,000
SALES (est): 611.4K **Privately Held**
SIC: 3451 Screw machine products

(G-3772)
TECHNO DESIGN INC
11 Erie St Ste 1 (07026-2302)
PHONE....................................973 478-0930
Reuben Diaz, *President*
Kris Krol, *Manager*
EMP: 5 **EST:** 1976
SQ FT: 8,000
SALES (est): 733.5K **Privately Held**
WEB: www.techno-design.com
SIC: 3556 Food products machinery

(G-3773)
TOBY-YANNI INCORPORATED
62 Plauderville Ave (07026-2242)
PHONE....................................973 253-9800
Elizabeth Tobias, *Principal*
Steven Karras, *Opers Staff*
EMP: 17
SALES (est): 1.9MM **Privately Held**
SIC: 3672 Printed circuit boards

(G-3774)
TOYDRIVER LLC
100 Outwater Ln (07026-2647)
PHONE....................................678 637-8500
Lauren Levy,
EMP: 1
SQ FT: 10,000
SALES (est): 2MM **Privately Held**
SIC: 3546 Drill attachments, portable

(G-3775)
US MAGIC BOX INC
Also Called: Designer
221 Macarthur Ave (07026-1215)
PHONE....................................973 772-2070
Sam Khattap, *President*
▼ **EMP:** 4
SALES (est): 481.8K **Privately Held**
WEB: www.usmagicbox.com
SIC: 2671 Packaging paper & plastics film, coated & laminated

(G-3776)
VENETIAN CORP
Also Called: Venetian Caterers, The
546 River Dr (07026-3818)
PHONE....................................973 546-2250
James Kourgelis, *President*
Christos Gourmos, *Principal*
EMP: 16
SALES (est): 3.4MM **Privately Held**
SIC: 2099 Food preparations

(G-3777)
WEARBEST SIL-TEX MILLS LTD (PA)
325 Midland Ave (07026-1718)
P.O. Box 589 (07026-0589)
PHONE....................................973 340-8844
Irwin Gasner, *President*
▲ **EMP:** 100 **EST:** 1940
SQ FT: 60,000
SALES (est): 21.3MM **Privately Held**
SIC: 2221 Broadwoven fabric mills, man-made

(G-3778)
WJJ AND COMPANY LLC
Also Called: Papertec
141 Lanza Ave Bldg 29 (07026-3530)
PHONE....................................973 246-7480
Kevin Bielen, *Vice Pres*
Theodore Bielen,
Todd Bielen,
EMP: 10
SALES (est): 3.1MM **Privately Held**
SIC: 2631 Paperboard mills

Garwood
Union County

(G-3779)
ACCURATE BUSHING COMPANY INC
Also Called: Smith Bearing
443 North Ave Ste 1 (07027-1090)
P.O. Box 52 (07027-0052)
PHONE....................................908 789-1121
Peter Dubinsky, *President*
Richard Picut, *Vice Pres*
Robert Picut, *Vice Pres*
Russel Picut, *Vice Pres*
Paul Robuck, *QC Mgr*
▲ **EMP:** 50
SQ FT: 45,000
SALES (est): 10.8MM **Privately Held**
WEB: www.accuratebushing.com
SIC: 3325 3562 3728 3568 Steel foundries; ball & roller bearings; aircraft parts & equipment; power transmission equipment; copper foundries

(G-3780)
ALMARK TOOL & MANUFACTURING CO
27 South Ave (07027-1337)
P.O. Box 189 (07027-0189)
PHONE....................................908 789-2440
Mark Bowman, *President*
Norma Bowman, *Treasurer*
EMP: 10
SQ FT: 6,000
SALES (est): 1.6MM **Privately Held**
WEB: www.almarktool.com
SIC: 3545 3544 Precision tools, machinists'; special dies, tools, jigs & fixtures

(G-3781)
BEN VENUTI
512 North Ave (07027-1017)
PHONE....................................908 389-9999
Jason White, *General Mgr*
Ben Venuti, *Principal*
EMP: 4 **EST:** 2008
SALES (est): 431.2K **Privately Held**
SIC: 3421 Table & food cutlery, including butchers'

(G-3782)
CASALE INDUSTRIES INC
50 Center St (07027-1242)
PHONE....................................908 789-0040
Edward Casale, *CEO*
Kenneth Casale, *President*
Susan Casale, *Corp Secy*
EMP: 50
SQ FT: 100,000
SALES (est): 6.9MM **Privately Held**
SIC: 3444 3443 Sheet metal specialties, not stamped; tanks for tank trucks, metal plate

(G-3783)
CREATIVE COLOR LITHOGRAPHERS
611 South Ave (07027-1238)
PHONE....................................908 789-2295
Frank Adams, *President*
Helen Christodoulou, *Vice Pres*
EMP: 15
SALES (est): 2MM **Privately Held**
WEB: www.creativecolor.net
SIC: 2752 2791 2789 2759 Commercial printing, offset; color lithography; typesetting; bookbinding & related work; commercial printing

(G-3784)
GRILL CREATIONS
100 North Ave Ste 8 (07027-1137)
PHONE....................................908 264-8426
Ivin Alvarez, *Manager*
EMP: 4
SALES (est): 301.9K **Privately Held**
SIC: 3949 Bowling alleys & accessories

(G-3785)
MOLD POLISHING COMPANY INC
45 North Ave Ste 3 (07027-1158)
P.O. Box 96 (07027-0096)
PHONE....................................908 518-9191
Joseph Guerrero, *President*
Susan Guerrero, *Vice Pres*
Alice Giler, *Manager*
EMP: 8
SQ FT: 8,000
SALES (est): 939.5K **Privately Held**
SIC: 3544 3471 Industrial molds; plating & polishing

(G-3786)
NEW JERSEY REPROGRAPHICS INC
Also Called: Precision Press
110 Center St (07027-1241)
PHONE....................................908 789-1616
Joseph M Bizzarro, *President*
EMP: 4
SQ FT: 3,500
SALES (est): 510K **Privately Held**
SIC: 2752 Commercial printing, offset

(G-3787)
NORCO INC
237 South Ave (07027-1341)
P.O. Box 186 (07027-0186)
PHONE....................................908 789-1550
Michael Rosenberg, *President*
Marc R Krattenstein, *Treasurer*
Marc Krattenstein, *Treasurer*
Adriana Curbelo, *Technology*
Elizabeth Ojeda, *Technology*
▲ **EMP:** 45
SQ FT: 18,000
SALES (est): 5.6MM **Privately Held**
WEB: www.norcopins.com
SIC: 3911 3499 2672 3961 Medals, precious or semiprecious metal; pins (jewelry), precious metal; novelties & giftware, including trophies; labels (unprinted), gummed: made from purchased materials; costume jewelry

(G-3788)
OCSIDOT INC
Also Called: Advance Printing Co
116 South Ave (07027-1340)
PHONE....................................908 789-3300
John Todisco, *President*
Ed Cristilles, *Vice Pres*
EMP: 17 **EST:** 1953
SQ FT: 17,000
SALES (est): 3.1MM **Privately Held**
SIC: 2752 2759 Commercial printing, offset; commercial printing

(G-3789)
P K WELDING LLC
520 South Ave (07027-1237)
PHONE....................................908 928-1002
Paul Gucker, *General Mgr*
Robert Parmentier,
EMP: 10
SQ FT: 2,000
SALES: 2.6MM **Privately Held**
SIC: 7692 Welding repair

(G-3790)
PEN COMPANY OF AMERICA LLC
502 South Ave (07027-1237)
PHONE....................................908 374-7949
EMP: 15
SALES (corp-wide): 294.5MM **Privately Held**
SIC: 3951 Pens & mechanical pencils
HQ: Pen Company Of America Llc
1401 S Park Ave
Linden NJ 07036

(G-3791)
PMC LIQUIFLO EQUIPMENT CO INC
443 North Ave (07027-1014)
PHONE....................................908 518-0666
Richard Picut, *CEO*
Marla Sattler, *Purch Mgr*
Cezary Elmanowski, *Technology*
▲ **EMP:** 25 **EST:** 1972

SALES (est): 5.3MM **Privately Held**
WEB: www.endurapumps.com
SIC: 3594 Fluid power pumps & motors
PA: Picut Industries Inc.
140 Mount Bethel Rd
Warren NJ 07059

(G-3792)
ROSCO INC
55 South Ave (07027-1337)
P.O. Box 427, Lanoka Harbor (08734-0427)
PHONE....................................908 789-1020
John K Burton, *President*
EMP: 5 **EST:** 1946
SQ FT: 3,700
SALES (est): 728.7K **Privately Held**
WEB: www.roscoincnj.com
SIC: 3365 Aluminum & aluminum-based alloy castings

(G-3793)
W A BUILDING MOVERS & CONTRS
246 North Ave Apt 1 (07027-1152)
PHONE....................................908 654-8227
Wayne Yarusi, *President*
Jason Yarusi, *Vice Pres*
EMP: 12
SALES: 550K **Privately Held**
WEB: www.buildingmoverswa.com
SIC: 1799 1542 3531 1522 Building mover, including houses; commercial & office building contractors; pile drivers (construction machinery); apartment building construction; excavation & grading, building construction; foundation & retaining wall construction

---

Gibbsboro
Camden County

(G-3794)
NICKS WORKSHOP INC
171 Clementon Rd W (08026-1107)
PHONE....................................856 784-6097
Nick Rulli, *President*
Mathew Rulli, *Vice Pres*
Rosemary Rulli, *Admin Sec*
EMP: 8
SALES (est): 1MM **Privately Held**
SIC: 2542 Fixtures: display, office or store: except wood

(G-3795)
PENN JERSEY PRESS INC
10 United States Ave E (08026-1125)
PHONE....................................856 627-2200
Richard Fichter, *President*
EMP: 5 **EST:** 1931
SQ FT: 5,400
SALES (est): 409.9K **Privately Held**
WEB: www.pennjerseypress.com
SIC: 2752 7334 2759 Commercial printing, offset; photocopying & duplicating services; commercial printing

(G-3796)
WILLIER ELC MTR REPR CO INC (PA)
1 Linden Ave (08026-1315)
P.O. Box 98 (08026-0098)
PHONE....................................856 627-3535
Donald P Willier Sr, *President*
Kathleen Willier, *Corp Secy*
James Willier, *Vice Pres*
Kurt Schneider, *Sales Staff*
Don Willier, *Executive*
EMP: 32 **EST:** 1954
SQ FT: 12,000
SALES: 9.7MM **Privately Held**
WEB: www.willierelectric.com
SIC: 5063 7694 Motors, electric; electric motor repair

(G-3797)
WILLIER ELC MTR REPR CO INC
Also Called: Willier Technical Services
3 Democrat Rd Ste Td (08026-1303)
P.O. Box 98 (08026-0098)
PHONE....................................856 627-2262
Don Willard, *Manager*
EMP: 40

SALES (corp-wide): 9.7MM **Privately Held**
WEB: www.willierelectric.com
SIC: 7694 Electric motor repair
PA: Willier Electric Motor Repair Co., Inc.
　　1 Linden Ave
　　Gibbsboro NJ 08026
　　856 627-3535

Gibbstown
Gloucester County

(G-3798)
MYCONE DENTAL SUPPLY CO INC (PA)
Also Called: Keystone Industries
480 S Democrat Rd　(08027-1239)
PHONE.................................856 663-4700
Fred Robinson, *Ch of Bd*
Cary Robinson, *President*
Sue Cary, *Info Tech Dir*
▲ EMP: 150
SQ FT: 45,000
SALES (est): 118.4MM **Privately Held**
SIC: 5047 3843 2844 Dental equipment & supplies; dental equipment & supplies; toilet preparations

(G-3799)
RAM DONUTS CORP
Also Called: Dunkin' Donuts
431 Harmony Rd　(08027-1722)
PHONE.................................856 599-0015
Bravin Patel, *Principal*
EMP: 5 **Privately Held**
SIC: 5461 2051 Doughnuts; doughnuts, except frozen
PA: Ram Donuts Corp
　　5751 Route 42
　　Blackwood NJ 08012

(G-3800)
WAGNER PROVISION CO INC
54 E Broad St　(08027-1475)
P.O. Box 95　(08027-0095)
PHONE.................................856 423-1630
Herbold Wagner Jr, *President*
Wagner Silveira, *Principal*
Caroline Wagner, *Corp Secy*
EMP: 10
SQ FT: 3,000
SALES (est): 3MM **Privately Held**
SIC: 2013 Sausages & other prepared meats

Gillette
Morris County

(G-3801)
ELEMENTS GLOBAL GROUP LLC
527 Meyersville Rd　(07933-1331)
PHONE.................................908 468-8407
▲ EMP: 5
SALES (est): 336.3K **Privately Held**
SIC: 2819 Industrial inorganic chemicals

(G-3802)
MITRONICS PRODUCTS INC
239 Morristown Rd Ste 1　(07933-1818)
P.O. Box 196　(07933-0196)
PHONE.................................908 647-5006
Eric Bergman, *President*
EMP: 8 EST: 1971
SQ FT: 2,750
SALES: 250K **Privately Held**
SIC: 3264 Insulators, electrical: porcelain

(G-3803)
SOUND CHICE ASSSTIVE LISTENING
498 Long Hill Rd　(07933-1345)
PHONE.................................908 647-2651
Phyllis R Wald, *President*
Lawrence Fast, *Vice Pres*
EMP: 4
SALES (est): 320K **Privately Held**
WEB: www.assistivelistening.net
SIC: 3651 Amplifiers: radio, public address or musical instrument

Gladstone
Somerset County

(G-3804)
HOBART GROUP HOLDINGS LLC
240 Main St　(07934-2016)
PHONE.................................908 470-1780
Dan Renick, *President*
Corinne Romero, *Senior VP*
Erin Foley, *Assoc VP*
Ralitsa Larsen, *Manager*
Martin Beatch, *Director*
EMP: 140
SALES (est): 12.1MM
SALES (corp-wide): 81.8MM **Privately Held**
SIC: 2834 Pharmaceutical preparations
PA: Precision Medicine Group, Llc
　　2 Bethesda Metro Ctr # 850
　　Bethesda MD 20814
　　240 654-0730

(G-3805)
WEXFORD INTERNATIONAL INC
190 Main St Ste 102　(07934-2064)
P.O. Box 715　(07934-0715)
PHONE.................................908 781-7200
Donald L Brown, *President*
Daniel T Kelly, *Partner*
▲ EMP: 5
SQ FT: 3,200
SALES (est): 2MM **Privately Held**
SIC: 2821 Molding compounds, plastics

Glassboro
Gloucester County

(G-3806)
ADVANTAGE DS LLC
8 Deptford Rd　(08028-2449)
PHONE.................................856 307-9600
James Madosky, *President*
EMP: 10
SALES: 700K **Privately Held**
SIC: 2395 2759 Embroidery products, except schiffli machine; screen printing

(G-3807)
ASTRO OUTDOOR ADVERTISING INC (PA)
Also Called: Astro Sign Co
230 E High St　(08028-2310)
PHONE.................................856 881-4300
Gerald H Painter, *CEO*
Joann Painter, *Corp Secy*
Jason Painter, *Accounts Mgr*
Michael Fratini, *Sales Staff*
EMP: 10
SQ FT: 3,500
SALES (est): 1.1MM **Privately Held**
SIC: 3993 Signs & advertising specialties

(G-3808)
CWI ARCHITECTURAL MILLWORK LLC
8 Deptford Rd Dept D　(08028-2449)
PHONE.................................856 307-7900
David Ganor, *Mng Member*
Kimberly Ganor,
EMP: 8
SQ FT: 6,200
SALES: 650K **Privately Held**
WEB: www.certainlywoodinc.com
SIC: 2431 5211 1751 Woodwork, interior & ornamental; millwork & lumber; cabinet & finish carpentry

(G-3809)
DEMOUNTABLE CONCEPTS INC
200 Acorn Rd　(08028-3299)
PHONE.................................856 863-3081
Frank Fisher, *CEO*
Rustin Cassway, *President*
David Fisher, *Vice Pres*
▼ EMP: 30
SQ FT: 50,000
SALES (est): 7.9MM **Privately Held**
WEB: www.demount.com
SIC: 3713 Truck bodies & parts

(G-3810)
ELRAY MANUFACTURING COMPANY
17 Liberty St　(08028-2305)
PHONE.................................856 881-1935
Edward Stopper, *President*
Betty Stopper, *Vice Pres*
EMP: 30 EST: 1952
SQ FT: 33,000
SALES (est): 6.1MM **Privately Held**
WEB: www.elrayman.com
SIC: 3469 3544 Machine parts, stamped or pressed metal; die sets for metal stamping (presses)

(G-3811)
FAZZIO MACHINE & STEEL INC
3278 Glassboro Crs Kys Rd　(08028-2716)
P.O. Box 232　(08028-0232)
PHONE.................................609 653-1098
Felix P Fazzio, *President*
James Fazzio, *Vice Pres*
Mike Fazzio, *Vice Pres*
EMP: 6 EST: 1943
SQ FT: 2,500
SALES (est): 2.2MM **Privately Held**
SIC: 5051 3599 Steel; machine shop, jobbing & repair

(G-3812)
GLASSBORO NEWS & FOOD STORE
255 E High St　(08028-2309)
PHONE.................................856 881-1181
Preg Shah, *Principal*
EMP: 4
SALES (est): 154.5K **Privately Held**
SIC: 2711 5411 Newspapers, publishing & printing; convenience stores

(G-3813)
KERK CABINETRY LLC
45 Dogwood Ave　(08028-2819)
PHONE.................................856 881-4213
Kristian Van Dexter, *Principal*
EMP: 4
SALES (est): 373K **Privately Held**
SIC: 2434 Wood kitchen cabinets

(G-3814)
MADHOUZ LLC
8 Deptford Rd Dept A　(08028-2449)
PHONE.................................609 206-8009
▲ EMP: 4
SALES (est): 487.6K **Privately Held**
SIC: 5199 3993 7319 7389 Gifts & novelties; signs & advertising specialties; display advertising service; embroidering of advertising on shirts, etc.; direct mail advertising services

(G-3815)
MCALISTER WELDING & FABG
112 Maple Leaf Ct　(08028-2644)
PHONE.................................856 740-3890
Dave McAlister, *Owner*
David McAlister, *Owner*
Lynn McAlister, *Co-Owner*
EMP: 15
SALES (est): 1.7MM **Privately Held**
SIC: 7692 3312 Welding repair; structural shapes & pilings, steel

(G-3816)
MRC GLOBAL (US) INC
70 Sewell St Ste J　(08028-2419)
PHONE.................................856 881-0345
Tim Fish, *Manager*
EMP: 4 **Publicly Held**
SIC: 1311 Crude petroleum & natural gas
HQ: Mrc Global (Us) Inc.
　　1301 Mckinney St Ste 2300
　　Houston TX 77010
　　877 294-7574

(G-3817)
NER DATA PRODUCTS INC (HQ)
307 Delsea Dr S　(08028-2647)
PHONE.................................888 637-3282
Francis C Oatway, *Ch of Bd*
Stephen F Oatway, *President*
Scott Steele, *Exec VP*
Robert Belvin, *Production*
Christopher Oatway, *CFO*
▲ EMP: 40

SQ FT: 60,000
SALES (est): 58.2MM
SALES (corp-wide): 73.2MM **Privately Held**
WEB: www.nerdata.com
SIC: 3577 3955 3861 3572 Computer peripheral equipment; carbon paper & inked ribbons; photographic equipment & supplies; computer storage devices; partitions & fixtures, except wood
PA: Ner Data Corporation
　　307 Delsea Dr S
　　Glassboro NJ 08028
　　856 881-5524

(G-3818)
S&W FABRICATORS INC
100 Delsea Dr S　(08028-2662)
P.O. Box 664　(08028-0664)
PHONE.................................856 881-7418
Andrea Sebastiani, *President*
EMP: 7
SALES (est): 1.1MM **Privately Held**
SIC: 3498 Fabricated pipe & fittings

(G-3819)
SPORTS STOP INC
Also Called: Two Vic's Sports Stop
31 Delsea Dr N　(08028-1930)
PHONE.................................856 881-2763
Fitz Duer, *President*
Maureen Duer, *Vice Pres*
EMP: 10
SQ FT: 3,800
SALES: 1MM **Privately Held**
WEB: www.twovics.com
SIC: 5941 5091 2759 Sporting goods & bicycle shops; sporting & recreation goods; screen printing

(G-3820)
WECOM INC
20 Warrick Ave　(08028-2500)
PHONE.................................856 863-8400
Eric Sprengle Sr, *President*
E Carl Sprengle Jr, *Vice Pres*
EMP: 29
SQ FT: 50,000
SALES: 3MM **Privately Held**
WEB: www.wecom.com
SIC: 3444 Sheet metal specialties, not stamped

Glen Gardner
Hunterdon County

(G-3821)
EASTERN CONCRETE MATERIALS INC
1 Railroad Ave　(08826-3537)
PHONE.................................908 537-2135
EMP: 4
SALES (corp-wide): 1.5B **Publicly Held**
SIC: 3273 1411 Ready-mixed concrete; granite dimension stone
HQ: Eastern Concrete Materials, Inc.
　　250 Pehle Ave Ste 503
　　Saddle Brook NJ 07663
　　201 797-7979

(G-3822)
FUEL OX LLC
117 Buffalo Hollow Rd　(08826-3209)
PHONE.................................908 747-4375
Randall Taylor, *President*
Jessica Schwarcz, *Manager*
EMP: 14 EST: 2013
SALES (est): 2.3MM **Privately Held**
SIC: 2911 Fuel additives

(G-3823)
HUP & SONS
10 White Tail Ln　(08826-3048)
PHONE.................................908 832-7878
Martin Hup Jr, *Owner*
EMP: 4
SALES (est): 480.1K **Privately Held**
SIC: 3292 1794 Floor tile, asphalt; excavation work

(G-3824)
VISION RAILINGS LTD LBLTY CO
Also Called: Ultimate Outdoors
213 Dee Dee Dr (08826-3220)
PHONE..................................908 310-8926
Andrea Nicolai,
EMP: 10
SALES (est): 790K **Privately Held**
SIC: 3441 Fabricated structural metal

Glen Ridge
Essex County

(G-3825)
G J HAERER CO INC (PA)
372 Ridgewood Ave (07028-1513)
PHONE..................................973 614-8090
Timothy J Kelleher, *President*
Richard B Colledge, *Vice Pres*
Sabina Prendergast, *Vice Pres*
EMP: 69
SQ FT: 15,000
SALES (est): 3.6MM **Privately Held**
WEB: www.gjhaerer.com
SIC: 2752 Commercial printing, offset

Glen Rock
Bergen County

(G-3826)
ARTIQUE GLASS STUDIO INC
483 S Broad St (07452-1309)
PHONE..................................201 444-3500
J De Mauro, *President*
EMP: 5
SALES (est): 572.5K **Privately Held**
SIC: 3211 5231 Antique glass; glass,
leaded or stained

(G-3827)
ASH INGREDIENTS INC
65 Harristown Rd Ste 307 (07452-3317)
PHONE..................................201 689-1322
Shawna Kriplani, *CEO*
Anil Kripalani, *President*
Steven Fantano, *Accounts Mgr*
Anish Joshi, *Director*
▲ **EMP:** 8
SQ FT: 1,500
SALES (est): 26MM **Privately Held**
SIC: 2834 Extracts of botanicals: pow-
dered, pilular, solid or fluid; powders,
pharmaceutical

(G-3828)
B E C MFG CORP
Also Called: Specialized Metal Stamping
649 Lincoln Ave (07452-2518)
PHONE..................................201 414-0000
Bart Sciaino, *President*
Jim Clavan, *Vice Pres*
Elizabeth Sciaino, *Admin Sec*
EMP: 25 **EST:** 1964
SQ FT: 60,000
SALES (est): 2.9MM **Privately Held**
WEB: www.becmfg.com
SIC: 3544 3469 Special dies & tools;
metal stampings

(G-3829)
CLASSIC DESIGNER
WOODWORK INC
60 Hazelhurst Ave (07452-2840)
PHONE..................................201 280-3711
Keith Richter, *Principal*
EMP: 4 **EST:** 2010
SALES (est): 260.2K **Privately Held**
SIC: 2431 Millwork

(G-3830)
COLIBRI SCENTIQUE LTD LBLTY
CO
68 Chadwick Pl (07452-3105)
PHONE..................................201 445-5715
Cheryl Sarno, *Mng Member*
EMP: 9
SALES (est): 1.2MM **Privately Held**
SIC: 2869 Industrial organic chemicals

(G-3831)
FIXTURE IT INC
397 Rock Rd (07452-1844)
P.O. Box 905 (07452-0905)
PHONE..................................201 445-0939
Dorothy O Neill, *President*
EMP: 26
SALES (est): 2.8MM **Privately Held**
SIC: 2542 2541 Partitions & fixtures, ex-
cept wood; store & office display cases &
fixtures

(G-3832)
MELISSA SPICE TRADING CORP
Also Called: Marian
123 Glen Ave (07452-2111)
PHONE..................................862 262-7773
Melissa Mifsud, *Mng Member*
▲ **EMP:** 12
SQ FT: 10,000
SALES (est): 3MM **Privately Held**
SIC: 5149 2099 Spices & seasonings;
spices, including grinding

(G-3833)
OPICI IMPORT CO INC
25 De Boer Dr (07452-3301)
PHONE..................................201 689-3256
Tom Hopper, *Principal*
Michael Proch, *Sales Mgr*
George Palmieri, *Sales Staff*
Ric Kinon, *Manager*
Steve Bailey, *Director*
▲ **EMP:** 39
SALES (est): 6.4MM **Privately Held**
SIC: 2084 Wines

(G-3834)
REGEN BIOLOGICS INC (PA)
233 Rock Rd (07452-1708)
PHONE..................................201 651-5140
Gerald E Bisbee Jr, *CEO*
Jeffrey Chandler, *Senior VP*
John Dichiara, *Senior VP*
William G Rodkey, *Vice Pres*
Dennis W O'Dowd, *CFO*
EMP: 10
SQ FT: 2,169
SALES (est): 1.3MM **Publicly Held**
WEB: www.regenbio.com
SIC: 3841 3842 Surgical & medical instru-
ments; orthopedic appliances

(G-3835)
WORLD ELECTRONICS INC
Also Called: Lowell Electronics
37 Hanover Pl (07452-2705)
PHONE..................................201 670-1177
EMP: 10
SQ FT: 5,200
SALES (est): 2MM **Privately Held**
SIC: 3671 5065 Whol Of Electronic Parts
Equipment & A Mfg Of Electron Tubes

(G-3836)
WORLD SOFTWARE
CORPORATION
Also Called: Worldox
266 Harristown Rd Ste 201 (07452-3321)
PHONE..................................201 444-3228
Thomas W Burke, *Ch of Bd*
Ray Zwiefelhofer, *President*
Kristina Burke, *Vice Pres*
Christian Homann, *Master*
EMP: 25
SALES (est): 4.2MM **Privately Held**
WEB: www.worldox.com
SIC: 7372 7371 Prepackaged software;
computer software development

Glendora
Camden County

(G-3837)
MK METALS INC
293 Lower Landing Rd (08029)
P.O. Box 103 (08029-0103)
PHONE..................................856 245-7033
EMP: 4
SALES (est): 374.7K **Privately Held**
SIC: 3441 Fabricated structural metal

(G-3838)
NICKOLAOS KAPPATOS ENTPS
INC
Also Called: Signpros
1215 Black Horse Pike (08029-1305)
PHONE..................................856 939-1099
Nickolaos Kappatos, *President*
EMP: 19
SQ FT: 9,000
SALES (est): 2MM **Privately Held**
SIC: 3993 Advertising artwork

(G-3839)
USV OPTICAL INC (DH)
Also Called: J C Penney Optical
1 Harmon Dr Glen Oaks Par (08029)
P.O. Box 124 (08029-0124)
PHONE..................................856 228-1000
William A Schwartz Jr, *CEO*
Carmen J Nepa III, *Exec VP*
Sue Hahn, *Human Res Dir*
David Pierson, *Director*
EMP: 412
SQ FT: 20,000
SALES (est): 241.5MM
SALES (corp-wide): 793.8MM **Privately
Held**
WEB: www.ntouchcomm.net
SIC: 5995 3851 Eyeglasses, prescription;
ophthalmic goods
HQ: U.S. Vision, Inc.
1 Harmon Dr
Blackwood NJ 08012
856 228-1000

Gloucester City
Camden County

(G-3840)
D&N MACHINE
MANUFACTURING INC
Also Called: D & N Machine Co
334 Nicholson Rd (08030-1229)
P.O. Box 67 (08030-0067)
PHONE..................................856 456-1366
Robert B Doble Jr, *President*
Sandy Doble, *Corp Secy*
EMP: 20 **EST:** 1949
SQ FT: 15,000
SALES (est): 3MM **Privately Held**
SIC: 3444 3556 3679 Sheet metal spe-
cialties, not stamped; food products ma-
chinery; electronic circuits

(G-3841)
G & M PRINTWEAR
549 S Broadway Ste 2 (08030-2455)
PHONE..................................856 742-5551
Rob Dill, *Owner*
EMP: 12
SQ FT: 4,800
SALES (est): 940K **Privately Held**
WEB: www.gmprintwear.com
SIC: 2759 Screen printing

(G-3842)
GLOUCESTER CITY BOX
WORKS LLC
775 Charles St (08030-2456)
P.O. Box 2 (08030-0002)
PHONE..................................856 456-9032
Kathleen White, *Mng Member*
EMP: 10
SALES (est): 1.3MM **Privately Held**
SIC: 3565 Packaging machinery

(G-3843)
H BARRON IRON WORKS INC
316 Water St (08030-2426)
PHONE..................................856 456-9092
Dennis Barron, *President*
Michael Barron, *Vice Pres*
EMP: 15 **EST:** 1955
SALES (est): 3.8MM **Privately Held**
SIC: 3441 1799 Building components,
structural steel; fence construction

(G-3844)
IMPERIAL DESIGN
729 Charles St (08030-2456)
PHONE..................................856 742-8480
Derek Cohen, *Owner*

EMP: 7
SALES (est): 472.2K **Privately Held**
SIC: 2542 Partitions & fixtures, except
wood

(G-3845)
MID-LANTIC PRECISION INC
940 Market St (08030-1861)
P.O. Box 105 (08030-0105)
PHONE..................................856 456-3810
Lauri Wilke, *President*
William Wilke, *Vice Pres*
EMP: 14
SQ FT: 5,000
SALES (est): 900K **Privately Held**
SIC: 3599 Machine shop, jobbing & repair

(G-3846)
NEWS INC GLOUCESTER CITY
34 S Broadway (08030-1710)
P.O. Box 151 (08030-0151)
PHONE..................................856 456-1199
Albert Countryman, *President*
Daniela Gallo, *Teacher*
Richard Maunz, *Teacher*
Erica McCabe, *Teacher*
EMP: 4
SALES (est): 250K **Privately Held**
SIC: 2711 Newspapers, publishing & print-
ing

(G-3847)
PIERANGELI GROUP INC
Also Called: Window Repairs & Restoration
221 Jersey Ave (08030-2027)
PHONE..................................856 582-4060
Raymond Depiano, *Div Sub Head*
EMP: 4
SALES (corp-wide): 18.9MM **Privately
Held**
WEB: www.strybuc.com
SIC: 7699 3211 Door & window repair; flat
glass
PA: Pierangeli Group, Inc.
2006 Elmwood Ave
Sharon Hill PA 19079
610 534-3200

(G-3848)
QUIK FLEX CIRCUIT INC
Also Called: Flextron Systems
85 Nicholson Rd (08030-1308)
PHONE..................................856 742-0550
Ishwar Chauhan, *President*
B Thakroe, *Vice Pres*
Piyush Patel, *Director*
H L Patel, *Admin Sec*
EMP: 15
SQ FT: 10,000
SALES: 620.9K **Privately Held**
WEB: www.flextronsystems.com
SIC: 3672 Printed circuit boards

(G-3849)
QUIK-FLEX CIRCUIT INC
85 Nicholson Rd (08030-1308)
PHONE..................................856 742-0550
Ishwar Chauhan, *President*
EMP: 20
SALES (est): 2.9MM **Privately Held**
SIC: 3625 Control circuit devices, magnet
& solid state

(G-3850)
REDKEYS DIES INC
1307 Market St (08030-1605)
P.O. Box 360 (08030-0360)
PHONE..................................856 456-7890
Morgan Reichner, *President*
▲ **EMP:** 6
SQ FT: 1,200
SALES (est): 807.6K **Privately Held**
WEB: www.redkeysdies.com
SIC: 3544 Dies, steel rule; special dies &
tools

(G-3851)
TELEFLEX INCORPORATED
860 Charles St (08030-2450)
PHONE..................................856 349-7234
Debra Gorges, *Manager*
EMP: 100
SALES (corp-wide): 2.4B **Publicly Held**
WEB: www.teleflex.com
SIC: 3841 3842 Surgical & medical instru-
ments; surgical appliances & supplies

PA: Teleflex Incorporated
550 E Swedesford Rd # 400
Wayne PA 19087
610 225-6800

(G-3852)
THERMOSEAL INDUSTRIES LLC (DH)
600 Jersey Ave (08030-2361)
PHONE.................................856 456-3109
Richard Chubb, *President*
Patrick McMullen, *CFO*
Jeffrey Stark, *Admin Sec*
Carlie Chubb, *Assistant*
◆ **EMP:** 60 **EST:** 1996
SQ FT: 45,000
SALES (est): 13.6MM
SALES (corp-wide): 8B **Privately Held**
WEB: www.thermoseal.com
SIC: 3231 Insulating glass: made from purchased glass
HQ: Chase Industries, Inc.
10021 Commerce Park Dr
West Chester OH 45246
513 860-5565

Great Meadows
Warren County

(G-3853)
CLASSIC IMPRESSIONS
2 Witte Ln (07838-2055)
PHONE.................................908 689-3137
Christine Witte, *President*
EMP: 4
SALES (est): 351.3K **Privately Held**
SIC: 2752 Commercial printing, lithographic

(G-3854)
D N D CORP
13 Cemetery Rd (07838-2012)
PHONE.................................908 637-4343
Robert Drechsel, *President*
William De Marco Jr, *General Mgr*
EMP: 8
SQ FT: 5,000
SALES (est): 510K **Privately Held**
SIC: 3599 7692 Machine shop, jobbing & repair; welding repair

(G-3855)
PARTAC PEAT CORP
95 Shades Of Death Rd (07838)
PHONE.................................908 637-4191
James Kelsey, *President*
EMP: 18
SQ FT: 45,000
SALES (est): 1.2MM **Privately Held**
WEB: www.partac.com
SIC: 0181 0782 1499 1459 Sod farms; turf installation services, except artificial; peat mining; clays (common) quarrying; sand mining; gravel mining

(G-3856)
PARTAC PEAT CORPORATION
Also Called: Kelsey Humus
95 Kelsey Park (07838)
PHONE.................................908 637-4631
Maria B Kelsey, *President*
Janes Kelsey, *President*
EMP: 15 **EST:** 1945
SALES (est): 1.1MM **Privately Held**
SIC: 1499 Peat mining

(G-3857)
PAUL ENGLEHARDT
Island Rd (07838)
P.O. Box 13 (07838-0013)
PHONE.................................908 637-4556
Paul Englehardt, *Owner*
EMP: 8
SQ FT: 2,000
SALES (est): 430K **Privately Held**
SIC: 2822 Silicone rubbers

(G-3858)
WORKS ENDURO RIDER INC
1 Jenny Jump Ave (07838-2415)
PHONE.................................908 637-6385
Andrew F Smith, *President*
▲ **EMP:** 6

SALES (est): 646.7K **Privately Held**
SIC: 3751 Motorcycles & related parts

Green Brook
Middlesex County

(G-3859)
ANDYS CUSTOM CABINETS
143 Jefferson Ave (08812-2607)
PHONE.................................732 752-6443
A Hopeck, *Principal*
EMP: 4
SALES (est): 363.1K **Privately Held**
SIC: 3553 Cabinet makers' machinery

(G-3860)
CORPORATE ENVELOPE & PRTG CO
299r Us Highway 22 (08812-1701)
PHONE.................................732 752-4333
Paul Psak, *President*
James Bidne, *Vice Pres*
EMP: 7
SQ FT: 8,000
SALES (est): 2MM **Privately Held**
WEB: www.corpenvelope.com
SIC: 2759 Commercial printing

(G-3861)
HOZRIC LLC
11 Ridge Rd (08812-1831)
PHONE.................................908 420-8821
Faizan Ahmed, *Vice Pres*
EMP: 4
SALES (est): 55.6K **Privately Held**
SIC: 7213 7371 7372 Linen supply, nonclothing; linen supply, clothing; computer software systems analysis & design, custom; computer software development & applications; prepackaged software

(G-3862)
IWC
12 Red Bud Ln (08812-1820)
PHONE.................................732 968-8122
Mark Kang, *General Mgr*
▲ **EMP:** 15
SALES (est): 1.3MM **Privately Held**
SIC: 3315 Wire & fabricated wire products

(G-3863)
J G SCHMIDT CO INC
Also Called: Jgs
354 U S Rt 22 (08812)
PHONE.................................732 563-9500
George R Schmidt, *CEO*
Thomas Schmidt, *President*
Theresa Schmidt, *Treasurer*
▲ **EMP:** 80 **EST:** 1920
SQ FT: 70,000
SALES (est): 14.4MM **Privately Held**
WEB: www.jgschmidt.com
SIC: 3469 Stamping metal for the trade

(G-3864)
K JABAT INC
342 Us Highway 22 (08812-1703)
P.O. Box 68, Middlesex (08846-0068)
PHONE.................................732 469-8177
Theresa Kulkaski, *President*
Shana Strange, *CFO*
Stanley Kulkaski, *Admin Sec*
▲ **EMP:** 15
SQ FT: 5,500
SALES (est): 3MM **Privately Held**
SIC: 3083 3082 Laminated plastics plate & sheet; tubes, unsupported plastic

(G-3865)
PAINTON STUDIOS INC
299 Us Highway 22 Ste 21 (08812-1716)
PHONE.................................732 302-0200
James M Painton, *President*
Joan S Painton, *Vice Pres*
EMP: 4
SQ FT: 2,000
SALES (est): 471.1K **Privately Held**
WEB: www.painton.com
SIC: 2791 Typesetting

(G-3866)
POOL TABLES PLUS INC (PA)
Also Called: Loree Jon Pool Tables Plus
299 Us Highway 22 Ste 24 (08812-1716)
PHONE.................................732 968-8228
Mark Ogonowski, *President*
Nancy Skalaski, *Vice Pres*
▲ **EMP:** 6
SQ FT: 10,000
SALES (est): 2.4MM **Privately Held**
SIC: 5941 5091 5021 2542 Pool & billiard tables; specialty sport supplies; billiard equipment & supplies; bar furniture; bar fixtures, except wood

(G-3867)
STAINLESS SURPLUS LLC
6 Pheasant Run (08812-2042)
PHONE.................................914 661-3800
Sam Desi,
◆ **EMP:** 5
SALES (est): 3.6MM **Privately Held**
SIC: 3341 Secondary nonferrous metals

Green Village
Morris County

(G-3868)
KLEEMEYER & MERKEL INC
Also Called: Green Village Packing Co
68 Britten Rd (07935-3000)
P.O. Box 204 (07935-0204)
PHONE.................................973 377-0875
William Kleemeyer Jr, *President*
Carl Kleemeyer, *Corp Secy*
EMP: 15
SQ FT: 5,000
SALES (est): 4MM **Privately Held**
SIC: 5147 5421 2011 Meats, fresh; meat markets, including freezer provisioners; meat packing plants

---

Grenloch
Gloucester County

(G-3869)
ENSINGER GRENLOCH INC (DH)
Also Called: Ensinger Hyde
1 Main St (08032)
PHONE.................................856 227-0500
Robert Racchini, *Vice Pres*
Chris Ranallo, *Vice Pres*
Larry Resavage, *Vice Pres*
▲ **EMP:** 75
SQ FT: 90,000
SALES (est): 36.7MM
SALES (corp-wide): 533.1MM **Privately Held**
WEB: www.insulbar.com
SIC: 3083 Thermoplastic laminates: rods, tubes, plates & sheet; thermosetting laminates: rods, tubes, plates & sheet
HQ: Ensinger Industries, Inc.
365 Meadowlands Blvd
Washington PA 15301
724 746-6050

Guttenberg
Hudson County

(G-3870)
ALAQUA INC
7004 Boulevard E Apt 28a (07093-5030)
PHONE.................................201 758-1580
Vital S Strumza, *President*
Fini Herscovitz, *Treasurer*
▲ **EMP:** 15
SALES: 18MM **Privately Held**
WEB: www.alaquainc.com
SIC: 3559 Chemical machinery & equipment

(G-3871)
O STITCH MATIC INC
Also Called: Deerbrook Fabrics
427 69th St (07093-2413)
PHONE.................................201 861-3045

Edward Parseghian, *President*
EMP: 6
SALES (corp-wide): 915.3K **Privately Held**
SIC: 2397 2395 Schiffli machine embroideries; pleating & stitching
PA: O Stitch Matic Inc
430 Walker St
Fairview NJ
201 945-4141

(G-3872)
SOFA DOCTOR INC
Also Called: Dr Sofa
148 71st St (07093-3410)
PHONE.................................718 292-6300
Shlomie Eini, *President*
EMP: 8 **EST:** 2004
SALES (est): 873.5K **Privately Held**
SIC: 2512 7641 Upholstered household furniture; furniture upholstery repair

(G-3873)
WELLS TRADING LLC
7000 Kennedy Blvd E M-9 (07093-4825)
PHONE.................................201 552-9909
David Acel,
◆ **EMP:** 10 **EST:** 2017
SALES (est): 1.1MM **Privately Held**
SIC: 2389 Costumes

Hackensack
Bergen County

(G-3874)
AAS TECHNOLOGIES INC
290 Lodi St (07601-3118)
PHONE.................................201 342-7300
Ralph Varano, *Ch of Bd*
EMP: 6
SALES (est): 663.9K **Privately Held**
SIC: 3699 5946 Security control equipment & systems; cameras

(G-3875)
ALKAZONE GLOBAL INC
200 S Newman St (07601-3124)
PHONE.................................201 880-7966
Robert Kim, *Principal*
EMP: 7
SALES (est): 210.5K **Privately Held**
SIC: 2086 Bottled & canned soft drinks

(G-3876)
ALLURE BOX & DISPLAY CO
216 Charles St (07601-3111)
PHONE.................................212 807-7070
Dov Baum, *Principal*
EMP: 10
SQ FT: 30,000
SALES (est): 1.1MM **Privately Held**
SIC: 2671 2631 2621 2541 Paper coated or laminated for packaging; container, packaging & boxboard; wrapping & packaging papers; store & office display cases & fixtures

(G-3877)
ARCADIA EQUIPMENT INC
140 Lawrence St (07601-4195)
PHONE.................................201 342-3308
Doug White, *President*
Sally White, *Admin Sec*
EMP: 12
SQ FT: 3,000
SALES (est): 8.8MM **Privately Held**
WEB: www.arcadiaequipment.com
SIC: 5034 3823 Pumps & pumping equipment; industrial instrmnts msrmnt display/control process variable

(G-3878)
ARTISAN OVEN INC
Also Called: Central Bakery
105 S State St (07601-3919)
PHONE.................................201 488-6261
Carlos A Garcia, *President*
EMP: 6 **EST:** 2010
SALES (est): 141.7K **Privately Held**
SIC: 5461 2051 Bread: bakery: wholesale or wholesale/retail combined

GEOGRAPHIC

(G-3879)
AURORA APPAREL INC
Also Called: Aurora Apparels
1 Riverside Sq Mall # 146 (07601-6358)
PHONE..............................201 646-4590
EMP: 4
SQ FT: 3,000
SALES (est): 330K Privately Held
SIC: 2211 Cotton Broadwoven Fabric Mill

(G-3880)
**B & S TOOL AND CUTTER
SERVICE**
99 John St (07601-4129)
PHONE..............................201 488-3545
Frederick Lindenau, President
Thomas Lindenau, Vice Pres
EMP: 9 EST: 1959
SQ FT: 5,000
SALES: 800K Privately Held
WEB: www.cncsharptools.com
SIC: 7699 3545 Knife, saw & tool sharpening & repair; cutting tools for machine tools

(G-3881)
**BASSIL BOOKBINDING
COMPANY INC**
535 S River St (07601-6621)
PHONE..............................201 440-4925
Elias Bassil, President
Christine Bassil, Managing Dir
▲ EMP: 27
SQ FT: 20,000
SALES (est): 4.6MM Privately Held
SIC: 2789 Binding only: books, pamphlets, magazines, etc.

(G-3882)
**BCG MARBLE GRAN
FABRICATORS CO**
167 Sussex St (07601-3317)
PHONE..............................201 343-8487
Guiseppe Guerini, President
◆ EMP: 10
SQ FT: 5,000
SALES (est): 1.3MM Privately Held
SIC: 3281 2511 2434 5032 Granite, cut & shaped; marble, building: cut & shaped; wood household furniture; wood kitchen cabinets; marble building stone

(G-3883)
BEACON OFFSET PRINTING LLC
204 Russell Pl (07601-3315)
PHONE..............................201 488-4241
Daniel Communali, President
Vivian Hollenbeck, Corp Secy
EMP: 5
SQ FT: 6,000
SALES: 600K Privately Held
SIC: 2752 Commercial printing, offset

(G-3884)
BETTER HEALTHLAB INC
Also Called: Alkazone
200 S Newman St Unit 1 (07601-3124)
P.O. Box 418, Alpine (07620-0418)
PHONE..............................201 880-7966
Robert Kim, President
William Kim, Opers Staff
Misook Kim, Treasurer
▲ EMP: 12
SQ FT: 12,000
SALES (est): 2MM Privately Held
WEB: www.betterhealthlab.com
SIC: 2086 Water, pasteurized: packaged in cans, bottles, etc.

(G-3885)
BIB AND TUCKER INC
51 Main St (07601-7001)
PHONE..............................201 489-9600
Ross Arrabito, President
Robin Arrabito, Vice Pres
EMP: 11
SQ FT: 5,000
SALES (est): 579.4K Privately Held
SIC: 2369 5641 Girls' & children's outerwear; infants' wear; children's wear

(G-3886)
BITRO GROUP INC
300 Lodi St (07601-3143)
PHONE..............................201 641-1004

Wha Lee, President
Tim Ahn, Opers Mgr
Charles Harder, Sales Staff
Greg Angier, Manager
▲ EMP: 25
SQ FT: 22,000
SALES (est): 6.3MM Privately Held
SIC: 3641 Electric lamps & parts for specialized applications

(G-3887)
**BRAINSTORM CELL
THRPEUTICS INC (PA)**
3 University Plaza Dr (07601)
PHONE..............................201 488-0460
Irit Arbel, Ch of Bd
Chaim Lebovits, President
Uri Yablonka, COO
Joseph Petroziello, Vice Pres
Mary Kay Turner, Vice Pres
EMP: 13
SALES (est): 2MM Publicly Held
SIC: 2836 Biological products, except diagnostic

(G-3888)
**C & K PUNCH & SCREW MCH
PDTS**
160 Hobart St (07601-3922)
PHONE..............................201 343-6750
Donald Kuder, President
Alan Conrad, Vice Pres
Carole Kuder, Treasurer
EMP: 6
SQ FT: 4,000
SALES (est): 910.2K Privately Held
WEB: www.candkpunches.com
SIC: 3544 3451 Special dies & tools; die sets for metal stamping (presses); jigs & fixtures; screw machine products

(G-3889)
CAD SIGNS LLC
169 Lodi St (07601-3942)
PHONE..............................201 267-0457
Oscar F Galeano,
EMP: 5 EST: 2005
SALES (est): 641.1K Privately Held
SIC: 3993 Electric signs

(G-3890)
CAD SIGNS NYC CORP
169 Lodi St (07601-3942)
PHONE..............................201 525-5415
Alex Galeano, President
EMP: 30 EST: 2013
SALES (est): 1.3MM Privately Held
SIC: 3993 Signs & advertising specialties

(G-3891)
CADENCE DISTRIBUTORS LLC
200 S Newman St Unit 8 (07601-3124)
PHONE..............................646 808-3031
Ankur Ahuja, Mng Member
▲ EMP: 3 EST: 2010
SALES (est): 1.7MM Privately Held
SIC: 2844 Perfumes & colognes

(G-3892)
**CALIFORNIA STUCCO
PRODUCTS**
85 Zabriskie St Ste 1 (07601-4934)
PHONE..............................201 457-1900
Edwin Gorter, President
EMP: 6 EST: 1927
SQ FT: 4,000
SALES (est): 676.5K Privately Held
WEB: www.californiastucco.net
SIC: 3299 Stucco

(G-3893)
**CALLAGHAN PUMP CONTROLS
INC**
106 Hobart St (07601-3911)
PHONE..............................201 621-0505
John Callaghan, CEO
Eileen Latona, Vice Pres
EMP: 4
SALES (est): 627.1K Privately Held
WEB: www.callaghanpump.com
SIC: 3561 Pumps & pumping equipment

(G-3894)
**CAMBRIDGE THERAPEUTIC
TECH LLC**
90 Main St Ste 107 (07601-7130)
PHONE..............................914 420-5555
John Klein, CEO
Mark Adams Jr, Exec VP
Barry Posner, Exec VP
EMP: 6
SALES (est): 315.6K Privately Held
SIC: 2834 Pharmaceutical preparations

(G-3895)
CAVALLA INC
111 Union St (07601-4083)
PHONE..............................201 343-3338
Arthur Pisani, President
Alfred Neri, Treasurer
Mirella Bortone, Finance Mgr
Bryan Kafka, Sales Engr
Robert Pisani, Admin Sec
▲ EMP: 20 EST: 1925
SQ FT: 12,000
SALES (est): 3.3MM Privately Held
WEB: www.cavalla.net
SIC: 3544 5084 Special dies & tools; packaging machinery & equipment

(G-3896)
CERAMIC PRODUCTS INC
221 Park St (07601-4215)
P.O. Box 105, Palisades Park (07650-0105)
PHONE..............................201 342-8200
Ante Vidaic, President
Susan Giacobone, President
Richard Giacobone, Vice Pres
Mark Vidaic, Manager
▲ EMP: 4
SQ FT: 800
SALES: 950K Privately Held
SIC: 3299 Ceramic fiber

(G-3897)
**CHAMPIONS ONCOLOGY INC
(PA)**
1 University Plz Ste 307 (07601-6205)
PHONE..............................201 808-8400
Ronnie Morris, CEO
Joel Ackerman, Ch of Bd
David Miller, CFO
EMP: 92
SALES: 27MM Publicly Held
WEB: www.championsbiotechnology.com
SIC: 2834 Pharmaceutical preparations

(G-3898)
CLIP STRIP CORP
241 Main St Fl 5 (07601-5711)
PHONE..............................201 342-9155
Edward Spitaletta, President
Buddy Mickolajczyk, Exec VP
Stuart Morrison, Sales Staff
▲ EMP: 6
SALES (est): 1.3MM Privately Held
WEB: www.clipstrip.com
SIC: 2542 Office & store showcases & display fixtures

(G-3899)
**CONCRETE CUTTING
PARTNERS INC**
508 Hudson St (07601-6608)
PHONE..............................201 440-2233
Barry Maillet, President
EMP: 8
SQ FT: 6,000
SALES (est): 995.7K Privately Held
SIC: 3559 1771 Concrete products machinery; concrete work

(G-3900)
CONTINENTAL COOKIES INC
185 S Newman St (07601-3125)
PHONE..............................201 498-1966
Steve Gavosto, President
EMP: 14
SQ FT: 15,000
SALES (est): 2.4MM Privately Held
WEB: www.continentalcookies.com
SIC: 2052 Cookies

(G-3901)
CONTRACT COATINGS INC
161 Beech St (07601-3424)
PHONE..............................201 343-3131
Jayant Amin, President
Bharat Patel, Vice Pres
EMP: 10
SQ FT: 6,700
SALES (est): 2.2MM Privately Held
WEB: www.contractcoatings.com
SIC: 2834 Pharmaceutical preparations

(G-3902)
CUTTING RECORDS INC
190 Main St Ste 403 (07601-7319)
PHONE..............................201 488-8444
Amado Marin, President
EMP: 7
SALES (est): 765.9K Privately Held
WEB: www.cuttingnyc.com
SIC: 2782 Record albums

(G-3903)
D & G LLC
Also Called: Hai Tai Boutique
29 1st St Apt 605 (07601-2067)
PHONE..............................201 289-5750
Ty Dobson, CEO
Madison Dey, Exec Sec
EMP: 5 EST: 2008
SQ FT: 2,200
SALES (est): 387.7K Privately Held
SIC: 2253 2341 2322 Knit outerwear mills; women's & children's underwear; underwear, men's & boys': made from purchased materials

(G-3904)
DAIRY DELUXE CORP
153 Lawrence St (07601-4111)
PHONE..............................845 549-0665
Jacob Breuer, President
EMP: 7
SALES: 450K Privately Held
SIC: 2038 Pizza, frozen

(G-3905)
DANSON SHEET METAL INC
Also Called: Hutcheon and Simon
140 Atlantic St (07601-4114)
PHONE..............................201 343-4876
Dan Cubicciotti Jr, President
EMP: 25 EST: 1922
SQ FT: 8,000
SALES: 4MM Privately Held
SIC: 3444 1761 Sheet metalwork; sheet metalwork

(G-3906)
DESIGN N STITCH INC
107 Pink St (07601-5207)
PHONE..............................201 488-1314
John Fitzpatrick, President
Robert Fitzpatrick, Corp Secy
EMP: 8
SQ FT: 2,000
SALES: 1MM Privately Held
WEB: www.design-n-stitch.com
SIC: 2262 2395 Screen printing: manmade fiber & silk broadwoven fabrics; embroidery products, except schiffli machine

(G-3907)
DIE TECH LLC
58 Mckinley St (07601-4007)
PHONE..............................201 343-8324
Jim Galbreath,
EMP: 8
SALES (est): 1MM Privately Held
SIC: 3544 Special dies & tools

(G-3908)
DISPLAY EQUATION LLC
135 Spring Valley Ave (07601-2947)
PHONE..............................201 343-4135
Frank J Cristiano,
Rosa Cristiano,
EMP: 6
SALES: 350K Privately Held
SIC: 2542 Office & store showcases & display fixtures

(G-3909)
DUCT MATE INC
190 Lexington Ave (07601-4021)
PHONE..............................201 488-8002

Joseph Tasca, *President*
Patricia Tasca, *Corp Secy*
EMP: 8
SALES: 900K **Privately Held**
WEB: www.ductmatehvac.com
SIC: 1711 3444 3585 Heating & air conditioning contractors; sheet metalwork; heating & air conditioning combination units

(G-3910)
EBSCO PUBLISHING INC
Also Called: Salem Press
2 University Plz Ste 310 (07601-6202)
PHONE..............................201 968-9899
Nancy Grimaldi, *Regl Sales Mgr*
Lapierre Deborah, *Accounts Exec*
Mooney Ryan, *Accounts Exec*
Richard Debenham, *Sales Staff*
Julia Colpitts, *Manager*
EMP: 8
SALES (corp-wide): 2.8B **Privately Held**
SIC: 2741 Miscellaneous publishing
HQ: Ebsco Publishing, Inc.
10 Estes St
Ipswich MA 01938
978 356-6500

(G-3911)
ELECTRO-CERAMIC INDUSTRIES
Also Called: Eci
75 Kennedy St (07601-5262)
PHONE..............................201 342-2630
Herbert Schlomann, *President*
Frank Floystad, *Vice Pres*
EMP: 25
SQ FT: 6,500
SALES (est): 3.1MM **Privately Held**
WEB: www.electroceramic.com
SIC: 3264 3675 3053 Porcelain parts for electrical devices, molded; electronic capacitors; gaskets, packing & sealing devices

(G-3912)
FENCE AMERICA NEW JERSEY INC
210 S Newman St Ste 1 (07601-3145)
PHONE..............................973 472-5121
EMP: 5 EST: 2014
SALES (est): 575K **Privately Held**
SIC: 4789 4212 3315 Pipeline terminal facilities, independently operated; local trucking, without storage; fencing made in wiredrawing plants

(G-3913)
FIFTY/FIFTY GROUP INC
Also Called: Lola Products
241 Main St Fl 5 (07601-5711)
PHONE..............................201 343-1243
Richard Spitaletta, *President*
Edward Spitaletta, *Chairman*
John Kakatsch, *Vice Pres*
Charles Spitaletta, *Vice Pres*
Eric Sun, *VP Opers*
▲ **EMP:** 35
SALES (est): 6.3MM **Privately Held**
WEB: www.lolaproducts.com
SIC: 3991 Brooms & brushes

(G-3914)
FIT GRAPHIX (PA)
390 Maple Hill Dr (07601-1411)
PHONE..............................201 488-4670
EMP: 8
SQ FT: 5,000
SALES: 810K **Privately Held**
SIC: 2759 Commercial Printing Specializing In Photo Boards

(G-3915)
FLEX MOULDING INC
22 E Lafayette St (07601-6831)
PHONE..............................201 487-8080
Milton Glicksman, *Principal*
EMP: 8 EST: 1965
SQ FT: 16,000
SALES: 1MM **Privately Held**
WEB: www.flexiblemoulding.com
SIC: 3089 2821 Injection molded finished plastic products; plastics materials & resins

(G-3916)
FORD FASTENERS INC
110 S Newman St (07601-3294)
PHONE..............................201 487-3151
Steve Cellary, *President*
Rossana Palatucci, *Office Mgr*
▲ **EMP:** 6 EST: 1963
SQ FT: 25,000
SALES (est): 2MM **Privately Held**
WEB: www.fordfasteners.com
SIC: 5072 3312 Screws; bolts; stainless steel

(G-3917)
FORDION PACKAGING LTD
185 Linden St Ste 3 (07601-4672)
PHONE..............................201 692-1344
Francis Harvey, *President*
John B Landers, *Vice Pres*
Brian Mc Manus, *Vice Pres*
Daniel J Ryan, *Vice Pres*
James Flanagan, *Treasurer*
EMP: 17
SQ FT: 2,000
SALES (est): 4.5MM **Privately Held**
SIC: 3081 Polypropylene film & sheet

(G-3918)
FOSTER ENGRAVING CORPORATION
174 S Main St Ste B (07601-5209)
PHONE..............................201 489-5979
Giovanni Osorio, *President*
EMP: 4 EST: 1959
SQ FT: 5,000
SALES: 300K **Privately Held**
SIC: 3089 3479 Engraving of plastic; etching & engraving

(G-3919)
FULL SERVICE MAILERS INC
123 S Newman St (07601-3211)
PHONE..............................973 478-8813
Evelio Velez Jr, *President*
EMP: 22
SQ FT: 154,000
SALES: 1.5MM **Privately Held**
SIC: 7331 2752 Mailing service; commercial printing, lithographic

(G-3920)
GENAVITE LLC
171 Beech St (07601-3424)
PHONE..............................201 343-3131
Bharat Patel, *President*
EMP: 10
SQ FT: 5,000
SALES (est): 1.8MM **Privately Held**
SIC: 2834 Vitamin preparations

(G-3921)
GENERAL AVIATION & ELEC MFG CO
Also Called: General A & E
30 Jersey Pl (07601-3103)
P.O. Box 2245, South Hackensack (07606-0845)
PHONE..............................201 487-1700
John Baker, *CEO*
Bella Baker, *Vice Pres*
Jeff Taney, *Sales Mgr*
Jeffrey Taney, *Sales Mgr*
EMP: 25 EST: 1954
SQ FT: 25,000
SALES (est): 2.9MM **Privately Held**
WEB: www.generalae.com
SIC: 3444 Sheet metal specialties, not stamped

(G-3922)
GERBINO COMPUTER SYSTEMS INC
Also Called: Innovative Computer Systems
200 Passaic St Ste 100 (07601-2761)
PHONE..............................201 342-8240
Steve Gerbino, *President*
Joy Demario, *CFO*
EMP: 8
SQ FT: 6,000

SALES: 1MM **Privately Held**
SIC: 7378 7379 7373 5045 Computer peripheral equipment repair & maintenance; computer related consulting services; value-added resellers, computer systems; computers, peripherals & software; custom computer programming services; prepackaged software

(G-3923)
GRAPHIC IMPRESSIONS INC
316 Prospect Ave Apt 10f (07601-2575)
PHONE..............................201 487-8788
Allan Bauer, *President*
Sharyn Bauer, *Treasurer*
▲ **EMP:** 9
SQ FT: 2,500
SALES (est): 857.5K **Privately Held**
WEB: www.graphic-impressions.com
SIC: 2752 Commercial printing, offset

(G-3924)
GREAT NOTCH INDUSTRIES INC
140 Liberty St (07601-3181)
PHONE..............................201 343-8110
Paul Galinski, *President*
James Galinski, *Vice Pres*
EMP: 5 EST: 1971
SQ FT: 3,200
SALES (est): 613.2K **Privately Held**
WEB: www.greatnotch.com
SIC: 3599 Machine shop, jobbing & repair

(G-3925)
GREY HOUSE PUBLISHING INC
Also Called: Salem Publishing
2 University Plz (07601-6202)
PHONE..............................201 968-0500
EMP: 8 **Privately Held**
SIC: 2741 Misc Publishing

(G-3926)
HARTMANN TOOL CO INC
147 Lodi St (07601-3928)
P.O. Box 405, Blairstown (07825-0405)
PHONE..............................201 343-8700
Thomas Hartmann, *Principal*
Dianne Hartmann, *Vice Pres*
EMP: 5
SQ FT: 1,300
SALES: 475K **Privately Held**
SIC: 3089 3544 Molding primary plastic; dies, plastics forming

(G-3927)
HIGH-TECHNOLOGY CORPORATION (PA)
144 South St (07601-3109)
PHONE..............................201 488-0010
Veronica Alroy, *President*
Aline Alroy, *Vice Pres*
Violeta Enciu, *Project Engr*
Elizabeth Bosniyak, *Admin Sec*
EMP: 18
SQ FT: 13,500
SALES (est): 4.4MM **Privately Held**
SIC: 8731 3542 Commercial physical research; machine tools, metal forming type

(G-3928)
HIRESPRINT LLC
225 Park St (07601-4215)
PHONE..............................201 488-1626
Cesar A Bonifacio,
EMP: 10
SALES (est): 738.8K **Privately Held**
SIC: 3993 Signs & advertising specialties

(G-3929)
HIROX - USA INC (HQ)
100 Commerce Way Ste 4 (07601-6307)
PHONE..............................201 342-2600
Yusuke Kajiro, *President*
Steve Buck, *General Mgr*
Yasuo Monno, *Sales Engr*
Christian Munoz, *Sales Staff*
Hideyuki Masui, *Manager*
EMP: 6
SALES (est): 1MM **Privately Held**
WEB: www.hirox-usa.com
SIC: 3944 Science kits: microscopes, chemistry sets, etc.

(G-3930)
HOFFMAN/NEW YORKER INC (PA)
46 Clinton Pl (07601-4523)
PHONE..............................201 488-1800
Terrance Rothlisberger, *General Mgr*
Terence V Rothlisberger, *Vice Pres*
Richard J Greco, *Treasurer*
Jeffrey A Rabinowitz, *Admin Sec*
▲ **EMP:** 7
SALES (est): 7.9MM **Privately Held**
WEB: www.hoffmanpressing.com
SIC: 3582 Pressing machines, commercial laundry & drycleaning

(G-3931)
INTERIOR ART & DESIGN INC
59 Oak St (07601-4927)
PHONE..............................201 488-8855
Ori Katzin, *President*
Ronit Katzin, *Treasurer*
EMP: 23 EST: 1991
SQ FT: 9,615
SALES: 1.2MM **Privately Held**
WEB: www.interiorart.com
SIC: 2392 2391 Household furnishings; curtains & draperies

(G-3932)
INTERNATIONAL CONTAINER CO
Also Called: Paper Board Products
409 S River St (07601-6616)
PHONE..............................201 440-1600
Jonathan A Marks, *President*
Peter L Kirsch, *Vice Pres*
Sean Searles, *Sales Staff*
Victoria Marks, *Admin Sec*
EMP: 46
SQ FT: 5,000
SALES (est): 9MM **Privately Held**
SIC: 2653 2657 Boxes, corrugated: made from purchased materials; folding paperboard boxes

(G-3933)
JACQUELINE EMBROIDERY CO
445 Thompson St Apt G (07601-1261)
P.O. Box 2562, Secaucus (07096-2562)
PHONE..............................732 278-8121
Frank Cervantes, *Owner*
EMP: 4
SQ FT: 5,000
SALES (est): 212.1K **Privately Held**
SIC: 2397 Schiffli machine embroideries

(G-3934)
JOHN COOPER COMPANY INC
Also Called: Beers Steel Erecting
250 Maywood Ave Ste C (07601)
PHONE..............................201 487-4018
Darby L Diedrich, *President*
EMP: 12
SQ FT: 20,000
SALES (est): 1.1MM **Privately Held**
SIC: 1761 1791 3441 Siding contractor; structural steel erection; fabricated structural metal

(G-3935)
KAYDEN MANUFACTURING INC
Also Called: Pool Ladder
83a Burlews Ct Ste A (07601-4839)
PHONE..............................201 880-9898
Jeff Kayden, *President*
Jess Kayden, *President*
Erika Kayden, *Vice Pres*
◆ **EMP:** 12
SQ FT: 3,500
SALES: 1MM **Privately Held**
WEB: www.kaydenmfg.com
SIC: 3949 Swimming pools, except plastic

(G-3936)
KEYPOINT INTELLIGENCE LLC
108 John St (07601-4130)
PHONE..............................201 489-6439
Dan Narbone, *Director*
EMP: 5 **Privately Held**
WEB: www.buyerslab.com
SIC: 2721 Statistical reports (periodicals): publishing only

HQ: Keypoint Intelligence Llc
80 Little Falls Rd
Fairfield NJ 07004
973 797-2100

(G-3937)
KRAISSL COMPANY INC
299 Williams Ave (07601-5225)
P.O. Box 2363, South Hackensack (07606-0963)
PHONE..............................201 342-0008
Richard C Michel, *Ch of Bd*
Angela Di Palma, *Controller*
EMP: 25
SQ FT: 13,000
SALES: 1.9MM **Privately Held**
WEB: www.kraissl.com
SIC: 3494 3561 3563 Valves & pipe fittings; pumps & pumping equipment; air & gas compressors including vacuum pumps

(G-3938)
LECO PLASTICS INC
130 Gameville St (07601)
PHONE..............................201 343-3330
Barry Schwartz, *President*
Seth Haubenstock, *Sales Dir*
Burt Schwartz, *Sales Staff*
▲ **EMP:** 10 EST: 1946
SQ FT: 20,000
SALES (est): 2.2MM **Privately Held**
WEB: www.lecoplastics.com
SIC: 3089 Extruded finished plastic products

(G-3939)
LIVEU INC
2 University Plz Ste 505 (07601-6210)
PHONE..............................201 742-5229
Avichai Cohen, *President*
EMP: 60 EST: 2008
SALES (est): 18.1MM **Privately Held**
SIC: 3861 Cameras & related equipment

(G-3940)
LOSURDO FOODS INC (PA)
Also Called: Bel-Capri
20 Owens Rd (07601-3297)
PHONE..............................201 343-6680
Marc Jx Losurdo, *President*
Marc Losurdo, *Vice Pres*
Maria Losurdo, *Treasurer*
Michael Losurdo Sr, *Officer*
Mary Losurdo, *Admin Sec*
▲ **EMP:** 50 EST: 1959
SQ FT: 20,000
SALES (est): 73.5MM **Privately Held**
WEB: www.losurdofoods.com
SIC: 5141 2022 2033 2045 Food brokers; natural cheese; tomato sauce: packaged in cans, jars, etc.; pizza doughs, prepared: from purchased flour

(G-3941)
M B C FOOD MACHINERY CORP
78 Mckinley St (07601-4009)
PHONE..............................201 489-7000
Mario Battaglia, *CEO*
John Battaglia, *President*
Chris Guilianti, *Foreman/Supr*
Rosa Battaglia, *Admin Sec*
EMP: 6
SQ FT: 4,410
SALES (est): 1.1MM **Privately Held**
WEB: www.mbcfoodmachinery.com
SIC: 3556 Food products machinery

(G-3942)
MACROMEDIA INCORPORATED (PA)
150 River St (07601-7110)
P.O. Box 75 (07602-0075)
PHONE..............................201 646-4000
Malcolm A Borg, *Ch of Bd*
Alfred Doblin, *Editor*
John Rowe, *Editor*
Stephen A Borg, *Vice Pres*
Susan Beard, *Human Res Dir*
EMP: 19
SQ FT: 360,000
SALES (est): 156.2MM **Privately Held**
WEB: www.mmsconnect.com
SIC: 2711 2721 Newspapers, publishing & printing; periodicals

(G-3943)
MASTER BOND INC
154 Hobart St (07601-3922)
PHONE..............................201 343-8983
James Brenner, *President*
Susan Edwards, *Corp Secy*
Michaels Robert, *Vice Pres*
Hillary Evans, *President*
Utsav Shah, *Engineer*
▲ **EMP:** 30
SQ FT: 16,000
SALES (est): 7.6MM **Privately Held**
SIC: 2891 2851 Adhesives; epoxy coatings

(G-3944)
MAVERICK CATERERS LLC
20 Railroad Ave (07601-3309)
PHONE..............................718 433-3776
AVI Moche,
Erik Gross,
EMP: 30
SQ FT: 4,000
SALES (est): 3.4MM **Privately Held**
SIC: 5149 2099 Natural & organic foods; food preparations

(G-3945)
MDJ INC
25 Dicarolis Ct 21 (07601-4115)
PHONE..............................201 457-9260
Donald Hahn, *President*
Peter Sowinski, *Vice Pres*
EMP: 40
SQ FT: 8,000
SALES (est): 4.1MM **Privately Held**
WEB: www.mdjco.com
SIC: 3672 Printed circuit boards

(G-3946)
MEDCO WEST ELECTRONICS INC
25 Dicarolis Ct 21 (07601-4115)
PHONE..............................201 457-9260
Guy Intoci, *President*
Peter Sowinski, *Vice Pres*
EMP: 6
SALES (est): 629.3K **Privately Held**
SIC: 3672 Printed circuit boards

(G-3947)
MERC USA INC
Also Called: Inserch By Merc U.Sa
41 Newman St (07601-3324)
PHONE..............................201 489-3527
Jahangir Astaneha, *President*
Mostafa Astaneha, *Vice Pres*
▲ **EMP:** 11
SALES (est): 2.8MM **Privately Held**
SIC: 5136 2329 Men's & boys' clothing; men's & boys' sportswear & athletic clothing

(G-3948)
MUL-T-LOCK USA INC
100 Commerce Way Ste 2 (07601-6307)
PHONE..............................973 778-3320
Nava Efrati, *President*
▲ **EMP:** 20
SQ FT: 10,000
SALES (est): 8.6MM
SALES (corp-wide): 9.3B **Privately Held**
WEB: www.mul-t-lockusa.com
SIC: 5072 3429 Security devices, locks; keys, locks & related hardware; padlocks; door locks, bolts & checks
HQ: Assa, Inc.
110 Sargent Dr
New Haven CT 06511
203 624-5225

(G-3949)
MULTI-PAK CORPORATION
180 Atlantic St (07601-3301)
PHONE..............................201 342-7474
Phil Cahill, *President*
Niel Cavanaugh, *Chairman*
EMP: 24 EST: 1956
SQ FT: 8,500
SALES (est): 5.4MM **Privately Held**
WEB: www.compactors1.com
SIC: 3589 3531 Garbage disposers & compactors, commercial; construction machinery

(G-3950)
MURRAY PAVING & CONCRETE LLC
210 S Newman St Ste 1 (07601-3145)
PHONE..............................201 670-0030
William Murray,
EMP: 35 EST: 2004
SALES: 26.8MM **Privately Held**
SIC: 1611 1771 1741 3281 Highway & street paving contractor; blacktop (asphalt) work; masonry & other stonework; concrete block masonry laying; curbing, paving & walkway stone

(G-3951)
NEI GOLD PRODUCTS OF NJ
Also Called: Nei House of Chains
44 Burlews Ct (07601-4829)
PHONE..............................201 488-5858
John Nanasi, *President*
Ernie Tacktill, *Exec VP*
Andy Kardos, *Vice Pres*
Ernie Reinetz, *Treasurer*
EMP: 30
SQ FT: 15,000
SALES (est): 369.8K **Privately Held**
SIC: 3911 Jewelry, precious metal

(G-3952)
NEI JEWELMASTERS OF NEW JERSEY (PA)
Also Called: Nanasi Enterprises
44 Burlews Ct (07601-4829)
PHONE..............................201 488-5858
John Nanasi, *President*
Norman Diamond, *Vice Pres*
Andy Kardos, *Vice Pres*
Sarah Nanasi, *Mktg Dir*
EMP: 15 EST: 1972
SQ FT: 15,000
SALES (est): 5.7MM **Privately Held**
SIC: 3911 Jewelry, precious metal

(G-3953)
NETWORK COMMUNICATIONS CONS
Also Called: Netcom
20 E Kennedy St (07601-6807)
PHONE..............................201 968-0684
Virginia Connors, *President*
James Tronolone, *Treasurer*
EMP: 10
SQ FT: 5,000
SALES: 1.3MM **Privately Held**
WEB: www.netcom-stl.com
SIC: 3663 8711 Radio & TV communications equipment; consulting engineer

(G-3954)
NJIW LIMITED LIABILITY COMPANY
Also Called: J A Visual Group
87 Burlews Ct (07601-4839)
PHONE..............................201 355-2955
Len Baum, *VP Sales*
Jeffrey Weissman, *Mng Member*
Terumi Uto,
EMP: 14
SALES (est): 187.7K **Privately Held**
SIC: 2759 8742 7389 Promotional printing; merchandising consultant;

(G-3955)
NORTH JERSEY MEDIA GROUP INC (HQ)
Also Called: North Jrsey Mdia Group Fndtion
150 River St (07601-7110)
PHONE..............................201 646-4000
Malcolm A Borg, *Ch of Bd*
John Cichowski, *Editor*
Lindsey Kelleher, *Editor*
Scott Muller, *Editor*
Sean Oates, *Editor*
▲ **EMP:** 1301 EST: 1964
SQ FT: 360,000
SALES (est): 349.5K
SALES (corp-wide): 156.2MM **Privately Held**
WEB: www.njmg.com
SIC: 2711 4813 Newspapers, publishing & printing;
PA: Macromedia Incorporated
150 River St
Hackensack NJ 07601
201 646-4000

(G-3956)
NU-EZ CUSTOM BINDERY LLC
111 Essex St Ste 1 (07601-4043)
PHONE..............................201 488-4140
Julia Paulucci,
EMP: 25
SALES (est): 7.2MM **Privately Held**
SIC: 2631 Binders' board

(G-3957)
OCEANIC GRAPHIC INTL INC
Also Called: Oceanic Graphic Printing
105 Main St Ste 1 (07601-8103)
PHONE..............................201 883-1816
David LI, *President*
Michael Lok, *Vice Pres*
EMP: 10
SALES (est): 933.8K **Privately Held**
WEB: www.ogprinting.com
SIC: 8742 2732 Marketing consulting services; book printing

(G-3958)
OSHEA SERVICES INC
Also Called: O'Shea's Printing Services
483 Main St (07601-5932)
PHONE..............................201 343-8668
Kathleen Bracken, *President*
Mildred O'Shea, *Director*
EMP: 9
SQ FT: 5,000
SALES: 800K **Privately Held**
SIC: 2752 2791 2789 2759 Commercial printing, offset; typesetting; bookbinding & related work; commercial printing

(G-3959)
OVEN ART LLC
Also Called: Oven Arts
200 S Newman St Unit 7 (07601-3124)
PHONE..............................973 910-2266
Manish Wadia,
EMP: 40
SQ FT: 20,000
SALES: 4.5MM **Privately Held**
SIC: 2052 5149 Cookies & crackers; crackers, cookies & bakery products

(G-3960)
P & A AUTO PARTS INC (PA)
530 River St (07601-5907)
PHONE..............................201 655-7117
Anne De Pasque, *President*
Bill Freedman, *VP Opers*
Robert Samarati, *Opers Mgr*
Steve Blitzstein, *Store Mgr*
Jackie De Pasque-Cupoli, *Treasurer*
EMP: 30
SQ FT: 13,000
SALES (est): 69.9MM **Privately Held**
WEB: www.paautoparts.com
SIC: 5531 5013 5015 3714 Automotive parts; automotive supplies & parts; motor vehicle parts, used; motor vehicle parts & accessories

(G-3961)
P L M MANUFACTURING COMPANY
Also Called: Progressive Machine Company
293 Hudson St (07601-6732)
P.O. Box 1663, South Hackensack (07606-0263)
PHONE..............................201 342-3636
Peter Wysocki, *President*
Kazmier Wysocki, *Vice Pres*
EMP: 27
SQ FT: 7,500
SALES (est): 3.6MM **Privately Held**
SIC: 3599 3444 Machine shop, jobbing & repair; sheet metalwork

(G-3962)
PATCHAMP INC
20 E Kennedy St (07601-6807)
PHONE..............................201 457-1504
Virginia Connors, *President*
James Tronolone, *Vice Pres*
EMP: 7
SQ FT: 5,000
SALES: 1MM **Privately Held**
WEB: www.patchamp.com
SIC: 3663 Television broadcasting & communications equipment

(G-3963)
PETNET SOLUTIONS INC
86-110 Orchard St Ste 2 (07601-4833)
PHONE.....................865 218-2000
Frank Chapman, *Branch Mgr*
EMP: 4
SALES (corp-wide): 95B **Privately Held**
SIC: 2835 Radioactive diagnostic substances
HQ: Petnet Solutions, Inc.
   810 Innovation Dr
   Knoxville TN 37932
   865 218-2000

(G-3964)
PMC INDUSTRIES INC
275 Hudson St (07601-6753)
P.O. Box 1663, South Hackensack (07606-0263)
PHONE.....................201 342-3684
Kazmier Wysocki, *President*
Peter Wysocki, *Vice Pres*
Mary Wysocki, *Treasurer*
Jim Harris, *Sales Executive*
Dominic Delia, *Manager*
EMP: 25
SQ FT: 10,000
SALES (est): 5.4MM **Privately Held**
WEB: www.pmc-industries.com
SIC: 3565 Packaging machinery

(G-3965)
PREFORM LABORATORIES INC
Also Called: Performance Laboratories Inc
34 George St (07601-3907)
P.O. Box 2208, South Hackensack (07606-0808)
PHONE.....................973 523-8610
Michael Bozzaotra, *CEO*
▲ EMP: 44
SQ FT: 5,400
SALES: 2.6MM **Privately Held**
WEB: www.performlab.com
SIC: 3842 Supports: abdominal, ankle, arch, kneecap, etc.

(G-3966)
RENNSTEIG TOOLS INC (DH)
411 Hackensack Ave # 200 (07601-6328)
PHONE.....................330 315-3044
Sascha Zmiskol, *President*
Mirko Reffke, *Vice Pres*
Andreas Heil, *Sales Staff*
Ralf Putsch, *Director*
Hans Michael Kraus, *Admin Sec*
▲ EMP: 3
SALES: 1.5MM
SALES (corp-wide): 153.4MM **Privately Held**
SIC: 5084 5251 3546 Machine tools & accessories; tools, power; cartridge-activated hand power tools
HQ: Rennsteig Werkzeuge Gmbh
   An Der Koppel 1
   Viernau 98547
   368 474-410

(G-3967)
ROY ANANIA
Also Called: South State Speed Shop
149 S State St (07601-3902)
PHONE.....................201 498-1555
Roy Anania, *Owner*
EMP: 6
SALES (est): 410K **Privately Held**
WEB: www.southstatespeed.com
SIC: 3519 Gasoline engines

(G-3968)
RUFFINO PAPER BOX MFG CO
Also Called: Ruffino Packaging Co
63 Green St (07601-4082)
PHONE.....................201 487-1260
Raymond Ruffino, *President*
Rosario Ruffino, *President*
EMP: 12
SQ FT: 12,000
SALES (est): 4.4MM **Privately Held**
SIC: 2652 Setup paperboard boxes

(G-3969)
S GOLDBERG & CO INC (PA)
Also Called: Sgfootwear Company
3 University Plz Ste 400 (07601-6222)
PHONE.....................201 342-1200
Matthew Feiner, *CEO*

Bernard Leifer, *President*
Helen B King, *Chairman*
Paul Kingslow, *COO*
Stanley Altscher, *CFO*
◆ EMP: 105 EST: 1896
SQ FT: 23,000
SALES (est): 25MM **Privately Held**
WEB: www.sgfootwear.com
SIC: 3149 3142 5139 Sandals, except rubber or plastic: children's; house slippers; slipper socks, made from purchased socks; footwear

(G-3970)
SAGE CHEMICAL INC
2 University Plz Ste 204 (07601-6211)
PHONE.....................201 489-5172
Daniel Newman, *President*
Nathan Barishan, *Vice Pres*
EMP: 4
SQ FT: 1,400
SALES (est): 516.1K **Privately Held**
SIC: 2899 5169 Chemical supplies for foundries; chemicals & allied products

(G-3971)
SAMUEL H FIELDS DENTAL LABS
Also Called: Fields Samuel H Dental Labs
197 Union St (07601-4236)
PHONE.....................201 343-4626
Samuel Fields, *President*
Robert Fields, *Corp Secy*
Richard Fields, *Vice Pres*
EMP: 25
SQ FT: 5,000
SALES (est): 1.8MM **Privately Held**
WEB: www.samfieldslab.com
SIC: 8072 8021 3843 Crown & bridge production; offices & clinics of dentists; dental equipment & supplies

(G-3972)
SGB PACKAGING GROUP INC
401 Hackensack Ave Fl 7 (07601-6411)
PHONE.....................201 488-3030
Shoshana Gibli, *President*
Lauren Gibli, *Director*
▲ EMP: 4
SALES (est): 658K **Privately Held**
WEB: www.sgbpackaging.com
SIC: 8748 2844 7389 Agricultural consultant; cosmetic preparations; cosmetic kits, assembling & packaging

(G-3973)
SGI APPAREL LTD
3 University Plz Ste 400 (07601-6222)
PHONE.....................201 342-1200
Bernard Leifer, *CEO*
Michael Diablo, *President*
Paul Kingslow, *Vice Pres*
Stanley Altscher, *CFO*
◆ EMP: 7
SQ FT: 23,000
SALES (est): 720.9K
SALES (corp-wide): 25MM **Privately Held**
WEB: www.sgfootwear.com
SIC: 2341 2322 Women's & children's nightwear; men's & boys' underwear & nightwear
PA: S. Goldberg & Co., Inc.
   3 University Plz Ste 400
   Hackensack NJ 07601
   201 342-1200

(G-3974)
SIGN A RAMA
Also Called: Sign-A-Rama
379 Main St (07601-5806)
PHONE.....................201 489-6969
Jonathan Sklar, *President*
Michael Fried, *Vice Pres*
EMP: 4
SALES (est): 383.6K **Privately Held**
SIC: 3993 Signs & advertising specialties

(G-3975)
SOMES UNIFORMS INC (PA)
Also Called: Heschel Some
314 Main St (07601-5707)
P.O. Box 68 (07602-0068)
PHONE.....................201 843-1199
Jerome S Some, *President*
Diane Some, *Treasurer*

Jason Some, *Sales Staff*
▲ EMP: 18
SQ FT: 40,000
SALES (est): 2.8MM **Privately Held**
SIC: 5699 2326 5961 Uniforms; men's & boys' work clothing; clothing, mail order (except women's); women's apparel, mail order

(G-3976)
SOUTH RIVER MACHINERY CORP
Also Called: South River Food Machinery
115 S River St (07601-6909)
PHONE.....................201 487-1736
Frank Chessari, *President*
Lisa Asala, *President*
EMP: 4
SALES (est): 310K **Privately Held**
SIC: 3599 Machine shop, jobbing & repair

(G-3977)
SPARTECH LLC
Also Called: Polycast
215 S Newman St (07601)
PHONE.....................201 489-4000
John Alfano, *General Mgr*
EMP: 35
SALES (corp-wide): 1.3B **Privately Held**
WEB: www.spartech.com
SIC: 2821 Plastics materials & resins
HQ: Spartech Llc
   120 Central
   Saint Louis MO 63105
   314 569-7400

(G-3978)
SPECTRUM INSTRUMENTATION CORP
401 Hackensack Ave Fl 4 (07601-6418)
PHONE.....................201 562-1999
Gisela Hassler, *CEO*
EMP: 20
SALES (est): 172.7K **Privately Held**
SIC: 3825 Oscillographs & oscilloscopes

(G-3979)
STOREMAXX INC
343 S River St (07601-6838)
PHONE.....................201 440-8800
Edward Spitaletta, *President*
◆ EMP: 11 EST: 2010
SALES (est): 1.5MM **Privately Held**
SIC: 3089 Plastic containers, except foam

(G-3980)
STUDIO L CONTRACTING LLC
18 Dicarolis Ct (07601-4115)
PHONE.....................201 837-1650
David Lehmann, *Mng Member*
EMP: 6
SQ FT: 2,400
SALES (est): 1MM **Privately Held**
SIC: 2434 2499 Wood kitchen cabinets; decorative wood & woodwork

(G-3981)
TECH ART INC
Also Called: Techart
25 Green St (07601-4003)
P.O. Box 1556, South Hackensack (07606-0156)
PHONE.....................201 525-0044
Gerald Pfund, *President*
Paul McDonald, *Vice Pres*
EMP: 10
SQ FT: 16,000
SALES (est): 790K **Privately Held**
SIC: 3999 Education aids, devices & supplies

(G-3982)
TESTRITE INSTRUMENT CO INC
Also Called: Testrite Visual Products
216 S Newman St (07601-3124)
PHONE.....................201 543-0240
Laurence S Rubin, *CEO*
Jeffrey Rubin, *President*
Ken Allen, *Vice Pres*
Juan Flores, *Plant Mgr*
Greg Green, *Opers Mgr*
◆ EMP: 130
SQ FT: 88,000

SALES (est): 32.2MM **Privately Held**
WEB: www.TESTRITE.com
SIC: 2542 5046 3599 3993 Fixtures: display, office or store: except wood; store fixtures & display equipment; tubing, flexible metallic; signs & advertising specialties

(G-3983)
TOTAL INK SOLUTIONS LLC
200 S Newman St Unit 4 (07601-3124)
PHONE.....................201 487-9600
Luis Uribe, *President*
Marc Jelinsky, *Vice Pres*
Andrew Maniotis, *VP Sales*
Michael D Savino, *Marketing Staff*
EMP: 10
SQ FT: 20,000
SALES (est): 1.9MM **Privately Held**
SIC: 2893 2396 Printing ink; screen printing on fabric articles

(G-3984)
TRAYCON MANUFACTURING CO INC
235 Main St Ste 204 (07601-7307)
PHONE.....................201 939-5555
August Pisto, *President*
Sandee Goldberg, *VP Admin*
EMP: 24 EST: 1963
SQ FT: 20,000
SALES (est): 4.7MM **Privately Held**
WEB: www.traycon.com
SIC: 3535 5084 Conveyors & conveying equipment; food product manufacturing machinery

(G-3985)
TRIUMPH KNITTING MACHINE SVC (PA)
Also Called: Truimph Knitting Mills
238 Main St Ste 102 (07601-7318)
PHONE.....................201 646-0022
Trudy Gerber, *President*
Steve Gerber, *Treasurer*
▲ EMP: 20
SQ FT: 20,000
SALES (est): 2.9MM **Privately Held**
WEB: www.triumphknittinginc.com
SIC: 2253 Knit outerwear mills

(G-3986)
TYPESTYLE INC
Also Called: Blue Dog Graphics
222 River St (07601-7516)
PHONE.....................201 343-3343
Donald Perlman, *President*
EMP: 5
SQ FT: 3,000
SALES (est): 791.7K **Privately Held**
SIC: 2752 Commercial printing, offset

(G-3987)
TYZ-ALL PLASTICS LLC
130 Gamewell St (07601-4230)
PHONE.....................201 343-1200
Burt Schwartz,
EMP: 8
SALES (est): 959.9K **Privately Held**
SIC: 3089 Food casings, plastic

(G-3988)
UNIVERSAL ELECTRIC MTR SVC INC
131 S Newman St (07601-3211)
PHONE.....................201 968-1000
Bill Stagg, *President*
John Kosuda, *Manager*
EMP: 44
SQ FT: 17,900
SALES (est): 2.3MM **Privately Held**
SIC: 7694 5063 3621 Electric motor repair; motors, electric; motors, electric; generators & sets, electric

(G-3989)
UPFIELD US INC
433 Hackensack Ave # 401 (07601-6319)
PHONE.....................201 894-2540
Michael Faherty, *General Mgr*
Carlos Dragonetti, *Finance*
EMP: 377
SALES: 177.4K
SALES (corp-wide): 58.3B **Privately Held**
SIC: 2079 Margarine-butter blends

PA: Unilever Plc
Unilever House
London EC4Y
207 822-5252

(G-3990)
WHAT A TEE 2 INC
82 Sussex St (07601-4104)
PHONE..................................201 457-0060
Craig Laskow, *President*
Harry Poulos, *President*
EMP: 16
SQ FT: 6,500
SALES (est): 1.4MM **Privately Held**
SIC: 2339 2329 Women's & misses' athletic clothing & sportswear; men's & boys' sportswear & athletic clothing

(G-3991)
WORLD SCIENTIFIC PUBLISHING CO
27 Warren St Ph 401 (07601-8918)
PHONE..................................201 487-9655
Doreen Phua, *President*
K K Phua, *Vice Pres*
Yubing Zhai, *Vice Pres*
Allan Barnett, *Sales Executive*
Calandra Braswell, *Manager*
▲ **EMP:** 10
SQ FT: 1,500
SALES (est): 1MM
SALES (corp-wide): 13.1MM **Privately Held**
WEB: www.wspc.com
SIC: 2741 Miscellaneous publishing
PA: World Scientific Publishing Co Pte Ltd
5 Toh Tuck Link
Singapore 59622
646 230-83

(G-3992)
ZAIYA INC
185 Kenneth St (07601)
PHONE..................................201 343-3988
EMP: 24
SALES (est): 1.7MM **Privately Held**
SIC: 2051 Mfg Bread/Related Products

Hackettstown
Warren County

(G-3993)
A AND P PHARMACY
Also Called: A&P
7 Naughright Rd Ste V (07840-5660)
PHONE..................................908 850-7640
EMP: 6
SALES (est): 380K **Privately Held**
SIC: 2834 Mfg Pharmaceutical Preparations

(G-3994)
ABB INSTALLATION PRODUCTS INC
1 Esna Park (07840-3906)
PHONE..................................908 852-1122
Allan Bordstrom, *General Mgr*
McNeel Ralph, *Production*
Joseph Luzasky, *Buyer*
EMP: 250
SALES (corp-wide): 36.4B **Privately Held**
WEB: www.tnb.com
SIC: 3643 3678 3644 3679 Connectors & terminals for electrical devices; solderless connectors (electric wiring devices); electronic connectors; electric conduits & fittings; raceways; insulators & insulation materials, electrical; electronic circuits
HQ: Abb Installation Products Inc.
860 Ridge Lake Blvd
Memphis TN 38120
901 252-5000

(G-3995)
AGRO FOODS INC
441 Schooleys Mountain Rd (07840-4023)
PHONE..................................201 954-9152
EMP: 4
SALES (est): 305.6K **Privately Held**
SIC: 1321 Natural gas liquids

(G-3996)
AJJ POWERNUTRITION LLC
Also Called: Nutrition Zone
1930 State Route 57 (07840-3484)
PHONE..................................908 452-5164
Jon Aid Anwar, *Owner*
Jawad Anwar,
Jonaid Anwar,
EMP: 7
SALES (est): 978.1K **Privately Held**
SIC: 2834 Vitamin, nutrient & hematinic preparations for human use

(G-3997)
ALMETEK INDUSTRIES INC
2 Joy Dr (07840-5331)
PHONE..................................908 850-9700
Lori Mc Mahon, *CEO*
Lori McMahon, *President*
Albert Burlando, *Principal*
Joyce Burlando, *Vice Pres*
Mike Quagliana, *Vice Pres*
EMP: 50
SQ FT: 42,000
SALES (est): 8.7MM **Privately Held**
WEB: www.almetek.com
SIC: 3999 3699 Identification badges & insignia; security devices

(G-3998)
ANDREX INC
101 Bilby Rd Ste E (07840-1753)
PHONE..................................908 852-2400
William T Pote, *President*
Thomas W Pote, *Vice Pres*
Marion Pote, *Admin Sec*
EMP: 15
SQ FT: 18,200
SALES (est): 2.3MM **Privately Held**
WEB: www.andrex.com
SIC: 3599 3679 3429 Hose, flexible metallic; harness assemblies for electronic use: wire or cable; manufactured hardware (general)

(G-3999)
ASTRODYNE CORPORATION (PA)
36 Newburgh Rd (07840-3904)
PHONE..................................908 850-5088
Peter Murphy, *President*
Marcus Grunwald, *Regional Mgr*
Jeff Snider, *Regional Mgr*
Kelly Atkinson, *Vice Pres*
Peter Resca, *VP Sls/Mktg*
▲ **EMP:** 53
SQ FT: 20,000
SALES (est): 208.5MM **Privately Held**
WEB: www.astrodyne.com
SIC: 3625 3621 3613 Switches, electric power; motors & generators; switchgear & switchboard apparatus

(G-4000)
B & H PRINTERS INC
Also Called: Jbq Printing & Marketing
470 Schooleys Mountain Rd # 1 (07840-4012)
PHONE..................................908 688-6990
Holly Harvey, *President*
Dana Harvey, *COO*
Robert Harvey, *Vice Pres*
EMP: 7
SQ FT: 4,000
SALES (est): 1.2MM **Privately Held**
SIC: 2752 Commercial printing, lithographic

(G-4001)
CEODEUX INCORPORATED
101 Bilby Rd Ste B (07840-1753)
PHONE..................................724 696-4340
Isabelle Schmitz, *President*
Shelli Martin, *Sales Staff*
▲ **EMP:** 25
SQ FT: 65,041
SALES (est): 4.8MM
SALES (corp-wide): 711.6K **Privately Held**
WEB: www.rotarex.com
SIC: 3494 5085 Valves & pipe fittings; valves & fittings
HQ: Ceodeux Sa
R. De Diekirch 24
Lintgen 7440
327 832-1

(G-4002)
CLASSIC CHESS AND GAMES INC
52 Main St (07840-1331)
PHONE..................................908 850-6553
Ken Tomchek, *President*
EMP: 4
SALES (est): 216.3K **Privately Held**
WEB: www.classicchessandgames.com
SIC: 3944 Board games, children's & adults'

(G-4003)
DALE BEHRE
Also Called: Dales's Custom Auto & Sign
108 East Ave Ste 6 (07840-2661)
PHONE..................................908 850-4225
Dale Behre, *Owner*
EMP: 5
SQ FT: 2,500
SALES (est): 484.2K **Privately Held**
WEB: www.dalescustomauto.com
SIC: 7532 3993 Body shop, automotive; signs & advertising specialties

(G-4004)
EDHARD CORP
279 Blau Rd (07840-5221)
PHONE..................................908 850-8444
Edgar Bars, *President*
Ilze Bars, *Vice Pres*
Henry Moskal, *Plant Mgr*
Gints Gulbis, *Prdtn Mgr*
EMP: 35
SQ FT: 33,000
SALES (est): 6.6MM **Privately Held**
WEB: www.edhard.com
SIC: 3599 Machine shop, jobbing & repair

(G-4005)
EMIL DIPALMA INC
182 Stephens State Pk Rd (07840-5007)
PHONE..................................973 477-2766
Emil Dipalma, *President*
EMP: 5 **EST:** 1978
SALES (est): 439.9K **Privately Held**
SIC: 1429 Trap rock, crushed & broken-quarrying

(G-4006)
EP SYSTEMS INC
470 Schooleys Mountain Rd (07840-4012)
PHONE..................................570 424-0581
EMP: 7
SALES (est): 655.6K **Privately Held**
SIC: 2842 Mfg Polish/Sanitation Goods

(G-4007)
EXPERT PROCESS SYSTEMS LLC
470 Schooleys Mountain Rd A (07840-4012)
PHONE..................................570 424-0581
EMP: 7
SQ FT: 6,500
SALES (est): 1.2MM **Privately Held**
SIC: 8711 3559 3556 1796 Engineering Services Mfg Misc Industry Mach Mfg Food Prdts Mach Bldg Equip Installation

(G-4008)
FRED S BURROUGHS NORTH JERSEY
6 Rushmore Ln (07840-2831)
PHONE..................................908 850-8773
Glen Zeeck, *Principal*
Tom Mount, *Principal*
John Nordstedt, *Principal*
Susan Reed, *Principal*
EMP: 99 **EST:** 2015
SALES (est): 2.8MM **Privately Held**
SIC: 3949 7389 Rods & rod parts, fishing;

(G-4009)
GREENE BROS SPCLTY COF RASTERS (PA)
Also Called: Greene's Beans Cafe
313 High St (07840-1955)
PHONE..................................908 979-0022
David Greene, *President*
Brian Greene, *Vice Pres*
EMP: 13
SQ FT: 1,200
SALES (est): 1.9MM **Privately Held**
SIC: 2095 5499 Roasted coffee; beverage stores

(G-4010)
HACKETTSTOWN PUBLIC WORKS
Also Called: Town of Hackettstown, The
309 E Plane St (07840-2015)
PHONE..................................908 852-2320
Thomas Kitchen, *Superintendent*
EMP: 8
SALES (est): 1.2MM **Privately Held**
SIC: 3531 1611 Road construction & maintenance machinery; highway & street construction

(G-4011)
HOMESTYLE KITCHENS & BATHS LLC
453 Route 46 E (07840-2693)
PHONE..................................908 979-9000
George Journey,
EMP: 5
SALES (est): 407.5K **Privately Held**
SIC: 2493 Reconstituted wood products

(G-4012)
INTEGRATED MICROWAVE TECH LLC (HQ)
Also Called: Vislink
101 Bilby Rd Ste 15 (07840-1753)
PHONE..................................908 852-3700
John Payne, *President*
Stephen Kitko, *Engineer*
Robert Chiarulli, *Controller*
Paul Norridge, *Finance*
EMP: 2
SQ FT: 40,000
SALES (est): 10.6MM **Publicly Held**
WEB: www.imt-solutions.com
SIC: 3663 Radio & TV communications equipment

(G-4013)
JEROME INDUSTRIES CORP (HQ)
36 Newburgh Rd (07840-3904)
PHONE..................................908 353-5700
Pete Kaczmarek, *CEO*
Theresa Di Girolamo, *Admin Sec*
▲ **EMP:** 38
SQ FT: 15,000
SALES (est): 4.9MM **Privately Held**
WEB: www.jeromeindustries.com
SIC: 3677 5065 3612 3674 Electronic coils, transformers & other inductors; electronic parts & equipment; transformers, except electric; semiconductors & related devices; power supplies, all types: static

(G-4014)
JS WELDING LLC (PA)
34 Brookside Ave (07840-4104)
PHONE..................................973 442-2202
John Szigeti, *Principal*
EMP: 5
SALES (est): 442.2K **Privately Held**
SIC: 7692 Welding repair

(G-4015)
KINGWOOD INDUSTRIAL PDTS INC
261 Main St Unit 12 (07840-2062)
PHONE..................................908 852-8655
Kevin Smith, *President*
EMP: 5
SALES (est): 37.8K **Privately Held**
WEB: www.kingwoodindustrial.com
SIC: 3842 Hearing aids

(G-4016)
LAMB PRINTING INC
700 Grand Ave (07840-1145)
PHONE..................................908 852-0837
Michael Lamb, *President*
Teresa Lamb, *Vice Pres*
EMP: 5
SQ FT: 2,500
SALES (est): 776.5K **Privately Held**
SIC: 5943 2759 2752 Office forms & supplies; directories (except telephone): printing; offset & photolithographic printing

---

(G-4017)
LIQUID METALWORKS LTD
LBLTY CO
700 Grand Ave Ste B (07840-1145)
PHONE..................................973 224-9710
Ryan Dempsey, *Principal*
EMP: 4 EST: 2008
SALES (est): 498.9K **Privately Held**
SIC: 3441 Fabricated structural metal

(G-4018)
LODI WELDING CO INC
133 Willow Grove St (07840-2017)
PHONE..................................908 852-8367
Donald W Buschgans, *President*
EMP: 4
SQ FT: 8,700
SALES (est): 576K **Privately Held**
SIC: 7692 Welding repair

(G-4019)
LORDON INC
453 Us Highway 46 E Ste 1 (07840-2694)
PHONE..................................908 813-1143
Donna Quagliana, *President*
Lori McMahon, *Vice Pres*
EMP: 6
SQ FT: 1,000
SALES (est): 650.2K **Privately Held**
WEB: www.britesidepanels.com
SIC: 3479 Coating of metals & formed
products

(G-4020)
MANGO CUSTOM CABINETS INC
216 W Stiger St (07840-1269)
PHONE..................................908 813-3077
Richard W Mango, *President*
EMP: 14
SQ FT: 14,000
SALES (est): 2.1MM **Privately Held**
SIC: 2511 5031 1751 Kitchen & dining
room furniture; kitchen cabinets; cabinet
& finish carpentry

(G-4021)
MARS INCORPORATED
Also Called: M & M Mars
700 High St (07840-1502)
PHONE..................................908 852-1000
Joanne Walker, *Manager*
EMP: 700
SALES (corp-wide): 34.2B **Privately Held**
SIC: 2064 2066 Candy & other confec-
tionery products; chocolate & cocoa prod-
ucts
PA: Mars, Incorporated
6885 Elm St Ste 1
Mc Lean VA 22101
703 821-4900

(G-4022)
MARS INCORPORATED
800 High St (07840-1552)
P.O. Box 731 (07840-0731)
PHONE..................................908 850-2420
Rick Hampton, *President*
EMP: 55
SALES (corp-wide): 34.2B **Privately Held**
SIC: 2066 2064 Chocolate & cocoa prod-
ucts; candy & other confectionery prod-
ucts
PA: Mars, Incorporated
6885 Elm St Ste 1
Mc Lean VA 22101
703 821-4900

(G-4023)
MARS CHOCOLATE NORTH
AMER LLC (HQ)
800 High St (07840-1552)
PHONE..................................908 852-1000
Todd R Lachman, *President*
◆ EMP: 850
SALES (est): 1.1B
SALES (corp-wide): 34.2B **Privately Held**
WEB: www.kilic-kalkan.com
SIC: 2064 2066 Candy & other confec-
tionery products; chocolate & cocoa prod-
ucts
PA: Mars, Incorporated
6885 Elm St Ste 1
Mc Lean VA 22101
703 821-4900

(G-4024)
MARS CHOCOLATE NORTH
AMER LLC
Masterfoods USA
700 High St (07840-1502)
PHONE..................................908 979-5070
David Prybylowski, *Branch Mgr*
EMP: 589
SALES (corp-wide): 34.2B **Privately Held**
WEB: www.kilic-kalkan.com
SIC: 2064 Candy & other confectionery
products
HQ: Mars Chocolate North America, Llc
800 High St
Hackettstown NJ 07840
908 852-1000

(G-4025)
MARS FOOD US LLC
800 High St (07840-1552)
PHONE..................................908 852-1000
Charlie Smith, *Branch Mgr*
EMP: 13
SALES (corp-wide): 34.2B **Privately Held**
SIC: 2047 Dog & cat food
HQ: Mars Food Us, Llc
2001 E Cashdan St Ste 201
Rancho Dominguez CA 90220
310 933-0670

(G-4026)
MARS WRIGLEY CONF US LLC
(HQ)
800 High St (07840-1552)
PHONE..................................908 852-1000
Cathryn Sleight, *President*
Grant Reid,
EMP: 150
SALES (est): 86.6MM
SALES (corp-wide): 34.2B **Privately Held**
SIC: 2064 Candy bars, including chocolate
covered bars
PA: Mars, Incorporated
6885 Elm St Ste 1
Mc Lean VA 22101
703 821-4900

(G-4027)
MOBILE POWER INC
392 Watters Rd (07840-5704)
PHONE..................................908 852-3117
Paul F Mitchell, *President*
EMP: 8
SALES: 550K **Privately Held**
WEB: www.mobilepowerinc.com
SIC: 3694 Alternators, automotive

(G-4028)
MS HEALTH SOFTWARE CORP
128 Willow Grove St (07840-2018)
PHONE..................................908 850-5564
Michael Sedita, *President*
Dorothy Higgins, *Vice Pres*
EMP: 7
SQ FT: 4,500
SALES: 735K **Privately Held**
WEB: www.mshealth.com
SIC: 7372 7371 Business oriented com-
puter software; computer software sys-
tems analysis & design, custom

(G-4029)
NORMS AUTO PARTS INC
Also Called: NAPA Auto Parts
135 Willow Grove St (07840-2017)
PHONE..................................908 852-5080
Norman Lemasters, *President*
EMP: 4
SALES (est): 364.8K **Privately Held**
SIC: 5531 3599 Automobile & truck equip-
ment & parts; machine shop, jobbing &
repair

(G-4030)
NORTHLAND TOOLING
TECHNOLOGIES
999 Willow Grove St Ste 2 (07840-5001)
PHONE..................................908 850-0023
Brian Zuber, *President*
EMP: 5
SQ FT: 3,250
SALES: 600K **Privately Held**
SIC: 3089 3599 Injection molding of plas-
tics; blow molded finished plastic prod-
ucts; machine shop, jobbing & repair

(G-4031)
PACKAGING CORPORATION
AMERICA
Also Called: PCA
101 Bilby Rd Bldg 1 (07840-1753)
PHONE..................................908 452-9271
EMP: 5
SQ FT: 9,000
SALES (corp-wide): 7B **Publicly Held**
SIC: 2653 Boxes, corrugated: made from
purchased materials
PA: Packaging Corporation Of America
1 N Field Ct
Lake Forest IL 60045
847 482-3000

(G-4032)
ROLLON CORPORATION
101 Bilby Rd Ste B (07840-1753)
PHONE..................................973 300-5492
Erlado Bianchessi, *President*
Rick Wood, *Managing Dir*
Marta Kalawur, *Purch Mgr*
Jose Barreto, *Engineer*
Ali Fritz, *Engineer*
▲ EMP: 26
SQ FT: 20,000
SALES (est): 7.9MM
SALES (corp-wide): 87.6MM **Privately
Held**
WEB: www.rolloncorp.com
SIC: 3562 Ball & roller bearings
PA: Rollon Spa
Via Trieste 26
Vimercate 20871
039 625-91

(G-4033)
ROTAREX INC NORTH AMERICA
Also Called: Rotarex Trade
101 Bilby Rd Ste B (07840-1753)
PHONE..................................724 696-3345
Jean Claude Schmitz, *President*
Bert Pistor, *Vice Pres*
▲ EMP: 100
SALES (est): 16.1MM **Privately Held**
SIC: 3592 5085 Valves; valves & fittings

(G-4034)
RUDOLPH RES ANALYTICAL
CORP (PA)
55 Newburgh Rd (07840-3903)
PHONE..................................973 584-1558
Richard C Spainer, *President*
Elizabeth Mintz, *Vice Pres*
Pete Postiglione, *Engineer*
Kathy Green, *Sales Staff*
Bob Taggart, *VP Info Sys*
EMP: 74
SQ FT: 30,000
SALES: 14.2MM **Privately Held**
WEB: www.rudolphresearch.com
SIC: 3827 Optical instruments & apparatus

(G-4035)
SALTOPIA INFUSED SEA SALT
LLC
9 Reservoir Rd (07840-5646)
PHONE..................................908 850-1926
Kimarie Santiago, *Mng Member*
EMP: 12 EST: 2012
SQ FT: 2,000
SALES: 275K **Privately Held**
SIC: 2899 5149 5999 Salt; salt, edible; al-
coholic beverage making equipment &
supplies

(G-4036)
SHARMATEK INC
999 Willow Grove St (07840-5001)
PHONE..................................908 852-5087
Vinay Sharma, *Ch of Bd*
Sonia Sharma, *President*
EMP: 7
SQ FT: 3,500
SALES (est): 490K **Privately Held**
SIC: 2834 Pharmaceutical preparations

(G-4037)
SMR RESEARCH CORPORATION
300 Valentine St Ste A (07840-2160)
PHONE..................................908 852-7677
Stuart Feldstein, *President*
EMP: 6
SQ FT: 10,450

SALES: 1.3MM **Privately Held**
WEB: www.smrresearch.com
SIC: 2721 8742 8732 7389 Statistical reports (periodicals): publishing only; business consultant; business research
service; financial services

(G-4038)
T C S TECHNOLOGIES INC
430 Sand Shore Rd Ste 1 (07840-5519)
PHONE..................................908 852-7555
Gerard W Fitzgerald, *President*
Pat Ward, *Vice Pres*
EMP: 12
SQ FT: 6,000
SALES (est): 1.4MM **Privately Held**
SIC: 3645 Residential lighting fixtures

(G-4039)
TRANSISTOR DEVICES INC (PA)
Also Called: Astrodyne Tdi
36 Newburgh Rd (07840-3904)
PHONE..................................908 850-5088
Chris Viola, *CEO*
James M Feely, *President*
Robert Smolinski, *COO*
Deedee Hanc, *Vice Pres*
Jeff Reed, *Vice Pres*
▲ EMP: 250 EST: 1951
SQ FT: 150,000
SALES (est): 216.8MM **Privately Held**
WEB: www.transdev.com
SIC: 3612 3625 3672 3812 Power trans-
formers, electric; switches, electric power;
printed circuit boards; search & navigation
equipment; measuring & controlling de-
vices

(G-4040)
TRANSISTOR DEVICES INC
Also Called: Astrodyne Tdi
36 Newburgh Rd (07840-3904)
PHONE..................................908 850-5088
James Feely, *Branch Mgr*
EMP: 250
SALES (corp-wide): 216.8MM **Privately
Held**
WEB: www.transdev.com
SIC: 3612 3679 Power transformers, elec-
tric; power supplies, all types: static
PA: Transistor Devices, Inc.
36 Newburgh Rd
Hackettstown NJ 07840
908 850-5088

(G-4041)
WOODTEC INC
300 W Stiger St (07840-1276)
PHONE..................................908 979-0180
John Marra, *President*
EMP: 7
SQ FT: 4,000
SALES (est): 990K **Privately Held**
SIC: 5712 2431 5211 Customized furni-
ture & cabinets; millwork; millwork & lum-
ber

(G-4042)
ZONE DEFENSE INC
428 Sand Shore Rd 7 (07840-5510)
PHONE..................................973 328-0436
George Mandas, *President*
EMP: 10
SQ FT: 7,500
SALES (est): 1.8MM **Privately Held**
SIC: 2431 3446 Interior & ornamental
woodwork & trim; bank fixtures, ornamen-
tal metal

Haddon Heights
Camden County

(G-4043)
ARTSIGN STUDIO
916 Kings Hwy Ste C (08035-1251)
PHONE..................................856 546-4889
Mark Zito, *Owner*
EMP: 5
SALES: 225K **Privately Held**
SIC: 3993 Signs, not made in custom sign
painting shops

(G-4044)
CHILDRENS RESEARCH & DEV CO
216 9th Ave (08035-1633)
PHONE..................................856 546-8814
Robert Petrillo, *President*
EMP: 4
SALES (est): 158.6K **Privately Held**
SIC: 2731 Textbooks: publishing only, not printed on site

(G-4045)
DEL BUONO BAKERY INC
319 Black Horse Pike (08035-1097)
PHONE..................................856 546-9585
Constantino Del Buono Jr, *Owner*
EMP: 30 EST: 1932
SQ FT: 7,500
SALES (est): 3.2MM **Privately Held**
SIC: 2051 5461 5149 Bread, all types (white, wheat, rye, etc): fresh or frozen; rolls, bread type: fresh or frozen; bakeries; groceries & related products

(G-4046)
MAXWELL MCKENNEY INC
116 White Horse Pike # 6 (08035-1936)
PHONE..................................856 310-0700
Larry Schultz, *President*
Kathleen Lawler, *Assistant*
Paul Brooker, *Associate*
Joanne Perniciaro, *Associate*
EMP: 6 EST: 1982
SALES (est): 770.6K **Privately Held**
SIC: 3731 Shipbuilding & repairing

(G-4047)
PEDIBRUSH LLC
211 7th Ave (08035-1623)
PHONE..................................856 796-2963
Christian Klemash, *CEO*
EMP: 6
SALES (est): 430K **Privately Held**
WEB: www.pedibrush.com
SIC: 3089 Handles, brush or tool: plastic

(G-4048)
RELAY SPECIALTIES INC
1810 Prospect Ridge Blvd (08035-1139)
PHONE..................................856 547-5000
Walter Woodward, *Manager*
EMP: 4
SALES (corp-wide): 9.9MM **Privately Held**
WEB: www.relayspec.com
SIC: 3625 Relays & industrial controls
PA: Relay Specialties, Inc.
    17 Raritan Rd
    Oakland NJ 07436
    201 337-1000

(G-4049)
SENSONICS INC
Also Called: Sensonics International
411 Black Horse Pike # 1 (08035-1051)
P.O. Box 112 (08035-0112)
PHONE..................................856 547-7702
Richard L Doty, *CEO*
▼ EMP: 11
SALES (est): 1.1MM **Privately Held**
WEB: www.smelltest.com
SIC: 2835 5999 8999 In vitro diagnostics; medical apparatus & supplies; scientific consulting

(G-4050)
W C DAVIS INC
126 W Atlantic Ave (08035-1902)
PHONE..................................856 547-4750
Richard Davis, *President*
EMP: 10
SALES (corp-wide): 1.5MM **Privately Held**
WEB: www.wcdavis.com
SIC: 3432 Plastic plumbing fixture fittings, assembly
PA: W C Davis Inc
    605 Station Ave
    Haddon Heights NJ 08035
    856 547-4750

Haddon Township
Camden County

(G-4051)
NEW JERSEY STEEL CORPORATION
2840 Mount Ephraim Ave (08104-3214)
P.O. Box 2506, Cherry Hill (08034-0205)
PHONE..................................856 337-0054
EMP: 18
SQ FT: 2,000
SALES (est): 2.1MM **Privately Held**
SIC: 3449 1541 Mfg Misc Structural Metalwork Industrial Building Construction

(G-4052)
NORWOOD INDUSTRIES INC
107 Norwood Ave (08108-3518)
P.O. Box 2056, Haddonfield (08033-0816)
PHONE..................................856 858-6195
Francis Kernan, *President*
Catherine Kernan, *Vice Pres*
EMP: 15
SALES: 500K **Privately Held**
WEB: www.norwoodind.com
SIC: 4783 5031 3952 Packing goods for shipping; lumber: rough, dressed & finished; palettes, artists'

Haddonfield
Camden County

(G-4053)
BERNARD D ASCENZO
61 Centre St (08033-1801)
PHONE..................................856 795-0511
Bernard Ascenzo, *Principal*
EMP: 4
SALES (est): 369.5K **Privately Held**
SIC: 3911 Jewelry, precious metal

(G-4054)
CELESTECH INC
221 Kngs Hwy W Hddonfield (08033)
PHONE..................................856 986-2221
Celeste Todaro, *President*
EMP: 7
SQ FT: 2,500
SALES: 4MM **Privately Held**
SIC: 3569 Centrifuges, industrial

(G-4055)
COMMUNITY NEWS NETWORK INC
Also Called: What's On In Haddonfield
6 S Haddon Ave Ste 1 (08033-1880)
PHONE..................................856 428-3399
David Hunter, *President*
Susan W Hunter, *Vice Pres*
EMP: 7
SALES (est): 285.4K **Privately Held**
SIC: 2711 Newspapers: publishing only, not printed on site

(G-4056)
DORADO SYSTEMS LLC
8 Kings Hwy E (08033-2002)
PHONE..................................856 354-0048
Michael Matt, *COO*
Margaret McGannon, *Vice Pres*
Corey Katzen, *Accounts Exec*
Neil Drummond, *Software Engr*
Brad Sillasen, *Software Dev*
EMP: 15
SALES (est): 1.6MM **Privately Held**
SIC: 2741 Business service newsletters: publishing & printing

(G-4057)
FROZEN DESSERTS LLC
39 Friends Ave (08033-1507)
PHONE..................................508 872-3573
EMP: 4
SALES (est): 228K **Privately Held**
SIC: 2024 Ice cream & frozen desserts

(G-4058)
GLOBAL DIRECT MARKETING GROUP
Also Called: Paramount Packaging
229 Kings Hwy E (08033-1909)
PHONE..................................856 427-6116
Curt J Byerley, *Principal*
Ed Strow, *Director*
Joseph Orlando, *Executive*
EMP: 3
SQ FT: 3,300
SALES: 2MM **Privately Held**
WEB: www.gdm-group.com
SIC: 2448 2653 2652 2657 Wood pallets & skids; corrugated & solid fiber boxes; setup paperboard boxes; folding paperboard boxes; bags: plastic, laminated & coated

(G-4059)
GOLDENS INC
Also Called: Ludovicos
9 Kings Hwy W (08033-2115)
PHONE..................................215 850-2512
Larry Maggio, *Vice Pres*
EMP: 9
SALES (est): 94.3K **Privately Held**
SIC: 7389 2032 ; Italian foods: packaged in cans, jars, etc.

(G-4060)
MEDALITY MEDICAL LLC
3 S Haddon Ave Ste 3 # 3 (08033-1882)
PHONE..................................215 990-0754
Tom Albright, *CEO*
EMP: 5
SALES (est): 447.3K **Privately Held**
SIC: 3845 Electromedical equipment

(G-4061)
PFK COACH PHYLLIS FLOOD KNERR
119 Walnut St (08033-1854)
PHONE..................................856 429-5425
Phyllis Knerr, *Principal*
EMP: 4 EST: 2010
SALES (est): 292.3K **Privately Held**
SIC: 3089 Organizers for closets, drawers, etc.: plastic

(G-4062)
PRINCETON HOSTED SOLUTIONS LLC
30 Washington Ave Ste D2 (08033-3400)
P.O. Box 2078 (08033-0836)
PHONE..................................856 470-2350
Brad Bono, *CEO*
Sara Trivedi, *Accounts Mgr*
Roman Slivinsky, *Manager*
EMP: 10 EST: 2011
SQ FT: 5,000
SALES (est): 1.3MM **Privately Held**
SIC: 8748 4812 3229 1731 Telecommunications consultant; cellular telephone services; fiber optics strands; telephone & telephone equipment installation

(G-4063)
PROFESSIONAL PRINTING SERVICES
116 N Haddon Ave Ste G (08033-2388)
PHONE..................................856 428-6300
Joseph Mc Elroy, *President*
EMP: 5
SALES (est): 490K **Privately Held**
SIC: 2752 Commercial printing, offset

(G-4064)
REVIVA LABS INC
705 Hopkins Rd (08033-3096)
PHONE..................................856 428-3885
Stephen Strassler, *President*
Terry French, *COO*
Melissa Baylis, *Vice Pres*
Charles Ricefield, *Vice Pres*
Judy Strassler, *Vice Pres*
EMP: 40 EST: 1973
SQ FT: 7,000
SALES (est): 7.3MM **Privately Held**
WEB: www.revivalabs.com
SIC: 5122 2844 Cosmetics; toilet preparations

(G-4065)
UM EQUITY CORP (HQ)
56 N Haddon Ave Ste 300 (08033-2438)
PHONE..................................856 354-2200
Joan Carter, *President*
John Aglialoro, *Chairman*
Arthur Hicks Jr, *Treasurer*
EMP: 3
SQ FT: 5,000
SALES (est): 13.1MM
SALES (corp-wide): 234MM **Privately Held**
SIC: 7371 3949 8099 8093 Custom computer programming services; treadmills; exercise equipment; physical examination service, insurance; specialty outpatient clinics
PA: Um Holding Company
    56 N Haddon Ave Ste 300
    Haddonfield NJ 08033
    856 354-2200

(G-4066)
W E WAMSLEY RESTORATIONS INC
26 Tanner St (08033-2404)
PHONE..................................856 795-4001
Wilbur E Wamsley, *President*
EMP: 6
SALES: 750K **Privately Held**
SIC: 5932 3931 7699 Musical instruments, secondhand; violins & parts; musical instrument repair services

Hainesport
Burlington County

(G-4067)
3 IS TECHNOLOGIES INC
4 Colfax Ln (08036-4818)
PHONE..................................609 238-8213
John Pettit, *President*
EMP: 5
SALES (est): 466.5K **Privately Held**
SIC: 3523 Farm machinery & equipment

(G-4068)
ACCURATE THERMAL SYSTEMS LLC
4104 Sylon Blvd (08036-3730)
PHONE..................................609 326-3190
Darren Sager, *President*
EMP: 5
SALES: 300K **Privately Held**
SIC: 3823 Temperature instruments: industrial process type

(G-4069)
ATLANTIC SWITCH GENERATOR LLC
4108 Sylon Blvd (08036-3730)
PHONE..................................609 518-1900
Steve Louden, *Partner*
Hank Bevillard, *Mng Member*
Steven Louden,
William Shields,
EMP: 10
SALES (est): 2.6MM **Privately Held**
SIC: 7694 7699 Electric motor repair; industrial machinery & equipment repair

(G-4070)
ATLANTIC WOOD INDUSTRIES INC
1517 Hwy 38 (08036)
PHONE..................................609 267-4700
Phil Taylor, *Manager*
EMP: 15
SALES (corp-wide): 87.8MM **Privately Held**
SIC: 2491 Preserving (creosoting) of wood
PA: Atlantic Wood Industries, Inc.
    405 E Perry St
    Savannah GA 31401
    912 966-7008

(G-4071)
CRYOVATION LLC (PA)
9b Mary Way (08036)
PHONE..................................609 914-4792
Joe Bernacki, *Director*
Ric Boyd,

GEOGRAPHIC

◆ **EMP:** 7
SQ FT: 5,000
SALES (est): 1.4MM **Privately Held**
WEB: www.cryovation.com
SIC: 3559 Cryogenic machinery, industrial

(G-4072)
HAINESPORT INDUSTRIAL RAILROAD
5900 Delaware Ave (08036-3667)
PHONE..................................609 261-8036
Ronald W Bridges, *President*
EMP: 10
SALES (est): 5.4MM **Privately Held**
SIC: 3743 Railroad equipment

(G-4073)
HOPPECKE BATTERIES INC
2 Berry Dr (08036-4858)
PHONE..................................856 616-0032
Marc Zoellner, *CEO*
Stefan Keuthen, *Vice Pres*
Lynda Johnston, *Sales Staff*
Susan Grout, *Office Mgr*
David Detjen, *Admin Sec*
▲ **EMP:** 33
SQ FT: 50,000
SALES: 20MM
SALES (corp-wide): 522.4MM **Privately Held**
WEB: www.hoppecke-us.com
SIC: 3691 Storage batteries
PA: Accumulatorenwerke Hoppecke Carl
      Zoellner & Sohn Gmbh
      Bontkirchener Str. 1
      Brilon 59929
      296 361-0

(G-4074)
INDEPENDENT METAL SALES INC
1900 Park Ave W (08036-3734)
P.O. Box 17 (08036-0017)
PHONE..................................609 261-8090
Edward Kligerman, *President*
John Davis, *General Mgr*
William Riddle, *Opers Staff*
Geoff Harper, *Sales Associate*
Jason Sheffield, *Manager*
EMP: 16
SQ FT: 48,000
SALES (est): 4.7MM **Privately Held**
WEB: www.independentmetalsales.com
SIC: 3444 5051 Sheet metalwork; metals
      service centers & offices

(G-4075)
JORDAN TOOLING & MANUFACTURING
1307 Maine Ave (08036-2957)
PHONE..................................609 261-2636
Fax: 609 267-2210
EMP: 7
SQ FT: 3,000
SALES (est): 390K **Privately Held**
SIC: 3599 Machine Shop

(G-4076)
PERRY PRODUCTS CORPORATION
25 Mount Laurel Rd (08036-2711)
P.O. Box 327 (08036-0327)
PHONE..................................609 267-1600
Jerome Epstein, *CEO*
Gregg Epstein, *President*
Kenneth Miller, *Exec VP*
Philip Wallace, *Vice Pres*
Annie Harris, *Project Mgr*
▲ **EMP:** 25
SQ FT: 190,000
SALES (est): 6.3MM **Privately Held**
SIC: 3443 Heat exchangers: coolers (after,
      inter), condensers, etc.

(G-4077)
SIGN A RAMA
Also Called: Sign-A-Rama
1413 Rte 38 (08036)
P.O. Box 360 (08036-0360)
PHONE..................................609 702-1444
Gary Kuffer, *Owner*
EMP: 4 EST: 2001
SALES (est): 359.9K **Privately Held**
SIC: 3993 Signs & advertising specialties

(G-4078)
SOUND PROFESSIONALS INC
3444 Sylon Blvd (08036-3664)
PHONE..................................609 267-4400
Chris Carfagno, *CEO*
Joseph Carfagno, *Technician*
EMP: 6
SALES (est): 1.6MM **Privately Held**
SIC: 5099 3651 Video & audio equipment;
      microphones

(G-4079)
T WIKER ENTERPRISES INC
Also Called: Total Logistics
5900 Delaware Ave (08036-3667)
P.O. Box 44 (08036-0044)
PHONE..................................609 261-9494
Thomas Wiker, *President*
EMP: 5
SQ FT: 46,500
SALES (est): 495.5K **Privately Held**
SIC: 4225 3325 General warehousing &
      storage; steel foundries

(G-4080)
TWO JAYS BINGO SUPPLY INC (PA)
Also Called: Two Jays Specialties
709 Park Ave E (08036-3656)
PHONE..................................609 267-4542
Donald Plucinski, *President*
Cynthia Plucinski, *Corp Secy*
EMP: 10
SQ FT: 3,500
SALES: 900K **Privately Held**
WEB: www.twojays.com
SIC: 5092 5021 3993 Amusement goods;
      office furniture; advertising novelties

<hr>
Haledon
Passaic County
<hr>

(G-4081)
DOORSILLS LLC
302 Legion Pl (07508-1420)
PHONE..................................973 904-0270
Donald Kuehn,
EMP: 5
SALES: 450K **Privately Held**
SIC: 3728 Aircraft assemblies, subassem-
      blies & parts

(G-4082)
E & W PIECE DYE WORKS
293 Morrissee Ave (07508-1436)
PHONE..................................973 942-8718
Joseph Pizzoli Jr, *President*
Joseph Pizzoli Sr, *Admin Sec*
EMP: 20 EST: 1959
SQ FT: 42,000
SALES: 3MM **Privately Held**
SIC: 2261 Dyeing cotton broadwoven fab-
      rics

(G-4083)
J P ROTELLA CO INC
20 E Barbour St (07508-1524)
P.O. Box 8438 (07538-0438)
PHONE..................................973 942-2559
John P Rotella, *President*
EMP: 12
SQ FT: 3,000
SALES: 500K **Privately Held**
SIC: 3679 3599 7692 3544 Electronic cir-
      cuits; machine shop, jobbing & repair;
      welding repair; special dies, tools, jigs &
      fixtures; gaskets, packing & sealing de-
      vices

(G-4084)
MRL MANUFACTURING CORP
59 Lee Ave (07508-1201)
P.O. Box 8440 (07538-0440)
PHONE..................................973 790-1744
John De Napoli, *President*
Lorraine Paone, *Vice Pres*
EMP: 16
SQ FT: 12,000
SALES (est): 2.6MM **Privately Held**
SIC: 3452 Bolts, nuts, rivets & washers

(G-4085)
STONE INDUSTRIES INC (PA)
Also Called: Braen Stone Company
400 Central Ave 402 (07508-1116)
P.O. Box 8310 (07538-8310)
PHONE..................................973 595-6250
Janet R Braen, *CEO*
Scott A Braen, *President*
Sam Braen III, *Vice Pres*
Charles Veldran, *Vice Pres*
Victor Coleson, *Mng Member*
EMP: 85
SQ FT: 6,000
SALES (est): 41.1MM **Privately Held**
WEB: www.braenstone.com
SIC: 1423 5032 2951 Crushed & broken
      granite; asphalt mixture; asphalt paving
      mixtures & blocks

(G-4086)
TEEFX SCREEN PRINTING LLC
250 Belmont Ave (07508-1404)
PHONE..................................973 942-6800
Mario Guarriello,
EMP: 3
SQ FT: 125,000
SALES: 1.2MM **Privately Held**
SIC: 2211 Print cloths, cotton

<hr>
Hamburg
Sussex County
<hr>

(G-4087)
ACCURATE FORMING LLC
24 Ames Blvd (07419-1518)
PHONE..................................973 827-7155
Rich Regole, *CEO*
R Mark Baker, *CFO*
◆ **EMP:** 47
SQ FT: 100,000
SALES (est): 10.8MM **Privately Held**
WEB: www.accurateforming.com
SIC: 3469 Stamping metal for the trade

(G-4088)
AMES RUBBER CORPORATION (PA)
19 Ames Blvd (07419-1514)
P.O. Box 15240, Newark (07192-5240)
PHONE..................................973 827-9101
Charles A Roberts, *President*
Timothy Marvil, *Principal*
William J Kovach, *CFO*
▲ **EMP:** 100 EST: 1949
SQ FT: 112,700
SALES (est): 30.6MM **Privately Held**
WEB: www.amesrubber.com
SIC: 3069 Rubber rolls & roll coverings;
      rubber automotive products

(G-4089)
DAUSON CORRUGATED CONTAINER
Also Called: Poly Bag Division
3627 State Rt 23 (07419-1821)
P.O. Box 331, Franklin (07416-0331)
PHONE..................................973 827-1494
Mark Taylor, *President*
EMP: 11
SALES: 5MM **Privately Held**
SIC: 2653 5113 Boxes, corrugated: made
      from purchased materials; boxes, solid
      fiber: made from purchased materials;
      boxes & containers

(G-4090)
EASTERN CONCRETE MATERIALS INC
3620 State Rt 23 N (07419-1426)
PHONE..................................973 827-7625
Michael Benza, *Manager*
EMP: 30
SALES (corp-wide): 1.5B **Publicly Held**
SIC: 1411 2951 1442 Dimension stone;
      asphalt & asphaltic paving mixtures (not
      from refineries); construction sand &
      gravel
HQ: Eastern Concrete Materials, Inc.
      250 Pehle Ave Ste 503
      Saddle Brook NJ 07663
      201 797-7979

(G-4091)
EASY STOP FOOD & FUEL CORP
19 Exeter Ln (07419-9662)
PHONE..................................973 517-0478
Kirit M Patel, *Owner*
EMP: 5
SALES (est): 369.2K **Privately Held**
SIC: 2869 Fuels

(G-4092)
EBELLE DEBELLE PHRM INC
Also Called: Ede Pharmaceutical
5 Witherwood Dr (07419-1273)
PHONE..................................973 823-0665
Renay Ebelle, *CEO*
Steve Alexander, *Vice Pres*
Jacqueline Williams-Phillips, *Vice Pres*
EMP: 10
SALES (est): 518.2K **Privately Held**
SIC: 2834 Drugs acting on the cardiovas-
      cular system, except diagnostic; drugs af-
      fecting parasitic & infective diseases;
      tablets, pharmaceutical

(G-4093)
ELASTOGRAF INC
19 Ames Blvd (07419-1514)
PHONE..................................973 209-3161
Charles Roberts, *Admin Sec*
EMP: 88
SALES (est): 2.4MM **Privately Held**
SIC: 3069 Molded rubber products

(G-4094)
LEVEL TEN PRODUCTS INC
3670 State Rt 94 (07419-9613)
PHONE..................................973 827-0900
Patrick Barrett, *President*
EMP: 18
SALES (est): 2.6MM **Privately Held**
SIC: 3714 Transmissions, motor vehicle

(G-4095)
ROBERTAS JEWELERS INC
Also Called: Roberta's Hut
175 State Rt 23 S Ste D (07419-1627)
PHONE..................................973 875-5318
Roberta Bootsma, *President*
Deborah Falanga, *Vice Pres*
Harry Bootsma, *Treasurer*
EMP: 4
SALES (est): 594K **Privately Held**
WEB: www.robertasjewelers.com
SIC: 5944 3911 Jewelry, precious stones
      & precious metals; jewelry, precious metal

(G-4096)
TRILLIUM US
3627 State Rt 23 (07419-1821)
PHONE..................................973 827-1661
▲ **EMP:** 6
SALES (est): 817.8K **Privately Held**
SIC: 3563 Air & gas compressors

(G-4097)
UNITED VACUUM LLC
Also Called: UNI-Vac
3627 State Rt 23 Bldg 3 (07419-1821)
PHONE..................................973 827-1661
Al Citarella, *Mng Member*
▲ **EMP:** 17
SQ FT: 3,000
SALES (est): 3MM
SALES (corp-wide): 46.3MM **Privately Held**
WEB: www.unitedvacuum.com
SIC: 3563 Vacuum pumps, except labora-
      tory
PA: Trillium Us Inc.
      13011 Se Jennifer St # 204
      Clackamas OR 97015
      503 607-0393

(G-4098)
WEB-COTE LTD
Also Called: Web-Cote Industries
141 Wheatsworth Rd (07419-2607)
P.O. Box 120 (07419-0120)
PHONE..................................973 827-2299
James Cowen, *President*
▲ **EMP:** 18
SQ FT: 16,000

SALES (est): 4.1MM **Privately Held**
SIC: 2672 Tape, pressure sensitive: made
from purchased materials
PA: L2f, Llc
1 Barker Ave
White Plains NY

(G-4099)
WILCOX PRESS
6 Main St (07419-1508)
PHONE...................................973 827-7474
Jodie Palmasano, *Partner*
Judy Ehrich, *Partner*
EMP: 5 EST: 1919
SQ FT: 2,400
SALES: 550K **Privately Held**
SIC: 2759 2752 5112 Letterpress printing;
commercial printing, offset; office supplies

Hamilton
Mercer County

(G-4100)
ACINO PRODUCTS LTD LBLTY CO
9b S Gold Dr (08691-1642)
P.O. Box 3093, Trenton (08619-0093)
PHONE...................................609 695-4300
Ravi Deshpande,
Sandy Desphande,
EMP: 10 EST: 2009
SALES (est): 1.4MM **Privately Held**
SIC: 2834 Medicines, capsuled or ampuled

(G-4101)
AFTEK INC
2960 E State Street Ext (08619-4504)
PHONE...................................609 588-0900
Dennis Cumbest, *General Mgr*
Gilbert Perez, *General Mgr*
Neville Richards, *Manager*
EMP: 4
SALES (est): 647.4K **Privately Held**
SIC: 3634 Sauna heaters, electric

(G-4102)
ANDLOGIC COMPUTERS
866 Nj 33 6 (08619)
PHONE...................................609 610-5752
Swapan Nandy, *Principal*
EMP: 4 EST: 2010
SALES (est): 230K **Privately Held**
SIC: 5734 3571 Computer & software
stores; personal computers (microcom-
puters)

(G-4103)
ASSA ABLOY ENTRANCE SYSTEMS US
Also Called: Besam Entrance Solutions
300 Horizon Center Blvd # 300
(08691-1919)
PHONE...................................609 528-2580
Cameron Cary, *Branch Mgr*
EMP: 22
SALES (corp-wide): 9.3B **Privately Held**
SIC: 3699 1796 3442 Door opening &
closing devices, electrical; installing build-
ing equipment; metal doors
HQ: Assa Abloy Entrance Systems Us Inc.
1900 Airport Rd
Monroe NC 28110
704 290-5520

(G-4104)
CONISTICS INC
1800 E State St Ste 148 (08609-2013)
PHONE...................................609 584-2600
Christian Leeser, *President*
▲ EMP: 4 EST: 2010
SALES (est): 429.4K **Privately Held**
SIC: 3829 Thermometers & temperature
sensors

(G-4105)
DENMATT INDUSTRIES LLC
Also Called: Closets By Dsign - Cntl Jersey
2080 E State Street Ext (08619-3308)
PHONE...................................609 689-0099
Dennis Mattessich, *Co-Owner*
EMP: 17
SALES (est): 701.8K **Privately Held**
SIC: 2522 Wallcases, office: except wood

(G-4106)
GRAM EQUIPMENT (PA)
1 S Gold Dr (08691-1606)
PHONE...................................201 750-6500
Neil Whyte, *President*
▲ EMP: 40
SALES (est): 11.2MM **Privately Held**
WEB: www.wcbicecream.com
SIC: 3565 3556 Packing & wrapping ma-
chinery; ice cream manufacturing machin-
ery

(G-4107)
HOUZER INC (HQ)
2605 Kuser Rd (08691-1805)
PHONE...................................609 584-1900
Tyler Byun, *President*
▲ EMP: 16
SQ FT: 43,000
SALES (est): 3.8MM
SALES (corp-wide): 120.2MM **Privately Held**
WEB: www.enexsink.com
SIC: 3431 5084 Sinks: enameled iron,
cast iron or pressed metal; industrial ma-
chinery & equipment
PA: Hamat Group Ltd
41 Hayozma
Ashdod 77524
885 138-88

(G-4108)
INTERSTATE PANEL LLC (PA)
67 Benson Ave (08610-4407)
PHONE...................................609 586-4411
Donald J Anderson,
Jerry R Turner,
EMP: 19
SQ FT: 9,000
SALES (est): 4MM **Privately Held**
SIC: 3446 Architectural metalwork

(G-4109)
LINEAR PHOTONICS LLC
3 Nami Ln Ste 7c (08619-1285)
PHONE...................................609 584-5747
Elen Catz, *President*
John McDonald, *Senior VP*
Eugene Hoffman, *Vice Pres*
Christopher Bruno, *Production*
Lou Pedrini, *Production*
EMP: 5
SQ FT: 2,500
SALES (est): 1.1MM **Privately Held**
WEB: www.linphotonic.com
SIC: 3671 Electronic tube parts, except
glass blanks

(G-4110)
LINEARIZER TECHNOLOGY INC (PA)
3 Nami Ln Unit C9 (08619-1285)
PHONE...................................609 584-5747
Allen Katz, *President*
Roger Dorval, *Vice Pres*
Eugene Hoffman, *Vice Pres*
Christie Luisi, *Purchasing*
Daniel P Chokola, *Engineer*
EMP: 56
SQ FT: 20,000
SALES (est): 10.4MM **Privately Held**
WEB: www.lintech.com
SIC: 3671 Electronic tube parts, except
glass blanks

(G-4111)
LINEARIZER TECHNOLOGY INC
3 Nami Ln Unit C9 (08619-1285)
PHONE...................................609 584-8424
John Macdonald, *President*
Roger Dorval, *VP Opers*
Dave Yousko, *Mfg Spvr*
Christie Soltis, *Purchasing*
Esther Lee, *Engineer*
EMP: 5 **Privately Held**
SIC: 3663 Radio & TV communications
equipment
PA: Linearizer Technology Inc.
3 Nami Ln Unit C9
Hamilton NJ 08619

(G-4112)
MEDAVANTE-PROPHASE INC (HQ)
100 American Metro Blvd (08619-2319)
PHONE...................................609 528-9400
Paul M Gilbert, *CEO*
Donna Salvucci, *Area Mgr*
Ian C Neilson, *Senior VP*
Peter Sorantin, *Senior VP*
Amir Elfar, *Vice Pres*
EMP: 11
SALES (est): 10MM
SALES (corp-wide): 87.2MM **Privately Held**
WEB: www.medavante.net
SIC: 2834 Solutions, pharmaceutical
PA: Wirb - Copernicus Group, Inc.
212 Carnegie Ctr Ste 301
Princeton NJ 08540
609 945-0101

(G-4113)
MEDICAL INDICATORS INC (PA)
16 Thmas J Rhdes Indus Dr (08619-1263)
PHONE...................................609 737-1600
Larry Gentile, *Principal*
Michael Minakowski, *Vice Pres*
Bedwuine Senatus, *QA Dir*
▼ EMP: 14
SQ FT: 10,500
SALES (est): 4.5MM **Privately Held**
WEB: www.medicalindicators.com
SIC: 5047 3829 Medical equipment & sup-
plies; thermometers, including digital: clin-
ical

(G-4114)
MEJ SIGNS INC
Also Called: Sign-A-Rama
3100 Quakerbridge Rd # 5 (08619-1658)
P.O. Box 9993, Trenton (08650-2993)
PHONE...................................609 584-6881
Mark Jarvis, *President*
EMP: 4
SALES: 360K **Privately Held**
SIC: 3993 Signs & advertising specialties

(G-4115)
MERCER C ALPHAGRAPHICS
100 Youngs Rd (08619-1025)
PHONE...................................609 921-0959
Mark Wilhelm, *President*
EMP: 6
SQ FT: 5,200
SALES (est): 1MM **Privately Held**
SIC: 2752 2759 Offset & photolithographic
printing; commercial printing

(G-4116)
MERLIN INDUSTRIES INC (PA)
2904 E State Street Ext (08619-4504)
PHONE...................................609 807-1000
Andrew Maggion, *President*
▲ EMP: 80
SQ FT: 30,000
SALES (est): 21.4MM **Privately Held**
SIC: 3999 5999 7389 Hot tub & spa cov-
ers; swimming pool chemicals, equipment
& supplies; swimming pool & hot tub serv-
ice & maintenance

(G-4117)
MILLNER KITCHENS INC
200b Whitehead Rd Ste 108 (08619-3283)
PHONE...................................609 890-7300
EMP: 4
SALES (est): 312.7K **Privately Held**
SIC: 2434 Wood kitchen cabinets

(G-4118)
NEU INC
1 N Johnston Ave Ste 2 (08609-1855)
PHONE...................................281 648-9751
Jack Morin, *President*
▲ EMP: 4
SALES (est): 2.1MM **Privately Held**
WEB: www.neu-inc.com
SIC: 3531 Railroad related equipment
HQ: Neu Railways
Neu Solids Handling & Processing
Marcq-En-Baroeul 59700
320 456-464

(G-4119)
OAVCO LTD LIABILITY COMPANY
Also Called: Oav Air Bearings
1800 E State St Ste 130 (08609-2013)
P.O. Box 7421, Princeton (08543-7421)
PHONE...................................609 454-5340
Murat Erturk, *CEO*
EMP: 12
SALES (corp-wide): 2MM **Privately Held**
SIC: 3366 Bushings & bearings
PA: Oavco Limited Liability Company
103 Carnegie Ctr
Princeton NJ 08540
855 535-4227

(G-4120)
POWER BROOKS CO LLC
Also Called: Brooks Power Systems
2 Marlen Dr (08691-1601)
PHONE...................................609 890-0100
Avinash Diwan,
Ambika Diwan,
Anuraj Diwan,
Veena Diwan,
EMP: 13
SQ FT: 6,000
SALES (est): 1.3MM **Privately Held**
SIC: 3699 Electrical equipment & supplies

(G-4121)
PRINCETEL INC (PA)
2560 E State Street Ext (08619-3318)
PHONE...................................609 588-8801
Barry Zhang, *President*
Craig Miller, *Design Engr*
Michael Oboyle, *Manager*
Maggie Yang, *Manager*
EMP: 30
SQ FT: 44,000
SALES: 11.6MM **Privately Held**
WEB: www.princetel.com
SIC: 3678 Electronic connectors

(G-4122)
PRINCETON IDENTITY INC
300 Horizon Center Blvd # 304
(08691-1919)
PHONE...................................609 256-6994
Mark Clifton, *CEO*
Lance Emmons, *CFO*
EMP: 20
SALES (est): 1MM **Privately Held**
SIC: 3571 Personal computers (microcom-
puters)

(G-4123)
ROMACO NORTH AMERICA INC
8 Commerce Way Ste 115 (08691-3373)
PHONE...................................609 584-2500
EMP: 8 EST: 2014
SALES (est): 824.1K **Privately Held**
SIC: 3053 3412 Packing materials; metal
barrels, drums & pails

Hammonton
Atlantic County

(G-4124)
AG&E HOLDINGS INC (PA)
223 Pratt St (08037-1719)
PHONE...................................609 704-3000
Robert M Pickus, *Ch of Bd*
Anthony R Tomasello, *President*
Anthony Tomasello, *President*
Francis X McCarthy, *CFO*
Francis McCarthy, *CFO*
▲ EMP: 34 EST: 1925
SQ FT: 15,000
SALES: 13.2MM **Publicly Held**
WEB: www.wellsgardner.com
SIC: 3944 7993 Video game machines,
except coin-operated; coin-operated
amusement devices; game machines

(G-4125)
AMERICAN FLUX & METAL LLC
352 Fleming Pike (08037-2522)
PHONE...................................609 561-7500
Joachim Rudoler, *Mng Member*
◆ EMP: 20 EST: 1993
SQ FT: 35,000

SALES (est): 9.9MM **Privately Held**
SIC: 2899 Fluxes: brazing, soldering, galvanizing & welding

(G-4126)
AMERICAN GALVANIZING CO INC
1919 S 12th St (08037)
P.O. Box 408 (08037-0408)
PHONE................................609 567-2090
John Gregor, *President*
George Cheesman, *Plant Mgr*
John Greenough, *Maint Spvr*
Allen Ivins, *Manager*
Jeff Scagnelli, *Manager*
EMP: 55 EST: 1965
SQ FT: 65,000
SALES: 9MM
SALES (corp-wide): 2.7B **Publicly Held**
SIC: 3479 Galvanizing of iron, steel or end-formed products
PA: Valmont Industries, Inc.
1 Valmont Plz Ste 500
Omaha NE 68154
402 963-1000

(G-4127)
AMERICAN GAMING & ELEC INC (HQ)
Also Called: Wells-Gardner
223 Pratt St (08037-1719)
PHONE................................609 704-3000
Anthony Tomasello, *President*
Renee Zimmerman, *CFO*
▲ EMP: 40
SALES: 6MM
SALES (corp-wide): 13.2MM **Publicly Held**
SIC: 3575 Computer terminals, monitors & components
PA: Ag&E Holdings Inc.
223 Pratt St
Hammonton NJ 08037
609 704-3000

(G-4128)
ARAWAK PAVING CO INC (PA)
Also Called: Aztek Sand Grav Cmpny-Division
7503 Weymouth Rd (08037-3410)
PHONE................................609 561-4100
Jack Barrett Sr, *President*
EMP: 23 EST: 1973
SQ FT: 5,000
SALES: 24MM **Privately Held**
WEB: www.arawakpci.com
SIC: 1611 2951 Highway & street paving contractor; resurfacing contractor; asphalt & asphaltic paving mixtures (not from refineries)

(G-4129)
BARRETT ASPHALT INC
7503 Weymouth Rd (08037-3410)
PHONE................................609 561-4100
John Barrett, *President*
Susan Barrett, *Admin Sec*
EMP: 25
SQ FT: 5,000
SALES (est): 6.7MM
SALES (corp-wide): 24MM **Privately Held**
WEB: www.arawakpci.com
SIC: 2951 Paving mixtures
PA: Arawak Paving Co., Inc.
7503 Weymouth Rd
Hammonton NJ 08037
609 561-4100

(G-4130)
BASIC COMMERCE & INDUSTRIES
Also Called: BCI
856 S Route 30 Ste 5a (08037-2032)
PHONE................................609 482-3740
Tom McParland, *Vice Pres*
EMP: 21
SALES (corp-wide): 31.6MM **Privately Held**
SIC: 7372 Prepackaged software
PA: Basic Commerce And Industries, Inc.
303 Harper Dr
Moorestown NJ 08057
856 778-1660

(G-4131)
BUCCI MANAGEMENT CO INC
Also Called: Marbleworld Manufacturing
603 N 1st Rd (08037-3124)
PHONE................................609 567-8808
Guy Bucci, *President*
Guy Bucci Jr, *Vice Pres*
Henrietta Bucci, *Treasurer*
EMP: 7
SQ FT: 1,000
SALES (est): 797.3K **Privately Held**
SIC: 3944 Marbles (toys)

(G-4132)
C & E CANNERS INC
1249 Mays Landing Rd (08037-2816)
P.O. Box 229 (08037-0229)
PHONE................................609 561-1078
Robert Cappuccio, *President*
▼ EMP: 15 EST: 1933
SQ FT: 40,000
SALES (est): 2.7MM **Privately Held**
SIC: 2033 Fruits & fruit products in cans, jars, etc.; vegetables & vegetable products in cans, jars, etc.

(G-4133)
CUSTOM SALES & SERVICE INC
Also Called: Custom Mobile Food Equipment
275 S 2nd Rd (08037-8445)
P.O. Box 635 (08037-0635)
PHONE................................609 561-6900
Lynda Sikora, *President*
Bill Sikora, *Plant Mgr*
David Kyle, *Project Leader*
▼ EMP: 48 EST: 1961
SQ FT: 22,000
SALES (est): 12.1MM **Privately Held**
WEB: www.foodcart.com
SIC: 3713 2599 Truck bodies (motor vehicles); carts, restaurant equipment

(G-4134)
GARVEY CORPORATION (PA)
208 S Route 73 (08037-9565)
PHONE................................609 561-2450
William Garvey, *President*
Sean Jackson, *General Mgr*
Frank Scancella, *Foreman/Supr*
Robert Schaeffer, *Production*
Domenic Salvatore, *Project Engr*
◆ EMP: 70 EST: 1926
SQ FT: 55,000
SALES (est): 30.9MM **Privately Held**
WEB: www.garvey.com
SIC: 3535 3444 Conveyors & conveying equipment; sheet metalwork

(G-4135)
HAMMONTON GAZETTE INC
14 Tilton St (08037-1951)
P.O. Box 1228 (08037-5228)
PHONE................................609 704-1939
Gabriel Donio, *President*
Gina Rullo, *Chief*
Frank Ingemi,
EMP: 5
SALES (est): 509.9K **Privately Held**
WEB: www.hammontongazette.com
SIC: 2711 Newspapers

(G-4136)
INTEGRITY MEDICAL DEVICES DEL
360 Fairview Ave (08037-1902)
PHONE................................609 567-8175
Carleton Kimber, *President*
George Hughes Sr, *Vice Pres*
Hector Rodriguez, *Plant Mgr*
Jeffrey Hunrath, *Maint Spvr*
Roe Capaccio, *Executive*
EMP: 87
SQ FT: 15,000
SALES (est): 12.8MM **Privately Held**
WEB: www.integritymedical.com
SIC: 2211 Bandages, gauzes & surgical fabrics, cotton

(G-4137)
KELLOGG COMPANY
Also Called: Kellogg's Eggo
322 S Egg Harbor Rd (08037-9439)
PHONE................................609 567-1688
Jeff Kirberg, *Branch Mgr*

EMP: 100
SALES (corp-wide): 13.5B **Publicly Held**
SIC: 2043 Cereal breakfast foods
HQ: Kellogg Usa Inc.
1 Kellogg Sq
Battle Creek MI 49017

(G-4138)
LUCCAS BAKERY INC
631 Egg Harbor Rd (08037-8507)
P.O. Box 97, Winslow (08095-0097)
PHONE................................609 561-5558
Anthony Lucca, *President*
Mary Ann Lucca, *Corp Secy*
EMP: 20 EST: 1959
SQ FT: 10,000
SALES: 900K **Privately Held**
SIC: 5149 2051 Bakery products; bread, cake & related products

(G-4139)
MASSARELLIS LAWN ORNAMENTS INC
500 S Egg Harbor Rd (08037-3341)
PHONE................................609 567-9700
Mario Massarelli, *President*
Gina Robeson, *General Mgr*
Christine L Massarelli, *Vice Pres*
Christine Massarelli, *Purchasing*
Arthur Noss, *Sales Mgr*
▲ EMP: 36
SALES (est): 6.7MM **Privately Held**
WEB: www.massarelli.com
SIC: 3272 Precast terrazo or concrete products

(G-4140)
NINSA LLC
125 Lincoln St (08037-1219)
PHONE................................609 561-7103
Greg Fondacaro, *President*
Olga Applegate, *CFO*
EMP: 8
SALES (est): 1.3MM **Privately Held**
SIC: 3315 Wire & fabricated wire products

(G-4141)
PLAGIDOS WINERY LLC
570 N 1st Rd (08037-9103)
PHONE................................609 567-4633
Ollie Tomasello,
EMP: 5
SALES (est): 413.4K **Privately Held**
SIC: 2084 Wines

(G-4142)
POLYVEL INC
100 9th St (08037-3362)
PHONE................................609 567-0080
Brian Tidwell, *President*
Gary Losasso, *Vice Pres*
Albert Losasso, *Admin Sec*
◆ EMP: 26
SQ FT: 46,000
SALES: 12MM **Privately Held**
WEB: www.polyvel.com
SIC: 2821 Plastics materials & resins

(G-4143)
PRECISION-TECH LLC
931 8th St (08037-8413)
PHONE................................609 517-2718
Michael Gazzara, *Principal*
EMP: 22
SALES (est): 3.5MM **Privately Held**
SIC: 3599 Machine shop, jobbing & repair

(G-4144)
SHARROTT WINE
370 S Egg Harbor Rd (08037-2460)
PHONE................................609 567-9463
Larry Sharrott, *Owner*
Evelyn Tisch, *Sales Staff*
EMP: 4 EST: 2007
SALES (est): 390K **Privately Held**
SIC: 2084 Wines

(G-4145)
TOMASELLO WINERY INC (PA)
225 N White Horse Pike (08037-1868)
P.O. Box 440 (08037-0440)
PHONE................................609 561-0567
Charles J Tomasello Sr, *Ch of Bd*
Charles J Tomasello Jr, *President*
John K Tomasello, *Vice Pres*
Margaret Tomasello, *Treasurer*

Stephen Smith, *Manager*
▲ EMP: 12 EST: 1933
SQ FT: 18,000
SALES (est): 3.8MM **Privately Held**
WEB: www.tomasellowinery.com
SIC: 2084 5812 Wine cellars, bonded: engaged in blending wines; eating places

┌─────────────────────────────┐
│   **Hampton**   │
│   *Hunterdon County*   │
└─────────────────────────────┘

(G-4146)
AMEC FOSTER WHEELER USA CORP
53 Frontage Rd (08827-4031)
P.O. Box 9000 (08827-9000)
PHONE................................713 929-5000
EMP: 29
SALES (corp-wide): 10B **Privately Held**
SIC: 8711 1629 3443 Engineering services; chemical plant & refinery construction; oil refinery construction; boilers: industrial, power, or marine
HQ: Amec Foster Wheeler Usa Corporation
17325 Park Row
Houston TX 77084
713 929-5000

(G-4147)
AMEC FSTER WHEELER N AMER CORP (HQ)
53 Frontage Rd (08827-4031)
P.O. Box 9000 (08827-9000)
PHONE................................936 448-6323
Gary Nedelka, *CEO*
Byron Roth, *President*
Peter Coppola, *Exec VP*
David Parham, *Exec VP*
Anthony Scerbo, *Exec VP*
◆ EMP: 59 EST: 1992
SQ FT: 72,000
SALES (est): 286.5MM
SALES (corp-wide): 10B **Privately Held**
WEB: www.fwcparts.com
SIC: 3433 3443 3532 3569 Steam heating apparatus; burners, furnaces, boilers & stokers; oil burners, domestic or industrial; gas burriers, industrial; condensers, steam; boilers: industrial, power, or marine; process vessels, industrial: metal plate; coal breakers, cutters & pulverizers; generators: steam, liquid oxygen or nitrogen
PA: John Wood Group Plc
15 Justice Mill Lane
Aberdeen AB12
122 485-1000

(G-4148)
BEHR TECHNOLOGY INC
223 State Route 31 (08827-5417)
PHONE................................908 537-9960
Thomas Behr, *President*
EMP: 4
SQ FT: 4,000
SALES: 2MM **Privately Held**
SIC: 5045 3577 Computers, peripherals & software; computer peripheral equipment

(G-4149)
CELLDEX THERAPEUTICS INC (PA)
53 Frontage Rd Ste 220 (08827-4034)
PHONE................................908 200-7500
Anthony S Marucci, *President*
Tibor Keler, *Exec VP*
Sarah Cavanaugh, *Senior VP*
Margo Heath-Chiozzi, *Senior VP*
Richard Wright, *Ch Credit Ofcr*
EMP: 144 EST: 1983
SQ FT: 49,600
SALES: 9.5MM **Publicly Held**
WEB: www.avantimmune.com
SIC: 2834 8731 Pharmaceutical preparations; biotechnical research, commercial

(G-4150)
ENPIRION INC
53 Frontage Rd Ste 210 (08827-4032)
PHONE................................908 575-7550
Ashraf Lotfi, *President*
Alan Smith, *Bd of Directors*
EMP: 50

SQ FT: 15,000
SALES (est): 6.3MM
SALES (corp-wide): 70.8B **Publicly Held**
WEB: www.enpirion.com
SIC: 3674 Semiconductor circuit networks
HQ: Altera Corporation
101 Innovation Dr
San Jose CA 95134
408 544-7000

(G-4151)
FOSTER WHEELER ARABIA LTD
53 Frontage Rd (08827-4031)
PHONE...................................908 730-4000
Umberto Della Sala, *CEO*
EMP: 5
SALES (est): 202.4K
SALES (corp-wide): 10B **Privately Held**
SIC: 8711 1629 3443 Engineering services; chemical plant & refinery construction; boiler shop products: boilers, smokestacks, steel tanks
HQ: Amec Foster Wheeler Limited
4th Floor Old Change House
Knutsford EC4V
207 429-7500

(G-4152)
FOSTER WHEELER INTL CORP (DH)
Also Called: Foster Wheeler
Perryville Corporate Pk 5 (08827)
PHONE...................................908 730-4000
Umberto Della Sala, *President*
Filippo Abba, *Exec VP*
Chris Covert, *Exec VP*
James Gibson, *Exec VP*
Marco Moresco, *Exec VP*
EMP: 11
SQ FT: 294,000
SALES (est): 3.8MM
SALES (corp-wide): 10B **Privately Held**
SIC: 8711 1629 3443 Engineering services; chemical plant & refinery construction; boiler shop products: boilers, smokestacks, steel tanks
HQ: Wheeler Foster International Holdings Inc
Perryville Corporate Pk 5
Hampton NJ 08827
908 730-4000

(G-4153)
FOSTER WHEELER ZACK INC (DH)
53 Frontage Rd (08827-4031)
P.O. Box 9000 (08827-9000)
PHONE...................................908 730-4000
Chris Covert, *President*
John Paul Archambault, *Vice Pres*
Jimmy Collins, *Vice Pres*
Michelle Davies, *Vice Pres*
Rakesh Jindal, *Vice Pres*
EMP: 70
SQ FT: 600,000
SALES (est): 50.1MM
SALES (corp-wide): 10B **Privately Held**
WEB: www.fwc.com
SIC: 8711 1629 3569 4931 Industrial engineers; industrial plant construction; oil refinery construction; chemical plant & refinery construction; generators: steam, liquid oxygen or nitrogen; electric & other services combined
HQ: Amec Foster Wheeler Limited
4th Floor Old Change House
London EC4V
207 429-7500

(G-4154)
FOSTER WHLER INTL HOLDINGS INC (DH)
Also Called: Foster Wheeler
Perryville Corporate Pk 5 (08827)
PHONE...................................908 730-4000
Kent Masters, *President*
Michelle Davies, *Exec VP*
Rakesh Jindal, *Vice Pres*
Peter Kuchler, *Vice Pres*
Lisa Wood, *Vice Pres*
EMP: 4 EST: 2001

SALES (est): 36.9MM
SALES (corp-wide): 10B **Privately Held**
SIC: 8711 3443 1629 Consulting engineer; boilers: industrial, power, or marine; chemical plant & refinery construction; oil refinery construction
HQ: Amec Foster Wheeler North America Corp.
53 Frontage Rd
Hampton NJ 08827
936 448-6323

(G-4155)
IKARIA THERAPEUTICS LLC
Perryvle 3 Corp Park Fl 3 (08827)
P.O. Box 9001 (08827-9001)
PHONE...................................908 238-6600
Douglas Greene, *Exec VP*
Bryan Ball, *Vice Pres*
Darrell Breaux, *Manager*
Dianne Burns, *Supervisor*
Jason Yackowski, *Info Tech Dir*
EMP: 6
SALES (est): 660K **Privately Held**
SIC: 2834 Pharmaceutical preparations

(G-4156)
INFINITI COMPONENTS INC (PA)
223 State Route 31 (08827-5417)
PHONE...................................908 537-9950
Thomas Behr, *President*
Andy Lifshin, *Vice Pres*
EMP: 4
SQ FT: 3,700
SALES (est): 2.3MM **Privately Held**
WEB: www.infiniticomponents.com
SIC: 5065 3679 Electronic parts; static power supply converters for electronic applications

(G-4157)
KAPPUS PLASTIC COMPANY INC
61 State Route 31 65 (08827-2751)
P.O. Box 151 (08827-0151)
PHONE...................................908 537-2288
Kathleen Plenkers, *CEO*
John Kappus, *Ch of Bd*
Annette Gormly, *President*
Noel Kappus, *Vice Pres*
Rob Slater, *Purch Agent*
EMP: 60
SQ FT: 35,000
SALES (est): 13.5MM **Privately Held**
WEB: www.kappusplastic.com
SIC: 3081 3069 Polyvinyl film & sheet; rubber rolls & roll coverings

(G-4158)
MALLINCKRODT LLC
Also Called: Mallinckrodt Parmaceuticals
53 Frontage Rd (08827-4031)
PHONE...................................908 238-6600
Dianne Burns, *Project Mgr*
Victor Ingraffia, *Accountant*
Roy Bjelquist, *Manager*
Brooke Mitch, *Manager*
Cecile Labossiere, *Senior Mgr*
EMP: 20 **Privately Held**
SIC: 3829 2834 2833 3841 Medical diagnostic systems, nuclear; pharmaceutical preparations; analgesics; codeine & derivatives; opium derivatives; catheters
HQ: Mallinckrodt Llc
675 Jmes S Mcdonnell Blvd
Hazelwood MO 63042
314 654-2000

(G-4159)
R & M CHEMICAL TECHNOLOGIES
7 Imlaydale Rd (08827-4500)
PHONE...................................908 537-9516
William Supplee, *President*
▲ EMP: 10
SQ FT: 12,800
SALES (est): 1.1MM **Privately Held**
SIC: 2819 4731 Nonmetallic compounds; freight forwarding

Hardwick
Warren County

(G-4160)
M T D INC
24 Slabtown Creek Rd (07825-3211)
PHONE...................................908 362-6807
Thomas Nichols, *President*
Mary Nichols, *Corp Secy*
Dave Nichols, *Vice Pres*
EMP: 3
SALES: 1.8MM **Privately Held**
SIC: 3844 X-ray apparatus & tubes

Harrington Park
Bergen County

(G-4161)
A M GRAPHICS INC
68 Schraalenburg Rd Ste 6 (07640-1932)
P.O. Box 2185, River Vale (07675-9005)
PHONE...................................201 767-5320
John Motta, *President*
Vera Motta, *Vice Pres*
EMP: 4
SQ FT: 2,000
SALES (est): 1MM **Privately Held**
SIC: 2752 2791 7336 Commercial printing, offset; hand composition typesetting; graphic arts & related design

(G-4162)
APPETITO PROVISIONS COMPANY
406 Lafayette Rd (07640-1324)
P.O. Box 715, Osprey FL (34229-0715)
PHONE...................................201 864-3410
Michael Tota, *President*
EMP: 35
SQ FT: 30,000
SALES (est): 6.8MM **Privately Held**
WEB: www.appetitosausage.com
SIC: 2013 Sausages from purchased meat

Harrison
Hudson County

(G-4163)
B & A GRAFX INC
1 Cape May St (07029-2402)
PHONE...................................646 302-8849
Jose Morales, *Principal*
EMP: 10
SQ FT: 800
SALES (est): 427.2K **Privately Held**
SIC: 3993 Signs & advertising specialties

(G-4164)
BARNETT MACHINE TOOLS INC
401 Supor Blvd Bldg 3n (07029-2059)
P.O. Box 189 (07029-0189)
PHONE...................................973 482-6222
Antonio Ferreira, *President*
Angelo Tamburri, *Vice Pres*
Steven Ferreira, *Manager*
▲ EMP: 17
SALES (est): 3MM **Privately Held**
WEB: www.barnettmachinetools.com
SIC: 3599 Machine shop, jobbing & repair

(G-4165)
BNG INDUSTRIES LLC
1 Cape May St Ste 2 (07029-2413)
PHONE...................................862 229-2414
Ian Grunes, *Mng Member*
EMP: 15
SALES: 250K **Privately Held**
SIC: 2511 4225 7922 Wood household furniture; miniwarehouse, warehousing; entertainment promotion

(G-4166)
CAMPBELL FOUNDRY COMPANY (PA)
Also Called: Campbell Group
800 Bergen St (07029-2034)
PHONE...................................973 483-5480

Chris Campbell, *President*
Greg Campbell, *Vice Pres*
John R Campbell III, *Vice Pres*
Beth A Skrenta, *Human Res Dir*
Ken Farrelly, *Sales Staff*
▲ EMP: 30
SQ FT: 5,000
SALES (est): 11.9MM **Privately Held**
WEB: www.campbellfoundry.com
SIC: 3321 Manhole covers, metal

(G-4167)
CEM INDUSTRIES INC
300 Somerset St Apt 217 (07029-2343)
PHONE...................................908 244-8080
Calvin Moore, *Principal*
EMP: 5
SALES (est): 175.5K **Privately Held**
SIC: 3999 Manufacturing industries

(G-4168)
CS OSBORNE & CO (PA)
Also Called: Parmelee Wrench
125 Jersey St (07029-1700)
PHONE...................................973 483-3232
I Jackson Angell III, *President*
D M Amador, *Vice Pres*
▲ EMP: 100 EST: 1826
SALES (est): 17.6MM **Privately Held**
WEB: www.csosborne.com
SIC: 3423 Hand & edge tools

(G-4169)
DOLCE VITA INTIMATES LLC (PA)
Also Called: Bebe Girdle
1000 1st St (07029-2332)
PHONE...................................973 482-8400
Jack Thekkekara, *President*
Diana Baragarian, *Principal*
Tara Perez-Cheatham, *Prdtn Mgr*
Suren Weerakoon, *Prdtn Mgr*
Cynthia Consentino, *Manager*
◆ EMP: 70
SALES (est): 8.1MM **Privately Held**
SIC: 2342 2341 Girdles & panty girdles; slips: women's, misses', children's & infants'

(G-4170)
E-LO SPORTSWEAR LLC
Also Called: Sharagano
1 Cape May St (07029-2402)
PHONE...................................862 902-5220
David Lomita, *Principal*
EMP: 15
SALES (corp-wide): 138.9MM **Privately Held**
SIC: 2337 Women's & misses' suits & skirts
PA: E-Lo Sportswear Llc
469 7th Ave Fl 15
New York NY 10018
212 300-0401

(G-4171)
EASTERN GLASS RESOURCES INC (PA)
770 Supor Blvd (07029-2035)
PHONE...................................973 483-8411
Phil Fisher, *President*
Cathy Hewitt, *Bookkeeper*
Richard Zmijewski, *Info Tech Mgr*
Joe Shary, *Technology*
▲ EMP: 35
SALES (est): 10.4MM **Privately Held**
SIC: 5023 3231 Glassware; products of purchased glass

(G-4172)
EMPORIA FOUNDRY INC
800 Bergen St (07029-2034)
PHONE...................................973 483-5480
Christopher Campbell, *President*
J Greg Campbell, *Vice Pres*
John R Campbell III, *Vice Pres*
EMP: 40
SQ FT: 30,000
SALES (est): 5.8MM
SALES (corp-wide): 11.9MM **Privately Held**
WEB: www.campbellfoundry.com
SIC: 3321 Manhole covers, metal

PA: Campbell Foundry Company
800 Bergen St
Harrison NJ 07029
973 483-5480

(G-4173)
FEDERAL CASTERS CORP (PA)
785 Harrison Ave (07029)
PHONE..................................973 483-6700
Salvatore Cumella, *Ch of Bd*
Charles Cumella, *President*
EMP: 58
SQ FT: 53,000
SALES (est): 21.1MM **Privately Held**
SIC: 5051 3562 Sheets, metal; casters

(G-4174)
FLEXO-CRAFT PRINTS INC
1000 1st St (07029-2332)
PHONE..................................973 482-7200
Mendel Klein, *Ch of Bd*
Abraham Klein, *President*
Dov Klein, *Senior VP*
Herschel Klein, *Vice Pres*
AVI Squire, *Sales Staff*
▲ **EMP:** 45 **EST:** 1978
SQ FT: 150,000
SALES (est): 12MM **Privately Held**
WEB: www.flexocraft.com
SIC: 2679 2759 2621 2674 Gift wrap,
paper: made from purchased material;
flexographic printing; wrapping & packag-
ing papers; shipping bags or sacks, in-
cluding multiwall & heavy duty

(G-4175)
FMB SYSTEMS INC
Also Called: F M B Systems
70 Supor Blvd (07029-1921)
PHONE..................................973 485-5544
Bradley A Yount, *President*
Boris Kromis, *Vice Pres*
Gary Paolella, *Vice Pres*
Michael Revolinsky, *Project Mgr*
▲ **EMP:** 70
SQ FT: 60,000
SALES (est): 19.6MM **Privately Held**
SIC: 3441 3446 Fabricated structural
metal; stairs, staircases, stair treads: pre-
fabricated metal

(G-4176)
**HOCKMEYER EQUIPMENT
CORP (PA)**
610 Supor Blvd (07029-1911)
PHONE..................................973 482-0225
Herman Hockmeyer Jr, *President*
Randall Seaman, *Vice Pres*
Rick Rimmer, *Technical Mgr*
Barry Cullens, *Webmaster*
Susan Hockmeyer, *Admin Sec*
◆ **EMP:** 67
SQ FT: 18,500
SALES (est): 16.7MM **Privately Held**
WEB: www.hockmeyer.com
SIC: 3559 7699 Refinery, chemical pro-
cessing & similar machinery; industrial
machinery & equipment repair

(G-4177)
**PRECISE CORPORATE
PRINTING INC**
Also Called: Precise Continental
1 Cape May St Ste 250 (07029-2409)
PHONE..................................973 350-0330
James P Donnelly, *CEO*
Frank Polizzi, *Vice Pres*
Willie Maldonado, *Prdtn Mgr*
EMP: 38
SQ FT: 35,000
SALES (est): 5.4MM **Privately Held**
WEB: www.precisecorp.com
SIC: 2759 Engraving; thermography

(G-4178)
PRETTY LIL CUPCAKES
317 Essex St (07029-2119)
PHONE..................................201 256-1205
Gabriela Sandwith, *President*
EMP: 4
SALES (est): 178.7K **Privately Held**
SIC: 2051 Bread, cake & related products

(G-4179)
R P BAKING LLC
Also Called: Pechter's
840 Jersey St (07029-2056)
PHONE..................................973 483-3374
Sal Battaglia, *President*
Anthony Battaglia, *Vice Pres*
Ignazio Battaglia,
Joseph Battaglia,
Mario Battaglia,
EMP: 22
SALES (est): 3.5MM **Privately Held**
SIC: 2051 Bread, cake & related products

(G-4180)
TRI-STATE BUNS LLC
Also Called: Tsb
808 Warren St 810 (07029-2022)
PHONE..................................973 418-8323
Anthony Bataglia,
Ignazio Battaglia,
EMP: 45
SQ FT: 1,000
SALES (est): 8.8MM **Privately Held**
SIC: 2051 Bread, cake & related products

Hasbrouck Heights
Bergen County

(G-4181)
**AMFINE CHEMICAL
CORPORATION (HQ)**
777 Perrace Ave Ste 602b (07604)
PHONE..................................201 818-0159
Koji Tajima, *President*
Takeyuki Mototani, *Exec VP*
Jay Kolaya, *Vice Pres*
Pete Goman, *Research*
Robert Weiler, *Sales Staff*
▲ **EMP:** 11
SQ FT: 5,000
SALES (est): 31.9MM **Privately Held**
WEB: www.amfine.com
SIC: 5169 2899 Industrial chemicals;
chemical preparations

(G-4182)
FUJIKIN OF AMERICA INC
777 Terrace Ave Ste 110 (07604-3111)
PHONE..................................201 641-1119
John Crawford, *Manager*
EMP: 7 **Privately Held**
SIC: 3592 Valves
HQ: Fujikin Of America, Inc.
454 Kato Ter
Fremont CA 94539

(G-4183)
GULF CABLE LLC (PA)
777 Terrace Ave Ste 101 (07604-3112)
PHONE..................................201 242-9906
Bonita Singh, *CFO*
Orin Brian Singh, *Mng Member*
Sherie Singh-Cho,
▲ **EMP:** 150
SQ FT: 70,000
SALES (est): 4.3MM **Privately Held**
SIC: 3351 Copper rolling & drawing

(G-4184)
H & L PRINTING CO
343 Boulevard Ste A (07604-1327)
PHONE..................................201 288-0877
Tossi Henry, *Owner*
EMP: 6
SALES (est): 520K **Privately Held**
SIC: 2759 Commercial printing

(G-4185)
JCDECAUX MALLSCAPE LLC
440 State Rt 17 Ste 9 (07604-3000)
PHONE..................................201 288-2024
Abraham Lee, *Branch Mgr*
EMP: 6
SALES (corp-wide): 9.5MM **Privately
Held**
SIC: 2531 Benches for public buildings
HQ: Jcdecaux Mallscape, Llc
350 5th Ave Fl 73
New York NY 10118
646 834-1200

(G-4186)
M & M PRINTING CORP
Also Called: Minuteman Press
216 Boulevard (07604-1920)
PHONE..................................201 288-7787
Steven Cifaldi, *President*
Joyce Cifaldi, *Principal*
EMP: 4
SALES (est): 537.9K **Privately Held**
SIC: 2752 2759 Commercial printing, litho-
graphic; commercial printing

(G-4187)
PABIN ASSOCIATES INC (PA)
Also Called: Gregory Associates
281 Springfield Ave (07604-1625)
PHONE..................................201 288-7216
John Pabin, *President*
EMP: 5
SALES (est): 584.5K **Privately Held**
SIC: 8742 3565 Materials mgmt. (purchas-
ing, handling, inventory) consultant; pack-
aging machinery

(G-4188)
SPINDLERS BAKE SHOP
247 Boulevard (07604-1902)
PHONE..................................201 288-1345
Vinnie Pertuzzella, *Partner*
Ippolita Pertuzzella, *Partner*
EMP: 6 **EST:** 1956
SQ FT: 1,500
SALES (est): 288.6K **Privately Held**
SIC: 5461 2051 Cakes; bakery: wholesale
or wholesale/retail combined

(G-4189)
TAPE GRAPHICS
208 Boulevard Ste A (07604-1839)
PHONE..................................201 393-9500
Joe Bassani, *President*
EMP: 4
SALES (est): 2.3MM **Privately Held**
SIC: 2752 Wrapper & seal printing, litho-
graphic

(G-4190)
**TOP RATED SHOPPING
BARGAINS**
92 Railroad Ave Ste 105 (07604-2887)
P.O. Box 272, Edgewater (07020-0272)
PHONE..................................800 556-5849
EMP: 10
SQ FT: 20,000
SALES (est): 356.3K **Privately Held**
SIC: 5014 3714 3911 2326 Whol
Toys/Hobby Goods Whol Tires/Tubes Mfg
Motor Vehicle Parts Mfg Precious Mtl
Jewelry

(G-4191)
TRACK SYSTEMS INC
Also Called: Mmp Ergonomics Co
174 Boulevard Ste 6 (07604-1844)
PHONE..................................201 462-0095
Robert Bogaczyk, *President*
Stuart Hirsh, *Vice Pres*
EMP: 12
SQ FT: 2,000
SALES (est): 3MM **Privately Held**
WEB: www.mmpergo.com
SIC: 3535 5046 Conveyors & conveying
equipment; commercial equipment

(G-4192)
UNIPLAST INDUSTRIES INC
1-5 Plant Rd (07604-2804)
P.O. Box 2367, South Hackensack (07606-
0967)
PHONE..................................201 288-4672
A Joel Goldman, *President*
Lawrence H Goldman, *Vice Pres*
Bertram Goldman, *Treasurer*
▲ **EMP:** 40
SQ FT: 50,000
SALES (est): 9MM **Privately Held**
WEB: www.uniplastindustries.com
SIC: 3089 Clothes hangers, plastic

(G-4193)
UNITED WIRE HANGER CORP
1-5 Plant Rd (07604-2804)
P.O. Box 2367, South Hackensack (07606-
0967)
PHONE..................................201 288-3212

Lawrence H Goldman, *President*
A Joel Goldman, *Exec VP*
Bertram Goldman, *Treasurer*
▲ **EMP:** 210 **EST:** 1962
SQ FT: 151,000
SALES (est): 33.9MM **Privately Held**
SIC: 3315 Hangers (garment), wire

Haskell
Passaic County

(G-4194)
AMERICAN BERYLLIA INC
16 1st Ave (07420-1502)
PHONE..................................973 248-8080
Dino Nicoletta, *President*
Nussy Brauner, *General Mgr*
Larry Feinsinger, *Shareholder*
Mark Feinsinger, *Shareholder*
Hirsch Wolf, *Shareholder*
▲ **EMP:** 20
SQ FT: 70,000
SALES (est): 5.7MM **Privately Held**
WEB: www.americanberyllia.com
SIC: 2869 Oxalic acid & metallic salts

(G-4195)
ARROW SHED LLC
1 3rd Ave (07420-1101)
PHONE..................................973 835-3200
Ed Paisker, *Vice Pres*
George Laski, *Technology*
EMP: 35
SALES (corp-wide): 121.5MM **Privately
Held**
WEB: www.spacemakersheds.com
SIC: 3448 3443 Buildings, portable: pre-
fabricated metal; fabricated plate work
(boiler shop)
HQ: Arrow Shed, Llc
1101 N 4th St
Breese IL 62230
618 526-4546

(G-4196)
GILBERT STORMS JR
Also Called: Gilbys
1456 Ringwood Ave Apt 1 (07420-1577)
PHONE..................................973 835-5729
Fax: 973 835-2941
EMP: 5
SQ FT: 2,500
SALES: 450K **Privately Held**
SIC: 2395 2262 5611 Mfg Embroidery &
Art Needlework Screen Printing Fabrics &
Ret Clothing Accessories

(G-4197)
**INTERNTNAL DMNSIONAL
STONE LLC**
14 Doty Rd Unit B (07420-1411)
PHONE..................................973 729-0359
Michael Nestico,
EMP: 4
SALES (est): 83.3K **Privately Held**
SIC: 3281 3272 Building stone products;
furniture, cut stone; building stone, artifi-
cial: concrete

(G-4198)
**LAKELAND TRANSFORMER
CORP**
6 Paul Pl (07420-1048)
PHONE..................................973 835-0818
Michael Golas, *Principal*
EMP: 5
SALES (est): 504.5K **Privately Held**
SIC: 3679 Cores, magnetic

(G-4199)
MACHINE PLUS INC
97 4th Ave (07420-1141)
PHONE..................................973 839-8884
Ford Robbins, *President*
Joyce Robbins, *Corp Secy*
Alan Pittelkow, *Vice Pres*
EMP: 8
SQ FT: 6,000
SALES (est): 660K **Privately Held**
SIC: 3599 7699 7692 Machine shop, job-
bing & repair; industrial machinery &
equipment repair; welding repair

(G-4200)
PHOENIX POWDER COATING LLC
400 Union Ave Ste 2 (07420-1554)
PHONE..................................973 907-7500
Steve Maus,
EMP: 4
SALES (est): 334.2K **Privately Held**
SIC: 3479 Coating of metals & formed products

(G-4201)
POLY MOLDING LLC
96 4th Ave (07420-1140)
PHONE..................................973 835-7161
Adam Corn, *Owner*
Damien Choma, *Sales Staff*
Joann Doty, *Office Mgr*
◆ EMP: 19
SQ FT: 30,000
SALES (est): 3.9MM **Privately Held**
WEB: www.polytek.com
SIC: 3086 Insulation or cushioning material, foamed plastic

(G-4202)
STAMPEX CORP
75 4th Ave (07420-1141)
PHONE..................................973 839-4040
Detmar Nieshalla, *President*
Tom Nieshalla, *Vice Pres*
EMP: 10
SQ FT: 4,000
SALES (est): 700K **Privately Held**
SIC: 3544 3469 Die sets for metal stamping (presses); metal.stampings

(G-4203)
TECHLINE EXTRUSION SYSTEMS
89 4th Ave (07420-1141)
PHONE..................................973 831-0317
Victor Norman, *President*
Wilma Norman, *Treasurer*
EMP: 9
SQ FT: 3,200
SALES: 900K **Privately Held**
SIC: 3565 Packaging machinery

Hawthorne
Passaic County

(G-4204)
ACCURACY DEVICES
321 Central Ave (07506-1223)
PHONE..................................973 427-8829
Dave Van Derzee, *Owner*
EMP: 6
SALES: 450K **Privately Held**
SIC: 3821 Laboratory equipment: fume hoods, distillation racks, etc.

(G-4205)
B & S SHEET METAL CO INC
60 5th Ave (07506-2140)
PHONE..................................973 427-3739
Robert Buchmann, *President*
Gary Buchmann, *Vice Pres*
EMP: 10 EST: 1960
SQ FT: 19,000
SALES (est): 1.8MM **Privately Held**
SIC: 3444 Sheet metal specialties, not stamped

(G-4206)
B WITCHING BATH COMPANY LLC (PA)
174 Lincoln Ave (07506-1302)
PHONE..................................973 423-1820
Barbara Ross,
EMP: 6
SALES (est): 559K **Privately Held**
SIC: 2844 Deodorants, personal; toilet preparations

(G-4207)
BASSANO PRTRS & LITHOGRAPHERS
Also Called: Bassano Graphics
67 Royal Ave (07506-1916)
PHONE..................................973 423-1400
Ronald C Bassano, *President*

Donna Bassano, *Treasurer*
EMP: 30 EST: 1978
SQ FT: 2,800
SALES (est): 5.1MM **Privately Held**
WEB: www.bassanoprinting.com
SIC: 2752 2759 Commercial printing, offset; letterpress printing

(G-4208)
BEAVER RUN FARMS (PA)
10 Wagaraw Rd (07506-2704)
PHONE..................................973 427-1000
Charles Shotmeyer, *President*
Henry Shotmeyer Jr, *Corp Secy*
EMP: 5
SQ FT: 20,000
SALES (est): 1.3MM **Privately Held**
SIC: 2951 Asphalt & asphaltic paving mixtures (not from refineries)

(G-4209)
BRAWER BROS INC (PA)
375 Diamond Bridge Ave (07506-1323)
P.O. Box 640 (07507-0640)
PHONE..................................973 238-0163
Shartel Smith, *President*
Adolfo Castillo, *Controller*
John Italia, *Manager*
◆ EMP: 10
SQ FT: 8,700
SALES (est): 18.5MM **Privately Held**
WEB: www.brawerbros.com
SIC: 2282 Textured yarn

(G-4210)
BROADHURST SHEET METAL WORKS
230 Warburton Ave (07506-1834)
PHONE..................................973 304-4001
Kris Lill, *President*
EMP: 8
SALES (est): 1.7MM **Privately Held**
SIC: 3444 Sheet metal specialties, not stamped

(G-4211)
CAKE SPECIALTY INC
255 Goffle Rd (07506-3606)
PHONE..................................973 238-0500
Joseph De Spirito, *President*
Nicholas De Spirito Fr, *Vice Pres*
Mike De Spirito, *Admin Sec*
EMP: 12 EST: 1965
SALES (est): 1.3MM **Privately Held**
WEB: www.cakespecialty.com
SIC: 2051 5461 Bakery: wholesale or wholesale/retail combined; bakeries

(G-4212)
COLLINS AND COMPANY LLC
121 Wagaraw Rd (07506-2711)
PHONE..................................973 427-4068
John Collins,
EMP: 9
SALES (est): 1.5MM **Privately Held**
SIC: 2679 Wallpaper

(G-4213)
COMMERCIAL PRODUCTS CO INC
117 Ethel Ave Ste 143 (07506-1526)
P.O. Box 504 (07507-0504)
PHONE..................................973 427-6887
Charles Arnoldi, *President*
Elaine Arnoldi, *Admin Sec*
EMP: 12 EST: 1944
SALES (est): 1.7MM **Privately Held**
SIC: 2843 2295 Softeners (textile assistants); resin or plastic coated fabrics

(G-4214)
COMPUTER CRAFTS INC
57 Thomas Rd N (07506-2717)
P.O. Box 645 (07507-0645)
PHONE..................................973 423-3500
John J Harkins, *Ch of Bd*
Donald Harkins, *President*
Robert Harkins, *Vice Pres*
▲ EMP: 250
SQ FT: 100,000
SALES (est): 35.9MM **Privately Held**
WEB: www.computer-crafts.com
SIC: 3679 3357 Harness assemblies for electronic use: wire or cable; fiber optic cable (insulated)

(G-4215)
CONTINENTAL AROMATICS
1 Thomas Rd S (07506-2701)
P.O. Box 567 (07507-0567)
PHONE..................................973 238-9300
Ira Schneider, *President*
Beatrice Spitzer, *Accountant*
EMP: 20
SQ FT: 22,000
SALES (est): 3.6MM **Privately Held**
WEB: www.continentalaromatics.com
SIC: 2844 Perfumes & colognes

(G-4216)
ENCORE INTERNATIONAL LLC
270 Lafayette Ave (07506-1920)
PHONE..................................973 423-3880
Linda Rosenblatt, *VP Business*
Mark Nichols, *VP Sales*
Peggi Geissler,
▲ EMP: 11
SQ FT: 2,500
SALES (est): 2.8MM **Privately Held**
WEB: www.encoreintl.com
SIC: 2844 Cosmetic preparations

(G-4217)
EPPLEY BUILDING & DESIGN INC
220 Goffle Rd Ste B (07506-3605)
PHONE..................................973 636-9499
Paul Eppley, *President*
David Rowell, *Project Mgr*
EMP: 25
SQ FT: 5,000
SALES: 4MM **Privately Held**
WEB: www.ebandd.com
SIC: 2434 Wood kitchen cabinets

(G-4218)
FISK ALLOY CONDUCTORS INC (HQ)
10 Thomas Rd N (07506-2716)
P.O. Box 26 (07507-0026)
PHONE..................................973 825-8500
Eric Fisk, *President*
Brian Fisk, *Vice Pres*
Aidan Din, *Engineer*
▲ EMP: 173
SQ FT: 65,000
SALES (est): 23MM **Privately Held**
WEB: www.fiskalloy.com
SIC: 3496 Miscellaneous fabricated wire products

(G-4219)
FISK ALLOY INC (PA)
10 Thomas Rd N (07506-2716)
P.O. Box 26 (07507-0026)
PHONE..................................973 427-7550
Eric Fisk, *President*
Jim Mentekidis, *Vice Pres*
Janet M Green, *CFO*
Maria Baba, *Sales Staff*
Bill Griglak, *Manager*
EMP: 22
SQ FT: 140,000
SALES: 48MM **Privately Held**
SIC: 3496 3356 3351 3339 Miscellaneous fabricated wire products; nonferrous rolling & drawing; copper rolling & drawing; primary nonferrous metals; steel wire & related products

(G-4220)
FISK ALLOY WIRE INCORPORATED
Also Called: Electro Plated Wire
10 Thomas Rd N (07506-2716)
P.O. Box 26 (07507-0026)
PHONE..................................973 949-4491
Eric Fisk, *President*
Brian Fisk, *Vice Pres*
Jim Mentekidis, *Vice Pres*
Brian Gerard, *Technical Mgr*
Ahmad Dodokh, *Engineer*
◆ EMP: 130
SQ FT: 140,000
SALES (est): 42.3MM **Privately Held**
SIC: 3496 3356 3351 3339 Miscellaneous fabricated wire products; nonferrous rolling & drawing; copper rolling & drawing; primary nonferrous metals; steel wire & related products

(G-4221)
FLAVOR ASSOCIATES INC
1 Thomas Rd N (07506-2717)
PHONE..................................973 238-9300
Ira Schneider, *President*
EMP: 15
SQ FT: 22,000
SALES (est): 1.5MM **Privately Held**
SIC: 2087 Extracts, flavoring

(G-4222)
GRAPHIC ARTS PRINTING
170 Parmelee Ave (07506-2925)
PHONE..................................201 343-6554
EMP: 5
SALES (est): 430K **Privately Held**
SIC: 2759 Commercial Printing

(G-4223)
HAWTHORNE KITCHENS INC
120 5th Ave (07506-2134)
PHONE..................................973 427-9010
Kia Olsen, *President*
Annelise Olsen, *Corp Secy*
EMP: 10
SQ FT: 40,000
SALES (est): 1.5MM **Privately Held**
SIC: 5712 2541 5719 1751 Cabinet work, custom; sink tops, plastic laminated; bath accessories; cabinet building & installation

(G-4224)
HAWTHORNE PRESS
463 Lafayette Ave (07506-2521)
P.O. Box 1 (07507-0001)
PHONE..................................973 427-3330
Linda Cmissonelli, *President*
Linda C Missonelli, *President*
EMP: 12
SALES (est): 500K **Privately Held**
SIC: 2711 Newspapers: publishing only, not printed on site

(G-4225)
HAWTHORNE RUBBER MFG CORP
35 4th Ave (07506-2150)
P.O. Box 171 (07507-0171)
PHONE..................................973 427-3337
Michael J Morton, *President*
Dennis Dec, *Managing Dir*
Donald Morton, *Chairman*
John Morton, *Vice Pres*
Charlotte Morton, *Admin Sec*
EMP: 50 EST: 1943
SQ FT: 14,000
SALES (est): 9MM **Privately Held**
WEB: www.hawthornerubber.com
SIC: 3069 3061 Molded rubber products; mechanical rubber goods

(G-4226)
INTEK PLASTICS INC
150 5th Ave (07506-2159)
PHONE..................................973 427-7331
Rich Theurer, *General Mgr*
EMP: 28
SALES (corp-wide): 43.8MM **Privately Held**
SIC: 3089 Injection molding of plastics
PA: Intek Plastics, Inc.
    1000 Spiral Blvd
    Hastings MN 55033
    651 437-3805

(G-4227)
IW TREMONT CO INC
Also Called: I W Tremont Co
18 Utter Ave (07506-2127)
PHONE..................................973 427-3800
Sal Averso, *President*
Andrew S Averso, *Vice Pres*
James Averso, *Vice Pres*
▲ EMP: 25
SQ FT: 17,000
SALES (est): 5.8MM **Privately Held**
WEB: www.iwtremont.com
SIC: 2621 Specialty or chemically treated papers

(G-4228)
J BLANCO ASSOCIATES INC
280 9th Ave 1 (07506-1549)
PHONE..................................973 427-0619

Victor Ramos, *President*
EMP: 11
SALES (est): 3.5MM **Privately Held**
WEB: www.jblanco.com
SIC: 3429 8711 Manufactured hardware (general); mechanical engineering

(G-4229)
JET PRECISION METAL INC
7 Schoon Ave (07506-1435)
PHONE................................973 423-4350
Nick Di Maggio, *President*
Luciano Iannucci, *Vice Pres*
Lou Iannucci, *Director*
Jill Vanhouten, *Admin Asst*
▲ **EMP:** 35
SQ FT: 30,000
SALES (est): 7MM **Privately Held**
WEB: www.jetprecision.com
SIC: 3444 Sheet metalwork

(G-4230)
LA FORCHETTA
27 Utter Ave (07506-2163)
PHONE................................973 304-4797
Peter Michienzi, *Owner*
EMP: 6
SALES (est): 594.3K **Privately Held**
SIC: 2273 Carpets & rugs

(G-4231)
MEDILOGIC GROUP LLC
275 Goffle Rd (07506-3606)
PHONE................................201 794-2166
Frank Occidantale, *Mng Member*
Frank Occidentale,
EMP: 8
SALES: 950K **Privately Held**
SIC: 3841 Surgical & medical instruments

(G-4232)
MIDDLEBURG YARN PROCESSING CO (PA)
375 Diamond Bridge Ave (07506-1323)
P.O. Box 639 (07507-0639)
PHONE................................973 238-1800
Shartel Smith, *CEO*
Howard Reece, *President*
▲ **EMP:** 33
SQ FT: 2,000
SALES (est): 9.9MM **Privately Held**
SIC: 2282 Throwing yarn; winding yarn; spooling yarn

(G-4233)
NATURALVERT LLC
150 Florence Ave Ste D (07506-2361)
P.O. Box 585 (07507-0585)
PHONE................................848 229-4600
Vetchay Vilvert, *Mng Member*
EMP: 4 **EST:** 2014
SQ FT: 600
SALES (est): 40K **Privately Held**
SIC: 5149 2043 Health foods; granola & muesli, except bars & clusters

(G-4234)
NEXUS PLASTICS INCORPORATED
1 Loretto Ave (07506-1300)
P.O. Box 667 (07507-0667)
PHONE................................973 427-3311
Marwan Sholakh, *President*
▼ **EMP:** 90
SQ FT: 82,000
SALES (est): 26.8MM **Privately Held**
WEB: www.nexusplastics.com
SIC: 3081 2673 Plastic film & sheet; plastic bags: made from purchased materials

(G-4235)
NYLOK CORPORATION
Also Called: Aerospace Nylok
S11 Thomas Rd S (07506)
P.O. Box 651 (07507-0651)
PHONE................................201 427-8555
John E Johnson, *Ch of Bd*
Richard Nolan, *President*
Leon Drake, *Vice Pres*
EMP: 16 **EST:** 1960
SQ FT: 10,000
SALES (est): 2.4MM **Privately Held**
SIC: 3452 Nuts, metal

(G-4236)
PASCACK DATA SERVICES INC
200 Central Ave Ste 100 (07506-1821)
PHONE................................973 304-4858
Howard Adler, *President*
EMP: 12 **EST:** 1971
SQ FT: 2,600
SALES (est): 3.1MM **Privately Held**
WEB: www.pascackdata.com
SIC: 7373 5045 7379 3571 Computer systems analysis & design; computer peripheral equipment; computer related consulting services; personal computers (microcomputers); computer installation; computer tape drives & components

(G-4237)
PEERLESS COATINGS LLC
Also Called: Peerless Coating Services
220a Goffle Rd (07506-3605)
PHONE................................973 427-8771
Richard Bottoni,
Joe Hyer,
EMP: 45
SALES (est): 5.2MM **Privately Held**
SIC: 3479 Coating of metals & formed products; painting, coating & hot dipping

(G-4238)
PETER YAGED
Also Called: Hawthorne Machine Products
58 Braen Ave (07506-2202)
P.O. Box 259 (07507-0259)
PHONE................................973 427-4219
Peter Yaged, *Owner*
EMP: 4 **EST:** 1948
SALES (est): 264.4K **Privately Held**
SIC: 3451 Screw machine products

(G-4239)
PHARMA SYSTEMS INC
662 Goffle Rd Ste 3 (07506-3420)
P.O. Box 194, Wyckoff (07481-0194)
PHONE................................973 636-9007
Bernard Giletta, *President*
EMP: 5
SALES (est): 500.5K **Privately Held**
WEB: www.pharmasystemsusa.com
SIC: 3559 Pharmaceutical machinery

(G-4240)
PREMIO FOODS INC (PA)
50 Utter Ave (07506-2117)
PHONE................................800 864-7622
Marc Cinque, *President*
Steven Cinque, *Vice Pres*
John Haug, *Plant Mgr*
Fely Brancato, *Purch Mgr*
Edwin Bolanos, *Engineer*
▲ **EMP:** 150 **EST:** 1978
SQ FT: 60,000
SALES (est): 34.4MM **Privately Held**
WEB: www.premiofoods.com
SIC: 2013 2011 Sausages from purchased meat; meat packing plants

(G-4241)
RADIANT ENERGY SYSTEMS INC
175 N Ethel Ave (07506-1515)
PHONE................................973 423-5220
Sarvejit Narang, *President*
Bob Narang, *President*
Rob Legrand, *Chief Engr*
Nicole Burchell, *Engineer*
Cornel Polnyj, *Project Engr*
▲ **EMP:** 30
SQ FT: 16,000
SALES (est): 8.4MM **Privately Held**
WEB: www.radiantenergy.com
SIC: 3567 Infrared ovens, industrial

(G-4242)
RUSH GRAPHICS INC
1122 Goffle Rd 32 (07506-2024)
PHONE................................973 427-9393
Zora Agheli, *President*
Manee Kassaii, *Marketing Mgr*
Sam Kassaii, *Officer*
EMP: 20
SQ FT: 10,000
SALES (est): 3.4MM **Privately Held**
WEB: www.rushgraphics.com
SIC: 2752 Commercial printing, offset

(G-4243)
SERVO-TEK PRODUCTS COMPANY INC
1096 Goffle Rd (07506-2009)
PHONE................................973 427-4249
Fax: 973 427-4249
EMP: 40
SQ FT: 25,000
SALES (est): 4.3MM **Privately Held**
SIC: 3625 3621 Mfg Relays/Industrial Controls Mfg Motors/Generators

(G-4244)
SIGNATURE MARKETING & MFG
Also Called: Signature Crafts
301 Wagaraw Rd (07506-1411)
PHONE................................973 427-3700
Michael Assile, *President*
Hala Assile, *Treasurer*
EMP: 8
SQ FT: 8,000
SALES (est): 1.3MM **Privately Held**
WEB: www.signaturecrafts.com
SIC: 2891 Glue

(G-4245)
STEALTHBITS TECHNOLOGIES INC (PA)
200 Central Ave (07506-1821)
PHONE................................201 301-9328
Stephen M Cochran, *President*
David Gordon, *President*
Jessie Wheeler, *Vice Pres*
Julie Muns, *Opers Staff*
Michael Burrofato, *QA Dir*
EMP: 85
SQ FT: 17,000
SALES (est): 32.5MM **Privately Held**
WEB: www.stealthbits.com
SIC: 7372 7371 Prepackaged software; custom computer programming services

(G-4246)
TEKNO INC
Also Called: Conexion Printing
86 5th Ave (07506-2138)
PHONE................................973 423-2004
Elliot Montalvo, *President*
Claudia Montalvo, *Manager*
EMP: 6
SQ FT: 10,000
SALES (est): 626.4K **Privately Held**
SIC: 2759 Letterpress printing

(G-4247)
ULMA FORM-WORKS INC (HQ)
58 5th Ave (07506-2160)
PHONE................................201 882-1122
Alberto Arocena, *President*
Frank Deluccia, *General Mgr*
Frank Cola, *Vice Pres*
Eugenio Pedrao, *CFO*
Mary Rambla, *Credit Staff*
▲ **EMP:** 52 **EST:** 1998
SQ FT: 9,500
SALES (est): 9.4MM
SALES (corp-wide): 134.7MM **Privately Held**
WEB: www.ulmaforms.com
SIC: 3443 3272 3444 Fabricated plate work (boiler shop); concrete stuctural support & building material; concrete forms, sheet metal
PA: Ulma C Y E S Coop
  Calle Otadui Zuhaiztia, 3 - Apdo 13
  Onati 20560
  943 034-900

(G-4248)
USSECURENET LLC
1086 Goffle Rd Ste 101 (07506-2012)
PHONE................................201 447-0130
Kathryn Zegarra, *Manager*
Debra Deffaa,
EMP: 4
SQ FT: 10,000
SALES (est): 569.2K **Privately Held**
SIC: 3663 4899 Satellites, communications; satellite earth stations

(G-4249)
VANDEREEMS MANUFACTURING CO
40 Schoon Ave (07506-1408)
PHONE................................973 427-2355

John Van Der Eems, *President*
EMP: 10 **EST:** 1933
SQ FT: 12,000
SALES (est): 1.4MM **Privately Held**
SIC: 2449 Shipping cases & drums, wood: wirebound & plywood; berry crates, wood: wirebound

(G-4250)
VIVITONE INC (PA)
111 Ethel Ave (07506-1528)
PHONE................................973 427-8114
Gerald Sandler, *President*
EMP: 18 **EST:** 1957
SQ FT: 35,000
SALES (est): 1MM **Privately Held**
SIC: 2816 2893 Inorganic pigments; printing ink

(G-4251)
VYRAL SYSTEMS INC
Also Called: Vyral Entertainment
300 Mountain Ave (07506-3314)
PHONE................................201 321-2488
David Kaplan, *CEO*
EMP: 5 **EST:** 2011
SQ FT: 650
SALES (est): 186.1K **Privately Held**
SIC: 7372 Application computer software

(G-4252)
WARP PROCESSING INC (PA)
375 Diamond Bridge Ave (07506-1323)
P.O. Box 640 (07507-0640)
PHONE................................973 238-1800
Shartel Smith, *President*
▲ **EMP:** 155
SQ FT: 7,000
SALES (est): 13.3MM **Privately Held**
SIC: 2282 Winding yarn

Hazlet
Monmouth County

(G-4253)
A SIGN OF EXCELLENCE INC
6 Surrey Dr (07730-1829)
PHONE................................732 264-0404
Sue Cosnoski, *President*
EMP: 4
SALES: 250K **Privately Held**
SIC: 3993 Signs & advertising specialties

(G-4254)
AAEON ELECTRONICS INC (HQ)
11 Crown Plz Ste 208 (07730-2496)
PHONE................................732 203-9300
Steve Hsu, *President*
Nancy Zimmerman, *Human Resources*
Tim Sterling, *Sales Mgr*
Bill Berry, *Accounts Exec*
Philip Sung, *Sales Staff*
▲ **EMP:** 33
SQ FT: 21,357
SALES (est): 8.8MM
SALES (corp-wide): 11.4B **Privately Held**
WEB: www.aaeonsystem.com
SIC: 3571 Electronic computers
PA: Asustek Computer Incorporation
  15, Lide Rd.,
  Taipei City TAP 11259
  228 943-447

(G-4255)
ADMARTEC INC
12 Crown Plz Ste 204 (07730-2441)
PHONE................................732 888-8248
Anatoly Nemiroski, *President*
EMP: 4
SQ FT: 2,500
SALES (est): 494.4K **Privately Held**
SIC: 3625 Control circuit devices, magnet & solid state

(G-4256)
ARGLEN INDUSTRIES INC
1 Bethany Rd Ste 44 (07730-1681)
PHONE................................732 888-8100
Andrew Strahl, *President*
EMP: 10

▲ = Import ▼=Export
◆ =Import/Export

SALES (est): 1.6MM **Privately Held**
WEB: www.arglen-us.com
SIC: 2752 Commercial printing, lithographic

(G-4257)
ASTRA CLEANERS OF HAZLET
35 Hazlet Ave (07730-1844)
PHONE....................................732 264-4144
David Lee, *Owner*
Paula Saeber, *Owner*
Ron Silver, *Owner*
EMP: 5
SALES (est): 103.4K **Privately Held**
SIC: 7216 2842 Curtain cleaning & repair; specialty cleaning, polishes & sanitation goods

(G-4258)
BURLINGTON ATLANTIC CORP
Burlington Battery
1 Crown Plz (07730-2441)
PHONE....................................732 888-7776
EMP: 5
SALES (corp-wide): 1.4MM **Privately Held**
SIC: 3692 Mfg Primary Batteries
PA: Burlington Atlantic Corporation
277 Frank Applegate Rd
Jackson NJ 08527
732 888-7799

(G-4259)
CIRCA PROMOTIONS INC
58 Village Ct (07730-1537)
P.O. Box 360, Atlantic Highlands (07716-0360)
PHONE....................................732 264-1200
Karen Kantor, *President*
EMP: 8
SQ FT: 3,000
SALES (est): 1.3MM **Privately Held**
WEB: www.circapromotions.com
SIC: 5199 2759 Advertising specialties; commercial printing

(G-4260)
GREEN LINE BOTANICALS LLC
8 Crown Plz Ste 103 (07730-2472)
PHONE....................................609 759-0221
EMP: 4
SALES (est): 182.3K **Privately Held**
SIC: 2833 Botanical products, medicinal: ground, graded or milled

(G-4261)
INDUSTRIAL WATER TECH INC
6 Village Ct (07730-1530)
PHONE....................................732 888-1233
Richard Demartino, *President*
EMP: 7
SQ FT: 2,000
SALES (est): 2MM **Privately Held**
WEB: www.iwtnj.com
SIC: 2899 8748 Water treating compounds; business consulting

(G-4262)
INTERNTNAL FLVORS FRGRNCES INC
Also Called: Interntonal Flavors Fragrances
600 Highway 36 (07730-1704)
PHONE....................................732 264-4500
Bob Papp, *Buyer*
David Smith, *Branch Mgr*
Analia Ferreira, *Manager*
EMP: 200
SALES (corp-wide): 3.9B **Publicly Held**
SIC: 2869 5999 2844 Flavors or flavoring materials, synthetic; perfumes & colognes; toilet preparations
PA: International Flavors & Fragrances Inc.
521 W 57th St
New York NY 10019
212 765-5500

(G-4263)
LAZAR TECHNOLOGIES INC
Also Called: LAZAR CAPPER
39 Evergreen St (07730-4033)
PHONE....................................732 739-9622
Carlos Gaviria, *President*
Isabel Gaviria, *Vice Pres*
Sabrina Gaviria, *Sales Staff*
▼ EMP: 10
SQ FT: 10,000

SALES (est): 1.8MM **Privately Held**
WEB: www.lazartec.com
SIC: 3599 Custom machinery

(G-4264)
LUMBER SUPER MART
State Hwy No 36 (07730)
P.O. Box 333 (07730-0333)
PHONE....................................732 739-1428
EMP: 4
SALES (est): 280K **Privately Held**
SIC: 5261 3089 Ret Nursery/Garden Supplies Mfg Plastic Products

(G-4265)
MID-STATE CONTROLS INC
8 Crown Plz Ste 102 (07730-2472)
PHONE....................................732 335-0500
Robert Rosko, *Principal*
EMP: 14
SALES (est): 2.2MM **Privately Held**
SIC: 3625 Control equipment, electric

(G-4266)
NAAVA INC (PA)
32 Appleton Dr (07730-2105)
PHONE....................................844 666-2282
Aki Soudunsaari, *CEO*
Niko Jarvinen, *President*
Jason Kahn, *Manager*
EMP: 5
SALES: 1.5MM **Privately Held**
SIC: 8742 3564 New products & services consultants; air purification equipment

(G-4267)
NOUVEAU PROSTHETICS LTD
984 State Route 36 (07730-1700)
PHONE....................................732 739-0888
Stuart Weiner, *President*
Camille Levin, *Administration*
EMP: 10
SQ FT: 3,200
SALES (est): 1MM **Privately Held**
SIC: 3842 5999 Limbs, artificial; braces, orthopedic; medical apparatus & supplies

(G-4268)
NOUVEAU PROSTHETICS ORTHOTICS
984 State Route 36 (07730-1700)
PHONE....................................732 739-0888
Stuart Weiner, *President*
Evett Weiner, *Corp Secy*
Camille Levin, *Asst Director*
EMP: 10
SQ FT: 1,400
SALES (est): 1.3MM **Privately Held**
SIC: 3842 Limbs, artificial; prosthetic appliances

(G-4269)
PETER MORLEY LLC
Also Called: Safeguard Business Systems
21 Village Ct (07730-1532)
P.O. Box 340, Sharon MA (02067-0340)
PHONE....................................732 264-0010
Peter Morley,
EMP: 4
SQ FT: 1,000
SALES (est): 590.9K **Privately Held**
SIC: 5112 2621 Business forms; stationery, envelope & tablet papers

(G-4270)
SILAB INC
1301 State Route 36 Ste 8 (07730-1751)
PHONE....................................732 335-1030
Jean Paufique, *CEO*
▲ EMP: 10
SALES (est): 1.3MM
SALES (corp-wide): 177.9K **Privately Held**
SIC: 2834 Extracts of botanicals: powdered, pilular, solid or fluid
HQ: Societe Industrielle Limousine D'application Biologique
Lieu Dit Madrias
Objat 19130
555 845-840

(G-4271)
TALENT INVESTMENT LLC
Also Called: Talent Technology Center
12 Crown Plz (07730-2441)
PHONE....................................732 931-0088

Yuhinin Hwang,
EMP: 7
SALES (est): 873.4K **Privately Held**
SIC: 2869 Silicones

(G-4272)
TRETINA PRINTING INC
1301 Concord Hwy 36 101 (07730)
PHONE....................................732 264-2324
Jan Tretina, *President*
Olga Tretina, *Corp Secy*
EMP: 15
SQ FT: 22,000
SALES (est): 2MM **Privately Held**
WEB: www.tretinaprinting.com
SIC: 2752 Photo-offset printing; commercial printing, offset

Hewitt
Passaic County

(G-4273)
A & A IRONWORK CO INC
955 Burnt Meadow Rd (07421-3503)
P.O. Box 1090 (07421-2090)
PHONE....................................973 728-4300
Adam G Muzer, *President*
Adam E Muzer, *Vice Pres*
Mark Muzer, *Vice Pres*
EMP: 14
SQ FT: 4,500
SALES (est): 3MM **Privately Held**
SIC: 3312 3446 Structural & rail mill products; architectural metalwork

(G-4274)
COM-FAB INC
921 Burnt Meadow Rd B (07421-3503)
PHONE....................................973 296-0433
Michael Fattal, *President*
EMP: 4
SQ FT: 1,875
SALES (est): 356.4K **Privately Held**
SIC: 3441 Building components, structural steel

(G-4275)
ECO-PLUG-SYSTEM LLC
1946 Union Valley Rd (07421-4100)
P.O. Box 12 (07421-0012)
PHONE....................................855 326-7584
Peter Esposito, *President*
▼ EMP: 6
SQ FT: 5,600
SALES: 156K **Privately Held**
SIC: 3559 Automotive related machinery

(G-4276)
MACK TRADING LLC
486 Lake Shore Dr (07421-1324)
PHONE....................................973 794-4904
EMP: 4 EST: 1999
SALES: 40K **Privately Held**
SIC: 2066 Mfg Chocolate/Cocoa Products

(G-4277)
NORTHEAST CON PDTS & SUP INC
937 Burnt Meadow Rd (07421-3503)
P.O. Box 963 (07421-0963)
PHONE....................................973 728-1667
Nancy Vitale, *President*
John Vitale, *Vice Pres*
EMP: 5
SALES (est): 785.7K **Privately Held**
SIC: 3272 Septic tanks, concrete

(G-4278)
NORTHEAST CONCRETE PDTS LLC
937 Burnt Meadow Rd (07421-3503)
PHONE....................................973 728-1667
John Vitale, *Owner*
Keith Plokhoy, *Project Mgr*
EMP: 5 EST: 2015
SALES (est): 147.1K **Privately Held**
SIC: 3272 Prestressed concrete products

(G-4279)
ROBERT YOUNG AND SON INC
830 Burnt Meadow Rd (07421-3506)
PHONE....................................973 728-8133
William Young, *President*

Karen Young, *Admin Sec*
EMP: 8
SQ FT: 100
SALES (est): 343.9K **Privately Held**
SIC: 3531 Asphalt plant, including gravel-mix type

High Bridge
Hunterdon County

(G-4280)
ADVANCED PRECISION SYSTEMS LLC
6 Sunset Dr (08829-1307)
PHONE....................................908 730-8892
Michael Manzella,
EMP: 5
SQ FT: 1,300
SALES (est): 230K **Privately Held**
WEB:
www.advancedprecisionsystems.com
SIC: 3499 Metal household articles

(G-4281)
CUSTOM ALLOY CORPORATION (PA)
3 Washington Ave Ste 5 (08829-2108)
PHONE....................................908 638-0257
Adam F Ambielli, *President*
Roger Carroll, *Maint Spvr*
Maritza Bauza, *Production*
Mary Snyder, *Purch Mgr*
Peter Fazio, *QC Mgr*
▲ EMP: 170
SQ FT: 150,000
SALES (est): 40.3MM **Privately Held**
WEB: www.customalloy.us
SIC: 3498 Fabricated pipe & fittings

(G-4282)
ENVIRO-CLEAR COMPANY INC
152 Cregar Rd (08829-1003)
PHONE....................................908 638-5507
J J Muldowney, *President*
Cindy Meyer, *President*
▲ EMP: 15
SQ FT: 15,000
SALES (est): 3.7MM **Privately Held**
WEB: www.enviro-clear.com
SIC: 3569 3532 Filters; clarifying machinery, mineral

(G-4283)
J & M MANUFACTURING INC
54 Main St (08829-1915)
P.O. Box 43 (08829-0043)
PHONE....................................908 638-4298
John Gargas, *President*
EMP: 8
SQ FT: 6,000
SALES (est): 912K **Privately Held**
SIC: 3599 Machine shop, jobbing & repair

(G-4284)
NORSAL DISTRIBUTION ASSOCIATES
150 Cregar Rd (08829-1003)
P.O. Box 264 (08829-0264)
PHONE....................................908 638-6430
Sal Moscato Sr, *Ch of Bd*
Sal Moscato Jr, *President*
Norma Moscato, *Vice Pres*
Russell Lown, *Opers Mgr*
EMP: 10
SQ FT: 11,700
SALES (est): 1MM **Privately Held**
WEB: www.norsalnda.com
SIC: 1731 3679 Electric power systems contractors; electronic circuits

---

Highland Lakes
Sussex County

(G-4285)
NORTH STAR SIGNS INC
3 Callan Ct (07422-1002)
PHONE....................................973 244-1144
Jesse Guzman, *Principal*
EMP: 9 EST: 2008

SALES (est): 133.6K **Privately Held**
SIC: 3993 Signs & advertising specialties

Highland Park
Middlesex County

(G-4286)
ALL COLORS SCREEN PRINTING LLC
176 Woodbridge Ave (08904-3767)
PHONE..................................732 777-6033
Stephen Mittler, *VP Mktg*
Gayle Brill Mittler, *Mng Member*
EMP: 6
SQ FT: 5,700
SALES (est): 821.3K **Privately Held**
SIC: 2759 3993 7389 5199 Screen printing; signs & advertising specialties; embroidering of advertising on shirts, etc.; advertising specialties

(G-4287)
BIRNN CHOCOLATES INC
314 Cleveland Ave (08904-1845)
PHONE..................................732 214-8680
John Cunnell, *President*
EMP: 4
SQ FT: 5,000
SALES (est): 424K **Privately Held**
WEB: www.birnnchocolates.com
SIC: 5441 5145 2066 Candy; candy; chocolate & cocoa products

(G-4288)
COLGATE-PALMOLIVE COMPANY
251 S 8th Ave (08904-3107)
PHONE..................................732 878-6062
Betty Won, *Research*
EMP: 279
SALES (corp-wide): 15.5B **Publicly Held**
SIC: 2844 Toothpastes or powders, dentifrices
PA: Colgate-Palmolive Company
300 Park Ave Fl 3
New York NY 10022
212 310-2000

(G-4289)
WATER MASTER CO
13 S 3rd Ave (08904-2509)
PHONE..................................732 247-1900
Marvin Cheiten, *Owner*
▼ **EMP:** 6 **EST:** 1947
SQ FT: 3,000
SALES (est): 380K **Privately Held**
SIC: 3069 3471 Molded rubber products; polishing, metals or formed products

(G-4290)
YAMATE CHOCOLATIER INC
320 Cleveland Ave (08904-1845)
PHONE..................................732 249-4847
EMP: 7
SALES (est): 716.6K **Privately Held**
SIC: 2026 Mfg Chocolate

Highlands
Monmouth County

(G-4291)
CERTIFIED CLAM CORP
190 Bay Ave Ste 1 (07732-1665)
P.O. Box 383 (07732-0383)
PHONE..................................732 872-6650
Cathy Armstrong, *President*
Janis Hartsgrove, *Sales Staff*
EMP: 14
SALES: 4.2MM **Privately Held**
SIC: 5146 2092 Seafoods; fresh or frozen packaged fish

(G-4292)
GARDNER RESOURCES INC
188 Bay Ave (07732-1624)
P.O. Box 363 (07732-0363)
PHONE..................................732 872-0755
Blair Lazar, *President*
Gary Tucker, *Sales Mgr*
Karin Swan, *Manager*

▲ **EMP:** 4
SALES (est): 476.9K **Privately Held**
SIC: 5499 5149 2033 Gourmet food stores; sauces; chili sauce, tomato: packaged in cans, jars, etc.

Hightstown
Mercer County

(G-4293)
ALLEGRO MFG
Also Called: Allegro Creative
150 Milford Rd (08520-6124)
PHONE..................................323 724-0101
EMP: 15
SALES (est): 3.3MM **Privately Held**
SIC: 3172 5199 Cosmetic bags; hairbrushes

(G-4294)
B-HIVE LTD LIABILITY COMPANY
10 Olivia Rd (08520-4762)
PHONE..................................302 438-2769
Tara Prabhakar,
EMP: 8
SALES: 100K **Privately Held**
SIC: 3572 Computer storage devices

(G-4295)
CCL LABEL INC
120 Stockton St (08520-3706)
PHONE..................................609 443-3700
Pat Moore, *Vice Pres*
Larry Joseph, *Facilities Mgr*
Dave Lore, *Purch Agent*
Joe Bair, *Sales Staff*
Jack Lang, *Branch Mgr*
EMP: 100
SALES (corp-wide): 3.9B **Privately Held**
SIC: 2679 2673 2672 Paper products, converted; paperboard products, converted; bags: plastic, laminated & coated; coated & laminated paper
HQ: Ccl Label, Inc.
161 Worcester Rd Ste 603
Framingham MA 01701
508 872-4511

(G-4296)
HIGHTS ELECTRIC MOTOR SERVICE
156 Stockton St (08520-3706)
PHONE..................................609 448-2298
Bernard E Stella Jr, *President*
Therese A Stella, *Corp Secy*
EMP: 4
SQ FT: 7,000
SALES (est): 1.4MM **Privately Held**
SIC: 5063 5084 7694 7699 Motors, electric; generators; pumps & pumping equipment; motor repair services; pumps & pumping equipment repair; generator repair

(G-4297)
NATIONAL CERTIFIED PRINTING
Also Called: Michael's Quick Printing
387 Mercer St A (08520-4407)
P.O. Box 271 (08520-0271)
PHONE..................................609 443-6323
Joseph Sharoff, *Owner*
EMP: 4
SALES (est): 423.1K **Privately Held**
SIC: 2752 Commercial printing, offset

(G-4298)
ROMULUS EMPRISES INC
60 Woodside Ave (08520-4900)
PHONE..................................609 683-4549
Harold D Romulus, *CEO*
Antoine Francis, *President*
Hymler Geffrard, *CFO*
EMP: 6
SALES: 70K **Privately Held**
SIC: 2076 Vegetable oil mills

Hillsborough
Somerset County

(G-4299)
4 WAY LOCK LLC
5 Ilene Ct Ste 12 (08844-1915)
PHONE..................................908 359-2002
Ann Magiash, *Mng Member*
EMP: 4
SQ FT: 25,000
SALES (est): 482.9K **Privately Held**
SIC: 3442 3429 Metal doors; keys, locks & related hardware

(G-4300)
ADAM GATES & COMPANY LLC
249 Homestead Rd Ste 5 (08844-1912)
P.O. Box 2248, East Millstone (08875-2248)
PHONE..................................908 829-3386
Chester Swasey,
EMP: 10
SQ FT: 5,000
SALES (est): 1.6MM **Privately Held**
WEB: www.adamgatescompany.com
SIC: 2899 8711 Chemical supplies for foundries; engineering services

(G-4301)
AEROPRES CORPORATION
318 Valley Rd (08844-4095)
PHONE..................................908 292-1240
Gordon R Sammis, *Plant Mgr*
Dan Martino, *Sales Mgr*
EMP: 9
SQ FT: 4,550
SALES (corp-wide): 37.2MM **Privately Held**
WEB: www.aeropres.com
SIC: 2813 Industrial gases
PA: Aeropres Corporation
1324 N Hearne Ave Ste 200
Shreveport LA 71107
318 429-6744

(G-4302)
AURA SIGNS INC
Also Called: Triaddisplay
6 Ilene Ct Ste 9 (08844-1921)
PHONE..................................866 963-7446
Deval Soni, *President*
EMP: 4
SALES (est): 465.2K **Privately Held**
SIC: 3993 Signs & advertising specialties

(G-4303)
BELLEMEAD HOT GLASS
884 Route 206 (08844-1509)
PHONE..................................908 281-5516
Robert Kuster, *Mng Member*
EMP: 6
SALES (est): 408.1K **Privately Held**
SIC: 3646 Chandeliers, commercial

(G-4304)
BELLEVUE PARFUMS USA LLC
2 Jill Ct Bldg 21 (08844-1935)
PHONE..................................908 262-7774
Narinder Manghani, *CEO*
EMP: 10 **EST:** 2016
SQ FT: 13,500
SALES (est): 997.3K **Privately Held**
SIC: 2844 Perfumes & colognes

(G-4305)
BEZWADA BIOMEDICAL LLC
15 Ilene Ct Ste 1 (08844-1920)
P.O. Box 6357 (08844-6357)
PHONE..................................908 281-7529
RAO S Bezwada, *President*
Sujata Moton, *CFO*
Neeti Srivastava, *Manager*
EMP: 4
SQ FT: 6,000
SALES (est): 559.3K **Privately Held**
WEB: www.bezwadabiomedical.com
SIC: 2822 8731 Ethylene-propylene rubbers, EPDM polymers; biotechnical research, commercial

(G-4306)
BNS ENTERPRISES INC
186 Wildflower Ln (08844-4868)
PHONE..................................908 285-6556
Bruce E Hemstock, *President*
EMP: 4
SALES (est): 100K **Privately Held**
SIC: 5063 3663 Batteries; radio & TV communications equipment

(G-4307)
BRENT RIVER CORP (DH)
Also Called: Tri-Delta Plastics
208 Cougar Ct (08844-4105)
PHONE..................................908 722-6021
Thomas J Dolan, *President*
Paul Rolando, *Opers Mgr*
Brian J Dolan, *VP Sls/Mktg*
▲ **EMP:** 33
SQ FT: 88,000
SALES (est): 17.6MM
SALES (corp-wide): 141MM **Privately Held**
SIC: 3089 Injection molding of plastics
HQ: Pretium Packaging, L.L.C.
15450 S Outer Forty Dr St
Chesterfield MO 63017
314 727-8200

(G-4308)
BRENT RIVER CORP
Tri Delta Technology
208 Cougar Ct (08844-4105)
PHONE..................................908 722-6021
Thomas J Dolan, *Branch Mgr*
EMP: 9
SALES (corp-wide): 141MM **Privately Held**
SIC: 3085 Plastics bottles
HQ: Brent River Corp.
208 Cougar Ct
Hillsborough NJ 08844
908 722-6021

(G-4309)
C AND C TOOL CO LLC
198 Us Highway 206 Ste 1 (08844-4138)
PHONE..................................908 431-0330
Steven A Calello,
EMP: 4
SQ FT: 1,600
SALES (est): 300K **Privately Held**
SIC: 3544 Industrial molds

(G-4310)
CLANTECH INC
198 Us Highway 206 Ste 10 (08844-4138)
PHONE..................................908 281-7667
John Gracie, *President*
David Gracie, *Admin Sec*
▲ **EMP:** 4 **EST:** 1975
SQ FT: 3,500
SALES: 1MM **Privately Held**
WEB: www.clantech.com
SIC: 3679 Power supplies, all types: static; commutators, electronic

(G-4311)
COUNTER EFX INC
301 Roycefield Rd Bldg 5 (08844-4097)
PHONE..................................908 203-0155
EMP: 9
SALES (est): 975K **Privately Held**
SIC: 2541 Contractor Specializing In Counter-Top

(G-4312)
DISTRIBUTOR LABEL PRODUCTS
Also Called: Certified Labeling Solutions
51 Old Camplain Rd (08844-4227)
PHONE..................................908 704-9997
Joseph Braun, *President*
Petra Braun, *Treasurer*
EMP: 25
SQ FT: 10,000
SALES (est): 5MM **Privately Held**
SIC: 2759 Labels & seals: printing

(G-4313)
EAST COAST ELECTRONICS INC
216 Us Highway 206 20a (08844-4384)
PHONE..................................908 431-7555
EMP: 3

SQ FT: 2,500
SALES: 1.5MM **Privately Held**
SIC: 5065 3643 Electronics Distr & Cable Mfg

(G-4314)
EAST COAST MEDIA LLC
14 Park Ave (08844-4125)
PHONE..................908 575-9700
Theresa Distasio, *President*
Andy Fresco III, *Mng Member*
Mark B Arnold,
▲ EMP: 22 EST: 1999
SQ FT: 20,000
SALES (est): 4.4MM **Privately Held**
WEB: www.companyflair.com
SIC: 2752 Commercial printing, lithographic

(G-4315)
ESCO PRECISION INC
71 Old Camplain Rd (08844-4297)
PHONE..................908 722-0800
Samy Elkholy, *President*
Ryan Elkholy, *Project Mgr*
Emir Elkholy, *Engineer*
▲ EMP: 20
SQ FT: 8,000
SALES: 2MM **Privately Held**
WEB: www.escoprecision.com
SIC: 3451 Screw machine products

(G-4316)
FISCHL MACHINE & TOOL
Also Called: F M T
5 Ilene Ct Ste 7 (08844-1915)
PHONE..................908 829-5621
Fax: 973 227-1867
EMP: 4
SQ FT: 2,500
SALES (est): 476.6K **Privately Held**
SIC: 3599 Mfg Industrial Machinery

(G-4317)
FREWITT USA INC
249 Homestead Rd (08844-1912)
PHONE..................908 829-5245
EMP: 20
SALES (est): 2.6MM **Privately Held**
SIC: 2041 Flour & other grain mill products

(G-4318)
G & J STEEL & TUBING INC
406 Roycefield Rd (08844-4099)
PHONE..................908 526-4445
John Tursky, *President*
Gary Borowicz, *Controller*
▲ EMP: 67
SQ FT: 25,000
SALES (est): 15.5MM **Privately Held**
WEB: www.gjsteel.com
SIC: 3498 Tube fabricating (contract bending & shaping)

(G-4319)
GENERAL TOOL SPECIALTIES INC
284 Sunnymeade Rd (08844-4630)
PHONE..................908 874-3040
John K Domici Jr, *President*
Susan Bittle, *Office Mgr*
EMP: 12
SQ FT: 7,000
SALES (est): 2.6MM **Privately Held**
SIC: 3544 Special dies, tools, jigs & fixtures

(G-4320)
GLEN-GERY CORPORATION
Also Called: Glen-Gery Brick
75 Hamilton Rd (08844-4671)
PHONE..................908 359-5111
Brendan Meagan, *Sales/Mktg Mgr*
EMP: 40
SALES (corp-wide): 1.2MM **Privately Held**
WEB: www.glengerybrick.com
SIC: 5032 3251 Brick, except refractory; brick & structural clay tile
HQ: Glen-Gery Corporation
1166 Spring St
Reading PA 19610
610 374-4011

(G-4321)
HANKIN ACQUISIONS INC
1 Harvard Way Ste 6 (08844-4294)
P.O. Box 5759 (08844-5759)
PHONE..................908 722-9595
David W Chou, *President*
Harshad Modi, *Vice Pres*
EMP: 13
SQ FT: 6,000
SALES (est): 1.6MM **Privately Held**
SIC: 3567 Incinerators, metal: domestic or commercial

(G-4322)
HANKIN ENVMTL SYSTEMS INC
1 Harvard Way Ste 6 (08844-4294)
P.O. Box 5759 (08844-5759)
PHONE..................908 722-9595
David W Chou, *CEO*
David C Chen, *President*
Harshad S Modi, *Exec VP*
Luis A Velazquez, *Vice Pres*
Richard Sun, *Controller*
EMP: 13
SQ FT: 6,000
SALES: 10MM
SALES (corp-wide): 274.7MM **Privately Held**
SIC: 3567 Incinerators, metal: domestic or commercial
PA: Cse Global Limited
202 Bedok South Avenue 1
Singapore 46933
651 203-33

(G-4323)
HERCULES ENTERPRISES LLC
321 Valley Rd (08844-4056)
PHONE..................908 369-0000
Carl Massaro,
▲ EMP: 100
SQ FT: 189,000
SALES (est): 26.6MM **Privately Held**
SIC: 3715 Truck trailers

(G-4324)
HILLSBOROUGH VACUUM LLC
54 Buckland Dr (08844-1127)
PHONE..................908 904-6600
Frank R Scrofani,
Patty G Scrofani,
EMP: 6
SQ FT: 2,000
SALES (est): 670K **Privately Held**
WEB: www.hillsboroughvacuum.com
SIC: 3635 5722 Household vacuum cleaners; vacuum cleaners

(G-4325)
HOT RUNNER TECHNOLOGY
216 Us Highway 206 (08844-4140)
PHONE..................908 431-5711
EMP: 9
SALES (est): 939.3K **Privately Held**
SIC: 3089 Injection molding of plastics

(G-4326)
ICOTE USA INC (PA)
465 Amwell Rd (08844-1207)
PHONE..................908 359-7575
Renata Jesionka, *President*
EMP: 4
SQ FT: 2,300
SALES (est): 89K **Privately Held**
SIC: 2952 Roofing materials

(G-4327)
IDEON LLC
249 Homestead Rd Ste 1 (08844-1912)
PHONE..................908 431-3126
Mikhail Laksin,
Brijesh Nigam,
Bhalendra Patel,
EMP: 4
SQ FT: 2,500
SALES (est): 1MM **Privately Held**
SIC: 2893 Printing ink

(G-4328)
INDUSTRIAL TUBE CORPORATION
297 Valley Rd (08844)
P.O. Box 957, Somerville (08876-0957)
PHONE..................908 369-3737
Gustav Imhauser, *President*

Lydia Imhauser, *Vice Pres*
Marion Imhauser, *Admin Sec*
▲ EMP: 40
SALES (est): 9.9MM **Privately Held**
WEB: www.industrialtubecorp.com
SIC: 3366 3351 3356 Brass foundry; tubing, copper & copper alloy; nickel

(G-4329)
INNOVATIVE MANUFACTURING INC
198 Us Highway 206 Ste 4 (08844-4138)
PHONE..................908 904-1884
Kevin J Lovell, *President*
Heather Lovell, *Vice Pres*
EMP: 18 EST: 1996
SALES (est): 3.4MM **Privately Held**
SIC: 3541 Machine tools, metal cutting type

(G-4330)
INSTRIDE SHOES LLC
29 Polhemus Dr (08844-1808)
PHONE..................908 874-6670
Erica Werremeyer,
▲ EMP: 20
SQ FT: 8,000
SALES: 13.5MM **Privately Held**
SIC: 3841 Surgical & medical instruments

(G-4331)
INTEGRATED PHOTONICS INC (HQ)
132 Stryker Ln Ste 1 (08844-1937)
PHONE..................908 281-8000
Robert T David, *CEO*
Ron Glass, *President*
Steve Licht, *Vice Pres*
Steven J Licht, *Vice Pres*
▼ EMP: 80 EST: 1999
SQ FT: 22,000
SALES (est): 5.4MM
SALES (corp-wide): 1.3B **Publicly Held**
WEB: www.integratedphotonics.com
SIC: 3827 Optical elements & assemblies, except ophthalmic
PA: Ii-Vi Incorporated
375 Saxonburg Blvd
Saxonburg PA 16056
724 352-4455

(G-4332)
INTEGRATED PHOTONICS INC
132 Stryker Ln Ste 1 (08844-1937)
PHONE..................908 281-8000
Robert Abbott, *Branch Mgr*
EMP: 4
SALES (corp-wide): 1.3B **Publicly Held**
WEB: www.integratedphotonics.com
SIC: 3827 Optical elements & assemblies, except ophthalmic
HQ: Integrated Photonics, Inc.
132 Stryker Ln Ste 1
Hillsborough NJ 08844
908 281-8000

(G-4333)
INTERGANIC FZCO LLC
Also Called: MII Organics
125 Stryker Ln Ste 3 (08844-1938)
PHONE..................224 436-0372
Craig Sirota, *CEO*
▲ EMP: 4 EST: 2014
SQ FT: 3,000
SALES: 1MM **Privately Held**
SIC: 2676 Infant & baby paper products

(G-4334)
J K DESIGN INC
Also Called: J K Print Management
465 Amwell Rd (08844-1207)
PHONE..................908 428-4700
Jerry Kaulius, *President*
Andrea Wolkofsky, *Vice Pres*
Joanna Karausz, *Project Mgr*
Hillary Sica, *Project Mgr*
Nick Guido, *Production*
EMP: 48
SQ FT: 900
SALES (est): 3.6MM **Privately Held**
SIC: 7336 2791 Graphic arts & related design; typesetting

(G-4335)
JOYCE LESLIE INC (PA)
401 Towne Centre Dr (08844-4698)
PHONE..................201 804-7800
Celia Clancy, *CEO*
Peter Left, *CFO*
Hermine Gewirtz, *Treasurer*
◆ EMP: 70 EST: 1947
SQ FT: 45,000
SALES (est): 284MM **Privately Held**
WEB: www.xion.com
SIC: 3087 Custom compound purchased resins

(G-4336)
K B ENTERPRISES OF NEW JERSEY
15 Ilene Ct Ste 1211 (08844-1920)
PHONE..................908 451-5282
Thomas Griffin, *President*
EMP: 4
SQ FT: 1,500
SALES: 900K **Privately Held**
SIC: 3911 Jewelry, precious metal

(G-4337)
KITCHEN DIRECT INC
739 Rte 206 (08844-1530)
PHONE..................908 359-1188
Ronald Tobia, *President*
EMP: 5
SALES (est): 517.4K **Privately Held**
WEB: www.kitchens-direct-nj.com
SIC: 2434 Wood kitchen cabinets

(G-4338)
KWG INDUSTRIES LLC
330 Roycefield Rd Unit B (08844-4148)
PHONE..................908 218-8900
Paul Taylor, *General Mgr*
Oguz Aydogan, *Engineer*
Kurt W Grimm,
EMP: 30
SQ FT: 25,000
SALES (est): 5.6MM **Privately Held**
SIC: 7389 5051 3354 3599 Metal cutting services; aluminum bars, rods, ingots, sheets, pipes, plates, etc.; steel; tubing, metal; aluminum extruded products; machine shop, jobbing & repair

(G-4339)
LIEDL
462 Long Hill Rd (08844-1012)
PHONE..................908 359-8335
EMP: 5
SALES (est): 469.8K **Privately Held**
SIC: 3272 Mfg Concrete Products

(G-4340)
NEWTON BIOPHARMA SOLUTIONS LLC
8 Fine Rd (08844-5268)
PHONE..................908 874-7145
Niya D Bowers, *Principal*
EMP: 5
SALES (est): 394.9K **Privately Held**
SIC: 2834 Pharmaceutical preparations

(G-4341)
NJ PAVER RESTORATIONS LLC
857 Amwell Rd (08844-3902)
PHONE..................732 558-6011
Pamela Mazuch, *Owner*
EMP: 4
SALES (est): 548.6K **Privately Held**
SIC: 3531 Pavers

(G-4342)
NU-STENT TECHNOLOGIES INC
1 Ilene Ct (08844-1916)
PHONE..................732 729-6270
EMP: 4
SALES (est): 260K **Privately Held**
SIC: 3841 Mfg Surgical/Medical Instruments

(G-4343)
ONYX GRAPHICS LLC
115 Stryker Ln Ste 4 (08844-1910)
PHONE..................908 281-0038
Robert Ceceri, *President*
David Perry, *Principal*
EMP: 5

SALES (est): 412.2K **Privately Held**
SIC: 7336 3089 Commercial art & graphic design; corrugated panels, plastic

(G-4344)
PERMADUR INDUSTRIES INC
Also Called: SISSCO DIVISION
186 Route 206 (08844-4123)
P.O. Box 1032, Somerville (08876-1032)
PHONE..........................908 359-9767
William A Schneider, *President*
Bill Schneider Jr, *VP Opers*
▲ **EMP:** 73 **EST:** 1972
SQ FT: 32,000
SALES: 27.9MM **Privately Held**
WEB: www.permadur.com
SIC: 5084 5072 5085 7699 Materials handling machinery; hardware; industrial supplies; construction equipment repair; magnets, permanent: metallic; industrial trucks & tractors

(G-4345)
PREMIUM SERVICE PRINTING
Also Called: B & L Printing Co
46 Old Camplain Rd (08844-4228)
PHONE..........................908 707-1311
Gerry Harris, *President*
EMP: 6
SQ FT: 6,000
SALES (est): 1MM **Privately Held**
SIC: 2752 Commercial printing, offset

(G-4346)
PRETIUM PACKAGING LLC
208 Cougar Ct (08844-4105)
PHONE..........................314 727-8200
EMP: 13
SALES (corp-wide): 141MM **Privately Held**
SIC: 3089 Garbage containers, plastic
HQ: Pretium Packaging, L.L.C.
15450 S Outer Forty Dr St
Chesterfield MO 63017
314 727-8200

(G-4347)
PROSCAPE TECHNOLOGIES INC
14 Dogwood Dr (08844-2516)
PHONE..........................215 441-0300
Timothy Healy, *President*
EMP: 49
SQ FT: 10,000
SALES (est): 5.7MM **Privately Held**
WEB: www.proscape.com
SIC: 7372 Business oriented computer software

(G-4348)
R & R PRINTING & COPY CENTER
46 Old Camplain Rd (08844-4228)
PHONE..........................732 249-9450
Robert Sepe, *President*
Maria Sepe, *Vice Pres*
EMP: 4
SQ FT: 500
SALES (est): 475.1K **Privately Held**
WEB: www.randrprinting.com
SIC: 2759 Screen printing

(G-4349)
R C FINE FOODS INC
139 Stryker Ln (08844-1930)
P.O. Box 236, Belle Mead (08502-0236)
PHONE..........................908 359-5500
Susan Goldman, *President*
Gary Cohen, *Vice Pres*
Jim Boganski, *Opers Staff*
Cathy Shaw, *Purchasing*
Ty Jones, *QC Mgr*
EMP: 70
SQ FT: 40,000
SALES (est): 13.3MM **Privately Held**
WEB: www.rcfinefoods.com
SIC: 2099 5149 2087 2045 Food preparations; groceries & related products; flavoring extracts & syrups; prepared flour mixes & doughs; pickles, sauces & salad dressings

(G-4350)
RB MANUFACTURING LLC
799 Us Highway 206 (08844-1530)
PHONE..........................908 533-2000

Ian Corkhill, *Engineer*
Karen Mintz, *Finance Mgr*
Karen White, *Hum Res Coord*
Rick Bay, *Branch Mgr*
EMP: 250
SALES (corp-wide): 16.1B **Privately Held**
WEB: www.reckittprofessional.com
SIC: 2035 2842 Mustard, prepared (wet); deodorants, nonpersonal; disinfectants, household or industrial plant; laundry cleaning preparations; specialty cleaning preparations
HQ: Rb Manufacturing Llc
399 Interpace Pkwy
Parsippany NJ 07054
973 404-2600

(G-4351)
REDKOH INDUSTRIES INC (PA)
Also Called: Redkoh Datatest Industries
300 Valley Rd (08844-4059)
P.O. Box 801, Belle Mead (08502-0801)
PHONE..........................908 369-1590
Paul Ford, *President*
Belinda Halloran, *General Mgr*
Phil Blockus, *Business Mgr*
John Jannone, *Exec VP*
Robert Prendeville, *Vice Pres*
EMP: 4
SQ FT: 10,000
SALES (est): 4.4MM **Privately Held**
WEB: www.redkoh.com
SIC: 3672 3625 7373 Printed circuit boards; industrial controls: push button, selector switches, pilot; computer systems analysis & design

(G-4352)
RICH DESIGNS
867 Amwell Rd (08844-3902)
PHONE..........................908 369-5035
April Dombey, *Principal*
EMP: 4
SALES (est): 354.2K **Privately Held**
SIC: 7532 5099 3993 Truck painting & lettering; signs, except electric; signs & advertising specialties

(G-4353)
S G A BUSINESS SYSTEMS INC
83 Haverford Ct (08844-5211)
PHONE..........................908 359-4626
Wayne Scarano, *President*
Nancy Spadavecchia, *Business Anlyst*
EMP: 5
SALES (est): 396.5K **Privately Held**
WEB: www.isga.com
SIC: 7374 3571 Data processing service; personal computers (microcomputers)

(G-4354)
SEBASTIAN & KING LTD LBLTY CO
816 Robin Rd (08844-4408)
PHONE..........................908 874-6953
Michael Sultan, *President*
Joanna Witas, *Vice Pres*
▲ **EMP:** 16
SALES: 39.5MM **Privately Held**
SIC: 2099 Sauces: gravy, dressing & dip mixes

(G-4355)
SPECIALTY TUBE FILLING LLC
1 Ilene Ct Bldg 8u6 (08844-1916)
PHONE..........................908 262-2219
Kevin Hagerman, *Mng Member*
EMP: 6
SALES (est): 617.1K **Privately Held**
SIC: 3565 Bottling machinery: filling, capping, labeling

(G-4356)
STERIS CORPORATION
10 Ilene Ct (08844-1922)
PHONE..........................908 904-1317
EMP: 5 **Privately Held**
SIC: 3842 Surgical appliances & supplies
HQ: Steris Corporation
5960 Heisley Rd
Mentor OH 44060
440 354-2600

(G-4357)
STERIS INSTRUMENT MGT SVCS INC
10 Ilene Ct (08844-1922)
PHONE..........................908 904-1317
Christian Mills, *President*
EMP: 4 **Privately Held**
SIC: 3841 Surgical & medical instruments
HQ: Steris Instrument Management Services, Inc.
3316 2nd Ave N
Birmingham AL 35222

(G-4358)
SULTAN FOODS INC
115 Stryker Ln Ste 13 (08844-1910)
P.O. Box 6293 (08844-6293)
PHONE..........................908 874-6953
Michael S Sultan, *President*
John Cummings, *Vice Pres*
EMP: 16
SQ FT: 5,800
SALES: 30MM **Privately Held**
SIC: 2099 Seasonings & spices

(G-4359)
SWISS ORTHOPEDIC INC
188 Us Highway 206 (08844-4123)
PHONE..........................908 874-5522
Peter Seitz, *President*
EMP: 8
SQ FT: 2,500
SALES (est): 978.6K **Privately Held**
SIC: 3842 5999 Prosthetic appliances; orthopedic & prosthesis applications

(G-4360)
THINFILMS INC
15 Ilene Ct Ste 6 (08844-1920)
PHONE..........................908 359-7014
Arshad Mumtaz, *President*
Meryl Seigel, *General Mgr*
Zareen Arshad, *Vice Pres*
Marc Diamond, *Engineer*
EMP: 14
SQ FT: 10,000
SALES: 2MM **Privately Held**
WEB: www.thinfilmsinc.com
SIC: 3674 Thin film circuits

(G-4361)
UAC PACKAGING LLC
330 Roycefield Rd Unit C (08844-4148)
PHONE..........................908 595-6890
Charles Bernius, *Mng Member*
EMP: 5
SALES (est): 430K **Privately Held**
SIC: 3499 Machine bases, metal

(G-4362)
Z SQUARED HG INC
1 Jill Ct Ste 7 (08844-1936)
PHONE..........................908 315-3646
Mehreen Husnain, *Principal*
EMP: 9
SALES (est): 343.2K **Privately Held**
SIC: 3714 Motor vehicle parts & accessories

(G-4363)
ZALA MACHINE CO INC
Also Called: Zala Machine Shop
109 Stryker Ln Ste 11 (08844-1911)
PHONE..........................908 431-9106
Stanislaw Zala, *President*
Elzeieta Zala, *Vice Pres*
EMP: 15
SQ FT: 16,000
SALES (est): 3.5MM **Privately Held**
SIC: 3599 Machine shop, jobbing & repair

Hillsdale
Bergen County

(G-4364)
BUILDING PERFORMANCE EQP INC
80 Broadway Ste 101 (07642-2745)
PHONE..........................201 722-1414
Klas Haglid, *CEO*
EMP: 10
SQ FT: 1,000

SALES (est): 1MM **Privately Held**
WEB: www.bpequip.com
SIC: 3564 3822 Ventilating fans: industrial or commercial; energy cutoff controls, residential or commercial types

(G-4365)
CAROL S MILLER CORPORATION
98 Saddlewood Dr (07642-1364)
PHONE..........................201 406-4578
Carol Schepker, *President*
▲ **EMP:** 4
SQ FT: 2,000
SALES (est): 190K **Privately Held**
SIC: 3171 Women's handbags & purses

(G-4366)
FORNAZOR INTERNATIONAL INC (PA)
455 Hillsdale Ave (07642-2710)
PHONE..........................201 664-4000
John Fornazor, *CEO*
Kevin Sinnott, *President*
◆ **EMP:** 25
SQ FT: 4,500
SALES (est): 25MM **Privately Held**
SIC: 0119 2034 2044 2045 Feeder grains; vegetable flour, meal & powder; rice milling; flours & flour mixes, from purchased flour; soybean oil, cake or meal; intracoastal (freight) transportation

(G-4367)
GENERAL GRAPHICS CORPORATION (PA)
63 Briarcliff Rd (07642-1358)
PHONE..........................201 664-4083
Evelyn F Meyer, *President*
EMP: 4
SALES (est): 833.3K **Privately Held**
SIC: 3841 Blood pressure apparatus

(G-4368)
KEN BAUER INC
Also Called: Ken Bauer & Sons
277 Broadway Ste A (07642-1436)
PHONE..........................201 664-6881
Ken Bauer, *President*
Sandy Martucci, *Treasurer*
Scott Bauer, *Admin Sec*
EMP: 21 **EST:** 1961
SQ FT: 12,000
SALES (est): 2MM **Privately Held**
WEB: www.kenbauer.com
SIC: 1521 1799 2434 2541 General remodeling, single-family houses; new construction, single-family houses; kitchen & bathroom remodeling; wood kitchen cabinets; wood partitions & fixtures

(G-4369)
OROSZLANY LASZLO
Also Called: Apollo Machine Shop
121 Patterson St (07642-2010)
PHONE..........................201 666-2101
EMP: 5
SQ FT: 5,000
SALES (est): 247.2K **Privately Held**
SIC: 5049 3541 3452 3451 Whol Professional Equip Mfg Machine Tool-Cutting Mfg Bolts/Screws/Rivets Mfg Screw Machine Prdts

(G-4370)
TEXX TEAM LLC
589 Hillsdale Ave (07642-2650)
P.O. Box 65, Carlstadt (07072-0065)
PHONE..........................201 289-1039
Teodor Stanchev, *COO*
▼ **EMP:** 23 **EST:** 2016
SQ FT: 3,000
SALES: 1MM
SALES (corp-wide): 2.1MM **Privately Held**
SIC: 2299 Textile mill waste & remnant processing
PA: Green Team Worldwide Recycling Group Limited Liability Company
589 Hillsdale Ave
Hillsdale NJ 07642
201 289-1039

▲ = Import ▼=Export
◆ =Import/Export

(G-4371)
U S LASER CORP
41 Crest Rd (07642-2638)
PHONE....................201 848-9200
Robert Regna, *President*
Eric Fink, *Manager*
EMP: 20
SALES (est): 3.2MM Privately Held
WEB: www.uslasercorp.com
SIC: 3699 Laser systems & equipment

Hillside
Union County

(G-4372)
ALL MERCHANDISE DISPLAY CORP
7 W Shelton Ter (07205-1126)
PHONE....................718 257-2221
Herman Klein, *CEO*
EMP: 30
SALES (est): 1.1MM Privately Held
SIC: 5411 2431 Grocery stores, chain; millwork

(G-4373)
AMERICAN STONE INC
215 Us Highway 22 (07205-1832)
PHONE....................973 318-7707
EMP: 26 Privately Held
SIC: 3281 Marble, building: cut & shaped
PA: American Stone Inc.
215 Us Highway 22
Hillside NJ 07205

(G-4374)
AMERICAN STONE INC (PA)
215 Us Highway 22 (07205-1832)
PHONE....................973 318-7707
Steven Young, *President*
EMP: 14
SALES (est): 3.9MM Privately Held
SIC: 3281 Marble, building: cut & shaped; granite, cut & shaped

(G-4375)
ARCH CROWN INC
460 Hillside Ave Ste 1 (07205-1100)
PHONE....................973 731-6300
Craig Meadow, *President*
Kinga Salierno, *President*
Norman Liebman, *Chairman*
Miriam Corcino, *Sales Staff*
Rose Liebman, *Shareholder*
◆ EMP: 36 EST: 1907
SALES (est): 6.6MM Privately Held
WEB: www.archcrown.com
SIC: 3081 2679 2791 2671 Unsupported plastics film & sheet; tags, paper (unprinted): made from purchased paper; labels, paper: made from purchased material; typesetting; packaging paper & plastics film, coated & laminated

(G-4376)
ARROW ENGINEERING CO INC
260 Pennsylvania Ave (07205-2636)
PHONE....................908 353-5229
Louis Spitzer, *President*
Ray Fluet, *Vice Pres*
Jenny Fluet, *Admin Sec*
EMP: 4 EST: 1920
SQ FT: 9,000
SALES (est): 630.6K Privately Held
WEB: www.arroweng.com
SIC: 3821 3826 Shakers & stirrers; analytical instruments

(G-4377)
ATLAS O LLC
378 Florence Ave (07205-1134)
PHONE....................908 687-9590
Tom Haedrich, *Mng Member*
EMP: 50 EST: 1950
SALES (est): 1.8MM Privately Held
WEB: www.atlaso.com
SIC: 7389 5945 3944 Convention & show services; hobby, toy & game shops; games, toys & children's vehicles

(G-4378)
AWARDS TROPHY COMPANY
611 Us Highway 22 (07205-1916)
PHONE....................908 687-5775
Mary Anne Kilgarriss, *President*
Steve Zall, *General Mgr*
▲ EMP: 7 EST: 1959
SALES (est): 1MM Privately Held
SIC: 3499 3479 Trophies, metal, except silver; engraving jewelry silverware, or metal

(G-4379)
BANNER DESIGN INC
600 N Union Ave Ste 11 (07205-1031)
PHONE....................908 687-5335
Peter Schapira, *President*
Gabriel Bodea, *Terminal Mgr*
Sam Bodea, *Terminal Mgr*
Paula Frederick, *Controller*
Ella Cojocaru, *Asst Mgr*
EMP: 35
SQ FT: 35,000
SALES (est): 3.2MM Privately Held
WEB: www.bannerdesignco.com
SIC: 1799 3993 2541 7336 Sign installation & maintenance; signs & advertising specialties; display fixtures, wood; store fixtures, wood; graphic arts & related design

(G-4380)
BEAU LABEL
385 Hillside Ave (07205-1123)
PHONE....................973 318-7800
Vincent Mela, *Owner*
Chiarina Affronti, *Controller*
Vincent Melapioni, *Executive*
EMP: 60 EST: 2008
SALES (est): 5.9MM Privately Held
SIC: 2241 Labels, woven

(G-4381)
BEAUTY-FILL LLC
1319 N Broad St (07205-2460)
PHONE....................908 353-1600
Gregory Harmon,
Robert Harmon,
Kurt Lueken,
▲ EMP: 30
SQ FT: 120,000
SALES (est): 5.3MM Privately Held
SIC: 3565 5999 5149 Bottling machinery: filling, capping, labeling; toiletries, cosmetics & perfumes; flavourings & fragrances

(G-4382)
BEST AMERICAN HANDS
475 Bloy St (07205-1707)
PHONE....................203 247-2028
Nitzy Cohen, *Mng Member*
EMP: 27
SALES (est): 853K Privately Held
SIC: 2599 Furniture & fixtures

(G-4383)
BRISTOL-MYERS SQUIBB COMPANY
171 Long Ave (07205-2350)
PHONE....................212 546-4000
Shuyan Du, *Branch Mgr*
EMP: 40
SALES (corp-wide): 22.5B Publicly Held
WEB: www.bms.com
SIC: 8731 2844 2834 Commercial physical research; toilet preparations; drugs acting on the cardiovascular system, except diagnostic
PA: Bristol-Myers Squibb Company
430 E 29th St Fl 14
New York NY 10016
212 546-4000

(G-4384)
CAMEO NOVELTY & PEN CORP
400 Hillside Ave (07205-1117)
PHONE....................973 923-1600
Sol Oberlander, *President*
▲ EMP: 20
SQ FT: 12,000
SALES (est): 2.5MM Privately Held
SIC: 3951 Pens & mechanical pencils

(G-4385)
CARTOLITH GROUP
28 Sager Pl (07205-1014)
PHONE....................908 624-9833
Roy Sayroo, *Manager*
▼ EMP: 5
SALES (est): 484.4K Privately Held
SIC: 2679 Paper products, converted

(G-4386)
CERTIFIED PROCESSING CORP
184 Us Highway 22 (07205-1895)
PHONE....................973 923-5200
Paul P Iacono, *President*
Kenneth P Iacono, *Treasurer*
EMP: 3 EST: 1960
SQ FT: 36,000
SALES: 1MM Privately Held
SIC: 2833 Caffeine & derivatives

(G-4387)
COOPER ALLOY CORPORATION
201 Sweetland Ave Ste 1 (07205-1756)
PHONE....................908 688-4120
Gerald Lewis, *President*
Stuart F Cooper, *Vice Pres*
John Brodeur, *Admin Sec*
EMP: 11 EST: 1931
SQ FT: 40,000
SALES (est): 2.2MM Privately Held
SIC: 5084 3561 Pumps & pumping equipment; industrial pumps & parts

(G-4388)
DESIGN FACTORY NJ INC
1210 Liberty Ave (07205-2023)
PHONE....................908 964-8833
Johnathon Simons, *Owner*
EMP: 4
SQ FT: 2,000
SALES (est): 529.6K Privately Held
SIC: 2752 7336 Commercial printing, offset; graphic arts & related design

(G-4389)
DIVERSIFIED DISPLAY PDTS LLC
Also Called: D D P
777 Ramsey Ave (07205-1011)
P.O. Box 913 (07205-0913)
PHONE....................908 686-2200
David Rosen,
EMP: 25
SQ FT: 5,600
SALES (est): 13.8MM Privately Held
WEB: www.ddpmsc.com
SIC: 5199 3577 Foams & rubber; printers & plotters

(G-4390)
DORAN SLING AND ASSEMBLY CORP
1285 Central Ave Ste 2 (07205-2645)
PHONE....................908 355-1101
Barry Lemberg, *President*
Michael Cuccinello, *Vice Pres*
EMP: 9
SQ FT: 60,000
SALES (est): 4.6MM Privately Held
SIC: 5051 3496 Rope, wire (not insulated); cable, wire; slings, lifting: made from purchased wire

(G-4391)
FLUETS CORP
260 Pennsylvania Ave (07205-2696)
PHONE....................908 353-5229
Ray Fluet, *President*
Raymond Fluet, *President*
Angie Fluet, *Vice Pres*
EMP: 30
SQ FT: 9,000
SALES (est): 5.3MM Privately Held
WEB: www.fluetscorp.com
SIC: 3599 Machine shop, jobbing & repair

(G-4392)
FREED FOODS INC
Also Called: Nurturme
225 Long Ave Ste 15 (07205-2356)
PHONE....................512 829-5535
Caroline Freedman, *CEO*
Lauren De La Rosa, *COO*
Sarah Jarvis, *Manager*
EMP: 6 EST: 2010

SALES (est): 2.7MM Privately Held
SIC: 2032 Baby foods, including meats: packaged in cans, jars, etc.

(G-4393)
G & H SHEET METAL WORKS INC
Also Called: G & H Metal Product
1423 Chestnut Ave (07205-1179)
PHONE....................973 923-1100
Eric H Heide, *President*
EMP: 9 EST: 1938
SQ FT: 18,000
SALES: 1.2MM Privately Held
WEB: www.ghsmw.com
SIC: 3446 3821 2599 Architectural metalwork; laboratory apparatus & furniture; factory furniture & fixtures

(G-4394)
GOLDEN METAL PRODUCTS CORP
100 Hoffman Pl Ste 1 (07205-1000)
PHONE....................973 399-1157
Thomas Abella, *President*
EMP: 41 EST: 1949
SQ FT: 16,000
SALES (est): 5.4MM Privately Held
WEB: www.goldenmetal.com
SIC: 3444 3469 Sheet metalwork; metal stampings

(G-4395)
H & H SWISS SCREW MACHINE PR
Also Called: H&H Swiss
1478 Chestnut Ave (07205-1174)
PHONE....................908 688-6390
Darryl Stacy, *President*
Diane Lucas, *Corp Secy*
John Auburger, *Opers Mgr*
Michael Jaffe, *QC Mgr*
EMP: 48 EST: 1943
SQ FT: 28,500
SALES (est): 11.5MM Privately Held
WEB: www.hhswiss.com
SIC: 3451 Screw machine products

(G-4396)
HERSHEY INDUSTRIES INC
1209 Central Ave (07205-2613)
PHONE....................908 353-3344
Henry Herbst, *President*
Miriam Herbst, *Corp Secy*
David Rubin, *Vice Pres*
EMP: 12 EST: 1975
SQ FT: 115,000
SALES (est): 1.1MM Privately Held
SIC: 2673 Plastic bags: made from purchased materials

(G-4397)
HILLSIDE BEVERAGE PACKING LLC
5 Evans Terminal (07205-2406)
PHONE....................908 353-6773
Sheree Linker, *Mng Member*
EMP: 8
SALES (est): 933.7K Privately Held
SIC: 2086 Soft drinks: packaged in cans, bottles, etc.

(G-4398)
HILLSIDE CANDY LLC (PA)
35 Hillside Ave (07205-1833)
PHONE....................973 926-2300
Ted Cohen, *President*
Henry Adamkowski, *Plant Mgr*
Ray Laconte, *CFO*
Dan Moore, *Manager*
Joanne Delvescovo, *IT/INT Sup*
▼ EMP: 10
SQ FT: 15,000
SALES (est): 6MM Privately Held
WEB: www.hillsidecandy.com
SIC: 2064 Candy & other confectionery products

(G-4399)
HILLSIDE PLASTICS CORPORATION
125 Long Ave (07205-2350)
P.O. Box 609 (07205-0609)
PHONE....................973 923-2700
Harold Kaufman, *President*

Maria Silva, *VP Business*
Karen Triebenbacher, *Sales Staff*
EMP: 60
SQ FT: 65,500
SALES (est): 22.5MM **Privately Held**
WEB: www.hillsideplasticscorp.com
SIC: 3081 Plastic film & sheet

(G-4400)
INB MANHATTAN DRUG
COMPANY INC (HQ)
225 Long Ave Ste 15 (07205-2356)
P.O. Box 278 (07205-0278)
PHONE....................973 926-0816
E Gerald Kay, *Chairman*
Christina Kay, *Vice Pres*
Riva Sheppard, *Vice Pres*
Dina Masi, *CFO*
Neil Reigrod, *Accounting Dir*
▼ **EMP:** 53
SQ FT: 40,000
SALES (est): 19.2MM
SALES (corp-wide): 49.9MM **Publicly
Held**
WEB: www.chemintl.com
SIC: 2834 Vitamin preparations
PA: Integrated Biopharma, Inc.
225 Long Ave Ste 13
Hillside NJ 07205
888 319-6962

(G-4401)
INB MANHATTAN DRUG
COMPANY INC
210 Route 22 (07205)
PHONE....................973 926-0816
EMP: 60
SALES (corp-wide): 49.9MM **Publicly
Held**
SIC: 2834 Pharmaceutical preparations
HQ: Inb Manhattan Drug Company, Inc.
225 Long Ave Ste 15
Hillside NJ 07205
973 926-0816

(G-4402)
INB MANHATTAN DRUG
COMPANY INC
225 Long Ave Ste 6 (07205-2356)
PHONE....................973 926-0816
EMP: 23
SALES (corp-wide): 49.9MM **Publicly
Held**
SIC: 2834 Vitamin preparations
HQ: Inb Manhattan Drug Company, Inc.
225 Long Ave Ste 15
Hillside NJ 07205
973 926-0816

(G-4403)
INTEGRATED BIOPHARMA INC
(PA)
225 Long Ave Ste 13 (07205-2368)
PHONE....................888 319-6962
E Gerald Kay, *Ch of Bd*
Christina Kay, *Co-CEO*
Riva Sheppard, *Co-CEO*
Dina L Masi, *CFO*
Dina Masi, *CFO*
EMP: 33
SQ FT: 76,161
SALES: 49.9MM **Publicly Held**
WEB: www.ibiopharma.com
SIC: 2834 Vitamin, nutrient & hematinic
preparations for human use

(G-4404)
INTERNATIONAL TOOL & MCH
LLC
Also Called: ITM
446 Hillside Ave (07205-1118)
PHONE....................908 687-5580
Chris Hoeker, *President*
▲ **EMP:** 5 **EST:** 1967
SQ FT: 12,000
SALES (est): 370K **Privately Held**
SIC: 3451 Screw machine products

(G-4405)
J R ENGINEERING & MACHINE
663 Ramsey Ave (07205-1009)
PHONE....................908 810-6300
Joseph E Kloss, *President*
Andrew Wakeman, *Vice Pres*
F Joseph Kilroy, *Director*

EMP: 10
SQ FT: 15,000
SALES: 1.6MM **Privately Held**
SIC: 3599 Machine shop, jobbing & repair

(G-4406)
JOMEL INDUSTRIES INC
140 Central Ave Ste 1 (07205-2377)
PHONE....................973 282-0300
Phillip Iuliano, *President*
Jeff Spitz, *Vice Pres*
◆ **EMP:** 10
SQ FT: 20,000
SALES (est): 1.3MM **Privately Held**
WEB: www.jomel.net
SIC: 2515 5712 2296 Mattresses & bed-
springs; mattresses; tire cord & fabrics

(G-4407)
JOMEL SEAMS REASONABLE
LLC (PA)
Also Called: J S R
140 Cent Ave (07205)
PHONE....................973 282-0300
Phil Iuliano, *President*
Jeffrey Spitz, *Vice Pres*
EMP: 14
SQ FT: 65,000
SALES (est): 16.4MM **Privately Held**
SIC: 2515 7389 Mattresses & bedsprings;
sewing contractor

(G-4408)
K & A ARCHITECTURAL MET GL
LLC
766b Ramsey Ave (07205-1039)
P.O. Box 544, Oceanport (07757-0544)
PHONE....................908 687-0247
Allen Jackson,
Kimberly Demott,
EMP: 15 **EST:** 2000
SQ FT: 3,000
SALES (est): 3.8MM **Privately Held**
SIC: 3446 Architectural metalwork

(G-4409)
LALLY-PAK INC
1209 Central Ave (07205-2613)
PHONE....................908 351-4141
Henry Herbst, *President*
▲ **EMP:** 75
SQ FT: 120,000
SALES (est): 18.8MM **Privately Held**
WEB: www.lallypak.com
SIC: 3081 2759 2671 Packing materials,
plastic sheet; bags, plastic: printing; plas-
tic film, coated or laminated for packaging

(G-4410)
LEOPARD INC
1 Montgomery St (07205-1106)
PHONE....................908 964-3600
Wendy Chen, *President*
Mark Merezio, *Vice Pres*
◆ **EMP:** 11 **EST:** 2000
SQ FT: 11,000
SALES (est): 2.3MM **Privately Held**
SIC: 3011 Truck or bus tires, pneumatic

(G-4411)
LOVE PALLET LLC
460 Mundet Pl (07205-1115)
P.O. Box 774 (07205-0774)
PHONE....................908 964-3385
Brenda Bardoza, *Managing Prtnr*
Susanne Lanzafama, *Managing Prtnr*
EMP: 7 **EST:** 1977
SQ FT: 700
SALES (est): 1.1MM **Privately Held**
WEB: www.lovepallet.com
SIC: 2448 Pallets, wood

(G-4412)
M DEITZ & SONS INC
Also Called: Deitz, Michael & Sons
490 Hillside Ave (07205-1119)
PHONE....................908 686-8800
Ken Deitz, *President*
Steve Deitz, *Vice Pres*
▲ **EMP:** 15 **EST:** 1921
SQ FT: 45,000
SALES (est): 2.5MM **Privately Held**
WEB: www.mdeitz.com
SIC: 2599 Bar, restaurant & cafeteria furni-
ture

(G-4413)
M S C PAPER PRODUCTS CORP
777 Ramsey Ave (07205-1011)
P.O. Box 913 (07205-0913)
PHONE....................908 686-2200
Edward Brody, *Vice Pres*
EMP: 20 **EST:** 1938
SQ FT: 34,000
SALES (est): 2MM **Privately Held**
SIC: 2679 2631 Gift wrap & novelties,
paper; paperboard mills

(G-4414)
MARK RONALD ASSOCIATES
INC (PA)
Also Called: R M A
1227 Central Ave (07205-2613)
P.O. Box 776 (07205-0776)
PHONE....................908 558-0011
Leslie J Satz, *CEO*
Michael Satz, *President*
Charles Riotto, *Vice Pres*
Ronald M Satz, *Vice Pres*
Howard Katuna, *Controller*
◆ **EMP:** 55
SQ FT: 80,000
SALES: 40MM **Privately Held**
WEB: www.ronaldmark.com
SIC: 3081 5162 Polyvinyl film & sheet;
plastics materials

(G-4415)
MCINTOSH INDUSTRIES INC
Also Called: Electro Mechanical Tech
676 Ramsey Ave (07205-1023)
PHONE....................908 688-7475
Peter McIntosh, *President*
▲ **EMP:** 21
SALES (est): 2.1MM **Privately Held**
WEB: www.mcintoshindustries.com
SIC: 7694 Electric motor repair

(G-4416)
MPM DISPLAY INC
1 Us Hwy Rt 22 W (07205)
PHONE....................973 374-3477
Michael A Bertko, *President*
EMP: 7
SQ FT: 10,762
SALES (est): 750K **Privately Held**
SIC: 2542 3496 Stands, merchandise dis-
play: except wood; miscellaneous fabri-
cated wire products

(G-4417)
NATURES RULE LLC
1319 N Broad St (07205-2460)
PHONE....................888 819-4220
Mohamad Hammod, *Mng Member*
▼ **EMP:** 11
SALES (est): 1.5MM **Privately Held**
SIC: 2834 Vitamin, nutrient & hematinic
preparations for human use; vitamin
preparations

(G-4418)
NEW YORK BLACKBOARD OF
NJ INC
83 Us Highway 22 (07205-1884)
PHONE....................973 926-1600
Henry Ruggiero, *President*
Kevin Ruggiero, *Sales Mgr*
Regina Ruggiero, *Admin Sec*
EMP: 6 **EST:** 1958
SQ FT: 12,000
SALES (est): 900K **Privately Held**
WEB: www.nyblackboard.com
SIC: 2493 Bulletin boards, cork; bulletin
boards, wood

(G-4419)
OASIS TRADING CO INC (DH)
Also Called: Aak Foodservice
635 Ramsey Ave (07205-1032)
PHONE....................908 964-0477
Anthony Alves, *President*
Liliana Ferreira, *Prdtn Mgr*
Vicky Veloso, *Buyer*
Brian Hennessy, *Sales Staff*
Jon Greenberg, *Manager*
◆ **EMP:** 150 **EST:** 1975
SQ FT: 200,000

SALES (est): 58.3MM
SALES (corp-wide): 3B **Privately Held**
WEB: www.oasisfoodsco.com
SIC: 2079 2035 4783 2084 Cooking oils,
except corn: vegetable refined; dressings,
salad: raw & cooked (except dry mixes);
mayonnaise; packing goods for shipping;
wines, brandy & brandy spirits; wines
HQ: Aak Sweden Ab
Vastra Kajen
Karlshamn 374 3
454 820-00

(G-4420)
POWER PHOTO CORP (PA)
Also Called: Powers Powershot Photo
40 Montgomery St (07205-1107)
PHONE....................732 200-1645
Louis Assoulin, *CEO*
▼ **EMP:** 60
SQ FT: 40,000
SALES (est): 16.5MM **Privately Held**
SIC: 3861 Photographic equipment & sup-
plies

(G-4421)
PTY LIGHTING LLC (PA)
Also Called: Pwg Lighting
100 Hoffman Pl (07205-1033)
PHONE....................855 303-4500
Joe Espinosa, *President*
▲ **EMP:** 8
SALES (est): 2.1MM **Privately Held**
SIC: 1731 3645 Lighting contractor; chan-
deliers, residential

(G-4422)
QUALITY FILMS CORP
500 Hillside Ave (07205-1119)
PHONE....................718 246-7150
Soloman Phillips, *President*
Moses Friedman, *Vice Pres*
▲ **EMP:** 5
SALES (est): 895.1K **Privately Held**
WEB: www.qualityshrinkfilm.com
SIC: 3861 Cameras & related equipment

(G-4423)
RAMCO EQUIPMENT CORP
Also Called: Randall Manufacturing Co
32 Montgomery St (07205-1107)
PHONE....................908 687-6700
Fred Randall, *President*
Jenny Ranall, *Vice Pres*
Oretta Tigges, *Materials Mgr*
▲ **EMP:** 22
SQ FT: 10,000
SALES: 671.7K **Privately Held**
SIC: 3559 Metal finishing equipment for
plating, etc.

(G-4424)
RANDALL MANUFACTURING CO
INC
Also Called: Ramco
32 Montgomery St (07205-1192)
PHONE....................973 746-2111
EMP: 20 **EST:** 1920
SQ FT: 20,000
SALES (est): 6MM **Privately Held**
SIC: 5072 3589 Whol Hardware Mfg Serv-
ice Industry Machinery

(G-4425)
RELIABLE PALLET SERVICES
LLC (PA)
460 Hillside Ave Ste 1 (07205-1100)
PHONE....................973 900-2260
EMP: 5
SALES (est): 1.4MM **Privately Held**
SIC: 2448 Pallets, wood

(G-4426)
SINGE CORPORATION
Also Called: Addressing Machine & Sup Div
1290 Central Ave (07205-2615)
PHONE....................908 289-7900
Herbert J Singe, *President*
Margaret Singe, *Treasurer*
▲ **EMP:** 9
SQ FT: 28,000
SALES (est): 1.1MM **Privately Held**
SIC: 5044 7629 3546 Mailing machines;
electronic equipment repair; power-driven
handtools

(G-4427)
SNAPCO MANUFACTURING CORP
140 Central Ave Ste 1 (07205-2377)
PHONE.................................973 282-0300
Arnold A Spitz, *Ch of Bd*
Jeffrey Spitz, *President*
Phillip Iuliano, *Vice Pres*
▲ EMP: 25 EST: 1941
SQ FT: 34,000
SALES (est): 3.9MM **Privately Held**
SIC: 2241 3965 3552 Fabric tapes; trimmings, textile; zipper; fasteners, snap; finishing machinery, textile

(G-4428)
SURVIVOR II INC
Also Called: Survirvor Windows II
1239 Central Ave (07205-2613)
PHONE.................................908 353-1155
Antonio Casas, *President*
EMP: 20
SQ FT: 14,000
SALES: 3MM **Privately Held**
SIC: 3089 Windows, plastic

(G-4429)
SUSAN MILLS INC (PA)
1285 Central Ave (07205-2645)
PHONE.................................908 355-1400
Luis Lee, *President*
▲ EMP: 10
SQ FT: 55,000 **Privately Held**
WEB: www.susanmills.com
SIC: 2257 Pile fabrics, circular knit

(G-4430)
THOMAS ERECTORS INC
630 Ramsey Ave (07205-1042)
PHONE.................................908 810-0030
Jeffrey Lukowiak, *Principal*
EMP: 8
SALES (est): 950.4K **Privately Held**
SIC: 3442 Window & door frames

(G-4431)
THOMAS MANUFACTURING INC
630 Ramsey Ave Ste 1 (07205-1042)
PHONE.................................908 810-0030
Thomas Lukowiak, *President*
Jeff Lukowiak, *COO*
Mitch Kapsaskis, *Vice Pres*
Jerry Doherty, *VP Finance*
▲ EMP: 20
SALES (est): 6.4MM **Privately Held**
WEB: www.thomasmfg.com
SIC: 3442 Window & door frames

(G-4432)
UNION BEVERAGE PACKERS LLC
600 N Union Ave Ste 7 (07205-1030)
PHONE.................................908 206-9111
Yaron Gohar, *CEO*
Dwight Deming, *Vice Pres*
Roy Gohar,
◆ EMP: 170
SALES (est): 33.9MM **Privately Held**
SIC: 2086 Soft drinks: packaged in cans, bottles, etc.

(G-4433)
UNIQUE WIRE WEAVING CO INC
762 Ramsey Ave (07205-1094)
PHONE.................................908 688-4600
Ken Beyer, *President*
Alex Cedeno, *Engineer*
Bill Bard, *Sales Executive*
Mary A Gibki, *Office Mgr*
▲ EMP: 20 EST: 1946
SQ FT: 10,000
SALES (est): 6MM **Privately Held**
WEB: www.uniquewire.com
SIC: 3496 3643 Woven wire products; current-carrying wiring devices

(G-4434)
UNITED FORMS FINISHING CORP
Also Called: Uff
1413 Chestnut Ave Ste 2 (07205-1132)
PHONE.................................908 687-0494
Elizabeth Demkin, *President*
Liz Demkin, *Vice Pres*
Paul A Dick Jr, *Vice Pres*

Paul Dick, *Vice Pres*
Janice Phemsint, *Human Res Dir*
EMP: 13
SQ FT: 30,000
SALES (est): 2.3MM **Privately Held**
WEB: www.uffcorp.net
SIC: 7331 2759 Mailing service; laser printing

(G-4435)
URBAN STATE
209 Hollywood Ave (07205-2446)
PHONE.................................646 836-4311
Jonathan Hunter,
Albertha Hunter,
EMP: 5
SALES (est): 216.1K **Privately Held**
SIC: 2111 7389 Cigarettes;

(G-4436)
VANTON PUMP & EQUIPMENT CORP
201 Sweetland Ave Ste 1 (07205-1756)
PHONE.................................908 688-4120
Larry Lewis, *President*
John Brodeur, *Corp Secy*
Kenneth Comerford, *Vice Pres*
Stuart Cooper, *Vice Pres*
Barbara Riscinti, *Treasurer*
▲ EMP: 39 EST: 1948
SQ FT: 30,000
SALES (est): 10MM **Privately Held**
WEB: www.vanton.com
SIC: 3561 Pump jacks & other pumping equipment

(G-4437)
WIREWORKS CORPORATION
380 Hillside Ave (07205-1339)
PHONE.................................908 686-7400
Gerald Krulewicz, *President*
Larry J Williams, *CFO*
Larry Williams, *CFO*
Richard Chilvers, *Sales Mgr*
EMP: 22
SQ FT: 4,500
SALES (est): 4.4MM **Privately Held**
WEB: www.wireworks.com
SIC: 3679 3672 3663 3651 Electronic circuits; printed circuit boards; radio & TV communications equipment; household audio & video equipment; nonferrous wiredrawing & insulating

(G-4438)
YALE HOOK & EYE CO INC
33 Race St (07205-2316)
PHONE.................................973 824-1440
Ann Roseman, *President*
Morton A Roseman, *Vice Pres*
▲ EMP: 10 EST: 1914
SQ FT: 54,000
SALES (est): 4.2MM **Privately Held**
WEB: www.snaptape.com
SIC: 3965 Fasteners, buttons, needles & pins

Ho Ho Kus
Bergen County

(G-4439)
ATOMIZING SYSTEMS INC
1 Hollywood Ave Ste 1 # 1 (07423-1438)
PHONE.................................201 447-1222
Michael Elkas, *President*
Thomas Pagliaroni, *Purchasing*
John Zhang, *Info Tech Dir*
▼ EMP: 14
SQ FT: 9,200
SALES (est): 2.6MM **Privately Held**
WEB: www.coldfog.com
SIC: 3822 3585 Air conditioning & refrigeration controls; refrigeration & heating equipment

(G-4440)
HO-HO-KUS SMKED DELICACIES LLC
320 Enos Pl (07423-1505)
PHONE.................................201 445-1677
David Feeney, *Principal*
EMP: 4 EST: 2010

SALES (est): 277.6K **Privately Held**
SIC: 2091 Fish, smoked

(G-4441)
JMP PRESS INC
Also Called: Minuteman Press
19 Sheridan Ave (07423-3507)
PHONE.................................201 444-0236
Prebin Karlsmark, *President*
Maja Karlsmark, *Vice Pres*
EMP: 6
SALES (est): 808.3K **Privately Held**
SIC: 2752 2791 2789 Commercial printing, lithographic; typesetting; bookbinding & related work

---

Hoboken
Hudson County

(G-4442)
A A SAYIA & COMPANY INC
1 Newark St Ste 29 (07030-5698)
P.O. Box M9 (07030-0009)
PHONE.................................201 659-1179
Garret Sayia, *President*
Peter Sayia, *Vice Pres*
Edward A Deep, *Treasurer*
◆ EMP: 8 EST: 1917
SQ FT: 2,000
SALES (est): 2.6MM **Privately Held**
WEB: www.aasayia.com
SIC: 5149 2087 Spices & seasonings; extracts, flavoring

(G-4443)
AF PHARMA LLC
1500 Garden St Apt 2i (07030-4493)
PHONE.................................908 769-7040
Lars Peitersen,
▲ EMP: 5
SALES (est): 780.7K **Privately Held**
SIC: 2834 Pharmaceutical preparations

(G-4444)
BURGISS GROUP LLC
111 River St Fl 10th (07030-5773)
PHONE.................................201 427-9600
Brian Schmid, *Managing Dir*
Fuhchun Tsay, *Controller*
Victor Kovatch, *Financial Analy*
Kagiso Rhenoster, *Financial Analy*
Alice Rutere, *Financial Analy*
EMP: 55
SQ FT: 30,000
SALES (est): 9.1MM **Privately Held**
WEB: www.burgiss.com
SIC: 7379 7372 7371 Computer related consulting services; prepackaged software; computer software development

(G-4445)
C M H HELE-SHAW INC
Also Called: Cunningham Marine Hydraulics
1714 Willow Ave (07030-3414)
PHONE.................................201 974-0570
EMP: 12
SQ FT: 10,000
SALES (est): 93.6K
SALES (corp-wide): 670.5K **Privately Held**
SIC: 3069 Mfg Hele-Shaw Pumps & Parts
PA: Cunningham Marine Hydraulics Co, Inc
1714 Willow Ave
Hoboken NJ
201 792-0500

(G-4446)
CARPATHIAN INDUSTRIES LLC
51 Newark St Ste 508 (07030-4543)
PHONE.................................201 386-5356
Paul Lichstein,
▲ EMP: 14
SQ FT: 1,500
SALES: 14.5MM **Privately Held**
WEB: www.carpathianinc.com
SIC: 3491 Industrial valves

(G-4447)
CHAMBORD PRINTS INC
38 Jackson St (07030-6072)
PHONE.................................201 795-2007
Dennis Shah, *President*
Mike Desai, *Admin Sec*

▲ EMP: 25 EST: 1945
SQ FT: 70,000
SALES (est): 2.5MM **Privately Held**
SIC: 2759 Screen printing

(G-4448)
COLLEGE SPUN MEDIA INC
95 River St Ste 408 (07030-5612)
PHONE.................................973 945-5040
Matthew Lombardi, *President*
EMP: 6
SALES: 900K **Privately Held**
SIC: 2741

(G-4449)
COSMOPOLITAN FOOD GROUP INC
50 Harrison St Ste 208 (07030-6087)
PHONE.................................908 998-1818
Baris Kantarci, *President*
◆ EMP: 5
SQ FT: 20,000
SALES: 15MM **Privately Held**
SIC: 5149 2079 2099 2035 Cooking oils; olive oil; vinegar; pickles, sauces & salad dressings

(G-4450)
D KWITMAN & SON INC (PA)
1015 Adams St (07030-2147)
PHONE.................................201 798-5511
Harold Kwitman, *President*
▲ EMP: 10 EST: 1934
SQ FT: 2,500
SALES (est): 4.8MM **Privately Held**
WEB: www.dkwitman.com
SIC: 5023 2391 2392 Curtains; curtains, window: made from purchased materials; bedspreads & bed sets: made from purchased materials

(G-4451)
FULL HOUSE PRINTING INC
303 1st St (07030-2433)
PHONE.................................201 798-7073
Rose Capaptorto, *President*
Larry Weiss, *President*
EMP: 5
SQ FT: 1,000
SALES: 250K **Privately Held**
WEB: www.fullhouseprinting.com
SIC: 2752 Commercial printing, offset

(G-4452)
GENDELL ASSOICATES PA
Also Called: Folditure
1031 Bloomfield St (07030-5203)
PHONE.................................201 656-4498
Alexander Gendell, *Principal*
EMP: 5 EST: 2005
SQ FT: 2,000
SALES (est): 100K **Privately Held**
SIC: 2519 Furniture, household: glass, fiberglass & plastic

(G-4453)
HARRISON SCOTT PBLICATIONS INC
Also Called: Asset Backed Alert
5 Marine View Plz Ste 400 (07030-5722)
PHONE.................................201 659-1700
Andrew Albert, *Ch of Bd*
Daniel Cowles, *President*
Thomas J Foderaro, *Editor*
Bob Mura, *Editor*
Michelle Lebowitz, *Opers Dir*
EMP: 34
SQ FT: 7,200
SALES: 19MM **Privately Held**
WEB: www.abalert.com
SIC: 2741 Newsletter publishing

(G-4454)
HOBOKEN EXECUTIVE ART INC
Also Called: Right Angle
320 Washington St Ste A (07030-4831)
PHONE.................................201 420-8262
Toni Sullivan, *President*
EMP: 6
SQ FT: 1,000
SALES (est): 685.7K **Privately Held**
SIC: 2499 8748 Picture & mirror frames, wood; business consulting

(G-4455)
HOBOKEN MARY LTD LIABILITY CO
1109 Washington St Apt 2 (07030-5327)
PHONE...............................201 234-9910
Ryan Grace, *Mng Member*
EMP: 4 EST: 2014
SALES (est): 155.5K **Privately Held**
SIC: 2085 5182 Cocktails, alcoholic; cocktails, alcoholic: premixed

(G-4456)
HORPHAG RESEARCH (USA) INC
5 Marine View Plz Ste 403 (07030-5722)
PHONE...............................201 459-0300
Bruce Nadler, *President*
Joel Melillo, *Vice Pres*
Peter Rohdewald, *Research*
Frank Assumma, *Mktg Dir*
EMP: 4 EST: 2010
SQ FT: 2,100
SALES (est): 16.2MM **Privately Held**
SIC: 2023 Dietary supplements, dairy & non-dairy based

(G-4457)
INTANGIBLE LABS INC
333 River St Apt 1144 (07030-5873)
PHONE...............................917 375-1301
Nader Al-Naji, *CEO*
EMP: 13
SALES (est): 300K
SALES (corp-wide): 570.5K **Privately Held**
SIC: 7372 Business oriented computer software
PA: Intangible Labs Llc
333 River St Apt 1144
Hoboken NJ 07030
917 375-1301

(G-4458)
JARDEN LLC (HQ)
Also Called: Newell Brands
221 River St (07030-5989)
PHONE...............................201 610-6600
Joe Cunningham, *Sales Staff*
◆ EMP: 20
SALES (est): 7.6B
SALES (corp-wide): 8.6B **Publicly Held**
WEB: www.jarden.com
SIC: 3089 3634 3631 Plastic containers, except foam; plastic kitchenware, tableware & houseware; electric housewares & fans; electric household cooking appliances; electric household cooking utensils; personal electrical appliances; barbecues, grills & braziers (outdoor cooking)
PA: Newell Brands Inc.
221 River St Ste 13
Hoboken NJ 07030
201 610-6600

(G-4459)
JOHN B STETSON COMPANY
86 Hudson St (07030-5617)
PHONE...............................212 563-1848
Paul Guilden, *Ch of Bd*
Steve Kantor, *President*
Richard Adler, *COO*
Jean Ebert, *Controller*
Kinao LI Tan, *Director*
EMP: 5
SQ FT: 900
SALES (est): 510K **Privately Held**
SIC: 5611 2353 Clothing, men's & boys': everyday, except suits & sportswear; hats, caps & millinery

(G-4460)
JOHN WILEY & SONS INC (PA)
111 River St Ste 2000 (07030-5790)
PHONE...............................201 748-6000
Jesse C Wiley, *Ch of Bd*
Brian A Napack, *President*
Aref Matin, *Exec VP*
Gary M Rinck, *Exec VP*
Judy Verses, *Exec VP*
◆ EMP: 100
SQ FT: 294,000
SALES: 1.8B **Publicly Held**
WEB: www.wiley.com
SIC: 2731 2721 Textbooks: publishing only, not printed on site; books: publishing only; statistical reports (periodicals): publishing only; trade journals: publishing only, not printed on site

(G-4461)
JOHN WILEY & SONS INC
111 River St Ste 4 (07030-5773)
PHONE...............................201 748-6000
Pamela Reh, *Manager*
EMP: 6
SALES (corp-wide): 1.8B **Publicly Held**
WEB: www.wiley.com
SIC: 2731 Textbooks: publishing only, not printed on site
PA: John Wiley & Sons, Inc.
111 River St Ste 2000
Hoboken NJ 07030
201 748-6000

(G-4462)
JOSEMI INC
1201 Hudson St Apt 216s (07030-7408)
PHONE...............................917 710-2110
Jonaf Tamir, *President*
EMP: 5
SALES (est): 338.8K **Privately Held**
SIC: 2387 Apparel belts

(G-4463)
L&W AUDIO/VIDEO INC
Also Called: Lowell / Edwards
1034 Clinton St Apt 101 (07030-3166)
PHONE...............................212 980-2862
Lowell Kaps, *President*
EMP: 7
SQ FT: 1,600
SALES: 1.2MM **Privately Held**
WEB: www.lowelledwards.com
SIC: 2511 2517 5031 5064 Wood household furniture; wood television & radio cabinets; lumber, plywood & millwork; kitchen cabinets; electrical appliances; television & radio; electrical work; sound equipment specialization; wood kitchen cabinets

(G-4464)
LIQUID HOLDINGS GROUP INC
111 River St Ste 1204 (07030-5777)
PHONE...............................212 293-1836
Peter R Kent, *CEO*
Victor Simone Jr, *Ch of Bd*
Robert O'Boyle, *Exec VP*
James Lee, *Officer*
Jose Ibietatorremendia, *Admin Sec*
EMP: 53
SALES: 4.8MM **Privately Held**
SIC: 7372 Business oriented computer software

(G-4465)
MANHATTAN NEON SIGN CORP
650 Newark St (07030-6009)
PHONE...............................212 714-0430
Marylin Tomasso, *President*
Pat Tomasso, *Vice Pres*
John Davi, *Supervisor*
EMP: 13
SALES (est): 1.7MM **Privately Held**
SIC: 3993 Neon signs

(G-4466)
MATISS INC (PA)
Also Called: City Window Fashions
51 Harrison St Fl 5 (07030-6038)
PHONE...............................201 648-0002
Mihaela Kalnins Cuceu, *President*
EMP: 20
SALES (est): 6.7MM **Privately Held**
SIC: 2591 Drapery hardware & blinds & shades

(G-4467)
MOSAIC GOLF LLC
900 Monroe St Apt 312 (07030-6245)
PHONE...............................201 906-6136
John Murphy, *Mng Member*
EMP: 6
SALES (est): 135.3K **Privately Held**
SIC: 7372 Application computer software

(G-4468)
NEWELL BRANDS INC (PA)
221 River St Ste 13 (07030-5990)
PHONE...............................201 610-6600
Christopher Peterson, *CEO*
Patrick D Campbell, *Ch of Bd*
Russell Torres, *President*
William A Burke III, *COO*
William Burke, *COO*
▲ EMP: 300
SALES: 8.6B **Publicly Held**
WEB: www.newell-rubbermaid.com
SIC: 3089 3469 2591 3951 Plastic kitchenware, tableware & houseware; household cooking & kitchen utensils, porcelain enameled; household cooking & kitchen utensils, metal; drapery hardware & blinds & shades; pens & mechanical pencils; markers, soft tip (felt, fabric, plastic, etc.); hair & hair-based products; power-driven handtools

(G-4469)
NRG BLUEWATER WIND LLC
22 Hudson Pl Ste 3 (07030-5512)
PHONE...............................201 748-5000
David Blazer, *Principal*
EMP: 5
SALES (est): 380K **Privately Held**
SIC: 3822 Temperature sensors for motor windings

(G-4470)
OBAGEL HOBOKEN LTD LBLTY CO
600 Washington St (07030-4908)
PHONE...............................201 683-8599
EMP: 4
SALES (est): 60.7K **Privately Held**
SIC: 5461 7372 Bagels; application computer software

(G-4471)
OBSERVER PARK
51 Garden St (07030-3558)
PHONE...............................201 798-7007
Jennifer Mortellaro, *Principal*
EMP: 10 EST: 2009
SALES (est): 676.6K **Privately Held**
SIC: 2711 Newspapers, publishing & printing

(G-4472)
PAN AMERICAN COFFEE COMPANY (PA)
500 16th St (07030-2336)
PHONE...............................201 963-2329
Roy Montes, *CEO*
EMP: 40 EST: 1964
SQ FT: 40,000
SALES (est): 46MM **Privately Held**
WEB: www.panamericancoffee.com
SIC: 5149 2095 Coffee, green or roasted; roasted coffee

(G-4473)
PEARSON EDUCATION INC (DH)
221 River St (07030-5989)
PHONE...............................201 236-7000
Will Ethridge, *CEO*
John Fallon, *President*
Leeanne Fisher, *President*
◆ EMP: 1583
SQ FT: 1,000
SALES (est): 2.5B
SALES (corp-wide): 5.3B **Privately Held**
WEB: www.phgenit.com
SIC: 2731 Book publishing
HQ: Pearson Education Holdings Inc.
330 Hudson St Fl 9
New York NY 10013
201 236-6716

(G-4474)
PEARSON EDUCATION INC
Also Called: Pearson Longman
221 River St (07030-5989)
PHONE...............................914 287-8000
Owen Mitchell, *President*
Joanne Dresner, *Manager*
EMP: 99
SALES (corp-wide): 5.3B **Privately Held**
WEB: www.phgenit.com
SIC: 2731 Book publishing

HQ: Pearson Education, Inc.
221 River St
Hoboken NJ 07030
201 236-7000

(G-4475)
PEARSON EDUCATION INC
Prentice Hall
221 River St Ste 200 (07030-5990)
PHONE...............................201 785-2721
Barbara Puegner, *Sales Staff*
Vanessa Stclair, *Business Anlyst*
Maria Gleason, *Manager*
Josh Richards, *Manager*
EMP: 19
SALES (corp-wide): 5.3B **Privately Held**
WEB: www.phgenit.com
SIC: 2731 Books: publishing only
HQ: Pearson Education, Inc.
221 River St
Hoboken NJ 07030
201 236-7000

(G-4476)
R NEUMANN & CO
300 Observer Hwy Ste 1 (07030-2412)
PHONE...............................201 659-3400
William Bernheim, *Vice Pres*
Richard Bernheim, *Manager*
▲ EMP: 14 EST: 1863
SQ FT: 30,000
SALES (est): 1.3MM **Privately Held**
WEB: www.rneumann.com
SIC: 3172 3199 Personal leather goods; novelties, leather

(G-4477)
RCDC CORPORATION
Also Called: Radiant Cut Diamond
59 Madison St 2 (07030-1805)
PHONE...............................212 382-0386
Stanley M Grossbard, *President*
Rebecca Grossbard, *Vice Pres*
EMP: 5
SQ FT: 1,600
SALES (est): 946.8K **Privately Held**
WEB: www.radiantcut.com
SIC: 5094 3915 Diamonds (gems); diamond cutting & polishing

(G-4478)
RELATIONAL ARCHITECTS INC
33 Newark St Ste 3a (07030)
PHONE...............................201 420-0400
Carl Feinberg, *Ch of Bd*
Max Gartner, *President*
Paul Verba, *Vice Pres*
EMP: 24
SQ FT: 6,800
SALES (est): 6.4MM **Privately Held**
WEB: www.relarc.com
SIC: 7372 Prepackaged software

(G-4479)
REUGE MANAGEMENT GROUP INC
Also Called: Retawa
89 River St Unit 1002 (07030-9643)
PHONE...............................888 306-3253
EMP: 4
SALES (est): 290K **Privately Held**
SIC: 3674 8331 Mfg Semiconductors/Related Devices Job Training/Related Services

(G-4480)
SIMS PUMP VALVE COMPANY INC
1314 Park Ave (07030-4404)
PHONE...............................201 792-0600
John A Kozel, *President*
Dr Charles Post, *Vice Pres*
Aaron Finney, *Sales Staff*
Patrick Ricciardi, *Applctn Conslt*
George Yochum, *Director*
EMP: 20 EST: 1919
SQ FT: 10,000
SALES (est): 5.7MM **Privately Held**
WEB: www.simsite.com
SIC: 3494 5085 Valves & pipe fittings; valves & fittings

(G-4481)
SLENDERTONE DISTRIBUTION INC
221 River St Ste 9 (07030-5990)
P.O. Box 5179 (07030-1502)
PHONE..........................732 660-1177
Andy Leyland, *CEO*
Michael Nohilly, *Vice Pres*
Devon Lineman, *Manager*
▲ EMP: 5
SALES: 10MM **Privately Held**
SIC: 3949 7311 Exercise equipment; advertising agencies
HQ: Bio-Medical Research Limited
Bmr House
Galway

(G-4482)
SMALL MOLECULES INC
38 Jackson St (07030-6072)
PHONE..........................201 918-4664
Julia Zhu, *Principal*
▲ EMP: 4
SALES (est): 305K **Privately Held**
SIC: 2869 Industrial organic chemicals

(G-4483)
SUMMIT PROFESSIONAL NETWORKS
33 41 Newark St Fl 2 (07030)
P.O. Box 770 (07030-0770)
PHONE..........................201 526-1230
John Whelan, *Manager*
EMP: 20
SALES (corp-wide): 181.8MM **Privately Held**
WEB: www.nationalunderwriter.com
SIC: 2711 Newspapers
HQ: Summit Professional Networks
4157 Olympic Blvd Ste 225
Erlanger KY 41018
859 692-2100

(G-4484)
TAXSTREAM LLC
95 River St Ste 5c (07030-5612)
PHONE..........................201 610-0390
Fax: 201 356-6521
EMP: 75
SQ FT: 10,000
SALES (est): 4.7MM
SALES (corp-wide): 3.2B **Publicly Held**
SIC: 7372 Prepackaged Software Services
HQ: Thomson Reuters Corporation
3 Times Sq
New York NY 10036
646 223-4000

(G-4485)
UNION DRY DOCK & REPAIR CO (PA)
51 Newark St Ste 504 (07030-4543)
P.O. Box 1539 (07030-1539)
PHONE..........................201 792-9090
Robert J Burke, *President*
Robert Ferrie, *Vice Pres*
Bruce Southern, *Vice Pres*
Carlotta Crissy, *Treasurer*
Carol A Barnes, *Admin Sec*
EMP: 4 EST: 1908
SQ FT: 1,500
SALES (est): 5.4MM **Privately Held**
SIC: 3731 Barges, building & repairing; scows, building & repairing; tugboats, building & repairing

(G-4486)
UNION DRY DOCK & REPAIR CO
Also Called: Yard
901 Sinatra Dr (07030-5797)
PHONE..........................201 963-5833
Bruce Southern, *General Mgr*
EMP: 45
SALES (corp-wide): 5.4MM **Privately Held**
SIC: 3731 3732 Shipbuilding & repairing; boat building & repairing
PA: Union Dry Dock & Repair Co Inc
51 Newark St Ste 504
Hoboken NJ 07030
201 792-9090

(G-4487)
W KODAK JEWELERS INC (PA)
Also Called: Kodak W Jewelers of Bayonne
60 Newark St (07030-4581)
PHONE..........................201 710-5491
Carol Kodak Walden, *President*
Bradley Kodak, *Vice Pres*
Creighton Kodak, *Vice Pres*
EMP: 5
SQ FT: 2,500
SALES (est): 2.1MM **Privately Held**
WEB: www.wkodakjewelers.com
SIC: 5944 3911 Jewelry, precious stones & precious metals; jewelry, precious metal

(G-4488)
WILEY PUBLISHING LLC (HQ)
Also Called: John Wiley and Sons
111 River St (07030-5773)
PHONE..........................201 748-6000
Stephen M Smith, *CEO*
Claudine McCarthy, *Editor*
William J Arlington, *Senior VP*
Ellis E Cousens, *Vice Pres*
Edward J Melando, *Vice Pres*
▲ EMP: 500
SALES (est): 476.1MM
SALES (corp-wide): 1.8B **Publicly Held**
WEB: www.mcp.com
SIC: 2731 Books: publishing & printing
PA: John Wiley & Sons, Inc.
111 River St Ste 2000
Hoboken NJ 07030
201 748-6000

(G-4489)
WILEY SUBSCRIPTION SERVICES
Also Called: Wiley-Interscience
111 River St (07030-5773)
PHONE..........................201 748-6000
Bradford Wiley II, *President*
EMP: 14
SQ FT: 230,000
SALES (est): 1.4MM
SALES (corp-wide): 1.8B **Publicly Held**
WEB: www.wiley.com
SIC: 2731 Textbooks: publishing only, not printed on site
PA: John Wiley & Sons, Inc.
111 River St Ste 2000
Hoboken NJ 07030
201 748-6000

(G-4490)
XCEPTIONAL INSTRUMENTS LLC
1200 Grand St Apt 423 (07030-2284)
PHONE..........................315 750-4345
Alberto Correa, *President*
EMP: 4
SALES (est): 158.3K **Privately Held**
SIC: 2047 Dog food

Holmdel
Monmouth County

(G-4491)
A&E PROMOTIONS LLC
118 Woodlake Ct A (07733-2544)
P.O. Box 355, Atlantic Highlands (07716-0355)
PHONE..........................732 382-2300
Mae Veltri,
Anthony Veltri,
Eugene Veltri,
EMP: 7
SQ FT: 20,000
SALES (est): 1.1MM **Privately Held**
SIC: 5199 2752 Advertising specialties; commercial printing, lithographic

(G-4492)
ACTION PRESS PARK SLOPE
5 Rustic Ln (07733-2318)
PHONE..........................718 624-3457
EMP: 4
SALES (est): 189.2K **Privately Held**
SIC: 2741 Miscellaneous publishing

(G-4493)
AER X DUST CORPORATION
12 Windingbrook Way (07733-2330)
P.O. Box 39, Tennent (07763-0039)
PHONE..........................732 946-9462
Guy D Cusumano, *President*
EMP: 6
SALES (est): 475K **Privately Held**
SIC: 5087 3564 3563 Vacuum cleaning systems; blowers & fans; air & gas compressors

(G-4494)
BKT EXIM US INC (HQ)
960 Holmdel Rd Ste 2-02 (07733-2138)
PHONE..........................732 817-1400
Shawn Rasey, *President*
EMP: 6
SALES (est): 5.3MM
SALES (corp-wide): 715.2MM **Privately Held**
SIC: 3011 Pneumatic tires, all types
PA: Balkrishna Industries Limited
Bkt House, C/15
Mumbai MH 40001
226 666-3800

(G-4495)
BKT TIRES INC
960 Holmdel Rd Ste 2 (07733-2100)
PHONE..........................844 258-8473
Minoo Mehta, *President*
EMP: 9
SQ FT: 2,000
SALES: 5.3MM
SALES (corp-wide): 715.2MM **Privately Held**
SIC: 3011 Pneumatic tires, all types
HQ: Bkt Exim Us, Inc.
960 Holmdel Rd Ste 2-02
Holmdel NJ 07733
732 817-1400

(G-4496)
CEI HOLDINGS INC (PA)
2182 State Route 35 (07733-1125)
PHONE..........................732 888-7788
John F Croddick, *President*
▲ EMP: 34
SALES (est): 243.4MM **Privately Held**
SIC: 2844 7389 4225 5122 Toilet preparations; cosmetic kits, assembling & packaging; general warehousing & storage; cosmetics, perfumes & hair products

(G-4497)
COSMETIC ESSENCE LLC (HQ)
2182 Hwy 35 (07733-1125)
PHONE..........................732 888-7788
Peter G Martin, *CEO*
Kurt Polinger, *General Mgr*
Tina Caputo, *Principal*
Christian Algarin, *Prdtn Mgr*
Teresa Grose, *Purch Agent*
▲ EMP: 237
SALES (est): 232.9MM
SALES (corp-wide): 243.4MM **Privately Held**
WEB: www.ceidistribution.com
SIC: 2844 7389 4225 Cosmetic preparations; cosmetic kits, assembling & packaging; general warehousing & storage
PA: Cei Holdings, Inc.
2182 State Route 35
Holmdel NJ 07733
732 888-7788

(G-4498)
COSMETIC ESSENCE INC
2182 State Route 35 (07733-1125)
PHONE..........................732 888-7788
EMP: 21 EST: 1982
SALES (est): 3.8MM **Privately Held**
SIC: 2844 7389 Mfg Toilet Preparations Business Services

(G-4499)
DRONE GO HOME LLC
Also Called: Aerodefense
101 Crawfords Corner Rd 4101r (07733-1976)
PHONE..........................732 991-3605
Linda Ziemba, *General Mgr*
EMP: 9
SALES (est): 205.8K **Privately Held**
SIC: 3721 3728 Autogiros; target drones

(G-4500)
EIGENT TECHNOLOGIES INC
10 Cindy Ln (07733-2027)
P.O. Box 710 (07733-0710)
PHONE..........................732 673-0402
Robert Warner, *President*
EMP: 8
SALES (est): 739.6K **Privately Held**
WEB: www.eigent.com
SIC: 3663 Radio & TV communications equipment

(G-4501)
FULLVIEW INC
3 Fieldpoint Dr (07733-1227)
PHONE..........................732 275-6500
Vic Nalwa, *President*
Joe Lazaroff, *Admin Sec*
▼ EMP: 5 EST: 2000
SALES: 1MM **Privately Held**
SIC: 3861 Cameras & related equipment

(G-4502)
HOLMDEL ACPNCTR & NTRL MED CTR
721 N Beers St Ste Suite (07733-1518)
PHONE..........................732 888-4910
Liping Wang, *Owner*
EMP: 8 EST: 2007
SALES (est): 700.2K **Privately Held**
SIC: 2834 8049 Medicines, capsuled or ampuled; acupuncturist

(G-4503)
J F C MACHINE WORKS LLC
2182 State Route 35 (07733-1125)
P.O. Box 133, Marlboro (07746-0133)
PHONE..........................732 203-2077
John F Croddick,
EMP: 12
SALES (est): 2MM **Privately Held**
SIC: 3565 Bag opening, filling & closing machines

(G-4504)
MAGNETIC PRODUCTS AND SVCS INC
Also Called: M P S
2135 State Route 35 Ste 1 (07733-1077)
PHONE..........................732 264-6651
Paul I Nippes, *President*
Marilyn B Nippes, *Corp Secy*
EMP: 9
SQ FT: 15,000
SALES (est): 1.3MM **Privately Held**
SIC: 8711 5049 3829 Engineering services; scientific & engineering equipment & supplies; measuring & controlling devices

(G-4505)
MAGRUDER COLOR COMPANY INC
14 Takolusa Dr (07733-1232)
PHONE..........................817 837-3293
EMP: 200
SQ FT: 250,000
SALES (est): 24.1MM **Privately Held**
WEB: www.magruder.com
SIC: 2865 Dyes & pigments

(G-4506)
METUCHEN CAPACITORS INC
2139 Highway 35 Ste 2 (07733-1095)
PHONE..........................800 899-6969
Gary Ficsor, *Ch of Bd*
Stephen P Ficsor, *President*
Sharon Petyo, *Purch Mgr*
Lydia Lyle, *Buyer*
Cathy Hoehl, *Accounting Dir*
EMP: 35
SQ FT: 20,000
SALES (est): 6.6MM **Privately Held**
WEB: www.metcaps.net
SIC: 3675 Electronic capacitors

(G-4507)
MOBILE INTELLIGENT ALERTS INC
72 Middletown Rd (07733-2206)
PHONE..........................201 410-5324
Tom Santora, *CEO*
EMP: 4 EST: 2013

SALES: 162K **Privately Held**
SIC: 3699 7371 7389 Security control
equipment & systems; software programming applications;

(G-4508)
MODELWARE INC
28 Red Coach Ln (07733-1137)
PHONE...................................732 264-3020
Anthony Dalleggio, *President*
EMP: 10 **EST:** 1995
SQ FT: 1,800
SALES (est): 994.3K
SALES (corp-wide): 3B **Publicly Held**
WEB: www.modelware.com
SIC: 3674 7372 3672 Microcircuits, inte-
grated (semiconductor); application com-
puter software; printed circuit boards
PA: Xilinx, Inc.
2100 All Programable
San Jose CA 95124
408 559-7778

(G-4509)
MTN GOVERNMENT SERVICES INC (DH)
200 Telegraph Rd (07733)
PHONE...................................703 443-6738
Peg Grayson, *President*
Margaret Grayson, *President*
Quais Hassan, *President*
Ty Narkmon, *President*
Catherine Melquist, *Vice Pres*
EMP: 15
SALES: 30MM **Publicly Held**
SIC: 3448 Prefabricated metal buildings
HQ: Emerging Markets Communications, Llc
3044 N Commerce Pkwy
Miramar FL 33025
954 538-4000

(G-4510)
MVN USA INC
960 Holmdel Rd (07733-2138)
PHONE...................................732 817-1400
Atul Nalhotra, *President*
EMP: 5
SALES (est): 308.4K **Privately Held**
SIC: 7372 Educational computer software

(G-4511)
NOVEGA VENTURE PARTNERS INC
Also Called: Vonage
23 Main St (07733-2136)
PHONE...................................732 528-2600
David Pearson, *President*
Gerald Maloney, *Treasurer*
Kurt Rogers, *Admin Sec*
EMP: 5
SALES: 436K
SALES (corp-wide): 1B **Publicly Held**
SIC: 7372 4813 Application computer soft-
ware; local & long distance telephone
communications
PA: Vonage Holdings Corp.
23 Main St
Holmdel NJ 07733
732 528-2600

(G-4512)
OPTHERIUM LABS OU
21 Riverside Ln (07733-2084)
PHONE...................................516 253-1777
Sergey Beck, *Principal*
EMP: 6
SALES (est): 135.3K **Privately Held**
SIC: 7372 7389 Application computer soft-
ware; financial services

(G-4513)
SAXA PHARMACEUTICALS LLC
22 Candlelight Dr (07733-2362)
PHONE...................................862 571-7630
Joseph Todisco, *Administration*
EMP: 4 **EST:** 2016
SALES (est): 216K **Privately Held**
SIC: 2834 Pharmaceutical preparations

(G-4514)
SPIRENT COMMUNICATIONS INC
101 Crawfords Corner Rd (07733-1976)
PHONE...................................732 946-4018

EMP: 5
SALES (corp-wide): 476.9MM **Privately Held**
SIC: 5065 4899 4813 3679 Telephone &
telegraphic equipment; data communication services; local & long distance telephone communications; electronic circuits
HQ: Spirent Communications Inc.
27439 Agoura Rd
Calabasas CA 91301
818 676-2300

(G-4515)
WILLOW TECHNOLOGY INC
12 Valley Point Dr (07733-1325)
PHONE...................................732 671-1554
William O Wurtz, *President*
EMP: 5
SALES (est): 400K **Privately Held**
WEB: www.willowtechnology.com
SIC: 3556 Mixers, commercial, food

(G-4516)
WORKWAVE LLC (DH)
101 Crawfords Corner Rd (07733-1976)
PHONE...................................866 794-1658
Chris Sullens, *President*
Shawn Cantor, *COO*
David Giannetto, *COO*
Zachary Pendleton, *Counsel*
Perry Pappas, *Senior VP*
EMP: 12 **EST:** 2006
SALES (est): 5.6MM **Privately Held**
SIC: 7372 Application computer software

Hopatcong
Sussex County

(G-4517)
ALLSTAR DISPOSAL
118 Hudson Ave (07843-1708)
PHONE...................................973 398-8808
Michael A Lombardi, *Principal*
EMP: 4
SALES (est): 314.1K **Privately Held**
SIC: 3089 Garbage containers, plastic

(G-4518)
ARCHLIT INC
42 Ithanell Rd (07843-1846)
PHONE...................................973 577-4400
Gaspar M Glusberg, *Principal*
EMP: 4
SALES (est): 513.7K **Privately Held**
SIC: 3648 Outdoor lighting equipment

(G-4519)
CORRVIEW INTERNATIONAL LLC
9 Pahaquarry Rd (07843-1419)
P.O. Box 8513, Landing (07850-8513)
PHONE...................................973 770-0571
William Duncan, *CEO*
EMP: 4
SQ FT: 2,000
SALES: 300K **Privately Held**
WEB: www.corrview.com
SIC: 7389 3531 Pipeline & power line in-
spection service; concrete grouting equip-
ment

(G-4520)
GREEN POWER CHEMICAL LLC
Also Called: Green Power Chemical Sciences
151 Sparta Stanhope Rd (07843)
PHONE...................................973 770-5600
Tom Hawkins, *Controller*
August Peter Dangelo, *Mng Member*
Peter D'Angelo, *Manager*
Jake Wilson, *Manager*
EMP: 10
SQ FT: 3,000
SALES: 1.5MM **Privately Held**
SIC: 2842 3559 Degreasing solvent; de-
greasing machines, automotive & indus-
trial

(G-4521)
HOPATCONG FUEL ON YOU LLC
107 Tulsa Trl (07843-1236)
PHONE...................................973 770-0854
John Corrente, *Principal*
EMP: 4

SALES (est): 280.1K **Privately Held**
SIC: 2869 Fuels

(G-4522)
SONRISE METAL INC
32 Shore Rd (07843-1328)
PHONE...................................973 423-4717
Fax: 973 423-0338
EMP: 18
SQ FT: 8,000
SALES (est): 3.1MM **Privately Held**
SIC: 3444 Mfg Sheet Metalwork

(G-4523)
WRA MANUFACTURING COMPANY INC
Also Called: Analytical Measurements
17 Portside Rd (07843-1424)
PHONE...................................908 416-2228
Warren R Adey, *President*
Bob Smith, *Manager*
EMP: 5 **EST:** 1945
SALES: 500K **Privately Held**
SIC: 3823 3826 PH instruments, industrial
process type; analytical instruments

Hope
Warren County

(G-4524)
CHRISTOPHER F MAIER
Also Called: Jenny Jump Farm
352 Great Meadows Rd (07844)
PHONE...................................908 459-5100
Christopher F Maier, *Owner*
EMP: 10 **EST:** 1947
SQ FT: 10,000
SALES (est): 1MM **Privately Held**
WEB: www.thelandofmakebelieve.org
SIC: 7999 3089 Tourist attraction, com-
mercial; novelties, plastic

Hopelawn
Middlesex County

(G-4525)
F & A SIGNS INC
Also Called: Stand Out Signs
49 W Pond Rd (08861-1540)
PHONE...................................732 442-9399
Joe Musuruca, *President*
EMP: 5
SQ FT: 6,000
SALES (est): 800K **Privately Held**
SIC: 3993 Signs & advertising specialties

Hopewell
Mercer County

(G-4526)
DOOR CENTER ENTERPRISES INC
Also Called: The Door Center Publishing
105 Crusher Rd (08525-2203)
PHONE...................................609 333-1233
Charles M Huebner, *President*
Louise Huebner, *Corp Secy*
Lucia Huebner, *Vice Pres*
EMP: 7
SQ FT: 2,000
SALES: 1MM **Privately Held**
WEB: www.doorposter.com
SIC: 5211 5031 5251 2741 Garage
doors, sale & installation; doors & win-
dows; door locks & lock sets; posters;
publishing only, not printed on site

(G-4527)
L & S CONTRACTING INC
259 Route 31 N (08525-2702)
PHONE...................................609 397-1281
Leon A Walters IV, *Principal*
Steven Walters, *Principal*
EMP: 6
SALES (est): 580K **Privately Held**
SIC: 4212 2875 5261 Local trucking, with-
out storage; compost; top soil

(G-4528)
ORAL FIXATION LLC
53 Railroad Pl A (08525-1826)
PHONE...................................609 937-9972
Eric Lybeck, *COO*
Jeremy H Kahn, *Mng Member*
Henry M Rich,
▲ **EMP:** 5
SQ FT: 1,000
SALES (est): 449.3K **Privately Held**
WEB: www.oralfix.com
SIC: 2064 Candy & other confectionery
products

(G-4529)
WELL MANAGER LLC
371 Route 31 N (08525-2802)
PHONE...................................609 466-4347
Daniel Serlenga, *Mng Member*
EMP: 4
SQ FT: 5,000
SALES: 500K **Privately Held**
SIC: 3714 Water pump, motor vehicle

Howell
Monmouth County

(G-4530)
AMERICAN BRAIDING & MFG CORP
247 Old Tavern Rd (07731-8814)
PHONE...................................732 938-6333
Jerry Bailey, *CEO*
Jason Bailey, *President*
Lara Nelson, *Manager*
▲ **EMP:** 11
SQ FT: 24,000
SALES (est): 1.1MM **Privately Held**
SIC: 3053 3069 Packing materials; gas-
kets, all materials; rubberized fabrics

(G-4531)
ARNOLD STEEL CO INC
79 Randolph Rd (07731-8611)
PHONE...................................732 363-1079
Felix Pflaster, *President*
Leon Pflaster, *Vice Pres*
Tina Pflaster, *CFO*
Pflaster Tina, *CFO*
EMP: 70
SQ FT: 60,000
SALES (est): 23.3MM **Privately Held**
WEB: www.arnoldsteel.com
SIC: 3441 2439 1791 Building compo-
nents, structural steel; structural wood
members; structural steel erection

(G-4532)
BR WELDING INC
3 Brook Rd (07731-8675)
PHONE...................................732 363-8253
Brandon REO, *President*
EMP: 19
SQ FT: 1,000
SALES (est): 3.4MM **Privately Held**
WEB: www.brwelding.com
SIC: 1799 7692 3444 Welding on site;
welding repair; sheet metalwork

(G-4533)
CHIPS ICE CREAM LLC
149 Newtons Corner Rd (07731-2890)
PHONE...................................732 840-6332
Robin Almeida,
EMP: 5
SALES (est): 272.3K **Privately Held**
SIC: 2052 Cones, ice cream

(G-4534)
CORNER STONE SOFTWARE INC
1246 Hwy 33 (07731)
P.O. Box 180 (07731-0180)
PHONE...................................732 938-5229
Paul Crooks, *CEO*
EMP: 4
SALES (est): 261.1K **Privately Held**
WEB: www.cornerstonesoft.com
SIC: 7372 Prepackaged software

(G-4535)
CUTTER DRILL & MACHINE INC
175 Ramtown Greenville Rd # 7
(07731-3829)
P.O. Box 140, Lakewood (08701-0140)
PHONE..................................732 206-1112
Michael C Tellier, *President*
William Young, *Corp Secy*
EMP: 7
SQ FT: 6,000
SALES (est): 2.1MM **Privately Held**
WEB: www.cutterdrill.com
SIC: 3541 3545 Machine tools, metal cutting type; drills (machine tool accessories)

(G-4536)
CUTTING EDGE GROWER SUPPLY LLC
97 Glen Arden Dr (07731-1639)
PHONE..................................732 905-9220
Jackie Barendregt, *Sales Executive*
Anthonie D Barendregt,
▲ **EMP:** 4
SALES (est): 1MM **Privately Held**
SIC: 5191 4971 3999 Greenhouse equipment & supplies; irrigation systems; atomizers, toiletry

(G-4537)
DON SHRTS PCTURE FRMES MOLDING
Also Called: Don Shurts Frames & Molding
294 Lanes Mill Rd (07731-2524)
PHONE..................................732 363-1323
EMP: 4
SQ FT: 8,000
SALES: 300K **Privately Held**
SIC: 2499 3089 Manufactures Wooden Picture Frames And Moldings

(G-4538)
EMIL A SCHROTH INC
Copper Av Yellow Brook Rd (07731)
P.O. Box 496, Farmingdale (07727-0496)
PHONE..................................732 938-5015
Emil A Schroth Jr, *President*
Benjamin U Jackson, *Vice Pres*
EMP: 40
SQ FT: 55,000
SALES (est): 7.3MM **Privately Held**
SIC: 5093 3341 Nonferrous metals scrap; secondary nonferrous metals

(G-4539)
ERVIN ADVERTISING CO INC (PA)
Also Called: Garden State Sign
4880 Us Hwy Rte 9 S (07731)
PHONE..................................732 363-7645
Joseph Ervin, *President*
Robert Ervin, *Vice Pres*
EMP: 6 **EST:** 1951
SQ FT: 4,000
SALES: 748.3K **Privately Held**
SIC: 3993 Electric signs; neon signs

(G-4540)
GOGREEN POWER INC
Also Called: Power By Gogreen
4675 Us Highway 9 (07731-3384)
PHONE..................................732 994-5901
James Murry, *CEO*
Elliot Buzil, *Exec VP*
Jessica Helmer, *Opers Mgr*
▲ **EMP:** 10
SALES: 4.5MM **Privately Held**
SIC: 3691 3699 3648 Alkaline cell storage batteries; extension cords; flashlights

(G-4541)
HOWELL TOWNSHIP POLICE
Also Called: HOWELL TOWNSHIP PAL
115 Kent Rd (07731-2420)
P.O. Box 713 (07731-0713)
PHONE..................................732 919-2805
Christopher Hill, *President*
John Stevens, *Exec Dir*
Chris Hill, *Exec Dir*
Rochelle Hill, *Administration*
EMP: 55
SALES (est): 3.1MM **Privately Held**
SIC: 2499 Policemen's clubs, wood

(G-4542)
JCH PARTNERS & CO LLC
8 Man O War Ln (07731-1161)
PHONE..................................732 664-6440
Timothy Harshaw,
EMP: 12
SALES (est): 553.1K **Privately Held**
SIC: 2899 Peppermint oil

(G-4543)
KARLA LANDSCAPING PAVERS
11 Woodland Dr (07731-1437)
PHONE..................................732 333-5852
Jorge Ortizdeorue, *Principal*
EMP: 4 **EST:** 2010
SALES (est): 561.5K **Privately Held**
SIC: 3531 Pavers

(G-4544)
KOEHLER INDUSTRIES INC
25 Arnold Blvd (07731-2792)
PHONE..................................732 364-2700
Raymond F Koehler, *President*
Patricia Koehler, *Corp Secy*
EMP: 4
SQ FT: 4,000
SALES: 300K **Privately Held**
WEB: www.flashlight.com
SIC: 3479 7336 Engraving jewelry silverware, or metal; etching on metals; silk screen design

(G-4545)
LAKEWOOD ELC MTR SLS & SVC
6850 Us Highway 9 (07731-3364)
PHONE..................................732 363-2865
Marc Lipman, *President*
EMP: 4
SALES (est): 310K **Privately Held**
SIC: 7694 5999 5063 Electric motor repair; motors, electric; motors, electric

(G-4546)
MARK-O-LITE SIGN CO INC
1420 Us Highway 9 (07731-3331)
PHONE..................................732 462-8530
Howard Mark, *President*
EMP: 10 **EST:** 1966
SQ FT: 3,000
SALES: 300K **Privately Held**
SIC: 3993 Electric signs; neon signs

(G-4547)
MULTALLOY LLC
Also Called: Multalloy 9070
507 Oak Glen Rd (07731-8933)
PHONE..................................732 961-1520
Tim Robert, *Manager*
EMP: 9
SALES (corp-wide): 381.4MM **Privately Held**
SIC: 2819 Elements
HQ: Multalloy Llc
3730 S Main St
Pearland TX 77581
713 943-3544

(G-4548)
PALUDE ENTERPRISES INC
1933 Hwy 35 Ste 105-144 (07731)
PHONE..................................732 241-5478
David Marsh, *President*
EMP: 5
SALES (est): 99K **Privately Held**
SIC: 3564 Air cleaning systems

(G-4549)
PHOENIX PACKING & GASKET CO
Also Called: Phoenix Pkg & Gasket Mfg Co
247 Old Tavern Rd (07731-8814)
PHONE..................................732 938-7377
Gerald D Bailey, *President*
EMP: 13
SQ FT: 24,000
SALES (est): 548.9K **Privately Held**
SIC: 3053 Gaskets, all materials; packing, metallic; packing, rubber

(G-4550)
SAWDUST DEPOT LLC
704 Hulses Corner Rd (07731-8551)
PHONE..................................973 344-5255
James Ippolito, *Mng Member*

EMP: 12
SALES (est): 1.2MM **Privately Held**
SIC: 2421 Sawdust & shavings

(G-4551)
SURBURBAN BUILDING PDTS INC (PA)
Also Called: Suburban Aluminum Mfg
1178 Lkwood Frmingdale Rd (07731-8659)
PHONE..................................732 901-8900
Vincent P Bochiaro, *President*
EMP: 30 **EST:** 1962
SQ FT: 25,000
SALES (est): 5MM **Privately Held**
WEB: www.suburbanbuildingproducts.com
SIC: 3442 5031 Storm doors or windows, metal; window frames, all materials

(G-4552)
UNITED ENERGY CORP (PA)
3598 Us Highway 9 Ste 303 (07731)
PHONE..................................732 994-5225
Jack Silver, *President*
Adam Hershey, *Corp Secy*
▼ **EMP:** 8
SQ FT: 4,800
SALES (est): 1.1MM **Publicly Held**
SIC: 2899 2911 Chemical preparations; solvents

Irvington
Essex County

(G-4553)
AGAPE INC
Also Called: Dairyland
487 Chancellor Ave (07111-4002)
PHONE..................................973 923-7625
Arthur Anastasio, *President*
EMP: 11
SQ FT: 6,000
SALES (est): 490K **Privately Held**
SIC: 2024 5812 Ice cream & ice milk; ice cream stands or dairy bars

(G-4554)
ALBERT PAPER PRODUCTS COMPANY
464 Coit St (07111-4607)
P.O. Box 989, Hillside (07205-0989)
PHONE..................................973 373-0330
Richard Kenah, *President*
Mark Kenah, *Vice Pres*
EMP: 25 **EST:** 1944
SQ FT: 38,500
SALES (est): 6.5MM **Privately Held**
SIC: 2657 2653 5199 Folding paperboard boxes; boxes, corrugated: made from purchased materials; packaging materials

(G-4555)
ALBOUM W HAT COMPANY INC
1439 Springfield Ave (07111-1357)
PHONE..................................201 399-4110
Stuart Alboum, *President*
Sophia Saketos, *Manager*
▲ **EMP:** 22
SQ FT: 30,000
SALES (est): 2.1MM **Privately Held**
SIC: 2353 Uniform hats & caps; hats: cloth, straw & felt; caps: cloth, straw & felt

(G-4556)
AMERICAN ALUMINUM CASTING CO (PA)
324 Coit St (07111-4087)
PHONE..................................973 372-3200
Robert W Hartl, *President*
Clifford Hartl, *Vice Pres*
EMP: 48 **EST:** 1921
SQ FT: 50,000
SALES (est): 8.4MM **Privately Held**
WEB: www.americanalum.com
SIC: 3363 Aluminum die-castings

(G-4557)
ARNOLD DESKS INC
Also Called: Arnolds Desk
120 Coit St (07111-4117)
P.O. Box 842, Hillside (07205-0842)
PHONE..................................908 686-5656
EMP: 35
SQ FT: 31,500

SALES (est): 4.4MM **Privately Held**
SIC: 2521 Cabinets, office: wood

(G-4558)
ARNOLD FURNITURE MFRS INC (PA)
400 Coit St (07111-4607)
PHONE..................................973 399-0505
Julius Arnold, *President*
EMP: 10 **EST:** 1962
SQ FT: 70,000 **Privately Held**
WEB: www.arnoldfurniture.com
SIC: 2521 3993 Wood office furniture; signs & advertising specialties

(G-4559)
ARNOLD KOLAX FURNITURE INC
Also Called: Arnold Gisler Furn Fabricators
120 Coit St Irvington (07111)
PHONE..................................973 375-3344
Eric Arnold, *President*
Benjamin Kolax, *Vice Pres*
EMP: 25
SQ FT: 18,000
SALES (est): 4.1MM **Privately Held**
WEB: www.arnoldkolax.com
SIC: 2521 Wood office furniture

(G-4560)
ARNOLD RECEPTION DESKS INC
120 Coit St (07111-4117)
PHONE..................................973 375-8101
William Kolax, *President*
Ben Kolax, *General Mgr*
Julius Arnold, *Vice Pres*
Jose Gonzalez, *Project Mgr*
Peter Branigan, *Sales Mgr*
▲ **EMP:** 26
SQ FT: 18,000
SALES (est): 3.9MM **Privately Held**
WEB: www.arnoldreceptiondesks.com
SIC: 2521 5712 Wood office desks & tables; custom made furniture, except cabinets

(G-4561)
BESTMARK NATIONAL LLC
171 Coit St (07111-4104)
PHONE..................................862 772-4863
Mark Weglicka, *President*
EMP: 30 **EST:** 2016
SALES (est): 72K **Privately Held**
SIC: 2431 Millwork

(G-4562)
BISTIS PRESS PRINTING CO
1310 Clinton Ave (07111-1403)
PHONE..................................973 373-8033
Matthew Bistis, *Partner*
Nicholas Bistis, *Partner*
EMP: 4 **EST:** 1939
SALES (est): 250K **Privately Held**
SIC: 2752 Commercial printing, offset

(G-4563)
BLEEMA MANUFACTURING CORP
517 Lyons Ave (07111-4717)
PHONE..................................973 371-1771
Bruce Bier, *President*
Robert Bier, *Vice Pres*
Steve Weinerman, *CFO*
EMP: 32
SQ FT: 36,000
SALES: 5MM **Privately Held**
SIC: 3643 Electric connectors

(G-4564)
DIVERSIFIED IMPRESSIONS INC
Also Called: Diversified Impressions
119 Coit St (07111-4104)
PHONE..................................973 399-9041
Richard Feldman, *President*
EMP: 4
SQ FT: 3,600
SALES: 500K **Privately Held**
SIC: 2752 Commercial printing, offset

(G-4565)
E J M STORE FIXTURES INC
460 Coit St (07111-4630)
PHONE..................................973 372-7907
Marcos Zos Santos, *Partner*

EMP: 6
SALES (est): 480K **Privately Held**
SIC: 2542 Fixtures, store: except wood

(G-4566)
ELECTRONIC TECHNOLOGY INC
Also Called: Eti
511 Lyons Ave (07111-4717)
PHONE................................973 371-5160
Victor Mohl, *President*
Bruce Bier, *Corp Secy*
Joseph Bier, *Vice Pres*
David Travis, *Vice Pres*
Mike De Oliveira, *Purchasing*
▲ **EMP:** 130
SQ FT: 23,000
SALES (est): 31.8MM **Privately Held**
WEB: www.eti-nj.com
SIC: 3625 Electric controls & control accessories, industrial

(G-4567)
ENGINE COMBO LLC
Also Called: TEC
300 Nye Ave (07111-4713)
PHONE................................201 290-4399
Kumal Pasawala, *Managing Prtnr*
▼ **EMP:** 16 **EST:** 2013
SQ FT: 25,000
SALES: 4.5MM **Privately Held**
SIC: 3465 Body parts, automobile: stamped metal

(G-4568)
FEHLBERG MFG INC
10 Renee Pl 16 (07111-4609)
PHONE................................973 399-1905
Harold Fehlberg, *President*
EMP: 6
SQ FT: 15,000
SALES: 500K **Privately Held**
SIC: 2522 Office furniture, except wood

(G-4569)
FLAME CUT STEEL INC
300 Coit St (07111-4006)
P.O. Box 524, Matawan (07747-0524)
PHONE................................973 373-9300
Ramesh Nuthi, *President*
EMP: 10
SALES (est): 1.1MM **Privately Held**
SIC: 3441 Fabricated structural metal for bridges

(G-4570)
FRONTLINE INDUSTRIES INC
990 Chancellor Ave (07111-1262)
PHONE................................973 373-7211
Alfredo A Ciotola, *President*
Alfred Ciotola, *Project Mgr*
David Hill, *Project Mgr*
Dan Gural, *Production*
EMP: 17
SQ FT: 15,000
SALES (est): 5.2MM **Privately Held**
SIC: 7699 5084 3053 Pumps & pumping equipment repair; pumps & pumping equipment; gaskets & sealing devices

(G-4571)
HARVESTER INC
Also Called: Harvester Chemical
31 Cordier St (07111-4035)
PHONE................................201 445-1122
Fax: 973 705-3255
EMP: 15
SALES (corp-wide): 5.9MM **Privately Held**
SIC: 2842 Mfg Polish/Sanitation Goods
PA: Harvester, Inc.
85 Carver Ave
Westwood NJ 07675
201 664-4884

(G-4572)
HIGH TECH MANUFACTURING INC
460 Coit St Bldg D (07111-4630)
PHONE................................973 372-7907
Azad Mehta, *CEO*
Victor Salgado, *President*
Jorge Salazar, *Vice Pres*
▲ **EMP:** 5
SQ FT: 8,000
SALES: 1MM **Privately Held**
SIC: 2542 Fixtures, office: except wood

(G-4573)
ICYKIDZ
539 Union Ave (07111-2855)
PHONE................................973 342-9665
Sharon Hand, *Owner*
EMP: 5
SALES: 12K **Privately Held**
SIC: 2024 Fruit pops, frozen; ices, flavored (frozen dessert); juice pops, frozen

(G-4574)
IMPERIAL SEWING MACHINE CO
584 S 21st St (07111-4202)
PHONE................................973 374-3405
Philip Pantusco, *President*
EMP: 5 **EST:** 1957
SQ FT: 14,000
SALES: 700K **Privately Held**
SIC: 3559 Sewing machines & attachments, industrial

(G-4575)
INTERNATIONAL VITAMIN CORP
209 40th St (07111-1154)
PHONE................................973 371-4400
Ray Mulbey, *Manager*
EMP: 203 **Privately Held**
WEB: www.invernessmedical.com
SIC: 2834 Vitamin preparations
PA: International Vitamin Corp
1 Park Plz Ste 800
Irvine CA 92614

(G-4576)
INTERNATIONAL VITAMIN CORP
191 40th St (07111-1184)
PHONE................................973 416-2000
Arthur Edell, *President*
EMP: 5
SQ FT: 30,000 **Privately Held**
WEB: www.invernessmedical.com
SIC: 2834 2899 Vitamin, nutrient & hematinic preparations for human use; gelatin capsules
PA: International Vitamin Corp
1 Park Plz Ste 800
Irvine CA 92614

(G-4577)
INTERNTNAL ARCHTCTRAL IRNWORKS
181 Coit St (07111-4104)
PHONE................................973 741-0749
Pedro Varela, *Owner*
▲ **EMP:** 40
SALES (est): 5.3MM **Privately Held**
SIC: 3446 Architectural metalwork

(G-4578)
JERSEY PLASTIC MOLDERS INC
Also Called: Primo Division
149 Shaw Ave (07111-4779)
PHONE................................973 926-1800
Joseph Zazzara, *President*
◆ **EMP:** 125
SQ FT: 120,000
SALES (est): 20.8MM **Privately Held**
SIC: 3089 Molding primary plastic

(G-4579)
M CHASEN & SON INC
123 S 20th St (07111-4704)
PHONE................................973 374-8956
Tedro Silveira, *Manager*
EMP: 19
SALES (corp-wide): 14.6MM **Privately Held**
SIC: 2299 Batting, wadding, padding & fillings
PA: M Chasen & Son Inc
117 S 20th St 123
Irvington NJ 07111
973 374-8956

(G-4580)
MANCO INDUSTRIES
673 S 21st St (07111-4101)
PHONE................................973 971-3131
Donald Mangione, *President*
EMP: 7
SQ FT: 5,200
SALES (est): 500K **Privately Held**
SIC: 3599 Machine shop, jobbing & repair

(G-4581)
P A K MANUFACTURING INC
704 S 21st St (07111-4109)
PHONE................................973 372-1090
Alex Even-Esh, *President*
Peter Wester, *Opers Mgr*
Peter Scranton, *VP Sls/Mktg*
▲ **EMP:** 19
SQ FT: 28,000
SALES (est): 5.5MM **Privately Held**
WEB: www.pakmanufacturing.com
SIC: 3841 Surgical instruments & apparatus

(G-4582)
PLASTICO PRODUCTS LLC
34 Loretto St (07111-4710)
PHONE................................973 923-1944
Edd Griffith,
EMP: 5
SQ FT: 45,000
SALES (est): 922.7K **Privately Held**
SIC: 3086 Cups & plates, foamed plastic

(G-4583)
PRINTMAKER INTERNATIONAL LTD (DH)
503 Chancellor Ave (07111-4002)
PHONE................................212 629-9260
Angus R Petrie, *Ch of Bd*
Edward Berkise, *President*
Paul Shen, *President*
▲ **EMP:** 8 **EST:** 1981
SQ FT: 10,000
SALES (est): 4.5MM **Privately Held**
WEB: www.printmakerintl.com
SIC: 5131 2335 2339 Textile converters; women's, juniors' & misses' dresses; sportswear, women's
HQ: First National Trading Co Inc
9114 90th St
Woodhaven NY 11421
917 359-3469

(G-4584)
RICHARDS MANUFACTURING CO INC
517 Lyons Ave (07111-4717)
P.O. Box 18109, Newark (07191-8109)
PHONE................................973 371-1771
Spencer Fox, *Senior VP*
EMP: 7
SALES (est): 495K **Privately Held**
SIC: 3674 Semiconductors & related devices

(G-4585)
RICHARDS MFG A NJ LTD PARTNR
517 Lyons Ave (07111-4717)
PHONE................................973 371-1771
Richards M Sales, *General Ptnr*
◆ **EMP:** 175
SQ FT: 80,000
SALES (est): 25.3MM **Privately Held**
SIC: 3643 Electric connectors

(G-4586)
RICHARDS MFG CO SALES INC
517 Lyons Ave (07111-4717)
PHONE................................973 371-1771
Bruce Bier, *CEO*
Joseph Bier, *President*
Steve Weinerman, *CFO*
Steven Weinerman, *CFO*
Robert Bier, *Treasurer*
▲ **EMP:** 25 **EST:** 1955
SQ FT: 36,000
SALES (est): 14.3MM **Privately Held**
WEB: www.richards-mfg.com
SIC: 5063 3678 3643 Lugs & connectors, electrical; electronic connectors; current-carrying wiring devices

(G-4587)
STUYVESANT PRESS INC
119 Coit St (07111-4104)
PHONE................................973 399-3880
Michael A Roesch, *President*
Theodore Roesch, *Vice Pres*
Lillian Roesch, *Admin Sec*
Mary Sandre, *Assistant*
EMP: 19
SQ FT: 10,000
SALES (est): 3.6MM **Privately Held**
WEB: www.stuyvesantpress.com
SIC: 2752 2761 2759 Commercial printing, offset; continuous forms, office & business; letterpress printing

(G-4588)
TIGER SUPPLIES INC
27 Selvage St (07111-4722)
P.O. Box 5395, Hillside (07205-5395)
PHONE................................973 854-8635
Herman Goldberger, *President*
Eva Rosa, *Sales Staff*
Mark Klagsbrun, *Chief Mktg Ofcr*
Christopher Dahlman, *Executive*
◆ **EMP:** 6
SALES (est): 2.2MM **Privately Held**
SIC: 3699 Laser systems & equipment

(G-4589)
WAYNE COUNTY FOODS INC
360 Coit St (07111-4627)
PHONE................................973 399-0101
Vincent P Nemeth, *President*
Josephine Nemeth, *Admin Sec*
EMP: 32
SQ FT: 7,500
SALES (est): 11.3MM **Privately Held**
WEB: www.waynecountyfoods.com
SIC: 5149 2033 Seasonings, sauces & extracts; juices; canned fruits & specialties

---

Iselin
Middlesex County

(G-4590)
ADVANSTAR COMMUNICATIONS INC
Also Called: Biopharm International
485 Us Highway 1 S # 200 (08830)
PHONE................................732 596-0276
Tom Brown, *Opers Mgr*
Jennifer S Markarian, *Mfg Staff*
Alison O'Connor, *Sales Mgr*
Derek R Hamilton, *Sales Staff*
Scott Vail, *Sales Staff*
EMP: 50
SALES (corp-wide): 1.3B **Privately Held**
WEB: www.advanstar.com
SIC: 2721 Magazines: publishing only, not printed on site
HQ: Advanstar Communications Inc.
2501 Colorado Ave Ste 280
Santa Monica CA 90404
310 857-7500

(G-4591)
AMERICAN BUS & COACH LLC
1020 Green St (08830-2146)
PHONE................................732 283-1982
George Dapper,
EMP: 34
SALES (est): 3.3MM **Privately Held**
SIC: 3713 Bus bodies (motor vehicles)

(G-4592)
ANSELL HAWKEYE INC (HQ)
111 Wood Ave S Ste 210 (08830-2700)
PHONE................................662 258-3200
Tablo Bebetti, *General Mgr*
Donald Rodenborn Jr, *Director*
James P Rodenborn, *Director*
EMP: 50
SQ FT: 28,000
SALES (est): 21.2MM **Privately Held**
WEB: www.hawkeyeglove.com
SIC: 3151 Gloves, leather: work

(G-4593)
ANSELL HEALTHCARE PRODUCTS LLC (DH)
111 Wood Ave S Ste 210 (08830-2700)
PHONE................................732 345-5400
Douglas Tough, *CEO*
Steve Genzer, *Vice Pres*
David Graham, *Vice Pres*
Dave Harrington, *Vice Pres*
Franois L Jeune, *Vice Pres*
◆ **EMP:** 200

SALES (est): 198.4MM **Privately Held**
SIC: **3069** 3842 2822 2326 Balloons, advertising & toy: rubber; birth control devices, rubber; finger cots, rubber; surgical appliances & supplies; synthetic rubber; men's & boys' work clothing

(G-4594)
ANSELL INC (DH)
Also Called: Ansell Alabama
111 Wood Ave S Ste 210 (08830-2700)
PHONE..................................334 794-4231
Fred Dietsch, *President*
Tim Presseler, *Business Mgr*
Mike Spitler, *Corp Secy*
Kerry Hoffman, *Vice Pres*
Justin Chance, *Manager*
◆ EMP: 100 EST: 1966
SQ FT: 150,000
SALES (est): 51.2MM **Privately Held**
SIC: **3069** 4225 3061 Birth control devices, rubber; balloons, advertising & toy: rubber; general warehousing & storage; mechanical rubber goods

(G-4595)
ANSELL LIMITED
111 Wood Ave S Ste 210 (08830-2700)
PHONE..................................732 345-5400
Magnus R Nicolin, *Branch Mgr*
William Gero, *Manager*
John Harper, *Manager*
Lucy Reday, *Manager*
Sayako Yamada, *Manager*
EMP: 26 **Privately Held**
SIC: **3842** Personal safety equipment
PA: Ansell Limited
  L 3 678 Victoria St
  Richmond VIC 3121

(G-4596)
ANSELL PROTECTIVE PRODUCTS LLC
111 Wood Ave S Ste 210 (08830-2700)
PHONE..................................732 345-5400
Douglas Tough, *President*
William Reed, *Senior VP*
William Reilly Jr, *Senior VP*
Rustom Jilla, *CFO*
Chris Azorr, *Accounts Mgr*
◆ EMP: 1900
SALES (est): 2.8MM **Privately Held**
WEB: www.ansellpro.com
SIC: **3842** 3069 Gloves, safety; rubber coated fabrics & clothing
HQ: Pacific Dunlop Holdings (Usa) Llc
  200 Schulz Dr
  Red Bank NJ 07701

(G-4597)
ARCH PARENT INC
Also Called: Staples
801 Us Highway 1 S (08830-2609)
PHONE..................................732 621-2873
EMP: 4 **Privately Held**
SIC: **2752** Commercial printing, lithographic
HQ: Arch Parent Inc.
  9 W 57th St Fl 31
  New York NY 10019
  212 796-8500

(G-4598)
AXIOM INGREDIENTS LLC
33 Wood Ave S Ste 600 (08830-2717)
PHONE..................................732 669-2458
Michael Desantis, *Mng Member*
EMP: 10
SALES (est): 2MM **Privately Held**
SIC: **1479** Mineral pigment mining

(G-4599)
BASF CATALYSTS LLC (DH)
Also Called: Engelhard
33 Wood Ave S (08830-2735)
P.O. Box 770 (08830-0770)
PHONE..................................732 205-5000
Fried-Walter M Nstermann, *CFO*
Jer Nimo Cruz, *Director*
Wayne Smith, *Bd of Directors*
◆ EMP: 100
SQ FT: 168,000

SALES (est): 316.2MM
SALES (corp-wide): 71.7B **Privately Held**
WEB: www.catalysts.basf.com
SIC: **2819** 2816 5094 3339 Catalysts, chemical; inorganic pigments; bullion, precious metals; precious metals
HQ: Basf Corporation
  100 Park Ave
  Florham Park NJ 07932
  973 245-6000

(G-4600)
BASF CORPORATION
Catalysts Division
25 Middlesex Tpke (08830-2721)
P.O. Box 770 (08830-0770)
PHONE..................................732 205-5086
Maurica Fedors, *Manager*
EMP: 163
SALES (corp-wide): 71.7B **Privately Held**
SIC: **2869** Industrial organic chemicals
HQ: Basf Corporation
  100 Park Ave
  Florham Park NJ 07932
  973 245-6000

(G-4601)
BASF CORPORATION
33 Wood Ave S Fl 2 (08830-2719)
PHONE..................................732 205-5000
EMP: 14
SALES (corp-wide): 71.7B **Privately Held**
SIC: **2819** Industrial inorganic chemicals
HQ: Basf Corporation
  100 Park Ave
  Florham Park NJ 07932
  973 245-6000

(G-4602)
BULKHAUL (USA) LIMITED (DH)
485 Us Highway 1 S E230b (08830)
PHONE..................................908 272-3100
Dennis McCullough, *Vice Pres*
Kevin Sneeden, *Regl Sales Mgr*
EMP: 11
SQ FT: 5,000
SALES (est): 3.2MM **Privately Held**
SIC: **4412** 4424 3443 Deep sea foreign transportation of freight; deep sea domestic transportation of freight; industrial vessels, tanks & containers
HQ: Bulkhaul Limited
  Brignell Road
  Middlesbrough TS2 1
  164 223-0423

(G-4603)
BUSINESS CONTROL SYSTEMS CORP
1173 Green St (08830-2011)
PHONE..................................732 283-1301
Alexander Want, *President*
Marc R Want, *Treasurer*
EMP: 12
SQ FT: 6,000
SALES (est): 2.3MM **Privately Held**
SIC: **3578** 7373 Point-of-sale devices; computer integrated systems design

(G-4604)
CISCO SYSTEMS INC
111 Wood Ave S Ste 2 (08830-2700)
PHONE..................................732 635-4200
Carl Wiese, *Vice Pres*
Genna Cargill, *Project Mgr*
Donna Taormina, *Opers Staff*
Omar Abdella, *Engineer*
Alan Benjamin, *Engineer*
EMP: 200
SALES (corp-wide): 51.9B **Publicly Held**
WEB: www.cisco.com
SIC: **3577** Data conversion equipment, media-to-media: computer
PA: Cisco Systems, Inc.
  170 W Tasman Dr
  San Jose CA 95134
  408 526-4000

(G-4605)
CLIENTSRVER TECH SOLUTIONS LLC
2 Austin Ave Fl 2 # 2 (08830-3058)
PHONE..................................732 710-4495
Srinivas Arra, *President*
EMP: 7
SQ FT: 1,000

SALES: 250K **Privately Held**
SIC: **7371** 7372 8748 Computer software development & applications; business oriented computer software; systems engineering consultant, ex. computer or professional

(G-4606)
COUNTRY OVEN
1585 Oak Tree Rd Ste 207 (08830-1555)
PHONE..................................732 494-4838
Sudhakar RAO Polsani, *Principal*
EMP: 5
SALES (est): 240.9K **Privately Held**
SIC: **2053** Cakes, bakery: frozen

(G-4607)
DOMINO FOODS INC (DH)
Also Called: Domino Sugar
99 Wood Ave S Ste 901 (08830-2733)
PHONE..................................732 590-1173
Brian O' Malley, *CEO*
Jack Giovinco, *Sales Staff*
John Damiano, *Manager*
▼ EMP: 125
SQ FT: 2,222
SALES (est): 594.9MM
SALES (corp-wide): 2B **Privately Held**
WEB: www.dominofoods.com
SIC: **5149** 2062 Sugar, honey, molasses & syrups; refined cane sugar from purchased raw sugar or syrup
HQ: American Sugar Refining, Inc.
  1 N Clematis St Ste 200
  West Palm Beach FL 33401
  561 366-5100

(G-4608)
ENGELHARD CORPORATION
101 Wood Ave S (08830-2749)
PHONE..................................732 205-5000
EMP: 19
SALES (est): 2.3MM **Privately Held**
SIC: **2819** Industrial inorganic chemicals

(G-4609)
FEDEX OFFICE & PRINT SVCS INC
1 Quality Way (08830-2924)
PHONE..................................732 636-3580
EMP: 20
SALES (corp-wide): 69.6B **Publicly Held**
WEB: www.kinkos.com
SIC: **7334** 2759 4731 Photocopying & duplicating services; commercial printing; freight transportation arrangement
HQ: Fedex Office And Print Services, Inc.
  7900 Legacy Dr
  Plano TX 75024
  800 463-3339

(G-4610)
HELSINN THERAPEUTICS US INC
170 Wood Ave S Fl 1 (08830-2742)
PHONE..................................908 231-1435
Riccardo Braglia, *CEO*
Franco De Vecchi, *Ch of Bd*
Paola Bonvicini, *President*
Paolo Guainazzi, *General Mgr*
Padraig Somers, *General Mgr*
EMP: 21
SALES (est): 6.5MM
SALES (corp-wide): 80MM **Privately Held**
SIC: **2834** Pharmaceutical preparations
PA: Helsinn Holding Sa
  Via Pian Scairolo 9
  Pazzallo TI 6912
  919 852-121

(G-4611)
IMMEDIS INC
485 Route 1 S Ste 330 (08830)
PHONE..................................212 239-2625
David Leboff, *Principal*
EMP: 17 EST: 2017
SALES (est): 1MM **Privately Held**
SIC: **7372** Business oriented computer software

(G-4612)
INFINEON TECH AMERICAS CORP
186 Wood Ave S (08830-2763)
PHONE..................................732 603-5914
Cheris Rickalla, *President*
EMP: 15
SALES (corp-wide): 8.7B **Privately Held**
WEB: www.infineon-ncs.com
SIC: **3674** Semiconductors & related devices
HQ: Infineon Technologies Americas Corp.
  101 N Pacific Coast Hwy
  El Segundo CA 90245
  310 726-8000

(G-4613)
LABNET INTERNATIONAL INC
33 Wood Ave S Ste 600 (08830-2717)
PHONE..................................732 417-0700
Gerald Cooney, *CEO*
▲ EMP: 30
SALES (est): 4.9MM
SALES (corp-wide): 11.2B **Publicly Held**
WEB: Www.labnetlink.com
SIC: **3821** Laboratory equipment: fume hoods, distillation racks, etc.
PA: Corning Incorporated
  1 Riverfront Plz
  Corning NY 14831
  607 974-9000

(G-4614)
MAGLIONES ITALIAN ICES LLC
Also Called: Little Jimmy's
111 Madison St (08830-1918)
PHONE..................................732 283-0705
Mike Maglione, *Mng Member*
George Maglione,
EMP: 10
SQ FT: 2,500
SALES: 900K **Privately Held**
SIC: **2024** 5143 5451 Ice cream & frozen desserts; ice cream & ices; ice cream (packaged)

(G-4615)
MAIDENFORM
485 Us Highway 1 S (08830)
PHONE..................................732 621-2216
Anthony Esposito, *Manager*
▲ EMP: 1200
SQ FT: 12,000
SALES (est): 47.6MM **Privately Held**
SIC: **2341** Women's & children's underwear

(G-4616)
MAIDENFORM BRANDS INC (HQ)
485 Us Highway 1 S (08830)
PHONE..................................888 573-0299
Maurice S Reznik, *CEO*
Malcolm Robinson, *President*
Christopher W Vieth, *COO*
Patrick J Burns, *Exec VP*
Nanci Prado, *Exec VP*
▲ EMP: 24
SQ FT: 81,300
SALES (est): 87.4MM
SALES (corp-wide): 6.8B **Publicly Held**
SIC: **2342** 5621 2341 Bras, girdles & allied garments; brassieres; foundation garments, women's; girdles & panty girdles; women's specialty clothing stores; ready-to-wear apparel, women's; women's & children's undergarments
PA: Hanesbrands Inc.
  1000 E Hanes Mill Rd
  Winston Salem NC 27105
  336 519-8080

(G-4617)
MICROSOFT CORPORATION
101 Wood Ave S Ste 900 (08830-2750)
PHONE..................................732 476-5600
Nilesh Parikh, *Engineer*
Paula Warfield, *Accounts Mgr*
Stephanie Mosticchio, *Sales Staff*
Donna Abrusci, *Branch Mgr*
Michael Glasser, *Manager*
EMP: 80

SALES (corp-wide): 125.8B **Publicly Held**
WEB: www.microsoft.com
SIC: 7372 Application computer software
PA: Microsoft Corporation
　1 Microsoft Way
　Redmond WA 98052
　425 882-8080

(G-4618)
NATIONAL LABNET CO
33 Wood Ave S Ste 600 (08830-2717)
PHONE..................................732 417-0700
Walter Demsia, *Owner*
▲ EMP: 22
SALES (est): 1.8MM **Privately Held**
WEB: www.labnetlink.com
SIC: 5049 3821 3826 Laboratory equipment, except medical or dental; scientific instruments; laboratory equipment: fume hoods, distillation racks, etc.; analytical instruments

(G-4619)
NOVAERA SOLUTIONS INC
33 Wood Ave S Ste 600 (08830-2717)
PHONE..................................732 452-3605
Dan Vaper, *President*
EMP: 81
SALES (est): 2.1MM **Privately Held**
SIC: 8748 7379 2836 Business consulting; computer related consulting services; ; biological products, except diagnostic

(G-4620)
OS33 SERVICES CORP (PA)
120 Wood Ave S Ste 505 (08830-2709)
PHONE..................................866 796-0310
David Matalon, *Principal*
EMP: 5 EST: 2014
SALES (est): 3.9MM **Privately Held**
SIC: 7372 7371 Prepackaged software; computer software development

(G-4621)
OTI AMERICA INC
517 Us Highway 1 S # 2150 (08830-3069)
PHONE..................................732 429-1900
Shlomi Cohen, *CEO*
Udi Abramovic, *Vice Pres*
Amir Eilam, *Vice Pres*
Yishay Curelaru, *CFO*
EMP: 9 EST: 1998
SALES (est): 2MM
SALES (corp-wide): 5.9MM **Privately Held**
SIC: 3571 Electronic computers
PA: On Track Innovations Ltd
　Industrial Zone
　Rosh Pina 12000
　468 680-00

(G-4622)
PARTH ENTERPRISES INC
665 State Route 27 (08830-1820)
PHONE..................................732 404-0665
EMP: 4
SALES: 500K **Privately Held**
SIC: 2752 Lithographic Commercial Printing

(G-4623)
POWER HOME RMDLG GROUP LLC
485 Us Highway 1 S C (08830)
PHONE..................................610 874-5000
Corey Schiller, *Branch Mgr*
EMP: 913 **Privately Held**
SIC: 3442 Window & door frames
PA: Power Home Remodeling Group, Llc.
　2501 Seaport Dr Lbby 1
　Chester PA 19013

(G-4624)
QUALITY SWEETS
1396 Oak Tree Rd (08830-1661)
PHONE..................................732 283-3799
Krishan Ram, *Owner*
EMP: 4
SALES (est): 302.4K **Privately Held**
SIC: 2869 Sweeteners, synthetic

(G-4625)
S S P ENTERPRISES INC
Also Called: Signs By Tomorrow
825 Us Highway 1 S (08830-2660)
PHONE..................................732 602-7878
Rajeez Krishna, *President*
EMP: 5
SQ FT: 1,700
SALES (est): 470K **Privately Held**
SIC: 3993 Signs & advertising specialties

(G-4626)
SENSIPLE INC (PA)
555 Us Highway 1 S # 330 (08830-3100)
PHONE..................................732 283-0499
Sadeesh Venugopal, *President*
Vivek Chaturvedi, *Vice Pres*
Christa Benedeto, *Opers Mgr*
Girish Can, *Manager*
Christa Di Benedetto, *Manager*
EMP: 12
SQ FT: 2,000
SALES (est): 8.1MM **Privately Held**
SIC: 7372 7379 Business oriented computer software; computer related consulting services

(G-4627)
SHOWCASE PRINTING OF ISELIN
181 E James Pl (08830-1226)
PHONE..................................732 283-0438
Vivian Hoppock, *President*
Glenn Hoppock, *Vice Pres*
EMP: 5
SALES: 250K **Privately Held**
SIC: 2752 Commercial printing, offset

(G-4628)
SIEMENS CORPORATION
170 Wood Ave S Fl 1 (08830-2726)
PHONE..................................732 590-6895
Thomas McCausland, *Manager*
Colleen Byrne, *Manager*
Helen Wong, *Manager*
Daryll Rouse, *Senior Mgr*
EMP: 80
SALES (corp-wide): 95B **Privately Held**
WEB: www.usa.siemens.com
SIC: 3612 Distribution transformers, electric
HQ: Siemens Corporation
　300 New Jersey Ave Nw # 10
　Washington DC 20001
　202 434-4800

(G-4629)
SMARTLINX SOLUTIONS LLC (PA)
111 Wood Ave S Ste 400 (08830-2700)
PHONE..................................732 385-5507
Marina Aslanyan, *CEO*
Susan Phillips, *Opers Mgr*
Kalpesh Patel, *QC Mgr*
Alex Gardner, *CFO*
Ranjan Dutta, *Controller*
EMP: 65
SALES: 13.9MM **Privately Held**
SIC: 7371 7372 7373 Computer software development; software programming applications; business oriented computer software; systems software development services

(G-4630)
SXWELL USA LLC
111 Wood Ave S Ste 210 (08830-2700)
PHONE..................................732 345-5400
EMP: 450
SALES (est): 851.8K **Privately Held**
SIC: 3069 Medical & laboratory rubber sundries & related products

(G-4631)
TDK ELECTRONICS INC (DH)
485b Us Highway 1 S # 200 (08830-3013)
PHONE..................................732 906-4300
Jon Nelson, *President*
Marlene Cortez, *Controller*
Richard Michelson, *Sales Mgr*
Tracey Dewitt, *Manager*
▲ EMP: 100
SQ FT: 22,477

SALES (est): 96.8MM **Privately Held**
SIC: 3679 3546 5065 3671 Electronic crystals; power-driven handtools; electronic parts & equipment; electron tubes
HQ: Tdk Electronics Ag
　Rosenheimer Str. 141e
　Munchen 81671
　895 402-00

(G-4632)
TECHENZYME INC
75 State Route 27 Ste 300 (08830-1536)
PHONE..................................732 632-8600
Manu Rajvanshi, *Branch Mgr*
EMP: 4
SALES (est): 272.6K
SALES (corp-wide): 1.4MM **Privately Held**
SIC: 2869 Enzymes
PA: Techenzyme Inc
　1091 Amboy Ave Ste A
　Edison NJ 08837
　732 662-3429

(G-4633)
THROMBOGENICS INC
101 Wood Ave S Ste 610 (08830-2750)
PHONE..................................732 590-2900
Patrick De Haes, *CEO*
Patrick D Haes, *CEO*
Claudia Alexandrou, *CFO*
Gabriel Almeida, *Finance*
Andreina De Sousa, *Finance*
EMP: 50
SALES (est): 10.2MM **Privately Held**
WEB: www.thrombogenics.com
SIC: 2834 Pharmaceutical preparations

(G-4634)
US NEWS & WORLD REPORT INC
99 Wood Ave S Ste 304 (08830-2715)
PHONE..................................212 716-6800
Mort Zuckerman, *Principal*
EMP: 12
SALES (corp-wide): 101.1MM **Privately Held**
SIC: 2721 Periodicals
PA: U.S. News & World Report, Inc.
　120 5th Ave Fl 7
　New York NY 10011
　212 716-6800

(G-4635)
VST CONSULTING INC
200 Middlesex Tpke # 102 (08830-2033)
PHONE..................................732 404-0025
Suresh Chatakondu, *President*
Priya Gupta, *Manager*
Subba RAO, *Manager*
Sandeeep Kumar, *IT/INT Sup*
EMP: 80
SQ FT: 2,500
SALES (est): 7.4MM **Privately Held**
SIC: 7372 7373 Application computer software; systems integration services

(G-4636)
XCHANGE SOFTWARE INC (PA)
10 Austin Ave Fl 2 (08830-2908)
PHONE..................................732 444-4943
Prabhakar R Yeruva, *President*
EMP: 6
SQ FT: 2,000
SALES (est): 3.8MM **Privately Held**
SIC: 7372 Application computer software

┌─────────────────────────┐
│ **Island Heights** │
│ *Ocean County* │
└─────────────────────────┘

(G-4637)
BEACHWOOD CANVAS WORKS LLC
39 Lake Ave (08732-7790)
P.O. Box 137 (08732-0137)
PHONE..................................732 929-1783
Dan Janquitto,
EMP: 10
SQ FT: 12,000
SALES (est): 944.7K **Privately Held**
SIC: 2394 Canvas & related products

┌─────────────────────────┐
│ **Jackson** │
│ *Ocean County* │
└─────────────────────────┘

(G-4638)
AMERIMOLD TECH INC
150 Park Ave (08527-3752)
PHONE..................................732 462-7577
EMP: 35
SQ FT: 17,500
SALES (est): 4.7MM **Privately Held**
SIC: 5085 3544 Whol Industrial Supplies Mfg Dies/Tools/Jigs/Fixtures

(G-4639)
ANJOYX LLC ◗
7 Elana Dr (08527-3130)
PHONE..................................323 505-2002
Brooke Fullman,
EMP: 6 EST: 2018
SALES: 500K **Privately Held**
SIC: 2741

(G-4640)
APPAREL STRGC ALLIANCES LLC
41 Greenwich Dr (08527-4878)
PHONE..................................732 833-7771
James Saar,
EMP: 15 EST: 2015
SALES: 10MM **Privately Held**
SIC: 2389 Apparel for handicapped

(G-4641)
BCG MARBLE & GRANITE SOUTH LLC
150 Faraday Ave (08527-5034)
PHONE..................................732 367-3788
Tony Cianvhetta, *President*
Pasquale Petrocelli, *Vice Pres*
▲ EMP: 8
SQ FT: 7,000
SALES (est): 968.2K **Privately Held**
SIC: 3281 5999 5032 Marble, building: cut & shaped; granite, cut & shaped; monuments & tombstones; marble building stone

(G-4642)
CENTRAL JERSEY HOT MIX ASP LLC
577 S Hope Chapel Rd (08527-5056)
PHONE..................................732 323-0226
James Johnson Jr,
Pamela Flockhart,
Carolyn Hordichuk,
David Johnson,
EMP: 4
SALES (est): 640K **Privately Held**
SIC: 5032 2951 Asphalt mixture; asphalt paving mixtures & blocks

(G-4643)
CLAYTON BLOCK COMPANY INC
Also Called: Clayton Concrete
1215 E Veterans Hwy (08527-5004)
PHONE..................................732 364-2404
EMP: 18
SALES (corp-wide): 46.8MM **Privately Held**
SIC: 3273 Mfg Ready-Mixed Concrete
PA: Clayton Block Company, Inc.
　1355 Campus Pkwy Ste 200
　Wall Township NJ 07753
　732 363-1995

(G-4644)
CLEANZONES LLC
640 Herman Rd Ste 2 (08527-3068)
PHONE..................................732 534-5590
David McClelland, *Mng Member*
Toni McClelland,
EMP: 10
SQ FT: 5,000
SALES (est): 1MM **Privately Held**
WEB: www.cleanzones.com
SIC: 3821 3564 Laboratory equipment: fume hoods, distillation racks, etc.; laboratory furniture; purification & dust collection equipment

(G-4645)
CREATIVE CONCEPTS OF NJ LLC
580 N County Line Rd (08527-4431)
PHONE.................................732 833-1776
Thomas Jonin, *Senior Partner*
Tyler Jonin, *Prdtn Mgr*
Michael Jonin, *Mktg Dir*
EMP: 4
SALES (est): 79.2K **Privately Held**
SIC: 2431 Interior & ornamental woodwork & trim

(G-4646)
CREATIVE WOOD PRODUCTS INC
370 Whitesville Rd Ste 8 (08527-5063)
PHONE.................................732 370-0051
George Tomaszewioz, *President*
Marion Romanowski, *Vice Pres*
EMP: 11
SQ FT: 8,000
SALES: 1.3MM **Privately Held**
SIC: 2431 Moldings, wood: unfinished & prefinished

(G-4647)
CUSTOM BARRES LLC
436 W Commodore Blvd # 28 (08527-5437)
PHONE.................................848 245-9464
Michal Pellicone, *Mng Member*
Scott Pellicone, *Mng Member*
EMP: 5
SQ FT: 3,600
SALES (est): 792.4K **Privately Held**
SIC: 2431 Brackets, wood

(G-4648)
D DEPASQUALE PAVING LLC
1 Reagan Dr (08527-5155)
PHONE.................................301 674-9775
Stephany Green,
EMP: 4 EST: 2012
SALES (est): 253.6K **Privately Held**
SIC: 2951 4212 Asphalt paving blocks (not from refineries); local trucking, without storage

(G-4649)
D J B WELDING INC
1461 Toms River Rd (08527-5211)
PHONE.................................732 657-7478
Daniel J Black, *President*
Vickie Black, *Manager*
EMP: 4
SALES (est): 250K **Privately Held**
SIC: 7692 Welding repair

(G-4650)
DESIGNER KITCHENS
250 Faraday Ave (08527-5035)
PHONE.................................732 370-5500
Edwin Rivera, *Partner*
Hector Rivera,
EMP: 10
SQ FT: 6,400
SALES (est): 640K **Privately Held**
SIC: 2511 2434 Kitchen & dining room furniture; wood kitchen cabinets

(G-4651)
DMD STAIRS & RAILS LLC
370 Whitesville Rd Ste 8 (08527-5063)
PHONE.................................732 901-0102
Douglas Diani, *Owner*
EMP: 7
SALES (est): 1MM **Privately Held**
SIC: 2431 Staircases, stairs & railings

(G-4652)
EARLE THE WALTER R CORP
655 S Hope Chapel Rd (08527-5202)
P.O. Box 757, Farmingdale (07727-0757)
PHONE.................................732 657-8551
Walter R Earle, *President*
EMP: 5
SALES (corp-wide): 3.8MM **Privately Held**
WEB: www.theearlecompanies.com
SIC: 2951 Concrete, bituminous
PA: Earle, The Walter R Corp
1800 State Route 34 # 205
Wall Township NJ 07719
732 308-1113

(G-4653)
EARLE ASPHALT COMPANY
655 S Hope Chapel Rd (08527-5202)
P.O. Box 757, Farmingdale (07727-0757)
PHONE.................................732 657-8551
Walter Earle, *Branch Mgr*
Grace Vanaartrijk, *Executive Asst*
EMP: 87
SALES (corp-wide): 40.5MM **Privately Held**
SIC: 2951 Asphalt & asphaltic paving mixtures (not from refineries)
PA: Earle Asphalt Company
1800 State Route 34 # 205
Wall Township NJ 07719
732 308-1113

(G-4654)
EAST COAST SALT DIST INC
621 Wright Debow Rd (08527-5425)
P.O. Box 283, Clarksburg (08510-0283)
PHONE.................................732 833-2973
David Macinnes, *President*
EMP: 4
SALES (est): 972.5K **Privately Held**
WEB: www.eastcoastsalt.com
SIC: 2819 4783 7389 Sodium compounds or salts, inorg., ex. refined sod. chloride; packing goods for shipping;

(G-4655)
ECS ENERGY LTD
16 Meadow Run Ct (08527-4070)
PHONE.................................201 341-5044
James Carbone, *President*
Peter Ramsey, *Exec VP*
EMP: 4 EST: 2007
SQ FT: 3,000
SALES: 1MM **Privately Held**
SIC: 3674 8742 Solar cells; management consulting services

(G-4656)
GALE NEWSON INC (PA)
460 Faraday Ave Ste 7 (08527-5072)
PHONE.................................732 961-7610
Graham Tyers, *President*
EMP: 24
SALES (est): 2.6MM **Privately Held**
SIC: 3599 Electrical discharge machining (EDM)

(G-4657)
INTELLIGENTPROJECT LLC
15 Walter Dr Ste 4 (08527-3419)
PHONE.................................732 928-3421
Jeffrey Raker,
EMP: 5
SALES (est): 320K **Privately Held**
WEB: www.intelligentproject.net
SIC: 1442 Construction sand & gravel

(G-4658)
MACHINE CONTROL SYSTEMS INC
47 Portchester Dr (08527-4395)
PHONE.................................732 529-6888
Frank Chipchase, *President*
EMP: 4 EST: 1998
SALES (est): 449.4K **Privately Held**
WEB: www.machinecontrolsys.com
SIC: 3556 Bakery machinery

(G-4659)
MBS INSTALLATIONS INC
29 Summerhill Ave (08527-4366)
PHONE.................................888 446-9135
Scott Shack, *CEO*
EMP: 10
SALES (est): 81.5K **Privately Held**
SIC: 7641 2521 Office furniture repair & maintenance; panel systems & partitions (free-standing), office: wood

(G-4660)
MILLENNIUM BROKERAGE SVCS LLC
156 E Commodore Blvd A (08527-3083)
PHONE.................................732 928-0900
John Griffith,
Pat Marcello,
Bob Recek,
EMP: 5

SALES (est): 2.4MM **Privately Held**
SIC: 1311 Crude petroleum & natural gas production

(G-4661)
OLD HIGHTS PRINT SHOP INC
16 Nancy Ct (08527-4669)
PHONE.................................609 443-4700
Cathy M Simmons, *President*
Richard J Simmons, *Vice Pres*
EMP: 7
SQ FT: 5,500
SALES (est): 808.6K **Privately Held**
SIC: 2752 2791 7384 Commercial printing, offset; typesetting; photograph developing & retouching

(G-4662)
PRESENTATION SOLUTIONS INC
432 Clearstream Rd (08527-2040)
PHONE.................................732 961-1960
Margo Sweeney, *President*
EMP: 4
SALES (est): 350K **Privately Held**
WEB: www.presentationsolution.com
SIC: 3993 Signs & advertising specialties

(G-4663)
PVH CORP
Also Called: Van Heusen
537 Monmouth Rd Ste 332 (08527-5368)
PHONE.................................732 833-9602
Rochelle Kuhn, *Branch Mgr*
EMP: 9
SALES (corp-wide): 9.6B **Publicly Held**
SIC: 2321 Men's & boys' dress shirts
PA: Pvh Corp.
200 Madison Ave Bsmt 1
New York NY 10016
212 381-3500

(G-4664)
SCHON J TOOL & MACHINE CO
Also Called: Schon Tool
150 Park Ave (08527-3752)
PHONE.................................732 928-6665
James B Schon, *President*
John O Schon, *Shareholder*
EMP: 5 EST: 1944
SALES (est): 416.5K **Privately Held**
SIC: 3069 Hard rubber & molded rubber products

(G-4665)
SIMI GRANOLA LLC
10 S New Prospect Rd (08527-1645)
PHONE.................................848 459-5619
Frank D'Angelo, *Principal*
EMP: 13
SALES (est): 1.3MM **Privately Held**
SIC: 2043 Granola & muesli, except bars & clusters

(G-4666)
T & B SPECIALTIES INC
479 Wright Debow Rd (08527-5420)
PHONE.................................732 928-4500
Thomas E Barchie, *President*
EMP: 5
SQ FT: 6,000
SALES (est): 2.3MM **Privately Held**
SIC: 5085 5087 5169 3052 Rubber goods, mechanical; hose, belting & packing; janitors' supplies; chemicals & allied products; rubber belting; rubber hose; mechanical rubber goods; extruded finished plastic products

(G-4667)
TRADEMARKSIGN
631 Herman Rd (08527-3009)
PHONE.................................848 223-4548
Thomas Menshouse, *Principal*
Sue Campbell, *Project Mgr*
EMP: 17 EST: 2016
SALES (est): 2.3MM **Privately Held**
SIC: 3993 Signs & advertising specialties

(G-4668)
VEP MANUFACTURING
575 S Hope Chapel Rd (08527-5056)
PHONE.................................732 657-0666
Robert Pfluger, *President*
Frances Pfluger, *Corp Secy*
Tom Pfluger, *Vice Pres*

Ryan Pfluger, *Plant Mgr*
Tim Pfluger, *Marketing Staff*
EMP: 10
SQ FT: 8,000
SALES (est): 1MM **Privately Held**
WEB: www.vepmfg.com
SIC: 3599 7692 Machine shop, jobbing & repair; welding repair

(G-4669)
VET CONSTRUCTION INC
29 N County Line Rd # 218 (08527)
PHONE.................................732 987-4922
EMP: 10
SALES: 500K **Privately Held**
SIC: 8741 1799 1389 Management Services Trade Contractor Oil/Gas Field Services

(G-4670)
YOGURT PARADISE LLC
10 S New Prospect Rd (08527-1645)
PHONE.................................732 534-6395
EMP: 4
SALES (est): 266.6K **Privately Held**
SIC: 2026 Mfg Fluid Milk

Jamesburg
Middlesex County

(G-4671)
CHEROKEE PHARMA LLC
1085 Cranbury S Riv 1 (08831-3410)
PHONE.................................732 422-7800
Suresh Balaswamy,
Suresh Palaniswamy,
EMP: 8
SALES (est): 660K **Privately Held**
SIC: 2834 Pharmaceutical preparations

(G-4672)
FORM TOPS LMINATORS OF TRENTON
37 Merlot Ct (08831-5307)
P.O. Box 389, Windsor (08561-0389)
PHONE.................................609 409-4357
Joseph Hadad, *President*
Sylvia Hadad, *Corp Secy*
John Dawes, *Vice Pres*
EMP: 6
SQ FT: 1,875
SALES: 250K **Privately Held**
SIC: 2541 5031 Cabinets, lockers & shelving; table or counter tops, plastic laminated; building materials, exterior; building materials, interior

(G-4673)
LESLI KATCHEN STEEL CNSTR INC
300 Buckelew Ave Ste 109 (08831-1400)
PHONE.................................732 521-2600
Leslie Katchen, *President*
EMP: 3
SALES (est): 1MM **Privately Held**
SIC: 3441 Fabricated structural metal

(G-4674)
MOLDERS FISHING PRESERVE
318 John Wall Rd (08831-3208)
PHONE.................................732 446-2850
John Genoese, *Manager*
EMP: 4
SALES (est): 331K **Privately Held**
SIC: 3089 Molding primary plastic

(G-4675)
MONROE MACHINE & DESIGN INC
566 Buckelew Ave (08831-2971)
PHONE.................................732 521-3434
Mozes Kovacs, *President*
Robert Kovacs, *Vice Pres*
Susan Kovacs, *Treasurer*
Ericka Kovacs, *Admin Sec*
EMP: 12
SQ FT: 3,500
SALES: 1MM **Privately Held**
WEB: www.monroemachine.com
SIC: 3599 Machine shop, jobbing & repair

GEOGRAPHIC

(G-4676)
RANX PHARMACEUTICALS INC
1085 Cranbury S River Rd (08831-3410)
PHONE................................571 214-8989
Sivakumar Rangasamy, *Principal*
EMP: 4
SALES (est): 249.5K Privately Held
SIC: 2834 Pharmaceutical preparations

(G-4677)
SWEET SIGN SYSTEMS INC
9 Davison Ave Ste 5 (08831-1373)
PHONE................................732 521-9300
Richard Dawson, *President*
EMP: 5 EST: 1920
SQ FT: 400
SALES (est): 697.1K Privately Held
SIC: 3993 Electric signs

Jersey City
Hudson County

(G-4678)
3DIMENSION DGNSTC SLUTION CORP
394 Union St Fl 1 (07304-1212)
PHONE................................201 780-4653
Farrukh Babar, *President*
EMP: 8 EST: 2009
SALES: 1MM Privately Held
SIC: 3845 Ultrasonic scanning devices, medical

(G-4679)
67 POLLOCK AVE CORP
Also Called: Willow Iron Works
67 Pollock Ave (07305-1109)
PHONE................................201 432-1156
Michael Zaccaria, *President*
Delores Zaccaria, *Treasurer*
EMP: 7
SQ FT: 2,500
SALES (est): 560K Privately Held
SIC: 1799 3446 3444 Ornamental metal work; architectural metalwork; sheet metalwork

(G-4680)
9001 CORPORATION
Also Called: Dunkin' Donuts
507 Summit Ave Ste 7 (07306-2933)
PHONE................................201 963-2233
Peter Matarazzo, *President*
EMP: 25
SALES (est): 837.4K Privately Held
SIC: 5461 2051 Doughnuts; doughnuts, except frozen

(G-4681)
9002 CORPORATION
Also Called: Dunkin' Donuts
318 Central Ave (07307-2911)
PHONE................................201 792-9595
Peter Matarazzo, *President*
EMP: 30
SALES (est): 815.9K Privately Held
SIC: 5461 2051 Doughnuts; doughnuts, except frozen

(G-4682)
A & R SEWING COMPANY INC
451 Communipaw Ave (07304-3601)
PHONE................................201 332-0622
Jerry Ragoobir, *President*
EMP: 12
SQ FT: 2,300
SALES: 100K Privately Held
SIC: 2392 5949 7389 Tablecloths & table settings; sewing, needlework & piece goods; sewing contractor

(G-4683)
A B TEES LLC
7 Sherman Ave Fl 3 (07307-2338)
PHONE................................201 239-0022
Anthony A Blunda, *Partner*
▲ EMP: 4 EST: 1998
SALES (est): 450.4K Privately Held
WEB: www.abtees1.com
SIC: 2759 Screen printing

(G-4684)
ACADIA SCENIC INC
150 Pacific Ave Ste 6 (07304-3201)
P.O. Box 197 (07303-0197)
PHONE................................201 653-8889
David Lawson, *President*
EMP: 30
SQ FT: 20,000
SALES (est): 3.6MM Privately Held
SIC: 3999 7922 7812 Theatrical scenery; equipment rental, theatrical; motion picture production & distribution, television

(G-4685)
ACRILEX INC (PA)
230 Culver Ave (07305-1122)
PHONE................................201 333-1500
Steve Sullivan, *President*
David Grunberg, *CFO*
Trevor Butler, *Sales Staff*
Dorothy Mlynarski, *Admin Sec*
▲ EMP: 45 EST: 1972
SQ FT: 50,000
SALES (est): 25.4MM Privately Held
WEB: www.acrilex.com
SIC: 5162 3081 Plastics materials; plastic film & sheet

(G-4686)
ADVANCE DIGITAL INC
185 Hudson St Ste 3100 (07311-1217)
PHONE................................201 459-2808
Peter Weinberger, *President*
Stuart Schauman, *Vice Pres*
Mike Schiller, *Technical Staff*
EMP: 250
SALES (est): 29.2MM Privately Held
WEB: www.advancecars.com
SIC: 7372 Publishers' computer software

(G-4687)
AFL TELECOMMUNICATIONS LLC
123 Town Square Pl (07310-1756)
PHONE................................864 486-7303
Kenny Nara, *Branch Mgr*
EMP: 69 Privately Held
SIC: 3357 Nonferrous wiredrawing & insulating
HQ: Afl Telecommunications Llc
    170 Ridgeview Center Dr
    Duncan SC 29334
    864 433-0333

(G-4688)
ALL AMRCAN RECYCL CORP CLIFTON
Also Called: Aarc
2 Hope St (07307-1306)
PHONE................................201 656-3363
Vincent M Ponte, *President*
Vincent F Ponte, *Vice Pres*
Charlie Jacobsen, *CFO*
EMP: 130 EST: 1998
SQ FT: 90,000
SALES (est): 37.1MM Privately Held
SIC: 4953 2611 Recycling, waste materials; pulp manufactured from waste or recycled paper

(G-4689)
ALPINE CUSTOM FLOORS
173 Sherman Ave (07307-2040)
P.O. Box 441, Elmwood Park (07407-0441)
PHONE................................201 533-0100
Paul Benson, *Owner*
EMP: 15
SALES (est): 1.4MM Privately Held
WEB: www.alpinegroupusa.com
SIC: 2426 Flooring, hardwood

(G-4690)
ALSTER IMPORT COMPANY INC
16 Burma Rd (07305-4634)
PHONE................................201 332-7245
Al Barletta, *President*
Paul Ling, *Vice Pres*
▲ EMP: 10
SQ FT: 10,000
SALES: 1.6MM Privately Held
SIC: 5094 3961 Jewelry; costume jewelry, ex. precious metal & semiprecious stones

(G-4691)
ANCRAFT PRESS CORP
234 16th St 8 (07310-1196)
PHONE................................201 792-9200
Marlon Curtis, *Principal*
Toni Andors, *Admin Sec*
▲ EMP: 15
SQ FT: 10,000
SALES (est): 1.1MM Privately Held
SIC: 2752 3555 2789 Commercial printing, lithographic; printing trades machinery; bookbinding & related work

(G-4692)
ANGELOS PANETTERIA INC
14 Wales Ave (07306-6412)
P.O. Box 1792, Englewood Cliffs (07632-1192)
PHONE................................201 435-4659
EMP: 6
SALES (est): 469K Privately Held
SIC: 2051 Manufactures Bread

(G-4693)
ANHEUSER-BUSCH LLC
30 Montgomery St Ste 700 (07302-3841)
PHONE................................973 645-7700
James Correll, *Manager*
Eugene Bocis, *Manager*
EMP: 162
SALES (corp-wide): 1.5B Privately Held
WEB: www.hispanicbud.com
SIC: 2082 Beer (alcoholic beverage)
HQ: Anheuser-Busch, Llc
    1 Busch Pl
    Saint Louis MO 63118
    800 342-5283

(G-4694)
ANTENNA SOFTWARE INC (HQ)
111 Town Square Pl # 520 (07310-1725)
PHONE................................201 217-3824
James J Hemmer, *President*
Adele Freedman, *Exec VP*
Ken Nicolson, *Exec VP*
Gregg Plekan, *Exec VP*
Pmp Arthur Punla, *Project Mgr*
EMP: 32
SQ FT: 13,000
SALES (est): 25.7MM
SALES (corp-wide): 891.5MM Publicly Held
WEB: www.antennasoftware.com
SIC: 7372 7371 Prepackaged software; computer software writing services
PA: Pegasystems Inc.
    1 Rogers St
    Cambridge MA 02142
    617 374-9600

(G-4695)
APPRENTICE FS INC
190 Chrstpher Columbus Dr (07302-3432)
PHONE................................973 960-0875
Angelo Stracquatanio, *CEO*
Gary Pignata, *Security Dir*
EMP: 30
SALES (est): 1MM Privately Held
SIC: 7372 Prepackaged software

(G-4696)
ARRAY SOLDERS LTD LIABILITY CO
329 Mercer Loop (07302-3232)
PHONE................................201 432-0095
Rolando Pavon, *Sales Staff*
Rosario Murillo,
Joseph Portelo,
EMP: 5
SQ FT: 14,000
SALES: 350K Privately Held
WEB: www.arraysolders.com
SIC: 3541 Machine tools, metal cutting type

(G-4697)
B2X CORPORATION
10 Exchange Pl Fl 25 (07302-4914)
PHONE................................201 714-2373
Joseph A Sorisi, *CEO*
Alessandra Coderoni, *President*
Mark Bonilla, *CFO*
▲ EMP: 6
SALES (est): 530K Privately Held
SIC: 2326 3571 Men's & boys' work clothing; electronic computers

(G-4698)
BANAREZ ENTERPRISES INC
175 Baldwin Ave (07306-1901)
PHONE................................201 222-7515
Miguel Banarez, *President*
EMP: 4
SALES: 185K Privately Held
SIC: 3565 Packaging machinery

(G-4699)
BANNON GROUP LTD
234 16th St 8 (07310-1196)
PHONE................................201 451-6500
Michael Falcone, *President*
EMP: 6 EST: 1996
SQ FT: 60,000
SALES (est): 1MM Privately Held
WEB: www.bannongroup.com
SIC: 2752 Commercial printing, offset

(G-4700)
BEL FUSE INC (PA)
206 Van Vorst St (07302-4421)
PHONE................................201 432-0463
Daniel Bernstein, *President*
Dennis Ackerman, *Vice Pres*
Raymond Cheung, *Vice Pres*
Craig Brosious, *CFO*
Marc Pryor, *Treasurer*
EMP: 139 EST: 1949
SQ FT: 19,000
SALES: 548.1MM Publicly Held
SIC: 3679 3674 3613 3677 Cores, magnetic; semiconductors & related devices; modules, solid state; fuses, electric; inductors, electronic

(G-4701)
BEL HYBRIDS & MAGNETICS INC
206 Van Vorst St (07302-4421)
PHONE................................201 432-0463
Daniel Bernstein, *President*
Peter Christopher, *Vice Pres*
Joyce Fitzpatrick, *Purch Agent*
Brian Gaultney, *Purchasing*
EMP: 10 EST: 1948
SQ FT: 12,600
SALES (est): 2.5MM
SALES (corp-wide): 548.1MM Publicly Held
SIC: 8731 8711 3677 Electronic research; engineering services; electronic coils, transformers & other inductors
PA: Bel Fuse Inc.
    206 Van Vorst St
    Jersey City NJ 07302
    201 432-0463

(G-4702)
BETHEL INDUSTRIES INC
3423 John F Kennedy Blvd (07307-4107)
PHONE................................201 656-8222
Sun Kim, *President*
▲ EMP: 250
SQ FT: 45,000
SALES (est): 49.5MM Privately Held
SIC: 2326 7389 Jackets, overall & work; sewing contractor

(G-4703)
BILLYKIRK (PA)
150 Bay St Fl 3 (07302-2900)
PHONE................................201 222-9092
Chris Bray, *Principal*
▲ EMP: 14
SALES (est): 1.7MM Privately Held
SIC: 3199 3172 Leather garments; leather cases

(G-4704)
BINDING PRODUCTS INC
430 Communipaw Ave Ste 1 (07304-3699)
PHONE................................212 947-1192
Freddie Brooks, *President*
EMP: 26
SQ FT: 16,000
SALES (est): 4.4MM Privately Held
SIC: 7334 2711 2732 5044 Photocopying & duplicating services; newspapers; book printing; office equipment; bookbinding & related work; electrical repair shops

(G-4705)
BORAK GROUP INC
255 Us Highway 1 And 9 (07306-6727)
PHONE..............................718 665-8500
Marc Borak, *President*
▲ EMP: 88
SALES (est): 36.1MM
SALES (corp-wide): 1.1B **Privately Held**
WEB: www.boraxpaper.com
SIC: 5113 2621 5085 Industrial & personal service paper; packaging paper; clean room supplies
PA: Imperial Bag & Paper Co. Llc
255 Route 1 And 9
Jersey City NJ 07306
201 437-7440

(G-4706)
BRUCE TELEKY INC
430 Communipaw Ave Ste 2 (07304-3699)
PHONE..............................718 965-9694
Bruce Teleky, *President*
EMP: 8
SQ FT: 14,000
SALES (est): 580K **Privately Held**
WEB: www.bruceteleky.com
SIC: 2741 Art copy & poster publishing

(G-4707)
C2 IMAGING LLC (HQ)
201 Plaza Two (07311-1100)
PHONE..............................646 557-6300
Tim Wieland, *President*
EMP: 20
SALES (est): 26.2MM
SALES (corp-wide): 128.5MM **Privately Held**
WEB: www.C2imagingllc.com
SIC: 7334 2759 7336 Photocopying & duplicating services; commercial printing; commercial art & graphic design
PA: Vomela Specialty Company
845 Minnehaha Ave E
Saint Paul MN 55106
651 228-2200

(G-4708)
CARLASCIO CUSTOM & ORTHOPEDIC (PA)
283 Grove St Apt 1 (07302-3660)
PHONE..............................201 333-8716
Louis Carlascio, *Owner*
EMP: 7 EST: 1923
SQ FT: 1,200
SALES (est): 587.5K **Privately Held**
WEB: www.carlorth.com
SIC: 5661 3143 3144 3149 Shoes, orthopedic; orthopedic shoes, men's; orthopedic shoes, women's; orthopedic shoes, children's

(G-4709)
CAROLE HCHMAN DESIGN GROUP INC (HQ)
Also Called: Sara Beth Division
90 Hudson St Fl 9 (07302-3900)
P.O. Box 101166, Atlanta GA (30392-1166)
PHONE..............................866 267-3945
Charlie Komar, *CEO*
Peter J Gabbe, *Ch of Bd*
Seth Morris, *President*
Carole Hochman, *Principal*
Paul Shreck, *Principal*
▲ EMP: 150
SQ FT: 26,000
SALES (est): 61.5MM
SALES (corp-wide): 255.4MM **Privately Held**
SIC: 2342 2341 2384 7389 Bras, girdles & allied garments; women's & children's underwear; nightgowns & negligees: women's & children's; women's & children's undergarments; bathrobes, men's & women's: made from purchased materials; interior designer; interior decorating
PA: Charles Komar & Sons, Inc.
90 Hudson St Fl 9
Jersey City NJ 07302
212 725-1500

(G-4710)
CENVEO WORLDWIDE LIMITED
25 Linden Ave E (07305-4726)
PHONE..............................201 434-2100
Vito Mazza, *Plant Mgr*

Melanie Mardirosian, *Human Res Mgr*
Calvin Boles, *Branch Mgr*
EMP: 65
SALES (corp-wide): 2.3B **Privately Held**
WEB: www.mail-well.com
SIC: 2677 2679 5112 Envelopes; tags, paper (unprinted): made from purchased paper; envelopes
HQ: Cenveo Worldwide Limited
200 First Stamford Pl # 2
Stamford CT 06902
203 595-3000

(G-4711)
CHARLES KOMAR & SONS INC (PA)
Also Called: Komar Company, The
90 Hudson St Fl 9 (07302-3900)
PHONE..............................212 725-1500
Charles Komar Jr, *CEO*
David Komar, *Ch of Bd*
Harold Komar, *Co-COB*
Herman Komar, *Co-COB*
Jay Harris, *COO*
◆ EMP: 475 EST: 1908
SALES (est): 255.4MM **Privately Held**
WEB: www.komar-ny.com
SIC: 2341 2384 5137 Women's & children's nightwear; nightgowns & negligees: women's & children's; robes & dressing gowns; nightwear: women's, children's & infants'

(G-4712)
CITY ENVELOPE INC
235 Orient Ave Apt 1 (07305-3658)
P.O. Box 15340 (07305-5340)
PHONE..............................201 792-9292
Randy Leif, *President*
EMP: 4
SALES (est): 764.9K **Privately Held**
SIC: 3555 2621 Presses, envelope, printing; stationery, envelope & tablet papers

(G-4713)
CITY OF JERSEY CITY
Also Called: Street Lights Dept
575 State Rt 440 (07305-4823)
PHONE..............................201 547-4470
Joe D'Souza, *Principal*
EMP: 15 **Privately Held**
WEB: www.cityofjerseycity.com
SIC: 3648 Street lighting fixtures
PA: City Of Jersey City
280 Grove St
Jersey City NJ 07302
201 547-5000

(G-4714)
COLOR CODED LLC
249 Thomas Mcgovern Dr # 3 (07305-4633)
PHONE..............................718 482-1063
EMP: 4
SALES (est): 370K **Privately Held**
SIC: 2752 Lithographic Commercial Printing

(G-4715)
COLUMBIA PAINT LAB INC
452 Communipaw Ave (07304-3659)
PHONE..............................201 435-4884
George Pahiakos, *President*
John Liapakis, *Admin Sec*
EMP: 20
SQ FT: 30,000
SALES (est): 4.2MM **Privately Held**
SIC: 2851 Paints & paint additives; varnishes

(G-4716)
CONNEAUT CREEK SHIP REPR INC
333 Washington St Ste 201 (07302-3095)
PHONE..............................212 863-9406
Joseph Craine, *President*
EMP: 4
SALES (est): 264.4K
SALES (corp-wide): 2.6B **Privately Held**
SIC: 3731 Shipbuilding & repairing
HQ: Rand Logistics, Inc.
333 Washington St Ste 201
Jersey City NJ 07302
212 863-9427

(G-4717)
CONNECTOR MFG CO
123 Town Square Pl (07310-1756)
PHONE..............................513 860-4455
EMP: 8 EST: 2017
SALES (est): 1.3MM **Privately Held**
SIC: 3999 Manufacturing industries

(G-4718)
CORGI SPIRITS LLC
150 Pacific Ave Bldg P (07304-3201)
PHONE..............................862 219-3114
Robert Hagemann, *Mng Member*
EMP: 6
SALES (est): 70.1K **Privately Held**
SIC: 2085 Distilled & blended liquors

(G-4719)
CRAFT SIGNS
136 Franklin St (07307-2330)
PHONE..............................201 656-1991
Michael Tepper, *President*
Robert Iezzi, *Owner*
EMP: 4
SQ FT: 2,000
SALES (est): 300K **Privately Held**
WEB: www.craftsigns.com
SIC: 3993 5999 Electric signs; decals

(G-4720)
DAILY NEWS LP
Also Called: New York Daily News
125 Theodore Conrad Dr (07305-4615)
PHONE..............................212 210-2100
Michael Aiello, *Branch Mgr*
EMP: 11
SALES (corp-wide): 1B **Publicly Held**
WEB: www.nydailynews.com
SIC: 2621 2759 2711 Catalog, magazine & newsprint papers; commercial printing; newspapers
HQ: Daily News, L.P.
4 New York Plz Fl 6
New York NY 10004

(G-4721)
DATAYOG INC
155 Morgan St (07302-2932)
PHONE..............................714 253-6558
Bharat Bhate,
EMP: 10
SQ FT: 4,500
SALES (est): 350.3K **Privately Held**
SIC: 7372 Prepackaged software

(G-4722)
DELIGHT FOODS USA LLC
Also Called: Impex
438 Saint Pauls Ave (07306-6126)
P.O. Box 1555, Livingston (07039-7155)
PHONE..............................201 369-1199
Joseph Parayil, *President*
Philip Parayil, *Vice Pres*
Mathew Parayil, *Director*
Alapatt Thomas, *Director*
◆ EMP: 11
SQ FT: 5,500
SALES (est): 5.6MM **Privately Held**
SIC: 5142 2092 Meat, frozen: packaged; fish, frozen: packaged; fish, frozen: prepared

(G-4723)
DESI TALK LLC (PA)
Also Called: Parikh Worldwide Media
35 Journal Sq Ste 204 (07306-4024)
PHONE..............................212 675-7515
Sudhir Parikh, *Chairman*
Ilayas Quraishi, *COO*
EMP: 8
SALES: 300K **Privately Held**
SIC: 2711 Newspapers, publishing & printing

(G-4724)
DG3 GROUP AMERICA INC (DH)
Also Called: Cgi North America
100 Burma Rd (07305-4623)
PHONE..............................201 793-5000
Steve Babat, *CEO*
Eric Genova, *Vice Pres*
Constantino Riviello, *Project Mgr*
Tim McAuliffe, *Opers Mgr*
Edward Andexler, *Production*
EMP: 11

SALES (est): 59.7MM
SALES (corp-wide): 1.3B **Privately Held**
WEB: www.cgii.net
SIC: 2752 Commercial printing, offset
HQ: Dg3 Holdings, Llc
100 Burma Rd
Jersey City NJ 07305
201 793-5000

(G-4725)
DG3 HOLDINGS LLC (HQ)
Also Called: Diversfied Globl Grphics Group
100 Burma Rd (07305-4623)
PHONE..............................201 793-5000
Tom Saggiomo, *CEO*
Angelo Autiero, *Vice Pres*
John D'Onofrio, *Vice Pres*
Michael D'Onofrio, *Vice Pres*
Phil Rybecky, *Vice Pres*
EMP: 8 EST: 2008
SALES (est): 147.7MM
SALES (corp-wide): 1.3B **Privately Held**
SIC: 2752 Commercial printing, offset
PA: Arsenal Capital Partners Lp
100 Park Ave Fl 31
New York NY 10017
212 771-1717

(G-4726)
DG3 NORTH AMERICA INC
Also Called: Diversfied Globl Grphics Group
100 Burma Rd (07305-4623)
PHONE..............................201 793-5000
Steven Babat, *CEO*
Arthur Baggot, *Vice Pres*
Bill Ballbach, *Vice Pres*
Peter Pantano, *Vice Pres*
Michael Roth, *CFO*
EMP: 405
SQ FT: 167,000
SALES: 160MM
SALES (corp-wide): 226.8MM **Privately Held**
WEB: www.dg3.com
SIC: 2752 Commercial printing, offset
PA: Resilience Capital Partners Llc
25101 Chagrin Blvd # 350
Cleveland OH 44122
216 292-0200

(G-4727)
DIACRITECH LLC
201 Marin Blvd Apt 1112 (07302-6499)
PHONE..............................732 238-1157
Madhu Rajamani,
Kavitha Rajamani,
EMP: 525
SQ FT: 18,000
SALES: 4MM **Privately Held**
WEB: www.diacritech.com
SIC: 7372 7313 Prepackaged software; radio, television, publisher representatives

(G-4728)
DIAMOND HUT JEWELRY EXCHANGE
Hudson Mall Rr 440 (07304)
PHONE..............................201 332-5372
Sachin Gupta, *Partner*
Neera Gupta, *General Mgr*
EMP: 7
SALES (est): 862.5K **Privately Held**
SIC: 3911 7631 5094 3479 Jewelry, precious metal; jewelry repair services; jewelry & precious stones; engraving jewelry silverware, or metal; jewelry stores

(G-4729)
DURABRITE LTG SOLUTIONS LLC
4 Beacon Way Apt 2003 (07304-6129)
PHONE..............................201 915-0555
Mark Larson, *VP Sales*
Steven Cronley, *Director*
EMP: 7
SALES (est): 662.2K **Privately Held**
SIC: 3646 7389 Commercial indusl & institutional electric lighting fixtures;

(G-4730)
EBAOTECH INC USA
101 Hudson St Ste 2100 (07302-3929)
PHONE..............................917 977-1145
Brenda Anaya, *Administration*
EMP: 4

SALES (est): 95.9K
SALES (corp-wide): 2.9MM **Privately Held**
SIC: 7372 Prepackaged software
HQ: Ebaotech Corporation
No.3 Building, Kic Plaza, No.270,
Songhu Road, Yangpu District
Shanghai 20043
216 140-7777

(G-4731)
ELECTROHEAT INDUCTION INC
81 Oakland Ave 3 (07306-2203)
PHONE..............................908 494-0726
Shame Prsna, *Principal*
▲ EMP: 4 EST: 2011
SALES (est): 266K **Privately Held**
SIC: 3567 Industrial furnaces & ovens

(G-4732)
ENTERPRISECC LTD LIABILITY CO
521 Palisade Ave (07307-1409)
PHONE..............................201 266-0020
Marco L Chaffiotte, *CEO*
EMP: 7
SALES (est): 807.6K **Privately Held**
SIC: 8711 3699 4813 5065 Construction & civil engineering; security devices; security control equipment & systems; telephone/video communications; communication equipment; telecommunications consultant

(G-4733)
FABRIC CHEMICAL CORPORATION
61 Cornelison Ave (07304-3403)
PHONE..............................201 432-0440
Andrew Jacobson, *President*
EMP: 9 EST: 1936
SQ FT: 15,000
SALES (est): 1.6MM **Privately Held**
SIC: 2842 Cleaning or polishing preparations

(G-4734)
FIZZY LIZZY LLC
64 Wayne St (07302-3518)
PHONE..............................212 966-3232
Elizabeth Morrill,
Abraham Bakal,
EMP: 5
SQ FT: 600
SALES (est): 394.8K **Privately Held**
SIC: 2086 Carbonated beverages, nonalcoholic: bottled & canned

(G-4735)
FLEXICIOUS LLC
57 Sip Ave Apt 4b (07306-3173)
P.O. Box 6350 (07306-0350)
PHONE..............................646 340-5066
Suha Ozal, *Partner*
EMP: 5
SALES (est): 207.4K **Privately Held**
SIC: 7372 Prepackaged software

(G-4736)
FLORENTINE PRESS INC
234 16th St Fl 4 (07310-1196)
PHONE..............................201 386-9200
Timothy Meredith, *Principal*
EMP: 4
SALES (est): 165.2K **Privately Held**
SIC: 2741 Miscellaneous publishing

(G-4737)
FORBES MEDIA LLC
Also Called: Forbes Magazine
499 Washington Blvd (07310-1995)
PHONE..............................212 620-2200
Mike Perlis, *President*
Ann Marinovich, *Vice Pres*
Jorge Consuegra, *Chief Mktg Ofcr*
James Lawrence, *Business Anlyst*
Mark Howard, *Risk Mgmt Dir*
EMP: 80
SALES (est): 20.7MM **Privately Held**
SIC: 2732 2752 Book printing; advertising posters, lithographed

(G-4738)
FOREST LABORATORIES LLC
185 Hudson St (07311-1209)
PHONE..............................631 436-4534
Taglietti Marco, *Branch Mgr*
EMP: 15 **Privately Held**
SIC: 2834 Pharmaceutical preparations
HQ: Forest Laboratories, Llc
909 3rd Ave Fl 23
New York NY 10022

(G-4739)
FOREST LABORATORIES LLC
1900 Plaza Five (07311-4032)
PHONE..............................631 501-5399
EMP: 35 **Privately Held**
SIC: 2834 Mfg Pharmaceutical Preparations
HQ: Forest Laboratories, Llc
909 3rd Ave Fl 23
New York NY 10022
212 421-7850

(G-4740)
FORSTERS CLEANING & TAILORING
Also Called: Hudson Drapery Service
248 Central Ave (07307-3084)
PHONE..............................201 659-4411
Robert Iezzi, *President*
EMP: 5 EST: 1898
SQ FT: 5,400
SALES (est): 202.2K **Privately Held**
SIC: 7216 7219 2391 Drycleaning collecting & distributing agency; curtain cleaning & repair; tailor shop, except custom or merchant tailor; draperies, plastic & textile: from purchased materials

(G-4741)
FROYO SKYVIEW LLC
42 Dales Ave (07306-6802)
PHONE..............................718 607-5656
Xuyan Chen, *CEO*
Xiang Wu, *Finance*
Jialin Zhang,
EMP: 8
SALES (est): 550.7K **Privately Held**
SIC: 3944 7389 Games, toys & children's vehicles;

(G-4742)
GENERAL PENCIL COMPANY INC (PA)
Also Called: Semi-Hex
67 Fleet St (07306-2213)
PHONE..............................201 653-5351
James S Weissenborn, *President*
Katie Vanconconi, *President*
Helmut Bode, *Vice Pres*
David Seeber, *Vice Pres*
Ingrid Abberton, *Human Res Mgr*
◆ EMP: 3 EST: 1888
SQ FT: 70,000
SALES (est): 4.5MM **Privately Held**
WEB: www.generalpencil.com
SIC: 3952 Pencil lead: black, indelible or colored: artists'; crayons: chalk, gypsum, charcoal, fusains, pastel, wax, etc.

(G-4743)
GL CONSULTING INC (PA)
Also Called: GL Associates
210 Hudson St Ste 1000 (07311-1208)
PHONE..............................201 938-0200
George Lambrianakos, *President*
Roger Elwell, *Vice Pres*
Amelia Ortiz, *Treasurer*
Dino Panayiotarakos, *Admin Sec*
EMP: 20
SALES (est): 3.6MM **Privately Held**
WEB: www.cetova.com
SIC: 7372 Business oriented computer software

(G-4744)
GLOCAL EXPERTISE LLC
185 Zabriskie St (07307-4316)
PHONE..............................718 928-3839
Yasmin Obriwala,
EMP: 5
SQ FT: 100

SALES: 5MM **Privately Held**
SIC: 3229 8748 5023 Glass furnishings & accessories; business consulting; decorative home furnishings & supplies

(G-4745)
GUM RUNNERS LLC
Also Called: Jolt Energy Gum
333 Washington St 2 (07302-3066)
P.O. Box 201, Lebanon (08833-0201)
PHONE..............................201 333-0756
Laurence Molloy,
Kevin M Gass,
▲ EMP: 12
SQ FT: 2,500
SALES (est): 1.5MM **Privately Held**
WEB: www.joltgum.com
SIC: 2067 Chewing gum

(G-4746)
HEALQU LLC
210 Fairmount Ave (07306-3304)
PHONE..............................844 443-2578
Yoel Katz, *Mng Member*
Stanley Salot,
EMP: 5 **Privately Held**
SIC: 3842 Ligatures, medical

(G-4747)
HMS MONACO ET CIE LTD
629 Grove St Fl 5 (07310-1249)
PHONE..............................201 533-0007
Ira Erstling, *President*
Steven Schulman, *Vice Pres*
▲ EMP: 25
SQ FT: 15,000
SALES: 4MM **Privately Held**
WEB: www.hmsmonaco.com
SIC: 3961 5199 Costume jewelry; gifts & novelties

(G-4748)
HOPE CENTER
43 Charles St (07307-2830)
PHONE..............................201 798-1234
Liz Vidal-Cintron, *President*
EMP: 10
SALES (est): 1.1MM **Privately Held**
SIC: 3669 8661 8299 Visual communication systems; Assembly of God Church; musical instrument lessons

(G-4749)
IMAAN TRADING INC
286 Bergen Ave (07305-1620)
PHONE..............................201 779-2062
Liza Azim, *President*
EMP: 5 EST: 2017
SALES (est): 270K **Privately Held**
SIC: 2844 Perfumes & colognes

(G-4750)
IPC SYSTEMS INC (PA)
Also Called: IPC Information Systems
3 2nd St Fl Plz10 (07311-4045)
PHONE..............................201 253-2000
Neil Barua, *CEO*
Robert Santella, *CEO*
David Brown, *Senior VP*
Rob Steets, *Vice Pres*
Irena Toh, *Project Mgr*
▲ EMP: 120
SQ FT: 35,000
SALES (est): 652.8MM **Privately Held**
SIC: 3661 Telephone & telegraph apparatus

(G-4751)
JON-DA PRINTING CO INC
234 16th St Fl 6 (07310-1196)
PHONE..............................201 653-6200
John Malluzzo, *President*
EMP: 15
SQ FT: 4,000
SALES (est): 2.1MM **Privately Held**
SIC: 2752 Commercial printing, offset

(G-4752)
JOSEPH C HANSEN COMPANY INC
Also Called: J C Hansen
234 16th St Fl 8 (07310-1196)
PHONE..............................201 222-1677
Harold Simon, *Principal*
EMP: 6 EST: 1980

SALES (est): 49.4K **Privately Held**
WEB: www.josephchansen.com
SIC: 3999 Theatrical scenery

(G-4753)
KENNAMETAL INC
123 Town Square Pl (07310-1756)
PHONE..............................412 248-8200
EMP: 126
SALES (corp-wide): 2.3B **Publicly Held**
SIC: 3545 Cutting tools for machine tools
PA: Kennametal Inc.
600 Grant St Ste 5100
Pittsburgh PA 15219
412 248-8000

(G-4754)
KOMAR INTIMATES LLC (HQ)
90 Hudson St (07302-3900)
P.O. Box 5227, New York NY (10087-5227)
PHONE..............................212 725-1500
Charles Komar, *CEO*
▲ EMP: 16
SQ FT: 2,400
SALES: 46.7MM
SALES (corp-wide): 255.4MM **Privately Held**
SIC: 2341 2254 5621 Panties: women's, misses', children's & infants'; nightwear (nightgowns, negligees, pajamas), knit; women's clothing stores; women's sportswear
PA: Charles Komar & Sons, Inc.
90 Hudson St Fl 9
Jersey City NJ 07302
212 725-1500

(G-4755)
KOMAR KIDS LLC (HQ)
90 Hudson St (07302-3900)
PHONE..............................212 725-1500
Charlie Komar, *CEO*
Jay Harris, *COO*
Harry Gaffney, *CFO*
David Komar, *Admin Sec*
▲ EMP: 9
SQ FT: 15,000
SALES (est): 6.6MM
SALES (corp-wide): 255.4MM **Privately Held**
SIC: 2254 Nightwear (nightgowns, negligees, pajamas), knit; underwear, knit
PA: Charles Komar & Sons, Inc.
90 Hudson St Fl 9
Jersey City NJ 07302
212 725-1500

(G-4756)
KOPPERS CHOCOLATE LLC
10 Exchange Pl Ste 2800 (07302-4914)
PHONE..............................212 243-0220
Lorie Alexander, *Ch of Bd*
Jeffrey Alexander, *Vice Pres*
Leslye Alexander, *Vice Pres*
▲ EMP: 100
SALES (est): 14.6MM **Privately Held**
WEB: www.kopperschocolate.com
SIC: 2064 2066 Candy & other confectionery products; chocolate & cocoa products

(G-4757)
L A S PRINTING CO
3035 John F Kennedy Blvd (07306-3669)
PHONE..............................201 991-5362
Joseph R Conti, *President*
Peter Miliotis, *Vice Pres*
EMP: 4
SQ FT: 6,000
SALES (est): 371.6K **Privately Held**
WEB: www.lasprinting.com
SIC: 2752 2791 Commercial printing, offset; photocomposition, for the printing trade

(G-4758)
LIBERTY PARK RACEWAY LLC
99 Caven Point Rd (07305-4605)
PHONE..............................201 333-7223
Eyal Farage, *Mng Member*
EMP: 12
SALES (est): 1.9MM **Privately Held**
SIC: 3644 Raceways

▲ = Import ▼=Export
◆ =Import/Export

(G-4759)
LINDER & COMPANY INC
Also Called: Linder Graphics
1183 W Side Ave (07306-6112)
PHONE..........................201 386-8788
George Linder, *President*
Camille Linder, *Treasurer*
EMP: 17 EST: 1852
SQ FT: 32,000
SALES (est): 3.3MM Privately Held
WEB: www.linderco.com
SIC: 2752 Photolithographic printing

(G-4760)
LOGOMANIA INC
Also Called: Composition Printing
110 1/2 Erie St (07302-2076)
P.O. Box 55 (07303-0055)
PHONE..........................201 798-0531
Allen Gradin, *President*
Lynn Gradin, *Admin Sec*
EMP: 4
SQ FT: 1,000
SALES: 400K Privately Held
SIC: 5943 2759 Stationery stores; commercial printing

(G-4761)
LOREAL USA PRODUCTS INC
Also Called: It Cosmetics
111 Town Square Pl # 317 (07310-1755)
PHONE..........................732 873-3520
Ashley Kaplan, *Manager*
Evelynda Rivera, *Senior Mgr*
Beth Winkler, *Senior Mgr*
Marigrace Mancini-Matts, *Director*
Victoria Sneden, *Relations*
EMP: 4
SALES (corp-wide): 4.4B Privately Held
SIC: 2844 Hair coloring preparations
HQ: L'oreal Usa Products, Inc.
10 Hudson Yards
New York NY 10001

(G-4762)
M LONDON INC (PA)
629 Grove St Fl 8 (07310-1264)
PHONE..........................201 459-6460
Michael Bannout, *President*
▲ EMP: 30
SQ FT: 30,000
SALES (est): 2.9MM Privately Held
SIC: 3171 3172 Women's handbags & purses; wallets; billfolds

(G-4763)
MAYA TRADING CORPORATION
Also Called: Maya Liquidation
746-748 Tonnelle Ave (07307)
PHONE..........................201 533-1400
Antounyous Gurguis, *President*
EMP: 5
SQ FT: 15,000
SALES (est): 507K Privately Held
SIC: 3253 Floor tile, ceramic

(G-4764)
MEDICO GRAPHICS SERVICES INC
683 Garfield Ave (07305-4213)
PHONE..........................201 216-1660
Robert Glickenhaus, *Principal*
EMP: 4
SALES (est): 451.6K Privately Held
SIC: 2752 Commercial printing, offset

(G-4765)
METAL MGT PITTSBURGH INC
Also Called: Sims Metal Management
1 Linden Ave E (07305-4726)
PHONE..........................201 333-2902
Galdino Claro, *CEO*
Bob Kelman, *President*
Dennis O'Loughlin, *President*
Leo Wasielewski, *QC Mgr*
Robert C Larry, *CFO*
▼ EMP: 43 EST: 1958
SQ FT: 12,000
SALES (est): 47.7MM Privately Held
WEB: www.mtlm.com
SIC: 5093 3341 Nonferrous metals scrap; secondary nonferrous metals
HQ: Metal Management, Inc.
200 W Madison St Ste 3600
Chicago IL 60606
312 645-0700

(G-4766)
MITSUBISHI TANABE PHARMA (DH)
525 Wshngton Blvd Fl 1400 Flr 1400 (07310)
PHONE..........................908 607-1950
Eiji Tanaka, *President*
Sam Shum, *Vice Pres*
Armand Famiglietti, *VP Opers*
Partha Banerjee, *Research*
Matthew Casey, *Manager*
EMP: 23
SALES (est): 18.9MM Privately Held
SIC: 2834 Pharmaceutical preparations

(G-4767)
MOJO ORGANICS INC
185 Hudson St Ste 2500 (07311-1215)
PHONE..........................201 633-6519
Glenn Simpson, *Ch of Bd*
Peter Spinner, *COO*
▲ EMP: 3
SALES: 1.6MM Privately Held
SIC: 2037 Fruit juices

(G-4768)
MOSCOVA ENTERPRISES INC
101 Hudson St (07302-3915)
PHONE..........................848 628-4873
Vickens Moscova, *Principal*
EMP: 10
SQ FT: 1,000
SALES (est): 464.6K Privately Held
SIC: 2741 8742 7311 ; management consulting services; new business start-up consultant; advertising consultant

(G-4769)
NESTLE WATERS NORTH AMER INC
Also Called: Poland Spring
111 Thomas Mcgovern Dr (07305-4620)
PHONE..........................201 451-4000
John Brophy, *Manager*
EMP: 64
SALES (corp-wide): 92B Privately Held
WEB: www.zephyronline.com
SIC: 5963 2086 Bottled water delivery; water, pasteurized: packaged in cans, bottles, etc.
HQ: Nestle Waters North America Inc.
900 Long Ridge Rd Bldg 2
Stamford CT 06902

(G-4770)
NICHOLAS GALVANIZING CO INC
120 Duffield Ave (07306-6123)
PHONE..........................201 795-1010
Robert Gregory, *President*
EMP: 30 EST: 1949
SQ FT: 18,000
SALES (est): 3.4MM Privately Held
SIC: 3479 Galvanizing of iron, steel or end-formed products

(G-4771)
NILSSON ELECTRICAL LABORATORY
333 W Side Ave (07305-1127)
PHONE..........................201 521-4860
John Brown, *President*
EMP: 6 EST: 1919
SQ FT: 4,500
SALES (est): 500K Privately Held
WEB: www.nilssoneleclab.com
SIC: 3612 5065 7629 Electronic meter transformers; electronic parts & equipment; electrical repair shops

(G-4772)
NIRWANA FOODS LLC
778 Newark Ave (07306-3807)
PHONE..........................201 659-2200
Jagdar Singh, *President*
▲ EMP: 11
SALES (est): 1.6MM Privately Held
SIC: 2086 Iced tea & fruit drinks, bottled & canned

(G-4773)
NORTH AMERICAN FRONTIER CORP
195 New York Ave (07307-1654)
PHONE..........................201 222-1931
Vincent Manz, *Principal*
EMP: 25
SQ FT: 27,000
SALES (est): 1.8MM Privately Held
SIC: 3199 Leather garments

(G-4774)
NSGV INC (HQ)
Also Called: Forbes Magazine
499 Washington Blvd Fl 9 (07310-2055)
PHONE..........................212 620-2200
Malcolm S Forbes Jr, *Ch of Bd*
Miguel Forbes, *President*
Robert L Forbes, *President*
Steve Forbes, *Chairman*
Timothy C Forbes, *COO*
EMP: 181 EST: 1917
SQ FT: 100,000
SALES (est): 70.2MM
SALES (corp-wide): 181.1MM Privately Held
WEB: www.forbes.com
SIC: 2721 Magazines: publishing only, not printed on site
PA: Forbes Management Company Inc
499 Washington Blvd Fl 9
Jersey City NJ 07310
212 620-2200

(G-4775)
NU GRAFIX INC
430 Communipaw Ave (07304-3663)
PHONE..........................201 413-1776
Charles Chaffey, *CEO*
EMP: 50
SALES (est): 4.9MM Privately Held
SIC: 2891 Laminating compounds

(G-4776)
NUTSCOM INC
Also Called: Newark Nut Company
10 Exchange Pl Ste 2800 (07302-4914)
PHONE..........................800 558-6887
Sanford Braverman, *President*
Kenneth Braverman, *Vice Pres*
Scott Bird, *Purch Mgr*
Ben Shakal, *CTO*
Stephanie Hart, *Relations*
EMP: 4
SALES: 58.8K Privately Held
SIC: 5441 2064 Candy; nuts, candy covered

(G-4777)
ORENS DAILY ROAST INC
430 Communipaw Ave Ste 13 (07304-3667)
PHONE..........................201 432-2008
Judd Meyerson, *Branch Mgr*
EMP: 15
SALES (corp-wide): 14.1MM Privately Held
SIC: 2095 5149 Roasted coffee; coffee & tea
PA: Oren's Daily Roast Inc
12 E 46th St Fl 6
New York NY 10017
212 348-5400

(G-4778)
ORIENT ORIGINALS INC
Also Called: Home Warehouse Outlet
55 Edward Hart Dr (07305-4607)
PHONE..........................201 332-5005
Rituraaj Baijal, *President*
▲ EMP: 30
SQ FT: 25,000
SALES (est): 5.9MM Privately Held
WEB: www.textileshop.com
SIC: 1541 2392 Industrial buildings & warehouses; cushions & pillows

(G-4779)
PEEL AWAY LABS INC
304 Newark Ave (07302-2312)
PHONE..........................516 603-3116
Maxwell H Cohen, *CEO*
EMP: 4
SALES (est): 140.1K Privately Held
SIC: 2392 Mattress protectors, except rubber

(G-4780)
PEEL AWAY LABS INC
304 Newark Ave (07302-2312)
PHONE..........................201 420-0051
Maxwell Cohen, *CEO*
EMP: 4
SALES (est): 404.6K Privately Held
SIC: 2211 Bed sheeting, cotton

(G-4781)
PENNETTA & SONS
428 Hoboken Ave (07306-2696)
PHONE..........................201 420-1693
May Pennetta, *President*
Victor Pennetta Jr, *Vice Pres*
EMP: 30
SQ FT: 18,000
SALES (est): 4.8MM Privately Held
WEB: www.pennetta.com
SIC: 1711 8748 7692 Mechanical contractor; warm air heating & air conditioning contractor; energy conservation consultant; welding repair

(G-4782)
PENTA DIGITAL INCORPORATED
234 16th St Fl 8 (07310-1196)
PHONE..........................201 839-5392
Jonathan Chung, *President*
EMP: 8
SALES (est): 509.8K Privately Held
WEB: www.pentadigitalinc.com
SIC: 2759 Commercial printing

(G-4783)
PIC GRAPHICS
926 Newark Ave Ste 400 (07306-6337)
PHONE..........................201 420-5040
Nat Zucker, *President*
Howard Zucker, *Vice Pres*
Julia Zucker, *Vice Pres*
Phillip Zucker, *Vice Pres*
▲ EMP: 32
SQ FT: 30,000
SALES: 9MM Privately Held
WEB: www.picgraphics.com
SIC: 3953 Marking devices

(G-4784)
POLAR TRUCK SALES
350 Sip Ave (07306-6525)
PHONE..........................201 246-1010
Raymond Higgins, *President*
EMP: 30
SALES (est): 5.2MM Privately Held
SIC: 5521 3711 Pickups & vans, used; truck & tractor truck assembly

(G-4785)
POLARIS CONSULTING & SVCS LTD
111 Town Square Pl # 340 (07310-1755)
PHONE..........................732 590-8151
EMP: 10 Privately Held
SIC: 7372 Prepackaged software
HQ: Polaris Consulting & Services Ltd.
20 Corporate Pl S
Piscataway NJ 08854

(G-4786)
POLY-VERSION INC
49 Fisk St (07305-1100)
PHONE..........................201 451-7600
Phillip Goldschmiedt, *President*
Teresa Mert, *Vice Pres*
▲ EMP: 35
SQ FT: 120,000
SALES (est): 6MM Privately Held
SIC: 3089 Work gloves, plastic

(G-4787)
POWERTRUNK INC (DH)
66 York St Ste 4 (07302-3839)
PHONE..........................201 630-4520
Jose Martin, *CEO*
Chris Ramsden, *Vice Pres*
Morne Stramrood, *Vice Pres*
Javier Murad, *Technical Mgr*
Diego Novellon, *Research*
EMP: 4
SALES (est): 384.7K Privately Held
SIC: 3663 Radio & TV communications equipment

HQ: Teltronic Sa
Calle F (Poligono Industrial Malpica)
(Oeste), Parc. 12
Zaragoza 50016
976 465-656

(G-4788)
PROGRESS PRINTING CO
338 Montgomery St (07302-4009)
P.O. Box 442 (07303-0442)
PHONE..................................201 433-3133
Manny Portnoy, *President*
Lois Porco, *Vice Pres*
EMP: 11
SQ FT: 6,000
SALES (est): 1.2MM **Privately Held**
WEB: www.progressprinting.com
SIC: 2752 Commercial printing, offset

(G-4789)
PROJECT FEED USA INC
127a Dwight St (07305-3227)
PHONE..................................201 443-7143
Kevin Wolfe, *Director*
EMP: 10
SALES (est): 283.4K **Privately Held**
SIC: 2032 Canned specialties

(G-4790)
PROTECTION INDUSTRIES CORP
107 York St (07302-3701)
P.O. Box 348 (07303-0348)
PHONE..................................201 333-8050
William J Hill, *Ch of Bd*
EMP: 17
SALES (corp-wide): 2.6MM **Privately Held**
SIC: 5063 3669 Control & signal wire & cable, including coaxial; fire detection systems, electric
PA: Protection Industries Corp
2897 Main St
Stratford CT 06614
203 375-9393

(G-4791)
PROXIMO DISTILLERS LLC
333 Washington St Fl 4 (07302-3066)
PHONE..................................201 204-1718
Mark Teasdale, *President*
EMP: 82
SALES (est): 11.9MM **Privately Held**
SIC: 2082 Malt beverages
PA: Proximo Spirits, Inc.
333 Washington St Ste 401
Jersey City NJ 07302

(G-4792)
PURELY ORGANIC SA LLC
142 Liberty Ave (07306-4920)
PHONE..................................201 942-0400
Raul Munoz, *CEO*
Raul Muoz, *CEO*
John Justiniano, *Principal*
Marcelo Muoz, *COO*
EMP: 4
SALES (est): 109.8K **Privately Held**
SIC: 2911 5191 Residues; fertilizers & agricultural chemicals; pesticides

(G-4793)
R WORLD ENTERPRISES
197 Congress St (07307-3415)
PHONE..................................201 795-2428
Marian Pacailler, *Partner*
Gene Pacailler, *Partner*
EMP: 5 EST: 1973
SALES (est): 497.6K **Privately Held**
SIC: 2048 5199 Bird food, prepared; pet supplies

(G-4794)
RAJBHOG FOODS INC
60 Amity St (07304-3510)
PHONE..................................551 222-4700
Ajit Mody, *Branch Mgr*
EMP: 5 **Privately Held**
SIC: 3556 Food products machinery
PA: Rajbhog Foods Inc.
812 Newark Ave
Jersey City NJ 07306

(G-4795)
RAJBHOG FOODS INC (PA)
812 Newark Ave (07306-3809)
PHONE..................................201 395-9400
Sanjiv Mod, *President*
Sachin Mody, *Vice Pres*
Satish Patel, *Sales Staff*
▲ EMP: 7
SQ FT: 37,000
SALES (est): 1.9MM **Privately Held**
SIC: 3556 Food products machinery

(G-4796)
RAJBHOG FOODS(NJ) INC
60 Amity St (07304-3510)
PHONE..................................551 222-4700
Sanjiv Mody, *President*
Sachin Mody, *Vice Pres*
Ajit Mody, *Admin Sec*
EMP: 125
SQ FT: 35,000
SALES (est): 8.8MM **Privately Held**
SIC: 2096 2013 5143 2038 Potato chips & similar snacks; frozen meats from purchased meat; frozen dairy desserts; breakfasts, frozen & packaged; dinners, frozen & packaged; ice cream & frozen desserts

(G-4797)
RAMBUSCH DECORATING COMPANY
Also Called: Rambusch Lighting
160 Cornelison Ave (07304-3513)
PHONE..................................201 333-2525
Martin V Rambusch, *Ch of Bd*
Edwin P Rambusch, *President*
▲ EMP: 41 EST: 1891
SQ FT: 5,000
SALES (est): 7.5MM **Privately Held**
WEB: www.rambusch.com
SIC: 3646 3231 3446 8742 Commercial indusl & institutional electric lighting fixtures; stained glass: made from purchased glass; architectural metalwork; industry specialist consultants

(G-4798)
RECRUIT CO LTD
Also Called: Recruit USA
111 Pavonia Ave (07310-1755)
PHONE..................................201 216-0600
Janet Chalmers, *Branch Mgr*
EMP: 35 **Privately Held**
SIC: 2721 6512 Magazines: publishing only, not printed on site; commercial & industrial building operation
PA: Recruit Holdings Co.,Ltd.
1-9-2, Marunouchi
Chiyoda-Ku TKY 100-0

(G-4799)
RELAYWARE INC
30 Montgomery St Ste 1210 (07302-3821)
PHONE..................................201 433-3331
Debra Padula, *Business Anlyst*
EMP: 12
SALES (est): 1.2MM
SALES (corp-wide): 6.6MM **Privately Held**
SIC: 7372 Business oriented computer software
HQ: Relayware, Inc.
303 Twin Dolphin Dr Fl 6
Redwood City CA 94065
650 632-4520

(G-4800)
RELIABLE PAPER RECYCLING INC
1 Caven Point Ave (07305-4603)
PHONE..................................201 333-5244
Leonard Pirrello, *President*
Gina Marquez, *Office Mgr*
▼ EMP: 105
SQ FT: 45,000
SALES (est): 21.7MM **Privately Held**
SIC: 4953 2611 5093 Recycling, waste materials; pulp mills; waste paper

(G-4801)
RONALD PERRY
Also Called: Uniquiwa's
14 Westervelt Pl 1 (07304-3428)
PHONE..................................201 702-2407
Ronald Perry, *Owner*
EMP: 10 EST: 2015
SALES (est): 319.7K **Privately Held**
SIC: 2326 Service apparel (baker, barber, lab, etc.), washable: men's

(G-4802)
S V PHARMA INC
227 Ocean Ave (07305-2613)
PHONE..................................201 433-1512
EMP: 4 EST: 2015
SALES (est): 267.6K **Privately Held**
SIC: 2834 Pharmaceutical preparations

(G-4803)
SAKSOFT INC (HQ)
30 Montgomery St Ste 1240 (07302-3834)
PHONE..................................201 451-4609
Aditya Krishna, *CEO*
Suman Kumar Mukherji, *Regl Sales Mgr*
EMP: 110
SQ FT: 950
SALES (est): 29.4MM **Privately Held**
WEB: www.saksoft.com
SIC: 7371 7372 Computer software development; prepackaged software

(G-4804)
SANDKAMP WOODWORKS LLC
430 Communipaw Ave Ste 1 (07304-3699)
PHONE..................................201 200-0101
Anthony Sandkamp,
EMP: 4
SALES (est): 497.8K **Privately Held**
WEB: www.sandkampwoodworks.com
SIC: 2434 Wood kitchen cabinets

(G-4805)
SARA EMPORIUM INC
833 Newark Ave (07306-3808)
PHONE..................................201 792-7222
Ahmed Akbary, *President*
EMP: 4 EST: 1997
SQ FT: 1,100
SALES: 3.5MM **Privately Held**
SIC: 3911 Jewelry, precious metal

(G-4806)
SCIVANTAGE INC (PA)
499 Washington Blvd Fl 11 (07310-2017)
PHONE..................................646 452-0001
Adnane Charchour, *CEO*
Nelson Suit, *Counsel*
Jennifer Cosenza, *Exec VP*
Christian J Farber, *Exec VP*
Susan Massaro, *Exec VP*
EMP: 80
SQ FT: 30,000
SALES (est): 46.7MM **Privately Held**
WEB: www.scivantage.com
SIC: 7372 Business oriented computer software

(G-4807)
SCYNEXIS INC
1 Evertrust Plz Fl 13 (07302-3051)
PHONE..................................201 884-5485
Guy Macdonald, *Ch of Bd*
Marco Taglietti, *President*
Nkechi Azie, *Vice Pres*
Ann Sanchez, *Buyer*
Eric Francois, *CFO*
EMP: 19 EST: 1999
SQ FT: 19,275
SALES: 257K **Privately Held**
WEB: www.scynexis.com
SIC: 2834 8731 Pharmaceutical preparations; commercial physical research; biological research

(G-4808)
SELFMADE LLC
Also Called: Selfmade Boutique
290 Hoboken Ave (07306-1692)
PHONE..................................201 792-8968
EMP: 5
SALES (est): 395.7K **Privately Held**
SIC: 2329 3161 5136 5621 Men's & boys' sportswear & athletic clothing; clothing & apparel carrying cases; men's & boys' clothing; boutiques

(G-4809)
SIGNS & CUSTOM METAL INC
62 Monitor St (07304-4019)
PHONE..................................201 200-0110
Shan Kumar, *President*
EMP: 12
SQ FT: 8,000
SALES (est): 1.8MM **Privately Held**
WEB: www.signscm.com
SIC: 5099 3993 Signs, except electric; signs & advertising specialties

(G-4810)
SIMS LEE INC (PA)
Also Called: Lee Sims Chocolates
743 Bergen Ave (07306-4795)
PHONE..................................201 433-1308
Nicholas Vlahakis, *CEO*
Allison McKernan, *President*
Valerie Vlahakis, *Corp Secy*
EMP: 10 EST: 1953
SQ FT: 2,000
SALES (est): 627.1K **Privately Held**
WEB: www.leesims.com
SIC: 5441 2064 Candy; chocolate candy, except solid chocolate

(G-4811)
SIRMA GROUP INC
1 Evertrust Plz Ste 1103 (07302-3086)
PHONE..................................646 357-3067
EMP: 400
SQ FT: 700
SALES (est): 3.9MM **Privately Held**
SIC: 7371 7372 Computer Programming Svc Prepackaged Software Svc

(G-4812)
SOH LLC
150 Bay St Apt 715 (07302-5917)
PHONE..................................646 943-4066
Song OH, *President*
Glen Conn, *Vice Pres*
EMP: 46 EST: 2009
SQ FT: 1,500
SALES (est): 665.5K **Privately Held**
SIC: 2231 Apparel & outerwear broadwoven fabrics

(G-4813)
STANLEY BLACK & DECKER INC
Also Called: Stanley Tools
123 Town Square Pl (07310-1756)
PHONE..................................860 225-5111
EMP: 11
SALES (corp-wide): 13.9B **Publicly Held**
WEB: www.stanleyworks.com
SIC: 3423 Hand & edge tools
PA: Stanley Black & Decker, Inc.
1000 Stanley Dr
New Britain CT 06053
860 225-5111

(G-4814)
STAR SNACKS CO LLC
111 Port Jersey Blvd (07305-4513)
PHONE..................................201 200-9820
Jacob Fleischer, *Site Mgr*
David Giuliani, *QC Mgr*
Rafie Miller, *CFO*
Zalmy Lieber, *Sales Associate*
Mendel Brachfeld, *Mng Member*
◆ EMP: 500
SQ FT: 160,000
SALES: 259.7MM **Privately Held**
SIC: 2068 Seeds: dried, dehydrated, salted or roasted

(G-4815)
STATEWIDE GRANITE AND MARBLE
Also Called: Statewide Granite & Marble
109 Carlton Ave (07306-3403)
PHONE..................................201 653-1700
Linda Coviello, *President*
Donato Capozza, *Vice Pres*
EMP: 11
SQ FT: 20,000
SALES (est): 1.2MM **Privately Held**
SIC: 5032 3281 Granite building stone; marble building stone; marble, building: cut & shaped; granite, cut & shaped; switchboard panels, slate

(G-4816)
STEPS CLOTHING INC
30 Mall Dr W Unit B59a (07310-1615)
PHONE..................................201 420-1496
Susan Yu, *Branch Mgr*

EMP: 21
SALES (corp-wide): 14.9MM **Privately Held**
SIC: 5137 2389 Women's & children's clothing; apparel for handicapped
PA: Steps Clothing, Inc.
662 Dell Rd
Carlstadt NJ 07072
201 438-9311

(G-4817)
STUDIO DELLARTE
234 16th St Fl 1 (07310-1196)
PHONE.................................718 599-3715
Jeremy Lebensohn, *Principal*
EMP: 5
SALES: 300K **Privately Held**
SIC: 3441 3446 Fabricated structural metal; gratings, tread: fabricated metal

(G-4818)
SURUCHI FOODS LLC
114 Baldwin Ave Ste A (07306-2050)
PHONE.................................201 432-2201
▲ EMP: 5
SALES (est): 340K **Privately Held**
SIC: 2099 Mfg Food Preparations

(G-4819)
TECHTRADE LLC
30 Montgomery St Ste 690 (07302-3862)
PHONE.................................201 706-8130
Tim Stark, *Warehouse Mgr*
Harvey T Bart,
▲ EMP: 6
SALES (est): 1.1MM **Privately Held**
WEB: www.techtradellc.com
SIC: 3841 Surgical & medical instruments

(G-4820)
THIS IS IT STAGEWORKS LLC
345 18th Street Jersey Cy (07310)
PHONE.................................201 653-2699
Mike Aug, *Sales Staff*
Ross Dombrowski, *Manager*
Scott Harrison,
EMP: 22
SQ FT: 30,000
SALES: 4.1MM **Privately Held**
SIC: 3999 3648 7922 Stage hardware & equipment, except lighting; stage lighting equipment; equipment rental, theatrical

(G-4821)
THOMAS RUSSO & SONS INC
854 Communipaw Ave (07304-1305)
PHONE.................................201 332-4159
Thomas Russo, *President*
Concetta Russo, *Admin Sec*
EMP: 5 EST: 1919
SQ FT: 5,500
SALES (est): 467.5K **Privately Held**
SIC: 3441 Fabricated structural metal

(G-4822)
TOTAL AMERICAN SERVICES INC (HQ)
100 Town Square Pl # 401 (07310-2778)
PHONE.................................206 626-3500
Ronald W Haddock, *President*
◆ EMP: 12 EST: 1999
SALES (est): 174.6MM
SALES (corp-wide): 8.4B **Publicly Held**
SIC: 2911 4612 5541 2895 Petroleum refining; crude petroleum pipelines; gasoline service stations; carbon black
PA: Total Sa
La Defense 6
Courbevoie 92400
964 410-926

(G-4823)
U I S INDUSTRIES INC (PA)
15 Exchange Pl Ste 1120 (07302-4937)
PHONE.................................201 946-2600
Andrew Pietrini, *President*
Joseph F Arrigo, *Vice Pres*
▲ EMP: 800
SQ FT: 6,000
SALES (est): 26.8MM **Privately Held**
SIC: 2064 Candy & other confectionery products

(G-4824)
U S TECH SOLUTIONS INC (PA)
10 Exchange Pl Ste 1710 (07302-4934)
PHONE.................................201 524-9600
Manoj Agarwal, *CEO*
Jaya Pratap, *Technology*
Debabrata Ghosh, *Technical Staff*
Shaik Mohsin, *Technical Staff*
Sunny Nalkari, *Technical Staff*
EMP: 95
SQ FT: 20,000
SALES: 166.2MM **Privately Held**
SIC: 7379 7372 Computer related consulting services; prepackaged software

(G-4825)
UTAX USA INC
30 Montgomery St Ste 1320 (07302-3858)
PHONE.................................201 433-1200
Yasuhiro Sasho, *President*
▲ EMP: 8
SQ FT: 1,700
SALES (est): 924K **Privately Held**
SIC: 3582 Commercial laundry equipment

(G-4826)
VIGILANT DESIGN
535 Communipaw Ave (07304-2940)
PHONE.................................201 432-3900
Darren Vigilant, *Owner*
EMP: 5
SALES (est): 648K **Privately Held**
WEB: www.vigilantdesign.com
SIC: 3471 Finishing, metals or formed products

(G-4827)
VIVIS LIFE LLC
Also Called: Partake Foods
25 Park Ln S Apt 709 (07310-3124)
P.O. Box 1108, Hoboken (07030-1108)
PHONE.................................201 798-1938
Denise Woodard, *Mng Member*
Jeremy Woodard,
EMP: 2 EST: 2016
SALES: 1MM **Privately Held**
SIC: 5149 2052 Cookies; cookies

(G-4828)
W W JEWELERS INC
Also Called: W W Manufacturing Jewelers
35 Journal Sq Ste 231 (07306-4024)
PHONE.................................718 392-4500
William Jacoby, *CEO*
David Bellman, *Vice Pres*
Stuart Kuropatkin, *Vice Pres*
Shirley Jacoby, *Treasurer*
Lynn Jacoby, *Admin Sec*
EMP: 75 EST: 1946
SQ FT: 20,000
SALES (est): 8.2MM **Privately Held**
WEB: www.wwjewelers.com
SIC: 3911 Rings, finger: precious metal

(G-4829)
WALTER MACHINE CO INC
84 Cambridge Ave 98 (07307-2101)
P.O. Box 7700 (07307-0700)
PHONE.................................201 656-5654
Donald R Chatrnuck, *President*
Donald W Chatrnuck, *Vice Pres*
Karen Chatrnuck, *Treasurer*
Elinor Chatrnuck, *Admin Sec*
◆ EMP: 30
SQ FT: 35,000
SALES (est): 5.9MM **Privately Held**
WEB: www.waltergear.com
SIC: 3566 3585 Gears, power transmission, except automotive; coolers, milk & water: electric

(G-4830)
WEINMAN BROS INC
111 Town Square Pl # 434 (07310-2766)
PHONE.................................212 695-8116
Robert Weinman, *President*
EMP: 25
SALES (est): 2.7MM **Privately Held**
SIC: 3911 Jewelry, precious metal

(G-4831)
WILLIAM ROBERT GRAPHICS INC
234 16th St Fl 7 (07310-1196)
PHONE.................................201 239-7400

Robert William Horneck, *President*
EMP: 6
SQ FT: 7,000
SALES (est): 750K **Privately Held**
SIC: 2752 Commercial printing, offset

(G-4832)
WILLOW RUN CONSTRUCTION INC
67 Pollock Ave (07305-1109)
PHONE.................................201 659-7266
Michael Zaccaria, *President*
Marilyn Zaccaria, *Admin Sec*
EMP: 10
SALES (est): 538.5K **Privately Held**
SIC: 7692 Welding repair

(G-4833)
WISELY PRODUCTS LLC
77 Hudson St Apt 2406 (07302-8525)
P.O. Box 308 (07303-0308)
PHONE.................................929 329-9188
Douglass Lee,
EMP: 6
SQ FT: 1,000
SALES: 9.9MM **Privately Held**
SIC: 3648 5021 Outdoor lighting equipment; outdoor & lawn furniture

(G-4834)
XCEEDIUM INC
30 Montgomery St Ste 1020 (07302-3836)
PHONE.................................201 536-1000
Glenn C Hazard, *CEO*
Richard Rose, *CFO*
EMP: 53
SQ FT: 5,000
SALES (est): 6.5MM **Privately Held**
WEB: www.xceedium.com
SIC: 3571 Electronic computers

Jobstown
Burlington County

(G-4835)
ALMA PARK ALPACAS
2800 Monmouth Rd (08041-2214)
PHONE.................................732 620-1052
Alma Park, *Principal*
EMP: 5
SALES (est): 492.7K **Privately Held**
SIC: 2231 Alpacas, mohair: woven

(G-4836)
ATLANTIC LINING CO INC
2206 Saylors Pond Rd 2 (08041-9990)
PHONE.................................609 723-2400
Nancy L Taylor, *President*
Francis Taylor, *Vice Pres*
Wayne Farrow, *CFO*
EMP: 45
SQ FT: 1,200
SALES (est): 12.9MM **Privately Held**
WEB: www.atlanticlining.com
SIC: 1799 2821 Protective lining installation, underground (sewage, etc.); polypropylene resins

Johnsonburg
Warren County

(G-4837)
RUBBER FAB & MOLDING INC
1100 Rte 519 (07846)
P.O. Box 412 (07846-0412)
PHONE.................................908 852-7725
William Washer, *President*
Sharon Washer, *Vice Pres*
EMP: 6
SQ FT: 4,000
SALES (est): 1.2MM **Privately Held**
WEB: www.rubber-fab.com
SIC: 3069 Medical & laboratory rubber sundries & related products

Keansburg
Monmouth County

(G-4838)
J AND S SPORTING APPAREL LLC
Also Called: Smitteez Sportswear
224 Main St (07734-1752)
P.O. Box 274 (07734-0274)
PHONE.................................732 787-5500
James W Smith, *Mng Member*
EMP: 4
SQ FT: 2,400
SALES: 250K **Privately Held**
SIC: 3949 2759 2395 Sporting & athletic goods; screen printing; embroidery & art needlework

Kearny
Hudson County

(G-4839)
5 STAR INDUSTRIES INC
2 Fish House Rd (07032-4320)
PHONE.................................862 255-2040
Jeffrey J Steele, *Principal*
EMP: 12
SALES (est): 1.4MM **Privately Held**
SIC: 3999 Barber & beauty shop equipment

(G-4840)
A L WILSON CHEMICAL CO
Also Called: Novel Technology Labs
1050 Harrison Ave (07032-5941)
P.O. Box 207 (07032-0207)
PHONE.................................201 997-3300
Fred G Schwarzmann Sr, *CEO*
Jeff Schwarz, *President*
Fred G Schwarzmann Jr, *President*
Christina Lang, *VP Admin*
Angel Carchi, *Purch Mgr*
▼ EMP: 17
SQ FT: 22,000
SALES (est): 4MM **Privately Held**
WEB: www.alwilson.com
SIC: 2842 Drycleaning preparations

(G-4841)
ALDEN - LEEDS INC
100 Hackensack Ave (07032-4657)
PHONE.................................973 344-7986
Jeffery Houtz, *Branch Mgr*
EMP: 4
SALES (est): 264.4K
SALES (corp-wide): 38MM **Privately Held**
SIC: 5091 3949 Swimming pools, equipment & supplies; water sports equipment
PA: Alden - Leeds, Inc.
55 Jacobus Ave Ste 1
Kearny NJ 07032
973 589-3544

(G-4842)
ALDEN - LEEDS INC (PA)
Also Called: Alden Leeds
55 Jacobus Ave Ste 1 (07032-4584)
PHONE.................................973 589-3544
Mark Epstein, *President*
Andy Epstein, *Vice Pres*
Lawrence Epstein, *Vice Pres*
Steven Epstein, *Vice Pres*
Steve Belvin, *Plant Mgr*
◆ EMP: 75
SQ FT: 180,000
SALES (est): 38MM **Privately Held**
WEB: www.aldenleeds.com
SIC: 2899 Water treating compounds

(G-4843)
AMERICAN INGREDIENTS INC
265 Harrison Tpke (07032-4315)
PHONE.................................714 630-6000
David A Holmes, *President*
Colin Mac Intyre, *Vice Pres*
Andrea Bauer, *Treasurer*
Catherine Holmes, *Admin Sec*
EMP: 15
SQ FT: 26,000

SALES (est): 1.1MM
SALES (corp-wide): 3.2B **Publicly Held**
SIC: 2833 Medicinals & botanicals
HQ: Pharmachem Laboratories, Llc
　265 Harrison Tpke
　Kearny NJ 07032
　201 246-1000

(G-4844)
APELIO INNOVATIVE INDS LLC
46 Sellers St (07032-4216)
PHONE....................................973 777-8899
Michael Bregman, *Managing Prtnr*
Denis Lyagushev, *Senior Engr*
Michael Zelenkoz, *Mng Member*
Boris Bregman,
Alison Hine,
EMP: 18
SALES (est): 2.2MM **Privately Held**
SIC: 3646 3645 3613 1731 Commercial
　indusl & institutional electric lighting fix-
　tures; residential lighting fixtures;
　switchgear & switchboard apparatus;
　electrical work

(G-4845)
ART PLAQUE CREATIONS INC
70 Arlington Ave (07032-4007)
PHONE....................................973 482-2536
Ed Marcus, *President*
Minerva Marquez, *Treasurer*
EMP: 10 **EST:** 1987
SQ FT: 11,100
SALES (est): 860K **Privately Held**
SIC: 3299 3263 3275 Statuary: gypsum,
　clay, papier mache, metal, etc.; semivitre-
　ous table & kitchenware; gypsum prod-
　ucts

(G-4846)
BELLEVILLE CORPORATION
Also Called: Gild-N-Son Manufacturing
328 Belleville Tpke (07032-3801)
PHONE....................................201 991-6222
Alan Gildenberg, *President*
EMP: 10 **EST:** 1947
SQ FT: 10,000
SALES (est): 1.6MM **Privately Held**
SIC: 3442 Screens, window, metal; screen
　doors, metal; storm doors or windows,
　metal

(G-4847)
BERNARDAUD NA INC
1 Jacobus Ave (07032-4532)
PHONE....................................973 274-3555
Isabelle Darocha, *Manager*
EMP: 4
SALES (corp-wide): 27.2MM **Privately
Held**
SIC: 3469 Table tops, porcelain enameled
HQ: Bernardaud Na, Inc.
　499 Park Ave
　New York NY 10022
　212 371-4300

(G-4848)
**BINDI NORTH AMERICA INC
(PA)**
Also Called: Bindi Dessert
630 Belleville Tpke (07032-4407)
PHONE....................................973 812-8118
Attilio Bindi, *President*
Marco Donnini, *Area Mgr*
Christopher Klemensowicz, *Opers Mgr*
Marco Marchese, *CFO*
Gianfranco Orlando, *Controller*
◆ **EMP:** 50
SALES (est): 13.3MM **Privately Held**
SIC: 2024 Dairy based frozen desserts

(G-4849)
**BOMBARDIER
TRANSPORTATION**
Also Called: Adtranz
1148 Newark Tpke (07032-4311)
PHONE....................................201 955-5874
Mark Ives, *Manager*
EMP: 4
SALES (corp-wide): 16.2B **Privately Held**
SIC: 3743 Train cars & equipment, freight
　or passenger

HQ: Bombardier Transportation (Holdings)
　Usa Inc.
　1251 Waterfront Pl
　Pittsburgh PA 15222
　412 655-5700

(G-4850)
**CAMPBELL FOUNDRY
COMPANY**
Campbell Materials
1235 Harrison Tpke (07032-4310)
PHONE....................................201 998-3765
John Pisciotto, *Branch Mgr*
EMP: 40
SALES (corp-wide): 11.9MM **Privately
Held**
WEB: www.campbellfoundry.com
SIC: 3321 Manhole covers, metal
PA: Campbell Foundry Company
　800 Bergen St
　Harrison NJ 07029
　973 483-5480

(G-4851)
**CP TEST & VALVE PRODUCTS
INC**
234 Sanford Ave (07032-5920)
P.O. Box 311 (07032-0311)
PHONE....................................201 998-1500
Pamela Krieg, *President*
Jim Krieg, *Vice Pres*
William Conklin, *Admin Sec*
▲ **EMP:** 8
SALES (est): 774.4K **Privately Held**
SIC: 3494 Pipe fittings

(G-4852)
**CRYSTAL BEVERAGE
CORPORATION (PA)**
174 Sanford Ave (07032-5920)
PHONE....................................201 991-2342
John Apolinario, *President*
Victor Apolinario, *Treasurer*
▲ **EMP:** 2
SQ FT: 14,000
SALES: 5MM **Privately Held**
SIC: 2086 Carbonated beverages, nonal-
　coholic: bottled & canned

(G-4853)
CUMMINS INC
435 Bergen Ave (07032-3938)
PHONE....................................973 491-0100
Whityeld Whylie, *General Mgr*
Richard Perry, *Manager*
EMP: 100
SALES (corp-wide): 23.7B **Publicly Held**
SIC: 5084 3519 Engines & parts, diesel;
　internal combustion engines
PA: Cummins Inc.
　500 Jackson St
　Columbus IN 47201
　812 377-5000

(G-4854)
DERV2000
420 Belgrove Dr (07032-1628)
PHONE....................................503 470-9158
Rosa Vernazza, *Vice Pres*
EMP: 4
SALES (est): 154.7K **Privately Held**
SIC: 3069 Reclaimed rubber (reworked by
　manufacturing processes)

(G-4855)
**FEED YOUR SOUL LTD LBLTY
CO**
78 John Miller Way # 100 (07032-6500)
PHONE....................................201 204-0720
Mya Zoracki, *Mng Member*
EMP: 4
SALES (est): 443.7K **Privately Held**
SIC: 2051 Bakery: wholesale or whole-
　sale/retail combined

(G-4856)
FUSAR TECHNOLOGIES INC
78 John Miller Way # 310 (07032-6531)
PHONE....................................201 563-0189
Ryan Shearman, *CEO*
Frank Bober, *Chairman*
Clayton Patton, *CFO*
Todd Rushing, *Exec Dir*
EMP: 9

SALES (est): 1.5MM **Privately Held**
SIC: 5045 7371 7372 Computer periph-
　eral equipment; custom computer pro-
　gramming services; application computer
　software

(G-4857)
**G & S MOTOR EQUIPMENT CO
INC**
Also Called: G & S Technologies
1800 Harrison Ave (07032)
P.O. Box 493 (07032-0493)
PHONE....................................201 998-9244
Gabor Newmark, *President*
Zoltan Lefkovits, *Corp Secy*
Jeffery Lefkovits, *Vice Pres*
George Newmark, *Vice Pres*
◆ **EMP:** 100
SQ FT: 60,000
SALES (est): 21.3MM **Privately Held**
WEB: www.gstechnologies.com
SIC: 3612 Distribution transformers, elec-
　tric

(G-4858)
**GALAXY SWITCHGEAR INDS
LLC**
46 Sellers St (07032-4216)
PHONE....................................914 668-8200
Isak Lamberg, *President*
Boris Bregman,
Charles Casquarelli,
Brett Sagona,
EMP: 30
SQ FT: 17,000
SALES (est): 5.4MM **Privately Held**
SIC: 3613 3645 Switchgear & switchboard
　apparatus; residential lighting fixtures

(G-4859)
**GARDEN STATE BTLG LTD
LBLTY CO**
174 Sanford Ave (07032-5920)
PHONE....................................201 991-2342
John Apolinario, *Ch of Bd*
Alan Silverstein, *Vice Pres*
EMP: 14
SQ FT: 14,000
SALES: 4.4MM
SALES (corp-wide): 5MM **Privately Held**
SIC: 2086 Carbonated beverages, nonal-
　coholic: bottled & canned
PA: Crystal Beverage Corporation
　174 Sanford Ave
　Kearny NJ 07032
　201 991-2342

(G-4860)
GIFFORD GROUP INC
Also Called: Just Plastics
35 Obrien St (07032-4212)
PHONE....................................212 569-8500
Robert C Vermann, *President*
Tammy Espaillat, *Vice Pres*
Lois Vermann, *Vice Pres*
EMP: 15
SQ FT: 25,000
SALES: 1.5MM **Privately Held**
WEB: www.justplastics.com
SIC: 3089 Injection molding of plastics

(G-4861)
GLW INC
78 John Miller Way # 447 (07032-6500)
PHONE....................................845 492-0476
Vadim Gurevich, *CEO*
Jan Heinsohn, *Director*
EMP: 5
SQ FT: 3,000
SALES: 200K **Privately Held**
SIC: 3841 Surgical & medical instruments

(G-4862)
GRAPHIC MANAGEMENT
21 Lafayette Pl (07032-2228)
PHONE....................................908 654-8400
Scott Wright, *President*
EMP: 40
SQ FT: 50,000
SALES (est): 4.8MM **Privately Held**
WEB: www.graphicmgt.com
SIC: 2752 Commercial printing, offset

(G-4863)
HONEYWARE INC (PA)
244 Dukes St (07032-3929)
PHONE....................................201 997-5900
Tony Sheng, *President*
Lambert Sheng, *Vice Pres*
Raymond Sheng, *Vice Pres*
James Sheng, *Shareholder*
◆ **EMP:** 65
SQ FT: 86,000
SALES (est): 11.5MM **Privately Held**
SIC: 3089 2899 2865 Injection molding of
　plastics; ink or writing fluids; dyes, syn-
　thetic organic

(G-4864)
HUDSON WEST PUBLISHING CO
Also Called: Observer, The
39 Seeley Ave (07032-1806)
P.O. Box 503 (07032-0503)
PHONE....................................201 991-1600
Mary Tortoreti, *President*
Lisa Pezzolla, *Publisher*
EMP: 15
SQ FT: 3,000
SALES (est): 1.1MM **Privately Held**
SIC: 2711 2741 Newspapers: publishing
　only, not printed on site; shopping news:
　publishing only, not printed on site

(G-4865)
HUGO NEU CORPORATION (PA)
78 John Miller Way Ste 1 (07032-6528)
PHONE....................................646 467-6700
Alan Ratner, *President*
Wendy Nue, *Principal*
John Neu, *Principal*
Peter Kelman, *Vice Pres*
Jeff Neu, *Vice Pres*
◆ **EMP:** 19
SQ FT: 15,186
SALES (est): 15.3MM **Privately Held**
WEB: www.hugoneu.com
SIC: 6531 3559 6719 Real estate agents
　& managers; recycling machinery; invest-
　ment holding companies, except banks

(G-4866)
HUGO NEU RECYCLING LLC
78 John Miller Way Ste 1 (07032-6528)
PHONE....................................914 530-2350
Robert Houghton, *CEO*
Jill Vaske, *President*
EMP: 25
SALES (est): 11MM
SALES (corp-wide): 15.3MM **Privately
Held**
SIC: 3399 5093 Staples, nonferrous metal
　or wire; laminating steel; metal scrap &
　waste materials
HQ: Sage Sustainable Electronics Llc
　2801 Charter St
　Columbus OH 43228
　844 472-4373

(G-4867)
INFINITE MFG GROUP INC
35 Obrien St (07032-4212)
PHONE....................................973 649-9950
Bernard Alloysius, *Branch Mgr*
EMP: 10
SALES (est): 901.9K
SALES (corp-wide): 6.6MM **Privately
Held**
SIC: 2542 Fixtures: display, office or store:
　except wood
PA: Infinite Manufacturing Group, Inc.
　35 Obrien St
　Kearny NJ 07032
　973 649-9950

(G-4868)
INFINITE MFG GROUP INC (PA)
Also Called: Infinite Sign
35 Obrien St (07032-4212)
PHONE....................................973 649-9950
Bernard Alloysius, *CEO*
▼ **EMP:** 30
SQ FT: 45,000

SALES (est): 6.6MM **Privately Held**
SIC: 2431 7389 2599 3441 Woodwork, interior & ornamental; styling of fashions, apparel, furniture, textiles, etc.; factory furniture & fixtures; fabricated structural metal; construction project management consultant; displays & cutouts, window & lobby

(G-4869)
INFINITE SIGN INDUSTRIES INC
35 Obrien St (07032-4212)
PHONE......................................973 649-9950
Bernard Alloysius, *President*
EMP: 50
SQ FT: 30,000
SALES (est): 6.8MM **Privately Held**
WEB: www.infinitesign.com
SIC: 3993 Signs, not made in custom sign painting shops

(G-4870)
INTELLICON INC
46 Sellers St (07032-4216)
PHONE......................................201 791-9499
Lenny Novikov, *President*
EMP: 4
SQ FT: 2,000
SALES (est): 820K **Privately Held**
WEB: www.intelliconinc.com
SIC: 3625 Industrial controls: push button, selector switches, pilot

(G-4871)
JAI GANESH FUEL LLC
815 Kearny Ave (07032-3147)
PHONE......................................201 246-8995
Jai Ganesh, *Mng Member*
EMP: 4 EST: 2010
SALES (est): 238.5K **Privately Held**
SIC: 2869 Fuels

(G-4872)
JIMENEZ PALLETS LLC
244 Dukes St (07032-3929)
PHONE......................................862 267-3900
Russell Jimenez, *Principal*
Alexander Jimenez, *Buyer*
EMP: 6 EST: 2013
SALES (est): 510K **Privately Held**
SIC: 2448 Pallets, wood

(G-4873)
JOSE MOREIRA
Also Called: Moreira, Jose B, Attorney
712 Kearny Ave (07032-3004)
PHONE......................................201 991-9001
Jose Moreira, *Owner*
EMP: 4
SALES (est): 348.8K **Privately Held**
WEB: www.josemoreira.com
SIC: 8111 2711 General practice attorney, lawyer; newspapers

(G-4874)
KEARNY SMELTING & REF CORP
936 Harrison Ave Ste 5 (07032-5999)
PHONE......................................201 991-7276
Francine Rothschild, *President*
EMP: 21 EST: 1945
SQ FT: 12,000
SALES (est): 3.6MM **Privately Held**
SIC: 3356 3351 3341 Nonferrous rolling & drawing; brass rolling & drawing; bronze rolling & drawing; brass smelting & refining (secondary); bronze smelting & refining (secondary)

(G-4875)
KENNEY STEEL TREATING CORP
100 Quincy Pl (07032-4012)
P.O. Box 6 (07032-0006)
PHONE......................................201 998-4420
John Patrick Dunphy Jr, *President*
James Dunphy, *Vice Pres*
EMP: 14
SQ FT: 16,000
SALES (est): 752K **Privately Held**
SIC: 3398 Metal heat treating

(G-4876)
KUEHNE CHEMICAL COMPANY INC (PA)
86 N Hackensack Ave (07032-4673)
PHONE......................................973 589-0700
Donald Nicolai, *President*
Kelly Ward, *General Mgr*
Manuel Cunha, *Vice Pres*
Bill Paulin, *CFO*
Mario Cifuentes, *Credit Mgr*
◆ EMP: 50
SQ FT: 10,000
SALES (est): 120.1MM **Privately Held**
SIC: 2819 4226 2812 Sodium & potassium compounds, exc. bleaches, alkalies, alum.; special warehousing & storage; alkalies & chlorine

(G-4877)
L & R MANUFACTURING CO INC (PA)
577 Elm St (07032-3699)
P.O. Box 607 (07032-0607)
PHONE......................................201 991-5330
James J Lazarus, *CEO*
Robert Lazarus, *President*
David Romanok, *Exec VP*
Carmen Distano, *Manager*
Joe Stickno, *Manager*
◆ EMP: 95 EST: 1928
SQ FT: 21,000
SALES (est): 18.9MM **Privately Held**
WEB: www.lrultrasonics.com
SIC: 2842 3841 3843 3699 Cleaning or polishing preparations; ultrasonic medical cleaning equipment; ultrasonic dental equipment; cleaning equipment, ultrasonic, except medical & dental

(G-4878)
L & R MANUFACTURING CO INC
John Hay Ave (07032)
P.O. Box 607 (07032-0607)
PHONE......................................201 991-5330
Robert J Lazarus, *President*
EMP: 110
SALES (corp-wide): 18.9MM **Privately Held**
WEB: www.lrultrasonics.com
SIC: 3699 Cleaning equipment, ultrasonic, except medical & dental
PA: L & R Manufacturing Co Inc
577 Elm St
Kearny NJ 07032
201 991-5330

(G-4879)
LA BELLA MOZZARELLA
15 Arlington Ave (07032-4006)
PHONE......................................201 997-1737
James Miller, *Partner*
David Miller, *Partner*
EMP: 5
SQ FT: 1,500
SALES (est): 1.2MM **Privately Held**
WEB: www.labellamozzarella.com
SIC: 2022 Processed cheese

(G-4880)
MAC PRODUCTS INC
Also Called: Mac Power
60 Pennsylvania Ave (07032-4595)
P.O. Box 469 (07032-0469)
PHONE......................................973 344-5149
Edward Gollob, *President*
Ed Russnow, *Vice Pres*
Christopher Oneill, *Purch Agent*
Eric Fefferman, *Design Engr*
Chirag Patel, *Manager*
◆ EMP: 60 EST: 1960
SQ FT: 195,000
SALES (est): 17.7MM **Privately Held**
WEB: www.macproducts.net
SIC: 3643 5063 3549 Connectors & terminals for electrical devices; electrical apparatus & equipment; metalworking machinery

(G-4881)
MAGOS AMERICA INC
78 John Miller Way # 309 (07032-6500)
PHONE......................................973 763-9597
Aviel Kislansky, *President*
Yaron Zussman, *General Mgr*
Gadi Dar-Ner, *Vice Pres*

Amit Isseroff, *Vice Pres*
EMP: 6
SQ FT: 1,200
SALES (est): 269.4K **Privately Held**
SIC: 3812 Antennas, radar or communications; radar systems & equipment
PA: Magosys Systems Ltd
Rehovot
Rehovot
774 140-155

(G-4882)
MARBLE ONLINE CORPORATION
260 Schuyler Ave Fl 1 (07032-4002)
PHONE......................................201 998-9100
Allan Lan, *President*
▲ EMP: 5 EST: 2014
SALES (est): 632.8K **Privately Held**
SIC: 3281 Marble, building: cut & shaped

(G-4883)
MARCOTEX INTERNATIONAL INC
Also Called: Ultimate Home Products Div
69 Sellers St (07032-4227)
PHONE......................................201 991-8200
Marc Moyal, *President*
▼ EMP: 35
SQ FT: 200,000
SALES (est): 4.8MM **Privately Held**
SIC: 5131 2211 Piece goods & other fabrics; sheets, bedding & table cloths: cotton

(G-4884)
MILLAR SHEET METAL
39 Rizzolo Rd Ste 2 (07032-4288)
PHONE......................................201 997-1990
Peter Millar, *President*
Margaret Millar, *Vice Pres*
EMP: 5
SQ FT: 3,000
SALES (est): 530K **Privately Held**
SIC: 1711 3444 Ventilation & duct work contractor; warm air heating & air conditioning contractor; sheet metalwork

(G-4885)
MIRACLE VERDE GROUP LLC
47 Sellers St (07032-4215)
PHONE......................................201 399-2222
Milton Dsouza, *Mng Member*
▼ EMP: 7
SQ FT: 35,000
SALES (est): 450.6K **Privately Held**
SIC: 2873 Fertilizers: natural (organic), except compost

(G-4886)
MULTI-TEX PRODUCTS CORP
54 2nd Ave (07032-4014)
PHONE......................................201 991-7262
Michaelene Dwulet, *President*
▲ EMP: 35 EST: 1971
SQ FT: 22,000
SALES (est): 4.1MM **Privately Held**
SIC: 2269 2299 2281 Finishing plants; yarns, specialty & novelty; yarn spinning mills

(G-4887)
NEW ENGLAND BEDDING TRNSPT INC
102 3rd Ave (07032-4028)
PHONE......................................631 484-0147
Douglas Daly, *President*
EMP: 8
SQ FT: 1,000
SALES (est): 1MM **Privately Held**
SIC: 2515 Mattresses & bedsprings

(G-4888)
OWENS CORNING SALES LLC
1249 Newark Tpke (07032-4398)
PHONE......................................201 998-5666
Tom Messlli, *Manager*
EMP: 125 **Publicly Held**
WEB: www.owenscorning.com
SIC: 3296 Mineral wool
HQ: Owens Corning Sales, Llc
1 Owens Corning Pkwy
Toledo OH 43659
419 248-8000

(G-4889)
PEPSI-COLA METRO BTLG CO INC
680 Belleville Tpke (07032-4407)
PHONE......................................201 955-2691
Tony Pessolano, *Branch Mgr*
EMP: 10
SALES (corp-wide): 64.6B **Publicly Held**
SIC: 2086 Carbonated soft drinks, bottled & canned
HQ: Pepsi-Cola Metropolitan Bottling Company, Inc.
1111 Westchester Ave
White Plains NY 10604
914 767-6000

(G-4890)
PERCEPTIONS INC
280 Central Ave (07032-4609)
PHONE......................................973 344-5333
Barry Pessar, *President*
Sy Blechman, *Vice Pres*
▲ EMP: 45
SQ FT: 5,600
SALES (est): 3.5MM **Privately Held**
WEB: www.perceptionsdress.com
SIC: 2335 Ensemble dresses: women's, misses' & juniors'; gowns, formal

(G-4891)
PERFECTO FOODS LLC
79 Stuyvesant Ave (07032-3139)
PHONE......................................201 889-5328
David P Perez, *Principal*
EMP: 5
SALES (est): 250.4K **Privately Held**
SIC: 2099 Food preparations

(G-4892)
PHARMACHEM LABORATORIES LLC (DH)
Also Called: Pharma Chem
265 Harrison Tpke (07032-4315)
PHONE......................................201 246-1000
David Holmes, *President*
Jasen Lavoie, *Vice Pres*
Jodie Adams, *Project Mgr*
Brian Wellenheider, *Prdtn Mgr*
Peter Kacur, *Warehouse Mgr*
◆ EMP: 70
SQ FT: 54,000
SALES (est): 111.3MM
SALES (corp-wide): 3.7B **Publicly Held**
WEB: www.pharmachem.com
SIC: 2099 2834 Food preparations; pharmaceutical preparations
HQ: Ashland Llc
50 E Rivercenter Blvd # 1600
Covington KY 41011
859 815-3333

(G-4893)
PICASSO LIGHTING INDS LLC
Also Called: Lightingindustries Picasso
46 Sellers St (07032-4216)
PHONE......................................201 246-8188
Lenny Novikov, *Vice Pres*
Andrew Bregman, *Engineer*
Joseph Dobosiewicz, *Engineer*
Yuri Khaskin, *Engineer*
Alister Mallet, *Engineer*
EMP: 20
SQ FT: 2,000
SALES (est): 3.3MM **Privately Held**
SIC: 3646 Commercial indusl & institutional electric lighting fixtures

(G-4894)
PRO SCREEN PRINTING INC
590 Belleville Tpke # 24 (07032-4241)
PHONE......................................201 246-7600
Fax: 201 246-9046
EMP: 6
SQ FT: 12,000
SALES (est): 580K **Privately Held**
SIC: 2752 Commercial Printer On Plastic Containers

(G-4895)
PROFESSIONAL ENVMTL SYSTEMS
1806 Harrison Ave (07032)
PHONE......................................201 991-3000
EMP: 24 EST: 1977
SQ FT: 54,000

SALES (est): 3.1MM **Privately Held**
SIC: 3444 1711 Mfg Sheet Metalwork
  Plumbing/Heating/Air Cond Contractor

(G-4896)
REFRIG-IT WAREHOUSE
77 Hackensack Ave (07032-4656)
PHONE..............................973 344-4545
Brian Doliner, *Branch Mgr*
EMP: 55
SALES (corp-wide): 12.4MM **Privately**
Held
SIC: 2673 Food storage & frozen food
  bags, plastic
PA: Refrig-It Warehouse
  80 Campus Dr
  Kearny NJ 07032
  973 344-4545

(G-4897)
S O S GASES INC (PA)
1100 Harrison Ave (07032-5998)
PHONE..............................201 998-7800
Steven De Phillips, *President*
Carmen J De Phillips, *Vice Pres*
EMP: 23 **EST:** 1961
SQ FT: 8,000
SALES (est): 7.8MM **Privately Held**
WEB: www.sosgasesinc.com
SIC: 2813 Industrial gases

(G-4898)
SMITH LIME FLOUR CO INC
60 Central Ave (07032-4603)
PHONE..............................973 344-1700
Mark Veca, *President*
Thomas Veca, *Corp Secy*
Robert Veca, *Vice Pres*
EMP: 18 **EST:** 1895
SQ FT: 14,000
SALES (est): 1.7MM **Privately Held**
SIC: 3274 Lime

(G-4899)
SOLID COLOR INC
78 John Miller Way # 420 (07032-6532)
PHONE..............................212 239-3930
Frank Ferreiras, *President*
Robert Ellis, *Treasurer*
EMP: 6
SQ FT: 5,000
SALES (est): 1MM **Privately Held**
SIC: 2752 Commercial printing, offset

(G-4900)
STANSON CORPORATION (PA)
2 N Hackensack Ave (07032-4611)
PHONE..............................973 344-8666
Robert Holuba, *President*
Angela Holuba, *Corp Secy*
Stanley Holuba Jr, *COO*
EMP: 75
SQ FT: 500,000
SALES (est): 6.5MM **Privately Held**
WEB: www.stanson.com
SIC: 2841 2842 Detergents, synthetic or-
  ganic or inorganic alkaline; specialty
  cleaning, polishes & sanitation goods

(G-4901)
TILCON NEW YORK INC
Also Called: Kearny Recycle
411 Bergen Ave (07032-3920)
PHONE..............................800 789-7625
EMP: 63
SALES (corp-wide): 30.6B **Privately Held**
SIC: 1429 Dolomitic marble, crushed &
  broken-quarrying
HQ: Tilcon New York Inc.
  9 Entin Rd
  Parsippany NJ 07054
  973 366-7741

(G-4902)
UNITED DIE COMPANY INC
Also Called: Udico
199 Devon Ter (07032-3916)
P.O. Box 490 (07032-0490)
PHONE..............................201 997-0250
John Kontra, *President*
Mary Kontra, *Vice Pres*
Marion Martin, *CFO*
EMP: 50 **EST:** 1940
SQ FT: 12,000

SALES (est): 8.7MM **Privately Held**
WEB: www.uniteddie.com
SIC: 3544 Wire drawing & straightening
  dies; special dies & tools

(G-4903)
WELDON MATERIALS INC
1100 Harrison Ave (07032-5922)
PHONE..............................201 991-3200
Todd Philips, *Manager*
EMP: 7 **Privately Held**
WEB: www.weldonmaterials.com
SIC: 2951 Road materials, bituminous (not
  from refineries)
PA: Weldon Materials, Inc.
  141 Central Ave
  Westfield NJ 07090

(G-4904)
WEST HUDSON LUMBER & MLLWK CO
60 Arlington Ave (07032-4007)
PHONE..............................201 991-7191
Johnathon Giordano, *President*
Patricia Giordano, *Vice Pres*
EMP: 5 **EST:** 1945
SQ FT: 7,500
SALES: 500K **Privately Held**
SIC: 2599 2431 Cabinets, factory; mill-
  work

(G-4905)
WESTERN PACIFIC FOODS INC
650 Belleville Tpke Ste 2 (07032-4409)
PHONE..............................908 838-0186
Zheng Cheo, *Managing Dir*
EMP: 14 **EST:** 2016
SQ FT: 23,000
SALES (est): 603.8K **Privately Held**
SIC: 2079 Margarine & margarine oils

(G-4906)
WILLIAMS SCOTSMAN INC
Also Called: Williams Scotsman - NY Cy
150 Western Rd (07032-6508)
PHONE..............................856 429-0315
Arnold Sobral, *Branch Mgr*
Carol Gorczyca, *Admin Mgr*
Terri Zentkovich, *Administration*
EMP: 8
SALES (corp-wide): 751.4MM **Publicly**
Held
WEB: www.willscot.com
SIC: 3412 3499 3542 Barrels, shipping:
  metal; fire- or burglary-resistive products;
  metal container making machines: cans,
  etc.
HQ: Williams Scotsman, Inc.
  901 S Bond St Ste 600
  Baltimore MD 21231
  410 931-6000

(G-4907)
WILPAK INDUSTRIES INC
244 Dukes St (07032-3929)
PHONE..............................201 997-7600
Tony Sheng, *President*
Raymond Sheng, *Corp Secy*
Lambert Sheng, *Vice Pres*
James Sheng, *Shareholder*
▲ **EMP:** 6
SQ FT: 3,000
SALES (est): 500K
SALES (corp-wide): 11.5MM **Privately**
Held
WEB: www.honeyware.com
SIC: 2899 3089 Ink or writing fluids; injec-
  tion molded finished plastic products
PA: Honeyware Inc.
  244 Dukes St
  Kearny NJ 07032
  201 997-5900

Keasbey
Middlesex County

(G-4908)
BAYSHORE RECYCLING CORP
75 Crows Mill Rd (08832-1004)
P.O. Box 290 (08832-0290)
PHONE..............................732 738-6000
Valerie Montecalvo, *President*
Stephen Thomas, *General Mgr*

Frank Montecalvo, *COO*
Al Ludwig, *Senior VP*
John Davies, *Vice Pres*
EMP: 25
SALES (est): 10.6MM **Privately Held**
WEB: www.bayshorerecycling.com
SIC: 4953 3087 Recycling, waste materi-
  als; custom compound purchased resins

(G-4909)
BRUCE SUPPLY CORP
300 Smith St (08832-1017)
PHONE..............................732 661-0500
EMP: 10
SALES (corp-wide): 168.3MM **Privately**
Held
SIC: 3432 Plumbing fixture fittings & trim
PA: Bruce Supply Corp.
  8805 18th Ave
  Brooklyn NY 11214
  718 259-4900

(G-4910)
CHARLES M JESSUP INC
177 Smith St (08832-1158)
PHONE..............................732 324-0430
Caren Jessup, *President*
Jay Jessup, *Vice Pres*
EMP: 6 **EST:** 1948
SQ FT: 7,000
SALES (est): 1.1MM **Privately Held**
SIC: 5084 3555 Screening machinery &
  equipment; printing trades machinery

(G-4911)
COASTAL METAL RECYCLING CORP
75 Crows Mill Rd (08832-1004)
PHONE..............................732 738-6000
Daniel A Scwartz Esq, *President*
EMP: 4
SALES (est): 400K **Privately Held**
SIC: 1081 Metal mining services

(G-4912)
MAINETTI USA INC (HQ)
300 Mac Ln (08832-1200)
PHONE..............................201 215-2900
Roberto Peruzzo, *President*
Gabriele Bosco, *General Mgr*
Steve Regino, *Co-President*
Keith Charlton, *Opers Dir*
Robert B Dennerlein, *CFO*
◆ **EMP:** 17
SALES (est): 12.5MM **Privately Held**
SIC: 3089 Clothes hangers, plastic
PA: Mainetti Americas, Inc.
  115 Enterprise Ave S
  Secaucus NJ 07094
  201 215-2900

(G-4913)
NESTLE USA INC
326 Smith St (08832-1029)
PHONE..............................973 390-9555
EMP: 132
SALES (corp-wide): 92B **Privately Held**
SIC: 2023 Evaporated milk
HQ: Nestle Usa, Inc.
  1812 N Moore St Ste 118
  Rosslyn VA 22209
  818 549-6000

(G-4914)
PRAXAIR INC
60 Crows Mill Rd (08832-1028)
P.O. Box 127 (08832-0127)
PHONE..............................732 738-4150
Mike Beaudrow, *Managing Dir*
Gary Wilson, *Branch Mgr*
EMP: 13
SQ FT: 100,000 **Privately Held**
SIC: 2813 Industrial gases
HQ: Praxair, Inc.
  10 Riverview Dr
  Danbury CT 06810
  203 837-2000

(G-4915)
PRAXAIR CRYOMAG SERVICES INC
Industrial Ave (08832)
PHONE..............................732 738-4000
Jack Quinn, *General Mgr*
▲ **EMP:** 10

SALES (est): 1.6MM **Privately Held**
SIC: 2813 Industrial gases
HQ: Praxair, Inc.
  10 Riverview Dr
  Danbury CT 06810
  203 837-2000

(G-4916)
WAKEFERN FOOD CORP (PA)
Also Called: Wakefern General Merchandise
5000 Riverside Dr (08832-1209)
PHONE..............................908 527-3300
Joseph Colalillo, *CEO*
Joe Amorim, *District Mgr*
Bill Mayo, *Senior VP*
Frank Rostan, *Senior VP*
Michael Ambrosio, *Vice Pres*
◆ **EMP:** 400
SALES (est): 890MM **Privately Held**
WEB: www.shoprite.com
SIC: 5411 5149 4213 2026 Co-operative
  food stores; groceries & related products;
  contract haulers; milk processing (pas-
  teurizing, homogenizing, bottling)

Kendall Park
Middlesex County

(G-4917)
ABRAZIL LLC
1 Jacques Ave (08824-1601)
PHONE..............................732 658-5191
Hugh Liang, *Purchasing*
Tony Chuang,
◆ **EMP:** 9
SALES (est): 1.2MM **Privately Held**
WEB: www.abrazil.com
SIC: 2833 Medicinals & botanicals

(G-4918)
COOLENHEAT INC
11 Clinton Ct (08824-1837)
PHONE..............................908 925-4473
Jeffrey Bossert, *President*
Randall Bossert, *Vice Pres*
Jonathan Bossert, *Treasurer*
EMP: 30
SQ FT: 18,000
SALES (est): 5.4MM **Privately Held**
SIC: 3498 3585 Fabricated pipe & fittings;
  evaporative condensers, heat transfer
  equipment

(G-4919)
NEWTECH GROUP CORP
Also Called: N G C
54 Inverness Dr (08824-7012)
PHONE..............................732 355-0392
Peggy Foung, *President*
Austin Yang,
EMP: 5
SALES: 50K **Privately Held**
WEB: www.newtechgc.com
SIC: 3357 2298 3678 3643 Nonferrous
  wiredrawing & insulating; cable, fiber;
  electronic connectors; current-carrying
  wiring devices

Kenilworth
Union County

(G-4920)
ALLOY CAST PRODUCTS INC
700 Swenson Dr (07033-1326)
PHONE..............................908 245-2255
Frank Panico Jr, *President*
EMP: 12
SQ FT: 14,850
SALES (est): 1.9MM **Privately Held**
WEB: www.alloycastproducts.com
SIC: 3369 3544 3545 Castings, except
  die-castings, precision; extrusion dies;
  cutting tools for machine tools

(G-4921)
ARBEE COMPANY INC
Also Called: Abbey Commemoratives
16 N 26th St (07033-1714)
PHONE..............................908 241-7717
Margaret A Beute, *Principal*
William M Beute, *Vice Pres*

Robert Boak, *Vice Pres*
EMP: 10
SQ FT: 3,500
SALES (est): 800K **Privately Held**
SIC: 3089 Laminating of plastic

(G-4922)
AUTO ACTION GROUP INC
Also Called: Installations Unlimited
121 N Michigan Ave Ste A (07033-1261)
PHONE....................908 964-6290
Jared Cohen, *CEO*
Chuck Graf, *General Mgr*
Greg Quinotas, *COO*
Karen Licciardi, *VP Sales*
Brenda Cohen, *Shareholder*
EMP: 50
SQ FT: 12,000
SALES (est): 9.8MM **Privately Held**
SIC: 3694 Automotive electrical equipment

(G-4923)
AYR GRAPHICS & PRINTING INC
Also Called: Proforma Ayr Graphics & Prtg
7 Mark Rd Ste A (07033-1000)
PHONE....................908 241-8118
Carl Gamba, *President*
Jennefer Chatman, *Admin Sec*
EMP: 6
SALES (est): 803.3K **Privately Held**
SIC: 2752 Commercial printing, lithographic

(G-4924)
B & B MILLWORK & DOORS INC
327 Monroe Ave (07033-1129)
PHONE....................973 249-0300
EMP: 6
SALES (est): 1.9MM **Privately Held**
SIC: 5031 2431 Millwork; millwork

(G-4925)
B & M FINISHERS INC
201 S 31st St (07033-1305)
PHONE....................908 241-5640
Robert Bramson, *President*
Donald Marcus, *Plant Mgr*
Kish Mody, *Production*
Wendy Frees, *Office Mgr*
Chris Nadolsky, *Manager*
▲ **EMP:** 35 **EST:** 1956
SALES (est): 4.5MM **Privately Held**
WEB: www.bmfinishers.com
SIC: 3471 Anodizing (plating) of metals or formed products

(G-4926)
B AND W PRINTING COMPANY INC
730 Fairfield Ave (07033-2012)
P.O. Box 65 (07033-0065)
PHONE....................908 241-3060
Claire Butler, *CEO*
Gary L Butler, *President*
EMP: 8 **EST:** 1950
SQ FT: 2,560
SALES (est): 450K **Privately Held**
WEB: www.bwprinting.com
SIC: 2752 2759 Commercial printing, offset; letterpress printing

(G-4927)
BEACON C M P CORP
295 N Michigan Ave Ste G (07033-1270)
P.O. Box 103 (07033-0103)
PHONE....................908 851-9393
Richard M Loncar, *President*
Lenore Rodino, *Vice Pres*
EMP: 5
SQ FT: 1,400
SALES (est): 744.2K **Privately Held**
SIC: 2899 Chemical preparations

(G-4928)
BELLA PALERMO PASTRY SHOP
541 Boulevard (07033-1656)
PHONE....................908 931-0298
Joe Oliveira, *Principal*
EMP: 23 **Privately Held**
SIC: 5461 2051 Pastries; cakes, pies & pastries
PA: Bella Palermo Pastry Shop
619 Elizabeth Ave
Elizabeth NJ 07206

(G-4929)
BENEDICT-MILLER LLC
100 N 12th St 5 (07033-1177)
PHONE....................908 497-1477
Richard Hayes, *Purch Mgr*
Nancy Nadolny, *Accounting Mgr*
Ed Halpin, *Sales Mgr*
Walter Las, *Marketing Staff*
Jeremiah H Shaw, *Mng Member*
EMP: 10
SALES (est): 2MM **Privately Held**
WEB: www.benedict-miller.com
SIC: 3312 5051 Plate, sheet & strip, except coated products; metals service centers & offices

(G-4930)
BLUE BLADE CORP
Also Called: Blue Blade Steel
123 N 8th St A (07033-1108)
PHONE....................908 272-2620
Jeremiah H Shaw Jr, *President*
Tony Casciano, *QC Mgr*
Gail Snyder, *Accounting Mgr*
Robert Van Laere, *Supervisor*
▲ **EMP:** 46 **EST:** 1933
SALES (est): 23.3MM **Privately Held**
WEB: www.blubladesteel.com
SIC: 3398 Metal heat treating

(G-4931)
BRENT MATERIAL COMPANY
308 N 14th St (07033-1168)
PHONE....................908 686-3832
Bill Fiorenzo, *Manager*
EMP: 8
SALES (corp-wide): 11.4MM **Privately Held**
SIC: 3272 5031 Sewer pipe, concrete; lumber, plywood & millwork
PA: Brent Material Company
325 Columbia Tpke Ste 308
Florham Park NJ 07932
973 325-3030

(G-4932)
CAMPTOWN TOOL & DIE CO INC
25 Sidney Cir (07033-1051)
P.O. Box 274 (07033-0274)
PHONE....................908 688-8406
Albert W Bossert Jr, *President*
Mary Ann Bossert, *Corp Secy*
Lee R Rosander, *Vice Pres*
EMP: 8
SQ FT: 18,000
SALES: 1MM **Privately Held**
WEB: www.camptownauto.com
SIC: 3544 3469 Dies & die holders for metal cutting, forming, die casting; stamping metal for the trade

(G-4933)
CUBIST PHARMACEUTICALS LLC (HQ)
2000 Galloping Hill Rd (07033-1310)
PHONE....................908 740-4000
Michael W Bonney, *CEO*
Robert Perez, *President*
Kerry A Flynn, *Owner*
Thomas Desrosier, *Exec VP*
Steven Gilman, *Exec VP*
◆ **EMP:** 176
SALES (est): 181.8MM
SALES (corp-wide): 42.2B **Publicly Held**
WEB: www.cubist.com
SIC: 2834 Pharmaceutical preparations
PA: Merck & Co., Inc.
2000 Galloping Hill Rd
Kenilworth NJ 07033
908 740-4000

(G-4934)
DAYSOL INC
Also Called: Display Pro Manufacturing
40 Boright Ave (07033-1015)
PHONE....................908 272-5900
Dennis Polvere, *President*
Dean Polvere, *Vice Pres*
William Silver, *Vice Pres*
EMP: 100
SQ FT: 60,000
SALES (est): 8.3MM **Privately Held**
SIC: 3993 Signs & advertising specialties

(G-4935)
DEWITT BROS TOOL CO INC
140 Market St (07033-2018)
PHONE....................908 298-3700
Michael De Witt, *President*
Wenny Dewitt, *Treasurer*
▲ **EMP:** 8 **EST:** 1923
SQ FT: 3,500
SALES (est): 1.9MM **Privately Held**
SIC: 5084 3545 Metalworking tools (such as drills, taps, dies, files); diamond cutting tools for turning, boring, burnishing, etc.

(G-4936)
DIGITRON ELECTRONIC CORP
144 Market St (07033-2018)
PHONE....................908 245-2012
Joel Schwartz, *President*
EMP: 30 **EST:** 1977
SQ FT: 25,000
SALES (est): 6.2MM **Privately Held**
WEB: www.digitroncorp.com
SIC: 3674 5065 Integrated circuits, semiconductor networks, etc.; semiconductor devices; transistors

(G-4937)
EXOTHERMIC MOLDING INC
50 Lafayette Pl (07033-1105)
PHONE....................908 272-2299
Paul K Steck, *President*
EMP: 25
SQ FT: 10,000
SALES (est): 6MM **Privately Held**
WEB: www.exothermic.com
SIC: 3089 Injection molding of plastics

(G-4938)
F & G TOOL & DIE INC
195 Sumner Ave (07033-1318)
PHONE....................908 241-5880
Norman Friedrich, *President*
John Friedrich, *Vice Pres*
EMP: 5
SQ FT: 14,000
SALES (est): 490K **Privately Held**
SIC: 3544 3469 Special dies & tools; stamping metal for the trade

(G-4939)
F & M MACHINE CO INC
751 Lexington Ave (07033-2015)
PHONE....................908 245-8830
Richard Rutledge, *President*
Norman Radick, *Vice Pres*
EMP: 10
SQ FT: 11,000
SALES (est): 1.7MM **Privately Held**
WEB: www.fmmachineco.com
SIC: 3469 3599 Stamping metal for the trade; machine shop, jobbing & repair

(G-4940)
FLEXLINE INC
Also Called: Service Seal Div
11 Columbus Ave (07033-1054)
PHONE....................908 486-3322
Jeffrey C Scheininger, *President*
▲ **EMP:** 18
SQ FT: 20,000
SALES (est): 4MM **Privately Held**
WEB: www.flexlineus.com
SIC: 3599 5085 Flexible metal hose, tubing & bellows; hose, belting & packing

(G-4941)
FOLEY-WAITE ASSOCIATES INC
746 Colfax Ave (07033-2051)
P.O. Box 164, Bloomfield (07003-0164)
PHONE....................908 298-0700
Kathryn W Schackner, *Partner*
James Kelley Conklin, *Partner*
EMP: 10
SQ FT: 8,000
SALES (est): 1.1MM **Privately Held**
SIC: 2434 2511 Wood kitchen cabinets; wood household furniture

(G-4942)
GAUER METAL PRODUCTS CO INC
175 N Michigan Ave (07033-1259)
P.O. Box 158 (07033-0158)
PHONE....................908 241-4080
Walter W Gauer, *CEO*

Dennis J Schultz, *President*
John Gotsch, *Senior VP*
Arturo Bermudez, *Engineer*
Brian Schultz, *Sales Staff*
EMP: 50 **EST:** 1946
SQ FT: 70,000
SALES (est): 10MM **Privately Held**
WEB: www.gauermetal.com
SIC: 3541 3535 3444 5051 Machine tools, metal cutting: exotic (explosive, etc.); conveyors & conveying equipment; sheet metalwork; bars, metal; racks, merchandise display or storage: except wood

(G-4943)
GR STONE LLC
91 Market St (07033-1723)
PHONE....................908 925-7290
Melvin Peralta, *Mng Member*
EMP: 8
SALES (est): 251.1K **Privately Held**
SIC: 3281 Marble, building: cut & shaped

(G-4944)
HI-GRADE PRODUCTS MFG CO
752 Jefferson Ave (07033-1718)
P.O. Box 273 (07033-0273)
PHONE....................908 245-4133
Jeffrey Pfingst, *President*
Donna Pfingst, *Admin Sec*
EMP: 10 **EST:** 1960
SQ FT: 5,000
SALES (est): 1.1MM **Privately Held**
SIC: 3451 Screw machine products

(G-4945)
IDL TECHNI-EDGE LLC
Also Called: Stanley Black Dcker Tchni-Edge
30 Boright Ave (07033-1086)
PHONE....................908 497-9818
Eric Carmichael, *Safety Mgr*
Mike Donath, *CFO*
Natasha Correa, *Marketing Staff*
Sean Quinn, *Mng Member*
▲ **EMP:** 140
SALES (est): 36MM
SALES (corp-wide): 13.9B **Publicly Held**
SIC: 3421 3425 3423 3841 Razor blades & razors; saw blades & handsaws; hand & edge tools; surgical & medical instruments
PA: Stanley Black & Decker, Inc.
1000 Stanley Dr
New Britain CT 06053
860 225-5111

(G-4946)
INK WELL PRINTERS LLC
38 S 21st St (07033-1626)
PHONE....................908 272-8090
Edward Ensslin III,
Elizabeth Ensslin,
EMP: 5
SQ FT: 1,500
SALES: 700K **Privately Held**
SIC: 2752 Commercial printing, lithographic

(G-4947)
INTERVET INC
2000 Galloping Hill Rd (07033-1310)
PHONE....................908 740-1182
Bernie Dotsey, *Manager*
EMP: 5
SALES (est): 409.2K
SALES (corp-wide): 42.2B **Publicly Held**
SIC: 2836 Biological products, except diagnostic
PA: Merck & Co., Inc.
2000 Galloping Hill Rd
Kenilworth NJ 07033
908 740-4000

(G-4948)
J M C TOOL & MFG CO
845 Fairfield Ave (07033-2013)
PHONE....................908 241-8950
Mario J Giaimo, *President*
Charles V Giaimo, *Corp Secy*
EMP: 9
SQ FT: 6,400
SALES (est): 1.2MM **Privately Held**
SIC: 3599 Machine shop, jobbing & repair

(G-4949)
J-MAC PLASTICS INC (PA)
40 Lafayette Pl (07033-1105)
PHONE..............................908 709-1111
John Mc Namara, *President*
Jill Farawell, *Vice Pres*
Dan Mc Namara, *Manager*
Elizabeth Mc Namara, *Admin Sec*
EMP: 20
SQ FT: 12,500
SALES (est): 3.5MM **Privately Held**
SIC: 3089 3544 Injection molding of plastics; industrial molds

(G-4950)
KELLES INCORPORATED
Also Called: Kelles Machining Center
20 Hoiles Dr Ste D (07033-1314)
PHONE..............................908 241-9300
Michael J Patrick, *President*
Tony Pace, *Vice Pres*
▲ EMP: 19
SALES (est): 1.6MM **Privately Held**
WEB: www.kelles.com
SIC: 3599 Machine shop, jobbing & repair

(G-4951)
KENECO INC
123 N 8th St (07033-1108)
P.O. Box 121 (07033-0121)
PHONE..............................908 241-3700
William Van Loan III, *President*
Thomas Hoefenkrieg, *Vice Pres*
EMP: 3
SQ FT: 800
SALES: 350MM **Privately Held**
WEB: www.kenecoinc.com
SIC: 3535 Conveyors & conveying equipment

(G-4952)
KENILWORTH ANODIZING CO
201 S 31st St Ste A (07033-1305)
PHONE..............................908 241-5640
Robert Bramson, *President*
EMP: 30 EST: 1957
SQ FT: 20,000
SALES (est): 2.7MM **Privately Held**
SIC: 3471 Anodizing (plating) of metals or formed products

(G-4953)
KNA GRAPHICS INC
Also Called: Sign-A-Rama
303 N 14th St (07033-1167)
PHONE..............................908 272-4232
Kamal Assad, *President*
Nada Assad, *Vice Pres*
EMP: 8
SQ FT: 4,000
SALES: 460K **Privately Held**
SIC: 3993 Signs & advertising specialties

(G-4954)
M & S HOLES CORP
20 Hoiles Dr Ste A1 (07033-1314)
PHONE..............................908 298-6900
EMP: 5
SQ FT: 3,000
SALES (est): 596.9K **Privately Held**
SIC: 3599 Mfg Industrial Machinery

(G-4955)
MAINGEAR INC
206 Market St (07033-2032)
PHONE..............................888 624-6432
Wallace Santos, *CEO*
Jake Vance, *Business Mgr*
EMP: 22
SQ FT: 5,000
SALES: 7.6MM **Privately Held**
SIC: 7373 3571 3575 3577 Turnkey vendors, computer systems; personal computers (microcomputers); computer terminals; computer peripheral equipment; computers & accessories, personal & home entertainment; computer & software stores

(G-4956)
MASTER DRAPERY WORKROOM INC
220 N 14th St (07033-1166)
PHONE..............................908 272-4404
Philip Ricca, *President*

Anne Ricca, *Corp Secy*
Philip A Ricca, *Vice Pres*
EMP: 10
SQ FT: 3,000
SALES (est): 520K **Privately Held**
SIC: 2391 Curtains & draperies

(G-4957)
MERCK & CO INC (PA)
2000 Galloping Hill Rd (07033-1310)
P.O. Box 100, Whitehouse Station (08889-0100)
PHONE..............................908 740-4000
Kenneth C Frazier, *Ch of Bd*
Richard R Deluca Jr, *President*
Roger M Perlmutter, *President*
Adam H Schechter, *President*
David King, *Counsel*
EMP: 277 EST: 1928
SALES: 42.2B **Publicly Held**
SIC: 2836 2844 5122 2834 Vaccines; veterinary biological products; suntan lotions & oils; animal medicines; druggists' preparations (pharmaceuticals)

(G-4958)
MERCK & CO INC
251 S 31st St (07033-1305)
PHONE..............................908 740-4000
EMP: 41
SALES (corp-wide): 42.2B **Publicly Held**
SIC: 2834 Pharmaceutical preparations
PA: Merck & Co., Inc.
　2000 Galloping Hill Rd
　Kenilworth NJ 07033
　908 740-4000

(G-4959)
MERCK & CO INC
2000 Galloping Hill Rd (07033-1310)
PHONE..............................908 298-4000
Fax: 908 822-7048
EMP: 56
SALES (corp-wide): 40.1B **Publicly Held**
SIC: 2834 Mfg Pharmaceutical Preparations
PA: Merck & Co., Inc.
　2000 Galloping Hill Rd
　Kenilworth NJ 07033
　908 740-4000

(G-4960)
MERCK SHARP & DOHME CORP (HQ)
2000 Galloping Hill Rd (07033-1310)
P.O. Box 982122, El Paso TX (79998-2122)
PHONE..............................908 740-4000
Kenneth C Frazier, *Ch of Bd*
Sanat Chattopadhyay, *Exec VP*
Richard R Deluca Jr, *Exec VP*
Julie L Gerberding, *Exec VP*
Mirian M Graddick-Weir, *Exec VP*
◆ EMP: 1600 EST: 1935
SALES: 2.6B
SALES (corp-wide): 42.2B **Publicly Held**
WEB: www.schering.com
SIC: 8741 2834 Management services; druggists' preparations (pharmaceuticals)
PA: Merck & Co., Inc.
　2000 Galloping Hill Rd
　Kenilworth NJ 07033
　908 740-4000

(G-4961)
MERCK SHARP & DOHME CORP
2000 Galloping Hill Rd (07033-1310)
PHONE..............................908 423-1000
Darlene Butler, *Counsel*
April Cobb, *Project Mgr*
Leif Matzon, *Project Mgr*
Laura Troast, *Project Mgr*
Stan Avery, *Research*
EMP: 275
SALES (corp-wide): 42.2B **Publicly Held**
SIC: 2834 Pharmaceutical preparations
HQ: Merck Sharp & Dohme Corp.
　2000 Galloping Hill Rd
　Kenilworth NJ 07033
　908 740-4000

(G-4962)
NATUREE NUTS INC
Also Called: Sungood
636 N Michigan Ave (07033-1042)
PHONE..............................732 786-4663

Abraham Rosman, *Vice Pres*
EMP: 10
SQ FT: 9,150
SALES (est): 409.3K **Privately Held**
SIC: 2064 2068 Nuts, glace; nuts: dried, dehydrated, salted or roasted

(G-4963)
NEW JERSEY AIR PRODUCTS INC
4 Mark Rd Ste D (07033-1025)
PHONE..............................908 964-9001
Pete Petracco, *President*
EMP: 10
SALES (est): 1.5MM **Privately Held**
SIC: 3999 Atomizers, toiletry

(G-4964)
NORDIC METAL LLC
500 S 31st St (07033-1398)
PHONE..............................908 245-8900
Bo Johansson,
Lars Johansson,
EMP: 4
SQ FT: 7,000
SALES (est): 800K **Privately Held**
SIC: 3444 Sheet metalwork

(G-4965)
OCEAN DRIVE INC
Also Called: Ocean Drive Clothing Co.
530 N Michigan Ave (07033-1023)
PHONE..............................908 964-2591
Abraham Shiloach, *President*
Joseph Shiloach, *Vice Pres*
◆ EMP: 7
SQ FT: 10,000
SALES (est): 1.1MM **Privately Held**
WEB: www.oceandriveclothing.com
SIC: 2339 Sportswear, women's

(G-4966)
OPTIMER PHARMACEUTICALS LLC
2000 Galloping Hill Rd (07033-1310)
PHONE..............................858 909-0736
Henry A McKinnell, *CEO*
John Womelsdorf, *President*
Eric Sirota, *COO*
Linda E Amper, *Senior VP*
Sherwood L Gorbach, *Senior VP*
EMP: 281
SQ FT: 24,000
SALES: 27.7MM
SALES (corp-wide): 42.2B **Publicly Held**
WEB: www.optimerpharma.com
SIC: 2834 Pharmaceutical preparations
HQ: Cubist Pharmaceuticals Llc
　2000 Galloping Hill Rd
　Kenilworth NJ 07033

(G-4967)
OPTIMUM PRECISION INC
Also Called: Optimum Precision Machine & Tl
147 N Michigan Ave (07033-1275)
PHONE..............................908 259-9017
Gregory Maroukian, *President*
EMP: 4
SALES (est): 242K **Privately Held**
SIC: 3599 Machine shop, jobbing & repair

(G-4968)
PETERSON STAMPING & MFG CO
75 N Michigan Ave (07033-1750)
P.O. Box 190 (07033-0190)
PHONE..............................908 241-0900
Robert Olsen, *President*
Laura M Peterson, *CFO*
Laura Peterson, *CFO*
Donna Olsen, *Treasurer*
EMP: 15 EST: 1945
SQ FT: 10,000
SALES (est): 1.5MM **Privately Held**
WEB: www.petersonstamping.com
SIC: 3469 Stamping metal for the trade

(G-4969)
PETRO PLASTICS COMPANY INC
500 Hoiles Dr (07033-1330)
PHONE..............................908 789-1200
Lewis Petrozzielo, *President*
EMP: 30
SQ FT: 24,000

SALES (est): 4.4MM **Privately Held**
SIC: 3089 Extruded finished plastic products; plastic processing

(G-4970)
PINNACLE COSMETIC PACKG LLC
Also Called: Pinnacle Cosmetics Packaging
80 Market St (07033-1722)
P.O. Box 733 (07033-0733)
PHONE..............................908 241-7777
Ed Halsch,
▲ EMP: 12
SQ FT: 25,000
SALES (est): 2.3MM **Privately Held**
WEB: www.pcp-llc.com
SIC: 2631 Container, packaging & boxboard

(G-4971)
PLASTPAC INC (PA)
30 Boright Ave (07033-1086)
PHONE..............................908 272-7200
Mark Porges, *President*
EMP: 15 EST: 2013
SALES (est): 9.3MM **Privately Held**
SIC: 3086 Packaging & shipping materials, foamed plastic

(G-4972)
PROGRESSIVE TOOL & MFG CORP
708 Fairfield Ave (07033-2012)
PHONE..............................908 245-7010
Gunther Heim, *President*
Willy Heim, *Corp Secy*
EMP: 4
SQ FT: 2,100
SALES (est): 270K **Privately Held**
SIC: 3544 Special dies & tools; jigs & fixtures

(G-4973)
RAMCO MANUFACTURING CO INC (PA)
365 Carnegie Ave (07033-2004)
P.O. Box 96 (07033-0096)
PHONE..............................908 245-4500
Kevin Nee, *President*
Gerald Nee, *Principal*
Virginia Nee, *Vice Pres*
Bryan Argenbright, *Sales Mgr*
EMP: 25 EST: 1938
SALES (est): 4.8MM **Privately Held**
WEB: www.ramco-safetyshields.com
SIC: 3494 3545 3463 Pipe fittings; files, machine tool; nonferrous forgings

(G-4974)
RESOURCES INC IN DISPLAY (PA)
Also Called: Unified Resources
40 Boright Ave (07033-1015)
PHONE..............................908 272-5900
Dennis Polvere, *President*
Dean Polvere, *Vice Pres*
William Silver, *Vice Pres*
John Pillarella, *Controller*
Gregory Gannon, *Shareholder*
▲ EMP: 30
SQ FT: 38,000
SALES (est): 3.8MM **Privately Held**
SIC: 3993 Displays & cutouts, window & lobby

(G-4975)
ROTECH TOOL & MOLD CO INC
824 Fairfield Ave (07033-2014)
PHONE..............................908 241-9669
Robert F Leschinski, *President*
Theresa J Leschinski, *Corp Secy*
EMP: 9
SQ FT: 5,018
SALES (est): 790K **Privately Held**
SIC: 3544 3542 Forms (molds), for foundry & plastics working machinery; industrial molds; machine tools, metal forming type

(G-4976)
SEAGRAVE COATINGS CORP
Also Called: Plextone
209 N Michigan Ave (07033-1264)
PHONE..............................201 933-1000
H Peter Tepperman, *CEO*

Ralph Mastriano, *Accounts Exec*
David Walden, *Accounts Exec*
Lisa Truesdale,
▲ EMP: 50 EST: 1846
SQ FT: 30,000
SALES (est): 9.9MM **Privately Held**
WEB: www.seagravecoatings.com
SIC: 2851 6794 Paints & allied products;
franchises, selling or licensing

(G-4977)
SECURITY FABRICATORS INC
321 Lafayette Ave (07033-1078)
P.O. Box 643 (07033-0643)
PHONE.....................................908 272-9171
Paul Cacicedo Sr, *Ch of Bd*
Paul Cacicedo Jr, *President*
Armando Orsini, *Corp Secy*
John De Rosa, *Exec VP*
Roseann De Rosa, *Vice Pres*
EMP: 18
SQ FT: 2,500
SALES (est): 7.6MM **Privately Held**
SIC: 3315 3496 3446 3354 Chain link
fencing; miscellaneous fabricated wire
products; architectural metalwork; alu-
minum extruded products

(G-4978)
SGS INTERNATIONAL INC
185 Sumner Ave Ste A (07033-1327)
PHONE.....................................718 836-1000
EMP: 4
SALES (corp-wide): 6.3MM **Privately
Held**
SIC: 2796 Gravure printing plates or cylin-
ders, preparation of
PA: Sgs International Inc.
185 Sumner Ave Ste A
Kenilworth NJ 07033
212 239-3655

(G-4979)
**STOLLEN MACHINE & TOOL
COMPANY**
761 Lexington Ave (07033-2015)
PHONE.....................................908 241-0622
Doug Stollen, *President*
EMP: 6 EST: 1954
SQ FT: 10,000
SALES: 500K **Privately Held**
SIC: 3599 Machine shop, jobbing & repair

(G-4980)
SYNRAY CORPORATION
209 N Michigan Ave (07033-1264)
PHONE.....................................908 245-2600
H Peter Tepperman, *CEO*
Stanley Lesnewski, *President*
Colleen Merendino, *Office Mgr*
Peter H Tepperman, *CTO*
▲ EMP: 25
SQ FT: 30,000
SALES (est): 7.7MM **Privately Held**
WEB: www.synray.com
SIC: 2821 Plastics materials & resins

(G-4981)
TASTE IT PRESENTS INC
200 Sumner Ave (07033-1319)
PHONE.....................................908 241-9191
John Alair, *President*
Paula Perlis, *Vice Pres*
Vincent Caminiti, *CFO*
Gina Concotilli, *Sales Mgr*
Mike Donato, *Sales Staff*
▲ EMP: 75
SQ FT: 85,000
SALES (est): 15.6MM **Privately Held**
WEB: www.tasteitpresents.com
SIC: 2099 Food preparations

(G-4982)
TOO COOL OF OCEAN CITY
530 N Michigan Ave (07033-1023)
PHONE.....................................908 810-6363
Eli Shiloach, *Manager*
EMP: 4
SALES (est): 355.1K **Privately Held**
SIC: 2389 Apparel & accessories

(G-4983)
TOP LINE SEATING INC
540 S 31st St (07033-1306)
PHONE.....................................908 241-9051
Carl Friedrich, *CEO*

Norman Friedrich, *President*
John Friedrich, *Vice Pres*
EMP: 15
SQ FT: 14,000
SALES: 1.5MM **Privately Held**
SIC: 2522 Office chairs, benches & stools,
except wood; chairs, office: padded or
plain, except wood; benches, office: ex-
cept wood; stools, office: except wood

(G-4984)
**UNION COUNTY SEATING & SUP
CO**
135 N Michigan Ave (07033-1269)
PHONE.....................................908 241-4949
Bruce Bussell, *President*
EMP: 26
SQ FT: 4,500
SALES: 1.2MM **Privately Held**
WEB: www.unioncountyseating.com
SIC: 2531 Seats, automobile

(G-4985)
VS SYSTEMATICS CORP
300 S Michigan Ave (07033-2036)
PHONE.....................................908 241-5110
Tony Esteves, *Principal*
EMP: 5
SQ FT: 5,000
SALES (est): 1.5MM **Privately Held**
WEB: www.vssystematics.com
SIC: 5999 3714 Motors, electric; motor ve-
hicle parts & accessories

(G-4986)
WAAGE ELECTRIC INC
720 Colfax Ave (07033-2050)
P.O. Box 337 (07033-0337)
PHONE.....................................908 245-9363
Curtis Marc Waage, *President*
Marc Waage, *President*
Bruce Waage, *Vice Pres*
EMP: 9 EST: 1908
SQ FT: 11,800
SALES: 1MM **Privately Held**
WEB: www.waage.com
SIC: 3567 7629 3821 3548 Heating units
& devices, industrial: electric; electrical
equipment repair services; laboratory ap-
paratus & furniture; welding apparatus;
fabricated plate work (boiler shop); heat-
ing equipment, except electric

(G-4987)
**WAGNER FOTO SCREEN
PROCESS**
4 Mark Rd (07033-1025)
PHONE.....................................908 624-0800
Jim Lucadema, *President*
Robert Mosucci, *Partner*
EMP: 4
SALES (est): 352.1K **Privately Held**
SIC: 2759 Screen printing

(G-4988)
**WELTON V JOHNSON
ENGINEERING**
22 N 26th St (07033-1724)
PHONE.....................................908 241-3100
Paul Damjanovic, *President*
EMP: 10 EST: 1946
SALES (est): 1.3MM **Privately Held**
SIC: 3451 Screw machine products

(G-4989)
**WESTFIELD SHTMTL WORKS
INC**
261 Monroe Ave (07033-1131)
P.O. Box 128 (07033-0128)
PHONE.....................................908 276-5500
Campbell Johnstone, *CEO*
Thomas Johnstone, *Vice Pres*
Gregg Wheatley, *CFO*
Greg Wheatley, *Human Res Dir*
EMP: 45
SQ FT: 50,000
SALES (est): 9.9MM **Privately Held**
WEB: www.westfieldsheetmetal.com
SIC: 3444 3441 Sheet metal specialties,
not stamped; fabricated structural metal

(G-4990)
WHITE HOME PRODUCTS INC
30 Boright Ave 4 (07033-1086)
PHONE.....................................908 226-2501

Donald Weiss, *CEO*
Tamara Owens, *President*
▲ EMP: 6
SALES (est): 570.7K **Privately Held**
SIC: 3634 Electric housewares & fans

(G-4991)
YUHL PRODUCTS INC
15 N 7th St (07033-1406)
PHONE.....................................908 276-5180
Ron Yuhl, *President*
EMP: 4
SQ FT: 1,000
SALES: 500K **Privately Held**
SIC: 5084 3089 Plastic products machin-
ery; injection molded finished plastic prod-
ucts

Kenvil
Morris County

(G-4992)
**COUNTY CONCRETE
CORPORATION (PA)**
Also Called: CCC
50 Railroad Ave (07847-2606)
P.O. Box F (07847-1005)
PHONE.....................................973 744-2188
John C Crimi, *President*
Peter Crimi, *Exec VP*
EMP: 80
SQ FT: 1,500
SALES (est): 30.2MM **Privately Held**
WEB: www.countyconcretenj.com
SIC: 3273 5032 Ready-mixed concrete;
sand, construction; stone, crushed or bro-
ken; gravel

(G-4993)
**MAJOR AUTO INSTALLATIONS
INC**
Also Called: Spectrum Communications
47 N Dell Ave Ste 10 (07847-2640)
PHONE.....................................973 252-4262
Edward A Windt, *CEO*
J Bradley Badal, *President*
Kent Meinhold, *COO*
EMP: 20
SQ FT: 4,500
SALES (est): 3.8MM **Privately Held**
SIC: 3663 5065 Radio broadcasting &
communications equipment; electronic
parts & equipment

(G-4994)
PINTO OF MONTVILLE INC
25 Pine St (07847-2603)
PHONE.....................................973 584-2002
John Pinto, *President*
EMP: 8
SQ FT: 5,000
SALES (est): 1.2MM **Privately Held**
SIC: 3589 Commercial cooking & food-
warming equipment

(G-4995)
PRO IMAGE PROMOTIONS INC
Also Called: Brian's Embroidery
480 Us Highway 46 (07847-2675)
PHONE.....................................973 252-8000
Brian Hewitt, *President*
EMP: 5
SALES (est): 454.4K **Privately Held**
SIC: 2395 Embroidery & art needlework

(G-4996)
TROY-ONIC INC
90 N Dell Ave (07847-2559)
P.O. Box 494 (07847-0494)
PHONE.....................................973 584-6830
Michael Murphy, *President*
Edna Murphy, *Corp Secy*
EMP: 40
SQ FT: 5,000
SALES (est): 3MM **Privately Held**
SIC: 3671 3545 Electron tubes; machine
tool accessories

Keyport
Monmouth County

(G-4997)
AMP CUSTOM RUBBER INC
3 Cass St Ste 8 (07735-1425)
P.O. Box 377, Hazlet (07730-0377)
PHONE.....................................732 888-2714
John Petrizzo, *President*
EMP: 12
SQ FT: 15,000
SALES (est): 1.6MM **Privately Held**
WEB: www.ampcustomrubber.com
SIC: 3061 2499 2493 Mechanical rubber
goods; cork & cork products; reconsti-
tuted wood products

(G-4998)
ENCUR INC
200 Division St (07735-1604)
P.O. Box 92 (07735-0092)
PHONE.....................................732 264-2098
Mark Curcio, *President*
Maureen Del Popolo, *Manager*
EMP: 7
SQ FT: 5,000
SALES (est): 1.8MM **Privately Held**
WEB: www.encur.com
SIC: 3564 5074 Air purification equipment;
heating equipment (hydronic)

(G-4999)
FAST COPY PRINTING CENTER
Also Called: Fast T'S
81 Broad St (07735-1242)
PHONE.....................................732 739-4646
William Sacks, *Owner*
EMP: 10
SQ FT: 4,500
SALES (est): 550K **Privately Held**
WEB: www.fastcopynj.com
SIC: 2752 Commercial printing, offset

(G-5000)
G & M CUSTOM FORMICA WORK
120 Francis St Ste 5 (07735-1363)
PHONE.....................................732 888-0360
George Macchia, *Partner*
James Macchia, *Partner*
Michael Macchia, *Partner*
EMP: 5
SALES: 150K **Privately Held**
WEB: www.sgprinting.net
SIC: 2434 Wood kitchen cabinets

(G-5001)
METHOD ASSOC INC
120 Francis St Ste 2 (07735-1363)
PHONE.....................................732 888-0444
Malcolm Will, *President*
Stephen Will, *General Mgr*
▲ EMP: 12
SQ FT: 20,000
SALES: 1.2MM **Privately Held**
WEB: www.methodassociates.com
SIC: 3543 7389 Industrial patterns; de-
sign, commercial & industrial

(G-5002)
**MR GREEN TEA ICE CREAM
CORP**
25 Church St Unit 104 (07735-1508)
P.O. Box 70255, Staten Island NY (10307-
0255)
PHONE.....................................732 446-9800
EMP: 21
SQ FT: 3,500
SALES: 2.5MM **Privately Held**
SIC: 2024 Mfg Ice Cream/Frozen Desert

(G-5003)
**MR GREEN TEA ICE CREAM
CORP**
42 E Front St (07735-1544)
PHONE.....................................732 446-9800
Richard Emanuele, *CEO*
Marcus Lemonis, *CEO*
Lori Emanuele, *Purch Dir*
EMP: 15
SQ FT: 10,000
SALES (est): 581.4K **Privately Held**
SIC: 2024 Ice cream & frozen desserts

(G-5004)
POLY-SMITH PTFE LLC
21 Industrial Dr (07735-6113)
PHONE..........................732 287-0610
Cathy Smith, *President*
Stephen Smith, *COO*
EMP: 10
SQ FT: 20,000
SALES: 7MM **Privately Held**
SIC: 3081 Packing materials, plastic sheet

(G-5005)
**TASK INTERNATIONAL (USA)
INC**
3 Cass St (07735-1425)
PHONE..........................732 739-0377
Richard Hopwood, *President*
Loretta Hopwood, *Corp Secy*
Thomas Saporita, *Vice Pres*
▲ **EMP:** 13
SQ FT: 5,000
SALES (est): 1.1MM **Privately Held**
SIC: 3585 Air conditioning equipment,
complete

(G-5006)
WCD ENTERPRISES INC
1 Main St (07735-1213)
PHONE..........................732 888-4422
Scott Delatush, *Opers Staff*
Hank Freeman, *CFO*
EMP: 9
SALES (est): 841K **Privately Held**
WEB: www.adultsights.com
SIC: 4813 2741

Kingston
Somerset County

(G-5007)
CIRCLEBLACK INC
4428 Route 27 Bldg C (08528-9613)
P.O. Box 371 (08528-0371)
PHONE..........................800 315-1241
John Donald Michel, *CEO*
Danny McGrory, *Engineer*
Matthew Valkovic, *Director*
EMP: 19
SALES (est): 209.6K **Privately Held**
SIC: 7389 7372 Financial services;
prepackaged software

(G-5008)
**CIVIC RESEARCH INSTITUTE
INC (PA)**
4478 Route 27 Ste 202 (08528-9613)
P.O. Box 585 (08528-0585)
PHONE..........................609 683-4450
Mark E Peel, *President*
Arthur H Rosenfeld, *Chairman*
Deborah J Launer, *Vice Pres*
Felicia A Rosenfeld, *Vice Pres*
EMP: 3
SQ FT: 1,000
SALES: 1.5MM **Privately Held**
WEB: www.civicresearchinstitute.com
SIC: 2721 Periodicals

(G-5009)
**JOSEPH AND WILLIAM
STAVOLA (PA)**
460 River Rd (08528)
P.O. Box 419 (08528-0419)
PHONE..........................609 924-0300
Joseph W Stavola, *President*
William Stavola, *Corp Secy*
EMP: 50
SQ FT: 5,000
SALES (est): 15.7MM **Privately Held**
SIC: 3273 2951 1429 1611 Ready-mixed
concrete; concrete, bituminous; trap rock,
crushed & broken-quarrying; highway &
street paving contractor

(G-5010)
KINGSTON NURSERIES LLC
Also Called: Mapleton Nurseries
140 Mapleton Rd (08528)
P.O. Box 396 (08528-0396)
PHONE..........................609 430-0366
Fax: 609 430-0367
EMP: 12

SALES (est): 880K **Privately Held**
SIC: 3299 Mfg Nonmetallic Mineral Products

(G-5011)
STA-SEAL INC (PA)
Promenade Blvd Rr 27 (08528)
P.O. Box 419 (08528-0419)
PHONE..........................609 924-0300
Joseph W Stavola, *President*
William H Stavola, *Corp Secy*
EMP: 7 **EST:** 1969
SQ FT: 5,000
SALES (est): 568.1K **Privately Held**
SIC: 3273 Ready-mixed concrete

(G-5012)
**TRAP ROCK INDUSTRIES INC
(PA)**
460 River Rd (08528)
P.O. Box 419 (08528-0419)
PHONE..........................609 924-0300
Joseph M Stavola, *President*
Wayne Byard, *Vice Pres*
Michael Crowley, *Vice Pres*
EMP: 300 **EST:** 1860
SQ FT: 90,000
SALES (est): 131.7MM **Privately Held**
WEB: www.traprock.com
SIC: 3273 3272 1429 1611 Ready-mixed
concrete; concrete products; trap rock,
crushed & broken-quarrying; highway &
street paving contractor

(G-5013)
TRAP ROCK INDUSTRIES LLC
460 River Rd (08528)
PHONE..........................609 924-0300
Michael Crowley, *Principal*
EMP: 99
SQ FT: 8,000
SALES (est): 3.4MM **Privately Held**
SIC: 1429 Trap rock, crushed & broken-
quarrying

Kinnelon
Morris County

(G-5014)
ACME WIRE FORMING LLC
18 Pepperidge Tree Ter (07405-2228)
PHONE..........................201 218-2912
Kevin Skvorecz,
EMP: 12
SALES (est): 851.7K **Privately Held**
SIC: 3496 Miscellaneous fabricated wire
products

(G-5015)
ARCHI-TREAD INC
191 Brook Valley Rd (07405-3326)
PHONE..........................973 725-5738
Scott Akin, *President*
EMP: 9
SALES (est): 920K **Privately Held**
SIC: 3534 Stair elevators, motor powered

(G-5016)
**DIAMEX INTERNATIONAL CORP
(PA)**
23 Birch Rd (07405-2504)
PHONE..........................973 838-8844
Andreas Ladjias, *President*
EMP: 7
SALES (est): 957.8K **Privately Held**
SIC: 2653 Corrugated & solid fiber boxes

(G-5017)
HILLCREST OPTICIANS
11 Kiel Ave Ste D-1 (07405-2557)
PHONE..........................973 838-6666
Eric Shnayder, *Owner*
EMP: 4
SALES (est): 190K **Privately Held**
SIC: 3851 5995 Ophthalmic goods; opti-
cians

(G-5018)
JTWO INC
Also Called: Storybook Knits
4 Birch Rd (07405-2505)
PHONE..........................201 410-1616
Jamie Gries, *President*

EMP: 4
SQ FT: 2,000
SALES (est): 1.9MM **Privately Held**
SIC: 2253 Sweaters & sweater coats, knit

(G-5019)
**LIFE RECOVERY SYSTEMS HD
LLC (PA)**
170 Kinnelon Rd Rm 5 (07405-2323)
PHONE..........................973 283-2800
John Diliddo, *President*
Robert Schock, *Managing Prtnr*
Rick Hettenbach, *Mng Member*
EMP: 4
SALES (est): 753.7K **Privately Held**
SIC: 3829 Personnel dosimetry devices

(G-5020)
OLYMPIC EDM SERVICES INC
Also Called: Olympic Custom Tools
20 Kiel Ave (07405-2552)
PHONE..........................973 492-0664
Donald Ferrante, *President*
EMP: 8
SQ FT: 4,000
SALES (est): 1.2MM **Privately Held**
SIC: 3544 3599 Special dies & tools; elec-
trical discharge machining (EDM)

(G-5021)
PUREVOLUTION
62 Fayson Lake Rd (07405-3124)
PHONE..........................973 919-4047
Jeffrey Schirripa, *CEO*
EMP: 10
SALES (est): 552.9K **Privately Held**
SIC: 2833 Medicinals & botanicals

(G-5022)
TUFF MUTTERS LLC
2 Kiel Ave Unit 155 (07405-2572)
PHONE..........................973 291-6679
Michelle Bonus, *Mng Member*
EMP: 4
SALES (est): 185.8K **Privately Held**
SIC: 2399 5199 5999 Horse & pet acces-
sories, textile; pet supplies; pet supplies

(G-5023)
TYPEN GRAPHICS INC
170 Kinnelon Rd Rm 12 (07405-2324)
PHONE..........................973 838-6544
Mary Weber, *President*
John Weber, *Vice Pres*
EMP: 8
SQ FT: 1,500
SALES (est): 797.4K **Privately Held**
WEB: www.typengraphics.com
SIC: 2791 Typesetting

Lafayette
Sussex County

(G-5024)
ACRYLICS UNLIMITED
11 Millpond Dr Unit 2 (07848-3826)
PHONE..........................973 862-6014
EMP: 7 **EST:** 2013
SALES (est): 985.8K **Privately Held**
SIC: 3089 Plastic processing

(G-5025)
BEAVER RUN FARMS
Also Called: Shotmeyer Bros
300 Beaver Run Rd (07848-3131)
PHONE..........................973 875-5555
Kevin Joan, *Manager*
EMP: 15
SALES (corp-wide): 1.3MM **Privately
Held**
SIC: 2951 Asphalt & asphaltic paving mix-
tures (not from refineries)
PA: Beaver Run Farms
10 Wagaraw Rd
Hawthorne NJ 07506
973 427-1000

(G-5026)
BON CHEF INC (PA)
205 State Route 94 (07848-4617)
PHONE..........................973 383-8848
Salvatore Torre, *President*
Tina Crowley, *General Mgr*

Kaya Gross, *Vice Pres*
Paul McGreevy, *Opers Mgr*
Chan William, *Engineer*
◆ **EMP:** 65 **EST:** 1973
SQ FT: 63,000
SALES: 34MM **Privately Held**
WEB: www.bonchef.com
SIC: 5046 3365 Commercial cooking &
food service equipment; aluminum
foundries

(G-5027)
F W BENNETT & SON INC
403 Sparta Rd (07848)
P.O. Box 724 (07848-0724)
PHONE..........................973 383-4050
Frank W Bennet, *President*
EMP: 4
SALES (est): 260.5K **Privately Held**
SIC: 1442 Common sand mining; gravel
mining

(G-5028)
**JAMES ZYLSTRA ENTERPRISES
INC**
Also Called: Fredon Welding & Iron Works
52 State Route 15 (07848-2424)
P.O. Box 260 (07848-0260)
PHONE..........................973 383-6768
James S Zylstra Jr, *President*
Laura Silvero, *Admin Asst*
EMP: 30
SQ FT: 9,200
SALES (est): 4.7MM **Privately Held**
WEB: www.fredonwelding.com
SIC: 3446 Architectural metalwork

(G-5029)
JORDAN MANUFACTURING LLC
28 Randazzo Rd (07848-2221)
P.O. Box 226 (07848-0226)
PHONE..........................973 383-8363
Gary Wilson, *Mayor*
Zdenek Fremund, *Manager*
EMP: 5
SQ FT: 6,000
SALES: 1MM
SALES (corp-wide): 326.6MM **Privately
Held**
WEB: www.jordanmanufacturing.com
SIC: 3469 3544 Stamping metal for the
trade; special dies & tools
HQ: Carl Stahl Sava Industries, Inc.
4 N Corporate Dr
Riverdale NJ 07457
973 835-0882

(G-5030)
**LIMECREST QUARRY
DEVELOPER LLC**
217 Limecrest Rd (07848-3646)
PHONE..........................973 383-7100
Pam Kelley, *General Mgr*
Howard Goddard, *Superintendent*
EMP: 15
SALES (est): 1.5MM **Privately Held**
WEB: www.limecrest.com
SIC: 1422 Crushed & broken limestone

(G-5031)
**METAPORT MANUFACTURING
LLC**
28 Randazzo Rd (07848-2221)
P.O. Box 226 (07848-0226)
PHONE..........................973 383-8363
Zdenek Fremund, *Mng Member*
EMP: 7
SALES (est): 750K **Privately Held**
SIC: 5084 3541 Machine tools & metal-
working machinery; machine tools, metal
cutting type

(G-5032)
RT COM USA INC
10 Millpond Dr Unit 2 (07848-3825)
P.O. Box 135, Ogdensburg (07439-0135)
PHONE..........................973 862-4210
Chanyi Ryu, *President*
Joon Ryu, *President*
EMP: 6
SALES (est): 577.8K **Privately Held**
WEB: www.rtcomusa.com
SIC: 3571 Electronic computers

2019 Harris New Jersey
Manufacturers Directory

▲ = Import ▼=Export
◆ =Import/Export

(G-5033)
SUSTAINABLE GARDENING INST INC
85 Lawrence Rd (07848)
PHONE....................................973 383-0497
Dan Freed, *Principal*
Eric Olsen, *Principal*
Lois J De Vries, *Exec Dir*
EMP: 4
SALES (est): 108.3K **Privately Held**
SIC: 2741

Lake Hiawatha
Morris County

(G-5034)
EMPIRICAL LABS INC
41 N Beverwyck Rd (07034-2605)
PHONE....................................973 541-9447
David Derr, *President*
Judith Saiya-Berr, *Vice Pres*
Judith Saiya-Berr, *Vice Pres*
EMP: 11
SALES (est): 2.5MM **Privately Held**
WEB: www.empiricallabs.com
SIC: 3651 5099 Audio electronic systems; video & audio equipment

Lake Hopatcong
Morris County

(G-5035)
CRETT CONSTRUCTION INC
18 Cella St (07849-2233)
PHONE....................................973 663-1184
John Starger, *President*
Ed Poskit, *Vice Pres*
EMP: 13
SALES (est): 1.1MM **Privately Held**
SIC: 1761 3444 Sheet metalwork; sheet metalwork

(G-5036)
DIGITIZE INC
158 Edison Rd (07849-2217)
PHONE....................................973 663-1011
Abraham Brecher, *President*
Linda Brecher, *Treasurer*
EMP: 17
SQ FT: 6,800
SALES (est): 3.2MM **Privately Held**
WEB: www.digitize-inc.com
SIC: 3669 3699 Fire alarm apparatus, electric; security devices

(G-5037)
STACKS ENVMTL LTD LBLTY CO
5 Crescent Dr (07849-1339)
P.O. Box 278 (07849-0278)
PHONE....................................973 885-2036
Raymond F Evans, *President*
EMP: 7
SQ FT: 30,000
SALES (est): 1.2MM **Privately Held**
SIC: 3443 Boiler shop products: boilers, smokestacks, steel tanks; breechings, metal plate

(G-5038)
WATER MARK TECHNOLOGIES INC
762 State Route 15 S 2d (07849-2410)
PHONE....................................973 663-3438
Phil Reilly, *President*
Kim Logsdon, *Vice Pres*
▲ EMP: 8
SALES (est): 1.5MM **Privately Held**
SIC: 2819 Brine

Lakehurst
Ocean County

(G-5039)
MICRO MEDIA PUBLICATIONS INC
Also Called: Berkeley Times
15 Union Ave (08733-3023)
P.O. Box 521 (08733-0521)
PHONE....................................732 657-7344
Stewart Swann, *President*
Chris Lundy, *Editor*
Robin Weather, *Vice Pres*
Allison Gradzki, *Prdtn Mgr*
Lorrie Toscano, *Sales Executive*
EMP: 7
SALES (est): 410K **Privately Held**
WEB: www.micromediapubs2.com
SIC: 2711 Newspapers: publishing only, not printed on site

(G-5040)
YERG INC
Also Called: Yerg Accounting Supplies
7 Fawnhollow Ln (08759-7312)
PHONE....................................973 759-4041
Kathleen Yerg-Marmo, *President*
Kathleen Yerg Marmo, *President*
Frank Marmo Jr, *Admin Sec*
EMP: 5 EST: 1909
SQ FT: 10,000
SALES (est): 567.6K **Privately Held**
WEB: www.yergpads.com
SIC: 2678 Stationery products

Lakewood
Ocean County

(G-5041)
10X DAILY LLC
10 Blue Jay Way (08701-4746)
PHONE....................................732 276-6407
Yitzchok Liebes, *Owner*
EMP: 4
SALES (est): 136.4K **Privately Held**
SIC: 2711 Newspapers, publishing & printing

(G-5042)
A&R PRINTING CORPORATION
Also Called: Printers Plus
421 W County Line Rd (08701-1204)
PHONE....................................732 886-0505
Jacob Stendig, *President*
EMP: 6
SQ FT: 5,700
SALES (est): 851K **Privately Held**
SIC: 2752 Commercial printing, offset

(G-5043)
ABSOLUME LLC (PA)
1153 Tiffany Ln (08701-5863)
PHONE....................................732 523-1231
Yisroel Berkowitz, *CEO*
Michael Greenberg, *COO*
EMP: 4
SQ FT: 300
SALES (est): 500K **Privately Held**
SIC: 3646 Commercial indusl & institutional electric lighting fixtures

(G-5044)
ACCUPAC INC
1700 Oak St (08701-5926)
PHONE....................................215 256-7094
Paul H Alvater, *Branch Mgr*
EMP: 144
SALES (corp-wide): 130.3MM **Privately Held**
SIC: 3823 Liquid analysis instruments, industrial process type
PA: Accupac, Inc.
1501 Indtl Blvd
Mainland PA 19451
215 256-7000

(G-5045)
ACKERSON DRAPERY DECORATOR SVC
500 James St Ste 14 (08701-4043)
PHONE....................................732 797-1967
Ronni L Leddy, *President*
Christina Ackerson, *Principal*
Michael K Leddy, *Vice Pres*
▲ EMP: 9
SQ FT: 6,500
SALES (est): 1.3MM **Privately Held**
WEB: www.ackersondrapery.com
SIC: 2391 2392 2591 Curtains & draperies; bedspreads & bed sets: made from purchased materials; slipcovers: made of fabric, plastic etc.; curtain & drapery rods, poles & fixtures; blinds vertical

(G-5046)
ADVANCED PRODUCTS LLC
1915 Swarthmore Ave (08701-4567)
PHONE....................................800 724-5464
Klink Stanley, *Mng Member*
Larry S Stanley, *Mng Member*
Andrew Davidson,
EMP: 20
SQ FT: 15,000
SALES: 5MM **Privately Held**
SIC: 3446 Architectural metalwork

(G-5047)
ALPHA ASSOCIATES INC
145 Lehigh Ave (08701-4527)
PHONE....................................732 730-1800
Steve Prinn, *Managing Prtnr*
Robert Antonius, *COO*
Kevin Burton, *Vice Pres*
Spyros Tsielepas, *Opers Mgr*
Susan Ferreira, *Purch Mgr*
EMP: 25
SALES (corp-wide): 31MM **Privately Held**
WEB: www.alphainc.com
SIC: 5131 3535 2295 Textile converters; conveyors & conveying equipment; coated fabrics, not rubberized
PA: Alpha Engineered Composites, Llc
145 Lehigh Ave
Lakewood NJ 08701
732 634-5700

(G-5048)
ALPHA ENGNEERED COMPOSITES LLC (PA)
145 Lehigh Ave (08701-4527)
PHONE....................................732 634-5700
Christopher J Avallone, *CEO*
John Baxter, *Vice Pres*
◆ EMP: 108
SQ FT: 112,000
SALES (est): 31MM **Privately Held**
WEB: www.alphainc.com
SIC: 2295 Resin or plastic coated fabrics

(G-5049)
AMERICAN BUSINESS PAPER INC
Also Called: American Graphic Solutions
222 River Ave (08701-4807)
PHONE....................................732 363-5788
Jeffrey Berger, *President*
EMP: 12
SALES (est): 1.6MM **Privately Held**
SIC: 2754 5113 Commercial printing, gravure; industrial & personal service paper

(G-5050)
AMERICAN VAN EQUIPMENT INC (PA)
149 Lehigh Ave (08701-4527)
PHONE....................................732 905-5900
Charles B Richter, *President*
Martin Richter, *Vice Pres*
Joseph Fallon, *VP Sales*
Richard Gebbia, *VP Mktg*
William Dempsey, *Info Tech Mgr*
▼ EMP: 140
SQ FT: 130,000
SALES (est): 74.7MM **Privately Held**
WEB: www.americanvan.com
SIC: 5531 3429 Automotive accessories; motor vehicle hardware

(G-5051)
AMERICHEM ENTERPRISES INC
6 Round Valley Ln (08701-5755)
PHONE....................................732 363-4840
Deanna Robinson, *President*
EMP: 7
SALES (est): 845.1K **Privately Held**
WEB: www.americanenterprisesllc.com
SIC: 5087 2842 Janitors' supplies; cleaning or polishing preparations; waxes for wood, leather & other materials

(G-5052)
AMETEK INC
485 Oberlin Ave S (08701-6904)
PHONE....................................732 370-9100
Scot Rapoza, *Purch Mgr*
Kim Murphy, *Branch Mgr*
EMP: 6
SALES (corp-wide): 4.8B **Publicly Held**
SIC: 3643 Current-carrying wiring devices
PA: Ametek, Inc.
1100 Cassatt Rd
Berwyn PA 19312
610 647-2121

(G-5053)
AMICO TECHNOLOGIES INC
Also Called: Keco Engineered Controls
1200 River Ave Ste 3a (08701-5657)
PHONE....................................732 901-5900
Joseph W Mitchell, *President*
EMP: 6
SQ FT: 1,000
SALES (est): 2.7MM **Privately Held**
WEB: www.kecocontrols.com
SIC: 5085 3823 Valves & fittings; industrial instrmnts msrmnt display/control process variable

(G-5054)
ARCHITECTURAL METAL AND GLASS
644 Cross St Unit 14 (08701-4654)
PHONE....................................732 994-7575
Anjennette Panebianco,
EMP: 4
SALES (est): 546.7K **Privately Held**
SIC: 5231 1542 3449 Glass; store front construction; curtain wall, metal

(G-5055)
AUGENBRAUNS BRIDAL PASSAIC LLC
200 Central Ave (08701-3134)
PHONE....................................845 425-3439
Joseph Augenbraun, *CEO*
Malky Augenbraun, *COO*
Chanie Coplowitz, *CFO*
Adina Fride, *CFO*
EMP: 7
SQ FT: 1,450
SALES (est): 516.4K **Privately Held**
SIC: 2335 Bridal & formal gowns

(G-5056)
AVANTEGARDE IMAGE LLC
535 E County Line Rd (08701-1486)
PHONE....................................732 363-8701
Sidney Welz,
EMP: 15
SALES (est): 794K **Privately Held**
WEB: www.avantgardeimage.com
SIC: 2514 Metal household furniture

(G-5057)
B P GRAPHICS INC
315 4th St (08701-3231)
PHONE....................................732 942-2315
Benjamin Heineman, *President*
EMP: 20
SQ FT: 6,000
SALES: 1.2MM **Privately Held**
SIC: 2759 Commercial printing

(G-5058)
BASIC LTD
575 Prospect St Ste 241 (08701-5040)
PHONE....................................718 871-6106
Harris Mermelstein, *President*
▲ EMP: 25
SALES (est): 5MM **Privately Held**
WEB: www.basic.net
SIC: 2673 Garment & wardrobe bags, (plastic film)

GEOGRAPHIC

(G-5059)
BBG SURGICAL LTD LIABILITY CO
1950 Rutgers Blvd D (08701-4537)
PHONE................................888 575-6277
Alan Berman,
Mark Bakst,
EMP: 8
SALES: 6MM **Privately Held**
SIC: 5047 3841 Instruments, surgical & medical; surgical instruments & apparatus

(G-5060)
BELAIR TIME CORPORATION
1995 Swarthmore Ave Ste 3 (08701-4572)
PHONE................................732 905-0100
Alan Grunwald, *President*
Adrienne Grunwald, *Principal*
Joan Grunwald, *Principal*
Bill Peak, *Natl Sales Mgr*
Johny Gupton, *VP Sales*
▲ **EMP:** 60 **EST:** 1945
SQ FT: 30,000
SALES (est): 9.8MM **Privately Held**
WEB: www.beltime.com
SIC: 3873 Watches & parts, except crystals & jewels

(G-5061)
BGS INC
Also Called: Buildgreen Solutions
910 E County Line Rd # 101 (08701-2092)
PHONE................................732 442-5000
Elkana Tombak, *CEO*
EMP: 15
SQ FT: 3,500
SALES: 2.8MM **Privately Held**
SIC: 3585 Parts for heating, cooling & refrigerating equipment

(G-5062)
BIMBO BAKERIES USA INC
160 Airport Rd Ste 4 (08701-6927)
PHONE................................732 886-1881
EMP: 56 **Privately Held**
SIC: 2051 Bakery: wholesale or wholesale/retail combined
HQ: Bimbo Bakeries Usa, Inc
　　255 Business Center Dr # 200
　　Horsham PA 19044
　　215 347-5500

(G-5063)
BORUCH TRADING LTD LBLTY CO
69 Gudz Rd (08701-2913)
PHONE................................718 614-9575
Boruch Kirschenbaum,
EMP: 8
SALES (est): 284.4K **Privately Held**
SIC: 3999 5064 Barber & beauty shop equipment; electric household appliances

(G-5064)
BP PRINT GROUP INC
315 4th St (08701-3231)
PHONE................................732 905-9830
Ben Heinemann, *President*
EMP: 70 **EST:** 2015
SQ FT: 9,000
SALES (est): 8.3MM **Privately Held**
SIC: 2752 Commercial printing, offset; letters, circular or form: lithographed; business form & card printing, lithographic; periodicals, lithographed

(G-5065)
BRAND AROMATICS INTL INC
1600 Oak St (08701-5924)
PHONE................................732 363-1204
Karl E Brand, *President*
Nancy Moore, *Purchasing*
Ed Heraty, *Manager*
Dianna Derosa, *Receptionist*
▲ **EMP:** 7
SQ FT: 100,000
SALES: 2.3MM
SALES (corp-wide): 5.4B **Publicly Held**
WEB: www.brandaromatics.com
SIC: 2087 Extracts, flavoring
PA: Mccormick & Company Incorporated
　　24 Schilling Rd Ste 1
　　Hunt Valley MD 21031
　　410 771-7301

(G-5066)
BRIGHT IDEAS USA LLC
890 Morris Ave (08701-5520)
PHONE................................732 886-8865
Deena Leiman,
▲ **EMP:** 4
SALES (est): 377.2K **Privately Held**
SIC: 2399 Fabricated textile products

(G-5067)
BRISCO APPAREL CO INC
575 Prospect St Ste 230 (08701-5075)
PHONE................................718 715-7110
Scott Gartner, *CEO*
EMP: 20
SALES (corp-wide): 14.9MM **Privately Held**
SIC: 2329 Shirt & slack suits: men's, youths' & boys'
PA: Brisco Apparel Co., Inc.
　　4315 13th Ave Fl 3
　　Brooklyn NY 11219
　　718 832-2080

(G-5068)
BSD INDUSTRIES LTD LIABILITY
110 Columbus Ave S (08701-2951)
PHONE................................732 534-4341
EMP: 5 **EST:** 2011
SALES (est): 174.5K **Privately Held**
SIC: 3999 Manufacturing industries

(G-5069)
CHERRI STONE INTERACTIVE LLC
Also Called: Zaffre
182 N Crest Pl (08701-3282)
PHONE................................844 843-7765
AMI Bielinki, *Mng Member*
EMP: 5
SALES: 350K **Privately Held**
SIC: 2844 7389 7311 8742 Deodorants, personal; face creams or lotions; ; advertising consultant; marketing consulting services

(G-5070)
CHURCH & DWIGHT CO INC
800 Airport Rd (08701-5909)
PHONE................................732 730-3100
Tom Volz, *Manager*
EMP: 14
SALES (corp-wide): 4.1B **Publicly Held**
WEB: www.churchdwight.com
SIC: 2812 Sodium bicarbonate
PA: Church & Dwight Co., Inc.
　　500 Charles Ewing Blvd
　　Ewing NJ 08628
　　609 806-1200

(G-5071)
CLAYTON ASSOCIATES INC
1650 Oak St (08701-5924)
PHONE................................732 363-2100
James Clayton, *President*
Brad Clayton, *Vice Pres*
Janice Clayton, *Vice Pres*
Margaret Candiano, *Office Mgr*
▲ **EMP:** 11
SQ FT: 18,500
SALES (est): 3.2MM **Privately Held**
WEB: www.jclayton.com
SIC: 3589 3569 Vacuum cleaners & sweepers, electric: industrial; brake burnishing or washing machines

(G-5072)
COMPONENT HARDWARE GROUP INC (PA)
1890 Swarthmore Ave (08701-4530)
P.O. Box 2020 (08701-8020)
PHONE................................800 526-3694
Partha Biswas, *President*
Chris Guarnieri, *Business Mgr*
Daniel Hazard, *Business Mgr*
Dan Keeley, *Business Mgr*
Lee Silverstone, *Business Mgr*
◆ **EMP:** 90
SQ FT: 85,000
SALES (est): 27.2MM **Privately Held**
WEB: www.componenthardware.com
SIC: 5251 3429 Hardware; manufactured hardware (general)

(G-5073)
CREATIVE FILM CORP
Also Called: Griff Decorative Film
700 Vassar Ave Ste 2 (08701-6957)
PHONE................................732 367-2166
Joseph Coburn, *CEO*
Gene Silvestro, *General Mgr*
Chip Adams, *Vice Pres*
EMP: 15
SALES (est): 2.4MM **Privately Held**
WEB: www.creativefilmcorp.net
SIC: 3081 Plastic film & sheet

(G-5074)
CREOH TRADING CORP
Also Called: Creoh Packaging
910 E County Line Rd (08701-2091)
PHONE................................718 821-0570
Daryl Hagler, *President*
Yuri Fromowitz, *COO*
Chany Mendlowitz, *Admin Sec*
▲ **EMP:** 13
SQ FT: 4,000
SALES: 6.5MM **Privately Held**
WEB: www.creoh.com
SIC: 3993 Signs & advertising specialties

(G-5075)
CREOH USA LLC
1771 Madison Ave Ste 7 (08701-1267)
PHONE................................718 821-0570
EMP: 5 **EST:** 2014
SALES (est): 226.8K **Privately Held**
SIC: 2653 Solid fiber boxes, partitions, display items & sheets

(G-5076)
CRIJUODAMA BAKING CORP T
1900 Highway 70 Ste 209 (08701-7324)
PHONE................................732 451-1250
EMP: 4
SALES (est): 197K **Privately Held**
SIC: 2051 Bread, cake & related products

(G-5077)
CUISINE INNVTONS UNLIMITED LLC
180 Lehigh Ave (08701-4526)
PHONE................................732 730-9310
Ron Rexroth,
EMP: 150
SALES (est): 21.1MM **Privately Held**
SIC: 2038 Frozen specialties

(G-5078)
CUSTOM EXTRUSION TECH INC
Also Called: CET Films
1650 Corporate Rd W (08701-5920)
PHONE................................732 367-5511
Paul Charapata, *CEO*
Guy Leigh, *Vice Pres*
Tom Kennedy, *CFO*
Tim Reimer, *Controller*
EMP: 15
SALES (est): 9.2MM **Privately Held**
SIC: 3544 Extrusion dies
HQ: R Tape Corporation
　　6 Ingersoll Rd
　　South Plainfield NJ 07080
　　908 753-5570

(G-5079)
CW INTERNATIONAL SALES LLC
Also Called: Crystal Ware
600 James St (08701-4023)
PHONE................................732 367-4444
Sam Greenwald, *Opers Staff*
Fred Katz, *Sales Dir*
Nisson Kugler, *Mng Member*
Tzaley Zombo, *Manager*
Camila Gomes, *Representative*
▲ **EMP:** 27
SQ FT: 145,000
SALES (est): 7.3MM **Privately Held**
SIC: 2621 2656 Towels, tissues & napkins: paper & stock; paper cups, plates, dishes & utensils

(G-5080)
D & A GRANULATION LLC
1970 Rutgers Univ Blvd (08701-4573)
PHONE................................732 994-7480
Tyson Pritchard, *President*
EMP: 4 **EST:** 2016
SALES (est): 124.1K **Privately Held**
SIC: 2833 Medicinals & botanicals

(G-5081)
DALEMARK INDUSTRIES INC
575 Prospect St Ste 211 (08701-5040)
PHONE................................732 367-3100
Michael Delli Gatti, *President*
EMP: 10 **EST:** 1955
SQ FT: 12,000
SALES (est): 1MM **Privately Held**
WEB: www.dalemark.com
SIC: 3953 3565 Marking devices; labeling machines, industrial

(G-5082)
DCM CLEAN AIR PRODUCTS INC
1650 Oak St (08701-5924)
PHONE................................732 363-2100
James Clayton, *President*
Brad Clayton, *Vice Pres*
EMP: 7 **EST:** 2012
SALES (est): 851.2K **Privately Held**
SIC: 3546 3589 Cartridge-activated hand power tools; vacuum cleaners & sweepers, electric: industrial

(G-5083)
DESTINY FOUNDATION
564 Marc Dr (08701-5115)
PHONE................................732 987-9008
Elaine Gilbert, *Principal*
Faigie Gilbert, *Executive Asst*
Nachum Amsel, *Education*
EMP: 5
SALES: 512.2K **Privately Held**
SIC: 3999 5999 Education aids, devices & supplies; education aids, devices & supplies

(G-5084)
DISPERSION TECHNOLOGY INC
1885 Swarthmore Ave (08701-4574)
P.O. Box 300 (08701-0300)
PHONE................................732 364-4488
Yogesh Parikh, *President*
Rosanne Heitner, *Admin Sec*
EMP: 10
SQ FT: 15,000
SALES (est): 1.2MM **Privately Held**
WEB: www.dispersion.com
SIC: 2816 Inorganic pigments

(G-5085)
DRAGON ASPHALT EQUIPMENT LLC
845 Towbin Ave (08701-5929)
PHONE................................732 922-9290
EMP: 10
SQ FT: 25,000
SALES (est): 2MM **Privately Held**
SIC: 3531 Mfg Construction Machinery

(G-5086)
DREAM CABINETRY
212 2nd St Unit 2 (08701-3424)
PHONE................................732 806-8444
Nechema Breilossky, *President*
Baila Berger, *Bookkeeper*
EMP: 7
SALES: 1.5MM **Privately Held**
SIC: 2434 Wood kitchen cabinets

(G-5087)
E P HOMIEK SHTMTL SUPS INC
1352 River Ave Ste 4 (08701-5646)
PHONE................................732 364-7644
Edward P Homiek, *President*
EMP: 20
SQ FT: 2,300
SALES (est): 9.9MM **Privately Held**
SIC: 3444 Metal ventilating equipment

(G-5088)
EAGLE RACING INC
810 Cross St Ste 4 (08701-4045)
PHONE................................732 367-8487
Dale Barlet, *President*
EMP: 4
SQ FT: 8,960
SALES (est): 489.3K **Privately Held**
SIC: 3559 Automotive related machinery

(G-5089)
ELECTRONIC CONNECTIONS INC (PA)
Also Called: Eci
195 Lehigh Ave Ste 3 (08701-4555)
PHONE...................................732 367-5588
Steven Jordan, *President*
Jim Greene, *Sales Staff*
EMP: 15
SQ FT: 8,100
SALES (est): 7.5MM **Privately Held**
WEB: www.ecinj.com
SIC: 5065 3679 Electronic parts; harness assemblies for electronic use: wire or cable

(G-5090)
ELITE EMRGNCY LIGHTS LTD LBLTY
1000 Bennett Blvd Ste 6 (08701-5944)
PHONE...................................732 534-2377
Nate Herskovits, *Principal*
EMP: 12
SALES (est): 253.9K **Privately Held**
SIC: 1731 3647 3711 3714 Standby or emergency power specialization; flasher lights, automotive; automobile assembly, including specialty automobiles; motor vehicle parts & accessories

(G-5091)
EOM WORLDWIDE SALES CORP
39 Harmony Dr (08701-5841)
PHONE...................................732 994-7352
David Teller, *President*
EMP: 1 EST: 2016
SQ FT: 1,100
SALES (est): 19.5MM **Privately Held**
SIC: 5946 3571 Cameras; personal computers (microcomputers)

(G-5092)
EPI GROUP LTD LIABILITY CO
410 Monmouth Ave (08701-3711)
PHONE...................................917 710-6607
Benjamin Klein, *President*
EMP: 5
SQ FT: 800
SALES: 4MM **Privately Held**
SIC: 3469 Kitchen fixtures & equipment: metal, except cast aluminum

(G-5093)
EROOMSYSTEM TECHNOLOGIES INC (PA)
150 Airport Rd Ste 1200 (08701-6924)
PHONE...................................732 730-0116
David A Gestetner, *Ch of Bd*
David Gestetner, *Technology*
EMP: 15
SQ FT: 1,600
SALES (est): 903.6K **Publicly Held**
WEB: www.eroomsystem.com
SIC: 7372 Business oriented computer software

(G-5094)
EVERGREEN KOSHER LLC
Also Called: Evergreen Lakewood
945 River Ave (08701-5659)
PHONE...................................732 370-4500
Yermy Freed,
EMP: 4 EST: 2017
SALES (est): 64.7K **Privately Held**
SIC: 5421 5411 2048 Meat & fish markets; grocery stores; fish food

(G-5095)
EXCLUSIVE MATERIALS LLC
Also Called: Exma Industries
1385 Pasadena St (08701-3922)
P.O. Box 1259 (08701-1008)
PHONE...................................732 886-9956
Yehudah Kirshenbaum,
▲ EMP: 8 EST: 2002
SALES (est): 557K **Privately Held**
SIC: 3494 Pipe fittings

(G-5096)
EZRIRX LLC (PA)
1525 Prospect St Ste 203 (08701-4662)
PHONE...................................718 502-6610
Ezriel Green, *CEO*
EMP: 2

SALES: 5MM **Privately Held**
SIC: 5122 7372 Pharmaceuticals; application computer software

(G-5097)
FASHION CENTRAL LLC
556 Warren Ave (08701-4813)
PHONE...................................732 887-7683
Yizhaq Chkory, *Manager*
▲ EMP: 8
SALES (est): 625.6K **Privately Held**
SIC: 2341 Women's & children's undergarments

(G-5098)
FEDPLAST INC
1174 Buckwald Ct (08701-1263)
PHONE...................................732 901-1153
Andre Grunberger, *President*
EMP: 14
SQ FT: 25,000
SALES (est): 1.1MM **Privately Held**
WEB: www.fedplast.com
SIC: 3083 Laminated plastics plate & sheet

(G-5099)
FLEXABAR CORPORATION (PA)
1969 Rutgers Blvd (08701-4538)
PHONE...................................732 901-6500
Andy Guglielmo, *CEO*
Richard J Guglielmo Sr, *President*
Anita Guglielmo, *Corp Secy*
Greg Devine, *Mktg Dir*
◆ EMP: 22 EST: 1955
SQ FT: 40,000
SALES (est): 7.7MM **Privately Held**
WEB: www.flexabar.com
SIC: 2851 Vinyl coatings, strippable

(G-5100)
FLEXDELL CORP
1969 Rutgers Blvd (08701-4538)
PHONE...................................732 901-7771
Richard Guglielmo Sr, *President*
EMP: 4 EST: 1952
SQ FT: 50,000
SALES (est): 395.2K
SALES (corp-wide): 7.7MM **Privately Held**
WEB: www.flexabar.com
SIC: 2851 Marine paints
PA: Flexabar Corporation
1969 Rutgers Blvd
Lakewood NJ 08701
732 901-6500

(G-5101)
FRANCIS METALS COMPANY INC
Also Called: Francis Cable Systems
687 Prospect St Ste 430 (08701-4747)
PHONE...................................732 761-0500
Matt Deiner, *President*
James Deiner, *Vice Pres*
EMP: 10
SQ FT: 24,000
SALES (est): 3.3MM **Privately Held**
SIC: 3441 3357 3699 Fabricated structural metal; nonferrous wiredrawing & insulating; electrical equipment & supplies

(G-5102)
G & S PRECISION PROTOTYPE
115 Somerset Ave (08701-3629)
P.O. Box 18, Allenwood (08720-0018)
PHONE...................................732 370-3010
Guenter K Schindler, *Owner*
EMP: 5
SALES (est): 320K **Privately Held**
SIC: 3429 Manufactured hardware (general)

(G-5103)
GATEWAY PROPERTY SOLUTIONS LTD
730 Airport Rd Unit 1 (08701-5994)
PHONE...................................732 901-9700
Eli Kessler, *CEO*
EMP: 20
SALES (est): 882.7K **Privately Held**
SIC: 1522 1389 1542 Hotel/motel & multi-family home construction; construction, repair & dismantling services; hospital construction; institutional building construction

(G-5104)
GLASSEAL PRODUCTS INC
485 Oberlin Ave S (08701-6996)
PHONE...................................732 370-9100
Ian McGavisk, *President*
William Hubbard, *Vice Pres*
EMP: 130
SQ FT: 50,000
SALES (est): 19.3MM
SALES (corp-wide): 4.8B **Publicly Held**
WEB: www.glasseal.com
SIC: 3643 3679 3471 3812 Connectors & terminals for electrical devices; hermetic seals for electronic equipment; plating of metals or formed products; search & navigation equipment; electronic connectors
HQ: Hcc Industries Inc.
4232 Temple City Blvd
Rosemead CA 91770
626 443-8933

(G-5105)
GOLDEN FLUFF INC
118 Monmouth Ave (08701-3347)
PHONE...................................732 367-5448
Ephraim Schwinder, *President*
Sara Schwinder, *Vice Pres*
▲ EMP: 13
SQ FT: 21,000
SALES (est): 1.5MM **Privately Held**
WEB: www.goldenfluff.com
SIC: 2096 5149 Potato chips & similar snacks; specialty food items

(G-5106)
GWENSTONE INC
Also Called: Big Dog Natural
1790 Swarthmore Ave (08701-4593)
P.O. Box 531 (08701-0531)
PHONE...................................732 785-2600
Christiane De Rijk, *Principal*
Carlo Van Bael, *Principal*
EMP: 5
SALES (est): 495.1K **Privately Held**
SIC: 2047 3999 Dog food; pet supplies

(G-5107)
HAROLD R HENRICH INC
300 Syracuse Ct (08701-6919)
PHONE...................................732 370-4455
Harold Henrich Jr, *CEO*
Tom Henrich, *President*
Mike Henrich, *Vice Pres*
Tom Sofia, *Plant Mgr*
Jeff Schmidt, *Engineer*
▲ EMP: 55 EST: 1929
SALES (est): 14.4MM **Privately Held**
WEB: www.haroldhenrich.com
SIC: 3441 3444 Fabricated structural metal; sheet metalwork

(G-5108)
HAT BOX
605 E County Line Rd # 1 (08701-1491)
PHONE...................................732 961-2262
Chester Golombeck, *Branch Mgr*
EMP: 23
SALES (corp-wide): 3.1MM **Privately Held**
SIC: 2389 5611 Men's miscellaneous accessories; men's & boys' clothing stores
PA: Hat Box
1837 Coney Island Ave
Brooklyn NY 11230
718 951-9533

(G-5109)
HERR FOODS INCORPORATED
100 Kenyon Dr (08701-4500)
PHONE...................................732 905-1600
Ike Neff, *Manager*
EMP: 38
SQ FT: 7,500
SALES (corp-wide): 392.5MM **Privately Held**
WEB: www.herrs.com
SIC: 2096 Potato chips & similar snacks
PA: Herr Foods Incorporated
20 Herr Dr
Nottingham PA 19362
610 932-9330

(G-5110)
HPI INTERNATIONAL INC
301 1st St (08701-3322)
PHONE...................................732 942-9900

Amy Berger, *Manager*
EMP: 10
SALES (corp-wide): 21.9MM **Privately Held**
WEB: www.hpi.com
SIC: 3861 Photographic equipment & supplies
PA: Hpi International Inc.
1040 E 17th St
Brooklyn NY 11230
718 768-8800

(G-5111)
IBOCO CORP
1205 Paco Way Ste B (08701-6126)
PHONE...................................732 417-0066
▲ EMP: 9
SQ FT: 10,000
SALES (est): 1.5MM
SALES (corp-wide): 2B **Privately Held**
WEB: www.iboco.com
SIC: 3357 Nonferrous wiredrawing & insulating
PA: Hager Se
Zum Gunterstal
Blieskastel 66440
684 294-50

(G-5112)
INCENTX LLC ✪
209 2nd St Ste 6 (08701-3326)
PHONE...................................302 202-2894
Hillel Zafir, *Mng Member*
Ariel Heitner,
Baruch Wolhendler,
EMP: 8 EST: 2018
SALES: 2.3MM **Privately Held**
SIC: 7371 7372 Custom computer programming services; computer software development & applications; prepackaged software; application computer software

(G-5113)
JA CISSEL MANUFACTURING CO
1995 Rutgers Blvd (08701-4774)
P.O. Box 2035 (08701-8035)
PHONE...................................732 901-0300
George Spisak, *President*
David Morgen, *President*
EMP: 20 EST: 1968
SALES (est): 2MM
SALES (corp-wide): 4.9MM **Privately Held**
WEB: www.jacissel.net
SIC: 3949 Golf equipment
PA: Century Sports, Inc.
1715 Oak St Ste 1
Lakewood NJ
732 905-4422

(G-5114)
JACQUARD FABRICS INC
Also Called: Jacquard Fabrics Co
1965 Swarthmore Ave (08701-4534)
PHONE...................................732 905-4545
Leonard Gliner, *President*
▲ EMP: 38 EST: 1985
SQ FT: 34,000
SALES (est): 6.3MM **Privately Held**
SIC: 2211 Jacquard woven fabrics, cotton

(G-5115)
JERSEY JACK PINBALL INC
1645 Oak St (08701-5925)
PHONE...................................732 364-9900
Jack Guarnieri, *President*
▲ EMP: 47
SALES (est): 7.6MM **Privately Held**
SIC: 3999 Coin-operated amusement machines

(G-5116)
JESEL INC
1985 Cedarbridge Ave # 2 (08701-7031)
PHONE...................................732 901-1800
Daniel Jesel, *President*
Mike Mullen, *Engineer*
Mike Caston, *Senior Engr*
EMP: 65
SQ FT: 40,000
SALES (est): 14.6MM **Privately Held**
WEB: www.jeselonline.com
SIC: 3714 Motor vehicle parts & accessories

(G-5117)
KOMO MACHINE INC
Also Called: Komo Innovative Cnc Solutions
1 Komo Dr (08701-5923)
P.O. Box 918801, Denver CO (80291-8801)
PHONE....................................732 719-6222
Mike Kolibas, *President*
John Foran, *Materials Mgr*
Doug Baird, *Production*
Steve Ostermann, *Engineer*
Joseph Shavit, *Engineer*
▲ EMP: 55 EST: 1999
SALES (est): 18.3MM
SALES (corp-wide): 2.5B **Privately Held**
WEB: www.komo.com
SIC: 3541 Machine tools, metal cutting
　type
PA: Pmc Global, Inc.
　12243 Branford St
　Sun Valley CA 91352
　818 896-1101

(G-5118)
**KRAEMER PROPERTIES INC
(PA)**
Also Called: Luminer Converting Group
1925 Swarthmore Ave Ste 1 (08701-4552)
PHONE....................................732 886-6557
Thomas N Spina, *CEO*
John Borelli, *Shareholder*
Paul Kraemer, *Shareholder*
▲ EMP: 35
SQ FT: 5,000
SALES (est): 6.4MM **Privately Held**
WEB: www.luminer.com
SIC: 2672 Labels (unprinted), gummed:
　made from purchased materials; tape,
　pressure sensitive: made from purchased
　materials

(G-5119)
**KRFC CUSTOM WOODWORKING
INC**
Also Called: Krfc Design Center
1328 River Ave Ste 25 (08701-5645)
PHONE....................................732 363-0522
Chris Cooper, *President*
Barbara Salerno, *Office Mgr*
EMP: 7 EST: 1998
SQ FT: 4,000
SALES (est): 730K **Privately Held**
SIC: 2499 Decorative wood & woodwork

(G-5120)
LAMINETICS INC
1151 River Ave (08701-5658)
PHONE....................................732 367-1116
Yechiel Malichy, *President*
EMP: 8
SQ FT: 3,700
SALES (est): 814K **Privately Held**
SIC: 2541 Table or counter tops, plastic
　laminated

(G-5121)
**LARDIERI CUSTOM
WOODWORKING**
1830 Swarthmore Ave Ste 6 (08701-4556)
PHONE....................................732 905-6334
Robert Lardieri, *President*
EMP: 11
SALES (est): 1.5MM **Privately Held**
SIC: 2499 Decorative wood & woodwork

(G-5122)
**LIFE SCIENCE LABORATORIES
LLC**
170 Oberlin Ave N Ste 26 (08701-4548)
PHONE....................................732 367-1900
Elke Isbee, *Purchasing*
Sam Brownstein, *VP Sales*
Miriam Brafman, *Marketing Mgr*
David Prichard, *Lab Dir*
Yochanan Bulka,
EMP: 9
SQ FT: 9,500
SALES (est): 2.3MM **Privately Held**
SIC: 2834 Vitamin preparations

(G-5123)
LIFE SCIENCE LABS MFG LLC
170 Oberlin Ave N Ste 26 (08701-4548)
PHONE....................................732 367-9937
Yochanan Bulka, *President*

EMP: 14
SQ FT: 9,000
SALES (est): 629K **Privately Held**
SIC: 2833 Vitamins, natural or synthetic:
　bulk, uncompounded

(G-5124)
**LIFE SCNCE LABS
SPPLEMENTS LLC**
Also Called: Lsl Supplements
216 River Ave (08701-4807)
PHONE....................................732 367-1749
Yochanan Bulka, *CEO*
EMP: 14
SQ FT: 18,000
SALES: 3.1MM **Privately Held**
SIC: 2834 Vitamin preparations

(G-5125)
LITTLE MISS CUPCAKE LLC
200 Tudor Ct (08701-1473)
PHONE....................................732 370-3083
Jonathan Platschek, *Principal*
EMP: 4
SALES (est): 205.7K **Privately Held**
SIC: 2051 Bread, cake & related products

(G-5126)
M AND R MANUFACTURING
Also Called: Mister Boardwalk
575 Prospect St Ste 202 (08701-5040)
PHONE....................................732 905-1061
Warren McLeod, *Principal*
EMP: 5
SALES (est): 212K **Privately Held**
SIC: 2499 Decorative wood & woodwork

(G-5127)
MAGNA INDUSTRIES INC
1825 Swarthmore Ave Ste 1 (08701-4570)
PHONE....................................732 905-0957
Walter Ostrowicki, *CEO*
Jerry Krzemiresk, *President*
▲ EMP: 28
SQ FT: 32,000
SALES (est): 6.1MM **Privately Held**
WEB: www.magnaindustries.com
SIC: 3556 Bakery machinery

(G-5128)
**MANLEY PERFORMANCE PDTS
INC (PA)**
1960 Swarthmore Ave (08701-4547)
PHONE....................................732 905-3366
Henry Manley, *President*
Pete Coleman, *Mfg Mgr*
Neil Vernarelli, *Opers Spvr*
Kari McNair, *Purch Mgr*
Gil Morejon, *CFO*
▲ EMP: 100
SQ FT: 40,000
SALES (est): 18.8MM **Privately Held**
WEB: www.manleyvalves.com
SIC: 3714 Motor vehicle engines & parts

(G-5129)
MASCO CABINETRY LLC
450 Oberlin Ave S (08701-6903)
PHONE....................................732 363-3797
EMP: 127
SALES (corp-wide): 7.1B **Publicly Held**
SIC: 2541 Mfg Wood Partitions/Fixtures
HQ: Masco Cabinetry Llc
　4600 Arrowhead Dr
　Ann Arbor MI 48105
　313 274-7400

(G-5130)
MASCO CABINETRY LLC
Also Called: Tfi OEM Commercial Group
440-450 Oberlin Ave S (08701)
PHONE....................................732 942-5138
EMP: 143
SALES (corp-wide): 7.1B **Publicly Held**
SIC: 2541 Mfg Wood Partitions/Fixtures
HQ: Masco Cabinetry Llc
　4600 Arrowhead Dr
　Ann Arbor MI 48105
　313 274-7400

(G-5131)
MASTER PRESENTATIONS INC
182 Hadassah Ln (08701-5561)
PHONE....................................732 239-7093
Maurice Pachtinger, *President*

▲ EMP: 10
SALES (est): 1MM **Privately Held**
SIC: 3915 Jewel preparing: instruments,
　tools, watches & jewelry

(G-5132)
**MAY NATIONAL ASSOCIATES NJ
INC**
Also Called: Sika
995 Towbin Ave (08701-5930)
PHONE....................................973 473-3330
Mark Yamout, *President*
▲ EMP: 55
SQ FT: 5,000
SALES (est): 12.8MM
SALES (corp-wide): 7.1B **Privately Held**
SIC: 2891 Caulking compounds
HQ: Sika Corporation
　201 Polito Ave
　Lyndhurst NJ 07071
　201 933-8800

(G-5133)
MDI MANUFACTURING INC
100 Syracuse Ct (08701-6909)
PHONE....................................732 994-5599
Mark Daugherty, *President*
Eileen Savage, *Executive Asst*
EMP: 19
SQ FT: 8,000
SALES (est): 3.9MM **Privately Held**
SIC: 3599 Machine shop, jobbing & repair

(G-5134)
**MEDICAL SCRUBS COLLECTN
NJ LLC (HQ)**
1655 Corporate Rd W (08701-5921)
PHONE....................................732 719-8600
Mark Bakst, *CEO*
EMP: 6
SALES: 2.8MM
SALES (corp-wide): 5MM **Privately Held**
SIC: 2211 Scrub cloths
PA: Avaline Medical Nj Limited Liability
　Company
　1665 Corporate Rd W
　Lakewood NJ 08701
　732 746-5030

(G-5135)
MILSPRAY LLC (HQ)
Also Called: Milspray Military Technologies
845 Towbin Ave (08701-5929)
PHONE....................................732 886-2223
Liz Shivers, *President*
Caroline Smith, *Marketing Staff*
Brian Matz, *Manager*
Courtney McBride, *Manager*
Matthew Johnston, *Director*
▲ EMP: 40
SQ FT: 18,000
SALES (est): 24.8MM
SALES (corp-wide): 360.7MM **Privately
Held**
SIC: 5169 2851 3812 Aerosols; paints &
　paint additives; defense systems & equip-
　ment
PA: R.A.F. Industries, Inc.
　165 Township Line Rd # 2100
　Jenkintown PA 19046
　215 572-0738

(G-5136)
**MIRACLE MILE AUTOMOTIVE
INC**
Also Called: Kraemer Koating
1925 Swarthmore Ave Ste 1 (08701-4552)
PHONE....................................732 886-6315
Paul Kraemer, *President*
Barbara Kraemer, *Vice Pres*
EMP: 5
SQ FT: 30,000
SALES (est): 5.1MM **Privately Held**
WEB: www.kraemerkoating.com
SIC: 3559 Chemical machinery & equip-
　ment

(G-5137)
MISTER COOKIE FACE INC
Also Called: Mrs Fieldbrook Food
1989 Rutgers Blvd (08701-4538)
P.O. Box 1318, Dunkirk NY (14048-6318)
PHONE....................................732 370-5533
Frank R Koenemund, *President*
Patty Napolitano, *QC Mgr*

Barbara Koenemund, *Office Mgr*
David Edelstein, *Director*
Ed Grosso, *Maintence Staff*
◆ EMP: 125
SQ FT: 40,000
SALES (est): 33.7MM
SALES (corp-wide): 779.5MM **Privately
Held**
WEB: www.cookieface.com
SIC: 2024 Ice cream, bulk
HQ: Fieldbrook Foods Corporation
　1 Ice Cream Dr
　Dunkirk NY 14048
　716 366-5400

(G-5138)
MJ GROSS COMPANY - NJ
Also Called: David Gross Group
2 Commonwealth Dr (08701-4163)
PHONE....................................212 542-3199
David Gross, *Owner*
EMP: 7
SQ FT: 1,500
SALES (est): 726.2K **Privately Held**
SIC: 5094 3911 Jewelry; jewelry, precious
　metal

(G-5139)
NITTO INC (HQ)
Also Called: Nitto Denko Automotive
1990 Rutgers Blvd (08701-4537)
PHONE....................................732 901-7905
Hideo Takasaki, *President*
Yoichiro Sakuma, *President*
Takei Nishioka, *General Mgr*
Toshihiko Omote, *Exec VP*
Toru Takeuchi, *Senior VP*
◆ EMP: 240
SALES: 144MM **Privately Held**
SIC: 2672 Tape, pressure sensitive: made
　from purchased materials

(G-5140)
NITTO INC
1975 Swarthmore Ave (08701-4534)
PHONE....................................732 901-0035
Kathy Biro, *Administration*
EMP: 12 **Privately Held**
SIC: 3714 Motor vehicle parts & acces-
　sories
HQ: Nitto, Inc.
　1990 Rutgers Blvd
　Lakewood NJ 08701
　732 901-7905

(G-5141)
NITTO INC
1990 Rutgers Blvd (08701-4537)
PHONE....................................732 901-7905
EMP: 11 **Privately Held**
SIC: 2672 3589 5162 5065 Tape, pres-
　sure sensitive: made from purchased ma-
　terials; water treatment equipment,
　industrial; plastics products; electronic
　parts
HQ: Nitto, Inc.
　1990 Rutgers Blvd
　Lakewood NJ 08701
　732 901-7905

(G-5142)
NOVASOM INDUSTRIES INC
15 Enclave Blvd (08701-5788)
PHONE....................................732 994-5652
Christian Carrieri, *CEO*
Terry Manton, *Vice Pres*
Francesca Carrieri, *Sales Staff*
▼ EMP: 1
SALES: 1MM **Privately Held**
SIC: 3571 Electronic computers

(G-5143)
**OLD FASHION KITCHEN INC
(PA)**
Also Called: Old Fashioned Kitchen
1045 Towbin Ave (08701-5931)
PHONE....................................732 364-4100
Jay Conzen, *President*
Jeff Brown, *CFO*
▲ EMP: 70
SQ FT: 30,000
SALES (est): 13.8MM **Privately Held**
WEB: www.oldfashionedkitchen.com
SIC: 2038 Ethnic foods, frozen

▲ = Import ▼=Export
◆ =Import/Export

(G-5144)
ORNATE MILLWORK LLC
15 Hazelwood Ln (08701-5131)
PHONE...................................866 464-5596
Tovia Halpern, *Mng Member*
EMP: 5
SALES (est): 250K **Privately Held**
SIC: 2431 Millwork

(G-5145)
PENN COPY CENTER INC
Also Called: Bernie's Copy Center
5 Morning Glory Ln (08701-5718)
PHONE...................................646 251-0313
Bernie Szimonowitz, *President*
EMP: 4
SALES (est): 569K **Privately Held**
SIC: 7334 2752 Photocopying & duplicating services; commercial printing, offset

(G-5146)
PERMA PURE LLC (DH)
1001 New Hampshire Ave (08701-6037)
PHONE...................................732 244-0010
Craig Sunada, *President*
Doug Hasbrouck, *General Mgr*
Kenneth Geiser, *Materials Mgr*
Tom Kmec, *Facilities Mgr*
Brian Fischer, *Engineer*
EMP: 5 EST: 1972
SQ FT: 25,000
SALES (est): 1.5MM
SALES (corp-wide): 1.5B **Privately Held**
WEB: www.permapure.com
SIC: 3826 Gas analyzing equipment
HQ: Halma Holdings Inc.
11500 Northlake Dr # 306
Cincinnati OH 45249
513 772-5501

(G-5147)
PLASTICS GALORE LLC
1970 Swarthmore Ave Ste 8 (08701-4553)
PHONE...................................732 363-8447
Chris Wollerman,
EMP: 8
SALES (est): 1MM **Privately Held**
SIC: 3089 Air mattresses, plastic

(G-5148)
POLARIS AMERICA LTD LBLTY CO
1985 Rutgers Blvd (08701-4569)
P.O. Box 486, Allenwood (08720-0486)
PHONE...................................614 540-1710
Chris Filos,
EMP: 35
SQ FT: 40,000
SALES (est): 6MM **Privately Held**
SIC: 3511 Turbines & turbine generator sets

(G-5149)
POWER APPAREL LLC
Also Called: So Nikki
40 Chestnut St Ste 13 (08701-5894)
PHONE...................................516 442-1333
Yehuda Roberts, *Mng Member*
Moshe Adams,
EMP: 10
SQ FT: 2,750
SALES: 2MM **Privately Held**
SIC: 2389 Men's miscellaneous accessories

(G-5150)
QUICK FAB ALUMINUM MFG CO
Also Called: Quik-Fab Aluminum Mfg
1830 Swarthmore Ave Ste 1 (08701-4556)
PHONE...................................732 367-7200
Joseph Leary, *President*
EMP: 25 EST: 1974
SQ FT: 52,000
SALES (est): 2.9MM **Privately Held**
WEB: www.quikfab.com
SIC: 3334 3442 Primary aluminum; metal doors, sash & trim

(G-5151)
REGAL LITHO PRTRS LTD LBLTY CO
1725 Oak St (08701-5927)
PHONE...................................732 901-1500
Simon Zeldes, *Mng Member*
Ben Zeldes,

EMP: 8 EST: 2013
SQ FT: 3,500
SALES: 700K **Privately Held**
SIC: 2752 Commercial printing, lithographic

(G-5152)
REGENCY CABINETRY LLC
525 Oberlin Ave S (08701-6906)
PHONE...................................732 363-5630
EMP: 4 **Privately Held**
WEB: www.regentcabinetry.com
SIC: 2434 Wood kitchen cabinets
PA: Regency Cabinetry Llc
525 Oberlin Ave S
Lakewood NJ 08701

(G-5153)
REGENCY CABINETRY LLC (PA)
Also Called: Regent
525 Oberlin Ave S (08701-7037)
PHONE...................................732 363-5630
Norman Shapiro, *Principal*
Leon Welcher, *Principal*
Reuvan Sternstein,
▲ EMP: 16
SALES (est): 2.3MM **Privately Held**
WEB: www.regentcabinetry.com
SIC: 2434 Wood kitchen cabinets

(G-5154)
REMOTE LANDLORD SYSTEMS LLC
525 E County Line Rd (08701-1405)
PHONE...................................732 534-4445
David Lieberman,
EMP: 6
SALES (est): 148.8K **Privately Held**
SIC: 7372 Business oriented computer software

(G-5155)
RENAISSANCE LAKEWOOD LLC (DH)
Also Called: Renaissance Pharmaceuticals
1200 Paco Way (08701-5938)
PHONE...................................732 901-2052
Serge Maltais, *President*
Mark Fite, *Senior VP*
Rick Bentzinger, *Vice Pres*
Kuljit Bhatia, *Vice Pres*
Gene Ciolfi, *Vice Pres*
▲ EMP: 11
SALES: 73.1MM
SALES (corp-wide): 248MM **Privately Held**
SIC: 2834 Druggists' preparations (pharmaceuticals); cold remedies; lip balms; ointments
HQ: Renaissance Ssp Holdings, Inc.
272 E Deerpath Ste 350
Lake Forest IL 60045
210 476-8194

(G-5156)
RENAISSANCE LAKEWOOD LLC
Also Called: Renaissance Pharmaceuticals
1720 Oak St (08701-5926)
PHONE...................................732 367-9000
Antonio Di Nicola, *Plant Mgr*
EMP: 440
SQ FT: 750,000
SALES (corp-wide): 248MM **Privately Held**
SIC: 2834 Druggists' preparations (pharmaceuticals)
HQ: Renaissance Lakewood, Llc
1200 Paco Way
Lakewood NJ 08701
732 901-2052

(G-5157)
REVIEW AND JUDGE LLC
910 E County Line Rd 202c (08701-2093)
PHONE...................................732 987-3905
Malky Paskes, *Mng Member*
EMP: 5
SALES: 92K **Privately Held**
SIC: 2741 Miscellaneous publishing

(G-5158)
ROBEN MANUFACTURING CO INC
760 Vassar Ave (08701-6907)
PHONE...................................732 364-6000
Gary R Huhn, *CEO*
Allen Hoffman, *Technical Staff*
Nev Heimall, *Admin Asst*
EMP: 31 EST: 1955
SQ FT: 30,000
SALES: 6.2MM **Privately Held**
WEB: www.robenmfg.com
SIC: 3443 Industrial vessels, tanks & containers

(G-5159)
ROELYNN LITHO INC
687 Prospect St Ste 410 (08701-4649)
PHONE...................................732 942-9650
Vincent J Praino, *President*
Rosemarie Praino, *Vice Pres*
▲ EMP: 15
SQ FT: 10,000
SALES (est): 2.4MM **Privately Held**
WEB: www.roelynn.com
SIC: 2752 Commercial printing, offset

(G-5160)
ROYAL SEAMLESS CORPORATION
1000 Airport Rd Ste 203 (08701-5960)
PHONE...................................732 901-9595
Hedwig Obara, *President*
Hedy Obara, *Vice Pres*
EMP: 14
SQ FT: 20,000
SALES (est): 1.7MM **Privately Held**
SIC: 3498 Fabricated pipe & fittings

(G-5161)
SEABOARD INDUSTRIES
1957 Rutgers University B (08701-4568)
PHONE...................................732 901-5700
Samtha Fullerton, *Manager*
EMP: 10
SALES (corp-wide): 19.9MM **Privately Held**
WEB: www.seaboard-usa.com
SIC: 5091 2899 Swimming pools, equipment & supplies; water treating compounds
PA: Seaboard Industries
185 Van Winkle Ave
Hawthorne NJ 07506
973 427-8500

(G-5162)
SHACHIHATA INC (USA)
525 Oberlin Ave S (08701-7037)
PHONE...................................732 905-7159
Youngsint Park, *Branch Mgr*
Maureen McGurk, *Manager*
Charles Duff, *CIO*
EMP: 12 **Privately Held**
WEB: www.xstamper.com
SIC: 3953 Embossing seals & hand stamps
HQ: Shachihata Inc. (U.S.A.)
20775 S Wstn Ave Ste 105
Torrance CA
310 530-4445

(G-5163)
SKAFFLES GROUP LTD LBLTY CO (PA)
139 Ocean Ave (08701-3668)
PHONE...................................732 901-2100
Steven Shwekey, *Mng Member*
Sam N Sasson,
▲ EMP: 2
SALES (est): 2.4MM **Privately Held**
SIC: 3999 Pet supplies

(G-5164)
SMARTPOOL LLC
1940 Rutgers Blvd (08701-4537)
PHONE...................................732 730-9880
Richard Holstein, *President*
Thomas Rahoche, *Controller*
Lewis Dubrofsky, *Mng Member*
◆ EMP: 24
SALES (est): 5MM **Privately Held**
WEB: www.smartpool.com
SIC: 3648 3569 Swimming pool lighting fixtures; heaters, swimming pool; electric

(G-5165)
SOFTWARE DEVELOPERS LLC
Also Called: Sellercloud
410 Monmouth Ave Apt 502 (08701-3747)
PHONE...................................888 315-6652
Jeremy Greenberg, *CEO*
Nussi Einhorn, *Analyst*
Melissa Borowicki, *Representative*
Esther Nierenberg, *Representative*
EMP: 25 EST: 2004
SQ FT: 3,600
SALES: 4.5MM **Privately Held**
SIC: 7372 Prepackaged software

(G-5166)
SR CUSTOM WOODCRAFT LTD LBLTY
1980 Swarthmore Ave (08701-4692)
PHONE...................................732 942-7601
Shlomo Ringel, *Mng Member*
EMP: 4
SALES (est): 372.6K **Privately Held**
SIC: 2511 Wood household furniture

(G-5167)
SS WHITE BURS INC
1145 Towbin Ave (08701-5932)
PHONE...................................732 905-1100
EMP: 180
SALES (corp-wide): 32.9MM **Privately Held**
WEB: www.sswhiteburs.com
SIC: 3843 7699 5047 Burs, dental; dental instrument repair; dental equipment & supplies
PA: Ss White Burs, Inc.
1145 Towbin Ave
Lakewood NJ 08701
732 905-1100

(G-5168)
STEICO USA INC
Also Called: Juvenile Planet
250 Carey St (08701-1836)
PHONE...................................732 364-6200
James Stein, *President*
EMP: 10
SQ FT: 2,000
SALES (est): 1.8MM **Privately Held**
SIC: 3944 5999 Games, toys & children's vehicles; infant furnishings & equipment

(G-5169)
STERN KNIT INC
3 Fillmore Ave (08701-5665)
PHONE...................................732 364-8055
Mark Stern, *President*
▲ EMP: 9 EST: 1950
SALES: 481.7K **Privately Held**
SIC: 2258 Warp & flat knit products

(G-5170)
TARYAG LEGACY FOUNDATION INC
1136 Somerset Ave (08701-2138)
PHONE...................................732 569-2467
Judy Wax, *CEO*
EMP: 15
SALES: 837.7K **Privately Held**
SIC: 2731 Book publishing

(G-5171)
TIPICO PRODUCTS CO INC
490 Oberlin Ave S (08701-6903)
PHONE...................................732 942-8820
William Gellert, *President*
Peggy Zimmerman, *Purchasing*
Richard Caridi, *Manager*
Deniss Sossa, *Technology*
▲ EMP: 81
SALES (est): 18MM **Privately Held**
WEB: www.tipicoproducts.com
SIC: 2022 5143 Cheese, natural & processed; cheese

(G-5172)
TLW BATH LTD LIABILITY COMPANY
Also Called: Quality Bath
1144 E Cnty Ln Rd (08701)
PHONE...................................732 942-7117
Steven Loeb, *Mktg Dir*
Mordi Lercher, *Mng Member*
Eli Golding, *Software Dev*
Bayla Nussbaum, *Software Dev*

▼ **EMP:** 30
SALES (est): 30MM **Privately Held**
SIC: 2499 5999 Kitchen, bathroom & household ware: wood; plumbing & heating supplies

(G-5173)
TWO 12 FASHION LLC
1525 Prospect St Ste 205 (08701-4662)
PHONE..........................848 222-1562
Aron S Weiner, *Administration*
EMP: 4 EST: 2015
SQ FT: 16,000
SALES: 550K **Privately Held**
SIC: 7389 2387 Apparel designers, commercial; apparel belts

(G-5174)
UNEX MANUFACTURING INC (PA)
691 New Hampshire Ave (08701-5452)
PHONE..........................732 928-2800
Brian Neuwirth, *President*
Mark Neuwirth, *Vice Pres*
Kevin Cupples, *Marketing Staff*
▲ **EMP:** 65 EST: 1965
SQ FT: 60,000
SALES (est): 18.3MM **Privately Held**
WEB: www.unex.com
SIC: 3535 Conveyors & conveying equipment

(G-5175)
VAEG LLC
Also Called: Alyce Intimate
1776 Avenue Of The States # 3 (08701-4591)
PHONE..........................917 533-0138
Victor Harari,
EMP: 5
SALES (est): 186.2K **Privately Held**
SIC: 2389 Apparel & accessories

(G-5176)
VINYLAST INC
Also Called: Quik-Sab
1830 Swarthmore Ave Ste 1 (08701-4556)
PHONE..........................732 367-7200
Joseph L Leary, *President*
▲ **EMP:** 20
SALES (est): 3.7MM **Privately Held**
WEB: www.vinylast.com
SIC: 3089 1521 Windows, plastic; single-family housing construction

(G-5177)
VITILLO & SONS INC
Also Called: Diversified Fixtures
1930 Swarthmore Ave (08701-4547)
PHONE..........................732 886-1393
Jerry Vitillo, *President*
Phil Vitillo, *Opers Staff*
Jerry Castoral, *Manager*
EMP: 18
SQ FT: 20,000
SALES (est): 3.6MM **Privately Held**
WEB: www.diversifiedfixture.com
SIC: 2542 3993 3841 2434 Office & store showcases & display fixtures; signs & advertising specialties; surgical & medical instruments; wood kitchen cabinets

(G-5178)
VOGEL PRECAST INC
1509 Prospect St (08701-4659)
PHONE..........................732 552-8837
Kathy Vogel, *President*
Timothy Vogel, *Vice Pres*
EMP: 6
SALES (est): 440K **Privately Held**
SIC: 3271 1711 Sewer & manhole block, concrete; septic system construction

(G-5179)
W G I CORP
Also Called: Webco Graphics
1875 Swarthmore Ave (08701-4772)
P.O. Box 1478 (08701-1016)
PHONE..........................732 370-2900
Glenn A Davis, *President*
Maureen Davis, *Admin Sec*
EMP: 15
SQ FT: 23,000
SALES (est): 1.8MM **Privately Held**
SIC: 2731 2752 Books: publishing & printing; commercial printing, lithographic

(G-5180)
WARDALE CORP
Also Called: Mister Boardwalk
575 Prospect St Ste 202 (08701-5040)
P.O. Box 736, Arkansas City KS (67005-0736)
PHONE..........................800 813-4050
Warren Mc Leod, *President*
Warren McLeod, *President*
Dale Mc Leod, *Corp Secy*
EMP: 20
SQ FT: 15,000
SALES (est): 1.6MM **Privately Held**
WEB: www.misterboardwalk.com
SIC: 2499 Fencing, docks & other outdoor wood structural products

(G-5181)
WEST PHRM SVCS LAKEWOOD INC
1200 Paco Way (08701-5938)
PHONE..........................732 730-3295
EMP: 5
SALES (est): 208K
SALES (corp-wide): 1.7B **Publicly Held**
SIC: 3069 Medical & laboratory rubber sundries & related products
PA: West Pharmaceutical Services, Inc.
530 Herman O West Dr
Exton PA 19341
610 594-2900

(G-5182)
WOODHAVEN LUMBER & MILLWORK (PA)
200 James St (08701-4103)
PHONE..........................732 901-0030
James T Robinson, *CEO*
Glenn Simons, *Vice Pres*
Louis Caruso, *Opers Staff*
Russell Gilbert, *Opers Staff*
Susan Ciemniecki, *Purchasing*
▲ **EMP:** 180
SALES (est): 48.5MM **Privately Held**
WEB: www.woodhavenlumber.com
SIC: 5211 2431 Millwork & lumber; cabinets, kitchen; paneling; interior & ornamental woodwork & trim

(G-5183)
WORTHINGTON BIOCHEMICAL CORP (PA)
730 Vassar Ave (08701-6907)
PHONE..........................732 942-1660
Von Worthington, *President*
Joseph M Berardo Sr, *Vice Pres*
Frederick Schmitz, *Vice Pres*
Rick Schmitz, *Vice Pres*
James Zacka, *Vice Pres*
EMP: 50
SQ FT: 30,000
SALES (est): 7.6MM **Privately Held**
WEB: www.worthington-biochem.com
SIC: 2835 2836 Enzyme & isoenzyme diagnostic agents; biological products, except diagnostic

(G-5184)
Y & J BAKERS INC
Also Called: Gelbsteins Bakery
415 Clifton Ave (08701-3235)
PHONE..........................732 363-3636
Joseph Gruenepaum, *President*
Joel Tesser, *Vice Pres*
EMP: 25
SQ FT: 4,000
SALES (est): 1MM **Privately Held**
SIC: 5461 5149 2051 Bakeries; bakery products; bread, cake & related products

(G-5185)
YATED NEEMAN INC
110 Shady Lane Dr (08701-2351)
PHONE..........................845 369-1600
Pinchos Lipschutz, *President*
▲ **EMP:** 12
SALES (est): 740.1K **Privately Held**
WEB: www.yated.com
SIC: 2711 Newspapers: publishing only, not printed on site

Lambertville
Hunterdon County

(G-5186)
ADVANCED CERAMETRICS INC (PA)
245 N Main St (08530-1416)
P.O. Box 128 (08530-0128)
PHONE..........................609 397-2900
Richard B Cass, *President*
Michael R Hendricks, *Exec VP*
Robert D Frawley, *Admin Sec*
EMP: 8
SQ FT: 20,000
SALES (est): 3.1MM **Privately Held**
WEB: www.advancedcerametrics.com
SIC: 3299 Ceramic fiber

(G-5187)
BREEN COLOR CONCENTRATES LLC
11 Kari Dr (08530-3411)
PHONE..........................609 397-8200
Howard Demonte, *President*
Scott Senour, *CFO*
◆ **EMP:** 10
SALES (est): 1MM **Privately Held**
SIC: 2821 2851 2816 Polyvinyl chloride resins (PVC); paints & allied products; inorganic pigments

(G-5188)
BUCKS COUNTY BREWING CO INC
80 Lambert Ln Ste 120 (08530-1920)
PHONE..........................609 929-0148
Jack Bryan, *President*
EMP: 5
SALES (est): 270K **Privately Held**
WEB: www.riverhorse.com
SIC: 2082 Beer (alcoholic beverage)

(G-5189)
G-FORCE RIVER SIGNS LLC
9 S Main St (08530-2135)
PHONE..........................609 397-4467
David Gerrity, *President*
EMP: 6
SALES (est): 253.7K **Privately Held**
SIC: 3993 Signs, not made in custom sign painting shops

(G-5190)
JOHNSON & JOHNSON
10 Stymiest Rd (08530-3107)
PHONE..........................732 524-0400
EMP: 80
SALES (corp-wide): 81.5B **Publicly Held**
SIC: 2676 Feminine hygiene paper products
PA: Johnson & Johnson
1 Johnson And Johnson Plz
New Brunswick NJ 08933
732 524-0400

(G-5191)
JULIUS E HOLLAND-MORITZ CO INC
Also Called: J.E. Holland-Moritz Co., Inc.
599 Brunswick Pike (08530-2720)
PHONE..........................609 397-1231
Jeanne Maier, *Corp Secy*
John Maier, *Vice Pres*
▲ **EMP:** 5
SQ FT: 3,200
SALES: 1MM **Privately Held**
WEB: www.jehmco.com
SIC: 3499 Aquarium accessories, metal

(G-5192)
KANSAS CITY DESIGN INC
201 S Main St (08530-1800)
PHONE..........................609 460-4629
William Arnold, *President*
EMP: 4
SALES (est): 567.9K **Privately Held**
SIC: 2671 Plastic film, coated or laminated for packaging

(G-5193)
L S P INDUSTRIAL CERAMICS INC
34 Mount Airy Village Rd (08530-3511)
P.O. Box 302 (08530-0302)
PHONE..........................609 397-8330
Frank D Smith, *President*
▲ **EMP:** 5
SQ FT: 900
SALES: 900K **Privately Held**
WEB: www.lspceramics.com
SIC: 3253 Floor tile, ceramic

(G-5194)
LOCAL WISDOM INC
287 S Main St Ste 2 (08530-1830)
PHONE..........................609 269-2320
Derrick Larane, *Principal*
Michael Alfaro, *Principal*
Pinaki Kathiari, *Principal*
Dan Spedaliere, *Accounts Mgr*
Ryan Czepiel, *Graphic Designe*
EMP: 35 EST: 2000
SQ FT: 5,000
SALES (est): 2.6MM **Privately Held**
SIC: 7371 7372 7379 Computer software development; prepackaged software;

(G-5195)
NXLEVEL INC
Also Called: NXLEVEL SOLUTIONS
201 S Main St Ste 5 (08530-1800)
PHONE..........................609 483-6900
Robert Christensen, *President*
Peter Sandford, *Exec VP*
Daniel Oconnor, *Vice Pres*
Pam Dorini, *Project Mgr*
Marc Lenzke, *Software Dev*
EMP: 20
SQ FT: 5,100
SALES: 3.4MM **Privately Held**
WEB: www.nxlevelsolutions.com
SIC: 7372 Educational computer software

(G-5196)
PULSETOR LLC
243 N Union St Ste 207 (08530-1521)
PHONE..........................609 303-0578
Nicholas C Barbi,
Richard B Mott,
James A Nicolino,
EMP: 5
SALES (est): 858.4K **Privately Held**
SIC: 3826 Analytical instruments

(G-5197)
SOUTH COUNTY SOCCER LEAGUE INC
3 Ferry St (08530-1802)
PHONE..........................908 310-9052
Regina Skrebel, *President*
Howard Young, *Vice Pres*
Richard Eyre, *Treasurer*
Robin Wedeking, *Admin Sec*
EMP: 4 EST: 2010
SALES (est): 132.7K **Privately Held**
SIC: 3949 Guards: football, basketball, soccer, lacrosse, etc.

(G-5198)
TRIUMPH BREWING OF PRINCETON
287 S Main St Ste 16 (08530-1869)
PHONE..........................609 773-0111
Torri Thompson, *Branch Mgr*
EMP: 5 **Privately Held**
WEB: www.triumphbrew.com
SIC: 2082 Malt beverages
PA: Triumph Brewing Company Of Princeton Inc
138 Nassau St Ste A
Princeton NJ 08542

Landing
Morris County

(G-5199)
34 WELDING LLC
95 Ford Rd (07850-1608)
PHONE..........................973 440-0116
EMP: 8

SALES (est): 88.7K **Privately Held**
SIC: 7692 Welding repair

(G-5200)
EDMUND KISS
Also Called: Ej Machine & Tool Co
12 Orben Dr Unit 1 (07850-1800)
PHONE...................................973 810-2312
Edmund Kiss, *Owner*
EMP: 5
SQ FT: 2,600
SALES (est): 605K **Privately Held**
SIC: 8711 3599 Machine tool design; machine shop, jobbing & repair

(G-5201)
GAMMA MACHINE & TOOL CO INC
32 Oneida Ave (07850-1318)
PHONE...................................973 398-8821
EMP: 4
SQ FT: 2,500
SALES (est): 280K **Privately Held**
SIC: 3599 Machine Shop

(G-5202)
ORCAS INTERNATIONAL INC
Also Called: Orcas Naturals
9 Lenel Rd (07850-1844)
PHONE...................................973 448-2801
K Gnaneshwar RAO, *President*
Kuldip RAO, *Vice Pres*
Vijay Khadse, *Opers Mgr*
Marlene Bencel, *Purch Mgr*
◆ **EMP:** 16
SQ FT: 10,000
SALES (est): 3.2MM **Privately Held**
SIC: 2023 5122 Dietary supplements, dairy & non-dairy based; drugs, proprietaries & sundries

(G-5203)
PRUDENT PUBLISHING CO INC
400 N Frontage Rd (07850-1516)
PHONE...................................973 347-4554
Sharon Ruthman, *Branch Mgr*
Yuhen Abreu, *CTO*
EMP: 22
SALES (corp-wide): 27.4MM **Privately Held**
WEB: www.bizgreetingcards.com
SIC: 2771 Greeting cards
PA: Prudent Publishing Co., Inc.
65 Challenger Rd Ste 501
Ridgefield Park NJ 07660
201 641-7900

(G-5204)
UNIQUE ENCAPSULATION TECH LLC
Also Called: Orcas Naturals
9 Lenel Rd (07850-1844)
PHONE...................................973 448-2801
Gnaneshwar K RAO, *Mng Member*
EMP: 27 EST: 2012
SQ FT: 12,000
SALES (est): 1.2MM **Privately Held**
SIC: 2023 Dietary supplements, dairy & non-dairy based

Landisville
Atlantic County

(G-5205)
BELLVIEW FARMS INC
Also Called: Bellview Winery
150 Atlantic St (08326-1204)
PHONE...................................856 697-7172
James Quarella, *President*
Sofia Zych, *Manager*
EMP: 7
SALES (est): 746.2K **Privately Held**
WEB: www.bellviewwinery.com
SIC: 2084 Wines

(G-5206)
FIBERTECH GROUP INC (DH)
Also Called: Pgi Nonwovens
450 N East Blvd (08326-1212)
PHONE...................................856 697-1600
Jerry Zucker, *Ch of Bd*
Jim Schaeffer, *COO*
Jay Tiedemann, *Vice Pres*

Gregg Wilkinson, *Vice Pres*
James Boyd, *Treasurer*
▲ **EMP:** 205
SQ FT: 240,000
SALES (est): 39.1MM **Publicly Held**
SIC: 2297 Spunbonded fabrics

Laurel Springs
Camden County

(G-5207)
J & R REBUILDERS INC
330 Washington Ave (08021-2050)
PHONE...................................856 627-1414
Robert Visconti, *President*
EMP: 8
SALES (est): 600K **Privately Held**
SIC: 7539 3714 3694 Automotive repair shops; motor vehicle parts & accessories; engine electrical equipment

(G-5208)
ORIGIN ALMOND CORPORATION
6 Grant Dr (08021-2705)
PHONE...................................609 576-5695
Jacob Deleon, *President*
EMP: 5
SALES (est): 139.9K **Privately Held**
SIC: 2087 Beverage bases, concentrates, syrups, powders & mixes

(G-5209)
VACUUM SALES INC
51 Stone Rd (08021-2137)
PHONE...................................856 627-7790
James Redstreake, *President*
Mike Downey, *Sales Staff*
Mike Vittese, *Sales Staff*
▼ **EMP:** 21
SQ FT: 10,000
SALES: 8MM **Privately Held**
WEB: www.vacuumsalesinc.com
SIC: 3713 Tank truck bodies

Laurence Harbor
Middlesex County

(G-5210)
TELCONTEL CORP
11 Industrial Dr (08879)
PHONE...................................732 441-0800
EMP: 10
SALES (est): 1MM **Privately Held**
SIC: 3661 3663 Manufactures Telecommunications Equipment

(G-5211)
VOLTA CORPORATION (PA)
11 Industrial Dr (08879)
P.O. Box 1027 (08879-4027)
PHONE...................................732 583-3300
Alexander R Norden, *President*
EMP: 22
SQ FT: 6,000
SALES (est): 2.9MM **Privately Held**
SIC: 3643 Connectors, electric cord

Lavallette
Ocean County

(G-5212)
SIGNAL SYSTEMS INTERNATIONAL (PA)
Also Called: Coastal Creations
1700 Grand Central Ave (08735-2432)
PHONE...................................732 793-4668
Tom M Kinney, *President*
William D Kinney, *Chairman*
Doris Kinney, *Vice Pres*
EMP: 4 EST: 1975
SQ FT: 3,750
SALES (est): 878K **Privately Held**
WEB: www.signalsystem.com
SIC: 3823 5699 3643 Liquid level instruments, industrial process type; bathing suits; current-carrying wiring devices

(G-5213)
Z LINE BEACHWEAR
Also Called: Z-Line
3263 Route 35 N (08735-1535)
PHONE...................................732 793-1234
Bruce Zabelski, *Owner*
Terry Zabelski, *Co-Owner*
EMP: 4
SQ FT: 3,000
SALES (est): 350.9K **Privately Held**
SIC: 7336 2396 Silk screen design; automotive & apparel trimmings

Lawrence Township
Mercer County

(G-5214)
AURO HEALTH LLC (DH)
2572 Brunswick Pike (08648-4128)
PHONE...................................732 839-9400
Nivaran Kapur, *President*
Gangadhar RAO Gorla, *Vice Pres*
Swami Iyer, *CFO*
Kiran Kumar Nagabandhi, *Controller*
EMP: 2 EST: 2012
SQ FT: 175,000
SALES (est): 5.3MM
SALES (corp-wide): 1.6B **Privately Held**
SIC: 2834 Pharmaceutical preparations
HQ: Aurobindo Pharma U.S.A., Inc.
279 Prnctn Hightstown Rd
East Windsor NJ 08520
732 839-9400

(G-5215)
BROOK METAL PRODUCTS INC
Also Called: Venture Shuffelbuard
16 Sunset Rd (08648-2712)
PHONE...................................908 355-1601
Russ McKay, *President*
Christopher McKay, *Exec VP*
▲ **EMP:** 14
SQ FT: 17,000
SALES (est): 1.8MM **Privately Held**
SIC: 3444 Sheet metalwork

(G-5216)
DKSH LUXURY & LIFESTYLE N AMER
9 Princess Rd Ste D (08648-2318)
PHONE...................................609 750-8800
Philipp Von Bueren, *President*
EMP: 6
SQ FT: 4,000
SALES (est): 740.5K **Privately Held**
SIC: 3873 5944 Watches, clocks, watchcases & parts; clock & watch stores

(G-5217)
MUALEMA LLC
Also Called: Sohha Savory Yogurt
2214 Town Ct N (08648-4736)
PHONE...................................609 820-6098
Angela Fout, *Mng Member*
John Fout,
EMP: 6
SALES: 600K **Privately Held**
SIC: 2026 Yogurt

(G-5218)
NASSAU COMMUNICATIONS INC
Also Called: Nassau Printers
650 Whitehead Rd (08648-4404)
PHONE...................................609 208-9099
Kenneth M Fisher, *President*
EMP: 10
SQ FT: 8,000
SALES (est): 1.2MM **Privately Held**
SIC: 2752 2791 2796 Lithographing on metal; typesetting, computer controlled; platemaking services

(G-5219)
RICHARD REIN
Also Called: U S 1 Publishing Co
15 Princess Rd K (08648-2301)
PHONE...................................609 452-7000
Richard Rein, *Owner*
Diana Riley, *Advt Staff*
EMP: 10

SALES (est): 390K **Privately Held**
WEB: www.princetoninfo.com
SIC: 2711 Newspapers: publishing only, not printed on site

(G-5220)
SOFTWARE SERVICES & SOLUTIONS
15 Laurel Wood Dr (08648-1043)
PHONE...................................203 630-2000
Elisabeth Masterson, *President*
Robert Masterson, *Vice Pres*
EMP: 10
SALES (est): 507.2K **Privately Held**
WEB: www.sss.com
SIC: 7379 7372 Computer related consulting services; prepackaged software

Lawrenceville
Mercer County

(G-5221)
A STITCH AHEAD
1770 Front Lake Ave (08648)
PHONE...................................609 586-1068
Glenn Mangee, *Owner*
EMP: 10
SALES (est): 662.1K **Privately Held**
WEB: www.astitchahead.com
SIC: 2395 Embroidery products, except schiffli machine

(G-5222)
ABI INC
227 Bakers Basin Rd (08648-3307)
PHONE...................................609 588-8225
James A Britton, *President*
EMP: 20 EST: 1998
SQ FT: 2,100
SALES (est): 1.5MM **Privately Held**
SIC: 3273 Ready-mixed concrete

(G-5223)
ADARE PHARMACEUTICALS INC (DH)
1200 Lenox Dr Ste 100 (08648-2329)
PHONE...................................877 731-5116
John Fraher, *CEO*
EMP: 37
SQ FT: 18,233
SALES (est): 75.5MM **Privately Held**
SIC: 2834 Pharmaceutical preparations
HQ: Allergan, Inc.
5 Giralda Farms
Madison NJ 07940
862 261-7000

(G-5224)
BOT LLC
Also Called: Bot Beverages
12 Clementon Way (08648-3742)
PHONE...................................609 439-1537
Cricket Allen, *Mng Member*
Brian Allen,
Craig Carlson,
Tom Connor,
EMP: 8
SQ FT: 225
SALES: 350K **Privately Held**
SIC: 2086 Bottled & canned soft drinks

(G-5225)
BRISTOL-MYERS SQUIBB COMPANY
3401 Princeton Pike (08648-1205)
PHONE...................................609 302-3000
Peter Dolan, *Branch Mgr*
Shari Leist, *Manager*
Leonard Procaccino, *Senior Mgr*
Brian Lee, *Director*
Caitlin Craparo, *Associate Dir*
EMP: 2500
SQ FT: 650,000
SALES (corp-wide): 22.5B **Publicly Held**
WEB: www.bms.com
SIC: 2834 Pharmaceutical preparations
PA: Bristol-Myers Squibb Company
430 E 29th St Fl 14
New York NY 10016
212 546-4000

(PA)=Parent Co (HQ)=Headquarters (DH)=Div Headquarters
✪ = New Business established in last 2 years   2019 Harris New Jersey
Manufacturers Directory   205

(G-5226)
CELSION CORPORATION (PA)
997 Lenox Dr Ste 100 (08648-2317)
PHONE.....................609 896-9100
Michael H Tardugno, *Ch of Bd*
Khursheed Anwer, *Exec VP*
Jason Fewell, *Vice Pres*
Jeffrey W Church, *CFO*
Nicholas Borys, *Chief Mktg Ofcr*
EMP: 21
SQ FT: 10,870
SALES: 500K **Publicly Held**
WEB: www.celsion.com
SIC: 2834 Pharmaceutical preparations

(G-5227)
COMMUNITY NEWS SERVICE LLC
15 Princess Rd K (08648-2301)
PHONE.....................609 396-1511
Joseph Emanski, *Manager*
EMP: 10
SALES (est): 648.1K **Privately Held**
SIC: 2711 Commercial printing & newspaper publishing combined

(G-5228)
CORE LABORATORIES LP
Core Lab Refinery Systems
11 Princess Rd Ste H (08648-2319)
PHONE.....................609 896-2673
Craig Tournay, *General Mgr*
Craig A Tournay, *Branch Mgr*
EMP: 10
SALES (corp-wide): 700.8MM **Privately Held**
SIC: 3829 Accelerometers
HQ: Core Laboratories Lp
6316 Windfern Rd
Houston TX 77040

(G-5229)
DATACOLOR INC (HQ)
Also Called: Applied Color Systems
5 Princess Rd (08648-2301)
P.O. Box 200834, Pittsburgh PA (15251-0834)
PHONE.....................609 924-2189
Albert Busch, *CEO*
Clifford Chuba, *Manager*
▲ EMP: 65
SQ FT: 72,000
SALES (est): 22.9MM
SALES (corp-wide): 81.1MM **Privately Held**
WEB: www.datacolor.com
SIC: 3827 3695 Optical test & inspection equipment; computer software tape & disks: blank, rigid & floppy
PA: Datacolor Ag
Waldstatterstrasse 12
Luzern LU 6003
448 353-711

(G-5230)
HALO FARM INC
Also Called: Milk Farm
970 Spruce St (08648-4548)
PHONE.....................609 695-3311
Jerry Reilly, *President*
Ann T Reilly, *Vice Pres*
EMP: 8
SQ FT: 2,500
SALES (est): 1MM **Privately Held**
WEB: www.milkfarm.com
SIC: 2033 5451 2026 5499 Fruit juices: packaged in cans, jars, etc.; dairy products stores; milk processing (pasteurizing, homogenizing, bottling); juices, fruit or vegetable

(G-5231)
HEL INC
4 Princess Rd Ste 208 (08648-2322)
PHONE.....................440 208-7360
Jasbir Singh, *President*
EMP: 6
SQ FT: 1,200
SALES: 4.2MM **Privately Held**
WEB: www.helgroup.com
SIC: 3821 Laboratory apparatus & furniture
HQ: Hel Limited
9-10 Capital Business Park
Borehamwood HERTS WD6 1
208 736-0640

(G-5232)
HYDROCRBON TECH INNOVATION LLC
1501 New York Ave (08648-4635)
PHONE.....................609 394-3102
Eric Caprani, *CEO*
Christian Vaute, *President*
Clementine Sarrazin, *Treasurer*
EMP: 27
SALES (est): 1MM
SALES (corp-wide): 45.8MM **Privately Held**
SIC: 2819 2899 Catalysts, chemical; water treating compounds
HQ: Axens North America, Inc.
650 College Rd E Ste 1200
Princeton NJ 08540
609 243-8700

(G-5233)
KIDCUTETURE LLC
5 Rosalind Dr (08648-3212)
PHONE.....................609 532-0149
Olga Pantelyat, *President*
Nataliya Pantelyat, *Vice Pres*
▲ EMP: 6
SALES (est): 518.9K **Privately Held**
SIC: 2335 Gowns, formal

(G-5234)
LAWRENCE MOLD AND TOOL CORP (PA)
1412 Ohio Ave (08648-4638)
PHONE.....................609 392-5422
George Lesenskyj Jr, *President*
◆ EMP: 45
SQ FT: 10,000
SALES (est): 6.9MM **Privately Held**
WEB: www.lawrencemold.net
SIC: 3544 Industrial molds

(G-5235)
LE BON MAGOT LTD LIABILITY CO
69 Lawrncvlle Pnnngton Rd (08648-1483)
PHONE.....................609 895-0211
Rohit Bansal,
EMP: 6
SALES (est): 203.6K **Privately Held**
SIC: 2099 Food preparations

(G-5236)
LMT MERCER GROUP INC
690 Puritan Ave (08648-4600)
PHONE.....................888 570-5252
Anthony Lesenskyj, *President*
Jim Fattori, *President*
Bernie Henry, *President*
Pete Fischel, *COO*
George Lesenskyj, *Vice Pres*
◆ EMP: 45
SQ FT: 40,000
SALES (est): 22.7MM **Privately Held**
WEB: www.lmtproducts.com
SIC: 3446 Fences, gates, posts & flagpoles

(G-5237)
MEADOWGATE FARM ALPACAS
Also Called: Meadowfarmalpacas Aolcom
3071 Lawrenceville Rd (08648-1108)
PHONE.....................609 219-0529
Diane Rosenberg, *Owner*
▲ EMP: 7
SALES (est): 500K **Privately Held**
WEB: www.meadowgatefarmalpacas.com
SIC: 2211 Alpacas, cotton

(G-5238)
MOA INSTRUMENTATION INC
20 Carla Way (08648-1500)
PHONE.....................215 547-8308
Marshall Borlaug, *Manager*
EMP: 7
SALES (est): 1.3MM
SALES (corp-wide): 2.6MM **Privately Held**
SIC: 3826 Spectrometers
PA: Moa Instrumentation, Inc.
1606 Manning Blvd Ste 1
Levittown PA 19057
609 352-9329

(G-5239)
NATIONAL REPROGRAPHICS INC
Bluedge
3175 Princeton Pike (08648-2331)
PHONE.....................609 896-4100
Frank Plum, *Vice Pres*
EMP: 42
SALES (corp-wide): 85MM **Privately Held**
SIC: 2759 Commercial printing
PA: National Reprographics Inc.
575 8th Ave Fl 8
New York NY 10018
212 366-7250

(G-5240)
NOAH LLC
610 Lawrenceville Rd (08648-4208)
PHONE.....................609 637-0039
Emery Cappola,
EMP: 5
SALES (est): 354.6K **Privately Held**
SIC: 3679 Electronic circuits

(G-5241)
ONO PHARMA USA INC
2000 Lenox Dr Ste 101 (08648-2314)
PHONE.....................609 219-1010
Wataru Kamoshima, *President*
Bryan Due, *Vice Pres*
Jon Fourre, *Research*
Julie Forte, *Manager*
Akira Fujiki, *Manager*
EMP: 12
SALES (est): 3.3MM **Privately Held**
WEB: www.ono-usa.com
SIC: 2834 Pharmaceutical preparations
PA: Ono Pharmaceutical Co., Ltd.
1-8-2, Kyutaromachi, Chuo-Ku
Osaka OSK 541-0

(G-5242)
PRINCETON POWER SYSTEMS INC
3175 Princeton Pike (08648-2331)
PHONE.....................609 955-5390
Ken McCauley, *President*
Darren Hammell, *President*
Ed Howell, *COO*
Ross Rampf, *Prdtn Mgr*
Neil Bradshaw, *Engineer*
▲ EMP: 55
SQ FT: 38,000
SALES (est): 14.8MM **Privately Held**
WEB: www.princetonpower.com
SIC: 3629 Power conversion units, a.c. to d.c.: static-electric

(G-5243)
SCIENTIFIC SALES INC
3 Glenbrook Ct (08648-5556)
P.O. Box 6725 (08648-0725)
PHONE.....................609 844-0055
Thomas Tesauro, *President*
Vicki Dyer, *Engineer*
◆ EMP: 12
SALES (est): 2.9MM **Privately Held**
WEB: www.scientificsales.com
SIC: 3829 Measuring & controlling devices

(G-5244)
TLG SIGNS INC
Also Called: Fastsigns
2901 Us Highway 1 Ste 3 (08648-2419)
PHONE.....................609 912-0500
William Belmont, *President*
Joan Belmont, *Vice Pres*
EMP: 8 EST: 1998
SALES: 1.2MM **Privately Held**
SIC: 3993 Signs & advertising specialties

(G-5245)
VARSITY SOFTWARE INC
124 Lwrncvlle Pnnngton Rd (08648)
PHONE.....................609 309-9955
John Weaver, *President*
EMP: 5
SALES (est): 210.4K **Privately Held**
SIC: 7372 Prepackaged software

(G-5246)
VINCH RECYCLING INC
1 Vinch Ave (08648-2811)
PHONE.....................609 393-0200
Joseph M Vinch, *President*
Charles J Vinch, *Vice Pres*
Gary Vinch, *Vice Pres*
Samuel Vinch, *Treasurer*
EMP: 10
SQ FT: 4,000
SALES (est): 813.7K **Privately Held**
SIC: 3444 Concrete forms, sheet metal

(G-5247)
WRIGHTWORKS ENGINEERING LLC
12 Rosetree Ln (08648-3233)
PHONE.....................609 882-8840
Craig Wright,
Lois Wright,
EMP: 8
SALES (est): 690K **Privately Held**
SIC: 3545 Precision tools, machinists'

(G-5248)
XYBION CORPORATION (PA)
2000 Lenox Dr Ste 101 (08648-2314)
PHONE.....................973 538-2067
Pradip K Banerjee, *President*
Kamal Biswas, *President*
David Chiaramonte, *Vice Pres*
Amy Carlson, *Manager*
Bob Friedman, *CTO*
EMP: 138
SQ FT: 11,000
SALES (est): 15.6MM **Privately Held**
SIC: 8731 3625 7371 3861 Electronic research; relays & industrial controls; computer software development; cameras, still & motion picture (all types); integrated circuits, semiconductor networks, etc.

Lebanon
Hunterdon County

(G-5249)
AIRSCAN INC
291 Rt 22 Ste 12 (08833)
PHONE.....................908 823-9425
Stephen Shoemaker, *President*
Sharon Dechant, *Manager*
EMP: 7
SQ FT: 3,000
SALES: 1MM **Privately Held**
WEB: www.airscan1.com
SIC: 3826 Gas testing apparatus

(G-5250)
ALAQUEST INTERNATIONAL INC
28 Molasses Hill Rd (08833-3206)
PHONE.....................908 713-9399
Marcia Magazzu, *President*
Ronald Magazzu, *Director*
EMP: 10
SALES (est): 750K **Privately Held**
WEB: www.alaquest.com
SIC: 7372 7373 7374 Prepackaged software; computer integrated systems design; service bureau, computer

(G-5251)
AUTODRILL LLC
1221 Us Highway 22 Ste 6 (08833-2228)
PHONE.....................908 542-0244
Joseph Agro,
▲ EMP: 6
SQ FT: 1,500
SALES (est): 1.1MM **Privately Held**
WEB: www.autodrill.com
SIC: 5084 3541 Machine tools & accessories; drilling machine tools (metal cutting)

(G-5252)
AVSTAR PUBLISHING CORP
3 Burlinghoff Ln (08833-4383)
PHONE.....................908 236-6210
Alvin Silverstein, *President*
Virginia Silverstein, *Vice Pres*
Laura Nunn, *Admin Sec*
EMP: 5
SALES (est): 400K **Privately Held**
SIC: 2731 Books: publishing & printing

(G-5253)
B & B PRESS INC
24 Cokesbury Rd Ste 11 (08833-2218)
PHONE......................................908 840-4093
Mark Bistis, *President*
Christopher Koch, *Prdtn Mgr*
John Bistis, *Treasurer*
EMP: 9 EST: 1922
SQ FT: 3,200
SALES: 1.5MM **Privately Held**
WEB: www.bbpress.com
SIC: 2752 2791 Commercial printing, off-set; typesetting, computer controlled

(G-5254)
CANDY TREASURE LLC
66 Welsh Rd (08833-4316)
P.O. Box 201 (08833-0201)
PHONE......................................201 830-3600
Oleg Yarmolenko,
▲ EMP: 8
SALES (est): 2.4MM **Privately Held**
SIC: 5947 2064 2066 Gift shop; candy & other confectionery products; chocolate & cocoa products

(G-5255)
CELIMMUNE
110 Old Driftway Ln (08833-4628)
PHONE......................................908 399-2954
EMP: 4 EST: 2016
SALES (est): 265.8K **Privately Held**
SIC: 2834 Pharmaceutical preparations

(G-5256)
CHATHAM CONTROLS CORPORATION
6 Corral Cir (08833-4021)
PHONE......................................908 236-6019
Richard H Perst, *President*
EMP: 6 EST: 1954
SALES (est): 1MM **Privately Held**
SIC: 3822 Thermostats, except built-in

(G-5257)
CONSTRUCTION SPECIALTIES INC (PA)
Also Called: C/S Corporate
3 Werner Way Ste 100 (08833-2230)
PHONE......................................908 236-0800
Tom Hakes, *President*
Timothy Cobbs, *Engineer*
Ailet Acosta, *Human Resources*
Chris Donohue, *Sales Staff*
Elizabeth Noble, *Business Anlyst*
▲ EMP: 50 EST: 1948
SQ FT: 20,000
SALES (est): 379MM **Privately Held**
WEB: www.c-sgroup.com
SIC: 3446 3354 3443 3272 Railings, pre-fabricated metal; railings, bannisters, guards, etc.: made from metal pipe; guards, made from pipe; aluminum ex-truded products; columns (fractioning, etc.): metal plate; floor slabs & tiles, pre-cast concrete; air conditioning units, complete: domestic or industrial

(G-5258)
CUTTING BOARD COMPANY (PA)
291 Route 22 E Bldg 6 (08833)
PHONE......................................908 725-0187
Theresa Pizzelanti, *Owner*
Tony Pizzelanti, *Co-Owner*
▲ EMP: 4
SQ FT: 5,000
SALES: 550K **Privately Held**
SIC: 3613 Distribution cutouts

(G-5259)
ENGINE FACTORY INC
24 Cokesbury Rd Ste 15 (08833-2218)
PHONE......................................908 236-9915
Bruce T Nelson, *Executive*
EMP: 4
SALES (est): 408.8K **Privately Held**
WEB: www.enginefactory.com
SIC: 3694 Engine electrical equipment

(G-5260)
ENPRO INC
1401 Us Highway 22 (08833-4215)
P.O. Box 418 (08833-0418)
PHONE......................................908 236-2137

Vincent Cioffi, *President*
Pearl Cioffi, *Corp Secy*
EMP: 30 EST: 1961
SQ FT: 7,500
SALES (est): 2.8MM **Privately Held**
SIC: 3589 Water treatment equipment, industrial

(G-5261)
FLEXBIOSYS INC
291 Us Highway 22 Ste 32 (08833-5071)
PHONE......................................908 300-3244
Gayle Tarry, *CEO*
Stanley Tarry, *President*
Bill Linney, *Vice Pres*
EMP: 12
SALES (est): 920.2K **Privately Held**
SIC: 2673 3085 Plastic bags: made from purchased materials; plastics bottles

(G-5262)
HOWMAN ELECTRONICS INC
Also Called: Howman Engineering
291 Us Highway 22 Ste 40 (08833-5072)
PHONE......................................908 534-2247
Salvatore Treppiccione, *President*
David Ward, *Vice Pres*
EMP: 15
SQ FT: 6,000
SALES: 2.5MM **Privately Held**
SIC: 3625 3643 Industrial controls: push button, selector switches, pilot; current-carrying wiring devices

(G-5263)
IAM INTERNATIONAL INC
4 Saddle Ridge Dr (08833-3249)
PHONE......................................908 713-9651
Neera Tulshian, *President*
Deen Tulshian, *CFO*
EMP: 2
SALES (est): 1.5MM **Privately Held**
SIC: 8748 2099 Business consulting; food preparations

(G-5264)
INTER CITY PRESS INC
143 Petticoat Ln (08833-4122)
PHONE......................................908 236-9911
Jack Aquila, *President*
EMP: 26 EST: 1905
SALES (est): 1.5MM **Privately Held**
SIC: 2759 Commercial printing

(G-5265)
INTREPID INDUSTRIES INC
291 Us Highway 22 Ste 3 (08833-5066)
PHONE......................................908 534-5300
A John Haley, *President*
Martha Lynn Haley, *Corp Secy*
EMP: 7 EST: 1972
SQ FT: 5,000
SALES (est): 1MM **Privately Held**
WEB: www.intrepidindustries.com
SIC: 3471 Plating & polishing

(G-5266)
JAEGER THOMAS & MELISSA DDS
1128 State Rd 31 (08833)
PHONE......................................908 735-2722
Thomas Jaeger, *Partner*
Melissa Jaeger, *Partner*
EMP: 14
SALES (est): 861.9K **Privately Held**
SIC: 8021 1799 3443 Orthodontist; sand-blasting of building exteriors; liners/lining

(G-5267)
JRH SERVICE & SALES LLC
30 Boulder Hill Rd (08833-4526)
PHONE......................................908 832-9266
EMP: 4 EST: 2008
SALES (est): 330K **Privately Held**
SIC: 3841 Mfg Surgical/Medical Instruments

(G-5268)
LEBANON CHEESE COMPANY INC
3 Railroad Ave (08833-2156)
P.O. Box 63 (08833-0063)
PHONE......................................908 236-2611
Joe Lotito, *President*
EMP: 8

SQ FT: 5,000
SALES: 3MM **Privately Held**
SIC: 2022 Natural cheese

(G-5269)
LEBANON DOOR LLC
Also Called: Lebanon Door Company
119 Main St (08833-2162)
P.O. Box 168 (08833-0168)
PHONE......................................908 236-2620
Glen G Coats,
EMP: 4
SQ FT: 2,000
SALES (est): 600K **Privately Held**
SIC: 5211 3442 Garage doors, sale & installation; doors, storm: wood or metal; garage doors, overhead: metal

(G-5270)
MDB CONSTRUCTION
236 Cokesbury Rd (08833-4538)
PHONE......................................908 628-8010
Michael Barnard, *Owner*
EMP: 5
SALES (est): 272.5K **Privately Held**
SIC: 5719 1522 1521 2452 Fireplaces & wood burning stoves; residential construction; single-family home remodeling, additions & repairs; farm & agricultural buildings, prefabricated wood; renovation, remodeling & repairs: industrial buildings; demolition, buildings & other structures

(G-5271)
MEDALCO METALS INC
5 Chrystal Dr (08833-3243)
PHONE......................................908 238-0513
Ken Booth, *Manager*
EMP: 4
SALES (est): 372.3K
SALES (corp-wide): 4.9MM **Privately Held**
SIC: 3364 Nonferrous die-castings except aluminum
PA: Medalco Metals, Inc.
23 College St Ste 3
South Hadley MA 01075
413 586-6010

(G-5272)
MOUNTAIN TOP LOGGING LLC
99 Main St (08833-2132)
P.O. Box 324 (08833-0324)
PHONE......................................908 413-2982
Matthew Good, *Principal*
EMP: 4 EST: 2010
SALES (est): 457.1K **Privately Held**
SIC: 2411 Logging camps & contractors

(G-5273)
PLATE CONCEPTS INC
Also Called: PCI
1221 Us Highway 22 Ste 3 (08833-2228)
PHONE......................................908 236-9570
James C Gooch, *President*
John Loiacona, *Principal*
Hank Shamsi, *Vice Pres*
Karl Duerwald, *Sales Staff*
EMP: 5
SQ FT: 5,000
SALES: 3MM **Privately Held**
WEB: www.plateconcepts.com
SIC: 3443 Heat exchangers, condensers & components

(G-5274)
RACEWELD CO INC
1120 Us Highway 22 (08833-4209)
P.O. Box 378 (08833-0378)
PHONE......................................908 236-6533
EMP: 4
SQ FT: 10,000
SALES: 175K **Privately Held**
SIC: 3499 3599 Mfgs Fabricated Metal Products & Job Machine Shop

(G-5275)
WEBER AND SCHER MFG CO INC
Also Called: George Scher Engineering
1231 Us Highway 22 (08833-2213)
P.O. Box 366 (08833-0366)
PHONE......................................908 236-8484
J William Scher, *CEO*
Gregory K Scher, *President*
J Douglas Scher, *Vice Pres*

Maryann Faethe, *Executive Asst*
Joan Scher, *Admin Sec*
▲ EMP: 24 EST: 1915
SALES: 5.3MM **Privately Held**
WEB: www.webscher.com
SIC: 3549 Metalworking machinery

Ledgewood
Morris County

(G-5276)
IDENTITY DEPOT INC
Also Called: Sign-A-Rama
244 Main St (07852-9615)
PHONE......................................973 584-9301
Micheal Grivalsky, *CEO*
Steven Grivalsky, *Vice Pres*
Carole Grivalsky, *Admin Sec*
EMP: 8
SQ FT: 5,800
SALES (est): 534.5K **Privately Held**
SIC: 3993 Signs & advertising specialties

(G-5277)
JT FUELS LLC
1470 Us Highway 46 (07852-9606)
PHONE......................................973 527-4470
John Farnsworth, *Manager*
EMP: 6
SALES (est): 504K **Privately Held**
SIC: 2869 Fuels

(G-5278)
PHILIPS ELEC N AMER CORP
1 Samsung Pl (07852-9760)
PHONE......................................973 804-2100
Glen McMail, *Exec VP*
EMP: 100
SALES (corp-wide): 20.8B **Privately Held**
WEB: www.usa.philips.com
SIC: 3651 Household audio & video equipment
HQ: Philips North America Llc
3000 Minuteman Rd Ms1203
Andover MA 01810
978 659-3000

(G-5279)
R B B CORP
Also Called: Adam Metal Products Company
7 Orben Dr (07852-9719)
P.O. Box 450 (07852-0450)
PHONE......................................973 770-1100
Raymond Bentley, *President*
Paul Groover, *IT/INT Sup*
▲ EMP: 35
SQ FT: 72,000
SALES (est): 7.5MM **Privately Held**
SIC: 3646 3645 Fluorescent lighting fixtures, commercial; ceiling systems, luminous; residential lighting fixtures

(G-5280)
RUDOLPH TECHNOLOGIES INC
1705 Us Highway 46 Ste 3 (07852-9720)
PHONE......................................973 448-4307
Jule Von Sternberg, *Branch Mgr*
EMP: 7
SALES (corp-wide): 273.7MM **Publicly Held**
WEB: www.rudolphtech.com
SIC: 3674 Transistors
PA: Rudolph Technologies, Inc.
16 Jonspin Rd
Wilmington MA 01887
978 253-6200

(G-5281)
STEB INC (PA)
Also Called: Castle Printing Center
1501 Us Highway 46 (07852-9718)
PHONE......................................973 584-0990
Kevin Ebner, *President*
James Storms, *Vice Pres*
EMP: 7
SQ FT: 1,400
SALES (est): 912.3K **Privately Held**
WEB: www.steb.com
SIC: 2752 2791 2789 Commercial printing, offset; typesetting; bookbinding & related work

G
E
O
G
R
A
P
H
I
C

(G-5282)
STEB INC
Also Called: Castle Printing
1501 Us Highway 46 (07852-9718)
PHONE.................................973 584-0990
Jim Storms, *Owner*
Wilkin Vargas, *Prdtn Mgr*
EMP: 11
SALES (est): 1.4MM
SALES (corp-wide): 912.3K **Privately Held**
WEB: www.steb.com
SIC: 2752 Commercial printing, offset
PA: Steb Inc.
　　1501 Us Highway 46
　　Ledgewood NJ 07852
　　973 584-0990

(G-5283)
TONYMACX86 LLC
23 Lookout Dr (07852-9730)
PHONE.................................973 584-5273
Michael Wallace, *Co-Owner*
Gabriel Rohmann, *Co-Owner*
EMP: 4
SALES (est): 27.3K **Privately Held**
SIC: 2741 7389　;

(G-5284)
VANDERMOLEN CORP
106 Hillcrest Ave (07852-9731)
PHONE.................................973 992-8506
Aldo H Vandermolen, *President*
EMP: 4
SQ FT: 9,000
SALES (est): 522.2K **Privately Held**
WEB: www.vandermolencorp.com
SIC: 3699 5083 Fly traps, electrical; lawn
　& garden machinery & equipment; agri-
　cultural machinery

(G-5285)
VERTELLUS LLC
1705 Us Highway 46 (07852-9720)
PHONE.................................973 440-4400
Rich Preziotti, *Manager*
EMP: 6
SALES (corp-wide): 487.6MM **Privately Held**
SIC: 2865 Cyclic crudes, coal tar
HQ: Vertellus Llc
　　1500 S Tibbs Ave
　　Indianapolis IN 46241
　　317 247-8141

Leesburg
Cumberland County

(G-5286)
ALLEN STEEL CO
202 High St (08327-2020)
P.O. Box 211 (08327-0211)
PHONE.................................856 785-1171
James P Allen III, *President*
Dorothy Allen, *Admin Sec*
EMP: 5 **EST:** 1952
SALES (est): 400K **Privately Held**
SIC: 3731 3556 Fishing vessels, large:
　building & repairing; food products ma-
　chinery

Leonia
Bergen County

(G-5287)
CARRY EASY INC
Also Called: Quality Medical Supplies
131 Fort Lee Rd Fl 2 (07605-2216)
PHONE.................................201 944-0042
EMP: 25
SALES: 950K **Privately Held**
SIC: 4119 5047 3842 Local Passenger
　Trans Whol Med/Hospital Equip Mfg Sur-
　gical Appliances

(G-5288)
EBIC PRPAREDNESS
SOLUTIONS LLC
236 Overlook Ave (07605-1519)
PHONE.................................719 244-6209

EMP: 4
SALES: 500K **Privately Held**
SIC: 7371 7372 Custom Computer Pro-
　graming Prepackaged Software Services

(G-5289)
LABRADA INC
41 Palmer Pl (07605-1314)
PHONE.................................201 461-2641
David Labrada, *President*
Orquidea La Brada, *Corp Secy*
Nidia La Brada, *Vice Pres*
EMP: 5 **EST:** 1967
SQ FT: 1,500
SALES (est): 430K **Privately Held**
WEB: www.labrada.com
SIC: 3911 Jewelry, precious metal

(G-5290)
MINMETALS INC (PA)
120 Schor Ave (07605-2208)
PHONE.................................201 809-1898
Shili Jing, *President*
David Cheng, *Managing Dir*
Zhou Addressing, *Vice Pres*
Qinglian Cui, *Vice Pres*
Feng Guiquan, *Vice Pres*
◆ **EMP:** 12
SQ FT: 25,000
SALES (est): 10.6MM **Privately Held**
WEB: www.minmetals.com
SIC: 5052 5051 3341 3295 Coal; steel;
　secondary nonferrous metals; minerals,
　ground or treated

(G-5291)
NATURALLY SCIENTIFIC INC
600 Willow Tree Rd (07605-2211)
PHONE.................................201 585-7055
EMP: 10 **EST:** 1998
SQ FT: 22,500
SALES: 2.7MM **Privately Held**
SIC: 2023 Mfg Dry/Evaporated Dairy Prod-
　ucts

(G-5292)
SUEZ TREATMENT SOLUTIONS
INC
600 Willow Tree Rd (07605-2211)
PHONE.................................201 676-2525
Martin Falkenberg, *Vice Pres*
Michael Bernhart, *Manager*
Pedro Dacruz, *Director*
EMP: 60
SALES (corp-wide): 94.7MM **Privately Held**
SIC: 3559 2834 Ozone machines; chlori-
　nation tablets & kits (water purification)
HQ: Suez Treatment Solutions Inc.
　　461 From Rd Ste 400
　　Paramus NJ 07652
　　201 767-9300

(G-5293)
TEKKOTE CORPORATION
580 Willow Tree Rd (07605-2211)
PHONE.................................201 585-1708
Lawrence Goldman, *President*
Matthew Cain, *Vice Pres*
Thomas Chanqanqui, *Vice Pres*
Irwin Kowal, *Vice Pres*
Jacinta Parker, *Traffic Mgr*
◆ **EMP:** 100
SQ FT: 65,000
SALES (est): 38.5MM **Privately Held**
SIC: 2679 Filter paper: made from pur-
　chased material
PA: Mondi Plc
　　Building 1 1st Floor Aviator Park
　　Addlestone KT15

(G-5294)
TURNING STAR INC
600 Willow Tree Rd (07605-2211)
PHONE.................................201 881-7077
Thomas Andrews, *President*
▼ **EMP:** 9 **EST:** 1998
SQ FT: 5,000
SALES (est): 1.9MM **Privately Held**
WEB: www.turningstar.com
SIC: 2899 Fire retardant chemicals

Liberty Corner
Somerset County

(G-5295)
NEW HORIZON PRESS
PUBLISHERS
34 Church St (07938)
P.O. Box 669, Far Hills (07931-0669)
PHONE.................................908 604-6311
Joan Dunphy, *President*
T J Dermot Dunphy, *Vice Pres*
EMP: 5
SALES (est): 568.7K **Privately Held**
WEB: www.newhorizonpressbooks.com
SIC: 2731 5942 Books: publishing only;
　book stores

(G-5296)
SEAL-SPOUT CORP
50 Allen Rd (07938)
P.O. Box 74 (07938-0074)
PHONE.................................908 647-0648
Fax: 908 647-0648
EMP: 12 **EST:** 1944
SQ FT: 16,000
SALES (est): 1.1MM **Privately Held**
SIC: 3549 3444 3089 Mfg Metalworking
　Machinery Mfg Sheet Metalwork Mfg
　Plastic Products

Lincoln Park
Morris County

(G-5297)
ACTION GRAPHICS INC (PA)
600 Ryerson Rd Ste G (07035-2054)
PHONE.................................973 633-6500
Leonard Wynbeek, *President*
David J Corby, *Vice Pres*
Dale Park, *Treasurer*
EMP: 28
SQ FT: 20,000
SALES (est): 5.8MM **Privately Held**
WEB: www.actiongraphicsnj.com
SIC: 2752 Catalogs, lithographed

(G-5298)
D S JH LLC
Also Called: Structural Steel Fabricators
107 Beaverbrook Rd Ste 3 (07035-1448)
PHONE.................................973 782-4086
Santosh Salvi, *Mng Member*
Jorge Hermida,
EMP: 20
SQ FT: 1,000
SALES: 1.2MM **Privately Held**
SIC: 3325 3441 Steel foundries; fabricated
　structural metal

(G-5299)
INDOOR ENVIRONMENTAL
TECH
Also Called: Tri-Dim Filter
600 Ryerson Rd Ste F (07035-2054)
PHONE.................................973 709-1122
John C Stanley Sr, *President*
EMP: 50
SALES (est): 4MM
SALES (corp-wide): 4.5B **Privately Held**
WEB: www.tridim.com
SIC: 8731 3564 Environmental research;
　blowers & fans
HQ: Tri-Dim Filter Corporation
　　93 Industrial Dr
　　Louisa VA 23093
　　540 967-2600

(G-5300)
J & S ENTERPRISES LLC
Also Called: Sports Factory
175 Beaverbrook Rd (07035-1411)
PHONE.................................973 696-9199
Jay Yang, *Mng Member*
Steve Beneventine,
EMP: 18
SQ FT: 38,000
SALES (est): 1.2MM **Privately Held**
WEB: www.sportsfactory.net
SIC: 3949 Guards: football, basketball,
　soccer, lacrosse, etc.

(G-5301)
MEDITERRANEAN CHEF INC
3 Borinski Dr (07035-2060)
PHONE.................................855 628-0903
Rafael Montekio, *Principal*
▲ **EMP:** 10
SQ FT: 10,000
SALES (est): 618.5K **Privately Held**
SIC: 2099 Food preparations

(G-5302)
NASA MACHINE TOOLS INC
1 Frassetto Way Ste B (07035-2056)
P.O. Box 157, Pompton Plains (07444-
0157)
PHONE.................................973 633-5200
Robert De George Sr, *President*
Moisey Korenblum, *Electrical Engi*
Robert George, *Marketing Mgr*
▲ **EMP:** 25
SQ FT: 16,200
SALES (est): 4.3MM **Privately Held**
WEB: www.nassamachine.com
SIC: 3541 Machine tools, metal cutting
　type

(G-5303)
NOVAPAC LABORATORIES INC
510 Ryerson Rd Ste 1 (07035-2016)
PHONE.................................973 414-8800
Jean Marc Perez, *President*
Jessie Desrouleaux, *Research*
▲ **EMP:** 27
SALES: 7.5MM **Privately Held**
SIC: 2844 Cosmetic preparations

(G-5304)
POLYTYPE AMERICA CORP
600 Ryerson Rd Ste M (07035-2054)
PHONE.................................201 995-1000
Pieter S Van Der Griendt, *President*
Marianne Mullaney, *Finance*
▲ **EMP:** 18 **EST:** 1946
SALES (est): 10.4MM
SALES (corp-wide): 81.8MM **Privately Held**
SIC: 3555 Printing trade parts & attach-
　ments
HQ: Polytype S.A.
　　Route De La Glane 26
　　Fribourg FR 1700
　　264 261-111

(G-5305)
ROMACO INC
6 Frassetto Way Ste D (07035-2055)
PHONE.................................973 709-0691
▲ **EMP:** 23
SALES: 5.5MM
SALES (corp-wide): 21.4B **Publicly Held**
SIC: 3565 Mfg Packaging Machinery
HQ: Robbins & Myers, Inc.
　　10586 N Highway 75
　　Willis TX 77378
　　936 890-1064

(G-5306)
TEKNICS INDUSTRIES INC
Also Called: Teknics Sales
170 Beaverbrook Rd Ste 1 (07035-1441)
PHONE.................................973 633-7575
Bruce T Robertson, *President*
David Robertson, *Vice Pres*
▲ **EMP:** 56
SQ FT: 20,000
SALES (est): 629.4K **Privately Held**
SIC: 3545 Machine tool attachments & ac-
　cessories

(G-5307)
TRANSMISSION TECHNOLOGY
CO
1 High Mountain Trl (07035-1937)
PHONE.................................973 305-3600
Dezi Folenta, *President*
Margaret Folenta, *Vice Pres*
EMP: 6
SQ FT: 1,000
SALES (est): 370K **Privately Held**
SIC: 3714 7389 Motor vehicle transmis-
　sions, drive assemblies & parts; design,
　commercial & industrial

(G-5308)
TRI-DIM FILTER CORPORATION
600 Ryerson Rd Ste F (07035-2054)
PHONE...................................973 709-1122
John Stanley, *Branch Mgr*
EMP: 10
SALES (corp-wide): 4.5B **Privately Held**
SIC: 3564 Blowers & fans
HQ: Tri-Dim Filter Corporation
93 Industrial Dr
Louisa VA 23093
540 967-2600

(G-5309)
UNGERER & COMPANY
4 Ungerer Way (07035-1449)
PHONE...................................973 628-0600
Kenneth G Voorhees, *CEO*
John Olsen, *Vice Pres*
Richard Dambres Jr, *CFO*
Hector Manrique, *Controller*
Joanne McGowan, *Controller*
EMP: 290
SALES (est): 99K
SALES (corp-wide): 96.5MM **Privately Held**
SIC: 2899 Chemical preparations; essential oils
PA: Ungerer Industries, Inc.
4 Ungerer Way
Lincoln Park NJ 07035
610 868-7266

Lincroft
Monmouth County

(G-5310)
AVAYA INC
307 Mddletown Lincroft Rd (07738-1526)
PHONE...................................732 852-2030
Tara Molnar, *Manager*
EMP: 250 **Publicly Held**
WEB: www.avaya.com
SIC: 3661 7372 Telephone & telegraph apparatus; business oriented computer software
HQ: Avaya Inc.
4655 Great America Pkwy
Santa Clara CA 95054
908 953-6000

(G-5311)
HOUSE OF PRILL INC
716 Newman Springs Rd # 303
(07738-1523)
PHONE...................................732 442-2400
Steven Lazar, *President*
Rachel Lazar, *Treasurer*
EMP: 20 EST: 1905
SQ FT: 11,500
SALES (est): 1.8MM **Privately Held**
WEB: www.houseofprill.com
SIC: 5023 5199 3264 Home furnishings; gifts & novelties; porcelain electrical supplies

(G-5312)
J & L CONTROLS INC
15 Leland Ter (07738)
PHONE...................................732 460-0380
John Stocker, *President*
EMP: 4
SQ FT: 1,200
SALES: 200K **Privately Held**
SIC: 3822 Building services monitoring controls, automatic

(G-5313)
NJ SERVICE TESTING & INSPTN
26 Oak St (07738-1821)
PHONE...................................732 221-6357
John Gillen, *Principal*
EMP: 4
SALES (est): 768.9K **Privately Held**
SIC: 3569 General industrial machinery

(G-5314)
SAINT LA SALLE AUXILIARY INC
850 Newman Springs Rd (07738-1608)
PHONE...................................732 842-4359
William Martin, *President*
EMP: 4 EST: 1956

SALES (est): 318.1K **Privately Held**
WEB: www.dlsaux.org
SIC: 2771 Greeting cards

Linden
Union County

(G-5315)
A&C CATALYSTS INC
Also Called: AC Catalyts
1600 W Blancke St (07036-6228)
PHONE...................................908 474-9393
Linnaea Nowold, *Materials Mgr*
David Rawlins, *Opers Staff*
John Wolfe, *Sales Executive*
Abe Goldstein, *Director*
◆ EMP: 23 EST: 1995
SQ FT: 26,000
SALES: 10MM **Privately Held**
WEB: www.ac-catalyst.com
SIC: 2819 Catalysts, chemical

(G-5316)
ADVANCE MACHINE INC
531 Pennsylvania Ave (07036-2898)
PHONE...................................908 486-7244
Richard J Walano Sr, *President*
Carl M Walano, *Vice Pres*
Robert Boccadutre, *Treasurer*
Richard J Walano Jr, *Admin Sec*
EMP: 11 EST: 1971
SQ FT: 4,800
SALES (est): 1.5MM **Privately Held**
SIC: 3599 Machine shop, jobbing & repair

(G-5317)
AIR PROTECTION PACKAGING CORP
Also Called: AP Packaging
1200 Fuller Rd Ste 2 (07036-5774)
PHONE...................................973 577-4343
Eli Green, *CEO*
Joel Green, *CEO*
EMP: 17
SALES: 8MM **Privately Held**
SIC: 3081 Packing materials, plastic sheet

(G-5318)
AJAY METAL FABRICATORS INC
355 Dalziel Rd (07036-6229)
PHONE...................................908 523-0557
Tony Zambell Jr, *President*
Carolyn Zambell, *Admin Sec*
EMP: 8
SALES (est): 1MM **Privately Held**
SIC: 3441 3444 Fabricated structural metal; sheet metalwork

(G-5319)
ALKON SIGNATURE INC
333 Cantor Ave (07036-6230)
PHONE...................................917 716-9137
EMP: 5
SALES (est): 363.6K **Privately Held**
SIC: 2434 Wood kitchen cabinets

(G-5320)
ALL RACKS INDUSTRIES INC
101 Roselle St (07036-2636)
PHONE...................................212 244-1069
Joseph Desimone, *President*
Charles Desimone, *Vice Pres*
EMP: 5 EST: 1978
SQ FT: 7,000
SALES: 500K **Privately Held**
SIC: 2542 Garment racks: except wood

(G-5321)
ALLIED FOOD PRODUCTS INC
1600 W Elizabeth Ave (07036-6325)
PHONE...................................908 357-2454
Isaac Stern, *Branch Mgr*
EMP: 25
SQ FT: 8,000 **Privately Held**
SIC: 2034 2045 2099 5149 Soup mixes; cake mixes, prepared: from purchased flour; dessert mixes & fillings; gravy mixes, dry; salad dressing; sauces
PA: Allied Food Products Inc.
251 Saint Marks Ave
Brooklyn NY 11238

(G-5322)
ALUMA SYSTEMS CON CNSTR LLC
1800 Lower Rd (07036-6512)
PHONE...................................908 418-5073
Martin Berger, *General Mgr*
EMP: 9
SALES (corp-wide): 3B **Privately Held**
SIC: 3444 1799 Forming machine work, sheet metal; shoring & underpinning work
HQ: Aluma Systems Concrete Construction, Llc
5045 N 12th St Ste 119
Phoenix AZ 85014
602 212-0350

(G-5323)
AMERICAN ENVELOPE
Also Called: American Micro Technologies
612 E Elizabeth Ave (07036-2662)
PHONE...................................908 241-9900
Edward Nodelman, *President*
▲ EMP: 4 EST: 1957
SQ FT: 4,200
SALES: 600K **Privately Held**
WEB: www.americanenvelope.com
SIC: 2752 Commercial printing, offset

(G-5324)
ANDERSON TOOL & DIE CORP
1430 W Blancke St (07036-6299)
PHONE...................................908 862-5550
▲ EMP: 30 EST: 1947
SQ FT: 28,000
SALES (est): 410.8K **Privately Held**
SIC: 3841 Mfg Surgical/Medical Instruments

(G-5325)
BAR FIELDS INC
Also Called: AB Aerospace
1400 W Elizabeth Ave (07036-6321)
PHONE...................................347 587-7795
Rose Ranna, *Ch of Bd*
EMP: 10 EST: 2011
SALES (est): 478.2K **Privately Held**
SIC: 3728 Aircraft parts & equipment

(G-5326)
BATHWARE HOUSE LTD LBLTY CO
524 W Edgar Rd (07036-6502)
PHONE...................................732 546-3220
Mario Talavera,
EMP: 4
SALES: 800K **Privately Held**
SIC: 2499 Kitchen, bathroom & household ware: wood

(G-5327)
BP CORPORATION NORTH AMER INC
Also Called: Air BP
Park And Brunswick Ave (07036)
PHONE...................................908 474-5000
Dan Murphy, *Manager*
EMP: 20
SALES (corp-wide): 298.7B **Privately Held**
WEB: www.bpamoco.com
SIC: 2911 2899 Petroleum refining; chemical preparations
HQ: Bp Corporation North America Inc.
501 Westlake Park Blvd
Houston TX 77079
281 366-2000

(G-5328)
BRODIE SYSTEM INC
1539 W Elizabeth Ave (07036-6322)
PHONE...................................908 862-8620
Thomas W Nielsen, *President*
Nicholas Lloyd, *Manager*
Jane Nielsen, *Administration*
▲ EMP: 16 EST: 1929
SQ FT: 22,000
SALES (est): 2.8MM **Privately Held**
WEB: www.brodiesystem.com
SIC: 3599 3479 Machine shop, jobbing & repair; painting, coating & hot dipping

(G-5329)
CAPITAL FOODS INC
1701 E Elizabeth Ave (07036-1726)
PHONE...................................908 587-9050

Joseph Falcone, *President*
EMP: 24 EST: 1992
SQ FT: 11,000
SALES (est): 3.9MM **Privately Held**
WEB: www.capitalfoods.com
SIC: 2022 Cheese, natural & processed

(G-5330)
CDI GROUP INC
1135 W Elizabeth Ave (07036-6314)
PHONE...................................908 862-1493
Jordan Ruddy, *CEO*
Norman L Constant, *Ch of Bd*
Bart Shulman, *President*
Richard Constant, *Vice Pres*
EMP: 18
SQ FT: 40,000
SALES (est): 4.3MM **Privately Held**
WEB: www.cdigroupinc.com
SIC: 5046 3993 Display equipment, except refrigerated; displays & cutouts, window & lobby

(G-5331)
CELLULAR EMPIRE INC
Also Called: Pom Gear
1400 W Elizabeth Ave (07036-6321)
PHONE...................................800 778-3513
Doris Mosseri, *President*
Steve Jacobs, *President*
EMP: 56
SQ FT: 8,500
SALES: 2MM **Privately Held**
SIC: 3629 Electronic generation equipment

(G-5332)
CENTRAL POLY-BAG CORP
2400 Bedle Pl (07036-1313)
PHONE...................................908 862-7570
Andrew Hoffer, *President*
Agnes Serhofer, *Treasurer*
▲ EMP: 14
SQ FT: 35,000
SALES: 9.9MM **Privately Held**
WEB: www.centralpoly.com
SIC: 2673 5113 Plastic bags: made from purchased materials; bags, paper & disposable plastic

(G-5333)
CHEMIQUIP PRODUCTS CO INC
109 Bradford Ave (07036-6339)
PHONE...................................201 868-4445
Jack Diamond, *President*
Kim C KY, *Admin Sec*
EMP: 9
SQ FT: 6,000
SALES (est): 1.7MM **Privately Held**
SIC: 3824 3491 Gauges for computing pressure temperature corrections; pressure valves & regulators, industrial

(G-5334)
CLEAN-TEX SERVICES INC (PA)
1420 E Linden Ave (07036-1506)
PHONE...................................908 912-2700
David Zahler, *CEO*
Jacob Zahler, *President*
Brian Powers, *Vice Pres*
Joseph Ferlisi, *VP Business*
Michael Kahan, *Info Tech Mgr*
EMP: 22 EST: 1995
SALES (est): 9.9MM **Privately Held**
SIC: 7231 7212 2299 Cosmetology & personal hygiene salons; pickup station, laundry & drycleaning; truck route, laundry & drycleaning; retail agent, laundry & drycleaning; crash, linen; towels & towelings, linen & linen-and-cotton mixtures

(G-5335)
COLORFLO INC
Also Called: Color Company
1261 W Elizabeth Ave (07036-6316)
P.O. Box 1398 (07036-0004)
PHONE...................................908 862-3010
Phillip Kasper, *President*
Christopher Bates, *General Mgr*
Jose M Garcia, *Vice Pres*
Diane Galgoci, *Office Mgr*
Kenneth Frenchu, *Shareholder*
EMP: 5
SQ FT: 7,000
SALES (est): 901.1K **Privately Held**
WEB: www.colorco-flo.com
SIC: 2851 Paints & allied products

(G-5336)
CORP AMERICAN MICA
1015 Pennsylvania Ave (07036-2240)
PHONE..................................908 587-5237
Ray Bailey, *Owner*
EMP: 6
SALES (est): 591.5K **Privately Held**
SIC: 3295 Mica, ground or otherwise
treated

(G-5337)
COUNTY GRAPHICS FORMS MGT LLC
2 Stercho Rd (07036-6222)
PHONE..................................908 474-9797
Gina Scarola, *Finance Mgr*
Robert Scarola, *VP Sales*
Fabienne Francois, *Sales Dir*
Robert Gaudiosi,
Rachael Gaudiosi,
EMP: 30 EST: 1976
SALES (est): 5.5MM **Privately Held**
WEB: www.countygraphics.com
SIC: 2752 Commercial printing, offset

(G-5338)
COX STATIONERS AND PRINTERS
1634 E Elizabeth Ave (07036-1725)
PHONE..................................908 928-1010
Michael Kaufman, *CEO*
Nick Caravassi, *Accounts Mgr*
Joanne Meurer, *Business Dir*
Danielle Sparacino,
EMP: 30
SALES (est): 2.6MM **Privately Held**
SIC: 7389 2396 Printers' services: folding,
collating; automotive & apparel trimmings

(G-5339)
CUSTOM FABRICATORS INC
400 Commerce Rd (07036-2429)
PHONE..................................908 862-4244
Joseph Bonanno, *President*
Chiffon Bonanno, *Corp Secy*
EMP: 7 EST: 1966
SQ FT: 12,000
SALES (est): 570K **Privately Held**
WEB: www.metalfab.net
SIC: 3444 Sheet metal specialties, not
stamped

(G-5340)
CUTTING EDGE CASTING INC
Also Called: Cutting Edge Industries
1233 W Saint Georges Ave (07036-6117)
PHONE..................................908 925-7500
Steve Filler, *President*
Tom Hazel, *Vice Pres*
Yvonne N Bryant, *Manager*
▲ EMP: 40
SQ FT: 40,000
SALES (est): 4.4MM **Privately Held**
WEB: www.cuttingedgecatalog.com
SIC: 3599 3645 Machine shop, jobbing &
repair; residential lighting fixtures

(G-5341)
DANGELO METAL PRODUCTS INC
360 Dalziel Rd (07036-6291)
PHONE..................................908 862-8220
John D'Angelo Jr, *President*
Rosemary Scamardella, *Treasurer*
Pauline Gajek, *Admin Sec*
EMP: 12
SQ FT: 14,000
SALES (est): 1.5MM **Privately Held**
SIC: 3471 3432 3494 3312 Plating of
metals or formed products; polishing,
metals or formed products; plumbing fix-
ture fittings & trim; valves & pipe fittings;
blast furnaces & steel mills

(G-5342)
DAVID LEIZ CUSTOM WOODWORK
Also Called: Leiz Custom Woodworking
2301 E Edgar Rd Bldg 5a (07036-1200)
PHONE..................................908 486-1533
David Leiz, *President*
EMP: 4 EST: 1975
SQ FT: 6,000
SALES: 500K **Privately Held**
SIC: 2434 Wood kitchen cabinets

(G-5343)
DIM INC
Also Called: Le BEC Fin Fine Foods
10 Grant St (07036-1735)
PHONE..................................908 925-2043
Daniel Monneaux, *President*
Irene Khlevner, *Vice Pres*
EMP: 10 EST: 1999
SALES (est): 1.2MM **Privately Held**
SIC: 2043 Cereal breakfast foods

(G-5344)
EASTSIDE EXPRESS CORPORATION
2025 E Linden Ave (07036-1147)
PHONE..................................908 486-3300
Michael Mac Farlane, *Owner*
EMP: 9
SALES (est): 785.6K **Privately Held**
SIC: 2741 Miscellaneous publishing

(G-5345)
EXCEL DIE SHARPENING CORP
19 Grant St (07036-1734)
PHONE..................................908 587-2606
Hanna Krysa, *President*
Jerry Krysa, *Manager*
EMP: 6
SQ FT: 3,400
SALES: 360K **Privately Held**
SIC: 7699 3444 Knife, saw & tool sharp-
ening & repair; sheet metalwork

(G-5346)
EXPRESS PRINTING INC
Also Called: Noble Metals
209 W Saint Georges Ave (07036-3948)
PHONE..................................908 925-6300
Arvind Patel, *President*
EMP: 4
SQ FT: 1,500
SALES (est): 526.8K **Privately Held**
SIC: 2752 Commercial printing, offset

(G-5347)
FAUST THERMOGRAPHIC SUPPLY
325 Cantor Ave (07036-6230)
P.O. Box 1277 (07036-0003)
PHONE..................................908 474-0555
Craig Schwartzer, *President*
▲ EMP: 14
SALES (est): 3.7MM **Privately Held**
WEB: www.faustusa.com
SIC: 2899 Ink or writing fluids

(G-5348)
FIVE STAR SUPPLIES NJ CORP
1301 W Elizabeth Ave A (07036-6389)
PHONE..................................908 862-8801
Maohua Dong, *President*
▲ EMP: 20
SALES (est): 3.5MM **Privately Held**
SIC: 2834 Pharmaceutical preparations

(G-5349)
G & S DESIGN & MANUFACTURING
Also Called: Galvanotech
330 Dalziel Rd (07036-6232)
PHONE..................................908 862-2444
Gennady Volkov, *President*
Sofya Volkov, *Vice Pres*
EMP: 15
SQ FT: 12,000
SALES (est): 2.7MM **Privately Held**
WEB: www.galvanotech.com
SIC: 3559 Electroplating machinery &
equipment

(G-5350)
G-TECH ELEVATOR ASSOCIATES LLC
12 Sherman St (07036-1954)
PHONE..................................866 658-9296
Brock Glenn,
▲ EMP: 14
SALES (est): 16.1MM **Privately Held**
SIC: 1796 3534 3446 7699 Elevator installation & conversion; elevators & moving stairways; elevators & equipment;
elevator guide rails; elevators: inspection,
service & repair; miscellaneous building
item repair services

(G-5351)
GENERAL MAGNAPLATE CORPORATION (PA)
1331 W Edgar Rd (07036-6496)
PHONE..................................908 862-6200
Candida C Aversenti, *Ch of Bd*
Edmund V Aversenti Jr, *President*
Larry Campbell, *Vice Pres*
EMP: 58
SQ FT: 90,000
SALES (est): 24.4MM **Privately Held**
WEB: www.magnaplate.com
SIC: 3479 3471 Coating of metals &
formed products; coating, rust preventive;
electroplating of metals or formed prod-
ucts

(G-5352)
GENERAL MAGNAPLATE WISCONSIN
1331 W Edgar Rd (07036-6496)
PHONE..................................800 441-6173
Candida C Aversenti, *CEO*
Edmund V Aversenti, *COO*
EMP: 15 EST: 1973
SQ FT: 30,000
SALES (est): 1.3MM
SALES (corp-wide): 24.4MM **Privately Held**
WEB: www.magnaplate.com
SIC: 3479 Coating of metals & formed
products; coating, rust preventive
PA: General Magnaplate Corporation
1331 W Edgar Rd
Linden NJ 07036
908 862-6200

(G-5353)
GINGKO TREE INC (PA)
601 W Linden Ave (07036-6500)
PHONE..................................973 652-9380
Jidong Pei, *President*
EMP: 4
SALES (est): 734.8K **Privately Held**
SIC: 2819 2869 2861 Hydrochloric acid;
sulfuric acid, oleum; ethyl alcohol,
ethanol; acetone, synthetic; acetone, nat-
ural; methanol, natural (wood alcohol)

(G-5354)
HANSOME ENERGY SYSTEMS INC (PA)
365 Dalziel Rd (07036-6292)
PHONE..................................908 862-9044
Albert Reposi, *Ch of Bd*
Selma Rossen, *President*
Thomas Costello, *Vice Pres*
▲ EMP: 40 EST: 1969
SQ FT: 30,000
SALES (est): 6.8MM **Privately Held**
SIC: 7629 8711 3625 3621 Electrical re-
pair shops; consulting engineer; noise
control equipment; motors & generators

(G-5355)
HEINZ GLAS USA INC
360 Hurst St (07036-6221)
PHONE..................................908 474-0300
Emanuele Mazzei, *CEO*
Carl August Heinz, *Ch of Bd*
▲ EMP: 13
SQ FT: 55,000
SALES (est): 2.1MM
SALES (corp-wide): 361.9MM **Privately Held**
SIC: 3221 3544 Cosmetic jars, glass; bot-
tles for packing, bottling & canning: glass;
industrial molds
PA: Heinz-Glas Gmbh & Co. Kgaa
Glashuttenplatz 1-7
Tettau 96355
926 977-0

(G-5356)
IFC PRODUCTS INC
568 E Elizabeth Ave (07036-2816)
P.O. Box 2175 (07036-0011)
PHONE..................................908 587-1221
Joseph Christiano, *President*
Maria Christiano, *Vice Pres*
EMP: 10
SQ FT: 6,000
SALES (est): 1.2MM **Privately Held**
SIC: 2087 Extracts, flavoring

(G-5357)
IFC SOLUTIONS INC
1601 E Linden Ave (07036-1508)
PHONE..................................908 862-8810
David J Dukes, *President*
Ted Palumbo, *Technology*
Judith Grossman, *Director*
▼ EMP: 25
SQ FT: 28,000
SALES (est): 6MM **Privately Held**
SIC: 2087 Food colorings

(G-5358)
INDUSTRIAL MACHINE & ENGRG CO
Also Called: Industrial Machine & Engrg Co
1807 W Elizabeth Ave (07036-6391)
PHONE..................................908 862-8874
Valeria Peti, *President*
Steven R Peti, *Treasurer*
Sheree Peti, *Shareholder*
EMP: 10
SQ FT: 25,000
SALES (est): 2.3MM **Privately Held**
SIC: 3599 Machine shop, jobbing & repair

(G-5359)
INFINEUM USA LP (DH)
1900 E Linden Ave (07036-1133)
PHONE..................................800 441-1074
Rick Finn, *Business Mgr*
Jacob Levine, *Counsel*
Bryan Boyle, *Opers Mgr*
Bill Parker, *Maint Spvr*
Jeff McPadden, *Opers Staff*
◆ EMP: 350
SQ FT: 300,000
SALES (est): 215.6MM
SALES (corp-wide): 1B **Privately Held**
WEB: www.infineum.com
SIC: 2899 Chemical preparations
HQ: Infineum International Limited
Milton Hill Business And Technology
Centre
Abingdon OXON OX13
123 554-9500

(G-5360)
INSULATION MATERIALS DISTRS
Also Called: Insulation Material Distrs
501 S Park Ave (07036-1192)
P.O. Box 2134 (07036-0010)
PHONE..................................908 925-2323
Harold Faske, *President*
EMP: 8
SALES (est): 750K **Privately Held**
SIC: 3296 Fiberglass insulation

(G-5361)
INTERLINK PRODUCTS INTL INC
1315 E Elizabeth Ave (07036-1951)
PHONE..................................908 862-8090
Eli Zhadanov, *President*
▲ EMP: 21
SQ FT: 5,000
SALES: 10MM **Privately Held**
SIC: 3431 Shower stalls, metal

(G-5362)
INTERMARK INC
601 E Linden Ave (07036-2413)
PHONE..................................908 474-1311
Fax: 908 474-1367
EMP: 6
SQ FT: 6,000
SALES: 1MM **Privately Held**
SIC: 3499 Metal Working Machinery Cnc

(G-5363)
INTERNATIONAL DESIGN & MFG LLC
1217 Pennsylvania Ave (07036-2050)
PHONE..................................908 587-2884
Heidi Bravo, *Mng Member*
▲ EMP: 5
SALES (est): 785K **Privately Held**
SIC: 3446 Architectural metalwork

(G-5364)
JJJ STRETCHERS INC
1628 E Elizabeth Ave (07036-1725)
PHONE..................................908 290-3505
EMP: 4

SALES (est): 126.9K **Privately Held**
SIC: **3842** Stretchers

(G-5365)
JOBE INDUSTRIES INC
1600 W Elizabeth Ave (07036-6325)
P.O. Box 1367 (07036-0004)
PHONE..................................908 862-0400
Sheila W Reicher, *President*
EMP: 8
SALES (est): 1.3MM **Privately Held**
WEB: www.jobe-industries.com
SIC: **2842** Specialty cleaning preparations

(G-5366)
JUST IN TIME CHEMICAL SALES
&
Also Called: Chemicals Services
1711 W Elizabeth Ave (07036-6326)
PHONE..................................908 862-7726
Stan Jakubowycz, *President*
Halyna Jakubowycz, *Vice Pres*
▲ EMP: 9
SALES (est): 6MM **Privately Held**
SIC: **5169 2869** Chemicals, industrial &
heavy; plasticizers, organic: cyclic &
acyclic

(G-5367)
JVM SALES CORP
3401a Tremley Point Rd (07036-3533)
PHONE..................................908 862-4866
Mary Beth Tomasino, *President*
Robert Boyle, *President*
Anthony Caliendo, *Vice Pres*
Douglas Kolacki, *Opers Staff*
EMP: 100 EST: 1983
SQ FT: 30,000
SALES (est): 29.1MM **Privately Held**
WEB: www.jvmsales.com
SIC: **2022** Natural cheese

(G-5368)
K & S INDUSTRIES INC
333 Dalziel Rd (07036-6229)
PHONE..................................908 862-3030
Peter Sklenar, *President*
Peter Korcasko, *Vice Pres*
▲ EMP: 14
SQ FT: 6,500
SALES: 2.1MM **Privately Held**
SIC: **3549 3565** Coil winding machines for
springs; packaging machinery

(G-5369)
KASHMIR CROWN BAKING LLC
(PA)
710 W Linden Ave (07036-6527)
PHONE..................................908 474-1470
Sajjad Ahmed, *Owner*
◆ EMP: 21
SALES (est): 9.1MM **Privately Held**
SIC: **2051** Bread, cake & related products

(G-5370)
KERNEY SERVICE GROUP INC
(PA)
Also Called: Kerney Ship Repair
1700 E Elizabeth Ave (07036-1727)
P.O. Box 1830, Tampa FL (33601-1830)
PHONE..................................908 486-2644
Frank Kerney Sr, *President*
Frank Karney Jr, *Vice Pres*
EMP: 25
SQ FT: 12,000
SALES (est): 6.5MM **Privately Held**
WEB: www.kerneyservice.com
SIC: **3731** Shipbuilding & repairing

(G-5371)
KT WELDING
328 Spruce St (07036-5066)
PHONE..................................908 862-7370
EMP: 4 EST: 1986
SALES (est): 170K **Privately Held**
SIC: **7692** Welding Repair

(G-5372)
LAEGER METAL SPINNING CO
INC
1514 E Elizabeth Ave (07036-1919)
PHONE..................................908 925-5530
Frederick W Laeger, *President*
Chris Sparrer, *General Mgr*
Mary Ann Laeger, *Vice Pres*

EMP: 7 EST: 1942
SQ FT: 6,000
SALES (est): 1MM **Privately Held**
SIC: **3469** Spinning metal for the trade

(G-5373)
LAMINATED INDUSTRIES INC
(PA)
2000 Brunswick Ave (07036-2400)
PHONE..................................908 862-5995
Chaim Schwimmer, *President*
Sam Schwimmer, *Vice Pres*
◆ EMP: 28
SQ FT: 100,000
SALES (est): 6.3MM **Privately Held**
SIC: **2679 2611** Paper products, con-
verted; pulp mills

(G-5374)
LAMINATED PAPERBOARD
CORP
2000 Brunswick Ave (07036-2400)
PHONE..................................908 862-5995
Mendel Schwimmer, *President*
Sam Schwimmer, *Vice Pres*
EMP: 7
SALES (est): 790K **Privately Held**
WEB: www.laminated-industries.com
SIC: **2679** Cardboard products, except die-
cut

(G-5375)
LENTINE SHEET METAL INC
Also Called: A Andersen Shtmtl Fabrication
1210 E Elizabeth Ave (07036-2049)
PHONE..................................908 486-8974
John Lentine, *President*
EMP: 12 EST: 1927
SQ FT: 16,000
SALES (est): 2.1MM **Privately Held**
WEB: www.aandersensheetmetal.com
SIC: **3444 5051** Sheet metal specialties,
not stamped; metals service centers & of-
fices

(G-5376)
LINDEN WELL DRILLING
2020 Clinton St (07036-3452)
P.O. Box 1247 (07036-0003)
PHONE..................................908 862-6633
Richard Lutz, *Principal*
Henry Lutz, *Vice Pres*
EMP: 25
SALES (est): 1.6MM **Privately Held**
SIC: **3443 8748** Liners/lining; environmen-
tal consultant

(G-5377)
LONGO ELCTRICAL-
MECHANICAL INC
1625 Pennsylvania Ave (07036-1761)
P.O. Box 1397 (07036-0004)
PHONE..................................973 537-0400
Bill Valente, *Manager*
EMP: 30
SALES (corp-wide): 21MM **Privately**
Held
WEB: www.longo-ind.com
SIC: **7629 7699 5999 7694** Electrical
equipment repair, high voltage; pumps &
pumping equipment repair; motors, elec-
tric; electric motor repair
PA: Longo Electrical-Mechanical, Inc.
1 Harry Shupe Blvd
Wharton NJ 07885
973 537-0400

(G-5378)
M C M CUSTOM FURNITURE INC
817 E Linden Ave (07036-2415)
PHONE..................................908 523-1666
Chris Degregoril, *Owner*
Cris Gregorio, *Owner*
EMP: 6
SALES (est): 542.9K **Privately Held**
SIC: **2434** Wood kitchen cabinets

(G-5379)
MAGNALUBE INC
1331 W Edgar Rd (07036-6402)
P.O. Box 1250 (07036-0003)
PHONE..................................718 729-1000
Kerby Saunders, *President*
Luke Saunders, *COO*
EMP: 8

SALES (est): 1.3MM **Privately Held**
WEB: www.magnalube.com
SIC: **2911** Greases, lubricating

(G-5380)
MATCHLESS UNITED
COMPANIES (HQ)
801 E Linden Ave Ste 1 (07036-2487)
PHONE..................................908 862-7300
Frank Ungari, *CEO*
Gary Slonski, *CFO*
EMP: 8
SQ FT: 30,000
SALES (est): 1.2MM
SALES (corp-wide): 14.7MM **Privately**
Held
SIC: **2842 5085** Specialty cleaning, pol-
ishes & sanitation goods; industrial sup-
plies
PA: The Matchless Metal Polish Company
840 W 49th Pl
Chicago IL 60609
773 924-1515

(G-5381)
MERCER COATING & LINING CO
INC
1410 E Linden Ave (07036-1506)
P.O. Box 1656 (07036-0006)
PHONE..................................908 925-5000
Mike Powers, *President*
EMP: 11 EST: 1964
SQ FT: 20,000
SALES (est): 1.6MM **Privately Held**
WEB: www.mercercoating.com
SIC: **3471** Sand blasting of metal parts

(G-5382)
MERLYN CABINETRY LLC
1801 W Edgar Rd Unit 2 (07036-6420)
PHONE..................................908 583-6950
Ankin Cheng, *General Mgr*
EMP: 7
SALES (est): 376K **Privately Held**
SIC: **2434** Wood kitchen cabinets

(G-5383)
METAL HOSE FABRICATORS
INC
1122 Fedirko Ct (07036-6137)
P.O. Box 3021, Clifton (07012-0321)
PHONE..................................908 925-7345
Charles Hartmann, *President*
Emanuele Dirubba, *Vice Pres*
EMP: 6
SQ FT: 6,000
SALES: 1.1MM **Privately Held**
SIC: **3599** Hose, flexible metallic

(G-5384)
METALS PLUS
200 Marion Ave (07036-6337)
PHONE..................................908 862-7677
Farid Mensi, *Owner*
Daniel Mensi, *Project Mgr*
EMP: 24
SALES (est): 2.4MM **Privately Held**
SIC: **3441** Fabricated structural metal

(G-5385)
MICROCAST TECHNOLOGIES
CORP (PA)
1611 W Elizabeth Ave (07036-6342)
PHONE..................................908 523-9503
Dean Fushcetti, *President*
Leonard Cordaro, *President*
Richard Fuschetti Jr, *Vice Pres*
Dean Fuschetti, *VP Opers*
Kasia Kozlowski, *VP Opers*
▲ EMP: 60
SQ FT: 20,000
SALES (est): 29.4MM **Privately Held**
WEB: www.mtcnj.com
SIC: **3364 8711 3089 5051** Zinc & zinc-
base alloy die-castings; engineering serv-
ices; injection molding of plastics;
stampings, metal; silk screen design; zinc
& zinc-base alloy castings, except die-
castings

(G-5386)
MIRE ENTERPRISES LLC
Also Called: Reggie's Roast Coffees
1501 W Blancke St Ste 3 (07036-6238)
PHONE..................................732 882-1010

Fax: 908 862-3711
▲ EMP: 4
SALES: 350K **Privately Held**
SIC: **2095** Mfg Roasted Coffee

(G-5387)
MM PACKAGING GROUP LLC
2401 E Linden Ave (07036-1121)
PHONE..................................908 759-0101
Moshe Sofer, *Principal*
▲ EMP: 6
SQ FT: 17,000
SALES: 500K **Privately Held**
SIC: **5199 2043** Packaging materials; ce-
real breakfast foods

(G-5388)
MNW LLC
301 Dalziel Rd (07036-6229)
PHONE..................................908 591-7277
Julie Pinho, *Mng Member*
Maxx Wattenderg, *Mng Member*
EMP: 20
SALES: 750K **Privately Held**
SIC: **2053** Frozen bakery products, except
bread

(G-5389)
MODERNLINEFURNITURE INC
531 N Stiles St (07036-5771)
PHONE..................................908 486-0200
Vladimir Spivak, *President*
Robert Deli, *Vice Pres*
EMP: 25
SQ FT: 70,000
SALES: 9MM **Privately Held**
SIC: **5712 2599** Office furniture; cabinets,
factory

(G-5390)
MOLDWORKS WORLDWIDE LLC
985 E Linden Ave (07036-2416)
PHONE..................................908 474-8082
Howard Hyams, *President*
Terry Hyams, *Chairman*
▲ EMP: 7
SQ FT: 6,500
SALES (est): 877.8K **Privately Held**
SIC: **2329** Men's & boys' sportswear & ath-
letic clothing

(G-5391)
NAPCO SEPARATION
EQUIPMENT INC
200 Marion Ave (07036-6337)
PHONE..................................908 862-7677
Farid E Mensi, *President*
EMP: 4
SQ FT: 10,000
SALES: 1.2MM **Privately Held**
SIC: **3441** Fabricated structural metal

(G-5392)
NATIONAL STEEL RULE
COMPANY (PA)
750 Commerce Rd (07036-2496)
PHONE..................................908 862-3366
Edmund Mucci Jr, *President*
Gregory Zimmer, *Senior VP*
Joseph E Bialoglow, *Vice Pres*
Bethann Bialoglow-Masiello, *Vice Pres*
John White, *Vice Pres*
▲ EMP: 90 EST: 1967
SALES (est): 38.3MM **Privately Held**
SIC: **3423 3546 3425** Rules or rulers,
metal; power-driven handtools; saw
blades & handsaws

(G-5393)
NATIONAL STEEL RULE
COMPANY
620 Commerce Rd (07036-2425)
PHONE..................................800 922-0885
Jim Lheureux, *Principal*
EMP: 10
SALES (corp-wide): 38.3MM **Privately**
Held
SIC: **3423** Rules or rulers, metal
PA: National Steel Rule Company
750 Commerce Rd
Linden NJ 07036
908 862-3366

(G-5394)
NATIONAL STEEL RULE COMPANY
712 Commerce Rd (07036-2423)
PHONE.................................908 862-3366
Ed Mucci, *President*
EMP: 100
SALES (corp-wide): 38.3MM **Privately Held**
SIC: 3423 Hand & edge tools
PA: National Steel Rule Company
   750 Commerce Rd
   Linden NJ 07036
   908 862-3366

(G-5395)
NEMA ASSOCIATES INC
408 E Elizabeth Ave (07036-3041)
PHONE.................................973 274-0052
Juan Lopez, *President*
EMP: 14
SALES (est): 2.6MM **Privately Held**
WEB: www.nemadesign.com
SIC: 7336 2752 7311 Commercial art & graphic design; creative services to advertisers, except writers; graphic arts & related design; package design; commercial printing, lithographic; advertising consultant

(G-5396)
NEW YORK POULTRY CO
3351 Tremley Point Rd # 2 (07036-3575)
PHONE.................................908 523-1600
Abdul Nasaoy, *President*
EMP: 15
SALES (est): 948.8K **Privately Held**
SIC: 2048 Poultry feeds

(G-5397)
NOBLE METALS CORP
Also Called: Ex-Press Printing
209 W Saint Georges Ave (07036-3948)
PHONE.................................908 925-6300
Arvind Patel, *President*
EMP: 4
SQ FT: 1,000
SALES (est): 279.3K **Privately Held**
SIC: 2752 Commercial printing, offset

(G-5398)
NVS INTERNATIONAL INC
1600 Lower Rd (07036-6516)
PHONE.................................908 523-0266
Natalie Soltys, *President*
◆ EMP: 25
SALES (est): 3.9MM **Privately Held**
SIC: 3731 Shipbuilding & repairing

(G-5399)
OIL TECHNOLOGIES SERVICES INC
Also Called: Seahawk Services
1177 W Elizabeth Ave (07036)
PHONE.................................856 845-4142
Wajdi Abdmessih, *President*
EMP: 6
SALES (corp-wide): 1MM **Privately Held**
SIC: 1389 5551 Testing, measuring, surveying & analysis services; oil consultants; marine supplies & equipment
PA: Oil Technologies Services Inc.
   1501 Grandview Ave Ste 1
   Paulsboro NJ 08066
   856 845-4142

(G-5400)
P & G LIGHTING & SIGN SERVICE
633 E Elizabeth Ave (07036-2661)
PHONE.................................908 925-3191
Paul Van Atten, *President*
EMP: 6
SQ FT: 10,000
SALES (est): 793.7K **Privately Held**
SIC: 3993 Signs & advertising specialties

(G-5401)
PALENQUE MEAT PROVISIONS LLC
23 Grant St (07036-1734)
PHONE.................................908 718-1557
Rasella Balbeuna, *Finance*
Sergio Leopoldo Mendez,
EMP: 25

SALES: 200K **Privately Held**
SIC: 2013 5147 Sausages & other prepared meats; meats & meat products; meats, fresh

(G-5402)
PANOS BRANDS LLC
Also Called: Walden Farms
1209 W Saint Georges Ave (07036-6117)
PHONE.................................800 229-1706
Santo Gonzalez, *Plant Mgr*
Richard Cerna, *Manager*
EMP: 22
SALES (corp-wide): 72.8MM **Privately Held**
SIC: 2035 2023 Dressings, salad: raw & cooked (except dry mixes); powdered cream
HQ: Panos Brands, Llc
   395 W Passaic St
   Rochelle Park NJ 07662

(G-5403)
PARAMOUNT METAL FINISHING CO
Also Called: Paramount Plating
1515 W Elizabeth Ave (07036-6322)
PHONE.................................908 862-0772
Vincent Fuschetti, *President*
Michael Fuschetti, *President*
Richard Fuschetti, *Corp Secy*
Richard Fuschetti Jr, *Vice Pres*
Monica Laskowski, *Purch Agent*
EMP: 120 EST: 1949
SQ FT: 54,000
SALES (est): 18.8MM **Privately Held**
WEB: www.pmf1.com
SIC: 3479 3471 1796 Coating of metals & formed products; finishing, metals or formed products; machinery installation

(G-5404)
PARAMOUNT PLATING CO INC
1515 W Elizabeth Ave (07036-6322)
PHONE.................................908 862-0772
Vincent Fuschetti, *President*
Richard A Fuschetti, *Corp Secy*
▲ EMP: 45
SQ FT: 54,000
SALES: 8.8MM **Privately Held**
SIC: 3471 Electroplating of metals or formed products; anodizing (plating) of metals or formed products

(G-5405)
PATWIN PLASTICS INC
2300 E Linden Ave (07036-1194)
PHONE.................................908 486-6600
Thomas Hannon Sr, *President*
Eva Hannon, *Corp Secy*
Thomas Hannon Jr, *Vice Pres*
Timothy Hannon, *Vice Pres*
Erin Hannen, *Sales Mgr*
▲ EMP: 45
SQ FT: 42,000
SALES (est): 11.5MM **Privately Held**
WEB: www.patwin.com
SIC: 3089 Extruded finished plastic products; plastic processing

(G-5406)
PEN COMPANY OF AMERICA LLC (HQ)
1401 S Park Ave (07036-1609)
PHONE.................................908 374-7949
Adam Bell, *President*
Mark Littwin, *Vice Pres*
EMP: 45
SQ FT: 20,000
SALES (est): 13.3MM
SALES (corp-wide): 294.5MM **Privately Held**
SIC: 3951 Pens & mechanical pencils
PA: Plaskolite, Llc
   400 W Nationwide Blvd # 400
   Columbus OH 43215
   614 294-3281

(G-5407)
PHILLIPS 66 COMPANY
Also Called: Bayway Refinery
1400 S Park Ave (07036-1610)
PHONE.................................908 296-0709
Dwight L Higgins, *President*
Deborah Lamond, *Plant Mgr*
Randy Austin, *Safety Mgr*

Frank Cicholski, *Human Res Mgr*
Cory Phillips, *Manager*
EMP: 5
SALES (corp-wide): 114.2B **Publicly Held**
WEB: www.phillips66.com
SIC: 5541 2911 Filling stations, gasoline; gasoline
HQ: Phillips 66 Company
   2331 Citywest Blvd
   Houston TX 77042
   281 293-6600

(G-5408)
PI METAL PRODUCTS INC
1717 Pennsylvania Ave (07036-1762)
PHONE.................................201 955-0800
Jincheng Wu, *President*
EMP: 6
SALES (est): 275.2K **Privately Held**
SIC: 3444 Sheet metalwork

(G-5409)
PIC CORPORATION
1101 W Elizabeth Ave (07036-6314)
P.O. Box 1458 (07036-0005)
PHONE.................................908 862-7977
Allen Rubel, *President*
David Lowe, *Vice Pres*
David Hennessey, *Project Mgr*
Joe Romano, *Facilities Mgr*
Sherri Daly, *Regl Sales Mgr*
▲ EMP: 30 EST: 1953
SQ FT: 45,000
SALES (est): 9.6MM **Privately Held**
WEB: www.pic-corp.com
SIC: 2879 5191 Insecticides, agricultural or household; insecticides

(G-5410)
PLASKOLITE NEW JERSEY LLC
1401 S Park Ave (07036-1609)
PHONE.................................908 486-1000
Adam Bell, *President*
EMP: 180
SALES (est): 81.8K
SALES (corp-wide): 294.5MM **Privately Held**
SIC: 2821 Plastics materials & resins
PA: Plaskolite, Llc
   400 W Nationwide Blvd # 400
   Columbus OH 43215
   614 294-3281

(G-5411)
PRAXAIR DISTRIBUTION INC
515 E Edgar Rd (07036-2403)
PHONE.................................908 862-7200
Michael Solomon, *Principal*
EMP: 18 **Privately Held**
SIC: 2813 5169 5084 Industrial gases; industrial gases; welding machinery & equipment
HQ: Praxair Distribution, Inc.
   10 Riverview Dr
   Danbury CT 06810
   203 837-2000

(G-5412)
PRO PLASTICS INC
1190 Sylvan St (07036-6417)
P.O. Box 1489 (07036-0005)
PHONE.................................908 925-5555
George C Sievewright, *President*
Dennis Krokosc, *Vice Pres*
John Scanlon, *Asst Sec*
EMP: 20
SQ FT: 10,000
SALES (est): 3.2MM **Privately Held**
WEB: www.proplasticsinc.com
SIC: 3089 5162 Injection molded finished plastic products; plastics materials

(G-5413)
PULASKI MEAT PRODUCTS CO
Also Called: Pulasky Meat Products Co
123 N Wood Ave (07036-4227)
PHONE.................................908 925-5380
Ronald Preiss, *President*
Else Preiss, *Corp Secy*
Preiss Judith, *Vice Pres*
Judith Preiss, *Vice Pres*
Paul Preiss, *Vice Pres*
EMP: 30
SQ FT: 18,000

SALES (est): 5MM **Privately Held**
SIC: 2013 2011 Sausages from purchased meat; ham, smoked: from purchased meat; meat packing plants

(G-5414)
RESEARCH & MFG CORP AMER (PA)
Also Called: Research Manufacturing
1130 W Elizabeth Ave (07036-6315)
PHONE.................................908 862-6744
Charles Semah, *President*
Shlomo Kanarek, *President*
▲ EMP: 12
SQ FT: 22,000
SALES (est): 3.3MM **Privately Held**
SIC: 3061 3714 3083 Mechanical rubber goods; motor vehicle parts & accessories; laminated plastics plate & sheet

(G-5415)
REX TOOL & MANUFACTURING INC
544 E Elizabeth Ave (07036-2816)
P.O. Box 1423 (07036-0005)
PHONE.................................908 925-2727
John Haydu, *President*
Patricia Haydu, *Corp Secy*
Jennifer Haydu, *Vice Pres*
EMP: 4 EST: 1953
SQ FT: 3,800
SALES (est): 496.7K **Privately Held**
SIC: 3544 Special dies & tools

(G-5416)
ROTUBA EXTRUDERS INC
1401 S Park Ave (07036-1698)
PHONE.................................908 486-1000
Adam Bell, *President*
Mark Littwin, *Vice Pres*
Jim Blumenfeld, *VP Opers*
Royce Ruggles, *Opers Staff*
Navin Dua, *Mfg Staff*
◆ EMP: 250 EST: 1948
SQ FT: 150,000
SALES (est): 54.4MM **Privately Held**
WEB: www.rotuba.com
SIC: 3089 3087 3951 Extruded finished plastic products; custom compound purchased resins; ball point pens & parts

(G-5417)
S & H R INC
Also Called: Furs By Severyn
401 N Wood Ave Ste 1 (07036-4156)
PHONE.................................908 925-3797
Chester Lebrow Severyn, *President*
Jadwiga Lobrow, *Vice Pres*
EMP: 5
SQ FT: 1,750
SALES (est): 472.1K **Privately Held**
WEB: www.lobrow.com
SIC: 5632 4226 2371 Furriers; fur storage; coats, fur

(G-5418)
SAKER SHOPRITES INC
Also Called: World Class Intl Kit 712
1911 Pennsylvania Ave (07036-1422)
PHONE.................................908 925-1550
Brant Walsh, *Manager*
EMP: 10 **Privately Held**
SIC: 5411 2099 Grocery stores; food preparations
HQ: Saker Shoprites, Inc.
   10 Centerville Rd
   Holmdel NJ 07733
   732 462-4700

(G-5419)
SAYBOLT LP
1026 W Elizabeth Ave # 5 (07036-6341)
PHONE.................................908 523-2000
EMP: 6
SALES (corp-wide): 700.8MM **Privately Held**
WEB: www.corelab.com
SIC: 1389 Testing, measuring, surveying & analysis services
HQ: Saybolt Lp
   6316 Windfern Rd
   Houston TX 77040
   713 328-2673

(G-5420)
SCREEN TECH INC OF NEW JERSEY
1800 W Blancke St (07036-6224)
PHONE..................................908 862-8000
Dennis Berthiaume, *President*
Jose Caria, *Treasurer*
Terri Krawec, *Executive*
▲ EMP: 60
SQ FT: 10,000
SALES (est): 7.7MM **Privately Held**
SIC: 2759 Screen printing

(G-5421)
SENTREX INGREDIENTS LLC
350 Cantor Ave (07036-6230)
PHONE..................................908 862-4440
Naushad Lalani,
Arthur Gurerrera,
▲ EMP: 5
SALES (est): 783.7K
SALES (corp-wide): 10.2MM **Privately Held**
SIC: 2087 Extracts, flavoring
PA: Flavor Producers, Llc
8521 Fllbrook Ave Ste 380
West Hills CA 91304
818 307-4062

(G-5422)
SHALLCROSS BOLT & SPECIALTIES
1 Mccandless St (07036-2318)
PHONE..................................908 925-4700
Jeffrey Kaden, *President*
Loretta Kaden, *Corp Secy*
Bob Eitner, *Sales Mgr*
Charles Meder, *Sales Staff*
Shirley Lake, *Info Tech Mgr*
EMP: 30
SQ FT: 18,000
SALES (est): 6.2MM **Privately Held**
WEB: www.shallcrossbolt.com
SIC: 3452 5072 Bolts, nuts, rivets & washers; bolts

(G-5423)
SHORT RUN STAMPING COMPANY INC (PA)
925 E Linden Ave (07036-2416)
PHONE..................................908 862-1070
Robert Speir, *CEO*
Randall Speir, *President*
Carol Speir, *Corp Secy*
Nigel F Hewett, *Vice Pres*
EMP: 25 EST: 1951
SQ FT: 20,000
SALES (est): 32MM **Privately Held**
WEB: www.shortrun.com
SIC: 3469 Patterns on metal; stamping metal for the trade

(G-5424)
SLYS EXPRESS LLC
518 Lindegar St (07036-5750)
PHONE..................................908 787-7516
Slawomir M Polchlopek, *Principal*
EMP: 4 EST: 2010
SALES (est): 330.4K **Privately Held**
SIC: 2655 Fiber shipping & mailing containers

(G-5425)
SOLAR COMPOUNDS CORPORATION
1201 W Blancke St (07036-6213)
P.O. Box 1097 (07036-1097)
PHONE..................................908 862-2813
Harry Bockus, *CEO*
Paula Kopcho, *Controller*
▼ EMP: 24 EST: 1920
SQ FT: 60,000
SALES (est): 6.4MM **Privately Held**
WEB: www.solarcompounds.com
SIC: 2891 Adhesives

(G-5426)
SOLUTIA INC
2000 Brunswick Ave (07036-2400)
PHONE..................................908 862-0278
EMP: 4
SALES (est): 158K **Publicly Held**
SIC: 2824 Organic fibers, noncellulosic

PA: Eastman Chemical Company
200 S Wilcox Dr
Kingsport TN 37660

(G-5427)
SOUTH BRUNSWICK FURNITURE INC
1015 Edward St (07036-6408)
PHONE..................................732 658-8850
William Schafer, *President*
EMP: 198
SQ FT: 60,000
SALES: 30MM **Privately Held**
SIC: 2519 5712 Household furniture, except wood or metal: upholstered; office furniture

(G-5428)
SS TOOL & MANUFACTURING CO
1 Garfield St (07036-1415)
PHONE..................................908 486-5497
Stephen Kanyo Sr, *President*
Stephen Kanyo Jr, *Corp Secy*
EMP: 4 EST: 1976
SQ FT: 4,000
SALES (est): 600K **Privately Held**
SIC: 3545 Machine tool attachments & accessories

(G-5429)
STAR METAL PRODUCTS
1125 W Elizabeth Ave (07036-6314)
PHONE..................................908 474-9860
Donald Eckloff, *President*
Robert Sarnecki, *Treasurer*
EMP: 38
SALES (est): 6MM **Privately Held**
WEB: www.starmetalproducts.com
SIC: 3444 Sheet metalwork

(G-5430)
STEED PERF6MANC3
1034 E Elizabeth Ave (07036-2230)
PHONE..................................908 583-5580
EMP: 4
SALES (est): 499.6K **Privately Held**
SIC: 3714 Motor vehicle parts & accessories

(G-5431)
STEEL MOUNTAIN FABRICATORS LLC (PA)
Also Called: Smf
1312 W Elizabeth Ave (07036-6319)
PHONE..................................908 862-2800
Michael Dell'aquila,
Joseph Dell'aquila,
Justin Heald,
EMP: 12
SALES (est): 2.5MM **Privately Held**
SIC: 3599 Machine & other job shop work

(G-5432)
STYLUS CUSTOM APPAREL INC
729 E Elizabeth Ave (07036-2621)
PHONE..................................908 587-0800
Domenico Muscillo, *President*
Yamira Montenegro, *Graphic Designe*
EMP: 5
SALES (est): 82.8K **Privately Held**
SIC: 2389 Men's miscellaneous accessories

(G-5433)
SUBURBAN SIGN CO INC
210 Marion Ave (07036-6337)
PHONE..................................908 862-7222
EMP: 20 EST: 1946
SQ FT: 12,000
SALES (est): 3.2MM **Privately Held**
SIC: 3993 Mfg Signs/Advertising Specialties

(G-5434)
TED-STEEL INDUSTRIES LTD
Also Called: Ted-Steel Indstries
101 Roselle St (07036-2636)
PHONE..................................212 279-3878
Charles Desimone, *President*
Joseph Desimone, *Vice Pres*
Saml T Grayburn,
EMP: 6 EST: 1959
SQ FT: 10,000

SALES (est): 711.5K **Privately Held**
SIC: 2542 Garment racks: except wood

(G-5435)
THOMAS H COX & SON INC
Also Called: Spectraform
1634 E Elizabeth Ave (07036-1725)
PHONE..................................908 928-1010
Michael Kaufman, *President*
Sally Kaufman, *CFO*
Todd Pifher, *Marketing Staff*
Jill Kaufman, *Admin Sec*
EMP: 28
SQ FT: 21,000
SALES: 4.2MM **Privately Held**
WEB: www.coxprinters.com
SIC: 5112 2752 Office supplies; commercial printing, offset

(G-5436)
TOTAL SPECIALTIES USA INC
Also Called: Total Lubricants USA
5 N Stiles St (07036-4208)
PHONE..................................908 862-9300
Barry Martin, *Plant Mgr*
Bernie Kordelski, *Safety Mgr*
Steve Daubert, *Human Res Mgr*
Michael Kane, *Sales Staff*
Karen Lin, *Manager*
EMP: 51
SALES (corp-wide): 8.4B **Publicly Held**
SIC: 2992 Oils & greases, blending & compounding
HQ: Total Specialties Usa, Inc.
1201 La St Ste 1800
Houston TX 77002

(G-5437)
TRIPLE S INDUSTRIES
1108 E Linden Ave (07036-2419)
P.O. Box 1293 (07036-0003)
PHONE..................................908 862-0110
Robert Schulte, *President*
John H Schulte, *Vice Pres*
Walter Bradshaw, *Treasurer*
Patricia Bradshaw, *Shareholder*
Ruth Schulte, *Admin Sec*
EMP: 7 EST: 1961
SALES (est): 905.8K **Privately Held**
SIC: 3599 Machine shop, jobbing & repair

(G-5438)
UNIQUE SCREEN PRINTING CORP
10 Mckinley St 16 (07036-1747)
PHONE..................................908 925-3773
Jose Grajeda, *President*
EMP: 50
SQ FT: 15,000
SALES (est): 5.5MM **Privately Held**
WEB: www.uniquescreenprinting.com
SIC: 2262 2261 2396 Screen printing: manmade fiber & silk broadwoven fabrics; screen printing of cotton broadwoven fabrics; automotive & apparel trimmings

(G-5439)
UNIVERSAL PARTS
1057 Pennsylvania Ave (07036-2240)
PHONE..................................908 601-6558
Mark Merezio, *Principal*
EMP: 4
SALES (est): 569K **Privately Held**
SIC: 3713 Truck bodies & parts

(G-5440)
VELOSO INDUSTRIES INC
1020 E Elizabeth Ave (07036-2230)
PHONE..................................908 925-0999
Carlos Veloso, *President*
▲ EMP: 5
SQ FT: 3,600
SALES (est): 697K **Privately Held**
SIC: 3089 Thermoformed finished plastic products

(G-5441)
WELL BILT INDUSTRIES INC
2 Maple Ave (07036-2820)
PHONE..................................908 486-6002
Les Zalewski, *President*
EMP: 15
SQ FT: 8,000

SALES (est): 3MM **Privately Held**
WEB: www.wellbiltind.com
SIC: 3469 3544 Stamping metal for the trade; special dies, tools, jigs & fixtures

(G-5442)
WGJF MANUFACTURING CORP
Also Called: Hammer Manufacturing
417 Commerce Rd (07036-2428)
P.O. Box 1340 (07036-0004)
PHONE..................................908 862-1730
William J Fig, *President*
William Fig, *Executive*
EMP: 26
SQ FT: 15,000
SALES (est): 5MM **Privately Held**
SIC: 3469 Stamping metal for the trade

Lindenwold
Camden County

(G-5443)
ACTION GRAPHICS INC
424 E Gibbsboro Rd (08021-1907)
PHONE..................................856 783-1825
Barry Balliet, *Owner*
EMP: 6
SALES (est): 515.9K **Privately Held**
WEB: www.actiongraphicsusa.com
SIC: 2759 Commercial printing

(G-5444)
ADVANCE SCALE COMPANY INC (PA)
2400 Egg Harbor Rd (08021-1431)
PHONE..................................856 784-4916
Jim Santarpio, *President*
Sheila Santarpio, *Vice Pres*
EMP: 30
SQ FT: 16,000
SALES (est): 11.1MM **Privately Held**
WEB: www.advancescale.com
SIC: 5046 3596 Scales, except laboratory; weighing machines & apparatus; industrial scales

(G-5445)
PAUL BURKHARDT & SONS INC
Also Called: Pe Burkhardt & Sons
648 7th Ave (08021-3549)
PHONE..................................856 435-2020
Paul Burkhardt Sr, *President*
Paul Burkhardt Jr, *President*
Winona Burkhardt, *Treasurer*
EMP: 6 EST: 1982
SQ FT: 600
SALES: 200K **Privately Held**
SIC: 5712 2434 Cabinet work, custom; wood kitchen cabinets

(G-5446)
PAVERART LLC
2512 Egg Harbor Rd Ste C (08021-1405)
PHONE..................................856 783-7000
Michael K Bull, *Vice Pres*
Kenneth R Bull,
John M Seroka,
EMP: 7
SQ FT: 10,000
SALES (est): 680K **Privately Held**
WEB: www.paverartllc.com
SIC: 3271 Concrete block & brick

(G-5447)
WILLIAM R HALL CO
901 E Gibbsboro Rd (08021-1209)
PHONE..................................856 784-6700
George Aho, *President*
EMP: 40
SQ FT: 22,000
SALES (est): 4.7MM
SALES (corp-wide): 9.3MM **Privately Held**
WEB: www.ecmoore.com
SIC: 3843 3291 Dental equipment & supplies; abrasive products
PA: E C Moore Company
13325 Leonard St
Dearborn MI 48126
313 581-7878

Linwood
Atlantic County

(G-5448)
ATLANTIC PRSTHTIC ORTHOTIC SVC
199 New Rd Ste 56 (08221-2025)
PHONE..................................609 927-6330
Rich Kathrins, *President*
Leonard Hollander, *President*
Joan Gatti, *Manager*
Jill Ojserkis, *Admin Sec*
EMP: 5
SALES: 1.4MM **Privately Held**
SIC: 3842 5999 Prosthetic appliances; limbs, artificial; orthopedic appliances; orthopedic & prosthesis applications; convalescent equipment & supplies

(G-5449)
HANGER PRSTHETCS & ORTHO INC
210 New Rd Ste 7 (08221-1371)
PHONE..................................609 653-8323
Thomas Delsey, *Manager*
EMP: 7
SALES (corp-wide): 1B **Publicly Held**
SIC: 3842 Orthopedic appliances
HQ: Hanger Prosthetics & Orthotics, Inc.
    10910 Domain Dr Ste 300
    Austin TX 78758
    512 777-3800

(G-5450)
PROCRETE LLC
4 Evergreen Rd (08221-1346)
P.O. Box 492 (08221-0592)
PHONE..................................609 365-2922
David McBride,
EMP: 4
SALES: 90K **Privately Held**
SIC: 1741 3271 7389 Masonry & other stonework; concrete block & brick;

Little Falls
Passaic County

(G-5451)
AMERICAN SOC OF MECH ENGINEERS
Also Called: Asme
150 Clove Rd Ste 6 (07424-2139)
PHONE..................................973 244-2282
Jim Barrett, *General Mgr*
Nicholas Jankowski, *Electrical Engi*
Anthony Martini, *Prgrmr*
Frank Parker, *Administration*
EMP: 82
SALES (corp-wide): 52.9MM **Privately Held**
WEB: www.asmestaff.org
SIC: 2741 8711 Technical manual & paper publishing; engineering services
PA: The American Society Of Mechanical Engineers
    2 Park Ave
    New York NY 10016
    212 591-7000

(G-5452)
ANDON BRUSH CO INC
1 Merrit Ave (07424-1145)
PHONE..................................973 256-6611
Robert Newell, *President*
Maria Goglia, *Production*
Kenneth Kuter, *VP Sales*
Laura Bizub, *Sales Mgr*
▲ EMP: 25
SALES (est): 5.4MM **Privately Held**
WEB: www.andonbrush.com
SIC: 5085 5113 3991 Brushes, industrial; closures, paper & disposable plastic; brooms & brushes

(G-5453)
ARTS WEEKLY INC
Also Called: The Aquarian Weekly
52 Sindle Ave (07424-1619)
P.O. Box 1140 (07424-8140)
PHONE..................................973 812-6766

Diane Casazza, *President*
Chris Farinas, *Vice Pres*
Mark Sterman, *Treasurer*
EMP: 50
SQ FT: 2,400
SALES (est): 1MM **Privately Held**
WEB: www.theaquarian.com
SIC: 2721 2711 Magazines: publishing & printing; newspapers

(G-5454)
CANTEL MEDICAL CORP (PA)
150 Clove Rd Ste 36 (07424-2100)
PHONE..................................973 890-7220
Charles M Diker, *Ch of Bd*
George L Fotiades, *President*
Peter G Clifford, *COO*
James Ackley, *Counsel*
Eric W Nodiff, *Exec VP*
◆ EMP: 8 EST: 1963
SALES: 918.1MM **Publicly Held**
WEB: www.cantelmedical.com
SIC: 3841 3589 Surgical & medical instruments; water purification equipment, household type

(G-5455)
CHEM FLOWTRONIC INC
195 Paterson Ave Ste 4 (07424-4656)
P.O. Box 4635, Wayne (07474-4635)
PHONE..................................973 785-0001
Kevin Mooney, *President*
▲ EMP: 8
SQ FT: 1,500
SALES (est): 1.7MM **Privately Held**
WEB: www.chem-flowtronics.com
SIC: 3824 Mechanical & electromechanical counters & devices

(G-5456)
HOFFMANN-LA ROCHE INC (DH)
150 Clove Rd Ste 88th (07424-2138)
PHONE..................................973 890-2268
Kurt Seiler, *President*
David McDede, *Principal*
Gregg Scheideler, *Principal*
Sean Johnston, *Vice Pres*
Tom Lyon, *Vice Pres*
◆ EMP: 3000 EST: 1905
SALES (est): 1B
SALES (corp-wide): 57.2B **Privately Held**
WEB: www.rocheusa.com
SIC: 2834 8733 Pharmaceutical preparations; medical research

(G-5457)
JOHN W KENNEDY COMPANY
60 Sindle Ave (07424-1649)
PHONE..................................973 256-5525
Dalton Pemberton, *Manager*
EMP: 5
SALES (corp-wide): 17.2MM **Privately Held**
SIC: 3559 Petroleum refinery equipment
PA: John W. Kennedy Co.
    990 Waterman Ave
    East Providence RI 02914
    401 434-1246

(G-5458)
JW PARR LEADBURING CO (PA)
Also Called: Parr, J W Leadburing Co
87 Parkway (07424-1227)
PHONE..................................973 256-8093
Gary Parr, *Owner*
EMP: 4 EST: 1969
SALES: 1MM **Privately Held**
WEB: www.garyparr.com
SIC: 7699 3443 8742 Tank repair; tanks, lined; metal plate; management consulting services

(G-5459)
LABEL GRAPHICS MFG INC (PA)
175 Paterson Ave (07424-1607)
PHONE..................................973 890-5665
Thomas Silvano, *President*
Denise Silvano, *Corp Secy*
Victor Paravati, *QC Mgr*
▲ EMP: 43
SQ FT: 26,000
SALES (est): 8.4MM **Privately Held**
WEB: www.labelgraphicsmfg.com
SIC: 2672 Labels (unprinted), gummed: made from purchased materials

(G-5460)
LITTLE FALLS SHOP RITE SUPER
171 Browertown Rd Ste 2 (07424-1718)
PHONE..................................973 256-0909
Charles M Infusino, *President*
Carol Tokar, *Corp Secy*
EMP: 282
SALES (est): 24.5MM **Privately Held**
SIC: 5912 5411 7384 5992 Drug stores; supermarkets, chain; photofinish laboratories; florists; cookies & crackers; bread, cake & related products

(G-5461)
METALIX INC
9 Villa Rd (07424-2315)
PHONE..................................973 546-2500
Gary Nardino, *President*
Charles Nardino, *Vice Pres*
EMP: 8 EST: 1951
SQ FT: 14,000
SALES (est): 42.9K **Privately Held**
SIC: 3444 Sheet metal specialties, not stamped

(G-5462)
OVADIA CORPORATION
101 E Main St Ste 501 (07424-2265)
PHONE..................................973 256-9200
Susan Ovadia, *President*
Steven Ovadia, *Vice Pres*
Michael Bender, *Mktg Dir*
Ed Ovadia, *Marketing Mgr*
▲ EMP: 50
SQ FT: 20,000
SALES (est): 7.5MM **Privately Held**
SIC: 3089 3993 Plastic containers, except foam; signs & advertising specialties

(G-5463)
PACKOM LLC
385 Main St (07424-1207)
PHONE..................................201 378-8382
Peter Dobirc, *Director*
EMP: 50
SQ FT: 12,000
SALES: 2.5MM **Privately Held**
SIC: 2064 Candy & other confectionery products

(G-5464)
PAPER CLIP COMMUNICATION INC
125 Paterson Ave Ste 4 (07424-4626)
PHONE..................................973 256-1333
Andy Mc Laughlin, *President*
Dorris Laughlin, *Vice Pres*
Jessica Stover, *Marketing Staff*
Christina Gillham, *Officer*
EMP: 10 EST: 1993
SQ FT: 1,600
SALES (est): 1.4MM **Privately Held**
WEB: www.paper-clip.com
SIC: 2759 Publication printing

(G-5465)
PRIORE CONSTRUCTION SVCS LLC
5 Peckman Rd (07424-1631)
PHONE..................................973 785-2262
Dominick Priore, *President*
Michael Priore, *Vice Pres*
EMP: 19
SQ FT: 13,000
SALES: 3MM **Privately Held**
SIC: 3441 Tower sections, radio & television transmission

(G-5466)
RUBIGO COSMETICS
101 E Main St Bldg 12 (07424-5608)
P.O. Box 647, Fair Lawn (07410-0647)
PHONE..................................973 636-6573
Jules Schlesinger, *President*
Carol Cozin, *Vice Pres*
Steve Schisrien, *Vice Pres*
Michael J Assante, *Treasurer*
EMP: 6
SQ FT: 10,000
SALES: 804.9K **Privately Held**
WEB: www.rubigo.com
SIC: 2844 5122 3991 Cosmetic preparations; cosmetics; brooms & brushes

(G-5467)
SIMTEK USA INC
13 Fairfield Ave (07424-1264)
PHONE..................................862 757-8130
EMP: 5
SALES (est): 484.3K **Privately Held**
SIC: 3728 Aircraft power transmission equipment

(G-5468)
SRE VENTURES LLC
Also Called: UPS Store, The
163 E Main St (07424-1711)
PHONE..................................973 785-0099
Steve Eldrige, *President*
EMP: 6
SQ FT: 2,000
SALES: 250K **Privately Held**
SIC: 7389 4215 4513 2621 Mailbox rental & related service; package delivery, vehicular; parcel delivery, vehicular; letter delivery, private air; package delivery, private air; parcel delivery, private air; printing paper

(G-5469)
STORY ELECTRIC MTR REPR CO INC
20 Francisco Ave (07424-2317)
P.O. Box 379 (07424-0379)
PHONE..................................973 256-1636
David R Wilberton, *President*
EMP: 6
SQ FT: 28,000
SALES: 3.5MM **Privately Held**
SIC: 1731 7694 General electrical contractor; electric motor repair

(G-5470)
TAURUS PRECISION INC
129 Paterson Ave (07424-1643)
PHONE..................................973 785-9254
Michael E Jakubas, *President*
EMP: 14
SQ FT: 5,000
SALES (est): 2.2MM **Privately Held**
SIC: 3599 3429 Machine shop, jobbing & repair; metal fasteners

(G-5471)
TSG INC
Also Called: Technical Systems Group
28 Muller Pl (07424-1133)
PHONE..................................973 785-1118
Peter Chin, *President*
EMP: 15
SALES (est): 1.4MM **Privately Held**
WEB: www.tompat.com
SIC: 3625 8711 Industrial controls: push button, selector switches, pilot; consulting engineer

(G-5472)
UTZ TECHNOLOGIES INC (PA)
4 Peckman Rd (07424-1631)
PHONE..................................973 339-1100
Dennis Curtis, *President*
Arthur Wein, *President*
Kristian Guidi, *General Mgr*
Donald Utz, *Chairman*
EMP: 30
SQ FT: 8,000
SALES: 5MM **Privately Held**
WEB: www.utz.com
SIC: 3679 Electronic circuits

(G-5473)
WTA GLOBAL LLC
125 Long Hill Rd Apt 3c (07424-2331)
PHONE..................................312 509-2559
Rustam Kencheshaov, *Mng Member*
EMP: 12
SALES: 1.8MM **Privately Held**
SIC: 3715 4789 Truck trailers; cargo loading & unloading services

Little Ferry
Bergen County

(G-5474)
ALTONA BLOWER & SHTMTL WORK
Also Called: Altona Blower & Shtmtl Works
23 N Washington Ave (07643-1602)
PHONE..................................201 641-3520
Walter Martin, *President*
Robert Class, *Vice Pres*
Chip Martin, *Vice Pres*
Abe Ingersoll, *Project Mgr*
Kelly B Battaglia, *Purch Mgr*
EMP: 9
SQ FT: 5,000
SALES (est): 1.5MM **Privately Held**
WEB: www.altonametal.com
SIC: 1711 3444 Ventilation & duct work contractor; pipe, sheet metal

(G-5475)
BRIX CITY BREWING
4 Alsan Way (07643-1001)
PHONE..................................201 440-0865
EMP: 5
SALES (est): 174.1K **Privately Held**
SIC: 2082 Beer (alcoholic beverage)

(G-5476)
CHIZZYS SERVICE CENTER
Also Called: Chizzy's Truck & Auto Repair
44 Bergen Tpke (07643-1609)
PHONE..................................201 641-7222
Mike Dizmadia, *President*
Matt Dizmadia, *Vice Pres*
EMP: 6
SALES (est): 624.8K **Privately Held**
SIC: 7538 7692 General truck repair; welding repair

(G-5477)
CITY DESIGN GROUP INC
201 Gates Rd Ste C (07643-1919)
PHONE..................................201 329-7711
Lee John, *President*
▲ EMP: 6
SALES (est): 631.9K **Privately Held**
SIC: 2339 Women's & misses' accessories

(G-5478)
CLINTON INDUSTRIES INC
207 Redneck Ave (07643-1320)
PHONE..................................201 440-0400
Harry Klein, *President*
Larry Paricio, *Vice Pres*
Dara Silver, *Vice Pres*
▲ EMP: 45
SQ FT: 25,000
SALES (est): 7MM **Privately Held**
WEB: www.clintonind.com
SIC: 3559 Sewing machines & attachments, industrial

(G-5479)
CLOVER BAGS & PAPER LLC
120 Industrial Ave (07643-1921)
PHONE..................................917 721-6783
EMP: 4
SALES (est): 455.6K **Privately Held**
SIC: 2621 Bag paper

(G-5480)
COMPCO ANALYTICAL INC
215 Gates Rd Ste U (07643-1928)
PHONE..................................201 641-3936
Mark Barenburg, *President*
Helene Barenburg, *Vice Pres*
EMP: 7
SQ FT: 2,500
SALES (est): 730K **Privately Held**
SIC: 7699 7372 5963 Hospital equipment repair services; prepackaged software; direct selling establishments

(G-5481)
DASSAULT AIRCRAFT SVCS CORP (DH)
200 Riser Rd (07643-1226)
PHONE..................................201 440-6700
Peter S Rothwell, *Principal*
Remy St-Martin, *COO*

Nicolas Roger, *Purchasing*
EMP: 11
SALES (est): 1.3MM
SALES (corp-wide): 41.6MM **Privately Held**
SIC: 3721 Aircraft
HQ: Dassault Falcon Jet Corp.
200 Riser Rd
Little Ferry NJ 07643
201 440-6700

(G-5482)
DASSAULT PROCUREMENT SVCS INC (DH)
200 Riser Rd (07643-1226)
PHONE..................................201 261-4130
Patrick Duterpre, *President*
Robin Willson, *Vice Pres*
Haywood Edmonds, *Manager*
EMP: 15
SQ FT: 4,500
SALES (est): 27.5MM
SALES (corp-wide): 41.6MM **Privately Held**
SIC: 5088 3812 Aircraft equipment & supplies; aircraft flight instruments
HQ: Dassault Aviation
Marcel Dassault
Paris 8e Arrondissement 75008
142 253-955

(G-5483)
DREW-WAL MACHINE & TOOL CORP
76 Monroe St (07643-2131)
PHONE..................................201 641-3887
Andrew J Kovach, *President*
Gloria Kovach, *Treasurer*
EMP: 4 EST: 1961
SALES (est): 468.3K **Privately Held**
SIC: 3599 Machine shop, jobbing & repair

(G-5484)
EASYFLEX EAST INC
101 Industrial Ave (07643-1936)
PHONE..................................201 853-9005
Sunmin Kim OH, *CEO*
Yoonsuk OH, *Principal*
▲ EMP: 4
SALES (est): 622K **Privately Held**
SIC: 3312 Stainless steel

(G-5485)
FERRY MACHINE CORP
75 Industrial Ave (07643-1996)
PHONE..................................201 641-9191
Louis Ferretti Jr, *President*
Tom Brock, *Vice Pres*
Susan Brock, *Treasurer*
EMP: 25 EST: 1952
SQ FT: 12,000
SALES (est): 5.2MM **Privately Held**
WEB: www.ferrymachine.com
SIC: 3599 7692 3841 3812 Machine shop, jobbing & repair; welding repair; surgical & medical instruments; search & navigation equipment

(G-5486)
FLAVOUR TEE INTERNATIONAL LLC
66 Industrial Ave (07643-1913)
PHONE..................................201 440-3281
Greg Carrandza, *General Mgr*
Cosmo Verni, *Principal*
EMP: 7
SQ FT: 5,000
SALES (est): 410K **Privately Held**
SIC: 2099 Food preparations

(G-5487)
GLOBE PHOTO ENGRAVING CO LLC
19 N Washington Ave Ste 1 (07643-1693)
PHONE..................................201 489-2300
Charles Mesropian, *Administration*
EMP: 25
SALES (est): 481.3K **Privately Held**
SIC: 2796 Platemaking services

(G-5488)
GLOBE PHOTO ENGRAVING CORP
19 N Washington Ave (07643-1693)
PHONE..................................201 489-2300

Charles Mesropian, *Principal*
Alan Soojian, *Principal*
EMP: 16
SQ FT: 30,000
SALES (est): 2.1MM **Privately Held**
SIC: 2796 7384 Photoengraving plates, linecuts or halftones; photographic services

(G-5489)
IMPACT PRINTING
15 Vogt Ln 1 (07643-1801)
PHONE..................................862 225-9167
Frank Corbiserie, *President*
EMP: 8
SALES (est): 385.4K **Privately Held**
SIC: 2752 Commercial printing, offset

(G-5490)
JJS OWN LTD LIABILITY COMPANY
71 Pickens St (07643-1911)
PHONE..................................551 486-8510
Joy Ortiz,
EMP: 8
SALES (est): 162.2K **Privately Held**
SIC: 2035 Pickles, sauces & salad dressings

(G-5491)
JNT TECHNICAL SERVICES INC
85 Industrial Ave (07643-1901)
PHONE..................................201 641-2130
Glenn F Jorgensen, *President*
EMP: 20
SQ FT: 10,000
SALES (est): 2.9MM **Privately Held**
WEB: www.jnt-tech-serv.com
SIC: 3545 5085 Machine tool accessories; industrial tools

(G-5492)
MAJOR PRODUCTS CO INC (HQ)
66 Industrial Ave (07643-1923)
P.O. Box 675 (07643-0675)
PHONE..................................201 641-5555
Daniel Derose Jr, *President*
Rich Eberhardt, *Business Mgr*
Valerie Leimer, *COO*
Ralph D Rose, *Vice Pres*
Ralph Rose, *Vice Pres*
▲ EMP: 20 EST: 1951
SQ FT: 54,000
SALES (est): 4.7MM **Privately Held**
SIC: 2034 7389 Soup mixes; packaging & labeling services
PA: Major International Limited
Major House, Higham Business Park
Rushden NORTHANTS
193 335-6012

(G-5493)
PAPER DOVE PRESS LLC
16 Monnett St (07643-1212)
PHONE..................................201 641-7938
Laurel Nakai, *Principal*
EMP: 4
SALES (est): 83.8K **Privately Held**
SIC: 2711 Newspapers

(G-5494)
REVERE PLASTICS INC
16 Industrial Ave (07643-1913)
P.O. Box 191480, Boston MA (02119-0028)
PHONE..................................201 641-0777
Fax: 201 641-1086
EMP: 6 EST: 1953
SQ FT: 10,000
SALES (est): 592.3K **Privately Held**
SIC: 3089 2394 Mfg Plastic Products Mfg Canvas/Related Products

(G-5495)
RIEDEL SIGN COMPANY INC
15 Warren St (07643-2006)
PHONE..................................201 641-9121
William F Riedel, *President*
EMP: 5
SALES (est): 549.8K **Privately Held**
WEB: www.riedelsignco.com
SIC: 3993 7389 Signs, not made in custom sign painting shops; sign painting & lettering shop

(G-5496)
SCIENTIFIC DESIGN COMPANY (PA)
49 Industrial Ave (07643-1922)
PHONE..................................201 641-0500
Paul R Lamb, *Principal*
Ashok S Padia, *Principal*
Allan S West, *Vice Pres*
Nabil Rizkalla, *Research*
Steve Allen, *Engineer*
◆ EMP: 126
SALES (est): 49.9MM **Privately Held**
WEB: www.scidesign.com
SIC: 8711 2819 Chemical engineering; catalysts, chemical

(G-5497)
SPIDENT USA INCORPORATED
205 Redneck Ave (07643-1320)
PHONE..................................201 944-0511
Kwang Soon Choi, *President*
▲ EMP: 4
SALES (est): 483.3K **Privately Held**
SIC: 3843 Dental equipment & supplies

(G-5498)
SPIRIT TEX LLC
201 Gates Rd Ste E (07643-1919)
PHONE..................................201 440-1113
Ammar Artani,
EMP: 6
SQ FT: 18,000
SALES (est): 800K **Privately Held**
SIC: 2325 2339 2369 2331 Jeans: men's, youths' & boys'; jeans: women's, misses' & juniors'; jeans: girls', children's & infants'; women's & misses' blouses & shirts; shirts, men's & boys'

Little Silver
Monmouth County

(G-5499)
ALL STRUCTURES LLC
Also Called: Yardworks
21 Rumson Rd (07739-1331)
PHONE..................................732 233-7071
James Mc Allister,
Jamie Mc Allister,
EMP: 5
SALES (est): 272.9K **Privately Held**
SIC: 2452 Panels & sections, prefabricated, wood

(G-5500)
SIMTRONICS CORPORATION
50 Birch Ave Ste 100 (07739-1107)
P.O. Box 38 (07739-0038)
PHONE..................................732 747-0322
Thomas B Judge, *President*
EMP: 10
SALES (est): 988.4K **Privately Held**
WEB: www.simtronics.com
SIC: 7371 3652 7372 Computer software writing services; compact laser discs, prerecorded; application computer software

---

Livingston
Essex County

(G-5501)
A C L EQUIPMENT CORP (PA)
Northfield Rd (07039)
PHONE..................................973 740-9800
Martin Reinfeld, *President*
Nancy Reinfeld, *Vice Pres*
Richard Greenburg, *Treasurer*
EMP: 7
SQ FT: 3,000
SALES (est): 549.3K **Privately Held**
WEB: www.aclequipment.com
SIC: 3993 3669 Electric signs; traffic signals, electric

(G-5502)
ACCESSION DATA SYSTEMS
25 Hickory Pl (07039-3614)
PHONE..................................973 992-7392
Ken Bernstein, *CEO*
EMP: 4

SALES: 200K **Privately Held**
WEB: www.accessiondata.com
SIC: 7372 Prepackaged software

(G-5503)
ALL SOLUTIONS INC
355 Eisenhower Pkwy # 210 (07039-1039)
PHONE.................................973 535-9100
Nalit Patel, *President*
Raj Gupta, *Sales Staff*
EMP: 39 EST: 1991
SQ FT: 7,500
SALES (est): 4.1MM **Privately Held**
WEB: www.aecsi.com
SIC: 8742 7376 7371 7372 Management
  consulting services; computer facilities
  management; custom computer program-
  ming services; prepackaged software;
  telephone communication, except radio

(G-5504)
ALLISON CORP (PA)
15-33 Okner Pkwy (07039-1626)
PHONE.................................973 992-3800
David Dennison, *President*
Stanley Saltz, *Controller*
Cheryl Dennison, *Admin Sec*
◆ EMP: 7 EST: 1960
SQ FT: 100,000
SALES (est): 1.1MM **Privately Held**
WEB: www.allisoncorp.com
SIC: 2211 2221 3714 2842 Automotive
  fabrics, cotton; automotive fabrics, man-
  made fiber; motor vehicle parts & acces-
  sories; deodorants, nonpersonal; motor
  vehicle supplies & new parts

(G-5505)
AMARK INDUSTRIES INC (PA)
Also Called: Kenlen Wire Products Division
293 Eisenhower Pkwy # 100 (07039-1719)
PHONE.................................973 992-8900
Mark Venturi, *CEO*
J P Venturi, *Vice Pres*
EMP: 2
SQ FT: 14,000
SALES: 1.5MM **Privately Held**
SIC: 3315 3451 Wire & fabricated wire
  products; screw machine products

(G-5506)
AMTOPP CORPORATION
9 Peach Tree Hill Rd (07039-5702)
PHONE.................................973 994-8074
Homer Sigh, *President*
John Young, *Principal*
Joanne Shiu, *Manager*
EMP: 900
SALES (est): 100.2MM **Privately Held**
SIC: 3081 Unsupported plastics film &
  sheet

(G-5507)
ATM AFICIONADO LLC
184 S Livingston Ave (07039-3014)
PHONE.................................973 251-2115
Mark Teitelbaum,
EMP: 7 EST: 2010
SALES (est): 707.7K **Privately Held**
SIC: 3629 Electrical industrial apparatus

(G-5508)
CAMPAK INC
Also Called: Tecnicam
119 Naylon Ave (07039-1005)
PHONE.................................973 994-4888
Thomas Miller, *CEO*
Donna Anderson, *Sales Mgr*
Brian Oliver, *Sales Engr*
▲ EMP: 9
SQ FT: 25,000
SALES (est): 3.6MM **Privately Held**
WEB: www.campak.com
SIC: 5084 3565 Packaging machinery &
  equipment; packaging machinery

(G-5509)
CUSTOM CONVERTERS INC
115 Naylon Ave (07039-1005)
PHONE.................................973 994-9000
Mark Krause, *President*
▲ EMP: 10 EST: 1982
SQ FT: 15,000
SALES (est): 2MM **Privately Held**
WEB: www.customconverters.com
SIC: 2679 Paper products, converted

(G-5510)
DMF ASSOCIATED ENGINES LLC
W Hobart Gap Rd (07039)
PHONE.................................973 535-9773
Dennis Bodor,
EMP: 100
SALES (est): 5.9MM **Privately Held**
SIC: 3694 Engine electrical equipment

(G-5511)
FORMOSA PLASTICS CORP USA (PA)
Also Called: Fpc USA
9 Peach Tree Hill Rd (07039-5702)
PHONE.................................973 992-2090
Jason Lin, *President*
Paula Ellentuch, *Editor*
Is Hwang, *Assistant VP*
Walter Chen, *Vice Pres*
Tony Chen, *Project Mgr*
◆ EMP: 340
SQ FT: 225,000
SALES (est): 1.2B **Privately Held**
WEB: www.fpcusa.com
SIC: 2821 Polyvinyl chloride resins
  (PVC); vinyl resins; caustic soda, sodium
  hydroxide

(G-5512)
FRANKLIN MILLER INC
60 Okner Pkwy (07039-1604)
PHONE.................................973 535-9200
William Galanty, *President*
Beth Rothenberg, *Corp Secy*
◆ EMP: 50 EST: 1918
SQ FT: 12,000
SALES (est): 15.2MM **Privately Held**
WEB: www.franklinmiller.com
SIC: 3559 3589 Refinery, chemical pro-
  cessing & similar machinery; sewage
  treatment equipment

(G-5513)
GEORGE PRESS INC
74 S Livingston Ave (07039-3009)
PHONE.................................973 992-7797
George Press, *President*
Shelley Hopmayer, *Sales Staff*
▲ EMP: 13
SALES (est): 1.7MM **Privately Held**
SIC: 5944 3911 Jewelry, precious stones
  & precious metals; jewelry, precious metal

(G-5514)
HYMAN W FISHER INC
121 E Northfield Rd (07039-4506)
PHONE.................................973 992-9155
Hyman Fisher, *President*
EMP: 7
SALES (est): 348.7K **Privately Held**
SIC: 8742 2741 7389 Incentive or award
  program consultant; technical papers:
  publishing only, not printed on site; con-
  vention & show services

(G-5515)
INTEPLAST GROUP CORPORATION (PA)
Also Called: Bopp Films
9 Peach Tree Hill Rd (07039-5702)
PHONE.................................973 994-8000
John Young, *Ch of Bd*
Homer Shieh, *President*
Marie Zagada, *President*
Andy Chen, *General Mgr*
Yiren Wang, *Business Mgr*
◆ EMP: 300
SQ FT: 20,000
SALES (est): 1.1B **Privately Held**
WEB: www.inteplast.com
SIC: 2673 Bags: plastic, laminated &
  coated

(G-5516)
INTRINSIQ SPCLTY SOLUTIONS INC
354 Eisenhower Pkwy # 2025
(07039-1022)
PHONE.................................973 251-2039
Michael Custode, *President*
Nestor Olivier, *CFO*
EMP: 42
SQ FT: 6,300

SALES (est): 2.4MM **Privately Held**
WEB: www.meridianemr.net
SIC: 7372 Business oriented computer
  software

(G-5517)
J-M MANUFACTURING COMPANY INC
Also Called: J-M Eagle
9 Peach Tree Hill Rd (07039-5702)
PHONE.................................800 621-4404
Walter Wang, *Manager*
EMP: 83
SALES (corp-wide): 1B **Privately Held**
PA: J-M Manufacturing Company, Inc.
  5200 W Century Blvd
  Los Angeles CA 90045
  800 621-4404
SIC: 2821 Polyvinyl chloride resins (PVC)

(G-5518)
LARACCAS MANUFACTURING INC
29 Manor Rd (07039-3848)
PHONE.................................973 571-1452
Anthony Laracca, *President*
EMP: 20
SALES (est): 3MM **Privately Held**
SIC: 2452 Prefabricated wood buildings

(G-5519)
LITHOS ESTIATORIO LTD LBLTY CO
405 Eisenhower Pkwy (07039-1000)
PHONE.................................973 758-1111
Lithos Estiatorio, *Principal*
EMP: 5
SALES (est): 337.6K **Privately Held**
SIC: 2752 Commercial printing, litho-
  graphic

(G-5520)
LIVINGSTON BAGEL WARREN INC
37 E Northfield Rd (07039-4501)
P.O. Box 1638 (07039-7238)
PHONE.................................973 994-1915
Sol Snyder, *President*
Rita Snyder, *Corp Secy*
EMP: 28 EST: 1969
SQ FT: 2,500
SALES (est): 1.6MM **Privately Held**
SIC: 5461 5149 5812 2051 Bagels; bak-
  ery products; delicatessen (eating
  places); bread, cake & related products

(G-5521)
LRK SEATING PRODUCTS LLC
Also Called: Seating Expert
15 Melrose Dr (07039-2430)
PHONE.................................973 462-2743
Edward Rakovsky, *President*
EMP: 4
SQ FT: 4,500
SALES (est): 155.8K **Privately Held**
SIC: 2599 Bar, restaurant & cafeteria furni-
  ture

(G-5522)
M4 MACHINE LLC
7 Industrial Pkwy Ste 18 (07039-1647)
PHONE.................................718 928-9695
Matthew Allen, *President*
EMP: 5
SALES (est): 167.6K **Privately Held**
SIC: 3599 Machine & other job shop work

(G-5523)
MAX PRO SERVICES LLC
Also Called: Total Relief Services
184 S Livingston Ave (07039-3014)
PHONE.................................973 396-2373
Donald Dauphin, *Mng Member*
EMP: 6
SALES (est): 244.5K **Privately Held**
WEB: www.maxproservices.com
SIC: 6531 6163 7389 3953 Selling agent,
  real estate; buying agent, real estate;
  agents, farm or business loan; legal & tax
  services; seal presses, notary & hand

(G-5524)
MILESTONE EDUCATION LLC
220 S Orange Ave (07039-5804)
PHONE.................................973 535-2717

EMP: 5 EST: 2013
SALES (est): 200.5K
SALES (corp-wide): 2.7MM **Privately Held**
SIC: 3843 Dental equipment & supplies
PA: Shenzhen Superline Technology Co.,
  Ltd.
  No.314, Suite B, Shaheshiji Holiday
  Square, N Anshan District
  Shenzhen 51805
  755 260-1615

(G-5525)
MILESTONE SCIENTIFIC INC (PA)
220 S Orange Ave Ste 102 (07039-5800)
PHONE.................................973 535-2717
Leonard A Osser, *CEO*
Leslie Bernhard, *Ch of Bd*
Joseph D'Agostino, *COO*
Keisha Harcum, *Controller*
Laura Kaunitz, *Office Mgr*
▲ EMP: 14 EST: 1989
SQ FT: 7,625
SALES: 9.6MM **Publicly Held**
WEB: www.milesci.com
SIC: 3843 Dental equipment & supplies;
  dental equipment; dental hand instru-
  ments; dental laboratory equipment

(G-5526)
MIND-ALLIANCE SYSTEMS LLC
21 Herbert Ter (07039-4803)
PHONE.................................212 920-1911
David Kamien, *Mng Member*
Romit Chatterjee, *Director*
EMP: 7
SALES (est): 433.1K **Privately Held**
SIC: 7372 8741 7379 Prepackaged soft-
  ware; business management; computer
  related consulting services

(G-5527)
MOBLTY INC
651 W Mount Pleasant Ave # 270
(07039-1600)
PHONE.................................973 535-3600
Rajesh Saggi, *CEO*
Rich Ullrich, *COO*
Ken Aufiero, *Exec VP*
Peter Dugan, *Exec VP*
Ankush Khurana, *Officer*
EMP: 20
SQ FT: 8,000
SALES: 1MM **Privately Held**
SIC: 7372 Business oriented computer
  software

(G-5528)
MORRIS PLAINS PIP INC
Also Called: PIP Printing
465 W Mount Pleasant Ave (07039-1720)
PHONE.................................973 533-9330
Steven Solotoss, *President*
Sandra Colyer, *Corp Secy*
EMP: 8
SQ FT: 1,800
SALES (est): 866.5K **Privately Held**
SIC: 2752 2791 2789 Commercial print-
  ing, offset; typesetting; bookbinding & re-
  lated work

(G-5529)
NAN YA PLASTICS CORP AMERICA (PA)
9 Peach Tree Hill Rd (07039-5702)
P.O. Box 478 (07039-0478)
PHONE.................................973 992-1775
Chia-Chau Wu, *President*
William Wong, *Chairman*
David Lin, *Treasurer*
George Chang, *Controller*
Harry Siazon, *Credit Mgr*
◆ EMP: 16
SQ FT: 5,000
SALES (est): 1B **Privately Held**
WEB: www.npcam.com
SIC: 2824 2869 3083 Polyester fibers;
  ethylene glycols; laminated plastics plate
  & sheet

(G-5530)
NAN YA PLASTICS CORP USA (HQ)
9 Peach Tree Hill Rd (07039-5702)
P.O. Box 478 (07039-0478)
PHONE....................................973 992-1775
William Wong, *Ch of Bd*
Chia-Chau Wu, *President*
David Lin, *Treasurer*
Alice Nightingale, *Admin Sec*
▲ EMP: 20
SQ FT: 5,000
SALES: 113MM
SALES (corp-wide): 10.7B **Privately Held**
WEB: www.npcusa.com
SIC: 2821 Plastics materials & resins
PA: Nan Ya Plastics Corporation
201, Dunhua N. Rd.,
Taipei City TAP 10508
227 122-211

(G-5531)
NANION TECHNOLOGIES INC
1 Naylon Pl Ste 3 (07039-1041)
PHONE....................................973 369-7960
Niels Fertig, *CEO*
Professor Jan Behrends, *Ch of Bd*
Rodolfo Haedo, *Senior VP*
Sonja Stlzle-Feix, *Director*
EMP: 8
SALES (est): 474.3K **Privately Held**
SIC: 3825 Instruments to measure electricity

(G-5532)
NIAFLEX CORPORATION
9 Peach Tree Hill Rd (07039-5702)
PHONE....................................407 851-6620
Jo Chen, *President*
James Smell, *Vice Pres*
EMP: 10 EST: 2010
SALES (est): 1.4MM **Privately Held**
SIC: 3081 Unsupported plastics film & sheet

(G-5533)
P D SALCO INC
61 Shrewsbury Dr (07039-3401)
PHONE....................................973 716-0517
Jeffrey Namer, *President*
Brandi Namer, *Vice Pres*
EMP: 11
SALES (est): 579.3K **Privately Held**
SIC: 2721 5192 Periodicals; books, periodicals & newspapers

(G-5534)
PENTA INTERNATIONAL CORP
Also Called: Penta Manufacturing Company
50 Okner Pkwy (07039-1604)
P.O. Box 1448, Caldwell (07007-1448)
PHONE....................................973 740-2300
Grace M Volpe, *President*
George Volpe Sr, *Senior VP*
Christine Tavares, *Vice Pres*
▲ EMP: 75
SQ FT: 100,000
SALES (est): 16MM **Privately Held**
WEB: www.pentamfg.com
SIC: 2087 Extracts, flavoring

(G-5535)
PET DEVICES LLC
184 S Livingston Ave (07039-3014)
PHONE....................................929 244-0012
Dimitri Vorona, *Mng Member*
EMP: 4
SQ FT: 1,000
SALES: 1MM **Privately Held**
SIC: 2048 Feed supplements

(G-5536)
PLASTPRO 2000 INC
Also Called: Plastpro Doors
9 Peach Tree Hill Rd (07039-5702)
PHONE....................................973 992-2090
Walter Wang, *Branch Mgr*
EMP: 6 **Privately Held**
WEB: www.plastproinc.com
SIC: 3089 Plastic hardware & building products
PA: Plastpro 2000, Inc.
5200 W Century Blvd Fl 9
Los Angeles CA 90045

(G-5537)
RECOMBINE LLC
3 Regent St Ste 301 (07039-1638)
PHONE....................................646 470-7422
Alicia Pagano, *Sales Mgr*
Stephanie Sehnert, *Marketing Staff*
Paul Fisher, *CTO*
Santiago Munne, *Officer*
Alexander Bisignano,
▲ EMP: 6 EST: 2011
SQ FT: 4,000
SALES (est): 300K **Privately Held**
SIC: 2835 In vitro diagnostics

(G-5538)
ROSEVILLE TOOL & MANUFACTURING
22 Okner Pkwy (07039-1604)
PHONE....................................973 992-5405
Gideon Schuftan, *President*
Louise Schuftan, *Corp Secy*
EMP: 25 EST: 1945
SQ FT: 13,000
SALES (est): 4.1MM **Privately Held**
SIC: 3469 3544 Stamping metal for the trade; special dies, tools, jigs & fixtures

(G-5539)
SERVICES EQUIPMENT COM LLC
4 Tamarack Dr (07039-1115)
P.O. Box 2032 (07039-7632)
PHONE....................................973 992-4404
Harvey Kahn, *Partner*
EMP: 4
SALES (est): 220.7K **Privately Held**
SIC: 3999 5131 Military insignia; flags & banners

(G-5540)
SHARKK LLC
70 S Orange Ave Ste 105 (07039-4916)
PHONE....................................302 377-3974
Dov Brafman, *CEO*
Isaac Rubinstein, *CTO*
Dovi Vogel, *Director*
EMP: 11 EST: 2011
SALES (est): 90.3K **Privately Held**
SIC: 3651 Speaker systems

(G-5541)
SIGNAL SIGN COMPANY LLC
105 Dorsa Ave (07039-1002)
PHONE....................................973 535-9277
Peggy Johnson, *Plant Mgr*
Bruce J Fish,
EMP: 12 EST: 1956
SQ FT: 15,000
SALES (est): 2MM **Privately Held**
WEB: www.signalsign.com
SIC: 3993 Electric signs; neon signs; letters for signs, metal

(G-5542)
STRIVR INC
20 Downing Pl (07039-3613)
PHONE....................................973 216-7379
Zachary Gray, *President*
Michael Manuccia, *COO*
Brian Murphy, *Vice Pres*
Zack Miller, *Opers Staff*
Veronique Lafargue, *VP Mktg*
EMP: 4
SALES (est): 235.5K **Privately Held**
SIC: 7372 7389 Application computer software;

(G-5543)
TRINITY PLASTICS INC (DH)
9 Peach Tree Hill Rd (07039-5702)
PHONE....................................973 994-8018
Joe Chen, *President*
▲ EMP: 135 EST: 2013
SALES (est): 98.5MM **Privately Held**
SIC: 2673 3081 Bags: plastic, laminated & coated; unsupported plastics film & sheet

(G-5544)
UTILITY DEVELOPMENT CORP
112 Naylon Ave (07039-1006)
PHONE....................................973 994-4334
Harry S Katz, *President*
Dr Radha Agarwal, *Vice Pres*
Toby Katz, *Shareholder*
EMP: 6

SQ FT: 5,000
SALES (est): 1MM **Privately Held**
SIC: 3086 8742 Packaging & shipping materials, foamed plastic; business consultant

(G-5545)
VANCO MILLWORK INC
18 Microlab Rd (07039-1639)
PHONE....................................973 992-3061
Lyn F Vanadia, *President*
Steven Vanadia, *Vice Pres*
EMP: 12
SALES (est): 1.4MM
SALES (corp-wide): 4.4MM **Privately Held**
WEB: www.vancoconstruction.com
SIC: 5211 2431 Millwork & lumber; millwork
PA: Vanco Construction Inc.
18 Microlab Rd
Livingston NJ 07039
973 994-0616

(G-5546)
VERSATILE DISTRIBUTORS INC
Also Called: American Jewel Window Systems
293 Eisenhower Pkwy # 100 (07039-1711)
PHONE....................................973 773-0550
Joel Cuccio, *CEO*
Todd Cuccio, *Plant Mgr*
EMP: 55 EST: 1946
SQ FT: 42,000
SALES (est): 9.4MM **Privately Held**
WEB: www.grovehomeproducts.com
SIC: 3089 Window frames & sash, plastic

(G-5547)
WEST ESSEX TRIBUNE INC
495 S Livingston Ave (07039-4327)
P.O. Box 65 (07039-0065)
PHONE....................................973 992-1771
Jennifer Cheiuk, *President*
Ellen Haerte, *Corp Secy*
EMP: 10 EST: 1929
SQ FT: 2,000
SALES (est): 680.4K **Privately Held**
SIC: 2711 Newspapers: publishing only, not printed on site

(G-5548)
WESTCHESTER LACE & TEXTILES
70 S Orange Ave Ste 220 (07039-4920)
PHONE....................................201 864-2150
Leonard Edelson, *President*
▲ EMP: 120
SALES (est): 9.9MM **Privately Held**
WEB: www.westchesterlace.com
SIC: 2258 Lace & lace products

(G-5549)
WIRE FABRICATORS & INSULATORS
20 Harding Pl (07039-1804)
PHONE....................................973 768-2839
Frank Basile, *President*
Tom Palmisano, *Manager*
EMP: 25 EST: 1963
SQ FT: 34,000
SALES: 952K **Privately Held**
SIC: 3357 3315 3496 Coaxial cable, nonferrous; cable, steel: insulated or armored; miscellaneous fabricated wire products

---

Lodi
Bergen County

(G-5550)
AERONAUTICAL INSTR & RDO CO (PA)
234 Garibaldi Ave (07644-2506)
P.O. Box 340 (07644-0340)
PHONE....................................973 473-0034
Abigail Burke, *CEO*
Wilfred Burke, *President*
Mario Lousada, *Controller*
Cyril Burke, *Manager*
Anne Burke, *Admin Sec*
EMP: 30
SQ FT: 10,000

SALES (est): 4.2MM **Privately Held**
SIC: 3812 3825 Radio magnetic instrumentation; test equipment for electronic & electrical circuits

(G-5551)
ALBA TRANSLATIONS CPA
436 Main St (07644-1856)
PHONE....................................973 340-1130
Alba Translations, *Principal*
EMP: 8
SALES (est): 88.7K **Privately Held**
SIC: 7692 Welding repair

(G-5552)
ALL STATE MEDAL CO INC
Also Called: Hock & Mandel
16 Adams Pl (07644-2928)
PHONE....................................973 458-1458
Richard J Micucci Sr, *President*
Richard J Micucci Jr, *Vice Pres*
EMP: 6
SALES (est): 490K **Privately Held**
SIC: 3499 5999 3911 Trophies, metal, except silver; trophies & plaques; jewelry, precious metal

(G-5553)
AMERIFAB CORP
196 Garibaldi Ave Ste 1 (07644-2506)
PHONE....................................973 777-2120
Tom Castell, *President*
EMP: 6
SQ FT: 4,000
SALES (est): 1MM **Privately Held**
SIC: 3444 Sheet metalwork

(G-5554)
BLUTEK POWER INC
300 1 State Rte 17 Ste B2 (07644)
PHONE....................................973 594-1800
Angelo Lopresti, *President*
▲ EMP: 10
SALES (est): 1.5MM **Privately Held**
WEB: www.blutekpower.com
SIC: 3621 Motors & generators

(G-5555)
BRIM ELECTRONICS INC
120 Home Pl (07644-1514)
P.O. Box 336, Fair Lawn (07410-0336)
PHONE....................................201 796-2886
Barry Danziger, *President*
EMP: 15
SQ FT: 5,000
SALES: 1MM **Privately Held**
WEB: www.brimelectronics.com
SIC: 3357 3678 3643 3429 Nonferrous wiredrawing & insulating; electronic connectors; current-carrying wiring devices; manufactured hardware (general)

(G-5556)
CHARLES DELUCA
Also Called: Associated Marble Co
239 Garibaldi Ave (07644-2505)
PHONE....................................973 778-5621
Charles Deluca, *Owner*
Charles De Luca Jr, *Manager*
EMP: 6
SQ FT: 4,600
SALES (est): 551.2K **Privately Held**
SIC: 3281 Marble, building: cut & shaped

(G-5557)
CRONOS-PRIM COLORADO LLC
Also Called: Cronos Design
300-2 State Rt 17 S Ste C (07644-3822)
P.O. Box 221762, Denver CO (80222-1020)
PHONE....................................303 369-7477
Gary Yurkovetskiy,
Mark Yurkovetskiy,
EMP: 5
SQ FT: 1,500
SALES (est): 521.8K **Privately Held**
SIC: 3442 2541 7389 Window & door frames; cabinets, lockers & shelving; interior design services

(G-5558)
DINA HERNANDEZ
Also Called: Orlando's Italian Bakery
236 Harrison Ave Ste A (07644-1051)
PHONE....................................973 772-8883
Dina Hernandez, *Partner*

EMP: 7
SQ FT: 6,000
SALES (est): 692.9K **Privately Held**
SIC: 2051 5461 Breads, rolls & buns; bakeries

(G-5559)
DO PRODUCTIONS LLC
11 Gregg St (07644-2704)
PHONE.....................856 866-3566
Christian Von Twinkle,
EMP: 80
SALES (est): 12.1MM
SALES (corp-wide): 8.4B **Privately Held**
SIC: 2038 Frozen specialties
HQ: Dr. Oetker Gmbh
Lutterstr. 14
Bielefeld 33617
521 155-0

(G-5560)
DUX PAINT LLC
18 Mill St (07644-2604)
PHONE.....................973 473-2376
Howard Goldstein, *President*
EMP: 10
SALES (est): 1.4MM **Privately Held**
SIC: 2851 1721 7532 Paints & paint additives; exterior residential painting contractor; truck painting & lettering

(G-5561)
DWILL AMERICA LLC
174 Terrace Ave (07644-2907)
PHONE.....................201 561-5737
Daniel Hong, *Mng Member*
EMP: 4
SALES (est): 407.1K **Privately Held**
SIC: 3679 Antennas, receiving

(G-5562)
FEDERAL EQUIPMENT & MFG CO INC
Also Called: Femco
194 Westervelt Pl (07644-1100)
PHONE.....................973 340-7600
Joan Giani, *President*
Douglas Howard, *Vice Pres*
EMP: 7
SQ FT: 3,400
SALES (est): 4.4MM **Privately Held**
SIC: 5085 2676 Industrial supplies; towels, napkins & tissue paper products

(G-5563)
H K METAL CRAFT MFG CORP
35 Industrial Rd (07644-2607)
PHONE.....................973 471-7770
Raymond Hopp, *President*
Nancy Hopp, *Corp Secy*
Robert Osborn, *COO*
▲ **EMP:** 38 EST: 1927
SQ FT: 58,000
SALES (est): 8.7MM **Privately Held**
WEB: www.hkmetalcraft.com
SIC: 3469 3452 3053 Stamping metal for the trade; washers, metal; gaskets & sealing devices

(G-5564)
HAWTHORNE PAINT COMPANY INC
18 Mill St (07644-2604)
PHONE.....................973 423-2335
Murray Greene, *CEO*
EMP: 9
SQ FT: 15,000
SALES (est): 1.9MM **Privately Held**
WEB: www.hawthornepaints.com
SIC: 2851 5231 Paints & paint additives; paint & painting supplies

(G-5565)
HOUSE PEARL FASHIONS (US) LTD (HQ)
300-2 D&E Rr 17 (07644)
PHONE.....................973 778-7551
Mehesh Seth, *President*
Paritosh Nath, *COO*
Sanjay Kapoor, *CFO*
▼ **EMP:** 15
SQ FT: 22,000

SALES: 15.5MM
SALES (corp-wide): 118.5MM **Privately Held**
SIC: 2329 2339 Coats (oiled fabric, leatherette, etc.): men's & boys'; women's & misses' outerwear
PA: Pearl Global Industries Limited
Pearl Tower, Plot No. 51, Sector 32
Gurgaon HR 12200
124 465-1000

(G-5566)
J D M ASSOCIATES INC
127 Kipp Ave (07644-3037)
PHONE.....................973 773-8699
Joseph Mastropaolo, *President*
Dorothy Mastropaolo, *Vice Pres*
EMP: 8
SALES (est): 892.8K **Privately Held**
SIC: 7336 2752 7313 2741 Art design services; promotional printing, lithographic; printed media advertising representatives; miscellaneous publishing

(G-5567)
LABEL MASTER INC
89 Dell Glen Ave (07644-1707)
PHONE.....................973 546-3110
Robert Mazzella, *President*
EMP: 9
SQ FT: 6,500
SALES (est): 1MM **Privately Held**
WEB: www.labelmaster.net
SIC: 2754 2672 Labels: gravure printing; tape, pressure sensitive: made from purchased materials

(G-5568)
LOBSTER LIFE SYSTEMS INC
10 Dell Glen Ave Ste 5a (07644-1759)
P.O. Box 839, Saddle Brook (07663-0839)
PHONE.....................201 398-0303
Thomas Olsen, *President*
EMP: 11 EST: 1987
SALES (est): 1.7MM **Privately Held**
WEB: www.lobsterlife.com
SIC: 3443 Water tanks, metal plate

(G-5569)
LODI CML COOPERATIVE LLC
170 Gregg St Ste 5 (07644-2620)
PHONE.....................201 820-2380
Wael Kioumji, *Principal*
EMP: 8
SALES (est): 987K **Privately Held**
SIC: 2051 Doughnuts, except frozen

(G-5570)
MARCO BOOK CO INC
Also Called: Everbind Marco
60 Industrial Rd (07644-2608)
P.O. Box 150, Greens Farms CT (06838-0150)
PHONE.....................973 458-0485
Stewart Penn, *CEO*
EMP: 50 EST: 1954
SQ FT: 52,000
SALES (est): 22.2MM **Privately Held**
SIC: 5192 2789 Books; bookbinding & related work

(G-5571)
MCCAIN ELLIOS FOODS INC
11 Gregg St (07644-2704)
PHONE.....................201 368-0600
Tim Driscoll, *President*
Van S Chaayk, *President*
Mark Bohen, *Vice Pres*
H McCain, *Vice Pres*
Peter Reijula, *Vice Pres*
EMP: 160
SQ FT: 150,000
SALES (est): 17.7MM
SALES (corp-wide): 19.5B **Privately Held**
SIC: 2038 Pizza, frozen
HQ: Mccain Usa, Inc.
1 Tower Ln Ste Uppr
Oakbrook Terrace IL 60181

(G-5572)
MINT PRINTING LLC
475 Westminster Pl (07644-1234)
PHONE.....................973 546-2060
Thomas Davis,
Nick Tarthelia,
EMP: 4

SALES: 978.3K **Privately Held**
SIC: 2752 Commercial printing, lithographic

(G-5573)
PRECIOUS COSMETICS PACKAGING
40 Meta Ln (07644-3807)
PHONE.....................973 478-4633
Sam Mikhail, *President*
Sanaa Mikhail, *Vice Pres*
▲ **EMP:** 14
SALES (est): 1.3MM **Privately Held**
SIC: 2844 5122 Cosmetic preparations; cosmetics

(G-5574)
RHINGO PRO LLC
32 Us Highway 46 E (07644-1309)
PHONE.....................201 728-9099
Kevin Jung, *CEO*
EMP: 4
SALES (est): 200.7K **Privately Held**
SIC: 3641 Electric lamps & parts for generalized applications; electric light bulbs, complete; tubes, electric light

(G-5575)
SILVERSTONE WIRELESS LLC (PA)
6 9 Park Pl (07644)
PHONE.....................845 458-5197
Jay Friedman, *CEO*
Joel Friedman,
▲ **EMP:** 8
SQ FT: 3,000
SALES (est): 8MM **Privately Held**
SIC: 3679 5271 Electronic circuits; mobile homes

(G-5576)
STAR NARROW FABRICS INC
Also Called: Star Group, The
80a Industrial Rd (07644-2619)
PHONE.....................973 778-8600
Michael Freidman, *President*
Marc Abeles, *Vice Pres*
Carolina Risso, *Accounts Exec*
▲ **EMP:** 6
SQ FT: 26,600
SALES (est): 722.5K **Privately Held**
SIC: 2759 2269 7336 2282 Labels & seals: printing; labels, cotton: printed; commercial art & graphic design; throwing & winding mills

(G-5577)
SUBURBAN AUTO SEAT CO INC (PA)
35 Industrial Rd (07644-2607)
PHONE.....................973 778-9227
Robert G Winfield, *President*
Jane Lee Winfield, *Admin Sec*
◆ **EMP:** 13 EST: 1945
SQ FT: 3,000
SALES (est): 1.7MM **Privately Held**
WEB: www.suburbanseats.com
SIC: 2531 5013 7532 Vehicle furniture; truck parts & accessories; interior repair services

(G-5578)
SUFFERN PLATING CORP
210 Garibaldi Ave (07644-2506)
P.O. Box 755 (07644-0755)
PHONE.....................973 473-4404
Philip Landau, *President*
Nilofar Khaledi, *QC Mgr*
David French, *CFO*
EMP: 42 EST: 1949
SQ FT: 25,000
SALES (est): 6.1MM **Privately Held**
SIC: 3471 Electroplating of metals or formed products

(G-5579)
SYNTHETIC GRASS SURFACES INC
Also Called: Synthetic Grass Surfaces NJ
6 Robert Ct (07644-3504)
PHONE.....................973 778-9594
Robert McLaren, *President*
EMP: 4
SALES: 15K **Privately Held**
SIC: 3999 Grasses, artificial & preserved

(G-5580)
TONY JONES APPAREL INC
Also Called: Clench
300-1 State Rt 17 S 1c (07644-3821)
PHONE.....................973 773-6200
John Yi, *President*
▲ **EMP:** 6
SALES: 5.4MM **Privately Held**
SIC: 2329 5136 Men's & boys' sportswear & athletic clothing; men's & boys' outerwear

(G-5581)
UVITEC PRINTING INK CO INC
14 Mill St (07644-2604)
PHONE.....................973 778-0737
George Dakos, *Ch of Bd*
Andrew Dakos, *President*
EMP: 20
SQ FT: 12,000
SALES (est): 4.1MM **Privately Held**
WEB: www.uvitec.com
SIC: 2893 2851 2821 Printing ink; coating, air curing; plastics materials & resins

(G-5582)
VITAMIA PASTA BOY INC
Also Called: Vitamia & Sons
206 Harrison Ave Ste 214 (07644-1013)
PHONE.....................973 546-1140
Anthony Vitamia, *President*
Maria Vitamia, *Vice Pres*
Joseph Vitamia, *Treasurer*
Paul Vitamia, *Admin Sec*
▲ **EMP:** 10
SQ FT: 2,500
SALES (est): 1MM **Privately Held**
SIC: 2026 2098 2099 5451 Pot cheese; macaroni & spaghetti; pasta, uncooked: packaged with other ingredients; cheese; bakery: wholesale or wholesale/retail combined; pickles, sauces & salad dressings

(G-5583)
WOOD & LAMINATES INC
102 Us Highway 46 E (07644-3608)
PHONE.....................973 773-7475
Gabriel Salazar, *President*
▲ **EMP:** 7
SQ FT: 5,000
SALES (est): 1MM **Privately Held**
WEB: www.wlbars.com
SIC: 1751 3083 Cabinet building & installation; laminated plastics plate & sheet

---

Logan Township
Gloucester County

(G-5584)
ADVANCED DRAINAGE SYSTEMS INC
Also Called: ADS
300 Progress Ct (08085-4539)
PHONE.....................856 467-4779
Bruce Schlichter, *Manager*
EMP: 60
SALES (corp-wide): 1.3B **Publicly Held**
WEB: www.ads-pipe.com
SIC: 3084 Plastics pipe
PA: Advanced Drainage Systems, Inc.
4640 Trueman Blvd
Hilliard OH 43026
614 658-0050

(G-5585)
ARYSTA LLC
Also Called: Arysta/ Labrea Bakery
11 Technology Dr (08085-1761)
PHONE.....................856 417-8100
Tom Bent, *General Mgr*
EMP: 7 EST: 2012
SALES (est): 928.8K **Privately Held**
SIC: 2052 Bakery products, dry

(G-5586)
CUSTOM BUILDING PRODUCTS INC
2115 High Hill Rd (08085-4529)
PHONE.....................856 467-9226
Steven Sabatino, *Manager*
EMP: 60 **Privately Held**
WEB: www.custombuildingproducts.com

SIC: 2891 Adhesives & sealants
HQ: Custom Building Products, Inc.
7711 Center Ave Ste 500
Huntington Beach CA 92647
800 272-8786

(G-5587)
ENGINRED ARRSTING SYSTEMS CORP
Also Called: Engineered Mtl Arresting Sys
2239 High Hill Rd (08085-4531)
PHONE..................................856 241-8620
John Matish, *Maint Spvr*
Kevin Quan, *Engineer*
Hong Zou, *Engineer*
EMP: 26
SALES (corp-wide): 833.4MM **Privately Held**
SIC: 3728 Aircraft landing assemblies & brakes
HQ: Engineered Arresting Systems Corporation
2550 Market St
Upper Chichester PA 19014
610 494-8000

(G-5588)
INFINITY COMPOUNDING LLC
Also Called: Infinity Ltl Engnred Compounds
2079 Center Square Rd (08085-1790)
PHONE..................................856 467-3030
Carlos Carreno, *President*
John Cusick, *Manager*
Dan Magee, *Technology*
▲ EMP: 40
SQ FT: 57,000
SALES: 15MM
SALES (corp-wide): 206MM **Privately Held**
WEB: www.infinitycompounding.com
SIC: 2821 Molding compounds, plastics
PA: Americhem, Inc.
2000 Americhem Way
Cuyahoga Falls OH 44221
330 929-4213

(G-5589)
UPTOWN BAKERIES
Also Called: Uptown Bagels
300 Eagle Ct (08085-1847)
PHONE..................................856 467-9552
Alfred Neuhauser, *Owner*
EMP: 150
SALES (est): 13MM **Privately Held**
SIC: 2051 5149 Bagels, fresh or frozen; bakery products

(G-5590)
VERONI USA INC
1110 Commerce Blvd # 200 (08085-1765)
PHONE..................................609 970-0320
Antonio Corsano, *CEO*
Marco Veroni, *President*
EMP: 28
SQ FT: 50,000
SALES (est): 105.9MM **Privately Held**
SIC: 2011 Cured meats from meat slaughtered on site

Long Beach Township
Ocean County

(G-5591)
MELTDOWN
13302 Long Beach Blvd (08008-2742)
PHONE..................................609 207-0527
Drew Merlo, *Manager*
EMP: 4
SALES (est): 287.8K **Privately Held**
SIC: 2052 Cones, ice cream

(G-5592)
NETX INFORMATION SYSTEMS INC (PA)
76 Auburn Rd (08008-7009)
PHONE..................................609 298-9118
Keith Saltstein, *President*
EMP: 19
SALES (est): 3.5MM **Privately Held**
WEB: www.netxinc.com
SIC: 7371 7372 Computer software development; educational computer software

Long Branch
Monmouth County

(G-5593)
ACCUCOLOR LLC (PA)
Also Called: Jamm Litho
185 Broadway (07740-7005)
PHONE..................................732 870-1999
Robert Labella, *President*
EMP: 4
SQ FT: 5,000
SALES (est): 613.9K **Privately Held**
SIC: 2752 Commercial printing, offset

(G-5594)
BRAD GARMAN DESIGNS
30 New Ct (07740-5103)
PHONE..................................732 229-6670
Brad Garman, *Owner*
EMP: 5
SALES (est): 220K **Privately Held**
SIC: 3911 Jewelry mountings & trimmings

(G-5595)
COOPER WHEELOCK INC
Also Called: Cooper Notification
273 Branchport Ave (07740-6830)
PHONE..................................732 222-6880
Scott Hearn, *President*
David Larry, *Vice Pres*
Brian Jones, *Purch Mgr*
Joe Kosich, *Engineer*
Simi Kaur, *Electrical Engi*
◆ EMP: 375 EST: 1833
SQ FT: 75,000
SALES (est): 60.1MM **Privately Held**
SIC: 3663 3669 Pagers (one-way); signaling apparatus, electric
HQ: Cooper Industries, Llc
600 Travis St Ste 5400
Houston TX 77002
713 209-8400

(G-5596)
CREATIVE PRODUCTS INC
92 Shrewsbury Dr (07740-7619)
PHONE..................................732 614-9035
Mary Amgers, *President*
Barry Papp, *Vice Pres*
EMP: 52
SALES: 65K **Privately Held**
SIC: 5083 3524 7389 Lawn & garden machinery & equipment; lawn & garden equipment;

(G-5597)
FRUTA LOCA LLC
547 Broadway Fl 1 (07740-5950)
PHONE..................................732 642-8233
Dalia Lopez, *Owner*
EMP: 4
SALES (est): 228.6K **Privately Held**
SIC: 2024 Ice cream & frozen desserts

(G-5598)
GAMIT FORCE ATHC LTD LBLTY CO
459 Atlantic Ave (07740-6807)
P.O. Box 303, West Long Branch (07764-0303)
PHONE..................................908 675-0733
Barbara Hill, *CEO*
Arlene Smith, *Vice Pres*
EMP: 10
SALES: 950K **Privately Held**
SIC: 5091 3949 Athletic goods; sporting & athletic goods

(G-5599)
INTER WORLD HIGHWAY LLC
Also Called: Touchboards
205 Westwood Ave (07740-6564)
PHONE..................................732 759-8235
EMP: 10
SALES (est): 1.5MM
SALES (corp-wide): 66.6MM **Privately Held**
SIC: 3699 5063 Electrical equipment & supplies; electrical supplies
PA: Inter World Highway, Llc
205 Westwood Ave
Long Branch NJ 07740
732 222-7077

(G-5600)
J & R FOODS INC
309 Morris Ave Ste 5 (07740-6580)
PHONE..................................732 229-4020
Rocco F Raimondi III, *President*
EMP: 10
SQ FT: 2,000
SALES: 1MM **Privately Held**
SIC: 2092 Seafoods, fresh: prepared

(G-5601)
JERSEY JOB GUIDE INC
422 Morris Ave Ste 5 (07740-6574)
PHONE..................................732 263-9675
Mike Beson, *President*
EMP: 5
SALES (est): 380K **Privately Held**
WEB: www.jerseyjobguide.com
SIC: 2741 Guides: publishing only, not printed on site

(G-5602)
LATINO U S A
Also Called: Latino USA Newspaper
647 Broadway (07740-5442)
PHONE..................................732 870-1475
Gio Simoes, *President*
EMP: 4 EST: 2003
SALES (est): 142.1K **Privately Held**
SIC: 2711 Newspapers

(G-5603)
LINK NEWS
176 Broadway (07740-7006)
P.O. Box 120 (07740-0120)
PHONE..................................732 222-4300
Patty Oneill, *Principal*
EMP: 5
SALES (est): 188.7K **Privately Held**
SIC: 2711 Newspapers

(G-5604)
MONMOUTH RUBBER CORP
Also Called: Monmouth Rubber & Plastics
75 Long Branch Ave (07740-7155)
PHONE..................................732 229-3444
John M Bonforte, *President*
▲ EMP: 48 EST: 1964
SQ FT: 30,000
SALES (est): 9.1MM **Privately Held**
WEB: www.monmouthrubber.com
SIC: 3061 3083 3053 Mechanical rubber goods; laminated plastic sheets; gasket materials

(G-5605)
RPM PRFRMNCE CATINGS GROUP INC (HQ)
280 West Ave (07740-6196)
PHONE..................................888 788-4323
David Reif, *CEO*
Peggy Fynan, *President*
Margaret Fynan, *Exec VP*
Frederick Pfaff, *Vice Pres*
Tony Abatto, *Director*
EMP: 17
SALES (est): 7.6MM
SALES (corp-wide): 5.5B **Publicly Held**
SIC: 2851 Coating, air curing
PA: Rpm International Inc.
2628 Pearl Rd
Medina OH 44256
330 273-5090

(G-5606)
SHORE MICROSYSTEMS INC (PA)
45 Memorial Pkwy (07740-6720)
PHONE..................................732 870-0800
Gordon Elam, *President*
Jiri Hlataey, *Vice Pres*
Thomas Bostwick, *Opers Staff*
EMP: 6
SALES (est): 1MM **Privately Held**
SIC: 3661 Telephones & telephone apparatus

Long Valley
Morris County

(G-5607)
ALL SEASONS CONSTRUCTION INC
43 Flocktown Rd (07853-3534)
PHONE..................................908 852-0955
Nina Dorlon, *President*
Kevin B Dorlon, *Vice Pres*
EMP: 4
SALES (est): 464.1K **Privately Held**
SIC: 1521 1799 1542 1389 New construction, single-family houses; building site preparation; commercial & office building, new construction; construction, repair & dismantling services; building construction consultant; snowplowing

(G-5608)
BLUE MARLIN SYSTEMS INC
2 Ranney Rd (07853-3169)
P.O. Box 241, Succasunna (07876-0241)
PHONE..................................973 722-0816
Dan Gupta, *President*
EMP: 55
SALES (est): 2.7MM **Privately Held**
WEB: www.bmsmail.com
SIC: 7372 Prepackaged software

(G-5609)
DIGITAL BINSCOM LLC
59 E Mill Rd Ste 1-103 (07853-6215)
PHONE..................................908 867-7055
Bruce Bender, *President*
EMP: 5 EST: 2008
SALES (est): 540K **Privately Held**
SIC: 3823 3829 Industrial process measurement equipment; measuring & controlling devices

(G-5610)
FRAZIER INDUSTRIAL COMPANY (PA)
91 Fairview Ave (07853-3381)
PHONE..................................908 876-3001
William L Mascharka, *CEO*
Donald Frazier, *Chairman*
Domenick Iellimo, *Vice Pres*
▼ EMP: 110 EST: 1949
SQ FT: 33,000
SALES: 281.2MM **Privately Held**
WEB: www.ecologic.com
SIC: 3441 Fabricated structural metal; pallet racks: except wood

(G-5611)
GARDEN STATE WOMAN MAG LLC
210 Parker Rd (07853-3055)
PHONE..................................908 879-7143
Judy Chapman, *Mng Member*
EMP: 5
SALES (est): 310K **Privately Held**
WEB: www.gswoman.com
SIC: 2721 Magazines: publishing only, not printed on site

(G-5612)
MILLENNIUM RESEARCH LLC
Also Called: Advanced Formulations
99 W Mill Rd (07853-3465)
PHONE..................................908 867-7646
Sean Campbell,
▲ EMP: 7
SALES (est): 1.3MM **Privately Held**
WEB: www.advancedformulations.com
SIC: 2844 Face creams or lotions

Ltl Egg Hbr
Ocean County

(G-5613)
ATLANTIC COAST WOODWORK INC
160 Country Club Blvd (08087-1832)
PHONE..................................609 294-2478
EMP: 7

G
E
O
G
R
A
P
H
I
C

SALES: 200K **Privately Held**
SIC: 2521 2599 2542 Mfg Custom Commercial Cabinets

(G-5614)
ATLANTIC FLOORING LLC
121 Middle Holly Ln (08087-2046)
PHONE....................................609 296-7700
Christopher King, *Principal*
EMP: 11
SALES (est): 1.8MM **Privately Held**
SIC: 3069 1771 2426 Flooring, rubber: tile or sheet; flooring contractor; flooring, hardwood

(G-5615)
BETHEL BINDERY
1500 Route 539 (08087-9754)
PHONE....................................609 296-5043
Thomas Giger, *President*
Velma Giger, *Corp Secy*
EMP: 10
SQ FT: 5,000
SALES: 500K **Privately Held**
WEB: www.bethelbindery.com
SIC: 2789 Binding only: books, pamphlets, magazines, etc.

(G-5616)
EAGLE FABRICATION INC
63 Ohio Dr (08087-1025)
PHONE....................................732 739-5300
Philip J De Caro Jr, *President*
Debra Decaro, *Vice Pres*
EMP: 30
SQ FT: 16,000
SALES (est): 4.5MM **Privately Held**
WEB: www.eaglefabrication.com
SIC: 2493 2821 2541 Marbleboard (stone face hard board); plastics materials & resins; wood partitions & fixtures

(G-5617)
MIEMIE DESIGN SERVICES INC
1341 Radio Rd (08087-1036)
PHONE....................................609 857-3688
Winston Chit, *CEO*
EMP: 25
SALES (est): 1.5MM **Privately Held**
SIC: 3599 Industrial machinery

(G-5618)
PINELANDS BREWING LTD LBLTY CO
140 7th Ave Unit 15 (08087-4259)
PHONE....................................609 296-6169
Lucas McCooley, *Mng Member*
Micheal Broderson,
Jason Chapman,
Sean Collin,
EMP: 10
SALES: 337K **Privately Held**
SIC: 2082 Beer (alcoholic beverage)

(G-5619)
REPRO TRONICS INC
348 Golf View Dr (08087-4230)
PHONE....................................201 722-1880
David Skrivanek, *President*
Janice Skrivanek, *Treasurer*
EMP: 5 EST: 1981
SQ FT: 1,800
SALES (est): 585K **Privately Held**
WEB: www.repro-tronics.com
SIC: 2752 Commercial printing, offset

(G-5620)
STEPHEN L FEILINGER
Also Called: Marlin Candle Co
655 Route 9 N (08087-3519)
P.O. Box 1068, Tuckerton (08087-5068)
PHONE....................................609 294-1884
Stephen L Feilinger, *Owner*
EMP: 2
SALES: 1MM **Privately Held**
WEB: www.marlincandle.com
SIC: 3999 Candles

Lumberton
Burlington County

(G-5621)
AAA PHARMACEUTICAL (PA)
681 Main St (08048-5013)
PHONE....................................609 288-6060
Shashikant Sheth, *President*
Tejash Sheth, *Vice Pres*
Thao Hanna, *Director*
EMP: 75
SQ FT: 31,000
SALES: 20MM **Privately Held**
WEB: www.aaapharm.com
SIC: 2834 Pharmaceutical preparations

(G-5622)
ABATETECH INC
30 Maple Ave (08048-2918)
P.O. Box 25 (08048-0025)
PHONE....................................609 265-2107
William J White, *President*
Robert Gunst, *Vice Pres*
John Mullarkey, *Vice Pres*
Elizabeth M Odonnell, *Treasurer*
EMP: 20
SQ FT: 6,500
SALES: 6.6MM **Privately Held**
WEB: www.abatetechinc.com
SIC: 1799 2431 8744 Asbestos removal & encapsulation; moldings & baseboards, ornamental & trim;

(G-5623)
BLUE RING STENCILS LLC (PA)
140 Mount Holly By Pass # 10 (08048-1114)
PHONE....................................866 763-3873
Fred Cox, *President*
EMP: 25 EST: 2017
SALES: 10MM **Privately Held**
SIC: 3953 Marking devices

(G-5624)
BURLINGTON CNTY ENDOSCOPY CTR
140 Mount Holly By Pass # 5 (08048-1114)
PHONE....................................609 267-1555
Elaine Lang, *Administration*
Karen Pepper, *Nurse*
EMP: 40
SALES (est): 4MM **Privately Held**
WEB: www.bcendoscopycenter.com
SIC: 3845 Endoscopic equipment, electromedical

(G-5625)
CCL LABEL INC
Also Called: CCL Label Tubedec
92 Ark Rd (08048-4103)
PHONE....................................856 273-0700
Lisa Robinson, *Purch Mgr*
Ronald Hoffman, *Engineer*
EMP: 31
SALES (corp-wide): 3.9B **Privately Held**
SIC: 2759 Labels & seals: printing
HQ: Ccl Label, Inc.
161 Worcester Rd Ste 603
Framingham MA 01701
508 872-4511

(G-5626)
CELEBRATION (US) INC
681 Main St (08048-5013)
P.O. Box 188, Sunman IN (47041-0188)
PHONE....................................609 261-5200
Tom Kleen, *President*
EMP: 180
SALES (est): 17.5MM
SALES (corp-wide): 3B **Privately Held**
SIC: 2796 Platemaking services
HQ: The Occasions Group Inc
1750 Tower Blvd
North Mankato MN 56003
800 296-9029

(G-5627)
CHAMPION FASTENERS INC (PA)
707 Smithville Rd (08048-5302)
PHONE....................................609 267-5222
Robert Santare, *President*
Ronald E Doane, *Chairman*

EMP: 25
SQ FT: 28,000
SALES (est): 4.5MM **Privately Held**
SIC: 3451 5085 Screw machine products; fasteners, industrial: nuts, bolts, screws, etc.

(G-5628)
DISTINCTIVE WOODWORK INC
70 Stacy Haines Rd Ste D (08048-4107)
PHONE....................................609 714-8505
Jim Cherubino, *President*
EMP: 7
SALES: 600K **Privately Held**
SIC: 2499 1751 Decorative wood & woodwork; cabinet & finish carpentry

(G-5629)
HEILIND ELECTRONICS INC
Also Called: Heilind Electronics Inc
120 Mount Holly Byp (08048)
PHONE....................................888 881-5420
Scott Jacobs, *President*
Miriam Jacobs, *Treasurer*
Craig Alan Jacobs, *Admin Sec*
▲ **EMP:** 93
SQ FT: 33,000
SALES: 45.4MM
SALES (corp-wide): 730.7MM **Privately Held**
WEB: www.5015.com
SIC: 5065 3678 Connectors, electronic; electronic connectors
PA: Heilind Electronics, Inc
58 Jonspin Rd
Wilmington MA 01887
978 657-4870

(G-5630)
HEILIND MIL-AERO LLC (HQ)
Also Called: Interstate Cnncting Components
100c Mount Holly Byp (08048)
P.O. Box 419186, Boston MA (02241-9186)
PHONE....................................856 722-5535
Robert Clapp, *President*
Christine Naddeo, *Purchasing*
Martha Veselka, *Engineer*
Cheryl Gordon, *Sales Staff*
Nicole Graboyes, *Graphic Designe*
▲ **EMP:** 110 EST: 2012
SALES (est): 24.6MM
SALES (corp-wide): 730.7MM **Privately Held**
SIC: 3678 Electronic connectors
PA: Heilind Electronics, Inc
58 Jonspin Rd
Wilmington MA 01887
978 657-4870

(G-5631)
IMPRINTZ CSTM PRINTED GRAPHICS
691 Main St (08048-5013)
PHONE....................................609 386-5673
Leah Arter, *President*
Don Arter, *Vice Pres*
EMP: 8
SQ FT: 5,000
SALES (est): 1MM **Privately Held**
WEB: www.imprintz.net
SIC: 5199 2759 Advertising specialties; screen printing

(G-5632)
MT HOLLY PHARMACY
1613 Rd 38th Unit 5 10 (08048)
PHONE....................................609 914-4890
EMP: 4
SALES (est): 180.1K **Privately Held**
SIC: 2834 Pharmaceutical preparations

(G-5633)
NEW JERSEY TECH GROUP LLC
Also Called: 1800iprint
1632 Route 38 (08048-2923)
PHONE....................................609 301-6405
Henry Vasquez,
EMP: 4
SALES (est): 273.9K **Privately Held**
SIC: 2759 Commercial printing

(G-5634)
PROCO INC
Also Called: Glass House, The
15 Queen St (08048-1111)
PHONE....................................609 265-8777

David Prouse, *President*
Ron Glembocki, *Vice Pres*
EMP: 4
SQ FT: 1,200
SALES (est): 380.1K **Privately Held**
SIC: 3231 Novelties, glass: fruit, foliage, flowers, animals, etc.

(G-5635)
RANSOME EQUIPMENT SALES LLC
106 Ark Rd (08048-4104)
PHONE....................................856 797-8100
Percy Ransome, *Principal*
◆ **EMP:** 7
SALES (est): 540.2K **Privately Held**
SIC: 3531 5082 Subgraders (construction equipment); road construction equipment

(G-5636)
TDK ELECTRONICS INC
Also Called: Epcos
120 Munt Holly Byp Unit 2 (08048)
PHONE....................................732 603-5941
Joann Melusky, *Principal*
EMP: 10 **Privately Held**
SIC: 3679 5065 3546 Electronic crystals; diskettes, computer; power-driven handtools; grinders, portable: electric or pneumatic
HQ: Tdk Electronics Inc.
485b Us Highway 1 S # 200
Iselin NJ 08830
732 906-4300

(G-5637)
UNITED STEEL PRODUCTS CO INC
130 Mount Holly By Pass # 5 (08048-1115)
PHONE....................................609 518-9230
Don Sitzer, *Branch Mgr*
EMP: 7
SALES (corp-wide): 225.3B **Publicly Held**
WEB: www.uspconnectors.com
SIC: 3441 Fabricated structural metal
HQ: United Steel Products Company, Inc.
703 Rogers Dr
Montgomery MN 56069
507 364-7333

(G-5638)
VU SOUND INCORPORATED
Also Called: Vu World
1 Cameron Ln (08048-5231)
PHONE....................................215 990-2864
Victor Stott Jr, *President*
▲ **EMP:** 16
SALES: 1.7MM **Privately Held**
SIC: 7812 7372 3822 7389 Audio-visual program production; home entertainment computer software; appliance controls except air-conditioning & refrigeration;

Lyndhurst
Bergen County

(G-5639)
ALPHA INDUSTRIES MGT INC (PA)
Also Called: Sigma Plastics Group, The
800 Page Ave (07071-2526)
P.O. Box 808 (07071-0808)
PHONE....................................201 933-6000
Alfred Teo, *Ch of Bd*
Daniel Murphy, *General Mgr*
William Lenchinsky, *Vice Pres*
Carvalho Mike, *Vice Pres*
John Teier, *CFO*
◆ **EMP:** 180
SQ FT: 205,000
SALES (est): 1.2B **Privately Held**
WEB: www.sigma-plastics.com
SIC: 2673 Plastic & pliofilm bags

(G-5640)
AMERIGEN PHARMACEUTICALS INC
9 Polito Ave Ste 900 (07071-3410)
PHONE....................................732 993-9826
John Lowry, *President*
Iva Klemick, *Vice Pres*

Karl Wagner, *CFO*
Michael Fortier, *Director*
Michelle Valsera, *Director*
EMP: 12
SALES (est): 2.8MM **Privately Held**
SIC: 2834 Pharmaceutical preparations
PA: Amerigen Pharmaceuticals Ltd
197 State Route 18
East Brunswick NJ 08816

(G-5641)
APEX SAW & TOOL CO INC
595 New York Ave (07071-1506)
P.O. Box 497 (07071-0497)
PHONE.................................201 438-8777
John Ferrie Jr, *President*
EMP: 8
SQ FT: 5,000
SALES (est): 590K **Privately Held**
SIC: 7699 3423 Knife, saw & tool sharpening & repair; hand & edge tools

(G-5642)
BARNES & NOBLE BOOKSELLERS INC
Also Called: Barnes & Noble.com
125 Chubb Ave Fl 3 (07071-3504)
PHONE.................................201 272-3635
Michelle Moscatello, *Business Anlyst*
Diedra Hughes, *Director*
Kate Griffin, *Analyst*
EMP: 30
SALES (corp-wide): 3.5B **Privately Held**
WEB: www.bnn.com
SIC: 5942 5961 2731 Book stores; catalog & mail-order houses; book publishing
HQ: Barnes & Noble Booksellers, Inc.
1166 Ave Americas Fl 18
New York NY 10036
212 403-2580

(G-5643)
BUZZBOARD INC (PA)
1050 Wall St W Ste 630 (07071-3600)
PHONE.................................415 906-6934
Umesh Tibrewal, *CEO*
Anil Bansal, *Chairman*
EMP: 6 EST: 2013
SALES (est): 1.3MM **Privately Held**
SIC: 7372 Application computer software

(G-5644)
CAMBRIDGE PAVERS INC
Also Called: Cambridge Pavingstones
1 Jerome Ave (07071-2915)
P.O. Box 157 (07071-0157)
PHONE.................................201 933-5000
Charles H Gamarekian, *President*
Chris Gamarekian, *Vice Pres*
Jack Callahan, *Opers Mgr*
Paul Bonilla, *Opers Staff*
Jim Latona, *Purch Mgr*
◆ **EMP:** 155
SQ FT: 65,000
SALES (est): 22MM **Privately Held**
WEB: www.cambridgepavers.com
SIC: 3281 Paving blocks, cut stone

(G-5645)
CAPITAL COOLING SYSTEMS LLC
1050 Wall St W Ste 202 (07071-3615)
PHONE.................................973 773-8700
Michael Chen,
EMP: 2
SALES: 2MM **Privately Held**
SIC: 3724 Cooling systems, aircraft engine

(G-5646)
CASE IT INC
1050 Valley Brook Ave B (07071-3634)
PHONE.................................800 441-4710
Adam Merzon, *Ch of Bd*
John Bogut, *Principal*
Howard Kaminsky, *Vice Pres*
Jeffrey Fine, *VP Prdtn*
Christopher Kracke, *VP Finance*
▲ **EMP:** 40
SQ FT: 35,000
SALES (est): 6.6MM **Privately Held**
WEB: www.caseit.com
SIC: 3965 2621 3952 3089 Zipper; bag paper; pencil holders; cases, plastic

(G-5647)
CCA INDUSTRIES INC
Also Called: Core Care America
1099 Wall St W Ste 275 (07071-3617)
PHONE.................................201 935-3232
Lance Funston, *Ch of Bd*
Brent Funston, *Vice Ch Bd*
Douglas Haas, *President*
Stephen A Heit, *CFO*
▲ **EMP:** 14
SQ FT: 1,751
SALES: 16.6MM **Privately Held**
WEB: www.ccaindustries.com
SIC: 2844 Cosmetic preparations; shampoos, rinses, conditioners: hair; toothpastes or powders, dentifrices; face creams or lotions

(G-5648)
CHASE MACHINE CO
127 Park Ave (07071-1419)
P.O. Box 148 (07071-0148)
PHONE.................................201 438-2214
Donald La Scola Jr, *President*
EMP: 15
SQ FT: 5,000
SALES (est): 2.2MM **Privately Held**
SIC: 3541 3491 Machine tools, metal cutting type; industrial valves

(G-5649)
COM TEK WRKPLACE SOLUTIONS LLC
Also Called: Drawbase Software
1099 Wall St W Ste 269 (07071-3617)
PHONE.................................973 927-6814
David Connors, *Vice Pres*
Evangelos Kontos,
EMP: 16
SQ FT: 2,000
SALES (est): 911.4K **Privately Held**
SIC: 7372 7373 7371 Prepackaged software; computer integrated systems design; custom computer programming services

(G-5650)
ELEGANT DESSERTS INC
275 Warren St (07071-2017)
PHONE.................................201 933-7309
John Mazur, *President*
Cindy Mazur, *Sales Staff*
EMP: 16
SQ FT: 10,000
SALES (est): 2.8MM **Privately Held**
SIC: 2024 Dairy based frozen desserts

(G-5651)
EPSILON PLASTICS INC (HQ)
Also Called: Alpha Industries
Page & Schuyler Ave 8 (07071)
P.O. Box 808 (07071-0808)
PHONE.................................201 933-6000
Mark Teo, *CEO*
Alfred S Teo, *CEO*
Greg Gallow, *General Mgr*
John Reier, *CFO*
EMP: 100
SALES (est): 21MM **Privately Held**
SIC: 2673 Bags: plastic, laminated & coated

(G-5652)
FABIAN COUTURE GROUP LLC
205 Chubb Ave Bldg C (07071-3520)
PHONE.................................800 367-6251
Kelly Sherman, *CFO*
Mark Harabedian, *Controller*
Brian Reedinger, *Accounts Exec*
Allan Weiss,
▲ **EMP:** 15
SALES (est): 2.2MM **Privately Held**
SIC: 2311 5136 Tailored suits & formal jackets; shirts, men's & boys'

(G-5653)
FABIAN FORMALS INC
Also Called: First Nighter Formals
205 Chubb Ave Ste 2 (07071-3520)
PHONE.................................201 460-7776
Allan Weiss, *President*
Mark Harabedian, *CFO*
Neil Weiss, *Treasurer*
▲ **EMP:** 50
SQ FT: 30,000

SALES (est): 5.4MM **Privately Held**
WEB: www.fabiancouture.com
SIC: 2311 Formal jackets, men's & youths': from purchased materials; tuxedos: made from purchased materials

(G-5654)
FACSIMILE CMMNCATIONS INDS INC
230 Clay Ave (07071-3507)
PHONE.................................201 672-0773
Larry Weiss, *Branch Mgr*
EMP: 4
SALES (corp-wide): 47.9MM **Privately Held**
SIC: 3861 Photocopy machines
PA: Facsimile Communications Industries, Inc.
134 W 26th St Fl 3
New York NY 10001
212 741-6400

(G-5655)
FER PLATING INC
Also Called: Imperial Electro-Plating
52 Park Ave (07071-1012)
PHONE.................................201 438-1010
Fred L Engelhardt, *President*
Richard Engelhardt, *Corp Secy*
Edward F Engelhardt, *Vice Pres*
EMP: 27 EST: 1950
SQ FT: 35,000
SALES (est): 3.1MM **Privately Held**
SIC: 3471 Electroplating of metals or formed products

(G-5656)
GRAYTOR PRINTING COMPANY INC
149 Park Ave (07071-1419)
PHONE.................................201 933-0100
Stephen Toron, *President*
Nissim Shenova, *COO*
Anthony De Benedetto, *CFO*
Lisa Gebhardt, *Admin Sec*
Armand S Toron, *Asst Sec*
EMP: 50 EST: 1948
SQ FT: 43,000
SALES (est): 3.5MM
SALES (corp-wide): 17.3MM **Privately Held**
WEB: www.graytor.com
SIC: 2752 Commercial printing, offset
PA: Dolce Brothers Printing, Inc
29 Brook Ave
Maywood NJ 07607
201 843-0400

(G-5657)
LEDONNE LEATHER CO INC
730 5th St (07071-3214)
PHONE.................................201 531-2100
Robert Le Donne, *President*
EMP: 10
SQ FT: 5,000
SALES (est): 1.6MM **Privately Held**
SIC: 5199 3171 3161 Leather, leather goods & furs; women's handbags & purses; luggage

(G-5658)
LONG ISLAND PIPE OF NJ
Also Called: Neill Supply Co
700 Schuyler Ave (07071-2913)
PHONE.................................201 939-1100
Robert Moss, *Principal*
EMP: 32
SALES (est): 8.8MM **Privately Held**
SIC: 3317 Steel pipe & tubes

(G-5659)
M & E PACKAGING CORP
900 Page Ave Fl 2 (07071-2534)
P.O. Box 808 (07071-0808)
PHONE.................................201 635-1381
Arezer Rosborough II, *General Mgr*
◆ **EMP:** 7
SALES (est): 892.1K **Privately Held**
SIC: 5199 2673 Packaging materials; plastic bags: made from purchased materials

(G-5660)
MAIL DIRECT PAPER COMPANY LLC
515 Vly Brook Ave Ste A (07071-1951)
PHONE.................................201 933-2782
Paul Cimicata,
Michele Cimicata,
EMP: 12
SALES (est): 1.8MM **Privately Held**
SIC: 2396 Fabric printing & stamping

(G-5661)
MARCHIONE INDUSTRIES INC
Also Called: Trylon
136 Park Ave (07071-1420)
PHONE.................................718 317-4900
Ralph Marchione, *President*
Barbara Marchione, *Vice Pres*
EMP: 15
SQ FT: 20,000
SALES (est): 2.2MM **Privately Held**
WEB: www.trylon.com
SIC: 3995 3446 Grave vaults, metal; architectural metalwork

(G-5662)
MEDIEVAL TIMES USA INC
Also Called: Meadowlands Castle
149 Polito Ave (07071-3601)
PHONE.................................201 933-2220
Jose Tejdor, *Manager*
EMP: 250
SALES (corp-wide): 31.5MM **Privately Held**
SIC: 2711 5813 5812 Newspapers; drinking places; eating places
PA: Medieval Times U.S.A., Inc.
6363 N State Highway 161 # 400
Irving TX 75038
214 596-7600

(G-5663)
MEGAS YEEROS LLC
165 Chubb Ave (07071-3503)
PHONE.................................212 777-6342
Nikos Stergiou, *General Mgr*
George Vanis, *Director*
◆ **EMP:** 20
SALES (est): 9.7MM **Privately Held**
SIC: 5147 2099 3556 Meats & meat products; food preparations; food products machinery

(G-5664)
MENASHA PACKAGING COMPANY LLC
160 Chubb Ave Ste 101 (07071-3526)
PHONE.................................973 893-1300
Jennifer McInerney, *Manager*
EMP: 146
SALES (corp-wide): 1.7B **Privately Held**
SIC: 2653 Display items, corrugated: made from purchased materials
HQ: Menasha Packaging Company, Llc
1645 Bergstrom Rd
Neenah WI 54956
920 751-1000

(G-5665)
MSC MARKETING & TECHNOLOGY
808 Page Ave 8 (07071)
PHONE.................................201 507-9100
Per Nylen, *President*
Bob Nocek, *President*
William Lenchinsky, *Executive*
Thomas Fowles, *Administration*
EMP: 30
SALES (est): 5.8MM **Privately Held**
SIC: 2671 Plastic film, coated or laminated for packaging

(G-5666)
NCS PEARSON INC
1099 Wall St W (07071-3678)
PHONE.................................201 896-1011
Isabella Elliott, *Manager*
EMP: 99
SALES (corp-wide): 5.3B **Privately Held**
SIC: 3577 Optical scanning devices
HQ: Ncs Pearson Inc
5601 Green Valley Dr # 220
Bloomington MN 55437
952 681-3000

(G-5667)
NORTHCOTT SILK USA INC
1099 Wall St W Ste 250 (07071-3605)
PHONE....................201 672-9600
Brian O'Rourke, *President*
▲ EMP: 8
SALES: 10.2MM **Privately Held**
SIC: 2399 Fabricated textile products

(G-5668)
OMEGA PLASTICS CORP (HQ)
Also Called: Sigma Plastics Group
Page & Schuyler Ave Ste 5 (07071)
PHONE....................201 507-9100
Alfred Teo, *President*
Stanley Band, *Exec VP*
John Reier, *CFO*
Robert Levine, *Sales Staff*
Chuck Magee, *Sales Staff*
▲ EMP: 100
SQ FT: 205,000
SALES (est): 73.9MM **Privately Held**
SIC: 2673 Plastic bags: made from purchased materials

(G-5669)
ON DEMAND PRINT GROUP
442 Valley Brook Ave (07071-1925)
PHONE....................201 636-2270
Allen Jack Fakhouri, *President*
EMP: 6
SQ FT: 6,000
SALES (est): 1MM **Privately Held**
SIC: 2752 Commercial printing, lithographic

(G-5670)
OPTICS PLASTICS
537 New York Ave (07071-1506)
P.O. Box 375 (07071-0375)
PHONE....................201 939-3344
Mike Mazzolla, *President*
EMP: 5 EST: 1999
SALES (est): 209.8K **Privately Held**
SIC: 3089 Plastics products

(G-5671)
OTIS GRAPHICS INC
290 Grant Ave (07071-1911)
PHONE....................201 438-7120
Patricia McKnight, *President*
Don Lyst, *Manager*
EMP: 11
SQ FT: 8,200
SALES (est): 1.3MM **Privately Held**
WEB: www.otisgraphics.com
SIC: 2791 2752 Typesetting; commercial printing, offset

(G-5672)
PM SWAPCO INC
Also Called: Select Records
1099 Wall St W Ste 390 (07071-3617)
PHONE....................201 438-7700
Fredrick Munao, *President*
▲ EMP: 10 EST: 1980
SALES (est): 1.1MM **Privately Held**
WEB: www.selectrecords.com
SIC: 3652 Pre-recorded records & tapes

(G-5673)
PRESTIGE INDUSTRIES LLC
1099 Wall St W Ste 353 (07071-3617)
PHONE....................866 492-2244
EMP: 28
SALES (est): 22.4K **Privately Held**
SIC: 3999 Advertising curtains
PA: Prestige Hospitality Services Llc
2 Wood St
Paterson NJ 07524

(G-5674)
RALPH LAUREN CORPORATION
Ralph Lauren Children's Wear
9 Polito Ave Fl 5 (07071-3406)
PHONE....................201 531-6000
Stephen Mannello, *President*
Robert Alexander, *Vice Pres*
Elizabeth Dipietro, *Vice Pres*
Cal McGee, *Vice Pres*
Elizabeth Moriarty, *Vice Pres*
EMP: 107

SALES (corp-wide): 6.3B **Publicly Held**
SIC: 2325 2321 2253 5621 Men's & boys' trousers & slacks; men's & boys' furnishings; men's & boys' sports & polo shirts; men's & boys' dress shirts; knit outerwear mills; shirts (outerwear), knit; sweaters & sweater coats, knit; women's clothing stores
PA: Ralph Lauren Corporation
650 Madison Ave Fl C1
New York NY 10022
212 318-7000

(G-5675)
ROLLS OFFSET GROUP INC (PA)
264 Castle Ter (07071-2002)
PHONE....................201 727-1110
Richard Schlanger, *CEO*
Carl Schlanger, *Vice Pres*
Stewart Avrick, *Shareholder*
Robert Fishbine, *Shareholder*
EMP: 20 EST: 1953
SQ FT: 250,000
SALES (est): 2MM **Privately Held**
WEB: www.rollsoffsetgroup.com
SIC: 2752 Commercial printing, offset

(G-5676)
SCAFA-TORNABENE ART PUBG CO
Also Called: Scafa Modern Art Group, The
165 Chubb Ave Ste 4 (07071-3503)
PHONE....................201 842-8500
John Bridgewater, *President*
Cyrus Bhote, *CFO*
▲ EMP: 25 EST: 1970
SQ FT: 25,000
SALES (est): 3.9MM
SALES (corp-wide): 149.2MM **Privately Held**
WEB: www.theartpublishinggroup.com
SIC: 5199 2741 Art goods; art copy: publishing & printing
PA: Quarto Group Inc(The)
The Old Brewery
London N7 9B
207 700-6700

(G-5677)
SIGMA EXTRUDING CORP (HQ)
Also Called: Sigma Stretch Film
Page & Schuyler Ave (07071)
P.O. Box 808 (07071-0808)
PHONE....................201 933-5353
Alfred S Teo, *CEO*
Stanley Band, *Vice Pres*
Kevin Plesa, *Sales Staff*
◆ EMP: 80
SQ FT: 38,000
SALES (est): 39.6MM **Privately Held**
WEB: www.sigmaplastics.com
SIC: 2673 Garment bags (plastic film): made from purchased materials

(G-5678)
SIKA CORPORATION (HQ)
201 Polito Ave (07071-3601)
P.O. Box 710 (07071-0710)
PHONE....................201 933-8800
Rick Montani, *President*
Jason Whitman, *Partner*
Kurt Anderson, *District Mgr*
Doug Smith, *District Mgr*
Martin Henricks, *Area Mgr*
◆ EMP: 258
SALES: 1.1B
SALES (corp-wide): 7.1B **Privately Held**
WEB: www.sikacorp.com
SIC: 2891 2899 2851 2821 Epoxy adhesives; chemical preparations; epoxy coatings; epoxy resins; concrete products
PA: Sika Ag
Zugerstrasse 50
Baar ZG 6341
584 366-800

(G-5679)
SIKA CORPORATION
875 Valley Brook Ave (07071)
PHONE....................201 933-8800
Steve Gill, *Principal*
Brian Blaquiere, *Marketing Staff*
EMP: 157

SALES (corp-wide): 7.1B **Privately Held**
WEB: www.sikacorp.com
SIC: 2899 2821 2851 2891 Concrete curing & hardening compounds; epoxy resins; epoxy coatings; sealants; epoxy adhesives
HQ: Sika Corporation
201 Polito Ave
Lyndhurst NJ 07071
201 933-8800

(G-5680)
SIKA FIBERS LLC
201 Polito Ave (07071-3601)
PHONE....................201 933-8800
Rick Montani, *Principal*
EMP: 50
SALES (est): 1.9MM
SALES (corp-wide): 7.1B **Privately Held**
SIC: 2221 Manmade & synthetic broadwoven fabrics
HQ: Sika Corporation
201 Polito Ave
Lyndhurst NJ 07071
201 933-8800

(G-5681)
TENEYCK INC
Also Called: Neill Supply Co., Inc.
700 Schuyler Ave (07071-2913)
PHONE....................201 939-1100
Brad Moss, *CEO*
Neil Shyman, *Vice Pres*
Alex Alvarado, *Sales Staff*
Tim Nowell, *Sales Staff*
EMP: 70
SQ FT: 56,000
SALES (est): 10.5MM
SALES (corp-wide): 2.6B **Privately Held**
WEB: www.neillsupply.com
SIC: 3569 5085 Sprinkler systems, fire: automatic; valves & fittings
HQ: Miles Moss Of Albany, Inc.
586 Commercial Ave
Garden City NY 11530
516 222-8008

(G-5682)
WACOAL AMERICA INC (DH)
1 Wacoal Plz (07071-3400)
PHONE....................201 933-8400
Robert Vitale, *President*
◆ EMP: 200 EST: 1952
SQ FT: 131,000
SALES (est): 145MM **Privately Held**
WEB: www.wacoal-america.com
SIC: 2342 2341 Brassieres; panties: women's, misses', children's & infants'; women's & children's nightwear
HQ: Wacoal International Corp
1 Wacoal Plz
Lyndhurst NJ 07071
201 933-8400

(G-5683)
WACOAL INTERNATIONAL CORP (DH)
1 Wacoal Plz (07071-3400)
PHONE....................201 933-8400
Ken Yamamoto, *President*
◆ EMP: 3
SQ FT: 50,000
SALES (est): 155MM **Privately Held**
SIC: 2341 Women's & children's undergarments

(G-5684)
YKK (USA) INC
1099 Wall St W Ste 244 (07071-3623)
PHONE....................201 935-4200
William Langley, *Manager*
EMP: 7 **Privately Held**
SIC: 3965 5131 Fasteners, slide zippers; zippers
HQ: Ykk (U.S.A.), Inc.
1300 Cobb Industrial Dr
Marietta GA 30066
770 427-5521

Madison
Morris County

(G-5685)
ACTAVIS ELIZABETH LLC
5 Giralda Farms (07940-1027)
PHONE....................973 442-3200
Elizabeth Cooper, *Manager*
Enzo Smeriglio, *Manager*
EMP: 193 **Privately Held**
SIC: 2834 Druggists' preparations (pharmaceuticals)
HQ: Actavis Elizabeth Llc
200 Elmora Ave
Elizabeth NJ 07202
908 527-9100

(G-5686)
ACTAVIS LLC (HQ)
Also Called: Allergan Finance
5 Giralda Farms (07940-1027)
PHONE....................862 261-7000
Brenton L Saunders, *CEO*
Brad Voinche, *District Mgr*
David A Buchen, *Exec VP*
David Buchen, *Exec VP*
William Meury, *Exec VP*
◆ EMP: 441
SALES (est): 4B **Privately Held**
WEB: www.watsonpharm.com
SIC: 2834 5122 Pharmaceutical preparations; pharmaceuticals

(G-5687)
ALLERGAN INC (HQ)
5 Giralda Farms (07940-1027)
P.O. Box 19534, Irvine CA (92623-9534)
PHONE....................862 261-7000
A Robert D Bailey, *Ch of Bd*
▲ EMP: 1300
SALES (est): 3.8B **Privately Held**
WEB: www.allergan.com
SIC: 2834 3841 Solutions, pharmaceutical; dermatologicals; drugs acting on the central nervous system & sense organs; proprietary drug products; surgical & medical instruments

(G-5688)
ALLERGAN SALES LLC
5 Giralda Farms (07940-1027)
PHONE....................973 442-3200
Andrew Fenton, *President*
Frank Rodriguez, *Vice Pres*
Roberto Hernandez, *Engineer*
Rigoberto Stevenson, *Engineer*
Brenton L Saunders, *Branch Mgr*
EMP: 13 **Privately Held**
SIC: 2834 Pharmaceutical preparations
HQ: Allergan Sales, Llc
2525 Dupont Dr
Irvine CA 92612
862 261-7000

(G-5689)
AMERICAN MICROSEMICONDUCTOR
133 Kings Rd (07940-2122)
P.O. Box 104 (07940-0104)
PHONE....................973 377-9566
William F Foley, *President*
Rosemarie Foley, *Corp Secy*
EMP: 45
SALES (est): 10.1MM **Privately Held**
WEB: www.americanmicrosemi.com
SIC: 5065 3674 Semiconductor devices; semiconductors & related devices

(G-5690)
CHATHAM BOOKSELLER INC
8 Green Village Rd (07940-1817)
PHONE....................973 822-1361
Frank Deodene, *President*
Carolyn Deodene, *Corp Secy*
EMP: 4
SQ FT: 2,000
SALES (est): 300K **Privately Held**
SIC: 5961 5932 2731 Book club, mail order; book stores, secondhand; books: publishing only

(G-5691)
E P HELLER COMPANY
21 Samson Ave 25 (07940-2261)
P.O. Box 26 (07940-0026)
PHONE................................973 377-2878
Eugene P Heller, *Ch of Bd*
August Daub, *President*
Stefan Koellmann, *Exec VP*
Douglas Heller, *Vice Pres*
Peter Heller, *Vice Pres*
EMP: 25
SQ FT: 10,000
SALES (est): 6.3MM **Privately Held**
WEB: www.ephco.com
SIC: 3545 5072 Cutting tools for machine
tools; power tools & accessories

(G-5692)
ELLIS INSTRUMENTS INC
4 Elmer St Ste 1 (07940-1941)
PHONE................................973 593-9222
Chuck Ellis, *President*
Andy Ellis, *Vice Pres*
EMP: 4
SALES: 2MM **Privately Held**
WEB: www.ellisinstruments.com
SIC: 5047 3841 Medical equipment & sup-
plies; surgical instruments & apparatus

(G-5693)
**GENERAL COMMIS ARCHIVES &
HSTR**
Also Called: Gcah
36 Madison Ave (07940-1434)
P.O. Box 127 (07940-0127)
PHONE................................973 408-3189
Rollins Jay, *Comms Dir*
Alfred Day, *Admin Sec*
Charles Yrigoyen Jr, *Admin Sec*
EMP: 1
SALES (est): 456.4K **Privately Held**
WEB: www.gcah.org
SIC: 2721 8412 Periodicals; museum; reli-
gious library

(G-5694)
HEALTHY ITALIA RETAIL LLC
55 Main St Apt 1 (07940-1881)
PHONE................................973 966-5200
Cristina Bossini, *Mng Member*
EMP: 15
SALES (est): 1MM **Privately Held**
SIC: 2032 8299 Italian foods: packaged in
cans, jars, etc.; cooking school

(G-5695)
IMPACT PROTECTIVE EQP LLC
8 Westerly Ave (07940-1606)
PHONE................................973 377-0903
Mark Monica,
Theodore Monica,
EMP: 8
SALES (est): 680K **Privately Held**
WEB: www.impactpads.com
SIC: 3949 Pads: football, basketball, soc-
cer, lacrosse, etc.

(G-5696)
J HARRIS COMPANY
57 Barnsdale Rd (07940-2807)
PHONE................................917 731-5080
Scott Goldstone, *President*
EMP: 4
SALES: 1MM **Privately Held**
SIC: 2329 Athletic (warmup, sweat & jog-
ging) suits: men's & boys'

(G-5697)
LEO PHARMA INC
7 Giralda Farms Ste 2 (07940-1051)
PHONE................................973 637-1690
John Koconis, *President*
Christian Antoni, *Senior VP*
Mitch Johnson, *Vice Pres*
Judit H Nyirady, *Vice Pres*
George Padden, *Vice Pres*
▲ EMP: 261
SALES (est): 117.8MM
SALES (corp-wide): 1.6B **Privately Held**
SIC: 5122 8731 2834 Pharmaceuticals;
biotechnical research, commercial; drugs
affecting parasitic & infective diseases
HQ: Leo Pharma A/S
Industriparken 55
Ballerup 2750
449 458-88

(G-5698)
MERCK & CO INC
2 Giralda Farms (07940-1026)
PHONE................................800 224-5318
Maureen Ngoh, *Manager*
Frank Zhang, *Associate Dir*
Craig Fancourt, *Associate*
Kim Novick, *Associate*
Diana Roselli, *Associate*
EMP: 38
SALES (corp-wide): 42.2B **Publicly Held**
SIC: 2834 Pharmaceutical preparations
PA: Merck & Co., Inc.
2000 Galloping Hill Rd
Kenilworth NJ 07033
908 740-4000

(G-5699)
PARKER PUBLICATIONS
Also Called: Madison Eagle
155 Main St (07940-2156)
PHONE................................908 766-3900
Steven Parker, *Owner*
Elizabeth K Parker, *Co-Owner*
EMP: 14
SQ FT: 1,800
SALES (est): 512.3K **Privately Held**
SIC: 2711 4215 Newspapers: publishing
only, not printed on site; courier services,
except by air

(G-5700)
PFIZER INC
1 Giralda Farms (07940-1021)
PHONE................................973 660-5000
Stephen Stanley, *Opers Staff*
Christopher O'Brien, *Engineer*
Christopher Glaab, *Manager*
Jordan Salit, *Manager*
Ghouse Shaik, *Consultant*
EMP: 14
SALES (corp-wide): 53.6B **Publicly Held**
SIC: 2833 2834 Antibiotics; drugs acting
on the cardiovascular system, except di-
agnostic
PA: Pfizer Inc.
235 E 42nd St
New York NY 10017
212 733-2323

(G-5701)
**ROBERT A EICK QLTY
BOOKBINDING**
Also Called: Eick-Rbert A Qulty Bookbinding
34 Central Ave (07940-1811)
PHONE................................973 822-2100
Robert A Eick, *Owner*
EMP: 15
SALES (est): 550K **Privately Held**
SIC: 2789 Binding only: books, pamphlets,
magazines, etc.

(G-5702)
SENSOR PRODUCTS INC
300 Madison Ave Ste 200 (07940-1868)
PHONE................................973 884-1755
Dimitri Raitzin, *CEO*
Paul Calado, *Engineer*
Charlie Manolio, *Engineer*
Jeffrey Stark, *Mng Member*
Gus Alvarez, *Technical Staff*
EMP: 23
SQ FT: 1,400
SALES (est): 3.9MM **Privately Held**
WEB: www.sensorprod.com
SIC: 3599 5084 Custom machinery; in-
struments & control equipment

(G-5703)
STEWART-MORRIS INC
71 Kings Rd Ste 1 (07940-2697)
PHONE................................973 822-2777
John R Morris, *President*
John Morris, *President*
EMP: 5
SQ FT: 3,000
SALES (est): 558.6K **Privately Held**
SIC: 5999 2399 Trophies & plaques; flags;
flags, fabric

(G-5704)
WYETH HOLDINGS LLC (DH)
Also Called: Wyeth Holdings Corporation
5 Giralda Farms (07940-1027)
PHONE................................973 660-5000
Greg Norden, *Ch of Bd*

Andre Petrunoff, *Director*
Lawrence V Stein, *Director*
▲ EMP: 42
SALES: 51MM
SALES (corp-wide): 53.6B **Publicly Held**
SIC: 2834 2836 Pharmaceutical preparations; analgesics; cough medicines; veterinary pharmaceutical preparations;
biological products, except diagnostic; al-
lergens, allergenic extracts; vaccines; veterinary biological products
HQ: Wyeth Llc
235 E 42nd St
New York NY 10017
212 733-2323

(G-5705)
WYETH LLC
5 Giralda Farms (07940-1027)
PHONE................................973 660-5000
Richard Hayes, *QC Mgr*
Anne Radestad, *Manager*
Chris Rand, *Manager*
Derek Breitenbach, *Administration*
EMP: 500
SALES (corp-wide): 53.6B **Publicly Held**
SIC: 2834 Pharmaceutical preparations
HQ: Wyeth Llc
235 E 42nd St
New York NY 10017
212 733-2323

(G-5706)
WYETH-AYERST (ASIA) LTD (DH)
5 Giralda Farms (07940-1027)
PHONE................................973 660-5500
Joan Chen, *Principal*
EMP: 4
SALES (est): 1.7MM
SALES (corp-wide): 53.6B **Publicly Held**
SIC: 2834 Pharmaceutical preparations
HQ: Wyeth Llc
235 E 42nd St
New York NY 10017
212 733-2323

Magnolia
Camden County

(G-5707)
GREASE N GO
334 S White Horse Pike (08049-1059)
PHONE................................856 784-6555
Joe Panchella, *General Mgr*
EMP: 4 EST: 2012
SALES (est): 167.6K **Privately Held**
SIC: 7549 3559 Lubrication service, auto-
motive; degreasing machines, automotive
& industrial

(G-5708)
J J L & W INC
Also Called: Komfort & Kare
424 N White Horse Pike (08049-1405)
PHONE................................856 854-3100
Seth Auerbach, *President*
EMP: 25
SQ FT: 3,600
SALES (est): 1.8MM **Privately Held**
WEB: www.komfortkare.com
SIC: 5999 3842 Hospital equipment &
supplies; prosthetic appliances

(G-5709)
**SAPPHIRE ENVELOPE &
GRAPHICS**
214 Davis Rd (08049-1215)
PHONE................................856 782-2227
Anthony Mellace, *President*
Stephen Bressi, *Vice Pres*
EMP: 20
SQ FT: 7,000
SALES (est): 3.5MM **Privately Held**
SIC: 2759 2752 Envelopes: printing; com-
mercial printing, lithographic

Mahwah
Bergen County

(G-5710)
ACUPAC PACKAGING INC
55 Ramapo Valley Rd (07430-1118)
PHONE................................201 529-3434
Rob Edmonds, *President*
Stephanie Hayano, *Vice Pres*
EMP: 200 EST: 1979
SQ FT: 66,000
SALES (est): 69MM
SALES (corp-wide): 603MM **Privately
Held**
WEB: www.acupac.com
SIC: 2844 Cosmetic preparations
PA: Knowlton Development Corporation Inc
255 Boul Roland-Therrien Bureau 100
Longueuil QC J4H 4
450 243-2000

(G-5711)
AIR WORLD INC
126 Christie Ave (07430-1351)
PHONE................................201 831-0700
Sam OH, *President*
Micheal OH, *Vice Pres*
▲ EMP: 20
SQ FT: 4,000
SALES: 3.8MM **Privately Held**
SIC: 3582 Commercial laundry equipment

(G-5712)
ALPHAGRAPHICS
1 Lethbridge Plz Ste 22 (07430-2113)
PHONE................................201 327-2200
John Chrisostomou, *President*
EMP: 5
SALES: 950K **Privately Held**
SIC: 2752 8743 Commercial printing, litho-
graphic; promotion service

(G-5713)
ALTIBASE INCORPORATED
1 International Blvd (07495-0027)
PHONE................................888 837-7333
Chris Chung, *CEO*
Jung Nahm, *Finance Mgr*
EMP: 6
SQ FT: 411
SALES (est): 449.9K **Privately Held**
SIC: 7372 Prepackaged software

(G-5714)
AMERICAN STENCYL INC
Also Called: American Sten-Cyl
37 Hillside Ave (07430-1815)
PHONE................................201 251-6460
Thomas Nardini, *President*
Mary Nardini, *Corp Secy*
EMP: 5 EST: 1982
SALES (est): 476.3K **Privately Held**
WEB: www.americansten-cyl.com
SIC: 3993 3953 Signs & advertising spe-
cialties; stencils, painting & marking

(G-5715)
**AT INFORMATION PRODUCTS
INC (PA)**
575 Corporate Dr Ste 401 (07430-3703)
PHONE................................201 529-0202
Joseph Traut, *Ch of Bd*
Roger Angrick, *President*
Joseph Rau, *Senior VP*
CJ Sgro, *Sales Mgr*
EMP: 8
SQ FT: 10,000
SALES: 3MM **Privately Held**
WEB: www.atip-usa.com
SIC: 3555 3565 5045 5084 Printing
trades machinery; labeling machines, in-
dustrial; computers; printing trades ma-
chinery, equipment & supplies

(G-5716)
BIMINI BAY OUTFITTERS LTD
43 Mckee Dr Ste 1 (07430-2122)
PHONE................................201 529-3550
Robert Feldsott, *President*
Edward Feldsott, *Vice Pres*
▼ EMP: 19
SQ FT: 15,000

SALES (est): 2.5MM **Privately Held**
WEB: www.biminibayoutfitters.com
SIC: 2311 2321 2329 5136 Tailored
dress & sport coats: men's & boys'; men's
& boys' sports & polo shirts; men's &
boys' sportswear & athletic clothing;
sportswear, men's & boys'

(G-5717)
BIONOMIC INDUSTRIES INC
777 Corporate Dr (07430-2008)
PHONE.................................201 529-1094
John Enhoffer, *President*
EMP: 12
SQ FT: 7,500
SALES (est): 3.6MM **Privately Held**
WEB: www.bionomicind.com
SIC: 3564 Air purification equipment

(G-5718)
BOGEN COMMUNICATIONS INC
1200 Macarthur Blvd # 303 (07430-2331)
PHONE.................................201 934-8500
Jonathan Guss, *CEO*
Michael P Fleischer, *President*
David Delbrocco, *Principal*
Jeffrey E Schwarz, *Chairman*
Yoav Stern, *Chairman*
◆ **EMP:** 100
SQ FT: 6,000
SALES (est): 20.3MM
SALES (corp-wide): 23.4MM **Privately
Held**
WEB: www.bogen-es.com
SIC: 3651 3661 3663 3669 Amplifiers:
radio, public address or musical instru-
ment; audio electronic systems; tele-
phone & telegraph apparatus; telephones
& telephone apparatus; radio broadcast-
ing & communications equipment; inter-
communication systems, electric;
communication equipment
PA: Bogen Corporation
50 Spring St Ste 1
Ramsey NJ 07446
201 934-8500

(G-5719)
BUHLER INC
40 Whitney Rd (07430-3130)
PHONE.................................201 847-0600
Rene Steiner, *President*
EMP: 21
SALES (corp-wide): 3.3B **Privately Held**
SIC: 3556 3542 3535 3564 Food prod-
ucts machinery; die casting machines;
conveyors & conveying equipment; dust
or fume collecting equipment, industrial
HQ: Buhler Inc.
13105 12th Ave N
Plymouth MN 55441
763 847-9900

(G-5720)
CASES BY SOURCE INC
Also Called: Source Packaging
215 Island Rd (07430-2130)
PHONE.................................201 831-0005
Alan Adler, *President*
Matthew Adler, *Vice Pres*
Jeff Chookazian, *Marketing Staff*
David Marshall, *Manager*
Lana Coffey, *Planning*
▲ **EMP:** 24
SQ FT: 7,500
SALES (est): 7.1MM **Privately Held**
WEB: www.casesbysource.com
SIC: 2653 Display items, solid fiber: made
from purchased materials

(G-5721)
CELCO
Also Called: Constantine Engrg Labs Co
14 Industrial Ave Ste 2 (07430-4201)
P.O. Box 555 (07430-0555)
PHONE.................................201 327-1123
Fax: 201 327-7047
EMP: 16 **EST:** 1947
SQ FT: 25,500
SALES (est): 3.4MM **Privately Held**
SIC: 3651 3677 3825 3823 Mfg Home
Audio/Video Eqp Mfg Elec Coil/Trans-
frmrs Mfg Elec Measuring Instr Mfg
Process Cntrl Instr

(G-5722)
CHEFMAN DIRECT INC
200 Performance Dr # 207 (07495-1101)
PHONE.................................888 315-8407
Ralph Newhouse, *CEO*
Eli Weiss, *Admin Sec*
EMP: 75
SALES (est): 1.1MM **Privately Held**
SIC: 3631 Indoor cooking equipment

(G-5723)
**CLEAR CUT WINDOW DISTRS
OF NJ**
127 Tam O Shanter Dr (07430-3270)
PHONE.................................201 512-1804
Stanley Freimark, *President*
EMP: 4
SALES: 175K **Privately Held**
SIC: 2431 Windows & window parts & trim,
wood

(G-5724)
CODA INC (PA)
30 Industrial Ave Ste 1 (07430-2207)
PHONE.................................201 825-7400
Lee Coda, *President*
Alfred Coda, *Vice Pres*
EMP: 24 **EST:** 1946
SQ FT: 45,000
SALES (est): 4MM **Privately Held**
WEB: www.codamount.com
SIC: 3861 Photographic equipment & sup-
plies

(G-5725)
CUPCAKE KITSCHEN
1042 Ash Dr (07430-2350)
PHONE.................................862 221-8872
EMP: 4
SALES (est): 178.9K **Privately Held**
SIC: 2051 Bread, cake & related products

(G-5726)
DATASCOPE CORP
Also Called: Datascope Patient Monitoring
800 Macarthur Blvd (07430-2001)
PHONE.................................201 995-8000
Don Southard, *Manager*
EMP: 34
SALES (corp-wide): 6.1B **Privately Held**
WEB: www.datascope.com
SIC: 3841 3845 Medical instruments &
equipment, blood & bone work; catheters;
electromedical equipment
HQ: Datascope Corp.
15 Law Dr
Fairfield NJ 07004
973 244-6100

(G-5727)
DATASCOPE CORP
Also Called: Maquet Cardiac Assist
1300 Macarthur Blvd (07430-2052)
PHONE.................................201 995-8700
Dan Pitkowski, *Principal*
Manish Godbole, *Opers Staff*
Marvin Fabor, *Production*
Patrick Adee, *Engineer*
Francis Cartey, *Engineer*
EMP: 9
SALES (corp-wide): 6.1B **Privately Held**
WEB: www.datascope.com
SIC: 3845 Electromedical equipment
HQ: Datascope Corp.
15 Law Dr
Fairfield NJ 07004
973 244-6100

(G-5728)
DIGITAL LIZARD LLC
500 Corporate Dr (07430-2005)
PHONE.................................201 684-0900
EMP: 4
SALES (est): 435.7K **Privately Held**
SIC: 2752 Commercial printing, litho-
graphic

(G-5729)
**DILIGAF ENTERPRISES INC
(DH)**
Also Called: Gsds
500 Corporate Dr (07430-2005)
PHONE.................................201 684-0900
Christopher Petro, *President*
Arthur Manzo, *COO*

John Poalillo, *Opers Staff*
Art Manzo, *Treasurer*
Kevin Dotson, *Manager*
▲ **EMP:** 40
SQ FT: 29,850
SALES (est): 10.7MM
SALES (corp-wide): 3.8B **Publicly Held**
WEB: www.globalsoftdigital.com
SIC: 2752 2759 Commercial printing, off-
set; commercial printing
HQ: Creel Printing, Llc
6330 W Sunset Rd
Las Vegas NV 89118
702 735-8161

(G-5730)
**DIMENSIONAL
COMMUNICATIONS INC**
1595 Macarthur Blvd (07430-3601)
PHONE.................................201 767-1500
Douglas Fixell, *President*
Steve Witzke, *Vice Pres*
Dan Cann, *Project Mgr*
Tim Higgins, *Prdtn Mgr*
Beverley Doughty, *Production*
▲ **EMP:** 80 **EST:** 1963
SQ FT: 75,000
SALES (est): 16.6MM **Privately Held**
WEB: www.dimcom.com
SIC: 3993 Signs & advertising specialties

(G-5731)
**DUN-RITE COMMUNICATIONS
INC**
31 Industrial Ave (07430-2223)
PHONE.................................201 444-0080
EMP: 6
SALES (est): 647.8K **Privately Held**
SIC: 1623 1799 2298 Water/Sewer/Utility
Construction Trade Contractor Mfg
Cordage/Twine

(G-5732)
DVASH FOODS USA INC
300 Corporate Dr (07430-3616)
PHONE.................................929 360-0758
Moshe Gertner, *Ch of Bd*
EMP: 4
SALES (est): 418.7K **Privately Held**
SIC: 5141 2096 Food brokers; potato
chips & similar snacks

(G-5733)
DXL ENTERPRISES INC
575 Corporate Dr Ste 420 (07430-2330)
PHONE.................................201 891-8718
Ulrich Gernhardt, *President*
Ralph Nitzl, *Facilities Mgr*
Patricia Clark Jones, *Assistant*
EMP: 11
SQ FT: 20,000
SALES (est): 2.8MM **Privately Held**
WEB: www.dxl.com
SIC: 3571 5094 7363 Electronic comput-
ers; precious metals; industrial help serv-
ice

(G-5734)
EDAX INC (HQ)
91 Mckee Dr (07430-2105)
PHONE.................................201 529-4880
Alan Devenish, *President*
James Abramson, *Corp Secy*
Jens Rafaelsen, *Engineer*
Mike Coy, *Marketing Staff*
EMP: 99
SALES (est): 26.1MM
SALES (corp-wide): 4.8B **Publicly Held**
WEB: www.edax.com
SIC: 3826 3829 Analytical instruments;
measuring & controlling devices
PA: Ametek, Inc.
1100 Cassatt Rd
Berwyn PA 19312
610 647-2121

(G-5735)
**ENVIRNMNTAL MGT CHEM
WSTE SVCS (PA)**
Also Called: Turnkey Solutions
45 Whitney Rd Bldg B (07430-3170)
PHONE.................................201 848-7676
David Lyman, *President*
EMP: 8
SQ FT: 10,000

SALES: 3MM **Privately Held**
WEB: www.turnkey-solutions-inc.com
SIC: 3589 5084 Water treatment equipment, industrial; industrial machinery &
equipment

(G-5736)
FECKEN-KIRFEL AMERICA INC
6 Leighton Pl Ste 1 (07430-3195)
PHONE.................................201 891-5530
Rudolf Schiffler, *President*
Michael Anders, *Vice Pres*
Marc Eskind, *Representative*
▲ **EMP:** 11
SQ FT: 22,000
SALES (est): 2.2MM
SALES (corp-wide): 48.7MM **Privately
Held**
WEB: www.fk-am.com
SIC: 3541 Machine tools, metal cutting
type
PA: Fecken - Kirfel Gmbh & Co. Kg
Prager Ring 1-15
Aachen 52070
241 182-020

(G-5737)
FLANAGAN HOLDINGS INC (PA)
Also Called: F & M Expressions Unlimited
211 Island Rd (07430-2130)
PHONE.................................201 512-3338
Frank E Flanagan, *President*
Buck Anderson, *Prdtn Mgr*
Nicole Anderson, *Accounts Mgr*
◆ **EMP:** 90 **EST:** 1983
SQ FT: 40,000
SALES (est): 9.9MM **Privately Held**
WEB: www.fmexpressions.com
SIC: 2759 Fashion plates: printing

(G-5738)
**FLAVOR & FRAGRANCE SPC
INC (PA)**
3 Industrial Ave (07430-2204)
PHONE.................................201 828-9400
Michael C Bloom, *President*
Bob Clemente, *Project Dir*
Jeffery Wichman, *Plant Mgr*
Ed Duderich, *Purch Mgr*
Jahna Tofts, *Project Engr*
▲ **EMP:** 100
SQ FT: 45,000
SALES (est): 23.9MM **Privately Held**
SIC: 2087 2869 2844 Extracts, flavoring;
perfumes, flavorings & food additives; toi-
let preparations

(G-5739)
FLOXITE COMPANY INC
31 Industrial Ave Ste 2 (07430-3591)
PHONE.................................201 529-2019
Bruce Pitot, *President*
Pat Ely, *Vice Pres*
▲ **EMP:** 15
SQ FT: 6,000
SALES (est): 5.6MM **Privately Held**
SIC: 3843 Dental equipment

(G-5740)
FMDK TECHNOLOGIES INC
Also Called: Merlin Controls
63 Ramapo Valley Rd 63w (07430-1133)
PHONE.................................201 828-9822
Frank Gallo, *President*
Bill Miller, *Consultant*
EMP: 8 **EST:** 1978
SQ FT: 5,000
SALES (est): 1.1MM **Privately Held**
WEB: www.fmdkinc.com
SIC: 3564 Blowers & fans

(G-5741)
GLASCO UV LLC
126 Christie Ave (07430-1351)
PHONE.................................201 934-3348
James Donnellan, *VP Opers*
Steven Martin, *Director*
Julie Donnellan,
EMP: 10
SALES: 2.5MM **Privately Held**
SIC: 3589 Water purification equipment,
household type

(G-5742)
GLENMARK PHRMCEUTICALS INC USA (HQ)
750 Corporate Dr (07430-2009)
PHONE...............................201 684-8000
Robert Mapsuk, *President*
Vijay Soni, *Exec VP*
Phumla Adesanya, *Manager*
Rajat Sharma, *Deputy Dir*
▲ EMP: 91
SQ FT: 68,627
SALES (est): 26.7MM
SALES (corp-wide): 865.2MM **Privately Held**
WEB: www.glenmark-generics.com
SIC: 2834 Pharmaceutical preparations
PA: Glenmark Pharmaceuticals Limited
Glenmark House, Wing-A, B. D.
Sawant Marg,
Mumbai MH 40009
224 018-9999

(G-5743)
GLENMARK THERAPEUTICS INC USA
750 Corporate Dr (07430-2009)
PHONE...............................201 684-8000
EMP: 307
SALES (est): 49.7MM
SALES (corp-wide): 865.2MM **Privately Held**
SIC: 2834 Pharmaceutical preparations
PA: Glenmark Pharmaceuticals Limited
Glenmark House, Wing-A, B. D.
Sawant Marg,
Mumbai MH 40009
224 018-9999

(G-5744)
GLOBE SCIENTIFIC INC
400 Corporate Dr (07430-3606)
PHONE...............................201 599-1400
Dara Diamond, *President*
Milton Diamond, *President*
Lisa Diamond Berger, *Vice Pres*
Beverly Diamond, *Admin Sec*
◆ EMP: 36
SQ FT: 40,000
SALES (est): 14MM **Privately Held**
WEB: www.globescientific.com
SIC: 5047 3841 Medical laboratory equipment; surgical & medical instruments

(G-5745)
GOLD BUYERS AT MALL LLC (PA)
1 International Blvd # 200 (07495-0027)
PHONE...............................201 512-5780
Danny Baruch,
EMP: 4
SALES (est): 1.5MM **Privately Held**
SIC: 3911 Jewelry, precious metal

(G-5746)
HEALTHSTAR COMMUNICATIONS INC (PA)
1000 Wyckoff Ave Ste 202 (07430-3164)
PHONE...............................201 560-5370
Jerry Brager, *CEO*
John Corcoran, *President*
Myron Holubiak, *President*
Peter Cossman, *Exec VP*
Patricia Brock, *Senior VP*
EMP: 39
SQ FT: 10,000
SALES (est): 75.9MM **Privately Held**
SIC: 7372 7311 6719 Prepackaged software; advertising agencies; personal holding companies, except banks

(G-5747)
HOWMEDICA OSTEONICS CORP (HQ)
Also Called: Stryker Orthopaedics
325 Corporate Dr (07430-2006)
PHONE...............................201 831-5000
Kevin A Lobo, *President*
David Floyd, *President*
Yin C Becker, *Vice Pres*
Steven P Benscoter, *Vice Pres*
Dean H Bergy, *Vice Pres*
▲ EMP: 153

SALES (est): 1B
SALES (corp-wide): 13.6B **Publicly Held**
SIC: 5047 3842 Orthopedic equipment & supplies; surgical appliances & supplies
PA: Stryker Corporation
2825 Airview Blvd
Portage MI 49002
269 385-2600

(G-5748)
I FCB HOLDINGS INC (HQ)
933 Macarthur Blvd (07430-2045)
PHONE...............................201 934-2000
Camille Shayka, *President*
EMP: 20
SALES (est): 1.1MM
SALES (corp-wide): 9.8MM **Privately Held**
SIC: 2834 Drugs acting on the cardiovascular system, except diagnostic
PA: Footstar, Inc.
45 Rockefeller Plz # 2260
New York NY 10111
201 934-2000

(G-5749)
I TRADE TECHNOLOGY LTD (PA)
115 Franklin Tpke Ste 144 (07430-1325)
PHONE...............................615 348-7233
Shia Lebreche, *President*
▲ EMP: 1
SALES: 1.5MM **Privately Held**
SIC: 3678 5999 5065 Electronic connectors; electronic parts & equipment; connectors, electronic

(G-5750)
JETYD CORPORATION
218 Island Rd (07430-2101)
PHONE...............................201 512-9500
Jason Junkers, *Branch Mgr*
EMP: 10
SALES (corp-wide): 2.6MM **Privately Held**
WEB: www.jetyd.com
SIC: 3423 3566 Wrenches, hand tools; torque converters, except automotive
PA: Jetyd Corporation
120 Wesley St
South Hackensack NJ 07606
201 343-4570

(G-5751)
JSN HOLDINGS LLC
1 International Blvd (07495-0027)
PHONE...............................201 857-5900
Brian Tedesco, *President*
▲ EMP: 10
SQ FT: 1,200
SALES: 5.2MM **Privately Held**
SIC: 3629 Battery chargers, rectifying or nonrotating

(G-5752)
LEVER MANUFACTURING CORP
420 State Rt 17 (07430-2135)
PHONE...............................201 684-4400
Irving V Gerstein, *President*
Mel B Gerstein, *Corp Secy*
William M Corbett, *Vice Pres*
David B Gerstein, *Vice Pres*
▲ EMP: 25 EST: 1905
SQ FT: 100,000
SALES (est): 4.6MM **Privately Held**
WEB: www.levercorp.com
SIC: 3552 3549 3541 Winders, textile machinery; metalworking machinery; machine tools, metal cutting type

(G-5753)
MICRO LOGIC INC (PA)
31 Industrial Ave Ste 7 (07430-2210)
PHONE...............................201 962-7510
James Lewis, *President*
Judy Recca, *Bookkeeper*
Diane Selja, *Accounts Mgr*
EMP: 15
SQ FT: 2,000
SALES (est): 1.8MM **Privately Held**
WEB: www.miclog.com
SIC: 7371 2741 Computer software development; technical manual & paper publishing

(G-5754)
MINDRAY DS USA INC (HQ)
Also Called: Mindray North America
800 Macarthur Blvd (07430-2001)
PHONE...............................201 995-8000
George Solomon, *President*
John Du, *President*
Leon LI, *General Mgr*
Maria Capuano-Weachoc, *Business Mgr*
Rich Cipolli, *Vice Pres*
◆ EMP: 277
SALES (est): 511.4MM
SALES (corp-wide): 1.9B **Privately Held**
WEB: www.mindray.com.cn
SIC: 2835 3841 3845 In vitro diagnostics; surgical & medical instruments; patient monitoring apparatus
PA: Shenzhen Mindray Bio-Medical Electronics Co., Ltd.
Mindray Building, Keji South No.12
Road, High-Tech Industrial Zo
Shenzhen 51805
755 818-8881

(G-5755)
MISSIONARY SOCIETY OF ST PAUL
Also Called: Polish Press
997 Macarthur Blvd (07430-2045)
PHONE...............................201 825-7300
EMP: 50
SALES (corp-wide): 6.5MM **Privately Held**
WEB: www.paulistpress.com
SIC: 2721 2731 Periodicals; book publishing
PA: The Missionary Society Of St Paul The Apostle In The State Of
8611 Midland Pkwy
Jamaica NY
312 922-3444

(G-5756)
MYAT INC (PA)
360 Franklin Tpke (07430-2258)
PHONE...............................201 529-0145
Philip Cindrich, *President*
Bea Porta, *Human Res Mgr*
Virginia Cindrich, *Director*
▲ EMP: 35 EST: 1951
SALES (est): 5.1MM **Privately Held**
WEB: www.myat.com
SIC: 3663 Transmitting apparatus, radio or television

(G-5757)
NEW YORK-NJ TRAIL CONFERENCE (PA)
600 Ramapo Valley Rd (07430-1633)
PHONE...............................201 512-9348
Jane Daniels, *Ch of Bd*
David Day, *Chief*
Monica Day, *Chief*
Mary Dodds, *Chief*
Daniel Hoberman, *Counsel*
EMP: 11
SQ FT: 5,200
SALES: 2.9MM **Privately Held**
WEB: www.nynjtc.org
SIC: 8699 2741 2731 Athletic organizations; atlas, map & guide publishing; book publishing

(G-5758)
NMP WATER SYSTEMS LLC
63 Ramapo Valley Rd # 103 (07430-1133)
PHONE...............................201 252-8333
Timothy Van Overloop, *Mng Member*
EMP: 7
SALES (est): 138.7K **Privately Held**
SIC: 7389 3589 3677 Water softener service; swimming pool filter & water conditioning systems; filtration devices, electronic

(G-5759)
NOBEL BIOCARE PROCERA LLC
800 Corporate Dr (07430-2011)
PHONE...............................201 529-7100
Richard Laube, *CEO*
▲ EMP: 40

SALES (est): 10.1MM
SALES (corp-wide): 19.8B **Publicly Held**
SIC: 3087 8021 Custom compound purchased resins; specialized dental practitioners
PA: Danaher Corporation
2200 Penn Ave Nw Ste 800w
Washington DC 20037
202 828-0850

(G-5760)
NORTH JERSEY MEDIA GROUP INC
6 Leighton Pl (07430-3198)
PHONE...............................201 485-7800
M O'Neill, *Owner*
EMP: 194
SQ FT: 10,000
SALES (corp-wide): 156.2MM **Privately Held**
WEB: www.njmg.com
SIC: 2711 Newspapers, publishing & printing
HQ: North Jersey Media Group Inc.
150 River St
Hackensack NJ 07601
201 646-4000

(G-5761)
PAULIST PRESS INC
997 Macarthur Blvd (07430-2096)
PHONE...............................201 825-7300
Lawrence Boadt, *President*
▲ EMP: 3
SQ FT: 76,665
SALES: 1.8MM **Privately Held**
SIC: 2731 Books: publishing only

(G-5762)
PRESCRIPTION DYNAMICS INC
310 Ridge Rd (07430-3613)
PHONE...............................201 746-6262
Michael De Giglio, *CEO*
EMP: 10
SALES (est): 1MM **Privately Held**
SIC: 2834 Medicines, capsuled or ampuled

(G-5763)
PRINTING & SIGNS EXPRESS INC
634 Wyckoff Ave (07430-3057)
PHONE...............................201 368-1255
Joseph Busto, *President*
EMP: 4
SALES (est): 454.6K **Privately Held**
SIC: 3993 2759 Signs & advertising specialties; commercial printing

(G-5764)
PTC ELECTRONICS INC
45 Whitney Rd Ste B9 (07430-3160)
P.O. Box 72, Wyckoff (07481-0072)
PHONE...............................201 847-0500
Alan Kicks, *President*
Alan F Kicks, *President*
Janet Kicks, *Vice Pres*
John Kicks, *Vice Pres*
Kenneth Ehrlich, *Warehouse Mgr*
EMP: 7
SQ FT: 2,000
SALES (est): 750K **Privately Held**
WEB: www.ptcelectronics.com
SIC: 5046 3052 3829 Scales, except laboratory; hose, pneumatic: rubber or rubberized fabric; pressure & vacuum indicators, aircraft engine; pressure transducers

(G-5765)
QUALITY CARTON INC (PA)
1 International Blvd # 610 (07495-0020)
PHONE...............................201 529-6900
Jack Bartta, *President*
Dan Baratta, *Vice Pres*
EMP: 5
SALES (est): 754K **Privately Held**
WEB: www.qualitycarton.com
SIC: 3565 Carton packing machines

(G-5766)
RADWIN INC
900 Corporate Dr (07430-3611)
PHONE...............................201 252-4224
Ilan Moshe, *President*
Danny Colbeci, *Vice Pres*
Eran Kaplan, *Vice Pres*

(PA)=Parent Co (HQ)=Headquarters (DH)=Div Headquarters
✪ = New Business established in last 2 years

2019 Harris New Jersey
Manufacturers Directory

225

GEOGRAPHIC

EMP: 5
SALES (est): 969.3K
SALES (corp-wide): 25.8MM **Privately Held**
SIC: 3663 Radio & TV communications equipment
PA: Radwin Ltd
27 Habarzel
Tel Aviv-Jaffa 69710
376 629-00

(G-5767)
REICH USA CORPORATION
300 Rte 17 Ste H (07430-2141)
P.O. Box 916 (07430-0916)
PHONE..............................201 684-9400
Joel G Poganski, *President*
Joel Poganski, *Vice Pres*
Loucas Nestoros, *Technology*
▲ **EMP:** 11
SALES (est): 1.9MM **Privately Held**
SIC: 3429 3568 Clamps, couplings, nozzles & other metal hose fittings; power transmission equipment

(G-5768)
RJ BRANDS LLC (PA)
Also Called: Chefman
200 Performance Dr # 207 (07495-1101)
PHONE..............................888 315-8407
Ralph Newhouse, *CEO*
Joseph Ritterman, *CFO*
Eli Weiss, *Officer*
▲ **EMP:** 140
SQ FT: 270,000
SALES (est): 135MM **Privately Held**
SIC: 3634 Electric household cooking appliances

(G-5769)
RUSSELL W ANDERSON INC
1 Fyke Rd (07430-2411)
PHONE..............................201 825-2092
Russell Anderson, *Principal*
EMP: 5 **EST:** 2013
SALES (est): 372.7K **Privately Held**
SIC: 3443 Tanks, lined: metal plate

(G-5770)
SCANDIA PACKAGING MACHINERY CO
30 Herlihy Dr (07430-2947)
PHONE..............................973 473-6100
W B Bronander III, *President*
Cecelia Bronander, *Vice Pres*
Paul De Ghetto, *Engineer*
▲ **EMP:** 26 **EST:** 1918
SALES (est): 6.6MM **Privately Held**
WEB: www.scandiapack.com
SIC: 3565 Packaging machinery

(G-5771)
SHOCK TECH INC (PA)
211 Island Rd (07430-2130)
PHONE..............................845 368-8600
Serge Seguin, *Ch of Bd*
Kevork Kayayan, *President*
Michael Alvarez, *Engineer*
Thomas Aspinwall, *CFO*
EMP: 40 **EST:** 1998
SQ FT: 50,000
SALES (est): 11.1MM **Privately Held**
WEB: www.shocktech.com
SIC: 8711 3061 3829 3714 Engineering services; mechanical rubber goods; measuring & controlling devices; motor vehicle parts & accessories; springs, shock absorbers & struts; automobiles

(G-5772)
SIX THIRTEEN ORIGINALS LLC
18 Industrial Ave Ste C (07430-2255)
PHONE..............................201 316-1900
Frank Flanagan,
▼ **EMP:** 50
SQ FT: 23,000
SALES: 8MM **Privately Held**
SIC: 2759 Screen printing

(G-5773)
SOUND UNITED LLC
100 Corporate Dr (07430-2041)
PHONE..............................201 762-6500
Kevin Zarow, *Branch Mgr*
EMP: 30 **Privately Held**

SIC: 3651 5065 Electronic kits for home assembly: radio, TV, phonograph; electronic parts & equipment
HQ: Sound United, Llc
1 Viper Way Ste 1 # 1
Vista CA 92081

(G-5774)
SPECTRO ANALYTICAL INSTRS INC (PA)
91 Mckee Dr (07430-2105)
PHONE..............................201 642-3000
Janet A King, *President*
Aron Thomas M, *Vice Pres*
E B King, *Admin Sec*
EMP: 10
SALES (est): 2.7MM **Privately Held**
WEB: www.spectro-ai.com
SIC: 6512 3844 3825 3823 Commercial & industrial building operation; X-ray apparatus & tubes; instruments to measure electricity; industrial instrmnts msrmnt display/control process variable

(G-5775)
STARNET BUSINESS SOLUTIONS
46 Industrial Ave Ste 2 (07430-2206)
PHONE..............................201 252-2863
Doug Arbolino, *CEO*
EMP: 50
SQ FT: 34,000
SALES (est): 9.3MM **Privately Held**
SIC: 2759 Bank notes: engraved

(G-5776)
STARNET PRINTING INC
46 Industrial Ave Ste 2 (07430-2206)
PHONE..............................201 760-2600
Lorraine Brink, *President*
EMP: 5
SALES (est): 171.1K **Privately Held**
SIC: 2732 2741 Book printing; catalogs: publishing & printing

(G-5777)
STRATEGIC MKTG PROMOTIONS INC (PA)
Also Called: S M P
1200 Macarthur Blvd # 251 (07430-2322)
PHONE..............................845 623-7777
Jennifer Pagels-Caglione, *Ch of Bd*
Robert Russo, *President*
Greg Caglione, *Vice Pres*
▼ **EMP:** 15
SQ FT: 3,000
SALES (est): 2.3MM **Privately Held**
SIC: 3999 Advertising display products

(G-5778)
STS TECHNOLOGIES LLC
282 Franklin Tpke (07430-1923)
PHONE..............................973 277-5416
Patricia Sciaino, *Principal*
Steven Sciaino, *Chief Engr*
EMP: 10 **EST:** 2012
SQ FT: 10,000
SALES (est): 555.8K **Privately Held**
SIC: 8711 3544 3599 Mechanical engineering; die sets for metal stamping (presses); crankshafts & camshafts, machining

(G-5779)
TAM METAL PRODUCTS INC
55 Whitney Rd (07430-3129)
PHONE..............................201 848-7800
Mark Cariddi, *President*
Thomas Clayton, *COO*
Frank Cariddi, *Vice Pres*
Jason Cariddi, *Vice Pres*
Ed Luzzi, *Purch Mgr*
EMP: 48
SQ FT: 50,000
SALES (est): 9.9MM **Privately Held**
WEB: www.tam-ind.com
SIC: 3599 3444 Machine shop, jobbing & repair; sheet metalwork

(G-5780)
THEORY DEVELOPMENT CORP
Also Called: Phillips Scientific Co
31 Industrial Ave Ste 1 (07430-2210)
PHONE..............................201 783-8770
Thomas M Phillips, *President*

EMP: 15
SQ FT: 13,000
SALES (est): 1.3MM **Privately Held**
WEB: www.phillipsscientific.com
SIC: 3829 3823 Nuclear radiation & testing apparatus; industrial instrmnts msrmnt display/control process variable

(G-5781)
THERMWELL PRODUCTS CO INC (PA)
Also Called: Frost King
420 Rte 17 (07430-2135)
PHONE..............................201 684-4400
David B Gerstein, *President*
Vincent Giarratana, *Exec VP*
Mel B Gerstein, *Vice Pres*
Chris Riccio, *VP Mfg*
Mark Heitlinger, *CFO*
◆ **EMP:** 400 **EST:** 1910
SQ FT: 100,000
SALES (est): 191.6MM **Privately Held**
WEB: www.frostking.com
SIC: 3442 Moldings & trim, except automobile: metal; weather strip, metal

(G-5782)
THERMWELL PRODUCTS CO INC
Filmco Industries
420 State Rt 17 (07430-2135)
PHONE..............................201 684-4400
Joe Scarpa, *Manager*
EMP: 5
SALES (corp-wide): 191.6MM **Privately Held**
WEB: www.frostking.com
SIC: 2672 Adhesive papers, labels or tapes: from purchased material
PA: Thermwell Products Co., Inc.
420 Rte 17
Mahwah NJ 07430
201 684-4400

(G-5783)
TRAFFIC SAFETY & EQUIPMENT CO
457 State Rt 17 (07430-2143)
PHONE..............................201 327-6050
Mark Simpson, *CEO*
Peter J Simpson, *President*
Robert Simpson, *Treasurer*
EMP: 10
SQ FT: 16,000
SALES (est): 1.4MM **Privately Held**
WEB: www.trafficsafetydirect.com
SIC: 3993 5084 Signs, not made in custom sign painting shops; industrial machinery & equipment

(G-5784)
TRANSPORTATION TECH SVCS INC
Also Called: Tandem Technologies
90 Mckee Dr (07430-2106)
PHONE..............................201 335-0238
Tim Rose, *CEO*
EMP: 28
SALES (est): 548.7K **Privately Held**
SIC: 7372 Application computer software

(G-5785)
UNION INSTITUTE INC
Also Called: National Tax Training School
67 Ramapo Valley Rd # 102 (07430-1170)
P.O. Box 767 (07430-0767)
PHONE..............................800 914-8138
Akiva J Eisenberg, *President*
Sarah Eisenberg, *Corp Secy*
EMP: 28 **EST:** 1952
SQ FT: 2,000
SALES (est): 1.1MM **Privately Held**
WEB: www.nattax.com
SIC: 8249 2721 Vocational schools; periodicals: publishing only

(G-5786)
WIND TUNNEL INC
60 Whitney Rd Ste 13 (07430-3180)
PHONE..............................201 485-7793
Jason Friedman, *CEO*
EMP: 5 **EST:** 2010
SALES (est): 571.1K **Privately Held**
SIC: 3443 Wind tunnels

(G-5787)
YOLO CANDY LLC
1 International Blvd # 208 (07495-0027)
PHONE..............................201 252-8765
John Budd, *Vice Pres*
Brent Greer, *Sales Staff*
Scott Silverstein, *Mng Member*
▲ **EMP:** 4 **EST:** 2012
SQ FT: 3,000
SALES: 1.5MM **Privately Held**
SIC: 2064 Chewing candy, not chewing gum

Malaga
Gloucester County

(G-5788)
HYPER BICYCLES INC (PA)
177 Malaga Park Dr (08328-4241)
P.O. Box 627 (08328-0627)
PHONE..............................856 694-0352
Clay Goldsmid, *President*
Joe Dechamp, *Vice Pres*
Eric Carter, *Manager*
▲ **EMP:** 2
SQ FT: 4,000
SALES (est): 1.5MM **Privately Held**
SIC: 3751 Bicycles & related parts

(G-5789)
R H VASSALLO INC
Us Rte 40 & State 47 (08328)
P.O. Box 375 (08328-0905)
PHONE..............................856 358-8841
Ron Vassallo, *President*
Diane Vassallo, *Treasurer*
EMP: 6
SQ FT: 5,000
SALES (est): 691.5K **Privately Held**
SIC: 2511 2452 5039 Lawn furniture: wood; prefabricated buildings, wood; prefabricated structures

Manahawkin
Ocean County

(G-5790)
ASAP POSTAL PRINTING
775 N Main St (08050-3025)
PHONE..............................609 597-7421
EMP: 6 **EST:** 2009
SALES (est): 390K **Privately Held**
SIC: 2759 Commercial Printing

(G-5791)
CLEARWATER WELL DRILLING CO
1073 Prospect Ave (08050-3049)
PHONE..............................609 698-1800
Leslie A Pascale, *President*
Yvonne Pascale, *Vice Pres*
EMP: 4
SQ FT: 3,500
SALES: 450K **Privately Held**
SIC: 3589 1781 Water filters & softeners, household type; water well drilling

(G-5792)
COPY-RITE PRINTING
378 N Main St Ste A (08050-3092)
PHONE..............................609 597-9182
Gail Moro, *Owner*
EMP: 4
SALES (est): 504.3K **Privately Held**
SIC: 2752 2791 Commercial printing, offset; typesetting

(G-5793)
JETTY LIFE LLC
509 N Main St 3 (08050-3021)
PHONE..............................800 900-6435
Edmund Townsend, *Manager*
Anthony Hediger, *Manager*
EMP: 5
SALES (est): 830.5K **Privately Held**
SIC: 3577 Printers & plotters

(G-5794)
NJ LOGO WEAR LLC
100 Mckinley Ave Ste 6 (08050-6056)
PHONE...............................609 597-9400
Keith Anderson,
EMP: 5
SQ FT: 2,500
SALES (est): 75K **Privately Held**
SIC: 7389 2759 2395 3499 Engraving
service; advertising, promotional & trade
show services; screen printing; embroi-
dery & art needlework; trophies, metal,
except silver

(G-5795)
PACE BUSINESS SOLUTIONS
INC
297 Route 72 W (08050-2890)
PHONE...............................908 451-0355
Joseph Tornabene, *President*
EMP: 33 EST: 2009
SALES (est): 3.8MM **Privately Held**
SIC: 7371 7372 7379 Computer software
systems analysis & design, custom;
prepackaged software; computer related
consulting services

(G-5796)
TAYLOR MADE CABINETS INC
516 E Bay Ave (08050-3325)
PHONE...............................609 978-6900
David Taylor, *President*
Chris Taylor, *Vice Pres*
EMP: 24
SQ FT: 10,000
SALES (est): 4.6MM **Privately Held**
WEB: www.taylormadecabinets.com
SIC: 2514 5031 5211 Metal kitchen & din-
ing room furniture; lumber, plywood &
millwork; cabinets, kitchen

(G-5797)
WEAVERS FIBERGLASS
19 Parker St (08050-3163)
PHONE...............................609 597-4324
Patrick Weaver, *President*
EMP: 5
SALES (est): 563K **Privately Held**
SIC: 2821 Plastics materials & resins

(G-5798)
WIRELESS EXPERIENCE OF PA
INC (PA)
Also Called: Wireless Experience, The
509 N Main St (08050-3021)
PHONE...............................732 552-0050
Brian Wainwright, *President*
Matt Langford, *Opers Staff*
Robert Shaver, *CFO*
Matt Mott, *Human Resources*
Chris Bulmer, *Manager*
EMP: 11 EST: 2008
SALES (est): 34.8MM **Privately Held**
SIC: 2451 1731 4812 Mobile homes; tele-
phone & telephone equipment installa-
tion; cellular telephone services

Manalapan
Monmouth County

(G-5799)
ABRIS DISTRIBUTION INC (PA)
522 Us Highway 9 Ste 377 (07726-8241)
PHONE...............................732 252-9819
Leonid Khegay, *President*
Albert Martirosyan, *Principal*
Vladimir Sim, *Vice Pres*
EMP: 25
SALES (est): 40MM **Privately Held**
SIC: 5045 3669 7629 Computer periph-
eral equipment; intercommunication sys-
tems, electric; telecommunication
equipment repair (except telephones)

(G-5800)
AIR PRODUCTS AND
CHEMICALS INC
405 Route 33 (07726-8308)
PHONE...............................732 446-5676
Dan Nettina, *Branch Mgr*
EMP: 23

SALES (corp-wide): 8.9B **Publicly Held**
WEB: www.airproducts.com
SIC: 2813 Industrial gases
PA: Air Products And Chemicals, Inc.
7201 Hamilton Blvd
Allentown PA 18195
610 481-4911

(G-5801)
ALWAYS BE SECURE LLC
195 Route 9 Ste 109 (07726-8294)
PHONE...............................917 887-2286
Michael Kaplun, *CEO*
Michael Zeidner, *COO*
EMP: 8
SQ FT: 2,500
SALES (est): 300.6K **Privately Held**
SIC: 3172 Wallets

(G-5802)
BASIC SOLUTIONS LTD
330 Adams Ct (07726-8701)
PHONE...............................201 978-7691
Lawrence Meltzer, *President*
Ken Kloff, *COO*
Bobby Choueke, *Vice Pres*
EMP: 4
SALES (est): 248.5K **Privately Held**
SIC: 2322 Men's & boys' underwear &
nightwear

(G-5803)
CCARD
Also Called: Manufacturing / Consultants
17 Belle Terre Dr (07726-4521)
PHONE...............................732 303-8264
Chris Cardinale, *President*
EMP: 6
SALES: 440K **Privately Held**
SIC: 3679 Electronic circuits

(G-5804)
COBYCO INC
65 Wilson Ave (07726-3813)
PHONE...............................732 446-4448
Coby Keinan, *President*
Elana Keinan, *Vice Pres*
◆ EMP: 4
SQ FT: 6,000
SALES: 310.5K **Privately Held**
SIC: 2284 Embroidery thread

(G-5805)
EAST COAST PALLETS LLC
17 Sweetmans Ln (07726-8349)
PHONE...............................732 308-3616
Enrique Martinez,
EMP: 4
SALES (est): 312.4K **Privately Held**
SIC: 2448 Pallets, wood & wood with metal

(G-5806)
EDESIA OIL LLC
225 County Road 522 B (07726-8824)
PHONE...............................732 851-7979
Joseph Calcagno, *Mng Member*
EMP: 10
SQ FT: 2,300
SALES (est): 1.3MM **Privately Held**
SIC: 2079 Olive oil

(G-5807)
ELKOM NORTH AMERICA INC
680 Madison Ave (07726-9594)
PHONE...............................732 786-0490
Angelika Uphoff, *Principal*
▲ EMP: 5
SALES (est): 457.3K **Privately Held**
SIC: 3353 Foil, aluminum

(G-5808)
EVERTLAST INTERIORS
52 Main St Ste 6 (07726)
PHONE...............................732 252-9965
EMP: 5
SALES (est): 287.4K **Privately Held**
SIC: 2431 Millwork

(G-5809)
EWC CONTROLS INC
385 State Route 33 (07726-8306)
PHONE...............................732 446-3110
Mike Reilly, *President*
Stan Plepis, *President*
David Imig, *Regional Mgr*
Dave Dreskin, *Purch Mgr*

Ric Kostbar, *QC Dir*
▲ EMP: 50
SQ FT: 26,000
SALES (est): 8.6MM **Privately Held**
WEB: www.ewccontrols.com
SIC: 3679 1711 3621 3585 Electronic cir-
cuits; plumbing, heating, air-conditioning
contractors; motors & generators; refrig-
ation & heating equipment; sheet metal-
work; heating equipment, except electric

(G-5810)
FERNANDES CUSTOM
CABINETS
233 Pease Rd (07726-2643)
PHONE...............................732 446-2829
Jonathan Fernandes, *Principal*
EMP: 5
SALES (est): 227.1K **Privately Held**
SIC: 2434 Wood kitchen cabinets

(G-5811)
FLOORING CONCEPTS NJ LLC
289 Highway 33 Ste 2c (07726-8365)
PHONE...............................732 409-7600
John Pilot,
EMP: 11
SALES (est): 227.9K **Privately Held**
SIC: 1752 3069 1771 2426 Floor laying
& floor work; flooring, rubber: tile or sheet;
flooring contractor; flooring, hardwood

(G-5812)
GPT INC
227 State Route 33 (07726-8362)
PHONE...............................732 446-2400
Michael Witt, *President*
Niels E Scholer, *Corp Secy*
Michael Monica, *Sales Staff*
EMP: 10
SQ FT: 2,200
SALES: 1MM **Privately Held**
WEB: www.gpt.net
SIC: 5169 3564 Industrial chemicals; pu-
rification & dust collection equipment

(G-5813)
HUB SIGN CRANE CORP
67 Wood Ave (07726-8062)
PHONE...............................732 252-9090
Chris Barber, *Principal*
EMP: 5
SALES (est): 540.9K **Privately Held**
SIC: 3993 Signs & advertising specialties

(G-5814)
INKWORKX CUSTOM SCREEN
PRTG
289 State Route 33 (07726-8364)
PHONE...............................609 898-5198
EMP: 4
SALES (est): 101.5K **Privately Held**
SIC: 2752 Commercial printing, litho-
graphic

(G-5815)
JACQUAR FUEL
107 Hawkins Rd (07726-8420)
PHONE...............................732 441-0700
Steve Pielli, *Principal*
EMP: 4 EST: 2009
SALES (est): 467.5K **Privately Held**
SIC: 2869 Fuels

(G-5816)
LEAD CONVERSION PLUS
Also Called: Intergrated Media Solutions
500 Craig Rd Ste 101 (07726-8748)
PHONE...............................802 497-1557
John Bean,
EMP: 15 EST: 2010
SALES (est): 903.7K **Privately Held**
SIC: 2721 Magazines: publishing only, not
printed on site

(G-5817)
MINUTEMAN PRESS
349 Us Highway 9 Ste 5 (07726-5105)
PHONE...............................732 536-8788
Joe Lorenz, *Partner*
Elaine Lorenz, *Partner*
EMP: 6

SALES (est): 1MM **Privately Held**
WEB: www.mmpmanalapan.com
SIC: 2752 Commercial printing, litho-
graphic

(G-5818)
NICE INSTRUMENTATION
205 Park Ave (07726-8372)
PHONE...............................732 851-4300
EMP: 14 EST: 2005
SQ FT: 5,000
SALES (est): 2MM **Privately Held**
SIC: 4941 3825 Water Supply Service Mfg
Electrical Measuring Instruments

(G-5819)
NJ GRASS CHOPPERS
254 Monmouth Rd (07726-8808)
PHONE...............................732 414-2850
Christopher Colosi, *Principal*
EMP: 7 EST: 2011
SALES (est): 975.7K **Privately Held**
SIC: 3751 Motorcycles & related parts

(G-5820)
NUTRI-PET RESEARCH INC
227 State Route 33 Ste 10 (07726-8363)
PHONE...............................732 786-8822
Janis Gianforte, *President*
Bruce Horner, *Principal*
EMP: 7
SQ FT: 1,200
SALES (est): 1.3MM **Privately Held**
WEB: www.nuprosupplements.com
SIC: 2834 Veterinary pharmaceutical
preparations

(G-5821)
ONE CLICK CLEANERS
43 Kipling Way (07726-3743)
PHONE...............................732 804-9802
EMP: 4
SALES (est): 41.8K **Privately Held**
SIC: 7219 3582 Hand laundries; commer-
cial laundry equipment

(G-5822)
ONWARDS INC
Also Called: Bestar
10 Connor Dr (07726-1662)
PHONE...............................732 309-7348
Yang Sup Cha, *President*
▲ EMP: 3
SALES: 1MM **Privately Held**
SIC: 2329 Men's & boys' sportswear & ath-
letic clothing

(G-5823)
PANATECH CORPORATION
5 Elkridge Way (07726-3179)
PHONE...............................732 331-5692
Jay Panchal, *President*
▲ EMP: 5
SALES (est): 608K **Privately Held**
SIC: 3433 1711 Solar heaters & collectors;
solar energy contractor

(G-5824)
REX LUMBER COMPANY
1 Station St (07726-1608)
PHONE...............................732 446-4200
Benjamin Forester, *Manager*
Steve Tagliamonte, *Representative*
EMP: 70
SALES (corp-wide): 57.3MM **Privately
Held**
WEB: www.rexlumber.com
SIC: 2421 2431 Custom sawmill; kiln dry-
ing of lumber; lumber: rough, sawed or
planed; millwork
PA: Rex Lumber Company
840 Main St
Acton MA 01720
800 343-0567

(G-5825)
S&A MOLDERS INC
75 Mount Vernon Rd (07726-8071)
PHONE...............................732 851-7770
EMP: 8 EST: 2015
SALES (est): 284.2K **Privately Held**
SIC: 3089 Injection molded finished plastic
products

(G-5826)
SUN PACIFIC POWER CORP
215 Gordons Corner Rd 1a (07726-3352)
PHONE................................888 845-0242
Nicholas Campanella, *President*
▲ EMP: 10
SQ FT: 2,000
SALES (est): 3.7MM Privately Held
SIC: 5074 3433 5719 5211 Heating
equipment & panels, solar; solar heaters
& collectors; lighting fixtures; solar heat-
ing equipment

Manasquan
Monmouth County

(G-5827)
AHERN BLUEPRINTING INC
Also Called: A1 Copying Center
231 Parker Ave (08736-2806)
PHONE................................732 223-1476
Matthew J Ahern, *President*
Patricia Ahern, *Vice Pres*
Patrick Ahern, *Vice Pres*
Edward Ahern, *Treasurer*
EMP: 11
SQ FT: 5,000
SALES (est): 1.9MM Privately Held
WEB: www.aherncopy.com
SIC: 7334 2759 Blueprinting service; com-
mercial printing

(G-5828)
APLNOW LLC (PA)
Also Called: Apl2000
2640 Highway 70 Ste 4 (08736-2610)
P.O. Box 361, Brielle (08730-0361)
PHONE................................732 223-5575
Douglas Masto, *Partner*
EMP: 9
SALES (est): 1.6MM Privately Held
SIC: 7371 7379 7372 Computer software
development; computer related consulting
services; business oriented computer
software

(G-5829)
ARMSTRONG & SONS
2335 Highway 34 (08736-1423)
PHONE................................732 223-1555
Linda Pietsch, *President*
Michael Pickell, *Vice Pres*
EMP: 5 EST: 1930
SQ FT: 2,200
SALES (est): 620.6K Privately Held
WEB: www.armstrongandsons.com
SIC: 7359 3541 Equipment rental & leas-
ing; cutoff machines (metalworking ma-
chinery)

(G-5830)
COAST STAR
13 Broad St (08736-2906)
PHONE................................732 223-0076
James Manser, *President*
Matt Koenig, *Manager*
EMP: 35 EST: 1877
SQ FT: 2,000
SALES (est): 2.2MM Privately Held
WEB: www.thecoaststar.com
SIC: 2711 2752 Newspapers: publishing
only, not printed on site; commercial print-
ing, lithographic

(G-5831)
**GAMMON TECHNICAL
PRODUCTS INC (PA)**
2300 Highway 34 (08736-1499)
P.O. Box 400 (08736-0400)
PHONE................................732 223-4600
James H Gammon, *President*
Howard M Gammon, *Vice Pres*
Howard Gammon, *Vice Pres*
Wanda Gammon, *Treasurer*
Elizabeth Eldridge, *Info Tech Mgr*
▲ EMP: 60 EST: 1960
SQ FT: 34,440
SALES (est): 12.2MM Privately Held
WEB: www.gammontech.com
SIC: 3823 Liquid analysis instruments, in-
dustrial process type; liquid level instru-
ments, industrial process type

(G-5832)
J & G GRAPHICS INC
Also Called: Doctor Tee Shirt
221 Parker Ave (08736-2806)
PHONE................................732 223-6660
Robert Giaquinto, *President*
Mary O'Brien, *Treasurer*
EMP: 4
SQ FT: 1,000
SALES (est): 550K Privately Held
WEB: www.jerseyrunner.com
SIC: 2759 Screen printing

(G-5833)
MC RENEWABLE ENERGY LLC
Also Called: Azimuth Renewable Energy
50 Fletcher Ave (08736-3132)
PHONE................................732 369-9933
Jim Alberts, *Vice Pres*
EMP: 14
SALES (est): 771.1K Privately Held
SIC: 1711 5211 5074 3674 Solar energy
contractor; solar heating equipment; heat-
ing equipment & panels, solar; solar cells

(G-5834)
MICHAEL LUBRICH
Also Called: Custom Kitchen By Lubrich
5 Mount Ln (08736-3600)
PHONE................................732 223-4235
Michael Lubrich, *Owner*
EMP: 5
SQ FT: 3,000
SALES (est): 395.7K Privately Held
SIC: 2434 Wood kitchen cabinets

(G-5835)
MR PAULS CUSTOM CABINETS
2416 Highway 35 Ste E (08736-1154)
PHONE................................732 528-9427
Paul Waltsak Jr, *President*
Claire Waltsak, *Treasurer*
▲ EMP: 6 EST: 1966
SQ FT: 8,000
SALES (est): 834.6K Privately Held
SIC: 2434 Wood kitchen cabinets

(G-5836)
**P L CUSTOM BODY & EQP CO
INC**
Also Called: Pl Custom Emergency Vehicles
2201 Atlantic Ave (08736-1097)
PHONE................................732 223-1411
Jean S Smock, *CEO*
Deborah Thomson, *President*
Nancy Buhagiar, *Vice Pres*
Daniel Feliciano, *Warehouse Mgr*
Lisa Croasmun, *QC Mgr*
EMP: 175 EST: 1946
SQ FT: 110,000
SALES (est): 44.5MM Privately Held
WEB: www.plcustom.com
SIC: 3711 5012 Ambulances (motor vehi-
cles), assembly of; automobiles & other
motor vehicles

(G-5837)
REDA FURNITURE LLC
25 Ocean Ave (08736-3219)
PHONE................................732 948-1703
Colin Wynd,
EMP: 12
SALES (est): 979.5K Privately Held
SIC: 2521 Wood office furniture

(G-5838)
SANFORD & BIRDSALL INC
Also Called: George Pnterman Kitchens
Baths
1704 Atlantic Ave (08736-1116)
PHONE................................732 223-6966
Virginia Sanford-Birdsall, *President*
John Birdsall, *Vice Pres*
EMP: 6 EST: 1950
SQ FT: 3,000
SALES (est): 620K Privately Held
WEB: www.penterman.com
SIC: 1799 3281 Kitchen & bathroom re-
modeling; bathroom fixtures, cut stone

(G-5839)
STAR NEWS GROUP
13 Broad St (08736-2906)
PHONE................................732 223-0076
EMP: 4

SALES (est): 144.6K Privately Held
SIC: 2711 Newspapers

(G-5840)
**SUSTANBLE BLDG
INNOVATIONS INC**
2435 Highway 34 Ste 204 (08736-1819)
PHONE................................800 560-4143
Tristram Collins, *President*
EMP: 7
SALES (est): 630K Privately Held
SIC: 2452 Prefabricated wood buildings

(G-5841)
TRIAD SCIENTIFIC INC
6 Stockton Lake Blvd (08736-3024)
PHONE................................732 292-1994
Tom Leskow, *President*
Bill Aronoff, *Vice Pres*
EMP: 5
SQ FT: 8,500
SALES (est): 1.2MM Privately Held
WEB: www.triadsci.com
SIC: 5049 3821 Laboratory equipment,
except medical or dental; laboratory ap-
paratus & furniture

(G-5842)
W F SHERMAN & SON INC
84 Broad St (08736-2907)
PHONE................................732 223-1505
Donald Lee Sherman Jr, *President*
Alan Lee Sherman, *Corp Secy*
EMP: 15 EST: 1878
SQ FT: 7,500
SALES (est): 1.9MM Privately Held
SIC: 2431 Doors, wood

(G-5843)
WINEMILLER PRESS INC
Also Called: Toadhall Promotions
2411 Atlantic Ave Ste 6 (08736-1030)
PHONE................................732 223-0100
Carol Hutchinson, *President*
EMP: 8
SQ FT: 10,000
SALES (est): 540K Privately Held
WEB: www.winemiller-press.com
SIC: 2754 3993 2759 Posters: gravure
printing; signs & advertising specialties;
engraving

(G-5844)
WITTICH BROS MARINE INC
25a Abe Voorhees Dr (08736-3560)
PHONE................................732 722-8656
George Wittich, *President*
Scott Wittich, *General Mgr*
William Wittich, *COO*
Luke Wittich, *Accounting Mgr*
EMP: 30
SALES (est): 2.2MM Privately Held
SIC: 4492 7389 3731 Towing & tugboat
service; ; dredges, building & repairing

Manchester
Ocean County

(G-5845)
**FIRST PRIORITY EMERGENCY
VHICL (HQ)**
Also Called: First Priority Specialty Pdts
2444 Ridgeway Blvd # 500 (08759-5703)
PHONE................................732 657-1104
Robert Freeman, *President*
Adam Grecco, *Info Tech Dir*
Greg Deforge, *Info Tech Mgr*
▼ EMP: 21
SQ FT: 12,000
SALES (est): 7.3MM Privately Held
SIC: 3711 Ambulances (motor vehicles),
assembly of
PA: First Priority Global Ltd.
160 Gold Mine Rd
Flanders NJ 07836
973 347-4321

(G-5846)
LUXFER MAGTECH INC
2590 Ridgeway Blvd (08759-5701)
PHONE................................803 610-9898
Jim Gardella, *CEO*
EMP: 48

SALES (est): 4.9MM
SALES (corp-wide): 487.9MM Privately
Held
SIC: 2819 3339 3274 Magnesium com-
pounds or salts, inorganic; primary non-
ferrous metals; lime
PA: Luxfer Holdings Plc
Ancorage Gateway
Salford LANCS M50 3
161 300-0611

(G-5847)
ORGO-THERMIT INC (PA)
3500 Colonial Dr (08759-5799)
PHONE................................732 657-5781
Michael Madden, *President*
Stephanie Amiano, *Human Resources*
Kathryn Hammesfahr, *Cust Mgr*
Bruce E Wylie, *Info Tech Mgr*
Ryan Chinn, *Technical Staff*
▲ EMP: 35
SQ FT: 60,000
SALES (est): 7.1MM Privately Held
WEB: www.orgothermit.com
SIC: 1799 3548 7692 Welding on site;
welding & cutting apparatus & acces-
sories; welding repair

(G-5848)
**READE MANUFACTURING
COMPANY (HQ)**
Also Called: Magnesium Elektron Powders
NJ
2590 Ridgeway Blvd (08759-5798)
PHONE................................732 657-6451
James Gardella, *President*
Nuala Kelly, *Human Res Mgr*
◆ EMP: 50
SALES (est): 13MM
SALES (corp-wide): 487.9MM Privately
Held
WEB: www.luxfer.com
SIC: 2819 5169 Industrial inorganic chem-
icals; chemicals & allied products
PA: Luxfer Holdings Plc
Ancorage Gateway
Salford LANCS M50 3
161 300-0611

(G-5849)
RED WALLET CONNECTION INC
Also Called: Barkin Expanding Envelope Co
106 Cardigan Ct (08759-4632)
PHONE................................201 223-2644
Linda Lafferty, *President*
Edward Lafferty, *Vice Pres*
EMP: 55
SALES (est): 9.6MM Privately Held
WEB: www.redwalletconnection.com
SIC: 2677 2675 Envelopes; folders, filing,
die-cut: made from purchased materials

Mantoloking
Ocean County

(G-5850)
JOHN J CHANDO JR INC (PA)
209 Downer Ave (08738)
P.O. Box 731, Normandy Beach (08739-
0731)
PHONE................................732 793-2122
John J Chando Jr, *President*
EMP: 7 EST: 1978
SQ FT: 1,200
SALES: 4MM Privately Held
SIC: 1521 8711 1542 2655 New construction, single-family houses; single-
family home remodeling, additions &
repairs; consulting engineer; nonresidential construction; fiber cans, drums & containers; radioactive waste materials,
disposal

Mantua
Gloucester County

(G-5851)
C BENNETT SCOPES INC
550 Bridgeton Pike (08051-1318)
PHONE................................856 464-6889
Carolyn Bennett, *President*

▲ = Import ▼=Export
◆ =Import/Export

EMP: 4
SALES (est): 270K **Privately Held**
SIC: **3999** 5199 5947 Fire extinguishers, portable; gifts & novelties; gift, novelty & souvenir shop

(G-5852)
KINNARNEY RUBBER CO INC
450 Main St (08051)
P.O. Box 37 (08051-0037)
PHONE..............................856 468-1320
Luke Kinnarney, *President*
Brian Kiannarney, *Vice Pres*
EMP: 12 EST: 1959
SQ FT: 6,000
SALES: 1MM **Privately Held**
WEB: www.kinnarney.com
SIC: **3069** 3061 Hard rubber & molded rubber products; boot or shoe products, rubber; mechanical rubber goods

(G-5853)
ORBIT ENERGY & POWER LLC
106 Mantua Blvd (08051-1057)
PHONE..............................800 836-3987
Sean Angelini, *Mng Member*
EMP: 45
SALES (est): 12MM **Privately Held**
SIC: **4911** 3691 ; storage batteries

Manville
Somerset County

(G-5854)
CREATIONSREWARDS NET LLC
116 S 19th Ave (08835-1634)
PHONE..............................908 526-3127
Christopher Basista, *President*
EMP: 7 EST: 2008
SALES (est): 474.4K **Privately Held**
SIC: **2741**

(G-5855)
ESTRIN CALABRESE SALES AGENCY
17 S Main St Ste 3 (08835-1966)
PHONE..............................908 722-9980
Michael Estrin, *President*
Frank Calabrese, *Vice Pres*
EMP: 7
SQ FT: 1,800
SALES (est): 1.1MM **Privately Held**
WEB: www.estrincalabrese.com
SIC: **3645** Residential lighting fixtures

(G-5856)
MANVILLE RUBBER PRODUCTS INC
1009 Kennedy Blvd (08835-2031)
PHONE..............................908 526-9111
Sophia Gajewski, *President*
▲ EMP: 35 EST: 1964
SQ FT: 7,500
SALES: 3.8MM **Privately Held**
WEB: www.manvillerubber.com
SIC: **3069** 3061 Molded rubber products; mechanical rubber goods

(G-5857)
MOLECU-WIRE CORPORATION
1215 Kennedy Blvd (08835-2035)
P.O. Box 5426, Somerset (08875-5426)
PHONE..............................908 429-0300
Vinod K Barot, *President*
Hung K Chan, *Vice Pres*
EMP: 12
SQ FT: 45,000
SALES (est): 1.7MM **Privately Held**
WEB: www.molecu.com
SIC: **3357** Nonferrous wiredrawing & insulating

Maple Shade
Burlington County

(G-5858)
A QUICK CUT STAMPING EMBOSSING
803 N Forklanding Rd (08052-1007)
PHONE..............................856 321-0050

Holly Zahradnick, *President*
John Zahradnick, *Principal*
EMP: 10
SALES: 175K **Privately Held**
SIC: **3953** Embossing seals & hand stamps

(G-5859)
ANSWERS IN MOTION LLC
204 S Lippincott Ave (08052-3251)
PHONE..............................732 267-7792
Gregg Pembleton, *Mng Member*
EMP: 5
SALES: 400K **Privately Held**
SIC: **3944** Games, toys & children's vehicles

(G-5860)
CITI-CHEM INC
122 E Kings Hwy Ste 503 (08052-3424)
PHONE..............................609 231-6655
Calvin King, *President*
Lafayette Turner, *Vice Pres*
EMP: 38
SQ FT: 7,000
SALES (est): 3.1MM **Privately Held**
SIC: **2819** Industrial inorganic chemicals

(G-5861)
CPS METALS INC
450 S Fellowship Rd (08052-1880)
PHONE..............................856 779-0846
Edwin Pelczarski, *President*
Paul Pelczarski, *Shareholder*
Thomas Pelczarski, *Shareholder*
EMP: 12
SQ FT: 12,000
SALES (est): 1.1MM **Privately Held**
WEB: www.cpsmetals.com
SIC: **3444** Sheet metalwork

(G-5862)
EMERALD PERFORMANCE MTLS LLC
Also Called: Cvc Thermoset Specialities
2980 Route 73 N (08052-1334)
PHONE..............................856 533-3000
EMP: 16
SALES (corp-wide): 557.5MM **Privately Held**
SIC: **2821** Thermosetting materials
PA: Emerald Performance Materials Llc
1499 Se Tech Center Pl
Vancouver WA 98683
360 954-7100

(G-5863)
FRANKS UPHOLSTERY & DRAPERIES
621 S Forklanding Rd (08052-2916)
PHONE..............................856 779-8585
Frank A Troso, *Owner*
Frank Troso, *Owner*
EMP: 4
SQ FT: 2,700
SALES: 350K **Privately Held**
SIC: **2391** 7641 1752 Curtains, window: made from purchased materials; reupholstery; carpet laying

(G-5864)
INNOVATIVE SFTWR SOLUTIONS INC
3000 S Lenola Rd (08052-1613)
PHONE..............................856 910-9190
Jim Barling, *President*
Larry Goldstein, *Vice Pres*
Steve Webb, *Vice Pres*
Mary Beth Imondi, *Manager*
EMP: 78
SQ FT: 13,000
SALES (est): 13.6MM **Privately Held**
WEB: www.issisystems.com
SIC: **7372** 7379 7378 Operating systems computer software; computer related consulting services; computer & data processing equipment repair/maintenance
PA: Advanced Solutions International, Inc.
901 N Pitt St Ste 200
Alexandria VA 22314

(G-5865)
LIQUID ELEMENTS
1000 E Park Ave (08052-1200)
PHONE..............................856 321-7646

Edward Moore, *Principal*
Micah Esposito, *Opers Mgr*
EMP: 4 EST: 2011
SALES: 211.1K **Privately Held**
SIC: **2819** Industrial inorganic chemicals

(G-5866)
MAIN STREET GRAPHICS INC
30 W Main St (08052-2432)
PHONE..............................856 755-3523
Eileen Cusumano, *President*
EMP: 4
SALES (est): 555.7K **Privately Held**
WEB: www.mainstreetgraphics.net
SIC: **2759** Commercial printing

(G-5867)
MARKS MANAGEMENT SYSTEMS INC
Also Called: Sir Speedy
590 E Kings Hwy (08052)
PHONE..............................856 866-0588
Dennis Marks, *President*
Darlene Marks, *Vice Pres*
EMP: 8
SQ FT: 2,000
SALES (est): 953.9K **Privately Held**
SIC: **2752** 2791 2789 Commercial printing, lithographic; typesetting; bookbinding & related work

(G-5868)
PIONEER MACHINE & TOOL CO INC
425 E Broadway (08052-1242)
PHONE..............................856 779-8800
Michael Czuzak, *President*
John Cuthbert, *Manager*
EMP: 26 EST: 1953
SQ FT: 20,000
SALES: 2.5MM **Privately Held**
WEB: www.pioneermachine.net
SIC: **3444** Sheet metal specialties, not stamped

(G-5869)
SJ MAGAZINE
1000 S Lenola Rd Ste 102 (08052-1630)
PHONE..............................856 722-9300
Marianne Aleardi, *Owner*
EMP: 10
SALES (est): 966.7K **Privately Held**
SIC: **2721** Magazines: publishing & printing

(G-5870)
STONCOR GROUP INC (DH)
Also Called: Stonhard
1000 E Park Ave (08052-1200)
P.O. Box 308 (08052-0308)
PHONE..............................800 257-7953
David Reif, *CEO*
Dan Ugarte, *General Mgr*
Ryan Engel, *Superintendent*
Dave Bentley, *Regional Mgr*
Ed Sabato, *Regional Mgr*
◆ EMP: 120
SQ FT: 75,000
SALES (est): 437.5MM
SALES (corp-wide): 5.5B **Publicly Held**
WEB: www.stoncor.com
SIC: **2851** Coating, air curing
HQ: Republic Powdered Metals, Inc.
2628 Pearl Rd
Medina OH 44256
330 225-3192

(G-5871)
STONHARD MANUFACTURING CO INC (DH)
1000 E Park Ave (08052-1200)
P.O. Box 308 (08052-0308)
PHONE..............................856 779-7500
Stork H Donald, *CEO*
Dave Reis, *CFO*
Beth Powers, *Human Res Mgr*
Sherri Groves, *Administration*
◆ EMP: 44
SALES (est): 13.5MM
SALES (corp-wide): 5.5B **Publicly Held**
WEB: www.stoncor.com
SIC: **2899** Chemical preparations
HQ: Stoncor Group, Inc.
1000 E Park Ave
Maple Shade NJ 08052
800 257-7953

(G-5872)
THOMSON LAMINATION CO INC
504 E Linwood Ave (08052-1213)
PHONE..............................856 779-8521
Sterling A Martin, *President*
Jim Tyson, *Info Tech Mgr*
▲ EMP: 88 EST: 1964
SQ FT: 75,000
SALES (est): 24.1MM **Privately Held**
WEB: www.tlclam.net
SIC: **3544** 3679 Special dies & tools; cores, magnetic

Maplewood
Essex County

(G-5873)
2A HOLDINGS INC
Also Called: Constitution Arms
12 Hoffman St (07040-1114)
PHONE..............................973 378-8011
EMP: 10
SALES (est): 961.9K **Privately Held**
SIC: **8748** 8742 3484 Business Consulting Svcs Mgmt Consulting Svcs Mfg Small Arms

(G-5874)
BARRASSO & BLASI INDUSTRIES
Also Called: Acme Ring Div
1581 Springfield Ave (07040-2474)
PHONE..............................973 761-0595
EMP: 10 EST: 1916
SALES (est): 700K **Privately Held**
SIC: **3911** Mfg Precious Metal Jewelry

(G-5875)
CUSTOM BEDDING CO
Also Called: Orange Mattress
1677 Springfield Ave (07040-2967)
PHONE..............................973 761-1100
Marcel Segal, *President*
EMP: 6
SQ FT: 12,500
SALES (est): 675.3K **Privately Held**
WEB: www.mycustombedding.com
SIC: **2515** 5712 Mattresses, innerspring or box spring; mattresses

(G-5876)
ELEMENTS ACCESSORIES INC
Also Called: Lava Lunch
16 Essex Rd (07040-2308)
PHONE..............................646 801-5187
Melissa Zimberg, *Principal*
▲ EMP: 4
SALES (est): 318.1K **Privately Held**
SIC: **2393** Bags & containers, except sleeping bags: textile

(G-5877)
GORDON FRGSON INTR DSIGNS SVCS
Also Called: Gordon Fergusson Intr Dctg Ser
205 Rutgers St (07040-3229)
PHONE..............................973 378-2330
Gary N Reusch, *President*
EMP: 6
SQ FT: 1,700
SALES: 500K **Privately Held**
SIC: **2391** 7389 Curtains & draperies; interior designer

(G-5878)
HAIR DEPOT LIMITED
53 Peachtree Rd (07040-1641)
PHONE..............................973 251-9924
Marlon Mendoza, *President*
EMP: 10
SALES (est): 480.2K **Privately Held**
SIC: **3999** Wigs, including doll wigs, toupees or wiglets; hair & hair-based products; hair curlers, designed for beauty parlors; hair driers, designed for beauty parlors

(G-5879)
IDEAL JACOBS CORPORATION
515 Valley St Bsmt 1 (07040-4301)
PHONE..............................973 275-5100
Andrew C Jacobs, *President*

GEOGRAPHIC

Wendy Jacobs, *Treasurer*
Vinnie Santoro, *Executive*
▲ EMP: 30
SQ FT: 16,000
SALES (est): 6.7MM **Privately Held**
WEB: www.idealjacobs.com
SIC: 2759 2431 Tags: printing; labels &
seals: printing; schedule, ticket & tag
printing & engraving; millwork

(G-5880)
MAPLEWOOD BEVERAGE
PACKERS LLC
Also Called: Arizona Iced Tea
45 Camptown Rd (07040-3034)
PHONE....................................973 416-4582
Nick De Maria,
▼ EMP: 165
SQ FT: 10,000
SALES (est): 48.8MM **Privately Held**
SIC: 2086 Carbonated beverages, nonal-
coholic: bottled & canned

(G-5881)
PEACOCK COMMUNICATIONS
INC (PA)
215 Rutgers St (07040-3229)
P.O. Box 339, Montville (07045-0339)
PHONE....................................973 763-3311
Bernard Cicirelli, *Chairman*
Loretta Cicirelli, *Treasurer*
EMP: 5
SQ FT: 13,000
SALES (est): 401.6K **Privately Held**
WEB: www.peacockcommunications.com
SIC: 2752 Commercial printing, offset

(G-5882)
R G DUNN ACQUISITIONS CO
INC
Also Called: Electronic Manufacturing Co
71 Newark Way (07040-3309)
PHONE....................................973 762-1300
Martin Peterson, *President*
EMP: 27 EST: 1935
SQ FT: 10,000
SALES (est): 5.1MM **Privately Held**
WEB: www.elecmfgco.com
SIC: 3599 Machine shop, jobbing & repair

(G-5883)
RAILS COMPANY INC (PA)
101 Newark Way (07040-3309)
PHONE....................................973 763-4320
Garwood N Burwell, *President*
Joan Maldonado, *Vice Pres*
Satish Shankar, *Purch Mgr*
Agnes Lee, *CFO*
Mik Kinda, *Treasurer*
▼ EMP: 30 EST: 1932
SQ FT: 31,000
SALES (est): 4.5MM **Privately Held**
WEB: www.railsco.com
SIC: 3743 3469 3444 Railroad equip-
ment; stamping metal for the trade; sheet
metalwork

(G-5884)
SUPERMEDIA LLC
Also Called: Verizon
50 Burnett Ave (07040-2968)
PHONE....................................973 649-9900
Joseph Gibbs, *Branch Mgr*
EMP: 254
SALES (corp-wide): 1.8B **Privately Held**
WEB: www.verizon.superpages.com
SIC: 2741 Directories, telephone: publish-
ing only, not printed on site
HQ: Supermedia Llc
2200 W Airfield Dr
Dfw Airport TX 75261
972 453-7000

(G-5885)
TOVATECH LLC
Also Called: Iultrasonic
205 Rutgers St (07040-3229)
PHONE....................................973 913-9734
Ed Murphy, *Manager*
Robert Sandor,
Rachel Kohn,
EMP: 5

SALES: 1.5MM **Privately Held**
SIC: 5047 3821 5049 Medical laboratory
equipment; laboratory equipment: fume
hoods, distillation racks, etc.; laboratory
equipment, except medical or dental

(G-5886)
TRIMARCO INC
Also Called: New Art Ring Co
1847 Springfield Ave # 1849 (07040-2904)
PHONE....................................973 762-7380
Nick Trimarco, *President*
EMP: 4
SQ FT: 4,000
SALES (est): 762.6K **Privately Held**
SIC: 5094 3911 Jewelry; diamonds
(gems); rings, finger: precious metal

(G-5887)
TURBOT HQ INC (PA)
105 Oakview Ave (07040-2303)
PHONE....................................973 922-0297
Nathan Wallace, *Principal*
EMP: 12
SALES (est): 2.4MM **Privately Held**
SIC: 7372 Prepackaged software

(G-5888)
UNION TOOL & MOLD CO INC
220 Rutgers St (07040-3228)
PHONE....................................973 763-6611
Bob Arrighi, *CEO*
Joyce Arrighi, *Corp Secy*
▲ EMP: 25 EST: 1956
SQ FT: 20,000
SALES (est): 6.1MM **Privately Held**
WEB: www.uniontool-mold.com
SIC: 3544 Industrial molds

(G-5889)
VISUAL IMPACT ADVERTISING
INC
Also Called: Matter Magazine
9 Highland Pl Apt 3 (07040-2568)
PHONE....................................973 763-4900
Karen Duncan, *President*
EMP: 10
SALES (est): 844.2K **Privately Held**
SIC: 2721 Magazines: publishing only, not
printed on site

Margate City
Atlantic County

(G-5890)
PET SALON INC
8510 Ventnor Ave (08402-2522)
PHONE....................................609 350-6480
Beth Simons, *President*
EMP: 11
SALES (corp-wide): 1.3MM **Privately**
Held
SIC: 3999 0752 Pet supplies; grooming
services, pet & animal specialties
PA: The Pet Salon Inc
3 S Franklin Ave
Margate City NJ 08402
609 350-6480

(G-5891)
PET SALON INC (PA)
Also Called: Groomershelper.com
3 S Franklin Ave (08402-2747)
PHONE....................................609 350-6480
Beth Simons, *President*
Charles Simons, *Vice Pres*
▲ EMP: 4
SALES: 1.3MM **Privately Held**
WEB: www.petshots.com
SIC: 3999 0752 Pet supplies; grooming
services, pet & animal specialties

Marlboro
Monmouth County

(G-5892)
A PLUS PRODUCTS
INCORPORATED
8 Timber Ln (07746-1444)
PHONE 732 866-9111

Mike Schriber, *Owner*
Jerry Carbonaro, *Purchasing*
Sonia Laul, *Engineer*
◆ EMP: 26 EST: 2007
SALES (est): 5.1MM **Privately Held**
SIC: 3469 Metal stampings

(G-5893)
CERTIFIED CABINET CORP
9 S Main St (07746-1539)
P.O. Box 201 (07746-0201)
PHONE....................................732 741-0755
Mark Forman, *President*
EMP: 4 EST: 2011
SALES (est): 442.6K **Privately Held**
SIC: 2434 Wood kitchen cabinets

(G-5894)
DA-GREEN ELECTRONICS   LTD
4 Timber Ln Ste B (07746-1481)
PHONE....................................732 254-2735
Marc Gable, *Partner*
Barry Greenberg, *Principal*
Ellen Gable, *Shareholder*
Arline Kane, *Shareholder*
Lillian Moore, *Shareholder*
EMP: 18
SALES (est): 2.7MM **Privately Held**
WEB: www.dgecorp.com
SIC: 3679 5065 3678 Harness assem-
blies for electronic use: wire or cable;
connectors, electronic; electronic connec-
tors

(G-5895)
DB DESIGNS INC
10 Damascus Dr (07746-1953)
PHONE....................................732 616-5018
David Belasco, *President*
EMP: 5
SALES (est): 210K **Privately Held**
SIC: 2326 Service apparel (baker, barber,
lab, etc.), washable: men's

(G-5896)
EFCO CORP
Also Called: Econ Forms
77 Vanderburg Rd (07746-1450)
PHONE....................................732 308-1010
Joe Capazi, *Manager*
EMP: 13
SALES (corp-wide): 256.4MM **Privately**
Held
SIC: 5051 5211 3444 Steel; masonry ma-
terials & supplies; concrete forms; sheet
metal
HQ: Efco Corp
1800 Ne Broadway Ave
Des Moines IA 50313
515 266-1141

(G-5897)
EXPERT APPLIANCE CENTER
LLC
460 County Road 520 (07746-1041)
PHONE....................................732 946-0999
Oleg Gampel, *Principal*
EMP: 4
SALES (est): 334K **Privately Held**
SIC: 5064 3634 Electrical appliances, tele-
vision & radio; housewares, excluding
cooking appliances & utensils

(G-5898)
FLEXCO BLDG PDTS LTD LBLTY
CO
15 Timber Ln (07746-1443)
PHONE....................................732 780-1700
Michael W O'Gorman, *Mng Member*
Robert Lombardi,
EMP: 15
SQ FT: 18,000
SALES: 3.6MM **Privately Held**
SIC: 3272 Building materials, except block
or brick: concrete

(G-5899)
GP ACOUSTICS (US) INC
Also Called: Kef America
10 Timber Ln (07746-1444)
PHONE....................................732 683-2356
▲ EMP: 21 EST: 1973
SALES (est): 3.6MM **Privately Held**
SIC: 3651 Loudspeakers, electrodynamic
or magnetic

PA: Gold Peak Industries (Holdings) Limited
9/F Bldg 12w Hong Kong Science
Park Ph 3
Sha Tin NT

(G-5900)
HILMAN INCORPORATED (PA)
Also Called: Hillman Rollers
12 Timber Ln (07746-1444)
P.O. Box 45 (07746-0045)
PHONE....................................732 462-6277
Norman A Hill, *Ch of Bd*
David A Hill, *Principal*
Susan Montgomery, *Vice Pres*
◆ EMP: 65 EST: 1953
SQ FT: 76,000
SALES (est): 20.5MM **Privately Held**
WEB: www.hilmaninc.com
SIC: 3537 Forklift trucks; dollies (hand or
power trucks), industrial except mining; lift
trucks, industrial: fork, platform, straddle,
etc.

(G-5901)
INSUL-STOP INC
240 Boundary Rd (07746-1478)
PHONE....................................732 706-1978
Harry Bussey III, *President*
EMP: 5
SQ FT: 150,000
SALES (est): 506.9K **Privately Held**
SIC: 2899 Insulating compounds

(G-5902)
INTERNTONAL RIDING
HELMETS INC
15 Timber Ln (07746-1443)
PHONE....................................732 772-0165
Frank Plastino, *President*
▲ EMP: 20
SQ FT: 23,000
SALES (est): 135.6K **Privately Held**
SIC: 3949 5699 Helmets, athletic; riding
apparel

(G-5903)
KEF AMERICA INC
10 Timber Ln (07746-1444)
PHONE....................................732 414-2074
Alec Chanin, *President*
▲ EMP: 24
SALES (est): 8.3MM **Privately Held**
WEB: www.kefamerica.com
SIC: 5065 3677 3663 3651 Electronic
parts & equipment; electronic coils, trans-
formers & other inductors; radio & TV
communications equipment; household
audio & video equipment

(G-5904)
MASTER STRAP LLC
20 Hastings Rd Ste B (07746-1365)
PHONE....................................888 503-7779
Abraham Ovadia, *President*
EMP: 4
SALES: 69K **Privately Held**
SIC: 3931 7389 Drums, parts & acces-
sories (musical instruments);

(G-5905)
MULTI-TECH INDUSTRIES INC
64 S Main St (07746-1893)
P.O. Box 159 (07746-0159)
PHONE....................................732 431-0550
James L Bernard, *President*
Cindy Stanziola, *Admin Sec*
▲ EMP: 10 EST: 1969
SQ FT: 8,000
SALES (est): 930K **Privately Held**
WEB: www.multi-tech-industries.com
SIC: 3644 3643 3812 3825 Noncurrent-
carrying wiring services; current-carrying
wiring devices; electric switches; detec-
tion apparatus: electronic/magnetic field,
light/heat; antennas, radar or communica-
tions; instruments to measure electricity;
semiconductors & related devices; motors
& generators

(G-5906)
NEW JERSEY GOLD BUYERS
CORP (PA)
460 County Road 520 (07746-1041)
PHONE....................................732 765-4653
Raymond Benz, *Owner*

EMP: 4
SALES (est): 294.9K **Privately Held**
SIC: 3356 Gold & gold alloy: rolling, drawing or extruding

(G-5907)
NYC WOODWORKING INC
39 Kingfisher Ct (07746-2504)
PHONE.................................718 222-1221
Mark Spelczak, *Owner*
EMP: 4
SALES (est): 381K **Privately Held**
SIC: 2431 Millwork

(G-5908)
PARKWAY PRINTING INC
52 N Main St Ste 11 (07746-1428)
PHONE.................................732 308-0300
Steven Meringolo, *President*
Robin Meringolo, *Admin Sec*
EMP: 5
SALES (est): 666.1K **Privately Held**
SIC: 2752 Commercial printing, offset

(G-5909)
PLASMA POWDERS & SYSTEMS INC
228 Boundary Rd Ste 2 (07746-1446)
P.O. Box 132 (07746-0132)
PHONE.................................732 431-0992
Peter Foy, *President*
◆ EMP: 7 EST: 1980
SQ FT: 6,000
SALES (est): 2.7MM **Privately Held**
WEB: www.plasmapowders.com
SIC: 5169 5051 3315 Metal polishes; metal wires, ties, cables & screening; steel wire & related products

(G-5910)
PRO SPORTS INC
Also Called: Champion Sports Products Co
1 Champion Way (07746-1457)
P.O. Box 368 (07746-0368)
PHONE.................................732 294-5561
Howard Meller, *President*
Steven Meller, *Vice Pres*
◆ EMP: 34
SQ FT: 150,000
SALES (est): 4.5MM **Privately Held**
SIC: 5941 3949 Specialty sport supplies; sporting & athletic goods

(G-5911)
PROFESSIONAL REPRODUCTIONS INC
75 Vanderburg Rd (07746-1450)
PHONE.................................212 268-1222
Dominic Manzi, *President*
Chris Manzi, *Vice Pres*
EMP: 14
SQ FT: 5,000
SALES (est): 2.3MM **Privately Held**
WEB: www.professionalrepro.com
SIC: 7334 2752 Blueprinting service; commercial printing, offset

(G-5912)
RTI DGE LLC
Also Called: Robert Technologies
4 Timber Ln Ste B (07746-1481)
PHONE.................................732 254-6389
Mike Scala,
Greg Lyons,
EMP: 19
SALES (est): 781.7K **Privately Held**
SIC: 3643 Current-carrying wiring devices

(G-5913)
SAM GRAPHICS INC
Also Called: Millenium Graphics
35 Vanderburg Rd (07746-1418)
PHONE.................................732 431-0440
Robert Klepner, *Principal*
EMP: 26
SQ FT: 8,000
SALES (est): 379.4K **Privately Held**
SIC: 2752 Commercial printing, lithographic

(G-5914)
SHOPINDIA INC
3 Topaz Ct (07746-2161)
PHONE.................................732 409-0656
Tarun Chandra, *CEO*

EMP: 5
SALES (est): 442K **Privately Held**
WEB: www.shopindia.com
SIC: 5023 3911 Decorative home furnishings & supplies; jewelry apparel

(G-5915)
SINE TRU TOOL COMPANY INC
238 Boundary Rd Ste 2 (07746-1485)
P.O. Box 280, Morganville (07751-0280)
PHONE.................................732 591-1100
Kenny Klawunn, *President*
Bruce Klawunn, *Production*
EMP: 6 EST: 1956
SQ FT: 12,000
SALES (est): 925.8K **Privately Held**
SIC: 3545 7692 3423 Cutting tools for machine tools; machine knives, metalworking; welding repair; hand & edge tools

(G-5916)
SYNERGETICA INTERNATIONAL INC
9 Inverness Dr (07746-2129)
PHONE.................................732 780-5865
Heng Michael Su, *President*
Nancy Yeh, *Accountant*
▲ EMP: 5
SALES: 8.5MM **Privately Held**
WEB: www.synergeticainc.com
SIC: 2834 Pharmaceutical preparations

(G-5917)
TOWN & COUNTRY PLASTICS INC
Also Called: T & C
10b Timber Ln (07746-1444)
P.O. Box 269, Morganville (07751-0269)
PHONE.................................732 780-5300
Harold Mermel, *President*
Leslie Mermel, *Vice Pres*
▲ EMP: 15
SQ FT: 5,000
SALES (est): 2.2MM **Privately Held**
SIC: 3089 3088 3822 Plastic processing; plastics plumbing fixtures; auto controls regulating residntl & coml environmt & applncs

(G-5918)
TUSCANY ESPECIALLY ITLN FOODS
13a S Main St Store 5 (07746)
PHONE.................................732 308-1118
Vincent Lafranca, *President*
Sal Faenza, *Vice Pres*
EMP: 10
SALES (est): 866.8K **Privately Held**
SIC: 2032 Italian foods: packaged in cans, jars, etc.

Marlton
Burlington County

(G-5919)
ABBOTT LABORATORIES
10000 Lincoln Dr E # 201 (08053-3108)
PHONE.................................856 988-5572
Stephen Fortino, *Branch Mgr*
EMP: 11
SALES (corp-wide): 30.5B **Publicly Held**
WEB: www.abbott.com
SIC: 2834 Pharmaceutical preparations
PA: Abbott Laboratories
    100 Abbott Park Rd
    Abbott Park IL 60064
    224 667-6100

(G-5920)
ACS QUALITY SERVICES INC
20 Elmgate Rd (08053-2402)
P.O. Box 266 (08053-0266)
PHONE.................................856 988-6550
Norm Skversky, *President*
EMP: 4
SALES (est): 619.7K **Privately Held**
SIC: 3823 Water quality monitoring & control systems

(G-5921)
ADEMCO INC
Also Called: ADI Global Distribution
1000 Lincoln Dr E (08053-1566)
PHONE.................................856 985-9050
EMP: 4
SALES (corp-wide): 4.8B **Publicly Held**
SIC: 5063 3669 3822 Electrical apparatus & equipment; emergency alarms; auto controls regulating residntl & coml environmt & applncs
HQ: Ademco Inc.
    1985 Douglas Dr N
    Golden Valley MN 55422
    800 468-1502

(G-5922)
BBM FAIRWAY INC
49 S Maple Ave (08053-2031)
PHONE.................................856 596-0999
Marykay Duff, *Branch Mgr*
EMP: 5
SQ FT: 1,900
SALES (corp-wide): 33.3MM **Privately Held**
WEB: www.bobit.com
SIC: 2721 Magazines: publishing only, not printed on site
PA: Bbm Fairway, Inc.
    3520 Challenger St
    Torrance CA 90503

(G-5923)
CAPE PROSTHETICS-ORTHOTICS
Also Called: Prosthetic Orthotic Solutions
100 Brick Rd Ste 315 (08053-2146)
PHONE.................................856 810-7900
Kevin Powers, *Principal*
EMP: 7 **Privately Held**
SIC: 3842 Limbs, artificial
HQ: Cape Prosthetics-Orthotics Inc
    855 Springdale Dr Ste 200
    Exton PA 19341
    610 644-7824

(G-5924)
CENTURUM INFORMATION TECH INC (HQ)
651 Route 73 N Ste 107 (08053-3445)
PHONE.................................856 751-1111
Robert M Matteucci, *CEO*
Samuel R Seymour, *Exec VP*
Thomas J Botulinski, *Vice Pres*
Steve Golle, *Vice Pres*
Jeffrey S Hughes Sr, *CFO*
EMP: 8
SQ FT: 2,000
SALES (est): 45MM
SALES (corp-wide): 57.1MM **Privately Held**
SIC: 8742 8711 3661 3663 Management consulting services; engineering services; telephone & telegraph apparatus; radio & TV communications equipment; commercial physical research; radio telephone communication
PA: Centurum Inc.
    651 Route 73 N Ste 107
    Marlton NJ 08053
    856 751-1111

(G-5925)
COVENTRY OF NEW JERSEY INC
10000 Lincoln Dr E # 201 (08053-3108)
PHONE.................................856 988-5521
Mark Recchiniti, *President*
Harry Orth, *Vice Pres*
EMP: 20
SALES (est): 1.1MM **Privately Held**
SIC: 2759 2752 Commercial printing; commercial printing, lithographic

(G-5926)
CUSTOM QUICK LABEL INC
300 Greentree Rd # 207 (08053-9418)
PHONE.................................856 596-7555
Judy Tagen, *President*
Martin Tagen, *Treasurer*
EMP: 7
SALES (est): 1.2MM **Privately Held**
SIC: 5131 2679 Labels; bridal supplies; labels, paper: made from purchased material

(G-5927)
DEFENSE SPPORT SVCS INTL 2 LLC
901 Lincoln Dr W Ste 200 (08053-3131)
PHONE.................................856 866-2200
Kathleen Bates, *Manager*
John Keating,
Clinton Bickett,
Paul W Cobb Jr,
Stephanie Finn, *Asst Sec*
EMP: 11
SALES (est): 957.7K **Privately Held**
SIC: 3721 4581 8711 8742 Airplanes, fixed or rotary wing; repairing; engineering services; management consulting services; systems analysis & engineering consulting services

(G-5928)
DEFENSE SUPPORT SVCS INTL LLC (DH)
901 Lincoln Dr W Ste 200 (08053-3131)
PHONE.................................850 390-4737
John F Keating, *Mng Member*
Donald W Smith,
EMP: 12
SALES (est): 8.9MM **Privately Held**
SIC: 4581 3728 8742 Airports, flying fields & services; aircraft parts & equipment; materials mgmt. (purchasing, handling, inventory) consultant
HQ: Pae Aviation And Technical Services Llc
    1320 N Courthouse Rd # 800
    Arlington VA 22201
    856 866-2200

(G-5929)
DOOLAN INDUSTRIES INCORPORATED (PA)
Also Called: Emc3
5 Blue Anchor St (08053-3011)
PHONE.................................856 985-1880
Timothy W Stein, *President*
EMP: 4
SQ FT: 5,000
SALES (est): 5.6MM **Privately Held**
SIC: 4959 3694 5051 7363 Environmental cleanup services; motor generator sets, automotive; metals service centers & offices; labor resource services

(G-5930)
DYNAMIC DEFENSE MATERIALS LLC
100 Sharp Rd (08053-5547)
P.O. Box 1339 (08053-6339)
PHONE.................................856 552-4150
Robert A Lipinski, *CEO*
John Yarsinsky, *CFO*
▲ EMP: 8
SQ FT: 5,000
SALES (est): 1.3MM **Privately Held**
WEB: www.ddmat.com
SIC: 3312 Armor plate

(G-5931)
FIVE MACS INC
Also Called: Business Card Express
8 E Stow Rd Ste 140 (08053-3161)
P.O. Box 728 (08053-0728)
PHONE.................................856 596-3150
John McTigue Jr, *President*
Madeline McTigue, *Vice Pres*
EMP: 31
SALES (est): 4.2MM **Privately Held**
WEB: www.bcex.com
SIC: 2754 5112 2759 Cards, except greeting: gravure printing; envelopes: gravure printing; stationery: gravure printing; invitations: gravure printing; envelopes; stationery; commercial printing

(G-5932)
GALLANT LABORATORIES INC
2407 Delancey Way (08053-8513)
PHONE.................................609 654-4146
Gary Gallant, *President*
Barbara Gallant, *Admin Sec*
EMP: 8
SQ FT: 6,000
SALES (est): 1MM **Privately Held**
SIC: 2844 Cosmetic preparations

(G-5933)
GLOBAL INDUSTRIES INC (PA)
Also Called: Global Furniture Group
17 W Stow Rd (08053-3116)
P.O. Box 562 (08053-0562)
PHONE..............................856 596-3390
Joel Appel, *Ch of Bd*
Jon Abraham, *Exec VP*
Alan Breslow, *Exec VP*
Jon Soll, *Exec VP*
Jailita Davis, *Project Mgr*
◆ EMP: 180 EST: 1990
SALES (est): 116MM Privately Held
WEB: www.evolvefurnituregroup.com
SIC: 2522 5021 Office furniture, except
wood; furniture

(G-5934)
INTERNTNAL BSCITS CNFCTONS INC
10000 Lincoln Dr E # 102 (08053-3108)
PHONE..............................856 813-1008
Don Demato, *Principal*
Monica Mattar, *Business Mgr*
Howard Abramovitz, *Director*
EMP: 4
SALES (est): 188.8K Privately Held
SIC: 2052 Biscuits, dry

(G-5935)
KAR INDUSTRIAL
906 Route 73 N (08053-1230)
PHONE..............................856 985-8730
Kevin Rose,
EMP: 7
SALES (est): 661.3K Privately Held
SIC: 7312 5046 3993 5099 Outdoor ad-
vertising services; signs, electrical; signs,
not made in custom sign painting shops;
signs, except electric

(G-5936)
LAWLESS JERKY LLC
37 N Maple Ave Apt 30 (08053-1758)
PHONE..............................310 869-5733
Matt Tolnick, *CEO*
EMP: 6 EST: 2013
SALES (est): 283.4K Privately Held
SIC: 2013 Snack sticks, including jerky:
from purchased meat

(G-5937)
LIBERTY COCA-COLA BEVS LLC
5 E Stow Rd Ste G (08053-3145)
PHONE..............................856 988-3844
Margaret Bailey, *Manager*
EMP: 20
SALES (corp-wide): 1.3B Privately Held
SIC: 2086 Bottled & canned soft drinks
PA: Liberty Coca-Cola Beverages Llc
725 E Erie Ave
Philadelphia PA 19134
215 427-4500

(G-5938)
LOCKHEED MARTIN
Also Called: Mission Systems & Training
3000 Lincoln Dr E Ste E (08053-1500)
PHONE..............................856 722-7782
Peggy Koenitzer, *Manager*
EMP: 100 Publicly Held
SIC: 3812 Search & navigation equipment
HQ: Lockheed Martin Integrated Systems,
Llc
6801 Rockledge Dr
Bethesda MD 20817

(G-5939)
LOCKHEED MARTIN
3000 Lincoln Dr E Ste E (08053-1500)
PHONE..............................856 722-2418
John R Busca, *Manager*
EMP: 250 Publicly Held
SIC: 3812 Search & navigation equipment
HQ: Lockheed Martin Integrated Systems,
Llc
6801 Rockledge Dr
Bethesda MD 20817

(G-5940)
LOCKHEED MARTIN CORPORATION
10000 Sagemore Dr # 10203 (08053-3944)
PHONE..............................856 988-1085
Sandra Ogbin, *Analyst*

EMP: 177 Publicly Held
SIC: 3812 Search & navigation equipment
PA: Lockheed Martin Corporation
6801 Rockledge Dr
Bethesda MD 20817

(G-5941)
MC DOES INC
Also Called: Fastsigns
906 Route 73 N (08053-1230)
PHONE..............................856 985-8730
Mark Esposito, *President*
John Downing, *Principal*
EMP: 9
SALES (est): 1.3MM Privately Held
SIC: 3993 Signs & advertising specialties

(G-5942)
MUNIPOL SYSTEMS
1 Eves Dr Ste 111 (08053-3125)
PHONE..............................856 985-2929
Jack Brownstein, *President*
Richmond Cooper, *Vice Pres*
James Mc Farland, *Vice Pres*
William Olsen, *Vice Pres*
EMP: 15
SALES (est): 700K Privately Held
WEB: www.munipol.com
SIC: 7372 Application computer software

(G-5943)
NETSCOUT SYSTEMS INC
2000 Lincoln Dr E (08053-1557)
PHONE..............................609 518-4100
Kevin Keough, *Vice Pres*
Bill Higgins, *Engineer*
Felix Houvig, *Engineer*
Charles Kuski, *Engineer*
Gene Litt, *Director*
EMP: 8
SALES (corp-wide): 909.9MM Publicly
Held
SIC: 7373 3577 Computer integrated sys-
tems design; computer peripheral equip-
ment
PA: Netscout Systems, Inc.
310 Littleton Rd
Westford MA 01886
978 614-4000

(G-5944)
OMNITESTER CORP (PA)
101 Flintlock Ln (08053-1111)
PHONE..............................856 985-8960
James M Lamy, *CEO*
James Wehman, *President*
EMP: 15
SQ FT: 5,000
SALES (est): 1.1MM Privately Held
SIC: 3825 Test equipment for electronic &
electrical circuits

(G-5945)
PACKAGING CORPORATION AMERICA
Also Called: Marlton Creative Design Center
8 E Stow Rd Ste 100 (08053-3161)
PHONE..............................856 596-5020
EMP: 4
SALES (corp-wide): 6.4B Publicly Held
SIC: 2653 Mfg Corrugated/Solid Fiber
Boxes
PA: Packaging Corporation Of America
1955 W Field Ct
Lake Forest IL 60045
847 482-3000

(G-5946)
PAPERY OF MARLTON LLC
300 Route 73 S Ste B (08053-3029)
PHONE..............................856 985-1776
Edmund Brandhorst,
Marylou Brandhorst,
EMP: 6
SALES: 600K Privately Held
SIC: 5943 5947 2759 Stationery stores;
greeting cards; gift shop; invitation & sta-
tionery printing & engraving

(G-5947)
PLESCIA & COMPANY INC
Also Called: Compliance Educational Sys-
tems
205 Shady Ln (08053-2718)
PHONE..............................856 793-0137
Gary Plescia, *President*

Joanne Plescia, *Vice Pres*
Christine Castile, *Treasurer*
EMP: 10
SALES (est): 844K Privately Held
SIC: 7372 Prepackaged software

(G-5948)
PREMIER PRODUCTS INC
1002 Lincoln Dr W Ste B (08053-1533)
PHONE..............................856 231-1800
Eric Alpert, *President*
Rich Holderman, *Vice Pres*
▲ EMP: 65
SQ FT: 3,000
SALES (est): 9.8MM Privately Held
SIC: 3714 Air conditioner parts, motor vehi-
cle

(G-5949)
REPCO INC
6 Eves Dr Unit 1 (08053-3147)
PHONE..............................856 762-0172
Ann Braytenbah, *President*
James Peter Gillin, *Treasurer*
Toni Atkinson, *Sales Staff*
Scott Tussey, *Consultant*
Cheryl Rockett, *Technology*
▲ EMP: 12
SQ FT: 20,000
SALES (est): 2.1MM Privately Held
WEB: www.repcoinc.com
SIC: 3699 Electrical equipment & supplies

(G-5950)
SCHURMAN FINE PAPERS
Also Called: Papyrus
300 State Hwy Rte 73 (08053)
PHONE..............................856 985-1776
EMP: 21
SALES (corp-wide): 366MM Privately
Held
SIC: 2679 2771 5947 5113 Gift wrap &
novelties, paper; greeting cards; gift, nov-
elty & souvenir shop; greeting cards;
paper & products, wrapping or coarse
PA: Schurman Fine Papers
300 Oak Bluff Ln
Goodlettsville TN 37072
707 425-8006

(G-5951)
SHEEX INC
Also Called: Sheex Performance Sleep
10000 Lincoln Dr E # 303 (08053-3108)
PHONE..............................856 334-3021
Michelle Brooke-Marciniak, *CEO*
Susan K Walvius, *President*
Kelle Giordano, *Vice Pres*
Denise Bearce, *Opers Staff*
Theresa Dalesandro, *Opers Staff*
▲ EMP: 20
SQ FT: 5,000
SALES (est): 4MM Privately Held
WEB: www.sheex.com
SIC: 2515 2392 Sleep furniture; house-
hold furnishings

(G-5952)
STONE MAR NATURAL STONE CO LLC (PA)
8 E Stow Rd Ste 200 (08053-3161)
PHONE..............................856 988-1802
Simon Katan, *President*
▲ EMP: 6
SALES (est): 1.2MM Privately Held
SIC: 3281 Cut stone & stone products

(G-5953)
TEST TECHNOLOGY INC (HQ)
5 E Stow Rd (08053-3145)
PHONE..............................856 596-1215
Linda A Austin, *President*
▲ EMP: 94
SQ FT: 71,000
SALES (est): 8.6MM
SALES (corp-wide): 15.4MM Privately
Held
WEB: www.testtech.com
SIC: 7629 3672 Electronic equipment re-
pair; printed circuit boards
PA: Revertech Solutions, Llc
4 E Stow Rd Ste 2
Marlton NJ 08053
877 207-2836

(G-5954)
THRYV INC
401 Route 73 N Bldg 20 (08053-3427)
PHONE..............................856 988-2700
Andrea Drioli, *Manager*
EMP: 42
SALES (corp-wide): 1.8B Privately Held
SIC: 2741 Telephone & other directory
publishing
PA: Thryv, Inc.
2200 W Airfield Dr
Dfw Airport TX 75261
972 453-7000

(G-5955)
VAN BRILL POOL & SPA CENTER
Also Called: All Seasons Pool & Spa
850 Route 70 W (08053-1646)
P.O. Box 844 (08053-0844)
PHONE..............................856 424-4333
Armand J Savaiano, *President*
Armand Savaiano, *President*
EMP: 8
SQ FT: 4,500
SALES (est): 1.7MM Privately Held
SIC: 5999 3272 Spas & hot tubs; fireplace
& chimney material: concrete

(G-5956)
WESTROCK RKT LLC
Also Called: Rock Team Alliance
5000 Lincoln Dr E (08053-1562)
PHONE..............................856 596-8604
Bill Atcheson, *Branch Mgr*
EMP: 161
SALES (corp-wide): 16.2B Publicly Held
SIC: 2631 Paperboard mills
HQ: Westrock Rkt, Llc
1000 Abernathy Rd Ste 125
Atlanta GA 30328
770 448-2193

(G-5957)
WISESORBENT TECHNOLOGY LLC
11 E Stow Rd (08053-3118)
PHONE..............................856 872-7713
Fei Shen,
EMP: 50
SALES (est): 5.7MM Privately Held
SIC: 2819 Industrial inorganic chemicals

Marmora
Cape May County

(G-5958)
LIBERTY COCA-COLA BEVS LLC
519 Route Us 9 S (08223-1258)
PHONE..............................609 390-5002
Jeff Glenn, *Branch Mgr*
EMP: 75
SQ FT: 35,000
SALES (corp-wide): 1.3B Privately Held
SIC: 2086 Bottled & canned soft drinks
PA: Liberty Coca-Cola Beverages Llc
725 E Erie Ave
Philadelphia PA 19134
215 427-4500

(G-5959)
SJSHORE MARKETING LTD LBLTY CO
Also Called: Allegra Marketing Print & Mail
533 S Shore Rd Ste 1 (08223-1258)
PHONE..............................609 390-1400
Nicholas Wieand,
Denise Wieand,
EMP: 15
SQ FT: 5,400
SALES (est): 907.5K Privately Held
SIC: 3993 7331 8742 2759 Signs & ad-
vertising specialties; mailing service; mar-
keting consulting services; advertising
literature: printing

(G-5960)
TEC ELEVATOR INC
510 Route Us 9 S (08223-1329)
PHONE..............................609 938-0647
Robert Shaw Jr, *CEO*
Jim McCabe, *Vice Pres*

Jim Koch, *Sales Staff*
Margaret Dromgoole, *Admin Sec*
EMP: 10
SALES (est): 2.3MM **Privately Held**
SIC: 3534 Elevators & equipment

Martinsville
Somerset County

(G-5961)
CHEMTRACT LLC
2144 Gilbride Rd (08836-2231)
PHONE....................732 820-0427
James Balkovec, *Owner*
EMP: 4 **EST:** 2012
SALES (est): 231.5K **Privately Held**
SIC: 2834 Pharmaceutical preparations

(G-5962)
COMPUTER DOC ASSOCIATES INC
2007 Washington Valley Rd (08836-2010)
P.O. Box 184, Gillette (07933-0184)
PHONE....................908 647-4445
Parveen Khattar, *President*
EMP: 68 **EST:** 1994
SALES (est): 6.8MM **Privately Held**
WEB: www.cdaus.com
SIC: 5734 7372 8243 8748 Computer & software stores; business oriented computer software; operating systems computer software; software training, computer; systems engineering consultant, ex. computer or professional

(G-5963)
MRS SULLIVANS INC (PA)
Also Called: Mrs. Sullivan's Pies
1990 Washington Valley Rd (08836-7000)
P.O. Box 446, Jackson TN (38302-0446)
PHONE....................908 246-8937
James Lawrence, *President*
Rodney Myrick, *President*
Ed Novy, *CFO*
EMP: 21
SQ FT: 12,000
SALES (est): 1.9MM **Privately Held**
WEB: www.mrssullivans.com
SIC: 2051 Cakes, pies & pastries

(G-5964)
RSR ENTERPRISES LLC
1480 Long Rd (08836-2030)
PHONE....................732 369-6053
Romeo Russo,
EMP: 11
SALES: 45K **Privately Held**
SIC: 2033 Spaghetti & other pasta sauce: packaged in cans, jars, etc.

(G-5965)
WINTERS STAMP MFG CO INC
Also Called: Winters Bank Signs
1024 Mayflower Ct (08836-2324)
P.O. Box 3, Elizabeth (07207-0003)
PHONE....................908 352-3725
J Carl Apsley Jr, *CEO*
Jane Apsley - Williams, *President*
▲ **EMP:** 10
SQ FT: 48,000
SALES (est): 836.8K **Privately Held**
SIC: 3953 3479 Marking devices; name plates: engraved, etched, etc.

Matawan
Monmouth County

(G-5966)
ADVANCE INTERNATIONAL INC (PA)
8 Willow Ridge Ct (07747-9662)
PHONE....................212 213-2229
Herbert Feinberg, *President*
Michael Minetti, *Vice Pres*
◆ **EMP:** 40 **EST:** 1954
SALES (est): 5.2MM **Privately Held**
SIC: 5199 3699 3999 Christmas novelties; Christmas tree lighting sets, electric; Christmas trees, artificial

(G-5967)
AGAU INC
Also Called: Print Shop, The
1077 State Route 34 Ste M (07747-2151)
PHONE....................732 583-4343
Paul Silvergold, *President*
EMP: 8 **EST:** 1979
SALES (est): 720K **Privately Held**
WEB: www.printshoppenj.com
SIC: 2752 Commercial printing, offset

(G-5968)
B SPINELLI FARM CONTAINERS
3992 Highway 516 (07747-7017)
PHONE....................732 616-7505
Benjamin Spinelli Jr, *President*
Benjamin Spinelli Sr, *Vice Pres*
Margaret Spinelli, *Vice Pres*
Helen Spinelli, *Admin Sec*
EMP: 6
SALES (est): 823.2K **Privately Held**
SIC: 2449 2653 Boxes, wood: wirebound; boxes, corrugated: made from purchased materials

(G-5969)
CARIB-DISPLAY CO (PA)
18 Northland Ln (07747-1321)
P.O. Box 306 (07747-0306)
PHONE....................732 583-1648
Cary Binder, *Owner*
EMP: 5
SALES (est): 497.2K **Privately Held**
WEB: www.caribdisplay.com
SIC: 2542 Partitions & fixtures, except wood

(G-5970)
CERONICS INC
5 Dock St (07747-2506)
P.O. Box 75 (07747-0075)
PHONE....................732 566-5600
Richard Patton, *President*
George Curchin, *Vice Pres*
EMP: 7
SQ FT: 3,000
SALES (est): 831.8K **Privately Held**
WEB: www.ceronicsinc.com
SIC: 3479 Coating of metals & formed products; painting, coating & hot dipping

(G-5971)
CODA RESOURCES LTD (PA)
Also Called: Cambridge Resources
100 Matawan Rd Ste 300 (07747-3915)
PHONE....................718 649-1666
Hillel Tropper, *CEO*
Steve Keilson, *General Mgr*
Kurtis Feil, *Vice Pres*
Larry Lasher, *Vice Pres*
Moshe Tropper, *Vice Pres*
▲ **EMP:** 102
SQ FT: 100,000
SALES (est): 30.5MM **Privately Held**
WEB: www.codaresources.com
SIC: 3469 2821 Metal stampings; molding compounds, plastics

(G-5972)
DIGIVAC COMPANY
105 B Church St Ste 4 (07747)
PHONE....................732 765-0900
Timothy Collins, *President*
Christine Diab, *Purchasing*
Heather Maitree, *Treasurer*
John Ennis, *Sales Staff*
Kerry Obrien, *Marketing Staff*
EMP: 12
SQ FT: 3,300
SALES (est): 1.3MM **Privately Held**
WEB: www.digivac.com
SIC: 3545 3823 3829 Gauges (machine tool accessories); industrial instrmnts msrmnt display/control process variable; measuring & controlling devices

(G-5973)
DULCE A DESSERT BAR LLC
609 S Atlantic Ave (07747-2225)
PHONE....................908 461-2418
Erica Townes,
EMP: 7
SALES (est): 210.5K **Privately Held**
SIC: 2099 Desserts, ready-to-mix

(G-5974)
DYNAMIC COATINGS LLC
253 Main St Ste 120 (07747-3222)
PHONE....................732 998-6625
Gregory Guga, *President*
EMP: 4 **EST:** 2015
SALES (est): 518.8K **Privately Held**
SIC: 3479 Metal coating & allied service

(G-5975)
ELIS HOT BAGELS INC
1055 Hwy 34 Ste C (07747-2192)
PHONE....................732 566-4523
Stuart Rauchman, *President*
EMP: 45
SQ FT: 4,000
SALES (est): 4MM **Privately Held**
SIC: 2051 5812 5149 5461 Bagels, fresh or frozen; eating places; groceries & related products; bakeries

(G-5976)
GEMTOR INC
1 Johnson Ave (07747-2595)
PHONE....................732 583-6200
Craig Neustater, *President*
Ruth Ullrich, *Admin Sec*
▲ **EMP:** 40
SQ FT: 18,000
SALES: 6MM **Privately Held**
WEB: www.gemtor.com
SIC: 3842 Personal safety equipment

(G-5977)
GOOSE COUNTRY LLC
10 Bramble Ln (07747-3801)
P.O. Box 2243, Edison (08818-2243)
PHONE....................646 860-8815
Deep Bhatia,
EMP: 3
SALES: 1.5MM **Privately Held**
SIC: 2386 Coats & jackets, leather & sheep-lined

(G-5978)
ITEC CONSULTANTS LLC
38 Hyer Ct (07747-1252)
PHONE....................732 784-8322
Robert Smith, *Mng Member*
Mario Rodrigues, *Mng Member*
EMP: 6
SALES (est): 570K **Privately Held**
SIC: 3651 Household audio & video equipment

(G-5979)
KITCHEN CRAFTERS PLUS
Also Called: B & B Custom Cabinets
1 Suydam Pl (07747-1024)
PHONE....................732 566-7995
Al Brisebois, *President*
Roger Buchko, *Vice Pres*
EMP: 4
SQ FT: 4,500
SALES (est): 330K **Privately Held**
WEB: www.kitchencraftersplus.com
SIC: 2434 1751 Wood kitchen cabinets; cabinet building & installation

(G-5980)
MODEL RECTIFIER CORPORATION
360 Main St Ste 2 (07747-3255)
PHONE....................732 225-2100
Frank Ritota, *President*
Roy C Gelber, *Chairman*
Anthony P Iati, *Vice Pres*
Akiko Kimura, *Vice Pres*
Debra Boyce, *Sales Staff*
▲ **EMP:** 35
SALES (est): 8MM **Privately Held**
WEB: www.modelrec.com
SIC: 3612 5092 Rectifier transformers; toy transformers; hobby goods

(G-5981)
NEW JERSEY STAIR AND RAIL INC
746 Lloyd Rd (07747-1401)
PHONE....................732 583-8400
Robert Barrett, *President*
Cathrine Barrett, *Corp Secy*
EMP: 5
SQ FT: 8,000

SALES (est): 467.1K **Privately Held**
SIC: 3446 Stairs, staircases, stair treads: prefabricated metal

(G-5982)
OPEN TERRA INC
20 Reddington Dr (07747-6647)
PHONE....................732 765-9600
David Sasson, *CEO*
Ted Bielenda, *CTO*
EMP: 7
SALES: 500K **Privately Held**
WEB: www.openterra.com
SIC: 3663 Mobile communication equipment

(G-5983)
PARWAN ELECTRONICS CORPORATION (PA)
Also Called: PEC
1230 Hwy 34 (07747-1952)
PHONE....................732 290-1900
Suraj Tschand, *President*
Vinay Tschand, *COO*
Kuwar Prashant, *Vice Pres*
Chand Tschand, *CFO*
Ajay Tschand, *CTO*
EMP: 23
SQ FT: 7,000
SALES (est): 5.6MM **Privately Held**
WEB: www.voicesaver.com
SIC: 3661 Carrier equipment, telephone or telegraph

(G-5984)
PENN POWER GROUP LLC
Also Called: Carrier Transicold of NJ
4118 Hiway 34 (07747)
PHONE....................732 441-1489
Gary Meyers, *Branch Mgr*
EMP: 10
SALES (corp-wide): 92MM **Privately Held**
SIC: 3519 Engines, diesel & semi-diesel or dual-fuel
PA: Penn Power Group, Llc
8330 State Rd
Philadelphia PA 19136
215 335-0500

(G-5985)
POMI USA INC
253 Main St Ste 380 (07747-3222)
PHONE....................732 541-4115
Constantino Vaia, *President*
▲ **EMP:** 7
SQ FT: 60
SALES (est): 470.9K
SALES (corp-wide): 286.5MM **Privately Held**
SIC: 2033 Canned fruits & specialties
PA: Consorzio Casalasco Del Pomodoro Societa' Agricola Cooperativa
Strada Provinciale 32
Rivarolo Del Re Ed Uniti CR 26036
037 553-6211

(G-5986)
RAZER SCANDINAVIA INC
432 State Route 34 Ste 1a (07747-2193)
PHONE....................732 441-1250
Charles Goodwin, *CFO*
▲ **EMP:** 4 **EST:** 2013
SALES: 158K **Privately Held**
SIC: 3462 Horseshoes

(G-5987)
ROSSOW COSMETIQUES - USA INC
Also Called: Rossow USA
100 Matawan Rd Ste 350 (07747-3902)
PHONE....................732 872-1464
Tara Tobin, *Opers Mgr*
Paul Kretzer, *Sales Dir*
Carrie Kutzkowski, *Office Mgr*
▲ **EMP:** 5
SQ FT: 1,200
SALES (est): 490K **Privately Held**
SIC: 2844 Cosmetic preparations

(G-5988)
SOUTH SHORE SIGN CO INC
Also Called: South Shore Signs
550 Morristown Rd (07747-3580)
PHONE....................718 984-5624
Anthony Nuzzolo, *Chairman*

GEOGRAPHIC

EMP: 12
SQ FT: 1,400
SALES (est): 1.2MM **Privately Held**
WEB: www.signbrothers.com
SIC: 3993 Advertising artwork

(G-5989)
STEELSTRAN INDUSTRIES INC
Also Called: A L Don Co
Foot Of Dock St (07747)
PHONE..............................732 566-5040
Bob Bauer, *Opers-Prdtn-Mfg*
EMP: 6
SQ FT: 9,000
SALES (corp-wide): 16.6MM **Privately Held**
SIC: 2499 3429 Poles, wood; ladders, wood; oars & paddles, wood; manufactured hardware (general)
PA: Steelstran Industries, Inc.
35 Mileed Way
Avenel NJ 07001
732 574-0700

(G-5990)
UNITED DIAM INC
12 Grenoble Ct (07747-9651)
PHONE..............................732 619-0950
Vivek Diora, *Exec Dir*
EMP: 5
SALES (est): 248.9K **Privately Held**
SIC: 3911 5094 Jewelry, precious metal; jewelry

Mauricetown
Cumberland County

(G-5991)
U S SILICA COMPANY
9035 Noble St (08329)
P.O. Box 254 (08329-0254)
PHONE..............................856 785-0720
Justo Lucena, *Plant Mgr*
Scott Eves, *Branch Mgr*
EMP: 50
SALES (corp-wide): 1.5B **Publicly Held**
WEB: www.u-s-silica.com
SIC: 1446 Foundry sand mining
HQ: U. S. Silica Company
24275 Katy Fwy Ste 100
Katy TX 77494
301 682-0600

Mays Landing
Atlantic County

(G-5992)
AMERICAN YOUTH ENTERPRISES INC
120 Marlin Ln (08330-1635)
P.O. Box 653 (08330-0653)
PHONE..............................609 909-1900
David Hagan Jr, *President*
EMP: 8
SQ FT: 5,000
SALES (est): 1MM **Privately Held**
WEB: www.americanyouth.org
SIC: 2759 Screen printing

(G-5993)
CASTELLANE MANUFACTURING CO
1405 Cantillon Blvd (08330-2023)
P.O. Box 921 (08330-0921)
PHONE..............................609 625-3427
Nicholas R Castellane, *President*
Elizabeth M Castellane, *Corp Secy*
EMP: 12 **EST:** 1958
SQ FT: 10,000
SALES (est): 1.2MM **Privately Held**
SIC: 2353 Uniform hats & caps

(G-5994)
INTEX MILLWORK SOLUTIONS LLC
45 Mill St (08330-1511)
PHONE..............................856 293-4100
Joe Umosella, *President*
Evan Krautwald, *Engineer*
Ned Lawrence, *Regl Sales Mgr*

Shea Kucenski, *Marketing Mgr*
Ted Amaniera, *Manager*
EMP: 40
SALES (est): 9.9MM **Privately Held**
SIC: 2431 Millwork

(G-5995)
NICKELS CARPET CLEANING
957 Morningside Dr (08330-1913)
PHONE..............................609 892-5783
Daniel Nickels, *Principal*
EMP: 6
SALES (est): 480.1K **Privately Held**
SIC: 3356 Nickel

(G-5996)
NORTH AMERICAN COMPOSITES CO
5450 Atlantic Ave (08330-2006)
PHONE..............................609 625-8101
Simon Bula, *Manager*
EMP: 14
SALES (corp-wide): 271.4MM **Privately Held**
SIC: 2821 Plastics materials & resins
HQ: North American Composites Company
300 Apollo Dr
Circle Pines MN 55014
651 766-6892

(G-5997)
PEPSI COLA CO
1440 Pinewood Blvd (08330-2096)
PHONE..............................609 476-5001
Joe Burns, *Principal*
Nancy Jones, *Purchasing*
Michael Nelson, *Administration*
EMP: 14
SALES (est): 2.2MM **Privately Held**
SIC: 2086 Carbonated soft drinks, bottled & canned

(G-5998)
PRECISION WELDING MACHINE
13th St (08330)
P.O. Box 216 (08330-0216)
PHONE..............................609 625-1465
Dave Birch, *Owner*
EMP: 6
SALES (est): 601.7K **Privately Held**
SIC: 7692 Welding repair

(G-5999)
VAN DUYNE BROS INC
5112 Oakwood Blvd (08330-2016)
PHONE..............................609 625-0299
Eileen Van Duyne, *President*
John L Van Duyne Jr, *Vice Pres*
Thomas Van Duyne, *Treasurer*
John L Van Duyne Sr, *Shareholder*
EMP: 5 **EST:** 1948
SALES (est): 607.2K **Privately Held**
SIC: 3732 1521 Lifeboats, building & repairing; new construction, single-family houses

(G-6000)
VANTAGE BUSINESS SYSTEMS INC
6019 Main St (08330-1845)
PHONE..............................609 625-7020
EMP: 6
SALES: 550K **Privately Held**
SIC: 7372 Prepackaged Software Services

Maywood
Bergen County

(G-6001)
ADLER INTERNATIONAL LTD (PA)
205 Maywood Ave (07607-1027)
PHONE..............................201 843-4525
Donald James Adler, *President*
▲ **EMP:** 7
SALES (est): 654K **Privately Held**
WEB: www.adlerinternational.com
SIC: 2678 5112 Stationery products; stationery & office supplies; writing instruments & supplies

(G-6002)
CIRCUIT REPRODUCTION CO
219 Hergesell Ave (07607-1140)
PHONE..............................201 712-9292
Paul Kabaria, *President*
Ashok Kabaria, *Vice Pres*
EMP: 12
SQ FT: 20,000
SALES (est): 1.6MM **Privately Held**
SIC: 3672 Printed circuit boards

(G-6003)
DE SAUSSURE EQUIPMENT CO INC
Also Called: Maywood Furniture
23 W Howcroft Rd (07607-1089)
PHONE..............................201 845-6517
Thomas McMullen, *CEO*
William P De Saussure IV, *President*
Jack Desaussure, *COO*
Kenneth Persson, *Vice Pres*
Barbara Jenkins, *CFO*
▲ **EMP:** 34
SQ FT: 44,700
SALES (est): 4.5MM **Privately Held**
WEB: www.maywood.com
SIC: 2514 Tables, household: metal

(G-6004)
DOLCE BROTHERS PRINTING INC (PA)
29 Brook Ave (07607-1130)
PHONE..............................201 843-0400
James Dolce, *President*
Glenn Dolce, *Vice Pres*
EMP: 80
SQ FT: 35,000
SALES (est): 17.3MM **Privately Held**
WEB: www.dolceprint.com
SIC: 2752 Commercial printing, offset

(G-6005)
DOLCE PRINTING
29 Brook Ave (07607-1130)
PHONE..............................201 843-0400
Matthew Yeranian, *President*
Bill Camarco, *General Mgr*
Aimee Cuevas, *Principal*
Bill Black, *Prdtn Mgr*
Jo-Ann Smolen, *Prdtn Mgr*
EMP: 16 **EST:** 2012
SALES (est): 2.3MM **Privately Held**
SIC: 2752 Commercial printing, offset

(G-6006)
INTERNATIONAL MOLASSES CORP
121 E Hunter Ave (07607-1831)
PHONE..............................201 368-8036
Ronald Targan, *President*
EMP: 30
SQ FT: 18,000
SALES (est): 2.8MM **Privately Held**
SIC: 2062 Blackstrap molasses from purchased raw sugar or syrup

(G-6007)
JACLYN HOLDINGS PARENT LLC (PA)
197 W Spring Valley Ave (07607-1730)
PHONE..............................201 909-6000
Robert Chestnov, *President*
EMP: 2
SALES (est): 34.6MM **Privately Held**
SIC: 3199 3111 2824 3172 Equestrian related leather articles; bag leather; vinyl fibers; cosmetic bags; investment holding companies, except banks

(G-6008)
JACLYN LLC
Bonnie International
197 W Spring Valley Ave # 101 (07607-1729)
PHONE..............................201 909-6000
Allan Ginsburg, *Branch Mgr*
EMP: 120
SALES (corp-wide): 34.6MM **Privately Held**
SIC: 2389 Costumes
HQ: Jaclyn Llc
500 7th Ave
New York NY 10018
201 909-6000

(G-6009)
JIMCAM PUBLISHING INC
Also Called: Our Town
19 W Pleasant Ave Fl 1 (07607-1320)
PHONE..............................201 843-5700
Jim Hornes, *President*
Camille Hornes, *CFO*
EMP: 5
SQ FT: 250
SALES (est): 440.5K **Privately Held**
SIC: 2759 Commercial printing

(G-6010)
JOSEPH CASTINGS INC
25 Brook Ave (07607-1130)
PHONE..............................201 712-0717
Albert Hess, *President*
Marion Hess, *Corp Secy*
Robert Hess, *Vice Pres*
EMP: 16 **EST:** 1957
SQ FT: 5,000
SALES (est): 1.7MM **Privately Held**
WEB: www.josephcastings.com
SIC: 3915 Jewelers' castings

(G-6011)
JP GROUP INTERNATIONAL LLC
Also Called: Lisabelle
525 Palmer Ave (07607-1325)
P.O. Box 748 (07607-0748)
PHONE..............................201 820-1444
Lisa Begega Mignano,
EMP: 4
SALES (est): 308.6K **Privately Held**
SIC: 2369 Girls' & children's outerwear

(G-6012)
MIDAS DESIGNS LTD
124 Lafayette Ave (07607-2035)
PHONE..............................201 567-2700
Adam Haber, *President*
Yvonne Wasilewski, *Corp Secy*
EMP: 6
SQ FT: 2,000
SALES: 1MM **Privately Held**
SIC: 3911 Jewelry, precious metal

(G-6013)
PARSELLS PRINTING INC
938 Spring Valley Rd # 1 (07607-1446)
PHONE..............................973 473-2700
James Parsells, *President*
Ron Parsells, *Vice Pres*
EMP: 4
SQ FT: 2,800
SALES (est): 270K **Privately Held**
WEB: www.parsellsprinting.com
SIC: 2752 Commercial printing, offset

(G-6014)
PRECISION PRODUCTS CO INC
219 Hergesell Ave (07607-1140)
PHONE..............................201 712-5757
Amit Kabaria, *President*
EMP: 25 **EST:** 1955
SQ FT: 13,000
SALES: 779.1K **Privately Held**
WEB: www.precisionproductsco.com
SIC: 3672 Printed circuit boards

(G-6015)
PRESTONE PRESS LLC
Also Called: Prestone Printing Company
29 Brook Ave 1 (07607-1130)
PHONE..............................347 468-7900
Brian Donovan, *Prdtn Mgr*
Alan Wechsler, *Sales Executive*
Robert Adler,
Steven Amoroso,
Thomas Politano,
EMP: 113
SALES (est): 24MM **Privately Held**
SIC: 2752 Commercial printing, offset

(G-6016)
STEPAN COMPANY
Maywood Division
100 W Hunter Ave (07607-1021)
PHONE..............................201 845-3030
Scott Behrens, *Vice Pres*
Janet A Catlett, *Vice Pres*
Joe Gartelmann, *Opers Mgr*
Warren Kaplan, *Research*
Phouvieng Xayariboun, *Research*
EMP: 91

▲ = Import ▼=Export
◆ =Import/Export

SALES (corp-wide): 1.9B **Publicly Held**
WEB: www.stepan.com
SIC: 2842 2899 Polishing preparations &
related products; sanitation preparations,
disinfectants & deodorants; chemical
preparations
PA: Stepan Company
22 W Frontage Rd
Northfield IL 60093
847 446-7500

(G-6017)
THYSSENKRUPP MATERIALS NA INC
Thyssnkrupp Mtllrgcal Pdts USA
25 E Spring Valley Ave (07607-2150)
PHONE..................................212 972-8800
Herr Thorsten Sorje, *Branch Mgr*
EMP: 11
SALES (corp-wide): 39.8B **Privately Held**
SIC: 3499 3313 Fire- or burglary-resistive
products; ferroalloys
HQ: Thyssenkrupp Materials Na, Inc.
22355 W 11 Mile Rd
Southfield MI 48033
248 233-5600

(G-6018)
VICTORS THREE-D INC
Also Called: Victors Settings
25 Brook Ave (07607-1130)
PHONE..................................201 845-4433
Albert Hess, *President*
Marion Hess, *Corp Secy*
Robert Hess, *Vice Pres*
Joseph De Poto, *Sales Staff*
Jim Cantilli, *Manager*
EMP: 100 EST: 1958
SQ FT: 27,000
SALES (est): 17.4MM **Privately Held**
WEB: www.victorsettings.com
SIC: 3339 3915 Primary nonferrous met-
als; jewelers' findings & materials

Medford
Burlington County

(G-6019)
AMEGA SCIENTIFIC CORPORATION
617 Stokes Rd (08055-3097)
PHONE..................................609 953-7295
Anthony Amato, *President*
Ron Cangro, *Engineer*
EMP: 12
SQ FT: 2,500
SALES (est): 1.6MM
SALES (corp-wide): 103.1MM **Publicly
Held**
WEB: www.amegascientific.com
SIC: 3822 5084 Auto controls regulating
residntl & coml environmt & applncs; in-
struments & control equipment
PA: Mesa Laboratories, Inc.
12100 W 6th Ave
Lakewood CO 80228
303 987-8000

(G-6020)
BERAT CORPORATION
Also Called: Shop Rite of Medford
208 Route 70 (08055-9522)
PHONE..................................609 953-7700
Anthony Massony, *Manager*
EMP: 200
SALES (corp-wide): 192.9MM **Privately
Held**
SIC: 5411 5992 5912 5812 Grocery
stores, independent; florists; drug stores
& proprietary stores; eating places; bread,
cake & related products
PA: Berat Corporation
1230 Blckwood Clmenton Rd
Clementon NJ 08021
856 627-6501

(G-6021)
CHEMTREAT INC
520 Stokes Rd Ste B11 (08055-2904)
PHONE..................................609 654-9522
EMP: 8
SALES (corp-wide): 19.1B **Publicly Held**
SIC: 2899 Ret Misc Merchandise

HQ: Chemtreat, Inc.
5640 Cox Rd Ste 300
Glen Allen VA 23060
804 965-0154

(G-6022)
FAULKNER INFORMATION SVCS LLC
143 Old Marlton Pike (08055-8750)
PHONE..................................856 662-2070
Tom Hogan, *President*
Michael Flaherty, *President*
Barbara Forkel, *Vice Pres*
Brady Hicks, *Assoc Editor*
EMP: 100
SQ FT: 14,000
SALES (est): 5.7MM
SALES (corp-wide): 20.3MM **Privately
Held**
WEB: www.faulkner.com
SIC: 2741 Technical manuals: publishing &
printing
PA: Information Today, Inc.
143 Old Marlton Pike
Medford NJ 08055
609 654-6266

(G-6023)
HOMAN COMMUNICATIONS INC
194 Route 70 Ste 9 (08055-2377)
PHONE..................................609 654-9594
Jack Acconey, *Owner*
EMP: 5
SALES (est): 395K **Privately Held**
WEB: www.homancom.com
SIC: 5731 7622 3663 Radios, two-way,
citizens' band, weather, short-wave, etc.;
home entertainment repair services; radio
broadcasting & communications equip-
ment

(G-6024)
INFORMATION TODAY INC (PA)
143 Old Marlton Pike (08055-8750)
PHONE..................................609 654-6266
Roger R Bilboul, *Ch of Bd*
Thomas H Hogan, *President*
Alison Trotta, *Editor*
Marydee Ojala, *Chief*
Stephen Faig, *Business Mgr*
EMP: 50 EST: 1979
SQ FT: 5,000
SALES (est): 20.3MM **Privately Held**
WEB: www.infotoday.com
SIC: 2721 7389 Trade journals: publishing
only, not printed on site; convention &
show services

(G-6025)
J & S PRECISION PRODUCTS CO
16 Medford Evesboro Rd (08055-9592)
PHONE..................................609 654-0900
Steven Janssen, *President*
Barbara Janssen, *Corp Secy*
David Janssen, *Vice Pres*
◆ EMP: 40 EST: 1964
SQ FT: 25,000
SALES (est): 7.5MM **Privately Held**
SIC: 3451 Screw machine products

(G-6026)
JOE MIKE PRECISION FABRICATION
6 Tidswell Ave (08055-2708)
PHONE..................................609 953-1144
Joseph Evans, *President*
EMP: 10
SALES (est): 750K **Privately Held**
SIC: 3541 3556 Gear cutting & finishing
machines; food products machinery

(G-6027)
L E ROSELLIS FOOD SPECIALTIES
Also Called: Roselli, L E
155 Church Rd (08055-9595)
P.O. Box 610 (08055-0610)
PHONE..................................609 654-4816
Dolores Roselli, *President*
Leo Roselli, *Vice Pres*
Leo P Roselli, *Vice Pres*
EMP: 10
SQ FT: 5,000

SALES (est): 1.5MM **Privately Held**
WEB: www.rosellisfood.com
SIC: 5411 2038 0161 2099 Frozen food
& freezer plans, except meat; ethnic
foods, frozen; vegetables & melons; food
preparations; macaroni & spaghetti

(G-6028)
LASER CONTRACTORS LLC
433 Mckendimen Rd (08055-9773)
PHONE..................................609 517-2407
Cheryl Ann Pereira, *Mng Member*
EMP: 4
SALES (est): 311.3K **Privately Held**
SIC: 3699 Laser systems & equipment

(G-6029)
LEOS ICE CREAM COMPANY
Also Called: Leo's Famous Yum Yum
7 Tomlinson Mill Rd Ste 5 (08055-3480)
PHONE..................................856 797-8771
Rick Cirelli, *CEO*
EMP: 7
SALES (est): 434.7K **Privately Held**
WEB: www.leosicecream.com
SIC: 2024 Ice cream & frozen desserts

(G-6030)
MFB SOFT PRETZELS INC
617 Stokes Rd (08055-3097)
PHONE..................................609 953-6773
Mark Butterfoss, *Principal*
EMP: 4
SALES (est): 302.7K **Privately Held**
SIC: 2051 Bakery: wholesale or whole-
sale/retail combined

(G-6031)
PLEXUS PUBLISHING INC
143 Old Marlton Pike (08055-8750)
PHONE..................................609 654-6500
Thomas H Hogan, *President*
Amy Reeve, *Vice Pres*
Rob Colding, *Marketing Staff*
▲ EMP: 30
SQ FT: 2,000
SALES (est): 3MM **Privately Held**
WEB: www.plexuspublishing.com
SIC: 2721 2731 Trade journals: publishing
only, not printed on site; book clubs: pub-
lishing only, not printed on site

(G-6032)
REILYS CANDY INC
719 Stokes Rd 721 (08055-3002)
PHONE..................................609 953-0040
Susan Pulkon, *President*
EMP: 10
SQ FT: 3,600
SALES (est): 250K **Privately Held**
SIC: 2064 5441 Candy & other confec-
tionery products; candy

(G-6033)
RPI INDUSTRIES INC
220 Route 70 (08055-9522)
PHONE..................................609 714-2330
Peter C Palko, *President*
P J Gavin, *Vice Pres*
▲ EMP: 100
SQ FT: 59,475
SALES (est): 22.1MM **Privately Held**
SIC: 2431 Doors, wood

(G-6034)
SOLV-TEC INCORPORATED
75 N Main St (08055-2718)
PHONE..................................609 261-4242
Patrick O'Brien, *President*
Michael Schult, *Vice Pres*
EMP: 8
SQ FT: 2,400
SALES: 3.5MM **Privately Held**
SIC: 2843 Surface active agents

(G-6035)
STAUTS PRINTING & GRAPHICS
12 Maine Trl (08055-8916)
PHONE..................................609 654-5382
Paul Stauts, *President*
EMP: 5
SQ FT: 700
SALES (est): 671.7K **Privately Held**
SIC: 2752 Commercial printing, offset

(G-6036)
TAURUS DEFENSE SOLUTIONS LLC
13 Butler Ct (08055-3911)
PHONE..................................617 916-6137
Tommy Dimona,
EMP: 4
SALES (est): 251.9K **Privately Held**
SIC: 3812 Defense systems & equipment

Medford Lakes
Burlington County

(G-6037)
FULFILLMENT PRINTING AND MAIL
77 Oswego Trl (08055-1110)
P.O. Box 1415, Medford (08055-6415)
PHONE..................................609 953-9500
Kathleen Schindler,
Irvin Chip Schindler,
EMP: 4
SALES (est): 733.8K **Privately Held**
SIC: 2752 Commercial printing, litho-
graphic

Mendham
Morris County

(G-6038)
ALLIED GROUP INC
5 Cold Hill Rd S Ste 19 (07945-3208)
P.O. Box 209 (07945-0209)
PHONE..................................973 543-4994
Vernon Pansmith, *President*
Edward Thomas, *Executive*
▲ EMP: 20
SQ FT: 1,400
SALES (est): 4.9MM **Privately Held**
WEB: www.alliedfilters.com
SIC: 2679 Filter paper: made from pur-
chased material

(G-6039)
JUDITH ROTH STUDIO COLLECTION
3 Stone House Rd (07945-3125)
P.O. Box 351 (07945-0351)
PHONE..................................973 543-4455
Judith Roth, *Owner*
▲ EMP: 6
SALES (est): 900K **Privately Held**
SIC: 2759 5199 Calendars: printing; cal-
endars

(G-6040)
MACIE PUBLISHING COMPANY
13 E Main St Ste 3 (07945-1537)
PHONE..................................973 983-8700
Edward Sueta Jr, *President*
Julie S Kaufmann, *Vice Pres*
▲ EMP: 12
SALES (est): 1.2MM **Privately Held**
SIC: 2741 Miscellaneous publishing

(G-6041)
MENDHAM GARDEN CENTER
11 W Main St (07945-1220)
PHONE..................................973 543-4178
Jack Broadhead, *Branch Mgr*
EMP: 5
SALES (corp-wide): 5.2MM **Privately
Held**
WEB: www.mendhamgardencenter.com
SIC: 5999 5261 3546 1799 Feed & farm
supply; lawn & garden supplies; lawn &
garden equipment; saws & sawing equip-
ment; fence construction
PA: Mendham Garden Center
1306 State Route 31 N
Annandale NJ
908 730-9664

(G-6042)
METRO SPORT INC
271 Hilltop Rd (07945-2906)
PHONE..................................973 879-3831
Xuming Wang, *President*
EMP: 35

SALES (est): 2MM **Privately Held**
SIC: 2253 Bathing suits & swimwear, knit

(G-6043)
SUETA MUSIC ED
PUBLICATIONS
13 E Main St Ste 3 (07945-1537)
PHONE...............................888 725-2333
Edward Sueta Sr, *President*
▲ EMP: 10
SALES (est): 802.1K **Privately Held**
SIC: 2741 7389 Music, sheet: publishing
　only, not printed on site; financial services

(G-6044)
SURVIVING LIFE CORP
Also Called: Sunshine Lane Mixed Media
3 Muirfield Ln (07945-1234)
PHONE...............................973 543-3370
Ronald C Striano PHD, *President*
EMP: 6
SALES: 360K **Privately Held**
SIC: 2732 Book printing

Metuchen
Middlesex County

(G-6045)
ACE ELECTRONICS INC
235 Liberty St (08840-1217)
P.O. Box 4215 (08840-4215)
PHONE (732) 603-9800
Edward Di Villa, *President*
Susan Di Vila, *Business Mgr*
Ashley Morris, *Business Mgr*
Vinn Patel, *Corp Secy*
Larry Pomasan, *Vice Pres*
EMP: 60
SQ FT: 15,000
SALES (est): 22.2MM **Privately Held**
WEB: www.aceelectronics.com
SIC: 3496 5051 Miscellaneous fabricated
　wire products; cable, wire

(G-6046)
AVANTIER INC (PA)
148 Main St (08840-2745)
PHONE...............................732 491-8150
Keng Stencer, *Principal*
EMP: 4
SALES (est): 852.2K **Privately Held**
SIC: 3827 Optical instruments & lenses

(G-6047)
BERKELEY VARITRONICS
SYSTEMS
Also Called: B V S
255 Liberty St (08840-1217)
PHONE...............................732 548-3737
Scott Schober, *CEO*
Gary W Schober, *President*
Eileen Schober, *Office Mgr*
EMP: 30
SQ FT: 20,000
SALES (est): 6MM **Privately Held**
WEB: www.bvsystems.com
SIC: 3577 8731 Computer peripheral
　equipment; computer (hardware) develop-
　ment

(G-6048)
BLUE PARACHUTE LLC
263 Amboy Ave Ste 1 (08840-2477)
PHONE...............................732 767-1320
David Frietberg, *Mng Member*
Angela Pineiro,
EMP: 4
SQ FT: 1,800
SALES (est): 471.2K **Privately Held**
SIC: 2752 7336 Commercial printing, litho-
　graphic; commercial art & illustration

(G-6049)
C & K PLASTICS INC
Also Called: CK
159 Liberty St (08840-1215)
PHONE...............................732 549-0011
Robert Carrier, *President*
Bridgette Carrier, *Project Mgr*
Mike O'Hara, *Production*
Tom Napolitano, *QC Mgr*
Roy Sorenson, *Engineer*
EMP: 80 EST: 1957

SQ FT: 85,000
SALES (est): 21.8MM **Privately Held**
WEB: www.candkplastics.com
SIC: 3089 3083 Plastic containers, except
　foam; laminated plastics plate & sheet

(G-6050)
CARBON FIBER ELEMENT LLC
690 New Durham Rd (08840-1757)
PHONE...............................973 809-9432
EMP: 4 EST: 2017
SALES (est): 331.4K **Privately Held**
SIC: 2819 Elements

(G-6051)
CHARTER MACHINE COMPANY
55 Wester Ave (08840-2537)
PHONE...............................732 494-5350
Michael Greenlaw, *Principal*
Heinz Goetz, *Engineer*
Anthony Tesoriero, *Design Engr*
Bill Wright, *Natl Sales Mgr*
Rick Jespersen, *Sales Engr*
EMP: 14 EST: 2014
SALES (est): 1.9MM **Privately Held**
SIC: 3599 Machine shop, jobbing & repair

(G-6052)
CHEM-IS-TRY INC
160 Liberty St Ste 4 (08840-1255)
PHONE...............................732 372-7311
Prafulla Kumar Porwal, *President*
▲ EMP: 5
SQ FT: 2,000
SALES: 1MM **Privately Held**
SIC: 2819 2833 2865 2869 Industrial in-
　organic chemicals; medicinals & botani-
　cals; cyclic crudes & intermediates;
　industrial organic chemicals; agricultural
　chemicals; chemical preparations

(G-6053)
CRITERION PUBLISHING CO
87 Forrest St (08840-1213)
P.O. Box 4278 (08840-4278)
PHONE...............................732 548-8300
William Crane Sr, *Owner*
EMP: 8 EST: 1952
SALES (est): 330K **Privately Held**
SIC: 2741 Miscellaneous publishing

(G-6054)
DIVINE PRINTING
131 Liberty St (08840-1215)
PHONE...............................732 632-8800
Devina Rodriguez, *Owner*
EMP: 4
SALES (est): 426.8K **Privately Held**
SIC: 2752 Commercial printing, offset

(G-6055)
ENAMEL ART STUDIO
120 Liberty St (08840-1216)
PHONE...............................732 321-0774
Helen Radchenko, *Principal*
EMP: 4
SALES (est): 379.2K **Privately Held**
SIC: 3911 5094 Jewelry, precious metal;
　jewelry & precious stones

(G-6056)
FRANCO MANUFACTURING CO
INC (PA)
555 Prospect St (08840-2271)
PHONE...............................732 494-0500
Louis D Franco, *President*
Jack D Franco, *Exec VP*
Jack Franco, *Exec VP*
Morris Franco, *Exec VP*
Edmund Rossi, *Senior VP*
◆ EMP: 175
SQ FT: 71,000
SALES (est): 130.7MM **Privately Held**
WEB: www.francomfg.com
SIC: 2392 2211 5023 5131 Towels, fabric
　& nonwoven: made from purchased mate-
　rials; washcloths & bath mitts: made from
　purchased materials; towels, dishcloths &
　washcloths: cotton; dishcloths; wash-
　cloths; towels & toweling, cotton; towels;
　textiles, woven; cotton goods; printing of
　narrow fabrics

(G-6057)
GLOBE DIE-CUTTING
PRODUCTS INC
76 Liberty St (08840-1237)
P.O. Box 4339 (08840-4339)
PHONE...............................732 494-7744
Irwin Brody, *President*
Bruce Brody, *Corp Secy*
▲ EMP: 200 EST: 1961
SQ FT: 30,000
SALES (est): 30.2MM **Privately Held**
SIC: 3544 2675 Special dies & tools; card-
　board cut-outs, panels & foundations: die-
　cut

(G-6058)
GRAPHIC EQUIPMENT
CORPORATION (PA)
Also Called: G E C
55 Wester Ave (08840-2590)
PHONE...............................732 494-5350
Karl Kuehnrich, *President*
Barbara Kuehnrich, *Corp Secy*
Michael Greenlaw, *Vice Pres*
Frank Markle, *Purch Mgr*
Heinz Goetz, *Engineer*
EMP: 45
SQ FT: 47,000
SALES (est): 9MM **Privately Held**
WEB: www.gecorp.com
SIC: 3599 3555 Machine shop, jobbing &
　repair; printing trades machinery

(G-6059)
GRAPHIC EQUIPMENT
CORPORATION
Also Called: Charter Machine
19 Wester Ave (08840-2537)
PHONE...............................732 548-4400
James A Vertes, *General Mgr*
James Vertes, *General Mgr*
Charlie Carson, *Foreman/Supr*
Heinz Goetz, *Engineer*
EMP: 48
SALES (corp-wide): 9MM **Privately Held**
WEB: www.gecorp.com
SIC: 3599 Machine shop, jobbing & repair
PA: Graphic Equipment Corporation
　55 Wester Ave
　Metuchen NJ 08840
　732 494-5350

(G-6060)
HARD CROME SOLUTIONS
195 Central Ave (08840-1848)
PHONE...............................732 500-2568
Frank Nicholas, *Owner*
▲ EMP: 5
SQ FT: 5,000
SALES (est): 170.5K **Privately Held**
SIC: 3471 Plating & polishing

(G-6061)
HOLLER METAL FABRICATORS
INC
215 Liberty St (08840-1217)
PHONE...............................732 635-9050
Dan Holler, *President*
EMP: 8
SQ FT: 20,000
SALES: 1.5MM **Privately Held**
SIC: 3441 Fabricated structural metal

(G-6062)
HYDRACORE INC
60 Liberty St (08840-1237)
PHONE...............................732 548-5500
Sam Lotfy, *President*
EMP: 5
SALES: 400K **Privately Held**
SIC: 3599 Machine shop, jobbing & repair

(G-6063)
IT WORQS LLC
16 Pearl St Ste 102 (08840-1962)
P.O. Box 513 (08840-0513)
PHONE...............................732 494-0009
Noorali Sonawalla, *Mng Member*
EMP: 50
SALES (est): 2.4MM **Privately Held**
WEB: www.itworqs.com
SIC: 7372 Prepackaged software

(G-6064)
J & E METAL FABRICATORS INC
1 Coan Pl (08840-2589)
PHONE...............................732 548-9650
Mark E Brazina, *President*
EMP: 28
SQ FT: 40,000
SALES: 2.2MM **Privately Held**
WEB: www.metalfab.com
SIC: 3444 Sheet metal specialties, not
　stamped

(G-6065)
MAXISIT INC
203 Main St (08840-2727)
PHONE...............................732 494-2005
Maulik Shah, *President*
Divya Reddy, *COO*
Arati Kaps, *Manager*
Dheeraj Reddy, *Manager*
Sristi Shrestha, *Manager*
EMP: 110
SQ FT: 5,000
SALES (est): 13.9MM **Privately Held**
WEB: www.maxisit.com
SIC: 7371 7373 7374 7372 Computer
　software development; computer inte-
　grated systems design; data processing &
　preparation; prepackaged software; infor-
　mation retrieval services

(G-6066)
MSI HOLDINGS LLC
203 Norcross Ave (08840-1253)
PHONE...............................732 549-7144
EMP: 4
SALES (est): 303.4K **Privately Held**
SIC: 3821 Mfg Laboratory Apparatus

(G-6067)
O S I INC
101 Hillside Ave (08840-1936)
PHONE...............................732 754-6271
Bogie Bosha, *President*
Martha Kelly, *Vice Pres*
EMP: 15
SQ FT: 10,000
SALES (est): 1.4MM **Privately Held**
WEB: www.osi-inc.com
SIC: 3699 Laser systems & equipment

(G-6068)
RELIABLE PALLET SERVICES
LLC
74 Liberty St (08840-1237)
PHONE...............................732 243-9642
EMP: 23
SALES (corp-wide): 1.4MM **Privately**
Held
SIC: 2448 Pallets, wood & wood with metal
PA: Reliable Pallet Services Llc
　460 Hillside Ave Ste 1
　Hillside NJ 07205
　973 900-2260

(G-6069)
SPEX CERTIPREP INC (PA)
203 Norcross Ave (08840-1253)
PHONE...............................732 549-7144
Michel Baudron, *Chairman*
Neil A Stein, *Chairman*
Lisa Petro, *Vice Pres*
Gilbert Hayat, *Treasurer*
▲ EMP: 53
SQ FT: 16,587
SALES (est): 13.1MM **Privately Held**
WEB: www.spexcsp.com
SIC: 3821 8734 2899 Chemical labora-
　tory apparatus; testing laboratories;
　chemical preparations

(G-6070)
SPEX CERTIPREP GROUP LLC
203 Norcross Ave (08840-1253)
PHONE...............................208 204-6656
Michel Baudron, *Chairman*
EMP: 11 EST: 2013
SALES (est): 1.7MM **Privately Held**
SIC: 3821 Chemical laboratory apparatus

(G-6071)
SPEX CERTPREP GROUP LLC
203 Norcross Ave (08840-1253)
PHONE...............................732 549-7144
William Hahn, *General Mgr*

Neil A Stein,
Ralph H Obenauf,
EMP: 9
SQ FT: 10,000
SALES (est): 1.1MM **Privately Held**
WEB: www.prostds.com
SIC: 2819 Industrial inorganic chemicals

(G-6072)
SPEX SAMPLE PREP LLC
65 Liberty St (08840-1221)
PHONE..................................732 549-7144
Ralph Obenauf, *Branch Mgr*
EMP: 17
SALES (corp-wide): 7.8MM **Privately Held**
SIC: 3821 Chemical laboratory apparatus
PA: Spex Sample Prep, Llc
203 Norcross Ave
Metuchen NJ 08840
732 549-7144

(G-6073)
SPEX SAMPLE PREP LLC (PA)
203 Norcross Ave (08840-1253)
PHONE..................................732 549-7144
Ralph Obenauf,
EMP: 55
SQ FT: 15,000
SALES (est): 7.8MM **Privately Held**
WEB: www.spexsampleprep.net
SIC: 3821 Chemical laboratory apparatus

(G-6074)
STELLAR DATA RECOVERY (PA)
48 Bridge St (08840-2277)
PHONE..................................877 778-6087
EMP: 3 **EST:** 2015
SALES (est): 1.9MM **Privately Held**
SIC: 7372 Prepackaged software

(G-6075)
SYNASIA INC
240 Amboy Ave (08840-2441)
PHONE..................................732 205-9880
Howard Z Qiu, *President*
Kevin Qiu, *Principal*
Jean Verfaillie, *Engineer*
Larry Qiu, *Finance Mgr*
Kevin Greene, *Mktg Dir*
▲ **EMP:** 4
SQ FT: 3,000
SALES (est): 520K **Privately Held**
WEB: www.synasia.com
SIC: 2819 5169 Industrial inorganic chemicals; chemicals & allied products

(G-6076)
T & E SALES OF MARLBORO INC
913 Middlesex Ave (08840-2201)
P.O. Box 791, Edison (08818-0791)
PHONE..................................732 549-7551
Martin Wachtel, *President*
EMP: 6
SALES (est): 1.1MM **Privately Held**
SIC: 3589 7542 Car washing machinery; washing & polishing, automotive

(G-6077)
TECHNOVISION INC
42 Bridge St (08840-2277)
PHONE..................................732 381-0200
Anju Aggarwal, *President*
Dinesh Goel, *Vice Pres*
EMP: 24
SALES: 3MM **Privately Held**
WEB: www.etechnovision.com
SIC: 7372 7379 Application computer software;

(G-6078)
TMC CORPORATION
335 High St Bldg B1 (08840-2285)
PHONE..................................609 860-1830
▲ **EMP:** 6
SQ FT: 5,000
SALES (est): 520K **Privately Held**
SIC: 3661 7389 Mfg Telephone Systems

(G-6079)
TRINITY MANUFACTURING LLC
60 Leonard St (08840-1220)
PHONE..................................732 549-2866
Randy Riley, *President*
Jay Myers, *President*

George Mitchell, *General Mgr*
George Cox Jr, *Exec VP*
John Farinola, *Exec VP*
◆ **EMP:** 120
SQ FT: 120,000
SALES (est): 34.3MM **Privately Held**
WEB: www.trinityinstore.com
SIC: 3646 3648 2541 Commercial indusl & institutional electric lighting fixtures; decorative area lighting fixtures; store & office display cases & fixtures

(G-6080)
WEST MACHINE WORKS INC
101 Liberty St (08840-1215)
PHONE..................................732 549-2183
Jan H Van Hoesen, *President*
Peter Van Hoesen, *Vice Pres*
EMP: 7 **EST:** 1945
SALES: 300K **Privately Held**
SIC: 3599 3544 Machine shop, jobbing & repair; special dies, tools, jigs & fixtures

(G-6081)
WINDOW SHAPES INC
225 Liberty St (08840-1217)
PHONE..................................732 549-0708
Tom Change, *President*
▲ **EMP:** 90 **EST:** 1997
SQ FT: 45,000
SALES (est): 12.9MM **Privately Held**
SIC: 3442 Storm doors or windows, metal

(G-6082)
WIRELESS COMMUNICATIONS INC
55 Liberty St (08840-1221)
PHONE..................................732 926-1000
EMP: 7 **Privately Held**
SIC: 3663 Radio broadcasting & communications equipment
PA: Wireless Communications, Inc.
1803 Old Slphur Spring Rd
Baltimore MD 21227

(G-6083)
WLXT LLC
Also Called: Wl Ring
16 Wernik Pl (08840-2422)
PHONE..................................732 906-7979
Mary Durocher, *Vice Pres*
Debbie Rabara, *Vice Pres*
Ethan Garr, *Comptroller*
Glenn Garr, *Director*
Howard Kaye,
EMP: 73
SALES (est): 6.2MM **Privately Held**
SIC: 3911 Jewelry, precious metal

(G-6084)
WORLD JOURNAL LLC
41a Bridge St (08840-2277)
PHONE..................................732 632-8890
Harver Lee, *Manager*
EMP: 12
SALES (corp-wide): 53.3MM **Privately Held**
WEB: www.wjnews.net
SIC: 2711 Newspapers, publishing & printing
HQ: World Journal Llc
14107 20th Ave Fl 2
Whitestone NY 11357
718 746-8889

(G-6085)
ZENITH ENERGY US LP (PA)
1 Highland Ave (08840-1956)
PHONE..................................732 515-7410
Jeffrey R Armstrong, *CEO*
Bryan Jackson, *Exec VP*
David Kinder, *Vice Pres*
Steve Mawer, *Engineer*
EMP: 4
SALES (est): 105.3MM **Privately Held**
SIC: 1311 Crude petroleum & natural gas

Mickleton
Gloucester County

(G-6086)
ATLAS FLASHER & SUPPLY CO INC
430 Swedesboro Ave (08056-1208)
P.O. Box 488 (08056-0488)
PHONE..................................856 423-3333
Karenanne Brown, *CEO*
Gary P Ottey, *Vice Pres*
Mike Scheufele, *Opers Mgr*
Brian Stevens, *Materials Mgr*
Jeremy Shaner, *Opers Spvr*
EMP: 30
SQ FT: 5,000
SALES (est): 7.1MM **Privately Held**
WEB: www.atlasflasher.com
SIC: 5999 7359 3993 Safety supplies & equipment; equipment rental & leasing; signs & advertising specialties

(G-6087)
MARTINS SPECIALTY SAUSAGE CO (PA)
150 Harmony Rd (08056-1210)
PHONE..................................856 423-4000
Martin Guinta, *President*
Tom Maschino, *Plant Engr*
Ed Hall, *Sales Mgr*
Robert Roselli, *Sales Staff*
EMP: 14
SQ FT: 8,800
SALES (est): 2.8MM **Privately Held**
SIC: 2013 Spiced meats from purchased meat

(G-6088)
SAINT-GOBAIN PRFMCE PLAS CORP
Also Called: Division Name Process Systems
210 Harmony Rd (08056-1209)
P.O. Box 248 (08056-0248)
PHONE..................................856 423-6630
Vincent Hurst, *Branch Mgr*
EMP: 75
SALES (corp-wide): 215.9MM **Privately Held**
SIC: 3083 3082 Thermoplastic laminates: rods, tubes, plates & sheet; unsupported plastics profile shapes
HQ: Saint-Gobain Performance Plastics Corporation
31500 Solon Rd
Solon OH 44139
440 836-6900

Middlesex
Middlesex County

(G-6089)
150 DEVELOPMENT GROUP LLC
242 Lincoln Blvd Ste 2 (08846-2361)
PHONE..................................732 546-3812
Massimo Pinelli, *Mng Member*
EMP: 5 **EST:** 2012
SALES (est): 673.6K **Privately Held**
SIC: 3572 Computer storage devices

(G-6090)
A D M CORPORATION
100 Lincoln Blvd (08846-1090)
PHONE..................................732 469-0900
Mary Mota, *Ch of Bd*
Susan Mota, *COO*
Joe Tattegrain, *QC Mgr*
Michael Turner, *CFO*
Edwin Yarber, *VP Sales*
▲ **EMP:** 100 **EST:** 1964
SQ FT: 100,000
SALES (est): 30MM **Privately Held**
WEB: www.packing-list.com
SIC: 2393 3081 2678 Bags & containers, except sleeping bags: textile; plastic film & sheet; writing paper & envelopes: made from purchased materials

(G-6091)
A T C COMPANIES INC
207 Blackford Ave (08846-2503)
P.O. Box 310 (08846-0310)
PHONE..................................732 560-0900
Stephen J Gajarsky, *President*
James Winship, *Opers Staff*
Elaine Gajarsky, *Admin Sec*
EMP: 38
SQ FT: 6,300
SALES (est): 6.5MM **Privately Held**
SIC: 3822 7629 Hydronic pressure or temperature controls; electrical equipment repair, high voltage

(G-6092)
ADSORPTECH INC (PA)
452 Lincoln Blvd (08846-2439)
PHONE..................................732 356-1000
James Flaherty, *President*
John Ambriano, *Vice Pres*
Ravi K Subramanian, *Vice Pres*
Apurva Maheshwary, *Director*
Ravi Subramanian, *Director*
▲ **EMP:** 5
SQ FT: 2,700
SALES (est): 1.1MM **Privately Held**
WEB: www.adsorptech.com
SIC: 3569 8711 Separators for steam, gas, vapor or air (machinery); consulting engineer

(G-6093)
ADSORPTECH LLC
452 Lincoln Blvd (08846-2439)
PHONE..................................732 491-7727
James Flaherty,
EMP: 6
SALES (est): 230.9K **Privately Held**
SIC: 3841 Oxygen tents

(G-6094)
ADVANCE MACHINE PLANNING INC
200 Egel Ave (08846-2506)
PHONE..................................732 356-4438
Henry A Phillips Sr, *President*
Susan Delaney, *Manager*
EMP: 10
SQ FT: 17,000
SALES (est): 640K **Privately Held**
SIC: 3559 8711 Rubber working machinery, including tires; engineering services

(G-6095)
AGATE LACQUER TRI-NAT LLC
824 South Ave (08846-2259)
PHONE..................................732 968-1080
Jane Natalini, *Mng Member*
▲ **EMP:** 5
SQ FT: 25,000
SALES (est): 989K **Privately Held**
SIC: 2851 2842 Lacquer: bases, dopes, thinner; lacquers, varnishes, enamels & other coatings; metal polish

(G-6096)
AMERICAN MADE FABRICATORS INC
84 Baekeland Ave (08846-2601)
PHONE..................................732 356-4306
EMP: 4
SALES (est): 523.8K **Privately Held**
SIC: 3542 Sheet metalworking machines

(G-6097)
ANALYTIC STRESS RELIEVING INC
190 Egel Ave (08846-2504)
PHONE..................................732 629-7232
David Herzog, *President*
EMP: 55
SALES (corp-wide): 225MM **Privately Held**
SIC: 3398 Metal heat treating
PA: Analytic Stress Relieving, Inc.
3118 W Pinhook Rd Ste 202
Lafayette LA 70508
337 237-8790

(G-6098)
ANSUN PROTECTIVE METALS INC
130 Lincoln Blvd (08846-1022)
P.O. Box 4260, Dunellen (08812-4260)
PHONE..............................732 302-0616
George Whalen, *President*
Anthony Mendel, *Vice Pres*
◆ **EMP:** 8
SQ FT: 10,000
SALES: 1MM **Privately Held**
WEB: www.ansunmetals.com
SIC: 3599 5051 Machine shop, jobbing & repair; metals service centers & offices

(G-6099)
ATC SYSTEMS INC
207 Blackford Ave (08846-2503)
P.O. Box 310 (08846-0310)
PHONE..............................732 560-0900
Stephen Gajarsky, *President*
James Winship, *COO*
Kevin O'Rourke, *Vice Pres*
EMP: 4 **EST:** 2009
SALES (est): 720.8K **Privately Held**
SIC: 3625 Control equipment, electric

(G-6100)
BAMCO INC (PA)
30 Baekeland Ave (08846-2601)
PHONE..............................732 302-0889
Michael Biviano, *President*
Scott Parneg, *Superintendent*
Allan Pasternak, *Corp Secy*
Bob Balaam, *Vice Pres*
Rick Marcavecchio, *Vice Pres*
▲ **EMP:** 80
SQ FT: 14,000
SALES (est): 14.2MM **Privately Held**
WEB: www.bamcoinc.org
SIC: 3446 Architectural metalwork

(G-6101)
BERRY GLOBAL INC
87 Lincoln Blvd (08846-1020)
PHONE..............................732 356-2870
Jim Deming, *Branch Mgr*
EMP: 127 **Publicly Held**
SIC: 3089 Bottle caps, molded plastic
HQ: Berry Global, Inc.
101 Oakley St
Evansville IN 47710
812 424-2904

(G-6102)
BOMAR EXO LTD LIABILITY CO
Also Called: Bomar Crystal Company
200b Wood Ave (08846-2553)
P.O. Box 10 (08846-0010)
PHONE..............................732 356-7787
Ermina Lirio, *CEO*
Dave Miskov, *Plant Mgr*
EMP: 11 **EST:** 1960
SQ FT: 20,000
SALES: 356.7K **Privately Held**
WEB: www.bomarcrystal.com
SIC: 3679 Quartz crystals, for electronic application

(G-6103)
CAPITAL PRINTING CORPORATION
420 South Ave (08846-2532)
PHONE..............................732 560-1515
Brett Russo, *President*
Nolan Russo Sr, *Principal*
Nolan Russo Jr, *CFO*
EMP: 80
SQ FT: 60,000
SALES (est): 25MM **Privately Held**
WEB: www.capitalprintingcorp.com
SIC: 2752 Commercial printing, offset

(G-6104)
CENTRAL COMPONENTS MFG LLC
440 Lincoln Blvd (08846-2439)
PHONE..............................732 469-5720
Greg Lane, *Opers Mgr*
Tom Stiff, *Accounting Mgr*
Tom Winfough,
Howard Chiou,
Gregg Lane,
▲ **EMP:** 6 **EST:** 1993

SALES (est): 1.3MM **Privately Held**
WEB: www.centralcm.com
SIC: 3678 8742 Electronic connectors; management consulting services

(G-6105)
CONTAINER MFG INC
Also Called: Container Manufacturing
50 Baekeland Ave (08846-2601)
P.O. Box 428 (08846-0428)
PHONE..............................732 563-0100
J Thomas Jennings, *President*
Robert Jennings, *Vice Pres*
EMP: 40
SQ FT: 32,000
SALES (est): 9.7MM **Privately Held**
WEB: www.containermanufacturing.com
SIC: 3089 Plastic containers, except foam

(G-6106)
CORE ACQUISITION LLC (PA)
215 Wood Ave Ste 215 # 215 (08846-2554)
PHONE..............................732 983-6025
Arpit Patel, *CEO*
Vithal Dhaduk, *President*
Payal Dhaduk, *CFO*
Ameeshi Chovatia,
EMP: 3
SQ FT: 32,000
SALES: 5MM **Privately Held**
SIC: 2834 Pills, pharmaceutical

(G-6107)
COREPHARMA LLC
215 Wood Ave Ste 215 # 215 (08846-2554)
PHONE..............................732 983-6025
Arpit Patel, *CEO*
Vithal Dhaduk, *President*
Payal Dhaduk, *CFO*
Rajendra Nagamalla, *Director*
▲ **EMP:** 3
SQ FT: 32,000
SALES (est): 5MM **Privately Held**
WEB: www.corepharma.com
PA: Core Acquisition, Llc
215 Wood Ave Ste 215 # 215
Middlesex NJ 08846
732 983-6025

(G-6108)
COVALNCE SPCALTY ADHESIVES LLC
87 Lincoln Blvd (08846-1020)
PHONE..............................732 356-2870
Seth Salano, *Branch Mgr*
EMP: 600 **Publicly Held**
SIC: 2891 Adhesives & sealants
HQ: Covalence Specialty Adhesives Llc
101 Oakley St
Evansville IN 47710

(G-6109)
COVALNCE SPCIALTY COATINGS LLC
Also Called: Tapes and Coatings
87 Lincoln Blvd (08846-1020)
PHONE..............................732 356-2870
Seth Salano, *Manager*
Elizabeth Curran,
EMP: 85
SALES (est): 4.8MM **Privately Held**
SIC: 2399 2821 2851 Fabricated textile products; plastics materials & resins; paints & allied products

(G-6110)
CRT INTERNATIONAL INC
260 Wagner St (08846-2501)
PHONE..............................973 887-7737
Carmine Tarantino, *President*
Rosa Tarantino, *Senior VP*
Mario Schiavone, *Finance Mgr*
Leonardo Orozco, *Webmaster*
Barbara Bihuniak, *Admin Asst*
EMP: 12
SALES (est): 1.8MM **Privately Held**
SIC: 2752 Business forms, lithographed

(G-6111)
DELISA PALLET CORP
116 South Ave (08846-2526)
PHONE..............................732 667-7070
John P Delisa, *President*

James A Chichelo, *Corp Secy*
David Colavita, *Manager*
▼ **EMP:** 11 **EST:** 1958
SQ FT: 5,000
SALES (est): 5.5MM **Privately Held**
WEB: www.delisapallet.com
SIC: 5031 2448 Pallets, wood; wood pallets & skids

(G-6112)
DISHMAN USA INC
476 Union Ave Ste 2 (08846-1968)
PHONE..............................732 560-4300
Bhavesh Oza, *CEO*
Jay R Vyas, *Chairman*
Nicola Giubellina, *Business Mgr*
▲ **EMP:** 10
SQ FT: 2,200
SALES (est): 2MM
SALES (corp-wide): 71.9MM **Privately Held**
WEB: www.dishman-usa.com
SIC: 2834 Pharmaceutical preparations
PA: Dishman Carbogen Amcis Limited
Bhadr-Raj Chambers, Swastik Cross Roads,
Ahmedabad GJ 38000
792 644-3053

(G-6113)
DOUBLE O MANUFACTURING INC
2b Smalley Ave (08846-2231)
PHONE..............................732 752-9423
Al Oslislo, *President*
Jim Oslislo, *Vice Pres*
EMP: 7
SQ FT: 7,500
SALES: 1MM **Privately Held**
WEB: www.doubleomfg.com
SIC: 3325 Steel foundries

(G-6114)
DYNAFLOW ENGINEERING INC
106 Egel Ave (08846-2504)
PHONE..............................732 356-9790
Ross Block, *President*
EMP: 5
SQ FT: 1,100
SALES (est): 1.1MM **Privately Held**
WEB: www.dynafloweng.com
SIC: 5084 3561 Pumps & pumping equipment; pumps & pumping equipment

(G-6115)
F S T PRINTING INC
1324 Bound Brook Rd (08846-1401)
PHONE..............................732 560-3749
Salvatore Buonocore, *President*
Frank Buonocore, *Vice Pres*
Timothy Hurley, *Vice Pres*
Patty Hurley, *Treasurer*
EMP: 5
SQ FT: 2,500
SALES: 600K **Privately Held**
SIC: 2759 Commercial printing, offset; business forms: printing; alcoholic beverage making equipment & supplies

(G-6116)
FLAVOR AND FD INGREDIENTS INC
256 Lackland Dr (08846-2511)
PHONE..............................201 298-6964
Sandy Feld, *Principal*
EMP: 21
SALES (corp-wide): 9.5MM **Privately Held**
WEB: www.summithillflavors.com
SIC: 2087 Flavoring extracts & syrups
PA: Flavor And Food Ingredients Inc.
21 Worlds Fair Dr
Somerset NJ 08873
732 805-0335

(G-6117)
FRAM TRAK INDUSTRIES INC
Also Called: Alpha Plastics
205 Hallock Ave (08846-2280)
PHONE..............................732 424-8400
Albert Santelli, *President*
Charlie Roberts, *Opers Mgr*
Paul Houston, *Admin Sec*
▲ **EMP:** 40
SQ FT: 66,000

SALES (est): 8.4MM **Privately Held**
WEB: www.framtrak.com
SIC: 3089 Injection molding of plastics

(G-6118)
GEMCO VALVE CO LLC
301 Smalley Ave (08846-2232)
PHONE..............................732 752-7900
John Muench, *Ch of Bd*
Jim Lenihan, *President*
Douglas Krok, *Engineer*
EMP: 20
SQ FT: 20,000
SALES (est): 2.4MM **Privately Held**
SIC: 3491 Industrial valves

(G-6119)
HAMAMATSU CORPORATION
250 Wood Ave (08846-2553)
PHONE..............................908 231-0960
Stilian Asenov, *Engineer*
Terry Matsushita, *Manager*
Seth Greenberg, *Manager*
EMP: 50 **Privately Held**
WEB: www.hps-industrial.com
SIC: 3827 5049 8731 3844 Optical instruments & lenses; optical goods; commercial physical research; X-ray apparatus & tubes
HQ: Hamamatsu Corporation
360 Foothill Rd
Bridgewater NJ 08807
908 231-0960

(G-6120)
HANDYTUBE CORPORATION
250 Lackland Dr Ste 1 (08846-2562)
PHONE..............................732 469-7420
Bill Glas, *Manager*
EMP: 50
SQ FT: 7,000
SALES (corp-wide): 1.5B **Publicly Held**
SIC: 3351 3498 Tubing, copper & copper alloy; fabricated pipe & fittings
HQ: Handytube Corporation
12244 Willow Grove Rd
Camden DE 19934

(G-6121)
IMAGE SCREEN PRINTING INC
532 Lincoln Blvd (08846-2441)
PHONE..............................732 560-1817
Nancy Mangee, *President*
Charles Mangee, *Corp Secy*
EMP: 8
SQ FT: 5,400
SALES: 640K **Privately Held**
SIC: 2759 Screen printing

(G-6122)
J G CARPENTER CONTRACTOR
Also Called: JG Tire
300 Lincoln Blvd (08846-2370)
P.O. Box 146 (08846-0146)
PHONE..............................732 271-8991
John Giaretta, *President*
John Giarretta, *Owner*
EMP: 8
SALES (est): 966K **Privately Held**
SIC: 4212 3011 Dump truck haulage; tires & inner tubes

(G-6123)
JEMA-AMERICAN INC
824 South Ave (08846-2259)
P.O. Box 206, Dunellen (08812-0206)
PHONE..............................732 968-5333
James Natalini, *President*
EMP: 7 **EST:** 1957
SQ FT: 10,000
SALES (est): 1.9MM **Privately Held**
WEB: www.jema-american.com
SIC: 3479 Coating of metals & formed products

(G-6124)
KOBA CORP
60 Baekeland Ave (08846-2601)
PHONE..............................732 469-0110
Joseph Koelmel Jr, *President*
Franz Bach, *Treasurer*
EMP: 60
SQ FT: 35,000

SALES (est): 10MM **Privately Held**
WEB: www.kobacorp.com
SIC: 3089 3544 Injection molding of plastics; special dies, tools, jigs & fixtures

(G-6125)
KRS AUTOMOTIVE DEV GROUP INC
Also Called: Phoenix Friction Products
278 Lincoln Blvd Ste 2 (08846-2373)
PHONE..................................732 667-7937
Louis Riveccio, *President*
William Sanders, *Vice Pres*
EMP: 10
SQ FT: 26,000
SALES (est): 1.3MM **Privately Held**
SIC: 3714 Clutches, motor vehicle

(G-6126)
L AND DS SAPORE RAVIOLI CHEESE
Also Called: Sapore Ravioli & Cheese
429b Lincoln Blvd (08846-2440)
PHONE..................................732 563-9190
Dominic Discenza, *President*
Anthony Florano, *Managing Prtnr*
Michael Discenza, *Vice Pres*
EMP: 15 EST: 1997
SQ FT: 1,500
SALES: 750K **Privately Held**
WEB: www.saporeravioli.com
SIC: 2099 Pasta, uncooked; packaged with other ingredients

(G-6127)
LOUIS N ROTHBERG & SON INC
550 Cedar Ave (08846-2433)
PHONE..................................732 356-9505
Louis N Rothberg, *President*
John Rothberg, *Vice Pres*
Dick Kimsey, *Controller*
Susan Rothberg, *Admin Sec*
EMP: 30
SQ FT: 12,200
SALES (est): 8.7MM **Privately Held**
WEB: www.lnrothberg.com
SIC: 1794 2951 Excavation & grading; building construction; asphalt paving mixtures & blocks

(G-6128)
LOWDER ELECTRIC AND CNSTR
250 Hallock Ave Ste B (08846-2281)
PHONE..................................732 764-6000
Jeremy Lowder, *President*
EMP: 5
SALES (est): 200.5K **Privately Held**
SIC: 7694 1731 Electric motor repair; general electrical contractor; electric power systems contractors; standby or emergency power specialization; voice, data & video wiring contractor

(G-6129)
MARITIME SOLUTIONS INC
Also Called: MSI
200 Pond Ave (08846-2219)
PHONE..................................732 752-3831
Richard Fredricks, *President*
Christopher Constantine, *Senior VP*
Gerard J Lynch, *VP Engrg*
EMP: 7 EST: 2007
SALES (est): 532.6K **Privately Held**
SIC: 3531 Marine related equipment

(G-6130)
MID STATE BINDERY
262 Lackland Dr (08846-2511)
PHONE..................................908 755-9388
Steve Stout, *Owner*
Sidney Stoddard, *Vice Pres*
EMP: 4
SALES (est): 140K **Privately Held**
SIC: 2789 Bookbinding & related work

(G-6131)
MORELLI CONTRACTING LLC
201 Egel Ave Ste B (08846-2574)
PHONE..................................732 356-8800
Anthony Morelli, *Mng Member*
Colleen Morelli,
EMP: 5 EST: 2004
SQ FT: 6,500
SALES: 600K **Privately Held**
SIC: 1411 Dimension stone

(G-6132)
MULBRO MANUFACTURING & SVC CO
488 Lincoln Blvd (08846-2439)
P.O. Box 386 (08846-0386)
PHONE..................................732 805-0290
Ray Mullen, *President*
EMP: 4 EST: 1954
SQ FT: 5,000
SALES (est): 310K **Privately Held**
WEB: www.mulbro.com
SIC: 7699 3949 5941 Bowling pins, refinishing or repair; sporting & athletic goods; bowling equipment & supplies

(G-6133)
NATIONAL MTAL FNSHNGS CORP INC (PA)
Also Called: National Metals
897 South Ave (08846-2569)
P.O. Box 486 (08846-0486)
PHONE..................................732 752-7770
Lou Fahsbender, *President*
▲ EMP: 15
SQ FT: 12,000
SALES (est): 2.9MM **Privately Held**
SIC: 3599 3471 Custom machinery; electroplating of metals or formed products

(G-6134)
NEW CENTURY MILLWORK INC
131 Lincoln Blvd (08846-1046)
PHONE..................................973 882-0222
EMP: 4 EST: 2014
SALES (est): 203K **Privately Held**
SIC: 2491 Millwork, treated wood

(G-6135)
NEWBOLD INC
Also Called: Newbold Target
200 Egel Ave (08846-2506)
PHONE..................................732 469-5654
Henry A Phillips Jr, *President*
Erin Mihalik, *Opers Staff*
EMP: 5
SALES (est): 180K **Privately Held**
WEB: www.newboldtargets.com
SIC: 3949 Target shooting equipment

(G-6136)
PETERSON BROTHERS MFG CO
10 Baekeland Ave (08846-2601)
PHONE..................................732 271-8240
Gary Lewis, *President*
Marlys Lewis, *Corp Secy*
EMP: 25 EST: 1951
SQ FT: 14,000
SALES (est): 3.8MM **Privately Held**
WEB: www.petersonbrothersmanufacturing.com
SIC: 3469 Stamping metal for the trade

(G-6137)
PETRO EXTRUSION TECH INC
Also Called: Petro Extrusion Technology
205 Hallock Ave Ste B (08846-2280)
P.O. Box 99, Garwood (07027-0099)
PHONE..................................908 789-3338
Robert Petrozziello, *President*
Frances Petrozziello, *Corp Secy*
Joseph Petrozziello, *Vice Pres*
Alan Pinsky, *Chief Engr*
Bill Gathercole, *Sales Staff*
EMP: 42
SQ FT: 20,000
SALES (est): 9.1MM **Privately Held**
WEB: www.petroextrusion.com
SIC: 3089 Extruded finished plastic products

(G-6138)
PHILLIPS SAFETY PRODUCTS INC
123 Lincoln Blvd Ste 2 (08846-1071)
PHONE..................................732 356-1493
Robert Phillips, *President*
William Brown, *Vice Pres*
Ryan Phillips, *Vice Pres*
Geri Baitz, *Accounts Mgr*
Mayura Satghare, *Manager*
▲ EMP: 20
SALES (est): 4MM **Privately Held**
WEB: www.phillips-safety.com
SIC: 3851 Ophthalmic goods

(G-6139)
POLISH NAIL
570 Union Ave (08846-1960)
PHONE..................................732 627-9799
Tuan Nguyen, *Owner*
EMP: 7
SALES: 420K **Privately Held**
SIC: 3999 Fingernails, artificial

(G-6140)
PREMIER SPECIALTIES INC
201 Egel Ave Ste 3a (08846-2574)
PHONE..................................732 469-6615
Roger Rich, *President*
▲ EMP: 19
SQ FT: 15,000
SALES (est): 5.7MM **Privately Held**
WEB: www.premierfragrances.com
SIC: 2087 2844 Flavoring extracts & syrups; cosmetic preparations

(G-6141)
PROMO GRAPHIC INC
Also Called: Graphic Impressions
112 Wood Ave (08846-2551)
PHONE..................................732 629-7300
Debra Rossello, *President*
EMP: 7
SQ FT: 3,500
SALES: 450K **Privately Held**
WEB: www.promographics.com
SIC: 2759 7336 Screen printing; commercial art & graphic design

(G-6142)
R & R IRRIGATION CO INC
283 Lincoln Blvd (08846-1734)
PHONE..................................732 271-7070
Stephen C Dobossy, *President*
Paul W Maiwaldt, *Vice Pres*
EMP: 18
SQ FT: 4,500
SALES (est): 2.6MM **Privately Held**
WEB: www.rrirrigation.com
SIC: 1731 3259 Electrical work; clay sewer & drainage pipe & tile

(G-6143)
SCARLET PRINTING
Also Called: Minuteman Press
253 Beechwood Ave (08846-1107)
PHONE..................................732 560-1415
Robert Oconner,
Erich Peter,
EMP: 6
SQ FT: 1,000
SALES (est): 300K **Privately Held**
WEB: www.mmpunion.net
SIC: 2752 2791 2789 Commercial printing, lithographic; typesetting; bookbinding & related work

(G-6144)
SCHIFANO CONSTRUCTION CORP
1 Smalley Ave (08846-2272)
P.O. Box 288 (08846-0288)
PHONE..................................732 752-3450
Dale Schifano, *President*
John Schifano, *Vice Pres*
Paul Schifano, *Treasurer*
Philip Schifano, *Admin Sec*
EMP: 12
SQ FT: 12,800
SALES (est): 3.7MM **Privately Held**
SIC: 1611 2951 Highway & street paving contractor; asphalt paving mixtures & blocks

(G-6145)
SCIENTIFIC MACHINE AND SUP CO
700 Cedar Ave (08846-2448)
P.O. Box 67 (08846-0067)
PHONE..................................732 356-1553
Elizabeth Landau, *President*
EMP: 20 EST: 1956
SQ FT: 10,000
SALES: 980K **Privately Held**
WEB: www.scientificmachine.com
SIC: 3821 3829 3494 Laboratory equipment: fume hoods, distillation racks, etc.; shakers & stirrers; evaporation apparatus, laboratory type; measuring & controlling devices; valves & pipe fittings

(G-6146)
SERMACH INC
Also Called: Service Machine Co
311 Lincoln Blvd Ste C (08846-2364)
PHONE..................................732 356-9021
Peter D'Elia, *President*
Richard Taylor, *General Mgr*
Teri Taylor, *General Mgr*
Lori D'Elia, *Treasurer*
EMP: 5
SQ FT: 3,500
SALES: 600K **Privately Held**
SIC: 3599 Machine shop, jobbing & repair

(G-6147)
SIGMA ENGINEERING & CONSULTING
220 Lincoln Blvd Ste A (08846-1738)
PHONE..................................732 356-3046
Robert Bruno, *President*
EMP: 18
SQ FT: 36,600
SALES (est): 2.5MM **Privately Held**
WEB: www.sigmaeca.com
SIC: 3599 1796 8711 3462 Machine shop, jobbing & repair; machinery installation; mechanical engineering; iron & steel forgings

(G-6148)
SILVER LINE BUILDING PDTS LLC
207 Pond Ave (08846-2220)
PHONE..................................732 752-8704
Brian Traynor, *Manager*
EMP: 220
SALES (corp-wide): 2B **Publicly Held**
WEB: www.silverlinewindow.com
SIC: 3089 3442 Windows, plastic; window frames & sash, plastic; awnings, fiberglass & plastic combination; injection molded finished plastic products; metal doors, sash & trim
HQ: Silver Line Building Products Llc
    1 Silverline Dr
    North Brunswick NJ 08902
    732 435-1000

(G-6149)
SOMA LABS INC
248 Wagner St 252 (08846-2501)
PHONE..................................732 271-3444
John Botzolakis, *President*
EMP: 17 EST: 1998
SQ FT: 11,000
SALES (est): 4MM **Privately Held**
WEB: www.somalabs.com
SIC: 2834 Vitamin preparations

(G-6150)
SPADIX TECHNOLOGIES INC
110 Egel Ave (08846-2504)
PHONE..................................732 356-6906
Albert Simone, *President*
Ann Marie Wolliver, *Manager*
Ann Wolliver, *Manager*
▲ EMP: 4 EST: 1995
SQ FT: 13,000
SALES (est): 200.4K **Privately Held**
WEB: www.spadixtechnologies.com
SIC: 3559 Glass cutting machinery

(G-6151)
SPIRAL WATER TECHNOLOGIES INC
200 Pond Ave (08846-2219)
PHONE..................................415 259-4929
Ashwin Gulati, *CEO*
EMP: 15
SALES (est): 733.7K **Privately Held**
SIC: 3589 Water treatment equipment, industrial

(G-6152)
SPRAY-TEK INC (PA)
344 Cedar Ave (08846-2433)
PHONE..................................732 469-0050
Mark Epstein, *Ch of Bd*
David Brand, *Vice Pres*
Melvin Denholtz, *Vice Pres*
EMP: 50
SQ FT: 22,000
SALES (est): 15.9MM **Privately Held**
SIC: 2834 Pharmaceutical preparations

GEOGRAPHIC

(G-6153)
STAINLESS STOCK
Also Called: Diamond Bright Metal Proc
333 Cedar Ave Ste 1 (08846-2400)
PHONE..................................732 564-1164
George Karpus, *President*
EMP: 8
SALES (est): 909.1K **Privately Held**
SIC: 3471 Polishing, metals or formed
products

(G-6154)
STIRLING AUDIO SERVICES LLC
201 Wood Ave (08846-2554)
PHONE..................................732 560-0707
Jim Ferrate Jr,
Mary Ann Mason,
EMP: 5
SALES (est): 612.5K **Privately Held**
WEB: www.stirlingaudioservices.com
SIC: 3651 Household audio & video equipment

(G-6155)
TESS-COM INC (PA)
400 South Ave Ste 11 (08846-2567)
PHONE..................................412 233-5782
Lou Colonna, *President*
David Colonna, *Vice Pres*
EMP: 20
SQ FT: 10,000
SALES (est): 5.2MM **Privately Held**
WEB: www.tesscom.com
SIC: 3826 5084 Environmental testing
equipment; pollution control equipment,
air (environmental)

(G-6156)
TOOLING ETC LLC
Also Called: Wagner Carbide Saw Division
250 Hallock Ave (08846-2281)
PHONE..................................732 752-8080
Ernest Jesacher, *Mng Member*
Erika Jesacher,
Markus Jesacher,
▲ EMP: 8 EST: 1980
SQ FT: 16,000
SALES (est): 1.1MM **Privately Held**
WEB: www.toolingetc.com
SIC: 3425 3541 7699 Saw blades for
hand or power saws; machine tools,
metal cutting type; knife, saw & tool
sharpening & repair

(G-6157)
UNIQUE AMRCN ALUM EXTRSION LLC
Also Called: Unalext
333 Cedar Ave Unit A (08846-2400)
PHONE..................................732 271-0006
Yechiel Munk, *Exec VP*
Ezriel Munk, *Mng Member*
EMP: 20
SQ FT: 30,000
SALES: 1.5MM **Privately Held**
SIC: 3354 Aluminum extruded products

(G-6158)
VEOLIA ES
125 Factory Ln (08846-1043)
PHONE..................................732 469-5100
James Nerger, *President*
EMP: 40
SALES (corp-wide): 600.9MM **Privately
Held**
WEB: www.marisolinc.com
SIC: 7389 5169 2869 Solvents recovery
service; chemicals & allied products; industrial organic chemicals
HQ: Veolia Environmental Services
125 Factory Ln
Middlesex NJ
732 469-5100

Middletown
Monmouth County

(G-6159)
AT&T SERVICES INC
200 S Laurel Ave (07748-1998)
PHONE..................................732 420-3131
Randall Stephensen, *CEO*
EMP: 1000

SALES (est): 73.9MM
SALES (corp-wide): 170.7B **Publicly
Held**
SIC: 3669 Intercommunication systems,
electric
HQ: At&t Communications Americas, Inc
900 Us Highway 202 206
Bedminster NJ 07921
404 861-9188

(G-6160)
BAY SHORE PRESS INC
Also Called: Courier Newspaper, The
320 Kings Hwy E (07748-3511)
PHONE..................................732 957-0070
Fax: 732 957-0143
EMP: 25
SALES (est): 1.3MM **Privately Held**
SIC: 2711 Newspapers-Publishing/Printing

(G-6161)
BIRDS BEWARE CORPORATION
Also Called: Paul Scammacca, Ceo
50 Townsend Dr (07748-3130)
PHONE..................................732 671-6377
Paul Scammacca, *CEO*
EMP: 7 EST: 2011
SALES (est): 301.4K **Privately Held**
SIC: 3089 0971 Garbage containers, plastic; wildlife management

(G-6162)
DREAMSTAR CONSTRUCTION LLC
248 Clubhouse Dr (07748-1325)
PHONE..................................732 393-2572
Ronald D Denig, *Mng Member*
EMP: 15 EST: 2006
SALES (est): 1.3MM **Privately Held**
WEB: www.dreamstarconstruction.com
SIC: 1541 1522 8741 2431 Industrial
buildings & warehouses; residential construction; construction management; millwork; doors & windows

(G-6163)
ENGINEERED PRECISION CAST CO
Also Called: Epco
952 Palmer Ave (07748-1255)
PHONE..................................732 671-2424
Walter Dubovick, *President*
William Dubovick, *General Mgr*
EMP: 90 EST: 1946
SQ FT: 55,000
SALES (est): 18.7MM **Privately Held**
WEB: www.epcast.com
SIC: 3324 3369 Commercial investment
castings, ferrous; nonferrous foundries

(G-6164)
GRAVITY VAULT LLC
37 Kanes Ln (07748-3501)
PHONE..................................732 856-9599
Nick Hohn, *Branch Mgr*
EMP: 5
SALES (corp-wide): 2.7MM **Privately
Held**
SIC: 3272 Burial vaults, concrete or precast terrazzo
PA: The Gravity Vault Llc
107 Pleasant Ave
Upper Saddle River NJ 07458
201 934-7625

(G-6165)
HEALTH CARE ALERT LLC
1715 State Route 35 # 208 (07748-1870)
PHONE..................................732 676-2630
Jerry Cariello, *CEO*
EMP: 10
SALES (est): 1.3MM **Privately Held**
SIC: 3841 Diagnostic apparatus, medical

(G-6166)
POWERWASH PLUS
25 Oriole Rd (07748-3236)
PHONE..................................732 671-6767
Christopher Nickel, *Principal*
Chris Nickel, *Principal*
EMP: 4
SALES (est): 346.9K **Privately Held**
SIC: 3589 High pressure cleaning equipment

(G-6167)
UNIVERSAL PARTS NEW JERSEY LLC
3 Chanowich Ct (07748-2200)
PHONE..................................732 615-0626
Mark T Merezio, *Principal*
EMP: 4
SALES (est): 245.2K **Privately Held**
SIC: 3715 Truck trailer chassis

Midland Park
Bergen County

(G-6168)
ACCURATE TANK TESTING LLC
Also Called: Accurate Oil
140 Greenwood Ave (07432-1417)
P.O. Box 366, Franklin Lakes (07417-0366)
PHONE..................................201 848-8224
Peter Woodard, *Mng Member*
EMP: 6
SALES (est): 292.6K **Privately Held**
WEB: www.oiltanktesting.com
SIC: 1389 Testing, measuring, surveying &
analysis services

(G-6169)
ALTECH MACHINE & TOOL INC
230 Bank St (07432-1708)
PHONE..................................201 652-4409
Ishmael Ciera, *President*
Pamela Sierra, *Vice Pres*
EMP: 6
SQ FT: 2,500
SALES: 416.7K **Privately Held**
WEB: www.altechmachine.com
SIC: 3599 Machine shop, jobbing & repair

(G-6170)
ATHLETIC ORGANIZATIONAL AIDS
54 Fairhaven Dr (07432-1017)
PHONE..................................201 652-1485
EMP: 26
SALES: 1.6MM **Privately Held**
WEB: www.starscheduler.com
SIC: 2732 7372 Book printing; prepackaged software

(G-6171)
BERGEN CNTY CRTRDGE XCHNGE LLC
268 Greenwood Ave (07432-1445)
PHONE..................................201 493-8182
Mark Giannella, *Principal*
EMP: 9
SALES (est): 867.1K **Privately Held**
SIC: 3955 Print cartridges for laser & other
computer printers
PA: American Internet Holdings L.L.C.
268 Greenwood Ave
Midland Park NJ 07432

(G-6172)
COMMERCE REGISTER INC
190 Godwin Ave (07432-1841)
PHONE..................................201 445-3000
Charles Greer, *President*
Tina Rodrigues, *Managing Dir*
Joel Rosano, *Vice Pres*
Donald Lettie, *Accounts Mgr*
Deb Rader, *Office Mgr*
EMP: 40
SQ FT: 7,500
SALES (est): 4MM **Privately Held**
WEB: www.comreg.com
SIC: 2741 7374 Directories: publishing &
printing; service bureau, computer

(G-6173)
CONVENTION NEWS COMPANY INC (PA)
Also Called: Aviation International News
214 Franklin Ave (07432-1842)
PHONE..................................201 444-5075
Wilson Leach, *President*
Nancy Obrien, *Publisher*
Jeff Burger, *Editor*
Kerry Lynch, *Editor*
Nigel Moll, *Editor*
EMP: 10
SQ FT: 4,800

SALES (est): 6.4MM **Privately Held**
WEB: www.ainonline.com
SIC: 2711 2721 8742 Newspapers, publishing & printing; periodicals; new products & services consultants

(G-6174)
DELUXE INNOVATIONS INC
140 Greenwood Ave Ste 2a (07432-1462)
P.O. Box 141 (07432-0141)
PHONE..................................201 857-5880
David Ferrari, *President*
Linda Ferrari, *Vice Pres*
EMP: 5
SQ FT: 2,550
SALES: 800K **Privately Held**
WEB: www.deluxeinnovations.com
SIC: 3944 Railroad models: toy & hobby

(G-6175)
GRAFWED INTERNET MEDIA STUDIOS
37 Millington Dr (07432-1110)
P.O. Box 121, Ridgewood (07451-0121)
PHONE..................................201 632-1771
Timothy Graf, *President*
EMP: 5
SALES (est): 410K **Privately Held**
WEB: www.grafweb.com
SIC: 4899 2741 7319 7389 Data communication services; miscellaneous publishing; transit advertising services; design
services

(G-6176)
HAFCO FOUNDRY & MACHINE CO
301 Greenwood Ave Ste 2 (07432-1484)
PHONE..................................201 447-0433
Michael J Fornaci, *President*
▲ EMP: 12 EST: 1969
SQ FT: 300
SALES (est): 2.7MM **Privately Held**
SIC: 3322 3462 3469 Malleable iron
foundries; iron & steel forgings; machine
parts, stamped or pressed metal

(G-6177)
HERITAGE INC
225 Franklin Ave Ste 4 (07432-1865)
PHONE..................................201 447-2600
Paul Mortola, *President*
EMP: 5
SQ FT: 1,300
SALES (est): 637.4K **Privately Held**
SIC: 2759 Screen printing

(G-6178)
IRON MOUNTAIN PLASTICS INC
112 Greenwood Ave (07432-1456)
PHONE..................................201 445-0063
Richard Ver Hage, *President*
Doris Ver Hage, *Corp Secy*
Glenn Ver Hage, *Vice Pres*
Henry Ver Hage, *Vice Pres*
EMP: 10
SQ FT: 10,000
SALES (est): 1.7MM **Privately Held**
SIC: 3089 Injection molded finished plastic
products; extruded finished plastic products

(G-6179)
MASTER REPRO INC
95 Greenwood Ave (07432-1423)
PHONE..................................201 447-4800
Mark Shishmanian, *President*
George Shismanian, *Vice Pres*
EMP: 7
SQ FT: 4,000
SALES: 700K **Privately Held**
WEB: www.masterrepro.com
SIC: 2752 Commercial printing, offset

(G-6180)
MC GINLEY PACKAGING METHODS
80 Greenwood Ave (07432-1413)
P.O. Box 150 (07432-0150)
PHONE..................................201 493-9330
John T Mc Ginley, *President*
EMP: 4
SQ FT: 7,500
SALES (est): 547.8K **Privately Held**
SIC: 2891 Adhesives

(G-6181)
MR QUICK SIGN
30 Dairy St (07432-1317)
PHONE....................................201 670-1690
Trena Greenfield, *Owner*
Bernard Greenfield, *Principal*
EMP: 4
SALES: 150K **Privately Held**
SIC: 3993 Signs & advertising specialties

(G-6182)
PINNACLE PRESS INC
41 Prospect St (07432-1645)
PHONE....................................201 652-0500
Howard Siegel, *President*
Ray Huber, *Vice Pres*
EMP: 5
SQ FT: 900
SALES: 750K **Privately Held**
WEB: www.printatpinnacle.com
SIC: 2752 Commercial printing, offset

(G-6183)
PIPER SERVICES LLC
Also Called: Piper Heating and Cooling
268 Greenwood Ave (07432-1445)
P.O. Box 734, Belleville (07109-0734)
PHONE....................................844 567-3900
Joe Rogers, *Mng Member*
John Celentano,
Kevin Frerich,
EMP: 17
SQ FT: 10,000
SALES: 2.5MM **Privately Held**
SIC: 3585 Parts for heating, cooling & re-frigerating equipment

(G-6184)
PRECISION MULTIPLE CONTRLS INC (PA)
Also Called: Ramsey Building Supply
33 Greenwood Ave (07432-1717)
PHONE....................................201 444-0600
Peter H Zecher, *President*
Darren Lilley, *Vice Pres*
Todd Zecher, *Vice Pres*
Jane Zecher, *Admin Sec*
▲ **EMP:** 50 **EST:** 1957
SQ FT: 70,000
SALES (est): 5.6MM **Privately Held**
WEB: www.precisionmulticontrols.com
SIC: 3625 3613 5211 5031 Electric controls & control accessories, industrial; time switches, electrical switchgear apparatus; lumber & other building materials; lumber, plywood & millwork; masons' materials

(G-6185)
PRECISION MULTIPLE CONTRLS INC
Also Called: PMC
33 Greenwood Ave (07432-1717)
PHONE....................................201 444-0600
Arnot Charles, *Branch Mgr*
EMP: 100
SALES (corp-wide): 5.6MM **Privately Held**
WEB: www.precisionmulticontrols.com
SIC: 3625 3613 5211 5031 Electric controls & control accessories, industrial; time switches, electrical switchgear apparatus; lumber & other building materials; masonry materials & supplies; tile, ceramic; lumber, plywood & millwork; building materials, exterior; building materials, interior; masons' materials; tile, clay or other ceramic, excluding refractory
PA: Precision Multiple Controls Inc.
33 Greenwood Ave
Midland Park NJ 07432
201 444-0600

(G-6186)
PRINTOLOGY
229 Godwin Ave (07432-1807)
PHONE....................................201 345-4632
Jon Bognar, *Owner*
Jonathan Boguar, *Principal*
EMP: 4
SALES (est): 567K **Privately Held**
SIC: 2759 Laser printing

(G-6187)
TASSEL TOPPERS LLC
445 Godwin Ave Ste 8 (07432-1507)
PHONE....................................855 827-7357
Marc Goldberg,
▲ **EMP:** 5
SALES (est): 200K **Privately Held**
SIC: 3499 Novelties & specialties, metal

(G-6188)
TECH PRODUCTS CO INC
300 Greenwood Ave (07432-1426)
PHONE....................................201 444-7777
Robert White, *President*
Robert Flournoy, *Vice Pres*
EMP: 10
SQ FT: 5,000
SALES (est): 1.1MM **Privately Held**
SIC: 8711 3599 3089 Mechanical engineering; machine shop, jobbing & repair; injection molding of plastics

(G-6189)
VAIRTEC CORPORATION
265 Greenwood Ave (07432-1446)
PHONE....................................201 445-6965
Robert Marlow, *President*
Johanna Poletti, *Treasurer*
Joan Miller, *Admin Sec*
EMP: 4 **EST:** 1958
SALES: 1.7MM **Privately Held**
WEB: www.nortechcorp.com
SIC: 3563 Vacuum (air extraction) systems, industrial

(G-6190)
WILKER GRAPHICS LLC
Also Called: AlphaGraphics
95 Greenwood Ave (07432-1423)
PHONE....................................201 447-4800
Nyree Shishmanian, *Consultant*
Bernie Wilker,
EMP: 6
SQ FT: 1,800
SALES (est): 741K **Privately Held**
SIC: 2752 2791 2789 Commercial printing, lithographic; typesetting; bookbinding & related work

(G-6191)
WOSTBROCK EMBROIDERY INC
11 Paterson Ave Ste 1 (07432-1873)
PHONE....................................201 445-3074
Henry Wostbrock, *President*
Barbara Wostbrock, *Corp Secy*
EMP: 4
SQ FT: 3,000
SALES (est): 200K **Privately Held**
WEB: www.chiefneckerchief.com
SIC: 2395 Embroidery products, except schiffli machine

Milford
Hunterdon County

(G-6192)
FLEMINGTON KNITTING MILLS
123 Dawn Rd (08848-1133)
PHONE....................................908 995-9590
Sven Klinge, *President*
EMP: 12 **EST:** 1993
SQ FT: 16,000
SALES: 1MM **Privately Held**
SIC: 2253 Knit outerwear mills

(G-6193)
GEORGIA-PACIFIC LLC
623 Riegelsville Rd (08848-1732)
PHONE....................................908 995-2228
Michael Diehl, *Project Engr*
Fred Huff, *Manager*
Brian Trapp, *Manager*
Arul Govindasami, *Director*
EMP: 112
SALES (corp-wide): 40.7B **Privately Held**
WEB: www.gp.com
SIC: 2653 2679 Boxes, corrugated: made from purchased materials; paper products, converted
HQ: Georgia-Pacific Llc
133 Peachtree St Nw
Atlanta GA 30303
404 652-4000

(G-6194)
PERMANORE ARCHTCTURAL FINISHES
3 Parkland Dr (08848-1976)
PHONE....................................908 797-4177
Monica Y Johnson, *President*
Robert Johnson, *Manager*
Robert J Johnson, *Officer*
EMP: 5
SQ FT: 3,000
SALES: 210K **Privately Held**
WEB: www.permanore.com
SIC: 3446 Architectural metalwork

Millburn
Essex County

(G-6195)
BEHRMAN HOUSE INC
241 Millburn Ave B (07041-1739)
PHONE....................................973 379-7200
David Behrman, *President*
▲ **EMP:** 15 **EST:** 1922
SQ FT: 23,400
SALES (est): 2.3MM **Privately Held**
WEB: www.behrmanhouse.com
SIC: 2731 5192 Books: publishing only; books

(G-6196)
ELIE TAHARI LTD (PA)
16 Bleeker St (07041-1415)
PHONE....................................973 671-6300
Elie Tahari, *Ch of Bd*
William Weimer, *Accountant*
Gary Wertheimer, *Accountant*
Ken Steneck, *Credit Staff*
Willie Rucker, *Sales Staff*
▲ **EMP:** 180
SALES (est): 171.9MM **Privately Held**
WEB: www.elietahari.com
SIC: 2331 2339 2335 2337 Blouses, women's & juniors': made from purchased material; slacks: women's, misses' & juniors'; women's, juniors' & misses' dresses; suits: women's, misses' & juniors'; jackets & vests, except fur & leather: women's; women's clothing stores; men's & boys' clothing stores

(G-6197)
ENFORSYS INC (PA)
Also Called: Enforsys Systems
27 Bleeker St 222 (07041-1414)
PHONE....................................973 515-8126
Lois Primovic, *CEO*
Lisa Klein, *CFO*
Colette Van Dyke, *Admin Asst*
William C Giordano,
Craig M Handschuch,
EMP: 35 **EST:** 2000
SALES (est): 3.9MM **Privately Held**
WEB: www.enforsys.com
SIC: 7372 Application computer software

(G-6198)
GRASSMAN-BLAKE INC
58 E Willow St (07041-1417)
P.O. Box 737 (07041-0737)
PHONE....................................973 379-6170
Richard Blake Jr, *President*
EMP: 25 **EST:** 1946
SALES (est): 3.9MM **Privately Held**
WEB: www.gbclasp.com
SIC: 3911 3915 Pearl jewelry, natural or cultured; jewelers' materials & lapidary work

(G-6199)
HUDSON MANUFACTURING CORP
12 E Willow St (07041-1417)
P.O. Box 683, New Providence (07974-0683)
PHONE....................................973 376-7070
Jeffrey Stapfer, *President*
Craig Stapfer, *Vice Pres*
EMP: 10 **EST:** 1940
SQ FT: 7,200
SALES (est): 814.3K **Privately Held**
SIC: 3544 Punches, forming & stamping

(G-6200)
INNOVI MOBILE LLC
45 Essex St Ste 201 (07041-1668)
PHONE....................................646 588-0165
Alex Zaltsman, *General Mgr*
David Robinson, *Software Dev*
EMP: 10
SALES (est): 524.2K **Privately Held**
SIC: 7371 7372 7379 Computer software development & applications; software programming applications; application computer software; computer related consulting services

(G-6201)
KASON CORPORATION (PA)
6771 E Willow St (07041)
PHONE....................................973 467-8140
Hossein Alamzad, *President*
◆ **EMP:** 60
SQ FT: 37,000
SALES (est): 18.9MM **Privately Held**
WEB: www.kason.com
SIC: 3569 Sifting & screening machines

(G-6202)
LENS MODE INC
Also Called: Contact Len Lab
150 Main St Ste 1 (07041-1179)
PHONE....................................973 467-2000
Daniel Strulowitz, *President*
EMP: 4
SQ FT: 5,000
SALES (est): 759.7K **Privately Held**
WEB: www.lensmode.com
SIC: 3851 Ophthalmic goods

(G-6203)
MCT DAIRIES INC (HQ)
Also Called: Trugman-Nash
15 Bleeker St Ste 103 (07041-1468)
P.O. Box 738 (07041-0738)
PHONE....................................973 258-9600
Ken Meyers, *President*
David Raff, *Exec VP*
Vincent McCann, *CFO*
Jennifer Dolan, *Accountant*
Jamie Loss, *Accounts Exec*
◆ **EMP:** 10
SQ FT: 2,000
SALES (est): 23.7MM **Privately Held**
WEB: www.mctdairies.com
SIC: 5084 5963 8999 3999 Food industry machinery; beverage services, direct sales; artists & artists' studios; barber & beauty shop equipment
PA: Allied Dairy Products, Inc.
15 Bleeker St Ste 103
Millburn NJ 07041
973 258-9600

(G-6204)
MCT MANUFACTURING INC
15 Bleeker St Ste 101 (07041-1463)
PHONE....................................877 258-9600
Ken Meyers, *President*
EMP: 4
SALES (est): 526.8K **Privately Held**
SIC: 3999 Manufacturing industries

(G-6205)
MILLBURN BAGEL INC
Also Called: Bagel Chateau
321 Millburn Ave Ste 14 (07041-1616)
PHONE....................................973 258-1334
Martin Wayne, *President*
EMP: 30
SQ FT: 3,000
SALES (est): 3.6MM **Privately Held**
SIC: 2051 5812 5461 Bagels, fresh or frozen; coffee shop; bakeries

(G-6206)
TAHARI ASL LLC (PA)
Also Called: Tahari Arthur S Levine
16 Bleeker St (07041-1415)
PHONE....................................888 734-7459
Mark Smith, *President*
Elie Tahari,
Arthur S Levine,
Lester E Schreiber,
▲ **EMP:** 41

SALES (est): 85.1MM **Privately Held**
SIC: 2331 2335 2339 Blouses, women's
& juniors': made from purchased material;
women's, juniors' & misses' dresses;
slacks: women's, misses' & juniors'

Millington
Morris County

(G-6207)
BLUEWATER INC
Also Called: Wild Bills Olde Fashioned Soda
50 Division Ave Ste 42 (07946-1377)
PHONE..................................973 532-1225
Christine Kropp, *CEO*
Derek Kropp, *Partner*
EMP: 13
SALES (est): 1.7MM **Privately Held**
SIC: 2087 Beverage bases

(G-6208)
RW DELIGHTS INC
Also Called: Heavenly Souffle
50 Division Ave Ste 44 (07946-1377)
PHONE..................................718 683-1038
Roxanne Kam, *President*
EMP: 5
SQ FT: 5,000
SALES: 550K **Privately Held**
SIC: 2024 Dairy based frozen desserts

Millstone Township
Monmouth County

(G-6209)
ARQUEST INC (PA)
14 Scotto Farm Ln (08535-9426)
PHONE..................................609 395-9500
John R Rinaldi, *CEO*
Matthew J Rinaldi, *President*
Paul Destefano, *Vice Pres*
Eddie Everett, *Vice Pres*
Reed Macfarland, *Vice Pres*
▲ EMP: 500
SQ FT: 7,000
SALES (est): 65.2MM **Privately Held**
WEB: www.arquest.com
SIC: 2676 Diapers, paper (disposable):
made from purchased paper; feminine hy-
giene paper products

(G-6210)
COBRA POWER SYSTEMS INC
(PA)
304 Monmouth Rd (08510-7936)
PHONE..................................908 486-1800
Doug Cohen, *President*
Gil Cohen, *Manager*
EMP: 7
SQ FT: 3,800
SALES: 2MM **Privately Held**
SIC: 3621 Motors & generators

(G-6211)
GREIF INC
200 Rike Dr (08535-8548)
PHONE..................................609 448-5300
Geoff Eaton, *Branch Mgr*
EMP: 40
SALES (corp-wide): 3.8B **Publicly Held**
WEB: www.greif.com
SIC: 2655 Fiber cans, drums & containers
PA: Greif, Inc.
   425 Winter Rd
   Delaware OH 43015
   740 549-6000

(G-6212)
**SAFEGAURD DOCUMENT
DESTRUCTION**
800 Rike Dr (08535-8526)
PHONE..................................609 448-6695
Frank Vitarelli, *Principal*
EMP: 4
SALES (est): 548.6K **Privately Held**
SIC: 3559 Tire shredding machinery

Millstone Twp
Monmouth County

(G-6213)
CHRISTOPHER SZUCO
Also Called: Westwood Construction
1061 Windsor Rd (08535-6017)
PHONE..................................732 684-7643
Christopher Szuco, *Owner*
EMP: 4
SALES (est): 365.6K **Privately Held**
SIC: 2514 1742 Frames for box springs or
bedsprings: metal; household furniture:
upholstered on metal frames; drywall

Milltown
Middlesex County

(G-6214)
BANNISTER COMPANY INC
216 Brook Dr (08850-1596)
PHONE..................................732 828-1353
EMP: 12 EST: 1956
SQ FT: 12,000
SALES (est): 1.5MM **Privately Held**
SIC: 3479 7389 Engraving & Signage

(G-6215)
FOCTEK PHOTONICS LLC
15 Birch St (08850-1342)
PHONE..................................732 828-8228
Larry Huang, *Principal*
EMP: 4
SALES (est): 243.6K **Privately Held**
SIC: 3661 Fiber optics communications
equipment

(G-6216)
**INTERNATIONAL PAPER
COMPANY**
101 Ford Ave (08850-1565)
P.O. Box 36 (08850-0036)
PHONE..................................732 828-1700
Richard Hostinsky, *Owner*
Bill Waldron, *Branch Mgr*
EMP: 60
SALES (corp-wide): 23.3B **Publicly Held**
WEB: www.tin.com
SIC: 2653 Corrugated & solid fiber boxes
PA: International Paper Company
   6400 Poplar Ave
   Memphis TN 38197
   901 419-9000

(G-6217)
JASON MILLS LLC
440 S Main St Ste 7 (08850-1727)
PHONE..................................732 651-7200
Michael L Lavroff, *President*
Brenda Stamboulian, *Sales Dir*
◆ EMP: 6
SQ FT: 2,000
SALES (est): 930.3K **Privately Held**
SIC: 2258 Lace & warp knit fabric mills

(G-6218)
OSSB AND L PHARMA LLC
6 Bel Air Ct (08850-2183)
PHONE..................................732 940-8701
Prabhavathi V K Maddula, *Principal*
EMP: 4
SALES (est): 227.4K **Privately Held**
SIC: 2834 Pharmaceutical preparations

(G-6219)
SALLY MILLER LLC
30 N Main St (08850-1549)
PHONE..................................732 729-4840
Sally Miller,
▲ EMP: 7
SALES (est): 1MM **Privately Held**
SIC: 2361 Girls' & children's dresses,
blouses & shirts

(G-6220)
SUNSHINE METAL & SIGN INC
Also Called: Sunshine Container
14 Louise Dr (08850-2155)
PHONE..................................973 676-4432
Jonathan W White, *President*

Karen J White, *Vice Pres*
EMP: 9
SALES (est): 1.8MM **Privately Held**
SIC: 2631 2653 Corrugating medium; cor-
rugated & solid fiber boxes

Millville
Cumberland County

(G-6221)
AAVOLYN CORP
207 Bogden Blvd Ste M (08332-4844)
P.O. Box 1097 (08332-8097)
PHONE..................................856 327-8040
Lynn Farrell, *President*
Carolyn Shourds, *Purch Mgr*
Venkat Koganti, *Engineer*
Melissa Dion, *Office Mgr*
Gerard Farrell, *Administration*
EMP: 25
SALES (est): 5MM **Privately Held**
WEB: www.aavolyn.com
SIC: 3563 Air & gas compressors

(G-6222)
**ABSOLUTE BUSINESS
SERVICES INC**
325 Maurice St (08332-4113)
PHONE..................................856 265-9447
Jaysen Rose, *President*
EMP: 4
SALES (est): 269K **Privately Held**
SIC: 2752 Business forms, lithographed

(G-6223)
**ADVANCED METAL
PROCESSING**
326 S Wade Blvd (08332-3544)
PHONE..................................856 327-0048
Shane Callahan, *General Mgr*
▲ EMP: 5
SALES (est): 572.8K **Privately Held**
SIC: 3471 Finishing, metals or formed
products

(G-6224)
AMCOR FLEXIBLES LLC
Also Called: Amcor Flexibles Mil
1633 Wheaton Ave (08332-2013)
PHONE..................................856 825-1400
Hutton Ward, *Director*
EMP: 135 **Privately Held**
SIC: 2671 2621 2821 3081 Plastic film,
coated or laminated for packaging; pack-
aging paper; plastics materials & resins;
packing materials, plastic sheet; closures,
stamped metal
HQ: Amcor Flexibles Llc
   2150 E Lake Cook Rd
   Buffalo Grove IL 60089
   224 313-7000

(G-6225)
AMCOR PHRM PACKG USA INC
Nipro Glass
1600 Malone St (08332-4831)
PHONE..................................856 825-3050
Jack Chebra, *Sales/Mktg Mgr*
EMP: 108 **Privately Held**
WEB: www.alcanpackaging.com
SIC: 3221 Glass containers
HQ: Amcor Pharmaceutical Packaging Usa,
   Llc
   625 Sharp St N
   Millville NJ 08332
   856 327-1540

(G-6226)
**AMCOR PHRM PACKG USA LLC
(DH)**
625 Sharp St N (08332-2862)
PHONE..................................856 327-1540
Peter Brues, *President*
Peter Bruess, *President*
David White, *President*
▲ EMP: 153 EST: 1888
SQ FT: 1,000,000
SALES (est): 629.3MM **Privately Held**
WEB: www.alcanpackaging.com
SIC: 3221 3085 Cosmetic jars, glass;
medicine bottles, glass; plastics bottles

(G-6227)
AMCOR PHRM PACKG USA LLC
1200 N 10th St (08332-2032)
PHONE..................................856 825-1400
Richard Calabro, *Manager*
EMP: 108 **Privately Held**
WEB: www.alcanpackaging.com
SIC: 3221 Cosmetic jars, glass
HQ: Amcor Pharmaceutical Packaging Usa,
   Llc
   625 Sharp St N
   Millville NJ 08332
   856 327-1540

(G-6228)
AMCOR PHRM PACKG USA LLC
Tube Drawing Division
1633 Wheaton Ave (08332-2013)
PHONE..................................856 825-1400
Bob Griffin, *Manager*
EMP: 150 **Privately Held**
WEB: www.alcanpackaging.com
SIC: 3221 Cosmetic jars, glass; medicine
bottles, glass
HQ: Amcor Pharmaceutical Packaging Usa,
   Llc
   625 Sharp St N
   Millville NJ 08332
   856 327-1540

(G-6229)
AMCOR PHRM PACKG USA LLC
Also Called: Wheaton Science Products
1501 N 10th St (08332-2038)
PHONE..................................856 825-1100
Steve Drozdow, *Manager*
Ade Adelakun, *Manager*
Wendy Whisler, *Supervisor*
Rob Nicke, *Analyst*
EMP: 200
SQ FT: 1,000 **Privately Held**
WEB: www.alcanpackaging.com
SIC: 3221 3829 3231 3229 Glass con-
tainers; measuring & controlling devices;
products of purchased glass; pressed &
blown glass
HQ: Amcor Pharmaceutical Packaging Usa,
   Llc
   625 Sharp St N
   Millville NJ 08332
   856 327-1540

(G-6230)
AMCOR PHRM PACKG USA LLC
Nipro Glass
1101 Wheaton Ave (08332-2003)
PHONE..................................856 825-1400
Walter Dolson, *Manager*
EMP: 22 **Privately Held**
WEB: www.alcanpackaging.com
SIC: 3559 Pharmaceutical machinery
HQ: Amcor Pharmaceutical Packaging Usa,
   Llc
   625 Sharp St N
   Millville NJ 08332
   856 327-1540

(G-6231)
**AMCOR RIGID PACKAGING USA
LLC**
625 Sharp St N (08332-2862)
PHONE..................................856 327-1540
Bill Bean, *QC Mgr*
Bruce Clungeon, *Branch Mgr*
Lisa Purdy, *Manager*
EMP: 58 **Privately Held**
SIC: 3085 Plastics bottles
HQ: Amcor Rigid Packaging Usa, Llc
   40600 Ann Arbor Rd E # 201
   Plymouth MI 48170

(G-6232)
**AMERICAN SIGN INSTLLATIONS
LLC**
209 S 15th St (08332-3446)
PHONE..................................856 506-0610
Stephen Armstrong, *CEO*
EMP: 4 EST: 2017
SALES (est): 138.4K **Privately Held**
SIC: 3993 Signs & advertising specialties

▲ = Import ▼=Export
◆ =Import/Export

(G-6233)
ARC INTERNATIONAL N AMER LLC (HQ)
Also Called: Cardinal Millville DC ARC Intl
601 S Wade Blvd (08332-3550)
PHONE...............................856 825-5620
Hubert Ibled, *President*
Olivier Malpel, *General Mgr*
Earleen Riggins, *Project Mgr*
Ken Turner, *Purch Agent*
Olga Grishina, *Engineer*
▲ **EMP:** 140
SQ FT: 750,000
SALES (est): 1B
SALES (corp-wide): 1.5MM **Privately Held**
SIC: 5023 2821 Glassware; plastics materials & resins
PA: Arc Holdings
104 Avenue Du General De Gaulle
Arques 62510
321 385-122

(G-6234)
ARCHITCTURAL METAL DESIGNS INC
Also Called: A M D
1505 Pineland Ave (08332-3505)
PHONE...............................856 765-3000
Martin J Schelmbach, *President*
Jennifer Schlembach, *Vice Pres*
Joe Paradise, *Project Mgr*
Michael Smith, *Manager*
Donna Louden, *Software Dev*
EMP: 35
SALES: 4MM **Privately Held**
SIC: 3444 Sheet metalwork

(G-6235)
BETCO GLASS INC
824 Columbia Ave (08332-3733)
P.O. Box 1099 (08332-8099)
PHONE...............................856 327-4301
Neil Betchner, *President*
EMP: 5
SALES (est): 386.6K **Privately Held**
SIC: 3229 Glass tubes & tubing

(G-6236)
BIG 3 PRECISION PRODUCTS INC
30 Gorton Rd (08332-6202)
PHONE...............................856 293-1400
Alan Scheidt, *Branch Mgr*
EMP: 8 **Privately Held**
SIC: 3089 Blow molded finished plastic products
HQ: Big 3 Precision Products, Inc.
2923 S Wabash Ave
Centralia IL 62801
618 533-3251

(G-6237)
BIG DADDYS SPORTS HAVEN
595 Sherman Ave (08332-7424)
PHONE...............................856 453-9009
EMP: 5 **EST:** 1999
SALES (est): 440K **Privately Held**
SIC: 3949 Fishing Hunting Guns & Atvs

(G-6238)
BODYBIO INC (PA)
45 Reese Rd (08332-6227)
PHONE...............................856 825-8338
Edward Kane, *CEO*
Patricia Kane MD, *Vice Pres*
EMP: 26
SALES (est): 3.2MM **Privately Held**
WEB: www.bodybio.com
SIC: 2833 Medicinal chemicals

(G-6239)
BREWSTER VAULTS & MONUMENTS
1017 Steep Run Rd (08332-7544)
PHONE...............................856 785-1412
Steven W Brewster, *President*
Joseph E Brewster, *Vice Pres*
Asa Brewster, *Treasurer*
EMP: 11
SALES (est): 1.7MM **Privately Held**
SIC: 3272 5999 Burial vaults, concrete or precast terrazzo; monuments, finished to custom order

(G-6240)
CAIN MACHINE INC
2248 E Main St (08332-3611)
PHONE...............................856 825-7225
Doug Cain, *President*
Jesse Cain, *Vice Pres*
Eleanor Cain, *Treasurer*
◆ **EMP:** 10
SALES (est): 1.6MM **Privately Held**
SIC: 3559 2821 3643 3444 Glass making machinery: blowing, molding, forming, etc.; polytetrafluoroethylene resins (teflon); current-carrying wiring devices; sheet metalwork

(G-6241)
CARLISLE MACHINE WORKS INC
412 S Wade Blvd Ste 5 (08332-3534)
P.O. Box 746 (08332-0746)
PHONE...............................856 825-0627
Mary Dougherty, *President*
Frank Hedges, *Marketing Staff*
Judi Doran, *Manager*
EMP: 24
SQ FT: 10,000
SALES (est): 4.6MM **Privately Held**
WEB: www.carlislemachine.com
SIC: 3433 3535 3823 Gas burners, domestic; conveyors & conveying equipment; combustion control instruments

(G-6242)
CHANKS USA LLC
2516 Mays Landing Rd (08332-1104)
PHONE...............................856 265-0203
Eric Ciancaglini,
EMP: 8
SALES (est): 235.3K **Privately Held**
SIC: 2045 5142 Prepared flour mixes & doughs; bakery products, frozen

(G-6243)
CREAMER GLASS LLC
2201 Quince Ln (08332-3661)
PHONE...............................856 327-2023
R Wayne Miskelly, *Owner*
Todd Miskelly, *General Mgr*
EMP: 8
SQ FT: 800
SALES (est): 430K **Privately Held**
WEB: www.creamerglass.com
SIC: 3229 Tubing, glass

(G-6244)
CREAMER GLASS LLC
411 N 10th St (08332-3145)
PHONE...............................856 327-2023
Todd Miskelly, *Mng Member*
EMP: 4
SALES: 500K **Privately Held**
SIC: 3229 1389 Tubing, glass; running, cutting & pulling casings, tubes & rods

(G-6245)
CUMBERLAND RCYCL CORP S JERSEY
Also Called: Luciano Brothers
N Delsea Dr (08332)
P.O. Box 2304, Vineland (08362-2304)
PHONE...............................856 825-4153
George Luciano Sr, *President*
EMP: 35
SALES (corp-wide): 7.8MM **Privately Held**
SIC: 4953 3341 3231 Recycling, waste materials; secondary nonferrous metals; products of purchased glass
PA: Cumberland Recycling Corporation Of South Jersey
702 S West Blvd
Vineland NJ 08360
856 692-7650

(G-6246)
DELTRONICS CORPORATION
22 Easterwood St (08332)
P.O. Box 446 (08332-0446)
PHONE...............................856 825-8200
Robert Hignutt, *President*
Kenneth Hignutt, *Vice Pres*
EMP: 15
SQ FT: 8,000

SALES: 1.6MM **Privately Held**
SIC: 7699 3625 5085 Mechanical instrument repair; industrial controls: push button, selector switches, pilot; industrial supplies

(G-6247)
DEMCO SCIENTIFIC GLASSWARE INC
25 N 6th St (08332-3341)
PHONE...............................856 327-7898
Clyde Demary, *President*
EMP: 8
SALES (est): 363K **Privately Held**
SIC: 3231 Medical & laboratory glassware: made from purchased glass; scientific & technical glassware: from purchased glass

(G-6248)
DURAND GLASS MFG CO INC
901 S Wade Blvd (08332-3531)
PHONE...............................856 327-1850
Susan Saidman, *CEO*
Ken Bell, *Vice Pres*
Emmanuel Gauffeny, *Vice Pres*
Steve Obrian, *Vice Pres*
Jay Branch, *Foreman/Supr*
▲ **EMP:** 1100
SQ FT: 800,000
SALES (est): 228.8MM
SALES (corp-wide): 1.5MM **Privately Held**
SIC: 3229 3269 5023 Tableware, glass or glass ceramic; kitchen articles, coarse earthenware; glassware
HQ: Arc International North America, Llc
601 S Wade Blvd
Millville NJ 08332
856 825-5620

(G-6249)
FRIEDRICH AND DIMMOCK INC
Also Called: F & D
2127 Wheaton Ave (08332-1421)
PHONE...............................856 825-0305
Joseph Plumbo, *CEO*
John T Plumbo, *CEO*
Bob Goffredi, *President*
Victor G Plumbo, *Chairman*
Steve Cimer, *CFO*
▲ **EMP:** 48 **EST:** 1919
SQ FT: 25,000
SALES (est): 7.6MM **Privately Held**
WEB: www.fdglass.com
SIC: 3229 5047 3231 3221 Scientific glassware; medical laboratory equipment; products of purchased glass; glass containers

(G-6250)
GARDEN STATE HIGHWAY PDTS INC (PA)
301 Riverside Dr D (08332-6717)
PHONE...............................856 692-7572
Sharon Green, *President*
Robert Green, *Vice Pres*
EMP: 46
SQ FT: 28,000
SALES (est): 11.9MM **Privately Held**
WEB: www.gardenstatehwy.com
SIC: 3993 5099 3499 Signs & advertising specialties; safety equipment & supplies; barricades, metal

(G-6251)
GENERAL POLYGON SYSTEMS INC
203 Peterson St (08332-4803)
PHONE...............................800 825-1655
Joseph Pitassi Jr, *President*
William Anderson, *Principal*
Rich Shea, *Principal*
Michael Sormanti, *Vice Pres*
Thomas Sole, *Mfg Mgr*
EMP: 10
SQ FT: 6,000
SALES (est): 1.6MM **Privately Held**
WEB: www.generalpolygon.com
SIC: 3599 Machine shop, jobbing & repair

(G-6252)
GLASS WAREHOUSE
Also Called: Wheaton Sands Products
1101 Wheaton Ave (08332-2003)
P.O. Box 1039 (08332-8039)
PHONE...............................856 825-1400
Steve Drozdow, *President*
James Smith, *Vice Pres*
▼ **EMP:** 8
SALES (est): 1MM **Privately Held**
WEB: www.glass-warehouse.com
SIC: 3229 Scientific glassware

(G-6253)
GROUPE SEB USA
2121 Eden Rd (08332-4060)
PHONE...............................856 825-6300
Cyril Buxtorf, *Senior VP*
Luc Gaudemard, *Senior VP*
Jacques Nadeau, *VP Finance*
Virginia Flower, *Accounting Mgr*
Xavier Sabourin, *Mktg Dir*
EMP: 10
SALES (corp-wide): 355.8K **Privately Held**
SIC: 3639 Floor waxers & polishers, electric: household
HQ: Groupe Seb Usa
5 Woodhollow Rd Fl 2
Parsippany NJ 07054

(G-6254)
HENDERSON AQUATIC INC (PA)
1 Whitall Ave (08332-3988)
PHONE...............................856 825-4771
Allan G Edmund, *President*
Joe Polak, *VP Sales*
◆ **EMP:** 25 **EST:** 1954
SQ FT: 15,000
SALES (est): 4.1MM **Privately Held**
WEB: www.hendersonusa.com
SIC: 3069 Wet suits, rubber

(G-6255)
HOLLY PACKAGING INC
1101 N 10th St (08332-2029)
P.O. Box 356 (08332-0356)
PHONE...............................856 327-8281
EMP: 50
SQ FT: 36,000
SALES (est): 11.9MM **Privately Held**
SIC: 2653 7389 Mfg Corrugated/Solid Fiber Boxes Business Services

(G-6256)
J AND J CONTRACTORS
604 5th St N (08332-2614)
PHONE...............................856 765-7521
Julian Mendez, *Owner*
Janet Mendez, *Co-Owner*
EMP: 10
SALES: 351K **Privately Held**
SIC: 3545 Drill bushings (drilling jig)

(G-6257)
JACQUET JONPAUL
25 E Main St Ste D (08332-4289)
PHONE...............................856 825-4259
Jon Paul Jacquet, *Principal*
EMP: 4
SALES (est): 368.6K **Privately Held**
SIC: 3843 Enamels, dentists'

(G-6258)
LAMONICA FINE FOODS LLC
Also Called: Cape May Foods
48 Gorton Rd (08332-6202)
P.O. Box 309 (08332-0309)
PHONE...............................856 776-2126
Danny Lavecchia, *President*
Steve Schwartz, *Regional Mgr*
Chris Douthett, *Vice Pres*
Michael Lavecchia, *Vice Pres*
Sandy Ritchie, *Buyer*
▲ **EMP:** 200 **EST:** 1949
SQ FT: 95,000
SALES (est): 38MM **Privately Held**
WEB: www.capemayfoods.com
SIC: 2091 2092 Clams: packaged in cans, jars, etc.; juice, clam: packaged in cans, jars, etc.; seafoods, fresh: prepared

(G-6259)
LLOYDS OF MILLVILLE INC
Also Called: Lloyd's Awnings
208 S Wade Blvd (08332-3542)
PHONE....................................856 825-0345
Benjamin H Lloyd Jr, *President*
Linda Lloyd, *Vice Pres*
EMP: 6
SALES: 250K **Privately Held**
SIC: 2394 Canvas & related products

(G-6260)
MCQUADE ENTERPRISES LLC
511 N 6th St (08332-2707)
PHONE....................................609 501-2437
Robert McQuade,
EMP: 5
SALES (est): 138.7K **Privately Held**
SIC: 6798 3524 6531 Real estate invest-
ment trusts; lawn & garden equipment;
real estate managers

(G-6261)
NIPRO GLASS AMERICAS CORP
1633 Wheaton Ave (08332-2013)
PHONE....................................856 825-1400
EMP: 11 **Privately Held**
SIC: 3221 Vials, glass
HQ: Nipro Pharmapackaging Americas
Corp.
1200 N 10th St
Millville NJ 08332

(G-6262)
NIPRO PHRMPCKGING
AMRICAS CORP (HQ)
Also Called: Millville Vials
1200 N 10th St (08332-2032)
PHONE....................................856 825-1400
Kurt Van Dal, *President*
Bob Luderitz, *Engineer*
Anthony Lieske, *Finance*
◆ EMP: 192
SQ FT: 4,000,000
SALES (est): 98.7MM **Privately Held**
SIC: 3221 Vials, glass

(G-6263)
NM KNIGHT CO INC
Also Called: Knight Gas Burner Co
1001 S 2nd St (08332-4234)
P.O. Box 1099 (08332-8099)
PHONE....................................856 327-4855
Jack Narbut, *President*
Connie Sparks, *Finance Mgr*
▲ EMP: 25
SQ FT: 12,000
SALES (est): 4.6MM **Privately Held**
WEB: www.nmknight.com
SIC: 3823 3433 5084 Combustion control
instruments; heating equipment, except
electric; industrial machinery & equipment

(G-6264)
NORTHEAST PRECAST LTD
LBLTY CO
92 Reese Rd (08332-6228)
PHONE....................................856 765-9088
John Ruga, *Principal*
Tom Talalaj, *Project Engr*
Robert Shanaman, *CFO*
Heidi Ahlquist, *Sales Staff*
Richard Hawk, *Marketing Staff*
EMP: 80
SQ FT: 65,000
SALES (est): 19.3MM **Privately Held**
SIC: 1799 3599 Fence construction; cus-
tom machinery

(G-6265)
OHM EQUIPMENT LLC
2525 S 2nd St (08332-9606)
PHONE....................................856 765-3011
Douglas OHM, *Principal*
EMP: 4
SALES (est): 308.3K **Privately Held**
WEB: www.ohmequipment.com
SIC: 3699 Electrical equipment & supplies

(G-6266)
PARKER-HANNIFIN
CORPORATION
525 Orange St (08332-4030)
PHONE....................................856 825-8900
EMP: 12

SALES (corp-wide): 14.3B **Publicly Held**
SIC: 3577 Computer peripheral equipment
PA: Parker-Hannifin Corporation
6035 Parkland Blvd
Cleveland OH 44124
216 896-3000

(G-6267)
RAILING DYNAMICS INC
1201 N 10th St (08332-2031)
PHONE....................................609 593-5400
Fax: 856 327-2343
EMP: 13
SALES (corp-wide): 94.2K **Privately Held**
SIC: 2411 Mfg And Distributes Vinyl Railing
And Fencing
HQ: Railing Dynamics Inc
135 Steelmanville Rd
Egg Harbor Township NJ 08226
609 601-1300

(G-6268)
REMINDER NEWSPAPER
2 W Vine St (08332-3823)
P.O. Box 1600 (08332-8600)
PHONE....................................856 825-8811
Darrell Kopp, *President*
EMP: 15
SALES (est): 845.8K **Privately Held**
WEB: www.nreminder.com
SIC: 2711 Newspapers

(G-6269)
RICHARD ANDRUS
Also Called: Andrus Bait Company
708 E Main St (08332-3441)
PHONE....................................856 825-1782
Richard Andrus, *Owner*
EMP: 5
SALES (est): 406.6K **Privately Held**
SIC: 2298 3949 Fishing lines, nets,
seines: made in cordage or twine mills;
lures, fishing: artificial

(G-6270)
SHURE-PAK CORPORATION
1500 N Ten St (08332)
P.O. Box 105 (08332-0105)
PHONE....................................856 825-0808
Aaron B Sheppard, *President*
Cynthia Sheppard, *Corp Secy*
George B Sheppard, *Vice Pres*
EMP: 8 EST: 1944
SQ FT: 22,000
SALES (est): 1.6MM **Privately Held**
WEB: www.shure-pak.com
SIC: 2631 2652 Folding boxboard; setup
paperboard boxes

(G-6271)
SOUTHWIND EQUESTRIAN
385 Lebanon Rd (08332-7446)
PHONE....................................856 364-9690
Jeannie Dickison Allan, *Owner*
EMP: 6
SALES: 150K **Privately Held**
SIC: 2084 Wines

Mine Hill
Morris County

(G-6272)
FIABILA USA INC
114 Iron Mountain Rd (07803-2300)
PHONE....................................973 659-9510
Pierre Miasnik, *President*
Mitchell Schlossman, *Vice Pres*
Anna Wnek, *Marketing Staff*
◆ EMP: 28
SQ FT: 11,000
SALES (est): 10.4MM **Privately Held**
WEB: www.fiabilausa.com
SIC: 5999 2841 Cosmetics; soap & other
detergents

(G-6273)
M2 ELECTRIC LLC
Also Called: M2 Enterprises
3 Iron Mountain Rd (07803-2312)
PHONE....................................973 770-4596
Aimee Oliva, *Mng Member*
Michael Oliva,
EMP: 14

SALES (est): 1.5MM **Privately Held**
WEB: www.m2enterprisesusa.com
SIC: 1731 2521 7389 General electrical
contractor; panel systems & partitions
(free-standing), office: wood;

(G-6274)
MINE HILL SPARTAN
274 Us Highway 46 (07803-3030)
PHONE....................................973 442-2280
Cengiz Unal, *Owner*
EMP: 5 EST: 2007
SALES (est): 417.8K **Privately Held**
SIC: 1389 Oil field services

(G-6275)
WIRE CLOTH MANUFACTURERS
INC (PA)
110 Iron Mountain Rd (07803-2300)
PHONE....................................973 328-1000
Kathleen Hegarty, *President*
Brian Blaber, *General Mgr*
Jim Beyer, *Managing Dir*
Kathleen H Blaber, *Vice Pres*
James P Hegarty Sr, *Vice Pres*
▲ EMP: 25 EST: 1965
SQ FT: 65,000
SALES: 4.9MM **Privately Held**
SIC: 3496 3564 3494 Wire cloth & woven
wire products; blowers & fans; valves &
pipe fittings

Monmouth Junction
Middlesex County

(G-6276)
ACCELEDEV CHEMICAL LLC
11 Deerpark Dr Ste 119 (08852-1923)
PHONE....................................732 274-1451
Charles Lewis, *President*
EMP: 5
SALES (corp-wide): 613K **Privately Held**
SIC: 2869 Laboratory chemicals, organic
PA: Acceledev Chemical, L.L.C.
18 Apple Ln
Wayne NJ 07470
862 239-1524

(G-6277)
ALCHEM PHARMTECH INC
1 Deerpark Dr Ste H2 (08852-1920)
PHONE....................................848 565-5694
EMP: 7
SALES (est): 809K **Privately Held**
SIC: 2834 Pharmaceutical preparations

(G-6278)
AMPERICON INC
1 Tamaron Ct (08852-2967)
PHONE....................................609 945-2591
Vivek Bhatnagar, *President*
EMP: 11
SALES (est): 211.7K **Privately Held**
SIC: 3433 Heating equipment, except elec-
tric

(G-6279)
BRIARS USA
891 Georges Rd (08852-3057)
P.O. Box 7092, North Brunswick (08902-
7092)
PHONE....................................732 821-7600
Joseph De Marco, *Ch of Bd*
Herbert Schloss, *President*
Guy Battaglia, *Vice Pres*
Maurie Motto, *Admin Sec*
EMP: 6 EST: 1921
SQ FT: 85,000
SALES (est): 919.1K **Privately Held**
WEB: www.briars.com
SIC: 2086 2087 Soft drinks: packaged in
cans, bottles, etc.; syrups, drink

(G-6280)
BWI CHEMICALS
Also Called: Aroma Chemicals
6 Libby Dr (08852-2921)
PHONE....................................732 689-0913
Yunus Bandukwala, *Owner*
▼ EMP: 2 EST: 2007
SALES: 1MM **Privately Held**
SIC: 2911 Aromatic chemical products

(G-6281)
CHEM-AQUA INC
34 Stouts Ln (08852-1911)
PHONE....................................972 438-0211
Bill Bolton, *President*
Kevin Battaglini, *District Mgr*
Jeffrey Kazio, *Consultant*
EMP: 11
SALES (corp-wide): 1B **Privately Held**
SIC: 3589 1629 Water treatment equip-
ment, industrial; waste water & sewage
treatment plant construction
HQ: Chem-Aqua, Inc.
2727 Chemsearch Blvd
Irving TX 75062
972 438-0232

(G-6282)
COCA COLA BOTTLING CO MID
AMER
Coca-Cola
60 Deans Rhode Hall Rd (08852-3031)
PHONE....................................732 398-4800
Ed Rowan, *Branch Mgr*
EMP: 10
SALES (corp-wide): 31.8B **Publicly Held**
WEB: www.phillycoke.com
HQ: Coca Cola Bottling Company Of Mid
America
435 Se 70th St
Topeka KS 66619
785 243-1071

(G-6283)
COCA-COLA REFRESHMENTS
USA INC
60 Deans Rhode Hall Rd (08852-3031)
PHONE....................................732 398-4800
Gina Kurdewan, *Manager*
EMP: 11
SALES (corp-wide): 31.8B **Publicly Held**
SIC: 2086 Bottled & canned soft drinks
HQ: Coca-Cola Refreshments Usa, Inc.
2500 Windy Ridge Pkwy Se
Atlanta GA 30339
770 989-3000

(G-6284)
COCA-COLA REFRESHMENTS
USA INC
60 Deans Rhode Hall Rd (08852-3031)
PHONE....................................201 635-6300
Ken Kaprowski, *Branch Mgr*
EMP: 300
SALES (corp-wide): 31.8B **Publicly Held**
WEB: www.cokecce.com
HQ: Coca-Cola Refreshments Usa, Inc.
2500 Windy Ridge Pkwy Se
Atlanta GA 30339
770 989-3000

(G-6285)
CYTOSORBENTS
CORPORATION (PA)
7 Deerpark Dr Ste K (08852-1977)
PHONE....................................732 329-8885
Phillip P Chan, *President*
Ronald Berger, *General Mgr*
Vincent J Capponi, *COO*
Matthew Sheahan, *Opers Mgr*
Kathleen P Bloch, *CFO*
EMP: 28
SQ FT: 15,745
SALES: 22.5MM **Publicly Held**
SIC: 3841 Surgical & medical instruments

(G-6286)
CYTOSORBENTS MEDICAL INC
(HQ)
7 Deerpark Dr Ste K (08852-1977)
PHONE....................................732 329-8885
Al W Kraus, *Ch of Bd*
Phillip P Chan, *President*
Vincent J Capponi, *COO*
Vincent Capponi, *COO*
Christopher Cramer, *Vice Pres*
EMP: 38
SQ FT: 12,400
SALES (est): 7.2MM
SALES (corp-wide): 22.5MM **Publicly
Held**
SIC: 3841 Surgical & medical instruments

PA: Cytosorbents Corporation
7 Deerpark Dr Ste K
Monmouth Junction NJ 08852
732 329-8885

(G-6287)
DOW JONES & COMPANY INC
Also Called: Wall Street Journal
4300 Us Highway 1 (08852-1963)
PHONE..............................609 520-4000
Georgie Fowler, *Finance*
Lauren Manuwald, *Personnel*
Florence Lefevre, *Sales Staff*
Danforth Austin, *Branch Mgr*
MO Malhotra, *Sr Project Mgr*
EMP: 4
SALES (corp-wide): 10B Publicly Held
SIC: 2711 Newspapers, publishing & print-
ing
HQ: Dow Jones & Company, Inc.
1211 Avenue Of The Americ
New York NY 10036
609 627-2999

(G-6288)
DOW JONES & COMPANY INC
4300 Us Highway 1 (08852-1963)
P.O. Box 300, Princeton (08543-0300)
PHONE..............................609 520-5238
EMP: 100
SQ FT: 3,000
SALES (corp-wide): 10B Publicly Held
SIC: 2711 Newspapers, publishing & print-
ing
HQ: Dow Jones & Company, Inc.
1211 Avenue Of The Americ
New York NY 10036
609 627-2999

(G-6289)
DRIVE TECHNOLOGY INC
2031 Us Highway 130 1I (08852-3014)
PHONE..............................732 422-6500
Thomas R Doscher, *President*
Marjorie Doscher, *Vice Pres*
EMP: 4 EST: 1975
SQ FT: 5,400
SALES: 800K Privately Held
SIC: 8711 5063 3566 Consulting engi-
neer; motor controls, starters & relays:
electric; motors, electric; speed changers,
drives & gears

(G-6290)
ELITE GRAPHIX LLC
45 Stouts Ln Ste 2 (08852-1914)
P.O. Box 1430, Belmar (07719-1430)
PHONE..............................732 274-2356
Joseph Angelone, *CEO*
EMP: 10
SALES (est): 1.1MM Privately Held
SIC: 2752 Business form & card printing,
lithographic

(G-6291)
FILTER TECHNOLOGIES INC
Also Called: Filter Process & Supply
45 Stouts Ln Ste 3 (08852-1914)
PHONE..............................732 329-2500
Peter Wojnarowicz, *President*
EMP: 5
SQ FT: 10,000
SALES: 400K Privately Held
WEB: www.filterselect.com
SIC: 5075 3589 5085 Air filters; water fil-
ters & softeners, household type; filters,
industrial

(G-6292)
I PHYSICIAN HUB
Also Called: Iphysicianhub
462 New Rd (08852-2653)
PHONE..............................732 274-0155
Ramdev Regulapati, *President*
EMP: 99
SALES (est): 2.8MM Privately Held
SIC: 7372 7379 8011 8099 Business ori-
ented computer software; ; group health
association; medical services organiza-
tion

(G-6293)
INFINOVA CORPORATION
Also Called: Infinova Networks
51 Stouts Ln Ste 1 (08852-1916)
PHONE..............................732 355-9100
Jeffrey Z Liu, *President*
Milind Borkar, *Vice Pres*
Stephan Cannellos, *Vice Pres*
Nathan Needel, *Vice Pres*
Adolph Salas, *Vice Pres*
▲ EMP: 50
SQ FT: 20,000
SALES (est): 10MM Privately Held
WEB: www.infinova.com
SIC: 3663 3661 3699 3625 Television
closed circuit equipment; fiber optics com-
munications equipment; security devices;
electric controls & control accessories, in-
dustrial

(G-6294)
INNOVTIVE PHTNICS SLUTION CORP
Also Called: Innovative Photonic Solutions
4250 Us Highway 1 Ste 1 (08852-1966)
PHONE..............................732 355-9300
Dieter Strohm, *President*
Nancy Morris, *Vice Pres*
Scott Rudder, *Vice Pres*
Tina Gong, *Sales Staff*
EMP: 8
SQ FT: 5,000
SALES (est): 1.6MM
SALES (corp-wide): 267.9K Privately
Held
WEB: www.innovativephotonics.com
SIC: 3648 Lighting equipment
HQ: Metrohm Ag
Ionenstrasse
Herisau AR 9100
713 538-585

(G-6295)
KAREBAY BIOCHEM INC
11 Deerpark Dr Ste 102a (08852-1923)
PHONE..............................732 823-1545
Lijun Dai, *Ch of Bd*
Drew Dai, *Vice Pres*
EMP: 4
SALES (est): 319.6K Privately Held
SIC: 2869 Laboratory chemicals, organic;
high purity grade chemicals, organic

(G-6296)
M G X INC
Also Called: Mastergraphx
45 Stouts Ln (08852-1914)
P.O. Box 567 (08852-0567)
PHONE..............................732 329-0088
Robert Townsend, *President*
Harry A Copeland, *Officer*
James G Copeland, *Officer*
Robert E Copeland, *Officer*
EMP: 11 EST: 1980
SQ FT: 5,000
SALES (est): 2.1MM Privately Held
WEB: www.mgxprint.com
SIC: 2752 Commercial printing, offset

(G-6297)
MEDCHEM EXPRESS LLC
11 Deerpark Dr (08852-1923)
PHONE..............................732 783-7915
James Dal, *Mng Member*
EMP: 5
SALES (est): 340.7K Privately Held
SIC: 2836 Biological products, except diag-
nostic

(G-6298)
NANONEX CORP
1 Deerpark Dr Ste O (08852-1962)
PHONE..............................732 355-1600
Lin W Chou, *President*
Hua Tan, *President*
Larry Koecher, *COO*
Lin Hu, *Engineer*
Yanjun Wang, *Engineer*
EMP: 12
SALES (est): 1.2MM Privately Held
WEB: www.nanonex.com
SIC: 3674 Semiconductors & related de-
vices

(G-6299)
PARABOLE LLC
1100 Cornwall Rd (08852-2410)
PHONE..............................609 917-8479
Rajib Kumar Saha, *CEO*
Manesh Murali, *President*
EMP: 9 EST: 2014

(G-6300)
PETRO PALLET LLC
575 Ridge Rd (08852-2638)
PHONE..............................732 230-3287
Anthony Lanza, *Mng Member*
EMP: 20
SQ FT: 1,000
SALES: 2MM Privately Held
SIC: 2448 Pallets, wood; pallets, wood &
wood with metal

(G-6301)
PHARMASEQ INC
11 Deerpark Dr Ste 104 (08852-1923)
PHONE..............................732 355-0100
Richard Morris, *CEO*
Wlodek Mandecki, *President*
▲ EMP: 5
SQ FT: 1,500
SALES (est): 1MM Privately Held
WEB: www.pharmaseq.com
SIC: 2835 8731 In vitro & in vivo diagnos-
tic substances; commercial physical re-
search

(G-6302)
PL A KADMONPHARMACEUTICALS
1 Deerpark Dr (08852-1920)
PHONE..............................732 230-3092
Ji-In Kim, *Owner*
EMP: 5
SALES (est): 400.6K Privately Held
SIC: 2834 Pharmaceutical preparations

(G-6303)
PRINCETON BIOMEDITECH CORP (PA)
Also Called: P B M
4242 Us Highway 1 (08852-1905)
P.O. Box 7139, Princeton (08543-7139)
PHONE..............................732 274-1000
Jemo Kang, *President*
Brian Lee, *Sales Executive*
Geun Lee, *Manager*
Sunny Suh, *Technology*
Nida Angeles, *Director*
▲ EMP: 100
SQ FT: 25,000
SALES (est): 18.3MM Privately Held
SIC: 2835 3826 In vitro diagnostics; preg-
nancy test kits; environmental testing
equipment

(G-6304)
PRINCETON ENDURING BIOTECH INC
190 Major Rd (08852-2303)
PHONE..............................732 406-3041
Shu-Min Liu, *CEO*
Howard Chen, *Principal*
Dechun Wu, *COO*
EMP: 4
SALES (est): 288.5K Privately Held
SIC: 2834 2836 Pharmaceutical prepara-
tions; biological products, except diagnos-
tic

(G-6305)
PRINCETON ENDURING BIOTECH INC
190 Major Rd (08852-2303)
PHONE...................,..........732 406-3041
EMP: 4
SALES (est): 180K Privately Held
SIC: 2836 2834 Mfg Biological Products
Mfg Pharmaceutical Preparations

(G-6306)
PRINCETONIAN GRAPHICS INC
45 Stouts Ln Ste 4 (08852-1914)
PHONE..............................732 329-8282
Jack E Norsworthy, *President*
Jack Norsworthy, *Prdtn Mgr*
EMP: 15 EST: 1969
SQ FT: 10,000
SALES (est): 2.4MM Privately Held
WEB: www.pringraph.com
SIC: 2752 Commercial printing, offset

(G-6307)
PROVID PHARMACEUTICALS INC
7 Deerpark Dr Ste M11 (08852-1981)
PHONE..............................732 565-1101
Gary L Olson, *Principal*
Edwin Thomas, *COO*
Christopher Self, *Vice Pres*
EMP: 6
SQ FT: 15,000
SALES (est): 1MM Privately Held
SIC: 2834 Pharmaceutical preparations

(G-6308)
REAL SOFT INC
Also Called: Diversity Direct
68 Culver Rd Ste 100 (08852-2820)
PHONE..............................609 409-3636
Rajan Desai, *President*
Joel Jerva, *Vice Pres*
Eabu Mathson, *Accounting Mgr*
Barkha Patni, *Accounting Mgr*
Anirban Singh, *Accounts Mgr*
EMP: 550
SQ FT: 58,000
SALES (est): 58.1MM Privately Held
WEB: www.realsoftinc.com
SIC: 7379 7373 7371 7372 Computer re-
lated consulting services; computer inte-
grated systems design; custom computer
programming services; computer software
systems analysis & design, custom; com-
puter software development; application
computer software; human resource con-
sulting services

(G-6309)
RIOGEN INC
1 Deerpark Dr Ste L3 (08852-1920)
PHONE..............................609 529-0503
Padmavathi Kanduri, *President*
EMP: 4 EST: 2013
SALES (est): 333.1K Privately Held
SIC: 2819 Industrial inorganic chemicals

(G-6310)
SALUS PHARMA LLC
11 Deerpark Dr Ste 118 (08852-1923)
PHONE..............................732 329-8089
Nuo Wang, *CEO*
Fan Zhou, *CFO*
▲ EMP: 10
SQ FT: 7,000
SALES (est): 1.6MM Privately Held
SIC: 2834 Druggists' preparations (phar-
maceuticals)

(G-6311)
SCIECURE PHARMA INC
11 Deerpark Dr Ste 120 (08852-1923)
PHONE..............................732 329-8089
Nuo Wang, *CEO*
Joeie Lee, *Supervisor*
▲ EMP: 34
SALES (est): 6.5MM
SALES (corp-wide): 5.1MM Privately
Held
SIC: 2834 Pharmaceutical preparations
PA: Beijing Sciecure Pharmaceutical Co.,
Ltd.
Zhongbei Industrial Park, Beishicao
Town, Shunyi District
Beijing 10130
106 044-7688

(G-6312)
SPENDYLOVE HOME CARE LLC
878 Georges Rd (08852-3011)
PHONE..............................732 430-5789
Maxwell Mensah,
EMP: 15 EST: 2015
SALES (est): 73.9K Privately Held
SIC: 8082 2741 Home health care serv-
ices; miscellaneous publishing

(G-6313)
SPHERE FLUIDICS INCORPORATED
11 Deerpark Dr Ste 210 (08852-1969)
PHONE..............................888 258-0226
Craig Cardella, *Vice Pres*
EMP: 4
SALES: 2.5MM Privately Held
SIC: 3821 Chemical laboratory apparatus

(G-6314)
SUVEN LIFE SCIENCES LTD
1100 Cornwall Rd Ste 5 (08852-2410)
PHONE................................732 274-0037
Venkat Jasti, *CEO*
Padmakumar Kumar, *Research*
Padma Kumar, *Director*
Pardha Uppalapati, *Director*
EMP: 10
SQ FT: 4,000
SALES (est): 1.7MM **Privately Held**
WEB: www.synthoncorp.com
SIC: 2899 Chemical preparations

(G-6315)
TRIS PHARMA INC
Also Called: Customer Complaint Dept
2031 Us Highway 130 Ste H (08852-3014)
PHONE................................732 940-0358
Ketan Mehta, *CEO*
Jeff Neubig, *Vice Pres*
Jessica Yoskowitz, *Buyer*
Marisol Santos, *Accounting Mgr*
Kristen Gilot-Dowd, *Sales Staff*
EMP: 76
SQ FT: 130,350 **Privately Held**
SIC: 2834 Syrups, pharmaceutical
PA: Tris Pharma, Inc.
    2033 Rte 130 Ste D
    Monmouth Junction NJ 08852

(G-6316)
TRIS PHARMA INC (PA)
2033 Rte 130 Ste D (08852)
PHONE................................732 940-2800
Ketan Mehta, *President*
Peter Ciano, *Senior VP*
Norma Cappetti, *Vice Pres*
Jeffery Palmer, *Vice Pres*
Richard Walton, *Vice Pres*
EMP: 249
SQ FT: 28,000
SALES (est): 120.2MM **Privately Held**
WEB: www.trispharma.com
SIC: 2834 Druggists' preparations (pharmaceuticals); drugs acting on the central nervous system & sense organs

(G-6317)
UNITED SILICON CARBIDE INC
7 Deerpark Dr Ste E (08852-1921)
PHONE................................732 355-0550
John Christopher Dries, *CEO*
Bhalla Anup, *President*
Betsy Cotton, *CFO*
EMP: 18
SALES (est): 5.2MM **Privately Held**
SIC: 8731 3674 Commercial research laboratory; transistors

(G-6318)
WALL STREET JOURNAL
4300 Us Highway 1 (08852-1906)
PHONE................................609 520-4000
Fax: 609 520-4274
EMP: 7
SALES (est): 429.8K **Privately Held**
SIC: 2711 Newspapers-Publishing/Printing

(G-6319)
WALLY ENTERPRISES INC
Also Called: Active Imprints
4266 Us Route 1 (08852)
PHONE................................732 329-2613
Duane Watlington, *President*
Nancy Watlington, *Vice Pres*
Steve Grennen, *Marketing Staff*
Jody Grzyb, *Consultant*
EMP: 12
SQ FT: 2,880
SALES (est): 1.7MM **Privately Held**
WEB: www.activeimprints.com
SIC: 7336 5199 5699 2395 Silk screen design; advertising specialties; T-shirts, custom printed; emblems, embroidered; embroidering of advertising on shirts, etc.; screen printing on fabric articles

(G-6320)
WYETH-AYERST PHARMACEUTICAL
865 Ridge Rd (08852-2718)
PHONE................................732 274-4221
EMP: 16

SALES (est): 2MM
SALES (corp-wide): 52.5B **Publicly Held**
SIC: 2834 Mfg Pharmaceutical Preparations
HQ: Wyeth Llc
    235 E 42nd St
    New York NY 10017
    973 660-5000

Monroe
Middlesex County

(G-6321)
EDISON DESIGN GROUP INC (PA)
95 Cobblestone Blvd (08831-7944)
PHONE................................732 993-3341
John Spicer, *President*
William Miller, *Design Engr*
Mike Herrick, *Software Dev*
EMP: 1
SALES: 1.6MM **Privately Held**
WEB: www.edg.com
SIC: 7372 Prepackaged software

(G-6322)
HRA INTERNATIONAL INC (PA)
489 Hillrose Way (08831-3778)
PHONE................................609 395-0939
Howard Rosenthal, *President*
EMP: 2
SQ FT: 2,000
SALES: 1MM **Privately Held**
WEB: www.hra-nca.org
SIC: 2323 5136 Neckties, men's & boys': made from purchased materials; scarves, men's & boys'

(G-6323)
UNIVERSAL SYSTEMS INSTALLERS
10 Red Oak Ct (08831-4067)
PHONE................................732 656-9002
Salvatore Filiano, *President*
Teresa Filiano, *Vice Pres*
EMP: 20
SALES (est): 2.6MM **Privately Held**
SIC: 2541 5031 1751 Store fixtures, wood; cabinets, lockers & shelving; lumber, plywood & millwork; millwork; cabinet & finish carpentry; store fixture installation

(G-6324)
WEBANNUITIESCOM INC (PA)
Also Called: United State Annuities
8 Talmadge Dr (08831-2910)
PHONE................................732 521-5110
Hersh Stern, *President*
EMP: 7
SQ FT: 1,600
SALES: 1.8MM **Privately Held**
WEB: www.webannuities.com
SIC: 6411 2721 Insurance brokers; trade journals; publishing only, not printed on site

---

Monroe Township
Middlesex County

(G-6325)
AKELA LASER CORPORATION
1095 Cranbury S Riv 14 (08831-3411)
PHONE................................732 305-7105
Bob Sellers, *President*
Mike Maiorov, *COO*
Mikhail Maiorov, *COO*
Vladimir Zeidel, *Mfg Dir*
Maria Kudryashova, *Controller*
EMP: 10
SQ FT: 6,200
SALES: 1MM **Privately Held**
WEB: www.akelalaser.com
SIC: 3674 Semiconductors & related devices

(G-6326)
AUGMA BIOMATERIALS USA INC
1989 Englishtown Rd Ste 1 (08831-3292)
PHONE................................201 509-4570

EMP: 4
SALES (est): 264.7K **Privately Held**
SIC: 3841 Surgical & medical instruments

(G-6327)
BERRY GLOBAL GROUP INC
34 Engelhard Dr (08831-3720)
PHONE................................732 469-2470
Wendy Hornich, *Human Res Mgr*
Jeanne Gonzalez, *Benefits Mgr*
Roman Dalessandro, *Branch Mgr*
EMP: 12 **Publicly Held**
SIC: 3089 Plastic containers, except foam
PA: Berry Global Group, Inc.
    101 Oakley St
    Evansville IN 47710

(G-6328)
BRACCO DIAGNOSTICS INC (DH)
259 Prospect Plains Rd (08831-3820)
PHONE................................609 514-2200
Vittorio Puppo, *President*
▲ EMP: 135
SQ FT: 59,500
SALES (est): 167.3MM **Privately Held**
WEB: www.diag.bracco.com
SIC: 2835 In vitro & in vivo diagnostic substances
HQ: Bracco U.S.A. Inc.
    259 Prospect Plains Rd
    Monroe Township NJ 08831
    609 514-2200

(G-6329)
BRACCO USA INC (HQ)
259 Prospect Plains Rd (08831-3820)
PHONE................................609 514-2200
Diana Bracco, *President*
Alberto Sana Maria, *Treasurer*
Dennis J Block, *Admin Sec*
Curtis Landherr,
Antonio Cantaluppi, *Asst Sec*
▲ EMP: 4
SQ FT: 66,187
SALES (est): 176MM **Privately Held**
SIC: 2835 In vitro & in vivo diagnostic substances
PA: Bracco Spa
    Via Caduti Di Marcinelle 13
    Milano MI
    022 177-1

(G-6330)
BROADWAY KLEER-GUARD CORP
Also Called: Shipmaster
1 S Middlesex Ave (08831-3726)
PHONE................................609 662-3970
Steve Kohn, *President*
▲ EMP: 30 EST: 1946
SQ FT: 30,000
SALES (est): 8.2MM **Privately Held**
WEB: www.shipmasterbags.com
SIC: 3081 5113 Packing materials, plastic sheet; bags, paper & disposable plastic

(G-6331)
DAILY DOLLAR LLC
48 E Sedgwick St (08831-1211)
PHONE................................732 236-9709
Krystina Mendez, *Principal*
EMP: 4
SALES (est): 157K **Privately Held**
SIC: 2711 Newspapers, publishing & printing

(G-6332)
FRAGRANCE EXCHANGE INC
1075 Cranbury Rd Ste 7 (08831-3409)
PHONE................................732 641-2210
▲ EMP: 5 EST: 2006
SALES (est): 995.2K **Privately Held**
SIC: 2844 Perfumes & colognes

(G-6333)
HORIZON GROUP USA INC
773 Cranbury S Rvr Rd 200 (08831-3032)
PHONE................................908 810-1111
EMP: 5
SALES (corp-wide): 180MM **Privately Held**
SIC: 3944 Games, toys & children's vehicles

PA: Horizon Group Usa, Inc.
    45 Technology Dr
    Warren NJ 07059
    908 810-1111

(G-6334)
LG ELECTRONICS USA INC
380 Deans Rhode Hall Rd (08831-3004)
PHONE................................732 605-0385
John Cummings, *Branch Mgr*
EMP: 6 **Privately Held**
SIC: 3679 Antennas, receiving
HQ: Lg Electronics U.S.A., Inc.
    1000 Sylvan Ave
    Englewood Cliffs NJ 07632
    201 816-2000

(G-6335)
METALWEST LLC
1 Fitzgerald Ave (08831-3729)
PHONE................................609 395-7007
Seth Wiener, *General Mgr*
Tony Hammes, *Vice Pres*
Brian Madison, *Vice Pres*
David Suchey, *Safety Dir*
Luke Babb, *Sales Staff*
EMP: 33
SALES (corp-wide): 213MM **Privately Held**
SIC: 5051 3441 Steel; fabricated structural metal
HQ: Metalwest, L.L.C.
    1229 Fulton St
    Brighton CO 80601
    303 654-0300

(G-6336)
METROPLEX PRODUCTS COMPANY INC
377 Deans Rhode Hall Rd (08831-3006)
PHONE................................732 249-0653
EMP: 8
SQ FT: 2,000
SALES (est): 4.7MM **Privately Held**
SIC: 5031 1751 2499 Whol Lumber/Plywood/Millwork Carpentry Contractor Mfg Wood Products

(G-6337)
NOODLE FAN
557 Englishtown Rd (08831-3042)
PHONE................................732 446-2820
EMP: 4
SALES (est): 149K **Privately Held**
SIC: 2098 Mfg Macaroni/Spaghetti

(G-6338)
NOVOTEC PHARMA LLC
Also Called: Accelis Pharma
20 Spruce Meadows Dr (08831-3103)
PHONE................................609 632-2239
Patrick Patel, *Managing Prtnr*
Snehal Patel, *Managing Prtnr*
EMP: 4
SQ FT: 5,000
SALES: 1MM **Privately Held**
SIC: 8731 2834 Commercial research laboratory; proprietary drug products

(G-6339)
OCEAN POWER TECHNOLOGIES INC (PA)
Also Called: Opt
28 Engelhard Dr Ste B (08831-3720)
PHONE................................609 730-0400
George H Kirby III, *CEO*
Terence J Cryan, *Ch of Bd*
Dean J Glover, *Vice Ch Bd*
Dean Glover, *Vice Chairman*
Mike Mekhiche, *VP Engrg*
◆ EMP: 28
SQ FT: 56,000
SALES: 632K **Publicly Held**
WEB: www.oceanpowertechnologies.com
SIC: 4911 3621 3629 Generation, electric power; distribution, electric power; generating apparatus & parts, electrical; electronic generation equipment

(G-6340)
PAGE STAMP LLC
110 Kings Mill Rd (08831-8903)
PHONE................................732 390-1700
EMP: 7
SALES: 700K **Privately Held**
SIC: 2759 Mfg Printing Equipment

(G-6341)
R & M MANUFACTURING INC
20 Abeel Rd (08831-2036)
PHONE..............................609 495-8032
Thomas Marvel, *President*
David Rudolph, *Vice Pres*
Gary Taylor, *Plant Mgr*
David G Rudolph, *Technology*
▲ EMP: 20
SQ FT: 30,000
SALES (est): 4MM **Privately Held**
SIC: 2434 2431 Wood kitchen cabinets;
millwork

(G-6342)
SETCO LLC
34 Engelhard Dr (08831-3796)
PHONE..............................610 321-9760
EMP: 7 **Publicly Held**
SIC: 3085 Plastics bottles
HQ: Setco, Llc
101 Oakley St
Evansville IN 47710
812 424-2904

(G-6343)
SHELAN CHEMICAL COMPANY INC
174 Tournament Dr (08831-2543)
PHONE..............................732 796-1003
Shelly Weiss, *President*
EMP: 9
SQ FT: 4,500
SALES (est): 8MM **Privately Held**
SIC: 5162 2493 2865 Resins; reconstituted wood products; dyes & pigments;
color pigments, organic

(G-6344)
SILVERTON PACKAGING CORP
75 Fairway Blvd (08831-2711)
PHONE..............................732 341-0986
Manolita Gadaleta, *President*
EMP: 1
SALES: 1MM **Privately Held**
WEB: www.silvertonpackagingcorp.com
SIC: 3081 Polyethylene film

(G-6345)
ST THOMAS CREATIONS (HQ)
3a S Middlesex Ave (08831-6809)
P.O. Box 100410, Pasadena CA (91189-0003)
PHONE..............................800 536-2284
▲ EMP: 42
SQ FT: 78,000
SALES (est): 6.9MM
SALES (corp-wide): 867.1MM **Privately Held**
SIC: 5023 3231 Whol Homefurnishings
Mfg Products-Purchased Glass
PA: Villeroy & Boch Ag
Saaruferstr. 1-3
Mettlach 66693
686 481-0

(G-6346)
STERLING PUBLISHING CO INC
Also Called: Sterling Publishing Warehouse
1 Barnes And Noble Way (08831-3417)
PHONE..............................732 248-6563
Joel Morales, *Accountant*
Robert A Ciofalo, *Manager*
Tony Romano, *Manager*
Lori Sgambati, *Director*
EMP: 17
SALES (corp-wide): 3.5B **Privately Held**
WEB: www.sterlingpub.com
SIC: 2731 5192 Books: publishing only;
books
HQ: Sterling Publishing Co., Inc.
1166 Avenue Of The Flr 17
New York NY 10036
212 532-7160

(G-6347)
STEVEN ORROS
Also Called: Winetree Publishing
106 Timber Hill Dr (08831-7961)
PHONE..............................732 972-1104
Steven Orros, *Owner*
EMP: 6
SALES (est): 258.7K **Privately Held**
SIC: 2741 Miscellaneous publishing

(G-6348)
TAYLOR COMMUNICATIONS INC
7 Costco Dr (08831-1129)
PHONE..............................732 561-8210
Mack Jim, *General Mgr*
EMP: 31
SALES (corp-wide): 3B **Privately Held**
SIC: 2754 Commercial printing, gravure
HQ: Taylor Communications, Inc.
1725 Roe Crest Dr
North Mankato MN 56003
507 625-2828

(G-6349)
TRICORBRAUN INC
111 Interstate Blvd (08831-3038)
PHONE..............................732 353-7104
EMP: 7
SALES (corp-wide): 467.8MM **Privately Held**
SIC: 5113 5084 3086 Industrial & personal service paper; food industry machinery; packaging & shipping materials,
foamed plastic
HQ: Tricorbraun Inc.
6 Cityplace Dr Ste 1000
Saint Louis MO 63141
314 569-3633

(G-6350)
VSAR RESOURCES LLC
30 Engelhard Dr (08831-3720)
PHONE..............................973 233-6000
Ashvin Vaghani, *Mng Member*
Vijay Vaghani,
▲ EMP: 15
SQ FT: 5,000
SALES (est): 3MM **Privately Held**
SIC: 2844 Face creams or lotions

Monroeville
Salem County

(G-6351)
GARDEN STATE FUEL
600 Buck Rd (08343-2534)
PHONE..............................856 442-0061
Baokar Saini, *President*
EMP: 6
SALES (est): 208.7K **Privately Held**
SIC: 1389 Oil & gas field services

(G-6352)
KRAMME CONSOLIDATED INC (PA)
Main St (08343)
PHONE..............................856 358-8151
Paul E Kramme Jr, *President*
Richard Kramme, *Treasurer*
Gerald A Kramme, *Admin Sec*
EMP: 3
SQ FT: 20,000
SALES (est): 19.4MM **Privately Held**
SIC: 4213 3229 Trucking, except local;
scientific glassware

(G-6353)
MONROEVILLE VINEYARD & WINERY
314 Richwood Rd (08343-1847)
PHONE..............................856 521-0523
Debra Basile, *CEO*
John Basile, *Owner*
EMP: 13
SALES (est): 100.4K **Privately Held**
SIC: 2084 Wines

Montague
Sussex County

(G-6354)
CRAIG ROBERTSON
Also Called: Robertson Industries
19 State Route 23 (07827-3303)
P.O. Box 720, New Hampton NY (10958-0720)
PHONE..............................973 293-8666
Craig Robertson, *Owner*
EMP: 9
SQ FT: 43,000

SALES (est): 1.1MM **Privately Held**
SIC: 3086 Packaging & shipping materials,
foamed plastic

(G-6355)
THOMPSON STONE
3 Myrtle Dr (07827-3024)
PHONE..............................973 293-7237
William Thompson, *Owner*
EMP: 5
SALES: 1MM **Privately Held**
WEB: www.thompsonstone.com
SIC: 3559 Stone working machinery

Montclair
Essex County

(G-6356)
ACTION COPY CENTERS INC
Also Called: Sir Speedy
590 Valley Rd Ste 2 (07043-1851)
PHONE..............................973 744-5520
Dave Pradip, *President*
Dave Moxa, *Vice Pres*
EMP: 6
SQ FT: 2,000
SALES (est): 907.7K **Privately Held**
SIC: 2752 2791 2789 Commercial printing, lithographic; typesetting; bookbinding
& related work

(G-6357)
ALCARO & ALCARO PLATING CO
112 Pine St (07042-4812)
P.O. Box 1215 (07042-1215)
PHONE..............................973 746-1200
Anthony Alcaro, *President*
EMP: 22
SQ FT: 2,500
SALES (est): 1.9MM **Privately Held**
WEB: www.platingservicesonline.com
SIC: 3471 Electroplating of metals or
formed products

(G-6358)
APPLEGATE FRM HMMADE ICE CREAM (PA)
616 Grove St (07043-2017)
PHONE..............................973 744-5900
Jason Street, *Owner*
Melinda Street, *Shareholder*
EMP: 10
SQ FT: 130,000
SALES (est): 925.4K **Privately Held**
SIC: 2024 Ice cream & frozen desserts

(G-6359)
ARCTIC GLACIER USA INC
363 Bloomfield Ave Ste 3b (07042-3655)
PHONE..............................973 771-3391
EMP: 11
SALES (corp-wide): 159.7MM **Privately Held**
SIC: 2097 Manufactured ice
HQ: Arctic Glacier U.S.A., Inc.
1654 Marthaler Ln
Saint Paul MN 55118
204 784-5873

(G-6360)
BEDLAM CORP
Also Called: Carpet Hardware Systems
33 Church St (07042-2701)
PHONE..............................973 774-8770
Richard Grabowsky, *President*
Jane Kaine, *General Mgr*
EMP: 13
SQ FT: 7,500
SALES: 767.7K **Privately Held**
WEB: www.bedlam.com
SIC: 3446 5051 Brasswork, ornamental:
structural; stairs, staircases, stair treads:
prefabricated metal; railings, prefabricated metal; metals service centers & offices

(G-6361)
CRAVE FOODS LLC
19 Club Rd (07043-2503)
PHONE..............................973 233-1220
Shahida Sayed,
Riaz Surti,

EMP: 12
SQ FT: 2,000
SALES (est): 970K **Privately Held**
WEB: www.cravefoods.com
SIC: 2032 Ethnic foods: canned, jarred,
etc.

(G-6362)
D L V LOUNGE INC
300 Bloomfield Ave (07042-3602)
PHONE..............................973 783-6988
George Marable Jr, *Treasurer*
EMP: 4
SQ FT: 1,200
SALES (est): 340K **Privately Held**
SIC: 2253 Lounge, bed & leisurewear; T-
shirts & tops, knit

(G-6363)
DOCBOX SOLUTIONS LTD LBLTY CO
140 Upper Mountain Ave (07042-1918)
PHONE..............................201 650-0970
Brian Cole, *CEO*
Stephanie Aranowitz, *COO*
Alain Espinosa, *CIO*
EMP: 6 EST: 2013
SALES: 100K **Privately Held**
SIC: 7372 7389 Business oriented computer software;

(G-6364)
DODDLE & CO LLC
41 Watchung Plz Ste 354 (07042-4117)
PHONE..............................917 836-1299
Nicki Radzely,
EMP: 7
SALES (est): 839.9K **Privately Held**
SIC: 3069 Baby pacifiers, rubber

(G-6365)
ELEMENTAL INTERIORS
204 Bellevue Ave (07043-1893)
PHONE..............................646 861-3596
Megan Downing, *Owner*
EMP: 4 EST: 2016
SALES (est): 297.5K **Privately Held**
SIC: 2819 Elements

(G-6366)
ENDOMEDIX INC
1 Normal Ave Cels404 (07043-1624)
PHONE..............................848 248-1883
Richard Russo, *President*
John M Abrahams MD, *Principal*
EMP: 5
SALES (est): 572.7K **Privately Held**
SIC: 3841 Surgical & medical instruments

(G-6367)
FLUOROPHARMA MEDICAL INC
8 Hillside Ave Ste 108 (07042-2129)
PHONE..............................973 744-1565
Walter Witoshkin, *Ch of Bd*
Thomas H Tulip, *President*
Tamara Rehin, *CFO*
Tamara Rhein, *CFO*
EMP: 4
SALES (est): 426K **Privately Held**
SIC: 2835 In vitro diagnostics

(G-6368)
HAL LEONARD LLC
Hal Leonard Publishing
33 Plymouth St Ste 302 (07042-2677)
P.O. Box 1520, Wayne (07474-1520)
PHONE..............................973 337-5034
Michael Mecina, *Branch Mgr*
EMP: 230
SALES (corp-wide): 173.9MM **Privately Held**
SIC: 2741 Music, sheet: publishing only,
not printed on site
PA: Hal Leonard Llc
7777 W Bluemound Rd
Milwaukee WI 53213
414 774-3630

(G-6369)
HYP HAIR INC
Also Called: Magna Publishing
372 Orange Rd (07042-4312)
PHONE..............................201 843-4004
EMP: 30
SALES (est): 2.8MM **Privately Held**
SIC: 2721 Publish Magazines

GEOGRAPHIC

(G-6370)
IMMTECH PHARMACEUTICALS INC
93 Prospect Ave (07042-1920)
PHONE........................212 791-2911
EMP: 24
SQ FT: 2,500
SALES (est): 3.9MM **Privately Held**
SIC: 2834 8731 Mfg Pharmaceutical Preparations Commercial Physical Research

(G-6371)
INTERCHANGE GROUP INC
Also Called: Soyka-Smith Design Research
52 Watchung Ave (07043-1338)
PHONE........................973 783-7032
Bridget Soyka-Smith, *President*
EMP: 10
SALES: 3.2MM **Privately Held**
SIC: 7389 2511 Design services; wood household furniture

(G-6372)
INTERCURE INC
Also Called: Intercure Limited and Resperat
356 Bloomfield Ave Ste 5 (07042-3625)
PHONE........................973 893-5653
Erez Gavish, *President*
Judy Chodirker, *Principal*
Arik Kleinstein, *CFO*
EMP: 20
SQ FT: 3,000
SALES (est): 2.3MM **Privately Held**
SIC: 3841 Blood pressure apparatus

(G-6373)
JERSEY CIDER WORKS LLC (PA)
42 Erwin Park Rd (07042-3020)
PHONE........................917 604-0067
Charles Rosen, *CEO*
EMP: 5
SQ FT: 10,000
SALES: 250K **Privately Held**
SIC: 2084 Wines

(G-6374)
LURE LASH SPA LLC
Also Called: Lure Lash
416 Bloomfield Ave (07042-3537)
PHONE........................973 783-5274
Anna Abraham, *Owner*
Carlean Martinez, *Co-Owner*
EMP: 10 EST: 2015
SQ FT: 2,000
SALES (est): 959.1K **Privately Held**
SIC: 5087 3949 Beauty salon & barber shop equipment & supplies; lures, fishing; artificial

(G-6375)
MONTCLAIR DISPATCH LLC
423 Bloomfield Ave (07042-3505)
PHONE........................973 509-8861
EMP: 4 EST: 2015
SALES (est): 137.1K **Privately Held**
SIC: 2711 Newspapers

(G-6376)
MONTCLAIR FUEL LLC
651 Bloomfield Ave (07042-2213)
PHONE........................973 744-4300
Barry's Flooring, *Administration*
EMP: 8
SALES (est): 731.6K **Privately Held**
SIC: 2869 Fuels

(G-6377)
NATIONAL HOUSING INSTITUTE
Also Called: Shelterforce Magazine
60 S Fullerton Ave # 206 (07042-2663)
PHONE........................973 509-1600
John Atlas, *President*
Bob Zdenek, *Vice Pres*
Harold Simon, *Exec Dir*
Patrick Morrissy, *Admin Sec*
EMP: 4
SQ FT: 1,200
SALES: 161.4K **Privately Held**
WEB: www.nhi.org
SIC: 2721 8733 Magazines: publishing only, not printed on site; noncommercial research organizations

(G-6378)
NORLO OF NEW JERSEY LLC
105 Alexander Ave (07043-2620)
PHONE........................646 492-3293
EMP: 6 EST: 2010
SALES (est): 358.6K **Privately Held**
SIC: 3089 Molding primary plastic

(G-6379)
NORTH JERSEY MEDIA GROUP INC
Also Called: Montclair Times Editorial
130 Valley Rd Ste D (07042-2355)
PHONE........................973 233-5000
Kathy Hivish, *Manager*
EMP: 30
SALES (corp-wide): 156.2MM **Privately Held**
WEB: www.njmg.com
SIC: 2711 Newspapers, publishing & printing
HQ: North Jersey Media Group Inc.
150 River St
Hackensack NJ 07601
201 646-4000

(G-6380)
OXFORD BIOCHRONOMETRICS LLC
153 Pine St (07042-4909)
PHONE........................201 755-5932
William Scheckel, *General Mgr*
EMP: 1 EST: 2016
SALES: 2.5MM **Privately Held**
SIC: 7372 Application computer software

(G-6381)
P O V INCORPORATED (PA)
Also Called: Pov Reports
29 Park St (07042-3407)
PHONE........................914 258-4361
David Ogden, *President*
Robert Hannan, *President*
Henry McCarter, *Vice Pres*
EMP: 15
SQ FT: 3,000
SALES (est): 1.1MM **Privately Held**
SIC: 2741 Newsletter publishing

(G-6382)
PAM OPTICAL CO
107 Park St (07042-3465)
PHONE........................973 744-8882
Kenneth Testa, *President*
Margaret Testa, *Vice Pres*
EMP: 4 EST: 1963
SQ FT: 100
SALES (est): 395.1K **Privately Held**
SIC: 3851 5995 Lenses, ophthalmic; optical goods stores

(G-6383)
PARSONS CABINETS INC
79 Beverly Rd (07043-1729)
PHONE........................973 279-4954
Winfield Parsons, *President*
Stephen Parsons, *Treasurer*
EMP: 8
SALES (est): 408.1K **Privately Held**
SIC: 2434 2541 1751 Wood kitchen cabinets; wood partitions & fixtures; wood television & radio cabinets; cabinet & finish carpentry

(G-6384)
PATTERSON SMITH PUBLISHING
23 Prospect Ter (07042-3204)
PHONE........................973 744-3291
Patterson Smith, *President*
Thomas Kelly, *Corp Secy*
EMP: 5
SQ FT: 5,000
SALES (est): 470.8K **Privately Held**
WEB: www.patterson-smith.com
SIC: 2731 Books: publishing only

(G-6385)
PRINTERS PLACE INC (PA)
8 S Fullerton Ave (07042-3359)
PHONE........................973 744-8889
Bill Coutts Sr, *President*
EMP: 5
SQ FT: 1,200

SALES (est): 1.3MM **Privately Held**
WEB: www.theprintersplace.com
SIC: 2752 5943 Commercial printing, offset; office forms & supplies

(G-6386)
PUENT-ROMER COMMUNICATIONS INC
Also Called: Studio042
423 Bloomfield Ave (07042-3505)
PHONE........................973 509-7591
Scott Kennedy, *CEO*
Pilar P Kennedy, *President*
Carol Castelluccio, *Graphic Designe*
EMP: 4
SQ FT: 3,200
SALES (est): 689.4K **Privately Held**
WEB: www.weprintfast.com
SIC: 2752 2789 2791 Commercial printing, offset; bookbinding & related work; typesetting

(G-6387)
RAOS SPECIALTY FOODS INC (HQ)
441 Bloomfield Ave (07042-3505)
PHONE........................212 269-0151
Eric Skae, *CEO*
Jim Morano, *President*
▲ EMP: 15
SQ FT: 8,000
SALES (est): 3.8MM
SALES (corp-wide): 8.4MM **Privately Held**
WEB: www.raos.com
SIC: 2033 2099 2079 2035 Tomato sauce: packaged in cans, jars, etc.; olives: packaged in cans, jars, etc.; mushrooms: packaged in cans, jars, etc.; pasta, uncooked: packaged with other ingredients; olive oil; dressings, salad: raw & cooked (except dry mixes)
PA: Sovos Brands Intermediate, Inc.
75 State St
Boston MA 02109
617 951-9400

(G-6388)
RETAIL MANAGEMENT PUBG INC
Also Called: Instore Magazine
28 Valley Rd (07042-2709)
PHONE........................212 981-0217
Fred Mouawad, *Ch of Bd*
EMP: 13
SALES (est): 1.8MM **Privately Held**
SIC: 2721 7313 8741 Magazines: publishing only, not printed on site; electronic media advertising representatives; management services

(G-6389)
SITETRACKER INC (PA)
491 Bloomfield Ave # 301 (07042-3406)
PHONE........................551 486-2087
Giuseppe Incitti, *CEO*
Irene Scher, *Vice Pres*
Tim May, *CTO*
Bob Amelung, *Director*
EMP: 17
SALES (est): 6.8MM **Privately Held**
SIC: 7372 Prepackaged software

(G-6390)
STERLING NET & TWINE CO INC (PA)
Also Called: Sterling Marine Products
18 Label St (07042-3823)
P.O. Box 411, Basking Ridge (07920-0411)
PHONE........................973 783-9800
James C Van Loon Jr, *President*
EMP: 10 EST: 1950
SQ FT: 12,000
SALES (est): 871.9K **Privately Held**
WEB: www.sterlingnets.com
SIC: 2399 3949 2298 Fishing nets; nets, launderers & dyers; sporting & athletic goods; nets, rope

(G-6391)
TEN ONE DESIGN LTD LBLTY CO
149 Chestnut St (07042-3062)
PHONE........................201 474-8232
Peter Skinner,

EMP: 4
SALES: 950K **Privately Held**
SIC: 3999 Manufacturing industries

(G-6392)
THATS HOW WE ROLL LLC (PA)
Also Called: Dippin Chips
214 Glenridge Ave (07042-3528)
PHONE........................973 240-0200
Aldo Zuppichini, *CEO*
Sam Kestenbaum, *Vice Pres*
Jason Ramjit, *Opers Staff*
EMP: 3
SALES (est): 1MM **Privately Held**
SIC: 2096 Corn chips & other corn-based snacks; tortilla chips

(G-6393)
WELLSPRING INFO INC
41 Watchung Plz Ste 506 (07042-4117)
PHONE........................800 268-3682
Scott Cohen, *President*
◆ EMP: 11 EST: 2010
SALES (est): 546.5K **Privately Held**
SIC: 2732 7371 Book printing; custom computer programming services; custom computer programming services; computer software development & applications; software programming applications

---

Montvale
Bergen County

(G-6394)
ACCURATE TOOL & DIE CO INC
Also Called: Accurate Transmissions
6 Westminster Ct (07645-1353)
PHONE........................201 476-9348
Dominick Costantino, *President*
Joseph Manderano, *Vice Pres*
▲ EMP: 4
SQ FT: 30,000
SALES (est): 744.1K **Privately Held**
SIC: 3714 3469 3544 Motor vehicle parts & accessories; metal stampings; special dies & tools

(G-6395)
ADVANSTAR COMMUNICATIONS INC
5 Paragon Dr (07645-1791)
PHONE........................973 944-7777
Claren Copany, *Manager*
EMP: 40
SALES (corp-wide): 1.3B **Privately Held**
WEB: www.advanstar.com
SIC: 2721 8742 Magazines: publishing only, not printed on site; sales (including sales management) consultant
HQ: Advanstar Communications Inc.
2501 Colorado Ave Ste 280
Santa Monica CA 90404
310 857-7500

(G-6396)
AMERICAN MEDICAL & DENTAL SUPS
240 W Grand Ave (07645-1716)
PHONE........................877 545-6837
Dinesh Sakhrani, *CEO*
EMP: 13 EST: 2008
SALES (est): 1.3MM **Privately Held**
SIC: 3843 Dental equipment & supplies

(G-6397)
AUTOMATED RESOURCE GROUP INC
135 Chestnut Ridge Rd # 2 (07645-1152)
PHONE........................201 391-8357
Ray Butkus, *CEO*
Thomas Amoriello Sr, *Ch of Bd*
Alexander Amoriello, *COO*
James N Slack, *CFO*
EMP: 60
SQ FT: 17,000
SALES (est): 3.7MM **Privately Held**
WEB: www.callargi.com
SIC: 7374 7372 Data processing service; publishers' computer software

(G-6398)
BEN HAMON MOORE CO
51 Chestnut Ridge Rd (07645-1862)
PHONE..................................800 344-0400
EMP: 23
SALES (est): 3.2MM **Privately Held**
SIC: 2851 Paints & allied products

(G-6399)
BENJAMIN MOORE & CO (HQ)
101 Paragon Dr (07645-1727)
PHONE..................................201 573-9600
Dan Calkins, *Ch of Bd*
Tim Little, *General Mgr*
Ken Marino, *VP Mfg*
Todd Kayhart, *Mfg Mgr*
Sherry Totaro, *Purch Mgr*
◆ EMP: 147 EST: 1891
SQ FT: 57,000
SALES (est): 845.3MM
SALES (corp-wide): 225.3B **Publicly Held**
WEB: www.benjaminmoore.com
SIC: 5231 2851 Paint; paints: oil or alkyd vehicle or water thinned
PA: Berkshire Hathaway Inc.
3555 Farnam St Ste 1140
Omaha NE 68131
402 346-1400

(G-6400)
BERRY GLOBAL FILMS LLC (DH)
95 Chestnut Ridge Rd (07645-1801)
P.O. Box 959, Evansville IN (47706-0959)
PHONE..................................201 641-6600
Tom Salmon, *CEO*
Jason K Greene, *Exec VP*
Mark W Miles, *CFO*
Tom Bradley, *Benefits Mgr*
Ken Ribe, *Info Tech Dir*
▼ EMP: 110 EST: 1970
SQ FT: 48,000
SALES (est): 887.6MM **Publicly Held**
WEB: www.aepinc.com
SIC: 2821 3081 Polyvinyl chloride resins (PVC); polyethylene resins; plastic film & sheet
HQ: Berry Global, Inc.
101 Oakley St
Evansville IN 47710
812 424-2904

(G-6401)
BFHJ HOLDINGS INC (PA)
26 Chestnut Ridge Rd (07645-1825)
PHONE..................................908 730-6280
EMP: 3 EST: 2015
SALES (est): 2MM **Privately Held**
SIC: 1731 3585 Energy management controls; heat pumps, electric

(G-6402)
CISCO SYSTEMS INC
1 Paragon Dr Ste 275 (07645-1751)
PHONE..................................201 782-0842
Michael Devito, *Regional Mgr*
Francois Negri, *Engineer*
Bob Musto, *Accounts Mgr*
Ken Orbach, *Business Anlyst*
Andrew Wozniak, *Branch Mgr*
EMP: 40
SALES (corp-wide): 51.9B **Publicly Held**
WEB: www.cisco.com
SIC: 3825 5063 3577 Network analyzers; electrical apparatus & equipment; computer peripheral equipment
PA: Cisco Systems, Inc.
170 W Tasman Dr
San Jose CA 95134
408 526-4000

(G-6403)
COINING INC
15 Mercedes Dr (07645-1815)
PHONE..................................201 791-4020
Peter Pachella, *General Mgr*
Maurice Mevissen, *Vice Pres*
Julie Scelzo, *Sales Mgr*
▲ EMP: 109 EST: 1963
SQ FT: 30,000
SALES (est): 14.4MM
SALES (corp-wide): 4.8B **Publicly Held**
WEB: www.coiningcorp.com
SIC: 3469 Stamping metal for the trade

HQ: Coining Holding Company
15 Mercedes Dr
Montvale NJ 07645

(G-6404)
COINING HOLDING COMPANY (HQ)
Also Called: Coining Manufactures
15 Mercedes Dr (07645-1815)
PHONE..................................201 791-4020
Ken Whited, *Vice Pres*
Paul Nikac, *Vice Pres*
Julie Scelzo, *Vice Pres*
Vito Tanzi, *Vice Pres*
Martin Oud, *Research*
▲ EMP: 15
SALES (est): 23.3MM
SALES (corp-wide): 4.8B **Publicly Held**
SIC: 3469 Stamping metal for the trade
PA: Ametek, Inc.
1100 Cassatt Rd
Berwyn PA 19312
610 647-2121

(G-6405)
COMPLEMENTARY COATINGS CORP (DH)
Also Called: Insl-X
101 Paragon Dr (07645-1727)
PHONE..................................845 786-5000
Stephen P O'Neill, *CEO*
Ross Laurie, *President*
Matthew Fuks, *Sales Staff*
Anthony Martinelli, *Sales Staff*
Kurt McClelland, *Sales Staff*
▼ EMP: 32
SALES (est): 35.3MM
SALES (corp-wide): 225.3B **Publicly Held**
SIC: 2851 Paints & allied products
HQ: Benjamin Moore & Co.
101 Paragon Dr
Montvale NJ 07645
201 573-9600

(G-6406)
CREATIVE PAVERS
45 Akers Ave (07645-2004)
PHONE..................................201 782-1661
Brett Unger, *Owner*
EMP: 8
SALES (est): 882.7K **Privately Held**
SIC: 3271 Paving blocks, concrete

(G-6407)
DATA CNTRUM COMMUNICATIONS INC
Also Called: Health Monitor Network
135 Chestnut Ridge Rd # 2 (07645-1152)
PHONE..................................201 391-1911
Eric Jensen, *President*
David Zuern, *Senior VP*
Dave Dolton, *Vice Pres*
Alex Dong, *Vice Pres*
Kim Vivas, *Prdtn Dir*
EMP: 18
SQ FT: 4,300
SALES (est): 4.1MM **Privately Held**
WEB: www.healthmonitor.com
SIC: 2721 Magazines: publishing only, not printed on site

(G-6408)
DOWDEN HEALTH MEDIA INC (HQ)
110 Summit Ave Ste 1 (07645-1776)
PHONE..................................201 740-6100
J Roger Friedman, *President*
Dobbs Obrien Sarah, *Editor*
Daniel J Mills, *CFO*
EMP: 60
SQ FT: 30,000
SALES (est): 7.1MM
SALES (corp-wide): 91.5MM **Privately Held**
WEB: www.dowdenhealthmedia.com
SIC: 2721 Magazines: publishing only, not printed on site
PA: Lebhar-Friedman, Inc.
4508 Oak Fair Blvd # 108
Tampa FL 33610
212 756-5000

(G-6409)
ECOCOM INC
221 W Grand Ave Ste 168 (07645-1729)
PHONE..................................201 393-0786
Stephen Shen, *President*
Lin LI, *Vice Pres*
▲ EMP: 6 EST: 1998
SALES: 10MM **Privately Held**
WEB: www.ecocom.com
SIC: 3496 Garment hangers, made from purchased wire

(G-6410)
EIGHT OCLOCK COFFEE COMPANY (DH)
155 Chestnut Ridge Rd # 2 (07645-1156)
PHONE..................................201 571-9214
Barbara Roth, *President*
EMP: 91
SQ FT: 13,000
SALES (est): 118.7MM
SALES (corp-wide): 470.2MM **Privately Held**
WEB: www.eightoclock.com
SIC: 5149 2095 Coffee & tea; roasted coffee

(G-6411)
EMPIRICAL GROUP LLC
155 Chestnut Ridge Rd (07645-1156)
PHONE..................................201 571-0300
John Petrizzo, *Principal*
▲ EMP: 25
SALES (est): 3.5MM
SALES (corp-wide): 470.2MM **Privately Held**
WEB: www.empiricalgroup.com
SIC: 2099 Tea blending
PA: Tata Global Beverages Limited
3rd Floor, Block C
Bengaluru KA 56002
806 717-1200

(G-6412)
GOOD EARTH TEAS INC
155 Chestnut Ridge Rd (07645-1156)
PHONE..................................831 423-7913
Ben Zaricor, *President*
Louise V Zaricor, *Corp Secy*
◆ EMP: 70
SQ FT: 41,000
SALES (est): 10.6MM
SALES (corp-wide): 470.2MM **Privately Held**
WEB: www.flagcollection.com
SIC: 2099 Tea blending; spices, including grinding
PA: Tata Global Beverages Limited
3rd Floor, Block C
Bengaluru KA 56002
806 717-1200

(G-6413)
HIGHLANDS ACQUISITION CORP
1 Paragon Dr Ste 125 (07645-1744)
PHONE..................................201 573-8400
Robert Pangia, *CEO*
EMP: 4
SALES (est): 271.2K **Privately Held**
SIC: 3845 Electromedical equipment

(G-6414)
INVESTMENT CASTING INSTITUTE
Also Called: INCAST
1 Paragon Dr Ste 110 (07645-1744)
PHONE..................................201 573-9770
Michael C Perry, *Exec Dir*
EMP: 5
SQ FT: 2,200
SALES: 1.4MM **Privately Held**
WEB: www.investmentcasting.org
SIC: 8621 2721 Education & teacher association; magazines: publishing only, not printed on site

(G-6415)
IVY CAPITAL PARTNERS LLC
102 Chestnut Ridge Rd # 1 (07645-1856)
PHONE..................................201 573-8400
Dennis O' Dowd, *Partner*
EMP: 5
SALES (est): 471.6K **Privately Held**
SIC: 3842 Orthopedic appliances

(G-6416)
IVY SPORTS MEDICINE LLC
102 Chestnut Ridge Rd # 1 (07645-1856)
PHONE..................................201 573-5423
Robert Pangia, *CEO*
EMP: 4
SALES (est): 745.2K
SALES (corp-wide): 13.6B **Publicly Held**
SIC: 3841 Surgical & medical instruments
PA: Stryker Corporation
2825 Airview Blvd
Portage MI 49002
269 385-2600

(G-6417)
KFT FIRE TRAINER LLC
Also Called: Kidde Fire Trainers
17 Philips Pkwy (07645-1810)
PHONE..................................201 300-8100
David Greer, *Chairman*
▲ EMP: 35
SQ FT: 25,755
SALES (est): 9.7MM
SALES (corp-wide): 2.3MM **Privately Held**
WEB: www.kiddeft.com
SIC: 3699 Electronic training devices
PA: Kft International, Llc
155 N Wacker Dr Ste 4150
Chicago IL

(G-6418)
KURT VERSEN INC
1 Paragon Dr Ste 157 (07645-1728)
PHONE..................................201 664-5283
Steve Siversten, *President*
▼ EMP: 15
SALES (est): 3.1MM
SALES (corp-wide): 4.4B **Publicly Held**
WEB: www.hubbell-ltg.com
SIC: 3645 Residential lighting fixtures
HQ: Hubbell Lighting, Inc.
701 Millennium Blvd
Greenville SC 29607

(G-6419)
LEADING PHARMA LLC
155 Chestnut Ridge Rd # 100 (07645-1156)
PHONE..................................201 746-9160
Ronald F Gold, *CEO*
EMP: 40
SALES (corp-wide): 10.6MM **Privately Held**
SIC: 5122 2834 Pharmaceuticals; pharmaceutical preparations
PA: Leading Pharma, Llc
3 Oak Rd
Fairfield NJ 07004
201 746-9160

(G-6420)
MICRONET ENERTEC TECH INC
28 W Grand Ave Ste 3 (07645-2100)
PHONE..................................201 225-0190
David Lucatz, *Ch of Bd*
EMP: 89
SALES: 14.1MM **Privately Held**
SIC: 3572 Computer storage devices

(G-6421)
PENTAX OF AMERICA INC
Pentax Medical Company
3 Paragon Dr (07645-1782)
PHONE..................................973 628-6200
John M Crump, *Vice Pres*
EMP: 45 **Privately Held**
WEB: www.pentaximaging.com
SIC: 3841 7371 Surgical instruments & apparatus; diagnostic apparatus, medical; computer software development & applications
HQ: Pentax Of America, Inc.
3 Paragon Dr
Montvale NJ 07645
201 571-2300

(G-6422)
PEOPLES EDUCATION INC
25 Philips Pkwy 105 (07645-1810)
PHONE..................................201 712-0090
Brian Beckwith, *CEO*
James Peoples, *Ch of Bd*
Diane Miller, *Vice Pres*
Matti Prima, *Vice Pres*
Michael Demarco, *CFO*

▲ **EMP:** 110
SALES (est): 9.2MM
SALES (corp-wide): 22.4MM **Publicly Held**
WEB: www.standardshelpdata.com
SIC: 2731 Textbooks: publishing only, not printed on site
PA: Peoples Educational Holdings, Inc.
25 Philips Pkwy 105
Montvale NJ 07645
201 712-0090

(G-6423)
PEOPLES EDUCTL HOLDINGS INC (PA)
Also Called: Mastery Education
25 Philips Pkwy 105 (07645-1810)
P.O. Box 513, Saddle Brook (07663-0513)
PHONE.................................201 712-0090
James J Peoples, *Ch of Bd*
Brian T Beckwith, *President*
Michael L Demarco, *CFO*
EMP: 4
SQ FT: 23,000
SALES (est): 22.4MM **Publicly Held**
WEB: www.peoplespublishing.com
SIC: 2731 Books: publishing & printing

(G-6424)
PIN PEOPLE LLC
1 Paragon Dr Ste 150 (07645-1751)
PHONE.................................888 309-7467
Andrew Dale,
EMP: 10
SQ FT: 12,000
SALES: 9.5MM **Privately Held**
WEB: www.thepinpeople.com
SIC: 3911 Pins (jewelry), precious metal

(G-6425)
RECKITT BENCKISER LLC
1 Philips Pkwy (07645-1810)
PHONE.................................973 404-2600
Sharon James, *Vice Pres*
Marcia Bole, *Research*
Aleksandra Kruszewska, *Research*
Lan Nguyen, *Research*
Geoffrey Woo, *Engineer*
EMP: 125
SALES (corp-wide): 16.1B **Privately Held**
WEB: www.reckittprofessional.com
SIC: 2842 2035 Specialty cleaning, polishes & sanitation goods; pickles, sauces & salad dressings
HQ: Reckitt Benckiser Llc
399 Interpace Pkwy # 101
Parsippany NJ 07054
973 404-2600

(G-6426)
RIDGEWOOD ENERGY O FUND LLC
14 Philips Pkwy (07645-1811)
PHONE.................................201 447-9000
Robert E Swanson, *CEO*
Edward Viterbo, *Manager*
EMP: 1
SALES: 16.9MM **Privately Held**
SIC: 1389 Gas field services; oil field services; servicing oil & gas wells

(G-6427)
RIDGEWOOD ENERGY S FUND LLC
14 Philips Pkwy (07645-1811)
PHONE.................................201 307-0470
Robert E Swanson, *CEO*
EMP: 1
SALES: 5.6MM
SALES (corp-wide): 17.8MM **Privately Held**
SIC: 1382 Oil & gas exploration services
PA: Ridgewood Energy Corporation
14 Philips Pkwy
Montvale NJ 07645
201 307-0470

(G-6428)
RIDGEWOOD ENERGY T FUND LLC
14 Philips Pkwy (07645-1811)
PHONE.................................800 942-5550
Robert E Swanson, *Principal*
EMP: 2

SALES: 6MM **Privately Held**
SIC: 1382 Oil & gas exploration services

(G-6429)
RIDGEWOOD ENERGY U FUND LLC
14 Philips Pkwy (07645-1811)
PHONE.................................201 447-9000
Robert E Swanson, *CEO*
EMP: 1
SALES: 5.3MM **Privately Held**
SIC: 1382 Oil & gas exploration services

(G-6430)
RIDGEWOOD ENERGY V FUND LLC
14 Philips Pkwy (07645-1811)
PHONE.................................800 942-5550
Jonathan Keehner, *Principal*
EMP: 2
SALES: 8MM **Privately Held**
SIC: 1382 Oil & gas exploration services

(G-6431)
RIDGEWOOD ENERGY Y FUND LLC
14 Philips Pkwy (07645-1811)
PHONE.................................201 447-9000
Robert E Swanson, *CEO*
EMP: 1
SALES: 11.3MM **Privately Held**
SIC: 1382 Oil & gas exploration services

(G-6432)
RODMAN MEDIA CORP
Also Called: Household and Per Pdts Indust
25 Philips Pkwy Fl 2 (07645-1810)
PHONE.................................201 825-2552
Rodman Zilenziger Jr, *President*
Jay Gorga, *Publisher*
Damaris Kope, *Publisher*
Art Largar, *Publisher*
Mark Weeks, *Publisher*
EMP: 45
SQ FT: 12,000
SALES (est): 9.1MM **Privately Held**
WEB: www.rodmanpublishing.com
SIC: 2721 Magazines: publishing only, not printed on site

(G-6433)
SHARP ELECTRONICS CORPORATION (HQ)
Also Called: Sharp Manufacturing Co Amer
100 Paragon Dr Ste 100 # 100 (07645-1780)
PHONE.................................201 529-8200
Tetsuji Kawamura, *CEO*
Toshiyiki Osawa, *Ch of Bd*
John Herrington, *President*
James Sanduski, *President*
Tim O'Brien, *Partner*
◆ **EMP:** 850
SQ FT: 500,000
SALES (est): 772.4MM **Privately Held**
WEB: www.sharp-usa.com
SIC: 5064 3651 3631 3861 Electrical appliances, television & radio; television sets; tape players & recorders; high fidelity equipment; television receiving sets; microwave ovens, including portable: household; projectors, still or motion picture, silent or sound; semiconductors & related devices; calcvlators, electronic

(G-6434)
SILBO INDUSTRIES INC
50 Chestnut Ridge Rd # 204 (07645-1845)
PHONE.................................201 307-0900
James Mullally, *President*
Alan Shalom, *Partner*
Howard Jakob, *Partner*
Jeff Shalom, *Partner*
Mitchell Shalom, *Partner*
◆ **EMP:** 14 **EST:** 1965
SQ FT: 5,700
SALES (est): 5.8MM **Privately Held**
SIC: 5085 3317 Valves & fittings; steel pipe & tubes

(G-6435)
SRS SOFTWARE LLC
Also Called: SRS Health Software
155 Chestnut Ridge Rd (07645-1156)
PHONE.................................201 802-1300
Khal Rai, *President*
Robert Harmonay, *COO*
Daniel McGraw, *Senior VP*
Ryan Newsome, *Vice Pres*
Lynn Scheps, *Vice Pres*
EMP: 32 **EST:** 2013
SALES (est): 2.8MM
SALES (corp-wide): 32.1MM **Privately Held**
SIC: 7372 Prepackaged software
PA: Nextech Systems, Llc
4221 W Boy Scout Blvd
Tampa FL 33607
813 425-9200

(G-6436)
THOMSOM HEALTH CARE INC
5 Paragon Dr (07645-1791)
PHONE.................................201 358-7300
Barry Gray, *Vice Pres*
EMP: 150
SALES (est): 5.8MM **Privately Held**
SIC: 8733 2741 Medical research; miscellaneous publishing

Montville
Morris County

(G-6437)
AIRZONE SYSTEMS
28 Valhalla Rd (07045-9760)
PHONE.................................201 207-6593
Tym Koda, *Owner*
EMP: 4 **EST:** 2010
SALES: 1.2MM **Privately Held**
SIC: 3443 Air coolers, metal plate

(G-6438)
BLAVOR INC
1 Mountain Ave (07045-9408)
PHONE.................................973 265-4165
Ratko Nedich, *President*
EMP: 5
SALES (est): 307.8K **Privately Held**
SIC: 3292 Asbestos products

(G-6439)
BOZZONE CUSTOM WOODWORK INC
4 Taylortown Rd (07045-9744)
PHONE.................................973 334-5598
EMP: 4
SQ FT: 3,000
SALES: 300K **Privately Held**
SIC: 2511 2541 5712 Mfg & Ret Custom Furniture

(G-6440)
COMPUTERADIO
7 Brittany Rd (07045-9549)
P.O. Box 282, Pine Brook (07058-0282)
PHONE.................................973 220-0087
Yurri Blanarovich, *Owner*
EMP: 5
SALES: 120K **Privately Held**
SIC: 3663 Radio & TV communications equipment

(G-6441)
DRUG DELIVERY TECHNOLOGY LLC
219 Changebridge Rd (07045-9514)
PHONE.................................973 299-1200
James N Czaban, *Partner*
Graham Reynolds, *Vice Pres*
Cornell Stamoran, *Vice Pres*
Sonya Clemmons, *Director*
Jack Aurora, *Officer*
EMP: 25
SALES (est): 2.5MM **Privately Held**
WEB: www.drugdeliverytech.com
SIC: 2721 Magazines: publishing & printing

(G-6442)
FILLIMERICA INC
170 Chngbrdge Rd Bldg A42 (07045)
PHONE.................................800 435-7257

Thomas Filliman, *President*
Lucille Filliman, *Vice Pres*
EMP: 5
SQ FT: 1,600
SALES: 433.5K **Privately Held**
SIC: 7379 3571 5734 Computer related consulting services; electronic computers; computer peripheral equipment

(G-6443)
HICKOK MATTHEWS CO INC
Also Called: Schroth's Gold & Silversmiths
337 Main Rd (07045-9729)
PHONE.................................973 335-3400
Win Schroth, *President*
Sue Schroth, *Treasurer*
Susan Schroth, *Admin Sec*
EMP: 4 **EST:** 1919
SQ FT: 4,200
SALES (est): 1MM **Privately Held**
WEB: www.hickokmatthews.com
SIC: 5944 3499 5094 3911 Jewelry, precious stones & precious metals; picture frames, metal; precious metals; jewelry apparel

(G-6444)
MAROTTA CONTROLS INC (PA)
78 Boonton Ave (07045)
P.O. Box 427 (07045-0427)
PHONE.................................973 334-7800
Thomas S Marotta, *Ch of Bd*
Steven A Fox, *Vice Pres*
Walter Gilmore, *Vice Pres*
Michael J Leahan, *Vice Pres*
Gordon Hartley, *Mfg Staff*
▲ **EMP:** 150 **EST:** 1943
SQ FT: 100,000
SALES (est): 29.8MM **Privately Held**
WEB: www.marotta.com
SIC: 3494 3823 Valves & pipe fittings; industrial instrmnts msrmnt display/control process variable

(G-6445)
P J MURPHY FOREST PDTS CORP (PA)
150 River Rd Ste L1 (07045-8924)
P.O. Box 300 (07045-0300)
PHONE.................................973 316-0800
Fred A Faehner, *President*
Roger Faehner, *Corp Secy*
Josh Faehnaer, *Vice Pres*
EMP: 6
SQ FT: 900
SALES: 25MM **Privately Held**
WEB: www.pjmurphy.net
SIC: 2421 Sawmills & planing mills, general

(G-6446)
ROCKLINE INDUSTRIES INC
1 Kramer Way (07045-9593)
P.O. Box 189 (07045-0189)
PHONE.................................973 257-2884
Lourdes Phr, *Human Res Mgr*
Chris Bruno, *Branch Mgr*
Lourdes Jesus, *Manager*
EMP: 135
SALES (corp-wide): 429.2MM **Privately Held**
WEB: www.rocklineind.com
SIC: 2679 5046 Filter paper: made from purchased material; coffee brewing equipment & supplies
PA: Rockline Industries, Inc.
4343 S Taylor Dr
Sheboygan WI 53081
800 558-7790

(G-6447)
SPERRO METAL PRODUCTS LLC
2 Skyline Dr (07045-9455)
P.O. Box 393, Kearny (07032-0393)
PHONE.................................973 335-2000
James Fernandez, *Mng Member*
Joseph Roman,
EMP: 25
SQ FT: 17,000
SALES (est): 4.9MM **Privately Held**
WEB: www.sperro.com
SIC: 3444 Sheet metalwork

(G-6448)
UNIVERSAL BUSINESS AUTOMATION
170 Changebridge Rd D3 (07045-9112)
PHONE.................................973 575-3568
Scott Liu, *President*
Ai-Ju Liu, *Vice Pres*
John Liu, *Vice Pres*
EMP: 7 **EST:** 1979
SQ FT: 3,000
SALES: 634.8K **Privately Held**
SIC: 7372 Application computer software

(G-6449)
WEB INDUSTRIES INC
5 Mars Ct (07045)
P.O. Box 237 (07045-0237)
PHONE.................................973 335-1200
William J Burgoyne, *President*
EMP: 14 **EST:** 1969
SQ FT: 24,000
SALES (est): 1MM **Privately Held**
SIC: 3541 Grinding, polishing, buffing, lapping & honing machines; grinding machines, metalworking

---

Moonachie
Bergen County

(G-6450)
4 OVER INC
4 Empire Blvd (07074-1303)
PHONE.................................201 440-1656
EMP: 12
SALES (corp-wide): 190.6MM **Privately Held**
SIC: 2759 7336 Commercial printing; commercial art & graphic design
HQ: 4 Over, Llc
5900 San Fernando Rd D
Glendale CA 91202
818 246-1170

(G-6451)
ACRISON INC (PA)
Also Called: Acrison International
20 Empire Blvd (07074-1382)
PHONE.................................201 440-8300
Ronald J Ricciardi, *President*
Ronald Ricciardi, *General Mgr*
Sal Pastino, *Managing Dir*
Charlie Paruta, *Production*
Joe Casini, *Controller*
◆ **EMP:** 95 **EST:** 1963
SQ FT: 65,000
SALES: 23MM **Privately Held**
WEB: www.acrison.com
SIC: 3823 3443 3545 Industrial process control instruments; hoppers, metal plate; hopper feed devices

(G-6452)
ALLMIKE METAL TECHNOLOGY INC
Also Called: Almike Metal Products
65 Anderson Ave (07074-1621)
PHONE.................................201 935-2306
Tom Fischetti, *President*
EMP: 19 **EST:** 1956
SQ FT: 20,000
SALES (est): 2.5MM **Privately Held**
SIC: 3444 Sheet metal specialties, not stamped

(G-6453)
ALU INC
240 Anderson Ave (07074-1632)
PHONE.................................201 935-2213
EMP: 25 **Privately Held**
WEB: www.alu.com
SIC: 4225 3993 General warehousing & storage; signs & advertising specialties
HQ: Alu Inc.
240 Anderson Ave
Moonachie NJ 07074

(G-6454)
AMKO DISPLAYS CORPORATION
Also Called: Alliance Store Fixture
7 Purcell Ct (07074-1606)
PHONE.................................201 460-7199

Hansang Lim, *CEO*
Heedeuk Lim, *President*
Eric Um, *General Mgr*
Roger Marcoux, *Vice Pres*
Dora Arnott, *Admin Asst*
▲ **EMP:** 15
SQ FT: 25,000
SALES (est): 3MM **Privately Held**
WEB: www.ahjunam.com
SIC: 2541 Store & office display cases & fixtures

(G-6455)
AVANTI LINENS INC (PA)
234 Moonachie Rd Ste 1 (07074-1391)
PHONE.................................201 641-7766
Arthur Tauber, *President*
◆ **EMP:** 159
SQ FT: 125,000
SALES (est): 41.9MM **Privately Held**
WEB: www.avantilinens.com
SIC: 2395 Decorative & novelty stitching, for the trade; embroidery & art needlework

(G-6456)
BERGEN HOMESTATE CORP
Also Called: All Smith Spinning and Turning
9 Willow St (07074-1502)
PHONE.................................201 372-9740
Michael Noback, *President*
Diane Van Blarcon, *Administration*
EMP: 7 **EST:** 1948
SQ FT: 4,500
SALES (est): 475.7K **Privately Held**
SIC: 3444 Forming machine work, sheet metal

(G-6457)
BIO COMPRESSION SYSTEMS INC
120 W Commercial Ave (07074-1703)
PHONE.................................201 939-0716
Robert Freidenrich, *CEO*
Donald Warren, *President*
◆ **EMP:** 24
SALES (est): 4.6MM **Privately Held**
WEB: www.biocompression.com
SIC: 3841 8011 3561 Surgical & medical instruments; offices & clinics of medical doctors; pumps & pumping equipment

(G-6458)
BULBRITE INDUSTRIES INC
145 W Commercial Ave (07074-1704)
P.O. Box 4108, South Hackensack (07606-4108)
PHONE.................................201 531-5900
Cathy Choi, *President*
Barbara Eun Choi, *Corp Secy*
Cynthia Bordes, *Vice Pres*
Addie Cinquino, *Vice Pres*
Rafael Rodas, *Vice Pres*
◆ **EMP:** 40
SALES (est): 8.7MM **Privately Held**
WEB: www.bulbrite.com
SIC: 3229 5063 Bulbs for electric lights; light bulbs & related supplies

(G-6459)
BYLADA FOODS LLC (PA)
140 W Commercial Ave (07074-1703)
PHONE.................................201 933-7474
Bob Silverman,
Donald Pompliano,
Eric Silverman,
Michael Silverman,
Robert Silverman,
▼ **EMP:** 4
SQ FT: 30,000
SALES (est): 9.4MM **Privately Held**
SIC: 2099 Food preparations

(G-6460)
CARLYLE CUSTOM CONVERTIBLES (PA)
6 Empire Blvd (07074-1303)
PHONE.................................973 546-4502
Albert De Matteo, *CEO*
Donna De Matteo, *President*
EMP: 60 **EST:** 1966
SQ FT: 28,000

SALES (est): 15.4MM **Privately Held**
SIC: 5712 2515 2512 2392 Furniture stores; sofa beds (convertible sofas); wood upholstered chairs & couches; household furnishings; comforters & quilts: made from purchased materials; sofas & couches; beds & bedding

(G-6461)
CARTER MANUFACTURING CO INC
55 Anderson Ave (07074-1677)
PHONE.................................201 935-0770
John Scholz, *Ch of Bd*
Mark Casatelli, *Vice Pres*
▲ **EMP:** 23
SQ FT: 15,000
SALES (est): 4.4MM **Privately Held**
SIC: 3469 Stamping metal for the trade

(G-6462)
DIAMOND WHOLESALE CO
30 Congress Dr (07074-1406)
PHONE.................................201 727-9595
David Rothenberg, *President*
▲ **EMP:** 35
SQ FT: 65,000
SALES (est): 6.6MM **Privately Held**
SIC: 1499 5094 Gemstone & industrial diamond mining; diamonds (gems)

(G-6463)
DU TECHNOLOGIES INC
300 W Commercial Ave (07074-1607)
PHONE.................................201 729-0070
Phil L Morar, *President*
▲ **EMP:** 15
SALES (est): 2.5MM **Privately Held**
SIC: 3089 Ducting, plastic

(G-6464)
ELECTRO-MINIATURES CORP (PA)
68 W Commercial Ave (07074-1703)
PHONE.................................201 460-0510
Mark Pollack, *President*
Jamie Pollack, *Vice Pres*
▼ **EMP:** 58 **EST:** 1952
SQ FT: 20,000
SALES: 9MM **Privately Held**
WEB: www.emcsales.com
SIC: 3621 Sliprings, for motors or generators

(G-6465)
FLEXI PRINTING PLATE CO INC
50 Commercial Ave (07074-1705)
PHONE.................................201 939-3600
John Moss, *Vice Pres*
Glendon Sabiel, *Sales Staff*
Joel Berlin, *Marketing Staff*
EMP: 18
SQ FT: 25,000
SALES (est): 3.9MM **Privately Held**
SIC: 2759 Commercial printing

(G-6466)
GALVANIC PRTG & PLATE CO INC
50 Commercial Ave (07074-1705)
PHONE.................................201 939-3600
John Moss, *President*
Lou Santiago, *Mfg Mgr*
Glendon Sabiel, *Sales Staff*
Paul Ragas, *Manager*
Larry Snyder, *Manager*
EMP: 25
SQ FT: 25,000
SALES (est): 5.5MM **Privately Held**
WEB: www.galvanicprinting.com
SIC: 2752 3555 Commercial printing, offset; printing plates

(G-6467)
GRANDI PASTAI ITALIANI INC
250 Moonachie Rd Ste 201 (07074-1319)
PHONE.................................201 786-5050
EMP: 8 **EST:** 2014
SALES (est): 235.7K **Privately Held**
SIC: 5812 2032 1541 Italian restaurant; Italian foods: packaged in cans, jars, etc.; food products manufacturing or packing plant construction

(G-6468)
H CROSS COMPANY
Also Called: Cross H Co
150 W Commercial Ave (07074-1706)
PHONE.................................201 964-9380
Edward McClary, *President*
Diane McClary, *Office Mgr*
EMP: 32 **EST:** 1939
SQ FT: 31,500
SALES (est): 7.2MM **Privately Held**
WEB: www.hcrosscompany.com
SIC: 3356 3351 3355 3353 Nickel & nickel alloy: rolling, drawing or extruding; zirconium & zirconium alloy bars, sheets, strip, etc.; strip, copper & copper alloy; coils, wire aluminum: made in rolling mills; coils, sheet aluminum

(G-6469)
HAIN CELESTIAL GROUP INC
Also Called: Terra Chips
50 Knickerbocker Rd (07074-1613)
PHONE.................................201 935-4500
Helene Miller, *Branch Mgr*
EMP: 29 **Publicly Held**
WEB: www.hain-celestial.com
SIC: 2096 Potato chips & similar snacks
PA: The Hain Celestial Group Inc
1111 Marcus Ave Ste 100
New Hyde Park NY 11042

(G-6470)
HIGHROAD PRESS LLC
220 Anderson Ave (07074-1632)
PHONE.................................201 708-6900
Eric Denburg, *VP Sales*
Hallie Denburg Satz,
EMP: 48
SQ FT: 38,000
SALES (est): 15.9MM **Privately Held**
WEB: www.highroadpress.com
SIC: 2752 Commercial printing, offset

(G-6471)
INOAC USA INC
Also Called: Crest Foam Industries
100 Carol Pl (07074-1300)
PHONE.................................201 807-0809
Amberley Babbage, *Plant Mgr*
Denise Sivnksty, *Buyer*
Cristian Tapia, *Train & Dev Mgr*
William Hughes, *Sales Mgr*
Akiko Eto, *Sales Staff*
EMP: 66
SALES (corp-wide): 342.6MM **Privately Held**
SIC: 3069 Foam rubber
PA: Inoac Usa, Inc.
1515 Equity Dr Ste 200
Troy MI 48084
248 619-7031

(G-6472)
INTERNATIONAL AROMATICS INC (PA)
200 Anderson Ave (07074-1632)
PHONE.................................201 964-0900
Gary Gerardi, *President*
EMP: 15
SALES (est): 3.8MM **Privately Held**
WEB: www.iaromatics.com
SIC: 2844 Perfumes & colognes

(G-6473)
JADE EASTERN TRADING INC (PA)
Also Called: Marquis
13 Division St Ste A (07074)
PHONE.................................201 440-8500
Jae R Lee, *President*
Stella Lee, *Co-Owner*
Edward Lee, *Vice Pres*
Lynn Chon, *Accountant*
Jaesung Park, *Office Mgr*
◆ **EMP:** 15
SQ FT: 41,000
SALES: 8MM **Privately Held**
SIC: 5136 2321 Trousers, men's & boys'; men's & boys' outerwear; shirts, men's & boys'; men's & boys' furnishings

(G-6474)
JOHN F PEARCE
76 Frederick St (07074-1007)
PHONE.................................201 440-8765

GEOGRAPHIC

John F Pearce, *Owner*
EMP: 5
SALES (corp-wide): 850K **Privately Held**
SIC: 3441 Fabricated structural metal
PA: John F Pearce
　155 S River St
　Hackensack NJ 07601
　201 488-0434

(G-6475)
JUNE JACOBS LABS LLC (PA)
46 Graphic Pl (07074-1106)
PHONE..............................201 329-9100
June Jacobs, *President*
Matthew E Silpe, *COO*
Charles Badalamente, *Opers Staff*
Matt Silpe, *Opers Staff*
Glenis Rosario, *QC Mgr*
▲ **EMP:** 2
SALES (est): 16.4MM **Privately Held**
SIC: 2844 Cosmetic preparations

(G-6476)
KEY HANDLING SYSTEMS INC
137 W Commercial Ave (07074-1704)
PHONE..............................201 933-9333
William E Stefan, *President*
Ron Baptista, *Senior VP*
Rudy Jaochico, *Vice Pres*
Steven V Melis, *Info Tech Dir*
Paul Hendrikse, *Director*
EMP: 40 **EST:** 1964
SQ FT: 53,350
SALES (est): 9.2MM **Privately Held**
WEB: www.keyhandling.com
SIC: 3535 Overhead conveyor systems

(G-6477)
LPS INDUSTRIES INC (PA)
Also Called: Lawrence Packaging
10 Caesar Pl (07074-1701)
P.O. Box 18858, Newark (07191-8858)
PHONE..............................201 438-3515
Madeleine D Robinson, *CEO*
Charles Ardman, *Vice Pres*
Carton Reducer, *Products*
▲ **EMP:** 150 **EST:** 1959
SQ FT: 164,000
SALES (est): 54.6MM **Privately Held**
WEB: www.lpsind.com
SIC: 2671 5046 3081 2673 Packaging
paper & plastics film, coated & laminated;
scales, except laboratory; packing materi-
als, plastic sheet; plastic bags: made from
purchased materials; labels: gravure
printing; packaging paper; bag paper

(G-6478)
MASSIMO ZANETTI BEVERAGE USA
10 Empire Blvd (07074-1303)
PHONE..............................201 440-1700
Jack Rush, *Principal*
Luis Jarrin, *Maintence Staff*
▲ **EMP:** 20 **EST:** 2011
SALES (est): 3.3MM **Privately Held**
SIC: 2095 Roasted coffee

(G-6479)
MATERIAL IMPORTS
10 Oxford Dr (07074-1010)
PHONE..............................201 229-1180
Shaheryar Irshad, *Owner*
Jaclyn Dasilva, *Sales Mgr*
▲ **EMP:** 6
SALES: 5MM **Privately Held**
SIC: 2211 2299 Towels & toweling, cotton;
batting, wadding, padding & fillings

(G-6480)
MEADOWLANDS BINDERY INC
146 W Commercial Ave (07074-1706)
PHONE..............................201 935-6161
Carmine Idone, *President*
Maria Molfetas, *Admin Sec*
EMP: 42
SQ FT: 12,000
SALES (est): 5.6MM **Privately Held**
WEB: www.meadowlandsbindery.com
SIC: 2789 Binding only: books, pamphlets,
magazines, etc.

(G-6481)
MODERN SPORTSWEAR CORPORATION
102 W Commercial Ave (07074-1704)
PHONE..............................201 804-2700
Chris Park, *President*
Holmshiek Park, *Corp Secy*
Scott Park, *Vice Pres*
▲ **EMP:** 10
SQ FT: 25,000
SALES (est): 1.9MM **Privately Held**
SIC: 3429 Aircraft & marine hardware, inc.
pulleys & similar items

(G-6482)
PACE PRESS INCORPORATED
1 Caesar Pl (07074-1702)
PHONE..............................201 935-7711
Jack Mangi, *President*
Seth Diamond, *Vice Pres*
Jonathan Vitale, *Vice Pres*
EMP: 75 **EST:** 1914
SQ FT: 78,000
SALES (est): 18.4MM **Privately Held**
SIC: 2752 Commercial printing, offset

(G-6483)
PERMAGRAPHICS INC
25 Graphic Pl (07074-1106)
PHONE..............................201 814-1200
Rita Caloni, *President*
Michael Caloni, *Vice Pres*
EMP: 13 **EST:** 1988
SQ FT: 25,000
SALES (est): 2.1MM **Privately Held**
SIC: 2752 2789 2791 Commercial print-
ing, offset; bookbinding & related work;
typesetting

(G-6484)
PRESIDENT CONT GROUP II LLC (PA)
200 W Commercial Ave (07074-1610)
PHONE..............................201 933-7500
Marvin Grossbard,
Lawrence Grossbard,
Richard Grossbard,
▲ **EMP:** 450
SALES (est): 203.8MM **Privately Held**
SIC: 2653 Boxes, corrugated: made from
purchased materials; sheets, corrugated:
made from purchased materials; display
items, corrugated: made from purchased
materials

(G-6485)
R SQUARED SLS & LOGISTICS LLC
Also Called: Zrike Brands
30 Congress Dr (07074-1406)
PHONE..............................201 329-9745
Dave Rothenberg, *President*
Gary Darwin, *Vice Pres*
Lee Rothman, *Vice Pres*
David Zrike, *Vice Pres*
▲ **EMP:** 8
SQ FT: 63,000
SALES (est): 1.2MM **Privately Held**
SIC: 3089 Plastic kitchenware, tableware &
houseware

(G-6486)
RAFFETTOS CORP
62 W Commercial Ave (07074-1703)
PHONE..............................201 372-1222
Richard Raffetto, *President*
EMP: 13
SALES (est): 1.5MM **Privately Held**
SIC: 2098 Macaroni & spaghetti

(G-6487)
ROYAL BAKING CO INC
Also Called: Leonard's Novelty Bakery
8 Empire Blvd (07074-1303)
PHONE..............................201 296-0888
Jack Di Piazza, *President*
Marann Carro, *Principal*
Darman Di Piazza, *Principal*
Leonard Di Piazza, *Vice Pres*
▲ **EMP:** 48 **EST:** 1945
SQ FT: 50,000
SALES: 12MM **Privately Held**
SIC: 2053 2052 Pastries (danish): frozen;
cakes, bakery: frozen; cookies

(G-6488)
SCREEN-TRANS DEVELOPMENT CORP
Also Called: Foil-On
100 Grand St (07074-1623)
PHONE..............................201 933-7800
Robert Devries, *President*
Roy Devries, *Shareholder*
EMP: 22
SQ FT: 18,800
SALES (est): 4.1MM **Privately Held**
WEB: www.screentrans.com
SIC: 2759 Screen printing

(G-6489)
SLI PRODUCTION CORP
Also Called: Its A Wig
7 Capital Dr (07074-1407)
PHONE..............................201 621-4260
Chul Park, *President*
▲ **EMP:** 6
SALES (est): 800.5K **Privately Held**
SIC: 3999 5199 Wigs, including doll wigs,
toupees or wiglets; wigs

(G-6490)
SUGAR AND PLUMM LLC
146 Redneck Ave (07074-1002)
PHONE..............................201 334-1600
Thierry Atlan, *Principal*
EMP: 7
SALES (est): 100.4K **Privately Held**
SIC: 2053 Frozen bakery products, except
bread

(G-6491)
SUN TAIYANG CO LTD
Also Called: Sun Trading
85 Oxford Dr (07074-1020)
PHONE..............................201 549-7100
Kyungja Park, *President*
◆ **EMP:** 90
SALES (est): 2.1MM **Privately Held**
SIC: 3999 Barber & beauty shop equip-
ment

(G-6492)
SUPPLY TECHNOLOGIES LLC
50 Graphic Pl (07074-1106)
PHONE..............................201 641-7600
EMP: 35
SALES (corp-wide): 1.4B **Publicly Held**
SIC: 3462 3732 Mfg Iron/Steel Forgings
Boatbuilding/Repairing
HQ: Supply Technologies Llc
　6065 Parkland Blvd Ste 1
　Cleveland OH 44124
　440 947-2100

(G-6493)
SWINTEC CORP (PA)
320 W Coml Ave Ste 1 (07074)
P.O. Box 356, Wood Ridge (07075-0356)
PHONE..............................201 935-0115
Dominic Vespia, *President*
Matt Arki, *Vice Pres*
◆ **EMP:** 15 **EST:** 1978
SQ FT: 38,000
SALES (est): 2.9MM **Privately Held**
WEB: www.swintec.com
SIC: 3579 3578 3661 Typewriters & parts;
calculators & adding machines; facsimile
equipment

(G-6494)
TEC CAST INC
2 W Commercial Ave (07074-1703)
P.O. Box 6596, Carlstadt (07072-0596)
PHONE..............................201 935-3885
Edgard Gotthold, *President*
EMP: 70
SALES (corp-wide): 7.5MM **Privately Held**
SIC: 3365 7389 Aluminum foundries; in-
spection & testing services
PA: Tec Cast Inc
　440 Meadow Ln
　Carlstadt NJ 07072
　201 935-3885

(G-6495)
ULTIMATE SPINNING TURNING CORP
9 Willow St (07074-1502)
PHONE..............................201 372-9740

Michael Novack, *President*
EMP: 7
SALES (est): 1.1MM **Privately Held**
SIC: 3542 3451 7389 Spinning machines,
metal; screw machine products;

(G-6496)
VICTORY PRESS
1 Caesar Pl (07074-1702)
P.O. Box 218, Rochelle Park (07662-0218)
PHONE..............................201 729-1007
Joe Damico,
EMP: 4
SALES (est): 230K **Privately Held**
WEB: www.victoryprint.com
SIC: 2741 Miscellaneous publishing

(G-6497)
WISE FOODS INC
150 Carol Pl (07074-1300)
PHONE..............................201 440-2876
Chris Raftery, *President*
EMP: 8 **Privately Held**
SIC: 2096 Potato chips & similar snacks
HQ: Wise Foods, Inc.
　228 Rasely St
　Berwick PA 18603

(G-6498)
WOODBRIDGE INOAC TECHNICAL
Also Called: Crest Foam Industries Inc
100 Carol Pl (07074-1300)
PHONE..............................201 807-0809
Kyle Schultz, *General Mgr*
Amberley Babbage, *Plant Mgr*
Florence Depippa, *Purch Mgr*
Kedar Muzumdar, *Engineer*
William Hughes, *Sales Mgr*
◆ **EMP:** 66
SQ FT: 65,000
SALES (est): 20.8MM
SALES (corp-wide): 342.6MM **Privately Held**
WEB: www.crestfoam.com
SIC: 3069 Foam rubber
PA: Inoac Usa, Inc.
　1515 Equity Dr Ste 200
　Troy MI 48084
　248 619-7031

(G-6499)
WOODBRIDGE INOAC TECHNICAL PRO
100 Carol Pl (07074-1300)
PHONE..............................201 807-0809
Yosuke Nakano, *Exec VP*
John Zianis, *Manager*
EMP: 64
SQ FT: 65,000
SALES (est): 2MM **Privately Held**
SIC: 3069 Foam rubber

Moorestown
Burlington County

(G-6500)
ACKLEY MACHINE CORPORATION
1273 N Church St Ste 106 (08057-1194)
PHONE..............................856 234-3626
Michael Ackley, *President*
Richard J Braemer, *Admin Sec*
▼ **EMP:** 34
SQ FT: 8,000
SALES (est): 8.3MM **Privately Held**
WEB: www.ackleymachine.com
SIC: 3555 3559 Printing trades machinery;
pharmaceutical machinery

(G-6501)
ALADDIN COLOR INC
19 E Main St Ste D (08057-3338)
P.O. Box 500, Lumberton (08048-0500)
PHONE..............................609 518-9858
David Bard, *Ch of Bd*
Eric Bard, *President*
EMP: 6
SQ FT: 5,000
SALES (est): 750K **Privately Held**
WEB: www.aladdincolor.com
SIC: 2752 Commercial printing, offset

(G-6502)
AMERICAN BILTRITE INC
Tape Products Division
105 Whittendale Dr (08057-1313)
PHONE....................................856 778-0700
Michel Merkx, *Vice Pres*
John Mauro, *Plant Mgr*
Shane Swafford, *Opers Staff*
Stanley Malinowski, *Purch Dir*
Feist Skip, *Purchasing*
EMP: 150
SQ FT: 119,000
SALES (corp-wide): 62.7MM **Publicly Held**
WEB: www.ambilt.com
SIC: 2672 Adhesive backed films, foams & foils
PA: American Biltrite Inc.
57 River St Ste 302
Wellesley MA 02481
781 237-6655

(G-6503)
AMERICAN HARLEQUIN CORPORATION
Also Called: Harlequin Floors
1531 Glen Ave (08057-1103)
PHONE....................................856 234-5505
Bob Dagger, *President*
Chantal Lagniau, *General Mgr*
Patricia A Basileo, *Exec VP*
Ray Lloyds, *VP Admin*
Lenny Basileo, *Opers Staff*
◆ **EMP:** 22
SQ FT: 24,000
SALES (est): 6.4MM **Privately Held**
WEB: www.harlequinfloors.com
SIC: 3069 5049 Mats or matting, rubber; theatrical equipment & supplies
PA: Harlequin Holdings International Limited
150 High Street
Sevenoaks

(G-6504)
AMERICAN PLASTIC WORKS INC
1270 Glen Ave (08057-1133)
PHONE....................................800 494-7326
Judith Zimmermann, *President*
EMP: 40
SALES (est): 3.4MM **Privately Held**
WEB: www.lwipromo.com
SIC: 2821 Plastics materials & resins

(G-6505)
ANDEK CORPORATION
850 Glen Ave (08057-1122)
P.O. Box 392 (08057-0392)
PHONE....................................856 866-7600
Harvey Liss, *President*
Andrew Liss, *Vice Pres*
Neil Shearer, *Vice Pres*
◆ **EMP:** 13
SALES (est): 1.6MM **Privately Held**
WEB: www.andek.com
SIC: 3479 2851 2891 Coating of metals & formed products; lacquers, varnishes, enamels & other coatings; adhesives & sealants

(G-6506)
AUNTIE ANNES SOFT PRETZELS
400 W Route 38 (08057-3219)
PHONE....................................856 722-0433
Mel Sickler, *Owner*
EMP: 20
SALES (est): 429.9K **Privately Held**
SIC: 5461 2096 2051 Pretzels; potato chips & similar snacks; bread, cake & related products

(G-6507)
AUTOMATION & CONTROL INC
Also Called: Aci
1491 Lancer Dr (08057-4207)
P.O. Box 386 (08057-0386)
PHONE....................................856 234-2300
Ron Iannacone, *President*
Randy Berry, *Engineer*
Tom George, *Engineer*
Greg Garwood, *Project Engr*
George Cramer, *Sales Staff*
EMP: 32

SQ FT: 4,500
SALES: 8MM **Privately Held**
WEB: www.automation-control.com
SIC: 8711 3613 1731 Electrical or electronic engineering; panel & distribution boards & other related apparatus; electrical work

(G-6508)
BIOMEDICON
30 E Central Ave (08057-2519)
PHONE....................................856 778-1880
Mark Singer, *Owner*
EMP: 19
SQ FT: 5,200
SALES: 1.7MM **Privately Held**
WEB: www.biomedicon.com
SIC: 3841 3826 5047 Surgical & medical instruments; analytical instruments; hospital equipment & furniture

(G-6509)
BODINE TOOL AND MACHINE CO INC
1273 N Church St Ste 104 (08057-1115)
PHONE....................................856 234-7800
William Lauth, *President*
Paul Donegan, *Vice Pres*
Eleanor Kerr, *Admin Sec*
EMP: 30 **EST:** 1937
SQ FT: 25,000
SALES (est): 6.4MM **Privately Held**
WEB: www.bodinetool.com
SIC: 3544 Special dies & tools; jigs & fixtures; industrial molds

(G-6510)
BRAINSTORM SOFTWARE CORP
16 Apple Orchard Rd (08057-3844)
PHONE....................................856 234-4945
Bruce Kratz, *President*
EMP: 4
SALES (est): 182.9K **Privately Held**
WEB: www.brainstorm-software.com
SIC: 7372 Prepackaged software

(G-6511)
C A SPALDING COMPANY
355 Crider Ave (08057-1238)
PHONE....................................267 550-9000
Javier Kuehnle, *President*
G Wesley Kuehnle, *President*
George Kuehnle, *Vice Pres*
EMP: 30 **EST:** 1932
SALES (est): 6.2MM **Privately Held**
WEB: www.caspalding.com
SIC: 3544 3444 7692 Special dies, tools, jigs & fixtures; sheet metalwork; welding repair

(G-6512)
CHEMIQUE INC
315 N Washington Ave (08057-2461)
PHONE....................................856 235-4161
EMP: 8 **EST:** 1976
SQ FT: 14,000
SALES (est): 1.7MM **Privately Held**
WEB: www.chemique.com
SIC: 5169 2842 Industrial chemicals; sanitation preparations

(G-6513)
CISCO SYSTEMS INC
308 Harper Dr Ste 100 (08057-3244)
PHONE....................................856 642-7000
Bill Moldovan, *Partner*
Fred Zalupski, *Partner*
Tom Franklin, *Regional Mgr*
David Brown, *Engineer*
Bill Didden, *Engineer*
EMP: 8
SALES (corp-wide): 51.9B **Publicly Held**
SIC: 3577 Computer peripheral equipment
PA: Cisco Systems, Inc.
170 W Tasman Dr
San Jose CA 95134
408 526-4000

(G-6514)
COCOA SERVICES INC
905 N Lenola Rd (08057-1042)
PHONE....................................856 234-1700
John Lyons, *President*
EMP: 10

SALES (est): 1.1MM **Privately Held**
SIC: 2066 Cocoa butter

(G-6515)
COMTREX SYSTEMS CORPORATION (PA)
101 Foster Rd B (08057-1118)
PHONE....................................856 778-0090
Nathan I Lipson, *Ch of Bd*
Jeffrey C Rice, *President*
Charles A Hardin, *Vice Pres*
Matthew R Carter, *VP Sales*
▲ **EMP:** 31
SQ FT: 19,000
SALES (est): 6.7MM **Publicly Held**
WEB: www.comtrex.com
SIC: 7373 3578 Computer integrated systems design; point-of-sale devices

(G-6516)
CR LAURENCE CO INC
Also Called: Thiladel Phia
1511 Lancer Dr (08057-4232)
PHONE....................................856 727-1022
Jason Key, *Manager*
EMP: 10
SALES (corp-wide): 30.6B **Privately Held**
WEB: www.crlaurence.com
HQ: C. R. Laurence Co., Inc.
2503 E Vernon Ave
Vernon CA 90058
323 588-1281

(G-6517)
CVC SPECIALTY CHEMICALS INC (HQ)
Also Called: Cvc Thermoset Specialties
844 N Lenola Rd V (08057-1052)
PHONE....................................856 533-3000
John Cech, *President*
◆ **EMP:** 19 **EST:** 1982
SQ FT: 20,400
SALES (est): 9.7MM
SALES (corp-wide): 557.5MM **Privately Held**
WEB: www.cvcchem.com
SIC: 2869 2821 5169 Industrial organic chemicals; epoxy resins; chemicals & allied products
PA: Emerald Performance Materials Llc
1499 Se Tech Center Pl
Vancouver WA 98683
360 954-7100

(G-6518)
DENTON VACUUM LLC
1259 N Church St (08057-1169)
PHONE....................................856 439-9100
EMP: 0
SQ FT: 80,000
SALES (est): 22.9MM **Privately Held**
SIC: 3821 Mfg Lab Apparatus/Furniture
PA: Denton Vacuum L.L.C.
1259 N Church St Bldg 3
Moorestown NJ 08057
856 439-9100

(G-6519)
EASTERN INSTRUMENTATION OF
710 E Main St Ste 1a (08057-3066)
PHONE....................................856 231-0668
Jerry Lomurno, *President*
EMP: 8
SALES (est): 890K **Privately Held**
WEB: www.eiphila.com
SIC: 3825 5065 3661 Instruments to measure electricity; electronic parts & equipment; fiber optics communications equipment

(G-6520)
ECOLAB INC
110 Marter Ave Ste 411 (08057-3124)
PHONE....................................856 596-4845
Ursula Carvale, *Branch Mgr*
EMP: 205
SALES (corp-wide): 14.6B **Publicly Held**
WEB: www.ecolab.com
SIC: 2841 Soap & other detergents
PA: Ecolab Inc.
1 Ecolab Pl
Saint Paul MN 55102
800 232-6522

(G-6521)
ELECTRO MAGNETIC PRODUCTS INC
355 Crider Ave (08057-1241)
PHONE....................................856 235-3011
Gordon Mason, *President*
Andrew Lipenta, *Vice Pres*
EMP: 40 **EST:** 1966
SQ FT: 30,000
SALES (est): 6.3MM **Privately Held**
WEB: www.empmags.com
SIC: 3544 Die sets for metal stamping (presses)

(G-6522)
EMS AVIATION INC
121 Whittendale Dr (08057-1373)
PHONE....................................856 234-5020
John Jarrell, *President*
John Byard Mowell, *Chairman*
Paul R Kuphal, *Senior VP*
EMP: 140
SQ FT: 34,000
SALES (est): 26.7MM
SALES (corp-wide): 41.8B **Publicly Held**
SIC: 3577 Computer peripheral equipment
PA: Honeywell International Inc.
300 S Tryon St
Charlotte NC 28202
973 455-2000

(G-6523)
ESSENTRA PACKAGING US INC
1224 N Church St (08057-1102)
PHONE....................................856 439-1700
EMP: 7
SALES (corp-wide): 1.3B **Privately Held**
SIC: 2673 Plastic bags: made from purchased materials
HQ: Essentra Packaging U.S. Inc.
2 Westbrook Corp Ctr
Westchester IL 60154
704 418-8692

(G-6524)
GRAYDON PRODUCTS INC
800 Glen Ave (08057-1122)
PHONE....................................856 234-9513
George Semanko, *President*
EMP: 35
SQ FT: 30,000
SALES (est): 5.4MM **Privately Held**
WEB: www.omnimedbeam.com
SIC: 3841 Surgical & medical instruments
PA: Omni Acquisition Corp
101 N Pine Ave
Maple Shade NJ

(G-6525)
GWYNN-E CO
222 Cedar St (08057-1709)
PHONE....................................215 423-6400
Michael L Gwynne, *Principal*
EMP: 6
SALES (est): 671.7K **Privately Held**
SIC: 2426 Hardwood dimension & flooring mills

(G-6526)
H G SCHAEVITZ LLC
Also Called: Alliance Sensors Group
102 Commerce Dr Ste 8 (08057-4205)
PHONE....................................856 727-0250
Harold Schaevitz, *President*
John Matmack, *Mng Member*
Howard Schaevitz, *Mng Member*
Ed Herceg, *CTO*
EMP: 6
SALES: 1,000K **Privately Held**
SIC: 3699 Electrical equipment & supplies

(G-6527)
HARRIS FREEMAN & CO INC
Also Called: Harris Tea Company
344 New Albany Rd (08057-1167)
PHONE....................................856 787-9026
Kishore Shah, *Partner*
Ram Amakant, *Info Tech Dir*
Tass Rupp, *Director*
EMP: 71
SALES (corp-wide): 292.1MM **Privately Held**
SIC: 5149 2099 2673 Tea; coffee, green or roasted; spices & seasonings; tea blending; food storage & trash bags (plastic)

PA: Harris Freeman & Co., Inc.
3110 E Miraloma Ave
Anaheim CA 92806
714 765-1190

(G-6528)
HILL-ROM HOLDINGS INC
202 Commerce Dr Ste 2 (08057-4226)
PHONE....................856 486-2117
Peter Soderberg, *CEO*
EMP: 8
SALES (corp-wide): 2.8B **Publicly Held**
SIC: 2599 Hospital furniture, except beds;
hospital beds
PA: Hill-Rom Holdings, Inc.
130 E Randolph St # 1000
Chicago IL 60601
312 819-7200

(G-6529)
HONEYWELL INTERNATIONAL INC
121 Whittendale Dr (08057-1373)
PHONE....................856 234-5020
EMP: 708
SALES (corp-wide): 41.8B **Publicly Held**
SIC: 3724 Aircraft engines & engine parts
PA: Honeywell International Inc.
300 S Tryon St
Charlotte NC 28202
973 455-2000

(G-6530)
INNOVASYSTEMS INC
1245 N Church St Ste 6 (08057-1142)
PHONE....................856 722-0410
John J Waters, *President*
Nick Schreier, *Vice Pres*
EMP: 12
SQ FT: 5,000
SALES (est): 2.6MM **Privately Held**
WEB: www.innovasystems.com
SIC: 3821 8711 Laboratory equipment:
fume hoods, distillation racks, etc.; chemical engineering

(G-6531)
JET PULVERIZER CO INC
1255 N Church St (08057-1136)
PHONE....................856 235-5554
Valentin Alvarez, *President*
William S Henry, *Vice Pres*
▲ EMP: 27
SQ FT: 20,000
SALES (est): 7.2MM **Privately Held**
WEB: www.jetpul.com
SIC: 3541 3559 Grinding machines, metalworking; chemical machinery & equipment

(G-6532)
KATIS KUPCAKES
233 Hedgeman Rd (08057-1308)
PHONE....................609 332-2172
Kati Angelini, *Owner*
EMP: 4 EST: 2010
SALES (est): 172K **Privately Held**
SIC: 2051 Biscuits, baked: baking powder
& raised

(G-6533)
KERN & SZALAI CO
Also Called: Kern & Szalai Machine Company
351 Crider Ave (08057-1238)
PHONE....................856 802-1500
Robert Santare, *President*
EMP: 14
SQ FT: 4,000
SALES (est): 1.6MM
SALES (corp-wide): 4.5MM **Privately Held**
WEB: www.champfast.com
SIC: 3599 Machine shop, jobbing & repair
PA: Champion Fasteners, Inc.
707 Smithville Rd
Lumberton NJ 08048
609 267-5222

(G-6534)
KETEC
1256 N Church St Ste A (08057-1146)
PHONE....................856 778-4343
Ronald Kenney, *President*
George Kaltner, *Vice Pres*
Bob Plizak, *Mfg Staff*
Bob Cantono, *Natl Sales Mgr*

Mike Vergilio, *Director*
EMP: 18
SQ FT: 2,000
SALES (est): 1.8MM **Privately Held**
WEB: www.ketec.com
SIC: 7382 3699 Protective devices, security; security control equipment & systems

(G-6535)
KRYDON GROUP INC
365 New Albany Rd Ste C (08057-1105)
PHONE....................877 854-1342
Jesus M Alvarez Jr, *President*
EMP: 4
SQ FT: 500
SALES: 1.4MM **Privately Held**
SIC: 3691 3612 8742 8741 Storage batteries; power transformers, electric; management consulting services; business management

(G-6536)
LANTIER CONSTRUCTION COMPANY
214 W Main St Ste 200 (08057-2345)
PHONE....................856 780-6366
Douglas Lantier, *Owner*
EMP: 35
SALES (est): 5MM **Privately Held**
SIC: 3479 4932 Name plates: engraved,
etched, etc.; gas & other services combined

(G-6537)
LIBERTY COCA-COLA BEVS LLC
1250 Glen Ave (08057-1112)
PHONE....................215 427-4500
Leon Ivey, *Manager*
EMP: 54
SALES (corp-wide): 1.3B **Privately Held**
SIC: 2086 Bottled & canned soft drinks
PA: Liberty Coca-Cola Beverages Llc
725 E Erie Ave
Philadelphia PA 19134
215 427-4500

(G-6538)
LOCKHEED MARTIN CORPORATION
199 Bortons Landing Rd (08057-3048)
PHONE....................856 722-7782
EMP: 99 **Publicly Held**
SIC: 3812 8711 3721 Search & navigation
equipment; engineering services; aircraft
PA: Lockheed Martin Corporation
6801 Rockledge Dr
Bethesda MD 20817

(G-6539)
LOCKHEED MARTIN CORPORATION
Lockheed Martin Naval Electron
199 Bortons Landing Rd (08057-3048)
P.O. Box 1027 (08057-0927)
PHONE....................856 722-3336
Robert Coutts, *Principal*
Mark Newkirk, *Engineer*
Tony Pellegrino, *Engineer*
Christine Gardling, *Personnel*
Gary Mietz, *Manager*
EMP: 230 **Publicly Held**
WEB: www.lockheedmartin.com
SIC: 8733 8734 3812 Research institute;
product testing laboratory, safety or performance; search & navigation equipment
PA: Lockheed Martin Corporation
6801 Rockledge Dr
Bethesda MD 20817

(G-6540)
LOCKHEED MARTIN CORPORATION
199 Bortons Landing Rd (08057-3048)
PHONE....................856 722-4100
Fred Moosally, *Division Pres*
Tom Yeaple, *Purch Agent*
Karen Donnelly, *Engineer*
Mark Hauser, *Engineer*
Adrian Knight, *Engineer*
EMP: 4500 **Publicly Held**
WEB: www.lockheedmartin.com
SIC: 3812 Defense systems & equipment
PA: Lockheed Martin Corporation
6801 Rockledge Dr
Bethesda MD 20817

(G-6541)
LOCKHEED MARTIN OVERSEAS LLC
199 Bortons Landing Rd (08057-3048)
PHONE....................856 787-3105
Richard D'Alesandro, *Manager*
EMP: 6
SALES (est): 156.8K **Publicly Held**
SIC: 3761 Space vehicles, complete
PA: Lockheed Martin Corporation
6801 Rockledge Dr
Bethesda MD 20817

(G-6542)
LONGPORT SHIELDS INC
Also Called: Shields Business Solutions
5 Twosome Dr (08057-1367)
PHONE....................856 727-0227
Richard Grossman, *CEO*
Bonnie Hill, *Controller*
EMP: 9
SALES (est): 910.6K
SALES (corp-wide): 1MM **Privately Held**
SIC: 3578 7699 Automatic teller machines
(ATM); automated teller machine (ATM)
repair
PA: Longport Shields Re Holdings, Llc
5 Twosome Dr
Moorestown NJ 08057
856 727-0227

(G-6543)
LUKOIL N ARLINGTON LTD LBLTY
302 Harper Dr Ste 303 (08057-4701)
PHONE....................856 722-6425
Julia Gureyea, *Office Mgr*
EMP: 20
SALES (est): 1MM **Privately Held**
SIC: 2396 Automotive & apparel trimmings

(G-6544)
MCLEAN PACKAGING CORPORATION (PA)
1504 Glen Ave (08057-1104)
PHONE....................856 359-2600
Joseph Fenkel, *CEO*
Stuart Fenkel, *President*
Jeffrey Besnick, *Vice Pres*
David Seidenberg, *Vice Pres*
Al Miller, *Plant Mgr*
▲ EMP: 100 EST: 1961
SQ FT: 110,000
SALES (est): 60MM **Privately Held**
SIC: 2652 2653 3089 2657 Setup paperboard boxes; boxes, corrugated: made from purchased materials; boxes, plastic; folding paperboard boxes

(G-6545)
MESA VETERANS POWER LLC
365 New Albany Rd Ste C (08057-1105)
PHONE....................856 222-1000
Sarah Armstrong, *CFO*
Howard B Gartland, *Manager*
EMP: 4
SALES (est): 364.3K **Privately Held**
SIC: 3612 Transformers, except electric

(G-6546)
MORGAN TOWERS INC
212 W Route 38 Ste 300 (08057-3271)
PHONE....................856 786-7200
Diane Lauro, *Manager*
EMP: 5
SALES (est): 376.4K **Privately Held**
SIC: 3441 Tower sections, radio & television transmission

(G-6547)
NW SIGN INDUSTRIES INC
Also Called: N W Sign Industries
360 Crider Ave (08057-1239)
P.O. Box 530, Oldwick (08858-0530)
PHONE....................856 802-1677
Chris Reedel, *Branch Mgr*
EMP: 30 **Privately Held**
SIC: 3993 Electric signs
PA: Nw Sign Industries, Inc.
360 Crider Ave
Moorestown NJ 08057

(G-6548)
NW SIGN INDUSTRIES INC (PA)
360 Crider Ave (08057-1239)
P.O. Box 530, Oldwick (08858-0530)
PHONE....................856 802-1677
Ronald Brodie, *President*
Joe Piemonte, *Controller*
Pat Scala, *Accountant*
Christopher Depaolo, *Manager*
EMP: 100
SQ FT: 65,000
SALES (est): 34.1MM **Privately Held**
SIC: 3993 Signs & advertising specialties

(G-6549)
OLDCASTLE BUILDINGENVELOPE INC
1500 Glen Ave (08057-1104)
PHONE....................856 234-9222
Dave Mailhiot, *General Mgr*
Dave Myer, *Branch Mgr*
Dan Kerr, *Director*
EMP: 100
SQ FT: 66,470
SALES (corp-wide): 30.6B **Privately Held**
WEB: www.oldcastleglass.com
SIC: 3231 5039 3211 Products of purchased glass; exterior flat glass: plate or window; flat glass
HQ: Oldcastle Buildingenvelope, Inc.
5005 Lndn B Jnsn Fwy 10
Dallas TX 75244
214 273-3400

(G-6550)
ONGUARD FENCE SYSTEMS LTD
355 New Albany Rd (08057-1117)
PHONE....................908 429-5522
Jinshan Gao, *Ch of Bd*
Thomas Chen, *President*
Karen Gao, *Vice Pres*
Thomas Roche, *Vice Pres*
▲ EMP: 30
SALES (est): 6.3MM **Privately Held**
SIC: 3089 Fences, gates & accessories:
plastic

(G-6551)
OPEX CORPORATION
835 Lancer Dr (08057-4225)
PHONE....................856 727-1100
Albert Stevens, *Owner*
Thomas Goraj, *Project Mgr*
EMP: 15
SALES (corp-wide): 221.8MM **Privately Held**
SIC: 3579 Mailing, letter handling & addressing machines
PA: Opex Corporation
305 Commerce Dr
Moorestown NJ 08057
856 727-1100

(G-6552)
OTIS ELEVATOR COMPANY
30 Twosome Dr Ste 4 (08057-1370)
PHONE....................856 235-5200
Joe Frask, *President*
EMP: 35
SALES (corp-wide): 66.5B **Publicly Held**
WEB: www.otis.com
SIC: 5084 3534 1796 Elevators; elevators
& moving stairways; installing building equipment
HQ: Otis Elevator Company
1 Carrier Pl
Farmington CT 06032
860 674-3000

(G-6553)
PARKEON INC
40 Twosome Dr Ste 7 (08057-1369)
PHONE....................856 234-8000
Naples A S, *CEO*
Yves Chambeau, *President*
Nadine Nel, *Project Mgr*
Robert Barnes, *Treasurer*
April Apfelbaum, *Human Resources*
▲ EMP: 50
SQ FT: 15,000

SALES (est): 13.7MM
SALES (corp-wide): 177.9K **Privately Held**
WEB: www.moorestown.parkeon.com
SIC: 3824 Parking meters
HQ: Flowbird
100 102
Paris 15e Arrondissement 75015
158 098-110

(G-6554)
PARTS LIFE INC (PA)
30 Twosome Dr Ste 1 (08057-1370)
PHONE..................................856 786-8675
Samuel Thevanayagam, *President*
Renee Lynn Schoppe, *Bookkeeper*
▲ EMP: 54
SALES: 3MM **Privately Held**
WEB: www.partslifeinc.com
SIC: 3799 3724 Electrocars for transporting golfers; aircraft engines & engine parts

(G-6555)
PERFECT PRINTING INC
1533 Glen Ave (08057-1103)
PHONE..................................856 787-1877
Joseph Olivo, *CEO*
Ann Olivo, *President*
Chris Buoni, *Vice Pres*
Charlie Olivo, *Vice Pres*
Brian Riggs, *Vice Pres*
EMP: 25
SALES (est): 4.3MM **Privately Held**
SIC: 2759 Commercial printing

(G-6556)
PETIT POIS CORP
Also Called: Sussex Wine Merchants
50 Twosome Dr Ste 3 (08057-1379)
PHONE..................................856 608-9644
James Weinrott, *President*
David Akry, *Treasurer*
▲ EMP: 7
SQ FT: 600
SALES (est): 1.8MM **Privately Held**
WEB: www.petitpois.net
SIC: 5182 2084 Wine; wines

(G-6557)
PIONEER & CO INC
97 Foster Rd Ste 5 (08057-1154)
PHONE..................................856 866-9191
Wolfgang Harms, *President*
Sven Harms, *Exec VP*
Bjorn Harms, *Vice Pres*
Patrick Morio, *CFO*
Karl Schuster, *Sales Staff*
◆ EMP: 20 EST: 1976
SQ FT: 7,200
SALES: 57.4K **Privately Held**
WEB: www.pioneer-research.com
SIC: 5699 3648 Sports apparel; underwater lighting fixtures

(G-6558)
POPLAR BINDERY INC
300 Mill St (08057-2522)
PHONE..................................856 727-8030
Steve Heisler, *President*
John Heisler, *Principal*
▲ EMP: 12
SALES (est): 1.4MM **Privately Held**
SIC: 2789 Binding only: books, pamphlets, magazines, etc.

(G-6559)
PRISM COLOR CORPORATION
31 Twosome Dr Ste 1 (08057-1390)
PHONE..................................856 234-7515
Edward Brown, *President*
Dennis O'Sullivan, *General Mgr*
Tom Krisak, *Vice Pres*
Bill Drexel Sr, *Plant Mgr*
Chris Elser, *Prdtn Mgr*
EMP: 84
SQ FT: 38,000
SALES (est): 14.3MM **Privately Held**
WEB: www.prismcolorcorp.com
SIC: 2752 7335 Commercial printing, offset; color separation, photographic & movie film

(G-6560)
PROTEUS DESIGNS LLC
900 N Lenola Rd Bldg 9 (08057-1043)
PHONE..................................215 519-0135
Joseph Herron, *Mng Member*
Patrick Barry,
Therese Barry,
Richard Skettini,
EMP: 4
SQ FT: 1,100
SALES: 360K **Privately Held**
SIC: 3944 Games, toys & children's vehicles

(G-6561)
QUANTUM COATING INC
1259 N Church St Bldg 1 (08057-1169)
PHONE..................................856 234-5444
Daniel Patriarca Jr, *CEO*
Valerie McKiernan, *Sales Staff*
EMP: 30
SQ FT: 15,000
SALES (est): 7.1MM **Privately Held**
WEB: www.quantumcoating.com
SIC: 3827 Optical instruments & lenses

(G-6562)
RAMSAY DAVID CABINETMAKERS
Also Called: David Ramsay
310 Mill St (08057-2536)
PHONE..................................856 234-7776
David Ramsay, *President*
EMP: 12
SQ FT: 8,000
SALES (est): 1.9MM **Privately Held**
WEB: www.ramsaycabinetmakers.com
SIC: 5712 3429 7389 Cabinet work, custom; furniture builders' & other household hardware; interior design services

(G-6563)
ROTARY DIE SYSTEMS INC
876 N Lenola Rd Ste 9a (08057-1046)
PHONE..................................856 234-3994
Robert Donahue, *President*
Maureen Donahue, *Shareholder*
EMP: 5
SQ FT: 9,000
SALES: 600K **Privately Held**
SIC: 3554 3599 Die cutting & stamping machinery; paper converting; machine shop, jobbing & repair

(G-6564)
S W ELECTRONICS & MFG (PA)
Also Called: Swemco
1215 N Church St (08057-1101)
PHONE..................................856 222-9900
Carl Szczepkowski, *CEO*
Albert Szczepkowski, *Ch of Bd*
Richard Szczepkowski, *President*
Christopher Ben, *Opers Dir*
Toan Vu, *QA Dir*
▲ EMP: 200 EST: 1965
SQ FT: 54,000
SALES (est): 69.3MM **Privately Held**
WEB: www.swemco.com
SIC: 3577 Computer peripheral equipment

(G-6565)
SCHINDLER ELEVATOR CORPORATION
840 N Lenola Rd Ste 4 (08057-1055)
PHONE..................................856 234-2220
Steve Ryan, *Branch Mgr*
EMP: 20
SALES (corp-wide): 10.9B **Privately Held**
WEB: www.us.schindler.com
SIC: 3534 7699 1796 Elevators & equipment; elevators: inspection, service & repair; miscellaneous building item repair services; elevator installation & conversion
HQ: Schindler Elevator Corporation
20 Whippany Rd
Morristown NJ 07960
973 397-6500

(G-6566)
SENTRY MFG LLC
351 Crider Ave (08057-1238)
PHONE..................................856 642-0480
Mike Vermes, *Principal*
EMP: 4 EST: 2001

SALES (est): 526.7K **Privately Held**
SIC: 3399 Primary metal products

(G-6567)
SPALDING AUTOMOTIVE INC (PA)
355 Crider Ave (08057-1238)
PHONE..................................215 638-3334
Javier Kuehnle, *President*
G Wesley Kuehnle Jr, *Vice Pres*
Andrew Horn CPA, *CFO*
Vince Florio, *Sales Staff*
▲ EMP: 37
SALES: 11.1MM **Privately Held**
WEB: www.spaldingautomotive.com
SIC: 3714 Motor vehicle parts & accessories

(G-6568)
STAR LINEN INC (PA)
Also Called: Linen Enterprises
1501 Lancer Dr (08057-4233)
PHONE..................................800 782-7999
Joseph W Ranieri, *President*
Louis A Gutman, *Vice Pres*
Cathy Allen, *Sales Associate*
Ellie Murphy, *Sales Associate*
Samantha Smith, *Marketing Mgr*
◆ EMP: 45
SQ FT: 64,500
SALES (est): 8.4MM **Privately Held**
WEB: www.starlinen.com
SIC: 2299 2392 Linen fabrics; blankets, comforters & beddings

(G-6569)
STUD WELDING CO THE INC
750 Glen Ave (08057-1124)
PHONE..................................856 866-9300
Ralph Kohart Jr, *President*
Douglas Oyama, *Sls & Mktg Exec*
EMP: 5
SQ FT: 8,000
SALES (est): 600K **Privately Held**
WEB: www.studweldingco.com
SIC: 5072 5085 5084 3699 Bolts; nuts (hardware); rivets; fasteners, industrial: nuts, bolts, screws, etc.; welding machinery & equipment; electrical welding equipment

(G-6570)
SWEMCO LLC (HQ)
121 Whittendale Dr Ste A (08057-1373)
PHONE..................................856 222-9900
Carl Szczepkowski,
Richard Szczepkowski,
EMP: 115
SQ FT: 30,000
SALES (est): 20.8MM
SALES (corp-wide): 69.3MM **Privately Held**
SIC: 3672 Printed circuit boards
PA: S W Electronics & Manufacturing Corp
1215 N Church St
Moorestown NJ 08057
856 222-9900

(G-6571)
SYMPHONY INC
Also Called: Symphony Pastries
1263 Glen Ave Ste 220 (08057-1178)
PHONE..................................856 727-9596
Yann Machard, *President*
Susan Cohen, *Opers Staff*
▲ EMP: 17
SQ FT: 2,500
SALES (est): 2.5MM **Privately Held**
WEB: www.symphonypastries.com
SIC: 2051 5461 Cakes, pies & pastries; pastries

(G-6572)
SYSCOM TECHNOLOGIES CORP
1537 Glen Ave (08057-1103)
PHONE..................................856 642-7661
Peter Anninos, *President*
Anthony Maladra, *Vice Pres*
EMP: 100
SQ FT: 36,000
SALES (est): 30.7MM **Privately Held**
SIC: 3672 Printed circuit boards

(G-6573)
THOMA INC (PA)
1640 Nixon Dr 323 (08057-2675)
PHONE..................................856 608-6887
Brian Thoma, *President*
▲ EMP: 14
SQ FT: 2,100
SALES (est): 2.3MM **Privately Held**
WEB: www.thomainc.com
SIC: 3821 Laboratory furniture

(G-6574)
V H EXACTA CORP
107 Whittendale Dr (08057-1364)
PHONE..................................856 235-7379
Francis A Hubler, *President*
Wayne Hubler, *Vice Pres*
Susan Hileman, *Treasurer*
Barbara Hubler, *Admin Sec*
EMP: 9
SQ FT: 10,000
SALES (est): 1.5MM **Privately Held**
SIC: 3469 Machine parts, stamped or pressed metal

(G-6575)
VERMES MACHINE CO INC
351 Crider Ave (08057-1238)
PHONE..................................856 642-9300
Erwin Vermes, *President*
Michael Vermes Jr, *Vice Pres*
▲ EMP: 25
SQ FT: 5,000
SALES (est): 5.1MM **Privately Held**
WEB: www.vermesmachine.com
SIC: 3599 7692 Machine shop, jobbing & repair; welding repair

(G-6576)
WAY IT WAS SPORTING SVC INC
620 Chestnut St (08057-2004)
PHONE..................................856 231-0111
Henry Peters, *President*
John R Peters, *Corp Secy*
EMP: 4
SQ FT: 1,000
SALES (est): 403.4K **Privately Held**
SIC: 5941 3484 Firearms; rifles or rifle parts, 30 mm. & below; shotguns or shotgun parts, 30 mm. & below

(G-6577)
WEILER LABELING SYSTEMS LLC
1256 N Church St (08057-1129)
PHONE..................................856 273-3377
Ted Geiselman, *President*
Mary Lawrence, *Parts Mgr*
Dana Breese, *Engineer*
Jim Esposito, *Engineer*
Paul Kotlyar, *Electrical Engi*
◆ EMP: 60
SQ FT: 33,000
SALES (est): 14MM
SALES (corp-wide): 585.6MM **Privately Held**
WEB: www.weilerls.com
SIC: 3565 Labeling machines, industrial
PA: Pro Mach, Inc.
50 E Rivercntr Blvd 180
Covington KY 41011
513 831-8778

(G-6578)
WILSONART LLC
11 Twosome Dr (08057-1367)
PHONE..................................800 822-7613
James Kane, *Manager*
EMP: 17
SALES (corp-wide): 14.7B **Publicly Held**
WEB: www.wilsonart.com
SIC: 2821 2541 Plastics materials & resins; table or counter tops, plastic laminated
HQ: Wilsonart Llc
2501 Wilsonart Dr
Temple TX 76504
254 207-7000

Morganville
Monmouth County

(G-6579)
ABLE GROUP TECHNOLOGIES INC
281 State Route 79 N (07751-1157)
PHONE.....................................732 591-9299
Alan Rogolsky, *Sales Staff*
EMP: 5
SALES (est): 602.9K **Privately Held**
SIC: 7378 7372 8731 Computer maintenance & repair; application computer software; computer (hardware) development

(G-6580)
ADS SALES CO INC
Also Called: Room Service Amenities
1010 Campus Dr (07751-1260)
PHONE.....................................732 591-0500
Ann Summer, *President*
Bob Luchenta, *Vice Pres*
Dennis Summer, *Vice Pres*
Marshall Summer, *Vice Pres*
Victoria McMillin, *Design Engr*
◆ EMP: 20
SQ FT: 7,000
SALES (est): 5MM **Privately Held**
WEB: www.roomserviceamenities.com
SIC: 5046 2844 5199 Hotel equipment & supplies; toilet preparations; advertising specialties

(G-6581)
AKZO NOBEL COATINGS INC
300 Campus Dr Ste B (07751-1281)
PHONE.....................................732 617-7734
Bill Garrison, *Manager*
EMP: 5
SALES (corp-wide): 11.3B **Privately Held**
WEB: www.nam.sikkens.com
SIC: 2869 Industrial organic chemicals
HQ: Akzo Nobel Coatings Inc.
　　8220 Mohawk Dr
　　Strongsville OH 44136
　　440 297-5100

(G-6582)
AMERICAN SOFT SOLUTIONS CORP
704 Ginesi Dr Ste 28a (07751-1249)
PHONE.....................................732 272-0052
Tariq Chaudhry, *President*
Yasmin Chaudhry, *Vice Pres*
EMP: 6
SALES (est): 264.2K **Privately Held**
SIC: 7372 Business oriented computer software

(G-6583)
AURORA MULTIMEDIA CORPORATION
205 Commercial Ct (07751-1070)
PHONE.....................................732 591-5800
Paul E Harris, *CEO*
Michael Twerdak, *COO*
Arielle Zebe, *Cust Mgr*
▲ EMP: 25
SQ FT: 11,000
SALES (est): 7.3MM **Privately Held**
WEB: www.auroramultimedia.com
SIC: 3669 Visual communication systems

(G-6584)
CENOGENICS CORPORATION (PA)
100 County Road 520 (07751-1270)
P.O. Box 308 (07751-0308)
PHONE.....................................732 536-6457
Michael Katz, *President*
Nitza Hernandez, *Vice Pres*
EMP: 25
SQ FT: 3,000
SALES (est): 3.7MM **Privately Held**
SIC: 3841 2835 Surgical & medical instruments; in vitro & in vivo diagnostic substances

(G-6585)
CHROMA TRADING USA INC
Also Called: Chroma Inks USA
18 Guest Dr (07751-1431)
PHONE.....................................732 956-4431
Shakher Puntambekar, *Manager*
EMP: 5
SALES (est): 634.2K **Privately Held**
SIC: 2893 Duplicating ink

(G-6586)
EMBROIDERY IN STITCHES INC
1020 Campus Dr (07751-1260)
PHONE.....................................732 460-2660
Harry Harkavy, *President*
Debra Harkavy, *Principal*
EMP: 16
SQ FT: 4,000
SALES (est): 910K **Privately Held**
SIC: 2395 Embroidery & art needlework

(G-6587)
HY-TEK MATERIAL HANDLING INC
704 Ginesi Dr Ste 25 (07751-1280)
PHONE.....................................732 490-6282
Thomas Mann, *President*
Sam Grooms, *Branch Mgr*
EMP: 33
SALES (corp-wide): 81.4MM **Privately Held**
SIC: 5084 3535 Materials handling machinery; belt conveyor systems, general industrial use; bulk handling conveyor systems; overhead conveyor systems; robotic conveyors
PA: Hy-Tek Material Handling, Inc.
　　2222 Rickenbacker Pkwy W
　　Columbus OH 43217
　　614 497-2500

(G-6588)
IDA AUTOMOTIVE INC
600 Texas Rd (07751-4128)
PHONE.....................................732 591-1245
Robert Ida, *President*
EMP: 4
SQ FT: 3,000
SALES (est): 550.1K **Privately Held**
SIC: 3714 5531 Motor vehicle parts & accessories; automotive & home supply stores

(G-6589)
INVITATION STUDIO
12 Hemingway Ct (07751-2017)
PHONE.....................................732 740-5558
Kira Kogan, *Principal*
EMP: 4
SALES (est): 223K **Privately Held**
SIC: 2221 Paper broadwoven fabrics

(G-6590)
JANAS LLC
3 Oxford Ct (07751-1626)
PHONE.....................................732 536-6719
Mitchell Newman, *Principal*
EMP: 5
SALES (est): 222.1K **Privately Held**
SIC: 2711 Newspapers

(G-6591)
LABORATORY DIAGNOSTICS CO INC (HQ)
100 County Road 520 (07751-1270)
P.O. Box 160 (07751-0160)
PHONE.....................................732 536-6300
Michael Katz, *President*
Nitza Hernandez, *Vice Pres*
EMP: 15
SALES (est): 2.3MM
SALES (corp-wide): 3.7MM **Privately Held**
WEB: www.cenogenics.com
SIC: 3841 2835 2295 Surgical & medical instruments; in vitro & in vivo diagnostic substances; coated fabrics, not rubberized
PA: Cenogenics Corporation
　　100 County Road 520
　　Morganville NJ 07751
　　732 536-6457

(G-6592)
LABORATORY DIAGNOSTICS CO INC
712 Ginesi Dr (07751-1206)
PHONE.....................................732 972-2145
Michael Katz, *Manager*
EMP: 7
SALES (corp-wide): 3.7MM **Privately Held**
WEB: www.cenogenics.com
SIC: 3841 Surgical & medical instruments
HQ: Laboratory Diagnostics Co Inc
　　100 County Road 520
　　Morganville NJ 07751
　　732 536-6300

(G-6593)
PAT BRY ADVERTISING SPC
Tennant Rd Rr 79 (07751)
P.O. Box 369 (07751-0369)
PHONE.....................................732 591-0999
Gary Bernie, *President*
Joseph Burn, *Treasurer*
EMP: 4
SQ FT: 1,250
SALES (est): 300K **Privately Held**
SIC: 3993 Signs & advertising specialties

(G-6594)
PLATYPUS PRINT PRODUCTIONS LLC
253 State Route 79 N (07751-2000)
PHONE.....................................732 772-1212
Jason Gerbsman,
Richard Trager,
EMP: 5
SQ FT: 2,000
SALES (est): 350K **Privately Held**
SIC: 2759 Catalogs: printing; circulars: printing

(G-6595)
POLARITY LLC
330 Mockingbird Ln (07751-4603)
PHONE.....................................732 970-3855
Al Belfer, *Principal*
EMP: 4
SALES (est): 223.6K **Privately Held**
SIC: 3827 Polarizers

(G-6596)
TRESKY CORP
704 Ginesi Dr Ste 11 (07751-1278)
PHONE.....................................732 536-8600
Thorlief Brandsberg, *CEO*
Alex Tresky, *President*
EMP: 4
SALES (est): 270K **Privately Held**
SIC: 3479 Bonderizing of metal or metal products

(G-6597)
TRILENIUM SALVAGE CO
147 Tennent Rd (07751-1131)
PHONE.....................................732 462-2909
Fred Smith, *Owner*
EMP: 4
SALES (est): 519.4K **Privately Held**
SIC: 3531 Automobile wrecker hoists

(G-6598)
VYTRAN CORPORATION
1400 Campus Dr (07751-1283)
PHONE.....................................732 972-2880
Eric Mies, *President*
Bernd Kaliske, *Prdtn Mgr*
Scott Bartolett, *Design Engr*
Kevin Lin, *Technician*
EMP: 45
SALES (est): 4.8MM **Privately Held**
SIC: 3661 Telephone & telegraph apparatus

(G-6599)
VYTRAN LLC
1400 Campus Dr (07751-1283)
PHONE.....................................732 972-2880
Jean Michel Pelaprat, *CEO*
John Hanogofsky, *Vice Pres*
George Jiarette, *Vice Pres*
Larry Winderg, *Vice Pres*
EMP: 27

SALES (est): 3.8MM
SALES (corp-wide): 205.9MM **Privately Held**
WEB: www.vytran.com
SIC: 3357 3661 Fiber optic cable (insulated); switching equipment, telephone
PA: Thorlabs, Inc.
　　56 Sparta Ave
　　Newton NJ 07860
　　973 579-7227

(G-6600)
ZIXEL LTD
4 Pegasus Ct (07751-1188)
PHONE.....................................732 972-3287
Zosim Ioffe, *President*
▲ EMP: 5
SQ FT: 750
SALES (est): 490K **Privately Held**
SIC: 3825 Test equipment for electronic & electric measurement

Morris Plains
Morris County

(G-6601)
ADEMCO I LLC
115 Tabor Rd (07950-2546)
PHONE.....................................973 455-2000
Jacqueline W Katzel, *President*
EMP: 4
SALES (est): 104.1K
SALES (corp-wide): 41.8B **Publicly Held**
SIC: 3724 Turbines, aircraft type
PA: Honeywell International Inc.
　　300 S Tryon St
　　Charlotte NC 28202
　　973 455-2000

(G-6602)
COTY US LLC
Also Called: Coty Research and Development
410 American Rd (07950-2461)
PHONE.....................................973 490-8700
Francesca P Pitsker, *COO*
Ralph Macchio, *Vice Pres*
Alan Farer, *Vice Pres*
James Flanagan, *Manager*
Elisheva Jasie, *Manager*
EMP: 100 **Publicly Held**
SIC: 2844 Perfumes & colognes; cosmetic preparations
HQ: Coty Us Llc
　　350 5th Ave
　　New York NY 10118

(G-6603)
DOUBLE CHECK
101 Gibraltar Dr Ste 1e (07950-1287)
PHONE.....................................973 984-2229
Joe Cincotta, *CEO*
Tim Ihde, *Principal*
Marianna Sullivan, *Engineer*
James Breslin, *Sr Software Eng*
Daniel Carlucci, *Director*
EMP: 6
SALES (est): 453.1K **Privately Held**
WEB: www.omnie.com
SIC: 7372 Application computer software

(G-6604)
DUCTS INC
8 Moraine Rd (07950-2711)
PHONE.....................................973 267-8482
Nicholas Roccaforte, *President*
Arlene Roccaforte, *Treasurer*
EMP: 8
SQ FT: 8,000
SALES (est): 600K **Privately Held**
WEB: www.ducts.com
SIC: 3444 Ducts, sheet metal

(G-6605)
ENCORE PHARMACEUTICAL INC
Also Called: Enspharma
49 Moraine Rd (07950-2721)
PHONE.....................................973 267-9331
Bhanu Godhani, *President*
Rakash Methpara, *General Mgr*
EMP: 7
SALES (est): 721.1K **Privately Held**
SIC: 2834 Pharmaceutical preparations

(G-6606)
HH SPINCO INC
115 Tabor Rd (07950-2546)
PHONE..................................973 455-2000
Jacqueline W Katzel, *President*
EMP: 4
SALES (est): 104.1K
SALES (corp-wide): 41.8B **Publicly Held**
SIC: 3724 Turbines, aircraft type
PA: Honeywell International Inc.
300 S Tryon St
Charlotte NC 28202
973 455-2000

(G-6607)
HONEYWELL ASIA PACIFIC INC
115 Tabor Rd (07950-2546)
PHONE..................................973 455-2000
John Tus, *President*
EMP: 72
SALES (est): 36.4MM
SALES (corp-wide): 41.8B **Publicly Held**
SIC: 3822 Auto controls regulating residntl
& coml environmt & applncs
PA: Honeywell International Inc.
300 S Tryon St
Charlotte NC 28202
973 455-2000

(G-6608)
HONEYWELL EAST ASIA INC
(HQ)
115 Tabor Rd (07950-2546)
PHONE..................................973 455-2000
John J Tus, *President*
EMP: 4
SALES (est): 10.4MM
SALES (corp-wide): 41.8B **Publicly Held**
SIC: 3812 Aircraft control systems, electronic
PA: Honeywell International Inc.
300 S Tryon St
Charlotte NC 28202
973 455-2000

(G-6609)
HONEYWELL INTERNATIONAL
INC
115 Tabor Rd (07950-2546)
PHONE..................................800 601-3099
Louis Vuoncino, *Branch Mgr*
EMP: 130
SALES (corp-wide): 41.8B **Publicly Held**
WEB: www.honeywell.com
SIC: 3724 Aircraft engines & engine parts
PA: Honeywell International Inc.
300 S Tryon St
Charlotte NC 28202
973 455-2000

(G-6610)
HONEYWELL INTERNATIONAL
INC
8 Waterloo Dr (07950-1438)
PHONE..................................973 285-5321
Michael Bonsignore, *Branch Mgr*
EMP: 48
SALES (corp-wide): 41.8B **Publicly Held**
WEB: www.honeywell.com
SIC: 3724 Aircraft engines & engine parts
PA: Honeywell International Inc.
300 S Tryon St
Charlotte NC 28202
973 455-2000

(G-6611)
HONEYWELL INTERNATIONAL
INC
115 Tabor Rd (07950-2546)
PHONE..................................973 455-2000
EMP: 70
SALES (corp-wide): 41.8B **Publicly Held**
SIC: 3724 Aircraft engines & engine parts
PA: Honeywell International Inc.
300 S Tryon St
Charlotte NC 28202
973 455-2000

(G-6612)
HONEYWELL INTERNATIONAL
INC
115 Tabor Rd (07950-2546)
PHONE..................................877 841-2840
John Hughes, *Branch Mgr*

EMP: 125
SALES (corp-wide): 41.8B **Publicly Held**
WEB: www.honeywell.com
SIC: 3724 Aircraft engines & engine parts
PA: Honeywell International Inc.
300 S Tryon St
Charlotte NC 28202
973 455-2000

(G-6613)
HONEYWELL INTERNATIONAL
INC
115 Tabor Rd (07950-2546)
PHONE..................................800 601-3099
Louis Vuoncino, *Branch Mgr*
EMP: 4
SALES (corp-wide): 41.8B **Publicly Held**
WEB: www.honeywell.com
SIC: 3724 Aircraft engines & engine parts
PA: Honeywell International Inc.
300 S Tryon St
Charlotte NC 28202
973 455-2000

(G-6614)
HONEYWELL INTERNATIONAL
INC
115 Tabor Rd (07950-2546)
PHONE..................................973 455-2000
EMP: 135
SALES (corp-wide): 41.8B **Publicly Held**
WEB: www.honeywell.com
SIC: 2999 5169 2819 Waxes, petroleum:
not produced in petroleum refineries;
waxes, except petroleum; industrial inorganic chemicals
PA: Honeywell International Inc.
300 S Tryon St
Charlotte NC 28202
973 455-2000

(G-6615)
HOUSES MAGAZINE INC
173 Morris St (07950)
PHONE..................................973 605-1877
Gene Petraglia, *President*
Peter Best, *Vice Pres*
EMP: 18
SALES (est): 1.4MM **Privately Held**
SIC: 2721 Periodicals: publishing only

(G-6616)
IBC PHARMACEUTICALS INC
300 The American Rd (07950-2460)
PHONE..................................973 540-9595
Cynthia Sullivan, *President*
Ken Chang, *Vice Pres*
EMP: 10
SALES (est): 895.3K
SALES (corp-wide): 2.1MM **Publicly Held**
WEB: www.immunomedics.com
SIC: 2834 Pharmaceutical preparations
PA: Immunomedics, Inc.
300 The American Rd
Morris Plains NJ 07950
973 605-8200

(G-6617)
IMMUNOMEDICS INC (PA)
300 The American Rd (07950-2460)
PHONE..................................973 605-8200
Behzad Aghazadeh, *Ch of Bd*
Usama Malik, *CFO*
Brendan P Delaney, *Ch Credit Ofcr*
Morris Rosenberg, *CTO*
Jared Freedberg, *General Counsel*
▲ **EMP:** 185
SQ FT: 85,000
SALES: 2.1MM **Publicly Held**
WEB: www.immunomedics.com
SIC: 2834 2835 Pharmaceutical preparations; in vitro diagnostics

(G-6618)
JOHNSON & JOHNSON
201 Tabor Rd (07950-2614)
PHONE..................................908 874-1000
Dawn Gabriel, *Research*
Cheryl Miller, *Branch Mgr*
Diane Hrozencik, *Manager*
Maureen Molina, *Director*
EMP: 147

SALES (corp-wide): 81.5B **Publicly Held**
WEB: www.jnj.com
SIC: 3842 3841 2834 2844 Surgical appliances & supplies; dressings, surgical; ligatures, medical; sutures, absorbable & non-absorbable; surgical & medical instruments; ophthalmic instruments & apparatus; diagnostic apparatus, medical; surgical instruments & apparatus; pharmaceutical preparations; drugs acting on the central nervous system & sense organs; dermatologicals; drugs affecting parasitic & infective diseases; toilet preparations; oral preparations; toilet preparations; powder: baby, face, talcum or toilet; feminine hygiene paper products; napkins, sanitary: made from purchased paper; panty liners: made from purchased paper; infant & baby paper products
PA: Johnson & Johnson
1 Johnson And Johnson Plz
New Brunswick NJ 08933
732 524-0400

(G-6619)
NOVARTIS PHARMACEUTICALS
CORP
220 E Hanover Ave (07950-2445)
PHONE..................................973 538-1296
Andrew S Sandler, *Vice Pres*
EMP: 15
SALES (corp-wide): 51.9B **Privately Held**
SIC: 2834 Pharmaceutical preparations
HQ: Novartis Pharmaceuticals Corporation
1 Health Plz
East Hanover NJ 07936
862 778-8300

(G-6620)
NPT PUBLISHING GROUP INC
Also Called: Non Profit Times
201 Littleton Rd Ste 2 (07950-2939)
PHONE..................................973 401-0202
John McIlquham, *President*
Ivan Goodinho, *Accounts Mgr*
Scott Vail, *Accounts Mgr*
Mary Ford, *Accounts Exec*
Mark Hrywna, *Senior Editor*
EMP: 15
SQ FT: 5,700
SALES (est): 2.4MM **Privately Held**
WEB: www.nptimes.com
SIC: 2721 8742 Magazines: publishing only, not printed on site; management consulting services

(G-6621)
PACIFIC MICROTRONICS INC
8 Laurel Ln (07950-3216)
PHONE..................................973 993-8665
Bob Grossman, *Principal*
EMP: 8
SALES (est): 340K **Privately Held**
SIC: 3721 Aircraft

(G-6622)
PALSGAARD INCORPORATED
101 Gibraltar Dr Ste 2b (07950-1287)
PHONE..................................973 998-7951
Rosa Regalado, *General Mgr*
▲ **EMP:** 19
SALES (est): 2.5MM
SALES (corp-wide): 219MM **Privately Held**
SIC: 2099 5145 Food preparations; snack foods
HQ: Palsgaard A/S
Palsgaardvej 10
Juelsminde 7130
768 276-82

(G-6623)
PFIZER INC
182 Tabor Rd (07950)
PHONE..................................973 993-0977
EMP: 146
SALES (corp-wide): 52.5B **Publicly Held**
SIC: 2834 Mfg Pharmaceutical Preps
PA: Pfizer Inc.
235 E 42nd St
New York NY 10017
212 733-2323

(G-6624)
Q&Q PHARMA RESEARCH
COMPANY
19 Meadow Bluff Rd (07950-1952)
PHONE..................................973 267-0160
Rui Yu, *Principal*
EMP: 7
SALES (est): 790.7K **Privately Held**
SIC: 2834 Pharmaceutical preparations

(G-6625)
RESIDEO FUNDING INC (HQ)
115 Tabor Rd (07950-2546)
PHONE..................................973 455-2000
EMP: 12
SALES (est): 27.4MM
SALES (corp-wide): 4.8B **Publicly Held**
SIC: 3699 High-energy particle physics equipment
PA: Resideo Technologies, Inc.
1985 Douglas Dr N
Golden Valley MN 55422
763 954-5204

(G-6626)
TEMPTIME CORPORATION (HQ)
116 The American Rd (07950-2443)
PHONE..................................973 984-6000
Renaat Van Den Hooff, *President*
Emily Moore, *President*
Katie Kraverath, *Business Mgr*
Mike Montana, *Business Mgr*
Steven Feldman, *Vice Pres*
▲ **EMP:** 74
SQ FT: 55,000
SALES (est): 12MM
SALES (corp-wide): 4.2B **Publicly Held**
WEB: www.heatmarker.com
SIC: 3826 Instruments measuring thermal properties
PA: Zebra Technologies Corporation
3 Overlook Pt
Lincolnshire IL 60069
847 634-6700

(G-6627)
UOP LLC
115 Tabor Rd (07950-2546)
PHONE..................................973 455-2096
Dennis Fenway, *Manager*
EMP: 7
SALES (corp-wide): 41.8B **Publicly Held**
WEB: www.uop.com
SIC: 2819 Catalysts, chemical
HQ: Uop Llc
25 E Algonquin Rd
Des Plaines IL 60016
847 391-2000

(G-6628)
WALPOLE WOODWORKERS
INC
540 Tabor Rd (07950-2726)
PHONE..................................973 539-3555
Ben Lowell, *Branch Mgr*
EMP: 25
SALES (corp-wide): 84.5MM **Privately Held**
WEB: www.walpolewoodworkers.com
SIC: 2499 5211 5712 2452 Fencing, wood; fencing; outdoor & garden furniture; prefabricated wood buildings; prefabricated metal buildings; wood household furniture
PA: Walpole Outdoors Llc
100 Rver Ridge Dr Ste 302
Norwood MA 02062
508 668-2800

(G-6629)
ZION INDUSTRIES INC
39 E Hanover Ave Ste G (07950-2456)
P.O. Box 362 (07950-0362)
PHONE..................................973 998-0162
Gilbert Carpete, *President*
EMP: 20
SALES (est): 720.7K **Privately Held**
SIC: 1389 8742 Construction, repair & dismantling services; maintenance management consultant

Morristown
Morris County

(G-6630)
ACTAVIS LLC
360 Mount Kemble Ave # 3 (07960-6662)
PHONE..................................800 272-5525
Diane Miranda, *VP Opers*
EMP: 150 **Privately Held**
WEB: www.watsonpharm.com
SIC: 2834 Pharmaceutical preparations
HQ: Actavis Llc
    5 Giralda Farms
    Madison NJ 07940
    862 261-7000

(G-6631)
ALLERGAN INC
16 Airport Rd (07960-4624)
PHONE..................................862 261-7000
George Hrichak II, *Principal*
EMP: 5 **Privately Held**
SIC: 2834 Drugs acting on the central
nervous system & sense organs
HQ: Allergan, Inc.
    5 Giralda Farms
    Madison NJ 07940
    862 261-7000

(G-6632)
ALLIED-SIGNAL CHINA LTD
101 Columbia Rd (07960-4640)
PHONE..................................973 455-2000
Lawrence Bossidy, *Principal*
EMP: 29
SALES (est): 3.8MM
SALES (corp-wide): 41.8B **Publicly Held**
WEB: www.honeywell.com
SIC: 3724 3714 3812 2824 Aircraft en-
gines & engine parts; motor vehicle parts
& accessories; search & navigation equip-
ment; organic fibers, noncellulosic; plas-
tics materials & resins
PA: Honeywell International Inc.
    300 S Tryon St
    Charlotte NC 28202
    973 455-2000

(G-6633)
**ALLIEDSIGNAL FOREIGN SLS
CORP**
101 Columbia Rd (07960-4640)
PHONE..................................973 455-2000
David Cote, *President*
G P Aloia, *Vice Pres*
Nahid Oloumi, *Program Mgr*
Emil Hensle, *CIO*
Ernie Park, *IT/INT Sup*
EMP: 4
SALES (est): 307.3K
SALES (corp-wide): 41.8B **Publicly Held**
WEB: www.honeywell.com
SIC: 3724 3714 3812 2824 Aircraft en-
gines & engine parts; motor vehicle parts
& accessories; search & navigation equip-
ment; organic fibers, noncellulosic; plas-
tics materials & resins
PA: Honeywell International Inc.
    300 S Tryon St
    Charlotte NC 28202
    973 455-2000

(G-6634)
ALMATICA PHARMA INC
44 Whippany Rd Ste 3 (07960-4558)
PHONE..................................877 447-7979
Douglas Drysdale, *CEO*
Robert Wessman, *Ch of Bd*
Kevin Dain, *CFO*
EMP: 21
SALES (est): 3MM **Privately Held**
SIC: 2834 Pharmaceutical preparations
PA: Alvogen Group, Inc.
    44 Whippany Rd Ste 300
    Morristown NJ 07960

(G-6635)
**ALPHAGRAPHICS PRINTSHOPS
OF TH**
60 Speedwell Ave (07960-6830)
PHONE..................................973 984-0066
Aaron Grohs, *President*
Brian Harrigan, *Chairman*

Tommy E Auger, *CFO*
EMP: 6
SQ FT: 8,000
SALES: 700K **Privately Held**
SIC: 2752 2759 Commercial printing, litho-
graphic; commercial printing

(G-6636)
ALVOGEN GROUP INC (PA)
44 Whippany Rd Ste 300 (07960-4558)
PHONE..................................973 796-3400
Robert Wessman, *CEO*
Darren Alkins, *President*
Elin Gabriel, *COO*
Georg Ingram, *Exec VP*
Chris Young, *Exec VP*
EMP: 42
SQ FT: 17,000
SALES (est): 388MM **Privately Held**
SIC: 2834 Pharmaceutical preparations

(G-6637)
ALVOGEN INC
44 Whippany Rd Ste 108 (07960-4558)
PHONE..................................973 796-3400
Lisa Graver, *Exec VP*
Kevin Bain, *CFO*
EMP: 110 EST: 2009
SQ FT: 43,000
SALES: 250MM **Privately Held**
SIC: 2834 Pharmaceutical preparations
PA: Alvogen Group, Inc.
    44 Whippany Rd Ste 300
    Morristown NJ 07960

(G-6638)
**ALVOGEN PB RESEARCH & DEV
LLC**
44 Whippany Rd Ste 300 (07960-4558)
PHONE..................................973 796-3400
Lisa Graver, *President*
EMP: 4
SALES (est): 90K **Privately Held**
SIC: 2834 Pharmaceutical preparations

(G-6639)
**ALVOGEN PHARMA US INC
(HQ)**
44 Whippany Rd Ste 300 (07960-4558)
PHONE..................................973 796-3400
Robert Wessman, *CEO*
Lisa Graver, *President*
Graham Baker, *CFO*
EMP: 500
SALES (est): 25MM **Privately Held**
SIC: 2834 Pharmaceutical preparations

(G-6640)
APPLETON GRP LLC
55 Madison Ave (07960-7337)
PHONE..................................973 285-3261
David Appleton, *Branch Mgr*
EMP: 108
SALES (corp-wide): 17.4B **Publicly Held**
SIC: 3823 Industrial instrmnts msrmnt dis-
play/control process variable
HQ: Appleton Grp Llc
    9377 W Higgins Rd
    Rosemont IL 60018
    847 268-6000

(G-6641)
**ASTRAZENECA
PHARMACEUTICALS LP**
Fl 2 Flr (07960)
PHONE..................................973 975-0324
Patrick Darken, *Vice Pres*
Ed Louie, *Mfg Staff*
Denny Himel, *Engineer*
Vance Kennedy, *Engineer*
Konstantine Lachaouri, *Auditor*
EMP: 10
SALES (corp-wide): 22B **Privately Held**
SIC: 2834 Druggists' preparations (phar-
maceuticals)
HQ: Astrazeneca Pharmaceuticals Lp
    1 Medimmune Way
    Gaithersburg MD 20878

(G-6642)
AVAYA CALA INC
350 Mount Kemble Ave (07960-6646)
PHONE..................................866 462-8292
EMP: 8 EST: 2000

SALES (est): 252.1K **Publicly Held**
SIC: 3661 Telephone & telegraph appara-
tus
HQ: Sierra Communication International Llc
    350 Mount Kemble Ave
    Morristown NJ 07960
    866 462-8292

(G-6643)
AVAYA INC
350 Mount Kemble Ave # 2 (07960-6646)
P.O. Box 1934 (07962-1934)
PHONE..................................908 953-6000
Robert Lesniak, *Business Mgr*
Alan Baratz PHD, *Vice Pres*
Mark Landers, *Vice Pres*
Todd Sheldon, *Opers Mgr*
Tibor Lukac, *Technical Mgr*
EMP: 310 **Publicly Held**
SIC: 3661 Telephone & telegraph appara-
tus
HQ: Avaya Inc.
    4655 Great America Pkwy
    Santa Clara CA 95054
    908 953-6000

(G-6644)
AVAYA WORLD SERVICES INC
350 Mount Kemble Ave (07960-6646)
PHONE..................................908 953-6000
Adele C Freeman, *Officer*
Nidal Abou-Itaif,
◆ EMP: 20
SALES (est): 1.7MM **Publicly Held**
SIC: 3661 7372 Telephone & telegraph
apparatus; prepackaged software
HQ: Avaya Inc.
    4655 Great America Pkwy
    Santa Clara CA 95054
    908 953-6000

(G-6645)
**AVIGDOR LTD LIABILITY
COMPANY**
Also Called: Avigdor Jewelry
25 Tikvah Way (07960-3607)
PHONE..................................973 898-4770
Ezra Solomon, *CEO*
EMP: 23 EST: 2012
SQ FT: 2,000
SALES (est): 1.7MM **Privately Held**
SIC: 3911 Jewelry, precious metal

(G-6646)
**BARRETT INDUSTRIES
CORPORATION (DH)**
73 Headquarters Plz (07960-3964)
PHONE..................................973 533-1001
Georges Ausseil, *President*
Zach Green, *Vice Pres*
Fred Shelton, *CFO*
Xiong Zeng, *Accountant*
Tina Davis, *Credit Staff*
EMP: 20
SALES (est): 362.6MM
SALES (corp-wide): 83.5MM **Privately
Held**
SIC: 1611 2951 4213 1799 Highway &
street paving contractor; road materials,
bituminous (not from refineries); trucking,
except local; building site preparation; ex-
cavation work
HQ: Colas Inc.
    73 Headquarters Plz 10t
    Morristown NJ 07960
    973 290-9082

(G-6647)
BAYER CONSUMER CARE INC
36 Columbia Rd (07960-4526)
PHONE..................................973 267-6198
Adrienne Pavan, *Principal*
Gregory Bitzas, *Business Mgr*
Stefan Hesse, *Vice Pres*
Willy Reissel, *Plant Mgr*
Kimberly Harris, *Project Mgr*
EMP: 488
SALES (est): 46.2MM **Privately Held**
SIC: 2834 Pharmaceutical preparations

(G-6648)
BAYER HEALTHCARE LLC
Qa Release Group
36 Columbia Rd (07960-4526)
PHONE..................................973 254-5000
EMP: 10

SALES (corp-wide): 45.3B **Privately Held**
SIC: 2834 Pharmaceutical preparations
HQ: Bayer Healthcare Llc
    100 Bayer Blvd
    Whippany NJ 07981
    862 404-3000

(G-6649)
BAYER HEALTHCARE LLC
Bayer Consumer Healthcare
36 Columbia Rd (07960-4526)
P.O. Box 1910 (07962-1910)
PHONE..................................973 254-5000
Gary Balkema, *Division Pres*
K S Lamberson, *Vice Pres*
Paul Moore, *Vice Pres*
Silvia Borghini, *Manager*
Andy Evans, *Manager*
EMP: 500
SALES (corp-wide): 45.3B **Privately Held**
SIC: 2834 Pharmaceutical preparations
HQ: Bayer Healthcare Llc
    100 Bayer Blvd
    Whippany NJ 07981
    862 404-3000

(G-6650)
BERTOT INDUSTRIES INC
23 Malcolm St Ste 1 (07960-4298)
PHONE..................................973 267-0006
Harold Jelonnek, *President*
Curtis Jelonnek, *Vice Pres*
Frank Gaden, *Admin Sec*
EMP: 9 EST: 1973
SQ FT: 10,000
SALES: 750K **Privately Held**
SIC: 3599 Machine shop, jobbing & repair

(G-6651)
CAPSUGEL INC (DH)
Also Called: Capsugel US
412 Mount Kemble Ave 200c (07960-6674)
PHONE..................................862 242-1700
Guido Driesen, *CEO*
Fradarique Bordes-Picard, *Business Mgr*
Dominik Mattern, *Business Mgr*
Fabrice Quaghebeur, *COO*
John Cullivan, *Vice Pres*
▲ EMP: 70
SALES (est): 630.2MM
SALES (corp-wide): 5.5B **Privately Held**
WEB: www.capsugel.com
SIC: 2834 Antibiotics, packaged

(G-6652)
**CAPSUGEL HOLDINGS US INC
(DH)**
412 Mount Kemble Ave 200c (07960-6666)
PHONE..................................862 242-1700
Guido Driesen, *CEO*
EMP: 9
SALES (est): 657.2MM
SALES (corp-wide): 5.5B **Privately Held**
SIC: 6799 2834 Investors; pharmaceutical
preparations

(G-6653)
CITY DIECUTTING INC
1 Cory Rd Ste C (07960-3112)
PHONE..................................973 270-0370
Eric Devos, *President*
EMP: 13
SALES (est): 2.1MM **Privately Held**
SIC: 3544 Special dies & tools

(G-6654)
COLAS INC (DH)
73 Headquarters Plz 10t (07960-3964)
PHONE..................................973 290-9082
Louis R Gabanna, *Ch of Bd*
Jean Vidal, *COO*
James E Weeks, *Senior VP*
Gordon R Crawley, *Vice Pres*
Anthony L Martino II, *Vice Pres*
▲ EMP: 1
SQ FT: 12,500
SALES (est): 1.6B
SALES (corp-wide): 83.5MM **Privately
Held**
SIC: 1611 1622 2951 Highway & street
paving contractor; bridge construction;
road materials, bituminous (not from re-
fineries)

▲ = Import ▼=Export
◆ =Import/Export

HQ: Colas Canada Inc
4950 Yonge St Suite 2400
Toronto ON M2N 6
416 293-5443

(G-6655)
CORENTEC AMERICA INC
60 Washington St Ste 202 (07960-6844)
PHONE..............................949 379-6227
Sung Taek Hong, *CEO*
EMP: 9
SALES (est): 991.3K **Privately Held**
SIC: 3845 Ultrasonic scanning devices,
medical

(G-6656)
COUNTY CONCRETE
CORPORATION
Ridgedale Ave (07960)
P.O. Box F, Kenvil (07847-1005)
PHONE..............................973 538-3113
Bill Space, *Manager*
EMP: 15
SALES (corp-wide): 30.2MM **Privately
Held**
WEB: www.countyconcretenj.com
SIC: 3273 1442 5039 5032 Ready-mixed
concrete; construction sand & gravel;
septic tanks; stone, crushed or broken
PA: County Concrete Corporation
50 Railroad Ave
Kenvil NJ 07847
973 744-2188

(G-6657)
CYPRESS PHARMACEUTICALS
INC
10 N Park Pl Ste 201 (07960-7101)
P.O. Box 399, Madison MS (39130-0399)
PHONE..............................601 856-4393
Max Draughn, *President*
Jason Sanderson, *CFO*
EMP: 125
SQ FT: 60,000
SALES (est): 15.7MM
SALES (corp-wide): 146MM **Privately
Held**
WEB: www.cypressrx.com
SIC: 2834 Pharmaceutical preparations
PA: Pernix Therapeutics Holdings, Inc.
10 N Park Pl Ste 201
Morristown NJ 07960

(G-6658)
DATASCAN GRAPHICS INC
55 Madison Ave Ste 400 (07960-7397)
PHONE..............................973 543-4803
Roy House, *President*
▲ EMP: 25
SQ FT: 8,500
SALES (est): 4.4MM **Privately Held**
SIC: 2752 Promotional printing, litho-
graphic

(G-6659)
DAYBROOK HOLDINGS INC
161 Madison Ave Ste 200 (07960-7329)
P.O. Box 1931 (07962-1931)
PHONE..............................973 538-6766
Gregory Holt, *President*
Steven Morganstern, *CFO*
Thomas Kenny, *Treasurer*
Joe Malin, *Admin Sec*
Leonard Guber, *Asst Sec*
EMP: 320
SQ FT: 2,700
SALES (est): 20.3MM **Privately Held**
SIC: 2077 Menhaden oil; fish meal, except
as animal feed

(G-6660)
DISCOVERY MAP
19 Wetmore Ave (07960-5243)
PHONE..............................973 868-4552
Debra King, *Principal*
EMP: 4
SALES (est): 149.7K **Privately Held**
SIC: 2741 Maps: publishing & printing

(G-6661)
DUSENBERY ENGINEERING CO
INC
309 E Hanover Ave (07960-4077)
P.O. Box 1001 (07962-1001)
PHONE..............................973 539-2200

Phillip N Williams, *President*
William Janus, *Vice Pres*
EMP: 9 EST: 1948
SQ FT: 10,000
SALES: 2MM **Privately Held**
SIC: 3443 Process vessels, industrial:
metal plate

(G-6662)
ENJOU CHOCOLAT
MORRISTOWN INC
8 Dehart St Ste 1 (07960-8205)
PHONE..............................973 993-9090
Wendy Jacobs Tafett, *President*
EMP: 6
SQ FT: 3,000
SALES (est): 706.1K **Privately Held**
SIC: 2064 5441 5812 Chocolate candy,
except solid chocolate; candy; ice cream
stands or dairy bars

(G-6663)
EPIC HOLDING INC
Also Called: Epic Industries
15 Footes Ln (07960-6304)
PHONE..............................732 249-6867
Ted Bustany, *President*
Sam Levine, *Vice Pres*
EMP: 40
SQ FT: 60,000
SALES (est): 9.8MM **Privately Held**
WEB: www.epicindustries.com
SIC: 2841 2869 2842 Detergents, syn-
thetic organic or inorganic alkaline; indus-
trial organic chemicals; floor waxes

(G-6664)
GARDEN STATE ORTHOPEDIC
CENTER
Also Called: Garden State Alnce Orthopaedic
95 Mount Kemble Ave (07960-5155)
PHONE..............................973 538-4948
Louis J Haberman, *Owner*
EMP: 5
SALES (est): 561.6K
SALES (corp-wide): 989.9K **Privately
Held**
SIC: 3842 5999 Limbs, artificial; orthope-
dic appliances; orthopedic & prosthesis
applications
PA: Garden State Orthopedic Center Inc
9 Post Rd Ste Op1
Oakland NJ 07436
201 337-5566

(G-6665)
GARRETT MOTION INC (PA)
89 Headquarters Plz (07960-6834)
PHONE..............................973 867-7016
Carlos Cardoso, *Ch of Bd*
Olivier Rabiller, *President*
Craig Balis, *Senior VP*
Daniel Deiro, *Senior VP*
Thierry Mabru, *Senior VP*
EMP: 11
SALES (est): 22.6MM **Privately Held**
SIC: 3714 Motor vehicle parts & acces-
sories

(G-6666)
GLASSWORKS STUDIO INC
151 South St Ste B103 (07960-9576)
PHONE..............................973 656-0800
Stacey Schlosser, *President*
EMP: 9
SQ FT: 3,500
SALES (est): 125K **Privately Held**
SIC: 3229 Glassware, art or decorative

(G-6667)
GRIFFEN LLC
44 Prospect St Apt 531 (07960-7816)
PHONE..............................973 723-5344
EMP: 5 EST: 2011
SQ FT: 1,500
SALES (est): 1.8MM **Privately Held**
SIC: 3089 Mfg Plastic Products

(G-6668)
HARRIS DRIVER CO (PA)
200 Madison Ave Ste 2 (07960-6167)
PHONE..............................973 267-8100
Frank L Driver IV, *Ch of Bd*
Lavinia Z Emery, *Admin Sec*
EMP: 4

SALES (est): 5.3MM **Privately Held**
SIC: 3357 Coaxial cable, nonferrous

(G-6669)
HEALTH SCIENCE FUNDING
LLC
55 Madison Ave (07960-7337)
PHONE..............................973 984-6159
EMP: 11 EST: 2004
SQ FT: 1,051
SALES (est): 890K **Privately Held**
SIC: 2834 Mfg Pharmaceutical Prepara-
tions

(G-6670)
HONEYWELL INTERNATIONAL
INC
20 Airport Rd (07960-4624)
PHONE..............................973 455-6633
Jerry Norton, *Director*
EMP: 30
SALES (corp-wide): 41.8B **Publicly Held**
WEB: www.honeywell.com
SIC: 3724 Aircraft engines & engine parts
PA: Honeywell International Inc.
300 S Tryon St
Charlotte NC 28202
973 455-2000

(G-6671)
HONEYWELL INTERNATIONAL
INC
101 Columbia Rd (07960-4640)
PHONE..............................973 455-5168
Donald Patton, *Engineer*
Jim Straub, *Engineer*
Gerry Whited, *Engineer*
John Sharkey, *Financial Analy*
Dan Stoltz, *Maintence Staff*
EMP: 5
SALES (corp-wide): 41.8B **Publicly Held**
SIC: 3724 Aircraft engines & engine parts
PA: Honeywell International Inc.
300 S Tryon St
Charlotte NC 28202
973 455-2000

(G-6672)
HONEYWELL INTERNATIONAL
INC
Columbia Tpke (07962)
PHONE..............................973 455-2000
EMP: 214
SALES (corp-wide): 41.8B **Publicly Held**
WEB: www.honeywell.com
SIC: 3714 3812 Motor vehicle parts & ac-
cessories; aircraft/aerospace flight instru-
ments & guidance systems
PA: Honeywell International Inc.
300 S Tryon St
Charlotte NC 28202
973 455-2000

(G-6673)
HONEYWELL SPAIN HOLDINGS
LLC (HQ)
101 Columbia Rd (07960-4640)
PHONE..............................973 455-2000
David M Cote,
EMP: 5
SALES (est): 849K
SALES (corp-wide): 41.8B **Publicly Held**
SIC: 3724 Aircraft engines & engine parts
PA: Honeywell International Inc.
300 S Tryon St
Charlotte NC 28202
973 455-2000

(G-6674)
HONEYWELL SPECLTY WAX &
ADDITV (HQ)
101 Columbia Rd (07960-4640)
PHONE..............................973 455-2000
David Cote, *CEO*
John Gottshall, *President*
George Paz, *Director*
◆ EMP: 13
SALES (est): 117.5MM
SALES (corp-wide): 41.8B **Publicly Held**
WEB:
www.honeywellspecialtymaterials.com
SIC: 2999 5169 Waxes, petroleum: not
produced in petroleum refineries; waxes,
except petroleum

PA: Honeywell International Inc.
300 S Tryon St
Charlotte NC 28202
973 455-2000

(G-6675)
ISDIN CORP
36 Cattano Ave (07960-9602)
PHONE..............................862 242-8129
Juan Emilio Naya Ariste, *CEO*
Robert Durso, *Principal*
EMP: 45
SALES (est): 6.2MM **Privately Held**
SIC: 2834 Chlorination tablets & kits (water
purification)

(G-6676)
KAHLE AUTOMATION
89 Headquarters Plz S (07960-6834)
PHONE..............................973 993-1850
EMP: 6
SALES (est): 155.2K
SALES (corp-wide): 19.4MM **Privately
Held**
SIC: 3559 Pharmaceutical machinery
PA: Kahle Automation Srl
Viale Europa Unita 57
Caravaggio BG 24043
036 335-5511

(G-6677)
LA PACE IMPORTS INC
3 Ascot Ln (07960-3202)
P.O. Box 337, Mendham (07945-0337)
PHONE..............................973 895-5420
Peter Carolan, *President*
Elena Carolan, *Vice Pres*
▲ EMP: 10
SQ FT: 5,000
SALES: 8MM **Privately Held**
WEB: www.pasta.com
SIC: 5149 2099 Pasta & rice; crackers,
cookies & bakery products; bakery prod-
ucts; cookies; pasta, uncooked: packaged
with other ingredients

(G-6678)
LEVY INNOVATION
3 Brigade Hill Rd (07960-4920)
PHONE..............................908 303-4492
Mark Levy, *Principal*
EMP: 4
SALES (est): 172K **Privately Held**
SIC: 2711 Newspapers, publishing & print-
ing

(G-6679)
LIGHTFOX INC
67 E Park Pl Ste 750 (07960-7103)
PHONE..............................973 209-9112
Tony Carrella, *CEO*
EMP: 20
SALES (est): 1MM **Privately Held**
SIC: 3648 Lighting equipment

(G-6680)
LONZA BIOLOGICS INC
412 Mount Kemble Ave # 200
(07960-6666)
PHONE..............................603 610-4809
Ronald French, *Mfg Spvr*
Jennifer Sprowl, *Mfg Spvr*
Daniel Grondin, *Production*
David Gandt, *Engineer*
Michael Mietzner, *Engineer*
EMP: 50
SALES (est): 17.6MM **Privately Held**
SIC: 2834 Pharmaceutical preparations

(G-6681)
LONZA INC (DH)
412 Mount Kemble Ave # 200
(07960-6666)
P.O. Box 1912 (07962-1912)
PHONE..............................201 316-9200
Jeanne Thomas, *CEO*
Paul Lemoi, *District Mgr*
Gary Abrizzani, *Business Mgr*
Mike Degennaro, *Vice Pres*
David Doles, *Vice Pres*
◆ EMP: 100 EST: 1958

G
E
O
G
R
A
P
H
I
C

SALES (est): 230.2MM
SALES (corp-wide): 5.5B **Privately Held**
WEB: www.riversidecap.com
SIC: 2899 2869 2819 Chemical preparations; industrial organic chemicals; industrial inorganic chemicals
HQ: Lonza America Inc.
412 Mount Kemble Ave 200s
Morristown NJ 07960
201 316-9200

(G-6682)
LONZA WALKERSVILLE INC
412 Mount Kemble Ave 200s (07960-6666)
PHONE.....................201 316-9259
Anja Fiedler, *Branch Mgr*
EMP: 4
SALES (corp-wide): 5.5B **Privately Held**
SIC: 2836 Biological products, except diagnostic
HQ: Lonza Walkersville, Inc.
8830 Biggs Ford Rd
Walkersville MD 21793
301 898-7025

(G-6683)
M J POWERS & CO PUBLISHERS
65 Madison Ave Ste 220 (07960-7307)
PHONE.....................973 898-1200
Michael J Powers, *President*
EMP: 4
SALES (est): 321.3K **Privately Held**
WEB: www.alertpubs.com
SIC: 2741 Business service newsletters: publishing & printing

(G-6684)
MAJESCO (HQ)
412 Mount Kemble Ave 110c (07960-6675)
PHONE.....................973 461-5200
Arun K Maheshwari, *Ch of Bd*
Ketan Mehta, *President*
Edward Ossie, *COO*
Prateek Kumar, *Exec VP*
Ganesh Pai, *Exec VP*
EMP: 7
SQ FT: 31,030
SALES (est): 139.8MM **Publicly Held**
WEB: www.majesco.com
SIC: 7372 7371 Prepackaged software; computer software development

(G-6685)
MENNEN COMPANY (HQ)
191 E Hanover Ave (07960-3100)
PHONE.....................973 630-1500
William S Shanahan, *President*
Andrew Hendry, *Vice Pres*
Brian J Heidtke, *Treasurer*
▲ **EMP:** 403 **EST:** 1878
SQ FT: 570,000
SALES (est): 24.5MM
SALES (corp-wide): 15.5B **Publicly Held**
SIC: 2844 2842 Toilet preparations; shampoos, rinses, conditioners: hair; lotions, shaving; deodorants, personal; deodorants, nonpersonal
PA: Colgate-Palmolive Company
300 Park Ave Fl 3
New York NY 10022
212 310-2000

(G-6686)
MFV INTERNATIONAL CORPORATION
89 Headquarters Plz (07960-6834)
PHONE.....................973 993-1687
Yoshiyuki Takahashi, *CEO*
Yoshifumi Tokuhara, *Chairman*
▲ **EMP:** 3
SQ FT: 280
SALES (est): 1.1MM **Privately Held**
SIC: 3089 3069 3999 Plastic containers, except foam; bags, rubber or rubberized fabric; atomizers, toiletry
PA: Mfv Co., Ltd.
15-8, Kashitahonmachi
Higashi-Osaka OSK 577-0

(G-6687)
MORRIS COUNTY IMAGING
310 Madison Ave Ste 110 (07960-6967)
PHONE.....................973 532-7900
Mary Ann Gomez, *Principal*
EMP: 5

SALES (est): 414.2K **Privately Held**
SIC: 3845 CAT scanner (Computerized Axial Tomography) apparatus

(G-6688)
MORRISTOWN CYCLE
103 Washington St (07960-8623)
PHONE.....................973 540-1244
David Shaw, *Owner*
EMP: 4 **EST:** 1971
SQ FT: 3,000
SALES (est): 440K **Privately Held**
SIC: 5571 7699 3751 Motorcycle parts & accessories; motorcycle repair service; motorcycles & related parts

(G-6689)
NEW JERSEY MONTHLY LLC
55 S Park Pl (07960-3924)
PHONE.....................973 539-8230
Kate Tomlinson, *Publisher*
Susan Brierly, *Editor*
Danielle Cortina, *Accounts Exec*
Christine Donga, *Accounts Exec*
Ann M Kramer, *Marketing Staff*
EMP: 40
SALES (est): 2.9MM **Privately Held**
SIC: 2721 Magazines: publishing & printing

(G-6690)
OMNIACTIVE HLTH TCHNLOGIES INC (HQ)
67 E Park Pl Ste 500 (07960-7138)
PHONE.....................866 588-3629
Hiren Doshi, *President*
Abhijit Bhattacharya, *President*
Chaitanya Desai, *COO*
Ashoke Roy, *CFO*
Jayant Deshpande, *CTO*
▲ **EMP:** 20
SALES (est): 2.4MM **Privately Held**
SIC: 2834 Vitamin, nutrient & hematinic preparations for human use

(G-6691)
PARADISE
1098 Mount Kemble Ave # 2 (07960-8004)
PHONE.....................973 425-0505
Paul Haley, *Principal*
EMP: 4
SALES (est): 140K **Privately Held**
SIC: 2389 5137 5621 Men's miscellaneous accessories; women's & children's outerwear; women's specialty clothing stores

(G-6692)
PERNIX THERAPEUTICS LLC
10 N Park Pl Ste 201 (07960-7101)
PHONE.....................800 793-2145
Cooper Collins, *President*
EMP: 45
SQ FT: 4,000
SALES (est): 6.6MM
SALES (corp-wide): 146MM **Privately Held**
WEB: www.zyberrx.com
SIC: 2834 5122 Pharmaceutical preparations; pharmaceuticals
PA: Pernix Therapeutics Holdings, Inc.
10 N Park Pl Ste 201
Morristown NJ 07960

(G-6693)
PICA PRINTINGS INC
Also Called: Digital Printed Communications
103 Ridgedale Ave Ste 4 (07960-4290)
PHONE.....................973 540-0420
Thomas Malphrus, *President*
EMP: 4
SQ FT: 1,400
SALES: 475K **Privately Held**
SIC: 2752 Commercial printing, offset

(G-6694)
PLUS PACKAGING INC
10 Mount Pleasant Rd (07960-3317)
P.O. Box 12, Madison (07940-0012)
PHONE.....................973 538-2216
Lee Dornfeld, *President*
◆ **EMP:** 6
SQ FT: 5,000

SALES (est): 1.1MM **Privately Held**
WEB: www.pluspackaging.com
SIC: 5199 2673 2672 Packaging materials; plastic bags: made from purchased materials; adhesive papers, labels or tapes: from purchased material

(G-6695)
PORTASEAL LLC
1 John St (07960-4237)
P.O. Box B, Convent Station (07961-0160)
PHONE.....................973 539-0100
Stanley Garbowy, *Principal*
EMP: 9 **EST:** 1959
SQ FT: 8,500
SALES (est): 1.1MM **Privately Held**
WEB: www.portaseal.com
SIC: 1799 5211 3442 Weather stripping; lumber & other building materials; garage doors, overhead: metal

(G-6696)
PTC INC
89 Headquarters Plz (07960-6834)
PHONE.....................973 631-6195
EMP: 19
SALES (corp-wide): 1.2B **Publicly Held**
WEB: www.ptc.com
SIC: 7372 Prepackaged software
PA: Ptc Inc.
121 Seaport Blvd
Boston MA 02210
781 370-5000

(G-6697)
RESTORTIONS BY PETER SCHICHTEL
10 New St (07960-4049)
PHONE.....................973 605-8818
Peter Schichtel, *Partner*
EMP: 9
SALES (est): 366.4K **Privately Held**
SIC: 7641 2499 1751 Antique furniture repair & restoration; decorative wood & woodwork; cabinet & finish carpentry

(G-6698)
SCHINDLER ELEVATOR CORPORATION (DH)
20 Whippany Rd (07960-4539)
P.O. Box 1935 (07962-1935)
PHONE.....................973 397-6500
Greg Ergenbright, *President*
John Kenner, *President*
John Albrecht, *General Mgr*
John Dull, *General Mgr*
Jim Ritter, *General Mgr*
◆ **EMP:** 325 **EST:** 1979
SQ FT: 162,500
SALES (est): 1.2B
SALES (corp-wide): 10.9B **Privately Held**
WEB: www.us.schindler.com
SIC: 3534 7699 1796 Elevators & equipment; elevators: inspection, service & repair; miscellaneous building item repair services; elevator installation & conversion
HQ: Schindler Enterprises Inc.
20 Whippany Rd
Morristown NJ 07960
973 397-6500

(G-6699)
SCHINDLER ENTERPRISES INC (HQ)
20 Whippany Rd (07960-4539)
PHONE.....................973 397-6500
David J Bauhs, *President*
John R Impellizeeri, *Vice Pres*
Mark Brauer, *Opers Staff*
Jujudhan Jena, *Treasurer*
Tom McCormack, *Manager*
◆ **EMP:** 10
SQ FT: 2,000
SALES (est): 1.2B
SALES (corp-wide): 10.9B **Privately Held**
SIC: 3534 7699 1796 Elevators & moving stairways; elevators: inspection, service & repair; elevator installation & conversion
PA: Schindler Holding Ag
Seestrasse 55
Hergiswil NW 6052
416 328-550

(G-6700)
SIERRA COMMUNICATION INTL LLC (DH)
350 Mount Kemble Ave (07960-6646)
PHONE.....................866 462-8292
Eric S Koza
EMP: 3
SALES (est): 17.3MM **Publicly Held**
SIC: 7372 3661 Prepackaged software; telephones & telephone apparatus
HQ: Avaya Inc.
4655 Great America Pkwy
Santa Clara CA 95054
908 953-6000

(G-6701)
SPEEDY SIGN-A-RAMA
166 Ridgedale Ave Ste 4 (07960-4085)
PHONE.....................973 605-8313
David Fan, *President*
EMP: 4
SQ FT: 2,500
SALES: 950K **Privately Held**
SIC: 3993 1799 Signs & advertising specialties; sign installation & maintenance

(G-6702)
TAISHO PHARMACEUTICAL R&D INC
350 Mount Kemble Ave # 4 (07960-6635)
PHONE.....................973 285-0870
Tetsuro Inoue, *President*
Shoji Yasuda, *Treasurer*
Kohji Shimasaki, *Admin Sec*
Helene Sabia, *Sr Associate*
EMP: 8
SALES (est): 1.2MM **Privately Held**
WEB: www.taisho.co.jp
SIC: 2834 Pharmaceutical preparations
PA: Taisho Pharmaceutical Co., Ltd.
3-24-1, Takada
Toshima-Ku TKY 171-0

(G-6703)
TECHNOLOGY CORP AMERICA INC
350 Mount Kemble Ave (07960-6646)
PHONE.....................866 462-8292
EMP: 4 **EST:** 1995
SALES (est): 190.8K **Publicly Held**
SIC: 3661 Telephones & telephone apparatus
HQ: Sierra Communication International Llc
350 Mount Kemble Ave
Morristown NJ 07960
866 462-8292

(G-6704)
TYCOM LIMITED (DH)
10 Park Ave (07960-4700)
PHONE.....................973 753-3040
Neil R Garvey, *President*
David Van Rossam, *CFO*
EMP: 250
SALES (est): 104.9MM **Privately Held**
SIC: 3643 1623 Current-carrying wiring devices; cable laying construction
HQ: Tyco International Management Company, Llc
9 Roszel Rd Ste 2
Princeton NJ 08540
609 720-4200

(G-6705)
U V INTERNATIONAL LLC (PA)
Also Called: U V International
360 Mount Kemble Ave # 2 (07960-6662)
PHONE.....................973 993-9454
Vinod Jhunjhunwala, *CEO*
▲ **EMP:** 8
SQ FT: 800
SALES (est): 5.4MM **Privately Held**
WEB: www.uvintl.com
SIC: 5074 3589 3498 Plumbing fittings & supplies; sewage & water treatment equipment; fabricated pipe & fittings

(G-6706)
VERMEER PHARMA LLC
36 Canfield Rd (07960-6933)
PHONE.....................973 270-0073
Mark Vanarendonk, *Principal*
EMP: 4 **EST:** 2014
SALES (est): 218.8K **Privately Held**
SIC: 2834 Pharmaceutical preparations

(G-6707)
VICTOR INTERNATIONAL MARKETING
35 Airport Rd Ste Ll25 (07960-4642)
PHONE.................................973 267-8900
Christopher Anderson, *President*
EMP: 4
SALES (est): 320K **Privately Held**
WEB: www.victorinternational.com
SIC: 8742 3559 Marketing consulting services; pharmaceutical machinery

(G-6708)
WARNER CHILCOTT (US) LLC
17 Airport Rd Ste 2 (07960-4665)
PHONE.................................973 442-3200
EMP: 4 **Privately Held**
SIC: 2834 Pharmaceutical preparations
HQ: Warner Chilcott (Us), Llc
400 Interpace Pkwy
Parsippany NJ 07054

(G-6709)
WASAK INC
45 S Park Pl Ste 224 (07960-3924)
PHONE.................................973 605-8122
Daryl Reigel, *President*
◆ EMP: 2
SALES: 1.2MM **Privately Held**
SIC: 2899 Water treating compounds

Mount Arlington
Morris County

(G-6710)
CABLETIME LTD
Also Called: Cabletime USA
100 Valley Rd Ste 203 (07856-1324)
PHONE.................................973 770-8070
Edward Carabetta, *General Mgr*
Ed Carabetta, *Vice Pres*
Chad Potenzone, *Technical Staff*
EMP: 4
SALES (est): 623.5K **Privately Held**
WEB: www.cabletime.com
SIC: 3695 Video recording tape, blank

(G-6711)
DOVE CHOCOLATE DISCOVERIES LLC
400 Valley Rd Ste 200 (07856-2316)
PHONE.................................866 922-3683
John Wyckoff, *President*
EMP: 20
SALES (est): 7.8MM
SALES (corp-wide): 34.2B **Privately Held**
SIC: 5141 2066 Groceries, general line; chocolate & cocoa products
PA: Mars, Incorporated
6885 Elm St Ste 1
Mc Lean VA 22101
703 821-4900

(G-6712)
EXODON LLC
111 Howard Blvd Ste 204 (07856-1315)
PHONE.................................973 398-2900
Gerald Tramontano,
EMP: 10
SALES (est): 1.4MM **Privately Held**
SIC: 3821 Clinical laboratory instruments, except medical & dental

(G-6713)
GRAY STAR INC
200 Valley Rd Ste 103 (07856-1320)
PHONE.................................973 398-3331
Martin H Stein, *President*
Russell Stein, *Vice Pres*
EMP: 4
SALES: 1MM **Privately Held**
WEB: www.graystarinc.com
SIC: 3844 Irradiation equipment

(G-6714)
KONGSBERG PROTECH
200 Valley Rd Ste 204 (07856-1320)
PHONE.................................973 770-0574
EMP: 5
SALES (corp-wide): 38.1MM **Privately Held**
SIC: 3489 Mfg Ordnance/Accessories

HQ: Kongsberg Protech Systems Usa Corporation
210 Industrial Park Rd # 105
Johnstown PA 15904
814 269-5700

(G-6715)
MARS RETAIL GROUP INC
Also Called: Ethel M Chocolates
400 Valley Rd Ste 204 (07856-2316)
PHONE.................................973 398-2078
Lowell Barry, *Branch Mgr*
EMP: 34
SALES (corp-wide): 34.2B **Privately Held**
SIC: 2066 Chocolate & cocoa products
HQ: Mars Retail Group, Inc.
2 Cactus Garden Dr
Henderson NV 89014
702 458-8864

(G-6716)
MICHELLE STE WINE ESTATES LTD
Also Called: Stimson Lane Wine & Spirit
200 Valley Rd Ste 200 # 200 (07856-1320)
PHONE.................................973 770-8100
Terry Adams, *Division Mgr*
Anthony Torrente, *COO*
Frank Genovese, *Vice Pres*
EMP: 5
SALES (corp-wide): 25.3B **Publicly Held**
WEB: www.columbia-crest.com
SIC: 2084 Wines
HQ: Michelle Ste Wine Estates Ltd
14111 Ne 145th St
Woodinville WA 98072
425 488-1133

(G-6717)
PDS PRCLNICAL DATA SYSTEMS INC
100 Valley Rd Ste 204 (07856-1324)
PHONE.................................973 398-2800
Sayed Badrawi, *CEO*
Maro Schuster, *Exec VP*
Jeffrey Oswald, *Opers Staff*
Michael Wasko, *Manager*
Carolyn Peters, *Administration*
EMP: 13
SQ FT: 4,000
SALES (est): 2.9MM
SALES (corp-wide): 2.5MM **Privately Held**
SIC: 7372 7371 8243 7374 Business oriented computer software; computer software development & applications; software training, computer; data processing & preparation; computer processing services; computer related maintenance services
PA: Pds Pathology Data Systems Ag
Durrenhubelstrasse 9
Pratteln BL 4133
613 778-777

(G-6718)
PRC LASER CORPORATION
111 Howard Blvd Ste 170 (07856-1315)
PHONE.................................973 347-0100
Walter Wilson, *President*
Guy Bauwens, *President*
Nancy Mc Namara, *Vice Pres*
William Ondish, *Opers Mgr*
Kelvin Tan, *Electrical Engi*
◆ EMP: 32
SALES: 8.7MM **Privately Held**
WEB: www.prclaser.com
SIC: 3699 Laser systems & equipment

(G-6719)
STORIS INC (PA)
Also Called: Storis Management Systems
400 Valley Rd Ste 302 (07856-2316)
PHONE.................................888 478-6747
Donald J Surdoval, *CEO*
Doug Culmone, *President*
Ryan Lindsley, *Business Mgr*
Lindsey Scapicchio, *Business Mgr*
Greg Strosnider, *Business Mgr*
EMP: 107
SQ FT: 24,000

SALES (est): 18.5MM **Privately Held**
WEB: www.storis.com
SIC: 3629 7372 5719 Battery chargers, rectifying or nonrotating; application computer software; bedding (sheets, blankets, spreads & pillows)

Mount Ephraim
Camden County

(G-6720)
BARBS HARLEY-DAVIDSON
Also Called: Harley Davidson Camden County
926 Black Horse Pike (08059-1815)
PHONE.................................856 456-4141
Barbara Boroweic, *President*
Mary Duffy, *General Mgr*
Jay Jaconetti, *Business Mgr*
Tom Beatty, *Manager*
Keith Rouleau, *Art Dir*
EMP: 24
SQ FT: 12,500
SALES (est): 6.6MM **Privately Held**
WEB: www.harleydavidsoncc.com
SIC: 5571 7699 3751 3519 Motorcycle dealers; motorcycle parts & accessories; motorcycle repair service; motorcycle accessories; diesel, semi-diesel or duel-fuel engines, including marine

(G-6721)
SELECT MACHINE TOOL INC
19 Thompson Ave (08059-2108)
PHONE.................................856 933-2100
Jay Brad, *President*
Margaret Brad, *Treasurer*
EMP: 9
SQ FT: 1,500
SALES (est): 600K **Privately Held**
SIC: 3599 Machine shop, jobbing & repair

(G-6722)
WINDOW FACTORY INC
603 N Black Horse Pike (08059-1319)
PHONE.................................856 546-5050
John D Merryfield, *President*
Joyce Merryfield, *Treasurer*
EMP: 25
SQ FT: 20,000
SALES (est): 3.3MM **Privately Held**
WEB: www.windowfactory.com
SIC: 2431 5211 1761 3442 Windows & window parts & trim, wood; door & window products; siding contractor; metal doors, sash & trim

Mount Holly
Burlington County

(G-6723)
AMCOR FLEXIBLES INC
Also Called: Amcor Flexibles Mount Holly
220 Shreve St (08060-2220)
PHONE.................................609 267-5900
Jim Lacanna, *Branch Mgr*
Nick Perez, *Manager*
EMP: 32 **Privately Held**
SIC: 3081 5199 3497 3353 Packing materials, plastic sheet; packaging materials; metal foil & leaf; aluminum sheet, plate & foil; packaging paper & plastics film, coated & laminated
HQ: Amcor Flexibles Llc
2150 E Lake Cook Rd
Buffalo Grove IL 60089
224 313-7000

(G-6724)
DEANS GRAPHICS
16 Mill St Ste D (08060-2154)
P.O. Box 809 (08060-0809)
PHONE.................................609 261-8817
Mark Deans, *Owner*
EMP: 5
SQ FT: 3,500
SALES (est): 526.5K **Privately Held**
WEB: www.deansgraphics.com
SIC: 2759 Screen printing

(G-6725)
EATON CORPORATION
96 Stemmers Ln (08060-5652)
PHONE.................................609 835-4230
Alexander Cutler, *CEO*
Douglas Sutton, *Engineer*
Philip Acone, *Sales Staff*
EMP: 40
SALES (est): 3MM **Privately Held**
WEB: www.eatoncutlerhammer.com
SIC: 3999 Barber & beauty shop equipment

(G-6726)
ELECTRONIC PARTS SPECIALTY CO
10 Eagle Ave Ste 1100 (08060-1602)
PHONE.................................609 267-0055
EMP: 9 EST: 1945
SQ FT: 30,000
SALES (est): 730K **Privately Held**
SIC: 3469 Mfg Metal Stampings

(G-6727)
EPICORE NETWORKS USA INC
4 Lina Ln (08060-5414)
PHONE.................................609 267-9118
William P Long, *President*
EMP: 20
SQ FT: 11,990
SALES: 11MM
SALES (corp-wide): 637K **Privately Held**
WEB: www.epicorebionet.com
SIC: 2077 2836 8731 Animal & marine fats & oils; biological products, except diagnostic; biotechnical research, commercial
PA: Epicore Bionetworks Inc
150 6 Ave Sw
Calgary AB T2P 3

(G-6728)
GLOBAL SPCLTY PRODUCTS-USA INC
10 Eagle Ave Ste 500 (08060-1601)
PHONE.................................609 518-7577
Davood Faghani, *President*
Cameron Faghani, *Natl Sales Mgr*
◆ EMP: 10
SQ FT: 15,000
SALES: 500K **Privately Held**
WEB: www.gsp-usa-inc.com
SIC: 5169 2842 Chemical additives; specialty cleaning, polishes & sanitation goods

(G-6729)
HAINESPORT TOOL & MACHINE CO
Also Called: Haineport Tools & Maintenance
1924 Ark Rd (08060)
PHONE.................................609 261-0016
Gerhard Zwick, *President*
EMP: 18 EST: 1950
SQ FT: 8,000
SALES (est): 2.7MM **Privately Held**
SIC: 3545 Machine tool attachments & accessories

(G-6730)
HIGH GATE CORP
Also Called: Mech-Tronics
100 Campus Dr (08060-9664)
PHONE.................................609 267-0680
Peter Reed, *President*
EMP: 10
SQ FT: 1,500
SALES (est): 1.6MM **Privately Held**
SIC: 3612 Specialty transformers

(G-6731)
INNOVATIVE METAL SOLUTIONS LLC
10 Eagle Ave Ste 400b (08060-1649)
PHONE.................................609 784-8406
Kevin Hocking,
EMP: 4
SQ FT: 1,800
SALES (est): 649.8K **Privately Held**
SIC: 3441 Fabricated structural metal

(G-6732)
METAL SPECIALTIES NEW JERSEY
1 Compass Ln (08060-5417)
PHONE...............................609 261-9277
Michael Ems, *Principal*
EMP: 8
SALES (est): 1.2MM **Privately Held**
SIC: 3444 7539 Sheet metal specialties, not stamped; machine shop, automotive

(G-6733)
R B BADAT LANDSCAPING INC
507 Woodlane Rd (08060-3808)
PHONE...............................609 877-7138
Robert B Badat, *President*
EMP: 5
SALES (est): 287K **Privately Held**
SIC: 1429 5032 Igneous rock, crushed & broken-quarrying; stone, crushed or broken

(G-6734)
R BARON ASSOCIATES INC
Also Called: Orthoessentials
10 Lippincott Ln Ste 6 (08060-1603)
PHONE...............................215 396-3803
Ronald Baron, *President*
EMP: 7
SALES: 750K **Privately Held**
SIC: 3843 Orthodontic appliances

(G-6735)
VERTIS INC
80 Stemmers Ln (08060-5652)
PHONE...............................215 781-1668
Steve King, *Manager*
EMP: 100
SALES (est): 10.6MM **Privately Held**
SIC: 2759 Commercial printing

Mount Laurel
Burlington County

(G-6736)
3 H TECHNOLOGY INSTITUTE LLC
Also Called: 3 Hti
3000 Atrium Way Ste 296 (08054-3928)
PHONE...............................866 624-3484
Garry Hossman, *Mng Member*
Vivek Madangeri, *Technical Staff*
EMP: 25
SALES (est): 360.4K **Privately Held**
SIC: 3559 5045 Plastics working machinery; computer software

(G-6737)
AMERICAN HARVEST BAKING CO INC (PA)
Also Called: Ahb Foods
823 E Gate Dr Ste 3 (08054-1202)
PHONE...............................856 642-9955
Jay Roseman, *President*
Barry Kratchman, *Vice Pres*
Betty Ann Peard, *Controller*
Betty Peard, *Controller*
EMP: 30
SALES (est): 13.7MM **Privately Held**
SIC: 2051 Bakery: wholesale or wholesale/retail combined

(G-6738)
AUS INC (PA)
Also Called: Valuation Services Group
155 Gaither Dr Ste A (08054-1753)
PHONE...............................856 234-9200
John L Ringwood, *President*
Jack Ringwood, *Principal*
Stuart G McDaniel, *Senior VP*
Pauline Ahern, *Vice Pres*
Barbara Marshall, *Vice Pres*
EMP: 5 EST: 1967
SALES (est): 60.8MM **Privately Held**
WEB: www.ingnews.com
SIC: 8742 2711 2752 8249 Business consultant; newspapers, publishing & printing; lithographing on metal; aviation school; janitorial service, contract basis; market analysis or research

(G-6739)
BAE SYSTEMS TECH SOL SRVC INC
Also Called: Technology Solutions Sector
8000 Midlantic Dr 700n (08054-1549)
PHONE...............................856 638-1003
John Bellanich, *Engineer*
Maurice Collins, *Manager*
EMP: 50
SALES (corp-wide): 21.6B **Privately Held**
SIC: 3812 Search & navigation equipment
HQ: Bae Systems Technology Solutions & Services Inc.
520 Gaither Rd
Rockville MD 20850
703 847-5820

(G-6740)
BASYS INC
1200 S Church St Ste 7 (08054-2936)
PHONE...............................732 616-5276
Jeffrey Marino, *President*
EMP: 3 EST: 2009
SALES: 1MM **Privately Held**
SIC: 7372 Prepackaged software

(G-6741)
BELLE PRINTING GROUP LLC (PA)
3838 Church Rd (08054-1106)
PHONE...............................856 235-5151
William C Shanley IV, *Mng Member*
Thomas R Shanley,
William C Shanley III,
EMP: 7
SALES (est): 5.7MM **Privately Held**
SIC: 3082 2759 8741 Unsupported plastics profile shapes; commercial printing; management services

(G-6742)
BLADES LANDSCAPING INC
Also Called: Blades Ldscpg Lawn Maint & Ir
2028 Briggs Rd (08054-4607)
P.O. Box 729, Marlton (08053-0729)
PHONE...............................856 779-7665
Keith Haitz, *President*
Joseph Butkus, *Admin Sec*
EMP: 13
SALES (est): 470K **Privately Held**
SIC: 0781 4959 0782 3271 Landscape services; snowplowing; lawn services; blocks, concrete; landscape or retaining wall

(G-6743)
BRIGHT LIGHTS USA INC (PA)
Also Called: Blusa Defense Manufacturing
11000 Midlantic Dr (08054-1566)
PHONE...............................856 546-5656
Daniel ARI Farber, *President*
Jennifer Telaar, *Purch Agent*
Carolyn Lohkemper, *Controller*
Sandy Brown, *Technology*
Debra Ginsberg, *Assistant*
▲ EMP: 55
SALES: 10MM **Privately Held**
WEB: www.brightlightsusa.com
SIC: 3728 Aircraft parts & equipment; aircraft body & wing assemblies & parts

(G-6744)
BSRM INC
691 Cornwallis Dr (08054-3216)
PHONE...............................888 509-0668
Bruce Rotkowitz, *President*
Matt Rotkowitz, *Vice Pres*
Russell Rotkowitz, *Vice Pres*
Scott Rotkowitz, *Vice Pres*
EMP: 4
SALES (est): 540.5K **Privately Held**
SIC: 3069 Reclaimed rubber (reworked by manufacturing processes)

(G-6745)
BURLINGTON DESIGN CENTER INC
3019 Marne Hwy (08054-2038)
PHONE...............................856 778-7772
Stephen F Tremain, *President*
Michael Keane, *Vice Pres*
John Keane, *Admin Sec*
EMP: 12
SQ FT: 3,300

SALES: 1.2MM **Privately Held**
SIC: 2679 Wallpaper

(G-6746)
CARILETHA COMPANY INC
2206 Sedgefield Dr (08054-1862)
PHONE...............................609 222-3055
Joseph M Doyle, *President*
EMP: 10
SALES (est): 261K **Privately Held**
SIC: 2741 Miscellaneous publishing

(G-6747)
CINCHSEAL ASSOCIATES INC
23b Roland Ave (08054-1011)
PHONE...............................856 662-5162
David M Pitchko, *President*
▲ EMP: 22
SQ FT: 10,000
SALES: 4MM **Privately Held**
WEB: www.cinchseal.com
SIC: 3053 Gaskets & sealing devices

(G-6748)
CLOVER GARDEN CTR LTD LBLTY CO
1017 S Church St (08054-2507)
PHONE...............................856 235-4625
Paula Brandimarte, *President*
Thal Le, *Partner*
EMP: 8 EST: 1947
SALES (est): 440.8K **Privately Held**
SIC: 5992 3999 0781 Flowers, fresh; plants, artificial & preserved; landscape planning services

(G-6749)
CONOPCO INC
305 Fellowship Rd Ste 114 (08054-1232)
PHONE...............................856 722-1664
Brentt Vandebovenkamp, *Manager*
EMP: 25
SALES (corp-wide): 58.3B **Privately Held**
SIC: 2844 Toilet preparations
HQ: Conopco, Inc.
700 Sylvan Ave
Englewood Cliffs NJ 07632
201 894-7760

(G-6750)
CUTMARK INC
102 Gaither Dr Ste 2 (08054-1714)
PHONE...............................856 234-3428
George Gibson, *President*
EMP: 4
SQ FT: 2,000
SALES (est): 560.4K **Privately Held**
WEB: www.cutmark.com
SIC: 3444 3599 Sheet metalwork; machine shop, jobbing & repair

(G-6751)
D & N SPORTING GOODS INC
Also Called: Sprint Screening
109 W Park Dr (08054-1260)
PHONE...............................856 778-0055
Dennis Boardman, *President*
Karin Barlow, *Vice Pres*
EMP: 18 EST: 1980
SQ FT: 28,000
SALES (est): 1.5MM **Privately Held**
SIC: 5941 7336 3993 5999 Sporting goods & bicycle shops; silk screen design; signs & advertising specialties; trophies & plaques

(G-6752)
DEL-VAL FOOD INGREDIENTS INC
3001 Irwin Rd Ste A (08054-4636)
PHONE...............................856 778-6623
George Shapirl, *President*
Thomas Clarkson, *Vice Pres*
▲ EMP: 15
SALES (est): 15.2MM **Privately Held**
SIC: 5141 2087 Groceries, general line; powders, flavoring (except drink)

(G-6753)
DELAWARE TECHNOLOGIES INC
641 Mount Laurel Rd (08054-9555)
PHONE...............................856 234-7692
Donald Dawson, *President*
Almeta Dawson, *Treasurer*

EMP: 10
SALES: 500K **Privately Held**
WEB: www.delawaretechnologies.com
SIC: 3821 3823 7629 Sample preparation apparatus; water quality monitoring & control systems; electronic equipment repair

(G-6754)
E & T PLASTIC MFG CO INC
824 E Gate Dr Ste E (08054-1254)
PHONE...............................856 787-0900
Bernie Delaney, *Human Res Mgr*
EMP: 8
SALES (corp-wide): 75MM **Privately Held**
SIC: 3089 Extruded finished plastic products; plastic processing
PA: E & T Plastic Manufacturing Co., Inc.
4545 37th St
Long Island City NY 11101
718 729-6226

(G-6755)
E & T SALES CO INC
824 E Gate Dr Ste E (08054-1254)
PHONE...............................856 787-0900
Ed Godshok, *Manager*
EMP: 9
SALES (corp-wide): 31.4MM **Privately Held**
SIC: 3089 5162 Plastic containers, except foam; plastics sheets & rods
PA: E. & T. Sales Co., Inc.
4545 37th St
Long Island City NY 11101
718 729-6226

(G-6756)
E BERKOWITZ & CO INC
Also Called: Security Systems Unlimited
520 Fellowship Rd B202 (08054-3407)
PHONE...............................856 608-1118
Eric Berkowitz, *President*
EMP: 7
SQ FT: 3,200
SALES (est): 680K **Privately Held**
SIC: 1731 2541 Sound equipment specialization; telephone & telephone equipment installation; fire detection & burglar alarm systems specialization; closed circuit television installation; store fixtures, wood

(G-6757)
E GROUP INC
129 Gaither Dr Ste M (08054-1708)
PHONE...............................856 320-9688
Wade Xu, *President*
EMP: 8
SQ FT: 18,000
SALES: 10MM **Privately Held**
SIC: 4812 3691 Radio telephone communication; storage batteries

(G-6758)
E LOC TOTAL LOGISTICS LLC
144 Canterbury Rd (08054-1416)
P.O. Box 1521 (08054-7521)
PHONE...............................609 685-6117
Robert Gittens, *Mng Member*
EMP: 6
SALES (est): 390.3K **Privately Held**
SIC: 3715 Truck trailers

(G-6759)
FAMOSA NORTH AMERICA INC
3000 Atrium Way Ste 101 (08054-3910)
PHONE...............................856 206-9844
Jose Dela Gandara, *CEO*
Ed Young, *President*
▲ EMP: 7
SQ FT: 2,200
SALES (est): 1MM **Privately Held**
SIC: 3944 Games, toys & children's vehicles

(G-6760)
FEDEX OFFICE & PRINT SVCS INC
1211 Route 73 Ste E (08054-2236)
PHONE...............................856 273-5959
Craig Weller, *Manager*
Jennifer Price, *Administration*
EMP: 15

SALES (corp-wide): 69.6B **Publicly Held**
WEB: www.kinkos.com
SIC: 7334 2791 2789 Photocopying & duplicating services; typesetting; bookbinding & related work
HQ: Fedex Office And Print Services, Inc.
7900 Legacy Dr
Plano TX 75024
800 463-3339

(G-6761)
FOOD SCIENCES CORP (PA)
Also Called: Robard
821 E Gate Dr (08054-1239)
PHONE...................................856 778-4192
Robert Schwartz, *President*
Jay Satinsky, *Business Mgr*
Steven Kaye, *Opers Mgr*
Scott Hoffman, *Maint Spvr*
Mary Hunsicker, *Purch Mgr*
EMP: 149
SQ FT: 58,000
SALES (est): 24MM **Privately Held**
WEB: www.foodsciences.com
SIC: 2023 Dietary supplements, dairy & non-dairy based

(G-6762)
FOX STEEL PRODUCTS LLC
8 Fox Run Dr (08054-3255)
PHONE...................................856 778-4661
Rose M Burns, *President*
EMP: 4
SALES (est): 280K **Privately Held**
SIC: 3312 3317 3316 3498 Blast furnaces & steel mills; steel pipe & tubes; cold finishing of steel shapes; fabricated pipe & fittings

(G-6763)
GLENBURNIE FEED & GRAIN
87 Chapel Hill Rd (08054-8510)
PHONE...................................856 986-8128
Charles E Connell Jr, *President*
David Estey, *Principal*
Marion J Connell, *Corp Secy*
EMP: 2
SALES: 1MM **Privately Held**
WEB: www.glenburniefeedandgrain.com
SIC: 5191 2048 Feed; prepared feeds

(G-6764)
GRAY HAIR SOFTWARE INC
124 Gaither Dr Ste 160 (08054-1719)
PHONE...................................866 507-9999
Cameron Bellamy, *President*
Joseph Carlantonio, *Project Mgr*
Scott Kushner, *CFO*
Valerie Capasso, *Accounts Mgr*
Adria Curcio, *Accounts Mgr*
EMP: 42
SQ FT: 3,000
SALES (est): 8.1MM **Privately Held**
WEB: www.grayhairsoftware.com
SIC: 7372 Business oriented computer software

(G-6765)
HOLMAN ENTERPRISES INC
Also Called: Holman Jaguar and Infinite
1311 Route 73 (08054-2215)
PHONE...................................609 383-6100
Ann Williams, *Manager*
EMP: 35
SALES (corp-wide): 1.6B **Privately Held**
WEB: www.holmanenterprises.com
SIC: 5511 7538 7532 7515 Automobiles, new & used; general automotive repair shops; top & body repair & paint shops; passenger car leasing; motor vehicle parts & accessories
PA: Holman Enterprises Inc.
244 E Kings Hwy
Maple Shade NJ 08052
856 663-5200

(G-6766)
INGERSOLL-RAND COMPANY
3001 Irwin Rd (08054-4636)
PHONE...................................856 793-7000
Tim Lowery, *Branch Mgr*
EMP: 50 **Privately Held**
WEB: www.ingersoll-rand.com

SIC: 3561 3429 3546 3563 Pumps & pumping equipment; furniture builders' & other household hardware; keys, locks & related hardware; power-driven hand-tools; air & gas compressors including vacuum pumps; winches; roller bearings & parts
HQ: Ingersoll-Rand Company
800 Beaty St Ste B
Davidson NC 28036
704 655-4000

(G-6767)
INJECTION WORKS INC
104 Gaither Dr (08054-1702)
PHONE...................................856 802-6444
Christopher A Rapacki, *President*
Irene Connolly, *General Mgr*
Robert Weiss, *General Mgr*
Dan Ferrante, *Opers Mgr*
Thomas O Kruse, *Treasurer*
▲ EMP: 35
SQ FT: 46,000
SALES (est): 7.1MM **Privately Held**
WEB: www.injectionworks.com
SIC: 3089 Injection molding of plastics

(G-6768)
INSTITUTE FOR RESPNSBLE ONLINE
82 Hillside Ln (08054-4517)
P.O. Box 1131 (08054-7131)
PHONE...................................856 722-1048
Richard Guerry, *Exec Dir*
Jacqueline Guerry,
EMP: 5
SALES (est): 489.3K **Privately Held**
SIC: 3669 Communications equipment

(G-6769)
INTERNTNAL INGRDENT SLTONS INC
3001 Irwin Rd Ste A (08054-4636)
PHONE...................................856 778-6623
George Shapirl, *President*
EMP: 25
SALES: 3MM **Privately Held**
SIC: 2099 5149 Seasonings & spices; spices, including grinding; spices & seasonings

(G-6770)
INTEST CORPORATION (PA)
804 E Gate Dr Ste 200 (08054-1209)
PHONE...................................856 505-8800
Joseph W Dews IV, *Ch of Bd*
James Pelrin, *President*
Dave Dao, *Engineer*
Richard Powell, *Engineer*
Chris West, *Engineer*
▲ EMP: 3
SQ FT: 54,897
SALES: 78.5MM **Publicly Held**
WEB: www.intest.com
SIC: 3825 3823 Digital test equipment, electronic & electrical circuits; semiconductor test equipment; temperature measurement instruments, industrial

(G-6771)
INVENTEK COLLOIDAL CLRS LLC
106 Gaither Dr (08054-1702)
PHONE...................................856 206-0058
Yasmin Andrecola,
Paul Andrecola,
EMP: 45
SQ FT: 25,000
SALES (est): 7.9MM **Privately Held**
SIC: 2841 Soap & other detergents

(G-6772)
J K P DONUTS INC
Also Called: Dunkin' Donuts
807 Route 73 (08054-1165)
PHONE...................................856 234-9844
Peter Amin, *President*
Vipul Patel, *Vice Pres*
Mukesh Patel, *Admin Sec*
EMP: 6
SALES (est): 270K **Privately Held**
SIC: 5461 2051 Doughnuts; doughnuts, except frozen

(G-6773)
JERSEY TEMPERED GLASS INC
2035 Briggs Rd (08054-4608)
P.O. Box 205 (08054-0205)
PHONE...................................856 273-8700
Nicholas Concio, *President*
EMP: 45
SQ FT: 48,000
SALES (est): 9.6MM **Privately Held**
WEB: www.jerseytemperedglass.com
SIC: 3211 3231 Tempered glass; products of purchased glass

(G-6774)
KUBIK MALTBIE INC
7000 Commerce Pkwy Ste C (08054-2288)
PHONE...................................856 234-0052
Sam Kohn, *CEO*
Chuck Maltbie, *President*
George Mayer, *President*
Gary Brooks, *Vice Pres*
A J Higgs, *Vice Pres*
◆ EMP: 40 EST: 1962
SQ FT: 36,000
SALES (est): 7.6MM
SALES (corp-wide): 66.1MM **Privately Held**
WEB: www.maltbie.com
SIC: 3993 2541 3231 Displays, paint process; displays & cutouts, window & lobby; wood partitions & fixtures; products of purchased glass
PA: Kubik Inc
1680 Mattawa Ave
Mississauga ON L4X 3
905 272-2818

(G-6775)
LINGO INC
Also Called: Acme Flagpole Division
10 Opal Ct (08054-3062)
PHONE...................................856 273-6594
John E Lingo Jr, *President*
Gail P Lingo, *Admin Sec*
EMP: 11
SQ FT: 12,000
SALES: 890K **Privately Held**
SIC: 3441 3446 Tower sections, radio & television transmission; flagpoles, metal

(G-6776)
LOCKHEED MARTIN CORPORATION
750 Centerton Rd (08054-1625)
PHONE...................................856 234-1261
Andrew Takacs, *Engineer*
EMP: 1265 **Publicly Held**
SIC: 3812 Aircraft/aerospace flight instruments & guidance systems
PA: Lockheed Martin Corporation
6801 Rockledge Dr
Bethesda MD 20817

(G-6777)
LOCKHEED MARTIN CORPORATION
532 Fellowship Rd (08054-3416)
P.O. Box 1027, Moorestown (08057-0927)
PHONE...................................856 787-3104
EMP: 435 **Publicly Held**
WEB: www.lockheedmartin.com
SIC: 3721 3761 3663 3764 Research & development on aircraft by the manufacturer; guided missiles & space vehicles, research & development; airborne radio communications equipment; guided missile & space vehicle engines, research & devel.; space vehicle guidance systems & equipment
PA: Lockheed Martin Corporation
6801 Rockledge Dr
Bethesda MD 20817

(G-6778)
LOCKHEED MARTIN CORPORATION
700 E Gate Dr Ste 200 (08054-3803)
PHONE...................................856 727-5800
Anthony Demarco, *President*
EMP: 5 **Publicly Held**
WEB: www.lockheedmartin.com
SIC: 3812 Search & navigation equipment
PA: Lockheed Martin Corporation
6801 Rockledge Dr
Bethesda MD 20817

(G-6779)
LTS NJ INC
109 W Park Dr Unit C (08054-1260)
PHONE...................................856 780-9888
Wing Pang, *Principal*
Kelly Breitton, *Accounts Mgr*
Sarah Dang, *Accounts Mgr*
Olivia Villari, *Accounts Mgr*
Nancy WEI, *Accounts Mgr*
EMP: 7
SALES: 1.4MM **Privately Held**
SIC: 3699 Security control equipment & systems

(G-6780)
MANNA GROUP LLC
137 Gaither Dr Ste F (08054-1711)
PHONE...................................856 881-7650
Dennis McCullough,
EMP: 10 EST: 2016
SALES (est): 215.9K **Privately Held**
SIC: 7379 2741 ;

(G-6781)
MDR DIAGNOSTICS LLC
199 6th Ave Ste C (08054-9749)
PHONE...................................609 396-0021
David Katz,
EMP: 20
SALES (est): 2.5MM **Privately Held**
SIC: 3829 Medical diagnostic systems, nuclear

(G-6782)
METROLOGIC INSTRUMENTS INC (HQ)
Also Called: Honeywell
534 Fellowship Rd (08054-3405)
PHONE...................................856 228-8100
Benny A Noens, *CEO*
Dipanjan Deb, *President*
Joseph Sawitsky, *Exec VP*
Mark Schmidt, *Exec VP*
Gregory Dinoia, *Vice Pres*
▲ EMP: 150
SQ FT: 116,000
SALES (est): 107.4MM
SALES (corp-wide): 41.8B **Publicly Held**
WEB: www.metrologic.com
SIC: 3577 3699 Magnetic ink & optical scanning devices; optical scanning devices; laser systems & equipment
PA: Honeywell International Inc.
300 S Tryon St
Charlotte NC 28202
973 455-2000

(G-6783)
MJ CORPORATE SALES INC
109 W Park Dr Unit A (08054-1260)
PHONE...................................856 778-0055
Robert Madosky, *Principal*
Toni Masciantonio, *Marketing Staff*
Penny Petty, *Manager*
Tim Trotman, *Manager*
▲ EMP: 25
SQ FT: 28,000
SALES (est): 4.3MM **Privately Held**
WEB: www.mjsales.com
SIC: 2759 5947 Screen printing; gifts & novelties

(G-6784)
MNEMONICS INC
102 Gaither Dr Ste 4 (08054-1714)
P.O. Box 877 (08054-0877)
PHONE...................................856 234-0970
Michael Negin, *President*
▼ EMP: 4
SQ FT: 1,600
SALES (est): 651.9K **Privately Held**
SIC: 3826 Laser scientific & engineering instruments

(G-6785)
MONARCH ART PLASTICS CO LLC
Also Called: Monarch Plastics
3838 Church Rd (08054-1106)
PHONE...................................856 235-5151
William C Shanley, *CEO*
Kimberton E Messner, *CFO*
Alex Marsh, *Sales Staff*
EMP: 25
SQ FT: 26,500

SALES (est): 4.5MM
SALES (corp-wide): 5.7MM **Privately Held**
WEB: www.monarchplastics.com
SIC: 2759 Screen printing
PA: Belle Printing Group Llc
　　3838 Church Rd
　　Mount Laurel NJ 08054
　　856 235-5151

(G-6786)
NETQUEST CORPORATION
523 Fellowship Rd Ste 205 (08054-3434)
PHONE..........................856 866-0505
Slobodan Pocek, *President*
Jesse Price, *Principal*
Ron Lill, *Engineer*
John Pye, *Design Engr*
Dan Pocek, *CFO*
EMP: 20
SQ FT: 10,000
SALES (est): 3.6MM **Privately Held**
WEB: www.netquestcorp.com
SIC: 3669 7371 3829 3823 Intercommunication systems, electric; custom computer programming services; measuring & controlling devices; industrial instrmnts msrmnt display/control process variable

(G-6787)
PAI SERVICES LLC
Also Called: Sage Payroll Services
305 Fellowship Rd Ste 300 (08054-1232)
PHONE..........................856 231-4667
William Scott,
EMP: 130
SALES (corp-wide): 2.3B **Privately Held**
SIC: 7371 7372 Computer software development & applications; business oriented computer software
HQ: Pai Services, Llc
　　305 Fellowship Rd Ste 300
　　Mount Laurel NJ

(G-6788)
PATIENTSTAR LLC
1000 Bishops Gate Blvd # 200 (08054-4634)
PHONE..........................856 722-0808
Lucine A King, *President*
Laureen Gonnella, *Opers Staff*
Hien Tran, *Sr Software Eng*
Kenneth S King,
EMP: 11
SALES (est): 1.1MM **Privately Held**
SIC: 7372 Business oriented computer software

(G-6789)
PENNY PLATE LLC (DH)
1400 Horizon Way Ste 300 (08054)
PHONE..........................856 429-7583
Paul Cobb, *President*
George Buff III, *Exec VP*
John Charles Buff, *Vice Pres*
▲ EMP: 75 EST: 1949
SQ FT: 40,000
SALES (est): 103.9MM
SALES (corp-wide): 294.6MM **Privately Held**
WEB: www.pennyplate.com
SIC: 3411 Food containers, metal
HQ: Replanet, Llc
　　800 N Haven Ave Ste 120
　　Ontario CA 91764
　　951 520-1700

(G-6790)
PLCS LLC
102 Gaither Dr Ste 1 (08054-1754)
PHONE..........................856 722-1333
David Payne, *President*
Kathleen Hatch, *CFO*
Richard Venesco, *Sales Mgr*
◆ EMP: 22
SQ FT: 14,000
SALES: 9.8MM **Privately Held**
WEB: www.plcsusa.com
SIC: 2891 5084 Sealing compounds for pipe threads or joints; industrial machinery & equipment

(G-6791)
PMC GROUP INC (PA)
1288 Route 73 Ste 401 (08054-2237)
PHONE..........................856 533-1866

Paritosh M Chakrabarti, *CEO*
Raj Chakrabarti, *Vice Pres*
Charles Yacomeni, *Vice Pres*
Richard Manthei, *Plant Mgr*
Terry Stapleton, *Opers Mgr*
◆ EMP: 15
SQ FT: 10,000
SALES (est): 297.9MM **Privately Held**
SIC: 3089 2812 Injection molding of plastics; plastic hardware & building products; alkalies & chlorine

(G-6792)
POLYMER PRODUCTS COMPANY INC
Also Called: PMC Group Polymer Products
1288 Route 73 Ste 401 (08054-2237)
P.O. Box 98, Stockertown PA (18083-0098)
PHONE..........................856 533-1866
Paritosh M Chakrabarti, *CEO*
Debtosh Chakrabarti, *President*
David Reinhart, *VP Opers*
Carroll Gower, *Accountant*
▲ EMP: 50
SQ FT: 80,000
SALES (est): 13.3MM **Privately Held**
SIC: 2819 Industrial inorganic chemicals
PA: Pmc Group, Inc.
　　1288 Route 73 Ste 401
　　Mount Laurel NJ 08054

(G-6793)
POLYTECHNIC INDUSTRIES INC
14 Roland Ave (08054-1012)
PHONE..........................856 235-6550
Alvin C Lanson, *President*
Steven Lanson, *Vice Pres*
Lori Miller, *Shareholder*
Eric Miller, *Admin Sec*
EMP: 10
SQ FT: 24,000
SALES (est): 2MM **Privately Held**
WEB: www.polytechnicind.com
SIC: 3728 Military aircraft equipment & armament

(G-6794)
PPG INDUSTRIES INC
823 E Gate Dr Ste 4 (08054-1202)
PHONE..........................856 273-7870
Amy Lee, *Branch Mgr*
EMP: 23
SALES (corp-wide): 15.3B **Publicly Held**
SIC: 2851 Shellac (protective coating)
PA: Ppg Industries, Inc.
　　1 Ppg Pl
　　Pittsburgh PA 15272
　　412 434-3131

(G-6795)
PRECISION PRINTING GROUP INC
606 Stamford Dr # 606 (08054-3515)
PHONE..........................856 753-0900
Joseph Cartafalsn, *President*
EMP: 45
SQ FT: 52,000
SALES (est): 10.3MM **Privately Held**
WEB: www.hamiltonpress.com
SIC: 2752 Commercial printing, lithographic

(G-6796)
PRODUCTIVE PLASTICS INC (PA)
103 W Park Dr (08054-1278)
PHONE..........................856 778-4300
Harold Gilham, *President*
John Zerillo, *Vice Pres*
Don Stiger, *Project Mgr*
Todd Mitchell, *VP Finance*
Don Steiger, *Sales Staff*
EMP: 78
SQ FT: 24,000
SALES (est): 17MM **Privately Held**
SIC: 3089 3083 3081 Thermoformed finished plastic products; laminated plastics plate & sheet; unsupported plastics film & sheet

(G-6797)
QAD INC
10000 Midlantic Dr 100w (08054-1542)
PHONE..........................856 273-1717
Jane Barrett, *Sales Staff*

Roland Desilets, *Branch Mgr*
George Bean, *Manager*
Albert Canez, *Technology*
Andy McGoff, *Sr Ntwrk Engine*
EMP: 150
SALES (corp-wide): 333MM **Publicly Held**
WEB: www.qad.com
SIC: 7372 5045 Application computer software; computers, peripherals & software
PA: Qad Inc.
　　100 Innovation Pl
　　Santa Barbara CA 93108
　　805 566-6000

(G-6798)
QELLUS LLC
309 Fellowship Rd (08054-1234)
PHONE..........................856 761-6575
Ihsan Hall, *CEO*
Greg Hocamp, *COO*
Todd Burn, *CIO*
EMP: 8
SQ FT: 500
SALES: 590.9K **Privately Held**
SIC: 7373 7372 7379 5734 Systems software development services; business oriented computer software; computer related consulting services; software, business & non-game

(G-6799)
RAMBLEWOOD CLEANERS INC (PA)
Also Called: Rumblewood Cleaners
1155 Route 73 Ste B (08054-2352)
PHONE..........................856 235-6051
Sung Kim, *President*
Fung Oak Kim, *President*
EMP: 4
SQ FT: 2,000
SALES: 200K **Privately Held**
SIC: 2842 Drycleaning preparations

(G-6800)
RHYTHMEDIX LLC
Also Called: Rmx
5000 Atrium Way Ste 1 (08054-3915)
PHONE..........................856 282-1080
Brian Pike, *Managing Prtnr*
Keith Gartland, *Vice Pres*
Ty McNeil, *Manager*
Dmitri Mezhevich, *CIO*
Kaye Bryson, *Administration*
▲ EMP: 6 EST: 2013
SQ FT: 13,000
SALES (est): 1MM **Privately Held**
SIC: 3845 Electromedical equipment

(G-6801)
S FRANKFORD & SONS INC
Also Called: Frankford Umbrellas
110 Gaither Dr Ste A (08054-1703)
PHONE..........................856 222-4134
Marc Kaufer, *Principal*
◆ EMP: 10 EST: 1898
SALES (est): 1.6MM **Privately Held**
WEB: www.umbrellasusa.com
SIC: 3999 5136 Garden umbrellas; umbrellas, men's & boys'

(G-6802)
SAGE SOFTWARE INC
305 Fellowship Rd Ste 300 (08054-1232)
PHONE..........................856 231-4667
Bryan Regan, *General Mgr*
EMP: 80
SALES (corp-wide): 2.3B **Privately Held**
SIC: 7372 8721 Prepackaged software; payroll accounting service
HQ: Sage Software, Inc.
　　271 17th St Nw Ste 1100
　　Atlanta GA 30363
　　866 996-7243

(G-6803)
SCIENTIFIX LLC
Also Called: Sfx Installations
520 Fellowship Rd E508 (08054-3417)
PHONE..........................856 780-5871
George F Lynch, *Mng Member*
Mike Simons, *Manager*
Brian Foresta,
▲ EMP: 8
SQ FT: 1,600

SALES (est): 2.1MM **Privately Held**
WEB: www.scientifix.net
SIC: 3821 Chemical laboratory apparatus

(G-6804)
SENSIGRAPHICS INC
105 W Park Dr (08054-1278)
PHONE..........................856 853-9100
Tony Ciccatelli, *Principal*
EMP: 6
SALES (est): 1.1MM **Privately Held**
WEB: www.sensigraphics.com
SIC: 3613 3679 Control panels, electric; electronic switches

(G-6805)
SFP SOFTWARE INC
162 Knotty Oak Dr (08054-2115)
PHONE..........................856 235-7778
Steven Pipe, *President*
Janeane Pipe, *Vice Pres*
EMP: 4 EST: 1997
SALES (est): 100K **Privately Held**
SIC: 7372 Prepackaged software

(G-6806)
SIEMENS INDUSTRY INC
Also Called: Siemens Fire Safety
2000 Crawford Pl Ste 300 (08054-3920)
PHONE..........................856 234-7666
Albert Melloni, *Manager*
EMP: 50
SALES (corp-wide): 95B **Privately Held**
WEB: www.sibt.com
SIC: 3822 5085 Air conditioning & refrigeration controls; industrial supplies
HQ: Siemens Industry, Inc.
　　1000 Deerfield Pkwy
　　Buffalo Grove IL 60089
　　847 215-1000

(G-6807)
SMITH ENTERPRISES
100 Hillside Ln (08054-4522)
PHONE..........................215 416-9881
Damian Smith, *Owner*
EMP: 4
SALES (est): 210K **Privately Held**
SIC: 2759 3993 Promotional printing; signs & advertising specialties

(G-6808)
SODASTREAM USA INC
136 Gaither Dr Ste 200 (08054-1725)
PHONE..........................856 755-3400
Daniel Birnbaum, *CEO*
Scott Guthrie, *President*
Jecka Glasman, *General Mgr*
Varda Shoham, *General Mgr*
Jack Thompson, *Senior VP*
▲ EMP: 72
SALES (est): 218.1MM
SALES (corp-wide): 154.6MM **Privately Held**
WEB: www.sodaclubusa.com
SIC: 2087 3585 Syrups, drink; soda fountain & beverage dispensing equipment & parts
PA: Sodastream International Ltd
　　1 Atirei Yeda
　　Kfar Saba 44643
　　397 623-23

(G-6809)
TELVUE CORPORATION (PA)
16000 Horizon Way Ste 100 (08054-4317)
PHONE..........................800 885-8886
Jesse Lerman, *President*
Paul Andrews, *Senior VP*
Ian Easter, *Engineer*
Henry Lisenbee, *Regl Sales Mgr*
Mark Steele, *CIO*
EMP: 26
SQ FT: 8,732
SALES (est): 6.8MM **Privately Held**
WEB: www.telvue.com
SIC: 3663 4813 Television broadcasting & communications equipment; studio equipment, radio & television broadcasting;

(G-6810)
UTAH INTERMEDIATE HOLDING CORP
1020 Briggs Rd (08054-4101)
PHONE..........................856 787-2700
Tom Gores, *CEO*

Marie Berdini, *Human Res Dir*
EMP: 203
SALES (est): 6.4MM **Privately Held**
SIC: 7372 7371 Business oriented computer software; software programming applications

(G-6811)
VILLA RADIOLOGY SYSTEMS LLC
124 Gaither Dr Ste 140 (08054-1712)
PHONE.................................203 262-8836
Walter F Schneider Sr, *Mng Member*
Claudio Portaluppi, *Manager*
▲ **EMP:** 7 EST: 2012
SALES (est): 879.3K **Privately Held**
SIC: 3844 Radiographic X-ray apparatus & tubes

(G-6812)
WHITTLE & MUTCH INC
712 Fellowship Rd (08054-1004)
PHONE.................................856 235-1165
John Mutch Jr, *President*
Samuel Mutch, *Vice Pres*
Richard Mutch, *Treasurer*
Peter Sauer, *Supervisor*
John Mutch III, *Admin Sec*
EMP: 14 EST: 1892
SQ FT: 20,000
SALES (est): 2.6MM **Privately Held**
WEB: www.wamiflavor.com
SIC: 2087 Extracts, flavoring

(G-6813)
WILLIAM SPENCER (PA)
Also Called: Spencer's
20 Lake Dr (08054-2077)
PHONE.................................856 235-1830
Valerie Houser, *President*
Orin G Houser, *Corp Secy*
Isabel Michalski, *Bookkeeper*
▼ **EMP:** 9
SQ FT: 15,800
SALES (est): 1.5MM **Privately Held**
SIC: 5712 3645 Furniture stores; residential lighting fixtures

(G-6814)
ZIMMER INC
Also Called: Tri-State Orthopedic
1001 Briggs Rd Ste 275 (08054-4105)
PHONE.................................856 778-8300
Stan Smoyer, *Branch Mgr*
EMP: 6
SALES (corp-wide): 7.9B **Publicly Held**
WEB: www.zimmer.com
SIC: 3842 Orthopedic appliances
HQ: Zimmer, Inc.
1800 W Center St
Warsaw IN 46580
800 348-9500

(G-6815)
ZOUNDS INC
Also Called: Zounds Hearing
3131 Route 38 Ste 19 (08054-9764)
PHONE.................................856 234-8844
EMP: 10 **Privately Held**
WEB: www.zoundshearing.com
SIC: 3842 3845 Surgical appliances & supplies; electromedical equipment
PA: Zounds, Inc.
6825 W Galveston St Ste 9
Chandler AZ 85226

Mount Royal
Gloucester County

(G-6816)
CW BROWN FOODS INC (PA)
Also Called: Bottos Gnine Itln Style Susage
161 Kings Hwy (08061-1011)
P.O. Box 243 (08061-0243)
PHONE.................................856 423-3700
Vince Botto, *President*
Dominic Botto, *Vice Pres*
Enrico Botto, *Treasurer*
Robert Botto Jr, *Admin Sec*
EMP: 50
SQ FT: 25,000
SALES: 10MM **Privately Held**
SIC: 2013 Sausages from purchased meat

(G-6817)
CW BROWN FOODS INC
Also Called: C W Brown & Company
161 Kings Hwy (08061-1011)
PHONE.................................856 423-3700
Vincent Botto, *Manager*
EMP: 14
SALES (corp-wide): 10MM **Privately Held**
SIC: 5411 2013 Grocery stores, independent; sausages & other prepared meats
PA: C.W. Brown Foods Inc.
161 Kings Hwy
Mount Royal NJ 08061
856 423-3700

(G-6818)
S GENO CARPET AND FLOORING
153 Sunset Dr (08061-1047)
PHONE.................................215 669-1400
Eugene Reilly, *Owner*
EMP: 4
SALES (est): 140K **Privately Held**
SIC: 3996 Hard surface floor coverings

Mountain Lakes
Morris County

(G-6819)
ACUSTRIP CO INC
10 Craven Rd (07046-1424)
P.O. Box 413 (07046-0413)
PHONE.................................973 299-8237
Ronald Schornstein, *Branch Mgr*
EMP: 4
SALES (corp-wide): 2.3MM **Privately Held**
WEB: www.acustrip.com
SIC: 3826 Liquid testing apparatus
PA: Acustrip Company, Inc
124 E Main St Apt 109b
Denville NJ 07834
973 299-8237

(G-6820)
ALEXANDER COMMUNICATIONS GROUP
Also Called: Alexander Marketing Services
36 Midvale Rd Ste 2e (07046-1330)
PHONE.................................973 265-2300
Lawrence Alexander, *President*
Margaret Dewitt, *Publisher*
EMP: 11
SQ FT: 5,000
SALES: 2MM **Privately Held**
WEB: www.alexcommgrp.com
SIC: 2721 2731 Periodicals: publishing & printing; book publishing

(G-6821)
CIRE TECHNOLOGIES INC
251 Boulevard (07046-1209)
PHONE.................................973 402-8301
Eric Becht, *President*
EMP: 5
SALES (est): 953.6K **Privately Held**
WEB: www.ciretechnologies.com
SIC: 3567 3552 8711 Incinerators, metal: domestic or commercial; drying machines, textile: for stock, yarn & cloth; consulting engineer

(G-6822)
DATA BASE ACCESS SYSTEMS INC
Also Called: Codenoll
60 Midvale Rd Ste 206 (07046-1309)
PHONE.................................973 335-0800
Michael Palazzi, *President*
John Bazin, *Vice Pres*
Frank Eppes, *Treasurer*
EMP: 14
SALES (est): 1.9MM **Privately Held**
WEB: www.dbasinc.com
SIC: 3577 Computer peripheral equipment

(G-6823)
DELUXE CORPORATION
Also Called: Deluxe Check Printers
105 Route 46 W (07046-1645)
PHONE.................................973 334-8000

Chris Strohler, *Sales Staff*
Steve Tenna, *Manager*
EMP: 167
SALES (corp-wide): 2B **Publicly Held**
WEB: www.dlx.com
SIC: 2782 Checkbooks
PA: Deluxe Corporation
3680 Victoria St N
Shoreview MN 55126
651 483-7111

(G-6824)
EUROIMMUN US INC
1 Bloomfield Ave 1 # 1 (07046-1429)
PHONE.................................973 656-1000
Hamid Ersanian, *CEO*
Theresa Gilosa, *Accounting Mgr*
Susan Goodhand, *Accountant*
Greg Stock, *Sales Mgr*
Lauren Basile, *Technical Staff*
▲ **EMP:** 20
SQ FT: 5,500
SALES (est): 4.4MM
SALES (corp-wide): 177.9K **Privately Held**
WEB: www.euroimmunus.com
SIC: 3829 Medical diagnostic systems, nuclear
HQ: Euroimmun Medizinische Labordiagnostika Ag
Seekamp 31
Lubeck 23560
451 585-50

(G-6825)
FBN NEW JERSEY MFG INC
8 Morris Ave (07046-1011)
P.O. Box 125 (07046-0125)
PHONE.................................973 402-1443
Phillip Motyka, *President*
Gary Petersen, *Vice Pres*
Cynthia Pensinger, *Project Mgr*
Raymond Grasso, *Mfg Staff*
Al Desrosiers, *Purch Agent*
▲ **EMP:** 32
SQ FT: 20,000
SALES (est): 3.7MM **Privately Held**
WEB: www.ocom.com
SIC: 3231 Products of purchased glass
HQ: Fabrinet Company Limited
5/6 Moo 6, Soi Khunpra, Phaholyothin Road
Khlong Luang 12120
252 496-00

(G-6826)
RED OAK SOFTWARE INC (PA)
115 Us Highway 46 F1000 (07046-1668)
PHONE.................................973 316-6064
George Cummings, *President*
EMP: 16
SQ FT: 4,300
SALES (est): 1.3MM **Privately Held**
WEB: www.redoaksw.com
SIC: 7372 Prepackaged software

(G-6827)
RICOH PRTG SYSTEMS AMER INC
Also Called: Ricoh Systems
115 Route 46 Bldg F (07046-1673)
PHONE.................................973 316-6051
Cheryl Taylor, *Branch Mgr*
EMP: 5 **Privately Held**
WEB: www.hitachi-printingsolutions.us
SIC: 3577 3861 3955 Printers, computer; toners, prepared photographic (not made in chemical plants); ribbons, inked: typewriter, adding machine, register, etc.
HQ: Ricoh Printing Systems America, Inc.
2390 Ward Ave Ste A
Simi Valley CA 93065
805 578-4000

(G-6828)
TIMES TIN CUP
35 Rainbow Trl (07046-1725)
PHONE.................................973 983-1095
Laurel Durenberger, *Principal*
EMP: 4
SALES (est): 410.2K **Privately Held**
SIC: 3356 Tin

(G-6829)
TURNER ENGINEERING INC
14 Morris Ave (07046-1011)
PHONE.................................973 263-1000
John J Turner Jr, *President*
Nancy Mattson, *Corp Secy*
EMP: 15
SQ FT: 2,200
SALES (est): 3.6MM **Privately Held**
WEB: www.turnereng.com
SIC: 3663 8711 Television closed circuit equipment; television monitors; engineering services; consulting engineer

(G-6830)
WESTERN SCIENTIFIC COMPUTERS
28 W Shore Rd (07046-1523)
PHONE.................................973 263-9311
Joseph Lutz, *President*
Jody Klinghoffer, *Vice Pres*
EMP: 13
SQ FT: 4,500
SALES: 1.8MM **Privately Held**
SIC: 3577 Computer peripheral equipment

Mountainside
Union County

(G-6831)
A K STAMPING CO INC
Also Called: Globe Manufacturing Sales Co
1159 Us Highway 22 (07092-2808)
P.O. Box 1213 (07092-0213)
PHONE.................................908 232-7300
Arthur A Kurz, *President*
Bernie Duetsch, *Prdtn Mgr*
Franklin Ozigbo, *Controller*
Diana Diaz, *Accountant*
Sarah Kurz, *Marketing Staff*
▲ **EMP:** 75 EST: 1954
SQ FT: 100,000
SALES (est): 17.5MM **Privately Held**
WEB: www.akstamping.com
SIC: 3469 3544 Stamping metal for the trade; special dies & tools; jigs & fixtures

(G-6832)
AIR & SPECIALTIES SHEET METAL
276 Sheffield St (07092-2303)
PHONE.................................908 233-8306
Kim Deitrich, *President*
Bruce Deitrich, *Vice Pres*
EMP: 15
SQ FT: 14,500
SALES (est): 3.7MM **Privately Held**
WEB: www.aircononline.com
SIC: 3549 3444 3441 Metalworking machinery; sheet metalwork; fabricated structural metal

(G-6833)
ALL PRINT RESOURCES GROUP INC
256 Sheffield St (07092-2303)
P.O. Box 1455 (07092-0455)
PHONE.................................201 994-0600
Joseph Dec, *President*
EMP: 4
SALES (est): 549.7K **Privately Held**
SIC: 2752 Commercial printing, offset

(G-6834)
AMERICAN ALUMINUM COMPANY
Also Called: Amalco
230 Sheffield St (07092-2303)
PHONE.................................908 233-3500
Robert Brucker, *President*
Daniel Osworth, *General Mgr*
Henry Brucker II, *Vice Pres*
Eldar Sukurlu, *Prdtn Mgr*
Rick Turner, *Facilities Mgr*
EMP: 70
SQ FT: 70,000
SALES (est): 18.7MM **Privately Held**
WEB: www.amalco.com
SIC: 3356 3489 3728 Battery metal; ordnance & accessories; aircraft parts & equipment

(G-6835)
AMERICAN TELETIMER CORP
1167 Globe Ave (07092-2903)
PHONE..................................908 654-4200
Joel Rosenzweig, *CEO*
Ron Couturier, *COO*
Matt Rosenzweig, *Manager*
Ford Cook, *Director*
EMP: 40
SQ FT: 6,400
SALES (est): 3.7MM **Privately Held**
WEB: www.teletimer.com
SIC: 3625 7384 Timing devices, electronic; photofinish laboratories

(G-6836)
CASE PRINCETON CO INC
615 Sherwood Pkwy Ste 5 (07092-2525)
PHONE..................................908 687-1750
Steve Parker, *President*
Steven Parker Jr, *Exec VP*
◆ **EMP:** 20 **EST:** 1964
SALES (est): 2.1MM **Privately Held**
WEB: www.princetoncase.com
SIC: 3089 3161 Cases, plastic; luggage

(G-6837)
CREATONE INC
1011 Us Highway 22 Ste 1 (07092-2803)
PHONE..................................908 789-8700
Arun Patel, *President*
Asha Patel, *Treasurer*
▲ **EMP:** 11
SQ FT: 6,000
SALES (est): 1.1MM **Privately Held**
WEB: www.assetor.net
SIC: 8711 3679 Electrical or electronic engineering; electronic circuits

(G-6838)
CSM ENVIRONMENTAL SYSTEMS LLC
269 Sheffield St Ste 1 (07092-2318)
PHONE..................................908 789-5431
Michael Torstrup, *Owner*
Jim Castillo, *Principal*
EMP: 12
SALES (est): 1.2MM **Privately Held**
SIC: 3564 Air purification equipment

(G-6839)
D PAGLIA & SONS INC
280 Sheffield St (07092-2303)
PHONE..................................908 654-5999
Daniel Paglia Sr, *President*
EMP: 14 **EST:** 1958
SQ FT: 2,500
SALES (est): 1.5MM **Privately Held**
WEB: www.dpaglia.com
SIC: 3911 Jewelry, precious metal

(G-6840)
DAVID E CONNOLLY INC
1091 Bristol Rd (07092-2301)
P.O. Box 2331, New Preston CT (06777-0331)
PHONE..................................908 654-4600
David E Connolly, *President*
Nora Connolly, *Vice Pres*
EMP: 18 **EST:** 1982
SQ FT: 3,000
SALES (est): 251.9K **Privately Held**
SIC: 3911 Jewelry, precious metal

(G-6841)
DE DITRICH PROCESS SYSTEMS INC (PA)
244 Sheffield St (07092-2303)
P.O. Box 345, Union (07083-0345)
PHONE..................................908 317-2585
Donald Doell, *CEO*
Adam Colucci, *Engineer*
Joseph Carnevale, *Controller*
Bob Stoerzer, *Human Res Mgr*
Sara Gerity, *Mktg Coord*
EMP: 35 **EST:** 1976
SQ FT: 100,000
SALES (est): 44.9MM **Privately Held**
WEB: www.ddpsinc.com
SIC: 8711 3443 Consulting engineer; industrial vessels, tanks & containers

(G-6842)
DIGITAL COLOR CONCEPTS INC
256 Sheffield St (07092-2303)
PHONE..................................908 264-0504
Don Cerwilliter, *Exec VP*
Michael Curcio, *VP Sales*
John Rock, *Sales Staff*
Ramona Pauley, *Executive*
EMP: 79 **Privately Held**
SIC: 2752 Commercial printing, lithographic
PA: Digital Color Concepts, Inc.
30 W 21st St Fl 5
New York NY 10010

(G-6843)
DORF FEATURE SERVICE INC
187 Mill Ln Ste 3 (07092-2919)
PHONE..................................908 518-1802
Sid Dorfman, *President*
EMP: 35
SALES (est): 1.8MM **Privately Held**
WEB: www.starledger.com
SIC: 7383 2711 News reporting services for newspapers & periodicals; newspapers

(G-6844)
EATON CORPORATION
1115 Globe Ave A (07092-2903)
PHONE..................................732 767-9600
Doug Carolan, *Manager*
EMP: 20 **Privately Held**
WEB: www.eaton.com
SIC: 3699 5065 Electrical equipment & supplies; electronic parts & equipment
HQ: Eaton Corporation
1000 Eaton Blvd
Cleveland OH 44122
440 523-5000

(G-6845)
ELENA CONSULTANTS & ELEC
1175 Globe Ave (07092-2903)
P.O. Box 1339 (07092-0339)
PHONE..................................908 654-8309
Rick Miller, *President*
Karen Miller, *Vice Pres*
EMP: 20
SQ FT: 15,000
SALES (est): 2.3MM **Privately Held**
SIC: 3674 8742 Solid state electronic devices; industrial consultant

(G-6846)
G & A COML SEATING PDTS CORP
152 Glen Rd (07092-2915)
PHONE..................................908 233-8000
Yuri Libson, *President*
◆ **EMP:** 9
SALES (est): 1.9MM **Privately Held**
SIC: 2521 Wood office furniture

(G-6847)
I-LIGHT USA INC
Also Called: Desisti Lighting
1011 Us Highway 22 Ste 3 (07092-2803)
PHONE..................................908 317-0020
Fabio Desisti, *Ch of Bd*
Mario Desisti, *Ch of Bd*
Greg Semper, *Treasurer*
▲ **EMP:** 9
SQ FT: 10,000
SALES (est): 6MM **Privately Held**
SIC: 5063 3648 Lighting fixtures; lighting equipment

(G-6848)
M P TUBE WORKS INC
237 Sheffield St (07092-2313)
P.O. Box 1430 (07092-0430)
PHONE..................................908 317-2500
Michael J McGinley, *President*
Paul W Kelman, *Vice Pres*
EMP: 8 **EST:** 1981
SQ FT: 15,000
SALES (est): 1.5MM **Privately Held**
SIC: 3498 5051 Tube fabricating (contract bending & shaping); cast iron pipe; tubing, metal

(G-6849)
NEWLINE PRTG & TECH SOLUTIONS
1011 Us Highway 22 Ste 1 (07092-2803)
PHONE..................................973 405-6133
John Luciano, *President*
▲ **EMP:** 10 **EST:** 1998
SALES: 3MM **Privately Held**
SIC: 2752 Commercial printing, offset

(G-6850)
NJ PRECISION TECH INC
1081 Bristol Rd (07092-2301)
PHONE..................................800 409-3000
Robert Tarantino, *President*
Michal Obloj, *Engineer*
Mohammad Oudeh, *Engineer*
EMP: 50
SQ FT: 10,500
SALES (est): 10.1MM **Privately Held**
WEB: www.njpt.com
SIC: 3599 Machine shop, jobbing & repair

(G-6851)
PRISM DGTAL COMMUNICATIONS LLC
1011 Us Highway 22 Ste A (07092-2803)
PHONE..................................973 232-5038
Jack Ayan, *Mng Member*
EMP: 10
SQ FT: 23,000
SALES (est): 2MM **Privately Held**
SIC: 2752 8742 Commercial printing, offset; marketing consulting services

(G-6852)
SPRINGFIELD HEATING & AC CO
Also Called: Spring Aire
217 Sheffield St (07092-2302)
PHONE..................................908 233-8400
Joseph Gallini Jr, *President*
Louis Gallini, *President*
George Gallini, *Vice Pres*
EMP: 11
SQ FT: 5,000
SALES (est): 1.2MM **Privately Held**
SIC: 1711 3444 Warm air heating & air conditioning contractor; sheet metalwork

(G-6853)
TRANO BRUCE PLUMBING & HEATING
872 Woodland Ave (07092-2524)
PHONE..................................908 654-3685
Bruce Trano, *Owner*
Craig Trano, *Partner*
EMP: 4
SALES (est): 290K **Privately Held**
SIC: 3431 1711 Plumbing fixtures: enameled iron cast iron or pressed metal; plumbing, heating, air-conditioning contractors

---

Mullica Hill
Gloucester County

(G-6854)
ALBERT FORTE NECKWEAR CO INC
127 Fellowship Ln (08062-2207)
P.O. Box 240, Paulsboro (08066-0240)
PHONE..................................856 423-2342
Albert Forte Jr, *President*
Brian Forte, *Admin Sec*
EMP: 6
SQ FT: 5,000
SALES (est): 662.7K **Privately Held**
SIC: 2323 Men's & boys' neckwear

(G-6855)
ANNA K PARK
50 N Main St (08062-9409)
PHONE..................................856 478-9500
Anna Park, *Principal*
EMP: 4
SALES (est): 327.3K **Privately Held**
SIC: 3843 Enamels, dentists'

(G-6856)
BOEING COMPANY
203 Churchill Way (08062-3608)
PHONE..................................314 232-1372
Kenneth Laubsch, *Branch Mgr*
EMP: 850
SALES (corp-wide): 101.1B **Publicly Held**
SIC: 3721 Aircraft
PA: The Boeing Company
100 N Riverside Plz
Chicago IL 60606
312 544-2000

(G-6857)
RANDOM 8 WOODWORKS LLC (PA)
459 Clems Run (08062-2807)
PHONE..................................856 417-3329
Randy Goodman, *Principal*
EMP: 4
SALES (est): 654K **Privately Held**
SIC: 2431 Millwork

(G-6858)
WJM TRUCKING INC
515 Macintosh Dr (08062-9475)
P.O. Box 54 (08062-0054)
PHONE..................................856 381-3635
William J Macmillan, *President*
EMP: 9
SALES (est): 750K **Privately Held**
SIC: 3715 Truck trailers

(G-6859)
ZIPPITYPRINT LLC
Also Called: Zippityprint.com
182 Harrisonville Rd (08062-2832)
PHONE..................................216 438-0001
Joseph P Dell Aquila, *CEO*
EMP: 12
SQ FT: 17,000
SALES: 1.7MM **Privately Held**
SIC: 2752 7331 7336 Commercial printing, offset; direct mail advertising services; graphic arts & related design

---

Murray Hill
Union County

(G-6860)
NOKIA INC
600-700 Mountain Ave (07974)
PHONE..................................908 582-3149
Khaled Ansari, *Partner*
Shashank Deulkar, *General Mgr*
Neil Scognamiglio, *General Mgr*
Nikolaus Singer, *Project Mgr*
Archana Gupta, *Engrg Mgr*
EMP: 17 **EST:** 1987
SALES (est): 2.9MM **Privately Held**
SIC: 3661 Telephone dialing devices, automatic

Neptune
Monmouth County

(G-6861)
5 KIDS GROUP LTD LIABILITY CO
37 State Route 35 N (07753-4745)
PHONE..................................732 774-5331
▲ **EMP:** 12
SALES (est): 809.7K **Privately Held**
SIC: 2284 Thread Mill

(G-6862)
A H HOFFMANN LLC
209 W Sylvania Ave (07753-6281)
PHONE..................................732 988-6000
Arthur Hoffmann,
EMP: 5
SQ FT: 9,600
SALES (est): 308.3K **Privately Held**
SIC: 1389 Oil consultants

(G-6863)
A PLUS POWERWASHING
503 Moore Rd (07753-5510)
PHONE..................................732 245-3816

Brian Hegarty, *Owner*
EMP: 4
SALES (est): 180K **Privately Held**
SIC: 3589 High pressure cleaning equipment

(G-6864)
ALLEGRO NUTRITION INC
Also Called: Gaspari Nutrition
1023 Waverly Ave (07753-3195)
PHONE.................................732 364-3777
Richard Gaspari, *President*
Oscar Iturralde, *Treasurer*
Troy Johnson, *Sales Staff*
Elizabeth Ritchie, *Mktg Dir*
Michael Maling, *Manager*
▼ **EMP:** 25
SQ FT: 65,000
SALES (est): 4.8MM **Privately Held**
SIC: 2023 Dietary supplements, dairy & non-dairy based
HQ: Allegro Limited
Jamestown House
Dublin D11 P
185 806-00

(G-6865)
ARTHUR A TOPILOW WILLIAM LRNER
Also Called: Atlantic Hemotology & Oncology
19 Davis Ave 2 (07753-4488)
PHONE.................................732 528-0760
Arthur Topilow MD, *Partner*
Carol Henningson, *Partner*
William Lerner MD, *Partner*
EMP: 23
SALES (est): 2.8MM **Privately Held**
SIC: 8011 2835 Oncologist; hemotology diagnostic agents

(G-6866)
ASBURY PARK PRESS INC
Also Called: Home News & Tribune
3600 Route 66 (07753-2605)
P.O. Box 1550 (07754-1550)
PHONE.................................732 922-6000
Thomas M Donovan, *President*
Robert T Collins, *Principal*
W Raymond Ollwerther, *Vice Pres*
Kristen Janet Materese, *Prdtn Mgr*
Brian Johnston, *Production*
▲ **EMP:** 1200 **EST:** 1879
SQ FT: 172,000
SALES (est): 198.6MM
SALES (corp-wide): 2.9B **Publicly Held**
WEB: www.app.com
SIC: 2711 2752 Commercial printing & newspaper publishing combined; commercial printing, lithographic
PA: Gannett Co., Inc.
7950 Jones Branch Dr
Mc Lean VA 22102
703 854-6000

(G-6867)
AUTOMATED CONTROL CONCEPTS INC (PA)
Also Called: A C C
3535 State Route 66 # 14 (07753-2625)
PHONE.................................732 922-6611
Robert J Tomasetta, *Ch of Bd*
Michael Blechman, *President*
Victor Ronchetti, *Vice Pres*
Jason Vandertuyn, *Prdtn Mgr*
Bill Coleman, *Engineer*
EMP: 32
SQ FT: 15,000
SALES: 10.2MM **Privately Held**
WEB: www.automated-control.com
SIC: 7373 3577 Systems integration services; computer peripheral equipment

(G-6868)
BROWNS WELDING SERVICE
105 Oxonia Ave (07753-4523)
PHONE.................................732 988-9530
Al Brown, *Owner*
EMP: 4
SALES (est): 200K **Privately Held**
SIC: 7692 Welding repair

(G-6869)
CARL STREIT & SON CO
703 Atkins Ave (07753-5169)
P.O. Box 157 (07754-0157)
PHONE.................................732 775-0803

James E Robinson Jr, *President*
Judith E Robinson, *Vice Pres*
EMP: 9
SQ FT: 1,344
SALES (est): 3.1MM **Privately Held**
SIC: 5147 2011 2015 Meats, fresh; meat packing plants; poultry slaughtering & processing

(G-6870)
CONTAINER GRAPHICS CORP
3535 Highway 66 Ste 2 (07753-2624)
PHONE.................................732 922-1180
Jeff McCready, *Branch Mgr*
EMP: 50
SQ FT: 5,000
SALES (corp-wide): 3MM **Privately Held**
WEB: www.containergraphics.com
SIC: 3953 3544 2796 Marking devices; special dies, tools, jigs & fixtures; platemaking services
PA: Container Graphics Corp.
114 Ednbrgh S Dr Ste 104
Cary NC 27511
919 481-4200

(G-6871)
COTTAGE LACE AND RIBBON CO INC (PA)
Also Called: Ribbon Bazaar
210 3rd Ave Ste 21 (07753)
PHONE.................................732 776-9353
Shahid Waseem, *President*
▲ **EMP:** 4
SALES (est): 1.1MM **Privately Held**
SIC: 5131 2241 Ribbons; ribbons

(G-6872)
CRAFTMASTER PRINTING INC (PA)
2024 State Route 33 (07753-6115)
PHONE.................................732 775-0011
Jeanne A Baumgartner, *President*
Robert Baumgartner, *Corp Secy*
Curtis Baumgartner, *Vice Pres*
EMP: 4
SQ FT: 1,200
SALES (est): 584.6K **Privately Held**
WEB: www.craftmasterprinting.com
SIC: 2752 Commercial printing, offset

(G-6873)
CREATIVE DISPLAY INC
349 Essex Rd (07753-2637)
PHONE.................................732 918-8010
Danette Bussey, *President*
David Longo, *Vice Pres*
▲ **EMP:** 7
SALES (est): 1.1MM **Privately Held**
SIC: 3999 Plants, artificial & preserved

(G-6874)
DYMAX SYSTEMS INC
3455 State Route 66 Ste 6 (07753-2759)
PHONE.................................732 918-2424
Ralph Barnhart, *President*
EMP: 15
SQ FT: 1,000
SALES (est): 922K **Privately Held**
WEB: www.dymaxsystems.com
SIC: 7379 7372 5045 Computer related consulting services; prepackaged software; computers

(G-6875)
EDMONDMARKS TECHNOLOGIES INC
3535 State Route 66 Ste 3 (07753-2624)
PHONE.................................732 643-0290
James Williams, *CEO*
Michael Marks, *President*
Susan Williams, *Vice Pres*
Kristy Capak, *Buyer*
Craig Abrams, *Info Tech Mgr*
EMP: 35
SQ FT: 11,600
SALES (est): 6.7MM **Privately Held**
SIC: 3699 8711 Electrical equipment & supplies; electrical or electronic engineering

(G-6876)
ELECTRO IMPULSE LABORATORY INC
1805 State Route 33 (07753-4847)
P.O. Box 278 (07754-0278)
PHONE.................................732 776-5800
Mark Rubin, *Ch of Bd*
Lucille P Gardner, *Vice Pres*
Carol Rubin, *Vice Pres*
Theresa Carmicheal, *Senior Buyer*
Steven P Pillsbury, *Admin Sec*
EMP: 45 **EST:** 1947
SQ FT: 53,000
SALES: 7.4MM **Privately Held**
WEB: www.electroimpulse.com
SIC: 3585 3825 Refrigeration equipment, complete; power measuring equipment, electrical

(G-6877)
EXCELSIOR MEDICAL LLC (HQ)
1933 Heck Ave (07753-4428)
PHONE.................................732 776-7525
James Abrams, *COO*
Sandra Rigopoulos, *CFO*
▲ **EMP:** 131
SALES (est): 68.2MM
SALES (corp-wide): 5.8B **Privately Held**
WEB: www.excelsiormedical.com
SIC: 3841 Surgical & medical instruments
PA: Medline Industries, Inc.
3 Lakes Dr
Northfield IL 60093
847 949-5500

(G-6878)
FIVE KIDS GROUP INC
37 Highway 35 N Fl 2 (07753-4745)
PHONE.................................732 774-5331
Glen Suchecki, *President*
EMP: 1
SQ FT: 8,500
SALES: 1.4MM **Privately Held**
SIC: 5699 3999 Uniforms & work clothing; embroidery kits

(G-6879)
G G TAUBER COMPANY INC
3535 State Route 66 Ste 1 (07753-2623)
PHONE.................................800 638-6667
Dana Belser Jr, *CEO*
Judith Bryant, *President*
EMP: 25 **EST:** 1947
SQ FT: 12,000
SALES (est): 1.8MM **Privately Held**
WEB: www.ggtauber.com
SIC: 3999 5699 5199 Identification badges & insignia; belts, apparel: custom; customized clothing & apparel; sports apparel; T-shirts, custom printed; advertising specialties

(G-6880)
GERIN CORPORATION INC
1109 7th Ave (07753-5189)
P.O. Box 307, Avon By The Sea (07717-0307)
PHONE.................................732 774-3256
Robert Gerin, *President*
EMP: 6
SQ FT: 4,550
SALES: 300K **Privately Held**
SIC: 3823 Viscosimeters, industrial process type

(G-6881)
GLUEFAST COMPANY INC
3535 State Route 66 Ste 1 (07753-2623)
PHONE.................................732 918-4600
Lester Mallet, *President*
Amy Altman, *Corp Secy*
Dawn Zic, *Bookkeeper*
Max Mallet, *Marketing Staff*
▲ **EMP:** 12 **EST:** 1939
SQ FT: 17,500
SALES (est): 3.5MM **Privately Held**
WEB: www.gluefast.com
SIC: 2891 3559 Glue; chemical machinery & equipment

(G-6882)
GOURMET KITCHEN LLC
1238 Corlies Ave (07753-5069)
PHONE.................................732 775-5222
Micheal Lacey, *President*
Ray Walsh, *Principal*

Pat Duffey, *Vice Pres*
Ryan Walsh, *Admin Sec*
▲ **EMP:** 140
SQ FT: 7,000
SALES (est): 26MM **Privately Held**
SIC: 2099 Food preparations

(G-6883)
GROEZINGER PROVISIONS INC
1200 7th Ave (07753-5190)
PHONE.................................732 775-3220
Laurie Cummins, *President*
EMP: 17 **EST:** 1982
SQ FT: 18,000
SALES (est): 3MM **Privately Held**
WEB: www.alexianpate.com
SIC: 2013 Sausages from purchased meat

(G-6884)
HINCK TURKEY FARM INC
3930 Belmar Blvd (07753-7111)
PHONE.................................732 681-0508
Robert Longo, *President*
EMP: 9
SQ FT: 12,000
SALES (est): 611.9K **Privately Held**
SIC: 2015 0253 Turkey processing & slaughtering; turkey farm

(G-6885)
HOLOCRAFT CORPORATION (PA)
Also Called: Flexcraft Company
50 Flexcraft Dr (07753-6276)
PHONE.................................732 502-9500
Ben Smith, *CEO*
Russ Smith Jr, *CFO*
David Schutzer, *Manager*
▼ **EMP:** 81
SQ FT: 34,000
SALES: 20MM **Privately Held**
WEB: www.flexcraftcompany.com
SIC: 3089 Blow molded finished plastic products; air mattresses, plastic

(G-6886)
KIRMS PRINTING CO INC
1520 Washington Ave (07753-4912)
P.O. Box 1067 (07754-1067)
PHONE.................................732 774-8000
Albert G Kirms, *President*
Norris D Kirms, *Corp Secy*
EMP: 20 **EST:** 1924
SQ FT: 9,600
SALES (est): 3MM **Privately Held**
SIC: 2752 2791 Commercial printing, offset; typesetting

(G-6887)
KRELL TECHNOLOGIES INC
11 Evergreen Ave (07753-6501)
PHONE.................................732 775-7355
Cuneyt Erdogan, *President*
Christine Kritch, *Accounts Mgr*
Christine Nodine, *Accounts Mgr*
EMP: 8
SQ FT: 1,300
SALES (est): 1.4MM **Privately Held**
SIC: 8711 3827 Engineering services; lens coating & grinding equipment

(G-6888)
LEES WOODWORKING INC
24 W Jumping Brook Rd (07753-3107)
PHONE.................................732 681-1002
Minh Lee, *Owner*
EMP: 5
SALES (est): 454.6K **Privately Held**
SIC: 2431 Millwork

(G-6889)
MALLETECH LLC
1107 11th Ave (07753-5165)
PHONE.................................732 774-0011
Leigh Stevens,
▲ **EMP:** 17
SALES (est): 2.4MM **Privately Held**
SIC: 3931 Musical instruments

(G-6890)
MARLO PLASTIC PRODUCTS INC
3535 State Route 66 Ste 1 (07753-2623)
PHONE.................................732 792-1988
Arthur Livingston, *President*

▲ **EMP:** 40 **EST:** 1945
SQ FT: 25,000
SALES (est): 6.7MM **Privately Held**
WEB: www.marloplastics.com
SIC: 3089 2759 Novelties, plastic; promotional printing

(G-6891)
MASTERCRAFT IRON INC
1111 10th Ave (07753-5130)
P.O. Box 748 (07754-0748)
PHONE................................732 988-3113
P Peter Stagaard III, *President*
Robert Van Norman, *Admin Sec*
EMP: 15
SQ FT: 3,500
SALES (est): 3MM **Privately Held**
SIC: 1761 3542 Sheet metalwork; punching, shearing & bending machines

(G-6892)
NEW DAWN INC
Also Called: Rex Sign
60 Steiner Ave (07753-6639)
PHONE................................732 774-1377
Jacqueline Janocha, *President*
EMP: 8
SALES (est): 937.3K **Privately Held**
SIC: 3993 Signs, not made in custom sign painting shops

(G-6893)
NJ PRESS MEDIA
3601 State Route 66 (07753-2604)
P.O. Box 1550 (07754-1550)
PHONE................................732 643-3604
Mary Kromer, *Accountant*
Jenna Intersimone, *Accounts Mgr*
Mary Klein, *Cust Mgr*
Bill Ditty, *Sales Staff*
Jonathan Pfeiffer, *Sales Staff*
EMP: 8 **EST:** 2012
SALES (est): 415.2K **Privately Held**
SIC: 2711 Newspapers, publishing & printing

(G-6894)
PARK STEEL & IRON CO (PA)
9 Evergreen Ave (07753-6501)
P.O. Box 365, Bradley Beach (07720-0365)
PHONE................................732 775-7500
Garet J Pilling, *CEO*
Scot Pilling, *Vice Pres*
EMP: 10
SQ FT: 19,000
SALES (est): 1.3MM **Privately Held**
SIC: 3441 3444 3341 Fabricated structural metal; sheet metalwork; secondary nonferrous metals

(G-6895)
SCAASIS ORIGINALS INC
Also Called: Oceanic Trading
1006 11th Ave (07753-5174)
PHONE................................732 775-7474
Brenda Saada, *President*
Esther Saada, *Treasurer*
▲ **EMP:** 30
SQ FT: 18,000
SALES (est): 4.3MM **Privately Held**
WEB: www.scaasis.com
SIC: 3961 5094 5199 Jewelry apparel, non-precious metals; costume jewelry, ex. precious metal & semiprecious stones; jewelry; gifts & novelties

(G-6896)
SCHOOL PUBLICATIONS CO INC
Also Called: Spc Publication
1520 Washington Ave (07753-4912)
P.O. Box 1067 (07754-1067)
PHONE................................732 988-1100
Albert G Kirms, *President*
Norris D Kirms, *Admin Sec*
EMP: 20
SALES (est): 1.3MM **Privately Held**
WEB: www.schoolpub.com
SIC: 2741 2752 2732 2731 Miscellaneous publishing; commercial printing, lithographic; book printing; book publishing; periodicals; newspapers

(G-6897)
SEAJAY MANUFACTURING CORP
9 Memorial Dr Ste 1 (07753-5083)
PHONE................................732 774-0900
Jeffrey Finn, *President*
Carl Flury, *President*
Robert Musanti, *Controller*
EMP: 11
SQ FT: 20,000
SALES (est): 800K **Privately Held**
SIC: 3089 3069 3559 3544 Blow molded finished plastic products; molded rubber products; plastics working machinery; special dies, tools, jigs & fixtures

(G-6898)
SHOP RITE SUPERMARKETS INC
Also Called: Shop Rite 299
2200 Highway 66 (07753-4062)
PHONE................................732 775-4250
Don Brennan, *Manager*
EMP: 180
SALES (corp-wide): 890MM **Privately Held**
SIC: 5411 5912 5992 2051 Supermarkets, chain; drug stores & proprietary stores; florists; bread, cake & related products
HQ: Shop Rite Supermarkets, Inc.
5000 Riverside Dr
Keasbey NJ 08832
908 527-3300

(G-6899)
STAR PROCESS HEAT SYSTEMS LLC
208 Iris Dr (07753-3654)
PHONE................................732 282-1002
Steven A Robinson,
Mary E Bass,
Steven A Robertson,
EMP: 5
SQ FT: 2,100
SALES (est): 500K **Privately Held**
WEB: www.starphs.com
SIC: 3599 Air intake filters, internal combustion engine, except auto

(G-6900)
TFH PUBLICATIONS INC
85 W Sylvania Ave (07753-6775)
PHONE................................732 897-6860
Marcy Cortez, *Controller*
EMP: 100
SALES (corp-wide): 2B **Publicly Held**
WEB: www.tfh.com
SIC: 2731 Books: publishing & printing
HQ: T.F.H. Publications, Inc.
85 W Sylvania Ave
Neptune NJ 07753
732 988-8400

(G-6901)
TFH PUBLICATIONS INC
211 W Sylvania Ave (07753-6296)
PHONE................................732 988-8400
Marcy Cortez, *Branch Mgr*
Albert Connelly, *Manager*
EMP: 40
SALES (corp-wide): 2B **Publicly Held**
WEB: www.tfh.com
SIC: 2731 Books: publishing & printing
HQ: T.F.H. Publications, Inc.
85 W Sylvania Ave
Neptune NJ 07753
732 988-8400

(G-6902)
TOLL COMPACTION SERVICE INC (PA)
Also Called: Toll Compaction Group
14 Memorial Dr (07753-5051)
PHONE................................732 776-8225
Paul B Pritchard, *CEO*
Tyson Pritchard, *President*
Brenda Buzzard, *Office Mgr*
Stacy Ritchie, *Admin Asst*
▲ **EMP:** 40
SQ FT: 23,000
SALES (est): 6.6MM **Privately Held**
WEB: www.tollcompaction.com
SIC: 2833 Medicinals & botanicals

(G-6903)
ZIMPLI KIDS INC
3301 Route 66 Ste 130 (07753-2705)
PHONE................................732 945-5995
Thomas Whale, *Principal*
EMP: 7
SALES (est): 231.3K **Privately Held**
SIC: 3944 Games, toys & children's vehicles

Neshanic Station
Somerset County

(G-6904)
AROME AMERICA LLC
2 Van Fleet Rd (08853-4300)
PHONE................................908 806-7003
John F Nobile, *Managing Prtnr*
▲ **EMP:** 7
SALES (est): 548.4K **Privately Held**
WEB: www.aromeamerica.com
SIC: 2099 Food preparations

(G-6905)
SOURLAND MOUNTAIN WDWKG LLC T
17 Higginsville Rd (08853-3612)
PHONE................................908 806-7661
EMP: 4 **EST:** 2009
SALES (est): 373.1K **Privately Held**
SIC: 2431 Millwork

(G-6906)
WESTCON ORTHOPEDICS INC
4 Craig Rd (08853-3504)
P.O. Box 342, Adelphia (07710-0342)
PHONE................................908 806-8981
Don Gordon, *President*
Robert Schultz, *Corp Secy*
Marcella Schultz, *Vice Pres*
EMP: 4
SALES: 250K **Privately Held**
SIC: 3841 Ophthalmic instruments & apparatus

Netcong
Morris County

(G-6907)
HOOKWAY ENTERPRISES INC
Also Called: Megasafe
130 Allen St (07857-1236)
PHONE................................973 691-0382
Michael J Hookway, *President*
EMP: 10
SQ FT: 5,000
SALES: 2MM **Privately Held**
SIC: 7382 3499 Protective devices, security; locks, safe & vault: metal

New Brunswick
Middlesex County

(G-6908)
ACCU SEAL RUBBER INC
18f Home News Row (08901-3644)
PHONE................................732 246-4333
Pravin Tejani, *President*
Surekse Tejani, *Accountant*
Manjula Tejani, *Admin Sec*
Dinesh Tejani, *Administration*
EMP: 4 **EST:** 2000
SQ FT: 4,200
SALES: 500K **Privately Held**
WEB: www.accusealrubber.com
SIC: 3069 Molded rubber products

(G-6909)
AKCROS CHEMICALS INC
500 Jersey Ave (08901)
PHONE................................800 500-7890
Paul Angus, *CEO*
Joe Trilone, *Safety Mgr*
Erin Maietta, *Human Res Mgr*
Charles Carraz, *Manager*
Vini Shah, *Manager*
◆ **EMP:** 72
SQ FT: 124,000

SALES (est): 25.5MM **Privately Held**
WEB: www.akcros.com
SIC: 2869 Industrial organic chemicals
HQ: Polymer Additives, Inc.
7500 E Pleasant Valley Rd
Independence OH 44131
216 875-7200

(G-6910)
ANS PLASTICS CORPORATION
625 Jersey Ave Ste 11a (08901-3679)
PHONE................................732 247-2776
Adel Samuel, *President*
Ramy Samuel, *Vice Pres*
▲ **EMP:** 14
SQ FT: 14,000
SALES (est): 3.9MM **Privately Held**
WEB: www.ansplastics.com
SIC: 2673 2671 5162 5113 Plastic bags: made from purchased materials; plastic film, coated or laminated for packaging; plastics film; bags, paper & disposable plastic

(G-6911)
AP DEAUVILLE LLC
594 Jersey Ave Ste 1 (08901-3569)
PHONE................................732 545-0200
Fred Horowitz, *CEO*
Bruce Lazare, *Senior VP*
Robert J Myszka, *Vice Pres*
Elmo Perez, *Technology*
▲ **EMP:** 49
SQ FT: 97,000
SALES: 40MM **Privately Held**
WEB: www.apdeauville.com
SIC: 2844 Cosmetic preparations

(G-6912)
AQUASPORTS POOLS LLC
999 Jersey Ave (08901-3609)
PHONE................................732 247-6298
EMP: 15
SALES (est): 1.3MM **Privately Held**
SIC: 3949 Swimming pools, plastic

(G-6913)
ART MATERIALS SERVICE INC
Also Called: AMS
625 Joyce Kilmer Ave (08901-3307)
PHONE................................732 545-8888
Joseph Eichert, *President*
Wilson Cubides, *President*
Gary Roark, *Admin Sec*
▲ **EMP:** 70 **EST:** 1977
SQ FT: 21,000
SALES (est): 12.5MM **Privately Held**
WEB: www.artmaterialsservice.com
SIC: 3429 Manufactured hardware (general)

(G-6914)
BUCKETS PLUS INC
Also Called: Mr Ice Buckets
345 Sandford St (08901-2320)
PHONE................................732 545-0420
Fred Haleluk, *President*
Sudesh Rajpal, *Opers Mgr*
◆ **EMP:** 6
SALES: 590K **Privately Held**
SIC: 3089 3229 Plastic kitchenware, tableware & houseware; barware

(G-6915)
CHALMERS & KUBECK INC
8 Jules Ln (08901-3636)
PHONE................................732 993-1251
Wayne Salvi, *Manager*
EMP: 7
SALES (corp-wide): 50.7MM **Privately Held**
WEB: www.candk.com
SIC: 3599 5085 Machine shop, jobbing & repair; valves & fittings
PA: Chalmers & Kubeck, Inc.
150 Commerce Dr
Aston PA 19014
610 494-4300

(G-6916)
CHANDLER PHARMACY LLC
Also Called: Chandler Pharmacy & Surgicals
272 George St (08901-1314)
PHONE................................732 543-1568
Janak Patel,
EMP: 5 **EST:** 2009

▲ = Import ▼=Export
◆ =Import/Export

SALES (est): 507.5K **Privately Held**
SIC: 2834 Pharmaceutical preparations

(G-6917)
CIELITO LINDO
224 French St (08901-2334)
PHONE..........................580 286-1127
Dari R Almonte Peralta, *Principal*
EMP: 4 EST: 2010
SALES (est): 232.9K **Privately Held**
SIC: 2024 Ice cream, bulk

(G-6918)
CORDIS INTERNATIONAL CORP
1 Johnson And Johnson Plz (08933-0001)
P.O. Box 25700, Miami FL (33102-5700)
PHONE..........................732 524-0400
Donald O'Dwer, *President*
Jesse Pin, *President*
Wayne C Casebolt, *Treasurer*
Daniel G Hall, *Admin Sec*
EMP: 531
SQ FT: 400,000
SALES (est): 120.8MM
SALES (corp-wide): 81.5B **Publicly Held**
WEB: www.jnj.com
SIC: 3841 Surgical & medical instruments
PA: Johnson & Johnson
1 Johnson And Johnson Plz
New Brunswick NJ 08933
732 524-0400

(G-6919)
DETERGENT 20 LLC
594 Jersey Ave (08901-3569)
PHONE..........................732 545-0200
Eddie Greenstein, *Director*
Fred Horowitz,
EMP: 10
SALES: 1MM **Privately Held**
SIC: 5169 2841 Detergents; soap & other
detergents

(G-6920)
DOWNTOWN PRINTING CENTER INC
46 Paterson St Ste 1 (08901-2092)
PHONE..........................732 246-7990
Juan E Ruiz, *President*
EMP: 14
SQ FT: 4,000
SALES (est): 1MM **Privately Held**
WEB: www.downtownprinting.com
SIC: 2752 2796 2791 2759 Photo-offset
printing; letterpress plates, preparation of;
typesetting; letterpress printing; thermography

(G-6921)
DREAM WELL COLLECTION INC
Also Called: Dreamwell
633 Nassau St (08902-2940)
PHONE..........................732 545-5900
Amanda Edna Srour, *Ch of Bd*
Isaac Srour, *Vice Pres*
▲ EMP: 12 EST: 2001
SQ FT: 20,000
SALES (est): 3.5MM **Privately Held**
SIC: 2515 Mattresses & bedsprings

(G-6922)
ECLIPSE SLEEP PRODUCTS LLC
1375 Jersey Ave Ste 1 (08902-1600)
PHONE..........................732 628-0002
Stuart Carlitz,
EMP: 80
SQ FT: 90,000
SALES (est): 5.6MM **Privately Held**
WEB: www.eclipsebedding.com
SIC: 2515 Mattresses & bedsprings

(G-6923)
ELAINE K JOSEPHSON INC
Also Called: Lawn Doctor of Mercer County
7f Jules Ln (08901-3675)
PHONE..........................609 259-2256
Elaine Josephson, *President*
Michael Josephson, *Vice Pres*
EMP: 5
SQ FT: 1,500
SALES (est): 590K **Privately Held**
SIC: 2034 Vegetables, dried or dehydrated
(except freeze-dried)

(G-6924)
ENERGY RECYCLING CO LLC
100 Jersey Ave Ste C8 (08901-3269)
P.O. Box 4762, Highland Park (08904-4762)
PHONE..........................732 545-6619
Larry Schrager, *President*
Rosella Sabatini, *Vice Pres*
EMP: 5
SALES: 700K **Privately Held**
WEB: www.energyrecyclingco.com
SIC: 3559 5084 Recycling machinery; recycling machinery & equipment

(G-6925)
EXCEL DISPLAY CORP
100 Jersey Ave Ste A6 (08901-3268)
P.O. Box 10045 (08906-0045)
PHONE..........................732 246-3724
Tony Chuang, *President*
EMP: 4 EST: 2003
SALES (est): 882.4K **Privately Held**
SIC: 3679 Liquid crystal displays (LCD)

(G-6926)
FEDEX OFFICE & PRINT SVCS INC
Also Called: Fedex Office Print & Ship Ctr
212 Rte 18 (08901)
PHONE..........................732 249-9222
EMP: 15
SALES (corp-wide): 69.6B **Publicly Held**
WEB: www.kinkos.com
SIC: 7334 2791 2789 Photocopying & duplicating services; typesetting; bookbinding & related work
HQ: Fedex Office And Print Services, Inc.
7900 Legacy Dr
Plano TX 75024
800 463-3339

(G-6927)
GATEHUSE MEDIA PA HOLDINGS INC
Snowden Pulications
104 Church St (08901-2002)
PHONE..........................732 246-7677
George Taber, *Branch Mgr*
Jessica Perry, *Director*
EMP: 28
SALES (corp-wide): 1.5B **Publicly Held**
WEB: www.journalpub.com
SIC: 2711 Newspapers: publishing only,
not printed on site
HQ: Gatehouse Media Pennsylvania Holdings, Inc.
175 Sullys Trl Fl 3
Pittsford NY 14534
585 598-0030

(G-6928)
GDB INTERNATIONAL INC (PA)
1 Home News Row (08901-3601)
PHONE..........................732 246-3001
Sanjeev Bagaria, *CEO*
Sunil Bagaria, *President*
Vanessa Downey, *Vice Pres*
Mani Palani, *Vice Pres*
Francisco Suarez, *Vice Pres*
◆ EMP: 100
SQ FT: 102,000
SALES (est): 114.9MM **Privately Held**
WEB: www.gdbinternational.com
SIC: 5162 5111 5093 2851 Plastics materials & basic shapes; printing & writing paper; plastics scrap; metal scrap & waste materials; paints & paint additives

(G-6929)
GLOBE PHARMA INC
2b Janine Pl (08901-3646)
PHONE..........................732 296-9700
Sanni Raju, *Owner*
Willie Pagsuyuin, *Director*
▲ EMP: 8
SALES (est): 1.1MM **Privately Held**
SIC: 2834 Pharmaceutical preparations

(G-6930)
GLOBEPHARMA INC
2b Janine Pl (08901-3646)
P.O. Box 7307, North Brunswick (08902-7307)
PHONE..........................732 296-9700
Sanni Raju, *President*

◆ EMP: 10
SQ FT: 5,000
SALES (est): 2.2MM **Privately Held**
WEB: www.globepharma.com
SIC: 3559 Pharmaceutical machinery

(G-6931)
GREENVILLE COLORANTS LLC (PA)
90 Paterson St (08901-2109)
PHONE..........................201 595-0200
Ronald M Weiss, *Mng Member*
▲ EMP: 14
SQ FT: 100,000
SALES (est): 35.8MM **Privately Held**
SIC: 5198 2865 Colors & pigments; dyes
& pigments

(G-6932)
GREENWAY PRODUCTS & SVCS LLC (PA)
14 Home News Row (08901-3602)
PHONE..........................732 442-0200
Jackie Wade, *Vice Pres*
Anthony Fabrizio, *CFO*
Dominick Davi, *Mng Member*
EMP: 41
SQ FT: 3,000
SALES (est): 38.8MM **Privately Held**
SIC: 2448 2499 3089 Pallets, wood &
wood with metal; mulch or sawdust products, wood; plastic processing

(G-6933)
I I GALAXY INC
235 Jersey Ave Ste 3 (08901-3281)
PHONE..........................732 828-2686
Earl Creighton II, *President*
Earl Creighton Sr, *Vice Pres*
EMP: 5
SALES: 200K **Privately Held**
SIC: 3599 Custom machinery

(G-6934)
ILLUMINATING EXPERIENCES LLC
625 Jersey Ave Ste 7 (08901-3679)
PHONE..........................800 734-5858
Donna Whittaker, *Accounting Mgr*
Stephen Blackman, *Mng Member*
▲ EMP: 7
SALES (est): 548.8K **Privately Held**
SIC: 3229 3646 Glass lighting equipment
parts; ceiling systems, luminous

(G-6935)
INTERNATIONAL SWIMMING POOLS
14c Van Dyke Ave (08901-3578)
P.O. Box 7367, Watchung (07069-0796)
PHONE..........................732 565-9229
Bradley Korbel, *President*
Nicholas J Pietrone, *Corp Secy*
Douglas F Colson, *Vice Pres*
Mary Turner, *Sales Executive*
Steven A Colson, *Shareholder*
▲ EMP: 25
SQ FT: 53,000
SALES (est): 4.3MM **Privately Held**
WEB:
www.internationalswimmingpools.com
SIC: 3444 Sheet metalwork

(G-6936)
INTERNTIONAL CNSLD CHEMEX CORP
235 Jersey Ave (08901-3281)
PHONE..........................732 828-7676
Walter M Geslak, *President*
Walter Geslak, *Principal*
EMP: 35
SQ FT: 48,974
SALES (est): 5.2MM **Privately Held**
SIC: 3589 2842 3561 5087 Car washing
machinery; cleaning or polishing preparations; pumps & pumping equipment; carwash equipment & supplies; soap & other
detergents

(G-6937)
J & G DIVERSIFIED
235 Jersey Ave Ste 5 (08901-3281)
PHONE..........................732 543-2537
Eli Komm, *President*
EMP: 5

SALES (est): 320K **Privately Held**
SIC: 3993 Signs & advertising specialties

(G-6938)
JETSTREAM OF HOUSTON LLP
Also Called: Fs Solutions
17 Jules Ln (08901-3643)
PHONE..........................732 448-7830
Alberto Albuquerque, *Opers Mgr*
EMP: 5
SALES (corp-wide): 1B **Publicly Held**
SIC: 5087 3563 Vacuum cleaning systems; spraying & dusting equipment
HQ: Jetstream Of Houston, Llp
5905 Thomas Rd
Houston TX 77041
832 590-1300

(G-6939)
JNJ INTERNATIONAL INV LLC
One Johnson/Johnson Plaza (08933-0001)
PHONE..........................732 524-0400
Zack Lemelle, *Vice Pres*
EMP: 6
SALES (est): 513.1K
SALES (corp-wide): 81.5B **Publicly Held**
SIC: 2676 2844 3841 3842 Feminine hygiene paper products; napkins, sanitary:
made from purchased paper; panty liners:
made from purchased paper; infant &
baby paper products; toilet preparations;
oral preparations; toilet preparations;
powder: baby, face, talcum or toilet; surgical & medical instruments; surgical instruments & apparatus; diagnostic apparatus,
medical; ophthalmic instruments & apparatus; surgical appliances & supplies; ligatures, medical; sutures, absorbable &
non-absorbable; dressings, surgical;
pharmaceutical preparations; drugs acting
on the central nervous system & sense
organs; dermatologicals; drugs affecting
parasitic & infective diseases
PA: Johnson & Johnson
1 Johnson And Johnson Plz
New Brunswick NJ 08933
732 524-0400

(G-6940)
JOHNSON & JOHNSON (PA)
1 Johnson And Johnson Plz (08933-0002)
P.O. Box 767, Neenah WI (54957-0767)
PHONE..........................732 524-0400
Alex Gorsky, *Ch of Bd*
Ashley McEvoy, *Chairman*
Jorge Mesquita, *Chairman*
Jennifer L Taubert, *Chairman*
Paulus Stoffels, *Exec VP*
EMP: 1000 EST: 1886
SALES: 81.5B **Publicly Held**
WEB: www.jnj.com
SIC: 2834 2676 3842 3841 Pharmaceutical preparations; drugs acting on the central nervous system & sense organs;
sanitary paper products; infant & baby
paper products; feminine hygiene paper
products; surgical appliances & supplies;
ligatures, medical; sutures, absorbable &
non-absorbable; dressings, surgical; surgical & medical instruments; surgical instruments & apparatus; diagnostic
apparatus, medical; ophthalmic instruments & apparatus; medical apparatus &
supplies; medical equipment & supplies

(G-6941)
JOHNSON & JOHNSON
100 Albany St Ste 100 # 100 (08901-1296)
PHONE..........................732 524-0400
Martes P Stepper, *Project Mgr*
Gabry Kuijten, *Manager*
Laura Zimmermann, *Admin Asst*
EMP: 147
SALES (corp-wide): 81.5B **Publicly Held**
WEB: www.jnj.com
SIC: 3842 3841 2834 2844 Surgical appliances & supplies; surgical & medical instruments; pharmaceutical preparations;
toilet preparations; feminine hygiene
paper products
PA: Johnson & Johnson
1 Johnson And Johnson Plz
New Brunswick NJ 08933
732 524-0400

(G-6942)
KVK USA INC
19 Home News Row Bldg A (08901-3601)
PHONE.....................................732 846-2355
Robert Sliner, *General Mgr*
◆ EMP: 10
SALES (est): 980K **Privately Held**
SIC: 2816 Inorganic pigments

(G-6943)
LASERWAVE GRAPHICS INC
24a Joyce Kilmer Ave N (08901-1950)
PHONE.....................................732 745-7764
Albert Hakim, *President*
Casey Antonucci, *Project Mgr*
Vince Lam, *Manager*
John Regina, *Director*
Jamie Hakim, *Teacher*
▲ EMP: 11
SQ FT: 2,000
SALES (est): 1.5MM **Privately Held**
WEB: www.laserwave.com
SIC: 2759 7336 2791 Commercial print-
ing; graphic arts & related design; type-
setting

(G-6944)
MANTTRA INC
1130 Somerset St (08901-3623)
PHONE.....................................877 962-6887
TT Jagannathan, *CEO*
S Ravichandran, *President*
T Jagannathan, *Principal*
K Shankaran, *Treasurer*
EMP: 4 EST: 1995
SALES: 2.6MM **Privately Held**
WEB: www.manttra.com
SIC: 3469 Pressure cookers, stamped or
drawn metal

(G-6945)
MCNICHOLS COMPANY
2 Home News Row (08901-3602)
PHONE.....................................877 884-4653
Arlene Schneier, *Sales Staff*
Glenn Stewart, *Branch Mgr*
EMP: 17
SALES (corp-wide): 177.1MM **Privately
Held**
SIC: 5051 3446 Steel; architectural metal-
work
PA: Mcnichols Company
2502 N Rocky Point Dr # 750
Tampa FL 33607
877 884-4653

(G-6946)
**MEDICAL DEVICE BUS SVCS
INC**
1 Johnson And Johnson Plz (08933-0001)
PHONE.....................................732 524-0400
Phil Bly, *Branch Mgr*
EMP: 5
SALES (corp-wide): 81.5B **Publicly Held**
SIC: 3842 Surgical appliances & supplies
HQ: Medical Device Business Services,
Inc.
700 Orthopaedic Dr
Warsaw IN 46582

(G-6947)
**METALLO GASKET COMPANY
INC**
16 Bethany St (08901-2324)
P.O. Box 550 (08903-0550)
PHONE.....................................732 545-7223
Frederick W Haleluk, *President*
N Lawrence Catanese, *Vice Pres*
EMP: 14
SQ FT: 16,000
SALES (est): 2.7MM **Privately Held**
WEB: www.metallogasket.com
SIC: 3053 5085 Gaskets, all materials; in-
dustrial supplies

(G-6948)
MISS SPORTSWEAR INC
745 Joyce Kilmer Ave (08901-3998)
PHONE.....................................212 391-2535
EMP: 9 **Privately Held**
SIC: 2329 Men's & boys' sportswear & ath-
letic clothing
PA: M.I.S.S. Sportswear, Inc.
1410 Broadway Rm 703
Brooklyn NY 10018

(G-6949)
**NBS GROUP SUP MED PDTS DIV
LLC**
Also Called: Nbs Medical
257 Livingston Ave Fl 3 (08901-3054)
P.O. Box 157, Milltown (08850-0157)
PHONE.....................................732 745-9292
Osman Boraie, *Mng Member*
EMP: 6
SQ FT: 2,000
SALES (est): 797.1K **Privately Held**
SIC: 3061 5047 Medical & surgical rubber
tubing (extruded & lathe-cut); medical &
hospital equipment

(G-6950)
NCONNEX INC
1 Richmond St Apt 3079 (08901-4508)
PHONE.....................................413 658-5582
Dan Xie, *Principal*
Yun Lin, *Principal*
EMP: 4
SALES (est): 270K **Privately Held**
SIC: 7372 Prepackaged software

(G-6951)
NETFRUITS INC
Also Called: Iweddingband.com
100 Jersey Ave (08901-3200)
PHONE.....................................732 249-2588
Hyun Yi, *President*
EMP: 4
SALES: 450K **Privately Held**
WEB: www.iweddingband.com
SIC: 3911 Jewelry, precious metal

(G-6952)
**NEW BRUNSWICK LAMP SHADE
CO**
7 Terminal Rd (08901-3615)
PHONE.....................................732 545-0377
◆ EMP: 26 EST: 1943
SALES (est): 2.7MM **Privately Held**
WEB: www.nbls.com
SIC: 3999 Shades, lamp or candle

(G-6953)
**NEW BRUNSWICK PLATING INC
(PA)**
596 Jersey Ave (08901-3502)
P.O. Box 7280, North Brunswick (08902-
7280)
PHONE.....................................732 545-6522
Robert Sica, *CEO*
Red Melchione, *President*
Brian Patterson, *COO*
Anthony Melchione, *Plant Mgr*
Bobbi Gumbinger, *CFO*
EMP: 52
SQ FT: 28,000
SALES (est): 6.9MM **Privately Held**
WEB: www.nbplating.com
SIC: 3471 Electroplating of metals or
formed products

(G-6954)
NIPPON BENKAN KAGYO
Also Called: Tube Line
475 Jersey Ave (08901-3297)
PHONE.....................................732 435-0777
Bob Sheldon, *Vice Pres*
EMP: 20 **Privately Held**
SIC: 3317 3494 Steel pipe & tubes; valves
& pipe fittings
PA: Nihon Bankin Kogyo K.K.
798-8, Shimokobashi, Sakaimachi
Sashima-Gun IBR 306-0

(G-6955)
**NOURYON SURFACE
CHEMISTRY**
500 Jersey Ave (08901)
PHONE.....................................312 544-7000
Jeff Simmonds, *Branch Mgr*
EMP: 65
SALES (corp-wide): 1.4B **Privately Held**
WEB: www.akzo-nobel.com
SIC: 2819 Catalysts, chemical
HQ: Nouryon Surface Chemistry
525 W Van Buren St # 1600
Chicago IL 60607
312 544-7000

(G-6956)
OHM LABORATORIES INC
14 Terminal Rd (08901-3616)
PHONE.....................................732 514-1072
John Foscolo, *Facilities Mgr*
Vasudeva Tatineni, *Research*
John Borja, *Engineer*
Phanindra Potineni, *Engineer*
Sanjay Shaw, *Branch Mgr*
EMP: 100
SALES (est): 1.3B **Privately Held**
WEB: www.ranbaxy.com
SIC: 2834 Pharmaceutical preparations
HQ: Ohm Laboratories, Inc.
1385 Livingston Ave
North Brunswick NJ 08902
732 418-2235

(G-6957)
**OMEGA CIRCUIT AND
ENGINEERING**
8 Terminal Rd (08901-3616)
PHONE.....................................732 246-1661
James C Genes, *President*
EMP: 30 EST: 1980
SQ FT: 16,000
SALES (est): 5.3MM **Privately Held**
WEB: www.omegacircuits.com
SIC: 3672 Circuit boards, television & radio
printed

(G-6958)
PLUMBING SUPPLY NOW LLC
167 Black Horse Ln (08902-4321)
PHONE.....................................732 228-8852
Evan Gartenberg,
EMP: 10
SQ FT: 250
SALES (est): 400.4K **Privately Held**
SIC: 3432 Plastic plumbing fixture fittings,
assembly

(G-6959)
POLVAC INC
235 Jersey Ave Ste 1 (08901-3281)
PHONE.....................................732 828-1662
Marek Ringwelski, *Owner*
EMP: 4
SQ FT: 2,600
SALES (est): 280K **Privately Held**
WEB: www.polvac.net
SIC: 3563 Vacuum pumps, except labora-
tory

(G-6960)
**PRESTIGE FORKLIFT MAINT
SVC**
31 Timber Ridge Rd (08902-5514)
PHONE.....................................732 297-1001
Phil Hill, *President*
EMP: 4 EST: 2001
SALES (est): 337.2K **Privately Held**
SIC: 3537 Forklift trucks

(G-6961)
**PRIMESOURCE BUILDING PDTS
INC**
20 Van Dyke Ave (08901-3253)
P.O. Box 6330, Edison (08818-6330)
PHONE.....................................732 296-0600
Dan Javitt, *Branch Mgr*
EMP: 25
SALES (corp-wide): 785.9MM **Privately
Held**
WEB: www.primesourcebp.com
SIC: 3965 Fasteners, buttons, needles &
pins
PA: Primesource Building Products, Inc.
1321 Greenway Dr
Irving TX 75038
972 999-8500

(G-6962)
PROCEDYNE CORP (PA)
11 Industrial Dr (08901-3657)
PHONE.....................................732 249-8347
Thomas R Parr, *President*
Bob Schulz, *Vice Pres*
EMP: 40
SQ FT: 60,000

SALES (est): 11.7MM **Privately Held**
WEB: www.procedyne.com
SIC: 3567 5065 8711 5051 Industrial furnaces & ovens; electronic parts & equipment; engineering services; metals
service centers & offices; chemical preparations

(G-6963)
PUBLISHING TECHNOLOGY INC
317 George St Ste 320 (08901-2091)
PHONE.....................................732 563-9292
EMP: 7
SALES (corp-wide): 15.4MM **Privately
Held**
WEB: www.publishingtechnology.com
SIC: 2711 Newspapers, publishing & print-
ing
PA: Ingenta Plc
8100 Alec Issigonis Way
Oxford OXON OX4 2
186 539-7800

(G-6964)
**R J BLEN GRPHIC ARTS
CNVERTING**
Also Called: Rj Bielan Graphic Arts
6 Jules Ln (08901-3636)
PHONE.....................................732 545-3501
Robert J Bielen, *President*
EMP: 22 EST: 1956
SQ FT: 18,000
SALES (est): 3.6MM **Privately Held**
SIC: 2675 2657 Paper die-cutting; paper-
board die-cutting; folding paperboard
boxes

(G-6965)
R K S PLASTICS INC
Also Called: All Size Polybags
100 Jersey Ave Ste B6 (08901-3271)
P.O. Box 836 (08903-0836)
PHONE.....................................732 435-8517
Sudhir Shah, *President*
Steve Levee, *Sales Mgr*
EMP: 8
SQ FT: 4,500
SALES (est): 2.7MM **Privately Held**
WEB: www.rksplastics.com
SIC: 5113 2673 Bags, paper & disposable
plastic; plastic bags: made from pur-
chased materials

(G-6966)
**RARITAN PACKAGING
INDUSTRIES**
Also Called: Raritan Container
570 Jersey Ave (08901-3502)
P.O. Box 7237, North Brunswick (08902-
7237)
PHONE.....................................732 246-7200
Bernard L Newman, *President*
Sandra Newman, *Vice Pres*
EMP: 26
SQ FT: 40,000
SALES: 3MM **Privately Held**
WEB: www.raritancontainer.com
SIC: 2653 5085 Boxes, corrugated: made
from purchased materials; packing, indus-
trial

(G-6967)
RELIABOTICS LLC
24 Van Dyke Ave (08901-3253)
PHONE.....................................732 791-5500
Mina Nassar, *Electrical Engi*
Steve Evers, *VP Sales*
Marci Tapper, *Office Mgr*
Juan Vega, *Mng Member*
EMP: 6
SALES (est): 786.7K **Privately Held**
SIC: 3535 Robotic conveyors

(G-6968)
RETRIEVEX
5 Home News Row (08901-3601)
PHONE.....................................732 247-3200
Leon Kroll, *CEO*
EMP: 5
SALES (est): 548.4K **Privately Held**
SIC: 3554 Cutting machines, paper

(G-6969)
ROYAL COSMETICS CORPORATION
Also Called: Royale Cosmetics
4 Jules Ln A (08901-3636)
PHONE...................................732 246-7275
Doodnauth Tulshi, *President*
Deancalli Tulshi, *Vice Pres*
▲ EMP: 14
SQ FT: 4,000
SALES (est): 2.2MM **Privately Held**
SIC: 2844 Toilet preparations

(G-6970)
SHERWOOD BRANDS CORPORATION
120 Jersey Ave (08901-3289)
PHONE...................................973 249-8200
Steve Deusch, *CEO*
EMP: 10
SALES (est): 552.2K **Privately Held**
SIC: 2064 Candy bars, including chocolate covered bars

(G-6971)
SPECTRUM LABORATORY PDTS INC (PA)
Also Called: Spectrum Chemicals & Lab Pdts
769 Jersey Ave (08901-3605)
PHONE...................................732 214-1300
Randy Burg, *President*
Nathalie Burg, *Principal*
Paul Burg, *Principal*
Rodica Cohen Burg, *Principal*
Vladimir Valentekovich, *VP Opers*
◆ EMP: 110 EST: 1971
SQ FT: 140,000
SALES (est): 60.4MM **Privately Held**
SIC: 2869 2899 5047 Laboratory chemicals, organic; chemical preparations; diagnostic equipment, medical

(G-6972)
SPECTRUM LABORATORY PDTS INC
Also Called: Spectrum Quality Products
755 769 & 777 Jersey Ave (08901)
PHONE...................................732 214-1300
Paul Burg, *Branch Mgr*
Adan Hernandez, *Manager*
Carlos Arbona, *Executive*
Nicole Quinlan-Lee, *Representative*
EMP: 35
SALES (corp-wide): 60.4MM **Privately Held**
SIC: 5169 2819 2869 2899 Organic chemicals, synthetic; industrial inorganic chemicals; laboratory chemicals, organic; chemical preparations
PA: Spectrum Laboratory Products, Inc.
769 Jersey Ave
New Brunswick NJ 08901
732 214-1300

(G-6973)
TARGUM PUBLISHING COMPANY
Also Called: Daily Targum
126 College Ave Ste 431 (08901-1166)
PHONE...................................732 247-1286
M Stefanelli, *Business Mgr*
Michelle Stefanelli, *Business Mgr*
Christopher Mahon, *Bd of Directors*
Selene Maugeri, *Bd of Directors*
Garret Bell, *Assistant*
EMP: 50
SQ FT: 1,000
SALES: 1.3MM **Privately Held**
WEB: www.dailytargum.com
SIC: 2711 Newspapers, publishing & printing

(G-6974)
TREK II PRODUCTS INC
400 Jersey Ave Ste 1 (08901-3589)
PHONE...................................732 214-9200
Michael Smokowicz, *Principal*
EMP: 7
SALES (est): 725.3K **Privately Held**
WEB: www.trekii.com
SIC: 8748 3931 Business consulting; musical instruments

(G-6975)
UNITED MIJOVI AMER LTD LBLTY
21 Roseland Pl (08902-2909)
PHONE...................................732 718-1001
Marcos Carrington, *President*
EMP: 10
SALES (est): 660K **Privately Held**
SIC: 2095 5149 Instant coffee; coffee & tea

(G-6976)
UNITED SILICON CARBIDE INC
100 Jersey Ave Bldg A (08901-3200)
PHONE...................................732 565-9500
Jhi Yong, *Principal*
EMP: 4 EST: 2010
SALES (est): 559.1K **Privately Held**
SIC: 2819 Carbides

(G-6977)
UNIVERSAL PRTEIN SPPLMNTS CORP (PA)
Also Called: Universal Labs
3 Terminal Rd (08901-3615)
PHONE...................................732 545-3130
Michael Rockoff, *CEO*
Clyde Rockoff, *President*
Juliet Janisz, *Editor*
Jordan Shallow, *Med Doctor*
◆ EMP: 100
SQ FT: 100,000
SALES (est): 40.4MM **Privately Held**
SIC: 2834 2032 Vitamin, nutrient & hematinic preparations for human use; vitamin preparations; canned specialties

(G-6978)
US PHARMA LAB INC (PA)
22 Van Dyke Ave (08901-3253)
PHONE...................................888 296-8775
Ashok Luhadia, *President*
Amol Luhadia, *Vice Pres*
Neha Shah, *Project Mgr*
Anil Shetty, *VP Finance*
Scott Specht, *Sales Staff*
▼ EMP: 125
SQ FT: 100,000
SALES (est): 44MM **Privately Held**
WEB: www.uspharmalab.com
SIC: 2834 Pharmaceutical preparations

(G-6979)
WATCHITUDE LLC
24a Joyce Kilmer Ave N (08901-1950)
PHONE...................................732 745-2626
Dan Hakim,
EMP: 5
SALES (est): 178.2K **Privately Held**
SIC: 3873 Watches & parts, except crystals & jewels

(G-6980)
WENNER BREAD PRODUCTS INC
571 Jersey Ave (08901-3501)
PHONE...................................631 563-6262
EMP: 104
SALES (corp-wide): 105.7MM **Privately Held**
SIC: 2051 2053 5461 Bread, all types (white, wheat, rye, etc); fresh or frozen; frozen bakery products, except bread; bakeries
PA: Wenner Bread Products, Inc.
2001 Orville Dr N
Ronkonkoma NY 11779
800 869-6262

(G-6981)
WHITE LOTUS HOME LTD LBLTY CO
745 Joyce Kilmer Ave (08901-3998)
PHONE...................................732 828-2111
Marlon Pando, *President*
EMP: 16
SQ FT: 6,000
SALES (est): 2.6MM **Privately Held**
WEB: www.whitelotus.net
SIC: 2392 5712 2515 Blankets, comforters & beddings; cushions & pillows; furniture stores; unfinished furniture; mattresses & foundations

(G-6982)
WOODLINE WORKS CORPORATION
625 Jersey Ave Ste 9 (08901-3679)
PHONE...................................732 828-9100
Song Wu, *President*
▲ EMP: 30
SQ FT: 24,000
SALES (est): 2.4MM **Privately Held**
SIC: 2511 Wood household furniture

New Egypt
Ocean County

(G-6983)
GO R DESIGN LLC
74 Hemlock Dr (08533-2738)
PHONE...................................609 286-2146
Tim Klein, *Mng Member*
EMP: 30
SQ FT: 3,000
SALES (est): 2.1MM **Privately Held**
SIC: 3499 3645 7336 Novelties & giftware, including trophies; residential lighting fixtures; commercial art & graphic design

(G-6984)
KINI PRODUCTS INC
7 Forest Hill Dr (08533-2731)
PHONE...................................732 299-5555
Nancy Gingrich, *President*
Neil B Gingrich Jr, *Vice Pres*
EMP: 5
SALES (est): 450K **Privately Held**
SIC: 2822 5099 Silicone rubbers; cases, carrying

(G-6985)
LITTLE HOUSE CANDLES INC
20 Province Line Rd (08533-1008)
PHONE...................................609 758-2996
Jennifer Ingalls, *President*
EMP: 5
SALES: 1MM **Privately Held**
WEB: www.littlehousecandles.com
SIC: 3999 5947 Candles; gift, novelty & souvenir shop

(G-6986)
VAHLCO RACING WHEELS LLC
849 Route 539 (08533-2004)
PHONE...................................609 758-7013
Fred Vahlsing, *President*
EMP: 4 EST: 2014
SALES (est): 442.4K **Privately Held**
SIC: 3714 Motor vehicle wheels & parts

(G-6987)
W2F INC (PA)
167 Archertown Rd (08533-1904)
P.O. Box 1291, Browns Mills (08015-8291)
PHONE...................................609 735-0135
Bob Jenkins, *President*
EMP: 6
SQ FT: 1,200
SALES: 980K **Privately Held**
SIC: 3449 3711 Miscellaneous metalwork; automobile assembly, including specialty automobiles

---

New Gretna
Burlington County

(G-6988)
VIKING YACHT COMPANY (PA)
On The Bass Riv Rr 9 (08224)
P.O. Box 308 (08224-0308)
PHONE...................................609 296-6000
Robert T Healey, *CEO*
Brian Keenan, *General Mgr*
Pat Healey, *Exec VP*
Patrick Healey, *Exec VP*
Joe Schwab, *Vice Pres*
▲ EMP: 271
SQ FT: 400,000
SALES: 280MM **Privately Held**
WEB: www.vikingyachts.com
SIC: 3732 Yachts, building & repairing

New Milford
Bergen County

(G-6989)
DMJ TECHNOLOGIES LLC
775 Maple St (07646-3005)
PHONE...................................201 261-5560
Steven Robert Lehr,
Julie Walder,
EMP: 6
SALES (est): 722.5K **Privately Held**
SIC: 3651 Audio electronic systems

(G-6990)
METRO PUBLISHING GROUP INC
Also Called: Metro Features
626 Mccarthy Dr (07646-1029)
PHONE...................................201 385-2000
Robert Nesoff, *President*
EMP: 10
SALES (est): 480K **Privately Held**
SIC: 2791 Typesetting

(G-6991)
PETER-LISAND MACHINE CORP
262 Voorhis Ave (07646-1924)
PHONE...................................201 943-5600
Peter Guasti, *President*
EMP: 4
SQ FT: 7,600
SALES: 200K **Privately Held**
WEB: www.peterlisand.com
SIC: 3651 3663 Household video equipment; radio & TV communications equipment

(G-6992)
SCOTT GRAPHICS PRINTING CO INC
690 River Rd Ste D (07646-2903)
PHONE...................................201 262-0473
Scott McNiff, *President*
Charles McNiff, *Vice Pres*
Joanne McNiff, *Treasurer*
Christie McNiff, *Art Dir*
Margaret McNiff, *Admin Sec*
EMP: 9
SQ FT: 6,000
SALES (est): 1.3MM **Privately Held**
WEB: www.scottgraphicsprinting.com
SIC: 2752 2791 2789 Commercial printing, offset; typesetting; bookbinding & related work

---

New Providence
Union County

(G-6993)
ALCATEL-LUCENT USA INC
600 Mountain Ave 700 (07974-2008)
PHONE...................................908 582-3275
Holly Anderson, *Partner*
Bob Verber, *Partner*
Sumeet Kaushal, *General Mgr*
Allison Cerra, *Vice Pres*
Marc Charriere, *Vice Pres*
EMP: 61
SALES (corp-wide): 25.8B **Privately Held**
SIC: 3661 7372 3663 3674 Telephone & telegraph apparatus; prepackaged software; radio broadcasting & communications equipment; integrated circuits, semiconductor networks, etc.
HQ: Nokia Of America Corporation
600 Mountain Ave Ste 700
New Providence NJ 07974

(G-6994)
APERAM STNLSS SVC & SOLUTNS
98 Floral Ave Ste 102 (07974-1542)
PHONE...................................908 988-0625
Ines Kolmsee, *CEO*
Guillaume Vercaemer, *General Mgr*
Shelley K Rome, *Purchasing*
David B Vu, *Engineer*
Ted R Niemiec, *Director*
◆ EMP: 43
SQ FT: 5,000

(PA)=Parent Co (HQ)=Headquarters (DH)=Div Headquarters
✪ = New Business established in last 2 years

2019 Harris New Jersey
Manufacturers Directory

271

G E O G R A P H I C

SALES (est): 54.7MM
SALES (corp-wide): 841.7MM **Privately Held**
SIC: **3312** Blast furnaces & steel mills
PA: Aperam
R. Guillaume Kroll 12c
Luxembourg 1882
273 627-00

(G-6995)
BOC GROUP INC
575 Mountain Ave (07974-2078)
PHONE...................................908 665-2400
Trevor J Burt, *President*
Mohamed Yussouf, *Engineer*
David L Brooks, *Treasurer*
James A Boyce, *Asst Treas*
Richard Jacobsen, *Manager*
▲ EMP: 856
SQ FT: 215,000
SALES (est): 406MM
SALES (corp-wide): 613.2MM **Privately Held**
SIC: **2813** 3569 3559 3561 Industrial gases; oxygen, compressed or liquefied; nitrogen; argon; gas producers, generators & other gas related equipment; cryogenic machinery, industrial; pumps & pumping equipment; turbines & turbine generator sets; flow instruments, industrial process type
HQ: B O C Holdings
The Priestley Centre,
Guildford GU2 7

(G-6996)
BOWMAR ENTERPRISES INC
Also Called: Accent Printing Solutions
558 Cent Ave (07974)
PHONE...................................908 277-3000
Michael Tan, *President*
EMP: 9
SQ FT: 3,500
SALES (est): 1.5MM **Privately Held**
SIC: **2752** 2791 Commercial printing, offset; photo-offset printing; typesetting

(G-6997)
CHEMETALL US INC (HQ)
Also Called: Chemetall Americas
675 Central Ave (07974-1560)
PHONE...................................908 464-6900
Ronald Felber, *President*
Mark Bruner, *President*
Gregory V Poff, *Vice Pres*
Kevin Filipski, *CFO*
▲ EMP: 80
SQ FT: 37,000
SALES (est): 114.5MM
SALES (corp-wide): 71.7B **Privately Held**
WEB: www.chemetall.com
SIC: **2842** 2899 2851 Specialty cleaning, polishes & sanitation goods; metal treating compounds; paints & allied products
PA: Basf Se
Carl-Bosch-Str. 38
Ludwigshafen Am Rhein 67056
621 600-

(G-6998)
FABLOK MILLS INC
140 Spring St (07974-1152)
P.O. Box 900 (07974-0900)
PHONE...................................908 464-1950
Alex Fisher, *President*
▲ EMP: 40 EST: 1952
SQ FT: 32,000
SALES (est): 5.3MM **Privately Held**
WEB: www.fablokmills.com
SIC: **2221** 2258 Broadwoven fabric mills, manmade; lace & warp knit fabric mills

(G-6999)
FLODYNE CONTROLS INC
48 Commerce Dr (07974-1142)
PHONE...................................908 464-6200
Carol Perrin, *President*
Michael Perrin, *Vice Pres*
Craig Kalugin, *Info Tech Mgr*
EMP: 25 EST: 1960
SQ FT: 30,000
SALES (est): 5.1MM **Privately Held**
WEB: www.flodynecontrols.com
SIC: **3491** Industrial valves

(G-7000)
FRC ELECTRICAL INDUSTRIES INC
705 Central Ave Ste 3 (07974-1151)
PHONE...................................908 464-3200
Ahmed El-Mahdawy, *Manager*
EMP: 44 **Privately Held**
SIC: **3679** 3444 3643 3053 Hermetic seals for electronic equipment; sheet metalwork; current-carrying wiring devices; gaskets, packing & sealing devices; electrical equipment & supplies
PA: Frc Electrical Industries Inc
1260 Clearmont St Ne
Palm Bay FL 32905

(G-7001)
FREEMAN TECHNICAL SALES INC
148 Maple St (07974-2405)
PHONE...................................908 464-4784
David Freeman, *President*
EMP: 1 EST: 2008
SQ FT: 400
SALES (est): 3.2MM **Privately Held**
SIC: **3999** Barber & beauty shop equipment

(G-7002)
GRAPHIC IMAGERY INC
556 Central Ave Ste 1 (07974-1563)
PHONE...................................908 755-2882
Linda Maher, *President*
EMP: 10
SQ FT: 1,600
SALES (est): 1.1MM **Privately Held**
WEB: www.graphicimagery.com
SIC: **7336** 2759 Graphic arts & related design; promotional printing

(G-7003)
GRAVER WATER SYSTEMS LLC (DH)
Also Called: Graver Water Division
675 Central Ave Ste 3 (07974-1560)
PHONE...................................908 516-1400
Robert Gluth,
Gregory Allemano,
Patrick Allen,
Michael O'Brien,
▼ EMP: 2
SQ FT: 40,000
SALES (est): 8.8MM
SALES (corp-wide): 225.3B **Publicly Held**
WEB: www.graver.com
SIC: **3589** Water treatment equipment, industrial
HQ: Marmon Industrial Llc
181 W Madison St Fl 26
Chicago IL 60602
312 372-9500

(G-7004)
INFORMATION TODAY INC
630 Central Ave Fl 2 (07974-1506)
PHONE...................................908 219-0279
Thomas Hogan Sr, *President*
John Yersak, *Vice Pres*
Nixon Carol, *Manager*
Bill Spence, *CIO*
EMP: 17
SALES (corp-wide): 20.3MM **Privately Held**
SIC: **2741** Directories: publishing only, not printed on site
PA: Information Today, Inc.
143 Old Marlton Pike
Medford NJ 08055
609 654-6266

(G-7005)
LAWYERS DIARY AND MANUAL LLC
890 Mountain Ave Ste 300 (07974-1218)
PHONE...................................973 642-1440
Andrew Strauss, *Chairman*
David Stein, *CFO*
EMP: 35
SALES (est): 2.7MM **Privately Held**
SIC: **2721** Periodicals: publishing only

(G-7006)
LINDE GLOBAL HELIUM INC
575 Mountain Ave (07974-2097)
PHONE...................................908 464-8100
Stephen Penn, *Principal*
▲ EMP: 24
SALES (est): 2.7MM **Privately Held**
SIC: **2813** Helium
HQ: Linde Gas North America Llc
200 Somerset Corp Blvd # 7000
Bridgewater NJ 08807

(G-7007)
LINDE NORTH AMERICA INC
575 Mountain Ave (07974-2097)
PHONE...................................908 464-8100
Christian Lafleur, *General Mgr*
Sebastian Elizagaray, *Business Mgr*
Shirley Kim, *Counsel*
Rob Capellman, *Vice Pres*
David Johnston, *Vice Pres*
EMP: 98
SALES (corp-wide): 1.4B **Privately Held**
SIC: **3569** 3559 3561 3511 Gas producers, generators & other gas related equipment; cryogenic machinery, industrial; pumps & pumping equipment; turbines & turbine generator sets; flow instruments, industrial process type; argon
HQ: Messer North America, Inc.
200 Somerset Corporate Bl
Bridgewater NJ 08807
908 464-8100

(G-7008)
LUCENT TECHNOLOGIES WORLD SVCS
600 Mountain Ave (07974-2008)
PHONE...................................908 582-3000
Holly Anderson, *Partner*
Dave Bolka, *Vice Pres*
Gil Harris, *Vice Pres*
George Hellmuth, *Vice Pres*
Rudy Hoebeke, *Vice Pres*
EMP: 200
SALES (est): 41MM
SALES (corp-wide): 25.8B **Privately Held**
WEB: www.bell-labs.com
SIC: **5065** 7622 3674 3663 Electronic parts & equipment; communication equipment repair; semiconductors & related devices; radio & TV communications equipment; telephone & telegraph apparatus; computer peripheral equipment
HQ: Alcatel-Lucent Technologies Holdings Inc.
600 Mountain Ave 700
New Providence NJ 07974
908 582-8500

(G-7009)
MARQUIS - WHOS WHO INC
Also Called: National Register Publishing
430 Mountain Ave Ste 403 (07974-2732)
PHONE...................................908 673-1006
Fred Marks, *Managing Dir*
Gene McGovern, *Principal*
James Finkelstein, *Principal*
Charles Lillis, *Vice Pres*
John Macdonald, *Vice Pres*
EMP: 80
SQ FT: 22,000
SALES (est): 9.9MM **Privately Held**
WEB: www.marquiswhoswho.com
SIC: **2741** Miscellaneous publishing

(G-7010)
MESSER LLC
100 Mountain Ave (07974-2069)
PHONE...................................908 464-8100
Claus Nussgruber, *Vice Pres*
Tom Pivonka, *Plant Mgr*
Carl Goode, *Opers Mgr*
Matthew Leong, *Facilities Mgr*
Cruz Bill, *Engineer*
EMP: 50
SALES (corp-wide): 1.4B **Privately Held**
SIC: **2813** Oxygen, compressed or liquefied
HQ: Messer Llc
200 Somerset Corp Blvd # 7000
Bridgewater NJ 08807
908 464-8100

(G-7011)
MESSER MERCHANT PRODUCTION LLC (DH)
Also Called: Linde Merchant Production, LLC
575 Mountain Ave (07974-2097)
PHONE...................................908 464-8100
Patrick F Murphy, *President*
EMP: 13
SALES (est): 2MM **Privately Held**
SIC: **2813** Oxygen, compressed or liquefied

(G-7012)
MGL PRINTING SOLUTION LLC
Also Called: Mgl Forms
154 South St Ste 1 (07974-2933)
PHONE...................................908 665-1999
Fred Smith, *CEO*
Darren Lowe, *General Ptnr*
Christopher Lowe,
Gregory Lowe,
Matthew Lowe,
EMP: 5
SQ FT: 2,300
SALES (est): 865.2K **Privately Held**
WEB: www.mglforms.com
SIC: **2752** Commercial printing, lithographic

(G-7013)
NEW VENTURE PARTNERS LLC
430 Mountain Ave Ste 404 (07974-2732)
P.O. Box 881 (07974-0881)
PHONE...................................908 464-8131
Anthony Abrahams, *CFO*
Chris Winter,
Harry Berry,
Dror Futter,
Franklin Rimalovski,
EMP: 600
SALES (est): 27MM **Privately Held**
WEB: www.nvpllc.com
SIC: **7372** Business oriented computer software

(G-7014)
NOKIA OF AMERICA CORPORATION (DH)
Also Called: Lucent
600 Mountain Ave Ste 700 (07974-2008)
P.O. Box 696526, San Antonio TX (78269-6526)
PHONE...................................908 582-3275
Michel Combes, *CEO*
Jeff Cortley, *President*
Satoshi Fujita, *President*
Frank Noviello, *President*
Shashank Deulkar, *General Mgr*
◆ EMP: 1300
SALES (est): 8.5B
SALES (corp-wide): 25.8B **Privately Held**
WEB: www.lucent.com
SIC: **3674** 7372 Integrated circuits, semiconductor networks, etc.; hybrid integrated circuits; prepackaged software
HQ: Alcatel Lucent
148 Route Nokia Paris Saclay
Nozay 91620
961 560-239

(G-7015)
ONTIMEWORKS LLC
Also Called: Everythingbenefits
1253 Springfield Ave (07974-2931)
PHONE...................................800 689-3568
Kevin Kelso, *Partner*
Dmitry Korsunsky, *CIO*
Rachel Lyubovitzky,
EMP: 19
SALES (est): 489.3K **Privately Held**
SIC: **7372** Business oriented computer software

(G-7016)
REEVES ENTERPRISES INC
Also Called: Templar Food Products
562 Central Ave (07974-1555)
PHONE...................................800 883-6752
Edward Reeves Jr, *President*
Ann Reeves, *Corp Secy*
Michael Murray, *Vice Pres*
Michael Eagan, *Opers Mgr*
▼ EMP: 7
SQ FT: 1,700

SALES (est): 943.6K Privately Held
WEB: www.icedtea.com
SIC: 2087 Beverage bases

(G-7017)
RR BOWKER LLC (HQ)
630 Central Ave (07974-1506)
PHONE.................................908 286-1090
Annie Callanan, *CEO*
Peter Ashekian, *Manager*
Gary Aiello,
Michael Cairns,
Robert N Snyder,
EMP: 155
SALES (est): 22.4MM
SALES (corp-wide): 345.3MM **Privately
Held**
WEB: www.bowker.com
SIC: 2731 Books: publishing only
PA: Cambridge Information Group, Inc.
    888 7th Ave Ste 1701
    New York NY 10106
    301 961-6700

(G-7018)
SKINDER-STRAUSS LLC (PA)
Also Called: Lawyers Diary & Manual
890 Mountain Ave Ste 300 (07974-1218)
P.O. Box 1027, Summit (07902-1027)
PHONE.................................973 642-1440
Andrew Strauss, *CEO*
Robert W Pladek, *President*
Karen Harris, *Partner*
Jerrold Krivitzky, *Partner*
Trudi Krivitzky, *Partner*
EMP: 125
SQ FT: 24,000
SALES (est): 28.7MM **Privately Held**
WEB: www.lawdiary.com
SIC: 2721 7389 Periodicals: publishing &
    printing; courier or messenger service

(G-7019)
SUNHAM HOME FASHIONS LLC
700 Central Park Ave (07974)
PHONE.................................908 363-1100
Christine Field, *Controller*
Richard Landis, *Manager*
Simon Lee, *Info Tech Mgr*
Tim Dong, *Technology*
EMP: 75 **Privately Held**
SIC: 2392 Blankets, comforters & beddings
PA: Sunham Home Fashions, Llc
    136 Madison Ave Fl 16
    New York NY 10016

(G-7020)
TAP INTO LLC
66 W 4th St (07974-1923)
P.O. Box 794 (07974-0794)
PHONE.................................908 370-1158
Michael Shapiro, *CEO*
Cheryl Brown, *Publisher*
Fred Smith, *Publisher*
Jonathan Sym, *Editor*
Natalie Hackett, *Manager*
EMP: 4 EST: 2013
SALES (est): 377.9K **Privately Held**
SIC: 7311 2741 7389 Advertising consult-
    ant; miscellaneous publishing;

(G-7021)
TAPINTONET
598 Central Ave Ste 7 (07974-1500)
PHONE.................................908 279-0303
Tim Lecras, *Director*
EMP: 9
SALES (est): 232.7K **Privately Held**
SIC: 2711 Newspapers

(G-7022)
TETLEY USA INC (HQ)
890 Mountain Ave Ste 105 (07974-1218)
PHONE.................................800 728-0084
Micheal Camp, *Principal*
Michael Fischle, *Principal*
▲ EMP: 28
SQ FT: 20,000
SALES (est): 35.6MM
SALES (corp-wide): 470.2MM **Privately
Held**
WEB: www.tetleyusa.com
SIC: 2099 Tea blending

PA: Tata Global Beverages Limited
    3rd Floor, Block C
    Bengaluru KA 56002
    806 717-1200

(G-7023)
UNISPHERE MEDIA LLC
630 Central Ave (07974-1506)
PHONE.................................908 795-3701
Thomas J Wilson,
Calvin Carr,
Daniel Fishman,
Elliot King,
EMP: 10
SQ FT: 800
SALES: 942.9K **Privately Held**
SIC: 2721 Magazines: publishing & printing

(G-7024)
VERTICE PHARMA LLC (PA)
630 Central Ave (07974-1506)
PHONE.................................877 530-1633
Don Degolyer, *President*
Scott Meyers, *COO*
Noel Greenberger, *Vice Pres*
Indranil Nandi, *Vice Pres*
Marc Padre, *Vice Pres*
EMP: 50
SALES (est): 63.8MM **Privately Held**
SIC: 2834 5122 Pharmaceutical prepara-
    tions; pharmaceuticals

(G-7025)
VISTAPHARM INC (HQ)
630 Central Ave (07974-1506)
PHONE.................................908 376-1622
Don Degolyer, *CEO*
Ozgur Kilic, *CFO*
▲ EMP: 200 EST: 1998
SALES (est): 49.6MM
SALES (corp-wide): 63.8MM **Privately
Held**
WEB: www.vistapharm.com
SIC: 2834 Proprietary drug products
PA: Vertice Pharma, Llc
    630 Central Ave
    New Providence NJ 07974
    877 530-1633

┌─────────────────────────┐
│   **Newark**   │
│   *Essex County*   │
└─────────────────────────┘

(G-7026)
24 HORAS INC
68 Madison St Ste A (07105-7109)
PHONE.................................973 817-7400
Victor Alves, *President*
EMP: 10
SALES (est): 487K **Privately Held**
WEB: www.24horasinc.com
SIC: 2711 1751 Newspapers: publishing
    only, not printed on site; carpentry work

(G-7027)
26 FLAVORS LLC
Also Called: Crazy Cups
29 Riverside Ave Bldg 2 (07104-4237)
PHONE.................................855 662-7299
Brian Sanders,
EMP: 8
SALES (est): 426.5K **Privately Held**
SIC: 2095 Roasted coffee

(G-7028)
A & L INDUSTRIES INC
Also Called: Ace Powder Coating
23 George St (07105-3526)
PHONE.................................973 589-8070
Elton Lima, *President*
EMP: 22
SQ FT: 35,000
SALES (est): 3MM **Privately Held**
SIC: 3471 Finishing, metals or formed
    products

(G-7029)
A C TRANSFORMER CORP
89 Madison St (07105-2191)
PHONE.................................973 589-8574
Robert Giangrande, *President*
Irene Giangrande, *Corp Secy*
EMP: 6 EST: 1949
SQ FT: 11,000

SALES (est): 780K **Privately Held**
WEB: www.actransformer.com
SIC: 3612 3677 Autotransformers, electric
    (power transformers); electronic coils,
    transformers & other inductors

(G-7030)
A V HYDRAULICS LTD LBLTY CO
2 Avenue C (07114-2602)
PHONE.................................973 621-6800
EMP: 5
SALES (est): 544.8K **Privately Held**
SIC: 3492 Control valves, aircraft: hy-
    draulic & pneumatic

(G-7031)
A-1 PLASTIC BAGS INC
136 Tichenor St (07105-1018)
PHONE.................................973 344-4441
Benjamin A Schwartz, *President*
▲ EMP: 75
SQ FT: 57,000
SALES (est): 13.5MM **Privately Held**
WEB: www.complast.com
SIC: 2673 Plastic bags: made from pur-
    chased materials

(G-7032)
**AARHUSKARLSHAMN USA INC
(PA)**
131 Marsh St (07114-3238)
PHONE.................................973 344-1300
Arne Frank, *CEO*
Terrence Thomas, *President*
Dennis Tagarelli, *Vice Pres*
Ann C Andersson, *Research*
Nick Birosik, *Engineer*
▲ EMP: 40 EST: 1998
SALES (est): 36.8MM **Privately Held**
SIC: 2079 Edible fats & oils

(G-7033)
ABCO DIE CASTERS INC
39 Tompkins Point Rd (07114-2814)
PHONE.................................973 624-7030
Joseph Vitollo, *President*
Steve Vitollo, *Vice Pres*
Fred Vitollo, *Treasurer*
▲ EMP: 80 EST: 1971
SQ FT: 60,000
SALES (est): 11.1MM **Privately Held**
SIC: 3479 3364 Coating of metals &
    formed products; zinc & zinc-base alloy
    die-castings

(G-7034)
**ACE BAG & BURLAP COMPANY
INC**
Also Called: Aceco Industrial Packaging Co
166 Frelinghuysen Ave (07114-1694)
PHONE.................................973 242-2200
Richard J Sherman, *President*
Linda Sherman, *Treasurer*
EMP: 12
SQ FT: 36,400
SALES (est): 2.3MM **Privately Held**
SIC: 5199 2393 Packaging materials; tex-
    tile bags

(G-7035)
ADCO CHEMICAL COMPANY INC
49 Rutherford St (07105-4820)
PHONE.................................973 589-0880
George Parker, *President*
Eleanor Parker, *Corp Secy*
Richard Carr, *Asst Sec*
EMP: 35 EST: 1936
SQ FT: 10,000
SALES (est): 6.1MM **Privately Held**
SIC: 2821 Plastics materials & resins

(G-7036)
ADVOCATE PUBLISHING CORP
Also Called: Directory & Almanac
171 Clifton Ave (07104-1019)
PHONE.................................973 497-4200
Isabel Kirchner, *Ch of Bd*
Archbishop John J Myers, *President*
Archbishop J Myers, *Principal*
EMP: 20
SQ FT: 8,000

SALES (est): 1MM
SALES (corp-wide): 62MM **Privately
Held**
WEB: www.ourladyofsorrowsschool.org
SIC: 2711 Newspapers: publishing only,
    not printed on site
PA: Roman Catholic Archdiocese Of
    Newark
    171 Clifton Ave
    Newark NJ 07104
    973 497-4000

(G-7037)
AIRMET INC
Also Called: Airmet Metal Works
794 N 6th St (07107-2717)
PHONE.................................973 481-5550
Stephen Yavorski, *President*
Cynthia Yavorski, *Office Mgr*
EMP: 7
SQ FT: 10,000
SALES (est): 731.9K **Privately Held**
WEB: www.airmet.com
SIC: 1711 3444 3446 3443 Mechanical
    contractor; sheet metalwork; architectural
    metalwork; fabricated plate work (boiler
    shop); fabricated structural metal

(G-7038)
ALL METAL POLISHING CO INC
23 George St (07105-3526)
PHONE.................................973 589-8070
Elton Lima, *President*
EMP: 25
SQ FT: 15,000
SALES (est): 1.7MM **Privately Held**
SIC: 3471 Polishing, metals or formed
    products; plating of metals or formed
    products

(G-7039)
ALLIED METAL INDUSTRIES INC
Also Called: Allied Steel Dist & Svc Ctr
118 Harper St 144 (07114-2804)
PHONE.................................973 824-7347
Toll Free:.................................888 -
Donald De Faria Jr, *CEO*
Donald De Faria Sr, *Ch of Bd*
Lynn Turiello, *Controller*
Lou Calderon, *Manager*
David Villamar, *Manager*
EMP: 43
SQ FT: 18,000
SALES (est): 37.3MM **Privately Held**
WEB: www.alliedsteel.com
SIC: 5051 3441 3444 Steel; fabricated
    structural metal for ships; sheet metal-
    work

(G-7040)
**ALLIED PLASTICS HOLDINGS
LLC (PA)**
560 Ferry St (07105-4402)
PHONE.................................718 729-5500
Menash Oratz, *Mng Member*
▼ EMP: 51
SQ FT: 70,000
SALES: 70K **Privately Held**
SIC: 3081 Plastic film & sheet

(G-7041)
**ALLSTATE PAPER BOX CO INC
(PA)**
223 Raymond Blvd (07105)
PHONE.................................973 589-2600
Matthew Elias, *President*
Robert Levine, *Vice Pres*
▲ EMP: 65
SQ FT: 138,000
SALES (est): 14.5MM **Privately Held**
WEB: www.allstatepaperbox.com
SIC: 2653 Boxes, corrugated: made from
    purchased materials

(G-7042)
ALM MEDIA LLC
New Jersey Law Journal
238 Mulberry St Fl 2 (07102-3528)
P.O. Box 20081 (07101-6081)
PHONE.................................973 642-0075
Robert Steinbaum, *Publisher*
Peter Arthur, *Systems Staff*
EMP: 45

SALES (corp-wide): 181.8MM **Privately Held**
WEB: www.alm.com
SIC: 2711 Newspapers
HQ: Alm Media, Llc
150 E 42nd St
New York NY 10017
212 457-9400

(G-7043)
ALVARO P ESCANDON INC
528 Ferry St (07105-4489)
PHONE....................................973 274-1040
Gary Escandon, *President*
EMP: 8
SALES: 3.5MM **Privately Held**
WEB: www.apescandon.com
SIC: 5199 2655 Bags, textile; reels (fiber), textile: made from purchased material

(G-7044)
AMERICAN FUR FELT LLC
53 Rome St (07105-3317)
PHONE....................................973 344-3026
Maria Dasilva, *Mng Member*
Lou Pereira,
▲ EMP: 19
SALES (est): 3.2MM **Privately Held**
SIC: 2299 Batting, wadding, padding & fillings

(G-7045)
AMERICAN SHALE OIL LLC (HQ)
520 Broad St Ste 1 (07102-3111)
PHONE....................................973 438-3500
Michael Jonas, *Exec VP*
Daniel Falik, *Vice Pres*
Joseph Giancaspro, *Controller*
William Ulrey, *Investment Ofcr*
Claude Popkin, *Mng Member*
EMP: 9
SALES (est): 2MM **Publicly Held**
SIC: 1382 Oil & gas exploration services

(G-7046)
AMROD CORP
305a Craneway St (07114-3114)
PHONE....................................973 344-3806
Mark Winkler, *President*
EMP: 60
SALES (corp-wide): 26.8MM **Privately Held**
WEB: www.amrod.com
SIC: 3351 3331 3366 3312 Extruded shapes, copper & copper alloy; primary copper; copper foundries; blast furnaces & steel mills
PA: Amrod Na Corporation
305a Craneway St
Newark NJ 07114
973 344-2978

(G-7047)
AMROD NA CORPORATION (PA)
305a Craneway St (07114-3114)
P.O. Box 445, Kearny (07032-0445)
PHONE....................................973 344-2978
Edward Gollob, *Ch of Bd*
Mark Woehnker, *President*
Randall Luebcke, *Mfg Spvr*
Manny Oliveira, *Opers Spvr*
▲ EMP: 80
SQ FT: 175,000
SALES (est): 26.8MM **Privately Held**
WEB: www.amrod.com
SIC: 3351 Extruded shapes, copper & copper alloy

(G-7048)
ANHYDRIDES & CHEMICALS INC
2 Margaretta St (07105)
PHONE....................................973 465-0077
Philip Rhodes, *President*
Micheal Rhodes, *President*
EMP: 8
SQ FT: 16,000
SALES (est): 690K **Privately Held**
SIC: 2821 Thermosetting materials

(G-7049)
ANTONIO MOZZARELLA FACTORY INC (PA)
631 Frelinghuysen Ave (07114-1330)
PHONE....................................973 353-9411
Thomas Pugliese, *President*

◆ EMP: 10
SQ FT: 51,000
SALES (est): 2.3MM **Privately Held**
WEB: www.antoniomozzarella.com
SIC: 5812 2032 Italian restaurant; Italian foods: packaged in cans, jars, etc.

(G-7050)
ANTONIO MOZZARELLA FACTORY INC
631 Frelinghuysen Ave # 2 (07114-1330)
PHONE....................................973 353-9411
Thomas Pugliese, *President*
EMP: 25
SALES (corp-wide): 2.3MM **Privately Held**
SIC: 5812 2032 Italian restaurant; Italian foods: packaged in cans, jars, etc.
PA: Antonio Mozzarella Factory Inc.
631 Frelinghuysen Ave
Newark NJ 07114
973 353-9411

(G-7051)
ARDMORE INC
29 Riverside Ave Bldg 14 (07104-4237)
PHONE....................................973 481-2406
Albert Sharphouse, *President*
EMP: 8
SQ FT: 18,000
SALES (est): 1.2MM **Privately Held**
WEB: www.ardmore.com
SIC: 2841 Soap & other detergents

(G-7052)
ARMETEC CORP
166 Abington Ave (07107-2633)
PHONE....................................973 485-2525
E Ginzburg, *Director*
EMP: 9
SALES (est): 993.6K **Privately Held**
SIC: 3446 Architectural metalwork

(G-7053)
AROL CHEMICAL PRODUCTS CO
649 Ferry St (07105-4601)
PHONE....................................973 344-1510
Sal Coppola, *President*
EMP: 8
SQ FT: 20,000
SALES (est): 1.6MM **Privately Held**
SIC: 2841 2842 2843 2899 Detergents, synthetic organic or inorganic alkaline; textile soap; degreasing solvent; textile finishing agents; textile processing assistants; oil treating compounds; oils & greases, blending & compounding; chemicals & allied products

(G-7054)
ARROW MACHINE COMPANY INC
117 Norfolk St (07103-3226)
PHONE....................................973 642-2430
George Ambandos, *President*
Sophie Ambandos, *Treasurer*
EMP: 6
SQ FT: 7,500
SALES: 350K **Privately Held**
SIC: 3519 Gas engine rebuilding; diesel engine rebuilding

(G-7055)
ASCOT TAG AND LABEL CO INC
577 3rd St (07107-2620)
PHONE....................................973 482-0900
Charles De Franza Sr, *President*
Charles De Franza Jr, *Vice Pres*
Michael De Franza, *Vice Pres*
EMP: 27 EST: 1976
SQ FT: 30,000
SALES: 2.5MM **Privately Held**
SIC: 2679 Tags & labels, paper

(G-7056)
ATLAS REFINERY INC
142 Lockwood St (07105-4776)
PHONE....................................973 589-2002
Steven Schroeder Sr, *CEO*
Steven Schroeder Jr, *President*
Joseph Gargano, *Technology*
Erin Fuller, *Admin Asst*
◆ EMP: 22 EST: 1887
SQ FT: 90,000

SALES (est): 15MM **Privately Held**
WEB: www.atlasrefinery.com
SIC: 2843 2899 Softeners (textile assistants); chemical preparations

(G-7057)
ATLAS WOODWORK INC
212 Wright St (07114-2629)
PHONE....................................973 621-9595
Antonio Martins, *President*
George Costa, *Vice Pres*
Rachel Martins, *Executive*
EMP: 12
SALES (est): 1.8MM **Privately Held**
WEB: www.atlaswoodwork.com
SIC: 2499 Decorative wood & woodwork

(G-7058)
AUDIO TECHNOLOGIES AND CODECS (PA)
Also Called: Atc Labs
105 Lock St Ste 411 (07103-3575)
PHONE....................................973 624-1116
Deepen Sinha, *President*
EMP: 17
SQ FT: 1,000
SALES (est): 1.7MM **Privately Held**
SIC: 7371 3651 Computer software development & applications; audio electronic systems

(G-7059)
AURA DETERGENT LLC
649 Ferry St (07105-4601)
PHONE....................................718 824-2162
EMP: 36
SALES (corp-wide): 1.2MM **Privately Held**
SIC: 2841 Soap & other detergents
PA: Aura Detergent, Llc
1746 Crosby Ave
Bronx NY 10461
718 824-2162

(G-7060)
AVANT INDUSTRIES LTD INC (PA)
780 Frelinghuysen Ave (07114-2294)
PHONE....................................973 242-1700
Rino Baranes, *President*
Bob De Prospo, *Vice Pres*
Antonio Matos, *Treasurer*
Edwardo Fernandez, *Admin Sec*
EMP: 4 EST: 1967
SQ FT: 78,000
SALES (est): 1.2MM **Privately Held**
SIC: 6512 3231 3221 Nonresidential building operators; products of purchased glass; glass containers

(G-7061)
AVITEX CO INC (PA)
461 Frelinghuysen Ave (07114-1404)
PHONE....................................973 242-2410
AVI N Lazarovitz, *President*
Angela Olivo, *Vice Pres*
▲ EMP: 30
SQ FT: 50,000
SALES (est): 4.2MM **Privately Held**
WEB: www.selectofficesuites.com
SIC: 2241 Trimmings, textile

(G-7062)
AVITEX CO INC
32 Noble St (07114-1363)
PHONE....................................973 242-2410
Ray Lindenberg, *Branch Mgr*
EMP: 4
SALES (corp-wide): 4.2MM **Privately Held**
SIC: 2241 Narrow fabric mills
PA: Avitex Co Inc
461 Frelinghuysen Ave
Newark NJ 07114
973 242-2410

(G-7063)
BABY TIME INTERNATIONAL INC
250 Passaic St (07104-3700)
PHONE....................................973 481-7400
Mandy Battap, *President*
▲ EMP: 5

SALES (est): 424.7K **Privately Held**
SIC: 3069 5137 Baby pacifiers, rubber; baby goods

(G-7064)
BELL CONTAINER CORP
615 Ferry St (07105-4404)
P.O. Box 5728 (07105-7728)
PHONE....................................973 344-4400
Arnold Kaplan, *Principal*
Richard Daspin, *Vice Pres*
Keith Jones, *Vice Pres*
Steven Jones, *Vice Pres*
Michael Schwarzmann, *CFO*
▲ EMP: 200
SQ FT: 220,000
SALES (est): 100.8MM **Privately Held**
WEB: www.bellcontainer.com
SIC: 2653 Boxes, corrugated: made from purchased materials; solid fiber boxes, partitions, display items & sheets

(G-7065)
BENJAMIN MOORE & CO
134 Lister Ave (07105-4566)
PHONE....................................973 344-1200
Glenn Cooper, *Principal*
EMP: 200
SALES (corp-wide): 225.3B **Publicly Held**
WEB: www.benjaminmoore.com
SIC: 2851 Varnishes
HQ: Benjamin Moore & Co.
101 Paragon Dr
Montvale NJ 07645
201 573-9600

(G-7066)
BENNETT HEAT TRTING BRZING INC (PA)
690 Ferry St (07105-4619)
PHONE....................................973 589-0590
David J Quaglia, *President*
Mark Fiore, *Vice Pres*
Lidia Galvez, *Vice Pres*
Peter Ciulla, *Controller*
EMP: 32 EST: 1954
SQ FT: 70,000
SALES (est): 6.4MM **Privately Held**
WEB: www.bennettheat.com
SIC: 3398 Brazing (hardening) of metal

(G-7067)
BLANKETS INC
26 Blanchard St (07105-4702)
PHONE....................................973 589-7800
Bruce Liroff, *President*
Harriet Liroff, *Treasurer*
▲ EMP: 20
SQ FT: 4,000
SALES (est): 3.5MM **Privately Held**
WEB: www.blankets.com
SIC: 3555 Printing trades machinery

(G-7068)
BOBS POLY TAPE PRINTERS INC
124 Orchard St (07102-3304)
PHONE....................................973 824-3005
Michael Hirtler, *President*
EMP: 4
SQ FT: 5,000
SALES: 500K **Privately Held**
SIC: 2752 Commercial printing, lithographic

(G-7069)
BOIRON AMERICA INC
1 Gateway Ctr Ste 2540114 (07102-5310)
PHONE....................................862 229-6770
Julien Blot, *Principal*
EMP: 7
SALES (est): 79.9K **Privately Held**
SIC: 2099 Food preparations

(G-7070)
BOMBARDIER TRANSPORTATION
60 Earhart Dr (07114-3703)
PHONE....................................973 624-9300
Raymond T Betler, *Branch Mgr*
EMP: 400

SALES (corp-wide): 16.2B **Privately Held**
SIC: 4111 3536 7538 4581 Monorails, regular route: except amusement & scenic; monorail systems; general automotive repair shops; airports, flying fields & services
HQ: Bombardier Transportation (Holdings) Usa Inc.
1251 Waterfront Pl
Pittsburgh PA 15222
412 655-5700

(G-7071)
BOYKO METAL FINISHING CO INC (PA)
100 Poinier St (07114-1711)
PHONE..................................973 623-4254
John Boyko Jr, *President*
John Boyko III, *Vice Pres*
EMP: 65
SQ FT: 2,500
SALES (est): 6.7MM **Privately Held**
SIC: 3479 3471 Coating of metals & formed products; plating & polishing

(G-7072)
BOYKO METAL FINISHING CO INC
100 Poinier St (07114-1711)
PHONE..................................973 623-4254
EMP: 5
SALES (corp-wide): 6.7MM **Privately Held**
SIC: 3471 Plating & polishing
PA: Boyko Metal Finishing Co Inc
100 Poinier St
Newark NJ 07114
973 623-4254

(G-7073)
BRAZILIAN PRESS & ADVERTISING
78 Fillmore St Ste 1 (07105-3682)
PHONE..................................973 344-4555
Silvio Desouza, *President*
EMP: 10
SALES (est): 650K **Privately Held**
WEB: www.brazilianpress.com
SIC: 2711 Newspapers: publishing only, not printed on site

(G-7074)
BRAZILIAN VOICE
412 Chestnut St (07105-2433)
P.O. Box 5686 (07105-0686)
PHONE..................................973 491-6200
Roberto Leman, *CEO*
Roberto Lima, *Editor*
Fabianne Lima, *Adv Mgr*
Lima Fablanne, *Manager*
EMP: 5
SALES (est): 230K **Privately Held**
SIC: 2711 Newspapers, publishing & printing

(G-7075)
BRICK CITY WHEELCHAIR RPS LLC
92 Hansbury Ave (07112-2205)
PHONE..................................862 371-4311
Bradford James Sr,
EMP: 5
SALES (est): 223.9K **Privately Held**
SIC: 3842 Wheelchairs

(G-7076)
BRISTOL-DONALD COMPANY INC
50 Roanoke Ave (07105-4398)
PHONE..................................973 589-2640
Robert P Greeley Jr, *President*
Daniel Greeley, *Vice Pres*
Johnathan Silva, *Purch Mgr*
EMP: 25 EST: 1945
SQ FT: 30,000
SALES (est): 5.7MM **Privately Held**
SIC: 3713 5012 5084 5088 Truck & bus bodies; truck bodies; hydraulic systems equipment & supplies; transportation equipment & supplies

(G-7077)
BROADVIEW TECHNOLOGIES INC
7-33 Amsterdam St (07105)
PHONE..................................973 465-0077
Philip S Rhodes, *President*
Phillip Rhodes, *Vice Pres*
Jason Tuerack, *Vice Pres*
◆ **EMP:** 20
SQ FT: 2,500
SALES (est): 5.6MM **Privately Held**
WEB: www.broadview-tech.com
SIC: 2851 Epoxy coatings

(G-7078)
BROADWAY EMPRESS ENTRMT INC
15-21 Oraton St (07104-4172)
PHONE..................................973 991-0009
Jean Rey, *CEO*
EMP: 8
SALES: 850K **Privately Held**
SIC: 3651 Household audio & video equipment

(G-7079)
C & Y GROUP EAST COAST INC
150 Saint Charles St (07105-3946)
PHONE..................................973 732-4816
EMP: 4
SALES (est): 308.8K **Privately Held**
SIC: 1081 Mine development, metal

(G-7080)
CALANDRA ITALIAN & FRENCH BKY
Also Called: Calandra's Bakery
204 1st Ave W (07107-2436)
PHONE..................................973 484-5598
Luciano Calandra Jr, *President*
Anthony Calandra, *Vice Pres*
Ortenza Calandra, *Vice Pres*
EMP: 60 EST: 1962
SQ FT: 30,000
SALES (est): 2.4MM **Privately Held**
SIC: 5461 2051 Bread; cakes; cookies; pastries; bread, cake & related products

(G-7081)
CAMBRIDGE INDUSTRIES CO INC
7 Amsterdam St 33 (07105-3801)
PHONE..................................973 465-4565
Philip Rhodes, *Vice Pres*
Philip Rhodes, *Vice Pres*
Joseph Stone, *Vice Pres*
EMP: 7
SQ FT: 10,000
SALES (est): 480K **Privately Held**
SIC: 2869 Plasticizers, organic: cyclic & acyclic

(G-7082)
CHARLES E GREEN & SON INC
625 3rd St (07107-2620)
P.O. Box 8277, Glen Ridge (07028-8277)
PHONE..................................973 485-3630
John V Green III, *President*
John V Green III, *President*
▲ **EMP:** 41 EST: 1870
SQ FT: 100,000
SALES (est): 7.9MM **Privately Held**
WEB: www.charlesegreen.com
SIC: 3429 3991 3544 3469 Manufactured hardware (general); paint rollers; special dies & tools; metal stampings

(G-7083)
CHEM-FLEUR INC
Also Called: Firmenich
150 Firmench Way (07114-3124)
P.O. Box 5880, Princeton (08543-5880)
PHONE..................................973 589-4266
David Shipman, *President*
James McKenna, *Plant Mgr*
Ron Kurtz, *Technology*
Isaac Mejias, *Technology*
▼ **EMP:** 80
SQ FT: 1,600
SALES (est): 6.1MM
SALES (corp-wide): 3.7B **Privately Held**
SIC: 2869 Industrial organic chemicals

HQ: Firmenich Incorporated
250 Plainsboro Rd
Plainsboro NJ 08536
609 452-1000

(G-7084)
CLEARWAY LLC
414 Wilson Ave (07105-4203)
PHONE..................................973 578-4578
Stephen Winer, *Principal*
▼ **EMP:** 2
SALES: 4MM **Privately Held**
SIC: 3728 Deicing equipment, aircraft

(G-7085)
COBON PLASTICS CORP
90 South St (07114-2719)
PHONE..................................973 344-6330
Michael Nelson, *President*
EMP: 10
SQ FT: 18,000
SALES (est): 1.2MM **Privately Held**
WEB: www.cobonplastics.com
SIC: 3082 Tubes, unsupported plastic

(G-7086)
COLOR SCREEN PROS INC
100 Verona Ave (07104-3608)
PHONE..................................973 268-5080
Oscar Cano, *CEO*
▲ **EMP:** 14
SQ FT: 5,000
SALES (est): 660K **Privately Held**
SIC: 2759 Screen printing

(G-7087)
CONDUENT STATE HEALTHCARE LLC
60 Park Pl Ste 605 (07102-5516)
PHONE..................................973 824-3250
Jacqueline Fischer, *Branch Mgr*
EMP: 5
SALES (corp-wide): 5.3B **Publicly Held**
SIC: 3577 8099 Computer peripheral equipment; blood related health services
HQ: Conduent State Healthcare, Llc
12410 Milestone Dr Ste 500
Germantown MD 20876
301 820-4200

(G-7088)
CORPORATE COMPUTER SYSTEMS
Also Called: C C S
33 Washington St Ste 1002 (07102-3129)
PHONE..................................732 739-5600
Mike D'Agostino, *Manager*
EMP: 19
SQ FT: 11,000
SALES (est): 3.2MM **Privately Held**
WEB: www.musicamusa.com
SIC: 3823 3577 7361 7371 Computer interface equipment for industrial process control; computer peripheral equipment; placement agencies; computer software development & applications

(G-7089)
COUNTING SHEEP COFFEE INC
41 Malvern St (07105-1510)
PHONE..................................973 589-4104
Deland Jessop, *CEO*
EMP: 4
SALES (est): 246.1K **Privately Held**
SIC: 2095 Roasted coffee

(G-7090)
COUSE & BOLTEN CO
90 S St Dock 5 (07114)
PHONE..................................973 344-6330
Michael Nelson, *President*
Charles Mans, *Vice Pres*
EMP: 9 EST: 1899
SQ FT: 18,000
SALES: 1MM **Privately Held**
SIC: 3052 Plastic hose; rubber hose; plastic belting; rubber belting

(G-7091)
CREATIVE EMBROIDERY CORP
305 3rd Ave W Ste 3 (07107-2387)
PHONE..................................973 497-5700
Steven Diamond, *President*
Marlene Diamond, *Corp Secy*
EMP: 20 EST: 1975

SQ FT: 65,000
SALES: 6MM **Privately Held**
SIC: 2395 2396 Embroidery products, except schiffli machine; automotive & apparel trimmings

(G-7092)
D & H PALLETS LLC
45 Verona Ave (07104-4409)
P.O. Box 8563, Elizabeth (07208-0563)
PHONE..................................973 481-2981
Hugo Munoz, *Principal*
Ramon Munoz,
EMP: 6 EST: 1999
SALES (est): 807.9K **Privately Held**
SIC: 2448 Pallets, wood & wood with metal

(G-7093)
DAMASCUS BAKERY INC
60 Mcclellan St (07114-2112)
PHONE..................................718 855-1456
Edward Mafoud, *President*
EMP: 49
SALES (corp-wide): 23.4MM **Privately Held**
SIC: 2051 5149 Bakery: wholesale or wholesale/retail combined; bread, all types (white, wheat, rye, etc): fresh or frozen; bakery products
PA: Damascus Bakery, Inc.
56 Gold St
Brooklyn NY 11201
718 855-1456

(G-7094)
DAMASCUS BAKERY NJ LLC
60 Mcclellan St (07114-2112)
PHONE..................................718 855-1456
James P Sweeney, *Principal*
▼ **EMP:** 55
SALES (est): 10.3MM **Privately Held**
SIC: 2051 Bakery: wholesale or wholesale/retail combined

(G-7095)
DARLING INGREDIENTS INC
Also Called: Quaker Soap Div
825 Wilson Ave (07105-4813)
PHONE..................................973 465-1900
Ed Schlagenhaft, *General Mgr*
William Frish, *Vice Pres*
John Latino, *Opers Staff*
EMP: 104
SALES (corp-wide): 3.3B **Publicly Held**
WEB: www.darlingii.com
SIC: 2077 2048 Animal & marine fats & oils; prepared feeds
PA: Darling Ingredients Inc.
5601 N Macarthur Blvd
Irving TX 75038
972 717-0300

(G-7096)
DCI SIGNS & AWNINGS INC
110 Riverside Ave (07104-4202)
PHONE..................................973 350-0400
Danny Castillo, *President*
EMP: 25
SQ FT: 12,000
SALES (est): 4.4MM **Privately Held**
WEB: www.dcisigns.com
SIC: 3993 1799 Electric signs; sign installation & maintenance

(G-7097)
DCM GROUP INC
Also Called: I3 Software
563 Broad St (07102-4503)
PHONE..................................732 516-1173
Kumar Chaluvadi, *President*
Sheshank Reddy, *Manager*
EMP: 6
SALES (est): 816.9K **Privately Held**
WEB: www.dcmgroup.com
SIC: 7372 Prepackaged software

(G-7098)
DEB EL FOOD PRODUCTS LLC (PA)
Also Called: Deb El Foods
520 Broad St Fl 6 (07102-3121)
P.O. Box 876, Elizabeth (07207-0876)
PHONE..................................908 351-0330
Elliott Gibber, *President*
Oscar Reyes, *General Mgr*
Monica James, *Opers Staff*

GEOGRAPHIC

Richard Mensh, *Buyer*
Michael Gibber, *Purchasing*
◆ **EMP:** 380
SQ FT: 30,000
SALES (est): 41.9MM **Privately Held**
SIC: 2015 Egg processing

(G-7099)
DEB-EL FOODS CORPORATION
520 Broad St (07102-3121)
P.O. Box 876, Elizabeth (07207-0876)
PHONE......................908 351-0330
Elliot Gibber, *President*
◆ **EMP:** 135
SQ FT: 30,000
SALES (est): 17.1MM **Privately Held**
SIC: 2015 Eggs, processed: dehydrated

(G-7100)
DEBORAH SALES & MFG CO
109 Meeker Ave (07114-1300)
PHONE......................973 344-8466
Carlos Rei, *President*
EMP: 4 EST: 1957
SQ FT: 5,000
SALES (est): 428.2K **Privately Held**
SIC: 3469 3496 Stamping metal for the
trade; miscellaneous fabricated wire prod-
ucts

(G-7101)
**DELEET MERCHANDISING
CORP (PA)**
Also Called: Prisco Printers Service
26 Blanchard St (07105-4784)
PHONE......................212 962-6565
Bruce Liroff, *President*
Richard Liroff, *Chairman*
Mauro Marcatili, *Business Mgr*
Jay Friedman, *Vice Pres*
David Gerson, *Vice Pres*
◆ **EMP:** 40
SQ FT: 30,000
SALES (est): 22MM **Privately Held**
SIC: 2869 5084 Industrial organic chemi-
cals; printing trades machinery, equip-
ment & supplies

(G-7102)
DELTECH RESINS CO (PA)
49 Rutherford St (07105-4820)
PHONE......................973 589-0880
Bob Elfante, *President*
▲ **EMP:** 20
SALES (est): 12.2MM **Privately Held**
WEB: www.deltechresins.com
SIC: 2821 Plastics materials & resins

(G-7103)
DORZAR CORPORATION
Also Called: New Great American Veal
50 Avenue L Ste 5 (07105-3841)
PHONE......................973 589-6363
Zarko Grgas, *President*
Dorothy Burke, *Treasurer*
EMP: 35
SQ FT: 9,500
SALES (est): 7.2MM **Privately Held**
SIC: 2011 Veal from meat slaughtered on
site

(G-7104)
DOSIS FRAGRANCE LLC
250 Passaic St (07104-3700)
PHONE......................718 874-0074
Abraham Hartman, *Manager*
▲ **EMP:** 4
SQ FT: 700
SALES (est): 671.8K **Privately Held**
SIC: 2844 5122 Perfumes & colognes;
perfumes

(G-7105)
DRS LEONARDO INC
95 William St (07102-1318)
PHONE......................973 775-4440
EMP: 28
SALES (corp-wide): 9.2B **Privately Held**
SIC: 3812 Navigational systems & instru-
ments
HQ: Leonardo Drs, Inc.
2345 Crystal Dr Ste 1000
Arlington VA 22202
703 416-8000

(G-7106)
**DURAAMEN ENGINEERED PDTS
INC (PA)**
457 Frelinghuysen Ave (07114-1426)
PHONE......................973 230-1301
Victor Pachade, *President*
EMP: 3 EST: 2010
SQ FT: 1,750
SALES: 1.2MM **Privately Held**
SIC: 3272 2851 Dry mixture concrete;
epoxy coatings; polyurethane coatings

(G-7107)
DURON CO INC
238 Emmet St (07114-2731)
PHONE......................973 242-5704
John A Dubicki, *President*
EMP: 11
SQ FT: 14,000
SALES (est): 1.3MM **Privately Held**
WEB: www.flatfile.com
SIC: 3469 Stamping metal for the trade

(G-7108)
DYNA VEYOR INC
10 Hudson St (07103-2804)
PHONE......................908 276-5384
Beverly Ayre, *CEO*
Stephen Ayre II, *President*
Stephen Ayre, *CFO*
Anthony M Ayre, *Treasurer*
EMP: 8
SQ FT: 26,000
SALES (est): 1.7MM **Privately Held**
WEB: www.dyna-veyor.com
SIC: 3535 3052 5085 Conveyors & con-
veying equipment; plastic belting; hose,
belting & packing

(G-7109)
**DYNAMIC DIE CUTTING &
FINSHG**
104-110 South St (07114-2719)
PHONE......................973 589-8338
Emilio Esteva, *President*
George Esteva, *Vice Pres*
EMP: 10 EST: 1958
SQ FT: 13,000
SALES: 500K **Privately Held**
SIC: 2675 3544 Die-cut paper & board;
special dies & tools

(G-7110)
E & G ROMAN CORP
14 Ogden St (07104-4010)
PHONE......................973 482-1123
Joseph Belott, *President*
EMP: 70
SALES: 26MM **Privately Held**
SIC: 3644 1623 Electric conduits & fit-
tings; gas main construction; sewer line
construction; underground utilities con-
tractor

(G-7111)
**ELAN FOOD LABORATORIES
INC**
Also Called: Elan Vanilla
268 Doremus Ave (07105-4879)
PHONE......................973 344-8014
Jerome Scharf, *President*
Ira Kapp, *Chairman*
Dr Jerry Guerrera, *Vice Pres*
David Weissman, *Vice Pres*
Lou Shragher, *VP Finance*
EMP: 15
SQ FT: 45,000
SALES (est): 3.4MM **Privately Held**
SIC: 2869 Vanillin, synthetic

(G-7112)
ELAN INC (PA)
268 Doremus Ave (07105-4879)
PHONE......................973 344-8014
David R Weisman, *CEO*
Ira Kapp, *Ch of Bd*
Jocelyn Manship, *President*
David Pimentel, *Vice Pres*
Phil Kapp, *QC Mgr*
▲ **EMP:** 67
SQ FT: 45,000

SALES (est): 15.1MM **Privately Held**
WEB: www.elan-chemical.com
SIC: 2087 2899 2869 Extracts, flavoring;
chemical preparations; industrial organic
chemicals

(G-7113)
**ELDON GLASS & MIRROR CO
INC**
Also Called: Luso Glass
58 Stockton St 76 (07105-3013)
PHONE......................973 589-2099
Carlos Firmino, *President*
Anna Firmino, *Admin Sec*
John Jroe, *Admin Sec*
EMP: 12
SALES (est): 1.4MM **Privately Held**
SIC: 1793 3229 Glass & glazing work;
glassware, art or decorative

(G-7114)
ELITE CABINETRY CORP
97 Main St (07105-3520)
PHONE......................973 583-0194
Marcio Rodrigues, *Principal*
EMP: 4 EST: 2009
SALES (est): 200.6K **Privately Held**
SIC: 2434 Wood kitchen cabinets

(G-7115)
**EMPIRE LUMBER & MILLWORK
CO**
Also Called: Empire Architectural Millwork
377 Frelinghuysen Ave (07114-1422)
P.O. Box 2070 (07114-0070)
PHONE......................973 242-2700
Ira Kent, *Ch of Bd*
Wayne Kent, *President*
Charlie Shields, *Vice Pres*
Ross Weinick, *Vice Pres*
EMP: 40 EST: 1949
SQ FT: 1,000
SALES (est): 7.9MM **Privately Held**
WEB: www.elmdoor.com
SIC: 2421 2431 3446 Lumber: rough,
sawed or planed; millwork; architectural
metalwork

(G-7116)
ENSEMBLEIQ INC
Also Called: Chain Store Age Magazine
1 Gateway Ctr 11-43 (07102-5310)
PHONE......................201 855-7600
John Kenlon, *Vice Pres*
EMP: 20
SALES (corp-wide): 28.6MM **Privately
Held**
SIC: 2731 Books: publishing only
PA: Ensembleiq, Inc.
8550 W Bryn Mawr Ave # 200
Chicago IL 60631
773 992-4450

(G-7117)
EPIQ SYSTEMS INC
50 Park Pl Ste 701 (07102-4308)
PHONE......................973 622-6111
Maria Celi, *Manager*
EMP: 7
SALES (corp-wide): 589.6MM **Privately
Held**
SIC: 3577 Computer peripheral equipment
HQ: Epiq Systems, Inc.
2 Ravinia Dr Ste 850
Atlanta GA 30346
913 621-9500

(G-7118)
EPOLIN CHEMICAL LLC (HQ)
358-364 Adams St (07105)
PHONE......................973 465-9495
Greg Amato, *CEO*
James Ivchenko, *President*
Morton Lefar, *Vice Pres*
▲ **EMP:** 8
SQ FT: 19,500
SALES (est): 1.4MM **Privately Held**
WEB: www.epolin.com
SIC: 2865 6512 Dyes & pigments; nonres-
idential building operators
PA: Polymathes Holdings I Llc
20 Nassau St Ste M
Princeton NJ 08542
609 945-1690

(G-7119)
EVERTILE FLOORING CO INC
127 Frelinghuysen Ave (07114-1631)
PHONE......................973 242-7474
EMP: 8
SALES (corp-wide): 1.4MM **Privately
Held**
WEB: www.locktile-usa.com
SIC: 3996 Hard surface floor coverings
PA: Evertile Flooring Co. Inc
127 Frelinghuysen Ave
Newark NJ 07114
973 242-7474

(G-7120)
EXTREME PALLET INC
315 Astor St (07114-2822)
PHONE......................973 286-1717
Eddie Sanchez, *President*
EMP: 9
SALES (est): 1.6MM **Privately Held**
SIC: 2448 Pallets, wood

(G-7121)
FABUWOOD CABINETRY CORP
69-95 Blanchard St (07105)
PHONE......................201 432-6555
Moshe Panzer, *CEO*
Solomon Eidlisz, *General Mgr*
Joel Epstein, *COO*
Peri Friedman, *Senior VP*
Joel Weinstein, *Senior VP*
◆ **EMP:** 750
SQ FT: 686,000
SALES (est): 139.2MM **Privately Held**
SIC: 2434 5031 Wood kitchen cabinets;
kitchen cabinets

(G-7122)
FAPS INC (PA)
371 Craneway St (07114-3114)
PHONE......................973 589-5656
Gary L Lobue, *President*
William Mazur, *General Mgr*
August Lobue, *Vice Pres*
Mike Mazzeo, *Opers Mgr*
James Graybush, *Warehouse Mgr*
▲ **EMP:** 200 EST: 1991
SQ FT: 6,000
SALES (est): 71.2MM **Privately Held**
WEB: www.fapsinc.com
SIC: 3499 3711 7538 Metal household ar-
ticles; motor vehicles & car bodies; gen-
eral automotive repair shops

(G-7123)
**FEDERAL BRONZE CAST INDS
INC (PA)**
9 Backus St (07105-3087)
PHONE......................973 589-7575
Douglas J Reichard, *CEO*
Raj Mittal, *Vice Pres*
Frank J Reilly, *Vice Pres*
Herminio Rodrigues, *Maint Spvr*
Carla Rodrigues, *Manager*
▲ **EMP:** 45
SQ FT: 40,000
SALES (est): 5.9MM **Privately Held**
SIC: 3366 Castings (except die): bronze

(G-7124)
FIRST FRIDAY GLOBAL INC
130 Mount Pleasant Ave (07104)
PHONE......................201 776-6709
Antonio M Francisco, *President*
EMP: 4
SALES (est): 219.4K **Privately Held**
SIC: 2711 Newspapers, publishing & print-
ing

(G-7125)
FLEXCRAFT INDUSTRIES INC
390 Adams St (07114-2802)
P.O. Box 2098 (07114-0098)
PHONE......................973 589-3403
Bruce Machleder, *President*
EMP: 6
SALES: 500K **Privately Held**
WEB: www.flexcraftindustries.com
SIC: 3479 2891 Coating of metals with
plastic or resins; adhesives & sealants

(G-7126)
FOREM PACKAGING INC
2 Joseph St (07105-4710)
P.O. Box 50090 (07105-8090)
PHONE..................................973 589-0402
Aron Forem, *President*
Mitchell Lewites, *CFO*
▲ EMP: 12
SQ FT: 70,000
SALES: 4.9MM **Privately Held**
SIC: 2671 Plastic film, coated or laminated
for packaging

(G-7127)
FORM CUT INDUSTRIES INC
195 Mount Pleasant Ave (07104-3814)
PHONE..................................973 483-5154
Charles M Alberto, *President*
Joan Alberto, *Corp Secy*
Steve Alberto, *Vice Pres*
Ken Degraaf, *Sales Mgr*
EMP: 49
SQ FT: 24,000
SALES (est): 8.8MM **Privately Held**
WEB: www.formcut.com
SIC: 3496 3451 Miscellaneous fabricated
wire products; screw machine products

(G-7128)
G & R FUEL CORP
822 Clinton Ave (07108-1031)
PHONE..................................973 732-0530
Sonny Singh, *Manager*
EMP: 5
SALES (est): 456.2K **Privately Held**
SIC: 2869 Fuels

(G-7129)
G BIG CORP
189 Frelinghuysen Ave (07114-1531)
PHONE..................................973 242-6521
Trevor Blackwell, *Principal*
EMP: 5 EST: 2010
SALES (est): 374.3K **Privately Held**
SIC: 3469 Metal stampings

(G-7130)
GAMBERT SHIRT CORP
Also Called: Gambert Custom Shirts
436 Ferry St Ste 2 (07105-3929)
PHONE..................................973 424-9105
Theodore Gambert, *CEO*
EMP: 50 EST: 1933
SQ FT: 7,200
SALES: 5.3MM **Privately Held**
SIC: 2321 2331 Men's & boys' furnishings;
women's & misses' blouses & shirts

(G-7131)
GANN LAW BOOKS INC
1 Washington Park # 1300 (07102-3194)
PHONE..................................973 268-1200
Michael Protzel, *President*
Howard Dubner, *Vice Pres*
Noemi Levine, *Office Mgr*
EMP: 19
SQ FT: 2,500
SALES (est): 1.7MM **Privately Held**
WEB: www.gannlaw.com
SIC: 2731 8111 Textbooks: publishing
only, not printed on site; legal services

(G-7132)
GLASSROOTS INC
10 Bleeker St (07102-1903)
PHONE..................................973 353-9555
Barbara Heisler, *Director*
Lisa Duggan, *Program Dir*
Jenny Pollack, *Program Dir*
Jason Minami, *Instructor*
Yazmine Graham, *Assistant*
EMP: 20
SALES: 1.3MM **Privately Held**
SIC: 3229 Pressed & blown glass

(G-7133)
**GLOBAL COMMODITIES
EXPORTACAO**
126 Jackson St (07105-2157)
PHONE..................................201 613-1532
Benjamin Allen, *CEO*
EMP: 8 EST: 2013

(G-7134)
GLOBAL MANUFACTURING LLC
Also Called: Global Force and Artic Bloc
35 William St Fl 2 (07102-2714)
PHONE..................................973 494-5413
David Slossberg, *Mng Member*
EMP: 4
SQ FT: 1,000
SALES (est): 458.1K **Privately Held**
WEB: www.globalmfgllc.com
SIC: 2389 Uniforms & vestments

(G-7135)
GLOBAL WEAVERS CORP
Also Called: J & S Housewares
9-13 Dey St (07103)
PHONE..................................973 824-5500
Simon Belfer, *President*
▲ EMP: 4
SALES (est): 226.3K **Privately Held**
SIC: 2392 5023 5712 Comforters & quilts:
made from purchased materials; home
furnishings; beds & accessories

(G-7136)
GOLDEN PLATTER FOODS INC
37 Tompkins Point Rd (07114-2814)
PHONE..................................973 344-8770
Scott Bennett, *CEO*
▲ EMP: 50
SQ FT: 20,000
SALES: 30MM **Privately Held**
SIC: 2015 Poultry, processed: frozen

(G-7137)
GOLDEN TROPICS LTD
1489-1495 Mccarter Hwy (07104-3966)
P.O. Box 9158 (07104-9158)
PHONE..................................973 484-0202
Carlos Favaro, *President*
Alicia Favaro, *Vice Pres*
▲ EMP: 25
SALES (est): 4.4MM **Privately Held**
SIC: 2099 2092 Food preparations; fresh
or frozen packaged fish

(G-7138)
GRAVER WATER SYSTEMS LLC
Also Called: Graver Chemical Products
72 Lockwood St (07105-4719)
PHONE..................................973 465-2380
Walter Bass, *VP Mfg*
Al Tavares, *Director*
EMP: 16
SALES (corp-wide): 225.3B **Publicly
Held**
WEB: www.graver.com
SIC: 3589 Water filters & softeners, house-
hold type
HQ: Graver Water Systems Llc
675 Central Ave Ste 3
New Providence NJ 07974
908 516-1400

(G-7139)
GREEN LABS LLC
211 Warren St Ste 206 (07103-3568)
PHONE..................................862 220-4845
Oscar Melancia De La Cruz Roma, *Vice
Pres*
David Guerrero, *Mng Member*
EMP: 6 EST: 2009
SALES: 1.4MM **Privately Held**
SIC: 2834 5149 2099 Extracts of botani-
cals: powdered, pilular, solid or fluid;
spices & seasonings; seasonings: dry
mixes

(G-7140)
GREWE PLASTICS INC
119 S 15th St (07107-1097)
PHONE..................................973 485-7602
Allen D Blum, *President*
EMP: 8
SALES (est): 1.2MM **Privately Held**
WEB: www.greweco.com
SIC: 3089 5162 Plastic processing; plas-
tics sheets & rods

(G-7141)
GROUP MARTIN LLC JJ
90 South St (07114-2719)
PHONE..................................862 240-1813
John Ra, *Principal*
▲ EMP: 10
SALES (est): 1MM **Privately Held**
SIC: 2082 2038 Ale (alcoholic beverage);
snacks, including onion rings, cheese
sticks, etc.

(G-7142)
**GUARDRITE STEEL DOOR
CORP**
81-87 Springdale Ave (07107-1232)
PHONE..................................973 481-4424
Todd Santana, *President*
▲ EMP: 6
SQ FT: 30,000
SALES (est): 965.5K **Privately Held**
SIC: 3442 1751 Rolling doors for industrial
buildings or warehouses, metal; window &
door installation & erection

(G-7143)
**HAENSSLER SHTMTL WORKS
INC**
592 Hawthorne Ave (07112-1122)
PHONE..................................973 373-6360
Wendy Haenssler, *President*
Richard Haenssler, *Vice Pres*
EMP: 14
SQ FT: 7,900
SALES (est): 1.2MM **Privately Held**
SIC: 3444 Sheet metalwork

(G-7144)
HALSEY NEWS
2 Prudential Dr (07102-3075)
PHONE..................................973 645-0017
EMP: 4
SALES (est): 92.2K **Privately Held**
SIC: 2711 Newspapers, publishing & print-
ing

(G-7145)
HAMMER BEDDING CORP
Also Called: Shifman Mattress Company
1 Mott St (07105-3712)
P.O. Box 5007 (07105-0007)
PHONE..................................973 589-2400
Michael Hammer, *President*
Phillip Zucker, *General Mgr*
Eileen Hammer, *Vice Pres*
Paula Nunes, *Human Resources*
Tim Wade, *Natl Sales Mgr*
▲ EMP: 35 EST: 1890
SQ FT: 50,000
SALES (est): 4MM **Privately Held**
WEB: www.shifmanmattresses.com
SIC: 2515 Mattresses, containing felt, foam
rubber, urethane, etc.; box springs, as-
sembled

(G-7146)
**HANDCRAFT MANUFACTURING
CORP**
640 Frelinghuysen Ave # 1 (07114-1360)
PHONE..................................973 565-0077
Erwin Mizrahy, *President*
EMP: 39
SALES (est): 3.9MM
SALES (corp-wide): 17.1MM **Privately
Held**
WEB: www.handcraftmfg.com
SIC: 2389 5137 5136 Men's miscella-
neous accessories; women's & children's
clothing; men's & boys' clothing
PA: Handcraft Manufacturing Corp.
34 W 33rd St Rm 401
New York NY 10001
212 251-0022

(G-7147)
HANDY STORE FIXTURES INC
337 Sherman Ave (07114-1507)
PHONE..................................973 242-1600
Paul Kurland, *President*
Richard Kurland, *Vice Pres*
Jim Lackey, *Regl Sales Mgr*
Jason Krane, *Director*
▼ EMP: 55 EST: 1952
SQ FT: 200,000

SALES (est): 10.3MM **Privately Held**
WEB: www.handysf.com
SIC: 2542 2541 Fixtures, store: except
wood; store fixtures, wood

(G-7148)
HAWK DAIRY INC
30 Jabez St (07105-3021)
PHONE..................................973 466-9030
Jack Taranto, *President*
EMP: 6
SQ FT: 16,000
SALES (est): 733K **Privately Held**
SIC: 2022 Natural cheese

(G-7149)
HEADWEAR CREATIONS INC
Also Called: Bold Hat Makers
200 Wright St (07114-2663)
PHONE..................................973 622-1144
Ruben Spitz, *President*
EMP: 48
SQ FT: 15,000
SALES (est): 4.8MM **Privately Held**
SIC: 2353 Hats & caps

(G-7150)
HILIN LIFE PRODUCTS INC
211 Warren St Ste 211 # 211 (07103-3568)
PHONE..................................917 250-3575
Helen Denise, *CEO*
EMP: 8
SALES (est): 779.5K **Privately Held**
SIC: 3845 Electromedical equipment

(G-7151)
HOLISTIC SOLAR USA INC
105 Lock St Ste 407 (07103-3567)
PHONE..................................732 757-5500
Scott Blow, *Corp Secy*
EMP: 5
SALES (est): 175K **Privately Held**
SIC: 3433 1711 3356 3674 Solar cells;
battery metal; ; solar heaters & collectors;
solar energy contractor

(G-7152)
**HONIG CHEMICAL & PROC
CORP**
414 Wilson Ave (07105-4203)
PHONE..................................973 344-0881
Robert Honig, *President*
Forest Goodman, *Exec VP*
Jim Cahill, *Manager*
Eloise Honig, *Admin Sec*
EMP: 32 EST: 1970
SQ FT: 70,000
SALES (est): 4.6MM **Privately Held**
SIC: 2869 Industrial organic chemicals

(G-7153)
HUDSON DISPLAYS CO
687 Frelinghuysen Ave # 1 (07114-1349)
PHONE..................................973 623-8255
Maggie Marin, *President*
Tito Marin, *Vice Pres*
Nelson Marin, *Treasurer*
EMP: 25
SQ FT: 20,000
SALES (est): 2.4MM **Privately Held**
WEB: www.hudsondisplays.com
SIC: 3999 Advertising display products

(G-7154)
IDT ENERGY INC (HQ)
520 Broad St Fl 9 (07102-3111)
PHONE..................................877 887-6866
Geoffrey Rochwarger, *CEO*
Alan Schwab, *COO*
Stuart Naftel, *Vice Pres*
Sara Miller, *Opers Staff*
Terrence P Stronz, *CFO*
EMP: 22
SALES (est): 2.4MM **Publicly Held**
SIC: 3679 Power supplies, all types: static

(G-7155)
**INDEPENDENT PRJ CONS LTD
LBLTY**
374 Chestnut St Ste C (07105-2495)
PHONE..................................973 780-8002
Omar Abdel Nieves,
EMP: 4

SALES (est): 142.8K **Privately Held**
SIC: 1389 1541 8742 Construction, repair & dismantling services; industrial buildings, new construction; steel building construction; construction project management consultant

(G-7156)
INDUSTRIAL HARD CHROMIUM CO
7 Rome St (07105-3317)
P.O. Box 605, Allendale (07401-0605)
PHONE.................................973 344-2265
Marilyn Foote, *President*
Craig Foote, *Vice Pres*
Rj Anderson, *Prdtn Mgr*
Nancy Lanzalott, *Controller*
EMP: 12
SQ FT: 13,000
SALES (est): 1.4MM **Privately Held**
WEB: www.ihcco.com
SIC: 3471 Chromium plating of metals or formed products; electroplating of metals or formed products

(G-7157)
INNOVATIVE RESIN SYSTEMS INC
257 Wilson Ave (07105-3826)
PHONE.................................973 465-6887
John Khosdeghian, *Manager*
EMP: 7
SALES (est): 956.8K
SALES (corp-wide): 7.1MM **Privately Held**
SIC: 2821 Epoxy resins
PA: Innovative Resin Systems, Inc.
70 Verkade Dr
Wayne NJ 07470
973 465-6887

(G-7158)
IPJUKEBOX LTD LIABILITY CO
211 Wrren St Ste 1022nwa (07103)
PHONE.................................201 286-4535
Ed Konchalski, *CEO*
EMP: 4
SALES (est): 222.9K **Privately Held**
SIC: 7372 8742 8249 7389 Application computer software; banking & finance consultant; banking school, training; financial services

(G-7159)
IRONBOUND EXPRESS INC
65 Jabez St (07105-3047)
PHONE.................................973 491-5151
Carmen Pizzuto, *Principal*
EMP: 4 **EST:** 1996
SALES (est): 518.6K **Privately Held**
SIC: 2655 Fiber cans, drums & similar products

(G-7160)
IRONBOUND INTERMODAL INDS INC
65 Jabez St (07105-3047)
PHONE.................................973 491-5151
Frank Borland, *President*
Danny Lastra, *Vice Pres*
Wendy Cruz, *Technology*
EMP: 15
SALES (est): 4.4MM **Privately Held**
SIC: 2655 Fiber cans, drums & containers

(G-7161)
IRONBOUND METAL
Also Called: Metal Fabrication
238 Emmet St (07114-2731)
PHONE.................................973 242-5704
John Dubicki, *Owner*
EMP: 4
SALES: 250K **Privately Held**
SIC: 3499 3699 Fabricated metal products; laser welding, drilling & cutting equipment

(G-7162)
IRONBOUND WELDING INC
156 Walnut St (07105-1216)
PHONE.................................973 589-3128
Louis J Tamasco Jr, *President*
Antoinette Tamasco, *Corp Secy*
EMP: 6
SQ FT: 4,000

SALES (est): 450K **Privately Held**
SIC: 7692 5211 5051 Welding repair; lumber & other building materials; steel

(G-7163)
IVEY KATRINA OWNER
Also Called: Fritnationalsupply
95 Montrose St (07106-2315)
PHONE.................................973 951-8328
Ivey Katrina, *Owner*
EMP: 4
SALES (est): 175.4K **Privately Held**
SIC: 3334 3366 3613 3612 Primary aluminum; bushings & bearings; control panels, electric; machine tool transformers

(G-7164)
J P EGAN INDUSTRIES INC
676 S 14th St (07103-1411)
PHONE.................................973 642-1500
Jan P Egan Jr, *President*
EMP: 8
SALES (est): 670K **Privately Held**
SIC: 2515 Mattresses & foundations

(G-7165)
J&S HOUSEWARE CORP
9 Dey St Ste 13 (07103)
PHONE.................................973 824-5500
Semen Belfer, *President*
◆ **EMP:** 8
SQ FT: 30,000
SALES (est): 1MM **Privately Held**
SIC: 2392 Comforters & quilts: made from purchased materials

(G-7166)
JARCHEM INDUSTRIES INC
Malec Don Specialty Chem Div
414 Wilson Ave (07105-4287)
PHONE.................................973 344-0600
Arnold Stern, *Branch Mgr*
EMP: 2
SALES (corp-wide): 5.9MM **Privately Held**
WEB: www.jarchem.com
SIC: 2869 Acetates: amyl, butyl & ethyl
PA: Jarchem Industries, Inc.
414 Wilson Ave
Newark NJ 07105
973 344-0600

(G-7167)
JED DISPLAY LLC
254-262 Wright St (07114)
PHONE.................................201 340-2329
Jim Howell, *Mng Member*
EMP: 9 **EST:** 2011
SALES (est): 1.1MM **Privately Held**
SIC: 2542 Racks, merchandise display or storage: except wood

(G-7168)
JEFFERSON PRINTING SERIVCE
184 Jefferson St (07105-1204)
PHONE.................................973 491-0019
Julio Depaula, *President*
EMP: 10
SALES (est): 2.9MM **Privately Held**
SIC: 2752 Commercial printing, lithographic

(G-7169)
JERSEY STEEL DOOR INC
95 N 11th St (07107-1117)
PHONE.................................973 482-4020
Rolin Gonzalez, *President*
EMP: 5
SALES (est): 671.6K **Privately Held**
SIC: 3442 1799 5211 Metal doors, sash & trim; antenna installation; door & window products

(G-7170)
JONAS MEDIA GROUP INC
520 Broad St Ste 400 (07102-3121)
PHONE.................................973 438-1900
Howard Jonas, *President*
EMP: 11
SALES (est): 550.8K **Publicly Held**
WEB: www.idt.net
SIC: 2721 2741 Magazines: publishing only, not printed on site; directories: publishing only, not printed on site

PA: Idt Corporation
520 Broad St 9
Newark NJ 07102

(G-7171)
JOYCE FOOD LLC (PA)
80 Avenue K (07105-3803)
PHONE.................................973 491-9696
Howard Freundlich,
Victor Ostreicher,
▲ **EMP:** 180 **EST:** 1945
SQ FT: 35,000
SALES (est): 15.9MM **Privately Held**
WEB: www.rokeach.com
SIC: 2034 2052 2099 2045 Soup mixes; cookies; crackers, dry; gelatin dessert preparations; seasonings & spices; pancake mixes, prepared: from purchased flour

(G-7172)
KAMPACK INC
100 Frontage Rd (07114-3718)
PHONE.................................973 589-7400
Karen Mehiel, *CEO*
Karen Aguerosmehiel, *President*
Denny Moran, *General Mgr*
Randy Baer, *Vice Pres*
Irving Levine, *Vice Pres*
EMP: 200 **EST:** 1959
SQ FT: 180,000
SALES (est): 73.2MM **Privately Held**
WEB: www.mannkraft.com
SIC: 2653 Sheets, corrugated: made from purchased materials; boxes, corrugated: made from purchased materials; display items, corrugated: made from purchased materials
HQ: U.S. Corrugated, Inc.
95 W Beau St Ste 430
Washington PA 15301
724 345-2050

(G-7173)
KEYSTONE FOLDING BOX COMPANY
367 Verona Ave (07104-1713)
PHONE.................................973 483-1054
Wade E Hartman, *President*
William Hartman, *Vice Pres*
Richard Rossbach, *QC Mgr*
Denise Persaud, *Accountant*
Glenn Boyd, *Sales Staff*
EMP: 75 **EST:** 1890
SQ FT: 85,000
SALES (est): 27MM **Privately Held**
WEB: www.keyboxco.com
SIC: 2657 Folding paperboard boxes

(G-7174)
KP FUEL CORPORATION
864 Mount Prospect Ave (07104-3620)
PHONE.................................973 350-1202
EMP: 4
SALES (est): 228.5K **Privately Held**
SIC: 2869 Fuels

(G-7175)
KRAFT TAPE PRINTERS INC
124 Orchard St (07102-3304)
PHONE.................................973 824-3005
Michael Hirtler, *President*
Dorinda Sceurman, *Admin Sec*
EMP: 9 **EST:** 1931
SQ FT: 5,000
SALES (est): 600K **Privately Held**
SIC: 2752 Commercial printing, offset

(G-7176)
L GAMBERT LLC
Also Called: L Gambert Shirts
61 Freeman St Ste 4 (07105-4000)
PHONE.................................973 344-3440
Lorraine Gambert, *Owner*
Bill Epps, *Controller*
EMP: 85
SQ FT: 9,000
SALES (est): 612.2K **Privately Held**
WEB: www.gambertshirts.com
SIC: 2321 Men's & boys' dress shirts; men's & boys' sports & polo shirts

(G-7177)
LANDEW SAWDUST CO INC
21 Poinier St (07114-1725)
PHONE.................................973 344-5255

Seymour Landew, *President*
EMP: 12 **EST:** 1914
SQ FT: 8,000
SALES: 400K **Privately Held**
SIC: 2421 Sawdust & shavings

(G-7178)
LEFT-HANDED LIBRA LLC
Also Called: Jane Carter Solution
50 Park Pl Ste 1001 (07102-4300)
PHONE.................................973 623-1112
Valli W APM, *Opers Mgr*
Jane Carter,
Michael Hellerman,
▼ **EMP:** 10
SALES: 4MM **Privately Held**
SIC: 3999 Hair & hair-based products

(G-7179)
LEXORA INC
Also Called: Lexora Home
425 Ferry St (07105-3903)
PHONE.................................855 453-9672
Andrey Bogan, *President*
EMP: 3
SALES: 1MM **Privately Held**
SIC: 2434 2499 Vanities, bathroom: wood; kitchen, bathroom & household ware: wood

(G-7180)
LIME ENERGY CO
100 Mulberry St 4 (07102-4056)
PHONE.................................732 791-5380
EMP: 6
SALES (corp-wide): 272.2MM **Publicly Held**
SIC: 3274 Lime
HQ: Lime Energy Co.
4 Gateway Ctr Fl 4 # 4
Newark NJ 07102
201 416-2575

(G-7181)
LION EXTRUDING CORP
106 Rutherford St (07105-4823)
PHONE.................................973 344-4648
Gary Demarco, *President*
Carl Demarco, *Vice Pres*
▼ **EMP:** 16
SQ FT: 15,000
SALES: 2.5MM **Privately Held**
SIC: 5093 3087 Plastics scrap; custom compound purchased resins

(G-7182)
LIPOID LLC
744 Broad St Ste 1801 (07102-3805)
PHONE.................................973 735-2692
C Matthias Rebmann, *Mng Member*
Michael Kahn, *Senior Mgr*
▼ **EMP:** 4
SALES (est): 380K **Privately Held**
WEB: www.lipoidllc.com
SIC: 2834 Pharmaceutical preparations

(G-7183)
LMC PRECISION INC
91 Rome St (07105-3405)
PHONE.................................973 522-0005
Manuel Lobo, *Owner*
Napoleon Cruz, *Vice Pres*
EMP: 10
SALES (est): 1.1MM **Privately Held**
SIC: 3469 Machine parts, stamped or pressed metal

(G-7184)
LOCKTILE INDUSTRIES LLC
127 Frelinghuysen Ave (07114-1631)
PHONE.................................888 562-5845
Nigel Mandel, *Mng Member*
Aaron Silberberg,
EMP: 10
SALES (est): 466K **Privately Held**
SIC: 3996 1752 Tile, floor: supported plastic; ceramic floor tile installation

(G-7185)
LOPES SAUSAGE CO
304 Walnut St (07105-1717)
PHONE.................................973 344-3063
Hermino R Lopes, *Owner*
EMP: 5 **EST:** 1967
SQ FT: 8,800

SALES: 400K **Privately Held**
SIC: 2013 Sausages from purchased meat

(G-7186)
LOUIS IRON WORKS INC
218 Lackawanna Ave (07103-3236)
PHONE..................................973 624-2700
Louis Velasco, *President*
EMP: 9
SALES (est): 640K **Privately Held**
WEB: www.louisironworks.com
SIC: 7692 Welding repair

(G-7187)
LUNA FOODS LLC
Also Called: Joey's Fine Foods
135 Manchester Pl (07104-1722)
PHONE..................................973 482-1400
Joseph Aihini, *President*
Joe Aihini, *Sales Executive*
EMP: 40
SQ FT: 18,000
SALES (est): 1.2MM
SALES (corp-wide): 2.4MM **Privately Held**
SIC: 2052 2051 Cookies & crackers; cakes, pies & pastries
PA: Indulge Desserts Holdings, Llc
666 5th Ave Fl 27
New York NY 10103
212 231-8600

(G-7188)
LUSO MACHINE NJ LLC
29 Avenue C (07114-2601)
PHONE..................................973 242-1717
Sergio Remelgado, *President*
EMP: 10
SALES (est): 798.9K **Privately Held**
SIC: 3449 3469 3599 Miscellaneous metalwork; metal stampings; custom machinery; machine shop, jobbing & repair

(G-7189)
LUSO-AMERICANO CO INC
66 Union St (07105-1417)
PHONE..................................973 344-3200
Antonio Matinho, *President*
Natalie Matinho, *Corp Secy*
Paul Matinho, *Vice Pres*
EMP: 23
SALES (est): 1.5MM **Privately Held**
WEB: www.lusoamericano.com
SIC: 2711 Newspapers: publishing only, not printed on site

(G-7190)
LUSOTECH LLC
82-84 Vanderpool St (07114-1765)
P.O. Box 237, Elizabeth (07207-0237)
PHONE..................................973 332-3861
Filipe M Daluz, *Mng Member*
EMP: 4
SALES: 500K **Privately Held**
SIC: 1711 7692 3449 Mechanical contractor; welding repair; bars, concrete reinforcing: fabricated steel

(G-7191)
LYCA TEL LLC (PA)
Also Called: Lycatel
24 Commerce St Ste 100 (07102-4060)
PHONE..................................973 286-0771
Allirajah Subaskaran, *Principal*
Somasuntharam Thayaparan, *Principal*
Nithiyananthasothy Vallipuram, *Principal*
Reginauld Wilson, *Business Mgr*
Hiral Patel, *Engineer*
EMP: 24
SQ FT: 4,000
SALES (est): 5.7MM **Privately Held**
WEB: www.lycatel.com
SIC: 3661 Telegraph & related apparatus

(G-7192)
LYONDELL CHEMICAL COMPANY
Also Called: Equistar Chemicals
300 Doremus Ave (07105-4882)
PHONE..................................973 578-2200
Josh Squillante, *Manager*
Joseph Squillante, *Manager*
EMP: 8

SALES (corp-wide): 39.1B **Privately Held**
WEB: www.lyondell.com
SIC: 2869 2822 Olefins; ethylene; polyethylene, chlorosulfonated (hypalon)
HQ: Lyondell Chemical Company
1221 Mckinney St Ste 300
Houston TX 77010
713 309-7200

(G-7193)
MAB ENTERPRISES INC
Also Called: Vibration Isolation Co
123 S 15th St (07107-1052)
PHONE..................................973 345-8282
Marlene Bennett, *President*
EMP: 15
SALES (est): 2.6MM **Privately Held**
WEB: www.vibrationiso.com
SIC: 3829 Vibration meters, analyzers & calibrators

(G-7194)
MACHINE PARTS INC
Also Called: M P I
17 Ferdon St (07105-3010)
PHONE..................................973 491-5444
Douglas Reicard, *President*
EMP: 10 EST: 1995
SALES (est): 1.3MM **Privately Held**
WEB: www.machineparts.com
SIC: 3599 Machine shop, jobbing & repair

(G-7195)
MANCO PLATING INCORPORATED
390 Park Ave (07107-1112)
P.O. Box 7025 (07107-0025)
PHONE..................................973 485-6800
Luis Garcia, *President*
EMP: 9 EST: 1966
SQ FT: 9,800
SALES: 700K **Privately Held**
SIC: 3471 Electroplating of metals or formed products; finishing, metals or formed products

(G-7196)
MARA POLISHING & PLATING CORP
105 W Peddie St (07112-2753)
PHONE..................................973 242-0800
Louis Galarza, *President*
Eugene Maykish, *Vice Pres*
EMP: 7
SQ FT: 5,000
SALES (est): 777.9K **Privately Held**
SIC: 3471 Plating of metals or formed products; polishing, metals or formed products

(G-7197)
MATTHEW BENDER & COMPANY INC (DH)
Also Called: Lexisnexis Matthew Bender
744 Broad St Fl 8 (07102-3803)
PHONE..................................518 487-3000
Andrew Prozes, *CEO*
EMP: 52 EST: 1915
SALES (est): 91.5MM
SALES (corp-wide): 9.6B **Privately Held**
SIC: 2731 Books: publishing only
HQ: Relx Inc.
230 Park Ave Ste 700
New York NY 10169
212 309-8100

(G-7198)
MEADOWS KNITTING CORP
Also Called: Safer Textiles
1875 Mccarter Hwy (07104-4211)
PHONE..................................973 482-6400
Albert Safer, *President*
EMP: 45 EST: 1977
SQ FT: 130,000
SALES (est): 7.2MM **Privately Held**
SIC: 2257 Weft knit fabric mills

(G-7199)
MEDITERRANEAN STUCCO CORP
111 Main St (07105-3520)
P.O. Box 5562 (07105-0562)
PHONE..................................973 491-0160
EMP: 12
SQ FT: 10,000

SALES (est): 1.1MM **Privately Held**
SIC: 3299 5032 Mfg Nonmetallic Mineral Products Whol Brick/Stone Material

(G-7200)
MERRILL CORPORATION
60 Park Pl Ste 400 (07102-5513)
PHONE..................................973 643-4403
Mike James, *Manager*
EMP: 87
SALES (corp-wide): 566.6MM **Privately Held**
SIC: 2759 Commercial printing
PA: Merrill Corporation
1 Merrill Cir
Saint Paul MN 55108
651 646-4501

(G-7201)
METALS USA PLATES & SHAPES INC
178-204 Frelinghuyen Ave (07114)
PHONE..................................973 242-1000
Pam Makarski, *Sales Mgr*
EMP: 50
SALES (corp-wide): 11.5B **Publicly Held**
SIC: 3441 Fabricated structural metal
HQ: Metals Usa Plates And Shapes, Inc.
50 Cabot Blvd E
Langhorne PA 19047
267 580-2100

(G-7202)
MIMEOCOM INC
158 Mount Olivet Ave (07114-2114)
PHONE..................................973 286-2901
Joseph Hanley, *Accounts Exec*
Steve Scott, *Manager*
Fisher John, *Director*
Vincent Rossi, *Director*
EMP: 15
SALES (corp-wide): 189MM **Privately Held**
SIC: 2759 Commercial printing
PA: Mimeo.Com, Inc.
3 Park Ave Fl 22
New York NY 10016
212 847-3000

(G-7203)
MITZI INTL HANDBAG & ACC LTD
Tucker Distribution
250 Passaic St (07104-3700)
PHONE..................................973 483-5015
Richard Freeman, *Opers-Prdtn-Mfg*
EMP: 125
SALES (corp-wide): 65.6MM **Privately Held**
WEB: www.beteshgroup.com
SIC: 4225 3171 General warehousing & storage; women's handbags & purses
PA: Mitzi International Handbag & Accessories, Ltd.
250 Passaic St
Newark NJ 07104
212 686-4666

(G-7204)
MONTANA ELECTRICAL DECORATING
Perdeco Displays
62 Mcwhorter St (07105-1413)
PHONE..................................973 344-1815
John Montano, *Manager*
EMP: 5
SQ FT: 10,000
SALES (corp-wide): 1.9MM **Privately Held**
SIC: 3993 Displays & cutouts, window & lobby
PA: Montana Electrical Decorating Corp
126 E 131st St 2
New York NY 10037
212 368-4600

(G-7205)
MOTION SYSTEMS LLC (HQ)
250 Passaic St (07104-3700)
PHONE..................................212 686-4666
Mike Betesh,
Elliot Betesh,
Steven Betesh,
Chris Cassidy,
EMP: 17

SALES (est): 6.5MM
SALES (corp-wide): 85.5MM **Privately Held**
SIC: 3161 Cases, carrying
PA: The Betesh Group Holding Corp
250 Passaic St
Newark NJ 07104
212 686-4666

(G-7206)
N & J MACHINE PRODUCTS CORP
222 Thomas St (07114-2614)
PHONE..................................973 589-0031
Nino Pereira, *President*
Philippe Moinot, *Electrical Engi*
EMP: 5
SQ FT: 5,000
SALES (est): 571.5K **Privately Held**
SIC: 3599 Machine shop, jobbing & repair

(G-7207)
N C CARPET BINDING & EQUIPMENT
Also Called: NC Carpet
858 Summer Ave (07104-3618)
PHONE..................................973 481-3500
Mark J Caplan, *President*
Mel Maher Jr, *Vice Pres*
Mal Maher, *Administration*
◆ EMP: 15
SQ FT: 25,000
SALES (est): 3.5MM **Privately Held**
WEB: www.n-ccarpet.com
SIC: 3559 Sewing machines & hat & zipper making machinery

(G-7208)
NEW COMMUNITY CORP
Also Called: Fashion Institute of Ncc
200 S Orange Ave (07103-2724)
PHONE..................................973 643-5300
Linda Arrell, *Manager*
Dorothy Artis, *Social Worker*
EMP: 30
SALES (corp-wide): 19MM **Privately Held**
SIC: 2326 2339 2337 2321 Work uniforms; women's & misses' outerwear; women's & misses' suits & coats; men's & boys' furnishings; men's & boys' suits & coats; broadwoven fabric mills, manmade
PA: New Community Corp
233 W Market St
Newark NJ 07103
973 623-2800

(G-7209)
NEW JERSEY HEADWEAR CORP
Also Called: Unionwear
305 3rd Ave W Ste 5 (07107-2387)
P.O. Box 7009 (07107-0009)
PHONE..................................973 497-0102
Mitchell Cahn, *President*
Mitch Cahn, *President*
Maria Guido, *Purch Mgr*
Gloria Montoya, *Accounting Mgr*
Abby Contreras, *Info Tech Mgr*
▲ EMP: 105
SQ FT: 50,000
SALES (est): 12.2MM **Privately Held**
WEB: www.unionwear.com
SIC: 2353 2331 2321 Baseball caps; women's & misses' blouses & shirts; men's & boys' furnishings

(G-7210)
NEW JRSY GLVNZNG & TNNNG WKS
139 Haynes Ave (07114-2207)
PHONE..................................973 242-3200
Robert Gregory, *President*
EMP: 53 EST: 1902
SQ FT: 2,500
SALES (est): 7MM **Privately Held**
SIC: 3479 Galvanizing of iron, steel or end-formed products

(G-7211)
NEWAGE PAINTING CORPORATION
78 Fillmore St Ste 7 (07105-3682)
PHONE..................................908 547-4734
Rossiny Dacosta, *President*

EMP: 6
SALES (est): 1.4K **Privately Held**
SIC: 2851 1799 1721 Paints, waterproof;
epoxy application; bridge painting

(G-7212)
NEWARK ASPHALT CORP
1500 Mccarter Hwy (07104-3997)
PHONE....................973 482-3503
Joseph Napp, *President*
Micheal Manno, *Vice Pres*
Raymond Lesoine, *Plant Supt*
Daniel Corvelli, *Admin Sec*
EMP: 9 **EST:** 1964
SQ FT: 5,000
SALES (est): 2.3MM
SALES (corp-wide): 17.6MM **Privately
Held**
WEB: www.napp-grecco.com
SIC: 2951 2952 Asphalt & asphaltic
paving mixtures (not from refineries); as-
phalt felts & coatings
PA: Napp-Grecco Company
1500 Mccarter Hwy
Newark NJ 07104
973 482-3500

(G-7213)
**NEWARK INDUSTRIAL
SPRAYING**
12 Amsterdam St (07105-3802)
PHONE....................973 344-6855
Richard D Wantz, *President*
Susan Farmen, *Corp Secy*
EMP: 15
SQ FT: 12,000
SALES (est): 1.7MM **Privately Held**
WEB: www.rwdi.com
SIC: 3479 Painting of metal products

(G-7214)
NEWARK IRONWORKS INC
Also Called: Newark Steel & Orna Sup Co
41 Frelinghuysen Ave # 43 (07114)
PHONE....................973 424-9790
Jose Martinez, *President*
EMP: 10
SQ FT: 5,000
SALES (est): 1.8MM **Privately Held**
SIC: 3441 5211 Fabricated structural
metal; lumber & other building materials

(G-7215)
NEWARK LINER & WASHER INC
819 Broadway (07104-4300)
PHONE....................973 482-5400
George Figueroa, *President*
Avelina Figueroa, *President*
Antonio Figueroa, *Vice Pres*
EMP: 12
SQ FT: 1,500
SALES (est): 1.8MM **Privately Held**
SIC: 3089 Bottle caps, molded plastic

(G-7216)
**NEWARK MORNING LEDGER CO
(PA)**
Also Called: Sunday Star Ledger
1 Gateway Ctr Ste 1100 (07102-5323)
PHONE....................973 392-4141
Donald E Newhouse, *President*
Glenn Hirsh, *CPA*
Peter Barash, *Manager*
Michael Antonio, *Analyst*
EMP: 500
SQ FT: 20,000
SALES (est): 217.5MM **Privately Held**
SIC: 2711 Commercial printing & newspa-
per publishing combined

(G-7217)
**NEWARK STAMP & DIE WORKS
INC**
35 Verona Ave (07104-4409)
PHONE 973 485-7111
Denis Bruce McNab, *President*
Barbara McNab, *Corp Secy*
EMP: 6
SQ FT: 10,000
SALES: 850K **Privately Held**
WEB: www.newarkstampdie.com
SIC: 3953 Embossing seals & hand
stamps

(G-7218)
NICHEM CO
750 Frelinghuysen Ave (07114-2221)
PHONE....................973 399-9810
Peigeng Lu, *President*
▲ **EMP:** 7
SALES (est): 2.6MM **Privately Held**
WEB: www.nichemcompany.com
SIC: 5199 3569 Smokers' supplies; filters

(G-7219)
NORPAK CORPORATION (PA)
70 Blanchard St (07105-4702)
PHONE....................973 589-4200
Anthony Coraci, *President*
James Coraci, *Vice Pres*
Andrew Crumrine, *Engineer*
Lara Basile, *Technology*
Michael Pacyna, *Director*
▲ **EMP:** 50
SQ FT: 140,000
SALES (est): 17.5MM **Privately Held**
WEB: www.norpak.net
SIC: 2671 Wrapping paper, waterproof or
coated; bread wrappers, waxed or lami-
nated: purchased material

(G-7220)
**PANASONIC CORP NORTH
AMERICA**
Panasonic Ind Dev Sales Co Div
2 Riverfront Plz Ste 200 (07102-5490)
PHONE....................201 348-7000
James French, *Vice Pres*
Erwin Wu, *Marketing Mgr*
EMP: 80 **Privately Held**
SIC: 5065 3625 Electronic parts & equip-
ment; relays, for electronic use
HQ: Panasonic Corporation Of North Amer-
ica
2 Riverfront Plz Ste 200
Newark NJ 07102
201 348-7000

(G-7221)
**PANASONIC CORP NORTH
AMERICA**
Panasonic Entp Solutions Co
2 Riverfront Plz Ste 200 (07102-5490)
PHONE....................201 348-7000
EMP: 4 **Privately Held**
SIC: 3663 Television broadcasting & com-
munications equipment
HQ: Panasonic Corporation Of North Amer-
ica
2 Riverfront Plz Ste 200
Newark NJ 07102
201 348-7000

(G-7222)
**PARAMOUNT BAKERIES INC
(PA)**
61 Davenport Ave (07107-2533)
PHONE....................973 482-6638
Shraga Zabludovsky, *President*
Linda Zabludovsky, *Admin Sec*
▲ **EMP:** 7 **EST:** 1920
SQ FT: 5,000
SALES (est): 10.8MM **Privately Held**
WEB: www.paramountbakeries.com
SIC: 2051 Bakery: wholesale or whole-
sale/retail combined

(G-7223)
**PARAMOUNT FIXTURE
CORPORATION**
Also Called: Paramount Fixture Sales
175 Mount Pleasant Ave (07104-3814)
PHONE....................973 485-1585
Danniel Moore, *President*
Steve Porcelli, *Corp Secy*
Jorge Lopes, *Vice Pres*
EMP: 38
SQ FT: 45,000
SALES (est): 6.2MM **Privately Held**
WEB: www.paramountfixturecorp.com
SIC: 2541 Store fixtures, wood

(G-7224)
PAUL DYEING COMPANY
626 Orange St (07107-1030)
P.O. Box C, Whippany (07981-0402)
PHONE....................973 484-1121
Laurie Braun, *President*
EMP: 15 **EST:** 1934

SQ FT: 7,000
SALES (est): 2MM **Privately Held**
WEB: www.pauldyeing.com
SIC: 2261 Dyeing cotton broadwoven fab-
rics

(G-7225)
**PEERLESS UMBRELLA CO INC
(PA)**
427 Ferry St (07105-3903)
PHONE....................973 578-4900
Gene Moscowitz, *President*
Peter Hiatrides, *Purch Agent*
Bryan McKatten, *Regl Sales Mgr*
Dan Edge, *Marketing Staff*
Rod Vaughn, *Manager*
◆ **EMP:** 110 **EST:** 1929
SQ FT: 100,000
SALES (est): 12.1MM **Privately Held**
WEB: www.peerlessumbrella.com
SIC: 3999 5136 Umbrellas, canes & parts;
candles; umbrellas, men's & boys'

(G-7226)
PENICK CORPORATION
33 Industrial Park Rd (07114)
PHONE....................856 678-3601
Dr Stuart A Rose, *President*
John Mc Roberts Jr, *Vice Pres*
Robert J Nilsen, *Treasurer*
EMP: 5
SQ FT: 100,000
SALES (est): 550.4K
SALES (corp-wide): 799.2MM **Privately
Held**
WEB: www.penickcorp.com
SIC: 2834 Pharmaceutical preparations
HQ: Siegfried Usa, Llc
33 Industrial Park Rd
Pennsville NJ 08070
856 678-3601

(G-7227)
**PERSONALITY
HANDKERCHIEFS INC**
Also Called: Hand Craft Mfg
640 Frelinghuysen Ave (07114-1360)
PHONE....................973 565-0077
Morris Mizrahi, *President*
Joseph I Mizrahi, *Corp Secy*
Irwin Mizrahi, *Exec VP*
Isaac Mizrahi, *Exec VP*
EMP: 30 **EST:** 1969
SQ FT: 65,000
SALES (est): 3.3MM **Privately Held**
SIC: 2389 5137 5136 Handkerchiefs, ex-
cept paper; men's miscellaneous acces-
sories; women's & children's clothing;
men's & boys' clothing

(G-7228)
**PHARMACEUTICAL
INNOVATIONS**
897 Frelinghuysen Ave (07114-2122)
PHONE....................973 242-2900
Gilbert Buchalter, *President*
▲ **EMP:** 25
SQ FT: 45,000
SALES (est): 6.2MM **Privately Held**
WEB: www.pharminnovations.com
SIC: 2834 Pharmaceutical preparations

(G-7229)
**PHARMCTCLPRSCRPTNSRVCLL
C LCNDA**
155 Jefferson St (07105-1706)
PHONE....................973 491-9000
Rita Lee Friedman, *President*
EMP: 4 **EST:** 2015
SALES (est): 336K **Privately Held**
SIC: 2834 Pharmaceutical preparations

(G-7230)
PITNEY BOWES INC
158 Mount Olivet Ave (07114-2114)
PHONE....................800 521-0080
Robert Divincenzo, *Principal*
EMP: 150
SALES (corp-wide): 3.5B **Publicly Held**
SIC: 3579 7359 Postage meters; business
machine & electronic equipment rental
services

PA: Pitney Bowes Inc.
3001 Summer St Ste 3
Stamford CT 06905
203 356-5000

(G-7231)
**PORTUGUESE BAKING
COMPANY INC**
Also Called: Teixeira's Bakery
221 Malvern St (07105-2424)
PHONE....................973 466-0118
Manuel Teixeira, *CEO*
EMP: 4 **EST:** 1991
SALES (est): 225.6K **Privately Held**
SIC: 2051 5149 5963 Bread, cake & re-
lated products; bakery products; bakery
goods, house-to-house

(G-7232)
PRAXAIR DISTRIBUTION INC
425 Avenue P (07105-4800)
PHONE....................973 589-7895
Mike Anuszewski, *Branch Mgr*
Tom Lanares, *Manager*
Kevin Thieu, *Manager*
EMP: 25 **Privately Held**
SIC: 5085 5169 2813 Welding supplies;
compressed gas; industrial gases
HQ: Praxair Distribution, Inc.
10 Riverview Dr
Danbury CT 06810
203 837-2000

(G-7233)
PREMIER RIBBON COMPANY
223 Raymond Blvd (07105)
PHONE....................973 589-2600
Matthew Elias, *President*
Robert Levine, *Vice Pres*
EMP: 9
SQ FT: 108,000
SALES (est): 621.3K
SALES (corp-wide): 14.5MM **Privately
Held**
WEB: www.allstatepaperbox.com
SIC: 2396 Ribbons & bows, cut & sewed
PA: Allstate Paper Box Co Inc
223 Raymond Blvd
Newark NJ 07105
973 589-2600

(G-7234)
**PRINCETON KEYNES GROUP
INC**
470 Mulberry St (07114-2738)
PHONE....................609 208-1777
Douglas Stewart, *Branch Mgr*
EMP: 10
SALES (corp-wide): 1.8MM **Privately
Held**
WEB: www.princetonkeynes.com
SIC: 2891 Adhesives & sealants
PA: The Princeton Keynes Group Inc
116 Village Blvd Ste 200
Princeton NJ 08540
609 951-2239

(G-7235)
PRINT POST
274 Chestnut St (07105)
PHONE....................973 732-0950
William Lion, *Principal*
EMP: 4
SALES (est): 487.8K **Privately Held**
SIC: 2752 Commercial printing, offset

(G-7236)
**PRINTERS SERVICE FLORIDA
INC (PA)**
26 Blanchard St (07105-4784)
PHONE....................973 589-7800
Richard Liroff, *Ch of Bd*
David Schwartz, *President*
Brian Blackburn, *Prdtn Mgr*
Daryll Engle, *Sales Staff*
▼ **EMP:** 2
SQ FT: 10,000
SALES (est): 3.8MM **Privately Held**
SIC: 5199 3555 Art goods; printing trades
machinery

(G-7237)
PRISCO DIGITAL LTD LBLTY CO (PA)
26 Blanchard St (07105-4702)
PHONE..................................973 589-7800
Eric Gutwillig, *Vice Pres*
EMP: 13
SALES: 6MM **Privately Held**
SIC: 2752 Commercial printing, offset

(G-7238)
PROFESSIONAL LAUNDRY SOLUTIONS
443 Orange St (07107-2901)
PHONE..................................973 392-0837
Francisco Mercado-Ebanks, *CEO*
EMP: 4
SALES (est): 187.3K **Privately Held**
SIC: 5719 5023 7349 3582 Beddings & linens; linens & towels; building & office cleaning services; washing machines, laundry: commercial, incl. coin-operated

(G-7239)
PSEG NUCLEAR LLC
80 Park Plz Ste 3 (07102-4194)
P.O. Box 232, Hancocks Bridge (08038-0232)
PHONE..................................973 430-5191
Ralph Izzo, *CEO*
Eric Carr, *President*
William Levis, *Vice Pres*
Marc Chastain, *Project Mgr*
Glenn Figueroa, *Opers Staff*
▲ EMP: 2013
SALES (est): 228.8MM
SALES (corp-wide): 9.7B **Publicly Held**
SIC: 3462 Nuclear power plant forgings, ferrous
HQ: Pseg Power Llc
80 Park Plz T-9
Newark NJ 07102

(G-7240)
PURE H2O TECHNOLOGIES INC
211 Warren St Ste 19 (07103-3571)
PHONE..................................973 622-0440
Matthew Rela, *President*
EMP: 10
SQ FT: 30,000
SALES: 2MM **Privately Held**
SIC: 3589 Water treatment equipment, industrial

(G-7241)
PYRAMID FOOD SERVICES CORP
93-105 Albert Ave (07105)
P.O. Box 248, Allentown (08501-0248)
PHONE..................................973 900-6513
Luis Ferreira, *President*
EMP: 17
SQ FT: 24,000
SALES (est): 645.4K **Privately Held**
SIC: 2099 Food preparations

(G-7242)
Q-PAK CORPORATION
2145 Mccarter Hwy (07104-4407)
PHONE..................................973 483-4404
Michael Formica, *President*
Anthony Formica, *Vice Pres*
EMP: 30 EST: 1964
SALES (est): 5MM **Privately Held**
WEB: www.qpakcorp.com
SIC: 3085 2842 Plastics bottles; ammonia, household; bleaches, household: dry or liquid

(G-7243)
R G SMITH TOOL & MFG CO
245 South St (07114-2990)
PHONE..................................973 344-1395
Edgar Blaus Jr, *President*
Christopher A Blaus, *Admin Sec*
EMP: 10 EST: 1921
SQ FT: 13,500
SALES (est): 1.3MM **Privately Held**
SIC: 3599 3544 Custom machinery; special dies, tools, jigs & fixtures

(G-7244)
RAB FOOD GROUP LLC (HQ)
Also Called: Horowitz
80 Avenue K (07105-3803)
PHONE..................................201 553-1100
Paul Bensabat, *CEO*
Alain Bankier, *President*
Mark Weinsten, *President*
David Rossi, *Vice Pres*
Michael Schrob, *Materials Mgr*
◆ EMP: 60 EST: 1888
SQ FT: 139,100
SALES (est): 50.6MM
SALES (corp-wide): 316.6MM **Privately Held**
SIC: 2052 2045 2032 2091 Matzos; cake mixes, prepared: from purchased flour; soups, except seafood: packaged in cans, jars, etc.; fish: packaged in cans, jars, etc.
PA: Tmci Holdings, Inc
80 Avenue K
Newark NJ 07105
201 553-1100

(G-7245)
RANDALL MFG CO INC
200 Sylvan Ave (07104-3691)
PHONE..................................973 482-8603
Cary S Tinfow, *President*
Deborah Tinfow, *Vice Pres*
Laurie A Holey, *Treasurer*
Charlotte S Tinfow, *Admin Sec*
▲ EMP: 36 EST: 1955
SQ FT: 33,000
SALES (est): 7.5MM **Privately Held**
SIC: 3442 2431 Moldings & trim, except automobile: metal; moldings, wood: unfinished & prefinished

(G-7246)
RAZAC PRODUCTS INC
Also Called: So Many Waves
25 Brenner St (07108-1610)
PHONE..................................973 622-3700
Darren Dowdy, *President*
Devon Dowdy, *Principal*
Jalil Dowdy, *Principal*
Madeline Dowdy, *Principal*
EMP: 5
SALES (est): 751.5K **Privately Held**
SIC: 3999 Hair, dressing of, for the trade; hair nets

(G-7247)
REAL KOSHER LLC
146 Christie St (07105-3916)
PHONE..................................973 690-5394
Irving Braun,
EMP: 6
SALES (est): 863.5K **Privately Held**
SIC: 2013 Sausages & other prepared meats

(G-7248)
REDDAWAY MANUFACTURING CO INC
32 Euclid Ave (07105-4599)
PHONE..................................973 589-1410
Pamela Barton, *Ch of Bd*
Todd Walker, *President*
Daisey Gonzalez, *Vice Pres*
▲ EMP: 15 EST: 1890
SQ FT: 60,000
SALES (est): 2.2MM **Privately Held**
SIC: 2241 Manmade fiber narrow woven fabrics
PA: Rossendale Reddaway Company Inc
32 Euclid Ave
Newark NJ

(G-7249)
REGINA WINE CO
Also Called: Rex Vinegar Co
828 Raymond Blvd (07105-2905)
PHONE..................................973 589-6911
B Vincent Carlesimo, *President*
▲ EMP: 5 EST: 1968
SQ FT: 10,000
SALES (est): 344.8K **Privately Held**
SIC: 2099 Vinegar

(G-7250)
REX WINE VINEGAR COMPANY
Also Called: Roma Vinegar
828 Raymond Blvd Ste 830 (07105-2905)
PHONE..................................973 589-6911
B Vincent Carlesimo, *President*
EMP: 8 EST: 1948
SQ FT: 10,000
SALES (est): 798K **Privately Held**
SIC: 2099 Vinegar

(G-7251)
ROBDEN ENTERPRISES INC
Also Called: Fastsigns
210 Market St (07102-3708)
PHONE..................................973 273-1200
Robert S Acquaye, *CEO*
Denise Acquaye, *President*
EMP: 7
SALES (est): 716.7K **Privately Held**
SIC: 3993 Signs & advertising specialties

(G-7252)
ROBERT YOUNG & SONS INC
25 Grafton Ave (07104-4239)
PHONE..................................973 483-0451
David Young, *President*
Nancy Young, *Admin Sec*
◆ EMP: 4 EST: 1885
SQ FT: 2,500
SALES: 650K **Privately Held**
SIC: 3281 5211 Granite, cut & shaped; paving stones

(G-7253)
ROYAL ALUMINUM CO INC
620 Market St Ste 1 (07105-3693)
PHONE..................................973 589-8880
John D Inelli, *President*
Pamela Inelli, *Corp Secy*
▲ EMP: 60
SQ FT: 45,000
SALES (est): 7.8MM **Privately Held**
SIC: 3089 1751 3442 Window frames & sash, plastic; carpentry work; storm doors or windows, metal

(G-7254)
RUGGIERO SEA FOOD INC (PA)
Also Called: Fisherman's Pride
474 Wilson Ave (07105-4833)
P.O. Box 5369 (07105-0369)
PHONE..................................973 589-0524
Rocco Ruggiero, *President*
Mario Pereira, *Admin Sec*
Ruggiero Seafood, *Products*
◆ EMP: 52
SALES (est): 51.5MM **Privately Held**
WEB: www.ruggieroseafood.com
SIC: 5146 5812 2092 Seafoods; eating places; fresh or frozen packaged fish

(G-7255)
RUGGIERO SEA FOOD INC
117 Avenue L (07105-3809)
PHONE..................................973 589-0524
Rocco Ruggiero, *Branch Mgr*
EMP: 8
SALES (est): 945.4K
SALES (corp-wide): 51.5MM **Privately Held**
SIC: 5146 5812 2092 Seafoods; eating places; fresh or frozen packaged fish
PA: Ruggiero Sea Food, Inc.
474 Wilson Ave
Newark NJ 07105
973 589-0524

(G-7256)
RUST-OLEUM CORPORATION
480 Frelinghuysen Ave (07114-1428)
PHONE..................................732 652-2378
EMP: 10
SALES (corp-wide): 5.5B **Publicly Held**
SIC: 2891 Adhesives & sealants
HQ: Rust-Oleum Corporation
11 E Hawthorn Pkwy
Vernon Hills IL 60061
847 367-7700

(G-7257)
S & G TOOL AID CORPORATION
43 E Alpine St (07114-1629)
PHONE..................................973 824-7730
George Gering, *President*
Steven Gering, *Vice Pres*
Brad Gering, *Plant Mgr*
▲ EMP: 61 EST: 1971
SQ FT: 15,000
SALES (est): 8.7MM
SALES (corp-wide): 60.3MM **Privately Held**
SIC: 3546 3829 3423 3714 Power-driven handtools; testing equipment: abrasion, shearing strength, etc.; hand & edge tools; motor vehicle parts & accessories
PA: M. Eagles Tool Warehouse, Inc.
178-192 Sherman Ave
Newark NJ 07114
973 824-6951

(G-7258)
S H P C INC
Also Called: Star National
187 Christie St (07105-3915)
PHONE..................................973 589-5242
Paul Sacks, *President*
Louis D Sacks, *President*
▲ EMP: 24 EST: 1950
SQ FT: 20,000
SALES (est): 3.3MM **Privately Held**
WEB: www.starheelplate.com
SIC: 3469 5072 Stamping metal for the trade; hardware

(G-7259)
SAFER HOLDING CORP
Also Called: Safer Textile
1875 Mccarter Hwy (07104-4211)
PHONE..................................973 485-1458
Albert Safer, *President*
Bill Garrity, *VP Admin*
Ray Dawson, *VP Sales*
Harvey Cohen, *Sales Staff*
▲ EMP: 700
SQ FT: 100,000
SALES (est): 78.2MM **Privately Held**
SIC: 2282 Knitting yarn: twisting, winding or spooling

(G-7260)
SAFER TEXTILE PROCESSING CORP
1875 Mccarter Hwy (07104-4211)
PHONE..................................973 482-6400
Albert Safer, *President*
Niso Barokas, *Vice Pres*
Stephen Hermann, *Vice Pres*
Richard Menken, *Vice Pres*
Martin Sohn, *Vice Pres*
EMP: 400
SQ FT: 100,000
SALES (est): 171.5K **Privately Held**
SIC: 7389 2396 2295 2261 Textile & apparel services; automotive & apparel trimmings; coated fabrics, not rubberized; finishing plants, cotton

(G-7261)
SAMAX ENTERPRISE INC
29-75 Riverside Ave Ste 2 (07104)
PHONE..................................973 350-9400
Pessy Fleischman, *President*
Aniko Lebowitz, *Vice Pres*
◆ EMP: 10
SALES (est): 2.1MM **Privately Held**
SIC: 2851 Lacquer: bases, dopes, thinner; varnishes; paint removers; varnish removers

(G-7262)
SANCON SERVICES INC
Also Called: Sancon Dumpster Rental Svcs
50 E Peddie St (07114-1411)
P.O. Box 466, Kenilworth (07033-0466)
PHONE..................................973 344-2500
Jose Conde, *President*
EMP: 4
SALES (est): 686.6K **Privately Held**
SIC: 3089 Garbage containers, plastic

(G-7263)
SCHIFFENHAUS INDUSTRIES INC (DH)
2013 Mccarter Hwy (07104-4301)
PHONE..................................973 484-5000
Steven C Voorhees, *President*
James A Rubright, *Chairman*
Robert B McIntosh, *Exec VP*
Paul W Stecher, *Senior VP*
EMP: 130
SQ FT: 170,000

SALES (est): 28.5MM
SALES (corp-wide): 16.2B **Publicly Held**
SIC: 2653 2679 Boxes, corrugated: made
from purchased materials; display items,
corrugated: made from purchased materials; corrugated paper: made from purchased material
HQ: Westrock - Southern Container, Llc
1000 Abernathy Rd Ste 125
Atlanta GA 30328
770 448-2193

(G-7264)
SCORIES INC
28 Vassar Ave (07112-2310)
P.O. Box 4223 (07112-0223)
PHONE...................................973 923-1372
William Hall, *President*
Yvonne Hall, *Vice Pres*
EMP: 10
SQ FT: 1,800
SALES (est): 1.1MM **Privately Held**
WEB: www.scories.com
SIC: 2844 7231 Hair preparations, includ-
ing shampoos; face creams or lotions;
beauty shops

(G-7265)
SEABRITE CORP
Also Called: Corte Provisions
574 Ferry St (07105-4402)
PHONE...................................973 491-0399
Antonio Seabra, *President*
Albano Seabra, *Vice Pres*
Rui Serra, *Mfg Staff*
EMP: 32
SALES (est): 4.4MM **Privately Held**
SIC: 2011 Meat packing plants

(G-7266)
SERRATELLI HAT COMPANY
INC
418 Central Ave (07107-3023)
P.O. Box 7069 (07107-0069)
PHONE...................................973 623-4133
Dean Serratelli, *President*
Peter Serratelli, *Vice Pres*
EMP: 5
SQ FT: 18,000
SALES (est): 3MM **Privately Held**
SIC: 2353 Hats & caps

(G-7267)
SHABAZZ FRUIT COLA
COMPANY LLC
24 Wyndmoor Ave (07112-1217)
PHONE...................................973 230-4641
Frankie Shabazz, *Principal*
EMP: 8
SALES (est): 360.7K **Privately Held**
SIC: 2086 Soft drinks: packaged in cans,
bottles, etc.

(G-7268)
SHAMROCK TECHNOLOGIES
INC (PA)
Foot Of Pacific St (07114)
PHONE...................................973 242-2999
William B Neuberg, *Ch of Bd*
Joon S Choo, *Vice Pres*
Manshi Sui, *Vice Pres*
◆ **EMP:** 90
SQ FT: 150,000
SALES: 70MM **Privately Held**
WEB: www.shamrocktechnologies.com
SIC: 2899 Chemical preparations

(G-7269)
SHEET METAL PRODUCTS INC
794 N 6th St (07107-2798)
PHONE...................................973 482-0450
William F Kovacs, *President*
James A Kovacs, *Corp Secy*
▲ **EMP:** 51
SQ FT: 27,000
SALES (est): 12.9MM **Privately Held**
SIC: 3443 3444 Plate work for the metal-
working trade; sheet metalwork

(G-7270)
SHERIS COOKERY INC
33 Delancey St (07105-1508)
PHONE...................................973 589-2060
Murray Forman, *President*
EMP: 15

SQ FT: 10,000
SALES (est): 2MM **Privately Held**
SIC: 2099 Salads, fresh or refrigerated;
cole slaw, in bulk

(G-7271)
SHEROY PRINTING INC
Also Called: Sir Speedy
40 Commerce St (07102-4003)
PHONE...................................973 242-4040
Roy Winters, *President*
Sherry Winters, *Admin Sec*
EMP: 15
SALES (est): 2.2MM **Privately Held**
SIC: 2752 2791 2789 Commercial print-
ing, lithographic; typesetting; bookbinding
& related work

(G-7272)
SIGNODE INDUSTRIAL GROUP
LLC
Angleboard
151-161 Buffington St (07112)
PHONE...................................201 741-2791
George Jarrin, *Manager*
EMP: 76
SALES (corp-wide): 11.1B **Publicly Held**
SIC: 3565 Packaging machinery
HQ: Signode Industrial Group Llc
3650 W Lake Ave
Glenview IL 60026
847 724-7500

(G-7273)
SILVER EDMAR
Also Called: G R P Signs
186 Van Buren St (07105-2638)
PHONE...................................973 817-7483
Edmar Silver, *Owner*
EMP: 5
SALES (est): 152.3K **Privately Held**
SIC: 7319 2759 Bus card advertising; pro-
motional printing

(G-7274)
SINAI MANUFACTURING CORP
Also Called: Jade Apparel Group
133 Kossuth St (07105-3485)
P.O. Box 50029 (07105-8029)
PHONE...................................973 522-1003
Florence Lee, *President*
Ajay Watts, *Controller*
EMP: 99
SALES (est): 3.6MM **Privately Held**
SIC: 2329 Field jackets, military

(G-7275)
SK & P INDUSTRIES INC (PA)
Also Called: Metrolab Division
73 Norfolk St (07103-3229)
PHONE...................................973 482-1864
Lynda Davidson, *President*
Edmund Davidson, *Vice Pres*
EMP: 8 **EST:** 1881
SALES (est): 1.2MM **Privately Held**
SIC: 3822 8734 3823 Auto controls regu-
lating residntl & coml environmt & ap-
plncs; testing laboratories; industrial
instrmnts msrmnt display/control process
variable

(G-7276)
SK & P INDUSTRIES INC
Also Called: Metrolab Div
73 Norfolk St (07103-3229)
PHONE...................................973 482-1864
Edmond Davidson, *Manager*
EMP: 8
SALES (corp-wide): 1.2MM **Privately**
Held
SIC: 3545 8734 7699 Machine tool ac-
cessories; testing laboratories; profes-
sional instrument repair services
PA: Sk & P Industries Inc
73 Norfolk St
Newark NJ 07103
973 482-1864

(G-7277)
SKIP GAMBERT & ASSOCIATES
INC
Also Called: S G A Custom Shirtmakers
436 Ferry St Ste 2 (07105-3929)
PHONE...................................973 344-3373
David G Gambert Jr, *President*
Claire Corcoran, *Manager*

Carla Pinheiro, *Director*
Skip Gambert, *Executive*
Patrice C Gambert, *Admin Sec*
EMP: 150
SQ FT: 28,000
SALES (est): 49.1MM **Privately Held**
SIC: 5136 2321 Shirts, men's & boys';
men's & boys' dress shirts

(G-7278)
SOCAFE LLC
41-43 Malvern St (07105)
PHONE...................................973 589-4104
EMP: 10
SALES (est): 1MM **Privately Held**
SIC: 2095 0179 Roasted coffee; coffee
farm

(G-7279)
SOWA CORP
223 Murray St (07114-2646)
PHONE...................................973 297-0008
Chris Garstka, *President*
EMP: 4
SALES (est): 540.2K **Privately Held**
SIC: 3469 Household cooking & kitchen
utensils, metal

(G-7280)
SPARTECH LLC
297 Ferry St (07105-3443)
PHONE...................................973 344-2700
John Alfano, *Plant Mgr*
Julie A McAlindon, *Manager*
EMP: 9
SALES (corp-wide): 1.3B **Privately Held**
SIC: 2821 Plastics materials & resins
HQ: Spartech Llc
120 Central
Saint Louis MO 63105
314 569-7400

(G-7281)
SPECTRUM FOILS INC
29 Riverside Ave Bldg 1 (07104-4237)
PHONE...................................973 481-0808
Carl Sowa, *President*
William Paczkowski, *Corp Secy*
William Huddleston, *Vice Pres*
Paul McCready, *Vice Pres*
EMP: 6
SQ FT: 11,000
SALES (est): 1.5MM **Privately Held**
SIC: 3497 Metal foil & leaf

(G-7282)
SPECTRUM PAINT APPLICATOR
425 Ferry St Fl 2 (07105-3903)
PHONE...................................973 732-9180
Arthur Edelson, *President*
Vicki Edelson, *Corp Secy*
▲ **EMP:** 40 **EST:** 1948
SQ FT: 25,000
SALES (est): 5.2MM **Privately Held**
WEB: www.spectrumbrush.com
SIC: 3991 Paint brushes; paint rollers

(G-7283)
SPRING EUREKA CO INC
9 Manufacturers Pl (07105-4405)
P.O. Box 5067 (07105-0067)
PHONE...................................973 589-4960
Jeffrey Suckow, *President*
Dorothy Cherry, *Shareholder*
Douglas Suckow, *Shareholder*
EMP: 20 **EST:** 1908
SQ FT: 13,000
SALES (est): 2.8MM **Privately Held**
SIC: 3493 3495 Coiled flat springs; flat
springs, sheet or strip stock; wire springs

(G-7284)
STANDARD EMBOSSING PLATE
MFG
129 Pulaski St (07105-2410)
PHONE...................................973 344-6670
Christian Fleissner IV, *President*
Richard Fleissner, *Vice Pres*
Susan Fleissner, *Admin Sec*
EMP: 5 **EST:** 1888
SQ FT: 15,000
SALES (est): 390K **Privately Held**
WEB: www.immigration-usa.com
SIC: 2796 Embossing plates for printing

(G-7285)
STAR EMBROIDERY CORP
305 3rd Ave W Ste 7 (07107-2387)
PHONE...................................973 481-4300
Uluwehi Lovell-Gannet, *President*
▲ **EMP:** 22
SALES (est): 1.6MM **Privately Held**
WEB: www.starembroidery.com
SIC: 2395 Embroidery & art needlework;
embroidery products, except schiffli ma-
chine

(G-7286)
STATE TOOL GEAR CO INC
211 Camden St (07103-2404)
PHONE...................................973 642-6181
Michael Insabella, *President*
Ross Insabella, *Vice Pres*
Camille Tedesco, *Treasurer*
EMP: 15 **EST:** 1962
SQ FT: 7,500
SALES (est): 2.4MM **Privately Held**
SIC: 3462 5085 3566 Gears, forged steel;
gears; speed changers, drives & gears;
reduction gears & gear units for turbines,
except automotive

(G-7287)
STIRRUP METAL PRODUCTS
CORP
215 Emmet St (07114-2732)
PHONE...................................973 824-7086
Todd Stirrup, *President*
George Stirrup, *Vice Pres*
▲ **EMP:** 18 **EST:** 1871
SQ FT: 20,000
SALES (est): 4.6MM **Privately Held**
WEB: www.stirrupmetal.com
SIC: 3469 3444 3471 3443 Stamping
metal for the trade; sheet metalwork; plat-
ing & polishing; fabricated plate work
(boiler shop); fabricated structural metal

(G-7288)
STR8LINE PUBLISHING
COMPANY
511 Frelinghuysen Ave (07114-1425)
P.O. Box 4240 (07112-0240)
PHONE...................................919 717-6740
Sonja Wilkerson, *CEO*
EMP: 4
SALES (est): 99.5K **Privately Held**
SIC: 2711 Newspapers

(G-7289)
SUBURBAN MONUMENT &
VAULT
203 Sherman Ave (07114-1611)
PHONE...................................973 242-7007
Clyde Brooks, *President*
EMP: 7 **EST:** 1968
SQ FT: 2,500
SALES: 500K **Privately Held**
SIC: 3272 Monuments, concrete

(G-7290)
SUCCESS SEWING INC
50 Columbia St Ste 2 (07102-4831)
PHONE...................................973 622-0328
Yalcin Mizrak, *President*
EMP: 5
SQ FT: 7,000
SALES: 300K **Privately Held**
WEB: www.mizrak.com
SIC: 2337 2335 Skirts, separate:
women's, misses' & juniors'; ensemble
dresses: women's, misses' & juniors'

(G-7291)
SUPERIOR PRINTING INK CO
INC
252 Wright St (07114-2631)
PHONE...................................973 242-5868
Jeff Simmons, *President*
EMP: 8
SALES (corp-wide): 137.8MM **Privately**
Held
SIC: 2893 2899 Printing ink; chemical
preparations
PA: Superior Printing Ink Co Inc
100 North St
Teterboro NJ 07608
201 478-5600

▲ = Import ▼=Export
◆ =Import/Export

(G-7292)
SUPREME INK CORP
65 Mcwhorter St (07105-1412)
PHONE..................................973 344-2922
John T Ahmed, *President*
EMP: 10
SQ FT: 8,000
SALES (est): 1.6MM **Privately Held**
WEB: www.supremeink.com
SIC: 2893 2752 Lithographic ink; commercial printing, lithographic

(G-7293)
SYMBIOMIX THERAPEUTICS LLC (DH)
105 Lock St Ste 409 (07103-3576)
PHONE..................................609 722-7250
David L Stern, *CEO*
Robert Jacks, *President*
Sharon Rwland, *Vice Pres*
David Palling, *VP Mfg*
Kristen Landon, *Marketing Staff*
EMP: 13
SQ FT: 1,083
SALES (est): 1.8MM
SALES (corp-wide): 1.5B **Privately Held**
SIC: 2834 Druggists' preparations (pharmaceuticals)
HQ: Lupin Inc.
111 S Calvert St Fl 21
Baltimore MD 21202
410 576-2000

(G-7294)
TBB INC (PA)
Also Called: Teixeira's Bakery
115-129 Kossuth St (07105)
PHONE..................................973 589-8875
Manuel Teixeira, *President*
Maria Teixeira, *Vice Pres*
▲ **EMP:** 5
SALES (est): 1.8MM **Privately Held**
SIC: 2051 Breads, rolls & buns

(G-7295)
TENAX FINISHING PRODUCTS CO
390 Adams St (07114-2899)
PHONE..................................973 589-9000
James A O'Neill, *President*
John F O'Neill, *Vice Pres*
Muriel Miller, *Manager*
EMP: 18 **EST:** 1948
SQ FT: 25,000
SALES (est): 2.9MM **Privately Held**
WEB: www.tenaxfp.com
SIC: 2851 Paints & allied products

(G-7296)
THIBAUT & WALKER CO INC
49 Rutherford St (07105-4820)
PHONE..................................973 589-3331
George Parker, *President*
Steven Holland, *Vice Pres*
EMP: 4 **EST:** 1880
SQ FT: 5,000
SALES (est): 970K **Privately Held**
SIC: 5162 2821 Resins; plastics materials & resins

(G-7297)
THIRTY-THREE QUEEN REALTY INC (PA)
Also Called: Flexon Industries
1 Flexon Plz (07114)
PHONE..................................973 824-5527
Joseph Folkman, *Ch of Bd*
David Rauch, *President*
Rickie Folkman, *Corp Secy*
Steve Pruitt, *Site Mgr*
Henry Rosenbaum, *Controller*
▲ **EMP:** 11
SQ FT: 2,000,000
SALES (est): 17.5MM **Privately Held**
WEB: www.flexonhose.com
SIC: 5085 3423 3052 Hose, belting & packing; hand & edge tools; rubber & plastics hose & beltings

(G-7298)
THOMSON REUTERS (MARKETS) LLC
Also Called: Thomson Financial
2 Gateway Ctr Fl 11 (07102-5006)
PHONE..................................973 286-7200

EMP: 5
SALES (corp-wide): 4.5B **Publicly Held**
SIC: 2731 Books-Publishing/Printing
HQ: Thomson Reuters (Markets) Llc
195 Broadway Fl 4
New York NY 10036
646 822-2000

(G-7299)
THOMSON REUTERS CORPORATION
Also Called: Research Institute of America
2 Gateway Ctr Fl 11 (07102-5006)
PHONE..................................212 337-4281
Robyn Staatorman, *Manager*
EMP: 500
SALES (corp-wide): 10.6B **Publicly Held**
SIC: 2731 Books: publishing only
HQ: Thomson Reuters Corporation
3 Times Sq
New York NY 10036
646 223-4000

(G-7300)
TITAN AMERICA LLC
178 Marsh St (07114-3237)
PHONE..................................973 690-5896
Ted Marousas, *Branch Mgr*
EMP: 5
SALES (corp-wide): 1.2MM **Privately Held**
SIC: 1499 Gypsum & calcite mining
HQ: Titan America Llc
5700 Lake Wright Dr # 300
Norfolk VA 23502
757 858-6500

(G-7301)
TOVLI INC
49 Hunter St (07114-1609)
P.O. Box 50320, Brooklyn NY (11205-0320)
PHONE..................................718 417-6677
Abraham Leser, *President*
Chana J Ostreicher, *Vice Pres*
▲ **EMP:** 50
SQ FT: 32,000
SALES (est): 4.8MM **Privately Held**
SIC: 2038 Frozen specialties

(G-7302)
TRADEMARK PLASTICS CORPORATION
494 Broad St Rm 202 (07102-3217)
PHONE..................................908 925-5900
Melvyn Schaffer, *CEO*
Robert Schaffer, *President*
Ann Schaffer, *Corp Secy*
▲ **EMP:** 30
SALES (est): 23.4MM **Privately Held**
WEB: www.trademarkplasticscorp.com
SIC: 2821 Plastics materials & resins

(G-7303)
TRUCKTECH PARTS & SERVICES
13 Avenue C (07114-2601)
PHONE..................................973 799-0500
Anderson Vieira, *Principal*
EMP: 4 **EST:** 2008
SALES (est): 822.1K **Privately Held**
SIC: 3537 7538 7539 7532 Industrial trucks & tractors; truck engine repair, except industrial; general truck repair; wheel alignment, automotive; trailer repair; body shop, trucks

(G-7304)
U J RAMELSON CO INC
165 Thomas St (07114-2709)
PHONE..................................973 589-5422
John Ramella, *President*
Daniel Ramella, *Vice Pres*
EMP: 8 **EST:** 1937
SQ FT: 2,400
SALES (est): 500K **Privately Held**
WEB: www.ramelson.com
SIC: 3952 Artists' materials, except pencils & leads

(G-7305)
U S SCREENING CORP
780 Frelinghuysen Ave (07114-2221)
PHONE..................................973 242-1110
Rino Baranes, *Ch of Bd*

Robert Deprospo, *Exec VP*
Carlos Matos, *Controller*
Carmen Peak, *Manager*
Maria Baranes, *Shareholder*
◆ **EMP:** 250
SQ FT: 140,000
SALES (est): 28.9MM **Privately Held**
SIC: 2759 2396 Screen printing; automotive & apparel trimmings

(G-7306)
UNION CONTAINER CORP
439 Frelinghuysen Ave (07114-1426)
P.O. Box 2159 (07114-0159)
PHONE..................................973 242-3600
A George Onufer, *President*
Robert Blakley, *Corp Secy*
EMP: 33 **EST:** 1940
SQ FT: 40,000
SALES (est): 3.4MM **Privately Held**
SIC: 2655 2631 Spools, fiber: made from purchased material; tubes, fiber or paper: made from purchased material; paperboard mills

(G-7307)
UNIPHY HEALTH HOLDINGS LLC
211 Warren St Ste 507 (07103-3568)
PHONE..................................844 586-4749
Adam Turinas, *CEO*
Chad Stoerp, *CFO*
Edward Guy, *CTO*
EMP: 20
SALES (est): 2.5MM
SALES (corp-wide): 3B **Privately Held**
SIC: 7372 Application computer software
HQ: Quadramed Corporation
2300 Corp Park Dr Ste 400
Herndon VA 20171
703 709-2300

(G-7308)
UNITED EQP FABRICATORS LLC
175 Orange St (07103-4009)
PHONE..................................973 242-2737
Robert Ayars, *President*
EMP: 6
SQ FT: 120,000
SALES (est): 570K **Privately Held**
SIC: 3089 3449 1799 5084 Plastic processing; miscellaneous metalwork; fiberglass work; pumps & pumping equipment; fiberglass fabrics

(G-7309)
UNITED LABEL CORP
65 Chambers St (07105-2893)
PHONE..................................973 589-6500
John O'Conner, *President*
EMP: 8 **EST:** 1965
SQ FT: 20,000
SALES: 1.5MM **Privately Held**
WEB: www.unitedlabelcorp.com
SIC: 2679 3479 2759 2672 Labels, paper: made from purchased material; name plates: engraved, etched, etc.; commercial printing; coated & laminated paper

(G-7310)
US WIRE & CABLE CORPORATION (PA)
Also Called: Flexon Inds Div US Wire Cable
366 Frelinghuysen Ave (07114-1424)
PHONE..................................973 824-5530
David Rauch, *President*
Joseph Folkman, *Vice Pres*
Alex Folkman, *Admin Sec*
◆ **EMP:** 482
SALES (est): 141.9MM **Privately Held**
WEB: www.uswireandcable.com
SIC: 3052 3315 Garden hose, plastic; cable, steel: insulated or armored

(G-7311)
VEHICLE SAFETY MFG LLC (HQ)
Also Called: V S M
408 Central Ave (07107-3021)
PHONE..................................973 643-3000
James Pineau, *CEO*
Fernando Columbro, *Senior VP*
Fernando Zambrano, *Safety Mgr*
Daviel Rivera, *CFO*
▲ **EMP:** 42
SQ FT: 50,000

SALES: 12MM
SALES (corp-wide): 24MM **Privately Held**
WEB: www.vehiclesafetymfg.com
SIC: 3647 Vehicular lighting equipment
PA: Aftermarket Controls Corp.
2519 Dana Dr
Laurinburg NC 28352
910 291-2500

(G-7312)
VIEIRAS BAKERY INC
34-48 Ave K (07105)
PHONE..................................973 589-7719
Carlos Vieira, *President*
◆ **EMP:** 60
SALES (est): 8.8MM **Privately Held**
WEB: www.vieirasbakery.com
SIC: 2051 Bread, all types (white, wheat, rye, etc): fresh or frozen

(G-7313)
WELDED PRODUCTS CO INC
330 Raymond Blvd Ste 336 (07105-4698)
PHONE..................................973 589-0180
Francis Zurica, *President*
EMP: 25 **EST:** 1930
SALES (est): 4MM **Privately Held**
SIC: 3312 7692 3443 3444 Sheet or strip, steel, hot-rolled; welding repair; tanks, standard or custom fabricated: metal plate; sheet metalwork

(G-7314)
WESTROCK RKT COMPANY
2013 Mccarter Hwy (07104-4301)
PHONE..................................973 484-5000
Steven Donohoe, *Branch Mgr*
EMP: 110
SALES (corp-wide): 16.2B **Publicly Held**
SIC: 5113 2653 Boxes & containers; corrugated & solid fiber boxes
HQ: Westrock Rkt, Llc
1000 Abernathy Rd Ste 125
Atlanta GA 30328
770 448-2193

(G-7315)
WICKR INC
211 Warren St Ste 34 (07103-3574)
PHONE..................................516 637-2882
EMP: 4
SALES (est): 241.6K **Privately Held**
SIC: 3699 Mfg Electrical Equipment/Supplies

(G-7316)
WINDOW 25 LLC
103 Van Buren St (07105-2851)
PHONE..................................973 817-9464
Natalina Costa, *Principal*
Joao Costa,
EMP: 4
SALES (est): 499.5K **Privately Held**
SIC: 5714 3495 5131 7641 Draperies; upholstery springs, unassembled; upholstery fabrics, woven; reupholstery & furniture repair

(G-7317)
XANTHUS INC
105 Lock St Ste 215 (07103-3565)
PHONE..................................973 643-0920
EMP: 5 **EST:** 1984
SALES: 500K **Privately Held**
SIC: 7372 Prepackaged Software Services

(G-7318)
ZAGO MANUFACTURING COMPANY
21 E Runyon St (07114-1510)
PHONE..................................973 643-6700
Gail Friedberg, *Vice Pres*
Jessica Reyes, *Purchasing*
Michele Marchak, *Accounts Mgr*
Alejandra Damacela, *Sales Staff*
EMP: 25
SQ FT: 8,000
SALES (est): 5.7MM **Privately Held**
WEB: www.flexibletrim.com
SIC: 3451 3679 3648 3452 Screw machine products; hermetic seals for electronic equipment; lighting equipment; bolts, nuts, rivets & washers; molded rubber products

(G-7319)
ZVONKO STULIC & SON INC
21 Main St (07105-3509)
PHONE..............................973 589-3773
Zvonko Stulic, *President*
EMP: 5
SQ FT: 5,000
SALES: 350K **Privately Held**
WEB: www.zssfabrication.com
SIC: 3556 Cutting, chopping, grinding, mixing & similar machinery

Newfield
Gloucester County

(G-7320)
CS INDUSTRIAL SERVICES LLC
303 Catawba Ave (08344-9515)
PHONE..............................609 381-4380
Carman Simonetti, *Mng Member*
EMP: 6
SALES (est): 899.9K **Privately Held**
SIC: 3441 Fabricated structural metal

(G-7321)
ERNEST R MILES CONSTRUCTION CO
Also Called: Miles Concrete Co
1445 Catawba Ave (08344-5332)
P.O. Box 39 (08344-0039)
PHONE..............................856 697-2311
Ernest Miles Jr, *President*
Ernest R Miles, *President*
Eleanor Miles, *Corp Secy*
EMP: 12
SQ FT: 8,000
SALES (est): 909.7K **Privately Held**
SIC: 1741 5032 3273 Foundation & retaining wall construction; stone masonry; concrete mixtures; ready-mixed concrete

(G-7322)
FENCEMAX
1624 Harding Hwy (08344-5221)
PHONE..............................609 646-2265
Mark Amechi, *Branch Mgr*
EMP: 5 **Privately Held**
SIC: 3089 Fences, gates & accessories: plastic
PA: Fencemax
664 Mantua Pike
Woodbury NJ 08096

(G-7323)
MILES CONCRETE COMPANY INC
1445 Catawba Ave (08344-5332)
P.O. Box 39 (08344-0039)
PHONE..............................856 697-2311
Ernest Miles Sr, *President*
Lisa Santoro, *Administration*
EMP: 17
SALES (est): 1.5MM **Privately Held**
SIC: 1771 3273 Concrete work; ready-mixed concrete

(G-7324)
NEW ERA ENTERPRISES INC
208 N West Blvd (08344-9556)
P.O. Box 747, Vineland (08362-0747)
PHONE..............................856 794-2005
Frank L Bosco, *President*
Lynda Bosco, *Treasurer*
EMP: 6
SQ FT: 1,700
SALES (est): 866.2K **Privately Held**
WEB: www.newera-spectro.com
SIC: 3826 Analytical instruments

(G-7325)
NOOPYS RESEARCH INC
108 Harding Hwy (08344-8409)
PHONE..............................856 358-6001
Lester Morgan, *President*
Pearl E Morgan, *Corp Secy*
EMP: 4
SQ FT: 9,500
SALES (est): 530.3K **Privately Held**
SIC: 2851 Paint removers; varnish removers

(G-7326)
PAUL BROS INC
113 Church St (08344-9595)
P.O. Box 10 (08344-0010)
PHONE..............................856 697-5895
Thomas D Paul, *President*
Nancy M Paul, *Treasurer*
William R Paul, *Admin Sec*
EMP: 25
SQ FT: 7,500
SALES: 2MM **Privately Held**
SIC: 3272 Concrete products

(G-7327)
RF VII INC
104 Church St (08344-9583)
PHONE..............................856 875-2121
Steve Barber, *CEO*
Kelly Barber, *President*
▲ EMP: 14 EST: 1994
SALES (est): 1.8MM **Privately Held**
WEB: www.rfvii.com
SIC: 7699 3825 Professional instrument repair services; precision instrument repair; mechanical instrument repair; radio frequency measuring equipment

(G-7328)
SOLID CAST STONE
470 Grubb Rd (08344-4813)
P.O. Box 343 (08344-0343)
PHONE..............................856 694-5245
Tiffany Brown, *President*
EMP: 4
SALES (est): 400K **Privately Held**
SIC: 3272 Concrete products

Newfoundland
Passaic County

(G-7329)
ATLANTIC RUBBER ENTERPRISES
Also Called: Hercules World Industries
35 Union Valley Rd (07435-1649)
PHONE..............................973 697-5900
Phillip Corbae, *President*
Josephine M Corbae, *Corp Secy*
▲ EMP: 8
SQ FT: 8,000
SALES (est): 1.5MM **Privately Held**
SIC: 5085 3053 3052 Hose, belting & packing; gaskets, packing & sealing devices; rubber & plastics hose & beltings

(G-7330)
ESP ASSOCIATES INC
Also Called: Electronic Specialty Products
2713 State Rt 23 Ste 8a (07435-1415)
P.O. Box 349 (07435-0349)
PHONE..............................973 208-9045
James R Johnson, *President*
EMP: 16
SALES (est): 2.5MM **Privately Held**
WEB: www.espnj.com
SIC: 3672 Printed circuit boards

(G-7331)
PHOENIX PRECISION CO
2963 State Rt 23 (07435-1419)
PHONE..............................973 208-8877
Edward Wolos III, *President*
Edward Wolos Jr, *Vice Pres*
EMP: 12
SQ FT: 10,000
SALES (est): 1.6MM **Privately Held**
SIC: 3599 Machine shop, jobbing & repair

(G-7332)
RGI INC
27 Union Valley Rd (07435-1649)
PHONE..............................973 697-2624
Barry Maloney, *President*
Raymond Christian, *Vice Pres*
EMP: 15
SQ FT: 11,000
SALES (est): 2.8MM **Privately Held**
WEB: www.rgi.net
SIC: 3494 Valves & pipe fittings

Newport
Cumberland County

(G-7333)
HANSON AGGREGATES BMC INC
1191 Railroad Ave (08345-2199)
PHONE..............................856 447-4294
Harry Zeller, *Manager*
EMP: 7
SALES (corp-wide): 20.6B **Privately Held**
SIC: 3273 Ready-mixed concrete
HQ: Hanson Aggregates Bmc, Inc.
852 Swamp Rd
Penns Park PA
215 598-3152

(G-7334)
MAYS LANDING SAND & GRAVEL CO (DH)
1101 Railroad Ave (08345-2199)
PHONE..............................856 447-4294
Dan Harrington, *President*
EMP: 1 EST: 1948
SQ FT: 2,000
SALES (est): 3.9MM
SALES (corp-wide): 20.6B **Privately Held**
SIC: 1442 Construction sand & gravel

Newton
Sussex County

(G-7335)
A B SCANTLEBURY CO INC
108 Phil Hardin Rd (07860-5223)
PHONE..............................973 770-3000
Arthur B Scantlebury, *President*
Lora Grant, *Vice Pres*
John Spinelli, *Finance Mgr*
EMP: 12
SQ FT: 5,000
SALES: 1MM **Privately Held**
WEB: www.absco.com
SIC: 3599 3444 Machine shop, jobbing & repair; sheet metal specialties, not stamped

(G-7336)
ALESSANDRA MISCELLANEOUS METAL
75 Mill St Ste B (07860-1453)
PHONE..............................973 786-6805
Scott Alessandra, *President*
EMP: 17
SQ FT: 3,000
SALES: 2.5MM **Privately Held**
SIC: 3446 Stairs, staircases, stair treads: prefabricated metal

(G-7337)
AUTOMATIC MACHINE PRODUCT
56 Paterson Ave (07860-2349)
PHONE..............................973 383-9929
Don Schanstra, *Owner*
EMP: 4
SQ FT: 2,000
SALES (est): 285.5K **Privately Held**
SIC: 3451 Screw machine products

(G-7338)
BACKROADS INC
160 County Road 521 (07860-6453)
PHONE..............................973 948-4176
Brian Rathjen, *President*
Shila Kamil, *Vice Pres*
EMP: 7
SALES (est): 300K **Privately Held**
WEB: www.backroadsusa.com
SIC: 2721 Magazines: publishing only, not printed on site

(G-7339)
CARSTENS PUBLICATIONS INC
Also Called: Flying Models
108 Phil Hardin Rd (07860-5223)
PHONE..............................973 383-3355
Harold H Carstens, *President*
Henry Carstens, *Treasurer*

George Riley, *Assoc Editor*
Chris Susicke, *Assoc Editor*
Phyllis Carstens, *Admin Sec*
EMP: 24
SQ FT: 11,000
SALES (est): 2.4MM **Privately Held**
WEB: www.carstens-publications.com
SIC: 2721 2731 Magazines: publishing only, not printed on site; books: publishing only

(G-7340)
CUSTOM WOOD FURNITURE INC
37 E Clinton St Ste 1 (07860-1870)
P.O. Box 3034 (07860-3034)
PHONE..............................973 579-4880
John K Kweselait, *President*
EMP: 19
SQ FT: 10,000
SALES (est): 2.6MM **Privately Held**
WEB: www.customwoodfurnitureinc.com
SIC: 2434 Wood kitchen cabinets

(G-7341)
EM SIGNS
80 Merriam Ave (07860-2420)
PHONE..............................973 300-9703
Eric M Martino, *Principal*
EMP: 5
SALES (est): 409.5K **Privately Held**
SIC: 3993 Signs, not made in custom sign painting shops

(G-7342)
ENGINEERED SILICONE PDTS LLC
Also Called: ESP
75 Mill St Ste 2 (07860-1453)
PHONE..............................973 300-5120
Louis Haberman, *Mng Member*
Lynn Snyder,
EMP: 5
SALES: 1.7MM **Privately Held**
WEB: www.weareesp.com
SIC: 2869 Silicones

(G-7343)
FREDON DEVELOPMENT INDS LLC
393 State Route 94 S (07860-5154)
PHONE..............................973 383-7576
Tom Krisanda, *Opers Staff*
Gerald Wildrick, *Mng Member*
EMP: 17
SQ FT: 11,000
SALES (est): 3MM **Privately Held**
SIC: 3089 Injection molding of plastics

(G-7344)
G A D INC
Also Called: Pro Gad Sales
914 Cedar Ridge Rd (07860-4400)
PHONE..............................973 383-3499
Patricia Barone, *President*
Vincent D Barone, *Corp Secy*
Vincent Barone, *Treasurer*
EMP: 4
SALES (est): 402.2K **Privately Held**
WEB: www.progadsales.com
SIC: 3949 Sporting & athletic goods

(G-7345)
GOETZ & RUSCHMANN INC
1 Brooks Plz (07860-2626)
P.O. Box 960, Bernardsville (07924-0960)
PHONE..............................973 383-9270
Harold A Sutton, *President*
Bertha Ruschmann, *Corp Secy*
EMP: 35 EST: 1933
SQ FT: 9,000
SALES (est): 1.5MM **Privately Held**
SIC: 2675 2673 2679 3354 Paper diecutting; bags: plastic, laminated & coated; foil board: made from purchased material; aluminum extruded products

(G-7346)
IMAGE POINT
69 Water St (07860-1414)
PHONE..............................908 684-1768
John Fernicola, *President*
EMP: 5
SALES (est): 401K **Privately Held**
SIC: 2396 Fabric printing & stamping

(G-7347)
J & S TOOL
56 Paterson Ave Ste 4 (07860-2350)
PHONE..................................973 383-5059
Roman Sleszar, *Owner*
EMP: 5 EST: 1941
SQ FT: 15,000
SALES (est): 900K **Privately Held**
WEB: www.jstool.com
SIC: 3541 5084 Machine tools, metal cutting type; industrial machinery & equipment

(G-7348)
KATIES CLOSETS
3 Lower Hill Rd (07860-5310)
PHONE..................................973 300-4007
Mike Higgins, *Owner*
EMP: 6
SALES (est): 583.6K **Privately Held**
SIC: 2673 Wardrobe bags (closet accessories): from purchased materials

(G-7349)
MAGAZINEXPERTS LLC
103 Spring St (07860-2145)
PHONE..................................973 383-0888
Donald Berry, *Mng Member*
Jennifir Pekarek, *Creative Dir*
EMP: 8
SALES: 792K **Privately Held**
SIC: 2741 Miscellaneous publishing

(G-7350)
MRI INTERNATIONAL
Also Called: Photographic Tech Intl
44 Clinton St (07860-1404)
P.O. Box 406 (07860-0406)
PHONE..................................973 383-3645
William Foltyn, *President*
Cynthia Dizeso, *Vice Pres*
▲ EMP: 7
SQ FT: 25,000
SALES (est): 1MM **Privately Held**
SIC: 5043 2899 Photographic processing - equipment; chemical preparations

(G-7351)
NATIONAL LECITHIM INC (PA)
93 Spring St Ste 303 (07860-2079)
PHONE..................................973 940-8920
Patricia Bruno, *President*
Glenn Geisler, *Vice Pres*
Jean Geisler, *Treasurer*
▲ EMP: 2
SALES: 1.3MM **Privately Held**
SIC: 2099 Emulsifiers, food

(G-7352)
NEW JERSEY HERALD (HQ)
2 Spring St (07860-2077)
P.O. Box 10 (07860-0010)
PHONE..................................973 383-1500
Thomas Oakley, *President*
Denise Minimi, *Sales Staff*
EMP: 130
SQ FT: 22,000
SALES (est): 48.7MM
SALES (corp-wide): 319.4MM **Privately Held**
WEB: www.njherald.com
SIC: 2711 Commercial printing & newspaper publishing combined
PA: Quincy Media, Inc.
130 S 5th St
Quincy IL 62301
217 223-5100

(G-7353)
PIN CANCER CAMPAIGN
34 County Road 519 (07860-6231)
PHONE..................................973 600-4170
EMP: 5 EST: 2011
SALES (est): 168.1K **Privately Held**
SIC: 3452 Pins

(G-7354)
RED OAK PACKAGING INC
Also Called: Four Star Color
52 Paterson Ave Ste 2 (07860-2363)
PHONE..................................862 268-8200
Charles Cioppa, *President*
EMP: 27 EST: 1963
SQ FT: 28,000

SALES (est): 6.5MM **Privately Held**
WEB: www.fourstarcolor.com
SIC: 2752 2631 Commercial printing, offset; milk carton board

(G-7355)
RIOTSOUND INC
Also Called: Millenium Worldwide
17 Hampton House Rd # 15 (07860-3404)
P.O. Box 3112 (07860-3112)
PHONE..................................917 273-5814
Alexander Shtaerman, *President*
Jennifer Shtaerman, *Vice Pres*
Jack Beierle, *VP Bus Dvlpt*
EMP: 4
SQ FT: 3,000
SALES: 1MM **Privately Held**
SIC: 5735 3651 5064 Records; audio electronic systems; high fidelity equipment

(G-7356)
SCHNEIDER & MARQUARD INC
Also Called: S & M Retaining Rings
112 Phil Hardin Rd (07860-5223)
P.O. Box 39 (07860-0039)
PHONE..................................973 383-2200
Michael O'Shea, *President*
Cheryl Foster, *Admin Sec*
EMP: 20
SQ FT: 23,000
SALES (est): 3.6MM **Privately Held**
WEB: www.schneidermarquard.com
SIC: 3544 Dies & die holders for metal cutting, forming, die casting; special dies & tools

(G-7357)
SCHRADER & COMPANY INC
188 Halsey Rd (07860-7058)
PHONE..................................973 579-1160
David Lake, *President*
Margaret Lake, *Treasurer*
EMP: 12
SALES (est): 1.6MM **Privately Held**
SIC: 3444 Sheet metalwork

(G-7358)
SKYLANDS PRESS
Also Called: Jmd Printing
57 Trinity St (07860-1824)
P.O. Box 809 (07860-0809)
PHONE..................................973 383-5006
John Daly, *Owner*
EMP: 4
SALES (est): 269.7K **Privately Held**
SIC: 2759 Commercial printing

(G-7359)
STUART MILLS INC (PA)
25 Stillwater Rd (07860-5037)
PHONE..................................973 579-5717
Stuart Mills, *President*
EMP: 6
SQ FT: 3,500
SALES: 500K **Privately Held**
SIC: 3599 Machine shop, jobbing & repair

(G-7360)
STUART MILLS INC
25 Stillwater Rd (07860-5037)
PHONE..................................973 579-5717
EMP: 4
SALES (corp-wide): 500K **Privately Held**
SIC: 3599 Machine shop, jobbing & repair
PA: Stuart Mills Inc
25 Stillwater Rd
Newton NJ 07860
973 579-5717

(G-7361)
T & M NEWTON CORPORATION
Also Called: Newton Tool
119 Fredon Springdale Rd (07860-5218)
PHONE..................................973 383-1232
Ralph Meola Jr, *President*
EMP: 7 EST: 1962
SQ FT: 11,000
SALES (est): 1.1MM **Privately Held**
SIC: 3089 Injection molding of plastics

(G-7362)
TECHNICAL OIL PRODUCTS CO INC (PA)
93 Spring St Ste 303 (07860-2079)
PHONE..................................973 940-8920

Alan S Geisler, *President*
Alan Geisler, *Owner*
Patricia Bruno, *Vice Pres*
Jean Geisler, *Admin Sec*
EMP: 9 EST: 1961
SALES (est): 828.5K **Privately Held**
SIC: 2079 2035 2869 Edible fats & oils; pickles, sauces & salad dressings; sorbitol

(G-7363)
THORLABS INC (PA)
56 Sparta Ave (07860-2402)
PHONE..................................973 579-7227
Alex Cable, *President*
David Beatson, *General Mgr*
Peter Heim, *General Mgr*
Dorothee Jennrich, *General Mgr*
Leo Beshada, *Superintendent*
▲ EMP: 128
SQ FT: 121,277
SALES (est): 205.9MM **Privately Held**
WEB: www.thorlabs.com
SIC: 3826 Analytical optical instruments

(G-7364)
VINE HILL FARM
100 Parsons Rd (07860-6340)
PHONE..................................973 383-0100
Andrew Napolitano, *Owner*
EMP: 4
SALES (est): 234.7K **Privately Held**
SIC: 5099 0115 2099 2511 Firewood; corn; maple syrup; cedar chests

Norma
Salem County

(G-7365)
B & B POULTRY CO INC
Almond Rd (08347)
P.O. Box 307 (08347-0307)
PHONE..................................856 692-8893
Benjamin Fisher, *President*
Dorothy Fisher, *Corp Secy*
Mark Fisher, *Vice Pres*
EMP: 175
SQ FT: 75,000
SALES (est): 28.8MM **Privately Held**
WEB: www.bandbpoultry.com
SIC: 2015 2011 Poultry, slaughtered & dressed; meat packing plants

North Arlington
Bergen County

(G-7366)
A-ONE MERCHANDISING CORP
170 Schuyler Ave (07031-5424)
PHONE..................................718 773-7500
Yakov Spritzer, *Ch of Bd*
▲ EMP: 13
SQ FT: 60,000
SALES (est): 3.9MM **Privately Held**
SIC: 3089 5113 Holders: paper towel, grocery bag, etc.: plastic; disposable plates, cups, napkins & eating utensils

(G-7367)
ALBERT H HOPPER INC
329 Ridge Rd (07031-5304)
PHONE..................................201 991-2266
Kenneth A Roberts, *President*
Doreen Schafer, *Manager*
Bernadeth Logan, *Admin Sec*
EMP: 6
SQ FT: 1,000
SALES: 150K **Privately Held**
WEB: www.ahhopper.com
SIC: 3281 5999 Monuments, cut stone (not finishing or lettering only); tombstones, cut stone (not finishing or lettering only); burial vaults, stone; monuments & tombstones

(G-7368)
ANGO ELECTRONICS CORPORATION
Also Called: Par Metal Products
29 Ewing Ave (07031-5001)
PHONE..................................201 955-0800

John Ango, *President*
▲ EMP: 10
SQ FT: 8,500
SALES (est): 1.9MM **Privately Held**
WEB: www.par-metal.com
SIC: 3679 3444 3354 Electronic circuits; sheet metalwork; aluminum extruded products

(G-7369)
ATLANTIC KENMARK ELECTRIC INC
11 Ewing Ave (07031-5001)
PHONE..................................201 991-2117
Salvatore Gaccione, *President*
Frank Gaccione, *Vice Pres*
Vincent Gaccione, *Treasurer*
▲ EMP: 17 EST: 1945
SQ FT: 5,000
SALES (est): 3.1MM **Privately Held**
SIC: 7694 Electric motor repair

(G-7370)
C & F BURNER CO
39 River Rd (07031-6101)
P.O. Box 7189 (07031-7189)
PHONE..................................201 998-8080
Robert A Dunn, *President*
Elizabeth Dunn, *Owner*
EMP: 34 EST: 1960
SQ FT: 1,000
SALES (est): 1.9MM **Privately Held**
SIC: 3433 Heating equipment, except electric

(G-7371)
CLAYTON BLOCK CO
2 Porete Ave (07031-6722)
PHONE..................................201 955-6292
John Cherchio, *President*
Richard Cherchio, *Treasurer*
EMP: 75
SQ FT: 15,000
SALES (est): 7.2MM
SALES (corp-wide): 31.8MM **Privately Held**
SIC: 3272 3271 Concrete products, precast; concrete block & brick
HQ: Clayton Block Company Llc
440 Hook Rd
Bayonne NJ 07002
201 339-8585

(G-7372)
FIRST INTERNET SYSTEMS
16 Geraldine Rd (07031-5407)
PHONE..................................201 991-1889
Balaji Modhagala, *Owner*
EMP: 13
SALES (est): 505.9K **Privately Held**
SIC: 7372 Prepackaged software

(G-7373)
FITTS SHEET METAL INC
44 Inman Pl (07031-6048)
PHONE..................................201 923-9239
Brian Szilva, *Principal*
EMP: 4 EST: 2010
SALES (est): 623.8K **Privately Held**
SIC: 3444 Sheet metalwork

(G-7374)
IDEAL DATA INC
420 River Rd (07031-5163)
PHONE..................................201 998-9440
Linda A Rueda, *President*
EMP: 15
SALES: 2MM **Privately Held**
WEB: www.idealdata.com
SIC: 7374 7331 3571 Data entry service; direct mail advertising services; electronic computers

(G-7375)
MINHURA INC
24 William St (07031-6153)
PHONE..................................862 763-4078
Jose Monteiro, *Owner*
EMP: 5
SALES (est): 285.4K **Privately Held**
SIC: 2064 Candy bars, including chocolate covered bars

(G-7376)
PAR METAL PRODUCTS INC
21 Ewing Ave (07031-5001)
PHONE..................................201 955-0800
John Ngo, *Principal*
EMP: 10
SALES (est): 1.3MM **Privately Held**
SIC: 3469 Electronic enclosures, stamped
or pressed metal

(G-7377)
PROACTIVE LTG SOLUTIONS
LLC
21 Ewing Ave (07031-5001)
PHONE..................................800 747-1209
Alfred Heyer, *CEO*
▼ EMP: 10
SQ FT: 25,000
SALES (est): 1.1MM **Privately Held**
SIC: 3648 Lighting equipment

(G-7378)
SCOTTS COMPANY LLC
125 Baler Blvd (07031-4415)
PHONE..................................201 246-0180
David Irwin, *Principal*
EMP: 15
SALES (corp-wide): 2.6B **Publicly Held**
WEB: www.scottscompany.com
SIC: 2873 Fertilizers: natural (organic), ex-
cept compost
HQ: The Scotts Company Llc
14111 Scottslawn Rd
Marysville OH 43040
937 644-0011

North Bergen
Hudson County

(G-7379)
A R C PLASMET CORP
4131 Bergen Tpke (07047-2509)
PHONE..................................201 867-8533
Ricardo Perez, *President*
Tony Palama, *President*
Genoveva Perez, *Corp Secy*
EMP: 11 EST: 1972
SQ FT: 8,000
SALES: 675K **Privately Held**
WEB: www.arcplasmet.com
SIC: 3089 Injection molding of plastics;
plastic processing

(G-7380)
ALCO TRIMMING
8608 Grand Ave Rear (07047-4337)
PHONE..................................201 854-8608
Michael Colon, *Partner*
Momeena Colon, *Partner*
EMP: 5
SQ FT: 7,000
SALES (est): 240K **Privately Held**
SIC: 2396 5131 Trimming, fabric; trim-
mings, apparel

(G-7381)
ALL-LACE PROCESSING CORP
1109 Grand Ave Ste 4 (07047-1628)
PHONE..................................201 867-1974
Achille Gaetano, *President*
Frank Gaetano, *Vice Pres*
EMP: 18
SQ FT: 15,000
SALES (est): 2.1MM **Privately Held**
WEB: www.alllace.com
SIC: 2258 Lace & warp knit fabric mills

(G-7382)
ALLIED SPECIALTY GROUP INC
(PA)
Also Called: Allied Metal
3223 Dell Ave (07047-2369)
PHONE..................................201 223-4600
Henry H Bilge, *President*
EMP: 19
SQ FT: 16,000
SALES (est): 2.3MM **Privately Held**
WEB: www.alliedmetal.com
SIC: 2819 Aluminum compounds

(G-7383)
ALVARO STAIRS LLC
4201 Tonnelle Ave Ste 12 (07047-2431)
PHONE..................................201 864-6754
Enrique Bernar,
EMP: 5
SALES (est): 470.8K **Privately Held**
SIC: 2431 Staircases & stairs, wood

(G-7384)
AMPERITE CO INC
4201 Tonnelle Ave Ste 6 (07047-2431)
P.O. Box 329 (07047-0329)
PHONE..................................201 864-9503
EMP: 35 EST: 1922
SQ FT: 12,000
SALES (est): 4.4MM **Privately Held**
WEB: www.amperite.com
SIC: 3679 3625 3647 3612 Delay lines;
industrial electrical relays & switches;
flasher lights, automotive; lamp ballasts;
voltage regulating transformers, electric
power; lighting equipment; current-carry-
ing wiring devices

(G-7385)
ARAFAT LAFI
7329 Broadway (07047-5738)
PHONE..................................201 854-7300
Lafi Arafat, *Owner*
EMP: 7
SALES (est): 400K **Privately Held**
SIC: 3999 Artificial flower arrangements

(G-7386)
ARMCO COMPRESSOR
PRODUCTS
Also Called: Armco Machine
2042 46th St (07047-2633)
P.O. Box 105 (07047-0105)
PHONE..................................201 866-6766
ARA Zadourian, *President*
Silva Zadourian, *Admin Sec*
▲ EMP: 4
SQ FT: 3,000
SALES (est): 738.1K **Privately Held**
WEB: www.armcocompressor.com
SIC: 3563 Air & gas compressors

(G-7387)
ARMEL ELECTRONICS INC
1601 75th St (07047-4094)
PHONE..................................201 869-4300
Ed Johnsen, *CEO*
EMP: 36
SQ FT: 27,000
SALES (est): 5.9MM **Privately Held**
WEB: www.armelelectronics.com
SIC: 3644 3643 3678 Terminal boards;
connectors & terminals for electrical de-
vices; electronic connectors

(G-7388)
BAL TOGS INC
Also Called: Bal-Togs
6605-09 Smith Ave (07047)
PHONE..................................201 866-0201
▲ EMP: 60
SQ FT: 40,000
SALES (est): 6.9MM **Privately Held**
SIC: 2339 Women's & misses' athletic
clothing & sportswear

(G-7389)
BERGEN MANUFACTURING &
SUPPLY
2025 85th St (07047-4714)
PHONE..................................201 854-3461
Ida Petrone, *President*
Michael Dimick, *Vice Pres*
EMP: 25 EST: 1975
SQ FT: 15,000
SALES (est): 3.1MM **Privately Held**
SIC: 5047 3949 2821 Medical equipment
& supplies; surgical equipment & sup-
plies; incontinent care products & sup-
plies; sporting & athletic goods; plastics
materials & resins

(G-7390)
BERGENLINE GELATO LLC
7903 Bergenline Ave (07047-4943)
PHONE..................................201 861-1100
EMP: 4

SALES (est): 202.9K **Privately Held**
SIC: 2024 Ice cream, bulk

(G-7391)
C3 CONCEPTS INC
Also Called: Christopher Fischer
1435 51st St Ste 2d (07047-3100)
PHONE..................................212 840-1116
Christopher Fischer, *President*
Charlene Kuo, *Vice Pres*
▲ EMP: 31 EST: 1996
SALES (est): 9.3MM **Privately Held**
WEB: www.c3concepts.com
SIC: 5137 2231 Women's & children's
clothing; broadwoven fabric mills, wool

(G-7392)
CAPITOL BOX CORP (PA)
1300 6th St (07047-1714)
PHONE..................................201 867-6018
Edward B Maleh, *President*
Shirley Maleh, *Vice Pres*
EMP: 23 EST: 1936
SQ FT: 12,700
SALES (est): 2.3MM **Privately Held**
WEB: www.capitolbox.com
SIC: 2652 5113 Setup paperboard boxes;
set-up paperboard boxes

(G-7393)
CAROL DAUPLAISE LTD
5901 W Side Ave (07047-6451)
PHONE..................................212 997-5290
Jeffrey Dauplaise, *Branch Mgr*
EMP: 20
SALES (est): 2MM
SALES (corp-wide): 7.2MM **Privately**
Held
WEB: www.dauplaisejewelry.com
SIC: 3911 5094 Jewelry, precious metal;
jewelry & precious stones
PA: Carol Dauplaise, Ltd.
29 W 36th St Fl 12
New York NY 10018
212 564-7301

(G-7394)
CHAMPION INK CO INC
2045 88th St (07047-4794)
PHONE..................................201 868-4100
Raymond Czorniewy, *President*
EMP: 5
SQ FT: 9,700
SALES (est): 951.8K **Privately Held**
SIC: 2893 Screen process ink

(G-7395)
CHIHA INC
Also Called: Chiha Sales
5711 Kennedy Blvd (07047-3202)
PHONE..................................201 861-2000
Edward Chiha, *President*
George A Chiha, *Vice Pres*
EMP: 12
SQ FT: 13,263
SALES (est): 1MM **Privately Held**
WEB: www.chiha.com
SIC: 2384 2253 Dressing gowns, men's &
women's: from purchased materials;
lounge, bed & leisurewear

(G-7396)
COLLECTION XIIX LTD
7001 Anpesil Dr Ste 2 (07047-4517)
PHONE..................................201 854-7740
Andrew Pizzo, *Branch Mgr*
EMP: 140
SALES (corp-wide): 22.9MM **Privately**
Held
WEB: www.collection18.com
SIC: 2339 Women's & misses' accessories
PA: Collection Xiix Ltd.
1370 Broadway Fl 17
New York NY 10018
212 686-8990

(G-7397)
COLONNA BROTHERS INC (PA)
4102 Bergen Tpke (07047-2510)
P.O. Box 808 (07047-0808)
PHONE..................................800 626-8384
Peter Colonna, *President*
Diane Maniscalco, *Corp Secy*
Mark Colonna, *Executive*
▲ EMP: 100 EST: 1918
SQ FT: 50,000

SALES (est): 32.3MM **Privately Held**
SIC: 2022 2099 5143 5149 Natural
cheese; seasonings & spices; cheese;
groceries & related products

(G-7398)
D3 LED LLC
1609 54th St (07047-3016)
PHONE..................................201 583-9486
EMP: 5
SALES (corp-wide): 14.5MM **Privately**
Held
SIC: 3993 Mfg Signs/Advertising Special-
ties
PA: D3 Led, Llc
11370 Sunrise Park Dr
Rancho Cordova CA 95742
916 669-7408

(G-7399)
DATA MEDICAL INC
2075 91st St (07047-4795)
P.O. Box 10124, Fairfield (07004-6124)
PHONE..................................800 790-9978
Chuck Ward, *CEO*
Harry Marmora, *President*
EMP: 12
SALES (est): 900K **Privately Held**
SIC: 3841 Surgical & medical instruments

(G-7400)
DERMARITE INDUSTRIES LLC
7777 W Side Ave (07047-6436)
PHONE..................................973 247-3491
Norman Braunstein, *President*
Mark Friedman, *Vice Pres*
Dominick Palmieri, *Vice Pres*
Hetal Sopariwala, *Materials Dir*
Barbara J Osborne, *Ch Credit Ofcr*
▲ EMP: 115
SQ FT: 14,000
SALES (est): 36.2MM **Privately Held**
WEB: www.dermarite.com
SIC: 2834 2841 Dermatologicals; oint-
ments; soap: granulated, liquid, cake,
flaked or chip

(G-7401)
DRAPERY & MORE INC
2321 Kennedy Blvd Ste 1 (07047-2039)
PHONE..................................201 271-9661
Ally Espana, *Owner*
EMP: 5
SALES (est): 420.3K **Privately Held**
SIC: 2391 Curtains, window: made from
purchased materials

(G-7402)
DRU WHITACRE MEDIA SVCS
LTD (PA)
Also Called: Drapekings
3200 Liberty Ave Ste 2c (07047-2394)
PHONE..................................201 770-9950
Drape Kings, *CEO*
Kevin Goodrich, *President*
Yossef Jackson, *General Mgr*
Whitney Taylor, *Business Mgr*
Jill Claps, *Prdtn Mgr*
▲ EMP: 85
SQ FT: 20,000
SALES (est): 19.2MM **Privately Held**
SIC: 2391 Draperies, plastic & textile: from
purchased materials

(G-7403)
EDISON LITHOG & PRTG CORP
(PA)
3725 Tonnelle Ave (07047-2421)
PHONE..................................201 902-9191
George Gross, *President*
Mel Schwartz, *General Mgr*
Joseph Ostreicher, *Vice Pres*
Ivy Newman, *Opers Mgr*
Carlos Sosa, *QC Mgr*
▲ EMP: 90 EST: 1958
SQ FT: 80,000
SALES: 36.2MM **Privately Held**
WEB: www.edisonlitho.com
SIC: 2752 Commercial printing, offset

(G-7404)
EUROPEAN PRETZEL ONE LLC
Also Called: Heidi's European Pretzel
1619 54th St (07047-3016)
PHONE..................................201 867-6117
Robert Johnson, *President*

EMP: 13
SALES (est): 760K **Privately Held**
WEB: www.heidispretzel.com
SIC: 2052 Pretzels

(G-7405)
FIVE STAR ALUMINUM PRODUCTS
Also Called: Five Star Building Products
2012 86th St (07047-4719)
PHONE..............................201 869-4181
Daniel Polito, *President*
EMP: 12
SQ FT: 18,300
SALES (est): 3.6MM **Privately Held**
SIC: 5031 3442 Metal doors, sash & trim; window frames, all materials; metal doors, sash & trim

(G-7406)
GENERAL ELECTRIC COMPANY
6001 Tonnelle Ave (07047-3307)
PHONE..............................201 866-2161
EMP: 200
SALES (corp-wide): 122B **Publicly Held**
SIC: 7694 4911 Armature Rewinding Electric Services
PA: General Electric Company
41 Farnsworth St
Boston MA 02210
617 443-3000

(G-7407)
GRAND DISPLAYS INC
3725 Tonnelle Ave (07047-2421)
PHONE..............................201 994-1500
EMP: 12 **Privately Held**
SIC: 2675 Die-cut paper & board
PA: Grand Displays, Inc.
1700 Suckle Hwy
Pennsauken NJ 08110

(G-7408)
GUILD & FACET LLC
Also Called: Guild Facet
3114 Tonnelle Ave (07047-2312)
PHONE..............................201 758-5368
Romil Shah, *Mng Member*
Mathew Agl,
EMP: 15
SALES: 200K **Privately Held**
SIC: 3911 Jewelry, precious metal

(G-7409)
HICKORY INDUSTRIES INC
4900 W Side Ave (07047-6411)
PHONE..............................201 223-4382
Steven Maroti, *President*
Aniko Heller, *Corp Secy*
Jeffrey Petrik, *CFO*
EMP: 25 EST: 1953
SQ FT: 43,000
SALES (est): 6.7MM **Privately Held**
WEB: www.hickorybbq.com
SIC: 3589 Cooking equipment, commercial

(G-7410)
I PRINT NB
9252 Kennedy Blvd (07047-9300)
PHONE..............................201 662-1133
Guillermo Melendrez, *Administration*
EMP: 4
SALES (est): 122.8K **Privately Held**
SIC: 2752 Commercial printing, lithographic

(G-7411)
INTERNATIONAL INSPIRATIONS LLC
8101 Tonnelle Ave (07047-4601)
PHONE..............................201 868-2000
Shaya Reiper, *Branch Mgr*
▲ EMP: 9
SALES (corp-wide): 7.8MM **Privately Held**
SIC: 3961 Costume jewelry
PA: International Inspirations, Llc
358 5th Ave Rm 501
New York NY 10001
212 465-8500

(G-7412)
K H MACHINE WORKS
4322 Grand Ave (07047-2622)
PHONE..............................201 867-2338

Bob Koehler, *Partner*
Grace Koehler, *Partner*
Shereelynn Koehler, *Partner*
EMP: 6 EST: 1918
SQ FT: 3,700
SALES: 450K **Privately Held**
WEB: www.pccom.net
SIC: 3469 7692 Machine parts, stamped or pressed metal; welding repair

(G-7413)
KATE SPADE & COMPANY
Also Called: Liz Claiborne
5901 W Side Ave (07047-6451)
PHONE..............................201 295-7569
EMP: 13
SALES (corp-wide): 1.2B **Publicly Held**
SIC: 2335 Mfg Women's/Misses' Dresses
PA: Kate Spade & Company
2 Park Ave Rm 8r
New York NY 10016
212 354-4900

(G-7414)
KATHY GIBSON DESIGNS INC (PA)
Also Called: Ansonia Bridal Veils
1435 51st St Ste 2 (07047-3100)
PHONE..............................201 420-0088
Ruth Wiener, *President*
Marie Sanchez, *Marketing Staff*
▲ EMP: 17 EST: 1946
SQ FT: 4,000
SALES (est): 1.9MM **Privately Held**
WEB: www.ansoniabridal.com
SIC: 2353 Millinery

(G-7415)
KHANNA PAPER INC
3135 Kennedy Blvd Ste 349 (07047-2379)
P.O. Box 1170, Little Falls (07424-8170)
PHONE..............................201 850-1707
Navdeep Singh, *Sales Staff*
Sandeep Pundir, *Asst Mgr*
Pawan Sharma, *Asst Mgr*
Saurbh Khanna, *Exec Dir*
Brij Mohan Khanna, *Director*
▼ EMP: 7
SALES: 40MM **Privately Held**
SIC: 5093 3554 Scrap & waste materials; paper industries machinery
PA: Khanna Paper Mills Limited
B-26, Infocity-1,
Gurgaon HR 12200

(G-7416)
LAWRENCE M GICHAN INCORPORATED
900 Dell Ave (07047-1555)
PHONE..............................201 330-3222
Larry Gichan, *President*
EMP: 12
SALES (est): 1MM **Privately Held**
SIC: 2448 Pallets, wood

(G-7417)
MARKS ICE CREAM
Also Called: Mark's Hmmade Ice Cream Dlghts
8205 Bergenline Ave (07047-5051)
PHONE..............................201 861-5099
Mark Russo, *Owner*
EMP: 4
SALES (est): 260.8K **Privately Held**
SIC: 2024 Ice cream & frozen desserts

(G-7418)
MARLENE TRIMMINGS LLC
Also Called: Marlene Lace
407 77th St (07047-5505)
PHONE..............................201 926-3108
Stephen Hepperle, *President*
EMP: 6
SALES: 68K **Privately Held**
SIC: 2241 8712 Trimmings, textile; house designer

(G-7419)
MARTY ANDERSON & ASSOC INC
4200 Grand Ave (07047-2518)
P.O. Box 1595, Hoboken (07030-1595)
PHONE..............................201 798-0507
Marty Anderson, *President*
EMP: 7

SQ FT: 1,100
SALES: 330K **Privately Held**
SIC: 1751 2431 Finish & trim carpentry; staircases, stairs & railings

(G-7420)
MAYABEQUE PRODUCTS INC
7424 Bergenline Ave Ste 1 (07047-5496)
PHONE..............................201 869-0531
Antonio Idavoy, *President*
Andre Idavoy, *President*
Rita Idavoy, *Admin Sec*
EMP: 7
SQ FT: 1,700
SALES (est): 720K **Privately Held**
SIC: 2013 5421 Sausages from purchased meat; meat markets, including freezer provisioners

(G-7421)
METRO WEB CORP
5901 Tonnelle Ave (07047-3221)
PHONE..............................201 553-0700
Tristan Vogel, *President*
William E Vogel, *Chairman*
Bob Irving, *Vice Pres*
Richard Moore, *CFO*
Chris Anne Hanson, *VP Human Res*
EMP: 50
SQ FT: 70,000
SALES (est): 8.8MM **Privately Held**
WEB: www.metrowebnj.com
SIC: 2752 Commercial printing, offset

(G-7422)
MIRIC INDUSTRIES INC
Also Called: Miric Revolving Swinging Doors
1516 Union Tpke (07047-2597)
PHONE..............................201 864-0233
Michael Petricko, *President*
EMP: 15 EST: 1976
SQ FT: 7,000
SALES (est): 3.4MM **Privately Held**
WEB: www.miricdoors.com
SIC: 7699 3442 3231 Door & window repair; metal doors, sash & trim; products of purchased glass

(G-7423)
ML METTLER CORP
Also Called: Mettler Mechanical
8905 Bergenwood Ave (07047-5309)
P.O. Box 161 (07047-0161)
PHONE..............................201 869-0170
Lawrence Mettler, *President*
EMP: 4
SALES (est): 395.4K **Privately Held**
SIC: 3585 5075 Refrigeration & heating equipment; air conditioning & ventilation equipment & supplies

(G-7424)
NAPA CONCEPTS LTD LIABILITY CO
36-3 Bergen Ridge Rd (07047-7235)
PHONE..............................201 673-2381
Fersun Senolsun, *Mng Member*
▲ EMP: 4
SALES (est): 206.5K **Privately Held**
SIC: 3714 Differentials & parts, motor vehicle

(G-7425)
NORCO MANUFACTURING INC
2025 85th St (07047-4714)
PHONE..............................201 854-3461
Steven Petrone, *President*
EMP: 10 EST: 1980
SQ FT: 2,500
SALES (est): 760K **Privately Held**
SIC: 3069 Hard rubber & molded rubber products

(G-7426)
NUCHAS TSQ LLC
5905 Kennedy Blvd (07047-3210)
PHONE..............................212 913-9682
Ariel Barbouth, *President*
EMP: 18
SQ FT: 160
SALES (est): 3.1MM **Privately Held**
SIC: 2051 5812 Pastries, e.g. danish: except frozen; eating places; fast food restaurants & stands

(G-7427)
PARTY CITY OF NORTH BERGEN
3111 Kennedy Blvd (07047-2378)
PHONE..............................201 865-0040
Phillip David, *President*
Michael Brent, *Vice Pres*
Lloyd Breslin, *Vice Pres*
EMP: 17
SQ FT: 7,300
SALES (est): 988K **Privately Held**
SIC: 5947 7299 2759 Gifts & novelties; costume rental; invitation & stationery printing & engraving

(G-7428)
PDM PACKAGING INC
4102 Bergen Tpke (07047-2510)
P.O. Box 808 (07047-0808)
PHONE..............................201 864-1115
Peter Colonna, *President*
Diane Maniscalco, *Corp Secy*
Mark Colonna, *Vice Pres*
▲ EMP: 10
SALES (est): 1.7MM **Privately Held**
WEB: www.pdmfoam.com
SIC: 2099 5149 5499 Spices, including grinding; spices & seasonings; spices & herbs

(G-7429)
PFIZER INC
8810 Durham Ave (07047-4434)
PHONE..............................201 294-8060
Corwin Nunez, *Principal*
EMP: 146
SALES (corp-wide): 53.6B **Publicly Held**
SIC: 2834 Pharmaceutical preparations
PA: Pfizer Inc.
235 E 42nd St
New York NY 10017
212 733-2323

(G-7430)
PRESTIGE BREAD JERSEY CY INC
Also Called: Hudson Bread
5601-5711 Tonnelle Ave (07047-3399)
PHONE..............................201 422-7900
Mariusz Kolodziej, *President*
◆ EMP: 60
SQ FT: 26,000
SALES (est): 12MM **Privately Held**
WEB: www.hudsonbread.com
SIC: 2051 Bread, all types (white, wheat, rye, etc): fresh or frozen

(G-7431)
QUES APRV A R KNITWEAR INC
2201 74th St (07047-6407)
PHONE..............................201 869-1333
Dionisio Garcia, *Principal*
EMP: 7
SALES (est): 698.6K **Privately Held**
SIC: 2258 Fabric finishing, warp knit

(G-7432)
RELIABLE WELDING & MCH WORK
Also Called: Reliable Rbr Plastic McHy Div
2008 Union Tpke (07047-2499)
PHONE..............................201 865-1073
Helga Liccardo, *President*
Joseph Liccardo III, *Vice Pres*
Thomas S Liccardo, *Vice Pres*
Zsolt Racz, *Engineer*
Louise Guerra, *Office Mgr*
▲ EMP: 20 EST: 1935
SQ FT: 125,000
SALES (est): 5.3MM **Privately Held**
SIC: 3559 3599 Rubber working machinery, including tires; machine shop, jobbing & repair

(G-7433)
REMCO PRESS INC
4201 Tonnelle Ave Ste 4 (07047-2431)
PHONE..............................201 751-5703
Anthony Skalicky Jr, *President*
EMP: 4
SQ FT: 5,000

GEOGRAPHIC

SALES: 900K Privately Held
WEB: www.remcopress.com
SIC: 2752 7336 2759 Business form & card printing, lithographic; commercial art & graphic design; invitation & stationery printing & engraving

(G-7434)
REUTHER CONTRACTING CO INC
Also Called: Reuther Material
5303 Tonnelle Ave 5311 (07047-3036)
P.O. Box 106 (07047-0106)
PHONE..........................201 863-3550
Andrew Reuther, *President*
Margaret Diehl, *Vice Pres*
Robert Diehl, *Vice Pres*
Lois Marrone, *Vice Pres*
EMP: 20
SQ FT: 4,500
SALES (est): 3.1MM Privately Held
SIC: 3271 Blocks, concrete or cinder: standard

(G-7435)
REUTHER MATERIAL CO INC
5303 Tonnelle Ave (07047-3090)
P.O. Box 106 (07047-0106)
PHONE..........................201 863-3550
Andrew Reuther, *President*
Bill Bringas, *Sales Mgr*
Noah Yunker, *Sales Staff*
Carmine Covello, *Manager*
Robert Diehl, *Bd of Directors*
EMP: 20 **EST:** 1927
SQ FT: 4,500
SALES (est): 4.9MM Privately Held
SIC: 3273 5032 Ready-mixed concrete; masons' materials

(G-7436)
SATEX FABRICS LTD
704 76th St (07047-4962)
PHONE..........................212 221-5555
Albert Abergel, *President*
▼ **EMP:** 6 **EST:** 1992
SALES (est): 940.9K Privately Held
WEB: www.satexfabrics.com
SIC: 5084 2221 Textile & leather machinery; textile mills, broadwoven: silk & manmade, also glass

(G-7437)
SEQUINS OF DISTINCTION INC
Also Called: Sequin City
1302 13th St (07047-1859)
PHONE..........................201 348-8111
Fax: 201 330-9050
EMP: 6 **EST:** 1971
SALES (est): 420K Privately Held
SIC: 2395 Mfg Embroidery Sequins On Fabric

(G-7438)
STEEL MOUNTAIN FABRICATORS LLC
2712 Secaucus Rd (07047-1549)
PHONE..........................201 741-3019
Michael Dell'aquila, *Branch Mgr*
EMP: 4
SALES (corp-wide): 2.5MM Privately Held
SIC: 3599 Machine & other job shop work
PA: Steel Mountain Fabricators Llc
1312 W Elizabeth Ave
Linden NJ 07036
908 862-2800

(G-7439)
SUUCHI INC
2321 Kennedy Blvd Ste S4 (07047-2039)
PHONE..........................201 284-0789
Suchitra Ramesh, *CEO*
Nick Yuen, *Opers Staff*
Miguel Astacio, *Production*
Al Gaviria, *Sales Staff*
Ben Yehooda, *CTO*
EMP: 109
SQ FT: 12,000
SALES: 1.2MM Privately Held
SIC: 7389 2331 Apparel designers, commercial; women's & misses' blouses & shirts

(G-7440)
TILCON NEW YORK INC
Also Called: North Bergen Asphalt
2414 95th St (07047-1414)
PHONE..........................800 789-7625
EMP: 63
SALES (corp-wide): 30.6B Privately Held
SIC: 2951 Asphalt paving mixtures & blocks
HQ: Tilcon New York Inc.
9 Entin Rd
Parsippany NJ 07054
973 366-7741

(G-7441)
TRIPP NYC INC
5200 W Side Ave (07047-6440)
PHONE..........................201 520-0420
Natharorn Daang Goodman, *President*
Ray Michael Goodman, *Vice Pres*
▲ **EMP:** 20
SQ FT: 9,000
SALES (est): 2.6MM Privately Held
WEB: www.trippnyc.com
SIC: 2339 Sportswear, women's

(G-7442)
VS HERCULES LLC (DH)
Also Called: Nutri-Force Nutrition
2101 91st St (07047-4731)
PHONE..........................201 868-5959
Colin Watts, *CEO*
Brenda Galgano, *CFO*
EMP: 6
SALES (est): 93.1MM Publicly Held
SIC: 2834 Vitamin, nutrient & hematinic preparations for human use
HQ: Vitamin Shoppe Industries Inc
300 Harmon Meadow Blvd
Secaucus NJ 07094
201 868-5959

(G-7443)
WALKER EIGHT CORP
Also Called: Universal Thd & Scallop Cutng
510 73rd St (07047-5407)
PHONE..........................201 861-4208
Joseph Simeone, *President*
Vinh Tran, *Corp Secy*
EMP: 5
SALES (est): 270K Privately Held
SIC: 2395 Scalloping, for the trade

(G-7444)
WY INDUSTRIES INC
Also Called: W Y Industries
2500 Secaucus Rd (07047-1553)
PHONE..........................201 617-8000
Bill Cheng, *President*
Brian Buchalski, *Plant Mgr*
◆ **EMP:** 75
SALES (est): 24.3MM Privately Held
WEB: www.wyindustries.com
SIC: 3089 Plastic containers, except foam

(G-7445)
XCESSORY LLC
5901 W Side Ave Fl 7n (07047-6451)
PHONE..........................917 647-7523
Darren Cohen, *President*
EMP: 5 **EST:** 2014
SALES (est): 201.3K Privately Held
SIC: 2389 Masquerade costumes

(G-7446)
ZEON US INC
5903 W Side Ave (07047-6451)
PHONE..........................516 532-7167
Charles Kreite, *President*
EMP: 2
SALES: 1MM Privately Held
SIC: 3873 Watches, clocks, watchcases & parts

North Brunswick
Middlesex County

(G-7447)
3R BIOPHARMA LLC
324 Perry Dr (08902-5594)
PHONE..........................914 486-1898
Suman Garlaphei,
EMP: 5

SALES (est): 81.8K Privately Held
SIC: 2834 Pharmaceutical preparations

(G-7448)
ABP INDUCTION LLC
1460 Livingston Ave 200-1 (08902-1873)
PHONE..........................732 932-6400
Boris Kon, *Engineer*
German M Gallegos, *Branch Mgr*
Andrew Perzanowski, *Manager*
EMP: 15
SALES (corp-wide): 8.1MM Privately Held
WEB: www.abpinduction.com
SIC: 3567 Industrial furnaces & ovens
PA: Abp Induction, Llc
1440 13th Ave
Union Grove WI 53182
262 317-5300

(G-7449)
ACHIEVEMENT JOURNAL LLC
5 Larson Ct (08902-9636)
PHONE..........................732 297-1570
Joseph Mancuso, *Principal*
EMP: 5
SALES (est): 255.5K Privately Held
SIC: 2711 Newspapers, publishing & printing

(G-7450)
ACTAVIS LLC
661 Us Highway 1 (08902-3390)
PHONE..........................732 843-4904
EMP: 130 **Privately Held**
SIC: 2834 Pharmaceutical preparations
HQ: Actavis Llc
5 Giralda Farms
Madison NJ 07940
862 261-7000

(G-7451)
AGRIUM ADVANCED TECH US INC
1470 Jersey Ave (08902-1659)
PHONE..........................732 296-8448
Gary Sosnowski, *Branch Mgr*
EMP: 12
SALES (corp-wide): 8.8B Privately Held
SIC: 2873 Nitrogenous fertilizers
HQ: Agrium Advanced Technologies (U.S.) Inc.
2915 Rocky Mountain Ave # 400
Loveland CO 80538

(G-7452)
ANICHEM LLC
195 Black Horse Ln (08902-4321)
PHONE..........................732 821-6500
Joe Zhang, *Safety Mgr*
Zhang Yichao, *Director*
Joe John, *Officer*
EMP: 6
SALES (est): 88.1K Privately Held
SIC: 2899 Acids

(G-7453)
ARTEGRAFT INC
206 N Center Dr (08902-4246)
P.O. Box 7305 (08902-7305)
PHONE..........................732 422-8333
Rick Gibson, *President*
Teddy Williams, *Sales Staff*
Cathleen Vanderveer, *Manager*
EMP: 14 **EST:** 1993
SQ FT: 5,000
SALES: 3MM Privately Held
WEB: www.artegraft.com
SIC: 3841 Surgical & medical instruments

(G-7454)
ASCENDIA PHARMACEUTICALS LLC
661 Us Highway 1 2 (08902-3390)
PHONE..........................732 640-0058
Jingjun Huang, *CEO*
EMP: 25 **EST:** 2012
SQ FT: 15,000
SALES (est): 1.1MM Privately Held
SIC: 2834 Druggists' preparations (pharmaceuticals)

(G-7455)
ATLANTIC PRECISION TECH LLC
432 Quarry Ln (08902-4727)
PHONE..........................732 658-3060
Carol Patrick,
EMP: 5
SALES: 700K Privately Held
SIC: 3441 Fabricated structural metal

(G-7456)
BASU GROUP INC
227 Us Hwy 1 162 (08902)
PHONE..........................908 517-9138
Bhaskar Basu, *President*
▼ **EMP:** 5
SALES (est): 780.2K Privately Held
SIC: 3171 Handbags, women's

(G-7457)
BOEHRINGER INGELHEIM ANIMAL
631 Us Highway 1 (08902-3390)
PHONE..........................732 729-5700
Heidi Tomenchok, *Opers Staff*
Dave Sirish, *Manager*
EMP: 30
SALES (corp-wide): 20B Privately Held
SIC: 2834 Pharmaceutical preparations
HQ: Boehringer Ingelheim Animal Health Usa Inc.
3239 Satellite Blvd # 50
Duluth GA 30096
800 325-9167

(G-7458)
BRUNSWICK SIGNS & EXHIBIT
1510 Jersey Ave (08902-1606)
PHONE..........................732 246-2500
Walter S Talan, *CEO*
EMP: 8
SQ FT: 15,000
SALES (est): 973.1K Privately Held
SIC: 3993 Displays & cutouts, window & lobby

(G-7459)
C D E INC
Also Called: Eastern Cold Drawn
950 Schweitzer Pl (08902-3235)
PHONE..........................732 297-2540
Anthony Russo, *President*
William Hughes, *Exec VP*
Cheryl Coelho, *Vice Pres*
Paul Finne, *Vice Pres*
▲ **EMP:** 55 **EST:** 1971
SQ FT: 100,000
SALES (est): 8.7MM Privately Held
SIC: 3315 Wire products, ferrous/iron: made in wiredrawing plants; wire, steel: insulated or armored

(G-7460)
CARL A VENABLE INC
Also Called: AlphaGraphics 321
65 Hidden Lake Dr (08902-1213)
PHONE..........................732 985-6677
Carl A Venable, *President*
EMP: 6
SQ FT: 1,610
SALES (est): 861.9K Privately Held
SIC: 2752 Commercial printing, lithographic

(G-7461)
CHEMSPEED TECHNOLOGIES INC
113 N Center Dr (08902-4909)
PHONE..........................732 329-1225
Rolf Gueller, *President*
Mark Meyers, *Vice Pres*
Tim Shay, *Director*
EMP: 12
SALES (est): 1.2MM
SALES (corp-wide): 6.8MM Privately Held
WEB: www.chemspeed.com
SIC: 3826 Analytical instruments
PA: Chemspeed Technologies Ag
Wolferstrasse 8
FUllinsdorf BL 4414
618 169-500

(G-7462)
CHROMOCELL CORPORATION (PA)
685 Us Highway 1 (08902-3390)
PHONE..................................732 565-1113
Christian Kopfli, *CEO*
Ken Rowe, *Vice Pres*
Marcus Sands, *Vice Pres*
Eni Entchev, *Purch Mgr*
Stuart Hayden, *Research*
EMP: 70
SALES (est): 32.5MM **Privately Held**
WEB: www.chromocell.com
SIC: 2834 Pharmaceutical preparations

(G-7463)
CLOUDAGEIT LTD LIABILITY CO
1308 Plymouth Rd (08902-4592)
PHONE..................................888 205-4128
Safia Djennane,
Donna Eastman,
EMP: 6 EST: 2012
SALES (est): 413.4K **Privately Held**
SIC: 7372 8748 7371 7389 Business oriented computer software; utility computer software; systems engineering consultant, ex. computer or professional; custom computer programming services;

(G-7464)
DAVION INC (PA)
2 Progress Rd (08902-4324)
PHONE..................................973 485-0793
James Placa Jr, *President*
Keith Blackmer, *Vice Pres*
Shanique Brown, *Manager*
◆ EMP: 20
SQ FT: 150,000
SALES (est): 16.2MM **Privately Held**
WEB: www.haba-davion.com
SIC: 2844 Cosmetic preparations

(G-7465)
DIAMOND FOODS USA INC
599 Nassau St (08902-2938)
PHONE..................................732 543-2186
Sardar M Sultani, *President*
▲ EMP: 3
SALES: 1.5MM **Privately Held**
SIC: 2044 5149 Rice milling; groceries & related products

(G-7466)
DISTEK INC
121 N Center Dr (08902-4910)
PHONE..................................732 422-7585
Gerald Brinker, *Founder*
Pierre Parks, *Opers Mgr*
Michael Baldino, *Prdtn Mgr*
Tracy Yu, *Senior Buyer*
Fausto Diaz, *Buyer*
EMP: 63
SALES (est): 16.3MM **Privately Held**
WEB: www.distekinc.com
SIC: 3826 5047 3999 Analytical instruments; medical equipment & supplies; atomizers, toiletry

(G-7467)
EASY SOFT INC
212 N Center Dr (08902-4246)
PHONE..................................732 398-1001
Mordechai Meles, *President*
Ralph Leo, *Vice Pres*
Manorama Savanur, *Vice Pres*
George Coleman, *Sales Staff*
Idrees Mbenga, *Sales Staff*
EMP: 12
SQ FT: 1,000
SALES (est): 2MM **Privately Held**
SIC: 7372 Prepackaged software
PA: Legal Software Developments Pty. Limited
L 8 201-217 Kent St
Sydney NSW 2000

(G-7468)
GENERAL FOUNDRIES INC (PA)
1 Progress Rd (08902-4325)
PHONE..................................732 951-9001
Rita J Todani, *President*
Alok Todani, *Principal*
Alex Todani, *Vice Pres*
▲ EMP: 30
SQ FT: 5,000

SALES: 22.5MM **Privately Held**
SIC: 3321 Gray iron castings

(G-7469)
IMAGE REMIT INC
205 N Center Dr (08902-4246)
PHONE..................................732 940-7900
Herman Velasquez, *Vice Pres*
EMP: 25
SALES (est): 3.8MM **Privately Held**
WEB: www.imageremit.com
SIC: 3861 7374 Trays, photographic printing & processing; data processing & preparation

(G-7470)
IN MOCEAN GROUP LLC
2400 Rte 1 (08902-4303)
PHONE..................................732 960-2415
EMP: 9
SALES (est): 1.1MM
SALES (corp-wide): 15.2MM **Privately Held**
SIC: 2369 Bathing suits & swimwear: girls', children's & infants'
PA: In Mocean Group, Llc
463 Fashion Ave Fl 21
New York NY 10018
212 944-0317

(G-7471)
INTENSE INC
1200 Airport Rd Ste A (08902-1892)
PHONE..................................732 249-2228
Kevin Laughlin, *CEO*
John Marsh, *CTO*
Martin Burdash, *IT/INT Sup*
EMP: 29
SALES (est): 6.4MM **Privately Held**
WEB: www.hpdinc.com
SIC: 3674 5995 Semiconductor diodes & rectifiers; contact lenses, prescription

(G-7472)
JOHN MALTESE IRON WORKS INC
1453 Jersey Ave (08902-1622)
P.O. Box 7161 (08902-7161)
PHONE..................................732 249-4350
Laurence Danza, *President*
Mary G Danza, *Corp Secy*
Lauren Kokinos, *Manager*
EMP: 21 EST: 1954
SQ FT: 50,000
SALES: 3.2MM **Privately Held**
WEB: www.jmiw.com
SIC: 3441 1791 Building components, structural steel; structural steel erection

(G-7473)
JOHNSON & JOHNSON
691 Rte 1 (08902-3390)
PHONE..................................732 422-5000
Steve Bowlan, *Manager*
EMP: 79
SALES (corp-wide): 81.5B **Publicly Held**
WEB: www.jnj.com
SIC: 2834 2844 2676 Pharmaceutical preparations; toilet preparations; sanitary paper products
PA: Johnson & Johnson
1 Johnson And Johnson Plz
New Brunswick NJ 08933
732 524-0400

(G-7474)
KAMAT PHARMATECH LLC
675 Us Highway 1 (08902-3378)
PHONE..................................732 406-6421
Madhav Kamat,
▲ EMP: 9 EST: 2013
SALES (est): 1.3MM **Privately Held**
SIC: 2834 Pharmaceutical preparations

(G-7475)
LIFE OF PARTY LLC
832 Ridgewood Ave Ste 4 (08902-2200)
PHONE..................................732 828-0886
Joann Soltis, *COO*
Robert Conner, *Plant Mgr*
Deb Rodriguez, *Executive*
Carol Krinsky,
▲ EMP: 40
SQ FT: 30,000

SALES (est): 7.8MM **Privately Held**
WEB: www.soapplace.com
SIC: 3089 2064 Molding primary plastic; candy & other confectionery products

(G-7476)
MATTRESS DEV CO DEL LLC
Also Called: Eclipse International
1375 Jersey Ave (08902-1600)
PHONE..................................732 628-0800
Sughra Zaidi, *Controller*
Stuart Carlitz,
EMP: 30
SQ FT: 80,000
SALES (est): 68.1K **Privately Held**
SIC: 2515 Mattresses & bedsprings

(G-7477)
MIDDLESEX PUBLICATIONS
Also Called: Suburban Parent Magazine
850 Us Highway 1 Fl 4 Flr 4 (08902)
PHONE..................................732 435-0005
EMP: 10
SALES (est): 1MM **Privately Held**
SIC: 2721 Sells Advertising Space & Publishes Monthly Publications

(G-7478)
MUSEAMI INC
2 King Arthur Ct Ste A (08902-3381)
PHONE..................................609 917-3000
Robert Taub, *President*
EMP: 14
SALES (est): 1.4MM **Privately Held**
SIC: 7372 Publishers' computer software

(G-7479)
NAUTICAL MARINE PAINT CORP (PA)
Also Called: National Paint Supply
1999 Elizabeth St (08902-4905)
PHONE..................................732 821-3200
Michael Schnurr, *President*
Donald Schnurr Jr, *Vice Pres*
Donald Schnurr Sr, *Director*
EMP: 25 EST: 1959
SQ FT: 87,000
SALES (est): 15.8MM **Privately Held**
SIC: 5198 2851 Paints; paints & paint additives

(G-7480)
NOBELUS LLC
1665 Jersey Ave (08902-1448)
PHONE..................................800 895-2747
EMP: 4
SALES (corp-wide): 23.1MM **Privately Held**
SIC: 5112 5084 3081 Blank books; cement making machinery; film base, cellulose acetate or nitrocellulose plastic
PA: Nobelus Llc
4841 Lumber Ln Ste 103
Knoxville TN 37921
800 895-2747

(G-7481)
OHM LABORATORIES INC (DH)
1385 Livingston Ave (08902-1829)
P.O. Box 7587, Princeton (08543-7587)
PHONE..................................732 418-2235
Dipak Chattaraj, *President*
Ganpat Desai, *Vice Pres*
Venkatachalam Krishnan, *Vice Pres*
Robert Patton, *Vice Pres*
Krishna Vakharia, *Engineer*
▲ EMP: 91
SQ FT: 90,000
SALES (est): 26.6MM
SALES (corp-wide): 1.3B **Privately Held**
WEB: www.ranbaxy.com
SIC: 2834 Druggists' preparations (pharmaceuticals)
HQ: Ranbaxy Inc.
2 Independence Way
Princeton NJ 08540
609 720-9200

(G-7482)
PARKWAY-KEW CORPORATION
2095 Excelsior Ave (08902-4431)
PHONE..................................732 398-2100
Gene Klein Sr, *President*
Eugene E Klein, *Principal*
Michael Hoffarth, *Vice Pres*
William Sibree, *Vice Pres*

EMP: 15 EST: 1953
SQ FT: 23,000
SALES (est): 3.2MM **Privately Held**
WEB: www.parkwaykew.com
SIC: 3599 8711 Machine shop, jobbing & repair; engineering services

(G-7483)
PRO TAPES & SPECIALTIES INC
621 Us Highway 1 (08902-6302)
P.O. Box 53026, Newark (07101-5326)
PHONE..................................732 346-0900
Arnold S Silver, *CEO*
Ed Miller, *President*
Barry Hart, *COO*
Chris Hart, *Vice Pres*
Barney Silver, *Vice Pres*
◆ EMP: 115
SQ FT: 142,000
SALES (est): 82.9MM **Privately Held**
WEB: www.protapes.com
SIC: 5113 2675 Pressure sensitive tape; die-cut paper & board

(G-7484)
QUICK BIAS BNDING TRMMING INDS
9 Creekside Ct (08902-4774)
PHONE..................................732 422-0123
Thomas Gagliano, *President*
Lorraine Gagliano, *Shareholder*
EMP: 11 EST: 1965
SQ FT: 15,000
SALES (est): 1MM **Privately Held**
SIC: 2396 Bindings, bias: made from purchased materials; trimming, fabric

(G-7485)
SCALA PASTRY
1896 Us Highway 130 (08902-3038)
PHONE..................................732 398-9808
Paul Scala, *Owner*
EMP: 5
SALES (est): 312.4K **Privately Held**
SIC: 2051 5311 Bread, cake & related products; department stores

(G-7486)
SOLVAY USA INC
219 Black Horse Ln (08902-4301)
P.O. Box 7500 (08902-7500)
PHONE..................................732 297-0100
Brian Wheeler, *Principal*
EMP: 250
SALES (corp-wide): 12.8MM **Privately Held**
WEB: www.food.us.rhodia.com
SIC: 2819 2812 2865 2869 Boric acid; phosphates, except fertilizers: defluorinated & ammoniated; soda ash, sodium carbonate (anhydrous); phenol, alkylated & cumene; diphenylamines; isocyanates; fluorinated hydrocarbon gases; silicones; plastics materials & resins; flavoring extracts & syrups
HQ: Solvay Usa Inc.
504 Carnegie Ctr
Princeton NJ 08540
609 860-4000

(G-7487)
SONGBIRD HEARING INC
210 N Center Dr (08902-4246)
PHONE..................................732 422-7203
Thomas E Gaedner, *Ch of Bd*
Thomas E Gardner, *Ch of Bd*
EMP: 46 EST: 1997
SQ FT: 20,000
SALES (est): 2.6MM **Privately Held**
SIC: 8731 3842 Medical research, commercial; electronic research; hearing aids

(G-7488)
SPECTRA MATTRESS INC
633 Nassau St (08902-2940)
PHONE..................................732 545-5900
Isaac Srour, *President*
EMP: 4
SQ FT: 50,000
SALES: 1MM **Privately Held**
SIC: 2515 Mattresses & bedsprings

(G-7489)
SUNRISE INTL EDUCATN INC
1542 Edly Cove Ct (08902-3074)
PHONE..................................917 525-0272

Gavin Newton-Taver, *CEO*
EMP: 54
SALES: 4MM **Privately Held**
SIC: 8299 7372 Educational services; educational computer software

(G-7490)
**THER-A-PEDIC SLEEP
PRODUCTS (PA)**
Also Called: Bedding Industries of America
1375 Jersey Ave (08902-1600)
PHONE............................732 628-0800
Stuart Carlitz, *CEO*
Greg Tanis, *Vice Pres*
◆ **EMP:** 81 **EST:** 1958
SQ FT: 90,000
SALES: 35MM **Privately Held**
WEB: www.therapedic.com
SIC: 2515 Mattresses, innerspring or box spring; box springs, assembled

(G-7491)
**URIGEN PHARMACEUTICALS
INC**
675 Us Highway 1 Ste 206b (08902-3378)
PHONE............................732 640-0160
Dan Vickery, *Branch Mgr*
EMP: 4 **Privately Held**
SIC: 2834 Pharmaceutical preparations
PA: Urigen Pharmaceuticals, Inc.
501 Silverside Rd Pmb 95
Wilmington DE 19809

(G-7492)
VESAG HEALTH INC
675 Us Highway 1 B202c (08902-3378)
PHONE............................732 333-1876
Rajendra Sadhu, *CEO*
Pradeep Karki, *Vice Pres*
Girija Rupakula, *Vice Pres*
EMP: 18 **EST:** 2011
SQ FT: 2,000
SALES: 200K **Privately Held**
SIC: 8099 3841 Health screening service; diagnostic apparatus, medical

(G-7493)
VISH LLC
Also Called: Vish Group
1605 Jersey Ave (08902-1448)
PHONE............................201 529-2900
Chris Hamilton, *Purch Mgr*
Mike Kukreja, *Sales Mgr*
Paul Hingorani, *Marketing Staff*
Vishal Kukreja, *Mng Member*
◆ **EMP:** 25
SQ FT: 48,000
SALES (est): 18.9MM **Privately Held**
SIC: 3081 Unsupported plastics film & sheet

North Haledon
Passaic County

(G-7494)
ACEY INDUSTRIES INC
Also Called: Bergen Screen Printing
9 Cranberry Ct (07508-2860)
PHONE............................973 595-1222
Uday Patel, *President*
EMP: 7 **EST:** 1998
SQ FT: 9,500
SALES: 405.7K **Privately Held**
SIC: 2396 Screen printing on fabric articles

(G-7495)
HOFER CONNECTORS CO INC
126 Linda Vista Ave (07508-2654)
PHONE............................973 427-1195
Allan P Hofer, *President*
EMP: 20
SALES (est): 2.3MM **Privately Held**
SIC: 5063 3643 Electrical fittings & construction materials; current-carrying wiring devices

(G-7496)
**HOFER MACHINE & TOOL CO
INC**
126 Linda Vista Ave (07508-2654)
PHONE............................973 427-1195
Alan P Hofer, *President*
EMP: 19 **EST:** 1947

SQ FT: 10,000
SALES (est): 3.2MM **Privately Held**
SIC: 3643 Connectors & terminals for electrical devices

(G-7497)
**MANNER TEXTILE PROCESSING
INC**
41 Oakdale Ct (07508-2948)
PHONE............................973 942-8718
Patrick Cupo, *President*
Anthony Cupo, *Treasurer*
EMP: 55 **EST:** 1959
SQ FT: 25,000
SALES (est): 4.9MM **Privately Held**
SIC: 2231 2269 2865 2261 Fabric finishing: wool, mohair or similar fibers; finishing plants; cyclic crudes & intermediates; finishing plants, cotton

(G-7498)
**MINI FROST FOODS
CORPORATION**
Also Called: Belmont Bakery
23 Willow Brook Ct (07508-2539)
PHONE............................973 427-4258
Katherine Parsells, *President*
EMP: 20
SQ FT: 5,000
SALES (est): 4.6MM **Privately Held**
SIC: 5142 5461 2052 2051 Bakery products, frozen; bakeries; cookies & crackers; bread, cake & related products

(G-7499)
PHOENIX SYSTEMS
39 Morningside Ave (07508-2507)
PHONE............................201 788-5511
Andrew Zaccaro, *Owner*
EMP: 3
SALES: 1.4MM **Privately Held**
WEB: www.phoenixsystemsglobal.com
SIC: 3651 Audio electronic systems

(G-7500)
SUN METAL FINISHING INC
5 Sicomac Rd 105 (07508-2972)
PHONE............................973 684-0119
Michael O'Brien, *President*
EMP: 20
SQ FT: 32,000
SALES (est): 1.4MM **Privately Held**
SIC: 3471 Finishing, metals or formed products

(G-7501)
**TOTOWA METAL FABRICATORS
INC**
40 Lee Dr (07508-3038)
PHONE............................973 423-1943
Frank Creegan, *CEO*
EMP: 15
SQ FT: 10,000
SALES (est): 1.2MM **Privately Held**
SIC: 3444 Metal ventilating equipment

North Middletown
Monmouth County

(G-7502)
**ADVANCED MICRO DEVICES
INC**
16 Snyder Dr (07748-5902)
PHONE............................732 787-2892
Michael Russo, *Manager*
EMP: 131
SALES (corp-wide): 6.4B **Publicly Held**
WEB: www.amd.com
SIC: 3674 Integrated circuits, semiconductor networks, etc.
PA: Advanced Micro Devices, Inc.
2485 Augustine Dr
Santa Clara CA 95054
408 749-4000

(G-7503)
**GUTTENPLANS FROZEN
DOUGH INC**
100 State Route 36 E (07748-5249)
PHONE............................732 495-9480
Abe Littenberg, *President*
Adam Guttenplan, *Vice Pres*

Jack Guttenplan, *Vice Pres*
Vivian Lee, *Finance Mgr*
Ed Kuhn, *Sales Staff*
EMP: 100
SQ FT: 54,000
SALES: 63.4MM **Privately Held**
WEB: www.guttenplan.com
SIC: 2041 Doughs, frozen or refrigerated

(G-7504)
QUALITY DIE SHOP INC
17 Argonne Pl (07748-5102)
PHONE............................732 787-0041
Kirk Harris, *President*
Suzanne Harris, *Vice Pres*
EMP: 7
SQ FT: 11,000
SALES (est): 490K **Privately Held**
SIC: 3544 Dies, steel rule

North Plainfield
Union County

(G-7505)
**GRANITE AND MARBLE ASSOC
INC**
Also Called: American Architectual Stone
310 Tremont Ave (07063-1669)
PHONE............................908 416-1100
John J Donatelli, *President*
John Donatelli, *President*
▲ **EMP:** 8
SALES (est): 606.4K **Privately Held**
SIC: 3281 Cut stone & stone products

(G-7506)
**J M S MELGAR TRANSPORT
LLC**
15 Pearl St (07060-4812)
PHONE............................908 834-1722
Manuel Melgar, *CEO*
EMP: 6
SALES (est): 438.6K **Privately Held**
SIC: 3743 Freight cars & equipment

(G-7507)
**ORLANDO SYSTEMS LTD LBLTY
CO**
375 North Dr Apt A10 (07060-3744)
PHONE............................908 400-5052
Theodor Basch, *President*
▼ **EMP:** 4
SALES: 1.5MM **Privately Held**
WEB: www.orlando-systems.com
SIC: 5049 5047 3829 3792 Laboratory equipment, except medical or dental; electro-medical equipment; whole body counters, nuclear; automobile house trailer chassis; automobile assembly, including specialty automobiles; telephone & telegraphic equipment

(G-7508)
RACEWAY PETROLEUM INC
643 Us Highway 22 (07060-3728)
PHONE............................908 222-2999
Gurbreed Singh, *Branch Mgr*
EMP: 16 **Privately Held**
SIC: 3644 Raceways
PA: Raceway Petroleum Inc
1411 Stelton Rd
Piscataway NJ 08854

Northfield
Atlantic County

(G-7509)
**ADVANCED SHORE IMAGING
ASSOCIA**
2605 Shore Rd (08225-2136)
P.O. Box 6750, Portsmouth NH (03802-6750)
PHONE............................732 678-0087
Thomas Yu, *President*
Laura Cougar, *COO*
EMP: 17
SQ FT: 10,500
SALES (est): 1.1MM **Privately Held**
SIC: 3829 Medical diagnostic systems, nuclear

(G-7510)
ARTISTIC HARDWARE
430 Tilton Rd Ste 2 (08225-1268)
PHONE............................609 383-1909
Tom Vassallo, *Opers Staff*
Carol Kelly, *Manager*
Patrick McCarthy,
EMP: 7
SQ FT: 3,800
SALES (est): 1.1MM **Privately Held**
SIC: 5251 3469 3429 1799 Builders' hardware; kitchen fixtures & equipment, porcelain enameled; cabinet hardware; kitchen & bathroom remodeling

(G-7511)
SUPERIOR JEWELRY CO
Also Called: Ocean-Craft International
430 Tilton Rd Ste 1 (08225-1268)
P.O. Box 188 (08225-0188)
PHONE............................215 677-8100
Howard Wiener, *President*
Ruth Wiener, *Vice Pres*
Barry Wiener, *Treasurer*
Howard W Pressales, *Manager*
▲ **EMP:** 11 **EST:** 1935
SQ FT: 5,000
SALES (est): 2.4MM **Privately Held**
WEB: www.superiorjewelry.com
SIC: 5094 3961 Jewelry; costume jewelry, ex. precious metal & semiprecious stones

(G-7512)
**ZEBRA TECHNOLOGIES
CORPORATION**
1501 Tilton Rd (08225-1876)
PHONE............................609 383-8743
Stacey Didonato, *Principal*
EMP: 400
SALES (corp-wide): 4.2B **Publicly Held**
SIC: 3577 Bar code (magnetic ink) printers
PA: Zebra Technologies Corporation
3 Overlook Pt
Lincolnshire IL 60069
847 634-6700

Northvale
Bergen County

(G-7513)
**A D M TRONICS UNLIMITED INC
(PA)**
224 Pegasus Ave Ste A (07647-1921)
PHONE............................201 767-6040
Andre Dimino, *President*
▲ **EMP:** 22
SQ FT: 16,000
SALES: 3MM **Publicly Held**
WEB: www.admtronics.com
SIC: 2891 2899 3841 2844 Adhesives & sealants; chemical preparations; surgical & medical instruments; cosmetic preparations

(G-7514)
ABON PHARMACEUTICALS LLC
140 Legrand Ave (07647-2403)
PHONE............................201 367-1702
Salah U Ahmed, *President*
Bruce L Downey, *Chairman*
Jennifer Barr, *QC Dir*
Himansu Pandya, *Manager*
Mahish Patel, *Director*
EMP: 38
SALES (est): 9.2MM **Privately Held**
SIC: 2834 Pharmaceutical preparations

(G-7515)
ACEDEPOTCOM (PA)
159 Paris Ave (07647-2029)
PHONE............................800 844-0962
EMP: 11
SALES (est): 2.7MM **Privately Held**
SIC: 3579 5112 5111 Address labeling machines; marking devices; fine paper

(G-7516)
**AIG INDUSTRIAL GROUP INC
(HQ)**
220 Pegasus Ave (07647-1904)
PHONE............................201 767-7300
Gerald Anderson, *President*

Melanie Kershaw, *Treasurer*
EMP: 12
SQ FT: 26,000
SALES: 5.4MM
SALES (corp-wide): 14.9MM **Privately Held**
SIC: 3829 2819 2843 Gas detectors; industrial inorganic chemicals; penetrants
PA: Meson Group, Inc
220 Pegasus Ave
Northvale NJ 07647
201 767-7300

(G-7517)
ALCAN BALTEK CORPORATION
108 Fairway Ct (07647-2401)
P.O. Box 16148, High Point NC (27261-6148)
PHONE..............................201 767-1400
Jacques Kohn, *CEO*
▲ **EMP:** 100
SALES (est): 14.5MM **Privately Held**
SIC: 2493 Reconstituted wood products

(G-7518)
AMERICAN GAS & CHEMICAL CO LTD
220 Pegasus Ave (07647-1904)
PHONE..............................201 767-7300
Gerald Anderson, *President*
James Zanosky, *General Mgr*
Melanie Kershaw, *Vice Pres*
Edouard Zuraik, *Technology*
EMP: 30
SQ FT: 26,000
SALES (est): 5.4MM
SALES (corp-wide): 14.9MM **Privately Held**
WEB: www.amgas.com
SIC: 2819 3829 2843 3812 Industrial inorganic chemicals; measuring & controlling devices; penetrants; search & navigation equipment
HQ: Aig Industrial Group Inc
220 Pegasus Ave
Northvale NJ 07647
201 767-7300

(G-7519)
BIPORE INC
31 Industrial Pkwy (07647-2203)
PHONE..............................201 767-1993
Durmus Koch, *President*
EMP: 16
SQ FT: 7,000
SALES (est): 2.7MM **Privately Held**
SIC: 3841 Catheters

(G-7520)
CELUS FASTENERS MFG INC (PA)
200 Paris Ave (07647-2205)
PHONE..............................800 289-7483
Frank C Lahnston, *President*
▲ **EMP:** 44
SQ FT: 27,000
SALES (est): 2.2MM **Privately Held**
SIC: 3429 3452 Metal fasteners; rivets, metal

(G-7521)
DELPHIAN CORPORATION
220 Pegasus Ave (07647-1900)
PHONE..............................201 767-7300
Gerald Anderson, *Ch of Bd*
Sherri Vollmer, *Accountant*
EMP: 145
SQ FT: 26,000
SALES: 9MM
SALES (corp-wide): 14.9MM **Privately Held**
WEB: www.delphian.com
SIC: 3823 3829 On-stream gas/liquid analysis instruments, industrial; gas detectors
PA: Meson Group, Inc
220 Pegasus Ave
Northvale NJ 07647
201 767-7300

(G-7522)
ELITE LABORATORIES INC
165 Ludlow Ave (07647-2305)
PHONE..............................201 750-2646
Bernard Berk, *CEO*
Mark Gittelman, *Corp Secy*

Doug Plassche, *Exec VP*
EMP: 38
SALES (est): 6.6MM
SALES (corp-wide): 7.5MM **Publicly Held**
WEB: www.elitepharma.com
SIC: 2834 Pharmaceutical preparations
PA: Elite Pharmaceuticals, Inc.
165 Ludlow Ave
Northvale NJ 07647
201 750-2646

(G-7523)
ELITE PHARMACEUTICALS INC (PA)
165 Ludlow Ave (07647-2305)
PHONE..............................201 750-2646
Nasrat Hakim, *President*
Douglas Plassche, *Exec VP*
Kenneth Smith, *Vice Pres*
Carter J Ward, *CFO*
Jeenarine Narine, *Director*
EMP: 37
SQ FT: 15,000
SALES: 7.5MM **Publicly Held**
WEB: www.elitepharma.com
SIC: 2834 Pharmaceutical preparations

(G-7524)
FEI-ELCOM TECH INC
260 Union St (07647-2208)
PHONE..............................201 767-8030
James Davis, *CEO*
Chuck Scheetz, *President*
Joe Milo, *General Mgr*
Cristina Rizzo, *Materials Mgr*
Janice Martini, *Purch Agent*
▲ **EMP:** 50
SALES (est): 8.2MM
SALES (corp-wide): 49.5MM **Publicly Held**
WEB: www.elcom-tech.com
SIC: 3663 Microwave communication equipment
PA: Frequency Electronics, Inc.
55 Charles Lindbergh Blvd # 2
Uniondale NY 11553
516 794-4500

(G-7525)
FILLO FACTORY INC
10 Fairway Ct (07647-2401)
P.O. Box 155, Dumont (07628-0155)
PHONE..............................201 439-1036
Ron Rexroth, *President*
Jay Winter, *Exec VP*
Mike Gillies, *Opers Mgr*
Domonic Lafarro, *Manager*
Melissa Rexroth, *Manager*
EMP: 50
SQ FT: 15,000
SALES (est): 12.1MM **Privately Held**
WEB: www.fillofactory.com
SIC: 2099 Food preparations

(G-7526)
GLOBTEK INC (PA)
186 Veterans Dr (07647-2303)
PHONE..............................201 784-1000
Anna Kaplan, *CEO*
Gino Cardillo, *Vice Pres*
Ellen McNamara, *Purch Agent*
Cheryl D'Amico, *Purchasing*
Steve Orecchio, *Engineer*
▲ **EMP:** 400
SQ FT: 25,000
SALES (est): 66.1MM **Privately Held**
WEB: www.globtek.com
SIC: 3612 Specialty transformers

(G-7527)
HAUSMANN ENTERPRISES LLC
Also Called: Hausmann Industries
130 Union St (07647-2207)
PHONE..............................201 767-0255
Kelvyn Cullimore, *CEO*
Dave Rogers, *Production*
Keith McHugh, *Sales Staff*
Stuart Freedman, *Manager*
◆ **EMP:** 95 EST: 1955
SQ FT: 60,000
SALES: 20.8MM
SALES (corp-wide): 62.5MM **Publicly Held**
WEB: www.hausmann.com
SIC: 2599 2531 Hospital furniture, except beds; public building & related furniture

PA: Dynatronics Corporation
7030 S Park Centre Dr
Salt Lake City UT 84121
801 568-7000

(G-7528)
INDUSTRIAL RIVET & FASTENER CO (PA)
200 Paris Ave (07647-2205)
PHONE..............................201 750-1040
William Goodman, *President*
Joanne Sherman, *Corp Secy*
▲ **EMP:** 54
SQ FT: 23,000
SALES (est): 22.9MM **Privately Held**
SIC: 5072 5085 3452 Miscellaneous fasteners; industrial supplies; bolts, nuts, rivets & washers

(G-7529)
INRAD OPTICS INC (PA)
181 Legrand Ave (07647-2498)
PHONE..............................201 767-1910
Amy Eskilson, *President*
Randy Clark, *Business Mgr*
William Foote, *Exec VP*
Bill Brucker, *Vice Pres*
Thomas A Caughey, *Vice Pres*
EMP: 63
SQ FT: 41,935
SALES: 11.4MM **Publicly Held**
WEB: www.ppgrpinc.com
SIC: 3699 3827 Laser systems & equipment; lenses, optical: all types except ophthalmic

(G-7530)
INTERPLEX NAS INC
232 Pegasus Ave (07647-1904)
PHONE..............................201 367-1300
Jack Seidler, *CEO*
Art Madgwick, *Principal*
▲ **EMP:** 55
SALES (est): 11.1MM **Privately Held**
SIC: 3679 Rheostats, for electronic end products
HQ: Interplex Industries, Inc.
231 Ferris Ave
Rumford RI 02916
718 961-6212

(G-7531)
JENTEC INC
20 Charles St Ste C (07647-2214)
PHONE..............................201 784-1031
Robert Jensen, *Ch of Bd*
Jarl Jensen, *President*
EMP: 3
SQ FT: 2,000
SALES: 1MM **Privately Held**
WEB: www.jentecinc.com
SIC: 8711 3842 Engineering services; surgical appliances & supplies

(G-7532)
JOHN G PAPAILIAS CO INC
Also Called: J G Papailias
245 Pegasus Ave (07647-1903)
PHONE..............................201 767-4027
George Papailias, *President*
Bob Surovich, *Engineer*
Robert P Surovich, *Marketing Staff*
▲ **EMP:** 8
SQ FT: 25,000
SALES (est): 870K **Privately Held**
WEB: www.papailias.com
SIC: 3823 3648 Liquid level instruments, industrial process type; flow instruments, industrial process type; lighting equipment

(G-7533)
LAB TECH INC (PA)
170 Legrand Ave (07647-2407)
PHONE..............................201 767-5613
Michael Pildes, *CEO*
▲ **EMP:** 8
SALES (est): 680.6K **Privately Held**
SIC: 3851 Lens grinding, except prescription: ophthalmic

(G-7534)
LEXI INDUSTRIES
252 Livingston St (07647-1906)
PHONE..............................201 297-7900
EMP: 10 EST: 2009

SALES (est): 1.1MM **Privately Held**
SIC: 3999 Manufacturing industries

(G-7535)
MAS MACHINE SHOP LLC
267 Livingston St (07647-1901)
P.O. Box 268 (07647-0268)
PHONE..............................201 768-9110
Marko Aleksich, *Mng Member*
EMP: 9
SQ FT: 4,800
SALES: 1.3MM **Privately Held**
SIC: 3599 Machine shop, jobbing & repair

(G-7536)
MESON GROUP INC (PA)
220 Pegasus Ave (07647-1904)
PHONE..............................201 767-7300
Gerald Anderson, *President*
Melanie Kershaw, *Vice Pres*
▲ **EMP:** 30
SQ FT: 26,000
SALES (est): 14.9MM **Privately Held**
WEB: www.mesongroup.com
SIC: 3823 3829 2819 2843 On-stream gas/liquid analysis instruments, industrial; gas detectors; industrial inorganic chemicals; penetrants

(G-7537)
MIDAS CHAIN INC
151 Veterans Dr (07647-2301)
PHONE..............................201 244-1150
Sam Samuel, *President*
Meredith Borowski, *Vice Pres*
Rob Asmar, *Sales Staff*
Robin Cole, *Receptionist*
▲ **EMP:** 3
SALES (est): 1MM **Privately Held**
WEB: www.midaschain.com
SIC: 5094 3915 Jewelry; jewelers' materials & lapidary work

(G-7538)
MRC PRECISION METAL OPTICS INC
Also Called: Inrad Optics
181 Legrand Ave (07647-2404)
PHONE..............................941 753-8707
Joe Rutherford, *President*
Joseph J Rutherford, *Vice Pres*
William J Foote, *CFO*
EMP: 30
SQ FT: 25,000
SALES (est): 3.9MM
SALES (corp-wide): 11.4MM **Publicly Held**
WEB: www.inradoptics.com
SIC: 3577 3827 Optical scanning devices; optical instruments & lenses
PA: Inrad Optics, Inc.
181 Legrand Ave
Northvale NJ 07647
201 767-1910

(G-7539)
MULTIMATIC LLC (PA)
Also Called: Multimatic Dry Cleaning Mch
162 Veterans Dr (07647-2300)
P.O. Box 156 (07647-0156)
PHONE..............................201 767-9660
Ronald Velli,
▲ **EMP:** 9 EST: 1968
SQ FT: 30,000
SALES (est): 1.4MM **Privately Held**
SIC: 3582 Drycleaning equipment & machinery, commercial

(G-7540)
NAOMI PET INTERNATIONAL INC
20 Charles St Ste D (07647-2214)
PHONE..............................201 660-7918
Sunkyu Lee, *Officer*
EMP: 4
SALES: 500K **Privately Held**
SIC: 3999 Pet supplies

(G-7541)
NEW YORK BOTANY INC
20 Charles St Ste B (07647-2214)
PHONE..............................201 564-7444
Younghoon Kim, *Officer*
EMP: 20

SALES: 1.2MM **Privately Held**
SIC: **2844** 5122 Cosmetic preparations; cosmetics

(G-7542)
ORTHOFEET INC
152 Veterans Dr Ste A (07647-2307)
PHONE....................................800 524-2845
Mark Koide, *CEO*
Michael Bar, *Vice Pres*
Rick Hynes, *CFO*
Jeremiah Sullivan, *CFO*
Zack Tanglao, *Accounts Mgr*
▲ EMP: 30
SQ FT: 30,000
SALES (est): 5.9MM **Privately Held**
WEB: www.orthofeet.com
SIC: **3842** Foot appliances, orthopedic

(G-7543)
PALM PRESS INC
Also Called: Minuteman Press
202 Livingston St (07647-1710)
PHONE....................................201 767-6504
Margaret Lorenzo, *President*
Vivian Abitabilo, *Treasurer*
EMP: 5 EST: 1980
SQ FT: 1,100
SALES: 650K **Privately Held**
WEB: www.minutemannorthvale.com
SIC: **2752** 2791 2789 2759 Commercial printing, lithographic; typesetting; bookbinding & related work; commercial printing

(G-7544)
RAB LIGHTING INC (PA)
170 Ludlow Ave (07647-2305)
PHONE....................................201 784-8600
Ross Barna, *Ch of Bd*
Terry Crawley, *Regional Mgr*
Vince Lostumbo, *District Mgr*
Ravi Parikh, *Business Mgr*
Rich Allis, *Vice Pres*
◆ EMP: 240 EST: 1946
SQ FT: 200,000
SALES (est): 69.7MM **Privately Held**
WEB: www.rabweb.com
SIC: **3625** 3648 3646 Electric controls & control accessories, industrial; outdoor lighting equipment; floodlights; commercial indusl & institutional electric lighting fixtures

(G-7545)
REMA CORROSION CONTROL
240 Pegasus Ave (07647-1923)
PHONE....................................201 256-8400
Charlie Altizer, *President*
Tom Moran, *Technical Mgr*
Raj Patel, *Marketing Staff*
Steve Byous, *Manager*
Dave Ormiston, *Technical Staff*
EMP: 10
SALES: 2MM
SALES (corp-wide): 3B **Privately Held**
SIC: **2851** Epoxy coatings
HQ: Rema Tip Top/North America, Inc.
240 Pegasus Ave Unit 2
Northvale NJ 07647
201 768-8100

(G-7546)
REMA TIP TOP/NORTH AMERICA INC (HQ)
240 Pegasus Ave Unit 2 (07647-1924)
P.O. Box 76 (07647-0076)
PHONE....................................201 768-8100
Olafur Gunnarsson, *President*
Sam Gerbasi, *Regional Mgr*
James McFadden, *Regional Mgr*
Adam Tillery, *Regional Mgr*
Mark Peavy, *Mfg Dir*
▲ EMP: 22 EST: 1923
SALES (est): 109MM
SALES (corp-wide): 3B **Privately Held**
WEB: www.rema.com
SIC: **5085** 3069 5014 Rubber goods, mechanical; liner strips, rubber; tire & tube repair materials
PA: Stahlgruber Otto Gruber Ag
Gruber Str. 65
Poing 85586
812 170-70

(G-7547)
RICH ART COLOR CO INC
202 Pegasus Ave (07647-1904)
PHONE....................................201 767-0009
Ben Horwitz, *President*
Erika Freed, *Director*
EMP: 10 EST: 1976
SQ FT: 30,000
SALES (est): 2.2MM **Privately Held**
WEB: www.richardwimmer.com
SIC: **3952** 2851 Artists' materials, except pencils & leads; paints & allied products

(G-7548)
S SWANSON LLC
157 Veterans Dr Ste B (07647-2310)
PHONE....................................201 750-5050
Lauren Levy,
EMP: 4
SALES (est): 156.7K **Privately Held**
SIC: **2844** Toilet preparations

(G-7549)
SHADE POWERS CO INC
Also Called: Window Designs By Powers
112 Paris Ave Ste C (07647-1544)
PHONE....................................201 767-3727
Barbara Powers, *President*
Gregory Powers Jr, *Corp Secy*
EMP: 12
SQ FT: 2,500
SALES (est): 1.5MM **Privately Held**
SIC: **5719** 3429 2591 Window furnishings; manufactured hardware (general); drapery hardware & blinds & shades

(G-7550)
SONOTRON MEDICAL SYSTEMS INC
Also Called: ADM Tronics
224 Pegasus Ave (07647-1920)
PHONE....................................201 767-6040
Andre Di Mino, *President*
Dominic Albi, *Vice Pres*
Vincent Di Mino, *Vice Pres*
▲ EMP: 8
SQ FT: 8,000
SALES (est): 1.4MM
SALES (corp-wide): 3MM **Publicly Held**
WEB: www.admtronics.com
SIC: **3845** Electromedical equipment
PA: A D M Tronics Unlimited, Inc.
224 Pegasus Ave Ste A
Northvale NJ 07647
201 767-6040

(G-7551)
TAKASAGO INTL CORP USA
Also Called: Fragrance Factory
267 Union St (07647-2210)
P.O. Box 932 (07647-0932)
PHONE....................................201 767-9001
Thibaut Madre, *President*
Gary Titus, *Vice Pres*
Ron Rand, *Branch Mgr*
EMP: 65 **Privately Held**
SIC: **2844** Concentrates, perfume
HQ: Takasago International Corporation (U.S.A)
4 Volvo Dr
Rockleigh NJ 07647
201 767-9001

(G-7552)
UNITED INSTRUMENT COMPANY LLC
207 Washington St Ste A (07647-2045)
PHONE....................................201 767-6000
George Petikas,
▲ EMP: 4
SALES (est): 661.8K **Privately Held**
SIC: **3545** 3829 Machine tool accessories; measuring & controlling devices

(G-7553)
VIZ MOLD & DIE LTD
210 Industrial Pkwy (07647-2219)
PHONE....................................201 784-8383
Dimitrios Lymberis, *President*
Georgia Lymberis, *Opers Mgr*
Joan Peters, *Admin Sec*
EMP: 10

SALES (est): 1.5MM **Privately Held**
WEB: www.vizmold.com
SIC: **3089** 3544 Molding primary plastic; special dies, tools, jigs & fixtures

(G-7554)
X-FACTOR CMMNCTONS HLDINGS INC (PA)
100 Stonehurst Ct (07647-2405)
PHONE....................................877 741-3727
Charles Saracino, *Ch of Bd*
Michael Piro, *Vice Pres*
Edwin F Heinen, *CFO*
Jeffrey Singman, *Sales Staff*
Brian Watts, *CIO*
EMP: 5
SQ FT: 1,500
SALES (est): 800.6K **Publicly Held**
SIC: **7372** Application computer software

(G-7555)
ZENITH LABORATORIES INC
140 Legrand Ave (07647-2403)
PHONE....................................201 767-1700
EMP: 4
SALES (corp-wide): 5B **Privately Held**
SIC: **2834** Pharmaceutical preparations
HQ: Zenith Laboratories, Inc
140 Legrand Ave
Northvale NJ 07647
201 767-1700

(G-7556)
ZENITH LABORATORIES INC (DH)
140 Legrand Ave (07647-2403)
PHONE....................................201 767-1700
William Schreck, *President*
Lenora C Gavalas, *Exec VP*
Veerappan S Sueramanian, *Vice Pres*
Richard H Friedman, *CFO*
Ruth H Wallestad, *Treasurer*
EMP: 245
SQ FT: 81,600
SALES (est): 24.4MM
SALES (corp-wide): 5B **Privately Held**
WEB: www.onxol.com
SIC: **2834** Drugs acting on the cardiovascular system, except diagnostic

┌─────────────────────────┐
│ **Norwood**   │
│ *Bergen County*   │
└─────────────────────────┘

(G-7557)
AEROJET ROCKETDYNE DE INC
500 Walnut St (07648-1316)
PHONE....................................201 440-1453
Scott Roy, *Branch Mgr*
EMP: 7
SALES (corp-wide): 1.9B **Publicly Held**
SIC: **3443** 2752 Industrial vessels, tanks & containers; commercial printing, lithographic
HQ: Inc Aerojet Rocketdyne Of De
8900 De Soto Ave
Canoga Park CA 91304
818 586-1000

(G-7558)
BON-JOUR GROUP LLC
Also Called: Bon Jour Promotions
1100 Blanch Ave (07648-1509)
PHONE....................................201 646-1070
Paul Tchertchian, *President*
Michael Tchertchian, *Vice Pres*
EMP: 12
SQ FT: 20,000
SALES: 1.3MM **Privately Held**
WEB: www.bon-jour.com
SIC: **2395** Embroidery products, except schiffli machine

(G-7559)
C & S SPECIALTY INC
121 Piermont Rd (07648-2317)
PHONE....................................201 750-7740
Soon K Chun, *President*
Seth Atkinson, *Director*
▲ EMP: 5
SALES (est): 1.8MM **Privately Held**
WEB: www.cs-sales.net
SIC: **2899** Chemical preparations

(G-7560)
CHERINGAL ASSOCIATES INC
Also Called: Control Group
500 Walnut St (07648-1316)
PHONE....................................201 784-8721
Lynne Levine, *General Mgr*
William Cheringal, *Co-President*
Jeffrey Levine, *Co-President*
Russell Vizzi, *Vice Pres*
Rob Gilbert, *Manager*
▲ EMP: 65
SQ FT: 58,000
SALES (est): 11.1MM **Privately Held**
WEB: www.controlgroupusa.com
SIC: **2759** 5999 3672 Flexographic printing; cosmetics; printed circuit boards

(G-7561)
CHIC BTQ DOLL DESIGN CO LLC
331 Piermont Rd Ste 8 (07648-1407)
PHONE....................................201 784-7727
Murray S Bass,
Allen Fu,
Sarah Nguyen,
EMP: 7
SALES (est): 540K **Privately Held**
SIC: **3942** Dolls & doll clothing

(G-7562)
CREATIVE CONCEPTS CORPORATION
70 Oak St Ste 202 (07648-1300)
PHONE....................................201 750-1234
EMP: 5 EST: 1990
SQ FT: 3,000
SALES (est): 890.7K **Privately Held**
SIC: **2844** Mfg Toilet Preparations

(G-7563)
GRUPPO EDITORIALE OGGI INC
Also Called: America Oggi
55 Walnut St Ste 209 (07648-1332)
PHONE....................................201 358-6582
Andrea Mantineo, *President*
Massimo Jaus, *Treasurer*
▲ EMP: 40
SALES (est): 3.1MM **Privately Held**
SIC: **2711** Newspapers: publishing only, not printed on site

(G-7564)
H GALOW CO INC
15 Maple St (07648-2003)
PHONE....................................201 768-0547
Michael Galow, *President*
Robert Galow, *Vice Pres*
EMP: 42
SALES (est): 8.1MM **Privately Held**
WEB: www.hgalowco.com
SIC: **3812** 3841 Aircraft flight instruments; medical instruments & equipment, blood & bone work

(G-7565)
INTAROME FRAGRANCE CORPORATION (PA)
370 Chestnut St (07648-2002)
PHONE....................................201 767-8700
D G Funsch, *CEO*
Marcia Rivera, *Sales Staff*
Betty Valdivia, *Manager*
EMP: 55 EST: 1969
SQ FT: 40,000
SALES (est): 13.8MM **Privately Held**
SIC: **2844** 5122 Cosmetic preparations; perfumes

(G-7566)
J B OFFSET PRINTING CORP
55 Walnut St Ste 209 (07648-1332)
PHONE....................................201 264-4400
Roy Steiger, *Principal*
EMP: 5 EST: 2014
SALES (est): 315.1K **Privately Held**
SIC: **2752** Commercial printing, lithographic

(G-7567)
J MEDIA LLC (PA)
Also Called: Luis Network
55 Walnut St Ste 105a (07648-1348)
PHONE....................................201 600-4573
Luis Jimenez,
Maria Alma-Jimenez,

EMP: 6
SALES: 623K **Privately Held**
SIC: 2741 7929 ; entertainment service

(G-7568)
LEMON INC
72 Mohawk Ave (07648-2417)
PHONE...................................201 417-5412
EMP: 4
SALES (est): 250K **Privately Held**
SIC: 2369 Mfg Girl/Youth Outerwear

(G-7569)
MT EMBROIDERY & PROMOTIONS LLC
Also Called: Bon Jour
70 Oak St Ste 103 (07648-1300)
PHONE...................................201 646-1070
Michael Tchertchian, *Owner*
Michael Tchectchian, *Mng Member*
EMP: 8
SALES: 750K **Privately Held**
SIC: 2395 2261 Embroidery & art needle-
work; screen printing of cotton broadwo-
ven fabrics

(G-7570)
NICOMAC SYSTEMS INC
54 Summit St (07648)
PHONE...................................201 871-0916
Paolo Nigris, *President*
EMP: 5
SALES (est): 463.8K **Privately Held**
SIC: 7372 Business oriented computer
software

(G-7571)
NICOS GROUP INC
80 Oak St Ste 201 (07648-1342)
PHONE...................................201 768-9501
Francesco Nigris, *President*
Claudio Castellarin, *Sales Mgr*
Jim Navarro, *Sales Engr*
Rosanne Cangialosi, *Manager*
Rosanne Candialosi, *Admin Sec*
▲ EMP: 6
SQ FT: 1,500
SALES: 6.1MM
SALES (corp-wide): 26.6K **Privately Held**
WEB: www.nicomac.com
SIC: 3559 1751 Pharmaceutical machin-
ery; carpentry work
PA: Nicomac Srl
Via Curiel 12
Liscate MI
029 542-041

(G-7572)
NORWOOD PRINTING INC
Also Called: Control Group
530 Walnut St (07648-1343)
PHONE...................................201 784-8721
William Cheringal, *President*
Rob Paglieri, *CFO*
Curtis Burns, *Manager*
Tony Sarno, *Director*
Jeff Levine, *Executive*
▲ EMP: 10
SQ FT: 21,000
SALES (est): 1.9MM **Privately Held**
SIC: 2752 Commercial printing, offset

(G-7573)
RAINMEN USA INCORPORATED (PA)
Also Called: AAA Umbrella Co
10 Maple St (07648-2004)
PHONE...................................201 784-3244
Jeffrey Nanus, *President*
Kelly Borre, *Regional Mgr*
Adam Scheps, *Vice Pres*
Lisa Hansell, *CFO*
Emily Nagel, *Regl Sales Mgr*
▲ EMP: 60
SQ FT: 60,000
SALES (est): 13.6MM **Privately Held**
WEB: www.rainmenusa.com
SIC: 3999 Garden umbrellas

(G-7574)
SOLENIS LLC
Ashland Water Technologies
49 Walnut St (07648-1329)
PHONE...................................201 767-7400
Steve Chookazian, *Manager*
EMP: 20

SALES (corp-wide): 783.4MM **Privately Held**
WEB: www.ashland.com
SIC: 2899 Water treating compounds
HQ: Solenis Llc
3 Beaver Valley Rd # 500
Wilmington DE 19803
866 337-1533

(G-7575)
TELESCRIPT INC (PA)
445 Livingston St (07648-1311)
PHONE...................................201 767-6733
Fax: 201 784-0323
EMP: 8
SQ FT: 3,000
SALES (est): 1MM **Privately Held**
SIC: 3663 Mfg Radio/Tv Communication
Equipment

(G-7576)
TRU MFG CORP
40 Oak St Ste 2 (07648-1315)
PHONE...................................201 768-4050
Angela Mastropietro, *President*
Paul Mastropaola, *President*
EMP: 23 EST: 1977
SQ FT: 24,000
SALES (est): 4.2MM **Privately Held**
WEB: www.trumfg.com
SIC: 3599 Machine shop, jobbing & repair

(G-7577)
ZENITH MFG & CHEMICAL CORP
Also Called: Zenith Ultrasonic
85 Oak St (07648-1313)
P.O. Box 412 (07648-0412)
PHONE...................................201 767-1332
Michael Pedzy, *President*
Maggie Miller, *Manager*
EMP: 15 EST: 1937
SALES: 1.5MM **Privately Held**
WEB: www.zenith-ultrasonics.com
SIC: 3699 Cleaning equipment, ultrasonic,
except medical & dental

Nutley
Essex County

(G-7578)
AMERICAN DIAGNSTC IMAGING INC
410 Centre St 2 (07110-1635)
PHONE...................................973 980-1724
Sadia Chaudhry, *President*
Danny Chaudhry, *Vice Pres*
EMP: 15
SALES (est): 1.2MM **Privately Held**
SIC: 3841 Diagnostic apparatus, medical

(G-7579)
AMY PUBLICATIONS LLC
11 Robert St (07110-1330)
PHONE...................................973 235-1800
Larry Mills,
Richard Miller,
EMP: 9
SALES: 1MM **Privately Held**
SIC: 2721 Magazines: publishing & printing

(G-7580)
BAUMAR INDUSTRIES INC
29 E Centre St (07110-3409)
PHONE...................................973 667-5490
Arthur Bautis, *President*
Daniel Marfino Jr, *Vice Pres*
EMP: 9
SQ FT: 6,000
SALES (est): 843.9K **Privately Held**
WEB: www.baumar.net
SIC: 2819 Industrial inorganic chemicals

(G-7581)
BSI CORP
52 E Centre St Ste 2 (07110-5406)
PHONE...................................631 589-1118
Jeremy Linder, *President*
◆ EMP: 22
SQ FT: 12,000
SALES: 3.1MM **Privately Held**
WEB: www.blockscientific.com
SIC: 5047 3821 Medical equipment & sup-
plies; laboratory apparatus & furniture

(G-7582)
CELTIC PASSIONS LLC
35 Park Dr (07110-2747)
PHONE...................................973 865-7046
Joanne Manley,
EMP: 10
SALES: 500K **Privately Held**
WEB: www.celticpassions.com
SIC: 2051 Bakery: wholesale or whole-
sale/retail combined

(G-7583)
COZY FORMAL WEAR INC (PA)
Also Called: Uniforms By Cozy
695 Passaic Ave (07110-1229)
PHONE...................................973 661-9781
Ralph Savastano, *President*
EMP: 9 EST: 1968
SQ FT: 8,250
SALES (est): 1.1MM **Privately Held**
WEB: www.cozytux.com
SIC: 7299 5699 2395 Tuxedo rental; uni-
forms & work clothing; embroidery prod-
ucts, except schiffli machine

(G-7584)
DANA AUTOMOTIVE INC
217 Darling Ave (07110-1034)
PHONE...................................973 667-1234
Laraine Fusaro, *President*
John Fusaro Jr, *Admin Sec*
Mark Fusaro, *Admin Sec*
EMP: 12
SQ FT: 45,000
SALES (est): 2.6MM **Privately Held**
SIC: 3714 Motor vehicle parts & acces-
sories

(G-7585)
DIETECH SERVICES LLC
40 Holmes St (07110-2616)
P.O. Box 641 (07110-0641)
PHONE...................................973 667-0798
Robin Rodriguez,
▲ EMP: 4
SQ FT: 3,000
SALES: 350K **Privately Held**
SIC: 3554 Paper industries machinery

(G-7586)
GRIFFITH SHADE COMPANY INC
308 Washington Ave Ste 1 (07110-1985)
PHONE...................................973 667-1474
John Griffith Jr, *President*
Mary Anne Griffith, *Vice Pres*
EMP: 4 EST: 1950
SQ FT: 2,250
SALES: 750K **Privately Held**
WEB: www.nutley.com
SIC: 2591 5719 Window shades; window
shades

(G-7587)
HOFFMANN-LA ROCHE INC
340 Kingsland St (07110-1199)
PHONE...................................973 235-3092
EMP: 61
SALES (corp-wide): 57.2B **Privately Held**
WEB: www.rocheusa.com
SIC: 2834 Pharmaceutical preparations
HQ: Hoffmann-La Roche Inc.
150 Clove Rd Ste 88th
Little Falls NJ 07424
973 890-2268

(G-7588)
HOFFMANN-LA ROCHE INC
500 Kingsland St (07110-1046)
PHONE...................................973 235-1016
Dianne Keel Atkins, *Branch Mgr*
EMP: 25
SALES (corp-wide): 57.2B **Privately Held**
WEB: www.rocheusa.com
SIC: 2834 Pharmaceutical preparations
HQ: Hoffmann-La Roche Inc.
150 Clove Rd Ste 88th
Little Falls NJ 07424
973 890-2268

(G-7589)
LANXESS SOLUTIONS US INC
10 Kingsland St (07110)
P.O. Box 610, Birdsboro PA (19508-0610)
PHONE...................................973 235-1800
George Cox, *Manager*
EMP: 150

SALES (corp-wide): 8.2B **Privately Held**
WEB: www.cromptoncorp.com
SIC: 2899 Chemical preparations
HQ: Lanxess Solutions Us Inc.
2 Armstrong Rd Ste 101
Shelton CT 06484
203 573-2000

(G-7590)
MANVA INDUSTRIES INC
Also Called: Printing Techniques
48 Franklin Ave (07110-3225)
PHONE...................................973 667-2606
Joseph Vitiello, *President*
Richard Vitiello, *Vice Pres*
Dan Vitiello, *Admin Sec*
EMP: 12
SQ FT: 3,500
SALES (est): 2.1MM **Privately Held**
SIC: 2752 Commercial printing, offset

(G-7591)
METRO BINDERY OF NEW JERSEY
187 Washington Ave (07110-3935)
PHONE...................................973 667-4190
Betty Ann Magnifico, *President*
EMP: 10
SQ FT: 18,000
SALES (est): 693K **Privately Held**
SIC: 2789 Bookbinding & related work

(G-7592)
PNC INC
115 E Centre St (07110-3400)
PHONE...................................973 284-1600
Sam Sangani, *President*
Bhavesh Sangani, *Prdtn Mgr*
Nicole Hurley, *Purchasing*
Ila Shah, *Finance Mgr*
▲ EMP: 200
SALES (est): 13.7MM **Privately Held**
WEB: www.pnconline.com
SIC: 3672 Circuit boards, television & radio
printed

(G-7593)
SECURITY DEFENSE SYSTEMS CORP
160 Park Ave Ste 1 (07110-2808)
PHONE...................................973 235-0606
Donna L Korkala, *President*
Jasmine Demerjian, *Corp Secy*
Gary Korkala, *Project Mgr*
EMP: 6 EST: 1980
SQ FT: 8,500
SALES (est): 590K **Privately Held**
WEB: www.securitydefense.com
SIC: 3844 X-ray apparatus & tubes

(G-7594)
THOMAS GRECO PUBLISHING INC (PA)
Also Called: New Jersey Automotive Mag
244 Chestnut St Ste 4 (07110-4318)
PHONE...................................973 667-6965
Thomas Greco, *President*
Lea Velocci, *Vice Pres*
Lealah Afif, *Associate*
Maria Casillas, *Associate*
Michael Durant, *Associate*
EMP: 10
SALES: 1MM **Privately Held**
WEB: www.nutleychamber.com
SIC: 2721 Magazines: publishing & printing

(G-7595)
THOMSON REUTERS CORPORATION
492 River Rd (07110-3609)
PHONE...................................973 662-3070
Jim McHugh, *Branch Mgr*
EMP: 15
SALES (corp-wide): 10.6B **Publicly Held**
SIC: 2741 8111 7372 7383 Miscella-
neous publishing; legal services; prepack-
aged software; news syndicates
HQ: Thomson Reuters Corporation
3 Times Sq
New York NY 10036
646 223-4000

G
E
O
G
R
A
P
H
I
C

(G-7596)
UNILITE INCORPORATED
151 River Rd　(07110-3513)
PHONE................................973 667-1674
Michael Foti, *President*
Quinto Foti, *Vice Pres*
Mario Foti, *Treasurer*
EMP: 5 **EST:** 1973
SQ FT: 3,000
SALES (est): 786.5K　**Privately Held**
SIC: 3469　Metal stampings

(G-7597)
WAFFLE WAFFLE LLC (PA)
43 River Rd　(07110-3411)
PHONE................................201 559-1286
Gennaro Mirabella, *Vice Pres*
Brian Samuels, *Vice Pres*
Bracken Abrams, *VP Sales*
Brittany Veres, *Marketing Mgr*
Justin Samuels, *Mng Member*
EMP: 12
SQ FT: 8,000
SALES (est): 2MM　**Privately Held**
SIC: 2038　Breakfasts, frozen & packaged

(G-7598)
ZINICOLA BAKING CO
127 King St　(07110-3340)
PHONE................................973 667-1306
John Zinicola Jr, *President*
EMP: 8
SQ FT: 5,000
SALES (est): 500K　**Privately Held**
SIC: 2051　5461　Bread, all types (white, wheat, rye, etc): fresh or frozen; bread

Oak Ridge
Passaic County

(G-7599)
A GIMENEZ TRADING LLC
5 Wegmann Way　(07438-9600)
PHONE................................973 697-2240
Melissa Laserna, *Mng Member*
Amy Laserna,
EMP: 8
SALES (est): 830K　**Privately Held**
SIC: 2013　Sausages & other prepared meats

(G-7600)
DUNBAR CONCRETE PRODUCTS INC
173 Oak Ridge Rd　(07438-8911)
P.O. Box 453　(07438-0453)
PHONE................................973 697-2525
Walter M Dunbar, *President*
EMP: 19
SALES (est): 2.3MM　**Privately Held**
SIC: 3272　3271　Concrete products, precast; covers, catch basin: concrete; sewer & manhole block, concrete

(G-7601)
DURA-CARB INC
204 Chamberlain Rd　(07438-8891)
P.O. Box 407　(07438-0407)
PHONE................................973 697-6665
Scott Beiermester, *President*
Joann Beiermeister, *Corp Secy*
Scott Beiermeister, *Vice Pres*
EMP: 8 **EST:** 1975
SQ FT: 5,000
SALES: 1.3MM　**Privately Held**
WEB: www.dura-carb.com
SIC: 3544　Special dies & tools

(G-7602)
ESCO PRODUCTS INC
Also Called: Esco Optics
95 Chamberlain Rd　(07438-8853)
PHONE................................973 697-3700
Gary Steneken, *President*
Linn Rossi, *Purch Mgr*
Ron Pietranowicz, *CFO*
Amanda Haught, *Manager*
Deanna Burd, *Director*
EMP: 45 **EST:** 1946
SQ FT: 20,000
SALES: 8MM　**Privately Held**
WEB: www.escoproducts.com
SIC: 3827　Lenses, optical: all types except ophthalmic; mirrors, optical; prisms, optical

(G-7603)
NORTH CHURCH GRAVEL INC
173 Oak Ridge Rd　(07438-8911)
P.O. Box 235　(07438-0235)
PHONE................................201 796-1556
Anthony Dell, *Principal*
EMP: 6 **EST:** 2005
SALES (est): 732.8K　**Privately Held**
SIC: 1442　Construction sand & gravel

(G-7604)
RAUE SCREW MACHINE PRODUCTS CO
173 Oak Ridge Rd　(07438-8911)
P.O. Box 207　(07438-0207)
PHONE................................973 697-7500
Carl Raue, *President*
Rod Raue, *Corp Secy*
Guy Raue, *Vice Pres*
EMP: 4
SQ FT: 3,200
SALES (est): 544.5K　**Privately Held**
SIC: 3599　Machine shop, jobbing & repair

(G-7605)
ROYAL OAK RAILINGS LLC
3 Field Ct　(07438-9129)
PHONE................................973 208-8900
Ernest Intorrella, *Principal*
EMP: 4
SALES (est): 453.8K　**Privately Held**
SIC: 2431　Staircases, stairs & railings

(G-7606)
RUNDING LLC
90 Greendale Dr　(07438-8971)
P.O. Box 118　(07438-0118)
PHONE................................973 277-8775
Glen Deleeuw,
Brittney Deleeuw,
EMP: 7
SQ FT: 2,000
SALES: 1.2MM　**Privately Held**
SIC: 3441　Fabricated structural metal

Oakhurst
Monmouth County

(G-7607)
ALKALINE CORPORATION
714 W Park Ave　(07755-1014)
P.O. Box 306　(07755-0306)
PHONE................................732 531-7830
Isadore Bale, *President*
Ron Kay, *Vice Pres*
Gabriella Cantella, *Admin Sec*
EMP: 21
SQ FT: 3,300
SALES (est): 3.8MM　**Privately Held**
WEB: www.allergyhelp.com
SIC: 2819　Elements

(G-7608)
EXHIBIT NETWORK INC
434 Brookside Ave　(07755-1402)
PHONE................................732 751-9600
EMP: 15
SQ FT: 30,000
SALES (est): 1.1MM　**Privately Held**
SIC: 3993　Mfg Of Custom Trade Show Exhibits

(G-7609)
FRIENDS HARDWOOD FLOORS INC
60 Monmouth Rd　(07755-1631)
P.O. Box 591　(07755-0591)
PHONE................................732 859-4019
Demir Santos, *Principal*
EMP: 6 **EST:** 2009
SALES (est): 818.1K　**Privately Held**
SIC: 2426　1771　1752　Flooring, hardwood; flooring contractor; floor laying & floor work

(G-7610)
KWIK ENTERPRISES LLC
Also Called: Vitamins For Life
1806 Bellmore St　(07755-2904)
P.O. Box 853　(07755-0853)
PHONE................................732 663-1559
Marcelo Gruberg,
Bernard Gruberg,
◆ **EMP:** 8
SQ FT: 2,000
SALES (est): 7.2MM　**Privately Held**
WEB: www.vitaminsforlife.net
SIC: 2834　Vitamin preparations

(G-7611)
OCEAN ENERGY INDUSTRIES INC
715 W Park Ave Unit 1073　(07755-8042)
PHONE................................954 828-2177
Robert Bado, *Owner*
Artem Madatov, *Owner*
EMP: 10
SALES (est): 419.5K　**Privately Held**
SIC: 1629　3699　3511　Dams, waterways, docks & other marine construction; electrical equipment & supplies; wheels, water

(G-7612)
R & K INDUSTRIES INC
Also Called: Waterloov
259 Overbrook Ave　(07755-1505)
PHONE................................732 531-1123
Richard Kuhns, *President*
EMP: 8 **EST:** 1997
SALES (est): 833K　**Privately Held**
SIC: 7299　3089　Home improvement & renovation contractor agency; gutters (glass fiber reinforced, fiberglass or plastic

(G-7613)
SWEET DELIGHT
65 Monmouth Rd　(07755-1667)
PHONE................................732 263-9100
Frida Fitzgerald, *Owner*
Michael Paolantonio, *Owner*
EMP: 10
SALES (est): 350.6K　**Privately Held**
WEB: www.sweetdelight.com
SIC: 2024　Ice cream & frozen desserts

Oakland
Bergen County

(G-7614)
AMERLUX LLC (DH)
Also Called: Amerlux Lighting Systems
178 Bauer Dr　(07436-3105)
PHONE................................973 882-5010
Chuck Campagna, *CEO*
Frank Diassi, *Chairman*
Don Knickerbocker, *Vice Pres*
Richard Lerner, *Vice Pres*
John Mamo, *Vice Pres*
◆ **EMP:** 197
SQ FT: 45,000
SALES (est): 42.1MM
SALES (corp-wide): 7.6B　**Privately Held**
WEB: www.amerlux.com
SIC: 3646　Commercial indusl & institutional electric lighting fixtures
HQ: Delta Electronics (Netherlands) B.V.
　Zandsteen 15
　Hoofddorp　2132
　206 550-900

(G-7615)
AZEGO TECHNOLOGY SVCS US INC (PA)
103 Bauer Dr Ste A　(07436-3102)
PHONE................................201 327-7500
Bob Gallagher, *President*
John Byrnes, *Vice Pres*
Bob Reynics, *Vice Pres*
Jackie Cohen, *Admin Sec*
EMP: 8
SQ FT: 8,000
SALES (est): 5MM　**Privately Held**
SIC: 3559　Electronic component making machinery

(G-7616)
BLOOMFIELD MANUFACTURING CO (PA)
29 Crosby Ln　(07436-3202)
P.O. Box 1266, Caldwell　(07007-1266)
PHONE................................973 575-8900
Susan Masinda, *President*
Linda Heberling, *Vice Pres*
EMP: 15
SQ FT: 30,000
SALES (est): 1.9MM　**Privately Held**
WEB: www.bloomfield.com
SIC: 3444　Sheet metalwork

(G-7617)
BROWN CHEMICAL CO INC (PA)
302 W Oakland Ave　(07436-1381)
P.O. Box 440　(07436-0440)
PHONE................................201 337-0900
Douglas A Brown, *CEO*
Douglas Brown, *COO*
Patrick Brown, *Vice Pres*
Dave Lyle, *Vice Pres*
▲ **EMP:** 35
SQ FT: 46,000
SALES (est): 21MM　**Privately Held**
WEB: www.brownchem.com
SIC: 5169　2869　Industrial chemicals; accelerators, rubber processing: cyclic or acyclic

(G-7618)
CAPTIVE FASTENERS CORP
19 Thornton Rd　(07436-3115)
PHONE................................201 337-6800
Joseph T Alderisio, *President*
Randy Carbora, *Vice Pres*
Ralph Rosario, *Plant Mgr*
Diane Struble, *Manager*
Maven Kudeimati, *Officer*
▲ **EMP:** 310 **EST:** 1974
SALES (est): 43.1MM　**Privately Held**
WEB: www.captive-fastener.com
SIC: 3965　5085　Fasteners; industrial supplies

(G-7619)
COLLAGEN MATRIX INC (PA)
15 Thornton Rd　(07436-3115)
PHONE................................201 405-1477
Bart J Doedens, *CEO*
Griselda Rodriguez, *Mfg Staff*
Liesa Denardo, *Purchasing*
Robert Villano, *Engineer*
Jennifer Duncan, *Accountant*
EMP: 78
SQ FT: 28,000
SALES (est): 15.5MM　**Privately Held**
WEB: www.collagenmatrix.com
SIC: 3841　8731　Surgical & medical instruments; commercial physical research

(G-7620)
CONCRETE ON DEMAND INC
45 Edison Ave Ste 1　(07436-1308)
PHONE................................201 337-0005
David Gross, *President*
EMP: 15
SQ FT: 10,000
SALES: 3.5MM　**Privately Held**
SIC: 3273　4213　Ready-mixed concrete; building materials transport

(G-7621)
CROWN EQUIPMENT CORPORATION
Also Called: Crown Lift Trucks
104 Bauer Dr　(07436-3105)
PHONE................................201 337-1211
Paul Almeida, *Branch Mgr*
Ray Milano, *Manager*
EMP: 61
SALES (corp-wide): 3.1B　**Privately Held**
SIC: 3537　Lift trucks, industrial: fork, platform, straddle, etc.
PA: Crown Equipment Corporation
　44 S Washington St
　New Bremen OH 45869
　419 629-2311

(G-7622)
CUSTOM CREATIONS (PA)
294 W Oakland Ave　(07436-1312)
PHONE................................201 651-9676
Charles Stoppiello, *Owner*

EMP: 8
SQ FT: 1,800
SALES (est): 770.4K **Privately Held**
WEB: www.custom-create.com
SIC: 2542 Cabinets: show, display or storage: except wood

(G-7623)
DBMCORP INC
32a Spruce St (07436-1811)
PHONE..................................201 677-0008
Dale Sydnor, *President*
Mike Cagney, *General Mgr*
William Pastor, *Vice Pres*
Michael Cagney, *VP Sls/Mktg*
Steve Dans, *Technology*
EMP: 15
SQ FT: 6,000
SALES (est): 3.2MM **Privately Held**
WEB: www.dbmcorp.com
SIC: 3825 Test equipment for electronic & electric measurement

(G-7624)
DEWEY ELECTRONICS CORPORATION (PA)
27 Muller Rd (07436-1375)
PHONE..................................201 337-4700
John H D Dewey, *CEO*
Edward L Proskey, *Senior VP*
EMP: 24 EST: 1955
SQ FT: 49,200
SALES (est): 3.3MM **Publicly Held**
WEB: www.deweyelectronics.com
SIC: 3621 3699 Motors & generators; electrical equipment & supplies

(G-7625)
DEWEY ELECTRONICS CORPORATION
Pitometer Log Division
27 Muller Rd (07436-1375)
PHONE..................................201 337-4700
John Dewey, *President*
EMP: 25
SALES (corp-wide): 3.3MM **Publicly Held**
WEB: www.deweyelectronics.com
SIC: 3812 Warfare counter-measure equipment
PA: The Dewey Electronics Corporation
27 Muller Rd
Oakland NJ 07436
201 337-4700

(G-7626)
DRS LEONARDO INC
Also Called: Drs Data & Imaging Systems
133 Bauer Dr (07436-3123)
PHONE..................................201 337-3800
David Stapley, *President*
EMP: 28
SALES (corp-wide): 9.2B **Privately Held**
SIC: 3812 Navigational systems & instruments
HQ: Leonardo Drs, Inc.
2345 Crystal Dr Ste 1000
Arlington VA 22202
703 416-8000

(G-7627)
ENGINEERING LABORATORIES INC
360 W Oakland Ave (07436-1249)
PHONE..................................201 337-8116
Daniel Mason, *President*
Marjorie Mason, *Corp Secy*
Adam Mason, *Vice Pres*
Jason Mason, *Vice Pres*
▲ EMP: 35 EST: 1935
SQ FT: 34,000
SALES (est): 7.2MM **Privately Held**
WEB: www.plasticball.com
SIC: 3089 Injection molded finished plastic products

(G-7628)
FIMS MANUFACTURING CORPORATION
8 Allerman Rd (07436-3324)
PHONE..................................201 845-7088
Sergio Facchini, *President*
Michael Facchini, *Vice Pres*
EMP: 24 EST: 1962
SQ FT: 20,000

SALES (est): 5.4MM **Privately Held**
SIC: 3599 Machine shop, jobbing & repair

(G-7629)
FREEDOM PLASTICS LLC
37 Edison Ave (07436-1301)
PHONE..................................201 337-9450
Charlie Romaniello, *President*
EMP: 12
SQ FT: 25,000
SALES (est): 2.2MM **Privately Held**
SIC: 2673 Bags: plastic, laminated & coated

(G-7630)
GOLDSTEIN & BURTON INC
Also Called: Nu Products Seasonings
20 Potash Rd (07436-3100)
PHONE..................................201 440-0065
Henry Goldstein, *President*
▼ EMP: 65 EST: 1949
SALES (est): 8.9MM **Privately Held**
WEB: www.nuproductsseasoning.com
SIC: 2099 Spices, including grinding; seasonings: dry mixes

(G-7631)
HOLIDAY BOWL INC
29 Spruce St (07436-1810)
PHONE..................................201 337-6516
Ed Dougherty, *President*
Gill Doltoy, *Manager*
EMP: 20 EST: 1960
SQ FT: 40,000
SALES (est): 1.5MM **Privately Held**
WEB: www.holidaybowl.com
SIC: 3949 7933 Bowling alleys & accessories; ten pin center

(G-7632)
ID TECHNOLOGY LLC
48 Spruce St (07436-1830)
PHONE..................................201 405-0767
Robert Zuilhof, *President*
EMP: 45
SALES (corp-wide): 585.6MM **Privately Held**
SIC: 3565 Labeling machines, industrial
HQ: Id Technology Llc
5051 N Sylvania Ave # 405
Fort Worth TX 76137
817 626-7779

(G-7633)
JOHN R ZABKA ASSOCIATES INC (PA)
Also Called: Hospital & Health Care Compen
3 Post Rd Ste 3 # 3 (07436-1610)
P.O. Box 376 (07436-0376)
PHONE..................................201 405-0075
Thomas Cioffe, *President*
Steve Welish, *Med Doctor*
Rosanne Cioffe, *Director*
EMP: 11
SALES (est): 1,000K **Privately Held**
WEB: www.hhcsinc.com
SIC: 2741 Miscellaneous publishing

(G-7634)
LABELING SYSTEMS LLC
48 Spruce St (07436-1830)
PHONE..................................201 405-0767
Robert Zuilhof, *President*
Jack Roe, *Vice Pres*
EMP: 45
SQ FT: 44,000
SALES (est): 8.1MM
SALES (corp-wide): 585.6MM **Privately Held**
WEB: www.labelingsystems.com
SIC: 3565 Labeling machines, industrial
PA: Pro Mach, Inc.
50 E Rivercntr Blvd 180
Covington KY 41011
513 831-8778

(G-7635)
METRONIC ENGINEERING CO INC
32 Iron Horse Rd (07436-1306)
PHONE..................................201 337-1266
D Lindsay Conner Jr, *President*
EMP: 17
SQ FT: 7,500

SALES (est): 1.1MM
SALES (corp-wide): 2.1MM **Privately Held**
WEB: www.tracermed.com
SIC: 3599 Machine shop, jobbing & repair
PA: Tracer Tool & Machine Co Inc
32 Iron Horse Rd
Oakland NJ 07436
201 337-6184

(G-7636)
METROPOLITAN VACUUM CLR CO INC
Also Called: METRO ELECTRIC DUSTER
5 Raritan Rd (07436-2709)
PHONE..................................201 405-2225
Jules Stern, *President*
Karen S Cohen, *VP Finance*
Kenneth Stern, *VP Sales*
David Stern, *VP Mktg*
▲ EMP: 70 EST: 1940
SQ FT: 60,000
SALES: 12MM **Privately Held**
WEB: www.metrovacworld.com
SIC: 3635 3589 3564 3563 Household vacuum cleaners; vacuum cleaners & sweepers, electric: industrial; blowers & fans; air & gas compressors

(G-7637)
MURRAY ELECTRONICS INC
12 Fox Ct (07436-3204)
PHONE..................................201 405-1158
Harold Murray, *President*
Kelly D Smith, *Treasurer*
EMP: 6
SQ FT: 2,400
SALES (est): 629.2K **Privately Held**
WEB: www.murrayelectronics.com
SIC: 3651 5065 7622 Household video equipment; video equipment, electronic; video repair

(G-7638)
NATIONAL ELECTRONIC ALLOYS INC (PA)
3 Fir Ct (07436-1884)
PHONE..................................201 337-9400
Richard Geoffrion, *President*
Edward Postolowski, *Vice Pres*
Karen Bertalotto, *Natl Sales Mgr*
Michael Sancetta, *Marketing Mgr*
Marie Gasser, *Office Mgr*
▲ EMP: 28
SQ FT: 20,000
SALES (est): 17.4MM **Privately Held**
WEB: www.nealloys.com
SIC: 5051 3341 3339 Steel; secondary nonferrous metals; primary nonferrous metals

(G-7639)
NICKEL SAVERS
90 Andrew Ave (07436-3802)
PHONE..................................201 405-1153
Robyn Sparacio, *President*
EMP: 6 EST: 2011
SALES (est): 467.8K **Privately Held**
SIC: 3356 Nickel

(G-7640)
P M C DINERS INC
Also Called: Paramount Modular Concepts
56 Spruce St (07436-1830)
PHONE..................................201 337-6146
Herbert G Enyart, *President*
EMP: 12 EST: 1970
SQ FT: 30,000
SALES (est): 2MM **Privately Held**
SIC: 3448 Prefabricated metal buildings

(G-7641)
PARK PLUS INC (PA)
Also Called: Romax Parking Solutions
31 Iron Horse Rd Ste 1 (07436-1305)
PHONE..................................201 651-8590
Ronald Astrup, *Ch of Bd*
▲ EMP: 7
SQ FT: 2,600
SALES: 10.4MM **Privately Held**
WEB: www.parkplusinc.com
SIC: 3559 Parking facility equipment & supplies

(G-7642)
RCM LTD INC
Also Called: Custom Golf
25 Cardinal Dr (07436-3910)
PHONE..................................201 337-3328
Bob Piccoli, *President*
EMP: 5
SALES (est): 400K **Privately Held**
SIC: 5941 3949 Golf goods & equipment; shafts, golf club

(G-7643)
REY CONSULTING INC
350 Ramapo Valley Rd (07436-2702)
PHONE..................................201 337-0051
Joe Rey, *President*
EMP: 10
SALES (est): 790K **Privately Held**
SIC: 7372 Prepackaged software

(G-7644)
RFF SERVICES LLC
40 Edison Ave Ste C (07436-1303)
PHONE..................................201 564-0040
Boris Burakov, *Mng Member*
EMP: 18
SQ FT: 3,300
SALES (est): 920K **Privately Held**
SIC: 7641 2512 Furniture repair & maintenance; upholstered household furniture

(G-7645)
ROYAL MASTER GRINDERS INC
143 Bauer Dr (07436-3103)
P.O. Box 630 (07436-0630)
PHONE..................................201 337-8500
John Memmelaar Jr, *President*
Rodney Allen, *Vice Pres*
▲ EMP: 51 EST: 1946
SQ FT: 24,000
SALES (est): 21.3MM **Privately Held**
WEB: www.royalmaster.com
SIC: 3541 5084 Grinding machines, metalworking; machine tools & metalworking machinery

(G-7646)
TOPCON AMERICA CORPORATION (HQ)
111 Bauer Dr (07436-3123)
PHONE..................................201 599-5100
David Mudrick, *President*
Sheng Liu, *Business Mgr*
Eric Chan, *Engineer*
Charlie Oschbach, *Business Anlyst*
Paulo E Stanga, *Consultant*
▲ EMP: 400
SALES (est): 274.1MM **Privately Held**
SIC: 3845 Laser systems & equipment, medical

(G-7647)
TOPCON MEDICAL SYSTEMS INC (DH)
111 Bauer Dr (07436-3123)
PHONE..................................201 599-5100
Shigehiro Ogino, *President*
David Mudrick, *President*
Alena Acosta, *Vice Pres*
Gene Borbone, *Vice Pres*
Elena Klyachman, *QA Dir*
▲ EMP: 100
SQ FT: 85,000
SALES: 74.1MM **Privately Held**
SIC: 3841 3826 3827 3829 Surgical & medical instruments; analytical instruments; optical instruments & apparatus; surveying instruments & accessories; ophthalmic goods; scientific instruments
HQ: Topcon America Corporation
111 Bauer Dr
Oakland NJ 07436
201 599-5100

(G-7648)
TRACER TOOL & MACHINE CO INC (PA)
32 Iron Horse Rd (07436-1392)
PHONE..................................201 337-6184
D Lindsay Conner Jr, *President*
Tina Tomat, *Sales Mgr*
EMP: 15 EST: 1960
SQ FT: 6,000

SALES (est): 2.1MM **Privately Held**
WEB: www.tracermed.com
SIC: 3599 3841 Machine shop, jobbing &
repair; surgical & medical instruments

(G-7649)
V G CONTROLS INC
17 Raritan Rd Ste 2 (07436-2743)
P.O. Box 7010 (07436-7010)
PHONE.................................973 764-6500
Vitaly Gelman, *President*
Elena Bubnova, *Manager*
EMP: 9
SALES (est): 3.1MM **Privately Held**
WEB: www.vgcontrols.com
SIC: 3823 8711 Industrial instrmnts
msrmnt display/control process variable;
engineering services

Oaklyn
Camden County

(G-7650)
ALLIANCE VINYL WINDOWS CO INC
301 Crescent Blvd (08107)
PHONE.................................856 456-4954
Paul Miraglia, *President*
EMP: 35
SALES (est): 6.9MM **Privately Held**
SIC: 5031 3442 Windows; metal doors,
sash & trim

Ocean
Monmouth County

(G-7651)
A C D CUSTOM GRANITE INC
1304 Roller Rd (07712-3904)
PHONE.................................732 695-2400
Cynthia Schomaker, *President*
EMP: 13
SQ FT: 13,000
SALES (est): 2MM **Privately Held**
SIC: 3281 Cut stone & stone products

(G-7652)
ACCESS RESPONSE INC
Also Called: Access Publishing Co
3321 Doris Ave (07712-4049)
P.O. Box 379, Asbury Park (07712-0379)
PHONE.................................732 660-0770
EMP: 8
SQ FT: 5,500
SALES: 1.5MM **Privately Held**
SIC: 2741 7331 7311 Misc Publishing Di-
rect Mail Advertising Services Advertising
Agency

(G-7653)
ADPRO IMPRINTS
Also Called: Budget Banners
1206 State Route 35 (07712-3515)
PHONE.................................732 531-2133
Peter Demaree, *Owner*
EMP: 6 EST: 1982
SALES (est): 673.1K **Privately Held**
WEB: www.adproimprints.com
SIC: 2759 Screen printing

(G-7654)
AKW INC
Also Called: A W Eurostile
1414 Roller Rd Rear (07712-3427)
PHONE.................................732 493-1883
Elizabeth Wyman, *Branch Mgr*
EMP: 7
SALES (corp-wide): 1.4MM **Privately Held**
WEB: www.aweurostile.com
SIC: 3443 5032 Fabricated plate work
(boiler shop); tile & clay products; marble
building stone
PA: Akw Inc
41 Newman Springs Rd E
Shrewsbury NJ 07702
732 530-9186

(G-7655)
ANDANTEX U S A INC
1705 Valley Rd (07712-3949)
PHONE.................................732 493-2812
Michael G Munn, *President*
Bruce Bradley, *Vice Pres*
Mary Ann Bradley, *Treasurer*
Mary Vaccarelli, *VP Finance*
Dave Potter, *Cust Mgr*
▲ EMP: 22
SQ FT: 8,800
SALES (est): 5.8MM **Privately Held**
WEB: www.andantex.com
SIC: 3568 Power transmission equipment

(G-7656)
ASBURY SYRUP COMPANY INC
3504 Rose Ave Ste 3 (07712-3983)
P.O. Box 2195, Asbury Park (07712-2195)
PHONE.................................732 774-5746
Anthony Sammarco Sr, *President*
EMP: 15
SALES (est): 3.8MM **Privately Held**
SIC: 5145 5113 2087 Syrups, fountain;
toppings, soda fountain; industrial & per-
sonal service paper; flavoring extracts &
syrups

(G-7657)
ATLANTIC PRTG & GRAPHICS LLC
1301 W Park Ave Ste D (07712-3190)
PHONE.................................732 493-4222
Edward Lawrence,
EMP: 5
SQ FT: 13,000
SALES (est): 532.9K **Privately Held**
SIC: 2752 Offset & photolithographic print-
ing

(G-7658)
CAROL PRODUCTS CO INC
1750 Brielle Ave Ste A1 (07712-3953)
PHONE.................................732 918-0800
Carol Hersh, *President*
David Hersh, *Vice Pres*
EMP: 60
SQ FT: 8,700
SALES (est): 7.4MM **Privately Held**
WEB: www.carolproducts.com
SIC: 3569 Filters

(G-7659)
COOPER POWER SYSTEMS LLC
42 Cindy Ln (07712-7250)
PHONE.................................732 481-4630
Paul Gruenebaum, *Manager*
EMP: 200 **Privately Held**
SIC: 3612 Power transformers, electric
HQ: Cooper Power Systems, Llc
2300 Badger Dr
Waukesha WI 53188
262 896-2400

(G-7660)
D L IMPRINTS
1701 Valley Rd Ste E (07712-3946)
PHONE.................................732 493-8555
Anthony L Lugo, *President*
Peter Demaree Jr, *Vice Pres*
EMP: 4
SALES: 235K **Privately Held**
SIC: 2759 Screen printing

(G-7661)
E L BAXTER CO INC
1227 Deal Rd (07712-2507)
P.O. Box 277, Long Branch (07740-0277)
PHONE.................................732 229-8219
Elwood L Baxter, *CEO*
Ron Eberhardt, *President*
Devra Budzik, *Director*
EMP: 15
SQ FT: 20,000
SALES (est): 2.3MM **Privately Held**
WEB: www.elbaxter.com
SIC: 2441 2653 Boxes, wood; boxes, cor-
rugated: made from purchased materials

(G-7662)
ECLEARVIEW TECHNOLOGIES INC
60 Barberry Dr (07712-8550)
PHONE.................................732 695-6999

EMP: 6
SQ FT: 100
SALES (est): 599K **Privately Held**
SIC: 3663 3572 7371 7372 Mfg Radio/Tv
Comm Equip Mfg Computer Storage Dvc
Computer Programming Svc Prepack-
aged Software Svc Computer Systems
Design

(G-7663)
EMC CORPORATION
Also Called: EMC Toy
8 The Fellsway (07712-3207)
PHONE.................................732 922-6353
EMP: 79
SALES (corp-wide): 78.6B **Publicly Held**
SIC: 3572 Mfg Computer Storage Devices
HQ: Emc Corporation
176 South St
Hopkinton MA 01748
508 435-1000

(G-7664)
GARDEN STATE IRON INC
3418 Sunset Ave (07712-3925)
PHONE.................................732 918-0760
Greg Andersen, *President*
EMP: 15
SALES (est): 1.8MM **Privately Held**
SIC: 1791 3446 Structural steel erection;
ornamental metalwork

(G-7665)
GARDEN STATE PROSTHETICS
3500 Sunset Ave (07712-3955)
PHONE.................................732 922-6650
Michael Dipersio, *Manager*
EMP: 4
SALES (est): 400K **Privately Held**
SIC: 3842 Prosthetic appliances

(G-7666)
I V MILLER & SONS
15 Cindy Ln (07712-7249)
PHONE.................................732 493-4040
George Miller, *President*
Jack Miller, *Vice Pres*
Juni Fraser, *Treasurer*
▲ EMP: 18 EST: 1949
SQ FT: 10,000
SALES (est): 2.2MM **Privately Held**
WEB: www.finalcut.com
SIC: 3479 Painting, coating & hot dipping

(G-7667)
KINETRON INC
1416 Roller Rd (07712-3496)
PHONE.................................732 918-7777
Judith Labrecque, *President*
James Gogan, *Principal*
Timothy Labrecque, *Principal*
EMP: 15 EST: 1960
SQ FT: 5,000
SALES (est): 1.5MM **Privately Held**
WEB: www.kinetron.com
SIC: 3444 Sheet metal specialties, not
stamped

(G-7668)
KMSCO INC
42a Cindy Ln (07712-7250)
PHONE.................................732 238-8666
Paul Van Anda, *President*
Alice Van Anda, *Vice Pres*
Bryan Finley, *Technology*
EMP: 12 EST: 1904
SQ FT: 13,000
SALES: 1.2MM **Privately Held**
WEB: www.logoknits.com
SIC: 2299 Fabrics: linen, jute, hemp, ramie

(G-7669)
LEIBROCK METAL PRODUCTS INC
1800 Brielle Ave (07712-3927)
PHONE.................................732 695-0326
William Vogel, *President*
EMP: 8
SQ FT: 10,000
SALES: 1MM **Privately Held**
SIC: 3469 3444 3316 Electronic enclo-
sures, stamped or pressed metal; sheet
metalwork; cold finishing of steel shapes

(G-7670)
ORYCON CONTROL TECHNOLOGY INC
3407 Rose Ave (07712-3968)
PHONE.................................732 922-2400
Salvatore Benenati, *President*
Thomas Miller, *Vice Pres*
Vincent Civale, *Treasurer*
David De Longe, *Admin Sec*
EMP: 26
SQ FT: 10,000
SALES (est): 4MM **Privately Held**
WEB: www.orycon.com
SIC: 3544 3823 Dies, plastics forming;
temperature instruments: industrial
process type

(G-7671)
PACENT ENGINEERING
3430 Sunset Ave Ste 18 (07712-3918)
PHONE.................................914 390-9150
EMP: 4
SALES (est): 133.2K **Privately Held**
SIC: 3999 Mfg Misc Products

(G-7672)
PEPSI-COLA METRO BTLG CO INC
3411 Sunset Ave (07712-3911)
PHONE.................................732 922-9000
Roseann Isasi, *Sales/Mktg Mgr*
Mark Barbara, *Sales Staff*
Paul Porcelli, *Sales Staff*
EMP: 160
SQ FT: 3,096
SALES (corp-wide): 64.6B **Publicly Held**
WEB: www.joy-of-cola.com
SIC: 2086 5149 Carbonated soft drinks,
bottled & canned; soft drinks
HQ: Pepsi-Cola Metropolitan Bottling Com-
pany, Inc.
1111 Westchester Ave
White Plains NY 10604
914 767-6000

(G-7673)
PETER L DEMAREE
1206 State Route 35 (07712-3515)
PHONE.................................732 531-2133
Peter Demaree Jr, *Owner*
Adam Kenter, *Co-Owner*
Anthony Lugo, *Co-Owner*
EMP: 8
SQ FT: 4,193
SALES (est): 300K **Privately Held**
SIC: 2261 Printing of cotton broadwoven
fabrics

(G-7674)
PHILLIPS ENTERPRISES INC
3600 Sunset Ave (07712-3915)
P.O. Box 2286, Asbury Park (07712-2286)
PHONE.................................732 493-3191
Joseph Phillips, *President*
Paul Phillips, *Vice Pres*
Brian Phillips, *Admin Sec*
EMP: 8
SQ FT: 12,000
SALES (est): 1.1MM **Privately Held**
WEB: www.phillipsentinc.com
SIC: 3315 3496 3469 Wire & fabricated
wire products; miscellaneous fabricated
wire products; metal stampings

(G-7675)
PHOENIX MANUFACTORING INC
1306 Brielle Ave (07712-3902)
PHONE.................................732 380-1666
Richard Sheridan, *President*
EMP: 9
SALES (est): 890K **Privately Held**
WEB: www.phoenixpvcrails.com
SIC: 2821 Polyvinyl chloride resins (PVC)

(G-7676)
Q P 195 INC
Also Called: Quikie Print & Copy Shop
827 W Park Ave (07712-7205)
PHONE.................................732 531-8860
Francine Goldstein, *President*
Jodie Rossi, *General Mgr*
Gerald Goldstein, *Corp Secy*
Katherine Bosco, *Manager*
EMP: 10
SQ FT: 3,000

SALES: 600K **Privately Held**
SIC: 2752 Commercial printing, lithographic

(G-7677)
Q P 500 INC
Also Called: Quickie Print & Copy Shop
827 W Park Ave (07712-7205)
PHONE..................................732 531-8860
Francine Goldstein, *President*
Gerald Goldstein, *Corp Secy*
EMP: 4
SALES (est): 573.2K **Privately Held**
SIC: 2752 Commercial printing, offset

(G-7678)
RAGAR CO INC
2106 Kings Hwy (07712-7204)
PHONE..................................732 493-1416
▲ **EMP:** 5
SALES (est): 360K **Privately Held**
SIC: 2499 Imports Exotic Woods

(G-7679)
RELIABILITY MAINTENANCE SVCS
823 W Park Ave Pmb 245 (07712-7205)
PHONE..................................732 922-8878
Alex B Johnston, *President*
EMP: 6
SALES: 150K **Privately Held**
SIC: 8734 3829 Testing laboratories; vibration meters, analyzers & calibrators

(G-7680)
SADWITH INDUSTRIES CORP
1015 Berkeley Ave (07712-3603)
P.O. Box 506, Matawan (07747-0506)
PHONE..................................732 531-3856
Jeff Sadwith, *President*
EMP: 5 **EST:** 1936
SQ FT: 30,000
SALES (est): 537.1K **Privately Held**
SIC: 3582 Commercial laundry equipment

(G-7681)
SCHALL MANUFACTURING INC
3501 Rose Ave (07712-3907)
PHONE..................................732 918-8800
Martin Schall, *President*
EMP: 6
SALES (est): 480K **Privately Held**
SIC: 3599 8742 Machine shop, jobbing & repair; manufacturing management consultant

(G-7682)
SELECTIVE COATINGS & INKS
Also Called: SCI
1750 Brielle Ave Ste B4 (07712-3953)
PHONE..................................732 493-0707
William Zak, *Branch Mgr*
EMP: 7
SALES (corp-wide): 1.9MM **Privately Held**
WEB: www.sci-inc-usa.com
SIC: 2893 Gravure ink
PA: Selective Coatings & Inks, Inc
5008 Industrial Rd
Wall Township NJ 07727
732 938-7677

(G-7683)
SIERRA PACKAGING INC
2106 Kings Hwy (07712-7204)
PHONE..................................732 571-2900
Paul Dorato, *President*
EMP: 12
SALES (est): 1.3MM **Privately Held**
WEB: www.sierrapackaging.com
SIC: 3086 Packaging & shipping materials, foamed plastic

(G-7684)
SPECIALTY LIGHTING INDS INC
1306 Doris Ave (07712-4041)
PHONE..................................732 517-0800
Ben Solomon, *Founder*
Neil Goldstein, *Vice Pres*
Jake Metz, *Vice Pres*
AWI Salomon, *Vice Pres*
Joey Basile, *Manager*
▲ **EMP:** 30

SALES (est): 86.8K **Privately Held**
WEB: www.specialtylightingindustries.com
SIC: 3646 Commercial indusl & institutional electric lighting fixtures

(G-7685)
STAMPING COM INC
Also Called: Molnar Tool and Dye
3600 Sunset Ave (07712-3915)
PHONE..................................732 493-4697
Chuck Molnar, *President*
EMP: 5 **EST:** 2009
SALES: 1.2MM **Privately Held**
SIC: 3469 Stamping metal for the trade

(G-7686)
UTE MICROWAVE INC
3500 Sunset Ave Ste D1 (07712-3956)
PHONE..................................732 922-1009
Lennart H Nilson, *President*
Mark McMorrow, *QC Mgr*
EMP: 20
SQ FT: 15,000
SALES (est): 3.2MM **Privately Held**
WEB: www.utemicrowave.com
SIC: 3679 Microwave components

(G-7687)
YEGHEN COMPUTER SYSTEM
Also Called: Y C S
5 Brook Dr Ste 101 (07712-3611)
PHONE..................................732 996-5500
J Yeghen, *President*
Pj N Yeghen, *President*
EMP: 10
SALES (est): 649K **Privately Held**
SIC: 7372 Prepackaged software

Ocean City
Cape May County

(G-7688)
COFFEE COMPANY LLC (PA)
Also Called: Ocean City Coffee Company
928 Boardwalk (08226-3537)
PHONE..................................609 399-5533
Joan Williamson,
Calvin Corvaia,
EMP: 6
SALES (est): 653.1K **Privately Held**
SIC: 2095 5812 Coffee roasting (except by wholesale grocers); coffee shop

(G-7689)
COFFEE COMPANY LLC
Also Called: Ocean City Coffee Company
917 Asbury Ave Unit A (08226-3587)
PHONE..................................609 398-2326
EMP: 7
SALES (est): 493.8K
SALES (corp-wide): 653.1K **Privately Held**
SIC: 2095 5812 Coffee roasting (except by wholesale grocers); coffee shop
PA: The Coffee Company L L C
928 Boardwalk
Ocean City NJ 08226
609 399-5533

(G-7690)
DAIRY MAID CONFECTIONERY CO
852 Boardwalk (08226-3633)
P.O. Box 899 (08226-0899)
PHONE..................................609 399-0100
Gene Arnone, *Controller*
EMP: 6
SALES (est): 370.3K **Privately Held**
SIC: 2064 Candy & other confectionery products

(G-7691)
M C SIGNS
323 Ocean Ave (08226-3684)
PHONE..................................609 399-7446
Mark Crego, *Owner*
EMP: 4
SQ FT: 4,500
SALES (est): 368.7K **Privately Held**
SIC: 3993 Signs, not made in custom sign painting shops; electric signs

(G-7692)
RAILING DYNAMICS INC (DH)
Also Called: R D I
3814 Waterview Blvd (08226-1836)
P.O. Box 319, Linwood (08221-0319)
PHONE..................................609 601-1300
Chris Terrels, *President*
Jonathan Gronow, *Exec VP*
Jay Penney, *Vice Pres*
Joe Russell, *Vice Pres*
Tim Meehan, *Plant Engr*
▲ **EMP:** 15
SQ FT: 22,000
SALES: 8MM
SALES (corp-wide): 1.5MM **Privately Held**
WEB: www.rdirail.com
SIC: 3315 Fence gates posts & fittings: steel
HQ: Barrette Outdoor Living, Inc.
7830 Freeway Cir
Middleburg Heights OH 44130
440 891-0790

(G-7693)
RAUHAUSERS INC
Also Called: Rauhauser's Own Make Candies
721 Asbury Ave Unit A (08226-3778)
PHONE..................................609 399-1465
Nancy Bloomdahl, *President*
Donald Bloomdahl, *Vice Pres*
EMP: 13
SQ FT: 1,500
SALES: 300K **Privately Held**
SIC: 2064 5441 Candy & other confectionery products; candy

(G-7694)
ROBERT BROWN
Also Called: Browns Awning Co
1125 West Ave 1 (08226-3078)
PHONE..................................609 398-6262
Robert Brown, *Owner*
EMP: 5
SQ FT: 950
SALES (est): 321.2K **Privately Held**
SIC: 2394 Canvas & related products

(G-7695)
SAMPLE MEDIA INC (PA)
Also Called: Ocean City Sentinel The
112 E 8th St (08226-3736)
P.O. Box 238 (08226-0238)
PHONE..................................609 399-5411
David Nahan, *President*
George Sample III, *Vice Pres*
EMP: 34 **EST:** 1881
SALES (est): 3.9MM **Privately Held**
SIC: 2752 2711 Commercial printing, lithographic; newspapers

(G-7696)
SHRIVERS SALT WTR TAFFY FUDGE
852 Boardwalk (08226-3633)
P.O. Box 899 (08226-0899)
PHONE..................................609 399-0100
Meryl Vangelov, *Principal*
EMP: 23
SALES (est): 6.2MM **Privately Held**
SIC: 5145 5441 2064 Candy; candy; chewing candy, not chewing gum

(G-7697)
TJS ICE CREAM
Also Called: T J'S Ice Cream Plus
100 E Atlantic Blvd (08226-4511)
PHONE..................................609 398-5055
Salvatore Pepe, *Owner*
EMP: 5
SALES (est): 245.6K **Privately Held**
WEB: www.tjsicecream.com
SIC: 2024 Ice cream & frozen desserts

(G-7698)
TRU TEMP SENSORS INC
113 Breton Ct (08226-2135)
PHONE..................................215 396-1550
Terry Hale, *President*
EMP: 4
SALES (est): 585.1K **Privately Held**
WEB: www.trutempsensors.com
SIC: 3823 3812 3357 Temperature measurement instruments, industrial; search & navigation equipment; nonferrous wire-drawing & insulating

---

Ocean Grove
Monmouth County

(G-7699)
COMFORT ZONE
44 Main Ave (07756-1546)
PHONE..................................732 869-9990
Steve Mandeville, *Owner*
EMP: 4 **EST:** 2000
SALES (est): 230K **Privately Held**
WEB: www.comfortzoneoceangrove.com
SIC: 7389 3231 Mounting merchandise on cards; stained glass: made from purchased glass

(G-7700)
FRANKLEN SHEET METAL CO INC
122 S Main St (07756-1014)
PHONE..................................732 988-0808
Steve Smith, *President*
Mindy Rebelo, *Office Mgr*
EMP: 10 **EST:** 1976
SQ FT: 2,000
SALES (est): 2MM **Privately Held**
SIC: 3444 Sheet metal specialties, not stamped

Ocean View
Cape May County

(G-7701)
ACTION SUPPLY INC
1413 Stagecoach Rd (08230-1305)
PHONE..................................609 390-0663
Thomas Tower, *President*
John Fennekohl, *Sales Dir*
EMP: 12
SQ FT: 5,000
SALES (est): 4.3MM **Privately Held**
WEB: www.actionsupplynj.com
SIC: 1442 5032 3273 Construction sand mining; masons' materials; ready-mixed concrete

(G-7702)
EARTHWORK ASSOCIATES INC
477 Corsons Tavern Rd (08230-1670)
PHONE..................................609 624-9395
EMP: 15 **EST:** 1947
SQ FT: 3,500
SALES (est): 1.4MM **Privately Held**
SIC: 1794 1442 Excavating Contractors & Sand And Gravel Washing

(G-7703)
MAGNETRAN INC
24 Elizabeth Ln (08230-1372)
PHONE..................................856 768-7787
George McCauley, *President*
EMP: 10 **EST:** 1979
SQ FT: 17,750
SALES (est): 890K **Privately Held**
WEB: www.magnetran.com
SIC: 3612 Electronic meter transformers

(G-7704)
OCEANVIEW MARINE WELDING LLC
414 Woodbine Ocean View R (08230-2007)
P.O. Box 516, South Seaville (08246-0516)
PHONE..................................609 624-9669
Andrew McDevitt, *Managing Prtnr*
EMP: 4
SALES (est): 334.9K **Privately Held**
SIC: 7692 3429 Welding repair; marine hardware

Oceanport
Monmouth County

(G-7705)
OUR TEAM FITNESS LLC
117 E Main St (07757-1238)
PHONE..................................848 208-5047

Jon Wells,
EMP: 4
SALES: 76.1K **Privately Held**
SIC: 7991 7372 7999 Physical fitness facilities; application computer software; physical fitness instruction

(G-7706)
ROY PRESS INC
Also Called: Roy Press Printers
57 Bridgewaters Dr Apt 17 (07757-1155)
PHONE.................................732 922-9460
Ralph Lawrence, *President*
EMP: 6 **EST:** 1886
SQ FT: 6,000
SALES (est): 625K **Privately Held**
SIC: 2752 Commercial printing, offset

(G-7707)
SHORE DRILLING INC
23 Branch Ave (07757-1016)
PHONE.................................732 935-1776
Kimberly Young Parent, *President*
Gary Parent, *Vice Pres*
EMP: 5
SALES: 700K **Privately Held**
SIC: 1381 Drilling oil & gas wells

Ogdensburg
Sussex County

(G-7708)
AJ SIRIS PRODUCTS CORP
Also Called: Accessories Plus
150 Main St (07439-1175)
P.O. Box 39 (07439-0039)
PHONE.................................973 823-0050
Donald F Ryan, *President*
John F Woods, *Corp Secy*
▲ **EMP:** 25 **EST:** 1918
SQ FT: 20,000
SALES: 10MM **Privately Held**
SIC: 5122 5199 3089 Cosmetics; bags, baskets & cases; caps, plastic

(G-7709)
CLEAR CONTROL LLC
93 Main St (07439-1236)
P.O. Box 155 (07439-0155)
PHONE.................................973 823-8200
Carl Flar, *Owner*
EMP: 6
SALES (est): 585.5K **Privately Held**
SIC: 2759 Screen printing

Old Bridge
Middlesex County

(G-7710)
ACCUMIX PHARMACEUTICALS LLC
42 Morris Dr (08857-3575)
PHONE.................................609 632-2225
Pishbhai Patel, *Managing Dir*
Patrick Patel, *Director*
Sam Patel, *Director*
EMP: 8
SALES: 1MM **Privately Held**
SIC: 8731 2834 Commercial research laboratory; proprietary drug products

(G-7711)
ALSTROM ENERGY GROUP LLC
11 Jocama Blvd Ste 11a (08857-3521)
PHONE.................................718 824-4901
EMP: 7
SALES (est): 142.3K **Privately Held**
SIC: 3621 Motors & generators

(G-7712)
BARMENSEN LABS LLC
2685 Hwy 516 (08857-2300)
PHONE.................................732 593-3515
Frank V Barone Jr,
EMP: 5
SALES (est): 575.8K **Privately Held**
SIC: 2844 Cosmetic preparations

(G-7713)
BLONDER TONGUE LABS INC (PA)
1 Jake Brown Rd (08857-1985)
PHONE.................................732 679-4000
Robert J Palle, *CEO*
Edward R Grauch, *President*
Donald Young, *Business Mgr*
Allen Horvath, *VP Mfg*
John Zirkel, *Technical Mgr*
▲ **EMP:** 117 **EST:** 1950
SQ FT: 130,000
SALES: 21.7MM **Publicly Held**
WEB: www.blondertongue.com
SIC: 3663 3699 Television broadcasting & communications equipment; television antennas (transmitting) & ground equipment; security control equipment & systems; security devices

(G-7714)
DELUXE GOURMET SPC LTD LBLTY
Also Called: Bea's Brooklyn's Best
85 Corona Ct (08857-2854)
PHONE.................................732 485-7519
Beatrissa Namm,
EMP: 14
SALES (est): 2MM **Privately Held**
SIC: 2099 Sauces: gravy, dressing & dip mixes

(G-7715)
FORMAN INDUSTRIES INC
Also Called: F I Companies
3150 Bordentown Ave (08857-9703)
PHONE.................................732 727-8100
Scott Forman, *CEO*
Ronald Sherry, *CFO*
EMP: 100
SQ FT: 39,000
SALES (est): 21.8MM **Privately Held**
WEB: www.ficompanies.com
SIC: 8711 2434 1542 1721 Consulting engineer; wood kitchen cabinets; custom builders, non-residential; interior commercial painting contractor; lighting maintenance service; safety inspection service

(G-7716)
ILKEM GRANITE & MARBLE 2 CORP
4420 Bordentown Ave (08857-1738)
PHONE.................................732 613-1457
EMP: 10
SALES (est): 1.3MM **Privately Held**
SIC: 3281 Building stone products

(G-7717)
JUST A TOUCH OF BAKING LLC
3141 Us Highway 9 (08857-2690)
PHONE.................................732 679-5123
EMP: 4
SALES (est): 269.4K **Privately Held**
SIC: 2051 Bread, cake & related products

(G-7718)
M&L POWER SYSTEMS MAINT INC
109 White Oak Ln Ste 82 (08857-1980)
PHONE.................................732 679-1800
Shriram Bagle, *Ch of Bd*
Milind Bagle, *President*
Lalita Bagle, *Admin Sec*
EMP: 25
SQ FT: 4,200
SALES: 3.7MM **Privately Held**
WEB: www.mlpower.com
SIC: 1731 3625 7629 3643 General electrical contractor; industrial electrical relays & switches; electrical equipment repair, high voltage; bus bars (electrical conductors)

(G-7719)
MADISON INDUSTRIES INC
554 Water Works Rd (08857-1731)
PHONE.................................732 727-2225
Bruce Bzura, *President*
Joel Bzura, *Vice Pres*
Phil Fusco, *Accounts Mgr*
EMP: 35 **EST:** 1963
SQ FT: 15,000

SALES (est): 7.3MM **Privately Held**
SIC: 2819 Zinc chloride; copper compounds or salts, inorganic; iron (ferric/ferrous) compounds or salts

(G-7720)
MIDHATTAN WOODWORKING CORP
3130 Bordentown Ave (08857-9703)
P.O. Box 163 (08857-0163)
PHONE.................................732 727-3020
Edmund Greco Sr, *CEO*
Edmund Greco Jr, *President*
Janine Bird, *Vice Pres*
George Greco, *Vice Pres*
Louis Marotta, *Project Mgr*
EMP: 50 **EST:** 1932
SQ FT: 112,000
SALES (est): 10.5MM **Privately Held**
WEB: www.midhattan.com
SIC: 2431 Woodwork, interior & ornamental

(G-7721)
NJ FUEL HAULERS INC
3617 Us Highway 9 (08857-3517)
PHONE.................................732 740-3681
Grigori Bruselovsky, *Principal*
EMP: 4
SALES (est): 213K **Privately Held**
SIC: 2869 Fuels

(G-7722)
OLD BRIDGE CHEMICALS INC
554 Water Works Rd (08857-1731)
PHONE.................................732 727-2225
Bruce Bzura, *President*
Joel Bzura, *Vice Pres*
Justin Bzura, *Manager*
Robert Coleman, *Manager*
Mary Paris, *Manager*
◆ **EMP:** 40 **EST:** 1968
SQ FT: 55,000
SALES (est): 15.5MM **Privately Held**
SIC: 2819 Copper compounds or salts, inorganic

(G-7723)
PFIZER INC
11 Erin Ln (08857-2756)
PHONE.................................732 591-2106
Duston Ndreu, *Associate*
EMP: 57
SALES (corp-wide): 53.6B **Publicly Held**
WEB: www.pfizer.com
SIC: 2834 Pharmaceutical preparations
PA: Pfizer Inc.
235 E 42nd St
New York NY 10017
212 733-2323

(G-7724)
PKM PANEL SYSTEMS CORP
4420 Bordentown Ave (08857-1738)
P.O. Box 272, South River (08882-0272)
PHONE.................................732 238-6760
Wallace Toto, *President*
EMP: 14 **EST:** 1971
SQ FT: 8,000
SALES (est): 2.4MM **Privately Held**
SIC: 3625 Relays & industrial controls

(G-7725)
PRIMARY SYSTEMS INC
30 State Route 18 (08857-1420)
PHONE.................................732 679-2200
Eric Alter, *President*
Scott Alter, *Vice Pres*
EMP: 13
SQ FT: 3,000
SALES (est): 3.2MM **Privately Held**
WEB: www.primarysys.com
SIC: 7373 8711 3699 Computer systems analysis & design; systems integration services; engineering services; electrical equipment & supplies

(G-7726)
QUALITY PLUS ONE CATERING INC (PA)
Also Called: Atlantic U S
10 Kerry Ct (08857-2610)
PHONE.................................732 967-1525
Joe Kowalski, *President*
Scott Kowalski, *Vice Pres*
EMP: 4

SQ FT: 7,600
SALES (est): 600K **Privately Held**
SIC: 7389 3589 Coffee service; water filters & softeners, household type

(G-7727)
REP TRADING ASSOCIATES INC
Also Called: Nifty Packaging
4 Jocama Blvd (08857-3513)
P.O. Box 161, Marlboro (07746-0161)
PHONE.................................732 591-1140
Norman Ferber, *President*
Audrey Tick, *Vice Pres*
Robyn Ferber, *Admin Sec*
▲ **EMP:** 15
SQ FT: 20,000
SALES (est): 2.5MM **Privately Held**
WEB: www.repmarkassoc.com
SIC: 3086 3842 Packaging & shipping materials, foamed plastic; adhesive tape & plasters, medicated or non-medicated

(G-7728)
SUPERIOR SIGNAL COMPANY LLC
Also Called: Superior Smoke
178 W Greystone Rd (08857-3426)
P.O. Box 96, Spotswood (08884-0096)
PHONE.................................732 251-0800
James Kovacs,
▲ **EMP:** 18 **EST:** 1943
SQ FT: 8,100
SALES (est): 3.8MM **Privately Held**
WEB: www.superiorsignal.com
SIC: 3829 7549 Measuring & controlling devices; emissions testing without repairs, automotive

(G-7729)
TRI-STATE GLASS & MIRROR INC (PA)
11a Jocama Blvd (08857-3513)
PHONE.................................732 591-5545
Michael Panebianco, *President*
EMP: 5
SQ FT: 7,100
SALES (est): 679.8K **Privately Held**
SIC: 3211 Flat glass

(G-7730)
YONKERS PLYWOOD MANUFACTURING
3130 Bordentown Ave (08857-9703)
P.O. Box 152 (08857-0152)
PHONE.................................732 727-1200
Edmund J Greco Jr, *President*
George Greco, *Vice Pres*
Steve Goldberg, *Executive*
EMP: 25
SQ FT: 112,000
SALES (est): 2.9MM **Privately Held**
SIC: 2435 Panels, hardwood plywood

Old Tappan
Bergen County

(G-7731)
ABC DIGITAL ELECTRONICS INC
Also Called: Automation Dynamics Systems
44 Country Squire Rd (07675-6837)
PHONE.................................201 666-6888
EMP: 6 **EST:** 1973
SQ FT: 10,000
SALES: 1.3MM **Privately Held**
SIC: 3825 7629 Manufactures & Services Computerized Electrical Test Systems

(G-7732)
AMERICAN COMPRESSED GASES INC (PA)
189 Central Ave (07675-7399)
P.O. Box 715 (07675-0715)
PHONE.................................201 767-3200
Ray Konrad, *Ch of Bd*
Arthur F Ramsdell Jr, *President*
Roger Hawkes, *Vice Pres*
Adam Konrad, *Vice Pres*
EMP: 21 **EST:** 1953
SQ FT: 6,000

SALES (est): 32.1MM **Privately Held**
WEB: www.dryicecorp.com
SIC: **5984** 3823 Liquefied petroleum gas
dealers; industrial instrmnts msrmnt dis-
play/control process variable

(G-7733)
ELYMAT CORP
180 Old Tappan Rd Ste 11 (07675-7048)
PHONE..............................201 767-7105
Robert Gardner, *President*
EMP: 20
SQ FT: 3,500
SALES (est): 3.9MM **Privately Held**
SIC: **3669** Intercommunication systems,
electric

(G-7734)
ELYMAT INDUSTRIES INC
180 Old Tappan Rd Ste 3 (07675-7052)
PHONE..............................201 767-7105
Robert Gardner, *President*
Roni Kaye, *Vice Pres*
Joanne Fontana, *Buyer*
Sandi Kohen, *Buyer*
Sandy McGrath, *Buyer*
EMP: 20
SQ FT: 3,500
SALES (est): 5.9MM **Privately Held**
WEB: www.elymat.com
SIC: **3669** Intercommunication systems,
electric

(G-7735)
**PEARSON TECHNOLOGY
CENTRE INC (HQ)**
Also Called: Pearson Business Services
200 Old Tappan Rd Ste 1 (07675-7005)
PHONE..............................201 767-5000
Gloria Samuels, *CEO*
Christina Rivas, *Principal*
Ken Lanfrank, *Vice Pres*
Edward Lewandowski, *Vice Pres*
Allison Longley, *Project Mgr*
▼ EMP: 2
SALES (est): 25.3MM
SALES (corp-wide): 5.3B **Privately Held**
WEB: www.informit.com
SIC: **2731** 8732 Textbooks: publishing
only, not printed on site; business re-
search service
PA: Pearson Plc
Shell Mex House
London WC2R
207 010-2000

(G-7736)
WOLF FORM CO INC
289 Orangeburgh Rd (07675-7484)
PHONE..............................201 567-6556
Bruno Ferri, *President*
Wendell Hunton, *Vice Pres*
Lorraine Hunton, *Treasurer*
EMP: 30 EST: 1928
SQ FT: 28,000
SALES (est): 2.4MM **Privately Held**
SIC: **3999** Forms: display, dress & show

(G-7737)
WORLDCAST NETWORK INC
20 Foxwood Sq S (07675-7358)
PHONE..............................201 767-2040
George Bukhbinder, *President*
Michael Galperin, *Principal*
EMP: 5
SALES (est): 610.6K **Privately Held**
SIC: **3364** Nonferrous die-castings except
aluminum

Oldwick
Hunterdon County

(G-7738)
AM BEST COMPANY INC (PA)
1 Ambest Rd (08858-7000)
PHONE..............................908 439-2200
Arthur Snyder, *President*
Douglas Woelfel, *President*
Vasilis Katsipis, *General Mgr*
Mark Dobrow, *Editor*
Caroline Saucer, *Editor*
▲ EMP: 525
SQ FT: 200,000

SALES (est): 160.8MM **Privately Held**
WEB: www.bestwire.com
SIC: **2731** 2721 2732 7323 Books: publishing only; magazines: publishing only,
not printed on site; book printing; credit
reporting services

(G-7739)
AM BEST COMPANY INC
Am Best Rd (08858)
PHONE..............................908 439-2200
Art Snyder, *Vice Pres*
EMP: 500
SALES (corp-wide): 160.8MM **Privately
Held**
WEB: www.bestwire.com
SIC: **2731** 2721 Book publishing; periodi-
cals
PA: A.M. Best Company, Inc.
1 Ambest Rd
Oldwick NJ 08858
908 439-2200

(G-7740)
MELICKS TOWN FARM INC (PA)
Old Turn Pike Rd (08858)
P.O. Box 73 (08858-0073)
PHONE..............................908 439-2318
John Melick, *CEO*
Peter Melick, *Principal*
Rebecca Melick, *Principal*
EMP: 11 EST: 1960
SALES (est): 2.5MM **Privately Held**
SIC: **0175** 0172 2099 0161 Apple or-
chard; peach orchard; grapes; cider, non-
alcoholic; vegetables & melons

Oradell
Bergen County

(G-7741)
CHR INTERNATIONAL INC
296 Kinderkamack Rd # 220 (07649-2147)
PHONE..............................201 262-8186
Catherine Huang, *President*
Arthur Rosenberg, *Vice Pres*
▲ EMP: 5
SALES (est): 1.9MM **Privately Held**
SIC: **5142** 2092 Vegetables, frozen;
seafoods, frozen: prepared

(G-7742)
**COMPUTECH APPLICATIONS
LLC**
768 Howard Ct E (07649-2419)
PHONE..............................201 261-5251
EMP: 5
SALES (est): 274.6K **Privately Held**
SIC: **7372** Prepackaged Software Services

(G-7743)
EMERSON SPEED PRINTING INC
379 Kinderkamack Rd (07649-2141)
PHONE..............................201 265-7977
Herb Kassab, *President*
EMP: 4
SQ FT: 3,000
SALES (est): 505.9K **Privately Held**
WEB: www.emersonspeedprinting.com
SIC: **2752** Photo-offset printing; commer-
cial printing, offset

(G-7744)
FULCRUM INC
660 Kinderkamack Rd # 203 (07649-1525)
PHONE..............................973 473-6900
James Maloy, *President*
Karl Nowosielski, *Vice Pres*
▲ EMP: 8
SQ FT: 3,900
SALES (est): 1.3MM **Privately Held**
WEB: www.fulcruminc.net
SIC: **3545** Scales, measuring (machinists'
precision tools)

(G-7745)
HEAD PIECE HEAVEN
449 2nd St (07649-1715)
PHONE..............................201 262-0788
Marcia Morris, *Owner*
EMP: 5
SALES (est): 420.4K **Privately Held**
SIC: **2335** Wedding gowns & dresses

(G-7746)
R T I INC
Also Called: Rti Computer Services
401 Hasbrouck Blvd (07649-2263)
PHONE..............................201 261-5852
Richard Tashjian, *President*
EMP: 25
SQ FT: 4,000
SALES: 1MM **Privately Held**
SIC: **3577** 5045 5734 7373 Computer
peripheral equipment; computers, periph-
erals & software; computer & software
stores; computer integrated systems de-
sign; computer peripheral equipment re-
pair & maintenance; computer related
consulting services

(G-7747)
S J T IMAGING INC
475 Kinderkamack Rd Ste 2 (07649-1545)
PHONE..............................201 262-7744
Harry J Abrahamsen, *President*
EMP: 92
SQ FT: 14,000
SALES: 25MM **Privately Held**
WEB: www.sjtimaging.com
SIC: **7335** 2759 8711 Commercial print-
ing; mechanical engineering; color sepa-
ration, photographic & movie film

(G-7748)
WEBER PACKAGING INC
494 Demarest Ave (07649-1703)
PHONE..............................201 262-6022
Lisa Weber, *President*
EMP: 4
SQ FT: 3,500
SALES (est): 648.7K **Privately Held**
WEB: www.webdesign.com
SIC: **2653** 5113 7336 Boxes, corrugated:
made from purchased materials; corru-
gated & solid fiber boxes; package design

Orange
Essex County

(G-7749)
**ALBERONA WELDING & IRON
WORKS**
452 Scotland Rd (07050-2205)
PHONE..............................973 674-3375
Anthony Prioletti, *President*
EMP: 6
SQ FT: 5,000
SALES: 1MM **Privately Held**
SIC: **1799** 3449 3446 Welding on site;
miscellaneous metalwork; architectural
metalwork

(G-7750)
**AMERICAN FOOD & BEV INDS
LLC**
50 S Center St Ste 20 (07050-3530)
PHONE..............................347 241-9827
EMP: 55
SALES (est): 1.7MM **Privately Held**
SIC: **2037** 5149 2099 Fruit juices; juices;
seasonings, sauces & extracts; vinegar

(G-7751)
**BELLEVILLE SCALE &
BALANCE LLC**
50 S Center St Ste 13 (07050-3530)
P.O. Box 540 (07051-0540)
PHONE..............................973 759-4487
Fax: 973 676-9778
▲ EMP: 5
SALES (est): 450K **Privately Held**
SIC: **3545** Mfg Machine Tool Accessories

(G-7752)
BERENNIAL INTERNATIONAL
Also Called: Instant Printing
355 Main St (07050-2703)
PHONE..............................973 675-6266
Bharati Tolia, *President*
EMP: 4
SQ FT: 1,000
SALES (est): 500K **Privately Held**
SIC: **2752** 7334 Commercial printing, off-
set; photocopying & duplicating services

(G-7753)
EAST TRADING WEST INV LLC
Also Called: American Traffic & St Sign Co
200 S Jefferson St (07050-1409)
PHONE..............................973 678-0800
M G Khaleeli, *President*
▲ EMP: 9
SQ FT: 7,500
SALES: 811.7K **Privately Held**
SIC: **3993** 5099 Signs, not made in cus-
tom sign painting shops; signs, except
electric

(G-7754)
LYCIRET CORP
377 Crane St (07050-2602)
P.O. Box 759 (07051-0759)
PHONE..............................973 882-0322
Morris Zelkha, *President*
Benjamin Regev, *CFO*
EMP: 46
SQ FT: 120,000
SALES (est): 3.6MM
SALES (corp-wide): 64.2B **Privately Held**
WEB: www.pharmachem.com
SIC: **5169** 2834 Chemicals & allied prod-
ucts; pharmaceutical preparations
HQ: Lycored Ltd
60 Hebron Rd.
Beer Sheva 84244
732 327-323

(G-7755)
LYCORED CORP (DH)
Also Called: Lycored USA
377 Crane St (07050-2602)
P.O. Box 759 (07051-0759)
PHONE..............................973 882-0322
Doug Lynch, *President*
Rony Patishi, *Chairman*
Michael Reuben, *Vice Pres*
Sarah Pullen, *Prdtn Mgr*
ADI Golan, *Purchasing*
◆ EMP: 49
SALES: 50MM
SALES (corp-wide): 64.2B **Privately Held**
SIC: **2023** Dietary supplements, dairy &
non-dairy based
HQ: Lycored Ltd
60 Hebron Rd.
Beer Sheva 84244
732 327-323

(G-7756)
METFAB STEEL WORKS LLC
560 Freeman St (07050-1325)
PHONE..............................973 675-7676
Edward Huneke, *Production*
Lorraine Murray,
EMP: 19
SQ FT: 5,000
SALES (est): 3.7MM **Privately Held**
SIC: **3441** Fabricated structural metal

(G-7757)
**NEWARK TRADE
TYPOGRAPHERS**
Also Called: Newark Trade Digital Graphics
177 Oakwood Ave (07050-3911)
P.O. Box 379 (07051-0379)
PHONE..............................973 674-3727
Robert Wislocky, *President*
EMP: 18 EST: 1938
SQ FT: 12,000
SALES (est): 2.3MM **Privately Held**
WEB: www.newarktrade.com
SIC: **2791** Typographic composition, for the
printing trade

(G-7758)
PRISM SHEET METAL INC
50 S Center St Ste 9 (07050-3530)
PHONE..............................973 673-0213
Nicholas Catone, *President*
Richard Smith, *Vice Pres*
EMP: 6
SALES: 2MM **Privately Held**
SIC: **3444** Sheet metalwork

(G-7759)
RESOLV CORPORATION
164 Elmwynd Dr (07050-3111)
PHONE..............................973 220-5141
Saif Aghi, *President*
Syed A Rizvi, *Vice Pres*
▲ EMP: 10 EST: 1995

SALES (est): 700K Privately Held
WEB: www.resolvcorp.com
SIC: 3544 Special dies, tools, jigs & fixtures

(G-7760)
SAVIGNANO FOOD CORP
Also Called: Andrea Company
107 S Jefferson St (07050-1512)
PHONE..................................973 673-3355
Michael Savignano, *President*
▲ EMP: 50
SQ FT: 3,000
SALES (est): 9.4MM Privately Held
WEB: www.andreafoods.com
SIC: 2038 5411 Ethnic foods, frozen; grocery stores, independent

(G-7761)
SERRANIS BAKERY
Also Called: Orange Sanitary
114 S Essex Ave (07050-2612)
PHONE..................................973 678-1777
William Serrani, *President*
Jeanne Serrani, *Vice Pres*
EMP: 12
SQ FT: 4,800
SALES (est): 1.6MM Privately Held
SIC: 5149 5461 2051 Bakery products; bread; bread, cake & related products

(G-7762)
SPS ALFACHEM INC (PA)
164 Elmwynd Dr (07050-3111)
PHONE..................................973 676-5141
Syed Rizvi, *President*
EMP: 7
SALES (est): 795.5K Privately Held
SIC: 8733 5047 2865 8731 Biotechnical research, noncommercial; diagnostic equipment, medical; food dyes or colors, synthetic; biotechnical research, commercial

(G-7763)
T & E INDUSTRIES INC
215 Watchung Ave (07050-1717)
PHONE..................................973 672-5454
Edward McEntee, *President*
Thomas Vanleet, *Manager*
▼ EMP: 45 EST: 1961
SQ FT: 30,000
SALES (est): 6.6MM Privately Held
WEB: www.teindustries.com
SIC: 3679 Hermetic seals for electronic equipment

(G-7764)
TRYCO TOOL & MFG CO INC
363 S Jefferson St (07050-1393)
PHONE..................................973 674-6867
Nelson Melillo Sr, *President*
Jim Heasty, *General Mgr*
Arthur Stasiuk, *General Mgr*
Vera Melillo, *Corp Secy*
Arthur Melillo, *VP Mfg*
EMP: 41 EST: 1940
SQ FT: 40,000
SALES (est): 10.6MM Privately Held
WEB: www.trycotool.com
SIC: 3544 3469 Die sets for metal stamping (presses); metal stampings

(G-7765)
UNICORP
291 Cleveland St (07050-2817)
P.O. Box 280 (07051-0280)
PHONE..................................973 674-1700
Steven Mercadante, *Owner*
Sireeta Brown, *Sales Staff*
▲ EMP: 150
SQ FT: 28,000
SALES (est): 23MM Privately Held
WEB: www.unicorpinc.com
SIC: 3678 3429 Electronic connectors; manufactured hardware (general)

Oxford
Warren County

(G-7766)
TILCON NEW YORK INC
Also Called: Oxford Quarry
Mount Pisgah Ave (07863)
P.O. Box 120 (07863-0120)
PHONE..................................800 789-7625
Tim Rooks, *Plant Mgr*
EMP: 45
SALES (corp-wide): 30.6B Privately Held
WEB: www.tilcon.com
SIC: 2951 Asphalt paving mixtures & blocks
HQ: Tilcon New York Inc.
9 Entin Rd
Parsippany NJ 07054
973 366-7741

Palisades Park
Bergen County

(G-7767)
BBM GROUP LLC
280 Broad Ave Fl 3 (07650-1574)
PHONE..................................201 482-6500
Chang Sik Kim, *President*
Dukwoo Lee, *Vice Pres*
▲ EMP: 7
SALES (est): 1.4MM Privately Held
SIC: 2342 Bras, girdles & allied garments

(G-7768)
BEAR USA INC (PA)
460 Bergen Blvd Ste 370 (07650-2358)
PHONE..................................201 943-4748
Thomas Hong, *President*
Albert Hong, *Vice Pres*
Robert Hong, *Vice Pres*
▲ EMP: 11
SQ FT: 34,000
SALES (est): 1MM Privately Held
WEB: www.bearusa.com
SIC: 2329 2339 3021 Men's & boys' leather, wool & down-filled outerwear; men's & boys' sportswear & athletic clothing; women's & misses' outerwear; women's & misses' athletic clothing & sportswear; shoes, rubber or plastic molded to fabric

(G-7769)
BERGEN INSTANT PRINTING INC
14 State Rt 5 1 (07650-1414)
PHONE..................................201 945-7303
Bill Ackerman, *President*
William Ackerman, *Vice Pres*
Louise Perlstein, *Office Mgr*
EMP: 6
SALES (est): 763.8K Privately Held
SIC: 2752 Commercial printing, offset

(G-7770)
BSC USA LLC
Also Called: World Impro
111 Grand Ave Ste 220 (07650-1035)
PHONE..................................908 487-4437
Namik Shakhpelangov, *Mng Member*
Fahad Sheikh, *Manager*
EMP: 10
SQ FT: 2,500
SALES (est): 1.2MM Privately Held
SIC: 2033 5141 Fruit juices: packaged in cans, jars, etc.; food brokers

(G-7771)
CHENILLE PRODUCTS INC
30 Henry Ave (07650-1114)
PHONE..................................201 703-1917
Alexander Dimant, *President*
Joan Dimant, *Vice Pres*
EMP: 11 EST: 1971
SQ FT: 10,000
SALES (est): 700K Privately Held
SIC: 2397 2395 Schiffli machine embroideries; emblems, embroidered; embroidery products, except schiffli machine

---

(G-7772)
DELTA CORRUGATED PPR PDTS CORP
199 W Ruby Ave (07650-1088)
PHONE..................................201 941-1910
Walter Lieb, *President*
Ira Parker, *Vice Pres*
Nick Canale, *Plant Mgr*
Michael Carle, *CFO*
Andrew Paer, *Info Tech Mgr*
▲ EMP: 190 EST: 1959
SQ FT: 150,000
SALES (est): 45.3MM Privately Held
SIC: 2653 Boxes, corrugated: made from purchased materials

(G-7773)
ESD PROFESSIONAL INC
Also Called: Izunami
468a Commercial Ave (07650-1270)
PHONE..................................212 300-7673
Jinwoo James Choi, *President*
EMP: 2 EST: 2014
SALES (est): 1.5MM Privately Held
SIC: 3999 5087 5961 Barber & beauty shop equipment; beauty parlor equipment & supplies; general merchandise, mail order

(G-7774)
MICROSIGNALS INC
Also Called: MSI
29 Fairview St Ste 1a (07650-1085)
PHONE..................................800 225-4508
EMP: 50
SALES (est): 1.5MM Privately Held
SIC: 3663 3677 3612 Mfg Radio/Tv Communication Equipment Mfg Electronic Coils/Transformers Mfg Transformers

(G-7775)
NORTH JRSEY PRSTHTICS ORTHTICS
39 Broad Ave (07650-1436)
PHONE..................................201 943-4448
Gary Marano, *President*
Anthony Marano, *Vice Pres*
EMP: 6
SALES (est): 640K Privately Held
SIC: 3842 Prosthetic appliances; orthopedic appliances

(G-7776)
PALISADES MAGNOLIA PRPTS LLC
169 Roosevelt Pl Unit B (07650-1152)
PHONE..................................201 424-7180
Jerry Milsap, *Principal*
EMP: 4 EST: 2015
SALES (est): 101.4K Privately Held
SIC: 2711 Newspapers

(G-7777)
PRECIOUS METAL PROCESSING CONS
430 Bergen Blvd (07650-2320)
PHONE..................................201 944-8053
Randy Epner, *President*
EMP: 4
SQ FT: 2,000
SALES (est): 400K Privately Held
WEB: www.preciousmetals-pmpc.com
SIC: 3549 Metalworking machinery

(G-7778)
ROYAL CREST HOME FASHIONS INC
170 Fair St (07650-1222)
PHONE..................................201 461-4600
Ron Haboush, *President*
▲ EMP: 5
SALES (est): 521.3K Privately Held
SIC: 2392 Shower curtains: made from purchased materials; tablecloths: made from purchased materials

(G-7779)
SUSHI HOUSE INC
Also Called: Gowasabi
225 Commercial Ave (07650-1109)
PHONE..................................201 482-0609
Alex Kim, *Ch of Bd*
Sung Choe, *Senior VP*
EMP: 25

SQ FT: 11,000
SALES: 10MM Privately Held
WEB: www.gowasabi.com
SIC: 2091 2092 5812 Canned & cured fish & seafoods; fresh or frozen packaged fish; caterers

(G-7780)
UNITED POS SOLUTIONS INC
Also Called: Up Solution
535 Broad Ave (07650-1607)
PHONE..................................800 303-2567
Lee Chang, *Manager*
EMP: 4 Privately Held
SIC: 3578 Cash registers
PA: United Pos Solutions Inc.
255 Route 17 S
Hackensack NJ 07601

Palmyra
Burlington County

(G-7781)
ARMOTEK INDUSTRIES INC
1 Roto Ave (08065)
PHONE..................................856 829-4585
John Burgess, *Vice Pres*
EMP: 48 EST: 1946
SQ FT: 70,000
SALES (est): 4.6MM Privately Held
WEB: www.armotek.com
SIC: 2759 Engraving
PA: Pamarco Technologies Llc
235 E 11th Ave
Roselle NJ 07203

(G-7782)
DEVECE & SHAFFER INC
400 Legion Ave (08065-2441)
P.O. Box 201 (08065-0201)
PHONE..................................856 829-7282
William De Vece Jr, *President*
EMP: 7
SQ FT: 5,000
SALES (est): 1.7MM Privately Held
SIC: 2752 2791 2789 Commercial printing, offset; typesetting; bookbinding & related work

(G-7783)
HERCULES WELDING & MACHINE CO
618 W 5th St (08065-2407)
PHONE..................................856 829-1820
Edward Beddall Jr, *President*
Francis B Beddall Jr, *Vice Pres*
Kathleen Beddall, *Corp Secy*
EMP: 4 EST: 1913
SQ FT: 4,000
SALES: 270K Privately Held
SIC: 3599 Machine shop, jobbing & repair

(G-7784)
LYDEM LLC
1 E Broad St (08065-1604)
PHONE..................................856 566-1419
Lily Shekhter, *Principal*
EMP: 5
SALES (est): 698.4K Privately Held
SIC: 2834 Solutions, pharmaceutical

(G-7785)
PAMARCO GLOBAL GRAPHICS INC
1 Roto Ave (08065)
PHONE..................................856 829-4585
John Stubblefield, *Vice Pres*
Kent Jones, *Technical Staff*
EMP: 10 Privately Held
SIC: 3555 Printing trades machinery
HQ: Pamarco Global Graphics, Inc.
235 E 11th Ave
Roselle NJ 07203
908 241-1200

(G-7786)
THEODORE E MOZER INC
14 E 4th St (08065-1503)
P.O. Box 25 (08065-0025)
PHONE..................................856 829-1432
Theodore E Mozer Jr, *President*
Thomas Mozer, *Vice Pres*
EMP: 20

▲ = Import ▼=Export
◆ =Import/Export

SQ FT: 16,000
SALES (est): 3.1MM **Privately Held**
WEB: www.theodoremozer.com
SIC: 3444 3443 3441 Sheet metal specialties, not stamped; fabricated plate work (boiler shop); fabricated structural metal

Paramus
Bergen County

(G-7787)
ADIDAS NORTH AMERICA INC
1 Garden State Plz (07652-2417)
PHONE.................................201 843-4555
EMP: 4
SALES (corp-wide): 25B **Privately Held**
SIC: 2329 Athletic (warmup, sweat & jogging) suits: men's & boys'
HQ: Adidas North America, Inc.
3449 N Anchor St Ste 500
Portland OR 97217
971 234-2300

(G-7788)
ALTERNATE SIDE STREET SUSPENDE
Also Called: Parking Survival Experts
16 Arcadian Way Ste C1 (07652-1291)
PHONE.................................201 291-7878
Glen Bulofsky, *President*
EMP: 5
SALES (est): 617.2K **Privately Held**
SIC: 2721 Periodicals

(G-7789)
AUSOME LLC
80 E State Rt 4 Ste 290 (07652-2661)
PHONE.................................732 951-8818
David Tsu, *CEO*
▲ EMP: 6
SALES (est): 121.5K **Privately Held**
SIC: 2064 Candy & other confectionery products

(G-7790)
AZAR INTERNATIONAL INC (PA)
Also Called: Azar Displays
80 W Century Rd Ste 400 (07652-1467)
P.O. Box 567 (07653-0567)
PHONE.................................845 624-8808
Elazar Cohen, *CEO*
▲ EMP: 50
SALES (est): 8.5MM **Privately Held**
WEB: www.azardisplays.com
SIC: 3993 Displays & cutouts, window & lobby

(G-7791)
B&B IMAGING LLC
Also Called: Cartridge World Paramus
733 Bush Pl (07652-4005)
PHONE.................................201 261-3131
Robert Doyle, *CEO*
Yong Cho, *COO*
EMP: 9
SQ FT: 700
SALES (est): 871.2K **Privately Held**
SIC: 3861 5085 7389 5045 Toners, prepared photographic (not made in chemical plants); ink, printers'; printers' services: folding, collating; printers, computer

(G-7792)
BARRINGTON PRESS INC (PA)
Also Called: PIP Printing
37 Spring Valley Ave (07652-2637)
PHONE.................................201 843-6556
Paul Ramirez, *CEO*
Paul E Ramirez, *President*
Linda Ramirez, *Corp Secy*
EMP: 11
SQ FT: 6,000
SALES: 1.9MM **Privately Held**
WEB: www.barringtonpress.com
SIC: 2752 Commercial printing, offset

(G-7793)
BNP MEDIA INC
Also Called: Stone World Magazine
210 E Rte 4 Ste 203 (07652-5103)
PHONE.................................201 291-9001

Alex Bachrach, *Branch Mgr*
EMP: 5
SQ FT: 3,700
SALES (corp-wide): 158.1MM **Privately Held**
SIC: 2721 Trade journals: publishing only, not printed on site
PA: Bnp Media, Inc.
2401 W Big Beaver Rd # 700
Troy MI 48084
248 362-3700

(G-7794)
COMMERCE ENTERPRISES INC
61 S Paramus Rd Ste 135 (07652-1266)
PHONE.................................201 368-2100
EMP: 12
SALES (est): 910K **Privately Held**
SIC: 2721 Magazine Publishing Not Printed On Site

(G-7795)
CRANIAL TECHNOLOGIES INC
115 W Century Rd Ste 280 (07652-1459)
PHONE.................................201 265-3993
Jeannie Pomatto, *President*
EMP: 50
SALES (est): 3.5MM **Privately Held**
WEB: www.cranialtechnologies.com
SIC: 2241 3841 Hat band fabrics; surgical & medical instruments
PA: Cranial Technologies, Inc.
1395 W Auto Dr
Tempe AZ 85284

(G-7796)
CREAMY CREATION LLC (DH)
61 S Paramus Rd Ste 535 (07652-1257)
PHONE.................................585 344-3300
Diederik C Van Dijk, *CFO*
EMP: 8
SALES (est): 844.3K
SALES (corp-wide): 13.2B **Privately Held**
WEB: www.creamy-creation.com
SIC: 2085 Ethyl alcohol for beverage purposes
HQ: Frieslandcampina Ingredients North America, Inc
61 S Paramus Rd Ste 535
Paramus NJ 07652
201 655-7780

(G-7797)
CURTISS-WRIGHT SURFC TECH LLC (HQ)
80 E Rte 4 Ste 310 (07652-2662)
PHONE.................................201 843-7800
Kevin Kobus, *General Mgr*
Helmut Watko, *VP Opers*
Rosemarie Finizio, *Human Resources*
Ed Weyand, *Accounts Mgr*
David Rivellini, *Mng Member*
EMP: 10
SQ FT: 7,500
SALES: 300MM
SALES (corp-wide): 2.4B **Publicly Held**
SIC: 3398 Metal heat treating
PA: Curtiss-Wright Corporation
130 Harbour Place Dr # 300
Davidson NC 28036
704 869-4600

(G-7798)
DMV-FNTERRA EXCIPIENTS USA LLC
61 S Paramus Rd Ste 535 (07652-1257)
PHONE.................................609 858-2111
Gerhard Pool, *COO*
Sam Steffan, *Officer*
Hermans Ermens,
◆ EMP: 4 EST: 2008
SQ FT: 1,982
SALES (est): 639K
SALES (corp-wide): 51MM **Privately Held**
SIC: 2834 Pharmaceutical preparations
PA: Dmv-Fonterra Excipients Gmbh & Co. Kg
Klever Str. 187
Goch 47574
282 392-8877

Alex Bachrach, *Branch Mgr*

(G-7799)
EUROPEAN IMPORTS OF LA INC
Also Called: Ebocent
25 Columbine Rd (07652-2144)
PHONE.................................973 536-1823
Jorge E Zuniga, *President*
EMP: 15
SQ FT: 700
SALES (est): 818.6K **Privately Held**
SIC: 3911 Jewelry, precious metal

(G-7800)
FANTASIA INDUSTRIES CORP
20 Park Pl (07652-3674)
PHONE.................................201 261-7070
Paul Bogosian, *Ch of Bd*
Archie Bogosian, *Corp Secy*
Juanita Bogosian, *Vice Pres*
Nick Parrilli, *Plant Mgr*
John Perrone, *VP Sales*
EMP: 25 EST: 1964
SQ FT: 28,000
SALES (est): 10.1MM **Privately Held**
WEB: www.fantasiahaircare.com
SIC: 2844 Hair coloring preparations

(G-7801)
GANZ BROTHERS INC
12 Mulberry Ct (07652-1350)
PHONE.................................201 820-1975
Christopher Ganz, *President*
Jonathan Ganz, *Vice Pres*
EMP: 14 EST: 1895
SQ FT: 20,000
SALES (est): 1MM **Privately Held**
WEB: www.ganzbrothers.com
SIC: 3565 5084 Packaging machinery; industrial machinery & equipment

(G-7802)
GASS CUSTOM WOODWORKING
169 Birchwood Rd (07652-1954)
PHONE.................................201 493-9282
Cynthia V Gass, *Principal*
EMP: 4
SALES (est): 446.3K **Privately Held**
SIC: 2431 Millwork

(G-7803)
GENERAL MCH EXPERIMENTAL WORKS
117 Gertrude Ave Ste 1 (07652-2593)
PHONE.................................201 843-9035
Paul Oelkrug, *President*
Regina Oelkrug, *Vice Pres*
EMP: 5
SQ FT: 3,400
SALES (est): 487.9K **Privately Held**
SIC: 3599 Machine shop, jobbing & repair

(G-7804)
GREAT EASTERN COLOR LITH
210 E State Rt 4 Ste 211 (07652-5103)
PHONE.................................201 843-5656
Lou Peretta, *Manager*
EMP: 7
SALES (corp-wide): 15.1MM **Privately Held**
WEB: www.magnapublishing.com
SIC: 5113 2752 Industrial & personal service paper; commercial printing, lithographic
PA: Great Eastern Color Lithographic Corporation
46 Violet Ave
Poughkeepsie NY 12601
845 454-7420

(G-7805)
HAYMARKET MEDIA INC
140 E Ridgewood Ave 370s (07652-3923)
PHONE.................................201 799-4800
Amey Bordikar, *President*
Nanisico Lee, *Owner*
Gemma Boyd, *General Mgr*
Simon Kanter, *Editor*
Rick Maffei, *Editor*
EMP: 5
SALES (corp-wide): 219.2MM **Privately Held**
SIC: 2721 Magazines: publishing only, not printed on site

HQ: Haymarket Media, Inc.
275 7th Ave Fl 10
New York NY 10001
646 638-6000

(G-7806)
HOSPITALITY GLASS BRANDS LLC
52 Forest Ave (07652-5200)
PHONE.................................800 869-8258
Chris Coursen, *President*
Tim Aid, *Regional Mgr*
Donald Miknis, *Vice Pres*
EMP: 20
SQ FT: 3,000
SALES (est): 1.6MM **Privately Held**
SIC: 3229 Glassware, industrial

(G-7807)
INFORMATION TECHNOLGY CORP
121 Gertrude Ave (07652-2515)
PHONE.................................201 556-1999
Cindy Garcia, *President*
EMP: 5
SALES (est): 544.7K **Privately Held**
SIC: 3575 Computer terminals

(G-7808)
IVY PHARAMA INC
140 E Ridgewood Ave # 415 (07652-3917)
PHONE.................................201 221-4179
EMP: 4
SALES (est): 275.1K **Privately Held**
SIC: 2834 Pharmaceutical preparations

(G-7809)
JAY-BEE LAMP & SHADE CO INC
Also Called: Liberty Lamp & Shade
540 Salem St (07652-5659)
PHONE.................................201 265-0762
Louis Schurman, *President*
Robert Schurman, *Asst Sec*
EMP: 5 EST: 1956
SQ FT: 12,000
SALES (est): 618.9K **Privately Held**
SIC: 3645 5719 Lamp & light shades; lamps & lamp shades

(G-7810)
JE TAIME SHOES
Garden State Plz Mall (07652)
PHONE.................................201 845-7463
David Vigilance, *Manager*
EMP: 5 EST: 2014
SALES (est): 286.1K **Privately Held**
SIC: 3144 Dress shoes, women's

(G-7811)
JOURNAL NEWS V INC
424 Acorn Dr (07652-4144)
PHONE.................................201 986-1458
Suresh Patel, *Principal*
EMP: 4
SALES (est): 200.5K **Privately Held**
SIC: 2711 Newspapers, publishing & printing

(G-7812)
KIEHLS SINCE 1851 INC
355 N Highway 17 (07652)
PHONE.................................201 843-1125
Klaus Heidegger, *Branch Mgr*
EMP: 8
SALES (corp-wide): 4.4B **Privately Held**
SIC: 2834 Pharmaceutical preparations
HQ: Kiehl's Since 1851, Inc.
435 Hudson St Fl 5
New York NY 10014
917 606-2740

(G-7813)
KINGSTER LLC
618 Mazur Ave (07652-1748)
PHONE.................................310 951-5127
Katie Donnelly, *Vice Pres*
EMP: 4
SALES (est): 126.8K **Privately Held**
SIC: 7372 Application computer software

(G-7814)
KOCH MDLAR PROCESS SYSTEMS LLC (PA)
45 Eisenhower Dr Ste 350 (07652-1416)
PHONE.................................201 368-2929

Len Miceli, *Vice Pres*
Chris Loftus, *Project Mgr*
Brendan Cross, *Engineer*
Roger Cuentas, *Engineer*
Jim Denoble, *Engineer*
◆ **EMP:** 70
SQ FT: 24,000
SALES (est): 29MM **Privately Held**
WEB: www.modularprocess.com
SIC: 3559 8711 Chemical machinery &
   equipment; consulting engineer; chemical
   engineering

(G-7815)
**LLOYD GERSTNER &
PARTNERS LLC**
Also Called: LG&p In-Store Agency
650 From Rd Ste 552 (07652-3553)
PHONE.....................201 634-9099
Paul Dundas, *Vice Pres*
Eileen Ford, *Vice Pres*
Sacha Joseph, *Vice Pres*
Tricia Kerr, *Vice Pres*
Bart Manion, *Vice Pres*
▲ **EMP:** 38
SQ FT: 6,000
SALES (est): 10MM **Privately Held**
SIC: 2542 8742 Fixtures, store: except
   wood; fixtures: display, office or store: ex-
   cept wood; merchandising consultant

(G-7816)
LUNET INC
Also Called: Sir Speedy
300 N State Rt 17 Ste 3 (07652-2918)
PHONE.....................201 261-3883
Louis Sallemi, *President*
Ronald Sallemi, *Vice Pres*
EMP: 7
SQ FT: 2,000
SALES (est): 990.6K **Privately Held**
SIC: 2752 2791 2789 Commercial print-
   ing, lithographic; typesetting; bookbinding
   & related work

(G-7817)
LUX HOME INC
Also Called: Pella Window Store
483 N Rte 17 (07652-3001)
PHONE.....................845 623-2821
Ellen Harmon, *Manager*
EMP: 7
SALES (corp-wide): 35.7MM **Privately
Held**
WEB: www.luxhome.com
SIC: 5211 2431 Door & window products;
   millwork
PA: Lux Home, Inc.
   4 Dedrick Pl
   West Caldwell NJ 07006
   973 575-0200

(G-7818)
METAL IMPROVEMENT CO INC
80 E Rte 4 Ste 310 (07652-2662)
PHONE.....................253 677-8604
David Adams, *President*
Paul Beeksma, *Sales Mgr*
EMP: 5
SALES (est): 287.5K **Privately Held**
SIC: 3398 Metal heat treating

(G-7819)
**METAL IMPROVEMENT
COMPANY LLC (HQ)**
Also Called: Curtiss-Wright Surface Tech
80 E Rte 4 Ste 310 (07652-2662)
PHONE.....................201 843-7800
David M Rivellini, *President*
William Bauer, *Senior VP*
Helmut Watko, *Senior VP*
David B Francis, *Vice Pres*
Gary Ogilby, *Vice Pres*
▲ **EMP:** 20
SQ FT: 5,000
SALES (est): 368.4MM
SALES (corp-wide): 2.4B **Publicly Held**
WEB: www.mic-houston.com
SIC: 3398 Shot peening (treating steel to
   reduce fatigue)
PA: Curtiss-Wright Corporation
   130 Harbour Place Dr # 300
   Davidson NC 28036
   704 869-4600

(G-7820)
**MICROWIZE TECHNOLOGY INC
(PA)**
1 Kalisa Way Ste 104 (07652-3538)
PHONE.....................800 955-0321
Robert Gabriel, *President*
Fred Dawli, *Vice Pres*
EMP: 18 **EST:** 1997
SALES (est): 4.3MM **Privately Held**
WEB: www.microwize.com
SIC: 7372 Prepackaged software

(G-7821)
ML WOODWORK INC
348 Bullard Ave (07652-4635)
PHONE.....................201 953-2175
Michal Lenczewski, *Principal*
EMP: 4
SALES (est): 400.7K **Privately Held**
SIC: 2431 Millwork

(G-7822)
MOVADO GROUP INC (PA)
650 From Rd Ste 375 (07652-3556)
PHONE.....................201 267-8000
Efraim Grinberg, *Ch of Bd*
Libby Diorio, *Area Mgr*
Alex Grinberg, *Senior VP*
Frank A Morelli, *Senior VP*
Mitchell C Sussis, *Senior VP*
◆ **EMP:** 277
SQ FT: 98,300
SALES (est): 679.5MM **Publicly Held**
WEB: www.movado-outlet.com
SIC: 3873 3915 7631 Watches, clocks,
   watchcases & parts; jewel preparing: in-
   struments, tools, watches & jewelry;
   watch repair

(G-7823)
MY HOUSE KITCHEN INC
492 N Rte 17 (07652-3004)
PHONE.....................201 262-9000
Okan Kinaci, *President*
EMP: 4
SALES (est): 217.7K **Privately Held**
SIC: 2511 Wood household furniture

(G-7824)
**NASSAUS WINDOW FASHIONS
INC**
799 N State Rt 17 (07652-3112)
PHONE.....................201 689-6030
Lewis Nassau, *President*
Bruce Heyman, *President*
Robert Mittenmaier, *Treasurer*
EMP: 23
SQ FT: 13,800
SALES (est): 2.3MM **Privately Held**
SIC: 5714 5719 2591 2391 Curtains;
   draperies; bedding (sheets, blankets,
   spreads & pillows); drapery hardware &
   blinds & shades; curtains & draperies

(G-7825)
NORMAN WEIL INC
Also Called: Norman Weil Textile
140 E Ridgewood Ave # 415 (07652-3917)
PHONE.....................201 940-7345
Norman Weil III, *President*
▲ **EMP:** 7
SALES (est): 5MM **Privately Held**
SIC: 2299 Batting, wadding, padding & fill-
   ings

(G-7826)
PAC TEAM AMERICA INC (PA)
205 Robin Rd Ste 200 (07652-1455)
PHONE.....................201 599-5000
Alain Borle, *CEO*
Eric Zuckerman, *President*
Dieter Pasewaldt, *CFO*
▲ **EMP:** 30
SALES (est): 25MM **Privately Held**
SIC: 2541 7336 Store & office display
   cases & fixtures; package design

(G-7827)
**POWER PACKAGING SERVICES
CORP**
20 Park Pl (07652-3617)
PHONE.....................201 261-2566
Don Simmons, *CEO*
EMP: 3
SQ FT: 400

SALES: 4MM **Privately Held**
SIC: 3999 Advertising display products

(G-7828)
RADCOM EQUIPMENT INC
10 Forest Ave (07652-5242)
PHONE.....................201 518-0033
AVI Zamir, *President*
Hilik Itman, *Vice Pres*
Amir N Mualem, *Engineer*
Ariella Michael, *Controller*
Yael Witting, *Controller*
EMP: 7
SQ FT: 6,500
SALES (est): 1.3MM
SALES (corp-wide): 9.1MM **Privately
Held**
WEB: www.radcomusa.com
SIC: 3825 3829 3577 Semiconductor test
   equipment; measuring & controlling de-
   vices; computer peripheral equipment
PA: Radcom Ltd
   24 Wallenberg Raul
   Tel Aviv-Jaffa 69719
   364 550-55

(G-7829)
RENELL LABEL PRINT INC
15 Sunflower Ave (07652-3701)
P.O. Box 403, Saddle River (07458-0403)
PHONE.....................201 652-6544
W Rene Huber, *President*
David Huber, *Vice Pres*
Melody L Huber, *Treasurer*
EMP: 9
SQ FT: 3,000
SALES (est): 980K **Privately Held**
WEB: www.renell.com
SIC: 2679 2672 Labels, paper: made from
   purchased material; coated & laminated
   paper

(G-7830)
ROYALE PIGMENTS & CHEM INC
Also Called: Awsm Industries
12 N State Rt 17 Ste 203 (07652-2644)
PHONE.....................201 845-4666
John Logue, *CEO*
Lindsay Logue, *President*
▲ **EMP:** 10
SQ FT: 4,000
SALES (est): 10.9MM **Privately Held**
SIC: 5169 2869 Chemicals, industrial &
   heavy; industrial organic chemicals

(G-7831)
SHO EYEWORKS
240 Frisch Ct Ste 104 (07652-5248)
PHONE.....................201 568-5500
Edward Choy, *Principal*
EMP: 7
SALES (est): 865.8K **Privately Held**
SIC: 3851 Eyeglasses, lenses & frames

(G-7832)
SIMEX MEDICAL IMAGING INC
68 Alden Rd (07652-3731)
PHONE.....................201 490-0204
Abraham Danan, *President*
EMP: 5
SALES (est): 470K **Privately Held**
SIC: 3845 Electromedical equipment

(G-7833)
SK LIFE SCIENCE INC
Also Called: Sklsi
461 From Rd Ste 100 (07652-3526)
PHONE.....................201 421-3800
Kee Choi, *Vice Pres*
Jaeyon Yoon, *Vice Pres*
Hunwoo Harry Shin, *Director*
▲ **EMP:** 30
SALES (est): 8.2MM **Privately Held**
SIC: 2833 Medicinals & botanicals
HQ: Sk Biopharmaceuticals Co., Ltd.
   221 Pangyoyeok-Ro, Bundang-Gu
   Seongnam 13494
   318 093-0114

(G-7834)
**SONY CORPORATION OF
AMERICA**
115 W Century Rd Ste 250 (07652-1459)
PHONE.....................201 930-1000
Hajime Kamata, *Business Mgr*
Javan Bernstein, *Counsel*

Robert Chaney, *Vice Pres*
Toshimoto Mitomo, *Vice Pres*
Tony Cheslick, *Accounts Mgr*
◆ **EMP:** 300 **Privately Held**
SIC: 3695 3652 3651 3577 Optical disks
   & tape, blank; compact laser discs, prerecorded; household audio & video equipment; computer peripheral equipment;
   computer storage devices
HQ: Sony Corporation Of America
   25 Madison Ave Fl 27
   New York NY 10010
   212 833-8000

(G-7835)
SONY ELECTRONICS INC
115 W Century Rd Ste 250 (07652-1459)
PHONE.....................201 930-1000
Alec Shapiro, *Branch Mgr*
EMP: 800 **Privately Held**
SIC: 3651 Household audio & video equip-
   ment
HQ: Sony Electronics Inc.
   16535 Via Esprillo Bldg 1
   San Diego CA 92127
   858 942-2400

(G-7836)
STERI-PHARMA LLC (PA)
120 N State Rt 17 (07652-2819)
PHONE.....................201 857-8210
Robert Giordanella,
EMP: 56
SALES (est): 18MM **Privately Held**
SIC: 2834 Pharmaceutical preparations

(G-7837)
SUEZ NORTH AMERICA INC
461 From Rd Ste 400 (07652-3526)
PHONE.....................201 767-9300
Axel Vayssiere, *President*
Thomas Anjoli, *Manager*
Sherry Corvino, *Executive Asst*
Kalpana Phulara, *Administration*
EMP: 14
SALES (corp-wide): 94.7MM **Privately
Held**
SIC: 3589 Sewage & water treatment
   equipment
HQ: Suez North America Inc.
   2000 First State Blvd
   Wilmington DE 19804
   302 633-5670

(G-7838)
**SUEZ TREATMENT SOLUTIONS
INC (DH)**
461 From Rd Ste 400 (07652-3526)
P.O. Box 1129 (07653-1129)
PHONE.....................201 767-9300
Maximilien Pellegrini, *Ch of Bd*
Vernon D Lucy, *Ch of Bd*
Paul G Davia, *Senior VP*
Albert A Pristera, *Vice Pres*
Robert W Winslow, *Treasurer*
◆ **EMP:** 173
SQ FT: 44,000
SALES (est): 152MM
SALES (corp-wide): 94.7MM **Privately
Held**
SIC: 3589 Sewage & water treatment
   equipment
HQ: Suez Groupe
   Tour Cb21
   Courbevoie 92400
   158 812-000

(G-7839)
**SWAROVSKI NORTH AMERICA
LTD**
700 Paramus Park (07652-3557)
PHONE.....................201 265-4888
EMP: 4
SALES (corp-wide): 4.7B **Privately Held**
SIC: 3961 Costume jewelry
HQ: Swarovski North America Limited
   1 Kenney Dr
   Cranston RI 02920
   401 463-6400

(G-7840)
SYNERON
707 Reeder Rd (07652-3721)
PHONE.....................201 599-9451
Richard Partridge, *President*
EMP: 4

SALES (est): 321K **Privately Held**
SIC: 3845 Electromedical equipment

(G-7841)
TESLA INC
Also Called: Tesla Motors
530 N Rte 17 (07652-3006)
PHONE.................................201 225-2544
EMP: 5
SALES (corp-wide): 21.4B **Publicly Held**
SIC: 3711 3714 Motor vehicles & car bodies; motor vehicle parts & accessories
PA: Tesla, Inc.
    3500 Deer Creek Rd
    Palo Alto CA 94304
    650 681-5000

(G-7842)
TWI PHARMACEUTICALS USA INC
115 W Century Rd Ste 180 (07652-1450)
PHONE.................................201 762-1410
Rick Pallokat, *Exec VP*
Rich Franchi, *Vice Pres*
Janice Busam, *Controller*
Linda Nesbitt, *Manager*
Kari Olson, *Manager*
EMP: 6
SALES (est): 294.2K **Privately Held**
SIC: 2834 Druggists' preparations (pharmaceuticals)

(G-7843)
VERSA PRODUCTS COMPANY INC
22 Spring Valley Rd (07652-4300)
PHONE.................................201 291-0379
Larsson Jan, *CEO*
Karl Larsson, *President*
Gramegna Gerry, *Vice Pres*
◆ EMP: 130 EST: 1949
SQ FT: 52,000
SALES (est): 30.4MM **Privately Held**
WEB: www.versa-valves.com
SIC: 3492 Control valves, fluid power: hydraulic & pneumatic

(G-7844)
WIRED PRODUCTS LLC
49 E Midland Ave Ste 6 (07652-2922)
PHONE.................................551 231-5800
Casey Dent,
Mark Barbalat,
EMP: 12
SALES: 100K **Privately Held**
SIC: 3449 Miscellaneous metalwork

(G-7845)
ZWIVEL LLC
45 Eisenhower Dr Ste 220 (07652-1416)
P.O. Box 97, Glen Rock (07452-0097)
PHONE.................................844 499-4835
Scott Kera, *President*
EMP: 20
SALES (est): 1.2MM **Privately Held**
SIC: 7372 Application computer software

Park Ridge
Bergen County

(G-7846)
AVIDA INCORPORATED
174 Kinderkamack Rd Ste A (07656-1364)
P.O. Box 2 (07656-0002)
PHONE.................................201 802-0749
Eric Kruegle, *CEO*
Herman Kruegle, *Vice Pres*
EMP: 4
SALES (est): 600K **Privately Held**
WEB: www.avida-sw.com
SIC: 3699 Electrical equipment & supplies

(G-7847)
DECORATING WITH FABRIC INC
1 Broadway (07656-2105)
PHONE.................................845 352-5064
Neil Gordon, *CEO*
Gino Ver Eecke, *Manager*
EMP: 6
SALES: 840K **Privately Held**
SIC: 5714 2261 Draperies; decorative finishing of cotton broadwoven fabrics

(G-7848)
DREAM MAKERS INC
53 Glendale Rd (07656-2011)
PHONE.................................201 248-5502
Susan Gerace, *President*
Lori Fields, *Vice Pres*
Rosina Hirsh, *CFO*
EMP: 4 EST: 2001
SALES (est): 450.5K **Privately Held**
SIC: 5092 3942 3069 Toys & hobby goods & supplies; dolls & stuffed toys; toys, rubber

(G-7849)
FARBEST-TALLMAN FOODS CORP (PA)
Also Called: Farbest Brands
1 Maynard Dr Ste 3101 (07656-1878)
PHONE.................................714 897-7199
Daniel M Meloro, *President*
Chip Jackson, *Senior VP*
Robert W Claire, *Treasurer*
Brent Lambert, *Sales Dir*
John Hemmingsen, *Sales Staff*
▲ EMP: 65
SQ FT: 6,600
SALES (est): 14.3MM **Privately Held**
WEB: www.farbest.com
SIC: 2023 2869 5149 5144 Dietary supplements, dairy & non-dairy based; sweeteners, synthetic; specialty food items; poultry & poultry products; food preparations; flavoring extracts & syrups

(G-7850)
FORINO KITCHEN CABINETS INC
33 S Maple Ave (07656-2146)
PHONE.................................201 573-0990
Charles Forino, *President*
Catherine Forino, *Corp Secy*
EMP: 9
SQ FT: 6,000
SALES: 840K **Privately Held**
SIC: 2499 2511 Woodenware, kitchen & household; kitchen & dining room furniture

(G-7851)
GORALSKI INC
Also Called: Goralski Embroidery
4 Marti Rd (07656-1023)
PHONE.................................201 573-1529
Victor F Goralski Jr, *President*
EMP: 25
SQ FT: 6,000
SALES (est): 1.7MM **Privately Held**
SIC: 2397 2395 Schiffli machine embroideries; pleating & stitching

(G-7852)
HALFWAY HOUNDS
108 E Main St (07656)
P.O. Box 132 (07656-0132)
PHONE.................................201 970-6235
Lynn Gregorski, *Principal*
EMP: 4
SALES (est): 224.9K **Privately Held**
SIC: 3999 Pet supplies

(G-7853)
INTERNATIONAL BUS MCHS CORP
Also Called: IBM
225 Brae Blvd (07656-1870)
PHONE.................................201 307-5136
Vince Ippolito, *Manager*
EMP: 20
SALES (corp-wide): 79.5B **Publicly Held**
WEB: www.ibm.com
SIC: 7372 Application computer software; operating systems computer software
PA: International Business Machines Corporation
    1 New Orchard Rd Ste 1 # 1
    Armonk NY 10504
    914 499-1900

(G-7854)
LETTIE PRESS INC
1 Evelyn St (07656-1804)
PHONE.................................201 391-6388
Theodore W Lettie, *President*
EMP: 5 EST: 1973

SALES (est): 320K **Privately Held**
WEB: www.lettieprell.com
SIC: 2752 Commercial printing, offset

(G-7855)
LEXMARK INTERNATIONAL INC
1 Maynard Dr Ste 3 (07656-1878)
PHONE.................................201 307-4600
Mindy Schlossman, *Branch Mgr*
EMP: 10
SALES (corp-wide): 441.3K **Privately Held**
WEB: www.lexmark.com
SIC: 3577 Printers, computer
HQ: Lexmark International Inc.
    740 W New Circle Rd
    Lexington KY 40511
    859 232-2000

(G-7856)
MILO RUNTAK WELDING MACHINERY
174 Kinderkamack Rd Ste A (07656-1364)
PHONE.................................201 391-0380
Milo Runtak, *Owner*
EMP: 5
SQ FT: 1,700
SALES (est): 280K **Privately Held**
SIC: 3599 Machine shop, jobbing & repair

(G-7857)
OPPENHEIM PLASTICS CO INC
27 Sherwood Downs (07656-2603)
P.O. Box 310, Saddle River (07458-0310)
PHONE.................................201 391-3811
Florence Oppenheim, *President*
Susan Mandell, *Treasurer*
EMP: 62 EST: 1950
SQ FT: 1,000
SALES (est): 3.1MM **Privately Held**
SIC: 3089 Plastic containers, except foam

(G-7858)
PLANET ASSOCIATES INC
24 Wampum Rd (07656-2161)
PHONE.................................201 693-8700
William Spencer, *President*
Fred Schlossberg, *CFO*
EMP: 25
SQ FT: 3,000
SALES (est): 2.5MM **Privately Held**
WEB: www.planetassoc.com
SIC: 7371 7372 8713 7373 Computer software development; prepackaged software; surveying services; computer systems analysis & design; software training, computer

(G-7859)
SEACUBE CONTAINER LEASING LTD
1 Maynard Dr (07656-1878)
PHONE.................................201 391-0800
EMP: 8 **Privately Held**
SIC: 3715 7359 Demountable cargo containers; equipment rental & leasing
PA: Seacube Container Leasing Ltd.
    123 Tice Blvd
    Woodcliff Lake NJ 07677

(G-7860)
TONI EMBROIDERY
185 W Leach Ave (07656-1845)
PHONE.................................201 664-6909
Tom Cornicelli, *Partner*
Louis Cornicelli, *Partner*
EMP: 5
SQ FT: 1,600
SALES (est): 307.8K **Privately Held**
SIC: 2395 Embroidery products, except schiffli machine

Parlin
Middlesex County

(G-7861)
ASHLAND LLC
50 S Minnisink Ave Ste 2 (08859-1082)
PHONE.................................732 353-7718
EMP: 75

SALES (corp-wide): 3.7B **Publicly Held**
SIC: 5169 1611 1622 2821 Alkalines & chlorine; alcohols & anti-freeze compounds; noncorrosive products & materials; chemical additives; highway & street construction; surfacing & paving; concrete construction: roads, highways, sidewalks, etc.; general contractor, highway & street construction; bridge construction; plastics materials & resins; ester gum; polyesters; thermoplastic materials; heavy distillates; oils, lubricating
HQ: Ashland Llc
    50 E Rivercenter Blvd # 1600
    Covington KY 41011
    859 815-3333

(G-7862)
ASHLAND SPCALTY INGREDIENTS GP
Ashland Aqlon Fnctnal Ingrdnts
50 S Minnisink Ave Ste 1 (08859-1082)
PHONE.................................732 353-7708
Paul Tuck, *Branch Mgr*
EMP: 50
SALES (corp-wide): 3.7B **Publicly Held**
SIC: 2869 2899 2851 Industrial organic chemicals; chemical preparations; paints & allied products
HQ: Ashland Specialty Ingredients G.P.
    5200 Laser Pkwy
    Dublin OH 43017
    302 594-5000

(G-7863)
E I DU PONT DE NEMOURS & CO
Also Called: Dupont
250 Cheesequake Rd (08859-1080)
PHONE.................................732 257-1579
Rajgopal Subramanian, *Research*
Charles P Richwine, *Corp Comm Staff*
Toichi Hamajima, *Branch Mgr*
Brian Stuver, *Technical Staff*
EMP: 50
SALES (corp-wide): 30.6B **Publicly Held**
WEB: www.dupont.com
SIC: 2819 2851 2796 Industrial inorganic chemicals; paints & allied products; platemaking services
HQ: E. I. Du Pont De Nemours And Company
    974 Centre Rd Bldg 735
    Wilmington DE 19805
    302 485-3000

(G-7864)
HITACHI CHEM DUPONT MICROSYST (PA)
Also Called: Hd Microsystems
Cheesequake Rd Bldg 424 (08859)
PHONE.................................732 613-2175
Kenya Misu, *President*
Toichi Hamajima, *Principal*
Steve Anderson, *Business Mgr*
Hitcahi Chemicals,
Dupont Industries,
▲ EMP: 28
SALES (est): 65.2MM **Privately Held**
WEB: www.hdmicrosystems.com
SIC: 5162 2821 Resins; polyimides (skybond, kaplon)

(G-7865)
INDUSTRIAL SUMMIT TECH CORP (HQ)
Also Called: I.S.t
250 Cheesequake Rd (08859-1080)
PHONE.................................732 238-2211
Yoshi Haramo, *CEO*
Asuka Nomura, *Manager*
Melissa Mazzei, *Director*
▲ EMP: 32
SALES (est): 9.7MM **Privately Held**
SIC: 2899 2851 Chemical preparations; paints & allied products

(G-7866)
JOHN E HERBST HEATING & COOLG
Also Called: Herbst John E Heating & Coolg
3143 Bordentown Ave 2b (08859-1163)
PHONE.................................732 721-0088
John E Herbst, *President*
EMP: 4 EST: 1973
SQ FT: 2,000

G E O G R A P H I C

SALES: 450K **Privately Held**
SIC: 1711 3444 Warm air heating & air
conditioning contractor; ventilation & duct
work contractor; sheet metalwork

(G-7867)
JOY-REI ENTERPRISES INC
Also Called: Joyrei Enterprises
3143 Bordentown Ave 5b (08859-1163)
P.O. Box 260 (08859-0260)
PHONE.....................................732 727-0742
James Reising, *President*
EMP: 9
SQ FT: 10,000
SALES (est): 770K **Privately Held**
SIC: 3542 3469 Mechanical (pneumatic or
hydraulic) metal forming machines; ma-
chine parts, stamped or pressed metal

(G-7868)
**MADISON PARK VOLUNTEER
FIRE CO**
3011 Cheesequake Rd (08859-1247)
PHONE.....................................732 727-1143
Mark Lebowitz, *Principal*
Nicholas Giugno, *Vice Pres*
Jim Ross, *Treasurer*
Anthony Guarnera, *Admin Sec*
EMP: 40
SQ FT: 12,000
SALES: 64.2K **Privately Held**
SIC: 3569 Firefighting apparatus & related
equipment

(G-7869)
XCHANGE SOFTWARE INC
499 Ernston Rd Ste A7 (08859-1406)
PHONE.....................................732 444-6666
Prabhakar R Yeruva, *President*
EMP: 36
SALES (corp-wide): 3.8MM **Privately
Held**
SIC: 7372 Application computer software
PA: Xchange Software Inc.
10 Austin Ave Fl 2
Iselin NJ 08830
732 444-4943

Parsippany
Morris County

(G-7870)
42 DESIGN SQUARE LLC
350 Parsippany Rd Apt 128 (07054-5162)
PHONE.....................................888 272-5979
Sapna Sheth, *Director*
Arpita Sheth,
EMP: 15
SALES: 500K **Privately Held**
SIC: 7336 8742 2721 Commercial art &
graphic design; training & development
consultant; periodicals

(G-7871)
**ACROW CORPORATION OF
AMERICA (PA)**
181 New Rd Ste 202 (07054-5645)
PHONE.....................................973 244-0080
William Killeen, *President*
Mark Joosten, *President*
Kenneth J Scott, *President*
John Brain, *Chief Engr*
Scott Patterson, *Chief Engr*
◆ EMP: 30 EST: 1951
SQ FT: 50,000
SALES (est): 38.2MM **Privately Held**
WEB: www.acrowusa.com
SIC: 3441 8711 Fabricated structural
metal; construction & civil engineering

(G-7872)
ACTAVIS INC
400 Interpace Pkwy # 400 (07054-1120)
PHONE.....................................973 394-8925
Yitzhak Peterburg, *CEO*
EMP: 5
SALES (est): 173.7K **Privately Held**
SIC: 2834 Pharmaceutical preparations

(G-7873)
ACTAVIS PHARMA INC (DH)
400 Interpace Pkwy Ste A1 (07054-1119)
PHONE.....................................862 261-7000

Paul M Bisaro, *CEO*
Carol Yeomans, *Vice Pres*
Lawrence Hill, *Exec Dir*
Jennifer Wang, *Exec Dir*
Victoria Di Santo, *Associate Dir*
▲ EMP: 95
SALES (est): 1.6B **Privately Held**
SIC: 2834 Pharmaceutical preparations
HQ: Actavis Llc
5 Giralda Farms
Madison NJ 07940
862 261-7000

(G-7874)
**ADARE PHARMACEUTICALS
INC**
400 Interpace Pkwy (07054-1120)
PHONE.....................................862 261-7000
Frank Verwiel, *CEO*
EMP: 441 **Privately Held**
SIC: 2834 Pharmaceutical preparations
HQ: Adare Pharmaceuticals, Inc.
1200 Lenox Dr Ste 100
Lawrenceville NJ 08648

(G-7875)
ADVANSIX INC (PA)
300 Kimball Dr Ste 101 (07054-2186)
PHONE.....................................973 526-1800
Erin N Kane, *President*
John M Quitmeyer, *Senior VP*
Christopher Gramm, *Vice Pres*
Michael Preston, *CFO*
Richard Dodd, *Manager*
EMP: 277
SALES: 1.5B **Publicly Held**
SIC: 2899 2821 5162 Chemical prepara-
tions; plastics materials & resins; resins

(G-7876)
AJ OSTER LLC
Alumet Supply
150 Lackawanna Ave (07054-1057)
PHONE.....................................973 673-5700
EMP: 6
SALES (corp-wide): 4.8MM **Privately
Held**
SIC: 3324 3353 Aerospace investment
castings, ferrous; aluminum sheet, plate &
foil
HQ: A.J. Oster, Llc
301 Metro Center Blvd # 204
Warwick RI 02886
401 736-2600

(G-7877)
ALFRED DUNNER INC
200 Walsh Dr (07054-1044)
PHONE.....................................212 944-6660
Ray Discher, *Manager*
EMP: 100
SQ FT: 90,000
SALES (corp-wide): 70.3MM **Privately
Held**
WEB: www.alfreddunner.com
SIC: 4225 2339 General warehousing &
storage; women's & misses' outerwear
PA: Alfred Dunner, Inc.
1333 Broadway Fl 11
New York NY 10018
212 478-4300

(G-7878)
ALLSTATE CAN CORPORATION
Also Called: Think Tin
1 Woodhollow Rd (07054-2821)
PHONE.....................................973 560-9030
David West, *President*
Richard Papera, *President*
Bob Cucci, *COO*
Louis Papera, *Vice Pres*
Stan Cherry, *Plant Mgr*
▲ EMP: 86
SQ FT: 135,000
SALES (est): 26MM **Privately Held**
WEB: www.allstatecan.com
SIC: 3411 Food containers, metal

(G-7879)
**ALTRIA GROUP DISTRIBUTION
CO**
9 Campus Dr Ste 3 (07054-4412)
PHONE.....................................804 274-2000
EMP: 150

SALES (corp-wide): 25.3B **Publicly Held**
WEB: www.philipmorrisusa.com
SIC: 2111 5194 Cigarettes; tobacco & to-
bacco products
HQ: Altria Group Distribution Company
6601 W Broad St
Richmond VA 23230

(G-7880)
AMG INTERNATIONAL INC (PA)
Also Called: Freeman Products Worldwide
71 Walsh Dr Ste 101 (07054-1010)
PHONE.....................................201 475-4800
Jean F Lefebvre, *CEO*
George Ercolino, *President*
Paul Raynor, *Vice Pres*
◆ EMP: 38
SALES (est): 13.5MM **Privately Held**
SIC: 3914 Trophies

(G-7881)
**APHENA PHRMA SLUTIONS - NJ
LLC**
2 Cranberry Rd Unit A3 (07054-1053)
PHONE.....................................973 947-5441
EMP: 91
SQ FT: 27,680
SALES (est): 3MM **Privately Held**
SIC: 2834 Mfg Pharmaceutical Prepara-
tions

(G-7882)
**AROUND CLOCK SWEEPING
LLC**
45 Essex Rd (07054-2662)
PHONE.....................................973 887-1144
Ronald A Natoli, *Principal*
EMP: 5
SALES (est): 15K **Privately Held**
SIC: 3991 Street sweeping brooms, hand
or machine

(G-7883)
ARTLINE HEAT TRANSFER INC
2 Eastmans Rd (07054-3703)
PHONE.....................................973 599-0104
Simone Parisi, *President*
EMP: 10
SALES (est): 930K **Privately Held**
SIC: 3999 Heating pads, nonelectric

(G-7884)
ASCEND LABORATORIES LLC
339 Jefferson Rd Ste 101 (07054-3707)
PHONE.....................................201 476-1977
Venkatesh Srinivasan, *President*
Allen Bagatsing, *Principal*
Grant Butler, *Vice Pres*
John Dillaway, *Vice Pres*
Schuyler Vanwinkle, *Vice Pres*
▲ EMP: 25
SQ FT: 3,600
SALES (est): 3.1MM
SALES (corp-wide): 794.7MM **Privately
Held**
WEB: www.ascendlaboratories.com
SIC: 2834 Pharmaceutical preparations
PA: Alkem Laboratories Limited
Devashish Building, Alkem House
Mumbai MH 40001
223 982-9999

(G-7885)
**ASCENSIA DIABETES CARE US
INC (DH)**
Also Called: Contour Next
5 Woodhollow Rd Ste 3 (07054-2832)
PHONE.....................................973 560-6500
Michael Kloss, *CEO*
Tetsuyuki Watanabe, *President*
Joseph Delahunty, *Vice Pres*
Steven Lynum, *Vice Pres*
Robert Schumm, *Vice Pres*
EMP: 150 EST: 2016
SALES: 400MM **Publicly Held**
SIC: 5047 2835 3841 Electro-medical
equipment; in vitro diagnostics; diagnostic
apparatus, medical
HQ: Ascensia Diabetes Care Holdings Ag
Peter Merian-Strasse 90
Basel BS 4052
444 658-355

(G-7886)
ASCO LP
7 Eastmans Rd (07054-3702)
PHONE.....................................973 386-9000
Robert Rafter, *Principal*
EMP: 25
SALES (corp-wide): 17.4B **Publicly Held**
WEB: www.rapcoassoc.com
SIC: 3443 Fabricated plate work (boiler
shop)
HQ: Asco, L.P.
160 Park Ave
Florham Park NJ 07932
800 972-2726

(G-7887)
ATLAS COPCO HURRICANE LLC
6 Century Dr Ste 85 (07054-4611)
PHONE.....................................800 754-7408
Ronnie Leten, *CEO*
Annika Berglund, *Senior VP*
Johan Halling, *Senior VP*
Hkan Osvald, *Senior VP*
Mats Rahmstrom, *Senior VP*
◆ EMP: 90
SALES (est): 14.2MM
SALES (corp-wide): 10.5B **Privately Held**
SIC: 3563 Air & gas compressors
HQ: Atlas Copco North America Llc
6 Century Dr Ste 85
Parsippany NJ 07054
973 397-3400

(G-7888)
**ATLAS COPCO NORTH
AMERICA LLC (DH)**
6 Century Dr Ste 85 (07054-4611)
PHONE.....................................973 397-3400
Eric Moore, *Mng Member*
EMP: 1
SALES (est): 1.6B
SALES (corp-wide): 10.5B **Privately Held**
SIC: 3312 Tool & die steel

(G-7889)
B&G FOODS INC (PA)
4 Gatehall Dr Ste 110 (07054-4522)
PHONE.....................................973 401-6500
Stephen C Sherrill, *Ch of Bd*
Robert C Cantwell, *President*
Kenneth G Romanzi, *COO*
Eric H Hart, *Exec VP*
Bill Herbes, *Exec VP*
EMP: 277 EST: 1996
SALES: 1.7B **Publicly Held**
WEB: www.bgfoods.com
SIC: 2013 2032 2035 Canned
meats (except baby food) from purchased
meat; beans & bean sprouts, canned,
jarred, etc.; Mexican foods: packaged in
cans, jars, etc.; canned fruits & special-
ties; pickles, sauces & salad dressings;
syrups; seasonings & spices

(G-7890)
B&G FOODS INC
4 Gatehall Dr Ste 110 (07054-4522)
PHONE.....................................973 401-6500
David L Wenner, *President*
EMP: 215
SALES (corp-wide): 1.7B **Publicly Held**
WEB: www.bgfoods.com
SIC: 2013 2032 2033 2035 Canned
meats (except baby food) from purchased
meat; beans & bean sprouts, canned,
jarred, etc.; Mexican foods: packaged in
cans, jars, etc.; canned fruits & specialties; pickles, sauces & salad dressings;
syrups; seasonings & spices
PA: B&G Foods, Inc.
4 Gatehall Dr Ste 110
Parsippany NJ 07054
973 401-6500

(G-7891)
**B&G FOODS NORTH AMERICA
INC (HQ)**
4 Gatehall Dr Ste 110 (07054-4522)
PHONE.....................................973 401-6500
Robert Cantwell, *President*
Thomas Crimmins, *CFO*
EMP: 21

▲ = Import ▼=Export
◆ =Import/Export

SALES (est): 47.3MM
SALES (corp-wide): 1.7B **Publicly Held**
SIC: 2013 Canned meats (except baby food) from purchased meat
PA: B&G Foods, Inc.
    4 Gatehall Dr Ste 110
    Parsippany NJ 07054
    973 401-6500

(G-7892)
BEDDING SHOPPE INC
811 Route 46 (07054-3405)
PHONE.............................973 334-9000
Michael Hatler, *President*
James Mascia, *Vice Pres*
EMP: 7
SQ FT: 12,500
SALES (est): 1.6MM **Privately Held**
WEB: www.beddingshoppe.com
SIC: 5712 7359 2515 Bedding & bedsprings; mattresses; furniture rental; chair beds

(G-7893)
BENCKISER N RECKITT AMER INC
Also Called: RB
399 Interpace Pkwy # 101 (07054-1133)
PHONE.............................973 404-2600
Alexander Lacik, *President*
Jiri Kulik, *General Mgr*
Erin Galyean, *Business Mgr*
Heather Allen, *Exec VP*
Rakesh Kapoor, *Exec VP*
▲ **EMP:** 1600
SQ FT: 13,000
SALES (est): 127.5K
SALES (corp-wide): 16.1B **Privately Held**
WEB: www.reckittbenckiser.com
SIC: 2035 2842 Pickles, sauces & salad dressings; specialty cleaning, polishes & sanitation goods
HQ: Reckitt Benckiser Holdings (Usa) Limited
    103-105 Bath Road
    Slough BERKS

(G-7894)
BIRDS EYE FOODS INC
Also Called: Agrilink Foods
399 Jefferson Rd (07054-3707)
PHONE.............................920 435-5300
Robb Lillibridge, *Manager*
EMP: 120
SALES (corp-wide): 9.5B **Publicly Held**
WEB: www.agrilinkfoods.com
SIC: 2037 Vegetables, quick frozen & cold pack, excl. potato products
HQ: Birds Eye Foods, Inc.
    121 Woodcrest Rd
    Cherry Hill NJ 08003
    585 383-1850

(G-7895)
BOONTON ELECTRONICS CORP
25 Eastmans Rd (07054-3702)
PHONE.............................973 386-9696
Timothy Whelan, *CEO*
Michael Kandell, *CFO*
EMP: 32
SQ FT: 50,000
SALES (est): 6.6MM
SALES (corp-wide): 52.7MM **Publicly Held**
WEB: www.boonton.com
SIC: 3825 3829 3621 Microwave test equipment; impedance measuring equipment; test equipment for electronic & electrical circuits; audiometers; measuring & controlling devices; motors & generators
PA: Wireless Telecom Group, Inc.
    25 Eastmans Rd
    Parsippany NJ 07054
    973 386-9696

(G-7896)
BUILDING MATERIALS MFG CORP (DH)
1 Campus Dr (07054-4404)
PHONE.............................973 628-3000
Richard A Nowak, *President*
Fabian Kulynych, *Technical Mgr*
Susan Card, *Executive Asst*
EMP: 1

SALES (est): 6.9MM
SALES (corp-wide): 2.5B **Privately Held**
SIC: 2493 Reconstituted wood products

(G-7897)
CASTLE CREEK PHRMCEUTICALS LLC
6 Century Dr Ste 2 (07054-4611)
PHONE.............................862 286-0400
Michael Derby, *CEO*
Amir Tavakkol, *Exec VP*
Mary Spellman, *Chief Mktg Ofcr*
EMP: 17
SALES (est): 894.8K **Privately Held**
SIC: 2834 Pharmaceutical preparations

(G-7898)
CELLEBRITE INC
7 Campus Dr Ste 201 (07054-4413)
PHONE.............................973 206-7763
Chris Shin, *President*
Jennifer Fernandez, *General Mgr*
Paul Borror, *Vice Pres*
Derek Brown, *Vice Pres*
Brendan Morgan, *Vice Pres*
EMP: 100
SALES (est): 19.7MM **Privately Held**
WEB: www.cellebriteusa.com
SIC: 3663 Cellular radio telephone

(G-7899)
CENTRAL PLASTICS INCORPORATED
Also Called: Plastic Profiles Co Div
333 New Rd Ste 3 (07054-4212)
PHONE.............................973 808-0990
Michelle Tripucka, *President*
Terry Taillon, *CFO*
EMP: 5
SQ FT: 10,000
SALES (est): 896.4K **Privately Held**
SIC: 3081 5162 Polypropylene film & sheet; polyvinyl film & sheet; plastics products; plastics sheets & rods; plastics film

(G-7900)
CEREXA INC
400 Interpace Pkwy Ste A1 (07054-1119)
PHONE.............................510 285-9200
Dennis Podlesak, *CEO*
George H Talbot MD, *Exec VP*
James G E MD PHD, *Vice Pres*
Bill Nelson PHD, *Vice Pres*
Stan E Abel, *CFO*
EMP: 22
SALES (est): 4.3MM **Privately Held**
SIC: 2834 Pharmaceutical preparations
HQ: Forest Laboratories, Llc
    909 3rd Ave Fl 23
    New York NY 10022

(G-7901)
CHEMTRADE CHEMICALS CORP (DH)
Also Called: General Performance Products
90 E Halsey Rd Ste 301 (07054-3709)
PHONE.............................973 515-0900
William E Redmond Jr, *CEO*
Greg Gilbert, *Vice Pres*
Douglas J Grierson, *Vice Pres*
James Imbriaco, *Vice Pres*
Douglas Mc Farland, *Vice Pres*
◆ **EMP:** 80
SQ FT: 50,000
SALES (est): 216.1MM
SALES (corp-wide): 1.2B **Privately Held**
SIC: 2819 Industrial inorganic chemicals
HQ: Chemtrade Gcc Holding Company
    90 E Halsey Rd Ste 301
    Parsippany NJ 07054
    973 515-0900

(G-7902)
CHEMTRADE CHEMICALS US LLC (DH)
Also Called: General Chemical Prfmce Pdts
90 E Halsey Rd (07054-3713)
PHONE.............................973 515-0900
Jeff Greene, *Mktg Dir*
William E Redmond Jr, *Mng Member*
Douglas Mc Farland, *Mng Member*
Joseph Leary, *Director*
Vincent Opalewski, *Director*
◆ **EMP:** 80

SALES (est): 216.1MM
SALES (corp-wide): 1.2B **Privately Held**
SIC: 2819 Industrial inorganic chemicals
HQ: Chemtrade Chemicals Corporation
    90 E Halsey Rd Ste 301
    Parsippany NJ 07054
    973 515-0900

(G-7903)
CHEMTRADE GCC HOLDING COMPANY (DH)
90 E Halsey Rd Ste 301 (07054-3709)
PHONE.............................973 515-0900
William E Redmond Jr, *President*
Douglas Mc Farland, *Vice Pres*
EMP: 2
SALES (est): 112.6MM
SALES (corp-wide): 1.2B **Privately Held**
SIC: 6719 2819 Investment holding companies, except banks; industrial inorganic chemicals
HQ: Chemtrade Water Chemical Inc.
    90 E Halsey Rd Ste 301
    Parsippany NJ 07054
    973 515-0900

(G-7904)
CHEMTRADE SOLUTIONS LLC (DH)
Also Called: General Chemical
90 E Halsey Rd Ste 301 (07054-3709)
PHONE.............................973 515-0900
Candice Soprano, *Business Mgr*
Douglas J Grierson, *Vice Pres*
Steve Bell, *Production*
Terri Sicsko, *Purchasing*
Ilia Romero, *Research*
▲ **EMP:** 1
SALES (est): 193MM
SALES (corp-wide): 1.2B **Privately Held**
SIC: 5169 2819 Chemicals & allied products; aluminum sulfate

(G-7905)
CHEMTRADE WATER CHEMICAL INC (HQ)
90 E Halsey Rd Ste 301 (07054-3709)
PHONE.............................973 515-0900
EMP: 0
SALES (est): 74.6MM
SALES (corp-wide): 1.2B **Privately Held**
SIC: 6719 2819 Investment holding companies, except banks; industrial inorganic chemicals
PA: Chemtrade Logistics Income Fund
    155 Gordon Baker Rd Suite 300
    North York ON M2H 3
    416 496-5856

(G-7906)
CLASSIC INDUSTRIES INC
50 Us Highway 46 Ste 100 (07054-2395)
PHONE.............................973 227-1366
Robert D H Luke, *President*
James Luke, *Corp Secy*
Ralph Loveys, *Vice Pres*
EMP: 5
SALES (est): 310K **Privately Held**
SIC: 3444 Sheet metalwork

(G-7907)
CLEAN AIR GROUP
6 Campus Dr Ste 2 (07054-4406)
PHONE.............................908 232-4200
Clara Rosales, *Manager*
EMP: 6
SALES (est): 693.6K **Privately Held**
SIC: 3559 Recycling machinery

(G-7908)
CONAGRAPHICS INC
Also Called: PIP Printing
1180 Us Highway 46 Ste 2 (07054-2153)
PHONE.............................973 331-1113
Martin Contzius, *President*
Janet Contzius, *Vice Pres*
EMP: 4
SQ FT: 1,150
SALES (est): 370K **Privately Held**
SIC: 2752 Commercial printing, offset

(G-7909)
CROLL-REYNOLDS CO INC (PA)
6 Campus Dr Ste 2 (07054-4406)
PHONE.............................908 232-4200

Samuel W Croll III, *CEO*
Henry Hage, *COO*
Phillip E Reynolds, *Vice Pres*
◆ **EMP:** 24 **EST:** 1917
SQ FT: 5,000
SALES (est): 9.5MM **Privately Held**
WEB: www.croll.com
SIC: 3563 3822 3564 Vacuum (air extraction) systems, industrial; air flow controllers, air conditioning & refrigeration; air cleaning systems

(G-7910)
CRONITE CO INC (PA)
120 E Halsey Rd (07054-3720)
P.O. Box 6330 (07054-7330)
PHONE.............................973 887-7900
Roberts Steffens, *Ch of Bd*
Thomas R Ward, *CFO*
▲ **EMP:** 35 **EST:** 1886
SQ FT: 30,300
SALES (est): 3.1MM **Privately Held**
WEB: www.cronite.com
SIC: 3555 5169 Engraving machinery & equipment, except plates; chemicals & allied products

(G-7911)
CROSS RIP OCEAN ENGRG LLC
Also Called: Cr Ocean Engineering, LLC
6 Campus Dr (07054-4406)
PHONE.............................973 455-0005
Samuel W Croll III, *CEO*
Nicholas Confuorto, *COO*
EMP: 5
SALES (est): 772.5K **Privately Held**
SIC: 3564 Purification & dust collection equipment

(G-7912)
CSC
168 Emily Pl (07054-3429)
P.O. Box 5670 (07054-6670)
PHONE.............................973 412-6339
EMP: 8
SALES (est): 2.3MM **Privately Held**
SIC: 3625 Motor controls & accessories

(G-7913)
DELAWARE PIPELINE COMPANY LLC
1 Sylvan Way Ste 2 (07054-3879)
PHONE.............................973 455-7500
EMP: 1
SALES: 12.5MM
SALES (corp-wide): 27.1B **Publicly Held**
SIC: 2911 Petroleum refining
HQ: Pbf Holding Company Llc
    1 Sylvan Way Ste 2
    Parsippany NJ 07054

(G-7914)
DENTAMACH INC
14 Walsh Dr Ste 102 (07054-1063)
PHONE.............................973 334-2220
Bill Pollack, *Ch of Bd*
Bruce Miller, *President*
EMP: 10
SALES (est): 884.7K **Privately Held**
SIC: 3843 Teeth, artificial (not made in dental laboratories)

(G-7915)
DEPENDABLE PRECISION PRODUCTS
42 Schindler Ct (07054-3300)
PHONE.............................973 887-3304
Donald Carlucci, *President*
EMP: 9
SQ FT: 4,800
SALES: 650K **Privately Held**
SIC: 3599 Machine shop, jobbing & repair

(G-7916)
DIALOGIC INC (DH)
4 Gatehall Dr Ste 9 (07054-4522)
PHONE.............................973 967-6000
Bill Crank, *President*
Christian Primeau, *COO*
Anthony Housefather, *Exec VP*
Kevin Gould, *Senior VP*
Jim Machi, *Senior VP*
EMP: 108

SALES (est): 104.5MM
SALES (corp-wide): 449.4K **Privately Held**
WEB: www.dialogic.com
SIC: 3661 3577 7371 Telephone & telegraph apparatus; data conversion equipment, media-to-media: computer; computer software development & applications
HQ: Groupe Dialogic Inc
    375 Boul Roland-Therrien Bureau 210
    Longueuil QC J4H 4
    450 651-5000

(G-7917)
DIGITAL PRINT SOLUTIONS INC
Also Called: Alphagraphics Printshops of th
5 Eastmans Rd (07054-3721)
PHONE..................................973 263-1890
Joseph Yutsus, *President*
Darin Hicks, *Vice Pres*
Tommy E Auger, *CFO*
EMP: 10
SQ FT: 7,500
SALES (est): 2MM **Privately Held**
SIC: 2752 Commercial printing, lithographic

(G-7918)
DONRAY PRINTING INC
2 Eastmans Rd (07054-3703)
PHONE..................................973 515-8100
Art Ferriola, *President*
Ray Ferriola, *Vice Pres*
▲ **EMP:** 35
SQ FT: 40,000
SALES (est): 6.9MM **Privately Held**
WEB: www.donrayprinting.com
SIC: 2752 2396 Color lithography; automotive & apparel trimmings

(G-7919)
DPI NEWCO LLC
Also Called: D P X
45 Waterview Blvd (07054-7611)
PHONE..................................973 257-8113
Jim Mullen, *Mng Member*
EMP: 41 EST: 1994
SALES (est): 72.3MM
SALES (corp-wide): 2.6B **Privately Held**
SIC: 2834 Pharmaceutical preparations
PA: Gpv Iii, Inc.
    245 Park Ave Rm 1601
    New York NY 10167
    212 286-8600

(G-7920)
DRS INFRARED TECHNOLOGIES LP
5 Sylvan Way Ste 305 (07054-3813)
PHONE..................................973 898-1500
Linda Zerpolo, *COO*
Matthew Green, *Vice Pres*
Matthew Brophy, *VP Opers*
Kristine Deciucis, *Senior Buyer*
Jeffrey Bicklein, *Engineer*
EMP: 5
SALES (est): 374K **Privately Held**
SIC: 3812 Search & navigation equipment

(G-7921)
DRS LEONARDO INC
5 Sylvan Way Ste 305 (07054-3813)
PHONE..................................973 898-1500
Mark Newman, *CEO*
Becky Rodrigues, *Program Mgr*
Tripodi Eric, *Technology*
EMP: 39
SALES (corp-wide): 9.2B **Privately Held**
SIC: 3812 Navigational systems & instruments
HQ: Leonardo Drs, Inc.
    2345 Crystal Dr Ste 1000
    Arlington VA 22202
    703 416-8000

(G-7922)
DSM NUTRITIONAL PRODUCTS LLC (DH)
Also Called: D S M
45 Waterview Blvd (07054-7611)
PHONE..................................800 526-0189
Richard Polacek, *President*
Jill Cohen, *Business Mgr*
Tim Shannon, *Vice Pres*
Hugh Welsh, *Vice Pres*

David Trussler, *Plant Mgr*
◆ **EMP:** 277
SQ FT: 106,000
SALES (est): 529MM
SALES (corp-wide): 10.6B **Privately Held**
WEB: www.nutraaccess.com
SIC: 2836 2834 Biological products, except diagnostic; vitamin, nutrient & hematinic preparations for human use

(G-7923)
DSM SIGHT & LIFE INC
45 Waterview Blvd (07054-7611)
PHONE..................................973 257-8208
Hugh Welsh, *President*
Roberto Boscio, *Principal*
James Hamilton, *Principal*
EMP: 4
SALES: 0
SALES (corp-wide): 10.6B **Privately Held**
SIC: 8699 2834 Charitable organization; vitamin preparations
HQ: Dsm Nutritional Products, Llc
    45 Waterview Blvd
    Parsippany NJ 07054
    800 526-0189

(G-7924)
E B R MANUFACTURING INC
10 Woodhaven Rd (07054-1468)
PHONE..................................973 263-8810
Herbert Wolf, *President*
Maxine Wolf, *Admin Sec*
EMP: 25
SQ FT: 42,000
SALES (est): 1.6MM **Privately Held**
SIC: 2395 Quilting, for the trade

(G-7925)
EARTH COLOR NEW YORK INC (HQ)
249 Pomeroy Rd (07054-3727)
PHONE..................................973 884-1300
Robert Kashan, *CEO*
Dennis Ganzak, *CFO*
EMP: 45
SALES (est): 67.4MM
SALES (corp-wide): 300.1MM **Privately Held**
SIC: 2752 7336 2791 Commercial printing, lithographic; graphic arts & related design; typesetting
PA: Mittera Group, Inc.
    1312 Locust St Ste 202
    Des Moines IA 50309
    515 343-5353

(G-7926)
EARTH THEBAULT INC (DH)
249 Pomeroy Rd (07054-3727)
PHONE..................................973 884-1300
J Brian Thebault, *CEO*
Wes Vanderwende, *President*
Kenneth Marino, *COO*
Don Seitz, *Senior VP*
Gerard Sittmann, *Vice Pres*
▲ **EMP:** 234 EST: 1930
SQ FT: 93,000
SALES (est): 81.6MM
SALES (corp-wide): 300.1MM **Privately Held**
WEB: www.thebault.com
SIC: 2752 Commercial printing, offset

(G-7927)
EARTHCOLOR INC
249 Pomeroy Rd (07054-3727)
PHONE..................................973 952-8360
EMP: 4
SALES (corp-wide): 300.1MM **Privately Held**
SIC: 2752 Commercial printing, lithographic
HQ: Earthcolor, Inc.
    249 Pomeroy Rd
    Parsippany NJ 07054

(G-7928)
EARTHCOLOR INC (HQ)
Also Called: Earth Digital
249 Pomeroy Rd (07054-3727)
PHONE..................................973 884-1300
Robert Kashan, *CEO*
Bruce Wexler, *President*
Cheryl Kahanec, *Exec VP*
Dennis Ganzak, *CFO*

Lucille Benezra, *VP Corp Comm*
EMP: 135
SQ FT: 93,000
SALES (est): 109.4MM
SALES (corp-wide): 300.1MM **Privately Held**
SIC: 2752 2759 Commercial printing, lithographic; business forms: printing
PA: Mittera Group, Inc.
    1312 Locust St Ste 202
    Des Moines IA 50309
    515 343-5353

(G-7929)
EBI LLC
Also Called: Biomet Bone Healing Tech
399 Jefferson Rd (07054-3707)
PHONE..................................800 526-2579
Bob Phelp, *President*
Bradley J Tandy, *Mng Member*
Jeffrey R Binder, *Mng Member*
Michael T Hodges, *Mng Member*
Eric Hayes, *Administration*
▲ **EMP:** 1504
SQ FT: 125,000
SALES (est): 155.7MM
SALES (corp-wide): 7.9B **Publicly Held**
WEB: www.ebimedical.com
SIC: 3842 Surgical appliances & supplies
HQ: Biomet, Inc.
    345 E Main St
    Warsaw IN 46580
    574 267-6639

(G-7930)
EBI LP
Also Called: Biomet Spine and Biomet Trauma
399 Jefferson Rd (07054-3707)
PHONE..................................973 299-9022
EMP: 29
SALES (est): 4.4MM
SALES (corp-wide): 7.9B **Publicly Held**
WEB: www.biomet.com
SIC: 3842 Surgical appliances & supplies
HQ: Biomet, Inc.
    345 E Main St
    Warsaw IN 46580
    574 267-6639

(G-7931)
EBI MEDICAL SYSTEMS LLC
100 Interpace Pkwy Ste 1 (07054-1149)
PHONE..................................973 299-3330
James Bechtold, *Principal*
EMP: 14
SALES (est): 2.1MM
SALES (corp-wide): 7.9B **Publicly Held**
WEB: www.biomet.com
SIC: 3842 Surgical appliances & supplies
HQ: Biomet, Inc.
    345 E Main St
    Warsaw IN 46580
    574 267-6639

(G-7932)
EDENBRIDGE PHARMACEUTICALS LLC
169 Lackawanna Ave # 110 (07054-1007)
PHONE..................................201 292-1292
Ryan Collins, *CEO*
Patrick Chu, *President*
EMP: 4
SALES (est): 964.1K **Privately Held**
SIC: 2834 Pharmaceutical preparations

(G-7933)
EFFICIENT LIGHTING INC
2 Cranberry Rd Ste 5b (07054-1053)
PHONE..................................973 846-8568
David Rivera, *President*
EMP: 16
SALES (est): 2.6MM **Privately Held**
SIC: 3645 5063 5719 Boudoir lamps; chandeliers, residential; desk lamps; floor lamps; lighting fixtures; lighting fixtures
PA: Efficient Lighting, Inc
    201 E Center St
    Anaheim CA 92805

(G-7934)
ELEVATE HR INC (PA)
1055 Parsippany Blvd # 511 (07054-1273)
PHONE..................................973 917-3230
David M Erickson, *President*
Lucy Rosendahl, *Vice Pres*

Ed Laplante, *Director*
EMP: 16
SALES (est): 2MM **Privately Held**
SIC: 7372 8742 Business oriented computer software; human resource consulting services

(G-7935)
ELUSYS THERAPEUTICS INC
4 Century Dr Ste 260 (07054-4612)
PHONE..................................973 808-0222
Elizabeth Posillico, *President*
Leslie Casey, *Vice Pres*
Stephen Haworth, *Vice Pres*
Jeremy Middleton, *Vice Pres*
James Porter, *Vice Pres*
EMP: 17
SQ FT: 13,000
SALES (est): 5.3MM **Privately Held**
WEB: www.elusys.com
SIC: 2834 8731 Pharmaceutical preparations; biotechnical research, commercial

(G-7936)
EMERSON RADIO CORP (PA)
35 Waterview Blvd Ste 140 (07054-7602)
PHONE..................................973 428-2000
Duncan Hon, *CEO*
Christopher Ho, *Ch of Bd*
Michael Binney, *CFO*
◆ **EMP:** 12 EST: 1912
SQ FT: 5,541
SALES (est): 8.9MM **Publicly Held**
WEB: www.emersonradio.com
SIC: 3651 Household audio & video equipment

(G-7937)
EPOCH EVERLASTING PLAY LLC
Also Called: International Playthings
75d Lackawanna Ave (07054-5700)
PHONE..................................973 316-2500
Rich Driscoll, *Warehouse Mgr*
Kelly Cardella, *Credit Mgr*
Brooke Visdomini, *Accountant*
Stacy Lobosco, *Sales Staff*
Stacey Bauman, *Director*
◆ **EMP:** 46 EST: 1967
SQ FT: 120,000
SALES (est): 13.1MM **Privately Held**
WEB: www.intplay.com
SIC: 3944 5092 Games, toys & children's vehicles; toys & hobby goods & supplies
PA: Epoch Co., Ltd.
    2-2-2, Komagata
    Taito-Ku TKY 111-0

(G-7938)
EVONIK CORPORATION (DH)
Also Called: Degussa
299 Jefferson Rd (07054-2827)
PHONE..................................973 929-8000
John Rolando, *President*
Joe Lally, *General Mgr*
Linda Keong, *Principal*
Sabine Fleming, *Business Mgr*
Lisa Mueller, *Business Mgr*
◆ **EMP:** 400
SQ FT: 150,500
SALES (est): 1.7B
SALES (corp-wide): 2.6B **Privately Held**
WEB: www.degussa.com
SIC: 2819 2869 2851 2816 Industrial inorganic chemicals; industrial organic chemicals; paints & allied products; inorganic pigments
HQ: Evonik Industries Ag
    Rellinghauser Str. 1-11
    Essen 45128
    201 177-01

(G-7939)
EVONIK FOAMS INC (DH)
299 Jefferson Rd (07054-2827)
PHONE..................................973 929-8000
Alexander Roth, *President*
▼ **EMP:** 24
SQ FT: 40,000
SALES (est): 4.1MM
SALES (corp-wide): 2.6B **Privately Held**
SIC: 3086 Insulation or cushioning material, foamed plastic

HQ: Evonik Corporation
299 Jefferson Rd
Parsippany NJ 07054
973 929-8000

(G-7940)
EXTREMITY MEDICAL LLC
300 Interpace Pkwy # 410 (07054-1148)
PHONE..................................973 588-8980
James Gannoe, *President*
Matthew Lyons, *President*
Ronald Stevenson, *General Mgr*
Brian Rowan, *Division VP*
Ray Penzimer, *Project Engr*
EMP: 14
SALES (est): 1.8MM **Privately Held**
SIC: 3842 Orthopedic appliances

(G-7941)
FAMCAM INC
3 Eastmans Rd (07054-3702)
PHONE..................................973 503-1600
Robert Perna, *President*
EMP: 28
SQ FT: 18,000
SALES: 3.2MM **Privately Held**
SIC: 3679 Electronic circuits

(G-7942)
FARMPLAST LLC
125 E Halsey Rd (07054-3723)
PHONE..................................973 287-6070
Mark Lomak,
◆ EMP: 28
SQ FT: 40,000
SALES (est): 7.2MM **Privately Held**
SIC: 3089 Injection molded finished plastic
products

(G-7943)
FERRERO U S A INC (DH)
7 Sylvan Way Fl 4 (07054-3805)
PHONE..................................732 764-9300
Bernard F Kreilmann, *CEO*
Pietro Ferrero, *Senior VP*
Glenn Lawse, *Vice Pres*
Dave Vennard, *Opers Mgr*
Hafsa Chawdry, *Opers Staff*
◆ EMP: 160
SQ FT: 150,000
SALES (est): 298.5MM
SALES (corp-wide): 230.1MM **Privately
Held**
WEB: www.ferrerousa.com
SIC: 5145 2064 Candy; candy & other
confectionery products
HQ: Ferrero Spa
Piazzale Pietro Ferrero 1
Alba CN
017 322-7500

(G-7944)
**FERRING PHARMACEUTICALS
INC (DH)**
100 Interpace Pkwy (07054-1149)
PHONE..................................973 796-1600
Aaron Graff, *President*
Mercia Van, *General Mgr*
Wanmei Wang, *General Mgr*
Michael Miles, *District Mgr*
Per Falk, *Exec VP*
▲ EMP: 216
SQ FT: 26,000
SALES (est): 108.9MM
SALES (corp-wide): 1.1B **Privately Held**
WEB: www.ferringusa.com
SIC: 2834 5122 Pharmaceutical prepara-
tions; pharmaceuticals
HQ: Ferring B.V.
Polarisavenue 144
Hoofddorp 2132
235 680-300

(G-7945)
FERRING PRODUCTION INC
100 Interpace Pkwy (07054-1149)
PHONE..................................973 796-1600
L P Brunse, *President*
Ahluwalia Lalit, *CFO*
L Ahluwalia, *Treasurer*
R Anderson, *Treasurer*
▲ EMP: 50 EST: 2011
SALES (est): 14MM
SALES (corp-wide): 1.1B **Privately Held**
SIC: 2834 Pharmaceutical preparations

HQ: Ferring Holding Inc.
100 Interpace Pkwy
Parsippany NJ 07054
973 796-1600

(G-7946)
FINLANDIA CHEESE INC (HQ)
2001 Us Highway 46 # 303 (07054-1315)
PHONE..................................973 316-6699
Emma Aer, *CEO*
Monique Charito, *COO*
Minyoung Cha, *QC Mgr*
Michael Restivo, *CFO*
Christine Chervenack, *Controller*
▲ EMP: 30 EST: 1998
SQ FT: 2,500
SALES (est): 4.1MM
SALES (corp-wide): 1.9B **Privately Held**
WEB: www.finlandiacheese.com
SIC: 2022 5143 Natural cheese; dairy
products, except dried or canned
PA: Valio Oy
Meijeritie 6
Helsinki 00370
103 811-21

(G-7947)
FLOWSERVE CORPORATION
333 Littleton Rd Ste 303 (07054-4866)
PHONE..................................973 334-9444
George Georgas, *Branch Mgr*
EMP: 6
SALES (corp-wide): 3.8B **Publicly Held**
SIC: 3561 Pumps & pumping equipment
PA: Flowserve Corporation
5215 N Oconnor Blvd Connor
Irving TX 75039
972 443-6500

(G-7948)
FLUOROTHERM POLYMERS INC
333 New Rd Ste 1 (07054-4212)
P.O. Box 123, Wyckoff (07481-0123)
PHONE..................................973 575-0760
Prabhat Shukla, *President*
Madhuri Shukla, *Vice Pres*
▲ EMP: 8
SQ FT: 5,000
SALES (est): 1.4MM **Privately Held**
SIC: 3082 3498 3317 3083 Unsupported
plastics profile shapes; fabricated pipe &
fittings; steel pipe & tubes; laminated
plastics plate & sheet; chemical prepara-
tions; paints & allied products

(G-7949)
FORESIGHT GROUP LLC
100 Ims Dr (07054-2957)
PHONE..................................888 992-8880
Vincent Budhai, *Manager*
Brian Dinardo, *Director*
Richard Dyer, *Sr Consultant*
Steve Runyon, *Sr Consultant*
EMP: 12
SALES (est): 1.5MM **Privately Held**
SIC: 2834 8731 Chlorination tablets & kits
(water purification); commercial research
laboratory

(G-7950)
**FOREST PHARMACEUTICALS
INC (DH)**
400 Interpace Pkwy Ste A1 (07054-1119)
PHONE..................................862 261-7000
Howard Solomon, *Ch of Bd*
Kenneth Goodman, *President*
William B Sparks, *Exec VP*
▲ EMP: 800
SQ FT: 87,000
SALES (est): 153.7MM **Privately Held**
WEB: www.forestpharm.com
SIC: 2834 Pharmaceutical preparations

(G-7951)
FREEMAN PRODUCTS INC (PA)
71 Walsh Dr Ste 101 (07054-1010)
PHONE..................................201 475-4800
George Ercolino, *President*
Vincent Cariello, *President*
George Ercolino, *CFO*
◆ EMP: 10
SQ FT: 40,000
SALES (est): 23.4MM **Privately Held**
SIC: 3914 Trophies

(G-7952)
**FRONTLINE MED
CMMNICATIONS INC (DH)**
Also Called: Frontline Med Communications
7 Century Dr Ste 302 (07054-4609)
PHONE..................................973 206-3434
Abigail Cruz, *Editor*
Robert Fee, *Editor*
Lori Laubach, *Editor*
Melissa Sears, *Editor*
Steven J Resnick, *Senior VP*
EMP: 70
SALES (est): 64MM
SALES (corp-wide): 705MM **Privately
Held**
WEB: www.cosderm.com
SIC: 2721 Trade journals: publishing &
printing
HQ: Webmd Health Corp.
395 Hudson St Fl 3
New York NY 10014
212 624-3700

(G-7953)
G HOLDINGS LLC (PA)
1 Campus Dr (07054-4404)
PHONE..................................973 628-3000
Robert B Tafaro, *CEO*
Adam Noble, *Senior VP*
Matthew Loncar, *Vice Pres*
Adel Collado, *Purchasing*
Richard Martinelli, *Credit Staff*
◆ EMP: 10
SALES (est): 2.5B **Privately Held**
SIC: 2869 2843 3295 6719 Solvents, or-
ganic; surface active agents; roofing gran-
ules; investment holding companies,
except banks

(G-7954)
GENERAL DYNAMICS MISSION
222 New Rd Ste 1 (07054-5626)
PHONE..................................973 335-2230
Mitchell L Dutton, *President*
Dale Kaminski, *Branch Mgr*
EMP: 48
SALES (corp-wide): 36.1B **Publicly Held**
WEB: www.axsys.com
SIC: 3562 Ball & roller bearings
HQ: General Dynamics Mission Systems,
Inc.
12450 Fair Lakes Cir # 200
Fairfax VA 22033
703 263-2800

(G-7955)
GENERAL ELECTRIC COMPANY
700 Parsippany Rd (07054-3712)
PHONE..................................973 887-6635
Linda Mason, *COO*
Aaron Arias, *Engineer*
Jerry D Darlington, *Sales Mgr*
John Lugbauer, *Sales Mgr*
Ted Wheeler, *IT/INT Sup*
EMP: 270
SALES (corp-wide): 121.6B **Publicly
Held**
SIC: 3599 3541 Machine shop, jobbing &
repair; milling machines
PA: General Electric Company
41 Farnsworth St
Boston MA 02210
617 443-3000

(G-7956)
GENTEK INC (DH)
90 E Halsey Rd Ste 301 (07054-3709)
PHONE..................................973 515-0900
William E Redmond, *President*
Vincent J Opalewski, *Vice Pres*
Paul Mikitik, *Purchasing*
Thomas B Testa, *CFO*
Walter Sparrowhood, *Technical Staff*
◆ EMP: 177
SALES (est): 151.4MM
SALES (corp-wide): 1.2B **Privately Held**
WEB: www.generalchemical.com/
SIC: 2869 2819 2844 3714 Industrial or-
ganic chemicals; industrial inorganic
chemicals; toilet preparations; motor vehi-
cle parts & accessories; cable, uninsu-
lated wire: made from purchased wire
HQ: Chemtrade Water Chemical Inc.
90 E Halsey Rd Ste 301
Parsippany NJ 07054
973 515-0900

(G-7957)
GSK CONSUMER HEALTHCARE
2 Sylvan Way (07054-3809)
PHONE..................................973 539-0645
EMP: 100
SALES (corp-wide): 36B **Privately Held**
SIC: 2834 Mfg Pharmaceutical Prepara-
tions
HQ: Gsk Consumer Healthcare
184 Liberty Corner Rd # 78
Warren NJ 07059
973 503-8000

(G-7958)
HAMMER PRESS PRINTERS INC
2 Cranberry Rd Ste 2 # 2 (07054-1053)
PHONE..................................973 334-4500
Susan Hammer, *CEO*
Sidney B Hammer, *President*
Kenneth Hammer, *Vice Pres*
EMP: 85 EST: 1929
SALES (est): 8.5MM **Privately Held**
WEB: www.hammerpress.net
SIC: 2752 Commercial printing, offset

(G-7959)
HARMS SOFTWARE INC
Also Called: Millennium Systems Intl
28 Eastmans Rd (07054-3703)
PHONE..................................973 402-9500
John Harms, *President*
EMP: 75
SQ FT: 13,000
SALES (est): 14.7MM **Privately Held**
WEB: www.harmssoftware.com
SIC: 7372 Business oriented computer
software

(G-7960)
ILLINOIS TOOL WORKS INC
ITW Thielex
6 Ringwood Dr (07054-1617)
PHONE..................................732 968-5300
Roger Cybert, *Manager*
EMP: 60
SQ FT: 45,000
SALES (corp-wide): 14.7B **Publicly Held**
SIC: 3082 5085 Tubes, unsupported plas-
tic; industrial supplies
PA: Illinois Tool Works Inc.
155 Harlem Ave
Glenview IL 60025
847 724-7500

(G-7961)
INDUSTRY PUBLICATIONS INC
Also Called: Spray Tech & Marketing
140 Littleton Rd Ste 320 (07054-1867)
PHONE..................................973 331-9545
Cynthia Vandervoort, *President*
Michael San Giovanni, *President*
Don Farrell, *Vice Pres*
EMP: 10 EST: 1922
SALES: 950K **Privately Held**
WEB: www.oilheating.com
SIC: 2721 Magazines: publishing only, not
printed on site

(G-7962)
**INTEGRATION INTERNATIONAL
INC (PA)**
160 Littleton Rd Ste 106 (07054-1871)
PHONE..................................973 796-2300
Pratap Jaykar, *President*
Suresh Patel, *CFO*
Parshuram Chenna, *Architect*
EMP: 31
SQ FT: 6,500
SALES (est): 14.4MM **Privately Held**
WEB: www.i3intl.com
SIC: 7379 7378 7372 Computer related
consulting services; computer mainte-
nance & repair; prepackaged software

(G-7963)
**INTEGRATION PARTNERS-NY
CORP**
1719 State Rt 10 Ste 114 (07054-4537)
PHONE..................................973 871-2100
Richard Schneider, *Manager*
EMP: 266
SALES (est): 12.3MM **Publicly Held**
SIC: 8741 7372 Management services;
prepackaged software

PA: Intercloud Systems, Inc.
1030 Broad St Ste 102
Shrewsbury NJ 07702

(G-7964)
INTERNTONAL MED NEWS GROUP LLC (DH)
Also Called: I M N G
7 Century Dr Ste 302 (07054-4609)
PHONE........................973 290-8237
Alan Imhoff, *President*
Gina Bennicasa, *Publisher*
Catherine Hackett, *Editor*
Sylvia Reitman, *Vice Pres*
Borden Therese, *Vice Pres*
EMP: 16
SQ FT: 6,100
SALES (est): 18.3MM
SALES (corp-wide): 9.6B **Privately Held**
WEB: www.imng.com
SIC: 2721 Magazines: publishing only, not printed on site

(G-7965)
INTERPACE DAGNOSTICS GROUP INC (PA)
300 Interpace Pkwy # 382 (07054-1100)
PHONE........................412 224-6100
Stephen J Sullivan, *Ch of Bd*
Jack E Stover, *President*
James Early, *CFO*
Gregory Richard, *Ch Credit Ofcr*
EMP: 42
SQ FT: 6,000
SALES: 21.9MM **Publicly Held**
SIC: 3841 8731 Diagnostic apparatus, medical; biotechnical research, commercial

(G-7966)
JHP GROUP HOLDINGS INC
1 Upper Pond Rd Ste 4 (07054-1050)
PHONE........................973 658-3569
Paul Campanelli, *CEO*
EMP: 957
SALES (est): 57.1MM **Privately Held**
SIC: 2834 Druggists' preparations (pharmaceuticals)
HQ: Par Pharmaceutical Companies, Inc.
1 Ram Ridge Rd
Chestnut Ridge NY 10977
845 573-5500

(G-7967)
JNBC ASSOCIATES LLC
100 Jefferson Rd (07054-3708)
PHONE........................973 560-5518
EMP: 5
SALES (est): 430K **Privately Held**
SIC: 3672 Mfg Printed Circuit Boards

(G-7968)
JODHPURI INC (PA)
260a Walsh Dr (07054-5702)
PHONE........................973 299-7009
Laxmi C Mehta, *President*
Sheila Mehta, *Vice Pres*
Becky Parris, *Office Mgr*
◆ EMP: 100 EST: 1989
SQ FT: 66,000
SALES (est): 18.2MM **Privately Held**
SIC: 2844 5023 Concentrates, perfume; decorative home furnishings & supplies

(G-7969)
KABEL N ELETTROTEK AMER INC
2 Cranberry Rd Ste 5a (07054-1053)
PHONE........................973 265-0850
Nicola Malaguti, *President*
▲ EMP: 5
SQ FT: 11,000
SALES: 9MM
SALES (corp-wide): 43.2MM **Privately Held**
SIC: 3315 1389 5063 Cable, steel: insulated or armored; oil & gas wells: building, repairing & dismantling; wire & cable
PA: Elettrotek Kabel Spa
Via Imerio Tondelli 10
Bagnolo In Piano RE 42011
052 295-6001

(G-7970)
KATENA PRODUCTS INC (PA)
6 Campus Dr Ste 310 (07054-4406)
PHONE........................973 989-1600
William Friedberg, *President*
Sheri Embleton, *Exec VP*
Nauman Chughtai, *Vice Pres*
Bryan Weinmann, *Vice Pres*
Raj Yerasi, *Vice Pres*
EMP: 40
SALES (est): 25MM **Privately Held**
WEB: www.katena.com
SIC: 3827 Optical instruments & lenses

(G-7971)
LAENNEC PUBLISHING INC
4 Woodhollow Rd Ste 1 (07054-2814)
PHONE........................973 882-9500
David Canfield, *President*
W P Harvey MD, *Vice Pres*
James McCarthy, *Vice Pres*
Heather Haselmann, *Associate Dir*
EMP: 5
SQ FT: 500
SALES: 45K **Privately Held**
SIC: 2741 Miscellaneous publishing

(G-7972)
LAFARGE ROAD MARKING INC
400 Lanidex Plz (07054-2722)
PHONE........................973 884-0300
Robert A Dirienzo, *President*
Anthony Cipolla, *Vice Pres*
Steve Shinners, *Vice Pres*
EMP: 250
SALES (est): 28.8MM **Privately Held**
SIC: 2851 3953 Paints & allied products; marking devices

(G-7973)
LANGAN ENGINEERING ENVIRONMEN (PA)
300 Kimball Dr Ste 4 (07054-2184)
PHONE........................973 560-4900
Andrew J Ciancia, *Ch of Bd*
David T Gockel, *President*
Nicholas De Rose, *Principal*
Rudolph P Frizzi, *Principal*
Ronald A Fuerst, *Principal*
EMP: 10 EST: 2012
SALES (est): 177.9MM **Privately Held**
SIC: 8711 8748 1389 0781 Consulting engineer; environmental consultant; testing, measuring, surveying & analysis services; landscape architects

(G-7974)
LP THEBAULT CO
249 Pomeroy Rd (07054-3727)
P.O. Box 169 (07054-0169)
PHONE........................973 884-1300
Bruce Wexler, *Exec VP*
EMP: 9
SALES (est): 1MM **Privately Held**
SIC: 2752 Commercial printing, offset

(G-7975)
MATHESON GAS PRODUCTS INC
959 Us Highway 46 (07054-3409)
PHONE........................201 867-4101
EMP: 15 EST: 1989
SALES (est): 35.8K **Privately Held**
SIC: 2813 Mfg Industrial Gases

(G-7976)
MAXIMUM MATERIAL HANDLING LLC
750 Edwards Rd (07054-4265)
PHONE........................973 227-1227
Renee Del, *Office Mgr*
Michael Dal Bon Jr,
EMP: 6
SALES (est): 1.5MM **Privately Held**
SIC: 3536 Hoists, cranes & monorails

(G-7977)
MEDICINES COMPANY (PA)
8 Sylvan Way (07054-3801)
PHONE........................973 290-6000
Clive A Meanwell, *CEO*
Fredric N Eshelman, *Ch of Bd*
Joseph Zelenski, *Partner*
Christopher T Cox, *Exec VP*
Nancye Green, *Exec VP*
EMP: 163 EST: 1996
SQ FT: 173,146
SALES: 6.1MM **Publicly Held**
WEB: www.themedicinescompany.com
SIC: 2834 Intravenous solutions

(G-7978)
MEDTRONIC USA INC
300 Interpace Pkwy # 340 (07054-1100)
PHONE........................973 331-7914
Janet Adamovic, *Principal*
EMP: 11 **Privately Held**
SIC: 3841 Surgical & medical instruments
HQ: Medtronic Usa, Inc.
710 Medtronic Pkwy
Minneapolis MN 55432
763 514-4000

(G-7979)
MSI TECHNOLOGIES LLC (PA)
1055 Parsippany Blvd 205a (07054-1230)
PHONE........................973 263-0080
Dale Baver, *Partner*
Jeffrey Herwitt, *Partner*
Darren Pico,
Darren Sammartino,
EMP: 10
SALES: 2.7MM **Privately Held**
WEB: www.msitechnologies.net
SIC: 7373 7372 Computer integrated systems design; business oriented computer software

(G-7980)
OHAUS CORPORATION (DH)
7 Campus Dr Ste 310 (07054-4413)
PHONE........................973 377-9000
Ted Xia, *President*
Jean-Yves Chever, *General Mgr*
Marty Colasurdo, *QC Mgr*
Bob Hansen, *Engineer*
Stethen Hrynkiewicz, *CFO*
▲ EMP: 53 EST: 1897
SQ FT: 130,000
SALES (est): 10.2MM
SALES (corp-wide): 2.9B **Publicly Held**
WEB: www.ohaus.com
SIC: 3821 3596 3423 Laboratory measuring apparatus; balances, laboratory; industrial scales; hand & edge tools
HQ: Mettler-Toledo, Llc
1900 Polaris Pkwy Fl 6
Columbus OH 43240
614 438-4511

(G-7981)
ONKOS SURGICAL INC
77 E Halsey Rd (07054-3714)
PHONE........................973 264-5400
Patrick Treacy, *President*
Gordon Ballard, *Vice Pres*
Charlie Christian, *Vice Pres*
Sean Curry, *Vice Pres*
Jerry Dalessio, *Vice Pres*
EMP: 27
SQ FT: 10,000
SALES: 2.2MM **Privately Held**
SIC: 3842 Implants, surgical

(G-7982)
PACIFICHEALTH LABORATORIES INC (PA)
800 Lanidex Plz Ste 220 (07054-2795)
PHONE........................732 739-2900
Fred Duffner, *President*
Stephen P Kuchen, *CFO*
▲ EMP: 9
SQ FT: 3,200
SALES: 6.9MM **Publicly Held**
WEB: www.pacifichealthlabs.com
SIC: 2834 2833 Vitamin, nutrient & hematinic preparations for human use; vitamins, natural or synthetic: bulk, uncompounded

(G-7983)
PACIRA PHARMACEUTICALS INC (PA)
5 Sylvan Way Ste 300 (07054-3813)
PHONE........................973 254-3560
David Stack, *Ch of Bd*
Max Reinhardt, *President*
Scott Braunstein, *COO*
Kristen Kaiser, *Exec VP*
James B Jones, *Senior VP*
EMP: 186

SQ FT: 42,000
SALES: 337.2MM **Publicly Held**
SIC: 2834 Pharmaceutical preparations

(G-7984)
PBF ENERGY COMPANY LLC (HQ)
1 Sylvan Way Ste 2 (07054-3879)
PHONE........................973 455-7500
Thomas J Nimbley, *Ch of Bd*
Matthew C Lucey, *President*
Trecia M Canty, *Senior VP*
T Paul Davis, *Senior VP*
Thomas L O'Connor, *Senior VP*
◆ EMP: 379
SQ FT: 58,000
SALES: 21.7B
SALES (corp-wide): 27.1B **Publicly Held**
WEB: www.pbfenergy.com
SIC: 2911 Petroleum refining
PA: Pbf Energy Inc.
1 Sylvan Way Ste 2
Parsippany NJ 07054
973 455-7500

(G-7985)
PBF ENERGY INC (PA)
1 Sylvan Way Ste 2 (07054-3879)
PHONE........................973 455-7500
Thomas J Nimbley, *Ch of Bd*
Matthew C Lucey, *President*
Gregory Eisentrager, *Superintendent*
Trecia Canty, *Senior VP*
Thomas L O'Connor, *Senior VP*
◆ EMP: 1714
SQ FT: 58,000
SALES: 27.1B **Publicly Held**
SIC: 2911 Petroleum refining

(G-7986)
PBF HOLDING COMPANY LLC (DH)
1 Sylvan Way Ste 2 (07054-3879)
PHONE........................973 455-7500
Thomas J Nimbley, *CEO*
Paul Davis, *President*
Matthew C Lucey, *President*
Trecia Canty, *Senior VP*
Thomas L O'Connor, *Senior VP*
◆ EMP: 379
SQ FT: 58,000
SALES: 27.1B
SALES (corp-wide): 27.1B **Publicly Held**
SIC: 2911 2992 Petroleum refining; lubricating oils

(G-7987)
PENSKE TRUCK LEASING CO LP
600 Edwards Rd (07054-4202)
PHONE........................973 575-0169
Terri Hymes, *CIO*
EMP: 30
SALES (corp-wide): 2.5B **Privately Held**
WEB: www.pensketruckleasing.com
SIC: 7513 4213 3519 Truck rental & leasing, no drivers; contract haulers; diesel engine rebuilding
PA: Penske Truck Leasing Co., L.P.
2675 Morgantown Rd
Reading PA 19607
610 775-6000

(G-7988)
PFIZER INC
400 Webro Rd (07054-2894)
PHONE........................973 739-0430
Tom Ladas, *Vice Pres*
Bob Van Andel, *Finance*
Anthony Corso, *Manager*
EMP: 100
SALES (corp-wide): 53.6B **Publicly Held**
WEB: www.pfizer.com
SIC: 2844 8741 Cosmetic preparations; management services
PA: Pfizer Inc.
235 E 42nd St
New York NY 10017
212 733-2323

(G-7989)
PIERRE FBRE PHRMACEUTICALS INC
8 Campus Dr Ste 2 (07054-4409)
PHONE........................973 898-1042

Jean-Luc Lowinski, *CEO*
Jean Jacques Bertrand, *Chairman*
EMP: 6
SALES (est): 960.6K
SALES (corp-wide): 400.4K **Privately Held**
SIC: 2834 Pharmaceutical preparations
HQ: Pierre Fabre Medicament
Labo Robopharm Pierre Fabre Pharmaceut
Boulogne-Billancourt 92100
149 108-000

(G-7990)
PINNACLE FOOD GROUP INC
399 Jefferson Rd (07054-3707)
PHONE..................................856 969-7100
Mark A Clouse, *CEO*
Craig Steeneck, *Exec VP*
Kelley Maggs Sr, *Senior VP*
Marc Mongulla, *Senior VP*
Phillip Barone, *Vice Pres*
EMP: 34 **EST:** 2014
SALES (est): 2.8MM **Privately Held**
SIC: 2038 Breakfasts, frozen & packaged

(G-7991)
PINNACLE FOODS FINANCE LLC (DH)
399 Jefferson Rd (07054-3707)
PHONE..................................973 541-6620
Robert J Gamgort, *CEO*
John Butler, *Exec VP*
Mary Beth Denooyer, *Exec VP*
Antonio F Fernandez, *Exec VP*
Duncan Hines, *Exec VP*
▲ **EMP:** 97
SALES: 2.4B
SALES (corp-wide): 9.5B **Publicly Held**
SIC: 2092 2099 2045 2038 Prepared fish or other seafood cakes & sticks; pancake syrup, blended & mixed; cake flour: from purchased flour; pancake mixes, prepared: from purchased flour; breakfasts, frozen & packaged

(G-7992)
PINNACLE FOODS GROUP LLC (DH)
399 Jefferson Rd (07054-3707)
PHONE..................................856 969-8238
Robert J Gamgort, *CEO*
Roger Deromedi, *Ch of Bd*
Mark L Schiller, *President*
Antonio F Fernandez, *Exec VP*
M Kelley Maggs, *Senior VP*
◆ **EMP:** 60
SALES (est): 673.7MM
SALES (corp-wide): 9.5B **Publicly Held**
WEB: www.aurorafoods.com
SIC: 2092 2099 2045 2038 Prepared fish or other seafood cakes & sticks; pancake syrup, blended & mixed; cake flour: from purchased flour; bread & bread type roll mixes: from purchased flour; pancake mixes, prepared: from purchased flour; breakfasts, frozen & packaged

(G-7993)
PINNACLE FOODS INC (HQ)
399 Jefferson Rd (07054-3707)
P.O. Box 3900, Peoria IL (61612-3900)
PHONE..................................973 541-6620
David S Marberger, *President*
Michael Barkley, *President*
Brittany Cole, *Partner*
Jill Denison, *General Mgr*
Michael Kelley Maggs, *Exec VP*
▼ **EMP:** 164
SALES: 3.1B
SALES (corp-wide): 9.5B **Publicly Held**
SIC: 2038 2035 Frozen specialties; pickles, sauces & salad dressings
PA: Conagra Brands, Inc.
222 Mdse Mart Plz
Chicago IL 60654
312 549-5000

(G-7994)
PINSONAULT ASSOCIATES LLC
5 Woodhollow Rd Ste 2 (07054-2832)
PHONE..................................800 372-9009
Tony Pinsonault, *Mktg Dir*
Christian Pinsonault,
Elizabeth Pinsonault,
EMP: 40

SQ FT: 10,000
SALES (est): 2.9MM
SALES (corp-wide): 518.1MM **Privately Held**
WEB: www.pinsonault.com
SIC: 7372 Business oriented computer software
HQ: Decision Resources, Inc.
100 District Ave Ste 213
Burlington MA 01803
781 993-2500

(G-7995)
PIRATE BRANDS LLC
Also Called: Pirates Booty
4 Gatehall Dr Ste 110 (07054-4522)
PHONE..................................973 401-6500
Mike Repole, *Mng Member*
Mel Ehrlich,
Jorgene Hertzwig,
EMP: 10
SALES (est): 962.4K
SALES (corp-wide): 7.7B **Publicly Held**
WEB: www.robertsamericangourmet.com
SIC: 2096 Potato chips & similar snacks
HQ: Amplify Snack Brands, Inc.
500 W 5th St Ste 1350
Austin TX 78701
512 600-9893

(G-7996)
PLASTIC PLUS GROUP LLC
7 Eastmans Rd (07054-3702)
PHONE..................................862 701-6981
Ryan Kurpat, *President*
Bill Bonzulak, *Warehouse Mgr*
Joe Waldman, *Mng Member*
Emil Michescu, *General Counsel*
AVI Berg,
▲ **EMP:** 15
SQ FT: 20,000
SALES: 10MM **Privately Held**
WEB: www.plasticplusgroup.com
SIC: 3081 Unsupported plastics film & sheet

(G-7997)
PNY TECHNOLOGIES INC (PA)
100 Jefferson Rd (07054-3708)
PHONE..................................973 515-9700
Gadi Cohen, *Ch of Bd*
John Hughes, *Senior VP*
Robert Stone, *Senior VP*
Jake Afber, *Vice Pres*
John P Hughes, *Vice Pres*
▲ **EMP:** 380
SALES (est): 128.1MM **Privately Held**
WEB: Www.pny.com
SIC: 3674 Semiconductors & related devices

(G-7998)
POLARIS PLATING INC
36 Teaneck Rd (07054-3642)
PHONE..................................973 278-0033
Frank J Zemo, *President*
EMP: 9
SQ FT: 20,000
SALES (est): 86.8K **Privately Held**
SIC: 3471 Electroplating of metals or formed products; finishing, metals or formed products

(G-7999)
PRECISION SPINE INC (PA)
5 Sylvan Way Ste 2 (07054-3813)
PHONE..................................601 420-4244
James R Pastena, *Ch of Bd*
Rich Dickerson, *President*
Christopher A Denicola, *COO*
Joe Deluca, *Senior VP*
Chris Denicola, *Vice Pres*
EMP: 10 **EST:** 2012
SALES (est): 1.9MM **Privately Held**
SIC: 3841 Anesthesia apparatus

(G-8000)
PREDICTIVE ANALYTCS DCISION
Also Called: Prads
2001 Route 46 Ste 310 (07054-1315)
PHONE..................................973 541-7020
Vivek Agarwal, *Exec Dir*
EMP: 2

SALES: 1MM
SALES (corp-wide): 4.9MM **Privately Held**
SIC: 7372 Prepackaged software
PA: Predictive Analytics Mauritius Holding Limited
C/O Dtos Ltd Raffles Tower, 19
Ebene
404 600-0

(G-8001)
PRINTING INDUSTRIES LLC
Also Called: D R Printing
1543 Us Hwy Rte 46 E (07054)
PHONE..................................973 334-9775
Deron Baumfeld, *Vice Pres*
Doug Rohlfing,
EMP: 8
SQ FT: 2,000
SALES (est): 450K **Privately Held**
SIC: 2752 Commercial printing, offset

(G-8002)
PRISMACOLOR CORP
Also Called: Colortec Printing Ink
120 E Halsey Rd (07054-3720)
P.O. Box 6330 (07054-7330)
PHONE..................................973 887-6040
Edward Ranno, *President*
EMP: 7
SALES (est): 860K **Privately Held**
SIC: 5085 2893 Ink, printers'; printing ink

(G-8003)
QUADRANT MEDIA CORP INC
7 Century Dr Ste 302 (07054-4609)
PHONE..................................973 701-8900
Stephen Stoneburn, *President*
EMP: 2
SALES (est): 42.8MM **Privately Held**
WEB: www.ptmg.com
SIC: 2721 Trade journals: publishing & printing

(G-8004)
RB MANUFACTURING LLC (DH)
399 Interpace Pkwy (07054-1133)
PHONE..................................973 404-2600
Alexander Lacik, *President*
Krista Davis, *Vice Pres*
Philippe Escoffier, *Vice Pres*
Abigail Powell, *Vice Pres*
Kelly M Slavitt, *Vice Pres*
▲ **EMP:** 277
SALES (est): 354.8MM
SALES (corp-wide): 16.1B **Privately Held**
SIC: 2035 2842 Mustard, prepared (wet); deodorants, nonpersonal; specialty cleaning preparations; laundry cleaning preparations; disinfectants, household or industrial plant
HQ: Reckitt Benckiser Llc
399 Interpace Pkwy # 101
Parsippany NJ 07054
973 404-2600

(G-8005)
RECKITT BENCKISER LLC (HQ)
399 Interpace Pkwy # 101 (07054-1133)
P.O. Box 225 (07054-0225)
PHONE..................................973 404-2600
Rakesh Kapoor, *CEO*
Helmut Albrecht, *Senior VP*
Ranjan Banerji, *Vice Pres*
Sunny Feng, *Project Mgr*
Pablo Delgado, *Prdtn Mgr*
◆ **EMP:** 400
SQ FT: 139,500
SALES (est): 814.4MM
SALES (corp-wide): 16.1B **Privately Held**
WEB: www.reckittprofessional.com
SIC: 2035 2842 Mustard, prepared (wet); deodorants, nonpersonal
PA: Reckitt Benckiser Group Plc
103-105 Bath Road
Slough BERKS SL1 3
845 769-7079

(G-8006)
REGENT CABINETS LLC (PA)
1719 State Rt 10 Ste 220 (07054-4537)
PHONE..................................732 363-5630
Reuvan Sternstein, *President*
▲ **EMP:** 10 **EST:** 2012
SQ FT: 25,000

SALES (est): 3.5MM **Privately Held**
SIC: 2434 Wood kitchen cabinets

(G-8007)
RESPIRONICS INC
Also Called: Respironics Healthscan
5 Woodhollow Rd Ste 1 (07054-2832)
PHONE..................................973 581-6000
Fax: 973 599-5646
EMP: 171
SALES (corp-wide): 26B **Privately Held**
SIC: 3842 3845 3841 3564 Mfg Surgical Appliances Mfg Electromedical Equip Mfg Surgical/Med Instr
HQ: Respironics, Inc.
1010 Murry Ridge Ln
Murrysville PA 15668
724 387-5200

(G-8008)
ROCKWELL AUTOMATION INC
299 Cherry Hill Rd # 200 (07054-1111)
PHONE..................................973 658-1500
Jim Tomamichel, *Branch Mgr*
EMP: 40 **Publicly Held**
SIC: 3625 Control equipment, electric
PA: Rockwell Automation, Inc.
1201 S 2nd St
Milwaukee WI 53204

(G-8009)
ROCKWELL AUTOMATION INC
700 Lanidex Plz Ste 101 (07054-2705)
PHONE..................................973 526-3901
EMP: 9 **Publicly Held**
SIC: 3625 Relays & industrial controls
PA: Rockwell Automation, Inc.
1201 S 2nd St
Milwaukee WI 53204

(G-8010)
ROHM AMERICA LLC (PA)
299 Jefferson Rd (07054-2827)
PHONE..................................973 929-8000
Jack Chenault, *President*
Johan Holleman, *Marketing Mgr*
◆ **EMP:** 100
SQ FT: 31,200
SALES (est): 195.9MM **Privately Held**
SIC: 2821 Acrylic resins

(G-8011)
ROSEMOUNT INC
1160 Parsippany Blvd # 102 (07054-1811)
PHONE..................................973 257-2300
Doug Viafora, *Manager*
EMP: 12
SALES (corp-wide): 17.4B **Publicly Held**
WEB: www.rosemount.com
SIC: 3823 Manometers, industrial process type
HQ: Rosemount Inc.
8200 Market Blvd
Chanhassen MN 55317
952 906-8888

(G-8012)
SENSOREDGE INC
140 Littleton Rd Ste 220 (07054-1896)
PHONE..................................973 975-4163
Igor Ofenbakh, *CEO*
Cornelius Cody, *Opers Mgr*
EMP: 7
SALES (est): 785.7K **Privately Held**
SIC: 2834 Medicines, capsuled or ampuled

(G-8013)
SEVERNA OPERATIONS INC
3 Eastmans Rd (07054-3702)
PHONE..................................973 503-1600
Samir Aboulhosn, *President*
Denise Masulli, *Human Res Mgr*
Mary Lauria, *Mktg Dir*
EMP: 28
SALES (est): 5.4MM **Privately Held**
SIC: 3678 Electronic connectors

(G-8014)
SHREE MELDI KRUPA LLC
Also Called: SMK Nutra Makers
71 Walsh Dr Ste B (07054-1010)
PHONE..................................732 407-5295
Avni Patel, *Mng Member*
Abhijit Patel,
Usha Patel,
EMP: 2

SQ FT: 1,500
SALES: 2MM **Privately Held**
SIC: 2023 Dietary supplements, dairy & non-dairy based

(G-8015)
SIGNIFY FINCL SOLUTIONS LLC
300 Interpace Pkwy Ste A (07054-1156)
PHONE 862 930-4682
Jeffrey Oulton, *CEO*
James Early, *CFO*
Olga Dovgan, *Business Anlyst*
EMP: 33 **EST:** 2013
SALES (est): 686.8K **Privately Held**
SIC: 7372 Publishers' computer software

(G-8016)
SIMON & SCHUSTER INC
1639 State Rt 10 Ste 200 (07054-4506)
PHONE 973 656-6000
Dave Upchurch, *Controller*
EMP: 50
SALES (corp-wide): 27.7B **Publicly Held**
WEB: www.digonsite.com
SIC: 2731 2741 7372 8732 Books: publishing only; textbooks: publishing only, not printed on site; miscellaneous publishing; technical manuals: publishing only, not printed on site; maps: publishing only, not printed on site; atlases: publishing only, not printed on site; business oriented computer software; business research service
HQ: Simon & Schuster, Inc.
1230 Ave Of The Americas
New York NY 10020
212 698-7000

(G-8017)
SOLAR TURBINES INCORPORATED
300 Kimball Dr Ste 4 (07054-2184)
PHONE 201 825-8200
Underwood James, *General Mgr*
Phaneuf David, *Area Mgr*
Alex Munoz, *Mfg Spvr*
Richard Pietras, *Purchasing*
Zhang Donghui, *Program Mgr*
EMP: 11
SALES (corp-wide): 54.7B **Publicly Held**
WEB: www.esolar.cat.com
SIC: 3511 Gas turbine generator set units, complete
HQ: Solar Turbines Incorporated
2200 Pacific Hwy
San Diego CA 92101
619 544-5000

(G-8018)
SONNEBORN LLC (DH)
600 Parsippany Rd Ste 100 (07054-3715)
PHONE 201 760-2940
Joe Brignola, *Vice Pres*
John Holloway, *Vice Pres*
Steve Puskas, *Project Engr*
Gregg Kam, *CFO*
Dominic Bellantuono, *Manager*
▼ **EMP:** 11
SALES (est): 66.4MM
SALES (corp-wide): 17.7B **Publicly Held**
SIC: 2869 Industrial organic chemicals
HQ: Sonneborn Us Holdings Llc
600 Parsippany Rd Ste 100
Parsippany NJ 07054
201 760-2940

(G-8019)
SONNEBORN HOLDING LLC
600 Parsippany Rd Ste 100 (07054-3715)
PHONE 201 760-2940
Luther Jones, *Vice Pres*
Gregg Kam, *CFO*
Roy Seib, *Marketing Mgr*
Paul C Raymond III, *Mng Member*
James Stiff,
EMP: 340
SALES (est): 69.6MM **Privately Held**
WEB: www.sonneborn.com
SIC: 2869 Fluorinated hydrocarbon gases

(G-8020)
SONNEBORN US HOLDINGS LLC (DH)
600 Parsippany Rd Ste 100 (07054-3715)
PHONE 201 760-2940
Paul Raymond III, *President*

Gregg Kam, *CFO*
EMP: 6
SALES (est): 66.4MM
SALES (corp-wide): 17.7B **Publicly Held**
SIC: 2869 Industrial organic chemicals
HQ: Hollyfrontier Lsp Holdings Llc
2828 N Harwood St # 1300
Dallas TX 75201
214 871-3555

(G-8021)
STANDARD INDUSTRIES INC (HQ)
Also Called: GAF
1 Campus Dr (07054-4404)
PHONE 973 628-3000
Robert B Tafaro, *President*
Richard A Nowak, *COO*
Daniel J Goldstein, *Senior VP*
Jan E Jerger-Stevens, *Senior VP*
Matti Kiik, *Senior VP*
◆ **EMP:** 1000
SALES (est): 1.2B
SALES (corp-wide): 2.5B **Privately Held**
SIC: 2493 Insulation & roofing material, reconstituted wood
PA: G Holdings Llc
1 Campus Dr
Parsippany NJ 07054
973 628-3000

(G-8022)
SUN CHEMICAL CORPORATION (HQ)
Also Called: US Advanced Materials Division
35 Waterview Blvd Ste 100 (07054-1285)
P.O. Box 32040, Cincinnati OH (45232-0040)
PHONE 973 404-6000
Rudi Lenz, *CEO*
Tony Cox, *Business Mgr*
Tony Searle, *Business Mgr*
John L McKeown, *Senior VP*
Jeffrey Berger, *Vice Pres*
◆ **EMP:** 100
SALES (est): 7.5B **Privately Held**
WEB: www.sunchemical.com
SIC: 2893 2865 Printing ink; color pigments, organic

(G-8023)
SYBASE INC
400 Interpace Pkwy Ste D1 (07054-1118)
PHONE 973 537-5700
EMP: 70
SALES (corp-wide): 22.5B **Publicly Held**
SIC: 7372 5045 Prepackaged Software Services Whol Computers/Peripherals
HQ: Sybase, Inc.
1 Sybase Dr
Dublin CA 94583
925 236-5000

(G-8024)
T & M TERMINAL COMPANY
1 Sylvan Way (07054-3887)
PHONE 419 902-2810
Neil Sahni, *Director*
EMP: 8
SALES (est): 487.2K
SALES (corp-wide): 27.1B **Publicly Held**
SIC: 2911 Petroleum refining
HQ: Pbf Holding Company Llc
1 Sylvan Way Ste 2
Parsippany NJ 07054

(G-8025)
TARGANTA THERAPEUTICS CORP (HQ)
8 Sylvan Way (07054-3801)
PHONE 973 290-6000
Mark W Leuchtenberger, *President*
Daniel S Char, *Vice Pres*
Roger D Miller, *VP Opers*
George A Eldridge, *CFO*
EMP: 70
SQ FT: 7,839
SALES (est): 3.1MM
SALES (corp-wide): 6.1MM **Publicly Held**
WEB: www.themedicinescompany.com
SIC: 2834 Pharmaceutical preparations
PA: The Medicines Company
8 Sylvan Way
Parsippany NJ 07054
973 290-6000

(G-8026)
TEVA API INC
400 Interpace Pkwy Ste A1 (07054-1119)
PHONE 201 307-6900
Kerri Wood, *President*
Aharon Yaari, *Vice Pres*
Sonny Say, *Buyer*
Erez Israeli, *Director*
▲ **EMP:** 23
SQ FT: 4,200
SALES (est): 8.1MM
SALES (corp-wide): 5B **Privately Held**
WEB: www.plantexusa.com
SIC: 2834 Pharmaceutical preparations
PA: Teva Pharmaceutical Industries Limited
5 Bazel
Petah Tikva 49510
392 672-67

(G-8027)
TEVA PHARMACEUTICALS
400 Interpace Pkwy Ste A1 (07054-1119)
PHONE 888 838-2872
Kare Schultz, *President*
Scott Smith, *District Mgr*
Renee Malaney, *Regl Sales Mgr*
Gil Feldman, *Marketing Staff*
Marc Andriola, *Manager*
▲ **EMP:** 13
SALES (est): 2.2MM **Privately Held**
SIC: 5912 2834 Drug stores & proprietary stores; pharmaceutical preparations

(G-8028)
TILCON NEW YORK INC (DH)
Also Called: Totowa Asphalt
9 Entin Rd (07054-5000)
PHONE 973 366-7741
Charles Clifton Morris, *President*
Joseph Dicarlo, *Manager*
▲ **EMP:** 270 **EST:** 1964
SALES (est): 393.7MM
SALES (corp-wide): 30.6B **Privately Held**
WEB: www.tilconny.com
SIC: 1429 5039 Trap rock, crushed & broken-quarrying; dolomitic marble, crushed & broken-quarrying; metal buildings
HQ: Tilcon Inc.
301 Hartford Ave
Newington CT 06111
860 223-3651

(G-8029)
TILCON NEW YORK INC
Also Called: Mount Hope Quarry
9 Entin Rd Ste 12 (07054-5000)
PHONE 800 789-7625
EMP: 8
SALES (corp-wide): 30.6B **Privately Held**
SIC: 1429 2911 Trap rock, crushed & broken-quarrying; asphalt or asphaltic materials, made in refineries
HQ: Tilcon New York Inc.
9 Entin Rd
Parsippany NJ 07054
973 366-7741

(G-8030)
TOYOTA MOTOR SALES
300 Webro Rd (07054-2825)
PHONE 973 515-5012
Bill Burris, *Marketing Staff*
EMP: 12
SALES (est): 862.9K **Privately Held**
SIC: 5511 5012 3711 Automobiles, new & used; automobile auction; motor vehicles & car bodies

(G-8031)
TOYSRUSCOM INC
Also Called: Toys "R" Us
5 Woodhollow Rd Ste 1 (07054-2832)
PHONE 973 617-3500
Antonio Urcelay, *CEO*
Wolfgang Link, *President*
Monika Merz, *President*
Richard Barry, *Exec VP*
Deborah Derby, *Exec VP*
EMP: 68
SALES (est): 33.8MM
SALES (corp-wide): 11.5B **Privately Held**
SIC: 3944 Electronic toys; blocks, toy
PA: Toys "r" Us, Inc.
1 Geoffrey Way
Wayne NJ 07470
973 617-3500

(G-8032)
UKRAINIAN NATIONAL ASSOCIATION (PA)
2200 State Rt 10 Ste 201 (07054-5305)
P.O. Box 280 (07054-0280)
PHONE 973 292-9800
Stefan Kaczaraj, *President*
Michael Koziupa, *Vice Pres*
Eugene Oscislawski, *Vice Pres*
Myron Groch, *Director*
Christine Kozak, *Admin Sec*
EMP: 41
SALES: 18.4MM **Privately Held**
WEB: www.ukrweekly.com
SIC: 6311 6512 6513 2711 Fraternal life insurance organizations; commercial & industrial building operation; apartment building operators; newspapers

(G-8033)
VALIDUS PHARMACEUTICALS LLC (PA)
119 Cherry Hill Rd # 310 (07054-1126)
PHONE 973 265-2777
Gina Walljasper, *Purchasing*
David Paznek, *QC Mgr*
Rick White, *Accountant*
Barbara A Cannizzaro, *Marketing Mgr*
James Hunter, *Mng Member*
EMP: 13
SALES (est): 4.4MM **Privately Held**
SIC: 2834 Pharmaceutical preparations

(G-8034)
VANDERBILT LLC
Also Called: Vanderbilt Industries
2 Cranberry Rd Ste 3b (07054-1053)
PHONE 973 316-3900
Mitchell Kane,
EMP: 35 **EST:** 2013
SALES (est): 4.7MM
SALES (corp-wide): 4.8MM **Privately Held**
SIC: 7382 3651 Security systems services; audio electronic systems
PA: A.C.R.E., Llc
300 State St
New London CT 06320
949 637-0423

(G-8035)
VENUS LABORATORIES INC
50 Lackawanna Ave (07054-1008)
PHONE 973 257-8983
EMP: 25
SALES (corp-wide): 93.5MM **Privately Held**
SIC: 2842 Mfg Polish/Sanitation Goods
PA: Venus Laboratories, Inc.
111 S Rohlwing Rd
Addison IL 60101
630 595-1900

(G-8036)
WARNER CHILCOTT (US) LLC (HQ)
Also Called: Warner Chilcott Laboratories
400 Interpace Pkwy (07054-1120)
PHONE 862 261-7000
Roger Boissonneault, *CEO*
Leland Cross, *Senior VP*
Izumi Hara, *Senior VP*
William Poll, *Vice Pres*
John Goll, *CFO*
▲ **EMP:** 52
SQ FT: 16,000
SALES (est): 90.8MM **Privately Held**
SIC: 2834 Pharmaceutical preparations

(G-8037)
WATERS TECHNOLOGIES CORP
1259 Route 46 Ste 3 (07054-4913)
PHONE 973 394-5660
John Antwerp, *Manager*
EMP: 10 **Publicly Held**
SIC: 3826 Chromatographic equipment, laboratory type
HQ: Waters Technologies Corporation,
34 Maple St
Milford MA 01757
508 478-2000

(G-8038)
WATSON LABORATORIES INC (DH)
Also Called: Allergan Pharmacy
400 Interpace Pkwy (07054-1120)
P.O. Box 1900, Corona CA (92878-1900)
PHONE..........................951 493-5300
Karin Shanahan, *President*
Paul M Bisaro, *Chairman*
Andy Boyer, *Vice Pres*
Weining Volinn, *Director*
Jeanette Dube, *Administration*
▲ EMP: 200
SQ FT: 100,000
SALES (est): 220.3MM **Privately Held**
SIC: 2834 Pharmaceutical preparations

(G-8039)
WINDOW TRENDS
194 Fieldcrest Rd (07054-2415)
PHONE..........................973 887-6676
Mike Ianndone, *Owner*
EMP: 4
SALES (est): 246.4K **Privately Held**
SIC: 2431 Window frames, wood

(G-8040)
WIRELESS TELECOM GROUP INC (PA)
25 Eastmans Rd (07054-3702)
PHONE..........................973 386-9696
Timothy Whelan, *CEO*
Alan L Bazaar, *Ch of Bd*
Michael Kandell, *CFO*
Daniel Monopoli, *CTO*
EMP: 88
SQ FT: 45,700
SALES: 52.7MM **Publicly Held**
WEB: www.willtek.com
SIC: 3625 3825 Noise control equipment; microwave test equipment; semiconductor test equipment; volt meters

(G-8041)
WIZDATA SYSTEMS INC
140 Littleton Rd Ste 220 (07054-1896)
PHONE..........................973 975-4113
Igor Ofenbakh, *President*
Aleksey Mazur, *Software Dev*
EMP: 12
SQ FT: 300
SALES: 1.2MM **Privately Held**
WEB: www.wdsystems.com
SIC: 8732 7372 Business analysis; prepackaged software

(G-8042)
WM STEINEN MFG CO (PA)
29 E Halsey Rd (07054-3704)
PHONE..........................973 887-6400
William Steinen, *CEO*
Thomas Keenan, *Vice Pres*
John Delaney, *Admin Sec*
EMP: 100 EST: 1907
SQ FT: 40,000
SALES (est): 15.3MM **Privately Held**
WEB: www.steinen.com
SIC: 3491 3432 3494 Process control regulator valves; plumbing fixture fittings & trim; plumbing & heating valves

(G-8043)
YUKON GRAPHICS INC
239 New Rd Ste B110 (07054-5614)
PHONE..........................973 575-5700
Alan Verbeke, *President*
Debbie Hanley, *Admin Sec*
EMP: 4
SQ FT: 16,000
SALES (est): 620.3K **Privately Held**
WEB: www.yukongraphics.com
SIC: 2752 Commercial printing, offset

(G-8044)
ZIMMER TRABECULAR MET TECH INC
10 Pomeroy Rd (07054-3722)
PHONE..........................973 576-0032
David Dvorak, *CEO*
Alex Khowaylo, *CEO*
Ajey Atre, *General Mgr*
EMP: 180
SQ FT: 100,000

SALES (est): 35.1MM
SALES (corp-wide): 7.9B **Publicly Held**
WEB: www.implex.com
SIC: 3841 3842 Veterinarians' instruments & apparatus; implants, surgical
PA: Zimmer Biomet Holdings, Inc.
345 E Main St
Warsaw IN 46580
574 267-6131

(G-8045)
ZOETIS INC (PA)
10 Sylvan Way Ste 105 (07054-3825)
PHONE..........................973 822-7000
Juan Ramon Alaix, *CEO*
Heidi C Chen, *Exec VP*
Andrew Fenton, *Exec VP*
Scott Brown, *Vice Pres*
Darryl Blum, *Opers Dir*
▲ EMP: 277
SALES: 5.8B **Publicly Held**
SIC: 2834 Pharmaceutical preparations

(G-8046)
ZOETIS LLC (HQ)
10 Sylvan Way Ste 105 (07054-3825)
P.O. Box 982163, El Paso TX (79998-2163)
PHONE..........................973 822-7000
Juan Ramon Alaix, *CEO*
Roxanne Lagano, *Exec VP*
Stefan Weiskopf, *Exec VP*
▲ EMP: 3 EST: 2012
SALES (est): 357.1MM
SALES (corp-wide): 5.8B **Publicly Held**
SIC: 2834 Pharmaceutical preparations
PA: Zoetis Inc.
10 Sylvan Way Ste 105
Parsippany NJ 07054
973 822-7000

Passaic
Passaic County

(G-8047)
3FORTY GROUP INC
90 Dayton Ave Ste 6a (07055-7014)
PHONE..........................973 773-1806
Jason Kin, *President*
EMP: 15
SQ FT: 13,000
SALES (est): 2.5MM **Privately Held**
SIC: 2253 Shirts (outerwear), knit

(G-8048)
A S A P NAMEPLATE & LABELING
Also Called: ASAP Printed Products
92 1st St (07055-6438)
PHONE..........................973 773-3934
EMP: 10
SALES (est): 690K **Privately Held**
SIC: 3479 2789 2396 Coating/Engraving Service Bookbinding/Related Work Mfg Auto/Apparel Trimming

(G-8049)
A W ROSS INC
297 Monroe St Ste 1 (07055-5293)
PHONE..........................973 471-5900
Vojtek Rys, *President*
EMP: 14 EST: 1968
SQ FT: 28,000
SALES (est): 1.8MM **Privately Held**
SIC: 2541 2434 Counters or counter display cases, wood; wood kitchen cabinets

(G-8050)
ACME ENGRAVING CO INC (PA)
19-37 Delaware Ave (07055-2099)
P.O. Box 1657 (07055-1657)
PHONE..........................973 778-0885
Roy Murat, *President*
EMP: 45 EST: 1947
SQ FT: 30,000
SALES (est): 4MM **Privately Held**
WEB: www.acmeengraving.com
SIC: 2796 2754 3479 3471 Platemaking services; rotogravure printing; etching & engraving; plating & polishing; printing trades machinery

(G-8051)
ARMADILLO METALWORKS INC
61 Willet St Ste 1 (07055-1971)
PHONE..........................973 777-2105
Jesse Krzywon, *President*
EMP: 23
SALES (est): 4.9MM **Privately Held**
SIC: 3479 Sherardizing of metals or metal products

(G-8052)
ATLANTIC MILLS INC
Also Called: Illinois Tools
1 Market St Ste 9 (07055-7364)
PHONE..........................973 344-2001
Michael O'Connell, *General Mgr*
▲ EMP: 65
SQ FT: 95,000
SALES (est): 6.8MM **Privately Held**
WEB: www.atlanticmills.com
SIC: 2211 Towels, dishcloths & washcloths: cotton

(G-8053)
BEARHANDS LTD
90 Dayton Ave Ste 9 (07055-7016)
PHONE..........................201 807-9898
Jeffrey Golden, *President*
Michael Wolinsky, *Vice Pres*
▲ EMP: 4
SALES (est): 363.1K **Privately Held**
WEB: www.bearhands.net
SIC: 2399 Hand woven apparel

(G-8054)
BETSY & ADAM LTD
Also Called: London Nite
90 Dayton Ave Ste 36 (07055-7017)
PHONE..........................212 302-3750
Michael Sklar, *Manager*
EMP: 15
SALES (corp-wide): 15.6MM **Privately Held**
WEB: www.betsyandadam.com
SIC: 5621 2335 Women's clothing stores; women's, juniors' & misses' dresses
PA: Betsy & Adam, Ltd.
525 Fashion Ave Fl 21
New York NY 10018
212 302-3750

(G-8055)
CENTRO ALTERNATIVO DE
21 Howe Ave (07055-4001)
PHONE..........................973 365-0995
Ricardo P Silva, *President*
Mariella Silva, *Owner*
EMP: 4
SALES (est): 177.7K **Privately Held**
SIC: 3221 Medicine bottles, glass

(G-8056)
COLONIAL - BENDE RIBBONS INC
180 Autumn St (07055-8511)
PHONE..........................973 777-8700
Andras Bende, *President*
Rene Rioux, *President*
▲ EMP: 7
SQ FT: 10,000
SALES (est): 420K **Privately Held**
SIC: 2396 Ribbons & bows, cut & sewed

(G-8057)
CROWN PRECISION CORP
61 Willet St Ste 6 (07055-1971)
PHONE..........................973 470-0097
Todd W Evans, *President*
Patricia Evans, *Vice Pres*
EMP: 4 EST: 1997
SQ FT: 1,800
SALES (est): 363K **Privately Held**
SIC: 3599 Machine shop, jobbing & repair

(G-8058)
CUSTOM COUNTERS BY PRECISION
11-17 Linden St (07055-2709)
PHONE..........................973 773-0111
William Pruseski, *President*
EMP: 25 EST: 1990
SALES (est): 3.9MM **Privately Held**
SIC: 2541 2821 2431 Counter & sink tops; plastics materials & resins; millwork

(G-8059)
DIMILO INDUSTRIES
90 Dayton Ave Ste 38 (07055-7017)
PHONE..........................973 955-0460
Richard Krauser, *President*
EMP: 8 EST: 2007
SALES (est): 440K **Privately Held**
SIC: 3694 Engine electrical equipment

(G-8060)
DISCOUNT PILLOW FACTORY LLC
90 Dayton Ave (07055-7035)
PHONE..........................973 444-1617
Usman Ahmad, *Mng Member*
EMP: 10
SQ FT: 12,000
SALES: 2MM **Privately Held**
SIC: 2392 Cushions & pillows

(G-8061)
DURAN CUTTING CORP
90 Dayton Ave Ste 6 (07055-7014)
PHONE..........................973 916-0006
Rafael Duran, *President*
◆ EMP: 14
SALES (est): 1.5MM **Privately Held**
SIC: 2335 Bridal & formal gowns

(G-8062)
E5 USA INC
61 Willet St Ste 24 (07055-1950)
PHONE..........................973 773-0750
Ron Koch, *President*
EMP: 7
SQ FT: 12,000
SALES: 700K **Privately Held**
SIC: 2389 Apparel for handicapped

(G-8063)
EMERALD ELECTRONICS USA INC
Also Called: E and E USA
90 Dayton Ave Ste 50 (07055-7019)
PHONE..........................718 872-5544
Elliot Tobal, *CEO*
EMP: 9
SQ FT: 6,500
SALES: 400K **Privately Held**
SIC: 3634 Electric household cooking appliances

(G-8064)
ET MANUFACTURING & SALES INC
Also Called: Ferber Plastics
90 Dayton Ave Ste C5 (07055-7014)
PHONE..........................973 777-6662
Michele Albo, *President*
John Vuolo, *Opers Mgr*
▲ EMP: 45 EST: 1948
SQ FT: 26,000
SALES (est): 4.2MM **Privately Held**
SIC: 3993 Signs & advertising specialties

(G-8065)
ETHAN ALLEN RETAIL INC
1 Market St Ste 1 # 1 (07055-7364)
PHONE..........................973 473-1019
Michael A Caffrey Jr, *Principal*
EMP: 125
SALES (corp-wide): 746.6MM **Publicly Held**
WEB: www.smyrna.ethanallen.com
SIC: 5712 3641 Furniture stores; electric lamps
HQ: Ethan Allen Retail, Inc.
25 Lake Avenue Ext
Danbury CT 06811
203 743-8000

(G-8066)
FALSTROM COMPANY
1 Falstrom Ct (07055)
PHONE..........................973 777-0013
Clifford F Lindholm III, *President*
EMP: 100 EST: 1870
SQ FT: 120,000
SALES (est): 23.3MM **Privately Held**
WEB: www.falstromcompany.com
SIC: 3441 Fabricated structural metal

GEOGRAPHIC

(G-8067)
GARYS KIDS
314 Monroe St (07055-8437)
PHONE..................................973 458-1818
Belkis D De Leon, *Principal*
EMP: 4
SALES (est): 318.5K **Privately Held**
SIC: 3672 Printed circuit boards

(G-8068)
GEIGER TOOL & MFG CO INC
50 Liberty St (07055-2737)
PHONE..................................973 777-2136
James Nogrady, *President*
Josef Schormann, *Vice Pres*
Debrah Heller, *Manager*
EMP: 16
SQ FT: 20,000
SALES: 2MM **Privately Held**
WEB: www.geigertool.com
SIC: 3599 Machine shop, jobbing & repair

(G-8069)
GEIGER TOOL CO INC
Also Called: LPI
50 Liberty St (07055-2737)
PHONE..................................973 777-5094
James Nogrady, *President*
Josef Schormann, *Vice Pres*
EMP: 18
SQ FT: 20,000
SALES (est): 1.8MM **Privately Held**
SIC: 3599 Machine shop, jobbing & repair

(G-8070)
GLOBAL WIRE & CABLE INC
61 Willet St Ste 4b (07055-1991)
PHONE..................................973 471-1000
George Szakacs, *President*
Leslie Kovach, *Vice Pres*
EMP: 45
SQ FT: 50,000
SALES (est): 886.3K **Privately Held**
SIC: 3315 3357 Wire, steel: insulated or
armored; cable, steel: insulated or ar-
mored; nonferrous wiredrawing & insulat-
ing

(G-8071)
GREENTREE PACKING INC
65 Central Ave (07055-8406)
P.O. Box 386 (07055-0386)
PHONE..................................212 675-2868
Michael P Waters, *President*
Don Waters, *Vice Pres*
EMP: 88 **EST:** 1894
SQ FT: 36,000
SALES (est): 26.3MM **Privately Held**
SIC: 2013 Sausages & other prepared
meats
PA: J A O Meat Packing Company, Inc
565 West St
New York NY 10014

(G-8072)
HAMPTON INDUSTRIES INC
1 Market St Ste 13 (07055-7364)
PHONE..................................973 574-8900
Carl Streit, *Ch of Bd*
Michael Streit, *President*
EMP: 40
SQ FT: 1,700
SALES: 10MM **Privately Held**
SIC: 2259 Curtains & bedding, knit; bed-
spreads, knit

(G-8073)
HOUSE OF HERBS I LLC
Also Called: Prime Choice Foods
38 Ann St (07055-5889)
P.O. Box 178 (07055-0178)
PHONE..................................973 779-2422
Adam Szala, *President*
EMP: 5
SQ FT: 15,000
SALES (est): 797.1K **Privately Held**
SIC: 2035 Pickles, sauces & salad dress-
ings

(G-8074)
INTERCHANGE EQUIPMENT INC
90 Dayton Ave Ste 120 (07055-7041)
PHONE..................................973 473-5005
Marc Herrmann, *President*
▲ **EMP:** 30
SQ FT: 30,000

SALES (est): 9.9MM **Privately Held**
SIC: 5084 3555 Printing trades machinery,
equipment & supplies; printing trades machinery

(G-8075)
J G SCHMIDT STEEL
Also Called: J G Schmidt Iron Works
211 Central Ave (07055-8613)
PHONE..................................973 473-4822
Raymond C Schlaier Jr, *President*
Robert Schlaier, *Vice Pres*
EMP: 19 **EST:** 1956
SQ FT: 20,000
SALES (est): 5.4MM **Privately Held**
SIC: 3441 3446 Building components,
structural steel; architectural metalwork

(G-8076)
JACKIE EVANS INC
Also Called: Jackie Evans Fashions
18 3rd St 26 (07055-7310)
PHONE..................................973 471-6991
Mario Monaco Sr, *President*
Mario Monaco Jr, *Vice Pres*
Domenick Monaco, *Admin Sec*
EMP: 150
SQ FT: 50,000
SALES (est): 13.2MM **Privately Held**
WEB: www.jackieevans.com
SIC: 2337 Women's & misses' suits &
coats

(G-8077)
JRM INDUSTRIES INC (PA)
1 Mattimore St (07055-7009)
PHONE..................................973 779-9340
Melvin Siegel, *Ch of Bd*
Lou Simon, *President*
Donna Simon, *Treasurer*
Arnold Gaudier, *Controller*
Maureen Franchino, *Office Mgr*
▲ **EMP:** 33 **EST:** 1920
SQ FT: 36,000
SALES (est): 6.7MM **Privately Held**
WEB: www.jrm.com
SIC: 2241 2672 2679 2759 Ribbons; fab-
ric tapes; labels, woven; tape, pressure
sensitive: made from purchased materi-
als; tags, paper (unprinted): made from
purchased paper; commercial printing;
packaging paper & plastics film, coated &
laminated; automotive & apparel trim-
mings

(G-8078)
K & K AUTOMOTIVE INC
979 Main Ave (07055-8620)
PHONE..................................973 777-2235
Abe Hazian, *President*
Imran Hazian, *Admin Sec*
EMP: 6 **EST:** 1966
SQ FT: 8,500
SALES (est): 510K **Privately Held**
WEB: www.kkautomotive.com
SIC: 3714 Motor vehicle engines & parts

(G-8079)
K-D INDUSTRIES INC
18 Falstrom Ct (07055-4465)
P.O. Box 118 (07055-0118)
PHONE..................................973 594-4800
Chris D'Alessandro, *President*
Glenn D'Alessandro, *Vice Pres*
Bruce Eklfon, *Bookkeeper*
Ajay Patel, *Manager*
EMP: 52
SQ FT: 12,000
SALES (est): 2.5MM **Privately Held**
SIC: 3599 Machine shop, jobbing & repair

(G-8080)
KINNERY PRECISION LLC
Also Called: Kinnery Metal
11 Exchange Pl (07055-4904)
PHONE..................................973 473-4664
Chaudhari Naresh, *Mng Member*
EMP: 5
SQ FT: 5,000
SALES (est): 410K **Privately Held**
SIC: 3523 Farm machinery & equipment

(G-8081)
LA MILAGROSA 1 LLC
100 8th St Bldg 400b (07055-7925)
PHONE..................................973 928-1799

Martha Bonola, *Mng Member*
▲ **EMP:** 15
SALES (est): 546.8K **Privately Held**
SIC: 3429 5251 5072 Keys, locks & re-
lated hardware; hardware; hardware

(G-8082)
LITTLE PRINTS DAY CARE II LLC
235 Lexington Ave (07055-6208)
PHONE..................................973 396-8989
German Lopez,
Maritza Lopez,
EMP: 10
SALES (est): 766.6K **Privately Held**
SIC: 2752 Commercial printing, litho-
graphic

(G-8083)
LOVELINE INDUSTRIES INC
90 Dayton Ave Ste 33 (07055-7017)
PHONE..................................973 928-3427
Martin Goldstein, *President*
Adam Goldstein, *Vice Pres*
Dan Goldstein, *Vice Pres*
▲ **EMP:** 20 **EST:** 1955
SQ FT: 10,400
SALES (est): 860K **Privately Held**
SIC: 2326 Work garments, except rain-
coats: waterproof

(G-8084)
MAJESTIC INDUSTRIES INC
2 Canal St (07055-6402)
PHONE..................................973 473-3434
Peter Ferentinos, *President*
Joe Ursini, *Vice Pres*
Michael Cattaneo, *Plant Mgr*
▲ **EMP:** 45
SQ FT: 100,000
SALES (est): 7.4MM **Privately Held**
SIC: 3944 Baby carriages & restraint seats

(G-8085)
MARTE CABINETS COUNTERTOPS LLC
48 Palmer St Apt 1 (07055-5420)
P.O. Box 1432 (07055-1432)
PHONE..................................973 525-9502
EMP: 4
SALES (est): 298.8K **Privately Held**
SIC: 2434 Wood kitchen cabinets

(G-8086)
MEGA INDUSTRIES LLC
79 South St (07055-7914)
P.O. Box 1565 (07055-1565)
PHONE..................................973 779-8772
Gilberto Estupinan, *Mng Member*
▲ **EMP:** 6
SQ FT: 4,500
SALES: 2.3MM **Privately Held**
SIC: 2024 Non-dairy based frozen
desserts; ices, flavored (frozen dessert);
juice pops, frozen

(G-8087)
MERCURY ADHESIVES INC
140 Dayton Ave (07055)
PHONE..................................973 472-3307
Joel Zeichner, *President*
EMP: 6
SQ FT: 10,000
SALES (est): 1.5MM **Privately Held**
SIC: 2891 Adhesives

(G-8088)
MERCURY PLASTIC BAG CO INC (PA)
168 7th St (07055-8216)
PHONE..................................973 778-7200
Marvin Rosen, *President*
Stuart Rosen, *Vice Pres*
Saundra Rosen, *Admin Sec*
EMP: 20 **EST:** 1961
SQ FT: 14,000
SALES (est): 1.8MM **Privately Held**
SIC: 2673 Plastic bags: made from pur-
chased materials

(G-8089)
METAL FINISHING CO LLC
25 Prospect St (07055-4914)
PHONE..................................973 778-9550
James Hakimi, *Principal*
EMP: 4

SALES (est): 379K **Privately Held**
SIC: 3559 3471 Metal finishing equipment
for plating, etc.; electroplating of metals or
formed products

(G-8090)
MIRROTEK INTERNATIONAL LLC
Also Called: Iron Chef
90 Dayton Ave (07055-7035)
PHONE..................................973 472-1400
Bezzi Boaz, *Info Tech Dir*
Joseph Bezborodko,
EMP: 45
SQ FT: 40,000
SALES: 7MM **Privately Held**
SIC: 3229 2035 Glass furnishings & ac-
cessories; seasonings & sauces, except
tomato & dry

(G-8091)
MWT MATERIALS INC
90 Dayton Ave Ste 6e (07055-7035)
PHONE..................................973 928-8300
Michael Katz, *President*
Paul Butler, *Vice Pres*
EMP: 12
SALES (est): 1.5MM **Privately Held**
WEB: www.mwt-materials.com
SIC: 3812 3679 Radar systems & equip-
ment; microwave components

(G-8092)
NORTHEAST PRO-TECH INC (PA)
61 Willet St Bldg L (07055-1971)
PHONE..................................973 777-5654
Frank De Work, *President*
Leslie De Work, *Vice Pres*
▲ **EMP:** 4
SALES: 1.3MM **Privately Held**
SIC: 2824 Organic fibers, noncellulosic

(G-8093)
OLDE GRANDAD INDUSTRIES INC
1 Market St Ste 15 (07055-7364)
PHONE..................................201 997-1899
Michael Kostak, *President*
▲ **EMP:** 6
SALES (est): 620K **Privately Held**
SIC: 3714 Motor vehicle parts & acces-
sories

(G-8094)
PATELLA CONSTRUCTION CORP
Also Called: Patella Woodworking
99 South St (07055)
PHONE..................................973 916-0100
Michael Ostroff, *President*
Richard Whitley, *COO*
Jens Sand, *VP Mfg*
Scott Glickman, *CFO*
EMP: 85
SQ FT: 80,000
SALES (est): 11MM **Privately Held**
WEB: www.patellawood.com
SIC: 2431 Interior & ornamental woodwork
& trim

(G-8095)
PLASTIC PLUS INC
184 Willet St (07055-1962)
PHONE..................................973 614-0271
Vijay Choksi, *President*
Viral Choksi, *Vice Pres*
▲ **EMP:** 4
SQ FT: 2,000
SALES: 1MM **Privately Held**
SIC: 3086 Plastics foam products

(G-8096)
PREMIUM IMPORTS INC
90 Dayton Ave Ste 98 (07055-7040)
PHONE..................................718 486-7125
Edward Fulop, *Ch of Bd*
Eugene Fulop, *CFO*
◆ **EMP:** 4
SALES (est): 1.9MM **Privately Held**
WEB: www.premiumimportsny.com
SIC: 2389 5699 Men's miscellaneous ac-
cessories; uniforms & work clothing

▲ = Import ▼=Export
◆ =Import/Export

(G-8097)
PUEBLA FOODS INC (PA)
26 Jefferson St (07055-6506)
PHONE..................................973 246-6311
Felix Sanchez, *President*
EMP: 22
SQ FT: 15,000
SALES (est): 2.7MM **Privately Held**
SIC: 2099 Tortillas, fresh or refrigerated

(G-8098)
PUEBLA FOODS INC
26 Jefferson St (07055-6506)
PHONE..................................973 473-4494
EMP: 10
SALES (corp-wide): 2.7MM **Privately Held**
SIC: 2099 Tortillas, fresh or refrigerated
PA: Puebla Foods Inc
    26 Jefferson St
    Passaic NJ 07055
    973 246-6311

(G-8099)
QUALCO INC
225 Passaic St (07055-6414)
PHONE..................................973 473-1222
John Ferentinos, *President*
Ed Solla, *General Mgr*
Paul Yager, *COO*
Thomas Ferentinos, *Vice Pres*
Juan Quintanar, *Opers Mgr*
▲ EMP: 50
SQ FT: 200,000
SALES (est): 19.9MM **Privately Held**
WEB: www.qualco.com
SIC: 2812 Alkalies & chlorine

(G-8100)
R L R FOIL STAMPING LLC
245 4th St Ste 4 (07055-7840)
PHONE..................................973 778-9464
Lawrence Vincent,
Richard Vincent,
EMP: 10
SQ FT: 15,000
SALES (est): 1.4MM **Privately Held**
WEB: www.rlrfoilstamping.com
SIC: 2679 2752 Paper products, con-
verted; commercial printing, offset

(G-8101)
RENAISSANCE CREATIONS LLC
95 8th St Fl 2 (07055-7905)
PHONE..................................551 206-1878
Arkadiusz Such,
EMP: 4 EST: 2011
SALES (est): 426.8K **Privately Held**
SIC: 2521 2531 2599 2511 Wood office
furniture; library furniture; school furniture;
bar furniture; kitchen & dining room furni-
ture

(G-8102)
**ROSALINDAS DISCOUNT
FURNITURE**
76 Lexington Ave (07055-5206)
PHONE..................................973 928-2838
EMP: 12
SQ FT: 8,000
SALES (est): 860K **Privately Held**
SIC: 2599 Mfg Furniture/Fixtures

(G-8103)
S&P MACHINE COMPANY INC
Also Called: Rehtek Machine Co.
135 Monroe St (07055-6513)
PHONE..................................973 365-2101
Stephen K Reh, *President*
Paul Reh, *Vice Pres*
EMP: 12
SQ FT: 9,000
SALES (est): 1.3MM **Privately Held**
WEB: www.rehtek.com
SIC: 3599 Machine shop, jobbing & repair

(G-8104)
SANDIK MANUFACTURING INC
100 8th St Ste 8 (07055-7980)
PHONE..................................973 779-0707
Girish Shah, *President*
Anup Shah, *Vice Pres*
EMP: 5 EST: 1978
SQ FT: 2,500

SALES: 800K **Privately Held**
SIC: 3469 Machine parts, stamped or
pressed metal

(G-8105)
SANIT TECHNOLOGIES LLC
Also Called: Durisan
90 Dayton Ave Ste 11 (07055-7016)
PHONE..................................862 238-7555
Arthur Wein, *VP Opers*
Joe Giovanniello, *Mng Member*
EMP: 12 EST: 2014
SQ FT: 20,000
SALES: 80K **Privately Held**
SIC: 2869 2819 2861 Industrial organic
chemicals; industrial inorganic chemicals;
gum & wood chemicals

(G-8106)
SENCO METALS LLC
90 Dayton Ave Ste 100 (07055-7040)
PHONE..................................973 342-1742
Filip Filipovski, *Mng Member*
EMP: 5
SALES (est): 441.7K **Privately Held**
SIC: 3441 7373 Fabricated structural
metal; computer-aided design (CAD) sys-
tems service

(G-8107)
SIGNMASTERS INC
217 Brook Ave Ste 2 (07055-3300)
PHONE..................................973 614-8300
Howard Muser, *CEO*
John Fernandez, *Vice Pres*
Marc Muser, *Project Mgr*
Carol Ballingall, *Accounts Exec*
Paul Fernandez, *Accounts Exec*
EMP: 72 EST: 1978
SQ FT: 75,000
SALES (est): 15.7MM **Privately Held**
SIC: 2759 Promotional printing

(G-8108)
**STAPLE SEWING AIDS
CORPORATION**
90 Dayton Ave Bldg 6c (07055-7041)
PHONE..................................973 249-0022
Jerome Zimmerman, *President*
Toby Zimmerman, *Vice Pres*
Steven Zimmerman, *Admin Sec*
EMP: 40 EST: 1974
SQ FT: 20,000
SALES (est): 4.1MM **Privately Held**
SIC: 2326 Aprons, work, except rubberized
& plastic: men's

(G-8109)
STERLING PRODUCTS INC
90 Dayton Ave Ste 77 (07055-7022)
PHONE..................................973 471-2858
Zipora Cartagena, *Principal*
EMP: 14
SALES (est): 1.8MM **Privately Held**
SIC: 3229 Glass lighting equipment parts

(G-8110)
SUNBRITE DYE CO INC (PA)
35 8th St Ste 6 (07055-7900)
P.O. Box 1076 (07055-1076)
PHONE..................................973 777-9830
Anthony Maltese Jr, *President*
EMP: 30 EST: 1961
SQ FT: 125,000
SALES (est): 13.5MM **Privately Held**
SIC: 2262 Dyeing: manmade fiber & silk
broadwoven fabrics

(G-8111)
TECHNICAL NAMEPLATE CORP
Also Called: ASAP Nameplate and Label Co
92 1st St (07055-6438)
PHONE..................................973 773-4256
Perla Navarro, *President*
Dominic Ciancitto, *General Mgr*
Harry Warshaw, *Admin Sec*
EMP: 20 EST: 1966
SQ FT: 10,000
SALES (est): 900K **Privately Held**
WEB: www.technicalnameplate.com
SIC: 3479 3993 2752 Name plates: en-
graved, etched, etc.; signs & advertising
specialties; commercial printing, litho-
graphic

(G-8112)
V M DISPLAY
90 Dayton Ave Ste 1g (07055-7035)
PHONE..................................973 365-8027
Victor Jimenez, *Owner*
EMP: 10
SQ FT: 2,500
SALES (est): 500K **Privately Held**
SIC: 2542 Stands, merchandise display:
except wood

(G-8113)
VALLE PRECISION MACHINE CO
58 Myrtle Ave (07055-3023)
PHONE..................................973 773-3037
Luis Valle, *President*
Carol Valle, *Vice Pres*
EMP: 8
SQ FT: 2,500
SALES: 1MM **Privately Held**
SIC: 3599 Machine shop, jobbing & repair

(G-8114)
VALUEWALK LLC
381 Terhune Ave (07055-2448)
PHONE..................................973 767-2181
Jacob Wolinsky,
EMP: 8
SALES (est): 517.1K **Privately Held**
SIC: 2711 Newspapers, publishing & print-
ing

(G-8115)
**WEES BEYOND PRODUCTS
CORP**
1 Market St Ste 6 (07055-7364)
PHONE..................................862 238-8800
Xia Zhou, *President*
William Bai, *Vice Pres*
EMP: 11
SQ FT: 30,000
SALES: 5MM **Privately Held**
SIC: 2499 Woodenware, kitchen & house-
hold

(G-8116)
WICK IT LLC
1 Gregory Ave (07055-5715)
P.O. Box 413, Windsor (08561-0413)
PHONE..................................973 249-2970
Joe Blythe, *Mng Member*
Danny Hughes, *Mng Member*
EMP: 8
SALES (est): 1.1MM **Privately Held**
WEB: www.wickit.com
SIC: 3292 Wick, asbestos

(G-8117)
**WINDOW PLUS HOME
IMPROVEMENT**
207 Monroe St (07055-5950)
PHONE..................................973 591-9993
Ismael Rodriquez, *President*
EMP: 15
SALES (est): 2.4MM **Privately Held**
SIC: 2591 1751 5211 Drapery hardware &
blinds & shades; window & door installa-
tion & erection; door & window products

Paterson
Passaic County

(G-8118)
**A C BAKERY DISTRIBUTORS
INC**
Also Called: AC Bakery
1 Industrial Plz (07503-2964)
PHONE..................................973 977-2255
Anthony Cipriano, *President*
Lena Johnson, *Admin Sec*
▲ EMP: 10
SQ FT: 5,000
SALES (est): 1.8MM **Privately Held**
SIC: 2051 Bread, cake & related products

(G-8119)
A S 4 PLASTIC INC
116 Getty Ave (07503-2807)
PHONE..................................973 925-5223
EMP: 4
SALES (est): 330.6K **Privately Held**
SIC: 3089 Plastic processing

(G-8120)
A S M TECHNICAL
34 Waite St (07524-1216)
PHONE..................................973 225-0111
EMP: 5
SALES: 400K **Privately Held**
SIC: 3559 Mfg Misc Industry Machinery

(G-8121)
ABBA METAL WORKS INC
337 River St (07524-2211)
PHONE..................................973 684-0808
Corrado Abbattista, *President*
Madaline Abbattista, *Vice Pres*
Mark Abbattista, *Project Mgr*
EMP: 7
SQ FT: 3,600
SALES (est): 1.3MM **Privately Held**
SIC: 3446 5719 1799 Stairs, staircases,
stair treads: prefabricated metal; metal-
ware; ornamental metal work

(G-8122)
ABCO METAL LLC
138 3rd Ave (07514-1513)
PHONE..................................973 772-8160
Todd Abrams,
EMP: 15
SALES (est): 1.4MM **Privately Held**
SIC: 3444 Sheet metalwork

(G-8123)
ABUELITO CHEESE INC
607 Main St (07503-3025)
PHONE..................................973 345-3503
Miguel Torres, *President*
Carolina Piaz, *General Mgr*
Senen Torres, *Plant Mgr*
EMP: 9
SALES (est): 1.3MM **Privately Held**
SIC: 2022 Cheese, natural & processed

(G-8124)
**ACCURATE BRONZE BEARING
CO**
64 Illinois Ave (07503-1707)
PHONE..................................973 345-2304
Roger Zito, *President*
Nancy Zito, *Corp Secy*
EMP: 5
SQ FT: 4,200
SALES: 500K **Privately Held**
SIC: 3568 5085 Power transmission
equipment; bearings

(G-8125)
**ACE REPROGRAPHIC SERVICE
INC**
74 E 30th St (07514-1855)
PHONE..................................973 684-5945
Toll Free:..................................888 -
Arthur M Scialla, *President*
Michael Avoletta, *Accounts Exec*
Kurt Biroc, *Manager*
EMP: 46 EST: 1933
SQ FT: 10,280
SALES (est): 10MM **Privately Held**
WEB: www.acereprographic.com
SIC: 2752 Commercial printing, litho-
graphic

(G-8126)
**AEROTECH PROC SOLUTIONS
LLC**
57 Wood St (07524-1007)
PHONE..................................973 782-4485
Glorianne Zyskowski, *Manager*
EMP: 4
SQ FT: 15,000
SALES (est): 275.7K **Privately Held**
SIC: 3471 Anodizing (plating) of metals or
formed products

(G-8127)
AFINA CORPORATION
40 Warren St (07524-2205)
PHONE..................................973 684-7650
Raymond Lombardo, *President*
Jacob Goren, *Vice Pres*
◆ EMP: 25
SQ FT: 20,000
SALES (est): 329.8K **Privately Held**
WEB: www.afinacorporation.com
SIC: 2541 Cabinets, except refrigerated:
show, display, etc.: wood

G E O G R A P H I C

(G-8128)
AHZANIS CASTLE LLC
134 E Main St (07522-1852)
PHONE................................973 874-3191
EMP: 6
SALES: 100K **Privately Held**
SIC: 2051 Cakes, bakery: except frozen

(G-8129)
AIRWORLD INC
70 Spruce St (07501-1734)
PHONE................................973 720-1008
Sam OH, *Owner*
John Rizzuto, *Vice Pres*
Joseph Chung, *Vice Pres*
EMP: 11
SQ FT: 5,000
SALES (est): 800K **Privately Held**
SIC: 3582 Commercial laundry equipment

(G-8130)
ALBEN METAL PRODUCTS INC
Also Called: V A Metal Products
11 Iowa Ave (07503-2516)
PHONE................................973 279-8891
Benjamin Vollero, *President*
Alexander Vollero, *Treasurer*
EMP: 4
SQ FT: 3,000
SALES: 340K **Privately Held**
SIC: 3599 3541 Machine shop, jobbing &
repair; machine tools, metal cutting type

(G-8131)
ALCHEMY BILLBOARDS LLC
125 5th Ave (07524-1204)
PHONE................................973 977-8828
George Wang,
EMP: 4
SALES (est): 398.5K **Privately Held**
SIC: 2396 Fabric printing & stamping

(G-8132)
ALL AMERICAN EXTRUSION INC
239 Lindbergh Pl (07503-2821)
PHONE................................973 881-9030
EMP: 5
SALES (est): 665.2K **Privately Held**
SIC: 2821 Plastics materials & resins

(G-8133)
ALL IN COLOR INC
132 Beckwith Ave (07503-2815)
PHONE................................973 626-0987
Daniel Parisi, *CEO*
Christopher Massa, *President*
EMP: 4
SALES: 300K **Privately Held**
SIC: 2732 8742 Book printing; marketing
consulting services

(G-8134)
ALLIED PLASTICS NEW JERSEY LLC
155 Sherman Ave (07502-1707)
PHONE................................973 956-9200
Menash Oratz, *CEO*
EMP: 85
SALES (est): 10MM
SALES (corp-wide): 70K **Privately Held**
WEB: www.alliedextruders.com
SIC: 2673 Bags: plastic, laminated &
coated
PA: Allied Plastics Holdings, Llc
560 Ferry St
Newark NJ 07105
718 729-5500

(G-8135)
AMB ENTERPRISES LLC (PA)
Also Called: Baker Adhesives
25 Lake St (07501-1516)
PHONE................................973 225-1070
Anthony Bucco, *Mng Member*
William Zelman,
EMP: 20
SQ FT: 40,000
SALES (est): 5.1MM **Privately Held**
SIC: 2891 Adhesives

(G-8136)
AMERICAN HOSE HYDRAULIC CO INC (PA)
700 21st Ave (07513-1145)
PHONE................................973 684-3225

Uri Dobriner, *President*
Danielle Dobriner, *Treasurer*
Idalee Ojeda, *Controller*
Scott Miller, *Manager*
John Scala, *Manager*
▲ EMP: 30
SALES (est): 23MM **Privately Held**
SIC: 5084 7699 3492 Hydraulic systems
equipment & supplies; hydraulic equip-
ment repair; hose & tube fittings & assem-
blies, hydraulic/pneumatic

(G-8137)
AMERICAN REFUSE SUPPLY INC (PA)
700 21st Ave (07513-1145)
PHONE................................973 684-3225
Uri Dobriner, *President*
Danielle Dobriner, *Treasurer*
Jerry Burns, *Manager*
EMP: 18
SQ FT: 10,000
SALES (est): 2.2MM **Privately Held**
SIC: 3714 Motor vehicle parts & acces-
sories

(G-8138)
AMERICARE LABORATORIES LTD
Also Called: Ameriderm Laboratories
126 Pennsylvania Ave # 104 (07503-2527)
PHONE................................973 279-5100
Bernard Elefant, *President*
Phyllis Elefant, *Treasurer*
▲ EMP: 20 EST: 1998
SQ FT: 15,000
SALES (est): 3.9MM **Privately Held**
WEB: www.ameriderm.com
SIC: 2844 5122 2841 Face creams or lo-
tions; toiletries; soap & other detergents

(G-8139)
ANDARN ELECTRO SERVICE INC
72 Michigan Ave (07503-1808)
P.O. Box 188 (07543-0188)
PHONE................................973 523-2220
Raman Patel, *President*
Chandra Patel, *Vice Pres*
Dinesh Patel, *Admin Sec*
EMP: 20 EST: 1956
SQ FT: 10,000
SALES (est): 2.4MM **Privately Held**
SIC: 3471 Anodizing (plating) of metals or
formed products

(G-8140)
ANNITTI ENTERPRISES INC
Also Called: E & H Laminating & Slitting Co
138 Grand St (07501-2639)
PHONE................................973 345-1725
Kenneth S Annitti, *President*
Ethel H Annitti, *Chairman*
Kevin W Annitti, *Vice Pres*
▲ EMP: 29 EST: 1976
SQ FT: 27,000
SALES (est): 8.5MM **Privately Held**
WEB: www.ehlam.com
SIC: 2891 Adhesives

(G-8141)
ARAB VOICE NEWSPAPER
956 Main St (07503-2307)
PHONE................................973 523-7815
Walid Rabah, *Owner*
EMP: 8
SALES (est): 389.4K **Privately Held**
SIC: 2711 Newspapers, publishing & print-
ing

(G-8142)
ARROW STEEL INC
629 E 19th St (07514-2800)
PHONE................................973 523-1122
Frank Tondo, *President*
Gail Tondo, *Corp Secy*
EMP: 10
SQ FT: 20,000
SALES (est): 2MM **Privately Held**
WEB: www.arrowcompactor.com
SIC: 3589 Garbage disposers & com-
pactors, commercial

(G-8143)
ATLANTIC STEEL SOLUTIONS LLC
74 Railroad Ave Bldg 102 (07501-2910)
PHONE................................973 978-0026
Weverton Palmieri, *Mng Member*
EMP: 10
SQ FT: 10,000
SALES (est): 364K **Privately Held**
SIC: 3462 Iron & steel forgings

(G-8144)
B L WHITE WELDING & STEEL CO
527 E 33rd St (07504-1746)
PHONE................................973 684-4111
Richard Haddad, *President*
EMP: 6 EST: 1951
SQ FT: 12,000
SALES (est): 778.6K **Privately Held**
SIC: 3441 7692 3446 Fabricated struc-
tural metal; welding repair; architectural
metalwork

(G-8145)
BAKER/TITAN ADHESIVES
25 Lake St (07501-1516)
PHONE................................973 225-1070
Tony Bucco, *President*
Morris Gialli, *General Mgr*
Bill Zelman, *Vice Pres*
▼ EMP: 20
SALES: 7MM
SALES (corp-wide): 5.1MM **Privately Held**
SIC: 2891 Adhesives
PA: Amb Enterprises Llc
25 Lake St
Paterson NJ 07501
973 225-1070

(G-8146)
BALTIMORE TRANSFORMER COMPANY
460 Totowa Ave (07522-1513)
PHONE................................973 942-2222
Daniel H Cezar, *President*
Frances Cezar, *Principal*
Cliff Markowitz, *Principal*
EMP: 38
SALES: 950K **Privately Held**
SIC: 3612 3677 Power transformers, elec-
tric; electronic transformers

(G-8147)
BASIC PLASTICS COMPANY INC (PA)
318 Mclean Blvd Bldg 5 (07504-1245)
PHONE................................973 977-8151
Erol Bulur, *President*
Paul Winakur, *Vice Pres*
EMP: 25
SQ FT: 40,000
SALES (est): 2.5MM **Privately Held**
WEB: www.basicplastics.com
SIC: 2673 2671 Plastic bags: made from
purchased materials; plastic film, coated
or laminated for packaging

(G-8148)
BIOGENESIS INC
Also Called: Biogenesis-Labs
444 Marshall St (07503-2909)
PHONE................................201 678-1992
Ann Rabbani, *President*
Kevin Rabbani, *COO*
▲ EMP: 10 EST: 1998
SALES (est): 2.5MM **Privately Held**
WEB: www.biogenesis-labs.com
SIC: 2844 Cosmetic preparations

(G-8149)
BREAD GUY INC
840 E 28th St (07513-1219)
P.O. Box 97 (07543-0097)
PHONE................................973 881-9002
EMP: 19 EST: 1996
SALES (est): 3MM **Privately Held**
SIC: 2051 5149 Mfg Bread/Related Prod-
ucts Whol Groceries

(G-8150)
BRISAR INDUSTRIES INC
Also Called: Brisar Delvco Packaging Svcs
76 Wood St (07524-1000)
PHONE................................973 278-2500
Mark Cohen, *President*
Adel Elsayed, *Vice Pres*
Karen Tuzzio, *Finance Mgr*
Kate Schultz, *Planning*
▲ EMP: 53
SALES: 9MM **Privately Held**
WEB: www.brisar.com
SIC: 7389 3089 7331 3544 Packaging &
labeling services; thermoformed finished
plastic products; direct mail advertising
services; special dies & tools

(G-8151)
BURLINGTON TEXTILE MACHINERY
Also Called: Btm
39 Mcbride Ave (07501-1715)
PHONE................................973 279-5900
Tom West, *President*
EMP: 17 EST: 1999
SALES (est): 1.7MM
SALES (corp-wide): 11.3MM **Privately Held**
WEB: www.glenro.com
SIC: 3552 5084 Textile machinery; textile
machinery & equipment
PA: Glenro, Inc.
39 Mcbride Ave
Paterson NJ 07501
973 279-5900

(G-8152)
C & S MACHINERY REBUILDING
636 E 19th St Ste 642 (07514)
PHONE................................973 742-7302
Cosmo Scardino, *President*
EMP: 4
SQ FT: 3,500
SALES (est): 380K **Privately Held**
SIC: 3542 Rebuilt machine tools, metal
forming types

(G-8153)
CACCIOLA IRON WORKS INC
65 N 9th St (07522-1109)
PHONE................................973 595-0854
Angelo Cacciola, *President*
Sal Cacciola, *Corp Secy*
Joe Cacciola, *Vice Pres*
▲ EMP: 6
SQ FT: 3,000
SALES: 350K **Privately Held**
SIC: 3446 Railings, bannisters, guards,
etc.: made from metal pipe

(G-8154)
CAPITAL SOAP PRODUCTS LLC
62 Kearney St (07522-1508)
P.O. Box 357 (07544-0357)
PHONE................................973 333-6100
A J Kretz, *President*
Kip Venezia, *Manager*
EMP: 18 EST: 1948
SQ FT: 50,000
SALES (est): 3.3MM **Privately Held**
SIC: 2842 2841 Sweeping compounds, oil
or water absorbent, clay or sawdust;
soap: granulated, liquid, cake, flaked or
chip

(G-8155)
CENTURY SERVICE AFFILIATES INC (PA)
Also Called: Carry Cases Plus
510 E 31st St (07504-2120)
PHONE................................973 742-3516
Steve Holand, *President*
Lawrence Holand, *Vice Pres*
Lizzie Roman, *Opers Staff*
Lizzie R Work, *Opers Staff*
▲ EMP: 30
SQ FT: 24,000
SALES (est): 5.2MM **Privately Held**
WEB: www.carrycasesplus.com
SIC: 3086 Packaging & shipping materials,
foamed plastic

(G-8156)
CERESIST INC
176 E 7th St Ste 2 (07524-1600)
P.O. Box 213, Hawthorne (07507-0213)
PHONE..................................973 345-3231
Dino Tsasaris, *President*
◆ EMP: 10
SALES (est): 2.3MM **Privately Held**
WEB: www.ceresist.com
SIC: 3272 Pipe, concrete or lined with concrete

(G-8157)
CHURCH VESTMENT MFG CO INC
41 Paterson Ave Ste 1 (07522-1460)
P.O. Box 2334 (07509-2334)
PHONE..................................973 942-2833
Gerard J Siccardi Jr, *President*
Michelle Siccardi, *Vice Pres*
Gerard J Siccardi Sr, *Treasurer*
EMP: 4 EST: 1955
SQ FT: 1,500
SALES (est): 219.6K **Privately Held**
SIC: 2389 Clergymen's vestments

(G-8158)
CLOVER STAMPING INC
60 Spruce St (07501-1727)
PHONE..................................973 278-4888
Robert Kellenberger, *President*
EMP: 9 EST: 1953
SQ FT: 15,000
SALES: 800K **Privately Held**
WEB: www.cloverstamping.com
SIC: 3469 3544 Stamping metal for the trade; special dies, tools, jigs & fixtures

(G-8159)
COLOR DECOR LTD LIABILITY CO
518 E 36th St (07504-1723)
PHONE..................................973 689-2699
Ed Velky,
EMP: 3
SALES: 3MM **Privately Held**
SIC: 2499 Yard sticks, wood

(G-8160)
COLUMBIAN ORNA IR WORKS INC
332 Vreeland Ave (07513-1014)
PHONE..................................973 697-0927
John Marogi, *President*
EMP: 4
SQ FT: 10,000
SALES (est): 716K **Privately Held**
SIC: 3446 Architectural metalwork

(G-8161)
COMMANDER IMAGING PRODUCTS INC
70 Spruce St Ste 8 (07501-1728)
PHONE..................................973 742-9298
Christine Brady, *President*
Richard A Brady, *Vice Pres*
Jose Marte, *Vice Pres*
Patricia Brady, *Admin Sec*
▲ EMP: 28
SQ FT: 32,000
SALES (est): 4.1MM **Privately Held**
WEB: www.commanderimaging.com
SIC: 3955 5112 Ribbons, inked: typewriter, adding machine, register, etc.; stationery & office supplies

(G-8162)
COMMUNICATION PRODUCTS CO
201 Mclean Blvd (07504-1000)
PHONE..................................973 977-8490
Joan Huang, *Manager*
EMP: 6
SALES (est): 367.9K **Privately Held**
SIC: 3679 Electronic components

(G-8163)
CONDUENT STATE HEALTHCARE LLC
Also Called: Mj Family Care
100 Hamilton Plz Ste 400 (07505-2104)
PHONE..................................973 754-6134
Naeil Hamdi, *Branch Mgr*
EMP: 5

SALES (corp-wide): 5.3B **Publicly Held**
SIC: 3577 Computer peripheral equipment
HQ: Conduent State Healthcare, Llc
12410 Milestone Dr Ste 500
Germantown MD 20876
301 820-4200

(G-8164)
CROWN ROLL LEAF INC (PA)
91 Illinois Ave (07503-1798)
P.O. Box 2305, Clifton (07015-2305)
PHONE..................................973 742-4000
Margaret Waitts, *CEO*
George Waitts, *COO*
James Waitts, *COO*
Manny Cueli, *Vice Pres*
Manuel Cueli, *Vice Pres*
▲ EMP: 151
SQ FT: 150,000
SALES (est): 63.4MM **Privately Held**
WEB: www.crownrollleaf.com
SIC: 3497 Metal foil & leaf

(G-8165)
CROWN ROLL LEAF INC
12 Columbia Ave (07503)
PHONE..................................973 684-2600
Maggy Waitts, *Branch Mgr*
EMP: 25
SALES (corp-wide): 63.4MM **Privately Held**
WEB: www.crownrollleaf.com
SIC: 7389 2759 Trading stamp promotion & redemption; commercial printing
PA: Crown Roll Leaf, Inc.
91 Illinois Ave
Paterson NJ 07503
973 742-4000

(G-8166)
CUSTOM LAMINATIONS INC
Also Called: Cli Group, The
932 Market St (07513-1129)
PHONE..................................973 279-9174
Daren Silverstein, *President*
Paul Harencak, *Vice Pres*
Carl Passaglia, *Manager*
Joyce Silverstein, *Admin Sec*
▲ EMP: 25
SQ FT: 50,000
SALES (est): 4.8MM **Privately Held**
WEB: www.customlaminations.com
SIC: 2295 2672 2396 Laminating of fabrics; coated & laminated paper; fabric printing & stamping

(G-8167)
DANIELLE DIE CUT PRODUCTS INC
238 Lindbergh Pl Ste 3 (07503-2823)
PHONE..................................973 278-3000
Daniel Dibetitto, *President*
▲ EMP: 32
SALES (est): 5.5MM **Privately Held**
SIC: 3423 2675 Cutting dies, except metal cutting; die-cut paper & board

(G-8168)
DANTCO CORP
Also Called: Dantco Mixers
9 Oak St (07501)
PHONE..................................973 278-8776
Michael Dantuono, *President*
Michael D Antuono, *President*
Lisa D Antuono, *Admin Sec*
▲ EMP: 10 EST: 1968
SQ FT: 6,000
SALES: 600K **Privately Held**
WEB: www.dantco.com
SIC: 3559 3679 3556 3613 Pharmaceutical machinery; paint making machinery; electronic circuits; dairy & milk machinery; control panels, electric

(G-8169)
DE JONG IRON WORKS INC
223 Godwin Ave 231 (07501-1602)
P.O. Box 532, Hawthorne (07507-0532)
PHONE..................................973 684-1633
Ed De Jong, *President*
John Sabilio, *Corp Secy*
Mark Boonstra, *Vice Pres*
Jerry De Jong, *Vice Pres*
EMP: 9 EST: 1908
SQ FT: 7,800

SALES (est): 1.2MM **Privately Held**
WEB: www.dejongiron.com
SIC: 3441 Fabricated structural metal

(G-8170)
DE LEON PLASTICS CORP
473 Getty Ave (07503-1815)
PHONE..................................973 653-3480
Mike Hamman, *CEO*
Hany Hammam, *President*
Hany Hamman, *President*
EMP: 15
SQ FT: 200
SALES: 1.2MM **Privately Held**
SIC: 3089 Plastic containers, except foam

(G-8171)
DELUXE FOODS INTERNATIONAL
29 E 25th St (07514-1503)
PHONE..................................862 257-1909
Elya Kraus, *CEO*
Ervin Silver, *President*
EMP: 5 EST: 2013
SALES: 2.2MM **Privately Held**
SIC: 2099 Food preparations

(G-8172)
DELVCO PHARMA PACKG SVCS INC
Also Called: Brisar Delvco
150 E 7th St (07524-1607)
PHONE..................................973 278-2500
Adel Elsayed, *President*
Mark Cohen, *COO*
Raul Martinez, *Info Tech Mgr*
Cristian Lopez, *Administration*
▲ EMP: 74
SALES (est): 11.4MM **Privately Held**
WEB: www.brisar.com
SIC: 3089 2653 Thermoformed finished plastic products; boxes, corrugated: made from purchased materials

(G-8173)
DICAR DIAMOND TOOL CORP
108 Kentucky Ave (07503-2508)
PHONE..................................973 684-0949
James Zambrano, *President*
Mark Zambrano, *Vice Pres*
EMP: 11
SALES: 200K **Privately Held**
WEB: www.dicardiamond.com
SIC: 5085 3423 Industrial tools; hand & edge tools

(G-8174)
DING MOO LLC
Also Called: Dingmans Dairy
18 Alabama Ave (07503-2107)
PHONE..................................973 881-8622
Marianna Powell, *Sales Staff*
Jim Allen, *Sales Associate*
Bill McCormick, *Sales Associate*
Joseph Belasco,
EMP: 35
SALES (est): 6.8MM **Privately Held**
SIC: 2024 Dairy based frozen desserts

(G-8175)
DYERICH FLOORING DESIGNS LTD
35 Dale Ave (07505-1906)
PHONE..................................973 357-0600
Richmond Eshaghoff, *President*
▲ EMP: 2
SALES: 4MM **Privately Held**
SIC: 3996 Hard surface floor coverings

(G-8176)
EDKO ELECTRONICS
460 Totowa Ave (07522-1513)
PHONE..................................973 942-2222
Martin Gorman, *Principal*
Cliff Markowitz, *Controller*
Frances Cezar, *Administration*
EMP: 38
SALES: 950K **Privately Held**
SIC: 3612 3677 Transformers, except electric; electronic transformers

(G-8177)
ELECTRONIC TRANSFORMER CORP
460 Totowa Ave (07522-1513)
PHONE..................................973 942-2222
Daniel Cezar, *President*
Cliff Markowitz, *Sales Mgr*
Frances Cezar, *Director*
EMP: 38 EST: 1961
SQ FT: 37,000
SALES (est): 6.1MM **Privately Held**
WEB: www.electronictransformercorp.com
SIC: 3677 Transformers power supply, electronic type; filtration devices, electronic

(G-8178)
ELEVATOR CABS OF NY INC
Also Called: Elevator Doors-Elevator Cabs
15 Jane St (07522-1197)
PHONE..................................973 790-9100
Cheryl Kozlowski, *CEO*
Thomas Aveni, *President*
EMP: 70 EST: 1960
SQ FT: 65,000
SALES (est): 19.1MM **Privately Held**
SIC: 3534 Elevators & equipment

(G-8179)
ELEVATOR DOORS INC
15 Jane St (07522-1197)
PHONE..................................973 790-9100
EMP: 35
SALES (est): 748.4K **Privately Held**
SIC: 3534 Elevators & equipment

(G-8180)
ELEVATOR ENTERANCES NY INC
15 Jane St (07522-1168)
PHONE..................................973 790-9100
Thomas Aveni, *President*
EMP: 25
SQ FT: 65,000
SALES (est): 3.3MM **Privately Held**
WEB: www.elevatordoors.com
SIC: 3534 Elevators & equipment

(G-8181)
ELEVATOR ENTRANCE INC
15 Jane St (07522-1168)
PHONE..................................973 790-9100
Thomas Aveni, *President*
EMP: 35 EST: 1945
SQ FT: 48,000
SALES (est): 7.9MM **Privately Held**
SIC: 3534 3442 Elevators & equipment; metal doors, sash & trim

(G-8182)
EMBROIDERY CONCEPTS
41 Paterson Ave 43 (07522-1460)
P.O. Box 2334 (07509-2334)
PHONE..................................973 942-8555
EMP: 4
SALES (est): 150K **Privately Held**
SIC: 2397 Embroidery

(G-8183)
EMPIRE INDUSTRIES INC
40 Warren St (07524-2205)
PHONE..................................973 279-2050
Jacob Goren, *President*
Bonnie Goren, *Treasurer*
▲ EMP: 52
SQ FT: 94,000
SALES (est): 7.8MM **Privately Held**
WEB: www.empire-industries.com
SIC: 2434 Wood kitchen cabinets

(G-8184)
ENA MEAT PACKING INC (PA)
240 E 5th St (07524-2109)
PHONE..................................973 742-4790
Ali Kucukkarca, *President*
Saffet Kucukkara, *Vice Pres*
Zatibeg Kucukkara, *Admin Sec*
EMP: 21
SQ FT: 100,000
SALES (est): 3.3MM **Privately Held**
SIC: 2011 2015 2013 Beef products from beef slaughtered on site; poultry slaughtering & processing; sausages & other prepared meats

(G-8185)
EVIVA LLC (PA)
30 Wood St (07524-1008)
PHONE..........................973 925-4028
Yahya Mohammad, *Mng Member*
EMP: 8
SQ FT: 20,000
SALES (est): 2.2MM **Privately Held**
SIC: 2499 1799 Kitchen, bathroom &
household ware: wood; kitchen & bath-
room remodeling

(G-8186)
EXALENT PACKAGING INC
55 1st Ave (07514-2035)
PHONE..........................973 742-9600
Fax: 973 742-9647
EMP: 22
SQ FT: 22,000
SALES (est): 2.3MM **Privately Held**
SIC: 2652 Mfg Setup Paperboard Boxes

(G-8187)
EXCEL HOBBY BLADES CORP
Also Called: Excel Blades
481 Getty Ave (07503-1313)
PHONE..........................973 278-4000
Mike Hamman, *President*
Kenda Hammam, *Sales Staff*
▲ EMP: 45
SQ FT: 18,000
SALES (est): 6.8MM **Privately Held**
SIC: 3423 3952 Hand & edge tools; lead
pencils & art goods

(G-8188)
F & R MACHINE CORP
41 Bleeker St (07524-1016)
P.O. Box 1262 (07509-1262)
PHONE..........................973 684-8139
Jack Liberzon, *President*
◆ EMP: 22
SQ FT: 18,000
SALES: 3.5MM **Privately Held**
SIC: 3599 Machine shop, jobbing & repair

(G-8189)
**FABRICOLOR HOLDING INTL
LLC**
24 1/2 Van Houten St (07505-1031)
P.O. Box 1856 (07509-1856)
PHONE..........................973 742-5800
Oleg Ponomarev, *Vice Pres*
Miro E Muzik, *Mng Member*
EMP: 5
SQ FT: 10,000
SALES: 2MM **Privately Held**
SIC: 2865 Dyes, synthetic organic

(G-8190)
FAIRFIELD TEXTILES CORP (PA)
Also Called: Paterson Laundry & Die Div
34 Waite St (07524-1216)
PHONE..........................973 227-1656
Otto Kuczynski, *President*
▲ EMP: 80 EST: 1976
SQ FT: 65,000
SALES: 13.9MM **Privately Held**
SIC: 2253 Jerseys, knit; dyeing & finishing
knit outerwear, excl. hosiery & glove

(G-8191)
FARAJ INC
107 Pennsylvania Ave (07503)
PHONE..........................201 313-4480
Zaher Faraj, *President*
Moe Samman, *General Mgr*
Raida Samman, *Vice Pres*
▲ EMP: 80
SQ FT: 10,000
SALES: 6.7MM **Privately Held**
WEB: www.farajinc.com
SIC: 2395 Embroidery & art needlework

(G-8192)
FELCO PRODUCTS LLC
18 Furler St (07512-1802)
PHONE..........................973 890-7979
▲ EMP: 5
SALES (est): 452.1K **Privately Held**
SIC: 3714 Mfg Motor Vehicle Parts/Acces-
sories

(G-8193)
FLECH PAPER PRODUCTS INC
55 1st Ave Ste 1 (07514-2036)
PHONE..........................973 357-8111
Douglas Kandel, *Co-President*
Stephen Echikson, *Co-President*
Doug Kandel, *Office Mgr*
◆ EMP: 15
SQ FT: 24,000
SALES: 2MM **Privately Held**
SIC: 2631 Specialty board

(G-8194)
FRANK ZOTYNIA & SON INC
38 Governor St (07501-1052)
P.O. Box 307, Stanhope (07874-0307)
PHONE..........................973 247-2800
Frank Zotynia, *Principal*
EMP: 1 EST: 2011
SQ FT: 20,000
SALES (est): 1.5MM **Privately Held**
SIC: 3548 Resistance welders, electric

(G-8195)
**FREED TRANSFORMER
COMPANY**
460 Totowa Ave (07522-1513)
PHONE..........................973 942-2222
Martin Gorman, *President*
Cliff Markowitz, *Controller*
Frances Cezar, *Administration*
EMP: 38
SQ FT: 40,000
SALES (est): 2MM **Privately Held**
SIC: 3677 Electronic coils, transformers &
other inductors

(G-8196)
G & H METAL FINISHERS INC
282 Dakota St (07503-2412)
PHONE..........................201 909-9808
George Grimm, *President*
Fred Grimm, *Corp Secy*
Henry Kunz, *Vice Pres*
EMP: 6 EST: 1956
SQ FT: 11,000
SALES (est): 1.1MM **Privately Held**
SIC: 3471 Electroplating of metals or
formed products; polishing, metals or
formed products

(G-8197)
**GENERAL CARBON
CORPORATION**
33 Paterson St (07501-1015)
PHONE..........................973 523-2223
Robert J Muller, *President*
Rob Murray, *Opers Mgr*
Mickey O'Shea, *Sales Mgr*
◆ EMP: 15
SQ FT: 20,000
SALES (est): 7.2MM **Privately Held**
WEB: www.generalcarbon.com
SIC: 2819 Charcoal (carbon), activated

(G-8198)
GIO VALI HANDBAG CORP
Also Called: Giovali Handbag
463 Grand St (07505-2036)
PHONE..........................973 279-3032
ARA Messrobian, *President*
EMP: 8
SQ FT: 7,500
SALES (est): 399.3K **Privately Held**
SIC: 3171 Handbags, women's

(G-8199)
GLENRO INC (PA)
39 Mcbride Ave (07501-1799)
P.O. Box 3052 (07509-3052)
PHONE..........................973 279-5900
Gary Van Denend, *President*
Jim Bilbrey, *Engineer*
Steven Baumgartner, *Officer*
◆ EMP: 14
SQ FT: 20,000
SALES (est): 11.3MM **Privately Held**
WEB: www.glenro.com
SIC: 3567 3672 Heating units & devices,
industrial: electric; printed circuit boards

(G-8200)
GLOBAL INGREDIENTS INC
317 9th Ave (07514-2310)
PHONE..........................973 278-6677

Frank Mountain, *President*
Harlie Mountain, *Vice Pres*
Griff Jones, *Opers Mgr*
James Minella, *Manager*
▲ EMP: 8
SQ FT: 15,000
SALES: 3MM **Privately Held**
WEB: www.globalingredients.net
SIC: 2099 Food preparations

(G-8201)
GORMAN INDUSTRIES INC
Also Called: Eagle Products Div
700 21st Ave (07513-1145)
PHONE..........................973 345-5424
Uri Dobriner, *President*
Danielle Dobriner, *Corp Secy*
EMP: 29
SQ FT: 10,000
SALES (est): 3.4MM **Privately Held**
SIC: 3714 5013 Motor vehicle parts & ac-
cessories; motor vehicle supplies & new
parts

(G-8202)
**GREENBAUM INTERIORS LLC
(PA)**
101 Washington St (07505-1301)
PHONE..........................973 279-3000
Joseph Jimmy Greenbaum,
Ellen Greenbaum,
Susan Greenbaum,
▲ EMP: 52
SQ FT: 123,000
SALES (est): 8.7MM **Privately Held**
WEB: www.greenbauminteriors.com
SIC: 5712 5021 2511 7389 Furniture
stores; furniture; wood household furni-
ture; interior decorating

(G-8203)
**GRIMALDI DEVELOPMENT
CORP**
65 1st Ave (07514-2000)
PHONE..........................973 345-0660
David Grimaldi, *President*
EMP: 5 EST: 1998
SQ FT: 6,000
SALES (est): 360K **Privately Held**
SIC: 3599 Machine shop, jobbing & repair

(G-8204)
GRIMCO PNEUMATIC CORP
65 1st Ave (07514-2030)
PHONE..........................973 345-0660
David Grimaldi, *President*
▼ EMP: 8
SQ FT: 14,000
SALES (est): 1.4MM **Privately Held**
WEB: www.grimcopresses.com
SIC: 3542 Machine tools, metal forming
type

(G-8205)
GROMMET MART INC
85-99 Hazel St (07503-2462)
PHONE..........................973 278-4100
Cilek Seker, *President*
EMP: 10
SALES (est): 1.2MM **Privately Held**
SIC: 3423 Hammers (hand tools)

(G-8206)
**GUERNSEY CREST ICE CREAM
CO**
134 19th Ave (07513-1208)
PHONE..........................973 742-4620
Margaret Cornwell, *President*
Joy Cornwell, *Vice Pres*
EMP: 4 EST: 1935
SQ FT: 3,200
SALES (est): 240K **Privately Held**
SIC: 2024 5812 Ice cream & frozen
desserts; ice cream stands or dairy bars

(G-8207)
**H C GRAPHICS
SCREENPRINTING**
238 Lindbergh Pl Ste 3 (07503-2823)
PHONE..........................973 247-0544
Thomas J Mueller, *President*
Carol Mueller, *Corp Secy*
▲ EMP: 8
SQ FT: 4,500

SALES (est): 1.5MM **Privately Held**
WEB: www.hcgraphics.com
SIC: 2759 2752 Screen printing; commer-
cial printing, offset

(G-8208)
HARMONY ELASTOMERS LLC
34 Trenton Ave (07513)
PHONE..........................973 340-4000
Arish Kiani, *President*
Sawib Toor, *CFO*
EMP: 20
SQ FT: 10,000
SALES: 5MM **Privately Held**
SIC: 2822 Synthetic rubber

(G-8209)
HILL MACHINE INC (PA)
Also Called: Hill Mixers Machine
295 Governor St (07501-1320)
PHONE..........................973 684-2808
Robert Brewer, *President*
Robert W Brewer Jr, *Corp Secy*
John Pullos, *Vice Pres*
Mike Titos, *Manager*
EMP: 5 EST: 1895
SQ FT: 11,500
SALES (est): 548.6K **Privately Held**
SIC: 3556 Homogenizing machinery: dairy,
fruit, vegetable

(G-8210)
HO-HO-KUS INC
189 Lyon St 201 (07524-2523)
PHONE..........................973 278-2274
Tom Nepola, *President*
EMP: 24
SQ FT: 5,300
SALES (est): 4.7MM **Privately Held**
WEB: www.hohokusinc.com
SIC: 3429 3812 3728 Manufactured hard-
ware (general); search & navigation
equipment; aircraft parts & equipment

(G-8211)
HY-TEST PACKAGING CORP
515 E 41st St (07504-1209)
PHONE..........................973 754-7000
John S Smith, *President*
Jackalyn Quazza, *Vice Pres*
Ted Smith, *Vice Pres*
EMP: 9
SQ FT: 34,000
SALES (est): 700K **Privately Held**
WEB: www.hy-testpackaging.com
SIC: 7389 2844 2841 Packaging & label-
ing services; toilet preparations; soap &
other detergents

(G-8212)
**IDEAL PLATING & POLISHING
CO**
107 Alabama Ave (07503-2108)
PHONE..........................973 759-5559
Ronald F Knigge, *President*
Constance Knigge, *Corp Secy*
Derek Thompson, *Admin Sec*
EMP: 10 EST: 1949
SQ FT: 18,000
SALES (est): 1MM **Privately Held**
SIC: 3471 Plating of metals or formed
products

(G-8213)
**INDEPENDENCE PLATING CORP
(PA)**
Also Called: Ideal Plating
107 Alabama Ave (07503-2199)
PHONE..........................973 523-1776
Ronald F Knigge, *President*
EMP: 23 EST: 1950
SQ FT: 28,000
SALES (est): 2.7MM **Privately Held**
WEB: www.independenceplating.com
SIC: 3471 Anodizing (plating) of metals or
formed products; electroplating of metals
or formed products

(G-8214)
INDUSTRIAL MACHINE CORP
44 Lehigh Ave (07503-1729)
PHONE..........................973 345-1800
Sam Szewzcyk, *President*
EMP: 9
SQ FT: 9,000

2019 Harris New Jersey
Manufacturers Directory

▲ = Import ▼=Export
◆ =Import/Export

SALES (est): 750K **Privately Held**
SIC: 3599 Machine shop, jobbing & repair

(G-8215)
INTERNTNAL PHARMA REMEDIES INC
244 Dixon Ave (07501-3308)
PHONE...................................201 417-3891
Nelson Herreira, *CEO*
EMP: 6
SALES (est): 477.8K **Privately Held**
SIC: 2834 Pharmaceutical preparations

(G-8216)
J KAUFMAN IRON WORKS INC
217 Godwin Ave (07501-1695)
P.O. Box 213, Elmwood Park (07407-0213)
PHONE...............................973 925-9972
Larry Kaufman, *President*
Joseph Kaufman, *Admin Sec*
EMP: 17
SALES (est): 3.1MM **Privately Held**
WEB: www.kaufmaniron.com
SIC: 3446 Gates, ornamental metal

(G-8217)
J V Q INC
245 E 17th St (07524-2012)
P.O. Box 2070, West Paterson (07424-7070)
PHONE...............................973 523-8806
Vic Amati, *President*
Quintin Amati, *Vice Pres*
Jim Reese, *Treasurer*
EMP: 14
SQ FT: 4,000
SALES (est): 900K **Privately Held**
WEB: www.jvq.com
SIC: 3544 Special dies, tools, jigs & fixtures

(G-8218)
JACHTS - COLUMBIA CAN LLC
90 6th Ave (07524-1406)
PHONE...............................973 925-8020
Darren Jachts, *CEO*
Eric Hammesfahr, *Regl Sales Mgr*
EMP: 17
SALES (est): 10.8MM **Privately Held**
SIC: 2655 Fiber cans, drums & containers

(G-8219)
JC PALLETS INC
354 E Marshall St (07503-3123)
PHONE...............................973 345-1102
Jose Cruz, *President*
EMP: 13
SALES (est): 1.4MM **Privately Held**
SIC: 2448 Pallets, wood & wood with metal

(G-8220)
JC PRINTING & ADVERTISING INC
168 8th Ave (07514-2218)
PHONE...............................973 881-8612
James Chappell, *President*
Cheryl Chappell, *Director*
Carlos Moscoso, *Graphic Designe*
EMP: 5
SQ FT: 2,000
SALES (est): 921.2K **Privately Held**
WEB: www.jcprintinginc.com
SIC: 2752 Commercial printing, offset

(G-8221)
JCC MILITARY SUPPLY LLC
125 5th Ave (07524-1204)
P.O. Box 1370, Twp Washinton (07676-1370)
PHONE...............................973 341-1314
Michael Cavallo,
▲ **EMP:** 5
SALES: 225K **Privately Held**
SIC: 3496 Miscellaneous fabricated wire products

(G-8222)
JEWM INC
Also Called: Tablecloth Co
514 Totowa Ave (07522-1541)
PHONE...............................973 942-1555
Judith Metzger, *President*
Michael Kramer, *Exec VP*
Bernie Kramer, *Vice Pres*
▼ **EMP:** 50

SQ FT: 18,000
SALES (est): 5MM **Privately Held**
WEB: www.tablecloth.com
SIC: 2392 5949 Tablecloths: made from purchased materials; sewing, needlework & piece goods

(G-8223)
JIT MANUFACTURING INC
50 Peel St (07524-1004)
PHONE...............................973 247-7300
John Norton, *President*
Andrew Graziano, *Vice Pres*
EMP: 12
SQ FT: 12,000
SALES (est): 2.4MM **Privately Held**
SIC: 2631 2675 Packaging board; die-cut paper & board

(G-8224)
JK INGREDIENTS INC
Also Called: J&K Ingredients
160 E 5th St (07524-1603)
PHONE...............................973 340-8700
James K Sausville, *President*
Halina McCabe, *Buyer*
Andy Madacsi, *Controller*
▲ **EMP:** 85
SQ FT: 37,000
SALES (est): 22.3MM **Privately Held**
WEB: www.jkingredients.net
SIC: 2099 2087 Food preparations; pie fillings, except fruit, meat & vegetable; powders, flavoring (except drink)

(G-8225)
JOHN ANTHONY BREAD DISTRIBUTOR
298 21st Ave (07501-3521)
PHONE...............................973 523-9258
John Imparato, *Owner*
Donna Imparato, *Partner*
EMP: 4
SALES (est): 260K **Privately Held**
SIC: 2051 Bread, cake & related products

(G-8226)
JOSEPH MONGA JR
Also Called: Decorative Iron Works
7383 Belmont Ave (07522)
PHONE...............................973 595-8517
Joseph Monga, *Owner*
EMP: 5
SALES (est): 569.2K
SALES (corp-wide): 570.3K **Privately Held**
SIC: 3446 Stairs, fire escapes, balconies, railings & ladders; stairs, staircases, stair treads: prefabricated metal
PA: Joseph Monga Jr
  300 Main St
  Little Ferry NJ 07643
  201 641-2431

(G-8227)
KB FOOD ENTERPRISES INC
19 E 5th St (07524)
PHONE...............................973 278-2800
Rick Paulso, *President*
EMP: 12
SQ FT: 14,500
SALES (est): 920K **Privately Held**
SIC: 2051 Bread, cake & related products

(G-8228)
KENNETEX INC
53 E 34th St (07514-1307)
PHONE...............................610 444-0600
Martin Rosen, *President*
Arthur Rosen, *Vice Pres*
▲ **EMP:** 57
SQ FT: 45,000
SALES (est): 6.3MM **Privately Held**
WEB: www.kennetex.com
SIC: 2281 2269 5949 Yarn spinning mills; finishing plants; sewing, needlework & piece goods

(G-8229)
KESSLER INDUSTRIES
40 Warren St (07524-2205)
PHONE...............................973 279-1417
Fax: 973 684-1139
EMP: 4

SALES (est): 700.2K **Privately Held**
SIC: 5074 3432 Whol Plumbing Equipment/Supplies Mfg Plumbing Fixture Fittings

(G-8230)
KLEIN RIBBON CORP
Also Called: Jeffrey Klein Ribbon Designs
176 E 7th St Ste 2 (07524-1600)
PHONE...............................973 684-4671
Raymond Klein, *President*
EMP: 36 EST: 1925
SQ FT: 25,000
SALES (est): 3.5MM **Privately Held**
WEB: www.myownribbon.com
SIC: 2241 2396 2297 Ribbons; automotive & apparel trimmings; nonwoven fabrics

(G-8231)
KOHLER INDUSTRIES INC
Also Called: Interfoam
155 Mcbride Ave Ste 1 (07501-2663)
PHONE...............................336 545-3289
Ronald Kohler, *President*
EMP: 5
SQ FT: 20,000
SALES (est): 478.4K **Privately Held**
SIC: 3086 Insulation or cushioning material, foamed plastic

(G-8232)
L & F GRAPHICS LTD LBLTY CO
Also Called: Lf Graphics
207 E 15th St (07524-2018)
PHONE...............................973 240-7033
Lenuare Foxworth, *Managing Prtnr*
Lenaure Foxworth Jr,
EMP: 5 EST: 2011
SQ FT: 2,900
SALES: 735K **Privately Held**
SIC: 3953 7336 7389 3993 Screens, textile printing; commercial art & graphic design; embroidering of advertising on shirts, etc.; signs & advertising specialties

(G-8233)
L & M MACHINE & TOOL CO INC
105 Lehigh Ave (07503-1218)
PHONE...............................973 523-5288
Francisco Moran, *President*
EMP: 5 EST: 1959
SQ FT: 5,500
SALES: 200K **Privately Held**
SIC: 3541 5084 3599 Machine tools, metal cutting type; metalworking tools (such as drills, taps, dies, files); machine shop, jobbing & repair

(G-8234)
L ARDEN CORP
72 Putnam St (07524-2206)
PHONE...............................973 523-6400
Luis Alvarez, *Owner*
EMP: 8
SALES (est): 750K **Privately Held**
SIC: 3531 Dozers, tractor mounted: material moving

(G-8235)
L D L TECHNOLOGY INC
137 Pennsylvania Ave (07503)
PHONE...............................973 345-9111
Daniel Laufer, *President*
Eleonore Tarricone, *Admin Sec*
EMP: 6
SQ FT: 5,000
SALES (est): 510K **Privately Held**
SIC: 3339 Zinc refining (primary), including slabs & dust; zinc smelting (primary), including zinc residue

(G-8236)
LA FAVORITE INDUSTRIES INC
33 Shady St (07524-1014)
PHONE...............................973 279-1266
Thomas Mastin, *President*
Eric Hague, *Vice Pres*
Linda Zisa, *Controller*
George Kenny, *Info Tech Mgr*
EMP: 14
SALES: 2MM **Privately Held**
WEB: www.lafavorite.com
SIC: 3069 2891 Expansion joints, rubber; sealing compounds, synthetic rubber or plastic

(G-8237)
LANCO-YORK INC (PA)
Also Called: Lanco Container
864 E 25th St (07513-1202)
PHONE...............................973 278-7400
Mitchell Leibowitz, *President*
Rochelle Leibowitz, *Corp Secy*
Denis Panza, *Exec VP*
Joshua Karlin, *Technical Staff*
▲ **EMP:** 22 EST: 1942
SQ FT: 50,000
SALES (est): 7.9MM **Privately Held**
SIC: 2653 Boxes, corrugated: made from purchased materials

(G-8238)
LBU INC
7 4th Ave 33 (07524-1202)
PHONE...............................973 773-4800
Jeffrey Mayer, *President*
Jerry Cong, *CFO*
Jim Black, *Financial Exec*
Fred King, *Office Mgr*
Melissa Hyseni, *Art Dir*
▲ **EMP:** 30
SQ FT: 30,000
SALES (est): 5.5MM **Privately Held**
WEB: www.lbuinc.com
SIC: 2392 3161 2393 Bags, laundry: made from purchased materials; ironing board pads: made from purchased materials; luggage; knapsacks, canvas: made from purchased materials

(G-8239)
LEVINE INDUSTRIES INC (PA)
Also Called: Levine Packaging Co
70 Levine St (07503)
PHONE...............................973 742-1000
Jeff Levine, *President*
Alan Levine, *President*
Theodore R Levine, *Vice Pres*
EMP: 35
SQ FT: 90,000
SALES (est): 8.1MM **Privately Held**
WEB: www.levineind.com
SIC: 2653 5113 Boxes, corrugated: made from purchased materials; shipping supplies

(G-8240)
LIBERTY ENVELOPE INC
45 E 5th St (07524-1101)
PHONE...............................973 546-5600
Ligia Guarderas, *President*
Kevin Guarderas, *CFO*
EMP: 16
SQ FT: 40,000
SALES (est): 1.7MM **Privately Held**
WEB: www.libertyenv.com
SIC: 2752 2759 7331 Commercial printing, offset; envelopes: printing; mailing service

(G-8241)
LINDSTROM & KING CO INC
108 Mclean Blvd (07514-1114)
PHONE...............................973 279-2511
Peter M Madsen, *President*
EMP: 5 EST: 1939
SQ FT: 6,000
SALES (est): 624.2K **Privately Held**
WEB: www.lindstromking.com
SIC: 3494 Valves & pipe fittings

(G-8242)
LINEN FOR TABLES
407 20th Ave (07513-1544)
PHONE...............................973 345-8472
Herbert Allen Jr, *Partner*
Victoria Allen, *Partner*
Wanda Vazquez, *Human Resources*
Margarita Diaz, *Admin Asst*
EMP: 7
SQ FT: 3,000
SALES (est): 440K **Privately Held**
WEB: www.allenlinen.com
SIC: 2392 5131 Napkins, fabric & nonwoven: made from purchased materials; tablecloths: made from purchased materials; linen piece goods, woven

(G-8243)
LITTLE FALLS ALLOYS INC (PA)
171-191 Caldwell Ave (07501)
PHONE...............................973 278-1666

Don Fellman, *President*
Donald P Fellman, *President*
Orlando Veltri, *Vice Pres*
Fred Walter, *Vice Pres*
Paul Veltri, *CFO*
▲ **EMP:** 32 **EST:** 1945
SQ FT: 30,000
SALES (est): 7.2MM **Privately Held**
WEB: www.lfa-wire.com
SIC: 3351 Wire, copper & copper alloy

(G-8244)
LMC-HB CORP
Also Called: Les Metalliers Champenois
23 27 East 23rd St (07514)
PHONE......................862 239-9814
Samuel Bonnet, *Director*
▲ **EMP:** 12
SALES: 12.7MM **Privately Held**
SIC: 8712 3442 3446 Architectural services; metal doors, sash & trim; architectural metalwork

(G-8245)
LO PRESTI & SONS LLC
Also Called: Giannella Bakery
298 21st Ave (07501-3521)
PHONE......................973 523-9258
Paul Lo Presti, *President*
▲ **EMP:** 32
SQ FT: 12,500
SALES (est): 1.5MM **Privately Held**
SIC: 5812 5149 5411 2052 Delicatessen (eating places); bakery products; supermarkets; cookies & crackers; bread, cake & related products

(G-8246)
LOTITO FOODS INC
510 E 35th St (07504-1720)
P.O. Box 39 (07543-0039)
PHONE......................973 684-2900
Michael Gali, *Manager*
EMP: 16
SALES (corp-wide): 37MM **Privately Held**
WEB: www.lotitofoods.com
SIC: 2022 Cheese, natural & processed
PA: Lotito Foods Inc.
    240 Carter Dr
    Edison NJ 08817
    732 248-0222

(G-8247)
M & S MACHINE & TOOL CORP
108 Maryland Ave (07503-2113)
PHONE......................973 345-5847
Nazim Sylejmanovski, *President*
Maksut Vebi, *Vice Pres*
EMP: 10
SALES (est): 1.8MM **Privately Held**
WEB: www.mandsmachine.com
SIC: 3599 3552 Machine shop, jobbing & repair; textile machinery

(G-8248)
MAJKA RAILING INC
125 Mcbride Ave (07501-2606)
PHONE......................973 247-7603
Mary Majka, *President*
Keith Majka, *Purch Dir*
EMP: 7
SALES: 250K **Privately Held**
SIC: 3446 1799 Railings, bannisters, guards, etc.: made from metal pipe; railings, prefabricated metal; home/office interiors finishing, furnishing & remodeling

(G-8249)
MANHATTAN SIGNS & DESIGNS LTD
130 Beckwith Ave Ste 2b (07503-2819)
PHONE......................973 278-3603
Eugene Nifenecker, *President*
EMP: 20
SALES (corp-wide): 2.4MM **Privately Held**
SIC: 3993 Signs & advertising specialties
PA: Manhattan Signs & Designs, Ltd.
    224 W 30th St
    New York NY 10001
    212 564-4400

(G-8250)
MAR MACHINE KEN MANUFACTURING
Also Called: Maria
477 E 30th St (07504-2110)
PHONE......................973 278-5827
Kenneth A Walder, *President*
Ewald Schlosser, *Vice Pres*
▲ **EMP:** 26 **EST:** 1940
SQ FT: 17,000
SALES (est): 3.9MM **Privately Held**
WEB: www.ken-mar-machine.com
SIC: 3842 Prosthetic appliances

(G-8251)
MARDON ASSOCIATES INC
Also Called: Bakers Puff Pastry
1 Industrial Plz (07503-2964)
PHONE......................973 977-2251
Anthony Cipriano, *President*
Orlie Parker, *Vice Pres*
Wolfgang Rathmann, *Vice Pres*
EMP: 11
SQ FT: 4,800
SALES (est): 782.1K **Privately Held**
SIC: 2053 Pastries (danish): frozen

(G-8252)
MASTER METAL POLISHING CORP
Also Called: Master Metal Finishers
57 Wood St (07524-1007)
PHONE......................973 684-0119
Gerardo Almeyda, *Ch of Bd*
Jeffrey Almeyda, *President*
Kevin Almeyda, *Vice Pres*
EMP: 20
SQ FT: 7,000
SALES: 2.5MM **Privately Held**
WEB: www.mastermetal.com
SIC: 3471 Anodizing (plating) of metals or formed products; polishing, metals or formed products; coloring & finishing of aluminum or formed products

(G-8253)
MEDICI INTERNATIONAL INC
85 5th Ave Build18 (07524-1110)
PHONE......................973 684-6084
Pierre Dabagh, *President*
EMP: 5
SALES (est): 744.3K **Privately Held**
SIC: 3171 8011 Women's handbags & purses; offices & clinics of medical doctors

(G-8254)
MENDELS MUFFINS AND STUFF INC
53 Jersey St (07501-1701)
PHONE......................973 881-9900
Mendel Neustadt, *Owner*
EMP: 6
SALES (est): 827.4K **Privately Held**
SIC: 2051 Bread, cake & related products

(G-8255)
MENDLES JUST BREAD INC
53 Jersey St (07501-1701)
PHONE......................973 881-9900
Mendle Nuestadt, *President*
EMP: 8
SALES (est): 239.7K **Privately Held**
SIC: 2051 Pies, bakery: except frozen

(G-8256)
METAL COMPONENTS INC
92 Maryland Ave Paterson (07503)
PHONE......................973 247-1204
Frank Mottola, *President*
Thomas Roskop, *Executive*
EMP: 24 **EST:** 1959
SQ FT: 22,000
SALES (est): 327.5K **Privately Held**
SIC: 3599 Machine shop, jobbing & repair

(G-8257)
METRO MILLS INC
Also Called: Fashion Windows Etc
151 Linwood Ave (07502-1895)
PHONE......................973 942-6034
Donald Kapit, *President*
Fred Pepe, *Treasurer*
EMP: 20
SQ FT: 17,000

SALES: 1.2MM **Privately Held**
SIC: 2391 2591 2211 Draperies, plastic & textile: from purchased materials; blinds vertical; window shades; bedspreads, cotton

(G-8258)
MICROSEAL INDUSTRIES INC
610 E 36th St (07513-1167)
P.O. Box 3054 (07509-3054)
PHONE......................973 523-0704
Michael Silverstein, *President*
Kenneth Lutz, *Controller*
Sheldon Silverstein, *Mktg Dir*
Rosie Sepulveda, *Office Mgr*
▲ **EMP:** 17
SQ FT: 25,000
SALES (est): 4.5MM **Privately Held**
WEB: www.microseal.com
SIC: 2672 Tape, pressure sensitive: made from purchased materials; coated paper, except photographic, carbon or abrasive

(G-8259)
MICROWAVE CONSULTING CORP
Also Called: McC Norsal
150 Railroad Ave (07501-2943)
P.O. Box 6040 (07509-6040)
PHONE......................973 523-6700
Scott Warner, *President*
EMP: 6
SALES: 350K **Privately Held**
SIC: 3679 Microwave components

(G-8260)
MIDLAND FARMS INC
845 E 25th St (07513-1201)
PHONE......................800 749-6455
Demetrios Haseotes, *Branch Mgr*
EMP: 24
SALES (corp-wide): 14.5MM **Privately Held**
SIC: 2026 Milk processing (pasteurizing, homogenizing, bottling)
PA: Midland Farms, Inc.
    375 Broadway
    Menands NY 12204
    518 436-7038

(G-8261)
MOCOCO PARTNERS CORP
439 E 22nd St (07514-2321)
PHONE......................347 768-3344
Daysi Duverge, *Principal*
EMP: 4 **EST:** 2016
SALES (est): 215.1K **Privately Held**
SIC: 2086 Bottled & canned soft drinks

(G-8262)
MPT DELIVERY SYSTEMS INC
Also Called: Pharmachem Laboratories
95 Prince St (07501-2905)
PHONE......................973 278-0283
Roger Herrell, *Principal*
▲ **EMP:** 6
SALES (est): 595.6K **Privately Held**
SIC: 2834 Pharmaceutical preparations

(G-8263)
MPT DELIVERY SYSTEMS INC
95 Prince St (07501-2905)
PHONE......................973 279-4132
David Holmes, *President*
Colin Mac Intyre, *Vice Pres*
Carson Normington, *Engineer*
Andrea Bauer, *Treasurer*
Catherine Holmes, *Admin Sec*
▲ **EMP:** 60
SQ FT: 26,000
SALES (est): 7.9MM
SALES (corp-wide): 3.7B **Publicly Held**
SIC: 2833 Vitamins, natural or synthetic: bulk, uncompounded
HQ: Pharmachem Laboratories, Llc
    265 Harrison Tpke
    Kearny NJ 07032
    201 246-1000

(G-8264)
NABLUS PASTRY & SWEETS
1050 Main St Fl 1 (07503-2212)
PHONE......................973 881-8003
Shar Abedravvo, *Owner*
▲ **EMP:** 5 **EST:** 1997

SALES (est): 292.4K **Privately Held**
SIC: 2051 Bakery: wholesale or wholesale/retail combined

(G-8265)
NEW ERA CONVERTING MCHY INC
235 Mclean Blvd (07504-1235)
P.O. Box 377, Hawthorne (07507-0377)
PHONE......................201 670-4848
Frank P Lembo, *CEO*
Robert Pasquale, *President*
Paul Lembo, *Exec VP*
Tom Lombardo, *Vice Pres*
John Pasquale, *Vice Pres*
▲ **EMP:** 40
SQ FT: 25,000
SALES (est): 11.2MM **Privately Held**
WEB: www.neweraconverting.com
SIC: 3599 Custom machinery

(G-8266)
NEW JERSEY BALANCING SVC INC
138 Michigan Ave Ste 40 (07503-1709)
PHONE......................973 278-5106
Francis Kennedy, *President*
EMP: 6 **EST:** 1964
SQ FT: 5,000
SALES (est): 500K **Privately Held**
WEB: www.njbalancinginc.com
SIC: 3599 Machine shop, jobbing & repair

(G-8267)
NEW JERSEY DIAMOND PRODUCTS CO
108 Kentucky Ave (07503-2508)
PHONE......................973 684-0949
Mark Zambrano, *President*
James G Zambrano, *Vice Pres*
EMP: 10 **EST:** 1966
SQ FT: 5,000
SALES: 1.5MM **Privately Held**
WEB: www.njdp.com
SIC: 3545 3291 5999 Diamond cutting tools for turning, boring, burnishing, etc.; abrasive products; alcoholic beverage making equipment & supplies

(G-8268)
NEW WORLD INTERNATIONAL INC
46 Lewis St (07501-3607)
PHONE......................973 881-8100
Carmen Bires, *President*
John J Bires, *Vice Pres*
▼ **EMP:** 10
SQ FT: 47,000
SALES: 2MM **Privately Held**
SIC: 2844 Cosmetic preparations

(G-8269)
NEXTWAVE WEB LLC
229 Marshall St (07503-3121)
PHONE......................973 742-4339
ISA Suqi,
Alia Suqi,
EMP: 11
SQ FT: 7,500
SALES (est): 2.1MM **Privately Held**
SIC: 2752 2741 Commercial printing, lithographic; miscellaneous publishing

(G-8270)
NORTH JERSEY SKEIN DYEING CO
Also Called: Hoof Fe Dye Works
152 Putnam St (07524-1913)
PHONE......................201 247-4202
Dominick H Aldi Sr, *President*
EMP: 8 **EST:** 1962
SQ FT: 5,000
SALES (est): 590.8K **Privately Held**
SIC: 2262 Dyeing: manmade fiber & silk broadwoven fabrics

(G-8271)
NORTHEAST TOMATO COMPANY INC
4 22 Erie St (07524)
PHONE......................973 684-4890
Gerald Pfund, *President*
EMP: 10

▲ = Import ▼=Export
◆ =Import/Export

SALES (est): 147.1K **Privately Held**
SIC: 2033 Vegetable pastes: packaged in cans, jars, etc.

(G-8272)
NORTHERN STATE PERIODICALS LLC
251 Vreeland Ave Ste B (07504-1736)
PHONE................................973 782-6100
Juan J Santos, *CEO*
EMP: 7
SALES: 200K **Privately Held**
SIC: 2741 Miscellaneous publishing

(G-8273)
OKONITE COMPANY
959 Market St (07513-1196)
PHONE................................201 825-0300
Thomas Scanlon, *Manager*
EMP: 85
SALES (corp-wide): 407MM **Privately Held**
WEB: www.okonite.com
SIC: 3357 Nonferrous wiredrawing & insulating
PA: The Okonite Company Inc
    102 Hilltop Rd
    Ramsey NJ 07446
    201 825-0300

(G-8274)
ORTHO-DYNAMICS INC
210 E 16th St (07524-2009)
PHONE................................973 742-4390
Steve Tushingham, *President*
Kurt Herron, *COO*
EMP: 9
SQ FT: 5,000
SALES (est): 730K **Privately Held**
WEB: www.ortho-dynamics.com
SIC: 3842 Foot appliances, orthopedic

(G-8275)
P & S BLIZZARD CORPORATION
Also Called: Blizzard Parts & Service
722 Madison Ave (07501-2407)
PHONE................................973 523-1700
Paul Kostovski, *President*
EMP: 6
SALES (est): 410K **Privately Held**
SIC: 2499 7699 7538 Snow fence, wood; recreational sporting equipment repair services; industrial equipment services; general automotive repair shops

(G-8276)
PAPER TUBES CORES & BOXES INC
Also Called: Paper Tube and Core
239 Lindbergh Pl (07503-2821)
PHONE................................973 977-8823
Russ Panzer, *President*
Howard Panzer, *Chairman*
Jeff Schindle, *Vice Pres*
▼ EMP: 14
SQ FT: 16,000
SALES (est): 3.6MM **Privately Held**
SIC: 2655 Fiber cans, drums & containers

(G-8277)
PARISER INDUSTRIES INC (PA)
91 Michigan Ave (07503-1807)
PHONE................................973 569-9090
Albert Pariser, *President*
Chad Dare, *Regional Mgr*
Craig Moser, *Regional Mgr*
Stephen Staum, *Regional Mgr*
Bill Little, *District Mgr*
◆ EMP: 27
SQ FT: 7,500
SALES (est): 11.1MM **Privately Held**
WEB: www.pariserchem.com
SIC: 2843 2899 Textile finishing agents; water treating compounds

(G-8278)
PARK AVENUE MEATS INC
194 Albion Ave (07502-1732)
PHONE................................718 731-4196
Ira Klein, *CEO*
EMP: 25
SALES (est): 1.8MM **Privately Held**
SIC: 2011 5141 2015 Meat packing plants; groceries, general line; poultry slaughtering & processing

(G-8279)
PATERSON BLEACHERY INC (PA)
207 E 15th St 219 (07524-2018)
PHONE................................973 684-1034
Antonio Armenante, *President*
George Armenante, *Vice Pres*
EMP: 15 EST: 1940
SQ FT: 35,000
SALES (est): 961.5K **Privately Held**
SIC: 2231 2241 2221 Broadwoven fabric mills, wool; fabric, animal fiber: narrow woven; broadwoven fabric mills, man-made

(G-8280)
PECATA ENTERPRISES INC
Also Called: Ultimate Textile
18 Market St (07501-1721)
PHONE................................973 523-9498
Roger Glickman, *President*
Lenny Kutner, *Vice Pres*
Stella Garzon, *Office Mgr*
◆ EMP: 50
SQ FT: 30,000
SALES (est): 8.4MM **Privately Held**
WEB: www.pecata.com
SIC: 2759 3552 Screen printing; textile machinery

(G-8281)
PERAGALLO ORGAN COMPANY OF NJ
Also Called: Peragallo Pipe Organ
306 Buffalo Ave (07503-1103)
PHONE................................973 684-3414
John Peragallo Jr, *President*
Frank Peragallo, *Vice Pres*
John Peragallo III, *Vice Pres*
EMP: 16 EST: 1918
SQ FT: 2,500
SALES (est): 2.1MM **Privately Held**
WEB: www.peragallo.com
SIC: 3931 7699 Organs, all types: pipe, reed, hand, electronic, etc.; synthesizers, music; organ tuning & repair; musical instrument repair services

(G-8282)
PETER GARAFANO & SON INC
Also Called: Garafano Tank Service
500 Marshall St (07503-2927)
PHONE................................973 278-0350
Peter Garafano, *President*
Daniel Garafano, *Admin Sec*
EMP: 24
SQ FT: 18,000
SALES (est): 8.2MM **Privately Held**
WEB: www.garafanotankservice.com
SIC: 5012 3441 7692 3713 Trailers for trucks, new & used; fabricated structural metal; welding repair; dump truck bodies

(G-8283)
PROMOTIONAL GRAPHICS INC
81 E 26th St (07514-1615)
PHONE................................973 423-3900
Diane Dopp, *President*
Wayne Dopp, *VP Prdtn*
Rodney Dopp, *CFO*
EMP: 16
SQ FT: 6,500
SALES (est): 1.6MM **Privately Held**
SIC: 2759 Labels & seals: printing

(G-8284)
QUALITY REMANUFACTURING INC
565 E 37th St (07504)
PHONE................................973 523-8800
Rick Waghorne, *President*
Brooks Reed, *Vice Pres*
EMP: 15
SQ FT: 15,000
SALES (est): 150.1K **Privately Held**
SIC: 3714 Transmission housings or parts, motor vehicle

(G-8285)
R A O CONTRACT SALES NY INC
Also Called: R A O Contract Sales
94 Fulton St Ste 4 (07501-1200)
PHONE................................201 652-1500
Brian Bergman, *President*
Brian B Bergman, *President*

Seth C Bergman, *Vice Pres*
Bruce E Bergman, *Treasurer*
Allison Ehrlich, *Office Mgr*
EMP: 9
SQ FT: 20,000
SALES (est): 1.2MM **Privately Held**
WEB: www.rao.com
SIC: 2499 3499 2493 3231 Picture & mirror frames, wood; picture frames, metal; bulletin boards, cork; bulletin boards, wood; mirrored glass

(G-8286)
RENTALIFT INC
Also Called: Jersey Lift Truck
48 Alabama Ave (07503-2107)
PHONE................................973 684-6111
Edward Gerena, *President*
EMP: 11
SALES (est): 2.9MM **Privately Held**
SIC: 3537 Forklift trucks

(G-8287)
RICO FOODS INC
Also Called: Rico Products
527 E 18th St (07514-2611)
PHONE................................973 278-0589
Emilio Hernandez, *President*
Lazara Fernandez, *Vice Pres*
Christine Hernandez, *Prdtn Mgr*
EMP: 41
SQ FT: 2,600
SALES (est): 9MM **Privately Held**
SIC: 2038 5999 Frozen specialties; packaging materials: boxes, padding, etc.

(G-8288)
RIGO INDUSTRIES INC
50 California Ave (07503-2518)
PHONE................................973 881-1780
Isaac Gorovitz, *President*
Zelieg Rivkin, *Vice Pres*
Mendel Karp, *Project Mgr*
Rachel Brook, *Admin Sec*
EMP: 40
SQ FT: 45,000
SALES (est): 8.7MM **Privately Held**
WEB: www.rigowall.com
SIC: 2621 Wallpaper (hanging paper)

(G-8289)
ROYCE ASSOCIATES A LTD PARTNR
Also Called: Passaic Color & Chemical
28 Paterson St (07501-1016)
PHONE................................973 279-0400
Adams Rice, *Manager*
EMP: 25
SALES (est): 5.7MM
SALES (corp-wide): 19.7MM **Privately Held**
SIC: 2865 Cyclic crudes & intermediates
PA: Royce Associates, A Limited Partnership
    35 Carlton Ave
    East Rutherford NJ 07073
    201 438-5200

(G-8290)
SABRE DIE CUTTING CO INC
68 Mill St (07501-1825)
PHONE................................973 357-9800
Michaqel Culver, *President*
Michael Culver, *President*
Elizabeth Flores, *Vice Pres*
Neil Feuerstein, *Sales Mgr*
EMP: 30
SQ FT: 35,000
SALES (est): 3.8MM **Privately Held**
SIC: 2675 7389 Paper die-cutting; packaging & labeling services

(G-8291)
SAHARA TEXTILE INC
52 Courtland St (07503-2947)
PHONE................................973 247-9900
Othman Jabbar, *President*
Nizar Jabbar, *Vice Pres*
▲ EMP: 20 EST: 1997
SQ FT: 90,000
SALES (est): 1.4MM **Privately Held**
SIC: 2392 Comforters & quilts: made from purchased materials

(G-8292)
SAMNA CNSTRCTN & STEEL FABRCTN
75 Dale Ave (07501-2903)
PHONE................................973 977-8400
Salem El Samna,
EMP: 10
SALES (est): 1.1MM **Privately Held**
SIC: 3441 Fabricated structural metal

(G-8293)
SAMSTUBEND INC
31 Maryland Ave (07503-2110)
PHONE................................973 278-2555
Steve Baresse, *President*
Sam Ajadi, *COO*
Arnold Virula, *Plant Mgr*
EMP: 12
SQ FT: 7,000
SALES (est): 2.7MM **Privately Held**
SIC: 3498 5074 Tube fabricating (contract bending & shaping); plumbing & hydronic heating supplies

(G-8294)
SAMUELSON FURNITURE INC
11-13 Maryland Ave (07503-2110)
PHONE................................973 278-4372
Lawrence Chaflin, *President*
Michael Chalfin, *Vice Pres*
Marianne San George, *Controller*
Larry Chlfin, *VP Human Res*
Florencia Pergament, *Sales Executive*
▲ EMP: 15
SALES (est): 3.5MM **Privately Held**
WEB: www.samuelsonfurniture.com
SIC: 3553 Furniture makers' machinery, woodworking

(G-8295)
SAPPHIRE BATH INC
93 Harrison St Ste 5 (07501-1251)
PHONE................................718 215-1262
Josh Leser, *CEO*
EMP: 5
SQ FT: 11,000
SALES: 1MM **Privately Held**
SIC: 3431 Bathroom fixtures, including sinks

(G-8296)
SEABOARD PAPER AND TWINE LLC
37 E 6th St (07524-1173)
PHONE................................973 413-8100
Mike Fiore, *Mng Member*
Robert Baretz,
Bill Mulligan,
▲ EMP: 26
SQ FT: 52,000
SALES (est): 4.2MM **Privately Held**
WEB: www.seaboardpaperandtwine.com
SIC: 2298 2679 3589 Twine; filter paper: made from purchased material; paperboard products, converted; commercial cleaning equipment

(G-8297)
SEALY MATTRESS CO N J INC
Also Called: Sealy Paterson
697 River St (07524-1538)
PHONE................................973 345-8800
David Hertz, *President*
Deek Medzadourian, *Opers Staff*
◆ EMP: 250 EST: 1881
SQ FT: 131,000
SALES: 100MM **Privately Held**
WEB: www.sealy.com
SIC: 2515 3493 Mattresses & foundations; steel springs, except wire

(G-8298)
SENAT POULTRY LLC
28 Warren St (07524-2104)
PHONE................................973 742-9316
Atabey Kucukkarca, *President*
EMP: 35
SALES (est): 4.7MM **Privately Held**
SIC: 2015 Poultry slaughtering & processing

(G-8299)
SKORR PRODUCTS LLC
90 George St (07503-2319)
P.O. Box 723, Butler (07405-0723)
PHONE................................973 523-2606
Robert Skvorecz, *Mng Member*
▲ EMP: 15
SALES (est): 2.5MM **Privately Held**
WEB: www.skorrproducts.com
SIC: 5051 3496 Metal wires, ties, cables &
screening; miscellaneous fabricated wire
products

(G-8300)
STARLITE WINDOW MFG CO INC
Also Called: Starlite Window Mfg Co
50 E 25th St (07514-1504)
PHONE................................973 278-9366
Juan D Rodriguez, *President*
Omar Rodriguez, *Sales Mgr*
Olivia Revira, *Manager*
EMP: 15
SQ FT: 7,500
SALES (est): 650K **Privately Held**
WEB: www.starlitewindows.com
SIC: 3442 5031 Window & door frames;
casements, aluminum; metal doors, sash
& trim

(G-8301)
STEPHCO SALES INC
238 Lindbergh Pl Ste 3 (07503-2823)
PHONE................................973 278-5454
Danny Dibetitto, *President*
Carmen Orasco, *Admin Sec*
▲ EMP: 32
SALES (est): 4.3MM **Privately Held**
SIC: 5087 3089 2675 Carpet & rug clean-
ing equipment & supplies, commercial;
plastic containers, except foam; die-cut
paper & board

(G-8302)
STEPHEN DOUGLAS PLASTICS INC
22 Green St 36 (07501-2825)
P.O. Box 2775 (07509-2775)
PHONE................................973 523-3030
Stewart Graff, *President*
Miriam Graff, *Corp Secy*
Douglas Graff, *Vice Pres*
Beshaw Paul, *CFO*
Fernando Surraco, *CTO*
◆ EMP: 135
SQ FT: 79,000
SALES (est): 38.7MM **Privately Held**
WEB: www.douglasstephen.com
SIC: 3089 Plastic containers, except foam;
plastic kitchenware, tableware & house-
ware

(G-8303)
STONEBRIDGE PAPER LLC
Also Called: Converting Resources
37 E 6th St (07524-1173)
P.O. Box 2571, Wayne (07474-2571)
PHONE................................973 413-8100
Robert Baretz, *Mng Member*
▲ EMP: 12
SQ FT: 42,000
SALES: 2MM **Privately Held**
SIC: 2679 Paper products, converted

(G-8304)
SUNGLO FABRICS INC
50 California Ave (07503-2503)
PHONE................................201 935-0830
Larry B Weissenberg, *President*
◆ EMP: 10 EST: 1932
SQ FT: 23,000
SALES (est): 1.6MM **Privately Held**
WEB: www.sunglofabrics.com
SIC: 2759 Screen printing

(G-8305)
SUNRISE SNACKS ROCKLAND INC
787 E 27th St (07504-2019)
PHONE................................845 352-2676
Simon Singer, *Branch Mgr*
EMP: 15
SALES (corp-wide): 1.4MM **Privately Held**
SIC: 2099 Food preparations

PA: Sunrise Snacks Of Rockland, Inc.
3 Sunrise Dr
Monsey NY 10952
845 352-2676

(G-8306)
SUPERTEX INC
860 Market St (07513-1127)
PHONE................................973 345-1000
EMP: 40
SQ FT: 30,000
SALES (est): 3.7MM **Privately Held**
WEB: www.meshtruckcovers.com
SIC: 2253 T-shirts & tops, knit

(G-8307)
SUPPLY PLUS NJ INC
3 E 26th St (07514-1505)
PHONE................................973 782-5930
Issac Greensfeld, *President*
▲ EMP: 40
SQ FT: 10,000
SALES (est): 9.7MM **Privately Held**
SIC: 3069 Sponge rubber & sponge rubber
products

(G-8308)
SUPPLY PLUS NY INC
3 E 26th St (07514-1505)
PHONE................................973 481-4800
Sam Neustein, *Ch of Bd*
Samuel Neustein Jr, *President*
Alex Neustein, *Vice Pres*
Murray Neustein, *Treasurer*
Hanna Neustein, *Admin Sec*
▲ EMP: 26
SQ FT: 66,000
SALES (est): 4.6MM **Privately Held**
SIC: 3291 5199 Pads, scouring: soap im-
pregnated; sponges, scouring: metallic;
foam rubber

(G-8309)
SUPPLYONE NEW YORK INC
143 Getty Ave (07503-2806)
PHONE................................718 392-7400
William T Leith, *Ch of Bd*
Jerry Gitelli, *President*
Jason Fuller, *CFO*
▲ EMP: 30 EST: 1934
SQ FT: 70,000
SALES (est): 15.9MM
SALES (corp-wide): 407.7MM **Privately
Held**
SIC: 3565 Carton packing machines
PA: Supplyone Holdings Company, Inc.
11 Campus Blvd Ste 150
Newtown Square PA 19073
484 582-5005

(G-8310)
SWEET POTATO PIE INC
140 Auburn St (07501-2035)
PHONE................................973 279-3405
Edgar Ramsey, *President*
Gwendolyn Ramsey, *Corp Secy*
EMP: 40
SQ FT: 6,500
SALES (est): 4.7MM **Privately Held**
WEB: www.classicpies.com
SIC: 2051 Pies, bakery: except frozen

(G-8311)
SYNERGY MICROWAVE CORP (PA)
201 Mclean Blvd (07504-1138)
PHONE................................973 881-8800
Ulrich L Rohde, *Ch of Bd*
Meta Rohde, *President*
Clark Heber, *QC Mgr*
Emma Anderson, *Accountant*
David P Lashinsky, *Manager*
▲ EMP: 100
SQ FT: 22,000
SALES (est): 15.7MM **Privately Held**
WEB: www.synergymwave.com
SIC: 3679 Microwave components

(G-8312)
TEC INSTALLATIONS INC
375 E 22nd St (07514-2312)
PHONE................................973 684-0503
Scott Crance, *President*
EMP: 10
SQ FT: 20,000

SALES (est): 2MM **Privately Held**
SIC: 3535 Conveyors & conveying equipment

(G-8313)
TEVCO ENTERPRISES INC
55 E 6th St (07524-1103)
PHONE................................908 754-7306
Marc Bergschneider, *President*
Jim Joyce, *President*
James Joyce, *Manager*
◆ EMP: 55 EST: 1987
SALES (est): 11.5MM
SALES (corp-wide): 5.5B **Publicly Held**
WEB: www.tevco.com
SIC: 2851 Enamels
PA: Rpm International Inc.
2628 Pearl Rd
Medina OH 44256
330 273-5090

(G-8314)
THEBGB INC (PA)
840 E 28th St (07513-1219)
PHONE................................917 749-5309
Jessica Sillaro, *President*
EMP: 1 EST: 2017
SQ FT: 10,000
SALES: 3MM **Privately Held**
SIC: 2051 Bread, cake & related products

(G-8315)
THERMA-TECH CORPORATION
300 Dakota St Ste 1 (07503-2448)
PHONE................................973 345-0076
Yonina Papka, *President*
Benjamin Papka, *Treasurer*
EMP: 10
SALES: 1.1MM **Privately Held**
SIC: 3567 Infrared ovens, industrial

(G-8316)
TRB ELECTRO CORP
6 Morris St (07501-1706)
P.O. Box 840 (07543-0840)
PHONE................................973 278-9014
Raman Patel, *Owner*
Dan Patel, *Corp Secy*
Chandra Patel, *Vice Pres*
EMP: 30 EST: 1964
SQ FT: 4,000
SALES (est): 3.7MM **Privately Held**
SIC: 3471 Anodizing (plating) of metals or
formed products

(G-8317)
TRINITY PRESS INC
655 Market St (07513-1228)
PHONE................................973 881-0690
Kevin Barnes, *President*
EMP: 40
SQ FT: 23,500
SALES (est): 9.2MM **Privately Held**
WEB: www.kevinbarnes.com
SIC: 2752 Commercial printing, offset

(G-8318)
TRISTATE CRATING PALLET CO INC
85 Fulton St (07501-1208)
PHONE................................973 357-8293
Marc Ellison, *President*
Maria Ellison, *President*
▲ EMP: 35
SQ FT: 30,000
SALES (est): 7.4MM **Privately Held**
WEB: www.tristatecrating.com
SIC: 2448 Pallets, wood

(G-8319)
UMETAL LLC
219 Lafayette St (07524-2494)
PHONE................................862 257-3032
Taylor Mackenzie, *Principal*
EMP: 5
SALES (est): 608.1K **Privately Held**
SIC: 3469 Metal stampings

(G-8320)
UNITED MACHINE INC
239 Lindbergh Pl Ste 2a (07503-2821)
PHONE................................973 345-4505
Yakov Opatzevfky, *President*
EMP: 4
SQ FT: 10,000

SALES: 200K **Privately Held**
SIC: 3599 Water leak detectors; weather
vanes

(G-8321)
URBAN MILLWORK & SUPPLY CORP
90 2nd Ave (07514-2025)
PHONE................................973 278-7072
Sheer Stundell, *President*
Brett Stundell, *Vice Pres*
EMP: 2 EST: 1964
SQ FT: 17,500
SALES: 1.3MM **Privately Held**
SIC: 2431 5211 Staircases & stairs, wood;
doors, storm: wood or metal

(G-8322)
VACS BANDAGE COMPANY INC
163 Pennsylvania Ave (07503)
P.O. Box 2582 (07509-2582)
PHONE................................973 345-3355
Anthony Vacca, *President*
EMP: 12
SQ FT: 7,000
SALES: 806.7K **Privately Held**
SIC: 2211 Bandage cloths, cotton

(G-8323)
VISION LIGHTING INC
48 N 2nd St (07522-1705)
PHONE................................973 720-1200
Barry Mabery, *President*
Frank Giarratana, *Vice Pres*
EMP: 5
SQ FT: 5,000
SALES (est): 490K **Privately Held**
WEB: www.fxlight.com
SIC: 3646 Commercial indusl & institu-
tional electric lighting fixtures

(G-8324)
YOLAND CORPORATION
924 E 25th St (07513)
PHONE................................862 257-9036
Roni Ginat, *General Mgr*
Ayal Adler, *Principal*
Tal Ganet, *Vice Pres*
ADI Ginat, *Manager*
EMP: 49
SQ FT: 8,000
SALES (est): 5.2MM
SALES (corp-wide): 3.4MM **Privately
Held**
WEB: www.yolandcorp.com
SIC: 2399 Parachutes
PA: D. Yoland Ltd.
17 Hamasger
Netanya 42378
986 161-03

(G-8325)
ZENEX PRECISION PRODUCTS CORP
69 George St (07503-2318)
PHONE................................973 523-6910
Zenon Wronski, *President*
Robert Wronski, *Vice Pres*
EMP: 10
SALES (est): 1MM **Privately Held**
WEB: www.zenexprecision.com
SIC: 3599 Machine shop, jobbing & repair

(G-8326)
ZULU FIRE DOORS LTD LBLTY CO
923 Market St (07513-1128)
PHONE................................973 569-9858
Harpal Singh Rai, *Mng Member*
EMP: 9
SALES (est): 1.1MM **Privately Held**
SIC: 3442 Metal doors, sash & trim

```
┌─────────────────────────┐
│        Paulsboro         │
│    Gloucester County     │
└─────────────────────────┘
```

(G-8327)
AAA PHARMACEUTICAL
157-160 W Jefferson St (08066)
PHONE................................856 423-2700
Tejash Sheth, *Vice Pres*
EMP: 15

SALES (corp-wide): 20MM **Privately
Held**
SIC: 2834 Pharmaceutical preparations
PA: Aaa Pharmaceutical
681 Main St
Lumberton NJ 08048
609 288-6060

(G-8328)
ACTIVE CONTROLS LLC
1501 Grandview Ave # 400 (08066-1865)
PHONE...................................856 669-0940
Michael Flowers, *President*
Jordan Flowers, *COO*
Russ Rolt, *Vice Pres*
▲ **EMP:** 4
SALES (est): 630.4K **Privately Held**
SIC: 3629 Electrical industrial apparatus

(G-8329)
ASTRAL DIAGNOSTICS INC
1224 Forest Pkwy Ste 200 (08066-1722)
PHONE...................................856 224-0900
Edward McCaffrey, *President*
EMP: 5
SQ FT: 8,000
SALES (est): 949.6K
SALES (corp-wide): 71.2MM **Privately
Held**
WEB: www.astraldiagnostics.com
SIC: 2835 In vitro & in vivo diagnostic sub-
stances
PA: Polysciences, Inc.
400 Valley Rd
Warrington PA 18976
215 343-6484

(G-8330)
BOSTIK INC
2000 Nolte Dr (08066-1700)
PHONE...................................856 848-8669
Theresa Honeycut, *Branch Mgr*
Joseph Weirich, *Executive*
Paul Dollard, *Planning*
EMP: 70
SALES (corp-wide): 98.4MM **Privately
Held**
WEB: www.bostik-us.com
SIC: 2891 2899 Adhesives; chemical
preparations
HQ: Bostik, Inc.
11320 W Wtertown Plank Rd
Wauwatosa WI 53226
414 774-2250

(G-8331)
COIM USA INC
Also Called: Air Products
675 Billingsport Rd (08066-1037)
PHONE...................................856 224-1668
Cathy Myers, *Principal*
EMP: 30
SQ FT: 20,000
SALES (corp-wide): 476.9MM **Privately
Held**
WEB: www.airproducts.com
SIC: 2813 2869 2819 Industrial gases; in-
dustrial organic chemicals; industrial inor-
ganic chemicals
HQ: Coim Usa Inc.
286 Mantua Grove Rd # 1
West Deptford NJ 08066
856 224-8560

(G-8332)
INTELCO
1927 Nolte Dr (08066-1727)
PHONE...................................856 384-8562
Grant Wells, *Branch Mgr*
EMP: 28 **Privately Held**
SIC: 2541 1799 2434 Table or counter
tops, plastic laminated; counter top instal-
lation; vanities, bathroom: wood
PA: Intelco
250 Harvard Ave
Westville NJ 08093

(G-8333)
LAMATEK INC (PA)
1226 Forest Pkwy (08066-1728)
PHONE...................................856 599-6000
G Robert Carlson, *CEO*
Laura Basara, *Vice Pres*
Jenna Hunsberger, *Purch Agent*
Fernando Gisone, *Buyer*
Terri Chicosky, *QC Mgr*

▼ **EMP:** 30
SQ FT: 13,000
SALES (est): 6.4MM **Privately Held**
SIC: 3069 3053 Weather strip, sponge
rubber; gaskets, packing & sealing de-
vices

(G-8334)
MATTHEY JOHNSON INC
2003 Nolte Dr (08066-1727)
PHONE...................................856 384-7022
Clint Zelst, *Vice Pres*
Anita Sargable, *Safety Mgr*
Tiffany Lee, *Buyer*
Frank Lord, *Buyer*
Jeff Jones, *Engineer*
EMP: 131
SALES (corp-wide): 13.8B **Privately Held**
SIC: 3341 Platinum group metals, smelting
& refining (secondary)
HQ: Johnson Matthey Inc.
435 Devon Park Dr Ste 600
Wayne PA 19087
610 971-3000

(G-8335)
MCGRORY GLASS INC
1400 Grandview Ave (08066-1801)
PHONE...................................856 579-3200
Christopher McGrory, *President*
Gary McGrory, *Corp Secy*
Charles McGrory, *Vice Pres*
Larry Walker, *Sales Staff*
▲ **EMP:** 60
SQ FT: 108,000
SALES (est): 17MM **Privately Held**
WEB: www.mcgrory-glass.com
SIC: 3211 5039 3231 3229 Construction
glass; glass construction materials; prod-
ucts of purchased glass; pressed & blown
glass; laminated plastics plate & sheet

(G-8336)
**OIL TECHNOLOGIES SERVICES
INC (PA)**
Also Called: Seahawk Services
1501 Grandview Ave Ste 1 (08066-1865)
PHONE...................................856 845-4142
Wajdi Abdmessih, *President*
Fabiola Abdmessih, *Vice Pres*
EMP: 6
SQ FT: 5,000
SALES: 1MM **Privately Held**
SIC: 1389 5551 Testing, measuring, sur-
veying & analysis services; oil consult-
ants; marine supplies & equipment

(G-8337)
**OIL TECHNOLOGIES SERVICES
INC**
Also Called: Seahawk Services
1501 Grandview Ave Ste 1 (08066-1865)
PHONE...................................856 845-4142
EMP: 6
SQ FT: 5,000
SALES: 1MM **Privately Held**
SIC: 1389 5551 Testing, measuring, sur-
veying & analysis services; oil consult-
ants; marine supplies & equipment

(G-8338)
**PAULSBORO REFINING
COMPANY LLC**
Also Called: Pbf Energy
800 Billingsport Rd (08066)
PHONE...................................973 455-7500
Thomas J Nimbley, *CEO*
Michael D Gayda, *President*
Donald F Lucey, *Exec VP*
Matthew C Lucey, *Exec VP*
Jeffrey Dill, *Senior VP*
▲ **EMP:** 1500
SALES (est): 17.1B
SALES (corp-wide): 27.1B **Publicly Held**
SIC: 2911 Oils, partly refined: sold for re-
running
HQ: Pbf Holding Company Llc
1 Sylvan Way Ste 2
Parsippany NJ 07054

(G-8339)
**PENNZOIL-QUAKER STATE
COMPANY**
1224 Forest Pkwy Ste 100 (08066-1722)
PHONE...................................856 423-1388

Ed Barney, *Manager*
EMP: 4
SALES (corp-wide): 388.3B **Privately
Held**
WEB: www.pzl.com
SIC: 2911 Petroleum refining
HQ: Pennzoil-Quaker State Company
150 N Dairy Ashford Rd
Houston TX 77079
713 245-4800

(G-8340)
**TRIANGLE TUBE/PHASE III CO
INC**
1240 Forest Pkwy Ste 100 (08066-1719)
PHONE...................................856 228-9940
Daniel Lasserre, *Ch of Bd*
Jack Weaver, *President*
◆ **EMP:** 51
SQ FT: 50,000
SALES (est): 11.3MM
SALES (corp-wide): 183.7K **Privately
Held**
WEB: www.triangletube.com
SIC: 3433 3639 3621 3443 Heating
equipment, except electric; hot water
heaters, household; motors & generators;
fabricated plate work (boiler shop)
HQ: Acv International
Oude Vijverweg 6
Beersel 1653
233 482-20

(G-8341)
**VALERO REF COMPANY-NEW
JERSEY**
800 Billingsport Rd (08066)
PHONE...................................856 224-6000
Paul Borbhu, *Manager*
EMP: 550
SALES (corp-wide): 117B **Publicly Held**
SIC: 2911 Petroleum refining
HQ: Valero Refining Company-New Jersey
1 Valero Way
San Antonio TX 78249
210 345-2000

Peapack
Somerset County

(G-8342)
PFIZER INC
100 Rte 206 N (07977)
P.O. Box 800 (07977-0800)
PHONE...................................908 901-8000
Juan C Perez, *Manager*
EMP: 146
SALES (corp-wide): 53.6B **Publicly Held**
WEB: www.pfizer.com
SIC: 2834 Antibiotics, packaged
PA: Pfizer Inc.
235 E 42nd St
New York NY 10017
212 733-2323

(G-8343)
**PHARMACIA & UPJOHN INC
(HQ)**
100 Route 206 N (07977)
PHONE...................................908 901-8000
Goran A Ando, *Exec VP*
Christopher J Coughlin, *CFO*
▲ **EMP:** 400
SALES (est): 825.6MM
SALES (corp-wide): 53.6B **Publicly Held**
WEB: www.pharmaciaupjohn.com
SIC: 2834 2833 Pharmaceutical prepara-
tions; medicinal chemicals
PA: Pfizer Inc.
235 E 42nd St
New York NY 10017
212 733-2323

(G-8344)
**PHARMACIA & UPJOHN
COMPANY LLC (HQ)**
Also Called: Pfizer
100 Rte 206 N (07977)
PHONE...................................908 901-8000
Ley S Smith, *President*
Shweta Jain, *Project Mgr*
Carla Wright, *Engineer*
Michael Lantigua, *Business Anlyst*

Marty Brown, *Manager*
◆ **EMP:** 277 **EST:** 1958
SQ FT: 300,000
SALES (est): 113.8MM
SALES (corp-wide): 53.6B **Publicly Held**
SIC: 2833 2048 2834 Medicinal chemicals; organic medicinal chemicals: bulk,
uncompounded; alkaloids & other botanical based products; agar-agar (ground);
feed supplements; druggists' preparations
(pharmaceuticals)
PA: Pfizer Inc.
235 E 42nd St
New York NY 10017
212 733-2323

(G-8345)
R P R GRAPHICS INC
87 Main St (07977-9801)
P.O. Box 118 (07977-0118)
PHONE...................................908 654-8080
Richard P Ruocco, *President*
Laura J Ruocco, *President*
Luis Velez, *President*
Frances Ruocco, *Corp Secy*
Susan J Arlington, *COO*
EMP: 50
SQ FT: 12,000
SALES (est): 5.6MM **Privately Held**
WEB: www.rprgraphicsinc.com
SIC: 3663 2796 Digital encoders; color
separations for printing

Pedricktown
Salem County

(G-8346)
CMI-PROMEX INC
7 Benjamin Green Rd (08067-3502)
PHONE...................................856 351-1000
Wayne Ligato, *President*
Michele S Barbara, *General Mgr*
Joseph Stefan, *Plant Mgr*
Andrew Corlett, *Engineer*
Bob Frawley, *Sales Dir*
EMP: 19
SQ FT: 10,000
SALES (est): 4.4MM **Privately Held**
WEB: www.cmi-promex.com
SIC: 3312 4013 7692 Tool & die steel;
switching & terminal services; welding re-
pair

(G-8347)
CST PAVERS
345 Route 130 (08067-3617)
PHONE...................................856 299-5339
David Guidi, *Principal*
EMP: 11
SALES (est): 1.4MM **Privately Held**
SIC: 3272 Concrete products

(G-8348)
DOCK RESINS CORPORATION
76 Porcupine Rd (08067-3509)
PHONE...................................908 862-2351
Howard Burke, *President*
James Robinson III, *Exec VP*
Joe Barbanel, *Senior VP*
A Warman, *Production*
▲ **EMP:** 46 **EST:** 1947
SQ FT: 24,000
SALES (est): 9.3MM
SALES (corp-wide): 225.3B **Publicly
Held**
WEB: www.lubrizol.com
SIC: 2821 Plastics materials & resins
HQ: The Lubrizol Corporation
29400 Lakeland Blvd
Wickliffe OH 44092
440 943-4200

(G-8349)
JE BERKOWITZ LP
1 Gateway Blvd (08067-3629)
P.O. Box 427 (08067-0427)
PHONE...................................856 456-7800
Chris Lewandowski, *President*
Arthur M Berkowitz, *Partner*
Alan Berkowitz, *Partner*
Edwin J Berkowitz, *Partner*
David B Byruch, *Partner*
▲ **EMP:** 200
SQ FT: 200,000

G
E
O
G
R
A
P
H
I
C

SALES (est): 80.3MM **Privately Held**
WEB: www.jeberkowitz.com
SIC: 3231 3211 Insulating glass: made from purchased glass; tempered glass: made from purchased glass; laminated glass

(G-8350)
LETTERING PLUS SIGN COMPANY
438 Perkintown Rd (08067-3106)
PHONE..................................856 299-0404
Bill Stouch, *President*
Sandra Stouch, *Treasurer*
EMP: 4
SALES (est): 392.3K **Privately Held**
SIC: 3993 7389 Signs, not made in custom sign painting shops; lettering & sign painting services

(G-8351)
LUBRIZOL ADVANCED MTLS INC
Also Called: B F Goodrich Performance Mtls
76 Porcupine Rd (08067-3509)
PHONE..................................856 299-3764
Joseph Lazevnick, *Manager*
EMP: 39
SALES (corp-wide): 225.3B **Publicly Held**
WEB: www.pharma.noveoninc.com
SIC: 2899 3087 Chemical preparations; custom compound purchased resins
HQ: Lubrizol Global Management, Inc
9911 Brecksville Rd
Brecksville OH 44141
216 447-5000

(G-8352)
PALLET SERVICES INC
66 Pennsgrve Pedrcktwn Rd (08067)
P.O. Box 9, Swedesboro (08085-0009)
PHONE..................................856 514-3908
Steve Sorbello Jr, *President*
EMP: 4 EST: 2012
SALES (est): 680.4K **Privately Held**
SIC: 2448 Pallets, wood

(G-8353)
PYLE PRECISION MACHINING LLC
175 Route 130 (08067-3612)
P.O. Box 5805, Deptford (08096-0805)
PHONE..................................856 376-3720
Don Pyle, *Owner*
EMP: 4 EST: 1998
SQ FT: 8,750
SALES (est): 148K **Privately Held**
SIC: 3599 Machine shop, jobbing & repair

(G-8354)
RANDOM 8 WOODWORKS LLC
32 W Mill St (08067-3531)
PHONE..................................856 364-7627
EMP: 6
SALES (corp-wide): 654K **Privately Held**
SIC: 2431 Millwork
PA: Random 8 Woodworks Llc
459 Clems Run
Mullica Hill NJ 08062
856 417-3329

(G-8355)
SALEM OAK VINEYARDS LTD LBLTY
62 N Railroad Ave (08067-3524)
PHONE..................................856 889-2121
Mandi Cassidy,
EMP: 5
SALES (est): 376.7K **Privately Held**
SIC: 2084 Wines

(G-8356)
WJV MATERIALS LLC
93 Pennsgrve Pedrcktwn (08067)
PHONE..................................856 299-8244
Dan Federanko,
EMP: 20
SALES (est): 2MM **Privately Held**
SIC: 3273 Ready-mixed concrete

Pemberton
Burlington County

(G-8357)
AZTECH MFG INC
147 W Hampton St (08068-1012)
PHONE..................................609 726-1212
Daniel R Murphy, *President*
EMP: 10
SALES (est): 962.3K **Privately Held**
SIC: 3599 Machine shop, jobbing & repair

(G-8358)
TOTALLY T SHIRTS & MORE INC
201 W Hampton St (08068-1014)
PHONE..................................609 894-0011
Tony Miraglia, *President*
EMP: 5
SQ FT: 1,000
SALES (est): 611.7K **Privately Held**
SIC: 2759 Screen printing

Pennington
Mercer County

(G-8359)
BRISTOL-MYERS SQUIBB COMPANY
311 Pnnington Rocky Hl Rd (08534-2130)
PHONE..................................212 546-4000
Chandra Shukla, *Manager*
Jennifer Karkas, *Associate*
EMP: 40
SALES (corp-wide): 22.5B **Publicly Held**
WEB: www.bms.com
SIC: 2834 Pills, pharmaceutical
PA: Bristol-Myers Squibb Company
430 E 29th St Fl 14
New York NY 10016
212 546-4000

(G-8360)
CERCIS INC
25 Route 31 S Ste C2030 (08534-2511)
PHONE..................................609 737-5120
Karen Kinsman, *Corp Secy*
EMP: 6
SQ FT: 1,500
SALES (est): 710K **Privately Held**
WEB: www.cercis.com
SIC: 3827 Light sources, standard

(G-8361)
CHRISTENSEN MANUFACTURING
11 Moores Mill Mt Rose Rd (08534-1840)
P.O. Box 592 (08534-0592)
PHONE..................................609 466-9700
Dave Christensen, *President*
John Healy, *Vice Pres*
EMP: 17
SQ FT: 6,000
SALES (est): 4.4MM **Privately Held**
WEB: www.christensenmfg.com
SIC: 3537 3713 Trucks, tractors, loaders, carriers & similar equipment; truck & bus bodies

(G-8362)
COMMERCIAL PDTS SVCS GROUP INC (PA)
Also Called: Green Building Solutions
1580 Reed Rd (08534-5000)
PHONE..................................609 730-4111
Robert A Rosenthal, *CEO*
Elizabeth Rosenthal, *President*
Sean Moriarity, *Opers Staff*
EMP: 8
SALES (est): 1.4MM **Privately Held**
SIC: 3699 Electrical equipment & supplies

(G-8363)
DIVERSATECH INC
1584 Reed Rd (08534-5003)
PHONE..................................609 730-9668
Haskel Zeloof, *President*
Sam Zeloof, *Maintence Staff*
EMP: 8
SQ FT: 4,000

SALES (est): 907.5K **Privately Held**
WEB: www.diversatech.com
SIC: 3599 Machine shop, jobbing & repair

(G-8364)
ELECTROCHEMICAL SOCIETY INC
Also Called: E C S
65 S Main St (08534-2827)
PHONE..................................609 737-1902
Paul Natishan, *President*
Becca J Compton, *General Mgr*
Linda Cannon, *Finance*
Jessica Wisniewski, *Human Resources*
Rob Gerth, *Mktg Dir*
EMP: 20
SQ FT: 6,000
SALES: 7MM **Privately Held**
WEB: www.electrochem.org
SIC: 8621 2741 Scientific membership association; miscellaneous publishing

(G-8365)
GENERAL SULLIVAN GROUP INC (PA)
Also Called: Sullivan Steel Service
85 Route 31 N (08534-3601)
PHONE..................................609 745-5004
Philip Trainer Jr, *Ch of Bd*
Alfred Deblasio Jr, *President*
◆ EMP: 26
SQ FT: 40,000
SALES: 19MM **Privately Held**
WEB: www.usatolerancerings.com
SIC: 5051 3316 Steel; corrugating iron & steel, cold-rolled

(G-8366)
GENERAL SULLIVAN GROUP INC
USA Tolerance Rings
85 Route 31 N (08534-3601)
PHONE..................................609 745-5000
Joseph Trainer, *Manager*
EMP: 18
SALES (corp-wide): 19MM **Privately Held**
SIC: 5051 3429 3452 Steel; metal fasteners; bolts, metal
PA: General Sullivan Group, Inc.
85 Route 31 N
Pennington NJ 08534
609 745-5004

(G-8367)
HOPEWELL VALLEY VINEYARDS LLC
46 Yard Rd (08534-3905)
PHONE..................................609 737-4465
Liz Radzki, *Purch Mgr*
Serjio Neri, *Mng Member*
Violeta Neri,
▲ EMP: 20
SALES (est): 3MM **Privately Held**
SIC: 2084 Wines

(G-8368)
JL PACKAGING GROUP CORP (PA)
2 Birch St (08534-3304)
PHONE..................................609 610-0286
Judy Chen, *CEO*
Kevin Chen, *Vice Pres*
Rachelle Blue, *Director*
Scott Peterson, *Director*
▲ EMP: 4
SALES: 9MM **Privately Held**
SIC: 3411 7389 Tin cans;

(G-8369)
KOOLTRONIC INC (PA)
30 Pennington Hopewell Rd (08534-3612)
PHONE..................................609 466-3400
Anne L Freedman, *CEO*
Barry J Freedman, *President*
Steve Coulton, *Business Mgr*
Deborah S Freedman, *Vice Pres*
Bill Green, *Opers Mgr*
▲ EMP: 120
SQ FT: 170,000

SALES (est): 35MM **Privately Held**
WEB: www.kooltronic.com
SIC: 3585 3564 3559 3443 Air conditioning equipment, complete; air conditioning units, complete: domestic or industrial; blowers & fans; blowing fans: industrial or commercial; recycling machinery; heat exchangers: coolers (after, inter), condensers, etc.

(G-8370)
LORNAN LITHO INC
130 Route 31 N Ste E (08534-3620)
PHONE..................................609 818-1198
Ronald Shankoff, *President*
Mike Shankoff, *Treasurer*
EMP: 10
SQ FT: 8,500
SALES (est): 143.2K **Privately Held**
SIC: 2752 Commercial printing, offset

(G-8371)
PENNINGTON FURNACE SUPPLY INC
6 Brookside Ave (08534-2209)
P.O. Box 218 (08534-0218)
PHONE..................................609 737-2500
Mark E Blackwell, *President*
Sarah Bregenzer, *Admin Sec*
EMP: 4 EST: 1960
SQ FT: 15,000
SALES: 429.4K **Privately Held**
SIC: 5075 1711 3567 Furnaces, warm air; heating systems repair & maintenance; induction heating equipment

(G-8372)
RLCT INDUSTRIES LLC
Also Called: Nanodesal
2 E Acres Dr (08534-2101)
PHONE..................................609 712-1318
Salatore Gaglio, *Mng Member*
EMP: 5 EST: 2017
SQ FT: 1,500
SALES (est): 317.5K **Privately Held**
SIC: 3589 2819 Commercial cooking & foodwarming equipment; elements

(G-8373)
ROLL TECH INDUSTRIES
55 Route 31 S Ste A (08534-2579)
PHONE..................................609 730-9500
John King, *Owner*
Meredith Murphy, *Office Mgr*
EMP: 18
SALES: 7MM **Privately Held**
SIC: 3315 Steel wire & related products

(G-8374)
SYMPATEC INC (HQ)
1600 Reed Rd C (08534-5002)
PHONE..................................609 303-0066
Stephan Roethele, *President*
Stefan Steigerwald, *COO*
Kay Mootz, *Sales Staff*
Hans Van Der Meer, *Mktg Dir*
EMP: 13
SQ FT: 4,000
SALES (est): 1.3MM
SALES (corp-wide): 29.4MM **Privately Held**
WEB: www.sympatec.com
SIC: 3826 Analytical instruments
PA: Sympatec Gmbh System-Partikel-Technik
Am Pulverhaus 1
Clausthal-Zellerfeld 38678
532 371-70

(G-8375)
TRAP ROCK INDUSTRIES INC
Pennington Hwy Rr 31 (08534)
P.O. Box 419, Kingston (08528-0419)
PHONE..................................609 924-0300
Mickey Stavola, *Principal*
EMP: 18
SALES (corp-wide): 131.7MM **Privately Held**
WEB: www.traprock.com
SIC: 1429 Igneous rock, crushed & broken-quarrying
PA: Trap Rock Industries, Inc.
460 River Rd
Kingston NJ 08528
609 924-0300

(G-8376)
UNCLE EDS CREAMERY
155 W Delaware Ave (08534-1602)
PHONE..................................609 818-0100
Edward P Gola, *Principal*
EMP: 5 EST: 2010
SALES (est): 375.7K **Privately Held**
SIC: 2024 Ice cream, bulk

Penns Grove
Salem County

(G-8377)
CST PRODUCTS LLC
345 Route 130 (08069)
PHONE..................................856 299-5339
Laurie Christy, *Sales Staff*
Ronald Krueger,
▲ EMP: 20
SALES (est): 2.9MM **Privately Held**
SIC: 3272 Paving materials, prefabricated
concrete

(G-8378)
EMPIRE SCALE & BALANCE
35 S Broad St Ste D (08069-1653)
PHONE..................................856 299-1651
Margery Deneis, *President*
EMP: 5 EST: 1990
SALES (est): 329.1K **Privately Held**
WEB: www.empirescalecorp.com
SIC: 3596 5046 Industrial scales; scales,
except laboratory

(G-8379)
U P N PALLET CO INC
305 N Virginia Ave (08069-1126)
PHONE..................................856 299-1192
Greg Massari, *President*
EMP: 10 EST: 1969
SQ FT: 6,000
SALES (est): 1MM **Privately Held**
SIC: 2448 Pallets, wood

Pennsauken
Camden County

(G-8380)
175 DEROUSSE LLC
175 Derousse Ave (08110-3851)
PHONE..................................856 662-0100
EMP: 4
SALES (est): 305.9K **Privately Held**
SIC: 3554 Mfg Paper Industrial Machinery

(G-8381)
ABC SIGN SYSTEMS INC
7970 National Hwy (08110-1412)
P.O. Box 622 (08110-0622)
PHONE..................................856 665-0950
Patrick Trifiletti, *President*
Stephen Trifiletti, *Vice Pres*
Michael Fulforth, *Purchasing*
Sharon Boyle, *Office Mgr*
EMP: 15 EST: 1952
SQ FT: 22,000
SALES (est): 2.3MM **Privately Held**
WEB: www.abcsignsystems.com
SIC: 3993 Electric signs

(G-8382)
ACRO DISPLAY INC (PA)
2250 Sherman Ave Unit A1 (08110-1539)
PHONE..................................215 229-1100
Paul Berenato Sr, *President*
EMP: 50
SQ FT: 150,000
SALES (est): 6.7MM **Privately Held**
WEB: www.acrodisplay.com
SIC: 2541 2542 Display fixtures, wood;
partitions & fixtures, except wood

(G-8383)
ADVANCED ABRASIVES
CORPORATION
7980 National Hwy (08110-1412)
PHONE..................................856 665-9300
Matthew Bees, *President*
Steven Ament, *QC Mgr*
Hodge Jones, *Marketing Staff*

Delia Caban, *Office Mgr*
▲ EMP: 15
SQ FT: 10,200
SALES (est): 1.7MM **Privately Held**
WEB: www.advancedabrasives.com
SIC: 3291 Abrasive products

(G-8384)
AFFORDABLE OFFSET
PRINTING INC
Also Called: Affordable Roofing
809 Hylton Rd Ste 11 (08110-1335)
PHONE..................................856 661-0722
Gary Coates, *CEO*
EMP: 6
SQ FT: 4,000
SALES (est): 961.1K **Privately Held**
WEB: www.affordableoffset.com
SIC: 2752 Commercial printing, offset

(G-8385)
AIRBORNE SYSTEMS N AMER
INC (HQ)
Also Called: Airborne Systems NA
5800 Magnolia Ave (08109-1309)
PHONE..................................856 663-1275
Elek Puskas, *CEO*
Vicki Panhuise, *President*
Brad Pedersen, *President*
JC Berland, *Exec VP*
Mike Garten, *Exec VP*
EMP: 5
SALES (est): 80.8MM **Privately Held**
SIC: 2426 3429 Textile machinery acces-
sories, hardwood; parachute hardware
PA: Transdigm Group Incorporated
1301 E 9th St Ste 3000
Cleveland OH 44114
216 706-2960

(G-8386)
AIRBORNE SYSTEMS N AMER
NJ INC
5800 Magnolia Ave (08109-1309)
PHONE..................................856 663-1275
Bryce Wiedeman, *President*
▼ EMP: 170
SQ FT: 44,400
SALES (est): 31.6MM **Privately Held**
WEB: www.paraflite.com
SIC: 2399 Parachutes
HQ: Airborne Systems North America Inc.
5800 Magnolia Ave
Pennsauken NJ 08109
856 663-1275

(G-8387)
ALUMINUM SHAPES INC
9000 River Rd (08110-3204)
PHONE..................................856 662-5500
Christopher V Boland, *Principal*
▲ EMP: 26
SALES (est): 6.8MM **Privately Held**
SIC: 3354 Aluminum extruded products

(G-8388)
AMER-RAC LLC
8128 River Rd (08110-2437)
PHONE..................................856 488-6210
Steven Shore,
EMP: 12
SQ FT: 15,000
SALES (est): 1.3MM **Privately Held**
WEB: www.amer-rac.com
SIC: 3317 Steel pipe & tubes

(G-8389)
APOLLO EAST LLC
7895 Airport Hwy (08109-4322)
PHONE..................................856 486-1882
Dora Ngan,
EMP: 50 EST: 2005
SQ FT: 70,000
SALES (est): 6MM
SALES (corp-wide): 5.3MM **Privately
Held**
WEB: www.apolloemb.com
SIC: 2395 8743 Embroidery products, ex-
cept schiffli machine; promotion service
PA: La Palm Furnitures & Accessories, Inc.
1650 W Artesia Blvd
Gardena CA 90248
310 217-2700

(G-8390)
APTAPHARMA CORPORATION
1533 Union Ave (08110-2489)
PHONE..................................856 665-0025
Ishwar Chauhan, *President*
Rakesh Lad, *Vice Pres*
Sivaramakrishna Nutalapati, *Treasurer*
EMP: 30
SQ FT: 30,000
SALES (est): 4MM **Privately Held**
SIC: 2834 Druggists' preparations (phar-
maceuticals)

(G-8391)
ARROW INFORMATION
PACKAGIG LLC
7100 Westfield Ave (08110-4021)
PHONE..................................856 317-9000
Brian Cassano, *General Mgr*
Margaret A Cassano,
EMP: 6
SALES (est): 1.4MM **Privately Held**
SIC: 2449 3086 2541 Rectangular boxes
& crates, wood; packaging & shipping
materials, foamed plastic; wood partitions
& fixtures

(G-8392)
ATLANTIC ASSOCIATES INTL
INC
Also Called: Hibrett Puratex
7001 Westfield Ave (08110-2633)
PHONE..................................856 662-1717
John P J Madden, *President*
EMP: 15 EST: 1959
SALES (est): 3.9MM **Privately Held**
SIC: 2842 2841 2819 Cleaning or polish-
ing preparations; soap & other deter-
gents; industrial inorganic chemicals

(G-8393)
BARRY CALLEBAUT USA LLC
1500 Suckle Hwy (08110-1423)
PHONE..................................856 663-2260
Jean-Marc Desheraud, *Facilities Mgr*
Magdalini Fliska, *Engineer*
Paul Lewis, *Sales Staff*
Michelle Trembley, *Manager*
Leclere Gilles, *Technology*
EMP: 37
SALES (corp-wide): 45.7MM **Privately
Held**
SIC: 2066 2099 Chocolate; cocoa & cocoa
products; food preparations
HQ: Barry Callebaut U.S.A. Llc
600 W Chicago Ave Ste 860
Chicago IL 60654

(G-8394)
BARRY CALLEBAUT USA LLC
1600 Suckle Hwy (08110-1444)
PHONE..................................856 663-2260
Lynn Bohl, *Sales Staff*
Ted Bertran, *Manager*
EMP: 92
SALES (corp-wide): 45.7MM **Privately
Held**
SIC: 2066 Chocolate; cocoa & cocoa prod-
ucts
HQ: Barry Callebaut U.S.A. Llc
600 W Chicago Ave Ste 860
Chicago IL 60654

(G-8395)
BEEF INTERNATIONAL INC
Also Called: B.I. Foods
7010 Central Hwy (08109-4367)
PHONE..................................856 663-6763
Kevin Ingraldi, *President*
Lee Gugenheim, *Accounts Exec*
Dan Naab, *Sales Executive*
Tom McMille, *Planning*
EMP: 60
SQ FT: 35,000
SALES (est): 11.5MM **Privately Held**
SIC: 2011 Beef products from beef slaugh-
tered on site

(G-8396)
BELL SUPPLY CO (PA)
7221 N Crescent Blvd (08110-1597)
PHONE..................................856 663-3900
Dominick Vittese, *President*
Carl Zuccarelli, *Opers Mgr*
Chase Campbell, *Purchasing*

Dorothy Vittese, *Treasurer*
EMP: 25 EST: 1946
SQ FT: 5,000
SALES (est): 13.8MM **Privately Held**
WEB: www.bellsupplyinc.com
SIC: 1742 3271 Drywall; blocks, concrete
or cinder: standard

(G-8397)
BON ARCHITECTUAL MILL
WORK LLC
9120 Pennsauken Hwy (08110-1206)
PHONE..................................856 320-2872
EMP: 4 EST: 2014
SALES (est): 335.9K **Privately Held**
SIC: 2431 Millwork

(G-8398)
BRAVO PACK INC
90 Twinbridge Dr (08110-4200)
PHONE..................................856 872-2937
Aibek Hakimov, *CEO*
Paul Vagnoni, *Executive*
▲ EMP: 4 EST: 2013
SALES (est): 945.5K **Privately Held**
SIC: 2677 5112 Envelopes; envelopes

(G-8399)
CAMPBELL HAUSFELD LLC
8550 Remington Ave (08110-1336)
PHONE..................................856 661-1800
Roy Raider, *Principal*
EMP: 134
SALES (corp-wide): 225.3B **Publicly
Held**
SIC: 3563 Air & gas compressors including
vacuum pumps
HQ: Campbell Hausfeld, Llc
225 Pictoria Dr Ste 210
Cincinnati OH 45246
513 367-4811

(G-8400)
CANADA DRY DEL VLY BTLG CO
Also Called: Canada Dry of Delaware Valley
8275 Us Hwy 130 (08110)
PHONE..................................856 662-6767
Harold Honickman, *Ch of Bd*
Joe Szarzynski, *General Mgr*
Nick Dicarlo, *Sales Mgr*
Kathy Strauss, *Supervisor*
▼ EMP: 200
SALES (est): 35.9MM **Privately Held**
SIC: 2086 Bottled & canned soft drinks

(G-8401)
CANADA DRY POTOMAC
CORPORATION
8275 Us Hwy 130 (08110)
PHONE..................................856 665-6200
John Jukus, *Manager*
EMP: 5
SALES (corp-wide): 78.3MM **Privately
Held**
SIC: 2086 Bottled & canned soft drinks
PA: Canada Dry Potomac Corporation
3600 Pennsy Dr
Hyattsville MD 20785
301 773-5500

(G-8402)
CETYLITE INDUSTRIES INC
9051 River Rd (08110-3293)
PHONE..................................856 665-6111
Stanley L Wachman, *Ch of Bd*
Keith Henry, *Prdtn Mgr*
Mike Harrington, *Controller*
Jeff Glassman, *Executive*
▲ EMP: 28
SQ FT: 22,400
SALES (est): 7.6MM **Privately Held**
WEB: www.cetylite.com
SIC: 2834 Pharmaceutical preparations

(G-8403)
CGS SALES AND SERVICE LLC
6950 River Rd (08110-2611)
PHONE..................................856 665-6154
Tony Pernicello, *Technical Staff*
Anthony W Pernicello,
▲ EMP: 5
SALES (est): 675.8K **Privately Held**
SIC: 2759 Screen printing

(G-8404)
CLARITY IMAGING TECH INC
4350 Haddonfield Rd # 300 (08109-3387)
PHONE.....................413 693-1234
EMP: 50
SALES (corp-wide): 439.3K Privately Held
WEB: www.clarityimaging.com
SIC: 3555 3861 Printing trade parts & attachments; photographic equipment & supplies
HQ: Clarity Imaging Technologies, Inc.
4350 Haddonfield Rd # 300
Pennsauken NJ 08109

(G-8405)
CLARITY IMAGING TECH INC (DH)
4350 Haddonfield Rd # 300 (08109-3387)
PHONE.....................877 272-4362
Peter Corritori, CEO
Justan Ham, Opers Mgr
Claire Walter, CFO
Duane Roush, Technical Staff
David Mac Isaac, Bd of Directors
▲ EMP: 6
SQ FT: 2,000
SALES (est): 10MM
SALES (corp-wide): 439.3K Privately Held
WEB: www.clarityimaging.com
SIC: 3555 Printing trade parts & attachments
HQ: Turbon Usa Inc.
4 Executive Campus # 104
Cherry Hill NJ 08002
856 665-6650

(G-8406)
COLORSOURCE INC
7025 Central Hwy (08109-4312)
PHONE.....................856 488-8100
Alfred Demarco, President
Murray Ellis, President
EMP: 8
SQ FT: 15,000
SALES (est): 3.1MM Privately Held
WEB: www.colorsource.com
SIC: 2752 Color lithography

(G-8407)
COMMERCIAL COMPOSITION & PRTG
1601 Sherman Ave Ste B (08110-2632)
PHONE.....................856 662-0557
EMP: 5 EST: 1983
SQ FT: 12,000
SALES (est): 230K Privately Held
SIC: 2791 Typesetting & Lithographic Printing

(G-8408)
CONNECTOR PRODUCTS INC
1300 John Tipton Blvd (08110-2315)
PHONE.....................856 829-9190
Mario Polidori, CEO
Thomas Polidori, President
Jessica Polidori, Treasurer
EMP: 13
SQ FT: 11,400
SALES (est): 3.5MM Privately Held
WEB: www.connectorproducts.com
SIC: 3643 Connectors, electric cord; rail bonds, electric: for propulsion & signal circuits

(G-8409)
CSL SERVICES INC
7905 Browning Rd Ste 316 (08109-4321)
PHONE.....................856 755-9440
Bruce Cohen, President
Alyson Lee, Business Mgr
Julie Oropallo, Project Mgr
Shari Snyder, Accountant
EMP: 14
SQ FT: 1,000
SALES (est): 3.5MM Privately Held
SIC: 3613 Metering panels, electric

(G-8410)
DATWYLER PHARMA PACKAGING
9012 Pennsauken Hwy (08110-1204)
PHONE.....................856 663-2202
Richard Gardner, Director

EMP: 50
SALES (corp-wide): 1.3B Privately Held
SIC: 3069 8731 3053 Druggists' rubber sundries; commercial physical research; gaskets, packing & sealing devices
HQ: Datwyler Pharma Packaging Usa Inc.
9012 Pennsauken Hwy
Pennsauken NJ 08110
856 663-2202

(G-8411)
DAYSEQUERRA CORPORATION (PA)
7209 Browning Rd (08109-4602)
PHONE.....................856 719-9900
David Day, President
Mike Pappas, Vice Pres
Sandy Martin, Opers Mgr
Cynthia Henderson, Sales Staff
EMP: 11
SQ FT: 4,000
SALES (est): 1.3MM Privately Held
WEB: www.daysequerra.com
SIC: 3663 Radio & TV communications equipment

(G-8412)
DELAIR LLC
Also Called: Delgard Premier Alum Fencing
9000 River Rd (08110-3204)
PHONE.....................856 663-2900
David Stewart, CEO
◆ EMP: 75
SQ FT: 400,000
SALES (est): 5.9MM Privately Held
SIC: 3949 3446 3496 3444 Swimming pools, except plastic; fences, gates, posts & flagpoles; miscellaneous fabricated wire products; sheet metalwork
PA: Shapes/Arch Holdings Llc
9000 River Rd
Delair NJ 08110

(G-8413)
DICALITE MINERALS CORP
9111 River Rd (08110-3205)
PHONE.....................856 320-2919
EMP: 7
SALES (corp-wide): 34.9MM Privately Held
SIC: 3295 2821 Diatomaceous earth, ground or otherwise treated; cellulose derivative materials
HQ: Dicalite Minerals Corp.
36994 Summit Lake Rd
Burney CA 96013

(G-8414)
DISC MAKERS INC
7905 N Crescent Blvd (08110-1402)
PHONE.....................800 468-9353
Tony Van Veen, President
Jeff Hurst, Editor
John Healy, Business Mgr
Rich Lawrenson, Business Mgr
Kathy Chevoor, COO
◆ EMP: 300
SALES (est): 3MM
SALES (corp-wide): 12.6MM Privately Held
SIC: 3652 Compact laser discs, prerecorded
PA: Diy Media Group, Inc.
7905 N Crescent Blvd
Pennsauken NJ 08110
856 663-9030

(G-8415)
DISPLAY IMPRESSIONS
8400a Remington Ave (08110-1348)
PHONE.....................856 488-1777
Karen Galasso, Owner
EMP: 12
SALES (est): 1.5MM Privately Held
SIC: 2759 Commercial printing

(G-8416)
E P R INDUSTRIES INC
Also Called: Dental Manufacturing
4576 S Crescent Blvd (08109-1828)
PHONE.....................856 488-1120
Robert Cherkas, President
Paul Cherkas, Vice Pres
EMP: 15 EST: 1976
SQ FT: 11,000

SALES (est): 2.4MM Privately Held
SIC: 3843 Dental materials; compounds, dental

(G-8417)
EAST COAST CABINETS INC
2250 Sherman Ave Unit A1 (08110-1539)
PHONE.....................856 488-9710
Joseph Romano, President
EMP: 15
SQ FT: 6,400
SALES (est): 142.8K Privately Held
WEB: www.eastcoastcabinets.net
SIC: 2511 Wood household furniture

(G-8418)
ENERTIA LLC
10471049 Thomas Busch (08110)
PHONE.....................856 330-4767
Eric Rivera,
EMP: 9
SALES (est): 849.2K Privately Held
SIC: 7372 7352 7371 7319 Application computer software; medical equipment rental; computer software development & applications; distribution of advertising material or sample services

(G-8419)
EVERITE MACHINE PRODUCTS CO
1555 Route 73 (08110-1325)
PHONE.....................856 330-6700
Daniel Stern, CEO
Mergenthal Bruce, President
Chris Zhu, General Mgr
Larry Lewandowski, QC Mgr
Bill Clipsham, Engineer
▲ EMP: 50 EST: 1950
SQ FT: 68,000
SALES (est): 11.4MM Privately Held
WEB: www.everite.net
SIC: 3541 3599 3613 Grinding machines, metalworking; machine shop, jobbing & repair; control panels, electric

(G-8420)
FLUIDYNE CORP
9100 Collins Ave (08110-1037)
PHONE.....................856 663-1818
William M Bloemker, President
Dennis Nelson, Vice Pres
EMP: 25
SQ FT: 15,000
SALES (est): 6.1MM Privately Held
WEB: www.fluidynecorp.com
SIC: 3494 Valves & pipe fittings

(G-8421)
FOULKROD ASSOCIATES
Also Called: Canada Dry of Delaware Valley
8275 N Crescent Blvd (08110-1435)
PHONE.....................856 662-6767
Harold Honickman, Chairman
EMP: 600 EST: 1976
SALES (est): 101.7MM Privately Held
SIC: 2086 5149 Bottled & canned soft drinks; groceries & related products

(G-8422)
FRANBETH INC
Also Called: Sir Speedy
5505 N Crescent Blvd (08110-1803)
PHONE.....................856 488-1480
Francis Gavin, President
EMP: 5
SQ FT: 3,000
SALES: 685K Privately Held
SIC: 7336 7334 2752 3993 Graphic arts & related design; photocopying & duplicating services; commercial printing, lithographic; signs & advertising specialties

(G-8423)
GARDEN STATE MGNTC IMAGING PC
6027 S Crescent Blvd (08110-6401)
PHONE.....................609 581-2727
Faizah Zuberi MD, President
EMP: 11
SQ FT: 5,000
SALES (est): 1.6MM Privately Held
SIC: 3826 Magnetic resonance imaging apparatus

(G-8424)
GARRISON PRINTING COMPANY INC
7155 Airport Hwy (08109-4301)
PHONE.....................856 488-1900
Jack Garrison, CEO
Jake Garrison III, President
William Fynes, Vice Pres
Daniel C Garrison, Vice Pres
Barbara Garrison, Treasurer
EMP: 32
SQ FT: 22,000
SALES: 5.5MM Privately Held
SIC: 2796 2752 Platemaking services; commercial printing, lithographic

(G-8425)
GOLDEN RULE INC
7150 N Park Dr Ste 620 (08109-4203)
PHONE.....................856 663-3074
John Liberto, President
EMP: 4
SQ FT: 1,800
SALES (est): 305.5K Privately Held
SIC: 3544 Special dies & tools

(G-8426)
GRAND DISPLAYS INC (PA)
1700 Suckle Hwy (08110-1427)
PHONE.....................201 994-1500
George Gross, CEO
Marjorie Sacino, COO
EMP: 33
SALES (est): 7.6MM Privately Held
SIC: 2675 Die-cut paper & board

(G-8427)
GREAT SOCKS LLC (PA)
Also Called: Standard Merchandising
7001 N Park Dr (08109-4399)
PHONE.....................856 964-9700
Katrina Bremer, Manager
Robyn Mohr, Director
Jordan Baatable,
▲ EMP: 50 EST: 1922
SQ FT: 4,902
SALES (est): 28.2MM Privately Held
SIC: 3949 2252 2339 2251 Sporting & athletic goods; hosiery; women's & misses' outerwear; women's hosiery, except socks

(G-8428)
GSC IMAGING LLC
7150 N Park Dr Ste 540 (08109-4203)
PHONE.....................856 317-9301
Ron Coutta, Vice Pres
Robert Sinatra, Vice Pres
William Gallagher, Mng Member
▲ EMP: 15
SQ FT: 16,000
SALES (est): 3.5MM Privately Held
WEB: www.gscimaging.com
SIC: 3955 5112 Print cartridges for laser & other computer printers; inked ribbons

(G-8429)
H & H INDUSTRIES INC
7612 N Crescent Blvd (08110-2594)
PHONE.....................856 663-4444
Gertrude Hajduk, President
Maryann Hajduk, Vice Pres
Walter Hajduk III, Vice Pres
EMP: 42 EST: 1950
SQ FT: 47,000
SALES (est): 7.8MM Privately Held
SIC: 3444 Sheet metalwork

(G-8430)
HAYS SHEET METAL INC
Also Called: H M Hays Sheet Metal Co
7070 Bldg B Kaighns Ave (08109)
PHONE.....................856 662-7722
Herbert M Hays, President
Michael Hays, President
EMP: 50
SQ FT: 9,000
SALES (est): 10MM Privately Held
SIC: 3444 Metal ventilating equipment

(G-8431)
HOLMAN ENTERPRISES INC
R M P Delaware Valley
9040 Burrough Dover Ln (08110-1033)
P.O. Box 615 (08110-0615)
PHONE..............................856 532-2410
Rodger Clyde, *Vice Pres*
Frank Lepore, *MIS Dir*
Ed N Hogan, *Analyst*
EMP: 196
SALES (corp-wide): 1.6B Privately Held
WEB: www.holmanenterprises.com
SIC: 3714 5013 Motor vehicle engines &
parts; motor vehicle supplies & new parts
PA: Holman Enterprises Inc.
244 E Kings Hwy
Maple Shade NJ 08052
856 663-5200

(G-8432)
HOSOKAWA MICRON
INTERNATIONAL
Also Called: Menardi-Criswell
751 Hylton Rd (08110-1357)
PHONE..............................866 507-4974
Alan Furraro, *Manager*
EMP: 17 Privately Held
WEB: www.hosokawa.com
SIC: 3559 Chemical machinery & equip-
ment
HQ: Hosokawa Micron International Inc.
10 Chatham Rd
Summit NJ 07901
908 273-6360

(G-8433)
HOUSE OF GOLD INC
1505 Suckle Hwy (08110-1468)
PHONE..............................856 665-0020
Leonard Solomon, *President*
EMP: 50
SQ FT: 23,000
SALES (est): 9MM Privately Held
WEB: www.houseofgold.com
SIC: 3469 Ash trays, stamped metal

(G-8434)
I ASSOCIATES LLC
9255 Commerce Hwy (08110-1201)
PHONE..............................215 262-7754
Jim Wolstenholme, *Principal*
EMP: 6
SALES (est): 390K Privately Held
SIC: 3993 Advertising artwork

(G-8435)
INCREASE BEVERAGE INTL INC
7250 Westfield Ave Ste M (08110-4093)
P.O. Box 5, Palmyra (08065-0005)
PHONE..............................609 303-3117
Joseph Roberts Jr, *President*
Daniel P Wergin, *Treasurer*
Terence P Fox, *Admin Sec*
◆ EMP: 15
SALES (est): 3.1MM Privately Held
SIC: 5149 2086 Soft drinks; bottled &
canned soft drinks

(G-8436)
INNOVATIVE POWDER
COATINGS LLC
9105 Burrough Dover Ln (08110-1003)
PHONE..............................856 661-0086
David Mac William,
Timothy Hhyde,
▲ EMP: 7
SQ FT: 20,000
SALES (est): 1.1MM Privately Held
SIC: 3479 Coating of metals & formed
products

(G-8437)
INSERTS EAST INCORPORATED
Also Called: G & F Graphic Services
7045 Central Hwy (08109-4312)
PHONE..............................856 663-8181
Nick Maiale, *Principal*
Jack Puccio, *Vice Pres*
John Defoney, *Plant Mgr*
Andy Kavulic, *CFO*
Michelle Baxter, *Manager*
EMP: 125
SQ FT: 104,000

SALES (est): 26.8MM Privately Held
WEB: www.gfgraphics.com
SIC: 8742 2791 2752 5043 Management
consulting services; typesetting; commercial printing, lithographic; printing apparatus, photographic

(G-8438)
INTERIOR SPECIALTIES LLC
6006 S Crescent Blvd (08109-1512)
PHONE..............................856 663-1700
Joseph Wood,
EMP: 12
SQ FT: 6,000
SALES (est): 1.6MM Privately Held
WEB: www.interior-specialties.com
SIC: 3231 3229 5719 Mirrored glass;
doors, glass: made from purchased glass;
glass furnishings & accessories; closet or-
ganizers & shelving units

(G-8439)
INTERNATIONAL PROCESS EQP
CO
Also Called: Ipec
9300 N Crescent Blvd (08110-1303)
PHONE..............................856 665-4007
Ronald Miller, *President*
EMP: 5
SQ FT: 14,000
SALES (est): 955.6K Privately Held
WEB: www.rotormill.com
SIC: 3532 Mining machinery

(G-8440)
J & J SNACK FOODS CORP (PA)
6000 Central Hwy (08109-4672)
PHONE..............................856 665-9533
Gerald B Shreiber, *Ch of Bd*
Alan Murphy, *General Mgr*
Mike Wallat, *Business Mgr*
Robert M Radano, *COO*
Gerard G Law, *Senior VP*
EMP: 300 EST: 1971
SQ FT: 70,000
SALES: 1.1B Publicly Held
WEB: www.jjsnack.com
SIC: 2087 2086 2024 2052 Syrups,
drink; mineral water, carbonated: pack-
aged in cans, bottles, etc.; ices, flavored
(frozen dessert); juice pops, frozen; cook-
ies; bread, cake & related products;
doughnuts, frozen

(G-8441)
J & J SNACK FOODS CORP PA
(HQ)
6000 Central Hwy (08109-4672)
PHONE..............................856 665-9533
Gerald B Shreiber, *President*
Robert M Radano, *COO*
Dennis G Moore, *Vice Pres*
Jorge Martinez, *Plant Mgr*
David Hughes, *Engineer*
EMP: 5
SQ FT: 70,000
SALES (est): 3MM
SALES (corp-wide): 1B Publicly Held
WEB: www.icee.net
SIC: 5145 2052 Pretzels; pretzels
PA: J & J Snack Foods Corp.
6000 Central Hwy
Pennsauken NJ 08109
856 665-9533

(G-8442)
J AND M PRECISION INC
Also Called: Jig Grinding Specialists
8103 River Rd (08110-2436)
PHONE..............................856 661-9595
Martin Moskag, *President*
Joseph H Gaynor, *Vice Pres*
EMP: 4
SQ FT: 1,600
SALES: 371.5K Privately Held
SIC: 3599 Machine shop, jobbing & repair

(G-8443)
J D CREW INC
Also Called: Krimstock Enterprises
1426 Union Ave (08110-2459)
PHONE..............................856 665-3676
Joseph Crew, *President*
Christina Crew, *Vice Pres*
EMP: 5 EST: 1945
SQ FT: 7,000

SALES: 500K Privately Held
SIC: 3953 3993 Marking devices; displays
& cutouts, window & lobby

(G-8444)
JARVIS ELECTRIC MOTORS INC
6001 S Crescent Blvd (08110-6401)
PHONE..............................856 662-7710
Carl Barner, *President*
Mariana Barner, *Admin Sec*
EMP: 5 EST: 1944
SQ FT: 2,500
SALES: 1MM Privately Held
SIC: 7694 5251 Electric motor repair;
tools, power

(G-8445)
JERSEY CAST STONE LTD
LBLTY CO
6845 Westfield Ave (08110-1527)
PHONE..............................856 333-6900
Anthony Ruggiero, *President*
EMP: 11 EST: 2014
SQ FT: 15,000
SALES: 2MM Privately Held
SIC: 3272 Stone, cast concrete

(G-8446)
JERSEY SPECIALTY CO INC
Also Called: Jsc Wire & Cable
7861 Airport Hwy (08110-4322)
P.O. Box 248, East Longmeadow MA
(01028-0248)
PHONE..............................413 525-2292
R D Foster, *CEO*
Jim Foster, *President*
▲ EMP: 20 EST: 1932
SQ FT: 40,000
SALES: 10MM Privately Held
WEB: www.jscwire.com
SIC: 3315 Steel wire & related products

(G-8447)
KEYSTONE ADJUSTABLE CAP
CO INC
1591 Hylton Rd Ste B (08110-1338)
PHONE..............................856 356-2809
Andrew Feinstein, *CEO*
Malcolm W George, *President*
Neal Woods, *VP Sales*
◆ EMP: 45 EST: 1925
SQ FT: 90,000
SALES (est): 11.6MM Privately Held
WEB: www.keystonecap.com
SIC: 2676 2389 Sanitary paper products;
disposable garments & accessories

(G-8448)
KOHLDER MANUFACTURING
INC
Also Called: Bush Refrigeration
1700 Admiral Wilson Blvd (08109-3988)
PHONE..............................856 963-1801
Jeffrey Bush, *CEO*
Jeffrey Kerber, *Vice Pres*
EMP: 5
SQ FT: 40,000
SALES (est): 881.1K Privately Held
WEB: www.bushrefrigeration.com
SIC: 3585 Refrigeration equipment, com-
plete

(G-8449)
KUSHNER DRAPERIES MFG LLC
5305 Marlton Pike (08109-4749)
PHONE..............................856 317-9696
Arthur Kushner, *Mng Member*
Boonie Kushner,
Carla Moore,
EMP: 30
SQ FT: 16,000
SALES: 2.1MM Privately Held
SIC: 2391 5023 7641 Draperies, plastic &
textile: from purchased materials; cur-
tains; draperies; slip covers (furniture);
upholstery work

(G-8450)
LATTICE INCORPORATED (PA)
7150 N Park Dr Ste 500 (08109-4203)
P.O. Box 536, Collingswood (08108-0536)
PHONE..............................856 910-1166
Paul Burgess, *Ch of Bd*
Joe Noto, *CFO*
EMP: 12

SQ FT: 4,000
SALES: 7.5MM Publicly Held
WEB: www.scidyn.com
SIC: 3661 8711 8742 7372 Telephone &
telegraph apparatus; engineering services; management consulting services;
application computer software

(G-8451)
LIDESTRI FOODS INC
Also Called: Lidestri Foods of New Jersey
1550 John Tipton Blvd (08110-2304)
PHONE..............................856 661-3218
Allison Plant, *Division Mgr*
Bud Heckler, *Manager*
EMP: 80
SALES (corp-wide): 247.9MM Privately
Held
WEB: www.francescorinaldi.com
SIC: 2099 Food preparations
PA: Lidestri Foods, Inc.
815 Whitney Rd W
Fairport NY 14450
585 377-7700

(G-8452)
MARSDEN INC
6800 Westfield Ave (08110-1532)
PHONE..............................856 663-2227
Thomas Smith, *President*
Suzanne Longacre, *Principal*
Melissa Lucidi, *Admin Sec*
EMP: 20
SQ FT: 20,000
SALES (est): 3.9MM Privately Held
WEB: www.marsdeninc.com
SIC: 3567 Driers & redriers, industrial
process

(G-8453)
MCALLISTER SERVICE
COMPANY (PA)
Also Called: Honeywell Authorized Dealer
7116 Park Ave (08109-3055)
P.O. Box 1327, Merchantville (08109-0327)
PHONE..............................856 665-4545
George McAllister, *CEO*
James McAllister, *President*
Donald McAllister, *Exec VP*
John Hammond, *Vice Pres*
Rick Becker, *Sales Staff*
EMP: 21 EST: 1917
SQ FT: 2,000
SALES (est): 9.7MM Privately Held
SIC: 5983 7629 7623 1711 Fuel oil deal-
ers; electrical repair shops; refrigeration
service & repair; heating & air condition-
ing contractors; petroleum refining

(G-8454)
MCCORMICKS BINDERY INC
5815 Magnolia Ave (08109-1308)
PHONE..............................856 663-8035
Dan McCormick, *President*
Dan Mc Cormick, *President*
Rod Mc Cormick, *Vice Pres*
Rod McCormick, *Vice Pres*
Steven Brown, *Manager*
EMP: 42
SALES: 3MM Privately Held
SIC: 2789 Pamphlets, binding

(G-8455)
MCKELLA 2-8-0 INC
Also Called: McKella 280
7025 Central Hwy (08109-4312)
PHONE..............................856 813-1153
Joseph Lagrossa, *President*
Jerry Camisa, *Business Mgr*
Rose M Balcavage, *Vice Pres*
Rose Balcabage, *CFO*
Bob Arthur, *VP Sales*
EMP: 85 EST: 1977
SQ FT: 45,000
SALES (est): 21MM Privately Held
WEB: www.citationgraphics.net
SIC: 2752 2791 7336 Commercial print-
ing, offset; typesetting; commercial art &
graphic design

(G-8456)
MCLEAN PACKAGING CORPORATION
Also Called: Mc Lean Corrugated Containers
1000 Thomas Busch Mem Hwy
(08110-2313)
PHONE....................856 359-2600
Stuart Fenkel, *Principal*
Shawn Hintosh, *Prdtn Mgr*
Denise Tyas, *Controller*
EMP: 75
SQ FT: 4,500
SALES (corp-wide): 60MM **Privately Held**
SIC: 2652 2653 Setup paperboard boxes; boxes, corrugated: made from purchased materials
PA: Mclean Packaging Corporation
   1504 Glen Ave
   Moorestown NJ 08057
   856 359-2600

(G-8457)
MENU EXPRESS
1053 Thomas Busch Mem Hwy
(08110-2312)
PHONE....................856 216-7777
EMP: 12
SALES (est): 1.5MM **Privately Held**
SIC: 2759 Commercial printing

(G-8458)
MOD-TEK CONVERTING LLC
Also Called: Modtek
2550 Haddonfield Rd Ste E (08110-1152)
PHONE....................856 662-6884
Shawn Borman,
EMP: 25
SQ FT: 33,000
SALES (est): 3.8MM **Privately Held**
SIC: 2679 Tags & labels, paper

(G-8459)
NATIONAL DISPLAY GROUP INC
6850 River Rd (08110-2609)
PHONE....................856 661-1212
Gene Gold, *Mng Member*
EMP: 20
SALES (est): 2.8MM **Privately Held**
WEB: www.nationaldisplaygroup.com
SIC: 2542 Office & store showcases & display fixtures

(G-8460)
NEWTEK SENSOR SOLUTIONS LLC
7300 N Route 130 Unit 7 (08110-1541)
PHONE....................856 406-6877
Tutul Rahman, *CEO*
EMP: 4
SALES (est): 302.1K **Privately Held**
SIC: 3823 Analyzers, industrial process type

(G-8461)
NEWTON TOOL & MFG INC
7249b Browning Rd (08109-4602)
PHONE....................856 241-1500
Kurt Joerger, *CEO*
Otto J Del Prado, *President*
▲ EMP: 90
SQ FT: 61,400
SALES (est): 8.8MM **Privately Held**
SIC: 3053 3569 3586 3544 Gaskets, packing & sealing devices; filters, general line: industrial; gasoline pumps, measuring or dispensing; special dies, tools, jigs & fixtures

(G-8462)
NOVELTY CONE CO INC
807 Sherman Ave (08110-2684)
PHONE....................856 665-9525
Steven Marinucci, *President*
Ron Marinucci, *Vice Pres*
Dawn Amatl, *Office Mgr*
Steve Marinucci, *Executive*
▲ EMP: 23 EST: 1902
SQ FT: 14,500
SALES (est): 4.8MM **Privately Held**
WEB: www.noveltycone.com
SIC: 2052 Cones, ice cream

(G-8463)
PARK PRINTING SERVICES INC
7300 N Crescent Blvd # 21 (08110-1542)
PHONE....................856 675-1600
Donald G Reed Sr, *President*
Margaret Reed, *Vice Pres*
Meredith Trimbur, *Graphic Designe*
EMP: 11 EST: 1934
SQ FT: 4,500
SALES (est): 2MM **Privately Held**
WEB: www.parkprintingco.com
SIC: 2752 Commercial printing, offset

(G-8464)
PENNOCK COMPANY
Also Called: Pennock Floral Co
7135 Colonial Ln (08109-4314)
PHONE....................215 492-7900
Robert Billings, *President*
Paul Schwegel, *General Mgr*
Timothy Dubell, *Sales Staff*
Alex Smith, *Administration*
EMP: 23
SALES (corp-wide): 76.4MM **Privately Held**
SIC: 5992 3999 Flowers, fresh; artificial trees & flowers
PA: Pennock Company
   5060 W Chester Pike
   Edgemont PA 19028
   215 492-7900

(G-8465)
PEPSI COLA BTLG CO PENNSAUKEN
8191 N Crescent Blvd (08110-1404)
PHONE....................856 665-6616
EMP: 9
SALES (est): 818.6K **Privately Held**
SIC: 2086 Carbonated soft drinks, bottled & canned

(G-8466)
PEPSI-COLA NAT BRND BEVS LTD (PA)
8275 N Crescent Blvd (08110-1435)
PHONE....................856 665-6200
Jeff Honickman, *CEO*
Harold Honickman, *Ch of Bd*
Marvin Goldstein, *Vice Ch Bd*
Walter Wilkinson, *CFO*
EMP: 300 EST: 1956
SQ FT: 90,000
SALES (est): 166.1MM **Privately Held**
SIC: 2086 Soft drinks: packaged in cans, bottles, etc.

(G-8467)
PEPSICO INC
8275 N Route 130 (08110-1435)
PHONE....................856 661-4604
Robert Brockway, *Branch Mgr*
EMP: 50
SALES (corp-wide): 64.6B **Publicly Held**
WEB: www.pepsico.com
SIC: 2086 Carbonated soft drinks, bottled & canned
PA: Pepsico, Inc.
   700 Anderson Hill Rd
   Purchase NY 10577
   914 253-2000

(G-8468)
PERMALITH PLASTICS LLC
6901 N Crescent Blvd (08110-1513)
PHONE....................215 925-5659
Cheryl Ruymen, *Controller*
William Callanan,
Thomas Leonard,
Robert O'Leary,
▲ EMP: 55 EST: 1956
SQ FT: 63,000
SALES (est): 13.7MM **Privately Held**
WEB: www.permalith.com
SIC: 3089 3993 Laminating of plastic; signs & advertising specialties

(G-8469)
PPG INDUSTRIES INC
Also Called: PPG Auto Glass
75 Twinbridge Dr Ste C (08110-4205)
PHONE....................856 662-9323
Cliff Nelson, *Branch Mgr*
EMP: 5

SALES (corp-wide): 15.3B **Publicly Held**
SIC: 3211 5013 Plate & sheet glass; automobile glass
PA: Ppg Industries, Inc.
   1 Ppg Pl
   Pittsburgh PA 15272
   412 434-3131

(G-8470)
PREFERRED PLASTICS INC
6512 Park Ave (08109-2430)
PHONE....................856 662-6250
Bob Gillon, *President*
Joseph Flood, *Treasurer*
EMP: 5 EST: 1996
SQ FT: 4,500
SALES: 400K **Privately Held**
SIC: 3089 Injection molding of plastics

(G-8471)
PREMIER PRESS INC
7120 Airport Hwy (08109-4302)
PHONE....................856 665-0722
Joseph Shipton, *President*
Mary Shipton, *Corp Secy*
EMP: 12
SQ FT: 10,000
SALES (est): 2.1MM **Privately Held**
WEB: www.premierpress.net
SIC: 2759 Commercial printing

(G-8472)
PRINCETON TECTONICS (PA)
1777 Hylton Rd (08110-1315)
P.O. Box 8057, Trenton (08650-0057)
PHONE....................609 298-9331
William Stephens, *President*
Richard Shenowski, *Vice Pres*
Mark Buehler, *Purch Mgr*
Rob Cash, *Cust Mgr*
Ryan Conklin, *Sales Staff*
▲ EMP: 120
SQ FT: 80,000
SALES: 20MM **Privately Held**
WEB: www.princetontec.com
SIC: 3648 3089 Flashlights; injection molding of plastics

(G-8473)
PRINT MAIL COMMUNICATIONS LLC
7025 Colonial Hwy Ste 2 (08109-4309)
PHONE....................856 488-0345
Julie Geary, *Production*
Ed Lincoln, *Production*
Greg Zweigle, *Production*
Paul Pollastrelli, *Sales Executive*
Scott Spruill, *Mng Member*
EMP: 22
SALES (est): 5.5MM **Privately Held**
WEB: www.printnmail.net
SIC: 2752 2759 Commercial printing, lithographic; commercial printing

(G-8474)
PRO WORLD
961 Bethel Ave (08110-2607)
PHONE....................856 406-1020
Debbie Dill, *Principal*
◆ EMP: 6
SALES (est): 350K **Privately Held**
SIC: 2326 Industrial garments, men's & boys'

(G-8475)
PURATOS CORPORATION (DH)
1705 Suckle Hwy (08110-1426)
PHONE....................856 428-4300
Karel Zimmermann, *President*
Fredric Duvauchelle, *President*
Annmarie Earle, *VP Finance*
◆ EMP: 140
SALES (est): 206.6MM
SALES (corp-wide): 30.1MM **Privately Held**
WEB: www.puratos.com
SIC: 2099 Food preparations
HQ: Puratos
   Industrialaan 25
   Dilbeek 1702
   248 144-44

(G-8476)
REBUILT PARTS CO LLC
Also Called: RPC Driveline Service
7929 River Rd (08110-2434)
PHONE....................856 662-3252
Henry Matznic, *Owner*
EMP: 12
SQ FT: 6,500
SALES: 2MM **Privately Held**
SIC: 5015 3714 5531 Automotive parts & supplies, used; motor vehicle parts & accessories; automotive accessories; automotive parts

(G-8477)
REDHAWK DISTRIBUTION INC
6835 Westfield Ave (08110-1527)
PHONE....................516 884-9911
Arvind Choudhary, *President*
Taram Singh, *Vice Pres*
EMP: 15
SALES (est): 1MM **Privately Held**
SIC: 2392 Cushions & pillows

(G-8478)
RHOADS METAL WORKS INC
1551 John Tipton Blvd (08110-2303)
PHONE....................856 486-1551
William Rhoads, *President*
EMP: 30
SQ FT: 36,000
SALES (est): 7MM **Privately Held**
WEB: www.rhoadsmetalworks.com
SIC: 3444 Sheet metal specialties, not stamped

(G-8479)
ROYER GROUP INC
7120 Airport Hwy (08109-4302)
PHONE....................856 324-0171
Amanda Schwartz, *CEO*
Frank Fareri, *Exec VP*
Michael Schwartz, *Production*
EMP: 20
SQ FT: 12,000
SALES (est): 3.6MM **Privately Held**
SIC: 2759 2789 2752 Commercial printing; bookbinding & related work; commercial printing, lithographic

(G-8480)
ROYERCOMM CORPORATION
Also Called: Royer Comm Graphics
7120 Airport Hwy (08109-4302)
PHONE....................856 665-6400
Royer Schwartz, *CEO*
Eric Schwartz, *President*
Frank Fareri, *Vice Pres*
EMP: 10 EST: 1996
SQ FT: 10,000
SALES (est): 520.1K **Privately Held**
SIC: 2759 Commercial printing

(G-8481)
S & S PRECISION COMPANY INC
Also Called: S&S Precision
2205 Sherman Ave (08110-1530)
PHONE....................856 662-0006
Gerald Spiece, *President*
EMP: 5
SQ FT: 5,000
SALES (est): 512.9K **Privately Held**
SIC: 3599 Machine shop, jobbing & repair

(G-8482)
SCOTT W SPRINGMAN
Also Called: Architectural Acrylics
7026 Camden Ave C (08110-1510)
PHONE....................856 751-2411
Scott W Springman, *Owner*
Barbara Springman, *Manager*
EMP: 7
SALES: 800K **Privately Held**
SIC: 2519 3089 Lawn & garden furniture, except wood & metal; plastic processing

(G-8483)
SEMINOLE WIRE & CABLE CO INC
Also Called: Seminole Wire Products
7861 Airport Hwy (08109-4322)
P.O. Box 123, Glendora (08029-0123)
PHONE....................856 324-2929
George H Genzel, *President*
Michael Genzel, *Vice Pres*

Janice Genzel, *Treasurer*
EMP: 18 **EST:** 1962
SQ FT: 7,800
SALES (est): 3.1MM **Privately Held**
SIC: 3699 3496 3357 Lead-in wires, electric lamp; miscellaneous fabricated wire products; aircraft wire & cable, nonferrous

(G-8484)
SIMMONS PET FOOD INC
9130 Griffith Morgan Ln (08110-3211)
PHONE..................................856 662-7412
EMP: 107
SALES (corp-wide): 600MM **Privately Held**
SIC: 2047 Dog & cat food
PA: Simmons Pet Food, Inc.
601 N Hico St
Siloam Springs AR 72761
479 524-8151

(G-8485)
SIMMONS PET FOOD NJ INC
9130 Griffith Morgan Ln (08110-3211)
PHONE..................................856 662-7412
◆ **EMP:** 285
SQ FT: 195,000
SALES: 152.5MM
SALES (corp-wide): 600MM **Privately Held**
WEB: www.menufoods.com
SIC: 2047 Dog food; cat food
PA: Simmons Pet Food, Inc.
601 N Hico St
Siloam Springs AR 72761
479 524-8151

(G-8486)
SISCO MANUFACTURING CO INC
7930 National Hwy (08110-1462)
PHONE..................................856 486-7550
Ken Smith, *CEO*
▲ **EMP:** 14
SALES (est): 2.2MM **Privately Held**
SIC: 3822 Hydronic pressure or temperature controls

(G-8487)
SOLIDSURFACE DESIGNS INC
1651 Sherman Ave (08110-2624)
PHONE..................................856 910-7720
Matthew Baiada, *CEO*
EMP: 26
SQ FT: 13,200
SALES (est): 3.7MM **Privately Held**
WEB: www.solidsurfacedesigns.com
SIC: 2821 5211 3281 1743 Plastics materials & resins; counter tops; marble, building: cut & shaped; granite, cut & shaped; marble installation, interior

(G-8488)
SPECTRUM NEON SIGN GROUP LLC
9130 Pennsauken Hwy Ste B (08110-1285)
PHONE..................................856 317-9223
Theresa String, *Principal*
EMP: 4
SQ FT: 4,000
SALES (est): 240.9K **Privately Held**
SIC: 3993 Neon signs; letters for signs, metal; signs, not made in custom sign painting shops

(G-8489)
TABLOID GRAPHIC SERVICES INC
7101 Westfield Ave (08110-4001)
PHONE..................................856 486-0410
Steve Brosious, *President*
Thomas Lynch, *Vice Pres*
Tom Lynch, *Vice Pres*
EMP: 55
SQ FT: 28,000
SALES (est): 9.1MM **Privately Held**
SIC: 2752 Commercial printing, offset

(G-8490)
TAYLOR MADE CUSTOM CABINETRY
7035 Central Hwy 200 (08109-4312)
PHONE..................................856 786-5433
Jay Taylor, *Owner*
EMP: 13

SALES: 1.2MM **Privately Held**
WEB: www.tmcc-inc.com
SIC: 1521 1751 7389 2499 Single-family home remodeling, additions & repairs; cabinet building & installation; exhibit construction by industrial contractors; decorative wood & woodwork

(G-8491)
THANKS FOR BEING GREEN LLC
Also Called: Magnum Computer Recycling
5070b Central Hwy (08109-4606)
PHONE..................................856 333-0991
Nicole Martorano, *General Mgr*
John Martorano Jr, *Principal*
EMP: 20
SQ FT: 28,000
SALES: 440K **Privately Held**
SIC: 3559 Recycling machinery

(G-8492)
THE CREATIVE PRINT GROUP INC
7905 Browning Rd Ste 112 (08109-4319)
PHONE..................................856 486-1700
Howard Friedman, *President*
Joel Mordecai, *Vice Pres*
EMP: 16
SQ FT: 3,800
SALES (est): 3MM **Privately Held**
WEB: www.creativeprintgroup.com
SIC: 2752 7374 8743 8742 Commercial printing, offset; data processing & preparation; public relations services; marketing consulting services

(G-8493)
TPG GRAPHICS LLC
Also Called: Clinton Envelope
9130 Pennsauken Hwy Ste C (08110-1285)
PHONE..................................856 314-0117
Robert Donner,
Robert C Donner,
EMP: 9
SALES (est): 1MM **Privately Held**
WEB: www.tpggraphics.com
SIC: 2677 Envelopes

(G-8494)
TURBO SOLUTIONS LLC (PA)
8500 Remington Ave Unit 1 (08110-1398)
PHONE..................................856 209-6900
Chris Marino, *Controller*
Warren Klein, *Mng Member*
EMP: 11 **EST:** 2015
SALES (est): 1.5MM **Privately Held**
SIC: 3714 Axles, motor vehicle

(G-8495)
UNIFIED DOOR & HDWR GROUP LLC
1650 Suckle Hwy (08110-1450)
PHONE..................................215 364-8834
Thomas Moser, *Branch Mgr*
EMP: 150
SALES (corp-wide): 170MM **Privately Held**
SIC: 3429 Manufactured hardware (general)
PA: Unified Door And Hardware Group, Llc
1650 Suckle Hwy
Pennsauken NJ 08110
856 320-4868

(G-8496)
WERKO MACHINE CO
9200 Collins Ave (08110-1039)
PHONE..................................856 662-0669
Robert Paul Mueller Jr, *Engineer*
Barbara Mueller, *Admin Sec*
EMP: 14 **EST:** 1946
SQ FT: 12,000
SALES (est): 2.5MM **Privately Held**
WEB: www.werkomachine.com
SIC: 3599 3549 Machine shop, jobbing & repair; metalworking machinery

(G-8497)
WINDMILL PRESS INC
1051 Thomas Busch Mem Hwy (08110-2312)
PHONE..................................856 663-8990
Burton Hurff, *President*

Helen Hurff, *Vice Pres*
EMP: 6
SALES: 450K **Privately Held**
SIC: 2789 7389 Bookbinding & related work; document embossing

(G-8498)
WURZ SIGNSYSTEMS LLC
2600 Haddonfield Rd (08110-1133)
PHONE..................................856 461-4397
Robert Wurz, *Owner*
EMP: 4
SALES: 950K **Privately Held**
SIC: 3993 Electric signs

(G-8499)
ZIN-TECH INC (PA)
Also Called: Z-Tech
1416 Union Ave (08110-2459)
PHONE..................................856 661-0900
Joseph Zingaro, *President*
Sylvester Rossi, *Vice Pres*
EMP: 22
SQ FT: 11,000
SALES (est): 3.2MM **Privately Held**
SIC: 3544 Dies, steel rule

Pennsville
Salem County

(G-8500)
JLB HAULING LTD LIABILITY CO
90 Dolbow Ave (08070-1706)
PHONE..................................856 514-2771
John Bruno Jr, *President*
Laird Bruno, *Vice Pres*
EMP: 6
SALES (est): 273.2K **Privately Held**
SIC: 4212 1481 Light haulage & cartage, local; mine & quarry services, nonmetallic minerals

(G-8501)
SIEGFRIED USA LLC (DH)
33 Industrial Park Rd (08070-3244)
PHONE..................................856 678-3601
Rudolf Hanko, *CEO*
Aaron Mercier, *Business Mgr*
Cyr Patrick, *Safety Mgr*
Jennifer Goodall, *Engineer*
Cecilia Guerrette, *Finance*
◆ **EMP:** 126 **EST:** 1928
SALES (est): 49.5MM
SALES (corp-wide): 799.2MM **Privately Held**
WEB: www.siegfried-usa.com
SIC: 2834 Pharmaceutical preparations
HQ: Siegfried Usa Holding , Inc.
33 Industrial Park Rd
Pennsville NJ 08070
856 678-3601

(G-8502)
SIEGFRIED USA HOLDING   INC (HQ)
33 Industrial Park Rd (08070-3244)
PHONE..................................856 678-3601
Michael Husler, *Chairman*
John Keenan, *Opers Staff*
Christopher Hood, *Mfg Staff*
Jason Troutman, *Engineer*
Robert Nilsen, *Finance*
▲ **EMP:** 43
SALES (est): 185MM
SALES (corp-wide): 799.2MM **Privately Held**
SIC: 2834 Druggists' preparations (pharmaceuticals)
PA: Siegfried Holding Ag
Untere Bruhlstrasse 4
Zofingen AG 4800
627 461-111

Pequannock
Morris County

(G-8503)
ALLEN CABINETS AND MILLWORK
60 Newark Pompton Tpke (07440-1624)
PHONE..................................973 694-0665
Len Vanderstad, *President*
EMP: 9
SQ FT: 2,500
SALES (est): 1.1MM **Privately Held**
WEB: www.allencabinets.com
SIC: 2434 Wood kitchen cabinets

(G-8504)
FLUENT DIAGNOSTICS
22 W Parkway (07440-1710)
PHONE..................................201 414-4516
Daniel Tanis,
Sheryl Carlson,
Stephen Morrison,
Paul Sullivan,
EMP: 4
SALES (est): 213.4K **Privately Held**
SIC: 3845 8082 Electromedical apparatus; respiratory analysis equipment, electromedical; home health care services

(G-8505)
FREEDOM VINYL SYSTEMS INC
67 2nd St (07440-1215)
PHONE..................................973 692-0332
Salvatore Anello, *President*
EMP: 5
SALES (est): 385.9K **Privately Held**
SIC: 3089 Fences, gates & accessories: plastic

(G-8506)
REEVES INTERNATIONAL INC (PA)
14 Industrial Rd (07440-1991)
PHONE..................................973 694-5006
Anthony Fleischmann, *President*
Diane Wheeler, *HR Admin*
Sandy Davick, *Technology*
Lisa Raimondo, *Information Mgr*
June Banker, *IT/INT Sup*
▲ **EMP:** 50
SQ FT: 53,000
SALES (est): 26.8MM **Privately Held**
WEB: www.breyerhorses.com
SIC: 5092 5199 3942 Dolls; gift baskets; stuffed toys, including animals

---

Perrineville
Monmouth County

(G-8507)
RDL MARKETING GROUP LLC
352a Sweetmans Ln (08535-1216)
PHONE..................................732 446-0817
Bob Levine,
EMP: 5
SALES (est): 400K **Privately Held**
SIC: 2741 Catalogs: publishing & printing

(G-8508)
SUCCESS PUBLISHERS LLC
29 Hampton Hollow Dr (08535-1004)
PHONE..................................609 443-0792
John F Abate, *Owner*
EMP: 6
SALES (est): 530K **Privately Held**
SIC: 2741 Miscellaneous publishing

Perth Amboy
Middlesex County

(G-8509)
ACE SIGN COMPANY INC
419 Summit Ave (08861-2016)
P.O. Box 66 (08862-0066)
PHONE..................................732 826-3858
Philip Smith, *President*
Patricia Smith, *Corp Secy*

G
E
O
G
R
A
P
H
I
C

EMP: 7
SQ FT: 5,000
SALES (est): 925.8K **Privately Held**
SIC: 3993 7389 Electric signs; sign paint-
ing & lettering shop

(G-8510)
ACOLYTE TECHNOLOGIES CORP
1000 Amboy Ave (08861-1951)
PHONE.....................................212 629-3239
EMP: 4
SALES (est): 255.1K **Privately Held**
SIC: 3674 Light emitting diodes

(G-8511)
ALL MECHANICAL SERVICES INC
430 High St (08861-3504)
P.O. Box 110 (08862-0110)
PHONE.....................................732 442-8292
Joe Auriemma, *President*
Greg Huhn, *Vice Pres*
Jeff Shelters, *Shareholder*
EMP: 13
SQ FT: 10,000
SALES (est): 2.2MM **Privately Held**
SIC: 3599 Machine shop, jobbing & repair

(G-8512)
AMT STITCH INC
257 New Brunswick Ave (08861-4024)
P.O. Box 2695 (08862-2695)
PHONE.....................................732 376-0009
Miladys Gomez, *President*
◆ EMP: 8
SALES (est): 851.6K **Privately Held**
SIC: 2211 Decorative trim & specialty fab-
rics, including twist weave

(G-8513)
CARDINAL FIBREGLASS INDUSTRIES
1050 State St (08861-2002)
PHONE.....................................718 625-4350
William J Weidmann, *President*
Mary Ellen Snow, *President*
EMP: 4
SQ FT: 17,000
SALES (est): 320K **Privately Held**
SIC: 3089 Plastic & fiberglass tanks

(G-8514)
CHEVRON PHILLIPS CHEM CO LP
1200 State St (08861-2003)
PHONE.....................................732 738-2000
Joe F Bromiley, *Branch Mgr*
EMP: 20
SALES (corp-wide): 8B **Privately Held**
WEB: www.cpchem.com
SIC: 2821 Plastics materials & resins
HQ: Chevron Phillips Chemical Company
　　Lp
　　10001 Six Pines Dr
　　The Woodlands TX 77380
　　832 813-4100

(G-8515)
CHEVRON USA INC
1200 State St (08861-2003)
PHONE.....................................732 738-2000
Scott Wooten, *Manager*
EMP: 100
SALES (corp-wide): 166.3B **Publicly Held**
SIC: 5541 2951 Filling stations, gasoline;
asphalt paving mixtures & blocks
HQ: Chevron U.S.A. Inc.
　　6001 Bollinger Canyon Rd D1248
　　San Ramon CA 94583
　　925 842-1000

(G-8516)
CROMPTON CORP
1000 Convery Blvd (08861-1932)
PHONE.....................................732 826-6600
Nick Lettieri, *Principal*
EMP: 5
SALES (est): 862.2K **Privately Held**
SIC: 2869 Industrial organic chemicals

(G-8517)
ENGLERT INC (PA)
1200 Amboy Ave (08861-1956)
PHONE.....................................800 364-5378
Debra Harnett, *CEO*
Joseph Turovach, *Vice Pres*
John Filippone, *Accountant*
Steven Del Popolo, *Manager*
◆ EMP: 150 EST: 1966
SQ FT: 176,000
SALES (est): 93.2MM **Privately Held**
WEB: www.englertinc.com
SIC: 3444 5033 Gutters, sheet metal; roof-
ing, siding & insulation

(G-8518)
EVANS MACHINE & TOOL CO
410 Summit Ave (08861-2017)
PHONE.....................................732 442-1144
Thomas Geslak, *Owner*
▲ EMP: 7
SQ FT: 10,000
SALES: 520K **Privately Held**
SIC: 3599 5051 Machine shop, jobbing &
repair; steel

(G-8519)
GOODLITE PRODUCTS INC
500 Division St (08861-3530)
PHONE.....................................718 697-7502
Nathan Meisels, *President*
▲ EMP: 10
SQ FT: 20,000
SALES (est): 2MM **Privately Held**
SIC: 3229 Bulbs for electric lights

(G-8520)
GRIMES MANUFACTURING INC
599 State St (08861-3542)
PHONE.....................................732 442-4572
Christopher Grimes, *President*
Mark Grimes, *Treasurer*
EMP: 6
SQ FT: 4,000
SALES (est): 660K **Privately Held**
WEB: www.grimesmanufacturing.com
SIC: 3599 Machine shop, jobbing & repair

(G-8521)
HOSEPHARM LTD LIABILITY CO
351 Smith St (08861-3921)
PHONE.....................................732 376-0044
EMP: 4
SALES (est): 312.4K **Privately Held**
SIC: 3052 Mfg Rubber/Plastic Hose/Belting

(G-8522)
HOT DIP GALVANIZING
1190 Amboy Ave (08861-1920)
PHONE.....................................732 442-7555
EMP: 9
SALES (est): 1MM **Privately Held**
SIC: 3479 Galvanizing of iron, steel or end-
formed products

(G-8523)
INTERNATIONAL PROCESSING CORP
1250 Amboy Ave (08861-1920)
PHONE.....................................732 826-4240
John Hawrylko, *President*
EMP: 14
SALES (est): 2.5MM **Privately Held**
SIC: 2048 Livestock feeds

(G-8524)
LANXESS SOLUTIONS US INC
1000 Coventry Blvd (08861)
PHONE.....................................732 826-1018
Rich Lissenden, *Manager*
EMP: 150
SQ FT: 50,000
SALES (corp-wide): 8.2B **Privately Held**
WEB: www.cromptoncorp.com
SIC: 2869 2821 Industrial organic chemi-
cals; plastics materials & resins
HQ: Lanxess Solutions Us Inc.
　　2 Armstrong Rd Ste 101
　　Shelton CT 06484
　　203 573-2000

(G-8525)
LINCOLN SIGNS & AWNINGS INC
895 State St (08861-2042)
PHONE.....................................732 442-3151

Julio Hernandez, *President*
Narda Hernandez, *Vice Pres*
EMP: 9
SQ FT: 2,000
SALES (est): 1.7MM **Privately Held**
SIC: 3993 Signs, not made in custom sign
painting shops

(G-8526)
MAYAB HAPPY TACOS INC
450 Florida Grove Rd (08861-3729)
PHONE.....................................732 293-0400
Jorge W Alamilla, *President*
Anna Alamilla, *Corp Secy*
Jorge M Alamilla, *Vice Pres*
EMP: 28 EST: 1976
SQ FT: 10,000
SALES (est): 5.9MM **Privately Held**
SIC: 2096 2032 Potato chips & similar
snacks; Mexican foods: packaged in
cans, jars, etc.

(G-8527)
MENDEZ DAIRY CO INC
450 Fayette St (08861-3805)
P.O. Box 1357 (08862-1357)
PHONE.....................................732 442-6337
Rafael Mendez, *President*
Sonal Patel, *General Mgr*
Michelle Farkas, *Admin Sec*
EMP: 100
SQ FT: 15,000
SALES (est): 9.4MM **Privately Held**
SIC: 2022 Cheese, natural & processed

(G-8528)
MONOGRAM CENTER INC
437 Amboy Ave (08861-3141)
PHONE.....................................732 442-1800
Bill Kraemer, *President*
Michael Kraemer, *Vice Pres*
EMP: 35
SQ FT: 14,000
SALES (est): 6.8MM **Privately Held**
WEB: www.monogramcenter.com
SIC: 5136 5137 7389 7336 Sportswear,
men's & boys'; sportswear, women's &
children's; lettering service; silk screen
design; automotive & apparel trimmings;
pleating & stitching

(G-8529)
POWER MAGNE-TECH CORP
Also Called: Power Magnetic
653 Sayre Ave (08861-3612)
PHONE.....................................732 826-4700
Leon Zelcer, *President*
Harold Tischler, *Sales Executive*
▲ EMP: 20
SQ FT: 11,000
SALES (est): 3.8MM **Privately Held**
WEB: www.quantummarketing.net
SIC: 3612 3621 Tripping transformers; in-
verters, rotating; electrical

(G-8530)
RECONSERVE INC
1250 Amboy Ave (08861-1920)
PHONE.....................................732 826-4240
Rick Brown, *Branch Mgr*
EMP: 6
SALES (corp-wide): 203.7MM **Privately Held**
SIC: 2048 Livestock feeds
HQ: Reconserve, Inc.
　　2811 Wilshire Blvd # 410
　　Santa Monica CA 90403
　　310 458-1574

(G-8531)
RIVERDALE COLOR MFG INC (PA)
1 Walnut St (08861-4531)
PHONE.....................................732 376-9300
Paul Maguire, *President*
Charles Irish, *Vice Pres*
Steve Maguire, *Vice Pres*
Brett Irish, *Opers Mgr*
Denise Mendez, *Purchasing*
▼ EMP: 33
SQ FT: 60,000
SALES (est): 8.6MM **Privately Held**
WEB: www.riverdalecolor.com
SIC: 2865 2816 Dyes & pigments; color
pigments

(G-8532)
SHIVA FUEL INC
737 New Brunswick Ave (08861-3649)
PHONE.....................................732 826-3228
EMP: 4
SALES (est): 218.9K **Privately Held**
SIC: 2869 Fuels

(G-8533)
SHOP RITE SUPERMARKETS INC
Also Called: Shoprite
Convery Blvd Fayette (08861)
PHONE.....................................732 442-1717
Arthur Hardardt, *Manager*
EMP: 150
SALES (corp-wide): 890MM **Privately Held**
SIC: 5411 5912 2051 Grocery stores;
drug stores & proprietary stores; bread,
cake & related products
HQ: Shop Rite Supermarkets, Inc.
　　5000 Riverside Dr
　　Keasbey NJ 08832
　　908 527-3300

(G-8534)
SKYCAM TECHNOLOGIES LLC
235 Kearny Ave (08861-4403)
PHONE.....................................908 205-5548
Arlen Encarnacion, *Mng Member*
EMP: 5
SALES (est): 500K **Privately Held**
SIC: 3699 Security devices

(G-8535)
SUPREME GRAPHICS AND PRTG INC
1027 State St (08861-2001)
PHONE.....................................718 989-9817
Abraham Greenwald, *CEO*
EMP: 1
SQ FT: 2,000
SALES (est): 1MM **Privately Held**
SIC: 2752 Commercial printing, litho-
graphic

(G-8536)
TOM JAMES COMPANY
Also Called: Tom James of Perth Amboy 2
581 Cortlandt St (08861-3354)
PHONE.....................................732 826-8400
Erica Orona, *Office Mgr*
Ames Turner, *Branch Mgr*
EMP: 20
SALES (corp-wide): 492.1MM **Privately Held**
WEB: www.englishamericanco.com
SIC: 2311 Suits, men's & boys': made from
purchased materials
PA: Tom James Company
　　263 Seaboard Ln
　　Franklin TN 37067
　　615 771-1122

(G-8537)
TROPICAL CHEESE INDUSTRIES (PA)
452 Fayette St (08861-3805)
P.O. Box 1357 (08862-1357)
PHONE.....................................732 442-4898
Rafael Mendez, *President*
Sonal Patel, *General Mgr*
Carlos Torres, *General Mgr*
Alejandro Lopez, *Vice Pres*
Luis Mendez, *Vice Pres*
▲ EMP: 320 EST: 1982
SQ FT: 73,000
SALES (est): 150.6MM **Privately Held**
SIC: 2022 5143 Natural cheese; cheese

(G-8538)
VIRA MANUFACTURING INC
1 Buckingham Ave (08861-3532)
PHONE.....................................732 771-8269
Alan Rabinowitz, *Exec VP*
Kenny Viviano, *Facilities Mgr*
Luis E Torres, *Mfg Staff*
Richard Walsh, *Sales Dir*
EMP: 26
SALES (est): 4MM **Privately Held**
SIC: 3999 Manufacturing industries

(G-8539)
VOIGT & SCHWEITZER LLC
Also Called: V & S Perth Amboy
1190 Amboy Ave (08861-1920)
PHONE.............................732 442-7555
Tammy Short, *Controller*
John Feeman, *Sales Staff*
Barry Helwig, *Sales Staff*
Carl Fristick, *Marketing Staff*
Robert Messler, *Manager*
EMP: 60
SALES (corp-wide): 819.3MM **Privately Held**
WEB: www.hotdipgalvanizing.com
SIC: 3479 Galvanizing of iron, steel or end-formed products
HQ: Voigt & Schweitzer Llc
987 Buckeye Park Rd
Columbus OH 43207
614 449-8281

Phillipsburg
Warren County

(G-8540)
ACCURATUS CERAMIC CORP
35 Howard St (08865-3060)
PHONE.............................908 213-7070
Raymond Tsao, *President*
Lorraine Simonof, *Sales Executive*
Stephen Zelnick, *Admin Sec*
▼ EMP: 20
SQ FT: 20,000
SALES: 3MM **Privately Held**
WEB: www.accuratus.com
SIC: 3545 3823 Diamond cutting tools for turning, boring, burnishing, etc.; industrial instrmnts msrmnt display/control process variable

(G-8541)
ARCHITCTRAL CBINETRY MLLWK LLC
1425 3rd Ave (08865-4605)
PHONE.............................908 213-2001
Cheryl Fortner,
EMP: 6 EST: 2013
SALES: 400K **Privately Held**
SIC: 2431 Millwork

(G-8542)
AVANTOR PERFORMANCE MTLS LLC
Also Called: J T Baker Chemical Co
600 N Broad St (08865-1271)
PHONE.............................908 859-2151
Matt Machalik, *Warehouse Mgr*
Craig Romanelli, *Manager*
Damon Debusk, *Manager*
Vinay Vasuki, *Manager*
EMP: 300
SALES (corp-wide): 1.4B **Publicly Held**
SIC: 2879 2899 2869 2819 Trace elements (agricultural chemicals); chemical preparations; industrial organic chemicals; industrial inorganic chemicals
HQ: Avantor Performance Materials, Llc
100 W Matsonford Rd
Radnor PA 19087
610 573-2600

(G-8543)
BAER AGGREGATES INC
454 River Rd (08865-7513)
PHONE.............................908 454-4412
Lou Mitschele, *President*
EMP: 13
SQ FT: 2,400
SALES (est): 1.9MM **Privately Held**
SIC: 1442 Construction sand & gravel

(G-8544)
BERRY GLOBAL INC
190 Strykers Rd (08865-9775)
PHONE.............................980 689-1660
EMP: 8 **Publicly Held**
SIC: 3089 Plastic containers, except foam
HQ: Berry Global, Inc.
101 Oakley St
Evansville IN 47710
812 424-2904

(G-8545)
BERRY GLOBAL INC
190 Strykers Rd (08865-9775)
PHONE.............................908 454-0900
EMP: 50 **Publicly Held**
WEB: www.captiveplastics.com
SIC: 3089 3081 Bottle caps, molded plastic; unsupported plastics film & sheet
HQ: Berry Global, Inc.
101 Oakley St
Evansville IN 47710
812 424-2904

(G-8546)
BIHLER OF AMERICA INC
85 Industrial Rd Bldg B (08865-4080)
PHONE.............................908 213-9001
Maxine Nordmeyer, *CEO*
Mathias Bihler, *President*
Barry Littlewood, *Vice Pres*
Michael El Kazzaz, *Project Mgr*
Vulgen Schoen, *Shareholder*
▲ EMP: 190
SQ FT: 200,000
SALES (est): 80.7MM **Privately Held**
WEB: www.bihler.com
SIC: 3679 5084 3544 Electronic circuits; metalworking machinery; special dies & tools

(G-8547)
CAPTIVE PLASTICS LLC
190 Strykers Rd (08865-9775)
PHONE.............................812 424-2904
Scott Bungert, *Branch Mgr*
EMP: 101 **Publicly Held**
SIC: 3089 Bottle caps, molded plastic
HQ: Captive Plastics, Llc
101 Oakley St
Evansville IN 47710
812 424-2904

(G-8548)
DAVID SISCO JR
Also Called: Treasure Hunt
1223 S Main St (08865-3730)
PHONE.............................908 454-0880
David Sisco Jr, *Owner*
EMP: 7
SQ FT: 800
SALES (est): 490.1K **Privately Held**
SIC: 7319 7313 2711 Transit advertising services; newspaper advertising representative; newspapers

(G-8549)
EDISON NATION INC (PA)
909 New Brunswick Ave (08865-4077)
PHONE.............................610 829-1039
Christopher B Ferguson, *Ch of Bd*
Kevin J Ferguson, *President*
Philip Anderson, *CFO*
Bruce R Bennett,
EMP: 3
SALES: 16.5MM **Publicly Held**
SIC: 3944 3086 Games, toys & children's vehicles; packaging & shipping materials, foamed plastic

(G-8550)
FERGUSON CONTAINERS CO INC
16 Industrial Rd (08865-4081)
P.O. Box 308 (08865-0308)
PHONE.............................908 454-9755
Kevin Ferguson, *Shareholder*
Scott Ferguson, *Shareholder*
Chris Ferguson, *Admin Sec*
EMP: 25 EST: 1960
SQ FT: 20,000
SALES (est): 5.6MM **Privately Held**
WEB: www.fergusoncontainers.com
SIC: 2653 Boxes, corrugated: made from purchased materials; boxes, solid fiber: made from purchased materials

(G-8551)
FLOWSERVE CORPORATION
222 Cameron Dr Ste 200 (08865-2777)
PHONE.............................908 859-7000
Robert Rajeski, *Principal*
Daniel Wright, *Data Proc Staff*
EMP: 200
SALES (corp-wide): 3.8B **Publicly Held**
SIC: 3561 Industrial pumps & parts

PA: Flowserve Corporation
5215 N Oconnor Blvd Connor
Irving TX 75039
972 443-6500

(G-8552)
G J OLIVER INC
50 Industrial Rd (08865-4083)
PHONE.............................908 454-9743
John G Oliver, *CEO*
Charles A Parker, *President*
Charles Parker, *Vice Pres*
Chuck Conroy, *Project Mgr*
Kevin Dishinger, *Project Mgr*
▲ EMP: 80
SQ FT: 120,000
SALES: 17MM **Privately Held**
WEB: www.gjoliver.com
SIC: 3441 3443 Fabricated structural metal; vessels, process or storage (from boiler shops): metal plate

(G-8553)
GRAPHIC ACTION INC
296 S Main St (08865-2825)
PHONE.............................908 213-0055
Frank T Geraghty, *President*
EMP: 6
SQ FT: 600
SALES: 350K **Privately Held**
SIC: 2752 7334 7336 Commercial printing, offset; photocopying & duplicating services; commercial art & graphic design

(G-8554)
GULCO INC
1 Riverside Way (08865-2340)
PHONE.............................908 238-2030
Donald Gulbrandsen, *President*
Vikram Singhal, *Managing Dir*
Robert Mikovitch, *Safety Mgr*
Rob Thurman, *Mfg Staff*
Jamie Adkins, *Production*
◆ EMP: 39
SQ FT: 20,000
SALES (est): 8.6MM **Privately Held**
SIC: 2819 2899 Aluminum chloride; chemical preparations
PA: Gulbrandsen Technologies Inc.
2 Main St
Clinton NJ 08809

(G-8555)
HARMONY SAND & GRAVEL INC
County Rd 519 (08865)
P.O. Box 277, Belvidere (07823-0277)
PHONE.............................908 475-4690
Richard L Hummer Jr, *President*
EMP: 30
SQ FT: 5,000
SALES (est): 7MM **Privately Held**
SIC: 1442 Construction sand & gravel

(G-8556)
J H M COMMUNICATIONS INC
Also Called: JHM Signs
1593 Springtown Rd (08865-4629)
PHONE.............................908 859-6668
John Maxman, *President*
Brenda Maxman, *Corp Secy*
EMP: 12
SALES: 1MM **Privately Held**
WEB: www.jhmsigns.com
SIC: 3993 2759 Signs & advertising specialties; promotional printing; circulars: printing

(G-8557)
JERSEY STRAND & CABLE INC
259 Center St Ste 3 (08865-3328)
PHONE.............................908 213-9350
Alfred Pratt Jr, *President*
Diane Pratt, *Vice Pres*
Michelle Johnson, *Payroll Mgr*
▲ EMP: 65 EST: 1978
SQ FT: 417
SALES (est): 12.7MM **Privately Held**
WEB: www.jerseystrandandcable.com
SIC: 3496 Cable, uninsulated wire: made from purchased wire

(G-8558)
KEYSTONE PACKAGING SERVICE
555 Warren St (08865-3230)
PHONE.............................908 454-8567

John R Schoeneck, *President*
Enoch Schoeneck, *Treasurer*
Norman Peil Jr, *Admin Sec*
EMP: 4 EST: 1937
SQ FT: 63,000
SALES: 400K **Privately Held**
SIC: 2673 Bags: plastic, laminated & coated

(G-8559)
LINDE GAS NORTH AMERICA LLC
225 Strykers Rd (08865-9486)
PHONE.............................908 777-9125
Dr Wolfgang Reitzle, *CEO*
EMP: 6 **Privately Held**
SIC: 2813 Industrial gases
HQ: Linde Gas North America Llc
200 Somerset Corp Blvd # 7000
Bridgewater NJ 08807

(G-8560)
MAGNETIKA INC
Also Called: Manufacturing Branch
300 Red School Ln (08865-2233)
PHONE.............................908 454-2600
Nick Defalco, *General Mgr*
Hernando Ortega, *Engineer*
John Greenleaf, *Branch Mgr*
James Haldeman, *MIS Dir*
EMP: 40
SALES (corp-wide): 40.4MM **Privately Held**
SIC: 3612 Ballasts for lighting fixtures; power transformers, electric
PA: Magnetika, Inc.
2041 W 139th St
Gardena CA 90249
310 527-8100

(G-8561)
MAIL TIME INC
224 Stockton St (08865-2948)
PHONE.............................908 859-5500
Mario Sgroi, *President*
Larry Still, *Accounting Mgr*
Charlie Sheng, *Chief Mktg Ofcr*
EMP: 25
SALES (est): 4.5MM **Privately Held**
SIC: 2752 Commercial printing, lithographic

(G-8562)
MCWANE INC
Atlantic States Cast Iron Pipe
183 Sitgreaves St (08865-3052)
PHONE.............................908 454-1161
Sara Courtney, *General Mgr*
David Hiestand, *Vice Pres*
Joe Carter, *Plant Mgr*
Shannon Brunner, *Safety Mgr*
Brendon Laport, *Safety Mgr*
EMP: 300
SALES (corp-wide): 1.2B **Privately Held**
WEB: www.mcwane.com
SIC: 3321 Pressure pipe & fittings, cast iron
PA: Mcwane, Inc.
2900 Highway 280 S # 300
Birmingham AL 35223
205 414-3100

(G-8563)
MED CONNECTION LLC
65 Howard St (08865-3101)
PHONE.............................908 213-7012
Robert K Kolonia, *President*
EMP: 4
SALES: 310K **Privately Held**
WEB: www.micromoldinginc.com
SIC: 2821 Molding compounds, plastics

(G-8564)
MOSER JEWEL COMPANY
518 State Route 57 (08865-9484)
PHONE.............................908 454-1155
Sharon L Duffield, *CEO*
Alexandre La Roche, *President*
Sharon Lobosco, *Legal Staff*
EMP: 7 EST: 1941
SQ FT: 6,300
SALES (est): 1MM **Privately Held**
WEB: www.mosercompany.com
SIC: 3915 3674 3568 Jewel bearings, synthetic; semiconductors & related devices; power transmission equipment

(G-8565)
N E R ASSOCIATES INC
Also Called: General Machine Kraft
45 Howard St (08865-3060)
PHONE..................................908 454-5955
Gene Cancelliere, *President*
Douglas Cancelliere, *Admin Sec*
EMP: 8
SQ FT: 4,000
SALES (est): 1.4MM **Privately Held**
SIC: 3449 Miscellaneous metalwork

(G-8566)
PHARM OPS INC
101 Broad St (08865-1208)
PHONE..................................908 454-7733
Shankar Musunuri, *Managing Dir*
Khurshid Iqbal, *Managing Dir*
EMP: 5
SALES (est): 723K **Privately Held**
SIC: 2834 Pharmaceutical preparations

(G-8567)
PHILIP MAMRAK
Also Called: P M Construction Co
531 Victory Ave (08865-3826)
PHONE..................................908 454-6089
Philip Mamrak, *Owner*
EMP: 8
SQ FT: 3,800
SALES (est): 514.9K **Privately Held**
WEB: www.pmconstructionco.com
SIC: 1623 1794 1611 2851 Water &
sewer line construction; excavation work;
highway & street paving contractor; epoxy
coatings

(G-8568)
PHILLIPSBURG MARBLE CO INC
1 Marble Hill Rd (08865-9331)
P.O. Box 172 (08865-0172)
PHONE..................................908 859-3435
Robert S Barron, *President*
▲ EMP: 22
SQ FT: 32,000
SALES (est): 4.4MM **Privately Held**
WEB: www.pburgmarble.com
SIC: 5032 3281 Marble building stone;
marble, building: cut & shaped

(G-8569)
PRECAST MANUFACTURING CO LLC
187 Strykers Rd (08865-9776)
PHONE..................................908 454-2122
Gregory P Fisher, *President*
Raymond M Fisher, *Vice Pres*
Vilma Delva, *Plant Mgr*
EMP: 36
SQ FT: 10,000
SALES (est): 6.2MM **Privately Held**
WEB: www.precastmfgco.com
SIC: 3272 Concrete products, precast

(G-8570)
PRESBYTERIAN REFORMED PUBG CO
Also Called: P & R Publishing
1102 Marble Hill Rd (08865)
P.O. Box 817 (08865-0817)
PHONE..................................908 454-0505
Bryce Craig, *President*
Virginia Horridge, *Vice Pres*
Ian Thompson, *Vice Pres*
Robert Den Dulk, *Treasurer*
Aaron Gottier, *Sr Project Mgr*
▲ EMP: 17 EST: 1930
SQ FT: 12,000
SALES (est): 1.5MM **Privately Held**
WEB: www.prpbooks.com
SIC: 2731 Books: publishing only

(G-8571)
R & H CO INC
Also Called: Metal Fabricators
1286 Strykers Rd (08865-9204)
PHONE..................................610 258-3177
William Kowalchuk Jr, *President*
EMP: 5
SQ FT: 6,000
SALES (est): 610K **Privately Held**
SIC: 3599 Machine shop, jobbing & repair

(G-8572)
RON BANAFATO INC
Also Called: Rbi Toys
1161 3rd Ave (08865-4708)
P.O. Box 288, Pluckemin (07978-0288)
PHONE..................................908 685-9447
Ron Banafato, *President*
▲ EMP: 8
SQ FT: 8,000
SALES (est): 1.2MM **Privately Held**
SIC: 3942 Stuffed toys, including animals

(G-8573)
RUTLER SCREEN PRINTING INC
169 Belview Rd (08865-2120)
PHONE..................................908 859-3327
John Shubert, *President*
Allen Shubert, *Vice Pres*
EMP: 13
SALES (est): 500K **Privately Held**
WEB: www.rutler.com
SIC: 2759 2396 Screen printing; automotive & apparel trimmings

(G-8574)
SCC CONCRETE INC
1051 River Rd (08865-8112)
P.O. Box 47 (08865-0047)
PHONE..................................908 859-2172
Richard Cornely, *President*
Patricia Cornely, *Corp Secy*
Francis Stine, *Vice Pres*
EMP: 13
SQ FT: 1,820
SALES (est): 2MM **Privately Held**
SIC: 3273 Ready-mixed concrete

(G-8575)
STARLIGHT ELECTRO-OPTICS INC
660 Hrmony Brass Cstle Rd (08865-9356)
PHONE..................................908 859-1362
Peter Curreri, *President*
EMP: 5
SALES (est): 610.9K **Privately Held**
SIC: 3699 3559 Laser systems & equipment; semiconductor manufacturing machinery

(G-8576)
STATELINE FABRICATORS LLC
100 Foul Rift Rd (08865-9533)
PHONE..................................908 387-8800
Edward Esposito, *President*
Frank Impeciati,
EMP: 40
SALES (est): 12MM **Privately Held**
SIC: 3441 5051 Building components,
structural steel; structural shapes, iron or
steel

(G-8577)
TITANIUM SMOKING KINGS LLC
509 March Blvd (08865-3908)
PHONE..................................908 339-8876
Robert William Ingraham Jr, *Principal*
EMP: 7
SALES (est): 146.3K **Privately Held**
SIC: 3356 Titanium

(G-8578)
TKL SPECIALTY PIPING INC
175 Broad St (08865-1208)
PHONE..................................908 454-0030
EMP: 5
SQ FT: 6,000
SALES (est): 1MM **Privately Held**
SIC: 3494 Valves And Pipe Fittings, Nec

(G-8579)
VILLA MILAGRO VINEYARDS LLC
33 Warren Glen Rd (08865)
PHONE..................................908 995-2072
Steve Gambino,
Audrey Gambino,
EMP: 4
SALES (est): 449.5K **Privately Held**
SIC: 0721 2084 Vines, cultivation of;
wines

Pilesgrove
Salem County

(G-8580)
RICHARD E PIERSON MTLS CORP (PA)
Also Called: R E Pierson Materials
426 Swedesboro Rd (08098-2534)
P.O. Box 430, Woodstown (08098-0430)
PHONE..................................856 467-4199
Richard E Pierson, *President*
EMP: 110
SALES (est): 38.2MM **Privately Held**
SIC: 2951 1611 1771 Asphalt paving mixtures & blocks; highway & street construction; concrete work

(G-8581)
TRIM FACTORY INC
1210 Route 40 (08098-3107)
PHONE..................................856 769-8746
Peggy Yurgin, *President*
Ida Yurgin, *Principal*
Phillip Yurgin, *Principal*
EMP: 6
SALES (est): 731.9K **Privately Held**
SIC: 2431 Exterior & ornamental woodwork & trim

Pine Beach
Ocean County

(G-8582)
CASTLE WOODCRAFT ASSOC LLC
161 Atlantic City Blvd (08741)
PHONE..................................732 349-1519
Ernest Guenzburger, *Mng Member*
Gerhart Frenz,
EMP: 15
SQ FT: 10,000
SALES: 1.5MM **Privately Held**
SIC: 2431 2434 5712 Millwork; wood
kitchen cabinets; cabinet work, custom

Pine Brook
Morris County

(G-8583)
ABOX AUTOMATION CORP
45 Us Highway 46 Ste 606 (07058-9390)
PHONE..................................973 659-9611
Harish Tailor, *President*
David Pfaff, *Vice Pres*
Steve Kanthan, *Treasurer*
Sean Keogh, *Admin Sec*
EMP: 4
SQ FT: 4,000
SALES (est): 1.7MM **Privately Held**
WEB: www.aboxautomation.com
SIC: 5084 3821 Packaging machinery &
equipment; laboratory apparatus & furniture

(G-8584)
AGSCO CORPORATION
60 Chapin Rd (07058-9216)
P.O. Box 669 (07058-0669)
PHONE..................................973 244-0005
Edward Plonsker, *Branch Mgr*
EMP: 23
SALES (corp-wide): 23.3MM **Privately Held**
SIC: 5085 3291 Bottler supplies; rouge,
polishing: abrasive
PA: Agsco Corporation
160 W Hintz Rd
Wheeling IL 60090
847 520-4455

(G-8585)
AMERICAN AERONAUTIC MFG CO
45 Us Highway 46 Ste 606 (07058-9390)
PHONE..................................973 442-8138
Wassim Ezzeddine, *Owner*
EMP: 5

SALES (est): 547.1K **Privately Held**
SIC: 3545 Machine tool attachments & accessories

(G-8586)
AMERICAN GARVENS CORPORATION
19a Chapin Rd (07058-9204)
PHONE..................................973 276-1093
Thomas Dudutis, *Vice Pres*
Thomas J Dudutis, *Vice Pres*
EMP: 4
SALES (est): 283.7K
SALES (corp-wide): 2.9B **Publicly Held**
WEB: www.mt.com
SIC: 3596 Scales & balances, except laboratory
PA: Mettler-Toledo International Inc.
1900 Polaris Pkwy Fl 6
Columbus OH 43240
614 438-4511

(G-8587)
BELAIR INSTRUMENT COMPANY LLC (PA)
Also Called: Avantik
19 Chapin Rd Bldg C (07058-9385)
P.O. Box 619, Springfield (07081-0619)
PHONE..................................973 912-8900
David L Patterson, *President*
Trevor Mornan, *CFO*
Diane Emtage, *Admin Sec*
Margaret J Patterson, *Admin Sec*
▲ EMP: 38
SQ FT: 4,000
SALES: 36.5MM **Privately Held**
SIC: 3826 3841 5047 Analytical instruments; surgical & medical instruments; surgical appliances & supplies;
medical & hospital equipment

(G-8588)
BELL-MARK SALES CO INC (PA)
331 Changebridge Rd Ste 1 (07058-9180)
P.O. Box 2007 (07058-2007)
PHONE..................................973 882-0202
John Marozzi, *President*
Bob Batesko, *Vice Pres*
Robert Batesko, *Vice Pres*
Thomas Pugh III, *Vice Pres*
Wayne Becker, *Engineer*
▲ EMP: 20 EST: 1960
SQ FT: 8,000
SALES (est): 17MM **Privately Held**
WEB: www.bell-mark.com
SIC: 3555 Printing trades machinery

(G-8589)
BGA CONSTRUCTION INC (PA)
321 Changebridge Rd (07058-9583)
PHONE..................................973 809-9745
Benjamin Gaudiosi, *President*
Hobart Carlton Price, *Opers Mgr*
▲ EMP: 55
SQ FT: 20,000
SALES: 12MM **Privately Held**
WEB: www.bgaconstruction.com
SIC: 2541 Garment racks, wood

(G-8590)
CHIRAL PHOTONICS INC
26 Chapin Rd Ste 1104 (07058-8802)
P.O. Box 694 (07058-0694)
PHONE..................................973 732-0030
Dan Neugroschl, *President*
Azriel Genack, *CTO*
▲ EMP: 10
SALES (est): 2.4MM **Privately Held**
WEB: www.chiralphotonics.com
SIC: 3577 Optical scanning devices

(G-8591)
CHIRAL PHOTONICS INC
26 Chapin Rd Ste 1104 (07058-8802)
P.O. Box 694 (07058-0694)
PHONE..................................973 732-0030
Dan Neugroschl, *President*
Jon Singer, *Director*
EMP: 15
SALES (est): 1.4MM **Privately Held**
SIC: 3827 Optical instruments & lenses

▲ = Import ▼ =Export
◆ =Import/Export

(G-8592)
CHRISTINE VALMY INC (PA)
285 Changebridge Rd Ste 1 (07058-9599)
PHONE...................................973 575-1050
Peter De Haydu, *President*
Christine Valmy, *Chairman*
Marina Dehaydu, *Vice Pres*
David Bickel, *CFO*
Ruchika Agarwal, *Manager*
▲ EMP: 21 EST: 1965
SQ FT: 20,000
SALES (est): 7.7MM **Privately Held**
WEB: www.christinevalmy.com
SIC: 2844 7231 Cosmetic preparations;
  cosmetology school

(G-8593)
CLARK EQUIPMENT COMPANY
Also Called: Doosan Machine Tools
19a Chapin Rd (07058-9204)
PHONE...................................973 618-2500
EMP: 2953 **Privately Held**
SIC: 3531 Construction machinery
HQ: Clark Equipment Company
  250 E Beaton Dr
  West Fargo ND 58078
  701 241-8700

(G-8594)
**COUNTY LINE
PHRMACEUTICALS LLC**
10 Bloomfield Ave Ste 3 (07058-9743)
PHONE...................................262 439-8109
Richard Losiniecki, *CEO*
Jeff Rumler,
Jon Thiel,
EMP: 9
SQ FT: 2,800
SALES (est): 3.4MM **Privately Held**
SIC: 2834 Pharmaceutical preparations

(G-8595)
CROWN TROPHY
101 Us Highway 46 Ste 136 (07058-9608)
PHONE...................................973 808-8400
Patricia May, *Owner*
EMP: 4
SQ FT: 1,400
SALES (est): 190K **Privately Held**
SIC: 5999 2499 2759 Trophies & plaques;
  trophy bases, wood; engraving

(G-8596)
DICAR INC (DH)
30 Chapin Rd Ste 1212 (07058-8902)
P.O. Box 643 (07058-0643)
PHONE...................................973 575-1377
Steve Warll, *President*
Daniel Freifeld, *President*
Ron Warll, *Principal*
Stephen Warll, *Principal*
Steven Sanfilippo, *COO*
◆ EMP: 50
SQ FT: 25,000
SALES (est): 41.6MM
SALES (corp-wide): 2.9MM **Privately
Held**
SIC: 2822 3081 Synthetic rubber; plastic
  film & sheet
HQ: Dicar B.V.
  De Boeg 8
  Drachten 9206
  512 582-682

(G-8597)
DICAR INC
5 Bader Rd (07058-9814)
P.O. Box 643 (07058-0643)
PHONE...................................973 575-4220
Dan Freifeld, *President*
Ira Sanders, *Technology*
Marina Sadikoska, *Prgrmr*
EMP: 72
SALES (corp-wide): 2.9MM **Privately
Held**
SIC: 2822 Synthetic rubber
HQ: Dicar, Inc.
  30 Chapin Rd Ste 1212
  Pine Brook NJ 07058
  973 575-1377

(G-8598)
DIOPSYS INC
16 Chapin Rd Ste 912 (07058-8900)
P.O. Box 672 (07058-0672)
PHONE...................................973 244-0622

Alberto Gonzlez Garcia, *Ch of Bd*
Tibor Szoke, *General Mgr*
John Siegfried, *Principal*
John Simon, *Principal*
Greg Adelsberg, *District Mgr*
▼ EMP: 39
SQ FT: 4,800
SALES (est): 11.1MM **Privately Held**
WEB: www.diopsys.com
SIC: 3841 Surgical & medical instruments

(G-8599)
**DOOSAN MACHINE TOOLS
AMER CORP (HQ)**
19a Chapin Rd (07058-9204)
PHONE...................................973 618-2500
Hyeong Joo Kim, *CEO*
Michael P Stanley, *President*
Kim Parkinson, *COO*
H S Lee, *CFO*
Yeong Su Yoon, *CFO*
◆ EMP: 60
SALES (est): 334.8MM **Privately Held**
WEB: www.doosanlift.com
SIC: 5084 5082 3545 Machine tools & ac-
  cessories; construction & mining machin-
  ery; machine tool accessories

(G-8600)
DRONE USA INC (PA)
330 Changebridge Rd # 101 (07058-9839)
PHONE...................................203 220-2296
Michael Bannon, *CEO*
Matthew Wiles, *VP Opers*
Rodrigo Kuntz Rangel, *CTO*
EMP: 11 EST: 1972
SALES (est): 12.2MM **Privately Held**
SIC: 3721 Motorized aircraft

(G-8601)
**FORD ATLANTIC FASTENER
CORP**
Also Called: Ford Atlanic
341 Changebridge Rd (07058-9717)
P.O. Box 733 (07058-0733)
PHONE...................................973 882-1191
Tony Innamarato, *President*
Ada Benedictis, *Info Tech Dir*
Thomas Schwarz, *Technology*
Parva Bakh, *IT/INT Sup*
▲ EMP: 27 EST: 1982
SQ FT: 15,000
SALES (est): 11.5MM **Privately Held**
SIC: 5072 3452 Bolts, nuts & screws;
  bolts, nuts, rivets & washers

(G-8602)
FRISCH PLASTICS CORP
81 Windsor Dr (07058-9636)
PHONE...................................973 685-5936
Ruth Lefkowitz, *Principal*
EMP: 7
SALES (est): 587.3K **Privately Held**
SIC: 3089 Injection molding of plastics

(G-8603)
I & J FISNAR INC
19 Chapin Rd Bldg C (07058-9385)
PHONE...................................973 646-5044
▲ EMP: 16
SALES (est): 4.7MM **Privately Held**
WEB: www.ijfisnar.com
SIC: 3569 Liquid automation machinery &
  equipment

(G-8604)
**II-VI ADVANCED MATERIALS
INC**
Also Called: Ii-VI Wide Band Gap, Inc.
20 Chapin Rd Ste 1007 (07058-9272)
P.O. Box 840 (07058-0840)
PHONE...................................973 227-1551
Fran Kramer, *President*
Craig Creaturo, *Treasurer*
EMP: 5
SALES (est): 26.8K
SALES (corp-wide): 1.3B **Publicly Held**
SIC: 3827 Optical instruments & lenses
PA: Ii-Vi Incorporated
  375 Saxonburg Blvd
  Saxonburg PA 16056
  724 352-4455

(G-8605)
II-VI INCORPORATED
Also Called: Ii-VI Advanced Materials Sic S
20 Chapin Rd Ste 1007 (07058-9272)
P.O. Box 840 (07058-0840)
PHONE...................................973 227-1551
Carl Johnson, *President*
EMP: 15
SALES (corp-wide): 1.3B **Publicly Held**
SIC: 3674 Silicon wafers, chemically
  doped
PA: Ii-Vi Incorporated
  375 Saxonburg Blvd
  Saxonburg PA 16056
  724 352-4455

(G-8606)
INGERSOLL-RAND COMPANY
26 Chapin Rd Ste 1107 (07058-8802)
PHONE...................................973 882-0924
EMP: 7 **Privately Held**
SIC: 3131 Rands
HQ: Ingersoll-Rand Company
  800 Beaty St Ste B
  Davidson NC 28036
  704 655-4000

(G-8607)
**INTERNATIONAL BEAUTY
PRODUCTS**
Also Called: Mauden International
39 Us Highway 46 Ste 804 (07058-8602)
P.O. Box 708 (07058-0708)
PHONE...................................973 575-6400
Henry Cho, *President*
Anthony Sehnaoui, *Vice Pres*
▲ EMP: 11 EST: 1989
SALES (est): 2.8MM **Privately Held**
SIC: 2844 Toilet preparations

(G-8608)
JIAHERB INC (HQ)
1 Chapin Rd Ste 1 # 1 (07058-9221)
PHONE...................................973 439-6869
Ying Chen, *President*
Scott Chen, *Vice Pres*
Guillaume Gigot, *Accounts Mgr*
Don Laforge, *Accounts Mgr*
◆ EMP: 22
SALES (est): 3.6MM
SALES (corp-wide): 96.4MM **Privately
Held**
SIC: 2833 Medicinals & botanicals
PA: Shaanxi Jiahe Phytochem Co., Ltd.
  A-6th Floor, No.66 Jinye 1st Road, Hi-
  Tech Zone
  Xian 71007
  298 834-8327

(G-8609)
**MECHANICAL TECHNOLOGIES
LLC**
10 Bloomfield Ave Ste 6 (07058-9743)
PHONE...................................973 616-3800
Chris Panza, *President*
Rich Fembleaux, *Vice Pres*
Lawrence Bovich, *Mng Member*
EMP: 38
SALES (est): 11.2MM **Privately Held**
SIC: 3585 Air conditioning equipment,
  complete; heating equipment, complete

(G-8610)
NATIONAL FUEL LLC
287 Changebridge Rd (07058-9560)
PHONE...................................973 227-4549
EMP: 5
SALES (est): 196.9K **Privately Held**
SIC: 2869 Fuels

(G-8611)
NEWARK MORNING LEDGER CO
Also Called: Star Ledger
26 Riverside Dr (07058-9758)
PHONE...................................973 882-6120
Bob Jared, *Manager*
Peter Finella, *Director*
EMP: 149
SALES (corp-wide): 217.5MM **Privately
Held**
SIC: 2782 2711 Ledgers & ledger sheets;
  newspapers, publishing & printing

PA: Newark Morning Ledger Co.
  1 Gateway Ctr Ste 1100
  Newark NJ 07102
  973 392-4141

(G-8612)
ODOWD ENTERPRISES INC
Also Called: O'Dowd Advertising
48 Us Highway 46 Ste 2 (07058-9298)
P.O. Box 108 (07058-0108)
PHONE...................................973 227-4607
Joseph P Odowd, *President*
Joseph P O'Dowd, *President*
Thomas O'Dowd, *Vice Pres*
EMP: 5
SQ FT: 4,400
SALES (est): 537.5K **Privately Held**
WEB: www.odowdadvertising.com
SIC: 2741 Miscellaneous publishing

(G-8613)
PCR TECHNOLOGIES INC
26 Chapin Rd Ste 1111 (07058-9211)
P.O. Box 868 (07058-0868)
PHONE...................................973 882-0017
Mark Vanzini, *President*
Peter Lemma, *Vice Pres*
EMP: 8
SQ FT: 7,000
SALES (est): 1.7MM **Privately Held**
WEB: www.pcrouting.com
SIC: 3672 3679 3444 3469 Circuit
  boards, television & radio printed; elec-
  tronic circuits; microwave components;
  sheet metalwork; metal stampings; vul-
  canized fiber plates, sheets, rods or tubes

(G-8614)
**PURE SOCCER ACADEMY LTD
LBLTY**
330 Changebridge Rd # 101 (07058-9839)
PHONE...................................877 945-6423
Nigel J W Nicholls, *President*
Ben Manning, *Director*
EMP: 5
SALES (est): 267.3K **Privately Held**
SIC: 3949 Sporting & athletic goods

(G-8615)
REFINE TECHNOLOGY LLC
26 Chapin Rd Ste 1107 (07058-8802)
P.O. Box 691 (07058-0691)
PHONE...................................973 952-0002
Sol Genauer, *CEO*
Jerry Shevitz, *President*
Edi Eliezer, *Vice Pres*
John B Carter, *VP Sales*
EMP: 18
SALES (est): 45.1K **Privately Held**
SIC: 3845 Laser systems & equipment,
  medical

(G-8616)
**SATO LBLING SOLUTIONS
AMER INC**
30 Chapin Rd Ste 1201 (07058-9398)
P.O. Box 777 (07058-0777)
PHONE...................................973 287-3641
Joseph Podsedly, *Branch Mgr*
EMP: 94
SALES (corp-wide): 20.3MM **Privately
Held**
SIC: 2759 Labels & seals: printing
PA: Sato Labeling Solutions America, Inc.
  1140 Windham Pkwy
  Romeoville IL 60446
  630 771-4200

(G-8617)
**SIGNATURE MARKETING
GROUP LTD (PA)**
25 Riverside Dr Ste 4 (07058-9391)
PHONE...................................973 575-7785
Thomas J Cioletti, *President*
Danielle Umstead, *Treasurer*
William Becher, *Accounts Mgr*
▲ EMP: 15
SQ FT: 24,000
SALES (est): 3MM **Privately Held**
WEB: www.signaturegroupltd.net
SIC: 3631 Household cooking equipment

G
E
O
G
R
A
P
H
I
C

(G-8618)
TRANE US INC
26 Chapin Rd Ste 1103 (07058-8802)
P.O. Box 154 (07058-0154)
PHONE.................................973 882-3220
Walter Macko, *Branch Mgr*
Bruce Hanna, *Manager*
EMP: 6 **Privately Held**
SIC: 3585 Refrigeration & heating equipment
HQ: Trane U.S. Inc.
    3600 Pammel Creek Rd
    La Crosse WI 54601
    608 787-2000

(G-8619)
VOLTA BELTING USA INC
60 Chapin Rd Ste 3 (07058-9217)
PHONE.................................973 276-7905
Zvika Avidan, *President*
▲ **EMP:** 17
SALES (est): 4.2MM **Privately Held**
SIC: 3535 Belt conveyor systems, general industrial use

(G-8620)
WEXCO INDUSTRIES INC
3 Barnet Rd (07058-9505)
PHONE.................................973 244-5777
Paula Lombard, *President*
William Clark, *General Mgr*
Steve Schwartz, *COO*
Mike Parmelee, *Vice Pres*
George Pollok, *Vice Pres*
◆ **EMP:** 20
SQ FT: 35,000
SALES (est): 7.3MM **Privately Held**
SIC: 5013 3714 Automotive supplies & parts; wipers, windshield, motor vehicle

---

Pine Hill
Camden County

(G-8621)
BRUCE MCCOY SR
Also Called: Wilcoy Press
5402 Tall Pnes (08021-7627)
PHONE.................................609 217-6153
EMP: 6 **EST:** 2006
SALES (est): 350K **Privately Held**
SIC: 2752 Lithographic Commercial Printing

(G-8622)
PINE HILL PRINTING INC
200 Erial Rd (08021-6212)
PHONE.................................856 346-2915
Edith Mc Cusker, *President*
Peter A Mc Cusker, *Vice Pres*
EMP: 9
SQ FT: 9,000
SALES: 1.5MM **Privately Held**
SIC: 2752 Commercial printing, offset

Piscataway
Middlesex County

(G-8623)
ABOUT OUR TOWN INC
2 Lakeview Ave Ste 312 (08854-2750)
PHONE.................................732 968-1615
Ronald Chilson, *President*
Ron Chilson, *Marketing Staff*
EMP: 6
SALES: 250K **Privately Held**
WEB: www.aboutourtown.com
SIC: 2711 7331 Newspapers, publishing & printing; direct mail advertising services

(G-8624)
ABSOLUTE PROTECTIVE SYSTEMS
51 Suttons Ln (08854-5716)
PHONE.................................732 287-4500
Paul Smoley, *President*
EMP: 30

SALES (est): 6.5MM **Privately Held**
WEB: www.absps.com
SIC: 1711 5063 3569 3999 Fire sprinkler system installation; alarm systems; sprinkler systems, fire: automatic; fire extinguishers, portable; access control systems specialization; closed circuit television installation; fire detection & burglar alarm systems specialization; closed circuit television services

(G-8625)
ACG NORTH AMERICA LLC
262 Old New Brunswick Rd A (08854-3756)
PHONE.................................908 757-3425
Ajit Singh, *President*
Nikunj Desai, *General Mgr*
Ganesh Shenoy, *Business Mgr*
Rajkunwar Singh, *Engineer*
Rakesh Sharma, *Sales Mgr*
▲ **EMP:** 25
SQ FT: 10,000
SALES (est): 3.1MM **Privately Held**
WEB: www.ucllc.net
SIC: 2834 Pharmaceutical preparations

(G-8626)
AFLEX EXTRUSION TECHNOLOGIES
240b N Randolphville Rd (08854-3127)
PHONE.................................732 752-0048
▲ **EMP:** 21
SQ FT: 12,500
SALES (est): 4.1MM **Privately Held**
SIC: 3089 Mfg Plastic Products

(G-8627)
AGILEX FLAVORS FRAGRANCES INC (HQ)
140 Centennial Ave (08854-3908)
PHONE.................................732 885-0702
Raymond J Hughes, *CEO*
Gail Guilbert, *Vice Pres*
Alice Rebeck, *Vice Pres*
Tony Trinco, *Vice Pres*
Florin-Joseph Vlad, *Vice Pres*
◆ **EMP:** 3
SALES (est): 55.4MM
SALES (corp-wide): 3.7B **Privately Held**
SIC: 2844 Toilet preparations
PA: Firmenich International Sa
    Route Des Jeunes 1
    Les Acacias GE 1227
    227 802-211

(G-8628)
ALL AMERICAN POLY CORP (PA)
40 Turner Pl (08854-3839)
P.O. Box 10148, New Brunswick (08906-0148)
PHONE.................................732 752-3200
Jack Klein, *President*
Joe Friedman, *Senior VP*
Neil Koenig, *Vice Pres*
Leon Ortega, *Plant Mgr*
Steve Pierson, *Prdtn Mgr*
▼ **EMP:** 250
SQ FT: 160,000
SALES (est): 75.8MM **Privately Held**
WEB: www.allampoly.com
SIC: 3081 2673 Unsupported plastics film & sheet; plastic bags: made from purchased materials

(G-8629)
AMERICAN HOME MFG LLC
4 Corporate Pl (08854-4120)
PHONE.................................732 465-1530
EMP: 9
SALES (corp-wide): 76.1MM **Privately Held**
SIC: 2299 Pillow fillings: curled hair, cotton waste, moss, hemp tow
HQ: American Home Manufacturing Llc
    302 5th Ave Fl 5
    New York NY 10001
    212 643-0680

(G-8630)
AMERICAN PHARMACEUTICAL LLC
1 New England Ave (08854-4128)
PHONE.................................732 645-3030

Ken Cappel, *Manager*
EMP: 6
SALES (est): 634.7K **Privately Held**
SIC: 2834 Pharmaceutical preparations

(G-8631)
AMERICAN STANDARD INTL INC
1 Centennial Ave Ste 101 (08854-3921)
P.O. Box 6820 (08855-6820)
PHONE.................................732 652-7100
Jay D Gould, *CEO*
Carol Houlik, *Director*
EMP: 25
SALES (est): 4.8MM **Privately Held**
SIC: 2499 Kitchen, bathroom & household ware: wood
HQ: Trane U.S. Inc.
    3600 Pammel Creek Rd
    La Crosse WI 54601
    608 787-2000

(G-8632)
AMNEAL PHARMACEUTICALS LLC
1 New England Ave Bldg A (08854-4128)
PHONE.................................908 947-3120
Ken Cappel, *Branch Mgr*
EMP: 17
SALES (corp-wide): 1.6B **Publicly Held**
SIC: 5122 2834 Pharmaceuticals; pharmaceutical preparations
HQ: Amneal Pharmaceuticals Llc
    400 Crossing Blvd Fl 3
    Bridgewater NJ 08807

(G-8633)
AMNEAL PHARMACEUTICALS LLC
47 Colonial Dr Bldg B (08854-4113)
PHONE.................................908 947-3120
Alpesh Patel, *Manager*
EMP: 14
SALES (corp-wide): 1.6B **Publicly Held**
SIC: 2834 Pharmaceutical preparations
HQ: Amneal Pharmaceuticals Llc
    400 Crossing Blvd Fl 3
    Bridgewater NJ 08807

(G-8634)
APICORE LLC (HQ)
15 Corporate Pl S Ste 110 (08854-6108)
PHONE.................................646 884-3765
Ravishanker Kovi, *President*
Sanjay Bhargav, *Opers Staff*
EMP: 40
SALES (est): 8.9MM
SALES (corp-wide): 22MM **Privately Held**
SIC: 2834 Solutions, pharmaceutical
PA: Medicure Inc
    1250 Waverley St Suite 2
    Winnipeg MB R3T 6
    204 487-7412

(G-8635)
APPCO PHARMA LLC
262 Old New Brunswick Rd (08854-3756)
PHONE.................................732 271-8300
Nagaraju Kanchanapalli, *Branch Mgr*
EMP: 35
SALES (corp-wide): 10MM **Privately Held**
SIC: 2834 Pharmaceutical preparations
PA: Appco Pharma Llc
    120 Belmont Dr
    Somerset NJ 08873
    732 271-8300

(G-8636)
AROMATIC TECHNOLOGIES INC (HQ)
Also Called: Agilex Fragrances
140 Centennial Ave (08854-3908)
PHONE.................................732 393-7300
Raymond Hughes, *CEO*
Kevin M Gilbert, *Senior VP*
Natalie L Hinden-Kuhles, *Senior VP*
Tony Trinco, *Senior VP*
Dan Freimuth, *Vice Pres*
▲ **EMP:** 55
SQ FT: 60,000

SALES (est): 12.7MM
SALES (corp-wide): 3.7B **Privately Held**
WEB: www.aromatec.com
SIC: 2869 Perfumes, flavorings & food additives
PA: Firmenich International Sa
    Route Des Jeunes 1
    Les Acacias GE 1227
    227 802-211

(G-8637)
AS AMERICA INC (HQ)
Also Called: American Standard Brands
1 Centennial Ave Ste 101 (08854-3921)
P.O. Box 6820 (08855-6820)
PHONE.................................732 980-3000
Steve Delarge, *President*
Chris Capone, *Vice Pres*
Jean L'Henaff, *Vice Pres*
Dan Harvey, *Opers Mgr*
Joe Ientile, *Engineer*
▲ **EMP:** 200
SALES (est): 2.4B **Privately Held**
SIC: 3261 3432 Vitreous plumbing fixtures; plumbing fixture fittings & trim

(G-8638)
ASD HOLDING CORP
Also Called: American Standard
1 Centennial Ave (08854-3921)
P.O. Box 6820 (08855-6820)
PHONE.................................800 442-1902
Steven P Delarge, *President*
EMP: 7 **EST:** 2007
SALES (est): 518.3K **Privately Held**
SIC: 3431 5047 Bathtubs: enameled iron, cast iron or pressed metal; bathroom fixtures, including sinks; plumbing fixtures: enameled iron cast iron or pressed metal; baths, whirlpool
HQ: Lixil Corporation
    3-2-5, Kasumigaseki
    Chiyoda-Ku TKY 100-0

(G-8639)
BCC (USA) INC
Also Called: Bearing Castings USA
143 Ethel Rd W (08854-5928)
PHONE.................................732 572-5450
Jimmy Chu, *President*
Andrew Doong, *General Mgr*
Marquis Yeh, *Treasurer*
▲ **EMP:** 5
SQ FT: 13,700
SALES (est): 805.8K **Privately Held**
SIC: 3568 5085 5045 Bearings, plain; bearings; computer peripheral equipment

(G-8640)
BEAUTY-PACK LLC
170 Circle Dr N (08854-3703)
P.O. Box 610, Gladstone (07934-0610)
PHONE.................................732 802-8200
Gregory Harmon,
EMP: 10 **EST:** 2013
SQ FT: 110,000
SALES (est): 670.2K **Privately Held**
SIC: 7389 2631 5084 Cosmetic kits, assembling & packaging; container, packaging & boxboard; processing & packaging equipment

(G-8641)
CAMBER PHARMACEUTICALS INC
1031 Centennial Ave (08854-4125)
PHONE.................................732 529-0430
Konstantin Ostaficiuk, *President*
▲ **EMP:** 47
SQ FT: 66,000
SALES (est): 34.3MM
SALES (corp-wide): 238.1MM **Privately Held**
SIC: 5122 2834 Pharmaceuticals; medicines, capsuled or ampuled
PA: Hetero Drugs Limited
    7-2-A2, Hetero Corporate Industrial Estate
    Hyderabad TS 50001
    402 370-4923

(G-8642)
CAPTIVE PLASTICS LLC
251 Circle Dr N (08854-3759)
PHONE.................................732 469-7900
R Beeler, *President*

EMP: 101 **Publicly Held**
SIC: **3089** Plastic containers, except foam
HQ: Captive Plastics, Llc
101 Oakley St
Evansville IN 47710
812 424-2904

(G-8643)
CATCHING ZZZ LLC
Also Called: Tanda Sleep
91 New England Ave (08854-4142)
PHONE..................................888 339-1604
Venkata Chinni, *Mng Member*
Janice Yates, *Director*
EMP: 6
SALES (est): 227.6K **Privately Held**
SIC: **2515** Mattresses & bedsprings

(G-8644)
CENTURY PRINTING CORP
10 New England Ave (08854-4101)
PHONE..................................732 981-0544
Guy T Greck, *President*
Michael Maroney, *Corp Secy*
EMP: 4
SQ FT: 2,000
SALES: 350K **Privately Held**
SIC: **2752** Commercial printing, offset

(G-8645)
CERAMI WOOD PRODUCTS INC
154 12th St (08854-1934)
PHONE..................................732 968-7222
Fax: 732 968-7227
EMP: 12 EST: 1979
SQ FT: 10,500
SALES: 1.5MM **Privately Held**
SIC: **2511** **2431** Mfg Wood Household Furniture Mfg Millwork

(G-8646)
CLASSIC PRINTERS & CONVERTERS
140 Ethel Rd W Ste K (08854-5951)
PHONE..................................732 985-1100
Sat Khurana, *President*
Rachna Khurana, *Vice Pres*
Raj Kumar, *Vice Pres*
EMP: 6
SQ FT: 4,500
SALES (est): 939.2K **Privately Held**
WEB: www.tapesandlabels.com
SIC: **2759** Labels & seals: printing

(G-8647)
CLEMS ORNEMENTAL IRON WORKS
Also Called: Clem's
110 11th St (08854-1508)
PHONE..................................732 968-7200
Clement L Carfaro Jr, *President*
Clem Carfaro III, *Vice Pres*
▼ EMP: 60
SQ FT: 20,500
SALES (est): 10MM **Privately Held**
WEB: www.clemsironworks.com
SIC: **2431** **3446** Staircases, stairs & railings; stair railings, wood; architectural metalwork; stairs, fire escapes, balconies, railings & ladders; railings, bannisters, guards, etc.: made from metal pipe

(G-8648)
COLGATE-PALMOLIVE COMPANY
909 River Rd (08854-5596)
P.O. Box 1343 (08855-1343)
PHONE..................................732 878-7500
Laren Addabbo, *Project Mgr*
Greg Schott, *Project Mgr*
Craig Buehner, *Purch Mgr*
Roger Lim, *Technical Mgr*
Tracey Aldrich, *Research*
EMP: 750
SALES (corp-wide): 15.5B **Publicly Held**
WEB: www.colgate.com
SIC: **2844** Toothpastes or powders, dentifrices
PA: Colgate-Palmolive Company
300 Park Ave Fl 3
New York NY 10022
212 310-2000

(G-8649)
COMPUPHARMA INC
242 Old New Brunswick Rd (08854-3754)
PHONE..................................973 227-6003
Barry Boyle, *Principal*
EMP: 5
SALES (est): 407.4K **Privately Held**
SIC: **2834** Pharmaceutical preparations

(G-8650)
CONTINENTAL PRECISION CORP (PA)
Also Called: Montrose Molders
25 Howard St (08854-1435)
P.O. Box 265, South Plainfield (07080-0265)
PHONE..................................908 754-3030
Judith Wilson, *Corp Secy*
William H Wilson, *Vice Pres*
▲ EMP: 195 EST: 1966
SQ FT: 940,000
SALES (est): 26.6MM **Privately Held**
WEB: www.montrosemolders.com
SIC: **3089** **3544** Injection molding of plastics; forms (molds), for foundry & plastics working machinery

(G-8651)
DAQ ELECTRONICS LLC
262 Old New Brunswick Rd B (08854-3756)
PHONE..................................732 981-0050
David Green, *President*
Christopher Sincock, *Vice Pres*
Robert Musumeci, *VP Opers*
Robert Kukoly, *QC Mgr*
Mike Schwartz, *Controller*
▼ EMP: 28
SQ FT: 25,000
SALES: 8MM **Privately Held**
WEB: www.daq.net
SIC: **3699** **3823** Security control equipment & systems; telemetering instruments, industrial process type; data loggers, industrial process type

(G-8652)
DATAPRO INTERNATIONAL INC
Also Called: Keydata International
201 Circle Dr N Ste 101 (08854-3723)
P.O. Box 1267, South Plainfield (07080-9267)
PHONE..................................732 868-0588
George Wu, *President*
▲ EMP: 36
SQ FT: 24,000
SALES (est): 4.4MM **Privately Held**
WEB: www.dataprocorp.com
SIC: **5045** **5961** **7373** **7379** Computers & accessories, personal & home entertainment; computers & peripheral equipment, mail order; computer integrated systems design; computer related consulting services; electronic computers

(G-8653)
DEOSEN USA INC
1140 Stelton Rd Ste 205 (08854-5291)
PHONE..................................908 382-6518
Lawrence Herbolsheimer, *CEO*
Roger Xu, *Sales Staff*
▲ EMP: 6
SQ FT: 1,500
SALES (est): 575.7K
SALES (corp-wide): 105.1MM **Privately Held**
SIC: **2099** Food preparations
PA: Deosen Biochemical Science And Technology Ltd.
No.89, An'ping Road, Linzi District
Zibo 25543
533 609-9627

(G-8654)
DESIGN & MOLDING SERVICES INC
25 Howard St (08854-1496)
PHONE..................................732 752-0300
John L Fontenelli, *Senior Partner*
Jerry Fontenelli, *Principal*
Robert Malenchek, *Principal*
EMP: 150
SQ FT: 73,000

SALES (est): 15.5MM **Privately Held**
WEB: www.designmold.com
SIC: **3089** Injection molding of plastics; molding primary plastic

(G-8655)
DFI AMERICA LLC
15 Corporate Pl S Ste 201 (08854-6107)
PHONE..................................732 562-0693
Ping Liu, *President*
Gavin Chan, *General Mgr*
David Lu, *General Mgr*
Eric Oo, *Engineer*
Kylie Chung, *Controller*
▲ EMP: 40
SQ FT: 82,000
SALES (est): 11.9MM **Privately Held**
WEB: www.itox.com
SIC: **5045** **3571** Computer peripheral equipment; electronic computers

(G-8656)
DIABETO INC
200 Centennial Ave # 200 (08854-3950)
PHONE..................................646 397-3175
Shreekant Pawar, *CEO*
Hemanshu Jain, *COO*
Kirk Treasure, *Sales Staff*
EMP: 5
SQ FT: 100
SALES (est): 351.4K **Publicly Held**
SIC: **3841** **3845** **7371** Diagnostic apparatus, medical; electromedical equipment; computer software development & applications
PA: Livongo Health, Inc.
150 W Evelyn Ave Ste 150 # 150
Mountain View CA 94041

(G-8657)
DPK CONSULTING LLC
220 Old New Brunswick Rd # 201 (08854-3757)
PHONE..................................732 764-0100
Steven Parents, *Owner*
Steven D Parent, *Mng Member*
EMP: 13
SQ FT: 900
SALES (est): 1.3MM **Privately Held**
SIC: **8713** **1389** Photogrammetric engineering; testing, measuring, surveying & analysis services

(G-8658)
DREAM ON ME INDUSTRIES INC (PA)
1532 S Washington Ave # 1 (08854-3947)
PHONE..................................732 752-7220
Mark Serure, *Ch of Bd*
Shareva Bacchus, *Opers Mgr*
Morris Srour, *Prdtn Mgr*
Charles Plittman, *CFO*
Jenny Keaveny, *Sales Mgr*
▲ EMP: 100
SQ FT: 150,000
SALES (est): 28.8MM **Privately Held**
WEB: www.babieskingdom.com
SIC: **2511** Children's wood furniture

(G-8659)
DYNAMIC METALS INC
1713 S 2nd St (08854-1741)
PHONE..................................908 769-0522
Michael Wright, *CEO*
Larry Parish, *President*
James R Moore, *Vice Pres*
Douglas D Parsons, *Vice Pres*
Mike Bagnara, *QC Mgr*
EMP: 25
SQ FT: 125,000
SALES (est): 6.2MM **Privately Held**
SIC: **3914** **5051** Stainless steel ware; steel

(G-8660)
ELVI PHARMA LLC
60 Ethel Rd W Ste 1 (08854-5995)
PHONE..................................732 640-2707
Yovanny Garcia, *Mng Member*
EMP: 10
SALES: 1.5MM **Privately Held**
SIC: **2834** Pharmaceutical preparations

(G-8661)
EMC PAVING LLC
57 Justice St (08854-5425)
PHONE..................................908 636-1054

John J Hanrahan, *Principal*
EMP: 7
SALES (est): 152.3K **Privately Held**
SIC: **3572** Computer storage devices

(G-8662)
EVONIK CORPORATION
2 Turner Pl (08854-3839)
PHONE..................................732 981-5000
Bob T W Lin, *Opers Mgr*
Marnie Phillips, *Export Mgr*
David Previs, *Technical Mgr*
Ashish Guha, *Research*
Maria Nargiello, *Branch Mgr*
EMP: 61
SALES (corp-wide): 2.6B **Privately Held**
SIC: **2869** Industrial organic chemicals
HQ: Evonik Corporation
299 Jefferson Rd
Parsippany NJ 07054
973 929-8000

(G-8663)
EXHIBIT CO INC
239 Old New Brunswick Rd (08854-3712)
PHONE..................................732 465-1070
Francesco Geraci, *President*
▲ EMP: 26
SQ FT: 60,000
SALES (est): 3.9MM **Privately Held**
WEB: www.exhibitcompanyinc.com
SIC: **3993** Signs & advertising specialties

(G-8664)
EXIM INCORPORATED (PA)
30 Thames Ave (08854-5229)
PHONE..................................908 561-8200
Harshad V Shah, *President*
Nirav H Shah, *Vice Pres*
Nirav Shah, *Vice Pres*
◆ EMP: 3
SQ FT: 2,000
SALES (est): 1.7MM **Privately Held**
SIC: **5093** **5162** **3569** **2611** Metal scrap & waste materials; waste paper; automotive wrecking for scrap; plastics materials & basic shapes; baling machines, for scrap metal, paper or similar material; pulp mills, mechanical & recycling processing; recycling machinery & equipment; recycling machinery

(G-8665)
FLAVOR SOLUTIONS INC
120 New England Ave (08854-4127)
PHONE..................................732 354-1931
William May, *President*
EMP: 5
SQ FT: 40,000
SALES (est): 1.1MM **Privately Held**
SIC: **2087** Extracts, flavoring

(G-8666)
G & W LABORATORIES INC
Also Called: G W Laboratories
1551 S Washington Ave (08854-6700)
PHONE..................................732 474-0729
EMP: 85
SALES (corp-wide): 241.2MM **Privately Held**
SIC: **2834** Pharmaceutical preparations
PA: G & W Laboratories, Inc.
301 Helen St
South Plainfield NJ 07080
908 753-2000

(G-8667)
GOLD SIGNATURE INCORPORATED
1260 Stelton Rd (08854-5282)
PHONE..................................732 777-9170
Raymond Morris, *President*
Gloria Morris, *Corp Secy*
EMP: 6
SALES (est): 490K **Privately Held**
SIC: **3911** **5094** Jewelry, precious metal; jewelry

(G-8668)
GORGIAS PRESS
46 Orris Ave (08854-5710)
PHONE..................................732 699-0343
George A Kiraz, *Partner*
Christine Kiraz, *Vice Pres*
▲ EMP: 6

SALES (est): 489.6K **Privately Held**
WEB: www.gorgiaspress.com
SIC: 2741 Miscellaneous publishing

(G-8669)
GORGIAS PRESS LLC
954 River Rd (08854-5504)
PHONE..............................732 885-8900
George Kiraz, *President*
EMP: 4
SALES (est): 130.8K **Privately Held**
SIC: 2731 Book publishing

(G-8670)
GRAPHIC PRESENTATIONS SYSTEMS
Also Called: Graphic Systems
262 Old New Brnswk Rd F (08854-3756)
PHONE..............................732 981-1120
Kevin Keizer, *President*
EMP: 19
SQ FT: 28,000
SALES (est): 2.7MM **Privately Held**
WEB: www.gpsinj.com
SIC: 3993 Displays & cutouts, window & lobby

(G-8671)
HEALTH AND NATURAL BEAUTY USA
Also Called: Health & Natural Beauty
140 Ethel Rd W Ste W (08854-5951)
PHONE..............................732 640-1830
Sayed Ibrahim, *President*
EMP: 12
SALES: 5MM **Privately Held**
SIC: 5999 2844 Toiletries, cosmetics & perfumes; oral preparations

(G-8672)
HERBAKRAFT INCORPORATED
121 Ethel Rd W Ste 6 (08854-5952)
P.O. Box 218 (08855-0218)
PHONE..............................732 463-1000
Nisha Khanijow, *President*
Denis Semana, *Business Mgr*
Liz Jaquez, *Exec VP*
Vinod Khanijow, *Exec VP*
Lissett Jaquez, *Vice Pres*
▲ **EMP:** 11
SQ FT: 6,000
SALES (est): 2.4MM **Privately Held**
SIC: 2833 Drugs & herbs: grading, grinding & milling

(G-8673)
HOMECO LLC
Also Called: Original Toy Company, The
739 South Ave (08854)
PHONE..............................732 802-7733
Schmiley Schick, *Mng Member*
Aaron Kedz,
◆ **EMP:** 22
SQ FT: 43,000
SALES: 17MM **Privately Held**
SIC: 3634 3942 Housewares, excluding cooking appliances & utensils; dolls & stuffed toys

(G-8674)
HORIBA INSTRUMENTS INC
Spex Forensics Group
20 Knightsbridge Rd (08854-3913)
PHONE..............................732 623-8335
Eric Teboul, *Branch Mgr*
EMP: 50 **Privately Held**
SIC: 3641 Ultraviolet lamps
HQ: Horiba Instruments Incorporated
9755 Research Dr
Irvine CA 92618
949 250-4811

(G-8675)
HORIBA INSTRUMENTS INC
Horiba Scientific
20 Knightsbridge Rd (08854-3913)
PHONE..............................732 494-8660
Sal Atzeni, *Exec VP*
EMP: 5 **Privately Held**
SIC: 3826 Spectrographs
HQ: Horiba Instruments Incorporated
9755 Research Dr
Irvine CA 92618
949 250-4811

(G-8676)
HUMANSCALE CORPORATION
220 Circle Dr N (08854-3705)
PHONE..............................732 537-2944
Raymond Agudo, *Plant Mgr*
Shiela Bowen, *Controller*
Michele Gerards, *Manager*
EMP: 220
SALES (corp-wide): 142.2MM **Privately Held**
SIC: 3577 Computer peripheral equipment
PA: Humanscale Corporation
1114 Avenue Of The Americ
New York NY 10036
212 725-4749

(G-8677)
INGERSOLL-RAND INTL INC
1 Centennial Ave Ste 101 (08854-3921)
PHONE..............................559 271-4625
Heather Foran, *Counsel*
Makila S Scruggs, *Counsel*
Sumanta Bhunia, *Vice Pres*
Michelle Trumpower, *Vice Pres*
Andrea Weiss, *Prdtn Dir*
EMP: 59
SALES (est): 1.3MM **Privately Held**
SIC: 3531 Construction machinery

(G-8678)
INGERSOLL-RAND US TRANE (HQ)
1 Centennial Ave Ste 101 (08854-3921)
P.O. Box 6820 (08855-6820)
PHONE..............................732 652-7100
Michael W Lamach, *CEO*
Michael Girard, *Area Mgr*
Susan Killion, *Area Mgr*
Trevor Joelson, *Business Mgr*
Bill Aiello, *Project Mgr*
◆ **EMP:** 83
SALES (est): 8.9B **Privately Held**
SIC: 3585 Refrigeration & heating equipment

(G-8679)
INNOVANCE INC
Also Called: Innovance Networks
15 Corporate Pl S Ste 101 (08854-6107)
PHONE..............................732 529-2300
EMP: 0 **EST:** 2000
SALES (est): 6.5MM **Privately Held**
SIC: 3661 Fiber Optic Communications

(G-8680)
INTELLECT DESIGN ARENA INC (HQ)
Also Called: INTELLECT SEEC
20 Corporate Pl S (08854-6144)
PHONE..............................732 769-1037
Pranav Pasricha, *CEO*
Ravindra Koka, *President*
Keith Keir, *Partner*
Uppili Srinivasan, *COO*
EMP: 18
SQ FT: 8,000
SALES: 20MM
SALES (corp-wide): 281.9MM **Privately Held**
SIC: 7372 Prepackaged software
PA: Polaris Consulting & Services Limited
Foundation, 34, It Highway
Kanchipuram TN 60310
443 987-4000

(G-8681)
JC MACELROY CO INC (PA)
91 Ethel Rd W (08854-5955)
P.O. Box 850 (08855-0850)
PHONE..............................732 572-7100
Scott J Spota, *President*
Douglas Steiner, *General Mgr*
Jeffrey Spota, *Vice Pres*
Julissa Auffant, *Project Mgr*
Justin Chirdon, *Project Mgr*
◆ **EMP:** 55 **EST:** 1932
SQ FT: 17,000
SALES (est): 29.9MM **Privately Held**
WEB: www.macelroy.com
SIC: 3441 5088 3452 3564 Fabricated structural metal; marine crafts & supplies; bolts, metal; blowers & fans; manufactured hardware (general)

(G-8682)
JOHNSON & JOHNSON
35 Azalea Pl (08854-7500)
PHONE..............................732 524-0400
Yash Shah, *IT/INT Sup*
EMP: 80
SALES (corp-wide): 81.5B **Publicly Held**
SIC: 2676 Feminine hygiene paper products
PA: Johnson & Johnson
1 Johnson And Johnson Plz
New Brunswick NJ 08933
732 524-0400

(G-8683)
KASHIV BIOSCIENCES LLC
20 New England Ave (08854-4101)
PHONE..............................732 475-0500
EMP: 25
SALES (corp-wide): 3.3MM **Privately Held**
SIC: 2834 Pharmaceutical preparations
PA: Kashiv Biosciences, Llc
995 Us Highway 202/206
Bridgewater NJ 08807
908 895-1520

(G-8684)
LUBRIZOL CORPORATION
377 Hoes Ln Ste 210 (08854-4153)
PHONE..............................732 981-0149
Jean Bryant, *CEO*
Qunhua Xu, *Research*
EMP: 7
SALES (corp-wide): 225.3B **Publicly Held**
SIC: 2899 Chemical preparations
HQ: The Lubrizol Corporation
29400 Lakeland Blvd
Wickliffe OH 44092
440 943-4200

(G-8685)
MACHINE ATOMATED CTRL TECH LLC
1308 Centennial Ave # 109 (08854-4324)
PHONE..............................732 921-8935
Carl Macalalad,
EMP: 4
SALES: 250K **Privately Held**
SIC: 7373 7372 Computer-aided engineering (CAE) systems service; business oriented computer software

(G-8686)
MARK ALAN PRINTING & GRAPHICS
Also Called: Sir Speedy
1032 Stelton Rd Ste 2 (08854-4333)
PHONE..............................732 981-9011
Mark Yanofsky, *President*
EMP: 4
SQ FT: 1,250
SALES (est): 584.8K **Privately Held**
SIC: 2752 Commercial printing, lithographic

(G-8687)
MARLABS INCORPORATED (PA)
1 Corporate Pl S Fl 3 (08854-6116)
PHONE..............................732 694-1000
Siby Vadakekkara, *CEO*
EMP: 55
SQ FT: 75,000
SALES (est): 104.4MM **Privately Held**
WEB: www.marlabs.com
SIC: 7372 Prepackaged software

(G-8688)
MARTEC ACCESS PRODUCTS INC
60 Kingsbridge Rd (08854-3919)
PHONE..............................908 233-0101
Charles B Engelstein, *President*
Isobel Wayrick, *Vice Pres*
Patty Cardinali, *Purchasing*
Adrian Gomez, *Design Engr*
Fred Knopp, *Treasurer*
▲ **EMP:** 60
SQ FT: 17,000
SALES (est): 1.2MM
SALES (corp-wide): 11.6MM **Privately Held**
WEB: www.martecaccess.com
SIC: 3663 Transmitter-receivers, radio

PA: Mars International, Inc.
60 Kingsbridge Rd
Piscataway NJ 08854
908 233-0044

(G-8689)
MEDISON PHARMACEUTICALS INC
201 Circle Dr N Ste 101 (08854-3723)
PHONE..............................856 304-8516
Vinay Patel, *CEO*
EMP: 12
SALES (est): 438.8K **Privately Held**
SIC: 2023 5149 Dietary supplements, dairy & non-dairy based; health foods

(G-8690)
MICHAEL ANTHONY SIGN DSIGN INC
Also Called: Michael Anthony Sign & Awng Co
250 Stelton Rd Ste 1 (08854-3285)
PHONE..............................732 453-6120
Michael Bradley, *President*
EMP: 25
SQ FT: 44,000
SALES (est): 3.8MM **Privately Held**
WEB: www.masign.com
SIC: 3993 3444 3446 Electric signs; awnings & canopies; architectural metalwork

(G-8691)
MILLSON PRECISION MACHINING
145 11th St (08854-1954)
PHONE..............................732 424-1700
Bryan Miller Sr, *President*
Bryan Miller Jr, *Vice Pres*
EMP: 6
SQ FT: 3,600
SALES (est): 500K **Privately Held**
WEB: www.mastercamedu.com
SIC: 3599 Machine shop, jobbing & repair

(G-8692)
MONTROSE MOLDERS CORPORATION
25 Howard St (08854-1435)
PHONE..............................908 754-3030
William Wilson, *Principal*
EMP: 31
SALES (est): 6.9MM **Privately Held**
SIC: 3089 Injection molding of plastics

(G-8693)
MSN PHARMACEUTICALS INC
20 Duke Rd (08854-3714)
PHONE..............................732 356-9900
Bharat Chintapathy, *President*
Linda Herzog, *Manager*
Steven Beagle, *Admin Sec*
▲ **EMP:** 6
SQ FT: 1,679
SALES (est): 962K **Privately Held**
SIC: 2834 Druggists' preparations (pharmaceuticals)
PA: Msn Laboratories Private Limited
Msn House, Plot No. C-24 ,Sanath Nagar ,Industrial Estate,
Hyderabad TS 50001

(G-8694)
NETWORK TYPESETTING INC
1637 Stelton Rd Ste B4 (08854-5961)
PHONE..............................732 819-0949
Marty Perzan, *President*
EMP: 4
SALES (est): 220K **Privately Held**
SIC: 2791 Typesetting

(G-8695)
NEWARK MORNING LEDGER CO
Also Called: Star Ledger
20 Duke Rd (08854-3714)
PHONE..............................732 560-1560
Joe Maker, *Manager*
EMP: 200
SALES (corp-wide): 217.5MM **Privately Held**
SIC: 2711 Newspapers, publishing & printing

▲ = Import ▼=Export
◆ =Import/Export

PA: Newark Morning Ledger Co.
1 Gateway Ctr Ste 1100
Newark NJ 07102
973 392-4141

(G-8696)
NGENIOUS SOLUTIONS INC
30 Knightsbridge Rd # 525 (08854-3948)
PHONE..............................732 873-3385
Nilesh Mehta, *CEO*
EMP: 7 **EST:** 2005
SQ FT: 100
SALES (est): 230.5K **Privately Held**
SIC: 7371 7372 Computer software development & applications; computer software systems analysis & design, custom; computer software development; software programming applications; application computer software

(G-8697)
PARKWAY PLASTICS INC
561 Stelton Rd (08854-3868)
PHONE..............................800 881-4996
Ed Rowan, *CEO*
Edward W Rowan III, *President*
Kirstin Rowan Kelly, *Treasurer*
Linda T Falzone, *Marketing Staff*
Kirstin Rowan, *Marketing Staff*
▼ **EMP:** 49 **EST:** 1954
SQ FT: 30,000
SALES: 6.2MM **Privately Held**
WEB: www.parkwayjars.com
SIC: 3089 Jars, plastic

(G-8698)
PEPSI-COLA METRO BTLG CO INC
Also Called: Pepsico
2200 New Brunswick Ave (08854-2746)
PHONE..............................732 424-3000
Christopher Brehm, *Sales Staff*
William Warren, *Marketing Staff*
Lou Allegretto, *Manager*
Todd Zayatz, *Admin Sec*
EMP: 400
SALES (corp-wide): 64.6B **Publicly Held**
WEB: www.pbg.com
SIC: 2086 Carbonated soft drinks, bottled & canned
HQ: Pepsi-Cola Metropolitan Bottling Company, Inc.
1111 Westchester Ave
White Plains NY 10604
914 767-6000

(G-8699)
PESTKA BIOMEDICAL LABS INC
Also Called: PBL Biomedical Laboratories
131 Ethel Rd W Ste 6 (08854-5900)
PHONE..............................732 777-9123
Robert Pestka, *CEO*
Bill Clark, *Vice Pres*
EMP: 40
SQ FT: 15,000
SALES (est): 6.7MM **Privately Held**
WEB: www.interferonsource.com
SIC: 8731 2836 2834 Biotechnical research, commercial; biological products, except diagnostic; pharmaceutical preparations

(G-8700)
PHARMASOURCE INTERNATIONAL LLC
1090 Stelton Rd (08854-5201)
PHONE..............................732 985-6182
EMP: 6
SALES (est): 510K **Privately Held**
SIC: 2834 3841 Mfg Pharmaceutical Preparations Mfg Surgical/Medical Instruments

(G-8701)
PREMIERE RACEWAY SYS LLC
230 Saint Nicholas Ave (08854)
PHONE..............................732 629-7715
William Wilson, *CEO*
Michael Sweeney, *COO*
Susan Linder,
James Williams,
EMP: 5
SALES (est): 410K **Privately Held**
SIC: 3089 Plastic hardware & building products

(G-8702)
PROSPECT GROUP LLC
Also Called: Yes Pac
260 Centennial Ave (08854-2947)
PHONE..............................718 635-4007
Eli Weinfeld,
EMP: 12 **EST:** 2005
SALES (est): 1.3MM **Privately Held**
SIC: 2656 Cups, paper: made from purchased material

(G-8703)
QUALITY SHEET METAL & WLDG INC
23 Clawson St (08854-2116)
PHONE..............................732 469-7111
Raymond Kavanagh, *President*
Ed Eager, *Vice Pres*
EMP: 16 **EST:** 1997
SQ FT: 8,600
SALES (est): 3.9MM **Privately Held**
SIC: 3444 Sheet metal specialties, not stamped

(G-8704)
RED DASH MEDIA LLC
Also Called: Meal Quik
30 Knightsbridge Rd # 525 (08854-3948)
PHONE..............................732 579-2396
Abhinav Chadha,
EMP: 5
SALES: 100K **Privately Held**
SIC: 7372 Application computer software

(G-8705)
RESEARCH & EDUCATION ASSN
61 Ethel Rd W (08854-5969)
PHONE..............................732 819-8880
Carl M Fuchs, *President*
Everett Scherrer, *President*
John Cording, *Vice Pres*
Yvette Fuchs, *Vice Pres*
Larry Kling, *Vice Pres*
EMP: 30
SQ FT: 40,000
SALES (est): 2.6MM
SALES (corp-wide): 3.8B **Publicly Held**
WEB: www.rea.com
SIC: 2731 Book publishing
HQ: Courier Communications Llc
15 Wellman Ave
North Chelmsford MA 01863
978 251-6000

(G-8706)
ROBERTET FLAVORS INC
Also Called: Robertet Flavors & Fragrances
10 Colonial Dr (08854-4114)
PHONE..............................732 271-1804
Bob Murphy, *Manager*
EMP: 10
SALES (corp-wide): 281.4MM **Privately Held**
SIC: 2087 2023 Powders, flavoring (except drink); dry, condensed, evaporated dairy products
HQ: Robertet Flavors, Inc.
10 Colonial Dr
Piscataway NJ 08854
732 981-8300

(G-8707)
SATURN BEAUTY GROUP LLC
140 Ethel Rd W Ste G (08854-5951)
P.O. Box 683, Edison (08818-0683)
PHONE..............................908 561-5000
Ravi Verg, *CEO*
Mira Verg, *Mng Member*
EMP: 4
SQ FT: 3,500
SALES: 12MM **Privately Held**
SIC: 2844 Toilet preparations

(G-8708)
SAVORX FLAVORS LLC
120 New England Ave (08854-4127)
PHONE..............................908 265-3033
Belayet Choudhury, *President*
EMP: 4
SALES (est): 150.3K **Privately Held**
SIC: 2087 Beverage bases, concentrates, syrups, powders & mixes

(G-8709)
SCALABLE SYSTEMS INC
15 Corporate Pl S Ste 222 (08854-6107)
PHONE..............................732 993-4320
Sam Biswal, *President*
Jack Francis, *Vice Pres*
Suman Bajaj, *Manager*
Suman Biswal, *Manager*
Anindya Jena, *Analyst*
EMP: 30
SALES (est): 3.4MM **Privately Held**
WEB: www.scalable-systems.com
SIC: 7372 8748 Application computer software; systems analysis & engineering consulting services

(G-8710)
SCOTTLINE LLC
15 Corporate Pl S Ste 402 (08854-6115)
PHONE..............................732 534-3123
Jyothi Kakumanu,
EMP: 20
SQ FT: 2,200
SALES (est): 1.4MM **Privately Held**
SIC: 7371 7361 7372 Computer software development; placement agencies; executive placement; business oriented computer software

(G-8711)
SHASUN USA INC
15 Corporate Pl S Ste 222 (08854-6107)
PHONE..............................732 465-0700
Abhaya Kumar Shankarlal, *CEO*
N Govindarajan, *CEO*
Jitesh Devendra, *President*
Michel Spagnol, *President*
▲ **EMP:** 13
SALES (est): 2.2MM **Privately Held**
WEB: www.shasun.com
SIC: 2834 Pharmaceutical preparations

(G-8712)
SIVANTOS INC (DH)
10 Constitution Ave (08854-6145)
PHONE..............................732 562-6600
Eric Timm, *CEO*
Brian Kinnerk, *CEO*
Annemarie Brennan, *Vice Pres*
Marie Hepola, *Vice Pres*
Thomas Hies, *Vice Pres*
▲ **EMP:** 357
SQ FT: 83,000
SALES (est): 268.7MM
SALES (corp-wide): 177.9K **Privately Held**
WEB: www.siemens-hearing.com
SIC: 3842 Orthopedic appliances
HQ: Sivantos Pte. Ltd.
18 Tai Seng Street
Singapore 53977
637 096-66

(G-8713)
SNACK INNOVATIONS INC (PA)
Also Called: Gourmet Basics
41 Ethel Rd W (08854-5969)
PHONE..............................718 509-9366
Allen Benz, *CEO*
Jack Benz, *Vice Pres*
▲ **EMP:** 20
SQ FT: 30,000
SALES (est): 4.6MM **Privately Held**
SIC: 2096 Potato chips & similar snacks

(G-8714)
SOLIDIA TECHNOLOGIES INC
11 Colonial Dr (08854-4113)
PHONE..............................908 315-5901
Thomas Schuler, *CEO*
Bo Boylan, *Vice Pres*
Dhamo Srinivasan, *Vice Pres*
Stephen Blackman, *Engineer*
Doug Robinson, *CFO*
▲ **EMP:** 29
SALES (est): 11.1MM **Privately Held**
SIC: 3531 Construction machinery

(G-8715)
SOZIO INC
Also Called: Je Sozio
51 Ethel Rd W (08854-5969)
PHONE..............................732 572-5600
Arnaud Moor, *President*
Melanie Ritter, *Purch Mgr*
Annette Peixoto, *Controller*
Geri Roman, *Marketing Mgr*
Michael Nina, *Marketing Staff*
◆ **EMP:** 60
SQ FT: 20,000
SALES (est): 14.8MM
SALES (corp-wide): 183.7K **Privately Held**
WEB: www.jesozio.com
SIC: 2844 Cosmetic preparations
HQ: Sozio J Et E -Descollonges
6 Rue Barbes
Levallois-Perret 92300
181 930-072

(G-8716)
SPECTRUM PLASTICS
250 Circle Dr N (08854-3705)
PHONE..............................732 564-1899
Ben Tran, *Owner*
Peter Hii, *CFO*
Gordon Lundene, *Credit Mgr*
Vera Lin, *Financial Analy*
Candace Verstuyft, *Marketing Staff*
EMP: 5
SALES (est): 881.7K **Privately Held**
SIC: 2673 Plastic bags: made from purchased materials

(G-8717)
SPEM CORPORATION
403 Bell St (08854-2349)
PHONE..............................732 356-3366
Satish Patel, *President*
John Seto, *Vice Pres*
Paul Ruggierio, *Admin Sec*
EMP: 23
SQ FT: 17,500
SALES (est): 1.7MM **Privately Held**
SIC: 3672 3679 3931 Printed circuit boards; harness assemblies for electronic use: wire or cable; synthesizers, music

(G-8718)
STAR CREATIONS INC (PA)
Also Called: Sumangel Jewellers
1506 Stelton Rd (08854-5915)
PHONE..............................212 221-3570
Kavita Khandelwal, *President*
Rekha Kenoongo, *Vice Pres*
EMP: 2
SQ FT: 2,500
SALES (est): 10MM **Privately Held**
WEB: www.starcreation.com
SIC: 1499 Gemstone & industrial diamond mining

(G-8719)
STARK PHARMA TECHNOLOGY INC
15 Corporate Pl S Ste 350 (08854-6112)
PHONE..............................848 217-4059
Latha Sudhir, *Exec Dir*
EMP: 11
SALES (est): 232.7K **Privately Held**
SIC: 7379 2834 Computer related services; pharmaceutical preparations

(G-8720)
STRATO INC
100 New England Ave Ste 1 (08854-4144)
PHONE..............................732 981-1515
Michael J Foxx, *CEO*
Steven Foxx, *Corp Secy*
Brian Cunkelman, *Vice Pres*
Dom Nuzzo, *Purch Mgr*
Michael Corridon, *CFO*
▲ **EMP:** 100
SQ FT: 100,000
SALES (est): 40.2MM **Privately Held**
WEB: www.stratoinc.com
SIC: 3743 Railroad equipment

(G-8721)
SWAPSHUB COMPANY INC
15 Corporate Pl S Ste 130 (08854-6117)
PHONE..............................732 529-4813
Mani Pillai, *President*
Jamal Mohamed, *Info Tech Mgr*
EMP: 6
SALES (est): 273.3K **Privately Held**
SIC: 7372 Business oriented computer software

(G-8722)
T & P MACHINE SHOP INC
600 Prospect Ave Ste E (08854-1414)
PHONE....................................732 424-9141
Tony Pasquale, *President*
EMP: 5
SALES (est): 550K **Privately Held**
SIC: 3599 Machine shop, jobbing & repair

(G-8723)
TECOGEN INC
417 Bell St (08854-2349)
PHONE....................................732 356-5601
EMP: 36
SALES (corp-wide): 35.8MM **Publicly Held**
SIC: 3585 Air conditioning units, complete: domestic or industrial
PA: Tecogen Inc.
　　45 1st Ave
　　Waltham MA 02451
　　781 622-1120

(G-8724)
TEKLTD (PA)
95 Mitchell Ave (08854-5556)
PHONE....................................732 463-2100
John C Lee, *President*
EMP: 8
SALES: 4MM **Privately Held**
WEB: www.tekltd.com
SIC: 3714 Motor vehicle parts & accessories

(G-8725)
THALES AVIONICS INC (HQ)
140 Centennial Ave (08854-3908)
PHONE....................................732 242-6300
Alan Pellegrini, *President*
Shyam Kumar, *General Mgr*
Ludovic Chouasne, *Finance Dir*
▲ EMP: 168 EST: 1977
SQ FT: 61,000
SALES (est): 83.1MM
SALES (corp-wide): 262.1MM **Privately Held**
SIC: 7699 3728 8711 Aircraft & heavy equipment repair services; aircraft parts & equipment; aviation &/or aeronautical engineering
PA: Thales
　　Tour Carpe Diem Esplanade Nord
　　Courbevoie 92400
　　157 778-000

(G-8726)
THERAPEUTIC PROTEINS INC
20 New England Ave (08854-4101)
PHONE....................................312 620-1500
Peter F Moesta, *CEO*
Zafeer Ahmad, *CEO*
Thomas L Flynn III, *President*
Sarfaraz K Niazi PHD, *Chairman*
Michael W Washabaugh, *Security Dir*
▲ EMP: 19
SALES (est): 6.8MM **Privately Held**
WEB: www.theraproteins.com
SIC: 2834 Pharmaceutical preparations

(G-8727)
TINGLEY RUBBER CORPORATION (PA)
1551 S Washington Ave # 403 (08854-6700)
PHONE....................................800 631-5498
William McCollum, *CEO*
Michael S Zedalis, *President*
Roger Brewer, *CFO*
John Alfano, *Sales Staff*
Michael Bender, *Sales Staff*
▲ EMP: 32 EST: 1929
SQ FT: 17,000
SALES (est): 9.7MM **Privately Held**
WEB: www.tingleyrubber.com
SIC: 3021 3069 Protective footwear, rubber or plastic; rubber coated fabrics & clothing

(G-8728)
TMG ENTERPRISES INC (PA)
200 Circle Dr N (08854-3705)
PHONE....................................732 469-2900
Dermot Murphy, *CEO*
Charles Zammit, *Vice Pres*
Letty Murphy, *Admin Sec*
EMP: 30

SQ FT: 11,300
SALES (est): 24.7MM **Privately Held**
WEB: www.tmg4mail.com
SIC: 7331 8744 2752 Mailing service; facilities support services; commercial printing, offset

(G-8729)
TOLLGRADE COMMUNICATIONS INC
30 Knightsbridge Rd # 602 (08854-3948)
PHONE....................................732 743-6720
EMP: 5
SALES (corp-wide): 264.8MM **Privately Held**
SIC: 3661 Telephone central office equipment, dial or manual
HQ: Tollgrade Communications, Inc.
　　260 Executive Dr Ste 150
　　Cranberry Township PA 16066
　　724 720-1400

(G-8730)
TRANE INC (DH)
1 Centennial Ave Ste 101 (08854-3921)
P.O. Box 6820 (08855-6820)
PHONE....................................732 652-7100
Michael W Lamach, *CEO*
Robert Hann, *District Mgr*
Michael Girard, *Area Mgr*
Willis Lovejoy, *Area Mgr*
Timothy McGinley, *Area Mgr*
▲ EMP: 277
SALES (est): 8.9B **Privately Held**
WEB: www.trane.com
SIC: 3585 Refrigeration & heating equipment

(G-8731)
TRANE US INC
1 Centennial Ave Ste 101 (08854-3921)
PHONE....................................732 652-7100
Christopher Coperchio, *Principal*
Clifford L Tomei, *Principal*
EMP: 140 **Privately Held**
SIC: 3585 Refrigeration & heating equipment
HQ: Trane U.S. Inc.
　　3600 Pammel Creek Rd
　　La Crosse WI 54601
　　608 787-2000

(G-8732)
TRANSACTION PUBLISHERS INC (PA)
Also Called: Society Trnsaction Periodicals
10 Corporate Pl S Ste 102 (08854-6148)
PHONE....................................732 445-2280
Mary Curtis, *President*
Scott Bramson, *President*
Frank Novak, *Vice Pres*
Michael Celletto, *Accounts Mgr*
Nancy Conine, *Cust Mgr*
◆ EMP: 42 EST: 1963
SQ FT: 5,000
SALES (est): 3.3MM **Privately Held**
WEB: www.transactionpub.com
SIC: 2721 2731 Periodicals: publishing only; book publishing

(G-8733)
TURQUOISE CHEMISTRY INC
537 New Durham Rd (08854-5314)
PHONE....................................908 561-0002
Teoman Mutlu, *President*
▲ EMP: 10
SALES (est): 1.3MM **Privately Held**
SIC: 2851 Removers & cleaners

(G-8734)
VALUEMOMENTUM INC (HQ)
220 Old New Brunswick Rd # 100 (08854-3757)
PHONE....................................908 755-0025
Kalyan Kodali, *CEO*
Gopimaniraju Samanthapudi, *Chairman*
Swarup Ghosh, *COO*
Rajesh Desingu, *Vice Pres*
Dinesh Banjan, *Engineer*
EMP: 60
SQ FT: 20,000

SALES (est): 76.5MM **Privately Held**
WEB: www.valuemomentum.com
SIC: 7373 7371 7372 Systems software development services; computer software development & applications; business oriented computer software

(G-8735)
VASCULOGIC LLC
37 E Burgess Dr (08854-6658)
PHONE....................................908 278-3573
Tim Maguire,
EMP: 5
SALES (est): 360K **Privately Held**
SIC: 3845 Electromedical equipment

(G-8736)
VASWANI INC
201 Circle Dr N Ste 114 (08854-3723)
PHONE....................................732 377-9794
Ishwar Vaswani, *Branch Mgr*
EMP: 10
SALES (corp-wide): 27MM **Privately Held**
WEB: www.vaswani.com
SIC: 2521 5021 Chairs, office: padded, upholstered or plain: wood; office & public building furniture
PA: Vaswani, Inc.
　　75 Carter Dr Ste 1
　　Edison NJ 08817
　　877 376-4425

(G-8737)
VIRA INSIGHT LLC
100 Ethel Rd W (08854-5967)
PHONE....................................732 442-6756
Jeff Jones, *CEO*
Chris Romano, *VP Bus Dvlpt*
EMP: 117
SQ FT: 50,000
SALES (corp-wide): 50.1MM **Privately Held**
SIC: 2542 Office & store showcases & display fixtures
PA: Vira Insight, Llc
　　120 Dividend Dr Ste 100
　　Coppell TX 75019
　　800 366-2345

(G-8738)
WILLIAM KENYON & SONS INC (HQ)
90 Ethel Rd W (08854-5929)
PHONE....................................732 985-8980
Christopher C Kenyon, *Ch of Bd*
William D Clark, *President*
Mike Wheaton, *COO*
Michael Wheaton, *Vice Pres*
Diane Sibilia, *Sales Staff*
▼ EMP: 20 EST: 1937
SQ FT: 42,000
SALES (est): 2.7MM
SALES (corp-wide): 18MM **Privately Held**
WEB: www.william-kenyon.com
SIC: 3599 2298 3829 3674 Custom machinery; rope, except asbestos & wire; measuring & controlling devices; semiconductors & related devices; miscellaneous fabricated wire products; chemical preparations
PA: William Kenyon & Sons Limited
　　Chapel Field Works
　　Hyde SK14
　　161 308-6030

(G-8739)
YC CABLE (EAST) INC
240 Circle Dr N (08854-3705)
PHONE....................................732 868-0800
Kai Cheng Hsu, *President*
Jean Shao, *General Mgr*
James Hsu, *Exec VP*
George Tellier, *Engineer*
Bruce Wilson, *Sales Staff*
▲ EMP: 20
SQ FT: 15,000
SALES (est): 6.4MM **Privately Held**
WEB: www.yceast.com
SIC: 3679 5065 5063 Harness assemblies for electronic use: wire or cable; electronic parts & equipment; electrical apparatus & equipment

(G-8740)
ZIEGLER CHEM & MINERAL CORP (PA)
600 Prospect Ave Ste A (08854-1414)
PHONE....................................732 752-4111
Gordon S Ziegler Jr, *Ch of Bd*
James Febo, *Vice Pres*
William Hyland, *Vice Pres*
Gordon S Ziegler III, *CFO*
Michael Hyland, *Controller*
▼ EMP: 14 EST: 1962
SQ FT: 3,000
SALES (est): 20.5MM **Privately Held**
WEB: www.zieglerchemical.com
SIC: 2911 1499 Asphalt or asphaltic materials, made in refineries; gilsonite mining

(G-8741)
ZIEGLER CHEM & MINERAL CORP
Also Called: Allied Asphalt Division
600 Prospect Ave Ste 1 (08854-1414)
PHONE....................................732 752-4111
Paul Gordman, *Plant Mgr*
Jim Febo, *Sales Executive*
Paul Gorman, *Branch Mgr*
EMP: 30
SALES (corp-wide): 20.5MM **Privately Held**
WEB: www.zieglerchemical.com
SIC: 1499 2951 Asphalt (native) mining; gilsonite mining; asphalt paving mixtures & blocks
PA: Ziegler Chemical & Mineral Corp.
　　600 Prospect Ave Ste A
　　Piscataway NJ 08854
　　732 752-4111

(G-8742)
ZXCHEM USA INC
255 Old New Brunswick Rd (08854-3734)
PHONE....................................732 529-6352
Zhiwei Zheng, *President*
Wade Zheng, *Vice Pres*
▲ EMP: 7
SALES (est): 773.6K
SALES (corp-wide): 29.3MM **Privately Held**
SIC: 5169 2099 Food additives & preservatives; food preparations
PA: Hainan Zhongxin Chemical Co.,Ltd
　　12c, Baifang Mansion, No.105 Binhai Avenue
　　Haikou 57010
　　898 685-4031

┌─────────────────────────┐
│　　　　**Pitman**　　　　│
│　　*Gloucester County*　　│
└─────────────────────────┘

(G-8743)
COMET TOOL COMPANY INC
651 Lambs Rd (08071-2042)
PHONE....................................856 256-1070
Frank L Maatje, *President*
Griff Noon, *Vice Pres*
EMP: 78 EST: 1973
SQ FT: 73,000
SALES (est): 26.7MM **Privately Held**
WEB: www.comet-tool.com
SIC: 3089 Injection molding of plastics

(G-8744)
CROSS MEDICAL SPECIALTIES INC
450 Andbro Dr Unit 7 (08071-1274)
PHONE....................................856 589-3288
EMP: 15
SQ FT: 1,200
SALES (est): 1.4MM **Privately Held**
SIC: 7699 3841 Repair Services Mfg Surgical/Medical Instruments

(G-8745)
INOX COMPONENTS
And 553 Rr 55 (08071)
PHONE....................................856 256-0800
Michael Duffy, *President*
EMP: 10
SQ FT: 10,000
SALES (est): 1.1MM **Privately Held**
SIC: 3444 Sheet metalwork

(G-8746)
KANE WOOD FUEL
512 Cedar Ave (08071-1815)
PHONE..............................856 589-3292
Frank Kane, *Owner*
Marguerite Kane, *Co-Owner*
EMP: 4
SALES (est): 520.8K **Privately Held**
SIC: 2411 5099 Logging; firewood

(G-8747)
REVIEW PRINTING INC
53 E Holly Ave 55 (08071-1198)
PHONE..............................856 589-7200
Douglas K Peterson, *President*
Carol Peterson, *Admin Sec*
EMP: 5 **EST:** 1898
SQ FT: 5,200
SALES (est): 380K **Privately Held**
SIC: 2752 Commercial printing, offset

(G-8748)
SALMON SIGNS
478 W Holly Ave (08071-1302)
PHONE..............................856 589-5600
Richard Salmon, *Owner*
EMP: 7 **EST:** 1960
SQ FT: 15,000
SALES: 488K **Privately Held**
WEB: www.richardsalmon.com
SIC: 7389 3993 Sign painting & lettering
shop; signs & advertising specialties

(G-8749)
SHERIDAN OPTICAL CO INC
Also Called: Sheridan Optical Lab
108 Clinton Ave (08071-1209)
P.O. Box 8 (08071-0008)
PHONE..............................856 582-0963
Edward F Sheridan, *President*
EMP: 21 **EST:** 1978
SQ FT: 2,000
SALES (est): 2.8MM **Privately Held**
SIC: 3851 Ophthalmic goods

Pittsgrove
Salem County

(G-8750)
PHOENIX GLASS LLC
615 Alvine Rd (08318-4128)
PHONE..............................856 692-0100
Charles R Everham, *Owner*
◆ **EMP:** 47
SALES (est): 7MM **Privately Held**
SIC: 5231 2396 Glass; automotive & ap-
parel trimmings

Pittstown
Hunterdon County

(G-8751)
AJG PACKAGING LLC
10 Northwood Dr (08867-5130)
PHONE..............................908 528-6052
Matthew Grimaldi, *Mng Member*
EMP: 5 **EST:** 2011
SALES: 3.2MM **Privately Held**
SIC: 3565 5084 7389 Bottling machinery:
filling, capping, labeling; packaging ma-
chinery & equipment;

(G-8752)
BENEDUCE VINEYARD
1 Jeremiah Ln (08867-5168)
PHONE..............................908 996-3823
Mike Beneduce Jr, *Principal*
Jen Pollard, *Manager*
EMP: 4 **EST:** 2011
SALES (est): 332.6K **Privately Held**
SIC: 2084 Wines

(G-8753)
**JANSSEN PHARMACEUTICALS
INC**
Km 0 Hm 5 Rr 362 (08867)
PHONE..............................908 735-4844
Thomas Varga, *Manager*
EMP: 7

SALES (corp-wide): 81.5B **Publicly Held**
WEB: www.ortho-mcneil.com
SIC: 2833 Medicinals & botanicals
HQ: Janssen Pharmaceuticals, Inc.
1125 Trnton Harbourton Rd
Titusville NJ 08560
609 730-2000

(G-8754)
MT SALEM ELECTRIC CO INC
79 Mount Salem Rd (08867-5137)
PHONE..............................908 735-6126
Frank J Hahola Jr, *President*
Linda A Hahola, *Vice Pres*
EMP: 10
SALES (est): 1.7MM **Privately Held**
SIC: 1731 5999 7694 General electrical
contractor; motors, electric; electric motor
repair

(G-8755)
SMITTYS DOOR SERVICE INC
170 Oak Grove Rd (08867-4006)
PHONE..............................908 284-0506
Tim Smith, *President*
Gwen Smith, *Admin Sec*
EMP: 8
SQ FT: 3,000
SALES (est): 1.5MM **Privately Held**
SIC: 2431 Doors, wood

Plainfield
Union County

(G-8756)
**A N LAGGREN AWNGS CANVAS
MFG**
Also Called: Mark I Interiors
1414 South Ave (07062-1941)
PHONE..............................908 756-1948
EMP: 15
SQ FT: 6,000
SALES (est): 1.9MM **Privately Held**
SIC: 2591 Mfg Awnings Draperies Window
Blinds And Shades

(G-8757)
**AMERICAN CODING AND MKG
INK CO**
1220 North Ave (07062-1796)
PHONE..............................908 756-0373
Thomas Sweet, *President*
Jamie Pedinoff, *Admin Sec*
EMP: 7
SQ FT: 5,000
SALES: 980K **Privately Held**
WEB: www.americancoding.com
SIC: 2893 Printing ink

(G-8758)
**ARCHITECTURAL IRON
DESIGNS**
Also Called: Duragates
950 S 2nd St (07063-1302)
PHONE..............................908 757-2323
Jayesh Shah, *President*
Allan R Papp, *Chairman*
Joseph Alves, *Sales Mgr*
▲ **EMP:** 6
SQ FT: 7,000
SALES (est): 1.3MM **Privately Held**
WEB: www.archirondesign.com
SIC: 3446 Architectural metalwork

(G-8759)
**ARROW PAPER COMPANY INC
(PA)**
633 North Ave (07060-1418)
P.O. Box 147, Millburn (07041-0147)
PHONE..............................908 756-1111
Jay Gutkin, *President*
Evelyn Gutkin, *Corp Secy*
Daniel Gutkin, *Vice Pres*
EMP: 9
SQ FT: 150,000
SALES (est): 702.6K **Privately Held**
SIC: 2679 5112 Paper products, con-
verted; stationery & office supplies

(G-8760)
**CAPITAL CONTRACTING &
DESIGN (PA)**
640 North Ave (07060-1419)
P.O. Box 1333 (07061-1333)
PHONE..............................908 561-8411
Donald W Finley, *President*
Mark McQuillan, *Vice Pres*
Michele Reese, *Office Mgr*
EMP: 26
SQ FT: 60,000
SALES: 3MM **Privately Held**
WEB: www.captlfix.com
SIC: 2541 2542 Display fixtures, wood; fix-
tures: display, office or store: except wood

(G-8761)
**DEK TRON INTERNATIONAL
CORP**
244 E 3rd St (07060-1848)
PHONE..............................908 226-1777
Salvador Diespensiera, *President*
Hector Vargas, *Principal*
EMP: 25
SQ FT: 12,000
SALES (est): 3.2MM **Privately Held**
WEB: www.dektroncorp.com
SIC: 3821 Laboratory measuring appara-
tus

(G-8762)
DUCTWORKS INC
434 W Front St (07060-1122)
P.O. Box 7031, Watchung (07069-0799)
PHONE..............................908 754-8190
Dianne Rocco, *Manager*
EMP: 12
SALES (est): 1.3MM **Privately Held**
SIC: 3444 Metal ventilating equipment

(G-8763)
EDWARD P PAUL & CO INC (PA)
525 South Ave (07060-1998)
PHONE..............................908 757-4212
Arthur Arditti, *Ch of Bd*
Andrew Arditi, *President*
EMP: 7
SQ FT: 100,000
SALES (est): 559K **Privately Held**
SIC: 2512 5023 Upholstered household
furniture; lamps: floor, boudoir, desk

(G-8764)
EDWIN LEONEL RAMIREZ
Also Called: Pin Express
918 Putnam Ave (07060-1842)
PHONE..............................732 648-5587
Edwin L Ramirez, *Principal*
EMP: 4
SALES (est): 251.9K **Privately Held**
SIC: 3452 Pins

(G-8765)
**F & C PROF ALUM RAILINGS
CORP**
1149 W Front St (07063-1130)
PHONE..............................908 753-8886
Segundo A Flores, *President*
Segundo B Flores, *Vice Pres*
EMP: 25
SALES (est): 5.9MM **Privately Held**
SIC: 3446 Architectural metalwork

(G-8766)
FLECK KNITWEAR CO INC
400 Leland Ave (07062-1606)
PHONE..............................908 754-8888
Peter Fleck, *President*
Heinz Fleck, *President*
Ursula Fleck, *Corp Secy*
EMP: 25
SQ FT: 30,000
SALES: 1MM **Privately Held**
SIC: 2253 Sweaters & sweater coats, knit;
collar & cuff sets, knit

(G-8767)
H & S FUEL INC
1100 South Ave (07062-1918)
PHONE..............................908 769-1362
EMP: 5 **EST:** 2009
SALES (est): 233.5K **Privately Held**
SIC: 2869 Mfg Industrial Organic Chemi-
cals

(G-8768)
HARSCO CORPORATION
709 Loretta Ter (07062-2104)
PHONE..............................908 454-7169
Jim Cook, *Branch Mgr*
EMP: 40
SQ FT: 500
SALES (corp-wide): 1.7B **Publicly Held**
WEB: www.ikgindustries.com
SIC: 5051 3446 Steel; architectural metal-
work
PA: Harsco Corporation
350 Poplar Church Rd
Camp Hill PA 17011
717 763-7064

(G-8769)
INJECTRON CORPORATION
Also Called: Detailed Designs
1000 S 2nd St (07063-1306)
P.O. Box 3012 (07063-0012)
PHONE..............................908 753-1990
Lou Pollak, *President*
Vincent Robinson, *COO*
Marvin Kaplan, *Vice Pres*
Larry Kettner, *Info Tech Dir*
Tony Cirello, *Technical Staff*
▲ **EMP:** 300 **EST:** 1959
SQ FT: 300,000
SALES (est): 56.4MM **Privately Held**
SIC: 3089 Injection molding of plastics

(G-8770)
LOB-STER INC
Also Called: Lobster Sports
1118 North Ave (07062-1633)
PHONE..............................818 764-6000
Leilani Makuakane, *Manager*
EMP: 5
SALES (est): 267.6K
SALES (corp-wide): 1.6MM **Privately
Held**
WEB: www.lobstersports.com
SIC: 3949 Tennis equipment & supplies
PA: Lob-Ster, Inc.
7340 Fulton Ave
North Hollywood CA 91605
818 764-6000

(G-8771)
NEUMANN SHEET METAL INC
759 North Ave (07062-1616)
PHONE..............................908 756-0415
William J McLean, *President*
Lora McLean, *Admin Sec*
EMP: 6
SQ FT: 5,200
SALES (est): 1.1MM **Privately Held**
SIC: 3444 Sheet metal specialties, not
stamped

(G-8772)
NEW INDUSTRIAL FOAM CORP
1355 W Front St Ste 3 (07063-1151)
P.O. Box 3120 (07063-0120)
PHONE..............................908 561-4010
Michael Weisman, *President*
Russell Kussner, *General Mgr*
Robert Weisman, *Corp Secy*
Bruce Klein, *Director*
EMP: 7 **EST:** 1960
SQ FT: 50,000
SALES (est): 980K **Privately Held**
SIC: 3086 Packaging & shipping materials,
foamed plastic

(G-8773)
NEW JERSEY HARDWOODS INC
1340 W Front St (07063-1127)
PHONE..............................908 754-0990
Ollie Herttua, *President*
Paula Herttua, *General Mgr*
EMP: 30 **EST:** 1981
SQ FT: 26,000
SALES (est): 5.6MM **Privately Held**
SIC: 5211 2431 Millwork & lumber; mill-
work

(G-8774)
O K TOOL CORPORATION
1233 North Ave (07062-1724)
PHONE..............................908 561-9920
Eric Kiesel, *President*
Theresa Kiesel, *Corp Secy*
Glen Kiesel, *Vice Pres*
▲ **EMP:** 5

SQ FT: 4,000
SALES (est): 410K **Privately Held**
WEB: www.glenmartech.com
SIC: 3599 Machine shop, jobbing & repair

(G-8775)
PAPP IRON WORKS INC
950 S 2nd St (07063-1302)
P.O. Box 3149 (07063-0149)
PHONE...908 731-1000
Allan Papp, *President*
Thomas Hale, *Project Mgr*
Jack Seltzer, *Controller*
Kirsten Froden, *Asst Controller*
EMP: 70 **EST:** 1948
SQ FT: 40,000
SALES (est): 17.3MM **Privately Held**
WEB: www.pappironworks.com
SIC: 3446 Architectural metalwork

(G-8776)
RAK FOAM SALES INC
1355 W Front St Ste 2 (07063-1151)
P.O. Box 3248 (07063-0248)
PHONE...908 668-1122
Robert Kussner, *President*
Russel Kussner, *Vice Pres*
EMP: 8
SQ FT: 3,000
SALES (est): 1MM **Privately Held**
SIC: 3069 Weather strip, sponge rubber

(G-8777)
REINCO INC
520 North Ave (07060-1417)
PHONE...908 755-0921
Erich Reinecker, *President*
Walter Reinecker, *Chairman*
George Braun, *Vice Pres*
▼ **EMP:** 12 **EST:** 1958
SQ FT: 8,000
SALES (est): 2.2MM **Privately Held**
WEB: www.reinco.com
SIC: 3531 Construction machinery

(G-8778)
SHUTTER DLIGHT LLC
970 Madison Ave (07060-2319)
PHONE...908 956-4206
Cai A King-Young, *Principal*
EMP: 4
SALES (est): 267.9K **Privately Held**
SIC: 3442 Shutters, door or window: metal

(G-8779)
UNITED BEDDING INDUSTRIES LLC
Also Called: Ubi
300 W 4th St (07060-4233)
PHONE...908 668-0220
Jose Furman,
EMP: 25
SQ FT: 60,000
SALES (est): 3MM **Privately Held**
SIC: 2392 Blankets, comforters & beddings

Plainsboro
Middlesex County

(G-8780)
BAGEL STREET
660 Plainsboro Rd Ste 18 (08536-3002)
PHONE...609 936-1755
James Rohr, *Owner*
Doug Rohr, *Co-Owner*
EMP: 25
SALES (est): 790.9K **Privately Held**
SIC: 5461 5812 2051 Bagels; eating places; bread, cake & related products

(G-8781)
BIOPHORE LLC
4510 Quail Ridge Dr (08536-4227)
PHONE...609 275-3713
EMP: 2
SALES: 3MM **Privately Held**
SIC: 8731 2834 8748 Coml Physical Research Mfg Pharmaceutical Preps Business Consulting Svcs

(G-8782)
COMMEATUS LLC
5216 Fox Run Dr (08536-3467)
PHONE...847 772-5314
Sibtain Shabbir, *CEO*
EMP: 10
SALES (est): 400.4K **Privately Held**
SIC: 3429 7389 Manufactured hardware (general);

(G-8783)
CSONKA WORLDWIDE
501 Plainsboro Rd Ph (08536-2070)
PHONE...609 514-2766
Michael Chunko, *President*
▲ **EMP:** 30 **EST:** 1996
SQ FT: 4,000
SALES (est): 4.2MM **Privately Held**
WEB: www.csonka.com
SIC: 5075 2121 5194 3564 Dehumidifiers, except portable; cigars; cigars; air purification equipment; humidifiers & dehumidifiers

(G-8784)
DERMA SCIENCES INC (HQ)
Also Called: Integra
311 Enterprise Dr (08536-3344)
PHONE...609 514-4744
Stephen T Wills, *CEO*
John Golden, *Regional Mgr*
Frederic Eigner, *Exec VP*
Brian Hoy, *Project Mgr*
Cheryl Luchento, *Project Mgr*
▲ **EMP:** 109
SQ FT: 15,065
SALES (est): 84.4MM **Publicly Held**
WEB: www.dermasciences.com
SIC: 2211 2834 3842 Bandages, gauzes & surgical fabrics, cotton; pharmaceutical preparations; ointments; bandages & dressings

(G-8785)
DOW JONES & COMPANY INC
5 Schalks Crossing Rd (08536-1620)
PHONE...609 520-5730
John Lynch, *Info Tech Dir*
EMP: 4
SALES (corp-wide): 10B **Publicly Held**
SIC: 2711 Newspapers, publishing & printing
HQ: Dow Jones & Company, Inc.
1211 Avenue Of The Americ
New York NY 10036
609 627-2999

(G-8786)
FEHU JEWEL LLC
2912 Quail Ridge Dr (08536-4070)
PHONE...609 297-5491
Jigar Narola,
EMP: 150
SALES (est): 3.7MM **Privately Held**
SIC: 3911 Jewelry, precious metal

(G-8787)
G S BABU & CO
57 Woodland Dr (08536-2053)
PHONE...732 939-5190
Prem Babu, *Owner*
Jayanthi Haribabu, *Mktg Dir*
EMP: 10
SALES (est): 370K **Privately Held**
SIC: 3199 Leggings or chaps, canvas or leather

(G-8788)
GADDE PHARMA LLC
41 Madison Dr (08536-2320)
PHONE...609 651-7772
Vijaya Gadde, *Principal*
EMP: 5
SALES (est): 325K **Privately Held**
SIC: 2834 Pharmaceutical preparations

(G-8789)
GLYSORTIA LLC
281 Hampshire Dr (08536-4336)
PHONE...715 426-5358
Rick Beardmore,
◆ **EMP:** 4
SALES (est): 621.2K **Privately Held**
SIC: 2879 Fungicides, herbicides

(G-8790)
INDOTRONIX INTERNATIONAL CORP
101 Morgan Ln Ste 210 (08536-3345)
PHONE...609 750-0700
Venkat Mantha, *Branch Mgr*
EMP: 4
SALES (corp-wide): 20.6MM **Privately Held**
WEB: www.iic.com
SIC: 7379 7371 7372 Computer related consulting services; custom computer programming services; computer software development; prepackaged software
HQ: Indotronix International Corp
687 Lee Rd Ste 250
Rochester NY 14606
845 473-1137

(G-8791)
INPHOT INC
13 Blossom Hill Dr (08536-3122)
PHONE...609 799-7172
Krishna Linga, *CEO*
EMP: 4
SALES (est): 462.5K **Privately Held**
SIC: 3674 Semiconductors & related devices

(G-8792)
INTEGRA LFSCNCES HOLDINGS CORP (PA)
311 Enterprise Dr (08536-3344)
PHONE...609 275-0500
Peter J Arduini, *President*
Robert T Davis Jr, *President*
Jerry Klawitter, *President*
Mari Klaseen, *Business Mgr*
Glenn Coleman, *COO*
▼ **EMP:** 200
SALES: 1.4B **Publicly Held**
WEB: www.integra-ls.com
SIC: 3841 2836 3842 Surgical & medical instruments; biological products, except diagnostic; surgical appliances & supplies; implants, surgical

(G-8793)
INTEGRA LIFESCIENCES CORP (HQ)
Also Called: Jarit
311 Enterprise Dr (08536-3344)
P.O. Box 639 (08536-0639)
PHONE...609 275-2700
Peter Arduini, *CEO*
Brian Larkin, *COO*
Maria Santiago, *COO*
Mark Augusti, *Vice Pres*
Jerry Backe, *Vice Pres*
EMP: 200 **EST:** 1994
SALES (est): 317.1MM **Publicly Held**
SIC: 3841 Surgical & medical instruments

(G-8794)
INTEGRA LIFESCIENCES CORP
Integra Neurosciences
311 Enterprise Dr (08536-3344)
PHONE...609 275-0500
John Henneman, *Manager*
Devon Zezza, *Senior Mgr*
EMP: 80 **Publicly Held**
SIC: 2834 3841 2836 Pharmaceutical preparations; surgical & medical instruments; biological products, except diagnostic
HQ: Integra Lifesciences Corporation
311 Enterprise Dr
Plainsboro NJ 08536
609 275-2700

(G-8795)
INTEGRA LIFESCIENCES CORP
105 Morgan Ln (08536-3339)
PHONE...609 275-2700
Marvin Fields, *Facilities Dir*
Thomas Kuczynski, *Project Engr*
Jeremy Howe-Smith, *Manager*
EMP: 20 **Publicly Held**
SIC: 3841 Surgical & medical instruments
HQ: Integra Lifesciences Corporation
311 Enterprise Dr
Plainsboro NJ 08536
609 275-2700

(G-8796)
INTEGRA LIFESCIENCES SALES LLC
311 Enterprise Dr (08536-3344)
PHONE...609 275-0500
Peter J Arduini, *CEO*
Patricia Dansbury, *Counsel*
Richard Gorelick, *Vice Pres*
Peter Fosbre, *Accountant*
Robert Fowler, *Sales Staff*
EMP: 300
SALES: 50.9MM **Publicly Held**
SIC: 3841 Surgical & medical instruments
HQ: Integra Lifesciences Corporation
311 Enterprise Dr
Plainsboro NJ 08536
609 275-2700

(G-8797)
INTELLISPHERE LLC (HQ)
Also Called: Targeted Healthcare
666 Plainsboro Rd Ste 300 (08536-3000)
PHONE...609 716-7777
Michael Hennessy,
EMP: 1
SALES (est): 3.2MM
SALES (corp-wide): 7.9MM **Privately Held**
WEB: www.mdnetguide.com
SIC: 2721 Magazines: publishing only, not printed on site
PA: Michael J. Hennessy And Associates Inc.
666 Plainsboro Rd Ste 300
Plainsboro NJ 08536
609 716-7777

(G-8798)
NOVO NORDISK INC (DH)
800 Scudders Mill Rd (08536-1606)
PHONE...609 987-5800
Doug Langa, *President*
Jesper Hiland, *President*
Martin Soeters, *President*
Frank Bigley, *Principal*
Rosemarie Wilk-Orescan, *Counsel*
◆ **EMP:** 277
SALES: 8B
SALES (corp-wide): 20.1B **Privately Held**
WEB: www.innolet-us.com
SIC: 2834 Pharmaceutical preparations
HQ: Novo Nordisk A/S
Novo Alle 1
BagsvArd 2880
444 488-88

(G-8799)
PHYSICANS EDUCATN RESOURCE LLC
666 Plainsboro Rd Ste 300 (08536-3000)
PHONE...609 378-3701
Neil Glasser, *Partner*
Leah Babitz, *Partner*
EMP: 8
SALES (est): 673.8K **Privately Held**
SIC: 2721 Trade journals: publishing only, not printed on site

(G-8800)
QUANTUM INTEGRATORS GROUP LLC
8 Madison Dr (08536-2315)
PHONE...609 632-0621
EMP: 55
SALES (corp-wide): 2.9MM **Privately Held**
SIC: 3572 Computer storage devices
PA: Quantum Integrators Group Llc
186 Princeton Hightstown
Princeton Junction NJ 08550
609 632-0621

(G-8801)
QUGEN INC
666 Plainsboro Rd Ste 215 (08536-3071)
PHONE...609 716-6300
Shirka Jain, *President*
Varun Suri, *Vice Pres*
▲ **EMP:** 3
SQ FT: 500
SALES: 6.7MM **Privately Held**
SIC: 2834 Pharmaceutical preparations

(G-8802)
ROSEMONT PUBLISHING & PRINTING
Also Called: Associated University Presses
10 Schalks Crossing Rd (08536-1612)
PHONE..............................609 269-8094
Julien Yoseloff, *President*
Darlene Yoseloff, *Vice Pres*
EMP: 10
SQ FT: 2,900
SALES (est): 610K **Privately Held**
SIC: 2731 Books: publishing only

(G-8803)
SPHINX SOFTWARE INC
2 Red Oak Dr (08536-3704)
PHONE..............................609 275-5085
Tariq Malik, *President*
Munazzah Malik, *CFO*
Darik Malik, *Treasurer*
EMP: 8
SQ FT: 1,500
SALES (est): 500K **Privately Held**
SIC: 7372 Prepackaged software

(G-8804)
T N T INFORMATION SYSTEMS
666 Plainsboro Rd Ste 100 (08536-3030)
PHONE..............................609 799-9488
Eali Pao, *Partner*
Yichun Zhang, *Partner*
EMP: 4
SQ FT: 1,000
SALES (est): 300K **Privately Held**
WEB: www.tntinfo.com
SIC: 7372 Application computer software

Pleasantville
Atlantic County

(G-8805)
ATLANTIC CITY WEEK
Also Called: Whoot Newspaper
8025 Black Horse Pike # 350 (08232-2900)
PHONE..............................609 646-4848
Lewis B Steiner, *President*
Christine Steiner, *Admin Sec*
EMP: 15 **EST:** 1974
SQ FT: 500
SALES (est): 737.6K **Privately Held**
WEB: www.whoot.com
SIC: 2711 5812 Newspapers: publishing only, not printed on site; eating places

(G-8806)
C & D SALES
Also Called: Screen Printing & Embroidery
73 E West Jersey Ave (08232-2753)
P.O. Box 1489 (08232-6489)
PHONE..............................609 383-9292
Catherine Carber, *Owner*
EMP: 6
SQ FT: 7,000
SALES (est): 495K **Privately Held**
SIC: 2759 2395 Screen printing; embroidery & art needlework

(G-8807)
C G I CSTM FIBERGLAS & DECKING
48 S Main St (08232-2728)
PHONE..............................609 646-5302
Gregory Fiore, *Owner*
EMP: 10
SALES (est): 675.6K **Privately Held**
SIC: 3089 1521 Plastics products; single-family home remodeling, additions & repairs

(G-8808)
COLONIAL UPHL & WIN TREATMENTS
425 S Main St (08232-3031)
PHONE..............................609 641-3124
Linda Tuccinardi, *Owner*
Lorenzo Tuccinardi, *Vice Pres*
EMP: 5 **EST:** 1948
SQ FT: 4,800

SALES (est): 220K **Privately Held**
WEB: www.interiordesign-concepts.com
SIC: 7641 2391 2392 Reupholstery & furniture repair; curtains & draperies; blankets, comforters & beddings

(G-8809)
CURRENT NEWSPAPER LLC
Also Called: Catamaran Media
1000 W Washington Ave (08232-3861)
PHONE..............................609 383-8994
Stacy Wagner, *Sales Associate*
Richard Travers,
EMP: 25
SALES (est): 1.1MM **Privately Held**
SIC: 2711 Newspapers, publishing & printing

(G-8810)
DAVIDMARK LLC
711 N Main St Ste 7 (08232-1590)
PHONE..............................609 277-7361
Mark Stubblefield,
EMP: 5
SALES (est): 225.3K **Privately Held**
SIC: 2339 Women's & misses' accessories

(G-8811)
FRANK & JIMS INC
Also Called: Frank Jims Storm Windows Doors
711 N Main St Ste 3 (08232-1590)
PHONE..............................609 646-1655
Michael Quinn, *President*
David Magill, *Vice Pres*
EMP: 4
SQ FT: 1,500
SALES (est): 520K **Privately Held**
SIC: 5211 1751 7699 2541 Door & window products; window & door installation & erection; door & window repair; shelving, office & store, wood

(G-8812)
HAYES MINDISH INC
1401 N Main St Ste 7 (08232-1096)
PHONE..............................609 641-9880
Sally Hayes, *President*
Michael Mindish, *Vice Pres*
EMP: 4
SALES: 600K **Privately Held**
SIC: 2759 Commercial printing

(G-8813)
ITS THE PITTS INC
Also Called: Lucky Dog Custom Apparel
619 Church St (08232-4208)
PHONE..............................609 645-7319
Richard Pitts, *President*
Cindy Pitts, *Vice Pres*
EMP: 8
SQ FT: 6,000
SALES (est): 519.5K **Privately Held**
SIC: 5699 2395 T-shirts, custom printed; emblems, embroidered

(G-8814)
JEWISH TIMES OF SOUTH JERSEY
21 W Delilah Rd (08232-1403)
PHONE..............................609 646-2063
Shy Kramer, *President*
EMP: 5
SALES (est): 230K **Privately Held**
WEB: www.jewishtimes-sj.com
SIC: 2711 Newspapers, publishing & printing

(G-8815)
MAINLAND PLATE GLASS COMPANY
53 E West Jersey Ave (08232-2753)
PHONE..............................609 277-2938
Richard Bozzelli, *President*
EMP: 10
SQ FT: 8,000
SALES (est): 960K **Privately Held**
SIC: 1793 3449 Glass & glazing work; miscellaneous metalwork

(G-8816)
NORTHROP GRUMMAN SYSTEMS CORP
8025 Black Horse Pike (08232-2900)
PHONE..............................609 272-9000

EMP: 138 **Publicly Held**
WEB: www.logicon.com
SIC: 3812 Search & navigation equipment
HQ: Northrop Grumman Systems Corporation
2980 Fairview Park Dr
Falls Church VA 22042
703 280-2900

(G-8817)
SALAD CHEF INC
Also Called: Green Fresh Fruit Salad
125 Shadeland Ave (08232-3623)
P.O. Box 244 (08232-0244)
PHONE..............................609 641-5455
Francis Green, *President*
Richard Green, *Vice Pres*
EMP: 11
SQ FT: 1,500
SALES: 300K **Privately Held**
SIC: 2099 5149 Salads, fresh or refrigerated; groceries & related products

(G-8818)
SEABOARD INSTRUMENT CO
4 N 1st St (08232-2604)
PHONE..............................609 641-5300
Thomas R Higbee, *President*
EMP: 5
SQ FT: 12,000
SALES: 250K **Privately Held**
SIC: 3825 Measuring instruments & meters, electric; tachometer generators; time code generators

(G-8819)
SOUTH JERSEY PUBLISHING CO (DH)
Also Called: Press of Atlantic City, The
1000 W Washington Ave (08232-3861)
PHONE..............................609 272-7000
Charles W Bitzer, *President*
Becky Hendricks, *Editor*
Keith L Dawn, *Vice Pres*
Charles Hanlon, *Treasurer*
Katie Macleod, *Advt Staff*
EMP: 335
SQ FT: 30,000
SALES (est): 45.2MM
SALES (corp-wide): 361.4MM **Privately Held**
WEB: www.pressofac.com
SIC: 2711 Newspapers: publishing only, not printed on site; newspapers, publishing & printing
HQ: Wilmington Trust Sp Services
1105 N Market St Ste 1300
Wilmington DE 19801
302 427-7650

(G-8820)
TRIBUNA HISPANA
1614 Dolphin Ave (08232-4657)
PHONE..............................609 646-9167
Jose Polo, *Owner*
EMP: 9
SALES (est): 280K **Privately Held**
SIC: 2711 Newspapers: publishing only, not printed on site

(G-8821)
WILMINGTON TRUST SP SERVICES
Also Called: Press of Atlantic City, The
1000 W Washington Ave (08232-3861)
PHONE..............................609 272-7000
Robert Buffone, *Sales Staff*
Bridget Fields, *Sales Staff*
Paul Merkoski, *Manager*
EMP: 175
SALES (corp-wide): 361.4MM **Privately Held**
SIC: 2759 2711 2752 Commercial printing; newspapers; commercial printing, lithographic
HQ: Wilmington Trust Sp Services
1105 N Market St Ste 1300
Wilmington DE 19801
302 427-7650

Pluckemin
Somerset County

(G-8822)
FRANKS CABINET SHOP INC
Also Called: Gbd Cabinet Shop
1992 Burnt Mills Rd (07978)
P.O. Box 78 (07978-0078)
PHONE..............................908 658-4396
John Darrow, *President*
Frank Klausz, *President*
Doug Boom,
EMP: 7
SQ FT: 4,000
SALES: 500K **Privately Held**
SIC: 2434 Wood kitchen cabinets

Point Pleasant Beach
Ocean County

(G-8823)
EAST COAST BREWING CO LLC
528 Arnold Ave (08742-2756)
PHONE..............................732 202-7782
Brian Ciriaco, *Owner*
EMP: 6
SALES (est): 523.8K **Privately Held**
SIC: 2082 Beer (alcoholic beverage)

(G-8824)
IDEAL KITCHENS INC
407 Route 35 (08742-4104)
PHONE..............................732 295-2780
Tony Cardone, *President*
EMP: 10 **EST:** 1969
SQ FT: 10,000
SALES (est): 1.5MM **Privately Held**
WEB: www.idealkitchens.com
SIC: 2434 Wood kitchen cabinets

(G-8825)
JUMP START PRESS
802 Cedar Ave (08742-2508)
PHONE..............................732 892-4994
Mary Pearce, *President*
Gari Fairweather, *Web Dvlpr*
EMP: 6
SALES (est): 189.7K **Privately Held**
SIC: 2741 Miscellaneous publishing

(G-8826)
KEEFE PRINTING INC
501 Atlantic Ave (08742-3077)
PHONE..............................732 295-2099
Kevin Keefe, *President*
Christopher Ehrhardt, *Vice Pres*
EMP: 6
SQ FT: 1,500
SALES (est): 480K **Privately Held**
WEB: www.kprint.com
SIC: 2759 Commercial printing

(G-8827)
LAURELTON WELDING SERVICE INC
117 Channel Dr (08742-2619)
PHONE..............................732 899-6348
Thomas Gallagher, *President*
Shelia Crane, *Admin Sec*
EMP: 7
SQ FT: 6,500
SALES (est): 470K **Privately Held**
SIC: 7692 Welding repair

(G-8828)
MCBRIDE AWNING CO
304 Richmond Ave (08742-2547)
PHONE..............................732 892-6256
Kerry Mc Bride, *Partner*
Brian Mc Bride, *Partner*
John Mc Bride, *Partner*
Kerry McBride, *Partner*
EMP: 5
SQ FT: 2,200
SALES (est): 709.1K **Privately Held**
SIC: 3089 1799 Awnings, fiberglass & plastic combination; awning installation

GEOGRAPHIC

(G-8829)
NORMA K CORPORATION
Also Called: Pleasant
30 Broadway (08742-2679)
PHONE....................................732 477-6441
Norma E Keller, *President*
Kenneth Keller, *Corp Secy*
John G Kennell, *Vice Pres*
Sharon Keller Hawryluk, *Admin Sec*
EMP: 5
SALES: 200K **Privately Held**
WEB: www.pleasant.com
SIC: 4493 3732 Marinas; fishing boats:
   lobster, crab, oyster, etc.: small

(G-8830)
OCEAN STAR
421 River Ave (08742-2569)
PHONE....................................732 899-7606
Jim Manser, *Owner*
EMP: 6
SALES (est): 172.8K **Privately Held**
SIC: 2711 Newspapers: publishing only,
   not printed on site

(G-8831)
POINT LOBSTER COMPANY INC
1 Saint Louis Ave (08742-2651)
PHONE....................................732 892-1718
Fax: 732 892-3928
EMP: 10
SALES (est): 1MM **Privately Held**
SIC: 2091 Mfg Canned/Cured
   Fish/Seafood

(G-8832)
**TBS INDUSTRIAL FLOORING
PDTS**
300 New Jersey Ave (08742-3328)
PHONE....................................732 899-1486
Thomas Brennan, *President*
EMP: 5
SALES (est): 400K **Privately Held**
SIC: 3996 1752 Hard surface floor cover-
   ings; floor laying & floor work

(G-8833)
**WOODHAVEN LUMBER &
MILLWORK**
1303 Richmond Ave (08742-3099)
PHONE....................................732 295-8800
Chuck Hessenaemter, *Manager*
John Moran, *Manager*
EMP: 20
SALES (corp-wide): 48.5MM **Privately
Held**
WEB: www.woodhavenlumber.com
SIC: 5251 2431 5211 Hardware; millwork;
   lumber products
PA: Woodhaven Lumber & Millwork Inc
   200 James St
   Lakewood NJ 08701
   732 901-0030

(G-8834)
YO GOT IT
606 Arnold Ave (08742-2531)
PHONE....................................732 475-7913
Scott Mizrahi, *Principal*
EMP: 4
SALES (est): 256.8K **Privately Held**
SIC: 2026 Yogurt

Point Pleasant Boro
Ocean County

(G-8835)
ALL SURFACE ASPHALT PAVING
528 Hardenberg Ave (08742-2827)
PHONE....................................732 295-3800
Lori Coe, *President*
EMP: 7
SQ FT: 650
SALES: 1MM **Privately Held**
SIC: 2951 Asphalt paving mixtures &
   blocks

(G-8836)
**ARNOLDS YACHT BASIN INC
(PA)**
1671 Beaver Dam Rd Ste 1 (08742-5161)
PHONE....................................732 892-3000

Arnold Dambrosa, *President*
David Dambrosa, *Vice Pres*
EMP: 6
SQ FT: 32,000
SALES (est): 490K **Privately Held**
SIC: 4493 5551 2759 Yacht basins; motor
   boat dealers; marine supplies; screen
   printing

(G-8837)
**ATLAS RECORDING MACHINES
CORP**
2140 Bridge Ave (08742-4916)
PHONE....................................732 295-3663
Anthony Hopcroft, *President*
Mary Hopcroft, *Corp Secy*
EMP: 8
SQ FT: 8,000
SALES (est): 172K **Privately Held**
SIC: 3599 Machine shop, jobbing & repair

(G-8838)
BLAZING VISUALS
2138 Bridge Ave (08742-4916)
PHONE....................................732 781-1401
EMP: 6 EST: 2013
SALES (est): 482.2K **Privately Held**
SIC: 3993 Signs & advertising specialties

(G-8839)
CARVER BOAT SALES INC
714 Canal St (08742-4509)
PHONE....................................732 892-0328
Christopher Carver, *President*
EMP: 4 EST: 1947
SALES (est): 290K **Privately Held**
SIC: 3732 5551 Boat building & repairing;
   boat dealers

(G-8840)
COLIE SAIL MAKERS INC
1649 Bay Ave (08742-4501)
PHONE....................................732 892-4344
Dev Colie, *President*
Stephanie Colie, *Corp Secy*
EMP: 7
SQ FT: 6,500
SALES (est): 672.3K **Privately Held**
WEB: www.coliesail.com
SIC: 2394 5551 Canvas & related prod-
   ucts; sailboats & equipment

(G-8841)
COURTNEY BOATLIFTS INC
Also Called: Atlantic Boatlifts
1209 Bay Ave (08742-4017)
P.O. Box 4381, Brick (08723-1581)
PHONE....................................732 892-8900
James R Courtney, *President*
EMP: 4
SALES (est): 410K **Privately Held**
SIC: 1629 3536 Dams, waterways, docks
   & other marine construction; boat lifts

(G-8842)
DAIRY QUEEN
2506 Bridge Ave (08742-4259)
PHONE....................................732 892-5700
Alex Zicelli, *Owner*
EMP: 16
SALES (est): 289.7K **Privately Held**
SIC: 5812 5143 2024 Ice cream stands or
   dairy bars; frozen dairy desserts; ice
   cream & frozen desserts

(G-8843)
DELICIOUS BAGELS INC (PA)
2259 Bridge Ave (08742-4920)
PHONE....................................732 892-9265
Tony Pontecorvo, *President*
Florence Pontecorvo, *Vice Pres*
EMP: 4
SQ FT: 1,800
SALES (est): 871.9K **Privately Held**
SIC: 2051 5461 Bagels, fresh or frozen;
   bagels

(G-8844)
**EAGLE ENGINEERING &
AUTOMATION**
Also Called: Eagle Drives & Controls
2111 Herbertsville Rd (08742-2255)
P.O. Box 924 (08742-0287)
PHONE....................................732 899-2292
Robert M Ryan, *President*

Maureen Akersten, *Controller*
EMP: 4
SQ FT: 8,000
SALES: 900K **Privately Held**
WEB: www.walker-eagle.com
SIC: 3621 3613 Motors, electric; control
   panels, electric

(G-8845)
GOLD ENTERPRISE LTD
1671 Beaver Dam Rd Ste 11 (08742-5161)
P.O. Box 538 (08742-0538)
PHONE....................................954 614-1001
Joel Gold, *President*
EMP: 130
SALES: 3MM **Privately Held**
SIC: 3679 7389 Electronic circuits; per-
   sonal service agents, brokers & bureaus

(G-8846)
TROPICAL EXPRESSIONS INC
2127 Bridge Ave (08742-4959)
PHONE....................................732 899-8680
Jack Lathrop McGuire, *President*
EMP: 4
SQ FT: 1,000
SALES (est): 250K **Privately Held**
WEB: www.tropicalislandimports.com
SIC: 3999 Lawn ornaments

(G-8847)
VASCURE NATURAL LLC
3828 River Rd (08742-2054)
PHONE....................................732 528-6492
Thomas McCrink,
EMP: 4
SALES (est): 399.6K **Privately Held**
SIC: 2834 Druggists' preparations (phar-
   maceuticals)

(G-8848)
WALKER ENGINEERING INC
2111 Herbertsville Rd (08742-2255)
P.O. Box 924 (08742-0924)
PHONE....................................732 899-2550
Jillian Leinen, *President*
Robert Ryan, *Vice Pres*
EMP: 11
SQ FT: 8,000
SALES (est): 3.3MM **Privately Held**
SIC: 5063 3625 Motors, electric; control
   equipment, electric

Pomona
Atlantic County

(G-8849)
SIGHT2SITE MEDIA LLC
269 W White Horse Pike (08240-1103)
PHONE....................................856 637-2479
EMP: 5 EST: 2011
SALES (est): 290K **Privately Held**
SIC: 2741 7389 Internet Publishing And
   Broadcasting

Pompton Lakes
Passaic County

(G-8850)
**AUTO TIG WELDING
FABRICATING**
88 Cannonball Rd Ste B (07442-1775)
PHONE....................................973 839-8877
John Pajenski, *President*
EMP: 4
SQ FT: 3,000
SALES (est): 300K **Privately Held**
SIC: 7692 Welding repair

(G-8851)
**GABRIEL SOUND LTD LIABILITY
CO**
138 Cannonball Rd (07442-1708)
P.O. Box 287 (07442-0287)
PHONE....................................973 831-7800
Erick Wain,
EMP: 7
SALES (est): 739.5K **Privately Held**
SIC: 3651 Speaker systems

(G-8852)
SOLAR PRODUCTS INC
228 Wanaque Ave (07442-2131)
PHONE....................................973 248-9370
Richard Eck, *Ch of Bd*
David Eck, *President*
Susan Robertson, *Corp Secy*
Tim Robertson, *Vice Pres*
John Schafer, *Vice Pres*
▲ **EMP:** 37
SQ FT: 30,000
SALES (est): 8.7MM **Privately Held**
WEB: www.solarproducts.com
SIC: 3567 3679 Heating units & devices,
   industrial: electric; quartz crystals, for
   electronic application

(G-8853)
**TANDEM COLOR IMAGING
GRAPHICS (PA)**
Also Called: Tandem Graphics
207 Wanaque Ave (07442-2103)
PHONE....................................973 513-9779
Michael Nass, *President*
EMP: 6
SQ FT: 4,500
SALES (est): 1.2MM **Privately Held**
WEB: www.tandemgraphics.net
SIC: 7336 2752 Film strip, slide & still film
   production; commercial printing, litho-
   graphic

(G-8854)
**TANDEM COLOR IMAGING
GRAPHICS**
Also Called: Tandem Graphics
207 Wanaque Ave (07442-2103)
PHONE....................................973 513-9779
EMP: 4
SALES (corp-wide): 1.2MM **Privately
Held**
SIC: 2752 Commercial printing, offset
PA: Tandem Color Imaging Graphics, Inc
   207 Wanaque Ave
   Pompton Lakes NJ 07442
   973 513-9779

(G-8855)
TILCON NEW YORK INC
Also Called: Pompton Lakes Quarry
Foot Of Broad St (07442)
PHONE....................................800 789-7625
Frank Jaluski, *Branch Mgr*
EMP: 27
SALES (corp-wide): 30.6B **Privately Held**
SIC: 1429 Trap rock, crushed & broken-
   quarrying
HQ: Tilcon New York Inc.
   9 Entin Rd
   Parsippany NJ 07054
   973 366-7741

Pompton Plains
Morris County

(G-8856)
**ALADDIN MANUFACTURING
CORP**
100 Alexander Ave (07444-1847)
PHONE....................................973 616-4600
Jeff Labinski, *Branch Mgr*
EMP: 260
SALES (corp-wide): 9.9B **Publicly Held**
SIC: 2273 5032 5023 Carpets, textile
   fiber; brick, stone & related material;
   home furnishings
HQ: Aladdin Manufacturing Corporation
   160 S Industrial Blvd
   Calhoun GA 30701
   706 629-7721

(G-8857)
AMMARK CORPORATION
230 W Parkway Ste 12 (07444-1060)
P.O. Box 519, Boonton (07005-0519)
PHONE....................................973 616-2555
John T Ford, *President*
Veronica Ford, *Vice Pres*
▲ **EMP:** 4

SALES (est): 515.4K **Privately Held**
WEB: www.ammarkcorp.com
SIC: 3494 3822 Valves & pipe fittings; air flow controllers, air conditioning & refrigeration

(G-8858)
AR2 PRODUCTS LLC
Also Called: Gopole
210 W Parkway Ste 9 (07444-1000)
PHONE..................................800 667-1263
Russell Van Zile, *CEO*
Ryan Vosburg, *Vice Pres*
Anthony Anari, *Opers Staff*
▲ EMP: 6
SQ FT: 5,000
SALES: 4.3MM **Privately Held**
SIC: 3861 Cameras & related equipment; lens shades, camera; light meters, camera; shutters, camera

(G-8859)
ASHLEY NORTON INC
210 W Parkway Ste 1 (07444-1000)
P.O. Box 374 (07444-0374)
PHONE..................................973 835-4027
Narendra Karnani, *President*
Ashish Karnani, *Vice Pres*
Joe Partington, *Opers Mgr*
Anthony Pacifico, *Sales Staff*
Samantha Sajban, *Sales Staff*
◆ EMP: 15
SQ FT: 18,000
SALES (est): 3.3MM **Privately Held**
SIC: 3429 Manufactured hardware (general)

(G-8860)
BAYVIEW ENTERTAINMENT LLC
210 W Parkway Ste 7 (07444-1000)
PHONE..................................201 880-5331
Seth Goldstein,
Peter Castro,
Sam Napolitano,
▲ EMP: 20
SALES (est): 3.2MM **Privately Held**
WEB: www.bayviewent.com
SIC: 3651 Household audio & video equipment

(G-8861)
CHILLER SOLUTIONS LLC
Also Called: Edwards Engineering
101 Alexander Ave Unit 3 (07444-1854)
PHONE..................................973 835-2800
Ala Uddin, *Manager*
Thomas Dellinger, *Bd of Directors*
Gene A Passaro,
EMP: 32
SALES (est): 7.4MM **Privately Held**
WEB: www.chillersolutions.com
SIC: 3585 Heating equipment, complete

(G-8862)
DEVON PRODUCTS
230 W Parkway Ste 3 (07444-1065)
PHONE..................................732 438-3855
EMP: 4
SALES: 300K **Privately Held**
SIC: 2844 Services-Misc

(G-8863)
EDWARDS COILS CORP
101 Alexander Ave Unit 3 (07444-1854)
P.O. Box 181, Hampton Falls NH (03844-0181)
PHONE..................................973 835-2800
Ernest M Cherry, *President*
Jose Mercedes, *Manager*
▲ EMP: 17
SQ FT: 35,000
SALES (est): 3.7MM **Privately Held**
SIC: 3443 Heat exchangers, condensers & components

(G-8864)
FRAGRANCE FACTORY INC
12 Peck Ave (07444-1429)
PHONE..................................973 835-2002
Robert Scherr, *Manager*
EMP: 4
SALES: 330K **Privately Held**
WEB: www.fragrancefactory.com
SIC: 3999 Candles

(G-8865)
GLOBAL BUSINESS DIMENSIONS INC (PA)
220 W Parkway Ste 8 (07444-1048)
PHONE..................................973 831-5866
Sanjay Prasad, *President*
Sam Phillips, *Vice Pres*
Lynn Rin, *Vice Pres*
Pacelli Sequeria, *Vice Pres*
Sarika Singh, *Human Resources*
EMP: 26
SQ FT: 11,000
SALES (est): 3.8MM **Privately Held**
WEB: www.globalbd.com
SIC: 3571 5063 Electronic computers; electrical supplies

(G-8866)
M C TECHNOLOGIES INC
4 Kinney Pl (07444-1608)
PHONE..................................973 839-2779
John M Chizacky, *President*
Melanie Chizacky, *Vice Pres*
EMP: 24
SALES (est): 2.1MM **Privately Held**
SIC: 3559 8731 8711 Automotive related machinery; engineering laboratory, except testing; consulting engineer

(G-8867)
MEDALLION INTERNATIONAL INC
233 W Parkway (07444-1028)
PHONE..................................973 616-3401
Michael Boudjouk, *President*
Paula Boudjouk, *President*
Amelia Boudjouk, *Treasurer*
◆ EMP: 15
SALES (est): 3MM **Privately Held**
SIC: 2087 2844 Extracts, flavoring; toilet preparations

(G-8868)
MORRIS INDUSTRIES INC (PA)
777 State Rt 23 (07444-1498)
P.O. Box 278 (07444-0278)
PHONE..................................973 835-6600
Robert Nochenson, *President*
Scott Ennis, *Sales Staff*
▲ EMP: 58
SQ FT: 30,000
SALES (est): 43.7MM **Privately Held**
WEB: www.morrispipe.com
SIC: 5051 5084 5074 3317 Pipe & tubing, steel; drilling equipment, excluding bits; drilling bits; pumps & pumping equipment; pipes & fittings, plastic; steel pipe & tubes; well casing, wrought: welded, lock joint or heavy riveted; service establishment equipment

(G-8869)
PENN ELCOM INC
232 W Parkway (07444-1029)
PHONE..................................973 839-7777
Helen Stratford, *Accounts Mgr*
Richard Stratford, *Branch Mgr*
EMP: 10 **Privately Held**
WEB: www.elcomhardware.com
SIC: 3429 5072 Manufactured hardware (general); hardware
HQ: Penn Elcom, Inc.
     7465 Lampson Ave
     Garden Grove CA 92841

(G-8870)
PHT AEROSPACE LLC (PA)
230 W Parkway Ste 2 (07444-1065)
PHONE..................................973 831-1230
Joe Wall, *General Mgr*
Iris Castello, *Purch Agent*
Roger P Antaki,
▲ EMP: 15
SQ FT: 5,000
SALES (est): 3.1MM **Privately Held**
SIC: 3621 Motors & generators

(G-8871)
STRONG MAN SAFETY PDTS CORP
240 W Parkway (07444-1029)
PHONE..................................973 831-1555
Jay Kinder, *President*
Robert Giannetti, *General Mgr*
Elaine Kinder, *Corp Secy*
▲ EMP: 8
SALES (est): 2.7MM **Privately Held**
WEB: www.strongman.com
SIC: 3444 Metal housings, enclosures, casings & other containers

(G-8872)
TRICOMP INC
230 W Parkway Ste 14 (07444-1060)
PHONE..................................973 835-1110
Thomas P Lospinoso, *President*
Joan L Graff, *Vice Pres*
Joan Graff, *Vice Pres*
EMP: 120
SQ FT: 5,000
SALES (est): 14.1MM **Privately Held**
WEB: www.tricomp.com
SIC: 3082 3061 3499 3053 Unsupported plastics profile shapes; mechanical rubber goods; magnets, permanent: metallic; gaskets, all materials; weather strip, metal; weather strip, sponge rubber

(G-8873)
TRIFORM PRODUCTS INC
164 W Parkway (07444-1255)
PHONE..................................973 278-2042
Doug Troast, *President*
David Troast, *Vice Pres*
EMP: 35 EST: 1975
SQ FT: 17,500
SALES (est): 4MM **Privately Held**
SIC: 3469 Metal stampings

(G-8874)
WATER WORKS SUPPLY COMPANY (PA)
660 State Rt 23 (07444-1422)
P.O. Box 306 (07444-0306)
PHONE..................................973 835-2153
James C Schmutz, *President*
Bill Braga, *VP Sales*
Craig Connolly, *Sales Staff*
John Mastrogiovanni, *Sales Associate*
EMP: 24
SQ FT: 7,000
SALES (est): 16MM **Privately Held**
SIC: 5051 3321 Cast iron pipe; cast iron pipe & fittings

(G-8875)
ZAXCOM INC
Also Called: Zaxcom Video
230 W Parkway Ste 9 (07444-1060)
PHONE..................................973 835-5000
Glen Sanders, *President*
Lisa Apriceno, *Finance Mgr*
EMP: 10
SQ FT: 6,700
SALES (est): 2.1MM **Privately Held**
WEB: www.zaxcom.com
SIC: 3663 Television broadcasting & communications equipment

(G-8876)
ZODIAC PAINTBALL INC
4 Sage Way (07444-1473)
PHONE..................................973 616-7230
Kenneth Hefferle, *Principal*
EMP: 4
SALES (est): 293.4K **Privately Held**
SIC: 3499 Nozzles, spray: aerosol, paint or insecticide

Port Elizabeth
Cumberland County

(G-8877)
WHIBCO INC
377 Port Commerland Rd (08348)
PHONE..................................856 825-5200
Marvin Blechen, *Manager*
EMP: 30
SALES (corp-wide): 18.3MM **Privately Held**
WEB: www.whibco.com
SIC: 3299 Insulsleeves (foundry materials)
PA: Whibco, Inc.
     87 E Commerce St
     Bridgeton NJ 08302
     856 455-9200

(G-8878)
WHIBCO OF NEW JERSEY INC
377 Port Cumberland Rd (08348)
PHONE..................................856 455-9200
Wade R Sjogren, *President*
Walter R Sjogren Jr, *Vice Pres*
Jane Sorgren, *Admin Sec*
EMP: 25
SALES (est): 2.2MM
SALES (corp-wide): 18.3MM **Privately Held**
SIC: 1446 1442 Industrial sand; sand mining
PA: Whibco, Inc.
     87 E Commerce St
     Bridgeton NJ 08302
     856 455-9200

Port Monmouth
Monmouth County

(G-8879)
PHOENIX ALLIANCE GROUP LLC
337 State Route 36 (07758-1367)
PHONE..................................732 495-4800
Rodney Cocuzza, *Mng Member*
EMP: 14
SQ FT: 1,000
SALES (est): 847.9K **Privately Held**
WEB: www.phoenixalliancegroup.net
SIC: 2759 Commercial printing

Port Murray
Warren County

(G-8880)
AMERICAN PROCESS SYSTEMS
131 Cherry Tree Bend Rd (07865-4112)
PHONE..................................908 216-6781
Carl Anderson, *Owner*
EMP: 6
SALES: 850K **Privately Held**
SIC: 5084 3999 Controlling instruments & accessories; dock equipment & supplies, industrial

(G-8881)
ANDREX SYSTEMS INC
17 Karrville Rd (07865-4118)
P.O. Box 115 (07865-0115)
PHONE..................................908 835-1720
William T Pote, *President*
Thomas Pote, *Vice Pres*
Rodger Johasen, *Product Mgr*
EMP: 8
SALES (est): 1.1MM **Privately Held**
WEB: www.andrex-sys.com
SIC: 3679 Harness assemblies for electronic use: wire or cable

(G-8882)
BOREALIS COMPOUNDS INC (DH)
176 Thomas Rd (07865-4014)
PHONE..................................908 850-6200
Kenneth Wiecoreck, *President*
Ernst Buchner, *General Mgr*
Helena Lukkarinen, *Managing Dir*
Willy Raymaekers, *Managing Dir*
Peter Neilsen, *Principal*
◆ EMP: 112
SQ FT: 10,000
SALES (est): 36.2MM **Privately Held**
SIC: 3087 Custom compound purchased resins
HQ: Borealis Ag
     Wagramer StraBe 17-19
     Wien 1220
     122 400-300

(G-8883)
FLEXCO MICROWAVE INC
17 Karrville Rd (07865-4118)
P.O. Box 115 (07865-0115)
PHONE..................................908 835-1720
William T Pote, *President*
Thomas W Pote, *Vice Pres*
Colene Thomas, *Vice Pres*
Kathleen Medina, *Admin Sec*

GEOGRAPHIC

▲ **EMP:** 35
SQ FT: 18,200
SALES (est): 7.5MM **Privately Held**
WEB: www.flexcomw.com
SIC: 3357 Coaxial cable, nonferrous

(G-8884)
PRINTING SERVICES
185 Old Turnpike Rd (07865-3221)
PHONE..............................908 269-8349
Michael Delacruz, *Partner*
Ernie Delacruz, *Partner*
EMP: 4
SQ FT: 3,100
SALES (est): 261.2K **Privately Held**
SIC: 2752 Commercial printing, lithographic

Port Norris
Cumberland County

(G-8885)
BIVALVE PACKING INC (HQ)
6957 Miller Ave (08349-3167)
P.O. Box 336 (08349-0336)
PHONE..............................856 785-0270
Steve Fleetwood, *President*
EMP: 4
SQ FT: 3,000
SALES (est): 2MM
SALES (corp-wide): 6.5MM **Privately Held**
SIC: 2092 Shellfish, fresh: shucked & packed in nonsealed containers

(G-8886)
HILLARD BLOOM PACKING CO INC
2601 Ogden Ave (08349-3141)
PHONE..............................856 785-0120
Hillard Bloom, *President*
Lena Hughes, *Corp Secy*
Harold Bickings, *Vice Pres*
EMP: 9
SQ FT: 5,000
SALES (est): 1MM **Privately Held**
WEB: www.bloombrothers.com
SIC: 2091 2092 Oysters: packaged in cans, jars, etc.; fresh or frozen packaged fish

(G-8887)
MILLER BERRY & SONS INC
2615 Robinstown Rd (08349)
P.O. Box 174 (08349-0174)
PHONE..............................856 785-1420
Dean Berry, *President*
Barbara Moore, *Corp Secy*
EMP: 11
SQ FT: 45,000
SALES (est): 1.3MM **Privately Held**
SIC: 2515 0139 Mattresses, containing felt, foam rubber, urethane, etc.; mattresses, innerspring or box spring; hay farm

(G-8888)
RICCI BROS SAND COMPANY INC
Also Called: Ricci Brothers Sand
2099 Dragston Rd (08349)
P.O. Box 664 (08349-0664)
PHONE..............................856 785-0166
Samuel J Ricci Sr, *President*
EMP: 24
SQ FT: 7,750
SALES (est): 6.3MM **Privately Held**
WEB: www.riccisand.com
SIC: 1442 Construction sand mining; gravel mining

(G-8889)
SURFSIDE FOODS LLC
Also Called: Surfside Products
1733 Main St (08349-3340)
P.O. Box 692 (08349-0692)
PHONE..............................856 785-2115
EMP: 8
SALES (est): 110.5K **Privately Held**
SIC: 2099 3556 Food preparations; food products machinery

Port Reading
Middlesex County

(G-8890)
A & D INDUS & MAR REPR INC
900 Port Reading Ave B2 (07064-1044)
PHONE..............................732 541-1481
Maryann Bryant, *Principal*
EMP: 21
SALES (est): 3.7MM **Privately Held**
SIC: 3732 3089 Boat building & repairing; plastic boats & other marine equipment

(G-8891)
ACME MANUFACTURING CO
900 Port Reading Ave A2 (07064-1044)
P.O. Box 70 (07064-0070)
PHONE..............................732 541-2800
Richard Morrone, *Partner*
Paul Morrone, *Partner*
Jose Rodriguez,
EMP: 5
SQ FT: 6,000
SALES (est): 634K **Privately Held**
WEB: www.acmecoating.com
SIC: 2542 Office & store showcases & display fixtures

(G-8892)
ALLIED OLD ENGLISH INC
100 Markley St (07064-1897)
PHONE..............................732 636-2060
Fred Ross, *Ch of Bd*
Sean Colon, *COO*
Bill Paskowski, *Exec VP*
Rick McGlynn, *Plant Engr*
Frank Gatti, *CFO*
◆ **EMP:** 45 EST: 1951
SQ FT: 63,000
SALES (est): 18MM **Privately Held**
WEB: www.alliedoldenglish.com
SIC: 2099 Sauces: gravy, dressing & dip mixes

(G-8893)
DURABOND DIVISION US GYPSUM
300 Markley St (07064-1819)
PHONE..............................732 636-7900
James Wilson, *Principal*
Bill Elser, *Plant Engr*
▲ **EMP:** 11 EST: 2007
SALES (est): 2.5MM **Privately Held**
SIC: 3275 Gypsum products

(G-8894)
NASCO STONE AND TILE LLC
200 Markley St (07064-1820)
PHONE..............................732 634-0589
Sammy Tawil, *Vice Pres*
Dianne Bailey, *Controller*
Ellen Schaed, *Sales Associate*
Christina Lamboy, *Manager*
Colleen Riley, *Manager*
◆ **EMP:** 30
SALES (est): 4.2MM **Privately Held**
SIC: 3253 Ceramic wall & floor tile

(G-8895)
SPEEDWAY LLC
750 Cliff Rd (07064-2201)
PHONE..............................732 750-7800
Darryl Harris, *Manager*
EMP: 300 **Publicly Held**
WEB: www.hess.com
SIC: 1311 2911 5172 Crude petroleum production; natural gas production; petroleum refining; petroleum products
HQ: Speedway Llc
   500 Speedway Dr
   Enon OH 45323
   937 864-3000

(G-8896)
UNITED STATES GYPSUM COMPANY
300 Markley St (07064-1895)
PHONE..............................732 636-7900
Peter Geedman, *Purch Mgr*
Deborah O'Dwyer, *Buyer*
Jordan Egg, *Engineer*
Michael Sencic, *Engineer*
James Wilson, *Manager*

EMP: 81
SALES (corp-wide): 8.2B **Privately Held**
WEB: www.usg.com
SIC: 3275 Gypsum products
HQ: United States Gypsum Company
   550 W Adams St Ste 1300
   Chicago IL 60661
   312 606-4000

Princeton
Mercer County

(G-8897)
ABBOTT LABORATORIES
400 College Rd E (08540-6607)
PHONE..............................609 443-9300
Troy Wessman, *Regional Mgr*
Barry Bass, *Branch Mgr*
Terry Weiner, *Admin Sec*
EMP: 21
SALES (corp-wide): 30.5B **Publicly Held**
SIC: 2834 Pharmaceutical preparations
PA: Abbott Laboratories
   100 Abbott Park Rd
   Abbott Park IL 60064
   224 667-6100

(G-8898)
ABBOTT POINT OF CARE INC (HQ)
400 College Rd E (08540-6607)
PHONE..............................609 454-9000
William P Moffitt, *President*
EMP: 240
SALES (est): 217.5MM
SALES (corp-wide): 30.5B **Publicly Held**
SIC: 3841 Diagnostic apparatus, medical
PA: Abbott Laboratories
   100 Abbott Park Rd
   Abbott Park IL 60064
   224 667-6100

(G-8899)
ACCELERATED TECHNOLOGIES INC
Also Called: Damco
2 Research Way Fl 2 # 2 (08540-6628)
PHONE..............................609 632-0350
Ranjan Chattopadhyay, *President*
Brahm Sharma, *CFO*
EMP: 4
SQ FT: 1,700
SALES (est): 174.8K **Privately Held**
SIC: 7372 Prepackaged software
PA: Damco Solutions Private Limited
   No.108, Hsidc Industrial Estate,
   Faridabad HR 12100

(G-8900)
ACQUEON TECHNOLOGIES INC
100 Overlook Ctr Fl 2 (08540-7814)
PHONE..............................609 945-3139
Parthasarathy Balasubramanian, *Technical Mgr*
Baskar Subramanian, *Branch Mgr*
EMP: 5
SALES (est): 321.7K
SALES (corp-wide): 263.9K **Privately Held**
WEB: www.acqueon.com
SIC: 7372 Business oriented computer software
PA: Acqueon Technologies, Inc.
   14785 Preston Rd Ste 550
   Dallas TX 75254
   888 946-6878

(G-8901)
ADVAXIS INC (PA)
305 College Rd E (08540-6608)
PHONE..............................609 452-9813
Anthony Lombardi, *CEO*
David Sidransky, *Ch of Bd*
Kenneth A Berlin, *President*
Keir Loiacono, *Owner*
Molly Henderson, *Exec VP*
EMP: 108
SQ FT: 48,500
SALES: 6MM **Publicly Held**
WEB: www.advaxis.com
SIC: 2834 Pharmaceutical preparations

(G-8902)
AGILE THERAPEUTICS INC
101 Poor Farm Rd (08540-1941)
PHONE..............................609 683-1880
Al Altomari, *Ch of Bd*
Dennis P Reilly, *CFO*
Joe D'Urso, *Controller*
Renee Selman, *Ch Credit Ofcr*
Elizabeth Garner, *Chief Mktg Ofcr*
EMP: 16
SQ FT: 7,000
SALES (est): 3.1MM **Privately Held**
WEB: www.agiletherapeutics.com
SIC: 2834 8733 Pharmaceutical preparations; medical research

(G-8903)
AICUMEN TECHNOLOGIES INC
11 Nestlewood Way (08540-6132)
PHONE..............................732 668-4204
Anantha Krishnan, *CEO*
EMP: 5 **Privately Held**
SIC: 3571 Computers, digital, analog or hybrid

(G-8904)
AKILA HOLDINGS INC
12 Hampstead Ct (08540-7074)
PHONE..............................609 454-5034
EMP: 5 EST: 2002
SALES (est): 13.2MM **Privately Held**
SIC: 2099 5153 Sugar; grain & field beans
PA: Akila Trading Private Limited
   S-9, 2nd Floor,
   New Delhi DL 11001

(G-8905)
ALAN PAUL ACCESSORIES INC
Also Called: Alan Paul Neckware
66 Witherspoon St # 3300 (08542-3239)
PHONE..............................609 924-4022
Alan Paul Spielholz, *President*
Amparo Spielholz, *Manager*
EMP: 5
SQ FT: 1,500
SALES (est): 331K **Privately Held**
SIC: 2253 Knit outerwear mills

(G-8906)
ALK TECHNOLOGIES INC (HQ)
1 Independence Way # 400 (08540-6662)
PHONE..............................609 683-0220
Katherine Kornhauser, *President*
Michael Kornhauser, *President*
Dave Ward, *Partner*
Mike Bodden, *Senior VP*
Barry J Glick, *Senior VP*
EMP: 147 EST: 1981
SQ FT: 12,000
SALES (est): 29.5MM
SALES (corp-wide): 3.1B **Publicly Held**
SIC: 3812 7372 Search & navigation equipment; prepackaged software
PA: Trimble Inc.
   935 Stewart Dr
   Sunnyvale CA 94085
   408 481-8000

(G-8907)
ALLOS THERAPEUTICS INC
302 Carnegie Ctr Ste 200 (08540-6376)
PHONE..............................609 936-3760
Mary McCalister, *Branch Mgr*
EMP: 4 **Publicly Held**
SIC: 2834 Pharmaceutical preparations
HQ: Allos Therapeutics, Inc.
   11000 Westmoor Cir # 150
   Westminster CO 80021

(G-8908)
APPEX INNOVATION SOLUTIONS LLC
103 Carnegie Ctr (08540-6235)
PHONE..............................215 313-3332
Pooja Vora, *President*
Manoj Vora, *Vice Pres*
Ankur Vora,
EMP: 5 EST: 2013
SALES (est): 129.8K **Privately Held**
SIC: 7379 7372 7371 7373 ; application computer software; computer software systems analysis & design, custom; systems software development services

(G-8909)
ARGYLE INTERNATIONAL INC
254 Wall St (08540-1511)
PHONE..............................609 924-9484
Arthur Gillman, *President*
Lian Shentu, *Vice Pres*
EMP: 7
SQ FT: 2,000
SALES (est): 894.2K **Privately Held**
WEB: www.argyleint.com
SIC: 3827 Optical instruments & lenses

(G-8910)
ARM & HAMMER ANIMAL NTRTN LLC (HQ)
Also Called: Arm & Hammer Animal & Fd Prod
469 N Harrison St (08540-3510)
PHONE..............................800 526-3563
Matthew Farrell, *CEO*
EMP: 10 EST: 2014
SALES (est): 228K
SALES (corp-wide): 4.1B **Publicly Held**
SIC: 3556 Dairy & milk machinery
PA: Church & Dwight Co., Inc.
500 Charles Ewing Blvd
Ewing NJ 08628
609 806-1200

(G-8911)
ARMKEL LLC
469 N Harrison St (08540-3510)
PHONE..............................609 683-5900
Robert A Davies III,
Bradley A Casper,
Zvi Eiref,
Adrian Huns,
Maureen K Usifer,
▲ EMP: 1500
SALES (est): 76.1MM
SALES (corp-wide): 4.1B **Publicly Held**
WEB: www.naircare.com
SIC: 2835 2844 Pregnancy test kits; depilatories (cosmetic)
PA: Church & Dwight Co., Inc.
500 Charles Ewing Blvd
Ewing NJ 08628
609 806-1200

(G-8912)
ARTEZIO LLC
195 Nassau St Rear 32 (08542-7004)
PHONE..............................609 786-2435
Pavel Adylin, *CEO*
Alexander Izosenkov, *Manager*
EMP: 4
SALES: 4.8MM
SALES (corp-wide): 6.3MM **Privately Held**
SIC: 7371 7379 7372 Computer software development & applications; ; business oriented computer software
PA: Artezio, Ooo
D. 36 Korp. 1, Shosse Pyatnitskoe
Moscow 12343
495 232-2683

(G-8913)
BATALLURE BEAUTY LLC (PA)
104 Carnegie Ctr Ste 202 (08540-6232)
PHONE..............................609 716-1200
Robin Burns McNeil, *Ch of Bd*
Amelia Romer, *Project Mgr*
Loren Zachau, *Purchasing*
Jeff Ghusson, *Marketing Mgr*
Amy Schinoff, *Marketing Mgr*
▲ EMP: 40
SQ FT: 4,000
SALES (est): 10.1MM **Privately Held**
WEB: www.batallure.com
SIC: 2844 Perfumes & colognes

(G-8914)
BERLITZ LANGUAGES US INC (DH)
7 Roszel Rd Fl 3 (08540-6257)
PHONE..............................609 759-5371
Yukako Uchinaga, *CEO*
Paul Weinstein, *Vice Pres*
Alistair Gatoff, *VP Finance*
EMP: 65
SQ FT: 62,275

SALES (est): 112.8MM **Privately Held**
WEB: www.berlitz.us
SIC: 8299 7389 2731 Language school; translation services; books: publishing only
HQ: Berlitz Corporation
7 Roszel Rd Fl 3
Princeton NJ 08540
207 828-3768

(G-8915)
BETA PHARMA INC
5 Vaughn Dr Ste 106 (08540-6313)
PHONE..............................609 436-4100
Don Zhang, *CEO*
Alysha Salandy, *Human Res Mgr*
Sharon Caja, *Legal Staff*
EMP: 16
SALES (est): 2.5MM **Privately Held**
SIC: 2834 Pharmaceutical preparations

(G-8916)
BIONPHARMA INC
600 Alexander Rd Ste 2-4b (08540-6013)
PHONE..............................609 380-3313
Venkat Krishman, *CEO*
Bill Winter, *Senior VP*
EMP: 5 EST: 2014
SALES (est): 575.3K **Privately Held**
SIC: 2834 Pharmaceutical preparations

(G-8917)
BLUECLONE NETWORKS LLC
103 Carnegie Ctr Ste 300 (08540-6235)
P.O. Box 241, Princeton Junction (08550-0241)
PHONE..............................609 944-8433
Milan Baria, *CEO*
EMP: 8
SQ FT: 10,000
SALES (est): 904.8K **Privately Held**
SIC: 3572 4813 7376 7373 Computer storage devices; voice telephone communications; computer facilities management; systems integration services; computer maintenance & repair

(G-8918)
BRISTOL-MYERS SQUIBB COMPANY
100 Nassau Park Blvd # 200 (08540-5997)
PHONE..............................609 419-5000
Bob Libbey, *Vice Pres*
Richard Wyzga, *Project Mgr*
Phyllis Hill, *Manager*
Kelliann Lorenz, *Manager*
Alim Macauley, *Manager*
EMP: 6
SALES (corp-wide): 22.5B **Publicly Held**
WEB: www.bms.com
SIC: 2834 Pharmaceutical preparations
PA: Bristol-Myers Squibb Company
430 E 29th St Fl 14
New York NY 10016
212 546-4000

(G-8919)
BRISTOL-MYERS SQUIBB COMPANY
Province Line Rd Rr 206 (08540)
P.O. Box 5200 (08543-5200)
PHONE..............................609 252-4875
Leon Rosenberg, *Principal*
Xiaomei Gu, *Research*
Michael Di Novi, *Admin Sec*
Cynthia Brogdon, *Oncology*
EMP: 4
SALES (corp-wide): 22.5B **Publicly Held**
SIC: 8731 2834 Commercial physical research; pharmaceutical preparations
PA: Bristol-Myers Squibb Company
430 E 29th St Fl 14
New York NY 10016
212 546-4000

(G-8920)
CALYPTUS PHARMACEUTICALS INC
174 Nassau St Ste 364 (08542-7005)
PHONE..............................908 720-6049
Sujeet Singh, *CEO*
EMP: 10 EST: 2017
SALES (est): 508.3K **Privately Held**
SIC: 2834 Pharmaceutical preparations

(G-8921)
CHEMICAL RESOURCES INC (PA)
Also Called: Chemres
103 Carnegie Ctr Ste 100 (08540-6235)
PHONE..............................609 520-0000
Paul Keimig, *President*
Jim Couture, *Vice Pres*
Bob Hamilton, *Vice Pres*
Diane Hogoboom, *Vice Pres*
Mike McFarland, *Vice Pres*
◆ EMP: 35
SQ FT: 5,000
SALES (est): 40.7MM **Privately Held**
WEB: www.chemicalresourcesinc.com
SIC: 5162 5169 2865 Plastics materials & basic shapes; chemicals & allied products; cyclic crudes & intermediates

(G-8922)
CHRYSLIS DATA SLTONS SVCS CORP (PA)
Also Called: Cdss
100 Overlook Ctr Fl 2 (08540-7814)
PHONE..............................609 375-2000
Subramani Somasundaram, *Ch of Bd*
Robert Grande, *Mng Member*
Seethalakshmi Vaidyanathan, *Admin Sec*
EMP: 5
SALES (est): 234.1K **Privately Held**
SIC: 7374 2741 7371 Data processing & preparation; ; computer software development & applications

(G-8923)
CHURCH & DWIGHT CO INC
Arm & Hammer
101 Thanet Cir Ste 1 (08540-3675)
PHONE..............................609 683-8021
Steven Kugini, *Branch Mgr*
Kristen Gates, *Manager*
Francine Valentino, *Manager*
Jim Balzano, *Sr Ntwrk Engine*
EMP: 9
SALES (corp-wide): 4.1B **Publicly Held**
WEB: www.churchdwight.com
SIC: 2812 Sodium bicarbonate
PA: Church & Dwight Co., Inc.
500 Charles Ewing Blvd
Ewing NJ 08628
609 806-1200

(G-8924)
CONJUPRO BIOTHERAPUETICS INC
302 Carnegie Ctr Ste 100 (08540-6376)
PHONE..............................609 356-0210
Qingxi Wang, *President*
Lily Liu, *Manager*
EMP: 13
SALES (est): 90K **Privately Held**
SIC: 2834 Pharmaceutical preparations

(G-8925)
CURRAN & CONNORS INC
5 Independence Way # 300 (08540-6627)
PHONE..............................609 514-0104
Shelley Feder, *Regional Mgr*
EMP: 5
SALES (corp-wide): 15.4MM **Privately Held**
SIC: 2721 Periodicals
PA: Curran & Connors, Inc.
140 Adams Ave Ste C20
Hauppauge NY 11779
631 435-0400

(G-8926)
CYBAGE SOFTWARE INC
500 College Rd E Ste 203 (08540-6635)
PHONE..............................848 219-1221
Gurvinder S Chhatwal, *Principal*
Nikhil Patel, *Software Engr*
Anurag Mishra, *Sr Software Eng*
Shruti Bhandari, *Analyst*
Sandip Gaikwad, *Analyst*
EMP: 5 **Privately Held**
SIC: 7372 Prepackaged software
HQ: Cybage Software, Inc.
4058 148th Ave Ne 1d
Redmond WA 98052
425 861-9190

(G-8927)
CYTEC INDUSTRIES INC
504 Carnegie Ctr (08540-6241)
PHONE..............................973 357-3100
EMP: 11
SALES (corp-wide): 12.8MM **Privately Held**
SIC: 2899 Chemical preparations
HQ: Cytec Industries Inc.
4500 Mcginnis Ferry Rd
Alpharetta GA 30005

(G-8928)
DAILY PLAN IT EXECUTIVE CENTER
707 Alexander Rd Ste 208 (08540-6331)
PHONE..............................609 514-9494
Michelle Stemmer, *Principal*
EMP: 4
SALES (est): 173K **Privately Held**
SIC: 2711 Newspapers, publishing & printing

(G-8929)
DATARAM MEMORY
777 Alexander Rd Ste 100 (08540-6300)
PHONE..............................609 799-0071
David A Moylan, *President*
Anthony M Lougee, *CFO*
EMP: 40 EST: 2017
SALES: 30.8MM
SALES (corp-wide): 28MM **Privately Held**
SIC: 3572 Computer storage devices
PA: Leading Testing Laboratories Llc
20823 Park Row Dr Ste 28c
Katy TX 77449
281 600-8227

(G-8930)
DIGITAL DOCUMENTS INC
Also Called: Document Depot
101 Main St (08540-5754)
PHONE..............................609 520-0094
Edward J Keenan Jr, *President*
Kim Keenan, *Admin Sec*
EMP: 4 EST: 1998
SQ FT: 1,000
SALES: 300K **Privately Held**
WEB: www.documentdepot.com
SIC: 7336 2752 Commercial art & graphic design; commercial printing, lithographic

(G-8931)
DOLAN LLC
Also Called: Virginia Lawyers Weekly
421 Executive Dr (08540-1526)
PHONE..............................800 451-9998
EMP: 4
SALES (corp-wide): 461MM **Privately Held**
SIC: 2711 Newspapers
HQ: Dolan Llc
222 S 9th St Ste 2300
Minneapolis MN 55402

(G-8932)
DOLCE TECHNOLOGIES LLC
90 Nassau St Fl 4 (08542-4529)
PHONE..............................609 497-7319
Jennifer Genovese, *General Mgr*
John C Dries,
Marshall Cohen,
Michael Ettenberg,
Michael Lange,
EMP: 4
SALES (est): 311.3K **Privately Held**
SIC: 3826 Mass spectroscopy instrumentation

(G-8933)
DR REDDYS LABORATORIES INC (HQ)
107 College Rd E Ste 100 (08540-6623)
PHONE..............................609 375-9900
Alok Sonig, *President*
Swaninathan Chandrasekaran, *Corp Secy*
Sunil Kumar Chebrolu, *Finance*
Prashanth Reddy, *Manager*
◆ EMP: 38
SQ FT: 1,742,400
SALES (est): 54.6MM **Privately Held**
SIC: 3089 5122 Cases, plastic; pharmaceuticals

(G-8934)
DVX LLC
2 Carter Brook Ln (08540-9508)
PHONE..............................609 924-3590
David Vilkomerson,
EMP: 4
SALES (est): 500K **Privately Held**
WEB: www.dvx.com
SIC: 3845 Ultrasonic medical equipment,
except cleaning

(G-8935)
E R SQUIBB & SONS INTER-AM
3551 Lawrenceville Rd (08540-4715)
P.O. Box 5400 (08543-5400)
PHONE..............................609 252-5144
Richard Gopstein, *Manager*
EMP: 13
SALES (corp-wide): 22.5B **Publicly Held**
SIC: 2834 Pharmaceutical preparations
HQ: E. R. Squibb & Sons Inter-American
Corporation
3551 Lawrenceville Rd
Princeton NJ 08540
609 252-4111

(G-8936)
E R SQUIBB & SONS INTER-AM
(HQ)
Also Called: Bristol-Myers Squibb
3551 Lawrenceville Rd (08540-4715)
P.O. Box 4000 (08543-4000)
PHONE..............................609 252-4111
Lamberto Andreotti, *CEO*
Quintan Oswald, *President*
James M Cornelius, *Chairman*
Rebecca Prince, *Counsel*
Donald Hayden, *Senior VP*
▲ EMP: 1
SQ FT: 735,000
SALES (est): 84.9MM
SALES (corp-wide): 22.5B **Publicly Held**
WEB: www.unitedinpurpose.com
SIC: 2834 Pharmaceutical preparations
PA: Bristol-Myers Squibb Company
430 E 29th St Fl 14
New York NY 10016
212 546-4000

(G-8937)
ECO LLC
344 Nassau St Ste F (08540-4622)
PHONE..............................609 683-9030
Kevin Stockdale,
EMP: 4
SALES (est): 333K **Privately Held**
SIC: 2834 Veterinary pharmaceutical
preparations

(G-8938)
EDDA TECHNOLOGY INC
5 Independence Way # 210 (08540-6627)
PHONE..............................609 919-9889
Jian-Zhong Qian, *President*
Xiaolan Zeng, *Exec VP*
George WEI, *Vice Pres*
EMP: 12
SALES (est): 1.8MM **Privately Held**
SIC: 3841 Diagnostic apparatus, medical

(G-8939)
ELECTEDFACE LLC
26 Snowden Ln (08540-3916)
PHONE..............................609 924-3636
EMP: 32 EST: 2010
SALES (est): 1.6MM **Privately Held**
SIC: 2741 Internet Publishing And Broad-
casting

(G-8940)
EMPTY WALLS INC
Also Called: Framesmith Gallery, The
3495 Us Highway 1 Ste 21 (08540-5933)
PHONE..............................609 452-8488
Paul Smith, *President*
Lisa Schwartz, *Vice Pres*
EMP: 5
SQ FT: 1,600
SALES (est): 300K **Privately Held**
SIC: 5999 3952 Art dealers; frames for
artists' canvases

(G-8941)
ENTERPRISE SERVICES LLC
989 Lenox Dr (08544-0001)
PHONE..............................609 259-9400
Larry Consalvoas, *Branch Mgr*
EMP: 53
SALES (corp-wide): 11.6B **Publicly Held**
WEB: www.eds.com
SIC: 7372 Prepackaged software
HQ: Perspecta Enterprise Solutions Llc
13600 Eds Dr A3s
Herndon VA 20171
703 245-9675

(G-8942)
EON LABS INC
506 Carnegie Ctr Ste 400 (08540-6243)
PHONE..............................609 627-8600
Bernhard Hampl, *President*
▲ EMP: 525
SQ FT: 20,000
SALES (est): 55.8MM **Privately Held**
WEB: www.eonlabs.com
SIC: 2834 Pharmaceutical preparations

(G-8943)
EVENUS PHARMACEUTICAL
LABS INC
506 Carnegie Ctr Ste 100 (08540-6243)
PHONE..............................609 395-8625
Jack Zheng, *CEO*
▲ EMP: 8
SQ FT: 5,732
SALES (est): 630K **Privately Held**
SIC: 2834 Pharmaceutical preparations

(G-8944)
EVEX ANALYTICAL
INSTRUMENTS
Also Called: Evex Instruments
857 State Rd (08540-1415)
P.O. Box 8439 (08543-8439)
PHONE..............................609 252-9192
EMP: 14
SQ FT: 15,000
SALES (est): 2.1MM **Privately Held**
SIC: 3826 Mfg Analytical Instruments

(G-8945)
EVOTEC (US) INC (HQ)
303b College Rd E (08540-6608)
PHONE..............................650 228-1400
Werner Lanthaler, *President*
Craig Johnstone, *COO*
Gary Depaolo, *Vice Pres*
Michael Jobling, *Vice Pres*
EMP: 35
SQ FT: 70,235
SALES (est): 10.6MM
SALES (corp-wide): 429.7MM **Privately**
Held
WEB: www.renovis.com
SIC: 2836 2834 Biological products, ex-
cept diagnostic; pharmaceutical prepara-
tions
PA: Evotec Se
Essener Bogen 7
Hamburg 22419
405 608-10

(G-8946)
EXCELL BRANDS LTD LIABILITY
CO
3 Independence Way # 114 (08540-6626)
PHONE..............................908 561-1130
EMP: 6
SALES (est): 724.2K **Privately Held**
SIC: 2844 5149 Perfumes & colognes;
flavourings & fragrances

(G-8947)
EYWA PHARMA INC
2 Research Way Fl 3 (08540-6628)
PHONE..............................609 751-9600
Srinivasan Seshan, *CEO*
Vince Suneja, *Senior VP*
Kavit Tyagi, *Senior VP*
Jayakumar Ramamoorthy, *Director*
Keith Giunta, *Surgery Dir*
EMP: 6
SQ FT: 2,500
SALES (est): 1.3MM **Privately Held**
SIC: 2834 Pharmaceutical preparations

(G-8948)
FELLOWSHIP IN PRAYER INC
291 Witherspoon St (08542-3227)
PHONE..............................609 924-6863
Howard Ende, *President*
EMP: 4
SALES: 57.2K **Privately Held**
SIC: 2721 Trade journals: publishing only,
not printed on site

(G-8949)
FINEX TRADE
315 Riverside Dr (08540-5429)
PHONE..............................609 921-2747
Cuneyt Buyukucak, *Owner*
▲ EMP: 1
SQ FT: 2,500
SALES (est): 5.7MM **Privately Held**
WEB: www.finextrade.com
SIC: 2079 1799 Olive oil; athletic & recre-
ation facilities construction

(G-8950)
FOUNDATION FOR STUDENT
COMM
Also Called: BUSINESS TODAY
48 University Pl Ste 305 (08540-5116)
PHONE..............................609 258-1111
Carol Klein, *President*
Jonathan Hastings, *President*
Michael Kratsios, *COO*
Dillon Smith, *Director*
EMP: 50
SALES: 1.2MM **Privately Held**
SIC: 2721 7389 Periodicals: publishing
only; convention & show services

(G-8951)
FRAUSCHER SENSOR TECH
USA INC
300 Carnegie Ctr Ste 320 (08540-6255)
PHONE..............................609 285-5492
Vivek Caroli, *Director*
EMP: 13 EST: 2015
SALES (est): 256.8K
SALES (corp-wide): 2.6MM **Privately**
Held
SIC: 3674 Radiation sensors
HQ: Frauscher Sensortechnik Gmbh
GewerbestraBe 1
St. Marienkirchen Bei SchArdinG
4774
771 129-200

(G-8952)
FREYR INC
150 College Rd W Ste 102 (08540-6659)
PHONE..............................908 483-7958
Srinivasa Sadhu, *President*
Sakshi Gaur, *Partner*
Avantika Mishra, *Partner*
Purvanshi Singh, *Partner*
Deepali Gaurav, *Manager*
EMP: 150
SALES: 6.5MM **Privately Held**
SIC: 7372 5045 Prepackaged software;
computer software

(G-8953)
FYX FLEET ROADSIDE
ASSISTANCE (DH)
Also Called: Trac Interstar LLC
750 College Rd E (08540-6646)
PHONE..............................609 452-8900
EMP: 11
SALES (est): 4.3MM **Privately Held**
SIC: 7359 3715 5012 Equipment rental &
leasing; truck trailers; trailers for passen-
ger vehicles
HQ: Trac Intermodal Llc
750 College Rd E
Princeton NJ 08540
609 452-8900

(G-8954)
GEISTLICH PHARMA NORTH
AMERICA
202 Carnegie Ctr Ste 103 (08540-6239)
PHONE..............................609 779-6560
Andreas Geistlich PHD, *CEO*
David Swanson, *General Mgr*
Jeffrey Lord, *Vice Pres*
Fotinos S Panagakos, *Vice Pres*
Alexandra Rodriguez, *Marketing Mgr*
EMP: 39

SQ FT: 3,500
SALES (est): 21.7MM
SALES (corp-wide): 53.3MM **Privately**
Held
SIC: 3843 Dental equipment & supplies
HQ: Geistlich Pharma Ag
Bahnhofstrasse 40
Wolhusen LU 6110
414 925-555

(G-8955)
GLOBAL IDS INC
182 Nassau St Ste 202 (08542-7000)
PHONE..............................609 683-1066
Arka Mukherjee, *CEO*
EMP: 100
SALES (est): 4.9MM **Privately Held**
SIC: 7372 Prepackaged software

(G-8956)
GUERBET LLC
821 Alexander Rd Ste 204 (08540-6352)
PHONE..............................812 333-0059
Massimo Carrara, *Mng Member*
Shannon Wehrendt, *Sr Associate*
▲ EMP: 21
SALES (est): 6.4MM
SALES (corp-wide): 554.5MM **Privately**
Held
WEB: www.guerbet-us.com
SIC: 2833 5122 Medicinals & botanicals;
drugs, proprietaries & sundries
PA: Guerbet
Paris Nord 2 Paris Nord 2
Villepinte 93420
145 915-000

(G-8957)
HALO PUB ICE CREAM
9 Hulfish St (08542-3709)
PHONE..............................609 921-1710
Jerry Reilly, *Owner*
EMP: 17
SALES (est): 992.8K **Privately Held**
SIC: 2024 Ice cream, bulk

(G-8958)
HEALTHPER INC (PA)
124 Brookstone Dr (08540-2404)
P.O. Box 110005, Trumbull CT (06611-
0005)
PHONE..............................888 257-1804
David Lenihan, *Ch of Bd*
Narinder Makin, *Vice Pres*
EMP: 1
SALES: 1MM **Privately Held**
SIC: 7372 Application computer software

(G-8959)
HENGRUI THERAPEUTICS INC
506 Carnegie Ctr Ste 102 (08540-6243)
PHONE..............................609 423-2155
EMP: 4
SALES (est): 90K **Privately Held**
SIC: 2834 Pharmaceutical preparations

(G-8960)
I-EXCEED TECH SOLUTIONS INC
103 Carnegie Ctr Ste 300 (08540-6235)
PHONE..............................917 693-3207
Joseph John, *President*
Anshuman Nayyrar, *Vice Pres*
Karthikeyan Sivaprakasam, *Vice Pres*
Kapil Gupta, *Treasurer*
Kritika Shukla, *Consultant*
EMP: 4 EST: 2011
SALES: 1.5MM **Privately Held**
SIC: 7372 7371 Application computer soft-
ware; computer software systems analy-
sis & design, custom

(G-8961)
INDO-MIM INC (PA)
214 Carnegie Ctr Ste 104 (08540-6244)
PHONE..............................734 327-9842
EMP: 8
SALES (est): 2.5MM **Privately Held**
SIC: 3841 Surgical & medical instruments

(G-8962)
INDO-US MIM TEC PRIVATE LTD
214 Carnegie Ctr Ste 104 (08540-6244)
PHONE..............................734 327-9842
Param Gutti, *Manager*
EMP: 5

SALES (corp-wide): 4.9MM **Privately
Held**
SIC: 3545 3544 3423 Machine tool ac-
cessories; special dies, tools, jigs & fix-
tures; hand & edge tools
HQ: Indo-Mim Private Limited
No 45, (P) Kiadb Industrial Area,
Bengaluru KA 56211

(G-8963)
INTELLIGENT MTL SOLUTIONS INC
Also Called: IMS
201 Washington Rd (08540-6449)
PHONE..................................609 514-4031
Howard Bell, *President*
Joe Dempsey, *CFO*
Ken Ehret, *Manager*
Josh Collins, *CTO*
EMP: 15
SQ FT: 12,000
SALES (est): 3.6MM **Privately Held**
SIC: 2819 Industrial inorganic chemicals

(G-8964)
IRON4U INC
5 Independence Way # 300 (08540-6627)
PHONE..................................609 514-5163
Odd Vaage-Nilsen, *President*
Lars Peitersen, *Vice Pres*
Christian Rode, *CFO*
EMP: 5
SALES (est): 301.4K **Privately Held**
SIC: 2834 Veterinary pharmaceutical
preparations

(G-8965)
JB ELECTRONICS
101 Wall St (08540-1522)
PHONE..................................609 497-2952
EMP: 10
SALES (est): 660K **Privately Held**
SIC: 3679 Design & Assemble Electronic
Circuits

(G-8966)
JIANGSU HENGRUI MEDICINE CO
506 Carnegie Ctr (08540-6243)
PHONE..................................609 395-8625
EMP: 6
SALES (est): 775.6K **Privately Held**
SIC: 2834 Pharmaceutical preparations

(G-8967)
JOHNSON & JOHNSON
51 Pettit Pl (08540-7645)
PHONE..................................732 524-0400
EMP: 80
SALES (corp-wide): 81.5B **Publicly Held**
SIC: 2676 Feminine hygiene paper prod-
ucts
PA: Johnson & Johnson
1 Johnson And Johnson Plz
New Brunswick NJ 08933
732 524-0400

(G-8968)
KYOWA HAKKO KIRIN CAL INC
212 Carnegie Ctr Ste 101 (08540-6236)
PHONE..................................609 580-7400
Kazuyoshi Tachibana, *President*
EMP: 5 **Privately Held**
SIC: 2834 Pharmaceutical preparations
HQ: Kyowa Kirin Pharmaceutical Research,
Inc.
9420 Athena Cir
La Jolla CA 92037

(G-8969)
LIGHTSCAPE MATERIALS INC
201 Washington Rd (08540-6449)
PHONE..................................609 734-2224
Gerard Frederickson, *CEO*
▲ EMP: 6
SALES (est): 950K **Privately Held**
SIC: 2816 Inorganic pigments

(G-8970)
LRK INC
Also Called: Lucy's Ravioli Kitchen
830 State Rd Ste 3 (08540-1443)
PHONE..................................609 924-6881
Caron Wendell, *President*
Joseph McLaughlin, *Vice Pres*

EMP: 14
SALES (est): 2MM **Privately Held**
SIC: 2099 5812 Pasta, uncooked: pack-
aged with other ingredients; eating places

(G-8971)
LUYE PHARMA USA LTD
502 Carnegie Ctr Ste 100 (08540-6289)
PHONE..................................609 799-7600
Liu Dian-Bo, *Chairman*
EMP: 23 EST: 2015
SALES: 4.3MM **Privately Held**
SIC: 2834 Druggists' preparations (phar-
maceuticals)

(G-8972)
MACLEODS PHARMA USA INC
103 College Rd E Ste 200 (08540-6611)
PHONE..................................609 269-5250
Pat O'Malley, *VP Opers*
▲ EMP: 13
SALES (est): 2.2MM **Privately Held**
SIC: 2834 Pharmaceutical preparations
PA: Macleods Pharmaceuticals Limited
304, Atlanta Arcade, Marol Church
Road
Mumbai MH 40005

(G-8973)
MARKUS WIENER PUBLISHERS INC
231 Nassau St (08542-4601)
PHONE..................................609 921-1141
Markus Wiener, *President*
Stacey Gartstein, *Manager*
EMP: 6
SALES: 1MM **Privately Held**
WEB: www.markuswiener.com
SIC: 2731 Books: publishing only

(G-8974)
MAYFAIR TECH LTD LBLTY CO
Also Called: Pendotech
66 Witherspoon St (08542-3239)
PHONE..................................609 802-1262
John Benson, *Design Engr*
James Furey,
EMP: 10
SALES: 2MM **Privately Held**
WEB: www.pendotech.com
SIC: 3823 Industrial instrmnts msrmnt dis-
play/control process variable

(G-8975)
MEDICURE PHARMA INC
116 Village Blvd Ste 200 (08540-5700)
PHONE..................................888 435-2220
Albert Friesen, *President*
Michael Janzen, *Principal*
EMP: 20
SALES (est): 2.5MM **Privately Held**
SIC: 2834 Pharmaceutical preparations

(G-8976)
MEGALITH PHARMACEUTICALS INC
302 Carnegie Ctr (08540-6374)
PHONE..................................877 436-7220
EMP: 4
SALES (est): 208.3K **Privately Held**
SIC: 2834 Pharmaceutical preparations

(G-8977)
METAL POWDER INDS FEDERATION
105 College Rd E Ste 101 (08540-6622)
PHONE..................................609 452-7700
C James Trambino, *CEO*
Jillaine K Regan, *Vice Pres*
EMP: 16
SQ FT: 7,100
SALES: 3.7MM **Privately Held**
SIC: 8611 2731 Trade associations; book
publishing

(G-8978)
MIKROS SYSTEMS CORPORATION (PA)
707 Alexander Rd (08540-6331)
P.O. Box 7189 (08543-7189)
PHONE..................................609 987-1513
Thomas J Meaney, *CEO*
Paul G Casner, *Ch of Bd*
Walter T Bristow, *COO*
Walter Bristow, *COO*

Patricia Kapp, *Vice Pres*
EMP: 2
SALES: 8.5MM **Publicly Held**
SIC: 3571 7371 8731 Personal computers (microcomputers); computer software
development; computer (hardware) development

(G-8979)
MILLENNIUM INFO TECH INC
4390 Us Highway 1 Ste 121 (08540-5747)
PHONE..................................609 750-7120
Ramana Krosuri, *President*
Santhosh Sagu, *Business Mgr*
Sunita Krosuri, *CFO*
Marcos Edghill, *Director*
EMP: 95
SQ FT: 2,000
SALES: 6MM **Privately Held**
WEB: www.mitiweb.com
SIC: 7372 Prepackaged software

(G-8980)
MIMO DISPLAY LLC (PA)
Also Called: Mimo Monitors
743 Alexander Rd Ste 15 (08540-6328)
PHONE..................................855 937-6466
David Anderson, *President*
Andre Liu, *COO*
Michael Wells, *Manager*
Tyler Wells, *Manager*
EMP: 9
SQ FT: 3,000
SALES (est): 2.5MM **Privately Held**
SIC: 3575 Computer terminals, monitors &
components

(G-8981)
MORSE METAL PRODUCTS CO INC (PA)
1 Hunters Run (08540-8646)
PHONE..................................732 422-3676
Carl H Geisler, *President*
Ceasar Leiva, *Manager*
EMP: 6 EST: 1945
SALES (est): 705.1K **Privately Held**
SIC: 3537 Industrial trucks & tractors

(G-8982)
MULTIFORCE SYSTEMS CORPORATION
101 Wall St (08540-1522)
PHONE..................................609 683-4242
Thomas Bates, *President*
W K Griesinger, *Chairman*
G Hallman, *Shareholder*
▼ EMP: 19 EST: 1981
SQ FT: 10,400
SALES (est): 4.4MM **Privately Held**
WEB: www.fuelforce.com
SIC: 3823 8748 7373 Gas flow comput-
ers, industrial process type; business con-
sulting; computer systems analysis &
design

(G-8983)
NEOPHARMA INC (HQ)
211 College Rd E Ste 101 (08540-6610)
PHONE..................................609 201-2185
Venu Gopala Krishna Gopa, *President*
Yasmin Saqib, *Principal*
EMP: 80 EST: 2017
SALES (est): 18.3MM
SALES (corp-wide): 156.5K **Privately
Held**
SIC: 2834 Pharmaceutical preparations

(G-8984)
NEWCARDIO INC
103 Carnegie Ctr Ste 300 (08540-6235)
PHONE..................................877 332-4324
Dr Jess Emery Jones, *CEO*
Michael E Hanson, *Principal*
James A Heisch, *Principal*
Greg Sadowski, *COO*
EMP: 11
SQ FT: 2,000
SALES (est): 838.1K **Privately Held**
SIC: 3845 Electromedical equipment

(G-8985)
NIKSUN INC (PA)
457 N Harrison St (08540-3510)
PHONE..................................609 936-9999
Parag Pruthi, *CEO*
Satish C Pruthi, *President*

Korwin Lee, *Vice Pres*
Charles Ng'ang'a, *Engineer*
Gil Galin, *Engineer*
EMP: 115 EST: 1997
SQ FT: 30,616
SALES (est): 33.8MM **Privately Held**
WEB: www.niksun.com
SIC: 7373 3571 Computer integrated sys-
tems design; electronic computers

(G-8986)
NONZERO FOUNDATION INC
321 Prospect Ave (08540-5330)
PHONE..................................609 688-0793
Robert Wright, *President*
Paul Glastris, *Trustee*
Jacqueline Shire, *Trustee*
EMP: 5
SALES (est): 280.4K **Privately Held**
SIC: 2741

(G-8987)
NOVO NORDISK INC
1100 Camput Rd (08540)
PHONE..................................609 987-5800
Joann Sufalko, *Vice Pres*
Terri Cherichello, *Administration*
EMP: 8
SALES (corp-wide): 20.1B **Privately Held**
SIC: 2834 Pharmaceutical preparations
HQ: Novo Nordisk Inc.
800 Scudders Mill Rd
Plainsboro NJ 08536
609 987-5800

(G-8988)
OAVCO LTD LIABILITY COMPANY (PA)
Also Called: Oav Air Bearing
103 Carnegie Ctr (08540-6235)
P.O. Box 7421 (08543-7421)
PHONE..................................855 535-4227
Murat Erturk, *Principal*
EMP: 10
SQ FT: 10,000
SALES (est): 2MM **Privately Held**
SIC: 3812 Omnibearing indicators

(G-8989)
OAVIATION CORPORATION
103 Carnegie Ctr Ste 212 (08540-6235)
PHONE..................................609 619-3060
Murat Erturk, *President*
EMP: 25
SQ FT: 25,000
SALES (est): 4.1MM **Privately Held**
SIC: 3812 Search & navigation equipment

(G-8990)
OHM LABORATORIES INC
Also Called: Ranbaxy Pharmaceuticals
2 Independence Way (08540-6620)
P.O. Box 8208 (08543-8208)
PHONE..................................609 720-9200
Bob Patton, *General Mgr*
Gursharan Singh, *General Mgr*
Jim Meehan, *Vice Pres*
Kishore Durga, *Production*
Carol Puhl, *Buyer*
EMP: 100
SALES (corp-wide): 1.3B **Privately Held**
WEB: www.ranbaxy.com
SIC: 2834 Pharmaceutical preparations
HQ: Ohm Laboratories, Inc.
1385 Livingston Ave
North Brunswick NJ 08902
732 418-2235

(G-8991)
OMTHERA PHARMACEUTICALS INC
Also Called: (A DEVELOPMENT-STAGE
COMPANY)
707 State Rd Ste 206 (08540-1437)
PHONE..................................908 741-4399
Gerald Wisler, *President*
Bernardus N Machielse, *COO*
Ramona M Lloyd, *Vice Pres*
Timothy J Maines, *Vice Pres*
Christian S Schade, *CFO*
EMP: 14
SALES (est): 1.9MM
SALES (corp-wide): 22B **Privately Held**
SIC: 2834 Pharmaceutical preparations

HQ: Astrazeneca Pharmaceuticals Lp
1 Medimmune Way
Gaithersburg MD 20878

(G-8992)
ORCHID PHARMACEUTICALS INC
Also Called: Orchid Chemicals
116 Village Blvd Ste 200 (08540-5700)
PHONE.................................609 951-2209
Satish Srinivasan, *President*
▲ EMP: 4
SALES (est): 324K **Privately Held**
SIC: 2834 Pharmaceutical preparations

(G-8993)
PATHEON BIOLOGICS LLC
201 College Rd E (08540-6610)
PHONE.................................609 919-3300
Mark R Bamforth, *CEO*
Jeff Strand, *General Mgr*
Robert J Broeze, *Senior VP*
Steven H Kasok, *CFO*
Jorge Villaverde, *Manager*
▲ EMP: 86
SQ FT: 60,000
SALES (est): 35.5MM
SALES (corp-wide): 242.1K **Privately Held**
WEB: www.laureatepharma.com
SIC: 5122 2834 Pharmaceuticals; pharmaceutical preparations
HQ: Patheon Biologics Llc
4766 Laguardia Dr
Saint Louis MO 63134

(G-8994)
PENETONE CORPORATION
1000 Herrontown Rd (08540-7716)
PHONE.................................609 921-0501
John McHale, *Branch Mgr*
EMP: 4
SALES (corp-wide): 25.3MM **Privately Held**
WEB: www.protectivecream.com
SIC: 2842 2048 Disinfectants, household or industrial plant; sanitation preparations; feed supplements
PA: Penetone Corporation
125 Kingsland Ave Ste 205
Clifton NJ 07014
201 567-3000

(G-8995)
PHILIP LIEF GROUP INC
371 Sayre Dr (08540-5860)
PHONE.................................609 430-1000
Philip Lief, *President*
EMP: 4
SQ FT: 2,500
SALES (est): 257.1K **Privately Held**
WEB: www.philipliefgroup.com
SIC: 2731 Book publishing

(G-8996)
POLYMATHES HOLDINGS I LLC (PA)
20 Nassau St Ste M (08542-4536)
PHONE.................................609 945-1690
Greg Amato, *CEO*
Murray S Cohen, *Ch of Bd*
James Ivchenko, *President*
EMP: 8 EST: 2012
SALES (est): 1.4MM **Privately Held**
SIC: 2865 6512 Dyes & pigments; nonresidential building operators

(G-8997)
PRINCETON BIOPHARMA STRATEGIES
660 Pretty Brook Rd (08540-7510)
PHONE.................................609 203-5303
Mark Altmeyer, *Principal*
EMP: 4
SALES (est): 319.4K **Privately Held**
SIC: 2834 Pharmaceutical preparations

(G-8998)
PRINCETON BLUE INC
5 Independence Way # 300 (08540-6627)
PHONE.................................908 369-0961
Pramod Sachdeva, *President*
Uma Sachdeva, *Vice Pres*
Balendu Mishra, *Manager*
Mike James, *Consultant*

Biswadeep Mukherjee, *Consultant*
EMP: 35
SQ FT: 250
SALES (est): 4.2MM **Privately Held**
WEB: www.princetonblue.com
SIC: 7372 Prepackaged software

(G-8999)
PRINCETON INFORMATION CENTER
Also Called: Applied Psychological Services
330 N Harrison St Ste 6 (08540-3500)
PHONE.................................609 924-7019
Robert Karlin, *President*
Barbara Scanna, *Business Mgr*
EMP: 4
SALES: 400K **Privately Held**
SIC: 2741 8999 Miscellaneous publishing; psychological consultant

(G-9000)
PRINCETON KEYNES GROUP INC (PA)
116 Village Blvd Ste 200 (08540-5700)
PHONE.................................609 951-2239
Douglas Stewart, *CEO*
▼ EMP: 13 EST: 1997
SQ FT: 25,000
SALES (est): 1.8MM **Privately Held**
WEB: www.princetonkeynes.com
SIC: 2891 8711 Adhesives & sealants; engineering services

(G-9001)
PRINCETON PACKET INC (HQ)
Also Called: Packet Publications
300 Witherspoon St (08542-3497)
P.O. Box 350 (08542-0350)
PHONE.................................609 924-3244
James B Kilgore, *President*
June Vogel, *Corp Secy*
Peg Gerke, *CFO*
EMP: 169
SQ FT: 21,000
SALES (est): 41.7MM **Privately Held**
WEB: www.packetmediaguide.com
SIC: 2711 3993 Commercial printing & newspaper publishing combined; signs & advertising specialties
PA: Packet Media, Llc
198 Us Highway 9 Ste 100
Englishtown NJ 07726
856 779-3800

(G-9002)
PRINCETON PUBLISHING GROUP
650 Rosedale Rd (08540-2218)
PHONE.................................609 577-0693
Adam Drake Baer, *President*
EMP: 5
SALES (est): 304.9K **Privately Held**
SIC: 2731 Book publishing

(G-9003)
PRINCETON QUADRANGLE CLUB
33 Prospect Ave (08540-5210)
PHONE.................................609 258-0376
Dinesh Maneyapanda, *Exec Dir*
Mary Eklund, *Admin Sec*
EMP: 7
SALES (est): 920.1K **Privately Held**
SIC: 8322 2099 Meal delivery program; food preparations

(G-9004)
PRINCETON RESEARCH INSTRUMENTS
Also Called: P R I
42 Cherry Valley Rd (08540-7640)
PHONE.................................609 924-0570
Charles A Crider, *President*
John McCaffrey, *Regional Mgr*
Bill Asher, *Vice Pres*
Robert Hyland, *Vice Pres*
Dana Kelly, *Vice Pres*
EMP: 4
SQ FT: 2,000
SALES (est): 320K **Privately Held**
WEB: www.prileeduhv.com
SIC: 3826 Analytical instruments

(G-9005)
PRINCETON SUPPLY CORP
301 N Harrison St Ste 473 (08540-3527)
PHONE.................................609 683-9100
John Astrab, *President*
EMP: 9
SALES (est): 2MM **Privately Held**
SIC: 2679 Paper products, converted

(G-9006)
PRINCETON TRADE AND TECHNOLOGY
1 Wall St (08540)
PHONE.................................609 683-0215
Mohammed Labib, *President*
EMP: 10
SQ FT: 4,000
SALES (est): 942.9K **Privately Held**
SIC: 3845 Medical cleaning equipment, ultrasonic

(G-9007)
PRINCETON UNIVERSITY PRESS (PA)
41 William St Ste 1 (08540-5223)
PHONE.................................609 258-4900
Harold T Shapiro, *President*
Mark Bellis, *Production*
Sara Lerner, *Production*
Lunsford Robert A, *Research*
Bortolon Alessandro, *Research*
▲ EMP: 85 EST: 1910
SQ FT: 26,000
SALES (est): 25.7MM **Privately Held**
WEB: www.pupress.princeton.edu
SIC: 2731 2741 Book publishing; miscellaneous publishing

(G-9008)
PRINCTON ALMNI PBLICATIONS INC
Also Called: Princeton Alumni Weekly
194 Nassau St Ste 38 (08542-7003)
PHONE.................................609 258-4885
Marilyn Mark, *President*
John I Merritt III, *President*
Nancy S Macmillan, *Admin Sec*
EMP: 8
SALES (est): 816.1K **Privately Held**
SIC: 2721 Magazines: publishing & printing

(G-9009)
PROMIA INCORPORATED
322 Commons Way (08540-1510)
PHONE.................................609 252-1850
Amy Reynolds, *Branch Mgr*
James Mullen, *Technology*
EMP: 5 **Privately Held**
SIC: 5734 7379 7371 7372 Computer software & accessories; computer related consulting services; computer software development; prepackaged software
PA: Promia Incorporated
20 Lauren Ave
Novato CA

(G-9010)
PROMIUS PHARMA LLC
107 College Rd E Ste 100 (08540-6623)
PHONE.................................609 282-1400
Anil Namboodiripad, *President*
Swaninathan Chandrasekaran, *Corp Secy*
Sunil Kumar Chebrolu, *Finance*
▲ EMP: 87
SALES (est): 24MM **Privately Held**
SIC: 2834 Pharmaceutical preparations
PA: Dr. Reddy's Laboratories Limited
Door No. 8-2-337, Road No. 3,
Hyderabad TS 50003

(G-9011)
QUANTUM SECURITY SYSTEMS INC
124 Fairfield Rd (08540-9579)
PHONE.................................609 252-0505
Harry Krotowski, *President*
EMP: 5
SALES (est): 681.2K **Privately Held**
SIC: 3699 Security control equipment & systems

(G-9012)
RAMCO SYSTEMS CORPORATION (HQ)
136 Main St Ste 305 (08540-5735)
PHONE.................................609 620-4800
Venkatesh Viswanathan, *CEO*
James Fitzgerald, *President*
Rajesh Kumar Ranganathan, *Finance*
EMP: 30
SALES: 17MM
SALES (corp-wide): 44.5MM **Privately Held**
WEB: www.rsc.ramco.com
SIC: 7372 Prepackaged software
PA: Ramco Systems Limited
No-64, Ramco Building,
Chennai TN 60011
446 653-4000

(G-9013)
RANBAXY USA INC
2 Independence Way (08540-6620)
PHONE.................................609 720-9200
EMP: 25
SALES: 3.5MM
SALES (corp-wide): 1.2B **Privately Held**
SIC: 2834 5122 Mfg Pharmaceutical Preparations Whol Drugs/Sundries
PA: Sun Pharmaceutical Industries Limited
Sun House, Cts No. 201 B/1,
Mumbai MH 40006
224 324-4324

(G-9014)
REFFERALS ONLY INC
Also Called: Roi Rnovations
3321 Lawrenceville Rd (08540-4719)
PHONE.................................609 921-1033
Linda Fahmie, *President*
EMP: 5
SALES (est): 432.4K **Privately Held**
SIC: 1389 Construction, repair & dismantling services

(G-9015)
REGENTREE LLC
116 Village Blvd Ste 200 (08540-5700)
PHONE.................................609 734-4328
Sunny Kim, *Manager*
EMP: 4
SALES (est): 213.5K **Privately Held**
SIC: 2834 Pharmaceutical preparations

(G-9016)
REPORTE HISPANO
42 Dorann Ave (08540-3906)
PHONE.................................609 933-1400
Kleibeel Sanandoval, *Principal*
Elizabeth Roca, *Sales Staff*
EMP: 4
SALES (est): 278.7K **Privately Held**
SIC: 2711 Newspapers

(G-9017)
ROCKWOOD HOLDINGS INC (HQ)
100 Overlook Ctr Ste 101 (08540-7814)
PHONE.................................609 514-0300
Seifi Ghasemi, *CEO*
Monika Engel-Bader, *President*
Andrew M Ross, *President*
Thomas J Riordan, *Exec VP*
Robert J Zatta, *CFO*
◆ EMP: 33
SALES (est): 1.3B **Publicly Held**
SIC: 2819 2816 Industrial inorganic chemicals; iron oxide pigments (ochers, siennas, umbers)

(G-9018)
ROCKWOOD SPECIALTIES GROUP INC (DH)
100 Overlook Ctr Ste 101 (08540-7814)
PHONE.................................609 514-0300
Seifi Ghasemi, *CEO*
Bob Zatta, *CFO*
◆ EMP: 10
SALES (est): 333.1MM **Publicly Held**
WEB: www.rockwoodadditives.com
SIC: 5169 2899 Industrial chemicals; chemical preparations
HQ: Rockwood Holdings, Inc.
100 Overlook Ctr Ste 101
Princeton NJ 08540
609 514-0300

▲ = Import ▼=Export
◆ =Import/Export

(G-9019)
SANDOZ INC (HQ)
100 College Rd W (08540-6604)
PHONE..................................609 627-8500
Benhard Hamel, *President*
Don Degolyer, *President*
Peter Goldschmidt, *President*
Robin Adelstein, *Vice Pres*
Ariel Alon, *Vice Pres*
▲ EMP: 140 EST: 1963
SQ FT: 240,000
SALES (est): 473.7MM
SALES (corp-wide): 51.9B **Privately Held**
WEB: www.sandoz.com
SIC: 2834 5122 Tablets, pharmaceutical;
pills, pharmaceutical; pharmaceuticals
PA: Novartis Ag
Lichtstrasse 35
Basel BS 4056
613 241-111

(G-9020)
SENSORS UNLIMITED INC
330 Carter Rd Ste 100 (08540-7438)
PHONE..................................609 333-8000
John Trezza, *Principal*
Robert Freeman,
▲ EMP: 64
SQ FT: 41,000
SALES (est): 17MM
SALES (corp-wide): 66.5B **Publicly Held**
WEB: www.sensorsinc.com
SIC: 3357 8731 3229 Fiber optic cable
(insulated); electronic research; pressed
& blown glass
HQ: Goodrich Corporation
2730 W Tyvola Rd 4
Charlotte NC 28217
704 423-7000

(G-9021)
SES ENGINEERING (US) INC
4 Research Way (08540-6707)
PHONE..................................609 987-4000
Michael Rist, *President*
Win Caldwell, *General Mgr*
Doug Clayton, *Vice Pres*
Deepak Mathur, *Vice Pres*
John Matlaga, *Vice Pres*
EMP: 99
SALES (est): 24.8MM
SALES (corp-wide): 19.2MM **Privately Held**
SIC: 3663 Satellites, communications
PA: Ses
Chat. De Betzdorf 22
Betzdorf
710 725-1

(G-9022)
SIGHTLOGIX INC
745 Alexander Rd Ste 5 (08540-6343)
PHONE..................................609 951-0008
Jim Hahn, *Ch of Bd*
John Romanowich, *President*
James Hahn, *Chairman*
Frank De Fina, *Exec VP*
Gabe Barbaro, *Mfg Dir*
▲ EMP: 21
SQ FT: 5,000
SALES (est): 3.2MM **Privately Held**
WEB: www.sightlogix.com
SIC: 7382 7373 3669 Protective devices,
security; computer-aided manufacturing
(CAM) systems service; visual communi-
cation systems

(G-9023)
SOLIGENIX INC (PA)
29 Emmons Dr Ste B10 (08540-5950)
PHONE..................................609 538-8200
Christopher J Schaber, *Ch of Bd*
Oreola Donini, *Senior VP*
Daniel P Ring, *Vice Pres*
Jonathan Guarino, *CFO*
Karen Krumeich, *CFO*
EMP: 18
SQ FT: 6,200
SALES: 5.2MM **Publicly Held**
WEB: www.dorbiopharma.com
SIC: 8731 2834 2836 Biological research;
biotechnical research, commercial; phar-
maceutical preparations; biological prod-
ucts, except diagnostic; vaccines

(G-9024)
SOLVAY HOLDING INC
Also Called: Rhodia
504 Carnegie Ctr (08540-6241)
P.O. Box 5203 (08543-5203)
PHONE..................................609 860-4000
James Harton, *President*
Jean Pierre Clamadieu, *Chairman*
John P Donahue, *Senior VP*
Karim Hajjar, *CFO*
Michel Defourny, *Admin Sec*
◆ EMP: 10389
SALES (est): 228.8MM
SALES (corp-wide): 330.1K **Privately
Held**
WEB: www.us.rhodia.com
SIC: 2819 2812 2865 2869 Boric acid;
soda ash, sodium carbonate (anhydrous);
phenol, alkylated & cumene; fluorinated
hydrocarbon gases
HQ: Rhodia Holdings Limited
Oak House
Watford HERTS WD24

(G-9025)
SOLVAY USA INC (HQ)
504 Carnegie Ctr (08540-6241)
P.O. Box 5203 (08543-5203)
PHONE..................................609 860-4000
Michael Lacey, *President*
Mark Dahlinger, *CFO*
Anthony Saviano, *Admin Sec*
◆ EMP: 350 EST: 1997
SQ FT: 94,500
SALES (est): 880.4MM
SALES (corp-wide): 12.8MM **Privately
Held**
WEB: www.food.us.rhodia.com
SIC: 2899 2869 2821 2087 Chemical
preparations; fluorinated hydrocarbon
gases; silicones; plastics materials &
resins; flavoring extracts & syrups; phe-
nol, alkylated & cumene; diphenylamines;
isocyanates
PA: Solvay
Rue De Ransbeek 310
Bruxelles 1120
226 421-11

(G-9026)
SONDPEX CORP AMERICA LLC
Also Called: Sondpex Electronics
4185 Route 27 (08540-8704)
PHONE..................................732 940-4430
Katie Wu,
Chuck Chen,
▲ EMP: 8
SQ FT: 6,500
SALES (est): 4MM **Privately Held**
WEB: www.sondpex.com
SIC: 3651 Audio electronic systems

(G-9027)
SPACETOUCH INC
34 Chambers St (08542-3739)
PHONE..................................609 712-6572
Yingzhe Hu, *CEO*
EMP: 5 EST: 2015
SQ FT: 5,000
SALES: 50K **Privately Held**
SIC: 3571 Electronic computers

(G-9028)
STEWARD LLC
Also Called: Steward Mag
345 Witherspoon St (08542-3405)
PHONE..................................609 816-8825
EMP: 5
SALES (est): 242.5K **Privately Held**
SIC: 7371 2721 Custom Computer Pro-
graming Periodicals-Publishing/Printing

(G-9029)
**SUN PHARMACEUTICAL INDS
INC**
2 Independence Way (08540-6620)
PHONE..................................313 871-8400
Subramanian Kalyanasundaram, *CEO*
Manjeet Bindra, *Officer*
Michelle Sabia, *Executive Asst*
EMP: 30
SALES (corp-wide): 1.3B **Privately Held**
SIC: 2834 Pharmaceutical preparations

HQ: Sun Pharmaceutical Industries, Inc.
270 Prospect Plains Rd
Cranbury NJ 08512
609 495-2800

(G-9030)
**SUREWAY PRTG & GRAPHICS
LLC**
338 Wall St (08540-1518)
P.O. Box 2213 (08543-2213)
PHONE..................................609 430-4333
George Bilgrav, *Sales Staff*
Christopher Sustak,
Pam Sustak,
EMP: 5
SALES (est): 627.6K **Privately Held**
SIC: 2752 Commercial printing, offset

(G-9031)
TAG OPTICS INC
200 N Harrison St (08540-3507)
P.O. Box 1572 (08542-1572)
PHONE..................................609 356-2142
Christian Theriault, *CEO*
EMP: 4
SALES (est): 443.5K **Privately Held**
SIC: 3827 Optical instruments & lenses

(G-9032)
TAREE PHARMA LLC
342 Herrontown Rd (08540-2931)
PHONE..................................609 252-9596
Scheire Raymond, *Principal*
EMP: 4
SALES (est): 219.4K **Privately Held**
SIC: 2834 Pharmaceutical preparations

(G-9033)
THINK BIG SOLUTIONS INC
14 Farber Rd (08540-5913)
PHONE..................................609 716-7343
Srinivas Meka, *Principal*
EMP: 7
SALES (corp-wide): 1.3MM **Privately
Held**
SIC: 7372 Business oriented computer
software
PA: Think Big Solutions Inc.
5 Jacob Dr
Princeton Junction NJ 08550
732 968-0211

(G-9034)
TRAC INTERMODAL LLC (HQ)
750 College Rd E (08540-6646)
PHONE..................................609 452-8900
Val T Noel, *COO*
Gregg Carpene, *Exec VP*
Inbal Arie, *Vice Pres*
James Bowe, *Vice Pres*
Rich Hediger, *Vice Pres*
EMP: 5 EST: 2012
SALES (est): 50.6MM **Privately Held**
SIC: 7359 3715 5012 Equipment rental &
leasing; truck trailers; trailers for passen-
ger vehicles

(G-9035)
TRENDMARK LLC
465 Meadow Rd Apt 10207 (08540-6366)
PHONE..................................551 226-7973
Tejas Vora, *CEO*
EMP: 4
SQ FT: 1,000
SALES (est): 148.7K **Privately Held**
SIC: 7372 Business oriented computer
software

(G-9036)
TRUE INFLUENCE LLC (PA)
103 Carnegie Ctr Ste 300 (08540-6235)
PHONE..................................888 223-1586
Brian Giese, *CEO*
Dennis Dale, *Vice Pres*
Peter Larkin, *Vice Pres*
Mike Rogers, *Vice Pres*
Ken Stout, *Vice Pres*
EMP: 10
SALES (est): 2.2MM **Privately Held**
SIC: 7372 Business oriented computer
software

(G-9037)
TWINPOD INC
252 Nassau St (08542-4600)
PHONE..................................908 758-5858

Jessy Dhanjal, *President*
Dion Cini, *Vice Pres*
EMP: 6 EST: 2008
SQ FT: 600
SALES (est): 345K **Privately Held**
WEB: www.twinpod.com
SIC: 5047 7372 7379 Diagnostic equip-
ment, medical; business oriented com-
puter software; computer related
consulting services

(G-9038)
**TYCO INTERNATIONAL MGT CO
LLC (DH)**
9 Roszel Rd Ste 2 (08540-6205)
PHONE..................................609 720-4200
George R Oliver, *CEO*
Edward D Breen, *President*
Paul Fitzhenry, *President*
Bill Evans, *General Mgr*
Jay Strohl, *General Mgr*
◆ EMP: 40 EST: 1962
SALES (est): 12.7B **Privately Held**
SIC: 3999 1711 1731 3669 Fire extin-
guishers, portable; fire sprinkler system
installation; safety & security specializa-
tion; fire detection & burglar alarm sys-
tems specialization; fire detection
systems, electric; smoke detectors; fire
alarm apparatus, electric; industrial
valves; automatic regulating & control
valves
HQ: Johnson Controls, Inc.
5757 N Green Bay Ave
Milwaukee WI 53209
414 524-1200

(G-9039)
UNISTAR INC
Also Called: Unistar Creations
61 Castleton Rd (08540-1644)
PHONE..................................212 840-2100
EMP: 4
SQ FT: 7,800
SALES: 1.5MM **Privately Held**
SIC: 5094 3911 Whol Jewelry/Precious
Stones Mfg Precious Metal Jewelry

(G-9040)
**VENSUN PHARMACEUTICALS
INC**
103 Carnegie Ctr Ste 300 (08540-6235)
PHONE..................................908 278-8386
George Sager, *Opers Staff*
EMP: 18
SALES (corp-wide): 216.9MM **Privately
Held**
SIC: 2834 Pharmaceutical preparations
HQ: Vensun Pharmaceuticals, Inc.
2 Tower Center Blvd # 1102
East Brunswick NJ
215 809-2015

(G-9041)
VENTURE INFO NETWORK
Also Called: The Vine
226 Linden Ln (08540-3449)
PHONE..................................609 279-0777
Micky Morgan, *Agent*
EMP: 5
SALES (est): 262.5K **Privately Held**
SIC: 2711 Newspapers

(G-9042)
**WESTERN DIGITAL
CORPORATION**
116 Village Blvd Ste 200 (08540-5700)
PHONE..................................609 734-7479
Tom Everett, *Manager*
EMP: 8
SALES (corp-wide): 16.5B **Publicly Held**
WEB: www.wdc.com
SIC: 3572 Disk drives, computer
PA: Western Digital Corporation
5601 Great Oaks Pkwy
San Jose CA 95119
408 717-6000

(G-9043)
WILSHIRE TECHNOLOGIES INC
243 Wall St (08540-1512)
PHONE..................................609 683-1117
Joe San Filippo, *CEO*
Rohit Deshpande, *Production*
Anthony Gargano, *Assistant*

G E O G R A P H I C

▲ EMP: 5
SQ FT: 600
SALES (est): 1.2MM Privately Held
WEB: www.wilshiretechnologies.com
SIC: 2899 8748 Chemical preparations;
business consulting

(G-9044)
WONG ROBINSON & CO INC (PA)
Also Called: Pequod Communications
743 Alexander Rd Ste 15 (08540-6328)
PHONE..................................609 951-0300
James Robertson, *President*
Andre Liu, *Vice Pres*
Patrick Wong, *Human Res Dir*
Ron Cohen, *Director*
▲ EMP: 20
SQ FT: 15,000
SALES (est): 3.1MM Privately Held
SIC: 2752 Commercial printing, offset

(G-9045)
ZULTNER & COMPANY
12 Wallingford Dr (08540-6428)
PHONE..................................609 452-0216
Richard Zultner, *Owner*
EMP: 10
SQ FT: 2,500
SALES (est): 640.2K Privately Held
WEB: www.zultner.com
SIC: 7372 Operating systems computer
software

(G-9046)
ZYCUS INC (HQ)
103 Carnegie Ctr Ste 321 (08540-6235)
PHONE..................................609 799-5664
Aatish Dedhia, *President*
Chiranjib Guha, *Vice Pres*
Sanjay Kadkol, *Vice Pres*
Hemant Nadkarni, *Vice Pres*
Mahesh Gosavi, *Project Mgr*
EMP: 32
SALES: 12.2MM Privately Held
WEB: www.zycus.com
SIC: 7372 Prepackaged software

Princeton Junction
Mercer County

(G-9047)
AEON CORPORATION
186 Princeton Hightstown (08550-1668)
PHONE..................................609 275-9003
Leo Spiekman, *Principal*
Zemer Mizrahi, *Vice Pres*
EMP: 9
SALES (est): 985.8K Privately Held
SIC: 3674 Semiconductors & related de-
vices

(G-9048)
AI TECHNOLOGY INC
Also Called: A I T
70 Washington Rd (08550-1012)
PHONE..................................609 799-9388
Kevin Chung, *CEO*
V Cirincione, *Principal*
Carol Redher, *Purch Mgr*
Maurice Leblon, *Advt Staff*
EMP: 40
SALES (est): 8.1MM Privately Held
SIC: 3678 Electronic connectors

(G-9049)
AIBENS IMORT
7 York Rd (08550-3273)
PHONE..................................609 902-9953
Tanmay Trivedi, *Owner*
EMP: 5
SALES (est): 238.2K Privately Held
SIC: 3312 Blast furnaces & steel mills

(G-9050)
AMERASIA INTL TECH INC
Also Called: A I T
70 Washington Rd (08550-1012)
P.O. Box 3081, Princeton (08543-3081)
PHONE..................................609 799-9388
Kevin Chung, *President*
Cynthia Chu, *Exec VP*
Jimmy Luo, *Project Engr*

Robinson Salguero, *Project Engr*
Ben Jakubovic, *Accountant*
EMP: 41
SQ FT: 52,000
SALES: 2.9MM Privately Held
WEB: www.aitechnology.com
SIC: 2891 Adhesives; sealants

(G-9051)
AMERITEX INDUSTRIES CORP
39 Everett Dr Ste 2 (08550-5393)
PHONE..................................609 502-0123
Richard Tuscano, *President*
EMP: 13
SALES (est): 1.2MM Privately Held
SIC: 3999 Barber & beauty shop equip-
ment

(G-9052)
AVANTE INTERNATIONAL TECH INC
70 Washington Rd (08550-1012)
PHONE..................................609 799-9388
Kevin Chung, *CEO*
Nabil Bensalah, *Business Mgr*
Cynthia Chu, *Exec VP*
Albert Chung, *Vice Pres*
Jeffery Douglass, *Project Mgr*
EMP: 40
SQ FT: 35,000
SALES (est): 7.1MM Privately Held
WEB: www.avantetech.com
SIC: 3579 Voting machines

(G-9053)
COMMUNITY PRIDE PUBLICATIONS
55 Prnceton Hightstown (08550-1110)
PHONE..................................609 921-8760
EMP: 10
SQ FT: 1,800
SALES (est): 690K Privately Held
SIC: 2741 Misc Publishing

(G-9054)
CURA BIOMED INC
103 S Longfellow Dr (08550-2237)
PHONE..................................609 647-1474
Jayasimha Raju, *Officer*
EMP: 4
SALES (est): 149.2K Privately Held
SIC: 3841 5047 Surgical & medical instru-
ments; medical equipment & supplies

(G-9055)
ENGILITY LLC
15 Roszel Rd (08550)
PHONE..................................703 633-8300
Anthony Smeraglinolo, *CEO*
Edward P Boykin, *Principal*
Darryll J Pines, *Principal*
Anthony Principi, *Principal*
Charles S Ream, *Principal*
EMP: 14
SALES (corp-wide): 4.6B Publicly Held
SIC: 3663 8733 Radio & TV communica-
tions equipment; noncommercial research
organizations
HQ: Engility Llc
4803 Stonecroft Blvd
Chantilly VA 20151
703 708-1400

(G-9056)
ENTOURAGE IMAGING INC
Also Called: Entourage Yearbooks
39 Everett Dr Ste 1-2 (08550-5393)
PHONE..................................888 926-6571
Elias Jo, *President*
Tianna Ellerbee, *Accounting Mgr*
Jayshree Kalwachwala, *Human Resources*
Allen Fowler, *Sales Staff*
Jessica Jones, *Sales Staff*
EMP: 28 EST: 2005
SQ FT: 4,000
SALES (est): 4.5MM Privately Held
SIC: 2741 Directories: publishing & printing

(G-9057)
EXCEL INDUSTRIAL CO INC
17 Huntington Dr (08550-2126)
PHONE..................................609 275-1748
Ben C Sun, *President*
EMP: 5

SALES: 100K Privately Held
WEB: www.excel-uae.com
SIC: 3552 Textile machinery

(G-9058)
FUCELTECH INC
11 Glengarry Way (08550-3033)
PHONE..................................609 275-0070
Chuni Ghosh, *CEO*
EMP: 4
SQ FT: 1,000
SALES (est): 10K Privately Held
SIC: 3674 Fuel cells, solid state

(G-9059)
FUNNIBONZ LLC
3 Lake View Ct (08550-4915)
PHONE..................................609 915-3685
James H Barbour III, *Mng Member*
James Barbour,
Fredrick Kurtz,
Ryan Marrone,
EMP: 5
SALES (est): 464.2K Privately Held
SIC: 2033 Barbecue sauce: packaged in
cans, jars, etc.

(G-9060)
HAIGHTS CROSS CMMNICATIONS INC (PA)
295 Prncton Hightstown Rd (08550-3123)
PHONE..................................212 209-0500
Rick Noble, *CEO*
Kevin R Brueggeman, *President*
Rich Freese, *President*
Julie Latzer, *Senior VP*
Diane Q Curtin, *Vice Pres*
▲ EMP: 41
SQ FT: 35,000
SALES (est): 83.8MM Privately Held
WEB: www.haightscross.com
SIC: 2731 Books: publishing only

(G-9061)
INNOLUTIONS INC
4 Wellesley Ct (08550-1829)
P.O. Box 384, Windsor (08561-0384)
PHONE..................................609 490-9799
Manoj Kumar-Patel, *President*
Piyushkumar Patel, *Vice Pres*
Michael Friedman, *Software Engr*
Smita Patel, *Admin Sec*
EMP: 9
SQ FT: 3,000
SALES: 2MM Privately Held
WEB: www.innoinc.com
SIC: 3625 Control equipment, electric

(G-9062)
MISTRAS GROUP INC (PA)
195 Clarksville Rd Ste 2 (08550-5392)
PHONE..................................609 716-4000
Sotirios J Vahaviolos, *Ch of Bd*
Michael J Lange, *Vice Ch Bd*
Dennis Bertolotti, *President*
Ricky Krebs, *General Mgr*
Joseph Schmidt, *General Mgr*
EMP: 135
SALES: 742.3MM Publicly Held
WEB: www.mistrasgroup.com
SIC: 8711 7372 3829 3825 Engineering
services; prepackaged software; measur-
ing & controlling devices; instruments to
measure electricity

(G-9063)
P S I CEMENT INC
12 Robert Dr (08550-3021)
PHONE..................................609 716-1515
Mike Ekladous, *President*
Samia Ekladous, *Vice Pres*
Mina Ekladous, *Admin Sec*
EMP: 6
SQ FT: 3,600
SALES (est): 1MM Privately Held
WEB: www.psicement.com
SIC: 5084 2674 Cement making machin-
ery; cement bags: made from purchased
materials

(G-9064)
PBA OF WEST WINDSOR
376 N Post Rd (08550-1325)
PHONE..................................609 799-6535
Keith Hillman, *Principal*
EMP: 40

SALES (est): 2.3MM Privately Held
SIC: 2499 Policemen's clubs, wood

(G-9065)
PHYSICAL ACOUSTICS CORPORATION
Also Called: Vibra-Metrics
195 Clarksville Rd (08550-5392)
PHONE..................................609 716-4000
Sotirios Vahaviolos, *President*
Mark Carlos, *Exec VP*
Leilani Cooper, *Engineer*
Jeff Donahue, *Engineer*
Kay Bickham, *Controller*
EMP: 135 EST: 2000
SQ FT: 50,000
SALES (est): 23.4MM Publicly Held
WEB: www.pacndt.com
SIC: 3829 Measuring & controlling devices
PA: Mistras Group, Inc.
195 Clarksville Rd Ste 2
Princeton Junction NJ 08550

(G-9066)
SCHLUMBERGER TECHNOLOGY CORP
Also Called: E M R Photoelectric Div
20 Wallace Rd (08550-1008)
P.O. Box 44 (08550-0044)
PHONE..................................609 275-3815
Patrice Ligneul, *Principal*
Andrew Mueller, *Engineer*
Ron Perez, *Engineer*
EMP: 115 Publicly Held
SIC: 1389 Oil field services
HQ: Schlumberger Technology Corp
300 Schlumberger Dr
Sugar Land TX 77478
281 285-8500

(G-9067)
SWEETLY SPIRITED CUPCAKES LTD
10 Newport Dr (08550-2224)
PHONE..................................917 846-4238
Cheryl G Ojeda, *Administration*
EMP: 7
SALES (est): 341.9K Privately Held
SIC: 2051 Bread, cake & related products

(G-9068)
THINK BIG SOLUTIONS INC (PA)
5 Jacob Dr (08550-5103)
PHONE..................................732 968-0211
Srinivas Meka, *Principal*
EMP: 4 EST: 2010
SALES (est): 1.3MM Privately Held
SIC: 7372 Business oriented computer
software

(G-9069)
VIBGYOR SOLUTIONS INC
14 Washington Rd Ste 623 (08550-1028)
PHONE..................................609 750-9158
Chandra Karnei, *President*
EMP: 6
SALES (est): 470K Privately Held
WEB: www.vibgyorsolutions.com
SIC: 7372 Prepackaged software

(G-9070)
WIZCOM CORPORATION
19 Washington Rd Ste D (08550-1030)
PHONE..................................609 750-0601
Nagarjuna Thota, *President*
Deepak Kotte, *Software Dev*
Aditya Pandiri, *Software Dev*
EMP: 20
SQ FT: 900
SALES (est): 10MM Privately Held
WEB: www.wizcomcorp.com
SIC: 7371 7372 Computer software devel-
opment; business oriented computer soft-
ware

(G-9071)
YOGO MIX
44 Normandy Dr (08550-3275)
PHONE..................................609 897-1379
Carlo Pugliese, *Principal*
EMP: 5
SALES (est): 524.2K Privately Held
SIC: 3273 Ready-mixed concrete

Prospect Park
Passaic County

(G-9072)
ADVANCED BREWING SYS LLC
91 Savoy Pl (07508-2228)
PHONE..................................973 633-1777
Vincent Fulco, *Principal*
▲ EMP: 7
SALES (est): 595.6K Privately Held
SIC: 2082 Malt beverages

(G-9073)
ENVELOPES & PRINTED PDTS INC
135 Fairview Ave (07508-1923)
PHONE..................................973 942-1232
William F Higgins, *President*
Christoper Higgins, *Admin Sec*
EMP: 9
SQ FT: 2,000
SALES (est): 1.1MM Privately Held
WEB: www.specialtyprinting.com
SIC: 2759 Invitation & stationery printing & engraving

(G-9074)
MICHELEX CORPORATION (PA)
204 Haledon Ave (07508-2023)
PHONE..................................201 977-1177
Albert Lacle, *CEO*
Venkat Kakani, *President*
EMP: 3
SALES (est): 2.4MM Privately Held
SIC: 7389 2834 Financial services; druggists' preparations (pharmaceuticals)

Rahway
Union County

(G-9075)
AIRTEC INC
Also Called: Airtec-Unique
17 W Scott Ave (07065-4529)
P.O. Box 1181 (07065-1181)
PHONE..................................732 382-3700
Joseph M Niemczyk, *President*
EMP: 8 EST: 1967
SQ FT: 20,000
SALES (est): 1.1MM Privately Held
SIC: 3444 Sheet metal specialties, not stamped

(G-9076)
AISHA&ANNA NATION OF TRENDS
2 Park Sq Apt 2210 (07065-4061)
PHONE..................................201 951-8197
Aisha Hale, *Principal*
▼ EMP: 4
SALES (est): 159.4K Privately Held
SIC: 2844 Toilet preparations

(G-9077)
API AMERICAS INC
329 New Brunswick Ave (07065-2928)
PHONE..................................732 382-6800
David A Walton, *President*
Bob Almer, *Vice Pres*
Scott Lewis, *Vice Pres*
Jeff Pendleton, *Opers Mgr*
Juan Blas, *Production*
EMP: 60 Privately Held
WEB: www.apifoils.com
SIC: 3497 2891 Metal foil & leaf; adhesives & sealants
HQ: Api Americas Inc.
3841 Greenway Cir
Lawrence KS 66046

(G-9078)
ARTISTIC BIAS PRODUCTS CO INC
1905 Elizabeth Ave (07065-4534)
PHONE..................................732 382-4141
Daniel Berg, *President*
▲ EMP: 50 EST: 1938

SALES (est): 5.1MM Privately Held
SIC: 2396 5131 2891 Trimming, fabric; piece goods & notions; adhesives & sealants

(G-9079)
ASSOCIATED PLASTICS INC
179 E Inman Ave (07065-4709)
PHONE..................................732 574-2800
Richard W Fisher Jr, *President*
Bruce Fisher, *Vice Pres*
EMP: 12 EST: 1962
SQ FT: 11,000
SALES (est): 1.7MM Privately Held
SIC: 3357 3089 Nonferrous wiredrawing & insulating; closures, plastic

(G-9080)
ASTRO TOOL & MACHINE CO INC
810 Martin St (07065-5410)
P.O. Box 1264 (07065-1264)
PHONE..................................732 382-2454
Gary Price, *President*
EMP: 26 EST: 1964
SQ FT: 20,000
SALES (est): 4.4MM Privately Held
WEB: www.astrotoolco.com
SIC: 3599 Machine shop, jobbing & repair

(G-9081)
ATLANTIC AIR ENTERPRISES INC
856 Elston St (07065-5408)
PHONE..................................732 381-4000
Darin Severino, *President*
EMP: 19 EST: 1941
SQ FT: 11,400
SALES (est): 3.9MM Privately Held
WEB: www.atlanticairent.com
SIC: 1761 3444 Sheet metalwork; sheet metalwork

(G-9082)
BARLICS MANUFACTURING CO INC
Also Called: Innan Molding
815 Martin St (07065-5409)
PHONE..................................732 381-6229
Glen Barlics, *President*
Mark Barlics, *Vice Pres*
EMP: 4
SALES (est): 1MM Privately Held
SIC: 5162 3544 Plastics products; special dies, tools, jigs & fixtures

(G-9083)
BRILLIANT BRDCSTG CONCEPT INC
800 New Brunswick Ave # 1 (07065-3847)
PHONE..................................732 287-9201
Annur Hamilton, *President*
EMP: 15
SALES (est): 649.5K Privately Held
SIC: 4832 3993 Radio broadcasting stations; signs & advertising specialties

(G-9084)
CAMEO METAL PRODUCTS INC
Also Called: Cameo Metal Forms
1745 Elizabeth Ave (07065-4532)
PHONE..................................732 388-4000
Fax: 732 388-4799
EMP: 12
SQ FT: 5,000
SALES (est): 870K Privately Held
SIC: 3471 Plating/Polishing Service

(G-9085)
CARBOLINE COMPANY
Also Called: Car Boline
842 Elston St (07065-5408)
PHONE..................................732 388-2912
EMP: 23
SALES (corp-wide): 5.5B Publicly Held
SIC: 2851 Lacquers, varnishes, enamels & other coatings
HQ: Carboline Company
2150 Schuetz Rd Fl 1
Saint Louis MO 63146
314 644-1000

(G-9086)
CLASSIC COOKING LLC
1600 St Grges Ave Ste 301 (07065)
PHONE..................................718 439-0200
Elliott Huss, *Mng Member*
▲ EMP: 100
SQ FT: 40,000
SALES: 15.8MM Privately Held
SIC: 2035 2037 2038 Pickles, sauces & salad dressings; vegetables, quick frozen & cold pack, excl. potato products; soups, frozen

(G-9087)
DASON STAINLESS PRODUCTS CO
1773 Elizabeth Ave (07065-4532)
PHONE..................................732 382-7272
William Thompson Jr, *President*
Rose Cummings, *Office Mgr*
EMP: 12 EST: 1961
SQ FT: 7,000
SALES (est): 1.6MM Privately Held
SIC: 3494 Pipe fittings

(G-9088)
DPJ INC
Also Called: Dpj Signs
245 E Inman Ave (07065-4704)
PHONE..................................732 499-8600
Derek Delhoyo, *President*
Jim Tozer, *Admin Sec*
EMP: 11
SQ FT: 6,500
SALES (est): 1.5MM Privately Held
SIC: 3993 Signs & advertising specialties

(G-9089)
ELECTRONIC MARINE SYSTEMS INC (PA)
Also Called: Engine Efficiency Associates
800 Ferndale Pl (07065-4909)
PHONE..................................732 680-4120
Thomas J Priola, *President*
▲ EMP: 15
SQ FT: 10,000
SALES: 4MM Privately Held
WEB: www.emsmarcon.com
SIC: 3669 Intercommunication systems, electric; fire alarm apparatus, electric; burglar alarm apparatus, electric

(G-9090)
ELECTRUM INC
Also Called: Electrum Recovery Works
827 Martin St (07065-5409)
PHONE..................................732 396-1616
Matthew Douglas, *President*
John A Silva Jr, *Vice Pres*
Alicia Kehler, *Regl Sales Mgr*
Adam Napell, *Regl Sales Mgr*
Bill Malcolm, *Sales Staff*
◆ EMP: 14
SQ FT: 20,000
SALES (est): 2.8MM Privately Held
WEB: www.electruminc.com
SIC: 3339 Precious metals

(G-9091)
ELIXENS AMERICA INC
1443 Pinewood St Bldg 4u (07065-5503)
PHONE..................................732 388-3555
Adrian America, *Chairman*
▲ EMP: 3
SALES: 2.3MM
SALES (corp-wide): 1MM Privately Held
WEB: www.elixensamerica.com
SIC: 5122 2899 Perfumes; oils & essential oils
HQ: Elixens
28 Boulevard Kellermann
Paris 13e Arrondissement 75013

(G-9092)
EXTRA OFFICE INC
580 Leesville Ave (07065-4822)
PHONE..................................732 381-9774
Louis Prince Jr, *President*
Louis Prince Sr, *Vice Pres*
EMP: 12
SQ FT: 16,000

SALES (est): 1.6MM Privately Held
WEB: www.extraoffice.net
SIC: 2522 1799 5046 7641 Office chairs, benches & stools, except wood; office bookcases, wallcases & partitions, except wood; office cabinets & filing drawers: except wood; office desks & tables: except wood; office furniture installation; partitions; office furniture repair & maintenance

(G-9093)
FELDWARE INC
900 Hart St (07065-5630)
P.O. Box 1883 (07065-7883)
PHONE..................................718 372-0486
Sidney Feldman, *President*
Charles Feldman, *Vice Pres*
▲ EMP: 25 EST: 1959
SQ FT: 15,000
SALES (est): 4.4MM Privately Held
SIC: 3469 Stamping metal for the trade

(G-9094)
FORTUNE RVRSIDE AUTO PARTS INC (PA)
Also Called: Fortune Metal Recycling
900 Leesville Ave (07065-4828)
PHONE..................................732 381-3355
Norman Ng, *CEO*
Chris Lam, *Vice Pres*
John Paik, *Vice Pres*
Simon Wong, *Vice Pres*
▼ EMP: 43
SQ FT: 12,000
SALES (est): 8.5MM Privately Held
WEB: www.fortuneriverside.com
SIC: 3324 Steel investment foundries

(G-9095)
FRANK B ROSS CO INC (PA)
970 New Brunswick Ave H (07065-3814)
P.O. Box 1241 (07065-1241)
PHONE..................................732 669-0810
Larry Powell, *President*
Donald Ayerlee, *Vice Pres*
Carmen Mangan, *Vice Pres*
Maryanne Willemsen, *Admin Sec*
▼ EMP: 16 EST: 1902
SQ FT: 77,000
SALES (est): 2.7MM Privately Held
WEB: www.rosswaxes.com
SIC: 2842 Beeswax, processing of; waxes for wood, leather & other materials

(G-9096)
FROST TECH INC
830 Elston St (07065-5408)
P.O. Box Ag (07065-0290)
PHONE..................................732 396-0071
Dennis P Berthiaame, *President*
EMP: 15
SALES (est): 1.2MM Privately Held
SIC: 1793 3211 Glass & glazing work; flat glass

(G-9097)
GENERAL ELECTRONIC ENGINEERING (PA)
132 W Main St (07065-4106)
PHONE..................................732 381-1144
William A Piegari, *President*
Ralph Eisenberge, *Vice Pres*
EMP: 9
SQ FT: 4,000
SALES (est): 2.1MM Privately Held
WEB: www.genelectronic.com
SIC: 3625 Electric controls & control accessories, industrial

(G-9098)
GRIGNARD COMPANY LLC
505 Capobianco Plz (07065-5401)
P.O. Box 1535 (07065-7535)
PHONE..................................732 340-1111
Kelly A Grignard, *Mng Member*
Etienne Grignard,
▲ EMP: 25
SQ FT: 40,000
SALES: 10MM Privately Held
WEB: www.grignard.com
SIC: 2899 4225 6519 Chemical preparations; general warehousing & storage; real property lessors

(G-9099)
HARBISONWALKER INTL INC
868 Elston St (07065-5408)
PHONE..................................732 388-8686
Ralph Turano, *Manager*
EMP: 8
SALES (corp-wide): 703.8MM **Privately Held**
SIC: 3255 Clay refractories
HQ: Harbisonwalker International, Inc.
1305 Cherrington Pkwy # 100
Moon Township PA 15108

(G-9100)
HARRISON ELECTRO MECHANICAL
1607 Coach St (07065-4103)
PHONE..................................732 382-6008
William Piegari, *President*
Arlene Piegari, *Corp Secy*
EMP: 12
SQ FT: 4,800
SALES (est): 2.1MM **Privately Held**
WEB: www.harrisonelectro.com
SIC: 3674 3672 3625 3357 Semiconductor diodes & rectifiers; circuit boards, television & radio printed; relays & industrial controls; nonferrous wiredrawing & insulating
PA: General Electronic Engineering Inc
132 W Main St
Rahway NJ 07065
732 381-1144

(G-9101)
HEALTH PHARMA USA LLC
1600 Hart St (07065-5519)
PHONE..................................732 540-8421
Hasmukh Patel,
Ankit Patel,
EMP: 12
SQ FT: 5,000
SALES (est): 53.6K **Privately Held**
SIC: 2899 Gelatin: edible, technical, photographic or pharmaceutical

(G-9102)
HONE-A-MATIC TOOL & CUTTER CO
187 Wescott Dr (07065-4706)
PHONE..................................732 382-6000
Anthony R Lamastra, *President*
Ken Lamastra, *Vice Pres*
EMP: 5 EST: 1961
SQ FT: 8,000
SALES (est): 567.3K **Privately Held**
SIC: 3541 3542 5084 Machine tools, metal cutting type; machine tools, metal forming type; metalworking tools (such as drills, taps, dies, files)

(G-9103)
INMAN MOLD AND MFG CO
273 E Inman Ave (07065-4704)
P.O. Box 1143 (07065-1143)
PHONE..................................732 381-3033
Glen Barlics, *President*
EMP: 8
SALES (corp-wide): 500K **Privately Held**
SIC: 3089 Injection molding of plastics
PA: Inman Mold And Manufacturing Co Inc
4 Commerce St
Springfield NJ 07081
732 381-3033

(G-9104)
INSTRUMENTATION TECHNOLOGY SLS
205 E Inman Ave (07065-4700)
PHONE..................................732 388-0866
Anna Sadowska, *President*
Stanley Lewand, *Vice Pres*
EMP: 7
SQ FT: 3,500
SALES (est): 760K **Privately Held**
SIC: 3625 Relays & industrial controls

(G-9105)
J C CONTRACTING INC
681 Mill St (07065-4812)
PHONE..................................973 748-5600
EMP: 16 EST: 2000
SQ FT: 20,000

SALES (est): 3MM **Privately Held**
SIC: 3661 3669 Mfg Telephone/Telegraph Apparatus Mfg Communications Equipment

(G-9106)
J VITALE SIGN CO INC
2204 Elizabeth Ave Ste 1 (07065-4601)
PHONE..................................732 388-8401
Joseph Frank Vitale, *President*
EMP: 6 EST: 1951
SQ FT: 2,000
SALES (est): 500K **Privately Held**
SIC: 7389 3993 Sign painting & lettering shop; lettering service; signs & advertising specialties

(G-9107)
JASON METAL PRODUCTS CORP
1072 Randolph Ave (07065-5526)
PHONE..................................732 396-1132
Richard Jaszyn, *President*
Chris Jaszyn, *Vice Pres*
EMP: 7 EST: 1979
SQ FT: 16,000
SALES (est): 1.1MM **Privately Held**
SIC: 3444 Sheet metalwork

(G-9108)
JM AHLE CO INC
625 Leesville Ave (07065-4821)
PHONE..................................732 388-5507
J Formisano, *General Mgr*
EMP: 4
SALES (corp-wide): 62MM **Publicly Held**
SIC: 3272 Building materials, except block or brick: concrete
HQ: J.M. Ahle Co., Inc.
190 William St Ste 2d
South River NJ 08882
732 238-1700

(G-9109)
JOSEPH BBINEC SHTMTL WORKS INC
774 Martin St (07065-5410)
PHONE..................................732 388-0155
Joseph T Babinec, *CEO*
Jason Babinec, *President*
Desiree Latorre, *Vice Pres*
EMP: 37 EST: 1955
SQ FT: 45,000
SALES (est): 7.3MM **Privately Held**
SIC: 1761 3444 Sheet metalwork; sheet metalwork

(G-9110)
JUICE HUB LLP
1555 Main St Ste A (07065-4068)
PHONE..................................732 784-8265
Arturo Ramirez, *Principal*
EMP: 4
SALES: 125K **Privately Held**
SIC: 2033 Fruit juices: fresh

(G-9111)
KAUFMAN STAIRS INC (PA)
150 E Inman Ave (07065-4702)
PHONE..................................908 862-3579
Alan Kaufman, *President*
Barbara Simon, *Vice Pres*
EMP: 50
SQ FT: 17,000
SALES (est): 7.5MM **Privately Held**
WEB: www.kaufmanstairs.com
SIC: 2431 3446 Staircases & stairs, wood; architectural metalwork

(G-9112)
KIDDESIGNS INC
1299 Main St (07065-5224)
PHONE..................................732 574-9000
Suzanne Fellows, *CEO*
Isaac E Ashkenazi, *President*
Edward Blanco, *Vice Pres*
Chabetaye Chraime, *Vice Pres*
Sean Chraime, *Vice Pres*
▲ EMP: 24
SQ FT: 55,000
SALES (est): 12.3MM **Privately Held**
WEB: www.kiddirect.com
SIC: 5092 3944 Toys & games; electronic toys

(G-9113)
LIEBERFARB INC
2100 Felver Ct (07065-5721)
PHONE..................................973 676-9090
Mark Schonwetter, *President*
Ann S Arnold, *Vice Pres*
Isabella Schonwetter, *Vice Pres*
Luba Schonwetter, *Vice Pres*
EMP: 18
SQ FT: 2,400
SALES (est): 2.5MM **Privately Held**
WEB: www.lieberfarb.com
SIC: 3911 Jewelry, precious metal

(G-9114)
LINDEN MOLD AND TOOL CORP
155 Wescott Dr (07065-4710)
P.O. Box C (07065-1215)
PHONE..................................732 381-1411
Vincent M Illuzzi, *President*
Steve Guzik, *Manager*
▲ EMP: 45
SQ FT: 15,000
SALES (est): 7.3MM **Privately Held**
WEB: www.lindenmold.com
SIC: 3544 3089 Industrial molds; injection molding of plastics

(G-9115)
LM AIR TECHNOLOGY INC
1467 Pinewood St (07065-5503)
PHONE..................................732 381-8200
Peter Daniele, *President*
Myron Szewczuk, *Vice Pres*
Susan Szewczuk, *Administration*
EMP: 20
SQ FT: 5,000
SALES (est): 4.7MM **Privately Held**
WEB: www.lmairtech.com
SIC: 3564 3821 Air purification equipment; laboratory apparatus & furniture

(G-9116)
M RAFI SONS GARMENT INDUSTRIES
1463 Pinewood St (07065-5503)
PHONE..................................732 381-7660
Zaheed Rafi, *Owner*
▲ EMP: 5
SALES (est): 450K **Privately Held**
SIC: 2326 Work garments, except raincoats: waterproof
PA: M. Rafi Sons Garments Industries (Pvt) Ltd.
'plot 10-A, Block-1,'
Lahore
427 466-988

(G-9117)
MERCK & CO INC
126 E Lincoln Ave (07065-4646)
P.O. Box 2000 (07065-0900)
PHONE..................................908 740-4000
John Hladick, *Technical Staff*
EMP: 100
SALES (corp-wide): 42.2B **Publicly Held**
SIC: 2836 2844 5122 2834 Vaccines; veterinary biological products; suntan lotions & oils; animal medicines; druggists' preparations (pharmaceuticals)
PA: Merck & Co., Inc.
2000 Galloping Hill Rd
Kenilworth NJ 07033
908 740-4000

(G-9118)
MERCK SHARP & DOHME CORP
126 E Lincoln Ave (07065-4607)
P.O. Box 2000 (07065-0900)
PHONE..................................732 594-4000
Thomas Zakszewski, *Buyer*
John Roosa, *Plant Engr*
Debra Smith, *VP Human Res*
Ron Maturo, *Manager*
Subashini Vedala, *Technology*
EMP: 100
SALES (corp-wide): 42.2B **Publicly Held**
SIC: 2834 Pharmaceutical preparations
HQ: Merck Sharp & Dohme Corp.
2000 Galloping Hill Rd
Kenilworth NJ 07033
908 740-4000

(G-9119)
MIGHTY MUG INCORPORATED
665 Martin St (07065-5409)
PHONE..................................732 382-3911
James Smaldone, *President*
Say Smaldone, *Vice Pres*
Danielle Vinci, *Sales Staff*
▲ EMP: 4
SALES: 15MM **Privately Held**
SIC: 3089 5085 Plastic kitchenware, tableware & houseware; plastic bottles

(G-9120)
NOVELL ENTERPRISES INC
Also Called: Novell Design Studio
2100 Felver Ct (07065-5721)
PHONE..................................732 428-8300
Victor Novogrodzki, *President*
Bruce Pucciarello, *Corp Secy*
Rick Mulholland, *Marketing Staff*
EMP: 52
SQ FT: 24,000
SALES (est): 20MM **Privately Held**
WEB: www.novelldesignstudio.com
SIC: 3911 Jewel settings & mountings, precious metal

(G-9121)
POLMAR IRON WORK INC
673 New Brunswick Ave (07065-3817)
PHONE..................................732 882-0900
Marek Wresilo, *President*
EMP: 12
SALES (est): 2.4MM **Privately Held**
SIC: 3441 Fabricated structural metal

(G-9122)
PREMAC INC
167 Wescott Dr (07065-4710)
P.O. Box 9 (07065-0009)
PHONE..................................732 381-7550
Edward H Schenker Sr, *President*
Eric L Schenker, *Vice Pres*
Fred Schenker, *Vice Pres*
Frieda Schenker, *Admin Sec*
EMP: 15 EST: 1950
SQ FT: 4,000
SALES (est): 2.3MM **Privately Held**
SIC: 3812 Instrument landing systems (ILS), airborne or ground

(G-9123)
R&R COSMETICS LLC
1140 Randolph Ave (07065-5507)
P.O. Box 1211 (07065-1211)
PHONE..................................732 340-1000
Musthafa E Kamal, *General Mgr*
EMP: 7
SALES (est): 1.1MM **Privately Held**
SIC: 2844 Face creams or lotions

(G-9124)
ROBERT MANSE DESIGNS LLC
Also Called: Bali Designs
2100 Felver Ct (07065-5721)
PHONE..................................732 428-8305
Robert Manse, *President*
Tess Griffin, *Merchandising*
EMP: 38
SQ FT: 24,000
SALES: 1.5MM **Privately Held**
SIC: 3911 Jewelry, precious metal

(G-9125)
ROYAL LACE CO INC
902 E Hazelwood Ave (07065-5608)
PHONE..................................718 495-9327
Moises Guttman, *Ch of Bd*
Aaron Guttman, *President*
Nathan Green, *Admin Sec*
▲ EMP: 20
SQ FT: 20,000
SALES (est): 3.7MM **Privately Held**
SIC: 2258 5131 Lace, knit; lace fabrics

(G-9126)
RSR ELECTRONICS INC
Also Called: Electronix Express
900 Hart St (07065-5630)
PHONE..................................732 381-8777
Eli Rosenbaum, *President*
Ajit Gulati, *Vice Pres*
Hitesh Vyas, *CFO*
Sol Kaye, *Marketing Mgr*
Victor Neumark, *Marketing Mgr*
▲ EMP: 45

▲ = Import ▼=Export
◆ =Import/Export

SQ FT: 32,750
SALES (est): 7.8MM **Privately Held**
WEB: www.rsrelectronics.com
SIC: 3999 5065 3825 3577 Education aids, devices & supplies; electronic parts & equipment; instruments to measure electricity; computer peripheral equipment

(G-9127)
SDI TECHNOLOGIES INC (PA)
1299 Main St (07065-5224)
PHONE....................732 574-9000
Ezra S Ashkenazi, *President*
Mark Chraime, *Senior VP*
Isaac Ashkenazi, *CFO*
Chabetaye Chraime, *CFO*
Geralyn Zamorski, *VP Human Res*
◆ **EMP:** 98 **EST:** 1956
SQ FT: 40,000
SALES (est): 35.5MM **Privately Held**
WEB: www.sdiworld.com
SIC: 3651 Sound reproducing equipment; tape recorders: cassette, cartridge or reel; household use; radio receiving sets

(G-9128)
SUNRISE PHARMACEUTICAL INC (PA)
665 E Lincoln Ave (07065-5711)
PHONE....................732 382-6085
Utpal Patel, *CEO*
Jayanti Patel, *President*
Gaurang Bhavsar, *Technology*
Deepak Bhalla, *Officer*
▲ **EMP:** 25
SQ FT: 33,000
SALES (est): 4.1MM **Privately Held**
SIC: 2834 Pharmaceutical preparations

(G-9129)
TRUCKEROS NEWS LLC
1720 Lawrence St (07065-5110)
P.O. Box 1646 (07065-7646)
PHONE....................732 340-1043
Cesar Vargas, *Owner*
EMP: 10
SALES (est): 738.9K **Privately Held**
SIC: 2731 Books: publishing & printing

(G-9130)
UNIQUE METAL PRODUCTS
17 W Scott Ave (07065-4529)
P.O. Box 1181 (07065-1181)
PHONE....................732 388-1888
Joseph Niemczyk Jr, *President*
EMP: 11 **EST:** 1959
SQ FT: 30,000
SALES (est): 1.2MM **Privately Held**
SIC: 3444 Sheet metal specialties, not stamped

(G-9131)
UNIQUE PRECISION CO INC
2095 Elizabeth Ave (07065-4624)
PHONE....................732 382-8699
Anthony Bobkoskie, *President*
Anthony Bobkowskie, *President*
EMP: 6
SQ FT: 3,200
SALES (est): 510K **Privately Held**
SIC: 3541 3599 Lapping machines; grinding castings for the trade

(G-9132)
WYTECH INDUSTRIES INC (PA)
960 E Hazelwood Ave (07065-5635)
PHONE....................732 396-3900
Anthony J Casalino, *CEO*
Michael Casalino, *President*
Clive James, *General Mgr*
Arthur Barry, *Vice Pres*
Michael Brown, *Vice Pres*
EMP: 65
SQ FT: 23,000
SALES (est): 30.1MM **Privately Held**
WEB: www.wytech.com
SIC: 3496 3315 Miscellaneous fabricated wire products; wire products, ferrous/iron: made in wiredrawing plants

---

Ramsey
Bergen County

(G-9133)
ACHILLES PROSTHETCS & ORTHOTCS
503 N Franklin Tpke # 12 (07446-1166)
PHONE....................201 785-9944
Peter R Buffington, *Principal*
EMP: 4
SALES (est): 304.7K **Privately Held**
SIC: 3842 Orthopedic appliances

(G-9134)
ADMA BIOLOGICS INC (PA)
465 State Rt 17 (07446-2049)
PHONE....................201 478-5552
Steven A Elms, *Ch of Bd*
Jerrold B Grossman, *Vice Ch Bd*
Adam S Grossman, *President*
Brian Lenz, *CFO*
James Mond, *Chief Mktg Ofcr*
EMP: 74
SQ FT: 4,200
SALES: 16.9MM **Publicly Held**
SIC: 2836 Biological products, except diagnostic

(G-9135)
AERO TEC LABORATORIES INC (PA)
Also Called: A T L
45 Spear Rd (07446-1221)
PHONE....................201 825-1400
Peter J Regna, *President*
Stephen White, *Managing Dir*
David Dack, *Vice Pres*
▼ **EMP:** 34 **EST:** 1969
SQ FT: 70,000
SALES (est): 13.1MM **Privately Held**
WEB: www.atlinc.com
SIC: 3069 8731 Rubber automotive products; commercial physical research

(G-9136)
ALTEON
170 Williams Dr (07446-2907)
PHONE....................201 934-1624
Marilyn Breslow, *Principal*
EMP: 5
SALES (est): 628.5K **Privately Held**
SIC: 2834 8731 Vitamin preparations; commercial physical research

(G-9137)
ANGELOS ITALIAN ICES ICECREAM
96 E Main St (07446-1925)
PHONE....................201 962-7575
Angelo Onello, *Owner*
EMP: 4
SALES (est): 213.4K **Privately Held**
SIC: 2024 Dairy based frozen desserts

(G-9138)
APOGEE SOUND INTERNATIONAL LLC
50 Spring St Ste 1 (07446-1131)
PHONE....................201 934-8500
Jonathan Guss, *CEO*
Maureen Flotard, *CFO*
EMP: 40
SALES (est): 5MM **Publicly Held**
WEB: www.apogeesound.com
SIC: 3651 Speaker systems
PA: Bogen Communications International, Inc.
1200 Macarthur Blvd # 303
Mahwah NJ 07430

(G-9139)
ARIES PRECISION TOOL INC
37 Orchard St (07446-1111)
P.O. Box 147, Westwood (07675-0147)
PHONE....................201 252-8550
Stephen Bachman, *President*
Lynn Bachman, *Vice Pres*
EMP: 7
SQ FT: 2,400
SALES: 1.2MM **Privately Held**
SIC: 3599 Machine shop, jobbing & repair

(G-9140)
ATL
45 Spear Rd (07446-1221)
PHONE....................201 825-1400
Peter Regna, *President*
EMP: 6 **EST:** 1975
SQ FT: 70,000
SALES (est): 596.2K
SALES (corp-wide): 13.1MM **Privately Held**
WEB: www.atlinc.com
SIC: 2869 Industrial organic chemicals
PA: Aero Tec Laboratories Inc.
45 Spear Rd
Ramsey NJ 07446
201 825-1400

(G-9141)
AYDIN JEWELRY MENUFECTURING
119 E Main St (07446-1926)
PHONE....................201 818-1002
Rick Aydin, *Principal*
EMP: 4
SALES (est): 285.7K **Privately Held**
SIC: 3911 Jewelry, precious metal

(G-9142)
BOGEN CORPORATION (PA)
50 Spring St Ste 1 (07446-1131)
PHONE....................201 934-8500
Johnathan Guss, *CEO*
Michael P Fleischer, *President*
Maureen A Flotard, *CFO*
EMP: 1
SQ FT: 70,000
SALES (est): 23.4MM **Privately Held**
SIC: 3651 3661 3663 3669 Amplifiers: radio, public address or musical instrument; audio electronic systems; telephone & telegraph apparatus; telephones & telephone apparatus; radio broadcasting & communications equipment; intercommunication systems, electric

(G-9143)
COMPTIME INC
Also Called: Comptime Print & Copy Center
385 N Franklin Tpke Ste 6 (07446-2820)
PHONE....................201 760-2400
Christopher Tausch, *President*
David Santulli, *Corp Secy*
EMP: 6
SQ FT: 1,250
SALES (est): 778.4K **Privately Held**
WEB: www.comptime.net
SIC: 7334 2791 Blueprinting service; typesetting

(G-9144)
FRELL CORP
Also Called: Buono Bagel-To The Max
885 State Rt 17 Ste 5 (07446-1654)
PHONE....................201 825-2500
Fred Greenberg, *President*
EMP: 10
SQ FT: 3,000
SALES (est): 430K **Privately Held**
SIC: 2051 5461 Bagels, fresh or frozen; bagels

(G-9145)
GENESIS BPS LLC
465 Route 17 S (07446-2012)
P.O. Box 331 (07446-0331)
PHONE....................201 708-1400
Jerrold Grossman, *Mng Member*
▲ **EMP:** 25
SQ FT: 30,000
SALES (est): 4.9MM
SALES (corp-wide): 988.7K **Privately Held**
WEB: www.genesisbps.com
SIC: 3841 Medical instruments & equipment, blood & bone work
PA: Genesis Bps International Sarl
C/O Harmannus Koeneman
Arnex-Sur-Nyon VD 1277
223 631-816

(G-9146)
GLEBAR OPERATING LLC
Also Called: Glebar Company
565 E Crescent Ave (07446-1219)
PHONE....................201 337-1500
Robert Baker, *CEO*

Adam Cook, *Ch of Bd*
John Bannayan, *President*
Mark Bannayan, *Vice Pres*
Robert Gleason, *Vice Pres*
▼ **EMP:** 61
SQ FT: 40,000
SALES (est): 22.7MM **Privately Held**
WEB: www.glebar.com
SIC: 3541 Grinding machines, metalworking

(G-9147)
INGUI DESIGN LLC
Also Called: Aurorae
46 N Central Ave (07446-1808)
PHONE....................201 264-9126
Michael Ingui, *Consultant*
Dennis Ingui,
Valerie Ingui,
EMP: 4
SQ FT: 3,000
SALES: 2MM **Privately Held**
SIC: 3949 Exercise equipment

(G-9148)
INNOVATIVE ART CONCEPTS LLC
Also Called: Cutting Edge Stencils
630 Swan St (07446-1014)
PHONE....................201 828-9146
John G Swisher, *Mng Member*
Janna Makaeva,
Harris M Recht,
EMP: 12 **EST:** 2009
SALES: 2.5MM **Privately Held**
SIC: 3953 Stencils, painting & marking

(G-9149)
LIQUID-SOLIDS SEPARATION CORP (HQ)
25 Arrow Rd (07446-1204)
PHONE....................201 236-4833
David J Painter, *President*
R Donald Peterson, *Treasurer*
EMP: 25
SQ FT: 24,000
SALES (est): 6.4MM **Privately Held**
WEB: www.leemlssfiltration.com
SIC: 3569 3089 5074 Filters, general line: industrial; plastic containers, except foam; water purification equipment

(G-9150)
LONGO ASSOCIATES INC
100 Hilltop Rd (07446-1119)
PHONE....................201 825-1500
Nat Longo, *President*
Anthony Stellatos, *Marketing Mgr*
▲ **EMP:** 13
SQ FT: 4,200
SALES (est): 2.7MM **Privately Held**
WEB: www.longoschools.com
SIC: 2531 School furniture

(G-9151)
MER MADE FILTER
25 Arrow Rd (07446-1204)
PHONE....................201 236-0217
Dave Painter, *President*
EMP: 5
SALES: 320K **Privately Held**
SIC: 5085 3564 Filters, industrial; blowers & fans

(G-9152)
MODEL ELECTRONICS INC (PA)
615 E Crescent Ave (07446-1220)
PHONE....................201 961-9200
Matthew Sasso, *President*
Peter Maroccia, *President*
Thomas Churchill, *Vice Pres*
EMP: 71
SALES (est): 21.2MM **Privately Held**
WEB: www.modelelectronicsinc.com
SIC: 3679 5064 5731 Recording & playback apparatus, including phonograph; radios; sound equipment, automotive

(G-9153)
MODEL ELECTRONICS INC
526 State Rt 17 (07446-2015)
PHONE....................201 961-1717
EMP: 36

SALES (corp-wide): 21.2MM **Privately Held**
SIC: 3679 Recording & playback apparatus, including phonograph
PA: Model Electronics, Inc.
    615 E Crescent Ave
    Ramsey NJ 07446
    201 961-9200

(G-9154)
OKONITE COMPANY INC (PA)
102 Hilltop Rd (07446-1171)
P.O. Box 340 (07446-0340)
PHONE..................................201 825-0300
Victor A Viggiano, *Ch of Bd*
Eric Canning, *District Mgr*
Dan Payton, *District Mgr*
Eric Thoreson, *District Mgr*
Harry Waters, *District Mgr*
◆ EMP: 200
SQ FT: 70,000
SALES (est): 407MM **Privately Held**
WEB: www.okonite.com
SIC: 3357 3315 3355 Nonferrous wire-drawing & insulating; cable, steel: insulated or armored; aluminum wire & cable

(G-9155)
PRONTO PRINTING & COPYING CTR
630 Swan St (07446-1014)
PHONE..................................201 426-0009
John Cortes, *President*
EMP: 6 EST: 1974
SQ FT: 3,000
SALES: 808K **Privately Held**
SIC: 2752 Commercial printing, offset

(G-9156)
TAURUS INTERNATIONAL CORP
275 N Franklin Tpke Ste 3 (07446-2812)
PHONE..................................201 825-2420
William J Coleman, *President*
Richard E Toth, *Vice Pres*
Jasen Toth, *VP Opers*
Bill Crable, *Engineer*
Lynette Castaldo, *Manager*
▲ EMP: 20
SQ FT: 5,000
SALES (est): 6.5MM **Privately Held**
WEB: www.taurusinternational.com
SIC: 5013 5082 5088 3462 Motor vehicle supplies & new parts; construction & mining machinery; transportation equipment & supplies; automotive & internal combustion engine forgings; automotive stampings

(G-9157)
TOILETTREE PRODUCTS INC
41 Orchard St Ste 1 (07446-1158)
PHONE..................................845 358-5316
Gary Parisi, *CEO*
Steve Parisi, *President*
Paul Parisi, *CFO*
▲ EMP: 6
SQ FT: 1,000
SALES (est): 4MM **Privately Held**
SIC: 5211 3261 Bathroom fixtures, equipment & supplies; bathroom accessories/fittings, vitreous china or earthenware

(G-9158)
WALDEN MOTT CORP
225 N Franklin Tpke Ste 1 (07446-1600)
PHONE..................................201 962-3704
Alfred F Walden, *President*
Charles Walden, *Vice Pres*
EMP: 5
SQ FT: 4,000
SALES: 425K **Privately Held**
WEB: www.papercatalog.com
SIC: 2721 2741 2711 Magazines: publishing only, not printed on site; directories: publishing only, not printed on site; newspapers: publishing only, not printed on site

---

Rancocas
Burlington County

(G-9159)
CONSARC CORPORATION (DH)
100 Indel Ave (08073)
P.O. Box 156 (08073-0156)
PHONE..................................609 267-8000
William J Marino, *President*
Lewis Jones, *Vice Pres*
Raymond J Roberts, *Vice Pres*
Gus John, *Plant Mgr*
Terrance O Malley, *Project Mgr*
◆ EMP: 50 EST: 1962
SQ FT: 62,000
SALES: 19.7MM
SALES (corp-wide): 1B **Privately Held**
WEB: www.consarc.com
SIC: 3567 Metal melting furnaces, industrial: electric
HQ: Indel, Inc.
    10 Indel Ave
    Rancocas NJ 08073
    609 267-9000

(G-9160)
ELECTRO-STEAM GENERATOR CORP
50 Indel Ave (08073)
P.O. Box 438 (08073-0438)
PHONE..................................609 288-9071
Robert A Murnane Jr, *President*
Brad Weigle, *Vice Pres*
EMP: 28
SALES (est): 54.4MM
SALES (corp-wide): 1B **Privately Held**
WEB: www.indelinc.com
SIC: 3621 Generators & sets, electric
HQ: Indel, Inc.
    10 Indel Ave
    Rancocas NJ 08073
    609 267-9000

(G-9161)
INDUCTOTHERM CORP (HQ)
10 Indel Ave (08073)
P.O. Box 157 (08073-0157)
PHONE..................................609 267-9000
Satyen N Prabhu, *President*
Paul C Webber, *General Mgr*
Trevor Heilman, *District Mgr*
Bill Newbold, *District Mgr*
Virginia R Smith, *Vice Pres*
◆ EMP: 180
SQ FT: 155,000
SALES (est): 43.6MM
SALES (corp-wide): 1B **Privately Held**
WEB: www.inductotherm.com
SIC: 3567 Induction heating equipment
PA: Rowan Technologies, Inc.
    10 Indel Ave
    Rancocas NJ 08073
    609 267-9000

(G-9162)
INDUCTOTHERM TECHNOLOGIES INC (HQ)
Also Called: Inductotherm Group
10 Indel Ave (08073)
PHONE..................................609 267-9000
Virginia Rowan Smith, *President*
EMP: 9
SALES (est): 1.7MM
SALES (corp-wide): 1B **Privately Held**
SIC: 3449 Bars, concrete reinforcing: fabricated steel
PA: Rowan Technologies, Inc.
    10 Indel Ave
    Rancocas NJ 08073
    609 267-9000

(G-9163)
PEMBERTON FABRICATORS INC
Also Called: Pemfab
30 Indel Ave (08073)
P.O. Box 227 (08073-0227)
PHONE..................................609 267-0922
Robert Murnane, *President*
Cheryl Parker, *Admin Sec*
◆ EMP: 2101 EST: 1962
SQ FT: 75,000

SALES: 11.3MM
SALES (corp-wide): 1B **Privately Held**
WEB: www.pemfab.com
SIC: 3444 3824 Sheet metal specialties, not stamped; fluid meters & counting devices
HQ: Indel, Inc.
    10 Indel Ave
    Rancocas NJ 08073
    609 267-9000

(G-9164)
PV/T INC
100 Indel Ave (08073)
P.O. Box 156 (08073-0156)
PHONE..................................609 267-3933
Brett Wenger, *Manager*
EMP: 4
SQ FT: 75,000
SALES (est): 442.7K
SALES (corp-wide): 1B **Privately Held**
WEB: www.pvt-vf.com
SIC: 3567 Heating units & devices, industrial: electric
HQ: Consarc Corporation
    100 Indel Ave
    Rancocas NJ 08073
    609 267-8000

(G-9165)
ROWAN TECHNOLOGIES INC (PA)
10 Indel Ave (08073)
P.O. Box 157 (08073-0157)
PHONE..................................609 267-9000
Virginia Rowan Smith, *President*
Charles Vivian, *District Mgr*
Manning J Smith, *Vice Pres*
Francis D Manley, *Treasurer*
◆ EMP: 100
SALES (est): 1B **Privately Held**
SIC: 3567 3548 3822 3541 Metal melting furnaces, industrial: fuel-fired; induction heating equipment; vacuum furnaces & ovens; welding & cutting apparatus & accessories; temperature controls, automatic; saws & sawing machines

(G-9166)
SQN PERIPHERALS INC (DH)
Also Called: Sqn Banking Systems
65 Indel Ave (08073)
P.O. Box 423 (08073-0423)
PHONE..................................609 261-5500
Joseph Uhland Jr, *President*
Jim Matusko, *Treasurer*
Lawrence A Krupnick, *Admin Sec*
EMP: 30
SQ FT: 5,000
SALES (est): 3.5MM
SALES (corp-wide): 1B **Privately Held**
WEB: www.sqnbankingsystems.com
SIC: 3577 Optical scanning devices
HQ: Indel, Inc.
    10 Indel Ave
    Rancocas NJ 08073
    609 267-9000

(G-9167)
TELEGENIX INC
71 Indel Ave (08073)
PHONE..................................609 265-3910
Henry M Rowan Jr, *Ch of Bd*
Joseph J Miller, *President*
Michael Gleeson, *Treasurer*
EMP: 16
SQ FT: 7,000
SALES (est): 3.1MM
SALES (corp-wide): 1B **Privately Held**
WEB: www.telegenix.com
SIC: 3669 3577 Transportation signaling devices; computer peripheral equipment
PA: Rowan Technologies, Inc.
    10 Indel Ave
    Rancocas NJ 08073
    609 267-9000

(G-9168)
WEL-FAB INC
50 Indel Ave (08073)
P.O. Box 86, Lumberton (08048-0086)
PHONE..................................609 261-1393
Dan O'Connor, *President*
Paul Elstone, *Vice Pres*
Bobby Clark, *VP Sales*
Charlie Branstetter, *Director*

EMP: 20
SQ FT: 4,875
SALES (est): 4MM **Privately Held**
WEB: www.wel-fab.com
SIC: 1799 7692 Welding on site; welding repair

Randolph
Morris County

(G-9169)
ADI AMERICAN DISTRIBUTORS LLC (PA)
2 Emery Ave Ste 1 (07869-1368)
PHONE..................................973 328-1181
David Beck, *CEO*
Heather Wynne, *Controller*
▲ EMP: 56
SQ FT: 28,000
SALES: 49MM **Privately Held**
WEB: www.americandistr.com
SIC: 5065 3679 3621 3672 Electronic parts & equipment; power supplies, all types: static; frequency converters (electric generators); printed circuit boards

(G-9170)
AFK MACHINE INC (PA)
50 High Ridge Rd (07869-4569)
PHONE..................................973 539-1329
John Klein, *Principal*
EMP: 4
SALES (est): 370K **Privately Held**
SIC: 3599 Machine shop, jobbing & repair

(G-9171)
AMERICAN MCH TOOL RPR RBLDG CO
12 Middlebury Blvd (07869-1111)
PHONE..................................973 927-0820
Alex Karoly, *President*
Olga Karoly, *Admin Sec*
EMP: 9
SALES (est): 1.2MM **Privately Held**
SIC: 3541 7699 Machine tool replacement & repair parts, metal cutting types; industrial machinery & equipment repair

(G-9172)
ARPAC TECHNOLOGY
45 Park Ave (07869-1705)
PHONE..................................973 252-0012
Pete Capra, *Principal*
EMP: 9
SALES (est): 1.2MM **Privately Held**
SIC: 3089 Plastic processing

(G-9173)
ARTISAN CONTROLS CORPORATION (PA)
111 Canfield Ave Ste B-18 (07869-1127)
PHONE..................................973 598-9400
John D Murray, *President*
Larry Affelt, *Vice Pres*
Leigh Ann Stevens, *Vice Pres*
Denise Maas, *Treasurer*
Deniese Moss, *Mktg Dir*
EMP: 21
SQ FT: 10,000
SALES (est): 3.2MM **Privately Held**
WEB: www.artisancontrols.com
SIC: 3625 Timing devices, electronic

(G-9174)
CHEN BROTHERS MACHINERY CO
Also Called: C.B.M. Co.
503 State Route 10 (07869-2152)
PHONE..................................973 328-0086
Kevin Chen, *CEO*
EMP: 5
SQ FT: 1,000
SALES (est): 137.2K **Privately Held**
SIC: 7699 3589 5087 Industrial equipment cleaning; car washing machinery; carwash equipment & supplies; laundry equipment & supplies

---

(G-9175)
DOUGLAS ELEC COMPONENTS INC
5 Middlebury Blvd (07869-1112)
PHONE..................................973 627-8230
Edward W Douglas, *President*
Karen Humphreys, *Materials Mgr*
Chuck Dean, *CFO*
Kim Tucci, *Human Res Mgr*
Joe Cowin, *Sales Staff*
▲ EMP: 60 EST: 1945
SALES (est): 14.4MM **Privately Held**
WEB: www.douglaselectrical.com
SIC: 3679 3699 Electronic circuits; electrical equipment & supplies

(G-9176)
ENVIROSIGHT LLC (PA)
Also Called: Pipeline Renewal Technologies
111 Canfield Ave Ste B-3 (07869-1129)
PHONE..................................973 970-9284
Richard Lindner, *President*
Robert Lindner, *COO*
Marie Weinberg, *Opers Staff*
Tammy Smith, *Production*
Justin Gehrlein, *Engineer*
EMP: 31
SQ FT: 2,800
SALES (est): 10.8MM **Privately Held**
WEB: www.envirosight.com
SIC: 5084 5046 3577 Industrial machinery & equipment; commercial equipment; computer peripheral equipment

(G-9177)
EUGENE KOZAK
Also Called: Kozak Precision Products
193 Franklin Rd (07869-1612)
PHONE..................................973 442-1001
Eugene Kozak, *Owner*
EMP: 4
SALES (est): 300K **Privately Held**
SIC: 3599 Machine shop, jobbing & repair

(G-9178)
FIRST JUICE INC
19 Tulip Ln (07869-4773)
PHONE..................................973 895-3085
David Glasser, *President*
Robert J Klausner, *VP Finance*
Cheryl Thomas, *VP Mktg*
Allan Carlin, *Admin Sec*
EMP: 9
SQ FT: 1,400
SALES (est): 630K **Privately Held**
WEB: www.tastebudtraining.com
SIC: 2086 Fruit drinks (less than 100% juice); packaged in cans, etc.

(G-9179)
GENERAL WIRE & STAMPING CO
1 Emery Ave Ste 3 (07869-1387)
PHONE..................................973 366-8080
Kenneth J Kelly, *President*
Patrick Egan, *Vice Pres*
EMP: 10
SQ FT: 12,000
SALES (est): 1.3MM **Privately Held**
WEB: www.generalwire.com
SIC: 3496 3469 Miscellaneous fabricated wire products; metal stampings

(G-9180)
GLENBROOK TECHNOLOGIES INC
11 Emery Ave (07869-1308)
PHONE..................................973 361-8866
Gilbert Zweig, *President*
Claire Zweig, *Exec VP*
Donna Miller, *Accounting Mgr*
Yvonne Coad, *Cust Mgr*
▼ EMP: 15
SQ FT: 13,300
SALES (est): 3.2MM **Privately Held**
WEB: www.glenbrooktech.com
SIC: 3844 Fluoroscopic X-ray apparatus & tubes

(G-9181)
GLOBAL MARKETING CORP
155 Canfield Ave (07869-1106)
PHONE..................................973 426-1088
Christopher D Boyhan, *President*
▲ EMP: 11 EST: 1981

SQ FT: 1,725
SALES (est): 1.9MM **Privately Held**
SIC: 3469 Household cooking & kitchen utensils, metal; household cooking & kitchen utensils, porcelain enameled

(G-9182)
GRANVILLE CONCRETE PRODUCTS
1076 State Route 10 (07869-1803)
PHONE..................................973 584-6653
Brian Peach, *President*
Bernard Peach, *Corp Secy*
Kevin Peach, *Vice Pres*
EMP: 4
SQ FT: 6,000
SALES: 900K **Privately Held**
SIC: 3272 Septic tanks, concrete

(G-9183)
GRAPHICS DEPOT INC
Also Called: Copy Depot, The
11 Middlebury Blvd Ste 4 (07869-1119)
PHONE..................................973 927-8200
David Bernstein, *President*
Robert Donohue, *Admin Sec*
EMP: 15
SALES (est): 1.7MM **Privately Held**
SIC: 2752 7334 Commercial printing, offset; photocopying & duplicating services

(G-9184)
GT MICROWAVE INC
2 Emery Ave Ste 2 # 2 (07869-1368)
PHONE..................................973 361-5700
Antonio C Baliotis, *President*
George Apsley, *Vice Pres*
Todd Zaleski, *Engineer*
Jacob Levy, *Manager*
Ellen Baliotis, *Admin Sec*
EMP: 20
SQ FT: 5,000
SALES (est): 4.1MM **Privately Held**
WEB: www.gtmicrowave.com
SIC: 3679 5199 Microwave components; packaging materials

(G-9185)
HAWK GRAPHICS INC
1248 Sussex Tpke (07869-2908)
P.O. Box 308, Mount Freedom (07970-0308)
PHONE..................................973 895-5569
Nicholas J Battaglino, *President*
Dorothy Battaglino, *Vice Pres*
Lorane Killer, *Administration*
EMP: 20
SQ FT: 20,000
SALES: 3MM **Privately Held**
SIC: 2752 Commercial printing, offset

(G-9186)
IMPERIAL COPY PRODUCTS INC
961 State Route 10 1ee (07869-1905)
PHONE..................................973 927-5500
Brian Abrams, *President*
David Abrams, *Vice Pres*
▲ EMP: 20
SQ FT: 20,000
SALES (est): 3.3MM **Privately Held**
WEB: www.imperialcopy.com
SIC: 5999 7699 5734 3674 Photocopy machines; photocopy machine repair; printers & plotters: computers; light emitting diodes; duplicating machines; office forms & supplies

(G-9187)
JAYGO INCORPORATED
7 Emery Ave (07869-1308)
PHONE..................................908 688-3600
John R Hayday, *President*
Joris Banning, *Vice Pres*
Jason Hayday, *Vice Pres*
Lauren Laverso, *Bookkeeper*
◆ EMP: 7
SQ FT: 35,000
SALES (est): 2.7MM **Privately Held**
WEB: www.jaygoinc.com
SIC: 3559 Chemical machinery & equipment; pharmaceutical machinery

(G-9188)
LANDICE INCORPORATED
Also Called: Landice Treadmills
111 Canfield Ave Ste A-1 (07869-1130)
PHONE..................................973 927-9010
Greg Savettiere, *President*
Andrew Taitel, *Vice Pres*
◆ EMP: 30
SQ FT: 22,000
SALES (est): 5.7MM **Privately Held**
WEB: www.landice.com
SIC: 3949 Treadmills

(G-9189)
LAROSE INDUSTRIES LLC (PA)
Also Called: Pen Master
1578 Sussex Tpke (07869-1833)
PHONE..................................973 543-2037
Joe Nardozza, *President*
Vito Amato, *Vice Pres*
Richard Ginelli, *VP Opers*
Tracy Namendorf, *Traffic Mgr*
Paige Rossnagel, *Production*
◆ EMP: 90
SQ FT: 125,000
SALES (est): 42.6MM **Privately Held**
SIC: 5092 3269 3944 Arts & crafts equipment & supplies; stationery articles, pottery; craft & hobby kits & sets

(G-9190)
MASTERCOOL USA INC
1 Aspen Dr Ste 1 # 1 (07869-1123)
PHONE..................................973 252-9119
Kia Nili, *President*
Michael Barjesteh, *Principal*
Bob Cacciabeve, *Vice Pres*
Steven Gillespie, *Engineer*
Walter Woronka, *Engineer*
◆ EMP: 45
SALES (est): 9.5MM **Privately Held**
WEB: www.mastercool.com
SIC: 3423 Hand & edge tools

(G-9191)
METRIE INC
1578 Sussex Tpke Ste 300 (07869-1833)
PHONE..................................973 584-0040
Bill Cody, *Branch Mgr*
EMP: 10
SALES (corp-wide): 183.4MM **Privately Held**
SIC: 3089 Molding primary plastic
HQ: Metrie Inc.
2200 140th Ave E Ste 600
Sumner WA 98390
253 470-5050

(G-9192)
NEWTYPE INC
447 State Route 10 Ste 14 (07869-2132)
PHONE..................................973 361-6000
Jo Ann Porto, *CEO*
Mark F Porto, *President*
Athena Theodosion, *Accountant*
EMP: 12
SALES: 720K **Privately Held**
WEB: www.newtypeinc.com
SIC: 7389 2791 Translation services; typesetting

(G-9193)
NORWALT DESIGN INC
961 Route 10 E Ste 2a (07869-1921)
PHONE..................................973 927-3200
Walter McDonald, *President*
Michael Seitel, *COO*
Norbert Seitel, *Vice Pres*
Lee Reilly, *Purchasing*
Ron Sawicki, *Engineer*
▲ EMP: 54
SQ FT: 40,000
SALES (est): 12.5MM **Privately Held**
WEB: www.norwalt.com
SIC: 3599 Custom machinery

(G-9194)
NYMAR MANUFACTURING COMPANY
215 State Route 10 2-4 (07869-2413)
PHONE..................................973 366-7265
Gerald Hughes, *President*
EMP: 15 EST: 1967
SQ FT: 7,500

SALES (est): 1.4MM **Privately Held**
WEB: www.nymar.com
SIC: 3599 Machine shop, jobbing & repair

(G-9195)
OMEGA SHIELDING PRODUCTS INC
9 Emery Ave (07869-1308)
PHONE..................................973 366-0080
Leon Komsa, *President*
Timothy Komsa, *Exec VP*
Andy Morris, *QC Mgr*
Chiungyao Chen, *Info Tech Dir*
Laurence R Niebling, *Admin Sec*
EMP: 12
SQ FT: 20,000
SALES (est): 2.3MM **Privately Held**
SIC: 3053 Gaskets, all materials

(G-9196)
PARTY CITY CORPORATION
477 State Route 10 # 102 (07869-2143)
PHONE..................................973 537-1707
Gordon Vanderhoff, *Manager*
EMP: 10
SALES (corp-wide): 2.4B **Publicly Held**
WEB: www.partycity.com
SIC: 5947 5199 7299 2759 Gifts & novelties; party favors, balloons, hats, etc.; costume rental; invitation & stationery printing & engraving
HQ: Party City Corporation
25 Green Pond Rd Ste 1
Rockaway NJ 07866

(G-9197)
RAME-HART INC
5 Emery Ave Ste 1 (07869-1300)
PHONE..................................973 335-0560
Thor Stadil, *CEO*
Ken Christiansen, *President*
Samuel Rich, *Treasurer*
EMP: 25 EST: 1961
SQ FT: 17,500
SALES: 9MM **Privately Held**
WEB: www.ramehart.com
SIC: 3826 Analytical instruments

(G-9198)
SCREENTEK MANUFACTURING CO LLC
220 Franklin Rd B (07869-1605)
PHONE..................................973 328-2121
James Rodimer,
▲ EMP: 15
SQ FT: 8,000
SALES (est): 2.7MM **Privately Held**
SIC: 5063 3315 Wire & cable; wire & fabricated wire products

(G-9199)
SERVOLIFT LLC
35 Righter Rd Ste A (07869-1707)
PHONE..................................973 442-7878
Marc Kaufman, *President*
Joachim Litterst, *Vice Pres*
Joe Litterst, *VP Opers*
Seth Ruckel, *Project Mgr*
Gregory Gil, *Engineer*
◆ EMP: 35
SQ FT: 15,000
SALES (est): 7MM **Privately Held**
WEB: www.servo-lift.com
SIC: 3821 5084 Chemical laboratory apparatus; chemical process equipment

(G-9200)
SOURCE MICRO LLC
5 Rolling Ridge Rd (07869-4506)
PHONE..................................973 328-1749
Robert Schaffer,
EMP: 10
SQ FT: 3,000
SALES: 5.1MM **Privately Held**
WEB: www.sourcemicro.com
SIC: 3577 Computer peripheral equipment

(G-9201)
SSI NORTH AMERICA INC
961 State Route 10 Ste 2i (07869-1927)
PHONE..................................973 598-0152
G Thomas Ennis, *CEO*
Lucas Lowenstein, *President*
Dennis Leberecht, *Vice Pres*
▲ EMP: 9

SALES (est): 8.8MM **Privately Held**
WEB: www.ssinorthamerica.com
SIC: 3081 Plastic film & sheet

(G-9202)
SURFACE SOURCE INTL INC
Also Called: Ssi North America
961 State Route 10 Ste 2i (07869-1927)
PHONE..............................973 598-0152
Lucas Marcus Lowenstein, *President*
Dennis Leberecht, *Vice Pres*
EMP: 12
SQ FT: 20,000
SALES (est): 8.1MM **Privately Held**
SIC: 2821 Polyvinyl chloride resins (PVC)

(G-9203)
TECHNOLOGY REVIEWS INC
Also Called: Technovations
14 Red Barn Ln (07869-3816)
PHONE..............................973 537-9511
Jaidev S Talwar, *President*
Robert Berger, *Principal*
Ramon Talwar, *Vice Pres*
EMP: 5
SALES (est): 720.2K **Privately Held**
SIC: 2821 8742 Plasticizer/additive based
plastic materials; industry specialist con-
sultants

(G-9204)
TROLEX CORPORATION
Also Called: Zone First
6 Aspen Dr (07869-1103)
PHONE..............................201 794-8004
Richard N Foster Jr, *President*
Joe Romyns, *General Mgr*
Amanda Delgado, *Vice Pres*
EMP: 40
SQ FT: 16,000
SALES (est): 8.2MM **Privately Held**
WEB: www.trolexcorp.com
SIC: 3822 Auto controls regulating residntl
& coml environmt & applncs

(G-9205)
ULTRAFLEX SYSTEMS FLORIDA INC
1578 Sussex Tpke Ste 400 (07869-1833)
PHONE..............................973 627-8608
John Schleicher, *President*
Jennifer Lauria, *Sales Staff*
Anthony Schneider, *Sales Staff*
Angela Elsier, *Director*
Alexa Schneider, *Director*
EMP: 37
SALES (est): 7.1MM
SALES (corp-wide): 15.6MM **Privately Held**
SIC: 2221 Manmade & synthetic broadwo-
ven fabrics
PA: Ultraflex Systems Of Florida, Inc.
6333 Pelican Creek Cir
Riverview FL 33578
973 664-6739

(G-9206)
UNETTE CORPORATION
1578 Sussex Tpke Ste 5 (07869-1833)
PHONE..............................973 328-6800
Joseph Hark, *President*
Carol Ann Hark, *Vice Pres*
Carol Hark, *Vice Pres*
Melissa Moran, *Opers Staff*
Tony Nugent, *VP Sales*
▲ **EMP:** 65
SQ FT: 115,000
SALES (est): 15MM **Privately Held**
WEB: www.unette.com
SIC: 3089 3085 Plastic containers, except
foam; plastics bottles

(G-9207)
VALLEY DIE CUTTING INC
100 Washington St (07869-1633)
PHONE..............................973 731-8884
Harold Lohse, *Manager*
EMP: 8
SALES (corp-wide): 5.6MM **Privately Held**
WEB: www.reel-parts.com
SIC: 4225 3544 General warehousing &
storage; special dies, tools, jigs & fixtures

PA: Valley Die Cutting, Inc
10 Park Ave
West Orange NJ
973 731-8884

Raritan
Somerset County

(G-9208)
BBK TECHNOLOGIES INC
Also Called: Fastsigns
13 Rte 206 S (08869)
PHONE..............................908 231-0306
Elizabeth Bowater, *President*
EMP: 7
SQ FT: 1,800
SALES (est): 736.9K **Privately Held**
SIC: 3993 Signs & advertising specialties

(G-9209)
D S F INC
Also Called: D S F Millwork
401 Us Highway 202 (08869-1529)
PHONE..............................908 218-5153
Simon Degirolamo, *President*
Janet Degirolamo, *Corp Secy*
EMP: 20
SALES (est): 2.9MM **Privately Held**
SIC: 2541 Wood partitions & fixtures

(G-9210)
DUET MICROELECTRONICS LLC
575 Route 28 Ste 100 (08869-1354)
PHONE..............................908 854-3838
John Van Sanders, *CEO*
EMP: 14
SALES (est): 1.1MM **Privately Held**
SIC: 3674 Semiconductors & related de-
vices

(G-9211)
JANSSEN GLOBAL SERVICES LLC
700 Route 202 (08869-1422)
PHONE..............................908 704-4000
Jeff Faris, *Director*
EMP: 9
SALES (est): 1.2MM
SALES (corp-wide): 81.5B **Publicly Held**
SIC: 2834 8731 Pharmaceutical prepara-
tions; commercial physical research
PA: Johnson & Johnson
1 Johnson And Johnson Plz
New Brunswick NJ 08933
732 524-0400

(G-9212)
JANSSEN RESEARCH & DEV LLC (HQ)
920 Us Highway 202 (08869-1420)
P.O. Box 300 (08869-0602)
PHONE..............................908 704-4000
P A Paterson MD, *Chairman*
Nicholas C Dracopoli, *Vice Pres*
Yusri A Elsayed, *Vice Pres*
Joseph Erhardt, *Vice Pres*
Michael Heftonrn MBA, *Vice Pres*
EMP: 1800
SALES (est): 861.8MM
SALES (corp-wide): 81.5B **Publicly Held**
WEB: www.jnjpharmarnd.com
SIC: 2834 8731 Pharmaceutical prepara-
tions; commercial physical research
PA: Johnson & Johnson
1 Johnson And Johnson Plz
New Brunswick NJ 08933
732 524-0400

(G-9213)
JOHNSON & JOHNSON
1000 Rte 202 (08869-1425)
P.O. Box 300 (08869-0602)
PHONE..............................908 722-9319
Christopher Bowers, *Division Mgr*
Adam Wieck, *Regional Mgr*
Kenneth J Dow, *Counsel*
Patricia Lukens, *Counsel*
Lynne M Szczepaniak, *Vice Pres*
EMP: 5

SALES (corp-wide): 81.5B **Publicly Held**
WEB: www.jnj.com
SIC: 3842 3841 2834 2844 Surgical appliances & supplies; ligatures, medical;
sutures, absorbable & non-absorbable;
dressings, surgical; surgical & medical instruments; surgical instruments & apparatus; diagnostic apparatus, medical;
ophthalmic instruments & apparatus;
pharmaceutical preparations; drugs acting
on the central nervous system & sense
organs; dermatologicals; drugs affecting
parasitic & infective diseases; toilet
preparations; oral preparations; toilet
preparations; powder: baby, face, talcum
or toilet; feminine hygiene paper products;
napkins, sanitary: made from purchased
paper; panty liners: made from purchased
paper; infant & baby paper products
PA: Johnson & Johnson
1 Johnson And Johnson Plz
New Brunswick NJ 08933
732 524-0400

(G-9214)
JOHNSON & JOHNSON
1101 Us Highway 202 (08869)
PHONE..............................908 704-6809
Elliot Millenson, *President*
Robert Boland, *Manager*
Jean Holland, *Associate Dir*
EMP: 79
SALES (corp-wide): 81.5B **Publicly Held**
WEB: www.jnj.com
SIC: 2834 Pharmaceutical preparations
PA: Johnson & Johnson
1 Johnson And Johnson Plz
New Brunswick NJ 08933
732 524-0400

(G-9215)
JOHNSON & JOHNSON
1003 Us Highway 202 P (08869-1424)
PHONE..............................908 526-5425
Fred Falk, *Manager*
Jason Hyska, *Manager*
Amrita Mandapati, *Manager*
Kathy Schnur, *Manager*
Michael Leyden, *Consultant*
EMP: 47
SALES (corp-wide): 81.5B **Publicly Held**
SIC: 2834 Pharmaceutical preparations
PA: Johnson & Johnson
1 Johnson And Johnson Plz
New Brunswick NJ 08933
732 524-0400

(G-9216)
OCD PHARMACEUTICALS
1001 Us Highway 202 (08869-1424)
PHONE..............................610 366-2314
EMP: 4 EST: 2017
SALES (est): 264.9K **Privately Held**
SIC: 2834 Pharmaceutical preparations

(G-9217)
ORTHO-CLINICAL DIAGNOSTICS INC (PA)
1001 Route 202 (08869-1424)
P.O. Box 350 (08869-0606)
PHONE..............................908 218-8000
Dr Martin D Madaus, *Ch of Bd*
Michael Beckstead, *Regional Mgr*
Robert Yates, *COO*
John Meckles, *Vice Pres*
Lisa Purdy, *Opers Spvr*
▲ **EMP:** 1000 EST: 1994
SQ FT: 335,000
SALES (est): 594MM **Privately Held**
WEB: www.orthoclinical.com
SIC: 2835 2834 Blood derivative diagnos-
tic agents; pharmaceutical preparations

(G-9218)
SOMERSET WOOD PRODUCTS CO
1 Johnson Dr (08869-1661)
PHONE..............................908 526-0030
Dorothy Bloch, *Ch of Bd*
Lester Bloch, *President*
EMP: 20 EST: 1967
SQ FT: 16,500
SALES (est): 3.4MM **Privately Held**
SIC: 2431 Interior & ornamental woodwork
& trim

Red Bank
Monmouth County

(G-9219)
ALL AMERICAN PRINT & COPY CTR
500 State Route 35 (07701-5038)
PHONE..............................732 758-6200
Ralph Cucinelli, *Vice Pres*
Barbara Cucinelli, *Graphic Designe*
EMP: 4
SALES (est): 386.4K **Privately Held**
SIC: 2752 7334 4822 Commercial print-
ing, offset; blueprinting service; facsimile
transmission services

(G-9220)
ANCHOR CONCRETE PRODUCTS INC (DH)
331 Newman Springs Rd # 236
(07701-6769)
PHONE..............................732 842-5010
Michael P O'Neill, *President*
John K O'Neill, *Vice Pres*
◆ **EMP:** 20 EST: 1955
SQ FT: 9,000
SALES (est): 44.4MM
SALES (corp-wide): 30.6B **Privately Held**
SIC: 3271 5032 Blocks, concrete or cin-
der: standard; masons' materials
HQ: Oldcastle Architectural, Inc.
3 Glenlake Pkwy
Atlanta GA 30328
770 804-3363

(G-9221)
ASTRIX SOFTWARE TECHNOLOGY (PA)
Also Called: Astrix Technology Group
125 Half Mile Rd Ste 200 (07701-6749)
PHONE..............................732 661-0400
Richard Albert, *CEO*
Robert Walla, *President*
Jennifer Best, *Managing Dir*
Richard Zepeda, *Managing Dir*
Dr Larry Hacker, *Vice Pres*
EMP: 15
SQ FT: 2,000
SALES (est): 8.4MM **Privately Held**
SIC: 7363 7372 Temporary help service;
prepackaged software

(G-9222)
B & C CUSTOM WD HANDRAIL CORP
Also Called: Stairshop
26 Sunset Ave (07701)
P.O. Box 2008 (07701-0901)
PHONE..............................732 530-6640
Christopher Kalkucki, *President*
Joyce Kalkucki, *Corp Secy*
EMP: 5
SQ FT: 5,000
SALES (est): 741.7K **Privately Held**
SIC: 2431 Woodwork, interior & ornamen-
tal

(G-9223)
CELLGAIN WIRELESS LLC
68 White St Ste 265 (07701-1656)
PHONE..............................732 889-4671
David Kho, *President*
Chigee Hsu, *Marketing Staff*
EMP: 10
SQ FT: 8,500
SALES (est): 935.1K **Privately Held**
SIC: 3663 8711 7539 Radio broadcasting
& communications equipment; engineer-
ing services; electrical services

(G-9224)
CRH AMERICAS INC
Also Called: Anchor
331 Newman Springs Rd (07701-5688)
PHONE..............................732 292-2500
Matt Lynch, *President*
EMP: 20
SALES (corp-wide): 30.6B **Privately Held**
SIC: 3271 Concrete block & brick

HQ: Crh Americas, Inc.
900 Ashwood Pkwy Ste 600
Atlanta GA 30338
770 804-3363

(G-9225)
DAB DESIGN INC
331 Newman Springs Rd # 143
(07701-5688)
PHONE...............................732 224-8686
Dana Barone, *President*
Neil Barone, *Vice Pres*
EMP: 5
SQ FT: 1,200
SALES (est): 359.8K **Privately Held**
SIC: 2511 Wood household furniture

(G-9226)
DENALI COMPANY LLC (PA)
211 Broad St (07701-2009)
PHONE...............................732 219-7771
Sholom Goldfeder, *Sales Mgr*
Kenneth A Lindemann,
Genith Copeland, *Admin Asst*
Keith Hawkins,
EMP: 20 EST: 1997
SALES (est): 2.2MM **Privately Held**
WEB: www.denalico.com
SIC: 2241 5699 Ribbons; marine apparel

(G-9227)
DYER COMMUNICATIONS INC
Also Called: Two River Times
75 W Front St Ste 2 (07701-1660)
PHONE...............................732 219-5788
Jody Calendar, *Principal*
Domenic Di Piero, *Principal*
Christina Johnson, *Editor*
Donna Rovere, *COO*
Lynette Wojcik, *VP Opers*
EMP: 25
SQ FT: 2,400
SALES (est): 1.7MM **Privately Held**
WEB: www.tworivertimes.com
SIC: 2711 Newspapers: publishing only,
not printed on site

(G-9228)
ES INDUSTRIAL
10 Mechanic St Ste 200 (07701-1855)
P.O. Box 843 (07701-0843)
PHONE...............................732 842-5600
Joe Alonzo, *Owner*
EMP: 53
SALES (est): 3.2MM **Privately Held**
SIC: 3589 Commercial cleaning equipment

(G-9229)
F T MILLWORK INC
Also Called: Custom Woodwork
9 Catherine St (07701-1205)
PHONE...............................732 741-1216
Frank Thomas, *President*
▲ EMP: 4 EST: 1982
SQ FT: 1,800
SALES (est): 340K **Privately Held**
SIC: 2431 Millwork

(G-9230)
INNOCOR INC (HQ)
Also Called: Sleep Innovations
200 Schulz Dr Ste 2 (07701-6745)
PHONE...............................732 945-6222
Carol S Eicher, *President*
Andy Soots, *General Mgr*
Steven Hajec, *Principal*
Nitin Chadda, *Exec VP*
Chris Lacorata, *Exec VP*
◆ EMP: 197
SQ FT: 28,000
SALES (est): 847.7MM
SALES (corp-wide): 224.3MM **Privately Held**
WEB: www.sleepinnovations.com
SIC: 2515 2392 3069 Mattresses & foundations; cushions & pillows; bathmats, rubber
PA: Comfort Holding, Llc
187 Rte 36 Ste 101
West Long Branch NJ 07764
732 263-0800

(G-9231)
INNOCOR FOAM TECH - ACP INC (DH)
Also Called: Flexible Foam
200 Schulz Dr Ste 2 (07701-6745)
PHONE...............................732 945-6222
Carol Eicher, *CEO*
Doug Vaughan, *CFO*
EMP: 82
SALES (est): 45.2MM
SALES (corp-wide): 224.3MM **Privately Held**
SIC: 3069 2515 2392 Bathmats, rubber; mattresses & foundations; cushions & pillows

(G-9232)
INNOCOR FOAM TECHNOLOGIES LLC (DH)
200 Schulz Dr Ste 2 (07701-6745)
PHONE...............................844 824-9348
Carol S Eicher, *CEO*
EMP: 185
SQ FT: 27,611
SALES (est): 227.3MM
SALES (corp-wide): 224.3MM **Privately Held**
SIC: 3086 Plastics foam products; carpet & rug cushions, foamed plastic; insulation or cushioning material, foamed plastic; padding, foamed plastic

(G-9233)
KULTUR INTERNATIONAL FILMS LTD
Also Called: Kultur Video
2 Bridge Ave Ste 633 (07701-4606)
PHONE...............................732 229-2343
Dennis Hedlund, *President*
Pearl Lee, *Principal*
EMP: 25
SQ FT: 10,000
SALES (est): 2.9MM **Privately Held**
SIC: 5099 3651 7812 Video cassettes, accessories & supplies; household video equipment; video tape production

(G-9234)
MAVERICK OIL CO
9 Central Ave (07701-1509)
PHONE...............................732 747-8637
Pat Mazuca, *Owner*
EMP: 26
SALES (est): 721K **Privately Held**
SIC: 1381 Drilling oil & gas wells

(G-9235)
MCGINNIS PRINTING
20 Monmouth St (07701-1614)
PHONE...............................732 758-0060
Dennis Mc Ginnis, *Owner*
EMP: 4
SQ FT: 1,000
SALES (est): 240K **Privately Held**
WEB: www.jasonsdreamsforkids.com
SIC: 2752 Commercial printing, offset

(G-9236)
MEDIA VISTA INC
Also Called: Mediavista News
60 Broad St Ste 100 (07701-1937)
PHONE...............................732 747-8060
Barry Weisbord, *CEO*
Steve Sherack, *Editor*
Sue Finley, *Vice Pres*
Michelle Benson, *Advt Staff*
EMP: 8
SALES (est): 724.2K **Privately Held**
SIC: 2721 Magazines: publishing only, not printed on site

(G-9237)
MONMOUTH JOURNAL
212 Maple Ave Ste 1 (07701-1758)
PHONE...............................732 747-7007
Gary Chapman, *Partner*
Douglas Paviluk, *Publisher*
EMP: 5
SALES (est): 457.8K **Privately Held**
WEB: www.themonmouthjournal.com
SIC: 2711 Newspapers, publishing & printing

(G-9238)
NALCO COMPANY LLC
66 Riverside Ave (07701-1071)
PHONE...............................609 617-2246
EMP: 10
SALES (corp-wide): 14.6B **Publicly Held**
SIC: 2992 Lubricating oils
HQ: Nalco Company Llc
1601 W Diehl Rd
Sugar Land TX 60563
630 305-1000

(G-9239)
PACIFIC DNLOP HOLDINGS USA LLC (DH)
200 Schulz Dr (07701-6776)
PHONE...............................732 345-5400
Doug Tough, *CEO*
Phil Corke, *Senior VP*
William Reed, *Senior VP*
Rustom Jilla, *Treasurer*
William Reilly Jr, *Admin Sec*
EMP: 7
SALES (est): 211.7MM **Privately Held**
SIC: 3069 3691 Balloons, advertising & toy: rubber; birth control devices, rubber; finger cots, rubber; storage batteries
HQ: Pacific Dunlop Investments (Usa) Inc
200 Schulz Dr
Red Bank NJ 07701
732 345-5400

(G-9240)
PACIFIC DUNLOP INVESTMENTS USA (HQ)
200 Schulz Dr (07701-6776)
PHONE...............................732 345-5400
Doug Tough, *President*
William Reed, *Vice Pres*
Rustom Jilla, *Treasurer*
William G Reilly Jr, *Admin Sec*
◆ EMP: 13
SALES (est): 275.9MM **Privately Held**
WEB: www.ap.ansell.com
SIC: 3069 3842 Rubber coated fabrics & clothing; gloves, safety

(G-9241)
QSA GLOBAL NATIONAL CORP
Also Called: Qsa National
331 Newman Springs Rd (07701-5688)
PHONE...............................865 888-6798
Leonard Becker, *President*
Jesse Telesz, *Vice Pres*
EMP: 3
SQ FT: 400
SALES (est): 2MM **Privately Held**
SIC: 8741 3699 7382 5043 Management services; security control equipment & systems; protective devices, security; identity recorders for photographing checks or fingerprints

(G-9242)
RED BANK GSTRNTROLOGY ASSOC PA
365 Broad St Ste 2e (07701-2151)
PHONE...............................732 842-4294
Brian Boyle MD, *President*
Howard Hampel, *Med Doctor*
Melissa Agosto, *Lic Prac Nurse*
EMP: 40
SALES (est): 4.7MM **Privately Held**
WEB: www.rbgastro.com
SIC: 8011 2711 Gastronomist; newspapers

(G-9243)
SEALS-EASTERN INCORPORATED
134 Pearl St (07701-1525)
P.O. Box 520 (07701-0520)
PHONE...............................732 747-9200
Daniel Hertz III, *CEO*
▲ EMP: 150 EST: 1960
SQ FT: 60,000
SALES (est): 15.6MM **Privately Held**
WEB: www.sealseastern.com
SIC: 3053 Gaskets, all materials

(G-9244)
SIC-NAICS LLC
Also Called: Siccode
331 Newman Springs Rd (07701-5688)
P.O. Box 25, Sea Girt (08750-0025)
PHONE...............................929 344-2633
Brian Kelly, *Director*
EMP: 5
SALES (est): 183.9K **Privately Held**
SIC: 2741 Telephone & other directory publishing

(G-9245)
STONEWORLD AT REDBANK INC
247 Cooper Rd (07701-6007)
PHONE...............................732 383-5110
Luis Pereira, *President*
EMP: 4
SALES: 1.2MM **Privately Held**
SIC: 3281 5999 Granite, cut & shaped; rock & stone specimens

(G-9246)
TOMMAX INC
65 Mechanic St Ste 205 (07701-1852)
PHONE...............................732 224-1046
Max Braverman, *Ch of Bd*
Thomas Langan, *President*
EMP: 7
SQ FT: 2,200
SALES: 1.7MM **Privately Held**
SIC: 2741 2721 5085 Catalogs: publishing & printing; magazines: publishing only, not printed on site; industrial supplies

(G-9247)
ULTRA CHEMICAL INC (PA)
2 Bridge Ave Ste 631 (07701-4606)
PHONE...............................732 224-0200
Arthur J Lynch, *President*
Brian Lynch, *Director*
Bryan Brown, *Admin Dir*
EMP: 14
SALES: 14MM **Privately Held**
SIC: 2869 5169 High purity grade chemicals, organic; organic chemicals, synthetic

(G-9248)
VALDEZ CREEK MIN LTD LBLTY CO
73 Broad St Ste 2 (07701-1979)
PHONE...............................732 704-1427
Megan Naputano, *Mng Member*
EMP: 8 EST: 2012
SALES (est): 482.3K **Privately Held**
SIC: 1041 1081 Underground gold mining; exploration, metal mining

---

Richland
Atlantic County

(G-9249)
BLUE CLAW MFG & SUPPLY COMPANY
118 Clover Ln (08350-2438)
PHONE...............................856 696-4366
Leonard Streeper, *President*
EMP: 7
SALES (est): 560K **Privately Held**
SIC: 3496 5091 Traps, animal & fish

Ridgefield
Bergen County

(G-9250)
BASHIAN BROS INC (PA)
Also Called: Bashian Rugs
65 Railroad Ave Ste 8 (07657-2130)
PHONE...............................201 330-1001
George G Bashian Jr, *Ch of Bd*
Garo Bashian, *Vice Pres*
Gary Bashian, *Vice Pres*
Michael Keleshian, *CFO*
Malcolm Samad, *Treasurer*
▲ EMP: 29 EST: 1959
SQ FT: 18,000

SALES (est): 4.4MM **Privately Held**
WEB: www.bashianrug.com
SIC: 2273 Carpets & rugs

(G-9251)
BIAZZO DAIRY PRODUCTS INC
1145 Edgewater Ave (07657-2102)
PHONE.................................201 941-6800
John Iapichino Sr, *President*
Ann Iapichino, *Corp Secy*
John Iapichino Jr, *Vice Pres*
Angel Mendez, *Buyer*
Mariela Dilev, *Human Res Mgr*
▲ **EMP:** 50 **EST:** 1940
SQ FT: 58,000
SALES (est): 12.9MM **Privately Held**
WEB: www.biazzo.com
SIC: 2022 Natural cheese

(G-9252)
BRUDERER MACHINERY INC (PA)
1200 Hendricks Cswy (07657-2106)
PHONE.................................201 941-2121
Alois Rupp, *CEO*
Alois J Rupp, *President*
Ronald Randall, *Vice Pres*
Jim Anderson, *Plant Mgr*
Anneli Martin, *Opers Mgr*
◆ **EMP:** 48
SQ FT: 29,000
SALES (est): 10.5MM **Privately Held**
WEB: www.bruderer.com
SIC: 3542 Punching & shearing machines

(G-9253)
CAROLACE EMBROIDERY CO INC (PA)
65 Railroad Ave Ste 3 (07657-2130)
PHONE.................................201 945-2151
Howard Mann, *President*
David Mann, *Chairman*
▲ **EMP:** 80 **EST:** 1951
SQ FT: 15,000
SALES (est): 46.4MM **Privately Held**
SIC: 2397 2395 2241 Schiffli machine
   embroideries; lace, burnt-out, for the
   trade; braids, textile

(G-9254)
COLORITE PLASTICS COMPANY (DH)
101 Railroad Ave (07657-2312)
PHONE.................................201 941-2900
Miguel Nistal, *Vice Pres*
Barbara O'Connell, *Purchasing*
Thomas V Gilboy, *CFO*
◆ **EMP:** 36
SALES (est): 14MM
SALES (corp-wide): 1.1B **Privately Held**
SIC: 3089 Blister or bubble formed pack-
   aging, plastic
PA: Tekni-Plex, Inc.
   460 E Swedesford Rd # 3000
   Wayne PA 19087
   484 690-1520

(G-9255)
COLORITE POLYMERS
101 Railroad Ave (07657-2312)
PHONE.................................800 631-1577
David Katz, *Principal*
◆ **EMP:** 11
SALES (est): 1.6MM
SALES (corp-wide): 1.1B **Privately Held**
SIC: 2821 Plastics materials & resins
PA: Tekni-Plex, Inc.
   460 E Swedesford Rd # 3000
   Wayne PA 19087
   484 690-1520

(G-9256)
COMFORT CONCEPTS INC
501 Broad Ave Ste 7 (07657-2348)
PHONE.................................201 941-6700
David Rersignato, *President*
Sandra Furnbach, *Vice Pres*
EMP: 5
SQ FT: 4,000
SALES (est): 501.1K **Privately Held**
SIC: 2391 Curtains & draperies

(G-9257)
COSMETIC ESSENCE LLC
Also Called: C E I
1135 Pleasantview Ter (07657-2310)
PHONE.................................201 941-9800
Joe Scuderi, *Plant Mgr*
James Mayo, *Warehouse Mgr*

Andy Catenzaro, *Branch Mgr*
EMP: 100
SALES (corp-wide): 243.4MM **Privately
Held**
WEB: www.ceidistribution.com
SIC: 2844 Cosmetic preparations
HQ: Cosmetic Essence, Llc
   2182 Hwy 35
   Holmdel NJ 07733
   732 888-7788

(G-9258)
DOLCO PACKAGING CORP (HQ)
101 Railroad Ave (07657-2312)
PHONE.................................201 941-2900
EMP: 50
SALES (est): 14.5MM
SALES (corp-wide): 1.1B **Privately Held**
SIC: 3089 Blister or bubble formed pack-
   aging, plastic
PA: Tekni-Plex, Inc.
   460 E Swedesford Rd # 3000
   Wayne PA 19087
   484 690-1520

(G-9259)
ENVELOPE FREEDOM HOLDINGS LLC (PA)
65 Railroad Ave (07657-2140)
PHONE.................................201 699-5800
Kenneth Bernstein, *CEO*
Michael Mento, *CFO*
EMP: 6
SQ FT: 30,000
SALES (est): 30.2MM **Privately Held**
SIC: 2752 2677 Commercial printing, litho-
   graphic; envelopes

(G-9260)
EYELET EMBROIDERIES INC
65 Railroad Ave Ste 3 (07657-2130)
PHONE.................................201 945-2151
EMP: 60
SQ FT: 15,000
SALES (est): 2.6MM
SALES (corp-wide): 54MM **Privately
Held**
SIC: 2397 Mfg Schiffli Embroidery
PA: Carolace Embroidery Co, Inc.
   65 Railroad Ave Ste 3
   Ridgefield NJ 07657
   201 945-2151

(G-9261)
FIS DATA SYSTEMS INC
1008 Virgil Ave (07657-1602)
PHONE.................................201 945-1774
Dan Liu, *Vice Pres*
EMP: 30
SALES (corp-wide): 8.4B **Publicly Held**
WEB: www.sungard.com
SIC: 7374 7372 Data processing service;
   prepackaged software
HQ: Fis Data Systems Inc.
   200 Campus Dr
   Collegeville PA 19426
   484 582-2000

(G-9262)
GARDEN STATE PRECISION INC
510 Church St (07657-2131)
PHONE.................................201 945-6410
Joseph Molino, *President*
EMP: 8
SQ FT: 5,000
SALES (est): 1.2MM **Privately Held**
WEB: www.gardenstateprecision.com
SIC: 3544 Special dies & tools

(G-9263)
GENZYME CORPORATION
Also Called: Genzyme Biosurgery
1125 Pleasantview Ter (07657-2310)
PHONE.................................201 313-9660
Don Woodhouse, *Vice Pres*
Steve Mottola, *VP Mfg*
John Frey, *Mfg Staff*
David Armistead, *Engineer*
Cyndi Klatt, *Manager*
EMP: 115 **Privately Held**
WEB: www.genzyme.com
SIC: 2834 Pharmaceutical preparations
HQ: Genzyme Corporation
   50 Binney St
   Cambridge MA 02142
   617 252-7500

(G-9264)
GROW COMPANY INC
Also Called: Vol Employees Beneficiary Assn
55 Railroad Ave (07657-2109)
PHONE.................................201 941-8777
Andrew Szalay, *CEO*
Magda Peck, *President*
Massoud Arvanaghi, *Vice Pres*
EMP: 20
SQ FT: 40,000
SALES (est): 3.3MM
SALES (corp-wide): 387.6MM **Privately
Held**
SIC: 2023 2834 2844 2087 Dietary sup-
   plements, dairy & non-dairy based; phar-
   maceutical preparations; cosmetic
   preparations; food colorings
PA: Frutarom Industries Ltd
   2 Hamanofim, Entrance
   Herzliya 46725
   747 177-126

(G-9265)
HITRONS TECH INC
1 Remsen Pl Ste 107 (07657-2321)
PHONE.................................201 941-0024
Serom Park, *Principal*
EMP: 5
SALES (est): 172.2K **Privately Held**
SIC: 3699 Electrical equipment & supplies

(G-9266)
HOLOGRAPHIC FINISHING INC
501 Hendricks Cswy (07657-2116)
P.O. Box 597 (07657-0597)
PHONE.................................201 941-4651
Michael Vulcano, *President*
Mariann Vulcano, *Corp Secy*
Charles Vulcano, *Vice Pres*
EMP: 13
SQ FT: 14,457
SALES (est): 1MM **Privately Held**
WEB: www.holographicfinishing.com
SIC: 3554 2752 2789 Die cutting &
   stamping machinery; paper converting;
   commercial printing, lithographic; book-
   binding & related work

(G-9267)
HR INDUSTRIES INC
605 Broad Ave Ste 102 (07657-1628)
PHONE.................................201 941-8000
Sylvia Siegal, *President*
Howard Rothbein, *Vice Pres*
EMP: 10
SQ FT: 1,800
SALES (est): 4MM **Privately Held**
SIC: 2653 Boxes, corrugated: made from
   purchased materials

(G-9268)
INTERNTNAL FOLDING PPR BOX SLS
1039 Hoyt Ave (07657-1507)
PHONE.................................201 941-3100
Stanley Shapiro, *Mng Member*
EMP: 26
SQ FT: 1,000
SALES (est): 3.2MM **Privately Held**
SIC: 5113 2657 Folding paperboard
   boxes; folding paperboard boxes

(G-9269)
JOHNSON & JOHNSON
472 Chestnut St (07657-2640)
PHONE.................................917 573-8007
John Yoon, *Branch Mgr*
EMP: 80
SALES (corp-wide): 81.5B **Publicly Held**
SIC: 2676 Feminine hygiene paper prod-
   ucts
PA: Johnson & Johnson
   1 Johnson And Johnson Plz
   New Brunswick NJ 08933
   732 524-0400

(G-9270)
K RON ART & MIRRORS INC
395 Broad Ave (07657-2333)
PHONE.................................201 313-7080
Albert Choi, *President*
EMP: 4
SQ FT: 14,500
SALES: 700K **Privately Held**
SIC: 5023 2499 Frames & framing, picture
   & mirror; picture & mirror frames, wood

(G-9271)
KIMBER MFG INC
161 Railroad Ave (07657-2312)
PHONE.................................201 840-5812
Leslie Edelman, *President*
Gloria Dillon, *Controller*
EMP: 64
SALES (corp-wide): 79.1MM **Privately
Held**
SIC: 3599 Machine shop, jobbing & repair
PA: Kimber Mfg., Inc.
   1120 Saw Mill River Rd
   Yonkers NY 10710
   888 243-4522

(G-9272)
KNG TEXTILE INC
478 Walnut St Fl 2 (07657-2602)
PHONE.................................704 564-0390
Nam Goo Kim, *President*
EMP: 2
SALES (est): 6.5MM **Privately Held**
SIC: 2281 Manmade & synthetic fiber
   yarns, spun

(G-9273)
LASERCAM LLC (PA)
1039 Hoyt Ave (07657-1507)
PHONE.................................201 941-1262
Karl Koether, *General Mgr*
Maryellen Alesso, *Controller*
David Shapiro, *Controller*
▲ **EMP:** 40
SQ FT: 12,000
SALES (est): 6.5MM **Privately Held**
WEB: www.lasercam.com
SIC: 3544 Dies, steel rule

(G-9274)
LYNN AMIEE INC
Also Called: Amiee Lynn Accessories
65 Railroad Ave Ste 209 (07657-2130)
PHONE.................................201 840-6766
Steven Spolansky, *Principal*
Stephanie Murphy, *Sales Associate*
Peggy Freedman, *Director*
EMP: 50 **Privately Held**
SIC: 2389 4213 Handkerchiefs, except
   paper; heavy machinery transport
PA: Lynn Amiee Inc
   366 5th Ave Fl 11
   New York NY 10001

(G-9275)
MDVIANI DESIGNS INC
724 Bergen Blvd Ste 2 (07657-1442)
PHONE.................................201 840-5410
Nelly Minassian, *Owner*
EMP: 4
SALES (est): 225.1K **Privately Held**
SIC: 3915 3911 Gems, real & imitation:
   preparation for settings; jewel settings &
   mountings, precious metal

(G-9276)
MISCHIEF INTERNATIONAL INC
501 Broad Ave Ste 12 (07657-2348)
PHONE.................................201 840-6888
Max Bhavnani, *President*
▲ **EMP:** 5
SALES (est): 5MM **Privately Held**
SIC: 2326 Men's & boys' work clothing

(G-9277)
MONTENA TARANTO FOODS INC
400 Victoria Ter (07657-2113)
PHONE.................................201 943-8484
Wade Montena, *President*
Joe Taranto, *Vice Pres*
▲ **EMP:** 20
SALES (est): 5.8MM **Privately Held**
WEB: www.montitrentini.com
SIC: 2022 Natural cheese

(G-9278)
MORSEMERE IRON WORKS INC
1085 Linden Ave Ste 2 (07657-1013)
PHONE.................................201 941-1133
Mark Candelitti, *President*
EMP: 10
SQ FT: 5,000
SALES: 1.1MM **Privately Held**
SIC: 3446 3449 Architectural metalwork;
   miscellaneous metalwork

(G-9279)
NES LIGHT INC
1179 Edgewater Ave (07657-2102)
PHONE.....................................201 840-0400
Daniel Shin, *Manager*
EMP: 6 EST: 2012
SQ FT: 1,500
SALES (est): 577.3K **Privately Held**
SIC: 3993 Electric signs

(G-9280)
NEW LIFE COLOR REPRODUCTIONS
610 Broad Ave (07657-1626)
PHONE.....................................201 943-7005
Dragomir Zivkovich, *President*
Kova Zivkovich, *Admin Sec*
EMP: 4
SQ FT: 12,000
SALES (est): 346.1K **Privately Held**
SIC: 7384 2752 Photographic services;
commercial printing, offset

(G-9281)
OLD UE LLC
Also Called: United Envelope
65 Railroad Ave (07657-2140)
PHONE.....................................800 752-4012
Kenneth Bernstein, *Mng Member*
Steve Bunker,
EMP: 400
SQ FT: 30,000
SALES (est): 79.6MM **Privately Held**
SIC: 2759 2677 Envelopes: printing; en-
velopes

(G-9282)
PC MARKETING INC (PA)
Also Called: Montego Bay
1040 Wilt Ave (07657-1512)
PHONE.....................................201 943-6100
Susan Miller, *President*
Eric Haynes, *Vice Pres*
Paul Manke, *Vice Pres*
Bruce Williams, *Vice Pres*
Korri Harris, *Cust Mgr*
▲ EMP: 44
SQ FT: 27,000
SALES (est): 18.5MM **Privately Held**
SIC: 5099 3639 Tanning salon equipment
& supplies; major kitchen appliances, ex-
cept refrigerators & stoves

(G-9283)
PIM LLC
742 Bergen Blvd (07657-1435)
PHONE.....................................646 225-6666
Anthony Kory,
EMP: 25
SALES (est): 3.7MM **Privately Held**
SIC: 3577 Computer peripheral equipment

(G-9284)
PLASTIC SPECIALTIES & TECH INC (HQ)
101 Railroad Ave (07657-2312)
PHONE.....................................201 941-2900
David Katz, *President*
Kenneth Baker, *CFO*
◆ EMP: 140
SQ FT: 9,900
SALES (est): 45.9MM
SALES (corp-wide): 1.1B **Privately Held**
WEB: www.coloritepolymers.tekni-plex.com
SIC: 3052 3082 2821 4953 Garden hose,
plastic; tubes, unsupported plastic; ther-
moplastic materials; recycling, waste ma-
terials; paints & allied products
PA: Tekni-Plex, Inc.
460 E Swedesford Rd # 3000
Wayne PA 19087
484 690-1520

(G-9285)
PURE TEC CORPORATION (HQ)
101 Railroad Ave (07657-2312)
PHONE.....................................201 941-2900
EMP: 4
SALES (est): 14MM
SALES (corp-wide): 1.1B **Privately Held**
SIC: 3089 Blister or bubble formed pack-
aging, plastic

PA: Tekni-Plex, Inc.
460 E Swedesford Rd # 3000
Wayne PA 19087
484 690-1520

(G-9286)
RAYBEAM MANUFACTURING CORP
700 Grand Ave Ste 5 (07657-1527)
P.O. Box 538 (07657-0538)
PHONE.....................................201 941-4529
Larry Muhlberg, *President*
Rose Wurst, *Corp Secy*
EMP: 3
SQ FT: 1,000
SALES: 1MM **Privately Held**
SIC: 2842 5169 Cleaning or polishing
preparations; industrial chemicals

(G-9287)
RQ FLOORS CORP (PA)
425 Victoria Ter (07657-2112)
PHONE.....................................201 654-3587
Leon Shekhets, *President*
Vera Shekhets, *Vice Pres*
Jan Maczuga, *Manager*
EMP: 27
SQ FT: 30,000
SALES: 7MM **Privately Held**
SIC: 2491 Flooring, treated wood block

(G-9288)
SAPORITO INC
959 Edgewater Ave (07657-2438)
PHONE.....................................201 265-8212
Caren Zahn, *President*
EMP: 5
SQ FT: 10,000
SALES: 500K **Privately Held**
SIC: 2022 Cheese, natural & processed

(G-9289)
STANDARD COATING CORPORATION
461 Broad Ave (07657-2391)
PHONE.....................................201 945-5058
David Roogh, *General Mgr*
Bernard Katz, *Admin Sec*
▲ EMP: 4 EST: 1937
SQ FT: 11,250
SALES (est): 692.7K **Privately Held**
WEB: www.nitrostan.com
SIC: 2851 Lacquer: bases, dopes, thinner;
enamels; coating, air curing

(G-9290)
SUPERIOR STAMPING PRODUCTS LLC
1200 Hendricks Cswy (07657-2106)
PHONE.....................................201 945-5874
Alois Rupp, *Mng Member*
EMP: 30
SALES (est): 1.7MM **Privately Held**
SIC: 3469 Metal stampings

(G-9291)
TOTAL IMAGE AND SIGN
719 Grand Ave Ste 1 (07657-1049)
PHONE.....................................201 941-2307
Seung Hee Kim, *President*
EMP: 7
SALES (est): 732.1K **Privately Held**
SIC: 3993 Signs & advertising specialties

(G-9292)
TOUFAYAN BAKERY INC (PA)
Also Called: Toufayan Bakeries
175 Railroad Ave (07657-2312)
PHONE.....................................201 941-2000
Harry Toufayan, *President*
Tony Fortunato, *Regional Mgr*
Paul Steinbach, *Prdtn Mgr*
Todd Germick, *Purchasing*
Suzanne Toufayan, *Treasurer*
▲ EMP: 135
SALES (est): 27MM **Privately Held**
SIC: 2051 Bakery: wholesale or whole-
sale/retail combined

(G-9293)
TREND PRINTING/INTL LABEL
1183 Edgewater Ave (07657-2102)
PHONE.....................................201 941-6611
David Fishbein, *President*
Arlene Fishbein, *Vice Pres*

EMP: 10
SQ FT: 10,000
SALES (est): 1.4MM **Privately Held**
SIC: 2752 Commercial printing, litho-
graphic

(G-9294)
UNION CITY FILAMENT CORP
1039 Hoyt Ave A (07657-1507)
P.O. Box 777 (07657-0777)
PHONE.....................................201 945-3366
Joseph Celia Jr, *President*
Constance Celia, *Vice Pres*
EMP: 40 EST: 1950
SQ FT: 11,000
SALES (est): 9MM **Privately Held**
WEB: www.ucfilament.com
SIC: 3356 3641 3671 Tungsten, basic
shapes; filaments, for electric lamps; elec-
tron tubes

(G-9295)
UNITED CITY ICE CUBE CO INC
695 Elm Ave (07657-1229)
PHONE.....................................201 945-8387
Salvina Palmadessa, *Principal*
EMP: 5
SALES (est): 264.1K **Privately Held**
SIC: 2097 Ice cubes

(G-9296)
UNITED ENVELOPE LLC (HQ)
65 Railroad Ave (07657-2140)
PHONE.....................................201 699-5800
Kenneth Bernstein, *President*
Stuart Grover, *Exec VP*
Michael Mento, *CFO*
EMP: 31
SQ FT: 30,000
SALES (est): 18.7MM
SALES (corp-wide): 30.2MM **Privately
Held**
SIC: 2752 2677 Commercial printing, litho-
graphic; envelopes
PA: Envelope Freedom Holdings, Llc
65 Railroad Ave
Ridgefield NJ 07657
201 699-5800

(G-9297)
WESTCHESTER DENIM BROTHERS INC
736 Slocum Ave (07657-1838)
PHONE.....................................203 260-1629
Mourad Elayan, *Principal*
EMP: 8
SALES (est): 598K **Privately Held**
SIC: 2211 Denims

Ridgefield Park
Bergen County

(G-9298)
ADVERTISERS SERVICE GROUP INC
65 Railroad Ave (07660-1321)
PHONE.....................................201 440-5577
Edward F Kelly, *President*
Patricia Kelly, *Corp Secy*
EMP: 12 EST: 1961
SQ FT: 15,000
SALES: 1MM **Privately Held**
WEB: www.advertisersservices.com
SIC: 7336 7311 2752 2796 Graphic arts
& related design; advertising agencies;
commercial printing, lithographic; com-
mercial printing, offset; platemaking serv-
ices

(G-9299)
ALPINE CORRUGATED MCHY INC
100 Challenger Rd Ste 304 (07660-2119)
PHONE.....................................201 440-3030
Linda Katsigeorgis, *President*
▼ EMP: 3
SQ FT: 30,000
SALES (est): 6.5MM **Privately Held**
WEB: www.alpinemachinery.com
SIC: 3554 Corrugating machines, paper

(G-9300)
CAOLION BNC CO LTD
65 Challenger Rd Ste 44 (07660-2103)
PHONE.....................................201 641-4709
James Jang, *CEO*
EMP: 146
SQ FT: 2,436
SALES: 4MM **Privately Held**
SIC: 2844 Cosmetic preparations

(G-9301)
CONSOLIDATED PACKG GROUP INC
30 Bergen Tpke (07660-2383)
P.O. Box 261 (07660-0261)
PHONE.....................................201 440-4240
Chaim Kaufman, *President*
Ben Kaufman, *Vice Pres*
Eli Kaufman, *Plant Mgr*
Bob Chambers, *Regl Sales Mgr*
EMP: 160
SQ FT: 120,000
SALES (est): 57.4MM **Privately Held**
SIC: 2673 2671 Plastic bags: made from
purchased materials; plastic film, coated
or laminated for packaging

(G-9302)
DATA COMMUNIQUE INC
65 Challenger Rd Fl 4 (07660-2103)
PHONE.....................................201 508-6000
Richard Plotka, *CEO*
Brian Essman, *CEO*
Ethan Kende, *President*
Gary Polanco, *President*
John Closson, *Principal*
EMP: 45
SQ FT: 7,500
SALES: 12MM
SALES (corp-wide): 78.1MM **Privately
Held**
SIC: 7313 8741 2791 2759 Printed
media advertising representatives; man-
agement services; typesetting; financial
note & certificate printing & engraving;
computer software development
HQ: Havas
29 30
Puteaux 92800
158 478-000

(G-9303)
DATA COMMUNIQUE INTL INC (DH)
65 Challenger Rd Ste 400 (07660-2122)
PHONE.....................................201 508-6000
Richard Posen, *Principal*
Wayne Tidswell, *Exec VP*
Sean Heffernan, *Vice Pres*
Amanatoulaye Bah, *Accountant*
Richard Plotka, *Officer*
EMP: 14
SALES (est): 2.6MM
SALES (corp-wide): 78.1MM **Privately
Held**
SIC: 2759 2752 Commercial printing;
commercial printing, lithographic
HQ: Havas
29 30
Puteaux 92800
158 478-000

(G-9304)
DMG AMERICA LLC
Also Called: Goldsmith & Revere
65 Challenger Rd Ste 340 (07660-2122)
PHONE.....................................201 894-5500
George Wolfe, *Mng Member*
Celia Basile, *Manager*
▲ EMP: 52
SQ FT: 10,000
SALES: 28MM **Privately Held**
WEB: www.zenithdmg.com
SIC: 3843 5047 Dental equipment & sup-
plies; medical & hospital equipment

(G-9305)
EQUIPMENT DISTRIBUTING CORP (PA)
3 Eucker St (07660-2335)
PHONE.....................................201 641-8414
Antonio S Limbardo, *President*
EMP: 7
SQ FT: 1,200

SALES (est): 1.1MM **Privately Held**
SIC: 3312 3441 Wire products, steel or iron; fabricated structural metal

(G-9306)
FLIR SECURITY INC
65 Challenger Rd (07660-2103)
PHONE.................................201 368-9700
Andrew C Teich, *President*
Todd M Duchene, *Senior VP*
Jeffrey D Frank, *Senior VP*
Shane R Harrison, *Senior VP*
Travis D Merrill, *Senior VP*
EMP: 5
SALES (est): 336.7K
SALES (corp-wide): 1.7B **Publicly Held**
SIC: 3663 5731 Digital encoders; video cameras & accessories
PA: Flir Systems, Inc.
27700 Sw Parkway Ave
Wilsonville OR 97070
503 498-3547

(G-9307)
FLIR SYSTEMS INC
65 Challenger Rd (07660-2103)
PHONE.................................201 368-9700
Reid Sullivan, *Vice Pres*
EMP: 4
SALES (corp-wide): 1.7B **Publicly Held**
SIC: 3861 Photographic equipment & supplies
PA: Flir Systems, Inc.
27700 Sw Parkway Ave
Wilsonville OR 97070
503 498-3547

(G-9308)
GRAPHIC SOLUTIONS & SIGNS LLC
200 Brinkerhoff St (07660-2020)
PHONE.................................201 343-7446
Felipe Alarcon,
EMP: 11
SALES (est): 1.2MM **Privately Held**
WEB: www.graphicsolutionsandsigns.com
SIC: 3993 Signs & advertising specialties

(G-9309)
HOSPITALITY GL BRANDS USA INC
185 Industrial Ave (07660-1333)
PHONE.................................800 869-5258
▲ EMP: 17
SALES (est): 2.1MM **Privately Held**
SIC: 3229 Novelty glassware

(G-9310)
KIRKWOOD NJ GLOBE ACQSTION LLC
1 Teaneck Rd (07660-2360)
PHONE.................................201 440-0800
Bob Coppinger, *CEO*
Stephan A Duncan, *President*
Eddie Kelley, *COO*
Christopher Noble, *Senior VP*
Craig Wenrich, *Vice Pres*
EMP: 5
SALES (est): 378K **Privately Held**
SIC: 3555 Printing presses

(G-9311)
KOLON USA INCORPORATED
Also Called: Scen'a Video Tape
65 Challenger Rd (07660-2103)
PHONE.................................201 641-5800
Edward Kang, *President*
Bruce Lee, *General Mgr*
Ivan Park, *General Mgr*
Jeffrey Hong, *Treasurer*
Debbie Hanlon, *Manager*
▲ EMP: 19
SQ FT: 58,000
SALES (est): 4.5MM
SALES (corp-wide): 2.9B **Privately Held**
WEB: www.kolonscena.com
SIC: 5199 3081 Packaging materials; unsupported plastics film & sheet
PA: Kolon Industries, Inc.
Kolon One&Only Tower
Seoul 07793
822 367-7311

(G-9312)
KUPELIAN FOODS INC
146 Bergen Tpke (07660-2323)
PHONE.................................201 440-8055
Edward Kupelian, *President*
EMP: 5
SQ FT: 1,500
SALES (est): 440K **Privately Held**
SIC: 2013 Sausages & other prepared meats

(G-9313)
OE SOLUTIONS AMERICA INC
Also Called: Moon
65 Challenger Rd Ste 240 (07660-2122)
PHONE.................................201 568-1188
Yong Kwan Park, *President*
Moonsoo Park, *Vice Pres*
Wanseok Seo, *Engineer*
Chuck Sinha, *VP Bus Dvlpt*
Moon Keum, *Accounting Mgr*
EMP: 15
SALES (est): 3MM **Privately Held**
SIC: 3661 Fiber optics communications equipment
PA: Oe Solutions Co., Ltd.
53 Cheomdanyeonsin-Ro 30beon-Gil, Buk-Gu
Gwangju 61080

(G-9314)
OUTPUT SERVICES GROUP INC (HQ)
Also Called: OSG Billing Services
100 Challenger Rd Ste 303 (07660-2119)
PHONE.................................201 871-1100
Scott W Bernstein, *CEO*
John Springthorpe III, *President*
Alan Connolly, *Exec VP*
John Delaney, *Exec VP*
Neil Metviner, *Exec VP*
◆ EMP: 34
SQ FT: 10,000
SALES (est): 199.7MM
SALES (corp-wide): 48.5MM **Privately Held**
WEB: www.osgbilling.com
SIC: 7372 Business oriented computer software
PA: Osg Group Holdings, Inc.
100 Challenger Rd Ste 303
Ridgefield Park NJ 07660
201 871-1100

(G-9315)
SAMSUNG SDS GLOBL SCL AMER INC (HQ)
100 Challenger Rd Ste 601 (07660-2121)
PHONE.................................201 229-4456
Sean Seung Gyo Kae, *CEO*
Ki Hyung Cho, *President*
Jong Moo Bae, *CFO*
Mario Lopez, *Sales Staff*
Ryan Park, *Manager*
EMP: 20
SALES (est): 173.5MM **Privately Held**
WEB: www.samsungsdsa.com
SIC: 7372 7371 Prepackaged software; computer software development

(G-9316)
SOFIELD MANUFACTURING CO INC
2 Main St (07660-2213)
PHONE.................................201 931-1530
EMP: 4
SQ FT: 5,000
SALES (est): 420K **Privately Held**
SIC: 3469 Mfg Metal Stampings

(G-9317)
SONOCO DISPLAY & PACKAGING LLC
Also Called: Sonoco Corrflex
55 Challenger Rd Ste 500 (07660-2107)
PHONE.................................201 612-4008
John Kinkella, *Director*
EMP: 8
SALES (corp-wide): 5.3B **Publicly Held**
SIC: 3086 Packaging & shipping materials, foamed plastic
HQ: Sonoco Display & Packaging, Llc
555 Aureole St
Winston Salem NC 27107

(G-9318)
STAR SOAP/STAR CANDLE/PRAYER C
Also Called: Star Candle Company
300 Industrial Ave (07660-1346)
PHONE.................................201 690-9090
Stanley Gurewitsch, *Mng Member*
Arnie Gurewitsch,
Steven Gurewitsch,
Sam Schwartz,
◆ EMP: 200 EST: 1939
SQ FT: 150,000
SALES (est): 42MM **Privately Held**
WEB: www.starcandle.com
SIC: 3999 Candles

(G-9319)
WEILING YANG
65 Challenger Rd (07660-2103)
PHONE.................................201 440-5329
Te Zhong, *President*
EMP: 6 EST: 2015
SALES (est): 148.1K **Privately Held**
SIC: 5499 2836 Spices & herbs; extracts

(G-9320)
WINIADAEWOO ELEC AMER INC (PA)
65 Challenger Rd Ste 360 (07660-2122)
PHONE.................................201 552-4950
Jung Han Kim, *President*
Siheon Song, *Vice Pres*
Michelle Yun, *CFO*
Byoung Kang, *Manager*
◆ EMP: 16
SQ FT: 10,000
SALES (est): 3.2MM **Privately Held**
SIC: 3634 5064 5722 Electric housewares & fans; electric household appliances; electric household appliances

---

Ridgewood
Bergen County

(G-9321)
ARAYA INC
Also Called: Araya Rebirth
10 Garber Sq Ste A (07450-3129)
PHONE.................................201 445-7005
Danella Musano, *President*
EMP: 5
SALES (est): 611.3K **Privately Held**
WEB: www.araya.com
SIC: 3842 Cosmetic restorations

(G-9322)
ARTISAN GARDENS LLC
76 N Maple Ave Ste 279 (07450-3212)
P.O. Box 761 (07451-0761)
PHONE.................................201 857-2600
Brian J Tauscher, *Principal*
EMP: 4
SALES (est): 356.4K **Privately Held**
SIC: 3633 Drycleaning machines, household: including coin-operated

(G-9323)
DOUGLAS LIVA MD
Also Called: Liva Eye Center
625 Franklin Tpke (07450-1913)
PHONE.................................201 444-7770
Douglas Liva, *Owner*
EMP: 7
SQ FT: 80,000
SALES (est): 775K **Privately Held**
WEB: www.eyemd.com
SIC: 3851 8011 Protectors, eye; ophthalmologist

(G-9324)
ERJ BAKING LLC
235 N Pleasant Ave (07450-2834)
PHONE.................................201 906-1300
Jeffrey Jayson, *Principal*
EMP: 4
SALES (est): 270.6K **Privately Held**
SIC: 2051 Bread, cake & related products

(G-9325)
NUTRA NUTS INC (PA)
Also Called: Grandpa Po's Nutra Nuts
247 Emmett Pl (07450-2803)
PHONE.................................323 260-7457
Mark Porro, *President*
Michael Porro, *CFO*
EMP: 4
SQ FT: 3,300
SALES: 200K **Privately Held**
WEB: www.nutranuts.com
SIC: 2064 Popcorn balls or other treated popcorn products

(G-9326)
PUBLISHERS PARTNERSHIP CO
23 N Pleasant Ave (07450-3920)
PHONE.................................201 689-1613
Molly Ledwith, *Partner*
EMP: 99
SALES (est): 2.8MM **Privately Held**
SIC: 2741 5942 Miscellaneous publishing; book stores

(G-9327)
QUALITY PRINT SOLUTIONS
589 Franklin Tpke (07450-1989)
PHONE.................................888 679-7237
Steve Fischgrund, *Partner*
EMP: 4 EST: 2013
SALES (est): 350K **Privately Held**
SIC: 2752 Commercial printing, lithographic

(G-9328)
RIDGEWOOD PRESS INC
609 Franklin Tpke (07450-1913)
PHONE.................................201 670-9797
Robert Modelski, *President*
John Pagluica, *Co-President*
Susan Burke, *Cust Mgr*
EMP: 12
SALES (est): 2.1MM **Privately Held**
WEB: www.rpress.com
SIC: 2752 7334 7336 Commercial printing, offset; photocopying & duplicating services; commercial art & graphic design

(G-9329)
SENSBL INC
615 Barnett Pl (07450-1601)
PHONE.................................862 225-3803
Bill Louttit, *President*
Cigdem Topaloglu, *Chief Mktg Ofcr*
Samil Ozavar, *Officer*
EMP: 10
SQ FT: 1,000
SALES: 250K **Privately Held**
SIC: 2086 5499 Carbonated beverages, nonalcoholic: bottled & canned; health & dietetic food stores

(G-9330)
STRONGWALL INDUSTRIES INC
107 Chestnut St (07450-2501)
P.O. Box 682 (07451-0682)
PHONE.................................201 445-4633
Nicole Kokoletsos, *President*
EMP: 7
SQ FT: 3,000
SALES (est): 1.1MM **Privately Held**
WEB: www.strongwall.com
SIC: 3297 3069 3272 High temperature mortar, nonclay; floor coverings, rubber; concrete products

(G-9331)
SUDARSHAN NORTH AMERICA INC
76 N Walnut St (07450-3224)
PHONE.................................201 652-2046
Rajesh Rathi, *CEO*
William Baker, *President*
◆ EMP: 7
SALES (est): 610MM
SALES (corp-wide): 198.9MM **Privately Held**
WEB: www.sudarshan.com
SIC: 2816 Color pigments
PA: Sudarshan Chemical Industries Limited
No-162, Wellesley Road,
Pune MH 41100
202 605-8888

(G-9332)
SVTC PHARMA INC
60 E Ridgewood Ave (07450-3810)
PHONE....................................201 652-0013
Purnachandra RAO Akkineni, *Principal*
EMP: 7 **EST:** 2011
SALES (est): 827.9K **Privately Held**
SIC: 2834 Pharmaceutical preparations

(G-9333)
UBERTESTERS INC
72 S Maple Ave (07450-4542)
PHONE....................................201 203-7903
Ran Rachlin, *CEO*
Sergey Eremenko, *Sales Mgr*
Alexey Taran, *Manager*
EMP: 14
SQ FT: 1,000
SALES (est): 349.8K **Privately Held**
SIC: 7372 Business oriented computer software

Ringoes
Hunterdon County

(G-9334)
ARGUS INTERNATIONAL INC (PA)
424 Route 31 N (08551-1409)
P.O. Box 559 (08551-0559)
PHONE....................................609 466-1677
Bernard J Costello, *President*
Maryellen Costello, *Executive*
EMP: 20
SQ FT: 25,000
SALES (est): 4.1MM **Privately Held**
WEB: www.argus-international.com
SIC: 3567 3672 3625 3563 Heating units & devices, industrial: electric; printed circuit boards; relays & industrial controls; air & gas compressors

(G-9335)
CATERING BY MADDALENAS INC
Also Called: Maddalenas Cheese Cake Catrg
415 Route 31 N (08551-1408)
PHONE....................................609 466-7510
Janet Maddalena, *President*
Eugene Maddalena, *Vice Pres*
EMP: 9
SQ FT: 5,000
SALES: 680K **Privately Held**
WEB: www.maddalenascatering.com
SIC: 5812 2051 5149 5461 Caterers; cakes, pies & pastries; bakery products; bakeries

(G-9336)
HED INTERNATIONAL INC
Also Called: Unique/Pereny
449 Route 31 N (08551-1408)
P.O. Box 246 (08551-0246)
PHONE....................................609 466-1900
James Dennis, *President*
John S Dennis, *CFO*
John Dennis, *Chief Mktg Ofcr*
Terrance Dennis, *Mktg Dir*
EMP: 15
SQ FT: 25,000
SALES (est): 4.3MM **Privately Held**
WEB: www.hed.com
SIC: 3567 Heating units & devices, industrial: electric

(G-9337)
INENERGY INC
293 Wertsville Rd (08551-1701)
PHONE....................................609 466-2512
Michael Kurtis, *President*
EMP: 25
SALES (est): 4MM **Privately Held**
SIC: 3433 Solar heaters & collectors

(G-9338)
JAY JARIWALA
Also Called: Dunkin' Donuts
1019 Us Highway 202 (08551-1049)
PHONE....................................908 806-8266
Jay Jariwala, *Owner*
EMP: 15
SALES (est): 304.1K **Privately Held**
SIC: 5461 2051 Doughnuts; doughnuts, except frozen

(G-9339)
MATTHEW WARREN INC
Also Called: Atlantic Spring
137 Us Highway 202 (08551-1909)
P.O. Box 650, Flemington (08822-0650)
PHONE....................................908 788-5800
Scott Solomon, *Exec VP*
EMP: 10
SALES (corp-wide): 185.9MM **Privately Held**
SIC: 3493 3495 Steel springs, except wire; wire springs
HQ: Matthew Warren, Inc.
9501 Tech Blvd Ste 401
Rosemont IL 60018
847 349-5760

(G-9340)
OLD YORK CELLARS
80 Old York Rd (08551-1309)
PHONE....................................908 284-9463
David Wolin, *Owner*
Narendra Haynes, *Mktg Dir*
Jan Barrie, *Manager*
Loren Dorman, *Manager*
EMP: 6
SALES (est): 386.2K **Privately Held**
SIC: 2084 Wines

(G-9341)
REAGENT CHEMICAL & RES INC
115 Us Highway 202 Ste E (08551-1913)
PHONE....................................908 284-2800
Stephen Finney, *CFO*
Larry Baggett, *Sales Mgr*
Robert Dritschel, *Branch Mgr*
EMP: 50
SALES (corp-wide): 517MM **Privately Held**
WEB: www.biotarget.com
SIC: 2819 3949 Sulfur, recovered or refined, incl. from sour natural gas; targets, archery & rifle shooting
PA: Reagent Chemical & Research, Inc.
115 Rte 202
Ringoes NJ 08551
908 284-2800

(G-9342)
UNIONVILLE VINEYARDS LLC
9 Rocktown Rd (08551-1214)
P.O. Box 104 (08551-0104)
PHONE....................................908 788-0400
Patricia Galloway, *Partner*
Kris Nielsen, *Partner*
John Cifelli, *General Mgr*
Jay Quilty, *Sales Staff*
Jackie Dezic, *Manager*
EMP: 8
SALES (est): 1MM **Privately Held**
WEB: www.unionvillevineyards.com
SIC: 2084 0172 Wines; grapes

Ringwood
Passaic County

(G-9343)
BACH TOOL PRECISION INC
51 Executive Pkwy (07456-1429)
PHONE....................................973 962-6224
Richard Ebersbach, *President*
Jane Ebersbach, *Office Admin*
EMP: 6
SALES (est): 590K **Privately Held**
WEB: www.bachtoolprecision.com
SIC: 3544 3545 Special dies & tools; precision tools, machinists'

(G-9344)
CIRCONIX TECHNOLOGIES LLC (DH)
29 Executive Pkwy (07456-1429)
PHONE....................................973 962-6160
Andre Icso, *President*
▲ **EMP:** 14
SQ FT: 15,000
SALES (est): 3.5MM **Privately Held**
WEB: www.circonix.com
SIC: 3613 7373 3823 Switchgear & switchboard apparatus; computer-aided engineering (CAE) systems service; industrial instrmnts msrmnt display/control process variable

(G-9345)
GB INDUSTRIES II INC
341 Margaret King Ave (07456-1415)
PHONE....................................973 728-5900
Gerard Barrere, *President*
John Barrere, *Vice Pres*
EMP: 6
SQ FT: 9,100
SALES (est): 1.2MM **Privately Held**
WEB: www.gbindustriesii.com
SIC: 3599 Machine shop, jobbing & repair

(G-9346)
ILL EAGLE ENTERPRISES LTD
Also Called: Ill-Eagle Enterprises
101 Miller Ln (07456-1208)
PHONE....................................973 237-1111
Darryl Sgroi, *President*
▲ **EMP:** 32
SQ FT: 20,000
SALES (est): 6MM **Privately Held**
WEB: www.illeagle.com
SIC: 3499 3914 2499 Novelties & giftware, including trophies; trophies, plated (all metals); picture frame molding, finished

(G-9347)
INOPAK LTD
24 Executive Pkwy (07456-1430)
PHONE....................................973 962-1121
John Polite, *President*
David Polite, *Corp Secy*
Nick Disarro, *Exec VP*
▲ **EMP:** 17
SQ FT: 17,500
SALES (est): 3.9MM **Privately Held**
WEB: www.inopak.com
SIC: 2841 3999 Soap & other detergents; soap dispensers

(G-9348)
MEMBRANES INTERNATIONAL INC
219 Margaret King Ave # 2 (07456-1440)
PHONE....................................973 998-5530
Dwight Loren, *CEO*
Jack Loren, *President*
EMP: 4
SALES (est): 837.9K **Privately Held**
WEB: www.membranesinternational.com
SIC: 3569 Filters

(G-9349)
MICROMAT CO
1165 Greenwood Lake Tpke E (07456-1416)
PHONE....................................201 529-3738
Erwin Eibert, *President*
EMP: 7 **EST:** 1963
SQ FT: 5,000
SALES (est): 1.1MM **Privately Held**
WEB: www.micromat.com
SIC: 3491 Pressure valves & regulators, industrial

(G-9350)
PRO-PAC SERVICE INC
15 Van Natta Dr (07456-1412)
PHONE....................................973 962-8080
Brian Douglas, *President*
▲ **EMP:** 12
SQ FT: 10,000
SALES (est): 2.4MM **Privately Held**
SIC: 3565 Packaging machinery

(G-9351)
PROGRESSIVE RUESCH INC
21 Van Natta Dr (07456-1412)
PHONE....................................973 962-7700
Stephen Honezarenko, *President*
▲ **EMP:** 30
SQ FT: 22,000
SALES (est): 7MM **Privately Held**
WEB: www.rueschmachinery.com
SIC: 3549 5084 Rotary slitters (metalworking machines); industrial machinery & equipment

(G-9352)
ROBERT NICHOLS CONTRACTING
407 Conklintown Rd (07456-2415)
PHONE....................................973 902-2632
EMP: 10
SALES (est): 900K **Privately Held**
SIC: 2899 Mfg Chemical Preparations

(G-9353)
SUSAN R BAUER INC
Also Called: Bauer Enterprises
427 Margaret King Ave (07456-1438)
PHONE....................................973 657-1590
Susan R Bauer, *President*
Mary Ellen Gutowski, *Manager*
Richard Bauer, *Admin Sec*
EMP: 8
SQ FT: 24,000
SALES (est): 950K **Privately Held**
SIC: 3441 Fabricated structural metal for bridges; expansion joints (structural shapes), iron or steel

(G-9354)
TERHUNE BROS WOODWORKING
58 Bearfort Ter (07456-2943)
PHONE....................................973 962-6686
Michael Terhune, *Principal*
EMP: 4
SALES (est): 324.6K **Privately Held**
SIC: 2431 Millwork

Rio Grande
Cape May County

(G-9355)
HANGER PRSTHETCS & ORTHO INC
1 Secluded Ln (08242-1546)
PHONE....................................609 889-8447
Virginia Millar, *Principal*
EMP: 7
SALES (corp-wide): 1B **Publicly Held**
SIC: 3842 Surgical appliances & supplies
HQ: Hanger Prosthetics & Orthotics, Inc.
10910 Domain Dr Ste 300
Austin TX 78758
512 777-3800

(G-9356)
MICHAELS CABINET CONNECTION
1054 Route 47 S (08242)
PHONE....................................609 889-6611
Michael Snow, *CEO*
EMP: 5
SQ FT: 5,000
SALES: 170K **Privately Held**
SIC: 2434 Wood kitchen cabinets

(G-9357)
RESDEL CORPORATION (PA)
Industrial Park (08242)
PHONE....................................609 886-1111
Nicholas Calio, *President*
Dave Beckas, *Prdtn Mgr*
Debbie Fazen, *Office Admin*
Charles Mannella, *Admin Sec*
EMP: 20 **EST:** 1957
SQ FT: 10,000
SALES (est): 2.3MM **Privately Held**
SIC: 3082 Tubes, unsupported plastic

(G-9358)
SEAWAVE CORP
Also Called: Cape May County Herald
1508 Route 47 (08242-1413)
P.O. Box 400 (08242-0400)
PHONE....................................609 886-8600
Arthur R Hall, *President*
Patricia Hall, *Admin Sec*
EMP: 29
SQ FT: 4,000
SALES (est): 2.2MM **Privately Held**
WEB: www.cmcherald.com
SIC: 2711 8611 Newspapers, publishing & printing; business associations

River Edge
Bergen County

(G-9359)
COLEMAX GROUP LLC (PA)
41 Grand Ave Ste 103 (07661-1947)
P.O. Box 103, Glen Rock (07452-0103)
PHONE..............................201 489-1080
Louie Valenti, *Accounts Mgr*
Richard Flashenberg,
▲ EMP: 5
SQ FT: 3,000
SALES (est): 4.4MM **Privately Held**
WEB: www.colemaxgroup.com
SIC: 3172 Cases, glasses

(G-9360)
CONTEMPOCORK LLC
175 Dorchester Rd (07661-1224)
PHONE..............................201 262-7738
EMP: 5
SALES (est): 380K **Privately Held**
SIC: 1752 2499 Floor Contractor

(G-9361)
FEDEX OFFICE & PRINT SVCS INC
1071 Main St (07661-2011)
PHONE..............................201 525-5070
EMP: 5
SALES (corp-wide): 69.6B **Publicly Held**
SIC: 2752 Commercial printing, lithographic
HQ: Fedex Office And Print Services, Inc.
7900 Legacy Dr
Plano TX 75024
800 463-3339

(G-9362)
JEWISH STANDARD INC
Also Called: Jewish Media Group
70 Grand Ave Ste 104 (07661-1936)
PHONE..............................201 837-8818
James Janoff, *Publisher*
Peggy Elias, *Accounts Exec*
Brenda Sutcliffe, *Accounts Exec*
Jane Carr, *Advt Staff*
Larry Yudelson, *Assoc Editor*
EMP: 15
SALES (est): 896.1K **Privately Held**
SIC: 2711 Newspapers, publishing & printing

(G-9363)
KELLOGG COMPANY
164 Monroe Ave (07661-2113)
PHONE..............................201 634-9140
J Volmar, *Principal*
EMP: 29
SALES (corp-wide): 13.5B **Publicly Held**
WEB: www.kelloggs.com
SIC: 2043 Cereal breakfast foods
PA: Kellogg Company
1 Kellogg Sq
Battle Creek MI 49017
269 961-2000

(G-9364)
ZSOMBOR ANTAL DESIGNS INC
Also Called: Best Cast
822 Kinderkamack Rd (07661-2324)
PHONE..............................201 225-1750
Zsombor Antal, *President*
Laura Antal, *Vice Pres*
▲ EMP: 15
SQ FT: 4,000
SALES (est): 1.6MM **Privately Held**
WEB: www.best-cast.com
SIC: 3471 3911 Decorative plating & finishing of formed products; gold plating; jewelry, precious metal

River Vale
Bergen County

(G-9365)
DOORTEC ARCHTCTURAL MET GL LLC (PA)
303 Martin St (07675-5610)
PHONE..............................201 497-5056

Jeffrey Bentzen, *Sales Staff*
Boris Barskiy,
EMP: 1
SALES: 4.8MM **Privately Held**
SIC: 3446 Architectural metalwork

(G-9366)
INTERTAPE POLYMER CORP
648 Athlone Ter (07675-6548)
PHONE..............................201 391-3315
EMP: 135
SALES (corp-wide): 1B **Privately Held**
SIC: 2672 Tape, pressure sensitive: made from purchased materials
HQ: Intertape Polymer Corp.
100 Paramount Dr Ste 300
Sarasota FL 34232
888 898-7834

(G-9367)
JOY JEWELERY AMERICA INC
228 Rivervale Rd Ste A (07675-6216)
PHONE..............................201 689-1150
Keith Lesser, *Principal*
EMP: 4
SALES (est): 400.7K **Privately Held**
SIC: 3911 Jewelry, precious metal

(G-9368)
UMBRELLAS UNLIMITED
808 Rivervale Rd (07675-6122)
PHONE..............................201 476-1011
Robert S Reiss, *Ch of Bd*
Ron Goldstein, *President*
Angela Sanfilippo, *Manager*
Raymond Lo, *Shareholder*
EMP: 2
SALES: 1.6MM **Privately Held**
SIC: 2211 Umbrella cloth, cotton

Riverdale
Morris County

(G-9369)
A & A CONCRETE PRODUCTS INC
2 S Corporate Dr (07457-1721)
P.O. Box 108 (07457-0108)
PHONE..............................973 835-2239
Sandra Alway, *President*
Dan Jiles, *Foreman/Supr*
EMP: 5
SQ FT: 6,000
SALES: 325K **Privately Held**
SIC: 5082 5039 3272 Concrete processing equipment; septic tanks; concrete products

(G-9370)
ALEXAM RIVERDALE
4000 Riverdale Rd (07457-1729)
PHONE..............................973 831-0065
EMP: 4
SALES (est): 433.7K **Privately Held**
SIC: 3713 Automobile wrecker truck bodies

(G-9371)
BER PLASTICS INC
5 Curtis St (07457-1113)
P.O. Box 2 (07457-0002)
PHONE..............................973 839-2100
Edward Ringley, *Ch of Bd*
Bernard Ewasko, *President*
EMP: 24 EST: 1965
SQ FT: 17,000
SALES (est): 3.6MM **Privately Held**
SIC: 3082 3081 Tubes, unsupported plastic; plastic film & sheet

(G-9372)
CAMFIL USA INC (HQ)
1 N Corporate Dr (07457-1715)
PHONE..............................973 616-7300
Armando Brunetti, *President*
Klaus Hassfurther, *General Mgr*
Carl Larochelle, *General Mgr*
Charles Seyffer, *General Mgr*
Paul Cleveland, *Managing Dir*
◆ EMP: 180
SQ FT: 106,000

SALES (est): 239.1MM
SALES (corp-wide): 921.6MM **Privately Held**
SIC: 3564 3569 Purification & dust collection equipment; filters, air: furnaces, air conditioning equipment, etc.; air purification equipment; dust or fume collecting equipment, industrial; filters; filters, general line: industrial
PA: Camfil Ab
Sveavagen 56e
Stockholm 111 3
854 512-500

(G-9373)
CARL STAHL SAVA INDUSTRIES INC (HQ)
4 N Corporate Dr (07457-1715)
P.O. Box 30 (07457-0030)
PHONE..............................973 835-0882
Zdenek A Fremund, *CEO*
Marc E Alterman, *President*
Gregory Soja, *Vice Pres*
Bruce R Staubitz, *Vice Pres*
▲ EMP: 85 EST: 1972
SQ FT: 70,000
SALES: 18.4MM
SALES (corp-wide): 326.6MM **Privately Held**
WEB: www.savacable.com
SIC: 3496 Miscellaneous fabricated wire products
PA: Carl Stahl Gmbh
Tobelstr. 2
SuBen 73079
716 240-070

(G-9374)
CVE INC
5 N Corporate Dr (07457-1715)
PHONE..............................201 770-0005
Kyu Taek Cho, *President*
Jae Joon, *General Mgr*
▲ EMP: 100
SQ FT: 63,000
SALES (est): 30.6MM **Privately Held**
WEB: www.cveusa.com
SIC: 3651 Household audio & video equipment

(G-9375)
DIVERSITECH INC
Also Called: K & E Components
18 Hamburg Tpke (07457-1116)
PHONE..............................973 835-2900
Keith Wolos, *President*
James Schmieder, *President*
Roy Wright, *Prdtn Mgr*
EMP: 28 EST: 1965
SQ FT: 27,000
SALES (est): 4.9MM **Privately Held**
WEB: www.sierrakd.com
SIC: 3599 Machine shop, jobbing & repair

(G-9376)
ELUXNET USA CORPORATION
3 S Corporate Dr Ste 2c (07457-1712)
PHONE..............................201 724-5986
Danniell Won, *Principal*
▲ EMP: 8
SALES (est): 746.4K **Privately Held**
SIC: 3646 Ornamental lighting fixtures, commercial

(G-9377)
EVS INTERACTIVE INC
Also Called: Redyref
100 Riverdale Rd (07457-1700)
PHONE..............................718 784-3690
Scott Berkowitz, *President*
Joseph Amico, *Vice Pres*
Fred Ravo, *Design Engr*
EMP: 15
SALES (est): 1.2MM **Privately Held**
SIC: 3444 Sheet metalwork

(G-9378)
GLASS CYCLE SYSTEMS INC
5 Mathews Ave (07457-1010)
P.O. Box 816, Butler (07405-0816)
PHONE..............................973 838-0034
David Bowlby, *President*
EMP: 4
SQ FT: 2,200

SALES: 150K **Privately Held**
SIC: 3559 4953 Recycling machinery; recycling, waste materials

(G-9379)
INDEPENDENT SHEET METAL CO INC
2 N Corporate Dr 2 # 2 (07457-1715)
PHONE..............................973 423-1150
Edward Rebenack, *President*
Stephen Pucilowski, *Vice Pres*
Scott Grant, *Project Mgr*
Jim Boniface, *Info Tech Mgr*
Steve Pucilowski, *Executive*
EMP: 100
SQ FT: 40,000
SALES (est): 24.4MM **Privately Held**
WEB: www.indsm.com
SIC: 3444 1761 Sheet metalwork; sheet metalwork

(G-9380)
P K PRECISION MACHINING INC
7 Mathews Ave (07457-1020)
PHONE..............................973 925-2020
Patricia Androvich, *President*
Kenneth F Androvich, *Vice Pres*
EMP: 4
SQ FT: 10,000
SALES: 275K **Privately Held**
WEB: www.pkprecision.com
SIC: 3599 Machine shop, jobbing & repair

(G-9381)
RAINBOW METAL UNITS CORP
Also Called: Dawnex Industries
1 Kenner Ct (07457-1500)
PHONE..............................718 784-3690
William Pymm, *President*
Edward Pymm, *Vice Pres*
EMP: 20
SQ FT: 30,000
SALES (est): 2.6MM **Privately Held**
WEB: www.redyref.com
SIC: 3444 Sheet metalwork

(G-9382)
RIVERDALE QUARRY LLC
125 Hamburg Tpke (07457-1000)
PHONE..............................973 835-0028
Gary Mahan, *General Mgr*
Charles Highler, *Manager*
EMP: 50
SALES (est): 2.1MM **Privately Held**
SIC: 1429 2951 Igneous rock, crushed & broken-quarrying; asphalt & asphaltic paving mixtures (not from refineries)

(G-9383)
SENTRY WATER MANAGEMENT
35 Newark Pompton Tpke (07457-1144)
PHONE..............................973 616-9000
Matt Copley, *General Mgr*
EMP: 40
SALES (est): 3.9MM **Privately Held**
SIC: 2899 Water treating compounds

(G-9384)
SETCON INDUSTRIES INC
5 Mathews Ave Ste 7 (07457-1034)
PHONE..............................973 283-0500
Glen Azzolino, *President*
Joseph Azzolino, *President*
Robert Azzolino, *Vice Pres*
EMP: 10 EST: 1961
SQ FT: 4,000
SALES (est): 1.6MM **Privately Held**
WEB: www.setconindustries.com
SIC: 2819 Industrial inorganic chemicals

(G-9385)
SIGMA-NETICS INC
2 N Corporate Dr (07457-1715)
PHONE..............................973 227-6372
Alan Glanzman, *CEO*
Claudio Dacal, *Vice Pres*
Rob Hishmeh, *Vice Pres*
Rose Nestor, *Buyer*
Avinash Patel, *Engineer*
◆ EMP: 35 EST: 1965
SQ FT: 55,000

SALES: 8MM **Privately Held**
WEB: www.sigmanetics.com
SIC: 3829 3625 3822 3613 Measuring &
controlling devices; switches, electric
power; auto controls regulating residntl &
coml environmt & applncs; power switching equipment

(G-9386)
SPECIALIZED FIRE & SEC INC
20 Cotluss Rd Ste 9 (07457-1400)
P.O. Box 110 (07457-0110)
PHONE....................................212 255-1010
Chris Kelly, *President*
Shawn Lawless, *Opers Staff*
Eric Greenwald, *VP Sales*
Justine Deselich, *Marketing Staff*
EMP: 20 EST: 1991
SQ FT: 5,500
SALES (est): 7.3MM **Privately Held**
SIC: 3699 Security control equipment &
systems

(G-9387)
TILCON NEW YORK INC
Also Called: Riverdale Quarry
125 Hamburg Tpke (07457-1003)
PHONE....................................973 835-0028
Frank Gelewski, *Manager*
EMP: 60
SALES (corp-wide): 30.6B **Privately Held**
WEB: www.tilconny.com
SIC: 1429 Boulder, crushed & broken-
quarrying
HQ: Tilcon New York Inc.
9 Entin Rd
Parsippany NJ 07054
973 366-7741

(G-9388)
**TTSS INTERACTIVE PRODUCTS
INC**
100 Riverdale Rd (07457-1700)
PHONE....................................301 230-1464
William Pymm, *President*
EMP: 20
SALES (est): 1.7MM **Privately Held**
SIC: 3679 Electronic circuits

Riverside
Burlington County

(G-9389)
**ALLISON SYSTEMS
CORPORATION**
220 Adams St (08075-3150)
PHONE....................................856 461-9111
Thomas K Allison Jr, *Principal*
Eve Allison, *Opers Mgr*
Tim Main, *Technology*
▲ EMP: 18 EST: 1968
SQ FT: 10,000
SALES (est): 3.9MM **Privately Held**
WEB: www.allisonblades.com
SIC: 3555 Presses, gravure

(G-9390)
**BEVERLY MANUFACTURING CO
INC**
Also Called: Beverly Transformers
63 Webster St (08075-3642)
PHONE....................................856 764-7898
Tony Cruz, *President*
Sonia Cruz, *Manager*
Filipe Cruz, *Info Tech Mgr*
EMP: 7
SALES (est): 847K **Privately Held**
WEB: www.beverlytransformers.com
SIC: 3612 Specialty transformers

(G-9391)
**C & C TOOL AND MACHINE CO
LLC**
38 W Scott St (08075-3602)
P.O. Box 407 (08075-7407)
PHONE....................................856 764-0911
Frank Canduci,
Nunzio Canduci,
EMP: 5
SQ FT: 4,500
SALES: 1.2MM **Privately Held**
SIC: 3599 Machine shop, jobbing & repair

(G-9392)
**CINDERELLA CHEESECAKE CO
INC**
Also Called: Cinderella Cheese Cake
208 N Fairview St (08075-3113)
P.O. Box 36 (08075-0036)
PHONE....................................856 461-6302
Joseph Makin, *President*
Bernadette Makin, *Corp Secy*
Alfred Rezende, *Vice Pres*
EMP: 15 EST: 1958
SQ FT: 20,000
SALES (est): 1.6MM **Privately Held**
SIC: 2053 2051 Cakes, bakery: frozen;
bread, cake & related products

(G-9393)
DEL BAKERS INC
Also Called: Delucca's Bakery
412 Kossuth St (08075-3234)
PHONE....................................856 461-0089
Nicola De Lucca, *President*
EMP: 20
SQ FT: 3,500
SALES (est): 2.4MM **Privately Held**
SIC: 2051 5149 Bread, cake & related
products; bakery products

(G-9394)
DRINK A TOAST COMPANY INC
Also Called: Boost Company, The
603 Harrison St (08075-3399)
P.O. Box 204 (08075-0204)
PHONE....................................856 461-1000
Daniel P McDonough, *President*
Nancy J Faunce, *President*
Daniel McDonough, *General Mgr*
Karen C Rogers, *Vice Pres*
Richard W Stockton, *Vice Pres*
EMP: 10
SQ FT: 18,000
SALES (est): 1.3MM **Privately Held**
WEB: www.boostevents.com
SIC: 2087 Syrups, drink

(G-9395)
GOOD IMPRESSIONS INC
Also Called: G I Trade Copy
28 E Scott St (08075-3616)
P.O. Box 409 (08075-7409)
PHONE....................................856 461-3232
Robert F Price, *President*
EMP: 7
SQ FT: 7,000
SALES (est): 1MM **Privately Held**
SIC: 2752 2759 7334 7389 Commercial
printing, offset; letterpress printing; photo-
copying & duplicating services; interior
designer; binding only: books, pamphlets,
magazines, etc.

(G-9396)
HOWARD LIPPINCOTT
Also Called: Lippincott Marine
74 Norman Ave (08075-1004)
PHONE....................................856 764-8282
Howard Lippincott, *Owner*
EMP: 4
SALES (est): 213.1K **Privately Held**
SIC: 5199 2394 2392 Canvas products;
canvas & related products; household fur-
nishings

(G-9397)
JAMCO MACHINE PRODUCTS
209 Adams St Ste 1 (08075-3147)
PHONE....................................856 461-2664
Joseph Molinari, *Owner*
EMP: 4 EST: 1984
SALES: 100K **Privately Held**
SIC: 3599 Machine & other job shop work

(G-9398)
**M & D PRCSION CNTRLESS
GRNDING**
120 Kossuth St (08075-3228)
PHONE....................................856 764-1616
Dave Speegle, *Owner*
EMP: 5
SALES (est): 195K **Privately Held**
SIC: 7389 3599 Grinding, precision: com-
mercial or industrial; machine shop. job-
bing & repair

(G-9399)
M AND D PRECISION GRINDING
120 Kossuth St (08075-3228)
PHONE....................................856 764-1616
Dave Speegle, *President*
Denise Daziani, *Corp Secy*
Frank Grasso, *Vice Pres*
EMP: 5
SQ FT: 6,700
SALES (est): 563.6K **Privately Held**
SIC: 3599 Grinding castings for the trade

(G-9400)
MELVILLE INDUSTRIES INC
Also Called: Cleardrain
219 Saint Mihiel Dr Ste 2 (08075-3028)
P.O. Box 555, Willingboro (08046-0555)
PHONE....................................856 461-0091
Frank Chille, *President*
EMP: 9 EST: 2010
SALES (est): 1MM **Privately Held**
SIC: 3561 Pumps & pumping equipment

(G-9401)
PER-FIL INDUSTRIES INC
407 Adams St (08075-3098)
P.O. Box 9 (08075-0009)
PHONE....................................856 461-5700
Horst E Boellmann, *Ch of Bd*
Shari Becker, *President*
Charlotte Boellmann, *Corp Secy*
◆ EMP: 23 EST: 1974
SQ FT: 20,000
SALES (est): 3.6MM **Privately Held**
WEB: www.per-fil.com
SIC: 3565 Packaging machinery

(G-9402)
**RICH PRODUCTS
CORPORATION**
100 American Legion Dr (08075-3054)
PHONE....................................800 356-7094
EMP: 750
SALES (corp-wide): 3.8B **Privately Held**
SIC: 2053 Frozen bakery products, except
bread
PA: Rich Products Corporation
1 Robert Rich Way
Buffalo NY 14213
716 878-8000

(G-9403)
**RIVERSIDE MARINA YACHT SLS
LLC**
74 Norman Ave Ste 1 (08075-1097)
PHONE....................................856 461-1077
Glenn Winter, *President*
Rebecca Winter, *Marketing Staff*
Bruce Woodington, *Director*
EMP: 15 EST: 1920
SQ FT: 30,000
SALES (est): 1.6MM **Privately Held**
WEB: www.riversideys.com
SIC: 4493 7699 3441 5551 Boat yards,
storage & incidental repair; boat repair;
boat & barge sections, prefabricated
metal; marine supplies

(G-9404)
US PIPE FABRICATION LLC
200 Rhawn St (08075-4680)
PHONE....................................856 461-3000
EMP: 19
SALES (corp-wide): 39.7MM **Privately
Held**
SIC: 3312 Blast Furnace- Steel Works
HQ: Us Pipe Fabrication, Llc
2 Chase Corporate Dr # 200
Hoover AL 35244
205 263-8540

Riverton
Burlington County

(G-9405)
ZENAS PATISSERIE
308 Broad St (08077-1304)
PHONE....................................856 303-8700
Zena Denirceeiren, *Owner*
EMP: 8
SALES (est): 568.1K **Privately Held**
SIC: 2051 5812 Bread, cake & related
products; coffee shop

Robbinsville
Mercer County

(G-9406)
ACCESS CONROL GROUP LLC
1226 Us Highway 130 (08691-1004)
PHONE....................................908 789-8700
Joanne Corniola, *Marketing Staff*
Arum Patel, *Mng Member*
EMP: 13
SALES (est): 1.8MM **Privately Held**
SIC: 3629 Electronic generation equipment

(G-9407)
**AMERICAN BANK NOTE
HOLOGRAPHIC (HQ)**
2 Applegate Dr (08691-2342)
PHONE....................................609 208-0591
Salvatore D'Amato, *Ch of Bd*
Kenneth H Traub, *President*
John Hynes, *Vice Pres*
Mark J Bonney, *CFO*
Michael T Banahan, *VP Sales*
▲ EMP: 100
SQ FT: 134,000
SALES (est): 4.9MM
SALES (corp-wide): 1.1B **Publicly Held**
WEB: www.abnh.com
SIC: 2759 Laser printing
PA: Viavi Solutions Inc.
6001 America Center Dr # 6
San Jose CA 95002
408 404-3600

(G-9408)
BIND-RITE ROBBINSVILLE LLC
1 Applegate Dr (08691-2341)
PHONE....................................609 208-1917
Paul Frontczak, *Vice Pres*
Tim Marsden, *Manager*
Harry Scharle, *Technology*
Steven Merson,
▲ EMP: 95
SALES (est): 19.1MM **Privately Held**
SIC: 2752 Commercial printing, offset

(G-9409)
CCL LABEL INC
104 N Gold Dr (08691-1602)
PHONE....................................609 586-1332
Christie Bailey, *Branch Mgr*
EMP: 190
SALES (corp-wide): 3.9B **Privately Held**
SIC: 2759 2679 Labels & seals: printing;
labels, paper: made from purchased ma-
terial
HQ: Ccl Label, Inc.
161 Worcester Rd Ste 603
Framingham MA 01701
508 872-4511

(G-9410)
**CJ TMI MANUFACTURING AMER
LLC**
2 Applegate Dr (08691-2342)
PHONE....................................609 669-0100
Feongjin Hwang,
EMP: 150
SALES (est): 258.3K
SALES (corp-wide): 5.3B **Privately Held**
SIC: 2099 Noodles, fried (Chinese)
HQ: Tmi Trading Corp.
7 Bushwick Pl
Brooklyn NY 11206

(G-9411)
ECLECTICISM PUBLISHING LLC
33 Stanwyck Ct (08691-3018)
PHONE....................................212 714-4714
Joseph A Halsey, *Principal*
EMP: 4
SALES (est): 222.7K **Privately Held**
SIC: 2741 Miscellaneous publishing

(G-9412)
GAUM INC (PA)
1080 Us Highway 130 (08691-1717)
PHONE....................................609 586-0132
Robert E Gaum, *President*
Tom Weiss, *Vice Pres*
Cheryl Gaum, *Admin Sec*

EMP: 38 EST: 1945
SQ FT: 11,000
SALES (est): 7.4MM **Privately Held**
WEB: www.gauminc.com
SIC: 3599 3544 Machine shop, jobbing & repair; special dies, tools, jigs & fixtures

(G-9413)
HARRISON HOSE AND TUBING INC
2705 Kuser Rd (08691-1807)
P.O. Box 9386, Trenton (08650-1386)
PHONE................................609 631-8804
James Logue, *President*
EMP: 20 EST: 1997
SQ FT: 12,000
SALES (est): 3.7MM **Privately Held**
WEB: www.harrisonhose.com
SIC: 3052 Plastic hose

(G-9414)
NORDSON EFD LLC
8 Applegate Dr (08691-2342)
PHONE................................609 259-9222
Jeff Pembroke, *President*
Curt Metzbower, *Opers Mgr*
Paul Bannwart, *Purchasing*
Anil Thakker, *Manager*
EMP: 180
SALES (corp-wide): 2.2B **Publicly Held**
SIC: 3823 Industrial instrmnts msrmnt display/control process variable
HQ: Nordson Efd Llc
40 Catamore Blvd
East Providence RI 02914
401 431-7000

(G-9415)
NOVACYL INC
1 Union St Ste 108 (08691-4219)
PHONE................................609 259-0444
Kimberly Jones, *President*
Carolyn Nicholas, *Vice Pres*
Robert Dollinger, *Treasurer*
▲ EMP: 9
SQ FT: 1,900
SALES (est): 1.6MM
SALES (corp-wide): 15.6MM **Privately Held**
SIC: 2834 Pharmaceutical preparations
HQ: Seqens
21 Ecully Parc
Ecully 69130
426 991-800

(G-9416)
RAS PROCESS EQUIPMENT
324 Meadowbrook Rd (08691-2503)
PHONE................................609 371-1000
John Bonacorda, *Owner*
Pat Horne, *Purchasing*
EMP: 26
SQ FT: 52,000
SALES (est): 5.2MM **Privately Held**
WEB: www.ras-inc.com
SIC: 3443 Reactor containment vessels, metal plate; heat exchangers, condensers & components; vessels, process or storage (from boiler shops): metal plate

(G-9417)
THOMAS A CASERTA INC
11 S Gold Dr Ste E (08691)
PHONE................................609 586-2807
Clifford Cicogna, *President*
Stanley P Rette, *Shareholder*
EMP: 14
SQ FT: 10,000
SALES (est): 2MM **Privately Held**
WEB: www.casertainc.com
SIC: 3069 3053 Washers, rubber; gaskets, packing & sealing devices

(G-9418)
TRI-STATE KNIFE GRINDING CORP
3 S Gold Dr (08691-1606)
PHONE................................609 890-4989
Scott Peterson, *President*
EMP: 20 EST: 2001

SALES (est): 2.5MM
SALES (corp-wide): 21.3MM **Privately Held**
WEB: www.colterpeterson.com
SIC: 7389 7699 3554 Grinding, precision: commercial or industrial; knife, saw & tool sharpening & repair; paper industries machinery
PA: Colter & Peterson, Inc.
19 Fairfield Pl
West Caldwell NJ 07006
973 684-0901

(G-9419)
WEBTECH INC
108 N Gold Dr (08691-1602)
PHONE................................609 259-2800
Stacey Evgeniadis, *General Mgr*
Art Maynard, *Corp Secy*
EMP: 25
SQ FT: 30,000
SALES (est): 5MM **Privately Held**
WEB: www.webtech-hts.com
SIC: 2679 Insulating paper: batts, fills & blankets

Rochelle Park
Bergen County

(G-9420)
ADD ROB LITHO LLC
11 W Passaic St Ste 1 (07662-3225)
PHONE................................201 556-0700
Harvey Ginsberg,
EMP: 5
SALES (est): 703.2K **Privately Held**
WEB: www.addroblitho.com
SIC: 2752 Commercial printing, offset

(G-9421)
ATLANTIC WASTE SERVICES
28 North Dr (07662-3602)
PHONE................................201 368-0428
William Covino, *Owner*
EMP: 14
SALES (est): 1.5MM **Privately Held**
SIC: 2655 Wastebaskets, fiber: made from purchased material

(G-9422)
DELL SOFTWARE INC
80 Parkway (07662-4204)
PHONE................................201 556-4600
Fax: 201 527-4699
EMP: 30
SALES (corp-wide): 23.2B **Publicly Held**
SIC: 7372 Prepackaged Software Services
HQ: Dell Software, Inc.
5 Polaris Way
Aliso Viejo CA 92656
949 754-8000

(G-9423)
FUTUREX INC
114 Essex St Ste 100 (07662-4348)
PHONE................................201 933-3943
Affonso Ze Aquino, *CEO*
Luiz Felipe Ze Aquino, *President*
Ninon Sanguesa, *Manager*
EMP: 11
SALES (est): 1.6MM **Privately Held**
SIC: 3821 Laboratory equipment: fume hoods, distillation racks, etc.

(G-9424)
INSTAPAK CORP SEALED AIR
80 Parker Ave Fl 2 (07662-3409)
PHONE................................201 791-7600
William Hickey, *President*
EMP: 60
SALES (est): 7.6MM
SALES (corp-wide): 4.7B **Publicly Held**
WEB: www.sealedair.com
SIC: 3086 Plastics foam products
PA: Sealed Air Corporation
2415 Cascade Pointe Blvd
Charlotte NC 28208
980 221-3235

(G-9425)
JMK TOOL DIE AND MFG CO INC (PA)
19 W Passaic St (07662-3213)
PHONE................................201 845-4710
John Kristofich, *President*
Mary Kristofich, *Corp Secy*
Robert Kristofich, *Vice Pres*
EMP: 7
SQ FT: 17,500
SALES (est): 1.8MM **Privately Held**
WEB: www.jmktool.com
SIC: 3469 3544 Stamping metal for the trade; special dies & tools

(G-9426)
LABEL SOLUTIONS INC
151 W Passaic St 2 (07662-3105)
PHONE................................201 599-0909
Ilana Weiss, *President*
EMP: 3
SQ FT: 700
SALES (est): 1MM **Privately Held**
WEB: www.labelsolutions.net
SIC: 2752 2759 Commercial printing, lithographic; labels & seals: printing

(G-9427)
ORBCOMM LLC (HQ)
395 W Passaic St Ste 3 (07662-3016)
PHONE................................703 433-6300
Jerome Eisenberg, *CEO*
John J Stolte, *Exec VP*
John Stolte Jr, *Exec VP*
Ashish Chona, *Vice Pres*
Joe Fazio, *Vice Pres*
EMP: 21
SALES (est): 15.5MM
SALES (corp-wide): 276.1MM **Publicly Held**
SIC: 3663 Satellites, communications
PA: Orbcomm Inc.
395 W Passaic St Ste 325
Rochelle Park NJ 07662
703 433-6300

(G-9428)
PANOS HOLDING COMPANY (HQ)
395 W Passaic St Ste 2 (07662-3016)
PHONE................................201 843-8900
Steven Grossman, *CEO*
EMP: 1
SALES (est): 9.2MM **Privately Held**
SIC: 5141 2099 Groceries, general line; food preparations

(G-9429)
REDFIELD CORPORATION
336 W Passaic St Ste 3 (07662-3027)
PHONE................................201 845-3990
Andrew Gould, *CEO*
EMP: 4
SQ FT: 2,600
SALES (est): 2.5MM **Privately Held**
WEB: www.redfieldcorp.com
SIC: 5047 3841 Medical equipment & supplies; surgical & medical instruments

(G-9430)
REMPAC FOAM CORP
370 W Passaic St (07662-3009)
PHONE................................973 881-8880
William Martin, *President*
Peter Pankiw, *CFO*
Steve Sobel, *HR Admin*
David Connell, *Executive*
◆ EMP: 13
SALES (est): 2MM **Privately Held**
SIC: 3086 Plastics foam products

(G-9431)
REMPAC LLC (PA)
Also Called: Tek-Pak Div
370 W Passaic St (07662-3009)
PHONE................................201 843-4585
William Salomon, *COO*
Tony Locklear, *Engineer*
Peter Pankiw, *CFO*
Alan Bushell,
Marc Bushell,
▲ EMP: 125
SQ FT: 10,000

SALES (est): 47.1MM **Privately Held**
WEB: www.memoryfoamfactory.com
SIC: 3086 3053 3061 Plastics foam products; gaskets, packing & sealing devices; mechanical rubber goods

(G-9432)
TRADE THERMOGRAPHERS INC
82 Chestnut Ave (07662-3821)
PHONE................................201 489-2060
Raymond Gramaglia, *President*
EMP: 15
SQ FT: 2,000
SALES (est): 850K **Privately Held**
SIC: 2759 2791 2752 Thermography; typesetting; commercial printing, lithographic

Rockaway
Morris County

(G-9433)
ABC PRINTING
20 Wall St Ste C (07866-2900)
PHONE................................973 664-1160
Yvonne Cook, *Owner*
EMP: 4
SALES (est): 100K **Privately Held**
SIC: 2752 Commercial printing, offset

(G-9434)
ABLE GEAR & MACHINE CO
91 Stickle Ave (07866-3127)
PHONE................................973 983-8055
Robert Hebrank, *Owner*
EMP: 5
SALES (est): 240K **Privately Held**
WEB: www.ablegear.com
SIC: 3599 3462 3566 Amusement park equipment; gear & chain forgings; speed changers, drives & gears

(G-9435)
ACCLIVITY LLC
300 Round Hill Dr Ste 2 (07866-1227)
PHONE................................973 586-2200
Scott Davisson, *Managing Prtnr*
Annette Brooks, *Engineer*
Melissa Thornley, *Mktg Coord*
Lauren Kasper, *Marketing Staff*
Ed Sherry, *Marketing Staff*
EMP: 45
SQ FT: 10,000
SALES (est): 3.9MM
SALES (corp-wide): 8.9MM **Privately Held**
SIC: 7372 Business oriented computer software
HQ: Priority-Software U.S. Llc
300 Round Hill Dr Ste 2
Rockaway NJ 07866
973 586-2200

(G-9436)
ADMIRAL FILTER COMPANY LLC
18 Green Pond Rd Ste 3 (07866-2054)
PHONE................................973 664-0400
Brian Hoffmann, *President*
Ira J Perlmuter,
EMP: 10
SQ FT: 10,000
SALES (est): 2.5MM **Privately Held**
SIC: 3569 Filters, general line: industrial

(G-9437)
ADMIRAL TECHNOLOGY LLC
18 Green Pond Rd Ste 3 (07866-2054)
PHONE................................973 698-5920
Ira Perlmuter, *Mng Member*
EMP: 38
SALES (est): 1.7MM **Privately Held**
SIC: 3491 Industrial valves

(G-9438)
ADVANCED PAVEMENT TECHNOLOGIES
195 Green Pond Rd (07866-1216)
PHONE................................973 366-8044
Ted Wilson, *Partner*
Andrew Muller, *Partner*
EMP: 12

SALES (est): 729K **Privately Held**
SIC: **1799** 1794 3272 Parking lot mainte-nance; excavation & grading, building construction; paving materials, prefabri-cated concrete

(G-9439)
ADVANCED TECHNOLOGY GROUP INC
Also Called: Atg
101 Round Hill Dr Ste 3 (07866-1214)
PHONE................................973 627-6955
LI Tao, *President*
Eric Maier, *Vice Pres*
Faithann McIver-Hanus, *Vice Pres*
EMP: 30
SQ FT: 12,000
SALES (est): 4.3MM **Publicly Held**
WEB: www.advtechgr.com
SIC: 3679 Electronic circuits
PA: Cognizant Technology Solutions Corpo-ration
500 Frank W Burr Blvd
Teaneck NJ 07666

(G-9440)
ALLIED CONCRETE CO INC (PA)
205 Franklin Ave (07866-3409)
PHONE................................973 627-6150
Kathryn Gallo, *President*
Michael C Gallo III, *Corp Secy*
EMP: 4 EST: 1951
SALES (est): 1.1MM **Privately Held**
SIC: 3273 Ready-mixed concrete

(G-9441)
ALLIED CONCRETE CO INC
205 Franklin Ave (07866-3409)
PHONE................................973 627-6150
EMP: 6
SQ FT: 500
SALES (corp-wide): 1.1MM **Privately Held**
SIC: 3273 Ready-mixed concrete
PA: Allied Concrete Co Inc
205 Franklin Ave
Rockaway NJ 07866
973 627-6150

(G-9442)
AMSCAN INC
25 Green Pond Rd (07866-2047)
PHONE................................973 983-0888
Lisa Laube, *Manager*
EMP: 52
SALES (corp-wide): 2.4B **Publicly Held**
SIC: 2656 Sanitary food containers
HQ: Amscan Inc.
80 Grasslands Rd Ste 3
Elmsford NY 10523
914 345-2020

(G-9443)
ASO SAFETY SOLUTIONS INC
300 Round Hill Dr Ste 6 (07866-1227)
PHONE................................973 586-9600
Helmet Freidrich, *CEO*
Simon Rocket, *Exec VP*
▲ EMP: 7
SQ FT: 12,000
SALES (est): 482.4K **Privately Held**
WEB: www.asnsafety.com
SIC: 3625 Relays & industrial controls

(G-9444)
ATLANTIC INTERNATIONAL TECH
114 Beach St Ste 3 (07866-3529)
PHONE................................973 625-0053
Robert Campbell, *CEO*
EMP: 15
SALES: 2MM **Privately Held**
SIC: 3231 Products of purchased glass

(G-9445)
AVADA SOFTWARE LLC
100 Enterprise Dr Ste 301 (07866-2129)
P.O. Box 2271, Oak Ridge (07438-2271)
PHONE................................973 697-1043
Sarah Brush, *Marketing Mgr*
Pete Dagosta, *Manager*
Tom Richardson, *Director*
Peter D'Agosta,
Robert Sordillo,
EMP: 15

SALES: 2.2MM **Privately Held**
WEB: www.avadasoftware.com
SIC: 7372 Business oriented computer software

(G-9446)
BAKERS PERFECTION INC
198 Green Pond Rd Ste 5 (07866-1219)
PHONE................................973 983-0700
Patrick S Amello Sr, *President*
EMP: 41
SQ FT: 11,200
SALES (est): 7.6MM **Privately Held**
WEB: www.bakersperfection.com
SIC: 2051 2052 2032 Cakes, pies & pas-tries; cookies & crackers; canned special-ties

(G-9447)
BRUCE KINDBERG
Also Called: Bmk Enterprises
305 Us Highway 46 (07866-3833)
PHONE................................973 664-0195
Bruce Kindberg, *Owner*
EMP: 5
SQ FT: 8,000
SALES: 2.7MM **Privately Held**
SIC: 3711 3714 3993 5531 Automobile assembly, including specialty automo-biles; motor vehicle parts & accessories; electric signs; speed shops, including race car supplies; automotive parts; auto-motive repair shops; radiator repair shop; automotive; radiators

(G-9448)
BTECH INC
Also Called: B Tech
10 Astro Pl Ste A (07866-4052)
PHONE................................973 983-1120
Manfred Laidig, *CEO*
Thomas Leonard, *President*
Christopher Ludeman, *Business Mgr*
Ed Martin, *Purchasing*
Itay Keren, *Electrical Engi*
◆ EMP: 23
SQ FT: 18,000
SALES (est): 6.8MM **Privately Held**
WEB: www.btechinc.com
SIC: 3825 3823 5063 Battery testers, electrical; industrial instrmnts msrmnt dis-play/control process variable; batteries

(G-9449)
CARSON & GEBEL RIBBON CO LLC
17 Green Pond Rd (07866-2001)
PHONE................................973 627-4200
Henry Gebel,
Richard Gebel,
▲ EMP: 40 EST: 1923
SQ FT: 50,000
SALES (est): 4.4MM
SALES (corp-wide): 382.2MM **Publicly Held**
SIC: 5131 2241 Ribbons; ribbons
HQ: Berwick Offray Llc
2015 W Front St
Berwick PA 18603
570 752-5934

(G-9450)
CBT SUPPLY INC
Also Called: Smart Desks
83 Jacobs Rd (07866-4603)
P.O. Box 391, Hibernia (07842-0391)
PHONE................................800 770-7042
Jeffery Korber, *President*
EMP: 7
SALES (est): 1.1MM **Privately Held**
SIC: 2521 Wood office furniture

(G-9451)
CREATIVE PATTERNS & MFG
114 Beach St Ste 4 (07866-3529)
P.O. Box 159 (07866-0159)
PHONE................................973 589-1391
David J Cummins, *President*
James Generoso, *Vice Pres*
EMP: 7
SQ FT: 5,400
SALES (est): 46.3MM **Privately Held**
SIC: 3543 Industrial patterns

(G-9452)
CSUS LLC
300 Forge Way Ste 3 (07866-2056)
PHONE................................973 298-8599
Juan Paez,
EMP: 6
SALES: 950K **Privately Held**
SIC: 3842 Surgical appliances & supplies

(G-9453)
DMG MORI USA INC
Also Called: Dmg Mori Seiki
400 Commons Way Ste A (07866-2030)
PHONE................................973 257-9620
Masaki Sasaki, *General Mgr*
EMP: 7 **Privately Held**
SIC: 3545 Measuring tools & machines, machinists' metalworking type
HQ: Dmg Mori Usa, Inc.
2400 Huntington Blvd
Hoffman Estates IL 60192
847 593-5400

(G-9454)
DYNASTY METALS INC
164 Franklin Ave (07866-3408)
P.O. Box 695 (07866-0695)
PHONE................................973 453-6630
Richard A Kolodin, *President*
John M Tolpa Jr, *Treasurer*
EMP: 45
SQ FT: 15,000
SALES (est): 5.4MM **Privately Held**
SIC: 3471 5051 Electroplating & plating; nonferrous metal sheets, bars, rods, etc.

(G-9455)
EMC SQUARED LLC
30 Rolling Ridge Dr (07866-4315)
PHONE................................973 586-8854
Ed Morgan, *Principal*
EMP: 5
SALES (est): 389.6K **Privately Held**
SIC: 3572 Computer storage devices

(G-9456)
ENDOT INDUSTRIES INC (PA)
60 Green Pond Rd (07866-2002)
PHONE................................973 625-8500
Gary Wellmann, *Ch of Bd*
Jennifer Wellmann Marin, *President*
Todne Wellmann, *Vice Pres*
EMP: 65
SQ FT: 52,000
SALES (est): 19MM **Privately Held**
SIC: 3084 3089 2823 Plastics pipe; duct-ing, plastic; cellulosic manmade fibers

(G-9457)
F G CLOVER COMPANY INC
40 Stickle Ave (07866-3128)
PHONE................................973 627-1160
Norman Iversen, *President*
EMP: 9
SQ FT: 14,000
SALES (est): 660K **Privately Held**
SIC: 3999 3469 Badges, metal: police-men, firemen, etc.; identification tags, ex-cept paper; spinning metal for the trade

(G-9458)
FABER PRECISION INC
198 Green Pond Rd Ste 6 (07866-1219)
PHONE................................973 983-1844
Kevin Faber, *President*
Stacey Faber, *Corp Secy*
EMP: 6
SQ FT: 8,400
SALES: 800K **Privately Held**
SIC: 3599 Machine shop, jobbing & repair

(G-9459)
FETTE COMPACTING AMERICA INC
400 Forge Way (07866-2033)
PHONE................................973 586-8722
Olaf Mueller, *President*
Anna Dewald, *Human Resources*
▲ EMP: 35
SQ FT: 28,000

SALES (est): 6.9MM
SALES (corp-wide): 471.1MM **Privately Held**
WEB: www.lmtfette.com
SIC: 3559 5084 Pharmaceutical machin-ery; industrial machinery & equipment
HQ: Lmt Usa, Inc.
1081 S Northpoint Blvd
Waukegan IL 60085
630 693-3270

(G-9460)
FIREFREEZE WORLDWIDE INC
272 Us Highway 46 (07866-3826)
PHONE................................973 627-0722
Evelyn Geisler, *President*
▲ EMP: 20
SALES (est): 4.2MM **Privately Held**
SIC: 2869 Hydraulic fluids, synthetic base

(G-9461)
FOOD MFG
100 Enterprise Dr (07866-2116)
PHONE................................973 920-7000
EMP: 200
SALES (est): 7MM **Privately Held**
SIC: 2754 Gravure Commercial Printing

(G-9462)
GANNETT STLLITE INFO NTWRK LLC
Daily Record, The
100 Commons Way (07866-2038)
PHONE................................973 428-6200
Walt Lafferty, *Manager*
EMP: 300
SALES (corp-wide): 2.9B **Publicly Held**
WEB: www.usatoday.com
SIC: 2711 Newspapers
HQ: Gannett Satellite Information Network, Llc
7950 Jones Branch Dr
Mc Lean VA 22102
703 854-6000

(G-9463)
GLITTERWRAP INC (DH)
701 Ford Rd Ste 1 (07866-2053)
PHONE................................800 745-4883
Alfred Scott, *CEO*
Melinda Scott, *President*
▲ EMP: 55
SQ FT: 81,000
SALES (est): 5.8MM
SALES (corp-wide): 576.8MM **Privately Held**
SIC: 2679 Gift wrap & novelties, paper
HQ: Ig Design Group Americas, Inc.
5555 Glenridge Connector # 300
Atlanta GA 30342
770 551-9727

(G-9464)
GLOBAL SEVEN INC
198 Green Pond Rd Ste 4 (07866-1219)
P.O. Box 367, Franklin (07416-0367)
PHONE................................973 209-7474
Jonathan Dean, *President*
EMP: 25
SQ FT: 100,000
SALES (est): 3.7MM **Privately Held**
SIC: 2899 Chemical preparations

(G-9465)
HTP CONNECTIVITY LLC
300 Round Hill Dr Ste 4 (07866-1227)
PHONE................................973 586-2286
▲ EMP: 4
SALES (est): 392.8K **Privately Held**
SIC: 3559 Electronic component making machinery

(G-9466)
IN THE SPOTLIGHTS
301 Mount Hope Ave # 2091 (07866-2130)
PHONE................................973 361-7768
EMP: 4
SALES (est): 480.2K **Privately Held**
SIC: 3648 Mfg Lighting Equipment

G
E
O
G
R
A
P
H
I
C

(G-9467)
INTERNET-SALES USA CORPORATION
Also Called: Greenproducts.info
65 Fleetwood Dr (07866-2220)
PHONE...............................775 468-8379
Samantha Schnurman, *Publisher*
David Schnurman, *Principal*
Arianne Schnurman, *Vice Pres*
Jordan Schnurman, *Project Mgr*
Michael Schnurman, *Finance Dir*
EMP: 6
SALES (est): 458.2K **Privately Held**
SIC: 1542 0139 0191 3444 Greenhouse construction; farm building construction; food crops; general farms, primarily crop; sheet metalwork;

(G-9468)
IONNI SIGN INC (PA)
14 White Meadow Ave (07866-2610)
P.O. Box 437 (07866-0437)
PHONE...............................973 625-3815
Joseph Ionni Jr, *President*
EMP: 5
SQ FT: 3,200
SALES (est): 937.7K **Privately Held**
WEB: www.ionnisign.com
SIC: 1799 3993 Sign installation & maintenance; signs & advertising specialties

(G-9469)
J & W SERVO SYSTEMS COMPANY
53 Green Pond Rd Ste 2 (07866-2044)
P.O. Box 97, Montville (07045-0097)
PHONE...............................973 335-1007
Anthony Villano, *President*
Phil Marshall, *Vice Pres*
Daniel Fox, *VP Sales*
Phil Gunn-Russell, *Technical Staff*
Bill Strickland, *Technical Staff*
EMP: 17
SQ FT: 30,000
SALES (est): 6.4MM **Privately Held**
WEB: www.servosystems.com
SIC: 5065 3823 Electronic parts & equipment; industrial instrmnts msrmnt display/control process variable

(G-9470)
J HEBRANK INC
Also Called: Linker Machines
20 Pine St (07866-3131)
PHONE...............................973 983-0001
Jean Hebrank, *President*
Robert Hebrank Sr, *Vice Pres*
Michael Hebrank, *Finance Dir*
EMP: 13 **EST:** 1939
SALES (est): 1.6MM **Privately Held**
WEB: www.linkermachines.com
SIC: 3556 Food products machinery

(G-9471)
JASON EQUIPMENT CORP
164 Franklin Ave (07866-3408)
P.O. Box 695 (07866-0695)
PHONE...............................973 983-7212
John Tolta, *President*
EMP: 21
SALES (est): 2.1MM **Privately Held**
SIC: 3559 Pharmaceutical machinery

(G-9472)
KESTREL CLOSETS LLC
29 Hillside Rd (07866-4404)
PHONE...............................973 586-1144
Craig Holzhauer, *Principal*
EMP: 7
SALES (est): 854.1K **Privately Held**
SIC: 2673 Wardrobe bags (closet accessories): from purchased materials

(G-9473)
KG SQUARED LLC
Also Called: Apw Company
5 Astro Pl Ste B (07866-4053)
PHONE...............................973 627-0643
Jason Kellenberger,
▼ **EMP:** 13
SQ FT: 5,000
SALES: 1MM **Privately Held**
SIC: 3679 3677 3612 Cores, magnetic; coil windings, electronic; transformers, except electric

(G-9474)
KOP-COAT INC
Kop-Coat Marine Group
36 Pine St (07866-3131)
PHONE...............................800 221-4466
James Mc Carthy, *Technical Mgr*
Linda Smith, *Branch Mgr*
EMP: 50
SALES (corp-wide): 5.5B **Publicly Held**
WEB: www.kop-coat.com
SIC: 2851 2891 5198 Paints & paint additives; adhesives & sealants; paints
HQ: Kop-Coat, Inc.
3040 William Pitt Way
Pittsburgh PA 15238
412 227-2426

(G-9475)
LMT USA INC
Also Called: Fette-America
400 Forge Way (07866-2033)
PHONE...............................973 586-8722
Philip Meyers, *Branch Mgr*
EMP: 6
SALES (corp-wide): 471.1MM **Privately Held**
WEB: www.lmtfette.com
SIC: 5084 3559 Machine tools & metalworking machinery; pharmaceutical machinery
HQ: Lmt Usa, Inc.
1081 S Northpoint Blvd
Waukegan IL 60085
630 693-3270

(G-9476)
MCWILLIAMS FORGE COMPANY (DH)
387 Franklin Ave (07866-4014)
PHONE...............................973 627-0200
Alexander M Mc Williams, *President*
Timothy C McWilliams, *Exec VP*
▲ **EMP:** 79 **EST:** 1945
SQ FT: 125,000
SALES: 60MM
SALES (corp-wide): 225.3B **Publicly Held**
WEB: www.mcwilliamsforge.com
SIC: 3462 3769 3463 Nuclear power plant forgings, ferrous; machinery forgings, ferrous; pump & compressor forgings, ferrous; aircraft forgings, ferrous; guided missile & space vehicle parts & auxiliary equipment; nonferrous forgings
HQ: Precision Castparts Corp.
4650 Sw Mcdam Ave Ste 300
Portland OR 97239
503 946-4800

(G-9477)
MODULAR PACKAGING SYSTEMS INC
385 Franklin Ave Ste C (07866-4037)
PHONE...............................973 970-9393
Clifford Smith, *President*
Bradford Smith, *Vice Pres*
EMP: 10
SQ FT: 15,000
SALES (est): 4.1MM **Privately Held**
WEB: www.modularpackaging.com
SIC: 5084 3599 Packaging machinery & equipment; amusement park equipment

(G-9478)
MONSTER COATINGS INC
12 Midway Ct (07866-1619)
P.O. Box 293 (07866-0293)
PHONE...............................973 983-7662
Denise B Tomahatsch, *President*
EMP: 4 **EST:** 2002
SALES: 400K **Privately Held**
SIC: 2631 Coated & treated board

(G-9479)
NICKEL ARTISTIC SERVICES LLC
39 Us Highway 46 (07866-4105)
PHONE...............................973 627-0390
Brett Nickel, *Mng Member*
Brian Nickel, *Mng Member*
Denise Nickel, *Mng Member*
Ken Nickel,
EMP: 4 **EST:** 2000

SALES (est): 425.4K **Privately Held**
SIC: 3993 Signs, not made in custom sign painting shops

(G-9480)
NOVA PRECISION PRODUCTS INC
160 Franklin Ave (07866-3429)
PHONE...............................973 625-1586
Chester Suhoski, *President*
Iris Suhoski, *Vice Pres*
EMP: 110
SQ FT: 6,500
SALES (est): 14MM **Privately Held**
WEB: www.novaprecisionproducts.com
SIC: 3451 3541 Screw machine products; machine tools, metal cutting type

(G-9481)
NUCLEAR DIAGNOSTIC PDTS INC
101 Round Hill Dr Ste 4 (07866-1214)
PHONE...............................973 664-9696
Frank Ruddy, *President*
Rodney Prosser, *Vice Pres*
EMP: 12
SQ FT: 10,000
SALES (est): 4.3MM **Privately Held**
SIC: 2834 Pharmaceutical preparations

(G-9482)
O O M INC
Also Called: Dunkin' Donuts
387 Us Highway 46 (07866-3806)
PHONE...............................973 328-9408
Dipak Patel, *President*
EMP: 6
SQ FT: 1,000
SALES (est): 215.6K **Privately Held**
SIC: 5461 2051 Doughnuts; doughnuts, except frozen

(G-9483)
PACKAGE DEVELOPMENT CO INC
100 Round Hill Dr Ste 8 (07866-1220)
PHONE...............................973 983-8500
Charles Schwester, *President*
Roberta Schwester, *Corp Secy*
Rick Folbrecht, *Senior VP*
Ron Demeo, *Vice Pres*
Summer Schwester, *Plant Mgr*
▼ **EMP:** 50
SQ FT: 55,000
SALES (est): 10MM **Privately Held**
WEB: www.pkgdev.com
SIC: 3081 4783 2653 Packing materials, plastic sheet; packing goods for shipping; display items, corrugated: made from purchased materials; display items, solid fiber: made from purchased materials

(G-9484)
PATRIOT AMERICAN SOLUTIONS LLC
5 Astro Pl (07866-4053)
PHONE...............................862 209-4772
William O'Cconnor, *President*
Richard Ferri, *Exec VP*
EMP: 61
SQ FT: 35,000
SALES: 7MM **Privately Held**
SIC: 3679 8711 Antennas, receiving; electrical or electronic engineering

(G-9485)
PHOENIX COLOR CORP
Also Called: Lehigh Phoenis
40 Green Pond Rd (07866-2002)
PHONE...............................800 632-4111
Marie Van Strander, *Financial Exec*
Rosa Dominguez, *Human Res Dir*
Mitchell Weiss, *Branch Mgr*
EMP: 30 **Publicly Held**
WEB: www.phoenixcolor.com
SIC: 2732 Books: printing only
HQ: Phoenix Color Corp.
18249 Phoenix Rd
Hagerstown MD 21742
301 733-0018

(G-9486)
PIERSON INDUSTRIES INC
7 Astro Pl (07866-4022)
PHONE...............................973 627-7945

Ted Pierson, *President*
Rich Carle, *Principal*
Maria Pierson, *Vice Pres*
Lisa Rodeiquez, *Manager*
Becky Custer, *Data Proc Dir*
▲ **EMP:** 145
SQ FT: 42,000
SALES (est): 36.4MM **Privately Held**
WEB: www.piersonindustries.com
SIC: 3089 Injection molding of plastics; molding primary plastic

(G-9487)
PLASTIFORM PACKAGING INC
114 Beach St Ste 6 (07866-3529)
P.O. Box 186 (07866-0186)
PHONE...............................973 983-8900
George Smith, *President*
Kathleen Smith, *Vice Pres*
EMP: 26
SQ FT: 21,000
SALES (est): 6MM **Privately Held**
SIC: 3089 Blister or bubble formed packaging, plastic

(G-9488)
POLYFIL CORPORATION
74 Green Pond Rd (07866-2002)
P.O. Box 130 (07866-0130)
PHONE...............................973 627-4070
AVI Zalcman, *President*
Juan Castaneda, *General Mgr*
Brenda Isherwood, *Financial Exec*
Jack Palmer, *VP Mktg*
Chimaroke Nworie, *Technical Staff*
EMP: 27
SQ FT: 60,000
SALES (est): 7.3MM
SALES (corp-wide): 225.9MM **Privately Held**
WEB: www.polyfilcorp.com
SIC: 2821 Polyethylene resins
PA: Kafrit Industries (1993) Ltd
Kibbutz
Kfar Azza 85142
868 098-45

(G-9489)
POWER HAWK TECHNOLOGIES INC
300 Forge Way Ste 2 (07866-2056)
PHONE...............................973 627-4646
William R Hickerson, *President*
John McCarthy, *Vice Pres*
◆ **EMP:** 17
SQ FT: 5,000
SALES (est): 2.1MM
SALES (corp-wide): 3.7B **Publicly Held**
WEB: www.powerhawk.com
SIC: 3423 5099 Hand & edge tools; safety equipment & supplies
PA: Snap-On Incorporated
2801 80th St
Kenosha WI 53143
262 656-5200

(G-9490)
PRIORITY-SOFTWARE US LLC (HQ)
300 Round Hill Dr Ste 2 (07866-1227)
PHONE...............................973 586-2200
Andres Richter, *CEO*
Scott Davisson, *Managing Dir*
Nadia Antanovskii, *Tech Recruiter*
David Wilson, *Sr Consultant*
EMP: 4
SALES (est): 3.9MM
SALES (corp-wide): 8.9MM **Privately Held**
SIC: 7372 Business oriented computer software
PA: Priority Software Ltd
12 Amal
Rosh Haayin 48092
392 510-00

(G-9491)
PRODUCT CLUB CORP
41 Pine St Ste 15 (07866-3139)
PHONE...............................973 664-0565
Eric B Polesuk, *President*
Mary Albanese, *VP Mktg*
Kristina Schulman, *Education*
▲ **EMP:** 10
SQ FT: 15,000

SALES (est): 1.3MM
SALES (corp-wide): 82.7MM **Privately Held**
WEB: www.productclub.com
SIC: 2844 Hair coloring preparations
PA: The Burmax Company Inc
28 Barretts Ave
Holtsville NY 11742
631 447-8700

(G-9492)
PURE RUBBER PRODUCTS CO
300 Round Hill Dr Ste 5 (07866-1227)
PHONE.................................973 784-3690
Virginia McCrink, *President*
Davis Pear, *Principal*
Hilliary McCrink, *Manager*
EMP: 8 EST: 1935
SQ FT: 5,090
SALES: 1.3MM **Privately Held**
WEB: www.purerubber.com
SIC: 3069 Molded rubber products

(G-9493)
RICCARR DISPLAYS INC
52 Green Pond Rd (07866-2002)
PHONE.................................973 983-6701
Paul Carr, *CEO*
Marc Niderman, *President*
EMP: 50
SQ FT: 100,000
SALES (est): 5.6MM **Privately Held**
WEB: www.tmird.com
SIC: 3993 Displays & cutouts, window &
lobby; displays, paint process

(G-9494)
RIDGE MANUFACTURING CORP
5 Astro Pl Ste A (07866-4053)
PHONE.................................973 586-2717
Richard Ferri, *President*
Kevin Garvin, *Vice Pres*
EMP: 75
SALES (est): 16.8MM **Privately Held**
SIC: 3559 Electronic component making
machinery

(G-9495)
RIVERSTONE INDUSTRIES CORP
65 Fleetwood Dr Ste 200 (07866-2220)
PHONE.................................973 586-2564
David Schnurman, *Vice Pres*
▲ EMP: 7 EST: 2010
SALES (est): 8.1MM **Privately Held**
SIC: 3999 Atomizers, toiletry

(G-9496)
ROYSONS CORPORATION
Also Called: Roysons Wall Covering
40 Vanderhoof Ave (07866-3138)
PHONE.................................973 625-5570
Roy Ritchie, *President*
Omega Larue, *COO*
Curt Hammaren, *Engineer*
Peter Cohan, *CFO*
Mussie Isaac, *Bookkeeper*
◆ EMP: 100 EST: 1978
SQ FT: 110,000
SALES (est): 27.4MM **Privately Held**
WEB: www.roysons.com
SIC: 3083 Plastic finished products, lami-
nated

(G-9497)
SAVIT CORPORATION
400 Commons Way Ste D (07866-2030)
PHONE.................................862 209-4516
Anthony Fabiano, *President*
EMP: 11
SQ FT: 7,000
SALES (est): 2MM **Privately Held**
WEB: www.savitcorporation.com
SIC: 3795 3761 Specialized tank compo-
nents, military; guided missiles & space
vehicles

(G-9498)
**SERVICE METAL FABRICATING
INC (PA)**
10 Stickle Ave (07866-3114)
PHONE.................................973 625-8882
Joseph Moretti Sr, *President*
David Lewin, *Opers Mgr*
Doug Reeve, *Engineer*
Kenneth Parisi, *Controller*

Colleen Reardon, *Receptionist*
◆ EMP: 65
SQ FT: 22,000
SALES (est): 16MM **Privately Held**
WEB: www.servicemetal.com
SIC: 3444 Sheet metal specialties, not
stamped

(G-9499)
**SKYLINE STL FBRCATRS &
ERCTRS**
419 Franklin Ave Ste 3 (07866-4051)
PHONE.................................973 957-0234
Mark Malek, *President*
EMP: 8 EST: 2000
SQ FT: 8,800
SALES (est): 1.4MM **Privately Held**
SIC: 3315 Steel wire & related products

(G-9500)
STAPLING MACHINES INC (PA)
41 Pine St Ste 101 (07866-3139)
PHONE.................................973 627-4400
Wade Howle, *President*
Doug Halkenhauser, *President*
Timothy Catton, *Vice Pres*
EMP: 30
SQ FT: 66,000
SALES (est): 3.2MM **Privately Held**
WEB: www.smcllc.com
SIC: 3553 Box making machines, for
wooden boxes

(G-9501)
STILES ENTERPRISES INC
114 Beach St (07866-3529)
P.O. Box 92 (07866-0092)
PHONE.................................973 625-9660
Richard Stiles, *President*
Diane Killiam, *Vice Pres*
Nancy Stiles, *Vice Pres*
▲ EMP: 10
SQ FT: 10,000
SALES (est): 2.9MM **Privately Held**
SIC: 5085 3061 3053 3052 Rubber
goods, mechanical; mechanical rubber
goods; gaskets, packing & sealing de-
vices; rubber & plastics hose & beltings;
synthetic rubber; carpets & rugs

(G-9502)
SUPERMATIC CORP
27 Old Beach Glen Rd (07866-1313)
PHONE.................................973 627-4433
Ted Kobrynowicz, *President*
Irene Kobrynowicz, *Vice Pres*
Maria Kobrynowicz, *Admin Sec*
EMP: 10
SQ FT: 6,000
SALES (est): 1.4MM **Privately Held**
WEB: www.supermaticnc.com
SIC: 3451 Screw machine products

(G-9503)
THERMO COTE INC
198 Green Pond Rd Ste 5 (07866-1219)
PHONE.................................973 464-3575
Chris Cordero, *Principal*
EMP: 4
SALES (est): 434.1K **Privately Held**
SIC: 2851 Vinyl coatings, strippable

(G-9504)
TITANIUM INDUSTRIES INC (PA)
18 Green Pond Rd Ste 1 (07866-2054)
PHONE.................................973 983-1185
Brett S Paddock, *President*
Dan Dinapoli, *General Mgr*
Debby Hazen, *General Mgr*
Jay Pudlock, *Regional Mgr*
Greg Himstead, *Vice Pres*
▲ EMP: 45
SALES (est): 76.6MM **Privately Held**
SIC: 5051 3542 3462 Iron & steel (fer-
rous) products; metal deposit forming ma-
chines; flange, valve & pipe fitting
forgings, ferrous

(G-9505)
TOCAD AMERICA INC (DH)
Also Called: Sunpak Division
53 Green Pond Rd Ste 4 (07866-2044)
PHONE.................................973 627-9600
Takeshi Fujikawa, *President*
Richard Darrow, *President*
Mitsuhiro Matsumoto, *CFO*

▲ EMP: 41
SQ FT: 35,000
SALES (est): 9.3MM **Privately Held**
WEB: www.tocad.com
SIC: 5043 5063 3691 Photographic cam-
eras, projectors, equipment & supplies;
batteries; storage batteries

(G-9506)
**TOLAN MACHINERY COMPANY
INC**
164 Franklin Ave (07866-3408)
P.O. Box 695 (07866-0695)
PHONE.................................973 983-7212
John Tolpa, *Owner*
Bill Ebbinghouser, *Principal*
John Staiber, *Principal*
Stephen Tolpa, *Principal*
Jeff Stoppelkamp, *Vice Pres*
EMP: 21 EST: 1945
SALES (est): 4.4MM **Privately Held**
SIC: 3443 Tanks, standard or custom fabri-
cated: metal plate

(G-9507)
**TOLAN MACHINERY POLISHING
CO**
164 Franklin Ave (07866-3408)
P.O. Box 695 (07866-0695)
PHONE.................................973 983-7212
John M Tolpa Jr, *President*
Christina Nieves, *Vice Pres*
EMP: 50
SQ FT: 90,000
SALES (est): 9.9MM **Privately Held**
WEB: www.tolanmachinery.com
SIC: 3443 Plate work for the metalworking
trade

(G-9508)
**TOM PONTE MODEL MAKERS
INC**
25 Pine St Ste 2 (07866-3143)
PHONE.................................973 627-5906
Mike Leone, *President*
Matt Malajko, *Vice Pres*
EMP: 5
SQ FT: 2,800
SALES (est): 525.7K **Privately Held**
WEB: www.pontemodels.com
SIC: 3999 Novelties, bric-a-brac & hobby
kits

(G-9509)
ULTIMATE TRADING CORP
Also Called: U T C
385 Franklin Ave Ste A (07866-4037)
PHONE.................................973 228-7700
James Geswelli, *President*
Todd Knichel, *Vice Pres*
Douglas Roberts, *Controller*
Stacie Androsky, *Director*
EMP: 100
SALES (est): 13.3MM **Privately Held**
SIC: 3911 5094 3961 3369 Jewelry, pre-
cious metal; jewelry & precious stones;
costume jewelry; nonferrous foundries

(G-9510)
UNITAO NUTRACEUTICALS LLC
6 Reservoir Pl (07866-1605)
PHONE.................................973 983-1121
Robert Colon, *Manager*
EMP: 2
SALES: 7.5MM **Privately Held**
SIC: 2834 Vitamin preparations

(G-9511)
VAPOR LOUNGE LLC
15 Van Duyne Ave (07866-4102)
PHONE.................................973 627-1277
Timothy Braun, *CEO*
Eric Totten, *CEO*
EMP: 6
SQ FT: 1,600
SALES (est): 651.3K **Privately Held**
SIC: 3634 Cigar lighters, electric

(G-9512)
WELDON ASPHALT CORP
311 W Main St Ste 1 (07866-3317)
PHONE.................................973 627-7500
Bob Weldon, *President*
EMP: 10

SALES (corp-wide): 6MM **Privately Held**
SIC: 2951 Asphalt paving mixtures &
blocks
PA: Weldon Asphalt Corp
141 Central Ave
Westfield NJ
908 233-4444

(G-9513)
WIDE BAND SYSTEMS INC
389 Franklin Ave (07866-4014)
P.O. Box 289 (07866-0289)
PHONE.................................973 586-6500
Frank Padula, *President*
Kevin Burns, *General Mgr*
Andy Prezuhy, *Production*
Debbie Shapiro, *Purch Agent*
Mark Stanley, *Engineer*
▼ EMP: 15
SQ FT: 9,300
SALES: 3.4MM **Privately Held**
WEB: www.widebandsystems.com
SIC: 3663 Microwave communication
equipment

(G-9514)
**WYMAN-GORDON FORGINGS
INC**
387 Franklin Ave (07866-4014)
PHONE.................................973 627-0200
Karen Norlin, *Manager*
EMP: 33
SALES (corp-wide): 225.3B **Publicly
Held**
SIC: 3462 Missile forgings, ferrous
HQ: Wyman-Gordon Forgings, Inc.
10825 Telge Rd
Houston TX 77095
281 856-9900

Rockleigh
Bergen County

(G-9515)
CARLEE CORPORATION
28 Piermont Rd (07647-2797)
PHONE.................................201 768-6800
Bruce A Burgermaster, *President*
Reggie Gencer, *General Mgr*
EMP: 25 EST: 1950
SQ FT: 47,000
SALES (est): 6.3MM **Privately Held**
WEB: www.carlee.com
SIC: 2299 Broadwoven fabrics: linen, jute,
hemp & ramie

(G-9516)
**CRESTRON ELECTRONICS INC
(PA)**
15 Volvo Dr (07647-2507)
PHONE.................................201 767-3400
Randy Klein, *President*
Dominick Accurso, *Partner*
Paul Riley, *Regional Mgr*
Dan Feldstein, *COO*
Joy Lemba, *Opers Mgr*
◆ EMP: 200 EST: 1971
SALES (est): 626.7MM **Privately Held**
SIC: 3571 3651 1731 3663 Minicomput-
ers; household audio & video equipment;
electrical work; radio & TV communica-
tions equipment; fire- or burglary-resistive
products; intercommunication systems,
electric

(G-9517)
GINSENG UP CORPORATION
24 Link Dr (07647-2503)
PHONE.................................800 446-7364
Paul Desilva, *Manager*
EMP: 12
SALES (corp-wide): 4.5MM **Privately
Held**
WEB: www.ginsengup.com
SIC: 2086 Bottled & canned soft drinks
PA: Ginseng Up Corporation
16 Plum St
Worcester MA 01604
508 799-6178

(G-9518)
HBC SOLUTIONS INC
Also Called: Harris Broadcast
22 Paris Ave Ste 110 (07647-2600)
PHONE.................................973 267-5990
EMP: 4
SALES (corp-wide): 2.2B Privately Held
SIC: 3663 Wholesales Electronic Parts
And Equipment
HQ: Hbc Solutions, Inc.
9800 S Meridian Blvd
Englewood CO 75034
303 476-4590

(G-9519)
IMAGE ACCESS CORP (PA)
22 Paris Ave Ste 210 (07647-2600)
PHONE.................................201 342-7878
Robert Feulner, President
William Bresnak Jr, Vice Pres
Claire Feulner, Vice Pres
Brent Bailey, Engineer
Paul Leake, Engineer
▼ EMP: 30
SQ FT: 4,000
SALES (est): 22.7MM Privately Held
WEB: www.imageaccesscorp.com
SIC: 5044 7389 7371 7372 Microfilm
equipment; microfilm recording & devel-
oping service; computer software devel-
opment & applications; prepackaged
software; computer peripheral equipment
repair & maintenance

(G-9520)
NEWARK FIBERS INC (PA)
28 Piermont Rd (07647-2712)
PHONE.................................201 768-6800
Bruce A Burgermaster, President
Charles Uchmanowicd, Vice Pres
EMP: 1
SQ FT: 18,000
SALES (est): 1.2MM Privately Held
SIC: 2299 2823 Batting, wadding, padding
& fillings; cellulosic manmade fibers

(G-9521)
ROYAL SOVEREIGN INTL INC (PA)
2 Volvo Dr (07647-2508)
PHONE.................................800 397-1025
T K Lim, CEO
Keung S Lim, President
◆ EMP: 45
SQ FT: 68,000
SALES (est): 13MM Privately Held
WEB: www.royalsovereign.com
SIC: 5044 3639 3083 Office equipment;
major kitchen appliances, except refriger-
ators & stoves; laminated plastics plate &
sheet

(G-9522)
TAKASAGO INTL CORP USA (HQ)
4 Volvo Dr (07647-2508)
P.O. Box 932 (07647-0932)
PHONE.................................201 767-9001
Sean G Traynor, Ch of Bd
Yoshiaki Suda, Exec VP
Brian Buck, Senior VP
Masayuki Mita, Senior VP
Sevi Adat, Vice Pres
◆ EMP: 170 EST: 1968
SQ FT: 50,000
SALES (est): 166.7MM Privately Held
SIC: 2844 Concentrates, perfume

(G-9523)
TIBURON LOCKERS INC
22 Paris Ave Ste 106 (07647-2600)
PHONE.................................201 750-4960
Jared Lowenthal, CEO
Carlos Rodriguez, Project Mgr
Steve Shipp, Opers Mgr
Steve Perdue, Opers Spvr
Michael Kreie, Accounts Mgr
EMP: 9
SALES (est): 174.5K Privately Held
SIC: 3429 Locks or lock sets

(G-9524)
VOLVO CAR NORTH AMERICA LLC (DH)
1 Volvo Dr (07647-2507)
PHONE.................................201 768-7300
Victor H Doolan, President
Chris Long, General Mgr
Elene Dube, Business Mgr
Ray Gallant, Vice Pres
Gregor Hembrough, Vice Pres
◆ EMP: 300 EST: 1957
SQ FT: 289,000
SALES (est): 647.4MM
SALES (corp-wide): 47.3B Privately Held
WEB: www.volvocars.com
SIC: 5511 5013 6159 7515 Automobiles,
new & used; automotive supplies & parts;
automobile finance leasing; passenger
car leasing; motor vehicle parts & acces-
sories
HQ: Volvo Personvagnar Ab
Tr Hb3s
Goteborg 405 3
315 900-00

Rocky Hill
Somerset County

(G-9525)
ENVIRNMNTAL DYNAMICS GROUP INC (PA)
5 Crscent Ave (08553)
PHONE.................................609 924-4489
Duke Wiser, President
Martin Cummins, Vice Pres
Ronald Knight, Vice Pres
EMP: 13
SQ FT: 5,000
SALES (est): 2.1MM Privately Held
WEB: www.environmentaldynamics.com
SIC: 3564 Filters, air: furnaces, air condi-
tioning equipment, etc.

Roebling
Burlington County

(G-9526)
MAGNATROL VALVE CORPORATION
Also Called: Clark Cooper
941 Hamilton Ave (08554-1707)
PHONE.................................856 829-4580
Chryssa Wilson, General Mgr
Dave Decaro, Buyer
John Busch, Branch Mgr
Gabe Cabasquini, Software Dev
EMP: 15
SALES (corp-wide): 11.9MM Privately
Held
WEB: www.magnatrol.com
SIC: 3561 3491 Pumps & pumping equip-
ment; solenoid valves
PA: Magnatrol Valve Corporation
67 5th Ave
Hawthorne NJ 07506
973 427-4341

Roosevelt
Monmouth County

(G-9527)
ACTION PACKAGING AUTOMATION
Also Called: A P A I
15 Oscar Dr (08555-7010)
P.O. Box 190 (08555-0190)
PHONE.................................609 448-9210
John Wojnicki, President
P J Wojnicki, Corp Secy
Robin Carroll, Mktg Dir
▲ EMP: 8
SQ FT: 18,000
SALES (est): 1.5MM Privately Held
WEB: www.apai-usa.com
SIC: 3565 3824 3542 Packaging machin-
ery; fluid meters & counting devices; ma-
chine tools, metal forming type

(G-9528)
DIAMOND MACHINE CO INC
30 N Valley Rd (08555-7017)
P.O. Box 420 (08555-0420)
PHONE.................................609 490-8940
George Pall, President
Ilona Pall, Admin Sec
EMP: 8
SALES (est): 665.5K Privately Held
SIC: 3599 Machine shop, jobbing & repair

(G-9529)
ICY COOLS INC
15 Oscar Dr (08555-7010)
P.O. Box 686 (08555-0686)
PHONE.................................609 448-0172
Paul Wojnicki, President
▲ EMP: 5 EST: 1996
SQ FT: 10,000
SALES (est): 352K Privately Held
WEB: www.icycools.com
SIC: 3585 5078 Room coolers, portable;
refrigeration equipment & supplies

Roseland
Essex County

(G-9530)
AMANO CINCINNATI INCORPORATED (DH)
Also Called: Amano Cincinnati Distributor
140 Harrison Ave (07068-1239)
PHONE.................................973 403-1900
Michael Lee, President
Osamu Okagaki, President
Kaushal Gokli, Vice Pres
Sabi Olyaie, Warehouse Mgr
Jodie Dooley, Mfg Spvr
◆ EMP: 100
SQ FT: 20,000
SALES (est): 39.1MM Privately Held
SIC: 3579 3559 Time clocks & time
recording devices; parking facility equip-
ment & supplies
HQ: Amano Usa Holdings, Inc.
140 Harrison Ave
Roseland NJ 07068
973 403-1900

(G-9531)
AMANO USA HOLDINGS INC (HQ)
140 Harrison Ave (07068-1239)
PHONE.................................973 403-1900
Tomoaki Hashimoto, President
Thomas M Benton, President
Yoshio Misumi, Vice Pres
Donna Mauriello, Manager
David Lopez, Info Tech Dir
◆ EMP: 2
SQ FT: 20,000
SALES (est): 104.4MM Privately Held
SIC: 3589 2842 3579 3559 Floor wash-
ing & polishing machines, commercial;
cleaning or polishing preparations; time
clocks & time recording devices; parking
facility equipment & supplies; industrial
chemicals; floor machinery, maintenance

(G-9532)
ANNIN & CO (PA)
Also Called: Annin Flag Makers
105 Eisenhower Pkwy # 203 (07068-1640)
PHONE.................................973 228-9400
Carter Beard, CEO
Lindley Scarlett, Exec VP
Sandra Van Lieu, Vice Pres
Tara Powell, Production
David Gregory, Purch Agent
▲ EMP: 50 EST: 1847
SALES (est): 163.7MM Privately Held
WEB: www.annin.com
SIC: 2399 Flags, fabric

(G-9533)
ARLO CORPORATION
119 Harrison Ave (07068)
PHONE.................................973 618-0030
Alan Aranowitz, President
EMP: 9
SQ FT: 5,000

(G-9534)
B&G FOODS INC
Also Called: Roseland Manufacturing
426 Eagle Rock Ave (07068-1719)
PHONE.................................973 403-6795
Florina Raro, Manager
EMP: 150
SALES (corp-wide): 1.7B Publicly Held
WEB: www.bgfoods.com
SIC: 2033 Jams, including imitation: pack-
aged in cans, jars, etc.; jellies, edible, in-
cluding imitation: in cans, jars, etc.
PA: B&G Foods, Inc.
4 Gatehall Dr Ste 110
Parsippany NJ 07054
973 401-6500

(G-9535)
BARRETT PAVING MATERIALS INC (DH)
3 Becker Farm Rd Ste 307 (07068-1726)
PHONE.................................973 533-1001
Robert Doucet, President
Jim M Meckstroth, Regional Mgr
Rod Russell, Regional Mgr
Ron Albers, Vice Pres
Dennis Luba, Vice Pres
◆ EMP: 20
SQ FT: 8,500
SALES (est): 209.7MM
SALES (corp-wide): 83.5MM Privately
Held
WEB: www.barrettpaving.com
SIC: 1611 2951 4213 1799 Highway &
street paving contractor; road materials,
bituminous (not from refineries); trucking,
except local; building site preparation; ex-
cavation work
HQ: Barrett Industries Corporation
73 Headquarters Plz
Morristown NJ 07960
973 533-1001

(G-9536)
BROTHERS SHEET METAL INC
15 Grand (07068)
PHONE.................................973 228-3221
Traci Dube, President
EMP: 14
SALES (est): 1.3MM Privately Held
SIC: 3444 Sheet metalwork

(G-9537)
EMISPHERE TECHNOLOGIES INC
4 Becker Farm Rd Ste 103 (07068-1734)
PHONE.................................973 532-8000
Timothy G Rothwell, Ch of Bd
Alan L Rubino, President
Alan Gallantar, CFO
EMP: 10
SQ FT: 4,100
SALES: 1.2MM Privately Held
WEB: www.emisphere.com
SIC: 2834 8731 Pharmaceutical prepara-
tions; biological research

(G-9538)
GLOBAL ECOLOGY CORPORATION (PA)
101 Eisenhower Pkwy # 300 (07068-1054)
PHONE.................................973 655-9001
Joseph Battiato, Ch of Bd
Peter Ubaldi, President
EMP: 4
SQ FT: 1,000
SALES (est): 63.1K Privately Held
WEB: www.hsni.us
SIC: 3589 Water treatment equipment, in-
dustrial

(G-9539)
GRANCO GROUP LLC
Also Called: Portable Container Services
101 Eisenhower Pkwy # 300 (07068-1032)
PHONE.................................973 515-4721
Walter Granco,
◆ EMP: 4
SQ FT: 1,000

SALES (est): 1.8MM Privately Held
SIC: 3965 5085 Fasteners; fasteners &
fastening equipment

▲ = Import ▼=Export
◆ =Import/Export

SALES (est): 858.7K **Privately Held**
SIC: **3715** 5085 5999 2448 Demountable
cargo containers; commercial containers;
packaging materials: boxes, padding,
etc.; cargo containers, wood & wood with
metal; milk (fluid) shipping containers,
metal; trucks, tractors & trailers: new &
used

(G-9540)
KNOW AMERICA MEDIA LLC
(PA)
Also Called: Diversity In Action
157 Eagle Rock Ave (07068-1353)
PHONE..................................770 650-1102
Larry Lebovitz, *CEO*
John Hanna, *Treasurer*
Marilyn Walker, *Comptroller*
EMP: 7
SQ FT: 3,495
SALES (est): 559K **Privately Held**
SIC: **2721** Magazines: publishing only, not
printed on site

(G-9541)
PAR CODE SYMBOLOGY INC
119 Harrison Ave (07068)
P.O. Box 87 (07068-0087)
PHONE..................................973 918-0550
David Aranowitz, *President*
Frankie Palmer, *Sales Dir*
EMP: 12
SQ FT: 8,000
SALES (est): 1.8MM **Privately Held**
WEB: www.parcode.com
SIC: **2672** 5046 Coated & laminated
paper; commercial equipment

(G-9542)
TDK ASSOCIATES CORP
Also Called: Signarama Roseland
12 Eisenhower Pkwy Ste 9 (07068-1638)
PHONE..................................862 210-8085
Tarek Eldakak, *President*
Joan Eldakak, *Vice Pres*
EMP: 5
SQ FT: 2,000
SALES (est): 300K **Privately Held**
SIC: **1799** 5046 3993 Sign installation &
maintenance; signs, electrical; signs &
advertising specialties

(G-9543)
TYSON FRESH MEATS INC
5 Becker Farm Rd Ste 408 (07068-1772)
PHONE..................................605 235-2061
Greg Charuka, *Branch Mgr*
EMP: 20
SALES (corp-wide): 40B **Publicly Held**
SIC: **2011** Meat packing plants
HQ: Tyson Fresh Meats, Inc.
800 Stevens Port Dr
Dakota Dunes SD 57049
605 235-2061

(G-9544)
WELDON CONCRETE CORP
Also Called: Asphalt Plant
1 Eisenhower Pkwy (07068-1607)
PHONE..................................973 228-7473
Joe Keppler, *Branch Mgr*
EMP: 4
SALES (corp-wide): 2.6MM **Privately
Held**
SIC: **3273** Ready-mixed concrete
PA: Weldon Concrete Corp
141 Central Ave
Westfield NJ
908 233-4444

(G-9545)
ZC UTILITY SERVICES LLC
Also Called: Carner Bros
10 Steel Ct (07068-1236)
P.O. Box 116 (07068-0116)
PHONE..................................973 226-1840
Kevin Corb, *Vice Pres*
Todd Zartman,
EMP: 8 EST: 2015
SALES (est): 1MM **Privately Held**
SIC: **1389** 7389 Excavating slush pits &
cellars; automobile recovery service

Roselle
Union County

(G-9546)
**ADVANCED CUTTING SERVICES
LLC**
169 E Highland Pkwy (07203-2643)
PHONE..................................908 241-5332
Bob Valchunnis,
EMP: 5
SALES (est): 728.4K **Privately Held**
WEB: www.acswaterjet.com
SIC: **3545** Cutting tools for machine tools

(G-9547)
**AMERICAN RIGGING & REPAIR
INC**
Also Called: Metro Industrial Supply
356 W 1st Ave (07203-1001)
PHONE..................................866 478-7129
Robert Banks, *President*
Tom Banks, *Treasurer*
▼ EMP: 10 EST: 1998
SQ FT: 12,000
SALES (est): 1.5MM **Privately Held**
SIC: **3731** Marine rigging

(G-9548)
**ART MOLD & POLISHING CO
INC**
220 Columbus Ave (07203-2018)
PHONE..................................908 518-9191
Michael Dellapia, *President*
Daniel Notarnicola, *Vice Pres*
Paulo Desousa, *Manager*
EMP: 10
SQ FT: 10,000
SALES (est): 1.3MM **Privately Held**
SIC: **3544** 3471 Industrial molds; polish-
ing, metals or formed products

(G-9549)
BINDGRAPHICS INC
490 W 1st Ave (07203-1041)
PHONE..................................908 245-1110
Eugene Trunzo, *President*
EMP: 22
SQ FT: 20,000
SALES (est): 3.4MM **Privately Held**
SIC: **2789** Binding only: books, pamphlets,
magazines, etc.

(G-9550)
**BODYCOTE THERMAL PROC
INC**
304 Cox St (07203-1704)
PHONE..................................908 245-0717
Bobby Lebell, *Manager*
EMP: 25
SALES (corp-wide): 935.8MM **Privately
Held**
WEB: www.mic-houston.com
SIC: **3398** Metal heat treating
HQ: Bodycote Thermal Processing, Inc.
12700 Park Central Dr # 700
Dallas TX 75251
214 904-2420

(G-9551)
**BODYCOTE THERMAL
PROCESSING**
304 Cox St (07203-1704)
PHONE..................................908 245-0717
Robert Lobell, *President*
Robert J Lobell, *President*
John S Ross, *President*
Lynn Cortese, *Accounting Mgr*
EMP: 30 EST: 1944
SQ FT: 12,000
SALES (est): 5.1MM **Privately Held**
WEB: www.metall.com
SIC: **3398** Metal heat treating

(G-9552)
CLENESCO PRODUCTS CORP
298 Cox St (07203-1704)
PHONE..................................908 245-5255
Ronald Globerman, *President*
Neil Salerno, *Admin Sec*
EMP: 12
SQ FT: 8,000

SALES (est): 1.5MM
SALES (corp-wide): 13.3MM **Privately
Held**
WEB: www.rmsllc.net
SIC: **2842** Specialty cleaning preparations
PA: Ronell Industries Inc
298 Cox St
Roselle NJ 07203
908 245-5255

(G-9553)
**CLIO FOODS & PROVISIONS
LLC**
145 E Highland Pkwy (07203-2644)
PHONE..................................908 505-2546
Andrea Sargeant, *Office Mgr*
Sergey Konchakovskiy,
EMP: 8
SALES (est): 623.2K **Privately Held**
SIC: **2024** Dairy based frozen desserts

(G-9554)
COMFORTFIT LABS INC
246 Columbus Ave (07203-2018)
PHONE..................................908 259-9100
Howell Schorr, *President*
Thomas J Calagna, *Vice Pres*
Randee Husik, *CFO*
Barbara Campbell, *Director*
EMP: 50
SALES (est): 7.6MM **Privately Held**
SIC: **3559** Sewing machines & hat & zipper
making machinery

(G-9555)
**CUBALAS EMERGENCY
LIGHTING LLC (PA)**
Also Called: C.E.S. Towing & Recovery
340 Cox St (07203-1704)
PHONE..................................908 514-0505
Robert Cubala, *Mng Member*
EMP: 5 EST: 2016
SALES (est): 823.5K **Privately Held**
SIC: **3648** 7549 7513 Lighting equipment;
towing services; truck rental & leasing, no
drivers

(G-9556)
CUSTOM ROLLER INC (PA)
240b Columbus Ave (07203-2088)
PHONE..................................908 298-7797
Elaine Ambrosio, *President*
Paul Materia, *Owner*
EMP: 8
SQ FT: 5,000
SALES (est): 1.1MM **Privately Held**
SIC: **3555** Printing trades machinery

(G-9557)
FARRELL EQP & CONTRLS INC
Also Called: Assured Automtn Flow Solutions
263 Cox St (07203-1703)
PHONE..................................732 770-4142
William Farrell, *President*
Brian Booth, *Vice Pres*
Mike O'Neill, *VP Sales*
Oneill Kim, *Marketing Mgr*
Vincent Collier, *Manager*
▲ EMP: 15
SQ FT: 10,000
SALES (est): 10.8MM **Privately Held**
WEB: www.flows.com
SIC: **5085** 3491 Valves & fittings; industrial
valves

(G-9558)
FORMIA MARBLE & STONE INC
219 E 11th Ave (07203-2015)
PHONE..................................908 259-0606
Filippo Berta, *President*
Ennio Grignolo, *Project Mgr*
Roy Ramotaur, *Project Mgr*
Melissa Knight, *Manager*
Philip Berta, *Supervisor*
◆ EMP: 40
SQ FT: 30,000
SALES (est): 2.7MM **Privately Held**
SIC: **3281** Table tops, marble

(G-9559)
**GIANT STL FABRICATORS
ERECTORS**
197 E Highland Pkwy (07203-2643)
PHONE..................................908 241-6766
John J Sorber Jr, *President*

Thomas A Fischetti, *Manager*
EMP: 4
SQ FT: 10,000
SALES (est): 399.1K **Privately Held**
SIC: **3441** 3444 Fabricated structural
metal; sheet metalwork

(G-9560)
HILLSIDE CANDY LLC
1112 Walnut St (07203-2024)
PHONE..................................908 241-4747
Socorro Nuguid, *QC Mgr*
Henry Adamkowski, *Branch Mgr*
William Young, *Web Dvlpr*
EMP: 25
SALES (corp-wide): 6MM **Privately Held**
WEB: www.hillsidecandy.com
SIC: **5441** 2064 Candy; candy & other
confectionery products
PA: Hillside Candy Llc
35 Hillside Ave
Hillside NJ 07205
973 926-2300

(G-9561)
HOWARD PRESS INC
Also Called: Fedex Office Commercial Press
450 W 1st Ave (07203-1095)
P.O. Box 379 (07203-0379)
PHONE..................................908 245-4400
Scott B Porter, *General Mgr*
Gordon E Eitel Jr, *Exec VP*
Gordon Eitel, *Vice Pres*
Matt Pagano, *Manager*
George Schnur, *MIS Dir*
▲ EMP: 60
SQ FT: 65,000
SALES (est): 10.3MM
SALES (corp-wide): 69.6B **Publicly Held**
WEB: www.howardpress.com
SIC: **2754** 2752 2796 2759 Letter, circu-
lar & form: gravure printing; commercial
printing, offset; platemaking services;
commercial printing; book printing; book
publishing
HQ: Fedex Office And Print Services, Inc.
7900 Legacy Dr
Plano TX 75024
800 463-3339

(G-9562)
**KRAFTWARE CORPORATION
(PA)**
270 Cox St (07203-1704)
PHONE..................................732 345-7091
Donald R Grant, *Ch of Bd*
D Rustin Grant, *President*
L Ripley Grant, *Exec VP*
▲ EMP: 25 EST: 1947
SQ FT: 30,000
SALES (est): 4.9MM **Privately Held**
WEB: www.kraftwareonline.com
SIC: **3499** 3229 5023 3914 Metal house-
hold articles; glassware, art or decorative;
kitchen tools & utensils; silverware &
plated ware; metal barrels, drums & pails

(G-9563)
**MANUFACTURERS BRUSH
CORP**
310 W 1st Ave (07203-1001)
PHONE..................................973 882-6966
Richard Draudt, *President*
EMP: 5
SALES (est): 300K **Privately Held**
SIC: **3991** Brushes, except paint & varnish

(G-9564)
**MATERIALS RESEARCH GROUP
INC**
244 W 1st Ave (07203-1102)
PHONE..................................908 245-3301
Walt Reed, *President*
Sharon Reed, *Vice Pres*
▲ EMP: 7
SQ FT: 8,000
SALES (est): 710K **Privately Held**
WEB: www.materialsresearchgroup.com
SIC: **3229** Pressed & blown glass

(G-9565)
MECHANITRON CORPORATION INC
Also Called: Mechanictron
310 W 1st Ave (07203-1001)
PHONE..........................908 620-1001
Dave Newman, *President*
EMP: 8
SQ FT: 3,000
SALES (est): 760K **Privately Held**
SIC: 3599 3452 Machine shop, jobbing & repair; bolts, nuts, rivets & washers

(G-9566)
MICHELLER & SON HYDRAULICS INC
534 W 1st Ave Ste 540 (07203-1028)
PHONE..........................908 687-1545
Birgetta Micheller, *Corp Secy*
John Micheller, *Vice Pres*
Patricia Waznica, *Office Mgr*
EMP: 10
SQ FT: 6,000
SALES: 1MM **Privately Held**
SIC: 3511 5084 7699 3599 Hydraulic turbines; hydraulic systems equipment & supplies; hydraulic equipment repair; machine shop, jobbing & repair; welding repair

(G-9567)
OILTEST INC
109 Aldene Rd Ste 4 (07203-1093)
PHONE..........................908 245-9330
Fax: 908 245-8972
EMP: 5
SALES (est): 616.8K **Privately Held**
SIC: 1389 Oil/Gas Field Services

(G-9568)
PAMARCO GLOBAL GRAPHICS INC (HQ)
Also Called: Memco
235 E 11th Ave (07203-2090)
PHONE..........................908 241-1200
Terry Ford, *President*
David Burgess, *Vice Pres*
Kimberly Parada, *CFO*
Mary Cantrell, *Supervisor*
Tony Tagiaferro, *Technology*
◆ EMP: 50 EST: 1946
SQ FT: 110,000
SALES (est): 32.9MM **Privately Held**
SIC: 3555 Printing trades machinery

(G-9569)
PAMARCO TECHNOLOGIES LLC (PA)
235 E 11th Ave (07203-2090)
PHONE..........................908 241-1200
Terrence W Ford, *CEO*
Dean Loria, *Production*
Kevin McAnally, *Engrg Mgr*
David Shumate, *Engineer*
Doug Johnson, *CFO*
▲ EMP: 37
SALES (est): 104.2MM **Privately Held**
WEB: www.armotek.com
SIC: 3555 Printing trades machinery

(G-9570)
PAR SHEET METAL INC
220 W 1st Ave (07203-1102)
PHONE..........................908 241-2477
Anthony Costa, *Vice Pres*
Andy Costa, *Vice Pres*
EMP: 10
SQ FT: 5,000
SALES (est): 650K **Privately Held**
SIC: 3444 Sheet metalwork

(G-9571)
RONELL INDUSTRIES INC (PA)
298 Cox St (07203-1798)
PHONE..........................908 245-5255
Ronald Globerman, *President*
Neil Salerno, *Vice Pres*
EMP: 482
SQ FT: 12,000
SALES (est): 13.3MM **Privately Held**
WEB: www.rmsllc.net
SIC: 7349 2842 Janitorial service, contract basis; specialty cleaning preparations

(G-9572)
SPECTRUM INTERNATIONAL LLC
109 Aldene Rd Ste 1 (07203-1093)
PHONE..........................908 998-9338
Edmund J Cienava,
EMP: 6
SALES (est): 340.7K **Privately Held**
SIC: 1389 Testing, measuring, surveying & analysis services

(G-9573)
STAMPLUS MANUFACTURING INC
654 W 1st Ave (07203-1026)
PHONE..........................908 241-8844
Jaromir Batka, *President*
EMP: 15
SQ FT: 19,000
SALES (est): 3.3MM **Privately Held**
SIC: 3469 Electronic enclosures, stamped or pressed metal

(G-9574)
SUPERFINE ONLINE INC
205 E 11th Ave (07203-2015)
PHONE..........................212 827-0063
EMP: 8
SQ FT: 4,000
SALES (est): 33.7K **Privately Held**
SIC: 2752 Lithographic Commercial Printing

(G-9575)
VICTORY BOX CORP
645 W 1st Ave (07203-1049)
P.O. Box 842, Cranford (07016-0842)
PHONE..........................908 245-5100
Alex Landy, *President*
Paul Bell, *Vice Pres*
Michael Radin, *Vice Pres*
Seymour Cohen, *Admin Sec*
EMP: 6 EST: 1996
SQ FT: 120,000
SALES (est): 810K **Privately Held**
SIC: 2653 Boxes, corrugated: made from purchased materials

(G-9576)
VITA-PURE INC (PA)
410 W 1st Ave (07203-1047)
PHONE..........................908 245-1212
Achyut Sahasra, *President*
▲ EMP: 25
SQ FT: 17,500
SALES: 8.4MM **Privately Held**
SIC: 2833 2834 Vitamins, natural or synthetic: bulk, uncompounded; pharmaceutical preparations

---

Roselle Park
Union County

(G-9577)
ACCURATE MACHINE & TOOL CO
135 W Clay Ave (07204-1946)
P.O. Box 187 (07204-0187)
PHONE..........................908 245-5545
Jeral Diehl, *President*
EMP: 6 EST: 1954
SQ FT: 5,000
SALES: 350K **Privately Held**
SIC: 3544 Special dies & tools

(G-9578)
AYR COMPOSITION INC
320 Chestnut St (07204-1904)
PHONE..........................908 241-8118
Carl Gamba, *President*
Jeanette Gamba, *President*
John Gamba, *Vice Pres*
Nick Gamba, *Vice Pres*
John A Gamba, *Treasurer*
EMP: 6
SQ FT: 2,800
SALES (est): 616.7K **Privately Held**
SIC: 2759 2791 Commercial printing; typesetting

(G-9579)
CASAS NEWS PUBLISHING CO
325 E Westfield Ave (07204-2317)
PHONE..........................908 245-6767
George Castro, *President*
EMP: 30
SALES (est): 1.3MM **Privately Held**
SIC: 2711 Newspapers, publishing & printing

(G-9580)
CROSSFIELD PRODUCTS CORP
Also Called: Dex-O-Tex Floor Coverings
140 Valley Rd (07204-1402)
P.O. Box 125 (07204-0125)
PHONE..........................908 245-2801
Charles R Watt, *Branch Mgr*
EMP: 75
SQ FT: 35,000
SALES (corp-wide): 17.2MM **Privately Held**
WEB: www.crossfieldproducts.com
SIC: 2821 3272 3089 Plastics materials & resins; concrete products; floor coverings, plastic
PA: Crossfield Products Corp.
3000 E Harcourt St
Compton CA 90221
310 886-9100

(G-9581)
CUSUMANO PERMA-RAIL CO
213 W Westfield Ave (07204-1894)
PHONE..........................908 245-9281
Vincent Cusumano, *Ch of Bd*
Jeffrey Cusumano, *President*
Joan Cusumano, *Corp Secy*
EMP: 8 EST: 1952
SQ FT: 5,000
SALES (est): 1.1MM **Privately Held**
WEB: www.cusumanorailings.com
SIC: 3446 5211 Architectural metalwork; lumber & other building materials

(G-9582)
D K TOOL & DIE WELDING GROUP (PA)
Also Called: D-K Tool & Die Welding
181 W Clay Ave (07204-1946)
PHONE..........................908 241-7600
Stanley W Dickerson, *President*
EMP: 22
SQ FT: 16,000
SALES (est): 1.8MM **Privately Held**
WEB: www.d-kwelding.com
SIC: 7692 Welding repair

(G-9583)
DELICIOUS FRESH PIEROGI INC
594 Chestnut St (07204-1320)
P.O. Box 109 (07204-0109)
PHONE..........................908 245-0550
Richard Jackiewicz, *President*
EMP: 17
SALES (est): 1.7MM **Privately Held**
SIC: 2038 5149 5499 Ethnic foods, frozen; specialty food items; gourmet food stores

(G-9584)
EXTRUDERS INTERNATIONAL INC
181 W Clay Ave (07204-1946)
PHONE..........................908 241-7750
Stanley W Dickerson, *President*
EMP: 5
SQ FT: 5,000
SALES (est): 420K **Privately Held**
SIC: 3469 Machine parts, stamped or pressed metal

(G-9585)
G CATALANO INC
222 Valley Rd (07204-1404)
PHONE..........................908 241-6333
Giordano Catalano, *President*
Catherine Catalano, *Admin Sec*
EMP: 4
SQ FT: 1,521
SALES: 150K **Privately Held**
SIC: 3599 Machine shop, jobbing & repair

(G-9586)
HEXACON ELECTRIC COMPANY INC
161 W Clay Ave (07204-1946)
PHONE..........................908 245-6200
Kathryn J Schwaiger, *President*
Nino Cilia, *Sales Mgr*
Rashonda Aiken, *Administration*
EMP: 50 EST: 1932
SQ FT: 70,844
SALES (est): 8.4MM **Privately Held**
WEB: www.hexaconelectric.com
SIC: 3423 3548 Soldering guns or tools, hand: electric; soldering equipment, except hand soldering irons

(G-9587)
INDUSTL ENVRNMNTL POLLUTN
176 W Westfield Ave (07204-1817)
PHONE..........................908 241-3830
Michael Mouracade, *President*
Alexander Mouracade, *Vice Pres*
EMP: 28
SQ FT: 15,000
SALES (est): 3.3MM **Privately Held**
SIC: 3556 Food products machinery

(G-9588)
MONTE PRINTING & GRAPHICS INC
540 W Westfield Ave (07204-1822)
P.O. Box 293 (07204-0293)
PHONE..........................908 241-6600
Philip A Montalto, *President*
EMP: 5
SQ FT: 2,300
SALES (est): 650K **Privately Held**
SIC: 2752 7336 Commercial printing, offset; commercial art & graphic design

(G-9589)
PRINTSMITH
253 W Westfield Ave (07204-1824)
PHONE..........................908 245-3000
Ray Smith, *Owner*
EMP: 4
SALES (est): 227.2K **Privately Held**
SIC: 2759 Screen printing

(G-9590)
R W WHEATON CO
215 W Clay Ave (07204-1909)
P.O. Box 4017 (07204-0517)
PHONE..........................908 241-4955
Christopher E Kern, *President*
Wendy W Kern, *Treasurer*
EMP: 5
SQ FT: 1,900
SALES: 2.7MM **Privately Held**
SIC: 3324 Commercial investment castings, ferrous

(G-9591)
SQUILLACE STL FABRICATORS LLC
240 W Westfield Ave (07204-1819)
PHONE..........................908 241-6424
Rick Squillace, *President*
EMP: 5
SALES (est): 592.9K **Privately Held**
SIC: 3441 Fabricated structural metal
PA: Squillace Steel Fabricators Llc
771 Amsterdam Ave
Roselle NJ 07203

Rosemont
Hunterdon County

(G-9592)
FREDERICKS MACHINE INC
99 Kingwood Stockton Rd (08556-9990)
P.O. Box 247 (08556-0247)
PHONE..........................609 397-4991
Peter Fredericks, *President*
Pete Fredericks, *President*
EMP: 5
SALES (est): 472.6K **Privately Held**
SIC: 3599 Machine shop, jobbing & repair

(G-9593)
MAGNETICS & CONTROLS INC
99 Kingwood Stockton Rd (08556-9990)
P.O. Box 127 (08556-0127)
PHONE..................................609 397-8203
Jonathan C Lamson, *President*
Charlene E Lamson, *Corp Secy*
EMP: 17
SQ FT: 7,500
SALES (est): 2.4MM **Privately Held**
WEB: www.magcon.com
SIC: 3679 Cores, magnetic

Rosenhayn
Cumberland County

(G-9594)
CUMBERLAND DAIRY INC (PA)
899 Landis Ave (08352)
P.O. Box 308 (08352-0308)
PHONE..................................800 257-8484
Carmine C Catalana IV, *President*
Frank Catalana, *COO*
David A Catalana, *Vice Pres*
Frank J Catalana, *Vice Pres*
Joe Plasha, *Plant Mgr*
▲ **EMP:** 65 **EST:** 1962
SQ FT: 24,000
SALES (est): 19.8MM **Privately Held**
SIC: 2026 Milk drinks, flavored; yogurt

(G-9595)
F&S PRODUCE COMPANY INC
730 Lebanon Rd (08352)
PHONE..................................856 453-0316
Salvatore Pipitone Jr, *President*
Andrea Wisniewski, *Controller*
EMP: 248
SALES (corp-wide): 107.5MM **Privately Held**
SIC: 0723 2099 2032 0181 Crop preparation services for market; food preparations; canned specialties; ornamental nursery products
PA: F&S Produce Company, Inc.
500 W Elmer Rd
Vineland NJ 08360
856 453-0316

(G-9596)
QIS INC
778 Vineland Ave (08352)
P.O. Box 517 (08352-0517)
PHONE..................................856 455-3736
Diane Rizzo Lodge, *President*
▲ **EMP:** 10
SQ FT: 5,000
SALES (est): 1.2MM **Privately Held**
SIC: 3229 Pressed & blown glass

(G-9597)
QUARK ENTERPRISES INC
320 Morton Ave (08352)
P.O. Box 2396, Vineland (08362-2396)
PHONE..................................856 455-0376
Doug Riley, *President*
Susan Burt, *Vice Pres*
Pearl Riley, *Treasurer*
EMP: 23
SQ FT: 10,000
SALES (est): 2.6MM **Privately Held**
WEB: www.quarkglass.com
SIC: 3229 3231 Scientific glassware; novelty glassware; products of purchased glass

(G-9598)
UNITED FARM PROCESSING CORP
458 Garrison Rd (08352)
P.O. Box 355 (08352-0355)
PHONE..................................856 451-4612
Fax: 856 451-4690
EMP: 10 **Privately Held**
SIC: 2035 Mfg Pickles/Sauces/Dressing
PA: United Farm Processing Corp
4366 Park Ave
Bronx NY 10457

Roxbury Township
Morris County

(G-9599)
CLASSIC MARKING PRODUCTS INC
3 Gold Mine Rd Ste 104 (07836-0579)
PHONE..................................973 383-2223
Fred Thornton, *President*
EMP: 6
SALES (est): 680.2K **Privately Held**
WEB: www.classicmarking.com
SIC: 3953 Marking devices

(G-9600)
PHOENIX MACHINE REBUILDERS INC
4 Gold Mine Rd (07836-9122)
PHONE..................................973 691-8029
Michael Coulson, *President*
EMP: 10
SQ FT: 6,000
SALES (est): 1.6MM **Privately Held**
SIC: 3599 Machine shop, jobbing & repair

Rumson
Monmouth County

(G-9601)
REISS CORPORATION (PA)
Also Called: Reiss Manufacturing
36 Bingham Ave (07760-1535)
P.O. Box 159 (07760-0159)
PHONE..................................732 446-6100
Carl Reiss, *President*
Ercan Akdogan, *Sales Staff*
Talar Sahagian, *Sales Staff*
▲ **EMP:** 125 **EST:** 1896
SQ FT: 135,000
SALES (est): 27.8MM **Privately Held**
WEB: www.reissmfg.com
SIC: 3061 Mechanical rubber goods

(G-9602)
REISS MANUFACTURING INC (HQ)
Also Called: Ronsil Silicone Rubber Div
36 Bingham Ave (07760-1535)
P.O. Box 159 (07760-0159)
PHONE..................................732 446-6100
Carl Reiss, *President*
Wayne Ruotolo, *Opers Staff*
Robert Geist, *Engineer*
Charles Stegura, *Asst Controller*
Doreen Santos, *Executive*
◆ **EMP:** 125
SQ FT: 135,000
SALES (est): 31.9MM
SALES (corp-wide): 27.8MM **Privately Held**
WEB: www.reissmfg.com
SIC: 3089 Injection molding of plastics
PA: Reiss Corporation
36 Bingham Ave
Rumson NJ 07760
732 446-6100

(G-9603)
RUMSONS KITCHENS INC
103 E River Rd (07760-1611)
PHONE..................................732 842-1810
Louis Gualtieri, *President*
Elizabeth Gualtieri, *Vice Pres*
EMP: 5
SQ FT: 2,500
SALES (est): 430K **Privately Held**
SIC: 2514 1521 Kitchen cabinets: metal; general remodeling, single-family houses

Runnemede
Camden County

(G-9604)
CAPITAL GASKET AND RUBBER INC
325 E Clements Bridge Rd (08078-1404)
P.O. Box 141, Glendora (08029-0141)
PHONE..................................856 939-3670
Dennis Iocono, *President*
EMP: 5
SQ FT: 2,990
SALES (est): 440K **Privately Held**
SIC: 3053 5199 5085 Gasket materials; packaging materials; gaskets

(G-9605)
DELAWARE VALLEY INSTALLATION
200 Evergreen Rd (08078)
PHONE..................................856 546-0097
Jo Ann Brooks, *President*
EMP: 7
SQ FT: 1,500
SALES (est): 621.7K **Privately Held**
SIC: 2541 Cabinets, lockers & shelving

(G-9606)
ICEE COMPANY
155 E 9th Ave (08078-1158)
PHONE..................................856 939-1540
EMP: 4
SALES (corp-wide): 1.1B **Publicly Held**
SIC: 2082 Malt beverages
HQ: The Icee Company
1205 S Dupont Ave
Ontario CA 91761
800 426-4233

(G-9607)
RAPID MODELS & PROTOTYPES INC
101 C Rose Ave (08078)
PHONE..................................856 933-2929
Angela Pizzo, *President*
Joseph Pizzo, *Vice Pres*
EMP: 4
SQ FT: 7,000
SALES (est): 350K **Privately Held**
WEB: www.rapidmodels.net
SIC: 8711 3999 Industrial engineers; models, general, except toy

(G-9608)
RISSE & RISSE GRAPHICS INC
901 E Clements Bridge Rd # 3 (08078-2000)
PHONE..................................856 751-7671
Rich Risse, *President*
Rob Risse, *Vice Pres*
EMP: 40
SALES (est): 5MM **Privately Held**
SIC: 2395 Embroidery & art needlework

(G-9609)
RUOFF & SONS INC
1030 Rose Ave (08078-1088)
P.O. Box 320 (08078-0320)
PHONE..................................856 931-2064
Steve Ruoff, *President*
Ray Ricciardi, *Purch Agent*
Victor Norbuts, *Manager*
Steffanie Smith, *Manager*
Nick Chiusolo, *Supervisor*
EMP: 30 **EST:** 1950
SQ FT: 27,000
SALES (est): 7MM **Privately Held**
SIC: 3599 Machine shop, jobbing & repair

(G-9610)
SILVERTOP ASSOCIATES INC (PA)
Also Called: Rasta Imposta
600 E Clements Bridge Rd (08078-1453)
P.O. Box 7 (08078-0007)
PHONE..................................856 939-9599
Robert Berman, *President*
Jodi Berman, *COO*
Tina Berman, *Ch Credit Ofcr*
▲ **EMP:** 35
SQ FT: 16,000
WEB: www.rastaimposta.com
SIC: 2389 2353 Costumes; hats, caps & millinery

(G-9611)
STRYKER CORPORATION
165 E 9th Ave Unit F (08078-1162)
PHONE..................................856 312-0046
Joe Nowicki, *Sales Staff*
Patti Coulter, *Branch Mgr*
Ken Bine, *Branch Mgr*
Lou Agoston, *Manager*
Matt Kissel, *Manager*
EMP: 7
SALES (corp-wide): 13.6B **Publicly Held**
SIC: 3841 Surgical & medical instruments
PA: Stryker Corporation
2825 Airview Blvd
Portage MI 49002
269 385-2600

(G-9612)
SUMMUS INC
521 Irish Hill Rd Ste A (08078-1490)
PHONE..................................215 820-3918
EMP: 4 **EST:** 2017
SALES (est): 336.6K **Privately Held**
SIC: 2511 Novelty furniture: wood

Rutherford
Bergen County

(G-9613)
APPLE AIR COMPRESSOR CORP (PA)
Also Called: Airtech Vacuum
301 Veterans Blvd (07070-2564)
PHONE..................................888 222-9940
Tom Latsos, *President*
Spencer Folsom, *Regional Mgr*
Jakob Mieritz, *Vice Pres*
Andriy Yakymenko, *Production*
Elias Rontogiannis, *Buyer*
▲ **EMP:** 13
SQ FT: 20,000
SALES (est): 5.7MM **Privately Held**
SIC: 5084 3561 Pumps & pumping equipment; pumps & pumping equipment

(G-9614)
ARCHITECTURAL WINDOW MFG CORP
359 Veterans Blvd (07070-2564)
PHONE..................................201 933-5094
Anthony M Laino Jr, *President*
Michael A Laino, *Vice Pres*
Ken Thompson, *Vice Pres*
Paul Laino, *CFO*
EMP: 200
SQ FT: 170,000
SALES (est): 44.3MM **Privately Held**
SIC: 3442 1751 Sash, door or window: metal; window & door (prefabricated) installation

(G-9615)
BEBUS CABINETRY LLC
12 Ames Ave (07070-1702)
PHONE..................................201 729-9300
Raul A Garcia, *Administration*
EMP: 4
SALES (est): 171.2K **Privately Held**
SIC: 2434 Wood kitchen cabinets

(G-9616)
CHERISHMET INC
301 State Rt 17 Ste 800 (07070-2581)
P.O. Box 1652 (07070-0652)
PHONE..................................201 842-7612
Adam Wang, *President*
▲ **EMP:** 10
SALES (est): 3.6MM **Privately Held**
WEB: www.cherishmet.com
SIC: 5051 1446 Ferroalloys; filtration sand mining

(G-9617)
DAIRY DELIGHT LLC
1 Industrial Dr (07070-2523)
PHONE..................................201 939-7878
Ariel Berger, *Mfg Staff*
Shulim Ostreicher, *Programmer Anys*

Victor Ostreicher,
Joe Sptizer,
▲ EMP: 10
SALES (est): 4.3MM **Privately Held**
SIC: 5084 2023 5149 Dairy products
manufacturing machinery; dry, con-
densed, evaporated dairy products; milk,
canned or dried

(G-9618)
**EAGLETRE-PUMP ACQUISITION
CORP**
301 Veterans Blvd (07070-2564)
PHONE..................................201 569-1173
Robert Fogelson, *President*
Nitin Singhal, *Admin Sec*
EMP: 85
SALES (est): 3.3MM **Privately Held**
SIC: 3563 Vacuum pumps, except labora-
tory

(G-9619)
EBSCO INDUSTRIES INC
Also Called: Vulcan Information Packaging
201 Highway 17 Ste 300 (07070-2583)
PHONE..................................201 933-1800
Marie Curcio, *Branch Mgr*
EMP: 15
SALES (corp-wide): 2.8B **Privately Held**
WEB: www.ebscoind.com
SIC: 2782 Looseleaf binders & devices
PA: Ebsco Industries, Inc.
　　5724 Highway 280 E
　　Birmingham AL 35242
　　205 991-6600

(G-9620)
FIELDVIEW CFD INC
301 Route 17 Fl 7 (07070-2575)
PHONE..................................425 460-8284
Damian McKay, *President*
John Billowits, *Principal*
Tom Chan, *Principal*
Elisa Simmonds, *Principal*
Brad Thompson, *Principal*
EMP: 6
SALES (est): 135.3K **Privately Held**
SIC: 7372 Prepackaged software

(G-9621)
FUNAI CORPORATION INC (HQ)
201 Route 17 Ste 903 (07070-2635)
PHONE..................................201 806-7635
Ryo Fukuda, *President*
George Kanazawa, *CFO*
▲ EMP: 25
SALES (est): 16.5MM **Privately Held**
SIC: 3651 Household audio & video equip-
ment

(G-9622)
GZGN INC
Also Called: Vrpark
301 Nj 17 Ste 800 (07070)
PHONE..................................201 842-7622
Mehmet Aksakal, *Founder*
EMP: 15
SQ FT: 1,000
SALES (est): 568K **Privately Held**
SIC: 3651 Home entertainment equipment,
electronic

(G-9623)
HIGHPONT CORPORATION
Also Called: Pierrepont & Co
63 E Pierrepont Ave (07070-2330)
P.O. Box 35, Lyndhurst (07071-0035)
PHONE..................................201 460-1364
Peter Paluch, *President*
EMP: 9
SALES (est): 560K **Privately Held**
SIC: 2013 Sausages from purchased meat

(G-9624)
JORY ENGRAVERS INC
23 W Erie Ave (07070-1299)
PHONE..................................201 939-1546
Gary Gagliardi, *President*
EMP: 5
SQ FT: 3,500
SALES (est): 837.4K **Privately Held**
SIC: 2752 7389 Commercial printing, litho-
graphic; engraving service

(G-9625)
JUNGANEW LLC
1 Orient Way Ste F104 (07070-2524)
PHONE..................................201 832-0892
Esther Giordano, *Mng Member*
EMP: 6
SALES (est): 304.6K **Privately Held**
SIC: 7372 Application computer software

(G-9626)
L-E-M PLASTICS AND SUPPLIES
255 Highland Cross Ste 4 (07070-2594)
PHONE..................................201 933-9150
Thomas Pietrowitz, *Principal*
Sally Burns, *Business Mgr*
Jon Leonard, *Purchasing*
EMP: 5
SALES (est): 1.4MM **Privately Held**
SIC: 5162 3089 Plastics sheets & rods; air
mattresses, plastic

(G-9627)
MAGPIE MARKETING INC
194 Woodland Ave (07070-2839)
PHONE..................................201 507-9155
Peter Hollingsworth, *President*
Laura White, *Vice Pres*
▲ EMP: 2
SQ FT: 3,000
SALES: 1.5MM **Privately Held**
WEB: www.magpiemarketing.com
SIC: 3251 Ceramic glazed brick, clay

(G-9628)
METAWATER USA INC (PA)
301 State Rt 17 Ste 504 (07070-2580)
PHONE..................................201 935-3436
Ken Akikawa, *CEO*
Ichiro Fukushima, *CEO*
EMP: 2
SALES (est): 67.7MM **Privately Held**
SIC: 3589 Water treatment equipment, in-
dustrial

(G-9629)
**NORTH JERSEY MEDIA GROUP
INC**
Also Called: South Bergenite Editorial
9 Lincoln Ave (07070-2112)
P.O. Box 471, Little Falls (07424-0471)
PHONE..................................201 933-1166
Jaime Winters, *Director*
EMP: 5
SALES (corp-wide): 156.2MM **Privately
Held**
WEB: www.njmg.com
SIC: 2711 Newspapers, publishing & print-
ing
HQ: North Jersey Media Group Inc.
　　150 River St
　　Hackensack NJ 07601
　　201 646-4000

(G-9630)
ORION MACHINERY CO LTD
301 Veterans Blvd (07070-2564)
PHONE..................................201 569-3220
Thomas Latsos, *President*
▲ EMP: 24
SQ FT: 20,000
SALES (est): 3.1MM **Privately Held**
WEB: www.orionmach.net
SIC: 3563 5084 3561 Vacuum pumps, ex-
cept laboratory; industrial machinery &
equipment; pumps & pumping equipment

(G-9631)
PEARL BAUMELL COMPANY INC
201 State Rt 17 Ste 302 (07070-2583)
PHONE..................................415 421-2113
Isaac Baum, *President*
Evelyn Baum, *Vice Pres*
EMP: 8
SQ FT: 1,500
SALES (est): 1.5MM **Privately Held**
SIC: 5094 3911 Pearls; precious stones
(gems); jewelry, precious metal

(G-9632)
SI PACKAGING LLC
1 Orient Way Ste F191 (07070-2524)
PHONE..................................973 869-9920
Peter S Rodriguez, *Mng Member*
EMP: 10 EST: 2013
SQ FT: 30,000

SALES: 8MM **Privately Held**
SIC: 2879 5169 2841 Exterminating products, for household or industrial use;
chemicals & allied products; detergents &
soaps, except specialty cleaning; soap &
other detergents

(G-9633)
SKUSKY INC
143 Vanderburgh Ave (07070-1433)
PHONE..................................732 912-7220
Ahmad Chavda, *President*
EMP: 27
SALES: 125K **Privately Held**
SIC: 2211 2258 Bed sheeting, cotton; cur-
tains & curtain fabrics, lace

(G-9634)
SONY MUSIC HOLDINGS INC
Also Called: Bmg Entertainment
301 State Rte Hwy (07070)
PHONE..................................201 777-3933
Andrew Lack, *Manager*
EMP: 400 **Privately Held**
SIC: 3652 8721 7929 5735 Pre-recorded
records & tapes; auditing services; enter-
tainers & entertainment groups; record &
prerecorded tape stores
HQ: Sony Music Holdings Inc.
　　25 Madison Ave Fl 26
　　New York NY 10010
　　212 833-8000

(G-9635)
**WORLD PLASTIC EXTRUDERS
INC**
41 Park Ave (07070-1713)
PHONE..................................201 933-2915
Charles Bierds, *President*
EMP: 75 EST: 1947
SQ FT: 31,500
SALES (est): 6.3MM
SALES (corp-wide): 533.1MM **Privately
Held**
WEB: www.alhyde.com
SIC: 3089 Extruded finished plastic prod-
ucts
HQ: Ensinger Grenloch, Inc.
　　1 Main St
　　Grenloch NJ 08032

Saddle Brook
Bergen County

(G-9636)
A A A STAMP AND SEAL MFG CO
361 N Midland Ave (07663-5701)
PHONE..................................201 796-1500
Barry Goldman, *President*
EMP: 5
SQ FT: 1,800
SALES (est): 560.5K **Privately Held**
WEB: www.aaastamp.com
SIC: 3953 5999 Embossing seals & hand
stamps; rubber stamps

(G-9637)
AA GRAPHICS INC
431 N Midland Ave (07663-5527)
PHONE..................................201 398-0710
Anthony Acocella, *President*
Francine Acocella, *Vice Pres*
EMP: 5
SQ FT: 4,000
SALES: 500K **Privately Held**
WEB: www.aagraphics.com
SIC: 2752 Commercial printing, litho-
graphic

(G-9638)
AARUBCO RUBBER CO INC
259 2nd St (07663-6201)
P.O. Box 8028 (07663-8028)
PHONE..................................973 772-8177
Stephen Wharton, *President*
Ruth Wharton, *Vice Pres*
Amber Wharton, *Technical Mgr*
Paul Dec, *Sales Staff*
EMP: 32 EST: 1964
SQ FT: 33,000

SALES (est): 7MM **Privately Held**
WEB: www.aarubco.com
SIC: 3052 3061 Rubber belting; mechani-
cal rubber goods

(G-9639)
ACETRIS HEALTH LLC
Park 80 West Plz 1 (07663)
PHONE..................................201 961-9000
Salvatore Guccion, *CEO*
EMP: 5
SALES (est): 1.9MM
SALES (corp-wide): 12MM **Privately
Held**
SIC: 2834 5122 Pharmaceutical prepara-
tions; drugs & drug proprietaries
HQ: Rising Pharmaceuticals, Inc.
　　250 Pehle Ave Ste 601
　　Saddle Brook NJ 07663

(G-9640)
ARROW FASTENER CO LLC
271 Mayhill St (07663-5395)
PHONE..................................201 843-6900
Gary Duboff, *President*
◆ EMP: 280 EST: 2009
SQ FT: 250,000
SALES (est): 108.9MM
SALES (corp-wide): 854.8MM **Privately
Held**
WEB: www.arrowfastener.com
SIC: 3579 3315 3452 3542 Stapling ma-
chines (hand or power); staples, steel:
wire or cut; rivets, metal; riveting ma-
chines
PA: Hangzhou Great Star Industrial Co.,
　　Ltd.
　　No. 35, 9th Ring Road, Jianggan Dis-
trict
　　Hangzhou 31001
　　571 816-0118

(G-9641)
B&M TECHNOLOGIES INC
109 5th St Ste 1 (07663-6157)
PHONE..................................201 291-8505
Brian Cho, *President*
EMP: 12
SQ FT: 5,000
SALES (est): 120.9K **Privately Held**
SIC: 2759 Laser printing

(G-9642)
**BLUE GAUNTLET FENCING
GEAR INC**
Also Called: Blue Gauntlet Fencing Co
280 N Midland Ave Ste 138 (07663-5751)
PHONE..................................201 797-3332
Jing Xi Chen, *President*
▲ EMP: 10
SQ FT: 3,600
SALES (est): 1.1MM **Privately Held**
WEB: www.blue-gauntlet.com
SIC: 3315 5039 5211 Fencing made in
wiredrawing plants; wire fence, gates &
accessories; fencing

(G-9643)
BLUE MONKEY INC
Also Called: Speed Center USA
456b Sylvan St (07663-6107)
PHONE..................................201 805-0055
Joseph Saade, *President*
EMP: 4
SQ FT: 5,000
SALES (est): 300K **Privately Held**
WEB: www.speedcenterusa.com
SIC: 2211 Denims

(G-9644)
CARPENTER & PATERSON INC
369 Jefferson St (07663-6240)
PHONE..................................973 772-1800
Dennis Bourrell, *Opers Mgr*
Tim Gonder, *Sales Staff*
Tom Ferraro, *Branch Mgr*
EMP: 35
SQ FT: 1,500
SALES (corp-wide): 32.3MM **Privately
Held**
WEB: www.carpenterandpaterson.com
SIC: 5085 8711 3429 Valves & fittings;
engineering services; manufactured hard-
ware (general)

PA: Carpenter & Paterson, Inc.
434 Latigue Rd
Westwego LA 70094
504 431-7722

(G-9645)
CHEFLER FOODS LLC
400 Lyster Ave (07663-5910)
PHONE..................................201 596-3710
Michael Leffler, *CEO*
Michael Kurland, *CFO*
EMP: 10 EST: 2016
SQ FT: 92,000
SALES (est): 583.5K **Privately Held**
SIC: 2833 3089 Vegetable oils, medicinal
grade: refined or concentrated; tubs, plastic (containers)

(G-9646)
CHEMAID LABORATORIES INC (DH)
100 Mayhill St (07663-5302)
P.O. Box 888 (07663-0888)
PHONE..................................201 843-3300
Roy Reiner, *President*
Marc Reiner, *Vice Pres*
▲ EMP: 111
SQ FT: 75,000
SALES (est): 33.2MM
SALES (corp-wide): 603MM **Privately Held**
WEB: www.chemaidlabs.com
SIC: 2844 Cosmetic preparations

(G-9647)
CLARITY IMAGING TECH INC
250 Pehle Ave Ste 402 (07663-5832)
PHONE..................................877 272-4362
EMP: 28
SALES (corp-wide): 439.3K **Privately Held**
SIC: 3555 Printing trade parts & attachments
HQ: Clarity Imaging Technologies, Inc.
4350 Haddonfield Rd # 300
Pennsauken NJ 08109

(G-9648)
CRESSI SUB USA
3 Rosol Ln (07663-5501)
PHONE..................................201 594-1450
Antonio Cressi, *President*
Robert Cooper, *Manager*
◆ EMP: 5 EST: 2002
SALES (est): 743.3K
SALES (corp-wide): 39.1MM **Privately Held**
SIC: 3949 Sporting & athletic goods
PA: Cressi Sub Spa
Via Gelasio Adamoli 501
Genova GE 16165
010 830-791

(G-9649)
DIAZ WHOLESALE & MFG CO INC
4 Rosol Ln (07663-5503)
PHONE..................................404 629-3616
Rene M Diaz, *Branch Mgr*
EMP: 100
SALES (corp-wide): 301.4MM **Privately Held**
SIC: 2038 Frozen specialties
PA: Diaz Wholesale & Mfg. Co., Inc.
5501 Fulton Indus Blvd Sw
Atlanta GA 30336
404 344-5421

(G-9650)
EASTERN CONCRETE MATERIALS INC (HQ)
Also Called: Nyc Concrete Materials
250 Pehle Ave Ste 503 (07663-5832)
PHONE..................................201 797-7979
Michael K Gentoso, *President*
William Steele, *Vice Pres*
EMP: 106
SALES (est): 56.2MM
SALES (corp-wide): 1.5B **Publicly Held**
SIC: 3273 1429 1442 Ready-mixed concrete; trap rock, crushed & broken-quarrying; construction sand mining; gravel mining

PA: U.S. Concrete, Inc.
331 N Main St
Euless TX 76039
817 835-4105

(G-9651)
ENTERPRISE CONTAINER LLC (PA)
575 N Midland Ave (07663-5505)
PHONE..................................201 797-7200
Gary Berkowitz,
Edward Berkowitz,
Rochelle Berkowitz,
EMP: 11
SALES (est): 2.4MM **Privately Held**
SIC: 2653 Boxes, corrugated: made from purchased materials; pads, solid fiber: made from purchased materials

(G-9652)
FASTPULSE TECHNOLOGY INC
Also Called: Lasermetrics Division
220 Midland Ave (07663-6404)
PHONE..................................973 478-5757
Robert Goldstein, *Ch of Bd*
Steven Goldstein, *President*
Mark Percevault, *Manager*
Marion Goldstein, *Admin Sec*
EMP: 14
SQ FT: 5,000
SALES: 1.5MM **Privately Held**
WEB: www.fastpulse.com
SIC: 3699 Laser systems & equipment

(G-9653)
GEL UNITED LTD LIABILITY CO
635 N Midland Ave 3184 (07663-5523)
PHONE..................................855 435-8683
Emad William Awadalla, *CEO*
EMP: 4
SALES (est): 226K **Privately Held**
SIC: 2822 Synthetic rubber

(G-9654)
GRATEFUL PED INC
Also Called: Levy & Rappel
339 10th St (07663-6315)
PHONE..................................973 478-6511
Robert Kramer, *President*
EMP: 16
SQ FT: 5,500
SALES: 1MM **Privately Held**
WEB: www.levyandrappel.com
SIC: 3842 8011 Orthopedic appliances; offices & clinics of medical doctors

(G-9655)
HISPANIC OUTLOOK IN HIGHER
299 Market St Ste 140 (07663-5312)
P.O. Box 68, Paramus (07653-0068)
PHONE..................................201 587-8800
Jose Lopez ISA, *President*
Nicole Lopez ISA, *Vice Pres*
EMP: 7
SQ FT: 28,000
SALES: 728.9K **Privately Held**
SIC: 2731 Book publishing

(G-9656)
INTERNATIONAL CHEFS INC
33 Bella Vista Ave (07663-4803)
PHONE..................................917 645-2900
Mike Khalil, *President*
Joseph Khalil, *Vice Pres*
EMP: 15 EST: 1970
SQ FT: 20,000
SALES: 8.5MM **Privately Held**
SIC: 2099 Ready-to-eat meals, salads & sandwiches

(G-9657)
INTERNATIONAL MOLASSES CORP
88 Market St Fl 2 (07663-4830)
PHONE..................................201 368-8036
Ronald Targan, *President*
Thomas McNiellie, *Vice Pres*
John Johansen, *Manager*
EMP: 20
SALES (est): 1.7MM **Privately Held**
SIC: 5149 2083 2061 Molasses, industrial; malt; raw cane sugar

(G-9658)
KAY WINDOW FASHIONS INC
271 2nd St (07663-6201)
PHONE..................................862 591-1554
Jeffrey Kleinstein, *CEO*
Sol Kleinstein, *President*
Joseph Kleinstein, *Vice Pres*
EMP: 10
SALES (est): 1.2MM **Privately Held**
SIC: 2591 7349 Window shades; blinds vertical; window blind cleaning

(G-9659)
MALT PRODUCTS CORPORATION (PA)
88 Market St (07663-4830)
P.O. Box 898 (07663-0898)
PHONE..................................201 845-4420
Ronald G Targen, *President*
Amy Targen, *President*
Joe Hickenbottom, *Vice Pres*
Nathan Mandelbaum, *Treasurer*
David Mandelbaum, *Admin Sec*
▼ EMP: 35
SALES (est): 141.7MM **Privately Held**
SIC: 2087 2083 Flavoring extracts & syrups; malt byproducts

(G-9660)
MALT PRODUCTS CORPORATION
88 Market St (07663-4830)
PHONE..................................201 845-9106
Chuck Stewart, *Superintendent*
EMP: 30
SALES (corp-wide): 141.7MM **Privately Held**
SIC: 2087 2083 Flavoring extracts & syrups; malt byproducts
PA: Malt Products Corporation
88 Market St
Saddle Brook NJ 07663
201 845-4420

(G-9661)
MEESE INC (HQ)
Also Called: Modroto
535 N Midland Ave (07663-5505)
PHONE..................................201 796-4490
William J Tingue, *Ch of Bd*
Ryan, *President*
John H Hurst, *CFO*
John Ortiz, *Controller*
Navin Indar, *Asst Controller*
▼ EMP: 10 EST: 1931
SQ FT: 35,000
SALES (est): 4.9MM
SALES (corp-wide): 119.6MM **Privately Held**
WEB: www.modroto.com
SIC: 3089 2394 3443 Plastic containers, except foam; canvas & related products; containers, shipping (bombs, etc.): metal plate
PA: Tingue, Brown & Co.
535 N Midland Ave
Saddle Brook NJ 07663
201 796-4490

(G-9662)
MIDLAND SCREEN PRINTING INC
280 N Midland Ave Ste 218 (07663-5708)
PHONE..................................201 703-0066
Robert Witrak, *President*
EMP: 15
SALES: 710K **Privately Held**
SIC: 2759 2395 Screen printing; embroidery products, except schiffli machine

(G-9663)
MJSE LLC
Also Called: Fairfield Stamping
374 N Midland Ave (07663-5702)
P.O. Box 8358 (07663-8358)
PHONE..................................201 791-9888
Steve Orkenyi,
Micheal Rebuth,
John Ross,
EMP: 10 EST: 1976
SQ FT: 5,500
SALES: 1MM **Privately Held**
WEB: www.fairfieldstamping.com
SIC: 3469 Metal stampings

(G-9664)
MS SIGNS INC
280 N Midland Ave Ste 128 (07663-5751)
PHONE..................................973 569-1111
MO Ladak, *President*
Kevin Cherashore, *Vice Pres*
▲ EMP: 7
SQ FT: 6,000
SALES (est): 1.4MM **Privately Held**
WEB: www.stgcorp.com
SIC: 3993 Signs & advertising specialties

(G-9665)
MUELLER DIE CUT SOLUTIONS INC
150 N Midland Ave (07663-5926)
P.O. Box 510 (07663-0510)
PHONE..................................201 791-5000
Pete Futia, *General Mgr*
EMP: 50
SALES (corp-wide): 19.7MM **Privately Held**
SIC: 3053 Gaskets, packing & sealing devices
PA: Mueller Die Cut Solutions, Inc.
10415 Westlake Dr
Charlotte NC 28273
704 588-3900

(G-9666)
NTT ELECTRONICS AMERICA INC
250 Pehle Ave Ste 706 (07663-5832)
PHONE..................................201 556-1770
Keiichi Kurakazu, *President*
Leonardo Castro, *Engineer*
Keigo Matsumura, *Treasurer*
Gerry Lacombe, *Sales Mgr*
EMP: 10
SQ FT: 2,500
SALES: 25MM **Privately Held**
WEB: www.nel-world.com
SIC: 3661 Switchboards, telephone or telegraph
HQ: Ntt Electronics Corporation
1-1-32, Shin-Urashimacho, Kanagawa-Ku
Yokohama KNG 221-0

(G-9667)
PAM INTERNATIONAL CO INC (PA)
45 Mayhill St (07663-5301)
PHONE..................................201 291-1200
Don E Kreiter, *Ch of Bd*
Karen Scholz, *President*
Deborah Kreiter, *Vice Pres*
▲ EMP: 90
SQ FT: 205,000
SALES (est): 4.9MM **Privately Held**
WEB: www.pamint.com
SIC: 2541 2542 Store & office display cases & fixtures; store fixtures, wood; office & store showcases & display fixtures; fixtures, store: except wood

(G-9668)
PARADIGM PACKAGING EAST LLC (DH)
141 5th St (07663-6125)
PHONE..................................201 909-3400
Robert Donnahoo, *President*
Mike Ross, *Manager*
▼ EMP: 200 EST: 1995
SALES (est): 56.5MM
SALES (corp-wide): 15.6MM **Privately Held**
WEB: www.paradigmpackaging.com
SIC: 3053 Packing materials
HQ: Comar, Llc
220 Laurel Rd Ste 201
Voorhees NJ 08043
856 692-6100

(G-9669)
PETER THOMAS ROTH LABS LLC
45 Mayhill St (07663-5301)
PHONE..................................201 329-9100
June Jacobs, *Manager*
EMP: 110
SALES (corp-wide): 28.2MM **Privately Held**
SIC: 2844 Cosmetic preparations

G
E
O
G
R
A
P
H
I
C

PA: Peter Thomas Roth Labs Llc
460 Park Ave Fl 16
New York NY 10022
212 581-5800

(G-9670)
PRIME INGREDIENTS INC
280 N Midland Ave Ste 340 (07663-5721)
PHONE....................201 791-6655
James Walsh, *President*
Tim Walsh, *Prdtn Mgr*
Walter Maurer, *Accounts Mgr*
Robin Tecchio, *Sales Staff*
Sandy Williams, *Sales Associate*
EMP: 9
SQ FT: 17,000
SALES (est): 1.3MM **Privately Held**
WEB: www.primeingredients.com
SIC: 2087 Food colorings; extracts, flavoring

(G-9671)
RFS COMMERCIAL INC
Also Called: Master Craft Interiors
280 N Midland Ave Bldg M (07663-5708)
PHONE....................201 796-0006
Anthony Pizzuto, *President*
Robert Pizzuto, *VP Opers*
EMP: 15
SQ FT: 7,500
SALES: 6.8MM **Privately Held**
WEB: www.rugandfloors.com
SIC: 5021 2591 1771 2531 Furniture;
window shades; concrete repair; flooring
contractor; school furniture; library furniture

(G-9672)
RIBBLE COMPANY INC
Also Called: Saddle Brook Controls
280 N Midland Ave Ste 380 (07663-5719)
P.O. Box 881 (07663-0881)
PHONE....................201 475-1812
Gary F Laurita, *President*
Mark Bastinck, *Vice Pres*
Alan Kowal, *Vice Pres*
Michael Montalbano, *Treasurer*
EMP: 19 **EST:** 1933
SQ FT: 10,700
SALES (est): 18MM **Privately Held**
WEB: www.saddlebrookcontrols.com
SIC: 5065 3823 Electronic parts & equipment; computer interface equipment for industrial process control

(G-9673)
RISING HEALTH LLC
Park 80 W Plz (07663)
PHONE....................201 961-9000
Walter Kaczmarek, *COO*
Steven S Rogers, *Officer*
EMP: 50 **EST:** 2016
SQ FT: 4,000
SALES (est): 2.4MM
SALES (corp-wide): 12MM **Privately Held**
SIC: 2834 5122 Pharmaceutical preparations; drugs & drug proprietaries
HQ: Rising Pharmaceuticals, Inc.
250 Pehle Ave Ste 601
Saddle Brook NJ 07663

(G-9674)
RISING PHARMA HOLDINGS INC (PA)
250 Pehle Ave Ste 601 (07663-5832)
PHONE....................201 961-9000
Venkateswarlu Jasti, *CEO*
EMP: 2
SALES (est): 12MM **Privately Held**
SIC: 2834 5122 Pharmaceutical preparations; drugs & drug proprietaries

(G-9675)
RISING PHARMACEUTICALS INC (HQ)
250 Pehle Ave Ste 601 (07663-5832)
PHONE....................201 961-9000
Albert L Eilender, *CEO*
Douglas Roth, *CFO*
▲ **EMP:** 50
SALES (est): 12MM **Privately Held**
SIC: 2834 5122 Pharmaceutical preparations; drugs & drug proprietaries

PA: Rising Pharma Holdings, Inc.
250 Pehle Ave Ste 601
Saddle Brook NJ 07663
201 961-9000

(G-9676)
SALERNOS KITCHEN CABINETS
Also Called: Salerno's Custom Cabinetry
599 N Midland Ave (07663-5505)
PHONE....................201 794-1990
Luciano Salerno, *President*
Peter Salerno, *Vice Pres*
Ben Salerno, *Manager*
EMP: 32
SQ FT: 4,000
SALES (est): 4.3MM **Privately Held**
WEB: www.salernos.com
SIC: 2511 2434 2431 Wood household
furniture; wood kitchen cabinets; millwork

(G-9677)
SCHEINERT & SONS INC
Also Called: Sidney Scheinert & Son
404 N Midland Ave 2 (07663-5707)
P.O. Box 527 (07663-0527)
PHONE....................201 791-4600
Richard P Scheinert, *Owner*
Irwin Scheinert, *Vice Pres*
Margaret Scheinert, *Treasurer*
Barbara Scheinert, *Admin Sec*
▲ **EMP:** 25 **EST:** 1902
SQ FT: 75,000
SALES (est): 6.1MM **Privately Held**
SIC: 5085 5072 3452 Fasteners, industrial: nuts, bolts, screws, etc.; bolts, nuts & screws; bolts, nuts, rivets & washers

(G-9678)
SCODIX INC
250 Pehle Ave Ste 101 (07663-5833)
PHONE....................855 726-3491
Kobi Bar, *CEO*
Roy Porat, *CEO*
Yaron Hermeche, *CFO*
Eli Grinberg, *CTO*
◆ **EMP:** 11
SALES (est): 78K **Privately Held**
SIC: 2752 Commercial printing, offset
PA: Scodix Ltd
13 Amal
Rosh Haayin
390 333-71

(G-9679)
SEALED AIR CORPORATION
301 Mayhill St (07663-5303)
PHONE....................201 712-7000
Richard Shanley, *Principal*
Ed Ackershoek, *Opers Mgr*
Simon Harper, *Mfg Mgr*
Luis Alcocer, *Purchasing*
Jay Liang, *Engineer*
EMP: 150
SALES (corp-wide): 4.7B **Publicly Held**
WEB: www.sealedair.com
SIC: 3086 Packaging & shipping materials,
foamed plastic
PA: Sealed Air Corporation
2415 Cascade Pointe Blvd
Charlotte NC 28208
980 221-3235

(G-9680)
SEALED AIR CORPORATION
301 Mayhill St (07663-5303)
PHONE....................973 890-4735
EMP: 75
SALES (corp-wide): 4.7B **Publicly Held**
WEB: www.sealedair.com
SIC: 3086 Packaging & shipping materials,
foamed plastic
PA: Sealed Air Corporation
2415 Cascade Pointe Blvd
Charlotte NC 28208
980 221-3235

(G-9681)
SKW QUAB CHEMICALS INC
250 Pehle Ave Ste 403 (07663-5832)
PHONE....................201 556-0300
Harold Feigenbaum, *President*
Karen Oneill, *Marketing Staff*
Thi M Thuy, *Manager*
Tai H Mak, *Director*
Karen O'Neill, *Director*
◆ **EMP:** 19

SQ FT: 2,700
SALES (est): 22.5MM
SALES (corp-wide): 177.9K **Privately
Held**
SIC: 2899 Chemical preparations
HQ: Skw Stahl-Metallurgie Holding Gmbh
Prinzregentenstr. 68
Munchen 81675
895 998-9230

(G-9682)
SYMRISE INC
250 Pehle Ave Ste 207 (07663-5832)
PHONE....................201 288-3200
John Cassidy, *Branch Mgr*
EMP: 5
SALES (corp-wide): 3.6B **Privately Held**
SIC: 2869 Perfume materials, synthetic;
flavors or flavoring materials, synthetic
HQ: Symrise Inc.
300 North St
Teterboro NJ 07608
201 288-3200

(G-9683)
TE WIRE & CABLE LLC
Also Called: PMC Thermocouple Division
107 5th St (07663-6125)
PHONE....................201 845-9400
Robert M Canny, *Principal*
Pat Durkin, *Vice Pres*
Michael Mescall, *CFO*
◆ **EMP:** 120
SQ FT: 84,000
SALES: 48MM
SALES (corp-wide): 225.3B **Publicly
Held**
SIC: 3357 Nonferrous wiredrawing & insulating
HQ: Marmon Holdings, Inc.
181 W Madison St Ste 2600
Chicago IL 60602
312 372-9500

(G-9684)
TOPPAN VINTAGE INC
109 5th St (07663-6157)
PHONE....................201 226-9220
David Kaye, *Vice Pres*
Bob Cesarano, *Branch Mgr*
EMP: 35 **Privately Held**
SIC: 8732 2759 Merger, acquisition & reorganization research; commercial printing; financial note & certificate printing & engraving; security certificates: engraved
HQ: Toppan Merrill Usa Inc.
747 3rd Ave Fl 7
New York NY 10017
212 596-7747

(G-9685)
UNILUX INC (HQ)
59 5th St (07663-6113)
PHONE....................201 712-1266
Steven A Hirsh, *Ch of Bd*
Steven Hirsh, *Ch of Bd*
Michael P Simonis, *President*
John Banek, *Vice Pres*
Art Mario, *Engineer*
▼ **EMP:** 28 **EST:** 1972
SQ FT: 20,000
SALES (est): 6.6MM
SALES (corp-wide): 3.6MM **Privately
Held**
WEB: www.unilux.com
SIC: 3648 Lighting equipment
PA: Astro Communications, Inc
630 Dundee Rd Ste 345
Northbrook IL
847 236-4121

(G-9686)
VIZIFLEX SEELS INC
406 N Midland Ave (07663-5707)
PHONE....................201 488-3446
Sergio Gonzalez, *President*
Devin Gonzalez, *Vice Pres*
EMP: 15
SQ FT: 20,000
SALES (est): 3MM **Privately Held**
WEB: www.viziflex.com
SIC: 3053 Gaskets, packing & sealing devices

(G-9687)
WESTLOCK CONTROLS CORPORATION (HQ)
280 N Midland Ave Ste 232 (07663-5717)
PHONE....................201 794-7650
Ronald Bozzo, *President*
Leo Minervini, *Vice Pres*
Joel Wittkamp, *Purch Mgr*
Alan Kerstner, *Engineer*
Ron Bozzo, *VP Finance*
▲ **EMP:** 120
SQ FT: 46,000
SALES (est): 35.6MM
SALES (corp-wide): 3.3B **Publicly Held**
WEB: www.westlockcontrols.com
SIC: 3492 Control valves, fluid power: hydraulic & pneumatic
PA: Crane Co.
100 1st Stamford Pl # 300
Stamford CT 06902
203 363-7300

(G-9688)
WISCO PROMO & UNIFORM INC
160 Us Highway 46 (07663-6228)
PHONE....................973 767-2022
Charlotte Yeon, *CEO*
▲ **EMP:** 5
SALES: 928.2K **Privately Held**
SIC: 2759 Screen printing

(G-9689)
ZIRTI LLC
296 Midland Ave Ste A (07663-6348)
PHONE....................201 509-8404
Gerald Sugerman, *Mng Member*
Jerald Sugarman,
EMP: 1
SQ FT: 35,000
SALES (est): 9.8MM **Privately Held**
SIC: 3089 Toilets, portable chemical: plastic

Saddle River
Bergen County

(G-9690)
ALLIANCE CORRUGATED BOX INC
10 E Saddle River Rd (07458-3205)
P.O. Box 1471, Secaucus (07096-1471)
PHONE....................877 525-5269
Eric Levine, *President*
EMP: 20 **EST:** 2015
SQ FT: 110,000
SALES (est): 333.8K **Privately Held**
SIC: 2653 5113 3086 5199 Boxes, corrugated: made from purchased materials; corrugated & solid fiber boxes; packaging & shipping materials, foamed plastic; packaging materials

(G-9691)
FUJIFILM MED SYSTEMS USA INC
155 Clearwater Rd (07458)
PHONE....................973 686-2631
EMP: 10 **Privately Held**
SIC: 3861 Photographic equipment & supplies
HQ: Fujifilm Medical Systems U.S.A., Inc.
81 Hartwell Ave Ste 300
Lexington MA 02421
203 324-2000

Salem
Salem County

(G-9692)
BLACKHAWK CRE CORPORATION (PA)
25 New Market St (08079)
PHONE....................856 887-0162
Don Zappley, *President*
Robert Keonopka, *Vice Pres*
John Scott, *CFO*
EMP: 10
SQ FT: 12,000

SALES: 5.6MM **Privately Held**
SIC: 3444 5013 3613 Sheet metalwork; automotive servicing equipment; switchgear & switchboard apparatus

(G-9693)
D AND M DISCOUNT FUELS
383 E Broadway (08079-1146)
PHONE................................856 935-0919
Dean Wood, *Principal*
EMP: 7 EST: 2011
SALES (est): 739.8K **Privately Held**
SIC: 2869 Fuels

(G-9694)
MANNINGTON MILLS INC (PA)
Also Called: Mannington Rsilient Floors Div
75 Mannington Mills Rd (08079-2009)
P.O. Box 30 (08079-0030)
PHONE................................856 935-3000
Russel Grizzel, *CEO*
Keith S Campbell, *Ch of Bd*
Dennis Bradway, *General Mgr*
Kim Speakman, *General Mgr*
Marty Adams, *District Mgr*
◆ EMP: 600 EST: 1915
SQ FT: 1,000,000
SALES (est): 722.8MM **Privately Held**
WEB: www.mannington.com
SIC: 3996 3253 2273 2435 Hard surface floor coverings; wall tile, ceramic; floor tile, ceramic; rugs, tufted; carpets, hand & machine made; veneer stock, hardwood; hardwood plywood, prefinished; panels, hardwood plywood; plywood, hardwood or hardwood faced

(G-9695)
MEDIANEWS GROUP INC
Also Called: Evening News, The
93 5th St (08079-1041)
P.O. Box 596, Bridgeton (08302-0490)
PHONE................................856 451-1000
Frank Gargano, *President*
Tina Rutledge, *Human Res Dir*
EMP: 85
SALES (corp-wide): 4.2B **Privately Held**
SIC: 2711 Newspapers: publishing only, not printed on site
HQ: Medianews Group, Inc.
101 W Colfax Ave Ste 1100
Denver CO 80202

(G-9696)
PRINTERS OF SALEM COUNTY LLC
38 Market St (08079-1902)
PHONE................................856 935-5032
Eric Pankok, *Owner*
EMP: 5
SALES (est): 622.8K **Privately Held**
SIC: 2759 Commercial printing

(G-9697)
SALEM PACKING CO
705 Salem Quinton Rd (08079-1288)
PHONE................................856 878-0002
Josephine Bonaccurso, *President*
Samuel Bonaccurso, *Vice Pres*
Anthony Bonaccurso, *Manager*
EMP: 20 EST: 1945
SQ FT: 3,000
SALES (est): 2.7MM **Privately Held**
SIC: 2011 Meat packing plants

(G-9698)
WIRE-PRO INC (DH)
Also Called: Wpi-Salem Division
90 W Broadway (08079-1301)
PHONE................................856 935-7560
Henry J Barbera, *President*
Gerald Eddis, *President*
Robert A Barbera, *Vice Pres*
Robert Oldstein, *CFO*
◆ EMP: 140 EST: 1971
SQ FT: 7,500
SALES (est): 43.8MM **Privately Held**
WEB: www.wpi-interconnect.com
SIC: 3678 3679 Electronic connectors; harness assemblies for electronic use: wire or cable
HQ: Cooper Crouse-Hinds, Llc
1201 Wolf St
Syracuse NY 13208
315 477-7000

Sandyston
Sussex County

(G-9699)
CUSTOM DOCKS INC
Also Called: Bob's Custom Docks
234 Us Highway 206 N (07826-8000)
PHONE................................973 948-3732
Robert Putera, *President*
EMP: 10
SQ FT: 12,000
SALES (est): 896.5K **Privately Held**
WEB: www.customdocks.net
SIC: 3999 5551 Dock equipment & supplies, industrial; boat dealers

---

Sayreville
Middlesex County

(G-9700)
AKAY USA LLC
500 Hartle St (08872-2770)
PHONE................................732 254-7177
Rajive Joseph, *General Mgr*
Shaji Vilson,
▲ EMP: 2
SALES: 8.5MM **Privately Held**
SIC: 2087 Powders, flavoring (except drink)

(G-9701)
ALL NATURAL PRODUCTS
4000 Bordentown Ave # 20 (08872-2752)
PHONE................................212 391-2870
Gene Davidovich, *Owner*
EMP: 10
SALES: 950K **Privately Held**
SIC: 2051 Bread, cake & related products

(G-9702)
ALZO INTERNATIONAL INC
650 Jernee Mill Rd (08872-1755)
PHONE................................732 254-1901
Albert Zofchak, *President*
Joyce Zofchak, *Vice Pres*
◆ EMP: 30
SQ FT: 71,000
SALES (est): 12.3MM **Privately Held**
WEB: www.alzointernational.com
SIC: 2869 2821 Industrial organic chemicals; amines, acids, salts, esters; ester gum

(G-9703)
BENCHMARK SCIENTIFIC INC
2600a Main St (08872-1462)
P.O. Box 709, Edison (08818-0709)
PHONE................................908 769-5555
Tony Damsia, *President*
◆ EMP: 50
SALES: 6.1MM **Privately Held**
SIC: 3821 Autoclaves, laboratory

(G-9704)
CHARIOT COURIER & TRANS SVCS
7 Parr Dr (08872-1084)
PHONE................................888 532-9125
Tina Marshall, *VP Opers*
Keith Marshall,
EMP: 10
SALES (est): 318.2K **Privately Held**
SIC: 4213 2759 7389 Automobiles, transport & delivery; contract haulers; heavy hauling; schedules, transportation: printing;

(G-9705)
CHEMO DYNAMICS INC
3 Crossman Rd S (08872-1404)
PHONE................................732 721-4700
Subir Chakraborty, *President*
Sunder N Bharathi, *Vice Pres*
Tao Jiang, *Research*
EMP: 10
SQ FT: 16,000
SALES (est): 1.9MM **Privately Held**
WEB: www.chemodynamics.com
SIC: 2869 8734 Perfumes, flavorings & food additives; food testing service

(G-9706)
COAST TO COAST LEA & VINYL INC (PA)
1 Crossman Rd S (08872-1488)
PHONE................................732 525-8877
Pamela Ross, *President*
Michael Ross, *Vice Pres*
▲ EMP: 9
SQ FT: 10,000
SALES (est): 2MM **Privately Held**
WEB: www.coast2coastleather.com
SIC: 3111 Mechanical leather

(G-9707)
CRA-Z WORKS CO INC
Also Called: East Coast Custom
242 Main St (08872-1190)
PHONE................................732 390-8238
Benjamin Pendleton, *President*
EMP: 6
SQ FT: 1,000
SALES (est): 849.8K **Privately Held**
SIC: 2329 5699 Athletic (warmup, sweat & jogging) suits: men's & boys'; sports apparel

(G-9708)
DMJ AND ASSOCIATES INC
27 William St (08872-1144)
PHONE................................732 613-7867
Daniel Vitti, *President*
James Morris, *Vice Pres*
EMP: 20
SALES (est): 2.2MM **Privately Held**
SIC: 4841 3663 1623 1711 Direct broadcast satellite services (DBS); multipoint distribution systems services (MDS); satellite master antenna systems services (SMATV); television broadcasting & communications equipment; water & sewer line construction; plumbing, heating, airconditioning contractors; installing building equipment; electrical apparatus & equipment; electronic wire & cable; electrical construction materials

(G-9709)
GREATER MEDIA NEWSPAPERS
201 Hartle St Ste B (08872-1883)
PHONE................................732 254-7004
Kevin Whitman, *Branch Mgr*
EMP: 4
SALES (corp-wide): 257.4MM **Publicly Held**
SIC: 2711 Newspapers, publishing & printing
HQ: Greater Media Newspapers
198 Us Highway 9 Ste 100
Englishtown NJ 07726
732 358-5200

(G-9710)
HOMESPUN GLOBAL LLC
4000 Bordentown Ave # 18 (08872-2752)
PHONE................................917 674-9684
Neeraj Jalan,
Manoj Purohit,
Rajat Srivastava,
EMP: 5
SQ FT: 1,000
SALES (est): 15MM **Privately Held**
SIC: 5719 5023 2211 Bedding (sheets, blankets, spreads & pillows); towels; sheets, textile; linens & towels; towels; sheets & sheetings, cotton

(G-9711)
INTEGRITY IRONWORKS CORP
33 Brookside Ave (08872-1236)
P.O. Box 129 (08871-0129)
PHONE................................732 254-2200
James Zagata, *President*
EMP: 5
SALES (est): 1MM **Privately Held**
SIC: 3441 Fabricated structural metal

(G-9712)
JAY FRANCO & SONS INC
115 Kennedy Dr (08872-1459)
PHONE................................732 721-0022
Shawn Glyn, *Vice Pres*
Paul Weldler, *VP Opers*
Hardat Rambaran, *Controller*
Sam Sutton, *Branch Mgr*
EMP: 100

SALES (corp-wide): 147.1MM **Privately Held**
SIC: 2211 5023 Towels & toweling, cotton; towels
PA: Jay Franco & Sons, Inc.
295 5th Ave Ste 312
New York NY 10016
212 679-3022

(G-9713)
KELKEN-GOLD INC
Also Called: Kelken Construction Systems
550 Hartle St Ste C (08872-2771)
PHONE................................732 416-6730
Ken Ginsky, *President*
Richard Gonzalez, *Vice Pres*
Peter Coutin, *Treasurer*
EMP: 5
SQ FT: 4,000
SALES: 1.2MM **Privately Held**
WEB: www.kelken.com
SIC: 3272 Concrete products

(G-9714)
LCI GRAPHICS INC
2400 Main St Ste 8 (08872-1474)
PHONE................................973 893-2913
Dan Seratelli Sr, *President*
Dan Seratelli Jr, *Exec VP*
Danielle Ross, *Manager*
EMP: 16
SQ FT: 5,000
SALES (est): 1.6MM **Privately Held**
WEB: www.lcigraphics.com
SIC: 2752 Commercial printing, offset

(G-9715)
LEETS STEEL INC
495 Raritan St (08872-1466)
PHONE................................917 416-7977
John Miranda, *President*
EMP: 6
SALES (est): 269.8K **Privately Held**
SIC: 3446 3441 1791 Ornamental metalwork; fabricated structural metal; structural steel erection

(G-9716)
LIVING FASHIONS LLC
602 Hartle St (08872)
PHONE................................732 626-5200
Yousuf Admani, *CEO*
EMP: 10
SALES (est): 383.1K **Privately Held**
SIC: 5023 2392 2252 Linens & towels; table mats, plastic & textile; men's, boys' & girls' hosiery

(G-9717)
LUNAR AUDIO VIDEO LLC (PA)
701 Hartle St Unit 703 (08872-2774)
P.O. Box 58, Pequannock (07440-0058)
PHONE................................973 233-7700
Chris Young, *Owner*
John Remelgado, *Project Mgr*
▲ EMP: 8
SALES: 1.1MM **Privately Held**
SIC: 3651 Household audio & video equipment

(G-9718)
MACTEC PACKAGING TECH LLC
550 Hartle St Ste A (08872-2771)
PHONE................................732 343-1607
Michael Castaldo, *Mng Member*
Daniel Luna,
EMP: 8
SQ FT: 5,000
SALES: 2.7MM **Privately Held**
SIC: 3565 Packaging machinery

(G-9719)
MAIN STREET AUTO & FUEL LLC
227 Main St (08872-1171)
PHONE................................732 238-0044
▲ EMP: 7
SALES (est): 798.5K **Privately Held**
SIC: 2869 Mfg Industrial Organic Chemicals

(G-9720)
OEG BUILDING MATERIALS INC
6001 Bordentown Ave (08872-2781)
PHONE................................732 667-3636
Oscar Rosner, *President*

GEOGRAPHIC

Asher Engel, *CFO*
Joel Lefkowitz, *VP Sales*
Yankee Eigner, *Officer*
Max Rydzewski, *Officer*
EMP: 25
SALES (est): 17.3MM **Privately Held**
SIC: 3444 3441 Sheet metalwork; fabricated structural metal

(G-9721)
PHARMETIC MFG COMPANY LLC
650 Jernee Mill Rd (08872-1755)
PHONE..............................732 254-1901
Albert A Zofchak,
Joyce Zofchak,
▲ **EMP:** 6
SALES (est): 850K **Privately Held**
SIC: 2869 Perfume materials, synthetic

(G-9722)
SABERT CORPORATION (PA)
2288 Main St (08872-1476)
PHONE..............................800 722-3781
Albert Salama, *President*
Robert Inlow, *Vice Pres*
Scott Carnie, *Warehouse Mgr*
Cindy Peterson, *Warehouse Mgr*
Cheryl Brown, *Purch Mgr*
◆ **EMP:** 200
SQ FT: 250,000
SALES (est): 195.6MM **Privately Held**
WEB: www.sabert.com
SIC: 3089 Trays, plastic

(G-9723)
SABERT CORPORATION
879 Main St Ste 899 (08872-1463)
PHONE..............................732 721-5544
Christian Gutierrez, *Vice Pres*
Michael Crockett, *Senior Buyer*
Linda Elsherbiny, *Engineer*
Tim Love, *VP Sales*
Sarah Boehnlein, *Sales Staff*
EMP: 42
SALES (corp-wide): 195.6MM **Privately Held**
SIC: 3089 Trays, plastic; plates, plastic; food casings, plastic
PA: Sabert Corporation
2288 Main St
Sayreville NJ 08872
800 722-3781

(G-9724)
STEIMLING & SON INC
7 Nickel Ave (08872-1717)
P.O. Box 283 (08871-0283)
PHONE..............................732 613-1550
Linda Steimling, *President*
EMP: 11
SQ FT: 15,000
SALES (est): 1.8MM **Privately Held**
SIC: 3599 Machine shop, jobbing & repair

(G-9725)
TMS INTERNATIONAL LLC
1 Crossman Rd N (08872-1402)
PHONE..............................732 721-7477
EMP: 5 **Privately Held**
SIC: 3312 Blast furnaces & steel mills
HQ: Tms International, Llc
12 Monongahela Ave
Glassport PA 15045
412 678-6141

(G-9726)
TURN-KEY TECHNOLOGIES INC
2400 Main St Ste 11 (08872-1474)
PHONE..............................732 553-9100
Craig Badrick, *President*
Stephen Murray, *Vice Pres*
Jay Prevost, *Engineer*
Robert Elgart, *Regl Sales Mgr*
Steve Badrick, *Exec Dir*
EMP: 18
SQ FT: 6,000
SALES (est): 22.4MM **Privately Held**
WEB: www.turn-keytechnologies.com
SIC: 5065 7622 3663 Paging & signaling equipment; radio repair shop; radio & TV communications equipment

(G-9727)
ZOOMESSENCE INC
550 Hartle St Ste B (08872-2771)
PHONE..............................732 416-6638
Bruce Leskanic, *Branch Mgr*
EMP: 7
SALES (corp-wide): 5.4MM **Privately Held**
SIC: 2899 2869 Chemical preparations; flavors or flavoring materials, synthetic
PA: Zoomessence, Inc.
1131 Victory Pl
Hebron KY 41048
859 534-5974

Scotch Plains
Union County

(G-9728)
ALL ENVMTL & TANK SVCS LLC
2560 Us Highway 22 346 (07076-1529)
PHONE..............................908 755-2962
EMP: 13
SALES (est): 2.4MM **Privately Held**
SIC: 3795 Tanks & tank components

(G-9729)
ANDERSON PUBLISHING LTD
180 Glenside Ave (07076-1518)
PHONE..............................908 301-1995
Oliver Anderson, *President*
Brenda Anderson, *Vice Pres*
Michael T Hearney, *Controller*
EMP: 6
SALES (est): 700K **Privately Held**
WEB: www.appliedradiology.com
SIC: 2721 Trade journals: publishing only, not printed on site

(G-9730)
ART DMENSIONS
1998 Us Highway 22 (07076-1014)
PHONE..............................908 322-8488
Bernice Pulido, *Owner*
EMP: 8
SALES (est): 847.4K **Privately Held**
WEB: www.artdmensions.com
SIC: 3993 Signs, not made in custom sign painting shops

(G-9731)
BE CU MANUFACTURING CO INC (PA)
2347 Beryllium Rd (07076-2194)
P.O. Box 429 (07076-0429)
PHONE..............................908 233-3342
Stephan Hoeckele, *President*
EMP: 25 EST: 1942
SQ FT: 18,000
SALES (est): 2.2MM **Privately Held**
SIC: 3469 Metal stampings

(G-9732)
GLEICHER MANUFACTURING CORP
851 Jerusalem Rd (07076-2039)
PHONE..............................908 233-2211
Charles Gleicher, *President*
Chick Gleicher, *President*
Maxine Gleicher, *Corp Secy*
EMP: 25 EST: 1937
SQ FT: 22,000
SALES (est): 7.9MM **Privately Held**
WEB: www.gleicher.com
SIC: 2675 2672 2671 2295 Die-cut paper & board; coated & laminated paper; packaging paper & plastics film, coated & laminated; coated fabrics, not rubberized

(G-9733)
HNT INDUSTRIES INC
Also Called: Westbrook Industries
233 Union Ave (07076-1254)
PHONE..............................908 322-0414
Kathleen Holmes, *CEO*
Mike Tatsch, *President*
EMP: 5 EST: 1945
SQ FT: 14,000
SALES (est): 500K **Privately Held**
SIC: 3469 Ornamental metal stampings

(G-9734)
HOBBY BLADE SPECIALTY INC
725 Jerusalem Rd (07076-2029)
PHONE..............................908 317-9306
Mike Torres, *President*
Ada Falcon, *Vice Pres*
EMP: 4
SALES (est): 505K **Privately Held**
SIC: 3421 Razor blades & razors

(G-9735)
IZZO ENTERPRISES INC
Also Called: PM Pool Service
2006 Route 22 (07076-1014)
PHONE..............................908 845-8200
Alfred Izzo, *President*
EMP: 25
SQ FT: 9,500
SALES (est): 82.1K **Privately Held**
SIC: 5999 3648 1799 Swimming pool chemicals, equipment & supplies; swimming pool lighting fixtures; swimming pool construction

(G-9736)
JEIVEN PHRM CONSULTING INC
6 Jacobs Ln (07076-4707)
PHONE..............................908 233-4508
Martin L Jeiven, *President*
Ash Sharma, *Vice Pres*
Nancy Levine, *Consultant*
Gregory Kushla, *Exec Dir*
Arvind Bhandari, *Director*
EMP: 9
SALES (est): 1.6MM **Privately Held**
WEB: www.jeiven.com
SIC: 2834 Pharmaceutical preparations

(G-9737)
NATURES BEAUTY MARBLE & GRAN
2476 Plainfield Ave (07076-2057)
PHONE..............................908 233-5300
Thelma Carinhas, *Owner*
EMP: 12
SALES (est): 1.1MM **Privately Held**
SIC: 5032 3281 Granite building stone; marble building stone; table tops, marble

(G-9738)
NEW SATELLITE NETWORK LLC
1942 Sunset Pl (07076-1207)
PHONE..............................908 922-0967
Vladimir Makarenko, *Principal*
EMP: 4
SALES (est): 165.3K **Privately Held**
SIC: 2711 Newspapers

(G-9739)
SALESCASTER DISPLAYS CORP
2095 Portland Ave (07076-1849)
P.O. Box 247 (07076-0247)
PHONE..............................908 322-3046
Dennis Tort, *President*
Mark Tort, *Vice Pres*
EMP: 5 EST: 1950
SQ FT: 10,000
SALES (est): 640K **Privately Held**
WEB: www.salescaster.com
SIC: 5046 3577 5063 Display equipment, except refrigerated; computer peripheral equipment; signaling equipment, electrical

(G-9740)
SECORD INC
1812 Front St (07076-1103)
PHONE..............................908 754-2147
Ria Williams, *President*
EMP: 11
SALES (est): 1.2MM **Privately Held**
SIC: 2834 Pharmaceutical preparations

(G-9741)
SHOOTING STAR INC
2500 Plainfield Ave (07076-2057)
PHONE..............................908 789-2500
Fred Andreae Jr, *President*
EMP: 4
SQ FT: 3,000
SALES (est): 527.4K **Privately Held**
WEB: www.shootingstar.net
SIC: 3999 Coin-operated amusement machines

(G-9742)
STRAHAN CONSULTING GROUP LLC
1290 Martine Ave (07076-2515)
PHONE..............................908 790-0873
Paul Strahan, *Owner*
EMP: 4
SALES (est): 500K **Privately Held**
SIC: 7379 3571 7374 4813 Computer related consulting services; electronic computers; computer graphics service;

(G-9743)
SYNTHETIC SURFACES INC (PA)
2450 Plainfield Ave (07076-2042)
P.O. Box 241 (07076-0241)
PHONE..............................908 233-6803
Norris Legue, *President*
Dorothy Legue, *Vice Pres*
EMP: 4
SQ FT: 1,700
SALES (est): 2MM **Privately Held**
WEB: www.syntheticsurfacesinc.com
SIC: 2891 2851 8742 Adhesives; epoxy adhesives; lacquers, varnishes, enamels & other coatings; industrial consultant

---

Sea Girt
Monmouth County

(G-9744)
140 MAIN STREET CORP
Also Called: Campbell's Pharmacy
2175 Highway 35 Ste 13 (08750-1009)
PHONE..............................732 974-2929
Dennis Campbell, *President*
Susan Baldasare, *Pharmacist*
EMP: 10 EST: 1990
SQ FT: 1,200
SALES (est): 2.1MM **Privately Held**
WEB: www.campbellspharmacy.com
SIC: 2834 5912 Pharmaceutical preparations; drug stores

(G-9745)
ADVANTAGE MOLDING PRODUCTS
2106 Highway 35 (08750-1002)
PHONE..............................732 303-8667
Jacqueline Cassidy, *President*
◆ **EMP:** 12
SQ FT: 5,000
SALES (est): 1.1MM **Privately Held**
SIC: 3089 Molding primary plastic

(G-9746)
NORTH SALES
Also Called: Bossett Sailmakers
11 Chicago Blvd (08750-2110)
PHONE..............................732 528-8899
Henry P Bossett, *Owner*
Ron Laneve, *Sales Associate*
EMP: 5 EST: 1979
SALES (est): 298.9K **Privately Held**
SIC: 2394 Sails: made from purchased materials

(G-9747)
ROCK SOLID WOODWORKING LLC
508 Washington Blvd Apt A (08750-2992)
PHONE..............................732 974-1261
Marie Marrone, *Principal*
EMP: 4
SALES (est): 334.9K **Privately Held**
SIC: 2431 Millwork

Sea Isle City
Cape May County

(G-9748)
LARSEN MARINE SERVICES LLC
333 45th Pl (08243-1847)
P.O. Box 12 (08243-0012)
PHONE..............................609 408-3564
Brian Larsen, *Mng Member*
Andrew Larsen,

EMP: 7
SALES: 800K **Privately Held**
SIC: 2499 Fencing, docks & other outdoor wood structural products

(G-9749)
SEA ISLE ICE CO INC (PA)
230 42nd St (08243-1952)
PHONE.................................609 263-8748
Sue Ann Romano, *Vice Pres*
Joseph A Romano Sr, *Treasurer*
EMP: 25 EST: 1960
SQ FT: 8,000
SALES: 950K **Privately Held**
SIC: 2097 Manufactured ice

Secaucus
Hudson County

(G-9750)
ACME COSMETIC COMPONENTS LLC
80 Seaview Dr Ste 1 (07094-1828)
P.O. Box 449, Woodside NY (11377)
PHONE.................................718 335-3000
Michael Roughton, *President*
David Wood,
▼ EMP: 39
SQ FT: 40,000
SALES (est): 9.3MM **Privately Held**
WEB: www.acmepans.com
SIC: 3469 Stamping metal for the trade

(G-9751)
AXG CORPORATION
700 Plaza Dr Ste 204 (07094-3604)
PHONE.................................212 213-3313
Vince Di Mattia, *President*
EMP: 5
SALES (est): 37.8MM **Privately Held**
SIC: 2542 Office & store showcases & display fixtures

(G-9752)
BEACHCARTS USA
296 Julianne Ter (07094-4013)
PHONE.................................201 319-0091
Lola Camacho, *Prgrmr*
◆ EMP: 4
SALES (est): 266.5K **Privately Held**
SIC: 3949 Sporting & athletic goods

(G-9753)
BIGFLYSPORTS INC
Also Called: Bigflysports Com
60 Metro Way Ste 2 (07094-1913)
PHONE.................................201 653-4414
Chris Maillet, *President*
Marc Weinman, *Mng Member*
Harran Holmes, *Associate*
▲ EMP: 7 EST: 2008
SALES (est): 6.9MM **Privately Held**
SIC: 5941 4783 3999 Team sports equipment; containerization of goods for shipping; barrettes

(G-9754)
BIND-RITE GRAPHICS INC
100 Castle Rd (07094-1602)
P.O. Box 2399 (07096-2399)
PHONE.................................201 863-8100
Alan Mirson, *President*
Elliot Ward, *Vice Pres*
EMP: 35
SQ FT: 47,000
SALES: 6MM **Privately Held**
SIC: 2789 2678 Binding only: books, pamphlets, magazines, etc.; binding & repair of books, magazines & pamphlets; stationery products

(G-9755)
CAMEO CHINA INC
Also Called: Cameo China East
501 Penhorn Ave Ste 12 (07094-2136)
PHONE.................................201 865-7650
Eric Lin, *Manager*
EMP: 5 **Privately Held**
WEB: www.cameochina.com
SIC: 3269 Figures: pottery, china, earthenware & stoneware

PA: Cameo China, Inc.
1938 Chico Ave
South El Monte CA 91733

(G-9756)
CLEVE SHIRTMAKERS INC
200 Meadowlands Pkwy # 2 (07094-2312)
P.O. Box 678, Saddle River (07458-0678)
PHONE.................................201 825-6122
David Stich, *President*
▲ EMP: 5
SALES (est): 390K **Privately Held**
WEB: www.cleveshirt.com
SIC: 2321 2331 Men's & boys' furnishings; women's & misses' blouses & shirts

(G-9757)
COMMAND WEB OFFSET COMPANY INC (PA)
100 Castle Rd (07094-1602)
P.O. Box 2399 (07096-2399)
PHONE.................................201 863-8100
Andrew Merson, *Ch of Bd*
Shirley Whitley, *President*
Paul Frontczak, *Exec VP*
Charles B Gardner, *Exec VP*
Steven Merson, *Vice Pres*
EMP: 136 EST: 1946
SALES (est): 107.3MM **Privately Held**
WEB: www.commandweb.com
SIC: 2732 2752 Books: printing only; lithographing on metal

(G-9758)
CR LAURENCE CO INC
70 Seaview Dr (07094-1807)
PHONE.................................201 770-1077
Peter Ascherl, *Branch Mgr*
EMP: 12
SALES (corp-wide): 30.6B **Privately Held**
WEB: www.crlaurence.com
SIC: 3231 Products of purchased glass
HQ: C. R. Laurence Co., Inc.
2503 E Vernon Ave
Vernon CA 90058
323 588-1281

(G-9759)
CREATIONS BY STEFANO INC
1261 Paterson Plank Rd (07094-3229)
PHONE.................................201 863-8337
Stefano Simone, *President*
EMP: 4
SALES (est): 340K **Privately Held**
SIC: 3911 Jewel settings & mountings, precious metal

(G-9760)
DELTA GALIL USA INC (HQ)
1 Harmon Plz Fl 5 (07094-2800)
PHONE.................................201 902-0055
Isaac Dabah, *CEO*
Colette Mynes, *President*
Noam Lautman, *Chairman*
Marcia Alfaiate, *Business Mgr*
Itzhak Weinstock, *COO*
▲ EMP: 100
SQ FT: 22,000
SALES (est): 476.1MM
SALES (corp-wide): 389.2MM **Privately Held**
SIC: 2341 Women's & children's undergarments; women's & children's nightwear
PA: Delta Galil Industries Ltd.
45 Haeshel
Caesarea 30889
768 177-229

(G-9761)
DESIGNCORE LTD
585 Windsor Dr Ste 1 (07094-2759)
PHONE.................................718 499-0337
Joseph F Ianno, *President*
▲ EMP: 70
SQ FT: 100,000
SALES (est): 14.4MM **Privately Held**
SIC: 2541 2431 2521 Wood partitions & fixtures; interior & ornamental woodwork & trim; wood office furniture

(G-9762)
EMPORIUM LEATHER COMPANY INC
Also Called: Royce Leather
501 Penhorn Ave Ste 9 (07094-2136)
PHONE.................................201 330-7720

Kathy Bauer, *President*
Harold Bauer, *Vice Pres*
Mark Tessler, *Controller*
Jean Saltos, *Cust Mgr*
Maria Izurieta, *Sales Executive*
▲ EMP: 20
SQ FT: 7,500
SALES: 5.3MM **Privately Held**
WEB: www.royceleathergifts.com
SIC: 3199 Equestrian related leather articles

(G-9763)
ESCADA US SUBCO LLC
55 Hartz Way Ste 17 (07094-2415)
PHONE.................................201 865-5200
Monica Arden, *Manager*
EMP: 328 **Privately Held**
SIC: 2339 5399 Service apparel, washable: women's; Army-Navy goods
PA: Escada America Llc
26 Main St
Chatham NJ 07928

(G-9764)
EUROPEAN AMRCN FOODS GROUP INC
425 Route 3 (07094-3737)
P.O. Box 2427 (07096-2427)
PHONE.................................201 583-1101
Antonio R Fasolino, *CEO*
EMP: 265
SALES (corp-wide): 33.1MM **Privately Held**
SIC: 2099 2079 Pasta, uncooked: packaged with other ingredients; edible oil products, except corn oil
PA: European American Foods Group Company Inc.
698 Kennedy Blvd
Bayonne NJ 07002
201 436-6106

(G-9765)
EVENING JOURNAL ASSOCIATION (HQ)
Also Called: Jersey Journal
1 Harmon Plz Ste 1000 (07094-2806)
PHONE.................................201 653-1000
Samuel Newhouse III, *President*
Daniel Canova, *Editor*
Lois Ditommaso, *Editor*
Steven Newhouse, *Vice Pres*
Agata Slota, *Sales Staff*
▲ EMP: 15
SQ FT: 100,000
SALES (est): 6.1MM
SALES (corp-wide): 1.3B **Privately Held**
WEB: www.jjournal.com
SIC: 2711 Job printing & newspaper publishing combined
PA: Advance Digital Inc.
3100 Harborside Fincl 3
Jersey City NJ 07311
201 459-2808

(G-9766)
FAST-PAK TRADING INC
375 County Ave Ste 2 (07094-2618)
PHONE.................................201 293-4757
Ivanco Ivanovski, *Co-Owner*
Kiro Ivanovski, *Co-Owner*
▲ EMP: 8
SQ FT: 75,000
SALES: 2.5MM **Privately Held**
WEB: www.fastpakstore.com
SIC: 5145 2032 5149 Snack foods; ethnic foods: canned, jarred, etc.; ethnic foods, frozen; health foods

(G-9767)
FH GROUP INTERNATIONAL INC
265 Secaucus Rd (07094-2117)
PHONE.................................201 210-2426
Jin Hao, *Vice Pres*
Samantha Fang, *Vice Pres*
Linda Jiang, *Manager*
▲ EMP: 30
SQ FT: 60,000
SALES (est): 4.3MM **Privately Held**
SIC: 2273 2211 Aircraft & automobile floor coverings; seat cover cloth, automobile: cotton

(G-9768)
FRESHPET INC (PA)
400 Plaza Dr Fl 1 (07094-3605)
P.O. Box 2157 (07096-2157)
PHONE.................................201 520-4000
William B Cyr, *CEO*
Charles A Norris, *Ch of Bd*
Scott Morris, *President*
Stephen Weise, *Exec VP*
Stephen Macchiaverna, *Senior VP*
EMP: 28
SQ FT: 20,000
SALES: 193.2MM **Publicly Held**
SIC: 2047 Dog & cat food

(G-9769)
FUJIKURA GRAPHICS INC
700 Penhorn Ave Ste 2 (07094-2158)
PHONE.................................201 420-5040
Koichi Kanai, *President*
Masahiro Takeda, *Admin Sec*
▲ EMP: 3 EST: 2009
SQ FT: 1,000
SALES: 7.3MM **Privately Held**
SIC: 3861 Printing equipment, photographic

(G-9770)
FURNITURE OF AMERICA NJ
50 Enterprise Ave N (07094-2525)
PHONE.................................201 605-8200
David Lin, *President*
◆ EMP: 36
SQ FT: 250,000
SALES (est): 200MM **Privately Held**
SIC: 5712 2512 Furniture stores; upholstered household furniture

(G-9771)
GAFAS SALES AND CONSULTING INC
114 Sandpiper Ky (07094-2210)
PHONE.................................862 368-5428
Leila Alfonso, *CEO*
EMP: 4
SALES (est): 406K **Privately Held**
SIC: 3851 Eyeglasses, lenses & frames

(G-9772)
GENERAL GLASS INTL CORP
Also Called: GCI
101 Venture Way (07094-1825)
PHONE.................................201 553-1850
Arthur Balik, *Ch of Bd*
Albert S Balik, *Vice Ch Bd*
David D Balik, *President*
Carol Balik, *Vice Pres*
Richard Balik, *Vice Pres*
◆ EMP: 125
SQ FT: 14,000
SALES (est): 8.9MM **Privately Held**
WEB: www.generalglass.com
SIC: 3211 3231 5039 Flat glass; mirrored glass; glass construction materials

(G-9773)
GENERAL TOOLS & INSTRS CO LLC (PA)
75 Seaview Dr (07094-1806)
PHONE.................................212 431-6100
Ralph Mallozzi, *President*
▲ EMP: 41
SQ FT: 40,000
SALES (est): 6.9MM **Privately Held**
WEB: www.generaltools.com
SIC: 3423 Hand & edge tools

(G-9774)
GENERAL TOOLS MFG CO LLC
75 Seaview Dr (07094-1806)
PHONE.................................201 770-1380
Gerry Weinstein, *Chairman*
▲ EMP: 6
SALES (est): 364K **Privately Held**
SIC: 3999 Manufacturing industries

(G-9775)
GOLDEN SEASON FASHION USA INC
Also Called: Dons Collection
555 Secaucus Rd Ste 1 (07094-2579)
PHONE.................................201 552-2088
Samuel Dong, *President*
Karry Zhang, *Vice Pres*
▲ EMP: 10

SQ FT: 1,800
SALES (est): 1.3MM **Privately Held**
WEB: www.gsfashion.com
SIC: 2339 Women's & misses' outerwear

(G-9776)
GOYA FOODS INC
100 Seaview Dr (07094-1887)
PHONE...................................201 348-4900
Robert Unanue, *President*
EMP: 289
SALES (corp-wide): 1.1B **Privately Held**
SIC: 2023 Canned specialties
PA: Goya Foods, Inc.
350 County Rd
Jersey City NJ 07307
201 348-4900

(G-9777)
GOYA FOODS INC
650 New County Rd (07094-1624)
PHONE...................................201 865-3470
Nelson Perez, *Branch Mgr*
EMP: 50
SALES (corp-wide): 1.1B **Privately Held**
SIC: 2032 Beans & bean sprouts, canned,
jarred, etc.; beans, baked with meat:
packaged in cans, jars, etc.
PA: Goya Foods, Inc.
350 County Rd
Jersey City NJ 07307
201 348-4900

(G-9778)
GRAMERCY PRODUCTS
INCORPORATED
600 Mdwlands Pkwy Ste 131 (07094-1637)
PHONE...................................212 868-2559
Rishi Gupta, *CEO*
Daniel R Troiano, *President*
▲ **EMP:** 20 **EST:** 2013
SALES: 3MM **Privately Held**
SIC: 3999 Pet supplies

(G-9779)
GREEN DISTRIBUTION LLC
565 Windsor Dr (07094-2716)
PHONE...................................201 293-4381
Robert Butters, *CEO*
◆ **EMP:** 85
SQ FT: 52,000
SALES (est): 14.3MM **Privately Held**
SIC: 2211 2396 5131 Apparel & outer-
wear fabrics, cotton; apparel findings &
trimmings; trimmings, apparel
PA: Falfurrias Capital Partners, L.P.
100 N Tryon St Ste 4100
Charlotte NC 28202

(G-9780)
HARTZ MOUNTAIN
CORPORATION (HQ)
400 Plaza Dr 400 # 400 (07094-3688)
P.O. Box 2488 (07096-2488)
PHONE...................................800 275-1414
Tatsuya Suto, *President*
Gumpei Futagami, *President*
Robert Calderone, *Business Mgr*
Steven Clegg, *Business Mgr*
Charlene Dave, *Business Mgr*
◆ **EMP:** 250 **EST:** 1971
SQ FT: 100,000
SALES (est): 728.9MM **Privately Held**
SIC: 5199 3999 Pet supplies; pet supplies

(G-9781)
HYGRADE BUSINESS GROUP
INC (PA)
30 Seaview Dr (07094-1826)
PHONE...................................800 836-7714
Victor Albetta, *President*
Joseph Molanelli, *COO*
Lewis Murilli, *COO*
Bob Isola, *Vice Pres*
Phil Masiell, *Vice Pres*
EMP: 30
SQ FT: 40,000
SALES: 20MM **Privately Held**
WEB: www.hygradebusiness.com
SIC: 2761 2759 Manifold business forms;
promotional printing

(G-9782)
JACMEL JEWELRY INC
401 Penhorn Ave Ste 1 (07094-2142)
PHONE...................................201 223-0435
Mark Clemente, *Branch Mgr*
EMP: 51
SALES (corp-wide): 90MM **Privately**
Held
SIC: 3961 Costume jewelry
PA: Jacmel Jewelry Inc.
1385 Broadway Fl 8
New York NY 10018
718 349-4300

(G-9783)
JUMP DESIGN GROUP INC
350 Old Secaucus Rd (07094)
PHONE...................................201 558-9191
EMP: 30 **Privately Held**
SIC: 2335 Women's, juniors' & misses'
dresses
PA: Jump Design Group Inc.
1400 Broadway Fl 2
New York NY 10018

(G-9784)
KAPSCH TRAFFICCOM USA INC
300 Lighting Way Ste 302 (07094-3646)
PHONE...................................201 528-9814
Jeff Dalusky, *Manager*
EMP: 16
SALES (corp-wide): 1.4B **Privately Held**
WEB: www.transdyn.com
SIC: 3625 Relays & industrial controls
HQ: Kapsch Trafficcom Usa, Inc.
8201 Greensboro Dr # 1002
Mc Lean VA 22102
703 885-1976

(G-9785)
KASHEE & SONS INC (PA)
600 Meadowlands Pkwy 21b (07094-1633)
PHONE...................................201 867-6900
Kashee Aslam, *President*
▲ **EMP:** 11 **EST:** 2011
SALES (est): 6.7MM **Privately Held**
SIC: 2273 Carpets & rugs

(G-9786)
KEURIG DR PEPPER INC
100 Electric Ave (07094-2616)
PHONE...................................201 832-0695
Mary Pepper, *Branch Mgr*
EMP: 99 **Publicly Held**
SIC: 2086 Soft drinks: packaged in cans,
bottles, etc.
PA: Keurig Dr Pepper Inc.
53 South Ave
Burlington MA 01803

(G-9787)
KYNC DESIGN LLC
701 Penhorn Ave Ste 1 (07094-2132)
PHONE...................................201 552-2067
Mehmet Tutuncu, *CEO*
Devi Shaheed, *President*
Isra Erbas, *Admin Sec*
EMP: 6
SALES (est): 948.4K **Privately Held**
SIC: 2273 5023 2841 2281 Carpets,
hand & machine made; carpets; soap &
other detergents; crochet yarn, spun

(G-9788)
L J LOEFFLER SYSTEMS INC
95 Centre Ave (07094-3250)
PHONE...................................212 924-7597
Jeanette Pioppi, *President*
John Pioppi, *Vice Pres*
Dominick Pioppi, *Treasurer*
EMP: 8 **EST:** 1977
SQ FT: 3,000
SALES: 650K **Privately Held**
SIC: 5065 3669 Intercommunication
equipment, electronic; intercommunica-
tion systems, electric

(G-9789)
LITTLEGIFTS INC
600 Mdwlands Pkwy Ste 131 (07094-1637)
PHONE...................................212 868-2559
Rishi Gupta, *CEO*
Daniel R Troiano, *President*
▲ **EMP:** 10

SALES: 2.5MM **Privately Held**
WEB: www.littlegifts.com
SIC: 3961 3911 3999 Costume jewelry;
jewelry, precious metal; pet supplies

(G-9790)
LYCORED CORP
300 Harmon Meadow Blvd # 440
(07094-3638)
PHONE...................................201 601-0060
EMP: 4
SALES (corp-wide): 64.2B **Privately Held**
SIC: 2023 Dietary supplements, dairy &
non-dairy based
HQ: Lycored Corp.
377 Crane St
Orange NJ 07050
973 882-0322

(G-9791)
MAINETTI AMERICAS INC (PA)
115 Enterprise Ave S (07094-1912)
PHONE...................................201 215-2900
Roberto Peruzzo, *President*
Steve Regino, *Co-President*
Claudia Gutierrez, *Manager*
▲ **EMP:** 4
SALES (est): 12.5MM **Privately Held**
SIC: 2759 3089 Bag, wrapper & seal print-
ing & engraving; clothes hangers, plastic

(G-9792)
MCM PRODUCTS USA INC
500 Plaza Dr Ste 101 (07094-3656)
PHONE...................................646 756-4090
Anthony Dimaso, *CFO*
EMP: 17
SALES (corp-wide): 26.2MM **Privately**
Held
SIC: 3171 3199 3149 Women's handbags
& purses; belt laces, leather; athletic
shoes, except rubber or plastic
PA: Mcm Products Usa Inc.
681 5th Ave Fl 10
New York NY 10022
646 756-4090

(G-9793)
MOOSAVI RUGS INC
Also Called: Moosavi Oriental Rugs
100 Park Plaza Dr 208n (07094-3635)
PHONE...................................201 617-9500
▲ **EMP:** 5
SQ FT: 5,500
SALES (est): 380K **Privately Held**
SIC: 2273 Mfg Carpets/Rugs

(G-9794)
NORTHSTAR TRAVEL MEDIA
LLC (PA)
100 Lighting Way Ste 200 (07094-3681)
PHONE...................................201 902-2000
Tom Kemp, *CEO*
Esther Lew, *Chief*
David Blansfield, *Exec VP*
Janine Bavoso, *Vice Pres*
Lori Cioffi, *Vice Pres*
EMP: 215
SQ FT: 32,000
SALES (est): 272.1MM **Privately Held**
WEB: www.northstartravelmedia.com
SIC: 2721 4789 4724 Magazines: pub-
lishing only, not printed on site; cargo
loading & unloading services; travel agen-
cies

(G-9795)
ORANGEHRM INC
538 Teal Plz (07094-2218)
PHONE...................................914 458-4254
Sujee Saparamadu, *President*
Mark Hudson, *Engineer*
Richie Blackwell, *Sales Staff*
Tina Harris, *Mktg Coord*
Shaun Bradley, *Manager*
EMP: 50
SALES (est): 4.5MM **Privately Held**
SIC: 7372 Prepackaged software

(G-9796)
PENN JERSEY ADVANCE INC
Also Called: Penn Jersey Advance Centl Svcs
1 Harmon Plz Fl 9 (07094-2804)
PHONE...................................201 775-6610
Richard Diamond, *Branch Mgr*
EMP: 100 **Privately Held**

SIC: 2711 Newspapers
PA: Penn Jersey Advance Inc.
18 Centre Sq
Easton PA 18042

(G-9797)
PERFORMANCE ALLOYS &
MATERIALS
462 Dunlin Plz (07094-2202)
P.O. Box 1191 (07096-1191)
PHONE...................................201 865-5268
Tatiana Svyadoz, *President*
Dove Goldman, *Vice Pres*
EMP: 4
SQ FT: 1,000
SALES: 100K **Privately Held**
SIC: 8711 3399 Engineering services;
metal powders, pastes & flakes

(G-9798)
PRG GROUP INC
915 Secaucus Rd (07094-2409)
PHONE...................................201 758-4000
Jeremiah Harris, *Ch of Bd*
Blair Lacorte, *President*
Nicole Scano-Schwiebert, *Exec VP*
Scott Hansen, *CFO*
EMP: 8 **EST:** 1997
SALES (est): 1.1MM **Privately Held**
SIC: 3646 1731 Commercial indusl & insti-
tutional electric lighting fixtures; lighting
contractor

(G-9799)
PRINT BY PREMIER LLC
Also Called: Premier Supplies
525 Windsor Dr (07094-2708)
PHONE...................................212 947-1365
Sheldon Lehman, *Mng Member*
EMP: 5
SALES (est): 1.3MM **Privately Held**
SIC: 2752 Publication printing, lithographic

(G-9800)
PROFORM ACOUSTIC
SURFACES LLC
307 Julianne Ter (07094-4012)
P.O. Box 1363 (07096-1363)
PHONE...................................201 553-9614
EMP: 5
SALES (est): 626.1K **Privately Held**
SIC: 3275 Acoustical plaster, gypsum

(G-9801)
QUEST DIAGNOSTICS
INCORPORATED (PA)
500 Plaza Dr Ste G (07094-3656)
PHONE...................................973 520-2700
Stephen H Rusckowski, *Ch of Bd*
James E Davis, *Exec VP*
Everett V Cunningham, *Senior VP*
Carrie Eglinton Manner, *Senior VP*
Michael E Prevoznik, *Senior VP*
▲ **EMP:** 2800
SALES: 7.5B **Publicly Held**
WEB: www.questdiagnostics.com
SIC: 8071 2835 Testing laboratories; in
vitro & in vivo diagnostic substances

(G-9802)
RANDY HANGERS LLC
115 Enterprise Ave S (07094-1912)
PHONE...................................201 215-2900
Ellen Stein, *Mng Member*
Andy Rupp,
▲ **EMP:** 9 **EST:** 1982
SQ FT: 600,000
SALES: 851.2K
SALES (corp-wide): 12.5MM **Privately**
Held
SIC: 3089 Clothes hangers, plastic
HQ: Mainetti Usa Inc.
300 Mac Ln
Keasbey NJ 08832
201 215-2900

(G-9803)
RELATIONAL SECURITY CORP
Also Called: Relsec
1 Harmon Plz Ste 700 (07094-2803)
PHONE...................................201 875-3456
Vivek Shivananda, *President*
Dawn Gustafson, *Partner*
Christopher Murphey, *Partner*
Andy Cooper, *Principal*

Phillip Woodward, *Principal*
EMP: 42
SQ FT: 3,500
SALES (est): 9.5MM
SALES (corp-wide): 39.1MM **Privately Held**
WEB: www.relsec.com
SIC: 7372 Application computer software
PA: Acl Services Ltd
    980 Howe St Suite 1500
    Vancouver BC V6Z 0
    604 669-4225

(G-9804)
ROSE BRAND WIPERS INC (PA)
Also Called: Rose Brand East
4 Emerson Ln (07094-2504)
P.O. Box 1536 (07096-1536)
PHONE....................201 809-1730
George M Jacobstein, *President*
Bertrand Bob, *General Mgr*
Tina Carlin, *General Mgr*
Rita Shapiro, *Vice Pres*
Tori Oggioni, *Production*
▲ **EMP:** 150 **EST:** 1921
SQ FT: 13,000
SALES (est): 106.4MM **Privately Held**
SIC: 5049 2399 Theatrical equipment &
    supplies; emblems, badges & insignia

(G-9805)
ROSE BRAND WIPERS INC
4 Emerson Ln (07094-2504)
PHONE....................201 770-1441
EMP: 150
SQ FT: 145,000
SALES (est): 13.7MM **Privately Held**
SIC: 2399 Mfg Fabricated Textile Products

(G-9806)
SANDER SALES ENTERPRISES LTD
Also Called: Cozy Home Fashions
200 Seaview Dr Fl 2 (07094-1830)
PHONE....................201 808-6705
Aron Weiss, *President*
Ronald J Aronne, *Controller*
▲ **EMP:** 30
SQ FT: 143,000
SALES (est): 4.9MM **Privately Held**
WEB: www.sandersales.net
SIC: 2299 Linen fabrics

(G-9807)
SARKLI-REPECHAGE LTD
300 Castle Rd (07094-1600)
PHONE....................201 549-4200
Lydia Sarfati, *President*
Val Cooper, *Managing Dir*
David Sarfati, *COO*
Shiri Sarfati, *Vice Pres*
Theresa Zazzera, *Opers Staff*
◆ **EMP:** 55 **EST:** 1980
SQ FT: 50,000
SALES (est): 15MM **Privately Held**
WEB: www.repechage.com
SIC: 2844 Cosmetic preparations

(G-9808)
SCHNEDER ELC BLDNGS AMRCAS INC
210 Meadowlands Pkwy (07094-2311)
PHONE....................201 348-9240
Greg Schumann, *Project Engr*
Daniel Riggle, *Accounts Exec*
Sam Belbina, *Manager*
EMP: 36
SALES (corp-wide): 177.9K **Privately Held**
SIC: 5084 3823 3822 Instruments & control equipment; industrial instrmnts msrmnt display/control process variable; auto controls regulating residntl & coml environmt & applncs
HQ: Schneider Electric Buildings Americas, Inc.
    1650 W Crosby Rd
    Carrollton TX 75006
    972 323-1111

(G-9809)
SCHOLASTIC INC
100 Plaza Dr Fl 4 (07094-3677)
PHONE....................201 633-2400
Carlos Jimenez, *Engineer*
EMP: 35

SALES (corp-wide): 1.6B **Publicly Held**
SIC: 2731 Books: publishing only; textbooks: publishing only, not printed on site
HQ: Scholastic Inc.
    557 Broadway Lbby 1
    New York NY 10012
    212 343-6100

(G-9810)
SCHOLASTIC UK GROUP LLC
Also Called: Scholastic National Field Off
100 Plaza Dr Fl 4 (07094-3677)
PHONE....................201 633-2400
Richard Robinson, *CEO*
Kevin Mc Enery, *President*
David J Walsh, *President*
Andrew Hedden, *Exec VP*
Maureen O'Connell, *Exec VP*
▲ **EMP:** 200
SALES (est): 36.7MM
SALES (corp-wide): 1.6B **Publicly Held**
WEB: www.scholastic.com
SIC: 2721 Magazines: publishing only, not printed on site
PA: Scholastic Corporation
    557 Broadway Lbby 1
    New York NY 10012
    212 343-6100

(G-9811)
SCOTT KAY INC
55 Hartz Way Ste 1 (07094-2425)
PHONE....................201 287-0100
David Minster, *CEO*
Scott Kay, *President*
Jeffrey Simon, *CFO*
Elaine Ye, *Controller*
EMP: 120
SQ FT: 12,000
SALES (est): 15MM **Privately Held**
WEB: www.scottkay.com
SIC: 3911 5944 Jewelry, precious metal; jewelry stores

(G-9812)
SCOTT KAY STERLING LLC
55 Hartz Way Ste 1 (07094-2425)
PHONE....................201 287-0100
Scott Kay, *CEO*
Jeffrey Somon, *COO*
EMP: 9
SQ FT: 4,000
SALES (est): 904K **Privately Held**
SIC: 5094 3911 Jewelry; jewelry, precious metal

(G-9813)
SEKISUI AMERICA CORPORATION (HQ)
Also Called: Voltek Division
333 Meadowlands Pkwy (07094-1804)
PHONE....................201 423-7960
Naofumi Negishi, *President*
Hirmou Mitsui, *Treasurer*
◆ **EMP:** 13
SQ FT: 4,400
SALES (est): 507.5MM **Privately Held**
SIC: 3086 Plastics foam products

(G-9814)
SIGN UP INC
Also Called: Fastsigns
255 State Rt 3 Ste 104a (07094-3857)
PHONE....................201 902-8640
Elizabeth Selbach, *President*
Rose Conklin, *Vice Pres*
EMP: 5
SQ FT: 2,600
SALES (est): 460K **Privately Held**
SIC: 3993 7532 Signs & advertising specialties; truck painting & lettering

(G-9815)
SMITH OPTICS INC
300 Lighting Way Ste 400 (07094-3672)
PHONE....................208 726-4477
Scott Macguffie, *Vice Pres*
EMP: 5 **EST:** 2016
SALES (est): 103K **Privately Held**
SIC: 3851 Ophthalmic goods

(G-9816)
SONATA GRAPHICS INC
Also Called: Minuteman Press
1247 Paterson Plank Rd # 65
(07094-3229)
PHONE....................201 866-0186
Tal Goldgraber, *President*
Brosh Goldgraber, *COO*
EMP: 5
SQ FT: 3,000
SALES (est): 785K **Privately Held**
WEB: www.sonatagraphics.com
SIC: 2752 2741 2789 2791 Commercial printing, lithographic; art copy & poster publishing; bookbinding & related work; typesetting

(G-9817)
SPRINGER SCNCE + BUS MEDIA LLC
333 Mdwlands Pkwy Fl 2 (07094-1814)
PHONE....................201 348-4033
Christian Staral, *Production*
Dennis Looney, *CFO*
Carol Bischoff, *Executive*
Sandy Vizzacchero, *Administration*
EMP: 60
SALES (corp-wide): 1.6B **Privately Held**
SIC: 2721 2731 Trade journals: publishing only, not printed on site; books: publishing only
HQ: Springer Science + Business Media, Llc
    233 Spring St Fl 6
    New York NY 10013
    212 460-1500

(G-9818)
ST JUDE MEDICAL LLC
333 Mdwlands Pkwy Ste 502 (07094-1822)
PHONE....................800 645-5368
Bob Marchetti, *Branch Mgr*
EMP: 43
SALES (corp-wide): 30.5B **Publicly Held**
WEB: www.sjm.com
SIC: 3845 Pacemaker, cardiac
HQ: St. Jude Medical, Llc
    1 Saint Jude Medical Dr
    Saint Paul MN 55117
    651 756-2000

(G-9819)
STRATEGIC CONTENT IMAGING
100 Castle Rd (07094-1602)
P.O. Box 2399 (07096-2399)
PHONE....................201 863-8100
Steven Murson, *Vice Pres*
EMP: 180 **EST:** 2001
SALES (est): 43MM **Privately Held**
WEB: www.sciimage.com/
SIC: 7334 7379 2752 7389 Photocopying & duplicating services; ; commercial printing, lithographic; printers' services: folding, collating

(G-9820)
THERMAL CONDUCTION ENGINEERING
Also Called: T C E
865 Roosevelt Ave (07094-3535)
PHONE....................201 865-1084
Jay Corrigan, *President*
Edward Perry, *President*
EMP: 9 **EST:** 1960
SQ FT: 9,000
SALES (est): 1.1MM **Privately Held**
SIC: 3567 Induction heating equipment

(G-9821)
TOSCANA CHEESE COMPANY INC
575 Windsor Dr (07094-2746)
PHONE....................201 617-1500
Victor J Paparazzo, *President*
Eric Felice, *VP Opers*
▲ **EMP:** 45
SQ FT: 42,500
SALES (est): 18MM **Privately Held**
WEB: www.toscanacheese.com
SIC: 2022 Natural cheese

(G-9822)
TRAVEL WEEKLY
100 Lighting Way Ste 200 (07094-3681)
PHONE....................201 902-1931

Dennis Schaal, *Principal*
Daisy Ouyang, *Editor*
Robert Silk, *Editor*
Wang Xinsheng, *Editor*
Diane Swiss, *Research*
EMP: 8
SALES (est): 812K **Privately Held**
SIC: 2759 Commercial printing

(G-9823)
TRIFLUENT PHARMA LLC
10-16 Aquarium Dr (07094-1919)
PHONE....................210 552-2057
Raul Garza, *CFO*
C Anthony Shippam,
EMP: 1
SQ FT: 20,000
SALES: 1MM **Privately Held**
SIC: 2834 Pharmaceutical preparations

(G-9824)
UNITED CABINET WORKS LLC
550 County Ave (07094-2607)
PHONE....................917 686-3395
Nick Roccaforte, *Mng Member*
EMP: 3
SALES (est): 2.3MM **Privately Held**
SIC: 2434 7389 Wood kitchen cabinets;

(G-9825)
US DISPLAY GROUP INC
100 Electric Ave (07094-2616)
PHONE....................931 455-9585
Al Rossi, *General Mgr*
EMP: 10 **Privately Held**
WEB: www.usdisplaygroup.com
SIC: 2653 Boxes, corrugated: made from purchased materials
HQ: U.S. Display Group, Inc.
    810 S Washington St
    Tullahoma TN 37388
    931 455-9585

(G-9826)
VITAMIN SHOPPE INDUSTRIES INC (HQ)
Also Called: Vitamin Shoppe, The
300 Harmon Meadow Blvd (07094-3642)
PHONE....................201 868-5959
Colin Watts, *CEO*
Tammi Aqueche, *District Mgr*
Patrick Rush, *District Mgr*
Tom Russo, *District Mgr*
Jim Schmidt, *District Mgr*
EMP: 540
SQ FT: 230,000
SALES (est): 797.7MM **Publicly Held**
WEB: www.ourmothernature.com
SIC: 5499 5961 2833 Vitamin food stores; pharmaceuticals, mail order; vitamins, natural or synthetic: bulk, uncompounded

(G-9827)
VITEC VIDEOCOM INC
700 Penhorn Ave Ste 1 (07094-2158)
PHONE....................908 852-3700
Sol Comerchero, *Partner*
Alan Hollis, *Senior VP*
Paul Weiser, *Vice Pres*
Robert Putkowski, *Purch Agent*
Fiorella Quiroz, *Hum Res Coord*
▲ **EMP:** 20
SALES (est): 2MM **Privately Held**
SIC: 3663 Microwave communication equipment

(G-9828)
WILENTA CARTING INC
46 Henry St (07094-2104)
P.O. Box 2596 (07096-2596)
PHONE....................201 325-0044
Peter Wilenta, *President*
Michael Wilenta, *COO*
EMP: 13
SQ FT: 1,700
SALES (est): 4.4MM **Privately Held**
SIC: 3555 5191 4953 Bronzing or dusting machines for the printing trade; animal feeds; recycling, waste materials

(G-9829)
WILENTA FEED INC
46 Henry St (07094-2104)
P.O. Box 2596 (07096-2596)
PHONE....................201 325-0044
Peter Wilenta, *President*

Michael Wilenta, *COO*
Jack Caffrey, *Manager*
Carmen Soto, *Asst Mgr*
◆ **EMP:** 13
SQ FT: 1,700
SALES (est): 2.2MM **Privately Held**
SIC: 3556 5191 4953 Bakery machinery;
animal feeds; recycling, waste materials

(G-9830)
ZOLLANVARI LTD
600 Mdwlands Pkwy Ste 130 (07094-1637)
PHONE..................................201 330-3344
Reza Zollanvari, *President*
▲ **EMP:** 11
SQ FT: 11,527
SALES (est): 1.4MM **Privately Held**
WEB: www.zollanvari.com
SIC: 2273 Carpets & rugs

Sewaren
Middlesex County

(G-9831)
**AUTOMATED MEDICAL PDTS
CORP**
440 Cliff Rd (07077-1408)
PHONE..................................732 602-7717
Janice Brown, *President*
EMP: 7
SQ FT: 2,000
SALES (est): 1.1MM **Privately Held**
WEB: www.ironintern.com
SIC: 3841 Surgical instruments & appara-
tus

(G-9832)
MOTIVA ENTERPRISES LLC
Also Called: Motiva Sales Terminal
111 State St (07077-1440)
PHONE..................................732 855-3266
Ralph Otis, *Manager*
EMP: 100 **Privately Held**
WEB: www.motivaenterprises.com
SIC: 2911 Petroleum refining
HQ: Motiva Enterprises Llc
500 Dallas St Fl 9
Houston TX 77002
713 277-8000

Sewell
Gloucester County

(G-9833)
ACE RESTORATION
24 Mariner Dr (08080-1946)
PHONE..................................267 897-2384
Matthew Gibson, *Owner*
EMP: 4
SALES (est): 154.7K **Privately Held**
SIC: 3088 Plastics plumbing fixtures

(G-9834)
**CONCORD PRODUCTS
COMPANY INC**
317 Salina Rd (08080-4103)
PHONE..................................856 933-3000
Erik Anthonsen, *Vice Pres*
Fran Tessing, *Office Mgr*
Ron Burke, *Training Spec*
◆ **EMP:** 47
SQ FT: 65,000
SALES (est): 8.8MM **Privately Held**
SIC: 2522 Office furniture, except wood

(G-9835)
COPERION CORPORATION (HQ)
590 Woodbury Glassboro Rd (08080-4558)
PHONE..................................201 327-6300
Thomas Kehl, *President*
Peter Hoffmann, *General Mgr*
Axel K Kiefer, *Managing Dir*
Steve Broes, *Business Mgr*
Chris Sturmey, *Business Mgr*
▲ **EMP:** 110
SQ FT: 89,000

SALES (est): 55.7MM **Publicly Held**
SIC: 3559 8711 3535 8734 Plastics working machinery; structural engineering;
bulk handling conveyor systems; testing
laboratories

(G-9836)
**COPERION K-TRON PITMAN
INC (DH)**
590 Woodbury Glassboro Rd (08080-4558)
PHONE..................................856 589-0500
Kevin C Bowen, *President*
Ulrich Bartel, *Plant Mgr*
Brandon Dohn, *Engineer*
Ronald Letizia, *Engineer*
Ralph Ungles, *Electrical Engi*
▲ **EMP:** 10
SQ FT: 92,000
SALES (est): 21.5MM **Publicly Held**
SIC: 3823 3829 3596 3535 Industrial
process control instruments; measuring &
controlling devices; scales & balances,
except laboratory; conveyors & conveying
equipment

(G-9837)
**COUNTY CONSERVATION CO
INC**
212 Blckwood Barnsboro Rd (08080-4202)
PHONE..................................856 227-6900
Francis Petrongolo Jr, *President*
John Petrongolo, *Owner*
Jeffrey Petrongolo, *Corp Secy*
EMP: 13
SALES (est): 3.7MM **Privately Held**
SIC: 3559 Recycling machinery

(G-9838)
CREATIVE COMPETITIONS INC
Also Called: Odyssey of The Mind
406 Ganttown Rd (08080-1862)
PHONE..................................856 256-2797
Samuel Micklus, *President*
Cheryl Micklus, *Treasurer*
Joy Stephenson, *Director*
EMP: 11
SQ FT: 4,000
SALES (est): 400K **Privately Held**
WEB: www.odysseyofthemind.com
SIC: 2731 Books: publishing only

(G-9839)
DELSEA PIPE INC
445 Delsea Dr (08080-9337)
PHONE..................................856 589-9374
Nick Bozine, *President*
Kim Ciemny, *Office Mgr*
EMP: 25
SQ FT: 8,000
SALES (est): 3.1MM **Privately Held**
SIC: 3317 Steel pipe & tubes

(G-9840)
EDWARD KURTH AND SON INC
220 Blckwood Barnsboro Rd (08080-4202)
PHONE..................................856 227-5252
Edward Kurth Jr, *President*
Andrew Kurth, *Vice Pres*
Robert B Kurth, *Admin Sec*
EMP: 30 **EST:** 1976
SQ FT: 28,000
SALES (est): 4.4MM **Privately Held**
WEB: www.edkurth.com
SIC: 7692 7699 Welding repair; boiler re-
pair shop

(G-9841)
EDWIN R BURGER & SON INC
732 Main St (08080-4546)
P.O. Box 184 (08080-0184)
PHONE..................................856 468-2300
Mark Burger, *President*
EMP: 30 **EST:** 1953
SQ FT: 8,000
SALES (est): 1.6MM **Privately Held**
SIC: 1799 3496 Fence construction; mis-
cellaneous fabricated wire products

(G-9842)
EKS PARTS INC
220 Blckwood Barnsboro Rd (08080-4202)
PHONE..................................856 227-8811
Edward F Kurth Jr, *Owner*
Robert B Kurth, *Corp Secy*
Andrew L Kurth, *Vice Pres*
EMP: 4

SALES (est): 390K **Privately Held**
SIC: 3443 Boiler shop products: boilers,
smokestacks, steel tanks

(G-9843)
**ELECTRIC MOBILITY
CORPORATION (PA)**
Also Called: Rascal Company, The
591 Mantua Blvd (08080-1032)
P.O. Box 36000, Louisville KY (40233-
6000)
PHONE..................................856 468-1000
Michael Flowers, *Ch of Bd*
Sanford Pearl, *COO*
Susan Flowers, *Treasurer*
Jordan Flowers, *Admin Sec*
▲ **EMP:** 110
SQ FT: 50,000
SALES (est): 37.4MM **Privately Held**
WEB: www.electricmobility.com
SIC: 5047 3842 Medical equipment & sup-
plies; wheelchairs

(G-9844)
**ELECTRIC MOBILITY
CORPORATION**
Also Called: Rascal Company, The
599 Mantua Blvd (08080-1016)
PHONE..................................856 468-1000
Michael Flowers, *Manager*
EMP: 200
SALES (corp-wide): 37.4MM **Privately
Held**
WEB: www.electricmobility.com
SIC: 3751 5999 Motor scooters & parts;
medical apparatus & supplies
PA: Electric Mobility Corporation
591 Mantua Blvd
Sewell NJ 08080
856 468-1000

(G-9845)
HUTCHINSON CABINETS
244 Bark Bridge Rd (08080-4612)
PHONE..................................856 468-5500
Etta Hutchinson, *Opers-Prdtn-Mfg*
George Hutchinson,
Lorrie Hutchinson, *Assistant*
EMP: 45 **EST:** 1976
SQ FT: 35,000
SALES (est): 4.9MM **Privately Held**
WEB: www.hutchinsoncabinets.com
SIC: 2434 2431 Wood kitchen cabinets;
millwork

(G-9846)
**IMPRESSIONS UNLIMITED PRTG
LLC**
638 Delsea Dr (08080-9399)
P.O. Box 386 (08080-0386)
PHONE..................................856 256-0200
Jeff Owens, *Plant Mgr*
Joseph G Layton, *Mng Member*
EMP: 6
SALES (est): 250K **Privately Held**
WEB: www.iuprint.com
SIC: 2752 Commercial printing, offset

(G-9847)
IRON ASYLUM INCORPORATED
233 Delsea Dr (08080-9401)
PHONE..................................856 352-4283
Victor Cohen, *President*
EMP: 14 **EST:** 2010
SQ FT: 1,000
SALES (est): 2MM **Privately Held**
SIC: 3441 Fabricated structural metal

(G-9848)
J & J MARINE INC
Also Called: J & J Tool & Die
1596 Hurffville Rd (08080-4270)
PHONE..................................856 228-4744
James Clauss, *President*
EMP: 14
SALES (est): 1.2MM **Privately Held**
SIC: 3544 1629 Special dies, tools, jigs &
fixtures; marine construction

(G-9849)
JANNETTI PUBLICATIONS
200 E Holly Ave (08080-2641)
P.O. Box 56, Pitman (08071-0056)
PHONE..................................856 256-2300
Anthony J Jannetti, *Owner*

Charlene Fuhrer, *Manager*
Craig Nelson, *Info Tech Mgr*
EMP: 53
SALES (est): 3MM **Privately Held**
WEB: www.medsurgnursing.net
SIC: 2721 8299 Periodicals: publishing
only; educational service, nondegree
granting: continuing educ.

(G-9850)
JVS COPY SERVICES INC
460 Main St (08080-4316)
PHONE..................................856 415-9090
Anthony Di Sciascio, *President*
Beverly Di Sciascio, *Vice Pres*
EMP: 10
SQ FT: 10,000
SALES (est): 1.5MM **Privately Held**
WEB: www.jvscopy.com
SIC: 7334 2752 Photocopying & duplicat-
ing services; commercial printing, litho-
graphic

(G-9851)
**K-TRON INTERNATIONAL INC
(HQ)**
Also Called: Pennsylvania Crusher
590 Woodbury Glassboro Rd (08080-4558)
PHONE..................................856 589-0500
Edward B Cloues II, *Ch of Bd*
Kevin C Bowen, *President*
Lukas Guenthardt, *Senior VP*
Donald W Melchiorre, *Senior VP*
Robert Zwart, *Mfg Staff*
◆ **EMP:** 59
SQ FT: 92,000
SALES (est): 123.1MM **Publicly Held**
WEB: www.ktron.com
SIC: 3532 3535 Feeders, ore & aggre-
gate; conveyors & conveying equipment

(G-9852)
OMEGA TOOL DIE
Also Called: International Roll Forms
8 International Ave (08080)
P.O. Box 5426, Deptford (08096-0426)
PHONE..................................856 228-7100
Jack Bosbikian, *President*
EMP: 8
SALES (est): 60.7K **Privately Held**
SIC: 3544 Special dies & tools

(G-9853)
**PASTARAMA DISTRIBUTORS
INC**
164 Center St (08080-1359)
PHONE..................................609 847-0378
Nicholas Z Pellicciotti, *President*
Barbara Pellicciotti, *Treasurer*
EMP: 4
SQ FT: 150
SALES (est): 240K **Privately Held**
SIC: 2099 Pasta, uncooked: packaged with
other ingredients

(G-9854)
YASHEEL INC
Also Called: Sir Speedy
11 Samantha Ct (08080-3151)
PHONE..................................856 275-6812
Shila Gohil, *President*
EMP: 4
SALES (est): 270K **Privately Held**
SIC: 2752 3993 2789 Commercial print-
ing, offset; signs & advertising specialties;
bookbinding & related work

Shamong
Burlington County

(G-9855)
**BROOK SADDLE RIDGE
EQUEST**
Also Called: Saddlebrook Ridge Equest Ctr
10 Saddle Brook Ct (08088-8225)
PHONE..................................609 953-1600
Gail Pratt, *Owner*
EMP: 10
SALES (est): 851K **Privately Held**
SIC: 3199 Equestrian related leather arti-
cles

(G-9856)
GLOW TUBE INC
83 Springers Brook Rd (08088-9567)
P.O. Box 725, Medford (08055-0725)
PHONE.................................609 268-7707
C W Keith, *President*
Dorthy Keith, *Treasurer*
Marique Keith, *Admin Sec*
EMP: 5
SALES: 150K **Privately Held**
SIC: 3825 Energy measuring equipment,
electrical

(G-9857)
HARRY SHAW MODEL MAKER INC
401 Stokes Rd (08088-8954)
P.O. Box 2087, Medford (08055-7087)
PHONE.................................609 268-0647
John W Kerby, *President*
William Jackman, *Corp Secy*
EMP: 4 **EST:** 1952
SQ FT: 7,500
SALES: 700K **Privately Held**
WEB: www.harryshawmodel.com
SIC: 3999 Models, general, except toy

(G-9858)
INOX STEEL CORP
48 Meetinghouse Ct (08088-9421)
PHONE.................................609 268-2334
John F Rebori, *President*
EMP: 7
SALES (est): 982.2K **Privately Held**
SIC: 3441 Fabricated structural metal

(G-9859)
SHAMONG MANUFACTURING COMPANY
33 Bunker Hill Rd (08088-8990)
PHONE.................................609 654-2549
Donald Autio, *President*
EMP: 34
SQ FT: 20,000
SALES (est): 6.6MM **Privately Held**
WEB: www.shamongmfg.com
SIC: 3444 Sheet metal specialties, not
stamped

(G-9860)
VALENZANO WINERY
1090 Route 206 (08088-9599)
PHONE.................................856 701-7871
EMP: 5
SALES (est): 641.1K **Privately Held**
SIC: 2084 Wines

(G-9861)
VALENZANO WINERY LLC
340 Forked Neck Rd (08088-9444)
PHONE.................................609 268-6731
Anthony Valenzano, *President*
Theresa Valenzano, *Sales Mgr*
Mark Valenzano,
EMP: 10
SALES (est): 886.4K **Privately Held**
WEB: www.valenzanowine.com
SIC: 2084 Wines

Ship Bottom
Ocean County

(G-9862)
RON JON SURF SHOP FLA INC
201 W 9th St (08008-4614)
PHONE.................................609 494-8844
Patty Gawronski, *Branch Mgr*
EMP: 14
SALES (corp-wide): 37.1MM **Privately Held**
WEB: www.rjss.com
SIC: 3949 5941 Surfboards; surfing equipment & supplies
PA: Ron Jon Surf Shop Of Fla., Inc.
4151 N Atlantic Ave
Cocoa Beach FL 32931
321 799-8888

Short Hills
Essex County

(G-9863)
AB SCIENCE USA LLC (HQ)
51 John F Kennedy Pkwy (07078-2704)
PHONE.................................973 218-2437
Alain Moussy, *Mng Member*
Albert Ahn,
EMP: 6
SQ FT: 1,500
SALES (est): 549.3K
SALES (corp-wide): 1.8MM **Privately Held**
SIC: 2834 Pharmaceutical preparations
PA: Ab Science
3 Avenue George V
Paris 8e Arrondissement 75008
140 701-629

(G-9864)
AGILIS CHEMICALS INC
830 Morris Tpke Fl 4 (07078-2625)
PHONE.................................973 910-2424
Jay Bhatia, *CEO*
EMP: 12
SALES: 15MM **Privately Held**
SIC: 2869 7371 2843 2834 Industrial organic chemicals; computer software development & applications; surface active agents; vitamin preparations; agricultural chemicals

(G-9865)
CAVALIER CHEMICAL CO INC
42 Colonial Way (07078-1813)
PHONE.................................908 558-0110
Norman Lubin, *President*
Mark Sherman, *Vice Pres*
EMP: 30
SQ FT: 52,000
SALES (est): 5.6MM **Privately Held**
WEB: www.cavalierchem.com
SIC: 2842 2841 Cleaning or polishing preparations; dishwashing compounds

(G-9866)
CHEESECAKE FACTORY INC
Also Called: Cheesecake Factory, The
1200 Morris Tpke Ste D103 (07078-0319)
PHONE.................................973 921-0930
EMP: 6 **Publicly Held**
SIC: 5812 2051 American restaurant; cakes, bakery: except frozen
PA: The Cheesecake Factory Incorporated
26901 Malibu Hills Rd
Calabasas Hills CA 91301

(G-9867)
CO-CO COLLABORATIVE LLC
61 Taylor Rd (07078-2256)
PHONE.................................917 685-5547
Suzanne Willian,
EMP: 5
SALES: 15K **Privately Held**
SIC: 7389 7372 Business services; application computer software

(G-9868)
DUN & BRADSTREET INC
Also Called: D&B
103 John F Kennedy Pkwy (07078-2708)
PHONE.................................973 921-5500
EMP: 50
SALES (corp-wide): 1.7B **Privately Held**
SIC: 7372 Business oriented computer software
HQ: Dun & Bradstreet, Inc
103 John F Kennedy Pkwy
Short Hills NJ 07078
973 921-5500

(G-9869)
GOLF ODYSSEY LLC
60 Woodcrest Ave (07078-2124)
PHONE.................................973 564-6223
David Baum, *Owner*
EMP: 4
SALES (est): 263.4K **Privately Held**
SIC: 2721 Magazines: publishing only, not printed on site

(G-9870)
JAMES COLUCCI ENTERPRISES LLC
150 Jfk Pkwy (07078-2703)
P.O. Box 1345, Summit (07902-1345)
PHONE.................................877 403-4900
James Colucci, *Principal*
EMP: 29
SALES: 11.5MM **Privately Held**
SIC: 3861 7371 Developers, photographic (not made in chemical plants); software programming applications

(G-9871)
M BLAUSTEIN INC (PA)
Also Called: Blaustein M Furs
516 Millburn Ave (07078-2523)
PHONE.................................973 379-1080
Lloyd Perkel, *CEO*
Julius Blaustein, *Ch of Bd*
Irene Blaustein, *Vice Pres*
Lauren Perkel, *Treasurer*
EMP: 4
SQ FT: 6,000
SALES (est): 458.7K **Privately Held**
SIC: 5632 2371 Furriers; fur apparel, made to custom order; apparel accessories; fur goods; coats, fur

(G-9872)
MALCAM US
51 John F Kennedy Pkwy (07078-2704)
PHONE.................................973 218-2461
Danny Moshe, *President*
EMP: 4
SALES (est): 205.6K **Privately Held**
SIC: 3823 Industrial process measurement equipment

(G-9873)
MORGAN CYCLE LLC
227 Old Short Hills Rd (07078-2133)
PHONE.................................973 218-9233
John Yen, *Mng Member*
▲ **EMP:** 2
SQ FT: 10,000
SALES: 1.2MM **Privately Held**
SIC: 3944 Wagons: coaster, express & play: children's

(G-9874)
PIKE MACHINE PRODUCTS INC
17 Clive Hills Rd (07078-1314)
PHONE.................................973 379-9128
Morton Weisman, *President*
Russell Weisman, *Vice Pres*
EMP: 100
SQ FT: 76,000
SALES (est): 11.7MM
SALES (corp-wide): 6.9B **Publicly Held**
WEB: www.pikedoors.com
SIC: 3231 Doors, glass: made from purchased glass
HQ: Anthony Doors, Inc.
12391 Montero Ave
Sylmar CA 91342
818 365-9451

(G-9875)
PRIORITY MEDICAL INC
748 Morris Tpke Ste 203 (07078-2617)
PHONE.................................973 376-5077
Russ Huizing, *President*
EMP: 5
SQ FT: 900
SALES (est): 572K **Privately Held**
SIC: 5999 3842 Medical apparatus & supplies; helmets, space

(G-9876)
RELATNSHIP CAPITL PARTNERS INC
51 Jfk Pkwy Fl 1 (07078-2713)
PHONE.................................908 962-4881
Martin Wise, *CEO*
EMP: 14
SQ FT: 1,000
SALES (est): 906.4K **Privately Held**
SIC: 7372 Application computer software

(G-9877)
RELPRO INC
51 Jfk Pkwy Fl 1w (07078-2702)
PHONE.................................908 962-4881
Martin Wise, *CEO*

Bob Summers, *Executive*
EMP: 8
SQ FT: 1,000
SALES (est): 186.1K **Privately Held**
SIC: 7372 Application computer software

(G-9878)
TAMIR BIOTECHNOLOGY INC
51 Jfk Pkwy Fl 1w (07078-2702)
PHONE.................................800 419-5061
David Sidransky, *Ch of Bd*
Jamie Sulley, *President*
Joanne M Barsa, *CFO*
EMP: 5 **EST:** 1981
SALES (est): 500K **Privately Held**
WEB: www.alfacell.com
SIC: 2836 8731 Culture media; commercial physical research

(G-9879)
VIATAR CTC SOLUTIONS INC
29 Clive Hills Rd (07078-1314)
PHONE.................................617 299-6590
Ilan K Reich, *CEO*
EMP: 5 **EST:** 2007
SALES (est): 278.6K **Privately Held**
SIC: 3841 Surgical & medical instruments

Shrewsbury
Monmouth County

(G-9880)
AKW INC (PA)
Also Called: A W Eurostile
41 Newman Springs Rd E (07702-4038)
PHONE.................................732 530-9186
Andrea Wyman, *President*
Elizabeth Wyman, *Corp Secy*
Michele Wyman, *Shareholder*
▲ **EMP:** 5
SQ FT: 30,000
SALES (est): 1.4MM **Privately Held**
WEB: www.aweurostile.com
SIC: 3443 5032 5211 Fabricated plate work (boiler shop); tile & clay products; marble building stone; tile, ceramic; masonry materials & supplies

(G-9881)
AMERTECH TOWERSERVICES LLC
149 Avenue At The Cmn (07702-4577)
PHONE.................................732 389-2200
Mark Gaeta, *President*
Robert Canino, *General Mgr*
EMP: 30
SQ FT: 10,000
SALES (est): 2.4MM **Privately Held**
SIC: 2499 Cooling towers, wood or wood & sheet metal combination

(G-9882)
ATHLETES ALLEY
Also Called: Imprint Ink
483 Broad St (07702-4003)
PHONE.................................732 842-1127
Nicholas Ford Jr, *Partner*
Greg Ford, *Partner*
EMP: 10 **EST:** 1976
SQ FT: 1,290
SALES (est): 1MM **Privately Held**
WEB: www.athletesalley.com
SIC: 5941 5699 2284 2893 Sporting goods & bicycle shops; sports apparel; embroidery thread; printing ink

(G-9883)
BEDROCK GRANITE INC
803 Shrewsbury Ave (07702-4307)
PHONE.................................732 741-0010
Joseph Iacono, *President*
Philip Vivolo, *Admin Sec*
EMP: 24
SQ FT: 12,000
SALES (est): 3.8MM **Privately Held**
WEB: www.bedrockgranite.net
SIC: 3281 1411 Granite, cut & shaped; dimension stone

(G-9884)
CEMP INC
Also Called: Detail Doctor
479 Broad St (07702-4003)
PHONE..................................732 933-1000
Sean Gatta, *President*
Matthew Cop, *Manager*
EMP: 13
SALES: 500K **Privately Held**
WEB: www.cemp.com
SIC: 3471 5511 Cleaning, polishing & finishing; new & used car dealers

(G-9885)
CHARTER FINCL PUBG NETWRK INC
Also Called: Financial Advisor Magazine
499 Broad St (07702-4043)
P.O. Box 7550 (07702-7550)
PHONE..................................732 450-8866
Charlie Stroller, *CEO*
EMP: 30
SQ FT: 4,000
SALES (est): 4.5MM **Privately Held**
WEB: www.financialadvisormagazine.com
SIC: 2721 Magazines: publishing & printing; magazines: publishing only, not printed on site

(G-9886)
CHISHOLM TECHNOLOGIES INC
450 Shrewsbury Plz # 301 (07702-4325)
PHONE..................................732 859-5578
Agnes Chisholm, *President*
Rosena Murray, *Vice Pres*
EMP: 4
SALES (est): 202.1K **Privately Held**
WEB: www.chisholmtech.com
SIC: 7372 Application computer software

(G-9887)
COUTURE EXCHANGE
703 Broad St Ste 1 (07702-4211)
PHONE..................................732 933-1123
Richard Patrick, *Owner*
Jennifer Patrick, *Co-Owner*
EMP: 5
SALES (est): 402.8K **Privately Held**
WEB: www.thecoutureexchange.com
SIC: 2389 Apparel & accessories

(G-9888)
DALA BEAUTY LLC
Also Called: Lavanila
1129 Broad St Ste 105 (07702-4314)
PHONE..................................732 380-7354
EMP: 5 **EST:** 2017
SALES (est): 473.6K **Privately Held**
SIC: 2844 Toilet preparations

(G-9889)
DCG PRINTING INC
Also Called: Omega Graphics
661 State Rte 35 (07702)
PHONE..................................732 530-4441
Douglas Godfrey, *President*
Stephanie Godfrey, *Admin Sec*
EMP: 4
SALES: 500K **Privately Held**
SIC: 2752 Commercial printing, offset

(G-9890)
DJEET
637 Broad St (07702-4150)
PHONE..................................732 224-8887
Casey Pesce, *Owner*
EMP: 6
SALES (est): 538.8K **Privately Held**
SIC: 2099 Food preparations

(G-9891)
EBSCO INDUSTRIES INC
Also Called: Ebsco Information Services
1151 Broad St Ste 212 (07702-4328)
P.O. Box 830625, Birmingham AL (35283-0625)
PHONE..................................732 542-8600
Stanley Terry, *General Mgr*
EMP: 50
SALES (corp-wide): 2.8B **Privately Held**
WEB: www.ebscoind.com
SIC: 2741 Miscellaneous publishing

PA: Ebsco Industries, Inc.
5724 Highway 280 E
Birmingham AL 35242
205 991-6600

(G-9892)
GAIL GERSONS WINE & DINE RESTA
812 Broad St (07702-4214)
PHONE..................................732 758-0888
Gail Gerson, *Principal*
EMP: 4
SALES (est): 232.7K **Privately Held**
SIC: 2711 7311 Newspapers, publishing & printing; advertising agencies

(G-9893)
INK ON PAPER COMMUNICATIONS (PA)
Also Called: Iop Communications
450 Shrewsbury Plz # 372 (07702-4325)
PHONE..................................732 758-6280
Gail De Nofa, *President*
Gail Denofa, *President*
Micheal E De Nofa Jr, *Vice Pres*
EMP: 1
SALES: 1MM **Privately Held**
WEB: www.iopcomm.com
SIC: 2752 Commercial printing, lithographic

(G-9894)
METALLIX DIRECT GOLD LLC
59 Avenue At The Cmn # 201 (07702-4806)
PHONE..................................732 544-0891
Pamela Rollins, *Principal*
EMP: 8
SALES (est): 873K **Privately Held**
SIC: 3339 Precious metals

(G-9895)
METALLIX REFINING INC (PA)
59 Avenue At The Cmn # 201 (07702-4806)
PHONE..................................732 936-0050
Eric Leiner, *President*
Maria Piastre, *President*
Jesus Rada, *Prdtn Mgr*
Leon Ratliff, *Buyer*
Lynn Falk, *CFO*
▲ **EMP:** 12 **EST:** 1970
SQ FT: 3,000
SALES (est): 12.8MM **Privately Held**
WEB: www.metallixrefining.com
SIC: 3339 Precious metals; gold refining (primary); platinum group metal refining (primary)

(G-9896)
MICHAEL DURU CLOTHIERS LLC
Also Called: Executive Clothiers
801 Broad St (07702-4201)
PHONE..................................732 741-1999
Michael Duru, *President*
Matt Duru, *Office Mgr*
Murat M Duru,
EMP: 7
SQ FT: 3,900
SALES: 1.1MM **Privately Held**
SIC: 2311 Tailored suits & formal jackets

(G-9897)
MISTER GOOD LUBE INC
Also Called: Mr Good Lube
473 Broad St (07702-4003)
PHONE..................................732 842-3266
Harideshi Kudo, *Manager*
EMP: 5
SALES (corp-wide): 2.5MM **Privately Held**
SIC: 1389 Construction, repair & dismantling services
PA: Mister Good Lube Inc
3411 Us Highway 9
Freehold NJ 07728
732 308-1111

(G-9898)
MONMOUTH TRUCK RAM DIV LLC
Also Called: Monmouth Hose & Hydraulics
799 Shrewsbury Ave (07702-4306)
PHONE..................................732 741-5001

Michele S Margiotta, *Mng Member*
EMP: 7
SALES (est): 176.6K **Privately Held**
SIC: 3599 Machine shop, jobbing & repair

(G-9899)
POLARIS PLATE HEAT EXCHNGERS L
Also Called: Polaris Thermal
1151 Broad St Ste 218 (07702-4328)
PHONE..................................732 345-7188
Jason Ryan, *Principal*
Barbara Blauth,
Steve Weintraub,
▼ **EMP:** 4
SQ FT: 1,400
SALES (est): 671.4K
SALES (corp-wide): 6.9B **Privately Held**
SIC: 3443 1711 Heat exchangers, condensers & components; plumbing, heating, air-conditioning contractors
HQ: Danfoss A/S
Nordborgvej 81
Nordborg 6430
748 822-22

(G-9900)
RAM HYDRAULICS INC
745 Shrewsbury Ave (07702-4306)
P.O. Box 416, Bayville (08721-0416)
PHONE..................................732 237-0904
Michael Mattei, *President*
EMP: 5
SQ FT: 6,200
SALES (est): 656.3K **Privately Held**
SIC: 3714 7538 Cylinder heads, motor vehicle; general truck repair

(G-9901)
RELAXZEN INC
621 Shrewsbury Ave (07702-4153)
PHONE..................................732 936-1500
▼ **EMP:** 10
SQ FT: 900
SALES (est): 690K **Privately Held**
SIC: 2086 Energy Drink Manufacturer

(G-9902)
STANGER ROBERT A & CO LP
1129 Broad St Fl 2 (07702-4333)
PHONE..................................732 389-3600
Keith D Allaire, *Principal*
Robert A Stanger, *Chairman*
Kevin Gannon, *Director*
EMP: 20
SALES (est): 2.2MM **Privately Held**
WEB: www.rastanger.com
SIC: 6726 6211 2741 Investment offices; security brokers & dealers; miscellaneous publishing

(G-9903)
SUPPLY CHAIN TECHNOLOGIES LLC
Also Called: Sct Software
1161 Broad St Ste 312 (07702-4362)
P.O. Box 14, Belmar (07719-0014)
PHONE..................................856 206-9849
David Henig, *CEO*
Rahul Agarwal, *President*
Jennifer Bygrave, *Mktg Coord*
EMP: 6
SALES (est): 358.2K **Privately Held**
SIC: 7372 Business oriented computer software

(G-9904)
VERTICAL PROTECTIVE AP LLC
830 Broad St Ste 3 (07702-4216)
PHONE..................................203 904-6099
Christopher Neary,
Phyllis Fee, *Administration*
EMP: 1
SQ FT: 1,000
SALES: 10MM **Privately Held**
SIC: 2326 Men's & boys' work clothing

(G-9905)
ZOONO USA LTD LIABILITY CO
1151 Broad St Ste 115 (07702-4312)
PHONE..................................732 722-8757
David Broadhead, *Prdtn Mgr*
Tom French,
Kim Bennet, *Executive Asst*
EMP: 4
SQ FT: 900

SALES: 400K **Privately Held**
SIC: 2842 Sanitation preparations, disinfectants & deodorants

---

Sicklerville
Camden County

(G-9906)
7TH SEVENTH DAY WELLNESS CTR
Also Called: Over The Rainbow Bridge Crysta
6 Sherwick Ct (08081-1317)
PHONE..................................856 308-0991
Lisa M Dottoli, *Owner*
EMP: 6
SALES: 150K **Privately Held**
SIC: 2833 Medicinals & botanicals

(G-9907)
ANVIL IRON WORKS INC
Little Mill Rd (08081)
PHONE..................................856 783-5959
William C Natoli Jr, *President*
EMP: 6
SALES (corp-wide): 882.9K **Privately Held**
SIC: 3441 Fabricated structural metal
PA: Anvil Iron Works Inc
1022 Washington Ave 26
Philadelphia PA 19147
215 468-8300

(G-9908)
AUTOACCESS LLC
451 Church Rd (08081-1772)
P.O. Box 529 (08081-0529)
PHONE..................................908 240-5919
Tunji Olabode, *CEO*
Olaide Olabode, *Vice Pres*
Olarenwaju Olabode, *Vice Pres*
EMP: 10
SALES (est): 447.9K **Privately Held**
SIC: 3711 5012 Motor vehicles & car bodies; automobiles & other motor vehicles

(G-9909)
ESI
Also Called: Electronic Assemblies, Inc Esi
1541 New Brooklyn Erial Rd (08081-3294)
PHONE..................................856 629-2492
Christine J Cunningham, *President*
James Cunningham, *Vice Pres*
EMP: 25
SQ FT: 5,000
SALES: 1.2MM **Privately Held**
SIC: 3643 3679 3672 3357 Power line cable; harness assemblies for electronic use: wire or cable; printed circuit boards; nonferrous wiredrawing & insulating

(G-9910)
GARY R MARZILI
Also Called: GM Precision Machine
840 Jarvis Rd (08081-2132)
PHONE..................................856 782-1546
Gary R Marzili, *Owner*
EMP: 4
SALES (est): 280K **Privately Held**
SIC: 3541 Machine tools, metal cutting type

(G-9911)
J & M CSTM SHTMTL LTD LBLTY CO
1331 New Brooklyn Erial Rd (08081-3292)
PHONE..................................856 627-6252
Janet Monitzer,
EMP: 9
SALES: 700K **Privately Held**
SIC: 3441 Fabricated structural metal

(G-9912)
NATIONAL COLOR GRAPHICS
1755 Williamstwn Erl Rd (08081-1238)
PHONE..................................856 435-6800
Jeffrey Hughes, *President*
Joseph Hughes, *Corp Secy*
EMP: 10
SQ FT: 5,000
SALES (est): 943.1K **Privately Held**
SIC: 7336 2759 Graphic arts & related design; commercial printing

(G-9913)
NICKOS CONSTRUCTION INC
17 Arcadian Dr (08081-3811)
PHONE..................................267 240-3997
Alex Nikolaenko, *President*
EMP: 17 **EST:** 2010
SALES: 3.3MM **Privately Held**
SIC: 1389 7389 Construction, repair & dis-
mantling services;

(G-9914)
PRO-MOTION INDUSTRIES LLC
102 Allied Pkwy (08081-9738)
PHONE..................................856 809-0040
Tom Dickerson, *General Mgr*
Kelly Cone,
▲ **EMP:** 10
SQ FT: 20,000
SALES (est): 3MM **Privately Held**
WEB: www.contractlabeling.com
SIC: 3565 Packaging machinery

(G-9915)
RIO SUPPLY
100 Allied Pkwy (08081-9738)
PHONE..................................856 719-0081
Renee Hastings, *Principal*
Dave Linden, *Area Mgr*
Megan Blackiston, *Bookkeeper*
Sean Rodgers, *Administration*
EMP: 7
SALES (est): 600K **Privately Held**
SIC: 3824 Fluid meters & counting devices

(G-9916)
**STORM CITY ENTERTAINMENT
INC**
700 Liberty Pl (08081-5715)
PHONE..................................856 885-6902
Susan Kain Jurgensen, *CEO*
Steve Newton, *President*
Raymond Pierce, *CFO*
EMP: 10
SQ FT: 3,300
SALES: 8MM **Privately Held**
SIC: 7372 Home entertainment computer
software

(G-9917)
**WASTEQUIP MANUFACTURING
CO**
1031 Hickstown Rd (08081-1091)
PHONE..................................856 784-5500
Andrew De Stefano, *President*
Eduardo Pagan, *Plant Mgr*
EMP: 100 **Privately Held**
WEB: www.rayfo.com
SIC: 3443 Dumpsters, garbage
HQ: Wastequip Manufacturing Company
Llc
6525 Morrison Blvd # 300
Charlotte NC 28211

Skillman
Somerset County

(G-9918)
CONNECTING PRODUCTS INC
186 Tamarack Cir (08558-2021)
PHONE..................................609 512-1121
Anthony Freakes, *President*
EMP: 10
SALES (est): 600.9K **Privately Held**
SIC: 8711 3699 Mechanical engineering;
electrical equipment & supplies

(G-9919)
CONNECTING PRODUCTS INC
194 Tamarack Cir Ste 1 (08558-2076)
PHONE..................................609 688-1808
▲ **EMP:** 7
SQ FT: 4,000
SALES (est): 2.4MM **Privately Held**
SIC: 3599 Mfg Industrial Machinery

(G-9920)
FORGE AHEAD LLC
1800 Route 206 (08558-1915)
PHONE..................................908 346-4794
Benton Camper, *CEO*
EMP: 4
SQ FT: 100

SALES (est): 98.3K **Privately Held**
SIC: 7372 Prepackaged software

(G-9921)
INGREDIENT HOUSE LLC
24 Vreeland Dr Ste 1 (08558-2621)
PHONE..................................609 285-5987
Graham Hall, *CEO*
Rudi Van Mol, *President*
EMP: 4
SALES (est): 324.9K **Privately Held**
SIC: 2099 Food preparations

(G-9922)
**JOHNSON & JOHNSON
CONSUMER INC (DH)**
199 Grandview Rd (08558-1303)
PHONE..................................908 874-1000
Kathleen Widmer, *President*
Michelle M Freyre, *Vice Pres*
Christopher Picariello, *Treasurer*
Alberto Guerrero, *Manager*
Lisa G Jenkins, *Admin Sec*
◆ **EMP:** 900 **EST:** 1879
SQ FT: 200,000
SALES (est): 423.9MM
SALES (corp-wide): 81.5B **Publicly Held**
SIC: 2834 Pharmaceutical preparations
HQ: Janssen Pharmaceuticals, Inc.
1125 Trnton Harbourton Rd
Titusville NJ 08560
609 730-2000

(G-9923)
**MIDLANTIC MEDICAL SYSTEMS
INC**
61 Fieldstone Rd (08558-1642)
PHONE..................................908 432-4599
Tom Devine, *President*
EMP: 3
SALES: 3MM **Privately Held**
SIC: 8099 3842 Medical services organi-
zation; implants, surgical

(G-9924)
MONTGOMERY NEWS
88 Orchard Rd Ste 10 (08558-2642)
PHONE..................................908 874-0020
Cliff Moore, *Owner*
EMP: 4
SALES (est): 308.8K **Privately Held**
WEB: www.montgomerynewsonline.com
SIC: 2711 Newspapers, publishing & print-
ing

(G-9925)
PERIBU GLOBAL SOURCING
Also Called: Peribu Collections LLC
5 Brookside Dr (08558-2104)
P.O. Box 130 (08558-0130)
PHONE..................................704 560-2035
Jessica Fogg, *Principal*
EMP: 10
SALES (est): 349.4K **Privately Held**
SIC: 2299 Textile goods

(G-9926)
**PRINCETON BIOMEDITECH
CORP**
75 Orchard Rd (08558-2609)
PHONE..................................908 281-0112
Caroline Christopher, *Branch Mgr*
EMP: 20
SALES (corp-wide): 18.3MM **Privately
Held**
SIC: 2835 In vitro diagnostics
PA: Princeton Biomeditech Corp
4242 Us Highway 1
Monmouth Junction NJ 08852
732 274-1000

(G-9927)
**VGYAAN PHARMACEUTICALS
LLC**
23 Orchard Rd Unit 180 (08558-2631)
PHONE..................................609 452-2770
Nailesh Bhatt, *CEO*
Nimisha Bhatt, *COO*
EMP: 4
SALES (est): 360.1K **Privately Held**
SIC: 2834 5122 Pharmaceutical prepara-
tions; pharmaceuticals

(G-9928)
VISIONWARE SYSTEMS INC
174 Tamarack Cir (08558-2021)
PHONE..................................609 924-0800
Larry Fridkis, *President*
Randolph Arends, *Project Mgr*
Christopher Barranco, *Opers Staff*
Kip Sullivan, *Corp Comm Staff*
Rachel Dagen, *Teacher*
EMP: 10
SQ FT: 1,700
SALES (est): 857.5K **Privately Held**
SIC: 7372 7335 Prepackaged software;
commercial photography

Somerdale
Camden County

(G-9929)
ACCURATE MOLD INC
900 Chestnut Ave Ste G (08083-1457)
PHONE..................................856 784-8484
Willard Miller, *President*
EMP: 32
SALES (est): 2.8MM **Privately Held**
WEB: www.accuratemold.net
SIC: 3089 3544 Injection molding of plas-
tics; special dies, tools, jigs & fixtures

(G-9930)
BISAGA INC
Also Called: Technique Precision
212 Ashland Ave (08083-1044)
PHONE..................................856 784-7966
Robert E Bisaga, *President*
Elizabeth J Bisaga, *Corp Secy*
EMP: 12
SQ FT: 14,000
SALES: 1.2MM **Privately Held**
WEB: www.techniqueprecision.com
SIC: 3599 Machine shop, jobbing & repair

(G-9931)
FIORE SKYLIGHTS INC
700 Grace St (08083-1446)
P.O. Box 160 (08083-0160)
PHONE..................................856 346-0118
Richard Materio, *President*
John Kennedy, *Treasurer*
EMP: 18
SQ FT: 10,000
SALES (est): 3MM **Privately Held**
WEB: www.fioreskylights.com
SIC: 3444 Skylights, sheet metal

(G-9932)
LINTHICUM SAILS
607 Grace St (08083-1435)
PHONE..................................856 783-4288
Bradford Linthicum, *Owner*
EMP: 5
SQ FT: 2,800
SALES (est): 230K **Privately Held**
SIC: 2394 Sails: made from purchased
materials

(G-9933)
**PEPCO MANUFACTURING CO
(PA)**
210 E Evergreen Ave (08083-1014)
P.O. Box 160 (08083-0160)
PHONE..................................856 783-3700
John M Kennedy, *CEO*
Frank A Reiss, *President*
Mark Berwick, *Purch Agent*
Beverly Winter, *CFO*
EMP: 85
SQ FT: 82,000
SALES: 7.5MM **Privately Held**
WEB: www.pepcosheetmetal.com
SIC: 3469 3444 Electronic enclosures,
stamped or pressed metal; metal hous-
ings, enclosures, casings & other contain-
ers

(G-9934)
**SANDOVAL GRAPHICS &
PRINTING**
Also Called: Sandoval Graphic Co
9 Minnetonka Rd (08083-2718)
PHONE..................................856 435-7320
Gilbert Sandoval, *Partner*
Anthony Sandoval, *Partner*

Chris Sandoval, *Partner*
EMP: 6 **EST:** 1968
SQ FT: 6,000
SALES: 300K **Privately Held**
WEB: www.sandovalgraphics.com
SIC: 2791 2752 7336 Typesetting; com-
mercial printing, lithographic; commercial
printing, offset; graphic arts & related de-
sign

(G-9935)
STAINES INC
Also Called: S & S Printing
610 S White Horse Pike (08083-1246)
PHONE..................................856 784-2718
Carolann Staines, *President*
William Staines, *Corp Secy*
EMP: 12
SQ FT: 5,000
SALES (est): 1.9MM **Privately Held**
SIC: 2752 2796 2791 Commercial print-
ing, lithographic; platemaking services;
typesetting

Somers Point
Atlantic County

(G-9936)
**ERCO CEILINGS SOMERS POINT
INC**
5 Chestnut St (08244-1130)
PHONE..................................609 517-2531
Esther Sykora, *Principal*
Donna Simon, *Accountant*
EMP: 30
SALES (est): 1.1MM **Privately Held**
SIC: 2591 Drapery hardware & blinds &
shades

(G-9937)
**INTERNTNAL ADHSIVE
COATING INC**
Also Called: International Tape Co
110 W New Jersey Ave (08244-1765)
PHONE..................................603 893-1894
Joseph V Curcio, *President*
▲ **EMP:** 38
SALES (est): 7.7MM **Privately Held**
WEB: www.itctapes.com
SIC: 2672 Tape, pressure sensitive: made
from purchased materials

(G-9938)
MOONBABIES LLC
505 New Rd Ste 7 (08244-2049)
PHONE..................................609 926-0201
Fax: 609 926-0957
EMP: 4
SALES (est): 230K **Privately Held**
SIC: 3911 Whole/Mfg Jewelry

(G-9939)
SEAVILLE MOTORSPORTS
Also Called: Easydook Midatlantic
65 Dockside Dr (08244-1010)
PHONE..................................609 624-0040
Ray Lepf, *Owner*
EMP: 10
SALES (est): 741K **Privately Held**
SIC: 3949 Water sports equipment

(G-9940)
**UNIVERSAL TAPE SUPPLY
CORP (PA)**
110 W New Jersey Ave (08244-1765)
PHONE..................................609 653-3191
Joseph V Curcio, *President*
Mario Curcio, *Vice Pres*
Bob Semet, *Vice Pres*
▲ **EMP:** 12
SQ FT: 2,000
SALES (est): 1.3MM **Privately Held**
WEB: www.universaltape.com
SIC: 2672 5113 3842 2891 Tape, pres-
sure sensitive: made from purchased ma-
terials; pressure sensitive tape; surgical
appliances & supplies; adhesives &
sealants

Somerset
Somerset County

(G-9941)
ACCESS BIO INC (PA)
65 Clyde Rd Ste A (08873-3485)
PHONE....................................732 873-4040
Young Ho Choi, *President*
Seungjae Baek, *Prdtn Mgr*
Sarg Han, *Research*
Jaean Jung, *CFO*
Jin Jung, *Manager*
◆ EMP: 19
SQ FT: 15,000
SALES (est): 10MM **Privately Held**
WEB: www.accessbio.net
SIC: 2835 2834 3674 In vitro diagnostics;
proprietary drug products; molecular de-
vices, solid state

(G-9942)
ADVANCED FOOD SYSTEMS INC
21 Roosevelt Ave (08873-5030)
PHONE....................................732 873-6776
Yongkeun Joh, *President*
Danny McMaster, *Maint Spvr*
Shakirah Dickens, *Opers Staff*
Chris Kelly, *Manager*
Rita O' Neill, *Manager*
EMP: 50
SQ FT: 26,800
SALES (est): 13.6MM **Privately Held**
SIC: 2087 8742 Flavoring extracts &
syrups; food & beverage consultant

(G-9943)
AEON INDUSTRIES INC
76 Veronica Ave (08873-3417)
PHONE....................................732 246-3224
John Baumann, *President*
Louis Bonapace, *Principal*
EMP: 5
SALES (est): 1.1MM **Privately Held**
SIC: 2679 2671 Labels, paper: made from
purchased material; packaging paper &
plastics film, coated & laminated

(G-9944)
AI-LOGIX INC
27 Worlds Fair Dr Ste 2 (08873-1353)
PHONE....................................732 469-0880
Moshe Tal, *President*
Mark Ringel, *CFO*
▲ EMP: 47
SQ FT: 19,500
SALES (est): 6.2MM
SALES (corp-wide): 47.5MM **Privately Held**
SIC: 3672 Circuit boards, television & radio
printed
HQ: Audiocodes, Inc.
200 Cottontail Ln A101e
Somerset NJ 08873
732 469-0880

(G-9945)
AKORN INC
275 Pierce St (08873-1261)
PHONE....................................732 532-1000
Rick Westerhoek Sr, *Branch Mgr*
EMP: 15
SALES (corp-wide): 694MM **Publicly Held**
SIC: 2834 Pharmaceutical preparations
PA: Akorn, Inc.
1925 W Field Ct Ste 300
Lake Forest IL 60045
847 279-6100

(G-9946)
AKORN INC
69 Veronica Ave Ste 6b (08873-3467)
PHONE....................................732 448-7043
Michael Stehn, *Vice Pres*
EMP: 6
SALES (corp-wide): 694MM **Publicly Held**
SIC: 2834 Pharmaceutical preparations
PA: Akorn, Inc.
1925 W Field Ct Ste 300
Lake Forest IL 60045
847 279-6100

(G-9947)
AKORN INC
72 Veronica Ave Ste 6 (08873-3426)
PHONE....................................732 846-8066
Eyal Mares, *VP Opers*
Hari Menon, *Exec Dir*
Steven Meyer, *Bd of Directors*
EMP: 60
SALES (corp-wide): 694MM **Publicly Held**
WEB: www.akorn.com
SIC: 2834 5047 Pharmaceutical prepara-
tions; surgical equipment & supplies
PA: Akorn, Inc.
1925 W Field Ct Ste 300
Lake Forest IL 60045
847 279-6100

(G-9948)
ALPHA ASSEMBLY SOLUTIONS INC (DH)
Also Called: Alpha Advanced Materials
300 Atrium Dr Fl 3 (08873-4160)
P.O. Box 206703, Dallas TX (75320-6703)
PHONE....................................908 791-3000
Rick Ertmann, *CEO*
Stephanie Beech, *HR Admin*
◆ EMP: 22
SALES (est): 102MM
SALES (corp-wide): 1.9B **Publicly Held**
WEB: www.alphametals.com
SIC: 3356 3341 3313 3339 Solder: wire,
bar, acid core, & rosin core; lead smelting
& refining (secondary); tin smelting & re-
fining (secondary); alloys, additive, except
copper: not made in blast furnaces; lead
smelting & refining (primary); tin refining
(primary); fluxes: brazing, soldering, gal-
vanizing & welding
HQ: Macdermid, Incorporated
245 Freight St
Waterbury CT 06702
203 575-5700

(G-9949)
ALPS TECHNOLOGIES INC
500 Memorial Dr Ste 1 (08873-1383)
PHONE....................................732 764-0777
Robert Wagner, *President*
EMP: 27
SQ FT: 24,000
SALES (est): 3.8MM **Privately Held**
WEB: www.alpstech.com
SIC: 3281 Cut stone & stone products

(G-9950)
ALTERA CORPORATION
106 Charles St (08873-2706)
PHONE....................................732 649-3477
John P Daane, *Branch Mgr*
EMP: 8
SALES (corp-wide): 70.8B **Publicly Held**
SIC: 3674 Semiconductors & related de-
vices
HQ: Altera Corporation
101 Innovation Dr
San Jose CA 95134
408 544-7000

(G-9951)
AMERICAN FIBERTEK INC
Also Called: Afi
120 Belmont Dr (08873-4243)
PHONE....................................732 302-0660
Jack Fernandes, *President*
Edward Davis, *Vice Pres*
EMP: 50
SQ FT: 10,800
SALES (est): 11MM **Privately Held**
WEB: www.americanfibertek.com
SIC: 3679 3577 Electronic circuits;
input/output equipment, computer

(G-9952)
AMERICAN POWER CORD CORP
4 Smalley Ave (08873)
PHONE....................................973 574-8301
Makil A Simon, *President*
EMP: 5
SALES (est): 177.6K **Privately Held**
SIC: 2298 Twine, cord & cordage

(G-9953)
ANALOG DEVICES INC
285 Davidson Ave Ste 402 (08873-4153)
PHONE....................................732 868-7100

John Kenney, *Manager*
EMP: 45
SALES (corp-wide): 6.2B **Publicly Held**
WEB: www.analog.com
SIC: 3674 Integrated circuits, semiconduc-
tor networks, etc.; hybrid integrated cir-
cuits
PA: Analog Devices, Inc.
1 Technology Way
Norwood MA 02062
781 329-4700

(G-9954)
API NANOFABRICATION & RES CORP
Also Called: Nanoopto
1600 Cottontail Ln Ste 1 (08873-5106)
PHONE....................................732 627-0808
EMP: 17
SALES (est): 1.8MM
SALES (corp-wide): 333.6MM **Privately Held**
SIC: 3827 Mfg Optical Instruments/Lenses
HQ: Api Technologies Corp.
400 Nickerson Rd
Marlborough MA 01752

(G-9955)
APPCO PHARMA LLC (PA)
Also Called: Appco Pharmaceuticals Corp.
120 Belmont Dr (08873-4243)
PHONE....................................732 271-8300
Rajendra P Appalaneni, *President*
Nagaraju Kanchanapalli, *General Mgr*
EMP: 47 EST: 2009
SQ FT: 25,000
SALES (est): 10MM **Privately Held**
SIC: 2834 Pharmaceutical preparations

(G-9956)
APPCO PHARMA LLC
120 Belmont Dr (08873-4243)
PHONE....................................732 271-8300
Nagaraju Kanchanapalli, *Branch Mgr*
EMP: 35
SALES (est): 2.3MM
SALES (corp-wide): 10MM **Privately Held**
SIC: 2834 Pharmaceutical preparations
PA: Appco Pharma Llc
120 Belmont Dr
Somerset NJ 08873
732 271-8300

(G-9957)
ASCENTTA INC
370 Campus Dr Ste 105 (08873-1128)
PHONE....................................732 868-1766
Shao H Liang, *Ch of Bd*
Shao Liang, *General Mgr*
Jennifer Ke, *Vice Pres*
Anna Rooney, *Sales Staff*
EMP: 15
SALES (est): 2.2MM **Privately Held**
WEB: www.ascentta.com
SIC: 3229 Fiber optics strands

(G-9958)
ASPIRE PHARMACEUTICALS INC (PA)
41 Veronica Ave (08873-6800)
PHONE....................................732 447-1444
Madhav Pai, *CEO*
Oscar Martinez, *Facilities Mgr*
Oksana Ivanova, *Opers Staff*
Jay Patel, *Accounts Mgr*
Mansing Korde, *Director*
▲ EMP: 77
SQ FT: 38,000
SALES (est): 24.3MM **Privately Held**
SIC: 2834 Pharmaceutical preparations

(G-9959)
AUDIOCODES INC
27 Worlds Fair Dr Ste 2 (08873-1353)
PHONE....................................732 469-0880
Ben Rabinowitz, *Vice Pres*
EMP: 8
SALES (corp-wide): 47.5MM **Privately Held**
SIC: 3823 7371 Transmitters of process
variables, stand. signal conversion; com-
puter software development

HQ: Audiocodes, Inc.
200 Cottontail Ln A101e
Somerset NJ 08873
732 469-0880

(G-9960)
AUDIOCODES INC (HQ)
200 Cottontail Ln A101e (08873-1273)
PHONE....................................732 469-0880
Shabtai Adlersberg, *President*
Bruce Gellman, *President*
Yossi Zilberfarb, *Vice Pres*
Kristy Boldt, *Vice Pres*
▲ EMP: 15
SQ FT: 3,000
SALES (est): 43MM
SALES (corp-wide): 47.5MM **Privately Held**
SIC: 3823 7371 Transmitters of process
variables, stand. signal conversion; com-
puter software development
PA: Audiocodes Ltd
1 Hayarden
Airport City 70199
397 640-00

(G-9961)
AUTOMANN INC (PA)
Also Called: Automann USA
850 Randolph Rd (08873-1288)
P.O. Box 6327 (08875-6327)
PHONE....................................201 529-4996
Thanwant Khanduja, *President*
Galo Ochoa, *General Mgr*
Chiranjeev Khanduja, *Vice Pres*
Jeev Khanduja, *Vice Pres*
Emanuel Manioudakis, *Facilities Mgr*
◆ EMP: 91
SQ FT: 80,000
SALES (est): 107.9MM **Privately Held**
WEB: www.automann.com
SIC: 5013 3715 Truck parts & acces-
sories; truck trailer chassis

(G-9962)
BERNAFON LLC
2501 Cottontail Ln # 102 (08873-5125)
PHONE....................................888 941-4203
Joseph Lugara, *President*
EMP: 4
SALES (est): 500.3K
SALES (corp-wide): 1.2MM **Privately Held**
SIC: 3841 Surgical & medical instruments
HQ: Demant A/S
Kongebakken 9
SmOrum 2765
391 771-00

(G-9963)
BLUE RIBBON AWARDS INC
12 Worlds Fair Dr Ste J (08873-1361)
PHONE....................................732 560-0046
Raymond F Zwigard, *President*
EMP: 4
SQ FT: 5,000
SALES (est): 448.4K **Privately Held**
SIC: 5999 2759 Trophies & plaques; en-
graving

(G-9964)
BUSINESS SOFTWARE APPLICATIONS
Also Called: Bsa Consulting
6 Sunny Ct (08873-5224)
PHONE....................................908 500-9980
Syed A Rahman, *President*
Khursheed Rahman, *Vice Pres*
EMP: 2
SALES: 1.2MM **Privately Held**
SIC: 7372 Prepackaged software

(G-9965)
CAMBRDGE INDS FOR VSLLY IMPRED
1230 Hamilton St (08873-3343)
PHONE....................................732 247-6668
Ben Tabatchnick, *Principal*
EMP: 8
SALES (est): 370.6K **Privately Held**
SIC: 3999 Manufacturing industries

(G-9966)
CARDINAL HEALTH SYSTEMS INC (HQ)
14 Schoolhouse Rd (08873-1213)
PHONE...............................732 537-6544
Jeff Henderson, *President*
Bhupinder Thomas, *Business Mgr*
Ivelisse Rivera, *Cust Mgr*
Anja Lowman, *Manager*
Stephen Kostic, *Supervisor*
EMP: 300 EST: 1988
SALES (est): 122.1MM
SALES (corp-wide): 145.5B **Publicly Held**
WEB: www.cardinal.com
SIC: 7372 2834 Prepackaged software; pharmaceutical preparations
PA: Cardinal Health, Inc.
7000 Cardinal Pl
Dublin OH 43017
614 757-5000

(G-9967)
CARTERET DIE-CASTING CORP
74 Veronica Ave (08873-3417)
P.O. Box 5610 (08875-5610)
PHONE...............................732 246-0070
John Burk, *President*
Gary Vogt, *Plant Mgr*
Mark Sirinathsingh, *Project Mgr*
John Mudrak, *VP Sales*
Paula Sirinathsingh, *Officer*
▲ EMP: 32 EST: 1960
SQ FT: 21,000
SALES (est): 8MM **Privately Held**
WEB: www.carteretdiecasting.com
SIC: 3364 Zinc & zinc-base alloy die-castings

(G-9968)
CATALENT INC (PA)
14 Schoolhouse Rd (08873-1213)
PHONE...............................732 537-6200
John R Chiminski, *CEO*
Alessandro Maselli, *President*
Steven L Fasman, *Senior VP*
Scott Gunther, *Senior VP*
Lance Miyamoto, *Senior VP*
EMP: 178
SQ FT: 265,000
SALES (est): 2.5B **Publicly Held**
SIC: 2834 Pharmaceutical preparations

(G-9969)
CATALENT CTS KANSAS CITY LLC
14 Schoolhouse Rd (08873-1213)
PHONE...............................732 537-6200
Scott Houlton, *Principal*
EMP: 4
SALES (est): 941.3K **Publicly Held**
SIC: 2834 Pharmaceutical preparations
PA: Catalent, Inc.
14 Schoolhouse Rd
Somerset NJ 08873

(G-9970)
CATALENT PHARMA SOLUTIONS LLC (DH)
14 Schoolhouse Rd (08873-1213)
P.O. Box 982106, El Paso TX (79998-2106)
PHONE...............................732 537-6200
Cornell Stamoran,
▲ EMP: 209
SALES (est): 81.3MM **Publicly Held**
SIC: 2834 Pharmaceutical preparations

(G-9971)
CATALENT PHARMA SOLUTIONS INC (HQ)
14 Schoolhouse Rd (08873-1213)
P.O. Box 982106, El Paso TX (79998-2106)
PHONE...............................732 537-6200
John R Chiminski, *President*
◆ EMP: 377
SQ FT: 265,000
SALES (est): 1.9B **Publicly Held**
SIC: 2834 3841 Pharmaceutical preparations; medical instruments & equipment, blood & bone work

(G-9972)
CATALENT US HOLDING I LLC
14 Schoolhouse Rd (08873-1213)
PHONE...............................877 587-1835
EMP: 5
SALES (est): 1.1MM **Publicly Held**
SIC: 2834 Pharmaceutical preparations
PA: Catalent, Inc.
14 Schoolhouse Rd
Somerset NJ 08873

(G-9973)
CAVAGNA NORTH AMERICA INC
50 Napoleon Ct (08873-1347)
PHONE...............................732 469-2100
Richard Darche, *Vice Pres*
Harry Tarsi, *Sales Mgr*
Nishant Patel, *Accounts Mgr*
Michael Toglia, *Manager*
Scott Littlewood, *Business Dir*
▲ EMP: 35
SQ FT: 27,000
SALES (est): 7.8MM
SALES (corp-wide): 2.7MM **Privately Held**
SIC: 3491 Gas valves & parts, industrial
HQ: Cavagna Group Spa
Via Statale 11/13
Calcinato BS 25011
030 966-3111

(G-9974)
CEDAR HILL LANDSCAPING
Also Called: Cedar Hill Topsoil
127 Cedar Grove Ln (08873-4718)
PHONE...............................732 469-1400
John E Janho Jr, *President*
Kelly Janho, *Office Mgr*
EMP: 20
SQ FT: 4,700
SALES (est): 3.4MM **Privately Held**
SIC: 4212 5261 1794 1429 Dump truck haulage; top soil; excavation work; trap rock, crushed & broken-quarrying

(G-9975)
COMPOSECURE LLC
309 Pierce St (08873-1229)
PHONE...............................908 518-0500
Michele Logan, *Mng Member*
EMP: 247 **Privately Held**
SIC: 2821 Plasticizer/additive based plastic materials
PA: Composecure L.L.C.
500 Memorial Dr Ste 4
Somerset NJ 08873

(G-9976)
COMPOSECURE LLC (PA)
500 Memorial Dr Ste 4 (08873-1383)
PHONE...............................908 518-0500
Luis Dasilva, *Vice Pres*
Stephen Luft, *Vice Pres*
Vincent Lombardo, *Mfg Mgr*
Jubeleen Gutierrez, *Purch Agent*
Barbara McQueary, *Purchasing*
▲ EMP: 200
SQ FT: 10,000
SALES (est): 126.3MM **Privately Held**
SIC: 2821 Plasticizer/additive based plastic materials

(G-9977)
CONSUMER GRAPHICS INC
18 Fordham Rd (08873-1064)
PHONE...............................732 469-4699
Ann Marie Dilorenzo, *President*
Mark Herzog, *Vice Pres*
EMP: 9
SQ FT: 7,500
SALES: 1.5MM **Privately Held**
SIC: 2741 2791 Miscellaneous publishing; typesetting

(G-9978)
COZZOLI MACHINE COMPANY (PA)
50 Schoolhouse Rd (08873-1289)
PHONE...............................732 564-0400
Joan Cozzoli Rooney, *President*
Pat Belefronte, *Human Res Mgr*
▲ EMP: 90 EST: 1919
SQ FT: 100,000

SALES (est): 18MM **Privately Held**
WEB: www.cozzoli.com
SIC: 3542 3565 Marking machines; bottle washing & sterilizing machines

(G-9979)
CSF CORPORATION (PA)
285 Davidson Ave Ste 103 (08873-4142)
PHONE...............................732 302-2222
Rich Scanlon, *President*
Melissa Spinola, *Business Mgr*
Raluca Iancu, *Controller*
Ashley Kaplan, *Marketing Mgr*
EMP: 50
SALES (est): 3.4MM **Privately Held**
SIC: 7372 Operating systems computer software

(G-9980)
CUSTOM ESSENCE
53 Veronica Ave (08873-3448)
PHONE...............................732 249-6405
Felix Buccellato, *President*
Christian Buccellato, *Exec VP*
Malini Amin, *Vice Pres*
Bob Diakon, *Vice Pres*
Raman Patel, *Vice Pres*
▼ EMP: 16
SQ FT: 5,000
SALES (est): 5.7MM **Privately Held**
WEB: www.customessence.com
SIC: 2844 Perfumes, natural or synthetic

(G-9981)
DAVIS-STANDARD LLC
220 Davidson Ave Ste 401 (08873-4146)
PHONE...............................908 722-6000
Frank Kennedy, *Branch Mgr*
EMP: 42 **Privately Held**
SIC: 3561 Pumps & pumping equipment
HQ: Davis-Standard, Llc
1 Extrusion Dr
Pawcatuck CT 06379

(G-9982)
DOW CHEMICAL COMPANY
1 Riverview Dr (08873-1139)
PHONE...............................800 258-2436
EMP: 71
SALES (corp-wide): 61.1B **Publicly Held**
SIC: 2821 3081 Thermoplastic materials; plastic film & sheet
HQ: The Dow Chemical Company
2211 H H Dow Way
Midland MI 48642
989 636-1000

(G-9983)
DYNAMIC SAFETY USA LLC
Also Called: Dynamic Safety International
400 Apgar Dr Ste H (08873-1154)
PHONE...............................844 378-7200
Rajeev S Emany, *President*
EMP: 4
SALES (est): 504K **Privately Held**
SIC: 3842 Personal safety equipment

(G-9984)
EFFEXOFT INC
1553 State Route 27 # 1100 (08873-3980)
PHONE...............................732 221-3642
Prasad Kunisetty, *President*
Llew Adal, *Administration*
Ginta Shaurina, *Administration*
Raj Sharan, *Recruiter*
EMP: 5 EST: 2007
SALES: 1MM **Privately Held**
SIC: 7372 7389 Business oriented computer software;

(G-9985)
EMMCO DEVELOPMENT CORP
243 Belmont Dr (08873-1286)
PHONE...............................732 469-6464
Linda Degaeta, *Vice Pres*
EMP: 15 EST: 1954
SQ FT: 16,000
SALES (est): 2.2MM **Privately Held**
SIC: 3562 3568 Ball bearings & parts; pivots, power transmission

(G-9986)
ENERSYS
80 Veronica Ave Ste 1 (08873-3498)
PHONE...............................800 719-7887
Fred Weber, *Branch Mgr*

EMP: 88
SALES (corp-wide): 2.8B **Publicly Held**
SIC: 3691 5063 Storage batteries; batteries
PA: Enersys
2366 Bernville Rd
Reading PA 19605
610 208-1991

(G-9987)
ENVIGO CRS INC (PA)
100 Mettlers Rd (08873-7378)
P.O. Box 2360, East Millstone (08875-2360)
PHONE...............................732 873-2550
Brian Cass, *CEO*
Joe Bedford, *Exec VP*
Carl John Michael Berg, *Vice Pres*
Michael Caulfield, *Vice Pres*
Nicki Iacono, *QC Mgr*
EMP: 183
SQ FT: 200,000
SALES (est): 94.1MM **Privately Held**
WEB: www.huntingdon.com
SIC: 2834 Pharmaceutical preparations

(G-9988)
EPIC MILLWORK LLC
1022 Hamilton St Ste J (08873-3387)
PHONE...............................732 296-0273
Jose Tabares, *Site Mgr*
Robert Epifano Jr, *Mng Member*
EMP: 40 EST: 2001
SALES: 2.8MM **Privately Held**
SIC: 1751 2431 Cabinet building & installation; millwork

(G-9989)
EQUIPMENT ERECTORS INC
15 Veronica Ave (08873-3489)
PHONE...............................732 846-1212
George Anderson, *President*
Rob Anderson, *Vice Pres*
Robert Anderson, *Vice Pres*
EMP: 50
SQ FT: 32,000
SALES (est): 9.9MM **Privately Held**
WEB: www.equipmenterectors.com
SIC: 3535 1796 Conveyors & conveying equipment; machinery installation

(G-9990)
EURODIA INDUSTRIE SA
Ameridia Div Eurodia Industrie
20 Worlds Fair Dr Ste F (08873-1362)
PHONE...............................732 805-4001
Daniel H Bar, *Vice Pres*
EMP: 4
SALES (corp-wide): 355.8K **Privately Held**
WEB: www.ameridia.com
SIC: 7389 3569 Design, commercial & industrial; sifting & screening machines
HQ: Eurodia Industrie
Eurodia Oenodia Zac Saint Martin
Pertuis 84120
490 087-500

(G-9991)
EXTRUSION TECHNIK USA INC
67 Veronica Ave Ste 15-16 (08873-3466)
PHONE...............................732 354-0177
Hemant Patel, *President*
▲ EMP: 10
SALES (est): 2.2MM **Privately Held**
SIC: 2821 Plastics materials & resins

(G-9992)
FALCON INDUSTRIES INC
371 Campus Dr (08873-1125)
PHONE...............................732 563-9889
Zig Michalski, *President*
Jim Harabedian, *Vice Pres*
Michael Miller, *Vice Pres*
Peter Wenzler, *VP Opers*
Peter Michalski, *Manager*
EMP: 60
SQ FT: 50,000
SALES (est): 13MM **Privately Held**
SIC: 3444 Sheet metalwork

(G-9993)
FANCYHEAT CORPORATION
40 Veronica Ave (08873-3417)
PHONE...............................973 589-1450
Fiore Masci, *President*

Jobee Ancona, *Vice Pres*
Joseph Diasparra, *Vice Pres*
▲ EMP: 16
SQ FT: 4,500
SALES (est): 4MM **Privately Held**
WEB: www.fancyheat.com
SIC: 2869 Fuels

(G-9994)
FLAVOR AND FD INGREDIENTS INC (PA)
Also Called: Summit Hill Flavors
21 Worlds Fair Dr (08873-1344)
PHONE..................................732 805-0335
Dwight Grenawalt, *Vice Pres*
▲ EMP: 38
SQ FT: 10,000
SALES (est): 9.5MM **Privately Held**
WEB: www.summithillflavors.com
SIC: 2087 Flavoring extracts & syrups

(G-9995)
FORTUNE INTERNATIONAL INC
56 Veronica Ave (08873-3417)
PHONE..................................732 214-0700
John Lai, *President*
Randell Wan, *Vice Pres*
◆ EMP: 8
SQ FT: 23,000
SALES (est): 1.5MM **Privately Held**
WEB: www.fortune-cnc.com
SIC: 3599 Machine shop, jobbing & repair

(G-9996)
G J CHEMICAL CO (PA)
40 Veronica Ave (08873-3417)
PHONE..................................973 589-1450
Diane Colonna, *President*
Arnold Colonna, *Purch Agent*
Gina Lopez, *Human Resources*
▲ EMP: 50
SQ FT: 45,000
SALES (est): 29.6MM **Privately Held**
SIC: 5169 2819 Industrial chemicals; chemicals, reagent grade: refined from technical grade

(G-9997)
GERICKE USA INC
14 Worlds Fair Dr Ste C (08873-1365)
PHONE..................................855 888-0088
Markus Gericke, *President*
Alberto Rodriguez, *Senior VP*
Alex Bickel, *Admin Sec*
◆ EMP: 4
SALES (est): 208.2K **Privately Held**
SIC: 3556 Dehydrating equipment, food processing

(G-9998)
GO FOTON CORPORATION (PA)
28 Worlds Fair Dr (08873-1391)
PHONE..................................732 412-7375
Simin Cai, *President*
Feng Tian, *Vice Pres*
Michael Zammit, *Vice Pres*
Alla Shtabnaya, *Engineer*
Joseph Stahley, *IT/INT Sup*
▲ EMP: 16 EST: 1983
SQ FT: 49,000
SALES (est): 2.5MM **Privately Held**
WEB: www.nsgamerica.com
SIC: 3229 Fiber optics strands

(G-9999)
HERR FOODS INCORPORATED
790 New Brunswick Rd (08873-5220)
PHONE..................................732 356-1295
Billy Esolda, *Branch Mgr*
Billy Esolida, *Manager*
EMP: 45
SQ FT: 10,000
SALES (corp-wide): 392.5MM **Privately Held**
WEB: www.herrs.com
SIC: 2096 Potato chips & similar snacks
PA: Herr Foods Incorporated
    20 Herr Dr
    Nottingham PA 19362
    610 932-9330

(G-10000)
HOUSE FOODS AMERICA CORP
801 Randolph Rd (08873-1224)
PHONE..................................732 537-9500
Tomio Uehara, *Manager*

EMP: 70 **Privately Held**
WEB: www.house-foods.com
SIC: 2099 Food preparations
HQ: House Foods America Corporation
    7351 Orangewood Ave
    Garden Grove CA 92841
    714 901-4350

(G-10001)
HOUSE OF CUPCAKES LLC
51 Suydam Rd (08873-7306)
PHONE..................................908 413-3076
Ruth Bzdewka, *Principal*
EMP: 8
SALES (est): 590.2K **Privately Held**
SIC: 2051 Bread, cake & related products

(G-10002)
HUAHAI US INC
700 Atrium Dr (08873-4107)
PHONE..................................609 655-1688
Jun Du, *President*
Qi Zhao, *Accountant*
Michelle Hu, *Manager*
EMP: 19
SALES (est): 3.4MM **Privately Held**
SIC: 2834 Pharmaceutical preparations

(G-10003)
HYDRATIGHT OPERATIONS INC
Also Called: Biach
12 Worlds Fair Dr Ste A (08873-1348)
PHONE..................................732 271-4100
Robert Boychuk, *General Mgr*
Paulette Weiss, *Vice Pres*
Richard Hill, *Branch Mgr*
EMP: 17
SALES (corp-wide): 1.1B **Publicly Held**
SIC: 3599 Machine & other job shop work
HQ: Hydratight Operations, Inc.
    1102 Hall Ct
    Deer Park TX 77536
    713 860-4200

(G-10004)
INDUSTRIAL COMBUSTION ASSN
20 Worlds Fair Dr Ste C (08873-1362)
PHONE..................................732 271-0300
Robert Peles, *President*
Regina Peles, *Corp Secy*
EMP: 11 EST: 1938
SQ FT: 5,600
SALES (est): 3.5MM **Privately Held**
WEB: www.icanj.com
SIC: 5074 5075 3594 Oil burners; warm air heating equipment & supplies; fluid power pumps & motors

(G-10005)
INVADERM CORPORATION
25 Worlds Fair Dr (08873-1344)
PHONE..................................732 307-7926
Nilesh Patel, *President*
EMP: 6
SALES (est): 2MM **Privately Held**
SIC: 2834 Pharmaceutical preparations

(G-10006)
IVOCLAR VIVADENT MFG INC
500 Memorial Dr (08873-1383)
PHONE..................................732 563-4755
Paul Panzera, *General Mgr*
Lou Alcuri, *Project Mgr*
Joe Dejesso, *Production*
Adam Pasierski, *Production*
Daniel Carroll, *Purch Mgr*
▲ EMP: 80 EST: 1961
SQ FT: 17,000
SALES (est): 16.4MM
SALES (corp-wide): 815MM **Privately Held**
WEB: www.ivoclarna.com
SIC: 3843 Dental materials
HQ: Ivoclar Vivadent, Inc.
    175 Pineview Dr
    Amherst NY 14228
    716 691-0010

(G-10007)
JANSSEN PHARMACEUTICALS INC
1 Campus Dr (08873)
PHONE..................................908 218-6908
Gloria Gibson, *Branch Mgr*
EMP: 80

SALES (corp-wide): 81.5B **Publicly Held**
WEB: www.ortho-mcneil.com
SIC: 2833 Medicinals & botanicals
HQ: Janssen Pharmaceuticals, Inc.
    1125 Trnton Harbourton Rd
    Titusville NJ 08560
    609 730-2000

(G-10008)
JANSSEN PHARMACEUTICALS INC
1 Cottontail Ln (08873-1135)
P.O. Box 300, Raritan (08869-0602)
PHONE..................................908 218-7701
George Weaver, *Director*
EMP: 80
SALES (corp-wide): 81.5B **Publicly Held**
WEB: www.ortho-mcneil.com
SIC: 2833 Medicinals & botanicals
HQ: Janssen Pharmaceuticals, Inc.
    1125 Trnton Harbourton Rd
    Titusville NJ 08560
    609 730-2000

(G-10009)
JERSEY METAL WORKS LLC
1022 Hamilton St Untid (08873)
PHONE..................................732 565-1313
Robert Epifano Jr, *Mng Member*
John Epifano, *Mng Member*
EMP: 8
SALES (est): 1.2MM **Privately Held**
SIC: 3441 Fabricated structural metal

(G-10010)
KAS ORIENTAL RUGS INC (PA)
62 Veronica Ave Ste A (08873-3484)
PHONE..................................732 545-1900
Prasadarao B Yarlagadda, *President*
Prasadarao Yarlagadda, *Principal*
Santhi Yarlagadda, *Vice Pres*
Lacy Estes, *Director*
Kasturibai Yarlagadda, *Admin Sec*
▲ EMP: 27
SQ FT: 100,000
SALES (est): 5.7MM **Privately Held**
WEB: www.kasrugs.com
SIC: 2392 2273 Cushions & pillows; carpets & rugs

(G-10011)
KRAUS & NAIMER INC (PA)
760 New Brunswick Rd (08873-5299)
PHONE..................................732 560-1240
Joachim Laurenz Naimer, *President*
Mark Farrell, *Managing Dir*
Ray Paella, *Vice Pres*
Ray Parello, *Vice Pres*
Agustin Muneton, *Electrical Engi*
EMP: 40 EST: 1950
SQ FT: 45,000
SALES (est): 15.8MM **Privately Held**
WEB: www.krausnaimer.com
SIC: 5063 3678 3643 Electrical supplies; electronic connectors; current-carrying wiring devices

(G-10012)
LA CASA DE TORTILLA
2017 State Route 27 (08873-3838)
PHONE..................................732 398-0660
Peter Chan, *Owner*
EMP: 6
SALES (est): 336.7K **Privately Held**
SIC: 2099 Tortillas, fresh or refrigerated

(G-10013)
LABVANTAGE SOLUTIONS INC (HQ)
265 Davidson Ave Ste 220 (08873-4120)
PHONE..................................908 707-4100
John Hesier, *President*
William Musil, *Technical Mgr*
EMP: 50
SQ FT: 15,000
SALES (est): 46.8MM **Privately Held**
WEB: www.labvantage.com
SIC: 7372 Prepackaged software

(G-10014)
LEAD BEAD PUBLISHING COMPANY
46 Shelly Dr (08873-1806)
PHONE..................................732 246-0410
James H Wiggins III, *Owner*

EMP: 4
SALES (est): 119.2K **Privately Held**
SIC: 2741 Music book & sheet music publishing

(G-10015)
LEVOMED INC
2 Rue Matisse (08873-4890)
PHONE..................................908 359-4804
Mohan Devineni, *President*
◆ EMP: 2
SALES: 1.5MM **Privately Held**
SIC: 2834 7389 Pills, pharmaceutical;

(G-10016)
LEWIS SCHELLER PRINTING CORP
Also Called: Scheller, Lewis Printing
1723 Hwy 27 (08873)
PHONE..................................732 843-5050
Lewis Scheller, *President*
Peggy Scheller, *Principal*
EMP: 6
SQ FT: 1,800
SALES (est): 94K **Privately Held**
WEB: www.lewprint.com
SIC: 2752 7334 Commercial printing, offset; photocopying & duplicating services

(G-10017)
LOGAN INSTRUMENTS CORPORATION
19c Schoolhouse Rd Ste C (08873)
P.O. Box 5785 (08875-5785)
PHONE..................................732 302-9888
Luke Lee, *President*
Vivian Lee, *Admin Sec*
◆ EMP: 17
SQ FT: 8,000
SALES: 30K **Privately Held**
SIC: 3559 Pharmaceutical machinery

(G-10018)
LOREAL USA PRODUCTS INC
Franklin Manufacturing
100 Commerce Dr (08873-3482)
PHONE..................................732 873-3520
Ed Allen, *Branch Mgr*
Yeji Shin, *Manager*
Kevin Stanton, *Manager*
Michael Dupey, *Director*
EMP: 600
SALES (corp-wide): 4.4B **Privately Held**
WEB: www.lorealparisusa.com
SIC: 2844 Toilet preparations
HQ: L'oreal Usa Products, Inc.
    10 Hudson Yards
    New York NY 10001

(G-10019)
LUMETA CORPORATION (PA)
300 Atrium Dr Ste 300 # 300 (08873-4160)
P.O. Box 822043, Philadelphia PA (19182-2043)
PHONE..................................732 357-3500
Michael Markulec, *President*
George Budd, *Principal*
Valerie Clayton, *Principal*
Constantine Malaxos, *Principal*
Matt Webster, *Vice Pres*
EMP: 25
SQ FT: 14,000
SALES (est): 3.7MM **Privately Held**
WEB: www.lumeta.com
SIC: 7372 Business oriented computer software

(G-10020)
LUPIN PHARMACEUTICALS INC
390 Campus Dr (08873-1102)
PHONE..................................908 603-6075
EMP: 4
SALES (est): 328.7K **Privately Held**
SIC: 2834 Pharmaceutical preparations

(G-10021)
LUPIN PHARMACEUTICALS INC
400 Campus Dr (08873-1145)
PHONE..................................908 603-6000
EMP: 21
SALES (corp-wide): 1.5B **Privately Held**
SIC: 2834 Pharmaceutical preparations
HQ: Lupin Pharmaceuticals, Inc.
    111 S Calvert St Fl 21
    Baltimore MD 21202
    410 576-2000

(G-10022)
MARIANO PRESS LLC
14 Veronica Ave (08873-3417)
PHONE...................................732 247-3659
Jerry Mariano, *Partner*
Joe Mariano, *Partner*
Jan Vreeland, *Opers Mgr*
▲ EMP: 12
SQ FT: 10,000
SALES (est): 2.3MM **Privately Held**
WEB: www.marianopress.com
SIC: 2752 2796 2789 2759 Commercial
printing, offset; platemaking services;
bookbinding & related work; commercial
printing

(G-10023)
MARMO ENTERPRISES INC
468 Elizabeth Ave (08873-5200)
PHONE...................................732 649-3011
Matthew Partsinevelos, *President*
EMP: 9
SQ FT: 9,400
SALES (est): 1.4MM **Privately Held**
WEB: www.marmoenterprises.com
SIC: 3281 Granite, cut & shaped

(G-10024)
MATERIALS TECHNOLOGY INC
Also Called: MTI Solar
220 Churchill Ave (08873-3441)
PHONE...................................732 246-1000
Sheldon L Soskin, *President*
Martin Stanko, *Vice Pres*
▲ EMP: 6
SQ FT: 26,800
SALES (est): 856K **Privately Held**
WEB: www.mtisolar.com
SIC: 3497 Copper foil
PA: Marshel Associates Inc
220 Churchill Ave
Somerset NJ 08873
732 246-1000

(G-10025)
MATRIX CONTROLS COMPANY INC
330 Elizabeth Ave (08873-7018)
PHONE...................................732 469-5551
Robert Lindeman, *Vice Pres*
EMP: 15 EST: 1958
SQ FT: 1,800
SALES (est): 1.9MM **Privately Held**
SIC: 3823 Controllers for process vari-
ables, all types

(G-10026)
MEDA PHARMACEUTICALS INC
265 Davidson Ave Ste 300 (08873-4120)
PHONE...................................732 564-2200
Joe Osborne, *District Mgr*
Jeffrey Hostler, *CFO*
Alfredo Quinones, *Accounts Mgr*
Matthew Holley, *Admin Sec*
▲ EMP: 150
SQ FT: 270,000
SALES (est): 126.4MM
SALES (corp-wide): 204.1K **Privately
Held**
WEB: www.medapharma.us
SIC: 2834 Pharmaceutical preparations
HQ: Mylan Inc
1000 Mylan Blvd
Canonsburg PA 15317
724 514-1800

(G-10027)
MEDICAL TRANSCRIPTION BILLING (PA)
Also Called: Mtbc
7 Clyde Rd (08873-5049)
PHONE...................................732 873-5049
Stephen A Snyder, *CEO*
A Hadi Chaudhry, *President*
Mahmud Haq, *Chairman*
Howard Clark, *Vice Chairman*
Loraine Goetsch, *Vice Pres*
▲ EMP: 10
SQ FT: 2,400
SALES (est): 50.5MM **Publicly Held**
WEB: www.mtbc.com
SIC: 7372 Prepackaged software

(G-10028)
MELILLO CONSULTING INC (PA)
285 Davidson Ave Ste 202 (08873-4153)
PHONE...................................732 563-8400
Mark J Melillo, *CEO*
Karen L Melillo, *Vice Pres*
Carolyn Borelly, *Project Mgr*
Angela Sutton, *Project Mgr*
Steven Branco, *Engineer*
EMP: 40
SQ FT: 21,000
SALES (est): 25.3MM **Privately Held**
WEB: www.mjm.com
SIC: 7371 7373 7372 5045 Computer
software development & applications;
computer integrated systems design;
prepackaged software; computers, pe-
ripherals & software

(G-10029)
MELLON D P M L L C (HQ)
2 Worlds Fair Dr Ste 310 (08873-1372)
PHONE...................................732 563-0030
Robert M Aaron, *President*
Steve R Diemer, *Vice Pres*
Guy Castranova, *CFO*
Charles Crow, *Asst Sec*
EMP: 5
SQ FT: 20,000
SALES (est): 30MM
SALES (corp-wide): 16.3B **Publicly Held**
SIC: 2421 Sawmills & planing mills, gen-
eral
PA: The Bank Of New York Mellon Corpora-
tion
240 E Greenwich St
New York NY 10007
212 495-1784

(G-10030)
MICRO STAMPING CORPORATION (PA)
Also Called: Micro Medical Technologies
140 Belmont Dr (08873-5113)
PHONE...................................732 302-0800
Brian Semcer, *President*
Frank Semcer, *Principal*
Frank J Semcer, *Chairman*
Jeffrey Drews, *Vice Pres*
Charles Edwards, *Vice Pres*
▲ EMP: 240 EST: 1945
SQ FT: 68,000
SALES (est): 51.2MM **Privately Held**
WEB: www.microstamping.com
SIC: 3841 3469 Surgical & medical instru-
ments; metal stampings

(G-10031)
MODULATION SCIENCES INC
12 Worlds Fair Dr Ste A (08873-1348)
PHONE...................................732 302-3090
Eric Small, *CEO*
EMP: 14
SQ FT: 7,500
SALES (est): 2.4MM **Privately Held**
WEB: www.modsci.com
SIC: 3663 Satellites, communications

(G-10032)
MRP NEW JERSEY LLC
17 Veronica Ave (08873-3514)
PHONE...................................732 873-7148
EMP: 4
SALES (est): 432.8K **Privately Held**
SIC: 3089 Plastics products

(G-10033)
MTBC ACQUISITION CORP (HQ)
7 Clyde Rd (08873-5049)
PHONE...................................732 873-5133
Mahmud Haq, *Principal*
EMP: 4
SALES (est): 33.5MM
SALES (corp-wide): 50.5MM **Publicly
Held**
SIC: 7372 Prepackaged software
PA: Medical Transcription Billing, Corp.
7 Clyde Rd
Somerset NJ 08873
732 873-5133

(G-10034)
MTBC HEALTH INC (HQ)
7 Clyde Rd (08873-5049)
PHONE...................................732 873-5133
Stephen Snyder, *CEO*

Bill Korn, *CFO*
EMP: 2
SALES (est): 3.4MM
SALES (corp-wide): 50.5MM **Publicly
Held**
SIC: 7372 Prepackaged software
PA: Medical Transcription Billing, Corp.
7 Clyde Rd
Somerset NJ 08873
732 873-5133

(G-10035)
MTBC PRACTICE MANAGEMENT CORP
7 Clyde Rd (08873-5049)
PHONE...................................732 873-5133
Stephen Snyder, *CEO*
Bill Korn, *CFO*
EMP: 120
SALES (est): 1.5MM
SALES (corp-wide): 50.5MM **Publicly
Held**
SIC: 7372 Prepackaged software
HQ: Mtbc Health, Inc.
7 Clyde Rd
Somerset NJ 08873
732 873-5133

(G-10036)
MULTILINK TECHNOLOGY CORP
300 Atrium Dr Fl 2 (08873-4160)
PHONE...................................732 805-9355
EMP: 45
SQ FT: 36,000
SALES (est): 3MM
SALES (corp-wide): 3.9B **Publicly Held**
SIC: 3674 Mfg Semiconductors/Related
Devices
HQ: Microsemi Communications, Inc.
4721 Calle Carga
Camarillo CA 93012
805 388-3700

(G-10037)
MYLAN API INC (DH)
49 Napoleon Ct (08873-1392)
PHONE...................................732 748-8882
John Miraglia, *President*
Alan Weiner, *Vice Pres*
Thomas Salus, *Admin Sec*
Kevin Macikowski, *Asst Sec*
EMP: 41 EST: 2014
SALES (est): 6.6MM
SALES (corp-wide): 204.1K **Privately
Held**
SIC: 2834 Solutions, pharmaceutical
HQ: Mylan Pharmaceuticals Inc.
781 Chestnut Ridge Rd
Morgantown WV 26505
304 599-2595

(G-10038)
MYLAN API US LLC
Also Called: Apicore US LLC
49 Napoleon Ct (08873-1392)
PHONE...................................732 748-8882
John Miraglia, *President*
Alan Weiner, *Vice Pres*
Thomas Salus, *Admin Sec*
Kevin Macikowski, *Asst Sec*
EMP: 40
SALES (est): 6.6MM
SALES (corp-wide): 204.1K **Privately
Held**
SIC: 2834 Pharmaceutical preparations
HQ: Mylan Api Inc.
49 Napoleon Ct
Somerset NJ 08873
732 748-8882

(G-10039)
NANOOPTO CORPORATION
1600 Cottontail Ln Ste 1 (08873-5106)
PHONE...................................732 627-0808
Fax: 732 627-9886
EMP: 31
SALES (est): 4.7MM **Privately Held**
SIC: 3827 Mfg Optical Instruments/Lenses

(G-10040)
NEW WORLD STAINLESS LLC
100 Randolph Rd Ste 5 (08873-1384)
PHONE...................................732 412-7137
Harry Stamateris, *Marketing Staff*
Cameron Zielinskie,
EMP: 40

SALES (est): 17.7MM **Privately Held**
SIC: 3317 Steel pipe & tubes

(G-10041)
NOVEL LABORATORIES INC
400 Campus Dr (08873-1145)
PHONE...................................908 603-6000
Veerappan Subramanian, *President*
Prasad Uv, *Opers Staff*
Rakesh Jambudi, *Production*
Venu Padmanabhan, *Production*
Devraj Swaminarayan, *Production*
▲ EMP: 175
SQ FT: 90,000
SALES (est): 82.4MM
SALES (corp-wide): 1.5B **Privately Held**
WEB: www.novellabs.net
SIC: 2834 Pharmaceutical preparations
HQ: Lupin Pharmaceuticals, Inc.
111 S Calvert St Fl 21
Baltimore MD 21202
410 576-2000

(G-10042)
ODIN PHARMACEUTICALS LLC
300 Franklin Square Dr (08873-4187)
PHONE...................................732 554-1100
Veerappan Subramanian,
EMP: 5
SQ FT: 70,000
SALES (est): 252.7K **Privately Held**
SIC: 2834 5122 Pharmaceutical prepara-
tions; pharmaceuticals

(G-10043)
OFS FITEL LLC
25 Schoolhouse Rd (08873-1207)
PHONE...................................732 748-7409
Peter Stupak, *Manager*
EMP: 30 **Privately Held**
WEB: www.ofsoptics.com
SIC: 3357 3661 Fiber optic cable (insu-
lated); telephone & telegraph apparatus
HQ: Ofs Fitel Llc
2000 Northeast Expy
Norcross GA 30071
888 342-3743

(G-10044)
OFS SPECIALTY PHOTONICS & LABS
25 Schoolhouse Rd (08873-1207)
PHONE...................................732 748-7401
EMP: 4
SALES (est): 270.6K **Privately Held**
SIC: 3661 Fiber optics communications
equipment

(G-10045)
OGURA INDUSTRIAL CORP (HQ)
100 Randolph Rd (08873-1384)
P.O. Box 5790 (08875-5790)
PHONE...................................586 749-1900
Frank J Flemming, *President*
▲ EMP: 13 EST: 1997
SALES (est): 1.9MM **Privately Held**
WEB: www.oguraclutch.com
SIC: 3714 Motor vehicle parts & acces-
sories

(G-10046)
ORION PRECISION INDUSTRIES
8 Veronica Ave (08873-3400)
PHONE...................................732 247-9704
John Sztankovits, *President*
Edith Sztankovits, *Vice Pres*
Paul Murcavage, *Plant Mgr*
Steve Foulon, *VP Sls/Mktg*
Bill Miicke, *Natl Sales Mgr*
EMP: 25
SQ FT: 8,000
SALES (est): 5.5MM **Privately Held**
WEB: www.orionprecision.com
SIC: 3451 Screw machine products

(G-10047)
OTICON INC (DH)
580 Howard Ave Ste B (08873-1136)
P.O. Box 6724 (08875-6724)
PHONE...................................732 560-1220
Niels Jacobsen, *CEO*
Svend Thomsen, *CFO*
Roger Peterson, *VP Sales*
Leanne Blair, *VP Mktg*
Robert Buchas, *Admin Sec*
▲ EMP: 145

G
E
O
G
R
A
P
H
I
C

SQ FT: 25,000
SALES (est): 33.3MM
SALES (corp-wide): 1.2MM **Privately Held**
WEB: www.oticonus.com
SIC: 3842 5047 Hearing aids; hearing aids
HQ: Demant A/S
   Kongebakken 9
   SmOrum 2765
   391 771-00

(G-10048)
OTICON MEDICAL LLC
580 Howard Ave (08873-1136)
PHONE..................................732 560-0727
Curt Gorman, *President*
John Sparacio, *President*
Cathy Van Evra, *QC Mgr*
▲ **EMP:** 23
SQ FT: 3,000
SALES (est): 2.8MM
SALES (corp-wide): 1.2MM **Privately Held**
SIC: 3842 Implants, surgical
HQ: Oticon Medical Ab
   Datavagen 37b
   Askim 436 3
   317 486-100

(G-10049)
P & R CASTINGS LLC
325 Pierce St (08873-1229)
PHONE..................................732 302-3600
Brian H Margulies,
Benjamin S Margulies,
▲ **EMP:** 25
SQ FT: 53,000
SALES (est): 2.9MM **Privately Held**
SIC: 3297 Castable refractories, nonclay

(G-10050)
P & R FASTENERS INC (PA)
325 Pierce St (08873-1229)
PHONE..................................732 302-3600
Benjamin S Margulies, *President*
Terry Carpenter, *General Mgr*
Phil Vesuvio, *General Mgr*
Bob Noonan, *CFO*
Jonathan Friedman, *Business Anlyst*
◆ **EMP:** 50 **EST:** 1970
SQ FT: 103,000
SALES (est): 24.5MM **Privately Held**
WEB: www.prfast.com
SIC: 5085 3452 Fasteners, industrial: nuts, bolts, screws, etc.; screws, metal

(G-10051)
PACON MANUFACTURING CORP
Also Called: Baumgartner Associates
400 Pierce St (08873)
PHONE..................................732 764-9070
Dorothy H Shannon, *Ch of Bd*
A Vernon Shannon III, *President*
Micheal Shannon, *President*
Lawrence H Shannon, *Vice Pres*
Richard Cuminale, *CFO*
▲ **EMP:** 125
SQ FT: 168,000
SALES (est): 43.7MM **Privately Held**
WEB: www.paconmfg.com
SIC: 2676 3821 3842 Sanitary paper products; incubators, laboratory; surgical appliances & supplies

(G-10052)
PERMABOND LLC (PA)
223 Churchill Ave (08873-3487)
PHONE..................................610 323-5003
Attilio Grossi, *CEO*
Amy Sutryn,
▲ **EMP:** 6
SALES: 3.6MM **Privately Held**
WEB: www.permabond.com
SIC: 2891 Adhesives & sealants

(G-10053)
PIM BRANDS LLC
500 Pierce St (08873-1270)
P.O. Box 8, Allentown (08501-0008)
PHONE..................................732 560-8300
Michael Rosenberg, *CEO*
Kevin Walsh, *President*
▲ **EMP:** 89
SQ FT: 180,000

SALES (est): 23MM **Privately Held**
WEB: www.promotioninmotion.com
SIC: 2064 Candy & other confectionery products

(G-10054)
POWER CONTAINER CORP
Also Called: PCC
33 Schoolhouse Rd Ste 2 (08873-1386)
PHONE..................................732 560-3655
Pittheus Molemans, *President*
Tim Brinkerhoff, *Maint Spvr*
Raphael Tacconi, *Mfg Staff*
Michael Ochieng, *Engineer*
Richard Tomasco, *Engineer*
◆ **EMP:** 32
SQ FT: 40,000
SALES (est): 6.4MM **Privately Held**
WEB: www.powercontainer.com
SIC: 3589 Commercial cooking & food-warming equipment

(G-10055)
PRESPERSE CORPORATION (PA)
19 Schoolhouse Rd (08873-1385)
PHONE..................................732 356-5200
Paulo Rodrigues, *President*
Joseph Macri, *CFO*
Tim Phillip, *Controller*
Stephen Doherty, *Technology*
Greg Delaney, *Planning*
◆ **EMP:** 20
SALES (est): 43.3MM **Privately Held**
WEB: www.presperse.com
SIC: 2844 Cosmetic preparations

(G-10056)
PRESTIGE CAMERA LLC
245 Belmont Dr (08873-1217)
PHONE..................................718 257-5888
Albert Houllou,
Frieda Stern,
▼ **EMP:** 50
SALES (est): 2.9MM **Privately Held**
SIC: 3861 Cameras & related equipment

(G-10057)
PROGENICS PHARMACEUTICALS INC
110 Clyde Rd Ste 4 (08873-3476)
PHONE..................................646 975-2500
Ben Osorio, *Manager*
EMP: 15
SALES (corp-wide): 15.6MM **Publicly Held**
SIC: 2834 Pharmaceutical preparations
PA: Progenics Pharmaceuticals Inc
   1 World Trade Ctr Fl 47
   New York NY 10007
   646 975-2500

(G-10058)
PROMOTION IN MOTION INC
500 Pierce St (08873-1270)
PHONE..................................732 560-8300
Frank McSorley, *Branch Mgr*
Susan O'Donnell, *Director*
EMP: 30
SALES (corp-wide): 146.5MM **Privately Held**
WEB: www.promotioninmotion.com
SIC: 2064 Candy & other confectionery products
PA: Promotion In Motion, Inc.
   25 Commerce Dr
   Allendale NJ 07401
   201 962-8530

(G-10059)
PTS INTERMEDIATE HOLDINGS LLC
14 Schoolhouse Rd (08873-1213)
PHONE..................................732 537-6200
EMP: 3000
SALES (est): 705.9MM **Publicly Held**
SIC: 2834 Pharmaceutical preparations
PA: Catalent, Inc.
   14 Schoolhouse Rd
   Somerset NJ 08873

(G-10060)
QUAD/GRAPHICS INC
13 Jensen Dr Ste 100 (08873-1393)
PHONE..................................732 469-0189

EMP: 50
SALES (corp-wide): 4.3B **Publicly Held**
SIC: 2752 Lithographic Commercial Printing
PA: Quad/Graphics Inc.
   N61w23044 Harrys Way
   Sussex WI 53089
   414 566-6000

(G-10061)
RARITAN INC (DH)
400 Cottontail Ln (08873-1238)
PHONE..................................732 764-8886
Doug Fikse, *President*
Henry Hsu, *Vice Pres*
Daniel Moran, *Vice Pres*
Ralf Ploenes, *Vice Pres*
Brian Fregeolle, *Warehouse Mgr*
▲ **EMP:** 41
SALES (est): 87.7MM
SALES (corp-wide): 21.2MM **Privately Held**
SIC: 3612 3577 Transformers, except electric; computer peripheral equipment
HQ: Legrand North America, Llc
   60 Woodlawn St
   West Hartford CT 06110
   860 233-6251

(G-10062)
RARITAN AMERICAS INC (DH)
Also Called: Raritan Computer
400 Cottontail Ln (08873-1238)
PHONE..................................732 764-8886
Ching-I Hsu, *President*
Stephen Gagliardo, *Technical Mgr*
Monica Madda, *Engineer*
Bob Dennerlein, *CFO*
Scott Helias, *Marketing Staff*
▲ **EMP:** 110
SQ FT: 55,000
SALES (est): 46.8MM
SALES (corp-wide): 21.2MM **Privately Held**
WEB: www.raritan.com
SIC: 3577 Computer peripheral equipment

(G-10063)
RED SQUARE FOODS INC
62 Berry St (08873-3505)
PHONE..................................732 846-0190
Boris Rapoport, *President*
Yuri Muzykozsky, *Vice Pres*
EMP: 12
SQ FT: 3,500
SALES (est): 2MM **Privately Held**
SIC: 2013 Head cheese from purchased meat products

(G-10064)
RENDAS TOOL & DIE INC
417 Elizabeth Ave (08873-1292)
P.O. Box 49, Martinsville (08836-0049)
PHONE..................................732 469-4670
Laszlo Rendas, *President*
Mary Ellen Rendas, *Admin Sec*
EMP: 25
SQ FT: 30,000
SALES (est): 1.6MM **Privately Held**
SIC: 3599 Machine shop, jobbing & repair

(G-10065)
REVENT INCORPORATED
22 Roosevelt Ave (08873-5031)
PHONE..................................732 777-5187
Daniel Lago, *CEO*
Charles Rampersaud, *Co-Owner*
Stefan Fallgren, *Vice Pres*
Stuart Hendry, *Vice Pres*
Lana Bildey, *Human Res Mgr*
◆ **EMP:** 40
SQ FT: 50,000
SALES: 18.6MM
SALES (corp-wide): 38.4MM **Privately Held**
WEB: www.revent.com
SIC: 3556 Ovens, bakery
PA: Revent International Ab
   Ekebyvagen 18
   Upplands Vasby 194 9
   859 000-600

(G-10066)
ROSENWACH TANK CO LLC
Also Called: Rosenwach Group
1100 Randolph Rd (08873-1291)
PHONE..................................732 563-4900
Andrew Rosenwach,
EMP: 30
SALES (est): 333.1K **Privately Held**
SIC: 3443 1711 Water tanks, metal plate; heating & air conditioning contractors

(G-10067)
ROTOR CLIP COMPANY INC (PA)
Also Called: Rotor Clamp
187 Davidson Ave (08873-4192)
PHONE..................................732 469-7707
Robert Slass, *President*
Jon Coiro, *General Mgr*
Benjamin Wetzel, *Counsel*
Henry Yates, *Vice Pres*
Jeff Van, *Plant Mgr*
▲ **EMP:** 290
SQ FT: 50,000
SALES (est): 76.6MM **Privately Held**
WEB: www.rotorclip.com
SIC: 3429 Metal fasteners; clamps & couplings, hose

(G-10068)
RUST-OLEUM CORPORATION
173 Belmont Dr (08873-1218)
PHONE..................................847 367-7700
Robert Nanes, *Plant Mgr*
Gail Gesicki, *Branch Mgr*
Andrew Talian, *Maintence Staff*
EMP: 28
SALES (corp-wide): 5.5B **Publicly Held**
WEB: www.rust-oleum.com
SIC: 2851 Paints & allied products
HQ: Rust-Oleum Corporation
   11 E Hawthorn Pkwy
   Vernon Hills IL 60061
   847 367-7700

(G-10069)
RUST-OLEUM CORPORATION
323 Campus Dr (08873-1138)
PHONE..................................732 469-8100
Rebecca Spencer, *Branch Mgr*
James Farrand, *Director*
EMP: 30
SALES (corp-wide): 5.5B **Publicly Held**
WEB: www.zinsser.com
SIC: 2851 2821 Shellac (protective coating); plastics materials & resins
HQ: Rust-Oleum Corporation
   11 E Hawthorn Pkwy
   Vernon Hills IL 60061
   847 367-7700

(G-10070)
SAINT-GOBAIN PRFMCE PLAS CORP
Also Called: Flexible Components
1600 Cottontail Ln (08873-5106)
PHONE..................................732 652-0910
George Carpenter, *Manager*
EMP: 75
SALES (corp-wide): 215.9MM **Privately Held**
SIC: 3599 3429 2891 2851 Flexible metal hose, tubing & bellows; manufactured hardware (general); adhesives & sealants; paints & allied products
HQ: Saint-Gobain Performance Plastics Corporation
   31500 Solon Rd
   Solon OH 44139
   440 836-6900

(G-10071)
SATURN OVERHEAD EQUIPMENT LLC
100 Apgar Dr (08873-1146)
PHONE..................................732 560-7210
Steven Gordan,
Eugenio Moutela,
▲ **EMP:** 11
SQ FT: 15,000
SALES (est): 3.5MM **Privately Held**
WEB: www.saturneng.com
SIC: 3537 3536 Industrial trucks & tractors; hoists

(G-10072)
SIGNIFY NORTH AMERICA CORP (DH)
Also Called: Color Kinetics
200 Franklin Square Dr (08873-4181)
P.O. Box 100285, Atlanta GA (30384-0285)
PHONE................................732 563-3000
Brent Shafer, *CEO*
Eugene De Lannoy, *CFO*
Raoul Gatzen, *CFO*
Philip O'Donnell, *Sales Staff*
Diego Campos, *Manager*
▲ EMP: 10
SQ FT: 20,000
SALES (est): 3.6B
SALES (corp-wide): 7.2B **Privately Held**
WEB: www.colorkinetics.com
SIC: 3646 Commercial indusl & institutional electric lighting fixtures
HQ: Signify Netherlands B.V.
High Tech Campus 48
Eindhoven 5656
402 791-111

(G-10073)
SOMERSET OUTPATIENT SURGERY
100 Franklin Square Dr # 100 (08873-4109)
PHONE................................781 635-2807
Sharon Bowen, *Principal*
EMP: 4
SALES (est): 310K **Privately Held**
SIC: 3841 Surgical & medical instruments

(G-10074)
SONIC INNOVATIONS INC
2501 Cottontail Ln (08873-5125)
P.O. Box 6779 (08875-6779)
PHONE................................888 423-7834
Joseph A Lugara, *President*
EMP: 8
SALES (est): 1.2MM **Privately Held**
SIC: 3842 Hearing aids
PA: Sonic Ag
Morgenstrasse 131b
Bern BE 3018
315 602-121

(G-10075)
STUART STEEL PROTECTION CORP
411 Elizabeth Ave (08873-1292)
P.O. Box 476, South Bound Brook (08880-0476)
PHONE................................732 469-5544
Gordon Stuart, *President*
◆ EMP: 20 EST: 1952
SALES (est): 12.6MM **Privately Held**
WEB: www.stusteel.com
SIC: 3599 3292 2899 Custom machinery; pipe covering (heat insulating material), except felt; chemical preparations

(G-10076)
STULL TECHNOLOGIES LLC
17 Veronica Ave (08873-3514)
PHONE................................732 873-5000
Gene Stull, *CEO*
Jason Stull, *VP Opers*
Vicky Clark, *Production*
Sanket Khandelwal, *Engineer*
Joe Sebastian, *Engineer*
▲ EMP: 95 EST: 1986
SQ FT: 189,000
SALES (est): 33.3MM **Privately Held**
WEB: www.stulltech.com
SIC: 3089 Closures, plastic
HQ: Mold-Rite Plastics, Llc
30 N La Salle St Ste 2425
Chicago IL 60602
518 561-1812

(G-10077)
SUNBIRD SOFTWARE INC
200 Cottontail Ln B106e (08873-1231)
PHONE................................732 993-4476
Herman Chan, *President*
EMP: 60 EST: 2015
SQ FT: 10,000
SALES (est): 7.6MM **Privately Held**
SIC: 7372 7371 Business oriented computer software; computer software development

(G-10078)
SYSCO GUEST SUPPLY LLC (HQ)
Also Called: Int'l Purchasing Exchange
300 Davidson Ave (08873-4175)
P.O. Box 6782 (08875-6782)
PHONE................................732 537-2297
Dave M Shattuck, *Vice Pres*
◆ EMP: 125
SALES (est): 1.4B
SALES (corp-wide): 60.1B **Publicly Held**
SIC: 5122 2844 5131 5139 Toilet soap; druggists' sundries; shampoos, rinses, conditioners: hair; toilet preparations; mouthwashes; sewing accessories; hair accessories; shoe accessories; hotels; casino hotel; hotel or motel management
PA: Sysco Corporation
1390 Enclave Pkwy
Houston TX 77077
281 584-1390

(G-10079)
TAKARA BELMONT USA INC (HQ)
101 Belmont Dr (08873-1293)
PHONE................................732 469-5000
Hidetaka Yoshikawa, *CEO*
Kunifousa Yashikawa, *Ch of Bd*
Toshi Hiraoka, *Exec VP*
Masahiro Kanaya, *Exec VP*
Rachel Delapena, *Human Res Mgr*
▲ EMP: 60
SQ FT: 100,000
SALES (est): 30.9MM **Privately Held**
WEB: www.belmontequip.com
SIC: 3843 3999 Dental chairs; barber & beauty shop equipment

(G-10080)
TAKARA BELMONT USA INC
Belmont Equipment Company
101 Belmont Dr (08873-1293)
PHONE................................732 469-5000
James Lowry, *General Mgr*
Luis Angulo, *Marketing Staff*
Belmont Takara, *Branch Mgr*
EMP: 50 **Privately Held**
WEB: www.belmontequip.com
SIC: 3843 Dental equipment
HQ: Takara Belmont Usa, Inc.
101 Belmont Dr
Somerset NJ 08873
732 469-5000

(G-10081)
TAYLOR COMMUNICATIONS INC
625 Pierce St Ste A (08873-1267)
PHONE................................732 560-3410
Peter Vanderzee, *Manager*
EMP: 55
SALES (corp-wide): 3B **Privately Held**
WEB: www.stdreg.com
SIC: 2761 Manifold business forms
HQ: Taylor Communications, Inc.
1725 Roe Crest Dr
North Mankato MN 56003
507 625-2828

(G-10082)
TEAM NISCA
100 Randolph Rd (08873-1384)
PHONE................................732 271-7367
Andrew Peterson, *Natl Sales Mgr*
Jayne Verbeyst, *Sales Staff*
Rob Miskelly, *Manager*
Tom Hudson, *Director*
EMP: 5
SALES (est): 411K **Privately Held**
SIC: 3089 Identification cards, plastic

(G-10083)
TECH BRAINS SOLUTIONS INC
Also Called: It Talent
220 Davidson Ave Ste 303 (08873-4144)
PHONE................................732 952-0552
Dheerta Kapoor, *President*
EMP: 40 EST: 2014
SALES: 6.6MM **Privately Held**
SIC: 7372 Application computer software

(G-10084)
TERUMO AMERICAS HOLDING INC (HQ)
265 Davidson Ave Ste 320 (08873-5115)
PHONE................................732 302-4900
Yutaro Shintaku, *CEO*
Jonathan Price, *Managing Dir*
Glenn Latham, *Vice Pres*
Hiroshi Matsumura, *Vice Pres*
Emily Miner, *Vice Pres*
▲ EMP: 75
SQ FT: 100,000
SALES (est): 866.9MM **Privately Held**
WEB: www.terumomedical.com
SIC: 3841 Needles, suture

(G-10085)
TERUMO MEDICAL CORPORATION (DH)
265 Davidson Ave Ste 320 (08873-5115)
PHONE................................732 302-4900
Jim Takeuchi, *President*
William Cahill, *Principal*
Ryota Sugimoto, *Business Mgr*
Bruce Canter, *Vice Pres*
Chris Pearson, *Vice Pres*
◆ EMP: 160
SALES (est): 52.4MM **Privately Held**
SIC: 3841 Needles, suture
HQ: Terumo Americas Holding, Inc.
265 Davidson Ave Ste 320
Somerset NJ 08873
732 302-4900

(G-10086)
TEVA WOMENS HEALTH INC
400 Campus Dr (08873-1145)
PHONE................................201 930-3300
Larry Downey, *Branch Mgr*
EMP: 5
SALES (corp-wide): 5B **Privately Held**
SIC: 2834 Pharmaceutical preparations
HQ: Teva Women's Health, Inc.
5040 Duramed Rd
Cincinnati OH 45213
513 731-9900

(G-10087)
THERMO FISHER SCIENTIFIC INC
265 Davidson Ave Ste 101 (08873-4120)
PHONE................................732 627-0220
Herb Kenny, *Vice Pres*
EMP: 15
SALES (corp-wide): 24.3B **Publicly Held**
WEB: www.thermo.com
SIC: 3826 Analytical instruments
PA: Thermo Fisher Scientific Inc.
168 3rd Ave
Waltham MA 02451
781 622-1000

(G-10088)
TOPPAN PRINTING CO AMER INC
Also Called: Peeq Media
1100 Randolph Rd (08873-5114)
PHONE................................732 469-8400
Shingo Ohkado, *President*
Phil Candura, *Vice Pres*
Jeffrey Snyder, *Vice Pres*
Toshiro Masuda, *Financial Exec*
Dennis Ascolese, *Manager*
EMP: 125 **Privately Held**
WEB: www.toppan.com
SIC: 2759 7336 2796 2789 Commercial printing; commercial art & graphic design; platemaking services; bookbinding & related work; commercial printing, lithographic; automotive & apparel trimmings
HQ: Toppan Printing Company (America), Inc.
2175 Greenhill Dr
Round Rock TX 78664
512 310-6212

(G-10089)
TRODAT USA INC (DH)
48 Heller Park Ln (08873-1206)
PHONE................................732 529-8500
Paul Demartini, *CEO*
Michelle Courtney, *Cust Mgr*
Shawn Chunn,
EMP: 11

SALES (est): 13.7MM
SALES (corp-wide): 2.6MM **Privately Held**
SIC: 3953 Marking devices
HQ: Trodat Gmbh
Linzer StraBe 156
Wels 4600
724 223-90

(G-10090)
TRODAT USA LLC
48 Heller Park Ln (08873-1206)
PHONE................................732 562-9500
Paul Demartini, *President*
May Yip, *Director*
◆ EMP: 90
SALES (est): 13.7MM
SALES (corp-wide): 2.6MM **Privately Held**
SIC: 3953 Embossing seals & hand stamps
HQ: Trodat Usa, Inc.
48 Heller Park Ln
Somerset NJ 08873

(G-10091)
UNITED PLASTICS GROUP INC
30 Commerce Dr (08873-3468)
PHONE................................732 873-8777
Chihming Wong, *President*
▲ EMP: 44 EST: 2001
SQ FT: 45,000
SALES (est): 9.4MM **Privately Held**
SIC: 2656 Sanitary food containers

(G-10092)
VEECO
Also Called: Mocvd Systems
394 Elizabeth Ave (08873-5117)
PHONE................................732 560-5300
John Peeler, *CEO*
David Glass, *Exec VP*
Bill Miller, *Exec VP*
Nino Federico, *Senior VP*
Herman Itzkowitz, *Senior VP*
EMP: 21
SALES (est): 3.9MM **Privately Held**
SIC: 3559 Semiconductor manufacturing machinery

(G-10093)
VEECO INSTRUMENTS INC
394 Elizabeth Ave (08873-5117)
PHONE................................732 560-5300
EMP: 34
SALES (corp-wide): 542MM **Publicly Held**
SIC: 3559 3572 3827 Semiconductor manufacturing machinery; computer storage devices; optical instruments & lenses; microscopes, except electron, proton & corneal
PA: Veeco Instruments Inc.
1 Terminal Dr
Plainview NY 11803
516 677-0200

(G-10094)
VEECO PROCESS EQUIPMENT INC
394 Elizabeth Ave (08873-5117)
PHONE................................732 560-5300
Malden Braun, *Branch Mgr*
EMP: 115
SQ FT: 5,600
SALES (corp-wide): 542MM **Publicly Held**
SIC: 3826 Analytical instruments
HQ: Veeco Process Equipment Inc.
1 Terminal Dr
Plainview NY 11803

(G-10095)
VENKATESHWARA INC
Also Called: Femto Calibrations
285 Davidson Ave Ste 100 (08873-4153)
PHONE................................908 964-4777
Sanjay Saxena, *President*
Madhu Saxena, *Admin Sec*
EMP: 10 EST: 1991
SQ FT: 2,000
SALES: 750K **Privately Held**
SIC: 3829 Measuring & controlling devices

(G-10096)
W A CLEARY CORPORATION (PA)
1049 Rte 27 (08873)
PHONE...................................732 247-8000
Margaret A Cleary, *Ch of Bd*
Mary Ellen Warwick, *President*
Evelyn Barnum, *Admin Sec*
EMP: 13
SQ FT: 1,400 **Privately Held**
WEB: www.waclearyproducts.com
SIC: 6719 2051 Investment holding companies, except banks; breads, rolls & buns

(G-10097)
W A CLEARY PRODUCTS INC
Also Called: W.A. Cleary Products
1049 Somerset St (08873-5014)
PHONE...................................732 246-2829
John Christman, *President*
EMP: 15
SALES (est): 2.1MM **Privately Held**
WEB: www.waclearyproducts.com
SIC: 2076 Vegetable oil mills
PA: W. A. Cleary Corporation
1049 Rte 27
Somerset NJ 08873
732 247-8000

(G-10098)
W R GRACE & CO-CONN
8 Heller Park Ln (08873-1206)
PHONE...................................732 868-6914
Bruce Robertson, *Manager*
EMP: 35
SALES (corp-wide): 1.9B **Publicly Held**
WEB: www.grace.com
SIC: 2899 Concrete curing & hardening compounds
HQ: W. R. Grace & Co.-Conn.
7500 Grace Dr
Columbia MD 21044
410 531-4000

Somerville
Somerset County

(G-10099)
A R BOTHERS WOODWORKING INC
236 Dukes Pkwy E (08876)
P.O. Box 127 (08876-0127)
PHONE...................................908 725-2891
EMP: 20
SQ FT: 20,000
SALES (est): 2.1MM **Privately Held**
SIC: 2434 Mfg Wood Kitchen Cabinets

(G-10100)
ACE ELECTRIC
3470 Us Highway 22 (08876-3446)
P.O. Box 160, Whitehouse Station (08889-0160)
PHONE...................................908 534-2404
John Chiappetta, *Owner*
EMP: 4 **EST:** 2011
SALES (est): 517.2K **Privately Held**
SIC: 3699 1731 Electrical equipment & supplies; electrical work

(G-10101)
ADIANT (PA)
92 E Main St Ste 405 (08876-2319)
PHONE...................................800 264-8303
Ash Nashed, *CEO*
Jon Carmen, *Senior VP*
Rafael Cosentino, *Senior VP*
EMP: 12
SALES (est): 3.1MM **Privately Held**
SIC: 3993 Advertising artwork

(G-10102)
AGFA CORPORATION
1318 State Hwy 31 (08876)
PHONE...................................908 231-5000
Perry Premdas, *Branch Mgr*
EMP: 5
SQ FT: 200,000
SALES (corp-wide): 494.6MM **Privately Held**
SIC: 2796 2893 Lithographic plates, positives or negatives; printing ink

HQ: Agfa Corporation
611 River Dr Ste 305
Elmwood Park NJ 07407
800 540-2432

(G-10103)
ALLIANCE SAND CO INC (PA)
51 Tannery Rd (08876-6040)
PHONE...................................908 534-4116
Ernest Renda, *President*
EMP: 3
SQ FT: 4,000
SALES (est): 1.8MM **Privately Held**
WEB: www.allpoconos.com
SIC: 1442 Common sand mining; construction sand mining; gravel mining

(G-10104)
BLUE CHIP INDUSTRIES INC
50 Old Camplain Rd (08876)
PHONE...................................908 704-1466
Carl A Inhoff, *President*
EMP: 6 **EST:** 1965
SQ FT: 4,500
SALES (est): 613.1K **Privately Held**
SIC: 3599 Machine shop, jobbing & repair

(G-10105)
CENTURY TUBE CORP
22 Tannery Rd (08876-6000)
PHONE...................................908 534-2001
Dominick De Angelo, *President*
Nick De Angelo, *Vice Pres*
▲ **EMP:** 40
SQ FT: 28,000
SALES (est): 14.8MM **Privately Held**
SIC: 3312 3317 3498 Tubes, steel & iron; steel pipe & tubes; tube fabricating (contract bending & shaping)

(G-10106)
CHOICE CABINETRY LLC
61 5th St (08876-3260)
PHONE...................................908 707-8801
Norman Pollock, *Mng Member*
▲ **EMP:** 50
SALES (est): 8MM **Privately Held**
SIC: 2434 Wood kitchen cabinets

(G-10107)
DEMAND LLC
36 S Adamsville Rd 1 (08876)
PHONE...................................908 526-2020
Joseph Kafara, *Mng Member*
EMP: 19
SALES (est): 3.5MM **Privately Held**
SIC: 3444 Sheet metalwork

(G-10108)
ETHICON INC (HQ)
Us Route 22 (08876)
P.O. Box 151 (08876-0151)
PHONE...................................732 524-0400
Steven Henn, *President*
Sarah G Brennan, *Vice Pres*
Kim Keller, *Engineer*
Robert J Decker, *Treasurer*
Freddy Garzon, *Sales Staff*
◆ **EMP:** 2500 **EST:** 1945
SQ FT: 772,000
SALES (est): 1.3B
SALES (corp-wide): 81.5B **Publicly Held**
WEB: www.ethiconinc.com
SIC: 3842 Sutures, absorbable & non-absorbable; ligatures, medical
PA: Johnson & Johnson
1 Johnson And Johnson Plz
New Brunswick NJ 08933
732 524-0400

(G-10109)
ETHICON LLC (HQ)
Rr 22 Box W (08876)
P.O. Box 16571, New Brunswick (08906-6571)
PHONE...................................908 218-3195
Clifford Holland, *President*
Mark Lambert, *Division Mgr*
Marjorie Medina, *Opers Staff*
Denise Dacey, *Engineer*
Maria Bradfish, *Senior Engr*
EMP: 55
SALES (est): 35.9MM
SALES (corp-wide): 81.5B **Publicly Held**
SIC: 3845 Endoscopic equipment, electromedical

PA: Johnson & Johnson
1 Johnson And Johnson Plz
New Brunswick NJ 08933
732 524-0400

(G-10110)
G & B MACHINE INC
35 N Middaugh St Ste B (08876-1827)
PHONE...................................908 707-1181
Gary Boccadutre, *President*
EMP: 5
SQ FT: 4,000
SALES (est): 500K **Privately Held**
WEB: www.gbmachineinc.com
SIC: 3599 Machine shop, jobbing & repair

(G-10111)
GALEN PUBLISHING LLC
Also Called: Advanced Studies In Medicine
166 W Main St (08876-2204)
P.O. Box 340 (08876-0340)
PHONE...................................908 253-9001
Jack Ciattarelli,
EMP: 25
SALES (est): 2.5MM **Privately Held**
SIC: 8011 2721 Offices & clinics of medical doctors; periodicals

(G-10112)
GANNETT CO INC
Also Called: Courier News
92 E Main St Ste 202 (08876-2319)
PHONE...................................908 243-6953
Jeffrey Phillips, *Vice Pres*
Julie Rosso, *Vice Pres*
Michael Sollecito, *Vice Pres*
Laurie Truitt, *Vice Pres*
Michael Deak, *Manager*
EMP: 77
SALES (corp-wide): 2.9B **Publicly Held**
SIC: 2711 Newspapers, publishing & printing
PA: Gannett Co., Inc.
7950 Jones Branch Dr
Mc Lean VA 22102
703 854-6000

(G-10113)
GLENTECH INC
46 4th St (08876-3206)
P.O. Box 7617, Hillsborough (08844-7617)
PHONE...................................908 685-2205
Scott Gordon, *President*
James Gordon, *Vice Pres*
Gregory Para, *Shareholder*
EMP: 12
SQ FT: 9,000
SALES (est): 1.6MM **Privately Held**
SIC: 3441 Fabricated structural metal

(G-10114)
HAMON CORPORATION (DH)
46 E Main St 300 (08876-2312)
P.O. Box 1500 (08876-1251)
PHONE...................................908 333-2000
William P Dillon, *CEO*
Carrie Torchio, *Partner*
Oliver Acheson, *COO*
Don Kawecki, *Exec VP*
H James Peters, *Exec VP*
◆ **EMP:** 95
SALES (est): 106.3MM **Privately Held**
WEB: www.hamonusa.com
SIC: 1629 3564 3499 5084 Industrial plant construction; blowers & fans; friction material, made from powdered metal; industrial machinery & equipment
HQ: Hamon & Cie (International)
Rue Emile Francqui 2
Mont-Saint-Guibert 1435
103 904-00

(G-10115)
HOME NEWS TRIBUNE
92 E Main St Ste 202 (08876-2319)
PHONE...................................908 243-6600
EMP: 20
SALES (est): 347.8K **Privately Held**
SIC: 2711 Newspapers, publishing & printing

(G-10116)
INDEPENDENCE TECHNOLOGY LLC
W Ethicon Bldg Rr 22 (08876)
PHONE...................................908 722-3767

PA: Johnson & Johnson
1 Johnson And Johnson Plz
New Brunswick NJ 08933
732 524-0400

Sandra Denarski, *CFO*
Kenneth Giason,
EMP: 12
SALES (est): 1.5MM
SALES (corp-wide): 81.5B **Publicly Held**
WEB: www.indetech.com
SIC: 3842 Wheelchairs
PA: Johnson & Johnson
1 Johnson And Johnson Plz
New Brunswick NJ 08933
732 524-0400

(G-10117)
INTERNATIONAL SHTMTL PLATE MFG
112 Veterans Mem Dr E (08876-2911)
P.O. Box 506 (08876-0506)
PHONE...................................908 722-6614
John Novak III, *President*
Andrew Novak, *Vice Pres*
Michelle Novak, *Office Mgr*
EMP: 32
SQ FT: 7,500
SALES (est): 7.6MM **Privately Held**
WEB: www.internationalsheetmetal.com
SIC: 3444 Sheet metal specialties, not stamped

(G-10118)
J & M AIR INC
189 S Bridge St (08876-3217)
PHONE...................................908 707-4040
Michael Favreau, *President*
Jamie Favreau, *Vice Pres*
EMP: 20
SQ FT: 5,000
SALES (est): 3MM **Privately Held**
SIC: 3589 5046 3444 Commercial cooking & foodwarming equipment; commercial cooking & food service equipment; sheet metalwork

(G-10119)
JOHNSON & JOHNSON MEDICAL INC (DH)
Us Rt 22 (08876)
PHONE...................................908 218-0707
William Clarke, *President*
EMP: 700 **EST:** 1949
SQ FT: 1,000,000
SALES (est): 169.4MM
SALES (corp-wide): 81.5B **Publicly Held**
SIC: 3842 Surgical appliances & supplies; drapes, surgical (cotton)
HQ: Ethicon Inc.
Us Route 22
Somerville NJ 08876
732 524-0400

(G-10120)
KOMPAC TECHNOLOGIES LLC
7 Commerce St (08876-6039)
PHONE...................................908 534-8411
Colin Hayes, *Electrical Engi*
Abby Archambault, *Marketing Staff*
Thomas Hayes, *Mng Member*
▲ **EMP:** 22 **EST:** 2006
SQ FT: 13,000
SALES (est): 6.2MM **Privately Held**
SIC: 3565 Labeling machines, industrial

(G-10121)
NEW JERSEY ELECTRIC MOTORS
84 Somerset St Ste A (08876-2842)
PHONE...................................908 526-5225
Salvatore Gambino, *President*
EMP: 6 **EST:** 1978
SQ FT: 800
SALES (est): 1MM **Privately Held**
SIC: 5999 7694 Motors, electric; electric motor repair

(G-10122)
NEXIRA INC
15 Somerset St (08876-2828)
PHONE...................................908 704-7480
Stephane Dondain, *President*
◆ **EMP:** 10
SQ FT: 6,000

SALES (est): 20.3MM
SALES (corp-wide): 355.8K **Privately Held**
WEB: www.cniworld.com
SIC: **2051** 5145 2099 Bakery: wholesale or wholesale/retail combined; confectionery; emulsifiers, food
HQ: Nexira
129 Chemin De Croisset
Rouen 76000
232 831-818

(G-10123)
POWERSPEC INC
25 4th St (08876-3205)
PHONE..................................732 494-9490
Laurie Elkoury, *President*
Peter Elkoury, *Vice Pres*
Peter E Koury, *Manager*
EMP: 30
SQ FT: 10,000
SALES (est): 3.5MM **Privately Held**
SIC: **6221** 5084 3629 Commodity contracts brokers, dealers; industrial machinery & equipment; power conversion units, a.c. to d.c.: static-electric

(G-10124)
ROAN PRINTING INC
Also Called: Minuteman Press
4 E Main St (08876-2308)
PHONE..................................908 526-5990
Sherman Feuer, *President*
Carole Feuer, *Vice Pres*
EMP: 10 EST: 1979
SQ FT: 3,750
SALES (est): 1.6MM **Privately Held**
WEB: www.mmprinting.com
SIC: **2752** 2791 7334 2789 Commercial printing, lithographic; typesetting; photocopying & duplicating services; bookbinding & related work; commercial printing

(G-10125)
SYMBOLOGY ENTERPRISES INC (PA)
50 Division St Ste 203 (08876-2943)
PHONE..................................908 725-1699
Gail Mc Inerney, *President*
Gail McInerney, *President*
Thomas McInerney, *Vice Pres*
Shaun McInerney, *Technology*
EMP: 10
SQ FT: 5,000
SALES: 3MM **Privately Held**
WEB: www.symbology.net
SIC: **3577** Verifiers, punch card; magnetic ink recognition devices

(G-10126)
TOP KNOBS USA INC (DH)
3 Millennium Way (08876-3876)
P.O. Box 779, Belle Mead (08502-0779)
PHONE..................................908 359-6174
Greg Gotleib, *CEO*
Mike Denvir, *Ch of Bd*
Warren Ramsland, *President*
Peter Suffredini, *Corp Secy*
Mike Perez, *Purch Mgr*
▲ EMP: 50
SQ FT: 30,000
SALES (est): 6.3MM
SALES (corp-wide): 843.1MM **Privately Held**
WEB: www.topknobsusa.com
SIC: **3264** Porcelain electrical supplies
HQ: Dimora Brands, Inc.
170 Township Line Rd
Hillsborough NJ 08844
908 359-6174

(G-10127)
TOWNE TECHNOLOGIES INC
6-10 Bell Ave (08876-1802)
P.O. Box 460 (08876-0460)
PHONE..................................908 722-9500
Dr Hercharan Dhillon, *President*
Daniel J Hughes, *Vice Pres*
Kuldip Dhillon, *Admin Sec*
▲ EMP: 15
SQ FT: 44,000
SALES: 1.5MM **Privately Held**
WEB: www.townetech.com
SIC: **3861** Photographic equipment & supplies

(G-10128)
WHITEHOUSE MACHINE & MFG CO
3585 Us Highway 22 (08876-3437)
PHONE..................................908 534-4722
Samuel Kessel, *President*
Mark Kessel, *Vice Pres*
Matthew Kessel, *Treasurer*
EMP: 7
SQ FT: 3,500
SALES: 400K **Privately Held**
SIC: **3599** Machine shop, jobbing & repair

South Amboy
Middlesex County

(G-10129)
ACE MOUNTINGS CO INC (PA)
11 Cross Ave (08879-1024)
PHONE..................................732 721-6200
Albert Chiang, *President*
Cindy Chiang, *Vice Pres*
Ll Liou, *Marketing Staff*
▲ EMP: 14
SQ FT: 5,000
SALES (est): 2.6MM **Privately Held**
WEB: www.acemount.com
SIC: **3674** Optical isolators

(G-10130)
ALL STATE PLASTICS INC
237 Raritan St (08879-1379)
PHONE..................................732 654-5054
John Vaccaro, *President*
Greg Vaccaro, *Vice Pres*
▲ EMP: 40
SQ FT: 25,000
SALES (est): 7.9MM **Privately Held**
WEB: www.allstateplastics.com
SIC: **3082** Unsupported plastics profile shapes

(G-10131)
BIOMED INNOVATIVE CONS LLC
104 N Broadway Apt D (08879-1882)
PHONE..................................732 599-7233
Anthony D'Antuono,
EMP: 4
SALES (est): 105K **Privately Held**
SIC: **5047** 3842 Orthopedic equipment & supplies; surgical appliances & supplies

(G-10132)
COMPLETE FILTER
3 Donamar Ln (08879-2900)
PHONE..................................732 441-0321
EMP: 4
SALES (est): 463.3K **Privately Held**
SIC: **3569** Filters

(G-10133)
GARDEN STATE TOOL & MOLD CORP
501 Bordentown Ave (08879-1500)
PHONE..................................908 245-2041
Thomas Dziedzic, *President*
EMP: 5
SQ FT: 2,100
SALES (est): 380K **Privately Held**
SIC: **3544** Industrial molds

(G-10134)
I-YELL-O FOODS INC
603 Washington Ave (08879-1263)
PHONE..................................732 525-2201
Alfonso Aiello, *President*
EMP: 5
SQ FT: 10,000
SALES: 2MM **Privately Held**
WEB: www.brooklyncannoli.com
SIC: **2053** Frozen bakery products, except bread

(G-10135)
KICKSONFIRECOM LLC
28 Lighthouse Dr (08879-3435)
PHONE..................................718 753-4248
Kevin Poux, *Accounts Mgr*
Furqan Khan,
EMP: 5

SALES: 300K **Privately Held**
SIC: **2721** 7371 Magazines: publishing & printing; computer software development & applications

(G-10136)
LOCKWOOD BOAT WORKS INC
1825 State Route 35 (08879-2525)
PHONE..................................732 721-1605
William Lockwood, *President*
William L Lockwood, *President*
Mary Lockwood, *Corp Secy*
Theresa Lockwood, *Manager*
EMP: 25
SQ FT: 13,000
SALES (est): 7.6MM **Privately Held**
WEB: www.lockwoodboatworks.com
SIC: **5551** 4493 4226 3732 Marine supplies; marinas; special warehousing & storage; boat building & repairing

(G-10137)
METALINE PRODUCTS COMPANY INC
101 N Feltus St (08879-1529)
PHONE..................................732 721-1373
Dolores Zilincar, *CEO*
August Zilincar III, *President*
▲ EMP: 25 EST: 1923
SQ FT: 25,000
SALES (est): 5.2MM **Privately Held**
SIC: **2542** 3993 Stands, merchandise display: except wood; signs & advertising specialties

(G-10138)
MORGAN PRINTING SERVICE INC
333 S Pine Ave (08879)
PHONE..................................732 721-2959
Robert Dein, *President*
Jason Madden, *Marketing Staff*
▲ EMP: 10
SQ FT: 4,500
SALES (est): 1.6MM **Privately Held**
SIC: **2752** 2791 Commercial printing, offset; typesetting

(G-10139)
PREMIER PRINTING SOLUTIONS LLC
513 S Pine Ave (08879-2129)
PHONE..................................732 525-0740
Carol Ciak, *Owner*
Edward Ciak, *Vice Pres*
Kevin Ciak, *Treasurer*
EMP: 5
SALES: 150K **Privately Held**
SIC: **2752** 7338 2261 2789 Commercial printing, offset; secretarial & typing service; printing of cotton broadwoven fabrics; bookbinding & related work

(G-10140)
ROBOKILLER LLC
101 S Broadway (08879-1707)
PHONE..................................723 838-1901
Meir Cohen, *CEO*
EMP: 40
SALES: 658.8K **Privately Held**
SIC: **7372** 7371 Application computer software; computer software development & applications
PA: Teltech Systems, Inc.
101 S Broadway
South Amboy NJ 08879

(G-10141)
SOUTH AMBOY DESIGNER T SHIRT L
603 Washington Ave Ste 5b (08879-1263)
PHONE..................................732 456-2594
Daniel Castillo,
EMP: 6
SALES (est): 339.9K **Privately Held**
SIC: **2752** 2395 Commercial printing, lithographic; embroidery products, except schiffli machine

(G-10142)
WHITE CASTLE
987 Us Highway 9 (08879-3302)
PHONE..................................732 721-3565
Janet Boehm, *Principal*
EMP: 25

SALES (est): 1.4MM **Privately Held**
SIC: **2085** Distilled & blended liquors

South Bound Brook
Somerset County

(G-10143)
CLEARY MACHINERY CO INC
24 Cedar St (08880-1352)
PHONE..................................732 560-3200
Gerard V Cleary, *President*
James A Cleary, *Vice Pres*
▲ EMP: 4
SQ FT: 4,200
SALES (est): 1.1MM **Privately Held**
WEB: www.clearymachinery.com
SIC: **5082** 3699 7699 General construction machinery & equipment; tractor-mounting equipment; laser systems & equipment; construction equipment repair

(G-10144)
TRI TECH TOOL & DESIGN CO INC
30 Cherry St (08880-1321)
PHONE..................................732 469-5433
Arthur Weber, *President*
Jason Weber, *Vice Pres*
EMP: 27 EST: 1978
SQ FT: 7,500
SALES: 6.5MM **Privately Held**
SIC: **3089** Injection molding of plastics

South Hackensack
Bergen County

(G-10145)
A-1 TABLECLOTH CO INC
450 Huyler St Ste 102 (07606-1563)
PHONE..................................201 727-4364
Robert Fox, *President*
▼ EMP: 150
SQ FT: 45,000
SALES (est): 9.6MM **Privately Held**
SIC: **7218** 2392 Industrial launderers; tablecloths & table settings

(G-10146)
ADCOMM INC
Also Called: Adcomm Government Systems
89 Leuning St Ste 9 (07606-1335)
PHONE..................................201 342-3338
Dennis Nathan, *President*
Gary Cofrancesco, *General Mgr*
Allen Cohen, *COO*
CP Nguyen, *Manager*
Joe Chen, *Info Tech Mgr*
EMP: 125
SQ FT: 60,000
SALES (est): 20.9MM **Privately Held**
SIC: **3679** Electronic circuits

(G-10147)
AEROSMITH
176 Saddle River Ave B (07606-1902)
PHONE..................................973 614-9392
David Lakin, *Owner*
Tim Lakin, *Owner*
EMP: 5 EST: 1999
SALES (est): 510.1K **Privately Held**
SIC: **3444** Sheet metalwork

(G-10148)
ALAN SCHATZBERG & ASSOCIATES
45 Ruta Ct (07606-1709)
PHONE..................................201 440-8855
Alan Schatzberg, *President*
Shira Reiz, *Sales Staff*
EMP: 11
SQ FT: 6,000
SALES (est): 1.6MM **Privately Held**
WEB: www.alanschatzberg.com
SIC: **2391** Curtains & draperies

(G-10149)
ALPRO INC
50 Romanelli Ave (07606-1424)
PHONE..................................201 342-4498
Girish Desai, *President*

EMP: 7
SALES (est): 620K **Privately Held**
SIC: 2834 Vitamin, nutrient & hematinic preparations for human use

(G-10150)
BIND-RITE SERVICES INC
16 Horizon Blvd (07606-1804)
PHONE..................................201 440-5585
Elliott Ward, *President*
Andrew Ward, *Principal*
Maria Ward, *Corp Secy*
John Petrosky, *Prdtn Mgr*
EMP: 150
SQ FT: 70,000
SALES (est): 20.9MM **Privately Held**
SIC: 2789 Binding only: books, pamphlets, magazines, etc.

(G-10151)
C W BRABENDER INSTRS INC
50 E Wesley St (07606-1416)
P.O. Box 2127 (07606-0727)
PHONE..................................201 343-8425
Richard Thoma, *President*
Ewald Heckmann, *Vice Pres*
Sirkka Vanderer, *Admin Sec*
▲ **EMP:** 28 **EST:** 1922
SQ FT: 20,000
SALES (est): 7.2MM
SALES (corp-wide): 240.3K **Privately Held**
WEB: www.cwbrabender.com
SIC: 3829 8734 3826 3821 Measuring & controlling devices; testing laboratories; analytical instruments; laboratory apparatus & furniture
HQ: C.W. Brabender Gesellschaft Mit Beschrankter Haftung
Kulturstr. 49-51
Duisburg 47055
203 778-80

(G-10152)
CASE MEDICAL INC
19 Empire Blvd (07606-1805)
P.O. Box 5069 (07606-4269)
PHONE..................................201 313-1999
Marcia Frieze, *CEO*
Allan Frieze, *President*
Steve Meredith, *Opers Staff*
Robert Chybicki, *Production*
Sudesh Kumar, *Buyer*
▲ **EMP:** 140 **EST:** 1943
SQ FT: 34,000
SALES (est): 28.4MM **Privately Held**
WEB: www.casemed.com
SIC: 5047 3469 Medical equipment & supplies; boxes, stamped metal

(G-10153)
CLEMENTS INDUSTRIES INC
Also Called: Tach-It
50 Ruta Ct (07606-1709)
PHONE..................................201 440-5500
Stephen Clements, *President*
Steven Clements, *President*
Arlene Peconio, *Credit Staff*
Jim Lyon, *Natl Sales Mgr*
Marilyn Clements, *Office Mgr*
◆ **EMP:** 25 **EST:** 1964
SQ FT: 15,000
SALES (est): 6MM **Privately Held**
WEB: www.clementsindustries.com
SIC: 3565 3599 5113 3552 Labeling machines, industrial; bread wrapping machinery; ties, form: metal; shipping supplies; textile machinery; miscellaneous fabricated wire products

(G-10154)
DANMAR PRESS INC
24 E Wesley St (07606-1416)
PHONE..................................201 487-4400
Danieal Stenchever, *President*
EMP: 12 **EST:** 1981
SQ FT: 4,050
SALES (est): 1.3MM **Privately Held**
SIC: 2752 Commercial printing, offset

(G-10155)
E & E GROUP CORP
7 Maple Ave 2 (07606-1605)
P.O. Box 1521 (07606-0121)
PHONE..................................201 814-0414
Hae K Cho, *President*

EMP: 4 **EST:** 1997
SALES (est): 567.6K **Privately Held**
SIC: 2671 Paper coated or laminated for packaging

(G-10156)
ECO LIGHTING USA LTD LBLTY CO
217 Huyler St (07606-1302)
PHONE..................................201 621-5661
Sean Blackman, *Mng Member*
◆ **EMP:** 8
SALES: 728K **Privately Held**
SIC: 3648 5063 Lighting equipment; lighting fixtures, commercial & industrial; lighting fixtures, residential

(G-10157)
EJZ FOODS LLC
21 Empire Blvd (07606-1805)
PHONE..................................201 229-0500
Matthew Berger, *Mng Member*
◆ **EMP:** 5
SALES (est): 139.9K
SALES (corp-wide): 145.2MM **Privately Held**
SIC: 2037 Fruit juices
PA: Dora's Naturals, Inc
21 Empire Blvd
South Hackensack NJ 07606
201 229-0500

(G-10158)
ENCORE ENTERPRISES INC (PA)
Also Called: Creative Safety Products
57 Leuning St (07606-1307)
PHONE..................................201 489-5044
Angelo C Congello Sr, *President*
Angelo Congelo Jr, *President*
Hala Saardi, *Accountant*
EMP: 5
SQ FT: 14,200
SALES (est): 1.2MM **Privately Held**
WEB: www.officerphil.com
SIC: 8299 7336 2752 Educational service, nondegree granting: continuing educ.; graphic arts & related design; commercial printing, lithographic

(G-10159)
ESSENTIAL DENTAL SYSTEMS INC
Also Called: EDS
89 Leuning St Ste 8 (07606-1334)
PHONE..................................201 487-9090
Dr Barry Musikant, *President*
Dr Allen Deutsch, *Exec VP*
Mary Allaire, *Human Res Mgr*
Sofia Dinneen, *Sales Staff*
Carrie Moncrieffe, *Marketing Mgr*
▲ **EMP:** 25
SQ FT: 10,000
SALES (est): 3.6MM **Privately Held**
WEB: www.edsdental.com
SIC: 3843 Dental materials; cement, dental; compounds, dental

(G-10160)
EUROPEAN STONE ART LLC
208 Huyler St (07606-1303)
PHONE..................................201 441-9116
Hiedi J Saville, *Mng Member*
Gary Saville,
EMP: 11
SALES (est): 1.3MM **Privately Held**
WEB: www.europeanstoneart.com
SIC: 3272 Concrete products

(G-10161)
F P SCHMIDT MANUFACTURING CO
143 Leuning St (07606-1385)
PHONE..................................201 343-4241
Robert F Schmidt, *Managing Prtnr*
Elizabeth L Butz, *Partner*
William P Schmidt, *Partner*
EMP: 15 **EST:** 1947
SQ FT: 20,000
SALES (est): 1MM **Privately Held**
SIC: 3451 Screw machine products

(G-10162)
IMAGINE GOLD LLC
60 Romanelli Ave (07606-1424)
PHONE..................................201 488-5988
Joe Curran, *President*
Karen Windfuhr,
◆ **EMP:** 20 **EST:** 1953
SQ FT: 22,000
SALES (est): 3.3MM **Privately Held**
WEB: www.imaginegold.com
SIC: 5199 3085 Pet supplies; plastics bottles

(G-10163)
J JOSEPHSON INC (HQ)
35 Horizon Blvd (07606-1804)
PHONE..................................201 440-7000
Mark Goodman, *President*
Dan Depasquale, *Principal*
Coit Edwards, *COO*
Efrain Nieves, *Engineer*
Teresa Messineo, *CFO*
◆ **EMP:** 122 **EST:** 1962
SQ FT: 160,000
SALES (est): 94.4MM
SALES (corp-wide): 49MM **Privately Held**
WEB: www.jjosephson.com
SIC: 2679 Wallpaper, embossed plastic: made on textile backing
PA: Coronet Wallpapers (Ontario) Limited
88 Ronson Dr
Etobicoke ON M9W 1
416 245-2900

(G-10164)
J JOSEPHSON INC
35 Empire Blvd (07606-1896)
PHONE..................................201 440-7000
Kin Bogg, *Manager*
EMP: 150
SALES (corp-wide): 49MM **Privately Held**
WEB: www.jjosephson.com
SIC: 2679 Wallpaper, embossed plastic: made on textile backing
HQ: J. Josephson, Inc.
35 Horizon Blvd
South Hackensack NJ 07606
201 440-7000

(G-10165)
J JOSEPHSON INC
14 Central Blvd (07606-1802)
PHONE..................................201 426-2646
Jeff Dugal, *Opers Staff*
Mark Goodman, *Branch Mgr*
EMP: 150
SALES (corp-wide): 49MM **Privately Held**
SIC: 2679 Wallpaper, embossed plastic: made on textile backing
HQ: J. Josephson, Inc.
35 Horizon Blvd
South Hackensack NJ 07606
201 440-7000

(G-10166)
JULIA CLEMENTE
120 Leuning St (07606-1317)
PHONE..................................201 488-2161
Julia Clemente, *Principal*
EMP: 4 **EST:** 2016
SALES (est): 306.1K **Privately Held**
SIC: 2051 Bread, cake & related products

(G-10167)
KDF REPROGRAPHICS INC
65 Worth St (07606-1422)
PHONE..................................201 784-9991
Stephen Hoey, *President*
John Dickson, *Corp Secy*
Kurt Flechsig, *Exec VP*
Tanya Berghuys, *Administration*
EMP: 10
SQ FT: 33,000
SALES (est): 1.5MM **Privately Held**
WEB: www.kdf-comp.com
SIC: 2759 3993 7922 7389 Commercial printing; electric signs; scenery design, theatrical; lettering & sign painting services; sign installation & maintenance

(G-10168)
LA FORGE DE STYLE LLC
57 Romanelli Ave (07606-1427)
PHONE..................................201 488-1955
Franck Chartrain,
David Gore,
EMP: 8
SQ FT: 8,000
SALES (est): 1.5MM **Privately Held**
SIC: 3446 Ornamental metalwork

(G-10169)
LYDON BROS CORP
254 Green St (07606-1429)
PHONE..................................201 343-4334
Timothy Mc Bride, *President*
S Mc Bride, *Vice Pres*
EMP: 22
SQ FT: 3,000
SALES (est): 1.6MM **Privately Held**
WEB: www.lydonoven.com
SIC: 3567 Driers & redriers, industrial process; enameling ovens

(G-10170)
M H OPTICAL SUPPLIES INC
Also Called: Quality Eyework
128 Leuning St (07606-1317)
PHONE..................................800 445-3090
Mitchel Hirsch, *President*
▲ **EMP:** 32
SQ FT: 20,000
SALES (est): 6.2MM **Privately Held**
SIC: 3827 Optical instruments & lenses

(G-10171)
MARINE ELECTRIC SYSTEMS INC
Also Called: Mesys
80 Wesley St (07606-1510)
PHONE..................................201 531-8600
Harry Epstein, *CEO*
Michael Epstein, *Chairman*
Carolyn Gould, *Purch Mgr*
Mark Biancolillo, *Engineer*
Scott Weeber, *CFO*
EMP: 21 **EST:** 1940
SQ FT: 25,000
SALES (est): 6.5MM **Privately Held**
WEB: www.marineelectricsystems.com
SIC: 3825 3823 3643 3612 Test equipment for electronic & electric measurement; industrial instrmnts msrmnt display/control process variable; current-carrying wiring devices; switchgear & switchboard apparatus

(G-10172)
NATUREX HOLDINGS INC (HQ)
375 Huyler St (07606-1532)
PHONE..................................201 440-5000
Olivier Rigaud, *Ch of Bd*
Gaetan Sourceau, *CFO*
EMP: 3
SALES (est): 237.7MM **Privately Held**
SIC: 2833 6719 Botanical products, medicinal: ground, graded or milled; investment holding companies, except banks

(G-10173)
NATUREX INC
125 Phillips Ave (07606-1585)
PHONE..................................201 440-5000
Thierry Lambert, *President*
EMP: 6 **Privately Held**
SIC: 2833 Botanical products, medicinal: ground, graded or milled
HQ: Naturex Inc.
375 Huyler St
South Hackensack NJ 07606
201 440-5000

(G-10174)
NATUREX INC (DH)
375 Huyler St (07606-1532)
PHONE..................................201 440-5000
Mary Clarke, *Ch of Bd*
◆ **EMP:** 200
SALES (est): 234.7MM **Privately Held**
SIC: 2833 Botanical products, medicinal: ground, graded or milled
HQ: Naturex Holdings Inc.
375 Huyler St
South Hackensack NJ 07606
201 440-5000

(G-10175)
NEW JERSEY LABEL LLC
30 Wesley St Unit 7 (07606-1509)
PHONE..................................201 880-5102
Steven Haedrich,
EMP: 12 **EST:** 1995
SALES (est): 1.2MM **Privately Held**
SIC: 2752 2791 2759 Commercial printing, lithographic; typesetting; commercial printing

(G-10176)
NO FIRE TECHNOLOGIES INC
5 James St (07606-1438)
PHONE..................................201 818-1616
Sam Oolie, *Ch of Bd*
Samuel Gottfried, *President*
◆ **EMP:** 7
SQ FT: 8,000
SALES (est): 1.1MM **Privately Held**
WEB: www.nofire.net
SIC: 2899 Fire retardant chemicals

(G-10177)
ON SITE COMMUNICATION
Also Called: Ess
15 Worth St (07606-1313)
P.O. Box 4103 (07606-4103)
PHONE..................................201 488-4123
T H Betz, *Partner*
Robert Dale, *Partner*
William Park, *Partner*
EMP: 50
SALES (est): 4.7MM **Privately Held**
SIC: 3663 Radio broadcasting & communications equipment

(G-10178)
OVERDRIVE HOLDINGS INC
540 Huyler St (07606-1544)
PHONE..................................201 440-1911
Ralph Guadagno, *Branch Mgr*
EMP: 12
SALES (corp-wide): 23.4MM **Privately Held**
SIC: 5013 3714 Trailer parts & accessories; automotive brakes; truck parts & accessories; wheels, motor vehicle; transmissions, motor vehicle; differentials & parts, motor vehicle
PA: Overdrive Holdings, Inc.
2501 Route 73
Cinnaminson NJ
856 665-4445

(G-10179)
PAINTING INC
60 Leuning St (07606-1317)
PHONE..................................201 489-6565
Lee Bronster, *CEO*
Wilson Richardson, *President*
EMP: 14
SQ FT: 5,000
SALES: 1.2MM **Privately Held**
SIC: 7532 2396 Lettering & painting services; automotive & apparel trimmings

(G-10180)
PHARMACHEM LABORATORIES INC
130 Wesley St (07606-1510)
..................................201 343-3611
Andrea Bauer, *Branch Mgr*
EMP: 30
SALES (corp-wide): 3.2B **Publicly Held**
SIC: 2099 2834 Food preparations; pharmaceutical preparations
HQ: Pharmachem Laboratories, Llc
265 Harrison Tpke
Kearny NJ 07032
201 246-1000

(G-10181)
PIONEER EMBROIDERY CO
Also Called: Fabric Bee
31 Saddle River Ave (07606)
PHONE..................................973 777-6418
EMP: 4
SQ FT: 1,200
SALES (est): 170K **Privately Held**
SIC: 2395 5949 Pleating/Stitching Services Ret Sewing Supplies/Fabrics

(G-10182)
PRINT GROUP INC
Also Called: Print Group The
24 E Wesley St (07606-1416)
PHONE..................................201 487-4400
Michael De Stefan, *President*
Anne De Stefan, *Admin Sec*
EMP: 10 **EST:** 1953
SALES (est): 1.8MM **Privately Held**
SIC: 2752 Commercial printing, offset

(G-10183)
REFUEL INC
150 Wesley St (07606-1510)
PHONE..................................917 645-2974
SRI Kasa, *Branch Mgr*
EMP: 4
SALES (corp-wide): 4MM **Privately Held**
SIC: 5091 5699 2211 Sporting & recreation goods; sports apparel; apparel & outerwear fabrics, cotton
HQ: Refuel Inc
1384 Broadway Rm 608
New York NY 10018
917 645-2974

(G-10184)
ROBERT J SMITH
Also Called: Mastercrafts
152 Louis St (07606-1721)
PHONE..................................201 641-6555
Robert J Smith, *Owner*
EMP: 6
SQ FT: 5,000
SALES: 500K **Privately Held**
SIC: 2521 2511 Wood office furniture; wood household furniture

(G-10185)
RQ FLOORS CORP
550 Huyler St (07606-1544)
PHONE..................................201 654-3587
Leon Shekhets, *President*
EMP: 14
SALES (corp-wide): 7MM **Privately Held**
SIC: 2491 Flooring, treated wood block
PA: Rq Floors Corp
425 Victoria Ter
Ridgefield NJ 07657
201 654-3587

(G-10186)
SALON INTERIORS INC
62 Leuning St (07606-1317)
PHONE..................................201 488-7888
Walter Siegordner, *President*
Keith Cauwenberghs, *Prdtn Mgr*
Marilyn Murphy, *CFO*
▲ **EMP:** 28 **EST:** 1979
SQ FT: 35,000
SALES (est): 6.3MM **Privately Held**
WEB: www.saloninteriors.com
SIC: 1542 5087 2541 Commercial & office building contractors; beauty parlor equipment & supplies; store & office display cases & fixtures

(G-10187)
SONDRA ROBERTS INC
3 Empire Blvd (07606-1806)
PHONE..................................212 684-3344
George Altirs, *CEO*
EMP: 20
SALES (est): 615.4K **Privately Held**
SIC: 2339 Women's & misses' accessories

(G-10188)
SPRING TIME MATTRESS MFG CORP (PA)
Also Called: Springtime Bedding
25 Saddle River Ave (07606-1922)
P.O. Box 4157 (07606-4157)
PHONE..................................973 473-5400
Isaac S Jakobovits, *CEO*
Isaac Jakobovits, *CEO*
Joel Wieder, *CFO*
EMP: 95
SALES (est): 8.3MM **Privately Held**
SIC: 2515 Mattresses & bedsprings

(G-10189)
TORQUE GUN COMPANY LLC
Also Called: Torque Gun Co, The
120 Wesley St (07606-1510)
PHONE..................................201 512-9800

EMP: 20
SALES (est): 2MM **Privately Held**
SIC: 3621 Torque motors, electric

(G-10190)
WELTER & KREUTZ PRINTING CO
51 Worth St (07606-1422)
P.O. Box 1834 (07606-0434)
PHONE..................................201 489-9098
Robert Kreutz, *President*
Barry R Kreutz, *Vice Pres*
EMP: 5
SQ FT: 3,000
SALES (est): 749.7K **Privately Held**
SIC: 2752 Commercial printing, offset

(G-10191)
YOUNIVERSAL LABORTORIES (PA)
Also Called: USA Head Office & Warehouse
100 Louis St (07606-1723)
PHONE..................................201 807-9000
Emir Agbas, *Owner*
Banu Basarir, *Opers Mgr*
▲ **EMP:** 5
SALES (est): 280.5K **Privately Held**
SIC: 2819 Industrial inorganic chemicals

South Orange
Essex County

(G-10192)
BIERMAN-EVERETT FOUNDRY CO
7 Speir Dr (07079-1023)
PHONE..................................973 373-8800
Robert Julius, *President*
Theresa Notoli, *Vice Pres*
EMP: 8
SQ FT: 36,000
SALES (est): 1MM **Privately Held**
SIC: 3321 3363 3366 3365 Gray iron castings; ductile iron castings; aluminum die-castings; copper foundries; aluminum foundries

(G-10193)
DANMOLA LARA
Also Called: Laras Designs
524 N Wyoming Ave (07079-1653)
P.O. Box 984 (07079-0984)
PHONE..................................973 762-7581
Lara Danmola, *Owner*
EMP: 5
SALES (est): 270K **Privately Held**
WEB: www.larasdesigns.com
SIC: 3911 Jewelry, precious metal

(G-10194)
ENDOTEC INC (PA)
20 Valley St Ste 210 (07079-2881)
PHONE..................................973 762-6100
Michael Pappas, *President*
Fred Buechel, *Vice Pres*
Stan Matlak, *VP Sales*
EMP: 15
SQ FT: 3,000
SALES (est): 1.2MM **Privately Held**
WEB: www.endotec.com
SIC: 3842 8011 Implants, surgical; offices & clinics of medical doctors

(G-10195)
FAN OF WORD
249 Waverly Pl (07079-2124)
PHONE..................................201 341-5474
Joseph Oniyama, *Partner*
EMP: 4
SALES (est): 224.5K **Privately Held**
SIC: 3499 7389 Novelties & giftware, including trophies;

(G-10196)
FLEET PACKAGING INC
75 S Orange Ave Ste 216 (07079-1743)
PHONE..................................866 302-0340
Gary Shippy, *President*
▲ **EMP:** 5
SQ FT: 400

SALES: 6.7MM **Privately Held**
SIC: 2674 3053 5199 Shipping & shopping bags or sacks; shopping bags: made from purchased materials; packing materials; packaging materials

(G-10197)
JEFFERSON PROSTHETIC ORTHOTIC
120 Prospect St Ste B (07079-2103)
PHONE..................................973 762-0780
Simon Chang, *President*
EMP: 5
SQ FT: 1,400
SALES (est): 340K **Privately Held**
SIC: 3842 Limbs, artificial; braces, orthopedic

(G-10198)
LEVEL DESIGNS GROUP LLC
495 W South Orange Ave (07079-1200)
PHONE..................................973 761-1675
Altair H Marques, *Mng Member*
EMP: 5 **EST:** 2011
SALES: 700K **Privately Held**
SIC: 7389 2653 2541 Design services; display items, solid fiber: made from purchased materials; display fixtures, wood

(G-10199)
MYERS GROUP LLC
Also Called: New World Leather
74 Blanchard Rd (07079-1341)
P.O. Box 1162, Maplewood (07040-0453)
PHONE..................................973 761-6414
Jay Myers, *Branch Mgr*
EMP: 7
SALES (corp-wide): 87MM **Privately Held**
SIC: 3111 Tanneries, leather
PA: The Myers Group Llc
257 W 38th St
New York NY 10018
973 761-6414

(G-10200)
NEPHROS INC (PA)
380 Lackawanna Pl (07079-1704)
PHONE..................................201 343-5202
Daron Evans, *President*
Andrew Astor, *COO*
Tim Nowicki, *Project Engr*
Jeff Hall, *Associate Dir*
◆ **EMP:** 15
SQ FT: 7,700
SALES: 5.6MM **Publicly Held**
WEB: www.nephros.com
SIC: 3841 8731 Surgical & medical instruments; medical research, commercial

(G-10201)
SNOTEX USA INC
116 Irvington Ave Apt 2f (07079-1973)
PHONE..................................973 762-0358
Kermit Lin, *President*
▲ **EMP:** 4
SALES: 1.2MM **Privately Held**
SIC: 2339 Women's & misses' outerwear

(G-10202)
TOTAL COVER IT LLC
223 Waverly Pl (07079-2124)
PHONE..................................973 342-4623
Greg Orgo, *Business Mgr*
Vivian Gaspar, *Accounts Exec*
David G Quick, *President*
EMP: 4
SALES (est): 121.2K **Privately Held**
SIC: 7372 Application computer software

(G-10203)
WORLD CONFECTIONS INC
14 S Orange Ave Ste A (07079-1754)
PHONE..................................718 768-8100
▲ **EMP:** 60
SQ FT: 20,000
SALES (est): 9.9MM **Privately Held**
SIC: 2064 5145 Candy & other confectionery products; candy

South Plainfield
Middlesex County

(G-10204)
A FRIERI MACHINE TOOL INC
1112 Belmont Ave (07080-4303)
PHONE...........................908 753-7555
Andrew Frieri, *President*
EMP: 6
SQ FT: 12,500
SALES: 650K **Privately Held**
SIC: 3599 3544 Machine shop, jobbing &
repair; special dies, tools, jigs & fixtures

(G-10205)
A&A COMPANY INC
Also Called: A & A Coating
2700 S Clinton Ave (07080-1428)
PHONE...........................908 561-2378
R Stewart Brunhouse Jr, *President*
EMP: 22 EST: 1944
SQ FT: 22,000
SALES (est): 4.2MM **Privately Held**
SIC: 3471 Plating & polishing

(G-10206)
ACCELERATED CNC LLC
2500 S Clinton Ave (07080-1414)
PHONE...........................908 561-8875
John Kologe, *Mng Member*
William Ehling,
EMP: 6
SQ FT: 100
SALES: 840K **Privately Held**
SIC: 3599 Machine shop, jobbing & repair

(G-10207)
ADEMCO INC
Also Called: ADI Global Distribution
107 Corporate Blvd (07080-2482)
PHONE...........................908 561-1888
Joseph Maselli, *Manager*
EMP: 6
SALES (corp-wide): 4.8B **Publicly Held**
WEB: www.honeywell.com
SIC: 5063 3669 3822 Electrical apparatus
& equipment; emergency alarms; auto
controls regulating residntl & coml envi-
ronmt & applncs
HQ: Ademco Inc.
1985 Douglas Dr N
Golden Valley MN 55422
800 468-1502

(G-10208)
ADMERA HEALTH LLC
126 Corporate Blvd (07080-2411)
PHONE...........................908 222-0533
Steve Sun, *CEO*
Zeil Rosenberg, *Vice Pres*
Ling Zhang, *Sales Staff*
Arthur Bolbirer, *Manager*
Jeffrey Mitchell, *Director*
EMP: 1
SALES (est): 1.1MM
SALES (corp-wide): 631.5MM **Publicly
Held**
SIC: 2835 8731 In vitro & in vivo diagnos-
tic substances; commercial physical re-
search
HQ: Genewiz, Llc
115 Corporate Blvd
South Plainfield NJ 07080
908 222-0711

(G-10209)
AIRBRASIVE JET TECH LLC
3461 S Clinton Ave (07080-1321)
PHONE...........................201 725-7340
Diane Cassetta, *General Mgr*
Joel Levine,
Bruce Berger,
Nat Wasserstein,
EMP: 5
SQ FT: 2,500
SALES (est): 697.7K **Privately Held**
SIC: 3545 Dressers, abrasive wheel: dia-
mond point or other

(G-10210)
**ALIRON INTERNATIONAL INC
(PA)**
1 Cragwood Rd Ste 101 (07080-2416)
PHONE...........................540 808-1615
Janaki Ram Ajjarapu, *President*
Joseph Mandour, *Senior VP*
Daniel Lynam, *Human Resources*
Megan Efthimiadis, *Manager*
Manisha Fnu, *Manager*
EMP: 20
SQ FT: 5,000
SALES (est): 5.8MM **Privately Held**
WEB: www.aliron.com
SIC: 7389 7371 4731 7372 Translation
services; custom computer programming
services; freight forwarding; business ori-
ented computer software; drugs & drug
proprietaries

(G-10211)
ALLEN FLAVORS INC (PA)
230 Saint Nicholas Ave (07080-1810)
PHONE...........................908 561-5995
Joey Allen, *President*
Bruce Weber, *General Mgr*
Michelle Allen, *Vice Pres*
Joe Harriman, *Vice Pres*
Alex Pereira, *Plant Mgr*
▲ EMP: 115
SALES (est): 29.3MM **Privately Held**
WEB: www.allenflavors.com
SIC: 2087 Extracts, flavoring; beverage
bases, concentrates, syrups, powders &
mixes

(G-10212)
ALLEN FLAVORS INC
220 Saint Nicholas Ave (07080-1810)
PHONE...........................908 753-0544
Joseph Allen, *Manager*
EMP: 13
SALES (est): 2.4MM
SALES (corp-wide): 29.3MM **Privately
Held**
SIC: 2087 Extracts, flavoring; beverage
bases, concentrates, syrups, powders &
mixes
PA: Allen Flavors, Inc.
230 Saint Nicholas Ave
South Plainfield NJ 07080
908 561-5995

(G-10213)
ALLIED TILE MFG CORP
631 Montrose Ave (07080-2601)
PHONE...........................718 647-2200
G Peter Gregor, *President*
▲ EMP: 9
SQ FT: 10,000
SALES (est): 1.3MM **Privately Held**
WEB: www.alliedtile.com
SIC: 3292 Tile, vinyl asbestos

(G-10214)
**ALPHA ASSEMBLY SOLUTIONS
INC**
109 Corporate Blvd (07080-2409)
PHONE...........................908 561-5170
Ravi Bhatkal, *Vice Pres*
EMP: 41
SALES (corp-wide): 1.9B **Publicly Held**
SIC: 3356 3341 3313 3339 Solder: wire,
bar, acid core, & rosin core; lead smelting
& refining (secondary); tin smelting & refining (secondary); alloys, additive, except
copper: not made in blast furnaces; lead
smelting & refining (primary); tin refining
(primary); fluxes: brazing, soldering, galvanizing & welding
HQ: Alpha Assembly Solutions Inc.
300 Atrium Dr Fl 3
Somerset NJ 08873
908 791-3000

(G-10215)
**AMERICAN HOME ESSENTIALS
INC**
600 Mont Rose Ave (07080)
PHONE...........................908 561-3200
Sohail Bari, *President*
Rashad H Hassan, *Vice Pres*
EMP: 8
SQ FT: 23,000

SALES: 5MM **Privately Held**
SIC: 2299 Linen fabrics

(G-10216)
**AMERICAN STRIP STEEL INC
(HQ)**
400 Metuchen Rd (07080-4807)
PHONE...........................800 526-1216
Le Roy Schecter, *President*
Lori Hagedorn, *CFO*
Jean Thomay, *Manager*
EMP: 17 EST: 1951
SQ FT: 90,000
SALES (est): 29.2MM
SALES (corp-wide): 107.9MM **Privately
Held**
SIC: 5051 3441 3316 Steel; fabricated
structural metal; cold finishing of steel
shapes
PA: Ware Industries Inc.
400 Metuchen Rd
South Plainfield NJ 07080
908 757-9000

(G-10217)
AMERIFAST CORP
104 Sylvania Pl (07080-1448)
PHONE...........................908 668-1959
James Peightel, *President*
▲ EMP: 10
SQ FT: 24,000
SALES: 1.7MM **Privately Held**
SIC: 3452 Nuts, metal

(G-10218)
**AMES ADVANCED MATERIALS
CORP**
3900 S Clinton Ave (07080-1316)
PHONE...........................908 226-2038
Frank Barber, *President*
Theresa Pagan, *Safety Mgr*
EMP: 160
SALES (corp-wide): 32.4MM **Privately
Held**
WEB: www.ferro.com
SIC: 3339 Silver refining (primary)
HQ: Ames Advanced Materials Corporation
50 Harrison Ave
South Glens Falls NY 12803
518 792-5808

(G-10219)
**ARCH PERSONAL CARE
PRODUCTS LP**
70 Tyler Pl (07080-1210)
PHONE...........................908 226-9329
Joseph Shaulson, *President*
Lisa Bouldin, *Vice Pres*
Steve Giuliano, *Vice Pres*
▼ EMP: 45
SQ FT: 30,000
SALES (est): 5.9MM
SALES (corp-wide): 5.5B **Privately Held**
WEB: www.archchemicals.com
SIC: 2844 Depilatories (cosmetic)
HQ: Arch Chemicals, Inc.
1200 Bluegrass Lakes Pkwy
Alpharetta GA 30004
678 624-5800

(G-10220)
ARIEL LABORATORIES LP
31 Davis St (07080-1429)
PHONE...........................908 755-4080
Peter Bohm, *Partner*
Ronni Bohm, *Partner*
Imperial Cosmetics, *General Ptnr*
Eric Bohm, *Business Dir*
Judith Amman, *Admin Asst*
▲ EMP: 6
SQ FT: 30,000
SALES (est): 1.3MM **Privately Held**
WEB: www.ariellabs.com
SIC: 2844 Cosmetic preparations; lipsticks;
face creams or lotions

(G-10221)
ASCENT AROMATICS INC
120 Case Dr (07080-5109)
PHONE...........................908 755-0120
John Pascame, *President*
Jem Unanth, *Vice Pres*
EMP: 5
SALES (est): 1MM **Privately Held**
SIC: 2844 Perfumes & colognes

(G-10222)
ATLAS ENTERPRISE
Also Called: Atlas Welders & Fabricators
2505 S Clinton Ave (07080-1425)
PHONE...........................908 561-1144
Ronald Eodice, *President*
Charles Percevault, *Corp Secy*
Joseph Novakowski, *Vice Pres*
EMP: 15 EST: 1977
SQ FT: 5,000
SALES (est): 1.6MM **Privately Held**
SIC: 7692 3441 Welding repair; fabricated
structural metal

(G-10223)
BANKER STEEL NJ LLC
1640 New Market Ave (07080-1641)
PHONE...........................732 968-6061
Donald Banker, *CEO*
EMP: 70
SQ FT: 34,300
SALES (est): 2.4MM
SALES (corp-wide): 2.9B **Privately Held**
SIC: 1791 3441 Structural steel erection;
fabricated structural metal
HQ: Banker Steel Co., L.L.C.
1619 Wythe Rd Ste B
Lynchburg VA 24501
434 847-4575

(G-10224)
BCSMACHINE & MFG CORP
3575 Kennedy Rd (07080-1996)
PHONE...........................908 561-1656
Salvatore Capparelli, *President*
Cynthia Bolesta, *Corp Secy*
Frank M Capparelli, *Vice Pres*
Debra Capparelli, *Shareholder*
Maria Farrell, *Shareholder*
EMP: 9 EST: 1964
SQ FT: 8,200
SALES (est): 870K **Privately Held**
SIC: 3599 3444 Machine shop, jobbing &
repair; sheet metalwork

(G-10225)
**BEATRICE HOME FASHIONS
INC (PA)**
151 Helen St (07080-3806)
P.O. Box 86 (07080-0086)
PHONE...........................908 561-7370
Sam N Gindi, *President*
▲ EMP: 20
SQ FT: 45,000
SALES (est): 5.2MM **Privately Held**
SIC: 2392 2391 Bedspreads & bed sets:
made from purchased materials;
draperies, plastic & textile: from pur-
chased materials

(G-10226)
BIOACTIVE RESOURCES LLC
138 Sylvania Pl (07080-1448)
PHONE...........................908 561-3114
Divya Desai, *CEO*
Mayur Desai,
▲ EMP: 13
SQ FT: 150,000
SALES (est): 4.3MM **Privately Held**
WEB: www.bioactiveresources.com
SIC: 2834 Vitamin preparations

(G-10227)
BRACO MANUFACTURING INC
4031b New Brunswick Ave (07080)
PHONE...........................732 752-7777
Jack Braha, *President*
Elliott Braha, *Vice Pres*
▲ EMP: 28
SQ FT: 40,000
SALES (est): 6.6MM **Privately Held**
WEB: www.bracomanufacturing.com
SIC: 2676 Diapers, paper (disposable):
made from purchased paper; napkins,
sanitary: made from purchased paper

(G-10228)
**BRENNTAG SPECIALTIES INC
(DH)**
1 Cragwood Rd Ste 302 (07080-2416)
PHONE...........................908 561-6100
Steve Brauer, *President*
Brendan Cullinan, *Vice Pres*
Bob Przybylowski, *Vice Pres*
Darren Birkelbach, *VP Opers*

Brad Owens, *Treasurer*
◆ **EMP:** 60 **EST:** 2003
SQ FT: 110,000
SALES (est): 312.7MM
SALES (corp-wide): 14.3B **Privately Held**
WEB: www.mpsi-sw.com
SIC: 5169 2816 2899 Industrial chemicals; color pigments; chemical preparations
HQ: Brenntag North America, Inc.
  5083 Pottsville Pike
  Reading PA 19605
  610 926-6100

(G-10229)
BUSCH LLC
Also Called: Busch Vacuum
39 Davis St (07080-1429)
PHONE..................................908 561-3233
Ted Dames, *Branch Mgr*
EMP: 6
SALES (corp-wide): 603.5MM **Privately Held**
WEB: www.buschpump.com
SIC: 3563 Air & gas compressors
HQ: Busch Llc
  516 Viking Dr
  Virginia Beach VA 23452
  757 463-7800

(G-10230)
BUSHWICK METALS LLC
1641 New Market Ave (07080-1634)
PHONE..................................908 604-1450
Dan De Silva, *General Mgr*
EMP: 5
SALES (corp-wide): 225.3B **Publicly Held**
SIC: 3315 Steel wire & related products
HQ: Bushwick Metals Llc
  1000 Bridgeport Ave # 208
  Shelton CT 06484
  888 399-4070

(G-10231)
BUSHWICK METALS LLC
Also Called: Azco Steel Company
1641 New Market Ave (07080-1634)
PHONE..................................908 754-8700
Roy Strandberg, *Branch Mgr*
EMP: 30
SALES (corp-wide): 225.3B **Publicly Held**
WEB: www.bushwickmetals.com
SIC: 5064 5051 3312 Irons; steel; pipes, iron & steel
HQ: Bushwick Metals Llc
  1000 Bridgeport Ave # 208
  Shelton CT 06484
  888 399-4070

(G-10232)
C M C STEEL FABRICATORS INC
Also Called: CMC Joist & Deck
14 Harmich Rd (07080-4804)
PHONE..................................908 561-3484
Keven Gennarelli, *Principal*
Mike Polesky, *Branch Mgr*
EMP: 140
SQ FT: 125,000
SALES (corp-wide): 4.6B **Publicly Held**
WEB: www.cmcsg.com
SIC: 3444 3441 Roof deck, sheet metal; fabricated structural metal
HQ: C M C Steel Fabricators, Inc.
  1 Steel Mill Dr
  Seguin TX 78155
  830 372-8200

(G-10233)
CANADA DRY BOTTLING CO NY LP
Also Called: Seven Up Bottle Co
1760 New Durham Rd (07080-2328)
PHONE..................................732 572-1660
Pat Burt, *Manager*
EMP: 60
SALES (corp-wide): 51.4MM **Privately Held**
SIC: 2086 5149 Bottled & canned soft drinks; soft drinks

PA: Canada Dry Bottling Company Of New York, L.P.
  11202 15th Ave
  College Point NY 11356
  718 358-2000

(G-10234)
CANDELA CORPORATION
Also Called: Applied Optronics
111 Corporate Blvd Ste I (07080-2480)
PHONE..................................908 753-6300
Bob Sellers, *General Mgr*
EMP: 12 **Privately Held**
WEB: www.candelalaser.com
SIC: 3674 3699 Integrated circuits, semiconductor networks, etc.; laser systems & equipment
HQ: Candela Corporation
  530 Boston Post Rd
  Wayland MA 01778
  508 969-1837

(G-10235)
CAST TECHNOLOGY INC
161 West St (07080-3812)
PHONE..................................908 753-5155
Kenneth Shilay Jr, *President*
Margaret Shilay, *Admin Sec*
EMP: 5
SALES: 700K **Privately Held**
WEB: www.castechnology.com
SIC: 3519 Diesel engine rebuilding

(G-10236)
CENTURY CONVEYOR SYSTEMS INC
4301 S Clinton Ave (07080-1216)
PHONE..................................908 205-0625
Robert Bruce Robbins, *President*
Beth Robbins, *Admin Sec*
EMP: 24
SALES (est): 1.1MM **Privately Held**
SIC: 3535 Conveyors & conveying equipment

(G-10237)
CHATHAM BRASS CO INC
1253 New Market Ave Ste D (07080-2033)
PHONE..................................908 668-0500
Allen Leighton, *President*
Gene Adamusik, *Vice Pres*
▲ **EMP:** 7 **EST:** 1956
SQ FT: 9,500
SALES: 1.6MM **Privately Held**
SIC: 3432 Plumbing fixture fittings & trim

(G-10238)
CHEMMARK DEVELOPMENT INC
70 Tyler Pl (07080-1210)
PHONE..................................908 561-0923
Robert C Mc Manus, *President*
Geoffrey Brooks, *Shareholder*
Ivar Malmstrom, *Shareholder*
EMP: 3
SQ FT: 200
SALES: 2.2MM **Privately Held**
WEB: www.cosmeticindex.com
SIC: 2869 Industrial organic chemicals

(G-10239)
COLOR TECHNIQUES INC
260 Ryan St (07080-4208)
PHONE..................................908 412-9292
Joseph Bolitsky, *President*
Jennifer Bolitsky, *Vice Pres*
◆ **EMP:** 12
SQ FT: 20,000
SALES (est): 1.8MM **Privately Held**
WEB: www.color-techniques.com
SIC: 2865 2816 Color pigments, organic; inorganic pigments

(G-10240)
COLORFUL STORY BOOKS INC
4301 New Brunswick Ave (07080-1205)
PHONE..................................908 561-3333
John J Blewitt III, *President*
EMP: 30
SQ FT: 34,000
SALES: 1.5MM **Privately Held**
SIC: 2789 Binding only: books, pamphlets, magazines, etc.

(G-10241)
CONFIRES FIRE PRTCTION SVC LLC
910 Oak Tree Ave (07080-5142)
PHONE..................................908 822-2700
Mark Calleo,
EMP: 15
SALES (est): 2.5MM **Privately Held**
SIC: 5087 3569 3429 3669 Service establishment equipment; sprinkler systems, fire: automatic; nozzles; fire fighting; emergency alarms

(G-10242)
CONVERSION TECHNOLOGY CO INC
4301 New Brunswick Ave A (07080-1205)
PHONE..................................732 752-5660
Karel Choteborsky, *General Mgr*
EMP: 10 **Privately Held**
WEB: www.fluidink.com
SIC: 2899 Ink or writing fluids
PA: Conversion Technology Co., Inc.
  5360 N Commerce Ave
  Moorpark CA 93021

(G-10243)
COSETTE PHARMACEUTICALS INC
111 Coolidge St (07080-3801)
PHONE..................................314 283-4776
Walt Kaczmarek, *CEO*
EMP: 250
SALES: 100MM **Privately Held**
SIC: 2834 Pharmaceutical preparations

(G-10244)
CULTECH INC
Also Called: AP Cultech
3500 Hadley Rd (07080-1152)
PHONE..................................732 225-2722
Isao Aiba, *President*
Diane Rivard, *QC Mgr*
David Monchy, *Manager*
◆ **EMP:** 130 **EST:** 1990
SQ FT: 140,000
SALES (est): 27.9MM
SALES (corp-wide): 6.9MM **Privately Held**
WEB: www.cultech.com
SIC: 2657 Folding paperboard boxes
HQ: Autajon Cs
  Petit Pelican Petit Pelican
  Montelimar 26200
  475 002-000

(G-10245)
DANMARK ENTERPRISES INC
Also Called: Designer Bagel
692 Oak Tree Ave (07080-5122)
PHONE..................................732 321-3366
Milton Celko, *President*
Linda Celko, *Treasurer*
EMP: 5
SQ FT: 2,500
SALES (est): 281.9K **Privately Held**
SIC: 2051 5461 Bagels, fresh or frozen; bagels

(G-10246)
DEER OUT ANIMAL REPELLANT LLC
3651 S Clinton Ave (07080-1322)
P.O. Box 290 (07080-0290)
PHONE..................................908 769-4242
Gregg Latorre, *Mng Member*
EMP: 3
SALES: 10MM **Privately Held**
WEB: www.deerout.com
SIC: 2879 Insecticides & pesticides

(G-10247)
DEFENSE PHOTONICS GROUP INC
126 Corporate Blvd Ste A (07080-2411)
PHONE..................................908 822-1075
John Husaim, *CEO*
▼ **EMP:** 18 **EST:** 2003
SQ FT: 7,500
SALES: 2MM **Privately Held**
SIC: 3721 5088 Aircraft; transportation equipment & supplies

(G-10248)
DUKERS APPLIANCE CO USA LTD
4475 S Clinton Ave # 115 (07080-1200)
PHONE..................................917 378-8866
Hang Sang TSE, *Manager*
EMP: 4 **Privately Held**
SIC: 3585 Refrigeration equipment, complete
HQ: Dukers Appliance Co., Usa Ltd.
  2488 Peck Rd
  Whittier CA 90601
  562 568-4060

(G-10249)
EMC CORPORATION
4041 Hadley Rd Ste F (07080-1111)
PHONE..................................908 226-0100
Gus Amegedzie, *Branch Mgr*
EMP: 18
SALES (corp-wide): 90.6B **Publicly Held**
WEB: www.emc.com
SIC: 3572 Computer storage devices
HQ: Emc Corporation
  176 South St
  Hopkinton MA 01748
  508 435-1000

(G-10250)
ENGO CO
128 Case Dr (07080-5199)
PHONE..................................908 754-6600
Robert Engo, *President*
Richard Engo, *Admin Sec*
▲ **EMP:** 35
SQ FT: 60,000
SALES (est): 5.4MM **Privately Held**
WEB: www.engo.com
SIC: 2542 Partitions & fixtures, except wood

(G-10251)
ENZON PHARMACEUTICALS INC
300 Corporate Ct Ste C (07080-2415)
PHONE..................................732 980-4500
Christopher Phillip, *Manager*
EMP: 95
SALES (corp-wide): 6.9MM **Publicly Held**
WEB: www.enzon.com
SIC: 2834 Pharmaceutical preparations
PA: Enzon Pharmaceuticals, Inc.
  20 Commerce Dr Ste 135
  Cranford NJ 07016
  732 980-4500

(G-10252)
EPOCH TIMES
50 Cragwood Rd Ste 305 (07080-2436)
PHONE..................................908 548-8026
Guangxun LI, *Principal*
▲ **EMP:** 3 **EST:** 2013
SALES: 2MM **Privately Held**
SIC: 2711 Newspapers

(G-10253)
EVERGARD STEEL CORP
3313 Revere Rd (07080-5120)
PHONE..................................908 925-6800
Connie Macellara, *President*
Catherine Smith, *Vice Pres*
EMP: 10 **EST:** 1961
SQ FT: 10,000
SALES (est): 1.3MM **Privately Held**
SIC: 3315 3496 Wire products, ferrous/iron: made in wiredrawing plants; miscellaneous fabricated wire products

(G-10254)
EVERLASTING VALVE COMPANY INC
108 Somogyi Ct (07080-4897)
PHONE..................................908 769-0700
Richard G Base, *President*
Frank Hawley, *Vice Pres*
Wilson Jim, *Vice Pres*
Roger Jensen, *VP Mfg*
Anthony Frusco, *Plant Mgr*
▼ **EMP:** 30 **EST:** 1906
SQ FT: 28,000
SALES: 11.2MM
SALES (corp-wide): 107.6MM **Privately Held**
WEB: www.everlastingvalve.com
SIC: 3494 Valves & pipe fittings

PA: Armstrong International, Inc.
816 Maple St
Three Rivers MI 49093
269 273-1415

(G-10255)
EXACTAL TOOL LTD INC
Also Called: Exactal Tool & Die
3586 Kennedy Rd Ste 3 (07080-1997)
PHONE..................................908 561-1177
Scott Kaese, *President*
EMP: 5
SQ FT: 4,500
SALES: 250K **Privately Held**
SIC: 3599 Machine shop, jobbing & repair

(G-10256)
F AND M EQUIPMENT LTD
Also Called: Komatsu Northeast
2820 Hamilton Blvd (07080-2518)
PHONE..................................215 822-0145
Ben Norris, *President*
EMP: 100
SALES (est): 127.2K **Privately Held**
SIC: 3537 3531 Lift trucks, industrial: fork,
platform, straddle, etc.; construction ma-
chinery
HQ: Komatsu America Corp.
1701 Golf Rd Ste 1-100
Rolling Meadows IL 60008
847 437-5800

(G-10257)
**FEDERAL METALS & ALLOYS
CO**
4216 S Clinton Ave (07080-1316)
PHONE..................................908 756-0900
Mark Scoda, *President*
Thomas C Dietz, *President*
Walter Adamczyk, *Corp Secy*
EMP: 20 **EST:** 1974
SALES (est): 1.5MM **Privately Held**
SIC: 3341 5093 Secondary nonferrous
metals; metal scrap & waste materials

(G-10258)
FERRO CORPORATION
2501 S Clinton Ave (07080-1425)
PHONE..................................908 226-2148
Carl Vogelzang, *Manager*
EMP: 4
SALES (corp-wide): 1.6B **Publicly Held**
SIC: 3479 Coating of metals & formed
products
PA: Ferro Corporation
6060 Parkland Blvd # 250
Mayfield Heights OH 44124
216 875-5600

(G-10259)
FINANCIAL INFORMATION INC
1 Cragwood Rd Ste 2 (07080-2448)
PHONE..................................908 222-5300
Elizabeth Kappel, *President*
Wayne Meszaros, *CFO*
Anthony Necci, *Manager*
Elaine Villani, *Manager*
Christy Deloatch, *Supervisor*
EMP: 40
SQ FT: 7,500
SALES (est): 3.1MM **Privately Held**
WEB: www.fiinet.com
SIC: 2711 2741 Newspapers, publishing &
printing; miscellaneous publishing

(G-10260)
FLAVOR DYNAMICS INC
640 Montrose Ave (07080-2602)
PHONE..................................888 271-8424
Dolf De Rovira, *President*
EMP: 24
SQ FT: 29,000
SALES (est): 4.2MM **Privately Held**
WEB: www.flavordynamics.com
SIC: 2087 Extracts, flavoring

(G-10261)
**FOURSCONSULTING LTD LBLTY
CO**
295 Durham Ave Ste 206 (07080-2548)
PHONE..................................732 599-4324
Soruba Subramanian, *Administration*
Ravi Rai, *Tech Recruiter*
Anuj Tyagi, *Tech Recruiter*
EMP: 6 **EST:** 2006

SALES (est): 418.9K **Privately Held**
SIC: 7372 Application computer software;
business oriented computer software

(G-10262)
FRAGRANCE SOLUTIONS CORP
3357 S Clinton Ave (07080-1303)
PHONE..................................732 832-7800
John Yorey, *President*
▼ **EMP:** 7 **EST:** 2011
SQ FT: 4,500
SALES (est): 542.6K **Privately Held**
SIC: 2844 Perfumes & colognes

(G-10263)
G & W LABORATORIES INC (PA)
301 Helen St (07080-3808)
PHONE..................................908 753-2000
Ronald Greenblatt, *CEO*
Greg Sherwood, *General Mgr*
James Coy, *Vice Pres*
Nihar Desai, *Vice Pres*
Philip Erickson, *Vice Pres*
▲ **EMP:** 300
SQ FT: 140,000
SALES (est): 241.2MM **Privately Held**
WEB: www.gwlabs.com
SIC: 2834 Suppositories; ointments

(G-10264)
G & W LABORATORIES INC
101 Coolidge St (07080-3801)
PHONE..................................908 753-2000
EMP: 85
SALES (corp-wide): 241.2MM **Privately
Held**
SIC: 2834 Suppositories; ointments
PA: G & W Laboratories, Inc.
301 Helen St
South Plainfield NJ 07080
908 753-2000

(G-10265)
G&W PA LABORATORIES LLC
111 Coolidge St (07080-3801)
PHONE..................................908 753-2000
Ronald Greenblatt, *Mng Member*
EMP: 9
SALES (corp-wide): 241.2MM **Privately
Held**
SIC: 2834 Pharmaceutical preparations
HQ: G&W Pa Laboratories, Llc
650 Cathill Rd
Sellersville PA 18960
215 799-5333

(G-10266)
GE HEALTHCARE INC
Also Called: Medi-Physics
900 Durham Ave (07080-2402)
PHONE..................................908 757-0500
Simon Steingart, *Opers Mgr*
Simon Eingart, *Manager*
Frank Mastromonica, *Manager*
William Batista, *IT/INT Sup*
EMP: 40
SALES (corp-wide): 121.6B **Publicly
Held**
SIC: 2834 Pharmaceutical preparations
HQ: Ge Healthcare Inc.
100 Results Way
Marlborough MA 01752
800 526-3593

(G-10267)
GLOPAK CORP
132 Case Dr (07080-5109)
PHONE..................................908 753-8735
Cydnee Martin, *CEO*
Barbara Martin, *Principal*
Harold Martin Jr, *Vice Pres*
EMP: 30
SQ FT: 100,000
SALES (est): 7.5MM **Privately Held**
SIC: 3069 3081 3086 2821 Bags, rubber
or rubberized fabric; polyethylene film;
plastics foam products; plastics materials
& resins

(G-10268)
**GOLDEN W PPR CONVERTING
CORP**
121 Helen St (07080-3806)
PHONE..................................908 412-8889
David Hooi, *Manager*
EMP: 20

SALES (est): 4.8MM
SALES (corp-wide): 27.5MM **Privately
Held**
SIC: 2621 Paper mills
PA: Golden West Paper Converting Corpo-
ration
2480 Grant Ave
San Lorenzo CA 94580
510 317-0646

(G-10269)
GREETINGTAP
Also Called: Tap For Message
832 Spicer Ave (07080-3949)
PHONE..................................347 731-4263
Kadeer Beg,
Ahmer Beg,
EMP: 6
SALES (est): 338.4K **Privately Held**
SIC: 2741 5045 2771 ; computers, pe-
ripherals & software; greeting cards

(G-10270)
GULTON G I D
116 Corporate Blvd Ste A (07080-2437)
PHONE..................................908 791-4622
Joan Srivastava, *Principal*
EMP: 5
SALES (est): 608.3K **Privately Held**
SIC: 3679 5065 Antennas, receiving; elec-
tronic parts & equipment

(G-10271)
GULTON INCORPORATED
116 Corporate Blvd Ste A (07080-2437)
PHONE..................................908 791-4622
Om Srivastava, *President*
Joan Srivastava, *Vice Pres*
Thomas Michalski, *CFO*
Ted Richardson, *CIO*
Donald Jennings, *Technician*
EMP: 20
SQ FT: 13,000
SALES (est): 4.8MM **Privately Held**
WEB: www.gulton.com
SIC: 3577 Printers & plotters

(G-10272)
**HARRIS STRUCTURAL STEEL
CO INC (PA)**
1640 New Market Ave (07080-1641)
PHONE..................................732 752-6070
Thomas Harris Jr, *Ch of Bd*
Marvin Strauss, *Exec VP*
EMP: 40 **EST:** 1910
SQ FT: 100,000
SALES (est): 8.3MM **Privately Held**
SIC: 3441 Fabricated structural metal

(G-10273)
**HARRIS STRUCTURAL STEEL
CO INC**
1640 New Market Ave (07080-1641)
PHONE..................................732 752-6070
EMP: 6
SALES (corp-wide): 8.3MM **Privately
Held**
SIC: 3441 1791 Fabricated structural
metal; structural steel erection
PA: Harris Structural Steel Co., Inc.
1640 New Market Ave
South Plainfield NJ 07080
732 752-6070

(G-10274)
HUMMEL CROTON INC
Also Called: Hummel Chemical
10 Harmich Rd (07080-4899)
PHONE..................................908 754-1800
Bernard F Schoen, *President*
Mark Dugan, *Vice Pres*
Michael Richard, *Opers Staff*
◆ **EMP:** 15
SQ FT: 20,000
SALES (est): 3.6MM **Privately Held**
WEB: www.hummelcroton.com
SIC: 2819 5169 Barium compounds; in-
dustrial chemicals

(G-10275)
IGI CORP
6 Ingersoll Rd (07080-1306)
PHONE..................................908 753-5570
Bud Philbrook, *President*
EMP: 5

SALES (est): 549.5K **Privately Held**
SIC: 2672 Coated & laminated paper

(G-10276)
ILEOS OF AMERICA INC
Also Called: Flexpaq
550 Hadley Rd (07080-2426)
PHONE..................................908 753-7300
Mark Andrei, *President*
▲ **EMP:** 200 **EST:** 1997
SQ FT: 150,000
SALES (est): 28.9MM **Privately Held**
WEB: www.flexpaq.com
SIC: 3559 2671 Semiconductor manufac-
turing machinery; packaging paper &
plastics film, coated & laminated
HQ: Ileos
100 102
Paris 15e Arrondissement 75015
147 340-950

(G-10277)
INNOVATIVE DISPOSABLES LLC
3611 Kennedy Rd (07080-1801)
PHONE..................................908 222-7111
Neal Schramm, *Mng Member*
Michael Schramm,
◆ **EMP:** 45 **EST:** 2000
SQ FT: 22,000
SALES (est): 13.7MM **Privately Held**
SIC: 2676 Diapers, paper (disposable):
made from purchased paper

(G-10278)
**INTELLGENT TRFFIC SUP PDTS
LLC**
Also Called: I T S Products
3005 Hadley Rd Ste 5 (07080-1108)
PHONE..................................908 791-1200
Edward Hanna, *Manager*
Kevin Flynn,
EMP: 5
SALES (est): 1.8MM **Privately Held**
WEB: www.its-products.com
SIC: 5063 3669 5085 Signaling equip-
ment, electrical; traffic signals, electric; in-
dustrial supplies

(G-10279)
INTERNATIONAL GRAPHICS INC
6 Ingersoll Rd (07080-1306)
PHONE..................................908 753-5570
Bud Philbrook, *President*
EMP: 165
SQ FT: 50,000
SALES (est): 12.4MM **Privately Held**
SIC: 2672 Coated & laminated paper

(G-10280)
**IPCA PHARMACEUTICALS INC
(HQ)**
51 Cragwood Rd Ste 307 (07080-2405)
PHONE..................................908 412-6561
Hasit Bhatt, *President*
Priyanka Yuvaraj, *President*
▲ **EMP:** 3
SALES (est): 7MM
SALES (corp-wide): 501.3MM **Privately
Held**
SIC: 2834 Druggists' preparations (phar-
maceuticals)
PA: Ipca Laboratories Limited
48, Kandivali Industrial Estate
Mumbai MH 40006
226 210-5200

(G-10281)
ISOMEDIX OPERATIONS INC
3459 S Clinton Ave (07080-1303)
PHONE..................................908 757-3727
Becky Aldhizer, *Manager*
EMP: 30 **Privately Held**
WEB: www.isomedix.com
SIC: 3842 Surgical appliances & supplies
HQ: Isomedix Operations Inc.
5960 Heisley Rd
Mentor OH 44060

(G-10282)
J R S TOOL & METAL FINISHING
Also Called: J R S Mch & Tl Sls Corp Ameri
107 Borman Rd (07080-2928)
P.O. Box 52 (07080-0052)
PHONE..................................908 753-2050
John Stopherd, *President*
Linda Stopherd, *Vice Pres*

▲ = Import ▼=Export
◆ =Import/Export

EMP: 4
SQ FT: 6,000
SALES: 199K **Privately Held**
SIC: 3599 5084 7375 3471 Machine
shop, jobbing & repair; machine tools &
accessories; information retrieval services; plating & polishing; hand & edge
tools; paints & allied products

(G-10283)
JERSEY TANK FABRICATORS INC
1271 New Market Ave Ste D (07080-2034)
P.O. Box 257, Cream Ridge (08514-0257)
PHONE..................................609 758-7670
Eric Turinsky, *Ch of Bd*
Arlene Turinsky, *Corp Secy*
Stacy Nownes, *Finance Mgr*
▲ EMP: 30
SALES (est): 5.1MM **Privately Held**
WEB: www.jerseytank.com
SIC: 1791 7699 3443 Storage tanks,
metal: erection; tank repair; fabricated
plate work (boiler shop)

(G-10284)
JORDACHE LTD
200 Helen St (07080-3800)
PHONE..................................908 226-4930
Scott Reichert, *Manager*
▲ EMP: 11
SALES (est): 1.1MM
SALES (corp-wide): 1.3B **Privately Held**
SIC: 2325 2339 2369 Jeans: men's,
youths' & boys'; men's & boys' jeans &
dungarees; jeans: women's, misses' &
juniors'; jeans: girls', children's & infants'
PA: Jordache Enterprises Inc.
1400 Broadway Rm 1400 # 1400
New York NY 10018
212 643-8400

(G-10285)
K & A INDUSTRIES INC
51 Cragwood Rd Ste 204 (07080-2405)
PHONE..................................908 226-7000
George Keelty, *President*
Robert Aitkens, *Vice Pres*
EMP: 6
SQ FT: 2,500
SALES (est): 720K **Privately Held**
WEB: www.kaindustries.com
SIC: 3699 Security control equipment &
systems

(G-10286)
KADAKIA INTERNATIONAL INC
Also Called: Kadakia International Group
669 Montrose Ave (07080-2601)
PHONE..................................908 754-4445
Sailesh Kadakia, *President*
Prital Kadakia, *Vice Pres*
Priti Kadakia, *Vice Pres*
▲ EMP: 6
SQ FT: 8,000
SALES (est): 2.1MM **Privately Held**
SIC: 5162 2851 Plastics film; enamels

(G-10287)
KEYSTONE PLASTICS INC
3451 S Clinton Ave (07080-1303)
PHONE..................................908 561-1300
Marvin J Naftal, *President*
Frances Gould-Naftal, *Corp Secy*
Michael Naftal, *Vice Pres*
◆ EMP: 60
SQ FT: 62,000
SALES (est): 14.5MM **Privately Held**
SIC: 3082 3991 Unsupported plastics pro-
file shapes; brooms & brushes

(G-10288)
KOBO PRODUCTS INC (PA)
3474 S Clinton Ave (07080-1320)
P.O. Box 36079, Newark (07188-6006)
PHONE..................................908 757-0033
David Schlossman, *President*
Yun Shao, *Vice Pres*
Frank Mazzella, *Plant Mgr*
Oreste Nuzzo, *Warehouse Mgr*
April Vandunk, *Export Mgr*
◆ EMP: 35
SQ FT: 11,000

SALES (est): 87.8MM **Privately Held**
WEB: www.koboproductsinc.com
SIC: 5122 2844 Cosmetics; cosmetic
preparations

(G-10289)
KOBO PRODUCTS INC
690 Montrose Ave (07080-2602)
P.O. Box 767 (07080-0767)
PHONE..................................908 941-3406
Julian Navarro, *Branch Mgr*
EMP: 25
SALES (corp-wide): 87.8MM **Privately Held**
SIC: 2844 Cosmetic preparations
PA: Kobo Products, Inc.
3474 S Clinton Ave
South Plainfield NJ 07080
908 757-0033

(G-10290)
KOBO PRODUCTS INC
234 Saint Nicholas Ave (07080-1810)
P.O. Box 767, Short Hills (07078)
PHONE..................................908 757-0033
Yun Shao, *Principal*
Denise Fishman, *Research*
Mark Sine, *Accounts Mgr*
Geminie Deasis, *Supervisor*
EMP: 30
SALES (corp-wide): 87.8MM **Privately Held**
SIC: 2844 Cosmetic preparations
PA: Kobo Products, Inc.
3474 S Clinton Ave
South Plainfield NJ 07080
908 757-0033

(G-10291)
LE PAPILLON LTD
Also Called: Le Papillon of New Jersey
500 Hadley Rd (07080-2426)
PHONE..................................908 753-7300
Watson Warriner, *President*
Mark Rosso, *Vice Pres*
▲ EMP: 15
SQ FT: 4,000
SALES (est): 3.5MM **Privately Held**
WEB: www.lepapillon.com
SIC: 3221 Bottles for packing, bottling &
canning: glass
HQ: Ileos
100 102
Paris 15e Arrondissement 75015
147 340-950

(G-10292)
LEHIGH UTILITY ASSOCIATES INC
1300 New Market Ave (07080-1452)
P.O. Box 398 (07080-0398)
PHONE..................................908 561-5252
Frank J Butrico, *President*
William A Butrico, *Vice Pres*
EMP: 16
SQ FT: 32,000
SALES (est): 4.3MM **Privately Held**
WEB: www.lehighutility.com
SIC: 3441 Fabricated structural metal

(G-10293)
LELAND LIMITED INC
2614 S Clinton Ave (07080-1427)
P.O. Box 466 (07080-0466)
PHONE..................................908 561-2000
Leland C Stanford, *President*
Dawn Klinger, *Vice Pres*
◆ EMP: 13
SQ FT: 10,000
SALES (est): 4MM **Privately Held**
WEB: www.lelandltd.com
SIC: 3443 3069 5063 Tanks, standard or
custom fabricated: metal plate; life jack-
ets, inflatable: rubberized fabric; lighting
fixtures, commercial & industrial

(G-10294)
LIME ENERGY CO
2100 S Clinton Ave (07080-1422)
PHONE..................................908 415-9469
Robert Gaylor, *Manager*
EMP: 4
SALES (corp-wide): 272.2MM **Publicly Held**
SIC: 3274 Lime

HQ: Lime Energy Co.
4 Gateway Ctr Fl 4 # 4
Newark NJ 07102
201 416-2575

(G-10295)
M & M INTERNATIONAL
3619 Kennedy Rd Ste A (07080-1891)
PHONE..................................908 412-8300
Min Lim, *Owner*
▲ EMP: 10
SALES (est): 940.2K **Privately Held**
WEB: www.mminternational.net
SIC: 3317 Steel pipe & tubes

(G-10296)
MADHU B GOYAL MD
908 Oak Tree Ave Ste C (07080-5100)
PHONE..................................908 769-0307
Madhu B Goyal, *Owner*
EMP: 4
SALES (est): 266.3K **Privately Held**
SIC: 8011 7631 3444 1711 Geriatric spe-
cialist, physician/surgeon; watch repair;
sheet metalwork; ventilation & duct work
contractor; malpractice & negligence law

(G-10297)
MARDEE COMPANY INC
Also Called: Mardee Video Company
242 Saint Nicholas Ave (07080-1810)
PHONE..................................908 753-4343
Mariano De Santis, *President*
Steve Saunders, *Manager*
▲ EMP: 50
SQ FT: 31,000
SALES (est): 7.8MM **Privately Held**
WEB: www.mardee.com
SIC: 3651 5099 Household audio & video
equipment; video & audio equipment

(G-10298)
MARINO BUILDING SYSTEMS CORP
Also Called: American Panel TEC
1640 New Market Ave 1a (07080-1641)
P.O. Box 70 (07080-0070)
PHONE..................................732 968-0555
John A Marino, *Ch of Bd*
John Marino, *Ch of Bd*
John Lanzilotta, *President*
Keith Sherman, *Plant Mgr*
Matthew Folkerts, *Project Mgr*
EMP: 125
SQ FT: 90,000
SALES (est): 21MM **Privately Held**
WEB: www.americanpaneltec.com
SIC: 3448 Trusses & framing: prefabri-
cated metal

(G-10299)
MARINO INTERNATIONAL CORP
1640 New Market Ave (07080-1641)
P.O. Box 178 (07080-0178)
PHONE..................................732 752-5100
John A Marino, *Chairman*
Tatyana Marino, *Vice Pres*
EMP: 2
SQ FT: 60,000
SALES: 1.2MM **Privately Held**
SIC: 2439 3444 3441 2452 Structural
wood members; sheet metalwork; fabri-
cated structural metal; prefabricated wood
buildings

(G-10300)
MICRODATA INSTRUMENT INC
1207 Hogan Dr (07080-2474)
PHONE..................................908 222-1717
George Cai, *President*
EMP: 10
SQ FT: 2,000
SALES (est): 850K **Privately Held**
WEB: www.microdatamdi.com
SIC: 3821 Laboratory apparatus, except
heating & measuring

(G-10301)
MONARCH TOWEL COMPANY INC (PA)
Also Called: Monarch Robe and Towel Com-
pany
301 Hollywood Ave (07080-4201)
PHONE..................................800 729-7623
Ashley Chadowitz, *President*
Myron Chadowitz, *General Mgr*

Marilyn Robillard, *Cust Mgr*
▲ EMP: 25
SQ FT: 40,000
SALES: 15MM **Privately Held**
WEB: www.kfn.com
SIC: 2384 Bathrobes, men's & women's:
made from purchased materials

(G-10302)
MONTROSE MOLDERS CORPORATION
230 Saint Nicholas Ave (07080-1810)
PHONE..................................908 754-3030
William H Wilson, *President*
Judith Wilson, *Corp Secy*
EMP: 120
SQ FT: 76,000
SALES (est): 8.1MM
SALES (corp-wide): 26.6MM **Privately Held**
WEB: www.montrosemolders.com
SIC: 3081 Unsupported plastics film &
sheet
PA: Continental Precision Corp
25 Howard St
Piscataway NJ 08854
908 754-3030

(G-10303)
MULTI PACKAGING SOLUTIONS INC
901 Durham Ave (07080-2401)
PHONE..................................908 757-6000
Jack Frank, *Prdtn Mgr*
Frank Figurelli, *Purch Agent*
Ted Rosario, *Engineer*
Bob S Pierre, *CFO*
John Weir, *Manager*
EMP: 200
SALES (corp-wide): 14.8B **Publicly Held**
SIC: 2631 2752 2671 2657 Folding
boxboard; commercial printing, litho-
graphic; packaging paper & plastics film,
coated & laminated; folding paperboard
boxes
HQ: Multi Packaging Solutions, Inc.
150 E 52nd St Fl 28
New York NY 10022

(G-10304)
NEKOOSA COATED PRODUCTS LLC
6 Ingersoll Rd (07080-1306)
PHONE..................................800 440-1250
Paul Charapata, *CEO*
EMP: 5 **Privately Held**
SIC: 2671 Packaging paper & plastics film,
coated & laminated
HQ: Nekoosa Coated Products, Llc
841 Market St
Nekoosa WI 54457
800 826-4886

(G-10305)
NEW JERSEY BINDERY SVCS LLC
4301 New Brunswick Ave (07080-1205)
PHONE..................................732 200-8024
EMP: 4
SALES (est): 129.1K **Privately Held**
SIC: 2789 Bookbinding & related work

(G-10306)
NMR MANUFACTURING LLC
25 Davis St (07080-1429)
PHONE..................................908 769-3234
Mary Rinaldi, *Principal*
▲ EMP: 4 EST: 2002
SALES (est): 220K **Privately Held**
SIC: 2844 Toilet preparations

(G-10307)
NOODLE GOGO
4811 Stelton Rd (07080-1194)
PHONE..................................908 222-8898
Phillip LI, *President*
EMP: 4
SALES (est): 241.9K **Privately Held**
SIC: 2098 Noodles (e.g. egg, plain &
water), dry

GEOGRAPHIC

(G-10308)
NU-MEAT TECHNOLOGY INC
601 Hadley Rd (07080-2403)
P.O. Box 897 (07080-0897)
PHONE..................................908 754-3400
John Sbraga, *CEO*
Manfred Unfried, *Ch of Bd*
Brian Dowd, *President*
Rob Barillari, *CFO*
Gary Raines, *Treasurer*
▲ EMP: 20
SQ FT: 6,532
SALES (est): 11MM **Privately Held**
WEB: www.nu-meat.com
SIC: 5147 2011 Meats & meat products;
   meat packing plants

(G-10309)
NUTRO LABORATORIES INC
650 Hadley Rd Ste C (07080-2477)
PHONE..................................908 755-7984
Michael Slade, *President*
▲ EMP: 210
SQ FT: 85,000
SALES (est): 32.2MM **Publicly Held**
WEB: www.nbty.com
SIC: 2834 Vitamin preparations; anal-
   gesics; antiseptics, medicinal; laxatives
HQ: The Nature's Bounty Co
   2100 Smithtown Ave
   Ronkonkoma NY 11779
   631 200-2000

(G-10310)
NYLTITE CORP OF AMERICA
3451 S Clinton Ave (07080-1303)
PHONE..................................908 561-1300
Frances Gould, *President*
Charna Gould, *Corp Secy*
EMP: 10
SQ FT: 67,000
SALES: 600K **Privately Held**
WEB: www.nyltite.com
SIC: 3965 2221 Fasteners; broadwoven
   fabric mills, manmade

(G-10311)
OMG ELECTRONIC CHEMICALS INC
Also Called: Fidelity Chemical Products Div
400 Corporate Ct Ste A (07080-2414)
PHONE..................................908 222-5800
Chris Vidoli, *Vice Pres*
Chris Bidoli, *Vice Pres*
Joseph Simioni, *Vice Pres*
▼ EMP: 205 EST: 1969
SQ FT: 15,000
SALES (est): 26.8MM
SALES (corp-wide): 1.4B **Privately Held**
SIC: 2899 2819 3339 Plating compounds;
   nickel compounds or salts, inorganic; zinc
   chloride; primary nonferrous metals
PA: Vectra Co.
   120 S Central Ave Ste 200
   Saint Louis MO 63105
   314 797-8600

(G-10312)
POLYMER DYNAMIX LLC
Also Called: Poly-Dyn International
1000 Coolidge St (07080-3805)
PHONE..................................732 381-1600
Zheng Qian, *Research*
Veerag Mehta, *Mng Member*
Viggy Mehta,
Vikas Mehta,
◆ EMP: 15
SALES (est): 4.4MM **Privately Held**
WEB: www.polymerdynamix.com
SIC: 2821 Plastics materials & resins

(G-10313)
PORTON USA LLC (HQ)
3001 Hadley Rd Ste 1-4 (07080-1134)
PHONE..................................908 791-9100
Bruce Jiang,
EMP: 30 EST: 2015
SALES (est): 4MM
SALES (corp-wide): 170.6MM **Privately Held**
SIC: 2834 Pharmaceutical preparations
PA: Porton Pharma Solutions Ltd.
   1 Fine Chemical Zone, Chongqing
   Chemical Industry Park, Changsho
   Chongqing 40122
   236 593-6900

(G-10314)
POWERHUSE FRMLTONS LTD LABILIT
150 Maple Ave Ste 216 (07080-3407)
PHONE..................................888 666-7715
EMP: 4 EST: 2009
SQ FT: 600
SALES (est): 350K **Privately Held**
SIC: 2834 Mfg Natural Food Supplements

(G-10315)
PRESTO PRINTING SERVICE INC
19 S Plainfield Ave (07080-3408)
PHONE..................................908 756-5337
Richard Depinto, *President*
Richard De Pinto, *President*
EMP: 4
SQ FT: 1,200
SALES (est): 330K **Privately Held**
SIC: 2752 Commercial printing, offset

(G-10316)
PROLONG PHARMACEUTICALS LLC
300 Corporate Ct Ste B (07080-2415)
PHONE..................................908 444-4660
Abraham Abuchowski, *CEO*
Glenn Kazo, *President*
Andy Burger, *Vice Pres*
Tom Flachmeyer, *Vice Pres*
Ron Jubin, *Vice Pres*
EMP: 51
SALES (est): 15MM **Privately Held**
SIC: 2834 Pharmaceutical preparations

(G-10317)
PTC THERAPEUTICS INC (PA)
100 Corporate Ct (07080-2400)
PHONE..................................908 222-7000
Stuart W Peltz, *CEO*
Michael Schmertzler, *Ch of Bd*
Marcio Souza, *COO*
Neil Almstead, *Exec VP*
Jay Barth, *Vice Pres*
EMP: 240
SALES: 264.7MM **Publicly Held**
WEB: www.ptcbio.com
SIC: 2834 8731 Pharmaceutical prepara-
   tions; biotechnical research, commercial

(G-10318)
QUALIS PACKAGING INC (PA)
550 Hadley Rd (07080-2426)
PHONE..................................908 782-0305
Julie Vandoren, *Vice Pres*
EMP: 10 EST: 2008
SQ FT: 50,000
SALES (est): 3.2MM **Privately Held**
SIC: 2844 Perfumes & colognes

(G-10319)
QUALITY COSMETICS MFG
4455 S Clinton Ave (07080-1213)
PHONE..................................908 755-9588
Anthony Richard Persaud, *President*
Teresa Persaud, *Vice Pres*
Theresa Persaud, *Purchasing*
▲ EMP: 40
SQ FT: 33,000
SALES (est): 8.4MM **Privately Held**
WEB: www.qualitycosmetics.com
SIC: 2844 Cosmetic preparations

(G-10320)
QUALITY GLASS INC
2300 S Clinton Ave Ste C (07080-1498)
PHONE..................................908 754-2652
Ronald Morris, *President*
Greg Morris, *Managing Dir*
Karen Morris, *Vice Pres*
EMP: 12
SALES (est): 1.7MM **Privately Held**
SIC: 7536 7699 3231 Automotive glass
   replacement shops; china & glass repair;
   door & window repair; products of pur-
   chased glass

(G-10321)
R & D CIRCUITS INC (PA)
Also Called: R&D Altanova
3601 S Clinton Ave (07080-1322)
PHONE..................................732 549-4554
Seyed Paransun, *President*
Jeff Bavaro, *Engineer*
Sharon Trueman, *Design Engr*
Deborah Bothwell, *CFO*
Kevin St Germaine, *CFO*
▲ EMP: 150 EST: 1971
SQ FT: 270,000
SALES (est): 36.8MM **Privately Held**
WEB: www.rdcircuits.com
SIC: 3672 Printed circuit boards

(G-10322)
R TAPE CORPORATION (DH)
6 Ingersoll Rd (07080-1306)
PHONE..................................908 753-5570
Paul Charapata, *CEO*
Joe Maisano, *Facilities Mgr*
Tim Reimer, *Controller*
Guy Leigh, *VP Sales*
◆ EMP: 125
SQ FT: 53,000
SALES (est): 30.2MM **Privately Held**
WEB: www.rtape.com
SIC: 2671 2241 Plastic film, coated or
   laminated for packaging; fabric tapes
HQ: Nekoosa Coated Products, Llc
   841 Market St
   Nekoosa WI 54457
   800 826-4886

(G-10323)
RADIANT COMMUNICATIONS CORP (PA)
5001 Hadley Rd (07080-1128)
P.O. Box 867 (07080-0867)
PHONE..................................908 757-7444
Tom Lewis, *President*
David Mandell, *Corp Secy*
Mike Whalen, *Prdtn Mgr*
Lyubomir Trayanov, *Engineer*
Rob Thaw, *Regl Sales Mgr*
▲ EMP: 41
SQ FT: 10,000
SALES (est): 7.6MM **Privately Held**
WEB: www.rccfiber.com
SIC: 3229 Fiber optics strands

(G-10324)
RECYCLE INC
20a Harmich Rd (07080-4824)
P.O. Box 340 (07080-0340)
PHONE..................................908 756-2200
Jeffrey Bey, *President*
Stanley Bey, *Chairman*
Jeanine Rutar, *CFO*
▲ EMP: 60
SQ FT: 85,000
SALES (est): 12.3MM **Privately Held**
SIC: 4953 3087 Recycling, waste materi-
   als; custom compound purchased resins

(G-10325)
RECYCLE INC EAST
20a Harmich Rd (07080-4824)
P.O. Box 340 (07080-0340)
PHONE..................................908 756-2200
Jeff Bey, *President*
EMP: 90
SQ FT: 80,000
SALES (est): 23.2MM
SALES (corp-wide): 1.1B **Privately Held**
SIC: 2655 3412 2821 Fiber cans, drums
   & containers; drums, fiber: made from
   purchased material; metal barrels, drums
   & pails; drums, shipping: metal; polyethyl-
   ene resins
HQ: National Container Group, Llc
   3620 W 38th St
   Chicago IL 60632

(G-10326)
SCONDA CANVAS PRODUCTS
Also Called: Main Attractions
20 Harmich Rd (07080-4804)
PHONE..................................732 225-3500
Rocky Sconda, *Owner*
Dean Dialfanso, *General Mgr*
Marie Zarra, *Business Mgr*
Thomas Ofarrell, *Engineer*
EMP: 26
SALES (est): 2.3MM **Privately Held**
WEB: www.mainattractions.com
SIC: 7359 2394 Party supplies rental serv-
   ices; tent & tarpaulin rental; sound & light-
   ing equipment rental; awnings, fabric:
   made from purchased materials

(G-10327)
SENSIENT TECHNOLOGIES CORP
Also Called: Sensient Cosmetics Technology
107 Wade Ave (07080-1311)
P.O. Box 705 (07080-0705)
PHONE..................................908 757-4500
Debby Keyes, *Mktg Coord*
Gregg White, *Manager*
EMP: 46
SQ FT: 18,000
SALES (corp-wide): 1.3B **Publicly Held**
WEB: www.sensient-tech.com
SIC: 2099 2816 2087 Yeast; inorganic
   pigments; beverage bases
PA: Sensient Technologies Corporation
   777 E Wisconsin Ave # 1100
   Milwaukee WI 53202
   414 271-6755

(G-10328)
SUKHADIAS SWEETS & SNACKS (PA)
Also Called: India Cafe
124 Case Dr (07080-5109)
PHONE..................................908 222-0069
Piyush Sukhadia, *President*
Jay Sukhadia, *Vice Pres*
Shaivi Sukhadia, *Director*
Bindu Sukhadia, *Admin Sec*
▲ EMP: 15
SQ FT: 6,000
SALES (est): 2.2MM **Privately Held**
SIC: 2051 Cakes, pies & pastries

(G-10329)
SUPERSEAL MANUFACTURING CO INC (DH)
125 Helen St (07080-3806)
PHONE..................................908 561-5910
Joseph Vespa Jr, *President*
Ronald A Vespa, *Vice Pres*
EMP: 19 EST: 1980
SQ FT: 128,000
SALES (est): 8.7MM
SALES (corp-wide): 1.2B **Privately Held**
SIC: 3089 Window frames & sash, plastic
HQ: Hwd Acquisition, Inc.
   575 S Whelen Ave
   Medford WI 54451
   800 433-4873

(G-10330)
TECHNICK PRODUCTS INC
1000 Coolidge St (07080-3805)
PHONE..................................908 791-0400
Amita Mehta, *President*
Veerag Mehta, *Vice Pres*
Marty Holden, *Sales Staff*
Erica Estrada, *Manager*
◆ EMP: 12
SALES (est): 4.9MM **Privately Held**
WEB: www.technickproducts.com
SIC: 2821 2841 Plastics materials &
   resins; soap & other detergents

(G-10331)
TOUCH DYNAMIC INC (PA)
121 Corporate Blvd (07080-2409)
PHONE..................................732 382-5701
Craig Paritz, *President*
▲ EMP: 75
SQ FT: 40,000
SALES (est): 20.2MM **Privately Held**
WEB: www.touchdynamic.com
SIC: 3575 3571 Computer terminals, mon-
   itors & components; personal computers
   (microcomputers)

(G-10332)
TWO RIVERS COFFEE LLC
Also Called: Brooklyn Bean Roastery
101 Kentile Rd Unit 13 (07080-4805)
P.O. Box 527 (07080-0527)
PHONE..................................908 205-0018
Steven Schreiber,
Mayer Koenig,
EMP: 5
SQ FT: 100,000
SALES (est): 1.1MM **Privately Held**
SIC: 2095 Coffee roasting (except by
   wholesale grocers)

(G-10333)
UMICORE PRECIOUS METALS NJ LLC
3950 S Clinton Ave (07080-1316)
PHONE.............................908 222-5006
Rick Holt, *Vice Pres*
Stephan Marczinkowski, *Vice Pres*
▲ EMP: 25
SALES (est): 12.5MM
SALES (corp-wide): 3.7B Privately Held
SIC: 3339 2869 Precious metals; industrial organic chemicals
PA: Umicore
Rue Du Marais 31
Bruxelles 1000
222 771-11

(G-10334)
UMICORE USA INC
3900 S Clinton Ave (07080-1316)
PHONE.............................908 226-2053
Gregory Hedden, *Branch Mgr*
EMP: 19
SALES (corp-wide): 3.7B Privately Held
SIC: 3339 Precious metals
HQ: Umicore Usa Inc.
3600 Glenwood Ave Ste 250
Raleigh NC 27612

(G-10335)
UNITED FUEL DISTRIBUTORS LLC
103 Spisso Ct (07080-2479)
PHONE.............................908 906-9053
Rajinder Kumar, *Principal*
EMP: 4 EST: 2010
SALES (est): 23K Privately Held
SIC: 2869 Fuels

(G-10336)
US PLASTIC SALES LLC
651 Metuchen Rd (07080-4820)
P.O. Box 617 (07080-0617)
PHONE.............................908 754-9404
Raphael Bilia,
▲ EMP: 5 EST: 1997
SQ FT: 50,000
SALES (est): 6MM Privately Held
SIC: 3081 Unsupported plastics film & sheet

(G-10337)
US SOFTWARE GROUP INC
Also Called: Ussg
1550 Park Ave Ste 202 (07080-5565)
P.O. Box 854, Edison (08818-0854)
PHONE.............................732 361-4636
Jake Kris, *Director*
EMP: 50
SALES (est): 4.8MM Privately Held
SIC: 7379 7372 4813 ; application computer software;

(G-10338)
VAN HYDRAULICS INC
110 Snyder Rd (07080-1915)
P.O. Box 320, Keasbey (08832-0320)
PHONE.............................732 442-5500
Arthur Fernandez Jr, *President*
Karen Fernandez, *Corp Secy*
Dean Reale, *Asst Mgr*
EMP: 40
SQ FT: 5,000
SALES (est): 7.1MM Privately Held
WEB: www.vanhydraulics.com
SIC: 3593 5084 7699 Fluid power cylinders & actuators; hydraulic systems equipment & supplies; hydraulic equipment repair

(G-10339)
VAN-NICK PALLET INC
104 Snyder Rd (07080-1915)
PHONE.............................908 753-1800
Bobby Ducalo, *Owner*
EMP: 8
SALES (est): 1.2MM Privately Held
SIC: 2448 Pallets, wood & wood with metal

(G-10340)
VANGUARD RESEARCH INDUSTRIES
239 Saint Nicholas Ave (07080-1809)
PHONE.............................908 753-2770
Harry F Sica Jr, *CEO*

Peter Costa, *President*
EMP: 23
SQ FT: 35,000
SALES (est): 3.1MM Privately Held
WEB: www.vanguardholdings.com
SIC: 3471 Electroplating of metals or formed products

(G-10341)
VIANT MEDICAL INC (DH)
6 Century Ln (07080-1323)
PHONE.............................908 561-0717
Dan Croteau, *CEO*
Justin Herbert, *Business Mgr*
John Porto, *Opers Mgr*
Thomas Testa, *CFO*
Shane Healy, *Sales Dir*
◆ EMP: 172
SQ FT: 40,000
SALES (est): 177.9MM
SALES (corp-wide): 368.7MM Privately Held
WEB: www.medtech-grp.com
SIC: 3841 Surgical & medical instruments

(G-10342)
VISUAL ARCHITECTURAL DESIGNS
Also Called: V A Design
15 Harmich Rd (07080-4804)
PHONE.............................908 754-3000
Sara Chrysanthopoulos, *CEO*
Matthew Weber, *Project Mgr*
Frank Nieves, *Sales Staff*
EMP: 19
SALES (est): 3.2MM Privately Held
SIC: 2541 2434 2531 2431 Store & office display cases & fixtures; wood kitchen cabinets; school furniture; millwork

(G-10343)
VITACARE PHARMA LLC
111 Skyline Dr (07080-1806)
PHONE.............................908 754-1792
Manav Shah,
Amrita Gupta,
Harendra Gupta,
EMP: 5
SALES (est): 1.1MM Privately Held
SIC: 2834 Pharmaceutical preparations

(G-10344)
WALL STREET GROUP INC
2 Hollywood Ct B (07080-4204)
PHONE.............................201 333-4784
Philip J Mc Gee, *President*
Alfred J Basile, *Vice Pres*
Charles Basile, *Vice Pres*
Mark Gorenstein, *Vice Pres*
Julie McGee Verbaro, *Vice Pres*
EMP: 60
SQ FT: 35,000
SALES (est): 11.6MM Privately Held
WEB: www.wallstreetgroup.com
SIC: 2759 Commercial printing

(G-10345)
WARE INDUSTRIES INC (PA)
Also Called: Marino Ware Division
400 Metuchen Rd (07080-4807)
P.O. Box 467 (07080-0467)
PHONE.............................908 757-9000
Leroy Schecter, *Ch of Bd*
Chip Gardner, *President*
Robert Jankowski, *General Mgr*
Richard Dargel, *COO*
John Farelli, *Vice Pres*
◆ EMP: 68 EST: 1972
SQ FT: 100,000
SALES (est): 107.9MM Privately Held
WEB: www.marinoware.com
SIC: 3444 Sheet metalwork

(G-10346)
WESTERLEIGH CONCEPTS INC
2 Hollywood Ct (07080-4204)
PHONE.............................908 205-8888
EMP: 12 EST: 2014
SALES (est): 1.7MM Privately Held
SIC: 2752 Commercial printing, offset

(G-10347)
XBOX EXCLUSIVE
111 Eleanor St (07080-4705)
PHONE.............................908 756-3731
Steven Melanson, *Owner*

EMP: 7
SALES (est): 381.7K Privately Held
WEB: www.xboxexclusive.com
SIC: 3651 7993 Household audio & video equipment; video game arcade

---

South River
Middlesex County

(G-10348)
ALLTITE GASKET CO
323 William St (08882-1077)
PHONE.............................732 254-2154
Ronald Dreger, *President*
John Graney, *Vice Pres*
EMP: 10 EST: 1947
SQ FT: 5,000
SALES: 1.2MM Privately Held
SIC: 3053 Gaskets, all materials

(G-10349)
BUCATI LEATHER INC
427 Whitehead Ave Ste 2 (08882-2595)
PHONE.............................732 254-0480
▲ EMP: 8 EST: 1993
SQ FT: 8,000
SALES: 2MM Privately Held
SIC: 3199 5199 Mfg Leather Goods Whol Nondurable Goods

(G-10350)
ENVIROCHEM INC
425 Whitehead Ave (08882-2536)
PHONE.............................732 238-6700
Deborah Gildersleeve, *President*
Sidney Fleisher, *Controller*
Tony Axley, *Sales Staff*
Diane Ciemiecki, *Office Mgr*
Bob Imparato, *Manager*
◆ EMP: 48 EST: 1975
SQ FT: 90,000
SALES (est): 15MM Privately Held
SIC: 2842 7389 Cleaning or polishing preparations; packaging & labeling services

(G-10351)
KYOSIS LLC
148 Whitehead Ave Ste 1 (08882-1735)
PHONE.............................908 202-8894
Rupesh Patel,
EMP: 6
SQ FT: 1,000
SALES (est): 192.8K Privately Held
SIC: 7379 1799 7521 3559 Computer related maintenance services; parking facility equipment & maintenance; parking facility equipment installation; parking garage; parking structure; parking facility equipment & supplies

(G-10352)
MAPEI CORPORATION
O Off (08882)
P.O. Box 105 (08882-0105)
PHONE.............................732 254-4830
Eddie Dilaurenzio, *Branch Mgr*
EMP: 40 Privately Held
SIC: 3531 2899 2891 Concrete grouting equipment; chemical preparations; adhesives & sealants
HQ: Mapei Corporation
1144 E Newport Center Dr
Deerfield Beach FL 33442
954 246-8888

(G-10353)
MAPEI CORPORATION
Whitehead (08882)
PHONE.............................732 254-4830
John Zimmerman, *Branch Mgr*
EMP: 12 Privately Held
SIC: 2891 Adhesives & sealants
HQ: Mapei Corporation
1144 E Newport Center Dr
Deerfield Beach FL 33442
954 246-8888

(G-10354)
MILLWOOD INC
7 Brick Plant Rd Ste C (08882-1145)
PHONE.............................732 967-8818
Chris Verbosky, *Manager*

EMP: 70 Privately Held
WEB: www.millwoodinc.com
SIC: 2448 Pallets, wood; skids, wood
PA: Millwood, Inc.
3708 International Blvd
Vienna OH 44473

(G-10355)
RELDAN METALS INC (PA)
396 Whitehead Ave 402 (08882-2900)
PHONE.............................732 238-8550
Alan Nadler, *President*
Howard Steinberg, *Senior VP*
EMP: 20
SALES (est): 12MM Privately Held
SIC: 3341 Gold smelting & refining (secondary)

(G-10356)
RELDAN METALS INC
396 Whitehead Ave 402 (08882-2900)
PHONE.............................732 238-8550
EMP: 180
SALES (corp-wide): 12MM Privately Held
SIC: 3341 Gold smelting & refining (secondary)
PA: Reldan Metals Inc.
396 Whitehead Ave 402
South River NJ 08882
732 238-8550

(G-10357)
SERIOUS WELDING & MECH LLC
427 Whitehead Ave Ste 3 (08882-2595)
P.O. Box 5241, Somerset (08875-5241)
PHONE.............................732 698-7478
Paul Bari, *President*
Paul Stevens, *Vice Pres*
EMP: 13
SQ FT: 2,000
SALES: 1.5MM Privately Held
SIC: 7699 7692 Mechanical instrument repair; welding repair

(G-10358)
SPORTSTAR WORLD WIDE INC
19 Thomas St (08882-1142)
PHONE.............................732 254-9214
Steve Kumar, *President*
Roger Thacar, *Owner*
EMP: 17
SALES: 1.1MM Privately Held
SIC: 2329 Athletic (warmup, sweat & jogging) suits: men's & boys'

Southampton
Burlington County

(G-10359)
ALPHA 1 STUDIO INC
3 Linda Ln (08088-9174)
PHONE.............................609 859-2200
Ray Witthauer, *President*
Michele Stow, *Director*
EMP: 8
SALES (est): 902K Privately Held
WEB: www.signstudio.com
SIC: 3993 7336 Signs & advertising specialties; commercial art & graphic design

(G-10360)
BENJAMIN BOOTH COMPANY
523 Meadowyck Ln (08088-9110)
PHONE.............................609 859-1995
David Frey, *President*
O Paul Frey, *Vice Pres*
Shirley Frey, *Treasurer*
▲ EMP: 12
SQ FT: 25,000
SALES (est): 1.3MM Privately Held
SIC: 3552 3991 Card clothing, textile machinery; brushes, household or industrial

(G-10361)
ESS GROUP INC
129 Eayrestown Rd (08088-9122)
PHONE.............................609 755-3139
Steven Szafara, *CEO*
EMP: 7

G
E
O
G
R
A
P
H
I
C

SALES (corp-wide): 34.6MM **Privately Held**
SIC: 2835 Electrolyte diagnostic agents
PA: The Ess Group Inc
    78 Carranza Rd
    Tabernacle NJ 08088
    609 268-1200

(G-10362)
EVERLAST ASSOCIATES INC
Also Called: Everlast Sheds
203 Route 530 (08088-1645)
PHONE..........................609 261-1888
Daniel Capocci, *President*
Daniel I Capocci, *President*
EMP: 8
SALES (est): 1.2MM **Privately Held**
WEB: www.everlastsheds.net
SIC: 3448 5211 5039 Buildings, portable:
prefabricated metal; lumber products; pre-
fabricated structures

(G-10363)
GENIE HOUSE CORP (PA)
139 Red Lion Rd (08088-8893)
P.O. Box 2478, Vincentown (08088-2478)
PHONE..........................609 859-0600
Lloyd Williams Jr, *President*
Deborah Ware, *General Mgr*
◆ EMP: 28 EST: 1967
SQ FT: 12,000
SALES (est): 5.2MM **Privately Held**
WEB: www.geniehouse.com
SIC: 3645 5719 Wall lamps; desk lamps;
floor lamps; lighting fixtures

(G-10364)
GMP PUBLICATIONS INC
4 Linda Ln Ste B (08088-9178)
P.O. Box 335, Medford (08055-0335)
PHONE..........................609 859-3400
John Cuspilich, *President*
Michael Van Horn, *President*
EMP: 4
SQ FT: 1,100
SALES (est): 532.2K **Privately Held**
WEB: www.pharmarecruiters.com
SIC: 2741 Miscellaneous publishing

(G-10365)
**IMAGES COSTUME
PRODUCTIONS**
881 Westminster Dr N (08088-1037)
PHONE..........................609 859-7372
Charles Veasey, *President*
Annette Veasey, *Vice Pres*
EMP: 5 EST: 1980
SALES: 500K **Privately Held**
SIC: 7922 2389 Costume & scenery de-
sign services; masquerade costumes

(G-10366)
JKA SPECIALTIES MFR INC
Also Called: J K A Specialties
157 Eayrestown Rd (08088-9122)
PHONE..........................609 859-2090
James F Young Sr, *President*
Kimnberly Brown, *President*
EMP: 15 EST: 1974
SQ FT: 7,500
SALES (est): 2.3MM **Privately Held**
SIC: 2297 3999 3993 Nonwoven fabrics;
badges, metal: policemen, firemen, etc.;
signs & advertising specialties

(G-10367)
L & L REDI-MIX INC (PA)
1939 Route 206 (08088-9593)
PHONE..........................609 859-2271
Linwood C Gerber, *President*
Larry Gerber, *Vice Pres*
Patrick Emmel, *Opers Staff*
Debora Doyle, *Controller*
EMP: 65
SQ FT: 9,000
SALES (est): 13.8MM **Privately Held**
WEB: www.llredimix.com
SIC: 3273 Ready-mixed concrete

(G-10368)
MCW PRECISION
137 Eayrestown Rd (08088-9122)
P.O. Box 2513, Vincentown (08088-2513)
PHONE..........................609 859-4400
Michael Wolfrom, *Owner*
Beth Wolfrom, *Office Mgr*

EMP: 10
SALES (est): 1.3MM **Privately Held**
SIC: 3399 Primary metal products

(G-10369)
**MEDFORD CEDAR PRODUCTS
INC**
59 Old Red Lion Rd (08088-2811)
PHONE..........................609 859-1400
Charline Scheibner, *CEO*
Albin E Scheibner Jr, *President*
EMP: 5
SQ FT: 5,000
SALES (est): 1MM **Privately Held**
WEB: www.medfordcedar.com
SIC: 5211 2499 5712 Planing mill prod-
ucts & lumber; flooring, wood; fencing,
docks & other outdoor wood structural
products; outdoor & garden furniture

(G-10370)
RCC FABRICATORS INC
2035 Route 206 (08088-3530)
PHONE..........................609 859-9350
Alfonso Daloisio Jr, *President*
EMP: 25
SALES (est): 6.4MM
SALES (corp-wide): 70.8MM **Privately
Held**
WEB: www.railroadconstruction.com
SIC: 3441 Building components, structural
steel
PA: Railroad Construction Company, Inc.
    75-77 Grove St
    Paterson NJ 07503
    973 684-0362

(G-10371)
SAFETY-KLEEN SYSTEMS INC
123 Red Lion Rd (08088-8830)
PHONE..........................609 859-2049
Keith Wilson, *Manager*
EMP: 19
SALES (corp-wide): 3.3B **Publicly Held**
SIC: 7359 4212 3559 4953 Equipment
rental & leasing; hazardous waste trans-
port; degreasing machines, automotive &
industrial; refuse systems
HQ: Safety-Kleen Systems, Inc.
    2600 N Central Expy # 400
    Richardson TX 75080
    972 265-2000

(G-10372)
**SAU-SEA SWIMMING POOL
PRODUCTS**
Also Called: Sausea Swimming Pool Enamels
1855 Route 206 (08088-3528)
P.O. Box 1419, Medford (08055-6419)
PHONE..........................609 859-8500
Mary Hunter, *President*
Steven Hunter, *Principal*
Thelma H Hunter, *Shareholder*
EMP: 12 EST: 1976
SQ FT: 5,000
SALES: 1MM **Privately Held**
WEB: www.sau-sea.com
SIC: 2851 5169 Paints, waterproof; chemi-
cals & allied products

(G-10373)
TRIPLE D ENTERPRISES INC
135 Eayrestown Rd (08088-9122)
PHONE..........................609 859-3000
David J Helgeson, *Director*
EMP: 6
SALES (est): 750K **Privately Held**
SIC: 3531 Plows: construction, excavating
& grading

(G-10374)
WOOD PRODUCTS INC
34 Allentown Rd (08088-8835)
PHONE..........................609 859-0303
John Taylor, *President*
Ronald G Taylor, *Vice Pres*
EMP: 6
SQ FT: 3,200
SALES (est): 731.3K **Privately Held**
SIC: 2431 Staircases & stairs, wood

┌─────────────────────┐
│   **Sparta**   │
│   *Sussex County*   │
└─────────────────────┘

(G-10375)
ADVANCED PRECISION INC
Also Called: API
15 Wilson Dr Ste B (07871-4409)
PHONE..........................800 788-9473
Vincent Fay, *CEO*
Anthony Falgares, *Opers Mgr*
Hugo Papa, *CFO*
Allyson Policastro, *Info Tech Mgr*
EMP: 25
SQ FT: 8,500
SALES (est): 4.9MM **Privately Held**
WEB: www.advancedprecision.com
SIC: 3841 Surgical & medical instruments

(G-10376)
AEROSPACE INDUSTRIES LLC
520 Lafayette Rd (07871-3447)
PHONE..........................973 383-9307
Robert J Lesko,
EMP: 5
SQ FT: 1,200
SALES: 500K **Privately Held**
SIC: 3724 5088 Aircraft engines & engine
parts; aircraft & parts

(G-10377)
ALPINE CREAMERY
14 White Deer Plz (07871-1858)
PHONE..........................973 726-0777
John Tulp, *Owner*
EMP: 4
SALES (est): 226.1K **Privately Held**
SIC: 2024 Ice cream, bulk

(G-10378)
ALTAFLO LLC
23 Wilson Dr Ste 1 (07871-4410)
PHONE..........................973 300-3344
Mary Hyde, *Mng Member*
Donald C Bishop,
EMP: 10
SQ FT: 15,000
SALES (est): 1.8MM **Privately Held**
WEB: www.altaflo.com
SIC: 2821 Plastics materials & resins

(G-10379)
AUTHENTICITY BREWING LLC
23 Kroghs Ln (07871-3444)
PHONE..........................862 432-9622
Aaron Buch,
EMP: 5
SALES (est): 150.7K **Privately Held**
SIC: 3999 Manufacturing industries

(G-10380)
B & W PLASTICS INC
20 Wilson Dr (07871-3400)
PHONE..........................973 383-0020
William Post, *President*
Louise Post, *VP Finance*
Christina Lordy, *VP Sales*
EMP: 7
SQ FT: 12,000
SALES (est): 1.3MM **Privately Held**
SIC: 3089 Injection molding of plastics

(G-10381)
CARL BUCK CORPORATION
14 Park Lake Rd Ste 3 (07871-3257)
PHONE..........................973 300-5575
Peter Gennaro, *President*
Cynthia Gennaro, *Vice Pres*
▼ EMP: 8 EST: 1946
SQ FT: 12,500
SALES: 1.5MM **Privately Held**
WEB: www.camacindustries.com
SIC: 3559 Metal finishing equipment for
plating, etc.; chemical machinery & equip-
ment

(G-10382)
**COLINEAR MACHINE & DESIGN
INC**
7 Wilson Dr (07871-3427)
PHONE..........................973 300-1681
John T San Giacomo Jr, *President*
John T S Giacomo Jr, *President*
Jae Castellana, *Opers Mgr*

John Sangiacomo, *Opers Mgr*
Michelle S Giacomo, *CFO*
EMP: 19
SQ FT: 13,000
SALES: 2.2MM **Privately Held**
WEB: www.colinearmachine.com
SIC: 3599 Machine shop, jobbing & repair

(G-10383)
**COMPACT FLUORESCENT
SYSTEMS**
Also Called: CFS
463 Stanhope Rd (07871-2816)
PHONE..........................908 475-8991
▲ EMP: 6
SALES: 120K **Privately Held**
SIC: 3646 Mfg Commercial Lighting Fix-
tures

(G-10384)
COUNTRY CLUB ICE CREAM
4 Tyler St (07871-2717)
P.O. Box 77 (07871-0077)
PHONE..........................973 729-5570
Maria E Rodriguez, *Director*
EMP: 7
SALES (est): 118.8K **Privately Held**
SIC: 5812 2024 Ice cream stands or dairy
bars; ice cream & frozen desserts

(G-10385)
CREATIVE METAL WORKS INC
22b Gail Ct (07871-3439)
P.O. Box 1068 (07871-5068)
PHONE..........................973 579-3717
Zoran Grubic, *President*
EMP: 10
SALES (est): 1.5MM **Privately Held**
SIC: 3446 Architectural metalwork

(G-10386)
DIAMOND CHIP REALTY LLC
Also Called: Diamond Sand & Gravel
33 Demarest Rd (07871-3441)
PHONE..........................973 383-4651
Frank Hunklene, *Mng Member*
EMP: 30
SALES (est): 1.1MM **Privately Held**
SIC: 3272 3273 Building stone, artificial:
concrete; ready-mixed concrete

(G-10387)
**FIREFIGHTER ONE LTD LBLTY
CO**
Also Called: Ff1 Professional Safety Svcs
34 Wilson Dr (07871-3400)
PHONE..........................973 940-3061
Jonathon Van Norman, *President*
Brian Kredatus, *Accounts Mgr*
Bryan Crawford, *Mktg Dir*
Ed Maines, *Manager*
Todd Rudloff, *Manager*
EMP: 6 EST: 2005
SALES (est): 1.6MM **Privately Held**
SIC: 2311 2899 3052 3429 Firemen's
uniforms: made from purchased materi-
als; fire extinguisher charges; fire hose,
rubber; nozzles, fire fighting; fire hydrant
valves

(G-10388)
GATE TECHNOLOGIES INC
Also Called: Cds.
27 Wilson Dr Unit C (07871-3484)
PHONE..........................973 300-0090
Robert Zaruba, *President*
Stephen Gough, *Manager*
▲ EMP: 6
SQ FT: 5,300
SALES (est): 1.2MM **Privately Held**
WEB: www.cdsindexers.com
SIC: 3443 3568 Heat exchangers, con-
densers & components; power transmis-
sion equipment

(G-10389)
H & H PRODUCTION MACHINING
Also Called: H & H Sheet Metal & Machining
30 White Lake Rd (07871-3249)
PHONE..........................973 383-6880
Eric Hohmann, *President*
David Hohmann, *President*
EMP: 6
SQ FT: 15,000

SALES (est): 1.7MM **Privately Held**
WEB: www.hhsmm.com
SIC: **3444** Sheet metalwork

(G-10390)
H I D SYSTEMS INC
520 Lafayette Rd (07871-3447)
PHONE.................................973 383-8535
Robert J Lesko, *President*
EMP: 7
SQ FT: 5,500
SALES (est): 861K **Privately Held**
WEB: www.hid.com
SIC: **3699 5063** Electrical equipment &
supplies; electrical apparatus & equip-
ment

(G-10391)
HCH INCORPORATED
99 Demarest Rd Ste 4 (07871-3489)
PHONE.................................973 300-4551
Gene Cinotti, *President*
EMP: 5
SQ FT: 3,000
SALES (est): 904.1K **Privately Held**
SIC: **5046 3556** Restaurant equipment &
supplies; food products machinery

(G-10392)
HID ULTRAVIOLET LLC
520 Lafayette Rd (07871-3447)
PHONE.................................973 383-8535
Robert Lesko, *President*
EMP: 11
SALES (est): 1MM **Privately Held**
SIC: **3641** Ultraviolet lamps

(G-10393)
ISTEC CORPORATION
Also Called: Istec Flow Measurement & Ctrl
5 Park Lake Rd Ste 6 (07871-3247)
PHONE.................................973 383-9888
Peter Johnson, *President*
Edward Bullis, *Vice Pres*
Justin Johnson, *Opers Mgr*
▲ EMP: 10
SQ FT: 6,000
SALES (est): 1.2MM **Privately Held**
SIC: **3823** Industrial instrmnts msrmnt dis-
play/control process variable

(G-10394)
KOMLINE-SANDERSON ENGRG CORP
34 White Lake Rd Ste C (07871-3233)
PHONE.................................973 579-0090
James Schutte, *CEO*
EMP: 5
SALES (corp-wide): 47.5MM **Privately
Held**
SIC: **3356** Battery metal
PA: Komline-Sanderson Corporation
12 Holland Ave
Peapack NJ 07977
908 234-1000

(G-10395)
LEHIGH CEMENT COMPANY
66 Demarest Rd (07871-3440)
PHONE.................................973 579-2111
Dan Harrington, *President*
Joe Lanardo, *Vice Pres*
Maryann Nied, *Sales Staff*
Richard Hertzog, *Admin Sec*
EMP: 8
SQ FT: 19,200
SALES (est): 1.7MM
SALES (corp-wide): 20.6B **Privately Held**
WEB: www.lehighcement.com
SIC: **5032 3241** Cement; cement, hy-
draulic
HQ: Lehigh Cement Company Llc
300 E John Carpenter Fwy
Irving TX 75062
877 534-4442

(G-10396)
MCKINLEY SCIENTIFIC LLC (PA)
33 Wilson Dr Ste C (07871-3493)
PHONE.................................973 579-4144
Paul Corcoran, *CEO*
Herb Lindsley, *COO*
Douglas Turk, *Vice Pres*
Ken Satz, *CFO*
Leigh Darbee, *Marketing Staff*
EMP: 10

SQ FT: 6,000
SALES (est): 2.4MM **Privately Held**
WEB: www.mckscientific.com
SIC: **3826 5049 7359** Analytical instru-
ments; scientific instruments; equipment
rental & leasing

(G-10397)
MEGA MEDIA CONCEPTS LTD LBLTY
26 Gail Ct Ste 1 (07871-3487)
PHONE.................................973 919-5661
Anthony Senatora, *Vice Pres*
Amy Pink,
▼ EMP: 4
SALES (est): 1MM **Privately Held**
WEB: www.megamediaconcepts.com
SIC: **3993 2759 8412** Signs & advertising
specialties; commercial printing; muse-
ums & art galleries

(G-10398)
MESSER LLC
Also Called: Boc Gases
20 Demarest Rd (07871-3440)
PHONE.................................973 579-2065
Michael Stevenson, *Branch Mgr*
EMP: 6
SALES (corp-wide): 1.4B **Privately Held**
SIC: **2813 3569 3561 3511** Oxygen,
compressed or liquefied; nitrogen; argon;
hydrogen; gas separators (machinery);
pumps & pumping equipment; turbines &
turbine generator sets; industrial flow &
liquid measuring instruments; anesthetics,
in bulk form
HQ: Messer Llc
200 Somerset Corp Blvd # 7000
Bridgewater NJ 08807
908 464-8100

(G-10399)
MOONLIGHT IMAGING LLC
286 Houses Corner Rd C (07871-4400)
PHONE.................................973 300-1001
EMP: 7
SALES (est): 55K **Privately Held**
SIC: **2759 7311 7336** Screen printing; ad-
vertising agencies; graphic arts & related
design

(G-10400)
MP PRODUCTION
Also Called: Applied Microphone Technology
104 Hillside Rd (07871-2015)
PHONE.................................973 729-9333
Martin Paglione, *Owner*
Ron Oswanski, *Executive*
▲ EMP: 15
SQ FT: 2,500
SALES (est): 1.4MM **Privately Held**
SIC: **3651** Microphones

(G-10401)
NATURES CHOICE CORPORATION (PA)
482 Houses Corner Rd (07871-3404)
PHONE.................................973 969-3299
James Schafle, *CEO*
James Panzini, *President*
EMP: 15
SQ FT: 6,000
SALES (est): 44.2MM **Privately Held**
WEB: www.enatureschoice.com
SIC: **4953 2824** Recycling, waste materi-
als; acrylic fibers

(G-10402)
NEWTON MEMORIAL HOSPITAL INC
89 Sparta Ave Ste 210 (07871-1792)
PHONE.................................973 726-0904
Michael Gallagher, *Branch Mgr*
EMP: 7 **Privately Held**
SIC: **3841 8062** Diagnostic apparatus,
medical; general medical & surgical hos-
pitals
HQ: Newton Memorial Hospital (Inc)
175 High St
Newton NJ 07860
973 383-2121

(G-10403)
NORTH AMERICA PRINTING
156 Woodport Rd (07871-2331)
PHONE.................................973 726-7713
EMP: 5 EST: 1998
SALES (est): 250K **Privately Held**
SIC: **2759** Commercial Printing

(G-10404)
NOVA CHEMICALS INC
56 Castlewood Trl (07871-3704)
PHONE.................................973 726-0056
Aroustamian Jean, *Branch Mgr*
EMP: 4 **Privately Held**
SIC: **2819** Industrial inorganic chemicals
HQ: Nova Chemicals Inc.
1555 Coraopolis Hts Rd
Moon Township PA 15108
412 490-4000

(G-10405)
PDS CONSULTANTS INC
22 Rainbow Trl (07871-1723)
PHONE.................................201 970-2313
Richard Murray, *President*
EMP: 20 EST: 2006
SALES (est): 1MM **Privately Held**
SIC: **8742 3851** Management consulting
services; ophthalmic goods

(G-10406)
PLX PHARMA INC
9 Fishers Ln Ste E (07871-2402)
PHONE.................................973 409-6541
Linda Lindquist, *Branch Mgr*
EMP: 8
SALES (corp-wide): 753.1K **Publicly
Held**
SIC: **2834** Pharmaceutical preparations
PA: Plx Pharma Inc.
8285 El Rio St Ste 130
Houston TX 77054
713 842-1249

(G-10407)
PRINTING CENTER INC
1 White Lake Rd (07871-3206)
PHONE.................................973 383-6362
Vince Perrella, *President*
Steve Guido, *President*
Donna Fern, *General Mgr*
Rick Breakstone, *Vice Pres*
Bill Locascio, *Vice Pres*
EMP: 38 EST: 1971
SALES (est): 7.9MM **Privately Held**
WEB: www.printcenter.com
SIC: **2752** Commercial printing, offset

(G-10408)
SUMMERLANDS INC
Also Called: Krogh's Restaurant
23 White Deer Plz (07871-1823)
PHONE.................................973 729-8428
Robert Fuchs, *President*
EMP: 50
SQ FT: 2,500
SALES (est): 1.9MM **Privately Held**
WEB: www.kroghs.com
SIC: **5812 5813 2082** American restau-
rant; tavern (drinking places); malt bever-
ages

(G-10409)
TECHFLEX INC (HQ)
104 Demarest Rd Ste 1 (07871-4407)
P.O. Box 119 (07871-0119)
PHONE.................................973 300-9242
William Dermody III, *President*
Vicki Greene, *General Mgr*
Mike Ballard, *Vice Pres*
Robert Reilly, *Prdtn Mgr*
Angelica Freykar, *Human Res Dir*
▲ EMP: 18
SQ FT: 40,000
SALES (est): 4.9MM
SALES (corp-wide): 7.7MM **Privately
Held**
WEB: www.techflex.com
SIC: **3089 3663 3651** Plastic containers,
except foam; radio broadcasting & com-
munications equipment; household audio
& video equipment
PA: Dermody Associates Inc
104 Demarest Rd Ste 1
Sparta NJ
973 300-9242

(G-10410)
TESA RENTALS LLC
286 Houses Corner Rd (07871-4400)
PHONE.................................973 300-0913
Christopher M Tiso,
Christopher Tiso,
EMP: 10
SQ FT: 3,000
SALES (est): 500K **Privately Held**
SIC: **3822** Auto controls regulating residntl
& coml environmt & applncs

(G-10411)
THERMOPLASTICS BIO-LOGICS LLC
Also Called: Tbl Performance Plastics
18 White Lake Rd (07871-3200)
PHONE.................................973 383-2834
Robert Dupont, *Partner*
Chris Ray, *Technical Mgr*
Diane Dupont, *Accounts Mgr*
EMP: 10
SALES (est): 2.6MM **Privately Held**
SIC: **3089** Extruded finished plastic prod-
ucts; plastic processing

(G-10412)
TIFFANY PACKAGING
270 Sparta Ave (07871-1122)
PHONE.................................973 726-8130
Sharon Willms, *Owner*
EMP: 8 EST: 1982
SALES (est): 754.7K **Privately Held**
SIC: **2673** Plastic & pliofilm bags

(G-10413)
TRI-COR FLEXIBLE PACKAGING INC
27 Brookfield Dr (07871-3212)
PHONE.................................973 940-1500
Guy Zimmermann, *President*
Donna Zimmermann, *Admin Sec*
▲ EMP: 24
SQ FT: 9,000
SALES: 14MM **Privately Held**
WEB: www.tri-cor.com
SIC: **3081** Polyethylene film

Spotswood
Middlesex County

(G-10414)
BP MACHINE CO INC
10 American Way Ste 3 (08884-1262)
PHONE.................................732 251-0449
Robert Provell, *President*
Steven Spennato, *Vice Pres*
EMP: 4
SQ FT: 1,500
SALES (est): 400K **Privately Held**
SIC: **3599** Machine shop, jobbing & repair

(G-10415)
INTERNATIONAL PAPER COMPANY
140 Summerhill Rd (08884-1235)
PHONE.................................732 251-2000
Margaret Guiliano, *Manager*
EMP: 163
SALES (corp-wide): 23.3B **Publicly Held**
SIC: **2631** Paperboard mills
PA: International Paper Company
6400 Poplar Ave
Memphis TN 38197
901 419-9000

(G-10416)
MJS OF SPOTSWOOD LLC
Also Called: Mjs Pizza Bar & Grill
19 Summerhill Rd (08884-1251)
PHONE.................................732 251-7400
EMP: 8 EST: 2015
SALES (est): 391.1K **Privately Held**
SIC: **2038 2045** Pizza, frozen; pizza
mixes: from purchased flour

(G-10417)
SCHWEITZER-MAUDUIT INTL INC
85 Main St (08884-1212)
PHONE.................................732 723-6100
Kevin Boland, *Manager*

EMP: 500 **Publicly Held**
SIC: 2141 2621 Tobacco stemming &
　redrying; paper mills
PA: Schweitzer-Mauduit International, Inc.
　100 N Point Ctr E Ste 600
　Alpharetta GA 30022

(G-10418)
SURATI NJ LLC
15 American Way (08884-1254)
PHONE..............................732 251-3404
Yashvantrai Sheth, *Principal*
Mahul Shah, *Manager*
▲ EMP: 13
SALES (est): 2MM **Privately Held**
SIC: 2035 Pickles, sauces & salad dress-
　ings

(G-10419)
SWM SPOTSWOOD MILL
85 Main St (08884-1212)
PHONE..............................732 723-6102
EMP: 5
SALES (est): 632.5K **Privately Held**
SIC: 3089 Injection molding of plastics

Spring Lake
Monmouth County

(G-10420)
BOZAK INC
204 State Route 71 Ste B1 (07762-1882)
PHONE..............................732 282-1556
Kenneth Bozak, *President*
EMP: 3
SALES: 8MM **Privately Held**
WEB: www.bozak.com
SIC: 3399 Laminating steel

(G-10421)
CROWN PRODUCTS INC
102 Pitney Ave (07762-1729)
PHONE..............................732 493-0022
Daria Tagliareni, *President*
▲ EMP: 35
SALES (est): 3.4MM **Privately Held**
SIC: 2392 5091 3949 Towels, fabric &
　nonwoven; made from purchased materi-
　als; golf equipment; sporting & athletic
　goods

(G-10422)
H T HALL INC (PA)
Also Called: Rock of Ages Monuments
1716 State Route 71 Ste 1 (07762-3225)
PHONE..............................732 449-3441
Harold T Hall Jr, *President*
Joan Hall, *Vice Pres*
Harold Hall III, *Admin Sec*
EMP: 16 EST: 1930
SQ FT: 20,000
SALES (est): 1.3MM **Privately Held**
WEB: www.hthall.com
SIC: 3272 3281 Monuments & grave
　markers, except terrazo; tombstones, pre-
　cast terrazzo or concrete; concrete prod-
　ucts, precast; cut stone & stone products

(G-10423)
MATRIX SALES GROUP LLC
Also Called: Matrix Apparel
309 Morris Ave Ste E (07762-1359)
PHONE..............................908 461-4148
Anthony Pristo, *Mng Member*
John Cottingham,
Dina Johannemann,
EMP: 80
SALES (est): 5.2MM **Privately Held**
SIC: 2326 2339 Men's & boys' work cloth-
　ing; women's & misses' athletic clothing &
　sportswear

(G-10424)
**THIRD AVE CHOCOLATE
SHOPPE**
1118 3rd Ave (07762-1329)
PHONE..............................732 449-7535
Matthew Magyar, *Owner*
EMP: 6
SALES (est): 210K **Privately Held**
SIC: 2066 5149 Chocolate; chocolate

Springfield
Union County

(G-10425)
**ALLMARK DOOR COMPANY LLC
(PA)**
15 Stern Ave (07081-2904)
PHONE..............................610 358-9800
Andrew Markham, *Vice Pres*
Ralph Markham, *Vice Pres*
Donald McKean, *Project Mgr*
Meghan King, *Accountant*
Lee Macdougall, *Regl Sales Mgr*
▲ EMP: 13
SQ FT: 8,000
SALES (est): 7MM **Privately Held**
SIC: 5031 3442 Doors; fire doors, metal

(G-10426)
**ANALYTICON INSTRUMENTS
CORP**
500 Morris Ave (07081-1027)
P.O. Box 92 (07081-0092)
PHONE..............................973 379-6771
Donald Vreeland, *President*
Wanda Vreeland, *Treasurer*
EMP: 5
SALES: 500K **Privately Held**
SIC: 3826 Analytical instruments

(G-10427)
APPLES & HONEY PRESS LLC
11 Edison Pl (07081-1310)
PHONE..............................973 379-7200
David Behrman, *President*
EMP: 17
SALES (est): 682.5K **Privately Held**
SIC: 2731 5942 Book publishing; chil-
　dren's books

(G-10428)
ATCO PRODUCTS INC
115 Victory Rd (07081-1314)
PHONE..............................973 379-3171
Martin Gornstein, *President*
Alan Gornstein, *Vice Pres*
▲ EMP: 50 EST: 1938
SQ FT: 28,800
SALES (est): 4.6MM **Privately Held**
WEB: www.atcoproducts.com
SIC: 3429 3312 3161 Luggage hardware;
　tool & die steel & alloys; luggage

(G-10429)
**AZTEC SOFTWARE
ASSOCIATES INC (PA)**
51 Commerce St (07081-3014)
PHONE..............................973 258-0011
Jonathan Blitt, *CEO*
Michael Kheyfets, *President*
Phyllis Schwartz, *President*
Geraldine Kaplan, *Vice Pres*
Raeann Sereno, *Accounts Mgr*
EMP: 27
SQ FT: 3,500
SALES (est): 3.2MM **Privately Held**
SIC: 7371 7372 5045 Computer software
　development; prepackaged software;
　computer software

(G-10430)
BARWORTH INC
Also Called: General Hydraulics
673 Morris Tpke (07081-1513)
P.O. Box 5343, Clinton (08809-0343)
PHONE..............................973 376-4883
Robert Swatsworth, *President*
John C Swathworth Jr, *Corp Secy*
EMP: 4 EST: 1953
SQ FT: 2,200
SALES: 1MM **Privately Held**
WEB: www.barworthinc.com
SIC: 3491 Gas valves & parts, industrial

(G-10431)
BIGELOW COMPONENTS CORP
74 Diamond Rd (07081)
PHONE..............................973 467-1200
Brett Harman, *President*
David Harman, *President*
EMP: 30
SQ FT: 15,000

SALES (est): 5.4MM **Privately Held**
SIC: 3452 3469 3316 Pins; rivets, metal;
　metal stampings; cold finishing of steel
　shapes

(G-10432)
BONNEY-VEHSLAGE TOOL CO
3 Dundar Rd (07081-3516)
PHONE..............................973 589-6975
Ramsay W Vehslage, *President*
Joseph R Krehel, *Vice Pres*
Ann B Vehslage, *Admin Sec*
EMP: 13
SQ FT: 6,000
SALES (est): 1.8MM **Privately Held**
WEB: www.bvtoolco.com
SIC: 3544 Punches, forming & stamping

(G-10433)
BRIGHTON AIR
21 Springfield Ave (07081-1312)
P.O. Box 1834, Cranford (07016-5834)
PHONE..............................973 258-1500
Daniel Ghanime, *Principal*
EMP: 8
SALES (est): 1.4MM **Privately Held**
SIC: 3822 Water heater controls

(G-10434)
**CG AUTOMATION SOLUTIONS
USA (PA)**
60 Fadem Rd (07081-3116)
PHONE..............................973 379-7400
Stephen Dalyai, *President*
Normand Lavoie, *President*
Omar Grandal, *Associate*
▼ EMP: 50 EST: 1975
SQ FT: 45,000
SALES (est): 7.8MM **Privately Held**
WEB: www.geiinc.com
SIC: 3823 Telemetering instruments, indus-
　trial process type

(G-10435)
**CINCINNATI THERMAL SPRAY
INC**
80 Fadem Rd (07081-3116)
PHONE..............................973 379-0003
Scot Crabtree, *Branch Mgr*
EMP: 25 **Privately Held**
SIC: 3479 3469 Coating of metals &
　formed products; machine parts, stamped
　or pressed metal
PA: Cincinnati Thermal Spray, Inc.
　10904 Deerfield Rd
　Blue Ash OH 45242

(G-10436)
COMTRON INC
12 Commerce St (07081-2903)
PHONE..............................732 446-7571
Guenther Wackerman, *President*
EMP: 15 EST: 1958
SQ FT: 10,000
SALES (est): 3.2MM **Privately Held**
SIC: 3663 Radio broadcasting & communi-
　cations equipment

(G-10437)
CORNELL MACHINE CO INC
45 Brown Ave (07081-2901)
PHONE..............................973 379-6860
Martin M Huska, *President*
Allan Huska, *Corp Secy*
EMP: 6
SQ FT: 7,400
SALES (est): 1MM **Privately Held**
WEB: www.cornellmachine.com
SIC: 3556 Mixers, commercial, food; ho-
　mogenizing machinery: dairy, fruit, veg-
　etable

(G-10438)
DANLINE INC
Also Called: Danline Quality Brushes
1 Silver Ct (07081-3113)
PHONE..............................973 376-1000
Suresh Seth, *President*
Brain Oleary, *Vice Pres*
Usha Seth, *Vice Pres*
▲ EMP: 30
SQ FT: 53,000
SALES (est): 3.5MM **Privately Held**
WEB: www.danlinebrushes.com
SIC: 3991 Brushes, household or industrial

(G-10439)
DRG INTERNATIONAL INC (PA)
841 Mountain Ave (07081-3437)
PHONE..............................973 564-7555
Cyril Geacintov, *President*
Sheila Dawson, *Sales Dir*
Malgorzata Fedosz, *Internal Med*
▲ EMP: 25
SQ FT: 7,500
SALES (est): 28.7MM **Privately Held**
WEB: www.drg-international.com
SIC: 5047 8071 3829 Medical equipment
　& supplies; diagnostic equipment, med-
　ical; medical laboratories; measuring &
　controlling devices

(G-10440)
EASY UNDIES LLC
Also Called: Easylving Brand, The
23 Springfield Ave (07081-1312)
PHONE..............................201 715-4909
Rochelle Denning,
EMP: 4 EST: 2000
SALES (est): 445.1K **Privately Held**
SIC: 5047 2211 Incontinent care products
　& supplies; underwear fabrics, cotton

(G-10441)
ELKAY PRODUCTS CO INC
35 Brown Ave (07081-2982)
P.O. Box 149 (07081-0149)
PHONE..............................973 376-7550
Steven Piller, *President*
EMP: 10
SQ FT: 25,000
SALES (est): 1.7MM **Privately Held**
SIC: 2299 5084 Padding & wadding, tex-
　tile; materials handling machinery

(G-10442)
F AND L MACHINERY
48 Commerce St (07081-3004)
PHONE..............................973 218-6216
Fred Villaverde, *Owner*
EMP: 5
SALES (est): 767.8K **Privately Held**
SIC: 5084 3599 Industrial machinery &
　equipment; machine shop, jobbing & re-
　pair

(G-10443)
**FEDEX OFFICE & PRINT SVCS
INC**
55 Route 22 (07081-3128)
PHONE..............................973 376-3966
EMP: 5
SALES (corp-wide): 69.6B **Publicly Held**
WEB: www.kinkos.com
SIC: 7334 2791 Photocopying & duplicat-
　ing services; typesetting
HQ: Fedex Office And Print Services, Inc.
　7900 Legacy Dr
　Plano TX 75024
　800 463-3339

(G-10444)
HUDSON ROBOTICS INC
10 Stern Ave (07081-2905)
PHONE..............................973 376-7400
Philip J Farrelly, *President*
John Celecki, *Prdtn Mgr*
Ron Majewski, *Design Engr*
Joseph Pulawski, *Regl Sales Mgr*
Tom Copeland, *Sales Staff*
EMP: 20
SQ FT: 12,000
SALES (est): 4.3MM **Privately Held**
WEB: www.hudsoncontrol.com
SIC: 3826 Analytical instruments

(G-10445)
I4 SUSTAINABILITY LLC
Also Called: Omniflow USA
140 Mountain Ave Ste 303 (07081-1725)
PHONE..............................732 618-3310
Luis Barros, *Mng Member*
EMP: 5
SQ FT: 5,000
SALES: 175K **Privately Held**
SIC: 5063 5074 3511 Lighting fixtures,
　commercial & industrial; heating equip-
　ment & panels, solar; turbines & turbine
　generator sets

(G-10446)
INMAN MOLD AND MFG CO (PA)
4 Commerce St (07081-2903)
PHONE..................................732 381-3033
Glen Barlics, *President*
Mark Barlics, *Corp Secy*
EMP: 9
SQ FT: 12,000
SALES: 500K **Privately Held**
SIC: 3089 3999 Injection molding of plastics; novelties, bric-a-brac & hobby kits

(G-10447)
J OBRIEN CO INC
40 Commerce St (07081-3004)
PHONE..................................973 379-8844
Sharmay O'Brien, *President*
Diane R O'Brien, *Corp Secy*
Christopher Droussiotis, *Technical Mgr*
Wesley Winters, *CIO*
▲ EMP: 20
SQ FT: 64,000
SALES (est): 5.1MM **Privately Held**
WEB: www.jobrien.com
SIC: 3089 5084 Plastic containers, except foam; identification cards, plastic; industrial machinery & equipment

(G-10448)
JEN ELECTRIC INC
631 Morris Ave (07081-1511)
PHONE..................................973 467-4901
Jennifer Daidone, *CEO*
John Daidone, *Vice Pres*
Frank Dobiszewski, *Chief Engr*
Jorge Doig, *Sales Staff*
EMP: 10
SQ FT: 2,800
SALES (est): 2MM **Privately Held**
SIC: 3669 Traffic signals, electric

(G-10449)
JURY VRDICT RVIEW PUBLICATIONS
Also Called: New Jersey Jury
45 Springfield Ave Ste 2 (07081-1316)
PHONE..................................973 376-9002
Ira Zarin, *President*
Gary Zarin, *Partner*
Jed Zarin, *Vice Pres*
Meredith Whelan, *Admin Sec*
EMP: 4
SQ FT: 5,000
SALES (est): 810K **Privately Held**
WEB: www.jvra.com
SIC: 2721 Magazines: publishing only, not printed on site

(G-10450)
KEMPAK INDUSTRIES
33 Fernhill Rd (07081-3708)
P.O. Box 2073, Union (07083-2073)
PHONE..................................908 687-4188
Joel Sacher, *President*
Susan Sacher, *Corp Secy*
EMP: 10 EST: 1970
SALES (est): 1.9MM **Privately Held**
SIC: 2841 Soap & other detergents

(G-10451)
KG SYSTEMS INC
765 Mountain Ave Ste 120 (07081-3231)
PHONE..................................973 515-4664
Daniel R Garlen, *CEO*
Marilyn K Garlen, *Treasurer*
EMP: 5
SQ FT: 3,000
SALES: 1MM **Privately Held**
WEB: www.kgsystems.com
SIC: 3545 Scales, measuring (machinists' precision tools)

(G-10452)
KREMENTZ & CO (PA)
Also Called: Krementz Gemstones
51 Commerce St (07081-3014)
P.O. Box 55, Ho Ho Kus (07423-0055)
PHONE..................................973 621-8300
Richard Krementz Jr, *Ch of Bd*
Michael Kheyfets, *COO*
EMP: 10
SQ FT: 160,000
SALES (est): 1.2MM **Privately Held**
SIC: 3911 Jewelry, precious metal

(G-10453)
LIFE SKILLS EDUCATION INC
51 Commerce St (07081-3014)
PHONE..................................507 645-2994
Robert Ciernia, *President*
Suzannah Cierna, *Manager*
EMP: 6
SQ FT: 2,500
SALES: 1.1MM **Privately Held**
WEB: www.lifeskillsed.com
SIC: 2731 8322 Pamphlets: publishing & printing; individual & family services
PA: Aztec Software Associates Inc
51 Commerce St
Springfield NJ 07081

(G-10454)
MIRANDA MTI INC
195 Mountain Ave (07081-1755)
PHONE..................................973 376-4275
Strath Goodship, *CEO*
EMP: 15
SALES (est): 1.9MM **Privately Held**
SIC: 3663 Television broadcasting & communications equipment

(G-10455)
NARVA INC
Also Called: New York Kitchen Specialist
101 Victory Rd (07081-1314)
PHONE..................................973 218-1200
Alex Morizou, *President*
EMP: 6
SQ FT: 10,000
SALES: 1.4MM **Privately Held**
WEB: www.narvakitchens.com
SIC: 5722 2499 1799 1751 Kitchens, complete (sinks, cabinets, etc.); decorative wood & woodwork; counter top installation; cabinet & finish carpentry

(G-10456)
NEWARK BRUSH COMPANY LLC
1 Silver Ct (07081-3113)
PHONE..................................973 376-1000
Brian O'Leary, *Exec VP*
Brian Oleary, *Exec VP*
Jeremy Glick,
▲ EMP: 18
SALES (est): 3.3MM **Privately Held**
SIC: 3991 Street sweeping brooms, hand or machine

(G-10457)
PACKAGED GAS SYSTEMS INC (PA)
18 Stern Ave (07081-2905)
PHONE..................................908 755-2780
Anthony Etimiraos, *President*
Catherine Atimiraos, *Corp Secy*
Laura Grasberger, *Office Admin*
EMP: 5
SQ FT: 800
SALES (est): 306.1K **Privately Held**
WEB: www.packagedgassystems.com
SIC: 3826 Gas analyzing equipment

(G-10458)
PAYLOCITY HOLDING CORPORATION
21 Fadem Rd Ste 10 (07081-3136)
PHONE..................................908 917-3027
EMP: 375
SALES (corp-wide): 467.6MM **Publicly Held**
SIC: 7372 Prepackaged software
PA: Paylocity Holding Corporation
1400 American Ln
Schaumburg IL 60173
847 463-3200

(G-10459)
PEMCO DENTAL CORPORATION
35 Stern Ave (07081-2904)
P.O. Box 249 (07081-0249)
PHONE..................................800 526-4170
Richard Balfour, *President*
Elizabeth Balfour, *Vice Pres*
Lawrence Balfour, *Vice Pres*
Liz Balfour, *Human Res Dir*
EMP: 35
SQ FT: 36,000

SALES: 6.4MM **Privately Held**
SIC: 5047 2521 Dental equipment & supplies; cabinets, office: wood

(G-10460)
PRINT MEDIA LLC
232 Morris Ave (07081-1212)
PHONE..................................973 467-0007
Robert Wallick, *Partner*
Sandy Walsh, *Partner*
EMP: 7 EST: 1999
SALES (est): 809.7K **Privately Held**
SIC: 2759 Commercial printing

(G-10461)
PRINT TECH LLC (PA)
49 Fadem Rd (07081-3115)
PHONE..................................908 232-2287
Russell F Evans, *CEO*
Frances Angiola, *Editor*
Gary Alessio,
▼ EMP: 70 EST: 2001
SQ FT: 18,100
SALES (est): 13.3MM **Privately Held**
SIC: 2752 Commercial printing, offset

(G-10462)
RAGS INTERNATIONAL INC
15 Tooker Ave (07081-1703)
PHONE..................................787 632-8447
Carlos Rivera, *CEO*
EMP: 8
SALES (est): 453.4K **Privately Held**
SIC: 5661 3949 Footwear, athletic; team sports equipment

(G-10463)
RAMSEY MACHINE & TOOL CO INC
60 Tooker Ave (07081-1704)
PHONE..................................973 376-7404
Ronald A Majewski Jr, *President*
EMP: 8 EST: 1950
SQ FT: 6,500
SALES: 600K **Privately Held**
SIC: 3599 Machine shop, jobbing & repair

(G-10464)
RENARD COMMUMNICATIONS INC
Also Called: Diversity/Careers In Enginrng
197 Mountain Ave (07081-1755)
P.O. Box 557 (07081-0557)
PHONE..................................973 912-8550
Roberta Renard, *President*
Jeff Wiener, *Vice Pres*
EMP: 32
SQ FT: 5,500
SALES: 6.4MM **Privately Held**
WEB: www.diversitycareers.com
SIC: 2721 Magazines: publishing & printing

(G-10465)
REVIVAL SASH & DOOR LLC
78 Diamond Rd (07081)
PHONE..................................973 500-4242
Mike Canizales, *Mng Member*
EMP: 6
SALES (corp-wide): 2.1MM **Privately Held**
SIC: 3442 Sash, door or window: metal
PA: Revival Sash & Door, Llc
135 E 57th St Bldg 15125
New York NY 10022
973 500-4242

(G-10466)
RING CONTAINER TECH LLC
50 Fadem Rd (07081-3116)
PHONE..................................973 258-0707
John Redman, *Branch Mgr*
EMP: 18
SALES (corp-wide): 293.5MM **Privately Held**
WEB: www.ringcontainer.com
SIC: 3089 Plastic containers, except foam
PA: Ring Container Technologies, Llc.
1 Industrial Park
Oakland TN 38060
800 280-7464

(G-10467)
SPRINGFIELD METAL PDTS CO INC
8 Commerce St (07081-2903)
PHONE..................................973 379-4600
John D Sommer, *President*
Lori M Perrine, *Treasurer*
Irene G Powell, *Admin Sec*
EMP: 10
SQ FT: 6,600
SALES (est): 1.3MM **Privately Held**
SIC: 3444 3443 3441 Sheet metal specialties, not stamped; fabricated plate work (boiler shop); fabricated structural metal

(G-10468)
TAYLOR COMMUNICATIONS INC
899 Mountain Ave Ste 2f (07081-3403)
PHONE..................................973 467-8259
EMP: 17
SALES (corp-wide): 3B **Privately Held**
SIC: 2754 Commercial printing, gravure
HQ: Taylor Communications, Inc.
1725 Roe Crest Dr
North Mankato MN 56003
507 625-2828

(G-10469)
TROPAION INC
955 S Springfield Ave C302 (07081-3570)
P.O. Box 1230, Mountainside (07092-1230)
PHONE..................................908 654-3870
Bruce Meyer, *President*
Elitza Meyer, *Vice Pres*
EMP: 4
SQ FT: 1,000
SALES: 300K **Privately Held**
WEB: www.tropaion.com
SIC: 8243 7372 7374 Software training, computer; prepackaged software; computer related consulting services

(G-10470)
UNITED WINDOW & DOOR MFG INC (PA)
24 Fadem Rd 36 (07081-3116)
PHONE..................................973 912-0600
Howard Rose, *President*
Nick Derrico, *Vice Pres*
Alan Schulman, *Vice Pres*
Saul Alfaro, *Prdtn Mgr*
Fernanda Castro, *Purch Agent*
EMP: 30
SQ FT: 110,000
SALES (est): 52.3MM **Privately Held**
SIC: 3089 Windows, plastic

(G-10471)
UNIVERSAL TOOLS & MFG CO
115 Victory Rd (07081-1376)
PHONE..................................973 379-4193
Dorothy Principe, *President*
Robin McElwee, *COO*
Helder Ruivo, *Plant Mgr*
Jessi McElwee, *Web Dvlpr*
▲ EMP: 27
SQ FT: 12,000
SALES (est): 4.6MM **Privately Held**
WEB: www.utmfg.com
SIC: 3469 3544 Stamping metal for the trade; special dies, tools, jigs & fixtures

(G-10472)
VALCOR ENGINEERING CORPORATION (PA)
2 Lawrence Rd (07081-3165)
PHONE..................................973 467-8400
Jody K Friedman, *Ch of Bd*
Lori K Klinghoffer, *Ch of Bd*
Robin K Walters, *Ch of Bd*
Hal Sorensen, *COO*
Nuno Dias, *Mfg Staff*
▲ EMP: 220
SQ FT: 176,000
SALES (est): 33.7MM **Privately Held**
WEB: www.valcor.com
SIC: 3492 3561 Fluid power valves & hose fittings; pumps & pumping equipment

GEOGRAPHIC

(PA)=Parent Co (HQ)=Headquarters (DH)=Div Headquarters
✪ = New Business established in last 2 years

2019 Harris New Jersey
Manufacturers Directory

401

(G-10473)
VALCOR ENGINEERING CORPORATION
Also Called: Electroid Co Div
45 Fadem Rd (07081-3115)
PHONE....................................973 467-8100
Steve Etter, *Branch Mgr*
EMP: 50
SALES (corp-wide): 33.7MM **Privately Held**
WEB: www.valcor.com
SIC: 3621 3714 3568 Control equipment for buses or trucks, electric; motor vehicle parts & accessories; power transmission equipment
PA: Valcor Engineering Corporation
2 Lawrence Rd
Springfield NJ 07081
973 467-8400

(G-10474)
VALCOR ENGINEERING CORPORATION
Electroid Company
2 Lawrence Rd (07081-3165)
PHONE....................................973 467-8400
EMP: 40
SALES (corp-wide): 33.7MM **Privately Held**
SIC: 3625 Actuators, industrial
PA: Valcor Engineering Corporation
2 Lawrence Rd
Springfield NJ 07081
973 467-8400

(G-10475)
WPI COMMUNICATIONS INC
Also Called: Atrium Publishing
55 Morris Ave Ste 312 (07081-1422)
P.O. Box 806, Short Hills (07078-0806)
PHONE....................................973 467-8700
Steven H Klinghoffer, *President*
Steve Klinghoffer, *Founder*
Lori K Klinghoffer, *Exec VP*
EMP: 15
SQ FT: 3,500
SALES (est): 1.6MM **Privately Held**
SIC: 2741 Newsletter publishing

Stanhope
Sussex County

(G-10476)
ALL IN ICING
24 Woods Edge Rd (07874-3242)
PHONE....................................973 896-5990
Donna Infantolino, *Owner*
EMP: 4
SALES (est): 282K **Privately Held**
SIC: 2051 Bread, cake & related products

(G-10477)
NEW YORK FOLDING BOX CO INC
20 Continental Dr (07874-2658)
PHONE....................................973 347-6932
Ken Kaplan, *Vice Pres*
Gregg Kaplan, *Vice Pres*
Mike Fiscella, *Controller*
EMP: 22 EST: 1918
SQ FT: 100,000
SALES (est): 5.2MM **Privately Held**
SIC: 2657 2653 Folding paperboard boxes; corrugated & solid fiber boxes

(G-10478)
PANEL COMPONENTS & SYSTEMS (PA)
Also Called: PC & S
149 Main St (07874-2667)
PHONE....................................973 448-9400
Tanja Lewit, *President*
Joseph Knolmayer, *Vice Pres*
EMP: 17
SQ FT: 6,000
SALES (est): 4.1MM **Privately Held**
WEB: www.pc-s.com
SIC: 5063 3825 Electrical supplies; instruments & control equipment; instruments to measure electricity

(G-10479)
TILCON NEW YORK INC
11 Lackawanna Dr (07874-3114)
PHONE....................................973 347-2405
John Brownell, *Manager*
EMP: 12
SALES (corp-wide): 30.6B **Privately Held**
WEB: www.tilconny.com
SIC: 1429 Crushed/Broken Stone
HQ: Tilcon New York Inc.
9 Entin Rd
Parsippany NJ 07054
973 366-7741

(G-10480)
UNITED STATES MINERAL PDTS CO (PA)
Also Called: US Minerals
41 Furnace St (07874-2624)
PHONE....................................973 347-1200
Russell Harvey, *District Mgr*
Rob Nicholoff, *Plant Mgr*
Mitz Patel, *Purch Agent*
Jason Cotton, *QA Dir*
Mike Brown, *Engineer*
◆ EMP: 65 EST: 1875
SQ FT: 50,000
SALES (est): 48.6MM **Privately Held**
WEB: www.cafco.com
SIC: 3296 Mineral wool insulation products

(G-10481)
WAGNER INDUSTRIES INC
51 Sparta Rd (07874-2881)
PHONE....................................973 347-0800
William S Wagner Sr, *President*
Michael Slavescu, *Engineer*
▼ EMP: 15
SQ FT: 10,000
SALES (est): 1MM **Privately Held**
WEB: www.wagner-industries.com
SIC: 3565 5084 3599 Packaging machinery; industrial machinery & equipment; machine shop, jobbing & repair

Stewartsville
Warren County

(G-10482)
D & H CUTOFF CO
2600 State Route 57 (08886-3158)
PHONE....................................908 454-4961
Eric Smith, *President*
Art Desaules, *President*
EMP: 7 EST: 1930
SQ FT: 4,000
SALES (est): 1MM **Privately Held**
WEB: www.dandhcutoff.com
SIC: 3599 Machine shop, jobbing & repair

(G-10483)
EAGLE STEEL & IRON LLC
102 Willever Way (08886-2011)
PHONE....................................908 587-1025
Karol Kulik,
EMP: 6
SALES (est): 545.6K **Privately Held**
SIC: 3441 3449 7389 Fabricated structural metal; bars, concrete reinforcing: fabricated steel;

(G-10484)
LINDE GAS NORTH AMERICA LLC
1 Greenwich St (08886-2020)
PHONE....................................908 329-9300
EMP: 35 **Privately Held**
SIC: 2813 Oxygen, compressed or liquefied
HQ: Linde Gas North America Llc
200 Somerset Corp Blvd # 7000
Bridgewater NJ 08807

(G-10485)
LINDE NORTH AMERICA INC
Also Called: Linde Elec & Specialty Gasses
1 Greenwich St Ste 100 (08886-2020)
PHONE....................................908 329-9700
Samuel Amaro, *Mfg Staff*
Andrew Dietz, *Branch Mgr*
EMP: 10
SALES (corp-wide): 1.4B **Privately Held**
SIC: 2813 Industrial gases

HQ: Messer North America, Inc.
200 Somerset Corporate Bl
Bridgewater NJ 08807
908 464-8100

(G-10486)
MESSER LLC
1 Greenwich St Ste 200 (08886-2020)
PHONE....................................908 329-9619
Todd Quintard, *Opers Staff*
Mark McGough, *Technical Mgr*
Roxanne Bailey, *Branch Mgr*
Joseph Beal, *Planning*
Elaine Bradford, *Analyst*
EMP: 22
SALES (corp-wide): 1.4B **Privately Held**
SIC: 2813 Nitrogen
HQ: Messer Llc
200 Somerset Corp Blvd # 7000
Bridgewater NJ 08807
908 464-8100

(G-10487)
PRINTPLUSCOM INC
452a County Road 519 (08886-2032)
PHONE....................................908 859-4774
Pamela Kresge, *President*
EMP: 4
SQ FT: 1,250
SALES (est): 513.7K **Privately Held**
SIC: 2752 Commercial printing, lithographic

(G-10488)
T & M PALLET CO INC
116 Edison Rd (08886-3123)
P.O. Box 177 (08886-0177)
PHONE....................................908 454-3042
Amos Tigar, *President*
Randy Tigar, *Treasurer*
EMP: 20
SQ FT: 4,305
SALES (est): 2.8MM **Privately Held**
SIC: 2448 7699 2441 Pallets, wood; pallet repair; nailed wood boxes & shook

Stirling
Morris County

(G-10489)
ENGINEERED PLASTIC PDTS INC (PA)
269 Mercer St (07980-1418)
P.O. Box 196 (07980-0196)
PHONE....................................908 647-3500
Chris Ratti, *President*
▲ EMP: 22
SQ FT: 25,000
SALES (est): 3.2MM **Privately Held**
WEB: www.engineeredplastic.com
SIC: 3089 Injection molding of plastics

(G-10490)
FIBERGUIDE INDUSTRIES INC (HQ)
1 Bay St Ste 1 # 1 (07980-1529)
PHONE....................................908 647-6601
Patricia Seniw, *President*
Ernest J Rich, *Corp Secy*
William Bozarth, *Vice Pres*
Kyle Ramirez, *Manager*
Akhil Trivedi, *Administration*
▼ EMP: 23
SQ FT: 13,500
SALES (est): 8MM
SALES (corp-wide): 1.5B **Privately Held**
WEB: www.fiberguide.com
SIC: 3229 Fiber optics strands
PA: Halma Public Limited Company
Misbourne Court
Amersham BUCKS HP7 0
149 472-1111

(G-10491)
INTERTEK LABORATORIES INC
340 Union St (07980-1312)
PHONE....................................908 903-1800
Denis R Rybkiewicz, *President*
Timmy Cutugno, *Technology*
Alan Scerri, *Technical Staff*
EMP: 30
SQ FT: 6,000

SALES (est): 6.7MM **Privately Held**
WEB: www.interteklabsinc.com
SIC: 3812 3823 3825 8711 Search & navigation equipment; industrial instrmnts msrmnt display/control process variable; instruments to measure electricity; electrical or electronic engineering; electronic research

(G-10492)
ISOLANTITE MANUFACTURING CO
337 Warren Ave (07980-1443)
P.O. Box 195 (07980-0195)
PHONE....................................908 647-3333
George W Lumpe, *President*
Mary Lou Hall, *Info Tech Mgr*
EMP: 30
SQ FT: 25,000
SALES (est): 3.8MM **Privately Held**
WEB: www.isolantite.com
SIC: 3264 Insulators, electrical: porcelain

(G-10493)
M & M WELDING & STEEL FABG
Also Called: M & M Welding & Machine
344 Essex St (07980-1342)
PHONE....................................908 647-6060
Oldrich Masek, *President*
Marie Masek, *Vice Pres*
EMP: 5
SQ FT: 6,000
SALES: 500K **Privately Held**
SIC: 7692 3599 Welding repair; machine shop, jobbing & repair

(G-10494)
P M Z TOOL INC
321 Warren Ave (07980-1442)
P.O. Box 201 (07980-0201)
PHONE....................................908 647-2125
Paul M Zuzak, *President*
EMP: 7
SQ FT: 3,400
SALES (est): 1.1MM **Privately Held**
SIC: 5084 3599 Machine tools & metalworking machinery; machine shop, jobbing & repair

(G-10495)
RECORDER PUBLISHING CO
Also Called: Recorder Newspaper
254 Mercer St (07980-1487)
PHONE....................................908 647-1180
Fax: 908 647-7679
EMP: 20
SALES (corp-wide): 15.4MM **Privately Held**
SIC: 2752 2711 Lithographic Commercial Printing Newspapers-Publishing/Printing
PA: Recorder Publishing Co
17 Morristown Rd 19
Bernardsville NJ 07981
908 766-3900

(G-10496)
SECURE SYSTEM INC
Also Called: Personal Secure
320 Essex St Ste 3 (07980-1339)
PHONE....................................732 922-3609
Gregory Lawson, *President*
Donald Ullery, *Vice Pres*
Stephen E Roman Jr, *CFO*
EMP: 25
SQ FT: 9,000
SALES: 4MM **Privately Held**
WEB: www.securesysteminc.com
SIC: 7382 3699 Protective devices, security; security control equipment & systems

(G-10497)
SUMAN REALTY LLC
103 Saint Josephs Dr (07980-1250)
PHONE....................................908 350-8039
Suman L Singh, *Principal*
EMP: 4
SALES (est): 271.9K **Privately Held**
SIC: 2869 Fuels

(G-10498)
TPI PARTNERS INC
Also Called: Thermoplastic Processes
1268 Valley Rd (07980-1425)
PHONE....................................908 561-3000
Lynn Kinney, *Administration*
EMP: 6

SALES (est): 566.4K
SALES (corp-wide): 17.2MM **Privately Held**
SIC: 3082 Tubes, unsupported plastic; rods, unsupported plastic
PA: Tpi Partners, Inc.
   21649 Cedar Creek Ave
   Georgetown DE 19947
   302 855-0139

(G-10499)
WORLD OF COFFEE INC
Also Called: World of Tea
328 Essex St (07980-1302)
PHONE....................................908 647-1218
Charles Newman, *President*
▲ EMP: 9
SQ FT: 7,500
SALES (est): 1.4MM **Privately Held**
SIC: 2095 Coffee roasting (except by wholesale grocers)

Stockholm
Sussex County

(G-10500)
RJTICECO LLC
Also Called: Crush Rite
4 Northwoods Trl (07460-1124)
P.O. Box 645 (07460-0645)
PHONE....................................973 697-0156
Bob Tice, *Mng Member*
Jeanne Tice,
EMP: 4
SALES (est): 472.7K **Privately Held**
SIC: 3634 Ice crushers, electric

Stockton
Hunterdon County

(G-10501)
GREEN LAND & LOGGING LLC
328 Rosemont Ringoes Rd (08559-1514)
PHONE....................................908 894-2361
Scott Green, *Principal*
EMP: 6 EST: 2010
SALES (est): 434.8K **Privately Held**
SIC: 2411 Logging

(G-10502)
ROBERT WALLACE
Also Called: Lucid Lighting
811 Rosemont Ringoes Rd (08559-1610)
PHONE....................................609 649-0596
Robert Wallace, *Owner*
EMP: 5
SQ FT: 900
SALES (est): 146.4K **Privately Held**
WEB: www.lucidlighting.com
SIC: 3645 3646 5719 5063 Residential lighting fixtures; commercial indusl & institutional electric lighting fixtures; lighting fixtures; lighting fixtures

Stone Harbor
Cape May County

(G-10503)
CAMP MARINE SERVICES INC
1000 Stone Harbor Blvd (08247-1423)
P.O. Box 35 (08247-0035)
PHONE....................................609 368-1777
Barry Camp, *President*
EMP: 4
SALES (est): 2MM **Privately Held**
SIC: 3732 5551 4493 Yachts, building & repairing; marine supplies; marinas

(G-10504)
CES IMPORTS LLC
252 93rd St (08247-2030)
PHONE....................................610 299-7930
Robert Ernst, *Mng Member*
Greg Ernst,
EMP: 4
SALES (est): 149.2K **Privately Held**
SIC: 3842 Clothing, fire resistant & protective

Stratford
Camden County

(G-10505)
CYPHER INSURANCE SOFTWARE
32 Sunnybrook Rd (08084-1650)
P.O. Box 433 (08084-0433)
PHONE....................................856 216-0575
EMP: 4
SALES: 118K **Privately Held**
SIC: 7372 Prepackaged Software Services

(G-10506)
PENNY PRESS
908 N White Horse Pike (08084-1002)
PHONE....................................856 547-1991
Joe Skeggs, *Partner*
Charlotte Skeggs, *Partner*
EMP: 7
SALES (est): 993.1K **Privately Held**
SIC: 2752 5199 7334 Commercial printing, offset; advertising specialties; photocopying & duplicating services

(G-10507)
SOUTH JERSEY PRETZEL INC
912 N White Horse Pike A (08084-1017)
PHONE....................................856 435-5055
George W Dudley, *President*
Robin Williams, *Manager*
EMP: 12
SALES (est): 1.3MM **Privately Held**
SIC: 2052 5142 5461 2024 Pretzels; poultry, frozen: packaged; pretzels; ices, flavored (frozen dessert); ice cream & ices; ice cream, soft drink & soda fountain stands

Succasunna
Morris County

(G-10508)
50 PLUS MONTHLY INC
5 Clearfield Rd (07876-1531)
P.O. Box 28, Nassau DE (19969-0028)
PHONE....................................973 584-7911
Lorraine Cintron, *President*
EMP: 5
SALES (est): 200K **Privately Held**
SIC: 2711 Newspapers

(G-10509)
C & N TOOLING & GRINDING INC
19 State Route 10 E # 14 (07876-1749)
PHONE....................................973 598-8411
Neil Rambaldi, *President*
Elmira Rambaldi, *Corp Secy*
EMP: 10
SQ FT: 3,000
SALES (est): 1.8MM **Privately Held**
SIC: 3599 7699 Machine shop, jobbing & repair; knife, saw & tool sharpening & repair

(G-10510)
COLFAJAS INC
5 West St (07876-1620)
PHONE....................................973 727-4813
Albeiro Ramirez, *President*
EMP: 4
SALES (est): 304.5K **Privately Held**
SIC: 2342 Bras, girdles & allied garments

(G-10511)
D & F WICKER IMPORT CO INC (PA)
295 State Route 10 E (07876-1321)
PHONE....................................973 736-5861
David Gruber, *President*
Jeffrey Gruber, *Vice Pres*
Frances Gruber, *Treasurer*
▲ EMP: 31
SQ FT: 40,000
SALES (est): 9MM **Privately Held**
WEB: www.dfwicker.com
SIC: 5021 2519 Household furniture; wicker & rattan furniture

(G-10512)
DAVIS CENTER INC
19 State Route 10 E # 25 (07876-1748)
PHONE....................................862 251-4637
Dorinne S Davis, *President*
EMP: 5
SALES (est): 450K **Privately Held**
WEB: www.thedaviscenter.com
SIC: 3845 8049 8299 5999 Audiological equipment, electromedical; audiologist; speech specialist; tutoring school; hearing aids

(G-10513)
HOLLAND MANUFACTURING CO INC (PA)
15 Main St (07876-1747)
P.O. Box 404 (07876-0404)
PHONE....................................973 584-8141
Jack Holland, *CEO*
Michael Pallante, *Vice Pres*
Paul Junas, *Mfg Staff*
Chase Holland, *Purchasing*
Edelina Zajac, *Human Res Mgr*
◆ EMP: 128
SQ FT: 150,000
SALES (est): 26.9MM **Privately Held**
WEB: www.hollandmfg.com
SIC: 2672 2621 2671 Gummed tape, cloth or paper base: from purchased materials; gummed paper: made from purchased materials; coated paper, except photographic, carbon or abrasive; specialty or chemically treated papers; building paper & felts; packaging paper & plastics film, coated & laminated

(G-10514)
JOSTENS INC
86 Roseville Rd (07876)
PHONE....................................973 584-5843
Lou Esposito, *General Mgr*
EMP: 6
SALES (corp-wide): 1.3B **Privately Held**
WEB: www.jostens.com
SIC: 3911 Rings, finger: precious metal
HQ: Jostens, Inc.
   7760 France Ave S Ste 400
   Minneapolis MN 55435
   952 830-3300

(G-10515)
MRI OF WEST MORRIS PA
66 Sunset Strip Ste 105 (07876-1362)
PHONE....................................973 927-1010
Michelle Dunn, *Manager*
Jeff Dunn, *Manager*
EMP: 11
SALES (est): 890K **Privately Held**
WEB: www.mriwestmorris.com
SIC: 3861 8011 X-ray film; radiologist

(G-10516)
PUSH BEVERAGES LLC
7 Longfellow Dr (07876-1165)
P.O. Box 343 (07876-0343)
PHONE....................................973 766-2663
Laurel Whitney,
EMP: 4 EST: 2013
SALES (est): 139.4K **Privately Held**
SIC: 2086 Bottled & canned soft drinks

(G-10517)
R P SMITH & SON INC
199 Main St (07876-1335)
P.O. Box 209 (07876-0209)
PHONE....................................973 584-4063
Robert P Smith, *President*
EMP: 10
SALES (est): 1.5MM **Privately Held**
SIC: 3271 Blocks, concrete or cinder: standard

(G-10518)
RAME-HART INSTRUMENT CO LLC
Also Called: Rame Hart Instrument
19 State Route 10 E # 11 (07876-1748)
P.O. Box 400, Netcong (07857-0400)
PHONE....................................973 448-0305
Carl Clegg, *Mng Member*
Ken Christiansen,
Rolf Pfeil,
EMP: 8

SALES: 2MM **Privately Held**
SIC: 3826 Analytical instruments

(G-10519)
S V O INC
Also Called: Single Vender Outsource
28 State Route 10 W (07876-1724)
PHONE....................................973 983-8380
Richard Spender, *President*
EMP: 4
SQ FT: 1,000
SALES (est): 535.4K **Privately Held**
SIC: 2759 Commercial printing

Summit
Union County

(G-10520)
ABRAXIS BIOSCIENCE INC (HQ)
86 Morris Ave (07901-3915)
PHONE....................................908 673-9000
Lonnie Moulder, *President*
Biplob Mitra, *Research*
Marian Pereira, *Research*
Mitchell Fogelman, *CFO*
Karen Legge, *Manager*
EMP: 100
SQ FT: 60,900
SALES (est): 102.2MM
SALES (corp-wide): 15.2B **Publicly Held**
SIC: 2834 Pharmaceutical preparations
PA: Celgene Corporation
   86 Morris Ave
   Summit NJ 07901
   908 673-9000

(G-10521)
ABRAXIS BIOSCIENCE INC
86 Morris Ave (07901-3915)
PHONE....................................908 673-9000
EMP: 100
SALES (corp-wide): 15.2B **Publicly Held**
SIC: 2834 Pharmaceutical preparations
HQ: Abraxis Bioscience, Inc.
   86 Morris Ave
   Summit NJ 07901

(G-10522)
ACETYLON PHARMACEUTICALS INC (HQ)
86 Morris Ave (07901-3915)
PHONE....................................908 673-9000
Mark Alles, *President*
Marc A Cohen, *Corp Secy*
Catherine A Wheeler, *Vice Pres*
EMP: 10
SALES (est): 848.3K
SALES (corp-wide): 15.2B **Publicly Held**
SIC: 2834 Pharmaceutical preparations
PA: Celgene Corporation
   86 Morris Ave
   Summit NJ 07901
   908 673-9000

(G-10523)
AHS HOSPITAL CORP
Also Called: Overlook Hospital, Summit Mri
99 Beauvoir Ave (07901-3533)
P.O. Box 220 (07902-0220)
PHONE....................................908 522-2000
Cathy Wasck, *Manager*
EMP: 35
SQ FT: 2,392 **Privately Held**
WEB: www.atlantichealth.org
SIC: 3845 3842 8062 Magnetic resonance imaging device, nuclear; surgical appliances & supplies; general medical & surgical hospitals
PA: Ahs Hospital Corp.
   465 South St
   Morristown NJ 07960

(G-10524)
AMERICAN ESTATES WINES INC
19 Hillside Ave (07901-1904)
PHONE....................................908 273-5060
George G Galey, *President*
Tom Jackson, *Sales Staff*
▲ EMP: 7
SALES (est): 755.4K **Privately Held**
SIC: 2084 Wines

G E O G R A P H I C

(G-10525)
ARTMOLDS JOURNAL LLC
18 Bank St Ste 1 (07901-3659)
PHONE..............................908 273-5600
Edmund McCormick,
Ed McCormick,
EMP: 4
SALES (est): 210.6K **Privately Held**
SIC: 2621 Catalog, magazine & newsprint
papers

(G-10526)
ASSOCIATE FIREPLACE
BUILDERS
Also Called: Fireplace Place Summit, The
331 Springfield Ave (07901-3626)
PHONE..............................908 273-5900
John Vierra, *President*
Dennis Miller, *Exec VP*
EMP: 7
SALES (est): 1MM **Privately Held**
SIC: 3272 5023 Fireplace & chimney ma-
terial: concrete; fireplace equipment & ac-
cessories

(G-10527)
BOURAS INDUSTRIES INC
25 Deforest Ave Ste 100 (07901-2140)
PHONE..............................908 918-9400
Nicholas J Bouras, *President*
Carl Koehler, *Exec VP*
Gary Ruckelshaus, *Vice Pres*
EMP: 650
SALES (est): 84.8MM **Privately Held**
WEB: www.bourasind.com
SIC: 5051 3444 4212 4214 Steel; roof
deck, sheet metal; flooring, cellular steel;
siding, sheet metal; local trucking, without
storage; local trucking with storage; fabri-
cated structural metal

(G-10528)
CELGENE CORPORATION
Also Called: US New Jersey Summit West
556 Morris Ave (07901-1330)
PHONE..............................908 897-4603
EMP: 24
SALES (corp-wide): 15.2B **Publicly Held**
SIC: 2834 Pharmaceutical preparations
PA: Celgene Corporation
86 Morris Ave
Summit NJ 07901
908 673-9000

(G-10529)
CELGENE CORPORATION (PA)
86 Morris Ave (07901-3915)
P.O. Box 421248, Indianapolis IN (46242-
1248)
PHONE..............................908 673-9000
Mark J Alles, *Ch of Bd*
Nadim Ahmed, *President*
Terrie J Curran, *President*
Alise Reicin, *President*
S J Rupert Vessey, *President*
EMP: 211
SALES: 15.2B **Publicly Held**
WEB: www.celgene.com
SIC: 2834 Pharmaceutical preparations

(G-10530)
COLTON INDUSTRIES INC
117 Colt Rd (07901-3039)
PHONE..............................908 277-2040
B G Colton, *CEO*
Brenda Colton, *Ch of Bd*
Stefanie Colton, *President*
EMP: 4
SALES: 6MM **Privately Held**
SIC: 2231 Fabric finishing: wool, mohair or
similar fibers

(G-10531)
ENVIRONMOLDS LLC
18 Bank St Ste 1 (07901-3659)
PHONE..............................908 273-5401
Ed McCormick, *Mng Member*
Hong Zhang,
▲ EMP: 10
SQ FT: 3,000
SALES (est): 710K **Privately Held**
SIC: 3299 5092 5999 Art goods: plaster
of paris, papier mache & scagliola; arts &
crafts equipment & supplies; art dealers

(G-10532)
GALLERY OF RUGS INC
447 Springfield Ave (07901-2615)
PHONE..............................908 934-0040
EMP: 5 EST: 2000
SALES (est): 460K **Privately Held**
SIC: 2273 Mfg Carpets/Rugs

(G-10533)
GSI
12 Princeton St (07901-4208)
PHONE..............................908 608-1325
Genevieve Spielberg, *Principal*
Toni Rhatican, *Office Mgr*
EMP: 4
SALES (est): 499.2K **Privately Held**
SIC: 3699 Laser systems & equipment

(G-10534)
HOSOKAWA MICRON
INTERNATIONAL
Also Called: Hosokawa Tech
10 Chatham Rd (07901-1310)
PHONE..............................908 273-6360
Bill Manzini, *Manager*
EMP: 150 **Privately Held**
WEB: www.hosokawa.com
SIC: 8711 8721 3532 Engineering serv-
ices; accounting, auditing & bookkeeping;
mining machinery
HQ: Hosokawa Micron International Inc.
10 Chatham Rd
Summit NJ 07901
908 273-6360

(G-10535)
HOSOKAWA MICRON
INTERNATIONAL
Also Called: Hosokawa Micron Powder Sys-
tems
10 Chatham Rd (07901-1310)
PHONE..............................908 273-6360
Rob Coorhees, *Branch Mgr*
EMP: 67 **Privately Held**
SIC: 3559 Chemical machinery & equip-
ment; plastics working machinery
HQ: Hosokawa Micron International Inc.
10 Chatham Rd
Summit NJ 07901
908 273-6360

(G-10536)
HOSOKAWA MICRON
INTERNATIONAL
Also Called: Micron Powder Systems
10 Chatham Rd (07901-1310)
PHONE..............................908 273-6360
Rob Voorhes, *Vice Pres*
EMP: 60 **Privately Held**
WEB: www.hosokawa.com
SIC: 3559 Chemical machinery & equip-
ment; plastics working machinery
HQ: Hosokawa Micron International Inc.
10 Chatham Rd
Summit NJ 07901
908 273-6360

(G-10537)
HOSOKAWA MICRON INTL INC
(HQ)
Also Called: Hosokawa Micron Powder Sys-
tems
10 Chatham Rd (07901-1310)
PHONE..............................908 273-6360
Robert Voorhees, *President*
Jodi Levine, *Buyer*
Ed Scannell, *Engineer*
Kris Thompson, *Engineer*
Judith Macgregor, *Finance*
◆ EMP: 70
SQ FT: 195,000
SALES (est): 98.5MM **Privately Held**
WEB: www.hosokawa.com
SIC: 3559 Chemical machinery & equip-
ment

(G-10538)
LITHOPTEK LLC (PA)
26 Ridge Rd (07901-2952)
PHONE..............................408 533-5847
Rudolf Hendel, *President*
Mark Schattenburg, *CTO*
EMP: 7
SALES (est): 307K **Privately Held**
SIC: 3827 Optical instruments & lenses

(G-10539)
MARKOV PROCESSES
INTERNATIONAL
475 Sprngfeld Ave Ste 401 (07901)
PHONE..............................908 608-1558
Michael Markov, *Ch of Bd*
EMP: 35 EST: 1992
SALES (est): 4.6MM **Privately Held**
SIC: 7372 Business oriented computer
software

(G-10540)
MERCK & CO INC
566 Morris Ave (07901-1311)
PHONE..............................908 298-4000
EMP: 48
SALES (corp-wide): 40.1B **Publicly Held**
SIC: 2834 Mfg Pharmaceutical Prepara-
tions
PA: Merck & Co., Inc.
2000 Galloping Hill Rd
Kenilworth NJ 07033
908 740-4000

(G-10541)
MYSUPERFOODS LTD LIABILITY
CO
371 Springfield Ave Ste 2 (07901-2708)
PHONE..............................646 283-7455
Katie Jesionowski, *President*
Silvia Gianni, *President*
EMP: 10
SALES (est): 1.2MM **Privately Held**
SIC: 2032 Baby foods, including meats:
packaged in cans, jars, etc.

(G-10542)
OPTIONS EDGE LLC
53 Division Ave Apt 12 (07901-2350)
PHONE..............................973 701-0051
Mark Guthner,
EMP: 4
SALES (est): 162K **Privately Held**
SIC: 2721 Periodicals

(G-10543)
PHARMION CORPORATION (HQ)
86 Morris Ave (07901-3915)
PHONE..............................908 673-9000
M James Barrett, *Ch of Bd*
Patrick J Mahaffy, *President*
Michael Cosgrave, *Exec VP*
Steven N Dupont, *Vice Pres*
Erle T Mast, *CFO*
EMP: 35
SQ FT: 29,000
SALES (est): 24.2MM
SALES (corp-wide): 15.2B **Publicly Held**
WEB: www.pharmion.com
SIC: 2834 Drugs affecting neoplasms &
endocrine systems
PA: Celgene Corporation
86 Morris Ave
Summit NJ 07901
908 673-9000

(G-10544)
SAFETY POWER INC
Also Called: SPI
55 Union Pl Ste 178 (07901-2563)
PHONE..............................908 277-1826
Robert Desnoyers, *President*
Bob Stelzer, *Chairman*
Randy Sadler, *VP Sls/Mktg*
EMP: 5
SQ FT: 200
SALES (est): 10MM
SALES (corp-wide): 2.9MM **Privately
Held**
SIC: 3564 Air purification equipment
PA: Safety Power Inc
26-5155 Spectrum Way
Mississauga ON L4W 5
416 477-2709

(G-10545)
SEQIRUS USA INC
25 Deforest Ave (07901-2140)
PHONE..............................908 739-0200
Brent Macgregor, *President*
Richard Culbert, *Treasurer*
John Minardo, *Admin Sec*
EMP: 10

SALES (est): 2.3MM
SALES (corp-wide): 6.9B **Privately Held**
SIC: 2836 Biological products, except diag-
nostic
PA: Csl Limited
45 Poplar Rd
Parkville VIC 3052
393 891-911

(G-10546)
SERVICE DATA CORP INC
Also Called: Service Data Forms
265 Oak Ridge Ave (07901-3258)
PHONE..............................908 522-0020
Ross Wagner, *President*
Katherine Wagner, *Corp Secy*
EMP: 6
SALES (est): 770K **Privately Held**
SIC: 5112 2732 2752 Business forms;
book printing; commercial printing, litho-
graphic

(G-10547)
SILICON PRESS INC
25 Beverly Rd (07901-1619)
PHONE..............................908 273-8919
Narain Gehani, *CEO*
Indu Gehani, *President*
EMP: 5
SALES (est): 370K **Privately Held**
WEB: www.silicon-press.com
SIC: 2731 5192 Book publishing; books,
periodicals & newspapers

(G-10548)
SOFTWARE PRACTICES AND
TECH
73 Stone Ridge Rd (07901-4156)
PHONE..............................908 464-2923
EMP: 6
SALES (est): 460K **Privately Held**
SIC: 7371 7372 Custom Computer Pro-
graming Prepackaged Software Services

(G-10549)
STESSL & NEUGEBAUER INC
9 Industrial Pl (07901-3512)
PHONE..............................908 277-3340
Wilfred Stessl, *President*
Carole Stessl, *Corp Secy*
EMP: 15
SALES (est): 1.8MM **Privately Held**
SIC: 2391 7641 Draperies, plastic & tex-
tile: from purchased materials; reuphol-
stery

(G-10550)
SUMMIT MILLWORK & SUPPLY
INC
235 Morris Ave (07901-5501)
P.O. Box 373 (07902-0373)
PHONE..............................908 273-1486
Aldo Curiale, *President*
Irene Curiale, *Admin Sec*
EMP: 4
SQ FT: 5,000
SALES (est): 664.3K **Privately Held**
SIC: 2431 Millwork

(G-10551)
SUMMIT TRUCK BODY INC (PA)
50 Franklin Pl (07901-3684)
PHONE..............................908 277-4342
Timothy Erday, *President*
EMP: 20 EST: 1953
SQ FT: 12,000
SALES (est): 2.9MM **Privately Held**
WEB: www.summittruckbody.com
SIC: 3713 7532 7538 Truck bodies &
parts; top & body repair & paint shops;
general truck repair

(G-10552)
SWEET ORANGE LLC
545 Morris Ave (07901-1325)
PHONE..............................908 522-0011
Dina Kim, *Principal*
EMP: 5
SALES (est): 250.6K **Privately Held**
SIC: 2024 Ice cream, bulk

(G-10553)
VENTURE APP LLC
12 Aubrey St (07901-1464)
PHONE..............................908 644-3985

Leonel Ayala,
EMP: 4 **EST:** 2017
SALES (est): 98.3K **Privately Held**
SIC: 7372 7389 Prepackaged software;

Surf City
Ocean County

(G-10554)
AMERICAN DIRECTORY PUBLISHING
Also Called: Regional Directory
1816 Long Beach Blvd (08008-5461)
PHONE................................609 494-4055
Michael Paul, *President*
EMP: 8
SQ FT: 1,000
SALES (est): 496.2K **Privately Held**
SIC: 2741 Telephone & other directory publishing

(G-10555)
JERSEY SHORE NEWS MGAZINES INC (PA)
Also Called: Beachcomber, The
1816 Long Beach Blvd (08008-5461)
PHONE................................609 494-5900
Curt Travers, *President*
Juliet Kaszas-Hoch, *Technical Staff*
EMP: 30
SQ FT: 5,000
SALES (est): 2.9MM **Privately Held**
WEB: www.thesandpaper.net
SIC: 2711 2741 Newspapers, publishing & printing; miscellaneous publishing

Sussex
Sussex County

(G-10556)
ANNETTE & JIM DIZENZO SLS LLC (PA)
Also Called: Kristino Handbags & ACC
6 Glenview Ln (07461-4848)
PHONE................................973 875-0895
Jim Dizenzo, *Mng Member*
Annette Dizenzo,
EMP: 4
SQ FT: 1,605
SALES (est): 384.7K **Privately Held**
SIC: 3171 Handbags, women's

(G-10557)
DEW ASSOCIATES INC
7 Armstrong Rd (07461-3005)
PHONE................................973 702-0545
Charles Mego, *COO*
EMP: 47
SALES (corp-wide): 7.8MM **Privately Held**
WEB: www.dewassoc.com
SIC: 3577 Computer peripheral equipment
PA: Dew Associates Inc
48 Woodport Rd
Sparta NJ
973 702-0545

(G-10558)
DOLAN ASSOC INC
71 Holland Rd A (07461-2838)
PHONE................................973 875-6408
Margaret Dolan, *President*
EMP: 5
SALES (est): 728K **Privately Held**
SIC: 3585 Heating & air conditioning combination units

(G-10559)
EASTERN CONCRETE MATERIALS INC
80 Estate Dr 23n (07461)
PHONE................................973 702-7866
Dave Besaw, *Manager*
EMP: 7
SALES (corp-wide): 1.5B **Publicly Held**
SIC: 1499 Asphalt mining & bituminous stone quarrying

HQ: Eastern Concrete Materials, Inc.
250 Pehle Ave Ste 503
Saddle Brook NJ 07663
201 797-7979

(G-10560)
GLASPLEX LLC
8 Estate Dr (07461-2710)
PHONE................................973 940-8940
Tiffany Dangelo, *Office Mgr*
EMP: 6 **EST:** 2013
SALES (est): 415.8K **Privately Held**
SIC: 3089 Air mattresses, plastic

(G-10561)
HIGH POINT PRECISION PRODUCTS
1 First St (07461-2509)
PHONE................................973 875-6229
Charles Stipo, *President*
Marilyn Stipo, *Treasurer*
EMP: 20 **EST:** 1971
SQ FT: 10,000
SALES (est): 3.7MM **Privately Held**
SIC: 3541 Screw machines, automatic

(G-10562)
INDUSTRIAL PROCESS & EQP INC (PA)
Also Called: Ipe
803 State Rt 23 (07461-3333)
P.O. Box 7068 (07461-7068)
PHONE................................973 702-0330
John Stearns, *President*
Joe Sandberg, *Project Engr*
EMP: 18
SQ FT: 400
SALES (est): 3.1MM **Privately Held**
SIC: 1711 1796 3444 Process piping contractor; machine moving & rigging; machinery installation; millwright; pipe, sheet metal

(G-10563)
J PAUL ALLEN INC
127 Sally Harden Rd (07461-3831)
PHONE................................973 702-1174
Jon Baker, *President*
EMP: 4
SALES (est): 271.5K **Privately Held**
SIC: 3546 Drills & drilling tools

(G-10564)
NEW HEAVEN CHEMICALS IOWA LLC
18 Jenny Ln (07461-4550)
PHONE................................201 506-9109
Ross N Cohen, *Principal*
EMP: 6
SALES (est): 374.5K **Privately Held**
SIC: 2819 Industrial inorganic chemicals

(G-10565)
RS PHILLIPS STEEL LLC
128 Lake Pochung Rd (07461-4127)
PHONE................................973 827-6464
Joseph Thomas, *General Mgr*
Mark Vanderwerf, *Business Mgr*
Rebecca Degroat, *Office Mgr*
Neil Phillips, *Mng Member*
Scott Phillips,
EMP: 25
SQ FT: 8,000
SALES (est): 9MM **Privately Held**
SIC: 1791 3441 3449 5051 Structural steel erection; fabricated structural metal; miscellaneous metalwork; metals service centers & offices

(G-10566)
TAMARAS EUROPEAN AMERICAN DELI
13 Essex Rd (07461-1109)
PHONE................................973 875-5461
Richard Stuckey, *Principal*
EMP: 6
SALES (est): 210K **Privately Held**
SIC: 2099 Food preparations

(G-10567)
TEK MOLDING
1440 County Rd 565 (07461-3135)
P.O. Box 735, Vernon (07462-0735)
PHONE................................973 702-0450
Tim Tanney, *Owner*

EMP: 6
SALES (est): 448.1K **Privately Held**
SIC: 3089 Molding primary plastic

(G-10568)
TIMPLEX CORP
1370 State Rt 23 (07461-3605)
PHONE................................973 875-5500
Ronald Slate, *President*
Marilyn Slate, *Corp Secy*
EMP: 18
SQ FT: 18,000
SALES (est): 3.1MM **Privately Held**
SIC: 2439 5211 Structural wood members; lumber & other building materials

(G-10569)
US OUTWORKERS LLC
6 Hunter Ridge Rd (07461-4600)
P.O. Box 453, Glenwood (07418-0453)
PHONE................................973 362-1458
Ryan Williams,
Robert Quaranta,
▲ **EMP:** 5
SALES (est): 585.2K **Privately Held**
SIC: 4959 3531 5033 Snowplowing; pavers; roofing, asphalt & sheet metal

Swedesboro
Gloucester County

(G-10570)
AMERICAN RENOLIT CORP LA
301 Berkeley Dr B (08085-1255)
PHONE................................856 241-4901
Fred Breidenbach, *General Mgr*
Pieter De Graaff, *Sales Staff*
EMP: 7
SALES (corp-wide): 2.2B **Privately Held**
SIC: 3081 Vinyl film & sheet
HQ: Solvay Draka, Inc.
6900 Elm St
Commerce CA 90040
323 725-7010

(G-10571)
ARTHUR H THOMAS COMPANY (PA)
Also Called: Thomas Scientific
1654 High Hill Rd (08085-1780)
P.O. Box 99 (08085-6099)
PHONE................................856 467-2000
Edward B Patterson Jr, *Principal*
Robert D Patterson, *Chairman*
Paul F Seliskar, *COO*
Lee Smith, *COO*
Robin Carroll, *Vice Pres*
▼ **EMP:** 263 **EST:** 1900
SQ FT: 140,000
SALES (est): 94.5MM **Privately Held**
SIC: 3821 5049 Laboratory equipment: fume hoods, distillation racks, etc.; scientific & engineering equipment & supplies

(G-10572)
BIOCHEMICAL SCIENCES INC
200 Commodore Dr (08085-1270)
PHONE................................856 467-1813
Doug Dowd, *General Mgr*
EMP: 4
SALES (est): 296.1K **Privately Held**
SIC: 2819 Industrial inorganic chemicals

(G-10573)
BOEING COMPANY
800 Arlington Blvd (08085-2502)
PHONE................................610 591-1978
Mark Kozachyn, *Engineer*
Dennis W Borgstrom, *Design Engr*
EMP: 996
SALES (corp-wide): 101.1B **Publicly Held**
SIC: 3721 Airplanes, fixed or rotary wing
PA: The Boeing Company
100 N Riverside Plz
Chicago IL 60606
312 544-2000

(G-10574)
BRASSCRAFT MANUFACTURING CO
Cobra Products
1 Warner Ct (08085-1743)
PHONE................................856 241-7700
Paul Sanderson, *CEO*
EMP: 5
SALES (corp-wide): 8.3B **Publicly Held**
SIC: 3423 2842 Hand & edge tools; drain pipe solvents or cleaners
HQ: Brasscraft Manufacturing Company
39600 Orchard Hill Pl
Novi MI 48375
248 305-6000

(G-10575)
CADDY CORPORATION OF AMERICA
509 Sharptown Rd (08085-3163)
P.O. Box 345, Bridgeport (08014-0345)
PHONE................................856 467-4222
Craig Cohen, *CEO*
Harry Schmidt, *President*
EMP: 52
SQ FT: 71,000
SALES (est): 16.6MM **Privately Held**
WEB: www.caddycorp.com
SIC: 3556 Food products machinery

(G-10576)
CENTRAL INK CORPORATION
2085 Center Square Rd A (08085-1790)
PHONE................................856 467-5562
Stephen Corson, *Branch Mgr*
EMP: 9
SALES (corp-wide): 34.4MM **Privately Held**
WEB: www.cicink.com
SIC: 2893 Letterpress or offset ink
PA: Central Ink Corporation
1100 Harvester Rd
West Chicago IL 60185
630 231-6500

(G-10577)
COBRA PRODUCTS INC
Also Called: Speedway
1 Warner Ct (08085-1743)
PHONE................................856 241-7700
Don Woody, *President*
▲ **EMP:** 77
SQ FT: 175,000
SALES (est): 12.7MM
SALES (corp-wide): 8.3B **Publicly Held**
WEB: www.cobraus.com
SIC: 1711 2842 Plumbing contractors; drain pipe solvents or cleaners
PA: Masco Corporation
17450 College Pkwy
Livonia MI 48152
313 274-7400

(G-10578)
DAMASK KANDIES
Also Called: Damask Candies
2255 Route 322 (08085-3633)
PHONE................................856 467-1661
Douglas Damask, *Owner*
EMP: 6
SALES (est): 445.4K **Privately Held**
SIC: 2064 5145 5441 Candy & other confectionery products; candy; candy

(G-10579)
DESIGN ASSISTANCE CORPORATION
3 Killdeer Ct Ste 301 (08085-1753)
P.O. Box 215 (08085-0215)
PHONE................................856 241-9500
Glenn Woerner, *President*
John Clements, *Division Mgr*
Mary Phelps, *Executive*
▼ **EMP:** 16
SALES (est): 3.6MM **Privately Held**
WEB: www.dac-3d.com
SIC: 3699 Electronic training devices

(G-10580)
DIGITAL PRODUCTIONS INC
100 Berkeley Dr Ste B (08085-9701)
P.O. Box 133 (08085-0133)
PHONE................................856 224-1111
Charles Budd, *President*
Ron Bruno, *Vice Pres*

Juli Gioia, *Director*
EMP: 12
SALES (est): 3.1MM **Privately Held**
SIC: 2752 Commercial printing, lithographic

(G-10581)
DIVERSIFIED FOAM PRODUCTS INC
Also Called: Diversified Industries
121 High Hill Rd (08085-1777)
PHONE............................856 662-1981
David Hoyt, *CEO*
Matthew Harris, *CEO*
Bruce Castor, *President*
Edward Janes, *Vice Pres*
Craig Kene, *Vice Pres*
◆ **EMP:** 60
SQ FT: 105,000
SALES (est): 24.5MM **Privately Held**
WEB: www.diversifiedindustries.com
SIC: 3069 Foam rubber

(G-10582)
DR SCHAR USA INC
305 Heron Dr (08085-1773)
PHONE............................856 803-5100
Martin Ziegler, *Manager*
EMP: 35
SALES (corp-wide): 181.3MM **Privately Held**
SIC: 2051 Bakery: wholesale or wholesale/retail combined
HQ: Dr. Schar Usa, Inc.
125 Chubb Ave Ste 1a
Lyndhurst NJ 07071

(G-10583)
EAGLEBURGMANN INDUSTRIES LP
614 Heron Dr Ste 8 (08085-1846)
PHONE............................856 241-7300
Patrick McCann, *General Mgr*
EMP: 10
SALES (corp-wide): 11B **Privately Held**
SIC: 3053 Gaskets, packing & sealing devices
HQ: Eagleburgmann Industries Lp
10035 Brookriver Dr
Houston TX 77040
713 939-9515

(G-10584)
ETHYLENE ATLANTIC CORP
136 Church St (08085-1123)
P.O. Box 1273, Kitty Hawk NC (27949-1273)
PHONE............................856 467-0010
Michael P Johnston, *President*
Kim Lamb, *General Mgr*
James Monaghan, *Corp Secy*
Barbara Johnston, *Vice Pres*
EMP: 25
SQ FT: 7,200
SALES (est): 3.2MM **Privately Held**
WEB: www.ethyleneatlantic.com
SIC: 3089 Injection molding of plastics

(G-10585)
FIOPLEX
49 Fredrick Blvd (08085-4245)
PHONE............................856 689-7213
Ronald Guittar, *President*
EMP: 4
SALES (est): 207K **Privately Held**
SIC: 3993 7389 Signs & advertising specialties;

(G-10586)
GINSEY INDUSTRIES INC
Also Called: Ginsey Home Solutions
2078 Center Square Rd (08085-1703)
PHONE............................856 933-1300
Herbert Briggs, *CEO*
George Valletti, *CFO*
▲ **EMP:** 75
SQ FT: 150,000
SALES (est): 21.6MM **Privately Held**
WEB: www.ginsey.com
SIC: 3261 Bathroom accessories/fittings, vitreous china or earthenware

(G-10587)
GREAT NORTHERN CORPORATION
500a Pedricktown Rd (08085-1729)
PHONE............................856 241-0080
Kris Achterberg, *Principal*
Mark Van, *Vice Pres*
Phil Brooks, *Manager*
James Bradshaw, *Manager*
EMP: 8
SALES (corp-wide): 522.4MM **Privately Held**
SIC: 2653 Boxes, corrugated: made from purchased materials
PA: Great Northern Corporation
395 Stroebe Rd
Appleton WI 54914
920 739-3671

(G-10588)
HEINKEL FILTERING SYSTEMS INC
520 Sharptown Rd (08085-3161)
PHONE............................856 467-3399
Allen Ferraro, *President*
Eckenroad Gary, *Vice Pres*
Dave Altum, *Engineer*
Sam An, *Project Engr*
Federico Juarez, *Regl Sales Mgr*
▲ **EMP:** 10
SQ FT: 20,000
SALES (est): 2.7MM
SALES (corp-wide): 288.4K **Privately Held**
WEB: www.heinkelusa.com
SIC: 3569 Centrifuges, industrial
HQ: Heinkel Process Technology Gmbh
Ferdinand-Porsche-Str. 8
Besigheim
714 396-920

(G-10589)
HERITAGE BAG COMPANY
2123 High Hill Rd (08085)
PHONE............................856 467-2247
Carl Allen, *President*
Donna Hubbard, *Sales Staff*
Bob Seidl, *Executive*
EMP: 70
SQ FT: 50,000
SALES (corp-wide): 2.9B **Privately Held**
WEB: www.heritage-bag.com
SIC: 2673 3081 Plastic bags: made from purchased materials; unsupported plastics film & sheet
HQ: Heritage Bag Company
501 Gateway Pkwy
Roanoke TX 76262
972 241-5525

(G-10590)
JOHN CRANE INC
Also Called: Smiths Group North America
301 Berkeley Dr Ste B (08085-1255)
PHONE............................856 467-6185
Mike Barnhard, *Sales Staff*
Don Williams, *Manager*
EMP: 80
SALES (corp-wide): 4.2B **Privately Held**
WEB: www.johncrane.com
SIC: 3053 Gaskets & sealing devices; packing materials
HQ: John Crane Inc.
227 W Monroe St Ste 1800
Chicago IL 60606
312 605-7800

(G-10591)
JP TECHNOLOGY INC
2150 High Hill Rd (08085-4530)
PHONE............................856 241-0111
Jinming Ding, *President*
Ray Chen, *Manager*
EMP: 15
SQ FT: 1,200
SALES (est): 688.2K **Privately Held**
SIC: 3441 Fabricated structural metal

(G-10592)
KENRIC INC
110 Richardson Ave (08085-1149)
P.O. Box 203 (08085-0203)
PHONE............................856 294-9161
Kennard J Sharr, *President*
Lisa M Scharr, *Admin Sec*

EMP: 5
SQ FT: 9,000
SALES (est): 1.8MM **Privately Held**
SIC: 3449 Bars, concrete reinforcing: fabricated steel

(G-10593)
L & L KILN MFG INC
505 Sharptown Rd (08085-3163)
P.O. Box 1898, Boothwyn PA (19061-7898)
PHONE............................856 294-0077
Stephen J Lewicki, *President*
Gregory D Lewicki, *Vice Pres*
▲ **EMP:** 20 EST: 1945
SQ FT: 28,000
SALES (est): 5MM **Privately Held**
WEB: www.hotkilns.com
SIC: 3567 Industrial furnaces & ovens

(G-10594)
MATTHIAS PAPER CORPORATION (PA)
301 Arlington Blvd (08085-1370)
P.O. Box 130 (08085-0130)
PHONE............................856 467-6970
John R Matthias, *CEO*
Warren E Storck, *Vice Pres*
Michael Dalessandro, *Manager*
Mark Secol, *Info Tech Mgr*
John R Matthias Jr, *Admin Sec*
◆ **EMP:** 28 EST: 1915
SQ FT: 46,000
SALES (est): 25.1MM **Privately Held**
WEB: www.matthiaspaper.com
SIC: 5113 2679 Paper & products, wrapping or coarse; paper products, converted

(G-10595)
MEDTRONIC INC
1130 Commerce Blvd # 100 (08085-1439)
PHONE............................908 289-5969
EMP: 173 **Privately Held**
SIC: 3841 Surgical & medical instruments
HQ: Medtronic, Inc.
710 Medtronic Pkwy
Minneapolis MN 55432
763 514-4000

(G-10596)
MISSA BAY CITRUS COMPANY
101 Arlington Blvd (08085-1265)
PHONE............................856 241-0900
Frank C Pollera, *President*
EMP: 19
SALES (est): 2.9MM **Privately Held**
SIC: 2099 Food preparations

(G-10597)
MISSA BAY LLC (DH)
101 Arlington Blvd (08085-1265)
PHONE............................856 241-0900
Frank C Pollera, *President*
Dennis Gertmenian,
Salvatore Tedesco,
▲ **EMP:** 51
SQ FT: 96,000
SALES (est): 39.1MM
SALES (corp-wide): 2.6MM **Privately Held**
WEB: www.missabay.com
SIC: 2099 5142 Food preparations; packaged frozen goods
HQ: Ready Pac Foods, Inc.
4401 Foxdale St
Irwindale CA 91706
626 856-8686

(G-10598)
MULTI-PLASTICS INC
210 Commodore Dr (08085-1292)
PHONE............................856 241-9014
Mike Budd, *COO*
Chad Grossman, *Plant Mgr*
Gary Keanry, *Foreman/Supr*
James Johnston, *Treasurer*
Robert Parsio, *Branch Mgr*
EMP: 30
SALES (corp-wide): 198MM **Privately Held**
WEB: www.multi-plastics.com
SIC: 5162 3089 Plastics materials; plastic processing
PA: Multi-Plastics, Inc.
7770 N Central Dr
Lewis Center OH 43035
740 548-4894

(G-10599)
OMEGA ENGINEERING INC
1 Killdeer Ct (08085-1845)
PHONE............................856 467-4200
Jim Ferguson, *President*
Jeff Pflieger, *Production*
EMP: 14
SALES (corp-wide): 2B **Privately Held**
SIC: 3823 Industrial instrmnts msrmnt display/control process variable
HQ: Omega Engineering, Inc.
800 Connecticut Ave 5n01
Norwalk CT 06854
203 359-1660

(G-10600)
PENNSYLVANIA MACHINE WORKS INC
U S Drop Forge Division
Rr 551 (08085)
P.O. Box 131 (08085-0131)
PHONE............................856 467-0500
Charles J Lafferty, *Manager*
EMP: 50
SALES (corp-wide): 35.9MM **Privately Held**
SIC: 3462 3494 Iron & steel forgings; pipe fittings
PA: Pennsylvania Machine Works, Inc.
201 Bethel Ave
Upper Chichester PA 19014
610 497-3300

(G-10601)
PHARMA SYNERGY LLC
103 Somerfield Rd (08085-2505)
PHONE............................856 241-2316
Antonio J Petillo, *Principal*
EMP: 4
SALES (est): 239.1K **Privately Held**
SIC: 2834 Pharmaceutical preparations

(G-10602)
POLYMER ADDITIVES INC
Also Called: Valtris Specialty Chemicals
170 Us 130 (08085)
PHONE............................856 467-8220
Bob Natan, *Plant Mgr*
EMP: 80 **Privately Held**
SIC: 2899 Fire retardant chemicals
HQ: Polymer Additives, Inc.
7500 E Pleasant Valley Rd
Independence OH 44131
216 875-7200

(G-10603)
PRECISE TECHNOLOGY INC
406 Heron Dr Ste A (08085-1755)
PHONE............................856 241-1760
William Finkley, *Branch Mgr*
EMP: 42
SALES (corp-wide): 11.6B **Publicly Held**
SIC: 3089 Injection molding of plastics
HQ: Rexam Limited
4 Millbank
London
158 240-8999

(G-10604)
RADIO SYSTEMS DESIGN INC
601 Heron Dr (08085-1741)
PHONE............................856 467-8000
Daniel J Braverman, *President*
Gerrett Conover, *CFO*
Dennis Greben, *Treasurer*
EMP: 23
SQ FT: 13,000
SALES (est): 2.4MM **Privately Held**
SIC: 3663 Radio & TV communications equipment

(G-10605)
RAJYSAN INCORPORATED
3 Hawk Ct (08085-1724)
PHONE............................800 433-1382
EMP: 23
SALES (corp-wide): 49.5MM **Privately Held**
SIC: 5084 5082 3621 Whol Industrial Equipment Whol Construction/Mining Equipment Mfg Motors/Generators
PA: Rajysan, Incorporated
4175 Guardian St
Simi Valley CA 93063
661 775-4920

(G-10606)
RASTELLI BROTHERS INC (PA)
Also Called: Rastelli Foods
300 Heron Dr (08085-1707)
PHONE....................................856 803-1100
Ray Rastelli III, *CEO*
Fabio Capone, *General Mgr*
Bassam Freiwat, *Regional Mgr*
Anthony Rastelli, *Exec VP*
Joseph Cangemi, *Facilities Mgr*
◆ EMP: 125
SQ FT: 40,000
SALES (est): 135.3MM **Privately Held**
WEB: www.rastellis.com
SIC: 5147 5421 2011 Meats, fresh; meat
markets, including freezer provisioners;
canned meats (except baby food), meat
slaughtered on site

(G-10607)
ROYAL INGREDIENTS LLC
510 Sharptown Rd (08085-3161)
PHONE....................................856 241-2004
EMP: 4
SALES (corp-wide): 8.1B **Privately Held**
SIC: 2099 2869 Sorghum syrups: for
sweetening; sweeteners, synthetic
HQ: Royal Ingredients, Llc
365 Canal St Ste 2929
New Orleans LA 70130
856 241-2004

(G-10608)
SAVITA NATURALS LTD
617 Heron Dr (08085-1741)
PHONE....................................856 467-4949
Richard Trout, *President*
Kevin Trout, *Director*
EMP: 20 EST: 1997
SQ FT: 380,000
SALES (est): 1.4MM **Privately Held**
SIC: 2066 Chocolate & cocoa products

(G-10609)
STANDARD INDUSTRIES INC
700 2nd St Ste C&D (08085-1138)
PHONE....................................856 241-0241
EMP: 119
SALES (corp-wide): 2.5B **Privately Held**
SIC: 2493 Insulation & roofing material, re-
constituted wood
HQ: Standard Industries Inc.
1 Campus Dr
Parsippany NJ 07054

(G-10610)
STECHER DAVE WELDING & FABG SP
1040 Township Line Rd (08085-1786)
PHONE....................................856 467-3558
Dave Stecher, *Owner*
EMP: 5
SQ FT: 4,000
SALES (est): 393.1K **Privately Held**
SIC: 7692 Welding repair

(G-10611)
STERIGENICS US LLC
303 Heron Dr (08085-1773)
PHONE....................................856 241-8880
Shaun Baburam, *Branch Mgr*
EMP: 9
SALES (corp-wide): 723.7MM **Privately Held**
SIC: 2842 Disinfectants, household or in-
dustrial plant
HQ: Sterigenics U.S., Llc
2015 Spring Rd Ste 650
Oak Brook IL 60523
630 928-1700

(G-10612)
SUPERIOR MARINE CANVAS
75 Belfiore Dr (08085-3613)
PHONE....................................856 241-1724
Brian Reed, *Owner*
EMP: 5
SALES (est): 257.8K **Privately Held**
WEB: www.superiorcanvas.com
SIC: 2394 Canvas & related products

(G-10613)
TAYLOR FARMS NEW JERSEY INC
406 Heron Dr Ste A (08085-1755)
PHONE....................................856 241-0097
Bruce Taylor, *CEO*
John Pulley, *Opers Mgr*
Dana Coughlin, *Production*
Marie Butler, *QA Dir*
Michael Guinto, *Engineer*
◆ EMP: 28
SALES (est): 13.2MM **Privately Held**
SIC: 2099 Food preparations
PA: Taylor Fresh Foods, Inc.
150 Main St Ste 400
Salinas CA 93901

(G-10614)
THOMAS SCIENTIFIC INC
1654 High Hill Rd (08085-1780)
P.O. Box 99 (08085-6099)
PHONE....................................800 345-2100
Richard Drew, *President*
Edward B Patterson Jr, *Principal*
Robert D Patterson, *Chairman*
Paul F Seliskar, *COO*
Craig D Kingery, *CFO*
EMP: 300
SQ FT: 140,000
SALES (est): 24.8MM
SALES (corp-wide): 94.5MM **Privately Held**
SIC: 5049 3821 Scientific & engineering
equipment & supplies; laboratory equip-
ment: fume hoods, distillation racks, etc.
PA: Arthur H. Thomas Company
1654 High Hill Rd
Swedesboro NJ 08085
856 467-2000

(G-10615)
THOMAS SCIENTIFIC LLC (HQ)
1654 High Hill Rd (08085-1780)
PHONE....................................800 345-2100
Charles Simmons, *CEO*
Robin Carroll, *Vice Pres*
Ricardo Martofel, *Vice Pres*
Kevin Lannan, *CFO*
Elizabeth Nolan, *Human Res Dir*
EMP: 6
SQ FT: 200,000
SALES (est): 260.2MM
SALES (corp-wide): 2.4B **Publicly Held**
SIC: 5049 3821 Scientific & engineering
equipment & supplies; laboratory equip-
ment: fume hoods, distillation racks, etc.
PA: The Carlyle Group L P
1001 Pennsylvania Ave Nw 220s
Washington DC 20004
202 729-5626

(G-10616)
UNIVEG LOGISTICS AMERICA INC
100 Dartmouth Dr Ste 400 (08085-2008)
PHONE....................................856 241-0097
Mayda Sotomayer, *President*
Vitor Figueiredo, *CFO*
Cordlee Penebad, *Admin Sec*
EMP: 9
SALES (est): 1.1MM **Privately Held**
SIC: 3086 Packaging & shipping materials,
foamed plastic

(G-10617)
WAGONHOUSE WINERY LLC
1401 State Highway 45 (08085-1657)
PHONE....................................609 780-8019
Dan Brown, *Principal*
Heather Brown, *Principal*
EMP: 5
SALES (est): 683.3K **Privately Held**
SIC: 2084 Wines

Tabernacle
Burlington County

(G-10618)
CONTE FARMS
299 Flyatt Rd (08088-9307)
PHONE....................................609 268-0513
Joseph Conte Jr, *Owner*
EMP: 12

SALES (est): 794.8K **Privately Held**
WEB: www.contefarms.com
SIC: 0161 0175 2051 Vegetables & melons; deciduous tree fruits; bread, cake &
related products

(G-10619)
JASCO SPECIALTIES AND FORMS
Also Called: Jasco Printing
86 Patty Bowker Rd (08088-9363)
PHONE....................................856 627-5511
EMP: 7
SALES (est): 700K **Privately Held**
SIC: 7336 2752 Commercial Art/Graphic
Design Lithographic Commercial Printing

(G-10620)
WATER RESOURCES NEW JERSEY LLC
Also Called: Water Resources of New Jersey
1609 Route 206 (08088-8837)
P.O. Box 2172, Vincentown (08088-2172)
PHONE....................................609 268-7965
Craig Cocco, *Mng Member*
Chris Cocco, *Manager*
EMP: 5
SALES: 500K **Privately Held**
WEB: www.waterresourcesnj.com
SIC: 3589 Sewage & water treatment
equipment; water treatment equipment,
industrial

Teaneck
Bergen County

(G-10621)
ADVANCING OPPORTUNITIES INC
Also Called: United Crbral Plsy Bldg Blocks
639 Teaneck Rd (07666-4258)
PHONE....................................201 907-0200
Lisa Camberery, *Branch Mgr*
EMP: 8
SALES (corp-wide): 11.6MM **Privately Held**
WEB: www.cpofnj.com
SIC: 3577 Computer peripheral equipment
PA: Advancing Opportunities, Inc.
1005 Whitehead Road Ext 1a
Ewing NJ 08638
609 882-4182

(G-10622)
ASSOCIATED CLEANING SYSTEMS
569 Oritani Pl (07666-1664)
PHONE....................................201 530-9197
Elizio Portes, *President*
Lourdes Mendoza-Portes, *Vice Pres*
EMP: 8
SALES: 400K **Privately Held**
SIC: 7699 2842 Cleaning services; spe-
cialty cleaning preparations

(G-10623)
AVACYN PHARMACEUTICALS INC
719 Downing St (07666-2220)
PHONE....................................201 836-2599
Allan Goldberg, *President*
EMP: 6
SALES (est): 344.2K **Privately Held**
SIC: 2834 Pharmaceutical preparations

(G-10624)
CIRCULITE INC
500 F W Burr Blvd Ste 40 (07666)
PHONE....................................201 478-7575
Eric Rose, *Ch of Bd*
Paul Southworth, *President*
Peter Pfreundschuh, *CFO*
EMP: 13
SALES (est): 1.3MM **Privately Held**
WEB: www.circulite.net
SIC: 3845 Electromedical equipment
HQ: Heartware International, Inc.
500 Old Connecticut Path
Framingham MA 01701

(G-10625)
COGNIZANT TECH SOLUTIONS CORP (PA)
500 Frank W Burr Blvd (07666-6804)
PHONE....................................201 801-0233
Francisco D'Souza, *CEO*
Michael Patsalos-Fox, *Ch of Bd*
Debashis Chatterjee, *President*
Sumithra Gomatam, *President*
Gajakarnan Vibushanan Kandiah, *President*
EMP: 80
SQ FT: 100,000
SALES: 16.1B **Publicly Held**
WEB: www.cognizant.com
SIC: 7371 7379 7372 Computer software
development & applications; computer re-
lated consulting services; business ori-
ented computer software

(G-10626)
DBC INC
Also Called: Photoscribe
300 Frank W Burr Blvd # 56 (07666-6704)
PHONE....................................212 819-1177
David Benderly, *President*
Carroll Dounn, *Vice Pres*
EMP: 60
SQ FT: 20,000
SALES (est): 7.8MM **Privately Held**
WEB: www.photoscribe.com
SIC: 3911 5944 Jewelry, precious metal;
jewelry stores

(G-10627)
DIAGNOSTIX PLUS INC
811 Queen Anne Rd (07666-4643)
PHONE....................................201 530-5505
Donald Bogustski, *President*
▲ EMP: 8
SQ FT: 500
SALES: 2MM **Privately Held**
WEB: www.diagplus.com
SIC: 5047 3841 Medical equipment & sup-
plies; diagnostic apparatus, medical

(G-10628)
DUNKIN DONUTS BASKIN ROBBINS
Also Called: Baskin-Robbins
332 Cedar Ln (07666-3418)
PHONE....................................201 692-1900
Mahdi Naeb, *General Mgr*
EMP: 4
SALES (est): 264.9K **Privately Held**
SIC: 2024 5461 5812 Ice cream, bulk;
bakeries; ice cream stands or dairy bars

(G-10629)
DYNA-SEA GROUP INC
765 Carroll Pl (07666-3303)
PHONE....................................201 928-0133
Daniel Berlin, *President*
▲ EMP: 6
SALES (est): 852.9K **Privately Held**
WEB: www.dyna-disk.com
SIC: 2099 Food preparations

(G-10630)
EMBROIDERIES UNLIMITED INC
532 Wyndham Rd (07666-2612)
PHONE....................................201 692-1560
Bruce Prince, *President*
EMP: 7
SQ FT: 3,500
SALES: 950K **Privately Held**
SIC: 2395 Embroidery products, except
schiffli machine

(G-10631)
EVANS CHEMETICS LP (HQ)
Glenpointe Center West 4 (07666)
PHONE....................................201 992-3100
Jelle Westra, *CEO*
Detlaf Schmidt, *General Ptnr*
Dave Spano, *Manager*
Anthony Moschetti, *Officer*
▲ EMP: 6
SQ FT: 2,500
SALES: 29.7MM
SALES (corp-wide): 91MM **Privately Held**
WEB: www.evanschemetics.com
SIC: 2899 Acids

PA: Bruno Bock Chemische Fabrik Gmbh &
Co. Kg
Eichholzer Str. 23
Marschacht 21436
417 690-980

(G-10632)
**GENESIS MARKETING GROUP
INC**
269 Edgemont Ter (07666-3405)
PHONE..................................201 836-1392
William Straus, *President*
EMP: 5
SQ FT: 1,800
SALES (est): 450K **Privately Held**
WEB: www.genesismkting.com
SIC: 3993 5199 8742 Signs & advertising
specialties; advertising specialties; incen-
tive or award program consultant

(G-10633)
**GREENER CORNERS LTD LBLTY
CO**
1178 W Laurelton Pkwy (07666-2749)
PHONE..................................201 638-2218
Aaron Klein, *Principal*
EMP: 5 EST: 2009
SALES (est): 376.9K **Privately Held**
SIC: 2833 Botanical products, medicinal:
ground, graded or milled

(G-10634)
H LAUZON FURNITURE CO INC
1098 Decatur Ave (07666-5709)
PHONE..................................201 837-7598
Francis Lauzon, *President*
Kenneth V Lauzon, *Corp Secy*
EMP: 12 EST: 1935
SQ FT: 12,500
SALES: 500K **Privately Held**
SIC: 2512 7641 5712 Chairs: upholstered
on wood frames; couches, sofas & daven-
ports: upholstered on wood frames; living
room furniture: upholstered on wood
frames; reupholstery; furniture stores

(G-10635)
JA HEILFERTY LLC
Also Called: Primepak Company
133 Cedar Ln (07666-4416)
PHONE..................................201 836-5060
John Verrier, *Partner*
William G Poppe Jr, *Principal*
William Poppe Jr, *Principal*
Christopher J Poppe, *COO*
Sue Clemente, *Sales Associate*
EMP: 31
SQ FT: 2,000
SALES: 36MM **Privately Held**
WEB: www.primepakcompany.com
SIC: 5162 3081 Plastics products; plastics
film; unsupported plastics film & sheet

(G-10636)
**LA MART MANUFACTURING
CORP**
Also Called: Lamart Manufacturing Co
1465 Palisade Ave (07666-3624)
PHONE..................................718 384-6917
Louis Spitzer, *President*
▲ **EMP:** 8 EST: 1989
SQ FT: 3,000
SALES (est): 1.5MM **Privately Held**
WEB: www.coverus.com
SIC: 3083 Plastic finished products, lami-
nated

(G-10637)
LEEWARD INTERNATIONAL INC
400 Frank W Burr Blvd # 68 (07666-6841)
PHONE..................................201 836-8830
Byungkuk Lee, *Ch of Bd*
◆ **EMP:** 11
SQ FT: 5,100
SALES (est): 7.5MM **Privately Held**
WEB: www.leewardinc.com
SIC: 5137 2339 2329 2369 Sportswear,
women's & children's; nightwear:
women's, children's & infants'; sports-
wear, women's; men's & boys' sportswear
& athletic clothing; bathing suits &
swimwear: girls', children's & infants'

(G-10638)
**LUST FOR LIFE FOOTWEAR
LLC (PA)**
1086 Teaneck Rd Ste 3d (07666-4858)
PHONE..................................646 732-9742
Steven Berend,
David Berend,
Karen Berend,
▲ **EMP:** 10
SQ FT: 2,500
SALES (est): 2.4MM **Privately Held**
SIC: 3021 5139 Protective footwear, rub-
ber or plastic; footwear

(G-10639)
MAJESTIC SIGNS LLC
951 Teaneck Rd (07666-4519)
PHONE..................................201 837-8104
Robert Hamburg, *Mng Member*
EMP: 4
SALES (est): 440.2K **Privately Held**
SIC: 3993 Signs & advertising specialties

(G-10640)
NIPPON PAINT (USA) INC (HQ)
Also Called: Nippon Paint America
400 Frank W Burr Blvd # 10 (07666-6726)
PHONE..................................201 692-1111
Hiroaki Ueno, *CEO*
Hidefumi Morita, *President*
Joan P Daniels, *CFO*
Joan Daniels, *VP Human Res*
▲ **EMP:** 10
SALES (est): 202.7MM **Privately Held**
SIC: 2851 Paints & allied products

(G-10641)
NITTO INC
400 Frank W Burr Blvd # 66 (07666-6841)
PHONE..................................201 645-4950
Keiko Iwabuchi, *Manager*
EMP: 16 **Privately Held**
SIC: 2672 3589 5162 5065 Tape, pressure sensitive: made from purchased materials; water treatment equipment,
industrial; plastics products; electronic
parts
HQ: Nitto, Inc.
1990 Rutgers Blvd
Lakewood NJ 08701
732 901-7905

(G-10642)
OCTAL CORPORATION
125 Galway Pl Ste B (07666-3633)
PHONE..................................201 862-1010
Dani Bar David, *President*
Zvi Davidzon, *Opers Staff*
Tony Dimitrov, *Engineer*
Danielle Mir, *Manager*
▲ **EMP:** 24
SQ FT: 1,500
SALES (est): 5.6MM **Privately Held**
WEB: www.octalcorporation.com
SIC: 3824 Mechanical & electromechanical
counters & devices

(G-10643)
**PHIBRO ANIMAL HEALTH CORP
(HQ)**
300 Frank W Burr Blvd (07666-6704)
PHONE..................................201 329-7300
Jack C Bendheim, *Ch of Bd*
Larry L Miller, *COO*
Daniel M Bendheim, *Exec VP*
Thomas G Dagger, *Senior VP*
Dean Warras, *Senior VP*
◆ **EMP:** 90 EST: 1946
SALES: 819.9MM **Publicly Held**
WEB: www.pahc.com
SIC: 2834 Veterinary pharmaceutical
preparations
PA: Bfi Co., Llc
300 Frank W Burr Blvd # 21
Teaneck NJ 07666
201 329-7300

(G-10644)
**PHIBRO ANMAL HLTH
HOLDINGS INC (DH)**
300 Frank W Burr Blvd (07666-6704)
PHONE..................................201 329-7300
Larry Miller, *President*
EMP: 5

SALES (est): 3MM
SALES (corp-wide): 819.9MM **Publicly
Held**
SIC: 2047 5191 Dog & cat food; animal
feeds
HQ: Phibro Animal Health Corporation
300 Frank W Burr Blvd
Teaneck NJ 07666
201 329-7300

(G-10645)
PHIBRO-TECH INC (DH)
Also Called: Phibro Animal Health Holdings
300 Frank W Burr Blvd # 21 (07666-6712)
PHONE..................................201 329-7300
Jack C Bendheim, *Ch of Bd*
W Dwight Glover, *President*
Gerald Carlson, *COO*
Daniel Welch, *Senior VP*
Don Lewis, *Vice Pres*
▲ **EMP:** 25
SQ FT: 23,000
SALES (est): 56MM
SALES (corp-wide): 819.9MM **Publicly
Held**
WEB: www.phibrochem.com
SIC: 4953 2819 Chemical detoxification;
nickel compounds or salts, inorganic
HQ: C P Chemicals, Inc.
65 Challenger Rd
Ridgefield Park NJ
201 329-7300

(G-10646)
PHIBROCHEM INC
300 Frank W Burr Blvd # 21 (07666-6704)
PHONE..................................201 329-7300
Jack Bendheim, *President*
Gerald Carlson, *COO*
Mark Chamberlin, *Vice Pres*
David Storbeck, *Vice Pres*
Daniel Welch, *Vice Pres*
▲ **EMP:** 5
SALES (est): 216.1K
SALES (corp-wide): 819.9MM **Publicly
Held**
SIC: 2819 Industrial inorganic chemicals
HQ: Phibro Animal Health Corporation
300 Frank W Burr Blvd
Teaneck NJ 07666
201 329-7300

(G-10647)
**PRIME TIME INTERNATIONAL
CO (PA)**
Also Called: Ptic
500 Frank W Burr Blvd # 24 (07666-6802)
PHONE..................................623 780-8600
John T Wertheim, *CEO*
James L Emery, *President*
James Emery, *President*
Bennet Lee Welchons, *Vice Pres*
Guillermo Nevarez, *Controller*
▲ **EMP:** 5
SALES (est): 19.5MM **Privately Held**
WEB: www.singlestick.com
SIC: 2121 Cigars

(G-10648)
**PRINCE AGRI PRODUCTS INC
(DH)**
300 Frank W Burr Blvd (07666-6704)
PHONE..................................201 329-7300
Jack Bendheim, *Ch of Bd*
Dean J Warras, *Division Pres*
Daniel Welch, *Senior VP*
Clayton Lamkin, *Vice Pres*
Richard Johnson, *CFO*
◆ **EMP:** 100
SALES (est): 86.3MM
SALES (corp-wide): 819.9MM **Publicly
Held**
WEB: www.princeagri.com
SIC: 2048 Feed supplements
HQ: Phibro Animal Health Corporation
300 Frank W Burr Blvd
Teaneck NJ 07666
201 329-7300

(G-10649)
RSD AMERICA INC
Also Called: Roger Software Distribution
300 Frank W Burr Blvd # 54 (07666-6713)
PHONE..................................201 996-1000
Pierre Van Beneden, *President*
Louis Pierre Roger, *Vice Pres*

Rich Carlo, *Engineer*
Mark Wurtzbacher, *Engineer*
Serge Quiniou, *Treasurer*
EMP: 18
SQ FT: 7,000
SALES: 5MM **Privately Held**
WEB: www.rsd-intl.com
SIC: 5045 7372 7379 Computer software;
prepackaged software; computer related
consulting services

(G-10650)
**SAMSUNG OPT-LCTRONICS
AMER INC**
Also Called: Hanwha Techwin America
500 Frank W Burr Blvd # 43 (07666-6804)
PHONE..................................201 325-2612
Ki Chul Kim, *President*
Lloyd Taylor, *Regl Sales Mgr*
◆ **EMP:** 150
SQ FT: 8,610
SALES: 188.5MM **Privately Held**
WEB: www.samsungcamerausa.com
SIC: 5043 7699 3861 Photographic cam-
eras, projectors, photographic supplies;
photographic & optical goods equipment
repair services; photographic instruments,
electronic
PA: Hanwha Aerospace Co., Ltd.
1204 Changwon-Daero, Seongsan-Gu
Changwon 51542

(G-10651)
SCJ GROUP LLC
492 Cedar Ln Ste 102c (07666-1713)
PHONE..................................201 289-5841
Sam Roney, *Mng Member*
EMP: 4
SALES (est): 330K **Privately Held**
SIC: 3651 Audio electronic systems

(G-10652)
SMARTEKG LLC
287 Rutland Ave (07666-2843)
PHONE..................................201 376-4556
Benjamin Strauss,
Lawrence Baruch,
Eric Forkosh,
Kalman Katlowitz,
EMP: 4
SALES (est): 235.6K **Privately Held**
SIC: 3841 Diagnostic apparatus, medical

(G-10653)
TROPHY KING INC
309 Queen Anne Rd (07666-3242)
PHONE..................................201 836-1482
James Walsh, *President*
Lorraine Walsh, *Treasurer*
EMP: 6
SALES: 525K **Privately Held**
WEB: www.trophyking.com
SIC: 3914 5999 5947 Trophies; trophies
& plaques; gift shop

(G-10654)
**VACUUM SOLUTIONS GROUP
INC**
555 Cedar Ln Ste 1 (07666-1743)
P.O. Box 2136 (07666-1536)
PHONE..................................781 762-0414
Robert Flynn, *President*
Lawrence Gilbert, *Treasurer*
EMP: 3
SQ FT: 200
SALES: 7MM **Privately Held**
WEB: www.vacuumsolutions.com
SIC: 3565 Vacuum packaging machinery

(G-10655)
**WORLDWIDE PT SL LTD LBLTY
CO**
Also Called: International Point of Sale
555 Cedar Ln Ste 7 (07666-1743)
PHONE..................................201 928-0222
Ed Levin,
EMP: 11
SALES (est): 1.3MM **Privately Held**
SIC: 3578 7371 Accounting machines &
cash registers; computer software devel-
opment & applications

▲ = Import ▼=Export
◆ =Import/Export

(G-10656)
WORLDWIDE SAFETY SYSTEMS LLC
Also Called: Durabak Depot
1297 Sussex Rd (07666-2805)
PHONE...............................888 613-4501
Aliza P Strauss,
Jacob Y Strauss,
EMP: 4
SALES (est): 814.7K Privately Held
SIC: 5169 2851 5198 2899 Polyurethane products; polyurethane coatings; paints, varnishes & supplies; chemical preparations

(G-10657)
ZESTOS FOODS LLC
1297 Sussex Rd (07666-2805)
PHONE...............................888 407-5852
AVI Aviner, CEO
Jacob Strauss, President
EMP: 4
SALES: 200K Privately Held
SIC: 5141 5145 5149 2096 Groceries, general line; snack foods; health foods; dried or canned foods; potato chips & similar snacks;

Tenafly
Bergen County

(G-10658)
ALL AMERICAN METAL FABRICATORS
34 Harold St (07670-1820)
PHONE...............................201 567-2898
Robert Leopold, President
EMP: 6
SQ FT: 2,500
SALES: 650K Privately Held
SIC: 3446 1799 3441 Stairs, staircases, stair treads: prefabricated metal; welding on site; fabricated structural metal

(G-10659)
ALPEX WHEEL CO INC (PA)
29 Atwood Ave (07670-1011)
P.O. Box 280 (07670-0280)
PHONE...............................201 871-1700
Richard S Baum, President
Charles Jonathan, Vice Pres
Barbara Baum, Treasurer
Jonathan Baum, VP Sales
Dave Angell, Regl Sales Mgr
▲ EMP: 16
SQ FT: 14,000
SALES (est): 3.7MM Privately Held
WEB: www.alpexwheel.com
SIC: 3291 3545 Wheels, abrasive; machine tool accessories

(G-10660)
BITWINE INC
4 Thatcher Rd (07670-3030)
PHONE...............................888 866-9435
Alon Cohen, Principal
EMP: 14
SALES (est): 902.4K Privately Held
SIC: 2741

(G-10661)
CHIC BEBE INC
53 Howard Park Dr (07670-2936)
PHONE...............................201 941-5414
Caren Karpik, President
EMP: 8
SQ FT: 1,600
SALES: 500K Privately Held
WEB: www.bebechic.com
SIC: 2392 2211 2221 Blankets, comforters & beddings; sheets, bedding & table cloths: cotton; bedding, manmade or silk fabric

(G-10662)
EXCITE VIEW LLC
4 Thatcher Rd Ste 2001 (07670-3030)
PHONE...............................201 227-7075
Alon Cohen,
Rafi Maslaton,
EMP: 50

SALES (est): 4.7MM Privately Held
SIC: 3651 Home entertainment equipment, electronic

(G-10663)
LES TOUT PETITE INC
24 W Railroad Ave (07670-1735)
PHONE...............................201 941-8675
Lois Letzt, President
Daniel Letzt, Vice Pres
EMP: 9
SALES (est): 1.3MM Privately Held
SIC: 2369 2339 Girls' & children's outerwear; sportswear, women's

(G-10664)
MATHEMATICS LEAGUE INC
Also Called: Math League Press
17 Lancaster Rd (07670-2307)
PHONE...............................201 568-6328
Daniel R Flegler, President
Steven R Conrad, Vice Pres
EMP: 4
SALES: 800K Privately Held
SIC: 2731 Book publishing

(G-10665)
PROGRAMATIC PLATERS INC
32 Laurel Ave (07670-2128)
PHONE...............................718 721-4330
Arnold Abbey, President
EMP: 12
SQ FT: 15,000
SALES (est): 1MM Privately Held
SIC: 3471 Plating of metals or formed products; electroplating of metals or formed products

(G-10666)
TIN CAN LIDS LLC
48 Lylewood Dr (07670-1909)
PHONE...............................201 503-0677
Nissim Gershon, Owner
EMP: 6
SALES (est): 260.7K Privately Held
SIC: 3411 Tin cans

(G-10667)
V AND S WOODWORKS INC
105 Piermont Rd (07670-1023)
PHONE...............................201 568-0659
Vincent Scroufari, President
Richard Vallejo, Vice Pres
EMP: 4
SQ FT: 2,500
SALES: 150K Privately Held
SIC: 2511 Wood household furniture

Tennent
Monmouth County

(G-10668)
REED & PERRINE INC
396 Main St (07763)
P.O. Box 100 (07763-0100)
PHONE...............................732 446-6363
Virginia Bulkowski, CEO
Ginny Bulkowski, President
Bob Bulkowski, Vice Pres
Robert Bulkowski, Vice Pres
▼ EMP: 23 EST: 1983
SQ FT: 100,000
SALES (est): 5.7MM Privately Held
SIC: 2873 2875 Fertilizers: natural (organic), except compost; fertilizers, mixing only

(G-10669)
REED & PERRINE SALES INC
396 Main St (07763)
PHONE...............................732 446-6363
Virginia Bulkowski, CEO
Ginny Bulkowski, President
Tammy Smith, Principal
Bob Bulkowski, Vice Pres
Keith Haines, Marketing Staff
EMP: 24 EST: 1983
SQ FT: 100,000
SALES: 18.7MM Privately Held
SIC: 2873 Fertilizers: natural (organic), except compost

Teterboro
Bergen County

(G-10670)
ADEMCO INC
Also Called: ADI Global Distribution
100 Hollister Rd (07608-1148)
PHONE...............................201 462-9570
Chris Mack, Manager
EMP: 10
SALES (corp-wide): 4.8B Publicly Held
WEB: www.adilink.com
SIC: 5063 3669 3822 Electrical apparatus & equipment; emergency alarms; auto controls regulating residntl & coml environt & applncs
HQ: Ademco Inc.
1985 Douglas Dr N
Golden Valley MN 55422
800 468-1502

(G-10671)
E & T PLASTIC MFG CO INC
200 Green St (07608-1208)
PHONE...............................201 596-5017
Ron Chiosse, Manager
EMP: 40
SALES (corp-wide): 75MM Privately Held
SIC: 3089 Extruded finished plastic products
PA: E & T Plastic Manufacturing Co., Inc.
4545 37th St
Long Island City NY 11101
718 729-6226

(G-10672)
E WORTMANN MACHINE WORKS INC
50 Hollister Rd (07608-1117)
PHONE...............................201 288-1654
Raymond Rogers, President
George Rogers Sr, Principal
EMP: 14 EST: 1937
SQ FT: 20,000
SALES (est): 2.8MM Privately Held
SIC: 3561 Pumps & pumping equipment

(G-10673)
EBIN NEW YORK INC
506 Us Highway 46 (07608-1104)
PHONE...............................201 288-8887
Joon Park, Principal
▲ EMP: 20 EST: 2014
SALES: 4.6MM Privately Held
SIC: 2844 Toilet preparations

(G-10674)
FOOD & BEVERAGE INC
Also Called: Chris's Cookies
100 Hollister Rd Unit C-1 (07608-1148)
PHONE...............................201 288-8881
Manish Wadia, CEO
Betty Osmanoglu, Exec VP
Christian Gargiulo, Vice Pres
EMP: 100
SQ FT: 40,000
SALES: 12MM Privately Held
WEB: www.chriscookies.com
SIC: 2052 5149 Cookies; crackers, cookies & bakery products

(G-10675)
FOOD INGREDIENT SOLUTIONS LLC (PA)
10 Malcolm Ave Ste 1 (07608-1054)
PHONE...............................201 440-4377
Jeff Greaves, President
Helen Greaves, Vice Pres
Sandeep Kulshrestha, Project Mgr
Marc Guistino, Facilities Mgr
Michele Lake, QC Mgr
▲ EMP: 9
SQ FT: 9,200
SALES (est): 7.6MM Privately Held
SIC: 2099 Food preparations

(G-10676)
FREESTREAM AIRCRAFT USA LTD
200 Fred Wehran Dr Ste 1 (07608-1107)
PHONE...............................201 365-6080

Rebecca P Cilli, President
Connie Marrero, Exec VP
Lucy Barkwell, Vice Pres
Jeremy Stumpf, Vice Pres
Kevin Crowe, CFO
EMP: 10
SALES (est): 128.1K Privately Held
SIC: 3721 Motorized aircraft

(G-10677)
FUTURE IMAGE SIGN & AWNING
Also Called: Future Image Signs
270 North St (07608-1214)
PHONE...............................201 440-1400
Peter Yang, Owner
EMP: 8
SALES (est): 811.6K Privately Held
SIC: 3993 Signs & advertising specialties

(G-10678)
GALVES AUTO PRICE LIST INC
430 Industrial Ave Ste 3 (07608-1046)
PHONE...............................201 393-0051
Paul Younger, President
Paul RAD, Sls & Mktg Exec
Sharon Masi, Manager
Daniel Ware, Manager
Brian Strada, Executive
EMP: 12 EST: 1957
SQ FT: 10,000
SALES (est): 1.5MM Privately Held
WEB: www.galves.com
SIC: 2731 2741 Books: publishing only; miscellaneous publishing

(G-10679)
GOTHAM INK OF NEW ENGLAND INC (HQ)
100 North St (07608-1202)
PHONE...............................201 478-5600
Jeffrey Simons, CEO
Harvey R Brice, President
EMP: 9
SQ FT: 50,000
SALES (est): 1.1MM
SALES (corp-wide): 137.8MM Privately Held
SIC: 2893 Gravure ink
PA: Superior Printing Ink Co Inc
100 North St
Teterboro NJ 07608
201 478-5600

(G-10680)
INTERFASHION COSMETICS CORP
32 Henry St (07608-1102)
PHONE...............................201 288-5858
James Chang, President
Wendy Chang, Vice Pres
▲ EMP: 50
SALES (est): 9.8MM Privately Held
WEB: www.ifcosmetics.com
SIC: 2844 Cosmetic preparations

(G-10681)
JET AVIATION ST LOUIS INC
Also Called: Jet Aviation Aircraft Maint
113 Chrles A Lindbergh Dr (07608-1009)
PHONE...............................201 462-4026
Michele Mizeski, President
Gary Dolski, Vice Pres
Robert Rodriguez, Opers Staff
Jennifer Gross, Buyer
Joe Sousan, Electrical Engi
EMP: 22
SALES (corp-wide): 36.1B Publicly Held
SIC: 4581 5172 3721 5088 Aircraft maintenance & repair services; petroleum products; aircraft; transportation equipment & supplies
HQ: Jet Aviation St. Louis, Inc.
6400 Curtiss Steinberg Dr
Cahokia IL 62206
618 646-8000

(G-10682)
JOHN S SWIFT COMPANY INC
375 North St Ste N (07608-1200)
PHONE...............................201 935-2002
Douglas Wilhelmy, Vice Pres
Rick Frydrych, Purch Agent
EMP: 6

GEOGRAPHIC

SALES (corp-wide): 15.7MM **Privately Held**
WEB: www.jssco.com
SIC: **2752** 2791 2789 Commercial printing, offset; typesetting; bookbinding & related work
PA: John S Swift Company Incorporated
999 Commerce Ct
Buffalo Grove IL 60089
847 465-3300

(G-10683)
JOHN S SWIFT PRINT OF NJ INC
Also Called: John S Swift Co
375 North St Ste N (07608-1200)
PHONE....................................201 678-3232
John S Swift III, *President*
EMP: 5
SQ FT: 5,400
SALES: 1.5MM **Privately Held**
SIC: **2752** Commercial printing, offset

(G-10684)
JOLT COMPANY INC (PA)
Also Called: Wet Planet Beverages
100 Hollister Rd Unit 1 (07608-1139)
PHONE....................................201 288-0535
C J Rapp, *President*
Lowell Patric, *CFO*
▲ EMP: 31
SQ FT: 4,000
SALES (est): 4.6MM **Privately Held**
WEB: www.wetplanet.com
SIC: **2086** Carbonated beverages, nonalcoholic: bottled & canned

(G-10685)
KERRY INC
Also Called: Kerry Ingredients and Flavours
546 Us Highway 46 (07608-1104)
PHONE....................................201 373-1111
Steve Raphel, *Manager*
EMP: 65 **Privately Held**
WEB: www.kerryingredients.com
SIC: **2023** Dry, condensed, evaporated dairy products
HQ: Kerry Inc.
3400 Millington Rd
Beloit WI 53511
608 363-1200

(G-10686)
MASTERTASTE INC
Also Called: Flavor and Fragrance Division
546 Us Highway 46 (07608-1104)
PHONE....................................201 373-1111
Edmond Scanlon, *Branch Mgr*
EMP: 10 **Privately Held**
WEB: www.mastertaste.com
SIC: **2087** 2844 Extracts, flavoring; perfumes, natural or synthetic
HQ: Mastertaste Inc.
160 Terminal Ave
Clark NJ 07066
732 882-0202

(G-10687)
MICROFOLD INC
375 North St Ste C (07608-1200)
PHONE....................................201 641-5052
Paul Perna, *President*
EMP: 4 EST: 2011
SALES (est): 415.1K **Privately Held**
SIC: **3554** Folding machines, paper

(G-10688)
NORTHERN ARCHITECTURAL SYSTEMS (PA)
111 Central Ave (07608-1123)
PHONE....................................201 943-6400
Robert Pecorella, *President*
Bipin Patel, *Engineer*
Stacey Shubsda, *Office Mgr*
Jared Grodner, *Technical Staff*
▲ EMP: 68
SQ FT: 127,000
SALES (est): 24.7MM **Privately Held**
WEB: www.northernwindow.com
SIC: **3442** Window & door frames

(G-10689)
PANTINA COSMETICS INC
30 Henry St (07608-1102)
PHONE....................................201 288-7767
Morris Chang, *President*
◆ EMP: 25

SQ FT: 22,000
SALES (est): 3.6MM **Privately Held**
SIC: **2844** Cosmetic preparations

(G-10690)
ROYLE SYSTEMS GROUP LLC
375 North St Ste M (07608-1200)
PHONE....................................201 644-0345
Gregory J Ramsey, *CEO*
John C Ramsey, *Ch of Bd*
Peter Ramsey, *General Mgr*
Peter M Ramsey, *Senior VP*
James Carbone, *VP Opers*
▲ EMP: 20
SQ FT: 85,000
SALES (est): 3.7MM **Privately Held**
WEB: www.roylesystems.com
SIC: **3542** Machine tools, metal forming type

(G-10691)
SUPERIOR PRINTING INK CO INC (PA)
100 North St (07608-1202)
PHONE....................................201 478-5600
Jeffrey Simons, *President*
Harvey R Brice, *Managing Dir*
Chris Vignola, *District Mgr*
Richard Killian, *Vice Pres*
Meyer Mandel, *Vice Pres*
▲ EMP: 175 EST: 1918
SALES (est): 137.8MM **Privately Held**
SIC: **2851** 2893 Varnishes; gravure ink

(G-10692)
SYMRISE INC (HQ)
300 North St (07608-1204)
PHONE....................................201 288-3200
Achim Daub, *CEO*
Natalia Khashkovskaya, *Business Mgr*
Elena Sakulina, *Business Mgr*
Andrew Woodland, *Business Mgr*
Kari Arienti, *Vice Pres*
◆ EMP: 320 EST: 1994
SQ FT: 125
SALES (est): 380.8MM
SALES (corp-wide): 3.6B **Privately Held**
WEB: www.symriseinc.com
SIC: **2869** Perfume materials, synthetic; flavors or flavoring materials, synthetic
PA: Symrise Ag
Muhlenfeldstr. 1
Holzminden 37603
553 190-0

(G-10693)
TAKASAGO INTL CORP USA
Also Called: TAKASAGO INTERNATIONAL CORPORATION (U.S.A.)
100 Green St (07608-1207)
PHONE....................................201 727-4200
Frank Jones, *General Mgr*
Nancy Escalante, *Purch Agent*
Sherri Keller, *QA Dir*
Deborah Ferrone, *Manager*
Deborah Rech, *Manager*
EMP: 45 **Privately Held**
SIC: **3996** 2087 Hard surface floor coverings; flavoring extracts & syrups
HQ: Takasago International Corporation (U.S.A)
4 Volvo Dr
Rockleigh NJ 07647
201 767-9001

(G-10694)
TAPIA ACCESSORY GROUP INC
Also Called: Tag
370 North St (07608-1209)
PHONE....................................201 393-0028
George Tapia, *President*
EMP: 50
SALES (est): 4.4MM **Privately Held**
SIC: **3911** 3961 Jewelry, precious metal; costume jewelry

(G-10695)
TRANE PARTS CENTER OF NJ
375 North St Ste J (07608-1200)
PHONE....................................201 489-9001
Fred Pose, *President*
Wally Macko, *General Mgr*
EMP: 5
SALES (est): 563.4K **Privately Held**
SIC: **3585** Refrigeration & heating equipment

(G-10696)
TRANSCORE LP
25 Central Ave (07608-1154)
PHONE....................................201 329-9200
George Sheppard, *Branch Mgr*
EMP: 13
SALES (corp-wide): 5.1B **Publicly Held**
WEB: www.transcore.com
SIC: **7373** 7622 3661 5065 Computer integrated systems design; communication equipment repair; toll switching equipment, telephone; communication equipment
HQ: Transcore, Lp
150 4th Ave N Ste 1200
Nashville TN 37219
615 988-8962

(G-10697)
TRUCKPRO LLC
Also Called: Truckpro 192
150 Central Ave (07608-1116)
PHONE....................................201 229-0599
Rich Poskorka, *Branch Mgr*
EMP: 20
SALES (corp-wide): 1.2B **Privately Held**
WEB: www.lightruck.com
SIC: **3714** Transmissions, motor vehicle
HQ: Truckpro, Llc
1900 Charles Bryan Rd
Cordova TN 38016
901 252-4200

Thorofare
Gloucester County

(G-10698)
ACCU-COTE INC
Also Called: Automatic Plating-Accu-Cote
3410 Jessup Rd (08086)
PHONE....................................856 845-7323
Ralph Dreyfuss, *President*
Paul Sanborn, *Vice Pres*
Edith Dreyfuss, *Treasurer*
Earl Curran, *VP Sales*
Anita Jones, *Technology*
EMP: 9 EST: 1976
SQ FT: 15,750
SALES (est): 701K **Privately Held**
SIC: **3471** Electroplating of metals or formed products

(G-10699)
GEISLERS LIQUOR STORE
195 Crown Point Rd (08086)
P.O. Box 146 (08086-0146)
PHONE....................................856 845-0482
Grace Geisler, *Owner*
EMP: 14
SQ FT: 2,500
SALES (est): 1.6MM **Privately Held**
SIC: **2082** 5921 7299 Ale (alcoholic beverage); liquor stores; beer (packaged); wine;

(G-10700)
GGB LLC (HQ)
1451 Metropolitan (08086)
P.O. Box 189 (08086-0189)
PHONE....................................856 848-3200
Susan Sweeney, *President*
Kenneth Walker, *General Mgr*
E Joseph Fults, *Vice Pres*
Linda O'Brien, *Production*
Andy Brown, *Sales Engr*
▲ EMP: 173
SQ FT: 120,000
SALES (est): 86.1MM
SALES (corp-wide): 1.5B **Publicly Held**
WEB: www.ggbearings.com
SIC: **3568** Bearings, bushings & blocks
PA: Enpro Industries, Inc.
5605 Carnegie Blvd # 500
Charlotte NC 28209
704 731-1500

(G-10701)
GGB LLC
Also Called: Ggb Bearing Technology
700 Mid Atlantic Pkwy (08086)
PHONE....................................856 848-3200
Karen Decker, *Cust Mgr*
Irma Fennal, *Sales Associate*

EMP: 13
SALES (corp-wide): 1.5B **Publicly Held**
SIC: **3568** Bearings, bushings & blocks
HQ: Ggb Llc
1451 Metropolitan
Thorofare NJ 08086
856 848-3200

(G-10702)
GGB LLC
Also Called: Ggb N.A.
1414 Metropolitan Ave (08086)
PHONE....................................856 686-2675
EMP: 6
SALES (corp-wide): 1.5B **Publicly Held**
SIC: **3568** Bearings, bushings & blocks
HQ: Ggb Llc
1451 Metropolitan
Thorofare NJ 08086
856 848-3200

(G-10703)
SLACK INCORPORATED
6900 Grove Rd (08086-9447)
PHONE....................................856 848-1000
Peter N Slack, *President*
Darrell Blood, *CFO*
EMP: 7
SALES (est): 2MM **Privately Held**
WEB: www.slackinc.com
SIC: **2741** Miscellaneous publishing
PA: The Wyanoke Group Inc
6900 Grove Rd
Thorofare NJ 08086

Three Bridges
Hunterdon County

(G-10704)
ENGINEERED COMPONENTS INC
546 Old York Rd (08887-2308)
P.O. Box 360 (08887-0360)
PHONE....................................908 788-8393
John M Liggett, *President*
Kevin McBrearty, *Vice Pres*
Tom Proctor, *Sales Mgr*
John Fiess, *Info Tech Mgr*
▲ EMP: 15 EST: 1977
SQ FT: 14,000
SALES (est): 4.5MM **Privately Held**
WEB: www.engrcomp.com
SIC: **5084** 3545 Industrial machine parts; machine tool attachments & accessories

Tinton Falls
Monmouth County

(G-10705)
ADIDAS NORTH AMERICA INC
Also Called: Adidas Outlet Store Tinton FLS
1 Premium Outlet Blvd (07753-7469)
PHONE....................................732 695-0085
EMP: 9
SALES (corp-wide): 25B **Privately Held**
SIC: **2329** Athletic (warmup, sweat & jogging) suits: men's & boys'; men's & boys' athletic uniforms; knickers, dress (separate): men's & boys'
HQ: Adidas North America, Inc.
3449 N Anchor St Ste 500
Portland OR 97217
971 234-2300

(G-10706)
C W GRIMMER & SONS INC
75 W Gilbert St (07701-4919)
PHONE....................................732 741-2189
William D Grimmer, *President*
Fulton W Hallowell III, *Vice Pres*
Arline Kinscherf, *Treasurer*
EMP: 10 EST: 1927
SQ FT: 10,000
SALES (est): 1.4MM **Privately Held**
SIC: **3446** 3441 Fire escapes, metal; railings, bannisters, guards, etc.: made from metal pipe; fabricated structural metal

(G-10707)
CLAYTON BLOCK COMPANY INC
100 Commerce Dr (07753)
PHONE..............................732 905-3234
Bill Grace, *Manager*
EMP: 13
SALES (corp-wide): 31.8MM **Privately Held**
WEB: www.claytononline.com
SIC: 3271 Blocks, concrete or cinder: standard
PA: Clayton Block Company, Inc.
1355 Campus Pkwy Ste 200
Wall Township NJ 07753
888 763-8665

(G-10708)
COMMVAULT AMERICAS INC
Also Called: Tinton Falls Systems
1 Commvault Way (07724-3096)
PHONE..............................888 746-3849
Robert Hammer, *President*
Miranda Lenning, *Senior Mgr*
Sam Grover, *Technology*
Miranda Foster, *Director*
Fred Lindstrom, *Director*
EMP: 6
SALES (est): 218K **Privately Held**
SIC: 7372 Prepackaged software

(G-10709)
COMMVAULT SYSTEMS INC (PA)
1 Commvault Way (07724-3096)
PHONE..............................732 870-4000
N Robert Hammer, *Ch of Bd*
Sanjay Mirchandani, *President*
Adam Bourke, *Partner*
Corey Wilensky, *Superintendent*
Jeremy Allen, *Principal*
EMP: 250
SALES: 710.9MM **Publicly Held**
WEB: www.commvault.com
SIC: 7373 7372 7376 Computer integrated systems design; prepackaged software; computer facilities management

(G-10710)
CURVON CORPORATION
34 Apple St (07724-2600)
PHONE..............................732 747-3832
Blake G Banta, *President*
▲ EMP: 20 EST: 1891
SQ FT: 16,350
SALES (est): 2.1MM **Privately Held**
WEB: www.curvon.com
SIC: 2399 Horse blankets

(G-10711)
DIGITAL OUTDOOR ADVG LLC
788 Shrewsbury Ave Ste 22 (07724-3080)
PHONE..............................732 616-2232
Christine Lanziano,
EMP: 7
SALES (est): 477.9K **Privately Held**
SIC: 3999 5199 7311 Advertising display products; advertising specialties; advertising consultant

(G-10712)
DIRECT DEVELOPMENT LLC
Also Called: Monitor Newspaper
97 Apple St 2 (07724-2637)
PHONE..............................732 739-8890
Clifford Moore, *Mng Member*
Lori Donnelly, *Creative Dir*
Shirley Stclair, *Executive Asst*
Erica Parker, *Graphic Designe*
Vinod Gopal,
EMP: 8
SALES (est): 250K **Privately Held**
SIC: 2711 Newspapers, publishing & printing

(G-10713)
EAST COAST PANELBOARD INC
Also Called: East Coast Power Systems
101 Tornillo Way (07712-7521)
PHONE..............................732 739-6400
Salvatore Rinaldi, *President*
Davina Stonack, *Project Mgr*
Peter Vallone, *Safety Mgr*
Mary Rinaldi, *Controller*
EMP: 40

SQ FT: 110,000
SALES (est): 22.2MM **Privately Held**
SIC: 5063 3699 Panelboards; electrical equipment & supplies

(G-10714)
EATON FILTRATION LLC
44 Apple St Ste 3 (07724-2672)
PHONE..............................732 767-4200
Craig Arnold, *COO*
Thomas S Gross, *COO*
Richard H Fearon, *CFO*
Alexander M Cutler,
Dwight Turner,
▲ EMP: 350
SALES (est): 51.9MM **Privately Held**
WEB: www.eaton.com
SIC: 3569 Filters & strainers, pipeline
HQ: Eaton Corporation
1000 Eaton Blvd
Cleveland OH 44122
440 523-5000

(G-10715)
EBSCO INDUSTRIES INC
30 Park Rd Ste 2 (07724-9794)
PHONE..............................201 569-2500
Alan Block, *Vice Pres*
EMP: 75
SALES (corp-wide): 2.8B **Privately Held**
WEB: www.ebscoind.com
SIC: 2741 Miscellaneous publishing
PA: Ebsco Industries, Inc.
5724 Highway 280 E
Birmingham AL 35242
205 991-6600

(G-10716)
ELITE STONE IMPORTERS LLC
45 Park Rd (07724-9716)
PHONE..............................732 542-7900
Courtney Larsen, *Sales Staff*
Chelsea Jorgensen, *Marketing Staff*
Michael Johnson, *Mng Member*
▲ EMP: 8
SALES (est): 1.2MM **Privately Held**
SIC: 3281 Cut stone & stone products

(G-10717)
FIS AVANTGARD LLC
106 Apple St Ste 110 (07724-2670)
PHONE..............................732 530-9303
Samuel Fensterstock, *Director*
EMP: 4
SALES (corp-wide): 8.4B **Publicly Held**
SIC: 7372 7378 7379 Business oriented computer software; computer maintenance & repair; computer related consulting services
HQ: Fis Avantgard Llc
680 E Swedesford Rd
Wayne PA 19087
484 582-2000

(G-10718)
HATTERAS PRESS INC
56 Park Rd (07724-9715)
PHONE..............................732 935-9800
Bill Duerr, *President*
Charles F Duerr, *Owner*
Vince Costanza, *COO*
Richard McKenna, *Senior VP*
Tom Ayala, *Vice Pres*
EMP: 260
SQ FT: 30,000
SALES (est): 93.2MM **Privately Held**
WEB: www.hatteraspress.com
SIC: 2752 2796 Commercial printing, offset; platemaking services

(G-10719)
HERMETIC SOLUTIONS GROUP INC (PA)
4000 State Route 66 # 310 (07753-7300)
PHONE..............................732 722-8780
Keith Barclay, *CEO*
EMP: 15
SQ FT: 3,000
SALES (est): 67.1MM **Privately Held**
SIC: 3679 Electronic circuits

(G-10720)
JSM CO
1052 Wayside Rd (07712-3146)
PHONE..............................732 695-9577
David J Paraskevas, *Owner*

EMP: 5
SQ FT: 3,000
SALES (est): 250K **Privately Held**
WEB: www.jerseyspeedskiffs.com
SIC: 3599 Machine & other job shop work; custom machinery

(G-10721)
KENNETH ASMAR CUSTOM INTERIORS
Also Called: Red Bank Cabinet
548 Shrewsbury Ave (07701-4907)
PHONE..............................732 544-6137
Kenneth Asmar, *President*
Christine Asmar, *Vice Pres*
EMP: 6 EST: 1994
SALES (est): 506K **Privately Held**
SIC: 2434 Wood kitchen cabinets

(G-10722)
LEVI STRAUSS & CO
1 Premium Outlet Blvd (07753-7469)
PHONE..............................732 493-4595
Stacy Blumenthal, *Branch Mgr*
EMP: 19
SALES (corp-wide): 5.5B **Publicly Held**
SIC: 2325 Jeans: men's, youths' & boys'
PA: Levi Strauss & Co.
1155 Battery St
San Francisco CA 94111
415 501-6000

(G-10723)
NIKE INC
1 Premium Outlet Blvd # 699 (07753-7479)
PHONE..............................732 695-0108
EMP: 38
SALES (corp-wide): 39.1B **Publicly Held**
SIC: 3021 Rubber & plastics footwear
PA: Nike, Inc.
1 Sw Bowerman Dr
Beaverton OR 97005
503 671-6453

(G-10724)
PAUSCH LLC
808 Shrewsbury Ave (07724-3002)
PHONE..............................732 747-6110
EMP: 4
SALES (est): 126.9K **Privately Held**
SIC: 3841 Diagnostic apparatus, medical

(G-10725)
RANGER INDUSTRIES INC (PA)
15 Park Rd (07724-9716)
PHONE..............................732 389-3535
Loretta Berry, *President*
Justin Russo, *General Mgr*
Deborah Distefano, *Credit Staff*
Patricia Behan, *Mktg Coord*
Alain Avrillon, *Marketing Staff*
▲ EMP: 40
SQ FT: 17,000
SALES (est): 10.1MM **Privately Held**
SIC: 3953 2893 Pads, inking & stamping; printing ink

(G-10726)
SCHELLMARK INC
Also Called: Schellmark Interactive
7 Thistledown St (07753-7589)
PHONE..............................732 345-7143
Bill Scheller, *President*
EMP: 5
SQ FT: 4,500
SALES: 500K **Privately Held**
WEB: www.comicgallery.com
SIC: 7311 2752 Advertising agencies; calendars, lithographed; cards, lithographed; post cards, picture: lithographed

(G-10727)
SENOR LOPEZ (PA)
15 Spring Ct (07724-3278)
PHONE..............................732 229-7622
Kim Lopez, *Partner*
Joseph Lopez, *Partner*
EMP: 1
SALES: 1.5MM **Privately Held**
WEB: www.senorlopez.com
SIC: 2329 Men's & boys' sportswear & athletic clothing

(G-10728)
STAVOLA ASPHALT COMPANY INC (PA)
Also Called: Stavola Paving Company
175 Drift Rd (07724-9701)
P.O. Box 482, Red Bank (07701-0482)
PHONE..............................732 542-2328
John Stavola, *President*
Joseph C Stavola, *Vice Pres*
Richard Stavola, *Vice Pres*
Joe Mahoney, *Manager*
James Stavola, *Admin Sec*
EMP: 22
SALES (est): 17.1MM **Privately Held**
SIC: 5033 2951 1611 Roofing & siding materials; asphalt paving mixtures & blocks; highway & street construction

(G-10729)
STAVOLA CONSTRUCTION MTLS INC (PA)
175 Drift Rd (07724-9701)
P.O. Box 482, Red Bank (07701-0482)
PHONE..............................732 542-2328
John Stavola, *President*
Frank Stavola Jr, *Vice Pres*
Joseph Stavola III, *Treasurer*
Dee Gill, *Sales Staff*
James Stavola Jr, *Admin Sec*
EMP: 49
SQ FT: 5,000
SALES (est): 9.3MM **Privately Held**
WEB: www.stavola.com
SIC: 3281 Stone, quarrying & processing of own stone products

(G-10730)
STAVOLA HOLDING CORPORATION
175 Drift Rd (07724-9701)
P.O. Box 482, Red Bank (07701-0482)
PHONE..............................732 542-2328
Joseph C Stavola III, *President*
John Stavola, *Principal*
Richard Stavola, *Vice Pres*
Joseph Stavola III, *Treasurer*
James Stavola Jr, *Admin Sec*
EMP: 250
SALES: 11.6MM **Privately Held**
SIC: 1611 2951 General contractor, highway & street construction; paving mixtures; paving blocks

(G-10731)
TDK-LAMBDA AMERICAS INC (DH)
Also Called: Tdk-Lmbda Amricas High Pwr Div
405 Essex Rd (07753-7701)
PHONE..............................732 922-9300
Frank Sweeney, *Ch of Bd*
Pascal Chauffson, *President*
Pascal Chausson, *Vice Pres*
David Norton, *Vice Pres*
Wayne Morrison, *Plant Mgr*
▲ EMP: 240
SQ FT: 90,250
SALES (est): 98.9MM **Privately Held**
WEB: www.lambda.com
SIC: 5065 3629 Electronic parts & equipment; power conversion units, a.c. to d.c.: static-electric

(G-10732)
TRF MUSIC INC
Also Called: Trf Production Music Libraries
106 Apple St Ste 302 (07724-2670)
PHONE..............................201 335-0005
Michael Nurko, *President*
Ann Marie Van Denheuvel, *Office Mgr*
EMP: 11
SQ FT: 3,000
SALES (est): 940K **Privately Held**
SIC: 2741 5736 Music, sheet: publishing only, not printed on site; musical instrument stores

(G-10733)
VANS INC
1 Premium Outlet Blvd # 815 (07753-7484)
PHONE..............................732 493-1516
Jeff Traub, *Branch Mgr*
EMP: 10
SALES (corp-wide): 13.8B **Publicly Held**
SIC: 3021 Canvas shoes, rubber soled

GEOGRAPHIC

HQ: Vans, Inc.
1588 S Coast Dr
Costa Mesa CA 92626
855 909-8267

(G-10734)
WEBB-MASON INC
628 Shrewsbury Ave Ste G　(07701-4912)
PHONE.............................732 747-6585
Kevin Brennan, *Manager*
EMP: 4
SALES (corp-wide): 113.5MM **Privately Held**
SIC: 2752 8742 8732 Business form & card printing, lithographic; marketing consulting services; market analysis or research
PA: Webb-Mason, Inc.
10830 Gilroy Rd
Hunt Valley MD 21031
410 785-1111

Titusville
Mercer County

(G-10735)
JANSSEN PHARMACEUTICALS INC (HQ)
1125 Trnton Harbourton Rd　(08560-1499)
P.O. Box 200　(08560-1002)
PHONE.............................609 730-2000
Jennifer Taubert, *President*
Laila Gagnon, *Engineer*
Lindsey Mault, *Sales Staff*
Laura Kessler, *Sr Project Mgr*
Linda Kapp, *Manager*
▲ EMP: 1100
SQ FT: 20,000
SALES (est): 601.4MM
SALES (corp-wide): 81.5B **Publicly Held**
WEB: www.janau.jnj.com
SIC: 2833 2834 Anesthetics, in bulk form; antihistamine preparations; astringents, medicinal
PA: Johnson & Johnson
1 Johnson And Johnson Plz
New Brunswick NJ 08933
732 524-0400

(G-10736)
TRAP ROCK INDUSTRIES INC
Rr 29　(08560)
P.O. Box 419, Kingston　(08528-0419)
PHONE.............................609 924-0300
Michael Stavola, *General Mgr*
EMP: 35
SALES (corp-wide): 131.7MM **Privately Held**
WEB: www.traprock.com
SIC: 1429 1442 Grits mining (crushed stone); gravel mining
PA: Trap Rock Industries, Inc.
460 River Rd
Kingston NJ 08528
609 924-0300

Toms River
Ocean County

(G-10737)
ABB LIGHTING INC
1501 Industrial Way　(08755-4955)
PHONE.............................866 222-8866
Guy Esposito, *President*
EMP: 4 EST: 2015
SQ FT: 12,000
SALES (est): 273.1K **Privately Held**
SIC: 3648 Public lighting fixtures

(G-10738)
ABOVE REST GLASS
2345 Route 9 Ste 31　(08755-0994)
PHONE.............................732 370-1616
William Mackay, *Owner*
EMP: 4
SALES (est): 170K **Privately Held**
SIC: 3231 1793 Products of purchased glass; glass & glazing work

(G-10739)
ADEMCO INC
Also Called: ADI Global Distribution
224 Route 37 E　(08753-5521)
PHONE.............................732 505-6688
EMP: 4
SALES (corp-wide): 4.8B **Publicly Held**
SIC: 5063 3669 3822 Electrical apparatus & equipment; emergency alarms; auto controls regulating residntl & coml environmt & applncs
HQ: Ademco Inc.
1985 Douglas Dr N
Golden Valley MN 55422
800 468-1502

(G-10740)
ALEX REAL LLC
Also Called: Superior Promotional Bags
1876 Lakewood Rd　(08755-1210)
PHONE.............................732 730-8770
Alexander Vorhand,
▲ EMP: 11 EST: 2007
SALES (est): 1.6MM **Privately Held**
SIC: 2759 5199 Screen printing; bags, textile

(G-10741)
ALL AMERICAN POWDERCOATING LLC
2002 Route 9　(08755-1644)
PHONE.............................732 349-7001
John Ciccone, *Principal*
EMP: 4
SALES (est): 342.8K **Privately Held**
SIC: 3479 Metal coating & allied service

(G-10742)
ALTANTIC PRINTING AND DESIGN
467 Lakehurst Rd　(08755-6342)
PHONE.............................732 557-9600
Jovi Flores, *President*
EMP: 17
SALES (est): 117K **Privately Held**
SIC: 2759 Commercial printing

(G-10743)
ANDREVIN INC
Also Called: Ideal Tile Company Toms River
792 Fischer Blvd　(08753-4667)
PHONE.............................732 270-2794
Vincent Elardo, *President*
Dianne Elardo, *Manager*
EMP: 8
SQ FT: 3,000
SALES (est): 745.7K **Privately Held**
SIC: 3253 Ceramic wall & floor tile

(G-10744)
ARTS WINDOWS INC
154537 W Unit 1 St 37　(08755)
PHONE.............................732 905-9595
Arthur Engel, *President*
Ronnie Engel, *Vice Pres*
EMP: 5
SQ FT: 12,000
SALES: 1MM **Privately Held**
WEB: www.artswindows.com
SIC: 2591 5719 5023 Window shade rollers & fittings; vertical blinds; vertical blinds

(G-10745)
AUTOSHRED LLC
1358 Hooper Ave　(08753-2882)
PHONE.............................732 244-0950
C Bruce Rush,
EMP: 4
SALES (est): 593.4K **Privately Held**
SIC: 3589 Shredders, industrial & commercial

(G-10746)
BAMBOO & RATTAN WORKS INC
1931 Silverton Rd　(08753-1414)
PHONE.............................732 255-4239
▲ EMP: 7 EST: 1880
SQ FT: 22,500
SALES (est): 1.6MM **Privately Held**
SIC: 5031 2541 3993 3496 Whol Lumber/Plywd/Millwk

(G-10747)
BANQUET SERVICES INTERNATIONAL
2214 Route 37 E Ste 1　(08753-6047)
PHONE.............................732 270-1188
Rosemarie Hansen, *President*
EMP: 5
SQ FT: 2,500
SALES (est): 411.5K **Privately Held**
SIC: 2731 Pamphlets: publishing only, not printed on site

(G-10748)
BARRY URNER PUBLICATIONS INC
1001 Corporate Cir　(08755-4815)
P.O. Box 389　(08754-0389)
PHONE.............................732 240-5330
Paul B Brown Jr, *President*
Brian W Quigley, *Controller*
Michael W O'Shaughnessy, *Admin Sec*
Michael O'Shaughnessy, *Admin Sec*
EMP: 63 EST: 1858
SQ FT: 16,000
SALES (est): 10.9MM **Privately Held**
WEB: www.urnerbarry.com
SIC: 2721 Trade journals: publishing & printing

(G-10749)
BASF CORPORATION
227 Oak Ridge Pkwy　(08755-4107)
P.O. Box 71　(08754-0071)
PHONE.............................848 221-2786
Ken Dupuis, *Manager*
EMP: 25
SALES (corp-wide): 71.7B **Privately Held**
WEB: www.cibasc.com
SIC: 2869 Industrial organic chemicals
HQ: Basf Corporation
100 Park Ave
Florham Park NJ 07932
973 245-6000

(G-10750)
BAY TREASURE SEAFOOD LLC
2002 Route 9 Unit 4　(08755-1214)
PHONE.............................732 240-3474
Jerry Centanni, *Mng Member*
EMP: 10
SALES: 3.5MM **Privately Held**
SIC: 2092 5146 Fresh or frozen packaged fish; seafoods

(G-10751)
BAYSIDE ORTHOPEDICS LLC
780 Route 37 W Ste 330　(08755-5064)
PHONE.............................732 691-4898
Erik S Larsen,
EMP: 8
SALES (est): 1MM **Privately Held**
SIC: 3842 Orthopedic appliances

(G-10752)
CICCONE INC
Also Called: Ciccone Brothers
2002 Route 9　(08755-1644)
PHONE.............................732 349-7071
Robyn Ciccone, *President*
John Ciccone, *Principal*
EMP: 6
SQ FT: 3,000
SALES: 500K **Privately Held**
SIC: 3446 Architectural metalwork

(G-10753)
CLAYTON BLOCK COMPANY INC
Also Called: Jersey Concrete
194 Chestnut St　(08753-5321)
P.O. Box 3015, Lakewood　(08701-9015)
PHONE.............................732 349-3700
Faith Skizewski, *Manager*
EMP: 18
SQ FT: 2,000
SALES (corp-wide): 31.8MM **Privately Held**
WEB: www.claytononline.com
SIC: 3273 3271 Ready-mixed concrete; concrete block & brick
PA: Clayton Block Company, Inc.
1355 Campus Pkwy Ste 200
Wall Township NJ 07753
888 763-8665

(G-10754)
COTTRELL GRAPHICS & ADVG SPC
2121 Route 9　(08755-1215)
PHONE.............................732 349-7430
David Cottrell, *President*
EMP: 7
SQ FT: 4,800
SALES (est): 453.7K **Privately Held**
SIC: 2752 Commercial printing, offset

(G-10755)
ENAILSUPPLY CORPORATION
Also Called: 911 Tatical Direct
2161 Whitesville Rd Ste C　(08755-1478)
PHONE.............................909 725-1698
Sudeep Arya, *President*
EMP: 6
SALES (est): 432.1K **Privately Held**
SIC: 2326 Work uniforms

(G-10756)
FERMAG TECHNOLOGIES INC
146 Village Rd　(08755-0904)
P.O. Box 1364, Edison　(08818-1364)
PHONE.............................732 985-7300
John Perkins, *President*
Peter Leddy, *Corp Secy*
▲ EMP: 8 EST: 1946
SQ FT: 30,000
SALES: 1.6MM **Privately Held**
WEB: www.fermagtechnologies.com
SIC: 3264 Ferrite & ferrite parts

(G-10757)
FIBER-SPAN INC
670 Commons Way　(08755-6431)
PHONE.............................908 253-9080
Hal Halpern, *CEO*
Henry Wojtunik, *President*
EMP: 40
SQ FT: 15,000
SALES (est): 10.5MM **Privately Held**
WEB: www.fiber-span.com
SIC: 3663 3661 Amplifiers, RF power & IF; fiber optics communications equipment

(G-10758)
FIRST NATIONAL SERVICING & DEV
102 Starc Rd　(08755-1329)
PHONE.............................732 341-5409
Bryan Grodzinski, *President*
EMP: 25
SQ FT: 6,000
SALES (est): 1.3MM **Privately Held**
SIC: 2834 5047 8071 Pharmaceutical preparations; medical & hospital equipment; medical laboratories

(G-10759)
FIX IT GUY
2562 Balfrey Dr　(08753-4607)
PHONE.............................732 278-9000
Al Pinerta, *Principal*
EMP: 4
SALES (est): 545K **Privately Held**
SIC: 3553 Cabinet makers' machinery

(G-10760)
FUEL MANAGEMENT SERVICES INC
13 Main Bayway　(08753-7019)
PHONE.............................732 929-1964
Mark Stellmach, *President*
Mary Kitchen, *Corp Secy*
EMP: 3
SALES (est): 1.5MM **Privately Held**
WEB: www.fuelmanagementservices.com
SIC: 5169 2899 Chemicals & allied products; chemical preparations

(G-10761)
GEORGE CIOCHER INC
1241 Birmingham Ave　(08757-1532)
PHONE.............................732 818-3495
George Ciocher, *President*
EMP: 7 EST: 1992
SALES (est): 671.4K **Privately Held**
SIC: 3446 1542 Architectural metalwork; religious building construction

▲ = Import ▼=Export
◆ =Import/Export

(G-10762)
GOOD AS GOLD JEWELERS INC
226 Route 37 W Ste 9 (08755-8047)
PHONE....................................732 286-1111
Robert Teufel, *President*
Todd Teufel, *Vice Pres*
EMP: 4
SQ FT: 980
SALES (est): 300K **Privately Held**
SIC: **5944** 7631 5932 3915 Jewelry, precious stones & precious metals; jewelry repair services; used merchandise stores; jewel cutting, drilling, polishing, recutting or setting

(G-10763)
HANSEN LITHOGRAPHY LTD
2214 Route 37 E Ste 1 (08753-6047)
PHONE....................................732 270-1188
Rose Hansen,
EMP: 5
SQ FT: 2,400
SALES (est): 325.4K **Privately Held**
SIC: **2752** Publication printing, lithographic

(G-10764)
HENRY DUDLEY
Also Called: Dudley Lab
1508 Wellington Ave (08757-1602)
PHONE....................................732 240-6895
Henry Dudley, *Owner*
EMP: 4 EST: 1970
SALES (est): 330K **Privately Held**
WEB: www.henrocks.com
SIC: **3559** Electronic component making machinery

(G-10765)
HEYCO MOLDED PRODUCTS INC (DH)
1800 Industrial Way (08755-4809)
P.O. Box 517 (08754-0517)
PHONE....................................732 286-4336
William H Jemison, *Ch of Bd*
William D Jemison, *President*
◆ EMP: 19
SALES (est): 10MM
SALES (corp-wide): 483.7MM **Privately Held**
SIC: **3089** 3469 3644 Injection molding of plastics; metal stampings; noncurrent-carrying wiring services

(G-10766)
HEYCO PRODUCTS CORP (DH)
1800 Industrial Way (08755-4809)
P.O. Box 517 (08754-0517)
PHONE....................................732 286-1800
Michael Jemison, *President*
Elliott Israel, *Corp Secy*
EMP: 6
SQ FT: 250,000
SALES: 17.3MM
SALES (corp-wide): 483.7MM **Privately Held**
SIC: **3351** 3679 Copper rolling & drawing; commutators, electronic
HQ: Penn Engineering & Manufacturing Corp.
5190 Old Easton Rd
Danboro PA 18916
215 766-8853

(G-10767)
HEYCO STAMPED PRODUCTS
1800 Industrial Way (08755-4809)
P.O. Box 517 (08754-0517)
PHONE....................................732 286-4336
Vincent L Fevola, *President*
Charles Lusk, *Treasurer*
EMP: 65
SQ FT: 40,000
SALES: 7MM
SALES (corp-wide): 483.7MM **Privately Held**
WEB: www.heyco.com
SIC: **3469** Stamping metal for the trade
HQ: Heyco Products Corp.
1800 Industrial Way
Toms River NJ 08755

(G-10768)
HUDSON VALLEY ENVIROMENTAL INC
Also Called: Hve
2063 Basswood Ct (08755-1391)
PHONE....................................732 967-0060
Frank Pasalano, *CEO*
Vincent Mastria, *Vice Pres*
EMP: 40 EST: 1995
SQ FT: 500
SALES: 7.6MM **Privately Held**
WEB: www.hvenvironmentalservices.com
SIC: **1389** 1795 1794 1629 Derrick building, repairing & dismantling; wrecking & demolition work; demolition, buildings & other structures; excavation work; timber removal

(G-10769)
IMWOTH LLC
Also Called: Autoshred
52 Hyers St Ste A-5 (08753-7465)
PHONE....................................732 244-0950
Peter Levitt,
EMP: 15
SQ FT: 2,500
SALES (est): 3.1MM **Privately Held**
SIC: **3559** Tire shredding machinery

(G-10770)
INSULITE INC
1890 Church Rd (08753-1499)
PHONE....................................732 255-1700
B Albert Horn, *President*
Shari Stein, *Finance Mgr*
EMP: 14 EST: 1960
SQ FT: 22,000
SALES: 1MM **Privately Held**
SIC: **3231** Insulating glass: made from purchased glass

(G-10771)
JERSEY COVER CORP
1746 Route 9 (08755-1208)
PHONE....................................732 286-6300
Kathleen Stern, *President*
EMP: 10
SQ FT: 5,000
SALES (est): 1.3MM **Privately Held**
SIC: **3949** Water sports equipment

(G-10772)
KITCHEN KING INC (PA)
1561 Route 9 Ste 9 (08755-3284)
PHONE....................................732 341-9660
Terry Barth, *President*
EMP: 19
SQ FT: 10,000
SALES (est): 1.4MM **Privately Held**
WEB: www.kitchenking.net
SIC: **2434** Wood kitchen cabinets

(G-10773)
KITCHENS BY FRANK INC
2345 Route 9 Ste 5 (08755-0966)
PHONE....................................732 364-1343
Frank Duelly, *President*
EMP: 5
SQ FT: 12,780
SALES: 1.5MM **Privately Held**
SIC: **2521** Cabinets, office: wood

(G-10774)
KUFALL PRINTING
4 Oak Ridge Pkwy (08755-8002)
PHONE....................................732 505-9847
Charles Kufall, *Partner*
Herbert Kufall, *Partner*
EMP: 6
SALES (est): 343.1K **Privately Held**
SIC: **2752** Commercial printing, offset; lithographing on metal

(G-10775)
LE-ED CONSTRUCTION INC
Also Called: Le-Ed Concrete & Supply Co
1609 Route 9 (08755-1205)
PHONE....................................732 341-4546
Edward Steitz, *President*
EMP: 20
SQ FT: 3,500
SALES (est): 8.5MM **Privately Held**
SIC: **5191** 3273 Farm supplies; ready-mixed concrete

(G-10776)
M E C TECHNOLOGIES INC
2200 Industrial Way S (08755-4945)
PHONE....................................732 505-0308
Richard Kulkaski, *President*
EMP: 48
SQ FT: 21,000
SALES (est): 7.2MM **Privately Held**
WEB: www.mectech.com
SIC: **3674** Semiconductor circuit networks

(G-10777)
MAX FLIGHT CORP
7 Executive Dr (08755-4947)
PHONE....................................732 281-2007
Frank McClintic, *President*
Lou Calao, *CFO*
EMP: 50
SQ FT: 30,000
SALES: 7MM **Privately Held**
WEB: www.maxflight.com
SIC: **3699** Flight simulators (training aids), electronic

(G-10778)
MECHANICAL COMPONENTS CORP
1 Executive Dr Unit B (08755-4947)
PHONE....................................732 938-3737
Ronald Fisher, *Vice Pres*
EMP: 4
SQ FT: 3,500
SALES: 320K **Privately Held**
SIC: **3469** Machine parts, stamped or pressed metal

(G-10779)
MULE ROAD PHARMACY
600 Mule Rd (08757-6460)
PHONE....................................732 244-3737
EMP: 8
SALES (est): 770.3K **Privately Held**
SIC: **2834** 5912 Pharmaceutical preparations; drug stores & proprietary stores

(G-10780)
MULTICOMM SOLUTIONS INC
1285 Rolls Ct (08755-1349)
PHONE....................................877 796-8480
Solomon Erenthal, *President*
EMP: 6
SALES (est): 943.6K **Privately Held**
SIC: **3699** Security control equipment & systems

(G-10781)
PAINTMASTER AUTO BODY
1920 Route 37 E Ste 1 (08753-8298)
P.O. Box 1608 (08754-1608)
PHONE....................................732 270-1700
Edward Jacobson, *President*
Ellen Jacobson, *Admin Sec*
EMP: 16
SQ FT: 37,500
SALES (est): 2.7MM **Privately Held**
SIC: **3714** Motor vehicle parts & accessories

(G-10782)
PENTACLE PUBLISHING CORP
Also Called: New Jersey 50 Plus
1830 Route 9 Ste 1 (08755-1487)
PHONE....................................732 240-3000
Patricia Jasin, *President*
EMP: 23
SQ FT: 2,800
SALES (est): 1.6MM **Privately Held**
SIC: **2721** 7929 Magazines: publishing only, not printed on site; entertainment service

(G-10783)
PHILIP PAPALIA
Also Called: CCA/Custom Change Aprons
21 Dugan Ln (08755-4025)
PHONE....................................732 349-5530
Philip Papalia, *Owner*
EMP: 15
SQ FT: 500
SALES (est): 880K **Privately Held**
SIC: **2339** 2389 2393 Aprons, except rubber or plastic: women's, misses', juniors'; men's miscellaneous accessories; bags & containers, except sleeping bags: textile

(G-10784)
PRESSTO GRAPHICS
109 Foxwood Ter (08755-7327)
P.O. Box 64 (08754-0064)
PHONE....................................732 286-9300
Bill Debernardis, *President*
EMP: 10
SALES (est): 908.3K **Privately Held**
WEB: www.presstographics.com
SIC: **2759** 2752 Commercial printing; commercial printing, lithographic

(G-10785)
PRIMAK PLUMBING & HEATING INC
904 Dorset Psge (08753-4019)
PHONE....................................732 270-6282
Michael Primak, *President*
EMP: 7
SALES (est): 1MM **Privately Held**
SIC: **3494** Plumbing & heating valves

(G-10786)
R V LIVOLSI INCORPORATED (PA)
Also Called: Triangle Reprocenter
20 E Water St (08753-7627)
PHONE....................................732 286-2200
Robert Livolsi, *President*
EMP: 7
SALES (est): 782.1K **Privately Held**
SIC: **2752** 7334 Commercial printing, offset; blueprinting service

(G-10787)
RAPID MANUFACTURING CO INC
25 Bay Point Dr (08753-2405)
PHONE....................................732 279-1252
Dante Cannella, *President*
Robert Gualtier, *Vice Pres*
Allen Cannella, *Treasurer*
EMP: 30 EST: 1955
SQ FT: 45,000
SALES (est): 3.8MM **Privately Held**
SIC: **3089** 3469 Injection molding of plastics; stamping metal for the trade

(G-10788)
S D L POWDER COATING INC
1591 Route 37 W Ste E4 (08755-4808)
PHONE....................................732 473-0800
Louis Russo, *Owner*
Louis Rossio, *Owner*
EMP: 5
SALES (est): 335.4K **Privately Held**
SIC: **3479** Coating of metals & formed products; painting, coating & hot dipping

(G-10789)
S L P ENGINEERING INC
Also Called: Slp Performance
1501 Industrial Way (08755-4955)
PHONE....................................732 240-3696
Edward Hamburger, *President*
EMP: 65
SALES (est): 11.1MM **Privately Held**
SIC: **3711** 8711 3714 Automobile assembly, including specialty automobiles; engineering services; motor vehicle parts & accessories

(G-10790)
SANTON INC
Also Called: Wasmund Bindery
128 Grand View Dr (08753-2018)
PHONE....................................201 444-9080
Anthony Prestifilippo, *President*
Lorraine Whalen, *Treasurer*
Sandra Prestifilippo, *Admin Sec*
EMP: 27
SQ FT: 8,000
SALES (est): 1.5MM **Privately Held**
WEB: www.wasmundbindery.com
SIC: **2789** 7434 Bookbinding & repairing: trade, edition, library, etc.; photocopying & duplicating services

(G-10791)
SHORE PRECISION MFG INC
1000 Industrial Way Ste D (08755-5057)
PHONE....................................732 914-0949
Wayne Cornwell, *President*
EMP: 10
SQ FT: 4,000

G E O G R A P H I C

SALES (est): 1MM **Privately Held**
SIC: 3599 Machine shop, jobbing & repair

(G-10792)
SHOWCASE PUBLICATIONS INC
Also Called: Auto Shopper
90 Irons St (08753-6534)
PHONE................................732 349-1134
Bob Draper, *President*
Donald F Hulucha, *Corp Secy*
Peggy Hickman, *Accounts Exec*
EMP: 80
SQ FT: 5,000
SALES (est): 10.4MM **Privately Held**
WEB: www.showpubs.org
SIC: 2721 Trade journals: publishing & printing

(G-10793)
SIGNATURE AUDIO VIDEO SYSTEMS
164 Kettle Creek Rd (08753-1858)
PHONE................................732 864-1039
Howard Cohen, *President*
Angela Marquini, *Vice Pres*
EMP: 4
SALES: 320K **Privately Held**
SIC: 3651 Household audio & video equipment

(G-10794)
SPECIALTY SYSTEMS INC (PA)
1451 Route 37 W Ste 1 (08755-4969)
PHONE................................732 341-1011
Emil Kaunitz, *President*
William Cabey, *Vice Pres*
Vincent Cervellieri, *Vice Pres*
George Galler, *Engineer*
Earl McDannell, *Engineer*
EMP: 36 **EST:** 1978
SQ FT: 9,000
SALES: 5.3MM **Privately Held**
WEB: www.specialtysystems.com
SIC: 7371 7379 7372 7373 Computer software development; computer related consulting services; prepackaged software; computer integrated systems design; engineering services

(G-10795)
STEEL RISER CORP
402 Marc Dr (08753-4228)
PHONE................................732 341-7031
Shawn Maguira, *President*
Charles Becella, *Vice Pres*
EMP: 5
SALES (est): 560K **Privately Held**
SIC: 3291 Grit, steel

(G-10796)
SUFFOLK COUNTY CONTRACTORS
Also Called: Suffolk Recycling
242 Dover Rd Unit 2 (08757-5157)
PHONE................................732 349-7726
William Major, *President*
Bill Clark, *Manager*
EMP: 30
SQ FT: 1,500
SALES (est): 3.9MM **Privately Held**
SIC: 1623 1611 3273 Sewer line construction; highway & street paving contractor; grading; ready-mixed concrete

(G-10797)
SUMMER SWEETS LLC
3071 Rt 35 N (08755)
PHONE................................732 240-9376
Beth Berruti, *Principal*
EMP: 5
SALES (est): 328.3K **Privately Held**
SIC: 2024 Ice cream & frozen desserts

(G-10798)
T L C SPECIALTIES INC
Also Called: TLC Signs & Banners
188 Walnut St (08753-5451)
PHONE................................732 244-4225
Timothy Snover, *President*
Cheryl Snover, *Vice Pres*
Snover Tim, *Production*
EMP: 18
SQ FT: 3,000

SALES (est): 2.1MM **Privately Held**
WEB: www.tlcsignandbanner.com
SIC: 5999 3993 Banners, flags, decals & posters; signs & advertising specialties

(G-10799)
TECHNIDYNE CORPORATION
2190 Route 9 Ste 9 (08755-0970)
PHONE................................732 363-1055
Frank Jehn, *President*
EMP: 8
SQ FT: 4,400
SALES (est): 700K **Privately Held**
WEB: www.technivet.com
SIC: 3596 7352 Scales & balances, except laboratory; medical equipment rental

(G-10800)
TRADEWINDS MARINE SERVICE
122 Eton Ct (08757-4447)
PHONE................................848 448-6888
Darrin Gordon, *Principal*
EMP: 8 **EST:** 2016
SALES (est): 362.1K **Privately Held**
SIC: 3732 Boat building & repairing

(G-10801)
UNIVERSAL INTERLOCK CORP
Also Called: Kitchenexpo
910 Hooper Ave (08753-8365)
PHONE................................732 818-8484
Brian Gordon, *President*
EMP: 4
SALES (est): 277K
SALES (corp-wide): 12.9MM **Privately Held**
WEB: www.gotokitchenexpo.com
SIC: 2599 5812 Cabinets, factory; eating places
PA: Universal Interlock Corporation
　950 New Durham Rd
　Edison NJ 08817
　732 650-9700

(G-10802)
WANASAVEALOTCOM LLC
524 Fielders Ln (08755-2146)
PHONE................................732 286-6956
Scott Gussin,
◆ **EMP:** 14
SQ FT: 15,000
SALES: 8.6MM **Privately Held**
WEB: www.wanasavealot.com
SIC: 5023 5064 3634 3639 Home furnishings; electrical appliances, television & radio; electric household cooking appliances; major kitchen appliances, except refrigerators & stoves

(G-10803)
WHE RESEARCH INC
Also Called: Atlantic Protective Pouches
1545 Route 37 W Ste 6 (08755-4985)
P.O. Box 1191 (08754-1191)
PHONE................................732 240-3871
Walter A Haine, *President*
Lorraine R Haine, *Vice Pres*
EMP: 5
SQ FT: 3,000
SALES (est): 340K **Privately Held**
WEB: www.wheresearch.com
SIC: 3089 Plastic processing

(G-10804)
WIZARD TECHNOLOGY INC
2165 Route 9 (08755-1215)
PHONE................................732 730-0800
Anthony Hesse, *President*
▼ **EMP:** 10
SALES (est): 880K **Privately Held**
SIC: 3552 Dyeing, drying & finishing machinery & equipment

(G-10805)
WOODSHOP INC
58 Flint Rd (08757-5117)
PHONE................................732 349-8006
Thomas Fantaccione, *President*
▲ **EMP:** 4
SQ FT: 2,500
SALES (est): 551.5K **Privately Held**
SIC: 2431 Millwork

(G-10806)
ZYCAL BIOCEUTICALS MFG LLC (PA)
5a Executive Dr (08755-4947)
PHONE................................888 779-9225
James J Scaffidi, *CEO*
EMP: 8 **EST:** 2013
SALES (est): 817K **Privately Held**
SIC: 3999 Barber & beauty shop equipment

Totowa
Passaic County

(G-10807)
ACCENT PRESS INC
132 Winifred Dr (07512-1144)
PHONE................................973 785-3127
Thomas Mostello, *President*
EMP: 5
SQ FT: 2,500
SALES (est): 460K **Privately Held**
SIC: 2752 Commercial printing, offset

(G-10808)
ADVANCED BIOTECH OVERSEAS LLC (PA)
Also Called: A B T
10 Taft Rd (07512-1006)
PHONE................................973 339-6242
Diana Robinson, *Accounts Exec*
Sid Arfa, *Manager*
James Mulligan, *Administration*
EMP: 5
SALES (est): 2.7MM **Privately Held**
SIC: 5149 8731 2869 Flavourings & fragrances; biotechnical research, commercial; perfumes, flavorings & food additives

(G-10809)
ALLIANCE DESIGN INC
Also Called: Alliance Design Group
434 Union Blvd (07512-2562)
PHONE................................973 904-9450
William Ng, *President*
Ej Davis, *VP Sales*
Dawn Dimartino, *Art Dir*
Susan Kluhspies, *Creative Dir*
Debra Faust, *Graphic Designe*
EMP: 12
SQ FT: 2,500
SALES (est): 1.3MM **Privately Held**
SIC: 7336 2759 Graphic arts & related design; commercial printing

(G-10810)
ALLOY STAINLESS PRODUCTS CO
611 Union Blvd (07512-2402)
PHONE................................973 256-1616
Annemarie Appleton, *President*
J Albert Dimauro, *President*
EMP: 100 **EST:** 1946
SQ FT: 14,000
SALES (est): 8.3MM
SALES (corp-wide): 15.9MM **Privately Held**
WEB: www.aspfitting.com
SIC: 3312 5051 Stainless steel; metals service centers & offices
PA: Knickerbocker Machine Shop Inc.
　611 Union Blvd
　Totowa NJ 07512
　973 256-1616

(G-10811)
AMERICAN TIRE DISTRIBUTORS
50 Us Highway 46 (07512-2302)
PHONE................................973 646-5600
William Berry, *President*
Debra Kokaj, *Manager*
EMP: 9
SALES (est): 1.1MM
SALES (corp-wide): 5B **Privately Held**
SIC: 5531 3011 Automotive tires; tires & inner tubes
HQ: American Tire Distributors Inc.
　12200 Herbert Wayne Ct # 150
　Huntersville NC 28078
　704 992-2000

(G-10812)
AMISH DAIRY PRODUCTS LLC
41 Vreeland Ave Ste 208 (07512-1120)
PHONE................................973 256-7676
Kenneth Tensen,
EMP: 7 **EST:** 1996
SALES (est): 816.7K **Privately Held**
SIC: 2023 Dietary supplements, dairy & non-dairy based

(G-10813)
APB-DYNASONICS INC
145 Shepherds Ln (07512-2130)
PHONE................................973 785-1101
Peter Patel, *President*
John Lee, *Managing Dir*
Charles Augustowski, *Principal*
Chuck Augustowski, *Vice Pres*
Taz Bhogal, *Engineer*
▲ **EMP:** 6
SQ FT: 25,000
SALES (est): 1.5MM **Privately Held**
WEB: www.apbdynasonics.com
SIC: 3651 Audio electronic systems

(G-10814)
ART OF NATURAL SOLUTION INC (PA)
45 Commerce Way Unit K (07512-1154)
PHONE................................973 812-0500
Alex Chang, *President*
EMP: 16
SALES: 500K **Privately Held**
SIC: 2844 Toilet preparations

(G-10815)
ART OF NATURAL SOLUTION INC
140 Commerce Way Unit A (07512-1158)
PHONE................................917 745-7894
Alex Chang, *Principal*
EMP: 48
SALES (corp-wide): 500K **Privately Held**
SIC: 2844 Toilet preparations
PA: The Art Of Natural Solution Inc
　45 Commerce Way Unit K
　Totowa NJ 07512
　973 812-0500

(G-10816)
ATLANTIC INERTIAL SYSTEMS INC
20f Commerce Way (07512-3111)
PHONE................................973 237-2713
Gerry Cordone, *Principal*
EMP: 315
SALES (corp-wide): 66.5B **Publicly Held**
WEB: www.condorpacific.com
SIC: 3812 Gyroscopes; navigational systems & instruments
HQ: Atlantic Inertial Systems Inc.
　250 Knotter Dr
　Cheshire CT 06410
　203 250-3500

(G-10817)
BAE SYSTEMS INFO & ELEC SYS
100 Campus Rd Ste 1 (07512-1212)
PHONE................................603 885-4321
Nissan Clark, *Engineer*
Richard Riley, *Engineer*
Dan Engheben, *Sr Software Eng*
Mitchell Sparrow, *Director*
EMP: 400
SALES (corp-wide): 21.6B **Privately Held**
WEB: www.iesi.na.baesystems.com
SIC: 3812 Search & navigation equipment
HQ: Bae Systems Information And Electronic Systems Integration Inc.
　65 Spit Brook Rd
　Nashua NH 03060
　603 885-4321

(G-10818)
BALLET MAKERS INC (PA)
Also Called: Capezio
1 Campus Rd (07512-1296)
PHONE................................973 595-9000
Lynn Shanahan, *CEO*
Donald Terlizzi, *Ch of Bd*
Anthony Giacoio, *Vice Ch Bd*
Nicholas Terlizzi Jr, *Vice Ch Bd*
Ann Kolenovic, *Regional Mgr*
◆ **EMP:** 1

▲ = Import ▼=Export
◆ =Import/Export

SQ FT: 80,000
SALES (est): 63.5MM **Privately Held**
SIC: 5661 3149 2389 5137 Shoe stores; ballet slippers; theatrical costumes; women's & children's sportswear & swimsuits; footwear, athletic; dancewear

(G-10819)
BEZERRA CORPORATION
232 Union Blvd (07512-2670)
PHONE.................................973 595-7775
Wilson Bezerra, *CEO*
Silvana A Bezerra, *President*
EMP: 6
SALES (est): 429.1K **Privately Held**
SIC: 3751 Motorcycles, bicycles & parts

(G-10820)
BIMBO BAKERIES USA INC
930 Riverview Dr Ste 100 (07512-1156)
PHONE.................................973 256-8200
John Coster, *Principal*
EMP: 175 **Privately Held**
WEB: www.gwbakeries.com
SIC: 2079 5149 Margarine, including imitation; groceries & related products
HQ: Bimbo Bakeries Usa, Inc
255 Business Center Dr # 200
Horsham PA 19044
215 347-5500

(G-10821)
CARAVAN INGREDIENTS INC
100 Adams Dr (07512-2200)
P.O. Box 1004 (07511-1004)
PHONE.................................973 256-8886
John Stone, *Branch Mgr*
EMP: 153
SALES (corp-wide): 1B **Privately Held**
SIC: 2045 Bread & bread type roll mixes: from purchased flour; blended flour: from purchased flour
HQ: Caravan Ingredients Inc.
8250 Flint St
Lenexa KS 66214
913 890-5500

(G-10822)
CENTROME INC
Also Called: Advanced Biotech
10 Taft Rd (07512-1006)
PHONE.................................973 339-6242
Augustin Isernia, *President*
Lopez Marylou, *Vice Pres*
Adam Arteaga, *Production*
Paolo Camara, *Production*
Yuri Moreno, *Purch Agent*
▲ EMP: 40
SQ FT: 40,000
SALES (est): 10.2MM **Privately Held**
WEB: www.adv-bio.com
SIC: 2087 Flavoring extracts & syrups

(G-10823)
CIBO VITA INC
12 Vreeland Ave (07512-1121)
PHONE.................................862 238-8020
Emre Imamoglu, *CEO*
Ahmet Celik, *President*
▲ EMP: 350 EST: 2009
SQ FT: 75,000
SALES (est): 221.8MM **Privately Held**
SIC: 5145 2041 2034 2068 Nuts, salted or roasted; grain cereals, cracked; dried & dehydrated fruits; nuts: dried, dehydrated, salted or roasted

(G-10824)
CORONET INC
Also Called: Coronet Led
55 Shepherds Ln (07512-2130)
PHONE.................................973 345-7660
Russel Osur, *CEO*
Steven Klauber, *COO*
John Dobbie, *Vice Pres*
Matthew Grasso, *Vice Pres*
John Duarte, *Senior Engr*
▲ EMP: 130 EST: 1946
SQ FT: 90,000
SALES (est): 18.9MM **Privately Held**
SIC: 3646 Fluorescent lighting fixtures, commercial

(G-10825)
ECI TECHNOLOGY INC
60 Gordon Dr (07512-2204)
PHONE.................................973 773-8686
Marianna Rabinovitch, *CEO*
James Abramson, *CFO*
▲ EMP: 175
SQ FT: 45,800
SALES (est): 33MM **Privately Held**
WEB: www.ecitechnology.com
SIC: 3826 Automatic chemical analyzers

(G-10826)
FABULOUS FABRICATORS LLC
Also Called: Source One
11 Jackson Rd (07512-1001)
PHONE.................................973 779-2400
Jay Schainholz,
▼ EMP: 50
SQ FT: 78,000
SALES (est): 6.7MM **Privately Held**
SIC: 3444 Sheet metalwork

(G-10827)
GABHEN INC
1 Maltese Dr (07512-1402)
PHONE.................................973 256-0666
EMP: 5
SALES (corp-wide): 70MM **Privately Held**
SIC: 3496 Mfg Mechanical Binding Wire
PA: Gabhen, Inc.
1 Maltese Dr
Totowa NJ 07512
800 631-3572

(G-10828)
GBW MANUFACTURING INC
20 W End Rd (07512-1406)
PHONE.................................973 279-0077
Ernest Relyea, *President*
EMP: 40
SQ FT: 25,000
SALES (est): 4.1MM **Privately Held**
SIC: 3229 3499 3231 Glass furnishings & accessories; metal household articles; novelties & specialties, metal; products of purchased glass

(G-10829)
GENZYME CORPORATION
25 Madison Rd (07512-1003)
PHONE.................................973 256-2106
EMP: 6 **Privately Held**
SIC: 2835 2834 8071 3842 Enzyme & isoenzyme diagnostic agents; pharmaceutical preparations; biological laboratory; surgical appliances & supplies; biological products, except diagnostic; drugs & drug proprietaries
HQ: Genzyme Corporation
50 Binney St
Cambridge MA 02142
617 252-7500

(G-10830)
GOODRICH CORPORATION
20 Commerce Way (07512-1154)
PHONE.................................973 237-2700
Calvin Purdin, *Branch Mgr*
EMP: 227
SALES (corp-wide): 66.5B **Publicly Held**
WEB: www.bfgoodrich.com
SIC: 3728 Aircraft parts & equipment
HQ: Goodrich Corporation
2730 W Tyvola Rd 4
Charlotte NC 28217
704 423-7000

(G-10831)
GRANDVIEW PRINTING CO INC
33 W End Rd (07512-1405)
PHONE.................................973 890-0006
Lewis De Marco, *President*
Jeffrey De Marco, *Vice Pres*
EMP: 10
SQ FT: 13,000
SALES (est): 1.6MM **Privately Held**
SIC: 2789 2796 2752 Bookbinding & related work; platemaking services; commercial printing, offset

(G-10832)
HOFFMANN-LA ROCHE INC
701 Union Blvd (07512-2207)
PHONE.................................973 235-8216

John Hemerick, *Branch Mgr*
EMP: 11
SALES (corp-wide): 57.2B **Privately Held**
WEB: www.rocheusa.com
SIC: 2834 Pharmaceutical preparations
HQ: Hoffmann-La Roche Inc.
150 Clove Rd Ste 88th
Little Falls NJ 07424
973 890-2268

(G-10833)
IPCO US LLC
21 Campus Rd (07512-1201)
PHONE.................................973 720-7000
Walter Miller, *President*
Charles Hillmann, *Sales Mgr*
Anders Ekelund, *Manager*
Anders Koijer, *Manager*
◆ EMP: 50
SQ FT: 50,000
SALES (est): 15.3MM
SALES (corp-wide): 11.1B **Privately Held**
SIC: 3823 3535 Industrial process measurement equipment; conveyors & conveying equipment
HQ: Sandvik, Inc.
17-02 Nevins Rd
Fair Lawn NJ 07410
201 794-5000

(G-10834)
KNICKERBOCKER MACHINE SHOP INC (PA)
Also Called: Alloy Stainless Products Co
611 Union Blvd (07512-2402)
PHONE.................................973 256-1616
John Simonelli, *President*
Flavian Simonelli, *Exec VP*
Anthony P Auferio, *Vice Pres*
Angel Caradonna, *Purch Agent*
Annemarie Appleton, *VP Bus Dvlpt*
EMP: 58 EST: 1944
SQ FT: 22,000
SALES (est): 15.9MM **Privately Held**
WEB: www.alloystainless.com
SIC: 3494 3432 Valves & pipe fittings; plumbing fixture fittings & trim

(G-10835)
LIGHTNING PRESS INC
140 Furler St (07512-1825)
PHONE.................................973 890-4422
Ron Balinski, *President*
Dana Balinski, *Vice Pres*
EMP: 12
SQ FT: 6,500
SALES (est): 1.9MM **Privately Held**
WEB: www.lightningpress.com
SIC: 2752 Commercial printing, offset

(G-10836)
MEDIN TECHNOLOGIES INC
11 Jackson Rd (07512-1001)
PHONE.................................973 779-2400
Bill Donaldson, *CEO*
▲ EMP: 101 EST: 2016
SALES (est): 35.9MM **Privately Held**
WEB: www.medin.com
SIC: 3914 3411 3841 Silverware & plated ware; metal cans; surgical instruments & apparatus

(G-10837)
MORENG METAL PRODUCTS INC
100 W End Rd (07512-1407)
P.O. Box 185 (07511-0185)
PHONE.................................973 256-2001
James R Moreng, *CEO*
Joseph H Moreng Jr, *Vice Pres*
EMP: 85
SQ FT: 45,000
SALES (est): 23.3MM **Privately Held**
WEB: www.morengmetal.com
SIC: 3444 3644 Sheet metal specialties, not stamped; noncurrent-carrying wiring services

(G-10838)
NATIONAL PLASTIC PRINTING
130 Furler St (07512-1825)
PHONE.................................973 785-1460
Richard Ullman, *President*
Kenneth D Ullman, *Vice Pres*
EMP: 30
SQ FT: 13,000

SALES (est): 3.5MM **Privately Held**
SIC: 3089 2759 Laminating of plastic; commercial printing

(G-10839)
O T D INC
Also Called: Unipro
18 Furler St (07512-1802)
PHONE.................................973 890-7979
Fax: 973 890-4898
▲ EMP: 8
SQ FT: 12,000
SALES (est): 690K **Privately Held**
SIC: 3714 Mfg Motor Vehicle Parts & Accessories

(G-10840)
OMEGA PACKAGING CORP
55 Kings Rd (07512-2205)
PHONE.................................973 890-9505
Larry Kalb, *President*
Bill Carr, *Vice Pres*
W M Prosser, *Vice Pres*
Jennifer Hartle, *Executive*
▲ EMP: 70
SQ FT: 40,000
SALES (est): 12.7MM **Privately Held**
SIC: 2844 2099 Cosmetic preparations; food preparations

(G-10841)
ORGANICS CORPORATION AMERICA
Also Called: Ambix Laboratories
55 W End Rd (07512-1405)
PHONE.................................973 890-9002
Elkin Serna, *President*
Alvin J Goren, *Chairman*
Michael Chanin, *Vice Pres*
▲ EMP: 40
SQ FT: 50,000
SALES (est): 11.3MM **Privately Held**
WEB: www.ambixlabs.com
SIC: 2844 2834 Cosmetic preparations; vitamin, nutrient & hematinic preparations for human use

(G-10842)
PCC ASIA LLC (PA)
200 Maltese Dr (07512-1404)
PHONE.................................973 890-3873
Peter Longo, *Mng Member*
Garrett Graven, *Manager*
▲ EMP: 5
SALES (est): 1.3MM **Privately Held**
SIC: 2295 Coated fabrics, not rubberized

(G-10843)
PHARMACHEM LABORATORIES INC
15 Adams Dr (07512-2201)
PHONE.................................973 256-1340
Andrea Bauer, *Branch Mgr*
EMP: 30
SALES (corp-wide): 3.2B **Publicly Held**
SIC: 2099 2834 Food preparations; pharmaceutical preparations
HQ: Pharmachem Laboratories, Llc
265 Harrison Tpke
Kearny NJ 07032
201 246-1000

(G-10844)
PHOENIX DOWN CORPORATION
85 Route 46 (07512-2301)
PHONE.................................973 812-8100
John Facatselis, *President*
Josie Molina, *Accountant*
Gaeton Dinapoli, *Human Res Mgr*
Kevin Miller, *Mktg Dir*
Ambiorix Hernandez, *Manager*
▼ EMP: 130
SQ FT: 60,000
SALES (est): 13.7MM **Privately Held**
WEB: www.phoenixdown.com
SIC: 2392 Pillows, bed: made from purchased materials; comforters & quilts: made from purchased materials

(G-10845)
PNC ELECTRONICS INC
20 W End Rd (07512-1411)
PHONE.................................973 237-0400
Peter Patel, *President*
Ila Sheh, *Corp Secy*
Sam Sangani, *Vice Pres*

▲ EMP: 30
SALES (est): 5.5MM **Privately Held**
SIC: 3577 Computer peripheral equipment

(G-10846)
PRECISION TEXTILES LLC (PA)
Also Called: P C C
200 Maltese Dr (07512-1404)
PHONE..............................973 890-3873
Dave Reaman, *Purch Agent*
Jack Higgins, *Controller*
Keith Martin, *Sales Mgr*
Peter Longo, *Mng Member*
Rino Baldecci, *Manager*
◆ EMP: 173
SQ FT: 210,000
SALES (est): 130.3MM **Privately Held**
WEB: www.pcc-usa.com
SIC: 2295 Coated fabrics, not rubberized

(G-10847)
PROTAMEEN CHEMICALS INC (PA)
375 Minnisink Rd (07512-1804)
P.O. Box 166 (07511-0166)
PHONE..............................973 256-4374
Emmanuel Balsamides Jr, *President*
Thomas Balsamides, *Vice Pres*
▲ EMP: 40
SQ FT: 40,000
SALES (est): 10.5MM **Privately Held**
WEB: www.protameen.com
SIC: 2819 7231 2869 Industrial inorganic
chemicals; beauty shops; industrial or-
ganic chemicals

(G-10848)
REDHEDINK LLC
135 Minnisink Rd (07512-1945)
PHONE..............................973 890-2320
Diane Byrne, *Principal*
EMP: 4
SALES (est): 209.4K **Privately Held**
SIC: 2711 Newspapers, publishing & print-
ing

(G-10849)
RELIANCE ELECTRONICS INC
145 Shepherds Ln (07512-2130)
PHONE..............................973 237-0400
Mamta Narkhede, *President*
Ramila Patel, *General Mgr*
Paresh Patel, *Vice Pres*
Yogesh Patel, *Treasurer*
Angela Carbone, *Sales Staff*
▲ EMP: 24
SALES (est): 6MM **Privately Held**
SIC: 3571 Electronic computers

(G-10850)
ROSS BICYCLES LLC
205 Us Highway 46 Ste 10 (07512-1815)
PHONE..............................888 392-5628
EMP: 13
SALES (corp-wide): 1.4MM **Privately
Held**
SIC: 3751 Motorcycles, bicycles & parts
PA: Ross Bicycles Llc
16192 Coastal Hwy
Lewes DE 19958
888 392-5628

(G-10851)
SE TYLOS USA
140 Commerce Way (07512-1158)
PHONE..............................973 837-8001
EMP: 4 EST: 2013
SALES (est): 321.4K **Privately Held**
SIC: 2869 Industrial organic chemicals

(G-10852)
SK CUSTOM CREATIONS INC
Also Called: S K
50 Furler St (07512-1802)
PHONE..............................973 754-9261
Ivan Acapana, *President*
Bov Radeliffe, *Vice Pres*
EMP: 50
SQ FT: 32,000
SALES (est): 8.2MM **Privately Held**
SIC: 2542 Office & store showcases & dis-
play fixtures

(G-10853)
SPIRAL BINDING LLC (PA)
1 Maltese Dr (07512-1413)
P.O. Box 286 (07511-0286)
PHONE..............................973 256-0666
Rob Roth, *CEO*
Jeff Pendleton, *Mfg Mgr*
Steven Kopesky, *Facilities Mgr*
Richard Christmas, *Opers Staff*
Anmol Advaney, *Purch Agent*
▲ EMP: 150 EST: 2017
SQ FT: 75,000
SALES (est): 25MM **Privately Held**
SIC: 2789 5112 3083 2891 Binding & re-
pair of books, magazines & pamphlets;
stationery & office supplies; laminated
plastics plate & sheet; adhesives &
sealants

(G-10854)
T F S INC
Also Called: United Federated Systems
40 Vreeland Ave Ste 101 (07512-1169)
PHONE..............................973 890-7651
Cathy Mostyn, *President*
Alan Rendfrey, *Controller*
Angle Ortiz, *Manager*
EMP: 29
SALES (est): 4.9MM **Privately Held**
SIC: 3699 7382 Security control equip-
ment & systems; security systems serv-
ices

(G-10855)
TOTOWA KICKBOXING LTD LBLTY CO
Also Called: Cko Kickboxing
1 Us Highway 46 (07512-2333)
PHONE..............................973 507-9106
Mauricio Barriga,
EMP: 18
SQ FT: 7,850
SALES (est): 467K **Privately Held**
SIC: 7941 3949 7991 Sports clubs, man-
agers & promoters; gloves, sport & ath-
letic: boxing, handball, etc.; physical
fitness facilities

(G-10856)
VECTRACOR INCORPORATED
785 Totowa Rd Ste 100 (07512-1500)
PHONE..............................973 904-0444
Brad S Schreck, *President*
Marcy Schreck, *Manager*
EMP: 11
SQ FT: 3,000
SALES (est): 1.3MM **Privately Held**
SIC: 3845 Electromedical equipment

(G-10857)
VERSABAR CORPORATION
100 Maltese Dr (07512-1403)
PHONE..............................973 279-8400
William E Taylor, *President*
Sarah Taylor, *Treasurer*
▲ EMP: 15 EST: 1945
SQ FT: 22,000
SALES (est): 3.1MM **Privately Held**
WEB: www.versabar.com
SIC: 3499 3429 Strapping, metal; manu-
factured hardware (general)

(G-10858)
VIBRA SCREW INC
755 Union Blvd (07512-2207)
P.O. Box 229 (07511-0229)
PHONE..............................973 256-7410
Eugene A Wahl Sr, *President*
Richard C Wahl, *Exec VP*
Joanne Young, *Purch Mgr*
Ellen Wahl Skibiak, *Treasurer*
Edward Giacobbe, *Regl Sales Mgr*
EMP: 40
SQ FT: 50,000
SALES: 10MM **Privately Held**
WEB: www.vibrascrew.com
SIC: 3535 3559 Conveyors & conveying
equipment;

(G-10859)
VIGOR INC
45 Frances St (07512-2471)
PHONE..............................973 851-9539
Victor Melnychuk, *Owner*
EMP: 4 EST: 2010

SALES: 140K **Privately Held**
SIC: 2431 Interior & ornamental woodwork
& trim

(G-10860)
VISKAL PRINTING LLC
Also Called: AlphaGraphics
40e Commerce Way (07512-3110)
PHONE..............................973 812-6600
Krishnan Thampi, *President*
EMP: 7
SALES (est): 1.2MM **Privately Held**
SIC: 2752 Commercial printing, litho-
graphic

(G-10861)
WESTROCK RKT LLC
29g Commerce Way (07512-3112)
PHONE..............................973 594-6000
EMP: 183
SALES (corp-wide): 16.2B **Publicly Held**
SIC: 2653 Corrugated & solid fiber boxes
HQ: Westrock Rkt, Llc
1000 Abernathy Rd Ste 125
Atlanta GA 30328
770 448-2193

(G-10862)
WG PRODUCTS INC
70 Maltese Dr (07512-1403)
P.O. Box 695 (07511-0695)
PHONE..............................973 256-5999
Kevin Cooney, *President*
▲ EMP: 8
SALES (est): 1.2MM **Privately Held**
SIC: 3999 Chairs, hydraulic, barber &
beauty shop

(G-10863)
WINDTREE THERAPEUTICS INC
710 Union Blvd (07512)
PHONE..............................973 339-2889
Ernest Tyler, *Branch Mgr*
EMP: 10
SALES (corp-wide): 1.7MM **Publicly Held**
WEB: www.discoverylabs.com
SIC: 2834 5122 Pharmaceutical prepara-
tions; pharmaceuticals
PA: Windtree Therapeutics, Inc.
2600 Kelly Rd Ste 100
Warrington PA 18976
215 488-9300

```
Towaco
Morris County
```

(G-10864)
APOGEE TECHNOLOGIES LLC
Also Called: R&L Sheet Metal
3 Cole Rd (07082)
PHONE..............................973 575-8448
Jerry Grieco,
EMP: 10
SALES (est): 862.7K **Privately Held**
SIC: 3499 Fabricated metal products

(G-10865)
BAUMER OF AMERICA INC
425 Main Rd (07082-1201)
P.O. Box 18 (07082-0018)
PHONE..............................973 263-1569
Philipp Schuster, *General Mgr*
Jesse Collinson, *General Mgr*
▲ EMP: 12
SQ FT: 10,000
SALES (est): 2.6MM
SALES (corp-wide): 78.5MM **Privately
Held**
WEB: www.baumerofamerica.com
SIC: 3423 Knives, agricultural or industrial
PA: Albrecht Baumer Gmbh & Co. Kg
Spezialmaschinenfabrik
Asdorfer Str. 96-106
Freudenberg 57258
273 428-90

(G-10866)
BOSCO PRODUCTS INC
441 Main Rd (07082-1201)
PHONE..............................973 334-7534
Steven Sanders, *President*
▼ EMP: 5
SQ FT: 40,000

SALES (est): 455K **Privately Held**
SIC: 2066 Chocolate

(G-10867)
CRAFT-PAK INC
1 Ashley Pl (07082-1447)
PHONE..............................718 763-0700
EMP: 16
SQ FT: 13,000
SALES (est): 2MM **Privately Held**
SIC: 2673 Mfg Plastic Bags

(G-10868)
DELMHORST INSTRUMENT COMPANY
51 Indian Ln E (07082-1025)
PHONE..............................973 334-2557
Aristide Laurenzi, *Ch of Bd*
Thomas Laurenzi, *President*
Alan Dlugasch, *Sales Staff*
Josh Rothman, *Mktg Coord*
▲ EMP: 28 EST: 1946
SQ FT: 13,970
SALES (est): 6MM **Privately Held**
WEB: www.delmhorst.com
SIC: 3829 Measuring & controlling devices

(G-10869)
DIVERSIFIED HEAT TRANSFER INC
439 Main Rd (07082-1369)
PHONE..............................800 221-1522
Norman Goldberg, *CEO*
James Colwell, *Vice Pres*
Thomas Franculo, *Vice Pres*
Jake Goldberg, *Vice Pres*
Jonathan Goldberg, *Vice Pres*
◆ EMP: 75 EST: 1932
SQ FT: 100,000
SALES (est): 26MM **Privately Held**
WEB: www.dhtnet.com
SIC: 3585 Evaporative condensers, heat
transfer equipment

(G-10870)
DROM INTERNATIONAL INC (HQ)
Also Called: Drom Fragrances
5 Jacksonville Rd (07082-1125)
PHONE..............................973 316-8400
Bertrand Lemont, *President*
Andreas Storp, *Principal*
Ferdinand Storp, *Principal*
John N Vargus, *Prdtn Mgr*
Angela Tomza, *Purch Mgr*
▲ EMP: 36
SQ FT: 22,000
SALES (est): 7.9MM
SALES (corp-wide): 123.7MM **Privately
Held**
SIC: 2869 Perfumes, flavorings & food ad-
ditives
PA: Drom Fragrances Gmbh & Co. Kg
Oberdiller Str. 18
Baierbrunn 82065
897 442-50

(G-10871)
ENGINEERED SECURITY SYSTEMS (PA)
Also Called: E S S
1 Indian Ln E (07082-1025)
PHONE..............................973 257-0555
Laurice R George, *CEO*
Angelo George, *Chairman*
EMP: 40 EST: 1971
SQ FT: 9,000
SALES (est): 8.6MM **Privately Held**
WEB: www.essi.net
SIC: 7382 3699 Burglar alarm mainte-
nance & monitoring; security control
equipment & systems

(G-10872)
GLOBAL GRAPHICS INTERGRATION
14 Willard Ln (07082-1517)
PHONE..............................973 334-9653
Julia Murray, *CEO*
EMP: 16
SQ FT: 60,000
SALES (est): 966.2K **Privately Held**
SIC: 2759 7311 8742 Commercial print-
ing; advertising agencies; marketing con-
sulting services

(G-10873)
JENISSE LEISURE PRODUCTS INC
5 Van Duyne Ct (07082-1439)
PHONE..................................973 331-1177
Richard Dehart, *President*
EMP: 10
SALES (est): 1.2MM **Privately Held**
SIC: 2899 Chemical preparations

(G-10874)
M D CARBIDE TOOL CORP
19 Old Jacksonville Rd (07082-1013)
PHONE..................................973 263-0104
Marian Depczynski, *President*
EMP: 21 EST: 1964
SALES: 85K **Privately Held**
SIC: 3599 3545 3369 Machine shop, jobbing & repair; machine tool accessories; nonferrous foundries

(G-10875)
MULTIPOWER INTERNATIONAL INC
7 Woodshire Ter (07082-1457)
P.O. Box 187 (07082-0187)
PHONE..................................973 727-0327
Qiang GE, *President*
▲ EMP: 7
SALES (est): 200K **Privately Held**
SIC: 3743 Engines, steam (locomotive)

(G-10876)
PANOVA INC
33 Jacksonville Rd Ste 2 (07082-1100)
PHONE..................................973 263-1700
Ehren A Dimitry, *CEO*
Ronald C Knauf, *President*
Deborah Ceglarski, *Controller*
Cheryl Gilberti, *Sales Executive*
Frieda Dimitry, *Admin Sec*
▲ EMP: 35
SQ FT: 12,500
SALES (est): 6MM **Privately Held**
WEB: www.amecorporation.com
SIC: 3069 3061 Molded rubber products; mechanical rubber goods

(G-10877)
PKC FINEWOODWORKING LLC
836 Main Rd (07082-1328)
PHONE..................................201 951-8880
Ciambruschini Paul, *Principal*
EMP: 4 EST: 2011
SALES (est): 357.9K **Privately Held**
SIC: 2431 Millwork

(G-10878)
PLASTINETICS INC
439 Main Rd (07082-1369)
PHONE..................................818 364-1611
Edward J Batta, *President*
EMP: 7
SQ FT: 6,500
SALES: 6.5MM **Privately Held**
WEB: www.plastinetics.com
SIC: 3089 Plastic containers, except foam; plastic kitchenware, tableware & houseware; plastic hardware & building products; boot or shoe products, plastic

(G-10879)
Q GLASS COMPANY INC
624 Rte 202 (07082)
PHONE..................................973 335-5191
Ellen Dotterweich, *President*
Daniel J Dotterweich III, *Vice Pres*
Daniel Dotterweich IV, *Manager*
EMP: 7 EST: 1947
SQ FT: 8,000
SALES: 1.1MM **Privately Held**
WEB: www.qglass.com
SIC: 3229 5023 5719 Glassware, industrial; glassware; glassware

(G-10880)
SEA BREEZE FRUIT FLAVORS INC
441 Main Rd (07082-1298)
PHONE..................................973 334-7777
Steven Sanders, *President*
Josh Sanders, *Vice Pres*
Joshua Sanders, *Vice Pres*
Deena Vreeland, *Marketing Mgr*
Vincent Saldutti, *Manager*

EMP: 70 EST: 1925
SQ FT: 40,000
SALES (est): 17.8MM **Privately Held**
SIC: 2087 5046 Syrups, drink; commercial equipment

(G-10881)
TELEDYNAMICS LLC
45 Indian Ln E Ste 1 (07082-1025)
PHONE..................................973 248-3360
Eric Witt, *Manager*
▼ EMP: 25
SQ FT: 18,000
SALES (est): 6.5MM **Privately Held**
SIC: 3536 Monorail systems

(G-10882)
TROY HILLS MANUFACTURING INC
2 Como Ct (07082-1128)
P.O. Box 98 (07082-0098)
PHONE..................................973 263-1885
Brian Melgaard, *President*
▲ EMP: 6
SALES (est): 908.4K **Privately Held**
SIC: 3632 3061 Freezers, home & farm; mechanical rubber goods

(G-10883)
UHLMANN PACKAGING SYSTEMS LP
44 Indian Ln E (07082-1032)
PHONE..................................973 402-8855
Markus Leuprecht, *Project Mgr*
Christian Mueller, *Project Mgr*
Maria Bumpus, *Purchasing*
Bogdan Nitulescu, *Engineer*
Abdon Villa, *Engineer*
▲ EMP: 75
SQ FT: 50,000
SALES (est): 18.7MM
SALES (corp-wide): 216.2MM **Privately Held**
WEB: www.uhlmann-usa.com
SIC: 3541 5084 Machine tool replacement & repair parts, metal cutting types; machine tools & metalworking machinery; instruments & control equipment
PA: Uhlmann Group Holding Gmbh & Co. Kg
Uhlmannstr. 14-18
Laupheim 88471
739 270-20

Tranquility
Sussex County

(G-10884)
TECHNODIAMANT USA INC
35a Kennedy Rd (07879)
P.O. Box 398 (07879-0398)
PHONE..................................908 850-8505
David Slaperud, *President*
Diane Cooke, *Manager*
EMP: 2
SQ FT: 1,000
SALES: 1.2MM
SALES (corp-wide): 367.4K **Privately Held**
WEB: www.technodiamant.com
SIC: 3545 5085 Diamond cutting tools for turning, boring, burnishing, etc.; dressers, abrasive wheel: diamond point or other; wheel turning equipment, diamond point or other; industrial supplies
HQ: Technodiamant Almere B.V.
De Vest 1 C
Valkenswaard

Trenton
Mercer County

(G-10885)
21ST CENTURY MEDIA NEWSPPR LLC (HQ)
Also Called: Journal Register Company
600 Perry St (08618-3934)
PHONE..................................215 504-4200
John Paton, *CEO*
Jeff Bairstow, *President*

Madeline Wood, *CTO*
EMP: 53
SALES (est): 18.2MM
SALES (corp-wide): 4.2B **Privately Held**
SIC: 2711 Newspapers
PA: Digital First Media, Llc
101 W Colfax Ave Fl 11
Denver CO 80202
212 257-7212

(G-10886)
A M GATTI INC
524 Tindall Ave (08610-5399)
PHONE..................................609 396-1577
Anthony Ursic, *Principal*
Chris Warner, *Manager*
Gina Soyka, *Office Admin*
EMP: 19 EST: 2010
SALES (est): 4.1MM **Privately Held**
SIC: 3568 Power transmission equipment

(G-10887)
A R J CUSTOM FABRICATION INC
151 Taylor St (08638-4320)
PHONE..................................609 695-6227
Anthony R Jones, *President*
Barbara Jones, *Treasurer*
EMP: 12
SQ FT: 15,000
SALES (est): 2.3MM **Privately Held**
SIC: 3444 Sheet metalwork

(G-10888)
A SIGN COMPANY
258 Old York Rd (08620)
PHONE..................................609 298-3388
EMP: 6
SQ FT: 9,000
SALES (est): 250K **Privately Held**
SIC: 3993 Mfg Signs/Advertising Specialties

(G-10889)
ALIGN SOURCING LTD LBLTY CO
46 Doe Dr (08620-1326)
P.O. Box 8482, Hamilton (08650-0482)
PHONE..................................609 375-8550
James Karas, *Mng Member*
▲ EMP: 2
SALES: 1MM **Privately Held**
SIC: 3823 7389 Thermal conductivity instruments, industrial process type;

(G-10890)
ALL COUNTY RECYCLING INC
391 Enterprise Ave (08638-4413)
PHONE..................................609 393-6445
Mark Barretti, *CEO*
EMP: 10 EST: 2007
SQ FT: 600
SALES (est): 1.8MM **Privately Held**
SIC: 4953 2631 Recycling, waste materials; cardboard

(G-10891)
ALLIANCE FOOD EQUIPMENT
Also Called: Gram Equipment
1 S Gold Dr (08691-1606)
P.O. Box 236, Northvale (07647-0236)
PHONE..................................201 784-1101
Neal E White, *President*
Jakob Hansen, *Principal*
EMP: 15
SQ FT: 28,000
SALES (est): 4.6MM **Privately Held**
SIC: 3565 Packaging machinery

(G-10892)
AMERICAN SCIENTIFIC LTG CORP
Also Called: A S L
725 E State St (08609-1409)
PHONE..................................718 369-1100
Yaakov Singer, *President*
▲ EMP: 25 EST: 1979
SQ FT: 25,000
SALES (est): 5.2MM **Privately Held**
WEB: www.asllighting.com
SIC: 3646 Commercial indusl & institutional electric lighting fixtures

(G-10893)
ANA DESIGN CORP
1 Ott St (08638-5196)
PHONE..................................609 394-0300
Fred Cohen, *CEO*
Donald Weeden, *Ch of Bd*
Frank Weeden, *President*
Elizabeth Barek, *Treasurer*
EMP: 12
SALES (est): 1.1MM **Privately Held**
WEB: www.anadesigncorp.com
SIC: 3999 Candles

(G-10894)
ANDREA AROMATICS INC
150 Enterprise Ave (08638-4404)
P.O. Box 3091, Princeton (08543-3091)
PHONE..................................609 695-7710
Michael D'Andrea, *President*
Janine Riggs, *Treasurer*
Susan D'Andrea, *Admin Sec*
▲ EMP: 20
SQ FT: 21,000
SALES: 7MM **Privately Held**
SIC: 2844 Toilet preparations

(G-10895)
AREA AUTO RACING NEWS INC
2831 S Broad St (08610-3603)
P.O. Box 8547 (08650-0547)
PHONE..................................609 888-3618
Leonard Sammons, *President*
EMP: 6 EST: 1961
SQ FT: 3,000
SALES: 570K **Privately Held**
WEB: www.aarn.com
SIC: 2711 2721 Newspapers, publishing & printing; magazines: publishing & printing; periodicals: publishing & printing

(G-10896)
ARM NATIONAL FOOD INC
539 Chestnut Ave (08611-1233)
PHONE..................................609 695-4911
Armando Rienzi, *Manager*
EMP: 5
SALES (corp-wide): 14MM **Privately Held**
SIC: 5141 5421 5147 5142 Groceries, general line; meat & fish markets; meats & meat products; packaged frozen goods; sausages & other prepared meats; meat packing plants
PA: Arm National Food, Inc.
1546 Lamberton Rd
Trenton NJ 08611
609 394-0431

(G-10897)
ASSA ABLOY ENTRANCE SYS US INC
Besam Entrance Solutions
300 Horizon Center Blvd # 302 (08691-1919)
PHONE..................................609 443-5800
Michael McCaslin, *Branch Mgr*
EMP: 50
SALES (corp-wide): 9.3B **Privately Held**
SIC: 3699 1796 3442 Door opening & closing devices, electrical; installing building equipment; metal doors
HQ: Assa Abloy Entrance Systems Us Inc.
1900 Airport Rd
Monroe NC 28110
704 290-5520

(G-10898)
AVANZATO JEWELERS LLC
2440 Whthrse Hmlton Sq Rd (08690-2820)
PHONE..................................609 890-0500
Raymond Whitehouse, *General Mgr*
Tom Avanzato, *Mng Member*
EMP: 7
SQ FT: 1,000
SALES (est): 722.1K **Privately Held**
SIC: 5944 3911 Jewelry, precious stones & precious metals; jewelry, precious metal

(G-10899)
AVONY ENTERPRISES INC
39 Meade St Ste 122 (08638-4321)
PHONE..................................212 242-8144
Jack Colon, *Principal*
EMP: 35 EST: 2017
SALES (est): 1.1MM **Privately Held**
SIC: 3599 Tubing, flexible metallic

(G-10900)
AZTEC GRAPHICS INC
420 Whitehead Rd (08619-3255)
PHONE....................609 587-1000
Ronald Balerno, *President*
Rob Malik, *Opers Mgr*
Eric Bonczkiewicz, *Graphic Designe*
EMP: 15
SQ FT: 9,500
SALES (est): 2.1MM **Privately Held**
WEB: www.aztecgraphics.com
SIC: **2261** 2791 2396 2395 Screen printing of cotton broadwoven fabrics; typesetting; automotive & apparel trimmings; pleating & stitching

(G-10901)
B & R PRINTING INC
Also Called: B & R Bindery Division
84 Hummingbird Dr (08690-3544)
PHONE....................609 448-3328
James Buckley Jr, *President*
EMP: 7
SQ FT: 9,500
SALES (est): 1MM **Privately Held**
SIC: **2752** 2789 Commercial printing, offset; photo-offset printing; binding only: books, pamphlets, magazines, etc.

(G-10902)
BARTLEY CRUCIBLE REFRACTORIES
15 Muirhead Ave (08638-5110)
P.O. Box 5464 (08638-0464)
PHONE....................609 393-0066
Dan Mischel, *President*
David Mischel, *Vice Pres*
▲ EMP: 13
SQ FT: 40,000
SALES (est): 1.8MM **Privately Held**
SIC: **3255** Clay refractories

(G-10903)
BENTON GRAPHICS INC
3 Industrial Dr (08619-3244)
PHONE....................609 587-4000
Mary A Benton, *President*
Margaret Linico, *Vice Pres*
EMP: 38
SQ FT: 22,500
SALES (est): 8.4MM **Privately Held**
WEB: www.bentongraphics.com
SIC: **3555** 3542 Printing trades machinery; machine tools, metal forming type

(G-10904)
BILLS PRINTING SERVICE INC
2829 S Broad St (08610-3603)
PHONE....................609 888-1841
William Mason, *President*
Patricia Mason, *Corp Secy*
EMP: 9
SQ FT: 4,000
SALES (est): 1.6MM **Privately Held**
SIC: **2759** Commercial printing

(G-10905)
BLACK LAGOON INC
78 Orourke Dr (08691-3913)
PHONE....................609 815-1654
Chris Borek, *President*
EMP: 5 EST: 2008
SALES (est): 379.9K **Privately Held**
SIC: **2782** Blankbooks & looseleaf binders

(G-10906)
BOLT WELDING & IRON WORKS
78 Wall St (08609-1106)
PHONE....................609 393-3993
Christopher Hiltey, *Owner*
EMP: 5
SQ FT: 1,500
SALES (est): 574K **Privately Held**
SIC: **3449** 3446 Miscellaneous metalwork; stairs, fire escapes, balconies, railings & ladders

(G-10907)
BUNN INDUSTRIES INCORPORATED (PA)
Also Called: Delaware Valley Box & Lbr Co
2651 E State Street Ext (08619-3319)
PHONE....................609 890-2900
Charles C Gould, *President*
EMP: 10
SQ FT: 15,000
SALES (est): 3.7MM **Privately Held**
SIC: **2653** 2441 2448 Boxes, corrugated: made from purchased materials; boxes, wood; wood pallets & skids

(G-10908)
BWAY CORPORATION
6 Litho Rd (08648-3304)
PHONE....................609 883-4300
Aren Millan, *Prdtn Mgr*
Berrdi James, *Branch Mgr*
Rich Shenowski, *Manager*
EMP: 17
SALES (corp-wide): 1.1B **Privately Held**
SIC: **3399** Metal powders, pastes & flakes
HQ: Bway Corporation
375 Northridge Rd Ste 600
Atlanta GA 30350

(G-10909)
CAPITOL STEEL INC
Also Called: Capitol Steel Products
10 Escher St (08609-1018)
PHONE....................609 538-9313
Sal Borgese, *President*
EMP: 11
SQ FT: 2,000
SALES (est): 2.3MM **Privately Held**
SIC: **3441** Building components, structural steel

(G-10910)
CARFARO INC
2075 E State Street Ext (08619-3323)
PHONE....................609 890-6600
Joseph Carfaro, *President*
Gayle L Carfaro, *Corp Secy*
Maria R Carfaro, *Vice Pres*
Charles Tilton, *Technology*
EMP: 50
SQ FT: 25,000
SALES (est): 16.8MM **Privately Held**
WEB: www.carfaro.com
SIC: **3446** Architectural metalwork

(G-10911)
CARPENTER LLC
Also Called: Carpenter Emergency Lighting
2 Marlen Dr (08691-1601)
PHONE....................609 689-3090
Avinash Diwan,
▲ EMP: 14
SALES (est): 2.9MM **Privately Held**
SIC: **3571** 3993 3648 Computers, digital, analog or hybrid; signs & advertising specialties; lighting equipment

(G-10912)
CASE PORK ROLL CO INC
644 Washington St (08611-3682)
P.O. Box 33019 (08629-3019)
PHONE....................609 396-8171
Thomas Grieb, *CEO*
Thomas Dolan, *President*
Richard Clem, *Corp Secy*
Arlene Greib, *Vice Pres*
Andrew Grieb, *Vice Pres*
EMP: 25 EST: 1950
SQ FT: 6,000
SALES (est): 4.9MM **Privately Held**
WEB: www.caseporkrollstore.com
SIC: **2013** Pork, cured: from purchased meat

(G-10913)
CB&I LLC
200 Horizon Center Blvd (08691-1904)
PHONE....................856 482-3000
EMP: 240
SALES (corp-wide): 6.7B **Publicly Held**
SIC: **3443** 3312 1791 Fabricated plate work (boiler shop); blast furnaces & steel mills; storage tanks, metal: erection
HQ: Cb&I Llc
3600 W Sam
Houston TX 77042
281 870-5000

(G-10914)
CCL LABEL (DELAWARE) INC
104 N Gold Dr (08691-1602)
PHONE....................609 259-1055
Craig Groendyk, *General Mgr*
Chris McQuiggan, *IT/INT Sup*
EMP: 150

SQ FT: 15,000
SALES (est): 3.7MM **Privately Held**
SIC: **2759** 2672 Flexographic printing; letterpress printing; coated & laminated paper
HQ: Ccl Label (Delaware), Inc.
15 Controls Dr
Shelton CT 06484
203 926-1253

(G-10915)
CENTRAL RECORD PUBLICATIONS
Also Called: Ad Lines
600 Perry St (08618-3934)
PHONE....................609 654-5000
Pat Haughey, *Manager*
EMP: 30 EST: 1896
SQ FT: 2,500
SALES (est): 1.3MM **Privately Held**
SIC: **2711** 2741 2721 Commercial printing & newspaper publishing combined; miscellaneous publishing; periodicals

(G-10916)
CIAO CUPCAKE
7 Wycklow Dr (08691-1204)
PHONE....................609 964-6167
Natalie Catalano, *Principal*
EMP: 4 EST: 2010
SALES (est): 214.1K **Privately Held**
SIC: **2051** Bread, cake & related products

(G-10917)
CLARICI GRAPHICS INC
88 Youngs Rd (08619-1013)
PHONE....................609 587-7204
Eugene S Clarici Sr, *President*
Eugene S Clarici Jr, *Vice Pres*
EMP: 20 EST: 1923
SQ FT: 2,000
SALES (est): 2.2MM **Privately Held**
WEB: www.clarici.com
SIC: **7336** 2396 Silk screen design; automotive & apparel trimmings

(G-10918)
CLAYTON BLOCK COMPANY INC
11111 Martins Ln (08620)
PHONE....................732 751-7600
Larry Reed, *Manager*
EMP: 15
SALES (corp-wide): 31.8MM **Privately Held**
WEB: www.claytononline.com
SIC: **3271** Concrete block & brick
PA: Clayton Block Company, Inc.
1355 Campus Pkwy Ste 200
Wall Township NJ 07753
888 763-8665

(G-10919)
CLAYTON BLOCK COMPANY INC
1200 New York Ave (08608)
PHONE....................609 695-0767
EMP: 13
SALES (corp-wide): 31.8MM **Privately Held**
WEB: www.claytononline.com
SIC: **3271** Blocks, concrete or cinder: standard
PA: Clayton Block Company, Inc.
1355 Campus Pkwy Ste 200
Wall Township NJ 07753
888 763-8665

(G-10920)
COCCO ENTERPRISES INC (PA)
3575 Quakerbridge Rd # 204 (08619-1271)
PHONE....................609 393-5939
Jan Saunders, *President*
Vicky Romanoski, *Vice Pres*
EMP: 15
SQ FT: 3,000
SALES (est): 1.4MM **Privately Held**
WEB: www.cocco-ent.com
SIC: **3842** Orthopedic appliances; prosthetic appliances

(G-10921)
CONGOLEUM CORPORATION (PA)
3500 Quakerbridge Rd (08619-1206)
P.O. Box 3127 (08619-0127)
PHONE....................609 584-3000
Christopher Oconnor, *President*
Tom McKay, *Vice Chairman*
Roy Parpart, *District Mgr*
Debbie Young, *Credit Staff*
Michael Marsteller, *Human Res Mgr*
◆ EMP: 36
SQ FT: 36,000
SALES (est): 116.7MM **Privately Held**
WEB: www.congoleum.com
SIC: **3081** Floor or wall covering, unsupported plastic; tile, unsupported plastic

(G-10922)
CONGOLEUM CORPORATION
3705 Quakerbridge Rd # 211 (08619-1288)
P.O. Box 3127 (08619-0127)
PHONE....................609 584-3601
Bob Agada, *Manager*
EMP: 100
SALES (corp-wide): 116.7MM **Privately Held**
SIC: **7389** 3081 3996 3253 Purchasing service; vinyl film & sheet; hard surface floor coverings; ceramic wall & floor tile
PA: Congoleum Corporation
3500 Quakerbridge Rd
Trenton NJ 08619
609 584-3000

(G-10923)
CONGOLEUM CORPORATION
1945 E State Street Ext (08619-3305)
P.O. Box 3127 (08619-0127)
PHONE....................609 584-3000
L Novak, *Engineer*
Wayne Neville, *Manager*
EMP: 313
SALES (corp-wide): 116.7MM **Privately Held**
WEB: www.congoleum.com
SIC: **3081** Floor or wall covering, unsupported plastic
PA: Congoleum Corporation
3500 Quakerbridge Rd
Trenton NJ 08619
609 584-3000

(G-10924)
CRAZY STEVES CONCOCTIONS LLC
Also Called: Crazy Steve's Pickles & Salsa
38 Herbert Rd (08691-2901)
PHONE....................908 787-2089
Steve Zielinski, *CEO*
EMP: 5 EST: 2009
SALES (est): 263.4K **Privately Held**
SIC: **2035** Pickled fruits & vegetables

(G-10925)
CREATIVE MACHINING SYSTEMS
124 Youngs Rd (08619-1097)
PHONE....................609 586-3932
Victor Scharko, *President*
Antonina Scharko, *Vice Pres*
EMP: 12
SQ FT: 13,000
SALES (est): 2.4MM **Privately Held**
WEB: www.creativemachining.com
SIC: **3599** 7692 Machine shop, jobbing & repair; welding repair

(G-10926)
CREST GROUP INC (HQ)
Also Called: Cresttek
Scotch Trenton Mercer Air (08628)
P.O. Box 7266 (08628-0266)
PHONE....................609 883-4000
J Michael Goodson, *CEO*
EMP: 10
SQ FT: 45,000
SALES (est): 4.5MM
SALES (corp-wide): 54.6MM **Privately Held**
WEB: www.thecrestgroup.com
SIC: **3699** Cleaning equipment, ultrasonic, except medical & dental

PA: Crestek, Inc.
18 Graphics Dr
Ewing NJ 08628
609 883-4000

(G-10927)
CYTOTHERM LP
110 Sewell Ave (08610-6059)
PHONE..................................609 396-1456
Roman Kuzyk, *Partner*
EMP: 6
SQ FT: 2,000
SALES: 1.5MM **Privately Held**
WEB: www.cytotherm.com
SIC: 3861 Processing equipment, photographic

(G-10928)
CZAR INDUSTRIES INC
Also Called: Rjd Machine Products
1424-1426 Heath Ave (08638)
PHONE..................................609 392-1515
Curtis P Duval, *President*
EMP: 9
SALES (est): 357.3K **Privately Held**
SIC: 3399 Primary metal products

(G-10929)
D A K OFFICE SERVICES INC
Also Called: Sir Speedy
3100 Quakerbridge Rd (08619-1658)
P.O. Box 511, Lakehurst (08733-0511)
PHONE..................................609 586-8222
David A Kaplan, *President*
Joanne Kaplan, *Treasurer*
Ira Kate, *Director*
EMP: 8
SQ FT: 5,000
SALES (est): 1.1MM **Privately Held**
SIC: 2752 2791 2789 Commercial printing, lithographic; typesetting; bookbinding & related work

(G-10930)
DEVATAL INC
644 Newkirk Ave (08610-4448)
PHONE..................................609 586-1575
Yair Devash, *Principal*
EMP: 4
SALES (est): 542.3K **Privately Held**
SIC: 2836 Biological products, except diagnostic

(G-10931)
DIGITAL ATELIER LLC
60 Sculptors Way Ste A (08619-3428)
PHONE..................................609 890-6666
Jon E Lash, *Mng Member*
EMP: 6
SALES: 867.3K **Privately Held**
SIC: 7336 3299 Art design services; art goods: plaster of paris, papier mache & scagliola

(G-10932)
E R SQUIBB & SONS INTER-AM
Also Called: Bristol-Myers Squibb
3 Hamilton Health Pl (08690-3542)
PHONE..................................609 818-3715
Pam Kagil, *Manager*
EMP: 7
SALES (corp-wide): 22.5B **Publicly Held**
WEB: www.unitedinpurpose.com
SIC: 2834 Pharmaceutical preparations
HQ: E. R. Squibb & Sons Inter-American Corporation
3551 Lawrenceville Rd
Princeton NJ 08540
609 252-4111

(G-10933)
EAST WEST SERVICE CO INC
2 Marlen Dr (08691-1601)
PHONE..................................609 631-9000
Avinash Diwan, *President*
▲ **EMP:** 25
SQ FT: 4,000
SALES (est): 3.3MM **Privately Held**
SIC: 3699 5065 Electrical equipment & supplies; electronic parts & equipment

(G-10934)
ELECTRICAL MOTOR REPR CO OF NJ
809 E State St (08609-1411)
P.O. Box 3787 (08629-0787)
PHONE..................................609 392-6149
Paul Doran, *President*
Joseph Castiglione, *Vice Pres*
EMP: 19
SQ FT: 3,800
SALES: 4MM **Privately Held**
WEB: www.elevatormotor.com
SIC: 7694 5063 Electric motor repair; motors, electric

(G-10935)
FAIRWAY BUILDING PRODUCTS LLC
Also Called: Carfaro
2075 E State Street Ext (08619-3323)
PHONE..................................609 890-6600
Joseph Carfaro, *Manager*
EMP: 50
SALES (corp-wide): 15.1MM **Privately Held**
SIC: 3446 Architectural metalwork
PA: Fairway Building Products, Llc
53 Eby Chiques Rd
Mount Joy PA 17552
717 653-6777

(G-10936)
GREATER NEW YORK BOX CO INC
1400 E State St (08609-1714)
PHONE..................................609 631-7900
Frederick Edelman, *President*
EMP: 4
SALES (est): 226.2K **Privately Held**
SIC: 2653 Corrugated & solid fiber boxes

(G-10937)
GRIFFITH ELECTRIC SUP CO INC (PA)
5 2nd St (08611-2293)
PHONE..................................609 695-6121
Meta Griffith, *President*
William Goodwin, *Principal*
Margaret Kline, *Exec VP*
Jack V Bok, *Marketing Staff*
EMP: 56
SQ FT: 65,000
SALES (est): 22.6MM **Privately Held**
WEB: www.griffithelec.com
SIC: 8711 3999 Electrical or electronic engineering; atomizers, toiletry

(G-10938)
HALO PUB INC
4617 Nottingham Way (08690-3819)
PHONE..................................609 586-1811
Jerry Reolie, *President*
EMP: 10
SALES (est): 590.8K **Privately Held**
SIC: 2024 Ice cream, bulk

(G-10939)
HODA INC
Also Called: Suburban Fence Company
532 Mulberry St (08638-3304)
PHONE..................................609 695-3000
David Solomon, *President*
Shirley Solomon, *Corp Secy*
EMP: 12
SQ FT: 3,500
SALES: 1MM **Privately Held**
WEB: www.hoda.com
SIC: 5031 5211 2499 Fencing, wood; trim, sheet metal; fencing; fencing, wood

(G-10940)
HUTCHINSON INDUSTRIES INC
251 Southard St (08609)
PHONE..................................609 394-1010
Bill Murray, *Branch Mgr*
EMP: 15
SALES (corp-wide): 8.4B **Publicly Held**
WEB: www.hutchinsoninc.com
SIC: 3069 3444 Rubber automotive products; sheet metalwork
HQ: Hutchinson Industries, Inc.
460 Southard St
Trenton NJ 08638
609 394-1010

(G-10941)
HUTCHINSON INDUSTRIES INC (DH)
460 Southard St (08638-4224)
PHONE..................................609 394-1010
Bob Graefe, *Opers Staff*
Shawn Riley, *Production*
Glen Weisman, *Purch Mgr*
Tom Marple, *QC Mgr*
Christopher Renson, *Engineer*
◆ **EMP:** 150
SQ FT: 300,000
SALES (est): 163.2MM
SALES (corp-wide): 8.4B **Publicly Held**
WEB: www.hutchinsoninc.com
SIC: 3069 Rubber automotive products
HQ: Hutchinson Corporation
460 Fuller Ave Ne
Grand Rapids MI 49503
616 459-4541

(G-10942)
HUTCHINSON INDUSTRIES INC
84 Parker Ave Ste 86 (08609-1624)
PHONE..................................609 394-1010
George Thomas, *Branch Mgr*
EMP: 14
SALES (corp-wide): 8.4B **Publicly Held**
WEB: www.hutchinsoninc.com
SIC: 3069 Rubber automotive products
HQ: Hutchinson Industries, Inc.
460 Southard St
Trenton NJ 08638
609 394-1010

(G-10943)
HUTCHINSON INDUSTRIES INC
106 108 Mulberry St (08609)
PHONE..................................609 394-1010
EMP: 4
SALES (corp-wide): 8.4B **Publicly Held**
SIC: 3999 Barber & beauty shop equipment
HQ: Hutchinson Industries, Inc.
460 Southard St
Trenton NJ 08638
609 394-1010

(G-10944)
INDUSTRIAL WATER INSTITUTE
33 Maitland Rd (08620-1014)
P.O. Box 1389, Hightstown (08520-0975)
PHONE..................................609 585-4880
Ray Kerollis, *President*
Joanne Taussig, *Vice Pres*
Eugene Sarafin, *Admin Sec*
EMP: 6
SALES: 275K **Privately Held**
SIC: 3999 Atomizers, toiletry

(G-10945)
INNOVATIVE AWARDS INC
634 Arena Dr Ste 102 (08610-3400)
PHONE..................................609 888-1400
George Tomko, *President*
EMP: 5
SQ FT: 2,800
SALES (est): 363K **Privately Held**
WEB: www.innovativeawards.org
SIC: 5999 2759 Trophies & plaques; screen printing

(G-10946)
JERSEY PRECAST CORPORATION INC
853 Nottingham Way (08638-4447)
PHONE..................................609 689-3700
M Amir Ulislam, *Ch of Bd*
Khurram Ansari, *Plant Mgr*
Suzan Sidhom, *Accountant*
Ray Chavez, *Director*
▲ **EMP:** 160
SQ FT: 250,000
SALES (est): 33.5MM **Privately Held**
WEB: www.jerseyprecast.com
SIC: 3272 Concrete products, precast

(G-10947)
JOHNSON & JOHNSON
205 Waverly Ct (08691-3033)
PHONE..................................732 524-0400
EMP: 80
SALES (corp-wide): 81.5B **Publicly Held**
SIC: 2676 Feminine hygiene paper products

PA: Johnson & Johnson
1 Johnson And Johnson Plz
New Brunswick NJ 08933
732 524-0400

(G-10948)
JPC MERGER SUB LLC
Also Called: Jersey Precast
853 Nottingham Way (08638-4447)
PHONE..................................609 890-4343
M Amir Ulislam, *Mng Member*
EMP: 131
SQ FT: 185,000
SALES: 37.4MM **Privately Held**
SIC: 3272 Concrete products, precast

(G-10949)
KAYLINE PROCESSING INC (PA)
31 Coates St (08611-2903)
PHONE..................................609 695-1449
Michael J Lebwohl, *President*
Rob Lebwohl, *Exec VP*
Thomas Spinner, *Manager*
Eric Whitehead, *Technology*
Kristin Schnee,
◆ **EMP:** 32 **EST:** 1972
SQ FT: 4,000
SALES: 5.5MM **Privately Held**
WEB: www.kayline.com
SIC: 3081 Polyvinyl film & sheet; vinyl film & sheet; plastic film & sheet

(G-10950)
KNF NEUBERGER INC (DH)
2 Black Forest Rd (08691-1810)
PHONE..................................609 890-8889
Martin Becker, *Principal*
Eric Wilson, *Production*
Jill Deblasio, *Buyer*
Thomas Rank, *Buyer*
Gerald Giraldi, *Engineer*
EMP: 100 **EST:** 1977
SQ FT: 40,000
SALES (est): 20.1MM
SALES (corp-wide): 139.7MM **Privately Held**
WEB: www.knf.com
SIC: 3821 3563 Vacuum pumps, laboratory; air & gas compressors including vacuum pumps
HQ: Knf Neuberger Gmbh
Alter Weg 3
Freiburg Im Breisgau 79112
766 459-090

(G-10951)
LENAPE PRODUCTS INC
610 Plum St (08638-3349)
PHONE..................................609 394-5376
Stephen M Bielawski, *President*
Thomas E Wenczel Jr, *Corp Secy*
Donald Bielawski, *Vice Pres*
◆ **EMP:** 50
SQ FT: 40,000
SALES: 5MM
SALES (corp-wide): 15.7MM **Privately Held**
WEB: www.lenapebath.com
SIC: 3261 Bathroom accessories/fittings, vitreous china or earthenware
PA: New Jersey Porcelain Co Inc
600 Plum St
Trenton NJ 08638
609 394-5376

(G-10952)
LINSEIS INC
109 N Gold Dr (08691)
PHONE..................................609 223-2070
Claus Linseis, *President*
Robert Ansel, *General Mgr*
Annellore Linseis, *Treasurer*
EMP: 5
SQ FT: 6,000
SALES (est): 1.3MM **Privately Held**
WEB: www.linseis.net
SIC: 3825 Analyzers for testing electrical characteristics

(G-10953)
LOCKWOODS ELECTRIC MOTOR SVC
2239 Nottingham Way (08619-3047)
PHONE..................................609 587-2333
Richard L Dey, *President*
Joanne Dey, *Corp Secy*

Kathleen Dey, *Corp Secy*
EMP: 34
SQ FT: 20,000
SALES (est): 5.7MM **Privately Held**
WEB: www.lockwoodselectricmotor.com
SIC: 7694 5999 Electric motor repair; motors, electric; electronic parts & equipment

(G-10954)
MAN-HOW INC
Also Called: Style Plus
1150 Southard St Ste 3 (08638-5042)
PHONE....................609 392-4895
Glen F Mangee, *President*
▲ **EMP:** 9
SQ FT: 35,000
SALES (est): 4.2MM **Privately Held**
SIC: 5139 2385 Footwear; raincoats, except vulcanized rubber: purchased materials

(G-10955)
MARANATHA NOW INC
Also Called: Atlas Bronze
445 Bunting Ave (08611-3207)
PHONE....................609 599-1402
Katherine Smith, *President*
Kris Frank, *Vice Pres*
Lois Mousley, *Treasurer*
Joshua Smith, *Admin Sec*
◆ **EMP:** 23
SQ FT: 10,000
SALES (est): 6.9MM **Privately Held**
WEB: www.atlasbronze.com
SIC: 3364 3366 Copper & copper alloy die-castings; brass & bronze die-castings; bushings & bearings, copper (nonmachined)

(G-10956)
MARSHALL MAINTENANCE (PA)
Also Called: Marshall Industrial Tech
529 S Clinton Ave (08611-1809)
PHONE....................609 394-7153
John Mako, *President*
Jim Milligan, *Project Mgr*
Ed Sauer, *Foreman/Supr*
Oscar Morel, *Buyer*
Rocco F Carnevale, *Treasurer*
EMP: 136 **EST:** 1951
SQ FT: 35,000
SALES (est): 34MM **Privately Held**
WEB: www.marshallindtech.com
SIC: 1796 1731 1711 3599 Machinery installation; electrical work; heating & air conditioning contractors; machine shop, jobbing & repair

(G-10957)
MERCER MACHINE & TOOL PRODUCTS
332 Darcy Ave (08629-1313)
PHONE....................609 587-1106
Tom Erni, *President*
EMP: 4 **EST:** 1945
SQ FT: 2,400
SALES (est): 515.9K **Privately Held**
SIC: 3599 Machine shop, jobbing & repair

(G-10958)
MILLNER KITCHENS INC
Also Called: Millner Lumber Co
200 Whitehead Rd Ste 108 (08619-3278)
PHONE....................609 890-7300
John Millner, *President*
EMP: 8
SALES (est): 1.1MM **Privately Held**
SIC: 2541 5211 Counters or counter display cases, wood; cabinets, kitchen

(G-10959)
MUIRHEAD RINGOES NJ INC
1040 Pennsylvania Ave (08638-3345)
PHONE....................609 695-7803
Edward Simpson, *President*
Doris Simpson, *Vice Pres*
EMP: 10
SQ FT: 2,500
SALES (est): 450.8K **Privately Held**
WEB: www.muirheadfoods.com
SIC: 5812 2099 Eating places; dressings, salad: dry mixes

(G-10960)
NEW HORIZON GRAPHICS INC
2 Christine Ave (08619-2906)
PHONE....................609 584-1301
Lyn Marlin, *President*
Richard Marlin, *Vice Pres*
EMP: 4
SALES: 125K **Privately Held**
SIC: 2752 Commercial printing, offset

(G-10961)
NEW JERSEY BUS & INDUST ASSN (PA)
Also Called: Njbia
10 W Lafayette St (08608-2002)
PHONE....................609 393-7707
Philip Kirschner, *President*
Steve Wilson, *President*
Betty Boros, *Vice Pres*
Frank Robinson, *Vice Pres*
Michael Wallace, *Vice Pres*
EMP: 57
SQ FT: 15,000
SALES (est): 9.2MM **Privately Held**
WEB: www.njbia.net
SIC: 8611 2721 Trade associations; magazines: publishing only, not printed on site

(G-10962)
NEW JERSEY DEPARTMENT TREASURY
Also Called: Print Shop
101 Carroll St (08609-1009)
P.O. Box 30 (08625-0030)
PHONE....................609 292-5133
Sandy Gallino, *Manager*
EMP: 25 **Privately Held**
WEB: www.tax.state.nj.us
SIC: 2754 9311 Commercial printing, gravure; finance, taxation & monetary policy;
HQ: New Jersey Department Of Treasury
    125 W State St
    Trenton NJ 08608

(G-10963)
NEW JERSEY PORCELAIN CO INC (PA)
600 Plum St (08638-3349)
PHONE....................609 394-5376
Stephen M Bielawski, *President*
Thomas E Wenczel Jr, *Corp Secy*
Donald A Bielawski, *Vice Pres*
◆ **EMP:** 15 **EST:** 1920
SQ FT: 100,000
SALES (est): 15.7MM **Privately Held**
SIC: 3261 3264 Plumbing fixtures, vitreous china; insulators, electrical: porcelain

(G-10964)
NEW JRSEY STATE LEAG MNCPLTIES
Also Called: New Jrsey State Leag Mncplitie
222 W State St (08608-1000)
PHONE....................609 695-3481
William G Dressel Jr, *Principal*
Kristin Lawrence, *Manager*
Brian Leszczak, *Info Tech Mgr*
Michael Cerra, *Director*
Suzanne Delany, *Director*
EMP: 19
SQ FT: 3,000
SALES (est): 4MM **Privately Held**
SIC: 8641 2721 Civic social & fraternal associations; magazines: publishing only, not printed on site

(G-10965)
NEWFUTUREVEST TWO LLC (PA)
17a Marlen Dr (08691-1648)
PHONE....................609 586-8004
Seth Harmening, *CFO*
Ron Gale,
Jan Gale,
EMP: 2
SALES (est): 1MM **Privately Held**
SIC: 2819 Industrial inorganic chemicals

(G-10966)
NINI DISPOSAL
410 Whitehead Rd (08619-3255)
PHONE....................609 587-2411
Sebastiano Nini, *Principal*

EMP: 7
SALES (est): 665.7K **Privately Held**
SIC: 3089 Garbage containers, plastic

(G-10967)
NORTH EASTERN BUSINESS FORMS
Also Called: Harrison Press
1111 Chestnut Ave (08611-2011)
PHONE....................609 392-1161
George Demeter, *Owner*
EMP: 5 **EST:** 1953
SALES (est): 313.5K **Privately Held**
SIC: 2761 2759 Manifold business forms; commercial printing

(G-10968)
OLD BARRACKS ASSOCIATION INC
Also Called: OLD BARRACKS MUSEUM
101 Barrack St (08608-2007)
PHONE....................609 396-1776
Richard Patterson, *Exec Dir*
Howard E Mitchell Jr,
EMP: 14
SQ FT: 15,000
SALES: 699.3K **Privately Held**
SIC: 8412 2741 Museum; newsletter publishing

(G-10969)
OMAHA STANDARD INC TR NJ
572 Whitehead Rd (08619-4804)
PHONE....................609 588-5400
EMP: 6
SALES (est): 456.3K **Privately Held**
SIC: 3965 Hooks, crochet

(G-10970)
PAHCO MACHINE INC (PA)
572 Whitehead Rd Ste 101 (08619-4804)
PHONE....................609 587-1188
Peter A Horvath Jr, *President*
Peter A Horvath Sr, *Chairman*
Judy Horvath, *Corp Secy*
EMP: 7
SQ FT: 8,000
SALES (est): 705.1K **Privately Held**
SIC: 3599 3544 Machine shop, jobbing & repair; industrial molds

(G-10971)
PALFINGER NORTH AMERICA
Also Called: Omaha Standards
572 Whitehead Rd Ste 301 (08619-4804)
P.O. Box 5757 (08638-0757)
PHONE....................609 588-5400
Warren Kimble, *General Mgr*
Dick Sullivan, *Technical Staff*
◆ **EMP:** 80
SALES (est): 22.5MM **Privately Held**
SIC: 3536 3537 Hoists, cranes & monorails; industrial trucks & tractors

(G-10972)
PERFORMANCE INDUSTRIES INC
Also Called: Davy Jnes Swmming Pool Pnt Div
51 Tucker St (08618-4705)
PHONE....................609 392-1450
Stewart Azarchi, *President*
Ginger Azarchi, *Treasurer*
EMP: 30 **EST:** 1946
SQ FT: 20,000
SALES (est): 2MM **Privately Held**
WEB: www.performanceindustries.com
SIC: 2851 Paints, waterproof

(G-10973)
PHOENIX CONTAINER INC
6 Litho Rd (08648-3304)
PHONE....................732 247-3931
Ken Sokoloff, *President*
Barry Zankel, *VP Finance*
▲ **EMP:** 110
SQ FT: 106,000
SALES (est): 10.8MM
SALES (corp-wide): 1.1B **Privately Held**
SIC: 3411 Pails, except shipping: metal
HQ: Bway Corporation
    375 Northridge Rd Ste 600
    Atlanta GA 30350

(G-10974)
PHOTO OFFSET PRTG & PUBG CO
536 Highway 33 (08619-4406)
PHONE....................609 587-4900
Robert A Perilli, *President*
EMP: 5
SQ FT: 18,000
SALES (est): 674.8K **Privately Held**
SIC: 2752 Photo-offset printing

(G-10975)
PMP COMPOSITES CORPORATION
572 Whitehead Rd Ste 101 (08619-4804)
PHONE....................609 587-1188
Peter A Horvath Sr, *Chairman*
EMP: 30
SALES (est): 4.4MM **Privately Held**
SIC: 3089 Injection molded finished plastic products; plastic processing

(G-10976)
PORFIRIO FOODS INC
320 Anderson St (08611-1106)
PHONE....................609 393-4116
Robert Calabro, *President*
Anthony Calabro, *Vice Pres*
EMP: 5 **EST:** 1965
SQ FT: 3,000
SALES (est): 516.3K **Privately Held**
SIC: 5411 2098 Grocery stores; macaroni products (e.g. alphabets, rings & shells), dry

(G-10977)
POWER MAGNETICS INC (PA)
377 Reservoir St (08618-3641)
PHONE....................609 695-1170
Ilene Pearl Bannwart, *CEO*
Carl A Bannwart, *President*
▲ **EMP:** 20
SQ FT: 17,000
SALES: 4MM **Privately Held**
WEB: www.powermagneticsinc.com
SIC: 3612 3621 Power transformers, electric; phase or rotary converters (electrical equipment)

(G-10978)
POWER MAGNETICS INC
Also Called: Icb Enterprises
377 Reservoir St (08618-3641)
PHONE....................800 747-0845
Ilene Pearl Bannwart, *Branch Mgr*
EMP: 20
SALES (corp-wide): 4MM **Privately Held**
SIC: 3612 3621 Power transformers, electric; phase or rotary converters (electrical equipment)
PA: Power Magnetics, Inc.
    377 Reservoir St
    Trenton NJ 08618
    609 695-1170

(G-10979)
POWER PRODUCTS AND ENGRG LLC
Also Called: Ppe
324 Meadowbrook Rd (08691-2503)
PHONE....................855 769-3751
Joe Polizzi, *Principal*
EMP: 30
SQ FT: 52,000
SALES (est): 1.3MM **Privately Held**
SIC: 3443 Condensers, steam; heat exchangers: coolers (after, inter), condensers, etc.; economizers (boilers); industrial vessels, tanks & containers

(G-10980)
PRESCRIPTION PODIATRY LABS
826 S Broad St (08611-1904)
PHONE....................609 695-1221
Robert Pagono, *President*
EMP: 6
SQ FT: 2,000
SALES: 300K **Privately Held**
SIC: 3842 Surgical appliances & supplies

(G-10981)
PRESS ROOM INC
100 Youngs Rd Ste 2 (08619-1025)
P.O. Box 2989 (08690-0189)
PHONE....................609 689-3817

Ted Altomari, *President*
EMP: 10
SALES (est): 1.3MM **Privately Held**
SIC: 2759 7334 Commercial printing; photocopying & duplicating services

(G-10982)
PRESTIGE ASSOCIATES INC
39 Meade St (08638-4321)
P.O. Box 3873 (08629-0873)
PHONE..................................609 393-1509
Robert McGuire, *President*
EMP: 50
SQ FT: 25,000
SALES (est): 8.7MM **Privately Held**
SIC: 2675 3081 Die-cut paper & board; floor or wall covering, unsupported plastic

(G-10983)
PRINCETON MICROWAVE TECHNOLOGY
5 Nami Ln Ste 1 (08619-1261)
PHONE..................................609 586-8140
Amar Kaur, *President*
Sarjit Singh, *Corp Secy*
EMP: 7
SQ FT: 2,500
SALES (est): 1.4MM **Privately Held**
WEB: www.princetonmicrowave.com
SIC: 3679 Microwave components; oscillators; passive repeaters

(G-10984)
PRO-DECK SUPPLY
3 Pembroke Ct (08648-2008)
PHONE..................................609 771-1100
Chad Mickley, *Manager*
EMP: 9 **Privately Held**
SIC: 3444 Roof deck, sheet metal
PA: Pro-Deck Supply
1608 5th St
Ewing NJ 08638

(G-10985)
R J D MACHINE PRODUCTS INC
1424-1428 Heath Ave (08638)
PHONE..................................609 392-1515
Richard Roslowski, *President*
Deborah Roslowski, *Corp Secy*
Roslowski Richard, *Treasurer*
EMP: 11
SQ FT: 10,000
SALES (est): 1.6MM **Privately Held**
WEB: www.rjdmachineproducts.com
SIC: 3599 Machine shop, jobbing & repair

(G-10986)
RALPH CLAYTON & SONS LLC
Also Called: Clayton Block
1144 New York Ave (08638-3308)
P.O. Box 3015, Lakewood (08701-9015)
PHONE..................................609 695-0767
Earl Brown, *Principal*
Joe Sweeney, *Manager*
EMP: 30
SALES (corp-wide): 106.4MM **Privately Held**
WEB: www.claytonco.com
SIC: 5032 3273 Concrete mixtures; gravel; sand, construction; ready-mixed concrete
PA: Ralph Clayton & Sons L.L.C.
1355 Campus Pkwy
Wall Township NJ 07753
732 363-1995

(G-10987)
RICZTONE INC
Also Called: Future Signs
19 Bow Hill Ave (08610-6509)
PHONE..................................609 695-6263
Rich Rutzler, *President*
Kimberly Arena, *Chairman*
EMP: 4
SQ FT: 2,200
SALES (est): 530.8K **Privately Held**
SIC: 3993 Signs, not made in custom sign painting shops

(G-10988)
ROCK DREAMS ELECTRONICS LLC
362 State Highway 33 (08619-4402)
PHONE..................................609 890-0808
EMP: 5
SQ FT: 8,000

SALES (est): 530K **Privately Held**
SIC: 3651 Mfg Household Audio & Video Equipment

(G-10989)
ROPER SCIENTIFIC INC (HQ)
3660 Quakerbridge Rd (08619-1208)
PHONE..................................941 556-2601
Jason Conley, *Vice Pres*
Norman Glitz, *Engineer*
Sathish Kuruvilla, *Engineer*
Daisy Xu, *Accountant*
Jack Mills, *Sales Dir*
EMP: 33
SQ FT: 20,000
SALES (est): 35.6MM
SALES (corp-wide): 5.1B **Publicly Held**
WEB: www.roperscientific.com
SIC: 3827 3861 8748 3829 Optical instruments & lenses; cameras & related equipment; systems analysis or design; measuring & controlling devices
PA: Roper Technologies, Inc.
6901 Prof Pkwy E Ste 200
Sarasota FL 34240
941 556-2601

(G-10990)
SCHOOL SPIRIT PROMOTIONS
3 Ely Ct (08690-2203)
PHONE..................................609 588-6902
Ron Thomson, *Principal*
EMP: 8
SALES (est): 583.1K **Privately Held**
SIC: 2389 Apparel & accessories

(G-10991)
SGW FUEL DELIVERY
353 Churchill Ave (08610-3220)
PHONE..................................609 209-8773
Scott M White, *Principal*
EMP: 4
SALES (est): 473.6K **Privately Held**
SIC: 2869 Fuels

(G-10992)
STEVEN MADOLA
Also Called: Park Ave Printing
2001 S Broad St (08610-6005)
PHONE..................................609 989-8022
Steven Madola, *Owner*
James Madola, *Exec Dir*
EMP: 9
SQ FT: 3,000
SALES: 400K **Privately Held**
SIC: 2752 Commercial printing, lithographic

(G-10993)
STONITE COIL CORPORATION
476 Route 156 (08620-9701)
P.O. Box 11036 (08620-0036)
PHONE..................................609 585-6600
William G Engel, *President*
Scott Root, *Vice Pres*
Kimberley Milec, *Controller*
Kimberley Cotner, *Accountant*
Carol Engel, *VP Human Res*
▲ **EMP:** 26 **EST:** 1950
SQ FT: 25,000
SALES (est): 8MM **Privately Held**
WEB: www.stonitecoil.com
SIC: 3677 Electronic coils, transformers & other inductors

(G-10994)
SWITLIK PARACHUTE COMPANY INC
Lalor & Hancock Sts (08609)
P.O. Box 1328 (08607-1328)
PHONE..................................609 587-3300
Richard Switlik, *Vice Pres*
Phuok Tran, *MIS Mgr*
EMP: 10
SALES (corp-wide): 21MM **Privately Held**
SIC: 3069 2399 3842 2326 Life jackets, inflatable: rubberized fabric; life rafts, rubber; parachutes; surgical appliances & supplies; men's & boys' work clothing
PA: Switlik Parachute Company, Inc.
1325 E State St
Trenton NJ 08609
609 587-3300

(G-10995)
TAC TECHNICAL INSTRUMENT CORP
Also Called: Tactic
21 W Piper Ave (08628-1310)
PHONE..................................609 882-2894
Kenneth H Beck, *Ch of Bd*
Frederick Beck, *President*
Howard Hunter, *Treasurer*
Ruth Kontura, *Admin Sec*
▼ **EMP:** 14
SQ FT: 10,000
SALES (est): 3MM **Privately Held**
WEB: www.tactictest.com
SIC: 3823 7389 3541 Industrial instrmnts msrmnt display/control process variable; inspection & testing services; machine tools, metal cutting type

(G-10996)
TAYLOR PROVISIONS COMPANY
63 Perrine Ave (08638-5114)
P.O. Box 5108 (08638-0108)
PHONE..................................609 392-1113
John T Cumbler, *Chairman*
George Cumbler, *CFO*
Elisabeth Cumbler, *Treasurer*
EMP: 75 **EST:** 1856
SQ FT: 1,500
SALES (est): 9.6MM **Privately Held**
SIC: 2011 2013 Meat packing plants; pork, cured: from purchased meat; pork, pickled: from purchased meat; pork, salted: from purchased meat

(G-10997)
TEKTITE INDUSTRIES INC
Also Called: Tektite Mfg Division
309 N Clinton Ave (08638-5122)
PHONE..................................609 656-0600
Scott Mele, *President*
Wayne Fowler, *COO*
▲ **EMP:** 9
SQ FT: 10,000
SALES (est): 1.5MM **Privately Held**
WEB: www.tek-tite.com
SIC: 3648 3089 3646 Lighting equipment; injection molding of plastics; commercial indusl & institutional electric lighting fixtures

(G-10998)
TIMES OF TRENTON PUBG CORP
413 River View Plz (08611-3427)
PHONE..................................609 989-5454
Richard Bilotti, *President*
Rachel Vallianos, *Advt Staff*
Kristin Bucci, *Manager*
EMP: 735 **EST:** 1882
SQ FT: 50,000
SALES (est): 29.2MM **Privately Held**
WEB: www.njtimes.com
SIC: 7313 2711 Newspaper advertising representative; newspapers

(G-10999)
TIMOTHY P BRYAN ELC CO INC
1926 Chestnut Ave (08611-2704)
PHONE..................................609 393-8325
Timothy P Bryan, *President*
Timothy Bryan Jr, *Vice Pres*
EMP: 9
SQ FT: 1,500
SALES (est): 2MM **Privately Held**
WEB: www.bryanelectricco.com
SIC: 1731 3629 General electrical contractor; battery chargers, rectifying or non-rotating

(G-11000)
TRANE US INC
2231 E State Street Ext (08619-3311)
PHONE..................................609 587-3400
Andy Stevenson, *General Mgr*
Brian Salay, *Buyer*
EMP: 61 **Privately Held**
SIC: 3585 Refrigeration & heating equipment
HQ: Trane U.S. Inc.
3600 Pammel Creek Rd
La Crosse WI 54601
608 787-2000

(G-11001)
TRENT BOX MANUFACTURING CO
1384 Yardville Ham Rd (08691-3343)
P.O. Box 2650 (08690-0150)
PHONE..................................609 587-7515
Carl A Angelini, *President*
Joyce Angelini, *Admin Sec*
EMP: 20 **EST:** 1959
SQ FT: 30,000
SALES (est): 4.3MM **Privately Held**
WEB: www.trent.com
SIC: 2653 Boxes, corrugated: made from purchased materials; boxes, solid fiber: made from purchased materials

(G-11002)
TRENTON PRINTING LLC
1150 Southard St Ste 2 (08638-5099)
PHONE..................................609 695-6485
Lucille Raymond, *CFO*
Steve Sadiwnyk, *Sales Mgr*
David Nugent, *Mng Member*
Bill Nugent, *Mng Member*
EMP: 17 **EST:** 1929
SQ FT: 17,500
SALES (est): 3.5MM **Privately Held**
WEB: www.trentonprinting.com
SIC: 2752 7331 Commercial printing, offset; mailing service

(G-11003)
TRENTON SHEET METAL INC
30 Adam Ave (08618-4108)
P.O. Box 1121 (08606-1121)
PHONE..................................609 695-6328
Robert Somogyi, *President*
Bob Somogyi, *President*
Marilyn Somogyi, *Corp Secy*
EMP: 30
SQ FT: 25,000
SALES (est): 5.3MM **Privately Held**
WEB: www.trentonsheetmetal.com
SIC: 3444 Sheet metal specialties, not stamped

(G-11004)
TRI-STEEL FABRICATORS INC
501 Prospect St (08618-3640)
P.O. Box 5756 (08638-0756)
PHONE..................................609 392-8660
James Werosta, *President*
Karl Werosta, *Principal*
EMP: 26 **EST:** 1949
SALES (est): 6.4MM **Privately Held**
SIC: 3441 1791 Building components, structural steel; structural steel erection

(G-11005)
TRIEFELDT STUDIOS INC
1115 Hamilton Ave (08629-1910)
PHONE..................................609 656-2380
Lauri Triefeldt, *President*
Wayne Triefeldt, *Corp Secy*
EMP: 4
SALES (est): 50K **Privately Held**
SIC: 2741 Directories: publishing & printing

(G-11006)
TUERFF SZIBER CAPITOL COPY SVC
116 W State St (08608-1102)
P.O. Box 72, Titusville (08560-0072)
PHONE..................................609 989-8776
Raymond Sziber, *President*
EMP: 7
SQ FT: 1,500
SALES (est): 899K **Privately Held**
WEB: www.capitol-copy.com
SIC: 2752 Commercial printing, offset

(G-11007)
UTHE TECHNOLOGY INC (HQ)
Scotch Rd (08628)
P.O. Box 7266 (08628-0266)
PHONE..................................609 883-4000
J Michael Goodson, *President*
EMP: 1 **EST:** 1966
SQ FT: 10,000
SALES (est): 1.8MM
SALES (corp-wide): 54.6MM **Privately Held**
SIC: 3679 Power supplies, all types: static

PA: Crestek, Inc.
18 Graphics Dr
Ewing NJ 08628
609 883-4000

(G-11008)
WHITE EAGLE PRINTING CO INC
2550 Kuser Rd (08691-3499)
P.O. Box 8363 (08650-0363)
PHONE..................................609 586-2032
Eric Bielawski, *President*
A Thad Bielawski Jr, *President*
Edward Krupa Jr, *Principal*
Lorretta Daunis, *Treasurer*
Laurie Smith, *Executive*
EMP: 25 EST: 1933
SQ FT: 1,500
SALES (est): 4.7MM **Privately Held**
WEB: www.whiteeagledistribution.co.uk
SIC: 2752 Commercial printing, offset

(G-11009)
WOODLAND MANUFACTURING COMPANY
1936 E State Street Ext (08619-3306)
PHONE..................................609 587-4180
Lawrence A Marcinkus Jr, *President*
Joseph Sciacca, *Accounts Mgr*
EMP: 15
SQ FT: 110,000
SALES (est): 3.8MM **Privately Held**
WEB: www.woodlandmfg.com
SIC: 2653 Boxes, corrugated: made from purchased materials

(G-11010)
WORD CENTER PRINTING
1905 Highway 33 Ste 10 (08690-1742)
PHONE..................................609 586-5825
Jerry Silverman, *Owner*
Marilyn Silverman, *Co-Owner*
Diane Heinz, *Sales Mgr*
EMP: 4
SQ FT: 1,500
SALES (est): 300K **Privately Held**
WEB: www.wordcenterprinting.com
SIC: 7338 2791 7334 Word processing service; hand composition typesetting; photocopying & duplicating services

(G-11011)
WT MEDIA LLC
4 Applegate Dr (08691-2342)
PHONE..................................609 921-3490
James Frintner, *Mng Member*
EMP: 17
SQ FT: 20,000
SALES (est): 1.8MM **Privately Held**
SIC: 2731 7311 Books: publishing & printing; advertising agencies

Tuckahoe
Cape May County

(G-11012)
MAUND ENTERPRISES INC
112 Buckhill Rd (08250)
P.O. Box 561 (08250-0561)
PHONE..................................609 628-2475
Keith Maund II, *President*
EMP: 5
SALES (est): 627.6K **Privately Held**
SIC: 3272 Burial vaults, concrete or precast terrazzo

(G-11013)
PIPE DREAMS MARINE LLC
251 Mill Rd (08250)
PHONE..................................609 628-9353
Donald Battin, *Owner*
EMP: 4
SALES (est): 482K **Privately Held**
SIC: 3499 Marine horns, compressed air or steam

(G-11014)
SUNSPLASH MARINA LLC
5 Mosquito Landing Rd (08250)
P.O. Box 87 (08250-0087)
PHONE..................................609 628-4445
John Yank,
EMP: 7

SALES (est): 794.2K **Privately Held**
SIC: 3732 Boat building & repairing

(G-11015)
YANK MARINE INC
7 Mosquito Landing Rd (08250)
PHONE..................................609 628-2928
John Yank, *President*
▲ EMP: 25
SQ FT: 18,000
SALES (est): 4.7MM **Privately Held**
SIC: 3732 Boat building & repairing

Turnersville
Camden County

(G-11016)
CDM ELECTRONICS INC (PA)
130 American Blvd (08012-1735)
PHONE..................................856 740-1200
Carmen De Leo, *President*
Christina Harrison, *Sales Staff*
Brian Kudlicki, *Sales Staff*
EMP: 108
SQ FT: 16,000
SALES (est): 51.7MM **Privately Held**
WEB: www.cdmelec.com
SIC: 3357 Aircraft wire & cable, nonferrous

Twp Washinton
Bergen County

(G-11017)
FLUIDSENS INTERNATIONAL INC
703 Beechwood Dr (07676-3802)
PHONE..................................914 338-3932
Arnon Scheflan, *CEO*
Irit Scheflan, *COO*
Gideon Vardi, *Vice Pres*
Alex Keinan, *Engineer*
Josef More, *CFO*
EMP: 5
SALES (est): 340K **Privately Held**
SIC: 3822 Auto controls regulating residntl & coml environmt & applncs

Union
Union County

(G-11018)
360 MEDIA INNOVATIONS LLC
1511a Stuyvesant Ave (07083)
PHONE..................................201 228-0941
Chima Gale, *President*
Jovita Gale, *Principal*
Abiose Gale,
EMP: 6
SQ FT: 900
SALES (est): 1.4MM **Privately Held**
SIC: 5065 4813 3651 Communication equipment; telephone communication, except radio; audio electronic systems

(G-11019)
ACUPOWDER INTERNATIONAL LLC (DH)
901 Lehigh Ave (07083-7632)
PHONE..................................908 851-4500
EMP: 8
SALES (est): 1.2MM
SALES (corp-wide): 31.8MM **Privately Held**
WEB: www.acupowder.com
SIC: 3399 Powder, metal

(G-11020)
ADAM TECH ASIA LLC (HQ)
909 Rahway Ave (07083-6549)
PHONE..................................908 687-5000
Vincent Devito, *CEO*
EMP: 3
SALES (est): 1.2MM
SALES (corp-wide): 5.2MM **Privately Held**
SIC: 3678 Electronic connectors

PA: Adam Technologies Inc.
909 Rahway Ave
Union NJ
908 687-5000

(G-11021)
ALL TOOL COMPANY INC
899 Rahway Ave (07083-6699)
PHONE..................................908 687-3636
John Vinciguerra, *President*
Scott Daniels, *General Mgr*
Dominick Rose, *Purch Agent*
Roselin Mutek, *Controller*
EMP: 11 EST: 1941
SQ FT: 15,000
SALES (est): 1.8MM **Privately Held**
SIC: 3599 Machine shop, jobbing & repair

(G-11022)
ALLARY CORPORATION
2204 Morris Ave Ste 209 (07083-5914)
P.O. Box 693, Livingston (07039-0693)
PHONE..................................908 851-0077
Alan B Sorrell, *President*
Larry Self, *Exec VP*
Lisa Gittleman, *Vice Pres*
Anita D Sorrell, *Vice Pres*
Jaina Naik, *Bookkeeper*
◆ EMP: 14
SQ FT: 3,000
SALES (est): 2.7MM **Privately Held**
SIC: 3965 Buckles & buckle parts; tape, hook-and-eye & snap fastener

(G-11023)
AMERICAN BRASS AND CRYSTAL INC
835 Lehigh Ave (07083-7631)
PHONE..................................908 688-8611
Ross Kirshenbaum, *President*
Lori Kirshenbaum, *Vice Pres*
▲ EMP: 20
SQ FT: 20,000
SALES (est): 3.5MM **Privately Held**
SIC: 3645 3646 Residential lighting fixtures; commercial indusl & institutional electric lighting fixtures

(G-11024)
AMERICAN INTR RESOURCES INC
Also Called: Locker Lady, The
1206 Francyne Way (07083-5800)
P.O. Box 3656 (07083-1894)
PHONE..................................908 851-0014
Grace Choe, *President*
EMP: 4
SALES (est): 879.2K **Privately Held**
SIC: 7389 2541 5021 Interior design services; cabinets, lockers & shelving; lockers

(G-11025)
AMERICAN PRODUCTS COMPANY INC
610 Rahway Ave Ste 1 (07083-6696)
PHONE..................................908 687-4100
Richard Picut, *President*
Christopher Walsh, *President*
Thea Lloyd, *General Mgr*
Russell Picut, *Vice Pres*
Bruno Garcia, *Production*
EMP: 95
SQ FT: 70,000
SALES (est): 16.6MM **Privately Held**
WEB: www.amerprod.com
SIC: 3491 Steam traps
PA: Picut Industries Inc.
140 Mount Bethel Rd
Warren NJ 07059

(G-11026)
ANISHA ENTERPRISES INC
Also Called: Axiam Printing
2165 Morris Ave Ste 1 (07083-5913)
PHONE..................................908 964-3380
Nisha Jhawar, *President*
Dan Maheshwari, *Exec VP*
Purushottam Jhawar, *Vice Pres*
Shakuntala Maheshwari, *Vice Pres*
EMP: 7
SQ FT: 4,000
SALES (est): 1MM **Privately Held**
WEB: www.axiamprinting.com
SIC: 2752 Commercial printing, offset

(G-11027)
ARMORPOXY INC
805 Lehigh Ave (07083-7626)
PHONE..................................908 810-9613
Daniel Blum, *President*
Elisabeth Speckhart, *Marketing Staff*
▲ EMP: 18
SALES (est): 5.6MM **Privately Held**
WEB: www.armorpoxy.com
SIC: 2851 5033 5023 5713 Epoxy coatings; roofing & siding materials; floor coverings; floor covering stores; floor laying & floor work

(G-11028)
B & G PLASTICS INC (PA)
Also Called: B & G International
1085 Morris Ave Ste 5d (07083-7136)
PHONE..................................973 824-9220
Chet Kolton, *President*
Michael Norman, *Exec VP*
▲ EMP: 45
SQ FT: 80,000
SALES (est): 5.7MM **Privately Held**
WEB: www.bgplastics.com
SIC: 3089 2679 Clothes hangers, plastic; paper products, converted

(G-11029)
BASF CORPORATION
2655 Route 22 W (07083-8505)
PHONE..................................732 205-2700
Thomas Anderson, *Branch Mgr*
EMP: 157
SALES (corp-wide): 71.7B **Privately Held**
SIC: 2869 Industrial organic chemicals
HQ: Basf Corporation
100 Park Ave
Florham Park NJ 07932
973 245-6000

(G-11030)
BEAUTY WOOD DESIGNS
284 Concord Ave (07083-4219)
PHONE..................................908 687-9697
Charles Potzer, *Owner*
EMP: 5 EST: 1988
SQ FT: 2,500
SALES: 250K **Privately Held**
SIC: 2759 Engraving

(G-11031)
BELTING INDUSTRIES GROUP LLC (HQ)
1090 Lousons Rd (07083-5030)
PHONE..................................908 272-8591
Susan Bender, *CEO*
Webb Scott Cooper, *President*
Gene Hobson, *COO*
Paul West, *CFO*
▲ EMP: 50
SQ FT: 33,000
SALES (est): 22.2MM **Privately Held**
WEB: www.beltingindustries.com
SIC: 5085 3052 2399 Hose, belting & packing; rubber belting; plastic belting; belting, fabric: made from purchased materials
PA: Passaic Rubber Co.
45 Demarest Dr
Wayne NJ 07470
973 696-9500

(G-11032)
BHAMRA CHAIN MANUFACTURING
1020 Springfield Rd (07083-8160)
PHONE..................................908 686-4555
Ajit Bhamra, *President*
Varmeet Bhamra, *Vice Pres*
EMP: 4
SQ FT: 2,500
SALES (est): 330K **Privately Held**
SIC: 3911 Necklaces, precious metal

(G-11033)
BUTTERFLY BOW TIES LLC
911 Garden St (07083-6557)
PHONE..................................973 626-2536
Edward Armah, *Owner*
EMP: 8
SQ FT: 5,000
SALES (est): 322.1K **Privately Held**
SIC: 2389 Men's miscellaneous accessories

(G-11034)
BUY BUY BABY INC (HQ)
650 Liberty Ave (07083-8107)
PHONE......................................908 688-0888
Shannan Macias, *Store Mgr*
Elizabeth Bennet, *Buyer*
Vickie Bingle, *Buyer*
Lilly Duryee, *Buyer*
Anna Pierle, *Sales Mgr*
◆ EMP: 15
SQ FT: 5,000
SALES (est): 100.5MM
SALES (corp-wide): 12B **Publicly Held**
SIC: 5641 5999 2023 Children's wear; infants' wear; baby carriages & strollers; high chairs; baby formulas
PA: Bed Bath & Beyond Inc.
650 Liberty Ave
Union NJ 07083
908 688-0888

(G-11035)
CE DE CANDY INC (PA)
Also Called: Smarties
1091 Lousons Rd (07083-5097)
PHONE......................................908 964-0660
Edward Dee, *Ch of Bd*
Michael Dee, *Vice Pres*
▲ EMP: 150 EST: 1949
SQ FT: 82,000
SALES (est): 59.3MM **Privately Held**
SIC: 2064 Candy & other confectionery products

(G-11036)
COMPREHENSIVE MKTG SYSTEMS
Also Called: Comprehensive Mktg Systems
850 Springfield Rd # 353 (07083-8614)
PHONE......................................908 810-9778
Carl Fazio, *President*
Sanford Greenman, *Vice Pres*
EMP: 5
SALES (est): 450K **Privately Held**
WEB: www.compmark.com
SIC: 7331 2752 Direct mail advertising services; commercial printing, offset

(G-11037)
CONTINNTAL CONCESSION SUPS INC
1135 Springfield Rd (07083-8120)
PHONE......................................516 629-4906
Reggie Leary, *Branch Mgr*
EMP: 25
SALES (corp-wide): 19.7B **Publicly Held**
WEB: www.ccsicandy.com
SIC: 5145 5113 2086 2096 Popcorn & supplies; candy; cups, disposable plastic & paper; napkins, paper; tea, iced: packaged in cans, bottles, etc.; fruit drinks (less than 100% juice): packaged in cans, etc.; popcorn, already popped (except candy covered)
HQ: Continental Concession Supplies, Inc.
575 Jericho Tpke Ste 300
Jericho NY 11753
516 739-8777

(G-11038)
CORONATION SHEET METAL CO
2198 Stanley Ter (07083-4315)
PHONE......................................908 686-0930
Joseph Cafiero, *President*
Stephen C Cafiero, *Treasurer*
Stephen Cafiero, *Admin Sec*
EMP: 9
SQ FT: 10,000
SALES: 1.1MM **Privately Held**
SIC: 3444 Sheet metal specialties, not stamped; ducts, sheet metal; ventilators, sheet metal

(G-11039)
CP EQUIPMENT SALES CO
1504 Oakland Ave (07083-5468)
P.O. Box 3723 (07083-1892)
PHONE......................................908 687-9621
Thomas J Kazalski, *President*
Susan Rice, *Treasurer*
EMP: 12
SALES (est): 1.1MM **Privately Held**
WEB: www.cpequip.com
SIC: 3589 Water treatment equipment, industrial

(G-11040)
D & D TECHNOLOGY INC
254 Elmwood Ave (07083-6775)
P.O. Box 3636 (07083-1894)
PHONE......................................908 688-5154
Roberta Varga, *CEO*
Ed G Varga, *President*
EMP: 9
SQ FT: 1,700
SALES (est): 3.5MM **Privately Held**
SIC: 5162 3544 Plastics materials & basic shapes; special dies, tools, jigs & fixtures

(G-11041)
DARTAGNAN INC (PA)
600 Green Ln (07083-8074)
PHONE......................................973 344-0565
Ariane Daguin, *President*
Kirk Eilers, *General Mgr*
Brian Hull, *General Mgr*
Padraic Doherty, *Vice Pres*
Gideon Brand, *Purch Mgr*
▲ EMP: 81
SQ FT: 36,000
SALES (est): 72.4MM **Privately Held**
WEB: www.dartagnan.com
SIC: 5147 5148 5149 2011 Meats, fresh; vegetables; natural & organic foods; canned meats (except baby food), meat slaughtered on site

(G-11042)
DEEP FOODS INC (PA)
Also Called: Inter Trend
1090 Springfield Rd Ste 1 (07083-8147)
PHONE......................................908 810-7500
Arvind Amin, *President*
Jeffrey Comitz, *Engineer*
◆ EMP: 150 EST: 1977
SQ FT: 60,000
SALES (est): 48.3MM **Privately Held**
WEB: www.deepfoods.com
SIC: 2038 2052 2024 5141 Dinners, frozen & packaged; bakery products, dry; ice milk, bulk; groceries, general line

(G-11043)
DORAN LLC
Also Called: Doran Company
599 Green Ln (07083-7701)
PHONE......................................908 289-9200
Randy Wojcik,
EMP: 4
SQ FT: 20,000
SALES (est): 350K **Privately Held**
SIC: 3542 Machine tools, metal forming type

(G-11044)
DUERR TOOL & DIE CO INC
1135 Springfield Rd (07083-8120)
PHONE......................................908 810-9035
Karl Duerr, *President*
Walter Duerr, *Corp Secy*
Jens Duerr, *Exec VP*
▲ EMP: 110 EST: 1945
SQ FT: 125,000
SALES (est): 9.4MM **Privately Held**
WEB: www.duerrinc.com
SIC: 3089 3544 Injection molding of plastics; special dies & tools

(G-11045)
DUREX INC (PA)
Also Called: Creative Serving
5 Stahuber Ave (07083-5086)
PHONE......................................908 688-0800
Robert Denholtz, *CEO*
Philip Feiner, *Vice Pres*
Jimy Castiglione, *Mfg Mgr*
Mike Danniballe, *Engineer*
Ruslan Leksin, *Engineer*
▲ EMP: 84 EST: 1946
SQ FT: 120,000
SALES (est): 26.9MM **Privately Held**
WEB: www.durexinc.com
SIC: 3469 3471 3444 Stamping metal for the trade; finishing, metals or formed products; sheet metalwork; metal housings, enclosures, casings & other containers

(G-11046)
DURO MANUFACTURING COMPANY
5 Stahuber Ave (07083-5037)
P.O. Box 1771 (07083-1771)
PHONE......................................908 810-9588
Robert Failla, *President*
Ann Marie Failla, *Admin Sec*
▲ EMP: 6
SQ FT: 8,000
SALES: 550K **Privately Held**
SIC: 3451 Screw machine products

(G-11047)
DYNA-LITE INC
1050 Commerce Ave Ste 2 (07083-5081)
P.O. Box 1554 (07083-1554)
PHONE......................................908 687-8800
Peter Poremba, *President*
Peter Roberts, *COO*
Orlando Dela Cruz, *Purchasing*
John Prazeres, *Research*
Terry Monahan, *CFO*
▲ EMP: 18
SQ FT: 12,000
SALES (est): 3.2MM **Privately Held**
WEB: www.dynalite.com
SIC: 3861 Flashlight apparatus for photographers, except bulbs

(G-11048)
EASY STREET PUBLICATIONS INC
1473 Ridgeway St (07083-5127)
P.O. Box 138, Vauxhall (07088-0138)
PHONE......................................917 699-7820
▲ EMP: 9
SQ FT: 2,000
SALES: 2.4MM **Privately Held**
SIC: 2771 Publishes Greeting Cards

(G-11049)
ECHO MOLDING INC
911 Springfield Rd Ste 1 (07083-8600)
PHONE......................................908 688-0099
Dieter Hekler, *President*
Gerhard Schlotterbeck, *Corp Secy*
▲ EMP: 38
SQ FT: 60,000
SALES: 9.3MM **Privately Held**
WEB: www.echomolding.com
SIC: 3089 Injection molding of plastics

(G-11050)
EL BATAL CORPORATION
Also Called: Grip Tight Tools
1060 Commerce Ave (07083-5026)
PHONE......................................908 964-3427
Walid Nakhla, *CEO*
▲ EMP: 18
SQ FT: 30,000
SALES (est): 2.4MM **Privately Held**
WEB: www.griptighttools.com
SIC: 5072 5032 3432 Hand tools; security devices, locks; building stone; granite building stone; plumbers' brass goods: drain cocks, faucets, spigots, etc.

(G-11051)
ELEMENTAL CONTAINER INC
860 Springfield Rd (07083-8614)
PHONE......................................908 687-7720
Luc Tournaire, *President*
Madelyn Cicalese, *General Mgr*
▲ EMP: 7
SQ FT: 22,000
SALES: 6MM **Privately Held**
WEB: www.elementalcontainer.com
SIC: 3411 Metal cans

(G-11052)
ERNEST SCHAEFER INC
731 Lehigh Ave (07083-7626)
PHONE......................................908 964-1280
Ernest Schaeffer III, *President*
EMP: 6 EST: 1922
SQ FT: 10,000
SALES: 1MM **Privately Held**
SIC: 5084 3555 Printing trades machinery, equipment & supplies; type, foundry (for printing)

(G-11053)
EVOQUA WATER TECHNOLOGIES LLC
Also Called: Electric Catalytic Pdts Group
2 Milltown Ct (07083-8108)
PHONE......................................908 851-4250
John Martin, *Manager*
EMP: 85
SALES (corp-wide): 1.3B **Publicly Held**
SIC: 3589 Water treatment equipment, industrial
HQ: Evoqua Water Technologies Llc
210 6th Ave Ste 3300
Pittsburgh PA 15222
724 772-0044

(G-11054)
FILTER HOLDINGS INC
Also Called: Summit Filter Corp
20 Milltown Rd (07083-8110)
PHONE......................................908 687-3500
Bernie Watson, *CEO*
Paul Silverthorne, *President*
EMP: 20 EST: 1945
SQ FT: 25,000
SALES (est): 6.2MM
SALES (corp-wide): 62.8K **Privately Held**
WEB: www.summitfilter.com
SIC: 3569 3564 2674 Filters, general line: industrial; blowers & fans; bags: uncoated paper & multiwall
PA: Hadley Capital Fund Ii Lp
1200 Central Ave Ste 300
Wilmette IL 60091
847 920-5300

(G-11055)
FLOW-TURN INC
1050 Commerce Ave (07083-5087)
PHONE......................................908 687-3225
Hermann Miedel, *President*
Dan Otero, *Opers Mgr*
Young Ran Miedel, *Director*
EMP: 25
SQ FT: 36,000
SALES: 2.5MM **Privately Held**
WEB: www.flow-turn.com
SIC: 3535 Belt conveyor systems, general industrial use

(G-11056)
FOREMOST MANUFACTURING CO INC
941 Ball Ave (07083-8799)
PHONE......................................908 687-4646
Herbert S Schiller, *CEO*
Patrick Curtin, *COO*
Michael Moritz, *Accounting Mgr*
Michael Franciosa, *Sales Executive*
Joan Schiller, *Admin Sec*
▲ EMP: 70 EST: 1957
SQ FT: 52,000
SALES (est): 11.7MM **Privately Held**
SIC: 3471 Finishing, metals or formed products

(G-11057)
FUEL STOP INC
2570 Us Highway 22 E (07083-8510)
PHONE......................................201 697-3319
EMP: 4
SALES (est): 307.1K **Privately Held**
SIC: 2869 Fuels

(G-11058)
GAVAN GRAHAM ELEC PDTS CORP (PA)
751 Rahway Ave (07083-6689)
PHONE......................................908 729-9000
Ron Regan, *President*
John Robak, *VP Opers*
Mike Donohue, *Sales Mgr*
Aj Metzger, *Sales Engr*
Christina Dobosiewicz, *Office Mgr*
EMP: 30
SQ FT: 42,000
SALES (est): 12.7MM **Privately Held**
WEB: www.gavangraham.com
SIC: 3441 Fabricated structural metal

(G-11059)
GEORGE J BENDER INC
Also Called: Bender Enterprises
1 Milltown Ct (07083-8108)
PHONE......................................908 687-0081

John Appicie, *President*
EMP: 35 **EST:** 1935
SQ FT: 6,700
SALES (est): 3.3MM **Privately Held**
SIC: 7694 5063 1731 Motor repair services; motors, electric; generators; electrical work

(G-11060)
GOLDSTEIN SETTING CO INC
Also Called: Dan Mar Jewelers
2464 Morris Ave (07083-5763)
PHONE..........................908 964-1034
Joseph Goldstein, *President*
Myrna Goldstein, *Admin Sec*
EMP: 12
SQ FT: 3,000
SALES (est): 460K **Privately Held**
SIC: 3911 5944 Jewel settings & mountings, precious metal; jewelry, precious stones & precious metals

(G-11061)
HASSELBLAD INC
Also Called: Hasselblad Bron Incorporated
1080a Garden State Rd (07083-8102)
PHONE..........................800 456-0203
Michael Hejtmanek, *President*
Sandra Strausser, *Finance Mgr*
Eric Peterson, *Sales Staff*
Maryann Murphy, *Administration*
▲ **EMP:** 21
SALES (est): 3MM **Privately Held**
SIC: 3861 Photographic equipment & supplies
PA: Hasselblad Ab

Goteborg

(G-11062)
HATHAWAY PLASTIC
911 Springfield Rd Ste 1 (07083-8600)
PHONE..........................908 688-9494
Robert Daniel, *Principal*
EMP: 7
SALES (est): 690.6K **Privately Held**
SIC: 3089 Injection molding of plastics

(G-11063)
HUMMEL DISTRIBUTING CORP
(PA)
850 Springfield Rd (07083-8614)
PHONE..........................908 688-5300
John Hummel, *President*
Lorraine Hummel, *Corp Secy*
Herbert Hummel Jr, *Vice Pres*
▲ **EMP:** 30
SQ FT: 33,000
SALES (est): 4.4MM **Privately Held**
WEB: www.hummelprintmail.com
SIC: 2759 7331 Commercial printing; mailing service

(G-11064)
HUMMEL PRINTING INC
850 Springfield Rd (07083-8614)
PHONE..........................908 688-5300
John Hummel, *President*
Lorraine Hummel, *Corp Secy*
Herbert Hummel Jr, *Vice Pres*
EMP: 30
SALES (est): 4.4MM **Privately Held**
SIC: 2759 7331 Commercial printing; mailing service
PA: Hummel Distributing Corp
850 Springfield Rd
Union NJ 07083
908 688-5300

(G-11065)
INSTRU-MET CORPORATION
931 Lehigh Ave (07083-7632)
PHONE..........................908 851-0700
Paul Metzger, *President*
Ward Ruoff, *Vice Pres*
Maria Silvia, *Admin Sec*
EMP: 8
SQ FT: 4,500
SALES (est): 860K **Privately Held**
WEB: www.instrumet.com
SIC: 3824 7629 3829 3825 Mechanical & electromechanical counters & devices; electronic equipment repair; testing equipment: abrasion, shearing strength, etc.; instruments to measure electricity

(G-11066)
JERSEY BOUND LATINO LLC
Also Called: Jersey Bound Latino Magazine
841 Hueston St (07083-7104)
P.O. Box 1230 (07083-1230)
PHONE..........................908 591-2830
Victor Nichols, *CEO*
Marlene Jauregui, *President*
EMP: 6
SALES (est): 259.1K **Privately Held**
SIC: 7389 8742 2741 5192 Subscription fulfillment services: magazine, newspaper, etc.; marketing consulting services; ; books, periodicals & newspapers; survey service: marketing, location, etc.

(G-11067)
JOHN CANARY CUSTOM WDWKG INC
Also Called: Canary' Closets & Cabinetry
697 Rahway Ave (07083-6683)
PHONE..........................908 851-2894
John Canary, *President*
Steve Seibert, *General Mgr*
Karol Weiland, *Bookkeeper*
Wayne Coe, *Sales Associate*
EMP: 18
SALES (est): 2MM **Privately Held**
WEB: www.canarycustom.com
SIC: 2434 Wood kitchen cabinets

(G-11068)
KALUSTYAN CORPORATION
(PA)
Also Called: Castle Foods
855 Rahway Ave (07083-6633)
PHONE..........................908 688-6111
Errol Karakash, *CEO*
John O Bas, *President*
Luis Ortriz, *Warehouse Mgr*
Manuel Castillo, *Human Res Mgr*
Carolina Montoya, *Administration*
◆ **EMP:** 80
SQ FT: 110,500
SALES (est): 15.1MM **Privately Held**
WEB: www.kalustyan.com
SIC: 2099 5149 5159 5153 Seasonings & spices; spices, including grinding; spices & seasonings; fruits, dried; nuts & nut by-products; beans, dry: bulk

(G-11069)
LINCOLN ELECTRIC PDTS CO INC
947 Lehigh Ave (07083-7632)
PHONE..........................908 688-2900
Bruce Leff, *President*
Peter Vallone, *Project Mgr*
Patrick Wallace, *Purch Agent*
Paul Iannacone, *Engineer*
George Vafakos, *Engineer*
EMP: 35 **EST:** 1949
SQ FT: 50,000
SALES (est): 15.4MM **Privately Held**
WEB: www.leproduct.com
SIC: 3613 Panelboards & distribution boards, electric; switchboards & parts, power

(G-11070)
LIONI LATTICINI INC (PA)
555 Lehigh Ave (07083-7976)
PHONE..........................908 686-6061
Giuseppe Salzarulo, *President*
Charlie Disalvo, *Vice Pres*
Sal Salzarulo, *Vice Pres*
Michelina Salzarulo, *Sales Mgr*
Andrea Salzarulo, *Office Mgr*
◆ **EMP:** 58
SALES (est): 13.7MM **Privately Held**
SIC: 2022 Cheese, natural & processed

(G-11071)
LIONI MOZZARELLA & SPCLTY
Also Called: Lioni Specialty Foods
555 Lehigh Ave (07083-7976)
PHONE..........................908 624-9450
Giuseppe Salzarulo, *President*
Charlie Disalvo, *Vice Pres*
Lori Church, *Sales Staff*
Michael Virga, *Admin Sec*
▲ **EMP:** 50

SALES (est): 5.3MM **Privately Held**
SIC: 2022 2099 5143 5149 Cheese spreads, dips, pastes & other cheese products; pasta, uncooked: packaged with other ingredients; cheese; pasta & rice; food brokers

(G-11072)
MAJOR PRINTING CO INC
934 Savitt Pl (07083-6759)
P.O. Box 1356 (07083-1356)
PHONE..........................908 686-7296
Joseph Stampone, *President*
John Stampone, *Vice Pres*
EMP: 4
SQ FT: 6,000
SALES (est): 600K **Privately Held**
WEB: www.majorprinting.com
SIC: 2752 Commercial printing, offset

(G-11073)
MANNING & LEWIS ENGRG CO INC
675 Rahway Ave Ste 1 (07083-6695)
PHONE..........................908 687-2400
Kurt Nelson, *President*
John R Hayday, *Vice Pres*
Alvin Matt, *Vice Pres*
▲ **EMP:** 60
SQ FT: 40,000
SALES (est): 7.1MM **Privately Held**
WEB: www.manninglewis.com
SIC: 3443 3559 Heat exchangers: coolers (after, inter), condensers, etc.; chemical machinery & equipment

(G-11074)
MARVIC CORP
Also Called: Marvic Formica In Design
2450 Iorio Ct (07083-8105)
PHONE..........................908 686-4340
Alfred D'Alessandro, *President*
Victoria D'Alessandro, *Corp Secy*
Mildred Carbone, *Vice Pres*
Al Dalessandro, *VP Opers*
Adriana Ross, *Accounts Mgr*
EMP: 50 **EST:** 1961
SQ FT: 10,000
SALES (est): 7.4MM **Privately Held**
SIC: 2541 3281 Counter & sink tops; cut stone & stone products

(G-11075)
MERRILL CORPORATION
649 Rahway Ave (07083-6683)
PHONE..........................908 810-3740
Tom Arnold, *President*
EMP: 100
SALES (corp-wide): 566.6MM **Privately Held**
WEB: www.merrillcorp.com
SIC: 2759 2752 Commercial printing; business form & card printing, lithographic
PA: Merrill Corporation
1 Merrill Cir
Saint Paul MN 55108
651 646-4501

(G-11076)
MORRE-TEC INDUSTRIES INC
Also Called: Extracts and Ingredients
1 Gary Rd (07083-5527)
PHONE..........................908 688-9009
Leonard Glass, *President*
Estelle Glass, *Admin Sec*
▲ **EMP:** 24
SQ FT: 20,000
SALES (est): 14.8MM **Privately Held**
WEB: www.morretec.com
SIC: 5169 2819 Industrial chemicals; industrial inorganic chemicals

(G-11077)
MR QUICKLY INC
Also Called: Quickly Printing
1965 Morris Ave (07083)
PHONE..........................908 687-6000
Larry Kovacs, *President*
EMP: 4
SQ FT: 1,000
SALES (est): 400K **Privately Held**
SIC: 2752 7334 Commercial printing, offset; photocopying & duplicating services

(G-11078)
MULBERRY METAL PRODUCTS INC (PA)
2199 Stanley Ter (07083-4399)
PHONE..........................908 688-8850
Richard Horn, *President*
Richard E Mueller, *Exec VP*
Kristina Hom, *Vice Pres*
Patricia Lynch, *Finance Mgr*
Robert Walker, *Sales Mgr*
EMP: 90 **EST:** 1927
SQ FT: 135,000
SALES: 24MM **Privately Held**
WEB: www.mulberrymetal.com
SIC: 3644 5065 Face plates (wiring devices); outlet boxes (electric wiring devices); switch boxes, electric; semiconductor devices

(G-11079)
NATIONAL WOODWORKING CO
985 Tinkettle Turn (07083-3499)
PHONE..........................908 851-9316
Richard Weber, *President*
Evelyn Weber, *Vice Pres*
EMP: 4
SQ FT: 7,500
SALES (est): 450K **Privately Held**
SIC: 2431 2511 Woodwork, interior & ornamental; wood household furniture

(G-11080)
PAIGE ELECTRIC COMPANY LP
(PA)
1160 Springfield Rd (07083-8121)
P.O. Box 368 (07083-0368)
PHONE..........................908 687-7810
James Coleman, *CEO*
David Coleman, *Vice Pres*
Joe Dobies, *Vice Pres*
Marty Fox, *Vice Pres*
Beata Kolodziej, *Opers Staff*
◆ **EMP:** 47
SQ FT: 47,000
SALES: 132.5MM **Privately Held**
WEB: www.paigewire.com
SIC: 5063 3699 Electronic wire & cable; electrical equipment & supplies

(G-11081)
PALMAROZZO BINDERY
850 Springfield Rd (07083-8614)
PHONE..........................908 688-5300
Tina Palmarozzo, *Owner*
EMP: 4
SALES (est): 150K **Privately Held**
SIC: 2789 Bookbinding & related work

(G-11082)
PATEL PRINTING PLUS CORP
1036 Commerce Ave (07083-5026)
PHONE..........................908 964-6422
Jawahar C Patel, *President*
Sharon Patel, *Vice Pres*
EMP: 10
SQ FT: 6,000
SALES (est): 1.2MM **Privately Held**
WEB: www.patelprintingplus.com
SIC: 2752 2791 Commercial printing, offset; typesetting

(G-11083)
PHILIP CRETER INC
20 Monroe St (07083-8192)
PHONE..........................908 686-2910
Doris Logan, *President*
Bruce Logan, *Vice Pres*
EMP: 6 **EST:** 1941
SQ FT: 10,000
SALES (est): 430K **Privately Held**
SIC: 3544 3599 3469 Special dies & tools; machine & other job shop work; machine parts, stamped or pressed metal

(G-11084)
PREMESCO INC
Also Called: Premesco Seamless Ring Co Div
2389 Vauxhall Rd (07083-5036)
PHONE..........................908 686-0513
EMP: 300
SQ FT: 40,000
SALES: 42.3MM **Privately Held**
SIC: 3911 3339 Rings, finger: precious metal; precious metals

(G-11085)
QUALITY INDEXING LLC
939 Lehigh Ave (07083-7632)
PHONE....................................908 810-0200
Daniel Blum, *Owner*
William E Ulrich, *Consultant*
EMP: 45 **EST:** 1920
SALES (est): 5.3MM **Privately Held**
SIC: 2675 Index cards, die-cut: made from
   purchased materials

(G-11086)
R M F ASSOCIATES INC
202 Carolyn Rd (07083-9403)
PHONE....................................908 687-9355
Roger M Furiness, *President*
Michael Rogers, *Vice Pres*
EMP: 140
SQ FT: 11,000
SALES: 10MM **Privately Held**
SIC: 3469 3444 Metal stampings; sheet
   metalwork

(G-11087)
S AND D FUEL LLC
1351 Magie Ave (07083-8070)
PHONE....................................908 248-8188
EMP: 4
SALES (est): 32.6K **Privately Held**
SIC: 2869 Fuels

(G-11088)
SATEC INC
10 Milltown Ct (07083-8108)
PHONE....................................908 258-0924
Ed Hoinowski, *President*
Esli Latorre, *General Mgr*
Shaun Olson, *Regional Mgr*
Bertil Christian, *Vice Pres*
Jeffrey Matthews, *Opers Mgr*
▲ **EMP:** 23
SALES (est): 5.2MM **Privately Held**
WEB: www.oksatec.com
SIC: 3825 Meters, power factor & phase
   angle

(G-11089)
SCHOTT NYC CORP
735 Rahway Ave (07083-6689)
PHONE....................................800 631-5407
Steven Colin, *CEO*
Roslyn Schott, *Corp Secy*
David Colin, *Vice Pres*
Maryann Schumacher, *Controller*
Calleson Edwards, *Accounts Exec*
▲ **EMP:** 100
SALES (est): 13.2MM
SALES (corp-wide): 13.4MM **Privately
Held**
WEB: www.schottnyc.com
SIC: 2386 2329 Coats & jackets, leather &
   sheep-lined; garments, leather; down-
   filled clothing: men's & boys'
PA: Schott Bros, Inc.
   735 Rahway Ave
   Union NJ 07083
   908 527-0011

(G-11090)
SHAFFER PRODUCTS INC
20 Milltown Rd (07083-8110)
P.O. Box 427 (07083-0427)
PHONE....................................908 206-1980
H Sabet, *Ch of Bd*
James K Shahidi, *President*
EMP: 25 **EST:** 1951
SQ FT: 10,000
SALES (est): 1.9MM **Privately Held**
WEB: www.shafferproducts.com
SIC: 2393 Bags & containers, except
   sleeping bags: textile

(G-11091)
SPINAL KINETICS LLC (PA)
950 W Chestnut St (07083-6966)
PHONE....................................908 687-2552
Steven Brownstein MD, *Partner*
Steven P Brownstein MD, *Partner*
Joseph Cioffi, *Opers Staff*
Donald Cioffi DC, *Mktg Dir*
EMP: 4 **EST:** 2008
SALES (est): 428.7K **Privately Held**
SIC: 8041 3842 8011 Offices & clinics of
   chiropractors; trusses, orthopedic & surgi-
   cal; neurosurgeon

(G-11092)
STERNVENT CO INC
No5 Stahuber Ave (07083)
P.O. Box 356, Bogota (07603-0356)
PHONE....................................908 688-0807
Philip Feiner, *President*
Gerson Feiner, *Vice Pres*
Penni Feiner, *Treasurer*
EMP: 35
SQ FT: 42,000
SALES (est): 5.5MM
SALES (corp-wide): 26.9MM **Privately
Held**
WEB: www.sternvent.com
SIC: 3564 Dust or fume collecting equip-
   ment, industrial
PA: Durex Inc.
   5 Stahuber Ave
   Union NJ 07083
   908 688-0800

(G-11093)
TARLTON C & T CO INC (PA)
Also Called: Nedco Conveyor Technology
967 Lehigh Ave (07083-7632)
PHONE....................................908 964-9400
Curtis Tarlton, *President*
Theresa Tarlton, *Corp Secy*
Daniel Oliva, *Sales Staff*
EMP: 40 **EST:** 1961
SQ FT: 23,000
SALES (est): 10MM **Privately Held**
SIC: 3535 Conveyors & conveying equip-
   ment

(G-11094)
**TESSLER & WEISS/PREMESCO
INC**
2389 Vauxhall Rd (07083-5091)
PHONE....................................800 535-3501
Mark Tessler, *President*
Esther Tessler, *Corp Secy*
EMP: 175 **EST:** 1936
SQ FT: 40,000
SALES (est): 19.8MM **Privately Held**
SIC: 3911 3915 Rings, finger: precious
   metal; jewelers' materials & lapidary work

(G-11095)
THERMO PLASTIC TECH INC
1119 Morris Ave (07083-3305)
PHONE....................................908 687-4833
Tino Quintanilla, *President*
Flor Quint, *Vice Pres*
▲ **EMP:** 30
SQ FT: 18,000
SALES (est): 5.1MM **Privately Held**
SIC: 3089 Molding primary plastic; plastic
   processing

(G-11096)
**UNION CASTING INDUSTRIES
INC (PA)**
Also Called: Industrial Ferguson Foundry
2365 Us Highway 22 W (07083-8517)
P.O. Box 531 (07083-0531)
PHONE....................................908 686-8888
Harvey Gross, *President*
Ken Kartodich, *Vice Pres*
EMP: 17
SALES (est): 3.2MM **Privately Held**
WEB: www.industrialferguson.com
SIC: 3364 3365 3366 Brass & bronze die-
   castings; copper & copper alloy die-cast-
   ings; zinc & zinc-base alloy die-castings;
   aluminum & aluminum-based alloy cast-
   ings; castings (except die): copper & cop-
   per-base alloy

(G-11097)
VALCONN ELECTRONICS INC
909 Rahway Ave (07083-6549)
PHONE....................................908 687-1600
Vince Devito, *CEO*
Joel Cohn, *President*
▲ **EMP:** 20
SQ FT: 16,000
SALES (est): 1.9MM **Privately Held**
SIC: 3679 3678 Electronic connectors;
   harness assemblies for electronic use:
   wire or cable

(G-11098)
VULCAN TOOL COMPANY INC
1080 Garden State Rd # 1 (07083-8181)
PHONE....................................908 686-0550
Anton Heldmann, *President*
EMP: 17 **EST:** 1967
SQ FT: 15,000
SALES (est): 3.5MM **Privately Held**
WEB: www.vulcantool.com
SIC: 3599 Machine shop, jobbing & repair

(G-11099)
WET-N-STICK LLC
Also Called: Duratape International
2816 Morris Ave Ste 21 (07083-4869)
PHONE....................................908 687-8273
Lee Goldman, *President*
▲ **EMP:** 7
SQ FT: 19,000
SALES (est): 971.5K **Privately Held**
WEB: www.duratape.com
SIC: 2672 Adhesive papers, labels or
   tapes: from purchased material

(G-11100)
**WILLIAM T HUTCHINSON
COMPANY**
453 Lehigh Ave (07083-7926)
PHONE....................................908 688-0533
Dean Roth, *President*
EMP: 13
SQ FT: 5,000
SALES: 1.8MM **Privately Held**
WEB: www.hssblanks.com
SIC: 3545 3546 Drilling machine attach-
   ments & accessories; power-driven hand-
   tools

Union Beach
Monmouth County

(G-11101)
**INTERNTNAL FLVORS
FRGRNCES INC**
800 Rose Ln (07735-3550)
PHONE....................................732 264-4500
Clint Brooks, *Manager*
Neil Da Costa, *Associate*
EMP: 250
SALES (corp-wide): 3.9B **Publicly Held**
SIC: 2869 Industrial organic chemicals
PA: International Flavors & Fragrances Inc.
   521 W 57th St
   New York NY 10019
   212 765-5500

(G-11102)
**INTERNTNAL FLVORS
FRGRNCES INC**
800 Rose Ln (07735-3550)
PHONE....................................732 264-4500
EMP: 126
SALES (corp-wide): 3.9B **Publicly Held**
WEB: www.iff.com
SIC: 2869 Flavors or flavoring materials,
   synthetic; perfume materials, synthetic
PA: International Flavors & Fragrances Inc.
   521 W 57th St
   New York NY 10019
   212 765-5500

(G-11103)
J R M PRODUCTS INC
701 Locust St (07735-1750)
PHONE....................................732 203-0200
Marianne Wichowski, *Branch Mgr*
EMP: 4
SALES (corp-wide): 320K **Privately Held**
SIC: 3469 Stamping metal for the trade
PA: J R M Products Inc
   15 Phillips Mills Dr
   North Middletown NJ 07748
   732 495-3092

Union City
Hudson County

(G-11104)
ALPINE BAKERY INC
521-523 30th St (07087-3863)
PHONE....................................201 902-0605
Danilo Torres, *President*
▲ **EMP:** 8
SALES (est): 836.4K **Privately Held**
SIC: 2051 Bread, cake & related products

(G-11105)
AMALIA CARRARA INC
2111 Kerrigan Ave (07087-2122)
PHONE....................................201 348-4500
Eve Muscio, *President*
EMP: 50 **EST:** 2001
SALES (est): 1.8MM **Privately Held**
WEB: www.amaliacarrara.com
SIC: 2335 Wedding gowns & dresses

(G-11106)
**ANDY GRAPHICS SERVICE
BUREAU**
3711 Park Ave (07087-6021)
PHONE....................................201 866-9407
Andy Nazarian, *Owner*
EMP: 4
SALES (est): 190K **Privately Held**
SIC: 2759 Commercial printing

(G-11107)
APHELION ORBITALS INC
540 39th St Ste 40 (07087-2500)
PHONE....................................321 289-0872
Matthew B Travis, *President*
Matthew Travis, *President*
Connor Givans, *Vice Pres*
Sihao Huang, *Vice Pres*
David Nagy, *Vice Pres*
EMP: 4
SALES (est): 197.4K **Privately Held**
SIC: 3663 2899 5088 3764 Space satel-
   lite communications equipment; pyrotech-
   nic ammunition: flares, signals, rockets,
   etc.; guided missiles & space vehicles;
   guided missile & space vehicle engines,
   research & devel.; propulsion units for
   guided missiles & space vehicles

(G-11108)
ATARA LLC
4315 Park Ave Apt 2i (07087-6566)
PHONE....................................916 765-2217
Kostyantyn Beynars, *Principal*
EMP: 4 **EST:** 2012
SALES (est): 220K **Privately Held**
SIC: 2844 7389 Shampoos, rinses, condi-
   tioners: hair;

(G-11109)
CUNY AND GUERBER INC
Also Called: C G Automation Group
2100 Kerrigan Ave (07087-2123)
P.O. Box 1192 (07087-1192)
PHONE....................................201 617-5800
David Matthews, *President*
Ray Cuny, *Vice Pres*
David B Matthews Sr, *Vice Pres*
David B Matthews Jr, *Vice Pres*
Steve Matthews, *Vice Pres*
EMP: 25
SQ FT: 22,500
SALES (est): 29.9MM **Privately Held**
WEB: www.cuny.biz
SIC: 5063 4783 3699 Lighting fixtures;
   containerization of goods for shipping;
   electrical equipment & supplies

(G-11110)
**DENGEN SCIENTIFIC
CORPORATION**
315 4th St (07087-4006)
PHONE....................................201 687-2983
Ysabel Depaul, *CFO*
EMP: 25
SALES (est): 903.2K **Privately Held**
SIC: 8711 8731 3812 3629 Engineering
   services; commercial physical research;
   defense systems & equipment; battery
   chargers, rectifying or nonrotating; prod-
   uct testing laboratories;

(G-11111)
DISCOUNT DIGITAL PRINT LLC
422 11th St (07087-4260)
PHONE...................201 659-9600
James Dilworth,
EMP: 12 EST: 2010
SALES (est): 937.9K Privately Held
SIC: 2752 Commercial printing, litho-
graphic

(G-11112)
**HAMILTON EMBROIDERY CO
INC**
907 21st St (07087-2104)
PHONE...................201 867-4084
Frank Blaso Sr, President
Frank Blaso Jr, Vice Pres
▲ EMP: 17
SQ FT: 25,000
SALES (est): 3.4MM Privately Held
WEB: www.hamiltonembroidery.com
SIC: 2397 2241 Schiffli machine embroi-
deries; narrow fabric mills

(G-11113)
**IMAGERY EMBROIDARY
CORPORATION**
2907 Jeannette St 2911 (07087-2333)
PHONE...................201 343-9333
Edison Cruz, President
EMP: 10
SQ FT: 4,500
SALES (est): 250K Privately Held
SIC: 2759 2395 Screen printing; embroi-
dery & art needlework

(G-11114)
J & T EMBROIDERY INC
646 36th St (07087-2511)
PHONE...................201 867-4897
Thomas Betancourt, President
EMP: 5
SALES (est): 300K Privately Held
SIC: 2395 Embroidery products, except
schiffli machine

(G-11115)
JARCO U S CASTING CORP
4407 Park Ave (07087-6345)
PHONE...................201 271-0003
Mario Herrera, President
Felix Disla, Vice Pres
▲ EMP: 45 EST: 1981
SQ FT: 14,000
SALES: 3MM Privately Held
WEB: www.jarcousa.com
SIC: 3993 3369 3272 Signs & advertising
specialties; castings, except die-castings,
precision; cast stone, concrete

(G-11116)
JCT DESIGN ENTERPRISES INC
1701 Summit Ave (07087-2020)
PHONE...................212 629-7412
Carlos Tapia, President
EMP: 25
SALES: 1.3MM Privately Held
SIC: 3911 Jewelry, precious metal

(G-11117)
KALEIDOSCOPE SOUND
514 Monastery Pl (07087-3389)
PHONE...................201 223-2868
Randy Craftone, Owner
EMP: 4
SALES (est): 363.2K Privately Held
SIC: 3663 Studio equipment, radio & tele-
vision broadcasting

(G-11118)
LA TRIBUNA PUBLICATION INC
300 36th St Apt 1 (07087-4724)
PHONE...................201 617-1360
Ruth M Molenaar, President
Soraya Molenaar, Vice Pres
EMP: 37 EST: 1988
SALES (est): 1.4MM Privately Held
SIC: 2711 8661 Newspapers: publishing
only, not printed on site; religious organi-
zations

(G-11119)
LICINI BROTHERS INC
Also Called: Licini Bros Provision
907 West St (07087-3007)
PHONE...................201 865-1130
Andrew Licini, President
Daniel Licini, Corp Secy
EMP: 9
SQ FT: 5,700
SALES (est): 925.8K Privately Held
SIC: 2013 5147 5421 Sausages & other
prepared meats; meats, fresh; meat & fish
markets

(G-11120)
LUSTERLINE INC
501 30th St Ste 1a (07087-3876)
PHONE...................201 758-5148
Devyani V Patel, President
Namesh Patel, Vice Pres
◆ EMP: 5
SQ FT: 1,200
SALES (est): 1.3MM Privately Held
SIC: 3911 Jewelry, precious metal

(G-11121)
MAXSYL LEATHER CO LLC
131 35th St (07087-5911)
PHONE...................201 864-0579
Walter Martillo Jr, President
John Bryant, General Mgr
EMP: 90
SALES (est): 5.4MM Privately Held
SIC: 3172 3111 Personal leather goods;
leather processing

(G-11122)
MSJ UNLIMITED SERVICES
519 35th St (07087-2501)
PHONE...................201 617-0764
Ruben Cruz, Owner
EMP: 5
SALES (est): 380.7K Privately Held
SIC: 3822 1711 Air conditioning & refriger-
ation controls; plumbing, heating, air-con-
ditioning contractors

(G-11123)
NICOLOSI FOODS INC
2214 Summit Ave (07087-2129)
PHONE...................201 624-1702
Robert Nicolosi, President
EMP: 9
SALES (est): 1.6MM Privately Held
SIC: 0751 2013 Slaughtering: custom live-
stock services; sausages & other pre-
pared meats

(G-11124)
NOBLEWORKS INC
500 Paterson Plank Rd (07087-3416)
PHONE...................201 420-0095
Ron Kanfi, President
▲ EMP: 12
SQ FT: 8,000
SALES: 1.6MM Privately Held
WEB: www.nobleworksinc.com
SIC: 2771 5112 Greeting cards; greeting
cards

(G-11125)
PUEBLO LATINO LAUNDRY LLC
1717 Bergenline Ave (07087-3232)
PHONE...................201 864-1666
EMP: 7
SQ FT: 1,800
SALES (est): 660K Privately Held
SIC: 2211 7215 Cotton Broadwoven Fab-
ric Mill Coin-Operated Laundry

(G-11126)
R & R FUEL INC
3205 Hudson Ave (07087-5803)
PHONE...................201 223-0786
Mussarat Shaheen, Principal
EMP: 5
SALES (est): 416.6K Privately Held
SIC: 2869 Fuels

(G-11127)
**S JARCO-U CASTINGS
CORPORATION**
109 45th St (07087-6311)
PHONE...................201 271-0003
Mario A Herrera, President

▲ EMP: 7
SALES (est): 851.1K Privately Held
SIC: 3369 Nonferrous foundries

(G-11128)
**SOCKS 47 LTD LIABILITY
COMPANY**
4620 Bergenline Ave (07087-5126)
PHONE...................201 866-2222
Abdulnaser Daaboul, Principal
EMP: 5
SALES (est): 107.4K Privately Held
SIC: 2252 Socks

(G-11129)
SONIA FASHION INC
422 11th St (07087-4260)
P.O. Box 8146 (07087-1846)
PHONE...................201 864-3483
Louis Taupier Jr, President
Lisa Taupier, Vice Pres
▲ EMP: 4
SQ FT: 10,500
SALES (est): 482.8K Privately Held
WEB: www.soniafashion.com
SIC: 2339 Jeans: women's, misses' & jun-
iors'

(G-11130)
U S A DISTRIBUTORS INC
Also Called: El Estelcil
3510 Bergenline Ave Ste 4 (07087-4775)
PHONE...................201 348-1959
Anthony Ibarria, President
EMP: 50
SQ FT: 7,000
SALES (est): 2.4MM Privately Held
SIC: 2711 Newspapers: publishing only,
not printed on site

(G-11131)
**UNION CITY MIRROR & TABLE
CO**
129 34th St (07087-5902)
PHONE...................201 867-0050
Lisa Russo, Corp Secy
Thomas Russo, Vice Pres
Gene Russo, Vice Pres
EMP: 48 EST: 1921
SQ FT: 55,000
SALES (est): 5.9MM Privately Held
SIC: 2511 3231 Tables, household: wood;
mirrored glass

(G-11132)
**UNION CITY WHIRLPOOL
REPAIR**
507 43rd St (07087-2611)
PHONE...................908 428-9146
Hilton Lehmann, Principal
EMP: 8 EST: 2016
SALES (est): 88.7K Privately Held
SIC: 7692 Welding repair

(G-11133)
**UNIQUE IMPRESSIONS LTD
LBLTY**
718 25th St (07087-2257)
PHONE...................201 751-4088
Frank Corbiserie,
EMP: 5
SALES (est): 301.3K Privately Held
SIC: 2759 Bag, wrapper & seal printing &
engraving

Upper Saddle River
Bergen County

(G-11134)
ATLANTIC EQP ENGINEERS INC
24 Industrial Ave (07458-2302)
P.O. Box 181 (07458-0181)
PHONE...................201 828-9400
Alan M Kessler, President
Barry E Kessler, Vice Pres
EMP: 11
SQ FT: 12,000
SALES: 6MM Privately Held
WEB: www.metal-powders.com
SIC: 3399 3324 3479 Powder, metal;
aerospace investment castings, ferrous;
coating of metals & formed products

(G-11135)
**BERGEN DIGITAL GRAPHICS
LLC**
Also Called: Fastsigns
346 State Rt 17 (07458-2308)
PHONE...................201 825-0011
William Miller,
Kevin Miller,
EMP: 4
SQ FT: 2,500
SALES (est): 623.6K Privately Held
SIC: 3993 Signs & advertising specialties

(G-11136)
BUSINESS CARDS TOMORROW
Also Called: B C T
11 Industrial Ave (07458-2301)
PHONE...................201 236-0088
John Cerdendino, Owner
Sue Negrin, Vice Pres
EMP: 20
SALES (est): 1.7MM Privately Held
SIC: 2752 Commercial printing, litho-
graphic

(G-11137)
**COMPONDING ENGRG
SOLUTIONS INC**
Also Called: C E S
72 Danebury Downs (07458-1536)
PHONE...................973 340-4000
Arash Kiani, President
EMP: 10
SALES (est): 2.2MM Privately Held
SIC: 8711 3089 Consulting engineer; pal-
lets, plastic

(G-11138)
CUSTOM LINERS INC
345 State Rt 17 (07458-2307)
PHONE...................732 940-0084
John Boag, Principal
EMP: 4
SALES (est): 553.5K Privately Held
SIC: 2844 Toilet preparations

(G-11139)
DIHCO INC
612 E Crescent Ave Ste A (07458-1859)
PHONE...................201 327-0518
Gus Hess, President
Peter Diamandea, Vice Pres
EMP: 4
SQ FT: 10,000
SALES: 700K Privately Held
SIC: 3599 Machine shop, jobbing & repair

(G-11140)
**HOFMANN TOOL & DIE
CORPORATION**
356 State Rt 17 (07458-2308)
PHONE...................201 327-0226
Charles Franco, President
EMP: 6
SQ FT: 5,000
SALES (est): 687.7K Privately Held
SIC: 3544 Special dies & tools

(G-11141)
INTEGRATE TECH INC
19 Barnfield Ct (07458-1201)
PHONE...................201 693-5625
Maxwell Witt, CEO
Kevin Celisca, CFO
EMP: 4
SALES (est): 108.2K Privately Held
SIC: 7372 Educational computer software

(G-11142)
MINWAX GROUP (INC)
10 Montinview Rd Ste N300 (07458)
PHONE...................201 818-7500
Peter Black, President
Stewart D Bill, President
Ridgely W Harrison III, President
Ann Allard, Vice Pres
Paul Gaynor, Vice Pres
EMP: 990
SALES (est): 116.7MM Privately Held
SIC: 2851 Stains: varnish, oil or wax

(G-11143)
MORE COPY PRINTING SERVICE
302 State Rt 17 (07458-2308)
PHONE...................201 327-1106

Felix Gomez, *Owner*
EMP: 4
SALES (est): 240K Privately Held
SIC: 2752 Commercial printing, lithographic

(G-11144)
PEARSON INC
1 Lake St (07458-1813)
PHONE....................201 236-7000
Leeanne Fisher, *President*
Wendy Craven, *Editor*
Gregory Doench, *Editor*
Katherine Rosenthal, *District Mgr*
Karen Abraham, *Counsel*
EMP: 22
SALES (corp-wide): 5.3B Privately Held
SIC: 2731 Books: publishing & printing; textbooks: publishing & printing
HQ: Pearson Inc.
    1330 Hudson St
    New York NY 10013
    212 641-2400

(G-11145)
PERKINS PLUMBING & HEATING
89 Fawnhill Rd (07458-1518)
PHONE....................201 327-2736
James Redmond, *President*
EMP: 4 EST: 1960
SALES (est): 390.1K Privately Held
SIC: 1711 1389 Plumbing contractors; bailing, cleaning, swabbing & treating of wells

(G-11146)
RED LETTER PRESS INC
16 Deerhorn Trl (07458-1131)
P.O. Box 393, Saddle River (07458-0393)
PHONE....................609 597-5257
Jack Kreismer, *President*
Robin Kreismer, *Admin Sec*
EMP: 3
SALES (est): 1.5MM Privately Held
SIC: 2759 2679 Letterpress printing; novelties, paper: made from purchased material

(G-11147)
TRIANGLE MANUFACTURING CO
116 Pleasant Ave (07458-2396)
PHONE....................201 962-7433
Fax: 201 825-0402
EMP: 8
SALES (est): 790K Privately Held
SIC: 3999 Mfg Misc Products

(G-11148)
TRIANGLE MANUFACTURING CO INC
120 Pleasant Ave (07458-2304)
PHONE....................201 825-1212
Neal Strohmeyer, *Branch Mgr*
EMP: 60
SALES (corp-wide): 45MM Privately Held
WEB: www.cyclonewinder.com
SIC: 3599 Machine & other job shop work; machine shop, jobbing & repair
PA: Triangle Manufacturing Co Inc
    25 Park Way
    Upper Saddle River NJ 07458
    201 825-1212

(G-11149)
WORLD PAC PAPER LLC
600 E Crescent Ave # 301 (07458-1842)
PHONE....................877 837-2737
Edgar L Smith Jr, *CEO*
EMP: 4 EST: 2004
SALES (est): 759K Privately Held
SIC: 2621 Book, bond & printing papers

(G-11150)
XTREME POWERTECH LLC
123 Pleasant Ave (07458-2303)
PHONE....................201 791-5050
Paul Hilfer, *Managing Prtnr*
Marty Lanning,
EMP: 11
SQ FT: 20,000
SALES (est): 1.7MM Privately Held
SIC: 3674 Semiconductor circuit networks; transistors

Vauxhall
Union County

(G-11151)
MELOVINO MEADERY
2933 Vauxhall Rd (07088-1260)
PHONE....................855 635-6846
EMP: 4
SALES (est): 339.2K Privately Held
SIC: 2084 Wines

Ventnor City
Atlantic County

(G-11152)
CAR WASH PARTS INC
6927 Atlantic Ave (08406-2504)
PHONE....................215 633-9250
Edward Eckelman, *President*
Ruth Eckleman, *Vice Pres*
Steven Krevitz, *Treasurer*
EMP: 4
SQ FT: 25,000
SALES (est): 671.4K Privately Held
SIC: 3589 5087 Car washing machinery; carwash equipment & supplies

(G-11153)
GPSCHARTSCOM
5021 Winchester Ave (08406-2459)
PHONE....................609 226-8842
Craig Bates, *Owner*
EMP: 4
SALES (est): 241K Privately Held
SIC: 2782 7389 Chart & graph paper, ruled;

(G-11154)
PHILDELPHIA-NEWSPAPERS-LLC
Also Called: Atlantic City News
109 S Dorset Ave (08406-2835)
PHONE....................609 823-0453
Brian Tierney, *Branch Mgr*
Bentley Alberts, *Executive*
Brendon Fitzsimons, *Executive*
EMP: 1001
SALES (corp-wide): 251.4MM Privately Held
SIC: 2711 Newspapers, publishing & printing
PA: Phildelphia-Newspapers-Llc
    801 Market St Ste 300
    Philadelphia PA 19107
    215 854-2000

(G-11155)
VOICINGS PUBLICATION INC
Also Called: Preachers Illustration Service
3 S Weymouth Ave Ste 2 (08406-2980)
PHONE....................609 822-9401
James Colainni Sr, *President*
James Colaianni Sr, *President*
Patricia Colaianni, *Vice Pres*
EMP: 5
SALES (est): 447.2K Privately Held
WEB: www.voicings.com
SIC: 2741 Miscellaneous publishing

Vernon
Sussex County

(G-11156)
ABOVE ENVIRONMENTAL SERVICES
57 Vernon Crossing Rd (07462-3209)
P.O. Box 801 (07462-0801)
PHONE....................973 702-7021
Thomas Bove, *President*
EMP: 5
SALES (est): 520.1K Privately Held
SIC: 1389 Oil field services

(G-11157)
BLISSFUL BITES
36 Butternut Dr (07462-3301)
PHONE....................973 670-6928

Dawn Mele, *Principal*
EMP: 4
SALES (est): 196K Privately Held
SIC: 2051 Bread, cake & related products

(G-11158)
CONGRUENT MACHINE CO INC
107 Maple Grange Rd (07462-3211)
P.O. Box 888 (07462-0888)
PHONE....................973 764-6767
Gerald Caiafa, *President*
EMP: 5
SQ FT: 12,000
SALES (est): 1MM Privately Held
SIC: 3599 3545 3952 3546 Machine shop, jobbing & repair; precision tools, machinists'; lead pencils & art goods; power-driven handtools; screw machine products

(G-11159)
INDEMAX INC
1 Industrial Dr (07462-3466)
PHONE....................973 209-2424
Alphonse Infurna, *President*
Patricia Infurna, *Vice Pres*
EMP: 7
SALES (est): 1.2MM Privately Held
WEB: www.indemax.com
SIC: 3547 Finishing equipment, rolling mill

(G-11160)
METALFAB INC
Prices Switch Rd (07462)
P.O. Box 9 (07462-0009)
PHONE....................973 764-2000
William Westdyk, *President*
Michael Randazzo, *COO*
Anthony R Bartello, *Vice Pres*
Cornelius De Bonte Jr, *Vice Pres*
Dave Eurich, *Purch Mgr*
▼ EMP: 30
SQ FT: 30,000
SALES (est): 7.2MM Privately Held
WEB: www.metalfabinc.com
SIC: 3444 3535 Sheet metal specialties, not stamped; conveyors & conveying equipment

(G-11161)
METALFAB MTL HDLG SYSTEMS LLC
11 Prices Switch Rd (07462-3311)
PHONE....................973 764-2000
Tony Manno,
Mike McMahon,
EMP: 30
SALES (est): 6MM Privately Held
SIC: 3535 Conveyors & conveying equipment

(G-11162)
NORTHWIND VENTURES INC
39 Woodland Dr (07462-3510)
PHONE....................917 509-1964
William Duffy, *President*
EMP: 4
SALES (est): 221.1K Privately Held
SIC: 7372 Prepackaged software

(G-11163)
TEO FABRICATIONS INC
95 Maple Grange Rd (07462-3206)
P.O. Box 232 (07462-0232)
PHONE....................973 764-5500
Robert Hearn, *President*
Elizabeth Hearn, *Vice Pres*
EMP: 4
SQ FT: 2,400
SALES (est): 605.6K Privately Held
WEB: www.teopro.com
SIC: 3711 Automobile assembly, including specialty automobiles

---

Verona
Essex County

(G-11164)
CAMECO INC
100 Pine St (07044-1346)
P.O. Box 209 (07044-0209)
PHONE....................973 239-2845
Jerome Perl, *CEO*

Richard Perl, *Corp Secy*
EMP: 70 EST: 1944
SQ FT: 25,000
SALES (est): 41.4MM Privately Held
SIC: 5147 5149 2011 2033 Meats, fresh; canned goods: fruit, vegetables, seafood, meats, etc.; meat packing plants; fruits & fruit products in cans, jars, etc.

(G-11165)
ELECTION GRAPHICS INC
15 Rockland Ter (07044-1607)
PHONE....................201 758-9966
Adam Perna, *President*
Louis Gelormini, *Vice Pres*
John Hollop, *Vice Pres*
EMP: 16
SQ FT: 2,700
SALES (est): 1.6MM Privately Held
SIC: 2752 Commercial printing, offset

(G-11166)
FARADAY PHOTONICS LLC
62 Depot St (07044-1338)
PHONE....................973 239-2005
EMP: 6
SALES (est): 618.6K Privately Held
SIC: 3661 Fiber optics communications equipment

(G-11167)
FERRANTE PRESS INC
Also Called: NJ Memorial Art
516 Bloomfield Ave (07044-2001)
PHONE....................609 239-4257
Vincent J Ferrante, *President*
Vincent Ferrante, *Manager*
EMP: 4
SQ FT: 2,600
SALES: 280K Privately Held
SIC: 2759 Letterpress printing

(G-11168)
GARDEN STATE WELDING LLC
89 Claremont Ave (07044-2805)
PHONE....................973 857-0792
Matthew Antolino, *Principal*
EMP: 8
SALES (est): 88.7K Privately Held
SIC: 7692 Welding repair

(G-11169)
INNOVATION PHOTONICS LLC
62 Depot St (07044-1338)
PHONE....................973 857-8380
EMP: 11
SQ FT: 13,000
SALES (corp-wide): 1MM Privately Held
SIC: 3827 Optical instruments & lenses
PA: Innovation Photonics Llc
    102 Hillside Ave
    West Caldwell NJ 07006
    973 228-4785

(G-11170)
M + P INTERNATIONAL INC
271 Grove Ave Ste G (07044-1729)
PHONE....................973 239-3005
Guido Bossaert, *Vice Pres*
Dale Schick, *Opers Mgr*
Chris Wilcox, *Manager*
Mao Yang, *Manager*
Irene Kennedy, *Officer*
EMP: 35
SALES (est): 5.3MM Privately Held
WEB: www.mpihome.com
SIC: 7373 7372 Computer integrated systems design; prepackaged software

(G-11171)
OZONE CONFECTIONERS BAKERS SUP
27 W Lincoln St (07044-1511)
PHONE....................201 791-4444
Patrick Lapone, *President*
Salvatore Lapone, *Corp Secy*
Louis Lapone, *Vice Pres*
EMP: 13 EST: 1947
SQ FT: 4,200
SALES (est): 1.5MM Privately Held
SIC: 2064 Candy & other confectionery products

(G-11172)
PROCLEAN SERVICES INC
Also Called: New Jersey Drapery Service
150 Linden Ave (07044-2204)
PHONE..................................973 857-5408
Robert Saeed, *President*
Patricia Bailey, *Vice Pres*
EMP: 11
SQ FT: 2,200
SALES: 900K **Privately Held**
SIC: 2211 5719 1799 7216 Draperies &
drapery fabrics, cotton; window furnish-
ings; window treatment installation; cur-
tain cleaning & repair

(G-11173)
RELIANCE GRAPHICS INC (PA)
80 Pompton Ave Ste 1 (07044-2913)
PHONE..................................973 239-5411
Robert Fetterly, *President*
EMP: 4
SQ FT: 1,000
SALES (est): 543.6K **Privately Held**
WEB: www.relianceballots.com
SIC: 2752 Commercial printing, offset

(G-11174)
SIRUI USA LLC
29 Commerce Ct (07044-1908)
PHONE..................................973 415-8082
EMP: 4
SALES (est): 381.4K **Privately Held**
SIC: 3827 Optical instruments & lenses

(G-11175)
**SOLMOR MANUFACTURING CO
INC**
3 Stonewood Pkwy (07044-5116)
PHONE..................................973 824-7203
Robert Ulmer, *President*
EMP: 4 EST: 1946
SALES: 500K **Privately Held**
SIC: 3915 Jewelers' findings & materials

(G-11176)
SUBITO MUSIC SERVICE INC
60 Depot St (07044-1338)
PHONE..................................973 857-3440
Stephen Culbertson, *President*
Michale Male, *Prdtn Mgr*
Christopher Haught, *Marketing Staff*
David Murray, *Manager*
Brian Vandenberge, *Manager*
▲ EMP: 7
SQ FT: 3,000
SALES (est): 450K **Privately Held**
WEB: www.subitomusic.com
SIC: 2741 Music book & sheet music pub-
lishing; music books: publishing only, not
printed on site; music, sheet: publishing
only, not printed on site

(G-11177)
**VERONA ALUMINUM PRODUCTS
INC**
320 Bloomfield Ave (07044-2497)
PHONE..................................973 857-4809
Christopher Cetruller, *President*
Joseph Cetruller, *Treasurer*
Patricia Maraviglia, *Human Resources*
EMP: 6
SALES (est): 592.2K **Privately Held**
SIC: 1751 1796 3442 Window & door
(prefabricated) installation; installing
building equipment; screens, window,
metal; sash, door or window: metal

Villas
Cape May County

(G-11178)
BEACH NUTTS MEDIA INC
Also Called: Shoppe
2503 Bayshore Rd (08251-1412)
PHONE..................................609 886-4113
Otto Jensch, *President*
Gene Nachel, *Manager*
EMP: 9
SALES (est): 660K **Privately Held**
SIC: 2621 Newsprint paper

(G-11179)
**MAJEWSKI PLUMBING & HTG
LLC**
14 E Miami Ave (08251-3115)
PHONE..................................609 374-6001
Michelle Cooper,
EMP: 5
SALES (est): 600K **Privately Held**
SIC: 3432 Plastic plumbing fixture fittings,
assembly

(G-11180)
RYDER TECHNOLOGY
Also Called: Ryder Global
36 E Drumbed Rd (08251-1907)
PHONE..................................215 817-7868
Ernest Ryder, *Owner*
▼ EMP: 5
SALES: 200K **Privately Held**
WEB: www.rydertechnology.com
SIC: 3585 Refrigeration & heating equip-
ment

(G-11181)
**SHOPPE CMC SHOPPERS
GUIDE (PA)**
2503 Bayshore Rd (08251-1412)
PHONE..................................609 886-4112
Gerry Jensch, *President*
Otto Jensch, *Publisher*
EMP: 6
SALES (est): 874.8K **Privately Held**
SIC: 7319 2741 Shopping news, advertis-
ing & distributing service; miscellaneous
publishing

Vincentown
Burlington County

(G-11182)
JAMES D MORRISSEY INC
Also Called: Ward Sand & Material
223 Sooy Place Rd (08088-6901)
PHONE..................................609 859-2860
Al Synder, *Office Mgr*
EMP: 12
SALES (corp-wide): 46.5MM **Privately
Held**
WEB: www.jdm-inc.com
SIC: 1446 Silica mining
PA: James D. Morrissey Inc.
9119 Frankford Ave
Philadelphia PA 19114
215 708-8420

Vineland
Cumberland County

(G-11183)
A M K GLASS INC
2880 Industrial Way (08360-1514)
PHONE..................................856 692-1488
Michael Kousmine, *President*
Kristine Kousmine, *President*
Marc Kousmine, *Vice Pres*
EMP: 8
SQ FT: 10,000
SALES (est): 1.1MM **Privately Held**
WEB: www.amkglass.com
SIC: 3231 8734 Medical & laboratory
glassware: made from purchased glass;
testing laboratories

(G-11184)
AGC PRODUCTS INC
Also Called: Andrews Glass
3740 N West Blvd (08360-1653)
PHONE..................................973 248-5039
Subramanian Natesan, *CEO*
EMP: 1
SQ FT: 30,000
SALES: 4MM **Privately Held**
SIC: 3231 Products of purchased glass

(G-11185)
ALLIED SPECIALTY FOODS INC
Also Called: Allied Steaks
1585 W Forest Grove Rd (08360-1570)
PHONE..................................856 507-1100
Paul Litten, *President*

EMP: 85
SQ FT: 20,000
SALES (est): 21MM
SALES (corp-wide): 40B **Publicly Held**
WEB: www.alliedsteaks.com
SIC: 2013 Sausages & other prepared
meats
HQ: Advancepierre Foods, Inc.
9990 Prnceton Glendale Rd
West Chester OH 45246
513 874-8741

(G-11186)
ALUSEAL LLC
1649 Castpa Pl (08360-3411)
PHONE..................................856 692-3355
Donald Bayer, *Owner*
▲ EMP: 4
SQ FT: 38,000
SALES (est): 572.1K **Privately Held**
SIC: 3354 Bars, extruded, aluminum

(G-11187)
ASSEM - PAK INC
1649 Castpa Pl (08360-3411)
PHONE..................................856 692-3355
Don Bayer Jr, *President*
Roseann Bayer, *Vice Pres*
Barbara George, *Production*
Jill Champion, *Purchasing*
▲ EMP: 140 EST: 2000
SQ FT: 40,000
SALES (est): 19.1MM **Privately Held**
SIC: 3221 2891 7389 Bottles for packing,
bottling & canning: glass; sealing com-
pounds, synthetic rubber or plastic; pack-
aging & labeling services

(G-11188)
ATCO RUBBER PRODUCTS INC
1480 N West Blvd (08360-2202)
PHONE..................................856 794-3393
Ray Savingel, *Manager*
EMP: 50
SALES (corp-wide): 2.5B **Publicly Held**
SIC: 3444 Metal ventilating equipment
HQ: Atco Rubber Products, Inc.
7101 Atco Dr
Fort Worth TX 76118
817 595-2894

(G-11189)
AUNT KITTYS FOODS INC
270 N Mill Rd (08360-3437)
P.O. Box 334, Hanover PA (17331-0334)
PHONE..................................856 691-2100
Gary Knisely, *Vice Pres*
Peitro Giraffa, *Vice Pres*
Pete Giraffa, *Vice Pres*
Steve Robertson, *Treasurer*
▲ EMP: 100
SQ FT: 100,000
SALES (est): 17.1MM
SALES (corp-wide): 292MM **Publicly
Held**
WEB: www.auntkittys.com
SIC: 2032 Soups & broths: canned, jarred,
etc.
PA: Hanover Foods Corporation
1486 York St
Hanover PA 17331
717 632-6000

(G-11190)
BABBITT MFG CO INC
719 E Park Ave (08360-3290)
PHONE..................................856 692-3245
Lois Gavigan, *President*
Steven Gavigan, *Vice Pres*
Brian G Gavigan, *Treasurer*
Ronald Gavigan, *Admin Sec*
EMP: 15
SQ FT: 19,400
SALES (est): 3.1MM **Privately Held**
SIC: 3444 5039 5031 5033 Sheet metal-
work; awnings; doors & windows; siding,
except wood; roofing, siding & sheet
metal work

(G-11191)
BARUFFI BROS INC (PA)
907 N Main Rd Bldg D (08360-8200)
PHONE..................................856 692-6400
Leonard Gagliarti Jr, *Ch of Bd*
Dominick Baruffi II, *President*
Micheal Jelinek, *General Mgr*

Arthur Baruffi Jr, *Vice Pres*
Michael Bertonazzi, *CFO*
EMP: 18
SALES: 984.8K **Privately Held**
SIC: 3275 Wallboard, gypsum

(G-11192)
BELLCO GLASS INC
340 Edrudo Rd (08360-3416)
P.O. Box 869 (08362-0869)
PHONE..................................800 257-7043
Steven Harker, *CEO*
Aaron Sackstein, *CFO*
Penny Taylor, *Sales Staff*
Emilia Puchliakow, *Marketing Mgr*
EMP: 85 EST: 1940
SQ FT: 55,000
SALES (est): 20.8MM **Privately Held**
SIC: 3821 3231 5047 Laboratory equip-
ment: fume hoods, distillation racks, etc.;
medical & laboratory glassware: made
from purchased glass; medical equipment
& supplies

(G-11193)
BEREZIN NILOLAI
402 E Wheat Rd (08360-2183)
PHONE..................................856 692-6191
Nilolai Berezin, *Owner*
EMP: 6
SALES (est): 250K **Privately Held**
SIC: 3599 Machine shop, jobbing & repair

(G-11194)
BERRY BLAST SMOOTHIES LLC
1194 Sharp Rd (08360-2460)
PHONE..................................856 692-6174
Brian M Buglio, *Principal*
EMP: 4
SALES (est): 191.1K **Privately Held**
SIC: 2037 Frozen fruits & vegetables

(G-11195)
**BIE REAL ESTATE HOLDINGS
LLC**
3539 Reilly Ct (08360-1500)
PHONE..................................856 691-9765
Alan Bierig, *Mng Member*
Daniel Bierig,
David Bierig,
Jacob Bierig,
EMP: 7
SQ FT: 100,000
SALES (est): 309.9K **Privately Held**
SIC: 2011 Meat packing plants

(G-11196)
BK MACHINE SHOP
586 N West Blvd (08360-2742)
PHONE..................................856 457-7150
EMP: 4
SALES (est): 208.2K **Privately Held**
SIC: 3599 Machine shop, jobbing & repair

(G-11197)
**CASA DI BERTACCHI
CORPORATION**
1910 Gallagher Dr (08360-1545)
P.O. Box 245, Buffalo NY (14240-0245)
PHONE..................................856 696-5600
Robert E Rich Jr, *President*
Basilio Gomez, *Production*
John Dougherty, *Treasurer*
EMP: 209 EST: 1966
SQ FT: 100,000
SALES (est): 26.6MM
SALES (corp-wide): 3.8B **Privately Held**
WEB: www.casadibertacchi.com
SIC: 2013 2098 Sausages from pur-
chased meat; macaroni & spaghetti
PA: Rich Products Corporation
1 Robert Rich Way
Buffalo NY 14213
716 878-8000

(G-11198)
CERVINIS INC
Also Called: Cervini's Auto Design
3656 N Mill Rd (08360-1528)
PHONE..................................856 691-1744
Danny Cervini, *President*
Jim Frie, *Managing Dir*
Lou Fava, *Mfg Staff*
Judy Coulter, *Human Res Dir*
▲ EMP: 10
SQ FT: 15,000

SALES (est): 2.1MM **Privately Held**
WEB: www.cervinis.com
SIC: 3714 5531 Motor vehicle body components & frame; automotive & home supply stores

(G-11199)
CHEMGLASS INC
3800 N Mill Rd (08360-1528)
PHONE..................................856 696-0014
Walter E Surdam, *CEO*
Steve Ware, *President*
David Surdam, *Vice Pres*
Philip Surdam, *Vice Pres*
Christopher Crawford, *Engineer*
▲ EMP: 225
SQ FT: 30,000
SALES (est): 27.7MM **Privately Held**
WEB: www.chemglass.com
SIC: 3826 Analytical instruments

(G-11200)
COMAR LLC
3100 N Mill Rd (08360-1524)
PHONE..................................856 507-5483
Don Hutchinson, *Branch Mgr*
EMP: 200
SALES (corp-wide): 15.6MM **Privately Held**
SIC: 3231 Products of purchased glass
HQ: Comar, Llc
220 Laurel Rd Ste 201
Voorhees NJ 08043
856 692-6100

(G-11201)
COMFORTAIRE LTD LIABILITY CO
Also Called: Comfortaire Htg & A Conditio
1435 E Sherman Ave (08361-7161)
P.O. Box 180 (08362-0180)
PHONE..................................856 692-5000
Robert Pizzo,
EMP: 4
SALES: 300K **Privately Held**
SIC: 3585 Refrigeration & heating equipment

(G-11202)
COMPASS WIRE CLOTH &
1942 N Mill Rd (08360-2030)
PHONE..................................856 853-7616
Mike McGrath Sr, *President*
Michael McGrath, *Vice Pres*
Chris Toppi, *Vice Pres*
Steve Elliott, *Finance*
Christopher Toppi, *Manager*
EMP: 40
SQ FT: 65,000
SALES (est): 6.4MM **Privately Held**
SIC: 3496 Miscellaneous fabricated wire products

(G-11203)
COMPASS WIRE CLOTH CORP
1942 N Mill Rd (08360-2030)
PHONE..................................856 853-7616
Michael Mc Grath, *President*
Bob Abate, *Vice Pres*
Robert Abate, *Vice Pres*
Chris Toppi, *Vice Pres*
Christopher Toppi, *Vice Pres*
▲ EMP: 32
SQ FT: 30,000
SALES (est): 7.9MM **Privately Held**
WEB: www.compasswire.com
SIC: 3496 Screening, woven wire: made from purchased wire

(G-11204)
CONTES PASTA COMPANY INC
310 Wheat Rd (08360-9627)
PHONE..................................856 697-3400
Michael Conte, *President*
Judy Sabella, *Vice Pres*
Tony Napoleon, *Research*
▲ EMP: 35
SQ FT: 28,000
SALES (est): 7.5MM **Privately Held**
WEB: www.contespasta.com
SIC: 2099 Pasta, uncooked: packaged with other ingredients

(G-11205)
CORNING PHARMACEUTICAL GL LLC
563 Crystal Ave (08360-3238)
PHONE..................................856 794-7100
Wendell P Weeks, *Mng Member*
EMP: 5 EST: 2015
SALES (est): 83.3K
SALES (corp-wide): 11.2B **Publicly Held**
SIC: 3229 Tubing, glass
PA: Corning Incorporated
1 Riverfront Plz
Corning NY 14831
607 974-9000

(G-11206)
CROWN CLOTHING CO
609 Paul St (08360-5699)
PHONE..................................856 691-0343
Howard Levin, *President*
Marsha Levin, *Corp Secy*
EMP: 152
SQ FT: 30,000
SALES (est): 13.6MM **Privately Held**
WEB: www.crownclothing.com
SIC: 2311 Military uniforms, men's & youths': purchased materials

(G-11207)
CUMBERLAND MARBLE & MONUMENT
Also Called: C M M Rentals
2858 S West Blvd (08360-7022)
PHONE..................................856 691-3334
Paul Presgrave III, *President*
Kim Presgraves, *Partner*
EMP: 4
SQ FT: 2,400
SALES (est): 511.2K **Privately Held**
WEB: www.indiadairy.com
SIC: 3272 7336 Art marble, concrete; silk screen design

(G-11208)
CUMBERLAND NEWS INC
603 E Landis Ave (08360-8004)
PHONE..................................856 691-2244
Paul DOE, *President*
Peter DOE, *Vice Pres*
EMP: 4
SALES: 350K **Privately Held**
SIC: 2711 Newspapers: publishing only, not printed on site

(G-11209)
CUSTOM GRAPHICS OF VINELAND
71 W Landis Ave (08360-8122)
PHONE..................................856 691-7858
James Mc Mahon, *President*
Russell Hull, *Corp Secy*
EMP: 27
SQ FT: 17,000
SALES (est): 3.1MM **Privately Held**
SIC: 2759 3993 2396 Screen printing; signs & advertising specialties; automotive & apparel trimmings

(G-11210)
D ELECTRIC MOTORS INC
94 W Sherman Ave (08360-7011)
P.O. Box 2367 (08362-2367)
PHONE..................................856 696-5959
Anthony L Desiere, *President*
Devin K Desiere, *Corp Secy*
Jim Ford, *Manager*
EMP: 9
SQ FT: 10,000
SALES (est): 2.3MM **Privately Held**
SIC: 7694 5063 Electric motor repair; electrical apparatus & equipment

(G-11211)
DDM STEEL CNSTR LTD LBLTY CO
3659 N Delsea Dr (08360-1664)
PHONE..................................856 794-9400
Rich Muckenfuss, *Mng Member*
EMP: 10
SALES (est): 2.1MM **Privately Held**
SIC: 3441 Building components, structural steel

(G-11212)
DE ROSSI & SON CO INC
411 S 6th St (08360)
PHONE..................................856 691-0061
Donald De Rossi, *President*
Debbie Pepper, *Director*
EMP: 170 EST: 1925
SQ FT: 50,000
SALES (est): 16.4MM **Privately Held**
SIC: 2311 Military uniforms, men's & youths': purchased materials

(G-11213)
DESIGNS BY JAMES
892 N Delsea Dr (08360-2744)
PHONE..................................856 692-1316
James J Crescenzeo, *Owner*
EMP: 4
SALES (est): 242K **Privately Held**
WEB: www.designsbyjames.com
SIC: 2396 2211 3993 Screen printing on fabric articles; print cloths, cotton; signs & advertising specialties

(G-11214)
DUN-RITE SAND & GRAVEL CO (PA)
573 E Grant Ave (08360-7109)
PHONE..................................856 692-2520
Peter Galetto, *President*
EMP: 4
SQ FT: 1,500
SALES: 10.9MM **Privately Held**
SIC: 1442 1411 Sand mining; gravel mining; dimension stone

(G-11215)
DUTRA SHEET METAL CO
1940 S West Blvd Ste E (08360-7088)
P.O. Box 2265 (08362-2265)
PHONE..................................856 692-8058
D'Lee Dutra, *President*
EMP: 9
SQ FT: 6,600
SALES: 1.5MM **Privately Held**
WEB: www.dutrasheetmetal.com
SIC: 3444 Sheet metalwork

(G-11216)
EATEM CORPORATION
Also Called: Eatem Foods
1829 Gallagher Dr (08360-1548)
PHONE..................................856 692-1663
Ron Savelli, *President*
Don Witherspoon, *Vice Pres*
Richard Garrison, *Opers Staff*
John Randazzi, *Research*
Mario Riviello, *Human Res Mgr*
◆ EMP: 80
SQ FT: 55,600
SALES (est): 25.3MM
SALES (corp-wide): 64.3B **Publicly Held**
WEB: www.eatemfoods.com
SIC: 2099 Food preparations
PA: Archer-Daniels-Midland Company
77 W Wacker Dr Ste 4600
Chicago IL 60601
312 634-8100

(G-11217)
EVEY VACUUM SERVICE
158 W Weymouth Rd (08360-2589)
PHONE..................................856 692-4779
Donald Calahan, *Owner*
Donald Callahan, *Manager*
EMP: 6
SALES (est): 931.6K **Privately Held**
SIC: 3561 8999 Industrial pumps & parts; artists & artists' studios

(G-11218)
F&S PRODUCE COMPANY INC (PA)
500 W Elmer Rd (08360-6314)
PHONE..................................856 453-0316
Salvatore Pipitone Jr, *President*
Colin Turner, *COO*
Debbie Rogers, *Human Res Mgr*
Nick Georgantas, *Director*
Bruce Siberski, *Director*
▲ EMP: 105
SQ FT: 675,000

SALES: 107.5MM **Privately Held**
WEB: www.freshcutproduce.com
SIC: 0723 2099 2032 0181 Vegetable crops market preparation services; vegetable packing services; vegetables, peeled for the trade; canned specialties; ornamental nursery products

(G-11219)
FRANK E GANTER INC
Also Called: R-Way Tooling Co
224 S Lincoln Ave (08361-7803)
P.O. Box 236 (08362-0236)
PHONE..................................856 692-2218
Frank E Ganter, *President*
Irene Ganter, *Vice Pres*
EMP: 8 EST: 1960
SQ FT: 6,500
SALES (est): 1.2MM **Privately Held**
SIC: 3599 5169 5084 7692 Machine shop, jobbing & repair; industrial gases; welding machinery & equipment; welding repair

(G-11220)
GANNETT STLLITE INFO NTWRK INC
Daily Journal, The
891 E Oak Rd (08360-2311)
PHONE..................................856 691-5000
Nancy Monaghan, *President*
Margaret Mays, *Production*
EMP: 175
SALES (corp-wide): 2.9B **Publicly Held**
WEB: www.usatoday.com
SIC: 2711 2752 8741 Newspapers; commercial printing, offset; management services
HQ: Gannett Satellite Information Network, Llc
7950 Jones Branch Dr
Mc Lean VA 22102
703 854-6000

(G-11221)
GANNETT STLLITE INFO NTWRK LLC
Also Called: Hammonton News, The
891 E Oak Rd Unit A (08360-2311)
P.O. Box 596, Hammonton (08037-0596)
PHONE..................................609 561-2300
Hushan Leiser, *Sales/Mktg Mgr*
EMP: 13
SALES (corp-wide): 2.9B **Publicly Held**
WEB: www.usatoday.com
SIC: 2711 Newspapers, publishing & printing
HQ: Gannett Satellite Information Network, Llc
7950 Jones Branch Dr
Mc Lean VA 22102
703 854-6000

(G-11222)
GARDELLAS RVIOLI ITLN DELI LLC
527 S Brewster Rd (08360-9621)
PHONE..................................856 697-3509
Diane Martine, *Mng Member*
EMP: 10 EST: 2005
SQ FT: 1,800
SALES (est): 1MM **Privately Held**
SIC: 2098 Macaroni & spaghetti

(G-11223)
GERRESHEIMER GLASS INC (DH)
537 Crystal Ave (08360-3238)
PHONE..................................856 692-3600
Uwe Rohrhoff, *CEO*
Axel Herberg, *Chairman*
Franck Langet, *Business Mgr*
Braden Miller, *Counsel*
Wolfgang Gruenauer, *Vice Pres*
▲ EMP: 350
SQ FT: 200,000
SALES: 500MM
SALES (corp-wide): 1.5B **Privately Held**
WEB: www.kimblescience.com
SIC: 3221 Medicine bottles, glass
HQ: Gerresheimer Glas Gmbh
Klaus-Bungert-Str. 4
Dusseldorf 40468
211 618-100

(G-11224)
GERRESHEIMER GLASS INC
91 W Forest Grove Rd (08360-2016)
PHONE.....................856 507-5852
Axel Herberg, *Chairman*
EMP: 350
SALES (corp-wide): 1.5B **Privately Held**
SIC: 3231 Products of purchased glass
HQ: Gerresheimer Glass Inc.
537 Crystal Ave
Vineland NJ 08360
856 692-3600

(G-11225)
GLASS DYNAMICS LLC
2662 Hance Bridge Rd (08361-7560)
PHONE.....................856 205-1503
Sharon Scudstill,
Kimberly Lawson,
▲ EMP: 6
SALES (est): 292.8K **Privately Held**
WEB: www.marketingtipsinprint.com
SIC: 3231 Stained glass: made from purchased glass

(G-11226)
GLASTRON INC
510 N West Blvd (08360-2896)
P.O. Box 687 (08362-0687)
PHONE.....................856 692-0500
Rex Gary, *Ch of Bd*
Bryan Wolcott, *President*
Alden Kille, *Corp Secy*
Ed Rohland, *Vice Pres*
Lynn Weiner, *Vice Pres*
EMP: 40
SQ FT: 12,000
SALES (est): 5.2MM **Privately Held**
WEB: www.glastroninc.com
SIC: 3231 3841 Products of purchased glass; surgical & medical instruments

(G-11227)
GRAPHICOLOR CORPORATION
1370 S Main Rd (08360-6501)
PHONE.....................856 691-2507
Robert W Stenger Jr, *President*
Cathy Stenger, *COO*
Patrick Procaccino, *Treasurer*
EMP: 22 EST: 1919
SQ FT: 10,000
SALES (est): 4.3MM **Privately Held**
WEB: www.graphicolorcorp.com
SIC: 2752 7336 Commercial printing, offset; chart & graph design

(G-11228)
GROVE SUPPLY INC
144 W Forest Grove Rd (08360-2017)
PHONE.....................856 205-0687
Matthew Grodsky, *Director*
EMP: 20
SALES (corp-wide): 64.1MM **Privately Held**
SIC: 3432 5074 Plumbing fixture fittings & trim; plumbing fittings & supplies
PA: Grove Supply, Inc.
106 Steamboat Dr
Warminster PA 18974
215 672-8666

(G-11229)
H P MACHINE SHOP INC
415 Oxford St (08360-2794)
PHONE.....................856 692-1192
John Petyan IV, *President*
Shirley Horvath, *Manager*
EMP: 9 EST: 1964
SQ FT: 7,000
SALES (est): 525K **Privately Held**
WEB: www.hp-machine.com
SIC: 3599 Machine shop, jobbing & repair

(G-11230)
H S MARTIN COMPANY INC
1149 S East Blvd (08360-6493)
P.O. Box 661 (08362-0661)
PHONE.....................856 692-8700
Nontas Kontes, *President*
John Trieres, *Vice Pres*
Cindy Dichino, *Purch Agent*
James E Kontes, *Treasurer*
Robert Ciesla, *Controller*
EMP: 15
SQ FT: 15,000

SALES (est): 2.4MM **Privately Held**
WEB: www.hsmartin.com
SIC: 3231 3829 Scientific & technical glassware: from purchased glass; medical & laboratory glassware: made from purchased glass; measuring & controlling devices

(G-11231)
HARRY J LAWALL & SON INC
3071 E Chestnut Ave C9 (08361-7847)
PHONE.....................856 691-7764
Harry Lawall, *Manager*
EMP: 7
SALES (corp-wide): 16.8MM **Privately Held**
SIC: 3842 5999 Limbs, artificial; artificial limbs
PA: Harry J. Lawall & Son, Inc.
8028 Frankford Ave
Philadelphia PA 19136
215 338-6611

(G-11232)
HONEYWELL INTERNATIONAL INC
2658 N West Blvd (08360-2057)
PHONE.....................856 691-5111
EMP: 673
SALES (corp-wide): 41.8B **Publicly Held**
SIC: 3724 Aircraft engines & engine parts
PA: Honeywell International Inc.
300 S Tryon St
Charlotte NC 28202
973 455-2000

(G-11233)
HOWES STANDARD PUBLISHING CO
1980 S West Blvd (08360-7018)
PHONE.....................856 691-2000
Barry Opromollo, *President*
EMP: 35 EST: 1892
SQ FT: 12,500
SALES (est): 5MM **Privately Held**
WEB: www.standard-publishing.com
SIC: 2752 2759 Commercial printing, offset; letterpress printing

(G-11234)
I S PARTS INTERNATIONAL INC
Also Called: Lattimer
3603 N Mill Rd (08360-1595)
PHONE.....................856 691-2203
Stephen Abernathy, *President*
Mark Hailwood, *Managing Dir*
Walt Martin, *CFO*
Walter Martin, *CFO*
▼ EMP: 36
SQ FT: 24,374
SALES (est): 6.9MM
SALES (corp-wide): 265.4K **Privately Held**
WEB: www.lattimer.com
SIC: 3443 3565 Metal parts; packaging machinery
HQ: Lattimer Holdings Limited
79-83 Shakespeare Street
Southport PR8 5

(G-11235)
INNOVA GROUP INC
327 Tuckahoe Rd (08360-9243)
PHONE.....................856 696-1053
John Tombleson, *President*
EMP: 4
SQ FT: 2,000
SALES (est): 460K **Privately Held**
SIC: 3089 Doors, folding: plastic or plastic coated fabric

(G-11236)
J D MACHINE PARTS INC
158 W Weymouth Rd (08360-2589)
PHONE.....................856 691-8430
Joseph D Mento, *President*
EMP: 11
SQ FT: 25,000
SALES (est): 600K **Privately Held**
WEB: www.jdmachineparts.com
SIC: 3599 7692 Machine shop, jobbing & repair; welding repair

(G-11237)
J F GILLESPIE INC
2547 Brunetta Dr (08360-7028)
PHONE.....................856 692-2233
Jerome F Gillespie, *President*
Dolores Gillespie, *Admin Sec*
EMP: 40
SQ FT: 10,000
SALES (est): 4.9MM **Privately Held**
WEB: www.jfgillespieinc.com
SIC: 3272 Concrete products

(G-11238)
JOFFE LUMBER & SUPPLY CO INC
Also Called: Joffe Millwork & Supply
18 Burns Ave (08360-7799)
P.O. Box 2309 (08362-2309)
PHONE.....................856 825-9550
Michael Bergen, *President*
EMP: 75 EST: 1933
SQ FT: 133,000
SALES (est): 34.1MM **Privately Held**
WEB: www.joffemillwork.com
SIC: 5031 2431 Lumber, plywood & millwork; doors & door parts & trim, wood

(G-11239)
KASHMIR
3926 N Delesa Dr (08360-1686)
PHONE.....................856 691-8969
Michael Radie, *Principal*
EMP: 4
SALES (est): 261.7K **Privately Held**
SIC: 2599 Bar, restaurant & cafeteria furniture

(G-11240)
KENNEDY CONCRETE INC
1969 S East Ave (08360-7141)
PHONE.....................856 692-8650
Thomas Towers, *President*
EMP: 50
SQ FT: 1,000
SALES (est): 8MM **Privately Held**
WEB: www.kennedyconcrete.com
SIC: 3273 Ready-mixed concrete

(G-11241)
LIMPERT BROTHERS INC
200 N West Blvd (08360-3794)
P.O. Box 1480 (08362-1480)
PHONE.....................856 691-1353
Pearl Giordano, *President*
Ruth Keller, *Admin Asst*
EMP: 24 EST: 1902
SQ FT: 70,000
SALES (est): 1.2MM **Privately Held**
WEB: www.limpertbrothers.com
SIC: 5812 2087 Eating places; fruits, crushed: for fountain use

(G-11242)
LT CHINI INC
Also Called: Gorgo Pallet Company
646 S Delsea Dr (08360-4459)
PHONE.....................856 692-0303
Louis Chini, *President*
Nick Biagi, *Vice Pres*
EMP: 9
SQ FT: 5,000
SALES (est): 1.8MM **Privately Held**
SIC: 2448 7699 Pallets, wood; pallet repair

(G-11243)
MUSIKRAFT LLC (PA)
Also Called: Applause Musical Products
528b N Harding Hwy (08360-8713)
P.O. Box 331, Landisville (08326-0331)
PHONE.....................856 697-8333
Gulab Gidwani, *Mng Member*
▲ EMP: 5
SALES (est): 450.1K **Privately Held**
SIC: 3931 Guitars & parts, electric & non-electric

(G-11244)
N B & SONS LLC
402 E Wheat Rd (08360-2183)
PHONE.....................856 692-6191
Maria Berezin, *Partner*
Nikolai Berezin Mg Mem, *Principal*
Annette Berezin,
EMP: 6

SQ FT: 2,500
SALES (est): 430K **Privately Held**
WEB: www.nbsons.com
SIC: 3599 Machine shop, jobbing & repair

(G-11245)
NATURE LABS LLC
46 N West Ave Ste B (08360-3611)
PHONE.....................856 839-0400
Louis Rivers, *CEO*
Johanna Guzman, *Opers Staff*
EMP: 7
SALES (est): 489.8K **Privately Held**
SIC: 2844 Toilet preparations

(G-11246)
NDS TECHNOLOGIES INC
891 E Oak Rd Unit B (08360-2311)
PHONE.....................856 691-0330
Norman Neill, *President*
Robert Degrazia, *Corp Secy*
Margaret Mays, *Production*
Keith Cooney, *Engineer*
Kimberly Swartz, *Cust Mgr*
EMP: 35
SQ FT: 6,000
SALES (est): 5.5MM **Privately Held**
WEB: www.ndstechnologiesinc.com
SIC: 3231 Products of purchased glass

(G-11247)
OMNI BAKING COMPANY LLC
2621 Freddy Ln Bldg 7 (08360-1559)
PHONE.....................856 205-1485
Lenny Amoroso Jr, *Partner*
Daniel Amoroso Jr, *Partner*
Lenny Amoroso Jr, *Partner*
John V Mulloy Sr, *Partner*
Dorria Creamer, *General Mgr*
EMP: 500
SQ FT: 55,000
SALES (est): 138.5MM
SALES (corp-wide): 1.2B **Publicly Held**
WEB: www.omnibaking.com
SIC: 2051 Bakery: wholesale or wholesale/retail combined
HQ: T.Marzetti Company
380 Polaris Pkwy Ste 400
Westerville OH 43082
614 846-2232

(G-11248)
P J GILLESPIE INC
Also Called: Gillespie Industries
2565 Brunetta Dr (08360-7028)
PHONE.....................856 327-2993
Paul J Gillespie Sr, *President*
Brigita Gillespie, *Vice Pres*
Donna Ruberti, *Vice Pres*
EMP: 20
SQ FT: 750
SALES (est): 3.1MM **Privately Held**
SIC: 3272 Septic tanks, concrete

(G-11249)
PACKAGING CORPORATION AMERICA
Also Called: PCA/Supply Services 302a
46 N West Ave Ste A (08360-3611)
PHONE.....................856 696-0114
Ron Capriotti, *Manager*
EMP: 4
SALES (corp-wide): 7B **Publicly Held**
SIC: 2653 Corrugated & solid fiber boxes
PA: Packaging Corporation Of America
1 N Field Ct
Lake Forest IL 60045
847 482-3000

(G-11250)
PARRISH SIGN CO INC
2242 S Delsea Dr (08360-7094)
PHONE.....................856 696-4040
Charles Parrish, *CEO*
Charles R Parrish Sr, *President*
Charles R Parrish Jr, *Vice Pres*
Craig S Parrish, *Treasurer*
Karen Parrish, *Admin Sec*
EMP: 8
SQ FT: 10,000
SALES (est): 1.2MM
SALES (corp-wide): 1.6MM **Privately Held**
WEB: www.parrishsign.com
SIC: 3993 Signs, not made in custom sign painting shops

PA: Charles R Parrish Inc
2242 S Delsea Dr
Vineland NJ 08360
856 691-4080

(G-11251)
PHIL DESIERE ELECTRIC MTR SVC
Also Called: Desiere Electric Motor Service
1338 Almond Rd (08360-2682)
PHONE...................................856 692-8442
Eugene Boston, *President*
Paul Cascia, *Vice Pres*
Lucinda Adams, *Treasurer*
EMP: 10
SQ FT: 11,000
SALES (est): 750K **Privately Held**
SIC: 7694 5063 Electric motor repair; motors, electric

(G-11252)
PHILCORR LLC
2317 Almond Rd (08360-3486)
PHONE...................................856 205-0557
Tom Fitzpatrick,
Peter Cadwallader,
Vernon Litzinger,
Mario Russo,
Ted Sidenburgh,
▲ **EMP:** 61
SALES (est): 14.6MM **Privately Held**
WEB: www.philcorr.com
SIC: 3089 Corrugated panels, plastic

(G-11253)
PHOENIX BUSINESS FORMS INC
2231 N East Blvd (08360-2174)
PHONE...................................856 691-2266
Joanne Buckalew, *President*
EMP: 5 **EST:** 1977
SQ FT: 5,500
SALES (est): 510K **Privately Held**
SIC: 2752 7389 Commercial printing, offset; advertising, promotional & trade show services

(G-11254)
PRECISION ELECTRONIC GLASS INC
Also Called: P E G
1013 Hendee Rd (08360-3295)
PHONE...................................856 691-2234
Phillip Rossi, *President*
▲ **EMP:** 75
SQ FT: 48,000
SALES (est): 12.6MM **Privately Held**
WEB: www.pegglass.com
SIC: 3231 Products of purchased glass

(G-11255)
R WAY TOOLING & MET WORKS LLC
Also Called: R-Way Machine and Fabrication
224 S Lincoln Ave (08361-7803)
PHONE...................................856 692-2218
James M Preziosi,
EMP: 14
SALES (est): 2MM **Privately Held**
SIC: 3599 3441 Machine shop, jobbing & repair; fabricated structural metal

(G-11256)
RENNOC CORPORATION
1450 E Chestnut Ave Ste B (08361-8467)
PHONE...................................856 327-5400
Michael Bruzzese, *President*
Richard W Conner, *Shareholder*
▲ **EMP:** 90 **EST:** 1954
SQ FT: 215,000
SALES (est): 7.9MM **Privately Held**
WEB: www.rennoc.com
SIC: 2329 Men's & boys' athletic uniforms

(G-11257)
RFC CONTAINER LLC (PA)
Also Called: Rfc Container Company
2066 S East Ave (08360-7129)
PHONE...................................856 692-0404
Mario Russo, *President*
Thomas Russo, *Vice Pres*
EMP: 74
SQ FT: 125,000

SALES (est): 18MM **Privately Held**
WEB: www.rfccontainer.com
SIC: 2653 Boxes, corrugated: made from purchased materials

(G-11258)
RHOADS OHARA ARCHITECTURAL
3690 N West Blvd (08360-1653)
P.O. Box 783, Newfield (08344-0783)
PHONE...................................856 692-4100
Lance Rhoads, *Mng Member*
Robert O'Hara,
EMP: 9
SQ FT: 10,000
SALES (est): 1.9MM **Privately Held**
SIC: 2435 Hardwood plywood, prefinished

(G-11259)
RICH PRODUCTS CORPORATION
1910 Gallagher Dr (08360-1545)
PHONE...................................856 696-5600
John Dougherty, *Branch Mgr*
EMP: 5
SALES (corp-wide): 3.8B **Privately Held**
SIC: 2038 Frozen specialties
PA: Rich Products Corporation
1 Robert Rich Way
Buffalo NY 14213
716 878-8000

(G-11260)
RICHARD E PIERSON MTLS CORP
Also Called: R E Pierson Materials
184 W Sherman Ave (08360-7011)
PHONE...................................856 691-0083
Richard E Pierson, *President*
EMP: 6 **Privately Held**
SIC: 2951 1611 1771 Asphalt paving mixtures & blocks; highway & street construction; concrete work
PA: Richard E. Pierson Materials Corp.
426 Swedesboro Rd
Pilesgrove NJ 08098

(G-11261)
RUDCO PRODUCTS INC (PA)
114 E Oak Rd (08360-2991)
P.O. Box 705 (08362-0705)
PHONE...................................856 691-0800
Robert A Rudolph, *President*
Mark Rudolph, *Purch Agent*
Deborah M Rudolph, *CFO*
Shannon Bowers, *Sales Staff*
Justin Johnson, *Sales Staff*
EMP: 85 **EST:** 1964
SQ FT: 25,000
SALES (est): 22.8MM **Privately Held**
SIC: 3443 3536 Dumpsters, garbage; hoists

(G-11262)
S P INDUSTRIES INC
AB Glass
1172 N West Blvd (08360-2201)
P.O. Box 610 (08362-0610)
PHONE...................................856 691-3200
Bill Downs, *CEO*
Cloud Volpe, *Branch Mgr*
EMP: 79
SALES (corp-wide): 1.5B **Privately Held**
WEB: www.virtis.com
SIC: 3231 Products of purchased glass
HQ: S P Industries, Inc.
935 Mearns Rd
Warminster PA 18974
215 672-7800

(G-11263)
SEREN INC
Also Called: Seren Industrial Power Systems
1670 Gallagher Dr (08360-1561)
PHONE...................................856 205-1131
Lawrence Hooper, *President*
Sharon Szumowski, *Associate*
EMP: 25
SQ FT: 10,000
SALES (est): 3.8MM **Privately Held**
SIC: 3825 Radio frequency measuring equipment

(G-11264)
SEREN INDUSTRIAL POWER SYSTEMS
1670 Gallagher Dr (08360-1561)
PHONE...................................856 205-1131
Larry Hooper, *President*
EMP: 13
SQ FT: 10,000
SALES: 3MM **Privately Held**
WEB: www.serenips.com
SIC: 3679 Electronic circuits

(G-11265)
SEREN IPS INC
1670 Gallagher Dr (08360-1561)
PHONE...................................856 205-1131
Lawrence Hooper, *President*
EMP: 55
SALES (est): 16.8MM **Privately Held**
SIC: 3699 Generators, ultrasonic

(G-11266)
SOUTH JERSEY PRECISION TL MOLD
4375 S Lincoln Ave (08361-7757)
PHONE...................................856 327-0500
Victor Rone, *President*
Robert G Rone, *Vice Pres*
Wyne Reeves, *Admin Sec*
EMP: 14
SQ FT: 9,000
SALES: 1.1MM **Privately Held**
WEB: www.southjerseyprecision.com
SIC: 3599 Machine shop, jobbing & repair

(G-11267)
SOUTH JERSEY PUBLISHING CO
Also Called: Press of Atlantic City
22 W Landis Ave (08360-8134)
PHONE...................................856 692-0455
Gary Campbell, *Manager*
EMP: 15
SALES (corp-wide): 361.4MM **Privately Held**
WEB: www.pressofac.com
SIC: 2711 2741 Commercial printing & newspaper publishing combined; miscellaneous publishing
HQ: South Jersey Publishing Company
1000 W Washington Ave
Pleasantville NJ 08232
609 272-7000

(G-11268)
SOUTHERN NEW JERSEY STL CO INC (PA)
Also Called: Southern NJ Steel
2591 N East Blvd (08360-1771)
PHONE...................................856 696-1612
Hugh Mc Caffrey, *President*
Carlo Gentilitti Sr, *President*
Chuck Yula, *Vice Pres*
Agnes Trummer, *Director*
Sue Dodds, *Admin Sec*
EMP: 40
SQ FT: 25,000
SALES (est): 5MM **Privately Held**
SIC: 3441 Fabricated structural metal

(G-11269)
TECTUBES USA INC
1299 W Forest Grove Rd (08360-1513)
PHONE...................................856 589-1250
Steven Wargo, *President*
Paul Diezel, *Department Mgr*
▲ **EMP:** 35
SQ FT: 29,000
SALES (est): 4MM
SALES (corp-wide): 902.2K **Privately Held**
WEB: www.norden.com
SIC: 2759 2752 Screen printing; commercial printing, lithographic
HQ: Emballator Tectubes Sweden Ab
Tubgatan 2
Hjo 544 5
503 326-00

(G-11270)
TJK MACHINE LLC
870 E Elmer Rd (08360-6466)
PHONE...................................856 691-7811
Nancy Parkin,
Jeffery Parkin,

EMP: 4
SALES: 300K **Privately Held**
SIC: 3599 Machine shop, jobbing & repair

(G-11271)
TUCKAHOE MANUFACTURING INC
327 Tuckahoe Rd (08360-9243)
PHONE...................................856 696-4100
John Tombleson, *President*
Robert Meighan, *Sales Mgr*
EMP: 6
SQ FT: 3,000
SALES (est): 700.1K **Privately Held**
SIC: 3442 Metal doors, sash & trim

(G-11272)
UNIVERSAL MOLD & TOOL INC
1200 S West Blvd Ste 4e (08360-6472)
PHONE...................................856 563-0488
Mile Kznaric, *President*
David Rainear, *Corp Secy*
Micheal Mitros, *Vice Pres*
EMP: 16
SQ FT: 6,000
SALES (est): 2MM **Privately Held**
SIC: 3544 Industrial molds

(G-11273)
URBAN SIGN & CRANE INC
527 E Chestnut Ave (08360-5620)
P.O. Box 640 (08362-0640)
PHONE...................................856 691-8388
Seth Davis, *President*
Maryann Gonyea, *Vice Pres*
EMP: 9
SALES (est): 1.5MM **Privately Held**
WEB: www.urbansigncompany.com
SIC: 3993 Electric signs

(G-11274)
V M GLASS CO
3231 N Mill Rd (08360-1525)
PHONE...................................856 794-9333
Michael Greico, *Owner*
EMP: 7
SQ FT: 5,000
SALES (est): 300K **Privately Held**
WEB: www.vmglass.com
SIC: 3231 Scientific & technical glassware: from purchased glass

(G-11275)
VINELAND KOSHER POULTRY INC (PA)
1050 S Mill Rd (08360-4376)
PHONE...................................856 692-1871
Israel Leifer, *President*
EMP: 159 **EST:** 1967
SQ FT: 30,000
SALES (est): 8.4MM **Privately Held**
WEB: www.vinelandkosherpoultry.com
SIC: 2015 Poultry slaughtering & processing

(G-11276)
VINELAND PACKAGING CORP
3602 N Mill Rd (08360-1508)
PHONE...................................856 794-3300
Joseph D Alessandro Jr, *President*
David D Alessandro, *Vice Pres*
EMP: 30
SQ FT: 33,000
SALES (est): 8.7MM **Privately Held**
WEB: www.vpcbox.com
SIC: 2653 Boxes, corrugated: made from purchased materials

(G-11277)
VINELAND SYRUP INC
723 S East Blvd (08360-5679)
P.O. Box 1326 (08362-1326)
PHONE...................................856 691-5772
Meilech Kornbluh, *President*
Jason Myers, *General Mgr*
EMP: 32
SQ FT: 30,000
SALES (est): 6.2MM **Privately Held**
WEB: www.vinelandsyrup.com
SIC: 2087 7359 Flavoring extracts & syrups; equipment rental & leasing

GEOGRAPHIC

(G-11278)
WORLDWIDE GLASS RESOURCES INC
1022 Spruce St (08360-2841)
PHONE..........................856 205-1508
James O Crawford, *President*
Edward Poisker, *Corp Secy*
▲ EMP: 25 EST: 2001
SQ FT: 6,000
SALES (est): 4.6MM Privately Held
WEB: www.wwglassresource.com
SIC: 3221 Vials, glass

Voorhees
Camden County

(G-11279)
ADVANCED ENERGY VOORHEES INC
1007 Laurel Oak Rd (08043-3515)
PHONE..........................856 627-1287
William A Ruff, *President*
Richard Beck, *Principal*
Doug Schatz, *Principal*
EMP: 90 EST: 1981
SQ FT: 78,000
SALES (est): 8.1MM
SALES (corp-wide): 718.8MM Publicly Held
WEB: www.advanced-energy.com
SIC: 3679 Power supplies, all types: static
PA: Advanced Energy Industries, Inc.
1625 Sharp Point Dr
Fort Collins CO 80525
970 221-4670

(G-11280)
ALLSTATE CONVEYOR SERVICE
256 Terrace Blvd (08043-4211)
P.O. Box 308, Medford (08055-0308)
PHONE..........................856 768-6566
Karla Porter, *President*
William J Porter, *Vice Pres*
EMP: 21
SALES (est): 5.2MM Privately Held
SIC: 3535 Conveyors & conveying equipment

(G-11281)
BURNS LINK MANUFACTURING CO
253 American Way (08043-1114)
P.O. Box 811, Cherry Hill (08003-0811)
PHONE..........................856 429-6844
Daniel Zoltowski, *President*
Stephen Zoltowski, *Vice Pres*
Darcy Veiock, *Bookkeeper*
Bob Knorr, *Sales Executive*
EMP: 16 EST: 1957
SQ FT: 20,000
SALES (est): 3.8MM Privately Held
WEB: www.linkburns.com
SIC: 3444 Sheet metal specialties, not stamped

(G-11282)
COMAR INC (PA)
Also Called: Comar Glass
201 Laurel Rd Fl 2 (08043-2329)
PHONE..........................856 692-6100
Mike Ruggieri, *CEO*
Dan Mullock, *President*
Mike Rozgony, *Vice Pres*
Jeff Schempp, *CFO*
Mark Valentino, *Sales Staff*
◆ EMP: 25
SQ FT: 7,000
SALES (est): 77.9MM Privately Held
SIC: 3089 3231 Plastic containers, except foam; products of purchased glass

(G-11283)
COMAR INC
Also Called: Innovation Design Center
201 Laurel Rd Fl 2 (08043-2329)
PHONE..........................856 507-5461
John Deli, *Manager*
EMP: 15
SALES (corp-wide): 77.9MM Privately Held
SIC: 2671 Plastic film, coated or laminated for packaging

PA: Comar, Inc.
201 Laurel Rd Fl 2
Voorhees NJ 08043
856 692-6100

(G-11284)
DAVID MITCHELL INC
3037 5th St (08043-3679)
PHONE..........................856 429-2610
David Mitchell, *President*
Edith Mitchell, *Admin Sec*
EMP: 20 EST: 1973
SALES (est): 3MM Privately Held
WEB: www.rmit.edu.au
SIC: 5144 2015 Poultry products; poultry slaughtering & processing

(G-11285)
FIS FINANCIAL SYSTEMS LLC
Also Called: Sungard
600 Laurel Oak Rd (08043-4456)
PHONE..........................856 784-7230
Charles Miller, *Branch Mgr*
EMP: 51
SALES (corp-wide): 8.4B Publicly Held
SIC: 7374 7372 Data processing service; business oriented computer software
HQ: Fis Financial Systems Llc
601 Riverside Ave
Jacksonville FL 32204
904 438-6000

(G-11286)
GOOD TO GO INC
Also Called: Sweet Eats Bakery
310 S Burnt Mill Rd (08043-1107)
PHONE..........................856 429-2005
Margaret Davidowich, *President*
Doug Davidowich, *Vice Pres*
Mike Davidowich, *Treasurer*
EMP: 20
SQ FT: 3,000
SALES (est): 2.1MM Privately Held
SIC: 2051 Bakery: wholesale or wholesale/retail combined

(G-11287)
GREENBUILT INTL BLDG CO
1081 Pndleton Ct Voorhees (08043)
P.O. Box 1361, Camden (08105-0361)
PHONE..........................609 300-9091
Dean Kriner, *President*
EMP: 124
SQ FT: 130,000
SALES: 22MM Privately Held
SIC: 1521 1522 2493 5031 Single-family housing construction; residential construction; multi-family dwelling construction; reconstituted wood products; building materials, exterior; building materials, interior; strawboard

(G-11288)
I SEE OPTICAL LABORATORIES
312 W Somerdale Rd (08043-2237)
PHONE..........................856 795-6435
Irv Palkovicz, *Branch Mgr*
EMP: 7
SALES (corp-wide): 1.3MM Privately Held
SIC: 3851 Eyeglasses, lenses & frames
PA: I See Optical Laboratories Inc
44 W Church St
Blackwood NJ 08012
856 227-9300

(G-11289)
IBC INC
1000 Main St Ste 309 (08043-4600)
PHONE..........................856 533-2806
EMP: 4 EST: 1998
SALES (est): 211.7K Privately Held
SIC: 3369 Nonferrous foundries

(G-11290)
ITALIAN TREASURES
1020 Voorhees Town Ctr (08043-1940)
PHONE..........................856 770-9188
Celeste J Cinalli, *Owner*
EMP: 4
SQ FT: 1,000
SALES (est): 100K Privately Held
SIC: 5947 2759 5099 Gift, novelty & souvenir shop; souvenir cards: printing; souvenirs

(G-11291)
MANTECH SYSTEMS ENGRG CORP
1000 Haddonfield Berlin R (08043-3520)
PHONE..........................856 566-9155
Gene Kiernan, *Manager*
EMP: 7
SALES (corp-wide): 1.9B Publicly Held
SIC: 3812 Defense systems & equipment
HQ: Mantech Systems Engineering Corporation
12015 Lee Jackson Hwy # 110
Fairfax VA 22033
703 218-6000

(G-11292)
PRODUCTIVE INDUSTRIAL FINSHG
103 American Way (08043-1112)
PHONE..........................856 427-9646
Diane Stoelker-Stern, *President*
Kevin Stern, *Vice Pres*
EMP: 7
SQ FT: 7,000
SALES (est): 462.2K Privately Held
WEB: www.xyzfinishing.com
SIC: 3479 3471 Painting of metal products; plating & polishing

(G-11293)
SENTRIMED LTD LIABILITY CO
49 Holly Oak Dr (08043-1511)
PHONE..........................914 582-8631
Ellen Marks, *President*
EMP: 5 EST: 2011
SALES (est): 479.5K Privately Held
SIC: 2834 Pharmaceutical preparations

(G-11294)
SULLIVAN-CARSON INC (PA)
1010 Hddonfield Berlin Rd (08043-3514)
PHONE..........................856 566-1400
James B Carson, *Ch of Bd*
James B Carson Sr, *Ch of Bd*
Paul Klapach, *Vice Pres*
EMP: 3 EST: 1853
SQ FT: 1,800
SALES (est): 4.9MM Privately Held
SIC: 2241 Elastic narrow fabrics, woven or braided; fabric tapes; webbing, woven

(G-11295)
TEMPTROL CORP
242 Terrace Blvd Ste E (08043-4209)
P.O. Box 5188, Riverside (08075-0588)
PHONE..........................856 461-7977
Robert R Schweder, *President*
Robin Nosari, *Vice Pres*
EMP: 21 EST: 1972
SQ FT: 4,000
SALES: 2.2MM Privately Held
SIC: 1711 3443 Warm air heating & air conditioning contractor; heat exchangers, condensers & components

(G-11296)
TOUCH OF CLASS PROMOTIONS LLC
19 Festival Dr (08043-4325)
PHONE..........................267 994-0860
Tammy Freedman, *President*
Stephen Kornfeld, *COO*
EMP: 4
SALES: 600K Privately Held
SIC: 3993 3951 5199 Advertising novelties; ball point pens & parts; badges

Waldwick
Bergen County

(G-11297)
BERTONE AROMATICS
26 Dora Ave (07463-2006)
P.O. Box 46, West Stockbridge MA (01266-0046)
PHONE..........................201 444-9821
Alan Birnbaum, *Owner*
EMP: 1
SALES: 2MM Privately Held
SIC: 2911 Aromatic chemical products

(G-11298)
CARTER PUMP INC
152d Franklin Tpke (07463-1802)
PHONE..........................201 568-9798
Kevin Powers, *President*
John McCarty, *Chairman*
EMP: 3
SQ FT: 35,000
SALES (est): 1.6MM
SALES (corp-wide): 10.6MM Privately Held
SIC: 3561 5084 Pumps, domestic: water or sump; industrial machinery & equipment
HQ: Coffin Turbo Pump, Inc.
326 S Dean St
Englewood NJ 07631
201 568-4700

(G-11299)
CORBETT INDUSTRIES INC
39 Hewson Ave Ste B (07463-1827)
P.O. Box 212 (07463-0212)
PHONE..........................201 445-6311
Richard Geier, *President*
Justin Krouse, *Vice Pres*
William Carman, *Treasurer*
Diane Procino, *Controller*
EMP: 11 EST: 1951
SQ FT: 10,000
SALES (est): 2.6MM Privately Held
WEB: www.corbettind.com
SIC: 7699 3567 Industrial machinery & equipment repair; heating units & devices, industrial: electric

(G-11300)
DESIGN PRODUCTIONS INC
9 Industrial Park (07463-1512)
PHONE..........................201 447-5656
Thomas Murphy, *President*
▲ EMP: 9
SQ FT: 15,000
SALES (est): 1.8MM Privately Held
WEB: www.designproductionsinc.com
SIC: 3993 Signs & advertising specialties

(G-11301)
DNP FOODS AMERICA LTD LBLTY CO
2 Dipippo Ct (07463-1025)
P.O. Box 128, Montvale (07645-0128)
PHONE..........................201 654-5581
Larry Mattessich, *Managing Dir*
EMP: 5
SALES (est): 266.9K Privately Held
SIC: 2844 3999 Toilet preparations; flowers, artificial & preserved

(G-11302)
EM ORTHODONTIC LABS INC
6 Lafayette Pl (07463-1711)
P.O. Box 112 (07463-0112)
PHONE..........................201 652-4411
Eva Macz, *President*
EMP: 8
SALES: 240K Privately Held
SIC: 3843 8072 Orthodontic appliances; orthodontic appliance production

(G-11303)
KOELLMANN GEAR CORPORATION
8 Industrial Park (07463-1512)
PHONE..........................201 447-0200
Michael Rasovic, *CEO*
▲ EMP: 250 EST: 1974
SQ FT: 15,000
SALES (est): 36.9MM Privately Held
WEB: www.koellmann.com
SIC: 3566 Gears, power transmission, except automotive; reduction gears & gear units for turbines, except automotive

(G-11304)
MENSHEN PACKAGING USA INC
21 Industrial Park (07463-1512)
PHONE..........................201 445-7436
Susan Kobernick, *Principal*
Jeff Dugal, *VP Opers*
George Flores, *Prdtn Mgr*
Ryan Frankle, *Mfg Mgr*
Darrin Taynor, *Safety Mgr*
▲ EMP: 98

SALES (est): 30MM
SALES (corp-wide): 591.9MM Privately Held
SIC: 2842 Industrial plant disinfectants or deodorants
HQ: Georg Menshen Gmbh & Co. Kg
Industriestr. 26
Finnentrop 57413
272 151-80

(G-11305)
MINERVA CUSTOM PRODUCTS LLC
49 Lockwood Dr (07463-1018)
PHONE.....................................201 447-4731
Deborah Dellavechia, Principal
EMP: 5
SALES (est): 334K Privately Held
SIC: 2441 2449 2542 7336 Cases, wood; shipping cases, wood: nailed or lock corner; shipping cases, wood: wirebound; counters or counter display cases: except wood; art design services

(G-11306)
MOSSTYPE CORPORATION
150 Franklin Tpke (07463-1897)
PHONE.....................................201 444-8000
Lester Moss, President
Lorraine Fiore, Sales Staff
Bruce Anderson, Manager
EMP: 4
SALES (est): 762.3K Privately Held
SIC: 3555 Printing plates

(G-11307)
MOSSTYPE HOLDING CORP (PA)
150 Franklin Tpke (07463-1802)
PHONE.....................................201 444-8000
Lester Moss, President
Richard Moss, Vice Pres
Bruce Anderson, Manager
EMP: 50 EST: 1896
SQ FT: 80,000
SALES (est): 4.7MM Privately Held
WEB: www.mosstype.com
SIC: 3555 2796 Printing plates; engraving machinery & equipment, except plates; platemaking services

(G-11308)
NEXTPHASE MEDICAL DEVICES LLC (PA)
Also Called: Meditron Devices
150 Hopper Ave (07463-1513)
PHONE.....................................201 968-9400
Milton Frank, President
Russ Van Zile, Opers Staff
▲ EMP: 30
SQ FT: 10,100
SALES (est): 7.7MM Privately Held
WEB: www.nexcoretech.com
SIC: 3845 Electromedical apparatus

(G-11309)
STAUFF CORPORATION (DH)
7 William Demarest Pl (07463-1511)
PHONE.....................................201 444-7800
Knut Menshen, Ch of Bd
Jeffrey Behlinger, President
Mike Thieleman, Business Mgr
Shawn Scott, Regl Sales Mgr
Keith Gloede, Cust Mgr
▲ EMP: 48
SQ FT: 40,000
SALES: 25MM
SALES (corp-wide): 591.9MM Privately Held
SIC: 3569 Liquid automation machinery & equipment
HQ: Walter Stauffenberg Gmbh & Co Kg
Im Ehrenfeld 4
Werdohl 58791
239 291-60

(G-11310)
SUPERIOR TRADEMARK INC
Also Called: Samson Sign Company
45 Zazzetti St (07463-1618)
P.O. Box 35 (07463-0035)
PHONE.....................................201 652-1900
Gordon D Mc Intire, President
Leslie Becher, Executive
Sue Mc Intire, Admin Sec

EMP: 8 EST: 1929
SQ FT: 6,000
SALES (est): 1.9MM Privately Held
SIC: 5084 2752 Printing trades machinery, equipment & supplies; transfers, decalcomania or dry: lithographed

(G-11311)
WALDWICK PLASTICS CORP
21 Industrial Park (07463-1512)
PHONE.....................................201 445-7436
George Flores, Plant Mgr
Anthony Vicale, Treasurer
◆ EMP: 6 EST: 2010
SALES (est): 723.1K Privately Held
SIC: 3089 Injection molding of plastics

(G-11312)
WALDWICK PRINTING CO
1 Harrison Ave (07463-1708)
PHONE.....................................201 652-5848
William R Cook, Owner
EMP: 4 EST: 1953
SQ FT: 2,700
SALES: 300K Privately Held
SIC: 2752 Commercial printing, offset

(G-11313)
WALDWICK VOLUNTEER
20 Whites Ln (07463-1716)
P.O. Box 244 (07463-0244)
PHONE.....................................201 445-8772
EMP: 25
SALES: 75.7K Privately Held
SIC: 3713 Ambulance bodies

Wall
Monmouth County

(G-11314)
AMERICAN PLUS PRINTERS INC
2604 Atlantic Ave Ste 300 (07719-9757)
PHONE.....................................732 528-2170
Dianne Strohmenger, President
Jim Heffernan, Executive
EMP: 28
SQ FT: 26,000
SALES (est): 3.3MM Privately Held
WEB: www.americanplusprinters.com
SIC: 2752 Commercial printing, offset

Wall Township
Monmouth County

(G-11315)
AIR CRUISERS COMPANY LLC (DH)
Also Called: Safran Aerosystems Evacuation
1747 State Route 34 (07727-3935)
PHONE.....................................732 681-3527
Chris Kimball, General Mgr
T Webb, Vice Pres
John Hendricksen, Manager
John O Donnell,
Angel Scardilli, Administration
◆ EMP: 321
SQ FT: 37,500
SALES (est): 476.6MM
SALES (corp-wide): 833.4MM Privately Held
WEB: www.aircruisers.com
SIC: 2531 3069 3728 2399 Seats, aircraft; air-supported rubber structures; fuel tanks, aircraft; parachutes
HQ: Zodiac Us Corporation
1747 State Route 34
Wall Township NJ 07727
732 681-3527

(G-11316)
ALTO DEVELOPMENT CORP (PA)
Also Called: A&E Medical
5206 Asbury Rd (07727-3609)
P.O. Box 758, Farmingdale (07727-0758)
PHONE.....................................732 938-2266
Eric Sklar, CEO
Michael Wojciechowicz, President
EMP: 62 EST: 1967
SQ FT: 25,000

SALES (est): 12.1MM Privately Held
WEB: www.aemedical.com
SIC: 3841 Surgical & medical instruments

(G-11317)
AP GLOBAL ENTERPRISES INC
Also Called: AP International
5044 Industrial Rd (07727-3629)
P.O. Box 601, Oakhurst (07755-0601)
PHONE.....................................732 919-6200
Andy Papiccio, CEO
EMP: 8 EST: 2010
SALES (est): 532K Privately Held
SIC: 3931 5099 Musical instruments; musical instruments parts & accessories

(G-11318)
APPLICAD INC
Also Called: Aci
5029 Industrial Rd (07727-3651)
PHONE.....................................732 751-2555
Paul Macmillan, CEO
John Macmillan, President
John Vowteras, Vice Pres
Erin Macmillan, Production
Erin Drumm, Purch Mgr
▲ EMP: 45
SQ FT: 20,000
SALES (est): 13.7MM Privately Held
WEB: www.aci-applicad.com
SIC: 3672 8711 Circuit boards, television & radio printed; engineering services

(G-11319)
ATLANTIS AROMATICS INC
5047 Industrial Rd Ste 4 (07727-4026)
PHONE.....................................732 919-1112
Phillip Abbot, President
EMP: 6
SQ FT: 6,000
SALES (est): 1MM Privately Held
WEB: www.atlantisaromatics.com
SIC: 2844 Perfumes & colognes

(G-11320)
BEL-RAY COMPANY INC (HQ)
1201 Bowman Ave (07727-3910)
P.O. Box 526, Farmingdale (07727-0526)
PHONE.....................................732 378-4000
Daryl Brosnan, CEO
Cody Wolf, Regional Mgr
Jeff Collier, Manager
Bret Jenkins, Manager
Keith Maurer, Manager
◆ EMP: 100 EST: 1946
SQ FT: 80,000
SALES (est): 21MM
SALES (corp-wide): 3.5B Publicly Held
WEB: www.belray.com
SIC: 2992 Re-refining lubricating oils & greases; rust arresting compounds, animal or vegetable oil base
PA: Calumet Specialty Products Partners Lp
2780 Wtrfront Pkwy E Dr S
Indianapolis IN 46214
317 328-5660

(G-11321)
BEVERAGE WORKS NY INC (PA)
1800 State Route 34 # 203 (07719-9145)
PHONE.....................................732 938-7600
Mark Ponsiglione, Ch of Bd
Sabato Satucci, Vice Pres
EMP: 15
SALES (est): 64.2MM Privately Held
WEB: www.beverageworks.com
SIC: 2086 Bottled & canned soft drinks

(G-11322)
BIO-KEY INTERNATIONAL INC (PA)
3349 Hwy 138 Ste E (07719-9671)
PHONE.....................................732 359-1100
Michael W Depasquale, Ch of Bd
Barbara Rivera, COO
James Sullivan, Senior VP
Renat Zhdanov, Vice Pres
Chris Collier, Engineer
EMP: 21
SQ FT: 4,517

SALES: 4MM Publicly Held
WEB: www.bio-key.com
SIC: 3699 3999 7372 7375 Electrical equipment & supplies; security control equipment & systems; fingerprint equipment; prepackaged software; information retrieval services

(G-11323)
CHAVANT INC
5043 Industrial Rd (07727-3651)
PHONE.....................................732 751-0003
Jack North, President
▲ EMP: 10 EST: 1870
SQ FT: 12,000
SALES (est): 1.8MM Privately Held
WEB: www.chavant.com
SIC: 3952 Modeling clay

(G-11324)
CHRISTIAN MSSONS IN MANY LANDS
Also Called: Cmml
2751 18th Ave (07719-9550)
P.O. Box 13, Spring Lake (07762-0013)
PHONE.....................................732 449-8880
Samuel E Robinson, President
Thomas J Turner, President
Paul Gilkensen, Vice Pres
John G Jeffers, Treasurer
Joe Cannata, Accounts Mgr
EMP: 6
SQ FT: 20,300
SALES (est): 12.8MM Privately Held
WEB: www.cmmlusa.org
SIC: 8661 2721 Non-church religious organizations; magazines: publishing only, not printed on site

(G-11325)
CLAYTON BLOCK COMPANY INC (PA)
1355 Campus Pkwy Ste 200 (07753-6832)
P.O. Box 3015, Lakewood (08701-9015)
PHONE.....................................888 763-8665
William R Clayton, President
Daniel Clayton, Vice Pres
Douglas Clayton, Vice Pres
Joe Forestieri, CFO
Carole Larrison, Administration
◆ EMP: 30
SALES (est): 31.8MM Privately Held
WEB: www.claytononline.com
SIC: 3273 Ready-mixed concrete

(G-11326)
CLAYTON BLOCK COMPANY INC
1601 18th Ave (07719-3783)
PHONE.....................................732 681-0186
Toni Sabatani, Manager
EMP: 26
SALES (corp-wide): 31.8MM Privately Held
WEB: www.claytononline.com
SIC: 3271 5211 5032 3272 Blocks, concrete or cinder: standard; concrete & cinder block; concrete & cinder block; concrete products
PA: Clayton Block Company, Inc.
1355 Campus Pkwy Ste 200
Wall Township NJ 07753
888 763-8665

(G-11327)
CLAYTON BLOCK COMPANY INC
1355 Campus Pkwy Ste 200 (07753-6832)
P.O. Box 3015, Lakewood (08701-9015)
PHONE.....................................732 751-1631
EMP: 13
SALES (corp-wide): 31.8MM Privately Held
WEB: www.claytononline.com
SIC: 3271 Concrete block & brick
PA: Clayton Block Company, Inc.
1355 Campus Pkwy Ste 200
Wall Township NJ 07753
888 763-8665

(G-11328)
CLAYTON SAND COMPANY
1355 Campus Pkwy (07753-6833)
P.O. Box 3015, Lakewood (08701-9015)
PHONE.....................................732 751-7600

GEOGRAPHIC

William Clayton, *Partner*
Daniel Clayton, *Partner*
Douglas Clayton, *Partner*
Jamie Huss, *Controller*
Donald Clayton, *Sales Mgr*
EMP: 45
SALES (est): 3.8MM **Privately Held**
SIC: 1442 5032 Construction sand & gravel; sand mining; sand, construction; gravel

(G-11329)
COATES INTERNATIONAL LTD (PA)
2100 Highway 34 (07719-9110)
PHONE.................................732 449-7717
George J Coates, *Ch of Bd*
Barry C Kaye, *CFO*
Gregory G Coates, *Admin Sec*
EMP: 4
SQ FT: 29,000
SALES: 19.2K **Publicly Held**
WEB: www.coatesengine.com
SIC: 3519 Parts & accessories, internal combustion engines

(G-11330)
COATES PRECISION ENGINEERING
2100 State Route 34 (07719-9110)
PHONE.................................732 449-9382
George Coates, *President*
Gregory Coates, *Vice Pres*
EMP: 6
SALES (est): 23K
SALES (corp-wide): 19.2K **Publicly Held**
WEB: www.coatesengine.com
SIC: 3599 Machine shop, jobbing & repair
PA: Coates International, Ltd.
    2100 Highway 34
    Wall Township NJ 07719
    732 449-7717

(G-11331)
COLUMBIA FUEL SERVICES INC
1717 Highway 34 (07727-3989)
PHONE.................................732 751-0044
Dave Oaks, *Manager*
EMP: 10
SALES (corp-wide): 9.1MM **Privately Held**
SIC: 2911 5084 Jet fuels; industrial machinery & equipment
PA: Columbia Fuel Services, Inc.
    175 Tower Ave
    Groton CT 06340
    860 449-1400

(G-11332)
CONCEPT PROFESSIONAL SYSTEMS
5005 Belmar Blvd Ste B1 (07727-4020)
PHONE.................................732 938-5321
Donald C Gspann, *President*
Jeff Etten, *Vice Pres*
George Bachar, *VP Bus Dvlpt*
EMP: 4
SQ FT: 1,800
SALES (est): 350K **Privately Held**
SIC: 3651 Audio electronic systems

(G-11333)
D & A ELECTRONICS MFG
5303 Asbury Rd (07727-3612)
PHONE.................................732 938-7400
Demetrios Tsoutsas, *President*
EMP: 12
SQ FT: 22,000
SALES (est): 980K **Privately Held**
SIC: 3822 Temperature controls, automatic

(G-11334)
DIALIGHT CORPORATION (DH)
1501 Hwy 34 (07727-3932)
P.O. Box 8500 S-7055, Philadelphia PA (19178-0001)
PHONE.................................732 751-5809
Roy Burton, *CEO*
Marty Rapp, *CEO*
John Doyle, *Vice Pres*
Gareth Eaton, *Vice Pres*
Dennis Geary, *Plant Mgr*
▲ **EMP:** 100
SQ FT: 35,000

SALES (est): 298.4MM
SALES (corp-wide): 217.8MM **Privately Held**
WEB: www.dialight.com
SIC: 3679 3674 Liquid crystal displays (LCD); electronic circuits; semiconductors & related devices
HQ: Roxboro Holdings Inc
    1501 State Route 34
    Wall Township NJ 07727
    732 919-3119

(G-11335)
EAGLE FIRE & SAFETY CORP
Also Called: Eagle Fire Protection
1604 Westminster Ln (07719-4731)
P.O. Box 943, Neptune (07754-0943)
PHONE.................................732 982-7388
Bill Vinsko, *President*
Justin Brett, *Vice Pres*
EMP: 8
SALES (est): 977.8K **Privately Held**
SIC: 5999 1711 3569 7389 Fire extinguishers; fire sprinkler system installation; sprinkler systems, fire: automatic; fire extinguisher servicing;

(G-11336)
EARLE THE WALTER R CORP (PA)
1800 State Route 34 # 205 (07719-9168)
P.O. Box 556, Farmingdale (07727-0556)
PHONE.................................732 308-1113
Walter R Earle, *President*
Marianne Earle, *Vice Pres*
▲ **EMP:** 1
SQ FT: 2,500
SALES (est): 3.8MM **Privately Held**
WEB: www.theearlecompanies.com
SIC: 2951 Concrete, bituminous

(G-11337)
EARLE ASPHALT COMPANY (PA)
Also Called: Earle Companies, The
1800 State Route 34 # 205 (07719-9168)
P.O. Box 556, Farmingdale (07727-0556)
PHONE.................................732 308-1113
Walter R Earle, *President*
Walter R Earle II, *President*
Marianne Earle, *Vice Pres*
Thomas J Earle, *Vice Pres*
William Mead, *Project Mgr*
EMP: 122 **EST:** 1968
SQ FT: 1,500
SALES (est): 40.5MM **Privately Held**
SIC: 2951 Asphalt paving mixtures & blocks

(G-11338)
EXALENZ BIOSCIENCE INC
1712 M St (07719-3452)
PHONE.................................732 232-4393
Lawrence Cohen, *CEO*
Dennis Boyle, *Principal*
Eitan Blank, *VP Opers*
EMP: 30
SALES (est): 3.2MM **Privately Held**
SIC: 3841 Diagnostic apparatus, medical

(G-11339)
FERMATEX VASCULAR TECH LLC
Also Called: Adam Spence Vascular Tech
1746 Rte 34 (07727-3937)
PHONE.................................732 681-7070
Mike Janish, *CEO*
EMP: 10
SALES (est): 103K
SALES (corp-wide): 8B **Privately Held**
SIC: 3061 Medical & surgical rubber tubing (extruded & lathe-cut)
HQ: Pexco Llc
    6470 E Johns Rssng 430
    Johns Creek GA 30097
    770 777-8540

(G-11340)
FIVE ELEMENTS ROBOTICS LLC
Also Called: 5 Elements Robotics
1333 Campus Pkwy (07753-6815)
PHONE.................................800 681-8514
Wendy Roberts, *CEO*
EMP: 6
SQ FT: 1,000

SALES: 800K **Privately Held**
SIC: 3571 5099 5045 Minicomputers; robots, service or novelty; computer software

(G-11341)
FIZZICS GROUP LLC
1775 State Route 34 D14 (07727-3961)
PHONE.................................917 545-4533
Philip Petracca, *CEO*
Roger An, *Principal*
Courtney Baldwin, *Principal*
Greg Taylor, *Principal*
Steve Balog, *CFO*
EMP: 7
SALES (est): 283.8K **Privately Held**
SIC: 2082 Beer (alcoholic beverage)

(G-11342)
FRED MCDOWELL INC
34 St Hwy (07753)
P.O. Box 118, Belmar (07719-0118)
PHONE.................................732 681-5000
Fred Mc Dowell Jr, *President*
Frank Fine, *Vice Pres*
Jean Mc Dowell, *Treasurer*
EMP: 6 **EST:** 1929
SQ FT: 2,000
SALES: 853.7K **Privately Held**
SIC: 3531 Asphalt plant, including gravel-mix type

(G-11343)
GARDEN STATE PRECAST INC
1630 Wyckoff Rd (07727-3921)
P.O. Box 702, Farmingdale (07727-0702)
PHONE.................................732 938-4436
J Kirby O Malley, *President*
Mike Vergona, *Plant Mgr*
Nick Papapietro, *Engineer*
Chris Tyler, *Manager*
Dave Schlameuss, *Director*
EMP: 70
SQ FT: 871,200
SALES: 12.5MM **Privately Held**
WEB: www.gardenstateprecast.com
SIC: 3272 Concrete products

(G-11344)
HANGER PRSTHETCS & ORTHO INC
5100 Belmar Blvd (07727-4027)
PHONE.................................732 919-7774
Sheryl Price, *Principal*
Brian Kleiberg, *Manager*
EMP: 5
SALES (corp-wide): 1B **Publicly Held**
SIC: 3842 Surgical appliances & supplies
HQ: Hanger Prosthetics & Orthotics, Inc.
    10910 Domain Dr Ste 300
    Austin TX 78758
    512 777-3800

(G-11345)
HANSON AGGREGATES WRP INC (DH)
Also Called: Western Rock Products
1333 Campus Pkwy (07753-6815)
PHONE.................................972 653-5500
Alan Murray, *President*
EMP: 34
SALES (est): 18.4MM
SALES (corp-wide): 20.6B **Privately Held**
SIC: 3281 3272 2951 1442 Cut stone & stone products; concrete products; asphalt paving mixtures & blocks; construction sand & gravel

(G-11346)
HONEYWELL INTERNATIONAL INC
5047 Industrial Rd Ste 2 (07727-4026)
PHONE.................................732 919-0010
Tom McMann, *Manager*
EMP: 657
SALES (corp-wide): 41.8B **Publicly Held**
WEB: www.honeywell.com
SIC: 3724 Aircraft engines & engine parts
PA: Honeywell International Inc.
    300 S Tryon St
    Charlotte NC 28202
    973 455-2000

(G-11347)
HUECK FOILS HOLDING CO (DH)
1955 State Route 34 3c (07719-9735)
PHONE.................................732 974-4100
Dietmar Wohlfart, *President*
Herbert Schwemmer, *Treasurer*
▲ **EMP:** 5
SALES (est): 77.3MM
SALES (corp-wide): 2.6MM **Privately Held**
WEB: www.hueckfoils.com
SIC: 3497 Zinc foil
HQ: Hc Beteiligungses. Mbh
    Pirkmuhle 14-16
    Pirk
    961 870-

(G-11348)
I 2 R CORP (PA)
Also Called: EMC Technologists
5033 Industrial Rd Ste 6 (07727-3946)
PHONE.................................732 919-1100
James Watts, *President*
William Watts, *President*
Steve Rust, *Sales Staff*
Jeanne Sass, *Network Mgr*
Marilyn Sally Watts, *Admin Sec*
◆ **EMP:** 6
SQ FT: 5,000
SALES (est): 923.3K **Privately Held**
WEB: www.emcceupen.com
SIC: 3699 8748 8711 5063 Electrical equipment & supplies; environmental consultant; consulting engineer; electrical supplies

(G-11349)
ICE COLD NOVELTY PRODUCTS INC
5005 Belmar Blvd Ste B2 (07727-4020)
PHONE.................................732 751-0011
Kevin Enright, *CEO*
Chris Ulrich, *President*
EMP: 7
SQ FT: 4,500
SALES (est): 966.2K **Privately Held**
SIC: 5046 2024 Commercial equipment; non-dairy based frozen desserts

(G-11350)
KATES-BYLSTON PUBLICATIONS INC
3349 State Route 138 D (07719-9671)
PHONE.................................732 746-0211
Allison Sullivan, *Publisher*
Nancy Becker, *Principal*
Patti Bartsche, *Editor*
Jeanne Petillo, *Natl Sales Mgr*
Amy Fidalgo, *Marketing Staff*
EMP: 8
SALES (est): 463.3K **Privately Held**
SIC: 2741 Miscellaneous publishing

(G-11351)
KAVON FILTER PRODUCTS CO
5022 Industrial Rd (07727-3650)
P.O. Box 1166 (07719-1166)
PHONE.................................732 938-3135
Douglas Von Bulow, *President*
Francis Cavanaugh, *Vice Pres*
Michael Cavanaugh, *Vice Pres*
Linda Von Bulow, *Exec Dir*
▼ **EMP:** 13 **EST:** 1962
SQ FT: 11,000
SALES (est): 2.8MM **Privately Held**
WEB: www.kavonfilter.com
SIC: 3599 3569 Machine & other job shop work; filters, general line: industrial

(G-11352)
KEMPTON WOOD PRODUCTS
2800 Ridgewood Rd Ste 2 (07719-2172)
PHONE.................................732 449-8673
Kevin Kempton, *Mng Member*
William Smith,
EMP: 5
SQ FT: 3,000
SALES (est): 1.3MM **Privately Held**
WEB: www.kemptonwoodproducts.com
SIC: 5211 2431 Millwork & lumber; millwork

(G-11353)
LOCKHEED MARTIN INTEGRTD SYSTM
1800 State Route 34 (07719-9168)
PHONE..................................856 762-2222
Ron Street, *Manager*
EMP: 104 **Publicly Held**
SIC: 3812 Search & navigation equipment
HQ: Lockheed Martin Integrated Systems, Llc
6801 Rockledge Dr
Bethesda MD 20817

(G-11354)
MACLEARIE PRINTING LLC
917 18th Ave (07719-3260)
PHONE..................................732 681-2772
James Maclearie, *Mng Member*
EMP: 6
SALES (est): 829K **Privately Held**
WEB: www.maclearie.com
SIC: 2752 Commercial printing, lithographic

(G-11355)
MELSTROM MANUFACTURING CORP
5303 Asbury Rd (07727-3612)
PHONE..................................732 938-7400
Demitrios Tsoutsas, *President*
EMP: 55
SQ FT: 25,000
SALES (est): 7.4MM **Privately Held**
SIC: 3679 Harness assemblies for electronic use: wire or cable

(G-11356)
MSG FIRE & SAFETY INC
5142 W Hurley Pond Rd # 1 (07727-1617)
PHONE..................................732 833-8500
Michael Granit, *President*
EMP: 6
SALES (est): 1MM **Privately Held**
SIC: 3432 5082 Lawn hose nozzles & sprinklers; construction & mining machinery

(G-11357)
MUSCO SPORTS LIGHTING LLC
Also Called: Musco Lighting
5146 W Hurley Pond Rd # 1 (07727-1622)
PHONE..................................732 751-9114
Dan Shalloo, *Sales Staff*
EMP: 7
SALES (corp-wide): 158.6MM **Privately Held**
SIC: 3648 Lighting equipment
HQ: Musco Sports Lighting, Llc
100 1st Ave W
Oskaloosa IA 52577
641 673-0411

(G-11358)
NICHOLAS OLIVER LLC
Also Called: BO&nic
1933 State Route 35 (07719-3502)
PHONE..................................732 690-7144
Nicholas Solazzo, *President*
Connie Dean Taylor, *Vice Pres*
EMP: 6
SALES (est): 520K **Privately Held**
SIC: 2331 2335 Blouses, women's & juniors': made from purchased material; women's, juniors' & misses' dresses

(G-11359)
ONCO INC
1551 Hwy 138 (07719-3705)
PHONE..................................732 292-7460
James Hendrickson, *President*
Eileen Williamson, *General Mgr*
Heidi Hendrickson, *Sales Staff*
EMP: 15
SALES (est): 1.4MM **Privately Held**
SIC: 7372 7371 Business oriented computer software; custom computer programming services

(G-11360)
OPDYKE AWNINGS INC
2036 State Route 35 (07719-3529)
PHONE..................................732 449-5940
James Opdyke, *President*
Andrew Opdyke, *Vice Pres*
EMP: 15

SALES (est): 1.2MM **Privately Held**
SIC: 2394 3993 Awnings, fabric: made from purchased materials; signs & advertising specialties

(G-11361)
PALUMBO MILLWORK INC
5033 Industrial Rd Ste 8 (07727-3946)
PHONE..................................732 938-3266
Nick Palumbo, *President*
EMP: 4
SQ FT: 5,000
SALES (est): 330K **Privately Held**
SIC: 2434 2431 Wood kitchen cabinets; millwork

(G-11362)
R & H SPRING & TRUCK REPAIR
4806 W Hurley Pond Rd (07719-9633)
PHONE..................................732 681-9000
Frank Todero, *President*
Elizabeth Todero, *Vice Pres*
Paul Botticelli, *Parts Mgr*
EMP: 10
SQ FT: 8,000
SALES: 1.5MM **Privately Held**
SIC: 7538 3531 3711 General truck repair; blades for graders, scrapers, dozers & snow plows; snow plow attachments; snow plows (motor vehicles), assembly of

(G-11363)
RFM PRINTING INC
1715 Hwy 34 (07727-3934)
P.O. Box 1430, Belmar (07719-1430)
PHONE..................................732 938-4400
Robert McKenna, *President*
Mike Surowiec, *General Mgr*
EMP: 10
SALES (est): 2.1MM **Privately Held**
WEB: www.rfmprinting.com
SIC: 2752 Commercial printing, offset

(G-11364)
RHEOMETER SERVICES
1933 Hwy 35 Ste 105283 (07719-3502)
PHONE..................................732 922-8899
William Pyburn, *President*
EMP: 6
SALES (est): 698.4K **Privately Held**
SIC: 3821 Laboratory equipment: fume hoods, distillation racks, etc.

(G-11365)
ROXBORO HOLDINGS INC (HQ)
1501 State Route 34 (07727-3932)
PHONE..................................732 919-3119
Roy Burton, *President*
Nick Gallogly, *Vice Pres*
▲ EMP: 100
SQ FT: 35,000
SALES (est): 298.2MM
SALES (corp-wide): 217.8MM **Privately Held**
SIC: 3643 3679 3993 3823 Current-carrying wiring devices; electronic circuits; signs & advertising specialties; industrial instrmnts msrmnt display/control process variable; semiconductors & related devices
PA: Dialight Plc
Tower 42 International Financial Centre
London EC2N
203 058-3540

(G-11366)
ROYAL PHARMACEUTICALS LLC
1967 Highway 34 Ste 103 (07719-9752)
PHONE..................................732 292-2661
Matthew Regan,
EMP: 5
SQ FT: 2,500
SALES (est): 504.6K **Privately Held**
SIC: 2834 Druggists' preparations (pharmaceuticals)

(G-11367)
SCREEN PRINTING & EMBROIDERY
5005 Belmar Blvd Ste B6 (07727-4020)
PHONE..................................732 256-9610
Timothy Dubrow, *Mng Member*
EMP: 4

SALES (est): 350.6K **Privately Held**
SIC: 2752 Commercial printing, lithographic

(G-11368)
SELECTIVE COATINGS & INKS (PA)
Also Called: SCI
5008 Industrial Rd (07727-3650)
PHONE..................................732 938-7677
William Zak, *President*
Joseph Bernardo, *Vice Pres*
Greg Beriont, *Plant Mgr*
Joan Zak, *Admin Sec*
▲ EMP: 15
SQ FT: 5,000
SALES (est): 1.9MM **Privately Held**
WEB: www.sci-inc-usa.com
SIC: 2893 Gravure ink

(G-11369)
SHORE AWNING CO
1933 State Route 35 # 126 (07719-3553)
P.O. Box 38, Avon By The Sea (07717-0038)
PHONE..................................732 775-3351
Michael Mc Clellan, *President*
Larry Gray, *Vice Pres*
EMP: 8 EST: 1946
SQ FT: 4,000
SALES: 965.4K **Privately Held**
SIC: 2394 Awnings, fabric: made from purchased materials

(G-11370)
SIMA S ENTERPRISES LLC
Also Called: Sima Enterprises
1298 Evans Rd (07719-4018)
PHONE..................................877 223-7639
Mordy Naftaly, *Mng Member*
▲ EMP: 5
SALES (est): 390.5K **Privately Held**
SIC: 2741 7389

(G-11371)
STONE GRAPHICS
5020 Industrial Rd (07727-3650)
PHONE..................................732 919-1111
Raymond C Stone Jr, *President*
▲ EMP: 13
SQ FT: 7,200
SALES (est): 600K **Privately Held**
WEB: www.signsbystone.com
SIC: 3993 2396 Signs, not made in custom sign painting shops; automotive & apparel trimmings

(G-11372)
SURE DESIGN
5027 Industrial Rd Ste 3 (07727-4040)
PHONE..................................732 919-3066
Ken Thomas, *Managing Prtnr*
EMP: 15
SALES (est): 2.5MM **Privately Held**
WEB: www.sure-design.com
SIC: 3672 Printed circuit boards

(G-11373)
SYMTERA ANALYTICS LLC
1806 State Route 35 (07719)
PHONE..................................718 696-9902
Haider Cheema, *CEO*
EMP: 10
SALES (est): 892.4K **Privately Held**
SIC: 3826 5049 Analytical instruments; analytical instruments

(G-11374)
SYNTIRO DYNAMICS LLC
1606 Cammar Dr (07719-4704)
PHONE..................................732 377-3307
EMP: 6
SALES (est): 583K **Privately Held**
SIC: 3494 Pipe fittings

(G-11375)
TOTAL GARAGE SOLUTIONS LLC
1709 State Route 34 Ste 2 (07727-4036)
PHONE..................................732 749-3993
Tara McSherry, *Office Mgr*
Tracy Yodice, *Manager*
EMP: 20

SALES (est): 1.4MM **Privately Held**
SIC: 2431 3699 Garage doors, overhead: wood; door opening & closing devices, electrical

(G-11376)
TRINITY HEATING & AIR INC (PA)
Also Called: Trinity Solar Systems
2211 Allenwood Rd (07719-9692)
PHONE..................................732 780-3779
Tom Pollock, *President*
Lauren English, *Partner*
Bill Condit, *General Mgr*
James Bradshaw, *District Mgr*
Kristian Calibuso, *District Mgr*
▲ EMP: 65
SQ FT: 145,000
SALES (est): 70.2MM **Privately Held**
WEB: www.trinityheatingandair.com
SIC: 3433 1731 1711 Solar heaters & collectors; electrical work; solar energy contractor

(G-11377)
VERNI VITO
Also Called: Minuteman Press
1818 State Route 35 Ste 8 (07719-3540)
PHONE..................................732 449-1760
Vito Verni, *Owner*
Detria Gallenger, *Bookkeeper*
EMP: 5
SQ FT: 1,500
SALES: 400K **Privately Held**
SIC: 2752 2791 2789 Commercial printing, lithographic; typesetting; bookbinding & related work

(G-11378)
WILLIAM OPDYKE AWNINGS INC (PA)
2036 State Route 35 (07719-3529)
PHONE..................................732 449-5940
James Opdyke, *President*
▲ EMP: 8 EST: 1914
SQ FT: 18,000
SALES (est): 1.5MM **Privately Held**
SIC: 5999 5712 2394 Awnings; furniture stores; canvas & related products

(G-11379)
ZODIAC US CORPORATION (HQ)
Also Called: Zodiac Aerosystems
1747 State Route 34 (07727-3935)
PHONE..................................732 681-3527
Jean-Louis Gerondeau, *CEO*
Mark Jeffers, *Vice Pres*
Robert Schalhoub, *Vice Pres*
Cathy Palmer, *Purch Mgr*
Lily Kua, *Buyer*
▲ EMP: 584
SALES (est): 1.3B
SALES (corp-wide): 833.4MM **Privately Held**
SIC: 3728 Aircraft landing assemblies & brakes
PA: Safran
2 Bd Du General Martial Valin
Paris 15e Arrondissement 75015
140 608-080

Wallington
Bergen County

(G-11380)
AEROSPACE MANUFACTURING INC
80 Van Winkle Ave (07057-1148)
P.O. Box 3398 (07057-0398)
PHONE..................................973 472-9888
Al Shafa, *President*
Lester Paszkowski, *Mfg Staff*
Amir Jabbarnia, *Manager*
James Hakimi, *Shareholder*
Vivian Hakimi, *Shareholder*
EMP: 50
SQ FT: 30,000
SALES (est): 7.9MM **Privately Held**
WEB: www.aero-space.us
SIC: 3728 Aircraft parts & equipment

(G-11381)
ALLIED WASTE PRODUCTS INC
61 Midland Ave Ste 61-71 (07057-1715)
PHONE..................................973 473-7638
John Macchiarelli, *President*
Mario Macchiarelli, *Treasurer*
EMP: 6 EST: 1950
SQ FT: 8,000
SALES (est): 590K **Privately Held**
SIC: 3559 Recycling machinery; boots,
shoes & leather working machinery

(G-11382)
**BRENNER METAL PRODUCTS
(PA)**
16 Main Ave (07057-1106)
P.O. Box 3517 (07057-0517)
PHONE..................................973 778-2466
Christine Brenner, *President*
EMP: 30
SQ FT: 18,000
SALES (est): 5.1MM **Privately Held**
SIC: 3842 5047 Surgical appliances &
supplies; medical & hospital equipment

(G-11383)
BRENNER METAL PRODUCTS
51 Paterson Ave (07057-1115)
PHONE..................................973 778-2466
Christine Brenner, *President*
EMP: 20
SALES (est): 1.2MM
SALES (corp-wide): 5.1MM **Privately
Held**
SIC: 3599 Machine & other job shop work
PA: Brenner Metal Products (Inc)
16 Main Ave
Wallington NJ 07057
973 778-2466

(G-11384)
DIJON ENTERPRISES LLC
Also Called: Make Wine With US
21 Curie Ave (07057-2233)
PHONE..................................201 876-9463
John Gizzi,
Dianne Greco,
EMP: 5
SQ FT: 12,000
SALES (est): 412.5K **Privately Held**
WEB: www.makewinewithus.com
SIC: 2084 Wines

(G-11385)
DRY BILGE SYSTEMS INC
460 Main Ave Ste C (07057-1851)
PHONE..................................862 257-1800
Patricia Tani, *President*
Peter Tani, *Project Mgr*
EMP: 22
SQ FT: 2,500
SALES (est): 1.2MM **Privately Held**
SIC: 3442 Metal doors, sash & trim

(G-11386)
GARFIELD MOLDING CO INC
10 Midland Ave (07057-1795)
PHONE..................................973 777-5700
EMP: 28 EST: 1908
SQ FT: 65,000
SALES (est): 4.6MM **Privately Held**
SIC: 3089 Mfg Plastic Products

(G-11387)
HYGLOSS PRODUCTS INC
45 Hathaway St (07057-1008)
PHONE..................................973 458-1700
Moshe Neurath, *President*
▲ EMP: 25
SQ FT: 19,000
SALES (est): 4.6MM **Privately Held**
WEB: www.hygloss.com
SIC: 3944 3999 5092 Craft & hobby kits &
sets; education aids, devices & supplies;
arts & crafts equipment & supplies

(G-11388)
**MERCHANTS ALARM SYSTEMS
INC**
203 Paterson Ave Ste 5 (07057-1344)
PHONE..................................973 779-1296
Walter Wargacki, *President*
Elizabeth Wargacki, *Vice Pres*
EMP: 30
SQ FT: 10,000

SALES (est): 3.3MM **Privately Held**
SIC: 1731 7381 3669 Fire detection &
burglar alarm systems specialization; burglary protection service; burglar alarm apparatus, electric

(G-11389)
R S RUBBER CORP
55 Paterson Ave (07057-1115)
P.O. Box 3400 (07057-0400)
PHONE..................................973 777-2200
Robert Buschgans, *President*
Bob Busch, *General Mgr*
EMP: 10
SQ FT: 15,000
SALES (est): 1.8MM **Privately Held**
SIC: 3053 5085 Gaskets, all materials;
gaskets

(G-11390)
TRIANGLE INK CO INC (PA)
53-57 Van Dyke St (07057)
PHONE..................................201 935-2777
Chester Bartolomei, *President*
EMP: 19 EST: 1978
SQ FT: 14,000
SALES (est): 4.1MM **Privately Held**
WEB: www.triangleink.com
SIC: 2893 Screen process ink

Wanaque
Passaic County

(G-11391)
BKH ELECTRONICS
9j Brookside Hts (07465-1620)
P.O. Box 247 (07465-0247)
PHONE..................................210 410-2757
Georgina Fabian, *Owner*
EMP: 4
SALES (est): 300K **Privately Held**
SIC: 3679 Electronic circuits

Waretown
Ocean County

(G-11392)
AMERILUBES LLC
5 Mantoloking Ln (08758-2354)
PHONE..................................704 399-7701
▼ EMP: 2
SALES: 5MM **Privately Held**
SIC: 3569 Mfg General Industrial Machin-
ery

(G-11393)
**CLAYTON BLOCK COMPANY
INC**
Rr 9 (08758)
PHONE..................................609 693-3000
EMP: 13
SALES (corp-wide): 31.8MM **Privately
Held**
WEB: www.claytononline.com
SIC: 3271 Blocks, concrete or cinder: stan-
dard
PA: Clayton Block Company, Inc.
1355 Campus Pkwy Ste 200
Wall Township NJ 07753
888 763-8665

(G-11394)
SUBURBAN GUIDES INC
97 Spring Lake Blvd (08758-2681)
PHONE..................................201 452-4989
David Bonynge, *President*
EMP: 4
SALES (est): 87.2K **Privately Held**
SIC: 2711 Newspapers

Warren
Somerset County

(G-11395)
3SHAPE INC
10 Independence Blvd # 150 (07059-2707)
PHONE..................................908 867-0144
Flemming Thorup, *President*

Henrik Vestermark, *Vice Pres*
Wendi Cohen, *Sales Mgr*
Michael Maccaquano, *Sales Mgr*
Rayah Khateeb, *Sales Staff*
EMP: 11
SALES (est): 84.1K
SALES (corp-wide): 300.8K **Privately
Held**
SIC: 3845 5045 CAT scanner (Computer-
ized Axial Tomography) apparatus; com-
puter software
HQ: 3shape A/S
Holmens Kanal 7, Sal 4
KObenhavn 1060
337 316-54

(G-11396)
**ACRELIC INTERACTIVE LLC
(PA)**
16 Mount Bethel Rd (07059-5604)
PHONE..................................908 222-2900
David A Rosen, *President*
Gordon S Smith, *President*
Garth A Rose, *COO*
Pamela M Hakim, *Director*
EMP: 4
SALES (est): 1.6MM **Privately Held**
WEB: www.acrelic.com
SIC: 7372 Business oriented computer
software

(G-11397)
AETERNA ZENTARIS INC
20 Independence Blvd # 401 (07059-2737)
PHONE..................................908 626-5428
Juergen Engel, *CEO*
David Mazzo, *President*
Ellen McDonald, *Vice Pres*
Mario Paradis, *Vice Pres*
Nicholas Pelliccione, *Vice Pres*
EMP: 8
SQ FT: 9,000
SALES (est): 2.3MM
SALES (corp-wide): 911K **Privately Held**
WEB: www.aeternazentaris.com
SIC: 5122 2834 Pharmaceuticals; phar-
maceutical preparations
PA: Aeterna Zentaris Inc
1 Place Ville-Marie Bureau 2500
Montreal QC

(G-11398)
**AQUESTIVE THERAPEUTICS
INC (PA)**
30 Technology Dr Ste 2a (07059-5167)
PHONE..................................908 941-1900
Santo Costa, *Ch of Bd*
Keith J Kendall, *President*
Daniel Barber, *COO*
Peter Boyd, *Senior VP*
Lori J Braender, *Senior VP*
EMP: 10
SQ FT: 16,454
SALES: 67.4MM **Publicly Held**
SIC: 2834 Pharmaceutical preparations

(G-11399)
BALLARD COLLECTION INC
Also Called: Karen Lee Ballard
221 Stirling Rd (07059-5238)
PHONE..................................908 604-0082
Karen Lee Engemann, *CEO*
Becky Sooy, *Vice Pres*
EMP: 7
SALES (est): 812.5K **Privately Held**
WEB: www.karenleeballard.com
SIC: 2392 Tablecloths & table settings

(G-11400)
**BELLEROPHON THERAPEUTICS
INC**
184 Liberty Corner Rd # 302 (07059-6868)
PHONE..................................908 574-4770
Fabian Tenenbaum, *CEO*
Jonathan M Peacock, *Ch of Bd*
Martin Dekker, *VP Engrg*
Megan Schoeps, *CFO*
Deborah A Quinn, *Chief Mktg Ofcr*
EMP: 20 EST: 2009
SQ FT: 22,000
SALES (est): 6.2MM **Privately Held**
SIC: 2834 Pharmaceutical preparations

(G-11401)
C S L WATER TREATMENT INC
Also Called: C S L Water Quality
156 Mount Bethel Rd (07059-5147)
P.O. Box 4246 (07059-0246)
PHONE..................................908 647-1400
John Truglio, *President*
Bernadette Truglio, *Admin Sec*
EMP: 12 EST: 1930
SQ FT: 8,000
SALES (est): 2.1MM **Privately Held**
WEB: www.cslwater.com
SIC: 2899 Water treating compounds

(G-11402)
**CELGENE CELLULAR
THERAPEUTICS**
33 Technology Dr (07059-5148)
PHONE..................................908 673-9000
EMP: 9
SALES (est): 729.2K
SALES (corp-wide): 15.2B **Publicly Held**
SIC: 2834 Pharmaceutical preparations
PA: Celgene Corporation
86 Morris Ave
Summit NJ 07901
908 673-9000

(G-11403)
CELGENE CORPORATION
Also Called: Celgene Cellular Therapeutics
7 Powderhorn Dr (07059-5190)
PHONE..................................732 271-1001
Kathy Davis, *General Mgr*
Larry Hamann, *Vice Pres*
Michelle McLaughlin, *Engineer*
Loic Faivre, *Accounting Mgr*
Wendy Moses, *HR Admin*
EMP: 30
SALES (corp-wide): 15.2B **Publicly Held**
SIC: 2834 Pharmaceutical preparations
PA: Celgene Corporation
86 Morris Ave
Summit NJ 07901
908 673-9000

(G-11404)
CHEMBIOPOWER INC
211 Warren St Ste 503 (07059)
PHONE..................................908 209-5595
Jeremiah Sullivan, *CFO*
EMP: 4
SALES (est): 156.7K **Privately Held**
SIC: 2869 Industrial organic chemicals

(G-11405)
CHROMIS FIBEROPTICS INC
6 Powderhorn Dr (07059-5105)
PHONE..................................732 764-0900
Frank Graziano, *President*
Miri Park, *COO*
Michael Bohrer, *Vice Pres*
Shiyu An, *Manager*
Lee Plyler, *CTO*
▲ EMP: 10
SQ FT: 12,100
SALES (est): 2.2MM **Privately Held**
WEB: www.chromisfiber.com
SIC: 3661 Fiber optics communications
equipment

(G-11406)
CIPLA USA INC (HQ)
10 Independence Blvd # 300 (07059-2730)
PHONE..................................908 356-8900
Nikhil Lalwani, *President*
Debeeak Agarwal, *CFO*
Sudip Jadhav, *Finance*
Biplab Mazumdar, *Admin Sec*
▲ EMP: 21
SQ FT: 6,000
SALES (est): 6.5MM
SALES (corp-wide): 1.6B **Privately Held**
SIC: 2834 Pharmaceutical preparations
PA: Cipla Limited
Cipla House, Peninsula Business Park
Mumbai MH 40001
222 308-2891

(G-11407)
DEALAMAN ENTERPRISES INC
214 Mountainview Rd (07059-5037)
PHONE..................................908 647-5533
George Dealaman, *President*
George Dealaman Jr, *Vice Pres*
Bruce Dealaman, *Treasurer*

Elizabeth Dealaman, *Admin Sec*
EMP: 30 **EST:** 1944
SQ FT: 1,751
SALES (est): 2.9MM **Privately Held**
SIC: 2011 4151 Pork products from pork slaughtered on site; school buses

(G-11408)
ELGEE MANUFACTURING COMPANY
Also Called: Elgee Power Vac Sweeper
225 Stirling Rd (07059-5238)
PHONE....................908 647-4100
Stephen Heinle, *President*
Rosie Uride, *Partner*
EMP: 8 **EST:** 1960
SQ FT: 10,000
SALES (est): 500K **Privately Held**
WEB: www.elgee.com
SIC: 3589 3444 Dirt sweeping units, industrial; roof deck, sheet metal

(G-11409)
EMERSON PROCESS MANAGEMENT
20 Independence Blvd (07059-2731)
PHONE....................908 605-4551
John Drisko, *General Mgr*
Dominique Driver, *General Mgr*
Joe Sweeney, *Regional Mgr*
Jeff Boedeker, *Business Mgr*
Mike Rooney, *Vice Pres*
EMP: 7
SALES (corp-wide): 17.4B **Publicly Held**
SIC: 3823 Industrial instrmnts msrmnt display/control process variable
HQ: Emerson Process Management Power & Water Solutions, Inc.
200 Beta Dr
Pittsburgh PA 15238
412 963-4000

(G-11410)
ESSILOR LABORATORIES AMER INC
Also Called: Eloa - New Jersey
5 Powderhorn Dr (07059-5105)
PHONE....................732 563-9884
Debra Case, *General Mgr*
Matt Swartz, *Med Doctor*
EMP: 15
SALES (corp-wide): 1.4MM **Privately Held**
WEB: www.crizal.com
SIC: 3851 Eyeglasses, lenses & frames
HQ: Essilor Laboratories Of America, Inc.
13515 N Stemmons Fwy
Dallas TX 75234
972 241-4141

(G-11411)
GLAXOSMITHKLINE CONSUMER (DH)
184 Libery Corner Rd (07059)
PHONE....................251 591-4188
Colin Mackenzie, *President*
Sherri Von Stein, *Human Res Mgr*
Tom Leeker, *Director*
◆ **EMP:** 400
SQ FT: 200,000
SALES (est): 395.6MM
SALES (corp-wide): 39.5B **Privately Held**
SIC: 2834 Pharmaceutical preparations
HQ: Glaxosmithkline Llc
5 Crescent Dr
Philadelphia PA 19112
215 751-4000

(G-11412)
GLAXOSMITHKLINE CONSUMER HLTH (DH)
184 Liberty Corner Rd (07059-6796)
PHONE....................215 751-5046
William Mosher, *Director*
◆ **EMP:** 9 **EST:** 2015
SALES (est): 61.2MM
SALES (corp-wide): 39.5B **Privately Held**
SIC: 2834 Druggists' preparations (pharmaceuticals)

(G-11413)
GSK CONSUMER HEALTH INC (HQ)
184 Liberty Corner Rd # 78 (07059-6796)
PHONE....................919 269-5000

Joseph Jimenez, *CEO*
John McKenna, *CFO*
Matthias Vogt, *Treasurer*
◆ **EMP:** 300
SALES (est): 325.8MM
SALES (corp-wide): 39.5B **Privately Held**
SIC: 2834 Pharmaceutical preparations
PA: Glaxosmithkline Plc
G S K House
Brentford MIDDX TW8 9
208 047-5000

(G-11414)
HILLARYS FASHION BOUTIQUE LLC
Also Called: Hillary's Fashions
177 Washington Valley Rd (07059-7210)
PHONE....................732 667-7733
Hillary Scharf,
EMP: 11
SALES (est): 825K **Privately Held**
SIC: 5621 5632 2335 Boutiques; women's accessory & specialty stores; women's, juniors' & misses' dresses

(G-11415)
HORIZON GROUP USA INC (PA)
45 Technology Dr (07059-5184)
PHONE....................908 810-1111
James H Cash, *CEO*
Cara Costa, *Exec VP*
Jim Neitzel, *Exec VP*
Michael Heyer, *Vice Pres*
Jeff Snyderman, *Vice Pres*
◆ **EMP:** 150 **EST:** 2000
SQ FT: 50,000
SALES (est): 180MM **Privately Held**
WEB: www.horizongroupusa.com
SIC: 3944 Games, toys & children's vehicles

(G-11416)
HUBER+SUHNER ASTROLAB INC
4 Powderhorn Dr (07059-5105)
PHONE....................732 560-3800
Andrew Weirback, *CEO*
Lisa Kiernan, *Controller*
EMP: 46
SQ FT: 21,000
SALES (est): 12.1MM
SALES (corp-wide): 890.5MM **Privately Held**
SIC: 2298 3678 Cable, fiber; electronic connectors
HQ: Huber + Suhner (North America) Corporation
8530 Steele Creek Pl
Charlotte NC 28273
704 790-7300

(G-11417)
II-VI OPTOELECTRONIC DVCS INC (HQ)
141 Mount Bethel Rd (07059-5128)
PHONE....................908 668-5000
Giovanni Barbarossa, *President*
Gary Ruland, *General Mgr*
Bob Cameron, *Engineer*
Tom Czirok, *Engineer*
Rajat Jain, *Engineer*
▲ **EMP:** 226
SQ FT: 150,000
SALES (est): 85.8MM
SALES (corp-wide): 1.3B **Publicly Held**
WEB: www.anadigics.com
SIC: 3674 Integrated circuits, semiconductor networks, etc.
PA: Ii-Vi Incorporated
375 Saxonburg Blvd
Saxonburg PA 16056
724 352-4455

(G-11418)
INLC TECHNOLOGY CORPORATION
30 Technology Dr Ste 1d (07059-5177)
PHONE....................908 834-8390
Clarel Thevenot, *General Mgr*
Seong W Suh,
EMP: 15
SQ FT: 1,400
SALES (est): 1.1MM **Privately Held**
SIC: 3827 3661 Polarizers; telephone & telegraph apparatus

(G-11419)
JENCKS SIGNS CORP
16 Geiger Ln (07059-5620)
PHONE....................908 542-1400
Patricia Herman, *President*
Barry Herman, *Admin Sec*
EMP: 4
SQ FT: 5,000
SALES (est): 360K **Privately Held**
SIC: 3993 Electric signs; signs, not made in custom sign painting shops

(G-11420)
LINCOLN MOLD & DIE CORP
13 Deerwood Trl (07059-5562)
PHONE....................908 241-3344
Vincent Comitini, *President*
Edward Drozd, *President*
John Raymonds, *Chairman*
Catherine Raymonds, *Corp Secy*
EMP: 55 **EST:** 1954
SQ FT: 25,000
SALES (est): 6.1MM **Privately Held**
WEB: www.lmold.com
SIC: 3544 Forms (molds), for foundry & plastics working machinery

(G-11421)
MEGAPLEX SOFTWARE INC
21 Broadway Rd (07059-5055)
PHONE....................908 647-3273
Dhiraj Sharma, *President*
EMP: 5
SALES: 1MM **Privately Held**
SIC: 7372 7379 Business oriented computer software; data processing consultant

(G-11422)
METRO RAILINGS LLC
2 Technology Dr Unit 4569 (07059-6625)
PHONE....................877 504-8300
Rickin Shah,
EMP: 4 **EST:** 2016
SALES (est): 602.1K **Privately Held**
SIC: 2431 Staircases, stairs & railings

(G-11423)
MOLNAR TOOLS INC
3 Stoningham Dr (07059-6740)
PHONE....................908 580-0671
Charles Molnar, *President*
Sophia Molnar, *Treasurer*
Charles Molnar Jr, *Admin Sec*
EMP: 11
SQ FT: 12,000
SALES (est): 1.6MM **Privately Held**
SIC: 3469 5251 Metal stampings; tools

(G-11424)
MOUNTAIN MILLWORK
142 Mountain Ave (07059-5260)
PHONE....................908 647-1100
Tom Guarino, *Principal*
EMP: 4
SALES (est): 522.7K **Privately Held**
SIC: 2431 Millwork

(G-11425)
PICUT INDUSTRIES INC (PA)
140 Mount Bethel Rd (07059-5280)
PHONE....................908 754-1333
Richard Picut, *President*
Ray Mattes, *Vice Pres*
EMP: 70
SQ FT: 170,000
SALES (est): 67.7MM **Privately Held**
SIC: 3491 Steam traps

(G-11426)
PICUT MFG CO INC
140 Mount Bethel Rd (07059-5280)
PHONE....................908 754-1333
Frederick R Picut, *President*
Walter Ryder, *Corp Secy*
Richard Picut, *Vice Pres*
Russell Picut, *Vice Pres*
Steve Tine, *Purch Mgr*
▲ **EMP:** 95 **EST:** 1966
SQ FT: 50,000
SALES (est): 17.5MM **Privately Held**
WEB: www.picut.com
SIC: 3599 Machine shop, jobbing & repair

(G-11427)
PITNEY BOWES INC
15 Mountainview Rd (07059-6711)
PHONE....................908 903-2870
Scott Powley, *Manager*
EMP: 13
SALES (corp-wide): 3.5B **Publicly Held**
SIC: 3579 7359 Postage meters; business machine & electronic equipment rental services
PA: Pitney Bowes Inc.
3001 Summer St Ste 3
Stamford CT 06905
203 356-5000

(G-11428)
REDPURO LLC
Also Called: Redpuro Import
106 Mount Horeb Rd Apt 8b (07059-5566)
PHONE....................908 370-4460
Alejandro Flores, *Owner*
EMP: 4
SQ FT: 900
SALES: 90K **Privately Held**
SIC: 2084 Wines

(G-11429)
SENSORY SOLUTIONS LLC
1 Ledgewood Ct (07059-6751)
PHONE....................973 615-7600
EMP: 4
SALES (est): 290.7K **Privately Held**
SIC: 2111 Cigarettes

(G-11430)
SHERRY INTERNATIONAL INC
31 Mountain Blvd Bldg M (07059-5647)
PHONE....................908 279-7255
Leilei Wang, *CEO*
Weixing Wang, *President*
▲ **EMP:** 10
SALES (est): 1.2MM **Privately Held**
SIC: 3825 Frequency meters: electrical, mechanical & electronic

(G-11431)
SIEMENS INDUSTRY INC
163 Washington Valley Rd (07059-7180)
PHONE....................732 302-1686
David B Blum, *Branch Mgr*
EMP: 4
SALES (corp-wide): 95B **Privately Held**
SIC: 3823 Electrodes used in industrial process measurement
HQ: Siemens Industry, Inc.
1000 Deerfield Pkwy
Buffalo Grove IL 60089
847 215-1000

(G-11432)
SUNRISE FOOD TRADING INC
163 Washington Valley Rd # 103 (07059-7181)
PHONE....................718 305-4388
Ping Song, *CEO*
◆ **EMP:** 15
SALES (est): 3.5MM **Privately Held**
SIC: 2092 5149 Seafoods, frozen: prepared; specialty food items

(G-11433)
SUPERIOR CUSTOM KITCHENS LLC
126 Mount Bethel Rd (07059-5129)
PHONE....................908 753-6005
John A Barna,
Joseph Borin,
EMP: 27
SQ FT: 4,000
SALES (est): 3.3MM **Privately Held**
WEB: www.superiorcustomkitchens.com
SIC: 5712 5211 2434 Cabinet work, custom; lumber & other building materials; wood kitchen cabinets

(G-11434)
UNIVERSAL PALLET INC
118 Smoke Rise Dr (07059-6821)
PHONE....................732 356-2624
Michael Dinardi, *Principal*
EMP: 7
SALES (est): 49.7K **Privately Held**
SIC: 2448 Pallets, wood & wood with metal

(G-11435)
VANTAGE TOOL & MFG INC
223 Stirling Rd (07059-5238)
PHONE................................908 647-1010
Stephen Heinle, *President*
Nancy D Heinle, *Vice Pres*
EMP: 4
SQ FT: 5,000
SALES (est): 330K **Privately Held**
SIC: 3544 3542 Special dies & tools; machine tools, metal forming type

(G-11436)
WARREN CAPITAL INC
6 Westwood Ct (07059-2704)
PHONE................................732 910-8134
Wendy Wu, *Principal*
EMP: 4
SALES (est): 250.7K **Privately Held**
SIC: 3442 Metal doors, sash & trim

Washington
Warren County

(G-11437)
ALBEA AMERICAS INC (DH)
191 State Route 31 N (07882-1529)
PHONE................................908 689-3000
Francois Luscan, *President*
Bruno Manach, *Exec VP*
Luc Rousselet, *Exec VP*
Arnaud Schuh, *Exec VP*
Franois Tassart, *Exec VP*
◆ **EMP:** 250
SALES (est): 169.1MM **Privately Held**
SIC: 3312 Pipes & tubes
HQ: Albea Services
   Zac Des Barbanniers Le Signac
   Gennevilliers 92230
   181 932-000

(G-11438)
ARCTIC FOODS INC
Also Called: Jmee Financial Division
251 E Washington Ave (07882-2405)
PHONE................................908 689-0590
Mark Rossi, *President*
Ezio Rossi, *Chairman*
Joseph Claps, *Vice Pres*
Carla Ditondo, *Office Mgr*
EMP: 24
SQ FT: 15,000
SALES (est): 2.4MM **Privately Held**
WEB: www.arcticfoods.com
SIC: 5421 5722 5147 5142 Meat markets, including freezer provisioners; food & freezer plans, meat; freezer provisioners, meat; household appliance stores; meats & meat products; packaged frozen goods; frozen specialties

(G-11439)
ARMIN KOSOSKI
Also Called: All Sports Stadium
297 State Route 31 S (07882-4068)
PHONE................................908 689-0411
Armin Kososki, *Owner*
EMP: 7
SQ FT: 2,100
SALES (est): 1.2MM **Privately Held**
SIC: 5091 5941 5699 5999 Sporting & recreation goods; sporting goods & bicycle shops; sports apparel; trophies & plaques; screen printing

(G-11440)
BASF CORPORATION
Washington New Jersey Site
2 Pleasant View Ave (07882-2320)
PHONE................................908 689-7470
Martha Brabston, *Branch Mgr*
EMP: 62
SALES (corp-wide): 71.7B **Privately Held**
WEB: www.basf.com
SIC: 2869 2843 Industrial organic chemicals; surface active agents
HQ: Basf Corporation
   100 Park Ave
   Florham Park NJ 07932
   973 245-6000

(G-11441)
BEMIS COMPANY INC
31 State St (07882)
PHONE................................908 689-3000
Eduardo Posada, *Business Mgr*
Angela Lowe, *Plant Mgr*
Wilton Brown, *Mfg Mgr*
Brower Mark, *Opers Staff*
Christopher Rogers, *Production*
EMP: 450
SALES (corp-wide): 256.8K **Privately Held**
WEB: www.pechineyplasticpackaging.com
SIC: 3498 Fabricated pipe & fittings
HQ: Bemis Company, Inc.
   2301 Industrial Dr
   Neenah WI 54956
   920 727-4100

(G-11442)
BIG BUCKS ENTERPRISES INC
Also Called: Massina Wildlife Management
55 Willow St (07882-2138)
P.O. Box 122, Chester (07930-0122)
PHONE................................908 320-7009
James Messina, *Vice Pres*
▲ **EMP:** 20
SALES (est): 193K **Privately Held**
SIC: 5191 2879 Fertilizer & fertilizer materials; fungicides, herbicides

(G-11443)
CANDLE ARTISANS INCORPORATED
253 E Washington Ave (07882-2405)
P.O. Box 190 (07882-0190)
PHONE................................908 689-2000
Robert Rumfield, *President*
▲ **EMP:** 20
SQ FT: 36,000
SALES (est): 2.4MM **Privately Held**
WEB: www.candleartisans.com
SIC: 3999 Candles

(G-11444)
CAPRA CUSTOM CABINETRY
259 E Washington Ave (07882-2405)
PHONE................................908 797-9848
John Capra, *Principal*
EMP: 4
SALES (est): 220K **Privately Held**
SIC: 2434 Wood kitchen cabinets

(G-11445)
GOOD IMPRESSIONS INC (PA)
325 W Washington Ave (07882-2153)
PHONE................................908 689-3071
Marian Kennedy, *President*
Wendy Witner, *Manager*
EMP: 10
SQ FT: 2,500
SALES (est): 1.3MM **Privately Held**
WEB: www.good-impressions.com
SIC: 2752 7334 Commercial printing, offset; photocopying & duplicating services

(G-11446)
HAZ LABORATORIES
39 Hartmans Corner Rd (07882-4378)
P.O. Box 67 (07882-0067)
PHONE................................908 453-3300
Henry Zajac Jr, *Owner*
EMP: 12
SQ FT: 10,000
SALES (est): 1.4MM **Privately Held**
WEB: www.mu-tron.com
SIC: 3679 3625 3841 Electronic circuits; industrial controls: push button, selector switches, pilot; surgical & medical instruments

(G-11447)
HERBALIST & ALCHEMIST INC
51 S Wandling Ave (07882-2192)
PHONE................................908 689-9020
Beth Lambert, *CEO*
David Winston, *President*
Elizabeth Lambert, *Treasurer*
Russell Chell, *Shareholder*
EMP: 10
SQ FT: 9,000
SALES (est): 1.4MM **Privately Held**
WEB: www.herbalist-alchemist.com
SIC: 2833 Medicinals & botanicals

(G-11448)
JOST BROTHERS JEWELRY MFG CORP
295 Jost Dr (07882)
PHONE................................908 453-2266
Stephen Jost, *President*
Charles Jost, *Vice Pres*
EMP: 13 **EST:** 1935
SALES (est): 1.7MM **Privately Held**
SIC: 3911 Jewelry, precious metal

(G-11449)
MYSTIC TIMBER LLC
95 Youmans Ave (07882-1807)
PHONE................................908 223-7878
Bruce Jorgensen,
Deb Jorgensen,
EMP: 4 **EST:** 2010
SALES (est): 325.4K **Privately Held**
SIC: 3443 Boiler shop products: boilers, smokestacks, steel tanks

(G-11450)
RDO INDUCTION LTD LIABILITY CO
2170 State Route 57 W (07882-3523)
PHONE................................908 835-7222
Robert Okner, *Principal*
◆ **EMP:** 6
SALES (est): 8.1K **Privately Held**
SIC: 3999 Heating pads, nonelectric

(G-11451)
SCHNEIDERS KITCHENS INC
252 State Route 31 N (07882-1550)
PHONE................................908 689-5649
Walter Schneider, *President*
Silvia Winiger, *Vice Pres*
Adolph Schneider, *Treasurer*
EMP: 7
SQ FT: 9,000
SALES (est): 910.8K **Privately Held**
SIC: 5712 2511 Cabinet work, custom; wood household furniture

(G-11452)
STEPHEN SWINTON STUDIO INC
49 New Hampton Rd (07882-4003)
PHONE................................908 537-9135
Stephen Swinton, *President*
EMP: 5
SALES (est): 275K **Privately Held**
WEB: www.swintonstudio.com
SIC: 7336 7374 7312 3993 Graphic arts & related design; service bureau, computer; poster advertising, outdoor; signs & advertising specialties; commercial photography; custom computer programming services

(G-11453)
T M BAXTER SERVICES LLC
1307 Washington Gdns (07882-2174)
PHONE................................908 500-9065
Thomas Zuchowski, *President*
EMP: 25
SQ FT: 2,500
SALES (est): 3.1MM **Privately Held**
SIC: 2499 1741 Veneer work, inlaid; masonry & other stonework

(G-11454)
WITTE CO INC
507 Rte 31 S (07882)
P.O. Box 47 (07882-0047)
PHONE................................908 689-6500
Richard B Witte, *CEO*
▲ **EMP:** 41
SQ FT: 5,600
SALES: 7.3MM **Privately Held**
WEB: www.witte.com
SIC: 3559 Chemical machinery & equipment

Watchung
Somerset County

(G-11455)
FANWOOD CRUSHED STONE COMPANY
Also Called: Welding Materials
1 New Providence Rd (07069-5015)
PHONE................................908 322-7840
Chuck Valley, *Manager*
EMP: 70
SALES (corp-wide): 31.4MM **Privately Held**
SIC: 1411 5032 Granite, dimension-quarrying; stone, crushed or broken
PA: Fanwood Crushed Stone Company Inc
   141 Central Ave
   Westfield NJ
   908 233-4444

(G-11456)
L & Z TOOL AND ENGINEERING INC
Also Called: La Marca Industries
1691 Us Highway 22 (07069-6501)
PHONE................................908 322-2220
Thomas Lamarca, *President*
Lena Lamarca, *Corp Secy*
Lance Lamonte, *Vice Pres*
Frank Cooper, *Marketing Staff*
EMP: 32
SQ FT: 20,000
SALES (est): 5.5MM **Privately Held**
WEB: www.lztool.com
SIC: 3544 Special dies & tools

(G-11457)
MEDISCOPE MANUFACTURING INC (PA)
744 Mountain Blvd Fl 2w (07069-6297)
PHONE................................908 756-2411
Dan Helme, *President*
Daniel Helme, *COO*
EMP: 45
SQ FT: 2,000
SALES (est): 4.3MM **Privately Held**
WEB: www.mediscope-mfg.com
SIC: 3599 Machine shop, jobbing & repair

(G-11458)
STANDARD TILE WATCHUNG CORP
1515 Us Highway 22 Ste 24 (07069-6516)
PHONE................................908 754-4200
Bill Spina, *President*
▲ **EMP:** 5 **EST:** 1942
SALES (est): 450K **Privately Held**
SIC: 3253 Ceramic wall & floor tile

(G-11459)
SUN PLASTICS CO INC
35 Blue Wolf Trl (07069-5425)
PHONE................................908 490-0870
Victoria Salerno, *President*
Jerry R Salerno, *Vice Pres*
EMP: 15
SQ FT: 13,000
SALES (est): 980K **Privately Held**
SIC: 3652 Phonograph record blanks; phonograph records, prerecorded

(G-11460)
SUPPLIES-SUPPLIES INC
85 Maple St (07069-6311)
P.O. Box 633, Kenilworth (07033-0633)
PHONE................................908 272-5100
Carl Streko, *President*
Bette Jo Streko, *Director*
EMP: 16
SQ FT: 2,300
SALES (est): 3.6MM **Privately Held**
WEB: www.ssofficesupplies.com
SIC: 5021 5112 5943 2752 Office furniture; school desks; stationery & office supplies; office forms & supplies; business form & card printing, lithographic

(G-11461)
WELDON ASPHALT CORP
1 New Providence Rd (07069-5015)
PHONE................................908 322-7840
Dick Meyers, *Manager*

EMP: 25
SALES (corp-wide): 6MM **Privately Held**
SIC: 3273 Ready-mixed concrete
PA: Weldon Asphalt Corp
141 Central Ave
Westfield NJ
908 233-4444

Waterford Works
Camden County

(G-11462)
JAMES R MACAULEY INC
1 Industrial Dr (08089)
PHONE.................................856 767-3474
George Macauley, *President*
EMP: 1
SQ FT: 13,000
SALES: 2MM **Privately Held**
SIC: 4953 5085 2842 Recycling, waste
materials; commercial containers; spe-
cialty cleaning, polishes & sanitation
goods

Wayne
Passaic County

(G-11463)
202 SMOOTHIE LLC
11 Danielle Dr (07470-2538)
PHONE.................................973 985-4973
Koushby Majagah, *Principal*
EMP: 5
SALES (est): 235.2K **Privately Held**
SIC: 2037 Frozen fruits & vegetables

(G-11464)
**AARISSE HEALTH CARE
PRODUCTS**
11 Robin Hood Way (07470-5427)
PHONE.................................973 686-1811
Jeff Behr, *Manager*
EMP: 6
SALES (est): 210.5K **Privately Held**
WEB: www.aarisse.com
SIC: 8082 3841 Home health care serv-
ices; surgical & medical instruments

(G-11465)
**ACCELEDEV CHEMICAL LLC
(PA)**
18 Apple Ln (07470-1964)
P.O. Box 3431 (07474-3431)
PHONE.................................862 239-1524
Charles Lewis, *President*
EMP: 5
SALES (est): 613K **Privately Held**
SIC: 8999 2899 Chemical consultant;
chemical preparations

(G-11466)
**ALAN CHEMICAL
CORPORATION INC**
573 Valley Rd Ste 1 (07470-3552)
PHONE.................................973 628-7777
Alan Braxton, *President*
EMP: 8
SALES (est): 1.1MM **Privately Held**
SIC: 2891 Adhesives & sealants

(G-11467)
**ALL AMERICAN OIL RECOVERY
CO**
1067 State Route 23 (07470-6649)
PHONE.................................973 628-9278
Roy R Vanvarick, *President*
Robert Vanvarick, *Treasurer*
Ann Billack, *Admin Sec*
EMP: 20
SALES (est): 3.3MM **Privately Held**
WEB: www.vanvarickandsons.com
SIC: 1382 4959 Oil & gas exploration
services; sanitary services

(G-11468)
**AMERICAN RENOLIT
CORPORATION**
1310 Hamburg Tpke Ste 5 (07470-4064)
PHONE.................................973 706-6912

EMP: 5
SALES (corp-wide): 2.2B **Privately Held**
SIC: 3081 5162 Plastic film & sheet; plas-
tics film
HQ: American Renolit Corporation
1207 E Lincolnway
La Porte IN 46350
219 324-6886

(G-11469)
**AMERICAN WOODCARVING
LLC**
1123 State Route 23 (07470-6608)
PHONE.................................973 835-8510
Michael Holst, *Mng Member*
EMP: 8
SQ FT: 3,500
SALES: 800K **Privately Held**
SIC: 3993 Signs & advertising specialties

(G-11470)
ANODIZING CORPORATION
Also Called: J E B Urban Renewal Associates
10 Legrande Ter (07470-6029)
PHONE.................................973 694-6449
Jack Lavorgna, *President*
EMP: 8 EST: 1974
SQ FT: 16,800
SALES (est): 460K **Privately Held**
SIC: 3471 Anodizing (plating) of metals or
formed products

(G-11471)
ANSCOTT CHEMICAL INDS INC
Also Called: Caled Chemical
26 Hanes Dr (07470-4722)
PHONE.................................973 696-7575
Jack Belluscio, *Executive*
EMP: 33
SALES (est): 16.3MM **Privately Held**
WEB: www.anscott.net
SIC: 2841 Detergents, synthetic organic or
inorganic alkaline

(G-11472)
**ATLANTIC EXTERIOR WALL
SYSTEMS**
25 Mansard Ct (07470-6040)
PHONE.................................973 646-8200
Joseph Farina, *President*
Nicholas D'Albo, *Vice Pres*
Salvatore D'Albo, *Vice Pres*
Naresh Shekhada, *Project Mgr*
Nicholas Caporuscio, *Opers Mgr*
▲ EMP: 55
SQ FT: 35,000
SALES (est): 11.5MM **Privately Held**
SIC: 2439 1791 Trusses, except roof: lam-
inated lumber; exterior wall system instal-
lation

(G-11473)
**BAE SYSTEMS INFO & ELEC
SYS**
150 Parish Dr (07470-9601)
PHONE.................................973 633-6000
Thomas Calabrase, *Purchasing*
Eric Bartscherer, *Engineer*
Kathleen Campolieto, *Engineer*
Charity Carter, *Engineer*
Michael Christoff, *Engineer*
EMP: 19
SALES (corp-wide): 21.6B **Privately Held**
SIC: 3812 Search & navigation equipment
HQ: Bae Systems Information And Elec-
tronic Systems Integration Inc.
65 Spit Brook Rd
Nashua NH 03060
603 885-4321

(G-11474)
**BAE SYSTEMS INFO & ELEC
SYS**
164 Totowa Rd (07470-3118)
PHONE.................................973 633-6000
Sabra Frankel, *Manager*
Alan Dewar, *Prgrmr*
EMP: 750
SALES (corp-wide): 21.6B **Privately Held**
WEB: www.iesi.na.baesystems.com
SIC: 3812 Aircraft/aerospace flight instru-
ments & guidance systems; defense sys-
tems & equipment

HQ: Bae Systems Information And Electronic Systems Integration Inc.
65 Spit Brook Rd
Nashua NH 03060
603 885-4321

(G-11475)
**BAYER HLTHCARE
PHRMCTICALS INC**
6 Westbelt (07470-6810)
PHONE.................................973 709-3545
EMP: 22
SALES (corp-wide): 45.3B **Privately Held**
SIC: 2834 3841 Drugs affecting neoplasms & endrocrine systems; drugs acting on the central nervous system &
sense organs; drugs acting on the cardiovascular system, except diagnostic; surgical & medical instruments
HQ: Bayer Healthcare Pharmaceuticals Inc.
100 Bayer Blvd
Whippany NJ 07981
862 404-3000

(G-11476)
BAYER U S LLC
6 Westbelt (07470-6810)
PHONE.................................973 709-3545
Xiomara Rios, *Business Mgr*
Fred Duchin, *Vice Pres*
Juan Nadal, *Vice Pres*
Joshua Yoskowitz, *Engineer*
Maria Pagan, *Accountant*
EMP: 10
SALES (est): 748.2K **Privately Held**
SIC: 2834 Pharmaceutical preparations

(G-11477)
BEL-ART PRODUCTS INC (DH)
661 Rte 23 (07470-6814)
PHONE.................................973 694-0500
David Landsberger, *President*
Brad Mahood, *COO*
Bradley N Mahood, *COO*
Jason Gidge, *Vice Pres*
Anthony Chiarella, *Purch Mgr*
◆ EMP: 40 EST: 1945
SQ FT: 62,000
SALES: 30MM
SALES (corp-wide): 1.5B **Privately Held**
WEB: www.nutechmfg.com
SIC: 3089 3479 Trays, plastic; coating of
metals with plastic or resins
HQ: S P Industries, Inc.
935 Mearns Rd
Warminster PA 18974
215 672-7800

(G-11478)
**BERGEN SIGN COMPANY INC
(PA)**
90 Newark Pompton Tpke (07470-6633)
PHONE.................................973 742-7755
Thomas Schneider, *CEO*
Richard Walker, *COO*
Ethel Lewis, *Office Mgr*
EMP: 23
SQ FT: 32,000
SALES: 6.1MM **Privately Held**
WEB: www.bergensign.com
SIC: 1799 3993 Sign installation & mainte-
nance; neon signs

(G-11479)
BIMBO BAKERIES USA INC
Also Called: Canada Bread
100 Riverview Dr (07470-3104)
PHONE.................................973 872-6167
EMP: 24 **Privately Held**
SIC: 2051 Bakery: wholesale or whole-
sale/retail combined
HQ: Bimbo Bakeries Usa, Inc
255 Business Center Dr # 200
Horsham PA 19044
215 347-5500

(G-11480)
**BMCA HOLDINGS
CORPORATION**
Also Called: Building Materials Corp Amer
1361 Alps Rd (07470-3700)
PHONE.................................973 628-3000
Robert Tasaro, *Ch of Bd*
Daniel Goldstein, *Senior VP*
Dave Rueter, *Senior VP*

Connie Goulding, *Vice Pres*
Dawn Skare, *Vice Pres*
EMP: 44
SALES (est): 467.5MM
SALES (corp-wide): 2.5B **Privately Held**
SIC: 2493 Insulation & roofing material, re-
constituted wood
HQ: G-I Holdings Inc.
1361 Alps Rd
Wayne NJ 07470
973 628-3000

(G-11481)
**BONLAND INDUSTRIES INC
(PA)**
50 Newark Pompton Tpke (07470-6698)
P.O. Box 200 (07474-0200)
PHONE.................................973 694-3211
William Boniface, *CEO*
Andrew Boniface, *President*
Linda West, *Exec VP*
John Rockwood, *Foreman/Supr*
Bill Hecht, *Opers Staff*
EMP: 99
SQ FT: 30,000
SALES (est): 70.5MM **Privately Held**
WEB: www.bonlandhvac.com
SIC: 1711 3444 Ventilation & duct work
contractor; warm air heating & air condi-
tioning contractor; mechanical contractor;
ventilators, sheet metal

(G-11482)
**BOSTON SCIENTIFIC
CORPORATION**
45 Barbour Pond Dr (07470-2094)
PHONE.................................973 709-7000
Paul Southworth, *President*
Faythe Williams, *Marketing Staff*
EMP: 40
SALES (corp-wide): 9.8B **Publicly Held**
WEB: www.bsci.com
SIC: 3841 3842 Surgical & medical instru-
ments; surgical appliances & supplies
PA: Boston Scientific Corporation
300 Boston Scientific Way
Marlborough MA 01752
508 683-4000

(G-11483)
**BP CORPORATION NORTH
AMER INC**
1500 Valley Rd (07470-2040)
PHONE.................................973 633-2200
Rodger Harris, *Manager*
EMP: 8
SALES (corp-wide): 298.7B **Privately
Held**
WEB: www.bpamoco.com
SIC: 2911 Petroleum refining
HQ: Bp Corporation North America Inc.
501 Westlake Park Blvd
Houston TX 77079
281 366-2000

(G-11484)
BP LUBRICANTS USA INC (DH)
Also Called: B P
1500 Valley Rd (07470-2040)
PHONE.................................973 633-2200
Marci Brand, *CEO*
Robert Meyers, *General Mgr*
Myriam Ordonez, *Project Mgr*
Emiliano Pasini, *Project Mgr*
John Veninger, *Project Mgr*
◆ EMP: 300
SQ FT: 90,000
SALES (est): 369MM
SALES (corp-wide): 298.7B **Privately
Held**
WEB: www.castrolna.com
SIC: 2992 Lubricating oils & greases
HQ: Bp America Inc.
4101 Winfield Rd Ste 200
Warrenville IL 60555
630 420-5111

(G-11485)
BROOKLINE CHEMICAL CORP
26 Hanes Dr (07470-4722)
PHONE.................................301 767-1177
Steve Hoh, *Branch Mgr*
EMP: 22

GEOGRAPHIC

SALES (corp-wide): 3.3MM Privately Held
WEB: www.brookline-chem.com
SIC: **2261** Chemical coating or treating of cotton broadwoven fabrics
PA: Brookline Chemical Corp.
    9817 Inglemere Dr
    Bethesda MD 20817
    301 767-1177

(G-11486)
C & N PACKAGING INC
Also Called: Suffolk Molds
155 Us Highway 46 Ste 200 (07470-6819)
PHONE..................................631 491-1400
Alain Mutschler, *CEO*
▲ EMP: 79
SQ FT: 32,000
SALES (est): 14.8MM
SALES (corp-wide): 7.5MM Privately Held
WEB: www.cnpkg.com
SIC: **3089** Closures, plastic
HQ: Mar-Lee Companies, Inc.
    180 Authority Dr
    Fitchburg MA 01420
    978 343-9600

(G-11487)
CARDINAL INTERNATIONAL INC
30 Corporate Dr (07470-3113)
P.O. Box 897, Pine Brook (07058-0897)
PHONE..................................973 628-0900
Bryan Ovouke, *President*
EMP: 18
SALES (est): 2.4MM
SALES (corp-wide): 1.5MM Privately Held
SIC: **3229** Pressed & blown glass
PA: Arc Holdings
    104 Avenue Du General De Gaulle
    Arques 62510
    321 385-122

(G-11488)
CLIFTON ADHESIVE INC
48 Burgess Pl (07470-6734)
PHONE..................................973 694-0845
Robert A Lefelar, *President*
Dan Higgins, *Engineer*
◆ EMP: 25
SQ FT: 22,000
SALES (est): 5.4MM Privately Held
WEB: www.cliftonadhesive.com
SIC: **2891** Adhesives, plastic

(G-11489)
COCO INTERNATIONAL INC
6 Highpoint Dr (07470-7423)
PHONE..................................973 694-1200
Don Lee, *CEO*
Bud Reisman, *Accounts Mgr*
▲ EMP: 20 EST: 2008
SALES: 3.5MM Privately Held
SIC: **2041** 5149 Grain cereals, cracked; breakfast cereals

(G-11490)
CREATIVE INDUSTRIAL KITCHENS
8 Leo Pl (07470-7272)
PHONE..................................973 633-0420
Tom Walsh, *Owner*
EMP: 5
SQ FT: 5,000
SALES: 500K Privately Held
SIC: **3564** 1711 Blowers & fans; ventilation & duct work contractor

(G-11491)
CYBEREXTRUDERCOM INC
1401 Valley Rd Ste 208 (07470-2074)
PHONE..................................973 623-7900
John Ives, *President*
EMP: 4
SALES (est): 1MM Privately Held
WEB: www.cyberextruder.com
SIC: **7372** 7371 7373 Prepackaged software; custom computer programming services; computer integrated systems design

(G-11492)
D & S COMPANIES LLC
10 Myrtle Ave (07470-6019)
PHONE..................................973 832-4959

Edward Slaska, *Mng Member*
EMP: 2 EST: 2005
SALES: 1MM Privately Held
SIC: **3524** Lawn & garden mowers & accessories

(G-11493)
DI-FERRARO INC
Also Called: Mead Wilbert
28 Burgess Pl (07470-6734)
PHONE..................................973 694-7200
Mario Ferraro Sr, *President*
Mario Ferraro Jr, *President*
Anna Ferraro, *Vice Pres*
EMP: 40 EST: 1937
SQ FT: 20,000
SALES (est): 7.7MM Privately Held
SIC: **3272** Burial vaults, concrete or precast terrazzo

(G-11494)
DMJ INDUSTRIAL SERVICES LLC
1 Hilltop Ter (07470-5807)
PHONE..................................973 692-8406
Stephen Sangle, *Owner*
EMP: 7
SALES: 120K Privately Held
SIC: **3441** Fabricated structural metal

(G-11495)
DOLAN & TRAYNOR INC
32 Riverview Dr (07470-3102)
PHONE..................................973 696-8700
Timothy J Traynor, *President*
B Michael Dolan, *Exec VP*
Tim Dolan, *Vice Pres*
Stephen G Wilkinson, *Vice Pres*
Gary Mastrache, *CFO*
EMP: 36
SQ FT: 40,000
SALES: 20MM Privately Held
WEB: www.dolan-traynor.com
SIC: **2421** 5032 Building & structural materials, wood; marble building stone

(G-11496)
DONNELLY INDUSTRIES INC
Also Called: DONNELLY CONSTRUCTION
557 Rte 23 (07470-6818)
PHONE..................................973 672-1800
Rod Donnelly, *CEO*
Gerard J Donnelly Jr, *President*
Chris Powers, *President*
Shahzad Khan, *COO*
Chris Donnelly, *Vice Pres*
▲ EMP: 95
SQ FT: 32,000
SALES: 48.1MM Privately Held
WEB: www.donnellyind.com
SIC: **1542** 2431 Commercial & office buildings, renovation & repair; millwork

(G-11497)
ENCORE LED LTG LTD LBLTY CO
155 Us Highway 46 (07470-6831)
PHONE..................................866 694-4533
William Dato,
EMP: 8
SALES (est): 644.5K Privately Held
SIC: **3646** 3645 3648 Commercial indusl & institutional electric lighting fixtures; garden, patio, walkway & yard lighting fixtures: electric; decorative area lighting fixtures; street lighting fixtures

(G-11498)
ESPERTECH INC
26 Hamilton Ave (07470-3059)
P.O. Box 3129 (07474-3129)
PHONE..................................973 577-6406
Thomas Bernhardt, *CTO*
EMP: 11
SALES (est): 637.9K Privately Held
SIC: **7372** Utility computer software

(G-11499)
EVA MARIA WOLFE
6 Westbelt (07470-6810)
PHONE..................................412 777-2000
Bayer Healthcare Phrm, *Principal*
EMP: 6 EST: 2010
SALES (est): 659.5K Privately Held
SIC: **2834** Pharmaceutical preparations

(G-11500)
EZ GENERAL CONSTRUCTION CORP
Also Called: Marble and Granite
155 Webster Dr (07470-5449)
PHONE..................................201 223-1101
Julio C Bonilla, *President*
Arturo Bonilla, *Vice Pres*
EMP: 6
SALES (est): 560.9K Privately Held
SIC: **3281** 1522 1521 Cut stone & stone products; residential construction; single-family home remodeling, additions & repairs

(G-11501)
FIDELITY INDUSTRIES INC (PA)
Also Called: Fidelity Wallcoverings
559 Rte 23 (07470-6832)
PHONE..................................973 696-9120
Dvosia Rivkin, *President*
Samuel Brook, *Vice Pres*
◆ EMP: 40 EST: 1974
SQ FT: 20,000
SALES (est): 18.9MM Privately Held
WEB: www.fidelitywall.com
SIC: **3069** Wallcoverings, rubber

(G-11502)
FILTREX INC
450 Hamburg Tpke Ste 2 (07470-8485)
P.O. Box 2273 (07474-2273)
PHONE..................................973 595-0400
Ken Bergstrom, *President*
Trish Koberowski, *Corp Secy*
EMP: 10
SQ FT: 8,000
SALES (est): 1.5MM Privately Held
SIC: **3589** Swimming pool filter & water conditioning systems; water treatment equipment, industrial

(G-11503)
FIN-TEK CORPORATION (PA)
Also Called: Fin-Tek Ozone
6 Leo Pl (07470-7272)
PHONE..................................973 628-2988
Donald Finnegan, *President*
Mary Finnegan, *Vice Pres*
Paul Finnegan, *Treasurer*
EMP: 7
SQ FT: 5,000
SALES (est): 2.5MM Privately Held
WEB: www.fin-tek.com
SIC: **8711** 3589 Engineering services; sewage & water treatment equipment

(G-11504)
FOREMOST CORP
2025 Hamburg Tpke Ste A (07470-6250)
PHONE..................................973 839-3360
William F Formosa Jr, *President*
Doris Formosa, *Corp Secy*
EMP: 3
SQ FT: 750
SALES: 1MM Privately Held
SIC: **5065** 3679 Electronic parts; electronic circuits

(G-11505)
FOUR WAY ENTERPRISES INC
Also Called: Butler Sign Co.
582 Fairfield Rd (07470-7354)
PHONE..................................973 633-5757
John Janis Jr, *President*
EMP: 16
SQ FT: 6,500
SALES (est): 2.1MM Privately Held
WEB: www.butlersignco.com
SIC: **3993** Electric signs; neon signs

(G-11506)
G T ASSOCIATES
440 Indian Rd (07470-4914)
P.O. Box 2005 (07474-2005)
PHONE..................................973 694-6040
Arthur L Tambe, *President*
Sam Giovino, *Admin Sec*
EMP: 8
SALES (est): 650K Privately Held
SIC: **3674** Semiconductors & related devices

(G-11507)
G-I HOLDINGS INC (HQ)
Also Called: G A F
1361 Alps Rd (07470-3700)
PHONE..................................973 628-3000
Robert B Tafaro, *CEO*
Peter Ganz, *President*
Susan Yoss, *President*
John M Sergey, *Exec VP*
Matti Kiik, *Vice Pres*
◆ EMP: 5
SALES (est): 1.3B
SALES (corp-wide): 2.5B Privately Held
SIC: **2869** 2843 3295 Solvents, organic; surface active agents; roofing granules
PA: G Holdings Llc
    1 Campus Dr
    Parsippany NJ 07054
    973 628-3000

(G-11508)
GAF ELK MATERIALS CORPORATION
1361 Alps Rd (07470-3700)
P.O. Box 402, Broadway (08808-0402)
PHONE..................................973 628-4083
Robert B Tafaro, *CEO*
Janssen Hunter, *Purch Mgr*
Tony Vallance, *Sales Staff*
Lisa Lambrix, *Director*
Robert Herschmann, *Maintence Staff*
▲ EMP: 137
SALES (est): 57.6MM Privately Held
SIC: **3271** 3272 3444 Roof ballast block, concrete; roofing tile & slabs, concrete; metal roofing & roof drainage equipment; roof deck, sheet metal

(G-11509)
GETINGE GROUP LOGISTICS AMERIC
45 Barbour Pond Dr (07470-2094)
PHONE..................................973 709-6000
Victor Guzman,
EMP: 40
SALES (est): 1.2MM Privately Held
SIC: **3841** 3845 Surgical & medical instruments; medical cleaning equipment, ultrasonic

(G-11510)
GETINGE USA INC (DH)
45 Barbour Pond Dr (07470-2094)
PHONE..................................800 475-9040
Charles Carrier, *President*
Terry D Cooke, *Vice Pres*
Michael Treude, *Vice Pres*
Andrew Prok, *Production*
Martin Pilcher, *Technical Mgr*
▲ EMP: 150 EST: 1971
SQ FT: 250,000
SALES (est): 205.1MM
SALES (corp-wide): 6.1B Privately Held
SIC: **3842** 3841 Sterilizers, hospital & surgical; surgical & medical instruments
HQ: Getinge Ab
    Lindholmspiren 7a
    Goteborg 417 5
    103 350-000

(G-11511)
GILL ASSOCIATES LLC
Also Called: Gill Assoc Idntfcation Systems
2025 Hamburg Tpke Ste M (07470-6250)
PHONE..................................973 835-5456
Alicia Zagorski, *Sales Executive*
John D Gill,
EMP: 6
SQ FT: 1,500
SALES (est): 844.2K Privately Held
SIC: **5043** 3089 5946 Photographic equipment & supplies; laminating of plastic; photographic supplies

(G-11512)
GRAPHIC PACKAGING INTL LLC
5 Haul Rd (07470-6624)
PHONE..................................973 709-9100
EMP: 7 **Publicly Held**
SIC: **2631** Container, packaging & boxboard
HQ: Graphic Packaging International, Llc
    1500 Riveredge Pkwy # 100
    Atlanta GA 30328

(G-11513)
GRAPHIC PACKAGING INTL LLC
Also Called: Altivity Packaging
5 Haul Rd (07470-6624)
PHONE..................................732 424-2100
Anthony Kolenski, *Manager*
EMP: 200 **Publicly Held**
SIC: 2631 Folding boxboard
HQ: Graphic Packaging International, Llc
1500 Riveredge Pkwy # 100
Atlanta GA 30328

(G-11514)
GRIMBILAS ENTERPRISES CORP
Also Called: Tornqvist Div
29 Hanes Dr (07470-4721)
PHONE..................................973 686-5999
John Grimbilas, *President*
Kenneth Grimbilas, *Vice Pres*
Peter Grimbilas, *Vice Pres*
Robert Grimbilas, *Vice Pres*
EMP: 20
SQ FT: 28,000
SALES (est): 2.8MM **Privately Held**
SIC: 3441 Building components, structural steel

(G-11515)
HAYDON CORPORATION (PA)
415 Hamburg Tpke Ste 1 (07470-2164)
PHONE..................................973 904-0800
Doug H Hillman, *President*
Giuseppe Testa, *Vice Pres*
Kenneth Rosa, *Materials Mgr*
Edward Quist, *Transportation*
Kathy Passaro, *Purch Mgr*
▲ EMP: 90
SQ FT: 105,000
SALES (est): 63MM **Privately Held**
WEB: www.2haydon.com
SIC: 3449 3634 3567 Miscellaneous metalwork; heating units, electric (radiant heat); baseboard or wall; industrial furnaces & ovens

(G-11516)
HERBERT J HINCHMAN & SON INC
26 Pike Dr (07470-2493)
PHONE..................................973 942-2063
Donald H Hinchman, *President*
Donald J Hinchman, *President*
EMP: 20
SQ FT: 7,500
SALES (est): 3MM **Privately Held**
SIC: 3273 5032 Ready-mixed concrete; gravel

(G-11517)
HEROS SALUTE AWARDS CO
1875 State Route 23 Ste 1 (07470-7528)
PHONE..................................973 696-5085
Robert Terry, *President*
EMP: 6
SQ FT: 1,125
SALES (est): 826.8K **Privately Held**
WEB: www.herossalute.com
SIC: 5999 3479 3993 Trophies & plaques; engraving jewelry silverware, or metal; signs & advertising specialties

(G-11518)
IMAGE MAKERS INSTANT PRINTING
1581 State Route 23 (07470-7506)
PHONE..................................973 633-1771
Gino Nuzzo, *President*
EMP: 5
SALES (est): 450K **Privately Held**
SIC: 2752 Commercial printing, offset

(G-11519)
INDUSTRIAL HABONIM VALVES & AC
22 Riverview Dr Ste 103 (07470-3100)
PHONE..................................201 820-3184
Josef Dotan, *President*
▲ EMP: 10 EST: 2008
SALES (est): 1.8MM **Privately Held**
SIC: 3491 3593 5085 Industrial valves; fluid power cylinders & actuators; valves, pistons & fittings

(G-11520)
INNOVATIVE RESIN SYSTEMS INC (PA)
70 Verkade Dr (07470-8215)
PHONE..................................973 465-6887
Pinakin Patel, *President*
John Khosdeghian, *CFO*
◆ EMP: 20
SQ FT: 3,500
SALES: 7.1MM **Privately Held**
WEB: www.innovativeresinsystems.com
SIC: 2821 Epoxy resins

(G-11521)
INNOVATIVE RESIN SYSTEMS INC
70 Verkade Dr (07470-8215)
PHONE..................................973 633-5342
Pinakin Patel, *President*
EMP: 15
SALES (corp-wide): 7.1MM **Privately Held**
WEB: www.innovativeresinsystems.com
SIC: 2821 Epoxy resins
PA: Innovative Resin Systems, Inc.
70 Verkade Dr
Wayne NJ 07470
973 465-6887

(G-11522)
INTERNTONAL SPECIALTY PDTS INC (DH)
Also Called: Ashland
1361 Alps Rd (07470-3700)
PHONE..................................859 815-3333
Sunil Kumar, *CEO*
Douglas Vaughan, *CFO*
Susan B Yoss, *Treasurer*
Leonora Gregory, *Manager*
◆ EMP: 725
SQ FT: 100,000
SALES (est): 414.3MM
SALES (corp-wide): 3.7B **Publicly Held**
WEB: www.ispcorp.com
SIC: 2869 2821 2843 2842 Amines, acids, salts, esters; plastics materials & resins; surface active agents; specialty cleaning, polishes & sanitation goods; chemical preparations
HQ: Ashland Llc
50 E Rivercenter Blvd # 1600
Covington KY 41011
859 815-3333

(G-11523)
ISP CHEMCO LLC (PA)
1361 Alps Rd (07470-3700)
PHONE..................................973 628-4000
Sunil Kumar, *CEO*
EMP: 2
SALES (est): 150.7MM **Privately Held**
SIC: 2869 Industrial organic chemicals

(G-11524)
ISP GLOBAL TECHNOLOGIES INC (DH)
1361 Alps Rd (07470-3700)
PHONE..................................973 628-4000
Sunil Kamar, *President*
Richard Weinberg, *Exec VP*
Susan Yoss, *Treasurer*
◆ EMP: 9
SQ FT: 100,000
SALES (est): 825.3MM
SALES (corp-wide): 3.7B **Publicly Held**
SIC: 3295 2869 Minerals, ground or treated; industrial organic chemicals
HQ: Ashland Llc
50 E Rivercenter Blvd # 1600
Covington KY 41011
859 815-3333

(G-11525)
ISP GLOBAL TECHNOLOGIES LLC (DH)
1361 Alps Rd (07470-3700)
PHONE..................................973 628-4000
Sunil Kamar, *CEO*
EMP: 3
SALES (est): 1.9MM
SALES (corp-wide): 3.2B **Publicly Held**
SIC: 3295 2869 Minerals, ground or treated; industrial organic chemicals

(G-11526)
JRZ ENTERPRISES LLC
Also Called: Precision
15 Corporate Dr Ste 5 (07470-3120)
P.O. Box 1121, Caldwell (07007-1121)
PHONE..................................973 962-6330
Patricia Zaino, *Controller*
Joseph Zaino, *Mng Member*
EMP: 7
SALES: 800K **Privately Held**
SIC: 5013 5087 7389 3559 Automotive supplies & parts; carwash equipment & supplies; packaging & labeling services; automotive related machinery

(G-11527)
JVC INDUSTRIAL AMERICA INC (DH)
1700 Valley Rd Ste 1 (07470-2045)
PHONE..................................800 247-3608
Fuji Sawa, *President*
Taka Nami, *Treasurer*
▼ EMP: 45 EST: 1996
SALES (est): 5.8MM **Privately Held**
SIC: 3651 8741 Television receiving sets; management services
HQ: Jvckenwood Usa Corporation
2201 E Dominguez St
Long Beach CA 90810
310 639-9000

(G-11528)
JVCKENWOOD USA CORPORATION
500 Valley Rd Ste 202 (07470-3528)
PHONE..................................973 317-5000
Kazuhiro Aigami, *CEO*
Takeshi Yamasaki, *Engineer*
EMP: 29 **Privately Held**
SIC: 3651 Home entertainment equipment, electronic
HQ: Jvckenwood Usa Corporation
2201 E Dominguez St
Long Beach CA 90810
310 639-9000

(G-11529)
KOP MARBLE GRANITE INC
155 Lions Head Dr W (07470-4002)
PHONE..................................973 283-8000
EMP: 5
SALES (est): 246K **Privately Held**
SIC: 1423 Diorite, crushed & broken-quarrying

(G-11530)
KROWNE METAL CORP
100 Haul Rd (07470-6616)
PHONE..................................973 305-3300
Roger Forman, *President*
Frank Bastante, *Exec VP*
Kyle Forman, *Natl Sales Mgr*
Nick Giella, *Natl Sales Mgr*
Lauren Lomoriello, *Executive Asst*
▲ EMP: 50 EST: 1948
SQ FT: 80,000
SALES (est): 13.1MM **Privately Held**
WEB: www.krowne.com
SIC: 3585 Soda fountain & beverage dispensing equipment & parts

(G-11531)
MADDAK INC (DH)
661 State Route 23 (07470-6814)
PHONE..................................973 628-7600
Kurt Landsberger, *Ch of Bd*
David Landsberger, *President*
Anny Landsberger, *Admin Sec*
▲ EMP: 4
SQ FT: 35,000
SALES: 4.2MM
SALES (corp-wide): 1.5B **Privately Held**
WEB: www.maddak.com
SIC: 5047 3841 Medical equipment & supplies; surgical & medical instruments
HQ: Bel-Art Products, Inc.
661 Rte 23
Wayne NJ 07470
973 694-0500

(G-11532)
MANE USA INC (DH)
60 Demarest Dr (07470-6702)
PHONE..................................973 633-5533
Michel Mane, *President*

Johnnattan Avendano, *Accounts Exec*
Renee Demary, *Manager*
◆ EMP: 120
SQ FT: 65,000
SALES (est): 162.1MM **Privately Held**
SIC: 2087 Flavoring extracts & syrups
HQ: V. Mane Fils
Quartier Notre Dame
Le Bar-Sur-Loup 06620
493 097-000

(G-11533)
MAQUET CARDIOVASCULAR LLC
45 Barbour Pond Dr (07470-2094)
PHONE..................................973 709-7000
Raoul Quintero, *CEO*
Chris Odom, *General Mgr*
Jason Soupiset, *Regional Mgr*
Philip Freed, *Senior VP*
Jeff Harris, *Vice Pres*
▲ EMP: 58
SALES (est): 18.1MM **Privately Held**
SIC: 3829 Medical diagnostic systems, nuclear

(G-11534)
MARTIN SPROCKET & GEAR INC
7 Highpoint Dr (07470-7432)
PHONE..................................973 633-5700
Fax: 973 633-7196
EMP: 10
SALES (corp-wide): 284.2MM **Privately Held**
SIC: 3566 3568 Mfg Speed Changers/Drives Mfg Power Transmission Equipment
PA: Martin Sprocket & Gear, Inc.
3100 Sprocket Dr
Arlington TX 76015
817 258-3000

(G-11535)
MP CUSTOM FL LLC
Also Called: Mp Millwork
624 Alps Rd (07470-3904)
PHONE..................................973 417-2288
Marek Pochwatka,
EMP: 10
SALES (est): 1MM **Privately Held**
SIC: 2431 2521 2599 2434 Planing mill, millwork; wood office furniture; hotel furniture; hospital furniture, except beds; wood kitchen cabinets

(G-11536)
NORTH JERSEY METAL FABRICATORS
130 Ryerson Ave Ste 107 (07470-8137)
PHONE..................................973 305-9830
Bela Ecker, *President*
EMP: 4
SQ FT: 5,000
SALES (est): 694.2K **Privately Held**
SIC: 3446 Railings, prefabricated metal

(G-11537)
ORSILLO & COMPANY
Also Called: Construction Services
189 Berdan Ave (07470-3233)
PHONE..................................973 248-1833
Pat Orsillo, *President*
EMP: 7 EST: 2013
SALES: 900K **Privately Held**
SIC: 1442 Construction sand & gravel

(G-11538)
PAGE 2 LLC
508 Hamburg Tpke Ste 108 (07470-8482)
PHONE..................................862 239-9830
Robert Richman,
Andrea Richman,
EMP: 6
SALES (est): 454.1K **Privately Held**
SIC: 2759 Advertising literature: printing

(G-11539)
PASSAIC COUNTY WELDERS INC
100 Parish Dr (07470-6099)
PHONE..................................973 696-1200
Robert Grimbilas, *Vice Pres*
Peter Grimbilas, *Vice Pres*
EMP: 30 EST: 1933
SQ FT: 24,000

SALES (est): 6.9MM **Privately Held**
WEB: www.passaiccountynj.org
SIC: 3441 Building components, structural
steel

(G-11540)
PASSAIC RUBBER CO (PA)
45 Demarest Dr (07470-6747)
P.O. Box 505 (07474-0505)
PHONE.............................973 696-9500
John Mathey, *President*
Jeffrey Leach, *COO*
▲ **EMP:** 93 **EST:** 1919
SQ FT: 70,000
SALES (est): 22.2MM **Privately Held**
WEB: www.passaic.com
SIC: 3061 3052 3069 2296 Mechanical
rubber goods; rubber belting; rolls, solid
or covered rubber; tire cord & fabrics

(G-11541)
PATRIOT PICKLE INC
20 Edison Dr (07470-4713)
PHONE.............................973 709-9487
William McEntee Jr, *President*
Bob Rento, *Vice Pres*
Amanda Mackey, *Office Mgr*
Kimberly Reinstra, *Office Mgr*
Bill Scully, *Maintence Staff*
EMP: 60
SALES (est): 12.8MM **Privately Held**
SIC: 2035 Pickles, sauces & salad dress-
ings

(G-11542)
PHOTOGRAPHIC ANALYSIS
COMPANY (PA)
190 Parish Dr (07470-4633)
PHONE.............................973 696-1000
Constance Mc Guire, *President*
L Arthur Jantzen, *Vice Pres*
Charles A Jantzen, *Treasurer*
EMP: 5
SQ FT: 1,500
SALES (est): 655.8K **Privately Held**
SIC: 3861 7699 Cameras & related equip-
ment; photographic equipment repair

(G-11543)
POLYMERIC RESOURCES CORP
(PA)
Also Called: A L M
55 Haul Rd Ste A (07470-6613)
P.O. Box 4237 (07474-4237)
PHONE.............................973 694-4141
Solomon Schlesinger, *President*
Shiraz Meghji, *Vice Pres*
Charlie Cook, *QC Mgr*
Arthur Quint, *CFO*
John Hardiman, *Accounts Mgr*
▲ **EMP:** 45
SQ FT: 200,000
SALES (est): 24.4MM **Privately Held**
WEB: www.polyconverting.com
SIC: 2821 3087 Plastics materials &
resins; custom compound purchased
resins

(G-11544)
PR PRODUCTS DISTRIBUTORS
INC
189 Berdan Ave Ste 281 (07470-3233)
PHONE.............................973 928-1120
Fernando Badillo, *President*
EMP: 7
SALES (est): 751.4K **Privately Held**
SIC: 2064 5145 Candy & other confec-
tionery products; confectionery

(G-11545)
QUARTERSPOT INC
145 Us Highway 46 Fl 3 (07470-6830)
PHONE.............................917 647-9170
Adam Cohen, *Branch Mgr*
EMP: 10
SALES (corp-wide): 4.6MM **Privately**
Held
SIC: 7372 Prepackaged software
PA: Quarterspot, Inc.
2751 Prosperity Ave # 330
Fairfax VA 22031
800 775-5143

(G-11546)
REED-LANE INC
359 Newark Pompton Tpke (07470-6600)
PHONE.............................973 709-1090
Frederick Clauss, *Ch of Bd*
Patricia Elvin, *President*
▲ **EMP:** 125
SQ FT: 135,000
SALES (est): 18.8MM **Privately Held**
WEB: www.reedlane.com
SIC: 7389 2834 Packaging & labeling
services; pharmaceutical preparations

(G-11547)
REEVES INTERNATIONAL INC
Also Called: Breyer Manufacturing
34 Owens Dr (07470-2341)
PHONE.............................973 956-9555
Frank Casamento, *Branch Mgr*
EMP: 30
SALES (est): 3.5MM
SALES (corp-wide): 26.8MM **Privately**
Held
WEB: www.breyerhorses.com
SIC: 3944 Games, toys & children's vehi-
cles
PA: Reeves International Inc.
14 Industrial Rd
Pequannock NJ 07440
973 694-5006

(G-11548)
REGAL CROWN FD SVC
SPECIALIST
20 Edison Dr (07470-4713)
PHONE.............................508 752-2679
Douglas Freund, *President*
EMP: 9
SQ FT: 20,000
SALES (est): 1MM **Privately Held**
SIC: 2035 Pickles, vinegar

(G-11549)
ROYAL ADHESIVES &
SEALANTS LLC
Also Called: Clifton Adhesives
48 Burgess Pl (07470-6734)
PHONE.............................973 694-0845
Dan Higgins, *Engineer*
Rod Alt, *Sales Staff*
Karl Huelsenbeck, *Branch Mgr*
Michael Edwards, *Manager*
James Fahey, *Manager*
EMP: 30
SALES (corp-wide): 3B **Publicly Held**
SIC: 2891 Sealants
HQ: Royal Adhesives And Sealants Llc
2001 W Washington St
South Bend IN 46628
574 246-5000

(G-11550)
SA BENDHEIM LTD (PA)
82 Totowa Rd Ste 1 (07470-3114)
PHONE.............................973 471-1733
Robert Jayson, *President*
Michael Cullinane, *General Mgr*
Doug Jones, *General Mgr*
Michael Tryon, *General Mgr*
Donald Jayson, *Vice Pres*
◆ **EMP:** 20
SALES (est): 25.4MM **Privately Held**
WEB: www.bendheimrestorationglass.com
SIC: 5039 5231 7389 2851 Glass con-
struction materials; glass, leaded or
stained; business services; undercoat-
ings, paint

(G-11551)
SAINT-GOBAIN PRFMCE PLAS
CORP
150 Dey Rd (07470-4670)
PHONE.............................973 696-4700
Rene Sarmiento, *Branch Mgr*
EMP: 162
SALES (corp-wide): 215.9MM **Privately**
Held
SIC: 3089 Plastic containers, except foam
HQ: Saint-Gobain Performance Plastics
Corporation
31500 Solon Rd
Solon OH 44139
440 836-6900

(G-11552)
SALOMONE REDI-MIX LLC
17 Demarest Dr (07470-6701)
PHONE.............................973 305-0022
Joseph Salomone, *Mng Member*
Paul Salomone, *Mng Member*
EMP: 28
SALES (est): 2.2MM **Privately Held**
SIC: 3273 4212 Ready-mixed concrete;
local trucking, without storage

(G-11553)
SCREENS INCORPORATED
130 Ryerson Ave Ste 219 (07470-8138)
P.O. Box 383, Pequannock (07440-0383)
PHONE.............................973 633-8558
Robert Vorndran, *President*
EMP: 4
SQ FT: 3,500
SALES (est): 320K **Privately Held**
WEB: www.screens-inc.com
SIC: 2431 Window screens, wood frame

(G-11554)
SWAROVSKI NORTH AMERICA
LTD
1400 Willowbrook Mall (07470-6905)
PHONE.............................973 812-7500
Lisa Briscuso, *Branch Mgr*
EMP: 4
SALES (corp-wide): 4.7B **Privately Held**
SIC: 3961 Costume jewelry
HQ: Swarovski North America Limited
1 Kenney Dr
Cranston RI 02920
401 463-6400

(G-11555)
T V L ASSOCIATES INC
3 Donna Ln (07470-2710)
PHONE.............................973 790-6766
EMP: 1
SALES: 1.4MM **Privately Held**
SIC: 4841 5051 3672 Cable/Pay Televi-
sion Service Metals Service Center Mfg
Printed Circuit Boards

(G-11556)
TEKTRONIX INC
1133 State Route 23 Ste 4 (07470-6682)
PHONE.............................973 628-1363
Matt Wood, *Manager*
EMP: 7
SALES (corp-wide): 6.4B **Publicly Held**
SIC: 3825 Instruments to measure electric-
ity
HQ: Tektronix, Inc.
14150 Sw Karl Braun Dr
Beaverton OR 97005
800 833-9200

(G-11557)
THIRD WAVE BUS SYSTEMS
LLC
1680 State Route 23 # 320 (07470-7520)
PHONE.............................201 703-2100
Korey Lind, *Partner*
Michael Cirillo, *Controller*
Jim Flynn, *Accounts Exec*
Michele Kovolesky, *Office Mgr*
Michael Nardini, *Manager*
EMP: 20
SALES (est): 2.8MM **Privately Held**
WEB: www.twbs.com
SIC: 7372 Prepackaged software

(G-11558)
TOSHIBA AMER CONSMR PDTS
INC
82 Totowa Rd (07470-3114)
PHONE.............................973 628-8000
Akio Ozaka, *CEO*
Tetsuya Sakaguchi, *Vice Pres*
EMP: 215
SQ FT: 100,000
SALES (est): 34.1K **Privately Held**
SIC: 3651 Television receiving sets; video
camera-audio recorders, household use
HQ: Toshiba America Inc
1251 Ave Of Ameri
New York NY 10020
212 596-0600

(G-11559)
TURBINE TEK INC
130 Ryerson Ave Ste 303 (07470-8139)
PHONE.............................973 872-0903
James Scageline, *Owner*
EMP: 6 **EST:** 2013
SALES (est): 175.1K **Privately Held**
SIC: 3714 Motor vehicle parts & acces-
sories

(G-11560)
UNIVERSAL METALCRAFT INC
24 Burgess Pl (07470-6734)
PHONE.............................973 345-3284
Viktor Wenstrom, *Ch of Bd*
Eric Wenstrom, *President*
Marlene Wenstrom, *Corp Secy*
Marc Wenstrom, *Vice Pres*
▲ **EMP:** 22
SQ FT: 42,000
SALES (est): 4.1MM **Privately Held**
WEB: www.umcraft.com
SIC: 3599 3452 3545 Machine shop, job-
bing & repair; bolts, nuts, rivets & wash-
ers; precision tools, machinists'

(G-11561)
US SIGN AND LIGHTING SVC
LLC
105 Dorsa Ave (07470-8107)
PHONE.............................973 305-8900
John Kelley, *Manager*
Michael P Kelly,
EMP: 7
SQ FT: 3,000
SALES: 430K **Privately Held**
SIC: 3993 Electric signs

(G-11562)
VACUMET CORP
22 Riverview Dr Ste 101 (07470-3115)
PHONE.............................973 628-0405
Robert T Korowicki, *CEO*
EMP: 4
SALES (est): 289.9K **Privately Held**
SIC: 3089 Plastics products

(G-11563)
VISION RESEARCH INC (HQ)
100 Dey Rd (07470-4604)
PHONE.............................973 696-4500
Charles A Jantzen, *President*
Jay Sepleton, *General Mgr*
Pat Pellicano, *Vice Pres*
Sean Wilson, *Engineer*
Dan Hafen, *Sales Mgr*
EMP: 93
SALES (est): 23.6MM
SALES (corp-wide): 4.8B **Publicly Held**
WEB: www.visionresearch.com
SIC: 3861 Cameras, still & motion picture
(all types)
PA: Ametek, Inc.
1100 Cassatt Rd
Berwyn PA 19312
610 647-2121

(G-11564)
WAYNE MOTORS INC
Also Called: Lincoln Mercury of Wayne
1910 State Route 23 (07470-6577)
PHONE.............................973 696-9710
Peter Spina, *President*
Gaspar J Spina, *Chairman*
Rona Spina, *Corp Secy*
Robert Spina, *Vice Pres*
Mark Siebenaler, *Sales Staff*
EMP: 90 **EST:** 1968
SQ FT: 9,700
SALES (est): 40.6MM **Privately Held**
WEB: www.waynelincolnmercury.com
SIC: 5511 7532 7538 3714 Automobiles,
new & used; body shop, automotive; gen-
eral automotive repair shops; motor vehi-
cle parts & accessories

(G-11565)
WILLOWBROOK GOLF CENTER
LLC
366 Us Highway 46 (07470-4822)
PHONE.............................973 256-6922
Song Hong,
EMP: 10

SALES (est): 935.1K **Privately Held**
WEB: www.willowbrookgolfcenter.com
SIC: 3949 Driving ranges, golf, electronic

(G-11566)
Z FAB LLC
24 Bodie Rd (07470-6102)
PHONE.....................................973 248-0686
Scott Silodor,
EMP: 6
SALES (est): 298.9K **Privately Held**
SIC: 2759 Commercial printing

Weehawken
Hudson County

(G-11567)
GLOBELA PHARMA LLC
62 Hauxhurst Ave (07086-6504)
P.O. Box 8236, Jersey City (07308-8236)
PHONE.....................................888 588-8511
Priyank Vaghashia,
EMP: 4
SALES (est): 99K **Privately Held**
SIC: 2834 Pharmaceutical preparations

(G-11568)
HANOVER DIRECT INC (PA)
Also Called: Hanover Direct Operating Group
1500 Harbor Blvd Ste 3 (07086-6782)
PHONE.....................................201 863-7300
Don Kelley, President
◆ EMP: 340
SQ FT: 56,700
SALES (est): 197.8MM **Privately Held**
WEB: www.hanoverdirect.com
SIC: 7389 5712 5961 2211 Telemarketing services; bedding & bedsprings; catalog & mail-order houses; pillow tubing; comforters & quilts, manmade fiber & silk

(G-11569)
MARKO ENGRAVING & ART CORP (PA)
19 Baldwin Ave (07086)
PHONE.....................................201 864-6500
Marko Melnitschenko, President
Ljubow Melnitschenko, Corp Secy
EMP: 15
SQ FT: 5,000
SALES (est): 1.2MM **Privately Held**
SIC: 3555 2796 Printing plates; platemaking services

(G-11570)
SWATCH GROUP LES BTQUES US INC
1200 Harbor Blvd (07086-6762)
PHONE.....................................201 271-1400
Caroline Faivet, President
Janet Cerutti, Vice Pres
John Kelley, Vice Pres
Jim Kenny, Vice Pres
Joe Mella, Vice Pres
EMP: 1
SALES (est): 4.7MM
SALES (corp-wide): 8.5B **Privately Held**
SIC: 3625 5094 3873 Timing devices, electronic; clocks, watches & parts; watches, clocks, watchcases & parts
HQ: The Swatch Group U S Inc
703 Nw 62nd Ave Ste 450
Miami FL 33126
201 271-1400

(G-11571)
TRUEFORT INC
3 W 18th St (07086-6601)
PHONE.....................................201 766-2023
Sameer Malhotra, Principal
EMP: 25
SALES (est): 222.7K **Privately Held**
SIC: 7372 Prepackaged software

Wenonah
Gloucester County

(G-11572)
51MAPS INC
500 E Mantua Ave (08090-2015)
PHONE.....................................800 927-5181
EMP: 7
SALES (est): 362K **Privately Held**
SIC: 7372 Prepackaged Software Services

(G-11573)
ALETE PRINTING LLC
722 Dartmouth Ct (08090-1003)
P.O. Box 371 (08090-0371)
PHONE.....................................856 468-3536
Patricia Koskinen, President
John Koskinen, Vice Pres
EMP: 4
SALES (est): 486.2K **Privately Held**
WEB: www.aleteprinting.com
SIC: 2752 Commercial printing, offset

(G-11574)
COTTERMAN INC
100 Hayes Ave (08090)
P.O. Box 278 (08090-0278)
PHONE.....................................856 415-0800
William M Thomas, President
Robert Flasher, Vice Pres
Michael Bonaventure, Treasurer
EMP: 15 EST: 1999
SALES (est): 2.3MM **Privately Held**
WEB: www.cottermaninc.com
SIC: 3548 Welding & cutting apparatus & accessories

(G-11575)
DOCUMENT CONCEPTS INC
1040 Mantua Pike (08090-1124)
P.O. Box 241, Woodbury (08096-7241)
PHONE.....................................856 251-1975
Greg Adair, President
EMP: 4 EST: 1998
SQ FT: 1,300
SALES (est): 552K **Privately Held**
WEB: www.documentconcepts.com
SIC: 2752 Commercial printing, lithographic

(G-11576)
S & J VILLARI LIVESTOCK LLC (HQ)
Also Called: Villari's
1481 Glassboro Rd (08090-1605)
P.O. Box 191 (08090-0191)
PHONE.....................................856 468-0807
Joseph P Villari Jr, Partner
Salvatore J Villari, Partner
EMP: 2
SALES (est): 1.6MM
SALES (corp-wide): 55.6MM **Privately Held**
WEB: www.villaris.com
SIC: 2011 Meat packing plants
PA: Villari Food Group, Llc
135 Carter Best Rd
Warsaw NC 28398
910 293-2157

West Berlin
Camden County

(G-11577)
ARTISTIC GLASS & DOORS INC
Also Called: Stained Glass Overlay
154 Cooper Rd Ste 201 (08091-9105)
PHONE.....................................856 768-1414
Michael Baron, President
EMP: 8
SQ FT: 2,200
SALES (est): 780K **Privately Held**
WEB: www.artisticglassanddoors.com
SIC: 5231 3231 5211 Glass, leaded or stained; stained glass: made from purchased glass; door & window products

(G-11578)
ASCALON STUDIOS INC
Also Called: Ascalon Art Studios
430 Cooper Rd (08091-3843)
PHONE.....................................856 768-3779
David Ascalon, President
Eric Ascalon, Vice Pres
EMP: 12
SQ FT: 3,000
SALES: 1.2MM **Privately Held**
WEB: www.ascalonstudios.com
SIC: 3231 Stained glass: made from purchased glass

(G-11579)
CAROLINA FLUID HANDLING INC
140 Bradford Dr (08091-9216)
PHONE.....................................248 228-8900
Fred Giuliano, Director
▲ EMP: 610
SALES (est): 53.5MM
SALES (corp-wide): 16.9B **Privately Held**
WEB: www.daycoinc.com
SIC: 3714 Fuel systems & parts, motor vehicle
PA: Sun Capital Partners, Inc.
5200 Town Center Cir # 600
Boca Raton FL 33486
561 962-3400

(G-11580)
CHAMPION OPCO LLC
Also Called: Champion Window Delaware Vly
414 Bloomfield Dr Ste 1 (08091-2416)
PHONE.....................................856 662-3400
Bruce Greenberg, Manager
EMP: 16
SALES (corp-wide): 516.4MM **Privately Held**
SIC: 3442 Window & door frames
PA: Champion Opco, Llc
12121 Champion Way
Cincinnati OH 45241
513 327-7338

(G-11581)
CHICK CAPOLI SALES
420 Commerce Ln Ste 7 (08091-9278)
PHONE.....................................856 768-4500
Chick Capoli, Owner
Angelo Capoli, Vice Pres
EMP: 20
SALES (est): 2.5MM **Privately Held**
SIC: 3714 Motor vehicle parts & accessories

(G-11582)
CHROMCRAFT REVINGTON INC (DH)
140 Bradford Dr Ste A (08091-9216)
PHONE.....................................662 562-8203
Ronald H Butler, CEO
E Michael Hanna, Senior VP
James M La Neve, CFO
◆ EMP: 37
SALES (est): 36.1MM
SALES (corp-wide): 70.7MM **Privately Held**
WEB: www.chromcraftrevington.com
SIC: 2511 2512 2521 2531 Wood household furniture; upholstered household furniture; wood office furniture; public building & related furniture
HQ: Sport-Haley, Inc.
200 Union Blvd Ste 400
Lakewood CO 80228
303 320-8800

(G-11583)
CIRCUIT TECH ASSEMBLY LLC
154 Cooper Rd Ste 101 (08091-9100)
PHONE.....................................856 231-0777
Bill Sherlock Jr, President
William Sherlock,
EMP: 15
SALES (est): 2.3MM **Privately Held**
WEB: www.circuittechassembly.com
SIC: 3672 Printed circuit boards

(G-11584)
COLORTEC PRINTING AND MAILING
424 Kelley Dr Ste A (08091-9285)
PHONE.....................................856 767-0108

Wayne Farlow, Owner
EMP: 5
SALES (est): 337K **Privately Held**
SIC: 2759 4731 Commercial printing; freight transportation arrangement

(G-11585)
COMPEX CORPORATION
439 Commerce Ln Ste 1 (08091-9206)
PHONE.....................................856 719-8657
David Gordon, President
▲ EMP: 30 EST: 1976
SQ FT: 5,000
SALES (est): 6.5MM **Privately Held**
WEB: www.compexcorp.com
SIC: 3679 Microwave components

(G-11586)
CONCEPT GROUP LLC (HQ)
380 Cooper Rd (08091-9203)
PHONE.....................................856 767-5506
Aarne Reid, CEO
David Reid, President
William Ethomas, General Mgr
Jennifer Kabis, Office Mgr
Ricard Riabko, Manager
EMP: 25
SQ FT: 13,000
SALES (est): 5.8MM
SALES (corp-wide): 2.6MM **Privately Held**
WEB: www.conceptgroupinc.com
SIC: 3599 Machine & other job shop work
PA: Conceptual Holdings Llc
593 Washington St
Wellesley MA 02482
561 320-9995

(G-11587)
COOPER POWER SYSTEMS LLC
402 Bloomfield Dr Ste 1 (08091-2405)
PHONE.....................................856 719-1100
EMP: 200 **Privately Held**
SIC: 3612 Power transformers, electric
HQ: Cooper Power Systems, Llc
2300 Badger Dr
Waukesha WI 53188
262 896-2400

(G-11588)
CROWFOOT ASSOCIATES INC
Also Called: Crowfoot Asphalt
Winslow Township (08091)
PHONE.....................................609 561-0107
Dennis E Powell, President
EMP: 8
SQ FT: 40,000
SALES (est): 1.1MM **Privately Held**
SIC: 2951 Asphalt paving mixtures & blocks

(G-11589)
DANIEL MAGUIRE
Also Called: Dan Maguire Electrical Contr
140 Collings Ave (08091-9121)
PHONE.....................................856 767-8443
Daniel Maguire, Owner
EMP: 23
SALES (est): 1.7MM **Privately Held**
SIC: 3699 Electrical equipment & supplies

(G-11590)
DYNASIL CORPORATION AMERICA
385 Cooper Rd (08091-9145)
PHONE.....................................856 767-4600
Craig Dunham, President
▲ EMP: 4
SALES (est): 633.7K **Privately Held**
SIC: 3827 Optical instruments & lenses

(G-11591)
E S INDUSTRIES INC
701 S Route 73 A (08091-2603)
PHONE.....................................856 753-8400
David A Kohler, President
Matthew Przybyciel, Vice Pres
EMP: 7
SQ FT: 8,500
SALES (est): 1.5MM **Privately Held**
WEB: www.esind.com
SIC: 3826 Chromatographic equipment, laboratory type

(G-11592)
EAST COAST PLASTICS INC
427 Commerce Ln Ste 7 (08091-9212)
PHONE..........................856 768-8700
David Lorenz, *President*
EMP: 9
SQ FT: 8,400
SALES (est): 1.5MM **Privately Held**
SIC: 3089 Injection molding of plastics

(G-11593)
ELECTRO PARTS INC
465 E Taunton Ave Ste 201 (08091-3847)
PHONE..........................856 767-5923
Esteban Sobrado, *President*
EMP: 7
SQ FT: 2,600
SALES: 900K **Privately Held**
WEB: www.electropartsinc.com
SIC: 5072 3312 Hardware; bar, rod & wire products

(G-11594)
FOODLINE PIPING PRODUCTS CO
225 Edgewood Ave (08091-2615)
PHONE..........................856 767-1177
Daniel Diadul, *President*
▼ EMP: 5
SALES (est): 635.5K **Privately Held**
SIC: 3498 Pipe sections fabricated from purchased pipe

(G-11595)
FOTOBRIDGE
154 Cooper Rd Ste 203 (08091-9105)
PHONE..........................856 809-9400
Paul Cooper, *Owner*
EMP: 5 EST: 2008
SALES (est): 667.4K **Privately Held**
SIC: 3577 Magnetic ink & optical scanning devices

(G-11596)
GALAXY TRANS & MAGNETICS LLC
386 Cooper Rd (08091-9203)
P.O. Box 27, Atco (08004-0027)
PHONE..........................856 753-4546
Will Curry, *Sales Staff*
James R Nancy Curry,
James R Curry,
Nancy Curry,
▲ EMP: 12 EST: 1998
SQ FT: 4,500
SALES (est): 1.9MM **Privately Held**
WEB: www.galaxytransformers.com
SIC: 3612 Power transformers, electric

(G-11597)
GARY R BANKS INDUSTRIAL GROUP
575 N Route 73 Ste C6 (08091-9292)
PHONE..........................856 687-2227
Gary Banks, *Mng Member*
EMP: 19
SALES: 397.9K **Privately Held**
SIC: 8748 1742 3479 Business consulting; plastering, drywall & insulation; coating, rust preventive

(G-11598)
GENERAL SIGN CO INC
105 Chestnut Ave (08091-3801)
PHONE..........................856 753-3535
Louis Brocco, *President*
Steven Brocco, *Vice Pres*
EMP: 7
SALES: 700K **Privately Held**
SIC: 3993 1799 Signs & advertising specialties; sign installation & maintenance

(G-11599)
HORIZON LABEL LLC
1049 Industrial Dr (08091-9136)
PHONE..........................856 767-0777
Ron Davis, *General Mgr*
August Roderick, *Sales Staff*
Paul Falkowski,
EMP: 16
SQ FT: 15,000
SALES (est): 2.8MM **Privately Held**
SIC: 2759 2672 Flexographic printing; coated & laminated paper

(G-11600)
JMJ PROFILE INC
154 Cooper Rd Ste 1303 (08091-9122)
PHONE..........................856 767-3930
Joseph M Colachi, *President*
Joseph A Colachi, *Vice Pres*
EMP: 7 EST: 1992
SALES (est): 1MM **Privately Held**
WEB: www.jmjprofile.com
SIC: 3083 Laminated plastic sheets

(G-11601)
JOHN B HORAY WELDING
399 Blaine Ave (08091-2131)
PHONE..........................856 336-2154
John B Horay Sr, *Owner*
Peter Horay, *Owner*
EMP: 5
SALES: 250K **Privately Held**
SIC: 7692 Welding repair

(G-11602)
KESSLER STEEL RULE DIE INC
Also Called: Dennis Kessler Steel Rule Die
1004 Industrial Dr Ste 10 (08091-9189)
PHONE..........................856 767-0231
Dennis Kessler, *President*
EMP: 6
SALES (est): 651.2K **Privately Held**
SIC: 3544 Dies, steel rule; special dies & tools

(G-11603)
LIGHTNING PRVNTION SYSTEMS INC
154 Cooper Rd Ste 1201 (08091-9116)
P.O. Box 353 (08091-0353)
PHONE..........................856 767-7806
Patricia McLaughlin, *CEO*
Ian Fawthrop, *President*
Deborah Minniti, *Managing Dir*
Jessica Jones, *Vice Pres*
EMP: 8
SQ FT: 2,500
SALES: 1.3MM **Privately Held**
WEB: www.lpsnet.com
SIC: 3643 3663 Lightning protection equipment; antennas, transmitting & communications

(G-11604)
LIQUID IRON INDUSTRIES INC
150 Cooper Rd Ste B4 (08091-9257)
PHONE..........................856 336-2639
Timothy Diekmann, *CEO*
EMP: 4
SALES (est): 321.6K **Privately Held**
SIC: 3999 7538 Manufacturing industries; general automotive repair shops

(G-11605)
LONGRUN PRESS INC
1002 Industrial Dr (08091-9164)
P.O. Box 1536, Cherry Hill (08034-0069)
PHONE..........................856 719-9202
Carl J Buehler III, *President*
Mary Beth Buehler, *Vice Pres*
EMP: 10
SQ FT: 12,000
SALES (est): 664.6K **Privately Held**
SIC: 7389 2752 Printing broker; offset & photolithographic printing

(G-11606)
M C CUSTOM SHTMTL FABRICATION
215 Old Egg Harbor Rd C (08091-1653)
PHONE..........................856 767-9509
Michael Carr Sr, *President*
Michael Carr Jr, *Vice Pres*
Shawn Carr, *Treasurer*
April Carr, *Admin Sec*
EMP: 6
SALES (est): 827.7K **Privately Held**
SIC: 3444 Ducts, sheet metal

(G-11607)
MEDPLAST WEST BERLIN INC (DH)
225 Old Egg Harbor Rd (08091-1602)
PHONE..........................856 753-7600
Harold Faig, *CEO*
Carl Dedtens, *President*
Mike Torti, *Vice Pres*
Kurt Massey, *CFO*
▲ EMP: 49
SQ FT: 65,000
SALES (est): 13MM
SALES (corp-wide): 368.7MM **Privately Held**
WEB: www.medplastgroup.com
SIC: 3089 Injection molding of plastics

(G-11608)
MOD-U-KRAF HOMES LLC (DH)
140 Bradford Dr Ste A (08091-9216)
PHONE..........................540 482-0273
Jeffery Powell,
EMP: 10
SQ FT: 104,000
SALES (est): 17.2MM **Privately Held**
WEB: www.mod-u-kraf.com
SIC: 1521 2452 Single-family housing construction; modular homes, prefabricated, wood
HQ: All American Group, Inc.
2831 Dexter Dr
Elkhart IN 46514
574 262-0123

(G-11609)
MODERN PRECISION TECH INC
225 Old Egg Harbor Rd (08091-1602)
PHONE..........................856 335-9303
Joe Lovallo, *CEO*
Douglas Cain, *Engineer*
EMP: 12
SALES (est): 435.7K **Privately Held**
SIC: 3599 Machine shop, jobbing & repair

(G-11610)
NEW DIMENSIONS INDUSTRIES LLC
151 Cooper Rd (08091-9244)
PHONE..........................201 531-1010
Michael Mozeika Jr, *President*
Robert Virella, *COO*
Judith Mozeika, *Admin Sec*
▲ EMP: 8
SQ FT: 40,000
SALES (est): 1.4MM **Privately Held**
WEB: www.newdimension-inc.com
SIC: 3086 Plastics foam products

(G-11611)
NOVA FLEX GROUP
1024 Industrial Dr (08091-9164)
PHONE..........................856 768-2275
EMP: 10 **Privately Held**
WEB: www.novaflexgroup.com
SIC: 3443 Ducting, metal plate
HQ: Nova Flex Group
1024 Industrial Dr
West Berlin NJ 08091

(G-11612)
NOVAFLEX INDUSTRIES INC
1024 Industrial Dr (08091-9164)
PHONE..........................856 768-2275
Melinda Donnelly, *President*
Kevin Donnelly, *Vice Pres*
Claire R Howard, *Admin Sec*
EMP: 11
SALES (est): 1.7MM **Privately Held**
SIC: 3492 3052 Hose & tube couplings, hydraulic/pneumatic; rubber & plastics hose & beltings

(G-11613)
PACKAGING GRAPHICS INC
435 Commerce Ln (08091-9254)
P.O. Box 160 (08091-0160)
PHONE..........................856 767-9000
Eileen Koff, *President*
Jason Clark, *President*
EMP: 28
SQ FT: 14,000
SALES (est): 4.8MM **Privately Held**
WEB: www.packaginggraphics.net
SIC: 3555 Printing plates

(G-11614)
PHOENIX TOOL & MACHINE INC
1044 Industrial Dr Ste 5 (08091-9104)
PHONE..........................856 753-5565
John R Dusak, *President*
EMP: 7 EST: 1997
SQ FT: 3,000
SALES (est): 750K **Privately Held**
SIC: 3599 Machine shop, jobbing & repair

(G-11615)
PHYTOBOLOGIC PHARMACEUTICS LLC
154 Cooper Rd Ste 202 (08091-9105)
PHONE..........................856 975-0444
Satish Kodavali,
Dr Samiran Bhadra,
Dr Lavanya Kodavali,
Tania Kodavali,
EMP: 5
SALES (est): 172.3K **Privately Held**
SIC: 2834 Pharmaceutical preparations

(G-11616)
PRINCETON TECTONICS
110 Collings Ave (08091-9121)
P.O. Box 8057, Trenton (08650-0057)
PHONE..........................609 298-9331
Richard Shenowski, *Branch Mgr*
EMP: 45
SALES (corp-wide): 20MM **Privately Held**
SIC: 3648 Outdoor lighting equipment
PA: Princeton Tectonics
1777 Hylton Rd
Pennsauken NJ 08110
609 298-9331

(G-11617)
PRINTING PLUS OF SOUTH JERSEY
406 N Route 73 (08091-2520)
PHONE..........................856 767-3941
Robert Behnke, *President*
EMP: 8
SQ FT: 3,500
SALES: 810.5K **Privately Held**
SIC: 2752 Commercial printing, offset

(G-11618)
RECYCLING N HENSEL AMER INC
1003 Industrial Dr (08091-9136)
PHONE..........................856 753-7614
Peter Lenz, *President*
Sebastian Hensel, *General Mgr*
Jason Tang, *Managing Dir*
Peter Ursprung, *Managing Dir*
Bob Henning, *Principal*
◆ EMP: 36
SALES: 10.2MM
SALES (corp-wide): 240.3K **Privately Held**
SIC: 3341 8742 Recovery & refining of nonferrous metals; business consultant
PA: Hensel Recycling International Gmbh
Muhlweg 10
Aschaffenburg
602 812-090

(G-11619)
RESINTECH INC (PA)
160 Cooper Rd (08091-9258)
PHONE..........................856 768-9600
Michael C Gottlieb, *President*
Michael Annocki, *Vice Pres*
Jeffrey H Gottlieb, *Vice Pres*
Lawrence Gottlieb, *Vice Pres*
Lynne Gottlieb, *Vice Pres*
◆ EMP: 120
SQ FT: 60,000
SALES (est): 91.7MM **Privately Held**
SIC: 5162 2819 3624 Resins; industrial inorganic chemicals; carbon & graphite products

(G-11620)
RUSSELL CAST STONE INC
Also Called: Continental Cast Stone East
400 Cooper Rd (08091-3843)
PHONE..........................856 753-4000
William Russell III, *CEO*
EMP: 58
SQ FT: 50,000
SALES: 6.4MM **Privately Held**
SIC: 3272 Concrete products

(G-11621)
SIGCO TOOL & MFG CO INC
110 Collings Ave (08091-9121)
PHONE..........................856 753-6565
Alfred Signor, *President*
Mark Cohen, *Corp Secy*
EMP: 26

▲ = Import ▼=Export
◆ =Import/Export

SALES (est): 4.2MM **Privately Held**
WEB: www.sigcotool.com
SIC: 3544 Forms (molds), for foundry & plastics working machinery

(G-11622)
SOUTH JERSEY COUNTERTOP CO
1044 Industrial Dr Ste 12 (08091-9126)
PHONE..............................856 768-7960
Ed Bader, *President*
EMP: 4
SALES (est): 256.6K **Privately Held**
SIC: 2541 1799 Counter & sink tops; counter top installation

(G-11623)
SPAGHETTI ENGINEERING CORP
Also Called: Digitails
150 Cooper Rd Ste C7 (08091-9223)
PHONE..............................856 719-9989
Michael Muhlbaier, *President*
Sbastian Clicharz, *Principal*
EMP: 11
SALES (est): 1.6MM **Privately Held**
SIC: 3647 Automotive lighting fixtures

(G-11624)
SULZER CHEMTECH USA INC
1008 Industrial Dr Ste F (08091-9190)
PHONE..............................856 768-2165
Kelvin Johnson, *Manager*
EMP: 162
SALES (corp-wide): 3.3B **Privately Held**
SIC: 3822 Electric air cleaner controls, automatic
HQ: Sulzer Chemtech Usa Inc.
1 Sulzer Way
Tulsa OK 74131
281 441-5200

(G-11625)
TAUNTON GRAPHICS INC
1049 Industrial Dr (08091-9136)
PHONE..............................856 719-8084
Paul Falkowski, *President*
EMP: 10
SALES (est): 990.6K **Privately Held**
WEB: www.horizonlabel.com
SIC: 2759 Labels & seals: printing

(G-11626)
TECHNITOOL INC
1028 Industrial Dr (08091-9164)
PHONE..............................856 768-2707
Sal Russomanno, *President*
Peter J Welding, *Vice Pres*
EMP: 30
SQ FT: 20,000
SALES (est): 6.1MM **Privately Held**
WEB: www.technitool.com
SIC: 3089 Injection molding of plastics

(G-11627)
TECHNOBOX INC
154 Cooper Rd Ste 901 (08091-9112)
PHONE..............................856 809-2306
Joseph P Norris, *President*
EMP: 8
SALES (est): 1.7MM **Privately Held**
WEB: www.technobox.com
SIC: 3577 Computer peripheral equipment

(G-11628)
TELECOM ASSISTANCE GROUP INC
Also Called: T A G
150 Cooper Rd Ste F15 (08091-9265)
PHONE..............................856 753-8585
John Humes, *Vice Pres*
Murray Kaplan, *Vice Pres*
EMP: 30
SQ FT: 5,500
SALES (est): 5.5MM **Privately Held**
WEB: www.tagcords.com
SIC: 3661 8748 Telephone & telegraph apparatus; communications consulting

(G-11629)
THWING-ALBERT INSTRUMENT CO
14 W Collings Ave (08091-9134)
PHONE..............................856 767-1000
Scott M Raab, *CEO*

Tom Boshore, *Manager*
Onesto Amodei, *Technology*
Donald Hudrick, *Software Engr*
Sandra Raab, *Admin Sec*
EMP: 55 EST: 1899
SALES (est): 14.1MM **Privately Held**
WEB: www.thwingalbert.com
SIC: 3829 Physical property testing equipment

(G-11630)
TOOL SHOP INC
335 Chestnut Ave (08091-9138)
P.O. Box 36 (08091-0036)
PHONE..............................856 767-8077
Paul Brunninghaus, *President*
EMP: 7
SQ FT: 4,000
SALES (est): 1.1MM **Privately Held**
WEB: www.toolshopinc.com
SIC: 3545 3541 3451 Cutting tools for machine tools; machine tools, metal cutting type; screw machine products

(G-11631)
TRIFLOW CORPORATION
Also Called: Triflow Specialties
150 Cooper Rd Ste A1 (08091-9256)
PHONE..............................856 768-7159
Mark E Goehring, *President*
EMP: 4
SALES (est): 2.5MM **Privately Held**
SIC: 5085 3491 3592 Valves & fittings; industrial valves; automatic regulating & control valves; valves, automatic control; pressure valves & regulators, industrial; valves

(G-11632)
TRIPLE-T CUTTING TOOLS INC
135 Edgewood Ave Ste A (08091-2601)
PHONE..............................856 768-0800
Steve Thomas, *President*
Mike Thomas, *Corp Secy*
Donna Gauntt, *QC Mgr*
Donna Scullin, *QC Mgr*
Matt Berghof, *Engineer*
EMP: 12
SQ FT: 2,000
SALES (est): 1.8MM **Privately Held**
WEB: www.triple-t.com
SIC: 3541 Machine tools, metal cutting type

(G-11633)
WESTAR TOOL LLC
427 Commerce Ln Ste 7 (08091-9212)
PHONE..............................856 507-8852
Robert Mason,
Edward Steafankiewick,
EMP: 4
SQ FT: 2,400
SALES: 300K **Privately Held**
SIC: 3089 Injection molding of plastics

(G-11634)
WIRELESS ELECTRONICS INC
Also Called: Wireless Communications & Elec
153 Cooper Rd (08091-9244)
PHONE..............................856 768-4310
Mike Travassos, *Branch Mgr*
EMP: 20 **Privately Held**
WEB: www.wirelessce.com
SIC: 7622 3663 Communication equipment repair; radio broadcasting & communications equipment
PA: Wireless Electronics, Inc.
2905 Southampton Rd
Philadelphia PA 19154

West Caldwell
Essex County

(G-11635)
21ST CENTURY MCH TLS CO INC
1140 Bloomfield Ave # 219 (07006-7126)
PHONE..............................973 808-2220
Angelo Pennetti, *President*
Charles Wilson, *Sales Mgr*
John Kusinko, *Sales Engr*
EMP: 5

SALES (est): 762K **Privately Held**
SIC: 3599 Machine shop, jobbing & repair

(G-11636)
ADHISA MOLDING
11 Patton Dr (07006-6404)
PHONE..............................862 324-5222
Carl Hurowitz, *President*
EMP: 4
SALES (est): 240K **Privately Held**
SIC: 2431 Moldings, wood: unfinished & prefinished

(G-11637)
ALFA WASSERMANN INC (PA)
Also Called: Schiapparelli Biosystems
4 Henderson Dr (07006-6608)
PHONE..............................973 882-8630
Irva Nordlicht, *President*
Peter Natoli, *Vice Pres*
James McClain, *VP Sales*
Frank Koubi, *Info Tech Mgr*
▲ EMP: 159
SQ FT: 50,000
SALES (est): 33MM **Privately Held**
WEB: www.awst.com
SIC: 3841 Diagnostic apparatus, medical

(G-11638)
ALFA WSSRMANN DAGNSTC TECH LLC
4 Henderson Dr (07006-6608)
PHONE..............................800 220-4488
Irva Nordlicht, *CEO*
EMP: 12
SALES (est): 1.7MM **Privately Held**
SIC: 3841 Diagnostic apparatus, medical
PA: Alfa Wassermann, Inc.
4 Henderson Dr
West Caldwell NJ 07006

(G-11639)
ALL MADINA INC
Also Called: Dunkin' Donuts
592 Passaic Ave (07006-6714)
PHONE..............................973 226-7772
Steven Huff, *Branch Mgr*
EMP: 10
SALES (est): 260.1K **Privately Held**
SIC: 5461 5499 2045 Doughnuts; coffee; doughnut mixes, prepared: from purchased flour
PA: All Madina Inc
199 Littleton Rd
Parsippany NJ 07054

(G-11640)
AMBRIOLA COMPANY INC
7 Patton Dr (07006-6404)
PHONE..............................973 228-3600
Alberto Auricchio, *President*
Anna Hauman, *Vice Pres*
Annmarie Hauman, *Vice Pres*
Phil Marfuggis, *Marketing Staff*
◆ EMP: 13
SALES (est): 3.1MM **Privately Held**
WEB: www.ambriola.com
SIC: 2022 Cheese spreads, dips, pastes & other cheese products
HQ: Gennaro Auricchio Spa
Via Dante Alighieri 27
Cremona CR 26100
037 240-3311

(G-11641)
AYERSPACE INC
25 Fairfield Ave (07006-7603)
PHONE..............................212 582-8410
EMP: 7 EST: 2001
SQ FT: 11,035
SALES (est): 450.2K **Privately Held**
SIC: 2515 6513 Mfg Mattresses/Bedsprings Apartment Building Operator

(G-11642)
BISHOP ASCENDANT INC
1083 Bloomfield Ave (07006-7105)
PHONE..............................201 572-7436
Justin Bishop, *CEO*
EMP: 5
SQ FT: 2,000

SALES (est): 57.1K **Privately Held**
SIC: 8999 8711 1629 3731 Inventor; engineering services; construction & civil engineering; dams, waterways, docks & other marine construction; submersible marine robots, manned or unmanned; water quality monitoring & control systems; sewage & water treatment equipment

(G-11643)
BLOOMFIELD NEWS LLC
172 Orton Rd (07006-8251)
PHONE..............................973 226-2127
Louis Venezia, *Principal*
EMP: 4
SALES (est): 97.7K **Privately Held**
SIC: 2711 Newspapers

(G-11644)
COLTER & PETERSON INC (PA)
19 Fairfield Pl (07006-6206)
PHONE..............................973 684-0901
James Colter, *Ch of Bd*
Bruce Peterson, *President*
Don Shields, *Exec VP*
Donald Sheilds, *Vice Pres*
Eric Peterson, *Treasurer*
◆ EMP: 45
SQ FT: 32,000
SALES (est): 21.3MM **Privately Held**
WEB: www.colter-peterson.com
SIC: 5084 3554 Printing trades machinery, equipment & supplies; paper industries machinery; cutting machines, paper

(G-11645)
CORPORATE MAILINGS INC (PA)
Also Called: Ccg Marketing Solutions
14 Henderson Dr (07006-6608)
PHONE..............................973 439-1168
Lois M Pinkin, *President*
Jeffrey T Lawshe, *Senior VP*
Jeffrey S Pinkin, *Senior VP*
Heather Pinkin, *Vice Pres*
James E Pinkin, *Vice Pres*
▲ EMP: 178
SQ FT: 375,000
SALES (est): 58.1MM **Privately Held**
WEB: www.corpcomm.com
SIC: 2752 7311 7331 7374 Promotional printing, lithographic; advertising agencies; mailing service; data processing service

(G-11646)
DIRECT PRTG IMPRESSIONS INC
Also Called: D P I
33 Fairfield Pl (07006-6206)
PHONE..............................973 227-6111
Rich Luggiero, *President*
Rosa Luggiero, *Vice Pres*
Dennis Pikaard, *Human Resources*
Frank Aresta, *Sales Staff*
Maria Lojo, *Office Mgr*
EMP: 18
SQ FT: 20,000
SALES (est): 3.9MM **Privately Held**
WEB: www.dpiprints.com
SIC: 2752 Commercial printing, offset

(G-11647)
DONNELLEY FINANCIAL LLC
5 Henderson Dr (07006-6607)
PHONE..............................973 882-7000
Russell Radil, *Manager*
EMP: 13
SALES (corp-wide): 963MM **Publicly Held**
WEB: www.bowne.com
SIC: 2752 Commercial printing, offset
HQ: Donnelley Financial, Llc
35 W Wacker Dr
Chicago IL 60601
844 866-4337

(G-11648)
ESSEX RISE CONVEYOR CORP
4 Fairfield Cres (07006-6205)
PHONE..............................973 575-7483
Charles V Wampler, *CEO*
Scott Swander, *Vice Pres*
Patty Spina, *Purch Agent*
EMP: 6

SQ FT: 25,000
SALES (est): 640K Privately Held
WEB: www.essexrise.com
SIC: 3535 Conveyors & conveying equip-

(G-11649)
EXIDE TECHNOLOGIES
Also Called: Exide Battery
1 Dodge Dr (07006-6713)
PHONE.................................973 439-9612
Mike Pucilowski, *Manager*
EMP: 7
SALES (corp-wide): 2.3B Privately Held
WEB: www.exideworld.com
SIC: 5063 5999 3629 Batteries; batteries, non-automotive; battery chargers, rectify-ing or nonrotating
PA: Exide Technologies
13000 Deerfield Pkwy # 200
Milton GA 30004
678 566-9000

(G-11650)
FANCORT INDUSTRIES INC
31 Fairfield Pl (07006-6286)
P.O. Box 565, Caldwell (07007-0565)
PHONE.................................973 575-0610
Ronald J Corey, *President*
Robert Antonelli, *Vice Pres*
Diane Buchanan, *Buyer*
Edgar R Garcia, *Engineer*
Eduardo G Rohwedder, *Sales Engr*
▲ **EMP:** 17 **EST:** 1973
SQ FT: 12,000
SALES (est): 4.5MM Privately Held
WEB: www.fancort.com
SIC: 3544 Special dies, tools, jigs & fix-tures

(G-11651)
FORTRESS GRAPHICS LLC
Also Called: Eastern Impressions
33 Fairfield Pl (07006-6206)
PHONE.................................973 276-0100
Jose Lojo, *Mng Member*
EMP: 23
SQ FT: 27,000
SALES: 350K Privately Held
SIC: 7389 2752 5999 5099 Printing bro-ker; photo-offset printing; alcoholic bever-age making equipment & supplies; brass goods

(G-11652)
GIA-TEK LLC
66 Westover Ave (07006-7723)
PHONE.................................973 228-0875
Robert Giannetti Jr, *Principal*
EMP: 5
SALES (est): 414K Privately Held
SIC: 3567 Heating units & devices, indus-trial: electric

(G-11653)
HOPE ELECTRICAL PRODUCTS CO
3 Fairfield Cres (07006-6204)
PHONE.................................973 882-7400
Margaret Hutchinson, *President*
Pete Hutchinson, *Vice Pres*
Travis Hutchinson, *Vice Pres*
Joe Kofler, *Plant Mgr*
EMP: 8 **EST:** 1933
SQ FT: 16,000
SALES (est): 1.3MM Privately Held
WEB: www.hopeelectricalproducts.com
SIC: 3644 5063 5999 Fuse boxes, elec-tric; fuses & accessories; electronic parts & equipment

(G-11654)
IMPACT INSTRUMENTATION INC
Also Called: Impact Medical
27 Fairfield Pl (07006-6206)
P.O. Box 508, Caldwell (07007-0508)
PHONE.................................973 882-1212
Leslie H Sherman, *President*
Mel Chettum, *Corp Secy*
▲ **EMP:** 150
SQ FT: 22,000
SALES (est): 26.9MM Privately Held
SIC: 3845 Respiratory analysis equipment, electromedical

HQ: Zoll Medical Corporation
269 Mill Rd
Chelmsford MA 01824
978 421-9655

(G-11655)
J R E INC
22 Fairfield Pl (07006-6207)
PHONE.................................973 808-0055
James Tuscano Jr, *Vice Pres*
Natalie Tuscano, *Vice Pres*
Terry Tuscano, *Vice Pres*
Danielle Tuscano, *Purchasing*
Danielle Conca, *Sales Mgr*
EMP: 32
SQ FT: 5,400
SALES (est): 5.8MM Privately Held
WEB: www.jreinc.com
SIC: 3672 Printed circuit boards

(G-11656)
JAK DIVERSIFIED II INC
Also Called: Multi-Pak Packaging
241 Clinton Rd (07006-6603)
PHONE.................................973 439-1182
John Culligan, *President*
Deborah Culligan, *COO*
Allyson Culligan, *Exec VP*
Brendan Sullivan, *Vice Pres*
Alexandra Oppel, *Accounting Mgr*
▲ **EMP:** 75
SQ FT: 55,000
SALES (est): 20.9MM Privately Held
SIC: 2834 Pharmaceutical preparations

(G-11657)
JAY GERISH COMPANY
2 York Ave (07006-6407)
PHONE.................................973 403-0655
Jay Gerish, *President*
Joan Gerish, *Corp Secy*
Joseph Gerish, *Vice Pres*
Kathleen Gerish Rieckert, *Vice Pres*
Kathy Gerish, *Finance*
▲ **EMP:** 8
SQ FT: 42,000
SALES (est): 1.1MM Privately Held
WEB: www.jaygerish.com
SIC: 2353 Hats & caps

(G-11658)
LTS LHMANN THRAPY SYSTEMS CORP
21 Henderson Dr (07006-6607)
PHONE.................................973 575-5170
Wolfgang Hartwig, *CEO*
Kenneth Rogers, *Vice Pres*
Dave Sacks, *Vice Pres*
Salvatore Sascatta, *Vice Pres*
Wolfgang Schafer, *Vice Pres*
▲ **EMP:** 1000
SQ FT: 150,000
SALES (est): 228.8MM
SALES (corp-wide): 577.3K Privately Held
WEB: www.ltslohmann.com
SIC: 2834 Pharmaceutical preparations
HQ: Lts Lohmann Therapie-Systeme Ag
Lohmannstr. 2
Andernach 56626
263 299-0

(G-11659)
LUMENARC INC
37 Fairfield Pl (07006-6206)
PHONE.................................973 882-5918
Harminder Bhalla, *President*
Ranbir Bhalla, *Vice Pres*
▲ **EMP:** 10
SQ FT: 25,000
SALES (est): 1.5MM Privately Held
SIC: 3643 Current-carrying wiring devices

(G-11660)
MARMAXX OPERATING CORP
Also Called: Marshalls
901 Bloomfield Ave (07006-7128)
PHONE.................................973 575-7910
Gwen O'Conner, *Manager*
EMP: 60
SALES (corp-wide): 38.9B Publicly Held
WEB: www.marshallsonline.com
SIC: 5311 5651 5641 2339 Department stores, discount; family clothing stores; children's & infants' wear stores; women's & misses' outerwear

HQ: Marmaxx Operating Corp.
770 Cochituate Rd
Framingham MA 01701

(G-11661)
MAXIMUM HUMN PRFMCE HLDNGS LLC (PA)
165 Clinton Rd (07006-6605)
PHONE.................................973 785-9055
Gerald Dente, *CEO*
EMP: 23 **EST:** 2010
SALES (est): 2.9MM Privately Held
SIC: 2834 Vitamin, nutrient & hematinic preparations for human use

(G-11662)
MAXLITE INC
10 York Ave (07006-6411)
PHONE.................................800 555-5629
EMP: 17 **Privately Held**
SIC: 3648 Arc lighting fixtures
PA: Maxlite, Inc.
12 York Ave
West Caldwell NJ 07006

(G-11663)
MAXLITE INC (PA)
12 York Ave (07006-6411)
PHONE.................................973 244-7300
Yon W Sung, *President*
Spencer Bolgard, *President*
Todd Kim, *General Mgr*
Jay Lee, *General Mgr*
Rick Schuett, *Senior VP*
▲ **EMP:** 70
SQ FT: 100,000
SALES: 134.6MM Privately Held
WEB: www.maxlite.com
SIC: 3699 5044 3641 5063 Electrical equipment & supplies; office equipment; electric lamps; electrical apparatus & equipment; semiconductors & related de-vices

(G-11664)
MERCURY SYSTEMS INC
2 Henderson Dr Ste B (07006-6608)
PHONE.................................973 244-1040
Ken Hermanny, *CEO*
Alexander Badalamenti, *Mfg Staff*
Christena Peters, *Buyer*
EMP: 36
SALES (corp-wide): 654.7MM Publicly Held
SIC: 3672 Printed circuit boards
PA: Mercury Systems, Inc.
50 Minuteman Rd
Andover MA 01810
978 256-1300

(G-11665)
MERRIMAC INDUSTRIES INC (HQ)
41 Fairfield Pl (07006-6287)
PHONE.................................973 575-1300
Bob Tavares, *President*
Greg Shaffer, *General Mgr*
Brendan Curran, *Principal*
Chad Corneil, *Business Mgr*
Reynold K Green, *COO*
▲ **EMP:** 100 **EST:** 1954
SQ FT: 71,200
SALES (est): 28.7MM
SALES (corp-wide): 3.3B Publicly Held
WEB: www.merrimacind.com
SIC: 3679 3663 3264 Microwave compo-nents; microwave communication equip-ment; amplifiers, RF power & IF; space satellite communications equipment; fer-rite & ferrite parts
PA: Crane Co.
100 1st Stamford Pl # 300
Stamford CT 06902
203 363-7300

(G-11666)
MICROGEN INC
33 Clinton Rd Ste 102 (07006-6790)
PHONE.................................973 575-9025
Robert G Prince, *President*
EMP: 5
SQ FT: 1,400

SALES: 2MM Privately Held
WEB: www.microgeninc.com
SIC: 2842 5169 Sanitation preparations, disinfectants & deodorants; specialty cleaning & sanitation preparations

(G-11667)
NEPTUNE RESEARCH & DEVELOPMENT
Also Called: N Research
267 Fairfield Ave (07006-6203)
PHONE.................................973 808-8811
Akos Sule, *President*
EMP: 20
SQ FT: 23,000
SALES (est): 3.7MM Privately Held
WEB: www.nresearch.com
SIC: 3491 Solenoid valves

(G-11668)
OCEAN POWER & EQUIPMENT CO
1140 Bloomfield Ave # 107 (07006-7126)
PHONE.................................973 575-5775
Richard A Russell, *President*
Jack Zhu, *General Mgr*
Vivian Zhang, *Sales Staff*
Chris Bergmann, *Contract Mgr*
◆ **EMP:** 5
SQ FT: 1,000
SALES (est): 967.2K Privately Held
WEB: www.ocean-power.us
SIC: 5088 3519 3731 Marine propulsion machinery & equipment; diesel, semi-diesel or duel-fuel engines, including ma-rine; commercial cargo ships, building & repairing; commercial passenger ships, building & repairing

(G-11669)
ORIGINAL BAGEL & BIALY CO INC
2 Fairfield Cres (07006-6205)
PHONE.................................973 227-5777
Bruce Levenbrook, *CEO*
Dave Harris, *President*
Bill Lasek, *COO*
Garrett Levenbrook, *Exec VP*
Alberto Pena, *Maintence Staff*
EMP: 43
SQ FT: 30,000
SALES (est): 16.2MM Privately Held
WEB: www.originalbagel.com
SIC: 2051 Bagels, fresh or frozen

(G-11670)
OSULLIVAN COMMUNICATIONS CORP (PA)
1 Fairfield Cres (07006-6204)
PHONE.................................973 227-5112
Elizabeth O'Sullivan, *Exec VP*
Joseph Bonis, *Senior VP*
Alison Fischer, *Vice Pres*
Cristina Sake, *Human Res Mgr*
Johanna Moore, *Manager*
▼ **EMP:** 23
SALES (est): 12.1MM Privately Held
SIC: 2752 Commercial printing, litho-graphic

(G-11671)
PCI INC
185 Fairfield Ave Ste 4c (07006-6417)
PHONE.................................973 226-8007
William J Murphy, *President*
Jack O'Dea, *Vice Pres*
EMP: 8
SQ FT: 3,000
SALES (est): 634.7K
SALES (corp-wide): 7.9MM Privately Held
WEB: www.advancedhorizons.com
SIC: 6531 3699 Rental agent, real estate; electrical equipment & supplies
PA: Advanced Horizons, Inc.
185 Fairfield Ave Ste 4c
West Caldwell NJ 07006
973 226-8007

(G-11672)
PLASTINETICS INC
195 Fairfield Ave (07006-6424)
PHONE.................................973 618-9090
Ed Batta, *Principal*
EMP: 4

SALES (est): 288.9K **Privately Held**
SIC: 3083 Plastic finished products, laminated

(G-11673)
POTDEVIN MACHINE CO
26 Fairfield Pl (07006-6207)
P.O. Box 1409, Caldwell (07007-1409)
PHONE..................................973 227-8828
Robert S Potdevin, *President*
Barbara Brose, *Bookkeeper*
Dominick Gagliano, *Sales Mgr*
EMP: 10
SQ FT: 25,000
SALES (est): 1.9MM **Privately Held**
WEB: www.potdevin.com
SIC: 3565 Packaging machinery

(G-11674)
QUAGEN PHARMACEUTICALS LLC (PA)
11 Patton Dr (07006-6404)
PHONE..................................973 228-9600
Ashish Shah,
EMP: 15
SALES: 789K **Privately Held**
SIC: 2834 Druggists' preparations (pharmaceuticals)

(G-11675)
QUAGEN PHARMACEUTICALS LLC
34 Fairfield Pl (07006-6209)
PHONE..................................973 228-9600
Ashish Shah, *President*
EMP: 10
SALES (corp-wide): 789K **Privately Held**
SIC: 2834 Pharmaceutical preparations
PA: Quagen Pharmaceuticals Llc
11 Patton Dr
West Caldwell NJ 07006
973 228-9600

(G-11676)
R R DONNELLEY & SONS COMPANY
5 Henderson Dr (07006-6607)
PHONE..................................973 439-8321
EMP: 200
SALES (corp-wide): 6.8B **Publicly Held**
WEB: www.rrdonnelley.com
SIC: 2754 Catalogs: gravure printing, not published on site
PA: R. R. Donnelley & Sons Company
35 W Wacker Dr
Chicago IL 60601
312 326-8000

(G-11677)
REGI US INC
8 Fairfield Cres Unit 1 (07006-6205)
PHONE..................................862 702-3901
Terry Gretsas, *Director*
EMP: 4
SQ FT: 35,000
SALES (est): 277.6K **Privately Held**
SIC: 2844 Toilet preparations
HQ: Regi Srl
Via Mattei 6-10-14
Bagnolo Cremasco CR 26010
037 331-861

(G-11678)
REVERE SURVIVAL PRODUCTS INC
3 Fairfield Cres (07006-6204)
PHONE..................................973 575-8811
Howard Koffman, *President*
◆ EMP: 10
SALES (est): 651.1K **Privately Held**
SIC: 3429 Manufactured hardware (general)

(G-11679)
RISE CORPORATION
Also Called: Richards Industries
4 Fairfield Cres (07006-6205)
PHONE..................................973 575-7480
Chester V Wampler II, *CEO*
Robert B Taylor, *President*
Carl Bondorff, *CFO*
Chuck Bechtel, *Info Tech Dir*
EMP: 20
SQ FT: 25,000

SALES (est): 3.8MM **Privately Held**
SIC: 3499 3537 Fire- or burglary-resistive products; pallets, metal; dollies (hand or power trucks), industrial except mining; skids, metal

(G-11680)
TIMELINE PROMOTIONS INC
19 Aldrin Dr (07006-7201)
PHONE..................................973 226-1512
Kim Meth, *President*
EMP: 4
SALES (est): 560K **Privately Held**
WEB: www.timelinepromotions.com
SIC: 8743 2759 Promotion service; commercial printing

(G-11681)
VITAQUEST INTERNATIONAL LLC (PA)
8 Henderson Dr (07006-6608)
PHONE..................................973 575-9200
Keith Frankel, *Ch of Bd*
Patrick Brueggman, *President*
David P Illingworth, *COO*
Yvonne York, *Wholesale*
Angela Van Houten, *Manager*
▲ EMP: 500
SQ FT: 150,000
SALES (est): 158.7MM **Privately Held**
WEB: www.gardenstatenutritionals.com
SIC: 2834 5149 5122 8742 Vitamin preparations; health foods; vitamins & minerals; marketing consulting services

(G-11682)
ZEISER INC
15 Patton Dr (07006-6404)
PHONE..................................973 228-0800
Thorsten Tritschler, *President*
Jeff Veksler, *President*
Rick Vandervliet, *General Mgr*
Jeff Vechsler, *Vice Pres*
Joseph Weber, *Vice Pres*
▲ EMP: 13
SQ FT: 45,000
SALES (est): 10.1MM
SALES (corp-wide): 266.5MM **Privately Held**
WEB: www.atlanticzeiser.com
SIC: 3578 5046 3555 2752 Calculating & accounting equipment; commercial equipment; printing trades machinery; commercial printing, lithographic
HQ: Zeiser Gmbh
Bogenstr. 6-8
Emmingen-Liptingen 78576
746 592-780

West Cape May
Cape May County

(G-11683)
FLYING FISH STUDIO
130 Park Blvd (08204-1239)
PHONE..................................609 884-2760
Susan B Lotozo, *Owner*
EMP: 5
SQ FT: 1,200
SALES: 350K **Privately Held**
WEB: www.flyingfishstudio.com
SIC: 7336 5947 5699 2326 Silk screen design; souvenirs; customized clothing & apparel; work apparel, except uniforms; service apparel (baker, barber, lab, etc.), washable: men's

---

West Creek
Ocean County

(G-11684)
BARNEGAT LIGHT FIBRGLS SUP LLC
304 Forge Rd Unit 12 (08092-3219)
PHONE..................................609 294-8870
Norma Bunkelberger, *Principal*
Thomas L Maher,
EMP: 3
SQ FT: 1,200

SALES (est): 2MM **Privately Held**
SIC: 5169 3732 3083 Chemicals & allied products; boat building & repairing; laminated plastics plate & sheet

(G-11685)
CLAYTON BLOCK COMPANY INC
Us Hwy 9 (08092)
PHONE..................................609 597-8128
EMP: 13
SALES (corp-wide): 31.8MM **Privately Held**
WEB: www.claytononline.com
SIC: 3271 Blocks, concrete or cinder: standard
PA: Clayton Block Company, Inc.
1355 Campus Pkwy Ste 200
Wall Township NJ 07753
888 763-8665

(G-11686)
DOWN SHORE PUBLISHING CORP
638 Teal St (08092)
P.O. Box 100 (08092-0100)
PHONE..................................609 978-1233
Raymond G Fisk, *President*
▲ EMP: 6
SALES (est): 660.4K **Privately Held**
WEB: www.down-the-shore.com
SIC: 2741 Miscellaneous publishing

(G-11687)
HORSETRACS
99 Oak Ave (08092-2816)
PHONE..................................732 228-7646
Barbara Frayman, *Owner*
EMP: 4
SALES (est): 210.6K **Privately Held**
SIC: 2399 Horse harnesses & riding crops, etc.: non-leather

(G-11688)
WOODWARD WOOD PRODUCTS DESIGN
Also Called: Handmade Furniture
612 Main St (08092-9757)
PHONE..................................609 597-2708
Richard Woodward, *President*
EMP: 15
SQ FT: 8,000
SALES: 2MM **Privately Held**
SIC: 2499 2512 Kitchen, bathroom & household ware: wood; wood upholstered chairs & couches

---

West Deptford
Gloucester County

(G-11689)
ACC FOODS LTD LIABILITY CO
280 Jessup Rd (08086-2128)
PHONE..................................856 848-8877
John D Ong, *Opers Mgr*
Dong John, *Sales Staff*
Hing Kong,
Kuang M Kwok,
Kai Chuen Wong,
◆ EMP: 106
SALES (est): 12.5MM **Privately Held**
SIC: 2099 Food preparations

(G-11690)
AKERS BIOSCIENCES INC
201 Grove Rd (08086-2231)
PHONE..................................856 848-8698
Howard R Yeaton, *CEO*
EMP: 32
SQ FT: 12,500
SALES: 1.6MM **Privately Held**
WEB: www.akersbiosciences.com
SIC: 2835 3829 In vitro diagnostics; measuring & controlling devices; medical diagnostic systems, nuclear

(G-11691)
ANDREW B DUFFY INC
322 Crown Point Rd (08086-2120)
P.O. Box 569, Thorofare (08086-0569)
PHONE..................................856 845-4900
Brian M Duffy, *President*
Sherri Veacock, *Office Mgr*

EMP: 15 EST: 1951
SQ FT: 12,000
SALES (est): 3.2MM **Privately Held**
WEB: www.abduffy.com
SIC: 3443 3444 3441 3412 Industrial vessels, tanks & containers; sheet metalwork; fabricated structural metal; metal barrels, drums & pails

(G-11692)
AQUATROLS CORP OF AMERICA
Also Called: Aqua Controls
1273 Imperial Way (08066-1808)
PHONE..................................856 537-6003
Tracy Jarman, *CEO*
Chris Parks, *Manager*
Tom Valentine, *Manager*
Robert Wilson, *Manager*
Robert A Moore Jr, *Admin Sec*
◆ EMP: 34 EST: 1955
SQ FT: 64,000
SALES (est): 11.5MM **Privately Held**
WEB: www.aquatrols.com
SIC: 2879 Agricultural chemicals

(G-11693)
ASSOCIATED ASPHALT MKTG LLC
400 Grove Rd (08066-1844)
PHONE..................................210 249-9988
Carol Streeper, *Branch Mgr*
EMP: 25 **Privately Held**
SIC: 1311 Crude petroleum & natural gas
PA: Associated Asphalt Partners, Llc
110 Franklin Rd Sw Fl 9
Roanoke VA 24011

(G-11694)
BOYLE TOOL & DIE CO INC
135 Crown Point Rd (08086-2173)
PHONE..................................856 853-1819
Thomas J Boyle, *President*
EMP: 10
SQ FT: 10,000
SALES (est): 966.3K **Privately Held**
SIC: 3544 3469 3496 3315 Special dies & tools; metal stampings; miscellaneous fabricated wire products; steel wire & related products

(G-11695)
BUMPER SPECIALTIES INC
1607 Imperial Way (08066-1816)
PHONE..................................856 345-7650
Leon Braunstein, *President*
Robert Steers, *Controller*
EMP: 149
SQ FT: 80,000
SALES (est): 25.8MM **Privately Held**
WEB: www.bumperspecialties.com
SIC: 3069 Hard rubber products

(G-11696)
CHECKPOINT SECURITY SYSTEMS GR
101 Wolf Dr (08066-2243)
PHONE..................................952 933-8858
George Off, *CEO*
Steve Champeau, *Vice Pres*
EMP: 125
SQ FT: 12,000
SALES (est): 8.4MM
SALES (corp-wide): 3.9B **Privately Held**
SIC: 1731 7382 3829 Fire detection & burglar alarm systems specialization; closed circuit television installation; fire alarm maintenance & monitoring; burglar alarm maintenance & monitoring; protective devices, security; measuring & controlling devices
HQ: Checkpoint Systems, Inc.
101 Wolf Dr
West Deptford NJ 08086
800 257-5540

(G-11697)
CHECKPOINT SYSTEMS INC (HQ)
101 Wolf Dr (08066-2243)
PHONE..................................800 257-5540
George Babich Jr, *President*
Per H Levin, *President*
David Murrihy, *Business Mgr*
Birgitta Pettersson, *Business Mgr*

Bernard Gremillet, *Exec VP*
◆ EMP: 104
SALES: 587.1MM
SALES (corp-wide): 3.9B **Privately Held**
WEB: www.checkpointsystems.com
SIC: 3699 3812 3663 Security control
equipment & systems; detection appara-
tus: electronic/magnetic field, light/heat;
television closed circuit equipment
PA: Ccl Industries Inc
　　111 Gordon Baker Rd Suite 801
　　Toronto ON M2H 3
　　800 563-2464

(G-11698)
CHECKPOINT SYSTEMS INC
201 Wolf Dr (08086-2245)
PHONE....................................856 848-1800
Erik N Cardinaal, *Managing Dir*
Michael Guiher, *Vice Pres*
George Babich Jr, *Branch Mgr*
Tim McMillan, *Manager*
Eric Turner, *Manager*
EMP: 114
SALES (corp-wide): 3.9B **Privately Held**
SIC: 3699 3812 3663 Security control
equipment & systems; detection appara-
tus: electronic/magnetic field, light/heat;
television closed circuit equipment
HQ: Checkpoint Systems, Inc.
　　101 Wolf Dr
　　West Deptford NJ 08086
　　800 257-5540

(G-11699)
CHECKPOINT SYSTEMS INC
101 Wolf Dr (08086-2243)
PHONE....................................952 933-8858
Nick Khalil, *President*
EMP: 125
SALES (corp-wide): 3.9B **Privately Held**
WEB: www.checkpointsystems.com
SIC: 1731 7382 3829 Fire detection &
burglar alarm systems specialization;
closed circuit television installation; fire
alarm maintenance & monitoring; burglar
alarm maintenance & monitoring; protective devices, security; measuring & controlling devices
HQ: Checkpoint Systems, Inc.
　　101 Wolf Dr
　　West Deptford NJ 08086
　　800 257-5540

(G-11700)
COIM USA INC (HQ)
Also Called: Novacote Flexpack
286 Mantua Grove Rd # 1 (08066-1738)
PHONE....................................856 224-8560
Lucio Siano, *CEO*
Michelangelo Cavallo, *President*
Angelo Macchi, *Principal*
Erann Dutton, *Purchasing*
Dave McDyer, *Engineer*
◆ EMP: 84
SALES (est): 30.3MM
SALES (corp-wide): 476.9MM **Privately
Held**
WEB: www.us.coimgroup.com
SIC: 2891 2821 Adhesives; polyesters;
elastomers, nonvulcanizable (plastics)
PA: C.O.I.M. Spa Chimica Organica Indus-
triale Milanese
　　Via Alessandro Manzoni 28
　　Settimo Milanese MI 20019
　　023 350-51

(G-11701)
EDWARDS BROTHERS INC
1301 Metropolitan Ave # 300 (08066-1862)
PHONE....................................856 848-6900
EMP: 5
SALES (corp-wide): 308.1MM **Privately
Held**
SIC: 2752 Lithographic Commercial Print-
ing
HQ: Edwards Brothers, Inc.
　　5411 Jackson Rd
　　Ann Arbor MI 48103
　　800 722-3231

(G-11702)
**HANGSTERFERS
LABORATORIES**
175 Ogden Rd (08051-1615)
PHONE....................................856 468-0216

Ann Jones, *CEO*
Pat Brewer, *Human Res Mgr*
Todd Pack, *Sales Mgr*
Skip Wolford, *Sales Mgr*
Cheryl Villanova, *Sales Staff*
◆ EMP: 30 EST: 1946
SQ FT: 30,000
SALES (est): 9.9MM **Privately Held**
WEB: www.hangsterfers.com
SIC: 2992 7389 Oils & greases, blending
& compounding;

(G-11703)
HUSSMANN CORPORATION
Also Called: Convenience Works
875 Kings Hwy Ste 205 (08096-3165)
PHONE....................................800 320-3510
Tim Lowery, *Manager*
EMP: 20 **Privately Held**
WEB: www.hussmann.com
SIC: 3585 Refrigeration & heating equip-
ment
HQ: Hussmann Corporation
　　12999 St Charles Rock Rd
　　Bridgeton MO 63044
　　314 291-2000

(G-11704)
ICS CORPORATION
100 Friars Blvd (08086-2141)
PHONE....................................215 427-3355
Richard Bastian, *President*
Matthew I Bastian, *President*
Richard Prendergast, *Vice Pres*
Catharine Radomicki, *Treasurer*
Keely Lavelle, *Controller*
EMP: 225 EST: 1965
SQ FT: 100,000
SALES (est): 34.2MM **Privately Held**
WEB: www.ics-corporation.com
SIC: 7374 2759 7331 Data processing &
preparation; commercial printing; direct
mail advertising services

(G-11705)
INSIGN INC
1709 Imperial Way (08066-1818)
PHONE....................................856 424-1161
Samuel A Miner, *President*
Ed McCann, *Vice Pres*
Harold Mas, *Project Mgr*
Chris Custren, *Graphic Designe*
EMP: 35
SALES (est): 5.6MM **Privately Held**
WEB: www.insigninc.com
SIC: 3993 2542 7389 Displays & cutouts,
window & lobby; partitions & fixtures, ex-
cept wood; interior designer; interior dec-
orating

(G-11706)
**INTERNATIONAL PAPER
COMPANY**
33 Phoenix Dr (08086-2156)
PHONE....................................856 853-7000
Rich Rosenbach, *President*
EMP: 21
SALES (corp-wide): 23.3B **Publicly Held**
WEB: www.internationalpaper.com
SIC: 2621 Paper mills
PA: International Paper Company
　　6400 Poplar Ave
　　Memphis TN 38197
　　901 419-9000

(G-11707)
JEROME GROUP INC
Also Called: Jerome Medical
1414 Metropolitan Ave (08066-1869)
PHONE....................................856 234-8600
Ronald S Kowalski, *President*
Anthony H Martinez, *Vice Pres*
Karen L Smith, *Vice Pres*
▲ EMP: 55 EST: 1947
SQ FT: 15,000
SALES (est): 5.7MM **Privately Held**
WEB: www.miamij.com
SIC: 3842 Splints, pneumatic & wood; sup-
ports: abdominal, ankle, arch, kneecap,
etc.
HQ: Ossur Americas, Inc.
　　27051 Towne Centre Dr # 100
　　Foothill Ranch CA 92610
　　949 362-3883

(G-11708)
JOHNSON MATTHEY INC
Also Called: Catalyst Chemicals and Ref Div
2001 Nolte Dr (08066-1795)
PHONE....................................856 384-7000
Martin D Turney, *Branch Mgr*
Daniel Cooper, *Executive*
Joe Molle, *Executive*
Nicole McFarland, *Clerk*
EMP: 235
SALES (corp-wide): 13.8B **Privately Held**
SIC: 3341 Secondary nonferrous metals
HQ: Johnson Matthey Inc.
　　435 Devon Park Dr Ste 600
　　Wayne PA 19087
　　610 971-3000

(G-11709)
LACROSSE REPUBLIC
711 Mantua Pike Ste 2 (08096-3357)
PHONE....................................856 853-8787
Bill Keane, *Owner*
EMP: 4
SALES (est): 364.4K **Privately Held**
SIC: 3949 Sporting & athletic goods

(G-11710)
MATTHEY JOHNSON INC
Also Called: Catalyst Chemicals and Ref Div
2001 Nolte Dr (08066-1727)
PHONE....................................856 384-7132
Brent Hackette, *Branch Mgr*
EMP: 230
SALES (corp-wide): 13.8B **Privately Held**
SIC: 3341 3339 3356 2834 Platinum
group metals, smelting & refining (secondary); gold smelting & refining (secondary); silver smelting & refining
(secondary); platinum group metal refining (primary); gold refining (primary); silver refining (primary); precious metals;
platinum group metals: rolling, drawing or
extruding; gold & gold alloy: rolling, drawing or extruding; powders, pharmaceutical; metal powders, pastes & flakes;
paste, metal; exhaust systems & parts,
motor vehicle
HQ: Johnson Matthey Inc.
　　435 Devon Park Dr Ste 600
　　Wayne PA 19087
　　610 971-3000

(G-11711)
MATTHEY JOHNSON INC
Also Called: Johnson Matthey Phrm Mtls
2003 Nolte Dr (08066-1727)
PHONE....................................856 384-7001
Joe Moy, *Sales Staff*
John Fowler, *Branch Mgr*
EMP: 43
SALES (corp-wide): 13.8B **Privately Held**
SIC: 2834 Pharmaceutical preparations
HQ: Johnson Matthey Inc.
　　435 Devon Park Dr Ste 600
　　Wayne PA 19087
　　610 971-3000

(G-11712)
OSSUR AMERICAS INC
680 Grove Rd (08066-1849)
PHONE....................................856 345-6000
Ron Kowalski, *Branch Mgr*
EMP: 4 **Privately Held**
SIC: 3842 Prosthetic appliances
HQ: Ossur Americas, Inc.
　　27051 Towne Centre Dr # 100
　　Foothill Ranch CA 92610
　　949 362-3883

(G-11713)
P W B OMNI INC
1319 Vallee Dr (08096-3139)
PHONE....................................856 384-1300
Elizabeth Foradori, *President*
EMP: 3
SALES (est): 5MM **Privately Held**
WEB: www.omnipwb.com
SIC: 5065 3672 Electronic parts & equip-
ment; wiring boards

(G-11714)
**PRECISION ORTHOTIC LAB OF
NJ**
1595 Imperial Way Ste 103 (08066-1864)
PHONE....................................856 848-6226
Aron Adams, *President*

EMP: 15
SQ FT: 1,500
SALES (est): 1.1MM **Privately Held**
WEB: www.precisionorthotic.com
SIC: 3842 Orthopedic appliances

(G-11715)
PUBLISHERS INC
Also Called: Fort Nassau Graphics
1757 Imperial Way (08066-1818)
PHONE....................................856 853-2800
Paul F Cipolone, *President*
Brian Francis, *Vice Pres*
Lorraine Gabbett, *Vice Pres*
EMP: 40 EST: 1957
SQ FT: 20,000
SALES (est): 10.7MM **Privately Held**
WEB: www.publishers.com
SIC: 2752 Commercial printing, offset

(G-11716)
**SOLVAY SPCLTY POLYMERS
USA LLC**
10 Leonard Ln (08086-2150)
PHONE....................................856 853-8119
Justin Gattuso, *Business Mgr*
Mahesh Padigala, *Engineer*
Charles Jones, *Branch Mgr*
EMP: 150
SQ FT: 5,000
SALES (corp-wide): 12.8MM **Privately
Held**
SIC: 2819 Industrial inorganic chemicals
HQ: Solvay Specialty Polymers Usa, L.L.C.
　　4500 Mcginnis Ferry Rd
　　Alpharetta GA 30005
　　770 772-8200

(G-11717)
USA WOOD DOOR INC
1475 Imperial Way (08066-1812)
P.O. Box 116, Thorofare (08086-0116)
PHONE....................................856 384-9663
John Krause, *President*
EMP: 50
SQ FT: 17,000
SALES (est): 7.6MM
SALES (corp-wide): 2.1B **Publicly Held**
WEB: www.usawooddoor.com
SIC: 2431 5211 Door frames, wood; door
sashes, wood; door trim, wood; doors &
door parts & trim, wood; door & window
products; doors, wood or metal, except
storm
PA: Masonite International Corporation
　　201 N Franklin St Ste 300
　　Tampa FL 33602
　　800 895-2723

(G-11718)
ZOO PRINTING INC
551 Mid Atlantic Pkwy (08066-1826)
PHONE....................................856 686-0800
EMP: 9
SALES (corp-wide): 18.9MM **Privately
Held**
SIC: 2759 Commercial printing
PA: Zoo Printing, Inc.
　　25152 Springfield Ct # 280
　　Valencia CA 91355
　　310 253-7751

┌─────────────────────────┐
│ **West Long Branch**   │
│ *Monmouth County*   │
└─────────────────────────┘

(G-11719)
ARTS EMBROIDERY LLC
175 Monmouth Rd (07764-1028)
PHONE....................................732 870-2400
Art Kraucis,
INA Kraucis,
EMP: 4
SALES (est): 231.2K **Privately Held**
SIC: 2395 2759 Embroidery & art needle-
work; screen printing

(G-11720)
BORO PRINTING INC
813 Broadway (07764-1542)
PHONE....................................732 229-1899
Evelyn Delatush, *President*
Gary Delatush, *Vice Pres*
EMP: 5

SQ FT: 3,500
SALES: 300K **Privately Held**
WEB: www.boroprinting.com
SIC: **2621** 2752 Printing paper; commercial printing, offset

(G-11721)
SHREM CONSULTING LTD LBLTY CO
Also Called: Nexxbrands
457 Monmouth Rd (07764-1263)
PHONE....................................917 371-0581
Abraham Shrem,
Talia Shrem,
EMP: 2
SALES: 1MM **Privately Held**
SIC: **2085** 2086 5149 5182 Cocktails, alcoholic; mineral water, carbonated: packaged in cans, bottles, etc.; mineral or spring water bottling; cocktails, alcoholic; premixed;

(G-11722)
SMB INTERNATIONAL LLC
Also Called: Vantage Brands
121 State Route 36 # 180 (07764-1436)
PHONE....................................732 222-4888
Scott Margulis, *Mng Member*
▼ EMP: 9 EST: 2009
SALES (est): 3.5MM **Privately Held**
SIC: **6141** 3915 Automobile & consumer finance companies; lapidary work, contract or other

(G-11723)
SPECIALTY PRODUCTS PLUS
215 Locust Ave (07764-1112)
PHONE....................................732 380-1188
Don Baldwin, *Owner*
EMP: 5
SALES (est): 535.9K **Privately Held**
SIC: **3432** Plumbing fixture fittings & trim

West Milford
Passaic County

(G-11724)
ALMOND BRANCH INC
Also Called: Agape Child Care Center
184 Marshall Hill Rd (07480-3512)
PHONE....................................973 728-3479
Cindy Palazzolo, *Pastor*
Rich Palazzolo, *Pastor*
Nicholas J Padovani, *Sr Pastor*
Ashley Druica, *Pub Rel Staff*
EMP: 25
SQ FT: 5,000
SALES: 700K **Privately Held**
WEB: www.agapechildcarecenter.com
SIC: **8661** 8351 7372 Assembly of God Church; preschool center; application computer software

(G-11725)
ANCHOR SALES & MARKETING INC
Also Called: Anchor Home Products
755 Macopin Rd 1 (07480-2608)
PHONE....................................973 545-2277
Frank G Petronzio, *President*
Linda Petronzio, *Vice Pres*
EMP: 13
SQ FT: 10,000
SALES (est): 1.3MM **Privately Held**
SIC: **2392** 5023 Towels, fabric & nonwoven: made from purchased materials; tablecloths: made from purchased materials; slip covers & pads; linens & towels; linens, table; towels

(G-11726)
BEL-TECH STAMPING INC
26 Industrial Rd Ste A (07480-4600)
PHONE....................................973 728-8229
Jim Beloch, *President*
EMP: 13
SQ FT: 4,500
SALES: 500K **Privately Held**
SIC: **3469** Metal stampings

(G-11727)
HYDRAULIC MANIFOLDS USA LLC
Also Called: Selling Precision
264 Marshall Hill Rd (07480-3511)
PHONE....................................973 728-1214
Nimit Patel, *Mng Member*
EMP: 30
SALES (est): 999.3K **Privately Held**
SIC: **3674** Integrated circuits, semiconductor networks, etc.

(G-11728)
LA DUCA TECHNICAL SERVICES LLC
51 Shadowy Ln (07480-1458)
PHONE....................................570 309-4009
Brian Laduca,
EMP: 4
SALES: 120K **Privately Held**
SIC: **3571** Electronic computers

(G-11729)
MARGARITAVILLE INC
Also Called: Pressure Wash
129 Lincoln Ave (07480-2136)
P.O. Box 371 (07480-0371)
PHONE....................................973 728-7562
Eric Hasting, *President*
EMP: 6
SALES: 300K **Privately Held**
SIC: **3589** High pressure cleaning equipment

(G-11730)
NEXTGEN EDGE INC
50 Beacon Hill Rd Apt A (07480-1255)
PHONE....................................610 507-6904
EMP: 4
SQ FT: 1,500
SALES (est): 217.6K **Privately Held**
SIC: **3841** Mfg Surgical/Medical Instruments

(G-11731)
SELLING PRECISION INC
264 Marshall Hill Rd (07480-3511)
PHONE....................................973 728-1214
William Calcagno Jr, *President*
Kenneth Calcagno, *Vice Pres*
Luis Granizo, *Design Engr*
EMP: 35
SQ FT: 9,000
SALES (est): 8MM **Privately Held**
WEB: www.sellingprecision.com
SIC: **3498** Manifolds, pipe: fabricated from purchased pipe

(G-11732)
SYMCON INC
Also Called: Symcon Controls
47 Cedar Ln (07480-2391)
PHONE....................................973 728-8661
Stella Scilingo, *President*
Michael Scilingo, *Vice Pres*
EMP: 4 EST: 1970
SALES: 27K **Privately Held**
SIC: **3613** 3498 3494 Panelboards & distribution boards, electric; fabricated pipe & fittings; valves & pipe fittings

(G-11733)
WALGREEN EASTERN CO INC
Also Called: Walgreens
1502 Union Valley Rd (07480-1354)
PHONE....................................973 728-3172
EMP: 30
SALES (corp-wide): 131.5B **Publicly Held**
SIC: **5912** 2834 Drug stores; pharmaceutical preparations
HQ: Walgreen Eastern Co., Inc.
200 Wilmot Rd
Deerfield IL 60015
847 940-2500

(G-11734)
WOODS INDUSTRIAL LLC
Also Called: Wood's Industrial Services
81 Hudson Dr (07480-4216)
PHONE....................................973 208-0664
Meredith Wood, *Managing Prtnr*
Robert J Wood, *Partner*
EMP: 10

SALES (est): 760K **Privately Held**
SIC: **3599** 1799 1796 Machine & other job shop work; welding on site; machine moving & rigging

West New York
Hudson County

(G-11735)
AIRCHARTERCOM LLC
6515 Kennedy Blvd E (07093-4231)
PHONE....................................212 999-4926
John Harrison, *CEO*
Imane Echouafni, *CFO*
Narjis Oughla, *Mng Member*
EMP: 42
SQ FT: 1,500
SALES (est): 5MM **Privately Held**
SIC: **7372** 4522 Application computer software; flying charter service

(G-11736)
CABIO NEWSPAPER
604 56th St (07093-1236)
PHONE....................................201 902-0811
Yamile Camacho, *Principal*
EMP: 5 EST: 2010
SALES (est): 160.2K **Privately Held**
SIC: **2711** Newspapers: publishing only, not printed on site

(G-11737)
CHRISTIAN ART
567 52nd St Ste 15 (07093-5623)
PHONE....................................201 867-8096
Anthony Ferrer, *Owner*
EMP: 5
SALES (est): 522.5K **Privately Held**
SIC: **2531** 3911 Church furniture; rosaries or other small religious articles, precious metal

(G-11738)
DU-MATT CORPORATION
12 65th St (07093-4104)
PHONE....................................201 861-4271
EMP: 6
SQ FT: 6,000
SALES (est): 798.5K **Privately Held**
SIC: **3423** Mfg Hand/Edge Tools

(G-11739)
ENTERPRISE SOLUTION PRODUCTS
28 Av At Pt Imperial 23 (07093)
PHONE....................................201 678-9200
Wayne Corion, *President*
EMP: 4
SQ FT: 1,800
SALES: 2.5MM **Privately Held**
SIC: **5112** 3861 Photocopying supplies; photocopy machines

(G-11740)
HILL CROSS CO INC
543 56th St (07093-8401)
P.O. Box 60 (07093-0060)
PHONE....................................201 864-3393
Christopher Hammer, *President*
Donald Rosegren, *Vice Pres*
EMP: 7
SQ FT: 18,000
SALES: 932.3K **Privately Held**
SIC: **3471** Electroplating of metals or formed products

(G-11741)
IMPERIAL DRUG & SPICE CORP
5620 Kennedy Blvd W (07093-1208)
P.O. Box 8624, Woodcliff Lake (07677-8624)
PHONE....................................201 348-1551
Francisco Gil, *President*
EMP: 5
SALES (est): 633.1K **Privately Held**
SIC: **2844** Hair preparations, including shampoos

(G-11742)
J & S FINISHING INC
443 62nd St Fl 1 (07093-2326)
PHONE....................................201 854-0338
Pedro A Calvo, *President*

EMP: 5
SALES (est): 363K **Privately Held**
SIC: **2395** Embroidery products, except schiffli machine; embroidery & art needlework

(G-11743)
JAV LATIN AMERICA EXPRESS
6321 Bergenline Ave (07093-1606)
PHONE....................................201 868-5004
Filomena Zaino, *Owner*
EMP: 4
SALES (est): 289.4K **Privately Held**
SIC: **2741** Miscellaneous publishing

(G-11744)
JID TRANSPORTATION LLC
158 61st St Apt 2 (07093-2925)
PHONE....................................201 362-0841
Jaile Luis Diaz, *Principal*
EMP: 1
SALES (est): 85MM **Privately Held**
SIC: **3713** 4212 7363 Truck cabs for motor vehicles; truck rental with drivers; truck driver services

(G-11745)
LENS LAB EXPRESS
5917 Bergenline Ave (07093-1306)
PHONE....................................201 861-0016
Howard Halle, *President*
EMP: 7
SALES (est): 861.7K **Privately Held**
SIC: **3851** 5995 5049 Ophthalmic goods; opticians; optical goods

(G-11746)
M & Z INTERNATIONAL INC
358 Oswego Ct (07093-8315)
PHONE....................................201 864-3331
Yuqiong Zhao, *President*
Liyu MA, *Director*
EMP: 5
SALES: 1MM **Privately Held**
WEB: www.mzinternational.com
SIC: **3699** Security devices

(G-11747)
MARLENE EMBROIDERY INC
6805 Madison St (07093-1818)
PHONE....................................201 868-1682
Ernest Hepperle, *President*
Marlene Hepperle, *Corp Secy*
James Hepperle, *Vice Pres*
EMP: 40
SQ FT: 5,000
SALES (est): 2.1MM **Privately Held**
SIC: **2397** Schiffli machine embroideries

(G-11748)
NESS PLASTICS INC
6040 Kennedy Blvd E 22f (07093-3825)
PHONE....................................201 854-4072
EMP: 10
SQ FT: 3,400
SALES (est): 590K **Privately Held**
SIC: **3069** 8711 Mfg Fabricated Rubber Products Engineering Services

(G-11749)
PRIAMO DESIGNS LTD
6614 Broadway (07093-3298)
PHONE....................................201 861-8808
Priamo Espaillat, *President*
▲ EMP: 7
SQ FT: 7,750
SALES: 600K **Privately Held**
SIC: **2341** Nightgowns & negligees: women's & children's

(G-11750)
PRINTING LAB LLC
609 55th St (07093-4636)
PHONE....................................201 305-0404
Julian Ospina,
Louis Ospina,
EMP: 17
SALES: 1.2MM **Privately Held**
SIC: **2759** Commercial printing

(G-11751)
PROMEKO INC
543 59th St (07093-1317)
PHONE....................................201 861-9446
Edalio Rondon, *President*
Ylia Rondon, *Corp Secy*

GEOGRAPHIC

EMP: 8
SQ FT: 15,000
SALES: 660K **Privately Held**
WEB: www.promekoinc.com
SIC: 2844 Cosmetic preparations

(G-11752)
QUADELLE TEXTILE CORP
573 56th St (07093-1233)
PHONE..................................201 865-1112
Rose Lenson, *President*
Harry Lenson, *Corp Secy*
EMP: 10 **EST:** 1957
SQ FT: 10,000
SALES: 110K **Privately Held**
SIC: 2397 2395 Schiffli machine embroideries; pleating & stitching

(G-11753)
ROYAL PRINTING SERVICE
441 51st St (07093)
P.O. Box 1000 (07093-1000)
PHONE..................................201 863-3131
Ralph S Passante Sr, *President*
Kevin Passante, *Vice Pres*
David Passante, *Admin Sec*
EMP: 43
SQ FT: 20,000
SALES (est): 6.6MM **Privately Held**
WEB: www.royalprintingnj.com
SIC: 2752 Commercial printing, offset

(G-11754)
SAUD & SON JEWELRY INC
Also Called: Saud Jewelry
441 60th St (07093-2211)
PHONE..................................201 866-4445
Jose Saud, *President*
EMP: 7
SQ FT: 2,000
SALES (est): 733.8K **Privately Held**
SIC: 5944 7631 3911 5094 Jewelry, precious stones & precious metals; jewelry repair services; jewelry, precious metal; jewelry

(G-11755)
SWISSTEX COMPANY
220 61st St Ste 2 (07093-2931)
PHONE..................................201 861-8000
Robert Wolfe, *Owner*
EMP: 20 **EST:** 1934
SQ FT: 10,000
SALES (est): 950K **Privately Held**
SIC: 2339 2341 2251 Sportswear, women's; bathing suits: women's, misses' & juniors'; women's & children's nightwear; women's hosiery, except socks

(G-11756)
WEBER & DOEBRICH INC
Also Called: Wedo
119 61st St (07093-2909)
PHONE..................................201 868-6122
Jane Zellweger, *President*
EMP: 9 **EST:** 1935
SALES: 400K **Privately Held**
SIC: 2397 Schiffli machine embroideries

West Orange
Essex County

(G-11757)
A & F ELECTROPLATING INC
106 Ashland Ave (07052-5401)
PHONE..................................973 983-2459
Frank Chabala, *President*
Lucille Chabala, *Corp Secy*
Barry Chabala, *Vice Pres*
EMP: 4 **EST:** 1968
SQ FT: 6,000
SALES: 600K **Privately Held**
SIC: 3471 Electroplating of metals or formed products

(G-11758)
ALL-STATE FENCE INC
347 Mount Pleasant Ave # 300 (07052-2730)
PHONE..................................732 431-4944
Scott Skrable, *President*
Michael Skrable, *Vice Pres*
EMP: 35

SQ FT: 3,000
SALES (est): 6.2MM **Privately Held**
WEB: www.allstatefence.com
SIC: 5031 5211 1799 2499 Fencing, wood; fencing; fence construction; fencing, wood

(G-11759)
ASAP CONTAINERS NJ NY CORP
25 Mountain Dr (07052-4016)
PHONE..................................732 659-4402
Ronen Barak, *President*
EMP: 10
SALES: 1MM **Privately Held**
SIC: 3715 Demountable cargo containers

(G-11760)
AURAPLAYER USA INC
21 Dale Dr (07052-2005)
PHONE..................................617 879-9013
Mia Urman, *President*
Gwen Edwards, *Exec VP*
Yossi Nakash, *CTO*
EMP: 11
SQ FT: 550
SALES: 146K **Privately Held**
SIC: 7372 7379 Business oriented computer software; computer related consulting services
PA: Auraplayer Ltd
  13 Kehilat Zhytomyr
  Tel Aviv-Jaffa
  522 934-361

(G-11761)
B T O INDUSTRIES INC
11 Lenox Ter (07052-2623)
P.O. Box 1845, Bloomfield (07003-1845)
PHONE..................................973 243-0011
Bruce Osborne, *President*
EMP: 9
SQ FT: 500
SALES (est): 1.1MM **Privately Held**
SIC: 7311 8748 2721 Advertising agencies; publishing consultant; magazines: publishing only, not printed on site

(G-11762)
BILDISCO MFG INC
Also Called: Bildisco Door Mfg
21 Central Ave (07052-5298)
PHONE..................................973 673-2400
Salvatore Valente, *President*
EMP: 15
SQ FT: 25,000
SALES (est): 2.8MM **Privately Held**
SIC: 3442 2431 3429 Metal doors; doors, wood; door locks, bolts & checks

(G-11763)
COR PRODUCTS INC
20 Standish Ave (07052-5519)
PHONE..................................973 731-4952
Cindy Douglas, *Principal*
EMP: 5
SALES (est): 522.5K **Privately Held**
SIC: 2542 Fixtures, office: except wood

(G-11764)
COZZOLINO FURNITURE DESIGN INC
Also Called: Cozzolino Inc.
20 Standish Ave (07052-5519)
PHONE..................................973 731-9292
Michael Cozzolino, *President*
Steven Cozzolino, *Vice Pres*
EMP: 38
SQ FT: 22,000
SALES (est): 6.1MM **Privately Held**
WEB: www.cozzolino.com
SIC: 5712 2521 2511 2431 Cabinet work, custom; custom made furniture, except cabinets; wood office furniture; wood household furniture; millwork

(G-11765)
D2CF LLC (PA)
108 Coccio Dr (07052-4119)
PHONE..................................973 699-4111
Amanda Zazoff, *Principal*
EMP: 2 **EST:** 2015
SALES (est): 1.3MM **Publicly Held**
SIC: 3669 Emergency alarms

(G-11766)
DATALINK SOLUTIONS INC
27 Fundus Rd (07052-3510)
PHONE..................................973 731-9373
Lenny Jacobs, *Manager*
EMP: 10
SALES (est): 935.6K **Privately Held**
SIC: 3825 Network analyzers

(G-11767)
FIRST MOUNTAIN CONSULTING
Also Called: Mostly Software Development
3 Colony Ct (07052-4613)
PHONE..................................973 325-8480
Simeon Berman MD, *President*
Rose Hutter, *Corp Secy*
Carol Berman, *Vice Pres*
Carol Bromberg, *Vice Pres*
EMP: 4
SQ FT: 4,000
SALES: 450K **Privately Held**
SIC: 7372 Prepackaged software

(G-11768)
GENOMESAFE LLC
4 Linden Ave (07052-4721)
PHONE..................................203 676-3752
Kurt Rohloff,
EMP: 4
SALES (est): 91.3K **Privately Held**
SIC: 8748 7371 7372 Systems engineering consultant, ex. computer or professional; computer software systems analysis & design, custom; utility computer software

(G-11769)
HANGER PRSTHETCS & ORTHO INC
59 Main St Ste 111 (07052-5333)
PHONE..................................973 736-0628
Thomas P Kirk, *Principal*
EMP: 7
SALES (corp-wide): 1B **Publicly Held**
SIC: 3842 Limbs, artificial
HQ: Hanger Prosthetics & Orthotics, Inc.
  10910 Domain Dr Ste 300
  Austin TX 78758
  512 777-3800

(G-11770)
KNOCK KNOCK GIVE A SOCK INC
60 Stanford Ave (07052-2048)
PHONE..................................917 885-6983
Adina Lichtman, *Founder*
EMP: 4
SALES (est): 427.8K **Privately Held**
SIC: 2252 Socks

(G-11771)
LESILU PRODUCTIONS INC
Also Called: Hey Doll
70 Winding Way (07052-3800)
PHONE..................................212 947-6419
Steven Sunshine, *CEO*
Lesli Sunshine, *President*
Luanne Trovato, *Corp Secy*
▲ **EMP:** 6 **EST:** 2000
SALES (est): 1.2MM **Privately Held**
SIC: 3961 Costume jewelry, ex. precious metal & semiprecious stones

(G-11772)
MDR LLC
401 Pleasant Valley Way # 2 (07052-2951)
PHONE..................................973 731-7100
Richard Heyderman, *Mng Member*
Cecelia Rampolla, *Admin Asst*
EMP: 4
SALES (est): 717.7K **Privately Held**
SIC: 2541 Store & office display cases & fixtures

(G-11773)
MEASUREMENT CONTROL CORP
Also Called: Measurement & Computing Co
9 Cummings Cir (07052-2255)
PHONE..................................800 504-9010
Robert Friedman, *CEO*
Michael Levin, *General Mgr*
EMP: 5

SALES (est): 739.3K **Privately Held**
SIC: 3823 Industrial process measurement equipment

(G-11774)
NATIONAL COMMUNICATIONS INC
69 Washington St (07052-5538)
PHONE..................................973 325-3151
Andy Brooke, *President*
Glen Kaufman, *Office Mgr*
EMP: 30
SQ FT: 22,000
SALES (est): 5MM **Privately Held**
WEB: www.trynci.com
SIC: 5065 5045 3357 Telephone equipment; terminals, computer; nonferrous wiredrawing & insulating

(G-11775)
OMEGA HEAT TRANSFER CO INC
36 Rock Spring Ave (07052-2633)
PHONE..................................732 340-0023
Steven Simon, *Owner*
▲ **EMP:** 18
SALES (est): 3.4MM **Privately Held**
SIC: 2672 Adhesive papers, labels or tapes: from purchased material

(G-11776)
PACKAGING MACHINERY & EQP CO
181 Watson Ave (07052-6050)
PHONE..................................973 325-2418
James Lyle Clark, *President*
Sandeep Mohan, *General Mgr*
EMP: 6
SQ FT: 6,000
SALES (est): 1.2MM **Privately Held**
SIC: 3565 Packaging machinery

(G-11777)
PANTHER PRINTING INC
29 Northfield Ave (07052-5358)
PHONE..................................239 542-1050
Thomas Cusmano, *President*
Anthony Cusmano, *Vice Pres*
Donald Cusmano, *Treasurer*
Tom Coveney, *Sales Staff*
EMP: 5 **EST:** 1994
SQ FT: 3,000
SALES: 500K **Privately Held**
SIC: 2752 Commercial printing, offset

(G-11778)
PROGRESSIVE 4 COLOR LTD LBLTY
24 Park Ave (07052-5553)
PHONE..................................973 736-5800
Andrea Risoli,
Michael Risoli,
EMP: 5
SQ FT: 5,000
SALES (est): 900K **Privately Held**
WEB: www.progressiveprintingcorp.com
SIC: 2752 Commercial printing, offset

(G-11779)
TELUCA INC
414 Eagle Rock Ave (07052-4229)
PHONE..................................973 232-0002
Karen Celleri, *President*
Albert Celleri, *COO*
◆ **EMP:** 5
SALES (est): 684.8K **Privately Held**
SIC: 3999 Hair & hair-based products

(G-11780)
UMC INC
24 Burnett Ter (07052-3810)
P.O. Box 21268, Sarasota FL (34276-4268)
PHONE..................................973 325-0031
Arthur Burgess, *President*
Alexa Weiss, *Accounts Exec*
EMP: 5
SALES (est): 251.7K **Privately Held**
SIC: 2322 Underwear, men's & boys': made from purchased materials

(G-11781)
URSO FUEL CORP
10 Rollinson St (07052-4602)
PHONE..................................973 325-3324
Janet Urso, *Principal*

EMP: 4
SALES (est): 271.5K **Privately Held**
SIC: 2869 Fuels

West Windsor
Mercer County

(G-11782)
ORGANICA WATER INC (PA)
61 Prnceton Hightstown Rd (08550-1120)
PHONE....................................609 651-8885
ARI Raivetz, *CEO*
Robert Freudenberg, *COO*
Attila Bodnr, *Vice Pres*
Robert Jaworski, *CFO*
EMP: 14 EST: 2013
SQ FT: 2,000
SALES (est): 8MM **Privately Held**
SIC: 3589 4953 Water treatment equipment, industrial;

Westampton
Burlington County

(G-11783)
ALCON PRODUCTS INC
161 Burrs Rd (08060-5507)
PHONE....................................609 267-3898
Joseph F Matarese Jr, *President*
Robert Perkins, *Superintendent*
EMP: 12
SQ FT: 8,000
SALES (est): 1.3MM **Privately Held**
SIC: 3354 Aluminum extruded products

(G-11784)
ATLANTIC CAN COMPANY
1200 Highland Dr (08060-5118)
PHONE....................................609 518-9950
EMP: 6 EST: 2011
SALES (est): 508K **Privately Held**
SIC: 3086 Packaging & shipping materials, foamed plastic

(G-11785)
DIANE MATSON INC
Also Called: Heidelberg Press
49 Brighton Rd (08060-2326)
PHONE....................................609 288-6833
Ray Vozdovic, *President*
Diane Vozdovic, *Corp Secy*
EMP: 10 EST: 1958
SQ FT: 8,000
SALES (est): 800K **Privately Held**
SIC: 2752 Commercial printing, offset; offset & photolithographic printing

(G-11786)
JAG FOOTWEAR ACC & RET CORP
32 Springside Rd (08060-5611)
PHONE....................................609 845-1700
Gabriellen Yin, *Associate*
EMP: 19 **Privately Held**
SIC: 3144 Dress shoes, women's
HQ: Jag Footwear, Accessories And Retail
Corporation
411 W Putnam Ave Fl 3
Greenwich CT 06830
239 301-3001

(G-11787)
JERSEY ORDNANCE INC
600 Highland Dr Ste 602 (08060-5124)
PHONE....................................609 267-2112
Frank S Key, *President*
EMP: 6
SALES (corp-wide): 1.9MM **Privately
Held**
WEB: www.purestcolloids.com
SIC: 2023 Dietary supplements, dairy & non-dairy based
PA: Jersey Ordnance Inc
600 Highland Dr Ste 602
Westampton NJ 08060
609 267-2112

(G-11788)
PARIS CORPORATION NEW JERSEY (PA)
800 Highland Dr (08060-5109)
PHONE....................................609 265-9200
Gerard Toscani, *Principal*
Sharon Hennelly, *Principal*
John Murray, *Principal*
Don Showmaker, *Principal*
Bob Fredericks, *Maint Spvr*
◆ EMP: 80 EST: 1994
SQ FT: 130,000
SALES (est): 101.9MM **Privately Held**
SIC: 5112 2752 5063 Computer paper; business forms, lithographed; commercial printing, offset; batteries

(G-11789)
PRIMEPOINT LLC
2 Springside Rd (08060-5644)
PHONE....................................609 298-7373
Jon Hoffman, *Opers Mgr*
Patrick Toner, *Engineer*
Fred Wainwright, *Controller*
Raquel Champion, *Finance Mgr*
April Weiss, *Human Resources*
EMP: 21 EST: 1975
SALES (est): 2.6MM **Privately Held**
WEB: www.eprimepoint.com
SIC: 7372 8721 Prepackaged software; accounting, auditing & bookkeeping

(G-11790)
PROTOFORM INC
112 Burrs Rd (08060-4405)
PHONE....................................609 261-6920
Jeffrey Gazzara, *President*
EMP: 5
SQ FT: 8,000
SALES: 1MM **Privately Held**
SIC: 2834 Pharmaceutical preparations

(G-11791)
QUAD/GRAPHICS INC
80 Stemmers Ln (08060-5652)
PHONE....................................609 534-7308
Jim Coss, *Director*
EMP: 50
SALES (corp-wide): 4.1B **Publicly Held**
SIC: 2752 Commercial printing, offset
PA: Quad/Graphics Inc.
N61w23044 Harrys Way
Sussex WI 53089
414 566-6000

(G-11792)
SUN BASKET INC
600 Highland Dr Ste 614 (08060-5124)
PHONE....................................408 669-4418
Todd Smith, *Branch Mgr*
EMP: 175
SALES (corp-wide): 76MM **Privately
Held**
SIC: 2099 Almond pastes
PA: Sun Basket, Inc.
1170 Olinder Ct
San Jose CA 95122
408 669-4418

Westfield
Union County

(G-11793)
AMANTE INTERNATIONAL LTD
510 Codding Rd (07090-4100)
PHONE....................................908 518-1688
LI Chen Fu, *President*
Grace Lee, *Vice Pres*
▼ EMP: 10
SALES (est): 581.1K **Privately Held**
SIC: 2329 2339 Men's & boys' sportswear & athletic clothing; women's & misses' athletic clothing & sportswear

(G-11794)
ARNHEM INC
Also Called: Arnhem Group, The
1 Elm St Ste 1 # 1 (07090-2194)
PHONE....................................908 709-4045
Michael Bonner, *President*
▲ EMP: 9

SALES (est): 1.2MM **Privately Held**
WEB: www.arnhemgroup.com
SIC: 2087 Flavoring extracts & syrups

(G-11795)
BRUNSWICK HOT MIX CORP
Also Called: Weldon Asphalt Division
141 Central Ave (07090-2149)
PHONE....................................908 233-4444
Richard Weldon, *President*
Bill Weldon, *Vice Pres*
William Weldon, *Vice Pres*
Robert Weldon III, *Treasurer*
Richard Myers, *Admin Sec*
EMP: 80
SALES (est): 4.3MM **Privately Held**
SIC: 1611 7513 2951 Surfacing & paving; truck rental & leasing, no drivers; asphalt paving mixtures & blocks

(G-11796)
CARBOLINE COMPANY
449 South Ave E (07090-1468)
PHONE....................................908 233-3150
Richard French, *Opers-Prdtn-Mfg*
EMP: 15
SALES (corp-wide): 5.5B **Publicly Held**
SIC: 2851 Paints & allied products
HQ: Carboline Company
2150 Schuetz Rd Fl 1
Saint Louis MO 63146
314 644-1000

(G-11797)
FOLDTEX II LTD
Also Called: Artistic Creations
705 E Broad St (07090-2001)
PHONE....................................908 928-0919
Bernard Formal, *President*
▲ EMP: 20
SQ FT: 61,000
SALES: 700K **Privately Held**
SIC: 3999 5131 Christmas trees, artificial; novelties, bric-a-brac & hobby kits; piece goods & notions

(G-11798)
GEORGE BRUMMER
Also Called: Brummer's Chocolates
125 E Broad St (07090-2275)
PHONE....................................908 232-1904
George Brummer, *Owner*
EMP: 4 EST: 1989
SQ FT: 2,000
SALES (est): 306K **Privately Held**
SIC: 2066 5441 Chocolate candy, solid; confectionery produced for direct sale on the premises

(G-11799)
HANDLER MANUFACTURING COMPANY
612 North Ave E (07090-1400)
P.O. Box 520 (07091-0520)
PHONE....................................908 233-7796
William A Lehman, *CEO*
Lorraine Lehman, *Corp Secy*
▲ EMP: 26 EST: 1920
SQ FT: 36,000
SALES (est): 5.8MM **Privately Held**
WEB: www.handlermfg.com
SIC: 3843 3545 3564 3821 Dental laboratory equipment; machine tool accessories; purification & dust collection equipment; laboratory apparatus & furniture

(G-11800)
HEARD WOODWORKING LLC
31 Normandy Dr (07090-3431)
PHONE....................................908 232-3978
Russell Heard, *President*
Annemarie Heard, *Partner*
EMP: 7
SALES (est): 646.4K **Privately Held**
SIC: 2431 Millwork

(G-11801)
PRINT TECH LLC
Also Called: Sign Tech
349 South Ave E (07090-1465)
PHONE....................................908 232-0767
John Szalkowski, *Manager*
EMP: 4

SALES (corp-wide): 13.3MM **Privately
Held**
SIC: 2752 Commercial printing, offset
PA: Print Tech Llc
49 Fadem Rd
Springfield NJ 07081
908 232-2287

(G-11802)
ROMARK LOGISTICS CES LLC (PA)
Also Called: Jtp Romark Logistics
822 South Ave W (07090-1460)
PHONE....................................908 789-2800
Marc D Lebovitz, *President*
Sharon McStine, *General Mgr*
Amy S Lebovitz, *Exec VP*
Rob Benz, *Transptn Dir*
Kevin Gamber, *Opers Mgr*
EMP: 29
SALES (est): 92.5MM **Privately Held**
SIC: 4225 4789 2631 General warehousing; cargo loading & unloading services; container, packaging & boxboard

(G-11803)
S M Z ENTERPRISES INC
Also Called: Bagel Chateau
223 South Ave E (07090-1456)
PHONE....................................908 232-1921
Scott Zilberberg, *President*
Mara Zilberberg, *Admin Sec*
EMP: 10 EST: 1980
SQ FT: 2,500
SALES: 530K **Privately Held**
SIC: 5812 2051 5461 American restaurant; bagels, fresh or frozen; bagels

(G-11804)
UNIVERSAL VENDING MGT LLC
425 North Ave E Ste 2 (07090-1537)
P.O. Box 130 (07091-0130)
PHONE....................................908 233-4373
Bruce Lipkin, *President*
Rudy Marano, *COO*
Robert Katz, *Exec VP*
Len Krieger, *CFO*
Janet Cullen, *Accounts Exec*
EMP: 18
SQ FT: 5,000
SALES: 13MM **Privately Held**
WEB: www.uvmweb.com
SIC: 8741 3581 Management services; automatic vending machines

(G-11805)
WATTHUNG COMMUNICATIONS INC
Also Called: The Westfield Leader
251 North Ave W Ste 7 (07090-1499)
P.O. Box 250 (07091-0250)
PHONE....................................908 232-4407
Horace R Corbin, *President*
David Corbin, *Sls & Mktg Exec*
EMP: 10
SQ FT: 2,000
SALES (est): 470K **Privately Held**
WEB: www.letitrip.org
SIC: 2711 Newspapers: publishing only, not printed on site

(G-11806)
WELDON MATERIALS INC (PA)
Also Called: Weldon Concrete Co.
141 Central Ave (07090-2189)
PHONE....................................908 233-4444
Richard T Weldon, *President*
William Weldon, *Vice Pres*
Eileen Mooney, *CIO*
EMP: 40
SQ FT: 3,000
SALES (est): 33.5MM **Privately Held**
WEB: www.weldonmaterials.com
SIC: 3273 Ready-mixed concrete

(G-11807)
WELDON QUARRY CO LLC
141 Central Ave (07090-2149)
PHONE....................................908 233-4444
Bill Annelli, *Executive*
William Weldon,
Norbert Weldon,
Richard T Weldon,
Robert F Weldon, ,
EMP: 50

SALES (est): 7.5MM **Privately Held**
SIC: 3273 Ready-mixed concrete

(G-11808)
WEST DRY INDUSTRIES INC
755 W Broad St (07090-4464)
P.O. Box 2595, Plainfield (07060-0595)
PHONE..........................908 757-4400
John Onacki, *President*
▲ EMP: 4
SALES (est): 560K **Privately Held**
SIC: 2819 Catalysts, chemical

Westville
Gloucester County

(G-11809)
ABC HOLDINGS INC
1000 Delsea Dr Ste F3 (08093-1567)
PHONE..........................856 219-3444
Christopher Smith, *Principal*
EMP: 12
SALES: 1.5MM **Privately Held**
SIC: 2431 Millwork

(G-11810)
ARTEX KNITTING MILLS INC
300 Harvard Ave (08093-1445)
P.O. Box 183 (08093-0183)
PHONE..........................856 456-2800
Arthur Pottash, *President*
Bernard Gerbarg, *Vice Pres*
◆ EMP: 80 EST: 1923
SQ FT: 80,000
SALES (est): 15.5MM **Privately Held**
WEB: www.artexknit.com
SIC: 2253 Hats & headwear, knit; scarves & mufflers, knit; neckties, knit

(G-11811)
CORNELL CRANE MFG LTD
224 Llenroc Ln (08093-1433)
P.O. Box 807 (08093)
PHONE..........................609 742-1900
Dolores Cornell, *President*
Thomas Kanzler, *Vice Pres*
Kevin Brockway, *Treasurer*
EMP: 10
SQ FT: 5,000
SALES: 1MM **Privately Held**
SIC: 3531 Cranes

(G-11812)
EAST COAST RUBBER PRODUCTS
1000 Delsea Dr Ste D2 (08093-1506)
PHONE..........................856 384-2747
John McDermott, *President*
EMP: 4
SQ FT: 2,400
SALES: 400K **Privately Held**
SIC: 3053 Oil seals, rubber

(G-11813)
EDGAR C BARCUS CO INC
416 Gateway Blvd (08093)
PHONE..........................856 456-0204
Leo Laskowski, *President*
Regina Laskowski, *Treasurer*
Lauren Laskowski, *Admin Sec*
EMP: 17 EST: 1949
SQ FT: 5,000
SALES (est): 1.7MM **Privately Held**
SIC: 3544 Dies, steel rule

(G-11814)
ENERGY COMPANY INC
Also Called: Energy Combustion Systems
50 Cutler Ave Ste 6 (08093-1577)
P.O. Box 68 (08093-0068)
PHONE..........................856 742-1916
Martin E Mittleman, *CEO*
Martin L Mittleman, *President*
Robert Smith, *Corp Secy*
Vincent Santangelo, *Vice Pres*
EMP: 20 EST: 1973
SALES: 3.7MM **Privately Held**
WEB: www.energycombustionsystems.com
SIC: 1799 3433 1711 Welding on site; burners, furnaces, boilers & stokers; boiler maintenance contractor

(G-11815)
HERITAGE SERVICE SOLUTIONS LLC
Also Called: Hawks and Co
1000 Delsea Dr Ste A1 (08093-1506)
PHONE..........................856 845-7311
Martin A Rosica, *Mng Member*
Kathy Lakutis, *Manager*
Dona Dymon,
EMP: 15 EST: 2005
SALES (est): 3.9MM **Privately Held**
WEB: www.hawksandco.com
SIC: 3585 Refrigeration & heating equipment

(G-11816)
HYDRO-MECHANICAL SYSTEMS INC
1030 Delsea Dr Unit 8 (08093-1590)
P.O. Box 87 (08093-0087)
PHONE..........................856 848-8888
Howard Rosenbloom, *President*
Anita Carney, *General Mgr*
Steve Rosenbloom, *General Mgr*
Mario Gematria, *Vice Pres*
Steven Rosenbloom, *Vice Pres*
▲ EMP: 17
SQ FT: 20,000
SALES (est): 3.7MM **Privately Held**
WEB: www.hydromechanical.com
SIC: 3292 3621 3568 3511 Clutch facings, asbestos; motors & generators; power transmission equipment; turbines & turbine generator set units, complete

(G-11817)
INTELCO (PA)
Also Called: Barkercraft
250 Harvard Ave (08093-1443)
P.O. Box 9 (08093-0009)
PHONE..........................856 456-6755
Michael E Wells, *President*
EMP: 69
SQ FT: 25,000
SALES (est): 20.2MM **Privately Held**
WEB: www.intelcousa.com
SIC: 2499 2821 2541 Kitchen, bathroom & household ware: wood; plastics materials & resins; wood partitions & fixtures

(G-11818)
LAWN MEDIC INC
Also Called: Lawn Medic of Delaware Valley
512 River Dr (08093-1024)
P.O. Box 310, Haddon Heights (08035-0310)
PHONE..........................856 742-1111
Peter Galantic, *Manager*
EMP: 4
SALES (est): 248.1K
SALES (corp-wide): 1.8MM **Privately Held**
WEB: www.lawnmedic.com
SIC: 0782 3524 2752 Lawn care services; lawn & garden equipment; commercial printing, offset
PA: Lawn Medic Inc
10 Gates St
Bergen NY 14416
585 494-1462

(G-11819)
RELIABLE WOOD PRODUCTS LLC
145 Broadway (08093-1148)
PHONE..........................856 456-6300
EMP: 79
SALES (corp-wide): 51.5MM **Privately Held**
WEB: www.reliablewoodproducts.com
SIC: 2611 Pulp manufactured from waste or recycled paper
PA: Reliable Wood Products, Llc
398 Lincoln Blvd Ste C2
Middlesex NJ 08846
973 969-3299

(G-11820)
ROYALTY PRESS INC
Also Called: Royalty Press Group
165 Broadway (08093-1148)
PHONE..........................856 663-2288
Scott Lang, *President*
Mike Kravitz, *Vice Pres*
EMP: 35

SALES (est): 5.3MM **Privately Held**
WEB: www.royaltypress.com
SIC: 2759 Commercial printing

(G-11821)
TECHNOL INC
1030 Delsea Dr Unit 8e (08093-1590)
P.O. Box 87 (08093-0087)
PHONE..........................856 848-5480
Howard Rosenbloom, *President*
Nathan Goodman, *Treasurer*
EMP: 18
SQ FT: 10,000
SALES (est): 2.3MM **Privately Held**
SIC: 3594 5084 Fluid power pumps & motors; hydraulic systems equipment & supplies

(G-11822)
THERMAL CHEK INC
912 Broadway (08093-1435)
PHONE..........................856 742-1200
Joseph E Heaton Sr, *President*
Joseph E Heaton Jr, *Vice Pres*
EMP: 24
SQ FT: 55,500
SALES (est): 4.2MM **Privately Held**
SIC: 3089 5031 Windows, plastic; fences, gates & accessories: plastic; lumber, plywood & millwork

(G-11823)
VINELAND SPECIALTY FOODS L L C
201 Harvard Ave (08093-1444)
P.O. Box 187 (08093-0187)
PHONE..........................856 742-5001
Marvin Raab,
EMP: 6
SQ FT: 19,300
SALES: 1.5MM **Privately Held**
SIC: 2038 Ethnic foods, frozen

Westwood
Bergen County

(G-11824)
ALLIANCE HAND & PHYSICAL
24 Booker St Ste 3 (07675-2632)
PHONE..........................201 822-0100
Pam Muscara, *President*
EMP: 16
SALES (est): 2.9MM **Privately Held**
SIC: 3842 Whirlpool baths, hydrotherapy equipment; hydrotherapy equipment

(G-11825)
ALPINE MACHINE & TOOL CORP
42 Bergenline Ave (07675-3115)
PHONE..........................201 666-0959
Thomas Wanner, *President*
EMP: 10
SQ FT: 3,000
SALES (est): 1.3MM **Privately Held**
SIC: 3965 3728 Fasteners; airframe assemblies, except for guided missiles

(G-11826)
AMERICAN MACHINE SPC NJ LLC
51 Bergenline Ave (07675-3105)
PHONE..........................201 664-0006
Brian Peltier,
EMP: 25
SALES (est): 4.4MM **Privately Held**
SIC: 3599 Machine shop, jobbing & repair

(G-11827)
ASIAMERICA GROUP INC
245 Old Hook Rd (07675-3172)
PHONE..........................201 497-5993
Yumin Zhang, *Principal*
EMP: 6
SALES (est): 108.9K **Privately Held**
SIC: 2834 Vitamin, nutrient & hematinic preparations for human use

(G-11828)
AUTO-STAK SYSTEMS INC (PA)
49 Old Hook Rd (07675-2406)
PHONE..........................201 358-9070
Mark Ritz, *President*
EMP: 5

SQ FT: 600
SALES (est): 520.9K **Privately Held**
WEB: www.autostak.com
SIC: 2542 Racks, merchandise display or storage: except wood

(G-11829)
CH TECHNOLOGIES USA INC
778 Carver Ave (07675-2605)
PHONE..........................201 666-2335
Rudolph Jaeger, *President*
Bridget Jaeger, *COO*
Janet Squilanti, *CFO*
EMP: 9 EST: 1987
SQ FT: 500
SALES (est): 1.1MM **Privately Held**
WEB: www.toxics.com
SIC: 3841 8748 0782 Surgical & medical instruments; business consulting; landscape contractors

(G-11830)
E-VENTS REGISTRATION LLC
40 Tillman St (07675-2611)
PHONE..........................201 722-9221
Vanessa Gollaher, *Sales Dir*
Jason Brookins, *Software Dev*
Alan Hanstein, *Director*
Jeffrey Posner,
EMP: 10
SQ FT: 2,000
SALES (est): 1.2MM **Privately Held**
SIC: 3999 Identification badges & insignia

(G-11831)
FRANKLIN GRAPHICS INC
Also Called: Franklin Press
60 Brickell Ave (07675-2044)
PHONE..........................201 935-5900
Stanley Baguchinsky, *President*
EMP: 6
SALES (est): 706K **Privately Held**
SIC: 2752 Commercial printing, lithographic

(G-11832)
JVS CHRISTMAS LIGHTING
15 Charles St Ste 4 (07675-2115)
PHONE..........................201 664-4022
EMP: 4 EST: 2014
SALES (est): 269.4K **Privately Held**
SIC: 3699 5023 Christmas tree lighting sets, electric; decorative home furnishings & supplies; decorating supplies

(G-11833)
KRISTINE DEER INC
Also Called: K-Deer
174 Westwood Ave (07675-1708)
PHONE..........................201 497-3333
Kristine Deer, *President*
EMP: 5 EST: 2013
SALES (est): 222.9K **Privately Held**
SIC: 7999 2389 Yoga instruction; men's miscellaneous accessories

(G-11834)
LIETH HOLDINGS LLC (PA)
Also Called: Westwood Sleep Centers
30 Westwood Ave Ste A (07675-1756)
PHONE..........................201 358-8282
Dion Vonderlieth, *Mng Member*
Leslie Vonderlieth, *Mng Member*
EMP: 9
SALES (est): 1.1MM **Privately Held**
SIC: 5712 2515 Mattresses; sleep furniture

(G-11835)
MEDTEC SERVICES LLC
67 Woodland Ave (07675-3114)
PHONE..........................201 722-9696
Vito Grisanti, *CEO*
EMP: 9
SALES (est): 565.4K **Privately Held**
SIC: 3841 Surgical & medical instruments

(G-11836)
OBERG & LINDQUIST CORP (PA)
671 Broadway (07675-1695)
PHONE..........................201 664-1300
John Oberg, *President*
Debra A Oberg, *Admin Sec*
EMP: 25 EST: 1945
SQ FT: 14,000

SALES (est): 2.6MM **Privately Held**
WEB: www.obergandlindquist.com
SIC: 2434 5722 Wood kitchen cabinets; household appliance stores

(G-11837)
PACKETSTORM COMMUNICATIONS INC
6 Sullivan St (07675-3171)
P.O. Box 18162, Sarasota FL (34276-1162)
PHONE..............................732 840-3871
Bill Luthy, *President*
Jim Grikas, *Sr Software Eng*
EMP: 10
SQ FT: 5,000
SALES: 4.3MM **Privately Held**
WEB: www.packetstorm.com
SIC: 3661 Telephone & telegraph apparatus

(G-11838)
PASCACK PRESS
69 Woodland Ave (07675-3114)
PHONE..............................201 664-2105
George Harcher, *President*
EMP: 7
SALES (est): 351.6K **Privately Held**
SIC: 2711 Newspapers, publishing & printing

(G-11839)
PASCACK VALLEY COPY CENTER
Also Called: Valley Prtg & Graphic Design
41 Bergenline Ave Ste 1 (07675-3179)
PHONE..............................201 664-1917
Shawn Jeffas, *President*
EMP: 6
SALES: 480K **Privately Held**
SIC: 2752 Commercial printing, offset

(G-11840)
QUANTUM VECTOR CORP
700 Broadway (07675-1683)
PHONE..............................201 870-1782
Isidor Farish, *President*
EMP: 4
SQ FT: 4,000
SALES (est): 365K **Privately Held**
SIC: 2211 3873 Apparel & outerwear fabrics, cotton; watches, clocks, watchcases & parts

(G-11841)
RADHA BEAUTY PRODUCTS LLC
220 Kinderkamack Rd Ste C (07675-3601)
PHONE..............................732 993-6242
Jose Bernardo De La Vega, *CEO*
Rebeka Letch, *Exec VP*
EMP: 7
SALES: 204.1K **Privately Held**
SIC: 2844 Perfumes, natural or synthetic

(G-11842)
RE SYSTEMS GROUP INC
700 Broadway Ste 204 (07675-1674)
PHONE..............................201 883-1572
Ira Gidon, *Treasurer*
EMP: 5
SQ FT: 4,000
SALES (est): 874.8K **Privately Held**
WEB: www.resystemsgroup.com
SIC: 7372 7379 Prepackaged software; computer related consulting services

(G-11843)
RINGFEDER PWR TRANSM USA CORP
165 Carver Ave (07675-2604)
PHONE..............................201 666-3320
Ross Rivard, *President*
Gordon Raspe, *CFO*
▲ EMP: 23
SQ FT: 15,840
SALES (est): 13.3MM
SALES (corp-wide): 4.7MM **Privately Held**
WEB: www.ringfeder.com
SIC: 5084 3545 Industrial machinery & equipment; machine tool attachments & accessories

HQ: Ringfeder Power-Transmission Gmbh
Werner-Heisenberg-Str. 18
GroB-Umstadt 64823
607 893-850

(G-11844)
SCANTRON CORPORATION
99 Kinderkamack Rd # 211 (07675-3012)
PHONE..............................201 666-7009
Bill Looney, *Principal*
EMP: 6 **Privately Held**
WEB: www.scantron.com
SIC: 3577 Optical scanning devices
HQ: Scantron Corporation
1313 Lone Oak Rd
Eagan MN 55121
651 683-6000

(G-11845)
SOCK COMPANY INC (PA)
40 Carver Ave (07675-3205)
P.O. Box 5122, Clinton (08809-0122)
PHONE..............................201 307-0675
Eileen J Tabano, *President*
Richard V Tabano, *Corp Secy*
Jennifer E Seamans, *Vice Pres*
James R Tabano, *Vice Pres*
Vincent R Tabano, *Vice Pres*
EMP: 24
SQ FT: 8,500
SALES (est): 4.8MM **Privately Held**
WEB: www.amerisox.com
SIC: 5632 5611 5621 5641 Dancewear; hosiery; lingerie (outerwear); lingerie & corsets (underwear); men's & boys' clothing stores; clothing, sportswear, men's & boys'; women's sportswear; children's & infants' wear stores; stockings: men's, women's & children's; hosiery

(G-11846)
US AIR POWER SYSTEMS
56 Otoole St (07675-3435)
PHONE..............................201 892-5235
Vijay Trivedi, *Principal*
EMP: 4
SALES (est): 522.5K **Privately Held**
SIC: 3822 Pressure controllers, air-conditioning system type

(G-11847)
VERIZON COMMUNICATIONS INC
285 Old Hook Rd (07675-3102)
PHONE..............................201 666-9934
John Eric, *Branch Mgr*
EMP: 45
SALES (corp-wide): 130.8B **Publicly Held**
WEB: www.verizon.com
SIC: 4813 4812 2741 8721 Data telephone communications; local telephone communications; voice telephone communications; cellular telephone services; directories, telephone: publishing only, not printed on site; billing & bookkeeping service; computer integrated systems design
PA: Verizon Communications Inc.
1095 Ave Of The Americas
New York NY 10036
212 395-1000

(G-11848)
YOURE SO INVITED LLC
260 Westwood Ave (07675-1716)
PHONE..............................201 664-8600
Linda Del Santo, *Owner*
EMP: 4 EST: 2009
SALES (est): 397.2K **Privately Held**
SIC: 2754 Stationery & invitation printing, gravure

(G-11849)
ZEKELMAN INDUSTRIES INC
Also Called: Wheatland Tube Co
90 Hurlbut St (07675-2915)
PHONE..............................724 342-6851
Bob Bussiere, *General Mgr*
Pat Shovlin, *Manager*
David Hoffman, *Manager*
EMP: 77 **Privately Held**
SIC: 3317 Steel pipe & tubes
PA: Zekelman Industries, Inc.
227 W Monroe St Ste 2600
Chicago IL 60606

(G-11850)
AMS PRODUCTS LLC
Also Called: Object Design
105 W Dewey Ave Ste 305 (07885-1659)
PHONE..............................973 442-5790
Amy Kim,
Mungjung Kim,
▲ EMP: 10
SQ FT: 14,000
SALES (est): 2MM **Privately Held**
WEB: www.laundrybagsny.com
SIC: 2393 2392 Textile bags; pillows, bed: made from purchased materials

(G-11851)
AMS TOY INTL INC
105 W Dewey Ave (07885-1660)
PHONE..............................973 442-5790
Amy Kim, *President*
Mong Jung Kim, *Vice Pres*
▲ EMP: 30
SQ FT: 12,000
SALES (est): 2.2MM **Privately Held**
WEB: www.amstoy.com
SIC: 2392 5092 Cushions & pillows; toys & hobby goods & supplies

(G-11852)
APPLIED RESOURCES CORP (PA)
105 W Dewey Ave Ste 311 (07885-1659)
PHONE..............................973 328-3882
Matthew Colello, *President*
George Haley, *QC Mgr*
▼ EMP: 20
SQ FT: 6,500
SALES: 3MM **Privately Held**
WEB: www.appliedresource.com
SIC: 3679 3825 3549 Electronic circuits; test equipment for electronic & electrical circuits; metalworking machinery

(G-11853)
BOLTTECH MANNINGS INC
Also Called: Bolttech-Mannings
321 Richard Mine Rd Ste 1 (07885-1838)
PHONE..............................973 537-1576
Peter Smith, *Branch Mgr*
EMP: 55
SALES (corp-wide): 462.1MM **Privately Held**
SIC: 3585 Heating equipment, complete
HQ: Bolttech Mannings, Inc.
501 Mosside Blvd
North Versailles PA 15137
724 872-4873

(G-11854)
CONVERTECH INC
353 Richard Mine Rd Ste 4 (07885-1800)
PHONE..............................973 328-1850
Larry Taitel, *President*
Robert Gensheimer, *General Mgr*
Celeste Recanati, *Production*
Frank Dolivera, *Engineer*
Lisa Dobak, *Controller*
▲ EMP: 38
SQ FT: 27,000
SALES (est): 10.3MM **Privately Held**
WEB: www.convertech.com
SIC: 3555 Printing trades machinery

(G-11855)
DEFINED PRO MACHINING LLC
105 W Dewey Ave Ste 419 (07885-1669)
PHONE..............................973 891-1038
Henrietta Fidler,
Mikheil Fidler,
EMP: 5
SQ FT: 4,000
SALES: 400K **Privately Held**
SIC: 3545 7389 Precision tools, machinists';

(G-11856)
DEZINE LINE INC
17 Robert St Ste B2 (07885-1922)
PHONE..............................973 989-1009
Steve Mattero, *President*

EMP: 10
SQ FT: 3,000
SALES: 593.6K **Privately Held**
WEB: www.dezineline.com
SIC: 2759 5699 2395 Screen printing; customized clothing & apparel; embroidery products, except schiffli machine

(G-11857)
EB MACHINE CORP
Also Called: Ebmachine
320 Richard Mine Rd (07885-1802)
PHONE..............................973 442-7729
Emil Boller, *President*
EMP: 7
SALES (est): 873.8K **Privately Held**
SIC: 3544 Industrial molds

(G-11858)
FOSSIL FUEL
105 W Dewey Ave (07885-1640)
PHONE..............................973 366-9111
Stephen Porcello, *Principal*
EMP: 5
SALES (est): 407.5K **Privately Held**
SIC: 2869 Fuels

(G-11859)
GAS DRYING INC
355 W Dewey Ave (07885-1305)
P.O. Box 504 (07885-0504)
PHONE..............................973 361-2212
Gary Behrens, *President*
EMP: 10 EST: 1957
SQ FT: 25,000
SALES (est): 1.7MM **Privately Held**
WEB: www.gasdrying.com
SIC: 3563 5084 Air & gas compressors including vacuum pumps; industrial machinery & equipment

(G-11860)
JAMES A STANLICK JR
Also Called: Precision Welding
845 Berkshire Valley Rd (07885-1525)
PHONE..............................973 366-7316
James Stanlick, *Owner*
Rich Campanella, *Manager*
Barbara Jacobson, *Manager*
EMP: 5
SQ FT: 6,500
SALES: 900K **Privately Held**
SIC: 3444 3446 1799 Sheet metalwork; stairs, staircases, stair treads: prefabricated metal; welding on site

(G-11861)
LONGO ELCTRICAL-MECHANICAL INC (PA)
Also Called: Longo Industries
1 Harry Shupe Blvd (07885-1646)
P.O. Box 511 (07885-0511)
PHONE..............................973 537-0400
Joseph M Longo, *Ch of Bd*
Andy Fuls, *Plant Engr*
Richard Dewalk, *Treasurer*
Pam Longo, *Admin Sec*
▲ EMP: 98
SQ FT: 60,000
SALES: 21MM **Privately Held**
WEB: www.longo-ind.com
SIC: 5063 5084 7694 Electrical supplies; pumps & pumping equipment; armature rewinding shops

(G-11862)
MARTIN TOOL COMPANY INC
60 State Route 15 S (07885-1227)
PHONE..............................973 361-9212
Lewis Martin, *President*
EMP: 12
SQ FT: 14,000
SALES (est): 1.6MM **Privately Held**
SIC: 3545 Precision tools, machinists'

(G-11863)
NATIONAL FLAG & DISPLAY CO INC
Also Called: Metro Flag Co
353 Richard Mine Rd Ste 5 (07885-1800)
PHONE..............................973 366-1776
Donald Bornstein, *Vice Pres*
EMP: 32

GEOGRAPHIC

SALES (corp-wide): 7.4MM **Privately Held**
WEB: www.nationalflag.com
SIC: 2399 Flags, fabric
PA: National Flag & Display Co., Inc.
　　30 E 21st St Apt 2b
　　New York NY 10010
　　212 228-6600

(G-11864)
NOWAK INC
17 Robert St (07885-1922)
PHONE..............................973 366-7208
Mark Nowak, *President*
EMP: 15
SQ FT: 5,000
SALES (est): 3.4MM **Privately Held**
SIC: 3556 3599 Food products machinery;
　　machine shop, jobbing & repair

(G-11865)
ODYSSEY AUTO SPECIALTY INC
317 Richard Mine Rd (07885-1837)
PHONE..............................973 328-2667
Laurence J Kahan, *President*
▲ EMP: 34
SQ FT: 19,000
SALES (est): 8MM **Privately Held**
WEB: www.odysseyauto.com
SIC: 3711 Automobile assembly, including
　　specialty automobiles

(G-11866)
PEACE MEDICAL INC
105 W Dewey Ave Unit 1-2 (07885-1643)
PHONE..............................800 537-9564
Tim Fegan, *President*
▲ EMP: 10
SQ FT: 10,000
SALES (est): 2.2MM **Privately Held**
WEB: www.peacemedical.com
SIC: 3842 Surgical appliances & supplies

(G-11867)
PHOENIX INDUSTRIES LLC
105 W Dewey Ave Ste 204 (07885-1642)
P.O. Box 416 (07885-0416)
PHONE..............................973 366-4199
Dean Mathews, *Accounts Mgr*
Brent Norcia, *Accounts Mgr*
Judith Morris, *Office Mgr*
Vincent Norcia,
Brent Nocrcia,
EMP: 5
SQ FT: 3,000
SALES: 1MM **Privately Held**
SIC: 2821 Plastics materials & resins

(G-11868)
PRO PACK INC
Also Called: Dynaclear Packaging
321 Richard Mine Rd Ste 1 (07885-1838)
PHONE..............................973 665-8333
Piero Quercia, *CEO*
Barbara Kaywork, *CFO*
▲ EMP: 18
SALES (est): 7.4MM **Privately Held**
WEB: www.shrinkfilm.com
SIC: 5084 5199 3565 Packaging machin-
　　ery & equipment; packaging materials;
　　packing & wrapping machinery

(G-11869)
REFRESCO US INC
92 N Main St (07885-1607)
PHONE..............................973 361-9794
Barbara Vance, *Production*
David Alexander, *Manager*
EMP: 100
SALES (corp-wide): 3.3B **Privately Held**
SIC: 2033 7389 Fruit juices: packaged in
　　cans, jars, etc.; packaging & labeling
　　services
HQ: Refresco Us, Inc.
　　6655 S Lewis Ave
　　Tulsa OK 74136
　　918 524-4029

(G-11870)
SAFE-STRAP COMPANY INC
105 W Dewey Ave Ste 410 (07885-1669)
PHONE..............................973 442-4623
Paul F Giampavolo, *President*
Raymond J Buonomo, *Vice Pres*
Rita Chapa, *Sales Staff*
Natalie Interdonato, *Sales Staff*

Cindi Falker, *Manager*
▲ EMP: 50
SALES (est): 8.9MM **Privately Held**
WEB: www.safestrap.com
SIC: 3199 Safety belts, leather

(G-11871)
SUNSET PRINTING AND ENGRV CORP
Also Called: Sunset Stationers
10 Kice Ave (07885-2217)
PHONE..............................973 537-9600
Mitchel Wainer, *Ch of Bd*
Deron Wainer, *Principal*
Jared Wainer, *Principal*
Robert Wainer, *Corp Secy*
Mitch Wainer, *Marketing Staff*
EMP: 49 EST: 1945
SQ FT: 24,000
SALES (est): 7MM **Privately Held**
WEB: www.sunsetcorpid.com
SIC: 2759 Engraving; commercial
　　printing, lithographic

(G-11872)
TREASURE CHEST CORP
10 N Main St Ste 1 (07885-2248)
PHONE..............................973 328-7747
Curtis P Morgan, *President*
James Harmke, *Vice Pres*
EMP: 4
SALES (est): 338.6K **Privately Held**
SIC: 2741 Miscellaneous publishing

(G-11873)
TRIANGLE AUTOMATIC INC
105 W Dewey Ave Ste 305 (07885-1659)
PHONE..............................973 625-3830
Zbigniew Rossa, *President*
EMP: 4
SQ FT: 2,000
SALES (est): 440K **Privately Held**
SIC: 3451 Screw machine products

(G-11874)
TURUL BOOKBINDERY INC
60 State Route 15 S (07885-1227)
PHONE..............................973 361-2810
Margit Rahill, *President*
EMP: 5 EST: 1932
SQ FT: 3,800
SALES: 220K **Privately Held**
WEB: www.thebookbindery.com
SIC: 2789 2759 3469 3544 Bookbinding
　　& repairing: trade, edition, library, etc.;
　　embossing on paper; metal stampings;
　　paper cutting dies

Whippany
Morris County

(G-11875)
3M COMPANY
140 Algonquin Pkwy (07981-1633)
PHONE..............................973 884-2500
Vic Ison, *Plant Mgr*
Julie Joy, *Branch Mgr*
EMP: 324
SALES (corp-wide): 32.7B **Publicly Held**
SIC: 3841 3842 3291 2842 Surgical in-
　　struments & apparatus; bandages &
　　dressings; bandages: plastic, muslin,
　　plaster of paris, etc.; dressings, surgical;
　　gauze, surgical; abrasive products;
　　coated abrasive products; pads, scouring:
　　soap impregnated; specialty cleaning,
　　polishes & sanitation goods
PA: 3m Company
　　3m Center
　　Saint Paul MN 55144
　　651 733-1110

(G-11876)
ABBOTT LABORATORIES PARSIPANNY
30 N Jefferson Rd (07981-1030)
PHONE..............................973 428-4000
Clive Bennett, *Principal*
◆ EMP: 5
SALES (est): 424.9K **Privately Held**
SIC: 2834 Pharmaceutical preparations

(G-11877)
AGWAY ENERGY SERVICES LLC
240 State Route 10 (07981-2105)
PHONE..............................973 887-5300
EMP: 28
SQ FT: 86,000
SALES (est): 2.2MM **Publicly Held**
WEB: www.hometownhearthandgrill.com
SIC: 1311 5261 Natural gas production;
　　nurseries & garden centers
HQ: Gas Connection, Llc
　　9801 Se 82nd Ave
　　Portland OR 97086

(G-11878)
BAYER HEALTHCARE LLC (DH)
100 Bayer Blvd (07981-1544)
P.O. Box 915 (07981-0915)
PHONE..............................862 404-3000
Gregory S Babe, *CEO*
Angie Toriggino, *Business Mgr*
Antje Woodman, *Business Mgr*
Susan Guzzo, *Counsel*
Michael Parrish, *VP Govt Rls*
◆ EMP: 800
SALES (est): 2B
SALES (corp-wide): 45.3B **Privately Held**
WEB: www.bayerhealthcare.com
SIC: 2834 8731 3845 3841 Pharmaceuti-
　　cal preparations; commercial physical re-
　　search; electromedical equipment;
　　surgical & medical instruments
HQ: Bayer Corporation
　　100 Bayer Rd Bldg 14
　　Pittsburgh PA 15205
　　412 777-2000

(G-11879)
BAYER HLTHCARE PHRMCTICALS INC
100 Bayer Blvd (07981-1544)
P.O. Box 915 (07981-0915)
PHONE..............................862 404-3000
Leslie Perrell, *Manager*
Willy Scherf, *Director*
Jennifer Korch, *Deputy Dir*
EMP: 773
SALES (corp-wide): 45.3B **Privately Held**
SIC: 2834 Drugs affecting neoplasms &
　　endrocrine systems
HQ: Bayer Healthcare Pharmaceuticals Inc.
　　100 Bayer Blvd
　　Whippany NJ 07981
　　862 404-3000

(G-11880)
BAYER HLTHCARE PHRMCTICALS INC (DH)
100 Bayer Blvd (07981-1544)
P.O. Box 915 (07981-0915)
PHONE..............................862 404-3000
Daniel Apel, *President*
Habib Dable, *Principal*
Richard K Heller, *Vice Pres*
Darara Dibabu, *Research*
Edna Johnson-Adams, *Regl Sales Mgr*
▲ EMP: 773
SALES (est): 548.6MM
SALES (corp-wide): 45.3B **Privately Held**
SIC: 2834 3841 Drugs affecting neo-
　　plasms & endrocrine systems; surgical &
　　medical instruments
HQ: Berlin Schering Inc
　　100 Bayer Blvd
　　Whippany NJ 07981
　　862 404-3000

(G-11881)
BIOMEDTRIX LLC
9 Whippany Rd Bldg B2-7 (07981-1530)
PHONE..............................973 331-7800
Christopher Sidebotham, *Mng Member*
Joseph Pych,
EMP: 17
SQ FT: 15,000
SALES: 6MM **Privately Held**
SIC: 5047 2835 Veterinarians' equipment
　　& supplies; veterinary diagnostic sub-
　　stances

(G-11882)
BLISPAK ACQUISITION CORP
1 Apollo Dr Ste 3 (07981-1424)
PHONE..............................973 884-4141
James Horan, *President*

EMP: 55
SQ FT: 20,000
SALES: 4MM **Privately Held**
WEB: www.blispakinc.com
SIC: 2671 5084 Plastic film, coated or
　　laminated for packaging; processing &
　　packaging equipment

(G-11883)
BREEZE-EASTERN LLC (HQ)
35 Melanie Ln (07981-1638)
PHONE..............................973 602-1001
Rodger Hahneman, *President*
Roger Hahneman, *General Mgr*
Gary Olson, *Vice Pres*
John Soehnlein, *Vice Pres*
John McKinley, *Opers Mgr*
▲ EMP: 6
SQ FT: 115,335
SALES (est): 14.6MM
SALES (corp-wide): 3.8B **Publicly Held**
WEB: www.transtechnology.com
SIC: 3563 3531 3728 Air & gas compres-
　　sors including vacuum pumps; winches;
　　aircraft armament, except guns
PA: Transdigm Group Incorporated
　　1301 E 9th St Ste 3000
　　Cleveland OH 44114
　　216 706-2960

(G-11884)
BREEZE-EASTERN LLC
35 Melanie Ln (07981-1638)
PHONE..............................973 602-1001
Rodger Hahneman, *Manager*
EMP: 100
SALES (corp-wide): 3.8B **Publicly Held**
WEB: www.transtechnology.com
SIC: 3728 3769 3536 3531 Aircraft parts
　　& equipment; guided missile & space ve-
　　hicle parts & auxiliary equipment; hoists,
　　cranes & monorails; construction machin-
　　ery
HQ: Breeze-Eastern Llc
　　35 Melanie Ln
　　Whippany NJ 07981
　　973 602-1001

(G-11885)
CHAMBERLAIN GROUP INC
35 Melanie Ln (07981-1638)
PHONE..............................201 472-4200
Mike Bado, *Principal*
EMP: 8
SALES (corp-wide): 1.4B **Privately Held**
SIC: 3699 Door opening & closing devices,
　　electrical
HQ: The Chamberlain Group Inc
　　300 Windsor Dr
　　Oak Brook IL 60523
　　630 279-3600

(G-11886)
COMBOCAP INC
125 Algonquin Pkwy (07981-1649)
PHONE..............................646 722-2743
Tobie Louw, *CEO*
Jacques Van Rooyen, *COO*
Richard Short, *CFO*
Andrea Fitting, *Chief Mktg Ofcr*
Teri Hartrum-Park, *Director*
EMP: 6
SALES (est): 335.7K **Privately Held**
SIC: 2834 Medicines, capsuled or ampuled

(G-11887)
CORPORATE MAILINGS INC
Also Called: United Shippers Associates
26 Parsippany Rd (07981-1447)
PHONE..............................973 808-0009
Jim Pinkin, *Branch Mgr*
EMP: 100
SALES (corp-wide): 58.1MM **Privately
Held**
WEB: www.corpcomm.com
SIC: 7331 7311 7374 2752 Mailing serv-
　　ice; advertising agencies; data processing
　　service; promotional printing, lithographic
PA: Corporate Mailings, Inc.
　　14 Henderson Dr
　　West Caldwell NJ 07006
　　973 439-1168

(G-11888)
DASCO SUPPLY LLC
150 Algonquin Pkwy (07981-1654)
P.O. Box 193 (07981-0193)
PHONE...............................973 884-1390
Robert Schwarzenbek, *President*
EMP: 12
SALES (corp-wide): 4.5B **Publicly Held**
WEB: www.dascosupply.com
SIC: 5075 3444 Whol Heat/Air Cond
Equipment/Supplies Mfg Sheet Metalwork
HQ: Dasco Supply, Llc
9 Whippany Rd Bldngd
Whippany NJ 07981
973 884-1390

(G-11889)
DOSCH-KING COMPANY INC (PA)
Also Called: Dosch-King Emulsions
16 Troy Hills Rd (07981-1529)
P.O. Box 260 (07981-0260)
PHONE...............................973 887-0145
David J King, *President*
Jeffrey King, *Corp Secy*
EMP: 15
SQ FT: 3,500
SALES (est): 6.5MM **Privately Held**
SIC: 1611 2951 Highway & street paving
contractor; asphalt & asphaltic paving
mixtures (not from refineries)

(G-11890)
ESSEX MORRIS SIGN CO
30 Troy Rd Ste 2 (07981-1641)
PHONE...............................973 386-1755
Michael Hoehn, *Partner*
Christopher Hoehn, *Partner*
EMP: 8
SQ FT: 2,000
SALES (est): 1.1MM **Privately Held**
SIC: 3993 7532 Signs, not made in cus-
tom sign painting shops; truck painting &
lettering

(G-11891)
FOODTEK INC (PA)
9 Whippany Rd Bldg C-2 (07981-1530)
P.O. Box 99, Hawthorne (07507-0099)
PHONE...............................973 257-4000
Victor Davila, *President*
Gilbert Finkel, *President*
Millicent Finkel, *Admin Sec*
EMP: 13 **EST:** 1972
SQ FT: 5,000
SALES (est): 2.5MM **Privately Held**
WEB: www.food-tek.com
SIC: 2045 2099 Prepared flour mixes &
doughs; food preparations

(G-11892)
GE AVIATION SYSTEMS LLC
110 Algonquin Pkwy (07981-1602)
PHONE...............................973 428-9898
Paul Hemingway, *Director*
EMP: 150
SALES (corp-wide): 121.6B **Publicly Held**
SIC: 4581 3812 3593 Aircraft mainte-
nance & repair services; search & naviga-
tion equipment; fluid power cylinders &
actuators
HQ: Ge Aviation Systems Llc
1 Neumann Way
Cincinnati OH 45215
937 898-9600

(G-11893)
GEL CONCEPTS LLC
30 Leslie Ct (07981-1635)
PHONE...............................973 884-8995
Bob Gould,
Bob N Gould,
▲ **EMP:** 25
SALES (est): 2.8MM **Privately Held**
WEB: www.gelconcepts.com
SIC: 2844 Cosmetic preparations

(G-11894)
HALO PHARMACEUTICAL INC (HQ)
30 N Jefferson Rd (07981-1030)
PHONE...............................973 428-4000
Lee Karras, *CEO*
Clive V Bennett, *President*

Vincent Tortoriello, *Research*
Mohd Asif, *CFO*
Michael Sadler, *Sales Staff*
▲ **EMP:** 100
SQ FT: 240,000
SALES (est): 27.5MM
SALES (corp-wide): 532MM **Publicly Held**
SIC: 2834 Pharmaceutical preparations
PA: Cambrex Corporation
1 Meadowlands Plz # 1510
East Rutherford NJ 07073
201 804-3000

(G-11895)
HERLEY INDUSTRIES INC
9 Whippany Rd (07981-1540)
PHONE...............................973 884-2580
Lloyd Kuhnle, *Engineer*
Earl Granville, *Administration*
EMP: 65
SALES (corp-wide): 984.8MM **Privately Held**
SIC: 3679 Microwave components
HQ: Herley Industries, Inc.
3061 Industry Dr
Lancaster PA 17603
717 397-2777

(G-11896)
HERLEY-CTI INC (DH)
Also Called: Ultra Electronics Herley
9 Whippany Rd (07981-1540)
PHONE...............................973 884-2580
Deanna Lund, *CEO*
Eric Demarco, *President*
Michael Fink, *Vice Pres*
Laura Siegal, *Treasurer*
Alan Veneri, *Accountant*
EMP: 10
SQ FT: 22,000
SALES (est): 98.2MM
SALES (corp-wide): 984.8MM **Privately Held**
WEB: www.cti-inc.com
SIC: 3679 Microwave components; oscilla-
tors
HQ: Herley Industries, Inc.
3061 Industry Dr
Lancaster PA 17603
717 397-2777

(G-11897)
MARK/TRECE INC
160 Algonquin Pkwy Ste 1 (07981-1691)
PHONE...............................973 884-1005
Matt Rachanow, *Sales Mgr*
Paul Rachanow, *Manager*
EMP: 45
SALES (corp-wide): 40.6MM **Privately Held**
SIC: 3555 2796 Printing plates; platemak-
ing services
PA: Mark/Trece, Inc.
2001 Stockton Rd
Joppa MD 21085
410 879-0060

(G-11898)
NEW JERSEY JEWISH NEWS (PA)
Also Called: Metrowest Jewish News
901 State Route 10 (07981-1105)
PHONE...............................973 887-3900
Lauri Sirois, *Supervisor*
Howard Rabner, *Director*
EMP: 28
SQ FT: 110,000
SALES: 18.6MM **Privately Held**
WEB: www.jhsmw.org
SIC: 8399 2711 Fund raising organization,
non-fee basis; newspapers

(G-11899)
NUTRA-MED PACKAGING INC
118 Algonquin Pkwy (07981-1602)
PHONE...............................973 625-2274
Mahesh Gupta, *Principal*
Kunal Gupta, *Vice Pres*
Sagar Chokshi, *Project Mgr*
Julie Callahan, *QA Dir*
Sushma Gupta, *Treasurer*
▲ **EMP:** 90
SQ FT: 100,000

(G-11900)
P-AMERICAS LLC
Also Called: Pepsico
15 Melanie Ln (07981-1652)
PHONE...............................973 739-4900
Mike Vanklingeren, *Safety Mgr*
Renee Ferguson, *Purch Agent*
Mark Optyke, *Manager*
EMP: 165
SALES (corp-wide): 64.6B **Publicly Held**
SIC: 2086 Carbonated soft drinks, bottled
& canned
HQ: P-Americas Llc
1 Pepsi Way
Somers NY 10589
336 896-5740

(G-11901)
PALMA INC
628 State Route 10 Ste 2 (07981-1522)
P.O. Box 2539, Bloomfield (07003-9339)
PHONE...............................973 429-1490
Federico Palma, *President*
Gregory Manton, *Vice Pres*
Fred Palma III, *Treasurer*
Michael Palma, *Admin Sec*
EMP: 15
SQ FT: 6,000
SALES: 2.5MM **Privately Held**
WEB: www.palmainc.com
SIC: 1752 2821 2851 Resilient floor lay-
ing; plastics materials & resins; epoxy
coatings

(G-11902)
PDR EQUITY LLC (PA)
Also Called: Pdr Network
200 Jefferson Park (07981-1069)
PHONE...............................201 358-7200
Mark Heinold, *CEO*
Ruth Williams, *Senior VP*
Mike Burnett, *CFO*
Salvatore Volpe, *Chief Mktg Ofcr*
David Cheng, *CTO*
EMP: 99
SQ FT: 42,000
SALES (est): 20.5MM **Privately Held**
SIC: 2834 5912 Pharmaceutical prepara-
tions; drug stores

(G-11903)
PERLIN CONVERTING LLC
Also Called: Perlen Packaging
135 Algonquin Pkwy (07981-1601)
PHONE...............................973 887-0257
Markus Haid, *Vice Pres*
Diana Catelotti, *Sales Mgr*
Fredy Brunner, *Sales Staff*
Spencer Dixon, *Sales Staff*
Douglas Vories, *Mng Member*
▲ **EMP:** 15
SALES (est): 2.8MM
SALES (corp-wide): 550.7MM **Privately Held**
SIC: 3081 Plastic film & sheet
HQ: Perlen Packaging Ag, Perlen
Perlenring 3
Perlen LU 6035
414 558-800

(G-11904)
POLY-GEL LLC
Also Called: Polygel
30 Leslie Ct (07981-1635)
PHONE...............................973 884-3300
Joel E Bickell, *Vice Pres*
Marty Vogel, *Vice Pres*
Laurie Karian, *Research*
Steve Tomlinson, *Sales Staff*
Leila Zain, *Sales Staff*
▲ **EMP:** 25
SALES (est): 3.9MM **Privately Held**
WEB: www.polygel.com
SIC: 2099 Gelatin dessert preparations

(G-11905)
POR-15 INC
Also Called: Restomotive Laboratories
64 S Jefferson Rd Ste 2 (07981-1014)
P.O. Box 1235, Morristown (07962-1235)
PHONE...............................973 887-1999

SALES (est): 25.5MM **Privately Held**
WEB: www.nutra-med.com
SIC: 2834 7389 Pharmaceutical prepara-
tions; packaging & labeling services

Tom Slutsker, *President*
Marion L Bechler, *Vice Pres*
EMP: 25 **EST:** 1975
SQ FT: 25,000
SALES (est): 3.7MM **Privately Held**
WEB: www.por15.com
SIC: 2899 5169 Rust resisting com-
pounds; rustproofing chemicals

(G-11906)
POWER DYNAMICS INC
145 Algonquin Pkwy Ste 2 (07981-1645)
PHONE...............................973 560-0019
James Papianni, *President*
Edward Grayson, *Chairman*
Michael Meehan, *Materials Mgr*
Frank W Petrillo, *Natl Sales Mgr*
Margaret Wojtala, *Sales Mgr*
▲ **EMP:** 50
SQ FT: 25,000
SALES (est): 9.3MM **Privately Held**
WEB: www.powerdynamics.com
SIC: 3629 5065 Electronic generation
equipment; electronic parts

(G-11907)
RECORDER PUBLISHING CO INC (PA)
Also Called: Parker Publications Corporated
100 S Jefferson Rd # 104 (07981-1009)
P.O. Box 687, Bernardsville (07924-0687)
PHONE...............................908 766-3900
Stephen Parker, *President*
Christine Lee, *Editor*
Philip Nardone, *Editor*
Walter Obrien, *Editor*
Jake Yaniak, *Prdtn Mgr*
EMP: 60 **EST:** 1896
SQ FT: 5,000
SALES (est): 16.1MM **Privately Held**
WEB: www.recordernewspapers.com
SIC: 2711 Commercial printing & newspa-
per publishing combined

(G-11908)
SCHERING BERLIN INC (DH)
100 Bayer Blvd (07981-1544)
PHONE...............................862 404-3000
Daniel Apel, *Officer*
▲ **EMP:** 1 **EST:** 1986
SALES (est): 899.9MM
SALES (corp-wide): 45.3B **Privately Held**
SIC: 2834 3841 Drugs affecting neoplasms & endocrine systems; drugs acting on the central nervous system &
sense organs; drugs acting on the cardiovascular system, except diagnostic; surgical & medical instruments
HQ: Bayer Healthcare Llc
100 Bayer Blvd
Whippany NJ 07981
862 404-3000

(G-11909)
SNO SKINS INC
622 State Route 10 Ste 19 (07981-1543)
PHONE...............................973 884-8801
Steve Weiss, *President*
Janine Weiss, *Vice Pres*
◆ **EMP:** 6
SALES (est): 973K **Privately Held**
WEB: www.snoskins.com
SIC: 2339 Women's & misses' athletic
clothing & sportswear

(G-11910)
STEPHEN GOULD CORPORATION (PA)
35 S Jefferson Rd (07981-1043)
PHONE...............................973 428-1500
Michael Golden, *CEO*
John Golden, *President*
Justin Golden, *President*
Peter V Slyke, *Vice Pres*
Edward Corbett, *Project Dir*
◆ **EMP:** 100 **EST:** 1939
SQ FT: 42,000
SALES: 678.7MM **Privately Held**
WEB: www.stephengould.com
SIC: 2631 2759 Container, packaging &
boxboard; labels & seals: printing

(G-11911)
V L V ASSOCIATES
34 Troy Rd (07981-1639)
PHONE...............................973 428-2884

Michael Vaillancourt, *President*
Mark Penna, *Human Res Mgr*
Gregory Dwyer, *Manager*
Michael Pfefferkorn, *Manager*
EMP: 12
SQ FT: 10,000
SALES (est): 2.2MM **Privately Held**
WEB: www.vlvassociates.com
SIC: 3845 Ultrasonic scanning devices, medical

(G-11912)
WATER DYNAMICS
INCORPORATED
9 Valley Forge Dr (07981-2214)
PHONE................973 428-8330
Kim Dwyer, *CEO*
Gregory Dwyer, *President*
EMP: 4 **EST:** 1999
SALES: 375K **Privately Held**
SIC: 2899 Water treating compounds

(G-11913)
WHIPPANY ACTUATION
SYSTEMS LLC
110 Algonquin Pkwy (07981-1602)
PHONE................973 428-9898
Gary Corde, *Business Mgr*
Fred Stokes, *Opers Mgr*
James Teehan, *Production*
Diane Dejesus, *Buyer*
Tara Hickey, *Buyer*
EMP: 236
SALES (est): 86.4MM
SALES (corp-wide): 3.8B **Publicly Held**
SIC: 3625 3728 Actuators, industrial; aircraft parts & equipment
PA: Transdigm Group Incorporated
1301 E 9th St Ste 3000
Cleveland OH 44114
216 706-2960

(G-11914)
WHIPTAIL TECHNOLOGIES LLC
Also Called: Whiptail Technologies Inc.
9 Whippany Rd Ste 67 (07981-1540)
PHONE................973 585-6375
Daniel Crain, *CEO*
Cristobal Conde, *Ch of Bd*
Cameron Pforr, *President*
Erik Hardy, *Exec VP*
EMP: 72
SQ FT: 12,000
SALES (est): 10.9MM
SALES (corp-wide): 51.9B **Publicly Held**
WEB: www.whiptailtech.com
SIC: 3572 Computer storage devices
PA: Cisco Systems, Inc.
170 W Tasman Dr
San Jose CA 95134
408 526-4000

Whitehouse
Hunterdon County

(G-11915)
DALLAS GROUP OF AMERICA
INC (PA)
374 Rte 22 (08888)
P.O. Box 489 (08888-0489)
PHONE................908 534-7800
David E Dallas, *CEO*
Robert H Dallas II, *President*
Clair Conzelman, *Business Mgr*
Zach Cummings, *Business Mgr*
Robert Gonzalez, *Business Mgr*
◆ **EMP:** 30
SQ FT: 12,000
SALES: 117.3MM **Privately Held**
SIC: 3339 2819 Primary nonferrous metals; industrial inorganic chemicals

(G-11916)
LARUE MANUFACTURING CORP
Also Called: American Display
291 Rte 22 E (08888)
P.O. Box 244 (08888-0244)
PHONE................908 534-2700
Keith Larue, *President*
Anita Thompson, *Vice Pres*
EMP: 5
SQ FT: 10,000

SALES: 1.5MM **Privately Held**
WEB: www.americandisplayusa.com
SIC: 3993 7336 7319 Signs & advertising specialties; commercial art & graphic design; display advertising service

(G-11917)
NAHALLAC LLC
6 Carman Ln (08888)
PHONE................908 635-0999
Dwayne Looney, *Principal*
Bruce Callahan, *Principal*
John Callahan, *Principal*
EMP: 7
SALES (est): 400K **Privately Held**
SIC: 3842 Sponges, surgical

(G-11918)
READINGTON FARMS INC
12 Mill Rd (08888)
PHONE................908 534-2121
Dominick V Romano, *Ch of Bd*
Donald Merrigan, *President*
Barry S Snyder, *Vice Pres*
Jason Maxham, *Engineer*
Ned Gladstein, *Admin Sec*
EMP: 89
SQ FT: 20,000
SALES: 190MM
SALES (corp-wide): 890MM **Privately Held**
WEB: www.readingtonfarms.com
SIC: 2026 Milk processing (pasteurizing, homogenizing, bottling)
PA: Wakefern Food Corp.
5000 Riverside Dr
Keasbey NJ 08832
908 527-3300

Whitehouse Station
Hunterdon County

(G-11919)
CE TECH LLC
8 Fairway Dr (08889-3369)
PHONE................908 229-3803
Tim Dywer, *President*
Tom Maresca, *General Mgr*
Todd Henderckson, *VP Sales*
EMP: 8
SALES (est): 204.7K **Privately Held**
SIC: 7372 7379 Prepackaged software; computer related consulting services

(G-11920)
HUNTERDON BREWING
COMPANY LLC
12 Coddington Rd (08889-3629)
P.O. Box 1050 (08889-1050)
PHONE................908 454-7445
Dave Masterson,
▲ **EMP:** 97 **EST:** 1996
SQ FT: 4,000
SALES (est): 16.6MM **Privately Held**
WEB: www.hunterdonbrewing.com
SIC: 2082 2084 Beer (alcoholic beverage); wines

(G-11921)
INSPIRE PHARMACEUTICALS
INC
1 Merck Dr (08889-3400)
PHONE................908 423-1000
John Canan, *President*
Mark McDonough, *Treasurer*
Juanita Lee, *Asst Treas*
EMP: 240
SQ FT: 43,278
SALES (est): 16.3MM
SALES (corp-wide): 694MM **Publicly Held**
WEB: www.inspirepharm.com
SIC: 2834 Pharmaceutical preparations
HQ: Oak Pharmaceuticals, Inc.
1925 W Field Ct Ste 300
Lake Forest IL 60045

(G-11922)
MERCK & CO INC
1 Merck Dr (08889-3497)
P.O. Box 100 (08889-0100)
PHONE................908 423-1000
Umesh Patel, *Marketing Staff*

Maryann Mendoza, *Office Mgr*
Linda Hunt, *Director*
EMP: 4
SALES (corp-wide): 42.2B **Publicly Held**
SIC: 2834 Pharmaceutical preparations
PA: Merck & Co., Inc.
2000 Galloping Hill Rd
Kenilworth NJ 07033
908 740-4000

(G-11923)
MERCK HOLDINGS LLC (DH)
1 Merck Dr (08889-3497)
PHONE................908 423-1000
Richard Henriques, *President*
Richard T Clark, *President*
Judy Lewent, *Senior VP*
Caroline Dorsa, *Treasurer*
Michael Hacker, *Asst Treas*
EMP: 10
SQ FT: 100,000
SALES (est): 269.7MM
SALES (corp-wide): 42.2B **Publicly Held**
SIC: 2834 6712 Proprietary drug products; bank holding companies
HQ: Merck Sharp & Dohme Corp.
2000 Galloping Hill Rd
Kenilworth NJ 07033
908 740-4000

(G-11924)
MERCK RESOURCE
MANAGEMENT INC
1 Merck Dr (08889-3497)
P.O. Box 100 (08889-0100)
PHONE................908 423-1000
W Merck, *President*
Troy Bussey, *Engineer*
Mark Hubly, *Sales Staff*
Ilia Slavov, *Manager*
Vladimir Svetnik, *Director*
EMP: 5
SALES (est): 598.3K **Privately Held**
SIC: 2834 Pharmaceutical preparations

(G-11925)
MERCK SHARP & DOHME (IA)
LLC (DH)
1 Merck Dr (08889-3497)
P.O. Box 100 (08889-0100)
PHONE................908 423-1000
Merri Baillargeon, *Vice Pres*
Grey F Warner,
Judy C Luwent,
Francis H Spiegel,
▲ **EMP:** 10
SQ FT: 100,000
SALES (est): 16.1MM
SALES (corp-wide): 42.2B **Publicly Held**
WEB: www.hairinfopark.com
SIC: 2834 Pharmaceutical preparations

(G-11926)
MERCK SHARP & DOHME CORP
Also Called: Merck Animal Health
2 Merck Dr (08889-3436)
PHONE................908 423-3000
Richard C Billups, *Counsel*
Richard Spotts, *Opers Mgr*
Olga D'Hennezel, *Opers Staff*
Stuart Waters, *Production*
Marshall Streeter, *Technical Mgr*
EMP: 32
SALES (corp-wide): 42.2B **Publicly Held**
SIC: 2834 Pharmaceutical preparations
HQ: Merck Sharp & Dohme Corp.
2000 Galloping Hill Rd
Kenilworth NJ 07033
908 740-4000

(G-11927)
MERCK SHARP DHME
ARGENTINA INC (DH)
1 Merck Dr (08889-3497)
P.O. Box 100 (08889-0100)
PHONE................908 423-1000
Grey F Warner, *President*
Ernesto Buesa, *Managing Dir*
Jared Chellevold, *Regional Mgr*
Axel Johnson, *Counsel*
Francis H Spiegel Jr, *Senior VP*
EMP: 1
SQ FT: 100,000
SALES (est): 1.1MM
SALES (corp-wide): 42.2B **Publicly Held**
SIC: 2834 Pharmaceutical preparations

HQ: Merck Sharp & Dohme (I.A.) Llc
1 Merck Dr
Whitehouse Station NJ 08889
908 423-1000

(G-11928)
MERCK SHARPE & DOHME DE
PR INC
1 Merck Dr (08889-3497)
P.O. Box 100 (08889-0100)
PHONE................908 423-1000
Kenneth C Frazier, *CEO*
Bruce N Kuhlik, *Exec VP*
Wolfgang Wein, *Exec VP*
Eliav Barr, *Vice Pres*
Stephen Tarnowski, *Finance*
▲ **EMP:** 5
SALES (est): 377K
SALES (corp-wide): 42.2B **Publicly Held**
SIC: 2834 Pharmaceutical preparations
HQ: Merck Sharp & Dohme Corp.
2000 Galloping Hill Rd
Kenilworth NJ 07033
908 740-4000

(G-11929)
MINALEX CORPORATION
25 Coddington Rd (08889-3630)
P.O. Box 247 (08889-0247)
PHONE................908 534-4044
James J Casey, *President*
Christopher Casey, *General Mgr*
James P Kowalski, *Vice Pres*
Ron Allen, *QC Mgr*
Robert Handel, *Manager*
EMP: 36 **EST:** 1965
SQ FT: 25,000
SALES (est): 10.6MM **Privately Held**
WEB: www.minalex.com
SIC: 3354 Aluminum extruded products

(G-11930)
ORGANON USA INC
1 Merck Dr (08889-3400)
PHONE................908 423-1000
Joanne Bollman, *Principal*
EMP: 5 **EST:** 2013
SALES (est): 536K
SALES (corp-wide): 42.2B **Publicly Held**
SIC: 2836 2834 Vaccines; veterinary biological products; druggists' preparations (pharmaceuticals)
PA: Merck & Co., Inc.
2000 Galloping Hill Rd
Kenilworth NJ 07033
908 740-4000

(G-11931)
PALUMBO ASSOCIATES INC
27 Ridge Rd (08889-3641)
PHONE................908 534-2142
Gary Palumbo, *President*
Anthony Braca, *Production*
Leslie Byron, *Office Admin*
EMP: 13
SQ FT: 5,000
SALES (est): 1.2MM **Privately Held**
SIC: 7389 3999 Exhibit construction by industrial contractors; preparation of slides & exhibits

(G-11932)
PHOENIX INDUSTRIAL LLC
531 Route 22 E 194 (08889)
PHONE................908 955-0114
ARI Falk, *Owner*
EMP: 5
SQ FT: 5,000
SALES (est): 313.1K **Privately Held**
SIC: 3423 Hand & edge tools

(G-11933)
SATELLITE PROS INC
148 Main St (08889-3692)
PHONE................908 823-9500
Andrew Hoffman, *President*
EMP: 7
SALES: 1.5MM **Privately Held**
SIC: 3663 Satellites, communications

(G-11934)
SCHERNG-PLOUGH PDTS
CARIBE INC
1 Merck Dr (08889-3400)
PHONE................908 423-1000
Scott Grandville, *Principal*

Gregory Hood, *Manager*
Delphine Gancel, *Senior Mgr*
Edgar Hamon, *Info Tech Mgr*
EMP: 9 **EST:** 2014
SALES (est): 959.5K **Privately Held**
SIC: 2834 Pharmaceutical preparations

(G-11935)
UNITED RING & SEAL INC
7 Blackberry Ln (08889-3119)
PHONE...................................610 253-3800
David Blackwood, *President*
Elizabeth Blackwood, *Corp Secy*
EMP: 9
SALES (est): 1.2MM **Privately Held**
WEB: www.unitedringandseal.com
SIC: 3599 Machine shop, jobbing & repair

(G-11936)
VALLEY TECH INC
295 Us Highway 22 E 201w (08889-3429)
P.O. Box 124 (08889-0124)
PHONE...................................908 534-5565
Richard A Schulley, *President*
Bill Linney, *Vice Pres*
EMP: 5
SQ FT: 1,000
SALES (est): 766.7K **Privately Held**
WEB: www.valleytechinc.com
SIC: 3561 7389 Pumps & pumping equipment; air pollution measuring service

Whiting
Ocean County

(G-11937)
BIG EYE LAMP INC
870 Route 530 Ste 2 (08759-3546)
PHONE...................................732 557-9400
EMP: 6
SQ FT: 3,000
SALES (est): 300K **Privately Held**
SIC: 3645 Mfg High Intensity Magnifying Lamps

(G-11938)
CMC COMPOSITES LLC
870 Route 530 Ste 12 (08759-3546)
PHONE...................................732 505-9400
Nicholas Taaffe, *Mng Member*
EMP: 20 **EST:** 2007
SQ FT: 2,500
SALES (est): 1.5MM **Privately Held**
SIC: 3353 Aluminum sheet, plate & foil

(G-11939)
JARAHIAN MILLWORK INC
870 Route 530 Ste 4 (08759-3546)
PHONE...................................732 240-5151
Harold Jarahian, *President*
EMP: 4
SQ FT: 5,000
SALES (est): 1MM **Privately Held**
SIC: 2431 Door trim, wood; moldings, wood: unfinished & prefinished

(G-11940)
LOGPOWERCOM LLC
47 Lacey Rd (08759-4439)
PHONE...................................732 350-9663
Todd Cooper, *President*
Marchia Ammons, *Vice Pres*
EMP: 5
SALES (est): 324.7K **Privately Held**
SIC: 3553 2421 Woodworking machinery; custom sawmill

Wildwood
Cape May County

(G-11941)
A B S SIGN COMPANY INC
3008 Park Blvd (08260-2496)
PHONE...................................609 522-6833
Randy Hentges, *President*
EMP: 7 **EST:** 1964
SQ FT: 2,750
SALES (est): 300K **Privately Held**
SIC: 3993 Neon signs

(G-11942)
CANTOL INC (HQ)
4701 Mediterranean Ave (08260-1651)
PHONE...................................609 846-7912
Elmer E Snethen, *President*
Richard Petsche, *Vice Pres*
Edward Berger, *Admin Sec*
EMP: 42
SQ FT: 40,000
SALES (est): 3.7MM
SALES (corp-wide): 13.8MM **Privately Held**
WEB: www.cantol.com
SIC: 2842 2899 2841 Cleaning or polishing preparations; chemical preparations; soap & other detergents
PA: Cantol Corp
199 Steelcase Rd W
Markham ON L3R 2
905 475-6141

(G-11943)
CUSTOM CABINETS BY JIM BUCKO
135 W Burk Ave (08260-1617)
PHONE...................................609 522-6646
James Bucko, *President*
EMP: 6
SALES (est): 900K **Privately Held**
SIC: 2434 Wood kitchen cabinets

(G-11944)
HALLCO INC
Also Called: Leader Printers
5914 New Jersey Ave (08260-1346)
PHONE...................................609 729-0161
Dennis O Hall, *President*
Arthur Hall, *Vice Pres*
Terri Hall, *Treasurer*
EMP: 6
SQ FT: 3,750
SALES (est): 440K **Privately Held**
SIC: 2752 Commercial printing, offset

(G-11945)
INDOOR ENTERTAINMENT OF NJ
5301 Ocean Ave (08260-4463)
P.O. Box 4 (08260-0004)
PHONE...................................609 522-6700
Richard Ramagosa, *President*
EMP: 20
SALES (est): 300K **Privately Held**
SIC: 3599 7999 3559 Carousels (merrygo-rounds); amusement & recreation; special industry machinery

(G-11946)
M S BROWN MFG JEWELERS (PA)
Also Called: M S Brown Jewelers
3304 Pacific Ave (08260-4824)
PHONE...................................609 522-7604
Gail Brown, *President*
Michael Brown, *Treasurer*
EMP: 4
SQ FT: 2,000
SALES (est): 452.6K **Privately Held**
WEB: www.msbrownjewelers.com
SIC: 5944 3911 Jewelry, precious stones & precious metals; jewelry, precious metal

(G-11947)
WALGREEN EASTERN CO INC
Also Called: Walgreens
5000 Park Blvd (08260-1428)
PHONE...................................609 522-1291
EMP: 30
SALES (corp-wide): 131.5B **Publicly Held**
SIC: 5912 2834 Drug stores; pharmaceutical preparations
HQ: Walgreen Eastern Co., Inc.
200 Wilmot Rd
Deerfield IL 60015
847 940-2500

Wildwood Crest
Cape May County

(G-11948)
NEDOHON INC (PA)
302 E Newark Ave (08260-3423)
PHONE...................................302 533-5512
Donna J Nedohon, *President*
Richard Nedohon, *Vice Pres*
EMP: 2 **EST:** 1963
SQ FT: 40,000
SALES (est): 2.2MM **Privately Held**
SIC: 5085 5051 3341 Valves & fittings; nonferrous metal sheets, bars, rods, etc.; secondary nonferrous metals

Williamstown
Gloucester County

(G-11949)
A-WIT TECHNOLOGIES INC
656 Ironwood Dr (08094-1686)
PHONE...................................800 985-2948
Orlando Hernadez, *President*
EMP: 7
SALES (est): 200K **Privately Held**
SIC: 3999 Education aids, devices & supplies

(G-11950)
AMCOR PHRM PACKG USA INC
918 E Malaga Rd (08094-3610)
P.O. Box 448 (08094-0448)
PHONE...................................856 728-9300
Ed Walsh, *Principal*
William Taylor, *Manager*
EMP: 120 **Privately Held**
WEB: www.alcanpackaging.com
SIC: 3221 2396 Cosmetic jars, glass; automotive & apparel trimmings
HQ: Amcor Pharmaceutical Packaging Usa, Llc
625 Sharp St N
Millville NJ 08332
856 327-1540

(G-11951)
APPLIED THERMAL SOLUTIONS INC
93 Eldridge Ave (08094-1343)
PHONE...................................856 818-8194
Jeffrey Bailey, *President*
Matt Dawkins, *Principal*
EMP: 5
SALES (est): 138K **Privately Held**
SIC: 3433 Burners, furnaces, boilers & stokers

(G-11952)
BETTER IMAGE GRAPHICS INC
1041 Glassboro Rd Ste E6 (08094-3545)
PHONE...................................856 262-0735
Lawrence E Faragalli, *President*
Prilscilla Faragalli, *Vice Pres*
Pat Preston, *Treasurer*
EMP: 6
SQ FT: 2,500
SALES (est): 300K **Privately Held**
SIC: 2752 Commercial printing, lithographic

(G-11953)
BLUE LIGHT WELDING & FABG LLC
2164 Grant Ave (08094-6132)
PHONE...................................856 629-5891
Vicky Hargesheimer, *Mng Member*
Michael Hargesheimer, *Principal*
EMP: 7
SALES (est): 1.6MM **Privately Held**
WEB: www.bluelightwelding.com
SIC: 7692 Welding repair

(G-11954)
COLOR COMP INC
1041 Glassboro Rd Ste E5 (08094-3545)
PHONE...................................856 262-3040
William Shisler, *President*
Donna Shisler, *Vice Pres*
Bill Shisler, *Manager*

EMP: 6
SALES (est): 731.8K **Privately Held**
WEB: www.colorcomp.net
SIC: 7336 2396 Graphic arts & related design; automotive & apparel trimmings

(G-11955)
COSMIC CUSTOM SCREEN PRTG LLC (PA)
935 S Black Horse Pike (08094-1900)
PHONE...................................856 629-8337
Debbie Bochaud,
EMP: 4
SALES (est): 250K **Privately Held**
SIC: 2759 Screen printing

(G-11956)
CREATIVE CMPT CONCEPTS LLC
2030 N Black Horse Pike (08094-9132)
PHONE...................................877 919-7988
Francis Peirce,
Raymond Nicloud,
EMP: 5
SALES (est): 125K **Privately Held**
SIC: 7373 7378 7371 5961 Systems software development services; local area network (LAN) systems integrator; computer maintenance & repair; computer software systems analysis & design, custom; computer equipment & electronics, mail order; computer installation; computer auxiliary storage units

(G-11957)
F P DEVELOPMENTS INC
402 S Main St (08094-1729)
PHONE...................................856 875-7100
Frederick W Pfleger Jr, *President*
Frederick W Pfleger Sr, *Chairman*
David Pfleger, *COO*
William Pfleger, *Treasurer*
Mary Pfleger, *Admin Sec*
EMP: 37 **EST:** 1963
SQ FT: 24,000
SALES (est): 9.5MM **Privately Held**
WEB: www.fpdevelopments.com
SIC: 3559 3565 Pharmaceutical machinery; packaging machinery

(G-11958)
FORMS & FLYERS OF NEW JERSEY
102 Sicklerville Rd (08094-1472)
PHONE...................................856 629-0718
Deborah Evangelista, *Owner*
Harry Evangelista, *Owner*
EMP: 4
SALES (est): 200K **Privately Held**
SIC: 2759 5943 Commercial printing; office forms & supplies

(G-11959)
GRAPHIC IMAGE
1401 N Blck Horse Pike A (08094-9164)
PHONE...................................856 262-8900
James McGhee Jr, *Partner*
Tim Geist, *Partner*
EMP: 5
SQ FT: 2,000
SALES (est): 260K **Privately Held**
SIC: 2759 Screen printing

(G-11960)
GREAT RAILING INC
1086 N Black Horse Pike (08094-9143)
PHONE...................................856 875-0050
Mario Conlin, *President*
Great Railing, *Principal*
EMP: 15
SQ FT: 12,200
SALES (est): 5MM **Privately Held**
SIC: 3444 5051 5211 Roof deck, sheet metal; steel decking; fencing

(G-11961)
INTERCOASTAL FABRICATORS INC
300 Thomas Ave Ste 301 (08094-3442)
PHONE...................................856 629-4105
Paul Daiber, *President*
EMP: 4
SALES: 250K **Privately Held**
SIC: 3444 Sheet metalwork

(G-11962)
JUST GLASS & MIRROR INC
1250 N Black Horse Pike (08094-2834)
PHONE...................................856 728-8383
Al Pfafman, *President*
EMP: 12
SQ FT: 2,000
SALES (est): 1.7MM **Privately Held**
WEB: www.justglassandmirror.net
SIC: 3211 5719 Insulating glass, sealed
    units; mirrors

(G-11963)
LETTS PLAY INC
1400 Sunset Ave (08094-4320)
PHONE...................................856 297-2530
Doris Letts, *President*
John Hunt, *Admin Sec*
EMP: 6
SALES (est): 307.1K **Privately Held**
SIC: 3942 5942 8999 7371 Dolls, except
    stuffed toy animals; children's books; au-
    thor; computer software development &
    applications

(G-11964)
MONROE TOOL & DIE INC
197 Sharp Rd (08094-7446)
PHONE...................................856 629-5164
Steven Kennedy, *President*
EMP: 5 **EST:** 1964
SQ FT: 4,400
SALES (est): 761.4K **Privately Held**
SIC: 3544 3469 Dies & die holders for
    metal cutting, forming, die casting; metal
    stampings

(G-11965)
MTS SYSTEMS CORPORATION
745 Debra Dr (08094-1641)
PHONE...................................856 875-4478
Chip Emery, *Manager*
EMP: 1000
SALES (corp-wide): 778MM **Publicly
Held**
WEB: www.mts.com
SIC: 8711 7699 3699 3577 Engineering
    services; hydraulic equipment repair;
    electrical equipment & supplies; computer
    peripheral equipment
PA: Mts Systems Corporation
    14000 Technology Dr
    Eden Prairie MN 55344
    952 937-4000

(G-11966)
**OLDCASTLE INFRASTRUCTURE
INC**
1920 12th St Rt 54 (08094)
PHONE...................................609 561-3400
Luis Matos, *Director*
EMP: 50
SALES (corp-wide): 30.6B **Privately Held**
WEB: www.oldcastle-precast.com
SIC: 3272 Concrete products, precast
HQ: Oldcastle Infrastructure, Inc.
    7000 Cntl Prkaway Ste 800
    Atlanta GA 30328
    470 602-2000

(G-11967)
PACE TARGET BROKERAGE INC
716 Clayton Rd (08094-3530)
P.O. Box 337 (08094-0337)
PHONE...................................856 629-2551
Joseph J Pace Jr, *President*
Regina Pace, *Vice Pres*
Nicholas Pace, *Treasurer*
Joe Pace III, *Admin Sec*
EMP: 25
SQ FT: 2,800
SALES (est): 3.5MM **Privately Held**
WEB: www.pacetarget.com
SIC: 2052 5145 Bakery products, dry;
    snack foods; candy; pretzels; potato chips

(G-11968)
PIPING SUPPLIES INC
18 E Black Horse Pike (08094-2613)
PHONE...................................609 561-9323
Nancy Walker, *President*
▲ **EMP:** 7
SQ FT: 79,500

SALES (est): 1.1MM **Privately Held**
SIC: 3494 3462 3463 Pipe fittings; flange,
    valve & pipe fitting forgings, ferrous;
    flange, valve or pipe fitting forgings, non-
    ferrous

(G-11969)
PIRAMAL GLASS - USA INC
918 E Malaga Rd (08094-3610)
PHONE...................................856 728-9300
Charles Macho, *Principal*
EMP: 130
SALES (corp-wide): 193.6MM **Privately
Held**
SIC: 3221 Glass containers
HQ: Piramal Glass - Usa, Inc.
    329 Herrod Blvd
    Dayton NJ 08810
    856 293-6400

(G-11970)
PIRAMAL GLASS - USA INC
Also Called: Decoration Operations
918 E Malaga Rd (08094-3610)
PHONE...................................856 293-6400
Charlie Macho, *Manager*
EMP: 365
SALES (corp-wide): 193.6MM **Privately
Held**
SIC: 3221 Glass containers
HQ: Piramal Glass - Usa, Inc.
    329 Herrod Blvd
    Dayton NJ 08810
    856 293-6400

(G-11971)
PRECISION BALL SPECIALTIES
1451 Glassboro Rd (08094-3300)
P.O. Box 132 (08094-0132)
PHONE...................................856 881-5646
John Williams, *President*
EMP: 10
SQ FT: 6,000
SALES (est): 1.2MM **Privately Held**
WEB: www.precisionballspecialties.com
SIC: 3545 3544 3496 Precision tools, ma-
    chinists'; special dies, tools, jigs & fix-
    tures; miscellaneous fabricated wire
    products

(G-11972)
**PRECISION METALCRAFTERS
INC**
17 Filbert St (08094-1897)
PHONE...................................856 629-1020
Frank Falconi, *President*
Joanna Buehler, *Opers Mgr*
Louise Falconi, *Admin Sec*
EMP: 25
SQ FT: 22,500
SALES (est): 4.3MM **Privately Held**
WEB: www.precisionmetalcrafters.net
SIC: 3599 3444 3441 Machine shop, job-
    bing & repair; sheet metalwork; fabricated
    structural metal

(G-11973)
**PREMIER ASSET LOGISTICS
NETWOR (PA)**
Also Called: Palnet
100 N Black Horse Pike # 100
    (08094-1483)
PHONE...................................877 725-6381
Michael L Smith, *Mng Member*
Bernie Bartley,
Darren Bronco,
Sean Crowe,
Mike Doyle,
EMP: 14
SALES (est): 2.6MM **Privately Held**
SIC: 2448 Pallets, wood

(G-11974)
**RESPONSE TIME
INCORPORATED**
1 Fiber Optic Ln (08094-4051)
PHONE...................................856 875-0025
Catrina Lancour Hahn, *CEO*
Frank Ross, *Opers Mgr*
EMP: 25
SALES (est): 3MM **Privately Held**
SIC: 3661 Fiber optics communications
    equipment

(G-11975)
**RICHARD E PIERSON MTLS
CORP**
Also Called: R E Pierson Materials
151 Industrial Dr (08094-7543)
PHONE...................................856 740-2400
Brian Hart, *Branch Mgr*
EMP: 6 **Privately Held**
SIC: 2951 1611 1771 Asphalt paving mix-
    tures & blocks; highway & street construc-
    tion; concrete work
PA: Richard E. Pierson Materials Corp.
    426 Swedesboro Rd
    Pilesgrove NJ 08098

(G-11976)
ROBERT J DONALDSON INC
1287 Glassboro Rd (08094-3507)
PHONE...................................856 629-2737
Douglas A Donaldson, *President*
W Scott Donaldson, *Vice Pres*
Benita Donaldson, *Shareholder*
Charles K Donaldson, *Shareholder*
Harold Oneio, *Shareholder*
EMP: 12
SQ FT: 10,000
SALES: 1.8MM **Privately Held**
WEB: www.donaldsonwire.com
SIC: 3496 3446 Miscellaneous fabricated
    wire products; gates, ornamental metal

(G-11977)
SCHUSTERS SHOES INC
1122 Rembrandt Way 1 (08094-6340)
PHONE...................................856 885-4551
Bill Nims, *President*
Joseph Watson, *Vice Pres*
EMP: 9 **EST:** 1958
SQ FT: 5,800
SALES (est): 1.2MM **Privately Held**
WEB: www.schustersshoes.com
SIC: 5661 3144 Footwear, athletic; ortho-
    pedic shoes, women's

(G-11978)
SNAP SET SPECIALISTS INC
300 Thomas Ave Bldg 6 (08094-3442)
P.O. Box 8074, Blackwood (08012-8074)
PHONE...................................856 629-9552
EMP: 4 **EST:** 1982
SQ FT: 2,500
SALES (est): 250K **Privately Held**
SIC: 2761 Mfg Manifold Business Forms

(G-11979)
SOUTH STATE INC
1340 Glassboro Rd (08094-8925)
PHONE...................................856 881-6030
EMP: 20
SALES (corp-wide): 12.3MM **Privately
Held**
SIC: 2951 5032 1611 Mfg Asphalt Mix-
    tures/Blocks Whol Brick/Stone Material
    Highway/Street Construction
PA: South State Inc
    202 Reeves Rd
    Bridgeton NJ
    856 451-5300

(G-11980)
SPECTACLE SHOPPE
Also Called: Precision Optical Lab
202 Dickens Ct (08094-1962)
PHONE...................................856 875-5046
George E Du Bois, *Owner*
EMP: 4 **EST:** 1976
SALES: 200K **Privately Held**
SIC: 5995 3851 Opticians; ophthalmic
    goods

(G-11981)
TOMWAR CORP
413 Paradise Rd (08094-3071)
PHONE...................................856 740-0111
Frances B Wark, *President*
Barbara Horn, *Vice Pres*
EMP: 20
SQ FT: 25,000
SALES (est): 963K **Privately Held**
SIC: 2782 Sample books

(G-11982)
TUBE CRAFT OF AMERICA INC
667 Lebanon Ave (08094-4003)
PHONE...................................856 629-5626

George Taniewski, *Vice Pres*
Diane Marino, *Office Mgr*
Ivan Taniewski, *Admin Sec*
EMP: 4
SALES (est): 370K **Privately Held**
WEB: www.tubecraftflange.com
SIC: 3498 Fabricated pipe & fittings

(G-11983)
**UNIVERSITY FASHIONS BY
JANET**
1888 Winslow Rd Bldg B (08094-4026)
PHONE...................................856 228-1615
Janet James, *Owner*
Ulysses James, *Co-Owner*
EMP: 7
SALES (est): 545K **Privately Held**
WEB: www.universityfashions.com
SIC: 2395 7336 Embroidery & art needle-
    work; silk screen design

(G-11984)
**VECTOR PRECISION
MACHINING**
1558 Janvier Rd (08094-3972)
PHONE...................................856 740-5131
Pawel Les, *President*
EMP: 5
SALES (est): 557.2K **Privately Held**
SIC: 3599 Machine shop, jobbing & repair

(G-11985)
VFI FABRICATORS INC
Also Called: V F I Fabricators
300 Thomas Ave Ste 101 (08094-3442)
P.O. Box 263 (08094-0263)
PHONE...................................856 629-8786
Alfred E Fabrico Sr, *President*
Alfred E Fabrico Jr, *Vice Pres*
Danielle Wilder, *Admin Sec*
EMP: 30
SQ FT: 15,000
SALES (est): 6.9MM **Privately Held**
WEB: www.vfifab.com
SIC: 3444 Sheet metal specialties, not
    stamped

(G-11986)
**WASTEQUIP MANUFACTURING
CO LLC**
New Brooklyn & Filbert St (08094)
PHONE...................................856 629-9222
Dominic Scardino, *Plant Mgr*
Andrew Stesanio, *Branch Mgr*
EMP: 49 **Privately Held**
WEB: www.rayfo.com
SIC: 3443 Dumpsters, garbage
HQ: Wastequip Manufacturing Company
    Llc
    6525 Morrison Blvd # 300
    Charlotte NC 28211

(G-11987)
WOOD WORKS
1111 N Black Horse Pike (08094-2838)
PHONE...................................856 728-4520
Robert B Bartling, *Partner*
Carol A Bartling, *Partner*
Dennis Drew, *Project Mgr*
Patricia McCarthy, *Technical Staff*
EMP: 8
SQ FT: 7,500
SALES: 1MM **Privately Held**
SIC: 2431 5031 5211 Millwork; millwork;
    millwork & lumber

Willingboro
Burlington County

(G-11988)
ALTERNATIVE AIR LLC (PA)
Also Called: Alternative Air Fixture
30 Echo Ln (08046-2247)
PHONE...................................609 261-5870
Jim Lunstead, *Partner*
Mike Banks, *Partner*
EMP: 5 **EST:** 1994
SALES (est): 646K **Privately Held**
WEB: www.airalternative.com
SIC: 2542 Fixtures, store: except wood

(G-11989)
BURLINGTON TIMES INC (HQ)
Also Called: Burlington County Times
4284 Route 130 (08046-2027)
PHONE..................................609 871-8000
Grover J Friend, *President*
Sandy V Fischer, *Purch Mgr*
Edward J Birch, *Treasurer*
EMP: 350 EST: 1958
SALES (est): 55.7MM
SALES (corp-wide): 1.5B **Publicly Held**
SIC: 2711 Commercial printing & newspaper publishing combined; newspapers, publishing & printing
PA: New Media Investment Group Inc.
1345 Avenue Of The Americ
New York NY 10105
212 479-3160

(G-11990)
COUNTER-FIT INC
1 Ironside Ct (08046-2533)
PHONE..................................609 871-8888
Michael Macaluso, *President*
Andrea Greerly, *Payroll Mgr*
▲ EMP: 135
SQ FT: 28,000
SALES (est): 11.5MM **Privately Held**
WEB: www.counter-fit.com
SIC: 2339 2337 3281 Sportswear, women's; women's & misses' suits & coats; cut stone & stone products

(G-11991)
HERMAN EICKHOFF
Also Called: Kennedy Shop N Bag
400 John F Kennedy Way (08046-2121)
PHONE..................................609 871-1809
Herman Eickhoff, *President*
Richard Eickhoff, *Vice Pres*
Karl Eickhoff, *Treasurer*
Bill Andrews, *Manager*
EMP: 104
SQ FT: 35,000
SALES (est): 7MM **Privately Held**
SIC: 5411 2051 Grocery stores; bread, cake & related products

(G-11992)
MAXTER CORPORATION
18 Chalford Ln (08046-3402)
PHONE..................................609 877-9700
John Mughal, *President*
Saida Mughal, *Vice Pres*
Rick Ruggerio, *Manager*
EMP: 4
SALES: 250K **Privately Held**
SIC: 3841 Surgical & medical instruments

(G-11993)
NATHJI PLUS INC
1 Rose St (08046-2537)
PHONE..................................609 877-7600
Hiren M Patel, *Principal*
EMP: 5
SALES (est): 668.1K **Privately Held**
SIC: 2836 Vaccines & other immunizing products

(G-11994)
PARADISE PUBLISHING GROUP LLC
25 Middlebury Ln Ste 3b (08046-2931)
PHONE..................................609 227-7642
Shema'yah Bey, *Principal*
EMP: 4
SALES (est): 83.8K **Privately Held**
SIC: 2711 Newspapers

Windsor
Mercer County

(G-11995)
DAVID BRADLEY CHOCOLATIER INC (PA)
92 N Main St Bldg 19 (08561-3209)
PHONE..................................609 443-4747
David Bradley, *Principal*
EMP: 14
SALES (est): 2.2MM **Privately Held**
SIC: 2066 2064 Chocolate & cocoa products; candy & other confectionery products

(G-11996)
HARWILL CORPORATION
Also Called: Harwill Express Press
92 N Main St (08561-3209)
P.O. Box 1645, East Windsor (08520-8945)
PHONE..................................609 895-1955
Steven Portrude, *President*
Harriet Portrude, *Admin Sec*
EMP: 7
SALES (est): 1.2MM **Privately Held**
WEB: www.harwill.net
SIC: 2759 7389 7336 Promotional printing; advertising literature: printing; advertising, promotional & trade show services; commercial art & graphic design; art design services; creative services to advertisers, except writers

(G-11997)
PYROMETER INSTRUMENT CO INC
92 N Main St Bldg 18d (08561-3209)
P.O. Box 479 (08561-0479)
PHONE..................................609 443-5522
Fax: 609 443-5590
EMP: 24 EST: 1928
SQ FT: 7,500
SALES (est): 4.4MM **Privately Held**
SIC: 3823 Mfg Process Control Instruments

(G-11998)
SILVER BRUSH LIMITED
92 N Main St Ste 19-I (08561-3209)
P.O. Box 414 (08561-0414)
PHONE..................................609 443-4900
Deirdra Silver, *President*
Edward Flax, *Corp Secy*
Ed Flax, *CFO*
▲ EMP: 5
SQ FT: 2,500
SALES (est): 972K **Privately Held**
WEB: www.silverbrush.com
SIC: 5199 3991 Artists' materials; paint brushes

(G-11999)
SPEC STEEL RULE DIES INC
92 N Main St Bldg 1b (08561-3209)
P.O. Box 33 (08561-0033)
PHONE..................................609 443-4435
John Nagy, *President*
Robert Margon, *Vice Pres*
Jessica Brown, *Admin Sec*
▲ EMP: 30
SQ FT: 7,000
SALES (est): 4.4MM **Privately Held**
WEB: www.specdies.com
SIC: 3544 Dies, steel rule

Wood Ridge
Bergen County

(G-12000)
ACADEMIA FURNITURE LLC
Also Called: Academia Furniture Industries
74 Passaic St (07075-1004)
PHONE..................................973 472-0100
Isaac Wagner, *CEO*
▲ EMP: 40
SQ FT: 140,000
SALES (est): 6.5MM **Privately Held**
SIC: 2531 5021 School furniture; office & public building furniture

(G-12001)
APPLE CORRUGATED BOX LTD
1 Passaic St Unit 76 (07075-1004)
PHONE..................................201 635-1269
Paul Belfiore, *Partner*
EMP: 16
SALES (est): 4.5MM **Privately Held**
SIC: 2653 Corrugated & solid fiber boxes

(G-12002)
CERTECH INC (DH)
Also Called: Morgan Technical Ceramics
1 Park Pl W (07075-2498)
PHONE..................................201 842-6800
John Stang, *CEO*
James McRickard, *President*
Ross Johnson, *Vice Pres*
Gilbert Carrasquillo, *Research*

Ron Delaney, *Executive*
▲ EMP: 114
SALES (est): 91.2MM
SALES (corp-wide): 1.3B **Privately Held**
SIC: 3364 Nonferrous die-castings except aluminum
HQ: Morganite Industries Inc.
4000 Westchase Blvd # 170
Raleigh NC 27607
919 821-1253

(G-12003)
KASANOVA INC
175 State Rt 17 (07075-2435)
PHONE..................................201 368-8400
Kathleen Campbell, *President*
▲ EMP: 6
SALES (est): 654.1K **Privately Held**
WEB: www.kasanova.com
SIC: 2434 Wood kitchen cabinets

(G-12004)
MEGA BRANDS AMERICA INC
68 Passaic St (07075-1004)
PHONE..................................973 535-1313
Chris Fraiser, *Technology*
EMP: 500
SALES (corp-wide): 75.8MM **Privately Held**
WEB: www.roseart.com
SIC: 2678 Stationery products
HQ: Mega Brands America, Inc.
333 Continental Blvd
El Segundo CA 90245
949 727-9009

(G-12005)
SKYLINE WINDOWS LLC
210 Park Pl E (07075-1808)
PHONE..................................201 531-9600
David Kraus, *President*
Samantha Falato, *Engineer*
EMP: 45
SALES (corp-wide): 88.9MM **Privately Held**
SIC: 2431 3442 Windows & window parts & trim, wood; metal doors, sash & trim
PA: Skyline Windows, Llc
220 E 138th St
Bronx NY 10451
212 491-3000

(G-12006)
STARFIRE LIGHTING INC
7 Donna Dr (07075-1915)
PHONE..................................201 438-9540
Zachary Gomes, *President*
Avinash Sanichar, *Engineer*
Craig Newman, *Treasurer*
Maggie Wisse, *Admin Asst*
▲ EMP: 50 EST: 1980
SQ FT: 50,000
SALES: 15.5MM **Privately Held**
WEB: www.starfirelighting.com
SIC: 3646 3645 Commercial indusl & institutional electric lighting fixtures; residential lighting fixtures

(G-12007)
TECH-PAK INC
3 Ethel Blvd (07075-2431)
PHONE..................................201 935-3800
Marvin Grossbard, *President*
EMP: 12
SALES (est): 1.4MM **Privately Held**
SIC: 3086 4226 3993 2672 Packaging & shipping materials, foamed plastic; special warehousing & storage; signs & advertising specialties; coated & laminated paper; bookbinding & related work

---

Woodbine
Cape May County

(G-12008)
BELLEPLAIN SUPPLY CO INC
Also Called: Belleplain Supply Gun Center
346 Hands Mill Rd (08270-3938)
PHONE..................................609 861-2345
Nicholas Germanio, *President*
Lou Ann Germanio, *Admin Sec*
EMP: 4 EST: 1967
SQ FT: 15,000

SALES (est): 595.6K **Privately Held**
WEB: www.browningguncenter.com
SIC: 3949 5699 Cases, gun & rod (sporting equipment); fishing equipment; sports apparel

(G-12009)
G & J SOLUTIONS INC
Also Called: Bill's Canvas Shop
419 Madison Ave (08270-2314)
PHONE..................................609 861-9838
John Dipompeo, *President*
Grace Dipompeo, *Corp Secy*
Yvonne Szafranski, *Sales Staff*
EMP: 13 EST: 1971
SQ FT: 7,300
SALES (est): 980K **Privately Held**
WEB: www.billscanvasshop.com
SIC: 2394 Awnings, fabric: made from purchased materials

(G-12010)
JMM STUDIOS
1524 Dehirsch Ave (08270-2412)
PHONE..................................609 861-3094
James Melonic, *Owner*
Adam Melonic, *Project Mgr*
EMP: 4
SALES (est): 250K **Privately Held**
SIC: 2531 Public building & related furniture

Woodbridge
Middlesex County

(G-12011)
35 FOOD CORP
Also Called: Antonio's Pasta
545 Us Highway 9 N (07095-1002)
PHONE..................................732 442-1640
Barbara Winant, *President*
Richard Winant, *Vice Pres*
EMP: 8
SQ FT: 3,800
SALES (est): 1MM **Privately Held**
SIC: 2099 5143 5149 Pasta, uncooked: packaged with other ingredients; cheese; pasta & rice

(G-12012)
ASCO
475 Us Highway 9 S (07095-1309)
PHONE..................................732 634-7017
Bill Goodliffe, *Principal*
EMP: 4 EST: 2009
SALES (est): 419.3K **Privately Held**
SIC: 3699 Electrical equipment & supplies

(G-12013)
ASCO POWER TECHNOLOGIES LP
1460 Us Highway 9 N # 209 (07095-1400)
PHONE..................................732 596-1733
Don Bachman, *Branch Mgr*
EMP: 11
SALES (corp-wide): 177.9K **Privately Held**
SIC: 3699 5063 Electrical equipment & supplies; electrical apparatus & equipment
HQ: Asco Power Technologies, L.P.
160 Park Ave
Florham Park NJ 07932

(G-12014)
AUTOMATIC SWITCH COMPANY
1460 Us Highway 9 N # 209 (07095-1408)
PHONE..................................732 596-1731
Ken Martin, *Manager*
EMP: 10
SALES (corp-wide): 17.4B **Publicly Held**
SIC: 3491 Solenoid valves
HQ: Automatic Switch Company
50-60 Hanover Rd
Florham Park NJ 07932
973 966-2000

(G-12015)
BOOKCODE CORP
2312 Plaza Dr (07095-1132)
PHONE..................................732 742-0481
Alok Mahapatra, *Director*
EMP: 9

SALES: 100K **Privately Held**
SIC: 2731 Book publishing

(G-12016)
GARDEN ST CHASIS REMANUF
1 Pennville Rd (07095)
PHONE.....................732 283-1910
Joseph Perez, *President*
Sabato Catucci, *Vice Pres*
Ronald Catucci, *Treasurer*
EMP: 50
SQ FT: 60,000
SALES (est): 6.4MM **Privately Held**
SIC: 3713 3711 Truck bodies (motor vehicles); chassis, motor vehicle

(G-12017)
HAIER AMERICA TRADING LLC
581 Main St 6 (07095-1148)
PHONE.....................212 594-3330
Lintau Lu, *Senior VP*
EMP: 4
SALES (corp-wide): 7.8K **Privately Held**
SIC: 3631 5064 Household cooking equipment; electrical appliances, television & radio
HQ: Haier America Trading, L.L.C.
50 Tice Blvd Ste 340
Woodcliff Lake NJ 07677
973 617-1800

(G-12018)
HARY MANUFACTURING INC
210 Grove Ave (07095-2337)
P.O. Box 187 (07095-0187)
PHONE.....................908 722-7100
Paul Hary, *President*
EMP: 10 EST: 2010
SQ FT: 10,000
SALES (est): 1.4MM **Privately Held**
SIC: 2759 3567 Screen printing; driers & redriers, industrial process

(G-12019)
MAUSER USA LLC
14 Convery Blvd (07095-2649)
PHONE.....................732 634-6000
Giovanni Balsano, *Plant Supt*
Monica McGrath, *Purch Mgr*
Herman Graff, *Branch Mgr*
Richard Richardson, *Maintence Staff*
EMP: 150
SALES (corp-wide): 1.1B **Privately Held**
WEB: www.mausergroup.com
SIC: 3412 Metal barrels, drums & pails
HQ: Mauser Usa, Llc
35 Cotters Ln Ste C
East Brunswick NJ 08816
732 353-7100

(G-12020)
RCLC INC (PA)
Also Called: Ra Liquidating
1480 Us Highway 9 N # 301 (07095-1407)
P.O. Box 3000 (07095-0995)
PHONE.....................732 877-1788
Louis V Aronson II, *President*
Daryl K Holcomb, *CFO*
Erwin M Ganz, *Treasurer*
Justin P Walder, *Admin Sec*
EMP: 16 EST: 1928
SALES (est): 4.6MM **Privately Held**
WEB: www.ronsoncorp.com
SIC: 3999 2899 3728 7363 Cigarette lighters, except precious metal; cigarette lighter flints; lighter fluid; aircraft parts & equipment; pilot service, aviation

(G-12021)
SNEAKER SWARM LLC
581 Main St Ste 640 (07095-1196)
PHONE.....................908 693-9262
Raheem Hardy, *Mng Member*
EMP: 11
SQ FT: 200,000
SALES (est): 350.1K **Privately Held**
SIC: 2721 Magazines: publishing & printing

(G-12022)
STONE MOUNTAIN PRINTING INC
Also Called: A-1 Thrifty Centers
74 Main St Fl 1 (07095-2963)
PHONE.....................732 636-8450
Steven Steinberg, *President*
Hank Steinberg, *Corp Secy*

EMP: 8
SQ FT: 24,000
SALES (est): 810K **Privately Held**
WEB: www.stonemountainprinting.com
SIC: 2752 Commercial printing, offset

(G-12023)
UNITED PREMIUM FOODS LLC
1 Amboy Ave (07095-2639)
PHONE.....................732 510-5600
Jim Kwon, *Mng Member*
EMP: 100
SQ FT: 5,000
SALES (est): 3.3MM **Privately Held**
SIC: 2011 5147 Meat packing plants; meats & meat products

(G-12024)
WOODBRIDGE MACHINE & TOOL CO
259 Bergen St (07095-1829)
PHONE.....................732 634-0179
Steve J Sepa, *President*
Irma Sepa, *Corp Secy*
EMP: 7
SQ FT: 2,500
SALES (est): 1MM **Privately Held**
SIC: 3599 Machine shop, jobbing & repair

Woodbury
Gloucester County

(G-12025)
AUNTIE ANNES SOFT PRETZELS
1750 Deptford Center Rd # 2086 (08096-5222)
PHONE.....................856 845-3667
Jane Hanson, *Manager*
Christine Aquelino, *Manager*
Melvin Sickler, *Admin Sec*
EMP: 35
SALES (est): 900.8K **Privately Held**
SIC: 5461 2052 Pretzels; pretzels

(G-12026)
BELLIA & SONS
1047 N Broad St (08096-3565)
PHONE.....................856 845-2234
Tom Bellia, *Owner*
Anthony Bellia, *Owner*
Carmen Dominguez, *Project Mgr*
EMP: 30
SQ FT: 3,000
SALES (est): 4.1MM **Privately Held**
SIC: 6513 7334 5943 5712 Apartment hotel operation; blueprinting service; office forms & supplies; office furniture; invitation & stationery printing & engraving

(G-12027)
DEWECHTER INC
Also Called: Constitution Co
58 S Broad St (08096-4629)
P.O. Box 358 (08096-7358)
PHONE.....................856 845-0225
Daniel Dewechter, *President*
EMP: 4 EST: 1946
SQ FT: 3,000
SALES (est): 360.3K **Privately Held**
SIC: 2759 Letterpress printing

(G-12028)
EP HENRY CORPORATION (PA)
201 Park Ave (08096-3599)
P.O. Box 615 (08096-7615)
PHONE.....................856 845-6200
James C Henry III, *CEO*
James C Henry Jr, *CEO*
Shafer Henry, *Vice Pres*
John Poignard, *Vice Pres*
Brian Trivelli, *Production*
▲ EMP: 100
SALES (est): 27.8MM **Privately Held**
WEB: www.ephenry.com
SIC: 3271 3281 5072 Blocks, concrete or cinder: standard; paving blocks, cut stone; builders' hardware

(G-12029)
FERRETT PRINTING INC
468 Warwick Rd (08096-6018)
PHONE.....................856 686-4896

Nicholas Ferrett, *President*
EMP: 5
SALES (est): 667.4K **Privately Held**
SIC: 2752 Commercial printing, lithographic

(G-12030)
GLOUCESTER COUNTY TIMES
309 S Broad St (08096-2406)
PHONE.....................856 845-7484
Frank Gargano, *President*
EMP: 5
SALES (est): 83.8K **Privately Held**
SIC: 2711 Newspapers, publishing & printing

(G-12031)
GTM MARKETING INC
1960 Harris Dr (08096-3863)
PHONE.....................856 227-2333
Karl R Baker, *President*
EMP: 6
SALES (est): 604.1K **Privately Held**
SIC: 2759 Screen printing

(G-12032)
HARRISBURG STAMP & STENCIL CO
10 Greenwood Ave Ste C (08096-3350)
PHONE.....................717 236-9000
John A Collins III, *President*
John A Collins Jr, *President*
EMP: 5
SALES: 500K
SALES (corp-wide): 10.3MM **Privately Held**
WEB: www.ams-stamps.com
SIC: 3953 Marking devices
PA: American Marking Systems Inc
1015 Paulison Ave
Clifton NJ 07011
973 478-5600

(G-12033)
NJ DEPT MILITARY VTRANS
Also Called: New Jersey National Guard
658 N Evergreen Ave (08096-3512)
PHONE.....................856 384-8831
EMP: 4 **Privately Held**
SIC: 9711 2731 National Security Books-Publishing/Printing
HQ: New Jersey Department Of Military And Veterans Affairs
101 Eggerts Crossing Rd
Lawrenceville NJ
609 530-6957

(G-12034)
ONE TWO THREE INC
537 Mantua Pike Ste B (08096-3257)
P.O. Box 123 (08096-7123)
PHONE.....................856 251-1238
Randy Rigley, *President*
EMP: 13
SALES (est): 1.7MM **Privately Held**
SIC: 2752 5199 Commercial printing, lithographic; advertising specialties

(G-12035)
PAUL FAGO CABINET MAKING INC
425 S Columbia St (08096-5733)
PHONE.....................856 384-0496
Susan Fago, *Executive*
EMP: 8
SALES (est): 704.6K **Privately Held**
SIC: 2434 Wood kitchen cabinets

(G-12036)
SECURITY 21 LLC
119 Steeplechase Ct (08096-6801)
PHONE.....................856 384-7474
Vince Reilly,
EMP: 6
SALES (est): 757.7K **Privately Held**
SIC: 3699 Security control equipment & systems

(G-12037)
SIGN SHOPPE INC
370 Glassboro Rd (08097-1009)
PHONE.....................856 384-2937
Janet Philphs, *President*
EMP: 5

SALES (est): 416K **Privately Held**
SIC: 3993 1799 7532 Signs & advertising specialties; sign installation & maintenance; truck painting & lettering

(G-12038)
SPECIALTY CASTING INC
42 Curtis Ave (08096-4636)
PHONE.....................856 845-3105
John F Cowgill, *President*
Daniel Cowgill, *Vice Pres*
EMP: 4
SQ FT: 5,000
SALES (est): 270K **Privately Held**
WEB: www.specialtycasting.com
SIC: 2821 Plastics materials & resins

(G-12039)
WORK N GEAR LLC
Also Called: Work'n Gear 8047
1692 Clements Bridge Rd H (08096-3028)
PHONE.....................856 848-7676
Lisa Grasso, *Manager*
EMP: 7
SALES (corp-wide): 46.1MM **Privately Held**
WEB: www.workngear.com
SIC: 5961 2759 Catalog & mail-order houses; screen printing
PA: Work 'n Gear, Llc
2300 Crown Colony Dr # 301
Quincy MA 02169
781 746-0100

Woodbury Heights
Gloucester County

(G-12040)
431 CONVERTERS INC
Also Called: Converter Company, The
230 Glassboro Rd (08097-1013)
PHONE.....................856 848-8949
Austin Bombaro, *President*
Ted Reinder, *Treasurer*
EMP: 6
SALES (est): 975.9K **Privately Held**
SIC: 3566 Torque converters, except automotive

(G-12041)
BILL CHAMBERS SHEET METAL
371 Glassboro Rd Ste 5 (08097-1026)
P.O. Box 172 (08097-0172)
PHONE.....................856 848-4774
William Chambers III, *Owner*
EMP: 3
SQ FT: 3,600
SALES: 1.5MM **Privately Held**
SIC: 3444 Sheet metalwork

(G-12042)
ELLENBY TECHNOLOGIES INC
412 Grandview Ave (08097-1556)
PHONE.....................856 848-2020
Bob Dobbins, *CEO*
Brian Stang, *Vice Pres*
Rick Morgan, *Purchasing*
Tom Carullo, *Engineer*
Andrea Mair, *Engineer*
▲ EMP: 45
SQ FT: 50,000
SALES (est): 9.6MM **Privately Held**
WEB: www.ellenbytech.com
SIC: 3699 8711 5063 Electrical equipment & supplies; consulting engineer; electrical apparatus & equipment

(G-12043)
EXCEL COLOR GRAPHICS INC
207 W Jersey Ave (08097-1035)
PHONE.....................856 848-3345
Jean-Paul Bonnette, *President*
Linda S Bonnette, *Corp Secy*
EMP: 6
SQ FT: 7,500
SALES: 650K **Privately Held**
SIC: 2752 Commercial printing, offset

(G-12044)
WOODBURY ROOF TRUSS INC
Also Called: Concord Truss Co
692 S Evergreen Ave (08097-1021)
PHONE.....................856 845-3848

Richard Phalines, *President*
John Gligor Sr, *Corp Secy*
EMP: 85
SQ FT: 40,000
SALES (est): 19.7MM **Privately Held**
SIC: 2439 Trusses, wooden roof; trusses, except roof: laminated lumber

Woodcliff Lake
Bergen County

(G-12045)
AMERICAN AUTO CARRIERS INC
188 Broadway Ste 1 (07677-8072)
PHONE..................................201 573-0371
Ray Ebeling, *President*
Arlen F Henock, *CFO*
EMP: 4
SALES (est): 256.2K **Privately Held**
WEB: www.walleniuslines.com
SIC: 3443 Industrial vessels, tanks & containers

(G-12046)
AMERICAN LOGISTICS NETWORK LLC
Also Called: Aln
188 Broadway Ste 1 (07677-8072)
PHONE..................................201 391-1054
Jhon Igltsias, *Principal*
Allison Pearsall, *Human Resources*
Robin Tarantino, *Director*
EMP: 8
SALES (est): 820K **Privately Held**
SIC: 3423 Jewelers' hand tools

(G-12047)
ATLANTEX INSTRUMENTS INC
7 Reeds Ln (07677-8348)
PHONE..................................201 391-5148
Hatcho A Fendian, *President*
Jessica Egler, *Software Engr*
EMP: 5
SALES (est): 736.3K **Privately Held**
SIC: 3699 Photographic control systems, electronic

(G-12048)
BMC SOFTWARE INC
50 Tice Blvd (07677-7654)
PHONE..................................703 761-0400
John Beischer, *Manager*
EMP: 8
SALES (corp-wide): 1.5B **Privately Held**
WEB: www.bmc.com
SIC: 7372 Prepackaged software
HQ: Bmc Software, Inc.
  2103 Citywest Blvd # 2100
  Houston TX 77042
  713 918-8800

(G-12049)
BMW OF NORTH AMERICA LLC (DH)
Also Called: BMW Group
300 Chestnut Ridge Rd (07677-7731)
P.O. Box 1227, Westwood (07675-1227)
PHONE..................................201 307-4000
Ludwig Willisch, *CEO*
Stefan Borbe, *General Mgr*
David Morrison, *General Mgr*
Markus Seidel, *General Mgr*
Joachim Steinle, *General Mgr*
◆ **EMP:** 700
SQ FT: 200,000
SALES (est): 1.8B
SALES (corp-wide): 111.6B **Privately Held**
WEB: www.detroitbmw.com
SIC: 5013 3751 5012 3711 Automotive supplies & parts; motorcycles, bicycles & parts; automobiles; motor vehicles & car bodies
HQ: Bmw (Us) Holding Corp.
  300 Chestnut Ridge Rd
  Woodcliff Lake NJ 07677
  201 307-4000

(G-12050)
BUTTONWOOD ENTERPRISES LLC
52 Winding Way (07677-7930)
PHONE..................................201 505-1901
Andrew Groh, *Mng Member*
Alan Edelman,
▲ **EMP:** 4
SALES: 500K **Privately Held**
SIC: 3825 7389 Internal combustion engine analyzers, to test electronics;

(G-12051)
CAST INC
Also Called: Computer Aided Software Tech
11 Stonewall Ct (07677-8412)
PHONE..................................201 391-8300
Nikolaos Zervas, *CEO*
Stephen Pollock, *President*
Harold Barbour, *Chairman*
Newton Abdala, *Vice Pres*
EMP: 9
SALES: 4MM **Privately Held**
WEB: www.cast-inc.com
SIC: 3674 Semiconductors & related devices

(G-12052)
CATALOGIC SOFTWARE INC
50 Tice Blvd Ste 110 (07677-7654)
PHONE..................................201 249-8980
Ken Barth, *President*
Mike Kuehn, *Vice Pres*
Rich Pappas, *Vice Pres*
Jeffery Chan, *Engineer*
CHI S Chang, *Engineer*
EMP: 120
SALES (est): 17.6MM **Privately Held**
SIC: 7372 Business oriented computer software

(G-12053)
CLIC TIME LLC
50 Tice Blvd Ste 340 (07677-7681)
PHONE..................................201 497-6743
James Richardson, *Managing Dir*
Mark Shell, *Mng Member*
◆ **EMP:** 22
SQ FT: 2,600
SALES: 14.9MM
SALES (corp-wide): 22.2MM **Privately Held**
SIC: 3873 5094 Watches, clocks, watchcases & parts; clocks, watches & parts
PA: Clic Time Holdings Limited
  The Old Police Station
  Newcastle-Upon-Tyne NE20

(G-12054)
EAGLE PHARMACEUTICALS INC (PA)
50 Tice Blvd Ste 315 (07677-7637)
PHONE..................................201 326-5300
Scott Tarriff, *CEO*
Michael Graves, *Ch of Bd*
David Pernock, *President*
Pete A Meyers, *CFO*
David E Riggs, *CFO*
▲ **EMP:** 43
SQ FT: 20,497
SALES: 213.3MM **Publicly Held**
SIC: 2834 Druggists' preparations (pharmaceuticals)

(G-12055)
EISAI INC (DH)
100 Tice Blvd (07677-8404)
PHONE..................................201 692-1100
Cynthia Schwalm, *President*
Lihua Yu, *President*
Jeffrey Granberry, *General Mgr*
Hideo Dan, *Senior VP*
Adriana Herrera, *Senior VP*
▲ **EMP:** 182
SALES (est): 161.5MM **Privately Held**
WEB: www.aciphex.com
SIC: 2834 Pharmaceutical preparations

(G-12056)
ESCO INDUSTRIES CORP
30 Stonewall Ct (07677-8413)
PHONE..................................973 478-5888
Leo Hsu, *President*
James Hsu, *General Mgr*
Jack Hsu, *Vice Pres*

Kathy Hsu, *Admin Sec*
▲ **EMP:** 25
SQ FT: 40,000
SALES (est): 5.3MM **Privately Held**
SIC: 3498 Fabricated pipe & fittings

(G-12057)
ID SYSTEMS INC (PA)
123 Tice Blvd (07677-7670)
PHONE..................................201 996-9000
Chris Wolfe, *CEO*
Norman L Ellis, *COO*
Roman Hlutkowsky, *Vice Pres*
Meg Otto, *Vice Pres*
Joey Pinzon, *Vice Pres*
▲ **EMP:** 101
SQ FT: 21,400
SALES: 53MM **Publicly Held**
WEB: www.id-systems.com
SIC: 3663 4812 ; radio telephone communication; cellular telephone services

(G-12058)
IVAX PHARMACEUTICALS LLC
400 Chestnut Ridge Rd (07677-7604)
PHONE..................................201 767-1700
Eric Mittleberg, *Branch Mgr*
EMP: 5
SALES (corp-wide): 5B **Privately Held**
WEB: www.ivaxpharmaceuticals.com
SIC: 2834 Pharmaceutical preparations
HQ: Ivax Pharmaceuticals, Llc
  74 Nw 176th St
  Miami FL 33169

(G-12059)
MEK INTERNATIONAL INC
3 Stonewall Ct (07677-8412)
PHONE..................................215 712-2490
Peter Kim, *President*
▲ **EMP:** 5
SALES (est): 553K **Privately Held**
SIC: 2311 2399 Policemen's uniforms: made from purchased materials; military insignia, textile

(G-12060)
PATAGONIA PHARMACEUTICALS LLC
50 Tice Blvd Ste A26 (07677-7682)
PHONE..................................201 264-7866
Rome Joshua, *Principal*
Zachary Rome, *Exec VP*
EMP: 5
SALES (est): 422.7K **Privately Held**
SIC: 2834 Pharmaceutical preparations

(G-12061)
PERFECT CLICKS LLC
172 Broadway Rear Bldg (07677-8077)
PHONE..................................845 323-6116
Chad Agrawal,
EMP: 4
SALES: 500K **Privately Held**
SIC: 2741

(G-12062)
PROFESSIONAL DISPOSABLES INC
400 Chestnut Ridge Rd (07677-7604)
PHONE..................................845 365-1700
Rozalia Gandelman, *Manager*
EMP: 948 **Privately Held**
SIC: 2676 Sanitary paper products
PA: Professional Disposables Inc.
  2 Nice Pak Park
  Orangeburg NY 10962

(G-12063)
ROLLS-ROYCE MOTOR CARS NA LLC
300 Chestnut Ridge Rd (07677-7739)
P.O. Box 1227, Westwood (07675-1227)
PHONE..................................201 307-4117
Pedro Moto, *President*
Sabine Brown, *General Mgr*
Scott Medley, *General Mgr*
Kyle Lippman, *Business Mgr*
Thomas Felbermair, *Vice Pres*
◆ **EMP:** 4293
SALES (est): 228.8MM
SALES (corp-wide): 111.6B **Privately Held**
SIC: 3711 Motor vehicles & car bodies

HQ: Bmw (Us) Holding Corp.
  300 Chestnut Ridge Rd
  Woodcliff Lake NJ 07677
  201 307-4000

(G-12064)
SKY GROWTH INTERMEDIATE
300 Tice Blvd (07677-8406)
PHONE..................................201 802-4000
Paul V Campanelli, *CEO*
Mike Burton, *President*
Joseph Barbarite, *Vice Pres*
Carlos Cruz, *Vice Pres*
Chad Gassert, *Vice Pres*
EMP: 350
SQ FT: 61,000
SALES (est): 28.1MM **Privately Held**
SIC: 2834 Druggists' preparations (pharmaceuticals)
HQ: Par Pharmaceutical, Inc.
  1 Ram Ridge Rd
  Chestnut Ridge NY 10977
  845 573-5500

(G-12065)
SONY CORPORATION OF AMERICA
123 Tice Blvd (07677-7670)
PHONE..................................201 930-1000
Jerry Kaplan, *Branch Mgr*
Dave Carson, *Manager*
Mike Pigoncelli, *Manager*
Noura Sen, *Manager*
EMP: 15 **Privately Held**
WEB: www.sony.com
SIC: 7812 7832 5064 3559 Motion picture production & distribution; motion picture production & distribution, television; motion picture theaters, except drive-in; television sets; radios; video cassette recorders & accessories; tape players & recorders; metal finishing equipment for plating, etc.; household audio equipment; household video equipment; software, computer games
HQ: Sony Corporation Of America
  25 Madison Ave Fl 27
  New York NY 10010
  212 833-8000

(G-12066)
TAB NETWORKS
50 Tice Blvd Ste 365 (07677-7673)
PHONE..................................201 746-0067
Thomas Plaut, *President*
Karen Richardson, *Accountant*
EMP: 5
SALES (est): 630.8K **Privately Held**
SIC: 7372 Prepackaged software

(G-12067)
UNIPORT INDUSTRIES CORPORATION
Also Called: Image Builder Appliques
23 Campbell Ave (07677-8061)
P.O. Box 8642 (07677-8642)
PHONE..................................201 391-6422
Diane Anderson, *President*
Harry Anderson, *Vice Pres*
EMP: 6
SQ FT: 2,000
SALES (est): 945.4K **Privately Held**
WEB: www.uniportind.com
SIC: 5131 2395 Piece goods & notions; emblems, embroidered

Woodland Park
Passaic County

(G-12068)
ACE METAL KRAFT CO INC
815 Mcbride Ave (07424-2892)
PHONE..................................973 278-6605
Richard Zega, *President*
John Lamanna, *Vice Pres*
EMP: 21
SQ FT: 6,400
SALES (est): 3.8MM **Privately Held**
SIC: 3599 Machine shop, jobbing & repair

(G-12069)
ADVANCED SEWER
10 Memorial Dr (07424-2515)
P.O. Box 2056, West Paterson (07424-7056)
PHONE..................................973 278-1948
Barbra Denora, *President*
EMP: 15
SALES (est): 1MM **Privately Held**
SIC: 1711 2842 Plumbing contractors; drain pipe solvents or cleaners

(G-12070)
AUTOPLAST SYSTEMS INC
Also Called: Asi
256 Bergen Blvd (07424-2502)
P.O. Box 312, Closter (07624-0312)
PHONE..................................973 785-8333
Elias Haber, *President*
EMP: 4
SALES (est): 428.9K **Privately Held**
SIC: 3559 Plastics working machinery

(G-12071)
BMB MACHINING LLC
86 Lackawanna Ave 208b (07424-2565)
PHONE..................................973 256-4010
Lawrence H Malone, *Owner*
Gennaro Minichino, *Owner*
EMP: 4
SALES (est): 155.1K **Privately Held**
SIC: 3451 Screw machine products

(G-12072)
BROMILOWS CANDY CO (PA)
350 Rifle Camp Rd (07424-2726)
PHONE..................................973 684-1496
Thomas Stewart, *President*
Ginny Monk, *General Mgr*
Ida Bromilow Stewart, *Vice Pres*
EMP: 6 EST: 1940
SQ FT: 5,000
SALES (est): 1.4MM **Privately Held**
WEB: www.bromilow.com
SIC: 5441 2064 2066 Candy; chocolate candy, except solid chocolate; chocolate & cocoa products

(G-12073)
CAMEO METAL FORMS INC
12 Andrews Dr (07424-2640)
PHONE..................................718 788-1106
Antonio Di Maio, *President*
Vito Di Maio, *Vice Pres*
EMP: 10
SALES (est): 780K **Privately Held**
SIC: 3951 3221 Ball point pens & parts; cosmetic jars, glass

(G-12074)
CENTURY BATHWORKS INC (PA)
Also Called: Century Shower Door
250 Lackawanna Ave Ste 2 (07424-2962)
PHONE..................................973 785-4290
Michael Macmillan, *President*
Ben Peschler, *Production*
Michael Russo, *Natl Sales Mgr*
Rosa Jurewicz, *Cust Mgr*
David Dixon, *Marketing Staff*
▲ EMP: 95 EST: 1946
SQ FT: 75,000
SALES (est): 22.1MM **Privately Held**
WEB: www.centuryshowerdoor-usa.com
SIC: 3231 3442 Doors, glass: made from purchased glass; screen doors, metal

(G-12075)
CENTURY BATHWORKS INC
Also Called: Screens & Fabricated Metals
250 Lackawanna Ave Ste 1 (07424-2962)
P.O. Box 647, West Paterson (07424-0647)
PHONE..................................201 785-1414
Phillip Bolchune, *Manager*
EMP: 30
SQ FT: 30,000
SALES (corp-wide): 22.1MM **Privately Held**
WEB: www.centuryshowerdoor-usa.com
SIC: 3442 3231 Metal doors; products of purchased glass
PA: Century Bathworks, Inc.
250 Lackawanna Ave Ste 2
Woodland Park NJ 07424
973 785-4290

(G-12076)
ELAINE INC
Also Called: Motomco
1 Hazel St (07424-3203)
PHONE..................................973 345-6200
Anthony Abbate, *President*
Elaine Abbate, *Admin Sec*
EMP: 6
SQ FT: 8,000
SALES: 500K **Privately Held**
WEB: www.njmeter.com
SIC: 5075 3823 Air filters; moisture meters, industrial process type

(G-12077)
EVERGREEN INFORMATION SVCS INC
8 Cedarwood Ter (07424-3709)
PHONE..................................973 339-9672
John Gilrain, *President*
Lisa Gilrain, *Vice Pres*
Karen Stuart, *Department Mgr*
EMP: 10 EST: 2008
SALES: 1.6MM **Privately Held**
SIC: 2731 2711 2721 Book publishing; newspapers: publishing only, not printed on site; magazines: publishing only, not printed on site

(G-12078)
F S R INC
244 Bergen Blvd (07424-2502)
PHONE..................................973 785-4347
William Fitzsimmons, *Chairman*
Dennis Kendzior, *Production*
Tom Damiano, *Purch Agent*
Brian Langbeen, *Engineer*
Scott Altieri, *Sales Mgr*
◆ EMP: 85
SQ FT: 27,000
SALES (est): 16.9MM **Privately Held**
SIC: 3663 3624 Radio & television switching equipment; electric carbons

(G-12079)
FMC CORPORATION
1130 Mcbride Ave (07424-3806)
PHONE..................................973 256-0768
Claire Sasak, *Branch Mgr*
EMP: 61
SALES (corp-wide): 4.7B **Publicly Held**
SIC: 2812 Soda ash, sodium carbonate (anhydrous)
PA: Fmc Corporation
2929 Walnut St
Philadelphia PA 19104
215 299-6000

(G-12080)
G & Y SPECIALTY FOODS LLC
2 Andrews Dr Ste 5 (07424-2604)
PHONE..................................956 821-9652
Jose Yvan Vazquez, *Mng Member*
Yusleidy Diaz, *Mng Member*
EMP: 8
SALES (est): 247.3K **Privately Held**
SIC: 5149 2037 Groceries & related products; fruit juices

(G-12081)
HERALD NEWS (PA)
Also Called: North Jersey Com. Newspaper
1 Garret Mountain Plz # 201 (07424-3398)
PHONE..................................973 569-7000
Malcom Borg, *Publisher*
Young West III, *Principal*
Leonard Robinson, *Advt Staff*
Gail Carlin, *Payroll Mgr*
John Flynn, *Art Dir*
EMP: 5
SALES (est): 2.1MM **Privately Held**
SIC: 2711 5521 2752 Newspapers, publishing & printing; used car dealers; commercial printing, lithographic

(G-12082)
IFORTRESS
228 Lackawanna Ave (07424-2996)
PHONE..................................973 812-6400
Karen Loughran, *Principal*
Robert Hayes, *Officer*
EMP: 4
SALES (est): 230K **Privately Held**
SIC: 3699 Security control equipment & systems

(G-12083)
KEARFOTT CORPORATION (HQ)
1150 Mcbride Ave Ste 1 (07424-2564)
PHONE..................................973 785-6000
Ronald E Zelazo, *President*
Middleton John, *General Mgr*
Natasha McLucas, *General Mgr*
Peter Boyfield, *Business Mgr*
Dominic Pascucci, *Business Mgr*
EMP: 220
SQ FT: 1,000,000
SALES (est): 213.7MM
SALES (corp-wide): 350.9MM **Privately Held**
WEB: www.ashfield.kearfott.com
SIC: 3812 Search & navigation equipment
PA: Astronautics Corporation Of America
4115 N Teutonia Ave
Milwaukee WI 53209
414 449-4000

(G-12084)
MAXELL CORPORATION OF AMERICA (HQ)
3 Garret Mountain Plz # 300 (07424-3352)
PHONE..................................973 653-2400
Steven Wafhio, *President*
Len Haine, *Vice Pres*
Kyoko Murakami, *Export Mgr*
Martin Lobkowicz, *Regl Sales Mgr*
Linda Pintard, *Cust Mgr*
◆ EMP: 30
SQ FT: 28,000
SALES (est): 680.4MM **Privately Held**
WEB: www.maxell.com
SIC: 3691 3652 3679 Storage batteries; pre-recorded records & tapes; headphones, radio

(G-12085)
NORTH JERSEY MEDIA GROUP INC
Also Called: Herald News
1 Garret Mountain Plz # 201 (07424-3318)
P.O. Box 471, West Paterson (07424-0471)
PHONE..................................973 569-7100
James Toolen, *Manager*
EMP: 40
SALES (corp-wide): 156.2MM **Privately Held**
WEB: www.njmg.com
SIC: 2711 2741 Newspapers; miscellaneous publishing
HQ: North Jersey Media Group Inc.
150 River St
Hackensack NJ 07601
201 646-4000

(G-12086)
POCHET OF AMERICA INC
Also Called: Art-Deco Division
1 Garret Mountain Plz # 502 (07424-3320)
PHONE..................................973 942-4923
Jean Claude Moreau, *President*
▲ EMP: 150
SQ FT: 73,000
SALES (est): 19.9MM
SALES (corp-wide): 28.7MM **Privately Held**
WEB: www.pochet.org
SIC: 3221 2759 Glass containers; engraving
HQ: Pochet Du Courval
44 46
Clichy 92110
964 439-556

(G-12087)
PREMIER COMPACTION SYSTEMS
264 Lackawanna Ave Ste 1 (07424-2959)
PHONE..................................718 328-5990
EMP: 10 EST: 2013
SALES (est): 1.9MM **Privately Held**
SIC: 5084 3589 Whol Industrial Equipment Mfg Service Industry Machinery

(G-12088)
QUALIPAC AMERICA CORP
1 Garret Mountain Plz # 502 (07424-3312)
PHONE..................................973 754-9920
Herve Robine, *President*
▲ EMP: 17
SQ FT: 30,000
SALES (est): 3MM
SALES (corp-wide): 28.7MM **Privately Held**
SIC: 3089 3085 Cases, plastic; bottle caps, molded plastic; closures, plastic; plastics bottles
HQ: Qualipac
44 46
Clichy 92110

(G-12089)
RBC DAIN RAUSCHER
3 Garret Mountain Plz # 201 (07424-3352)
PHONE..................................973 778-7300
Stan Golderberg, *Principal*
EMP: 15
SALES (est): 1.9MM **Privately Held**
SIC: 3324 Steel investment foundries

(G-12090)
RELX INC
1167 Mcbride Ave Ste 3 (07424-2543)
PHONE..................................973 812-1900
Robert Sikora, *Research*
EMP: 60
SALES (corp-wide): 9.6B **Privately Held**
WEB: www.lexis-nexis.com
SIC: 2721 Periodicals
HQ: Relx Inc.
230 Park Ave Ste 700
New York NY 10169
212 309-8100

(G-12091)
SKS FUEL INC
941 Mcbride Ave (07424-2618)
PHONE..................................973 200-0796
EMP: 4
SALES (est): 210.2K **Privately Held**
SIC: 2869 Fuels

(G-12092)
TECHNIQUES INC
14 Alexandria Ct (07424-3410)
PHONE..................................973 256-0947
Arvind Patel, *President*
EMP: 29 EST: 1955
SQ FT: 15,000
SALES: 1.7MM **Privately Held**
SIC: 3672 3613 Printed circuit boards; time switches, electrical switchgear apparatus

(G-12093)
TOMCEL MACHINE INC
86 Lackawanna Ave Ste 301 (07424-3805)
PHONE..................................973 256-8257
Frederick Foy, *President*
EMP: 5
SQ FT: 2,100
SALES: 250K **Privately Held**
SIC: 3599 Machine shop, jobbing & repair

Woodstown
Salem County

(G-12094)
A1 CUSTOM COUNTERTOPS INC
20 Old Salem Rd (08098-9474)
PHONE..................................856 200-3596
Thomas Matteo, *President*
Steve Matteo, *Vice Pres*
Elaine Matteo, *Treasurer*
Everett Matteo, *Admin Sec*
EMP: 10
SALES (est): 603.8K **Privately Held**
SIC: 2541 Counter & sink tops

(G-12095)
P W PERKINS CO INC
221 Commissioners Pike (08098-2032)
PHONE..................................856 769-3525
Charles B Perkins III, *CEO*
EMP: 7
SQ FT: 2,500
SALES (est): 831.8K **Privately Held**
WEB: www.pwperkins.com
SIC: 2819 Industrial inorganic chemicals

(G-12096)
SOUTH JERSEY FARMERS EXCHANGE
101 East Ave (08098-1318)
PHONE................................856 769-0062
Lee C Williams Jr, *President*
Sara Williams, *Treasurer*
EMP: 7
SQ FT: 35,000
SALES (est): 1MM **Privately Held**
SIC: 2873 3523 Fertilizers: natural (organic), except compost; turf equipment, commercial

Woolwich Township
Gloucester County

(G-12097)
GRASSO FOODS INC
9 Ogden Rd (08085-3435)
P.O. Box 427, Swedesboro (08085-0427)
PHONE................................856 467-2223
EMP: 4
SALES (est): 258.4K **Privately Held**
SIC: 2037 Frozen fruits & vegetables

(G-12098)
SHANI AUTO FUEL CORP
541 Kings Hwy (08085-5057)
PHONE................................856 241-9767
EMP: 4
SALES (est): 309K **Privately Held**
SIC: 2869 Fuels

Wrightstown
Burlington County

(G-12099)
MARANATHA CERAMIC TILE & MARBL
Also Called: Maranatha Stairs
253 Cokstown New Egypt Rd
(08562-1722)
PHONE................................609 758-1168
Thomas Raab, *President*
Patricia Raab, *Treasurer*
EMP: 20
SQ FT: 12,000
SALES (est): 4.7MM **Privately Held**
WEB: www.maranathastairs.net
SIC: 5211 1743 1799 2431 Tile, ceramic; tile installation, ceramic; home/office interiors finishing, furnishing & remodeling; staircases & stairs, wood

(G-12100)
SPECIALTY FABRICATORS LLC
118 Meany Rd (08562-1612)
PHONE................................609 758-6995
Buddy Wilkins, *Purch Mgr*
Ken Austin, *Design Engr*
Jim Christman, *Sales Staff*
Ed Symbouras, *Mng Member*
Ross Varra, *Manager*
EMP: 40
SQ FT: 20,000
SALES (est): 9MM **Privately Held**
WEB: www.specialtyfabricators.com
SIC: 3585 Refrigeration & heating equipment

Wyckoff
Bergen County

(G-12101)
AIR & HYDRAULIC POWER INC
555 Goffle Rd (07481-2937)
P.O. Box 159 (07481-0159)
PHONE................................201 447-1589
Robert A Main Jr, *President*
Susan Main, *Corp Secy*
Timothy Den Bleyker, *Vice Pres*
Bill Main, *Vice Pres*
William Main, *Vice Pres*
EMP: 8
SQ FT: 32,000
SALES: 550K
SALES (corp-wide): 35.5MM **Privately Held**
SIC: 3492 Valves, hydraulic, aircraft
PA: Main, Robert A & Sons Holding Company Inc
555 Goffle Rd
Wyckoff NJ 07481
201 447-3700

(G-12102)
ALADEN ATHLETIC WEAR LLC
465 W Main St Ste 5 (07481-1452)
PHONE................................973 838-2425
Ron L Blaustein, *President*
Carlos A Arco, *Vice Pres*
Rafael A Arco, *Vice Pres*
EMP: 25
SQ FT: 11,000
SALES (est): 1.5MM **Privately Held**
SIC: 2329 Men's & boys' sportswear & athletic clothing

(G-12103)
BARRETT BRONZE INC
540 Ravine Ct (07481-2921)
PHONE................................914 699-6060
Eli Ross, *President*
Jamie Ross, *Principal*
Jeff Hirshon, *Prdtn Mgr*
▲ EMP: 20
SALES (est): 2.2MM **Privately Held**
WEB: www.barrettbronze.com
SIC: 3299 2821 Statuary: gypsum, clay, papier mache, metal, etc.; plastics materials & resins

(G-12104)
BEALL TECHNOLOGIES INC
210 Braen Ave (07481-2948)
PHONE................................201 689-2130
Purnendu Chatterjee, *President*
George Soros,
EMP: 20 EST: 1970
SALES (est): 1.5MM **Privately Held**
SIC: 3577 3643 Computer peripheral equipment; current-carrying wiring devices

(G-12105)
BIG COLOR SYSTEM INC
681 Lawlins Rd Unit 30 (07481-1443)
PHONE................................201 236-0404
Mike Bognar, *Owner*
EMP: 12
SALES (est): 1.9MM **Privately Held**
SIC: 2759 Commercial printing

(G-12106)
C J ELECTRIC
327 Franklin Ave (07481-2041)
PHONE................................201 891-0739
EMP: 5
SALES (est): 92.4K **Privately Held**
SIC: 4911 3699 1731 Electric services; electrical equipment & supplies; electrical work

(G-12107)
CORDES PRINTING INC
460 Braen Ave (07481-2949)
PHONE................................201 652-7272
Mark Cordes, *President*
Linda March, *Technology*
EMP: 6
SALES (est): 1MM **Privately Held**
WEB: www.cordesprinting.com
SIC: 2752 2791 Commercial printing, offset; typesetting

(G-12108)
DAF PRODUCTS INC
Also Called: D A F
420 Braen Ave (07481-2949)
PHONE................................201 251-1222
Thomas P Palmer, *President*
Mario Fusco, *Vice Pres*
▲ EMP: 18
SALES: 15MM **Privately Held**
SIC: 2295 3552 Laminating of fabrics; textile machinery

(G-12109)
DLITE PRODUCTS INC
540 Ravine Ct (07481-2921)
PHONE................................201 444-0822
Bill Hennessy, *President*
Roger Mayfarth, *Vice Pres*
▲ EMP: 6
SALES (est): 338.7K **Privately Held**
WEB: www.dlite.com
SIC: 3999 Magic equipment, supplies & props

(G-12110)
DMA DATA INDUSTRIES INC
479 Goffle Rd (07481-3003)
PHONE................................201 444-5733
Louis Ciarlo, *President*
EMP: 5
SQ FT: 2,000
SALES (est): 291K **Privately Held**
SIC: 7372 Prepackaged software

(G-12111)
FACTONOMY INC
459 Oldwoods Rd (07481-1448)
P.O. Box 14 Wall St, New York NY (10005)
PHONE................................201 848-7812
Philip Rugani, *CEO*
Neil Jordan, *COO*
EMP: 11
SQ FT: 4,500
SALES (est): 525.2K **Privately Held**
SIC: 7371 7372 Computer software development & applications; application computer software

(G-12112)
GARDEN STATE IRRIGATION
500 W Main St Ste 5 (07481-1406)
PHONE................................201 848-1300
Mark Nidowizz, *Owner*
Joel Perales, *Technician*
EMP: 15
SALES (est): 2.6MM **Privately Held**
WEB: www.gardenstateirrigation.com
SIC: 3648 Outdoor lighting equipment

(G-12113)
ICEBOXX LLC
600 Braen Ave (07481-2914)
PHONE................................201 857-0404
Kevin Schimidt,
EMP: 6
SALES (est): 790K **Privately Held**
SIC: 3585 Ice making machinery

(G-12114)
M B R ORTHOTICS INC
579 Goffle Rd (07481-2946)
PHONE................................201 444-7750
Michael Rebarber, *President*
EMP: 4
SQ FT: 800
SALES (est): 554.4K **Privately Held**
SIC: 3842 Orthopedic appliances

(G-12115)
M K ENTERPRISES INC
Also Called: Van Grouw Welding & Fabg
430 W Main St (07481-1420)
PHONE................................201 891-4199
Mark Pouzzuli, *President*
Ken Vandenberg, *Admin Sec*
EMP: 4
SQ FT: 6,000
SALES (est): 564K **Privately Held**
SIC: 3441 7699 Fabricated structural metal; welding equipment repair

(G-12116)
MAIN ROBERT A & SONS HOLDG CO (PA)
555 Goffle Rd (07481-2937)
P.O. Box 159 (07481-0159)
PHONE................................201 447-3700
Robert A Main Jr, *Principal*
Susan Main, *Corp Secy*
William Main, *Vice Pres*
EMP: 27
SQ FT: 29,000
SALES (est): 35.5MM **Privately Held**
SIC: 3496 3535 3443 3441 Miscellaneous fabricated wire products; conveyors & conveying equipment; cylinders, pressure: metal plate; tower sections, radio & television transmission; screw machine products; metal stampings

(G-12117)
MARKBILT INC
308 Canterbury Ln (07481-2304)
P.O. Box 32, Hawthorne (07507-0032)
PHONE................................201 891-7842
Plutarco Leyva, *General Mgr*
EMP: 55
SALES (corp-wide): 4.4MM **Privately Held**
SIC: 2259 Convertors, knit goods
PA: Markbilt Inc
55 Thomas Rd N
Hawthorne NJ
973 423-0556

(G-12118)
RADIATION SYSTEMS INC
455 W Main St (07481-1419)
PHONE................................201 891-7515
Richard Ver Hage, *President*
Glenn Ver Hage, *Vice Pres*
Henry Ver Hage, *Vice Pres*
William Van Dyke Jr, *Vice Pres*
EMP: 7
SQ FT: 9,000
SALES (est): 740K **Privately Held**
WEB: www.radiationsystems.com
SIC: 3567 3444 Infrared ovens, industrial; sheet metal specialties, not stamped

(G-12119)
RICHARD J BELL CO INC
Also Called: Rjb Design Group Co.
465 W Main St (07481-1453)
PHONE................................201 847-0887
Richard J Bell, *President*
EMP: 10
SQ FT: 10,000
SALES (est): 1.2MM **Privately Held**
SIC: 2542 Counters or counter display cases: except wood

(G-12120)
RONY INC
393 Crescent Ave Ste 12 (07481-2837)
PHONE................................201 891-2551
Manuel Pires, *CEO*
Ronald Pires, *President*
▼ EMP: 5
SQ FT: 5,000
SALES (est): 807.2K **Privately Held**
WEB: www.rony.com
SIC: 3714 5013 Motor vehicle parts & accessories; motor vehicle supplies & new parts

(G-12121)
STRAPS MANUFACTURING NJ INC
Also Called: Titan Trading Co
480 Braen Ave (07481-2949)
PHONE................................201 368-5201
Joel Rothstein, *President*
EMP: 16
SQ FT: 12,000
SALES (est): 1.3MM **Privately Held**
WEB: www.titan-trading.com
SIC: 2387 3965 Apparel belts; fasteners

(G-12122)
TRAP-ZAP ENVIRONMENTAL SYSTEMS
255 Braen Ave (07481-2948)
PHONE................................201 251-9970
Robert Belle, *President*
EMP: 40
SQ FT: 3,000
SALES (est): 8MM **Privately Held**
WEB: www.trapzap.com
SIC: 3272 2842 Grease traps, concrete; specialty cleaning, polishes & sanitation goods

(G-12123)
TYPELINE
506 Spencer Dr (07481-2925)
PHONE................................201 251-2201
Fax: 201 836-8337
EMP: 10
SQ FT: 2,000
SALES: 500K **Privately Held**
SIC: 2791 7336 2759 2752 Typesetting Services Coml Art/Graphic Design Commercial Printing Lithographic Coml Print

(G-12124)
VICTORY IRON WORKS INC
780 Mountain Ave (07481-1098)
PHONE...................................201 485-7181
Theresa Edson, *President*
Mae Marchese, *Vice Pres*
EMP: 6 **EST:** 1926
SQ FT: 5,000
SALES (est): 823.4K **Privately Held**
SIC: 3441 Fabricated structural metal

SIC INDEX

Standard Industrial Classification Alphabetical Index

SIC NO	PRODUCT

A

3291 Abrasive Prdts
2891 Adhesives & Sealants
3563 Air & Gas Compressors
3585 Air Conditioning & Heating Eqpt
3721 Aircraft
3724 Aircraft Engines & Engine Parts
3728 Aircraft Parts & Eqpt, NEC
2812 Alkalies & Chlorine
3363 Aluminum Die Castings
3354 Aluminum Extruded Prdts
3365 Aluminum Foundries
3355 Aluminum Rolling & Drawing, NEC
3353 Aluminum Sheet, Plate & Foil
3483 Ammunition, Large
3826 Analytical Instruments
2077 Animal, Marine Fats & Oils
2389 Apparel & Accessories, NEC
2387 Apparel Belts
3446 Architectural & Ornamental Metal Work
7694 Armature Rewinding Shops
3292 Asbestos products
2952 Asphalt Felts & Coatings
3822 Automatic Temperature Controls
3581 Automatic Vending Machines
3465 Automotive Stampings
2396 Automotive Trimmings, Apparel Findings, Related Prdts

B

2673 Bags: Plastics, Laminated & Coated
2674 Bags: Uncoated Paper & Multiwall
3562 Ball & Roller Bearings
2836 Biological Prdts, Exc Diagnostic Substances
2782 Blankbooks & Looseleaf Binders
3312 Blast Furnaces, Coke Ovens, Steel & Rolling Mills
3564 Blowers & Fans
3732 Boat Building & Repairing
3452 Bolts, Nuts, Screws, Rivets & Washers
2732 Book Printing, Not Publishing
2789 Bookbinding
2731 Books: Publishing & Printing
3131 Boot & Shoe Cut Stock & Findings
2342 Brassieres, Girdles & Garments
2051 Bread, Bakery Prdts Exc Cookies & Crackers
3251 Brick & Structural Clay Tile
3991 Brooms & Brushes
3995 Burial Caskets
2021 Butter

C

3578 Calculating & Accounting Eqpt
2064 Candy & Confectionery Prdts
2033 Canned Fruits, Vegetables & Preserves
2032 Canned Specialties
2394 Canvas Prdts
3624 Carbon & Graphite Prdts
2895 Carbon Black
3955 Carbon Paper & Inked Ribbons
3592 Carburetors, Pistons, Rings & Valves
2273 Carpets & Rugs
2823 Cellulosic Man-Made Fibers
3241 Cement, Hydraulic
3253 Ceramic Tile
2043 Cereal Breakfast Foods
2022 Cheese
1479 Chemical & Fertilizer Mining
2899 Chemical Preparations, NEC
2067 Chewing Gum
2361 Children's & Infants' Dresses & Blouses
3261 China Plumbing Fixtures & Fittings
3262 China, Table & Kitchen Articles
2066 Chocolate & Cocoa Prdts
2111 Cigarettes
2121 Cigars
2257 Circular Knit Fabric Mills
3255 Clay Refractories
1459 Clay, Ceramic & Refractory Minerals, NEC
1241 Coal Mining Svcs
3479 Coating & Engraving, NEC
2095 Coffee
3316 Cold Rolled Steel Sheet, Strip & Bars
3582 Commercial Laundry, Dry Clean & Pressing Mchs
2759 Commercial Printing
2754 Commercial Printing: Gravure
2752 Commercial Printing: Lithographic
3646 Commercial, Indl & Institutional Lighting Fixtures

3669 Communications Eqpt, NEC
3577 Computer Peripheral Eqpt, NEC
3572 Computer Storage Devices
3575 Computer Terminals
3271 Concrete Block & Brick
3272 Concrete Prdts
3531 Construction Machinery & Eqpt
1442 Construction Sand & Gravel
2679 Converted Paper Prdts, NEC
3535 Conveyors & Eqpt
2052 Cookies & Crackers
3366 Copper Foundries
1021 Copper Ores
2298 Cordage & Twine
2653 Corrugated & Solid Fiber Boxes
3961 Costume Jewelry & Novelties
2261 Cotton Fabric Finishers
2211 Cotton, Woven Fabric
3466 Crowns & Closures
1311 Crude Petroleum & Natural Gas
1423 Crushed & Broken Granite
1422 Crushed & Broken Limestone
1429 Crushed & Broken Stone, NEC
3643 Current-Carrying Wiring Devices
2391 Curtains & Draperies
3087 Custom Compounding Of Purchased Plastic Resins
3281 Cut Stone Prdts
3421 Cutlery
2865 Cyclic-Crudes, Intermediates, Dyes & Org Pigments

D

3843 Dental Eqpt & Splys
2835 Diagnostic Substances
2675 Die-Cut Paper & Board
3544 Dies, Tools, Jigs, Fixtures & Indl Molds
1411 Dimension Stone
2047 Dog & Cat Food
3942 Dolls & Stuffed Toys
2591 Drapery Hardware, Window Blinds & Shades
2381 Dress & Work Gloves
2034 Dried Fruits, Vegetables & Soup
1381 Drilling Oil & Gas Wells

E

3263 Earthenware, Whiteware, Table & Kitchen Articles
3634 Electric Household Appliances
3641 Electric Lamps
3694 Electrical Eqpt For Internal Combustion Engines
3629 Electrical Indl Apparatus, NEC
3699 Electrical Machinery, Eqpt & Splys, NEC
3845 Electromedical & Electrotherapeutic Apparatus
3313 Electrometallurgical Prdts
3675 Electronic Capacitors
3677 Electronic Coils & Transformers
3679 Electronic Components, NEC
3571 Electronic Computers
3678 Electronic Connectors
3676 Electronic Resistors
3471 Electroplating, Plating, Polishing, Anodizing & Coloring
3534 Elevators & Moving Stairways
3431 Enameled Iron & Metal Sanitary Ware
2677 Envelopes
2892 Explosives

F

2241 Fabric Mills, Cotton, Wool, Silk & Man-Made
3499 Fabricated Metal Prdts, NEC
3498 Fabricated Pipe & Pipe Fittings
3443 Fabricated Plate Work
3069 Fabricated Rubber Prdts, NEC
3441 Fabricated Structural Steel
2399 Fabricated Textile Prdts, NEC
2295 Fabrics Coated Not Rubberized
2297 Fabrics, Nonwoven
3523 Farm Machinery & Eqpt
3965 Fasteners, Buttons, Needles & Pins
2875 Fertilizers, Mixing Only
2655 Fiber Cans, Tubes & Drums
2091 Fish & Seafoods, Canned & Cured
2092 Fish & Seafoods, Fresh & Frozen
3211 Flat Glass
2087 Flavoring Extracts & Syrups
2045 Flour, Blended & Prepared
2041 Flour, Grain Milling
3824 Fluid Meters & Counters
3593 Fluid Power Cylinders & Actuators

3594 Fluid Power Pumps & Motors
3492 Fluid Power Valves & Hose Fittings
2657 Folding Paperboard Boxes
3556 Food Prdts Machinery
2099 Food Preparations, NEC
3149 Footwear, NEC
2053 Frozen Bakery Prdts
2037 Frozen Fruits, Juices & Vegetables
2038 Frozen Specialties
2371 Fur Goods
2599 Furniture & Fixtures, NEC

G

3944 Games, Toys & Children's Vehicles
3524 Garden, Lawn Tractors & Eqpt
3053 Gaskets, Packing & Sealing Devices
2369 Girls' & Infants' Outerwear, NEC
3221 Glass Containers
3231 Glass Prdts Made Of Purchased Glass
1041 Gold Ores
3321 Gray Iron Foundries
2771 Greeting Card Publishing
3769 Guided Missile/Space Vehicle Parts & Eqpt, NEC
3764 Guided Missile/Space Vehicle Propulsion Units & parts
3761 Guided Missiles & Space Vehicles
2861 Gum & Wood Chemicals
3275 Gypsum Prdts

H

3423 Hand & Edge Tools
3425 Hand Saws & Saw Blades
3171 Handbags & Purses
3429 Hardware, NEC
2426 Hardwood Dimension & Flooring Mills
2435 Hardwood Veneer & Plywood
2353 Hats, Caps & Millinery
3433 Heating Eqpt
3536 Hoists, Cranes & Monorails
2252 Hosiery, Except Women's
2251 Hosiery, Women's Full & Knee Length
2392 House furnishings: Textile
3142 House Slippers
3639 Household Appliances, NEC
3651 Household Audio & Video Eqpt
3631 Household Cooking Eqpt
2519 Household Furniture, NEC
3633 Household Laundry Eqpt
3632 Household Refrigerators & Freezers
3635 Household Vacuum Cleaners

I

2097 Ice
2024 Ice Cream
2819 Indl Inorganic Chemicals, NEC
3823 Indl Instruments For Meas, Display & Control
3569 Indl Machinery & Eqpt, NEC
3567 Indl Process Furnaces & Ovens
3537 Indl Trucks, Tractors, Trailers & Stackers
2813 Industrial Gases
2869 Industrial Organic Chemicals, NEC
3543 Industrial Patterns
1446 Industrial Sand
3491 Industrial Valves
2816 Inorganic Pigments
3825 Instrs For Measuring & Testing Electricity
3519 Internal Combustion Engines, NEC
3462 Iron & Steel Forgings

J

3915 Jewelers Findings & Lapidary Work
3911 Jewelry: Precious Metal

K

1455 Kaolin & Ball Clay
2253 Knit Outerwear Mills
2254 Knit Underwear Mills
2259 Knitting Mills, NEC

L

3821 Laboratory Apparatus & Furniture
2258 Lace & Warp Knit Fabric Mills
3952 Lead Pencils, Crayons & Artist's Mtrls
2386 Leather & Sheep Lined Clothing
3151 Leather Gloves & Mittens
3199 Leather Goods, NEC
3111 Leather Tanning & Finishing
3648 Lighting Eqpt, NEC

S I C

SIC INDEX

SIC NO	PRODUCT

10 metal mining
1021 Copper Ores
1041 Gold Ores
1044 Silver Ores
1081 Metal Mining Svcs

12 coal mining
1241 Coal Mining Svcs

13 oil and gas extraction
1311 Crude Petroleum & Natural Gas
1321 Natural Gas Liquids
1381 Drilling Oil & Gas Wells
1382 Oil & Gas Field Exploration Svcs
1389 Oil & Gas Field Svcs, NEC

14 mining and quarrying of nonmetallic minerals, except fuels
1411 Dimension Stone
1422 Crushed & Broken Limestone
1423 Crushed & Broken Granite
1429 Crushed & Broken Stone, NEC
1442 Construction Sand & Gravel
1446 Industrial Sand
1455 Kaolin & Ball Clay
1459 Clay, Ceramic & Refractory Minerals, NEC
1479 Chemical & Fertilizer Mining
1481 Nonmetallic Minerals Svcs, Except Fuels
1499 Miscellaneous Nonmetallic Mining

20 food and kindred products
2011 Meat Packing Plants
2013 Sausages & Meat Prdts
2015 Poultry Slaughtering, Dressing & Processing
2021 Butter
2022 Cheese
2023 Milk, Condensed & Evaporated
2024 Ice Cream
2026 Milk
2032 Canned Specialties
2033 Canned Fruits, Vegetables & Preserves
2034 Dried Fruits, Vegetables & Soup
2035 Pickled Fruits, Vegetables, Sauces & Dressings
2037 Frozen Fruits, Juices & Vegetables
2038 Frozen Specialties
2041 Flour, Grain Milling
2043 Cereal Breakfast Foods
2044 Rice Milling
2045 Flour, Blended & Prepared
2046 Wet Corn Milling
2047 Dog & Cat Food
2048 Prepared Feeds For Animals & Fowls
2051 Bread, Bakery Prdts Exc Cookies & Crackers
2052 Cookies & Crackers
2053 Frozen Bakery Prdts
2061 Sugar, Cane
2062 Sugar, Cane Refining
2064 Candy & Confectionery Prdts
2066 Chocolate & Cocoa Prdts
2067 Chewing Gum
2068 Salted & Roasted Nuts & Seeds
2075 Soybean Oil Mills
2076 Vegetable Oil Mills
2077 Animal, Marine Fats & Oils
2079 Shortening, Oils & Margarine
2082 Malt Beverages
2083 Malt
2084 Wine & Brandy
2085 Liquors, Distilled, Rectified & Blended
2086 Soft Drinks
2087 Flavoring Extracts & Syrups
2091 Fish & Seafoods, Canned & Cured
2092 Fish & Seafoods, Fresh & Frozen
2095 Coffee
2096 Potato Chips & Similar Prdts
2097 Ice
2098 Macaroni, Spaghetti & Noodles
2099 Food Preparations, NEC

21 tobacco products
2111 Cigarettes
2121 Cigars
2141 Tobacco Stemming & Redrying

22 textile mill products
2211 Cotton, Woven Fabric
2221 Silk & Man-Made Fiber

2231 Wool, Woven Fabric
2241 Fabric Mills, Cotton, Wool, Silk & Man-Made
2251 Hosiery, Women's Full & Knee Length
2252 Hosiery, Except Women's
2253 Knit Outerwear Mills
2254 Knit Underwear Mills
2257 Circular Knit Fabric Mills
2258 Lace & Warp Knit Fabric Mills
2259 Knitting Mills, NEC
2261 Cotton Fabric Finishers
2262 Silk & Man-Made Fabric Finishers
2269 Textile Finishers, NEC
2273 Carpets & Rugs
2281 Yarn Spinning Mills
2282 Yarn Texturizing, Throwing, Twisting & Winding Mills
2284 Thread Mills
2295 Fabrics Coated Not Rubberized
2296 Tire Cord & Fabric
2297 Fabrics, Nonwoven
2298 Cordage & Twine
2299 Textile Goods, NEC

23 apparel and other finished products made from fabrics and similar material
2311 Men's & Boys' Suits, Coats & Overcoats
2321 Men's & Boys' Shirts
2322 Men's & Boys' Underwear & Nightwear
2323 Men's & Boys' Neckwear
2325 Men's & Boys' Separate Trousers & Casual Slacks
2326 Men's & Boys' Work Clothing
2329 Men's & Boys' Clothing, NEC
2331 Women's & Misses' Blouses
2335 Women's & Misses' Dresses
2337 Women's & Misses' Suits, Coats & Skirts
2339 Women's & Misses' Outerwear, NEC
2341 Women's, Misses' & Children's Underwear & Nightwear
2342 Brassieres, Girdles & Garments
2353 Hats, Caps & Millinery
2361 Children's & Infants' Dresses & Blouses
2369 Girls' & Infants' Outerwear, NEC
2371 Fur Goods
2381 Dress & Work Gloves
2384 Robes & Dressing Gowns
2385 Waterproof Outerwear
2386 Leather & Sheep Lined Clothing
2387 Apparel Belts
2389 Apparel & Accessories, NEC
2391 Curtains & Draperies
2392 House furnishings: Textile
2393 Textile Bags
2394 Canvas Prdts
2395 Pleating & Stitching For The Trade
2396 Automotive Trimmings, Apparel Findings, Related Prdts
2397 Schiffli Machine Embroideries
2399 Fabricated Textile Prdts, NEC

24 lumber and wood products, except furniture
2411 Logging
2421 Saw & Planing Mills
2426 Hardwood Dimension & Flooring Mills
2431 Millwork
2434 Wood Kitchen Cabinets
2435 Hardwood Veneer & Plywood
2439 Structural Wood Members, NEC
2441 Wood Boxes
2448 Wood Pallets & Skids
2449 Wood Containers, NEC
2451 Mobile Homes
2452 Prefabricated Wood Buildings & Cmpnts
2491 Wood Preserving
2493 Reconstituted Wood Prdts
2499 Wood Prdts, NEC

25 furniture and fixtures
2511 Wood Household Furniture
2512 Wood Household Furniture, Upholstered
2514 Metal Household Furniture
2515 Mattresses & Bedsprings
2517 Wood T V, Radio, Phono & Sewing Cabinets
2519 Household Furniture, NEC
2521 Wood Office Furniture
2522 Office Furniture, Except Wood
2531 Public Building & Related Furniture
2541 Wood, Office & Store Fixtures
2542 Partitions & Fixtures, Except Wood
2591 Drapery Hardware, Window Blinds & Shades

2599 Furniture & Fixtures, NEC

26 paper and allied products
2611 Pulp Mills
2621 Paper Mills
2631 Paperboard Mills
2652 Set-Up Paperboard Boxes
2653 Corrugated & Solid Fiber Boxes
2655 Fiber Cans, Tubes & Drums
2656 Sanitary Food Containers
2657 Folding Paperboard Boxes
2671 Paper Coating & Laminating for Packaging
2672 Paper Coating & Laminating, Exc for Packaging
2673 Bags: Plastics, Laminated & Coated
2674 Bags: Uncoated Paper & Multiwall
2675 Die-Cut Paper & Board
2676 Sanitary Paper Prdts
2677 Envelopes
2678 Stationery Prdts
2679 Converted Paper Prdts, NEC

27 printing, publishing, and allied industries
2711 Newspapers: Publishing & Printing
2721 Periodicals: Publishing & Printing
2731 Books: Publishing & Printing
2732 Book Printing, Not Publishing
2741 Misc Publishing
2752 Commercial Printing: Lithographic
2754 Commercial Printing: Gravure
2759 Commercial Printing
2761 Manifold Business Forms
2771 Greeting Card Publishing
2782 Blankbooks & Looseleaf Binders
2789 Bookbinding
2791 Typesetting
2796 Platemaking & Related Svcs

28 chemicals and allied products
2812 Alkalies & Chlorine
2813 Industrial Gases
2816 Inorganic Pigments
2819 Indl Inorganic Chemicals, NEC
2821 Plastics, Mtrls & Nonvulcanizable Elastomers
2822 Synthetic Rubber (Vulcanizable Elastomers)
2823 Cellulosic Man-Made Fibers
2824 Synthetic Organic Fibers, Exc Cellulosic
2833 Medicinal Chemicals & Botanical Prdts
2834 Pharmaceuticals
2835 Diagnostic Substances
2836 Biological Prdts, Exc Diagnostic Substances
2841 Soap & Detergents
2842 Spec Cleaning, Polishing & Sanitation Preparations
2843 Surface Active & Finishing Agents, Sulfonated Oils
2844 Perfumes, Cosmetics & Toilet Preparations
2851 Paints, Varnishes, Lacquers, Enamels
2861 Gum & Wood Chemicals
2865 Cyclic-Crudes, Intermediates, Dyes & Org Pigments
2869 Industrial Organic Chemicals, NEC
2873 Nitrogenous Fertilizers
2874 Phosphatic Fertilizers
2875 Fertilizers, Mixing Only
2879 Pesticides & Agricultural Chemicals, NEC
2891 Adhesives & Sealants
2892 Explosives
2893 Printing Ink
2895 Carbon Black
2899 Chemical Preparations, NEC

29 petroleum refining and related industries
2911 Petroleum Refining
2951 Paving Mixtures & Blocks
2952 Asphalt Felts & Coatings
2992 Lubricating Oils & Greases
2999 Products Of Petroleum & Coal, NEC

30 rubber and miscellaneous plastics products
3011 Tires & Inner Tubes
3021 Rubber & Plastic Footwear
3052 Rubber & Plastic Hose & Belting
3053 Gaskets, Packing & Sealing Devices
3061 Molded, Extruded & Lathe-Cut Rubber Mechanical Goods
3069 Fabricated Rubber Prdts, NEC
3081 Plastic Unsupported Sheet & Film
3082 Plastic Unsupported Profile Shapes
3083 Plastic Laminated Plate & Sheet
3084 Plastic Pipe

S I C

SIC NO	PRODUCT

3085 Plastic Bottles
3086 Plastic Foam Prdts
3087 Custom Compounding Of Purchased Plastic Resins
3088 Plastic Plumbing Fixtures
3089 Plastic Prdts

31 leather and leather products

3111 Leather Tanning & Finishing
3131 Boot & Shoe Cut Stock & Findings
3142 House Slippers
3143 Men's Footwear, Exc Athletic
3144 Women's Footwear, Exc Athletic
3149 Footwear, NEC
3151 Leather Gloves & Mittens
3161 Luggage
3171 Handbags & Purses
3172 Personal Leather Goods
3199 Leather Goods, NEC

32 stone, clay, glass, and concrete products

3211 Flat Glass
3221 Glass Containers
3229 Pressed & Blown Glassware, NEC
3231 Glass Prdts Made Of Purchased Glass
3241 Cement, Hydraulic
3251 Brick & Structural Clay Tile
3253 Ceramic Tile
3255 Clay Refractories
3259 Structural Clay Prdts, NEC
3261 China Plumbing Fixtures & Fittings
3262 China, Table & Kitchen Articles
3263 Earthenware, Whiteware, Table & Kitchen Articles
3264 Porcelain Electrical Splys
3269 Pottery Prdts, NEC
3271 Concrete Block & Brick
3272 Concrete Prdts
3273 Ready-Mixed Concrete
3274 Lime
3275 Gypsum Prdts
3281 Cut Stone Prdts
3291 Abrasive Prdts
3292 Asbestos products
3295 Minerals & Earths: Ground Or Treated
3296 Mineral Wool
3297 Nonclay Refractories
3299 Nonmetallic Mineral Prdts, NEC

33 primary metal industries

3312 Blast Furnaces, Coke Ovens, Steel & Rolling Mills
3313 Electrometallurgical Prdts
3315 Steel Wire Drawing & Nails & Spikes
3316 Cold Rolled Steel Sheet, Strip & Bars
3317 Steel Pipe & Tubes
3321 Gray Iron Foundries
3322 Malleable Iron Foundries
3324 Steel Investment Foundries
3325 Steel Foundries, NEC
3331 Primary Smelting & Refining Of Copper
3334 Primary Production Of Aluminum
3339 Primary Nonferrous Metals, NEC
3341 Secondary Smelting & Refining Of Nonferrous Metals
3351 Rolling, Drawing & Extruding Of Copper
3353 Aluminum Sheet, Plate & Foil
3354 Aluminum Extruded Prdts
3355 Aluminum Rolling & Drawing, NEC
3356 Rolling, Drawing-Extruding Of Nonferrous Metals
3357 Nonferrous Wire Drawing
3363 Aluminum Die Castings
3364 Nonferrous Die Castings, Exc Aluminum
3365 Aluminum Foundries
3366 Copper Foundries
3369 Nonferrous Foundries: Castings, NEC
3398 Metal Heat Treating
3399 Primary Metal Prdts, NEC

34 fabricated metal products, except machinery and transportation equipment

3411 Metal Cans
3412 Metal Barrels, Drums, Kegs & Pails
3421 Cutlery
3423 Hand & Edge Tools
3425 Hand Saws & Saw Blades
3429 Hardware, NEC
3431 Enameled Iron & Metal Sanitary Ware
3432 Plumbing Fixture Fittings & Trim, Brass
3433 Heating Eqpt
3441 Fabricated Structural Steel
3442 Metal Doors, Sash, Frames, Molding & Trim
3443 Fabricated Plate Work
3444 Sheet Metal Work
3446 Architectural & Ornamental Metal Work
3448 Prefabricated Metal Buildings & Cmpnts

3449 Misc Structural Metal Work
3451 Screw Machine Prdts
3452 Bolts, Nuts, Screws, Rivets & Washers
3462 Iron & Steel Forgings
3463 Nonferrous Forgings
3465 Automotive Stampings
3466 Crowns & Closures
3469 Metal Stampings, NEC
3471 Electroplating, Plating, Polishing, Anodizing & Coloring
3479 Coating & Engraving, NEC
3482 Small Arms Ammunition
3483 Ammunition, Large
3484 Small Arms
3489 Ordnance & Access, NEC
3491 Industrial Valves
3492 Fluid Power Valves & Hose Fittings
3493 Steel Springs, Except Wire
3494 Valves & Pipe Fittings, NEC
3495 Wire Springs
3496 Misc Fabricated Wire Prdts
3497 Metal Foil & Leaf
3498 Fabricated Pipe & Pipe Fittings
3499 Fabricated Metal Prdts, NEC

35 industrial and commercial machinery and computer equipment

3511 Steam, Gas & Hydraulic Turbines & Engines
3519 Internal Combustion Engines, NEC
3523 Farm Machinery & Eqpt
3524 Garden, Lawn Tractors & Eqpt
3531 Construction Machinery & Eqpt
3532 Mining Machinery & Eqpt
3533 Oil Field Machinery & Eqpt
3534 Elevators & Moving Stairways
3535 Conveyors & Eqpt
3536 Hoists, Cranes & Monorails
3537 Indl Trucks, Tractors, Trailers & Stackers
3541 Machine Tools: Cutting
3542 Machine Tools: Forming
3543 Industrial Patterns
3544 Dies, Tools, Jigs, Fixtures & Indl Molds
3545 Machine Tool Access
3546 Power Hand Tools
3547 Rolling Mill Machinery & Eqpt
3548 Welding Apparatus
3549 Metalworking Machinery, NEC
3552 Textile Machinery
3553 Woodworking Machinery
3554 Paper Inds Machinery
3555 Printing Trades Machinery & Eqpt
3556 Food Prdts Machinery
3559 Special Ind Machinery, NEC
3561 Pumps & Pumping Eqpt
3562 Ball & Roller Bearings
3563 Air & Gas Compressors
3564 Blowers & Fans
3565 Packaging Machinery
3566 Speed Changers, Drives & Gears
3567 Indl Process Furnaces & Ovens
3568 Mechanical Power Transmission Eqpt, NEC
3569 Indl Machinery & Eqpt, NEC
3571 Electronic Computers
3572 Computer Storage Devices
3575 Computer Terminals
3577 Computer Peripheral Eqpt, NEC
3578 Calculating & Accounting Eqpt
3579 Office Machines, NEC
3581 Automatic Vending Machines
3582 Commercial Laundry, Dry Clean & Pressing Mchs
3585 Air Conditioning & Heating Eqpt
3586 Measuring & Dispensing Pumps
3589 Service Ind Machines, NEC
3592 Carburetors, Pistons, Rings & Valves
3593 Fluid Power Cylinders & Actuators
3594 Fluid Power Pumps & Motors
3596 Scales & Balances, Exc Laboratory
3599 Machinery & Eqpt, Indl & Commercial, NEC

36 electronic and other electrical equipment and components, except computer

3612 Power, Distribution & Specialty Transformers
3613 Switchgear & Switchboard Apparatus
3621 Motors & Generators
3624 Carbon & Graphite Prdts
3625 Relays & Indl Controls
3629 Electrical Indl Apparatus, NEC
3631 Household Cooking Eqpt
3632 Household Refrigerators & Freezers
3633 Household Laundry Eqpt
3634 Electric Household Appliances
3635 Household Vacuum Cleaners
3639 Household Appliances, NEC

3641 Electric Lamps
3643 Current-Carrying Wiring Devices
3644 Noncurrent-Carrying Wiring Devices
3645 Residential Lighting Fixtures
3646 Commercial, Indl & Institutional Lighting Fixtures
3647 Vehicular Lighting Eqpt
3648 Lighting Eqpt, NEC
3651 Household Audio & Video Eqpt
3652 Phonograph Records & Magnetic Tape
3661 Telephone & Telegraph Apparatus
3663 Radio & T V Communications, Systs & Eqpt, Broadcast/Studio
3669 Communications Eqpt, NEC
3671 Radio & T V Receiving Electron Tubes
3672 Printed Circuit Boards
3674 Semiconductors
3675 Electronic Capacitors
3676 Electronic Resistors
3677 Electronic Coils & Transformers
3678 Electronic Connectors
3679 Electronic Components, NEC
3691 Storage Batteries
3692 Primary Batteries: Dry & Wet
3694 Electrical Eqpt For Internal Combustion Engines
3695 Recording Media
3699 Electrical Machinery, Eqpt & Splys, NEC

37 transportation equipment

3711 Motor Vehicles & Car Bodies
3713 Truck & Bus Bodies
3714 Motor Vehicle Parts & Access
3715 Truck Trailers
3721 Aircraft
3724 Aircraft Engines & Engine Parts
3728 Aircraft Parts & Eqpt, NEC
3731 Shipbuilding & Repairing
3732 Boat Building & Repairing
3743 Railroad Eqpt
3751 Motorcycles, Bicycles & Parts
3761 Guided Missiles & Space Vehicles
3764 Guided Missile/Space Vehicle Propulsion Units & parts
3769 Guided Missile/Space Vehicle Parts & Eqpt, NEC
3792 Travel Trailers & Campers
3795 Tanks & Tank Components
3799 Transportation Eqpt, NEC

38 measuring, analyzing and controlling instruments; photographic, medical an

3812 Search, Detection, Navigation & Guidance Systs & Instrs
3821 Laboratory Apparatus & Furniture
3822 Automatic Temperature Controls
3823 Indl Instruments For Meas, Display & Control
3824 Fluid Meters & Counters
3825 Instrs For Measuring & Testing Electricity
3826 Analytical Instruments
3827 Optical Instruments
3829 Measuring & Controlling Devices, NEC
3841 Surgical & Medical Instrs & Apparatus
3842 Orthopedic, Prosthetic & Surgical Appliances/Splys
3843 Dental Eqpt & Splys
3844 X-ray Apparatus & Tubes
3845 Electromedical & Electrotherapeutic Apparatus
3851 Ophthalmic Goods
3861 Photographic Eqpt & Splys
3873 Watch & Clock Devices & Parts

39 miscellaneous manufacturing industries

3911 Jewelry: Precious Metal
3914 Silverware, Plated & Stainless Steel Ware
3915 Jewelers Findings & Lapidary Work
3931 Musical Instruments
3942 Dolls & Stuffed Toys
3944 Games, Toys & Children's Vehicles
3949 Sporting & Athletic Goods, NEC
3951 Pens & Mechanical Pencils
3952 Lead Pencils, Crayons & Artist's Mtrls
3953 Marking Devices
3955 Carbon Paper & Inked Ribbons
3961 Costume Jewelry & Novelties
3965 Fasteners, Buttons, Needles & Pins
3991 Brooms & Brushes
3993 Signs & Advertising Displays
3995 Burial Caskets
3996 Linoleum & Hard Surface Floor Coverings, NEC
3999 Manufacturing Industries, NEC

73 business services

7372 Prepackaged Software

76 miscellaneous repair services

7692 Welding Repair
7694 Armature Rewinding Shops

SIC SECTION

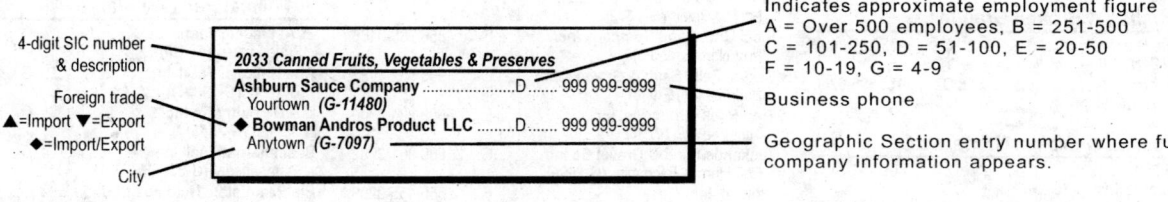

2033 Canned Fruits, Vegetables & Preserves

- 4-digit SIC number & description
- Foreign trade
  ▲=Import ▼=Export
  ◆=Import/Export
- City

Ashburn Sauce Company ....D 999 999-9999
Yourtown *(G-11480)*
◆ **Bowman Andros Product LLC** ....D 999 999-9999
Anytown *(G-7097)*

Indicates approximate employment figure
A = Over 500 employees, B = 251-500
C = 101-250, D = 51-100, E = 20-50
F = 10-19, G = 4-9

Business phone

Geographic Section entry number where full company information appears.

See footnotes for symbols and codes identification.

- The SIC codes in this section are from the latest Standard Industrial Classification manual published by the U.S. Government's Office of Management and Budget. For more information regarding SICs, see the Explanatory Notes.
- Companies may be listed under multiple classifications.

10 METAL MINING

1021 Copper Ores

Freeport-Mcmoran Inc ....G 908 558-4361
Elizabeth *(G-2738)*

1041 Gold Ores

Freeport-Mcmoran Inc ....G 908 558-4361
Elizabeth *(G-2738)*
Valdez Creek Min Ltd Lblty Co ....G 732 704-1427
Red Bank *(G-9248)*

1044 Silver Ores

Freeport-Mcmoran Inc ....G 908 558-4361
Elizabeth *(G-2738)*

1081 Metal Mining Svcs

C & Y Group East Coast Inc ....G 973 732-4816
Newark *(G-7079)*
Coastal Metal Recycling Corp ....G 732 738-6000
Keasbey *(G-4911)*
◆ Connell Mining Products LLC ....D 908 673-3700
Berkeley Heights *(G-395)*
Demaio Inc ....E 609 965-4094
Egg Harbor City *(G-2657)*
Industrial Stl & Fastener Corp ....G 610 667-2220
Cherry Hill *(G-1377)*
Kp Excavation LLC ....E 201 933-4200
Carlstadt *(G-1178)*
Valdez Creek Min Ltd Lblty Co ....G 732 704-1427
Red Bank *(G-9248)*

12 COAL MINING

1241 Coal Mining Svcs

◆ Asbury Carbons Inc ....G 908 537-2155
Asbury *(G-60)*
Starfuels Inc ....G 201 685-0400
Englewood *(G-2944)*
◆ Tof Energy Corporation ....D 908 691-2422
Bedminster *(G-280)*

13 OIL AND GAS EXTRACTION

1311 Crude Petroleum & Natural Gas

Agway Energy Services LLC ....E 973 887-5300
Whippany *(G-11877)*
Associated Asphalt Mktg LLC ....E 210 249-9988
West Deptford *(G-11693)*
◆ JM Huber Corporation ....D 732 603-3630
Edison *(G-2540)*
Millennium Brokerage Svcs LLC ....G 732 928-0900
Jackson *(G-4660)*
MRC Global (us) Inc ....G 856 881-0345
Glassboro *(G-3816)*
MRC Global (us) Inc ....F 732 225-4005
East Brunswick *(G-2158)*
Njr Clean Energy Ventures Corp ....B 732 938-1000
Belmar *(G-351)*
Speedway LLC ....B 732 750-7800
Port Reading *(G-8895)*
Zenith Energy US LP ....G 732 515-7410
Metuchen *(G-6085)*

1321 Natural Gas Liquids

Agro Foods Inc ....G 201 954-9152
Hackettstown *(G-3995)*

M G S ....G 609 698-7000
Barnegat *(G-160)*
Pipeline Eqp Resources Co LLC ....G 888 232-7372
Boonton *(G-564)*

1381 Drilling Oil & Gas Wells

Foundation Monitoring ....G 856 829-0410
Cinnaminson *(G-1457)*
Jay-Bee Oil & Gas Inc ....D 908 686-1493
Clark *(G-1499)*
Maverick Oil Co ....E 732 747-8637
Red Bank *(G-9234)*
Shore Drilling Inc ....G 732 935-1776
Oceanport *(G-7707)*
◆ Tof Energy Corporation ....D 908 691-2422
Bedminster *(G-280)*
UNI-Tech Drilling Company Inc ....E 856 694-4200
Franklinville *(G-3641)*

1382 Oil & Gas Field Exploration Svcs

All American Oil Recovery Co ....E 973 628-9278
Wayne *(G-11467)*
American Shale Oil LLC ....G 973 438-3500
Newark *(G-7045)*
Foresight Enviroprobe Inc ....G 609 259-1244
Clarksburg *(G-1520)*
Hess Corporation ....G 609 882-8477
Ewing *(G-3035)*
Masouleh Corp ....E 973 470-8900
Clifton *(G-1664)*
Ridgewood Energy S Fund LLC ....G 201 307-0470
Montvale *(G-6427)*
Ridgewood Energy T Fund LLC ....G 800 942-5550
Montvale *(G-6428)*
Ridgewood Energy U Fund LLC ....G 201 447-9000
Montvale *(G-6429)*
Ridgewood Energy V Fund LLC ....G 800 942-5550
Montvale *(G-6430)*
Ridgewood Energy Y Fund LLC ....G 201 447-9000
Montvale *(G-6431)*

1389 Oil & Gas Field Svcs, NEC

A H Hoffmann LLC ....G 732 988-6000
Neptune *(G-6862)*
Above Environmental Services ....G 973 702-7021
Vernon *(G-11156)*
Accurate Tank Testing LLC ....G 201 848-8224
Midland Park *(G-6168)*
All Seasons Construction Inc ....G 908 852-0955
Long Valley *(G-5607)*
Conti-Robert and Co JV ....D 732 520-5000
Edison *(G-2483)*
Creamer Glass LLC ....G 856 327-2023
Millville *(G-6244)*
Dpk Consulting LLC ....F 732 764-0100
Piscataway *(G-8657)*
Environmental Technical Drlg ....G 732 938-3222
Farmingdale *(G-3385)*
Garden State Fuel ....G 856 442-0061
Monroeville *(G-6351)*
Gateway Property Solutions Ltd ....E 732 901-9700
Lakewood *(G-5103)*
Hudson Valley Enviromental Inc ....E 732 967-0060
Toms River *(G-10768)*
Independent Prj Cons Ltd Lblty ....G 973 780-8002
Newark *(G-7155)*
▲ Kabel N Elettrotek Amer Inc ....G 973 265-0850
Parsippany *(G-7969)*

Langan Engineering Environmen ....F 973 560-4900
Parsippany *(G-7973)*
Mine Hill Spartan ....G 973 442-2280
Mine Hill *(G-6274)*
Mister Good Lube Inc ....G 732 842-3266
Shrewsbury *(G-9897)*
Nickos Construction Inc ....F 267 240-3997
Sicklerville *(G-9913)*
Oil Technologies Services Inc ....G 856 845-4142
Paulsboro *(G-8336)*
Oil Technologies Services Inc ....G 856 845-4142
Paulsboro *(G-8337)*
Oil Technologies Services Inc ....G 856 845-4142
Linden *(G-5399)*
Oiltest Inc ....G 908 245-9330
Roselle *(G-9567)*
Perkins Plumbing & Heating ....G 201 327-2736
Upper Saddle River *(G-11145)*
Refferals Only Inc ....G 609 921-1013
Princeton *(G-9014)*
Ridgewood Energy O Fund LLC ....G 201 447-9000
Montvale *(G-6426)*
Robert Weidener ....G 201 703-5700
Fair Lawn *(G-3119)*
Saybolt LP ....G 908 523-2000
Linden *(G-5419)*
Schlumberger Technology Corp ....C 609 275-3815
Princeton Junction *(G-9066)*
Shelby Mechanical Inc ....E 856 665-4540
Cinnaminson *(G-1484)*
Spectrum International LLC ....G 908 998-9338
Roselle *(G-9572)*
◆ Tof Energy Corporation ....D 908 691-2422
Bedminster *(G-280)*
Vet Construction Inc ....F 732 987-4922
Jackson *(G-4669)*
Zc Utility Services LLC ....G 973 226-1840
Roseland *(G-9545)*
Zion Industries Inc ....E 973 998-0162
Morris Plains *(G-6629)*

14 MINING AND QUARRYING OF NONMETALLIC MINERALS, EXCEPT FUELS

1411 Dimension Stone

◆ Ankur International Inc ....F 609 409-6009
Cranbury *(G-1811)*
Bedrock Granite Inc ....E 732 741-0010
Shrewsbury *(G-9883)*
Dun-Rite Sand & Gravel Co ....G 856 692-2520
Vineland *(G-11214)*
Eastern Concrete Materials Inc ....E 973 827-7625
Hamburg *(G-4090)*
Eastern Concrete Materials Inc ....G 908 537-2135
Glen Gardner *(G-3821)*
Fanwood Crushed Stone Company ......D 908 322-7840
Watchung *(G-11455)*
Morelli Contracting LLC ....G 732 356-8800
Middlesex *(G-6131)*
S J Quarry Materials Inc ....D 856 691-3133
Elmer *(G-2803)*
▲ Stone Surfaces Inc ....D 201 935-8803
East Rutherford *(G-2321)*

1422 Crushed & Broken Limestone

Legacy Vulcan LLC ....E 973 253-8828
Clifton *(G-1656)*

Limecrest Quarry Developer LLC..........F 973 383-7100
Lafayette (G-5030)

1423 Crushed & Broken Granite

Kop Marble Granite Inc..........................G...... 973 283-8000
Wayne (G-11529)
Stone Industries Inc................................D...... 973 595-6250
Haledon (G-4085)

1429 Crushed & Broken Stone, NEC

A E Stone Inc......................................E 609 641-2781
Egg Harbor Township (G-2673)
Cedar Hill Landscaping ....E 732 469-1400
Somerset (G-9974)
Eastern Concrete Materials Inc ....C...... 201 797-7979
Saddle Brook (G-9650)
Emil Dipalma Inc ....G...... 973 477-2766
Hackettstown (G-4005)
Joseph and William Stavola ....E 609 924-0300
Kingston (G-5009)
Millington Quarry Inc ....D...... 908 542-0055
Basking Ridge (G-192)
R B Badat Landscaping Inc ....G...... 609 877-7138
Mount Holly (G-6733)
Riverdale Quarry LLC ....E 973 835-0028
Riverdale (G-9382)
▲ Stone Surfaces Inc ....D...... 201 935-8803
East Rutherford (G-2321)
▲ Tilcon New York Inc ....B...... 973 366-7741
Parsippany (G-8028)
Tilcon New York Inc ....D...... 973 835-0028
Riverdale (G-9387)
Tilcon New York Inc ....E 800 789-7625
Pompton Lakes (G-8855)
Tilcon New York Inc ....D...... 800 789-7625
Kearny (G-4901)
Tilcon New York Inc ....E 800 789-7625
Parsippany (G-8029)
Tilcon New York Inc ....F 973 347-2405
Stanhope (G-10479)
Trap Rock Industries Inc ....F 609 924-0300
Pennington (G-8375)
Trap Rock Industries Inc ....E 609 924-0300
Titusville (G-10736)
Trap Rock Industries Inc ....B...... 609 924-0300
Kingston (G-5012)
Trap Rock Industries LLC ....D...... 609 924-0300
Kingston (G-5013)

1442 Construction Sand & Gravel

Action Supply Inc.................................F 609 390-0663
Ocean View (G-7701)
Alliance Sand Co Inc ....G...... 908 534-4116
Somerville (G-10103)
Baer Aggregates Inc ....F 908 454-4412
Phillipsburg (G-8543)
Clayton Sand Company ....E 732 751-7600
Wall Township (G-11328)
Control Industries Inc ....G...... 201 437-3826
Bayonne (G-212)
County Concrete Corporation ....F 973 538-3113
Morristown (G-6656)
Dun-Rite Sand & Gravel Co...................G...... 856 692-2520
Vineland (G-11214)
Earthwork Associates Inc ....F 609 624-9395
Ocean View (G-7702)
Eastern Concrete Materials Inc ....C...... 201 797-7979
Saddle Brook (G-9650)
Eastern Concrete Materials Inc ....E 973 827-7625
Hamburg (G-4090)
F W Bennett & Son Inc ....G...... 973 383-4050
Lafayette (G-5027)
Hanson Aggregates Wrp Inc..................E 972 653-5500
Wall Township (G-11345)
Harmony Sand & Gravel Inc...................E 908 475-4690
Phillipsburg (G-8555)
Intelligentproject LLC ....G...... 732 928-3421
Jackson (G-4657)
J Gennaro Trucking ....F 973 773-0805
Garfield (G-3749)
Mays Landing Sand & Gravel Co............G...... 856 447-4294
Newport (G-7334)
New Jersey Pulverizing Co Inc...............F 732 269-1400
Bayville (G-249)
North Church Gravel Inc ....G...... 201 796-1556
Oak Ridge (G-7603)
Orsillo & Company................................G...... 973 248-1833
Wayne (G-11537)
Partac Peat Corp ....F 908 637-4191
Great Meadows (G-3855)

Pinnacle Materials Inc ....E 732 254-7676
East Brunswick (G-2165)
Pioneer Concrete Corp ....E 609 693-6151
Forked River (G-3542)
Ricci Bros Sand Company Inc ....E 856 785-0166
Port Norris (G-8888)
Saxton Falls Sand & Gravel Co ....E 908 852-0121
Budd Lake (G-936)
Trap Rock Industries Inc ....E 609 924-0300
Titusville (G-10736)
Tuckahoe Sand & Gravel Co Inc ....E 609 861-2082
Egg Harbor Township (G-2699)
Whibco Inc..E 856 455-9200
Bridgeton (G-779)
Whibco of New Jersey Inc ....E 856 455-9200
Port Elizabeth (G-8878)

1446 Industrial Sand

▲ Cherishmet Inc ....F 201 842-7612
Rutherford (G-9616)
Covia Holdings Corporation ....E 856 785-2700
Dividing Creek (G-2069)
Covia Holdings Corporation ....E 856 451-6400
Bridgeton (G-756)
▲ Inversand Company Inc ....F 856 881-2345
Clayton (G-1526)
James D Morrissey Inc ....E 609 859-2860
Vincentown (G-11182)
New Jersey Pulverizing Co Inc ....F 732 269-1400
Bayville (G-249)
U S Silica Company ....E 856 785-0720
Mauricetown (G-5991)
Whibco Inc..E 856 455-9200
Bridgeton (G-779)
Whibco of New Jersey Inc ....E 856 455-9200
Port Elizabeth (G-8878)

1455 Kaolin & Ball Clay

◆ JM Huber Corporation ....D...... 732 603-3630
Edison (G-2540)

1459 Clay, Ceramic & Refractory Minerals, NEC

▼ Eaglevision Usa LLC ....G...... 908 322-1892
Fanwood (G-3372)
Partac Peat Corp ....F 908 637-4191
Great Meadows (G-3855)

1479 Chemical & Fertilizer Mining

Axiom Ingredients LLC ....F 732 669-2458
Iselin (G-4598)

1481 Nonmetallic Minerals Svcs, Except Fuels

Jersey Boring & Drlg Co Inc ....E 973 242-3800
Fairfield (G-3244)
Jlb Hauling Ltd Liability Co......................G...... 856 514-2771
Pennsville (G-8500)
Tag Minerals Inc ....G...... 732 252-5146
Freehold (G-3701)

1499 Miscellaneous Nonmetallic Mining

◆ Asbury Carbons Inc ....G...... 908 537-2155
Asbury (G-60)
▲ Diamond Wholesale Co ....E 201 727-9595
Moonachie (G-6462)
Eastern Concrete Materials Inc ....G...... 973 702-7866
Sussex (G-10559)
▼ Hungerford & Terry Inc ....E 856 881-3200
Clayton (G-1525)
Innovative Cutng Concepts LLC ....G...... 609 484-9960
Egg Harbor Township (G-2684)
Mteixeira Soapstone VA LLC ....G...... 201 757-8608
Fort Lee (G-3574)
Partac Peat Corp ....F 908 637-4191
Great Meadows (G-3855)
Partac Peat Corporation ....F 908 637-4631
Great Meadows (G-3856)
Star Creations Inc ....G...... 212 221-3570
Piscataway (G-8718)
Sussex Humus & Supply Inc ....G...... 973 779-8812
Clifton (G-1727)
Titan America LLC ....G...... 973 690-5896
Newark (G-7300)
Ziegler Chem & Mineral Corp ....E 732 752-4111
Piscataway (G-8741)
▼ Ziegler Chem & Mineral Corp ....F 732 752-4111
Piscataway (G-8740)

20 FOOD AND KINDRED PRODUCTS

2011 Meat Packing Plants

▲ Applegate Farms LLC ....C...... 908 725-2768
Bridgewater (G-790)
Arm National Food Inc ....G...... 609 695-4911
Trenton (G-10896)
B & B Poultry Co Inc ....C...... 856 692-8893
Norma (G-7365)
Beef International Inc ....D...... 856 663-6763
Pennsauken (G-8395)
Bie Real Estate Holdings LLC..................G...... 856 691-9765
Vineland (G-11195)
Bringhurst Bros Inc ....E 856 767-0110
Berlin (G-418)
Buckhead Meat Company ....C...... 732 661-4900
Edison (G-2471)
▲ Burger Maker Inc ....E 201 939-4747
Carlstadt (G-1133)
Cameco Inc ....D...... 973 239-2845
Verona (G-11164)
Carl Streit & Son Co ....G...... 732 775-0803
Neptune (G-6869)
Carnegie Deli Products Inc ....D...... 201 507-5557
Carlstadt (G-1136)
Comarco Products Inc ....D...... 856 342-7557
Camden (G-1053)
▲ DArtagnan Inc ....G...... 973 344-0565
Union (G-11041)
Dealaman Enterprises Inc ....E 908 647-5533
Warren (G-11407)
Dorzar Corporation ....E 973 589-6363
Newark (G-7103)
Ena Meat Packing Inc ....E 973 742-4790
Paterson (G-8184)
Katzs Delicatessen Mfg ....E 212 254-2246
Carlstadt (G-1173)
Kleemeyer & Merkel Inc ....F 973 377-0875
Green Village (G-3868)
Mamamancinis Holdings Inc ....G...... 201 532-1212
East Rutherford (G-2299)
▲ Nourhan Trading Group Inc ....G...... 732 381-8110
Carteret (G-1261)
▲ Nu-Meat Technology Inc ....E 908 754-3400
South Plainfield (G-10308)
Park Avenue Meats Inc ....E 718 731-4196
Paterson (G-8278)
▲ Premio Foods Inc ....C...... 800 864-7622
Hawthorne (G-4240)
Pulaski Meat Products Co ....E 908 925-5380
Linden (G-5413)
◆ Rastelli Brothers Inc ....C...... 856 803-1100
Swedesboro (G-10606)
S & J Villari Livestock LLC......................G...... 856 468-0807
Wenonah (G-11576)
Salem Packing Co ....E 856 878-0002
Salem (G-9697)
Seabrite Corp ....E 973 491-0399
Newark (G-7265)
Smithfield Packaged Meats Corp ....E 908 354-2674
Elizabeth (G-2776)
Taylor Provisions Company ....D...... 609 392-1113
Trenton (G-10996)
Tyson Fresh Meats Inc ....E 605 235-2061
Roseland (G-9543)
United Premium Foods LLC ....D...... 732 510-5600
Woodbridge (G-12023)
Veroni Usa Inc ....E 609 970-0320
Logan Township (G-5590)
York Street Caterers Inc ....C...... 201 868-9088
Englewood (G-2955)

2013 Sausages & Meat Prdts

A Gimenez Trading LLC ....G...... 973 697-2240
Oak Ridge (G-7599)
◆ Al and John Inc ....B...... 973 742-4990
Caldwell (G-1020)
Allied Specialty Foods Inc ....D...... 856 507-1100
Vineland (G-11185)
Appetito Provisions Company ....E 201 864-3410
Harrington Park (G-4162)
▲ Applegate Farms LLC ....C...... 908 725-2768
Bridgewater (G-790)
Arm National Food Inc ....G...... 609 695-4911
Trenton (G-10896)
B&G Foods Inc ....B...... 973 401-6500
Parsippany (G-7889)
B&G Foods Inc ....C...... 973 401-6500
Parsippany (G-7890)

- **B&G Foods North America Inc** ... E ... 973 401-6500 — Parsippany *(G-7891)*
- **Bringhurst Bros Inc** ... E ... 856 767-0110 — Berlin *(G-418)*
- **Buckhead Meat Company** ... C ... 732 661-4900 — Edison *(G-2471)*
- **Campbell Soup Supply Co LLC** ... G ... 856 342-4800 — Camden *(G-1049)*
- **Casa Di Bertacchi Corporation** ... C ... 856 696-5600 — Vineland *(G-11197)*
- **Case Pork Roll Co Inc** ... E ... 609 396-8171 — Trenton *(G-10912)*
- **CW Brown Foods Inc** ... E ... 856 423-3700 — Mount Royal *(G-6816)*
- **CW Brown Foods Inc** ... F ... 856 423-3700 — Mount Royal *(G-6817)*
- **Dubon Corp** ... G ... 212 812-2171 — Elizabeth *(G-2730)*
- **Ena Meat Packing Inc** ... E ... 973 742-4790 — Paterson *(G-8184)*
- ◆ **Fratelli Beretta Usa Inc** ... D ... 201 438-0723 — Budd Lake *(G-923)*
- **Greentree Packing Inc** ... D ... 212 675-2868 — Passaic *(G-8071)*
- **Groezinger Provisions Inc** ... F ... 732 775-3220 — Neptune *(G-6883)*
- **Highpont Corporation** ... G ... 201 460-1364 — Rutherford *(G-9623)*
- **Kupelian Foods Inc** ... G ... 201 440-8055 — Ridgefield Park *(G-9312)*
- **Lawless Jerky LLC** ... G ... 310 869-5733 — Marlton *(G-5936)*
- **Licini Brothers Inc** ... G ... 201 865-1130 — Union City *(G-11119)*
- **Lopes Sausage Co** ... G ... 973 344-3063 — Newark *(G-7185)*
- **Mamamancinis Holdings Inc** ... G ... 201 532-1212 — East Rutherford *(G-2299)*
- ▲ **Marathon Enterprises Inc** ... F ... 201 935-3330 — Englewood *(G-2921)*
- **Martins Specialty Sausage Co** ... F ... 856 423-4000 — Mickleton *(G-6087)*
- **Mayabeque Products Inc** ... G ... 201 869-0531 — North Bergen *(G-7420)*
- **Nicolosi Foods Inc** ... G ... 201 624-1702 — Union City *(G-11123)*
- ▼ **Nitta Casings Inc** ... C ... 800 526-3970 — Bridgewater *(G-857)*
- **Palenque Meat Provisions LLC** ... E ... 908 718-1557 — Linden *(G-5401)*
- ▲ **Premio Foods Inc** ... C ... 800 864-7622 — Hawthorne *(G-4240)*
- **Pulaski Meat Products Co** ... E ... 908 925-5380 — Linden *(G-5413)*
- **Rajbhog Foods(nj) Inc** ... C ... 551 222-4700 — Jersey City *(G-4796)*
- **Real Kosher LLC** ... G ... 973 690-5394 — Newark *(G-7247)*
- **Red Square Foods Inc** ... F ... 732 846-0190 — Somerset *(G-10063)*
- **Shahnawaz Food LLC** ... F ... 908 413-4206 — Edison *(G-2606)*
- **Taylor Provisions Company** ... D ... 609 392-1113 — Trenton *(G-10996)*
- **Thumann Incorporated** ... C ... 201 935-3636 — Carlstadt *(G-1229)*
- **Wagner Provision Co Inc** ... F ... 856 423-1630 — Gibbstown *(G-3800)*

2015 Poultry Slaughtering, Dressing & Processing

- **B & B Poultry Co Inc** ... C ... 856 692-8893 — Norma *(G-7365)*
- **Carl Streit & Son Co** ... G ... 732 775-0803 — Neptune *(G-6869)*
- **David Mitchell Inc** ... E ... 856 429-2610 — Voorhees *(G-11284)*
- **Deb El Food Products LLC** ... D ... 908 409-0010 — Elizabeth *(G-2727)*
- ◆ **Deb El Food Products LLC** ... B ... 908 351-0330 — Newark *(G-7098)*
- ◆ **Deb-El Foods Corporation** ... C ... 908 351-0330 — Newark *(G-7099)*
- **Ena Meat Packing Inc** ... E ... 973 742-4790 — Paterson *(G-8184)*
- ▲ **Golden Platter Foods Inc** ... E ... 973 344-8770 — Newark *(G-7136)*
- **Hinck Turkey Farm Inc** ... G ... 732 681-0508 — Neptune *(G-6884)*
- **Mamamancinis Holdings Inc** ... G ... 201 532-1212 — East Rutherford *(G-2299)*
- ▲ **Nema Food Distribution Inc** ... G ... 973 256-4415 — Fairfield *(G-3276)*
- ▼ **Papettis Hygrade Egg Pdts Inc** ... A ... 908 282-7900 — Elizabethport *(G-2790)*
- **Park Avenue Meats Inc** ... E ... 718 731-4196 — Paterson *(G-8278)*
- **Perdue Farms Inc** ... G ... 609 298-4100 — Bridgeton *(G-768)*
- **Senat Poultry LLC** ... E ... 973 742-9316 — Paterson *(G-8298)*
- **Vineland Kosher Poultry Inc** ... C ... 856 692-1871 — Vineland *(G-11275)*

2021 Butter

- **Cookman Creamery LLC** ... G ... 732 361-5215 — Brielle *(G-906)*

2022 Cheese

- **Abuelito Cheese Inc** ... G ... 973 345-3503 — Paterson *(G-8123)*
- ◆ **Ambriola Company Inc** ... F ... 973 228-3600 — West Caldwell *(G-11640)*
- ◆ **Arthur Schuman Inc** ... D ... 973 227-0030 — Fairfield *(G-3146)*
- ▲ **Biazzo Dairy Products Inc** ... E ... 201 941-6800 — Ridgefield *(G-9251)*
- **Capital Foods Inc** ... E ... 908 587-9050 — Linden *(G-5329)*
- ▲ **Colonna Brothers Inc** ... D ... 800 626-8384 — North Bergen *(G-7397)*
- ▲ **Finlandia Cheese Inc** ... E ... 973 316-6699 — Parsippany *(G-7946)*
- **Hawk Dairy Inc** ... G ... 973 466-9030 — Newark *(G-7148)*
- **Jvm Sales Corp** ... D ... 908 862-4866 — Linden *(G-5367)*
- **La Bella Mozzarella** ... G ... 201 997-1737 — Kearny *(G-4879)*
- **Lebanon Cheese Company Inc** ... G ... 908 236-2611 — Lebanon *(G-5268)*
- ◆ **Lioni Latticini Inc** ... D ... 908 686-6061 — Union *(G-11070)*
- ▲ **Lioni Mozzarella & Spclty** ... E ... 908 624-9450 — Union *(G-11071)*
- ▲ **Losurdo Foods Inc** ... E ... 201 343-6680 — Hackensack *(G-3940)*
- **Lotito Foods Inc** ... F ... 973 684-2900 — Paterson *(G-8246)*
- **Mendez Dairy Co Inc** ... D ... 732 442-6337 — Perth Amboy *(G-8527)*
- **Mondelez International Inc** ... E ... 973 503-2000 — East Hanover *(G-2222)*
- ▲ **Montena Taranto Foods Inc** ... E ... 201 943-8484 — Ridgefield *(G-9277)*
- **Saporito Inc** ... G ... 201 265-8212 — Ridgefield *(G-9288)*
- **Saputo Cheese USA Inc** ... E ... 201 508-6400 — Carlstadt *(G-1212)*
- **South American Imports Corp** ... G ... 201 941-2020 — Cliffside Park *(G-1544)*
- ▲ **Tipico Products Co Inc** ... D ... 732 942-8820 — Lakewood *(G-5171)*
- ▲ **Toscana Cheese Company Inc** ... E ... 201 617-1500 — Secaucus *(G-9821)*
- ▲ **Tropical Cheese Industries** ... B ... 732 442-4898 — Perth Amboy *(G-8537)*

2023 Milk, Condensed & Evaporated

- **Advanced Orthomolecular RES Inc** ... G ... 317 292-9013 — Clifton *(G-1557)*
- ▼ **Allegro Nutrition Inc** ... E ... 732 364-3777 — Neptune *(G-6864)*
- ▲ **American Casein Company** ... E ... 609 387-2988 — Burlington *(G-947)*
- ▲ **American Custom Drying Co** ... E ... 609 387-3933 — Burlington *(G-948)*
- **Amish Dairy Products LLC** ... G ... 973 256-7676 — Totowa *(G-10812)*
- **Arla Foods Ingredients N Amer** ... F ... 908 604-8551 — Basking Ridge *(G-175)*
- **Biofarma Us LLC** ... F ... 609 301-6446 — East Windsor *(G-2346)*
- ◆ **Buy Buy Baby Inc** ... F ... 908 688-0888 — Union *(G-11034)*
- ▲ **Dairy Delight LLC** ... F ... 201 939-7878 — Rutherford *(G-9617)*
- ▲ **Farbest-Tallman Foods Corp** ... D ... 714 897-7199 — Park Ridge *(G-7849)*
- **Food Sciences Corp** ... C ... 856 778-4192 — Mount Laurel *(G-6761)*
- ◆ **Gerber Products Company** ... C ... 973 593-7500 — Florham Park *(G-3508)*
- **Gold Star Distribution LLC** ... F ... 973 882-5300 — East Hanover *(G-2216)*
- **Grow Company Inc** ... E ... 201 941-8777 — Ridgefield *(G-9264)*
- **Horphag Research (usa) Inc** ... G ... 201 459-0300 — Hoboken *(G-4456)*
- ▲ **Icelandirect Inc** ... F ... 800 763-4690 — Clifton *(G-1638)*
- **Jersey Ordnance Inc** ... G ... 609 267-2112 — Westampton *(G-11787)*
- **Kerry Inc** ... D ... 201 373-1111 — Teterboro *(G-10685)*
- **Lycored Corp** ... G ... 201 601-0060 — Secaucus *(G-9790)*
- ◆ **Lycored Corp** ... E ... 973 882-0322 — Orange *(G-7755)*
- **Medison Pharmaceuticals Inc** ... F ... 856 304-8516 — Piscataway *(G-8689)*
- **Naturally Scientific Inc** ... F ... 201 585-7055 — Leonia *(G-5291)*
- **Nestle Usa Inc** ... C ... 973 390-9555 — Keasbey *(G-4913)*
- ▲ **Nutri Sport Pharmacal Inc** ... F ... 973 827-9287 — Franklin *(G-3608)*
- ◆ **Orcas International Inc** ... F ... 973 448-2801 — Landing *(G-5202)*
- **Panos Brands LLC** ... E ... 800 229-1706 — Linden *(G-5402)*
- **Robertet Flavors Inc** ... F ... 732 271-1804 — Piscataway *(G-8706)*
- **Shree Meldi Krupa LLC** ... G ... 732 407-5295 — Parsippany *(G-8014)*
- ▼ **Syncom Pharmaceuticals Inc** ... E ... 973 787-2405 — Fairfield *(G-3321)*
- **Unique Encapsulation Tech LLC** ... E ... 973 448-2801 — Landing *(G-5204)*
- ▲ **V E N Inc** ... C ... 973 786-7862 — Andover *(G-52)*
- **Willings Nutraceutical Corp** ... F ... 856 424-9088 — Cherry Hill *(G-1427)*
- **Yinlink International Inc** ... C ... 973 818-4664 — Cranbury *(G-1894)*

2024 Ice Cream

- **Agape Inc** ... F ... 973 923-7625 — Irvington *(G-4553)*
- **Alpine Creamery** ... G ... 973 726-0777 — Sparta *(G-10377)*
- **Angelos Italian Ices Icecream** ... G ... 201 962-7575 — Ramsey *(G-9137)*
- **Applegate Frm Hmmade Ice Cream** ... F ... 973 744-5900 — Montclair *(G-6358)*
- **Arctic Products Co Inc** ... F ... 609 393-4264 — Ewing *(G-3016)*
- **Bergenline Gelato LLC** ... G ... 201 861-1100 — North Bergen *(G-7390)*
- **Bertolotti LLC** ... F ... 201 941-3116 — Fairview *(G-3357)*
- **Best of Farms LLC** ... G ... 201 512-8400 — Fair Lawn *(G-3091)*
- ◆ **Bindi North America Inc** ... E ... 973 812-8118 — Kearny *(G-4848)*
- **Cielito Lindo** ... G ... 580 286-1127 — New Brunswick *(G-6917)*
- **Clio Foods & Provisions LLC** ... G ... 908 505-2546 — Roselle *(G-9553)*
- **Confectionately Yours LLC** ... E ... 732 821-6863 — Franklin Park *(G-3633)*
- **Conopco Inc** ... C ... 920 499-2509 — Englewood Cliffs *(G-2965)*
- **Country Club Ice Cream** ... G ... 973 729-5570 — Sparta *(G-10384)*
- **Cumberland Dairy Inc** ... E ... 856 451-1300 — Bridgeton *(G-757)*
- **Dairy Queen** ... F ... 732 892-5700 — Point Pleasant Boro *(G-8842)*
- ◆ **Deep Foods Inc** ... C ... 908 810-7500 — Union *(G-11042)*
- **Ding Moo LLC** ... E ... 973 881-8622 — Paterson *(G-8174)*
- **Dunkin Donuts Baskin Robbins** ... G ... 201 692-1900 — Teaneck *(G-10628)*
- **Elegant Desserts Inc** ... F ... 201 933-7309 — Lyndhurst *(G-5650)*
- ◆ **Eveready Trading Inc** ... G ... 201 944-6484 — Fort Lee *(G-3557)*

Frozen Desserts LLC G 508 872-3573
Haddonfield *(G-4057)*

Fruta Loca LLC G 732 642-8233
Long Branch *(G-5597)*

Gelotti Confections LLC G 973 403-9968
Caldwell *(G-1025)*

Guernsey Crest Ice Cream Co G 973 742-4620
Paterson *(G-8206)*

Halo Pub Ice Cream F 609 921-1710
Princeton *(G-8957)*

Halo Pub Inc F 609 586-1811
Trenton *(G-10938)*

Heavenly Havens Creamery LLC G 609 259-6600
Allentown *(G-27)*

Ice Cold Novelty Products Inc G 732 751-0011
Wall Township *(G-11349)*

Icykidz G 973 342-9665
Irvington *(G-4573)*

J & J Snack Foods Corp B 856 665-9533
Pennsauken *(G-8440)*

J & J Snack Foods Corp C 856 467-9552
Bridgeport *(G-740)*

Kwality Foods Ltd Liability Co G 732 906-1941
Edison *(G-2547)*

Leos Ice Cream Company G 856 797-8771
Medford *(G-6029)*

Magliones Italian Ices LLC F 732 283-0705
Iselin *(G-4614)*

Marks Ice Cream G 201 861-5099
North Bergen *(G-7417)*

Mars Incorporated F 973 691-3500
Budd Lake *(G-929)*

▲ Mega Industries LLC G 973 779-8772
Passaic *(G-8086)*

◆ Mister Cookie Face Inc C 732 370-5533
Lakewood *(G-5137)*

Mr Green Tea Ice Cream Corp E 732 446-9800
Keyport *(G-5002)*

Mr Green Tea Ice Cream Corp F 732 446-9800
Keyport *(G-5003)*

Piemonte & Liebhauser LLC F 973 937-6200
Florham Park *(G-3519)*

Rajbhog Foods(nj) Inc C 551 222-4700
Jersey City *(G-4796)*

Rolo Systems E 973 627-4214
Denville *(G-2055)*

Rw Delights Inc G 718 683-1038
Millington *(G-6208)*

South Jersey Pretzel Inc F 856 435-5055
Stratford *(G-10507)*

Summer Sweets LLC G 732 240-9376
Toms River *(G-10797)*

Sweet Delight F 732 263-9100
Oakhurst *(G-7613)*

Sweet Orange LLC G 908 522-0011
Summit *(G-10552)*

Talenti Gelato LLC E 800 298-4020
Englewood Cliffs *(G-2990)*

▲ Taylor Products Inc E 732 225-4620
Edison *(G-2631)*

Tjs Ice Cream G 609 398-5055
Ocean City *(G-7697)*

▼ Tofutti Brands Inc G 908 272-2400
Cranford *(G-1928)*

Uncle Eds Creamery G 609 818-0100
Pennington *(G-8376)*

◆ Unilever United States Inc A 201 735-9661
Englewood Cliffs *(G-2995)*

2026 Milk

▲ Cumberland Dairy Inc D 800 257-8484
Rosenhayn *(G-9594)*

Cumberland Dairy Inc E 856 451-1300
Bridgeton *(G-757)*

Frozen Falls LLC G 908 350-3939
Basking Ridge *(G-184)*

Garelick Farms LLC C 609 499-2600
Burlington *(G-970)*

Georges Wine and Spirits Galle G 973 948-9950
Branchville *(G-707)*

Halo Farm Inc G 609 695-3311
Lawrenceville *(G-5230)*

▲ Johanna Foods Inc B 908 788-2200
Flemington *(G-3452)*

Midland Farms Inc E 800 749-6455
Paterson *(G-8260)*

Mualema LLC G 609 820-6098
Lawrence Township *(G-5217)*

Readington Farms Inc D 908 534-2121
Whitehouse *(G-11918)*

Tuscan/Lehigh Dairies Inc D 570 385-1884
Burlington *(G-989)*

▲ Vitamia Pasta Boy Inc F 973 546-1140
Lodi *(G-5582)*

Wakefern Food Corp B 732 819-0140
Edison *(G-2645)*

◆ Wakefern Food Corp B 908 527-3300
Keasbey *(G-4916)*

Wwf Operating Company F 856 459-3890
Bridgeton *(G-780)*

Yamate Chocolatier Inc G 732 249-4847
Highland Park *(G-4290)*

Yo Got It G 732 475-7913
Point Pleasant Beach *(G-8834)*

Yogurt Paradise LLC G 732 534-6395
Jackson *(G-4670)*

2032 Canned Specialties

◆ Antonio Mozzarella Factory Inc F 973 353-9411
Newark *(G-7049)*

Antonio Mozzarella Factory Inc E 973 353-9411
Newark *(G-7050)*

▲ Aunt Kittys Foods Inc D 856 691-2100
Vineland *(G-11189)*

B&G Foods Inc B 973 401-6500
Parsippany *(G-7889)*

B&G Foods Inc C 973 401-6500
Parsippany *(G-7890)*

Bakers Perfection Inc E 973 983-0700
Rockaway *(G-9446)*

▲ Bono USA Inc G 973 978-7361
Fairfield *(G-3159)*

Campbell Company of Canada G 856 342-4800
Camden *(G-1046)*

Campbell Soup Company A 856 342-4800
Camden *(G-1047)*

Crave Foods LLC F 973 233-1220
Montclair *(G-6361)*

CSC Brands LP F 800 257-8443
Camden *(G-1056)*

F&S Produce Company Inc C 856 453-0316
Rosenhayn *(G-9595)*

▲ F&S Produce Company Inc C 856 453-0316
Vineland *(G-11218)*

▲ Fast-Pak Trading Inc G 201 293-4757
Secaucus *(G-9766)*

Freed Foods Inc G 512 829-5535
Hillside *(G-4392)*

Goldens Inc G 215 850-2512
Haddonfield *(G-4059)*

Goya Foods Inc B 201 348-4900
Secaucus *(G-9776)*

Goya Foods Inc E 201 865-3470
Secaucus *(G-9777)*

Grandi Pastai Italiani Inc G 201 786-5050
Moonachie *(G-6467)*

Healthy Italia Retail LLC F 973 966-5200
Madison *(G-5694)*

Mayab Happy Tacos Inc E 732 293-0400
Perth Amboy *(G-8526)*

▲ Mrs Mazzulas Food Products G 732 248-0555
Edison *(G-2570)*

▲ Mushroom Wisdom Inc F 973 470-0010
East Rutherford *(G-2305)*

Mysuperfoods Ltd Liability Co F 646 283-7455
Summit *(G-10541)*

▲ Nema Food Distribution Inc G 973 256-4415
Fairfield *(G-3276)*

◆ Nestle Healthcare Ntrtn Inc C 800 422-2752
Bridgewater *(G-856)*

◆ Novartis Corporation E 212 307-1122
East Hanover *(G-2226)*

Project Feed Usa Inc F 201 443-7143
Jersey City *(G-4789)*

◆ RAB Food Group LLC D 201 553-1100
Newark *(G-7244)*

▲ Sanket Corporation F 732 287-0201
Edison *(G-2604)*

Tuscany Especially Itln Foods F 732 308-1118
Marlboro *(G-5918)*

◆ Universal Prtein Spplmnts Corp D 732 545-3130
New Brunswick *(G-6977)*

2033 Canned Fruits, Vegetables & Preserves

B&G Foods Inc C 973 403-6795
Roseland *(G-9534)*

B&G Foods Inc B 973 401-6500
Parsippany *(G-7889)*

B&G Foods Inc C 973 401-6500
Parsippany *(G-7890)*

BSC USA LLC F 908 487-4437
Palisades Park *(G-7770)*

▼ C & E Canners Inc F 609 561-1078
Hammonton *(G-4132)*

Cameco Inc D 973 239-2845
Verona *(G-11164)*

Campbell Company of Canada G 856 342-4800
Camden *(G-1046)*

Campbell Soup Company A 856 342-4800
Camden *(G-1047)*

Campbell Soup Company G 856 342-4759
Camden *(G-1048)*

▲ European Amrcn Foods Group Inc E 201 436-6106
Bayonne *(G-215)*

Funnibonz LLC G 609 915-3685
Princeton Junction *(G-9059)*

▲ Gardner Resources Inc G 732 872-0755
Highlands *(G-4292)*

Garelick Farms LLC C 609 499-2600
Burlington *(G-970)*

Halo Farm Inc G 609 695-3311
Lawrenceville *(G-5230)*

Ingrasselino Products LLC G 800 960-1316
Clifton *(G-1640)*

▲ Johanna Foods Inc B 908 788-2200
Flemington *(G-3452)*

Juice Hub LLP G 732 784-8265
Rahway *(G-9110)*

◆ Lassonde Pappas and Co Inc D 856 455-1000
Carneys Point *(G-1242)*

Lassonde Pappas and Co Inc E 856 455-1001
Bridgeton *(G-762)*

▲ Losurdo Foods Inc E 201 343-6680
Hackensack *(G-3940)*

Northeast Tomato Company Inc F 973 684-4890
Paterson *(G-8271)*

Pappas Lassonde Holdings Inc G 856 455-1000
Carneys Point *(G-1243)*

▲ Pomi USA Inc G 732 541-4115
Matawan *(G-5985)*

▲ Raos Specialty Foods Inc F 212 269-0151
Montclair *(G-6387)*

Refresco Us Inc D 973 361-9794
Wharton *(G-11869)*

RSR Enterprises LLC F 732 369-6053
Martinsville *(G-5964)*

Wayne County Foods Inc E 973 399-0101
Irvington *(G-4589)*

2034 Dried Fruits, Vegetables & Soup

Allied Food Products Inc E 908 357-2454
Linden *(G-5321)*

▲ Cibo Vita Inc B 862 238-8020
Totowa *(G-10823)*

Elaine K Josephson Inc G 609 259-2256
New Brunswick *(G-6923)*

◆ Fornazor International Inc E 201 664-4000
Hillsdale *(G-4366)*

▲ Joyce Food LLC C 973 491-9696
Newark *(G-7171)*

▲ Major Products Co Inc E 201 641-5555
Little Ferry *(G-5492)*

▲ Mrs Mazzulas Food Products G 732 248-0555
Edison *(G-2570)*

▲ Osem USA Inc G 201 871-4433
Englewood Cliffs *(G-2985)*

2035 Pickled Fruits, Vegetables, Sauces & Dressings

B&G Foods Inc B 973 401-6500
Parsippany *(G-7889)*

B&G Foods Inc C 973 401-6500
Parsippany *(G-7890)*

▲ Benckiser N Reckitt Amer Inc A 973 404-2600
Parsippany *(G-7893)*

◆ Birds Eye Foods Inc C 585 383-1850
Cherry Hill *(G-1346)*

▼ Chelten House Products Inc C 856 467-1600
Bridgeport *(G-735)*

▲ Classic Cooking LLC D 718 439-0200
Rahway *(G-9086)*

Conopco Inc G 201 894-7760
Englewood Cliffs *(G-2964)*

◆ Cosmopolitan Food Group Inc G 908 998-1818
Hoboken *(G-4449)*

Crazy Steves Concoctions LLC G 908 787-2089
Trenton *(G-10924)*

▼ Dee & L LLC F 201 858-0138
Bayonne *(G-213)*

House of Herbs I LLC ....G 973 779-2422
Passaic *(G-8073)*

Ingrasselino Products LLC ....G 800 960-1316
Clifton *(G-1640)*

Jjs Own Ltd Liability Company............G 551 486-8510
Little Ferry *(G-5490)*

Kaplan & Zubrin ....E 856 964-1083
Camden *(G-1073)*

Mamamancinis Holdings Inc ....G 201 532-1212
East Rutherford *(G-2299)*

Mirrotek International LLC ....E 973 472-1400
Passaic *(G-8090)*

◆ Oasis Trading Co Inc ....C 908 964-0477
Hillside *(G-4419)*

Panos Brands LLC ....G 800 229-1706
Linden *(G-5402)*

Patriot Pickle Inc ....D 973 709-9487
Wayne *(G-11541)*

▼ Pinnacle Foods Inc ....C 973 541-6620
Parsippany *(G-7993)*

R C Fine Foods Inc ....G 908 359-5500
Hillsborough *(G-4349)*

▲ Raos Specialty Foods Inc ....F 212 269-0151
Montclair *(G-6387)*

RB Manufacturing LLC ....C 908 533-2000
Hillsborough *(G-4350)*

▲ RB Manufacturing LLC ....B 973 404-2600
Parsippany *(G-8004)*

◆ Reckitt Benckiser LLC ....B 973 404-2600
Parsippany *(G-8005)*

Reckitt Benckiser LLC ....C 973 404-2600
Montvale *(G-6425)*

Regal Crown Fd Svc Specialist ....G 508 752-2679
Wayne *(G-11548)*

Rutgers Food Innovation Center ....F 856 459-1900
Bridgeton *(G-771)*

◆ Silver Palate Kitchens Inc.............E 201 568-0110
Cresskill *(G-1944)*

▲ Surati NJ LLC ....F 732 251-3404
Spotswood *(G-10418)*

Technical Oil Products Co Inc ....G 973 940-8920
Newton *(G-7362)*

Unilever United States Inc................G 800 298-5018
Englewood Cliffs *(G-2996)*

◆ Unilever United States Inc ....A 201 735-9661
Englewood Cliffs *(G-2995)*

United Farm Processing Corp ....F 856 451-4612
Rosenhayn *(G-9598)*

▲ Vitamia Pasta Boy Inc ....F 973 546-1140
Lodi *(G-5582)*

▲ Yipin Food Products Inc ....F 718 788-3059
Edison *(G-2648)*

Yunta USA Inc ....G 614 835-6588
Cranbury *(G-1896)*

2037 Frozen Fruits, Juices & Vegetables

202 Smoothie LLC...............................G 973 985-4973
Wayne *(G-11463)*

American Food & Bev Inds LLC ....D 347 241-9827
Orange *(G-7750)*

Bart Foods Group LLC ....G 973 650-8837
Fairfield *(G-3152)*

Berry Blast Smoothies LLC ....G 856 692-6174
Vineland *(G-11194)*

Birds Eye Foods Inc ....C 920 435-5300
Parsippany *(G-7894)*

◆ Birds Eye Foods Inc ....C 585 383-1850
Cherry Hill *(G-1346)*

▲ Classic Cooking LLC ....D 718 439-0200
Rahway *(G-9086)*

◆ Ejz Foods LLC ....G 201 229-0500
South Hackensack *(G-10157)*

G & Y Specialty Foods LLC ....G 956 821-9652
Woodland Park *(G-12080)*

◆ Gerber Products Company ....C 973 593-7500
Florham Park *(G-3508)*

Grasso Foods Inc................................G 856 467-2223
Woolwich Township *(G-12097)*

▲ Mojo Organics Inc ....G 201 633-6519
Jersey City *(G-4767)*

▲ Seabrook Brothers & Sons Inc ....C 856 455-8080
Bridgeton *(G-772)*

2038 Frozen Specialties

Amys Omelette Hse Burlington............F 609 386-4800
Burlington *(G-949)*

Appetizers Made Easy Inc ....E 201 531-1212
East Rutherford *(G-2271)*

Arctic Foods Inc ....E 908 689-0590
Washington *(G-11438)*

Battistini Foods................................G 609 476-2184
Egg Harbor Township *(G-2680)*

◆ Birds Eye Foods Inc ....C 585 383-1850
Cherry Hill *(G-1346)*

▲ Caesars Pasta LLC ....E 856 227-2585
Blackwood *(G-462)*

Campbell Soup Company ....A 856 342-4800
Camden *(G-1047)*

Campbell Soup Company ....G 856 342-4759
Camden *(G-1048)*

▲ Classic Cooking LLC ....D 718 439-0200
Rahway *(G-9086)*

Cuisine Innvtons Unlimited LLC ....C 732 730-9310
Lakewood *(G-5077)*

Dairy Deluxe Corp ....G 845 549-0665
Hackensack *(G-3904)*

◆ Deep Foods Inc ....C 908 810-7500
Union *(G-11042)*

Delicious Fresh Pierogi Inc..................F 908 245-0550
Roselle Park *(G-9583)*

Dewy Meadow Farms Inc ....F 908 218-5655
Bridgewater *(G-818)*

Diaz Wholesale & Mfg Co Inc ....D 404 629-3616
Saddle Brook *(G-9649)*

DO Productions LLC ....D 856 866-3566
Lodi *(G-5559)*

▲ Dr Pregers Sensible Foods Inc.........D 201 703-1300
Elmwood Park *(G-2823)*

▲ Fast-Pak Trading Inc ....G 201 293-4757
Secaucus *(G-9766)*

▲ Group Martin LLC Jj ....F 862 240-1813
Newark *(G-7141)*

L E Rosellis Food Specialties ....F 609 654-4816
Medford *(G-6027)*

McCain Ellios Foods Inc....................C 201 368-0600
Lodi *(G-5571)*

Mjs of Spotswood LLC ....G 732 251-7400
Spotswood *(G-10416)*

▲ Old Fashion Kitchen Inc..................D 732 364-4100
Lakewood *(G-5143)*

Peak Finance Holdings LLC..................E 856 969-7100
Cherry Hill *(G-1406)*

Pinnacle Food Group Inc ....E 856 969-7100
Parsippany *(G-7990)*

▲ Pinnacle Foods Finance LLC............D 973 541-6620
Parsippany *(G-7991)*

Pinnacle Foods Group LLC ....C 856 969-7100
Cherry Hill *(G-1409)*

◆ Pinnacle Foods Group LLC ....D 856 969-8238
Parsippany *(G-7992)*

▼ Pinnacle Foods Inc ....C 973 541-6620
Parsippany *(G-7993)*

Rajbhog Foods(nj) Inc ....C 551 222-4700
Jersey City *(G-4796)*

Rich Products Corporation ....D 856 696-5600
Vineland *(G-11259)*

Rico Foods Inc ....E 973 278-0589
Paterson *(G-8287)*

▲ Savignano Food Corp.......................E 973 673-3355
Orange *(G-7760)*

Severino Pasta Mfg Co Inc ....E 856 854-3716
Collingswood *(G-1771)*

Seviroli Foods Inc ....G 856 931-1900
Bellmawr *(G-343)*

▲ Tovli Inc...E 718 417-6677
Newark *(G-7301)*

◆ Unilever United States Inc ....A 201 735-9661
Englewood Cliffs *(G-2995)*

Vineland Specialty Foods L L C ....G 856 742-5001
Westville *(G-11823)*

Waffle Waffle LLC...............................F 201 559-1286
Nutley *(G-7597)*

2041 Flour, Grain Milling

A & S Frozen Inc ....E 201 672-0510
East Rutherford *(G-2268)*

Bay State Milling Company ....D 973 772-3400
Clifton *(G-1572)*

▲ Cibo Vita Inc ....B 862 238-8020
Totowa *(G-10823)*

▲ Coco International Inc ....E 973 694-1200
Wayne *(G-11489)*

Frewitt USA Inc ....E 908 829-5245
Hillsborough *(G-4317)*

Guttenplans Frozen Dough Inc............G 732 495-9480
North Middletown *(G-7503)*

J Spinelli & Sons Inc...........................E 856 691-3133
Elmer *(G-2799)*

2043 Cereal Breakfast Foods

Dim Inc...F 908 925-2043
Linden *(G-5343)*

◆ Gerber Products Company ....C 973 593-7500
Florham Park *(G-3508)*

Kellogg Company ....E 201 634-9140
River Edge *(G-9363)*

Kellogg Company ....D 609 567-1688
Hammonton *(G-4137)*

▲ Mm Packaging Group LLC ....G 908 759-0101
Linden *(G-5387)*

Naturalvert LLC ....G 848 229-4600
Hawthorne *(G-4233)*

◆ Silver Palate Kitchens Inc ....E 201 568-0110
Cresskill *(G-1944)*

Simi Granola LLC...............................F 848 459-5619
Jackson *(G-4665)*

2044 Rice Milling

▲ Diamond Foods USA Inc ....G 732 543-2186
North Brunswick *(G-7465)*

◆ Fornazor International Inc ....E 201 664-4000
Hillsdale *(G-4366)*

2045 Flour, Blended & Prepared

All Madina Inc....................................F 973 226-7772
West Caldwell *(G-11639)*

Allied Food Products Inc.....................E 908 357-2454
Linden *(G-5321)*

Caravan Ingredients Inc ....C 973 256-8886
Totowa *(G-10821)*

Chanks USA LLC ....G 856 265-0203
Millville *(G-6242)*

Foodtek Inc...F 973 257-4000
Whippany *(G-11891)*

◆ Fornazor International Inc ....E 201 664-4000
Hillsdale *(G-4366)*

Jimmys Cookies LLC ....C 973 779-8500
Clifton *(G-1647)*

▲ Joyce Food LLC................................C 973 491-9696
Newark *(G-7171)*

▲ Losurdo Foods Inc..........................E 201 343-6680
Hackensack *(G-3940)*

Mjs of Spotswood LLC ....G 732 251-7400
Spotswood *(G-10416)*

Nijama Corporation.............................G 973 272-3223
Clifton *(G-1678)*

Peak Finance Holdings LLC..................G 856 969-7100
Cherry Hill *(G-1406)*

▲ Pinnacle Foods Finance LLC............D 973 541-6620
Parsippany *(G-7991)*

◆ Pinnacle Foods Group LLC ....D 856 969-8238
Parsippany *(G-7992)*

Procter & Gamble Mfg Co ....D 732 602-4500
Avenel *(G-143)*

R C Fine Foods Inc ....D 908 359-5500
Hillsborough *(G-4349)*

◆ RAB Food Group LLC ....D 201 553-1100
Newark *(G-7244)*

◆ Slt Foods Inc ....F 732 661-1030
Dayton *(G-1988)*

William R Tatz Industries.....................G 973 751-0720
Belleville *(G-325)*

2046 Wet Corn Milling

◆ Amerchol Corporation ....C 732 248-6000
Edison *(G-2452)*

Ingredion Incorporated.......................D 908 685-5000
Bridgewater *(G-836)*

▼ National Strch Chem Holdg Corp .....A 908 685-5000
Bridgewater *(G-854)*

2047 Dog & Cat Food

Freshpet Inc.......................................E 201 520-4000
Secaucus *(G-9768)*

Gwenstone Inc ....G 732 785-2600
Lakewood *(G-5106)*

Mars Incorporated.............................F 973 691-3500
Budd Lake *(G-929)*

Mars Food Us LLC ....F 908 852-1000
Hackettstown *(G-4025)*

Phibro Anmal Hlth Holdings Inc ....G 201 329-7300
Teaneck *(G-10644)*

Simmons Pet Food Inc........................C 856 662-7412
Pennsauken *(G-8484)*

◆ Simmons Pet Food Nj Inc................B 856 662-7412
Pennsauken *(G-8485)*

Xceptional Instruments LLC ....G 315 750-4345
Hoboken *(G-4490)*

2048 Prepared Feeds For Animals & Fowls

Buckhead Meat Company C 732 661-4900
Edison *(G-2471)*
Darling Ingredients Inc C 973 465-1900
Newark *(G-7095)*
Evergreen Kosher LLC G 732 370-4500
Lakewood *(G-5094)*
Glenburnie Feed & Grain G 856 986-8128
Mount Laurel *(G-6763)*
International Processing Corp F 732 826-4240
Perth Amboy *(G-8523)*
New York Poultry Co F 908 523-1600
Linden *(G-5396)*
Penetone Corporation G 609 921-0501
Princeton *(G-8994)*
Pet Devices LLC G 929 244-0012
Livingston *(G-5535)*
◆ **Pharmacia & Upjohn Company LLC** B 908 901-8000
Peapack *(G-8344)*
◆ **Prince Agri Products Inc** D 201 329-7300
Teaneck *(G-10648)*
R World Enterprises G 201 795-2428
Jersey City *(G-4793)*
Reconserve Inc G 732 826-4240
Perth Amboy *(G-8530)*

2051 Bread, Bakery Prdts Exc Cookies & Crackers

9001 Corporation E 201 963-2233
Jersey City *(G-4680)*
9002 Corporation E 201 792-9595
Jersey City *(G-4681)*
▲ **A C Bakery Distributors Inc** F 973 977-2255
Paterson *(G-8118)*
Ability2work A NJ Nnprfit Corp F 908 782-3458
Flemington *(G-3427)*
Acme Markets Inc E 609 884-7217
Cape May *(G-1091)*
Ahzanis Castle LLC G 973 874-3191
Paterson *(G-8128)*
All In Icing G 973 896-5990
Stanhope *(G-10476)*
All Natural Products F 212 391-2870
Sayreville *(G-9701)*
▲ **Alpine Bakery Inc** G 201 902-0605
Union City *(G-11104)*
American Harvest Baking Co Inc E 856 642-9955
Mount Laurel *(G-6737)*
▼ **Amorosos Baking Co** B 215 471-4740
Bellmawr *(G-327)*
Angelos Panetteria Inc G 201 435-4659
Jersey City *(G-4692)*
Angels Bakery USA LLC E 718 389-1400
Carteret *(G-1245)*
▲ **Anthony & Sons Bakery Itln Bky** D 973 625-2323
Denville *(G-2031)*
Artisan Oven Inc G 201 488-6261
Hackensack *(G-3878)*
Auntie Annes Soft Pretzels E 856 722-0433
Moorestown *(G-6506)*
Aversas Italian Bakery Inc E 856 227-8005
Blackwood *(G-460)*
Bagel Club F 908 806-6022
Flemington *(G-3432)*
Bagel Street E 609 936-1755
Plainsboro *(G-8780)*
Bakers Perfection Inc E 973 983-0700
Rockaway *(G-9446)*
Barbeitos Inc G 732 726-9543
Avenel *(G-123)*
Bella Palermo Pastry Shop E 908 931-0298
Kenilworth *(G-4928)*
Berat Corporation C 609 953-7700
Medford *(G-6020)*
Bimbo Bakeries Usa Inc D 732 886-1881
Lakewood *(G-5062)*
Bimbo Bakeries Usa Inc D 732 390-7715
East Brunswick *(G-2129)*
Bimbo Bakeries Usa Inc D 856 435-0500
Clementon *(G-1531)*
Bimbo Bakeries Usa Inc E 973 872-6167
Wayne *(G-11479)*
Blissful Bites G 973 670-6928
Vernon *(G-11157)*
Branchville Bagels Inc G 973 948-7077
Branchville *(G-704)*
Bread & Bagels F 856 667-2333
Cherry Hill *(G-1349)*
Bread Guy Inc F 973 881-9002
Paterson *(G-8149)*
Cake Specialty Inc F 973 238-0500
Hawthorne *(G-4211)*
Calandra Italian & French Bky D 973 484-5598
Newark *(G-7080)*
Cambridge Bagels Inc F 973 743-5683
Bloomfield *(G-494)*
Campbell Soup Company A 856 342-4800
Camden *(G-1047)*
Campbell Soup Company G 856 342-4759
Camden *(G-1048)*
Carnegie Deli Products Inc D 201 507-5557
Carlstadt *(G-1136)*
Catering By Maddalenas Inc G 609 466-7510
Ringoes *(G-9335)*
Celtic Passions LLC F 973 865-7046
Nutley *(G-7582)*
Cheesecake Factory Inc G 973 921-0930
Short Hills *(G-9866)*
Chocolate Face Cupcake G 609 624-2253
Cape May Court House *(G-1109)*
Ciao Cupcake G 609 964-6167
Trenton *(G-10916)*
Cinderella Cheesecake Co Inc F 856 461-6302
Riverside *(G-9392)*
Conte Farms F 609 268-0513
Tabernacle *(G-10618)*
Cravings F 732 531-7122
Allenhurst *(G-21)*
Creative Desserts G 732 477-0808
Brick *(G-715)*
Crijuodama Baking Corp T G 732 451-1250
Lakewood *(G-5076)*
Crust and Crumb Bakery G 609 492-4966
Beach Haven *(G-255)*
Cupcake Celebrations G 973 885-0826
Columbus *(G-1799)*
Cupcake Kitschen G 862 221-8872
Mahwah *(G-5725)*
Damascus Bakery Inc E 718 855-1456
Newark *(G-7093)*
▼ **Damascus Bakery NJ LLC** D 718 855-1456
Newark *(G-7094)*
Danmark Enterprises Inc G 732 321-3366
South Plainfield *(G-10245)*
Del Bakers Inc E 856 461-0089
Riverside *(G-9393)*
Del Buono Bakery Inc E 856 546-9585
Haddon Heights *(G-4045)*
Delicious Bagels Inc G 732 892-9265
Point Pleasant Boro *(G-8843)*
Dell Aquila Baking Company G 201 886-0613
Englewood *(G-2896)*
Dina Hernandez G 973 772-8883
Lodi *(G-5558)*
Dr Schar Usa Inc E 856 803-5100
Swedesboro *(G-10582)*
Ecce Panis Inc G 877 706-0510
Carlstadt *(G-1155)*
Elis Hot Bagels Inc E 732 566-4523
Matawan *(G-5975)*
Erj Baking LLC G 201 906-1300
Ridgewood *(G-9324)*
Excellence In Baking Inc G 732 287-1313
Edison *(G-2508)*
Feed Your Soul Ltd Lblty Co G 201 204-0720
Kearny *(G-4855)*
Food Circus Super Markets Inc D 732 291-4079
Atlantic Highlands *(G-106)*
Fragales Bakery Inc F 973 546-0327
Garfield *(G-3744)*
Frell Corp F 201 825-2500
Ramsey *(G-9144)*
G N J Inc F 856 786-1127
Cinnaminson *(G-1458)*
Good To Go Inc E 856 429-2005
Voorhees *(G-11286)*
Herman Eickhoff C 609 871-1809
Willingboro *(G-11991)*
House of Cupcakes LLC G 908 413-3076
Somerset *(G-10001)*
▲ **International Delights LLC** C 973 928-5431
Clifton *(G-1642)*
J & J Snack Foods Corp C 856 933-3597
Bellmawr *(G-336)*
J & J Snack Foods Corp B 856 665-9533
Pennsauken *(G-8440)*
J & J Snack Foods Corp C 856 467-9552
Bridgeport *(G-740)*
J K P Donuts Inc G 856 234-9844
Mount Laurel *(G-6772)*
Jad Bagels LLC G 201 567-4500
Englewood *(G-2915)*
Jay Jariwala F 908 806-8266
Ringoes *(G-9338)*
John Anthony Bread Distributor G 973 523-9258
Paterson *(G-8225)*
Julia Clemente G 201 488-2161
South Hackensack *(G-10166)*
Just A Touch of Baking LLC G 732 679-5123
Old Bridge *(G-7717)*
◆ **Kashmir Crown Baking LLC** E 908 474-1470
Linden *(G-5369)*
Katis Kupcakes G 609 332-2172
Moorestown *(G-6532)*
KB Food Enterprises Inc F 973 278-2800
Paterson *(G-8227)*
Kohouts Bakery G 973 772-7270
Garfield *(G-3750)*
Lithuanian Bakery T J Inc F 908 354-0970
Elizabeth *(G-2754)*
Little Falls Shop Rite Super B 973 256-0909
Little Falls *(G-5460)*
Little Miss Cupcake LLC G 732 370-3083
Lakewood *(G-5125)*
Livingston Bagel Warren Inc E 973 994-1915
Livingston *(G-5520)*
▲ **Lo Presti & Sons LLC** E 973 523-9258
Paterson *(G-8245)*
Lodi Cml Cooperative LLC G 201 820-2380
Lodi *(G-5569)*
Luccas Bakery Inc E 609 561-5558
Hammonton *(G-4138)*
Luna Foods LLC E 973 482-1400
Newark *(G-7187)*
Mendels Muffins and Stuff Inc G 973 881-9900
Paterson *(G-8254)*
Mendles Just Bread Inc G 973 881-9900
Paterson *(G-8255)*
Mfb Soft Pretzels Inc G 609 953-6773
Medford *(G-6030)*
Millburn Bagel Inc E 973 258-1334
Millburn *(G-6205)*
Minardi Baking Co Inc E 973 742-1107
Denville *(G-2048)*
Mini Frost Foods Corporation E 973 427-4258
North Haledon *(G-7498)*
Mondelez Global LLC A 201 794-4000
Fair Lawn *(G-3111)*
Mrs Sullivans Inc E 908 246-8937
Martinsville *(G-5963)*
▲ **Nablus Pastry & Sweets** G 973 881-8003
Paterson *(G-8264)*
Nan Bread Distribution G 201 475-9311
Elmwood Park *(G-2844)*
◆ **Nexira Inc** F 908 704-7480
Somerville *(G-10122)*
Northeast Foods Inc D 732 549-2243
Edison *(G-2578)*
Nuchas Tsq LLC F 212 913-9682
North Bergen *(G-7426)*
O O M Inc G 973 328-9408
Rockaway *(G-9482)*
Omni Baking Company LLC B 856 205-1485
Vineland *(G-11247)*
Original Bagel & Bialy Co Inc E 973 227-5777
West Caldwell *(G-11669)*
Orthodox Baking Co Inc E 973 844-9393
Belleville *(G-305)*
Pao Ba Avo LLC G 908 962-9090
Elizabeth *(G-2767)*
▲ **Paramount Bakeries Inc** G 973 482-6638
Newark *(G-7222)*
Paramount Bakeries Inc G 973 482-6638
East Orange *(G-2257)*
Pechters Southern NJ LLC G 856 786-8000
Cinnaminson *(G-1479)*
Perk & Pantry G 856 451-4333
Bridgeton *(G-769)*
Portuguese Baking Company Inc G 973 466-0118
Newark *(G-7231)*
◆ **Prestige Bread Jersey Cy Inc** D 201 422-7900
North Bergen *(G-7430)*
Pretty Lil Cupcakes G 201 256-1205
Harrison *(G-4178)*
Provence LLC C 201 503-9717
Englewood *(G-2935)*
R P Baking LLC E 973 483-3374
Harrison *(G-4179)*
Ram Donuts Corp G 856 599-0015
Gibbstown *(G-3799)*

Rombiolo LLC ....G...... 973 680-0405
Bloomfield (G-517)

S M Z Enterprises Inc ....F...... 908 232-1921
Westfield (G-11803)

Scala Pastry ....G...... 732 398-9808
North Brunswick (G-7485)

Serranis Bakery ....F...... 973 678-1777
Orange (G-7761)

Shop Rite Supermarkets Inc ....C...... 732 442-1717
Perth Amboy (G-8533)

Shop Rite Supermarkets Inc ....C...... 732 775-4250
Neptune (G-6898)

Shop-Rite Supermarkets Inc ....C...... 609 646-2448
Absecon (G-4)

Sibi Distributors ....G...... 908 658-4448
Basking Ridge (G-197)

Spindlers Bake Shop ....G...... 201 288-1345
Hasbrouck Heights (G-4188)

Springdale Farm Market Inc ....E...... 856 424-8674
Cherry Hill (G-1416)

▲ Sukhadias Sweets & Snacks .....F...... 908 222-0069
South Plainfield (G-10328)

Sweet Potato Pie Inc ....E...... 973 279-3405
Paterson (G-8310)

Sweetly Spirited Cupcakes Ltd ....G...... 917 846-4238
Princeton Junction (G-9067)

▲ Symphony Inc ....F...... 856 727-9596
Moorestown (G-6571)

Tasty Baking Company ....G...... 609 641-8588
Egg Harbor Township (G-2698)

Tasty Cake South Jersey ....G...... 856 428-8414
Cherry Hill (G-1422)

▲ Tbb Inc ....G...... 973 589-8875
Newark (G-7294)

Terrignos Bakery ....E...... 856 451-6368
Bridgeton (G-774)

Thebgb Inc ....G...... 917 749-5309
Paterson (G-8314)

▲ Toufayan Bakery Inc ....C...... 201 941-2000
Ridgefield (G-9292)

Tri-State Buns LLC ....E...... 973 418-8323
Harrison (G-4180)

Uptown Bakeries ....C...... 856 467-9552
Logan Township (G-5589)

◆ Vieiras Bakery Inc ....D...... 973 589-7719
Newark (G-7312)

▲ Vitamia Pasta Boy Inc ....F...... 973 546-1140
Lodi (G-5582)

W A Cleary Corporation ....F...... 732 247-8000
Somerset (G-10096)

Wenner Bread Products Inc ....C...... 631 563-6262
New Brunswick (G-6980)

Y & J Bakers Inc ....E...... 732 363-3636
Lakewood (G-5184)

Zaiya Inc ....E...... 201 343-3988
Hackensack (G-3992)

Zenas Patisserie ....G...... 856 303-8700
Riverton (G-9405)

Zinicola Baking Co ....G...... 973 667-1306
Nutley (G-7598)

2052 Cookies & Crackers

A & A Soft Pretzel Company ....G...... 856 338-0208
Camden (G-1038)

Arysta LLC ....G...... 856 417-8100
Logan Township (G-5585)

Auntie Annes Soft Pretzels ....E...... 856 845-3667
Woodbury (G-12025)

Bakers Perfection Inc ....E...... 973 983-0700
Rockaway (G-9446)

◆ Birds Eye Foods Inc ....C...... 585 383-1850
Cherry Hill (G-1346)

Caliz - Malko LLC ....G...... 973 207-5200
Fairfield (G-3162)

Campbell Soup Company ....A...... 856 342-4800
Camden (G-1047)

Campbell Soup Company ....C...... 856 342-4759
Camden (G-1048)

Chips Ice Cream LLC ....G...... 732 840-6332
Howell (G-4533)

Continental Cookies Inc ....F...... 201 498-1966
Hackensack (G-3900)

◆ Deep Foods Inc ....C...... 908 810-7500
Union (G-11042)

Direct Sales and Services Inc ....E...... 973 340-4480
Garfield (G-3739)

European Pretzel One LLC ....E...... 201 867-6117
North Bergen (G-7404)

◆ Fairfield Gourmet Food Corp .....D...... 973 575-4365
Cedar Grove (G-1278)

Federal Pretzel Baking Co ....E...... 215 467-0505
Bridgeport (G-737)

Food & Beverage Inc ....D...... 201 288-8881
Teterboro (G-10674)

◆ Gerber Products Company ....C...... 973 593-7500
Florham Park (G-3508)

Interntnal Bscits Cnfctons Inc ....G...... 856 813-1008
Marlton (G-5934)

J & J Snack Foods Corp ....C...... 856 933-3597
Bellmawr (G-336)

J & J Snack Foods Corp ....B...... 856 665-9533
Pennsauken (G-8440)

J & J Snack Foods Corp ....C...... 856 467-9552
Bridgeport (G-740)

J & J Snack Foods Corp PA ....B...... 856 665-9533
Pennsauken (G-8441)

Jassmine Corp ....G...... 848 565-0515
Clifton (G-1646)

Jimmys Cookies LLC ....C...... 973 779-8500
Clifton (G-1647)

▲ John Wm Macy Cheesesticks Inc ..D...... 201 791-8036
Elmwood Park (G-2833)

▲ Joyce Food LLC ....C...... 973 491-9696
Newark (G-7171)

Kitchen Table Bakers Inc ....E...... 516 931-5113
Fairfield (G-3252)

Little Falls Shop Rite Super ....B...... 973 256-0909
Little Falls (G-5460)

▲ Lo Presti & Sons LLC ....E...... 973 523-9258
Paterson (G-8245)

Luna Foods LLC ....E...... 973 482-1400
Newark (G-7187)

Meltdown ....G...... 609 207-0527
Long Beach Township (G-5591)

Millstone Dq Inc ....G...... 609 259-6733
Clarksburg (G-1522)

Mini Frost Foods Corporation ....E...... 973 427-4258
North Haledon (G-7498)

Mondelez Global LLC ....A...... 201 794-4000
Fair Lawn (G-3111)

Mondelez Global LLC ....A...... 201 794-4080
Fair Lawn (G-3112)

Nabisco Royal Argentina Inc ....G...... 973 503-2000
East Hanover (G-2224)

▲ Novelty Cone Co Inc ....E...... 856 665-9525
Pennsauken (G-8462)

Oven Art LLC ....E...... 973 910-2266
Hackensack (G-3959)

Pace Target Brokerage Inc ....E...... 856 629-2551
Williamstown (G-11967)

◆ RAB Food Group LLC ....D...... 201 553-1100
Newark (G-7244)

▲ Royal Baking Co Inc ....E...... 201 296-0888
Moonachie (G-6487)

▲ Silk City Snacks LLC ....E...... 973 928-3161
Clifton (G-1720)

South Jersey Pretzel Inc ....F...... 856 435-5055
Stratford (G-10507)

Vivis Life LLC ....G...... 201 798-1938
Jersey City (G-4827)

2053 Frozen Bakery Prdts

A & S Frozen Inc ....E...... 201 672-0510
East Rutherford (G-2268)

Cinderella Cheesecake Co Inc ....F...... 856 461-6302
Riverside (G-9392)

Country Oven ....G...... 732 494-4838
Iselin (G-4606)

I-Yell-O Foods Inc ....G...... 732 525-2201
South Amboy (G-10134)

J & J Snack Foods Corp ....C...... 856 467-9552
Bridgeport (G-740)

J & J Snack Foods Corp ....C...... 856 933-3597
Bellmawr (G-336)

J & J Snack Foods Corp ....B...... 856 665-9533
Pennsauken (G-8440)

Mardon Associates Inc ....F...... 973 977-2251
Paterson (G-8251)

Mnw LLC ....E...... 908 591-7277
Linden (G-5388)

▲ Nema Food Distribution Inc ....G...... 973 256-4415
Fairfield (G-3276)

Rich Products Corporation ....A...... 800 356-7094
Riverside (G-9402)

▲ Royal Baking Co Inc ....E...... 201 296-0888
Moonachie (G-6487)

Sugar and Plumm LLC ....G...... 201 334-1600
Moonachie (G-6490)

Wenner Bread Products Inc ....C...... 631 563-6262
New Brunswick (G-6980)

2061 Sugar, Cane

Global Commodities Exportacao ....G...... 201 613-1532
Newark (G-7133)

International Molasses Corp ....E...... 201 368-8036
Saddle Brook (G-9657)

2062 Sugar, Cane Refining

▼ Domino Foods Inc ....C...... 732 590-1173
Iselin (G-4607)

International Molasses Corp ....E...... 201 368-8036
Maywood (G-6006)

2064 Candy & Confectionery Prdts

Al Richrds Homemade Chocolates ...F...... 201 436-0915
Bayonne (G-201)

Amys Omelette Hse Burlington ......F...... 609 386-4800
Burlington (G-949)

▲ Ausome LLC ....G...... 732 951-8818
Paramus (G-7789)

▲ Bergen Marzipan & Chocolate .....G...... 201 385-8343
Bergenfield (G-373)

Bromilows Candy Co ....G...... 973 684-1496
Woodland Park (G-12072)

▲ Cadbury Adams USA LLC ....E...... 973 503-2000
East Hanover (G-2197)

▲ Candy Treasure LLC ....G...... 201 830-3600
Lebanon (G-5254)

▲ Ce De Candy Inc ....C...... 908 964-0660
Union (G-11035)

▲ Cns Confectionery Products LLC ...F...... 201 823-1400
Bayonne (G-211)

Dairy Maid Confectionery Co ....G...... 609 399-0100
Ocean City (G-7690)

Damask Kandies ....G...... 856 467-1661
Swedesboro (G-10578)

David Bradley Chocolatier Inc ....F...... 609 443-4747
Windsor (G-11995)

David Bradley Chocolatier Inc ....E...... 732 536-7719
Englishtown (G-3001)

Enjou Chocolat Morristown Inc ......G...... 973 993-9090
Morristown (G-6662)

◆ Ferrero U S A Inc ....C...... 732 764-9300
Parsippany (G-7943)

Fralingers Inc ....G...... 609 345-2177
Atlantic City (G-91)

Fralingers Inc ....E...... 609 345-2177
Atlantic City (G-90)

Genevieves Inc ....F...... 973 772-8816
Garfield (G-3746)

Giambris Quality Sweets Inc ....G...... 856 783-1099
Clementon (G-1533)

Growtech LLC ....D...... 732 993-8683
Cranbury (G-1837)

▼ Hillside Candy LLC ....F...... 973 926-2300
Hillside (G-4398)

Hillside Candy LLC ....E...... 908 241-4747
Roselle (G-9560)

▲ James Candy Company ....E...... 609 344-1519
Atlantic City (G-95)

Joy Snacks LLC ....F...... 732 272-0707
Avenel (G-132)

▲ Koppers Chocolate LLC ....D...... 212 243-0220
Jersey City (G-4756)

Krauses Homemade Candy Inc ......F...... 201 943-4790
Fairview (G-3362)

▲ Life of Party LLC ....E...... 732 828-0886
North Brunswick (G-7475)

Lucas World Inc ....G...... 832 293-3770
Budd Lake (G-926)

◆ Mafco Worldwide Corporation .....C...... 856 964-8840
Camden (G-1075)

Marlow Candy & Nut Co Inc ....E...... 201 569-7606
Englewood (G-2922)

Mars Incorporated ....A...... 908 852-1000
Hackettstown (G-4021)

Mars Incorporated ....D...... 908 850-2420
Hackettstown (G-4022)

◆ Mars Chocolate North Amer LLC ...A...... 908 852-1000
Hackettstown (G-4023)

Mars Chocolate North Amer LLC ....A...... 908 979-5070
Hackettstown (G-4024)

Mars Wrigley Conf US LLC ....C...... 908 852-1000
Hackettstown (G-4026)

Minhura Inc ....G...... 862 763-4078
North Arlington (G-7375)

Naturee Nuts Inc ....F...... 732 786-4663
Kenilworth (G-4962)

▲ Nova Distributors LLC ....F...... 908 222-1010
Edison (G-2580)

SIC

Nutra Nuts Inc ....G...... 323 260-7457
Ridgewood (G-9325)
Nutscom Inc ....G...... 800 558-6887
Jersey City (G-4776)
Old Monmouth Peanut Brittle Co ....G...... 732 462-1311
Freehold (G-3684)
▲ Oral Fixation LLC ....G...... 609 937-9972
Hopewell (G-4528)
Ozone Confectioners Bakers Sup ....F...... 201 791-4444
Verona (G-11171)
Packom LLC ....E...... 201 378-8382
Little Falls (G-5463)
▲ Pim Brands LLC ....D...... 732 560-8300
Somerset (G-10053)
PR Products Distributors Inc ....G...... 973 928-1120
Wayne (G-11544)
◆ Promotion In Motion Inc ....D...... 201 962-8530
Allendale (G-14)
Promotion In Motion Inc ....E...... 732 560-8300
Somerset (G-10058)
Rauhausers Inc ....F...... 609 399-1465
Ocean City (G-7693)
Reilys Candy Inc ....F...... 609 953-0040
Medford (G-6032)
Sherwood Brands Corporation ....F...... 973 249-8200
New Brunswick (G-6970)
Shrivers Salt Wtr Taffy Fudge ....E...... 609 399-0100
Ocean City (G-7696)
Sims Lee Inc ....F...... 201 433-1308
Jersey City (G-4810)
▲ U I S Industries Inc ....A...... 201 946-2600
Jersey City (G-4823)
Webers Candy Store ....G...... 856 455-8277
Bridgeton (G-778)
William R Tatz Industries ....G...... 973 751-0720
Belleville (G-325)
▲ World Confections Inc ....D...... 718 768-8100
South Orange (G-10203)
▲ Yolo Candy LLC ....G...... 201 252-8765
Mahwah (G-5787)

2066 Chocolate & Cocoa Prdts

Barry Callebaut USA LLC ....E...... 856 663-2260
Pennsauken (G-8393)
Barry Callebaut USA LLC ....D...... 856 663-2260
Pennsauken (G-8394)
▲ Bergen Marzipan & Chocolate ....G...... 201 385-8343
Bergenfield (G-373)
Birnn Chocolates Inc ....G...... 732 214-8680
Highland Park (G-4287)
▼ Bosco Products Inc ....G...... 973 334-7534
Towaco (G-10866)
Bromilows Candy Co ....G...... 973 684-1496
Woodland Park (G-12072)
▲ Candy Treasure LLC ....G...... 201 830-3600
Lebanon (G-5254)
▲ Chocmod USA Inc ....E...... 201 585-8730
Fort Lee (G-3552)
Cocoa Services Inc ....F...... 856 234-1700
Moorestown (G-6514)
David Bradley Chocolatier Inc ....F...... 609 443-4747
Windsor (G-11995)
David Bradley Chocolatier Inc ....E...... 732 536-7719
Englishtown (G-3001)
Dove Chocolate Discoveries LLC........E...... 866 922-3683
Mount Arlington (G-6711)
Forget ME Not Chocolates By NA ....G...... 856 753-8916
Atco (G-86)
Fralingers Inc ....E...... 609 345-2177
Atlantic City (G-90)
Genevieves Inc ....F...... 973 772-8816
Garfield (G-3746)
George Brummer ....G...... 908 232-1904
Westfield (G-11798)
K K S Criterion Chocolates ....E...... 732 542-7847
Eatontown (G-2406)
▲ Koppers Chocolate LLC ....D...... 212 243-0220
Jersey City (G-4756)
Mack Trading LLC ....G...... 973 794-4904
Hewitt (G-4276)
Mars Incorporated ....D...... 908 850-2420
Hackettstown (G-4022)
Mars Incorporated ....A...... 908 852-1000
Hackettstown (G-4021)
Mars Incorporated ....F...... 973 691-3500
Budd Lake (G-929)
◆ Mars Chocolate North Amer LLC .....A...... 908 852-1000
Hackettstown (G-4023)
Mars Retail Group Inc ....E...... 973 398-2078
Mount Arlington (G-6715)

Matisse Chocolatier Inc ....G...... 201 568-2288
Englewood (G-2923)
Nouveautes Inc ....F...... 973 882-8850
Fairfield (G-3283)
◆ Promotion In Motion Inc ....D...... 201 962-8530
Allendale (G-14)
Savita Naturals Ltd ....E...... 856 467-4949
Swedesboro (G-10608)
Third Ave Chocolate Shoppe ....G...... 732 449-7535
Spring Lake (G-10424)
Undercover Chocolate Co LLC ....G...... 973 668-5000
East Hanover (G-2244)

2067 Chewing Gum

▲ Gum Runners LLC ....F...... 201 333-0756
Jersey City (G-4745)
▲ L A Dreyfus Co ....C...... 732 549-1600
Edison (G-2548)

2068 Salted & Roasted Nuts & Seeds

◆ Cibo Vita Inc ....B...... 862 238-8020
Totowa (G-10823)
▲ Cns Confectionery Products LLC .....F...... 201 823-1400
Bayonne (G-211)
▲ Naturee Nuts Inc ....F...... 732 786-4663
Kenilworth (G-4962)
▲ Nutsco Inc ....F...... 856 966-6400
Camden (G-1081)
◆ Star Snacks Co LLC ....B...... 201 200-9820
Jersey City (G-4814)

2075 Soybean Oil Mills

◆ Fornazor International Inc ....E...... 201 664-4000
Hillsdale (G-4366)

2076 Vegetable Oil Mills

Romulus Emprises Inc ....G...... 609 683-4549
Hightstown (G-4298)
Textron Inc ....E...... 201 945-1500
Edgewater (G-2441)
W A Cleary Products Inc ....G...... 732 246-2829
Somerset (G-10097)

2077 Animal, Marine Fats & Oils

Bringhurst Bros Inc ....E...... 856 767-0110
Berlin (G-418)
Darling Ingredients Inc ....C...... 973 465-1900
Newark (G-7095)
Daybrook Holdings Inc ....B...... 973 538-6766
Morristown (G-6659)
Epicore Networks USA Inc ....E...... 609 267-9118
Mount Holly (G-6727)

2079 Shortening, Oils & Margarine

◆ Aak USA Inc ....D...... 973 344-1300
Edison (G-2444)
▲ Aarhuskarlshamn USA Inc ....D...... 973 344-1300
Newark (G-7032)
Bimbo Bakeries USA Inc ....C...... 973 256-8200
Totowa (G-10820)
◆ Cosmopolitan Food Group Inc ....G...... 908 998-1818
Hoboken (G-4449)
Edesia Oil LLC ....F...... 732 851-7979
Manalapan (G-5806)
▲ European Amrcn Foods Group Inc ...E...... 201 436-6106
Bayonne (G-215)
European Amrcn Foods Group Inc ......B...... 201 583-1101
Secaucus (G-9764)
▲ Finex Trade ....G...... 609 921-2747
Princeton (G-8949)
▲ Hojiblanca USA Inc ....G...... 201 384-3007
Dumont (G-2113)
◆ Oasis Trading Co Inc ....C...... 908 964-0477
Hillside (G-4419)
▲ Olivos USA Inc ....G...... 201 893-0142
Fort Lee (G-3580)
Procter & Gamble Mfg Co ....D...... 732 602-4500
Avenel (G-143)
▲ Raos Specialty Foods Inc ....F...... 212 269-0151
Montclair (G-6387)
Technical Oil Products Co Inc ....G...... 973 940-8920
Newton (G-7362)
Upfield US Inc ....B...... 201 894-2540
Hackensack (G-3989)
Western Pacific Foods Inc ....F...... 908 838-0186
Kearny (G-4905)

2082 Malt Beverages

▲ Advanced Brewing Sys LLC ....G...... 973 633-1777
Prospect Park (G-9072)
Anheuser-Busch LLC ....C...... 973 645-7700
Jersey City (G-4693)
Brewers Apprentice The Inc ....G...... 732 863-9411
Freehold (G-3654)
Brix City Brewing ....G...... 201 440-0865
Little Ferry (G-5475)
Bucks County Brewing Co Inc ....G...... 609 929-0148
Lambertville (G-5188)
Cape May Brewing Ltd Lblty Co ....F...... 609 849-9933
Cape May (G-1092)
Cape May Brewing Ltd Lblty Co ....G...... 609 849-9933
Cape May (G-1093)
▲ Carton Brewing Company LLC ....G...... 732 654-2337
Atlantic Highlands (G-105)
Core 3 Brewery Ltd Lblty Co ....G...... 856 562-0386
Franklinville (G-3636)
Dark City Brewery LLC ....G...... 917 273-4995
Asbury Park (G-74)
East Coast Brewing Co LLC ....G...... 732 202-7782
Point Pleasant Beach (G-8823)
Fizzics Group LLC ....G...... 917 545-4533
Wall Township (G-11341)
Geislers Liquor Store ....F...... 856 845-0482
Thorofare (G-10699)
▲ Group Martin LLC Jj ....F...... 862 240-1813
Newark (G-7141)
Headquarters Pub LLC ....E...... 609 347-2579
Atlantic City (G-94)
▲ High Point Brewing Co Inc ....G...... 973 838-7400
Butler (G-1003)
▲ Hunterdon Brewing Company LLC ..D...... 908 454-7445
Whitehouse Station (G-11920)
ICEE Company ....G...... 856 939-1540
Runnemede (G-9606)
Pinelands Brewing Ltd Lblty Co ....F...... 609 296-6169
Ltl Egg Hbr (G-5618)
Proximo Distillers LLC ....D...... 201 204-1718
Jersey City (G-4791)
River Horse Brewery Co Inc ....F...... 609 883-0890
Ewing (G-3063)
▲ Shore Point Distrg Co Inc ....C...... 732 308-3334
Freehold (G-3700)
Summerlands Inc ....E...... 973 729-8428
Sparta (G-10408)
▲ Sunco & Frenchie Ltd Lblty Co ......G...... 973 478-1011
Clifton (G-1726)
Triumph Brewing of Princeton ....G...... 609 773-0111
Lambertville (G-5198)
Tuckahoe Brewing Company LLC ....F...... 609 645-2739
Egg Harbor Twp (G-2703)

2083 Malt

International Molasses Corp ....E...... 201 368-8036
Saddle Brook (G-9657)
▼ Malt Products Corporation ....E...... 201 845-4420
Saddle Brook (G-9659)
Malt Products Corporation ....E...... 201 845-9106
Saddle Brook (G-9660)

2084 Wine & Brandy

▲ American Estates Wines Inc ....G...... 908 273-5060
Summit (G-10524)
Aslegacy Spirits LLC ....G...... 609 784-8383
Eastampton (G-2371)
Bellview Farms Inc ....G...... 856 697-7172
Landisville (G-5205)
Beneduce Vineyard ....G...... 908 996-3823
Pittstown (G-8752)
Brook Hollow Winery LLC ....G...... 908 496-8200
Columbia (G-1792)
Cream Ridge Winery ....G...... 609 259-9797
Cream Ridge (G-1933)
Dijon Enterprises LLC ....G...... 201 876-9463
Wallington (G-11384)
GP Wine Works LLC ....G...... 201 997-6055
Bayonne (G-221)
Grape Bginnings Handson Winery ......G...... 732 380-7356
Eatontown (G-2394)
▲ Hojiblanca USA Inc ....G...... 201 384-3007
Dumont (G-2113)
▲ Hopewell Valley Vineyards LLC ......E...... 609 737-4465
Pennington (G-8367)
▲ Hunterdon Brewing Company LLC ..D...... 908 454-7445
Whitehouse Station (G-11920)
Jersey Cider Works LLC ....G...... 917 604-0067
Montclair (G-6373)

Jersey Cider Works LLC ....G...... 908 940-4115
Asbury *(G-65)*

◆ Laird & Company ....E...... 732 542-0312
Eatontown *(G-2408)*

Melovino Meadery ....G...... 855 635-6846
Vauxhall *(G-11151)*

Michelle Ste Wine Estates Ltd ....G...... 973 770-8100
Mount Arlington *(G-6716)*

Monroeville Vineyard & Winery ....F...... 856 521-0523
Monroeville *(G-6353)*

Natali Vineyards LLC ....G...... 609 465-0075
Cape May Court House *(G-1113)*

◆ Oasis Trading Co Inc ....G...... 908 964-0477
Hillside *(G-4419)*

Old York Cellars ....G...... 908 284-9463
Ringoes *(G-9340)*

▲ Opici Import Co Inc ....E...... 201 689-3256
Glen Rock *(G-3833)*

▲ Petit Pois Corp ....G...... 856 608-9644
Moorestown *(G-6556)*

Plagidos Winery LLC ....G...... 609 567-4633
Hammonton *(G-4141)*

Redpuro LLC ....G...... 908 370-4460
Warren *(G-11428)*

▲ Renault Winery Inc ....E...... 609 965-2111
Egg Harbor City *(G-2666)*

Ripe Life Wines LLC ....G...... 201 560-3233
Franklin Lakes *(G-3630)*

◆ Royal Wine Corporation ....C...... 718 384-2400
Bayonne *(G-233)*

Royal Wine Corporation ....G...... 201 535-9006
Bayonne *(G-234)*

Salem Oak Vineyards Ltd Lblty ....G...... 856 889-2121
Pedricktown *(G-8355)*

Sharrott Wine ....G...... 609 567-9463
Hammonton *(G-4144)*

Southwind Equestrian ....G...... 856 364-9690
Millville *(G-6271)*

▲ Tomasello Winery Inc ....F...... 609 561-0567
Hammonton *(G-4145)*

Unionville Vineyards LLC ....G...... 908 788-0400
Ringoes *(G-9342)*

Valenzano Winery ....G...... 856 701-7871
Shamong *(G-9860)*

Valenzano Winery LLC ....F...... 609 268-6731
Shamong *(G-9861)*

Villa Milagro Vineyards LLC ....G...... 908 995-2072
Phillipsburg *(G-8579)*

W J R B Inc ....G...... 609 884-1169
Cape May *(G-1104)*

Wagonhouse Winery LLC ....G...... 609 780-8019
Swedesboro *(G-10617)*

Willow Creek Winery Inc ....G...... 609 770-8782
Cape May *(G-1105)*

Winery Pak LLC ....G...... 800 434-4599
Cedar Knolls *(G-1316)*

2085 Liquors, Distilled, Rectified & Blended

Aslegacy Spirits LLC ....G...... 609 784-8383
Eastampton *(G-2371)*

Claremont Distilled Spirits ....F...... 973 227-7027
Fairfield *(G-3169)*

Corgi Spirits LLC ....G...... 862 219-3114
Jersey City *(G-4718)*

Creamy Creation LLC ....G...... 585 344-3300
Paramus *(G-7796)*

Custom Blends Inc ....G...... 215 934-7080
Ewing *(G-3025)*

Ganter Distillers Liabilit ....G...... 609 344-7867
Atlantic City *(G-92)*

Hoboken Mary Ltd Liability Co ....G...... 201 234-9910
Hoboken *(G-4455)*

Island Beach Distillery ....G...... 609 242-5054
Forked River *(G-3541)*

▲ Prince Black Distillery Inc ....E...... 212 695-6187
Clifton *(G-1699)*

Shrem Consulting Ltd Lblty Co ....G...... 917 371-0581
West Long Branch *(G-11721)*

Skunktown Distillery LLC ....G...... 908 824-7754
Flemington *(G-3468)*

White Castle ....E...... 732 721-3565
South Amboy *(G-10142)*

2086 Soft Drinks

Alkazone Global Inc ....G...... 201 880-7966
Hackensack *(G-3875)*

B-Tea Beverage LLC ....E...... 201 512-8400
Fair Lawn *(G-3089)*

Bai Brands LLC ....G...... 609 586-0500
Bordentown *(G-577)*

▲ Better Healthlab Inc ....F...... 201 880-7966
Hackensack *(G-3884)*

Beverage Works Nj Inc ....F...... 973 439-5700
Fairfield *(G-3157)*

Beverage Works Ny Inc ....F...... 732 938-7600
Wall Township *(G-11321)*

Bot LLC ....G...... 609 439-1537
Lawrenceville *(G-5224)*

Briars Usa ....G...... 732 821-7600
Monmouth Junction *(G-6279)*

Canada Dry Bottling Co NY LP ....D...... 732 572-1660
South Plainfield *(G-10233)*

▼ Canada Dry Del Vly Btlg Co ....C...... 856 662-6767
Pennsauken *(G-8400)*

Canada Dry Dstrg Wilmington De ....E...... 609 645-7070
Egg Harbor Township *(G-2681)*

Canada Dry Potomac Corporation ....G...... 856 665-6200
Pennsauken *(G-8401)*

Ccbcc Operations LLC ....D...... 609 324-7424
Bordentown *(G-579)*

Coca Cola Bottling Co Mid Amer ....F...... 732 398-4800
Monmouth Junction *(G-6282)*

Coca-Cola Refreshments USA Inc ....F...... 732 398-4800
Monmouth Junction *(G-6283)*

Coca-Cola Refreshments USA Inc ....B...... 201 635-6300
Monmouth Junction *(G-6284)*

◆ Continental Food & Bev Inc ....F...... 973 815-1600
Clifton *(G-1588)*

Continntal Concession Sups Inc ....E...... 516 629-4906
Union *(G-11037)*

Crescent Bottling Co Inc ....G...... 856 964-2268
Camden *(G-1055)*

▲ Crystal Beverage Corporation ....G...... 201 991-2342
Kearny *(G-4852)*

◆ Evereast Trading Inc ....G...... 201 944-6484
Fort Lee *(G-3557)*

First Juice Inc ....G...... 973 895-3085
Randolph *(G-9178)*

Fizzy Lizzy LLC ....G...... 212 966-3232
Jersey City *(G-4734)*

Foulkrod Associates ....A...... 856 662-6767
Pennsauken *(G-8421)*

Garden State Btlg Ltd Lblty Co ....F...... 201 991-2342
Kearny *(G-4859)*

◆ Gerber Products Company ....C...... 973 593-7500
Florham Park *(G-3508)*

Ginseng Up Corporation ....F...... 800 446-7364
Rockleigh *(G-9517)*

Hillside Beverage Packing LLC ....G...... 908 353-6773
Hillside *(G-4397)*

Iceberg Coffee LLC ....G...... 908 675-6972
Freehold *(G-3669)*

◆ Increase Beverage Intl Inc ....F...... 609 303-3117
Pennsauken *(G-8435)*

J & J Snack Foods Corp ....B...... 856 665-9533
Pennsauken *(G-8440)*

J & J Snack Foods Corp ....C...... 856 467-9552
Bridgeport *(G-740)*

▲ Jolt Company Inc ....E...... 201 288-0535
Teterboro *(G-10684)*

Keurig Dr Pepper Inc ....D...... 908 684-4400
Andover *(G-48)*

Keurig Dr Pepper Inc ....F...... 732 969-1600
Carteret *(G-1258)*

Keurig Dr Pepper Inc ....D...... 201 933-0070
Carlstadt *(G-1174)*

Keurig Dr Pepper Inc ....D...... 201 832-0695
Secaucus *(G-9786)*

Keurig Dr Pepper Inc ....D...... 732 388-5545
Avenel *(G-134)*

Liberty Coca-Cola Bevs LLC ....D...... 215 427-4500
Moorestown *(G-6537)*

Liberty Coca-Cola Bevs LLC ....D...... 609 390-5002
Marmora *(G-5958)*

Liberty Coca-Cola Bevs LLC ....E...... 856 988-3844
Marlton *(G-5937)*

▼ Maplewood Beverage Packers LLC ....C...... 973 416-4582
Maplewood *(G-5880)*

Mococo Partners Corp ....G...... 347 768-3344
Paterson *(G-8261)*

Mosse Beverage Industries LLC ....G...... 732 977-5558
Bayville *(G-248)*

Nestle Waters North Amer Inc ....D...... 201 451-4000
Jersey City *(G-4769)*

▲ Nirwana Foods LLC ....F...... 201 659-2200
Jersey City *(G-4772)*

P-Americas LLC ....G...... 973 739-4900
Whippany *(G-11900)*

Pepsi ....G...... 732 238-1598
East Brunswick *(G-2163)*

Pepsi Cola Btlg Co Pennsauken ....G...... 856 665-6616
Pennsauken *(G-8465)*

Pepsi Cola Co ....F...... 609 476-5001
Mays Landing *(G-5997)*

Pepsi-Cola Metro Btlg Co Inc ....F...... 201 955-2691
Kearny *(G-4889)*

Pepsi-Cola Metro Btlg Co Inc ....C...... 732 922-9000
Ocean *(G-7672)*

Pepsi-Cola Metro Btlg Co Inc ....B...... 732 424-3000
Piscataway *(G-8698)*

Pepsi-Cola Nat Brnd Bevs Ltd ....B...... 856 665-6200
Pennsauken *(G-8466)*

Pepsico Inc ....E...... 856 661-4604
Pennsauken *(G-8467)*

Push Beverages LLC ....G...... 973 766-2663
Succasunna *(G-10516)*

▼ Relaxzen Inc ....F...... 732 936-1500
Shrewsbury *(G-9901)*

Sensbl Inc ....F...... 862 225-3803
Ridgewood *(G-9329)*

Shabazz Fruit Cola Company LLC ....G...... 973 230-4641
Newark *(G-7267)*

Shrem Consulting Ltd Lblty Co ....G...... 917 371-0581
West Long Branch *(G-11721)*

Snapple Beverage Corp ....D...... 201 933-0070
Carlstadt *(G-1218)*

▲ Snapple Distributors Inc ....E...... 732 815-2800
Avenel *(G-146)*

◆ Supreme Manufacturing Co Inc ....E...... 732 254-0087
East Brunswick *(G-2183)*

Tuscan/Lehigh Dairies Inc ....D...... 570 385-1884
Burlington *(G-989)*

Two Little Guys Co ....G...... 973 744-7502
Elizabeth *(G-2783)*

◆ Unilever United States Inc ....A...... 201 735-9661
Englewood Cliffs *(G-2995)*

◆ Union Beverage Packers LLC ....C...... 908 206-9111
Hillside *(G-4432)*

▲ V E N Inc ....C...... 973 786-7862
Andover *(G-52)*

Water On Time Bottled ....G...... 862 252-9798
East Orange *(G-2267)*

2087 Flavoring Extracts & Syrups

▼ 201 Food Packing Inc ....F...... 973 463-0777
East Hanover *(G-2192)*

◆ A A Sayia & Company Inc ....G...... 201 659-1179
Hoboken *(G-4442)*

Adron Inc ....E...... 973 334-1600
Boonton *(G-536)*

Advanced Food Systems Inc ....E...... 732 873-6776
Somerset *(G-9942)*

▲ Akay USA LLC ....G...... 732 254-7177
Sayreville *(G-9700)*

▲ Allen Flavors Inc ....C...... 908 561-5995
South Plainfield *(G-10211)*

Allen Flavors Inc ....F...... 908 753-0544
South Plainfield *(G-10212)*

▲ Arnhem Inc ....G...... 908 709-4045
Westfield *(G-11794)*

Asbury Syrup Company Inc ....F...... 732 774-5746
Ocean *(G-7656)*

Bluewater Inc ....F...... 973 532-1225
Millington *(G-6207)*

▲ Brand Aromatics Intl Inc ....G...... 732 363-1204
Lakewood *(G-5065)*

Briars Usa ....G...... 732 821-7600
Monmouth Junction *(G-6279)*

Cargill Incorporated ....G...... 908 820-9800
Elizabeth *(G-2719)*

▲ Centrome Inc ....E...... 973 339-6242
Totowa *(G-10822)*

◆ Citroil Enterprises Inc ....F...... 201 933-8405
Carlstadt *(G-1140)*

◆ Citromax Flavors Inc ....G...... 201 933-8405
Carlstadt *(G-1141)*

Citromax Usa Inc ....E...... 201 933-8405
Carlstadt *(G-1142)*

▲ Del-Val Food Ingredients Inc ....F...... 856 778-6623
Mount Laurel *(G-6752)*

Drink A Toast Company Inc ....F...... 856 461-1000
Riverside *(G-9394)*

▲ Elan Inc ....D...... 973 344-8014
Newark *(G-7112)*

▲ Farbest-Tallman Foods Corp ....D...... 714 897-7199
Park Ridge *(G-7849)*

▲ Flavor & Fragrance Spc Inc ....D...... 201 828-9400
Mahwah *(G-5738)*

Flavor and Fd Ingredients Inc ....E...... 201 298-6964
Middlesex *(G-6116)*

▲ Flavor and Fd Ingredients Inc ....E 732 805-0335	Vineland Syrup Inc ....E 856 691-5772	▲ Massimo Zanetti Beverage USA ......E 201 440-1700
Somerset (G-9994)	Vineland (G-11277)	Moonachie (G-6478)

▲ Flavor and Fd Ingredients Inc ....E 732 805-0335
Somerset *(G-9994)*

Flavor Associates Inc ....F 973 238-9300
Hawthorne *(G-4221)*

Flavor Dynamics Inc ....E 888 271-8424
South Plainfield *(G-10260)*

Flavor Solutions Inc ....G 732 354-1931
Piscataway *(G-8665)*

Flavors of Origin Inc ....G 201 460-8306
Carlstadt *(G-1157)*

◆ Flavors of Origin Inc ....E 732 499-9700
Avenel *(G-127)*

Givaudan Flavors Corporation ....D 609 409-6200
Cranbury *(G-1836)*

Givaudan Flavors Corporation ....C 973 386-9800
East Hanover *(G-2212)*

Givaudan Fragrances Corp ....C 973 386-9800
East Hanover *(G-2213)*

Grow Company Inc ....E 201 941-8777
Ridgefield *(G-9264)*

Ifc Products Inc ....F 908 587-1221
Linden *(G-5356)*

▼ Ifc Solutions Inc ....E 908 862-8810
Linden *(G-5357)*

Innophos LLC ....G 973 808-5900
East Hanover *(G-2217)*

Interbahm International Inc ....E 732 499-9700
Avenel *(G-131)*

Interntnal Flvors Frgrnces Inc ....D 732 329-4600
Dayton *(G-1972)*

J & J Snack Foods Corp ....B 856 665-9533
Pennsauken *(G-8440)*

J & J Snack Foods Corp ....C 856 467-9552
Bridgeport *(G-740)*

▲ Jk Ingredients Inc ....D 973 340-8700
Paterson *(G-8224)*

Kerry Flavor Systems Us LLC ....C 513 771-4682
Clark *(G-1502)*

Kerry Inc ....D 908 237-1595
Flemington *(G-3453)*

Limpert Brothers Inc ....E 856 691-1353
Vineland *(G-11241)*

▼ Malt Products Corporation ....E 201 845-4420
Saddle Brook *(G-9659)*

Malt Products Corporation ....E 201 845-9106
Saddle Brook *(G-9660)*

◆ Mane USA Inc ....C 973 633-5533
Wayne *(G-11532)*

◆ Mastertaste Inc ....C 732 882-0202
Clark *(G-1508)*

Mastertaste Inc ....F 201 373-1111
Teterboro *(G-10686)*

◆ Medallion International Inc ....F 973 616-3401
Pompton Plains *(G-8867)*

Origin Almond Corporation ....G 609 576-5695
Laurel Springs *(G-5208)*

▲ Penta International Corp ....D 973 740-2300
Livingston *(G-5534)*

▲ Premier Specialties Inc ....F 732 469-6615
Middlesex *(G-6140)*

Prime Ingredients Inc ....G 201 791-6655
Saddle Brook *(G-9670)*

R C Fine Foods Inc ....D 908 359-5500
Hillsborough *(G-4349)*

▼ Reeves Enterprises Inc ....G 800 883-6752
New Providence *(G-7016)*

▲ Robertet Inc ....E 201 405-1000
Budd Lake *(G-932)*

Robertet Flavors Inc ....F 732 271-1804
Piscataway *(G-8706)*

Sapphire Flvors Fragrances LLC ....F 973 200-8849
Fairfield *(G-3307)*

Savorx Flavors LLC ....G 908 265-3033
Piscataway *(G-8708)*

Savoury Systems Intl LLC ....E 908 526-2524
Branchburg *(G-680)*

Sea Breeze Fruit Flavors Inc ....D 973 334-7777
Towaco *(G-10880)*

Sensient Technologies Corp ....E 908 757-4500
South Plainfield *(G-10327)*

▲ Sentrex Ingredients LLC ....G 908 862-4440
Linden *(G-5421)*

▲ Sodastream USA Inc ....D 856 755-3400
Mount Laurel *(G-6808)*

◆ Solvay USA Inc ....B 609 860-4000
Princeton *(G-9025)*

Solvay USA Inc ....C 732 297-0100
North Brunswick *(G-7486)*

Takasago Intl Corp USA ....E 201 727-4200
Teterboro *(G-10693)*

Vineland Syrup Inc ....E 856 691-5772
Vineland *(G-11277)*

Whittle & Mutch Inc ....F 856 235-1165
Mount Laurel *(G-6812)*

Wild Flavors Inc ....F 908 820-9800
Elizabeth *(G-2786)*

2091 Fish & Seafoods, Canned & Cured

◆ Gerber Products Company ....C 973 593-7500
Florham Park *(G-3508)*

Hillard Bloom Packing Co Inc ....G 856 785-0120
Port Norris *(G-8886)*

Ho-Ho-Kus Smked Delicacies LLC ....G 201 445-1677
Ho Ho Kus *(G-4440)*

▲ Lamonica Fine Foods LLC ....C 856 776-2126
Millville *(G-6258)*

Point Lobster Company Inc ....F 732 892-1718
Point Pleasant Beach *(G-8831)*

◆ RAB Food Group LLC ....D 201 553-1100
Newark *(G-7244)*

Sea Harvest Inc ....E 609 884-3000
Cape May *(G-1102)*

Sushi House Inc ....E 201 482-0609
Palisades Park *(G-7779)*

2092 Fish & Seafoods, Fresh & Frozen

Bay Treasure Seafood LLC ....F 732 240-3474
Toms River *(G-10750)*

Bivalve Packing Inc ....G 856 785-0270
Port Norris *(G-8885)*

Black Sea Fisheries ....G 973 553-1580
Fort Lee *(G-3551)*

Certified Clam Corp ....F 732 872-6650
Highlands *(G-4291)*

▲ CHR International Inc ....G 201 262-8186
Oradell *(G-7741)*

◆ Delight Foods USA LLC ....F 201 369-1199
Jersey City *(G-4722)*

▲ Golden Tropics Ltd ....E 973 484-0202
Newark *(G-7137)*

Hillard Bloom Packing Co Inc ....G 856 785-0120
Port Norris *(G-8886)*

J & R Foods Inc ....F 732 229-4020
Long Branch *(G-5600)*

▲ Lamonica Fine Foods LLC ....C 856 776-2126
Millville *(G-6258)*

▲ Lm Foods LLC ....D 732 855-9500
Carteret *(G-1259)*

New Jrsey Sfood Mktg Group LLC ....G 609 296-7026
Egg Harbor City *(G-2665)*

Peak Finance Holdings LLC ....G 856 969-7100
Cherry Hill *(G-1406)*

◆ Pinnacle Foods Finance LLC ....D 973 541-6620
Parsippany *(G-7991)*

◆ Pinnacle Foods Group LLC ....D 856 969-8238
Parsippany *(G-7992)*

◆ Ruggiero Sea Food Inc ....G 973 589-0524
Newark *(G-7254)*

Ruggiero Sea Food Inc ....G 973 589-0524
Newark *(G-7255)*

◆ Sunrise Food Trading Inc ....F 718 305-4388
Warren *(G-11432)*

Sushi House Inc ....E 201 482-0609
Palisades Park *(G-7779)*

2095 Coffee

26 Flavors LLC ....G 855 662-7299
Newark *(G-7027)*

◆ Adagio Teas Inc ....G 973 253-7400
Elmwood Park *(G-2807)*

Arias Mountain-Coffee LLC ....F 973 927-9595
Flanders *(G-3401)*

▼ Coffee Associates Inc ....E 201 945-1060
Edgewater *(G-2436)*

Coffee Company LLC ....G 609 399-5533
Ocean City *(G-7688)*

Coffee Company LLC ....G 609 398-2326
Ocean City *(G-7689)*

▲ Corim International Coffee Imp ....D 800 942-4201
Brick *(G-714)*

Counting Sheep Coffee Inc ....G 973 589-4104
Newark *(G-7089)*

Eight OClock Coffee Company ....D 201 571-9214
Montvale *(G-6410)*

▲ European Coffee Classics Inc ....E 856 428-7202
Cherry Hill *(G-1360)*

Greene Bros Spclty Cof Rasters ....F 908 979-0022
Hackettstown *(G-4009)*

Longview Coffee Co NJ Inc ....G 908 788-4186
Frenchtown *(G-3715)*

▲ Massimo Zanetti Beverage USA ......E 201 440-1700
Moonachie *(G-6478)*

Melitta Usa Inc ....E 856 428-7202
Cherry Hill *(G-1393)*

▲ Mire Enterprises LLC ....G 732 882-1010
Linden *(G-5386)*

Nestle Usa Inc ....C 732 462-1300
Freehold *(G-3682)*

Orens Daily Roast Inc ....F 201 432-2008
Jersey City *(G-4777)*

Pan American Coffee Company ....E 201 963-2329
Hoboken *(G-4472)*

Socafe LLC ....F 973 589-4104
Newark *(G-7278)*

Two Rivers Coffee LLC ....G 908 205-0018
South Plainfield *(G-10332)*

United Mijovi Amer Ltd Lblty ....F 732 718-1001
New Brunswick *(G-6975)*

▲ World of Coffee Inc ....G 908 647-1218
Stirling *(G-10499)*

2096 Potato Chips & Similar Prdts

Auntie Annes Soft Pretzels ....E 856 722-0433
Moorestown *(G-6506)*

◆ Birds Eye Foods Inc ....C 585 383-1850
Cherry Hill *(G-1346)*

Campbell Soup Company ....A 856 342-4800
Camden *(G-1047)*

Campbell Soup Company ....C 856 342-4759
Camden *(G-1048)*

Continntal Concession Sups Inc ....E 516 629-4906
Union *(G-11037)*

Dvash Foods USA Inc ....G 929 360-0758
Mahwah *(G-5732)*

▲ Golden Fluff Inc ....F 732 367-5448
Lakewood *(G-5105)*

Hain Celestial Group Inc ....E 201 935-4500
Moonachie *(G-6469)*

Herr Foods Incorporated ....E 732 356-1295
Somerset *(G-9999)*

Herr Foods Incorporated ....E 732 905-1600
Lakewood *(G-5109)*

Ktb Foods Inc ....G 973 240-0200
Fairfield *(G-3253)*

Mayab Happy Tacos Inc ....E 732 293-0400
Perth Amboy *(G-8526)*

Pirate Brands LLC ....F 973 401-6500
Parsippany *(G-7995)*

Planet Popcorn LLC ....G 732 294-8680
Freehold *(G-3687)*

Rajbhog Foods(nj) Inc ....C 551 222-4700
Jersey City *(G-4796)*

▲ Snack Innovations Inc ....E 718 509-9366
Piscataway *(G-8713)*

Thats How We Roll LLC ....G 973 240-0200
Montclair *(G-6392)*

Wise Foods Inc ....G 201 440-2876
Moonachie *(G-6497)*

Zestos Foods LLC ....G 888 407-5852
Teaneck *(G-10657)*

Ziggy Snack Foods LLC ....E 917 662-6038
Clifton *(G-1744)*

2097 Ice

Arctic Glacier USA Inc ....F 973 771-3391
Montclair *(G-6359)*

Artic Ice Manufacturing Co ....G 973 772-7000
Garfield *(G-3729)*

Cold Spring Ice Inc ....E 609 884-3405
Cape May *(G-1096)*

Sea Isle Ice Co Inc ....E 609 263-8748
Sea Isle City *(G-9749)*

United City Ice Cube Co Inc ....G 201 945-8387
Ridgefield *(G-9295)*

◆ United States Cold Storage Inc ....B 856 354-8181
Camden *(G-1089)*

2098 Macaroni, Spaghetti & Noodles

◆ A Zeregas Sons Inc ....C 201 797-1400
Fair Lawn *(G-3080)*

Casa Di Bertacchi Corporation ....C 856 696-5600
Vineland *(G-11197)*

Gardellas Rvioli ltln Deli LLC ....C 856 697-3509
Vineland *(G-11222)*

L E Rosellis Food Specialties ....F 609 654-4816
Medford *(G-6027)*

Noodle Fan ....G 732 446-2820
Monroe Township *(G-6337)*

Noodle Gogo ....G 908 222-8898
South Plainfield *(G-10307)*

Porfirio Foods Inc ....G 609 393-4116
Trenton (G-10976)

Raffettos Corp ....F 201 372-1222
Moonachie (G-6486)

Severino Pasta Mfg Co Inc ....E 856 854-3716
Collingswood (G-1771)

◆ Silver Palate Kitchens Inc ....E 201 568-0110
Cresskill (G-1944)

▲ Sun Noodle New Jersey LLC ......G 201 530-1100
Carlstadt (G-1224)

▲ Vitamia Pasta Boy Inc ....F 973 546-1140
Lodi (G-5582)

2099 Food Preparations, NEC

35 Food Corp ....G 732 442-1640
Woodbridge (G-12011)

▲ A Cheerful Giver Inc ....F 856 358-4438
Elmer (G-2792)

◆ ACC Foods Ltd Liability Co ....C 856 848-8877
West Deptford (G-11689)

Akila Holdings Inc ....G 609 454-5034
Princeton (G-8904)

Allied Food Products Inc ....E 908 357-2454
Linden (G-5321)

◆ Allied Old English Inc ....E 732 636-2060
Port Reading (G-8892)

▲ American Custom Drying Co ....E 609 387-3933
Burlington (G-948)

American Food & Bev Inds LLC .....D 347 241-9827
Orange (G-7750)

Applied Nutrition Corp ....E 973 734-0023
Cedar Knolls (G-1299)

▲ Arome America LLC ....G 908 806-7003
Neshanic Station (G-6904)

B&G Foods Inc ....B 973 401-6500
Parsippany (G-7889)

B&G Foods Inc ....C 973 401-6500
Parsippany (G-7890)

Barry Callebaut USA LLC ....E 856 663-2260
Pennsauken (G-8393)

Boiron America Inc ....G 862 229-6770
Newark (G-7069)

Boulevard Lunch Service Inc ....F 732 381-5772
Clark (G-1495)

Buona Vita Inc ....D 856 453-7972
Bridgeton (G-754)

▼ Bylada Foods LLC ....G 201 933-7474
Moonachie (G-6459)

Bylada Foods LLC ....F 201 933-7474
East Rutherford (G-2280)

Caravan Ingredients Inc ....E 201 672-0510
East Rutherford (G-2284)

CJ TMI Manufacturing Amer LLC ...C 609 669-0100
Robbinsville (G-9410)

▲ Colonna Brothers Inc ....D 800 626-8384
North Bergen (G-7397)

▲ Contes Pasta Company Inc ....E 856 697-3400
Vineland (G-11204)

◆ Cosmopolitan Food Group Inc .....G 908 998-1818
Hoboken (G-4449)

Croces Pasta Poducts ....G 856 795-6000
Cherry Hill (G-1354)

Daves Salad House Inc ....G 908 965-0773
Elizabeth (G-2725)

Deluxe Foods International ....G 862 257-1909
Paterson (G-8171)

Deluxe Gourmet Spc Ltd Lblty ....F 732 485-7519
Old Bridge (G-7714)

▲ Deosen Usa Inc ....G 908 382-6518
Piscataway (G-8653)

DJeet ....G 732 224-8887
Shrewsbury (G-9890)

DOrazio Foods Inc ....D 856 931-1900
Bellmawr (G-330)

Dulce A Dessert Bar LLC ....G 908 461-2418
Matawan (G-5973)

▲ Dyna-Sea Group Inc ....G 201 928-0133
Teaneck (G-10629)

◆ Eatem Corporation ....D 856 692-1663
Vineland (G-11216)

▲ Empire Specialty Foods Inc ....G 646 773-2630
East Brunswick (G-2143)

▲ Empirical Group LLC ....E 201 571-0300
Montvale (G-6411)

▲ European Amrcn Foods Group Inc ..E 201 436-6106
Bayonne (G-215)

European Amrcn Foods Group Inc ...B 201 583-1101
Secaucus (G-9764)

F&S Produce Company Inc ....C 856 453-0316
Rosenhayn (G-9595)

▲ F&S Produce Company Inc ....C 856 453-0316
Vineland (G-11218)

▲ Farbest-Tallman Foods Corp ....D 714 897-7199
Park Ridge (G-7849)

Fillo Factory Inc ....E 201 439-1036
Northvale (G-7525)

▲ Firma Foods USA Corporation .....G 201 794-1181
Englewood (G-2905)

Flavour Tee International LLC ....G 201 440-3281
Little Ferry (G-5486)

▲ Food Ingredient Solutions LLC .....G 201 440-4377
Teterboro (G-10675)

Foodtek Inc ....F 973 257-4000
Whippany (G-11891)

◆ Gel Spice Co Inc ....E 201 339-0700
Bayonne (G-218)

Gel Spice Co LLC ....C 201 339-0700
Bayonne (G-219)

▲ Global Ingredients Inc ....E 973 278-6677
Paterson (G-8200)

▲ Golden Tropics Ltd ....E 973 484-0202
Newark (G-7137)

▼ Goldstein & Burton Inc ....D 201 440-0065
Oakland (G-7630)

◆ Good Earth Teas Inc ....D 831 423-7913
Montvale (G-6412)

▲ Gourmet Kitchen LLC ....C 732 775-5222
Neptune (G-6882)

Green Labs LLC ....G 862 220-4845
Newark (G-7139)

Harris Freeman & Co Inc ....D 856 787-9026
Moorestown (G-6527)

▲ Hojiblanca USA Inc ....G 201 384-3007
Dumont (G-2113)

House Foods America Corp ....D 732 537-9500
Somerset (G-10000)

Iam International Inc ....G 908 713-9651
Lebanon (G-5263)

Ingredient House LLC ....G 609 285-5987
Skillman (G-9921)

International Chefs Inc ....F 917 645-2900
Saddle Brook (G-9656)

▲ International Coconut Corp ....F 908 289-1555
Elizabeth (G-2751)

Interntnal Ingrdent Sltons Inc ....E 856 778-6623
Mount Laurel (G-6769)

J & J Snack Foods Corp ....C 856 933-3597
Bellmawr (G-336)

▲ Jk Ingredients Inc ....D 973 340-8700
Paterson (G-8224)

▲ Joyce Food LLC ....C 973 491-9696
Newark (G-7171)

◆ Kalustyan Corporation ....D 908 688-6111
Union (G-11068)

Kerry Inc ....C 845 584-3081
Clark (G-1503)

L and Ds Sapore Ravioli Cheese .....F 732 563-9190
Middlesex (G-6126)

L E Rosellis Food Specialties ....F 609 654-4816
Medford (G-6027)

La Casa De Tortilla ....G 732 398-0660
Somerset (G-10012)

▲ La Pace Imports Inc ....F 973 895-5420
Morristown (G-6677)

Le Bon Magot Ltd Liability Co ....G 609 895-0211
Lawrenceville (G-5235)

▲ Leng-Dor USA Inc ....F 732 254-4300
Cranbury (G-1857)

Lidestri Foods Inc ....D 856 661-3218
Pennsauken (G-8451)

▲ Lioni Mozzarella & Spclty ....E 908 624-9450
Union (G-11071)

Longview Coffee Co NJ Inc ....E 908 788-4186
Frenchtown (G-3715)

Lorenzo Food Group Inc ....E 201 868-9088
Englewood (G-2920)

Lrk Inc ....F 609 924-6881
Princeton (G-8970)

Maverick Caterers LLC ....E 718 433-3776
Hackensack (G-3944)

MCI Service Parts ....G 732 967-9081
East Brunswick (G-2156)

▲ Mediterranean Chef Inc ....F 855 628-0903
Lincoln Park (G-5301)

◆ Megas Yeeros LLC ....E 212 777-6342
Lyndhurst (G-5663)

Melicks Town Farm Inc ....F 908 439-2318
Oldwick (G-7740)

▲ Melissa Spice Trading Corp ....F 862 262-7773
Glen Rock (G-3832)

▲ Metropolitan Foods Inc ....C 973 672-9400
Clifton (G-1668)

▲ Mincing Trading Corporation ....E 732 355-9944
Dayton (G-1980)

Missa Bay Citrus Company ....F 856 241-0900
Swedesboro (G-10596)

▲ Missa Bay LLC ....D 856 241-0900
Swedesboro (G-10597)

Muirhead Ringoes NJ Inc ....G 609 695-7803
Trenton (G-10959)

▲ Mushroom Wisdom Inc ....F 973 470-0010
East Rutherford (G-2305)

▲ National Lecithim Inc ....G 973 940-8920
Newton (G-7351)

Nestle Usa Inc ....C 732 462-1300
Freehold (G-3682)

◆ Nexira Inc ....F 908 704-7480
Somerville (G-10122)

▲ Omega Packaging Corp ....D 973 890-9505
Totowa (G-10840)

Organica Aromatics Corp ....G 609 443-3333
East Windsor (G-2357)

▲ Palsgaard Incorporated ....F 973 998-7951
Morris Plains (G-6622)

Panda Plates Inc ....E 917 848-8777
Englewood (G-2930)

Panos Holding Company ....G 201 843-8900
Rochelle Park (G-9428)

◆ Papa Johns New Jersey ....D 609 395-0045
Cranbury (G-1869)

Pastarama Distributors Inc ....G 609 847-0378
Sewell (G-9853)

▲ Paulaur Corporation ....D 609 395-8844
Cranbury (G-1870)

▲ PDM Packaging Inc ....F 201 864-1115
North Bergen (G-7428)

Peak Finance Holdings LLC ....E 856 969-7100
Cherry Hill (G-1406)

Pennant Ingredients Inc ....E 856 428-4300
Cherry Hill (G-1407)

▲ Pereg Gourmet Spices Ltd ....G 718 261-6767
Clifton (G-1689)

Perfecto Foods LLC ....G 201 889-5328
Kearny (G-4891)

Pharmachem Laboratories Inc ....E 973 256-1340
Totowa (G-10843)

Pharmachem Laboratories Inc ....E 201 343-3611
South Hackensack (G-10180)

◆ Pharmachem Laboratories LLC ....D 201 246-1000
Kearny (G-4892)

▲ Pinnacle Foods Finance LLC ....D 973 541-6620
Parsippany (G-7991)

◆ Pinnacle Foods Group LLC ....D 856 969-8238
Parsippany (G-7992)

▲ Poly-Gel LLC ....E 973 884-3300
Whippany (G-11904)

Prince Chikovani Inc ....G 347 622-2789
Bayonne (G-232)

Princeton Quadrangle Club ....G 609 258-0376
Princeton (G-9003)

Procter & Gamble Mfg Co ....D 732 602-4500
Avenel (G-143)

Puebla Foods Inc ....E 973 246-6311
Passaic (G-8097)

Puebla Foods Inc ....F 973 473-4494
Passaic (G-8098)

◆ Puratos Corporation ....C 856 428-4300
Pennsauken (G-8475)

Pyramid Food Services Corp ....F 973 900-6513
Newark (G-7241)

R C Fine Foods Inc ....D 908 359-5500
Hillsborough (G-4349)

▲ Raos Specialty Foods Inc ....F 212 269-0151
Montclair (G-6387)

Ready Pac Produce Inc ....D 609 499-1900
Florence (G-3477)

▲ Regina Wine Co ....G 973 589-6911
Newark (G-7249)

Rex Wine Vinegar Company ....G 973 589-6911
Newark (G-7250)

Royal Ingredients LLC ....G 856 241-2004
Swedesboro (G-10607)

Saker Shoprites Inc ....F 908 925-1550
Linden (G-5418)

Salad Chef Inc ....F 609 641-5455
Pleasantville (G-8817)

▲ Sebastian & King Ltd Lblty Co .....F 908 874-6953
Hillsborough (G-4354)

Sensient Technologies Corp ....E 908 757-4500
South Plainfield (G-10327)

Sheris Cookery Inc ....F 973 589-2060
Newark *(G-7270)*

◆ Silver Palate Kitchens Inc ....E 201 568-0110
Cresskill *(G-1944)*

Spice Chain Corporation ....D 800 584-0422
East Brunswick *(G-2178)*

Sultan Foods Inc ....F 908 874-6953
Hillsborough *(G-4358)*

Sun Basket Inc ....C 408 669-4418
Westampton *(G-11792)*

Sunrise Snacks Rockland Inc ......F 845 352-2676
Paterson *(G-8305)*

Surfside Foods LLC ....G 856 785-2115
Port Norris *(G-8889)*

▲ Suruchi Foods LLC ....G 201 432-2201
Jersey City *(G-4818)*

Tamaras European American Deli ....G 973 875-5461
Sussex *(G-10566)*

▲ Taste It Presents Inc ....D 908 241-9191
Kenilworth *(G-4981)*

Taste Italy Manufacturing LLC ....G 856 223-0707
Egg Harbor City *(G-2668)*

◆ Taylor Farms New Jersey Inc ....E 856 241-0097
Swedesboro *(G-10613)*

▲ Tetley USA Inc 800 728-0084
New Providence *(G-7022)*

Tin Man Snacks LLC ....E 732 329-9100
Dayton *(G-1992)*

▼ Tofutti Brands Inc ....G 908 272-2400
Cranford *(G-1928)*

▲ United Natural Trading Co ....D 732 650-9905
Edison *(G-2636)*

Venetian Corp ....F 973 546-2250
Garfield *(G-3776)*

Vine Hill Farm ....G 973 383-0100
Newton *(G-7364)*

▲ Vitamia Pasta Boy Inc ....F 973 546-1140
Lodi *(G-5582)*

Zinas Salads Inc ....E 973 428-0660
East Hanover *(G-2249)*

▲ Zxchem USA Inc ....G 732 529-6352
Piscataway *(G-8742)*

21 TOBACCO PRODUCTS

2111 Cigarettes

Altria Group Distribution Co ....C 804 274-2000
Parsippany *(G-7879)*

Philip Morris USA Inc ....F 908 781-6400
Bedminster *(G-276)*

Sensory Solutions LLC ....G 973 615-7600
Warren *(G-11429)*

Sherman Group Holdings ....G 201 735-9000
Fort Lee *(G-3587)*

◆ Sherman Nat Inc ....E 201 735-9000
Englewood *(G-2940)*

Shermans 1400 Brdway N Y C Ltd .....D 201 735-9000
Englewood *(G-2941)*

Urban State ....G 646 836-4311
Hillside *(G-4435)*

2121 Cigars

▲ Csonka Worldwide ....E 609 514-2766
Plainsboro *(G-8783)*

Itg Brands LLC ....G 973 386-9087
East Hanover *(G-2219)*

▲ Prime Time International Co ....G 623 780-8600
Teaneck *(G-10647)*

◆ Sherman Nat Inc ....E 201 735-9000
Englewood *(G-2940)*

2141 Tobacco Stemming & Redrying

Schweitzer-Mauduit Intl Inc ....B 732 723-6100
Spotswood *(G-10417)*

22 TEXTILE MILL PRODUCTS

2211 Cotton, Woven Fabric

▲ Absecon Mills Inc ....C 609 965-5373
Cologne *(G-1773)*

◆ Allison Corp ....G 973 992-3800
Livingston *(G-5504)*

◆ Amt Stitch Inc ....G 732 376-0009
Perth Amboy *(G-8512)*

▲ Atlantic Mills Inc ....D 973 344-2001
Passaic *(G-8052)*

Aurora Apparel Inc ....G 201 646-4590
Hackensack *(G-3879)*

Avail Inc ....G 732 560-2222
Bridgewater *(G-796)*

Bai Lar Interior Services Inc ....G 732 738-0350
Fords *(G-3530)*

Blue Monkey Inc ....G 201 805-0055
Saddle Brook *(G-9643)*

Chic Bebe Inc ....G 201 941-5414
Tenafly *(G-10661)*

Country Club Products Inc ....G 908 352-5400
Elizabeth *(G-2723)*

▲ Derma Sciences Inc ....C 609 514-4744
Plainsboro *(G-8784)*

Designs By James ....G 856 692-1316
Vineland *(G-11213)*

Easy Undies LLC ....G 201 715-4909
Springfield *(G-10440)*

▲ Fh Group International Inc ....E 201 210-2426
Secaucus *(G-9767)*

◆ Franco Manufacturing Co Inc ......C 732 494-0500
Metuchen *(G-6056)*

Gene Mignola Inc ....G 732 775-9291
Asbury Park *(G-77)*

◆ Green Distribution LLC ....G 201 293-4381
Secaucus *(G-9779)*

◆ Hanover Direct Inc ....G 201 863-7300
Weehawken *(G-11568)*

Homespun Global LLC ....G 917 674-9684
Sayreville *(G-9710)*

Integrity Medical Devices Del ....D 609 567-8175
Hammonton *(G-4136)*

▲ Jacquard Fabrics Inc ....E 732 905-4545
Lakewood *(G-5114)*

Jay Franco & Sons Inc ....D 732 721-0022
Sayreville *(G-9712)*

Leggs Hns Bli Plytx Fctry Outl ......G 908 289-7262
Elizabeth *(G-2753)*

▼ Marcotex International Inc ....E 201 991-8200
Kearny *(G-4883)*

▲ Material Imports ....E 201 229-1180
Moonachie *(G-6479)*

▲ Meadowgate Farm Alpacas ....G 609 219-0529
Lawrenceville *(G-5237)*

Medical Scrubs Collectn NJ LLC ....G 732 719-8600
Lakewood *(G-5134)*

Metro Mills Inc ....E 973 942-6034
Paterson *(G-8257)*

Peel Away Labs Inc ....G 201 420-0051
Jersey City *(G-4780)*

Picture Knits Inc ....E 973 340-3131
Clifton *(G-1691)*

Proclean Services Inc ....F 973 857-5408
Verona *(G-11172)*

Pueblo Latino Laundry LLC ....G 201 864-1666
Union City *(G-11125)*

Quantum Vector Corp ....G 201 870-1782
Westwood *(G-11840)*

Refuel Inc ....G 917 645-2974
South Hackensack *(G-10183)*

Skusky Inc ....E 732 912-7220
Rutherford *(G-9633)*

▲ Stanbee Company Inc ....E 201 933-9666
Carlstadt *(G-1221)*

Teefx Screen Printing LLC ....G 973 942-6800
Haledon *(G-4086)*

▲ Tex Gul Inc ....G 973 857-3200
Cedar Grove *(G-1293)*

Trimtex Company Inc ....D 201 945-2151
Englewood Cliffs *(G-2994)*

Umbrellas Unlimited : ....G 201 476-1011
River Vale *(G-9368)*

Vacs Bandage Company Inc ....F 973 345-3355
Paterson *(G-8322)*

Westchester Denim Brothers Inc ......G 203 260-1629
Ridgefield *(G-9297)*

2221 Silk & Man-Made Fiber

▲ Absecon Mills Inc ....C 609 965-5373
Cologne *(G-1773)*

◆ Allison Corp ....G 973 992-3800
Livingston *(G-5504)*

Chic Bebe Inc ....G 201 941-5414
Tenafly *(G-10661)*

◆ Fablok Mills Inc ....E 908 464-1950
New Providence *(G-6998)*

◆ Hanover Direct Inc ....B 201 863-7300
Weehawken *(G-11568)*

Invitation Studio ....G 732 740-5558
Morganville *(G-6589)*

◆ Kt America Corp ....E 609 655-5333
Cranbury *(G-1853)*

◆ L&M Architectural Graphics Inc ......F 973 575-7665
Fairfield *(G-3254)*

New Community Corp ....E 973 643-5300
Newark *(G-7208)*

Nyltite Corp of America ....F 908 561-1300
South Plainfield *(G-10310)*

▲ Nyp Corp (frmr Ny-Pters Corp) ......D 908 351-6550
Elizabeth *(G-2763)*

Paterson Bleachery Inc ....F 973 684-1034
Paterson *(G-8279)*

Picture Knits Inc ....E 973 340-3131
Clifton *(G-1691)*

▼ Satex Fabrics Ltd ....G 212 221-5555
North Bergen *(G-7436)*

Sika Fibers LLC ....E 201 933-8800
Lyndhurst *(G-5680)*

Tex-Net Inc ....E 609 499-9111
Florence *(G-3478)*

Thomas Clark Fiberglass LLC ....G 609 492-9257
Barnegat *(G-163)*

Ultraflex Systems Florida Inc ....E 973 627-8608
Randolph *(G-9205)*

United Eqp Fabricators LLC ....G 973 242-2737
Newark *(G-7308)*

▲ Wearbest Sil-Tex Mills Ltd ....E 973 340-8844
Garfield *(G-3777)*

2231 Wool, Woven Fabric

Alma Park Alpacas ....G 732 620-1052
Jobstown *(G-4835)*

▲ C3 Concepts Inc ....E 212 840-1116
North Bergen *(G-7391)*

Colton Industries Inc ....G 908 277-2040
Summit *(G-10530)*

◆ Dollfus Mieg Company Inc ....C 732 662-1005
Edison *(G-2492)*

Manner Textile Processing Inc ....D 973 942-8718
North Haledon *(G-7497)*

Paterson Bleachery Inc ....F 973 684-1034
Paterson *(G-8279)*

Soh LLC ....E 646 943-4066
Jersey City *(G-4812)*

2241 Fabric Mills, Cotton, Wool, Silk & Man-Made

▲ Avitex Co Inc ....E 973 242-2410
Newark *(G-7061)*

Avitex Co Inc ....G 973 242-2410
Newark *(G-7062)*

Beau Label ....D 973 318-7800
Hillside *(G-4380)*

Brian Lenhart Interactive LLC ....G 610 737-5314
Berkeley Heights *(G-391)*

▲ Carolace Embroidery Co Inc ....D 201 945-2151
Ridgefield *(G-9253)*

▲ Carson & Gebel Ribbon Co LLC ......E 973 627-4200
Rockaway *(G-9449)*

◆ Cottage Lace and Ribbon Co Inc ......G 732 776-9353
Neptune *(G-6871)*

Cranial Technologies Inc ....E 201 265-3993
Paramus *(G-7795)*

Denali Company LLC ....E 732 219-7771
Red Bank *(G-9226)*

▲ Hamilton Embroidery Co Inc ....F 201 867-4084
Union City *(G-11112)*

▲ Jrm Industries Inc ....E 973 779-9340
Passaic *(G-8077)*

Klein Ribbon Corp ....E 973 684-4671
Paterson *(G-8230)*

Marlene Trimmings LLC ....G 201 926-3108
North Bergen *(G-7418)*

▲ Otex Specialty Narrow Fabrics ......G 908 879-3636
Bernardsville *(G-440)*

Paterson Bleachery Inc ....F 973 684-1034
Paterson *(G-8279)*

◆ R Tape Corporation ....C 908 753-5570
South Plainfield *(G-10322)*

▲ Reddaway Manufacturing Co Inc ......F 973 589-1410
Newark *(G-7248)*

▲ Snapco Manufacturing Corp ....E 973 282-0300
Hillside *(G-4427)*

Sullivan-Carson Inc ....G 856 566-1400
Voorhees *(G-11294)*

▲ Textol Systems Inc ....E 201 935-1220
Carlstadt *(G-1227)*

Trimtex Company Inc ....D 201 945-2151
Englewood Cliffs *(G-2994)*

Wingold Embroidery LLC ....G 732 845-9802
Freehold *(G-3705)*

2251 Hosiery, Women's Full & Knee Length

▲ Great Socks LLC ....E....... 856 964-9700
Pennsauken (G-8427)

Swisstex Company ....E....... 201 861-8000
West New York (G-11755)

2252 Hosiery, Except Women's

▲ Great Socks LLC ....E....... 856 964-9700
Pennsauken (G-8427)

J T Murdoch Shoes ....F....... 973 748-6484
Bloomfield (G-503)

Knock Knock Give A Sock Inc ....G....... 917 885-6983
West Orange (G-11770)

Living Fashions Llc ....F....... 732 626-5200
Sayreville (G-9716)

Sock Company Inc ....E....... 201 307-0675
Westwood (G-11845)

Sock Drawer and More LLC ....G....... 888 637-3399
Edison (G-2615)

Socks 47 Ltd Liability Company ....G....... 201 866-2222
Union City (G-11128)

2253 Knit Outerwear Mills

3forty Group Inc ....F....... 973 773-1806
Passaic (G-8047)

Alan Paul Accessories Inc ....G....... 609 924-4022
Princeton (G-8905)

◆ Artex Knitting Mills Inc ....D....... 856 456-2800
Westville (G-11810)

Chiha Inc ....F....... 201 861-2000
North Bergen (G-7395)

D & G LLC ....G....... 201 289-5750
Hackensack (G-3903)

D L V Lounge Inc ....G....... 973 783-6988
Montclair (G-6362)

▲ Elegant Headwear Co Inc ....C....... 908 558-1200
Elizabeth (G-2732)

▲ Fairfield Textiles Corp ....D....... 973 227-1656
Paterson (G-8190)

Fleck Knitwear Co Inc ....E....... 908 754-8888
Plainfield (G-8766)

Flemington Knitting Mills ....F....... 908 995-9590
Milford (G-6192)

Jtwo Inc ....G....... 201 410-1616
Kinnelon (G-5018)

Metro Sport Inc ....E....... 973 879-3831
Mendham (G-6042)

Ralph Lauren Corporation ....C....... 201 531-6000
Lyndhurst (G-5674)

Supertex Inc ....E....... 973 345-1000
Paterson (G-8306)

▲ Triumph Knitting Machine Svc ....E....... 201 646-0022
Hackensack (G-3985)

2254 Knit Underwear Mills

▲ Komar Intimates LLC ....F....... 212 725-1500
Jersey City (G-4754)

▲ Komar Kids LLC ....G....... 212 725-1500
Jersey City (G-4755)

2257 Circular Knit Fabric Mills

Meadows Knitting Corp ....E....... 973 482-6400
Newark (G-7198)

▲ Susan Mills Inc ....F....... 908 355-1400
Hillside (G-4429)

Trimtex Company Inc ....D....... 201 945-2151
Englewood Cliffs (G-2994)

2258 Lace & Warp Knit Fabric Mills

All-Lace Processing Corp ....F....... 201 867-1974
North Bergen (G-7381)

▲ Endurance Net Inc ....F....... 609 499-3450
Florence (G-3475)

▲ Fablok Mills Inc ....E....... 908 464-1950
New Providence (G-6998)

◆ Jason Mills LLC ....G....... 732 651-7200
Milltown (G-6217)

▲ Keystone Dyeing and Finishing ......G....... 718 482-7780
Dayton (G-1975)

Ques Aprv A R Knitwear Inc ....G....... 201 869-1333
North Bergen (G-7431)

Rebtex Inc ....C....... 908 722-3549
Branchburg (G-676)

▲ Royal Lace Co Inc ....G....... 718 495-9327
Rahway (G-9125)

Skusky Inc ....E....... 732 912-7220
Rutherford (G-9633)

▲ Stern Knit Inc ....G....... 732 364-8055
Lakewood (G-5169)

▲ Westchester Lace & Textiles ....C....... 201 864-2150
Livingston (G-5548)

World Class Marketing Corp ....E....... 201 313-0022
Fort Lee (G-3595)

2259 Knitting Mills, NEC

Curtain Care Plus Inc ....G....... 800 845-6155
Clifton (G-1594)

◆ Dollfus Mieg Company Inc ....C....... 732 662-1005
Edison (G-2492)

Hampton Industries Inc ....E....... 973 574-8900
Passaic (G-8072)

Markbilt Inc ....D....... 201 891-7842
Wyckoff (G-12117)

2261 Cotton Fabric Finishers

Anne Alanna Inc ....G....... 609 465-3787
Cape May Court House (G-1106)

Aztec Graphics Inc ....F....... 609 587-1000
Trenton (G-10900)

Brookline Chemical Corp ....E....... 301 767-1177
Wayne (G-11485)

Chartwell Promotions Ltd Inc ....G....... 732 780-6900
Freehold (G-3657)

Decorating With Fabric Inc ....G....... 845 352-5064
Park Ridge (G-7847)

E & W Piece Dye Works ....E....... 973 942-8718
Haledon (G-4082)

▲ Finn & Emma LLC ....G....... 973 227-7770
Fairfield (G-3201)

▲ Hanes Companies - NJ LLC ....F....... 201 729-9100
Edison (G-2525)

◆ Hydromer Inc ....E....... 908 526-2828
Branchburg (G-646)

▲ Keystone Dyeing and Finishing ......G....... 718 482-7780
Dayton (G-1975)

▲ Lacoa Inc ....G....... 973 754-1000
Elmwood Park (G-2837)

Manner Textile Processing Inc ....D....... 973 942-8718
North Haledon (G-7497)

Martin Corporation ....F....... 856 451-0900
Bridgeton (G-764)

Mt Embroidery & Promotions LLC ......G....... 201 646-1070
Norwood (G-7569)

Paul Dyeing Company ....F....... 973 484-1121
Newark (G-7224)

Peter L Demaree ....G....... 732 531-2133
Ocean (G-7673)

Premier Printing Solutions LLC ....G....... 732 525-0740
South Amboy (G-10139)

Rebtex Inc ....C....... 908 722-3549
Branchburg (G-676)

Rolferrys Specialties Inc ....G....... 856 456-2999
Brooklawn (G-915)

Safer Textile Processing Corp ....B....... 973 482-6400
Newark (G-7260)

Screened Images Inc ....E....... 732 651-8181
East Brunswick (G-2175)

Unique Screen Printing Corp ....E....... 908 925-3773
Linden (G-5438)

2262 Silk & Man-Made Fabric Finishers

Chartwell Promotions Ltd Inc ....G....... 732 780-6900
Freehold (G-3657)

Design N Stitch Inc ....G....... 201 488-1314
Hackensack (G-3906)

Dye Into Print Inc ....D....... 973 772-8019
Clifton (G-1606)

Gilbert Storms Jr ....G....... 973 835-5729
Haskell (G-4196)

▲ Keystone Dyeing and Finishing ......G....... 718 482-7780
Dayton (G-1975)

Life Liners Inc ....G....... 973 635-9234
Chatham (G-1326)

Marijon Dyeing & Finishing Co ....C....... 201 933-9770
East Rutherford (G-2300)

Martin Corporation ....F....... 856 451-0900
Bridgeton (G-764)

North Jersey Skein Dyeing Co ....G....... 201 247-4202
Paterson (G-8270)

Screened Images Inc ....E....... 732 651-8181
East Brunswick (G-2175)

▲ Stefan Enterprises Inc ....E....... 973 253-6005
Garfield (G-3770)

Sunbrite Dye Co Inc ....G....... 973 777-9830
Passaic (G-8110)

Unique Screen Printing Corp ....E....... 908 925-3773
Linden (G-5438)

2269 Textile Finishers, NEC

◆ Asha44 LLC ....E....... 201 306-3600
Fairfield (G-3147)

Dye Into Print Inc ....D....... 973 772-8019
Clifton (G-1606)

◆ Franco Manufacturing Co Inc ....C....... 732 494-0500
Metuchen (G-6056)

▲ Kennetex Inc ....D....... 610 444-0600
Paterson (G-8228)

Manner Textile Processing Inc ....D....... 973 942-8718
North Haledon (G-7497)

▲ Multi-Tex Products Corp ....E....... 201 991-7262
Kearny (G-4886)

▲ Star Narrow Fabrics Inc ....G....... 973 778-8600
Lodi (G-5576)

2273 Carpets & Rugs

A & J Carpets Inc ....G....... 856 227-1753
Blackwood (G-458)

Aladdin Manufacturing Corp ....B....... 973 616-4600
Pompton Plains (G-8856)

▲ Amici Imports Inc ....F....... 908 272-8300
Cranford (G-1900)

▲ Bamboo & Rattan Works Inc ....G....... 732 255-4239
Toms River (G-10746)

▲ Banilivy Rug Corp ....G....... 212 684-3629
Englewood (G-2880)

▲ Bashian Bros Inc ....E....... 201 330-1001
Ridgefield (G-9250)

▲ Ben-Aharon & Son Inc ....G....... 201 541-2388
Englewood (G-2881)

Cno Corporation ....G....... 732 785-5799
Brick (G-713)

▲ Fh Group International Inc ....E....... 201 210-2426
Secaucus (G-9767)

Gallery of Rugs Inc ....G....... 908 934-0040
Summit (G-10532)

Hakakian Behzad ....E....... 973 267-2506
Cedar Knolls (G-1306)

▲ Kas Oriental Rugs Inc ....E....... 732 545-1900
Somerset (G-10010)

▲ Kashee & Sons Inc ....F....... 201 867-6900
Secaucus (G-9785)

Kync Design LLC ....G....... 201 552-2067
Secaucus (G-9787)

La Forchetta ....G....... 973 304-4797
Hawthorne (G-4230)

◆ Mannington Mills Inc ....A....... 856 935-3000
Salem (G-9694)

▲ Moosavi Rugs Inc ....G....... 201 617-9500
Secaucus (G-9793)

Newark Auto Top Co Inc ....F....... 973 677-9935
East Orange (G-2256)

▲ Samad Brothers Inc ....F....... 201 372-0909
East Rutherford (G-2318)

▲ Seldom Seen Designs LLC ....G....... 973 535-8805
Caldwell (G-1030)

Shaw Industries Inc ....B....... 609 655-8300
Cranbury (G-1882)

▲ SNS Oriental Rugs LLC ....G....... 201 355-8786
Carlstadt (G-1219)

▲ Stiles Enterprises Inc ....F....... 973 625-9660
Rockaway (G-9501)

▲ Worldwide Whl Flr Cvg Inc ....E....... 732 906-1400
Edison (G-2647)

▲ Zollanvari Ltd ....F....... 201 330-3344
Secaucus (G-9830)

2281 Yarn Spinning Mills

▲ Kennetex Inc ....D....... 610 444-0600
Paterson (G-8228)

Kng Textile Inc ....G....... 704 564-0390
Ridgefield (G-9272)

Kync Design LLC ....G....... 201 552-2067
Secaucus (G-9787)

▲ Multi-Tex Products Corp ....E....... 201 991-7262
Kearny (G-4886)

World Class Marketing Corp ....E....... 201 313-0022
Fort Lee (G-3595)

2282 Yarn Texturizing, Throwing, Twisting & Winding Mills

◆ Brawer Bros Inc ....F....... 973 238-0163
Hawthorne (G-4209)

Family Screen Printing Inc ....F....... 856 933-2780
Bellmawr (G-332)

Kairos Enterprises LLC ....F....... 201 731-3181
Englewood Cliffs (G-2979)

▲ Middleburg Yarn Processing Co......E 973 238-1800
Hawthorne *(G-4232)*
▲ Safer Holding Corp......A 973 485-1458
Newark *(G-7259)*
▲ Star Narrow Fabrics Inc......G 973 778-8600
Lodi *(G-5576)*
▲ Warp Processing Inc......C 973 238-1800
Hawthorne *(G-4252)*

2284 Thread Mills

▲ 5 Kids Group Ltd Liability Co ......F 732 774-5331
Neptune *(G-6861)*
Athletes Alley ......F 732 842-1127
Shrewsbury *(G-9882)*
◆ Cobyco Inc ......G 732 446-4448
Manalapan *(G-5804)*

2295 Fabrics Coated Not Rubberized

Alpha Associates Inc ......E 732 730-1800
Lakewood *(G-5047)*
◆ Alpha Engneered Composites LLC ..C 732 634-5700
Lakewood *(G-5048)*
◆ Butler Prtg & Laminating Inc ......C 973 838-8550
Butler *(G-997)*
Commercial Products Co Inc ......F 973 427-6887
Hawthorne *(G-4213)*
▲ Custom Laminations Inc ......E 973 279-9174
Paterson *(G-8166)*
▲ Daf Products Inc ......F 201 251-1222
Wyckoff *(G-12108)*
◆ DMS Inc ......G 973 928-3040
Cedar Grove *(G-1275)*
Gleicher Manufacturing Corp ......E 908 233-2211
Scotch Plains *(G-9732)*
Laboratory Diagnostics Co Inc ......F 732 536-6300
Morganville *(G-6591)*
▲ PCC Asia LLC ......G 973 890-3873
Totowa *(G-10842)*
Plastic By All LLC ......G 732 785-5900
Brick *(G-729)*
◆ Precision Textiles LLC ......C 973 890-3873
Totowa *(G-10846)*
Safer Textile Processing Corp ......B 973 482-6400
Newark *(G-7260)*
▲ W C Omni Incorporated ......E 732 248-0999
Edison *(G-2643)*

2296 Tire Cord & Fabric

◆ Jomel Industries Inc ......F 973 282-0300
Hillside *(G-4406)*
▲ Passaic Rubber Co ......D 973 696-9500
Wayne *(G-11540)*

2297 Fabrics, Nonwoven

◆ Fabrictex LLC ......G 732 225-3990
Edison *(G-2510)*
▲ Fibertech Group Inc ......C 856 697-1600
Landisville *(G-5206)*
JKA Specialties Mfr Inc ......F 609 859-2090
Southampton *(G-10366)*
Klein Ribbon Corp ......E 973 684-4671
Paterson *(G-8230)*

2298 Cordage & Twine

American Power Cord Corp ......G 973 574-8301
Somerset *(G-9952)*
Contemporary Cabling Company ......G 732 382-5064
Clark *(G-1496)*
Dun-Rite Communications Inc ......G 201 444-0080
Mahwah *(G-5731)*
Egg Harbor Rope Products Inc ......G 609 965-2435
Egg Harbor City *(G-2659)*
French Textile Co Inc ......F 973 471-5000
Clifton *(G-1622)*
Huber+suhner Astrolab Inc ......E 732 560-3800
Warren *(G-11416)*
▲ Motion Control Tech Inc ......F 973 361-2226
Dover *(G-2098)*
Newtech Group Corp ......G 732 355-0392
Kendall Park *(G-4919)*
Richard Andrus ......G 856 825-1782
Millville *(G-6269)*
▲ Seaboard Paper and Twine LLC ......E 973 413-8100
Paterson *(G-8296)*
▲ Steelstran Industries Inc ......E 732 574-0700
Avenel *(G-147)*
Sterling Net & Twine Co Inc ......F 973 783-9800
Montclair *(G-6390)*

▼ William Kenyon & Sons Inc ......E 732 985-8980
Piscataway *(G-8738)*

2299 Textile Goods, NEC

▲ AMD Fine Linens LLC ......G 201 568-5255
Englewood *(G-2875)*
American Dawn Inc ......G 856 467-9211
Bridgeport *(G-734)*
▲ American Fur Felt LLC ......F 973 344-3026
Newark *(G-7044)*
American Home Essentials Inc ......G 908 561-3200
South Plainfield *(G-10215)*
American Home Mfg LLC ......G 732 465-1530
Piscataway *(G-8629)*
Carlee Corporation ......E 201 768-6800
Rockleigh *(G-9515)*
Classic Silks Com I ......G 908 204-0940
Bernardsville *(G-436)*
Clean-Tex Services Inc ......E 908 912-2700
Linden *(G-5334)*
Crescent Uniforms LLC ......F 732 398-1866
Franklin Park *(G-3634)*
▼ Douglass Industries Inc ......E 609 804-6040
Egg Harbor City *(G-2658)*
Elkay Products Co Inc ......F 973 376-7550
Springfield *(G-10441)*
◆ Halsted Corporation ......E 201 333-0670
Cranbury *(G-1838)*
Jubili Bead & Yarn Shoppe ......F 856 858-7844
Collingswood *(G-1769)*
Kmsco Inc ......F 732 238-8666
Ocean *(G-7668)*
M Chasen & Son Inc ......F 973 374-8956
Irvington *(G-4579)*
▲ Material Imports ......E 201 229-1180
Moonachie *(G-6479)*
▲ Multi-Tex Products Corp ......E 201 991-7262
Kearny *(G-4886)*
Newark Fibers Inc ......E 201 768-6800
Rockleigh *(G-9520)*
▲ Norman Weil Inc ......G 201 940-7345
Paramus *(G-7825)*
Peribu Global Sourcing ......F 704 560-2035
Skillman *(G-9925)*
▲ Sander Sales Enterprises Ltd ......E 201 808-6705
Secaucus *(G-9806)*
◆ Something Different Linen Inc ......C 973 272-0601
Clifton *(G-1722)*
★ Star Linen Inc ......E 800 782-7999
Moorestown *(G-6568)*
▼ Texx Team LLC ......E 201 289-1039
Hillsdale *(G-4370)*

23 APPAREL AND OTHER FINISHED PRODUCTS MADE FROM FABRICS AND SIMILAR MATERIAL

2311 Men's & Boys' Suits, Coats & Overcoats

▼ Bimini Bay Outfitters Ltd ......F 201 529-3550
Mahwah *(G-5716)*
Burlington Coat Factory ......D 908 994-9562
Elizabeth *(G-2718)*
Crown Clothing Co ......C 856 691-0343
Vineland *(G-11206)*
De Rossi & Son Co Inc ......C 856 691-0061
Vineland *(G-11212)*
▲ Fabian Couture Group LLC ......F 800 367-6251
Lyndhurst *(G-5652)*
▲ Fabian Formals Inc ......E 201 460-7776
Lyndhurst *(G-5653)*
Firefighter One Ltd Lblty Co ......G 973 940-3061
Sparta *(G-10387)*
Fordham Inc ......E 973 575-7840
Fairfield *(G-3205)*
▲ Mek International Inc ......G 215 712-2490
Woodcliff Lake *(G-12059)*
Michael Duru Clothiers LLC ......G 732 741-1999
Shrewsbury *(G-9896)*
New Community Corp ......E 973 643-5300
Newark *(G-7208)*
Tom James Company ......E 732 826-8400
Perth Amboy *(G-8536)*

2321 Men's & Boys' Shirts

▼ Bimini Bay Outfitters Ltd ......F 201 529-3550
Mahwah *(G-5716)*
▲ Central Mills Inc ......B 732 329-2009
Dayton *(G-1960)*

▲ Cleve Shirtmakers Inc ......G 201 825-6122
Secaucus *(G-9756)*
Drifire LLC ......E 866 266-4035
East Brunswick *(G-2136)*
Gambert Shirt Corp ......E 973 424-9105
Newark *(G-7130)*
◆ Jade Eastern Trading Inc ......F 201 440-8500
Moonachie *(G-6473)*
L Gambert LLC ......D 973 344-3440
Newark *(G-7176)*
New Community Corp ......E 973 643-5300
Newark *(G-7208)*
▲ New Jersey Headwear Corp ......C 973 497-0102
Newark *(G-7209)*
◆ New Top Inc ......E 201 438-3990
Carlstadt *(G-1191)*
Pvh Corp ......G 908 685-0050
Elizabeth *(G-2771)*
Pvh Corp ......G 609 344-6273
Atlantic City *(G-101)*
Pvh Corp ......G 732 833-9602
Jackson *(G-4663)*
Pvh Corp ......G 908 685-0050
Bridgewater *(G-872)*
Pvh Corp ......G 908 685-0148
Bridgewater *(G-873)*
Pvh Corp ......F 908 788-5880
Flemington *(G-3465)*
Pvh Corp ......G 908 685-0050
Bridgewater *(G-871)*
Ralph Lauren Corporation ......C 201 531-6000
Lyndhurst *(G-5674)*
Saad Collection Inc ......G 732 763-4015
Edison *(G-2603)*
Skip Gambert & Associates Inc ......C 973 344-3373
Newark *(G-7277)*

2322 Men's & Boys' Underwear & Nightwear

Basic Solutions Ltd ......G 201 978-7691
Manalapan *(G-5802)*
▲ Central Mills Inc ......B 732 329-2009
Dayton *(G-1960)*
D & G LLC ......G 201 289-5750
Hackensack *(G-3903)*
◆ Sgi Apparel Ltd ......G 201 342-1200
Hackensack *(G-3973)*
Umc Inc ......G 973 325-0031
West Orange *(G-11780)*

2323 Men's & Boys' Neckwear

Albert Forte Neckwear Co Inc ......G 856 423-2342
Mullica Hill *(G-6854)*
HRA International Inc ......G 609 395-0939
Monroe *(G-6322)*
▲ Robert Stewart Inc ......G 973 751-5151
Belleville *(G-313)*

2325 Men's & Boys' Separate Trousers & Casual Slacks

▲ Eddie Domani Inc ......G 908 469-8863
Elizabethport *(G-2787)*
Guess Inc ......E 201 941-3683
Edgewater *(G-2439)*
▲ Jordache Ltd ......F 908 226-4930
South Plainfield *(G-10284)*
Levi Strauss & Co ......F 732 493-4595
Tinton Falls *(G-10722)*
Ralph Lauren Corporation ......C 201 531-6000
Lyndhurst *(G-5674)*
Spirit Tex LLC ......G 201 440-1113
Little Ferry *(G-5498)*

2326 Men's & Boys' Work Clothing

◆ Ansell Healthcare Products LLC ......C 732 345-5400
Iselin *(G-4593)*
▲ B2x Corporation ......G 201 714-2373
Jersey City *(G-4697)*
Bestwork Inds For The Blind ......D 856 424-2510
Cherry Hill *(G-1345)*
▲ Bethel Industries Inc ......C 201 656-8222
Jersey City *(G-4702)*
Db Designs Inc ......G 732 616-5018
Marlboro *(G-5895)*
◆ Eagle Work Clothes Inc ......E 908 964-8888
Florham Park *(G-3502)*
Enailsupply Corporation ......G 909 725-1698
Toms River *(G-10755)*
Flying Fish Studio ......G 609 884-2760
West Cape May *(G-11683)*

▼ Happy Chef Inc ....E 973 492-2525
Butler (G-1002)

Janet Shops Inc ....F 973 748-4992
Bloomfield (G-504)

▲ Loveline Industries Inc ....G 973 928-3427
Passaic (G-8083)

Luxury and Trash Ltd Lblty Co ....G 201 315-4018
Closter (G-1760)

▲ M Rafi Sons Garment Industries ....G 732 381-7660
Rahway (G-9116)

Matrix Sales Group LLC ....D 908 461-4148
Spring Lake (G-10423)

▲ Mischief International Inc ....G 201 840-6888
Ridgefield (G-9276)

New Community Corp ....E 973 643-5300
Newark (G-7208)

◆ Pro World ....G 856 406-1020
Pennsauken (G-8474)

Ronald Perry ....F 201 702-2407
Jersey City (G-4801)

▲ Somes Uniforms Inc ....F 201 843-1199
Hackensack (G-3975)

Staple Sewing Aids Corporation ....E 973 249-0022
Passaic (G-8108)

Switlik Parachute Company Inc ....F 609 587-3300
Trenton (G-10994)

Tellas Ltd ....E 201 399-8888
Englewood Cliffs (G-2991)

▲ Todd Shelton LLC ....G 844 626-6355
East Rutherford (G-2326)

Top Rated Shopping Bargains ....F 800 556-5849
Hasbrouck Heights (G-4190)

Vertical Protective AP LLC ....G 203 904-6099
Shrewsbury (G-9904)

2329 Men's & Boys' Clothing, NEC

39 Idea Factory Row LLC ....G 908 244-8631
Flemington (G-3425)

Adidas North America Inc ....G 201 843-4555
Paramus (G-7787)

Adidas North America Inc ....G 732 695-0085
Tinton Falls (G-10705)

Aladen Athletic Wear LLC ....E 973 838-2425
Wyckoff (G-12102)

▼ Amante International Ltd ....F 908 518-1688
Westfield (G-11793)

▲ Bear USa Inc ....F 201 943-4748
Palisades Park (G-7768)

▼ Bimini Bay Outfitters Ltd ....F 201 529-3550
Mahwah (G-5716)

Brisco Apparel Co Inc ....E 718 715-7110
Lakewood (G-5067)

Central Mills Inc ....G 732 329-2009
Dayton (G-1959)

▲ Central Mills Inc ....B 732 329-2009
Dayton (G-1960)

CRA-Z Works Co Inc ....G 732 390-8238
Sayreville (G-9707)

▲ Daman International Inc ....G 917 945-9708
Cherry Hill (G-1355)

Evh LLC ....F 973 257-0076
Boonton (G-553)

▲ Finn & Emma LLC ....G 973 227-7770
Fairfield (G-3201)

▼ House Pearl Fashions (us) Ltd ....F 973 778-7551
Lodi (G-5565)

J Harris Company ....G 917 731-5080
Madison (G-5696)

Kmba Fashions Inc ....G 973 789-1652
East Orange (G-2255)

▲ Leather Works NJ Ltd Lblty Co ....G 732 452-1100
Edison (G-2549)

◆ Leeward International Inc ....F 201 836-8830
Teaneck (G-10637)

▲ Merc USA Inc ....F 201 489-3527
Hackensack (G-3947)

MISS Sportswear Inc ....G 212 391-2535
New Brunswick (G-6948)

▲ Moldworks Worldwide LLC ....G 908 474-8082
Linden (G-5390)

▲ Onwards Inc ....G 732 309-7348
Manalapan (G-5822)

▲ Rennoc Corporation ....D 856 327-5400
Vineland (G-11256)

▲ Safire Silk Inc ....G 201 636-4061
Carlstadt (G-1211)

▲ Schott Nyc Corp ....D 800 631-5407
Union (G-11089)

Selfmade LLC ....G 201 792-8968
Jersey City (G-4808)

Senor Lopez ....G 732 229-7622
Tinton Falls (G-10727)

Sinai Manufacturing Corp ....D 973 522-1003
Newark (G-7274)

Sportstar World Wide Inc ....F 732 254-9214
South River (G-10358)

▲ Tony Jones Apparel Inc ....G 973 773-6200
Lodi (G-5580)

What A Tee 2 Inc ....F 201 457-0060
Hackensack (G-3990)

2331 Women's & Misses' Blouses

▲ Chic LLC ....G 732 354-0035
East Brunswick (G-2132)

▲ Cleve Shirtmakers Inc ....G 201 825-6122
Secaucus (G-9756)

▲ Elie Tahari Ltd ....C 973 671-6300
Millburn (G-6196)

Gambert Shirt Corp ....E 973 424-9105
Newark (G-7130)

Luxury and Trash Ltd Lblty Co ....G 201 315-4018
Closter (G-1760)

▲ Metropolitan Manufacturing Inc ....D 201 933-8111
East Rutherford (G-2302)

▲ New Jersey Headwear Corp ....C 973 497-0102
Newark (G-7209)

Nicholas Oliver LLC ....G 732 690-7144
Wall Township (G-11358)

Saad Collection Inc ....G 732 763-4015
Edison (G-2603)

Spirit Tex LLC ....G 201 440-1113
Little Ferry (G-5498)

Suuchi Inc ....C 201 284-0789
North Bergen (G-7439)

▲ Tahari ASL LLC ....E 888 734-7459
Millburn (G-6206)

2335 Women's & Misses' Dresses

Amalia Carrara Inc ....E 201 348-4500
Union City (G-11105)

Augenbrauns Bridal Passaic LLC ....G 845 425-3439
Lakewood (G-5055)

Betsy & Adam Ltd ....F 212 302-3750
Passaic (G-8054)

Donna Karan International Inc ....G 609 345-3402
Atlantic City (G-89)

◆ Duran Cutting Corp ....F 973 916-0006
Passaic (G-8061)

▲ Elie Tahari Ltd ....C 973 671-6300
Millburn (G-6196)

Haddad Bros Inc ....E 718 377-5505
Bloomfield (G-502)

Head Piece Heaven ....G 201 262-0788
Oradell (G-7745)

Hillarys Fashion Boutique LLC ....F 732 667-7733
Warren (G-11414)

Infinity Sourcing Services LLC ....G 212 868-2900
Englewood Cliffs (G-2976)

Jump Design Group Inc ....E 201 558-9191
Secaucus (G-9783)

Kate Spade & Company ....F 201 295-7569
North Bergen (G-7413)

Kate Spade & Company ....G 609 395-3109
Dayton (G-1974)

▲ Kidcuteture LLC ....G 609 532-0149
Lawrenceville (G-5233)

▲ Liz Fields Llc ....G 201 408-5640
Englewood (G-2919)

▲ Metropolitan Manufacturing Inc ....D 201 933-8111
East Rutherford (G-2302)

Nicholas Oliver LLC ....G 732 690-7144
Wall Township (G-11358)

▲ Perceptions Inc ....F 973 344-5333
Kearny (G-4890)

▲ Printmaker International Ltd ....G 212 629-9260
Irvington (G-4583)

Success Sewing Inc ....G 973 622-0328
Newark (G-7290)

▲ Tahari ASL LLC ....E 888 734-7459
Millburn (G-6206)

2337 Women's & Misses' Suits, Coats & Skirts

▲ Chic LLC ....G 732 354-0035
East Brunswick (G-2132)

▲ Counter-Fit Inc ....C 609 871-8888
Willingboro (G-11990)

E-Lo Sportswear LLC ....F 862 902-5220
Harrison (G-4170)

◆ Eagle Work Clothes Inc ....E 908 964-8888
Florham Park (G-3502)

▲ Elie Tahari Ltd ....C 973 671-6300
Millburn (G-6196)

Fordham Inc ....E 973 575-7840
Fairfield (G-3205)

Fyi Marketing Inc ....G 646 546-5226
Englewood Cliffs (G-2971)

▼ Happy Chef Inc ....E 973 492-2525
Butler (G-1002)

Jackie Evans Inc ....C 973 471-6991
Passaic (G-8076)

▲ Metropolitan Manufacturing Inc ....D 201 933-8111
East Rutherford (G-2302)

Nana Creations Inc ....F 201 263-1112
Fort Lee (G-3577)

New Community Corp ....E 973 643-5300
Newark (G-7208)

Nine West Holdings Inc ....G 908 354-8895
Elizabeth (G-2760)

Nine West Holdings Inc ....G 201 541-7004
Englewood (G-2928)

Success Sewing Inc ....G 973 622-0328
Newark (G-7290)

2339 Women's & Misses' Outerwear, NEC

39 Idea Factory Row LLC ....G 908 244-8631
Flemington (G-3425)

Alfred Dunner Inc ....D 212 944-6660
Parsippany (G-7877)

▼ Amante International Ltd ....F 908 518-1688
Westfield (G-11793)

▲ Attitudes In Dressing Inc ....B 908 354-7214
Elizabeth (G-2713)

▲ Bal Togs Inc ....D 201 866-0201
North Bergen (G-7388)

▲ Bear USa Inc ....F 201 943-4748
Palisades Park (G-7768)

Bestwork Inds For The Blind ....D 856 424-2510
Cherry Hill (G-1345)

Blue Fish Clothing Inc ....C 908 996-3720
Frenchtown (G-3709)

▲ Central Mills Inc ....B 732 329-2009
Dayton (G-1960)

▲ Chic LLC ....G 732 354-0035
East Brunswick (G-2132)

▲ City Design Group Inc ....G 201 329-7711
Little Ferry (G-5477)

Collection Xiix Ltd ....C 201 854-7740
North Bergen (G-7396)

▲ Counter-Fit Inc ....C 609 871-8888
Willingboro (G-11990)

Davidmark LLC ....G 609 277-7361
Pleasantville (G-8810)

▲ Elie Tahari Ltd ....C 973 671-6300
Millburn (G-6196)

Escada US Subco LLC ....B 201 865-5200
Secaucus (G-9763)

Fordham Inc ....E 973 575-7840
Fairfield (G-3205)

Fyi Marketing Inc ....G 646 546-5226
Englewood Cliffs (G-2971)

Garylin Togs ....D 908 354-7218
Elizabeth (G-2741)

▲ Golden Season Fashion USA Inc ....F 201 552-2088
Secaucus (G-9775)

▲ Great Socks LLC ....E 856 964-9700
Pennsauken (G-8427)

▼ Happy Chef Inc ....E 973 492-2525
Butler (G-1002)

Helen Morley LLC ....E 201 348-6459
Cresskill (G-1942)

▼ House Pearl Fashions (us) Ltd ....F 973 778-7551
Lodi (G-5565)

▲ Jordache Ltd ....F 908 226-4930
South Plainfield (G-10284)

Kmba Fashions Inc ....G 973 789-1652
East Orange (G-2255)

◆ Leeward International Inc ....F 201 836-8830
Teaneck (G-10637)

Les Tout Petite Inc ....G 201 941-8675
Tenafly (G-10663)

Marmaxx Operating Corp ....D 973 575-7910
West Caldwell (G-11660)

Matrix Sales Group LLC ....D 908 461-4148
Spring Lake (G-10423)

▲ Metropolitan Manufacturing Inc ....D 201 933-8111
East Rutherford (G-2302)

New Community Corp ....E 973 643-5300
Newark (G-7208)

◆ Ocean Drive Inc ....G.... 908 964-2591
   Kenilworth (G-4965)
Philip Papalia ....F.... 732 349-5530
   Toms River (G-10783)
▲ Printmaker International Ltd ....G.... 212 629-9260
   Irvington (G-4583)
◆ Sno Skins Inc ....G.... 973 884-8801
   Whippany (G-11909)
▲ Snotex USA Inc ....G.... 973 762-0358
   South Orange (G-10201)
Sondra Roberts Inc ....E.... 212 684-3344
   South Hackensack (G-10187)
▲ Sonia Fashion Inc ....G.... 201 864-3483
   Union City (G-11129)
Spirit Tex LLC ....G.... 201 440-1113
   Little Ferry (G-5498)
Swisstex Company ....E.... 201 861-8000
   West New York (G-11755)
▲ Tahari ASL LLC ....E.... 888 734-7459
   Millburn (G-6206)
Tellas Ltd ....E.... 201 399-8888
   Englewood Cliffs (G-2991)
▲ Tripp Nyc Inc ....E.... 201 520-0420
   North Bergen (G-7441)
What A Tee 2 Inc ....F.... 201 457-0060
   Hackensack (G-3990)

2341 Women's, Misses' & Children's Under-wear & Nightwear

▲ Carole Hchman Design Group Inc....C.... 866 267-3945
   Jersey City (G-4709)
▲ Central Mills Inc ....B.... 732 329-2009
   Dayton (G-1960)
◆ Charles Komar & Sons Inc ....B.... 212 725-1500
   Jersey City (G-4711)
D & G LLC ....G.... 201 289-5750
   Hackensack (G-3903)
▲ Delta Galil USA Inc ....D.... 201 902-0055
   Secaucus (G-9760)
◆ Dolce Vita Intimates LLC ....D.... 973 482-8400
   Harrison (G-4169)
▲ Fashion Central LLC ....G.... 732 887-7683
   Lakewood (G-5097)
▲ Komar Intimates LLC ....F.... 212 725-1500
   Jersey City (G-4754)
▲ Maidenform ....A.... 732 621-2216
   Iselin (G-4615)
▲ Maidenform Brands Inc ....E.... 888 573-0299
   Iselin (G-4616)
▲ Priamo Designs Ltd ....G.... 201 861-8808
   West New York (G-11749)
◆ Sgi Apparel Ltd ....G.... 201 342-1200
   Hackensack (G-3973)
Swisstex Company ....E.... 201 861-8000
   West New York (G-11755)
◆ Wacoal America Inc ....C.... 201 933-8400
   Lyndhurst (G-5682)
◆ Wacoal International Corp ....G.... 201 933-8400
   Lyndhurst (G-5683)

2342 Brassieres, Girdles & Garments

▲ Bbm Group LLC ....G.... 201 482-6500
   Palisades Park (G-7767)
▲ Carole Hchman Design Group Inc....C.... 866 267-3945
   Jersey City (G-4709)
Colfajas Inc ....G.... 973 727-4813
   Succasunna (G-10510)
◆ Dolce Vita Intimates LLC ....D.... 973 482-8400
   Harrison (G-4169)
▲ Maidenform Brands Inc ....E.... 888 573-0299
   Iselin (G-4616)
◆ Wacoal America Inc ....C.... 201 933-8400
   Lyndhurst (G-5682)

2353 Hats, Caps & Millinery

▲ Alboum W Hat Company Inc ....E.... 201 399-4110
   Irvington (G-4555)
American Baby Headwear Co Inc......D.... 908 558-0017
   Elizabeth (G-2710)
Castellane Manufacturing Co ....F.... 609 625-3427
   Mays Landing (G-5993)
Headwear Creations Inc ....E.... 973 622-1144
   Newark (G-7149)
▲ Impact Design Inc ....E.... 908 289-2900
   Elizabethport (G-2789)
▲ Jay Gerish Company ....G.... 973 403-0655
   West Caldwell (G-11657)
John B Stetson Company ....G.... 212 563-1848
   Hoboken (G-4459)

▲ Kathy Gibson Designs Inc ....F.... 201 420-0088
   North Bergen (G-7414)
▲ Kathy Jeanne Inc ....F.... 973 575-9898
   Fairfield (G-3248)
Mod Hatter ....G.... 609 492-0999
   Beach Haven (G-256)
Nes Enterprises Inc ....G.... 201 964-1400
   Carlstadt (G-1190)
▲ New Jersey Headwear Corp ....C.... 973 497-0102
   Newark (G-7209)
Serratelli Hat Company Inc ....G.... 973 623-4133
   Newark (G-7266)
▲ Silvertop Associates Inc ....E.... 856 939-9599
   Runnemede (G-9610)

2361 Children's & Infants' Dresses & Blouses

Haddad Bros Inc ....E.... 718 377-5505
   Bloomfield (G-502)
▲ Jasper Fashion Ltd Lblty Co ....F.... 917 561-4533
   Elizabeth (G-2752)
Lollytogs Ltd ....F.... 732 438-5500
   Dayton (G-1978)
▲ Sally Miller LLC ....G.... 732 729-4840
   Milltown (G-6219)

2369 Girls' & Infants' Outerwear, NEC

American Baby Headwear Co Inc......D.... 908 558-0017
   Elizabeth (G-2710)
▲ Attitudes In Dressing Inc ....B.... 908 354-7218
   Elizabeth (G-2713)
Bib and Tucker Inc ....F.... 201 489-9600
   Hackensack (G-3885)
Blue Fish Clothing Inc ....G.... 908 996-3720
   Frenchtown (G-3709)
▲ Central Mills Inc ....B.... 732 329-2009
   Dayton (G-1960)
Frenchtoastcom LLC ....F.... 732 438-5500
   Dayton (G-1964)
Garylin Togs ....D.... 908 354-7218
   Elizabeth (G-2741)
Haddad Bros Inc ....E.... 718 377-5505
   Bloomfield (G-502)
In Mocean Group LLC ....G.... 732 960-2415
   North Brunswick (G-7470)
▲ Jordache Ltd ....F.... 908 226-4930
   South Plainfield (G-10284)
JP Group International LLC ....G.... 201 820-1444
   Maywood (G-6011)
◆ Leeward International Inc ....F.... 201 836-8830
   Teaneck (G-10637)
Lemon Inc ....G.... 201 417-5412
   Norwood (G-7568)
Les Tout Petite Inc ....E.... 201 941-8675
   Tenafly (G-10663)
Lollytogs Ltd ....D.... 732 438-5500
   Dayton (G-1979)
Lollytogs Ltd ....F.... 732 438-5500
   Dayton (G-1978)
Spirit Tex LLC ....G.... 201 440-1113
   Little Ferry (G-5498)

2371 Fur Goods

M Blaustein Inc ....G.... 973 379-1080
   Short Hills (G-9871)
S & H R Inc ....G.... 908 925-3797
   Linden (G-5417)

2381 Dress & Work Gloves

American Baby Headwear Co Inc......D.... 908 558-0017
   Elizabeth (G-2710)

2384 Robes & Dressing Gowns

▲ Carole Hchman Design Group Inc....C.... 866 267-3945
   Jersey City (G-4709)
◆ Charles Komar & Sons Inc ....B.... 212 725-1500
   Jersey City (G-4711)
Chiha Inc ....F.... 201 861-2000
   North Bergen (G-7395)
▲ Monarch Towel Company Inc ....E.... 800 729-7623
   South Plainfield (G-10301)
Peach Boutique LLC ....G.... 908 351-0739
   Elizabeth (G-2768)

2385 Waterproof Outerwear

A J P Scientific Inc ....G.... 973 472-7200
   Clifton (G-1551)
▲ Man-How Inc ....G.... 609 392-4895
   Trenton (G-10954)

2386 Leather & Sheep Lined Clothing

Cockpit Usa Inc ....F.... 212 575-1616
   Elizabeth (G-2721)
G-III Apparel Group Ltd ....D.... 732 438-0209
   Dayton (G-1965)
G-III Leather Fashions Inc ....D.... 212 403-0500
   Dayton (G-1966)
Goose Country LLC ....G.... 646 860-8815
   Matawan (G-5977)
▲ Prime Fur & Leather Inc ....F.... 201 941-9600
   Fairview (G-3368)
▲ Schott Nyc Corp ....D.... 800 631-5407
   Union (G-11089)

2387 Apparel Belts

Josemi Inc ....G.... 917 710-2110
   Hoboken (G-4462)
Straps Manufacturing NJ Inc ....F.... 201 368-5201
   Wyckoff (G-12121)
Two 12 Fashion LLC ....G.... 848 222-1562
   Lakewood (G-5173)

2389 Apparel & Accessories, NEC

Apparel Strgc Alliances LLC...........F.... 732 833-7771
   Jackson (G-4640)
◆ Ballet Makers Inc ....G.... 973 595-9000
   Totowa (G-10818)
Better Team USA Corporation ....F.... 973 365-0947
   Clifton (G-1574)
Blu-J2 LLC ....G.... 201 750-1407
   Demarest (G-2024)
Butterfly Bow Ties LLC ....G.... 973 626-2536
   Union (G-11033)
Church Vestment Mfg Co Inc ....G.... 973 942-2833
   Paterson (G-8157)
▲ Costume Gallery Inc ....G.... 609 386-6601
   Delanco (G-2005)
Couture Exchange ....G.... 732 933-1123
   Shrewsbury (G-9887)
E5 Usa Inc ....G.... 973 773-0750
   Passaic (G-8062)
Fine Wear U S A ....G.... 201 313-3777
   Fort Lee (G-3558)
Global Manufacturing LLC ....G.... 973 494-5413
   Newark (G-7134)
Handcraft Manufacturing Corp ....E.... 973 565-0077
   Newark (G-7146)
Hat Box ....E.... 732 961-2262
   Lakewood (G-5108)
Images Costume Productions ....G.... 609 859-7372
   Southampton (G-10365)
Jaclyn LLC ....C.... 201 909-6000
   Maywood (G-6008)
▲ Jese Apparel LLC ....F.... 732 969-3200
   Dayton (G-1973)
◆ Keystone Adjustable Cap Co Inc ...E.... 856 356-2809
   Pennsauken (G-8447)
Kristine Deer Inc ....G.... 201 497-3333
   Westwood (G-11833)
Lion Sales Corp ....G.... 732 417-9363
   Edison (G-2551)
Lynn Amiee Inc ....E.... 201 840-6766
   Ridgefield (G-9274)
▲ New York Popular Inc ....D.... 718 499-2020
   Carteret (G-1260)
Paradise ....G.... 973 425-0505
   Morristown (G-6691)
Peach Boutique LLC ....G.... 908 351-0739
   Elizabeth (G-2768)
Personality Handkerchiefs Inc ....E.... 973 565-0077
   Newark (G-7227)
▲ Pets First Inc ....E.... 908 289-2900
   Elizabethport (G-2791)
Philip Papalia ....F.... 732 349-5530
   Toms River (G-10783)
Power Apparel LLC ....F.... 516 442-1333
   Lakewood (G-5149)
◆ Premium Imports Inc ....G.... 718 486-7125
   Passaic (G-8096)
▲ Robert F Gaiser Inc ....F.... 973 838-9254
   Butler (G-1013)
School Spirit Promotions ....G.... 609 588-6902
   Trenton (G-10990)
▲ Silvertop Associates Inc ....E.... 856 939-9599
   Runnemede (G-9610)
Steps Clothing Inc ....E.... 201 420-1496
   Jersey City (G-4816)
Stylus Custom Apparel Inc ....G.... 908 587-0800
   Linden (G-5432)

Too Cool of Ocean City .... G 908 810-6363
  Kenilworth *(G-4982)*

Vaeg LLC .... G 917 533-0138
  Lakewood *(G-5175)*

◆ Wells Trading LLC .... F 201 552-9909
  Guttenberg *(G-3873)*

Xcessory LLC .... G 917 647-7523
  North Bergen *(G-7445)*

2391 Curtains & Draperies

▲ Ackerson Drapery Decorator Svc ... G 732 797-1967
  Lakewood *(G-5045)*

Alan Schatzberg & Associates ..... F 201 440-8855
  South Hackensack *(G-10148)*

▲ Beatrice Home Fashions Inc ..... E 908 561-7370
  South Plainfield *(G-10225)*

Beltor Manufacturing Corp .... G 856 768-5570
  Berlin *(G-415)*

Bloomfield Drapery Co Inc .... F 973 777-3566
  East Rutherford *(G-2278)*

Colonial Uphl & Win Treatments ... G 609 641-3124
  Pleasantville *(G-8808)*

Comfort Concepts Inc .... G 201 941-6700
  Ridgefield *(G-9256)*

▲ D Kwitman & Son Inc .... F 201 798-5511
  Hoboken *(G-4450)*

Drapery & More Inc .... G 201 271-9661
  North Bergen *(G-7401)*

▲ Dru Whitacre Media Svcs Ltd ..... D 201 770-9950
  North Bergen *(G-7402)*

Forsters Cleaning & Tailoring ..... G 201 659-4411
  Jersey City *(G-4740)*

Franks Upholstery & Draperies ..... G 856 779-8585
  Maple Shade *(G-5863)*

Gordon Frgson Intr Dsigns Svcs ... G 973 378-2330
  Maplewood *(G-5877)*

Interior Art & Design Inc .... E 201 488-8855
  Hackensack *(G-3931)*

Kushner Draperies Mfg LLC .... E 856 317-9696
  Pennsauken *(G-8449)*

Master Drapery Workroom Inc .... G 908 272-4404
  Kenilworth *(G-4956)*

Metro Mills Inc .... E 973 942-6034
  Paterson *(G-8257)*

Nassaus Window Fashions Inc .... G 201 689-6030
  Paramus *(G-7824)*

Stessl & Neugebauer Inc .... F 908 277-3340
  Summit *(G-10549)*

▲ Tankleff Inc .... E 201 402-6500
  Fairview *(G-3369)*

▲ W Gerriets International Inc ..... F 609 771-8111
  Ewing *(G-3077)*

2392 House furnishings: Textile

A & R Sewing Company Inc .... F 201 332-0622
  Jersey City *(G-4682)*

▼ A-1 Tablecloth Co Inc .... C 201 727-4364
  South Hackensack *(G-10145)*

▲ Ackerson Drapery Decorator Svc ... G 732 797-1967
  Lakewood *(G-5045)*

American Dawn Inc .... G 856 467-9211
  Bridgeport *(G-734)*

▲ AMS Products LLC .... F 973 442-5790
  Wharton *(G-11850)*

▲ AMS Toy Intl Inc .... E 973 442-5790
  Wharton *(G-11851)*

Anchor Sales & Marketing Inc ..... F 973 545-2277
  West Milford *(G-11725)*

B T Partners Inc .... G 609 652-6511
  Galloway *(G-3720)*

Ballard Collection Inc .... G 908 604-0082
  Warren *(G-11399)*

▲ Beatrice Home Fashions Inc ..... E 908 561-7370
  South Plainfield *(G-10225)*

▲ Better Sleep Inc .... F 908 464-2200
  Branchburg *(G-625)*

Carlyle Custom Convertibles .... D 973 546-4502
  Moonachie *(G-6460)*

Chic Bebe Inc .... G 201 941-5414
  Tenafly *(G-10661)*

Colonial Uphl & Win Treatments ... G 609 641-3124
  Pleasantville *(G-8808)*

▲ Crown Products Inc .... E 732 493-0022
  Spring Lake *(G-10421)*

▲ D Kwitman & Son Inc .... F 201 798-5511
  Hoboken *(G-4450)*

Discount Pillow Factory LLC .... F 973 444-1617
  Passaic *(G-8060)*

◆ Drake Corp .... G 732 254-1530
  East Brunswick *(G-2135)*

Fine Linen Inc .... F 908 469-3634
  Elizabeth *(G-2736)*

◆ Franco Manufacturing Co Inc ..... C 732 494-0500
  Metuchen *(G-6056)*

◆ Global Weavers Corp .... G 973 824-5500
  Newark *(G-7135)*

Howard Lippincott .... G 856 764-8282
  Riverside *(G-9396)*

◆ Innocor Inc .... C 732 945-6222
  Red Bank *(G-9230)*

Innocor Foam Tech - Acp Inc .... D 732 945-6222
  Red Bank *(G-9231)*

Interior Art & Design Inc .... E 201 488-8855
  Hackensack *(G-3931)*

◆ J&S Houseware Corp .... G 973 824-5500
  Newark *(G-7165)*

◆ Janico Inc .... F 732 370-2223
  Freehold *(G-3672)*

▼ Jewm Inc .... E 973 942-1555
  Paterson *(G-8222)*

▲ Kas Oriental Rugs Inc .... E 732 545-1900
  Somerset *(G-10010)*

▲ Lbu Inc .... E 973 773-4800
  Paterson *(G-8238)*

Linen For Tables .... G 973 345-8472
  Paterson *(G-8242)*

Living Fashions Llc .... F 732 626-5200
  Sayreville *(G-9716)*

Marketing Administration Assoc ... G 732 840-3021
  Brick *(G-726)*

▲ Orient Originals Inc .... E 201 332-5005
  Jersey City *(G-4778)*

Peel Away Labs Inc .... G 516 603-3116
  Jersey City *(G-4779)*

◆ Pegasus Home Fashions Inc .... C 908 965-1919
  Elizabeth *(G-2769)*

▼ Phoenix Down Corporation .... C 973 812-8100
  Totowa *(G-10844)*

▲ R L Plastics Inc .... G 732 340-1100
  Avenel *(G-144)*

Redhawk Distribution Inc .... F 516 884-9911
  Pennsauken *(G-8477)*

▲ Royal Crest Home Fashions Inc ... G 201 461-4600
  Palisades Park *(G-7778)*

▲ Sahara Textile Inc .... E 973 247-9900
  Paterson *(G-8291)*

◆ Sheex Inc .... E 856 334-3021
  Marlton *(G-5951)*

Stanlar Enterprises Inc .... E 973 680-4488
  Bloomfield *(G-518)*

◆ Star Linen Inc .... E 800 782-7999
  Moorestown *(G-6568)*

Starlight One Corp .... G 862 684-0561
  Clifton *(G-1725)*

Sunham Home Fashions LLC .... D 908 363-1100
  New Providence *(G-7019)*

▲ Tatara Group Inc .... G 732 231-6031
  Avenel *(G-149)*

▲ Triangle Home Fashions LLC ..... G 732 355-9800
  East Brunswick *(G-2187)*

United Bedding Industries LLC ..... E 908 668-0220
  Plainfield *(G-8779)*

White Lotus Home Ltd Lblty Co ..... F 732 828-2111
  New Brunswick *(G-6981)*

2393 Textile Bags

▲ A D M Corporation .... D 732 469-0900
  Middlesex *(G-6090)*

Ace Bag & Burlap Company Inc ..... F 973 242-2200
  Newark *(G-7034)*

American Dawn Inc .... G 856 467-9211
  Bridgeport *(G-734)*

▲ AMS Products LLC .... F 973 442-5790
  Wharton *(G-11850)*

▲ Elements Accessories Inc .... G 646 801-5187
  Maplewood *(G-5876)*

◆ Halsted Corporation .... E 201 333-0670
  Cranbury *(G-1838)*

◆ Kt America Corp .... F 609 655-5333
  Cranbury *(G-1853)*

▲ Lbu Inc .... E 973 773-4800
  Paterson *(G-8238)*

▲ Nyp Corp (frmr Ny-Pters Corp) ... D 908 351-6550
  Elizabeth *(G-2763)*

Philip Papalia .... F 732 349-5530
  Toms River *(G-10783)*

Shaffer Products Inc .... E 908 206-1980
  Union *(G-11090)*

2394 Canvas Prdts

Awning Design Inc .... G 908 462-1131
  Freehold *(G-3651)*

Beachwood Canvas Works LLC .... F 732 929-1783
  Island Heights *(G-4637)*

Blacher Canvas Products Inc .... G 732 968-3666
  Dunellen *(G-2121)*

▲ Canvas Creations .... G 609 465-8428
  Cape May Court House *(G-1108)*

Colie Sail Makers Inc .... G 732 892-4344
  Point Pleasant Boro *(G-8840)*

Costa Mar Cnvas Enclosures LLC ... E 609 965-1538
  Egg Harbor City *(G-2656)*

Fisher Canvas Products Inc .... G 609 239-2733
  Burlington *(G-967)*

G & J Solutions Inc .... F 609 861-9838
  Woodbine *(G-12009)*

Harold F Fisher & Sons Inc .... G 800 624-2868
  Cinnaminson *(G-1462)*

Howard Lippincott .... G 856 764-8282
  Riverside *(G-9396)*

Hudson Awning Co Inc .... E 201 339-7171
  Bayonne *(G-223)*

▼ Kerry Wilkens Inc .... G 732 787-0070
  Belford *(G-283)*

Linthicum Sails .... G 856 783-4288
  Somerdale *(G-9932)*

Lion Visual Ltd Liability Co ...... G 973 278-3802
  Fairfield *(G-3264)*

Lloyds of Millville Inc .... G 856 825-0345
  Millville *(G-6259)*

▼ Meese Inc .... F 201 796-4490
  Saddle Brook *(G-9661)*

North Sales .... G 732 528-8899
  Sea Girt *(G-9746)*

Opdyke Awnings Inc .... F 732 449-5940
  Wall Township *(G-11360)*

Polyair Inter Pack Inc .... D 201 804-1700
  Carlstadt *(G-1204)*

Pv Deroche LLC .... G 908 475-2266
  Belvidere *(G-365)*

Revere Plastics Inc .... G 201 641-0777
  Little Ferry *(G-5494)*

Robert Brown .... G 609 398-6262
  Ocean City *(G-7694)*

Sconda Canvas Products .... E 732 225-3500
  South Plainfield *(G-10326)*

Shore Awning Co .... G 732 775-3351
  Wall Township *(G-11369)*

Superior Marine Canvas .... G 856 241-1724
  Swedesboro *(G-10612)*

Texas Canvas Co Inc .... G 973 278-3802
  Fairfield *(G-3326)*

▲ William Opdyke Awnings Inc ..... G 732 449-5940
  Wall Township *(G-11378)*

2395 Pleating & Stitching For The Trade

A Stitch Ahead .... F 609 586-1068
  Lawrenceville *(G-5221)*

Advantage Ds LLC .... F 856 307-9600
  Glassboro *(G-3806)*

Ambro Manufacturing Inc .... F 908 806-8337
  Flemington *(G-3429)*

Apollo East LLC .... E 856 486-1882
  Pennsauken *(G-8389)*

Arts Embroidery LLC .... G 732 870-2400
  West Long Branch *(G-11719)*

◆ Avanti Linens Inc .... C 201 641-7766
  Moonachie *(G-6455)*

Aztec Graphics Inc .... F 609 587-1000
  Trenton *(G-10900)*

Bauer Sport Shop .... G 201 384-6522
  Dumont *(G-2111)*

Bon-Jour Group LLC .... F 201 646-1070
  Norwood *(G-7558)*

C & D Sales .... G 609 383-9292
  Pleasantville *(G-8806)*

▲ Carolace Embroidery Co Inc ..... D 201 945-2151
  Ridgefield *(G-9253)*

CDK Industries LLC .... G 856 488-5456
  Cherry Hill *(G-1352)*

▲ Central Safety Equipment Co ..... E 609 386-6448
  Burlington *(G-958)*

Chenille Products Inc .... E 201 703-1917
  Palisades Park *(G-7771)*

Cozy Formal Wear Inc .... G 973 661-9781
  Nutley *(G-7583)*

Creative Embroidery Corp .... E 973 497-5700
  Newark *(G-7091)*

Design N Stitch Inc ....G ... 201 488-1314
Hackensack *(G-3906)*

Dezine Line Inc ....F ... 973 989-1009
Wharton *(G-11856)*

E B R Manufacturing Inc ....E ... 973 263-8810
Parsippany *(G-7924)*

Embroideries Unlimited Inc ....G ... 201 692-1560
Teaneck *(G-10630)*

Embroidery In Stitches Inc ....F ... 732 460-2660
Morganville *(G-6586)*

Family Screen Printing Inc ....F ... 856 933-2780
Bellmawr *(G-332)*

▲ Faraj Inc ....D ... 201 313-4480
Paterson *(G-8191)*

Gilbert Storms Jr ....G ... 973 835-5729
Haskell *(G-4196)*

Golden Rule Creations Inc ....G ... 201 337-4050
Franklin Lakes *(G-3625)*

Goralski Inc ....E ... 201 573-1529
Park Ridge *(G-7851)*

Imagery Embroidary Corporation .....F ... 201 343-9333
Union City *(G-11113)*

▲ Innovative Design Inc ....G ... 201 227-2555
Cresskill *(G-1943)*

Its The Pitts Inc ....G ... 609 645-7319
Pleasantville *(G-8813)*

J & S Finishing Inc ....G ... 201 854-0338
West New York *(G-11742)*

J & T Embroidery Inc ....G ... 201 867-4897
Union City *(G-11114)*

J and S Sporting Apparel LLC ....G ... 732 787-5500
Keansburg *(G-4838)*

Mary Bridget Enterprises ....E ... 609 267-4830
Cinnaminson *(G-1471)*

Midland Screen Printing Inc ....F ... 201 703-0066
Saddle Brook *(G-9662)*

Monogram Center Inc ....E ... 732 442-1800
Perth Amboy *(G-8528)*

Mt Embroidery & Promotions LLC ....G ... 201 646-1070
Norwood *(G-7569)*

NJ Logo Wear LLC ....G ... 609 597-9400
Manahawkin *(G-5794)*

O Stitch Matic Inc ....G ... 201 861-3045
Guttenberg *(G-3871)*

Patchworks Co Inc ....G ... 973 627-2002
Dover *(G-2103)*

Peach Boutique LLC ....G ... 908 351-0739
Elizabeth *(G-2768)*

Pioneer Embroidery Co ....G ... 973 777-6418
South Hackensack *(G-10181)*

Pro Image Promotions Inc ....G ... 973 252-8000
Kenvil *(G-4995)*

Quadelle Textile Corp ....F ... 201 865-1112
West New York *(G-11752)*

Red Diamond Co - Athc Letering ......G ... 973 759-2005
Belleville *(G-310)*

Risse & Risse Graphics Inc ....E ... 856 751-7671
Runnemede *(G-9608)*

Semels Embroidery Inc ....F ... 973 473-6868
Clifton *(G-1713)*

Sequins of Distinction Inc ....G ... 201 348-8111
North Bergen *(G-7437)*

Sgh Inc ....G ... 609 698-8868
Barnegat *(G-161)*

Sniderman John ....F ... 201 569-5482
Englewood *(G-2942)*

South Amboy Designer T Shirt L ......G ... 732 456-2594
South Amboy *(G-10141)*

▲ Star Embroidery Corp ....E ... 973 481-4300
Newark *(G-7285)*

▲ Tone Embroidery Corp ....E ... 201 943-1082
Fairview *(G-3371)*

Toni Embroidery ....G ... 201 664-6909
Park Ridge *(G-7860)*

Uniport Industries Corporation ....G ... 201 391-6422
Woodcliff Lake *(G-12067)*

Unique Embroidery Inc ....F ... 201 943-9191
Elmwood Park *(G-2859)*

University Fashions By Janet ....G ... 856 228-1615
Williamstown *(G-11983)*

Walker Eight Corp ....G ... 201 861-4208
North Bergen *(G-7443)*

Wally Enterprises Inc ....F ... 732 329-2613
Monmouth Junction *(G-6319)*

William Cromley ....G ... 856 881-6019
Clayton *(G-1530)*

World Class Marketing Corp ....E ... 201 313-0022
Fort Lee *(G-3595)*

Wostbrock Embroidery Inc ....G ... 201 445-3074
Midland Park *(G-6191)*

2396 Automotive Trimmings, Apparel Findings, Related Prdts

A S A P Nameplate & Labeling ....F ... 973 773-3934
Passaic *(G-8048)*

Acey Industries Inc ....G ... 973 595-1222
North Haledon *(G-7494)*

Alchemy Billboards LLC ....E ... 973 977-8828
Paterson *(G-8131)*

Alco Trimming ....G ... 201 854-8608
North Bergen *(G-7380)*

Ambro Manufacturing Inc ....F ... 908 806-8337
Flemington *(G-3429)*

Amcor Phrm Packg USA Inc ....C ... 856 728-9300
Williamstown *(G-11950)*

Art Flag Co Inc ....F ... 212 334-1890
Fair Haven *(G-3078)*

▲ Artistic Bias Products Co Inc ....E ... 732 382-4141
Rahway *(G-9078)*

▲ Associated Fabrics Corporation ...E ... 201 300-6053
Fair Lawn *(G-3086)*

Aztec Graphics Inc ....F ... 609 587-1000
Trenton *(G-10900)*

Budget Print Center ....G ... 973 743-0073
Bloomfield *(G-492)*

C Q Corporation ....F ... 201 935-8488
East Rutherford *(G-2281)*

C S Hot Stamping ....G ... 201 840-4004
Edgewater *(G-2435)*

◆ Circle Visual Inc ....E ... 212 719-5153
Carlstadt *(G-1139)*

Clarici Graphics Inc ....E ... 609 587-7204
Trenton *(G-10917)*

▲ Colonial - Bende Ribbons Inc ....G ... 973 777-8700
Passaic *(G-8056)*

Color Comp Inc ....G ... 856 262-3040
Williamstown *(G-11954)*

Cox Stationers and Printers ....E ... 908 928-1010
Linden *(G-5338)*

Creative Embroidery Corp ....E ... 973 497-5700
Newark *(G-7091)*

Custom Graphics of Vineland ....E ... 856 691-7858
Vineland *(G-11209)*

▲ Custom Laminations Inc ....E ... 973 279-9174
Paterson *(G-8166)*

Designs By James ....G ... 856 692-1316
Vineland *(G-11213)*

▲ Donray Printing Inc ....E ... 973 515-8100
Parsippany *(G-7918)*

Family Screen Printing Inc ....F ... 856 933-2780
Bellmawr *(G-332)*

French Textile Co Inc ....F ... 973 471-5000
Clifton *(G-1622)*

◆ Green Distribution LLC ....D ... 201 293-4381
Secaucus *(G-9779)*

Image Point ....G ... 908 684-1768
Newton *(G-7346)*

▲ Jrm Industries Inc ....E ... 973 779-9340
Passaic *(G-8077)*

Klein Ribbon Corp ....E ... 973 684-4671
Paterson *(G-8230)*

Lukoil N Arlington Ltd Lblty ....E ... 856 722-6425
Moorestown *(G-6543)*

Mail Direct Paper Company LLC ....F ... 201 933-2782
Lyndhurst *(G-5660)*

Mar-Kal Products Corp ....F ... 973 783-7155
Carlstadt *(G-1185)*

McLain Studios Inc ....G ... 732 775-0271
Asbury Park *(G-80)*

Monogram Center Inc ....E ... 732 442-1800
Perth Amboy *(G-8528)*

Nes Enterprises Inc ....G ... 201 964-1400
Carlstadt *(G-1190)*

Newark Auto Top Co Inc ....F ... 973 677-9935
East Orange *(G-2256)*

Painting Inc ....F ... 201 489-6565
South Hackensack *(G-10179)*

▲ Papillon Ribbon & Bow Inc ....E ... 973 928-6128
Clifton *(G-1683)*

◆ Phoenix Glass LLC ....E ... 856 692-0100
Pittsgrove *(G-8750)*

Premier Ribbon Company ....G ... 973 589-2600
Newark *(G-7233)*

Quick Bias Bnding Trmming Inds ......F ... 732 422-0123
North Brunswick *(G-7484)*

R & B Printing Inc ....G ... 908 766-4073
Bernardsville *(G-443)*

Red Diamond Co - Athc Letering ......G ... 973 759-2005
Belleville *(G-310)*

Rutler Screen Printing Inc ....F ... 908 859-3327
Phillipsburg *(G-8573)*

Safer Textile Processing Corp ....B ... 973 482-6400
Newark *(G-7260)*

Scher Fabrics Inc ....F ... 212 382-2266
Freehold *(G-3699)*

Screened Images Inc ....E ... 732 651-8181
East Brunswick *(G-2175)*

Semels Embroidery Inc ....F ... 973 473-6868
Clifton *(G-1713)*

Sniderman John ....F ... 201 569-5482
Englewood *(G-2942)*

▲ Stefan Enterprises Inc ....E ... 973 253-6005
Garfield *(G-3770)*

▲ Stone Graphics ....F ... 732 919-1111
Wall Township *(G-11371)*

Suzie Mac Specialties Inc ....E ... 732 238-3500
East Brunswick *(G-2184)*

Toppan Printing Co Amer Inc ....C ... 732 469-8400
Somerset *(G-10088)*

Total Ink Solutions LLC ....F ... 201 487-9600
Hackensack *(G-3983)*

◆ U S Screening Corp ....C ... 973 242-1110
Newark *(G-7305)*

Unique Screen Printing Corp ....E ... 908 925-3773
Linden *(G-5438)*

Wally Enterprises Inc ....F ... 732 329-2613
Monmouth Junction *(G-6319)*

Z Line Beachwear ....G ... 732 793-1234
Lavallette *(G-5213)*

Zone Two Inc ....F ... 732 237-0766
Bayville *(G-254)*

2397 Schiffli Machine Embroideries

▲ Carolace Embroidery Co Inc ....D ... 201 945-2151
Ridgefield *(G-9253)*

Chenille Products Inc ....F ... 201 703-1917
Palisades Park *(G-7771)*

Embroidery Concepts ....G ... 973 942-8555
Paterson *(G-8182)*

Eyelet Embroideries Inc ....D ... 201 945-2151
Ridgefield *(G-9260)*

Goralski Inc ....E ... 201 573-1529
Park Ridge *(G-7851)*

▲ Hamilton Embroidery Co Inc ....F ... 201 867-4084
Union City *(G-11112)*

Jacqueline Embroidery Co ....G ... 732 278-8121
Hackensack *(G-3933)*

John M Sniderman Inc ....G ... 201 450-4291
Fairview *(G-3361)*

Marlene Embroidery Inc ....E ... 201 868-1682
West New York *(G-11747)*

O Stitch Matic Inc ....G ... 201 861-3045
Guttenberg *(G-3871)*

Quadelle Textile Corp ....F ... 201 865-1112
West New York *(G-11752)*

▲ Tone Embroidery Corp ....E ... 201 943-1082
Fairview *(G-3371)*

Tri-Chem Inc ....F ... 973 751-9200
Belleville *(G-317)*

Weber & Doebrich Inc ....E ... 201 868-6122
West New York *(G-11756)*

2399 Fabricated Textile Prdts, NEC

◆ Air Cruisers Company LLC ....B ... 732 681-3527
Wall Township *(G-11315)*

▼ Airborne Systems N Amer NJ Inc ..C ... 856 663-1275
Pennsauken *(G-8386)*

▲ Annin & Co ....E ... 973 228-9400
Roseland *(G-9532)*

Art Flag Co Inc ....F ... 212 334-1890
Fair Haven *(G-3078)*

Atlas Auto Trim Inc ....G ... 732 985-6800
Edison *(G-2463)*

▲ Bearhands Ltd ....G ... 201 807-9898
Passaic *(G-8053)*

▲ Belting Industries Group LLC ....E ... 908 272-8591
Union *(G-11031)*

▲ Bright Ideas Usa LLC ....G ... 732 886-8865
Lakewood *(G-5066)*

Clothes Horse International ....F ... 856 829-8460
Cinnaminson *(G-1446)*

Colorcraft Sign Co ....F ... 609 386-1115
Beverly *(G-1115)*

Covalnce Spcialty Coatings LLC ....D ... 732 356-2870
Middlesex *(G-6109)*

▲ Curvon Corporation ....E ... 732 747-3832
Tinton Falls *(G-10710)*

Horsetracs ....G ... 732 228-7646
West Creek *(G-11687)*

▲ Mek International Inc ....G ... 215 712-2490
Woodcliff Lake *(G-12059)*

National Flag & Display Co Inc ....E 973 366-1776
  Wharton *(G-11863)*

▲ Northcott Silk USA Inc ....G....... 201 672-9600
  Lyndhurst *(G-5667)*

Patchworks Co Inc ....G....... 973 627-2002
  Dover *(G-2103)*

Rose Brand Wipers Inc ....C....... 201 770-1441
  Secaucus *(G-9805)*

▲ Rose Brand Wipers Inc ....C....... 201 809-1730
  Secaucus *(G-9804)*

Sterling Net & Twine Co Inc ....F 973 783-9800
  Montclair *(G-6390)*

Stewart-Morris Inc ....G....... 973 822-2777
  Madison *(G-5703)*

Switlik Parachute Company Inc......F 609 587-3300
  Trenton *(G-10994)*

Tri G Manufacturing LLC ....F 732 460-1881
  Colts Neck *(G-1789)*

Tuff Mutters LLC ....G....... 973 291-6679
  Kinnelon *(G-5022)*

▲ Union Hill Corp ....G....... 732 786-9422
  Englishtown *(G-3010)*

◆ Weatherbeeta USA Inc ....G....... 732 287-1182
  Edison *(G-2646)*

Yoland Corporation ....E 862 257-9036
  Paterson *(G-8324)*

24 LUMBER AND WOOD PRODUCTS, EXCEPT FURNITURE

2411 Logging

▲ Bamboo & Rattan Works Inc.......G....... 732 255-4239
  Toms River *(G-10746)*

Green Land & Logging LLC ....G....... 908 894-2361
  Stockton *(G-10501)*

Kane Wood Fuel ....G....... 856 589-3292
  Pitman *(G-8746)*

Mountain Top Logging LLC ....G....... 908 413-2982
  Lebanon *(G-5272)*

New Jersey Fence & Guardrail ....F 973 786-5400
  Andover *(G-50)*

Railing Dynamics Inc ....F 609 593-5400
  Millville *(G-6267)*

2421 Saw & Planing Mills

Dolan & Traynor Inc ....E 973 696-8700
  Wayne *(G-11495)*

Empire Lumber & Millwork Co.........E 973 242-2700
  Newark *(G-7115)*

John H Abbott Inc ....G....... 609 561-0303
  Egg Harbor City *(G-2662)*

Landew Sawdust Co Inc ....F 973 344-5255
  Newark *(G-7177)*

Logpowercom LLC ....G....... 732 350-9663
  Whiting *(G-11940)*

Mellon D P M L L C ....G....... 732 563-0030
  Somerset *(G-10029)*

P J Murphy Forest Pdts Corp ....G....... 973 316-0800
  Montville *(G-6445)*

Rex Lumber Company ....D....... 732 446-4200
  Manalapan *(G-5824)*

Riephoff Saw Mill Inc ....F 609 259-7265
  Allentown *(G-30)*

Sawdust Depot LLC ....F 973 344-5255
  Howell *(G-4550)*

Schairer Brothers ....G....... 609 965-0996
  Egg Harbor City *(G-2667)*

Thomas Cobb & Sons...................G....... 856 451-0671
  Bridgeton *(G-775)*

Ufp Berlin LLC ....C....... 856 767-0596
  Berlin *(G-431)*

2426 Hardwood Dimension & Flooring Mills

Airborne Systems N Amer Inc ....G....... 856 663-1275
  Pennsauken *(G-8385)*

Alpine Custom Floors....................F 201 533-0100
  Jersey City *(G-4689)*

Atlantic Flooring LLC ....F 609 296-7700
  Ltl Egg Hbr *(G-5614)*

Flooring Concepts Nj LLC ....F 732 409-7600
  Manalapan *(G-5811)*

Friends Hardwood Floors Inc ....G....... 732 859-4019
  Oakhurst *(G-7609)*

Gwynn-E Co..............................G....... 215 423-6400
  Moorestown *(G-6525)*

2431 Millwork

Abatetech Inc ....E 609 265-2107
  Lumberton *(G-5622)*

ABC Holdings Inc ....F 856 219-3444
  Westville *(G-11809)*

Adhisa Molding ....G....... 862 324-5222
  West Caldwell *(G-11636)*

All Merchandise Display Corp ....E 718 257-2221
  Hillside *(G-4372)*

▲ All Seasons Door & Window Inc....E 732 238-7100
  East Brunswick *(G-2124)*

Alvaro Stairs LLC ....G....... 201 864-6754
  North Bergen *(G-7383)*

AM Wood Inc ....F 732 246-1506
  East Brunswick *(G-2126)*

Architctral Cbinetry Mllwk LLC ....G....... 908 213-2001
  Phillipsburg *(G-8541)*

Architectural Wdwkg Assoc ....G....... 908 996-7866
  Frenchtown *(G-3708)*

◆ Artistic Doors and Windows Inc ...E 732 726-9400
  Avenel *(G-121)*

B & B Millwork & Doors Inc...........G....... 973 249-0300
  Kenilworth *(G-4924)*

B & C Custom WD Handrail Corp ....G....... 732 530-6640
  Red Bank *(G-9222)*

Bell arte Inc ....F 908 355-1199
  Elizabeth *(G-2715)*

Bestmark National LLC ....E 862 772-4863
  Irvington *(G-4561)*

Bildisco Mfg Inc ....F 973 673-2400
  West Orange *(G-11762)*

Bon Architectual Mill Work LLC ....G....... 856 320-2872
  Pennsauken *(G-8397)*

Cabinet Tronics Inc ....F 609 267-2625
  Birmingham *(G-455)*

Castle Woodcraft Assoc LLC ....F 732 349-1519
  Pine Beach *(G-8582)*

Caw LLC ....F 973 429-7004
  Bloomfield *(G-495)*

Cerami Wood Products Inc ....F 732 968-7222
  Piscataway *(G-8645)*

Classic Designer Woodwork Inc ......G....... 201 280-3711
  Glen Rock *(G-3829)*

Clear Cut Window Distrs of NJ ....G....... 201 512-1804
  Mahwah *(G-5723)*

▼ Clems Ornemental Iron Works ......D....... 732 968-7200
  Piscataway *(G-8647)*

Cozzolino Furniture Design Inc ....E 973 731-9292
  West Orange *(G-11764)*

Creative Concepts of NJ LLC ....G....... 732 833-1776
  Jackson *(G-4645)*

Creative Wood Products Inc ....F 732 370-0051
  Jackson *(G-4646)*

Crincoli Woodwork Co Inc ....F 908 352-9332
  Elizabeth *(G-2724)*

Custom Barres LLC ....G....... 848 245-9464
  Jackson *(G-4647)*

Custom Counters By Precision ....E 973 773-0111
  Passaic *(G-8058)*

Cwi Architectural Millwork LLC ....G....... 856 307-7900
  Glassboro *(G-3808)*

▲ Design of Tomorrow Inc ....F 973 227-1000
  Fairfield *(G-3185)*

▲ Designcore Ltd ....D....... 718 499-0337
  Secaucus *(G-9761)*

DMD Stairs & Rails LLC.................G....... 732 901-0102
  Jackson *(G-4651)*

▲ Donnelly Industries Inc ....G....... 973 672-1800
  Wayne *(G-11496)*

Door Stop LLC ....F 718 599-5112
  Carlstadt *(G-1153)*

Dor-Win Manufacturing Co ....E 201 796-4300
  Elmwood Park *(G-2821)*

Dreamstar Construction LLC ....F 732 393-2572
  Middletown *(G-6162)*

Empire Lumber & Millwork Co ....E 973 242-2700
  Newark *(G-7115)*

Epic Millwork LLC ....E 732 296-0273
  Somerset *(G-9988)*

Evertlast Interiors ....G....... 732 252-9965
  Manalapan *(G-5808)*

F L Feldman Associates ....F 732 776-8544
  Asbury Park *(G-76)*

▲ F T Millwork Inc ....G....... 732 741-1216
  Red Bank *(G-9229)*

Gass Custom Woodworking ....G....... 201 493-9282
  Paramus *(G-7802)*

Glen Rock Stair Corp....................E 201 337-9595
  Franklin Lakes *(G-3624)*

Greenbrook Stairs Inc ....G....... 908 221-9145
  Bernardsville *(G-438)*

Hahns Woodworking ....F 908 722-2742
  Branchburg *(G-645)*

Heard Woodworking LLC ....G....... 908 232-3978
  Westfield *(G-11800)*

Hutchinson Cabinets ....E 856 468-5500
  Sewell *(G-9845)*

Iacovelli Stairs Incorporated ....F 609 693-3476
  Forked River *(G-3540)*

▲ Ideal Jacobs Corporation ....E 973 275-5100
  Maplewood *(G-5879)*

▼ Infinite Mfg Group Inc ....E 973 649-9950
  Kearny *(G-4868)*

Intex Millwork Solutions LLC ....E 856 293-4100
  Mays Landing *(G-5994)*

Jarahian Millwork Inc....................G....... 732 240-5151
  Whiting *(G-11939)*

Joffe Lumber & Supply Co Inc ....D....... 856 825-9550
  Vineland *(G-11238)*

Joseph Naticchia ....F 609 882-7709
  Ewing *(G-3039)*

K2 Millwork Ltd Liability Co ....G....... 609 379-6411
  Columbus *(G-1801)*

Katadin Inc ....G....... 908 526-0166
  Branchburg *(G-651)*

Kaufman Stairs Inc ....E 908 862-3579
  Rahway *(G-9111)*

Kempton Wood Products ....G....... 732 449-8673
  Wall Township *(G-11352)*

Lauderdale Millwork Inc ....F 908 508-9550
  Berkeley Heights *(G-406)*

Lees Woodworking Inc ....G....... 732 681-1002
  Neptune *(G-6888)*

Lukach Interiors Inc ....F 973 777-1499
  Clifton *(G-1662)*

Lux Home Inc ....G....... 845 623-2821
  Paramus *(G-7817)*

M K Woodworking Inc ....G....... 609 771-1350
  Ewing *(G-3044)*

M R C Millwork & Trim Inc ....G....... 201 954-2176
  Franklin Lakes *(G-3627)*

Manhattan Door Corp ....D....... 718 963-1111
  Carlstadt *(G-1184)*

Maranatha Ceramic Tile & Marbl ......E 609 758-1168
  Wrightstown *(G-12099)*

Marty Anderson & Assoc Inc ....G....... 201 798-0507
  North Bergen *(G-7419)*

Metro Railings LLC ....G....... 877 504-8300
  Warren *(G-11422)*

Midhattan Woodworking Corp ....E 732 727-3020
  Old Bridge *(G-7720)*

Midlantic Shutter & Milwork ....G....... 908 806-3400
  Flemington *(G-3457)*

ML Woodwork Inc ....G....... 201 953-2175
  Paramus *(G-7821)*

Mountain Millwork ....G....... 908 647-1100
  Warren *(G-11424)*

Mp Custom FL LLC ....F 973 417-2288
  Wayne *(G-11535)*

National Woodworking Co ....G....... 908 851-9316
  Union *(G-11079)*

New Jersey Hardwoods Inc ....E 908 754-0990
  Plainfield *(G-8773)*

Nyc Woodworking Inc ....G....... 718 222-1221
  Marlboro *(G-5907)*

Ornate Millwork LLC ....G....... 866 464-5596
  Lakewood *(G-5144)*

Palumbo Millwork Inc ....G....... 732 938-3266
  Wall Township *(G-11361)*

Patella Construction Corp ....D....... 973 916-0100
  Passaic *(G-8094)*

Pkc Finewoodworking LLC ....G....... 201 951-8880
  Towaco *(G-10877)*

Precision Dealer Services Inc ....E 908 237-1100
  Flemington *(G-3461)*

▲ Prestige Millwork LLC ....E 908 526-5100
  Bridgewater *(G-868)*

Progress Woodwork ....G....... 732 906-8680
  Edison *(G-2593)*

▲ R & M Manufacturing Inc ....E 609 495-8032
  Monroe Township *(G-6341)*

▲ Randall Mfg Co Inc ....E 973 482-8603
  Newark *(G-7245)*

Random 8 Woodworks LLC ....G....... 856 417-3329
  Mullica Hill *(G-6857)*

Random 8 Woodworks LLC ....G....... 856 364-7627
  Pedricktown *(G-8354)*

Rex Lumber Company ....D....... 732 446-4200
  Manalapan *(G-5824)*

Rock Solid Woodworking LLC ....G 732 974-1261
 Sea Girt (G-9747)
Royal Oak Railings LLC ....G 973 208-8900
 Oak Ridge (G-7605)
▲ RPI Industries Inc ....D 609 714-2330
 Medford (G-6033)
▲ Rsl LLC ....D 609 484-1600
 Egg Harbor Township (G-2695)
Rsl LLC ....E 609 645-9777
 Egg Harbor Township (G-2696)
Salernos Kitchen Cabinets ....E 201 794-1990
 Saddle Brook (G-9676)
Screens Incorporated ....G 973 633-8558
 Wayne (G-11553)
Skyline Windows LLC ....E 201 531-9600
 Wood Ridge (G-12005)
Smittys Door Service Inc ....G 908 284-0506
 Pittstown (G-8755)
Somerset Wood Products Co ....E 908 526-0030
 Raritan (G-9218)
Sourland Mountain Wdwkg LLC T ....G 908 806-7661
 Neshanic Station (G-6905)
Stairworks Inc ....G 908 276-2829
 Cranford (G-1927)
Summit Millwork & Supply Inc ....G 908 273-1486
 Summit (G-10550)
Tea Elle Woodworks ....G 732 938-9660
 Farmingdale (G-3394)
Terhune Bros Woodworking ....G 973 962-6686
 Ringwood (G-9354)
Total Garage Solutions LLC ....E 732 749-3993
 Wall Township (G-11375)
▲ Trim and Tassels LLC ....G 973 808-1566
 Fairfield (G-3333)
Trim Factory Inc ....G 856 769-8746
 Pilesgrove (G-8581)
Urban Millwork & Supply Corp ....G 973 278-7072
 Paterson (G-8321)
USA Wood Door Inc ....E 856 384-9663
 West Deptford (G-11717)
V Custom Millwork Inc ....F 732 469-9600
 Bridgewater (G-901)
Vanco Millwork Inc ....F 973 992-3061
 Livingston (G-5545)
Vigor Inc ....G 973 851-9539
 Totowa (G-10859)
Visual Architectural Designs ....F 908 754-3000
 South Plainfield (G-10342)
W F Sherman & Son Inc ....F 732 223-1505
 Manasquan (G-5842)
West Hudson Lumber & Mllwk Co ....G 201 991-7191
 Kearny (G-4904)
Window Factory Inc ....E 856 546-5050
 Mount Ephraim (G-6722)
Window Trends ....G 973 887-6676
 Parsippany (G-8039)
▲ Wohners ....G 201 568-7307
 Englewood (G-2954)
Wood Products Inc ....G 609 859-0303
 Southampton (G-10374)
Wood Works ....G 856 728-4520
 Williamstown (G-11987)
▲ Woodhaven Lumber & Millwork ....C 732 901-0030
 Lakewood (G-5182)
Woodhaven Lumber & Millwork ....E 732 295-8800
 Point Pleasant Beach (G-8833)
▲ Woodshop Inc ....G 732 349-8006
 Toms River (G-10805)
Woodtec Inc ....G 908 979-0180
 Hackettstown (G-4041)
Zone Defense Inc ....F 973 328-0436
 Hackettstown (G-4042)

2434 Wood Kitchen Cabinets

▲ 10-31 Incorporated ....E 908 496-4946
 Columbia (G-1791)
A & J Carpets Inc ....G 856 227-1753
 Blackwood (G-458)
A R Bothers Woodworking Inc ....E 908 725-2891
 Somerville (G-10099)
A W Ross Inc ....F 973 471-5900
 Passaic (G-8049)
Alkon Signature Inc ....G 917 716-9137
 Linden (G-5319)
Allen Cabinets and Millwork ....G 973 694-0665
 Pequannock (G-8503)
◆ Bcg Marble Gran Fabricators Co ....F 201 343-8487
 Hackensack (G-3882)
Bebus Cabinetry LLC ....G 201 729-9300
 Rutherford (G-9615)

Bennett Cabinets ....G 732 548-1616
 Edison (G-2467)
Bernard Miller Fabricators ....G 856 541-9499
 Camden (G-1041)
Capra Custom Cabinetry ....G 908 797-9848
 Washington (G-11444)
Castle Woodcraft Assoc LLC ....F 732 349-1519
 Pine Beach (G-8582)
Certified Cabinet Corp ....G 732 741-0755
 Marlboro (G-5893)
▲ Choice Cabinetry LLC ....G 908 707-8801
 Somerville (G-10106)
CPB Inc ....E 856 697-2700
 Buena (G-939)
Custom Cabinets By Jim Bucko ....G 609 522-6646
 Wildwood (G-11943)
Custom Wood Furniture Inc ....F 973 579-4880
 Newton (G-7340)
David Leiz Custom Woodwork ....G 908 486-1533
 Linden (G-5342)
Designer Kitchens ....G 732 370-5500
 Jackson (G-4650)
Dream Cabinetry ....G 732 806-8444
 Lakewood (G-5086)
Elite Cabinetry Corp ....G 973 583-0194
 Newark (G-7114)
▲ Empire Industries Inc ....D 973 279-2050
 Paterson (G-8183)
Eppley Building & Design Inc ....E 973 636-9499
 Hawthorne (G-4217)
F L Feldman Associates ....F 732 776-8544
 Asbury Park (G-76)
◆ Fabuwood Cabinetry Corp ....A 201 432-6555
 Newark (G-7121)
Fernandes Custom Cabinets ....G 732 446-2829
 Manalapan (G-5810)
Foley-Waite Associates Inc ....F 908 298-0700
 Kenilworth (G-4941)
Forman Industries Inc ....D 732 727-8100
 Old Bridge (G-7715)
Frank Burton & Sons Inc ....G 856 455-1202
 Bridgeton (G-758)
Franks Cabinet Shop Inc ....G 908 658-4396
 Pluckemin (G-8822)
G & M Custom Formica Work ....G 732 888-0360
 Keyport (G-5000)
Gemcraft Inc ....G 732 449-8944
 Belmar (G-349)
Hanssem ....G 732 425-7695
 Edison (G-2527)
Hutchinson Cabinets ....E 856 468-5500
 Sewell (G-9845)
Ideal Kitchens Inc ....F 732 295-2780
 Point Pleasant Beach (G-8824)
Intelco ....E 856 384-8562
 Paulsboro (G-8332)
J & R Custom Woodworking Inc ....G 973 625-4114
 Denville (G-2041)
John Canary Custom Wdwkg Inc ....F 908 851-2894
 Union (G-11067)
▲ Kasanova Inc ....G 201 368-8400
 Wood Ridge (G-12003)
Ken Bauer Inc ....E 201 664-6881
 Hillsdale (G-4368)
Kenneth Asmar Custom Interiors ....G 732 544-6137
 Tinton Falls (G-10721)
Kerk Cabinetry LLC ....G 856 881-4213
 Glassboro (G-3813)
Kinzee Industries Inc ....F 201 408-4301
 Englewood (G-2916)
Kitchen and More Inc ....F 908 272-3388
 Cranford (G-1914)
Kitchen Crafters Plus ....G 732 566-7995
 Matawan (G-5979)
Kitchen Direct Inc ....G 908 359-1188
 Hillsborough (G-4337)
Kitchen King Inc ....F 732 341-9660
 Toms River (G-10772)
Kobolak & Son Inc ....G 856 829-6106
 Cinnaminson (G-1468)
L&W Audio/Video Inc ....G 212 980-2862
 Hoboken (G-4463)
Lexora Inc ....G 855 453-9672
 Newark (G-7179)
M C M Custom Furniture Inc ....G 908 523-1666
 Linden (G-5378)
M K Woodworking Inc ....G 609 771-1350
 Ewing (G-3044)
Marte Cabinets Countertops LLC ....G 973 525-9502
 Passaic (G-8085)

Masterpiece Kitchens Inc ....G 609 518-7887
 Cherry Hill (G-1390)
Merlyn Cabinetry LLC ....G 908 583-6950
 Linden (G-5382)
Michael Lubrich ....G 732 223-4235
 Manasquan (G-5834)
Michaels Cabinet Connection ....G 609 889-6611
 Rio Grande (G-9356)
Millner Kitchens Inc ....G 609 890-7300
 Hamilton (G-4117)
▲ Mk Wood Inc ....G 973 450-5110
 Belleville (G-302)
Mp Custom FL LLC ....F 973 417-2288
 Wayne (G-11535)
▲ Mr Pauls Custom Cabinets ....G 732 528-9427
 Manasquan (G-5835)
Oberg & Lindquist Corp ....E 201 664-1300
 Westwood (G-11836)
Palumbo Millwork Inc ....G 732 938-3266
 Wall Township (G-11361)
Parsons Cabinets Inc ....G 973 279-4954
 Montclair (G-6383)
Paul Burkhardt & Sons Inc ....G 856 435-2020
 Lindenwold (G-5445)
Paul Fago Cabinet Making Inc ....G 856 384-0496
 Woodbury (G-12035)
Platinum Designs LLC ....G 908 782-4010
 Flemington (G-3459)
▲ Platon Interiors ....G 201 567-5533
 Englewood (G-2932)
▲ R & M Manufacturing Inc ....E 609 495-8032
 Monroe Township (G-6341)
Regency Cabinetry LLC ....G 732 363-5630
 Lakewood (G-5152)
▲ Regency Cabinetry LLC ....F 732 363-5630
 Lakewood (G-5153)
▲ Regent Cabinets LLC ....F 732 363-5630
 Parsippany (G-8006)
Royal Cabinet Company Inc ....E 908 203-8000
 Bound Brook (G-605)
Salernos Kitchen Cabinets ....E 201 794-1990
 Saddle Brook (G-9676)
Sandkamp Woodworks LLC ....G 201 200-0101
 Jersey City (G-4804)
Shearman Cabinets ....G 973 677-0071
 East Orange (G-2263)
▲ Shekia Group LLC ....E 732 372-7668
 Edison (G-2608)
St Martin Cabinetry Inc ....G 732 902-6020
 Edison (G-2619)
Studio L Contracting LLC ....G 201 837-1650
 Hackensack (G-3980)
Superior Custom Kitchens LLC ....E 908 753-6005
 Warren (G-11433)
Theberge Cabinets Inc ....G 201 941-1141
 Fairview (G-3370)
Tsg LLC ....G 732 372-7668
 Edison (G-2634)
United Cabinet Works LLC ....G 917 686-3395
 Secaucus (G-9824)
Visual Architectural Designs ....F 908 754-3000
 South Plainfield (G-10342)
Vitillo & Sons Inc ....F 732 886-1393
 Lakewood (G-5177)

2435 Hardwood Veneer & Plywood

▲ Essex Coatings LLC ....F 732 855-9400
 Avenel (G-126)
◆ Mannington Mills Inc ....A 856 935-3000
 Salem (G-9694)
Rhoads OHara Architectural ....G 856 692-4100
 Vineland (G-11258)
Woodhut LLC ....F 732 414-6440
 Freehold (G-3706)
Yonkers Plywood Manufacturing ....E 732 727-1200
 Old Bridge (G-7730)

2439 Structural Wood Members, NEC

Arnold Steel Co Inc ....D 732 363-1079
 Howell (G-4531)
▲ Atlantic Exterior Wall Systems ....D 973 646-8200
 Wayne (G-11472)
Marino International Corp ....G 732 752-5100
 South Plainfield (G-10299)
Thomas Smock Woodworking ....G 732 542-9167
 Eatontown (G-2426)
Timplex Corp ....F 973 875-5500
 Sussex (G-10568)
Truss Engineering ....G 201 871-4800
 Englewood (G-2948)

Woodbury Roof Truss Inc ....D....... 856 845-3848
  Woodbury Heights *(G-12044)*

2441 Wood Boxes

Boxworks Inc ....G....... 856 456-9030
  Bellmawr *(G-328)*
Bunn Industries Incorporated.............F....... 609 890-2900
  Trenton *(G-10907)*
Cutler Bros Box & Lumber Co ....E....... 201 943-2535
  Fairview *(G-3359)*
E L Baxter Co Inc ....F....... 732 229-8219
  Ocean *(G-7661)*
Minerva Custom Products LLC ....G....... 201 447-4731
  Waldwick *(G-11305)*
T & M Pallet Co Inc...............................E....... 908 454-3042
  Stewartsville *(G-10488)*

2448 Wood Pallets & Skids

Atco Pallet Company ....E....... 856 461-8141
  Delanco *(G-2003)*
Atlantic Indus WD Pdts LLC ....G....... 609 965-4555
  Egg Harbor City *(G-2652)*
Avenel Pallet Co Inc.............................F....... 732 752-0500
  Dunellen *(G-2119)*
Bunn Industries Incorporated.............F....... 609 890-2900
  Trenton *(G-10907)*
Cutler Bros Box & Lumber Co ....E....... 201 943-2535
  Fairview *(G-3359)*
D & H Pallets LLC..................................G....... 973 481-2981
  Newark *(G-7092)*
▼ Delisa Pallet Corp ....F....... 732 667-7070
  Middlesex *(G-6111)*
East Coast Pallets LLC..........................G....... 732 308-3616
  Manalapan *(G-5805)*
Extreme Pallet Inc ....G....... 973 286-1717
  Newark *(G-7120)*
F & R Pallets Inc ....E....... 856 964-8516
  Camden *(G-1062)*
General Pallet LLC ....G....... 732 549-1000
  Flemington *(G-3446)*
Global Direct Marketing Group ....G....... 856 427-6116
  Haddonfield *(G-4058)*
◆ Granco Group LLC ....G....... 973 515-4721
  Roseland *(G-9539)*
Greenway Products & Svcs LLC ....E....... 732 442-0200
  New Brunswick *(G-6932)*
Isco ....G....... 856 672-9182
  Barrington *(G-174)*
JC Pallets Inc...G....... 973 345-1102
  Paterson *(G-8219)*
Jimenez Pallets LLC ....G....... 862 267-3900
  Kearny *(G-4872)*
Lawrence M Gichan Incorporated ....F....... 201 330-3222
  North Bergen *(G-7416)*
Love Pallet LLC......................................G....... 908 964-3385
  Hillside *(G-4411)*
Lt Chini Inc..G....... 856 692-0303
  Vineland *(G-11242)*
Millwood Inc ....D....... 732 967-8818
  South River *(G-10354)*
North Eastern Pallet Exchange...........E....... 908 289-0018
  Elizabeth *(G-2761)*
Notie Corp...G....... 609 259-3477
  Allentown *(G-28)*
Pallet Services Inc ....G....... 856 514-3908
  Pedricktown *(G-8352)*
Pedestal Pallet Inc ....G....... 732 968-7488
  Dunellen *(G-2122)*
Petro Pallet LLC ....E....... 732 230-3287
  Monmouth Junction *(G-6300)*
Poor Boy Pallet LLC ....E....... 856 451-3771
  Bridgeton *(G-770)*
Premier Asset Logistics Networ ....F....... 877 725-6381
  Williamstown *(G-11973)*
Reliable Pallet Services LLC.................G....... 973 900-2260
  Hillside *(G-4425)*
Reliable Pallet Services LLC.................G....... 732 243-9642
  Metuchen *(G-6068)*
Riephoff Saw Mill Inc ....F....... 609 259-7265
  Allentown *(G-30)*
Royal Pallet Inc ....G....... 973 299-0445
  Boonton *(G-566)*
Select Enterprises Inc ....G....... 732 287-8622
  Edison *(G-2605)*
T & M Pallet Co Inc...............................E....... 908 454-3042
  Stewartsville *(G-10488)*
Tommys Pallet Yard LLC ....G....... 609 424-3996
  Bordentown *(G-596)*
▲ Tristate Crating Pallet Co Inc ....E....... 973 357-8293
  Paterson *(G-8318)*

U P N Pallet Co Inc...............................F....... 856 299-1192
  Penns Grove *(G-8379)*
Universal Pallet Inc...............................G....... 732 356-2624
  Warren *(G-11434)*
Van-Nick Pallet Inc ....G....... 908 753-1800
  South Plainfield *(G-10339)*
Warren Pallet Company Inc ....F....... 908 995-7172
  Bloomsbury *(G-532)*
Wm Leiber Inc ....G....... 732 938-2080
  Farmingdale *(G-3396)*

2449 Wood Containers, NEC

Arrow Information Packagig LLC ....G....... 856 317-9000
  Pennsauken *(G-8391)*
B Spinelli Farm Containers ....G....... 732 616-7505
  Matawan *(G-5968)*
Boxworks Inc ....G....... 856 456-9030
  Bellmawr *(G-328)*
Builders Firstsource Inc ....E....... 856 767-3153
  Berlin *(G-419)*
Caudalie Usa Inc ....G....... 201 939-4969
  Carlstadt *(G-1137)*
Cutler Bros Box & Lumber Co ....E....... 201 943-2535
  Fairview *(G-3359)*
Jan Packaging Inc ....D....... 973 361-7200
  Dover *(G-2091)*
Minerva Custom Products LLC ....G....... 201 447-4731
  Waldwick *(G-11305)*
Vandereems Manufacturing Co ....F....... 973 427-2355
  Hawthorne *(G-4249)*

2451 Mobile Homes

Acton Mobile Industries Inc ....G....... 610 485-5100
  Burlington *(G-946)*
Wireless Experience of PA Inc ....F....... 732 552-0050
  Manahawkin *(G-5798)*

2452 Prefabricated Wood Buildings & Cmpnts

All Structures LLC ....G....... 732 233-7071
  Little Silver *(G-5499)*
Laraccas Manufacturing Inc ....E....... 973 571-1452
  Livingston *(G-5518)*
Marino International Corp ....G....... 732 752-5100
  South Plainfield *(G-10299)*
Mdb Construction ....G....... 908 628-8010
  Lebanon *(G-5270)*
Mod-U-Kraf Homes LLC ....F....... 540 482-0273
  West Berlin *(G-11608)*
R H Vassallo Inc ....G....... 856 358-8841
  Malaga *(G-5789)*
Sustanble Bldg Innovations Inc ....G....... 800 560-4143
  Manasquan *(G-5840)*
Walpole Woodworkers Inc ....E....... 973 539-3555
  Morris Plains *(G-6628)*

2491 Wood Preserving

Atlantic Wood Industries Inc ....F....... 609 267-4700
  Hainesport *(G-4070)*
New Century Millwork Inc ....G....... 973 882-0222
  Middlesex *(G-6134)*
Rq Floors Corp ....E....... 201 654-3587
  Ridgefield *(G-9287)*
Rq Floors Corp ....F....... 201 654-3587
  South Hackensack *(G-10185)*

2493 Reconstituted Wood Prdts

▲ Alcan Baltek Corporation ....D....... 201 767-1400
  Northvale *(G-7517)*
AMP Custom Rubber Inc ....F....... 732 888-2714
  Keyport *(G-4997)*
Bmca Holdings Corporation ....E....... 973 628-3000
  Wayne *(G-11480)*
Building Materials Mfg Corp ....G....... 973 628-3000
  Parsippany *(G-7896)*
Eagle Fabrication Inc ....E....... 732 739-5300
  Ltl Egg Hbr *(G-5616)*
Greenbuilt Intl Bldg Co ....C....... 609 300-9091
  Voorhees *(G-11287)*
Homasote Company ....C....... 609 883-3300
  Ewing *(G-3036)*
Homestyle Kitchens & Baths LLC ....G....... 908 979-9000
  Hackettstown *(G-4011)*
◆ JM Huber Corporation ....D....... 732 603-3630
  Edison *(G-2540)*
Johns Manville Corporation ....E....... 732 225-9190
  Edison *(G-2542)*
New York Blackboard of NJ Inc ....G....... 973 926-1600
  Hillside *(G-4418)*

R A O Contract Sales NY Inc ....G....... 201 652-1500
  Paterson *(G-8285)*
Shelan Chemical Company Inc.............G....... 732 796-1003
  Monroe Township *(G-6343)*
Standard Industries Inc ....C....... 856 241-0241
  Swedesboro *(G-10609)*
◆ Standard Industries Inc ....A....... 973 628-3000
  Parsippany *(G-8021)*

2499 Wood Prdts, NEC

All-State Fence Inc ....E....... 732 431-4944
  West Orange *(G-11758)*
American Standard Intl Inc ....E....... 732 652-7100
  Piscataway *(G-8631)*
Amertech Towerservices LLC................E....... 732 389-2200
  Shrewsbury *(G-9881)*
AMP Custom Rubber Inc ....F....... 732 888-2714
  Keyport *(G-4997)*
Anthony Excavating & Dem ....G....... 609 926-8804
  Egg Harbor Township *(G-2676)*
Architectural Wdwkg Assoc ....G....... 908 996-7866
  Frenchtown *(G-3708)*
▲ Atlantic Coolg Tech & Svcs LLC ....E....... 201 939-0900
  Carlstadt *(G-1127)*
Atlas Woodwork Inc...............................F....... 973 621-9595
  Newark *(G-7057)*
Bathware House Ltd Lblty Co ....G....... 732 546-3220
  Linden *(G-5326)*
Best Value Rugs & Carpets Inc ....G....... 732 752-3526
  Dunellen *(G-2120)*
Canac Kitchens of NJ Inc ....F....... 201 567-9585
  Englewood *(G-2890)*
Color Decor Ltd Liability Co ....G....... 973 689-2699
  Paterson *(G-8159)*
Comprelli Equipment and Svc ....G....... 973 428-8687
  East Hanover *(G-2201)*
Contempocork LLC ....G....... 201 262-7738
  River Edge *(G-9360)*
Crown Trophy ....G....... 973 808-8400
  Pine Brook *(G-8595)*
Denby USA Limited................................G....... 800 374-6479
  Bridgewater *(G-817)*
Distinctive Wdwrk By Rob Hoffm ....G....... 609 877-8122
  Beverly *(G-450)*
Distinctive Woodwork Inc ....G....... 609 714-8505
  Lumberton *(G-5628)*
Doerre Fence Co LLC.............................F....... 732 751-9700
  Farmingdale *(G-3384)*
Don Shrts Pcture Frmes Molding ....G....... 732 363-1323
  Howell *(G-4537)*
Edison Finishing ....G....... 732 287-6660
  Edison *(G-2500)*
Eviva LLC..G....... 973 925-4028
  Paterson *(G-8185)*
Forino Kitchen Cabinets Inc ....G....... 201 573-0990
  Park Ridge *(G-7850)*
Frameco Inc...E....... 973 989-1424
  Dover *(G-2084)*
◆ Frameware Inc ....F....... 800 582-5608
  Fairfield *(G-3207)*
▲ General Metal Manufacturing Co ......E....... 973 386-1818
  East Hanover *(G-2211)*
Greenway Products & Svcs LLC ....E....... 732 442-0200
  New Brunswick *(G-6932)*
▲ HB Technik USA Ltd Lblty Prtnr ....G....... 973 875-8688
  Branchville *(G-708)*
Hoboken Executive Art Inc ....G....... 201 420-8262
  Hoboken *(G-4454)*
Hoda Inc ....F....... 609 695-3000
  Trenton *(G-10939)*
Howell Township Police ....D....... 732 919-2805
  Howell *(G-4541)*
▲ III Eagle Enterprises Ltd ....E....... 973 237-1111
  Ringwood *(G-9346)*
Intelco ....D....... 856 456-6755
  Westville *(G-11817)*
Jorgensen Carr Ltd ....G....... 201 792-2278
  East Orange *(G-2253)*
K Ron Art & Mirrors Inc ....G....... 201 313-7080
  Ridgefield *(G-9270)*
Krfc Custom Woodworking Inc ....G....... 732 363-0522
  Lakewood *(G-5119)*
Lardieri Custom Woodworking ....F....... 732 905-6334
  Lakewood *(G-5121)*
Larsen Marine Services LLC...................G....... 609 408-3564
  Sea Isle City *(G-9748)*
Larson-Juhl US LLC ....E....... 973 439-1801
  Caldwell *(G-1026)*
Lexora Inc ....G....... 855 453-9672
  Newark *(G-7179)*

SIC

M and R Manufacturing ....G....... 732 905-1061
Lakewood *(G-5126)*

Medford Cedar Products Inc ....G....... 609 859-1400
Southampton *(G-10369)*

Metroplex Products Company Inc .....G....... 732 249-0653
Monroe Township *(G-6336)*

Narva Inc ....G....... 973 218-1200
Springfield *(G-10455)*

▼ National Fence Systems Inc ....D....... 732 636-5600
Avenel *(G-139)*

P & S Blizzard Corporation ....G....... 973 523-1700
Paterson *(G-8275)*

Pba of West Windsor ....E....... 609 799-6535
Princeton Junction *(G-9064)*

Perk & Pantry ....G....... 856 451-4333
Bridgeton *(G-769)*

R A O Contract Sales NY Inc ....G....... 201 652-1500
Paterson *(G-8285)*

▲ Ragar Co Inc ....G....... 732 493-1416
Ocean *(G-7678)*

Randells Cstm Fniture Kitchens ......F....... 856 216-9400
Cherry Hill *(G-1412)*

Restortions By Peter Schichtel ....G....... 973 605-8818
Morristown *(G-6697)*

Revelation Gallery Inc ....G....... 973 627-6558
Denville *(G-2052)*

Roma Moulding Inc ....F....... 732 346-0999
Edison *(G-2600)*

Steelstran Industries Inc ....G....... 732 566-5040
Matawan *(G-5989)*

Studio L Contracting LLC ....G....... 201 837-1650
Hackensack *(G-3980)*

Swiss Madison LLC ....F....... 434 623-4766
Dayton *(G-1991)*

T M Baxter Services LLC ....E....... 908 500-9065
Washington *(G-11453)*

Taylor Made Custom Cabinetry ....F....... 856 786-5433
Pennsauken *(G-8490)*

▼ Tlw Bath Ltd Liability Company ....E....... 732 942-7117
Lakewood *(G-5172)*

◆ Vaswani Inc ....D....... 877 376-4425
Edison *(G-2637)*

Walpole Woodworkers Inc ....E....... 973 539-3555
Morris Plains *(G-6628)*

Wardale Corp ....E....... 800 813-4050
Lakewood *(G-5180)*

Wees Beyond Products Corp ....F....... 862 238-8800
Passaic *(G-8115)*

Woodward Wood Products Design .....G....... 609 597-2708
West Creek *(G-11688)*

25 FURNITURE AND FIXTURES

2511 Wood Household Furniture

▲ 10-31 Incorporated ....E....... 908 496-4946
Columbia *(G-1791)*

◆ Bcg Marble Gran Fabricators Co ....F....... 201 343-8487
Hackensack *(G-3882)*

▲ Berg East Imports Inc ....D....... 908 354-5252
Barrington *(G-168)*

Bernard Miller Fabricators ....G....... 856 541-9499
Camden *(G-1041)*

Bng Industries LLC ....F....... 862 229-2414
Harrison *(G-4165)*

Bozzone Custom Woodwork Inc ....G....... 973 334-5598
Montville *(G-6439)*

▲ Central Shippee Inc ....E....... 973 838-1100
Bloomingdale *(G-526)*

Cerami Wood Products Inc ....F....... 732 968-7222
Piscataway *(G-8645)*

◆ Chromcraft Revington Inc ....E....... 662 562-8203
West Berlin *(G-11582)*

Cozzolino Furniture Design Inc ....E....... 973 731-9292
West Orange *(G-11764)*

Creative Cabinet Designs Inc ....F....... 973 402-5886
Boonton *(G-547)*

Dab Design Inc ....G....... 732 224-8686
Red Bank *(G-9225)*

Designer Kitchens ....F....... 732 370-5500
Jackson *(G-4650)*

▲ Dream On ME Industries Inc ....D....... 732 752-7220
Piscataway *(G-8658)*

East Coast Cabinets Inc ....E....... 856 488-9710
Pennsauken *(G-8417)*

Foley-Waite Associates Inc ....F....... 908 298-0700
Kenilworth *(G-4941)*

Forino Kitchen Cabinets Inc ....G....... 201 573-0990
Park Ridge *(G-7850)*

▲ Greenbaum Interiors LLC ....D....... 973 279-3000
Paterson *(G-8202)*

Interchange Group Inc ....F....... 973 783-7032
Montclair *(G-6371)*

L&W Audio/Video Inc ....G....... 212 980-2862
Hoboken *(G-4463)*

Mango Custom Cabinets Inc ....F....... 908 813-3077
Hackettstown *(G-4020)*

My House Kitchen Inc ....G....... 201 262-9000
Paramus *(G-7823)*

National Woodworking Co ....G....... 908 851-9316
Union *(G-11079)*

R H Vassallo Inc ....G....... 856 358-8841
Malaga *(G-5789)*

Rainbow Closets Inc ....D....... 973 882-3800
Fairfield *(G-3297)*

Renaissance Creations LLC ....G....... 551 206-1878
Passaic *(G-8101)*

Robert J Smith ....G....... 201 641-6555
South Hackensack *(G-10184)*

Salernos Kitchen Cabinets ....E....... 201 794-1990
Saddle Brook *(G-9676)*

Sawitz Studios Inc ....G....... 201 842-9444
Carlstadt *(G-1213)*

Schneiders Kitchens Inc ....G....... 908 689-5649
Washington *(G-11451)*

Sr Custom Woodcraft Ltd Lblty ....G....... 732 942-7601
Lakewood *(G-5166)*

Starphil Inc ....G....... 908 353-8943
Elizabeth *(G-2777)*

Summus Inc ....G....... 215 820-3918
Runnemede *(G-9612)*

Union City Mirror & Table Co ....E....... 201 867-0050
Union City *(G-11131)*

V and S Woodworks Inc ....G....... 201 568-0659
Tenafly *(G-10667)*

Vine Hill Farm ....G....... 973 383-0100
Newton *(G-7364)*

Walpole Woodworkers Inc ....E....... 973 539-3555
Morris Plains *(G-6628)*

▲ Woodline Works Corporation ....E....... 732 828-9100
New Brunswick *(G-6982)*

◆ Woodpeckers Inc ....F....... 973 751-4744
Belleville *(G-326)*

2512 Wood Household Furniture, Upholstered

Carlyle Custom Convertibles ....D....... 973 546-4502
Moonachie *(G-6460)*

◆ Chromcraft Revington Inc ....E....... 662 562-8203
West Berlin *(G-11582)*

Custom Decorators Service ....G....... 973 625-0516
Denville *(G-2033)*

Edward P Paul & Co Inc ....G....... 908 757-4212
Plainfield *(G-8763)*

◆ Furniture of America NJ ....E....... 201 605-8200
Secaucus *(G-9770)*

H Lauzon Furniture Co Inc ....E....... 201 837-7598
Teaneck *(G-10634)*

Masters Interiors Inc ....E....... 973 253-0784
Clifton *(G-1665)*

Rff Services LLC ....G....... 201 564-0040
Oakland *(G-7644)*

Sofa Doctor Inc ....G....... 718 292-6300
Guttenberg *(G-3872)*

Woodward Wood Products Design .....F....... 609 597-2708
West Creek *(G-11688)*

2514 Metal Household Furniture

Avantegarde Image LLC ....F....... 732 363-8701
Lakewood *(G-5056)*

Christopher Szuco ....G....... 732 684-7643
Millstone Twp *(G-6213)*

▲ De Saussure Equipment Co Inc .....E....... 201 845-6517
Maywood *(G-6003)*

▼ Knickerbocker Bed Company ....E....... 201 933-3100
Carlstadt *(G-1176)*

◆ NPS Public Furniture Corp ....D....... 973 594-1100
Clifton *(G-1679)*

Rumsons Kitchens Inc ....G....... 732 842-1810
Rumson *(G-9603)*

South Jersey Metal Inc ....E....... 856 228-0642
Deptford *(G-2066)*

Taylor Made Cabinets Inc ....E....... 609 978-6900
Manahawkin *(G-5796)*

2515 Mattresses & Bedsprings

Ayerspace Inc ....G....... 212 582-8410
West Caldwell *(G-11641)*

Bedding Shoppe Inc ....G....... 973 334-9000
Parsippany *(G-7892)*

Carlyle Custom Convertibles ....D....... 973 546-4502
Moonachie *(G-6460)*

Catching Zzz LLC ....G....... 888 339-1604
Piscataway *(G-8643)*

◆ Comfort Rvolution Holdings LLC .....F....... 732 272-9111
Eatontown *(G-2385)*

Custom Bedding Co ....G....... 973 761-1100
Maplewood *(G-5875)*

▲ Dream Well Collection Inc ....F....... 732 545-5900
New Brunswick *(G-6921)*

Eclipse Sleep Products LLC ....D....... 732 628-0002
New Brunswick *(G-6922)*

Grand Life Inc ....G....... 201 556-8975
Carlstadt *(G-1160)*

▲ Hammer Bedding Corp ....G....... 973 589-2400
Newark *(G-7145)*

◆ Innocor Inc ....C....... 732 945-6222
Red Bank *(G-9230)*

Innocor Foam Tech - Acp Inc ....D....... 732 945-6222
Red Bank *(G-9231)*

J P Egan Industries Inc ....G....... 973 642-1500
Newark *(G-7164)*

◆ Jomel Industries Inc ....F....... 973 282-0300
Hillside *(G-4406)*

Jomel Seams Reasonable LLC ....F....... 973 282-0300
Hillside *(G-4407)*

Leggett & Platt Incorporated ....D....... 732 225-2440
Edison *(G-2550)*

Lieth Holdings LLC ....G....... 201 358-8282
Westwood *(G-11834)*

Mattress Dev Co Del LLC ....E....... 732 628-0800
North Brunswick *(G-7476)*

Miller Berry & Sons Inc ....F....... 856 785-1420
Port Norris *(G-8887)*

New England Bedding Trnspt Inc ......G....... 631 484-0147
Kearny *(G-4887)*

◆ Sealy Mattress Co N J Inc ....C....... 973 345-8800
Paterson *(G-8297)*

▲ Sheex Inc ....E....... 856 334-3021
Marlton *(G-5951)*

Spectra Mattress Inc ....G....... 732 545-5900
North Brunswick *(G-7488)*

Spring Time Mattress Mfg Corp ....D....... 973 473-5400
South Hackensack *(G-10188)*

◆ Ther-A-Pedic Sleep Products ....D....... 732 628-0800
North Brunswick *(G-7490)*

White Lotus Home Ltd Lblty Co ....F....... 732 828-2111
New Brunswick *(G-6981)*

2517 Wood T V, Radio, Phono & Sewing Cabinets

Bernard Miller Fabricators ....G....... 856 541-9499
Camden *(G-1041)*

Imagine Audio LLC ....G....... 856 488-1466
Cherry Hill *(G-1375)*

L&W Audio/Video Inc ....G....... 212 980-2862
Hoboken *(G-4463)*

Parsons Cabinets Inc ....G....... 973 279-4954
Montclair *(G-6383)*

2519 Household Furniture, NEC

▲ Casual Classics Inc ....G....... 916 294-9880
Barnegat *(G-156)*

▲ D & F Wicker Import Co Inc ....E....... 973 736-5861
Succasunna *(G-10511)*

Gendell Assoicates PA ....G....... 201 656-4498
Hoboken *(G-4452)*

Scott W Springman ....G....... 856 751-2411
Pennsauken *(G-8482)*

South Brunswick Furniture Inc ....C....... 732 658-8850
Linden *(G-5427)*

2521 Wood Office Furniture

Arnold Desks Inc ....E....... 908 686-5656
Irvington *(G-4557)*

Arnold Furniture Mfrs Inc ....F....... 973 399-0505
Irvington *(G-4558)*

Arnold Kolax Furniture Inc ....E....... 973 375-3344
Irvington *(G-4559)*

▲ Arnold Reception Desks Inc ....E....... 973 375-8101
Irvington *(G-4560)*

Arthur Gordon Associates Inc ....F....... 732 431-3361
Freehold *(G-3649)*

Atlantic Coast Woodwork Inc ....G....... 609 294-2478
Ltl Egg Hbr *(G-5613)*

Cbt Supply Inc ....G....... 800 770-7042
Rockaway *(G-9450)*

◆ Chromcraft Revington Inc ....E....... 662 562-8203
West Berlin *(G-11582)*

Cozzolino Furniture Design Inc ....E 973 731-9292
West Orange *(G-11764)*

▲ Designcore Ltd ....D 718 499-0337
Secaucus *(G-9761)*

▲ Fu WEI Inc ....G 732 937-8388
East Brunswick *(G-2147)*

◆ G & A Coml Seating Pdts Corp ....G 908 233-8000
Mountainside *(G-6846)*

Kitchens By Frank Inc ....G 732 364-1343
Toms River *(G-10773)*

La Cour Inc ....E 973 227-3300
Fairfield *(G-3255)*

M2 Electric LLC ....F 973 770-4596
Mine Hill *(G-6273)*

Mbs Installations Inc ....F 888 446-9135
Jackson *(G-4659)*

Mp Custom FL LLC ....F 973 417-2288
Wayne *(G-11535)*

Pemco Dental Corporation ....E 800 526-4170
Springfield *(G-10459)*

Reda Furniture LLC ....F 732 948-1703
Manasquan *(G-5837)*

Renaissance Creations LLC ....G 551 206-1878
Passaic *(G-8101)*

Robert J Smith ....G 201 641-6555
South Hackensack *(G-10184)*

Vaswani Inc ....F 877 376-4425
Edison *(G-2638)*

Vaswani Inc ....F 732 377-9794
Piscataway *(G-8736)*

Zacs International LLC ....F 609 368-3482
Burlington *(G-994)*

2522 Office Furniture, Except Wood

◆ Concord Products Company Inc ......E 856 933-3000
Sewell *(G-9834)*

Creative Innovations Inc ....F 973 636-9060
Fair Lawn *(G-3094)*

▲ Daco Limited Partnership ....D 973 263-1100
Boonton *(G-548)*

Denmatt Industries LLC ....F 609 689-0099
Hamilton *(G-4105)*

Extra Office Inc ....F 732 381-9774
Rahway *(G-9092)*

Fehlberg Mfg Inc ....G 973 399-1905
Irvington *(G-4568)*

Gaw Associates Inc ....F 856 608-1428
Cherry Hill *(G-1367)*

◆ Global Industries Inc ....C 856 596-3390
Marlton *(G-5933)*

La Cour Inc ....E 973 227-3300
Fairfield *(G-3255)*

◆ Stylex Inc ....C 856 461-5600
Delanco *(G-2007)*

Top Line Seating Inc ....F 908 241-9051
Kenilworth *(G-4983)*

2531 Public Building & Related Furniture

▲ Academia Furniture LLC ....E 973 472-0100
Wood Ridge *(G-12000)*

◆ Air Cruisers Company LLC ....B 732 681-3527
Wall Township *(G-11315)*

Archer Plastics Inc ....G 856 692-0242
Elmer *(G-2794)*

Christian Art ....G 201 867-8096
West New York *(G-11737)*

◆ Chromcraft Revington Inc ....E 662 562-8203
West Berlin *(G-11582)*

◆ Hausmann Enterprises LLC ....D 201 767-0255
Northvale *(G-7527)*

Jcdecaux Mallscape LLC ....E 201 288-2024
Hasbrouck Heights *(G-4185)*

Jmm Studios ....G 609 861-3094
Woodbine *(G-12010)*

Johnson Controls Inc ....E 856 245-9977
Blackwood *(G-472)*

▲ Longo Associates Inc ....F 201 825-1500
Ramsey *(G-9150)*

Renaissance Creations LLC ....G 551 206-1878
Passaic *(G-8101)*

RFS Commercial Inc ....E 201 796-0006
Saddle Brook *(G-9671)*

◆ Suburban Auto Seat Co Inc ....F 973 778-9227
Lodi *(G-5577)*

Union County Seating & Sup Co ....E 908 241-4949
Kenilworth *(G-4984)*

Visual Architectural Designs ....F 908 754-3000
South Plainfield *(G-10342)*

2541 Wood, Office & Store Fixtures

▲ 10-31 Incorporated ....E 908 496-4946
Columbia *(G-1791)*

A W Ross Inc ....F 973 471-5900
Passaic *(G-8049)*

A1 Custom Countertops Inc ....F 856 200-3596
Woodstown *(G-12094)*

Acro Display Inc ....E 215 229-1100
Pennsauken *(G-8382)*

◆ Afina Corporation ....E 973 684-7650
Paterson *(G-8127)*

Allure Box & Display Co ....F 212 807-7070
Hackensack *(G-3876)*

American Intr Resources Inc ....G 908 851-0014
Union *(G-11024)*

▲ Amko Displays Corporation ....F 201 460-7199
Moonachie *(G-6454)*

Arrow Information Packagig LLC ....G 856 317-9000
Pennsauken *(G-8391)*

▲ Bamboo & Rattan Works Inc ....G 732 255-4239
Toms River *(G-10746)*

Banner Design Inc ....E 908 687-5335
Hillside *(G-4379)*

Bernard Miller Fabricators ....G 856 541-9499
Camden *(G-1041)*

▲ Bga Construction Inc ....D 973 809-9745
Pine Brook *(G-8589)*

Bossen Architectural Millwork ....F 856 786-1100
Cinnaminson *(G-1444)*

Bozzone Custom Woodwork Inc ....G 973 334-5598
Montville *(G-6439)*

Capital Contracting & Design ....E 908 561-8411
Plainfield *(G-8760)*

Costa Custom Cabinets Inc ....F 973 429-7004
Bloomfield *(G-499)*

Counter Efx Inc ....G 908 203-0155
Hillsborough *(G-4311)*

CPB Inc ....E 856 697-2700
Buena *(G-939)*

Cronos-Prim Colorado LLC ....G 303 369-7477
Lodi *(G-5557)*

Custom Counters By Precision ....E 973 773-0111
Passaic *(G-8058)*

D S F Inc ....G 908 218-5153
Raritan *(G-9209)*

Delaware Valley Installation ....G 856 546-0097
Runnemede *(G-9605)*

▲ Design Display Group Inc ....C 201 438-6000
Carlstadt *(G-1150)*

▲ Designcore Ltd ....D 718 499-0337
Secaucus *(G-9761)*

E Berkowitz & Co Inc ....G 856 608-1118
Mount Laurel *(G-6756)*

Eagle Fabrication Inc ....E 732 739-5300
Ltl Egg Hbr *(G-5616)*

East Coast Storage Eqp Co Inc ....E 732 451-1316
Brick *(G-716)*

Fixture It Inc ....E 201 445-0939
Glen Rock *(G-3831)*

Form Tops Lminators of Trenton ....G 609 409-4357
Jamesburg *(G-4672)*

Frank & Jims Inc ....G 609 646-1655
Pleasantville *(G-8811)*

Garley Inc ....G 215 788-5756
Burlington *(G-971)*

▼ Handy Store Fixtures Inc ....D 973 242-1600
Newark *(G-7147)*

Hawthorne Kitchens Inc ....E 973 427-9010
Hawthorne *(G-4223)*

▲ Impact Unlimited Inc ....C 732 274-2000
Dayton *(G-1970)*

Intelco ....E 856 384-8562
Paulsboro *(G-8332)*

Intelco ....D 856 456-6755
Westville *(G-11817)*

Ken Bauer Inc ....E 201 664-6881
Hillsdale *(G-4368)*

◆ Kubik Maltbie Inc ....E 856 234-0052
Mount Laurel *(G-6774)*

Laminetics Inc ....G 732 367-1116
Lakewood *(G-5120)*

Level Designs Group LLC ....E 973 761-1675
South Orange *(G-10198)*

Lyle/Carlstrom Associates Inc ....E 908 526-2270
Branchburg *(G-658)*

Marvic Corp ....G 908 686-4340
Union *(G-11074)*

Masco Cabinetry LLC ....C 732 363-3797
Lakewood *(G-5129)*

Masco Cabinetry LLC ....C 732 942-5138
Lakewood *(G-5130)*

Mdr LLC ....G 973 731-7100
West Orange *(G-11772)*

▲ Medlaurel Inc ....E 856 461-6600
Delanco *(G-2006)*

Millner Kitchens Inc ....G 609 890-7300
Trenton *(G-10958)*

Obare Services Ltd Lblty Co ....G 908 456-1887
Elizabeth *(G-2764)*

▲ Pac Team America Inc ....E 201 599-5000
Paramus *(G-7826)*

▲ Pam International Co Inc ....D 201 291-1200
Saddle Brook *(G-9667)*

Paramount Fixture Corporation ....E 973 485-1585
Newark *(G-7223)*

Parsons Cabinets Inc ....G 973 279-4954
Montclair *(G-6383)*

Precision Dealer Services Inc ....E 908 237-1100
Flemington *(G-3461)*

S L Enterprises Inc ....G 908 272-8145
Ewing *(G-3064)*

▲ Salon Interiors Inc ....E 201 488-7888
South Hackensack *(G-10186)*

Sawitz Studios Inc ....E 201 842-9444
Carlstadt *(G-1213)*

Showtech Inc ....G 973 249-6336
Clifton *(G-1717)*

South Jersey Countertop Co ....G 856 768-7960
West Berlin *(G-11622)*

◆ Trinity Manufacturing LLC ....C 732 549-2866
Metuchen *(G-6079)*

Universal Systems Installers ....E 732 656-9002
Monroe *(G-6323)*

Visual Architectural Designs ....F 908 754-3000
South Plainfield *(G-10342)*

Wagner Rack Inc ....E 973 278-6966
Clifton *(G-1737)*

Warehouse Solutions Inc ....F 201 880-1110
Fair Lawn *(G-3128)*

Wilsonart LLC ....F 800 822-7613
Moorestown *(G-6578)*

2542 Partitions & Fixtures, Except Wood

Acme Manufacturing Co ....G 732 541-2800
Port Reading *(G-8891)*

Acro Display Inc ....E 215 229-1100
Pennsauken *(G-8382)*

All Racks Industries Inc ....G 212 244-1069
Linden *(G-5320)*

Alternative Air LLC ....G 609 261-5870
Willingboro *(G-11988)*

Atlantic Coast Woodwork Inc ....G 609 294-2478
Ltl Egg Hbr *(G-5613)*

Auto-Stak Systems Inc ....G 201 358-9070
Westwood *(G-11828)*

Axg Corporation ....G 212 213-3313
Secaucus *(G-9751)*

Benco Inc ....F 973 575-4440
Fairfield *(G-3154)*

Capital Contracting & Design ....E 908 561-8411
Plainfield *(G-8760)*

Carib-Display Co ....G 732 583-1648
Matawan *(G-5969)*

▲ Clip Strip Corp ....G 201 342-9155
Hackensack *(G-3898)*

Cor Products Inc ....G 973 731-4952
West Orange *(G-11763)*

Custom Creations ....G 201 651-9676
Oakland *(G-7622)*

Display Equation LLC ....G 201 343-4135
Hackensack *(G-3908)*

E J M Store Fixtures Inc ....G 973 372-7907
Irvington *(G-4565)*

East Coast Storage Eqp Co Inc ....E 732 451-1316
Brick *(G-716)*

▲ Engo Co ....E 908 754-6600
South Plainfield *(G-10250)*

Fixture It Inc ....E 201 445-0939
Glen Rock *(G-3831)*

▼ Frazier Industrial Company ....C 908 876-3001
Long Valley *(G-5610)*

Gauer Metal Products Co Inc ....E 908 241-4080
Kenilworth *(G-4942)*

▼ Handy Store Fixtures Inc ....D 973 242-1600
Newark *(G-7147)*

▲ High Tech Manufacturing Inc ....G 973 372-7907
Irvington *(G-4572)*

Imperial Design ....G 856 742-8480
Gloucester City *(G-3844)*

Infinite Mfg Group Inc ....F 973 649-9950
  Kearny *(G-4867)*

Insign Inc ....E 856 424-1161
  West Deptford *(G-11705)*

Jed Display LLC ....G 201 340-2329
  Newark *(G-7167)*

Leo Prager Inc ....G 201 266-8888
  Englewood *(G-2918)*

▲ Lloyd Gerstner & Partners LLC ....E 201 634-9099
  Paramus *(G-7815)*

Lyle/Carlstrom Associates Inc ....E 908 526-2270
  Branchburg *(G-658)*

▲ Metaline Products Company Inc .....E 732 721-1373
  South Amboy *(G-10137)*

Minerva Custom Products LLC ....G 201 447-4731
  Waldwick *(G-11305)*

▲ Modern Showcase Inc ....F 201 935-2929
  Carlstadt *(G-1188)*

Modern Store Equipment ....F 609 241-7438
  Burlington *(G-980)*

Mpm Display Inc ....G 973 374-3477
  Hillside *(G-4416)*

National Display Group Inc ....E 856 661-1212
  Pennsauken *(G-8459)*

▲ Ner Data Products Inc ....F 888 637-3282
  Glassboro *(G-3817)*

Nicks Workshop Inc ....G 856 784-6097
  Gibbsboro *(G-3794)*

North Bergen Marble & Granite ....G 201 945-9988
  Cliffside Park *(G-1543)*

▲ Pam International Co Inc ....D 201 291-1200
  Saddle Brook *(G-9667)*

▲ Pool Tables Plus Inc ....G 732 968-8228
  Green Brook *(G-3866)*

Rbdel Inc ....G 609 324-0040
  Bordentown *(G-594)*

Richard J Bell Co Inc ....F 201 847-0887
  Wyckoff *(G-12119)*

S L Enterprises Inc ....G 908 272-8145
  Ewing *(G-3064)*

Sk Custom Creations Inc ....E 973 754-9261
  Totowa *(G-10852)*

Spark Wire Products Co Inc ....G 973 773-6945
  Clifton *(G-1723)*

Ted-Steel Industries Ltd ....G 212 279-3878
  Linden *(G-5434)*

◆ Testrite Instrument Co Inc ....C 201 543-0240
  Hackensack *(G-3982)*

Toltec Products LLC ....G 908 832-2131
  Califon *(G-1035)*

V M Display ....F 973 365-8027
  Passaic *(G-8112)*

Vira Insight LLC ....C 732 442-6756
  Piscataway *(G-8737)*

Vitillo & Sons Inc ....F 732 886-1393
  Lakewood *(G-5177)*

2591 Drapery Hardware, Window Blinds & Shades

A N Laggren Awngs Canvas Mfg ....F 908 756-1948
  Plainfield *(G-8756)*

A Plus Installs LLC ....G 201 255-4412
  Bloomfield *(G-488)*

▲ Ackerson Drapery Decorator Svc ...G 732 797-1967
  Lakewood *(G-5045)*

▲ Acme Drapemaster America Inc .....G 732 512-0613
  Edison *(G-2446)*

Arts Windows Inc ....G 732 905-9595
  Toms River *(G-10744)*

Best Draperies Inc ....G 856 429-5453
  Cherry Hill *(G-1343)*

Best Drapery Inc ....G 856 429-2242
  Cherry Hill *(G-1344)*

C & M Shade Corp ....E 201 807-1200
  Fairfield *(G-3160)*

Erco Ceilings Somers Point Inc ....E 609 517-2531
  Somers Point *(G-9936)*

Glasscare Inc ....F 201 943-1122
  Cliffside Park *(G-1539)*

Griffith Shade Company Inc ....G 973 667-1474
  Nutley *(G-7586)*

Kay Window Fashions Inc ....F 862 591-1554
  Saddle Brook *(G-9658)*

Matiss Inc ....E 201 648-0002
  Hoboken *(G-4466)*

Metro Mills Inc ....E 973 942-6034
  Paterson *(G-8257)*

Nassaus Window Fashions Inc ....E 201 689-6030
  Paramus *(G-7824)*

▲ Newell Brands Inc ....B 201 610-6600
  Hoboken *(G-4468)*

RFS Commercial Inc ....F 201 796-0006
  Saddle Brook *(G-9671)*

SF Lutz LLC ....G 609 646-9490
  Egg Harbor Township *(G-2697)*

Shade Powers Co Inc ....F 201 767-3727
  Northvale *(G-7549)*

Spotless Venetian Blind Servic ....G 732 548-1711
  Edison *(G-2618)*

Uncle Jimmys Cheesecakes ....G 201 248-1820
  Cliffside Park *(G-1545)*

Window Plus Home Improvement ....F 973 591-9993
  Passaic *(G-8117)*

▲ Worldwide Whl Flr Cvg Inc ....G 732 906-1400
  Edison *(G-2647)*

2599 Furniture & Fixtures, NEC

Acorn Industry Inc ....F 732 536-6256
  Englishtown *(G-2999)*

Atlantic Coast Woodwork Inc ....G 609 294-2478
  Ltl Egg Hbr *(G-5613)*

Best American Hands ....E 203 247-2028
  Hillside *(G-4382)*

▼ Custom Sales & Service Inc ....E 609 561-6900
  Hammonton *(G-4133)*

G & H Sheet Metal Works Inc ....G 973 923-1100
  Hillside *(G-4393)*

◆ Hausmann Enterprises LLC ....D 201 767-0255
  Northvale *(G-7527)*

Hill-Rom Holdings Inc ....G 856 486-2117
  Moorestown *(G-6528)*

▼ Infinite Mfg Group Inc ....E 973 649-9950
  Kearny *(G-4868)*

Kashmir ....G 856 691-8969
  Vineland *(G-11239)*

Lbd Corp ....E 201 541-6760
  Englewood *(G-2917)*

Lrk Seating Products LLC ....G 973 462-2743
  Livingston *(G-5521)*

▲ M Deitz & Sons Inc ....F 908 686-8800
  Hillside *(G-4412)*

Modernlinefurniture Inc ....G 908 486-0200
  Linden *(G-5389)*

Mp Custom FL LLC ....F 973 417-2288
  Wayne *(G-11535)*

◆ Organize It-All Inc ....E 201 488-0808
  Bogota *(G-534)*

◆ Outwater Plstcs/Industries Inc ....D 201 498-8750
  Bogota *(G-535)*

Renaissance Creations LLC ....G 551 206-1878
  Passaic *(G-8101)*

Rosalindas Discount Furniture ....F 973 928-2838
  Passaic *(G-8102)*

Universal Interlock Corp ....G 732 818-8484
  Toms River *(G-10801)*

West Hudson Lumber & Mllwk Co ....G 201 991-7191
  Kearny *(G-4904)*

▲ Wood Textures ....G 732 230-5005
  Dayton *(G-1996)*

26 PAPER AND ALLIED PRODUCTS

2611 Pulp Mills

All Amrcan Recycl Corp Clifton ....C 201 656-3363
  Jersey City *(G-4688)*

County of Somerset ....C 732 469-3363
  Bridgewater *(G-814)*

◆ Exim Incorporated ....G 908 561-8200
  Piscataway *(G-8664)*

Garden State Recycl Edison LLC ....F 732 393-0200
  Edison *(G-2519)*

◆ Laminated Industries Inc ....E 908 862-5995
  Linden *(G-5373)*

▼ Reliable Paper Recycling Inc ....E 201 333-5244
  Jersey City *(G-4800)*

Reliable Wood Products LLC ....D 856 456-6300
  Westville *(G-11819)*

2621 Paper Mills

Allure Box & Display Co ....F 212 807-7070
  Hackensack *(G-3876)*

Amcor Flexibles LLC ....C 856 825-1400
  Millville *(G-6224)*

Arthur A Kaplan Co Inc ....E 201 806-2100
  East Rutherford *(G-2273)*

Artmolds Journal LLC ....G 908 273-5600
  Summit *(G-10525)*

Beach Nutts Media Inc ....G 609 886-4113
  Villas *(G-11178)*

▲ Borak Group Inc ....D 718 665-8500
  Jersey City *(G-4705)*

Boro Printing Inc ....G 732 229-1899
  West Long Branch *(G-11720)*

▲ Case It Inc ....E 800 441-4710
  Lyndhurst *(G-5646)*

Cell Distributors Inc ....E 718 473-0162
  Dayton *(G-1958)*

City Envelope Inc ....G 201 792-9292
  Jersey City *(G-4712)*

Clover Bags & Paper LLC ....G 917 721-6783
  Little Ferry *(G-5479)*

▲ Cw International Sales LLC ....E 732 367-4444
  Lakewood *(G-5079)*

Daily News LP ....F 212 210-2100
  Jersey City *(G-4720)*

Delta Paper Corporation ....E 856 532-0333
  Burlington *(G-963)*

▲ Flexo-Craft Prints Inc ....E 973 482-7200
  Harrison *(G-4174)*

◆ G R Impex Ltd Liability Co ....F 301 873-5333
  Avenel *(G-129)*

Glue Fold Inc ....D 973 575-8400
  Clifton *(G-1627)*

Golden W Ppr Converting Corp ....E 908 412-8889
  South Plainfield *(G-10268)*

H S Folex Schleussner Inc ....G 973 575-7626
  Fairfield *(G-3220)*

◆ Holland Manufacturing Co Inc ....C 973 584-8141
  Succasunna *(G-10513)*

Institutational Edge LLC ....G 201 944-5447
  Englewood Cliffs *(G-2977)*

International Paper Company ....E 856 853-7000
  West Deptford *(G-11706)*

International Paper Company ....C 856 931-8000
  Bellmawr *(G-335)*

International Paper Company ....C 856 546-7000
  Barrington *(G-173)*

International Paper Company ....C 973 405-2400
  Clifton *(G-1643)*

▲ IW Tremont Co Inc ....E 973 427-3800
  Hawthorne *(G-4227)*

Lodor Offset Corporation ....F 201 935-7100
  Carlstadt *(G-1182)*

▲ Lps Industries Inc ....C 201 438-3515
  Moonachie *(G-6477)*

Peter Morley LLC ....G 732 264-0010
  Hazlet *(G-4269)*

Printwrap Corporation ....F 973 239-1144
  Cedar Grove *(G-1289)*

Retrographics Publishing Inc ....G 201 501-0505
  Closter *(G-1762)*

Rigo Industries Inc ....E 973 881-1780
  Paterson *(G-8288)*

Schweitzer-Mauduit Intl Inc ....B 732 723-6100
  Spotswood *(G-10417)*

Screen Reproductions Co Inc ....E 201 935-0830
  Carlstadt *(G-1214)*

Sealed Air Holdings ....G 201 791-7600
  Elmwood Park *(G-2855)*

Sre Ventures LLC ....G 973 785-0099
  Little Falls *(G-5468)*

Victor Securities Inc ....G 646 481-4835
  Englewood *(G-2952)*

World Pac Paper LLC ....G 877 837-2737
  Upper Saddle River *(G-11149)*

2631 Paperboard Mills

All County Recycling Inc ....F 609 393-6445
  Trenton *(G-10890)*

Allure Box & Display Co ....F 212 807-7070
  Hackensack *(G-3876)*

Beauty-Pack LLC ....F 732 802-8200
  Piscataway *(G-8640)*

◆ Flech Paper Products Inc ....F 973 357-8111
  Paterson *(G-8193)*

Graphic Packaging Intl LLC ....G 973 709-9100
  Wayne *(G-11512)*

Graphic Packaging Intl LLC ....C 732 424-2100
  Wayne *(G-11513)*

Greenbuilt Intl Bldg Co ....C 609 300-9091
  Voorhees *(G-11287)*

International Paper Company ....C 732 251-2000
  Spotswood *(G-10415)*

JIT Manufacturing Inc ....F 973 247-7300
  Paterson *(G-8223)*

◆ Lamitech Inc ....E 609 860-8037
  Cranbury *(G-1854)*

M S C Paper Products Corp ....E 908 686-2200
Hillside (G-4413)
Monster Coatings Inc ....G....... 973 983-7662
Rockaway (G-9478)
Multi Packaging Solutions Inc ....C....... 908 757-6000
South Plainfield (G-10303)
Nu-EZ Custom Bindery LLC ....E 201 488-4140
Hackensack (G-3956)
Packageman 201 898-1922
Belleville (G-306)
▲ Pinnacle Cosmetic Packg LLC ......F 908 241-7777
Kenilworth (G-4970)
▲ Qualserv Imports Inc ....G....... 973 620-9234
Denville (G-2050)
Red Oak Packaging Inc 862 268-8200
Newton (G-7354)
Romark Logistics CES LLC ....E 908 789-2800
Westfield (G-11802)
▲ Shell Packaging Corporation ....E 908 871-7000
Berkeley Heights (G-412)
Shure-Pak Corporation.......................G....... 856 825-0808
Millville (G-6270)
◆ Stephen Gould Corporation ....D....... 973 428-1500
Whippany (G-11910)
Sunshine Metal & Sign Inc ....G....... 973 676-4432
Milltown (G-6220)
Union Container Corp...........................E 973 242-3600
Newark (G-7306)
▼ United States Box Corp ....E 973 481-2000
Fairfield (G-3336)
Westrock Cp LLC..................................D....... 732 866-1890
Colts Neck (G-1790)
Westrock Cp LLC..................................E 973 594-6000
Clifton (G-1739)
Westrock Rkt LLC ....C....... 856 596-8604
Marlton (G-5956)
Wjj and Company LLC..........................F 973 246-7480
Garfield (G-3778)

2652 Set-Up Paperboard Boxes

Capitol Box Corp.................................E.......201 867-6018
North Bergen (G-7392)
Cross Country Box Co Inc ....F 973 673-8349
Clifton (G-1592)
Exalent Packaging Inc ....E 973 742-9600
Paterson (G-8186)
Global Direct Marketing Group.............G....... 856 427-6116
Haddonfield (G-4058)
▲ McLean Packaging Corporation ......D....... 856 359-2600
Moorestown (G-6544)
McLean Packaging Corporation ....D....... 856 359-2600
Pennsauken (G-8456)
Ruffino Paper Box Mfg Co ....F 201 487-1260
Hackensack (G-3968)
Shure-Pak Corporation.......................G....... 856 825-0808
Millville (G-6270)
▼ United States Box Corp ....E 973 481-2000
Fairfield (G-3336)

2653 Corrugated & Solid Fiber Boxes

Ace Box Landau Co Inc ....G....... 201 871-4776
Englewood Cliffs (G-2956)
Albert Paper Products Company...........E 973 373-0330
Irvington (G-4554)
▲ Algar/Display Connection Corp ....D....... 201 438-1000
Garfield (G-3726)
Alliance Corrugated Box Inc ....E 877 525-5269
Saddle River (G-9690)
▲ Allstate Paper Box Co Inc ....D....... 973 589-2600
Newark (G-7041)
Apple Corrugated Box Ltd ....F 201 635-1269
Wood Ridge (G-12001)
B Spinelli Farm Containers ....G....... 732 616-7505
Matawan (G-5968)
▲ Bell Container Corp ....C....... 973 344-4400
Newark (G-7064)
Boxworks Inc.......................................G....... 856 456-9030
Bellmawr (G-328)
Bunn Industries Incorporated.............F 609 890-2900
Trenton (G-10907)
▲ Cases By Source Inc ....E 201 831-0005
Mahwah (G-5720)
Creoh Usa LLC ....G....... 718 821-0570
Lakewood (G-5075)
Dauson Corrugated Container.............F 973 827-1494
Hamburg (G-4089)
▲ Delta Corrugated Ppr Pdts Corp......C....... 201 941-1910
Palisades Park (G-7772)
▲ Delvco Pharma Packg Svcs Inc........D....... 973 278-2500
Paterson (G-8172)

Diamex International Corp ....G....... 973 838-8844
Kinnelon (G-5016)
E L Baxter Co Inc ....F 732 229-8219
Ocean (G-7661)
Enterprise Container LLC ....F 201 797-7200
Saddle Brook (G-9651)
Ferguson Containers Co Inc................EZ....... 908 454-9755
Phillipsburg (G-8550)
Georgia-Pacific LLC.............................C....... 908 995-2228
Milford (G-6193)
Global Direct Marketing Group.............G....... 856 427-6116
Haddonfield (G-4058)
Graphcorr LLC......................................F 732 355-0088
Dayton (G-1967)
Great Northern Corporation ....E 856 241-0080
Swedesboro (G-10587)
Greater New York Box Co Inc ....G....... 609 631-7900
Trenton (G-10936)
Holly Packaging Inc ....E 856 327-8281
Millville (G-6255)
HR Industries Inc ....F 201 941-8000
Ridgefield (G-4058)
International Container Co ....E 201 440-1600
Hackensack (G-3932)
International Paper Company ....D....... 732 828-1700
Milltown (G-6216)
Kampack Inc ....C....... 973 589-7400
Newark (G-7172)
▲ Lanco-York Inc ....E 973 278-7400
Paterson (G-8237)
Level Designs Group LLC ....G....... 973 761-1675
South Orange (G-10198)
Levine Industries Inc ....E 973 742-1000
Paterson (G-8239)
Levine Packaging Supply Corp ....E 973 575-3456
Fairfield (G-3261)
▲ McLean Packaging Corporation ....D....... 856 359-2600
Moorestown (G-6544)
McLean Packaging Corporation ....D....... 856 359-2600
Pennsauken (G-8456)
Menasha Packaging Company LLC ......C....... 973 893-1300
Lyndhurst (G-5664)
Menasha Packaging Company LLC ......C....... 732 985-0800
Edison (G-2562)
New York Folding Box Co Inc ....E 973 347-6932
Stanhope (G-10477)
Orora Packaging Solutions ....E 609 249-5200
Cranbury (G-1866)
▼ Package Development Co Inc ....E 973 983-8500
Rockaway (G-9483)
Packaging Corporation America ....G....... 856 596-5020
Marlton (G-5945)
Packaging Corporation America ....G....... 908 452-9271
Hackettstown (G-4031)
Packaging Corporation America ....G....... 856 696-0114
Vineland (G-11249)
▼ Paige Company Containers Inc ....E 201 461-7800
Elmwood Park (G-2846)
Pin Point Container Corp ....F 856 848-2115
Deptford (G-2065)
Pratt Industries USA Inc......................D....... 201 934-1900
Allendale (G-13)
▲ President Cont Group II LLC ....B....... 201 933-7500
Moonachie (G-6484)
Raritan Packaging Industries ....E 732 246-7200
New Brunswick (G-6966)
Rectico Inc ....F 973 575-0009
Fairfield (G-3298)
Rfc Container LLC 856 692-0404
Vineland (G-11257)
SA Richards Inc ....G....... 201 947-3850
Fort Lee (G-3585)
Schiffenhaus Industries Inc ....C....... 973 484-5000
Newark (G-7263)
Squire Corrugated Cont Corp ....D....... 908 862-9111
Basking Ridge (G-198)
Sunshine Metal & Sign Inc ....G....... 973 676-4432
Milltown (G-6220)
Sutherland Packaging Inc ....D....... 973 786-5141
Andover (G-51)
Trent Box Manufacturing Co ....C....... 609 587-7515
Trenton (G-11001)
Trenton Corrugated Products ....E 609 695-0808
Ewing (G-3070)
US Display Group Inc ....F 931 455-9585
Secaucus (G-9825)
Victory Box Corp.................................D....... 908 245-5100
Roselle (G-9575)
Vineland Packaging Corp......................C....... 856 794-3300
Vineland (G-11276)

Weber Packaging Inc ....G....... 201 262-6022
Oradell (G-7748)
Westrock Rkt LLC ....C....... 973 594-6000
Totowa (G-10861)
Westrock Rkt Company.........................D....... 732 274-2500
Dayton (G-1994)
Westrock Rkt Company.........................C....... 973 484-5000
Newark (G-7314)
Woodland Manufacturing Company .....F 609 587-4180
Trenton (G-11009)

2655 Fiber Cans, Tubes & Drums

Alvaro P Escandon Inc 973 274-1040
Newark (G-7043)
Atlantic Waste Services ....F 201 368-0428
Rochelle Park (G-9421)
Caraustar Industries Inc......................E 908 782-0505
Frenchtown (G-3710)
Greif Inc ....E 609 448-5300
Millstone Township (G-6211)
▲ Hicube Coating LLC ....G....... 973 883-7404
Clifton (G-1634)
Ironbound Express Inc ....G....... 973 491-5151
Newark (G-7159)
Ironbound Intermodal Inds Inc ....F 973 491-5151
Newark (G-7160)
Jachts - Columbia Can LLC ....F 973 925-8020
Paterson (G-8218)
John J Chando Jr Inc ....G....... 732 793-2122
Mantoloking (G-5850)
▲ JRC Web Accessories ....F 973 625-3888
Fairfield (G-3247)
◆ Mauser Usa LLC ....E 732 353-7100
East Brunswick (G-2155)
▼ Paper Tubes Cores & Boxes Inc......F 973 977-8823
Paterson (G-8276)
Recycle Inc East..................................D....... 908 756-2200
South Plainfield (G-10325)
▲ Schutz Container Systems Inc ....D....... 908 429-1637
Branchburg (G-682)
◆ Schutz Corp ....D....... 908 526-6161
Branchburg (G-683)
Slys Express LLC ....G....... 908 787-7516
Linden (G-5424)
Sonoco Products Company ....D....... 609 655-0300
Dayton (G-1989)
▲ Tunnel Barrel & Drum Co Inc ....E 201 933-1444
Carlstadt (G-1233)
Union Container Corp...........................E 973 242-3600
Newark (G-7306)

2656 Sanitary Food Containers

◆ American International Cont ....F 973 917-3331
Boonton (G-541)
Amscan Inc ....D....... 973 983-0888
Rockaway (G-9442)
Continental Cup Company LLC ....G....... 602 803-4666
Bernardsville (G-437)
▲ Cw International Sales LLC...............E 732 367-4444
Lakewood (G-5079)
Heavenly Havens Creamery LLC...........G....... 609 259-6600
Allentown (G-27)
Prospect Group LLC............................F 718 635-4007
Piscataway (G-8702)
▲ Soundview Paper Holdings LLC.......A....... 201 796-4000
Elmwood Park (G-2856)
▲ United Plastics Group Inc ....E 732 873-8777
Somerset (G-10091)

2657 Folding Paperboard Boxes

Albert Paper Products Company...........E 973 373-0330
Irvington (G-4554)
Contemprary Grphics Bndery Inc ....C....... 856 663-7277
Camden (G-1054)
◆ Cultech Inc ....C....... 732 225-2722
South Plainfield (G-10244)
Global Direct Marketing Group.............G....... 856 427-6116
Haddonfield (G-4058)
International Container Co ....E 201 440-1600
Hackensack (G-3932)
Interntnal Folding Ppr Box Sls ....E 201 941-3100
Ridgefield (G-9268)
Keystone Folding Box Company............D....... 973 483-1054
Newark (G-7173)
▲ McLean Packaging Corporation ....D....... 856 359-2600
Moorestown (G-6544)
Multi Packaging Solutions Inc ....C....... 908 757-6000
South Plainfield (G-10303)
New York Folding Box Co Inc ....E 973 347-6932
Stanhope (G-10477)

R J Blen Grphic Arts Cnverting	E	732 545-3501
New Brunswick *(G-6964)*		

2671 Paper Coating & Laminating for Packaging

Aeon Industries Inc	G	732 246-3224
Somerset *(G-9943)*		
Allure Box & Display Co	F	212 807-7070
Hackensack *(G-3876)*		
Amcor Flexibles Inc	E	609 267-5900
Mount Holly *(G-6723)*		
Amcor Flexibles LLC	C	856 825-1400
Millville *(G-6224)*		
▲ ANS Plastics Corporation	F	732 247-2776
New Brunswick *(G-6910)*		
◆ Arch Crown Inc	E	973 731-6300
Hillside *(G-4375)*		
Basic Plastics Company Inc	E	973 977-8151
Paterson *(G-8147)*		
Blispak Acquisition Corp	D	973 884-4141
Whippany *(G-11882)*		
Comar Inc	F	856 507-5461
Voorhees *(G-11283)*		
Consolidated Packg Group Inc	C	201 440-4240
Ridgefield Park *(G-9301)*		
Delta Paper Corporation	E	856 532-0333
Burlington *(G-963)*		
E & E Group Corp	G	201 814-0414
South Hackensack *(G-10155)*		
Employment Horizons Inc	B	973 538-8822
Cedar Knolls *(G-1304)*		
▲ Forem Packaging Inc	F	973 589-0402
Newark *(G-7126)*		
Gleicher Manufacturing Corp	E	908 233-2211
Scotch Plains *(G-9732)*		
◆ Holland Manufacturing Co Inc	C	973 584-8141
Succasunna *(G-10513)*		
Homasote Company	C	609 883-3300
Ewing *(G-3036)*		
▲ Ileos of America Inc	C	908 753-7300
South Plainfield *(G-10276)*		
▲ Jrm Industries Inc	E	973 779-9340
Passaic *(G-8077)*		
Kansas City Design Inc	G	609 460-4629
Lambertville *(G-5192)*		
▲ Lally-Pak Inc	D	908 351-4141
Hillside *(G-4409)*		
▲ Lps Industries Inc	C	201 438-3515
Moonachie *(G-6477)*		
LV Adhesive Inc	E	201 507-0080
Carlstadt *(G-1183)*		
MSC Marketing & Technology	E	201 507-9100
Lyndhurst *(G-5665)*		
Multi Packaging Solutions Inc	C	908 757-6000
South Plainfield *(G-10303)*		
Nekoosa Coated Products LLC	G	800 440-1250
South Plainfield *(G-10304)*		
▲ Norpak Corporation	E	973 589-4200
Newark *(G-7219)*		
Polyair Inter Pack Inc	D	201 804-1725
Carlstadt *(G-1203)*		
◆ R Tape Corporation	C	908 753-5570
South Plainfield *(G-10322)*		
▼ US Magic Box Inc	G	973 772-2070
Garfield *(G-3775)*		

2672 Paper Coating & Laminating, Exc for Packaging

American Biltrite Inc	C	856 778-0700
Moorestown *(G-6502)*		
Avery Dennison Corporation	G	201 956-6100
Fair Lawn *(G-3088)*		
Capital Label and Affixing Co	G	856 786-1700
Cinnaminson *(G-1445)*		
CCL Label Inc	D	609 443-3700
Hightstown *(G-4295)*		
CCL Label (delaware) Inc	C	609 259-1055
Trenton *(G-10914)*		
▲ Custom Laminations Inc	E	973 279-9174
Paterson *(G-8166)*		
◆ Dikeman Laminating Corporation	E	973 473-5696
Clifton *(G-1598)*		
Fedex Office & Print Svcs Inc	E	856 427-0099
Cherry Hill *(G-1361)*		
Gleicher Manufacturing Corp	E	908 233-2211
Scotch Plains *(G-9732)*		
Graphic Express Menu Co Inc	E	973 685-0022
Clifton *(G-1629)*		

◆ Holland Manufacturing Co Inc	C	973 584-8141
Succasunna *(G-10513)*		
Horizon Label LLC	F	856 767-0777
West Berlin *(G-11599)*		
Igi Corp	G	908 753-5570
South Plainfield *(G-10275)*		
International Graphics Inc	C	908 753-5570
South Plainfield *(G-10279)*		
▲ Interntnal Adhsive Coating Inc	E	603 893-1894
Somers Point *(G-9937)*		
Intertape Polymer Corp	C	201 391-3315
River Vale *(G-9366)*		
▲ Jrm Industries Inc	E	973 779-9340
Passaic *(G-8077)*		
▲ Kraemer Properties Inc	E	732 886-6557
Lakewood *(G-5118)*		
▲ Label Graphics Mfg Inc	E	973 890-5665
Little Falls *(G-5459)*		
Label Graphics Mfg Inc	G	973 276-1555
Fairfield *(G-3257)*		
Label Master Inc	G	973 546-3110
Lodi *(G-5567)*		
▲ Lacoa Inc	G	973 754-1000
Elmwood Park *(G-2837)*		
▲ Lamart Corporation	E	973 772-6262
Clifton *(G-1654)*		
LV Adhesive Inc	E	201 507-0080
Carlstadt *(G-1183)*		
◆ Main Tape Company Inc	C	609 395-1704
Cranbury *(G-1862)*		
▲ Microseal Industries Inc	F	973 523-0704
Paterson *(G-8258)*		
◆ Nitto Inc	C	732 901-7905
Lakewood *(G-5139)*		
Nitto Inc	G	732 901-7905
Lakewood *(G-5141)*		
Nitto Inc	F	201 645-4950
Teaneck *(G-10641)*		
▲ Norco Inc	C	908 789-1550
Garwood *(G-3787)*		
▲ Omega Heat Transfer Co Inc	F	732 340-0023
West Orange *(G-11775)*		
Par Code Symbology Inc	F	973 918-0550
Roseland *(G-9541)*		
◆ Plus Packaging Inc	G	973 538-2216
Morristown *(G-6694)*		
Renell Label Print Inc	E	201 652-6544
Paramus *(G-7829)*		
Tech-Pak Inc	F	201 935-3800
Wood Ridge *(G-12007)*		
Thermwell Products Co Inc	G	201 684-4400
Mahwah *(G-5782)*		
▲ Trek Inc	G	732 269-6300
Bayville *(G-252)*		
▲ Unifoil Corporation	D	973 244-9900
Fairfield *(G-3335)*		
United Label Corp	G	973 589-6500
Newark *(G-7309)*		
▲ Universal Tape Supply Corp	F	609 653-3191
Somers Point *(G-9940)*		
▲ Web-Cote Ltd	F	973 827-2299
Hamburg *(G-4098)*		
▲ Wet-N-Stick LLC	G	908 687-8273
Union *(G-11099)*		

2673 Bags: Plastics, Laminated & Coated

▲ A-1 Plastic Bags Inc	D	973 344-4441
Newark *(G-7031)*		
Ace Box Landau Co Inc	D	201 871-4776
Englewood Cliffs *(G-2956)*		
▼ All American Poly Corp	C	732 752-3200
Piscataway *(G-8628)*		
Allied Plastics New Jersey LLC	D	973 956-9200
Paterson *(G-8134)*		
◆ Alpha Industries MGT Inc	C	201 933-6000
Lyndhurst *(G-5639)*		
American Transparent Plastic	E	732 287-3000
Edison *(G-2455)*		
▲ ANS Plastics Corporation	F	732 247-2776
New Brunswick *(G-6910)*		
Apco Extruders Inc	E	732 287-3000
Edison *(G-2458)*		
▲ Basic Ltd	E	718 871-6106
Lakewood *(G-5058)*		
Basic Plastics Company Inc	E	973 977-8151
Paterson *(G-8147)*		
Beta Plastics	D	201 933-1400
Carlstadt *(G-1129)*		
CCL Label Inc	D	609 443-3700
Hightstown *(G-4295)*		

▲ Central Poly-Bag Corp	F	908 862-7570
Linden *(G-5332)*		
Consolidated Packg Group Inc	C	201 440-4240
Ridgefield Park *(G-9301)*		
Craft-Pak Inc	F	718 763-0700
Towaco *(G-10867)*		
Dana Poly Corp	E	800 474-1020
Dover *(G-2082)*		
Duro Bag Manufacturing Company	C	908 351-2400
Elizabeth *(G-2731)*		
Epsilon Plastics Inc	D	201 933-6000
Lyndhurst *(G-5651)*		
Essentra Packaging US Inc	C	856 439-1700
Moorestown *(G-6523)*		
Ez-Dumpster LLC	G	908 752-2787
Bridgewater *(G-824)*		
Flexbiosys Inc	F	908 300-3244
Lebanon *(G-5261)*		
Freedom Plastics LLC	F	201 337-9450
Oakland *(G-7629)*		
Gemini Plastic Films Corp	E	973 340-0700
Garfield *(G-3745)*		
General Film Products Inc	E	908 351-0454
Elizabeth *(G-2742)*		
Global Direct Marketing Group	C	856 427-6116
Haddonfield *(G-4058)*		
Goetz & Ruschmann Inc	E	973 383-9270
Newton *(G-7345)*		
◆ Halsted Corporation	E	201 333-0670
Cranbury *(G-1838)*		
Harris Freeman & Co Inc	D	856 787-9026
Moorestown *(G-6527)*		
Heritage Bag Company	D	856 467-2247
Swedesboro *(G-10589)*		
Hershey Industries Inc	F	908 353-3344
Hillside *(G-4396)*		
◆ Inteplast Group Corporation	B	973 994-8000
Livingston *(G-5515)*		
Katies Closets	G	973 300-4007
Newton *(G-7348)*		
Kestrel Closets LLC	G	973 586-1144
Rockaway *(G-9472)*		
Keystone Packaging Service	G	908 454-8567
Phillipsburg *(G-8558)*		
▲ Lps Industries Inc	C	201 438-3515
Moonachie *(G-6477)*		
◆ M & E Packaging Corp	G	201 635-1381
Lyndhurst *(G-5659)*		
M S Plastics and Packg Co	F	973 492-2400
Butler *(G-1007)*		
Mercury Plastic Bag Co Inc	E	973 778-7200
Passaic *(G-8088)*		
▼ Nexus Plastics Incorporated	D	973 427-3311
Hawthorne *(G-4234)*		
▲ Nova Distributors LLC	F	908 222-1010
Edison *(G-2580)*		
▲ Omega Plastics Corp	D	201 507-9100
Lyndhurst *(G-5668)*		
◆ Plus Packaging Inc	G	973 538-2216
Morristown *(G-6694)*		
Potti-Bags Inc	G	201 796-5555
Elmwood Park *(G-2851)*		
Power Bag and Film LLC	F	908 832-6648
Califon *(G-1033)*		
R K S Plastics Inc	G	732 435-8517
New Brunswick *(G-6965)*		
Refrig-It Warehouse	D	973 344-4545
Kearny *(G-4896)*		
◆ Sigma Extruding Corp	D	201 933-5353
Lyndhurst *(G-5677)*		
▲ Source Direct Inc	F	856 768-7445
Cinnaminson *(G-1486)*		
Spectrum Plastics	G	732 564-1899
Piscataway *(G-8716)*		
Tiffany Packaging	G	973 726-8130
Sparta *(G-10412)*		
▲ Trinity Plastics Inc	C	973 994-8018
Livingston *(G-5543)*		
▲ X-L Plastics Inc	C	973 777-9400
Clifton *(G-1741)*		

2674 Bags: Uncoated Paper & Multiwall

Filter Holdings Inc	E	908 687-3500
Union *(G-11054)*		
▲ Fleet Packaging Inc	G	866 302-0340
South Orange *(G-10196)*		
▲ Flexo-Craft Prints Inc	E	973 482-7200
Harrison *(G-4174)*		
P S I Cement Inc	G	609 716-1515
Princeton Junction *(G-9063)*		

2675 Die-Cut Paper & Board

American Bindery Depot Inc ....C 732 287-2370
Edison (G-2453)
▲ Danielle Die Cut Products Inc ....E 973 278-3000
Paterson (G-8167)
Dynamic Die Cutting & Finshg ....F 973 589-8338
Newark (G-7109)
Gleicher Manufacturing Corp ....E 908 233-2211
Scotch Plains (G-9732)
▲ Globe Die-Cutting Products Inc ....C 732 494-7744
Metuchen (G-6057)
Goetz & Ruschmann Inc......................E 973 383-9270
Newton (G-7345)
Grand Displays Inc ....F 201 994-1500
North Bergen (G-7407)
Grand Displays Inc ....E 201 994-1500
Pennsauken (G-8426)
JIT Manufacturing Inc ....F 973 247-7300
Paterson (G-8223)
Prestige Associates Inc ....E 609 393-1509
Trenton (G-10982)
◆ Pro Tapes & Specialties Inc ....C 732 346-0900
North Brunswick (G-7483)
Quality Indexing LLC ....E 908 810-0200
Union (G-11085)
R J Blen Grphic Arts Cnverting ....E 732 545-3501
New Brunswick (G-6964)
Recycled Pprbd Inc Clifton ....E 201 768-7468
Clifton (G-1706)
Red Wallet Connection Inc ....D 201 223-2644
Manchester (G-5849)
Rush Index Tabs Inc ....D 800 914-3036
East Rutherford (G-2317)
Sabre Die Cutting Co Inc ....E 973 357-9800
Paterson (G-8290)
▲ Stephco Sales Inc ....E 973 278-5454
Paterson (G-8301)
Vmc Die Cutting Corp ....F 973 450-4655
Belleville (G-323)

2676 Sanitary Paper Prdts

▲ Arquest Inc ....B 609 395-9500
Millstone Township (G-6209)
▲ Braco Manufacturing Inc ....E 732 752-7777
South Plainfield (G-10227)
Federal Equipment & Mfg Co Inc...........G 973 340-7600
Lodi (G-5562)
◆ Innovative Disposables LLC ....E 908 222-7111
South Plainfield (G-10277)
▲ Interganic Fzco LLC ....G 224 436-0372
Hillsborough (G-4333)
Jnj International Inv LLC ....G 732 524-0400
New Brunswick (G-6939)
Johnson & Johnson ....D 732 524-0400
Piscataway (G-8682)
Johnson & Johnson ....D 732 524-0400
Princeton (G-8967)
Johnson & Johnson ....D 917 573-8007
Ridgefield (G-9269)
Johnson & Johnson ....D 732 524-0400
Lambertville (G-5190)
Johnson & Johnson ....D 732 524-0400
Branchburg (G-650)
Johnson & Johnson ....D 732 524-0400
Trenton (G-10947)
Johnson & Johnson ....A 732 524-0400
New Brunswick (G-6940)
Johnson & Johnson ....D 732 422-5000
North Brunswick (G-7473)
Johnson & Johnson ....G 908 722-9319
Raritan (G-9213)
Johnson & Johnson ....C 908 874-1000
Morris Plains (G-6618)
Johnson & Johnson ....C 732 524-0400
New Brunswick (G-6941)
◆ Keystone Adjustable Cap Co Inc ......E 856 356-2809
Pennsauken (G-8447)
◆ Marcal Manufacturing LLC ....F 201 796-4000
Elmwood Park (G-2839)
Marcal Paper Mills LLC.......................A 800 631-8451
Elmwood Park (G-2840)
▲ Pacon Manufacturing Corp ....C 732 764-9070
Somerset (G-10051)
Professional Disposables Inc ....A 845 365-1700
Woodcliff Lake (G-12062)
▲ Samseng Tissue Co ....F 609 479-3997
Burlington (G-984)
▲ Soundview Paper Holdings LLC ....A 201 796-4000
Elmwood Park (G-2856)

2677 Envelopes

▲ Bravo Pack Inc ....G 856 872-2937
Pennsauken (G-8398)
Cenveo Worldwide Limited ....D 201 434-2100
Jersey City (G-4710)
Envelope Freedom Holdings LLC ....G 201 699-5800
Ridgefield (G-9259)
Old Ue LLC ....B 800 752-4012
Ridgefield (G-9281)
Red Wallet Connection Inc ....D 201 223-2644
Manchester (G-5849)
Tpg Graphics LLC ....G 856 314-0117
Pennsauken (G-8493)
United Envelope LLC ....E 201 699-5800
Ridgefield (G-9296)
Washington Stamp Exchange Inc ....F 973 966-0001
Florham Park (G-3526)
Watonka Printing Inc ....G 732 974-8878
Belmar (G-356)

2678 Stationery Prdts

▲ A D M Corporation ....D 732 469-0900
Middlesex (G-6090)
▲ Adler International Ltd ....G 201 843-4525
Maywood (G-6001)
Arna Marketing Group Inc ....G 908 625-7395
Branchburg (G-621)
Bind-Rite Graphics Inc ....E 201 863-8100
Secaucus (G-9754)
Mega Brands America Inc ....B 973 535-1313
Wood Ridge (G-12004)
▲ Officemate International Corp ....D 732 225-7422
Edison (G-2583)
Yerg Inc ....G 973 759-4041
Lakehurst (G-5040)

2679 Converted Paper Prdts, NEC

Aeon Industries Inc..............................G 732 246-3224
Somerset (G-9943)
▲ Allied Group Inc ....E 973 543-4994
Mendham (G-6038)
◆ Arch Crown Inc ....E 973 731-6300
Hillside (G-4375)
Arrow Paper Company Inc ....G 908 756-1111
Plainfield (G-8759)
Ascot Tag and Label Co Inc ....E 973 482-0900
Newark (G-7055)
▲ B & G Plastics Inc ....G 973 824-9220
Union (G-11028)
Burlington Design Center Inc ....F 856 778-7772
Mount Laurel (G-6745)
Caraustar Clifton Primary Pack ....C 973 472-4900
Clifton (G-1580)
▼ Cartolith Group ....G 908 624-9833
Hillside (G-4385)
CCL Label Inc ....D 609 443-3700
Hightstown (G-4295)
CCL Label Inc ....E 609 586-1332
Robbinsville (G-9409)
Cenveo Worldwide Limited ....D 201 434-2100
Jersey City (G-4710)
Collins and Company LLC ....G 973 427-4068
Hawthorne (G-4212)
▲ Custom Converters Inc ....F 973 994-9000
Livingston (G-5509)
Custom Quick Label Inc ....G 856 596-7555
Marlton (G-5926)
◆ Flexo-Craft Prints Inc ....G 973 482-7200
Harrison (G-4174)
Georgia-Pacific LLC.............................C 908 995-2228
Milford (G-6193)
▲ Glitterwrap Inc ....D 800 745-4883
Rockaway (G-9463)
Goetz & Ruschmann Inc......................E 973 383-9270
Newton (G-7345)
▲ Icup Inc ....E 856 751-2045
Cherry Hill (G-1373)
◆ J Josephson Inc ....G 201 440-7000
South Hackensack (G-10163)
J Josephson Inc ....C 201 440-7000
South Hackensack (G-10164)
J Josephson Inc ....D 201 426-2646
South Hackensack (G-10165)
▲ Jrm Industries Inc ....E 973 779-9340
Passaic (G-8077)
◆ Laminated Industries Inc ....E 908 862-5995
Linden (G-5373)
Laminated Paperboard Corp ....G 908 862-5995
Linden (G-5374)

▲ Legacy Converting Inc ....E 609 642-7020
Cranbury (G-1856)
M S C Paper Products Corp ....E 908 686-2200
Hillside (G-4413)
Magnetic Ticket & Label Corp ....E 973 759-6500
Belleville (G-299)
◆ Matthias Paper Corporation ....E 856 467-6970
Swedesboro (G-10594)
Mod-Tek Converting LLC ....E 856 662-6884
Pennsauken (G-8458)
Princeton Supply Corp ....G 609 683-9100
Princeton (G-9005)
R L R Foil Stamping LLC ....F 973 778-9464
Passaic (G-8100)
Red Letter Press Inc ....G 609 597-5257
Upper Saddle River (G-11146)
Renell Label Print Inc ....G 201 652-6544
Paramus (G-7829)
Rockline Industries Inc.........................C 973 257-2884
Montville (G-6446)
Schiffenhaus Industries Inc ....C 973 484-5000
Newark (G-7263)
Schurman Fine Papers ....E 856 985-1776
Marlton (G-5950)
▲ Seaboard Paper and Twine LLC ....E 973 413-8100
Paterson (G-8296)
Specialty Kraft Converters LLC ....G 732 225-2080
Edison (G-2617)
▲ Stonebridge Paper LLC ....E 973 413-8100
Paterson (G-8303)
◆ Tekkote Corporation ....D 201 585-1708
Leonia (G-5293)
United Label Corp ....E 973 589-6500
Newark (G-7309)
Webtech Inc ....E 609 259-2800
Robbinsville (G-9419)

27 PRINTING, PUBLISHING, AND ALLIED INDUSTRIES

2711 Newspapers: Publishing & Printing

10x Daily LLC ....G 732 276-6407
Lakewood (G-5041)
21st Century Media Newsppr LLC ....D 215 504-4200
Trenton (G-10885)
24 Horas Inc ....F 973 817-7400
Newark (G-7026)
50 Plus Monthly Inc ....G 973 584-7911
Succasunna (G-10508)
About Our Town Inc ....G 732 968-1615
Piscataway (G-8623)
Achievement Journal LLC......................G 732 297-1570
North Brunswick (G-7449)
Advocate Publishing Corp ....E 973 497-4200
Newark (G-7036)
Ainsworth Media ....G 856 854-1400
Collingswood (G-1766)
Alm Media LLC ....E 973 642-0075
Newark (G-7042)
Andis Inc ....G 973 627-0400
Denville (G-2030)
Arab Voice Newspaper ....G 973 523-7815
Paterson (G-8141)
Area Auto Racing News Inc ....G 609 888-3618
Trenton (G-10895)
Arts Weekly Inc ....E 973 812-6766
Little Falls (G-5453)
▲ Asbury Park Press Inc ....A 732 922-6000
Neptune (G-6866)
Atlantic City Week................................F 609 646-4848
Pleasantville (G-8805)
Aus Inc ....G 856 234-9200
Mount Laurel (G-6738)
Bay Shore Press Inc ....E 732 957-0070
Middletown (G-6160)
Bayonne Community News.....................E 201 437-2460
Bayonne (G-205)
Bernardsville News ....G 908 766-3900
Bernardsville (G-435)
Binding Products Inc ....E 212 947-1192
Jersey City (G-4704)
Bloomfield Life Inc ....F 973 233-5001
Cedar Grove (G-1270)
Bloomfield News LLC ....G 973 226-2127
West Caldwell (G-11643)
Borton Enterprises ....F 856 453-9221
Bridgeton (G-752)
Brazilian Press & Advertising ....F 973 344-4555
Newark (G-7073)

Brazilian Voice	G	973 491-6200	
Newark *(G-7074)*			
Burlington Times Inc	B	609 871-8000	
Willingboro *(G-11989)*			
Cabio Newspaper	G	201 902-0811	
West New York *(G-11736)*			
Casas News Publishing Co	E	908 245-6767	
Roselle Park *(G-9579)*			
Catholic Star Herald	G	856 583-6142	
Camden *(G-1050)*			
Central Record Publications	E	609 654-5000	
Trenton *(G-10915)*			
Cgw News LLC	G	973 473-3972	
Clifton *(G-1581)*			
Coast Star	E	732 223-0076	
Manasquan *(G-5830)*			
Coaster Inc	F	732 775-3010	
Asbury Park *(G-73)*			
Community News Network Inc	G	856 428-3399	
Haddonfield *(G-4055)*			
Community News Service LLC	F	609 396-1511	
Lawrenceville *(G-5227)*			
Convention News Company Inc	F	201 444-5075	
Midland Park *(G-6173)*			
Cumberland News Inc	G	856 691-2244	
Vineland *(G-11208)*			
Current Newspaper LLC	E	609 383-8994	
Pleasantville *(G-8809)*			
Daily Dollar LLC	G	732 236-9709	
Monroe Township *(G-6331)*			
Daily News LP	F	212 210-2100	
Jersey City *(G-4720)*			
Daily Plan It Executive Center	G	609 514-9494	
Princeton *(G-8928)*			
David Sisco Jr	G	908 454-0880	
Phillipsburg *(G-8548)*			
Desi Talk LLC	G	212 675-7515	
Jersey City *(G-4723)*			
Diocese of Camden New Jersey	A	856 756-7900	
Camden *(G-1058)*			
Diocese of Paterson	F	973 279-8845	
Clifton *(G-1599)*			
Direct Development LLC	G	732 739-8890	
Tinton Falls *(G-10712)*			
Dolan LLC	G	800 451-9998	
Princeton *(G-8931)*			
Dorf Feature Service Inc	E	908 518-1802	
Mountainside *(G-6843)*			
Dow Jones & Company Inc	G	609 520-4000	
Monmouth Junction *(G-6287)*			
Dow Jones & Company Inc	F	609 520-4000	
Cranbury *(G-1830)*			
Dow Jones & Company Inc	G	609 520-5730	
Plainsboro *(G-8785)*			
Dow Jones & Company Inc	D	609 520-5238	
Monmouth Junction *(G-6288)*			
Dyer Communications Inc	E	732 219-5788	
Red Bank *(G-9227)*			
Elmer Times Co Inc	G	856 358-6171	
Elmer *(G-2796)*			
▲ Epoch Times	G	908 548-8026	
South Plainfield *(G-10252)*			
▲ Evening Journal Association	F	201 653-1000	
Secaucus *(G-9765)*			
Evergreen Information Svcs Inc	F	973 339-9672	
Woodland Park *(G-12077)*			
Financial Information Inc	E	908 222-5300	
South Plainfield *(G-10259)*			
First Friday Global Inc	G	201 776-6709	
Newark *(G-7124)*			
Gail Gersons Wine & Dine Resta	G	732 758-0888	
Shrewsbury *(G-9892)*			
Gannett Co Inc	D	908 243-6953	
Somerville *(G-10112)*			
Gannett Stllite Info Ntwrk Inc	C	856 691-5000	
Vineland *(G-11220)*			
Gannett Stllite Info Ntwrk LLC	B	973 428-6200	
Rockaway *(G-9462)*			
Gannett Stllite Info Ntwrk LLC	F	609 561-2300	
Vineland *(G-11221)*			
Gannett Stllite Info Ntwrk LLC	D	856 663-6000	
Cherry Hill *(G-1366)*			
Gatehuse Media PA Holdings Inc	E	732 246-7677	
New Brunswick *(G-6927)*			
Glassboro News & Food Store	G	856 881-1181	
Glassboro *(G-3812)*			
Gloucester County Times	G	856 845-7484	
Woodbury *(G-12030)*			
Greater Media Newspapers	E	732 358-5200	
Englishtown *(G-3003)*			
Greater Media Newspapers	G	732 254-7004	
Sayreville *(G-9709)*			
▲ Gruppo Editoriale Oggi Inc	E	201 358-6582	
Norwood *(G-7563)*			
Halsey News	G	973 645-0017	
Newark *(G-7144)*			
Hammonton Gazette Inc	G	609 704-1939	
Hammonton *(G-4135)*			
Hawthorne Press	F	973 427-3330	
Hawthorne *(G-4224)*			
Herald News	G	973 569-7000	
Woodland Park *(G-12081)*			
Home News Tribune	G	908 243-6600	
Somerville *(G-10115)*			
Hudson West Publishing Co	F	201 991-1600	
Kearny *(G-4864)*			
Hunterdon County Democrat Inc	D	908 782-4747	
Flemington *(G-3449)*			
Hunterdon County Democrat Inc	G	908 996-4047	
Frenchtown *(G-3713)*			
James Kinkade	F	856 451-1177	
Bridgeton *(G-760)*			
Janas LLC	G	732 536-6719	
Morganville *(G-6590)*			
Jersey Shore News Mgazines Inc	G	609 494-5900	
Surf City *(G-10555)*			
Jewish Standard Inc	F	201 837-8818	
River Edge *(G-9362)*			
Jewish Times of South Jersey	G	609 646-2063	
Pleasantville *(G-8814)*			
Jose Moreira	G	201 991-9001	
Kearny *(G-4873)*			
Journal News V Inc	G	201 986-1458	
Paramus *(G-7811)*			
La Tribuna Publication Inc	G	201 617-1360	
Union City *(G-11118)*			
Latino U S A	G	732 870-1475	
Long Branch *(G-5602)*			
Levy Innovation	G	908 303-4492	
Morristown *(G-6678)*			
Link News	G	732 222-4300	
Long Branch *(G-5603)*			
Luso-Americano Co Inc	E	973 344-3200	
Newark *(G-7189)*			
Macromedia Incorporated	F	201 646-4000	
Hackensack *(G-3942)*			
Medianews Group Inc	D	856 451-1000	
Salem *(G-9695)*			
Medieval Times USA Inc	G	201 933-2220	
Lyndhurst *(G-5662)*			
Micro Media Publications Inc	G	732 657-7344	
Lakehurst *(G-5039)*			
Monmouth Journal	G	732 747-7007	
Red Bank *(G-9237)*			
Montclair Dispatch LLC	G	973 509-8861	
Montclair *(G-6375)*			
Montgomery News	G	908 874-0020	
Skillman *(G-9924)*			
Muse Monthly LLC	G	609 443-3509	
East Windsor *(G-2355)*			
New Jersey Herald	C	973 383-1500	
Newton *(G-7352)*			
New Jersey Jewish News	G	973 887-3900	
Whippany *(G-11898)*			
New Satellite Network LLC	G	908 922-0967	
Scotch Plains *(G-9738)*			
New View Media	E	973 691-3002	
Budd Lake *(G-931)*			
Newark Morning Ledger Co	B	973 392-4141	
Newark *(G-7216)*			
Newark Morning Ledger Co	C	732 560-1560	
Piscataway *(G-8695)*			
Newark Morning Ledger Co	G	973 882-6120	
Pine Brook *(G-8611)*			
News Inc Gloucester City	G	856 456-1199	
Gloucester City *(G-3846)*			
Newspaper Media Group LLC	E	856 779-3800	
Cherry Hill *(G-1399)*			
Newspaper Media Group LLC	E	201 798-7800	
Califon *(G-1032)*			
NJ Advance Media LLC	D	732 902-4300	
Edison *(G-2575)*			
NJ Press Media	G	732 643-3604	
Neptune *(G-6893)*			
▲ North Jersey Media Group Inc	A	201 646-4000	
Hackensack *(G-3955)*			
North Jersey Media Group Inc	G	201 933-1166	
Rutherford *(G-9629)*			
North Jersey Media Group Inc	E	973 233-5000	
Montclair *(G-6379)*			
North Jersey Media Group Inc	E	973 569-7100	
Woodland Park *(G-12085)*			
North Jersey Media Group Inc	C	201 485-7800	
Mahwah *(G-5760)*			
Observer Park	F	201 798-7007	
Hoboken *(G-4471)*			
Ocean Star	G	732 899-7606	
Point Pleasant Beach *(G-8830)*			
Packet Media LLC	E	856 779-3800	
Englishtown *(G-3007)*			
Palisades Magnolia Prpts LLC	G	201 424-7180	
Palisades Park *(G-7776)*			
Paper Dove Press LLC	G	201 641-7938	
Little Ferry *(G-5493)*			
Paradise Publishing Group LLC	G	609 227-7642	
Willingboro *(G-11994)*			
Parker Publications	F	908 766-3900	
Madison *(G-5699)*			
Parker Publications Inc	E	908 766-3900	
Bernardsville *(G-441)*			
Pascack Press	G	201 664-2105	
Westwood *(G-11838)*			
Penn Jersey Advance Inc	D	201 775-6610	
Secaucus *(G-9796)*			
Philadelphia Inquirer	E	856 779-3840	
Cherry Hill *(G-1408)*			
Phildelphia-Newspapers-Llc	A	609 823-0453	
Ventnor City *(G-11154)*			
Princeton Packet Inc	C	609 924-3244	
Princeton *(G-9001)*			
Publishing Technology Inc	G	732 563-9292	
New Brunswick *(G-6963)*			
Recorder Newspaper	G	973 226-4000	
Caldwell *(G-1029)*			
Recorder Publishing Co	G	908 647-1180	
Stirling *(G-10495)*			
Recorder Publishing Co Inc	D	908 766-3900	
Whippany *(G-11907)*			
Red Bank Gstrntrology Assoc PA	E	732 842-4294	
Red Bank *(G-9242)*			
Redhedink LLC	G	973 890-2320	
Totowa *(G-10848)*			
Reminder Newspaper	F	856 825-8811	
Millville *(G-6268)*			
Reporte Hispano	G	609 933-1400	
Princeton *(G-9016)*			
Richard Rein	F	609 452-7000	
Lawrence Township *(G-5219)*			
Sample Media Inc	G	609 884-2021	
Cape May *(G-1101)*			
Sample Media Inc	E	609 399-5411	
Ocean City *(G-7695)*			
School Publications Co Inc	E	732 988-1100	
Neptune *(G-6896)*			
Seawave Corp	E	609 886-8600	
Rio Grande *(G-9358)*			
South Jersey Publishing Co	B	609 272-7000	
Pleasantville *(G-8819)*			
South Jersey Publishing Co	F	856 692-0455	
Vineland *(G-11267)*			
Star News Group	G	732 223-0076	
Manasquan *(G-5839)*			
Str8line Publishing Company	G	919 717-6740	
Newark *(G-7288)*			
Suburban Guides Inc	G	201 452-4989	
Waretown *(G-11394)*			
Summit Professional Networks	E	201 526-1230	
Hoboken *(G-4483)*			
Tapintonet	G	908 279-0303	
New Providence *(G-7021)*			
Targum Publishing Company	E	732 247-1286	
New Brunswick *(G-6973)*			
Times of Trenton Pubg Corp	A	609 989-5454	
Trenton *(G-10998)*			
Tribuna Hispana	G	609 646-9167	
Pleasantville *(G-8820)*			
U S A Distributors Inc	E	201 348-1959	
Union City *(G-11130)*			
Ukrainian National Association	E	973 292-9800	
Parsippany *(G-8032)*			
Valuewalk LLC	G	973 767-2181	
Passaic *(G-8114)*			
Venture Info Network	G	609 279-0777	
Princeton *(G-9041)*			
Vicinity Media Group Inc	F	973 276-1688	
Fairfield *(G-3343)*			
Walden Mott Corp	E	201 962-3704	
Ramsey *(G-9158)*			
Wall Street Journal	G	609 520-4000	
Monmouth Junction *(G-6318)*			

Watthung Communications Inc ....F 908 232-4407
Westfield *(G-11805)*
West Essex Tribune Inc ....F 973 992-1771
Livingston *(G-5547)*
Wilmington Trust Sp Services ....C 609 272-7000
Pleasantville *(G-8821)*
World Journal LLC ....F 732 632-8890
Metuchen *(G-6084)*
Worrall Community Newspapers ....G 973 743-4040
Bloomfield *(G-522)*
▲ **Yated Neeman Inc** ....F 845 369-1600
Lakewood *(G-5185)*

2721 Periodicals: Publishing & Printing

42 Design Square LLC ....F 888 272-5979
Parsippany *(G-7870)*
Advanstar Communications Inc ....E 973 944-7777
Montvale *(G-6395)*
Advanstar Communications Inc ....E 732 596-0276
Iselin *(G-4590)*
▲ **Airbrush Action Inc** ....G 732 223-7878
Barnegat *(G-155)*
Alexander Communications Group ....F 973 265-2300
Mountain Lakes *(G-6820)*
Alternate Side Street Suspende ....G 201 291-7878
Paramus *(G-7788)*
▲ **AM Best Company Inc** ....A 908 439-2200
Oldwick *(G-7738)*
AM Best Company Inc ....B 908 439-2200
Oldwick *(G-7739)*
American Foreclosures Inc ....F 201 501-0200
Bergenfield *(G-370)*
Amy Publications LLC ....G 973 235-1800
Nutley *(G-7579)*
Anderson Publishing Ltd ....G 908 301-1995
Scotch Plains *(G-9729)*
Area Auto Racing News Inc ....G 609 888-3618
Trenton *(G-10895)*
Arts Weekly Inc ....E 973 812-6766
Little Falls *(G-5453)*
B T O Industries Inc ....G 973 243-0011
West Orange *(G-11761)*
Backroads Inc ....G 973 948-4176
Newton *(G-7338)*
Barry Urner Publications Inc ....D 732 240-5330
Toms River *(G-10748)*
▲ **Bauer Publishing Company LP** ....G 201 569-6699
Englewood Cliffs *(G-2960)*
Bbm Fairway Inc ....G 856 596-0999
Marlton *(G-5922)*
BNP Media Inc ....G 201 291-9001
Paramus *(G-7793)*
Bondi Digital Publishing LLC ....G 212 405-1655
Edgewater *(G-2434)*
Carstens Publications Inc ....E 973 383-3355
Newton *(G-7339)*
Casino Player Publishing LLC ....E 609 404-0600
Galloway *(G-3721)*
Central Record Publications ....E 609 654-5000
Trenton *(G-10915)*
Charter Fincl Pubg Netwrk Inc ....E 732 450-8866
Shrewsbury *(G-9885)*
Christian Mssons In Many Lands ....G 732 449-8880
Wall Township *(G-11324)*
Civic Research Institute Inc ....G 609 683-4450
Kingston *(G-5008)*
Commerce Enterprises Inc ....F 201 368-2100
Paramus *(G-7794)*
Convention News Company Inc ....F 201 444-5075
Midland Park *(G-6173)*
Curran & Connors Inc ....G 609 514-0104
Princeton *(G-8925)*
Data Cntrum Communications Inc ....F 201 391-1911
Montvale *(G-6407)*
Dentistry Today Inc ....E 973 882-4700
Fairfield *(G-3184)*
Dowden Health Media Inc ....D 201 740-6100
Montvale *(G-6408)*
Drug Delivery Technology LLC ....E 973 299-1200
Montville *(G-6441)*
E W Williams Publications ....F 201 592-7007
Fort Lee *(G-3556)*
Evergreen Information Svcs Inc ....F 973 339-9672
Woodland Park *(G-12077)*
Excerpta Medica Inc ....D 908 547-2100
Bridgewater *(G-822)*
Fellowship In Prayer Inc ....G 609 924-6863
Princeton *(G-8948)*
Foundation For Student Comm ....E 609 258-1111
Princeton *(G-8950)*
Friday Morning Quarterback ....E 856 424-6873
Cherry Hill *(G-1363)*
Frontline Med Cmmnications Inc ....D 973 206-3434
Parsippany *(G-7952)*
Galen Publishing LLC ....E 908 253-9001
Somerville *(G-10111)*
Garden State Woman Mag LLC ....G 908 879-7143
Long Valley *(G-5611)*
General Commis Archives & Hstr ....G 973 408-3189
Madison *(G-5693)*
Global Strategy Institute A ....G 973 615-7447
Bloomfield *(G-501)*
Golf Odyssey LLC ....G 973 564-6223
Short Hills *(G-9869)*
Haymarket Media Inc ....G 201 799-4800
Paramus *(G-7805)*
Heinrich Bauer Publishing LP ....F 201 569-6699
Englewood *(G-2911)*
Heinrich Bauer Verlag ....E 201 569-0006
Englewood Cliffs *(G-2973)*
▲ **Hobby Publications Inc** ....E 732 536-5160
Freehold *(G-3668)*
Houses Magazine Inc ....F 973 605-1877
Morris Plains *(G-6615)*
Hsh Assoc Financial Publishers ....G 973 838-3330
Butler *(G-1004)*
Hyp Hair Inc ....E 201 843-4004
Montclair *(G-6369)*
Industry Publications Inc ....F 973 331-9545
Parsippany *(G-7961)*
Information Today Inc ....E 609 654-6266
Medford *(G-6024)*
Innovation In Medtech LLC ....G 888 202-5939
Chatham *(G-1321)*
Intellisphere LLC ....G 609 716-7777
Plainsboro *(G-8797)*
International Data Group Inc ....F 732 460-9404
Eatontown *(G-2405)*
Interntonal Med News Group LLC ....F 973 290-8237
Parsippany *(G-7964)*
Investment Casting Institute ....G 201 573-9770
Montvale *(G-6414)*
J S Paluch Co Inc ....F 732 516-1900
Edison *(G-2537)*
Jannetti Publications ....D 856 256-2300
Sewell *(G-9849)*
◆ **John Wiley & Sons Inc** ....D 201 748-6000
Hoboken *(G-4460)*
Jonas Media Group Inc ....F 973 438-1900
Newark *(G-7170)*
Jury Vrdict Rview Publications ....G 973 376-9002
Springfield *(G-10449)*
Keypoint Intelligence LLC ....G 201 489-6439
Hackensack *(G-3936)*
Keypoint Intelligence LLC ....E 973 797-2100
Fairfield *(G-3249)*
Kicksonfirecom LLC ....G 718 753-4248
South Amboy *(G-10135)*
Know America Media LLC ....G 770 650-1102
Roseland *(G-9540)*
Lawyers Diary and Manual LLC ....E 973 642-1440
New Providence *(G-7005)*
Lead Conversion Plus ....F 802 497-1557
Manalapan *(G-5816)*
Macromedia Incorporated ....F 201 646-4000
Hackensack *(G-3942)*
McMunn Associates ....E 856 858-3440
Collingswood *(G-1770)*
Media Vista Inc ....G 732 747-8060
Red Bank *(G-9236)*
Middlesex Publications ....F 732 435-0005
North Brunswick *(G-7477)*
Mindwise Media LLC ....G 973 701-0685
Chatham *(G-1327)*
Missionary Society of St Paul ....E 201 825-7300
Mahwah *(G-5755)*
Modern Drummer Publications ....F 973 239-4140
Fairfield *(G-3272)*
Music Trades Corp ....G 201 871-1965
Englewood *(G-2927)*
▼ **N J W Magazine** ....F 201 886-2185
Fort Lee *(G-3575)*
National Housing Institute ....G 973 509-1600
Montclair *(G-6377)*
New Jersey Bus & Indust Assn ....D 609 393-7707
Trenton *(G-10961)*
New Jersey Business Magazine ....G 973 882-5004
Fairfield *(G-3278)*
New Jersey Monthly LLC ....E 973 539-8230
Morristown *(G-6689)*
New Jrsey State Leag Mncplties ....F 609 695-3481
Trenton *(G-10964)*
Northstar Travel Media LLC ....C 201 902-2000
Secaucus *(G-9794)*
Npt Publishing Group Inc ....F 973 401-0202
Morris Plains *(G-6620)*
Nsgv Inc ....C 212 620-2200
Jersey City *(G-4774)*
Options Edge LLC ....G 973 701-0051
Summit *(G-10542)*
P D Salco Inc ....F 973 716-0517
Livingston *(G-5533)*
Pentacle Publishing Corp ....E 732 240-3000
Toms River *(G-10782)*
Physicans Educatn Resource LLC ....G 609 378-3701
Plainsboro *(G-8799)*
Pioneer Associates Inc ....E 201 592-7007
Fort Lee *(G-3581)*
▲ **Plexus Publishing Inc** ....E 609 654-6500
Medford *(G-6031)*
Princton Almni Pblications Inc ....G 609 258-4885
Princeton *(G-9008)*
Quadrant Media Corp Inc ....G 973 701-8900
Parsippany *(G-8003)*
▲ **Quick Frozen Foods Intl** ....E 201 592-7007
Fort Lee *(G-3583)*
Recruit Co Ltd ....E 201 216-0600
Jersey City *(G-4798)*
Relx Inc ....D 973 812-1900
Woodland Park *(G-12090)*
Renard Commmunications Inc ....E 973 912-8550
Springfield *(G-10464)*
Retail Management Pubg Inc ....F 212 981-0217
Montclair *(G-6388)*
Rodman Media Corp ....E 201 825-2552
Montvale *(G-6432)*
▲ **Scholastic Uk Group LLC** ....C 201 633-2400
Secaucus *(G-9810)*
School Publications Co Inc ....E 732 988-1100
Neptune *(G-6896)*
Showcase Publications Inc ....D 732 349-1134
Toms River *(G-10792)*
Sino Monthly New Jersey Inc ....F 732 650-0688
Edison *(G-2611)*
Sj Magazine ....F 856 722-9300
Maple Shade *(G-5869)*
Skinder-Strauss LLC ....C 973 642-1440
New Providence *(G-7018)*
SMR Research Corporation ....G 908 852-7677
Hackettstown *(G-4037)*
Sneaker Swarm LLC ....F 908 693-9262
Woodbridge *(G-12021)*
Sports Impact Inc ....G 732 257-1451
East Brunswick *(G-2179)*
Springer Scnce + Bus Media LLC ....D 201 348-4033
Secaucus *(G-9817)*
Steppin Out Magazine ....G 201 703-0911
Fair Lawn *(G-3122)*
Steward LLC ....G 609 816-8825
Princeton *(G-9028)*
T3i Group LLC ....E 856 424-1100
Cherry Hill *(G-1420)*
Thomas Greco Publishing Inc ....F 973 667-6965
Nutley *(G-7594)*
Thomas Publishing Company LLC ....E 973 543-4994
Chester *(G-1435)*
Tommax Inc ....G 732 224-1046
Red Bank *(G-9246)*
◆ **Transaction Publishers Inc** ....E 732 445-2280
Piscataway *(G-8732)*
Union Institute Inc ....E 800 914-8138
Mahwah *(G-5785)*
Unisphere Media LLC ....F 908 795-3701
New Providence *(G-7023)*
US Frontline News Inc ....E 646 284-6233
Demarest *(G-2026)*
US News & World Report Inc ....F 212 716-6800
Iselin *(G-4634)*
Vicinity Publications Inc ....G 973 276-1688
Fairfield *(G-3344)*
Visual Impact Advertising Inc ....F 973 763-4900
Maplewood *(G-5889)*
Vitamin Retailer Magazine Inc ....G 732 432-9600
East Brunswick *(G-2191)*
Walden Mott Corp ....G 201 962-3704
Ramsey *(G-9158)*
Webannuitiescom Inc ....G 732 521-5110
Monroe *(G-6324)*

SIC

2731 Books: Publishing & Printing

Africa World Press G 609 695-3200
Ewing *(G-3013)*

Alexander Communications Group F 973 265-2300
Mountain Lakes *(G-6820)*

▲ AM Best Company Inc A 908 439-2200
Oldwick *(G-7738)*

AM Best Company Inc B 908 439-2200
Oldwick *(G-7739)*

Apples & Honey Press LLC F 973 379-7200
Springfield *(G-10427)*

Avstar Publishing Corp G 908 236-6210
Lebanon *(G-5252)*

Banquet Services International G 732 270-1188
Toms River *(G-10747)*

Barnes & Noble Booksellers Inc E 201 272-3635
Lyndhurst *(G-5642)*

▲ Behrman House Inc F 973 379-7200
Millburn *(G-6195)*

Berlitz Languages US Inc D 609 759-5371
Princeton *(G-8914)*

Blue Dome Inc G 646 415-9331
Clifton *(G-1576)*

Bon Venture Services LLC D 973 584-5699
Flanders *(G-3402)*

Bookcode Corp G 732 742-0481
Woodbridge *(G-12015)*

Carstens Publications Inc E 973 383-3355
Newton *(G-7339)*

Chatham Bookseller Inc G 973 822-1361
Madison *(G-5690)*

Childrens Research & Dev Co G 856 546-8814
Haddon Heights *(G-4044)*

CNG Publishing Company G 973 768-0978
Burlington *(G-959)*

Colt Media Inc G 732 946-3276
Colts Neck *(G-1779)*

Comex Systems Inc G 800 543-6959
Chester *(G-1432)*

Creative Competitions Inc F 856 256-2797
Sewell *(G-9838)*

Dawn Bible Students Assn G 201 438-6421
East Rutherford *(G-2285)*

Ensembleiq Inc E 201 855-7600
Newark *(G-7116)*

Evergreen Information Svcs Inc F 973 339-9672
Woodland Park *(G-12077)*

Excerpta Medica Inc D 908 547-2100
Bridgewater *(G-822)*

◆ Franklin Electronic Publs Inc D 609 386-2500
Burlington *(G-969)*

◆ Franklin Mint LLC E 800 843-6468
Fort Lee *(G-3559)*

Galves Auto Price List Inc F 201 393-0051
Teterboro *(G-10678)*

Gann Law Books Inc F 973 268-1200
Newark *(G-7131)*

Gorgias Press LLC G 732 885-8900
Piscataway *(G-8669)*

▲ Haights Cross Cmmnications Inc E 212 209-0500
Princeton Junction *(G-9060)*

Hispanic Outlook In Higher G 201 587-8800
Saddle Brook *(G-9655)*

Hispanic Outlook-12 Mag Inc G 201 587-8800
Fair Lawn *(G-3104)*

▲ Howard Press Inc D 908 245-4400
Roselle *(G-9561)*

▲ Hudson Group (hg) Inc B 201 939-5050
East Rutherford *(G-2292)*

J S Paluch Co Inc F 732 516-1900
Edison *(G-2537)*

J S Paluch Co Inc E 732 238-2412
East Brunswick *(G-2153)*

◆ John Wiley & Sons Inc D 201 748-6000
Hoboken *(G-4460)*

John Wiley & Sons Inc D 732 302-2265
Edison *(G-2541)*

John Wiley & Sons Inc G 201 748-6000
Hoboken *(G-4461)*

▲ Just US Books Inc G 973 672-7701
East Orange *(G-2254)*

Learning Links-Usa Inc G 516 437-9071
Cranbury *(G-1855)*

Life Skills Education Inc G 507 645-2994
Springfield *(G-10453)*

▲ Manning Publication Co F 856 375-2597
Cherry Hill *(G-1388)*

Markus Wiener Publishers Inc G 609 921-1141
Princeton *(G-8973)*

Mathematics League Inc G 201 568-6328
Tenafly *(G-10664)*

Matthew Bender & Company Inc D 518 487-3000
Newark *(G-7197)*

McGraw-Hill Glbl Edctn Hldngs D 609 371-8301
East Windsor *(G-2354)*

Metal Powder Inds Federation F 609 452-7700
Princeton *(G-8977)*

Missionary Society of St Paul E 201 825-7300
Mahwah *(G-5755)*

Modern Drummer Publications F 973 239-4140
Fairfield *(G-3272)*

New Horizon Press Publishers G 908 604-6311
Liberty Corner *(G-5295)*

New York-NJ Trail Conference F 201 512-9348
Mahwah *(G-5757)*

NJ Dept Military Vtrans G 856 384-8831
Woodbury *(G-12033)*

Patterson Smith Publishing G 973 744-3291
Montclair *(G-6384)*

▲ Paulist Press Inc G 201 825-7300
Mahwah *(G-5761)*

◆ Pearson Education Inc A 201 236-7000
Hoboken *(G-4473)*

Pearson Education Inc D 914 287-8000
Hoboken *(G-4474)*

Pearson Education Inc E 609 395-6000
Cranbury *(G-1871)*

Pearson Education Inc F 201 785-2721
Hoboken *(G-4475)*

Pearson Inc E 201 236-7000
Upper Saddle River *(G-11144)*

▼ Pearson Technology Centre Inc G 201 767-5000
Old Tappan *(G-7735)*

Pegasus Group Publishing Inc F 973 884-9100
East Hanover *(G-2234)*

▲ Peoples Education Inc C 201 712-0090
Montvale *(G-6422)*

Peoples Eductl Holdings Inc G 201 712-0090
Montvale *(G-6423)*

Philip Lief Group Inc G 609 430-1000
Princeton *(G-8995)*

▲ Plexus Publishing Inc E 609 654-6500
Medford *(G-6031)*

▲ Presbyterian Reformed Pubg Co F 908 454-0505
Phillipsburg *(G-8570)*

Princeton Publishing Group G 609 577-0693
Princeton *(G-9002)*

▲ Princeton University Press D 609 258-4900
Princeton *(G-9007)*

Railpace Co Inc G 732 388-4984
Clark *(G-1514)*

Red Sea Press Inc G 609 695-3200
Ewing *(G-3059)*

▲ Renaissance House G 201 408-4048
Englewood *(G-2937)*

Research & Education Assn E 732 819-8880
Piscataway *(G-8705)*

Rosemont Publishing & Printing F 609 269-8094
Plainsboro *(G-8802)*

RR Bowker LLC C 908 286-1090
New Providence *(G-7017)*

Scholastic Inc E 201 633-2400
Secaucus *(G-9809)*

School Publications Co Inc E 732 988-1100
Neptune *(G-6896)*

Silicon Press Inc G 908 273-8919
Summit *(G-10547)*

Simon & Schuster Inc E 973 656-6000
Parsippany *(G-8016)*

Springer Scnce + Bus Media LLC D 201 348-4033
Secaucus *(G-9817)*

Sterling Publishing Co Inc F 732 248-6563
Monroe Township *(G-6346)*

Taryag Legacy Foundation Inc F 732 569-2467
Lakewood *(G-5170)*

Techsetters Inc E 856 240-7905
Collingswood *(G-1772)*

TFH Publications Inc D 732 897-6860
Neptune *(G-6900)*

TFH Publications Inc E 732 988-8400
Neptune *(G-6901)*

Thomson Reuters (markets) LLC G 973 286-7200
Newark *(G-7298)*

Thomson Reuters Corporation B 212 337-4281
Newark *(G-7299)*

◆ Transaction Publishers Inc E 732 445-2280
Piscataway *(G-8732)*

Trilogy Publications LLC G 201 816-1211
Englewood Cliffs *(G-2993)*

Truckeros News LLC F 732 340-1043
Rahway *(G-9129)*

W G I Corp F 732 370-2900
Lakewood *(G-5179)*

▲ Wiley Publishing LLC B 201 748-6000
Hoboken *(G-4488)*

Wiley Subscription Services F 201 748-6000
Hoboken *(G-4489)*

Wordmasters G 201 327-4201
Allendale *(G-20)*

Wt Media LLC F 609 921-3490
Trenton *(G-11011)*

2732 Book Printing, Not Publishing

All In Color Inc G 973 626-0987
Paterson *(G-8133)*

▲ AM Best Company Inc A 908 439-2200
Oldwick *(G-7738)*

Aramani Inc G 201 945-1160
Fairview *(G-3356)*

Athletic Organizational Aids E 201 652-1485
Midland Park *(G-6170)*

Binding Products Inc E 212 947-1192
Jersey City *(G-4704)*

Command Web Offset Company Inc C 201 863-8100
Secaucus *(G-9757)*

Forbes Media LLC D 212 620-2200
Jersey City *(G-4737)*

▲ G & H Soho Inc F 201 216-9400
Elmwood Park *(G-2826)*

▲ Howard Press Inc D 908 245-4400
Roselle *(G-9561)*

NJ Copy Center LLC G 973 788-1600
Fairfield *(G-3281)*

Oceanic Graphic Intl Inc F 201 883-1816
Hackensack *(G-3957)*

Phoenix Color Corp E 800 632-4111
Rockaway *(G-9485)*

School Publications Co Inc E 732 988-1100
Neptune *(G-6896)*

Service Data Corp Inc G 908 522-0020
Summit *(G-10546)*

Starnet Printing Inc G 201 760-2600
Mahwah *(G-5776)*

Surviving Life Corp G 973 543-3370
Mendham *(G-6044)*

◆ Wellspring Info Inc F 800 268-3682
Montclair *(G-6393)*

Wheal-Grace Corp E 973 450-8100
Belleville *(G-324)*

2741 Misc Publishing

Access Response Inc G 732 660-0770
Ocean *(G-7652)*

Action Press Park Slope G 718 624-3457
Holmdel *(G-4492)*

Altare Publishing Inc G 727 237-1330
Ewing *(G-3014)*

American Directory Publishing G 609 494-4055
Surf City *(G-10554)*

American Soc of Mech Engineers D 973 244-2282
Little Falls *(G-5451)*

Anjoyx LLC G 323 505-2002
Jackson *(G-4639)*

Arthur A Kaplan Co Inc E 201 806-2100
East Rutherford *(G-2273)*

Beterrific Corp G 201 735-7711
Fort Lee *(G-3549)*

Bitwine Inc F 888 866-9435
Tenafly *(G-10660)*

◆ Bookazine Co Inc D 201 339-7777
Bayonne *(G-207)*

Bruce Teleky Inc G 718 965-9694
Jersey City *(G-4706)*

Cape Publishing Inc G 609 898-4500
Cape May *(G-1094)*

Captivate Internationalllc G 732 734-0403
Edison *(G-2473)*

Cariletha Company Inc F 609 222-3055
Mount Laurel *(G-6746)*

Catalogue Publishers Inc F 973 423-3600
Fair Lawn *(G-3093)*

Central Record Publications E 609 654-5000
Trenton *(G-10915)*

Charles Kerr Enterprises Inc G 732 738-6500
Edison *(G-2476)*

Chryslis Data Sltons Svcs Corp G 609 375-2000
Princeton *(G-8922)*

Clyde Otis Music Group G 845 425-8198
Englewood *(G-2893)*

Cohansey Cove	G	609 884-7726	
Cape May (G-1095)			
College Spun Media Inc	G	973 945-5040	
Hoboken (G-4448)			
Commerce Register Inc	E	201 445-3000	
Midland Park (G-6172)			
Community Pride Publications	F	609 921-8760	
Princeton Junction (G-9053)			
Consumer Graphics Inc	G	732 469-4699	
Somerset (G-9977)			
Creationsrewards Net LLC	G	908 526-3127	
Manville (G-5854)			
Criterion Publishing Co	G	732 548-8300	
Metuchen (G-6053)			
Crossfire Publications	G	516 352-9087	
Caldwell (G-1021)			
Discovery Map	G	973 868-4552	
Morristown (G-6660)			
Door Center Enterprises Inc	G	609 333-1233	
Hopewell (G-4526)			
Dorado Systems LLC	F	856 354-0048	
Haddonfield (G-4056)			
▲ Down Shore Publishing Corp	G	609 978-1233	
West Creek (G-11686)			
Dune Grass Publishing LLC	G	609 774-6562	
Blackwood (G-464)			
Eastside Express Corporation	G	908 486-3300	
Linden (G-5344)			
Ebsco Industries Inc	E	732 542-8600	
Shrewsbury (G-9891)			
Ebsco Industries Inc	D	201 569-2500	
Tinton Falls (G-10715)			
Ebsco Publishing Inc	E	201 968-9899	
Hackensack (G-3910)			
Eclecticism Publishing LLC	E	212 714-4714	
Robbinsville (G-9411)			
Electedface LLC	E	609 924-3636	
Princeton (G-8939)			
Electrochemical Society Inc	E	609 737-1902	
Pennington (G-8364)			
Entourage Imaging Inc	E	888 926-6571	
Princeton Junction (G-9056)			
Excerpta Medica Inc	D	908 547-2100	
Bridgewater (G-822)			
Faulkner Information Svcs LLC	D	856 662-2070	
Medford (G-6022)			
Financial Information Inc	E	908 222-5300	
South Plainfield (G-10259)			
Florentine Press Inc	G	201 386-9200	
Jersey City (G-4736)			
◆ Franklin Electronic Publs Inc	D	609 386-2500	
Burlington (G-969)			
Friday Morning Quarterback	E	856 424-6873	
Cherry Hill (G-1363)			
Galves Auto Price List Inc	F	201 393-0051	
Teterboro (G-10678)			
Geolytics Inc	G	908 707-1505	
Branchburg (G-644)			
Gmp Publications Inc	G	609 859-3400	
Southampton (G-10364)			
Go Waddle Inc	G	301 452-5084	
Berkeley Heights (G-399)			
▲ Gorgias Press	G	732 699-0343	
Piscataway (G-8668)			
Grafwed Internet Media Studios	G	201 632-1771	
Midland Park (G-6175)			
Greetingtap	G	347 731-4263	
South Plainfield (G-10269)			
Grey House Publishing Inc	G	201 968-0500	
Hackensack (G-3925)			
Hal Leonard LLC	C	973 337-5034	
Montclair (G-6368)			
Harrison Scott Pblications Inc	E	201 659-1700	
Hoboken (G-4453)			
Heritage Publishing	G	732 747-7770	
Colts Neck (G-1785)			
Hudson West Publishing Co	F	201 991-1600	
Kearny (G-4864)			
Hyman W Fisher Inc	G	973 992-9155	
Livingston (G-5514)			
Information Today Inc	F	908 219-0279	
New Providence (G-7004)			
Iws License Corp	F	732 872-0014	
Atlantic Highlands (G-107)			
J D M Associates Inc	G	973 773-8699	
Lodi (G-5566)			
J Media LLC	G	201 600-4573	
Norwood (G-7567)			
J S Paluch Co Inc	E	732 238-2412	
East Brunswick (G-2153)			

J S Paluch Co Inc	F	732 516-1900	
Edison (G-2537)			
Jav Latin America Express	G	201 868-5004	
West New York (G-11743)			
Jem Printing Inc	G	908 782-9986	
Flemington (G-3450)			
Jersey Bound Latino LLC	G	908 591-2830	
Union (G-11066)			
Jersey Job Guide Inc	G	732 263-9675	
Long Branch (G-5601)			
Jersey Shore News Mgazines Inc	E	609 494-5900	
Surf City (G-10555)			
Jersey Shore Publications	G	732 892-1276	
Brick (G-723)			
▲ Jigsaw Publishing LLC	G	973 838-4838	
Butler (G-1006)			
John Patrick Publishing LLC	D	609 883-2700	
Ewing (G-3038)			
John R Zabka Associates Inc	F	201 405-0075	
Oakland (G-7633)			
Jonas Media Group Inc	F	973 438-1900	
Newark (G-7170)			
Jump Start Press	G	732 892-4994	
Point Pleasant Beach (G-8825)			
Kabab & Curry Express	G	732 416-6560	
Edison (G-2544)			
Kates-Bylston Publications Inc	G	732 746-0211	
Wall Township (G-11350)			
Laennec Publishing Inc	G	973 882-9500	
Parsippany (G-7971)			
Lead Bead Publishing Company	G	732 246-0410	
Somerset (G-10014)			
▲ Light Inc	G	973 777-2704	
Clifton (G-1659)			
Little Fox Inc	G	609 919-9691	
Englewood Cliffs (G-2984)			
▲ Lympha Press USA	G	732 792-9677	
Freehold (G-3678)			
M J Powers & Co Publishers	G	973 898-1200	
Morristown (G-6683)			
M/C Communications LLC	F	908 766-0402	
Basking Ridge (G-188)			
▲ Macie Publishing Company	G	973 983-8700	
Mendham (G-6040)			
Magazinexperts LLC	G	973 383-0888	
Newton (G-7349)			
Manna Group LLC	F	856 881-7650	
Mount Laurel (G-6780)			
Marquis - Whos Who Inc	D	908 673-1006	
New Providence (G-7009)			
Micro Logic Inc	F	201 962-7510	
Mahwah (G-5753)			
Moscova Enterprises Inc	F	848 628-4873	
Jersey City (G-4768)			
National Home Planning Service	G	973 376-3200	
Chatham (G-1328)			
New York-NJ Trail Conference	F	201 512-9348	
Mahwah (G-5757)			
Nextwave Web LLC	F	973 742-4339	
Paterson (G-8269)			
Nighthawk Interactive LLC	G	732 243-9922	
Edison (G-2574)			
Nonzero Foundation Inc	G	609 688-0793	
Princeton (G-8986)			
North Jersey Media Group Inc	G	973 569-7100	
Woodland Park (G-12085)			
Northern State Periodicals LLC	G	973 782-6100	
Paterson (G-8272)			
Oasis Entertainment Group	G	973 256-7077	
Cedar Grove (G-1285)			
Odowd Enterprises Inc	G	973 227-4607	
Pine Brook (G-8612)			
Old Barracks Association Inc	F	609 396-1776	
Trenton (G-10968)			
P O V Incorporated	F	914 258-4361	
Montclair (G-6381)			
Pavexpress	G	201 330-8300	
Clifton (G-1686)			
Perfect Clicks LLC	G	845 323-6116	
Woodcliff Lake (G-12061)			
Physicians Weekly LLC	G	908 766-0421	
Basking Ridge (G-195)			
Princeton Information Center	G	609 924-7019	
Princeton (G-8999)			
▲ Princeton University Press	D	609 258-4900	
Princeton (G-9007)			
Publishers Partnership Co	D	201 689-1613	
Ridgewood (G-9326)			
Raphel Marketing Inc	G	609 348-6646	
Atlantic City (G-102)			

Rdl Marketing Group LLC	G	732 446-0817	
Perrineville (G-8507)			
Review and Judge LLC	G	732 987-3905	
Lakewood (G-5157)			
Rockwood Corporation	G	908 355-8600	
Frenchtown (G-3717)			
▲ Scafa-Tornabene Art Pubg Co	E	201 842-8500	
Lyndhurst (G-5676)			
Scholastic Book Fairs Inc	G	609 578-4142	
Cranbury (G-1880)			
School Publications Co Inc	E	732 988-1100	
Neptune (G-6896)			
Seven Mile Pubg & Creative	F	609 967-7707	
Avalon (G-116)			
Sheridan Printing Company Inc	E	908 454-0700	
Alpha (G-42)			
Shoppe CMC Shoppers Guide	G	609 886-4112	
Villas (G-11181)			
Sic-Naics LLC	G	929 344-2633	
Red Bank (G-9244)			
Sight2site Media LLC	G	856 637-2479	
Pomona (G-8849)			
▲ Sima S Enterprises LLC	G	877 223-7639	
Wall Township (G-11370)			
Simon & Schuster Inc	B	856 461-6500	
Delran (G-2020)			
Simon & Schuster Inc	E	973 656-6000	
Parsippany (G-8016)			
Slack Incorporated	G	856 848-1000	
Thorofare (G-10703)			
Sonata Graphics Inc	G	201 866-0186	
Secaucus (G-9816)			
South Jersey Publishing Co	F	856 692-0455	
Vineland (G-11267)			
Spendylove Home Care LLC	F	732 430-5789	
Monmouth Junction (G-6312)			
Squash Beef LLC	G	917 577-8723	
Colts Neck (G-1788)			
Stanger Robert A & Co LP	E	732 389-3600	
Shrewsbury (G-9902)			
Starnet Printing Inc	G	201 760-2600	
Mahwah (G-5776)			
Steven Orros	G	732 972-1104	
Monroe Township (G-6347)			
▲ Subito Music Service Inc	G	973 857-3440	
Verona (G-11176)			
Success Publishers LLC	G	609 443-0792	
Perrineville (G-8508)			
▲ Sueta Music Ed Publications	F	888 725-2333	
Mendham (G-6043)			
Supermedia LLC	B	973 649-9900	
Maplewood (G-5884)			
Sustainable Gardening Inst Inc	G	973 383-0497	
Lafayette (G-5033)			
T3i Group LLC	E	856 424-1100	
Cherry Hill (G-1420)			
Tap Into LLC	G	908 370-1158	
New Providence (G-7020)			
Teckchek	G	919 497-0136	
East Brunswick (G-2186)			
Thepositive Press	G	856 266-8765	
Cinnaminson (G-1490)			
Thomas Publishing Company LLC	E	973 543-4994	
Chester (G-1435)			
Thomsom Health Care Inc	C	201 358-7300	
Montvale (G-6436)			
Thomson Reuters Corporation	F	973 662-3070	
Nutley (G-7595)			
Thryv Inc	F	908 237-0956	
Flemington (G-3471)			
Thryv Inc	E	856 988-2700	
Marlton (G-5954)			
Token Torch Ltd Liability Co	F	973 629-1805	
East Orange (G-2266)			
Tommax Inc	G	732 224-1046	
Red Bank (G-9246)			
Tonymacx86 LLC	G	973 584-5273	
Ledgewood (G-5283)			
Treasure Chest Corp	G	973 328-7747	
Wharton (G-11872)			
Trf Music Inc	F	201 335-0005	
Tinton Falls (G-10732)			
Triefeldt Studios Inc	G	609 656-2380	
Trenton (G-11005)			
Verizon Communications Inc	E	201 666-9934	
Westwood (G-11847)			
Verizon Communications Inc	D	609 646-9939	
Egg Harbor Township (G-2700)			
Victory Press	G	201 729-1007	
Moonachie (G-6496)			

SIC

Voicings Publication Inc .... G 609 822-9401
  Ventnor City *(G-11155)*

Walden Mott Corp .... G 201 962-3704
  Ramsey *(G-9158)*

Wcd Enterprises Inc .... G 732 888-4422
  Keyport *(G-5006)*

▲ World Scientific Publishing Co .... F 201 487-9655
  Hackensack *(G-3991)*

Wpi Communications Inc .... F 973 467-8700
  Springfield *(G-10475)*

2752 Commercial Printing: Lithographic

A M Graphics Inc .... G 201 767-5320
  Harrington Park *(G-4161)*

A To Z Printing & Promotion .... G 973 916-9995
  Clifton *(G-1552)*

A&E Promotions LLC .... G 732 382-2300
  Holmdel *(G-4491)*

A&R Printing Corporation .... G 732 886-0505
  Lakewood *(G-5042)*

AA Graphics Inc .... G 201 398-0710
  Saddle Brook *(G-9637)*

ABC Printing .... G 973 664-1160
  Rockaway *(G-9433)*

Aboudi Printing LLC .... G 732 542-2929
  Eatontown *(G-2373)*

Absolute Business Services Inc .... G 856 265-9447
  Millville *(G-6222)*

Accent Press Inc .... G 973 785-3127
  Totowa *(G-10807)*

Accucolor LLC .... G 732 870-1999
  Long Branch *(G-5593)*

▲ Accurate Plastic Printers LLC .... E 973 591-0180
  Clifton *(G-1554)*

Ace Reprographic Service Inc .... E 973 684-5945
  Paterson *(G-8125)*

Action Copy Centers Inc .... G 973 744-5520
  Montclair *(G-6356)*

Action Graphics Inc .... E 973 633-6500
  Lincoln Park *(G-5297)*

Adams Bill Printing & Graphics .... G 856 455-7177
  Bridgeton *(G-749)*

Add Rob Litho LLC .... G 201 556-0700
  Rochelle Park *(G-9420)*

Advertisers Service Group Inc .... F 201 440-5577
  Ridgefield Park *(G-9298)*

AE Litho Offset Printers Inc .... D 609 239-0700
  Beverly *(G-445)*

Aerojet Rocketdyne De Inc .... G 201 440-1453
  Norwood *(G-7557)*

Affordable Offset Printing Inc .... G 856 661-0722
  Pennsauken *(G-8384)*

Agau Inc .... G 732 583-4343
  Matawan *(G-5967)*

AGFA Corporation .... E 201 440-0111
  Carlstadt *(G-1119)*

AGFA Corporation .... E 201 288-4101
  Carlstadt *(G-1120)*

Aladdin Color Inc .... G 609 518-9858
  Moorestown *(G-6501)*

Alete Printing LLC .... G 856 468-3536
  Wenonah *(G-11573)*

All American Print & Copy Ctr .... G 732 758-6200
  Red Bank *(G-9219)*

All Print Resources Group Inc .... G 201 994-0600
  Mountainside *(G-6833)*

Allegro Printing Corporation .... G 609 641-7060
  Galloway *(G-3719)*

▲ Allied Envelope Co Inc .... E 201 440-2000
  Carlstadt *(G-1122)*

Allied Printing-Graphics Inc .... G 973 227-0520
  Fairfield *(G-3139)*

AlphaGraphics .... G 201 327-2200
  Mahwah *(G-5712)*

AlphaGraphics .... F 856 761-8000
  Cherry Hill *(G-1339)*

AlphaGraphics Printshops of Th .... G 973 984-0066
  Morristown *(G-6635)*

▲ American Envelope .... G 908 241-9900
  Linden *(G-5323)*

American Graphic Systems Inc .... G 201 796-0666
  Fair Lawn *(G-3084)*

American Plus Printers Inc .... E 732 528-2170
  Wall *(G-11314)*

▲ Ancraft Press Corp .... F 201 792-9200
  Jersey City *(G-4691)*

Andrew P Mc Hugh Inc .... G 856 547-8953
  Barrington *(G-167)*

Anisha Enterprises Inc .... G 908 964-3380
  Union *(G-11026)*

Anuco Inc .... F 973 887-9465
  East Hanover *(G-2194)*

Arch Parent Inc .... G 732 621-2873
  Iselin *(G-4597)*

Arglen Industries Inc .... F 732 888-8100
  Hazlet *(G-4256)*

Arna Marketing Group Inc .... D 908 625-7395
  Branchburg *(G-621)*

▲ Asbury Park Press Inc .... A 732 922-6000
  Neptune *(G-6866)*

◆ Asha44 LLC .... E 201 306-3600
  Fairfield *(G-3147)*

Atlantic Prtg & Graphics LLC .... G 732 493-4222
  Ocean *(G-7657)*

Aus Inc .... G 856 234-9200
  Mount Laurel *(G-6738)*

Ayr Graphics & Printing Inc .... G 908 241-8118
  Kenilworth *(G-4923)*

B & B Press Inc .... G 908 840-4093
  Lebanon *(G-5253)*

B & H Printers Inc .... G 908 688-6990
  Hackettstown *(G-4000)*

B & R Printing Inc .... G 609 448-3328
  Trenton *(G-10901)*

B and W Printing Company Inc .... G 908 241-3060
  Kenilworth *(G-4926)*

Bab Printing Jan Service .... G 908 272-6224
  Cranford *(G-1901)*

Bannon Group Ltd .... G 201 451-6500
  Jersey City *(G-4699)*

Bar Lan Inc .... G 856 596-2330
  Brigantine *(G-911)*

Barrington Press Inc .... F 201 843-6556
  Paramus *(G-7792)*

Bartlett Printing & Graphic .... G 609 386-1525
  Burlington *(G-952)*

Barton & Cooney LLC .... D 609 747-9300
  Burlington *(G-953)*

Bassano Prtrs & Lithographers .... E 973 423-1400
  Hawthorne *(G-4207)*

Beacon Offset Printing LLC .... G 201 488-4241
  Hackensack *(G-3883)*

Berennial International .... G 973 675-6266
  Orange *(G-7752)*

Bergen Instant Printing Inc .... G 201 945-7303
  Palisades Park *(G-7769)*

Berry Business Procedure Co .... G 908 272-6464
  Cranford *(G-1903)*

Better Image Graphics Inc .... G 856 262-0735
  Williamstown *(G-11952)*

Big Red Pin LLC .... G 732 993-9765
  Edison *(G-2469)*

▲ Bind-Rite Robbinsville LLC .... D 609 208-1917
  Robbinsville *(G-9408)*

Bistis Press Printing Co .... G 973 373-8033
  Irvington *(G-4562)*

Bittner Industries Inc .... G 856 817-8400
  Cherry Hill *(G-1347)*

Blue Parachute LLC .... G 732 767-1320
  Metuchen *(G-6048)*

Bobs Poly Tape Printers Inc .... G 973 824-3005
  Newark *(G-7068)*

Boro Printing Inc .... G 732 229-1899
  West Long Branch *(G-11720)*

Bowmar Enterprises Inc .... G 908 277-3000
  New Providence *(G-6996)*

BP Print Group Inc .... D 732 905-9830
  Lakewood *(G-5064)*

Bravo Print & Mail Inc .... G 201 806-3750
  Carlstadt *(G-1131)*

Bruce McCoy Sr .... G 609 217-6153
  Pine Hill *(G-8621)*

Budget Print Center .... G 973 743-0073
  Bloomfield *(G-492)*

Burdol Inc .... G 856 453-0336
  Bridgeton *(G-755)*

Burlington Press Corporation .... F 609 387-0030
  Burlington *(G-955)*

Business Cards Tomorrow .... E 201 236-0088
  Upper Saddle River *(G-11136)*

Business Cards Tomorrow Inc .... F 609 965-0808
  Egg Harbor City *(G-2654)*

C Harry Marean Printing .... G 609 965-4708
  Egg Harbor City *(G-2655)*

C Jackson Associates Inc .... E 856 761-8000
  Cherry Hill *(G-1351)*

Cantone Press Inc .... E 201 569-3435
  Englewood *(G-2891)*

Capital Printing Corporation .... D 732 560-1515
  Middlesex *(G-6103)*

Carl A Venable Inc .... G 732 985-6677
  North Brunswick *(G-7460)*

Catholic Star Herald .... G 856 583-6142
  Camden *(G-1050)*

Century Printing Corp .... G 732 981-0544
  Piscataway *(G-8644)*

▲ Challenge Printing Co Inc .... C 973 471-4700
  Clifton *(G-1582)*

CIC Letter Service Inc .... D 201 896-1900
  Carlstadt *(G-1138)*

Classic Graphic Inc .... G 856 753-0055
  Berlin *(G-420)*

Classic Impressions .... G 908 689-3137
  Great Meadows *(G-3853)*

Cmyk Printing Inc .... F 201 458-1300
  Carlstadt *(G-1144)*

Coast Star .... E 732 223-0076
  Manasquan *(G-5830)*

Color Coded LLC .... G 718 482-1063
  Jersey City *(G-4714)*

Colorsource Inc .... G 856 488-8100
  Pennsauken *(G-8406)*

Columbia Press Inc .... E 973 575-6535
  Fairfield *(G-3171)*

Command Web Offset Company Inc .... C 201 863-8100
  Secaucus *(G-9757)*

Comprehensive Mktg Systems .... G 908 810-9778
  Union *(G-11036)*

Conagraphics Inc .... G 973 331-1113
  Parsippany *(G-7908)*

Conkur Printing Co Inc .... E 212 541-5980
  Englewood *(G-2894)*

Contemprary Grphics Bndery Inc .... C 856 663-7277
  Camden *(G-1054)*

Copy-Rite Printing .... G 609 597-9182
  Manahawkin *(G-5792)*

Corbi Printing Co Inc .... G 856 547-2444
  Audubon *(G-112)*

Cordes Printing Inc .... G 201 652-7272
  Wyckoff *(G-12107)*

Cornerstone Prints Imaging LLC .... G 908 782-7966
  Flemington *(G-3434)*

▲ Corporate Mailings Inc .... C 973 439-1168
  West Caldwell *(G-11645)*

Corporate Mailings Inc .... D 973 808-0009
  Whippany *(G-11887)*

Cottrell Graphics & Advg Spc .... G 732 349-7430
  Toms River *(G-10754)*

County Graphics Forms MGT LLC .... E 908 474-9797
  Linden *(G-5337)*

Coventry of New Jersey Inc .... E 856 988-5521
  Marlton *(G-5925)*

Craftmaster Printing Inc .... G 732 775-0011
  Neptune *(G-6872)*

Craftsmen Photo Lithographers .... E 973 316-5791
  East Hanover *(G-2204)*

Creative Color Lithographers .... F 908 789-2295
  Garwood *(G-3783)*

Crt International Inc .... F 973 887-7737
  Middlesex *(G-6110)*

Csg Systems Inc .... E 973 337-4400
  Bloomfield *(G-500)*

Custom Book Bindery Inc .... F 973 815-1400
  Clifton *(G-1595)*

D & I Printing Co Inc .... E 201 871-3620
  Englewood *(G-2895)*

D A K Office Services Inc .... G 609 586-8222
  Trenton *(G-10929)*

D L Printing Co Inc .... G 732 750-1917
  Avenel *(G-125)*

Danmar Press Inc .... F 201 487-4400
  South Hackensack *(G-10154)*

Data Communique Intl Inc .... F 201 508-6000
  Ridgefield Park *(G-9303)*

▲ Datascan Graphics Inc .... E 973 543-4803
  Morristown *(G-6658)*

▲ Dato Company Inc .... G 732 225-2272
  Cranbury *(G-1829)*

Dcg Printing Inc .... G 732 530-4441
  Shrewsbury *(G-9889)*

Dee Jay Printing Inc .... G 973 227-7787
  Fairfield *(G-3182)*

Delgen Press Inc .... G 973 472-2266
  Clifton *(G-1597)*

Design Factory Nj Inc .... G 908 964-8833
  Hillside *(G-4388)*

Devece & Shaffer Inc .... G 856 829-7282
  Palmyra *(G-7782)*

Dg3 Group America Inc .... F 201 793-5000
  Jersey City *(G-4724)*

Dg3 Holdings LLC	G	201 793-5000	
Jersey City *(G-4725)*			
Dg3 North America Inc	B	201 793-5000	
Jersey City *(G-4726)*			
Diane Matson Inc	F	609 288-6833	
Westampton *(G-11785)*			
Digital Color Concepts Inc	D	908 264-0504	
Mountainside *(G-6842)*			
Digital Documents Inc	G	609 520-0094	
Princeton *(G-8930)*			
Digital Lizard LLC	G	201 684-0900	
Mahwah *(G-5728)*			
Digital Print Solutions Inc	F	973 263-1890	
Parsippany *(G-7917)*			
Digital Productions Inc	F	856 224-1111	
Swedesboro *(G-10580)*			
▲ **Diligaf Enterprises Inc**	E	201 684-0900	
Mahwah *(G-5729)*			
Direct Prtg Impressions Inc	F	973 227-6111	
West Caldwell *(G-11646)*			
Discount Digital Print LLC	F	201 659-9600	
Union City *(G-11111)*			
Diversified Impressions Inc	G	973 399-9041	
Irvington *(G-4564)*			
Divine Printing	G	732 632-8800	
Metuchen *(G-6054)*			
Document Concepts Inc	G	856 251-1975	
Wenonah *(G-11575)*			
Dohrman Printing Co Inc	G	201 933-0346	
Carlstadt *(G-1152)*			
Dolce Brothers Printing Inc	D	201 843-0400	
Maywood *(G-6004)*			
Dolce Printing	F	201 843-0400	
Maywood *(G-6005)*			
Donnelley Financial LLC	F	973 882-7000	
West Caldwell *(G-11647)*			
▲ **Donray Printing Inc**	E	973 515-8100	
Parsippany *(G-7918)*			
Douglas Maybury Assoc	G	908 879-5878	
Chester *(G-1433)*			
Downtown Printing Center Inc	F	732 246-7990	
New Brunswick *(G-6920)*			
Dpi Copies Prtg & Graphics Inc	F	856 874-1355	
Cherry Hill *(G-1357)*			
Dynamic Printing & Graphics	F	973 473-7177	
Clifton *(G-1608)*			
Earth Color New York Inc	E	973 884-1300	
Parsippany *(G-7925)*			
▲ **Earth Thebault Inc**	C	973 884-1300	
Parsippany *(G-7926)*			
Earthcolor Inc	G	973 952-8360	
Parsippany *(G-7927)*			
Earthcolor Inc	C	973 884-1300	
Parsippany *(G-7928)*			
▲ **East Coast Media LLC**	E	908 575-9700	
Hillsborough *(G-4314)*			
▲ **Edison Lithog & Prtg Corp**	D	201 902-9191	
North Bergen *(G-7403)*			
Edwards Brothers Inc	G	856 848-6900	
West Deptford *(G-11701)*			
Elbee Litho Inc	G	732 698-7738	
East Brunswick *(G-2139)*			
Election Graphics Inc	F	201 758-9966	
Verona *(G-11165)*			
Elite Graphix LLC	F	732 274-2356	
Monmouth Junction *(G-6290)*			
Elmwood Press Inc	F	201 794-6273	
Elmwood Park *(G-2824)*			
Emerson Speed Printing Inc	G	201 265-7977	
Oradell *(G-7743)*			
Encore Enterprises Inc	G	201 489-5044	
South Hackensack *(G-10158)*			
Envelope Freedom Holdings LLC	G	201 699-5800	
Ridgefield *(G-9259)*			
Esquire Business Forms	G	609 883-1155	
Ewing *(G-3029)*			
Excel Color Graphics Inc	G	856 848-3345	
Woodbury Heights *(G-12043)*			
Excellent Prtg & Graphics LLC	F	973 773-6661	
Clifton *(G-1617)*			
Express Printing Inc	G	908 925-6300	
Linden *(G-5346)*			
Express Printing Services Inc	G	973 585-7355	
Fairfield *(G-3197)*			
Extreme Digital Graphics Inc	F	973 227-5599	
Fairfield *(G-3198)*			
Falcon Graphics Inc	G	908 232-1991	
Clark *(G-1497)*			
Falcon Printing & Graphics	G	732 462-6862	
Freehold *(G-3665)*			

Fast Copy Printing Center	F	732 739-4646	
Keyport *(G-4999)*			
Fedex Office & Print Svcs Inc	G	201 525-5070	
River Edge *(G-9361)*			
Ferrett Printing Inc	G	856 686-4896	
Woodbury *(G-12029)*			
FLM Graphics Corporation	D	973 575-9450	
Fairfield *(G-3202)*			
Flortek Corporation	E	201 436-7700	
Bayonne *(G-216)*			
Forbes Media LLC	D	212 620-2200	
Jersey City *(G-4737)*			
Fortress Graphics LLC	E	973 276-0100	
West Caldwell *(G-11651)*			
Franbeth Inc	G	856 488-1480	
Pennsauken *(G-8422)*			
Franklin Graphics Inc	G	201 935-5900	
Westwood *(G-11831)*			
Fulfillment Printing and Mail	G	609 953-9500	
Medford Lakes *(G-6037)*			
Full House Printing Inc	G	201 798-7073	
Hoboken *(G-4451)*			
Full Service Mailers Inc	G	973 478-8813	
Hackensack *(G-3919)*			
G J Haerer Co Inc	D	973 614-8090	
Glen Ridge *(G-3825)*			
Galvanic Prtg & Plate Co Inc	E	201 939-3600	
Moonachie *(G-6466)*			
Gangi Graphics Inc	G	732 840-8680	
Brick *(G-719)*			
Gannett Stllite Info Ntwrk Inc	C	856 691-5000	
Vineland *(G-11220)*			
Garrison Printing Company Inc	E	856 488-1900	
Pennsauken *(G-8424)*			
Genua & Mulligan Printing	E	973 894-1500	
Clifton *(G-1624)*			
Gerardi Press Inc	G	973 627-2600	
Denville *(G-2039)*			
Gmpc Printing	G	973 546-6060	
Clifton *(G-1628)*			
Gms Litho Corp	G	973 575-9400	
Fairfield *(G-3216)*			
Goffco Industries LLC	G	973 492-0150	
Butler *(G-1001)*			
Good Impressions Inc	G	856 461-3232	
Riverside *(G-9395)*			
Good Impressions Inc	F	908 689-3071	
Washington *(G-11445)*			
Grandview Printing Co Inc	F	973 890-0006	
Totowa *(G-10831)*			
Graph Tech Sales & Service	F	201 218-1749	
Fairfield *(G-3218)*			
Graphic Action Inc	G	908 213-0055	
Phillipsburg *(G-8553)*			
▲ **Graphic Impressions Inc**	G	201 487-8788	
Hackensack *(G-3923)*			
Graphic Impressions Prtg Co	G	856 728-2266	
Blackwood *(G-468)*			
Graphic Management	E	908 654-8400	
Kearny *(G-4862)*			
Graphicolor Corporation	E	856 691-2507	
Vineland *(G-11227)*			
Graphics Depot Inc	F	973 927-8200	
Randolph *(G-9183)*			
Graytor Printing Company Inc	D	201 933-0100	
Lyndhurst *(G-5656)*			
Great Eastern Color Lith	G	201 843-5656	
Paramus *(G-7804)*			
Great Northern Commercial Svcs	G	908 475-8855	
Belvidere *(G-364)*			
▲ **Green Horse Media LLC**	C	856 933-0222	
Bellmawr *(G-333)*			
Gross Printing Associates Inc	F	718 832-1110	
Clifton *(G-1630)*			
▲ **H C Graphics Screenprinting**	G	973 247-0544	
Paterson *(G-8207)*			
Hallco Inc	G	609 729-0161	
Wildwood *(G-11944)*			
Hammer Press Printers Inc	D	973 334-4500	
Parsippany *(G-7958)*			
Hansen Lithography Ltd	G	732 270-1188	
Toms River *(G-10763)*			
Happle Printing	G	609 476-0100	
Dorothy *(G-2071)*			
Harvard Printing Group	D	973 672-0800	
Fairfield *(G-3222)*			
Hatteras Press Inc	B	732 935-9800	
Tinton Falls *(G-10718)*			
Hawk Graphics Inc	E	973 895-5569	
Randolph *(G-9185)*			

Herald News	G	973 569-7000	
Woodland Park *(G-12081)*			
Hermitage Press of New Jersey	D	609 882-3600	
Ewing *(G-3034)*			
Highroad Press LLC	E	201 708-6900	
Moonachie *(G-6470)*			
Holographic Finishing Inc	F	201 941-4651	
Ridgefield *(G-9266)*			
Hometown Office Sups & Prtg Co	G	609 298-9020	
Bordentown *(G-583)*			
▲ **Howard Press Inc**	D	908 245-4400	
Roselle *(G-9561)*			
Howes Standard Publishing Co	E	856 691-2000	
Vineland *(G-11233)*			
Hub Print & Copy Center LLC	G	201 585-7887	
Fort Lee *(G-3563)*			
I Print Nb	G	201 662-1133	
North Bergen *(G-7410)*			
Image Makers Instant Printing	G	973 633-1771	
Wayne *(G-11518)*			
Imagine Screen Prtg & Prod LLC	C	732 329-2009	
Dayton *(G-1969)*			
Impact Printing	G	862 225-9167	
Little Ferry *(G-5489)*			
Impressions Unlimited Prtg LLC	G	856 256-0200	
Sewell *(G-9846)*			
Ink On Paper Communications	G	732 758-6280	
Shrewsbury *(G-9893)*			
Ink Well Printers LLC	G	908 272-8090	
Kenilworth *(G-4946)*			
Inkworkx Custom Screen Prtg	G	609 898-5198	
Manalapan *(G-5814)*			
Inserts East Incorporated	C	856 663-8181	
Pennsauken *(G-8437)*			
Instant Imprints	G	973 252-9500	
Flanders *(G-3413)*			
Instant Printing of Dover Inc	G	973 366-6855	
Dover *(G-2090)*			
J B Offset Printing Corp	G	201 264-4400	
Norwood *(G-7566)*			
J D M Associates Inc	G	973 773-8699	
Lodi *(G-5566)*			
Jasco Specialties and Forms	G	856 627-5511	
Tabernacle *(G-10619)*			
JC Printing & Advertising Inc	G	973 881-8612	
Paterson *(G-8220)*			
Jefferson Printing Serivce	F	973 491-0019	
Newark *(G-7168)*			
Jem Printing Inc	G	908 782-9986	
Flemington *(G-3450)*			
Jersey Printing Associates Inc	E	732 872-9654	
Atlantic Highlands *(G-108)*			
Jli Marketing & Printing Corp	F	732 828-8877	
Cranbury *(G-1848)*			
Jmc Design & Graphics Inc	G	973 276-9033	
Fairfield *(G-3245)*			
Jmp Press Inc	G	201 444-0236	
Ho Ho Kus *(G-4441)*			
John S Swift Company Inc	G	201 935-2002	
Teterboro *(G-10682)*			
John S Swift Print of NJ Inc	G	201 678-3232	
Teterboro *(G-10683)*			
Johnston Letter Co Inc	G	973 482-7535	
Flanders *(G-3414)*			
Jon-Da Printing Co Inc	F	201 653-6200	
Jersey City *(G-4751)*			
Jory Engravers Inc	G	201 939-1546	
Rutherford *(G-9624)*			
Jvs Copy Services Inc	F	856 415-9090	
Sewell *(G-9850)*			
K R B Printing For Business	F	856 751-5200	
Cherry Hill *(G-1379)*			
Kay Printing & Envelope Co Inc	E	973 330-3000	
Clifton *(G-1649)*			
Keskes Printing LLC	G	856 767-4733	
Berlin *(G-425)*			
Keystone Printing Inc	G	201 387-7252	
Dumont *(G-2114)*			
Killian Graphics	G	973 635-5844	
Chatham *(G-1325)*			
Kirms Printing Co Inc	E	732 774-8000	
Neptune *(G-6886)*			
Knock Out Graphics Inc	F	732 774-3331	
Asbury Park *(G-78)*			
Kraft Tape Printers Inc	G	973 824-3005	
Newark *(G-7175)*			
Kufall Printing	G	732 505-9847	
Toms River *(G-10774)*			
L A S Printing Co	G	201 991-5362	
Jersey City *(G-4757)*			

S
I
C

Label Solutions Inc ....G.... 201 599-0909
Rochelle Park *(G-9426)*
Lamb Printing Inc ....G.... 908 852-0837
Hackettstown *(G-4016)*
Latta Graphics Inc ....E.... 201 440-4040
Carlstadt *(G-1181)*
Laureate Press ....G.... 609 646-1545
Egg Harbor City *(G-2663)*
Lawn Medic Inc ....G.... 856 742-1111
Westville *(G-11818)*
LCI Graphics Inc ....F.... 973 893-2913
Sayreville *(G-9714)*
Lettie Press Inc ....G.... 201 391-6388
Park Ridge *(G-7854)*
Lewis Scheller Printing Corp ....G.... 732 843-5050
Somerset *(G-10016)*
Lexington Graphics Corp ....G.... 973 345-2493
Clifton *(G-1658)*
Liberty Envelope Inc ....F.... 973 546-5600
Paterson *(G-8240)*
Lightning Press Inc ....F.... 973 890-4422
Totowa *(G-10835)*
Linder & Company Inc ....F.... 201 386-8788
Jersey City *(G-4759)*
Lithos Estiatorio Ltd Lblty Co ....G.... 973 758-1111
Livingston *(G-5519)*
Little Prints Day Care II LLC ....F.... 973 396-8989
Passaic *(G-8082)*
Lmp Printing Corp ....G.... 973 428-1987
Clifton *(G-1660)*
Longrun Press Inc ....F.... 856 719-9202
West Berlin *(G-11605)*
Lornan Litho Inc ....F.... 609 818-1198
Pennington *(G-8370)*
LP Thebault Co ....G.... 973 884-1300
Parsippany *(G-7974)*
Lunet Inc ....G.... 201 261-3883
Paramus *(G-7816)*
M & M Printing Corp ....G.... 201 288-7787
Hasbrouck Heights *(G-4186)*
M G X Inc ....F.... 732 329-0088
Monmouth Junction *(G-6296)*
Maclearie Printing LLC ....G.... 732 681-2772
Wall Township *(G-11354)*
Mail Time Inc ....E.... 908 859-5500
Phillipsburg *(G-8561)*
Major Printing Co Inc ....G.... 908 686-7296
Union *(G-11072)*
Manva Industries Inc ....F.... 973 667-2606
Nutley *(G-7590)*
Manzi Printing ....G.... 732 542-1927
Eatontown *(G-2409)*
▲ **Mariano Press LLC** ....F.... 732 247-3659
Somerset *(G-10022)*
Mark Alan Printing & Graphics ....G.... 732 981-9011
Piscataway *(G-8686)*
Mark Lithography Inc ....E.... 973 538-5557
Cedar Knolls *(G-1309)*
Marks Management Systems Inc ....G.... 856 866-0588
Maple Shade *(G-5867)*
Master Printing Inc ....E.... 201 842-9100
Carlstadt *(G-1186)*
Master Repro Inc ....G.... 201 447-4800
Midland Park *(G-6179)*
McGinnis Printing ....G.... 732 758-0060
Red Bank *(G-9235)*
McKella 2-8-0 Inc ....D.... 856 813-1153
Pennsauken *(G-8455)*
Medico Graphics Services Inc ....G.... 201 216-1660
Jersey City *(G-4764)*
◆ **Menu Solutions Inc** ....D.... 718 575-5160
Belleville *(G-300)*
Mercer C AlphaGraphics ....G.... 609 921-0959
Hamilton *(G-4115)*
Merrill Corporation ....D.... 908 810-3740
Union *(G-11075)*
Metro Prtg & Promotions LLC ....F.... 973 316-1600
Boonton *(G-563)*
Metro Seliger Industries Inc ....C.... 201 438-4530
Carlstadt *(G-1187)*
Metro Web Corp ....E.... 201 553-0700
North Bergen *(G-7421)*
Mgl Printing Solution LLC ....G.... 908 665-1999
New Providence *(G-7012)*
Mid Atlantic Graphix Inc ....G.... 609 569-9990
Egg Harbor Township *(G-2690)*
Mint Printing LLC ....G.... 973 546-2060
Lodi *(G-5572)*
Minuteman Press ....G.... 973 403-0146
Caldwell *(G-1027)*
Minuteman Press ....G.... 732 536-8788
Manalapan *(G-5817)*
Monte Printing & Graphics Inc ....G.... 908 241-6600
Roselle Park *(G-9588)*
More Copy Printing Service ....G.... 201 327-1106
Upper Saddle River *(G-11143)*
▲ **Morgan Printing Service Inc** ....F.... 732 721-2959
South Amboy *(G-10138)*
◆ **Morris County Duplicating** ....D.... 973 993-8484
Cedar Knolls *(G-1310)*
Morris Plains Pip Inc ....G.... 973 533-9330
Livingston *(G-5528)*
Morrison Press Inc ....F.... 201 488-4848
Closter *(G-1761)*
▲ **Mountain Printing Company Inc** ....E.... 856 767-7600
Berlin *(G-427)*
Mr Quickly Inc ....G.... 908 687-6000
Union *(G-11077)*
Multi Packaging Solutions Inc ....C.... 908 757-6000
South Plainfield *(G-10303)*
My Way Prints Inc ....G.... 973 492-1212
Butler *(G-1010)*
Nassau Communications Inc ....F.... 609 208-9099
Lawrence Township *(G-5218)*
National Certified Printing ....G.... 609 443-6323
Hightstown *(G-4297)*
Nema Associates Inc ....F.... 973 274-0052
Linden *(G-5395)*
New Horizon Graphics Inc ....G.... 609 584-1301
Trenton *(G-10960)*
New Jersey Label LLC ....F.... 201 880-5102
South Hackensack *(G-10175)*
New Jersey Reprographics Inc ....G.... 908 789-1616
Garwood *(G-3786)*
New Life Color Reproductions ....G.... 201 943-7005
Ridgefield *(G-9280)*
New Standard Printing Corp ....G.... 973 366-0006
Dover *(G-2101)*
▲ **Newline Prtg & Tech Solutions** ....F.... 973 405-6133
Mountainside *(G-6849)*
Nextwave Web LLC ....F.... 973 742-4339
Paterson *(G-8269)*
Nitka Graphics Inc ....F.... 201 797-3000
Fair Lawn *(G-3114)*
Noble Metals Corp ....G.... 908 925-6300
Linden *(G-5397)*
▲ **Norwood Printing Inc** ....F.... 201 784-8721
Norwood *(G-7572)*
Nu-Plan Business Systems Inc ....G.... 732 231-6944
Clark *(G-1510)*
Ocsidot Inc ....F.... 908 789-3300
Garwood *(G-3788)*
Old Hights Print Shop Inc ....G.... 609 443-4700
Jackson *(G-4661)*
On Demand Print Group ....G.... 201 636-2270
Lyndhurst *(G-5669)*
One Two Three Inc ....F.... 856 251-1238
Woodbury *(G-12034)*
Orora Visual LLC ....G.... 973 916-2804
Clifton *(G-1681)*
OShea Services Inc ....G.... 201 343-8668
Hackensack *(G-3958)*
▼ **OSullivan Communications Corp** ....E.... 973 227-5112
West Caldwell *(G-11670)*
Otis Graphics Inc ....F.... 201 438-7120
Lyndhurst *(G-5671)*
Pace Press Incorporated ....D.... 201 935-7711
Moonachie *(G-6482)*
Pad and Publ Assembly Corp ....E.... 856 424-0158
Cherry Hill *(G-1404)*
Palm Press Inc ....G.... 201 767-6504
Northvale *(G-7543)*
Panther Printing Inc ....G.... 239 542-1050
West Orange *(G-11777)*
▲ **Paravista Inc** ....E.... 732 752-1222
Fairfield *(G-3289)*
◆ **Paris Corporation New Jersey** ....D.... 609 265-9200
Westampton *(G-11788)*
Park Printing Services Inc ....F.... 856 675-1600
Pennsauken *(G-8463)*
Parkway Printing Inc ....G.... 732 308-0300
Marlboro *(G-5908)*
Parsells Printing Inc ....G.... 973 473-2700
Maywood *(G-6013)*
Parth Enterprises Inc ....G.... 732 404-0665
Iselin *(G-4622)*
Pascack Valley Copy Center ....G.... 201 664-1917
Westwood *(G-11839)*
Patel Printing Plus Corp ....F.... 908 964-6422
Union *(G-11082)*
PDM Litho Inc ....E.... 718 301-1740
Clifton *(G-1687)*
PDQ Print & Copy Inc ....F.... 201 569-2288
Englewood *(G-2931)*
Peacock Communications Inc ....G.... 973 763-3311
Maplewood *(G-5881)*
Peeq Imaging ....D.... 212 490-3850
Carlstadt *(G-1198)*
Penn Copy Center Inc ....G.... 646 251-0313
Lakewood *(G-5145)*
Penn Jersey Press Inc ....G.... 856 627-2200
Gibbsboro *(G-3795)*
Penny Press ....G.... 856 547-1991
Stratford *(G-10506)*
Permagraphics Inc ....F.... 201 814-1200
Moonachie *(G-6483)*
▲ **Pharmaceutic Litho Label Inc** ....C.... 336 785-4000
Cranford *(G-1923)*
Philip Holzer and Assoc LLC ....E.... 212 691-9500
Carlstadt *(G-1201)*
Phillip Balderose ....G.... 732 574-1330
Clark *(G-1512)*
Phoenix Business Forms Inc ....G.... 856 691-2266
Vineland *(G-11253)*
Photo Offset Prtg & Pubg Co ....G.... 609 587-4900
Trenton *(G-10974)*
Pica Printings Inc ....G.... 973 540-0420
Morristown *(G-6693)*
Pine Hill Printing Inc ....G.... 856 346-2915
Pine Hill *(G-8622)*
Pinnacle Press Inc ....G.... 201 652-0500
Midland Park *(G-6182)*
Pinto Printing ....G.... 856 232-2550
Blackwood *(G-477)*
Pirolli Printing Co Inc ....F.... 856 933-1285
Bellmawr *(G-341)*
Precision Printing Group Inc ....E.... 856 753-0900
Mount Laurel *(G-6795)*
Premier Graphics Inc ....E.... 732 872-9933
Atlantic Highlands *(G-110)*
Premier Printing Solutions LLC ....G.... 732 525-0740
South Amboy *(G-10139)*
Premium Service Printing ....G.... 908 707-1311
Hillsborough *(G-4345)*
Pressto Graphics ....F.... 732 286-9300
Toms River *(G-10784)*
Presto Printing Service Inc ....G.... 908 756-5337
South Plainfield *(G-10315)*
Prestone Press LLC ....C.... 347 468-7900
Maywood *(G-6015)*
Princetonian Graphics Inc ....F.... 732 329-8282
Monmouth Junction *(G-6306)*
Print By Premier LLC ....G.... 212 947-1365
Secaucus *(G-9799)*
Print Factory Ltd Liability Co ....G.... 973 866-5230
Clifton *(G-1700)*
Print Group Inc ....F.... 201 487-4400
South Hackensack *(G-10182)*
Print Mail Communications LLC ....E.... 856 488-0345
Pennsauken *(G-8473)*
Print Peel ....E.... 201 507-0080
Carlstadt *(G-1208)*
Print Post ....G.... 973 732-0950
Newark *(G-7235)*
Print Shoppe Inc ....G.... 908 782-9213
Flemington *(G-3463)*
▼ **Print Tech LLC** ....D.... 908 232-2287
Springfield *(G-10461)*
Print Tech LLC ....G.... 908 232-0767
Westfield *(G-11801)*
Printers Place Inc ....G.... 973 744-8889
Montclair *(G-6385)*
Printing Center Inc ....E.... 973 383-6362
Sparta *(G-10407)*
Printing Delite Inc ....G.... 973 676-3033
East Orange *(G-2260)*
Printing Industries LLC ....G.... 973 334-9775
Parsippany *(G-8001)*
Printing Plus of South Jersey ....G.... 856 767-3941
West Berlin *(G-11617)*
Printing Services ....G.... 908 269-8349
Port Murray *(G-8884)*
Printpluscom Inc ....G.... 908 859-4774
Stewartsville *(G-10487)*
Printwrap Corporation ....F.... 973 239-1144
Cedar Grove *(G-1289)*
Prisco Digital Ltd Lblty Co ....F.... 973 589-7800
Newark *(G-7237)*
Prism Color Corporation ....D.... 856 234-7515
Moorestown *(G-6559)*

Prism Dgtal Communications LLC ......F 973 232-5038
Mountainside *(G-6851)*

Pro Screen Printing Inc ....G 201 246-7600
Kearny *(G-4894)*

Product Identification Co Inc ....F 973 227-7770
Garfield *(G-3762)*

Professional Printing Services ....G 856 428-6300
Haddonfield *(G-4063)*

Professional Reproductions Inc ....F 212 268-1222
Marlboro *(G-5911)*

Progress Printing Co ....F 201 433-3133
Jersey City *(G-4788)*

Progressive 4 Color Ltd Lblty ....G 973 736-5800
West Orange *(G-11778)*

Progressive Offset Inc ....E 201 569-3900
Englewood *(G-2934)*

Prohaska & Co Inc ....G 732 238-3420
East Brunswick *(G-2169)*

Pronto Printing & Copying Ctr ....G 201 426-0009
Ramsey *(G-9155)*

Publishers Inc ....E 856 853-2800
West Deptford *(G-11715)*

Puent-Romer Communications Inc .....G 973 509-7591
Montclair *(G-6386)*

Q P 195 Inc ....G 732 531-8860
Ocean *(G-7676)*

Q P 500 Inc ....G 732 531-8860
Ocean *(G-7677)*

Quad/Graphics Inc ....E 609 534-7308
Westampton *(G-11791)*

Quad/Graphics Inc ....E 732 469-0189
Somerset *(G-10060)*

Quality Print Solutions ....G 888 679-7237
Ridgewood *(G-9327)*

R & B Printing Inc ....G 908 766-4073
Bernardsville *(G-443)*

R L R Foil Stamping LLC ....F 973 778-9464
Passaic *(G-8100)*

R V Livolsi Incorporated ....G 732 286-2200
Toms River *(G-10786)*

Rays Reproduction Inc ....G 201 666-5650
Emerson *(G-2868)*

Recorder Publishing Co ....E 908 647-1180
Stirling *(G-10495)*

Red Oak Packaging Inc ....E 862 268-8200
Newton *(G-7354)*

Redmond Bcms Inc ....D 973 664-2000
Denville *(G-2051)*

Regal Litho Prtrs Ltd Lblty Co ....G 732 901-1500
Lakewood *(G-5151)*

Register Lithographers Ltd ....D 973 916-2804
Clifton *(G-1707)*

Reliable Envelope and Graphics ....E 201 794-7756
Elmwood Park *(G-2854)*

Reliance Graphics Inc ....G 973 239-5411
Verona *(G-11173)*

Remco Press Inc ....G 201 751-5703
North Bergen *(G-7433)*

Repro Tronics Inc ....G 201 722-1880
Ltl Egg Hbr *(G-5619)*

Repromatic Printing Inc ....G 973 239-7610
Cedar Grove *(G-1291)*

Review Printing Inc ....G 856 589-7200
Pitman *(G-8747)*

Rfm Printing Inc ....F 732 938-4400
Wall Township *(G-11363)*

Ridgewood Press Inc ....F 201 670-9797
Ridgewood *(G-9328)*

Riegel Holding Company Inc ....D 609 771-0361
Ewing *(G-3062)*

Roan Printing Inc ....F 908 526-5990
Somerville *(G-10124)*

▲ Roelynn Litho Inc ....F 732 942-9650
Lakewood *(G-5159)*

Rolls Offset Group Inc ....E 201 727-1110
Lyndhurst *(G-5675)*

Roned Printing & Reproduction ....G 973 386-1848
East Hanover *(G-2236)*

Roy D Smith Inc ....G 201 384-4163
Bergenfield *(G-383)*

Roy Press Inc ....G 732 922-9460
Oceanport *(G-7706)*

Royal Printing Service ....E 201 863-3131
West New York *(G-11753)*

Royer Graphics Inc ....G 856 344-7935
Clementon *(G-1535)*

Royer Group Inc ....E 856 324-0171
Pennsauken *(G-8479)*

Rush Graphics Inc ....E 973 427-9393
Hawthorne *(G-4242)*

SAM Graphics Inc ....E 732 431-0440
Marlboro *(G-5913)*

Sample Media Inc ....E 609 399-5411
Ocean City *(G-7695)*

Sandoval Graphics & Printing ....G 856 435-7320
Somerdale *(G-9934)*

▼ Sandy Alexander Inc ....C 973 470-8100
Clifton *(G-1710)*

Sapphire Envelope & Graphics ....G 856 782-2227
Magnolia *(G-5709)*

Scarlet Printing ....G 732 560-1415
Middlesex *(G-6143)*

Schellmark Inc ....G 732 345-7143
Tinton Falls *(G-10726)*

School Publications Co Inc ....E 732 988-1100
Neptune *(G-6896)*

◆ Scodix Inc ....F 855 726-3491
Saddle Brook *(G-9678)*

Scott Graphics Printing Co Inc ....G 201 262-0473
New Milford *(G-6992)*

Screen Printing & Embroidery ....G 732 256-9610
Wall Township *(G-11367)*

Service Data Corp Inc ....G 908 522-0020
Summit *(G-10546)*

Sherman Printing Co Inc ....G 973 345-2493
Clifton *(G-1715)*

Sheroy Printing Inc ....F 973 242-4040
Newark *(G-7271)*

Shindo International Inc ....E 973 470-8100
Clifton *(G-1716)*

Showcase Printing of Iselin ....G 732 283-0438
Iselin *(G-4627)*

Shree Ji Printing Corporation ....E 201 842-9500
Carlstadt *(G-1216)*

Signs of Security Inc ....E 973 340-8404
Garfield *(G-3768)*

Solid Color Inc ....G 212 239-3930
Kearny *(G-4899)*

Sonata Graphics Inc ....G 201 866-0186
Secaucus *(G-9816)*

South Amboy Designer T Shirt L ......G 732 456-2594
South Amboy *(G-10141)*

Staines Inc ....F 856 784-2718
Somerdale *(G-9935)*

Standard Prtg & Mail Svcs Inc ....F 973 790-3333
Fairfield *(G-3314)*

Star Litho Inc ....G 973 641-1603
Fairfield *(G-3315)*

Star Promotions Inc ....F 732 356-5959
Bound Brook *(G-607)*

Stauts Printing & Graphics ....G 609 654-5382
Medford *(G-6035)*

Steb Inc ....G 973 584-0990
Ledgewood *(G-5281)*

Steb Inc ....F 973 584-0990
Ledgewood *(G-5282)*

Steven Madola ....G 609 989-8022
Trenton *(G-10992)*

Stobbs Printing Co Inc ....G 973 748-4441
Bloomfield *(G-519)*

Stone Mountain Printing Inc ....G 732 636-8450
Woodbridge *(G-12022)*

Strategic Content Imaging ....C 201 863-8100
Secaucus *(G-9819)*

Stuyvesant Press Inc ....F 973 399-3880
Irvington *(G-4587)*

Sunset Printing and Engrv Corp ....E 973 537-9600
Wharton *(G-11871)*

Superfine Online Inc ....E 212 827-0063
Roselle *(G-9574)*

Superior Trademark Inc ....G 201 652-1900
Waldwick *(G-11310)*

Supplies-Supplies Inc ....F 908 272-5100
Watchung *(G-11460)*

Supreme Graphics and Prtg Inc ....G 718 989-9817
Perth Amboy *(G-8535)*

Supreme Ink Corp ....F 973 344-2922
Newark *(G-7292)*

Sureway Prtg & Graphics LLC ....G 609 430-4333
Princeton *(G-9030)*

Suzie Mac Specialties Inc ....E 732 238-3500
East Brunswick *(G-2184)*

T G Type-O-Graphics Inc ....G 973 253-3333
Fair Lawn *(G-3125)*

Tabloid Graphic Services Inc ....D 856 486-0410
Pennsauken *(G-8489)*

Tandem Color Imaging Graphics ....G 973 513-9779
Pompton Lakes *(G-8854)*

Tandem Color Imaging Graphics ....G 973 513-9779
Pompton Lakes *(G-8853)*

Tangent Graphics Inc ....G 201 488-2840
Englewood *(G-2946)*

Tanter Inc ....G 732 382-3555
Clark *(G-1516)*

Tanzola Printing Inc ....G 973 779-0858
Clifton *(G-1729)*

Tape Graphics ....G 201 393-9500
Hasbrouck Heights *(G-4189)*

Technical Nameplate Corp ....E 973 773-4256
Passaic *(G-8111)*

▲ Tectubes USA Inc ....E 856 589-1250
Vineland *(G-11269)*

Tedco Inc ....G 609 883-0799
Ewing *(G-3069)*

The Creative Print Group Inc ....F 856 486-1700
Pennsauken *(G-8492)*

Thermo X-Press Printing LLC ....G 973 585-6505
East Hanover *(G-2241)*

▲ Thermo-Graphics Inc ....G 908 486-0100
Avenel *(G-150)*

Thewal Inc ....F 973 635-1880
Chatham *(G-1330)*

Thomas H Cox & Son Inc ....E 908 928-1010
Linden *(G-5435)*

Tmg Enterprises Inc ....E 732 469-2900
Piscataway *(G-8728)*

Toms River Printing Corp ....G 732 240-2033
Brielle *(G-909)*

Toppan Printing Co Amer Inc ....C 732 469-8400
Somerset *(G-10088)*

Trade Thermographers Inc ....F 201 489-2060
Rochelle Park *(G-9432)*

Tremont Printing Co ....G 973 227-0742
Fairfield *(G-3332)*

Trend Printing/Intl Label ....F 201 941-6611
Ridgefield *(G-9293)*

Trenton Printing LLC ....F 609 695-6485
Trenton *(G-11002)*

Trentypo Inc ....G 609 883-5971
Ewing *(G-3071)*

Tretina Printing Inc ....F 732 264-2324
Hazlet *(G-4272)*

Trinity Press Inc ....E 973 881-0690
Paterson *(G-8317)*

Trukmanns Inc ....G 973 538-7718
Cedar Knolls *(G-1314)*

Tuerff Sziber Capitol Copy Svc ....G 609 989-8776
Trenton *(G-11006)*

Twill Inc ....F 908 665-1700
Berkeley Heights *(G-413)*

Typeline ....F 201 251-2201
Wyckoff *(G-12123)*

Typestyle Inc ....G 201 343-3343
Hackensack *(G-3986)*

United Envelope LLC ....E 201 699-5800
Ridgefield *(G-9296)*

Unity Graphics & Engraving Co ....E 201 541-5462
Englewood *(G-2950)*

Vanguard Printing ....G 856 358-2665
Elmer *(G-2806)*

Verni Vito ....G 732 449-1760
Wall Township *(G-11377)*

Vernw Printing Company ....G 973 751-6462
Belleville *(G-321)*

Vestal Publishing Co Inc ....G 732 583-3232
Cliffwood *(G-1549)*

▲ Vintage Print Gallery ....F 201 501-0505
Closter *(G-1764)*

Viskal Printing LLC ....G 973 812-6600
Totowa *(G-10860)*

W B Mason Co Inc ....D 888 926-2766
Bellmawr *(G-345)*

W B Mason Co Inc ....E 888 926-2766
Egg Harbor Township *(G-2701)*

W G I Corp ....F 732 370-2900
Lakewood *(G-5179)*

Waldwick Printing Co ....G 201 652-5848
Waldwick *(G-11312)*

Washington Stamp Exchange Inc ....F 973 966-0001
Florham Park *(G-3526)*

Watonka Printing Inc ....G 732 974-8878
Belmar *(G-356)*

Webb-Mason Inc ....G 732 747-6585
Tinton Falls *(G-10734)*

Welter & Kreutz Printing Co ....G 201 489-9098
South Hackensack *(G-10190)*

Westbury Press Inc ....D 201 894-0444
Englewood *(G-2953)*

Westerleigh Concepts Inc ....F 908 205-8888
South Plainfield *(G-10346)*

SIC

White Eagle Printing Co Inc ....E 609 586-2032
Trenton *(G-11008)*

Wilcox Press ....G 973 827-7474
Hamburg *(G-4099)*

Wilker Graphics LLC ....G 201 447-4800
Midland Park *(G-6190)*

William Robert Graphics Inc ....G 201 239-7400
Jersey City *(G-4831)*

Wilmington Trust Sp Services ....C 609 272-7000
Pleasantville *(G-8821)*

▲ Wong Robinson & Co Inc ....E 609 951-0300
Princeton *(G-9044)*

Yasheel Inc ....G 856 275-6812
Sewell *(G-9854)*

Your Printer V20 Ltd ....E 609 771-4000
Cranbury *(G-1895)*

Yukon Graphics Inc ....G 973 575-5700
Parsippany *(G-8043)*

▲ Zeiser Inc ....F 973 228-0800
West Caldwell *(G-11682)*

Zippityprint LLC ....F 216 438-0001
Mullica Hill *(G-6859)*

Zwier Corp ....G 973 748-4009
Bloomfield *(G-524)*

2754 Commercial Printing: Gravure

Acme Engraving Co Inc ....E 973 778-0885
Passaic *(G-8050)*

▲ All-State International Inc ....C 908 272-0800
Cranford *(G-1899)*

American Business Paper Inc ....F 732 363-5788
Lakewood *(G-5049)*

Arna Marketing Inc ....E 908 231-1100
Branchburg *(G-622)*

Brandmuscle Inc ....G 973 685-0022
Clifton *(G-1577)*

▲ Challenge Printing Co Inc ....C 973 471-4700
Clifton *(G-1582)*

Constant Services Inc ....E 973 227-2990
Fairfield *(G-3173)*

East Coast Distributors Inc ....F 732 223-5995
Eatontown *(G-2389)*

Five Macs Inc ....E 856 596-3150
Marlton *(G-5931)*

Food Mfg ....C 973 920-7000
Rockaway *(G-9461)*

▲ Howard Press Inc ....D 908 245-4400
Roselle *(G-9561)*

Label Master Inc ....G 973 546-3110
Lodi *(G-5567)*

▲ Link Color NA Inc ....G 201 438-8222
East Rutherford *(G-2295)*

▲ Lps Industries Inc ....G 201 438-3515
Moonachie *(G-6477)*

Lrp and P Graphics ....E 856 424-0158
Cherry Hill *(G-1385)*

New Jersey Department Treasury ...E 609 292-5133
Trenton *(G-10962)*

Pad and Publ Assembly Corp ....E 856 424-0158
Cherry Hill *(G-1404)*

▲ Pantone LLC ....C 201 935-5500
Carlstadt *(G-1196)*

R R Donnelley & Sons Company ...C 973 439-8321
West Caldwell *(G-11676)*

◆ Tadbik NJ Inc ....E 973 882-9595
Fairfield *(G-3322)*

Taylor Communications Inc ....E 732 561-8210
Monroe Township *(G-6348)*

Taylor Communications Inc ....F 973 467-8259
Springfield *(G-10468)*

Wheal-Grace Corp ....E 973 450-8100
Belleville *(G-324)*

Winemiller Press Inc ....G 732 223-0100
Manasquan *(G-5843)*

Youre So Invited LLC ....E 201 664-8600
Westwood *(G-11848)*

2759 Commercial Printing

224 Graphics Inc ....F 973 433-9224
Fairfield *(G-3132)*

4 Over Inc ....F 201 440-1656
Moonachie *(G-6450)*

▲ A B Tees LLC ....G 201 239-0022
Jersey City *(G-4683)*

Abbott Artkives LLC ....G 201 232-9477
Belleville *(G-288)*

Action Graphics Inc ....G 856 783-1825
Lindenwold *(G-5443)*

Active Learning Associates ....G 908 284-0404
Flemington *(G-3428)*

Adpro Imprints ....G 732 531-2133
Ocean *(G-7653)*

Advantage Ds LLC ....F 856 307-9600
Glassboro *(G-3806)*

Ahern Blueprinting Inc ....F 732 223-1476
Manasquan *(G-5827)*

Alcop Adhesive Label Co ....G 609 871-4400
Beverly *(G-446)*

▲ Alex Real LLC ....G 732 730-8770
Toms River *(G-10740)*

All Colors Screen Printing LLC .....G 732 777-6033
Highland Park *(G-4286)*

▲ All-State International Inc ....C 908 272-0800
Cranford *(G-1899)*

Alliance Design Inc ....F 973 904-9450
Totowa *(G-10809)*

AlphaGraphics Printshops of Th ...G 973 984-0066
Morristown *(G-6635)*

Altantic Printing and Design ....F 732 557-9600
Toms River *(G-10742)*

▲ American Bank Note Holographic ...D 609 208-0591
Robbinsville *(G-9407)*

American Graphic Systems Inc .....G 201 796-0666
Fair Lawn *(G-3084)*

American Youth Enterprises Inc ....G 609 909-1900
Mays Landing *(G-5992)*

Andy Graphics Service Bureau .....G 201 866-9407
Union City *(G-11106)*

▲ Applied Image Inc ....E 732 410-2444
Freehold *(G-3647)*

Armin Kososki ....G 908 689-0411
Washington *(G-11439)*

Armotek Industries Inc ....E 856 829-4585
Palmyra *(G-7781)*

Arnolds Yacht Basin Inc ....G 732 892-3000
Point Pleasant Boro *(G-8836)*

Artistic Typography Corp ....G 845 783-1990
Englewood *(G-2877)*

Arts Embroidery LLC ....G 732 870-2400
West Long Branch *(G-11719)*

ASAP Postal Printing ....G 609 597-7421
Manahawkin *(G-5790)*

Avail Inc ....G 732 560-2222
Bridgewater *(G-796)*

Ayr Composition Inc ....G 908 241-8118
Roselle Park *(G-9578)*

B and W Printing Company Inc .....G 908 241-3060
Kenilworth *(G-4926)*

B P Graphics Inc ....E 732 942-2315
Lakewood *(G-5057)*

B&M Technologies Inc ....F 201 291-8505
Saddle Brook *(G-9641)*

Bassano Prtrs & Lithographers .....E 973 423-1400
Hawthorne *(G-4207)*

Beauty Wood Designs ....G 908 687-9697
Union *(G-11030)*

Belle Printing Group LLC ....G 856 235-5151
Mount Laurel *(G-6741)*

Bellia & Sons ....E 856 845-2234
Woodbury *(G-12026)*

Big Color System Inc ....F 201 236-0404
Wyckoff *(G-12105)*

Bills Printing Service Inc ....G 609 888-1841
Trenton *(G-10904)*

Blue Ribbon Awards Inc ....G 732 560-0046
Somerset *(G-9963)*

Branded Screen Printing ....G 908 879-7411
Chester *(G-1431)*

Brimar Industries Inc ....E 973 340-7889
Garfield *(G-3733)*

Brite Concepts Inc ....G 201 270-8544
Englewood *(G-2886)*

Burdol Inc ....G 856 453-0336
Bridgeton *(G-755)*

◆ Butler Prtg & Laminating Inc .....C 973 838-8550
Butler *(G-997)*

C & D Sales ....G 609 383-9292
Pleasantville *(G-8806)*

C and R Printing Corporation ....F 201 528-8912
Carlstadt *(G-1134)*

C Harry Marean Printing ....G 609 965-4708
Egg Harbor City *(G-2655)*

C2 Imaging LLC ....E 646 557-6300
Jersey City *(G-4707)*

Campbell Converting Corp ....G 609 835-2720
Beverly *(G-448)*

Campus Coordinates LLC ....G 732 866-6060
Freehold *(G-3655)*

CCL Label Inc ....C 609 586-1332
Robbinsville *(G-9409)*

CCL Label Inc ....E 856 273-0700
Lumberton *(G-5625)*

CCL Label (delaware) Inc ....C 609 259-1055
Trenton *(G-10914)*

Central Mills Inc ....G 732 329-2009
Dayton *(G-1959)*

▲ Cgs Sales and Service LLC ....G 856 665-6154
Pennsauken *(G-8403)*

▲ Chambord Prints Inc ....E 201 795-2007
Hoboken *(G-4447)*

Chariot Courier & Trans Svcs ....F 888 532-9125
Sayreville *(G-9704)*

▲ Cheringal Associates Inc ....D 201 784-8721
Norwood *(G-7560)*

Circa Promotions Inc ....G 732 264-1200
Hazlet *(G-4259)*

Classic Printers & Converters ......G 732 985-1100
Piscataway *(G-8646)*

Clear Control LLC ....G 973 823-8200
Ogdensburg *(G-7709)*

▲ Color Screen Pros Inc ....G 973 268-5080
Newark *(G-7086)*

Colorcraft Sign Co ....F 609 386-1115
Beverly *(G-449)*

Colortec Printing and Mailing ....G 856 767-0108
West Berlin *(G-11584)*

Commercial Business Forms Inc ...G 973 682-9000
Cedar Knolls *(G-1302)*

Corporate Envelope & Prtg Co ......G 732 752-4333
Green Brook *(G-3860)*

Cosmic Custom Screen Prtg LLC ...G 856 629-8337
Williamstown *(G-11955)*

Coventry of New Jersey Inc ....E 856 988-5521
Marlton *(G-5925)*

Creative Color Lithographers ....F 908 789-2295
Garwood *(G-3783)*

Crown Roll Leaf Inc ....E 973 684-2600
Paterson *(G-8165)*

Crown Trophy ....G 973 808-8400
Pine Brook *(G-8595)*

Custom Graphics of Vineland ....E 856 691-7858
Vineland *(G-11209)*

Custom Labels Inc ....G 973 473-1934
Fairfield *(G-3177)*

D L Imprints ....G 732 493-8555
Ocean *(G-7660)*

Daily News LP ....F 212 210-2100
Jersey City *(G-4720)*

Data Communique Inc ....E 201 508-6000
Ridgefield Park *(G-9302)*

Data Communique Intl Inc ....F 201 508-6000
Ridgefield Park *(G-9303)*

Deans Graphics ....G 609 261-8817
Mount Holly *(G-6724)*

Delgen Press Inc ....G 973 472-2266
Clifton *(G-1597)*

Dewechter Inc ....G 856 845-0225
Woodbury *(G-12027)*

Dezine Line Inc ....F 973 989-1009
Wharton *(G-11856)*

▲ Diligaf Enterprises Inc ....E 201 684-0900
Mahwah *(G-5729)*

Display Impressions ....F 856 488-1777
Pennsauken *(G-8415)*

Distributor Label Products ....E 908 704-9997
Hillsborough *(G-4312)*

DOT Graphix Inc ....F 609 994-3416
Barnegat *(G-158)*

Downtown Printing Center Inc ....F 732 246-7990
New Brunswick *(G-6920)*

Driscoll Label Company Inc ....F 973 585-7291
East Hanover *(G-2206)*

Dye Into Print Inc ....D 973 772-8019
Clifton *(G-1606)*

E C D Ventures Inc ....E 856 875-1100
Blackwood *(G-465)*

Earthcolor Inc ....C 973 884-1300
Parsippany *(G-7928)*

Engraved Images Ltd ....G 908 234-0323
Far Hills *(G-3375)*

Envelopes & Printed Pdts Inc ....G 973 942-1232
Prospect Park *(G-9073)*

Envirnmntal Dsign Grphic Entps ...G 973 361-1829
Dover *(G-2083)*

F S T Printing Inc ....G 732 560-3749
Middlesex *(G-6115)*

Fedex Office & Print Svcs Inc ....G 201 672-0508
East Rutherford *(G-2288)*

Fedex Office & Print Svcs Inc ....E 732 636-3580
Iselin *(G-4609)*

Ferrante Press Inc	G	609 239-4257	
Verona (G-11167)			
Fischlers Dawnpoint	G	856 428-2092	
Cherry Hill (G-1362)			
Fit Graphix	G	201 488-4670	
Hackensack (G-3914)			
Five Macs Inc	E	856 596-3150	
Marlton (G-5931)			
◆ Flanagan Holdings Inc	D	201 512-3338	
Mahwah (G-5737)			
Flexi Printing Plate Co Inc	F	201 939-3600	
Moonachie (G-6465)			
▲ Flexo-Craft Prints Inc	E	973 482-7200	
Harrison (G-4174)			
Fordham Inc	E	973 575-7840	
Fairfield (G-3205)			
Forms & Flyers of New Jersey	G	856 629-0718	
Williamstown (G-11958)			
Foto Fantasy	G	732 548-8446	
Edison (G-2514)			
Frank J Zechman	G	732 495-0077	
Belford (G-282)			
Frontend Graphics Inc	G	856 547-1600	
Cherry Hill (G-1364)			
▲ Fu WEI Inc	G	732 937-8388	
East Brunswick (G-2147)			
G & M Printwear	F	856 742-5551	
Gloucester City (G-3841)			
Global Graphics Intergration	F	973 334-9653	
Towaco (G-10872)			
Good Impressions Inc	G	856 461-3232	
Riverside (G-9395)			
Graphic Arts Printing	G	201 343-6554	
Hawthorne (G-4222)			
Graphic Image	G	856 262-8900	
Williamstown (G-11959)			
Graphic Imagery Inc	F	908 755-2882	
New Providence (G-7002)			
GTM Marketing Inc	G	856 227-2333	
Woodbury (G-12031)			
H & H Graphic Printing Inc	G	201 369-9700	
Carlstadt (G-1162)			
H & L Printing Co	G	201 288-0877	
Hasbrouck Heights (G-4184)			
▲ H C Graphics Screenprinting	G	973 247-0544	
Paterson (G-8207)			
Harwill Corporation	G	609 895-1955	
Windsor (G-11996)			
Hary Manufacturing Inc	F	908 722-7100	
Woodbridge (G-12018)			
Hayes Mindish Inc	G	609 641-9880	
Pleasantville (G-8812)			
Heritage Inc	G	201 447-2600	
Midland Park (G-6177)			
▲ Hit Promo LLC	C	800 237-6305	
Bellmawr (G-334)			
Horizon Label LLC	F	856 767-0777	
West Berlin (G-11599)			
▲ Howard Press Inc	D	908 245-4400	
Roselle (G-9561)			
Howes Standard Publishing Co	E	856 691-2000	
Vineland (G-11233)			
▲ Hummel Distributing Corp	E	908 688-5300	
Union (G-11063)			
Hummel Printing Inc	E	908 688-5300	
Union (G-11064)			
Hygrade Business Group Inc	E	800 836-7714	
Secaucus (G-9781)			
Ics Corporation	C	215 427-3355	
West Deptford (G-11704)			
▲ Ideal Jacobs Corporation	E	973 275-5100	
Maplewood (G-5879)			
Illinois Tool Works Inc	E	609 395-5600	
Cranbury (G-1839)			
Image Screen Printing Inc	C	732 560-1817	
Middlesex (G-6121)			
Imagery Embroidary Corporation	F	201 343-9333	
Union City (G-11113)			
Important Papers Inc	G	856 751-4544	
Cherry Hill (G-1376)			
Imprintz Cstm Printed Graphics	G	609 386-5673	
Lumberton (G-5631)			
Industrial Lbeling Systems Inc	E	973 808-8188	
Fairfield (G-3238)			
Innovative Awards Inc	G	609 888-1400	
Trenton (G-10945)			
Instant Printing of Dover Inc	G	973 366-6855	
Dover (G-2090)			
Inter City Press Inc	E	908 236-9911	
Lebanon (G-5264)			

Italian Treasures	G	856 770-9188	
Voorhees (G-11290)			
J & G Graphics Inc	G	732 223-6660	
Manasquan (G-5832)			
J and S Sporting Apparel LLC	G	732 787-5500	
Keansburg (G-4838)			
J F I Printing	G	973 759-3444	
Belleville (G-297)			
J H M Communications Inc	G	908 859-6668	
Phillipsburg (G-8556)			
J&E Business Services LLC	G	973 984-8444	
Clifton (G-1645)			
Jimcam Publishing Inc	G	201 843-5700	
Maywood (G-6009)			
John Patrick Publishing LLC	D	609 883-2700	
Ewing (G-3038)			
▲ Jrm Industries Inc	E	973 779-9340	
Passaic (G-8077)			
▲ Judith Roth Studio Collection	G	973 543-4455	
Mendham (G-6039)			
K M Media Group LLC	G	973 330-3000	
Clifton (G-1648)			
Kdf Reprographics Inc	F	201 784-9991	
South Hackensack (G-10167)			
Keefe Printing Inc	G	732 295-2099	
Point Pleasant Beach (G-8826)			
Keskes Printing LLC	G	856 767-4733	
Berlin (G-425)			
Koday Press Inc	F	201 387-0001	
Dumont (G-2116)			
Kraftwork Custom Design	F	609 883-8444	
Ewing (G-3043)			
Label Solutions Inc	G	201 599-0909	
Rochelle Park (G-9426)			
▲ Lacoa Inc	G	973 754-1000	
Elmwood Park (G-2837)			
▲ Lally-Pak Inc	D	908 351-4141	
Hillside (G-4409)			
Lamb Printing Inc	G	908 852-0837	
Hackettstown (G-4016)			
▲ Laserwave Graphics Inc	F	732 745-7764	
New Brunswick (G-6943)			
Latta Graphics Inc	E	201 440-4040	
Carlstadt (G-1181)			
Liberty Envelope Inc	F	973 546-5600	
Paterson (G-8240)			
Licensee Services Inc	F	609 465-2003	
Cape May Court House (G-1112)			
▲ Lizard Label Co	F	973 808-3322	
Fairfield (G-3265)			
Logomania Inc	G	201 798-0531	
Jersey City (G-4760)			
M & M Printing Corp	G	201 288-7787	
Hasbrouck Heights (G-4186)			
Maggio Printing LLC	E	856 931-7805	
Bellmawr (G-338)			
Magic Printing Corp	F	732 726-0620	
Avenel (G-135)			
Main Street Graphics Inc	G	856 755-3523	
Maple Shade (G-5866)			
▲ Mainetti Americas Inc	E	201 215-2900	
Secaucus (G-9791)			
▲ Mariano Press LLC	F	732 247-3659	
Somerset (G-10022)			
▲ Marlo Plastic Products Inc	E	732 792-1988	
Neptune (G-6890)			
Mary Bridget Enterprises	E	609 267-4830	
Cinnaminson (G-1471)			
Med-Con Tech Ltd Lblty Co	G	888 654-0856	
Clinton (G-1747)			
▼ Mega Media Concepts Ltd Lblty	G	973 919-5661	
Sparta (G-10397)			
Menu Express	F	856 216-7777	
Pennsauken (G-8457)			
Mercer C AlphaGraphics	G	609 921-0959	
Hamilton (G-4115)			
Merrill Corporation	D	973 643-4403	
Newark (G-7200)			
Merrill Corporation	D	908 810-3740	
Union (G-11075)			
Midland Screen Printing Inc	F	201 703-0066	
Saddle Brook (G-9662)			
Midlantic Color Graphics LLC	G	856 786-3113	
Cinnaminson (G-1474)			
Mike Dolly Screen Printing	F	732 294-8979	
Freehold (G-3679)			
Mimeocom Inc	F	973 286-2901	
Newark (G-7202)			
▲ Mj Corporate Sales Inc	E	856 778-0055	
Mount Laurel (G-6783)			

Monarch Art Plastics Co LLC	E	856 235-5151	
Mount Laurel (G-6785)			
Moonlight Imaging LLC	G	973 300-1001	
Sparta (G-10399)			
National Color Graphics	F	856 435-6800	
Sicklerville (G-9912)			
National Plastic Printing	E	973 785-1460	
Totowa (G-10838)			
National Reprographics Inc	E	609 896-4100	
Lawrenceville (G-5239)			
New Jersey Label LLC	F	201 880-5102	
South Hackensack (G-10175)			
New Jersey Tech Group LLC	G	609 301-6405	
Lumberton (G-5633)			
New Line Prtg & Tech Solutions	G	973 405-6133	
Clifton (G-1676)			
Newton Screen Printing Co	G	973 827-0486	
Franklin (G-3606)			
NJ Logo Wear LLC	G	609 597-9400	
Manahawkin (G-5794)			
Njiw Limited Liability Company	F	201 355-2955	
Hackensack (G-3954)			
North America Printing	G	973 726-7713	
Sparta (G-10403)			
North Eastern Business Forms	G	609 392-1161	
Trenton (G-10967)			
O Berk Company LLC	E	201 941-1610	
Fairview (G-3365)			
Ocsidot Inc	F	908 789-3300	
Garwood (G-3788)			
Office Needs Inc	G	732 381-7770	
Clark (G-1511)			
Old Ue LLC	B	800 752-4012	
Ridgefield (G-9281)			
OShea Services Inc	G	201 343-8668	
Hackensack (G-3958)			
Outfront Media LLC	D	973 575-6900	
Fairfield (G-3286)			
Output Services Group Inc	G	201 871-1100	
Carlstadt (G-1193)			
Page 2 LLC	G	862 239-9830	
Wayne (G-11538)			
Page Stamp LLC	G	732 390-1700	
Monroe Township (G-6340)			
Palm Press Inc	G	201 767-6504	
Northvale (G-7543)			
Paper Clip Communication Inc	F	973 256-1333	
Little Falls (G-5464)			
Papery of Marlton LLC	G	856 985-1776	
Marlton (G-5946)			
Party City Corporation	F	973 537-1707	
Randolph (G-9196)			
Party City of North Bergen	F	201 865-0040	
North Bergen (G-7427)			
Patchworks Co Inc	G	973 627-2002	
Dover (G-2103)			
▲ Peacock Products Inc	F	201 385-5585	
Bergenfield (G-382)			
◆ Pecata Enterprises Inc	E	973 523-9498	
Paterson (G-8280)			
Penn Jersey Press Inc	G	856 627-2200	
Gibbsboro (G-3795)			
Penta Digital Incorporated	G	201 839-5392	
Jersey City (G-4782)			
Perco Inc	F	908 464-3000	
Berkeley Heights (G-410)			
Perfect Printing Inc	E	856 787-1877	
Moorestown (G-6555)			
▲ Pharmaceutic Litho Label Inc	C	336 785-4000	
Cranford (G-1923)			
Phoenix Alliance Group LLC	F	732 495-4800	
Port Monmouth (G-8879)			
Platypus Print Productions LLC	G	732 772-1212	
Morganville (G-6594)			
▲ Pochet of America Inc	C	973 942-4923	
Woodland Park (G-12086)			
Precise Corporate Printing Inc	E	973 350-0330	
Harrison (G-4177)			
Premier Press Inc	F	856 665-0722	
Pennsauken (G-8471)			
Premium Color Group LLC	E	973 472-7007	
Carlstadt (G-1207)			
Press Room Inc	F	609 689-3817	
Trenton (G-10981)			
Pressto Graphics	F	732 286-9300	
Toms River (G-10784)			
▲ Pressworks	G	856 427-9001	
Cherry Hill (G-1411)			
Print Communications Group Inc	D	973 882-9444	
Fairfield (G-3295)			

Print Mail Communications LLC............E....... 856 488-0345
Pennsauken (G-8473)
Print Media LLC..............................G....... 973 467-0007
Springfield (G-10460)
Print Solutions LLC ....F....... 201 567-9622
Englewood (G-2933)
Printers of Salem County LLC..............G....... 856 935-5032
Salem (G-9696)
Printing & Signs Express Inc................G....... 201 368-1255
Mahwah (G-5763)
Printing Lab LLC ....F....... 201 305-0404
West New York (G-11750)
Printology ....G....... 201 345-4632
Midland Park (G-6186)
Printsmith ....G....... 908 245-3000
Roselle Park (G-9589)
Product Identification Co Inc ....F....... 973 227-7770
Garfield (G-3762)
Promo Graphic Inc................................G....... 732 629-7300
Middlesex (G-6141)
Promotional Graphics Inc ....F....... 973 423-3900
Paterson (G-8283)
R & R Printing & Copy Center...............G....... 732 249-9450
Hillsborough (G-4348)
Ramsey Graphics and Printing.............G....... 201 300-2912
Elmwood Park (G-2852)
Red Diamond Co - Athc Letering..........G....... 973 759-2005
Belleville (G-310)
Red Letter Press Inc ....G....... 609 597-5257
Upper Saddle River (G-11146)
Redmond Bcms Inc ....D....... 973 664-2000
Denville (G-2051)
Reliable Envelope and Graphics ....E....... 201 794-7756
Elmwood Park (G-2854)
Remco Press Inc..................................G....... 201 751-5703
North Bergen (G-7433)
▼ Riegel Cmmunications Group Inc ....E....... 609 771-0555
Ewing (G-3061)
Riverside Graphics Inc ....F....... 201 876-9000
Belleville (G-311)
Roan Printing Inc ....F....... 908 526-5990
Somerville (G-10124)
Rolferrys Specialties Inc ....G....... 856 456-2999
Brooklawn (G-915)
Royalty Press Inc..................................E....... 856 663-2288
Westville (G-11820)
Royer Group Inc...................................E....... 856 324-0171
Pennsauken (G-8479)
Royercomm Corporation.......................F....... 856 665-6400
Pennsauken (G-8480)
Rutler Screen Printing Inc.....................F....... 908 859-3327
Phillipsburg (G-8573)
S J T Imaging Inc ....D....... 201 262-7744
Oradell (G-7747)
S V O Inc ....G....... 973 983-8380
Succasunna (G-10519)
▲ Sabrimax Corp ....F....... 201 871-0808
Englewood (G-2938)
Samuel Elliott Inc..................................E....... 856 773-6000
Cinnaminson (G-1483)
Sapphire Envelope & Graphics ....E....... 856 782-2227
Magnolia (G-5709)
Sato Lbling Solutions Amer Inc............D....... 973 287-3641
Pine Brook (G-8616)
Screen Play Inc ....G....... 973 227-9014
Fairfield (G-3309)
▲ Screen Tech Inc of New Jersey ....D....... 908 862-8000
Linden (G-5420)
Screen-Trans Development Corp ....E....... 201 933-7800
Moonachie (G-6488)
Semels Embroidery Inc ....F....... 973 473-6868
Clifton (G-1713)
Sharp Impressions Inc ....G....... 201 573-4943
Garfield (G-3767)
Sherman Printing Co Inc.......................G....... 973 345-2493
Clifton (G-1715)
Signmasters Inc....................................D....... 973 614-8300
Passaic (G-8107)
Silver Edmar...G....... 973 817-7483
Newark (G-7273)
▼ Six Thirteen Originals LLC ....E....... 201 316-1900
Mahwah (G-5772)
Sjshore Marketing Ltd Lblty Co............F....... 609 390-1400
Marmora (G-5959)
Skylands Press ....G....... 973 383-5006
Newton (G-7358)
Smith Enterprises ....G....... 215 416-9881
Mount Laurel (G-6807)
Sports Stop Inc ....F....... 856 881-2763
Glassboro (G-3819)

▲ Star Narrow Fabrics Inc....................G....... 973 778-8600
Lodi (G-5576)
Starnet Business Solutions ....E....... 201 252-2863
Mahwah (G-5775)
◆ Stephen Gould Corporation ....D....... 973 428-1500
Whippany (G-11910)
Stewart Business Forms Inc.................F....... 856 768-2011
Blackwood (G-481)
Stuyvesant Press Inc............................F....... 973 399-3880
Irvington (G-4587)
◆ Sunglo Fabrics Inc ....F....... 201 935-0830
Paterson (G-8304)
Sunset Printing and Engrv Corp ....E....... 973 537-9600
Wharton (G-11871)
Taunton Graphics Inc ....F....... 856 719-8084
West Berlin (G-11625)
Tbc Color Imaging Inc ....E....... 973 470-8100
Clifton (G-1731)
▲ Tectubes USA Inc.............................E....... 856 589-1250
Vineland (G-11269)
Tekno Inc ....G....... 973 423-2004
Hawthorne (G-4246)
Terminal Printing Co.............................G....... 201 659-5924
Belleville (G-316)
Timeline Promotions Inc.......................G....... 973 226-1512
West Caldwell (G-11680)
Toppan Printing Co Amer Inc...............C....... 732 469-8400
Somerset (G-10088)
Toppan Vintage Inc ....E....... 201 226-9220
Saddle Brook (G-9684)
Totally T Shirts & More Inc...................G....... 609 894-0011
Pemberton (G-8358)
Trade Thermographers Inc....................F....... 201 489-2060
Rochelle Park (G-9432)
Travel Weekly ....G....... 201 902-1931
Secaucus (G-9822)
Tremont Printing Co ....G....... 973 227-0742
Fairfield (G-3332)
Trentypo Inc..F....... 609 883-5971
Ewing (G-3071)
Trico Web LLC......................................G....... 201 438-3860
Carlstadt (G-1232)
Trukmanns Inc......................................E....... 973 538-7718
Cedar Knolls (G-1314)
Turul Bookbindery Inc...........................G....... 973 361-2810
Wharton (G-11874)
Typecom LLC ....G....... 201 969-1901
Fort Lee (G-3591)
Typeline..F....... 201 251-2201
Wyckoff (G-12123)
◆ U S Screening Corp ....C....... 973 242-1110
Newark (G-7305)
▲ Unimac Graphics LLC ....C....... 201 372-1000
Carlstadt (G-1234)
Unique Impressions Ltd Lblty ....G....... 201 751-4088
Union City (G-11133)
United Forms Finishing Corp ....F....... 908 687-0494
Hillside (G-4434)
United Label Corp.................................G....... 973 589-6500
Newark (G-7309)
University Publications Inc...................G....... 212 268-4222
Belford (G-284)
Unlimited Print Products Inc.................F....... 609 882-0653
Ewing (G-3075)
Vernon Display Graphics Inc ....E....... 201 935-7117
Carlstadt (G-1235)
Vernw Printing Company ....G....... 973 751-6462
Belleville (G-321)
Vertis Inc..D....... 215 781-1668
Mount Holly (G-6735)
Wagner Foto Screen Process ....G....... 908 624-0800
Kenilworth (G-4987)
Wall Street Group Inc ....D....... 201 333-4784
South Plainfield (G-10344)
Watonka Printing Inc ....G....... 732 974-8878
Belmar (G-356)
Whitehouse Prtg & Labeling LLC.........G....... 973 521-7648
Fairfield (G-3353)
Wilcox Press...G....... 973 827-7474
Hamburg (G-4099)
Wilmington Trust Sp Services ....C....... 609 272-7000
Pleasantville (G-8821)
Winemiller Press Inc.............................G....... 732 223-0100
Manasquan (G-5843)
▲ Winsome Digital Inc..........................F....... 609 645-2211
Egg Harbor Township (G-2702)
▲ Wisco Promo & Uniform Inc ....G....... 973 767-2022
Saddle Brook (G-9688)
Work n Gear LLC..................................G....... 856 848-7676
Woodbury (G-12039)

Z Fab LLC ....G....... 973 248-0686
Wayne (G-11566)
Zeeks Tees...F....... 732 291-2700
Belford (G-285)
Zone Two Inc ....F....... 732 237-0766
Bayville (G-254)
Zoo Printing Inc....................................G....... 856 686-0800
West Deptford (G-11718)
Zwier Corp ....G....... 973 748-4009
Bloomfield (G-524)

2761 Manifold Business Forms

▲ All-State International Inc................C....... 908 272-0800
Cranford (G-1899)
▲ Drew & Rogers Inc ....E....... 973 575-6210
Fairfield (G-3187)
Hygrade Business Group Inc................E....... 800 836-7714
Secaucus (G-9781)
◆ Infoseal LLC.....................................D....... 201 569-4500
Englewood (G-2913)
North Eastern Business Forms ....G....... 609 392-1161
Trenton (G-10967)
Snap Set Specialists Inc.......................G....... 856 629-9552
Williamstown (G-11978)
Stewart Business Forms Inc.................F....... 856 768-2011
Blackwood (G-481)
Stuyvesant Press Inc............................F....... 973 399-3880
Irvington (G-4587)
Taylor Communications Inc ....D....... 732 560-3410
Somerset (G-10081)
Watonka Printing Inc ....G....... 732 974-8878
Belmar (G-356)
Webb Press ....G....... 609 386-0100
Burlington (G-992)

2771 Greeting Card Publishing

▲ Amaryllis Inc......................................G....... 973 635-0500
Chatham (G-1318)
▲ Easy Street Publications Inc............G....... 917 699-7820
Union (G-11048)
Greetingtap...G....... 347 731-4263
South Plainfield (G-10269)
Magnetic Ticket & Label Corp..............E....... 973 759-6500
Belleville (G-299)
▲ Nobleworks Inc ....F....... 201 420-0095
Union City (G-11124)
Prudent Publishing Co Inc ....E....... 973 347-4554
Landing (G-5203)
Saint La Salle Auxiliary Inc ....G....... 732 842-4359
Lincroft (G-5314)
Schurman Fine Papers ....E....... 856 985-1776
Marlton (G-5950)

2782 Blankbooks & Looseleaf Binders

Black Lagoon Inc ....G....... 609 815-1654
Trenton (G-10905)
Cutting Records Inc..............................G....... 201 488-8444
Hackensack (G-3902)
Deluxe Corporation...............................C....... 973 334-8000
Mountain Lakes (G-6823)
Ebsco Industries Inc.............................F....... 201 933-1800
Rutherford (G-9619)
Flortek Corporation ....E....... 201 436-7700
Bayonne (G-216)
Gpschartscom.......................................G....... 609 226-8842
Ventnor City (G-11153)
Johnthan Leasing Corp.........................E....... 908 226-3434
Asbury (G-66)
Newark Morning Ledger Co ....C....... 973 882-6120
Pine Brook (G-8611)
Reed Presentations Inc ....F....... 908 832-0007
Asbury (G-69)
Star Bindery Inc ....E....... 609 519-5732
Franklinville (G-3640)
Tomwar Corp ....E....... 856 740-0111
Williamstown (G-11981)
Walden Lang In-Pak Service ....E....... 973 595-5250
Clifton (G-1738)

2789 Bookbinding

A S A P Nameplate & Labeling.............F....... 973 773-3934
Passaic (G-8048)
Action Copy Centers Inc ....G....... 973 744-5520
Montclair (G-6356)
Allegro Printing Corporation ....G....... 609 641-7060
Galloway (G-3719)
American Bindery Depot Inc.................C....... 732 287-2370
Edison (G-2453)

American Graphic Systems Inc	G	201 796-0666
Fair Lawn *(G-3084)*
▲ Ancraft Press Corp	F	201 792-9200
Jersey City *(G-4691)*
B & R Printing Inc	G	609 448-3328
Trenton *(G-10901)*
Bar Lan Inc	G	856 596-2330
Brigantine *(G-911)*
▲ Bassil Bookbinding Company Inc	E	201 440-4925
Hackensack *(G-3881)*
Benton Bindery Inc	F	732 431-9064
Freehold *(G-3653)*
Berk Gold Stamping Corporation	E	973 786-6052
Andover *(G-45)*
Bethel Bindery	F	609 296-5043
Ltl Egg Hbr *(G-5615)*
Bind-Rite Graphics Inc	E	201 863-8100
Secaucus *(G-9754)*
Bind-Rite Services Inc	C	201 440-5585
South Hackensack *(G-10150)*
Bindgraphics Inc	E	908 245-1110
Roselle *(G-9549)*
Binding Products Inc	E	212 947-1192
Jersey City *(G-4704)*
Budget Print Center	G	973 743-0073
Bloomfield *(G-492)*
C Jackson Associates Inc	E	856 761-8000
Cherry Hill *(G-1351)*
Capitol Bindery Inc	E	609 883-5971
Ewing *(G-3018)*
Colorful Story Books Inc	E	908 561-3333
South Plainfield *(G-10240)*
Cornerstone Prints Imaging LLC	G	908 782-7966
Flemington *(G-3434)*
Craftsmen Photo Lithographers	E	973 316-5791
East Hanover *(G-2204)*
Creative Color Lithographers	F	908 789-2295
Garwood *(G-3783)*
Custom Book Bindery Inc	F	973 815-1400
Clifton *(G-1595)*
D & I Printing Co Inc	F	201 871-3620
Englewood *(G-2895)*
D A K Office Services Inc	G	609 586-8222
Trenton *(G-10929)*
Devece & Shaffer Inc	G	856 829-7282
Palmyra *(G-7782)*
Dm Graphic Center LLC	F	973 882-8990
Fairfield *(G-3186)*
E & M Bindery Inc	C	973 777-9300
Clifton *(G-1609)*
Fedex Office & Print Svcs Inc	F	732 249-9222
New Brunswick *(G-6926)*
Fedex Office & Print Svcs Inc	F	856 273-5959
Mount Laurel *(G-6760)*
Fedex Office & Print Svcs Inc	E	856 427-0099
Cherry Hill *(G-1361)*
Good Impressions Inc	E	856 461-3232
Riverside *(G-9395)*
Grandview Printing Co Inc	F	973 890-0006
Totowa *(G-10831)*
Holographic Finishing Inc	F	201 941-4651
Ridgefield *(G-9266)*
Hub Print & Copy Center LLC	G	201 585-7887
Fort Lee *(G-3563)*
Instant Printing of Dover Inc	G	973 366-6855
Dover *(G-2090)*
Jersey Printing Associates Inc	E	732 872-9654
Atlantic Highlands *(G-108)*
Jmp Press Inc	G	201 444-0236
Ho Ho Kus *(G-4441)*
John S Swift Company Inc	G	201 935-2002
Teterboro *(G-10682)*
Johnston Letter Co Inc	G	973 482-7535
Flanders *(G-3414)*
Latta Graphics Inc	E	201 440-4040
Carlstadt *(G-1181)*
▲ Lb Book Bindery LLC	F	973 244-0442
Fairfield *(G-3258)*
Lo Gatto Bookbinding	G	201 438-4344
East Rutherford *(G-2297)*
Lunet Inc	G	201 261-3883
Paramus *(G-7816)*
Marco Book Co Inc	C	973 458-0485
Lodi *(G-5570)*
▲ Mariano Press LLC	F	732 247-3659
Somerset *(G-10022)*
Marks Management Systems Inc	G	856 866-0588
Maple Shade *(G-5867)*
McCormicks Bindery Inc	E	856 663-8035
Pennsauken *(G-8454)*

Meadowlands Bindery Inc	E	201 935-6161
Moonachie *(G-6480)*
Metro Bindery of New Jersey	F	973 667-4190
Nutley *(G-7591)*
Mid State Bindery	G	908 755-9388
Middlesex *(G-6130)*
Miniature Folding Inc	F	201 773-6477
Elmwood Park *(G-2843)*
Morris Plains Pip Inc	G	973 533-9330
Livingston *(G-5528)*
Myriams Dream Book Bindery	G	609 345-5555
Atlantic City *(G-99)*
▲ Nb Bookbinding Inc	G	973 247-1200
Clifton *(G-1673)*
New Jersey Bindery Svcs LLC	G	732 200-8024
South Plainfield *(G-10305)*
Northeast Bindery Inc	F	908 436-3737
Elizabeth *(G-2762)*
Ont Sutter	G	201 265-0262
Emerson *(G-2867)*
OShea Services Inc	G	201 343-8668
Hackensack *(G-3958)*
Pad and Publ Assembly Corp	E	856 424-0158
Cherry Hill *(G-1404)*
Palm Press Inc	G	201 767-6504
Northvale *(G-7543)*
Palmarozzo Bindery	G	908 688-5300
Union *(G-11081)*
Permagraphics Inc	F	201 814-1200
Moonachie *(G-6483)*
Philip Holzer and Assoc LLC	E	212 691-9500
Carlstadt *(G-1201)*
▲ Poplar Bindery Inc	F	856 727-8030
Moorestown *(G-6558)*
Premier Printing Solutions LLC	G	732 525-0740
South Amboy *(G-10139)*
Puent-Romer Communications Inc	G	973 509-7591
Montclair *(G-6386)*
R & B Printing Inc	G	908 766-4073
Bernardsville *(G-443)*
Redmond Bcms Inc	D	973 664-2000
Denville *(G-2051)*
Roan Printing Inc	G	908 526-5990
Somerville *(G-10124)*
Robert A Eick Qlty Bookbinding	G	973 822-2100
Madison *(G-5701)*
Royer Group Inc	E	856 324-0171
Pennsauken *(G-8479)*
Santon Inc	G	201 444-9080
Toms River *(G-10790)*
Scarlet Printing	G	732 560-1415
Middlesex *(G-6143)*
Scott Graphics Printing Co Inc	G	201 262-0473
New Milford *(G-6992)*
Sheroy Printing Inc	F	973 242-4040
Newark *(G-7271)*
Sonata Graphics Inc	G	201 866-0186
Secaucus *(G-9816)*
▲ Spiral Binding LLC	C	973 256-0666
Totowa *(G-10853)*
Standard Prtg & Mail Svcs Inc	F	973 790-3333
Fairfield *(G-3314)*
Star Promotions Inc	F	732 356-5959
Bound Brook *(G-607)*
Steb Inc	G	973 584-0990
Ledgewood *(G-5281)*
Tanter Inc	G	732 382-3555
Clark *(G-1516)*
Tanzola Printing Inc	G	973 779-0858
Clifton *(G-1729)*
Tech-Pak Inc	F	201 935-3800
Wood Ridge *(G-12007)*
Tedco Inc	G	609 883-0799
Ewing *(G-3069)*
Thewal Inc	F	973 635-1880
Chatham *(G-1330)*
Toppan Printing Co Amer Inc	G	732 469-8400
Somerset *(G-10088)*
Turul Bookbindery Inc	G	973 361-2810
Wharton *(G-11874)*
Verni Vito	G	732 449-1760
Wall Township *(G-11377)*
Washington Stamp Exchange Inc	F	973 966-0001
Florham Park *(G-3526)*
Westbury Press Inc	D	201 894-0444
Englewood *(G-2953)*
Wilker Graphics LLC	G	201 447-4800
Midland Park *(G-6190)*
Windmill Press Inc	G	856 663-8990
Pennsauken *(G-8497)*

Yasheel Inc	G	856 275-6812
Sewell *(G-9854)*

2791 Typesetting

A M Graphics Inc	G	201 767-5320
Harrington Park *(G-4161)*
Action Copy Centers Inc	G	973 744-5520
Montclair *(G-6356)*
American Graphic Systems Inc	G	201 796-0666
Fair Lawn *(G-3084)*
◆ Arch Crown Inc	E	973 731-6300
Hillside *(G-4375)*
Ayr Composition Inc	G	908 241-8118
Roselle Park *(G-9578)*
Aztec Graphics Inc	F	609 587-1000
Trenton *(G-10900)*
B & B Press Inc	G	908 840-4093
Lebanon *(G-5253)*
Bar Lan Inc	G	856 596-2330
Brigantine *(G-911)*
Bartlett Printing & Graphic	G	609 386-1525
Burlington *(G-952)*
Bowmar Enterprises Inc	G	908 277-3000
New Providence *(G-6996)*
Budget Print Center	G	973 743-0073
Bloomfield *(G-492)*
Commercial Composition & Prtg	G	856 662-0557
Pennsauken *(G-8407)*
Comptime Inc	G	201 760-2400
Ramsey *(G-9143)*
Consumer Graphics Inc	G	732 469-4699
Somerset *(G-9977)*
Copy-Rite Printing	G	609 597-9182
Manahawkin *(G-5792)*
Cordes Printing Inc	G	201 652-7272
Wyckoff *(G-12107)*
Cornerstone Prints Imaging LLC	G	908 782-7966
Flemington *(G-3434)*
Craftsmen Photo Lithographers	E	973 316-5791
East Hanover *(G-2204)*
Creative Color Lithographers	F	908 789-2295
Garwood *(G-3783)*
D A K Office Services Inc	G	609 586-8222
Trenton *(G-10929)*
Data Communique Inc	E	201 508-6000
Ridgefield Park *(G-9302)*
Devece & Shaffer Inc	G	856 829-7282
Palmyra *(G-7782)*
Downtown Printing Center Inc	F	732 246-7990
New Brunswick *(G-6920)*
Earth Color New York Inc	E	973 884-1300
Parsippany *(G-7925)*
Fedex Office & Print Svcs Inc	F	732 249-9222
New Brunswick *(G-6926)*
Fedex Office & Print Svcs Inc	F	856 273-5959
Mount Laurel *(G-6760)*
Fedex Office & Print Svcs Inc	G	973 376-3966
Springfield *(G-10443)*
Fedex Office & Print Svcs Inc	E	856 427-0099
Cherry Hill *(G-1361)*
Gangi Graphics Inc	G	732 840-8680
Brick *(G-719)*
Hub Print & Copy Center LLC	G	201 585-7887
Fort Lee *(G-3563)*
Inserts East Incorporated	C	856 663-8181
Pennsauken *(G-8437)*
Instant Printing of Dover Inc	G	973 366-6855
Dover *(G-2090)*
J K Design Inc	E	908 428-4700
Hillsborough *(G-4334)*
Jem Printing Inc	G	908 782-9986
Flemington *(G-3450)*
Jmp Press Inc	G	201 444-0236
Ho Ho Kus *(G-4441)*
John S Swift Company Inc	G	201 935-2002
Teterboro *(G-10682)*
Johnston Letter Co Inc	G	973 482-7535
Flanders *(G-3414)*
Kirms Printing Co Inc	E	732 774-8000
Neptune *(G-6886)*
L A S Printing Co	G	201 991-5362
Jersey City *(G-4757)*
▲ Laserwave Graphics Inc	F	732 745-7764
New Brunswick *(G-6943)*
Lunet Inc	G	201 261-3883
Paramus *(G-7816)*
Marks Management Systems Inc	G	856 866-0588
Maple Shade *(G-5867)*
McKella 2-8-0 Inc	D	856 813-1153
Pennsauken *(G-8455)*

SIC

Metro Publishing Group Inc ....F 201 385-2000
New Milford **(G-6990)**

▲ Morgan Printing Service Inc ....F 732 721-2959
South Amboy **(G-10138)**

Morris Plains Pip Inc ....G 973 533-9330
Livingston **(G-5528)**

Nassau Communications Inc ....F 609 208-9099
Lawrence Township **(G-5218)**

Network Typesetting Inc ....G 732 819-0949
Piscataway **(G-8694)**

New Jersey Label LLC ....F 201 880-5102
South Hackensack **(G-10175)**

Newark Trade Typographers ....F 973 674-3727
Orange **(G-7757)**

Newtype Inc ....F 973 361-6000
Randolph **(G-9192)**

Old Hights Print Shop Inc ....G 609 443-4700
Jackson **(G-4661)**

OShea Services Inc ....G 201 343-8668
Hackensack **(G-3958)**

Otis Graphics Inc ....F 201 438-7120
Lyndhurst **(G-5671)**

Pad and Publ Assembly Corp ....E 856 424-0158
Cherry Hill **(G-1404)**

Painton Studios Inc ....G 732 302-0200
Green Brook **(G-3865)**

Palm Press Inc ....G 201 767-6504
Northvale **(G-7543)**

Patel Printing Plus Corp ....F 908 964-6422
Union **(G-11082)**

Permagraphics Inc ....F 201 814-1200
Moonachie **(G-6483)**

Philip Holzer and Assoc LLC ....E 212 691-9500
Carlstadt **(G-1201)**

Printing Delite Inc ....G 973 676-3033
East Orange **(G-2260)**

Puent-Romer Communications Inc ....G 973 509-7591
Montclair **(G-6386)**

Redmond Bcms Inc ....D 973 664-2000
Denville **(G-2051)**

Roan Printing Inc ....F 908 526-5990
Somerville **(G-10124)**

Sandoval Graphics & Printing ....G 856 435-7320
Somerdale **(G-9934)**

Scarlet Printing ....G 732 560-1415
Middlesex **(G-6143)**

Scott Graphics Printing Co Inc ....G 201 262-0473
New Milford **(G-6992)**

Sheroy Printing Inc ....F 973 242-4040
Newark **(G-7271)**

Sign On Inc ....G 201 384-7714
Bloomingdale **(G-530)**

Sonata Graphics Inc ....G 201 866-0186
Secaucus **(G-9816)**

Staines Inc ....F 856 784-2718
Somerdale **(G-9935)**

Standard Prtg & Mail Svcs Inc ....F 973 790-3333
Fairfield **(G-3314)**

Star Promotions Inc ....F 732 356-5959
Bound Brook **(G-607)**

Steb Inc ....G 973 584-0990
Ledgewood **(G-5281)**

Tangent Graphics Inc ....G 201 488-2840
Englewood **(G-2946)**

Tanter Inc ....G 732 382-3555
Clark **(G-1516)**

Techsetters Inc ....E 856 240-7905
Collingswood **(G-1772)**

Tedco Inc ....G 609 883-0799
Ewing **(G-3069)**

Thewal Inc ....F 973 635-1880
Chatham **(G-1330)**

Trade Thermographers Inc ....F 201 489-2060
Rochelle Park **(G-9432)**

Trentypo Inc ....F 609 883-5971
Ewing **(G-3071)**

Typeline ....F 201 251-2201
Wyckoff **(G-12123)**

Typen Graphics Inc ....G 973 838-6544
Kinnelon **(G-5023)**

Verni Vito ....G 732 449-1760
Wall Township **(G-11377)**

Wilker Graphics LLC ....F 201 447-4800
Midland Park **(G-6190)**

Word Center Printing ....G 609 586-5825
Trenton **(G-11010)**

Zwier Corp ....G 973 748-4009
Bloomfield **(G-524)**

2796 Platemaking & Related Svcs

Acme Engraving Co Inc ....E 973 778-0885
Passaic **(G-8050)**

Advertisers Service Group Inc ....F 201 440-5577
Ridgefield Park **(G-9298)**

AGFA Corporation ....G 908 231-5000
Somerville **(G-10102)**

Celebration (us) Inc ....C 609 261-5200
Lumberton **(G-5626)**

Container Graphics Corp ....E 732 922-1180
Neptune **(G-6870)**

Downtown Printing Center Inc ....F 732 246-7990
New Brunswick **(G-6920)**

E I Du Pont De Nemours & Co ....E 732 257-1579
Parlin **(G-7863)**

Essex West Graphics Inc ....D 973 227-2400
Fairfield **(G-3192)**

Garrison Printing Company Inc ....E 856 488-1900
Pennsauken **(G-8424)**

Globe Photo Engraving Co LLC ....E 201 489-2300
Little Ferry **(G-5487)**

Globe Photo Engraving Corp ....F 201 489-2300
Little Ferry **(G-5488)**

Grandview Printing Co Inc ....F 973 890-0006
Totowa **(G-10831)**

Hatteras Press Inc ....B 732 935-9800
Tinton Falls **(G-10718)**

▲ Howard Press Inc ....D 908 245-4400
Roselle **(G-9561)**

▲ Lacoa Inc ....G 973 754-1000
Elmwood Park **(G-2837)**

▲ Mariano Press LLC ....F 732 247-3659
Somerset **(G-10022)**

Mark/Trece Inc ....E 973 884-1005
Whippany **(G-11897)**

Marko Engraving & Art Corp ....F 201 864-6500
Weehawken **(G-11569)**

Marko Engraving & Art Corp ....F 201 945-6555
Fairview **(G-3363)**

Mosstype Holding Corp ....E 201 444-8000
Waldwick **(G-11307)**

Nassau Communications Inc ....F 609 208-9099
Lawrence Township **(G-5218)**

Pan Graphics Inc ....D 973 478-2100
Garfield **(G-3753)**

R P R Graphics Inc ....E 908 654-8080
Peapack **(G-8345)**

SGS International Inc ....G 718 836-1000
Kenilworth **(G-4978)**

Staines Inc ....F 856 784-2718
Somerdale **(G-9935)**

Standard Embossing Plate Mfg ....G 973 344-6670
Newark **(G-7284)**

Tangent Graphics Inc ....G 201 488-2840
Englewood **(G-2946)**

Toppan Printing Co Amer Inc ....C 732 469-8400
Somerset **(G-10088)**

Unity Graphics & Engraving Co ....E 201 541-5462
Englewood **(G-2950)**

28 CHEMICALS AND ALLIED PRODUCTS

2812 Alkalies & Chlorine

Church & Dwight Co Inc ....F 732 730-3100
Lakewood **(G-5070)**

Church & Dwight Co Inc ....F 609 655-6101
Cranbury **(G-1822)**

Church & Dwight Co Inc ....G 609 683-8021
Princeton **(G-8923)**

Church & Dwight Co Inc ....B 609 806-1200
Ewing **(G-3021)**

FMC Corporation ....D 973 256-0768
Woodland Park **(G-12079)**

FMC Corporation ....D 732 541-3000
Carteret **(G-1253)**

◆ Formosa Plastics Corp USA ....B 973 992-2090
Livingston **(G-5511)**

◆ Kuehne Chemical Company Inc ......E 973 589-0700
Kearny **(G-4876)**

◆ PMC Group Inc ....F 856 533-1866
Mount Laurel **(G-6791)**

▲ Qualco Inc ....D 973 473-1222
Passaic **(G-8099)**

◆ Solvay Holding Inc ....A 609 860-4000
Princeton **(G-9024)**

Solvay USA Inc ....C 732 297-0100
North Brunswick **(G-7486)**

2813 Industrial Gases

Aeropres Corporation ....G 908 292-1240
Hillsborough **(G-4301)**

Air Liquide Advanced Materials ....F 908 231-9060
Branchburg **(G-612)**

Air Products and Chemicals Inc ....E 732 446-5676
Manalapan **(G-5800)**

Airgas Usa LLC ....F 609 685-4241
Cherry Hill **(G-1337)**

Airgas Usa LLC ....E 856 829-7878
Cinnaminson **(G-1440)**

American Spraytech LLC ....E 908 725-6060
Branchburg **(G-617)**

▲ Boc Group Inc ....A 908 665-2400
New Providence **(G-6995)**

Coim USA Inc ....E 856 224-1668
Paulsboro **(G-8331)**

◆ Concorde Specialty Gases Inc ....E 732 544-9899
Eatontown **(G-2386)**

Linde Gas North America LLC ....E 908 329-9300
Stewartsville **(G-10484)**

Linde Gas North America LLC ....G 908 777-9125
Phillipsburg **(G-8559)**

Linde Gas North America LLC ....F 732 438-9977
Dayton **(G-1977)**

◆ Linde Gas North America LLC ....A 908 508-3000
Bridgewater **(G-844)**

◆ Linde Gas USA LLC ....D 908 464-8100
Bridgewater **(G-845)**

▲ Linde Global Helium Inc ....E 908 464-8100
New Providence **(G-7006)**

Linde North America Inc ....D 908 454-7455
Alpha **(G-39)**

Linde North America Inc ....F 908 329-9700
Stewartsville **(G-10485)**

Linde North America Inc ....E 908 464-8100
New Providence **(G-7007)**

Matheson Gas Products Inc ....F 201 867-4101
Parsippany **(G-7975)**

◆ Matheson Tri-Gas Inc ....D 908 991-9200
Basking Ridge **(G-189)**

Matheson Tri-Gas Inc ....E 908 991-9200
Basking Ridge **(G-190)**

◆ Messer LLC ....C 908 464-8100
Bridgewater **(G-849)**

Messer LLC ....E 908 329-9619
Stewartsville **(G-10486)**

Messer LLC ....B 512 330-0153
Bridgewater **(G-850)**

Messer LLC ....E 908 464-8100
New Providence **(G-7010)**

Messer LLC ....G 973 579-2065
Sparta **(G-10398)**

Messer Merchant Production LLC ....F 908 464-8100
New Providence **(G-7011)**

◆ Messer North America Inc ....B 908 464-8100
Bridgewater **(G-851)**

Praxair Inc ....F 732 738-4150
Keasbey **(G-4914)**

▲ Praxair Cryomag Services Inc ....F 732 738-4000
Keasbey **(G-4915)**

Praxair Distribution Inc ....F 908 862-7200
Linden **(G-5411)**

Praxair Distribution Inc ....F 973 589-7895
Newark **(G-7232)**

S O S Gases Inc ....E 201 998-7800
Kearny **(G-4897)**

2816 Inorganic Pigments

◆ BASF Catalysts LLC ....D 732 205-5000
Iselin **(G-4599)**

◆ Breen Color Concentrates LLC ....F 609 397-8200
Lambertville **(G-5187)**

◆ Brenntag Specialties Inc ....D 908 561-6100
South Plainfield **(G-10228)**

◆ Color Techniques Inc ....F 908 412-9292
South Plainfield **(G-10239)**

Custom Chemicals Corp ....A 201 791-5100
Elmwood Park **(G-2820)**

Dispersion Technology Inc ....F 732 364-4488
Lakewood **(G-5084)**

Elementis Specialties Inc ....F 201 432-0800
East Windsor **(G-2370)**

◆ Elementis Specialties Inc ....C 609 443-2000
East Windsor **(G-2369)**

◆ Evonik Corporation ....B 973 929-8000
Parsippany **(G-7938)**

Ferro Corporation ....E 732 287-4925
Edison **(G-2511)**

◆ French Color Fragrance Co Inc.........E 201 567-6883
Englewood *(G-2907)*
Kronos Worldwide Inc ....E 609 860-6200
Cranbury *(G-1852)*
◆ Kvk Usa Inc ....F 732 846-2355
New Brunswick *(G-6942)*
▲ Lightscape Materials Inc ....G 609 734-2224
Princeton *(G-8969)*
▼ Riverdale Color Mfg Inc.....................E 732 376-9300
Perth Amboy *(G-8531)*
◆ Rockwood Holdings Inc......................E 609 514-0300
Princeton *(G-9017)*
Ruichem Usa Inc ....G 978 992-1811
Fort Lee *(G-3584)*
Sensient Technologies Corp..................E 908 757-4500
South Plainfield *(G-10327)*
◆ Sudarshan North America Inc ....G 201 652-2046
Ridgewood *(G-9331)*
Vivitone Inc...F 973 427-8114
Hawthorne *(G-4250)*

2819 Indl Inorganic Chemicals, NEC

◆ A&C Catalysts Inc...............................E 908 474-9393
Linden *(G-5315)*
Affinity Chemical Woodbine LLC ....F 973 873-4070
Flanders *(G-3398)*
AIG Industrial Group Inc ....F 201 767-7300
Northvale *(G-7516)*
Airgas Usa LLC ....F 609 685-4241
Cherry Hill *(G-1337)*
Airgas Usa LLC ....E 856 829-7878
Cinnaminson *(G-1440)*
Alkaline Corporation................................E 732 531-7830
Oakhurst *(G-7607)*
Allied Specialty Group Inc ....F 201 223-4600
North Bergen *(G-7382)*
American Gas & Chemical Co Ltd.........E 201 767-7300
Northvale *(G-7518)*
Atlantic Associates Intl Inc ....F 856 662-1717
Pennsauken *(G-8392)*
Avantor Performance Mtls LLC ....G 610 573-2759
Bridgewater *(G-797)*
Avantor Performance Mtls LLC ....B 908 859-2151
Phillipsburg *(G-8542)*
◆ BASF Catalysts LLC...........................D 732 205-5000
Iselin *(G-4599)*
BASF Catalysts LLC ....C 732 205-5000
Carteret *(G-1249)*
BASF Corporation...................................F 732 205-5000
Iselin *(G-4601)*
◆ BASF Corporation ....B 973 245-6000
Florham Park *(G-3491)*
◆ Basfin Corporation..............................A 973 245-6000
Florham Park *(G-3493)*
Baumar Industries Inc ....G 973 667-5490
Nutley *(G-7580)*
Bd Biscnces Systems Rgents Inc ....G 201 847-6800
Franklin Lakes *(G-3614)*
Biochemical Sciences Inc.......................G 856 467-1813
Swedesboro *(G-10572)*
Carbon Fiber Element LLC.....................G 973 809-9432
Metuchen *(G-6050)*
▲ Chem-Is-Try Inc ....G 732 372-7311
Metuchen *(G-6052)*
◆ Chemtrade Chemicals Corp ....D 973 515-0900
Parsippany *(G-7901)*
◆ Chemtrade Chemicals US LLC..........D 973 515-0900
Parsippany *(G-7902)*
Chemtrade Gcc Holding Company........G 973 515-0900
Parsippany *(G-7903)*
Chemtrade Solutions LLC......................F 908 464-1500
Berkeley Heights *(G-394)*
▲ Chemtrade Solutions LLC..................G 973 515-0900
Parsippany *(G-7904)*
Chemtrade Water Chemical Inc.............G 973 515-0900
Parsippany *(G-7905)*
Chessco Industries Inc..........................E 609 882-0400
Ewing *(G-3020)*
Church & Dwight Co Inc........................B 609 806-1200
Ewing *(G-3021)*
Citi-Chem Inc...E 609 231-6655
Maple Shade *(G-5860)*
CMS Technology Inc...............................F 512 913-1898
Bridgewater *(G-812)*
Coim USA Inc ....E 856 224-1668
Paulsboro *(G-8331)*
◆ Dallas Group of America Inc ....E 908 534-7800
Whitehouse *(G-11915)*
E I Du Pont De Nemours & Co...............E 732 257-1579
Parlin *(G-7863)*

East Coast Salt Dist Inc.........................G 732 833-2973
Jackson *(G-4654)*
Elemental Interiors..................................G 646 861-3596
Montclair *(G-6365)*
Elementis Chromium Inc........................C 609 443-2000
East Windsor *(G-2367)*
▲ Elements Global Group LLC.............G 908 468-8407
Gillette *(G-3801)*
◆ Elkem Silicones USA Corp ....E 732 227-2060
East Brunswick *(G-2141)*
Engelhard Corporation...........................F 732 205-5000
Iselin *(G-4608)*
◆ Evonik Corporation.............................B 973 929-8000
Parsippany *(G-7938)*
Evoqua Water Technologies LLC ....F 908 353-7400
Elizabeth *(G-2733)*
Foster and Company Inc........................E 973 267-4100
Cedar Knolls *(G-1305)*
▲ Futurrex Inc ....F 973 209-1563
Franklin *(G-3603)*
▲ G J Chemical Co ....E 973 589-1450
Somerset *(G-9996)*
◆ General Carbon Corporation..............F 973 523-2223
Paterson *(G-8197)*
◆ Gentek Inc...C 973 515-0900
Parsippany *(G-7956)*
Gingko Tree Inc.......................................G 973 652-9380
Linden *(G-5353)*
◆ Gulco Inc...E 908 238-2030
Phillipsburg *(G-8554)*
Holtec International ....B 856 797-0900
Camden *(G-1069)*
Honeywell International Inc ....C 973 455-2000
Morris Plains *(G-6614)*
◆ Hummel Croton Inc ....F 908 754-1800
South Plainfield *(G-10274)*
Hydrocrbon Tech Innovation LLC ....E 609 394-3102
Lawrenceville *(G-5232)*
Innophos Inc...G 973 587-8735
Cranbury *(G-1840)*
◆ Innophos LLC ....G 609 495-2495
Cranbury *(G-1841)*
Innophos Holdings Inc............................D 609 495-2495
Cranbury *(G-1842)*
◆ Innophos Inc...A 609 495-2495
Cranbury *(G-1843)*
Innophos Investments II Inc...................G 609 495-2495
Cranbury *(G-1844)*
Innophos Invstmnts Hldings Inc ....G 609 495-2495
Cranbury *(G-1845)*
Intelligent Mtl Solutions Inc ....F 609 514-4031
Princeton *(G-8963)*
◆ JM Huber Corporation ....D 732 603-3630
Edison *(G-2540)*
◆ Kuehne Chemical Company Inc.......E 973 589-0700
Kearny *(G-4876)*
Ligno Tech USA Inc ....G 908 429-6660
Bridgewater *(G-843)*
Liquid Elements ....G 856 321-7646
Maple Shade *(G-5865)*
◆ Lonza Inc...D 201 316-9200
Morristown *(G-6681)*
Luxfer Magtech Inc ....E 803 610-9898
Manchester *(G-5846)*
Madison Industries Inc............................E 732 727-2225
Old Bridge *(G-7719)*
Mateson Chemical Corporation..............G 215 423-3200
Cinnaminson *(G-1472)*
▲ Mel Chemicals Inc...............................C 908 782-5800
Flemington *(G-3455)*
▲ Meson Group Inc.................................E 201 767-7300
Northvale *(G-7536)*
▲ Morre-TEC Industries Inc ....E 908 688-9009
Union *(G-11076)*
Multalloy LLC ....G 732 961-1520
Howell *(G-4547)*
New Heaven Chemicals Iowa LLC........G 201 506-9109
Sussex *(G-10564)*
Newfuturevest Two LLC ....G 609 586-8004
Trenton *(G-10965)*
▲ Northeast Chemicals Inc ....E 508 634-6900
East Brunswick *(G-2160)*
Northeast Chemicals Inc.........................E 732 227-0100
East Brunswick *(G-2161)*
Northeast Chemicals Inc.........................F 732 673-6966
East Brunswick *(G-2162)*
Nouryon Surface Chemistry ....D 312 544-7000
New Brunswick *(G-6955)*
Nouryon Surface Chemistry ....D 732 985-6262
Edison *(G-2579)*

Nova Chemicals Inc................................G 973 726-0056
Sparta *(G-10404)*
◆ Old Bridge Chemicals Inc ....E 732 727-2225
Old Bridge *(G-7722)*
▼ Omg Electronic Chemicals Inc ....C 908 222-5800
South Plainfield *(G-10311)*
P W Perkins Co Inc.................................G 856 769-3525
Woodstown *(G-12095)*
Perimeter Solutions LP ....C 732 541-3000
Carteret *(G-1264)*
▲ Phibro-Tech Inc ....E 201 329-7300
Teaneck *(G-10645)*
▲ Phibrochem Inc ....G 201 329-7300
Teaneck *(G-10646)*
▲ Polymer Products Company Inc.......E 856 533-1866
Mount Laurel *(G-6792)*
PQ Corporation ....E 732 750-9040
Avenel *(G-141)*
▲ Protameen Chemicals Inc ....E 973 256-4374
Totowa *(G-10847)*
▲ R & M Chemical Technologies..........F 908 537-9516
Hampton *(G-4159)*
◆ Reade Manufacturing Company........E 732 657-6451
Manchester *(G-5848)*
Reagent Chemical & RES Inc.................E 908 284-2800
Ringoes *(G-9341)*
◆ Resintech Inc ....C 856 768-9600
West Berlin *(G-11619)*
Riogen Inc...G 609 529-0503
Monmouth Junction *(G-6309)*
Rlct Industries LLC ....G 609 712-1318
Pennington *(G-8372)*
◆ Rockwood Holdings Inc......................E 609 514-0300
Princeton *(G-9017)*
Sanit Technologies LLC ....F 862 238-7555
Passaic *(G-8105)*
◆ Scientific Design Company ....C 201 641-0500
Little Ferry *(G-5496)*
Setcon Industries Inc...............................F 973 283-0500
Riverdale *(G-9384)*
◆ Solvay Holding Inc ....A 609 860-4000
Princeton *(G-9024)*
Solvay Spclty Polymers USA LLC.........C 856 853-8119
West Deptford *(G-11716)*
Solvay USA Inc...C 732 297-0100
North Brunswick *(G-7486)*
Solvay USA Inc...D 609 860-4000
Cranbury *(G-1883)*
◆ Somerville Acquisitions Co Inc.........C 908 782-9500
Flemington *(G-3469)*
Spectrum Laboratory Pdts Inc................E 732 214-1300
New Brunswick *(G-6972)*
Spex Certprep Group LLC.....................G 732 549-7144
Metuchen *(G-6071)*
▲ Synasia Inc ....G 732 205-9880
Metuchen *(G-6075)*
Totalcat Group Inc ....G 908 497-9610
Cranford *(G-1929)*
United Silicon Carbide Inc ....G 732 565-9500
New Brunswick *(G-6976)*
UOP LLC ....G 973 455-2096
Morris Plains *(G-6627)*
W R Grace & Co-Conn ....C 732 777-4877
Edison *(G-2644)*
▲ Water Mark Technologies Inc...........G 973 663-3438
Lake Hopatcong *(G-5038)*
▲ West Dry Industries Inc ....G 908 757-4400
Westfield *(G-11808)*
Wisesorbent Technology LLC ....E 856 872-7713
Marlton *(G-5957)*
▲ Youniversal Labortories ....G 201 807-9000
South Hackensack *(G-10191)*

2821 Plastics, Mtrls & Nonvulcanizable Elastomers

Adco Chemical Company Inc ....E 973 589-0880
Newark *(G-7035)*
Advansix Inc...B 973 526-1800
Parsippany *(G-7875)*
All American Extrusion Inc ....G 973 881-9030
Paterson *(G-8132)*
Allied-Signal China Ltd...........................E 973 455-2000
Morristown *(G-6632)*
Alliedsignal Foreign Sls Corp.................G 973 455-2000
Morristown *(G-6633)*
Alpine Group Inc......................................B 201 549-4400
East Rutherford *(G-2269)*
Altaflo LLC..F 973 300-3344
Sparta *(G-10378)*

S I C

◆ Alzo International Inc ....E ... 732 254-1901
  Sayreville (G-9702)
	Innovative Resin Systems Inc ....F ... 973 633-5342
	  Wayne (G-11521)
		Thibaut & Walker Co Inc ....G ... 973 589-3331
		  Newark (G-7296)

Amcor Flexibles LLC ....C ... 856 825-1400
  Millville (G-6224)
	Intelco ....D ... 856 456-6755
	  Westville (G-11817)
		▲ Trademark Plastics Corporation ....E ... 908 925-5900
		  Newark (G-7302)

American Plastic Works Inc ....E ... 800 494-7326
  Moorestown (G-6504)
	◆ Interntonal Specialty Pdts Inc ......A ... 859 815-3333
	  Wayne (G-11522)
		United Resin Inc ....F ... 856 358-2574
		  Elmer (G-2805)

Anhydrides & Chemicals Inc ....G ... 973 465-0077
  Newark (G-7048)
	▲ Interplast Inc ....F ... 609 386-4990
	  Burlington (G-975)
		Uvitec Printing Ink Co Inc ....E ... 973 778-0737
		  Lodi (G-5581)

▼ Anti Hydro International Inc ....F ... 908 284-9000
  Flemington (G-3430)
	J-M Manufacturing Company Inc ......D ... 800 621-4404
	  Livingston (G-5517)
		Weavers Fiberglass ....G ... 609 597-4324
		  Manahawkin (G-5797)

▲ ARC International N Amer LLC .....C ... 856 825-5620
  Millville (G-6233)
	Kairos Enterprises LLC ....G ... 201 731-3181
	  Englewood Cliffs (G-2979)
		▲ Wexford International Inc ....G ... 908 781-7200
		  Gladstone (G-3805)

Ashland LLC ....G ... 908 243-3500
  Bridgewater (G-794)
	Lanxess Solutions US Inc ....C ... 732 826-1018
	  Perth Amboy (G-8524)
		Wilsonart LLC ....F ... 800 822-7613
		  Moorestown (G-6578)

Ashland LLC ....D ... 732 353-7718
  Parlin (G-7861)
	Louis A Nelson Inc ....F ... 973 743-7404
	  Bloomfield (G-506)
		Zahk Sales Inc ....G ... 516 633-9179
		  Branchburg (G-697)

Atlantic Lining Co Inc ....E ... 609 723-2400
  Jobstown (G-4836)
	Med Connection LLC ....G ... 908 213-7012
	  Phillipsburg (G-8563)	

▲ Barrett Bronze Inc ....E ... 914 699-6060
  Wyckoff (G-12103)
	Multi-Plastics Extrusions Inc ....F ... 732 388-2300
	  Avenel (G-138)
		2822 Synthetic Rubber (Vulcanizable Elastomers)

Bergen Manufacturing & Supply .....E ... 201 854-3461
  North Bergen (G-7389)
	▲ Nan Ya Plastics Corp USA ....F ... 973 992-1775
	  Livingston (G-5530)
		◆ Ansell Healthcare Products LLC ....C ... 732 345-5400
		  Iselin (G-4593)

▼ Berry Global Films LLC ....C ... 201 641-6600
  Montvale (G-6400)
	North American Composites Co ....F ... 609 625-8101
	  Mays Landing (G-5996)
		Bezwada Biomedical LLC ....G ... 908 281-7529
		  Hillsborough (G-4305)

◆ Breen Color Concentrates LLC .....F ... 609 397-8200
  Lambertville (G-5187)
	Nouryon Surface Chemistry ....D ... 732 985-6262
	  Edison (G-2579)
		◆ Dicar Inc ....E ... 973 575-1377
		  Pine Brook (G-8596)

◆ Cain Machine Inc ....F ... 856 825-7225
  Millville (G-6240)
	Palma Inc ....F ... 973 429-1490
	  Whippany (G-11901)
		Dicar Inc ....D ... 973 575-4220
		  Pine Brook (G-8597)

◆ Cary Compounds LLC ....E ... 732 274-2626
  Dayton (G-1957)
	Petro Packaging Co Inc ....E ... 908 272-4054
	  Cranford (G-1922)
		Gel United Ltd Liability Co ....G ... 855 435-8683
		  Saddle Brook (G-9653)

Chevron Phillips Chem Co LP ....E ... 732 738-2000
  Perth Amboy (G-8514)
	Phoenix Industries LLC ....G ... 973 366-4199
	  Wharton (G-11867)
		Harmony Elastomers LLC ....E ... 973 340-4000
		  Paterson (G-8208)

Clausen Company Inc ....F ... 732 738-1165
  Fords (G-3531)
	Phoenix Manufactoring Inc ....G ... 732 380-1666
	  Ocean (G-7675)
		Kini Products Inc ....G ... 732 299-5555
		  New Egypt (G-6984)

▲ Coda Resources Ltd ....C ... 718 649-1666
  Matawan (G-5971)
	Phoenix Resins Inc ....F ... 888 627-3769
	  Cinnaminson (G-1482)
		Lyondell Chemical Company ....G ... 973 578-2200
		  Newark (G-7192)

◆ Coim USA Inc ....D ... 856 224-8560
  West Deptford (G-11700)
	Plaskolite New Jersey LLC ....C ... 908 486-1000
	  Linden (G-5410)
		Newark Auto Top Co Inc ....F ... 973 677-9935
		  East Orange (G-2256)

◆ Colorite Polymers ....F ... 800 631-1577
  Ridgefield (G-9255)
	◆ Plastic Specialties & Tech Inc ......C ... 201 941-2900
	  Ridgefield (G-9284)
		Paul Englehardt ....G ... 908 637-4556
		  Great Meadows (G-3857)

Composecure LLC ....C ... 908 518-0500
  Somerset (G-9975)
	Plastics For Chemicals Inc ....G ... 609 242-9100
	  Forked River (G-3543)
		Pierce-Roberts Rubber Company .....F ... 609 394-5245
		  Ewing (G-3052)

▲ Composecure LLC ....C ... 908 518-0500
  Somerset (G-9976)
	Polyfil Corporation ....G ... 973 627-4070
	  Rockaway (G-9488)
		▲ Stiles Enterprises Inc ....F ... 973 625-9660
		  Rockaway (G-9501)

Covalnce Spclalty Coatings LLC .....D ... 732 356-2870
  Middlesex (G-6109)
	◆ Polymer Dynamix LLC ....G ... 732 381-1600
	  South Plainfield (G-10312)	

Crossfield Products Corp ....D ... 908 245-2801
  Roselle Park (G-9580)
	▲ Polymer Technologies Inc ....D ... 973 778-9100
	  Clifton (G-1695)
		2823 Cellulosic Man-Made Fibers

Custom Counters By Precision ....E ... 973 773-0111
  Passaic (G-8058)
	▲ Polymeric Resources Corp ....E ... 973 694-4141
	  Wayne (G-11543)
		Endot Industries Inc ....D ... 973 625-8500
		  Rockaway (G-9456)

Custom Molders Group LLC ....G ... 908 218-7997
  Branchburg (G-635)
	◆ Polyvel Inc ....E ... 609 567-0080
	  Hammonton (G-4142)
		Newark Fibers Inc ....G ... 201 768-6800
		  Rockleigh (G-9520)

◆ Cvc Specialty Chemicals Inc ....F ... 856 533-3000
  Moorestown (G-6517)
	▲ Pure Tech International Inc ....G ... 908 722-4800
	  Branchburg (G-674)	

▲ Deltech Resins Co ....E ... 973 589-0880
  Newark (G-7102)
	Recycle Inc East ....G ... 908 756-2200
	  South Plainfield (G-10325)
		2824 Synthetic Organic Fibers, Exc Cellulosic

Dicalite Minerals Corp ....G ... 856 320-2919
  Pennsauken (G-8413)
	◆ Rimtec Manufacturing Corp ....D ... 609 387-0011
	  Burlington (G-983)
		Allied-Signal China Ltd ....E ... 973 455-2000
		  Morristown (G-6632)

▲ Dock Resins Corporation ....E ... 908 862-2351
  Pedricktown (G-8348)
	◆ Rohm America LLC ....D ... 973 929-8000
	  Parsippany (G-8010)
		Alliedsignal Foreign Sls Corp ....G ... 973 455-2000
		  Morristown (G-6633)

Dow Chemical Company ....D ... 800 258-2436
  Somerset (G-9982)
	Rust-Oleum Corporation ....E ... 732 469-8100
	  Somerset (G-10069)
		Jaclyn Holdings Parent LLC ....G ... 201 909-6000
		  Maywood (G-6007)

E-Beam Services Inc ....E ... 513 933-0031
  Cranbury (G-1831)
	▲ Safas Corporation ....E ... 973 772-5252
	  Clifton (G-1709)
		◆ Nan Ya Plastics Corp America ......F ... 973 992-1775
		  Livingston (G-5529)

Eagle Fabrication Inc ....E ... 732 739-5300
  Ltl Egg Hbr (G-5616)
	Sika Corporation ....E ... 856 298-2313
	  Audubon (G-114)
		Natures Choice Corporation ....F ... 973 969-3299
		  Sparta (G-10401)

Emerald Performance Mtls LLC ......F ... 856 533-3000
  Maple Shade (G-5862)
	Sika Corporation ....C ... 201 933-8800
	  Lyndhurst (G-5679)
		▲ Northeast Pro-Tech Inc ....G ... 973 777-5654
		  Passaic (G-8092)

▲ Extrusion Technik USA Inc ....F ... 732 354-0177
  Somerset (G-9991)
	◆ Sika Corporation ....B ... 201 933-8800
	  Lyndhurst (G-5678)
		Solutia Inc ....G ... 908 862-0278
		  Linden (G-5426)

▲ Federal Plastics Corporation ....E ... 908 272-5800
  Cranford (G-1910)
	Solidsurface Designs Inc ....E ... 856 910-7720
	  Pennsauken (G-8487)	

Flex Moulding Inc ....G ... 201 487-8080
  Hackensack (G-3915)
	◆ Solvay USA Inc ....B ... 609 860-4000
	  Princeton (G-9025)
		2833 Medicinal Chemicals & Botanical Prdts

Foam Rubber Fabricators Inc ....E ... 973 751-1445
  Belleville (G-296)
	Solvay USA Inc ....C ... 732 297-0100
	  North Brunswick (G-7486)
		7th Seventh Day Wellness Ctr ....G ... 856 308-0991
		  Sicklerville (G-9906)

◆ Formosa Plastics Corp USA ....B ... 973 992-2090
  Livingston (G-5511)
	Spartech LLC ....E ... 201 489-4000
	  Hackensack (G-3977)
		◆ Abrazil LLC ....G ... 732 658-5191
		  Kendall Park (G-4917)

Glopak Corp ....E ... 908 753-8735
  South Plainfield (G-10267)
	Spartech LLC ....G ... 973 344-2700
	  Newark (G-7280)
		American Ingredients Inc ....F ... 714 630-6000
		  Kearny (G-4843)

▲ Hitachi Chem Dupont Microsyst ....E ... 732 613-2175
  Parlin (G-7864)
	Specialty Casting Inc ....G ... 856 845-3105
	  Woodbury (G-12038)
		Bodybio Inc ....E ... 856 825-8338
		  Millville (G-6238)

Illinois Tool Works Inc ....E ... 609 395-5600
  Cranbury (G-1839)
	Surface Source Intl Inc ....G ... 973 598-0152
	  Randolph (G-9202)
		Certified Processing Corp ....G ... 973 923-5200
		  Hillside (G-4386)

▲ Infinity Compounding LLC ....E ... 856 467-3030
  Logan Township (G-5588)
	▲ Synray Corporation ....G ... 908 245-2600
	  Kenilworth (G-4980)
		Chefler Foods LLC ....F ... 201 596-3710
		  Saddle Brook (G-9645)

Innovative Resin Systems Inc ....G ... 973 465-6887
  Newark (G-7157)
	◆ Technick Products Inc ....F ... 908 791-0400
	  South Plainfield (G-10330)
		▲ Chem-Is-Try Inc ....G ... 732 372-7311
		  Metuchen (G-6052)

◆ Innovative Resin Systems Inc ....E ... 973 465-6887
  Wayne (G-11520)
	Technology Reviews Inc ....G ... 973 537-9511
	  Randolph (G-9203)
		▲ Cyalume Specialty Products Inc .....E ... 732 469-7760
		  Bound Brook (G-601)

		D & A Granulation LLC ....G ... 732 994-7480 Lakewood (G-5080)
		Eleison Pharmaceuticals Inc ....G ... 215 416-7620 Bordentown (G-580)

Fisher Scientific Company LLC ....B 201 796-7100
Fair Lawn (G-3102)
Green Line Botanicals LLC ....G 609 759-0221
Hazlet (G-4260)
Greener Corners Ltd Lblty Co ....G 201 638-2218
Teaneck (G-10633)
▲ Guerbet LLC ....E 812 333-0059
Princeton (G-8956)
▲ Herbakraft Incorporated ....F 732 463-1000
Piscataway (G-8672)
Herbalist & Alchemist Inc ....F 908 689-9020
Washington (G-11447)
Herborium Group Inc ....G 201 849-4431
Fort Lee (G-3560)
Ivc Industries Inc ....B 732 308-3000
Freehold (G-3671)
Ivy-Dry Inc ....G 973 575-1992
Fairfield (G-3242)
▲ Janssen Pharmaceuticals Inc ....A 609 730-2000
Titusville (G-10735)
Janssen Pharmaceuticals Inc ....D 908 218-6908
Somerset (G-10007)
Janssen Pharmaceuticals Inc ....D 908 218-7701
Somerset (G-10008)
Janssen Pharmaceuticals Inc ....G 908 735-4844
Pittstown (G-8753)
◆ Jiaherb Inc ....E 973 439-6869
Pine Brook (G-8608)
Kingchem Life Science LLC ....F 201 825-9988
Allendale (G-10)
Life Science Labs Mfg LLC ....F 732 367-9937
Lakewood (G-5123)
Mallinckrodt LLC ....E 908 238-6600
Hampton (G-4158)
Matinas Biopharma Inc ....F 908 443-1860
Bedminster (G-272)
Messer LLC ....G 973 579-2065
Sparta (G-10398)
▲ Mpt Delivery Systems Inc ....D 973 279-4132
Paterson (G-8263)
Naturex Holdings Inc ....G 201 440-5000
South Hackensack (G-10172)
Naturex Inc ....G 201 440-5000
South Hackensack (G-10173)
◆ Naturex Inc ....C 201 440-5000
South Hackensack (G-10174)
▲ Navinta LLC ....F 609 883-1135
Ewing (G-3048)
Nouryon Surface Chemistry ....D 732 985-6262
Edison (G-2579)
Novel Ingrdent Inv Hldings Inc ....F 973 808-5900
East Hanover (G-2232)
Novel Ingredient Holdings Inc ....F 973 808-5900
East Hanover (G-2233)
▲ Pacifichealth Laboratories Inc ....G 732 739-2900
Parsippany (G-7982)
Pfizer Inc ....F 973 660-5000
Madison (G-5700)
Pfizer Inc ....C 212 733-2323
Bridgewater (G-864)
▲ Pharmacia & Upjohn Inc ....B 908 901-8000
Peapack (G-8343)
◆ Pharmacia & Upjohn Company LLC .B 908 901-8000
Peapack (G-8344)
Prime Coding Services LLC ....G 732 254-3036
East Brunswick (G-2168)
Purevolution ....F 973 919-4047
Kinnelon (G-5021)
Sanherb Biotech Inc ....F 347 946-5896
Belle Mead (G-287)
Savient Pharmaceuticals Inc ....F 732 418-9300
Bridgewater (G-887)
◆ Shanghai Freemen Americas LLC ...E 732 981-1288
Edison (G-2607)
▲ Sk Life Science Inc ....E 201 421-3800
Paramus (G-7833)
Sunflower Seed ....G 908 735-3822
Clinton (G-1750)
◆ Sytheon Ltd ....G 973 988-1075
Boonton (G-569)
▲ Toll Compaction Service Inc ....E 732 776-8225
Neptune (G-6902)
▲ Vita-Pure Inc ....G 908 245-1212
Roselle (G-9576)
Vitamin Shoppe Industries Inc ....A 201 868-5959
Secaucus (G-9826)
Yinlink International Inc ....G 973 818-4664
Cranbury (G-1894)
◆ Zoetis Products LLC ....C 973 660-5000
Florham Park (G-3528)

2834 Pharmaceuticals

140 Main Street Corp ....F 732 974-2929
Sea Girt (G-9744)
3r Biopharma LLC ....G 914 486-1898
North Brunswick (G-7447)
A and P Pharmacy ....G 908 850-7640
Hackettstown (G-3993)
AAA Pharmaceutical ....F 856 423-2700
Paulsboro (G-8327)
AAA Pharmaceutical ....D 609 288-6060
Lumberton (G-5621)
AB Science Usa LLC ....G 973 218-2437
Short Hills (G-9863)
Abbott Laboratories ....G 732 346-6649
Edison (G-2445)
Abbott Laboratories ....E 609 443-9300
Princeton (G-8897)
Abbott Laboratories ....F 856 988-5572
Marlton (G-5919)
◆ Abbott Laboratories Parsipanny ....G 973 428-4000
Whippany (G-11876)
ABG Lab LLC ....G 973 559-5663
Fair Lawn (G-3081)
Abon Pharmaceuticals LLC ....E 201 367-1702
Northvale (G-7514)
Abraxis Bioscience Inc ....D 908 673-9000
Summit (G-10520)
Abraxis Bioscience Inc ....G 908 673-9000
Summit (G-10521)
Accelrx Labs LLC ....G 609 301-6446
East Windsor (G-2333)
◆ Access Bio Inc ....F 732 873-4040
Somerset (G-9941)
Accumix Pharmaceuticals LLC ....G 609 632-2225
Old Bridge (G-7710)
Acetris Health LLC ....G 201 961-9000
Saddle Brook (G-9639)
Acetylon Pharmaceuticals Inc ....F 908 673-9000
Summit (G-10522)
▲ Acg North America LLC ....G 908 757-3425
Piscataway (G-8625)
Acino Products Ltd Lblty Co ....F 609 695-4300
Hamilton (G-4100)
Actavis Inc ....G 973 394-8925
Parsippany (G-7872)
▲ Actavis Elizabeth LLC ....B 908 527-9100
Elizabeth (G-2706)
Actavis Elizabeth LLC ....C 908 527-9100
Fort Lee (G-3544)
Actavis Elizabeth LLC ....C 973 442-3200
Madison (G-5685)
Actavis LLC ....C 800 272-5525
Morristown (G-6630)
Actavis LLC ....C 732 843-4904
North Brunswick (G-7450)
◆ Actavis LLC ....B 862 261-7000
Madison (G-5686)
Actavis LLC ....D 732 947-5300
Edison (G-2447)
▲ Actavis Pharma Inc ....D 862 261-7000
Parsippany (G-7873)
Activus Solutions LLC ....F 973 713-0696
Cranford (G-1897)
Adare Pharmaceuticals Inc ....B 862 261-7000
Parsippany (G-7874)
Adare Pharmaceuticals Inc ....E 877 731-5116
Lawrenceville (G-5223)
Adlers Pharmacy Ltc Inc ....E 856 685-7440
Cherry Hill (G-1332)
Advantice Health LLC ....F 973 946-7550
Cedar Knolls (G-1296)
Advaxis Inc ....G 609 452-9813
Princeton (G-8901)
Aerie Pharmaceuticals Inc ....D 908 470-4320
Bedminster (G-258)
Aeterna Zentaris Inc ....G 908 626-5428
Warren (G-11397)
▲ AF Pharma LLC ....G 908 769-7040
Hoboken (G-4443)
Aflag Pharmaceuticals LLC ....G 732 609-4139
Edison (G-2449)
Agile Therapeutics Inc ....F 609 683-1880
Princeton (G-8902)
Agilis Chemicals Inc ....F 973 910-2424
Short Hills (G-9864)
Agno Pharma ....G 609 223-0638
Allentown (G-23)
Ajj Powernutrition LLC ....G 908 452-5164
Hackettstown (G-3996)

Akorn Inc ....E 609 662-9100
Cranbury (G-1807)
Akorn Inc ....F 732 532-1000
Somerset (G-9945)
Akorn Inc ....G 732 448-7043
Somerset (G-9946)
Akorn Inc ....D 732 846-8066
Somerset (G-9947)
▼ Akrimax Pharmaceuticals LLC ....D 908 372-0506
Cranford (G-1898)
Aks Pharma Inc ....G 856 521-0710
Elmer (G-2793)
Alcami New Jersey Corporation ....D 732 346-5100
Edison (G-2451)
Alchem Pharmtech Inc ....B 848 565-5694
Monmouth Junction (G-6277)
Alembic Pharmaceuticals Inc ....G 908 393-9604
Bridgewater (G-783)
Alere Inc ....B 732 620-4244
Freehold (G-3645)
▲ Align Pharmaceuticals LLC ....G 908 834-0960
Berkeley Heights (G-387)
Allergan Inc ....D 908 306-0374
Bedminster (G-259)
Allergan Inc ....G 862 261-7000
Morristown (G-6631)
▲ Allergan Inc ....A 862 261-7000
Madison (G-5687)
Allergan Sales LLC ....F 973 442-3200
Madison (G-5688)
Allied Pharma Inc ....G 732 738-3295
Fords (G-3529)
Allos Therapeutics Inc ....G 609 936-3760
Princeton (G-8907)
Almatica Pharma Inc ....E 877 447-7979
Morristown (G-6634)
▲ Alpharma US Inc ....E 201 228-5090
Bridgewater (G-784)
Alpro Inc ....G 201 342-4498
South Hackensack (G-10149)
Alteon ....G 201 934-1624
Ramsey (G-9136)
Altima Innovations Inc ....G 732 474-1500
Branchburg (G-615)
Alvogen Group Inc ....E 973 796-3400
Morristown (G-6636)
Alvogen Inc ....C 973 796-3400
Morristown (G-6637)
Alvogen Pb Research & Dev LLC ....G 973 796-3400
Morristown (G-6638)
Alvogen Pharma Us Inc ....B 973 796-3400
Morristown (G-6639)
Amarin Corporation PLC ....E 908 719-1315
Bedminster (G-260)
Amarin Pharma Inc ....D 908 719-1315
Bridgewater (G-785)
Amas Pharmaceuticals LLC ....E 908 883-1129
Berkeley Heights (G-388)
American Pharmaceutical LLC ....G 732 645-3030
Piscataway (G-8630)
Amerigen Pharmaceuticals Inc ....F 732 993-9826
Lyndhurst (G-5640)
Amerigen Pharmaceuticals Ltd ....F 732 993-9826
East Brunswick (G-2127)
Amicus Therapeutics Inc ....C 609 662-2000
Cranbury (G-1809)
Amicus Therapeutics Us Inc ....G 609 662-2000
Cranbury (G-1810)
Amneal Pharmaceuticals Inc ....A 908 409-6822
Bridgewater (G-786)
Amneal Pharmaceuticals Inc ....F 908 947-3120
Bridgewater (G-787)
Amneal Pharmaceuticals LLC ....F 908 947-3120
Piscataway (G-8633)
Amneal Pharmaceuticals LLC ....G 908 409-6823
Branchburg (G-618)
▲ Amneal Pharmaceuticals LLC ....E 908 947-3120
Bridgewater (G-788)
Amneal Pharmaceuticals LLC ....E 908 231-1911
Branchburg (G-619)
Amneal Pharmaceuticals LLC ....F 908 947-3120
Piscataway (G-8632)
Amneal-Agila LLC ....F 908 947-3120
Bridgewater (G-789)
Ans Nutrition Inc ....E 212 235-5205
Farmingdale (G-3377)
Antares Pharma Inc ....C 609 359-3020
Ewing (G-3015)
Aphena Phrma Slutions - NJ LLC ....D 973 947-5441
Parsippany (G-7881)

S
I
C

Company		Phone
API Inc	F	973 227-9335
Fairfield (G-3144)		
Apicore LLC	E	646 884-3765
Piscataway (G-8634)		
Appco Pharma LLC	E	732 271-8300
Somerset (G-9955)		
Appco Pharma LLC	E	732 271-8300
Piscataway (G-8635)		
Appco Pharma LLC	E	732 271-8300
Somerset (G-9956)		
Aprecia Pharmaceuticals Co	E	215 359-3300
East Windsor (G-2335)		
Aptapharma Corporation	E	856 665-0025
Pennsauken (G-8390)		
Aquarius Biotechnologies Inc	G	908 443-1860
Bedminster (G-261)		
Aquestive Therapeutics Inc	F	908 941-1900
Warren (G-11398)		
▲ Arcadia Consmr Healthcare Inc	F	800 824-4894
Bridgewater (G-791)		
▲ Archon Vitamin LLC	D	732 537-1220
Edison (G-2459)		
Archon Vitamin LLC	G	973 371-1700
Edison (G-2460)		
Arno Therapeutics Inc	G	862 703-7170
Flemington (G-3431)		
▲ Ascend Laboratories LLC	E	201 476-1977
Parsippany (G-7884)		
Ascendia Pharmaceuticals LLC	E	732 640-0058
North Brunswick (G-7454)		
▲ Ash Ingredients Inc	G	201 689-1322
Glen Rock (G-3827)		
Asiamerica Group Inc	G	201 497-5993
Westwood (G-11827)		
▲ Aspire Pharmaceuticals Inc	D	732 447-1444
Somerset (G-9958)		
Astrazeneca Pharmaceuticals LP	F	973 975-0324
Morristown (G-6641)		
Aurex Labs Ltd Lblty Co	F	609 308-2304
East Windsor (G-2337)		
Auro Health LLC	G	732 839-9400
Lawrence Township (G-5214)		
Auro Packaging LLC	E	732 839-9408
East Windsor (G-2338)		
Aurobindo Pharma USA Inc	G	732 839-9402
Dayton (G-1952)		
Aurobindo Pharma USA Inc	G	732 839-9400
East Windsor (G-2339)		
Aurobindo Pharma USA Inc	G	732 839-9400
Dayton (G-1953)		
▲ Aurobindo Pharma USA Inc	E	732 839-9400
East Windsor (G-2340)		
Aurobindo Pharma USA Inc	G	609 409-6774
Cranbury (G-1813)		
Aurobindo Pharma USA LLC	E	732 839-9400
East Windsor (G-2341)		
Aurolife Pharma LLC	E	732 839-9746
Dayton (G-1954)		
Aurolife Pharma LLC	G	732 839-9408
East Windsor (G-2342)		
▲ Aurolife Pharma LLC	C	732 839-4377
Dayton (G-1955)		
Auromedics Pharma LLC	F	732 823-4122
East Windsor (G-2343)		
▲ Auromedics Pharma LLC	E	732 839-9400
East Windsor (G-2344)		
◆ Austarpharma LLC	D	732 225-2930
Edison (G-2464)		
Avacyn Pharmaceuticals Inc	G	201 836-2599
Teaneck (G-10623)		
▲ Aventis Inc	A	800 981-2491
Bridgewater (G-798)		
Aventis Phrmcticals Foundation	F	908 981-5000
Bridgewater (G-799)		
◆ BASF Corporation	B	973 245-6000
Florham Park (G-3491)		
◆ Basfin Corporation	A	973 245-6000
Florham Park (G-3493)		
◆ Bausch & Lomb Incorporated	B	585 338-6000
Bridgewater (G-800)		
▲ Bausch Health Americas Inc	B	908 927-1400
Bridgewater (G-802)		
Bausch Health Us LLC	E	908 927-1400
Bridgewater (G-803)		
Bausch Health Us LLC	G	908 927-1400
Bridgewater (G-804)		
Bayer Consumer Care Inc	B	973 267-6198
Morristown (G-6647)		
Bayer Healthcare LLC	F	973 254-5000
Morristown (G-6648)		

Company		Phone
◆ Bayer Healthcare LLC	A	862 404-3000
Whippany (G-11878)		
Bayer Healthcare LLC	B	973 254-5000
Morristown (G-6649)		
Bayer Hlthcare Phrmcticals Inc	A	862 404-3000
Whippany (G-11879)		
Bayer Hlthcare Phrmcticals Inc	E	973 709-3545
Wayne (G-11475)		
▲ Bayer Hlthcare Phrmcticals Inc	A	862 404-3000
Whippany (G-11880)		
Bayer U S LLC	E	973 709-3545
Wayne (G-11476)		
Bellerophon Therapeutics Inc	E	908 574-4770
Warren (G-11400)		
Beta Pharma Inc	F	609 436-4100
Princeton (G-8915)		
▲ Bioactive Resources LLC	F	908 561-3114
South Plainfield (G-10226)		
Bionpharma Inc	G	609 380-3313
Princeton (G-8916)		
Biophore LLC	G	609 275-3713
Plainsboro (G-8781)		
Biovail Distribution Company	G	908 927-1400
Bridgewater (G-805)		
Boehringer Ingelheim Animal	E	732 729-5700
North Brunswick (G-7457)		
Boyds Pharmacy Inc	F	609 499-0100
Florence (G-3473)		
Bracco Research USA Inc	E	609 514-2517
Cranbury (G-1815)		
Bristol-Myers Squibb Company	G	609 419-5000
Princeton (G-8918)		
Bristol-Myers Squibb Company	E	212 546-4000
Pennington (G-8359)		
Bristol-Myers Squibb Company	E	908 218-3700
Bridgewater (G-807)		
Bristol-Myers Squibb Company	A	609 302-3000
Lawrenceville (G-5225)		
Bristol-Myers Squibb Company	G	609 252-4875
Princeton (G-8919)		
Bristol-Myers Squibb Company	E	212 546-4000
Hillside (G-4383)		
Bta Pharmaceuticals Inc	E	908 927-1400
Bridgewater (G-809)		
Caladrius Biosciences Inc	E	908 842-0100
Basking Ridge (G-177)		
Calyptus Pharmaceuticals Inc	F	908 720-6049
Princeton (G-8920)		
▲ Camber Pharmaceuticals Inc	E	732 529-0430
Piscataway (G-8641)		
Cambrex Corporation	C	201 804-3000
East Rutherford (G-2282)		
Cambridge Therapeutic Tech LLC	G	914 420-5555
Hackensack (G-3894)		
▲ Capsugel Inc	D	862 242-1700
Morristown (G-6651)		
Capsugel Holdings Us Inc	E	862 242-1700
Morristown (G-6652)		
Caraco Pharmaceutical Labs	G	609 819-8200
Cranbury (G-1820)		
Cardinal Health Systems Inc	B	732 537-6544
Somerset (G-9966)		
Carnegie Pharmaceuticals LLC	E	732 783-7013
Delran (G-2013)		
Castle Creek Phrmceuticals LLC	F	862 286-0400
Parsippany (G-7897)		
Catalent Inc	C	732 537-6200
Somerset (G-9968)		
Catalent Cts LLC	C	201 785-0275
Allendale (G-6)		
Catalent CTS Kansas City LLC	G	732 537-6200
Somerset (G-9969)		
▲ Catalent Pharma Solutions LLC	C	732 537-6200
Somerset (G-9970)		
◆ Catalent Pharma Solutions Inc	B	732 537-6200
Somerset (G-9971)		
Catalent US Holding I LLC	G	877 587-1835
Somerset (G-9972)		
Celator Pharmaceuticals Inc	E	609 243-0123
Ewing (G-3019)		
Celgene Cellular Therapeutics	G	908 673-9000
Warren (G-11402)		
Celgene Corporation	F	908 464-8101
Berkeley Heights (G-392)		
Celgene Corporation	G	732 271-1001
Warren (G-11403)		
Celgene Corporation	F	908 967-1432
Berkeley Heights (G-393)		
Celgene Corporation	G	908 897-4603
Summit (G-10528)		

Company		Phone
Celgene Corporation	C	908 673-9000
Summit (G-10529)		
Celgene Corporation	A	908 673-9000
Cedar Knolls (G-1301)		
Celgene Corporation	G	908 673-9000
Basking Ridge (G-179)		
Celimmune	G	908 399-2954
Lebanon (G-5255)		
Celldex Therapeutics Inc	C	908 200-7500
Hampton (G-4149)		
Cellectar Biosciences Inc	G	608 441-8120
Florham Park (G-3496)		
Cellular Sciences Inc	G	908 237-1561
Flemington (G-3433)		
Celsion Corporation	E	609 896-9100
Lawrenceville (G-5226)		
Central Admxture Phrm Svcs Inc	E	201 541-0080
Englewood (G-2892)		
Cerexa Inc	E	510 285-9200
Parsippany (G-7900)		
▲ Cetylite Industries Inc	E	856 665-6111
Pennsauken (G-8402)		
Champions Oncology Inc	D	201 808-8400
Hackensack (G-3897)		
Chandler Pharmacy LLC	G	732 543-1568
New Brunswick (G-6916)		
Chemtract LLC	G	732 820-0427
Martinsville (G-5961)		
Cherokee Pharma Llc	G	732 422-7800
Jamesburg (G-4671)		
Chromocell Corporation	D	732 565-1113
North Brunswick (G-7462)		
▲ Cipla USA Inc	E	908 356-8900
Warren (G-11406)		
▲ Cispharma Inc	F	609 235-9807
Cranbury (G-1823)		
Citius Pharmaceuticals Inc	G	978 938-0338
Cranford (G-1904)		
Cmic Cmo USA Corporation	E	609 395-9700
Cranbury (G-1825)		
Combocap Inc	G	646 722-2743
Whippany (G-11886)		
▲ Command Nutritionals LLC	E	973 227-8210
Fairfield (G-3172)		
Compupharma Inc	G	973 227-6003
Piscataway (G-8649)		
Conjupro Biotherapeutics Inc	F	609 356-0210
Princeton (G-8924)		
Contract Coatings Inc	F	201 343-3131
Hackensack (G-3901)		
Core Acquisition LLC	G	732 983-6025
Middlesex (G-6106)		
▲ Corepharma LLC	G	732 983-6025
Middlesex (G-6107)		
Cormedix Inc	G	908 517-9500
Berkeley Heights (G-396)		
Corrigan Center For Integrativ	G	973 239-0700
Cedar Grove (G-1273)		
Cosette Pharmaceuticals Inc	C	314 283-4776
South Plainfield (G-10243)		
County Line Phrmaceuticals LLC	G	262 439-8109
Pine Brook (G-8594)		
◆ Cubist Pharmaceuticals LLC	C	908 740-4000
Kenilworth (G-4933)		
▲ Cyalume Specialty Products Inc	E	732 469-7760
Bound Brook (G-601)		
Cyclacel Pharmaceuticals Inc	F	908 517-7330
Berkeley Heights (G-397)		
Cyclase Dynamics Inc	G	973 420-3259
Barnegat Light (G-165)		
Cypress Pharmaceuticals Inc	C	601 856-4393
Morristown (G-6657)		
D&E Nutraceuticals Inc	E	212 235-5200
Farmingdale (G-3383)		
Daiichi Sankyo Inc	G	908 992-6400
Basking Ridge (G-180)		
▲ Dainippon Sumitomo Pharma Amer	E	201 592-2050
Fort Lee (G-3554)		
▲ Derma Sciences Inc	C	609 514-4744
Plainsboro (G-8784)		
▲ Dermarite Industries LLC	C	973 247-3491
North Bergen (G-7400)		
Dermatological Soc of NJ Inc	G	856 546-5600
Barrington (G-171)		
Difco Laboratories Inc	G	410 316-4113
Franklin Lakes (G-3619)		
▲ Dishman Usa Inc	F	732 560-4300
Middlesex (G-6112)		
◆ Dmv-Fnterra Excipients USA LLC	G	609 858-2111
Paramus (G-7798)		

Dpi Newco LLC......E...... 973 257-8113
Parsippany (G-7919)
▲ Dse Healthcare Solutions LLC......G...... 732 417-1870
Edison (G-2494)
DSM Nutritional Products LLC......B...... 908 475-0150
Belvidere (G-361)
DSM Nutritional Products LLC......C...... 908 475-5300
Belvidere (G-362)
DSM Nutritional Products LLC......C...... 908 475-5300
Belvidere (G-363)
DSM Nutritional Products LLC......C...... 908 475-7093
Belvidere (G-360)
◆ DSM Nutritional Products LLC......B...... 800 526-0189
Parsippany (G-7922)
DSM Sight & Life Inc......G...... 973 257-8208
Parsippany (G-7923)
E R Squibb & Sons LLC......G...... 732 246-3195
East Brunswick (G-2137)
E R Squibb & Sons Inter-AM......F...... 609 252-5144
Princeton (G-8935)
E R Squibb & Sons Inter-AM......G...... 609 818-3715
Trenton (G-10932)
▲ E R Squibb & Sons Inter-AM......G...... 609 252-4111
Princeton (G-8936)
▲ Eagle Pharmaceuticals Inc......E...... 201 326-5300
Woodcliff Lake (G-12054)
Ebelle Debelle Phrm Inc......F...... 973 823-0665
Hamburg (G-4092)
Eco LLC......G...... 609 683-9030
Princeton (G-8937)
Edenbridge Pharmaceuticals LLC......G...... 201 292-1292
Parsippany (G-7932)
Edgemont Pharmaceuticals LLC......G...... 908 375-8039
Far Hills (G-3374)
▲ Eisai Inc......C...... 201 692-1100
Woodcliff Lake (G-12055)
Ekr Therapeutics Incorporated......C...... 877 435-2524
Bedminster (G-263)
Eli Lillybranchburg......G...... 908 541-8000
Branchburg (G-637)
Elite Laboratories Inc......E...... 201 750-2646
Northvale (G-7522)
Elite Pharmaceuticals Inc......E...... 201 750-2646
Northvale (G-7523)
Elusys Therapeutics Inc......F...... 973 808-0222
Parsippany (G-7935)
Elvi Pharma LLC......F...... 732 640-2707
Piscataway (G-8660)
Emisphere Technologies Inc......F...... 973 532-8000
Roseland (G-9537)
Enaltec Labs Inc......G...... 908 864-8000
Bridgewater (G-819)
Encore Pharmaceutical Inc......G...... 973 267-9331
Morris Plains (G-6605)
Endo Phrmaceuticals Valera Inc......F...... 609 235-3230
Cranbury (G-1832)
Enteris Biopharma Inc......G...... 973 453-3518
Boonton (G-551)
Envigo Crs Inc......C...... 732 873-2550
Somerset (G-9987)
▲ Enzon Pharmaceuticals Inc......G...... 732 980-4500
Cranford (G-1909)
Enzon Pharmaceuticals Inc......D...... 732 980-4500
South Plainfield (G-10251)
▲ Eon Labs Inc......A...... 609 627-8600
Princeton (G-8942)
Esjay Pharma LLC......G...... 609 469-5920
East Windsor (G-2350)
Esjay Pharma LLC......F...... 732 438-1816
Allentown (G-26)
Eva Maria Wolfe......G...... 412 777-2000
Wayne (G-11499)
▲ Evenus Pharmaceutical Labs Inc......G...... 609 395-8625
Princeton (G-8943)
Evotec (us) Inc......E...... 650 228-1400
Princeton (G-8945)
▲ Exeltis Usa Inc......D...... 973 324-0200
Florham Park (G-3503)
Exeltis USA Dermatology LLC......E...... 973 805-4060
Florham Park (G-3504)
Exemplify Biopharma Inc......G...... 732 500-3208
Cranbury (G-1833)
Eyetech Inc......F...... 646 454-1779
Bridgewater (G-823)
Eywa Pharma Inc......G...... 609 751-9600
Princeton (G-8947)
▲ Faubel Pharma Services......G...... 908 730-7563
Bordentown (G-581)
Faulding Holdings Inc......C...... 908 527-9100
Elizabeth (G-2734)
▲ Ferring Pharmaceuticals Inc......C...... 973 796-1600
Parsippany (G-7944)
▲ Ferring Production Inc......E...... 973 796-1600
Parsippany (G-7945)
First National Servicing & Dev......E...... 732 341-5409
Toms River (G-10758)
▲ Five Star Supplies NJ Corp......E...... 908 862-8801
Linden (G-5348)
Fordoz Pharma Corp......F...... 609 469-5949
East Windsor (G-2351)
Foresight Group LLC......F...... 888 992-8880
Parsippany (G-7949)
Forest Laboratories LLC......F...... 631 436-4534
Jersey City (G-4738)
Forest Laboratories LLC......E...... 631 501-5399
Jersey City (G-4739)
▲ Forest Pharmaceuticals Inc......A...... 862 261-7000
Parsippany (G-7950)
Fougera Pharmaceuticals Inc......E...... 973 514-4241
East Hanover (G-2210)
Fractal Solutions Corp......G...... 201 608-6828
Edgewater (G-2438)
▲ G & W Laboratories Inc......B...... 908 753-2000
South Plainfield (G-10263)
G & W Laboratories Inc......D...... 732 474-0729
Piscataway (G-8666)
G & W Laboratories Inc......D...... 908 753-2000
South Plainfield (G-10264)
G&W PA Laboratories LLC......G...... 908 753-2000
South Plainfield (G-10265)
Gadde Pharma LLC......G...... 609 651-7772
Plainsboro (G-8788)
GE Healthcare Inc......E...... 908 757-0500
South Plainfield (G-10266)
Genavite LLC......F...... 201 343-3131
Hackensack (G-3920)
Generon Biomed Inc......G...... 908 203-4701
Bridgewater (G-827)
Genzyme Corporation......C...... 201 313-9660
Ridgefield (G-9263)
Genzyme Corporation......G...... 973 256-2106
Totowa (G-10829)
◆ Glaxosmithkline Consumer......B...... 251 591-4188
Warren (G-11411)
◆ Glaxosmithkline Consumer Hlth......G...... 215 751-5046
Warren (G-11412)
Glaxosmithkline LLC......E...... 856 952-6023
Collingswood (G-1768)
Glaxosmithkline LLC......E...... 609 472-8175
Cherry Hill (G-1368)
▲ Glenmark Phrmceuticals Inc USA......D...... 201 684-8000
Mahwah (G-5742)
Glenmark Therapeutics Inc USA......B...... 201 684-8000
Mahwah (G-5743)
▲ Glenwood LLC......C...... 201 569-0050
Englewood (G-2910)
▲ Globe Pharma Inc......G...... 732 296-9700
New Brunswick (G-6929)
Globela Pharma LLC......G...... 888 588-8511
Weehawken (G-11567)
Grant Industries Inc......D...... 201 791-8700
Elmwood Park (G-2828)
◆ Grant Industries Inc......D...... 201 791-6700
Elmwood Park (G-2829)
Grant Industries Inc......F...... 201 791-6700
Elmwood Park (G-2830)
Granulation Technology Inc......F...... 973 276-0740
Fairfield (G-3217)
Green Labs LLC......G...... 862 220-4845
Newark (G-7139)
Grow Company Inc......E...... 201 941-8777
Ridgefield (G-9264)
◆ Gsk Consumer Health Inc......B...... 919 269-5000
Warren (G-11413)
Gsk Consumer Healthcare......D...... 973 539-0645
Parsippany (G-7957)
▲ Guardian Drug Company Inc......D...... 609 860-2600
Dayton (G-1968)
▲ Halo Pharmaceutical Inc......D...... 973 428-4000
Whippany (G-11894)
Health Science Funding LLC......F...... 973 984-6159
Morristown (G-6669)
Helsinn Therapeutics US Inc......E...... 908 231-1435
Iselin (G-4610)
Hengrui Therapeutics Inc......G...... 609 423-2155
Princeton (G-8959)
Hepion Pharmaceuticals Inc......E...... 732 902-4000
Edison (G-2529)
Heritage Pharma Holdings Inc......G...... 732 429-1000
East Brunswick (G-2148)
Heritage Pharma Labs Inc......F...... 732 238-7880
East Brunswick (G-2149)
▲ Heritage Pharma Labs Inc......C...... 732 238-7880
East Brunswick (G-2150)
▲ Heritage Pharmaceuticals Inc......E...... 732 429-1000
East Brunswick (G-2151)
Hikma Injectables USA Inc......G...... 732 542-1191
Eatontown (G-2398)
◆ Hikma Pharmaceuticals USA Inc......B...... 732 542-1191
Eatontown (G-2399)
Hikma Pharmaceuticals USA Inc......F...... 732 542-1191
Eatontown (G-2400)
Hikma Pharmaceuticals USA Inc......C...... 856 424-3700
Cherry Hill (G-1372)
▲ Hill Pharma Inc......F...... 973 521-7400
Fairfield (G-3228)
Hisamitsu Phrm Co Inc......F...... 973 765-0122
Florham Park (G-3510)
Hobart Group Holdings LLC......C...... 908 470-1780
Gladstone (G-3804)
◆ Hoffmann-La Roche Inc......A...... 973 890-2268
Little Falls (G-5456)
Hoffmann-La Roche Inc......F...... 973 235-8216
Totowa (G-10832)
Hoffmann-La Roche Inc......D...... 973 235-3092
Nutley (G-7587)
Hoffmann-La Roche Inc......E...... 973 235-1016
Nutley (G-7588)
Holmdel Acpnctr & Ntrl Med Ctr......G...... 732 888-4910
Holmdel (G-4502)
▲ Hovione LLC......D...... 609 918-2600
East Windsor (G-2352)
HRP Capital Inc......G...... 201 242-4938
Fort Lee (G-3562)
Huahai US Inc......F...... 609 655-1688
Somerset (G-10002)
Hutchison Medipharma (us) Inc......G...... 973 567-3254
Florham Park (G-3512)
I Fcb Holdings Inc......E...... 201 934-2000
Mahwah (G-5748)
IBC Pharmaceuticals Inc......F...... 973 540-9595
Morris Plains (G-6616)
Ikaria Therapeutics LLC......G...... 908 238-6600
Hampton (G-4155)
Imclone Systems LLC......G...... 908 541-8100
Branchburg (G-648)
◆ Imclone Systems LLC......C...... 908 541-8000
Bridgewater (G-833)
Imclone Systems LLC......D...... 908 218-0147
Branchburg (G-647)
Immtech Pharmaceuticals Inc......E...... 212 791-2911
Montclair (G-6370)
▲ Immunomedics Inc......C...... 973 605-8200
Morris Plains (G-6617)
Impax Laboratories LLC......F...... 732 595-4600
Bridgewater (G-834)
▼ INB Manhattan Drug Company Inc......D...... 973 926-0816
Hillside (G-4400)
INB Manhattan Drug Company Inc......D...... 973 926-0816
Hillside (G-4401)
INB Manhattan Drug Company Inc......E...... 973 926-0816
Hillside (G-4402)
◆ Ino Therapeutics LLC......D...... 908 238-6600
Bedminster (G-266)
Insmed Incorporated......C...... 908 977-9900
Bridgewater (G-837)
Inspire Pharmaceuticals Inc......C...... 908 423-1000
Whitehouse Station (G-11921)
Integra Lifesciences Corp......D...... 609 275-0500
Plainsboro (G-8794)
Integrated Biopharma Inc......E...... 888 319-6962
Hillside (G-4403)
Intellect Neurosciences Inc......G...... 201 608-5101
Englewood Cliffs (G-2978)
International Vitamin Corp......C...... 973 371-4400
Irvington (G-4575)
International Vitamin Corp......G...... 973 416-2000
Irvington (G-4576)
Interntnal Pharma Remedies Inc......G...... 201 417-3891
Paterson (G-8215)
Invaderm Corporation......G...... 732 307-7926
Somerset (G-10005)
Inventiv Health Clinical LLC......G...... 973 348-1000
Basking Ridge (G-186)
▲ Ipca Pharmaceuticals Inc......G...... 908 412-6561
South Plainfield (G-10280)
Iron4u Inc......G...... 609 514-5163
Princeton (G-8964)
Isdin Corp......E...... 862 242-8129
Morristown (G-6675)

SIC

Ivax Pharmaceuticals LLC	G	201 767-1700	Woodcliff Lake *(G-12058)*
Ivc Industries Inc	B	732 308-3000	Freehold *(G-3671)*
Ivy Pharama Inc	G	201 221-4179	Paramus *(G-7808)*
▲ Jak Diversified II Inc	D	973 439-1182	West Caldwell *(G-11656)*
Jamol Laboratories Inc	G	201 262-6363	Emerson *(G-2865)*
Janssen Global Services LLC	G	908 704-4000	Raritan *(G-9211)*
▲ Janssen Pharmaceuticals Inc	A	609 730-2000	Titusville *(G-10735)*
Janssen Research & Dev LLC	A	908 704-4000	Raritan *(G-9212)*
Jeiven Phrm Consulting Inc	G	908 233-4508	Scotch Plains *(G-9736)*
Jems Pharma LLC	G	609 386-0141	Burlington *(G-976)*
Jhp Group Holdings Inc	A	973 658-3569	Parsippany *(G-7966)*
Jiangsu Hengrui Medicine Co	G	609 395-8625	Princeton *(G-8966)*
Jnj International Inv LLC	G	732 524-0400	New Brunswick *(G-6939)*
Johnson & Johnson	A	732 524-0400	New Brunswick *(G-6940)*
Johnson & Johnson	D	908 704-6809	Raritan *(G-9214)*
Johnson & Johnson	E	908 526-5425	Raritan *(G-9215)*
Johnson & Johnson	D	732 422-5000	North Brunswick *(G-7473)*
Johnson & Johnson	G	908 722-9319	Raritan *(G-9213)*
Johnson & Johnson	C	908 874-1000	Morris Plains *(G-6618)*
Johnson & Johnson	C	732 524-0400	New Brunswick *(G-6941)*
◆ Johnson & Johnson Consumer Inc	A	908 874-1000	Skillman *(G-9922)*
Juventio LLC	G	973 908-8097	Chatham *(G-1324)*
▲ Kamat Pharmatech LLC	G	732 406-6421	North Brunswick *(G-7474)*
Kashiv Biosciences LLC	E	732 475-0500	Piscataway *(G-8683)*
Kiehls Since 1851 Inc	G	201 843-1125	Paramus *(G-7812)*
Klus Pharma Inc	F	609 662-1913	Cranbury *(G-1850)*
▲ Kos Pharmaceuticals Inc	E	609 495-0500	Cranbury *(G-1851)*
◆ Kwik Enterprises LLC	G	732 663-1559	Oakhurst *(G-7610)*
Kyowa Hakko Kirin Cal Inc	G	609 580-7400	Princeton *(G-8968)*
Kyowa Kirin Inc	D	908 234-1096	Bedminster *(G-267)*
▲ Lab Express Inc	F	973 227-1700	Fairfield *(G-3256)*
Leading Pharma LLC	E	201 746-9160	Fairfield *(G-3259)*
Leading Pharma LLC	E	201 746-9160	Montvale *(G-6419)*
▲ Leo Pharma Inc	B	973 637-1690	Madison *(G-5697)*
◆ Levomed Inc	G	908 359-4804	Somerset *(G-10015)*
Lexicon Pharmaceuticals Inc	F	609 466-5500	Basking Ridge *(G-187)*
Life Science Laboratories LLC	G	732 367-1900	Lakewood *(G-5122)*
Life Scnce Labs Spplements LLC	F	732 367-1749	Lakewood *(G-5124)*
Lifecell Corporation	F	908 947-1100	Bridgewater *(G-842)*
Lifecell Corporation	F	908 947-1100	Branchburg *(G-655)*
▲ Lifecell Corporation	C	908 947-1100	Branchburg *(G-656)*
▼ Lipoid LLC	G	973 735-2692	Newark *(G-7182)*
LLC Dunn Meadow	F	201 297-4603	Fort Lee *(G-3569)*
Lonza Biologics Inc	E	603 610-4809	Morristown *(G-6680)*
▲ LTS Lhmann Thrapy Systems Corp	A	973 575-5170	West Caldwell *(G-11658)*

Lupin Pharmaceuticals Inc	G	908 603-6075	Somerset *(G-10020)*
Lupin Pharmaceuticals Inc	E	908 603-6000	Somerset *(G-10021)*
Luye Pharma USA Ltd	E	609 799-7600	Princeton *(G-8971)*
Lyciret Corp	E	973 882-0322	Orange *(G-7754)*
Lydem LLC	G	856 566-1419	Palmyra *(G-7784)*
▲ Macleods Pharma Usa Inc	F	609 269-5250	Princeton *(G-8972)*
Mafco Worldwide LLC	F	856 964-8840	Camden *(G-1076)*
▲ Magnifica Inc	G	323 202-0386	Cranbury *(G-1861)*
Mallinckrodt Ard Inc	G	510 400-0700	Bedminster *(G-268)*
Mallinckrodt Ard LLC	F	908 238-6600	Bedminster *(G-269)*
Mallinckrodt Hospital Pdts Inc	G	908 238-6600	Bedminster *(G-270)*
▲ Mallinckrodt Hospital Pdts Inc	G	314 654-2000	Bedminster *(G-271)*
Mallinckrodt LLC	E	908 238-6600	Hampton *(G-4158)*
Matinas Biopharma Holdings Inc	F	908 443-1860	Bedminster *(G-273)*
Matrixx Initiatives Inc	E	877 942-2626	Bridgewater *(G-847)*
Matthey Johnson Inc	E	856 384-7001	West Deptford *(G-11711)*
Matthey Johnson Inc	C	856 384-7132	West Deptford *(G-11710)*
Maximum Humn Prfmce Hldngs LLC	E	973 785-9055	West Caldwell *(G-11661)*
▲ Meda Pharmaceuticals Inc	C	732 564-2200	Somerset *(G-10026)*
Medavante-Prophase Inc	F	609 528-9400	Hamilton *(G-4112)*
Medicines Company	C	973 290-6000	Parsippany *(G-7977)*
◆ Medicis Pharmaceutical Corp	F	866 246-8245	Bridgewater *(G-848)*
Medicon Inc	G	201 669-7456	Allendale *(G-12)*
Medicure Pharma Inc	E	888 435-2220	Princeton *(G-8975)*
Medimtriks Pharmaceuticals Inc	E	973 882-7512	Fairfield *(G-3267)*
Megalith Pharmaceuticals Inc	G	877 436-7220	Princeton *(G-8976)*
Memomind Pharma Inc	G	201 302-9020	Fort Lee *(G-3571)*
Merck & Co Inc	E	908 740-4000	Kenilworth *(G-4958)*
Merck & Co Inc	E	800 224-5318	Madison *(G-5698)*
Merck & Co Inc	D	908 298-4000	Kenilworth *(G-4959)*
Merck & Co Inc	E	908 298-4000	Summit *(G-10540)*
Merck & Co Inc	G	908 423-1000	Whitehouse Station *(G-11922)*
Merck & Co Inc	G	609 771-8790	Ewing *(G-3045)*
Merck & Co Inc	B	908 740-4000	Kenilworth *(G-4957)*
Merck & Co Inc	D	908 740-4000	Rahway *(G-9117)*
Merck Holdings LLC	F	908 423-1000	Whitehouse Station *(G-11923)*
Merck Resource Management Inc	G	908 423-1000	Whitehouse Station *(G-11924)*
▲ Merck Sharp & Dohme (ia) LLC	F	908 423-1000	Whitehouse Station *(G-11925)*
Merck Sharp & Dohme Corp	B	908 423-1000	Kenilworth *(G-4961)*
Merck Sharp & Dohme Corp	G	908 423-3000	Whitehouse Station *(G-11926)*
Merck Sharp & Dohme Corp	D	732 594-4000	Rahway *(G-9118)*
Merck Sharp & Dohme Corp	G	908 685-3892	Branchburg *(G-659)*
◆ Merck Sharp & Dohme Corp	A	908 740-4000	Kenilworth *(G-4960)*
Merck Sharp Dhme Argentina Inc	G	908 423-1000	Whitehouse Station *(G-11927)*
▲ Merck Sharpe & Dohme De PR Inc	G	908 423-1000	Whitehouse Station *(G-11928)*

Michelex Corporation	G	201 977-1177	Prospect Park *(G-9074)*
Mitsubishi Tanabe Pharma	E	908 607-1950	Jersey City *(G-4766)*
Mountain LLC	G	908 409-6823	Bridgewater *(G-853)*
▲ Mpt Delivery Systems Inc	G	973 278-0283	Paterson *(G-8262)*
▲ Msn Pharmaceuticals Inc	G	732 356-9900	Piscataway *(G-8693)*
Mt Holly Pharmacy	G	609 914-4890	Lumberton *(G-5632)*
Mule Road Pharmacy	G	732 244-3737	Toms River *(G-10779)*
Mylan API Inc	E	732 748-8882	Somerset *(G-10037)*
Mylan API US LLC	E	732 748-8882	Somerset *(G-10038)*
▲ Myos Rens Technology Inc	G	973 509-0444	Cedar Knolls *(G-1311)*
▼ Natures Rule LLC	F	888 819-4220	Hillside *(G-4417)*
Nautilus Neurosciences Inc	G	908 437-1320	Bedminster *(G-275)*
Neopharma Inc	D	609 201-2185	Princeton *(G-8983)*
Newton Biopharma Solutions LLC	G	908 874-7145	Hillsborough *(G-4340)*
▲ Nextron Medical Tech Inc	D	973 575-0614	Fairfield *(G-3279)*
Njs Associates Company	G	973 960-8688	Bridgewater *(G-858)*
▲ Novacyl Inc	G	609 259-0444	Robbinsville *(G-9415)*
Novartis Corporation	D	862 778-8300	East Hanover *(G-2227)*
Novartis Corporation	B	973 503-7488	East Hanover *(G-2228)*
◆ Novartis Corporation	E	212 307-1122	East Hanover *(G-2226)*
◆ Novartis Pharmaceuticals Corp	A	862 778-8300	East Hanover *(G-2229)*
Novartis Pharmaceuticals Corp	F	973 538-1296	Morris Plains *(G-6619)*
Novartis Pharmaceuticals Corp	G	862 778-8300	East Hanover *(G-2231)*
Novartis Pharmaceuticals Corp	G	862 778-8300	East Hanover *(G-2230)*
▲ Novel Laboratories Inc	C	908 603-6000	Somerset *(G-10041)*
Novitium Pharma LLC	G	609 469-5920	East Windsor *(G-2356)*
◆ Novo Nordisk Inc	B	609 987-5800	Plainsboro *(G-8798)*
Novo Nordisk Inc	G	609 987-5800	Princeton *(G-8987)*
Novotec Pharma LLC	G	609 632-2239	Monroe Township *(G-6338)*
Nuclear Diagnostic Pdts Inc	F	973 664-9696	Rockaway *(G-9481)*
Nuclear Diagnostic Products of	F	856 489-5733	Cherry Hill *(G-1401)*
▲ Nutra-Med Packaging Inc	D	973 625-2274	Whippany *(G-11899)*
▲ Nutri Sport Pharmacal Inc	F	973 827-9287	Franklin *(G-3608)*
Nutri-Pet Research Inc	G	732 786-8822	Manalapan *(G-5820)*
▲ Nutro Laboratories Inc	C	908 755-7984	South Plainfield *(G-10309)*
Ocd Pharmaceuticals	G	610 366-2314	Raritan *(G-9216)*
Odin Pharmaceuticals LLC	G	732 554-1100	Somerset *(G-10042)*
▲ OHM Laboratories Inc	D	732 418-2235	North Brunswick *(G-7481)*
OHM Laboratories Inc	D	609 720-9200	Princeton *(G-8990)*
OHM Laboratories Inc	D	732 514-1072	New Brunswick *(G-6956)*
▲ Omniactive Hlth Tchnlogies Inc	E	866 588-3629	Morristown *(G-6690)*
Omthera Pharmaceuticals Inc	F	908 741-4399	Princeton *(G-8991)*
Ono Pharma USA Inc	F	609 219-1010	Lawrenceville *(G-5241)*
Onpharma Inc	G	408 335-6850	Bridgewater *(G-859)*
Optimer Pharmaceuticals LLC	B	858 909-0736	Kenilworth *(G-4966)*

▲ **Orchid Pharmaceuticals Inc**............G....... 609 951-2209
Princeton ***(G-8992)***
▲ **Organics Corporation America**.........E....... 973 890-9002
Totowa ***(G-10841)***
Organon USA Inc.................................G....... 908 423-1000
Whitehouse Station ***(G-11930)***
Ortho Biotech Products LP..................D....... 908 541-4000
Bridgewater ***(G-861)***
▲ **Ortho-Clinical Diagnostics Inc**..........A....... 908 218-8000
Raritan ***(G-9217)***
▲ **Osmotica Pharmaceutical Corp**........C....... 908 809-1300
Bridgewater ***(G-862)***
Osmotica Pharmaceuticals PLC............G....... 908 809-1300
Bridgewater ***(G-863)***
Ossb and L Pharma LLC.......................G....... 732 940-8701
Milltown ***(G-6218)***
Outlook Therapeutics Inc.....................D....... 609 619-3990
Cranbury ***(G-1867)***
▲ **Pacifichealth Laboratories Inc**..........G....... 732 739-2900
Parsippany ***(G-7982)***
Pacira Pharmaceuticals Inc.................C....... 973 254-3560
Parsippany ***(G-7983)***
Palatin Technologies Inc.....................F....... 609 495-2200
Cranbury ***(G-1868)***
Parker Labs...G....... 973 276-9500
Fairfield ***(G-3290)***
Patagonia Pharmaceuticals LLC..........G....... 201 264-7866
Woodcliff Lake ***(G-12060)***
▲ **Patheon Biologics LLC**.....................D....... 609 919-3300
Princeton ***(G-8993)***
▼ **Paw Bioscience Products LLC**........G....... 732 460-0088
Eatontown ***(G-2416)***
Pdr Equity LLC......................................D....... 201 358-7200
Whippany ***(G-11902)***
Pds Biotechnology Corporation............F....... 800 208-3343
Berkeley Heights ***(G-409)***
Penick Corporation...............................G....... 856 678-3601
Newark ***(G-7226)***
Pernix Therapeutics LLC.......................E....... 800 793-2145
Morristown ***(G-6692)***
Pestka Biomedical Labs Inc..................E....... 732 777-9123
Piscataway ***(G-8699)***
Pfizer Inc...D....... 732 591-2106
Old Bridge ***(G-7723)***
Pfizer Inc...C....... 973 993-0977
Morris Plains ***(G-6623)***
Pfizer Inc...C....... 201 294-8060
North Bergen ***(G-7429)***
Pfizer Inc...C....... 908 251-5685
Dunellen ***(G-2123)***
Pfizer Inc...E....... 609 434-4920
Ewing ***(G-3050)***
Pfizer Inc...C....... 908 901-8000
Peapack ***(G-8342)***
Pfizer Inc...C....... 212 733-2323
Bridgewater ***(G-864)***
Pfizer Inc...F....... 973 660-5000
Madison ***(G-5700)***
Pharm Ops Inc.......................................G....... 908 454-7733
Phillipsburg ***(G-8566)***
Pharma Synergy LLC.............................G....... 856 241-2316
Swedesboro ***(G-10601)***
▲ **Pharmaceutical Innovations**.............E....... 973 242-2900
Newark ***(G-7228)***
Pharmachem Laboratories Inc.............E....... 973 256-1340
Totowa ***(G-10843)***
Pharmachem Laboratories Inc.............E....... 201 343-3611
South Hackensack ***(G-10180)***
◆ **Pharmachem Laboratories LLC**.......D....... 201 246-1000
Kearny ***(G-4892)***
▲ **Pharmacia & Upjohn Inc**..................B....... 908 901-8000
Peapack ***(G-8343)***
◆ **Pharmacia & Upjohn Company LLC**.B....... 908 901-8000
Peapack ***(G-8344)***
Pharmasource International LLC..........G....... 732 985-6182
Piscataway ***(G-8700)***
Pharmatech International Inc................F....... 973 244-0393
Fairfield ***(G-3291)***
Pharmctclprscrptnsrvcllc Lcnda...........G....... 973 491-9000
Newark ***(G-7229)***
Pharmedium Services LLC....................E....... 847 457-2362
Dayton ***(G-1983)***
Pharming Healthcare Inc.......................E....... 908 524-0888
Bridgewater ***(G-865)***
Pharmion Corporation...........................E....... 908 673-9000
Summit ***(G-10543)***
◆ **Phibro Animal Health Corp**...............D....... 201 329-7300
Teaneck ***(G-10643)***
Phytobologic Pharmaceutics LLC.........G....... 856 975-0444
West Berlin ***(G-11615)***

▲ **Phytoceuticals Inc**...............................G....... 201 791-2255
Elmwood Park ***(G-2850)***
Pierre Fbre Phrmaceuticals Inc.............G....... 973 898-1042
Parsippany ***(G-7989)***
Pl A Kadmonpharmaceuticals................G....... 732 230-3092
Monmouth Junction ***(G-6302)***
Plantfusion...G....... 732 537-1220
Edison ***(G-2590)***
Plx Pharma Inc.......................................G....... 973 409-6541
Sparta ***(G-10406)***
Pmv Pharmaceuticals Inc......................G....... 650 241-2822
Cranbury ***(G-1873)***
Porton Usa LLC.....................................E....... 908 791-9100
South Plainfield ***(G-10313)***
Powerhuse Frmltons Ltd Labilit...........G....... 888 666-7715
South Plainfield ***(G-10314)***
Prescription Dynamics Inc....................F....... 201 746-6262
Mahwah ***(G-5762)***
▼ **Prince Sterilization Svcs LLC**..........E....... 973 227-6882
Fairfield ***(G-3294)***
Princeton Biopharma Strategies...........G....... 609 203-5303
Princeton ***(G-8997)***
Princeton Enduring Biotech Inc............G....... 732 406-3041
Monmouth Junction ***(G-6304)***
Princeton Enduring Biotech Inc............G....... 732 406-3041
Monmouth Junction ***(G-6305)***
Progenics Pharmaceuticals Inc............F....... 646 975-2500
Somerset ***(G-10057)***
Prolong Pharmaceuticals LLC..............D....... 908 444-4660
South Plainfield ***(G-10316)***
▲ **Promius Pharma LLC**.......................D....... 609 282-1400
Princeton ***(G-9010)***
Protoform Inc..G....... 609 261-6920
Westampton ***(G-11790)***
Provid Pharmaceuticals Inc..................G....... 732 565-1101
Monmouth Junction ***(G-6307)***
Ptc Therapeutics Inc.............................C....... 908 222-7000
South Plainfield ***(G-10317)***
Pts Intermediate Holdings LLC.............A....... 732 537-6200
Somerset ***(G-10059)***
Purdue Pharma LP.................................G....... 203 588-8000
Ewing ***(G-3055)***
Q&Q Pharma Research Company.........G....... 973 267-0160
Morris Plains ***(G-6624)***
Qrx Pharma Incorporated......................F....... 908 506-2900
Bedminster ***(G-277)***
Quagen Pharmaceuticals LLC...............F....... 973 228-9600
West Caldwell ***(G-11674)***
Quagen Pharmaceuticals LLC...............F....... 973 228-9600
West Caldwell ***(G-11675)***
▲ **Qugen Inc**..G....... 609 716-6300
Plainsboro ***(G-8801)***
Rafael Pharmaceuticals Inc..................E....... 609 409-7050
Cranbury ***(G-1876)***
Ranbaxy USA Inc...................................E....... 609 720-9200
Princeton ***(G-9013)***
Ranx Pharmaceuticals Inc....................G....... 571 214-8989
Jamesburg ***(G-4676)***
▲ **Raritan Phrmctcals Incoporated**.......C....... 732 238-1685
East Brunswick ***(G-2173)***
▲ **Rasi Laboratories Inc**.......................D....... 732 873-8500
Cranbury ***(G-1878)***
▲ **Reed-Lane Inc**.....................................C....... 973 709-1090
Wayne ***(G-11546)***
Regado Biosciences Inc.........................G....... 908 580-2109
Basking Ridge ***(G-196)***
Regentree LLC.......................................G....... 609 734-4328
Princeton ***(G-9015)***
Reliance Vitamin LLC............................C....... 732 537-1220
Edison ***(G-2596)***
▲ **Renaissance Lakewood LLC**..........F....... 732 901-2052
Lakewood ***(G-5155)***
Renaissance Lakewood LLC.................B....... 732 367-9000
Lakewood ***(G-5156)***
Riconpharma LLC...................................E....... 973 627-4685
Denville ***(G-2054)***
Rising Health LLC..................................E....... 201 961-9000
Saddle Brook ***(G-9673)***
Rising Pharma Holdings Inc..................G....... 201 961-9000
Saddle Brook ***(G-9674)***
▲ **Rising Pharmaceuticals Inc**.............E....... 201 961-9000
Saddle Brook ***(G-9675)***
Roche Diagnostics Corporation............F....... 908 253-0707
Branchburg ***(G-678)***
Rouses Pt Pharmaceuticals LLC...........G....... 239 390-1495
Cranford ***(G-1926)***
Royal Pharmaceuticals LLC...................G....... 732 292-2661
Wall Township ***(G-11366)***
S V Pharma Inc......................................G....... 201 433-1512
Jersey City ***(G-4802)***

▲ **Sabinsa Corporation**...........................E....... 732 777-1111
East Windsor ***(G-2359)***
▲ **Salix Pharmaceuticals Ltd**................D....... 866 246-8245
Bridgewater ***(G-879)***
▲ **Salus Pharma LLC**............................F....... 732 329-8089
Monmouth Junction ***(G-6310)***
▲ **Sandoz Inc**..C....... 609 627-8500
Princeton ***(G-9019)***
Sandoz Inc...A....... 862 778-8300
East Hanover ***(G-2237)***
▲ **Sanofi US Services Inc**.....................A....... 336 407-4994
Bridgewater ***(G-880)***
Sanofi US Services Inc...........................G....... 336 407-4994
Bridgewater ***(G-881)***
Sanofi US Services Inc...........................E....... 908 231-4000
Bridgewater ***(G-882)***
Sanofi US Services Inc...........................F....... 908 231-4000
Bridgewater ***(G-883)***
▲ **Sanofi-Aventis US LLC**.....................D....... 908 981-5000
Bridgewater ***(G-884)***
◆ **Sanofi-Synthelabo Inc**.......................B....... 908 981-5000
Bridgewater ***(G-886)***
Sanofi-Synthelabo Inc.............................A....... 908 231-2000
Bridgewater ***(G-885)***
Saxa Pharmaceuticals LLC....................G....... 862 571-7630
Holmdel ***(G-4513)***
▲ **Schering Berlin Inc**............................G....... 862 404-3000
Whippany ***(G-11908)***
Schering-Plough Corp.............................G....... 908 595-3638
Branchburg ***(G-681)***
Scherng-Plough Pdts Caribe Inc...........G....... 908 423-1000
Whitehouse Station ***(G-11934)***
▲ **Sciecure Pharma Inc**.........................E....... 732 329-8089
Monmouth Junction ***(G-6311)***
Scynexis Inc...F....... 201 884-5485
Jersey City ***(G-4807)***
Secord Inc..F....... 908 754-2147
Scotch Plains ***(G-9740)***
Sensoredge Inc...G....... 973 975-4163
Parsippany ***(G-8012)***
Sentrimed Ltd Liability Co......................G....... 914 582-8631
Voorhees ***(G-11293)***
Sharmatek Inc...G....... 908 852-5087
Hackettstown ***(G-4036)***
▲ **Shasun USA Inc**..................................F....... 732 465-0700
Piscataway ***(G-8711)***
◆ **Siegfried Usa LLC**..............................C....... 856 678-3601
Pennsville ***(G-8501)***
▲ **Siegfried USA Holding Inc**...............E....... 856 678-3601
Pennsville ***(G-8502)***
▲ **Silab Inc**...F....... 732 335-1030
Hazlet ***(G-4270)***
Sky Growth Intermediate..........................B....... 201 802-4000
Woodcliff Lake ***(G-12064)***
Solaris Pharma Corporation.....................G....... 908 864-0404
Bridgewater ***(G-891)***
Solgen Pharmaceuticals Inc....................E....... 732 983-6025
Edison ***(G-2616)***
Soligenix Inc..F....... 609 538-8200
Princeton ***(G-9023)***
Soma Labs Inc...F....... 732 271-3444
Middlesex ***(G-6149)***
Speciality Pharma Mfg LLC.....................G....... 201 675-3411
Carlstadt ***(G-1220)***
Spray-Tek Inc...E....... 732 469-0050
Middlesex ***(G-6152)***
Star Pharma Inc..G....... 718 466-1790
East Brunswick ***(G-2180)***
Stark Pharma Technology Inc..................F....... 848 217-4059
Piscataway ***(G-8719)***
Steri-Pharma LLC......................................D....... 201 857-8210
Paramus ***(G-7836)***
Strides Pharma Inc.....................................G....... 609 773-5000
East Brunswick ***(G-2181)***
Strive Pharmaceuticals Inc........................G....... 609 269-2001
East Brunswick ***(G-2182)***
Suez Treatment Solutions Inc...................D....... 201 676-2525
Leonia ***(G-5292)***
Sun Pharmaceutical Inds Inc.....................E....... 313 871-8400
Princeton ***(G-9029)***
Sun Pharmaceutical Inds Inc.....................E....... 609 495-2800
Cranbury ***(G-1884)***
▲ **Sun Pharmaceutical Inds Inc**.............B....... 609 495-2800
Cranbury ***(G-1885)***
Sunovion Pharmaceuticals Inc..................D....... 201 592-2050
Fort Lee ***(G-3590)***
▲ **Sunrise Pharmaceutical Inc**...............E....... 732 382-6085
Rahway ***(G-9128)***
Sv Pharma Inc..G....... 732 651-1336
East Brunswick ***(G-2185)***

SIC

Svtc Pharma Inc ....G. 201 652-0013
Ridgewood (G-9332)

Symbiomix Therapeutics LLC ....F 609 722-7250
Newark (G-7293)

▲ Synergetica International Inc..........G. 732 780-5865
Marlboro (G-5916)

Taisho Pharmaceutical R&D Inc..........G. 973 285-0870
Morristown (G-6702)

Tap Pharmaceutical Products..........G. 908 470-9700
Bedminster (G-279)

Taree Pharma LLC ....G. 609 252-9596
Princeton (G-9032)

Targanta Therapeutics Corp ....D 973 290-6000
Parsippany (G-8025)

Taro Pharmaceuticals USA Inc ....E 609 655-9002
Cranbury (G-1886)

Teligent Inc ....C. 856 697-1441
Buena (G-942)

Teligent Inc ....F. 856 697-1441
Buena (G-943)

▲ Teva Api Inc ....E. 201 307-6900
Parsippany (G-8026)

▲ Teva Pharmaceuticals ....F 888 838-2872
Parsippany (G-8027)

Teva Pharmaceuticals Usa Inc ....C 973 575-2775
Fairfield (G-3325)

Teva Womens Health Inc ....G 201 930-3300
Somerset (G-10086)

▲ Therapeutic Proteins Inc ....F 312 620-1500
Piscataway (G-8726)

Thrombogenics Inc ....E 732 590-2900
Iselin (G-4633)

Topifram Laboratories Inc..........E 201 894-9020
Englewood Cliffs (G-2992)

Torrent Pharma Inc ....E 269 544-2299
Basking Ridge (G-199)

Triarco Industries LLC ....G. 973 942-5100
Cranbury (G-1887)

Trifluent Pharma LLC ....G 210 552-2057
Secaucus (G-9823)

▲ Trigen Laboratories LLC ....A 732 721-0070
Bridgewater (G-898)

Tris Pharma Inc ....D 732 940-0358
Monmouth Junction (G-6315)

Tris Pharma Inc ....C 732 940-2800
Monmouth Junction (G-6316)

▲ Tulex Pharmaceuticals Inc ....F 609 619-3098
Cranbury (G-1890)

TWI Pharmaceuticals Usa Inc ....G 201 762-1410
Paramus (G-7842)

Unipack Inc ....F 973 450-9880
Belleville (G-318)

Unitao Nutraceuticals LLC ....G 973 983-1121
Rockaway (G-9510)

◆ Universal Prtein Spplmnts Corp ....D 732 545-3130
New Brunswick (G-6977)

Urigen Pharmaceuticals Inc ....G 732 640-0160
North Brunswick (G-7491)

▼ US Pharma Lab Inc ....C 888 296-8775
New Brunswick (G-6978)

Valeritas Holdings Inc.............D 908 927-9920
Bridgewater (G-902)

Validus Pharmaceuticals LLC ....F 973 265-2777
Parsippany (G-8033)

Vascular Therapies Inc ....G 201 266-8310
Cresskill (G-1946)

Vascure Natural LLC ....G 732 528-6492
Point Pleasant Boro (G-8847)

Vensun Pharmaceuticals Inc ....F 908 278-8386
Princeton (G-9040)

Vermeer Pharma LLC.............G 973 270-0073
Morristown (G-6706)

▲ Vertical Pharmaceuticals LLC..........D 732 721-0070
Bridgewater (G-903)

Vertical/Trigen Holdings LLC..........F 732 721-0070
Bridgewater (G-904)

Vertice Pharma LLC ....E 877 530-1633
New Providence (G-7024)

Vgyaan Pharmaceuticals LLC.............G 609 452-2770
Skillman (G-9927)

▲ Vistapharm Inc ....C 908 376-1622
New Providence (G-7025)

▲ Vita-Pure Inc ....E 908 245-1212
Roselle (G-9576)

Vitacare Pharma LLC ....G 908 754-1792
South Plainfield (G-10343)

Vitaquest International LLC..........F 973 787-9900
Fairfield (G-3345)

Vitaquest International LLC..........F 973 575-9200
Fairfield (G-3346)

▲ Vitaquest International LLC ....B 973 575-9200
West Caldwell (G-11681)

Vs Hercules LLC ....G 201 868-5959
North Bergen (G-7442)

Walgreen Eastern Co Inc ....E 973 728-3172
West Milford (G-11733)

Walgreen Eastern Co Inc ....E 609 522-1291
Wildwood (G-11947)

Warner Chilcott (us) LLC ....G 973 442-3200
Morristown (G-6708)

▲ Warner Chilcott (us) LLC ....D 862 261-7000
Parsippany (G-8036)

▲ Watson Laboratories Inc ....C 951 493-5300
Parsippany (G-8038)

Windsor Labs LLC ....G 609 301-6446
East Windsor (G-2364)

Windtree Therapeutics Inc ....F 973 339-2889
Totowa (G-10863)

▲ Wyeth Holdings LLC ....E 973 660-5000
Madison (G-5704)

Wyeth LLC ....G 973 660-5000
Madison (G-5705)

Wyeth-Ayerst (asia) Ltd ....G 973 660-5500
Madison (G-5706)

Wyeth-Ayerst Pharmaceutical ....F 732 274-4221
Monmouth Junction (G-6320)

Wynnpharm Inc ....G 732 409-1005
Freehold (G-3707)

Zenia Pharma LLC ....G 973 246-9718
Clifton (G-1743)

Zenith Laboratories Inc ....G 201 767-1700
Northvale (G-7555)

Zenith Laboratories Inc ....C 201 767-1700
Northvale (G-7556)

▲ Zoetis Inc ....B 973 822-7000
Parsippany (G-8045)

▲ Zoetis LLC ....G 973 822-7000
Parsippany (G-8046)

◆ Zoetis Products LLC ....G 973 660-5000
Florham Park (G-3528)

Zoetis Products LLC ....F 973 660-5000
Bridgewater (G-905)

2835 Diagnostic Substances

◆ Access Bio Inc ....F 732 873-4040
Somerset (G-9941)

Admera Health LLC.............G 908 222-0533
South Plainfield (G-10208)

Akers Biosciences Inc ....E 856 848-8698
West Deptford (G-11690)

Alere Inc ....B 732 620-4244
Freehold (G-3645)

Alere Inc ....B 732 358-5921
Freehold (G-3646)

▲ Armkel LLC ....A 609 683-5900
Princeton (G-8911)

Arthur A Topilow William Lrner ....E 732 528-0760
Neptune (G-6865)

Ascensia Diabetes Care US Inc ....G 973 560-6500
Parsippany (G-7885)

Astral Diagnostics Inc ....G 856 224-0900
Paulsboro (G-8329)

Avalon Globocare Corp ....G 732 780-4400
Freehold (G-3650)

Baxter Healthcare Corporation..........C 732 225-4700
Edison (G-2466)

Bioalert Technologies LLC..........G 551 655-2939
Englewood Cliffs (G-2961)

Biomedtrix LLC ....F 973 331-7800
Whippany (G-11881)

▲ Biotech Atlantic Inc ....F 732 389-4789
Eatontown (G-2380)

▲ Bracco Diagnostics Inc ....C 609 514-2200
Monroe Township (G-6328)

▲ Bracco USA Inc ....G 609 514-2200
Monroe Township (G-6329)

Cenogenics Corporation ....E 732 536-6457
Morganville (G-6584)

DMS Laboratories Inc ....G 908 782-3353
Flemington (G-3438)

Dpc Cirrus ....F 973 927-2828
Flanders (G-3406)

▲ Dsrv Inc ....F 973 631-1200
Budd Lake (G-921)

Ess Group Inc ....G 609 755-3139
Southampton (G-10361)

Fluoropharma Medical Inc ....G 973 744-1565
Montclair (G-6367)

Foundation For Embryonic ....G 973 656-2847
Basking Ridge (G-183)

Genzyme Corporation.............G 973 256-2106
Totowa (G-10829)

▲ Immunomedics Inc ....C 973 605-8200
Morris Plains (G-6617)

Laboratory Diagnostics Co Inc ....F 732 536-6300
Morganville (G-6591)

Medica ....G 760 634-5440
Dover (G-2096)

◆ Mindray Ds Usa Inc ....B 201 995-8000
Mahwah (G-5754)

▲ Ortho-Clinical Diagnostics Inc..........A 908 218-8000
Raritan (G-9217)

Petnet Solutions Inc ....G 865 218-2000
Hackensack (G-3963)

▲ Pharmaseq Inc ....G 732 355-0100
Monmouth Junction (G-6301)

Princeton Biomeditech Corp ....E 908 281-0112
Skillman (G-9926)

▲ Princeton Biomeditech Corp ....D 732 274-1000
Monmouth Junction (G-6303)

▲ Quest Diagnostics Incorporated ....A 973 520-2700
Secaucus (G-9801)

▲ Recombine LLC ....G 646 470-7422
Livingston (G-5537)

▼ Sensonics Inc ....F 856 547-7702
Haddon Heights (G-4049)

Virid Biosciences Limited ....F 732 410-9573
Cherry Hill (G-1426)

Worthington Biochemical Corp ....E 732 942-1660
Lakewood (G-5183)

2836 Biological Prdts, Exc Diagnostic Substances

A J P Scientific Inc ....G 973 472-7200
Clifton (G-1551)

Adma Biologics Inc.............D 201 478-5552
Ramsey (G-9134)

Brainstorm Cell Thrpeutics Inc..........F 201 488-0460
Hackensack (G-3887)

Devatal Inc ....G 609 586-1575
Trenton (G-10930)

Difco Laboratories Inc ....G 410 316-4113
Franklin Lakes (G-3619)

DSM Nutritional Products LLC ....C 908 475-7093
Belvidere (G-360)

◆ DSM Nutritional Products LLC ....B 800 526-0189
Parsippany (G-7922)

Epicore Networks USA Inc ....E 609 267-9118
Mount Holly (G-6727)

Evotec (us) Inc ....E 650 228-1400
Princeton (G-8945)

Genzyme Corporation.............G 973 256-2106
Totowa (G-10829)

◆ Imclone Systems LLC ....C 908 541-8000
Bridgewater (G-833)

Imclone Systems LLC.............D 908 218-0147
Branchburg (G-647)

▼ Integra Lfscnces Holdings Corp..........C 609 275-0500
Plainsboro (G-8792)

Integra Lifesciences Corp ....D 609 275-0500
Plainsboro (G-8794)

Intervet Inc ....G 908 740-1182
Kenilworth (G-4947)

Kedrion Biopharma Inc ....D 201 242-8900
Fort Lee (G-3567)

Lonza Walkersville Inc.............G 201 316-9259
Morristown (G-6682)

Medchem Express LLC ....G 732 783-7915
Monmouth Junction (G-6297)

Merck & Co Inc.............B 908 740-4000
Kenilworth (G-4957)

Merck & Co Inc.............D 908 740-4000
Rahway (G-9117)

Monmouth Bioproducts LLC ....G 732 863-0300
Freehold (G-3680)

Nathji Plus Inc ....G 609 877-7600
Willingboro (G-11993)

Novaera Solutions Inc ....D 732 452-3605
Iselin (G-4619)

Organon USA Inc ....G 908 423-1000
Whitehouse Station (G-11930)

Pestka Biomedical Labs Inc..........E 732 777-9123
Piscataway (G-8699)

Pharming Healthcare Inc ....E 908 524-0888
Bridgewater (G-865)

Princeton Enduring Biotech Inc..........G 732 406-3041
Monmouth Junction (G-6305)

Princeton Enduring Biotech Inc..........G 732 406-3041
Monmouth Junction (G-6304)

Seqirus Inc ....G...... 919 577-5000
East Hanover *(G-2238)*

Seqirus USA Inc ....F...... 908 739-0200
Summit *(G-10545)*

Soligenix Inc ....F...... 609 538-8200
Princeton *(G-9023)*

Tamir Biotechnology Inc ....G...... 800 419-5061
Short Hills *(G-9878)*

Teligent Inc ....F...... 856 697-1441
Buena *(G-943)*

Weiling Yang ....G...... 201 440-5329
Ridgefield Park *(G-9319)*

Worthington Biochemical Corp ....E...... 732 942-1660
Lakewood *(G-5183)*

▲ Wyeth Holdings LLC ....E...... 973 660-5000
Madison *(G-5704)*

2841 Soap & Detergents

◆ Amerchol Corporation ....C...... 732 248-6000
Edison *(G-2452)*

▲ Americare Laboratories Ltd ....E...... 973 279-5100
Paterson *(G-8138)*

Anscott Chemical Inds Inc ....E...... 973 696-7575
Wayne *(G-11471)*

Ardmore Inc ....G...... 973 481-2406
Newark *(G-7051)*

Arol Chemical Products Co ....G...... 973 344-1510
Newark *(G-7053)*

Atlantic Associates Intl Inc ....F...... 856 662-1717
Pennsauken *(G-8392)*

Aura Detergent LLC ....E...... 718 824-2162
Newark *(G-7059)*

Cantol Inc ....E...... 609 846-7912
Wildwood *(G-11942)*

Capital Soap Products LLC ....F...... 973 333-6100
Paterson *(G-8154)*

Cavalier Chemical Co Inc ....E...... 908 558-0110
Short Hills *(G-9865)*

Church & Dwight Co Inc ....B...... 609 806-1200
Ewing *(G-3021)*

▲ Dermarite Industries LLC ....C...... 973 247-3491
North Bergen *(G-7400)*

Detergent 20 LLC ....F...... 732 545-0200
New Brunswick *(G-6919)*

Dynamic Blending Company Inc ......F...... 856 541-6626
Camden *(G-1059)*

Ecolab Inc ....C...... 856 596-4845
Moorestown *(G-6520)*

Epic Holding Inc ....E...... 732 249-6867
Morristown *(G-6663)*

◆ Fiabila USA Inc ....E...... 973 659-9510
Mine Hill *(G-6272)*

Hy-Test Packaging Corp ....G...... 973 754-7000
Paterson *(G-8211)*

▲ Inopak Ltd ....F...... 973 962-1121
Ringwood *(G-9347)*

Interntional Cnsld Chemex Corp ......E...... 732 828-7676
New Brunswick *(G-6936)*

Inventek Colloidal Clrs LLC ....E...... 856 206-0058
Mount Laurel *(G-6771)*

Kempak Industries ....F...... 908 687-4188
Springfield *(G-10450)*

Kync Design LLC ....G...... 201 552-2067
Secaucus *(G-9787)*

Made Solutions LLC ....G...... 201 254-3693
Fair Lawn *(G-3110)*

Magnuson Products ....F...... 973 472-9292
Clifton *(G-1663)*

Pilot Chemical Company Ohio ....F...... 732 634-6613
Avenel *(G-140)*

Procter & Gamble Mfg Co ....D...... 732 602-4500
Avenel *(G-143)*

S W I International Inc ....G...... 973 334-2525
Boonton *(G-567)*

Si Packaging LLC ....F...... 973 869-9920
Rutherford *(G-9632)*

Stanson Corporation ....D...... 973 344-8666
Kearny *(G-4900)*

◆ Technick Products Inc ....F...... 908 791-0400
South Plainfield *(G-10330)*

◆ Unilever United States Inc ....A...... 201 735-9661
Englewood Cliffs *(G-2995)*

2842 Spec Cleaning, Polishing & Sanitation Preparations

3M Company ....B...... 973 884-2500
Whippany *(G-11875)*

▼ A L Wilson Chemical Co ....F...... 201 997-3300
Kearny *(G-4840)*

Advanced Sewer ....F...... 973 278-1948
Woodland Park *(G-12069)*

▲ Agate Lacquer Tri-Nat LLC ....G...... 732 968-1080
Middlesex *(G-6095)*

◆ Allison Corp ....G...... 973 992-3800
Livingston *(G-5504)*

◆ Amano USA Holdings Inc ....G...... 973 403-1900
Roseland *(G-9531)*

Americhem Enterprises Inc ....G...... 732 363-4840
Lakewood *(G-5051)*

▼ Aqua Products Inc ....E...... 856 829-8444
Cinnaminson *(G-1441)*

Arol Chemical Products Co ....G...... 973 344-1510
Newark *(G-7053)*

Associated Cleaning Systems ....G...... 201 530-9197
Teaneck *(G-10622)*

Astra Cleaners of Hazlet ....G...... 732 264-4144
Hazlet *(G-4257)*

Atlantic Associates Intl Inc ....F...... 856 662-1717
Pennsauken *(G-8392)*

▲ Benckiser N Reckitt Amer Inc ......A...... 973 404-2600
Parsippany *(G-7893)*

Brasscraft Manufacturing Co ....G...... 856 241-7700
Swedesboro *(G-10574)*

Cantol Inc ....E...... 609 846-7912
Wildwood *(G-11942)*

Capital Soap Products LLC ....F...... 973 333-6100
Paterson *(G-8154)*

Cavalier Chemical Co Inc ....E...... 908 558-0110
Short Hills *(G-9865)*

▲ Chemetall US Inc ....D...... 908 464-6900
New Providence *(G-6997)*

Chemique Inc ....G...... 856 235-4161
Moorestown *(G-6512)*

Church & Dwight Co Inc ....B...... 609 806-1200
Ewing *(G-3021)*

Clenesco Products Corp ....F...... 908 245-5255
Roselle *(G-9552)*

◆ Cobra Products Inc ....D...... 856 241-7700
Swedesboro *(G-10577)*

Edwards Creative Products Inc ....F...... 856 665-3200
Cherry Hill *(G-1358)*

◆ Envirochem Inc ....E...... 732 238-6700
South River *(G-10350)*

Ep Systems Inc ....G...... 570 424-0581
Hackettstown *(G-4006)*

Epic Holding Inc ....E...... 732 249-6867
Morristown *(G-6663)*

Fabric Chemical Corporation ....G...... 201 432-0440
Jersey City *(G-4733)*

▼ Frank B Ross Co Inc ....E...... 732 669-0810
Rahway *(G-9095)*

◆ Global Spclty Products-Usa Inc ......F...... 609 518-7577
Mount Holly *(G-6728)*

Green Power Chemical LLC ....G...... 973 770-5600
Hopatcong *(G-4520)*

Harvester Inc ....F...... 201 445-1122
Irvington *(G-4571)*

Houghton Chemical Corporation ......F...... 201 460-8071
Carlstadt *(G-1166)*

International Products Corp ....F...... 609 386-8770
Burlington *(G-974)*

Interntional Cnsld Chemex Corp ......E...... 732 828-7676
New Brunswick *(G-6936)*

◆ Interntional Specialty Pdts Inc ......A...... 859 815-3333
Wayne *(G-11522)*

James R Macauley Inc ....G...... 856 767-3474
Waterford Works *(G-11462)*

Jobe Industries Inc ....G...... 908 862-0400
Linden *(G-5365)*

◆ L & R Manufacturing Co Inc ....D...... 201 991-5330
Kearny *(G-4877)*

Made Solutions LLC ....G...... 201 254-3693
Fair Lawn *(G-3110)*

Magnuson Products ....F...... 973 472-9292
Clifton *(G-1663)*

Matchless United Companies ....G...... 908 862-7300
Linden *(G-5380)*

▲ Mennen Company ....B...... 973 630-1500
Morristown *(G-6685)*

▲ Menshen Packaging USA Inc ....D...... 201 445-7436
Waldwick *(G-11304)*

Microgen Inc ....G...... 973 575-9025
West Caldwell *(G-11666)*

National Auto Detailing Netwrk ....E...... 856 931-5529
Bellmawr *(G-340)*

Penetone Corporation ....E...... 201 567-3000
Clifton *(G-1688)*

Penetone Corporation ....G...... 609 921-0501
Princeton *(G-8994)*

PQ Corporation ....E...... 732 750-9040
Avenel *(G-141)*

▲ Prestige Laboratories Inc ....E...... 973 772-8922
East Rutherford *(G-2311)*

Q-Pak Corporation ....E...... 973 483-4404
Newark *(G-7242)*

Ramblewood Cleaners Inc ....G...... 856 235-6051
Mount Laurel *(G-6799)*

Raybeam Manufacturing Corp ....G...... 201 941-4529
Ridgefield *(G-9286)*

RB Manufacturing LLC ....C...... 908 533-2000
Hillsborough *(G-4350)*

▲ RB Manufacturing LLC ....B...... 973 404-2600
Parsippany *(G-8004)*

Reckitt Benckiser LLC ....C...... 973 404-2600
Montvale *(G-6425)*

◆ Reckitt Benckiser LLC ....B...... 973 404-2600
Parsippany *(G-8005)*

Ronell Industries Inc ....B...... 908 245-5255
Roselle *(G-9571)*

▲ Royce Associates A Ltd Partnr ......D...... 201 438-5200
East Rutherford *(G-2315)*

Schulke Inc ....G...... 973 521-7163
Fairfield *(G-3308)*

Stanson Corporation ....D...... 973 344-8666
Kearny *(G-4900)*

Stepan Company ....D...... 201 845-3030
Maywood *(G-6016)*

Stepan Company ....D...... 609 298-1222
Bordentown *(G-595)*

Sterigenics US LLC ....G...... 856 241-8880
Swedesboro *(G-10611)*

Trap-Zap Environmental Systems ......E...... 201 251-9977
Wyckoff *(G-12122)*

Trim Brush Company Inc ....G...... 973 887-2525
East Hanover *(G-2243)*

Venus Laboratories Inc ....E...... 973 257-8983
Parsippany *(G-8035)*

Zoono USA Ltd Liability Co ....G...... 732 722-8757
Shrewsbury *(G-9905)*

2843 Surface Active & Finishing Agents, Sulfonated Oils

Agilis Chemicals Inc ....F...... 973 910-2424
Short Hills *(G-9864)*

AIG Industrial Group Inc ....F...... 201 767-7300
Northvale *(G-7516)*

American Gas & Chemical Co Ltd ......E...... 201 767-7300
Northvale *(G-7518)*

Arol Chemical Products Co ....G...... 973 344-1510
Newark *(G-7053)*

◆ Atlas Refinery Inc ....E...... 973 589-2002
Newark *(G-7056)*

BASF Corporation ....D...... 908 689-7470
Washington *(G-11440)*

◆ BASF Corporation ....B...... 973 245-6000
Florham Park *(G-3491)*

◆ Basfin Corporation ....A...... 973 245-6000
Florham Park *(G-3493)*

Commercial Products Co Inc ....F...... 973 427-6887
Hawthorne *(G-4213)*

◆ G Holdings LLC ....F...... 973 628-3000
Parsippany *(G-7953)*

◆ G-I Holdings Inc ....G...... 973 628-3000
Wayne *(G-11507)*

◆ Interntional Specialty Pdts Inc ......A...... 859 815-3333
Wayne *(G-11522)*

◆ Lanxess Sybron Chemicals Inc ......C...... 609 893-1100
Birmingham *(G-457)*

▲ Meson Group Inc ....E...... 201 767-7300
Northvale *(G-7536)*

Nutech Corp ....G...... 908 707-2097
Franklin Lakes *(G-3629)*

◆ Pariser Industries Inc ....E...... 973 569-9090
Paterson *(G-8277)*

▲ Pflaumer Brothers Inc ....G...... 609 883-4610
Ewing *(G-3051)*

Solv-TEC Incorporated ....G...... 609 261-4242
Medford *(G-6034)*

Stepan Company ....D...... 609 298-1222
Bordentown *(G-595)*

2844 Perfumes, Cosmetics & Toilet Preparations

▲ 3lab Inc ....F...... 201 227-4742
Englewood *(G-2871)*

▲ A D M Tronics Unlimited Inc ....E...... 201 767-6040
Northvale *(G-7513)*

ABG Lab LLC	G	973 559-5663	
Fair Lawn *(G-3081)*			
Acupac Packaging Inc	C	201 529-3434	
Mahwah *(G-5710)*			
Adorage Inc	G	201 886-7000	
Edgewater *(G-2432)*			
Adron Inc	E	973 334-1600	
Boonton *(G-536)*			
◆ ADS Sales Co Inc	E	732 591-0500	
Morganville *(G-6580)*			
◆ Agilex Flavors Fragrances Inc	G	732 885-0702	
Piscataway *(G-8627)*			
▼ AlSha&anna Nation of Trends	G	201 951-8197	
Rahway *(G-9076)*			
Alkaline Corporation	G	732 531-7830	
Eatontown *(G-2375)*			
Aloe Science Inc	E	908 231-8888	
Branchburg *(G-614)*			
◆ Amerchol Corporation	C	732 248-6000	
Edison *(G-2452)*			
American Prvate Label Pdts LLC	G	845 733-8151	
Franklin *(G-3598)*			
American Spraytech LLC	G	908 725-6060	
Branchburg *(G-617)*			
▲ Americare Laboratories Ltd	E	973 279-5100	
Paterson *(G-8138)*			
Anatolian Naturals Inc	G	201 893-0142	
Fort Lee *(G-3546)*			
▲ Andrea Aromatics Inc	E	609 695-7710	
Trenton *(G-10894)*			
▲ AP Deauville LLC	E	732 545-0200	
New Brunswick *(G-6911)*			
▼ Arch Personal Care Products LP	E	908 226-9329	
South Plainfield *(G-10219)*			
▲ Ariel Laboratories LP	G	908 755-4080	
South Plainfield *(G-10220)*			
▲ Armkel LLC	A	609 683-5900	
Princeton *(G-8911)*			
Art of Natural Solution Inc	F	973 812-0500	
Totowa *(G-10814)*			
Art of Natural Solution Inc	E	917 745-7894	
Totowa *(G-10815)*			
Art of Shaving - Fl LLC	G	732 410-2520	
Freehold *(G-3648)*			
Ascent Aromatics Inc	G	908 755-0120	
South Plainfield *(G-10221)*			
Atara LLC	G	916 765-2217	
Union City *(G-11108)*			
Atlantis Aromatics Inc	G	732 919-1112	
Wall Township *(G-11319)*			
Avon Products Inc	G	973 779-5590	
Clifton *(G-1569)*			
B Witching Bath Company LLC	G	973 423-1820	
Hawthorne *(G-4206)*			
Barmensen Labs LLC	G	732 593-3515	
Old Bridge *(G-7712)*			
▲ Batallure Beauty LLC	E	609 716-1200	
Princeton *(G-8913)*			
▲ Beilis Development LLC	F	862 203-3650	
Fair Lawn *(G-3090)*			
Bellevue Parfums USA LLC	F	908 262-7774	
Hillsborough *(G-4304)*			
Bellwood Aeromatics Inc	G	201 670-4617	
Fairfield *(G-3153)*			
▲ Bentley Laboratories LLC	C	732 512-0200	
Edison *(G-2468)*			
▼ Bio-Nature Labs Ltd Lblty Co	E	732 738-5550	
Edison *(G-2470)*			
▲ Biogenesis Inc	F	201 678-1992	
Paterson *(G-8148)*			
Bristol-Myers Squibb Company	E	212 546-4000	
Hillside *(G-4383)*			
▲ Caboki LLC	G	609 642-2108	
Cranbury *(G-1819)*			
▲ Cadbury Adams USA LLC	E	973 503-2000	
East Hanover *(G-2197)*			
▲ Cadence Distributors LLC	G	646 808-3031	
Hackensack *(G-3891)*			
Caolion BNC Co Ltd	C	201 641-4709	
Ridgefield Park *(G-9300)*			
Caret Corporation	F	973 423-6098	
Fairfield *(G-3165)*			
▲ CCA Industries Inc	E	201 935-3232	
Lyndhurst *(G-5647)*			
▲ Cei Holdings Inc	E	732 888-7788	
Holmdel *(G-4496)*			
▲ Charabot & Co Inc	F	201 812-2762	
Budd Lake *(G-920)*			
▲ Chemaid Laboratories Inc	C	201 843-3300	
Saddle Brook *(G-9646)*			
Cherri Stone Interactive LLC	G	844 843-7765	
Lakewood *(G-5069)*			
Cheveux Cosmetics Corporation	D	732 446-7516	
Englishtown *(G-3000)*			
Christian Dior Perfumes LLC	G	609 409-3628	
Cranbury *(G-1821)*			
▲ Christine Valmy Inc	E	973 575-1050	
Pine Brook *(G-8592)*			
Church & Dwight Co Inc	B	609 806-1200	
Ewing *(G-3021)*			
Cococare Products Inc	E	973 989-8880	
Dover *(G-2078)*			
Colgate-Palmolive Company	B	732 878-6062	
Highland Park *(G-4288)*			
Colgate-Palmolive Company	A	732 878-7500	
Piscataway *(G-8648)*			
Colgate-Palmolive Company	G	609 239-6001	
Burlington *(G-961)*			
Conair Corporation	C	609 426-1300	
East Windsor *(G-2348)*			
Conopco Inc	E	856 722-1664	
Mount Laurel *(G-6749)*			
Continental Aromatics	G	973 238-9300	
Hawthorne *(G-4215)*			
▲ Contract Filling Inc	C	973 433-0053	
Cedar Grove *(G-1272)*			
Cosmetic Coatings Inc	E	201 438-7150	
Carlstadt *(G-1146)*			
▲ Cosmetic Concepts Inc	C	973 546-1234	
Garfield *(G-3736)*			
▲ Cosmetic Essence LLC	C	732 888-7788	
Holmdel *(G-4497)*			
Cosmetic Essence LLC	G	201 941-9800	
Ridgefield *(G-9257)*			
Cosmetic Essence Inc	C	732 888-7788	
Holmdel *(G-4498)*			
▲ Cosrich Group Inc	E	866 771-7473	
Bloomfield *(G-498)*			
Coty US LLC	C	973 490-8700	
Morris Plains *(G-6602)*			
Coughlan Products LLC	G	973 845-6440	
Flanders *(G-3403)*			
Creative Concepts Corporation	G	201 750-1234	
Norwood *(G-7562)*			
▼ Custom Essence	F	732 249-6405	
Somerset *(G-9980)*			
Custom Liners Inc	G	732 940-0084	
Upper Saddle River *(G-11138)*			
Dala Beauty LLC	G	732 380-7354	
Shrewsbury *(G-9888)*			
◆ Davion Inc	E	973 485-0793	
North Brunswick *(G-7464)*			
▲ Davlyn Industries Inc	C	609 655-5974	
East Windsor *(G-2349)*			
Devon Products	G	732 438-3855	
Pompton Plains *(G-8862)*			
◆ Disposable Hygiene LLC	C	973 779-1982	
Clifton *(G-1600)*			
▲ Dnp Foods America Ltd Lblty Co	G	201 654-5581	
Waldwick *(G-11301)*			
▲ Dosis Fragrance LLC	G	718 874-0074	
Newark *(G-7104)*			
▲ Ebin New York Inc	E	201 288-8887	
Teterboro *(G-10673)*			
Edgewell Personal Care LLC	G	973 753-3000	
Cedar Knolls *(G-1303)*			
Edgewell Personal Care LLC	G	201 785-8000	
Allendale *(G-8)*			
▲ Encore International LLC	F	973 423-3880	
Hawthorne *(G-4216)*			
▲ Englewood Lab LLC	C	201 567-2267	
Englewood *(G-2901)*			
◆ ET Browne Drug Co Inc	D	201 894-9020	
Englewood Cliffs *(G-2970)*			
Excell Brands Ltd Liability Co	G	908 561-1130	
Princeton *(G-8946)*			
Fantasia Industries Corp	E	201 261-7070	
Paramus *(G-7800)*			
▲ Flavor & Fragrance Spc Inc	D	201 828-9400	
Mahwah *(G-5738)*			
▲ Fragrance Exchange Inc	G	732 641-2210	
Monroe Township *(G-6332)*			
▼ Fragrance Solutions Corp	G	732 832-7800	
South Plainfield *(G-10262)*			
◆ French Color Fragrance Co Inc	E	201 567-6883	
Englewood *(G-2907)*			
Gallant Laboratories Inc	G	609 654-4146	
Marlton *(G-5932)*			
▲ Gel Concepts LLC	G	973 884-8995	
Whippany *(G-11893)*			
◆ Gentek Inc	C	973 515-0900	
Parsippany *(G-7956)*			
Givaudan Fragrances Corp	C	973 448-6500	
Budd Lake *(G-924)*			
Grow Company Inc	E	201 941-8777	
Ridgefield *(G-9264)*			
▲ Hair Systems Inc	D	732 446-2202	
Englishtown *(G-3004)*			
Health and Natural Beauty USA	F	732 640-1830	
Piscataway *(G-8671)*			
Hudson Cosmetic Mfg Corp	D	973 472-2323	
Clifton *(G-1637)*			
Hy-Test Packaging Corp	G	973 754-7000	
Paterson *(G-8211)*			
Imaan Trading Inc	G	201 779-2062	
Jersey City *(G-4749)*			
▼ Imperial Dax Co Inc	E	973 227-6105	
Fairfield *(G-3234)*			
Imperial Drug & Spice Corp	G	201 348-1551	
West New York *(G-11741)*			
▲ Innovative Cosmtc Concepts LLC	F	212 391-8110	
Edison *(G-2534)*			
▲ Innovative Cosmtc Concepts LLC	D	973 225-0264	
Clifton *(G-1641)*			
Intarome Fragrance Corporation	D	201 767-8700	
Norwood *(G-7565)*			
Inter Parfums Inc	E	609 860-1967	
Dayton *(G-1971)*			
▲ Interfashion Cosmetics Corp	E	201 288-5858	
Teterboro *(G-10680)*			
International Aromatics Inc	F	201 964-0900	
Moonachie *(G-6472)*			
▲ International Beauty Products	F	973 575-6400	
Pine Brook *(G-8607)*			
Interntnal Flvors Frgrnces Inc	C	732 264-4500	
Hazlet *(G-4262)*			
Isp Chemicals LLC	E	973 635-1551	
Chatham *(G-1323)*			
Jersey Shore Cosmetics LLC	F	908 500-9954	
Flemington *(G-3451)*			
Jnj International Inv LLC	G	732 524-0400	
New Brunswick *(G-6939)*			
◆ Jodhpuri Inc	D	973 299-7009	
Parsippany *(G-7968)*			
Johnson & Johnson	D	732 422-5000	
North Brunswick *(G-7473)*			
Johnson & Johnson	G	908 722-9319	
Raritan *(G-9213)*			
Johnson & Johnson	C	908 874-1000	
Morris Plains *(G-6618)*			
Johnson & Johnson	C	732 524-0400	
New Brunswick *(G-6941)*			
▲ June Jacobs Labs LLC	G	201 329-9100	
Moonachie *(G-6475)*			
Keystone Europe LLC	G	856 663-4700	
Cherry Hill *(G-1380)*			
Klabin Fragrances Inc	F	973 857-3600	
Cedar Grove *(G-1280)*			
Kobo Products Inc	E	908 941-3406	
South Plainfield *(G-10289)*			
Kobo Products Inc	E	908 757-0033	
South Plainfield *(G-10290)*			
◆ Kobo Products Inc	E	908 757-0033	
South Plainfield *(G-10288)*			
LOreal Usa Inc	C	732 499-6617	
Clark *(G-1504)*			
LOreal Usa Inc	D	212 818-1500	
Clark *(G-1505)*			
LOreal Usa Inc	D	732 499-6690	
Clark *(G-1506)*			
LOreal Usa Inc	G	732 499-2809	
Clark *(G-1507)*			
LOreal Usa Inc	A	609 860-7500	
Cranbury *(G-1858)*			
LOreal USA Products Inc	G	732 873-3520	
Jersey City *(G-4761)*			
LOreal USA Products Inc	A	732 873-3520	
Somerset *(G-10018)*			
Lux Naturals LLC	G	848 229-2950	
Edison *(G-2554)*			
Lvmh Fragrance Brands US LLC	G	212 931-2668	
Edison *(G-2555)*			
MAC Cosmetics Inc	F	856 661-9024	
Cherry Hill *(G-1387)*			
Mastertaste Inc	F	201 373-1111	
Teterboro *(G-10686)*			
◆ Medallion International Inc	F	973 616-3401	
Pompton Plains *(G-8867)*			
▲ Mennen Company	B	973 630-1500	
Morristown *(G-6685)*			

Merck & Co Inc ....B 908 740-4000
Kenilworth **(G-4957)**

Merck & Co Inc ....D 908 740-4000
Rahway **(G-9117)**

▲ Millennium Research LLC ....G 908 867-7646
Long Valley **(G-5612)**

▲ Mycone Dental Supply Co Inc ....C 856 663-4700
Gibbstown **(G-3798)**

Nature Labs LLC ....G 856 839-0400
Vineland **(G-11245)**

Nellsam Group Inc ....G 201 951-9459
Cliffside Park **(G-1542)**

▼ New World International Inc ....F 973 881-8100
Paterson **(G-8268)**

New York Botany Inc ....E 201 564-7444
Northvale **(G-7541)**

▲ Nmr Manufacturing LLC ....G 908 769-3234
South Plainfield **(G-10306)**

▲ Novapac Laboratories Inc ....E 973 414-8800
Lincoln Park **(G-5303)**

▲ Nu-World Corporation ....C 732 541-6300
Carteret **(G-1262)**

Nu-World Corporation ....G 732 541-6300
Edison **(G-2582)**

▲ Omega Packaging Corp ....D 973 890-9505
Totowa **(G-10840)**

▲ Organics Corporation America ....E 973 890-9002
Totowa **(G-10841)**

◆ Pantina Cosmetics Inc ....E 201 288-7767
Teterboro **(G-10689)**

▲ Paramount Cosmetics Inc ....D 973 472-2323
Clifton **(G-1684)**

Peter Thomas Roth Labs LLC ....C 201 329-9100
Saddle Brook **(G-9669)**

Pfizer Inc ....D 973 739-0430
Parsippany **(G-7988)**

▲ Precious Cosmetics Packaging ....F 973 478-4633
Lodi **(G-5573)**

▲ Premier Specialties Inc ....F 732 469-6615
Middlesex **(G-6140)**

◆ Presperse Corporation ....E 732 356-5200
Somerset **(G-10055)**

Procter & Gamble Mfg Co ....D 732 602-4500
Avenel **(G-143)**

▲ Product Club Corp ....F 973 664-0565
Rockaway **(G-9491)**

Promeko Inc ....G 201 861-9446
West New York **(G-11751)**

Qualis Packaging Inc ....F 908 782-0305
South Plainfield **(G-10318)**

▲ Quality Cosmetics Mfg ....E 908 755-9588
South Plainfield **(G-10319)**

◆ Quest Intl Flavors Fragrances ....B 973 576-9500
East Hanover **(G-2235)**

R&R Cosmetics LLC ....G 732 340-1000
Rahway **(G-9123)**

Radha Beauty Products LLC ....G 732 993-6242
Westwood **(G-11841)**

Regi US Inc ....G 862 702-3901
West Caldwell **(G-11677)**

Revel Nail LLC ....E 855 738-3501
Blackwood **(G-480)**

Reviva Labs Inc ....E 856 428-3885
Haddonfield **(G-4064)**

Revlon Inc ....E 732 287-1400
Edison **(G-2598)**

Revlon Consumer Products Corp ....D 732 287-1400
Edison **(G-2599)**

▲ Robertet Inc ....E 201 405-1000
Budd Lake **(G-932)**

▲ Robertet Fragrances Inc ....E 201 405-1000
Budd Lake **(G-933)**

Robertet Fragrances Inc ....E 973 575-4550
Fairfield **(G-3302)**

▲ Rossow Cosmetiques - Usa Inc ....G 732 872-1464
Matawan **(G-5987)**

▲ Royal Cosmetics Corporation ....F 732 246-7275
New Brunswick **(G-6969)**

Rubigo Cosmetics ....G 973 636-6573
Little Falls **(G-5466)**

S Swanson LLC ....G 201 750-5050
Northvale **(G-7548)**

◆ Sarkli-Repechage Ltd ....D 201 549-4200
Secaucus **(G-9807)**

Saturn Beauty Group LLC ....G 908 561-5000
Piscataway **(G-8707)**

Scories Inc ....F 973 923-1372
Newark **(G-7264)**

▲ SGB Packaging Group Inc ....G 201 488-3030
Hackensack **(G-3972)**

▲ Shiseido America Inc ....C 609 371-5800
East Windsor **(G-2360)**

Shiseido Americas Corporation ....G 609 371-5800
East Windsor **(G-2361)**

▲ Siloa Inc ....G 908 234-9040
Bedminster **(G-278)**

◆ Sozio Inc ....D 732 572-5600
Piscataway **(G-8715)**

Suite K Value Added Svcs LLC ....F 732 590-0647
Edison **(G-2622)**

Suite K Value Added Svcs LLC ....F 609 655-6890
Edison **(G-2623)**

▲ Suite K Value Added Svcs LLC ....D 609 655-6890
Edison **(G-2624)**

◆ Sysco Guest Supply LLC ....C 732 537-2297
Somerset **(G-10078)**

▲ Takasago Intl Corp USA ....C 201 767-9001
Rockleigh **(G-9522)**

Takasago Intl Corp USA ....E 201 767-9001
Northvale **(G-7551)**

Topifram Laboratories Inc ....E 201 894-9020
Englewood Cliffs **(G-2992)**

◆ Unilever United States Inc ....A 201 735-9661
Englewood Cliffs **(G-2995)**

▲ Victory International USA LLC ....F 732 417-5900
Eatontown **(G-2429)**

▲ Vsar Resources LLC ....F 973 233-6000
Monroe Township **(G-6350)**

▲ World Wide Packaging LLC ....E 973 805-6500
Florham Park **(G-3527)**

▲ Yankee Tool Inc ....F 973 664-0878
Denville **(G-2062)**

2851 Paints, Varnishes, Lacquers, Enamels

◆ Actega North America Inc ....C 856 829-6300
Delran **(G-2008)**

Actega North America Inc ....F 856 829-6300
Cinnaminson **(G-1439)**

▼ Advanced Protective Products ....F 201 794-2000
Fair Lawn **(G-3082)**

Affordable Lead Solutions LLC ....G 856 207-1348
Bridgeton **(G-750)**

▲ Agate Lacquer Tri-Nat LLC ....G 732 968-1080
Middlesex **(G-6095)**

American Chemical & Coating Co ....G 908 353-2260
Elizabeth **(G-2711)**

◆ Andek Corporation ....F 856 866-7600
Moorestown **(G-6505)**

▲ Armorpoxy Inc ....F 908 810-9613
Union **(G-11027)**

Ashland LLC ....G 908 243-3500
Bridgewater **(G-794)**

Ashland Spcalty Ingredients GP ....E 732 353-7708
Parlin **(G-7862)**

Ben Hamon Moore Co ....E 800 344-0400
Montvale **(G-6398)**

Benjamin Moore & Co ....C 973 344-1200
Newark **(G-7065)**

◆ Benjamin Moore & Co ....C 201 573-9600
Montvale **(G-6399)**

Benjamin Moore & Co ....D 973 569-5000
Clifton **(G-1573)**

◆ Breen Color Concentrates LLC ....F 609 397-8200
Lambertville **(G-5187)**

◆ Broadview Technologies Inc ....E 973 465-0077
Newark **(G-7077)**

Carboline Company ....F 908 233-3150
Westfield **(G-11796)**

Carboline Company ....G 732 388-2912
Rahway **(G-9085)**

▲ Chemetall US Inc ....D 908 464-6900
New Providence **(G-6997)**

Clausen Company Inc ....E 732 738-1165
Fords **(G-3531)**

Colorflo Inc ....G 908 862-3010
Linden **(G-5335)**

Columbia Paint Lab Inc ....E 201 435-4884
Jersey City **(G-4715)**

▼ Complementary Coatings Corp ....E 845 786-5000
Montvale **(G-6405)**

Covalnce Spcialty Coatings LLC ....D 732 356-2870
Middlesex **(G-6109)**

Custom Chemicals Corp ....A 201 791-5100
Elmwood Park **(G-2820)**

Dunbar Sales Company Inc ....G 201 437-6500
Bayonne **(G-2827)**

Duraamen Engineered Pdts Inc ....G 973 230-1301
Newark **(G-7106)**

Dux Paint LLC ....F 973 473-2376
Lodi **(G-5560)**

E I Du Pont De Nemours & Co ....E 732 257-1579
Parlin **(G-7863)**

◆ Elementis Specialties Inc ....C 609 443-2000
East Windsor **(G-2369)**

Elementis Specialties Inc ....F 201 432-0800
East Windsor **(G-2370)**

◆ Evonik Corporation ....B 973 929-8000
Parsippany **(G-7938)**

Ferro Corporation ....E 732 287-4925
Edison **(G-2511)**

◆ Flexabar Corporation ....E 732 901-6500
Lakewood **(G-5099)**

Flexdell Corp ....G 732 901-7771
Lakewood **(G-5100)**

▲ Fluorotherm Polymers Inc ....G 973 575-0760
Parsippany **(G-7948)**

◆ Fti Inc ....G 973 443-0004
Florham Park **(G-3506)**

◆ Gdb International Inc ....D 732 246-3001
New Brunswick **(G-6928)**

Hartin Paint & Filler Corp ....E 201 438-3300
Carlstadt **(G-1164)**

Hawthorne Paint Company Inc ....G 973 423-2335
Lodi **(G-5564)**

Hempel (usa) Inc ....E 201 939-2801
Clifton **(G-1633)**

▲ Industrial Summit Tech Corp ....E 732 238-2211
Parlin **(G-7865)**

J R S Tool & Metal Finishing ....G 908 753-2050
South Plainfield **(G-10282)**

▲ Kadakia International Inc ....G 908 754-4445
South Plainfield **(G-10286)**

Kop-Coat Inc ....E 800 221-4466
Rockaway **(G-9474)**

Lafarge Road Marking Inc ....C 973 884-0300
Parsippany **(G-7972)**

▲ Master Bond Inc ....E 201 343-8983
Hackensack **(G-3943)**

▲ Milspray LLC ....E 732 886-2223
Lakewood **(G-5135)**

Minwax Group (inc) ....A 201 818-7500
Upper Saddle River **(G-11142)**

◆ Muralo Company Inc ....C 201 437-0770
Bayonne **(G-229)**

Nautical Marine Paint Corp ....E 732 821-3200
North Brunswick **(G-7479)**

Newage Painting Corporation ....G 908 547-4734
Newark **(G-7211)**

▲ Nippon Paint (usa) Inc ....F 201 692-1111
Teaneck **(G-10640)**

Noopys Research Inc ....G 856 358-6001
Newfield **(G-7325)**

North Jersey Specialists Inc ....G 973 927-1616
Flanders **(G-3416)**

Palma Inc ....F 973 429-1490
Whippany **(G-11901)**

Penn Metal Finishing Co Inc ....G 609 387-3400
Burlington **(G-981)**

Performance Industries Inc ....E 609 392-1450
Trenton **(G-10972)**

Philip Mamrak ....G 908 454-6089
Phillipsburg **(G-8567)**

◆ Plastic Specialties & Tech Inc ....C 201 941-2900
Ridgefield **(G-9284)**

PPG Industries Inc ....E 856 273-7870
Mount Laurel **(G-6794)**

Prem-Khichi Enterprises Inc ....F 973 242-0300
East Brunswick **(G-2167)**

◆ Protech Powder Coatings Inc ....D 973 276-1292
Fairfield **(G-3296)**

Rema Corrosion Control ....F 201 256-8400
Northvale **(G-7545)**

Rich Art Color Co Inc ....F 201 767-0009
Northvale **(G-7547)**

Ricks Cleanouts Inc ....E 973 340-7454
Garfield **(G-3763)**

▲ Royce Associates A Ltd Partnr ....D 201 438-5200
East Rutherford **(G-2315)**

RPM Prfrmnce Catings Group Inc ....F 888 788-4323
Long Branch **(G-5605)**

Rust-Oleum Corporation ....E 847 367-7700
Somerset **(G-10068)**

Rust-Oleum Corporation ....E 732 469-8100
Somerset **(G-10069)**

◆ SA Bendheim Ltd ....E 973 471-1733
Wayne **(G-11550)**

Saint-Gobain Prfmce Plas Corp ....D 732 652-0910
Somerset **(G-10070)**

◆ Samax Enterprise Inc ....F 973 350-9400
Newark **(G-7261)**

S I C

Sau-Sea Swimming Pool Products ....F 609 859-8500
Southampton *(G-10372)*

▲ Seagrave Coatings Corp ....E 201 933-1000
Kenilworth *(G-4976)*

◆ Sika Corporation ....B 201 933-8800
Lyndhurst *(G-5678)*

Sika Corporation ....C 201 933-8800
Lyndhurst *(G-5679)*

▲ Standard Coating Corporation ....G 201 945-5058
Ridgefield *(G-9289)*

Steven Industries Inc ....E 201 437-6500
Bayonne *(G-235)*

◆ Stoncor Group Inc ....G 800 257-7953
Maple Shade *(G-5870)*

▲ Superior Printing Ink Co Inc ....C 201 478-5600
Teterboro *(G-10691)*

Synthetic Surfaces Inc ....G 908 233-6803
Scotch Plains *(G-9743)*

▼ Target Coatings Inc ....G 800 752-9922
Fair Lawn *(G-3127)*

Technical Coatings Co ....E 973 927-8600
Flanders *(G-3422)*

Tenax Finishing Products Co ....F 973 589-9000
Newark *(G-7295)*

◆ Tevco Enterprises Inc ....D 908 754-7306
Paterson *(G-8313)*

Thermo Cote Inc ....G 973 464-3575
Rockaway *(G-9503)*

▲ Tq3 north America Inc ....G 973 882-7900
Fairfield *(G-3331)*

▲ Turquoise Chemistry Inc ....F 908 561-0002
Piscataway *(G-8733)*

Uvitec Printing Ink Co Inc ....E 973 778-0737
Lodi *(G-5581)*

Worldwide Safety Systems LLC ....G 888 613-4501
Teaneck *(G-10656)*

2861 Gum & Wood Chemicals

Gingko Tree Inc ....G 973 652-9380
Linden *(G-5353)*

◆ Importers Service Corp ....E 732 248-1946
Edison *(G-2533)*

Sanit Technologies LLC ....F 862 238-7555
Passaic *(G-8105)*

2865 Cyclic-Crudes, Intermediates, Dyes & Org Pigments

American Chemical & Coating Co ....G 908 353-2260
Elizabeth *(G-2711)*

Carib Chemical Co Inc ....F 201 791-6700
Elmwood Park *(G-2814)*

▲ Carib Chemical Co Inc ....F 201 791-6700
Elmwood Park *(G-2815)*

▲ Chem-Is-Try Inc ....G 732 372-7311
Metuchen *(G-6052)*

◆ Chemical Resources Inc ....E 609 520-0000
Princeton *(G-8921)*

◆ Color Techniques Inc ....F 908 412-9292
South Plainfield *(G-10239)*

Coloron Plastics Corporation ....E 908 685-1210
Branchburg *(G-631)*

◆ Dominion Colour Corp USA ....F 973 279-9591
Clifton *(G-1603)*

◆ Elementis Specialties Inc ....C 609 443-2000
East Windsor *(G-2369)*

▲ Epolin Chemical LLC ....G 973 465-9495
Newark *(G-7118)*

Fabricolor Holding Intl LLC ....G 973 742-5800
Paterson *(G-8189)*

Ferro Corporation ....C 856 467-3000
Bridgeport *(G-738)*

Ferro Corporation ....E 732 287-4925
Edison *(G-2511)*

◆ French Color Fragrance Co Inc ....E 201 567-6883
Englewood *(G-2907)*

▲ Greenville Colorants LLC ....F 201 595-0200
New Brunswick *(G-6931)*

◆ Honeyware Inc ....D 201 997-5900
Kearny *(G-4863)*

Magruder Color Company Inc.........C 817 837-3293
Holmdel *(G-4505)*

Manner Textile Processing Inc ....D 973 942-8718
North Haledon *(G-7497)*

◆ Novartis Corporation ....E 212 307-1122
East Hanover *(G-2226)*

▲ Orient Corporation of America ....G 908 298-0990
Cranford *(G-1920)*

Penn Color Inc ....C 201 791-5100
Elmwood Park *(G-2848)*

Polymathes Holdings I LLC ....G 609 945-1690
Princeton *(G-8996)*

Primex Color Compounding ....E 800 282-7933
Garfield *(G-3758)*

▼ Riverdale Color Mfg Inc ....E 732 376-9300
Perth Amboy *(G-8531)*

Royce Associates A Ltd Partnr ....E 973 279-0400
Paterson *(G-8289)*

Shelan Chemical Company Inc ....G 732 796-1003
Monroe Township *(G-6343)*

◆ Solvay Holding Inc ....A 609 860-4000
Princeton *(G-9024)*

Solvay USA Inc ....C 732 297-0100
North Brunswick *(G-7486)*

◆ Solvay USA Inc ....B 609 860-4000
Princeton *(G-9025)*

SPS Alfachem Inc ....G 973 676-5141
Orange *(G-7762)*

◆ Sun Chemical Corporation ....D 973 404-6000
Parsippany *(G-8022)*

Vertellus LLC ....G 973 440-4400
Ledgewood *(G-5285)*

William R Tatz Industries ....G 973 751-0720
Belleville *(G-325)*

2869 Industrial Organic Chemicals, NEC

Acceledev Chemical LLC ....G 732 274-1451
Monmouth Junction *(G-6276)*

Adron Inc ....G 973 334-1600
Boonton *(G-536)*

Advanced Biotech Overseas LLC ....G 973 339-6242
Totowa *(G-10808)*

Agilis Chemicals Inc ....F 973 910-2424
Short Hills *(G-9864)*

◆ Akcros Chemicals Inc ....D 800 500-7890
New Brunswick *(G-6909)*

Akzo Nobel Coatings Inc ....G 732 617-7734
Morganville *(G-6581)*

▲ Alzo International Inc ....G 732 254-1901
Sayreville *(G-9702)*

▲ Amerchol Corporation ....C 732 248-6000
Edison *(G-2452)*

▲ American Beryllia Inc ....G 973 248-8080
Haskell *(G-4194)*

▲ Aromatic Technologies Inc ....D 732 393-7300
Piscataway *(G-8636)*

▲ Aromiens Inc ....G 732 225-8689
Edison *(G-2461)*

Ashland Spcalty Ingredients GP ....C 908 243-3500
Bridgewater *(G-795)*

Ashland Spcalty Ingredients GP ....E 732 353-7708
Parlin *(G-7862)*

ATL ....G 201 825-1400
Ramsey *(G-9140)*

Avantor Performance Mtls LLC ....B 908 859-2151
Phillipsburg *(G-8542)*

Bal-Edge Corporation ....G 973 895-8826
Eatontown *(G-2379)*

▲ Barnet Products LLC ....F 201 346-4620
Englewood Cliffs *(G-2959)*

◆ BASF Americas Corporation ....F 973 245-6000
Florham Park *(G-3488)*

◆ BASF California Inc ....G 973 245-6000
Florham Park *(G-3489)*

BASF Catalysts Holdg China LLC ......G 973 245-6000
Florham Park *(G-3490)*

◆ BASF Corporation ....B 973 245-6000
Florham Park *(G-3491)*

BASF Corporation ....G 908 689-7470
Washington *(G-11440)*

BASF Corporation ....E 848 221-2786
Toms River *(G-10749)*

BASF Corporation ....C 732 205-5086
Iselin *(G-4600)*

BASF Corporation ....C 732 205-2700
Union *(G-11029)*

BASF Corporation ....E 973 426-5429
Budd Lake *(G-919)*

BASF Corporation ....C 973 245-6000
Edison *(G-2465)*

◆ Basfin Corporation ....A 973 245-6000
Florham Park *(G-3493)*

◆ Berje Incorporated ....D 973 748-8980
Carteret *(G-1250)*

Biotech Support Group LLC ....G 732 613-1967
East Brunswick *(G-2130)*

▲ Brown Chemical Co Inc ....E 201 337-0900
Oakland *(G-7617)*

Cambridge Industries Co Inc ....G 973 465-4565
Newark *(G-7081)*

▼ Chem-Fleur Inc ....D 973 589-4266
Newark *(G-7083)*

▲ Chem-Is-Try Inc ....G 732 372-7311
Metuchen *(G-6052)*

Chembiopower Inc ....G 908 209-5595
Warren *(G-11404)*

Chemmark Development Inc.........G 908 561-0923
South Plainfield *(G-10238)*

Chemo Dynamics Inc.........F 732 721-4700
Sayreville *(G-9705)*

Coim USA Inc ....E 856 224-1668
Paulsboro *(G-8331)*

Colibri Scentique Ltd Lblty Co ....G 201 445-5715
Glen Rock *(G-3830)*

Crompton Corp ....G 732 826-6600
Perth Amboy *(G-8516)*

◆ Cvc Specialty Chemicals Inc ....F 856 533-3000
Moorestown *(G-6517)*

D and M Discount Fuels ....G 856 935-0919
Salem *(G-9693)*

◆ Deleet Merchandising Corp ....E 212 962-6565
Newark *(G-7101)*

▲ Drom International Inc ....G 973 316-8400
Towaco *(G-10870)*

Easy Stop Food & Fuel Corp ....G 973 517-0478
Hamburg *(G-4091)*

Elan Food Laboratories Inc.........F 973 344-8014
Newark *(G-7111)*

▲ Elan Inc ....D 973 344-8014
Newark *(G-7112)*

▲ Energy Chem America Inc.........D 201 816-2307
Englewood Cliffs *(G-2969)*

Engineered Silicone Pdts LLC ....G 973 300-5120
Newton *(G-7342)*

Epic Holding Inc ....E 732 249-6867
Morristown *(G-6663)*

Evonik Corporation.........D 732 981-5000
Piscataway *(G-8662)*

◆ Evonik Corporation ....B 973 929-8000
Parsippany *(G-7938)*

▲ Fancyheat Corporation ....F 973 589-1450
Somerset *(G-9993)*

▲ Farbest-Tallman Foods Corp ....D 714 897-7199
Park Ridge *(G-7849)*

▲ Firefreeze Worldwide Inc ....E 973 627-0722
Rockaway *(G-9460)*

▲ Flavor & Fragrance Spc Inc ....D 201 828-9400
Mahwah *(G-5738)*

Flavor Development Corp ....F 201 784-8188
Closter *(G-1755)*

FMC Corporation.........C 609 963-6200
Ewing *(G-3031)*

Fossil Fuel ....G 973 366-9111
Wharton *(G-11858)*

Fuel One Inc ....G 732 726-9500
Avenel *(G-128)*

Fuel Stop Inc ....G 201 697-3319
Union *(G-11057)*

G & R Fuel Corp ....G 973 732-0530
Newark *(G-7128)*

◆ G Holdings LLC ....F 973 628-3000
Parsippany *(G-7953)*

◆ G-I Holdings Inc ....G 973 628-3000
Wayne *(G-11507)*

◆ Gentek Inc ....C 973 515-0900
Parsippany *(G-7956)*

Gingko Tree Inc.........G 973 652-9380
Linden *(G-5353)*

Givaudan Flavors Corporation ....C 973 463-8192
Cranbury *(G-1835)*

Givaudan Flavors Corporation ....C 973 386-9800
East Hanover *(G-2212)*

Givaudan Fragrances Corp ....C 973 576-9500
East Hanover *(G-2214)*

Givaudan Fragrances Corp ....C 973 560-1939
East Hanover *(G-2215)*

Givaudan Fragrances Corp ....C 973 448-6500
Budd Lake *(G-924)*

Glamorous Glo ....G 732 361-3235
Eatontown *(G-2393)*

H & S Fuel Inc ....G 908 769-1362
Plainfield *(G-8767)*

Honig Chemical & Proc Corp ....E 973 344-0881
Newark *(G-7152)*

Hopatcong Fuel On You LLC ....G 973 770-0854
Hopatcong *(G-4521)*

Interntnal Flvors Frgrnces Inc.........G 732 264-4500
Union Beach *(G-11101)*

Interntnal Flvors Frgrnces Inc.........C 732 264-4500
Union Beach *(G-11102)*

Interntnal Flvors Frgrnces Inc ....C 732 264-4500
Hazlet (G-4262)
◆ Interntonal Specialty Pdts Inc ....A 859 815-3333
Wayne (G-11522)
Isp Chemco LLC ....G 973 628-4000
Wayne (G-11523)
Isp Chemicals LLC ....E 973 635-1551
Chatham (G-1323)
◆ Isp Global Technologies Inc ....G 973 628-4000
Wayne (G-11524)
Isp Global Technologies LLC ....G 973 628-4000
Wayne (G-11525)
Jacquar Fuel ....G 732 441-0700
Manalapan (G-5815)
Jai Ganesh Fuel LLC ....G 201 246-8995
Kearny (G-4871)
Jarchem Industries Inc ....F 973 344-0600
Newark (G-7166)
Jt Fuels LLC ....G 973 527-4470
Ledgewood (G-5277)
▲ Just In Time Chemical Sales & ....G 908 862-7726
Linden (G-5366)
Karebay Biochem Inc ....G 732 823-1545
Monmouth Junction (G-6295)
▲ Kenrich Petrochemicals Inc ....E 201 823-9000
Bayonne (G-226)
Kp Fuel Corporation ....G 973 350-1202
Newark (G-7174)
Lanxess Solutions US Inc ....G 732 826-1018
Perth Amboy (G-8524)
Lanxess Solutions US Inc ....C 973 887-7411
East Hanover (G-2221)
Lanxess Solutions US Inc ....C 732 738-1000
Fords (G-3533)
Ligno Tech USA Inc ....G 908 429-6660
Bridgewater (G-843)
◆ Lonza Inc ....D 201 316-9200
Morristown (G-6681)
Lyondell Chemical Company ....G 973 578-2200
Newark (G-7192)
Lyondell Chemical Company ....F 732 985-6262
Edison (G-2556)
Main Fuel LLC ....G 201 941-2707
Cliffside Park (G-1541)
▲ Main Street Auto & Fuel LLC ....G 732 238-0044
Sayreville (G-9719)
Modern Fuel Inc ....G 973 471-1501
Clifton (G-1670)
Montclair Fuel LLC ....G 973 744-4300
Montclair (G-6376)
◆ Nan Ya Plastics Corp America ....F 973 992-1775
Livingston (G-5529)
National Fuel LLC ....G 973 227-4549
Pine Brook (G-8610)
▼ National Strch Chem Holdg Corp .....A 908 685-5000
Bridgewater (G-854)
NJ Fuel Haulers Inc..............................G 732 740-3681
Old Bridge (G-7721)
▲ Northeast Chemicals Inc ....E 508 634-6900
East Brunswick (G-2160)
Northeast Chemicals Inc ....E 732 227-0100
East Brunswick (G-2161)
Northeast Chemicals Inc ....F 732 673-6966
East Brunswick (G-2162)
▲ Pharmetic Mfg Company LLC ....G 732 254-1901
Sayreville (G-9721)
▲ Phoenix Chemical Inc ....F 908 707-0232
Branchburg (G-667)
Pilot Chemical Company Ohio ....F 732 634-6613
Avenel (G-140)
Prospect Transportation Inc ....D 201 933-9999
Carlstadt (G-1209)
▲ Protameen Chemicals Inc ....E 973 256-4374
Totowa (G-10847)
Quality Sweets ....G 732 283-3799
Iselin (G-4624)
R & R Fuel Inc ....G 201 223-0786
Union City (G-11126)
Route 22 Fuel LLC ....G 908 526-5270
Bridgewater (G-877)
Royal Ingredients LLC ....G 856 241-2004
Swedesboro (G-10607)
▲ Royale Pigments & Chem Inc ....E 201 845-4666
Paramus (G-7830)
▲ Royce Associates A Ltd Partnr ....D 201 438-5200
East Rutherford (G-2315)
Royce International Corp ....G 201 438-5200
East Rutherford (G-2316)
S and D Fuel LLC ....G 908 248-8188
Union (G-11087)

Sanit Technologies LLC ....F 862 238-7555
Passaic (G-8105)
Scher Chemicals Inc ....A 973 471-1300
Clifton (G-1711)
SE Tylos USA ....G 973 837-8001
Totowa (G-10851)
Sgw Fuel Delivery ....G 609 209-8773
Trenton (G-10991)
Shani Auto Fuel Corp ....G 856 241-9767
Woolwich Township (G-12098)
Shiva Fuel Inc ....G 732 826-3228
Perth Amboy (G-8532)
Sks Fuel Inc ....G 973 200-0796
Woodland Park (G-12091)
▲ Small Molecules Inc ....G 201 918-4664
Hoboken (G-4482)
◆ Solvay Holding Inc ....A 609 860-4000
Princeton (G-9024)
◆ Solvay USA Inc ....B 609 860-4000
Princeton (G-9025)
Solvay USA Inc ....C 732 297-0100
North Brunswick (G-7486)
▼ Sonneborn LLC ....F 201 760-2940
Parsippany (G-8018)
Sonneborn Holding LLC ....G 201 760-2940
Parsippany (G-8019)
Sonneborn US Holdings LLC ....G 201 760-2940
Parsippany (G-8020)
◆ Spectrum Laboratory Pdts Inc ....C 732 214-1300
New Brunswick (G-6971)
Spectrum Laboratory Pdts Inc ....E 732 214-1300
New Brunswick (G-6972)
Stepan Company ....D 609 298-1222
Bordentown (G-595)
Suman Realty LLC ....G 908 350-8039
Stirling (G-10497)
▲ Surface Technology Inc ....F 609 259-0099
Ewing (G-3068)
▲ Sweet Solutions Inc ....G 732 512-0777
Edison (G-2628)
◆ Symrise Inc ....B 201 288-3200
Teterboro (G-10692)
Symrise Inc ....G 201 288-3200
Saddle Brook (G-9682)
Symrise Inc ....D 908 429-6824
Branchburg (G-686)
Talent Investment LLC ....G 732 931-0088
Hazlet (G-4271)
Techenzyme Inc ....G 732 632-8600
Iselin (G-4632)
Technical Oil Products Co Inc ....G 973 940-8920
Newton (G-7362)
◆ Troy Corporation ....D 973 443-4200
Florham Park (G-3524)
Ultra Chemical Inc ....F 732 224-0200
Red Bank (G-9247)
▲ Umicore Precious Metals NJ LLC .....E 908 222-5006
South Plainfield (G-10333)
United Fuel Distributors LLC ....G 908 906-9053
South Plainfield (G-10335)
▲ Unitex International Inc ....E 856 786-5000
Cinnaminson (G-1494)
Urso Fuel Corp ....G 973 325-3324
West Orange (G-11781)
Veolia Es ....E 732 469-5100
Middlesex (G-6158)
Viva Chemical Corporation ....G 201 461-5281
Fort Lee (G-3594)
Zoomessence Inc ....G 732 416-6638
Sayreville (G-9727)

2873 Nitrogenous Fertilizers

Agrium Advanced Tech US Inc ....F 732 296-8448
North Brunswick (G-7451)
Growmark Fs LLC ....F 609 267-7054
Eastampton (G-2372)
▼ Miracle Verde Group LLC ....G 201 399-2222
Kearny (G-4885)
▼ Plant Food Company Inc ....E 609 448-0935
Cranbury (G-1872)
▼ Polyorganic Technoligies Corp ....G 609 288-8233
East Brunswick (G-2166)
▼ Reed & Perrine Inc ....E 732 446-6363
Tennent (G-10668)
Reed & Perrine Sales Inc ....E 732 446-6363
Tennent (G-10669)
Scotts Company LLC ....F 201 246-0180
North Arlington (G-7378)
South Jersey Farmers Exchange ....G 856 769-0062
Woodstown (G-12096)

2874 Phosphatic Fertilizers

Growmark Fs LLC ....F 609 267-7054
Eastampton (G-2372)
Innophos Inc ....G 973 587-8735
Cranbury (G-1840)
Innophos Holdings Inc ....D 609 495-2495
Cranbury (G-1842)
Innophos Investments II Inc ....G 609 495-2495
Cranbury (G-1844)
Innophos Invstmnts Hldings Inc ....G 609 495-2495
Cranbury (G-1845)
◆ Missry Associates Inc ....C 732 752-7500
Edison (G-2568)

2875 Fertilizers, Mixing Only

Growmark Fs LLC ....F 609 267-7054
Eastampton (G-2372)
L & S Contracting Inc ....G 609 397-1281
Hopewell (G-4527)
▼ Reed & Perrine Inc ....E 732 446-6363
Tennent (G-10668)

2879 Pesticides & Agricultural Chemicals, NEC

Agilis Chemicals Inc ....F 973 910-2424
Short Hills (G-9864)
◆ AP&g Co Inc ....D 718 492-3648
Bayonne (G-202)
◆ Aquatrols Corp of America ....E 856 537-6003
West Deptford (G-11692)
▲ Arcadia Consmr Healthcare Inc ....F 800 824-4894
Bridgewater (G-791)
Avantor Performance Mtls LLC ....B 908 859-2151
Phillipsburg (G-8542)
◆ BASF Corporation ....B 973 245-6000
Florham Park (G-3491)
BASF Plant Science LP ....G 973 245-3238
Florham Park (G-3492)
◆ Basfin Corporation ....A 973 245-6000
Florham Park (G-3493)
▲ Big Bucks Enterprises Inc ....E 908 320-7009
Washington (G-11442)
▲ Chem-Is-Try Inc ....G 732 372-7311
Metuchen (G-6052)
Deer Out Animal Repellant LLC ....G 908 769-4242
South Plainfield (G-10246)
◆ Flottec LLC ....G 973 588-4717
Boonton (G-554)
◆ Glysortia LLC ....G 715 426-5358
Plainsboro (G-8789)
Healios Inc ....G 908 731-5061
Flemington (G-3447)
◆ Novartis Corporation ....E 212 307-1122
East Hanover (G-2226)
▲ Pic Corporation ....E 908 862-7977
Linden (G-5409)
Residex LLC ....G 856 232-0880
Blackwood (G-479)
Si Packaging LLC ....F 973 869-9920
Rutherford (G-9632)

2891 Adhesives & Sealants

▲ A D M Tronics Unlimited Inc ....E 201 767-6040
Northvale (G-7513)
Alan Chemical Corporation Inc ....G 973 628-7777
Wayne (G-11466)
▲ Alva-Tech Inc ....F 609 747-1133
Burlington Township (G-995)
Amb Enterprises LLC ....E 973 225-1070
Paterson (G-8135)
Amerasia Intl Tech Inc ....E 609 799-9388
Princeton Junction (G-9050)
▲ American Casein Company ....E 609 387-2988
Burlington (G-947)
American Chemical & Coating Co ....G 908 353-2260
Elizabeth (G-2711)
◆ Andek Corporation ....F 856 866-7600
Moorestown (G-6505)
▲ Annitti Enterprises Inc ....E 973 345-1725
Paterson (G-8140)
Aos Thermal Compounds LLC ....F 732 389-5514
Eatontown (G-2378)
API Americas Inc ....D 732 382-6800
Rahway (G-9077)
▲ Artistic Bias Products Co Inc ....E 732 382-4141
Rahway (G-9078)
▲ Assem - Pak Inc ....C 856 692-3355
Vineland (G-11187)

▼ Baker/Titan Adhesives ....E 973 225-1070
Paterson *(G-8145)*

Bostik Inc ....D 856 848-8669
Paulsboro *(G-8330)*

Clark Stek-O Corp ....D 201 437-0770
Bayonne *(G-209)*

◆ Clifton Adhesive Inc ....E 973 694-0845
Wayne *(G-11488)*

◆ Coim USA Inc ....D 856 224-8560
West Deptford *(G-11700)*

Compounders Inc ....G 732 938-5007
Farmingdale *(G-3381)*

Covalnce Spcalty Adhesives LLC .....A 732 356-2870
Middlesex *(G-6108)*

CR Laurence Co Inc ....F 856 727-1022
Moorestown *(G-6516)*

Custom Building Products Inc ......D 856 467-9226
Logan Township *(G-5586)*

Dritac Flooring Products LLC ......F 973 614-9000
Clifton *(G-1604)*

◆ Dritac Flooring Products LLC .....D 973 614-9000
Clifton *(G-1605)*

Elektromek Inc ....F 973 614-9000
Clifton *(G-1615)*

Essentra Plastics LLC ....G 518 437-5138
Edison *(G-2507)*

Flexcraft Industries Inc ....G 973 589-3403
Newark *(G-7125)*

◆ Frimpeks Inc ....F 201 266-0116
Fairfield *(G-3208)*

▲ Gluefast Company Inc ....F 732 918-4600
Neptune *(G-6881)*

HB Fuller Company ....E 732 287-8330
Edison *(G-2528)*

Henkel US Operations Corp ....E 908 685-7000
Bridgewater *(G-830)*

Hercules LLC ....G 732 777-4697
Edison *(G-2530)*

▲ Hudson Industries Corporation ...G 973 402-0100
Fairfield *(G-3231)*

Kop-Coat Inc ....E 800 221-4466
Rockaway *(G-9474)*

La Favorite Industries Inc ....F 973 279-1266
Paterson *(G-8236)*

Mapei Corporation ....F 732 254-4830
South River *(G-10353)*

Mapei Corporation ....E 732 254-4830
South River *(G-10352)*

▲ Master Bond Inc ....E 201 343-8983
Hackensack *(G-3943)*

▲ May National Associates NJ Inc ..D 973 473-3330
Lakewood *(G-5132)*

Mc Ginley Packaging Methods ......G 201 493-9330
Midland Park *(G-6180)*

Mercury Adhesives Inc ....G 973 472-3307
Passaic *(G-8087)*

Mon-Eco Industries Inc ....F 732 257-7942
East Brunswick *(G-2157)*

National Casein New Jersey Inc ....E 856 829-1880
Cinnaminson *(G-1476)*

▼ National Strch Chem Holdg Corp ..A 908 685-5000
Bridgewater *(G-854)*

▲ Natl Adhesies Div of Henke ....G 908 685-7000
Bridgewater *(G-855)*

Norland Products Inc ....E 609 395-1966
Cranbury *(G-1865)*

Nu Grafix Inc ....E 201 413-1776
Jersey City *(G-4775)*

Palmetto Adhesives Company ......F 856 451-0400
Bridgeton *(G-767)*

▲ Permabond LLC ....G 610 323-5003
Somerset *(G-10052)*

▲ Petronio Shoe Products Corp .....F 973 751-7579
Belleville *(G-307)*

◆ Plcs LLC ....E 856 722-1333
Mount Laurel *(G-6790)*

▼ Princeton Keynes Group Inc ....F 609 951-2239
Princeton *(G-9000)*

Princeton Keynes Group Inc ....F 609 208-1777
Newark *(G-7234)*

Royal Adhesives & Sealants LLC ....E 973 694-0845
Wayne *(G-11549)*

Rust-Oleum Corporation ....F 732 652-2378
Newark *(G-7256)*

Saint-Gobain Prfmce Plas Corp .....D 732 652-0910
Somerset *(G-10070)*

Sap-Seal Products Inc ....G 201 385-5553
Bergenfield *(G-384)*

Signature Marketing & Mfg ....G 973 427-3700
Hawthorne *(G-4244)*

◆ Sika Corporation ....B 201 933-8800
Lyndhurst *(G-5678)*

Sika Corporation ....C 201 933-8800
Lyndhurst *(G-5679)*

▼ Solar Compounds Corporation .....E 908 862-2813
Linden *(G-5425)*

▲ Spiral Binding LLC ....C 973 256-0666
Totowa *(G-10853)*

Steven Industries Inc ....E 201 437-6500
Bayonne *(G-235)*

Synthetic Surfaces Inc ....G 908 233-6803
Scotch Plains *(G-9743)*

▲ Universal Tape Supply Corp ....F 609 653-3191
Somers Point *(G-9940)*

Zymet Inc ....F 973 428-5245
East Hanover *(G-2250)*

2892 Explosives

Cartridge Actuated Devices ....E 973 575-8760
Fairfield *(G-3166)*

Cartridge Actuated Devices ....E 973 347-2281
Byram Township *(G-1017)*

▼ Mjg Technologies Incorporated ...G 856 228-6118
Blackwood *(G-475)*

2893 Printing Ink

AGFA Corporation ....G 908 231-5000
Somerville *(G-10102)*

American Coding and Mkg Ink Co ....G 908 756-0373
Plainfield *(G-8757)*

Athletes Alley ....F 732 842-1127
Shrewsbury *(G-9882)*

Central Ink Corporation ....G 856 467-5562
Swedesboro *(G-10576)*

Champion Ink Co Inc ....G 201 868-4100
North Bergen *(G-7394)*

Chroma Trading Usa Inc ....G 732 956-4431
Morganville *(G-6585)*

Custom Chemicals Corp ....A 201 791-5100
Elmwood Park *(G-2820)*

Flint Group US LLC ....G 732 329-4627
Dayton *(G-1962)*

Gotham Ink of New England Inc .....G 201 478-5600
Teterboro *(G-10679)*

Ideon LLC ....G 908 431-3126
Hillsborough *(G-4327)*

Kohl & Madden Prtg Ink Corp ....E 201 935-8666
Carlstadt *(G-1177)*

Lodor Offset Corporation ....F 201 935-7100
Carlstadt *(G-1182)*

▲ Pan Technology Inc ....E 201 438-7878
Carlstadt *(G-1195)*

Prismacolor Corp ....G 973 887-6040
Parsippany *(G-8002)*

▲ Ranger Industries Inc ....E 732 389-3535
Tinton Falls *(G-10725)*

▲ Selective Coatings & Inks ....F 732 938-7677
Wall Township *(G-11368)*

Selective Coatings & Inks ....G 732 493-0707
Ocean *(G-7682)*

Sun Chemical Corporation ....C 201 933-4500
Carlstadt *(G-1222)*

◆ Sun Chemical Corporation ....D 973 404-6000
Parsippany *(G-8022)*

Sun Chemical Corporation ....E 201 438-4831
East Rutherford *(G-2322)*

Sun Chemical Corporation ....F 201 935-8666
Carlstadt *(G-1223)*

Superior Printing Ink Co Inc ....G 973 242-5868
Newark *(G-7291)*

▲ Superior Printing Ink Co Inc .....C 201 478-5600
Teterboro *(G-10691)*

Supreme Ink Corp ....F 973 344-2922
Newark *(G-7292)*

Total Ink Solutions LLC ....F 201 487-9600
Hackensack *(G-3983)*

Toyo Ink America LLC ....F 201 804-0620
Carlstadt *(G-1230)*

Triangle Ink Co Inc ....F 201 935-2777
Wallington *(G-11390)*

Uvitec Printing Ink Co Inc ....E 973 778-0737
Lodi *(G-5581)*

Vivitone Inc ....F 973 427-8114
Hawthorne *(G-4250)*

2895 Carbon Black

◆ Total American Services Inc ......F 206 626-3500
Jersey City *(G-4822)*

2899 Chemical Preparations, NEC

▲ A D M Tronics Unlimited Inc ......E 201 767-6040
Northvale *(G-7513)*

A J P Scientific Inc ....G 973 472-7200
Clifton *(G-1551)*

Acceledev Chemical LLC ....G 862 239-1524
Wayne *(G-11465)*

Adam Gates & Company LLC ....F 908 829-3386
Hillsborough *(G-4300)*

▲ Advanced Polymer Inc ....F 201 964-3000
Carlstadt *(G-1118)*

Advansix Inc ....B 973 526-1800
Parsippany *(G-7875)*

Airdye Solutions LLC ....E 540 433-9101
Cedar Grove *(G-1266)*

◆ Alden - Leeds Inc ....D 973 589-3544
Kearny *(G-4842)*

Alpha Assembly Solutions Inc ......E 908 561-5170
South Plainfield *(G-10214)*

Alpha Assembly Solutions Inc ......E 908 791-3000
Somerset *(G-9948)*

◆ Amerchol Corporation ....C 732 248-6000
Edison *(G-2452)*

◆ American Flux & Metal LLC ....E 609 561-7500
Hammonton *(G-4125)*

▲ American Water - Pridesa LLC .....G 856 435-7711
Camden *(G-1039)*

▲ Amfine Chemical Corporation .....F 201 818-0159
Hasbrouck Heights *(G-4181)*

Anichem LLC ....G 732 821-6500
North Brunswick *(G-7452)*

Aphelion Orbitals Inc ....G 321 289-0872
Union City *(G-11107)*

Arol Chemical Products Co ....G 973 344-1510
Newark *(G-7053)*

Ashland LLC ....G 908 243-3500
Bridgewater *(G-794)*

Ashland Spcalty Ingredients GP ....E 732 353-7708
Parlin *(G-7862)*

◆ Atlas Refinery Inc ....E 973 589-2002
Newark *(G-7056)*

Avantor Performance Mtls LLC ......B 908 859-2151
Phillipsburg *(G-8542)*

◆ BASF Corporation ....B 973 245-6000
Florham Park *(G-3491)*

◆ Basfin Corporation ....A 973 245-6000
Florham Park *(G-3493)*

Beacon C M P Corp ....G 908 851-9393
Kenilworth *(G-4927)*

Bergen International LLC ....G 201 299-4499
East Rutherford *(G-2276)*

Bostik Inc ....D 856 848-8669
Paulsboro *(G-8330)*

BP Corporation North Amer Inc .....E 908 474-5000
Linden *(G-5327)*

◆ Brenntag Specialties Inc ....D 908 561-6100
South Plainfield *(G-10228)*

▲ C & S Specialty Inc ....G 201 750-7740
Norwood *(G-7559)*

C S L Water Treatment Inc ....F 908 647-1400
Warren *(G-11401)*

Caloric Color Co Inc ....F 973 471-4748
Garfield *(G-3734)*

Cantol Inc ....E 609 846-7912
Wildwood *(G-11942)*

◆ CC Packaging LLC ....G 732 213-9008
Bayville *(G-242)*

▲ Chem-Is-Try Inc ....G 732 372-7311
Metuchen *(G-6052)*

▲ Chemetall US Inc ....D 908 464-6900
New Providence *(G-6997)*

Chemtreat Inc ....G 609 654-9522
Medford *(G-6021)*

Conversion Technology Co Inc ......F 732 752-5660
South Plainfield *(G-10242)*

◆ Croda Inc ....D 732 417-0800
Edison *(G-2486)*

Croda Investments Inc ....G 732 417-0800
Edison *(G-2487)*

Custom Blends Inc ....G 215 934-7080
Ewing *(G-3025)* .

Cytec Industries Inc ....F 973 357-3100
Princeton *(G-8927)*

◆ Delta Procurement Inc ....G 201 623-9353
Carlstadt *(G-1149)*

▲ Elan Inc ....D 973 344-8014
Newark *(G-7112)*

◆ Elementis Global LLC ....C 609 443-2000
East Windsor *(G-2368)*

◆ Elementis Specialties Inc ....C 609 443-2000
   East Windsor *(G-2369)*

▲ Elixens America Inc ....G 732 388-3555
   Rahway *(G-9091)*

EMD Performance Materials Corp ....B 908 429-3500
   Branchburg *(G-638)*

Euclid Chemical Company ....F 732 390-9770
   East Brunswick *(G-2145)*

▲ Evans Chemetics LP ....G 201 992-3100
   Teaneck *(G-10631)*

▲ Faust Thermographic Supply ......F 908 474-0555
   Linden *(G-5347)*

Ferro Corporation ....C 856 467-3000
   Bridgeport *(G-738)*

Firefighter One Ltd Lblty Co ....G 973 940-3061
   Sparta *(G-10387)*

Fisher Scientific Company LLC ....B 201 796-7100
   Fair Lawn *(G-3102)*

◆ Flavors of Origin Inc ....E 732 499-9700
   Avenel *(G-127)*

▲ Fluorotherm Polymers Inc ....G 973 575-0760
   Parsippany *(G-7948)*

Fuel Management Services Inc ....G 732 929-1964
   Toms River *(G-10760)*

Full Circle Mfg Group ....F 908 353-8933
   Elizabeth *(G-2740)*

Gamka Sales Co Inc ....E 732 248-1400
   Edison *(G-2518)*

Garratt-Callahan Company ....G 732 287-2200
   Edison *(G-2520)*

Global Seven Inc ....E 973 209-7474
   Rockaway *(G-9464)*

▲ Grignard Company LLC ....F 732 340-1111
   Rahway *(G-9098)*

▼ Gulbrandsen Technologies Inc .....E 908 735-5458
   Clinton *(G-1746)*

◆ Gulco Inc ....E 908 238-2030
   Phillipsburg *(G-8554)*

Health Pharma USA LLC ....F 732 540-8421
   Rahway *(G-9101)*

◆ Honeyware Inc ....D 201 997-5900
   Kearny *(G-4863)*

Houghton Chemical Corporation .....E 201 460-8071
   Carlstadt *(G-1166)*

▲ Hudson Industries Corporation ....G 973 402-0100
   Fairfield *(G-3231)*

▲ Hychem Corporation ....G 732 280-8803
   Belmar *(G-350)*

Hydrocrbon Tech Innovation LLC ....E 609 394-3102
   Lawrenceville *(G-5232)*

▲ Industrial Summit Tech Corp ....E 732 238-2211
   Parlin *(G-7865)*

Industrial Water Tech Inc ....G 732 888-1233
   Hazlet *(G-4261)*

◆ Infineum USA LP ....B 800 441-1074
   Linden *(G-5359)*

Insul-Stop Inc ....G 732 706-1978
   Marlboro *(G-5901)*

Interbahm International Inc ....E 732 499-9700
   Avenel *(G-131)*

International Vitamin Corp ....G 973 416-2000
   Irvington *(G-4576)*

◆ Interntonal Specialty Pdts Inc .....A 859 815-3333
   Wayne *(G-11522)*

Jch Partners & Co LLC ....F 732 664-6440
   Howell *(G-4542)*

Jenisse Leisure Products Inc ....F 973 331-1177
   Towaco *(G-10873)*

Krohn Technical Products Inc ....F 201 933-9696
   Carlstadt *(G-1179)*

Kronos Worldwide Inc ....E 609 860-6200
   Cranbury *(G-1852)*

Lanxess Solutions US Inc ....C 973 235-1800
   Nutley *(G-7589)*

◆ Lanxess Sybron Chemicals Inc ....C 609 893-1100
   Birmingham *(G-457)*

Lodor Offset Corporation ....E 201 935-7100
   Carlstadt *(G-1182)*

◆ Lonza Inc ....D 201 316-9200
   Morristown *(G-6681)*

Lubrizol Advanced Mtls Inc ....E 856 299-3764
   Pedricktown *(G-8351)*

Lubrizol Corporation ....G 732 981-0149
   Piscataway *(G-8684)*

Lubrizol Global Management ....F 973 471-1300
   Clifton *(G-1661)*

Mapei Corporation ....E 732 254-4830
   South River *(G-10352)*

▲ Mel Chemicals Inc ....C 908 782-5800
   Flemington *(G-3455)*

Morgan Advanced Ceramics Inc ....E 973 808-1621
   Fairfield *(G-3273)*

▲ Mri International ....G 973 383-3645
   Newton *(G-7350)*

▼ No Fire Technologies Inc ....G 201 818-1616
   South Hackensack *(G-10176)*

Norland Products Inc ....E 609 395-1966
   Cranbury *(G-1865)*

Nouryon Surface Chemistry ....D 732 985-6262
   Edison *(G-2579)*

▲ Nova Distributors LLC ....G 908 222-1010
   Edison *(G-2580)*

Nutech Corp ....G 908 707-2097
   Franklin Lakes *(G-3629)*

Olon USA Inc ....F 973 577-6038
   Florham Park *(G-3518)*

▼ Omg Electronic Chemicals Inc ......C 908 222-5800
   South Plainfield *(G-10311)*

◆ Pariser Industries Inc ....E 973 569-9090
   Paterson *(G-8277)*

▼ Plant Food Company Inc ....E 609 448-0935
   Cranbury *(G-1872)*

Polymer Additives Inc ....D 856 467-8220
   Swedesboro *(G-10602)*

Polymer Additives Inc ....F 856 467-8247
   Bridgeport *(G-743)*

Por-15 Inc ....E 973 887-1999
   Whippany *(G-11905)*

Prestone Products Corporation ....E 732 577-7800
   Freehold *(G-3693)*

Prestone Products Corporation ....E 732 431-8200
   Freehold *(G-3692)*

Procedyne Corp ....E 732 249-8347
   New Brunswick *(G-6962)*

Rclc Inc ....F 732 877-1788
   Woodbridge *(G-12020)*

Robert Nichols Contracting ....F 973 902-2632
   Ringwood *(G-9352)*

◆ Rockwood Specialties Group Inc ....F 609 514-0300
   Princeton *(G-9018)*

▲ Royce Associates A Ltd Partnr ....D 201 438-5200
   East Rutherford *(G-2315)*

Sage Chemical Inc ....G 201 489-5172
   Hackensack *(G-3970)*

Saltopia Infused Sea Salt LLC ....F 908 850-1926
   Hackettstown *(G-4035)*

Seaboard Industries ....F 732 901-5700
   Lakewood *(G-5161)*

Sentry Water Management ....E 973 616-9000
   Riverdale *(G-9383)*

Serene House USA Inc ....G 609 980-1214
   Cherry Hill *(G-1414)*

◆ Shamrock Technologies Inc ....D 973 242-2999
   Newark *(G-7268)*

Sika Corporation ....E 201 933-8800
   Lyndhurst *(G-5679)*

◆ Sika Corporation ....B 201 933-8800
   Lyndhurst *(G-5678)*

◆ SKW Quab Chemicals Inc ....F 201 556-0300
   Saddle Brook *(G-9681)*

Solenis LLC ....E 201 767-7400
   Norwood *(G-7574)*

◆ Solvay USA Inc ....B 609 860-4000
   Princeton *(G-9025)*

◆ Spectrum Laboratory Pdts Inc ......C 732 214-1300
   New Brunswick *(G-6971)*

Spectrum Laboratory Pdts Inc ....E 732 214-1300
   New Brunswick *(G-6972)*

▲ Spex Certiprep Inc ....D 732 549-7144
   Metuchen *(G-6069)*

Stepan Company ....D 201 845-3030
   Maywood *(G-6016)*

◆ Stonhard Manufacturing Co Inc ....E 856 779-7500
   Maple Shade *(G-5871)*

◆ Stuart Steel Protection Corp ....G 732 469-5544
   Somerset *(G-10075)*

Sun Chemical Corporation ....E 201 438-4831
   East Rutherford *(G-2322)*

Superior Printing Ink Co Inc ....G 973 242-5868
   Newark *(G-7291)*

Suven Life Sciences Ltd ....F 732 274-0037
   Monmouth Junction *(G-6314)*

Sylvan Chemical Corporation ....E 201 934-4224
   Fair Lawn *(G-3124)*

▲ Torpac Inc ....E 973 244-1125
   Fairfield *(G-3330)*

▼ Turning Star Inc ....G 201 881-7077
   Leonia *(G-5294)*

Ungerer & Company ....B 973 628-0600
   Lincoln Park *(G-5309)*

▼ United Energy Corp ....G 732 994-5225
   Howell *(G-4552)*

W R Grace & Co-Conn ....E 732 868-6914
   Somerset *(G-10098)*

◆ Wasak Inc ....G 973 605-8122
   Morristown *(G-6709)*

Water Dynamics Incorporated ....G 973 428-8330
   Whippany *(G-11912)*

▼ William Kenyon & Sons Inc ....E 732 985-8980
   Piscataway *(G-8738)*

▲ Wilpak Industries Inc ....G 201 997-7600
   Kearny *(G-4907)*

▲ Wilshire Technologies Inc ....G 609 683-1117
   Princeton *(G-9043)*

Worldwide Safety Systems LLC ....G 888 613-4501
   Teaneck *(G-10656)*

Zoomessence Inc ....G 732 416-6638
   Sayreville *(G-9727)*

29 PETROLEUM REFINING AND RELATED INDUSTRIES

2911 Petroleum Refining

Ashland LLC ....G 908 243-3500
   Bridgewater *(G-794)*

Ashland LLC ....D 732 353-7718
   Parlin *(G-7861)*

BASF Plant Science LP ....G 973 245-3238
   Florham Park *(G-3492)*

Bertone Aromatics ....G 201 444-9821
   Waldwick *(G-11297)*

BP Corporation North Amer Inc ....G 973 633-2200
   Wayne *(G-11483)*

BP Corporation North Amer Inc ....E 908 474-5000
   Linden *(G-5327)*

▼ Bwi Chemicals ....G 732 689-0913
   Monmouth Junction *(G-6280)*

Columbia Fuel Services Inc ....F 732 751-0044
   Wall Township *(G-11331)*

Delaware Pipeline Company LLC ....G 973 455-7500
   Parsippany *(G-7913)*

Fuel Bio Holdings Ltd Lblty Co ....G 908 344-6875
   Elizabeth *(G-2739)*

Fuel Ox LLC ....F 908 747-4375
   Glen Gardner *(G-3822)*

Intertek USA Inc ....E 732 969-5200
   Carteret *(G-1257)*

Magnalube Inc ....G 718 729-1000
   Linden *(G-5379)*

McAllister Service Company ....E 856 665-4545
   Pennsauken *(G-8453)*

Motiva Enterprises LLC ....D 732 855-3266
   Sewaren *(G-9832)*

▲ Paulsboro Refining Company LLC ...A 973 455-7500
   Paulsboro *(G-8338)*

◆ Pbf Energy Company LLC ....B 973 455-7500
   Parsippany *(G-7984)*

◆ Pbf Energy Inc ....A 973 455-7500
   Parsippany *(G-7985)*

◆ Pbf Holding Company LLC ....B 973 455-7500
   Parsippany *(G-7986)*

Pennzoil-Quaker State Company ....G 856 423-1388
   Paulsboro *(G-8339)*

Phillips 66 Company ....G 908 296-0709
   Linden *(G-5407)*

Purely Organic SA LLC ....G 201 942-0400
   Jersey City *(G-4792)*

Speedway LLC ....G 732 750-7800
   Port Reading *(G-8895)*

Starfuels Inc ....G 201 685-0400
   Englewood *(G-2944)*

T & M Terminal Company ....G 419 902-2810
   Parsippany *(G-8024)*

Tilcon New York Inc ....G 800 789-7625
   Parsippany *(G-8029)*

◆ Total American Services Inc ....F 206 626-3500
   Jersey City *(G-4822)*

▼ United Energy Corp ....G 732 994-5225
   Howell *(G-4552)*

Valero Ref Company-New Jersey ....A 856 224-6000
   Paulsboro *(G-8341)*

▼ Ziegler Chem & Mineral Corp ....F 732 752-4111
   Piscataway *(G-8740)*

2951 Paving Mixtures & Blocks

A E Stone Inc ....E 609 641-2781
   Egg Harbor Township *(G-2673)*

All Surface Asphalt Paving ....G 732 295-3800
   Point Pleasant Boro *(G-8835)*

Arawak Paving Co Inc ....E 609 561-4100
Hammonton *(G-4128)*
Barrett Asphalt Inc ....E 609 561-4100
Hammonton *(G-4129)*
Barrett Industries Corporation ....E 973 533-1001
Morristown *(G-6646)*
◆ Barrett Paving Materials Inc ....E 973 533-1001
Roseland *(G-9535)*
Beaver Run Farms ....G 973 427-1000
Hawthorne *(G-4208)*
Beaver Run Farms ....F 973 875-5555
Lafayette *(G-5025)*
Brick-Wall Corp ....E 732 787-0226
Atlantic Highlands *(G-104)*
Brick-Wall Corp ....E 609 693-6223
Forked River *(G-3536)*
Brunswick Hot Mix Corp ....D 908 233-4444
Westfield *(G-11795)*
Central Jersey Hot Mix Asp LLC ....G 732 323-0226
Jackson *(G-4642)*
Chevron USA Inc ....D 732 738-2000
Perth Amboy *(G-8515)*
▲ Colas Inc ....G 973 290-9082
Morristown *(G-6654)*
Crowfoot Associates Inc ....G 609 561-0107
West Berlin *(G-11588)*
D Depasquale Paving LLC ....G 301 674-9775
Jackson *(G-4648)*
Dosch-King Company Inc ....F 973 887-0145
Whippany *(G-11889)*
▲ Earle The Walter R Corp ....G 732 308-1113
Wall Township *(G-11336)*
Earle The Walter R Corp ....G 732 657-8551
Jackson *(G-4652)*
Earle Asphalt Company ....D 732 657-8551
Jackson *(G-4653)*
Earle Asphalt Company ....C 732 308-1113
Wall Township *(G-11337)*
Eastern Concrete Materials Inc ....E 973 827-7625
Hamburg *(G-4090)*
Flemington Bituminous Corp ....F 908 782-2722
Flemington *(G-3442)*
Hanson Aggregates Wrp Inc ....E 972 653-5500
Wall Township *(G-11345)*
Joseph and William Stavola ....E 609 924-0300
Kingston *(G-5009)*
Louis N Rothberg & Son Inc ....E 732 356-9505
Middlesex *(G-6127)*
Newark Asphalt Corp ....G 973 482-3503
Newark *(G-7212)*
Richard E Pierson Mtls Corp ....G 856 740-2400
Williamstown *(G-11975)*
Richard E Pierson Mtls Corp ....G 856 691-0083
Vineland *(G-11260)*
Richard E Pierson Mtls Corp ....C 856 467-4199
Pilesgrove *(G-8580)*
Riverdale Quarry LLC ....E 973 835-0028
Riverdale *(G-9382)*
Rosano Asphalt LLC ....G 732 620-8400
Farmingdale *(G-3391)*
Schifano Construction Corp ....F 732 752-3450
Middlesex *(G-6144)*
South State Inc ....E 856 881-6030
Williamstown *(G-11979)*
Stavola Asphalt Company Inc ....E 732 542-2328
Tinton Falls *(G-10728)*
Stavola Construction Mtls Inc ....E 732 356-5700
Bound Brook *(G-608)*
Stavola Contracting Co Inc ....G 732 935-0156
Englishtown *(G-3009)*
Stavola Holding Corporation ....C 732 542-2328
Tinton Falls *(G-10730)*
Stone Industries Inc ....D 973 595-6250
Haledon *(G-4085)*
Tilcon New York Inc ....E 800 789-7625
North Bergen *(G-7440)*
Tilcon New York Inc ....E 800 789-7625
Oxford *(G-7766)*
Weldon Asphalt Corp ....F 973 627-7500
Rockaway *(G-9512)*
Weldon Materials Inc ....G 201 991-3200
Kearny *(G-4903)*
Ziegler Chem & Mineral Corp ....E 732 752-4111
Piscataway *(G-8741)*

2952 Asphalt Felts & Coatings

◆ Actega North America Inc ....C 856 829-6300
Delran *(G-2008)*
◆ Fti Inc ....G 973 443-0004
Florham Park *(G-3506)*

Icote USA Inc ....G 908 359-7575
Hillsborough *(G-4326)*
▲ Karnak Corporation ....D 732 388-0300
Clark *(G-1500)*
Karnak Midwest LLC ....G 732 388-0300
Clark *(G-1501)*
Koadings Inc ....G 732 517-0784
Allenhurst *(G-22)*
Lodor Offset Corporation ....F 201 935-7100
Carlstadt *(G-1182)*
Newark Asphalt Corp ....G 973 482-3503
Newark *(G-7212)*
▲ United Asphalt Company ....E 856 753-9811
Berlin *(G-432)*
▲ Vector Foiltec LLC ....G 862 702-8909
Fairfield *(G-3340)*

2992 Lubricating Oils & Greases

American Oil & Supply Co ....F 732 389-5514
Eatontown *(G-2377)*
Arol Chemical Products Co ....G 973 344-1510
Newark *(G-7053)*
◆ Bel-Ray Company Inc ....E 732 378-4000
Wall Township *(G-11320)*
◆ BP Lubricants USA Inc ....B 973 633-2200
Wayne *(G-11484)*
Chemours Company ....G 856 540-3398
Deepwater *(G-1998)*
Federal Lorco Petroleum LLC ....D 908 352-0542
Elizabeth *(G-2735)*
◆ Fti Inc ....G 973 443-0004
Florham Park *(G-3506)*
Gordon Terminal Service Co PA ....D 201 437-8300
Bayonne *(G-220)*
◆ Hangsterfers Laboratories ....E 856 468-0216
West Deptford *(G-11702)*
International Products Corp ....F 609 386-8770
Burlington *(G-974)*
Lanxess Solutions US Inc ....C 973 887-7411
East Hanover *(G-2221)*
Lanxess Solutions US Inc ....C 732 738-1000
Fords *(G-3533)*
Marine Oil Service Inc ....G 908 282-6440
Elizabeth *(G-2755)*
Mil-Comm Products Company Inc ....F 201 935-8561
East Rutherford *(G-2304)*
Nalco Company LLC ....F 609 617-2246
Red Bank *(G-9238)*
◆ Pbf Holding Company LLC ....B 973 455-7500
Parsippany *(G-7986)*
Penetone Corporation ....E 201 567-3000
Clifton *(G-1688)*
▲ Pflaumer Brothers Inc ....E 609 883-4610
Ewing *(G-3051)*
Total Specialties Usa Inc ....D 908 862-9300
Linden *(G-5436)*

2999 Products Of Petroleum & Coal, NEC

Honeywell International Inc ....C 973 455-2000
Morris Plains *(G-6614)*
◆ Honeywell Speclty Wax & Additv ......F 973 455-2000
Morristown *(G-6674)*

30 RUBBER AND MISCELLANEOUS PLASTICS PRODUCTS

3011 Tires & Inner Tubes

American Tire Distributors ....G 973 646-5600
Totowa *(G-10811)*
Bkt Exim Us Inc ....G 732 817-1400
Holmdel *(G-4494)*
Bkt Tires Inc ....G 844 258-8473
Holmdel *(G-4495)*
Coilhose Pneumatics Inc ....E 732 432-7177
East Brunswick *(G-2133)*
J G Carpenter Contractor ....G 732 271-8991
Middlesex *(G-6122)*
◆ Leopard Inc ....F 908 964-3600
Hillside *(G-4410)*

3021 Rubber & Plastic Footwear

▲ Bear USa Inc ....F 201 943-4748
Palisades Park *(G-7768)*
▲ Lust For Life Footwear LLC ....F 646 732-9742
Teaneck *(G-10638)*
Nike Inc ....G 732 695-0108
Tinton Falls *(G-10723)*

▲ Tingley Rubber Corporation ....E 800 631-5498
Piscataway *(G-8727)*
Vans Inc ....F 732 493-1516
Tinton Falls *(G-10733)*

3052 Rubber & Plastic Hose & Belting

Aarubco Rubber Co Inc ....E 973 772-8177
Saddle Brook *(G-9638)*
▲ Atlantic Rubber Enterprises ....G 973 697-5900
Newfoundland *(G-7329)*
▲ Belting Industries Group LLC ....E 908 272-8591
Union *(G-11031)*
▲ Brecoflex Co LLC ....D 732 460-9500
Eatontown *(G-2381)*
Couse & Bolten Co ....G 973 344-6330
Newark *(G-7090)*
Daniel C Herring Co Inc ....F 732 530-6557
Eatontown *(G-2387)*
Dyna Veyor Inc ....G 908 276-5384
Newark *(G-7108)*
Firefighter One Ltd Lblty Co ....G 973 940-3061
Sparta *(G-10387)*
Firetrainer Symtron ....G 201 794-0200
Fair Lawn *(G-3100)*
Forbo Siegling LLC ....F 201 567-6100
Englewood *(G-2906)*
Harrison Hose and Tubing Inc ....E 609 631-8804
Robbinsville *(G-9413)*
Hosepharm Ltd Liability Co ....F 732 376-0044
Perth Amboy *(G-8521)*
◆ Jason Industrial Inc ....E 973 227-4904
Fairfield *(G-3243)*
Minor Rubber Co Inc ....E 973 338-6800
Bloomfield *(G-511)*
Novaflex Industries Inc ....F 856 768-2275
West Berlin *(G-11612)*
▲ Passaic Rubber Co ....D 973 696-9500
Wayne *(G-11540)*
◆ Plastic Specialties & Tech Inc ....C 201 941-2900
Ridgefield *(G-9284)*
▲ Polytech Designs Inc ....F 973 340-1390
Clifton *(G-1696)*
Ptc Electronics Inc ....G 201 847-0500
Mahwah *(G-5764)*
Pure Tech International Inc ....G 908 722-4968
Branchburg *(G-673)*
▲ Pure Tech International Inc ....G 908 722-4800
Branchburg *(G-674)*
▲ Stiles Enterprises Inc ....F 973 625-9660
Rockaway *(G-9501)*
▲ Superflex Ltd ....E 718 768-1400
Elizabeth *(G-2778)*
T & B Specialties Inc ....G 732 928-4500
Jackson *(G-4666)*
Targa Industries Inc ....F 973 584-3733
Flanders *(G-3421)*
▲ Thirty-Three Queen Realty Inc ....F 973 824-5527
Newark *(G-7297)*
◆ US Wire & Cable Corporation ....B 973 824-5530
Newark *(G-7310)*

3053 Gaskets, Packing & Sealing Devices

Alltite Gasket Co ....F 732 254-2154
South River *(G-10348)*
▲ American Braiding & Mfg Corp ....F 732 938-6333
Howell *(G-4530)*
▼ Arcy Manufacturing Co Inc ....F 201 635-1910
Carlstadt *(G-1124)*
Aspe Inc ....E 973 808-1155
Fairfield *(G-3148)*
▲ Atlantic Rubber Enterprises ....G 973 697-5900
Newfoundland *(G-7329)*
Banks Bros Corporation ....D 973 680-4488
Bloomfield *(G-491)*
Capital Gasket and Rubber Inc ....G 856 939-3670
Runnemede *(G-9604)*
▲ Cinchseal Associates Inc ....E 856 662-5162
Mount Laurel *(G-6747)*
Coast Rubber and Gasket Inc ....G 609 747-0110
Burlington *(G-960)*
Cryopak Verification Tech Inc ....F 732 346-9200
Edison *(G-2488)*
Custom Gasket Mfg LLC ....F 201 331-6363
Englewood Cliffs *(G-2966)*
Datwyler Pharma Packaging ....E 856 663-2202
Pennsauken *(G-8410)*
Eagleburgmann Industries LP ....F 856 241-7300
Swedesboro *(G-10583)*
East Coast Rubber Products ....G 856 384-2747
Westville *(G-11812)*

Eastern Molding Co Inc ....G..... 973 759-0220
Belleville *(G-294)*

Electro-Ceramic Industries ....E..... 201 342-2630
Hackensack *(G-3911)*

▲ Fleet Packaging Inc ....G..... 866 302-0340
South Orange *(G-10196)*

Frc Electrical Industries Inc ....E..... 908 464-3200
New Providence *(G-7000)*

Frontline Industries Inc ....F..... 973 373-7211
Irvington *(G-4570)*

▲ H K Metal Craft Mfg Corp ....E..... 973 471-7770
Lodi *(G-5563)*

J P Rotella Co Inc ....F..... 973 942-2559
Haledon *(G-4083)*

Ja-Bar Silicone Corp ....D..... 973 786-5000
Andover *(G-47)*

John Crane Inc ....D..... 856 467-6185
Swedesboro *(G-10590)*

▼ Lamatek Inc ....E..... 856 599-6000
Paulsboro *(G-8333)*

Ls Rubber Industries Inc ....F..... 973 680-4488
Bloomfield *(G-507)*

▲ Mercer Rubber Company ....E..... 856 931-5000
Bellmawr *(G-339)*

Metallo Gasket Company Inc ....F..... 732 545-7223
New Brunswick *(G-6947)*

▲ Monmouth Rubber Corp ....E..... 732 229-3444
Long Branch *(G-5604)*

Mueller Die Cut Solutions Inc ....E..... 201 791-5000
Saddle Brook *(G-9665)*

▲ Newton Tool & Mfg Inc ....D..... 856 241-1500
Pennsauken *(G-8461)*

Omega Shielding Products Inc ....F..... 973 366-0080
Randolph *(G-9195)*

▼ Paradigm Packaging East LLC ....C..... 201 909-3400
Saddle Brook *(G-9668)*

Phoenix Packing & Gasket Co ....F..... 732 938-7377
Howell *(G-4549)*

R S Rubber Corp ....F..... 973 777-2200
Wallington *(G-11389)*

▲ Rempac LLC ....C..... 201 843-4585
Rochelle Park *(G-9431)*

Romaco North America Inc ....G..... 609 584-2500
Hamilton *(G-4123)*

▲ Seals-Eastern Incorporated ....C..... 732 747-9200
Red Bank *(G-9243)*

Specialty Rubber Inc ....G..... 609 704-2555
Elwood *(G-2860)*

▲ Sprialseal Inc ....G..... 732 738-6113
Cliffwood *(G-1547)*

▲ Stiles Enterprises Inc ....F..... 973 625-9660
Rockaway *(G-9501)*

Thomas A Caserta Inc ....F..... 609 586-2807
Robbinsville *(G-9417)*

Tricomp Inc ....C..... 973 835-1110
Pompton Plains *(G-8872)*

Viziflex Seels Inc ....F..... 201 488-3446
Saddle Brook *(G-9686)*

3061 Molded, Extruded & Lathe-Cut Rubber Mechanical Goods

Aarubco Rubber Co Inc ....E..... 973 772-8177
Saddle Brook *(G-9638)*

AMP Custom Rubber Inc ....F..... 732 888-2714
Keyport *(G-4997)*

◆ Ansell Inc ....D..... 334 794-4231
Iselin *(G-4594)*

Eastern Molding Co Inc ....G..... 973 759-0220
Belleville *(G-294)*

Fermatex Vascular Tech LLC ....F..... 732 681-7070
Wall Township *(G-11339)*

Hawthorne Rubber Mfg Corp ....E..... 973 427-3337
Hawthorne *(G-4225)*

Kinnarney Rubber Co Inc ....F..... 856 468-1320
Mantua *(G-5852)*

▲ Manville Rubber Products Inc ....E..... 908 526-9111
Manville *(G-5856)*

Mid-State Enterprises Inc ....F..... 973 427-6040
Bloomfield *(G-510)*

Minor Rubber Co Inc ....E..... 973 338-6800
Bloomfield *(G-511)*

▲ Monmouth Rubber Corp ....E..... 732 229-3444
Long Branch *(G-5604)*

Nbs Group Sup Med Pdts Div LLC ....G..... 732 745-9292
New Brunswick *(G-6949)*

▲ Panova Inc ....E..... 973 263-1700
Towaco *(G-10876)*

▲ Passaic Rubber Co ....D..... 973 696-9500
Wayne *(G-11540)*

Pierce-Roberts Rubber Company ....F..... 609 394-5245
Ewing *(G-3052)*

▲ Reiss Corporation ....C..... 732 446-6100
Rumson *(G-9601)*

▲ Rempac LLC ....C..... 201 843-4585
Rochelle Park *(G-9431)*

▲ Research & Mfg Corp Amer ....F..... 908 862-6744
Linden *(G-5414)*

Shock Tech Inc ....E..... 845 368-8600
Mahwah *(G-5771)*

▲ Stiles Enterprises Inc ....F..... 973 625-9660
Rockaway *(G-9501)*

T & B Specialties Inc ....G..... 732 928-4500
Jackson *(G-4666)*

Tricomp Inc ....C..... 973 835-1110
Pompton Plains *(G-8872)*

▲ Troy Hills Manufacturing Inc ....G..... 973 263-1885
Towaco *(G-10882)*

3069 Fabricated Rubber Prdts, NEC

Accu Seal Rubber Inc ....G..... 732 246-4333
New Brunswick *(G-6908)*

▼ Aero TEC Laboratories Inc ....E..... 201 825-1400
Ramsey *(G-9135)*

Aerogroup Retail Holdings Inc ....D..... 732 819-9843
Edison *(G-2448)*

◆ Air Cruisers Company LLC ....B..... 732 681-3527
Wall Township *(G-11315)*

▲ American Braiding & Mfg Corp ......F..... 732 938-6333
Howell *(G-4530)*

◆ American Harlequin Corporation ....E..... 856 234-5505
Moorestown *(G-6503)*

▲ Ames Rubber Corporation ....D..... 973 827-9101
Hamburg *(G-4088)*

◆ Ansell Healthcare Products LLC ....C..... 732 345-5400
Iselin *(G-4593)*

◆ Ansell Inc ....D..... 334 794-4231
Iselin *(G-4594)*

◆ Ansell Protective Products LLC ......A..... 732 345-5400
Iselin *(G-4596)*

◆ Asbury Carbons Inc ....G..... 908 537-2155
Asbury *(G-60)*

Atlantic Flooring LLC ....F..... 609 296-7700
Ltl Egg Hbr *(G-5614)*

▲ Baby Time International Inc ....G..... 973 481-7400
Newark *(G-7063)*

Banks Bros Corporation ....D..... 973 680-4488
Bloomfield *(G-491)*

Bsrm Inc ....G..... 888 509-0668
Mount Laurel *(G-6744)*

Bumper Specialties Inc ....C..... 856 345-7650
West Deptford *(G-11695)*

C M H Hele-Shaw Inc ....F..... 201 974-0570
Hoboken *(G-4445)*

Datwyler Pharma Packaging ....D..... 856 663-2202
Pennsauken *(G-8410)*

Derv2000 ....G..... 503 470-9158
Kearny *(G-4854)*

◆ Diversified Foam Products Inc ....D..... 856 662-1981
Swedesboro *(G-10581)*

Doddle & Co LLC ....G..... 917 836-1299
Montclair *(G-6364)*

Dream Makers Inc ....G..... 201 248-5502
Park Ridge *(G-7848)*

▲ Dso Fluid Handling Co Inc ....E..... 732 225-9100
Edison *(G-2495)*

Eastern Molding Co Inc ....G..... 973 759-0220
Belleville *(G-294)*

Elastograf Inc ....D..... 973 209-3161
Hamburg *(G-4093)*

◆ Fidelity Industries Inc ....E..... 973 696-9120
Wayne *(G-11501)*

Fidelity Industries Inc ....F..... 973 777-2592
Clifton *(G-1620)*

Flooring Concepts Nj LLC ....F..... 732 409-7600
Manalapan *(G-5811)*

Glopak Corp ....E..... 908 753-8735
South Plainfield *(G-10267)*

Hawthorne Rubber Mfg Corp ....E..... 973 427-3337
Hawthorne *(G-4225)*

◆ Henderson Aquatic Inc ....E..... 856 825-4771
Millville *(G-6254)*

Hutchinson Industries Inc ....F..... 609 394-1010
Trenton *(G-10940)*

◆ Hutchinson Industries Inc ....C..... 609 394-1010
Trenton *(G-10941)*

Hutchinson Industries Inc ....F..... 609 394-1010
Trenton *(G-10942)*

◆ Innocor Inc ....C..... 732 945-6222
Red Bank *(G-9230)*

Innocor Foam Tech - Acp Inc ....D..... 732 945-6222
Red Bank *(G-9231)*

Inoac Usa Inc ....D..... 201 807-0809
Moonachie *(G-6471)*

Kappus Plastic Company Inc ....D..... 908 537-2288
Hampton *(G-4157)*

Kinnarney Rubber Co Inc ....F..... 856 468-1320
Mantua *(G-5852)*

La Favorite Industries Inc ....F..... 973 279-1266
Paterson *(G-8236)*

▼ Lamatek Inc ....E..... 856 599-6000
Paulsboro *(G-8333)*

◆ Leland Limited Inc ....F..... 908 561-2000
South Plainfield *(G-10293)*

Linoleum Sales Company Inc ....G..... 201 438-1844
East Rutherford *(G-2296)*

Ls Rubber Industries Inc ....F..... 973 680-4488
Bloomfield *(G-507)*

▲ Manville Rubber Products Inc ....E..... 908 526-9111
Manville *(G-5856)*

Mat Logo Central LLC ....G..... 973 433-0311
Cedar Grove *(G-1281)*

▲ Mfv International Corporation ....F..... 973 993-1687
Morristown *(G-6686)*

Miroad Rubber USA LLC ....G..... 480 280-2543
Edison *(G-2567)*

Ness Plastics Inc ....F..... 201 854-4072
West New York *(G-11748)*

Norco Manufacturing Inc ....F..... 201 854-3461
North Bergen *(G-7425)*

Pacific Dnlop Holdings USA LLC ......G..... 732 345-5400
Red Bank *(G-9239)*

◆ Pacific Dunlop Investments USA ....F..... 732 345-5400
Red Bank *(G-9240)*

▲ Panova Inc ....E..... 973 263-1700
Towaco *(G-10876)*

▲ Passaic Rubber Co ....D..... 973 696-9500
Wayne *(G-11540)*

Pierce-Roberts Rubber Company ....F..... 609 394-5245
Ewing *(G-3052)*

Pure Rubber Products Co ....G..... 973 784-3690
Rockaway *(G-9492)*

Rak Foam Sales Inc ....G..... 908 668-1122
Plainfield *(G-8776)*

▲ Rema Tip Top/North America Inc ....E..... 201 768-8100
Northvale *(G-7546)*

▲ Rp Products LLC ....G..... 732 254-4222
East Brunswick *(G-2174)*

▲ Rubber & Silicone Products Co ....E..... 973 227-2300
Fairfield *(G-3305)*

Rubber Fab & Molding Inc ....G..... 908 852-7725
Johnsonburg *(G-4837)*

Schon J Tool & Machine Co ....G..... 732 928-6665
Jackson *(G-4664)*

Seajay Manufacturing Corp ....F..... 732 774-0900
Neptune *(G-6897)*

▲ Star-Glo Industries LLC ....C..... 201 939-6162
East Rutherford *(G-2319)*

Strongwall Industries Inc ....G..... 201 445-4633
Ridgewood *(G-9330)*

▲ Supply Plus NJ Inc ....E..... 973 782-5930
Paterson *(G-8307)*

Switlik Parachute Company Inc ....F..... 609 587-3300
Trenton *(G-10994)*

Sxwell USA LLC ....B..... 732 345-5400
Iselin *(G-4630)*

Thomas A Caserta Inc ....F..... 609 586-2807
Robbinsville *(G-9417)*

▲ Tingley Rubber Corporation ....E..... 800 631-5498
Piscataway *(G-8727)*

Top Rated Shopping Bargains ....F..... 800 556-5849
Hasbrouck Heights *(G-4190)*

Transport Products Inc ....G..... 973 857-6090
Cedar Grove *(G-1294)*

Tricomp Inc ....C..... 973 835-1110
Pompton Plains *(G-8872)*

▲ Vibration Muntings Contrls Inc ......D..... 800 569-8423
Bloomingdale *(G-531)*

▼ Water Master Co ....G..... 732 247-1900
Highland Park *(G-4289)*

West Phrm Svcs Lakewood Inc ....G..... 732 730-3295
Lakewood *(G-5181)*

◆ Woodbridge Inoac Technical ....D..... 201 807-0809
Moonachie *(G-6498)*

Woodbridge Inoac Technical Pro ......D..... 201 807-0809
Moonachie *(G-6499)*

Zago Manufacturing Company ....E..... 973 643-6700
Newark *(G-7318)*

S I C

3081 Plastic Unsupported Sheet & Film

▲ A D M Corporation ....D 732 469-0900
Middlesex (G-6090)
▲ Acrilex Inc ....E 201 333-1500
Jersey City (G-4685)
Air Protection Packaging Corp ....F 973 577-4343
Linden (G-5317)
▼ All American Poly Corp ....C 732 752-3200
Piscataway (G-8628)
▼ Allied Plastics Holdings LLC ....D 718 729-5500
Newark (G-7040)
Amcor Flexibles Inc ....E 609 267-5900
Mount Holly (G-6723)
Amcor Flexibles LLC ....C 856 825-1400
Millville (G-6224)
American Renolit Corp La ....G 856 241-4901
Swedesboro (G-10570)
American Renolit Corporation ....G 973 706-6912
Wayne (G-11468)
American Transparent Plastic ....E 732 287-3000
Edison (G-2455)
Amtopp Corporation ....A 973 994-8074
Livingston (G-5506)
◆ Arch Crown Inc ....E 973 731-6300
Hillside (G-4375)
Ber Plastics Inc ....E 973 839-2100
Riverdale (G-9371)
Berry Global Inc ....C 908 353-3850
Elizabeth (G-2716)
Berry Global Inc ....E 908 454-0900
Phillipsburg (G-8545)
Berry Global Inc ....C 609 395-4199
Cranbury (G-1814)
▼ Berry Global Films LLC ....C 201 641-6600
Montvale (G-6400)
▲ Broadway Kleer-Guard Corp ....E 609 662-3970
Monroe Township (G-6330)
Caloric Color Co Inc ....F 973 471-4748
Garfield (G-3734)
Central Plastics Incorporated ....G 973 808-0990
Parsippany (G-7899)
◆ Congoleum Corporation ....E 609 584-3000
Trenton (G-10921)
Congoleum Corporation ....B 609 584-3000
Trenton (G-10923)
Congoleum Corporation ....D 609 584-3601
Trenton (G-10922)
Corbco Inc ....G 609 549-6299
Forked River (G-3538)
Creative Film Corp ....F 732 367-2166
Lakewood (G-5073)
◆ Dicar Inc ....E 973 575-1377
Pine Brook (G-8596)
Dow Chemical Company ....D 800 258-2436
Somerset (G-9982)
Fordion Packaging Ltd ....F 201 692-1344
Hackensack (G-3917)
Gemini Plastic Films Corp ....E 973 340-0700
Garfield (G-3745)
◆ Glitterex Corp ....D 908 272-9121
Cranford (G-1911)
Glopak Corp ....E 908 753-8735
South Plainfield (G-10267)
H S Folex Schleussner Inc ....G 973 575-7626
Fairfield (G-3220)
Heritage Bag Company ....D 856 467-2247
Swedesboro (G-10589)
Hillside Plastics Corporation ....D 973 923-2700
Hillside (G-4399)
JA Heilferty LLC ....E 201 836-5060
Teaneck (G-10635)
Kappus Plastic Company Inc ....D 908 537-2288
Hampton (G-4157)
◆ Kayline Processing Inc ....E 609 695-1449
Trenton (G-10949)
▲ Kolon USA Incorporated ....F 201 641-5800
Ridgefield Park (G-9311)
▲ Lally-Pak Inc ....D 908 351-4141
Hillside (G-4409)
▲ Lps Industries Inc ....C 201 438-3515
Moonachie (G-6477)
◆ Mark Ronald Associates Inc ....D 908 558-0011
Hillside (G-4414)
Montrose Molders Corporation ....C 908 754-3030
South Plainfield (G-10302)
▼ Nexus Plastics Incorporated ....D 973 427-3311
Hawthorne (G-4234)
Niaflex Corporation ....F 407 851-6620
Livingston (G-5532)
Nobelus LLC ....G 800 895-2747
North Brunswick (G-7480)
▼ Package Development Co Inc ....E 973 983-8500
Rockaway (G-9483)
Pegasus Products Inc ....E 908 707-1122
Branchburg (G-666)
▲ Perlin Converting LLC ....F 973 887-0257
Whippany (G-11903)
Petro Packaging Co Inc ....E 908 272-4054
Cranford (G-1922)
▲ Plastic Plus Group LLC ....F 862 701-6981
Parsippany (G-7996)
Poly-Smith Ptfe LLC ....F 732 287-0610
Keyport (G-5004)
Prestige Associates Inc ....E 609 393-1509
Trenton (G-10982)
Primex Plastics Corporation ....C 973 470-8000
Garfield (G-3759)
Productive Plastics Inc ....D 856 778-4300
Mount Laurel (G-6796)
Silverton Packaging Corp ....G 732 341-0986
Monroe Township (G-6344)
▲ Ssi North America Inc ....G 973 598-0152
Randolph (G-9201)
▲ Tri-Cor Flexible Packaging Inc ....E 973 940-1500
Sparta (G-10413)
▲ Trinity Plastics Inc ....C 973 994-8018
Livingston (G-5543)
Up United LLC ....E 718 383-5700
Bridgewater (G-900)
▲ US Plastic Sales LLC ....G 908 754-9404
South Plainfield (G-10336)
◆ Vish LLC ....E 201 529-2900
North Brunswick (G-7493)
Zack Painting Co Inc ....E 732 738-7900
Fords (G-3534)

3082 Plastic Unsupported Profile Shapes

▲ Accessrec LLC ....G 973 955-0514
Clifton (G-1553)
▲ All State Plastics Inc ....E 732 654-5054
South Amboy (G-10130)
Alpha Wire Corporation ....C 908 925-8000
Elizabeth (G-2709)
Belle Printing Group LLC ....G 856 235-5151
Mount Laurel (G-6741)
Ber Plastics Inc ....E 973 839-2100
Riverdale (G-9371)
Cobon Plastics Corp ....F 973 344-6330
Newark (G-7085)
▲ Fluorotherm Polymers Inc ....G 973 575-0760
Parsippany (G-7948)
Illinois Tool Works Inc ....D 732 968-5300
Parsippany (G-7960)
▲ K Jabat Inc ....F 732 469-8177
Green Brook (G-3864)
◆ Keystone Plastics Inc ....D 908 561-1300
South Plainfield (G-10287)
▲ Plast-O-Matic Valves Inc ....D 973 256-3000
Cedar Grove (G-1287)
◆ Plastic Specialties & Tech Inc ....C 201 941-2900
Ridgefield (G-9284)
▲ Pure Tech International Inc ....G 908 722-4800
Branchburg (G-674)
Resdel Corporation ....E 609 886-1111
Rio Grande (G-9357)
Saint-Gobain Prfmce Plas Corp ....D 856 423-6630
Mickleton (G-6088)
Tpi Partners Inc ....G 908 561-3000
Stirling (G-10498)
Tricomp Inc ....C 973 835-1110
Pompton Plains (G-8872)
▲ X-L Plastics Inc ....C 973 777-9400
Clifton (G-1741)
Zeus Industrial Products Inc ....C 908 292-6500
Branchburg (G-698)

3083 Plastic Laminated Plate & Sheet

Barnegat Light Fibrgls Sup LLC ....G 609 294-8870
West Creek (G-11684)
C & K Plastics Inc ....D 732 549-0011
Metuchen (G-6049)
▲ Dikeman Laminating Corporation ....E 973 473-5696
Clifton (G-1598)
▲ Ensinger Grenloch Inc ....D 856 227-0500
Grenloch (G-3869)
▲ Federal Plastics Corporation ....E 908 272-5800
Cranford (G-1910)
Fedplast Inc ....F 732 901-1153
Lakewood (G-5098)
Flex Products LLC ....D 201 440-1570
Carlstadt (G-1158)
▲ Fluorotherm Polymers Inc ....G 973 575-0760
Parsippany (G-7948)
Graphic Express Menu Co Inc ....E 973 685-0022
Clifton (G-1629)
JMJ Profile Inc ....G 856 767-3930
West Berlin (G-11600)
▲ K Jabat Inc ....F 732 469-8177
Green Brook (G-3864)
▲ La Mart Manufacturing Corp ....G 718 384-6917
Teaneck (G-10636)
▲ McGrory Glass Inc ....D 856 579-3200
Paulsboro (G-8335)
▲ Monmouth Rubber Corp ....E 732 229-3444
Long Branch (G-5604)
◆ Nan Ya Plastics Corp America ....F 973 992-1775
Livingston (G-5529)
Owens Plastic Products Inc ....G 856 447-3500
Cedarville (G-1317)
▲ Plast-O-Matic Valves Inc ....D 973 256-3000
Cedar Grove (G-1287)
Plastinetics Inc ....G 973 618-9090
West Caldwell (G-11672)
Productive Plastics Inc ....D 856 778-4300
Mount Laurel (G-6796)
▲ Research & Mfg Corp Amer ....F 908 862-6744
Linden (G-5414)
◆ Royal Sovereign Intl Inc ....E 800 397-1025
Rockleigh (G-9521)
◆ Roysons Corporation ....D 973 625-5570
Rockaway (G-9496)
Saint-Gobain Prfmce Plas Corp ....D 856 423-6630
Mickleton (G-6088)
▲ Spiral Binding LLC ....C 973 256-0666
Totowa (G-10853)
Washington Stamp Exchange Inc ....F 973 966-0001
Florham Park (G-3526)
▲ Wood & Laminates Inc ....G 973 773-7475
Lodi (G-5583)

3084 Plastic Pipe

Advanced Drainage Systems Inc ....D 856 467-4779
Logan Township (G-5584)
Endot Industries Inc ....D 973 625-8500
Rockaway (G-9456)

3085 Plastic Bottles

▲ Amcor Phrm Packg USA LLC ....C 856 327-1540
Millville (G-6226)
Amcor Rigid Packaging Usa LLC ....D 856 327-1540
Millville (G-6231)
Brent River Corp ....G 908 722-6021
Hillsborough (G-4308)
Flexbiosys Inc ....F 908 300-3244
Lebanon (G-5261)
◆ Imagine Gold LLC ....E 201 488-5988
South Hackensack (G-10162)
Q-Pak Corporation ....E 973 483-4404
Newark (G-7242)
▲ Qualipac America Corp ....F 973 754-9920
Woodland Park (G-12088)
Setco LLC ....G 610 321-9760
Monroe Township (G-6342)
Shriji Polymers LLC ....E 609 906-2355
Ewing (G-3065)
▲ Unette Corporation ....D 973 328-6800
Randolph (G-9206)

3086 Plastic Foam Prdts

A & S Packaging & Display ....F 201 531-1900
Carlstadt (G-1117)
Alliance Corrugated Box Inc ....E 877 525-5269
Saddle River (G-9690)
Arrow Information Packagig LLC ....G 856 317-9000
Pennsauken (G-8391)
Atlantic Can Company ....G 609 518-9950
Westampton (G-11784)
Capitol Foam Products Inc ....E 201 933-5277
East Rutherford (G-2283)
▲ Century Service Affiliates Inc ....E 973 742-3516
Paterson (G-8155)
Craig Robertson ....G 973 293-8666
Montague (G-6354)
Edison Nation Inc ....G 610 829-1039
Phillipsburg (G-8549)
▼ Evonik Foams Inc ....E 973 929-8000
Parsippany (G-7939)
Fxi Inc ....D 201 933-8540
East Rutherford (G-2290)

Glopak Corp	E	908 753-8735
South Plainfield (G-10267)		
Innocor Foam Technologies LLC	C	844 824-9348
Red Bank (G-9232)		
Instapak Corp Sealed Air	D	201 791-7600
Rochelle Park (G-9424)		
Integrated Packaging Inds Inc	E	973 839-0500
Butler (G-1005)		
Johns Manville Corporation	E	732 225-9190
Edison (G-2542)		
Kohler Industries Inc	G	336 545-3289
Paterson (G-8231)		
▲ New Dimensions Industries LLC	G	201 531-1010
West Berlin (G-11610)		
New Industrial Foam Corp	G	908 561-4010
Plainfield (G-8772)		
Ocean Foam Fabricators LLC	E	973 745-1445
Belleville (G-304)		
▲ Pacor Inc	E	609 324-1100
Bordentown (G-592)		
▲ Plastic Plus Inc	G	973 614-0271
Passaic (G-8095)		
Plastico Products LLC	G	973 923-1944
Irvington (G-4582)		
Plastpac Inc	F	908 272-7200
Kenilworth (G-4971)		
Pmc Inc	B	201 933-8540
East Rutherford (G-2310)		
◆ Poly Molding LLC	E	973 835-7161
Haskell (G-4201)		
◆ Rempac Foam Corp	F	973 881-8880
Rochelle Park (G-9430)		
▲ Rempac LLC	C	201 843-4585
Rochelle Park (G-9431)		
▲ Rep Trading Associates Inc	F	732 591-1140
Old Bridge (G-7727)		
Sealed Air Corporation	C	201 712-7000
Saddle Brook (G-9679)		
Sealed Air Corporation	D	973 890-4735
Saddle Brook (G-9680)		
◆ Sekisui America Corporation	F	201 423-7960
Secaucus (G-9813)		
▲ Shell Packaging Corporation	E	908 871-7000
Berkeley Heights (G-412)		
Sierra Packaging Inc	F	732 571-2900
Ocean (G-7683)		
Sonoco Display & Packaging LLC	G	201 612-4008
Ridgefield Park (G-9317)		
▲ T C P Reliable Manufacturing	E	732 346-9200
Edison (G-2630)		
▲ Tcp Reliable Inc	G	848 229-2466
Edison (G-2632)		
Tech-Pak Inc	F	201 935-3800
Wood Ridge (G-12007)		
Tricorbraun Inc	G	732 353-7104
Monroe Township (G-6349)		
Univeg Logistics America Inc	G	856 241-0097
Swedesboro (G-10616)		
▲ US Propack Inc	G	732 294-4500
Freehold (G-3702)		
Utility Development Corp	G	973 994-4334
Livingston (G-5544)		
Willings Nutraceutical Corp	F	856 424-9088
Cherry Hill (G-1427)		

3087 Custom Compounding Of Purchased Plastic Resins

Bayshore Recycling Corp	E	732 738-6000
Keasbey (G-4908)		
◆ Borealis Compounds Inc	C	908 850-6200
Port Murray (G-8882)		
Diamond Sg Intl Ltd Lblty Co	G	732 861-9850
Eatontown (G-2388)		
▲ Federal Plastics Corporation	E	908 272-5800
Cranford (G-1910)		
◆ Joyce Leslie Inc	D	201 804-7800
Hillsborough (G-4335)		
▼ Lion Extruding Corp	F	973 344-4648
Newark (G-7181)		
Lubrizol Advanced Mtls Inc	E	856 299-3764
Pedricktown (G-8351)		
▲ Nobel Biocare Procera LLC	E	201 529-7100
Mahwah (G-5759)		
▲ Polymeric Resources Corp	E	973 694-4141
Wayne (G-11543)		
▲ Recycle Inc	D	908 756-2200
South Plainfield (G-10324)		
◆ Rotuba Extruders Inc	C	908 486-1000
Linden (G-5416)		

3088 Plastic Plumbing Fixtures

Ace Restoration	G	267 897-2384
Sewell (G-9833)		
Sell All Properties LLC	F	856 963-8800
Camden (G-1087)		
▲ Town & Country Plastics Inc	F	732 780-5300
Marlboro (G-5917)		

3089 Plastic Prdts

A & D Indus & Mar Repr Inc	E	732 541-1481
Port Reading (G-8890)		
A R C Plasmet Corp	F	201 867-8533
North Bergen (G-7379)		
A S 4 Plastic Inc	G	973 925-5223
Paterson (G-8119)		
▲ A-One Merchandising Corp	F	718 773-7500
North Arlington (G-7366)		
Accurate Mold Inc	E	856 784-8484
Somerdale (G-9929)		
Acrylics Unlimited	G	973 862-6014
Lafayette (G-5024)		
◆ Advantage Molding Products	G	732 303-8667
Sea Girt (G-9745)		
Advantage Molding Products	G	732 303-8667
Freehold (G-3643)		
▲ Aflex Extrusion Technologies	E	732 752-0048
Piscataway (G-8626)		
▲ AJ Siris Products Corp	F	973 823-0050
Ogdensburg (G-7708)		
Allgrind Plastics Inc	F	908 479-4400
Asbury (G-57)		
Allstar Disposal	F	973 398-8808
Hopatcong (G-4517)		
▲ Alva-Tech Inc	F	609 747-1133
Burlington Township (G-995)		
Arbee Company Inc	F	908 241-7717
Kenilworth (G-4921)		
Arpac Technology	A	973 252-0012
Randolph (G-9172)		
Artus Corp	E	201 568-1000
Englewood (G-2878)		
Associated Plastics Inc	F	732 574-2800
Rahway (G-9079)		
▲ B & G Plastics Inc	F	973 824-9220
Union (G-11028)		
B & W Plastics Inc	G	973 383-0020
Sparta (G-10380)		
Be & K Plastics LLC	F	609 386-3200
Burlington (G-954)		
◆ Bel-Art Products Inc	E	973 694-0500
Wayne (G-11477)		
Berry Global Inc	C	732 356-2870
Middlesex (G-6101)		
Berry Global Inc	C	908 353-3850
Elizabeth (G-2716)		
Berry Global Inc	G	980 689-1660
Phillipsburg (G-8544)		
Berry Global Inc	C	908 454-0900
Phillipsburg (G-8545)		
Berry Global Inc	C	609 395-4199
Cranbury (G-1814)		
Berry Global Inc	C	718 205-3115
Elizabeth (G-2717)		
Berry Global Group Inc	F	732 469-2470
Monroe Township (G-6327)		
Big 3 Precision Products Inc	G	856 293-1400
Millville (G-6236)		
Birds Beware Corporation	G	732 671-6377
Middletown (G-6161)		
▲ Brent River Corp	E	908 722-6021
Hillsborough (G-4307)		
▲ Brisar Industries Inc	D	973 278-2500
Paterson (G-8150)		
◆ Buckets Plus Inc	G	732 545-0420
New Brunswick (G-6914)		
◆ Butler Prtg & Laminating Inc	G	973 838-8550
Butler (G-997)		
C & K Plastics Inc	D	732 549-0011
Metuchen (G-6049)		
▲ C & N Packaging Inc	D	631 491-1400
Wayne (G-11486)		
C G I Cstm Fiberglas & Decking	F	609 646-5302
Pleasantville (G-8807)		
Camtec Industries Inc	F	732 332-9800
Colts Neck (G-1777)		
Captive Plastics LLC	C	812 424-2904
Phillipsburg (G-8547)		
Captive Plastics LLC	C	732 469-7900
Piscataway (G-8642)		

Cardinal Fibreglass Industries	G	718 625-4350
Perth Amboy (G-8513)		
Carecam International Inc	E	973 227-0720
Fairfield (G-3164)		
▲ Case It Inc		800 441-4710
Lyndhurst (G-5646)		
◆ Case Princeton Co Inc	E	908 687-1750
Mountainside (G-6836)		
Chefler Foods LLC	F	201 596-3710
Saddle Brook (G-9645)		
Christopher F Maier	F	908 459-5100
Hope (G-4524)		
◆ Colorite Plastics Company	E	201 941-2900
Ridgefield (G-9254)		
◆ Comar Inc	E	856 692-6100
Voorhees (G-11282)		
Comet Tool Company Inc	D	856 256-1070
Pitman (G-8743)		
Competech Smrtcard Sltions Inc	G	201 256-4184
Englewood Cliffs (G-2963)		
Componding Engrg Solutions Inc	F	973 340-4000
Upper Saddle River (G-11137)		
Consolidated Cont Holdings LLC	D	609 655-0855
Cranbury (G-1827)		
Consolidated Container Co LP	D	908 289-5862
Elizabeth (G-2722)		
Container Mfg Inc	E	732 563-0100
Middlesex (G-6105)		
▲ Continental Precision Corp	C	908 754-3030
Piscataway (G-8650)		
Crossfield Products Corp	D	908 245-2801
Roselle Park (G-9580)		
Custom Molders Corp	D	908 218-7997
Branchburg (G-634)		
De Leon Plastics Corp	F	973 653-3480
Paterson (G-8170)		
▲ Delvco Pharma Packg Svcs Inc	D	973 278-2500
Paterson (G-8172)		
Design & Molding Services Inc	C	732 752-0300
Piscataway (G-8654)		
▲ Design Display Group Inc	C	201 438-6000
Carlstadt (G-1150)		
Dolco Packaging Corp	E	201 941-2900
Ridgefield (G-9258)		
Domtar		201 942-2077
Delran (G-2015)		
Don Shrts Pcture Frmes Molding	G	732 363-1323
Howell (G-4537)		
Dor-Win Manufacturing Co	E	201 796-4300
Elmwood Park (G-2821)		
◆ Dr Reddys Laboratories Inc	E	609 375-9900
Princeton (G-8933)		
▲ Du Technologies Inc	F	201 729-0070
Moonachie (G-6463)		
▲ Duerr Tool & Die Co Inc	C	908 810-9035
Union (G-11044)		
E & T Plastic Mfg Co Inc	E	201 596-5017
Teterboro (G-10671)		
E & T Plastic Mfg Co Inc		856 787-0900
Mount Laurel (G-6754)		
E & T Sales Co Inc	G	856 787-0900
Mount Laurel (G-6755)		
East Coast Plastics Inc	G	856 768-8700
West Berlin (G-11592)		
▲ Echo Molding Inc	E	908 688-0099
Union (G-11049)		
Edwards Creative Products Inc	F	856 665-3200
Cherry Hill (G-1358)		
Emdeon Corporation	A	201 703-3400
Elmwood Park (G-2825)		
Endot Industries Inc	D	973 625-8500
Rockaway (G-9456)		
▲ Engineered Plastic Pdts Inc	C	908 647-3500
Stirling (G-10489)		
▲ Engineering Laboratories Inc	E	201 337-8116
Oakland (G-7627)		
◆ Enor Corporation	C	201 750-1680
Englewood (G-2902)		
Ethylene Atlantic Corp		856 467-0010
Swedesboro (G-10584)		
Exothermic Molding Inc	E	908 272-2299
Kenilworth (G-4937)		
◆ Farmplast LLC	E	973 287-6070
Parsippany (G-7942)		
Fencemax	G	609 646-2265
Newfield (G-7322)		
Flex Moulding Inc	G	201 487-8080
Hackensack (G-3915)		
Flex Products LLC	D	201 440-1570
Carlstadt (G-1158)		

Foster Engraving Corporation ....G 201 489-5979
Hackensack (G-3918)

▲ Fram Trak Industries Inc ....E 732 424-8400
Middlesex (G-6117)

Fredon Development Inds LLC ....F 973 383-7576
Newton (G-7343)

Freedom Vinyl Systems Inc ....G 973 692-0332
Pequannock (G-8505)

Frisch Plastics Corp ....G 973 685-5936
Pine Brook (G-8602)

Garden State Fabricators ....G 732 928-5006
Cream Ridge (G-1935)

Garfield Molding Co Inc ....E 973 777-5700
Wallington (G-11386)

Gifford Group Inc ....G 212 569-8500
Kearny (G-4860)

Gill Associates LLC ....G 973 835-5456
Wayne (G-11511)

Glasplex LLC ....G 973 940-8940
Sussex (G-10560)

◆ Globe Packaging Co Inc ....G 201 896-1144
Carlstadt (G-1159)

Graham Packaging Company LP ....E 717 849-8500
Bordentown (G-582)

Greco Industries LLC ....G 732 919-6200
Colts Neck (G-1784)

Greenway Products & Svcs LLC ....E 732 442-0200
New Brunswick (G-6932)

Grewe Plastics Inc ....G 973 485-7602
Newark (G-7140)

Griffen LLC ....G 973 723-5344
Morristown (G-6667)

Hartmann Tool Co Inc ....G 201 343-8700
Hackensack (G-3926)

Hathaway Plastic ....G 908 688-9494
Union (G-11062)

◆ Hayward Industrial Products ....C 908 351-5400
Elizabeth (G-2745)

◆ Hayward Industries Inc ....B 908 351-5400
Elizabeth (G-2746)

◆ Heyco Molded Products Inc ....F 732 286-4336
Toms River (G-10765)

Highland Products Inc ....G 973 366-0156
Dover (G-2086)

▼ Holocraft Corporation ....D 732 502-9500
Neptune (G-6885)

Home Organization LLC ....F 201 351-2121
Closter (G-1757)

◆ Honeyware Inc ....D 201 997-5900
Kearny (G-4863)

Hot Runner Technology ....G 908 431-5711
Hillsborough (G-4325)

▲ Icup Inc ....E 856 751-2045
Cherry Hill (G-1373)

▲ Injection Works Inc ....E 856 802-6444
Mount Laurel (G-6767)

▲ Injectron Corporation ....B 908 753-1990
Plainfield (G-8769)

Inman Mold and Mfg Co ....G 732 381-3033
Springfield (G-10446)

Inman Mold and Mfg Co ....G 732 381-3033
Rahway (G-9103)

Innova Group Inc ....G 856 696-1053
Vineland (G-11235)

Intek Plastics Inc ....E 973 427-7331
Hawthorne (G-4226)

Iron Mountain Plastics Inc ....F 201 445-0063
Midland Park (G-6178)

▲ J OBrien Co Inc ....E 973 379-8844
Springfield (G-10447)

J-Mac Plastics Inc ....E 908 709-1111
Kenilworth (G-4949)

◆ Janico Inc ....F 732 370-2223
Freehold (G-3672)

◆ Jarden LLC ....E 201 610-6600
Hoboken (G-4458)

◆ Jerhel Plastics Inc ....G 201 436-6662
Bayonne (G-225)

◆ Jersey Plastic Molders Inc ....C 973 926-1800
Irvington (G-4578)

Kinect Auto Parts Corporation ....G 862 702-8252
Fairfield (G-3251)

Koba Corp ....D 732 469-0110
Middlesex (G-6124)

L-E-M Plastics and Supplies ....G 201 933-9150
Rutherford (G-9626)

Lamart Corp ....F 973 772-6262
Clifton (G-1653)

Lamart Corporation ....G 973 772-6262
Clifton (G-1655)

▲ Leco Plastics Inc ....F 201 343-3330
Hackensack (G-3938)

▲ Life of Party LLC ....E 732 828-0886
North Brunswick (G-7475)

Linden Mold and Tool Corp ....E 732 381-1411
Rahway (G-9114)

Liquid-Solids Separation Corp ....E 201 236-4833
Ramsey (G-9149)

LNS Inc ....F 609 927-6656
Egg Harbor Township (G-2688)

Lumber Super Mart ....G 732 739-1428
Hazlet (G-4264)

Madan Plastics Inc ....D 908 276-8484
Cranford (G-1915)

▲ Mainetti Americas Inc ....G 201 215-2900
Secaucus (G-9791)

◆ Mainetti USA Inc ....F 201 215-2900
Keasbey (G-4912)

Mamrout Paper Group Corp ....G 718 510-5484
Edison (G-2558)

▲ Marlo Plastic Products Inc ....E 732 792-1988
Neptune (G-6890)

McBride Awning Co ....G 732 892-6256
Point Pleasant Beach (G-8828)

▲ McLean Packaging Corporation ....D 856 359-2600
Moorestown (G-6544)

▲ Medplast West Berlin Inc ....E 856 753-7600
West Berlin (G-11607)

▼ Meese Inc ....F 201 796-4490
Saddle Brook (G-9661)

Metrie Inc ....F 973 584-0040
Randolph (G-9191)

▲ Mfv International Corporation ....G 973 993-1687
Morristown (G-6686)

▲ Microcast Technologies Corp ....D 908 523-9503
Linden (G-5385)

▲ Mighty Mug Incorporated ....G 732 382-3911
Rahway (G-9119)

Molders Fishing Preserve ....G 732 446-2850
Jamesburg (G-4674)

Montrose Molders Corporation ....E 908 754-3030
Piscataway (G-8692)

Mrp New Jersey LLC ....G 732 873-7148
Somerset (G-10032)

Multi-Plastics Inc ....E 856 241-9014
Swedesboro (G-10598)

National Casein New Jersey Inc ....E 856 829-1880
Cinnaminson (G-1476)

National Diversified Sales Inc ....G 559 562-9888
Bordentown (G-590)

National Plastic Printing ....E 973 785-1460
Totowa (G-10838)

Newark Liner & Washer Inc ....F 973 482-5400
Newark (G-7215)

▲ Newell Brands Inc ....B 201 610-6600
Hoboken (G-4468)

Nini Disposal ....G 609 587-2411
Trenton (G-10966)

Norlo of New Jersey LLC ....G 646 492-3293
Montclair (G-6378)

Northland Tooling Technologies ....G 908 850-0023
Hackettstown (G-4030)

▲ Novembal USA Inc ....E 732 947-3030
Edison (G-2581)

▲ Onguard Fence Systems Ltd ....E 908 429-5522
Moorestown (G-6550)

Onguard Fence Systems Ltd ....E 908 429-5522
Branchburg (G-663)

Onyx Graphics LLC ....G 908 281-0038
Hillsborough (G-4343)

Oppenheim Plastics Co Inc ....D 201 391-3811
Park Ridge (G-7857)

Optics Plastics ....G 201 939-3344
Lyndhurst (G-5670)

▲ Ovadia Corporation ....E 973 256-9200
Little Falls (G-5462)

Owens Plastic Products Inc ....G 856 447-3500
Cedarville (G-1317)

P D Q Plastics Inc ....G 201 823-0270
Bayonne (G-230)

▼ Parkway Plastics Inc ....E 800 881-4996
Piscataway (G-8697)

▲ Patwin Plastics Inc ....E 908 486-6600
Linden (G-5405)

Pcr Technologies Inc ....G 973 882-0017
Pine Brook (G-8613)

Pedibrush LLC ....G 856 796-2963
Haddon Heights (G-4047)

▲ Pelco Packaging Corporation ....F 973 675-4994
East Orange (G-2259)

▲ Permalith Plastics LLC ....D 215 925-5659
Pennsauken (G-8468)

Petro Extrusion Tech Inc ....E 908 789-3338
Middlesex (G-6137)

Petro Plastics Company Inc ....E 908 789-1200
Kenilworth (G-4969)

Pfk Coach Phyllis Flood Knerr ....G 856 429-5425
Haddonfield (G-4061)

▲ Philcorr LLC ....D 856 205-0557
Vineland (G-11252)

▲ Pierson Industries Inc ....C 973 627-7945
Rockaway (G-9486)

Plastasonics Inc ....F 732 998-8361
Bayville (G-250)

Plasti Foam ....D 908 722-5254
Branchburg (G-668)

▲ Plastic Reel Corp of America ....E 201 933-5100
Carlstadt (G-1202)

Plastics Galore LLC ....G 732 363-8447
Lakewood (G-5147)

Plastiform Packaging Inc ....E 973 983-8900
Rockaway (G-9487)

Plastinetics Inc ....G 818 364-1611
Towaco (G-10878)

Plastpro 2000 Inc ....G 973 992-2090
Livingston (G-5536)

◆ PMC Group Inc ....F 856 533-1866
Mount Laurel (G-6791)

Pmp Composites Corporation ....E 609 587-1188
Trenton (G-10975)

Poly Source Enterprises LLC ....G 732 580-5409
Freehold (G-3688)

▲ Poly-Version Inc ....E 201 451-7600
Jersey City (G-4786)

Polycel Structural Foam Inc ....D 908 722-5254
Branchburg (G-669)

▲ Polycel Structural Foam Inc ....E 908 722-5254
Branchburg (G-670)

Polymer Molded Products ....G 732 907-1990
Bound Brook (G-604)

Precise Technology Inc ....E 856 241-1760
Swedesboro (G-10603)

Preferred Plastics Inc ....G 856 662-6250
Pennsauken (G-8470)

Premiere Raceway Sys LLC ....G 732 629-7715
Piscataway (G-8701)

Pretium Packaging LLC ....F 314 727-8200
Hillsborough (G-4346)

▲ Princeton Tectonics ....C 609 298-9331
Pennsauken (G-8472)

Pro Plastics Inc ....E 908 925-5555
Linden (G-5412)

Productive Plastics Inc ....D 856 778-4300
Mount Laurel (G-6796)

▲ Protec Secure Card Ltd Lblty ....E 732 542-0700
Eatontown (G-2417)

Pure TEC Corporation ....G 201 941-2900
Ridgefield (G-9285)

▲ Pure Tech International Inc ....G 908 722-4800
Branchburg (G-674)

▲ Qualipac America Corp ....F 973 754-9920
Woodland Park (G-12088)

R & K Industries Inc ....G 732 531-1123
Oakhurst (G-7612)

▲ R Squared Sls & Logistics LLC ....G 201 329-9745
Moonachie (G-6485)

▲ Randy Hangers LLC ....G 201 215-2900
Secaucus (G-9802)

Rapid Manufacturing Co Inc ....E 732 279-1252
Toms River (G-10787)

◆ Reiss Manufacturing Inc ....C 732 446-6100
Rumson (G-9602)

◆ Revere Industries LLC ....C 856 881-3600
Clayton (G-1528)

Revere Plastics Inc ....G 201 641-0777
Little Ferry (G-5494)

Ring Container Tech LLC ....F 973 258-0707
Springfield (G-10466)

◆ Rotuba Extruders Inc ....C 908 486-1000
Linden (G-5416)

▲ Royal Aluminum Co Inc ....D 973 589-8880
Newark (G-7253)

▲ Royce Associates A Ltd Partnr ....D 201 438-5200
East Rutherford (G-2315)

Russo Seamless Gutter LLC ....G 732 836-0151
Brick (G-730)

S&A Molders Inc ....G 732 851-7770
Manalapan (G-5825)

◆ Sabert Corporation ....C 800 722-3781
Sayreville (G-9722)

Sabert Corporation ....E 732 721-5544
　Sayreville (G-9723)
Saint-Gobain Prfmce Plas Corp ....C ... 973 696-4700
　Wayne (G-11551)
▼ Sama Plastics Corp ....E 973 239-7200
　Cedar Grove (G-1292)
Sancon Services Inc ....G ... 973 344-2500
　Newark (G-7262)
Scott W Springman ....G 856 751-2411
　Pennsauken (G-8482)
Seajay Manufacturing Corp ....F 732 774-0900
　Neptune (G-6897)
Seal-Spout Corp ....F 908 647-0648
　Liberty Corner (G-5296)
Sealed Air Holdings ....G 201 791-7600
　Elmwood Park (G-2855)
Silver Line Building Pdts LLC ......C 732 752-8704
　Middlesex (G-6148)
Sinclair and Rush Inc ....G 862 262-8189
　Carlstadt (G-1217)
▲ Sonetronics Inc ....D 732 681-5016
　Belmar (G-354)
▲ Stephco Sales Inc ....E 973 278-5454
　Paterson (G-8301)
◆ Stephen Douglas Plastics Inc ....C 973 523-3030
　Paterson (G-8302)
◆ Storemaxx Inc ....F 201 440-8800
　Hackensack (G-3979)
▲ Stull Technologies LLC ....D 732 873-5000
　Somerset (G-10076)
Superseal Manufacturing Co Inc .....F 908 561-5910
　South Plainfield (G-10329)
Survivor II Inc ....E 908 353-1155
　Hillside (G-4428)
Swm Spotswood Mill ....G 732 723-6102
　Spotswood (G-10419)
T & B Specialties Inc ....G 732 928-4500
　Jackson (G-4666)
T & M Newton Corporation ....G 973 383-1232
　Newton (G-7361)
Team Nisca ....G 732 271-7367
　Somerset (G-10082)
Tech Products Co Inc ....F 201 444-7777
　Midland Park (G-6188)
▲ Techflex Inc ....F 973 300-9242
　Sparta (G-10409)
Technimold Inc ....F 908 232-8331
　Flemington (G-3470)
Technitool Inc ....E 856 768-2707
　West Berlin (G-11626)
Tek Molding ....G 973 702-0450
　Sussex (G-10567)
▲ Tektite Industries Inc ....G 609 656-0600
　Trenton (G-10997)
Thermal Chek Inc ....E 856 742-1200
　Westville (G-11822)
▲ Thermo Plastic Tech Inc ....E 908 687-4833
　Union (G-11095)
Thermoplastics Bio-Logics LLC .....F 973 383-2834
　Sparta (G-10411)
▲ Town & Country Plastics Inc ......F 732 780-5300
　Marlboro (G-5917)
Tri Tech Tool & Design Co Inc ......E 732 469-5433
　South Bound Brook (G-10144)
Triumph Plastics LLC ....G 973 584-5500
　Flanders (G-3424)
Tyz-All Plastics LLC ....G 201 343-1200
　Hackensack (G-3987)
▲ Unette Corporation ....D 973 328-6800
　Randolph (G-9206)
▲ Uniplast Industries Inc ....E 201 288-4672
　Hasbrouck Heights (G-4192)
United Eqp Fabricators LLC ....G 973 242-2737
　Newark (G-7308)
▼ United States Box Corp ....E 973 481-2000
　Fairfield (G-3336)
United Window & Door Mfg Inc ......E 973 912-0600
　Springfield (G-10470)
Vacumet Corp ....G 973 628-0405
　Wayne (G-11562)
Valley Plastic Molding Co ....F 973 334-2100
　Boonton (G-572)
◆ Van Ness Plastic Molding Co ......C 973 778-9500
　Clifton (G-1734)
Vanguard Container Corp ....E 732 651-9717
　East Brunswick (G-2189)
▲ Veloso Industries Inc ....G 908 925-0999
　Linden (G-5440)
Versatile Distributors Inc ....D 973 773-0550
　Livingston (G-5546)

▲ Vinylast Inc ....E 732 367-7200
　Lakewood (G-5176)
Viz Mold & Die Ltd ....F 201 784-8383
　Northvale (G-7553)
◆ Waldwick Plastics Corp ....G 201 445-7436
　Waldwick (G-11311)
▲ Weiss-Aug Co Inc ....C 973 887-7600
　East Hanover (G-2246)
Westar Tool LLC ....G 856 507-8852
　West Berlin (G-11633)
Whe Research Inc ....G 732 240-3871
　Toms River (G-10803)
▲ Whole Year Trading Co Inc ....G 732 238-1196
　Dayton (G-1995)
Willings Nutraceutical Corp ....F 856 424-9088
　Cherry Hill (G-1427)
▲ Wilpak Industries Inc ....G 201 997-7600
　Kearny (G-4907)
World Plastic Extruders Inc ....D 201 933-2915
　Rutherford (G-9635)
◆ WY Industries Inc ....G 201 617-8000
　North Bergen (G-7444)
Yuhl Products Inc ....G 908 276-5180
　Kenilworth (G-4991)
Zirti LLC ....G 201 509-8404
　Saddle Brook (G-9689)

31 LEATHER AND LEATHER PRODUCTS

3111 Leather Tanning & Finishing

Buonaventura Bag and Cases LLC .....G 212 960-3442
　Clifton (G-1579)
▲ Cejon Inc ....E 201 437-8780
　Bayonne (G-208)
▲ Coast To Coast Lea & Vinyl Inc .....G 732 525-8877
　Sayreville (G-9706)
▲ Dani Leather USA Inc ....G 973 598-0890
　Flanders (G-3404)
Disys Commerce Inc ....G 201 567-0457
　Englewood (G-2898)
Jaclyn Holdings Parent LLC ....G 201 909-6000
　Maywood (G-6007)
Maxsyl Leather Co LLC ....D 201 864-0579
　Union City (G-11121)
Myers Group LLC ....G 973 761-6414
　South Orange (G-10199)

3131 Boot & Shoe Cut Stock & Findings

Cross Counter Inc ....G 973 677-0600
　East Orange (G-2251)
Ingersoll-Rand Company ....G 973 882-0924
　Pine Brook (G-8606)

3142 House Slippers

◆ S Goldberg & Co Inc ....C 201 342-1200
　Hackensack (G-3969)

3143 Men's Footwear, Exc Athletic

▲ Bm USA Incorporated ....E 800 624-5499
　Carlstadt (G-1130)
Carlascio Custom & Orthopedic ......G 201 333-8716
　Jersey City (G-4708)
Vf Outdoor LLC ....G 908 352-5390
　Elizabeth (G-2785)

3144 Women's Footwear, Exc Athletic

Carlascio Custom & Orthopedic ......G 201 333-8716
　Jersey City (G-4708)
Jag Footwear ACC & Ret Corp ....F 609 845-1700
　Westampton (G-11786)
Je TAime Shoes ....G 201 845-7463
　Paramus (G-7810)
Schusters Shoes Inc ....G 856 885-4551
　Williamstown (G-11977)

3149 Footwear, NEC

◆ Ballet Makers Inc ....G 973 595-9000
　Totowa (G-10818)
Carlascio Custom & Orthopedic ......G 201 333-8716
　Jersey City (G-4708)
McM Products USA Inc ....F 646 756-4090
　Secaucus (G-9792)
◆ S Goldberg & Co Inc ....C 201 342-1200
　Hackensack (G-3969)

3151 Leather Gloves & Mittens

Ansell Hawkeye Inc ....E 662 258-3200
　Iselin (G-4592)

3161 Luggage

▲ Atco Products Inc ....E 973 379-3171
　Springfield (G-10428)
◆ Case Princeton Co Inc ....E 908 687-1750
　Mountainside (G-6836)
▲ Gibbons Company Ltd ....E 441 294-5047
　Elizabeth (G-2743)
Iacobucci USA Inc ....G 732 935-6633
　Eatontown (G-2401)
▲ Lbu Inc ....E 973 773-4800
　Paterson (G-8238)
Ledonne Leather Co Inc ....F 201 531-2100
　Lyndhurst (G-5657)
Mirage Wholesale Group LLC ....G 718 757-6590
　Elizabeth (G-2759)
Motion Systems LLC ....F 212 686-4666
　Newark (G-7205)
Naluco Inc ....D 800 601-8198
　Clifton (G-1672)
Quiet Tone Inc ....G 732 431-2826
　Freehold (G-3696)
Selfmade LLC ....G 201 792-8968
　Jersey City (G-4808)
▲ Transglobe Usa Inc ....G 973 465-1998
　Carlstadt (G-1231)
Tumi Holdings Inc ....D 908 756-4400
　Edison (G-2635)
◆ Wisdom USA Inc ....F 201 933-1998
　Carlstadt (G-1240)
Xstatic Pro Inc ....F 718 237-2299
　Bayonne (G-237)

3171 Handbags & Purses

Annette & Jim Dizenzo Sls LLC ......G 973 875-0895
　Sussex (G-10556)
▼ Basu Group Inc ....G 908 517-9138
　North Brunswick (G-7456)
▲ Carol S Miller Corporation ....G 201 406-4578
　Hillsdale (G-4365)
Gio Vali Handbag Corp ....G 973 279-3032
　Paterson (G-8198)
Ledonne Leather Co Inc ....F 201 531-2100
　Lyndhurst (G-5657)
▲ M London Inc ....E 201 459-6460
　Jersey City (G-4762)
McM Products USA Inc ....F 646 756-4090
　Secaucus (G-9792)
Medici International Inc ....G 973 684-6084
　Paterson (G-8253)
Mitzi Intl Handbag & ACC Ltd ....C 973 483-5015
　Newark (G-7203)
Tapestry Inc ....F 856 488-2220
　Cherry Hill (G-1421)

3172 Personal Leather Goods

Allegro Mfg ....F 323 724-0101
　Hightstown (G-4293)
Always Be Secure LLC ....G 917 887-2286
　Manalapan (G-5801)
▲ Billykirk ....F 201 222-9092
　Jersey City (G-4703)
▲ Colemax Group LLC ....G 201 489-1080
　River Edge (G-9359)
G-III Leather Fashions Inc ....D 212 403-0500
　Dayton (G-1966)
Jaclyn Holdings Parent LLC ....G 201 909-6000
　Maywood (G-6007)
▲ M London Inc ....E 201 459-6460
　Jersey City (G-4762)
Maxsyl Leather Co LLC ....D 201 864-0579
　Union City (G-11121)
▲ R Neumann & Co ....F 201 659-3400
　Hoboken (G-4476)
Tumi Holdings Inc ....D 908 756-4400
　Edison (G-2635)

3199 Leather Goods, NEC

Adventure Industries LLC ....G 609 426-1777
　East Windsor (G-2334)
▲ Billykirk ....F 201 222-9092
　Jersey City (G-4703)
Brook Saddle Ridge Equest ....F 609 953-1600
　Shamong (G-9855)
▲ Bucati Leather Inc ....G 732 254-0480
　South River (G-10349)

S
I
C

▲ Emporium Leather Company Inc ....E 201 330-7720
Secaucus (G-9762)

G S Babu & Co ....F 732 939-5190
Plainsboro (G-8787)

Jaclyn Holdings Parent LLC ....G 201 909-6000
Maywood (G-6007)

McM Products USA Inc ....F 646 756-4090
Secaucus (G-9792)

North American Frontier Corp ....E 201 222-1931
Jersey City (G-4773)

▲ R Neumann & Co ....F 201 659-3400
Hoboken (G-4476)

▲ Safe-Strap Company Inc ....E 973 442-4623
Wharton (G-11870)

32 STONE, CLAY, GLASS, AND CONCRETE PRODUCTS

3211 Flat Glass

Artique Glass Studio Inc ....G 201 444-3500
Glen Rock (G-3826)

◆ Edmund Optics Inc ....C 856 547-3488
Barrington (G-172)

Elco Glass Industries Co Inc ....E 732 363-6550
Freehold (G-3662)

▲ Europrojects Intl Inc ....G 201 408-5215
Englewood (G-2903)

Floral Glass Industries Inc ....E 201 939-4600
East Rutherford (G-2289)

Frost Tech Inc ....F 732 396-0071
Rahway (G-9096)

◆ General Glass Intl Corp ....G 201 553-1850
Secaucus (G-9772)

▲ JE Berkowitz LP ....C 856 456-7800
Pedricktown (G-8349)

Jersey Tempered Glass Inc ....E 856 273-8700
Mount Laurel (G-6773)

Just Glass & Mirror Inc ....F 856 728-8383
Williamstown (G-11962)

▲ McGrory Glass Inc ....D 856 579-3200
Paulsboro (G-8335)

Oldcastle Buildingenvelope Inc ....D 856 234-9222
Moorestown (G-6549)

Pierangeli Group Inc ....G 856 582-4060
Gloucester City (G-3847)

Pilkington North America Inc ....C 973 470-5703
Clifton (G-1692)

PPG Industries Inc ....G 856 662-9323
Pennsauken (G-8469)

Tri-State Glass & Mirror Inc ....G 732 591-5545
Old Bridge (G-7729)

3221 Glass Containers

Amcor Phrm Packg USA Inc ....C 856 825-3050
Millville (G-6225)

Amcor Phrm Packg USA Inc ....C 856 728-9300
Williamstown (G-11950)

▲ Amcor Phrm Packg USA LLC...........C 856 327-1540
Millville (G-6226)

Amcor Phrm Packg USA LLC ....C 856 825-1400
Millville (G-6227)

Amcor Phrm Packg USA LLC ....C 856 825-1400
Millville (G-6228)

Amcor Phrm Packg USA LLC ....C 856 825-1100
Millville (G-6229)

Ardagh Glass Inc ....C 508 478-2500
Bridgeton (G-751)

Ardagh Glass Inc ....B 732 969-0827
Carteret (G-1248)

▲ Assem - Pak Inc ....C 856 692-3355
Vineland (G-11187)

Avant Industries Ltd Inc ....G 973 242-1700
Newark (G-7060)

Cameo Metal Forms Inc ....F 718 788-1106
Woodland Park (G-12073)

Centro Alternativo De ....G 973 365-0995
Passaic (G-8055)

◆ Friedrich and Dimmock Inc ....E 856 825-0305
Millville (G-6249)

▲ Gerresheimer Glass Inc ....B 856 692-3600
Vineland (G-11223)

▲ Heinz Glas USA Inc ....F 908 474-0300
Linden (G-5355)

▲ Le Papillon Ltd ....F 908 753-7300
South Plainfield (G-10291)

◆ Leone Industries Inc ....B 856 455-2000
Bridgeton (G-763)

Nipro Glass Americas Corp ....C 856 825-1400
Millville (G-6261)

◆ Nipro Phrmpckging Amricas Corp....C 856 825-1400
Millville (G-6262)

▲ Piramal Glass - Usa Inc ....E 856 293-6400
Dayton (G-1984)

Piramal Glass - Usa Inc ....C 856 728-9300
Williamstown (G-11969)

Piramal Glass - Usa Inc ....B 856 293-6400
Williamstown (G-11970)

◆ Pochet of America Inc ....C 973 942-4923
Woodland Park (G-12086)

Vivreau Advanced Water Systems ......F 212 502-3749
Fairfield (G-3347)

▲ Worldwide Glass Resources Inc .....E 856 205-1508
Vineland (G-11278)

3229 Pressed & Blown Glassware, NEC

Amcor Phrm Packg USA LLC ....C 856 825-1100
Millville (G-6229)

Ascentta Inc ....F 732 868-1766
Somerset (G-9957)

Betco Glass Inc ....G 856 327-4301
Millville (G-6235)

◆ Buckets Plus Inc ....G 732 545-0420
New Brunswick (G-6914)

◆ Bulbrite Industries Inc ....E 201 531-5900
Moonachie (G-6458)

C Technologies Inc ....E 908 707-1009
Bridgewater (G-810)

▲ Cardinal International Inc ....F 973 628-0900
Wayne (G-11487)

Corning Pharmaceutical GL LLC.........C 856 794-7100
Vineland (G-11205)

Creamer Glass LLC ....E 856 327-2023
Millville (G-6243)

Creamer Glass LLC ....E 856 327-2023
Millville (G-6244)

▲ Crystal World Inc ....E 201 488-0909
Carlstadt (G-1148)

▲ Daum Inc ....G 862 210-8522
Fairfield (G-3179)

▲ Durand Glass Mfg Co Inc ....A 856 327-1850
Millville (G-6248)

◆ E G L Company Inc ....C 908 508-1111
Berkeley Heights (G-398)

Eldon Glass & Mirror Co Inc ....F 973 589-2099
Newark (G-7113)

▼ Fiberguide Industries Inc ....E 908 647-6601
Stirling (G-10490)

Folio Art Glass Inc ....G 732 431-0044
Colts Neck (G-1783)

▲ Friedrich and Dimmock Inc ....E 856 825-0305
Millville (G-6249)

Gbw Manufacturing Inc ....E 973 279-0077
Totowa (G-10828)

▼ Glass Warehouse ....G 856 825-1400
Millville (G-6252)

Glassblowerscom LLC ....G 856 232-7898
Blackwood (G-467)

Glassroots Inc ....E 973 353-9555
Newark (G-7132)

Glassworks Studio Inc ....G 973 656-0800
Morristown (G-6666)

Glocal Expertise Llc ....G 718 928-3839
Jersey City (G-4744)

▲ Go Foton Corporation ....F 732 412-7375
Somerset (G-9998)

▲ Goodlite Products Inc ....F 718 697-7502
Perth Amboy (G-8519)

▲ Hospitality GL Brands USA Inc ......F 800 869-5258
Ridgefield Park (G-9309)

Hospitality Glass Brands LLC ....G 800 869-8258
Paramus (G-7806)

▲ Icup Inc ....E 856 751-2045
Cherry Hill (G-1373)

▲ Illuminating Experiences LLC ....G 800 734-5858
New Brunswick (G-6934)

Interior Specialties LLC ....F 856 663-1700
Pennsauken (G-8438)

▲ Kraftware Corporation ....E 732 345-7091
Roselle (G-9562)

Kramme Consolidated Inc ....G 856 358-8151
Monroeville (G-6352)

▲ Lumiko USA Inc ....G 609 409-6900
Cranbury (G-1860)

M D Laboratory Supplies Inc ....E 732 322-0773
Franklin Park (G-3635)

▲ Materials Research Group Inc ....G 908 245-3301
Roselle (G-9564)

▲ McGrory Glass Inc ....D 856 579-3200
Paulsboro (G-8335)

Metro Optics LLC ....F 908 413-0004
Flemington (G-3456)

▲ Mg Decor LLC ....F 201 923-5493
East Rutherford (G-2303)

Mirrotek International LLC ....E 973 472-1400
Passaic (G-8090)

Partners In Vision Inc ....G 888 748-1112
Edison (G-2587)

Princeton Hosted Solutions LLC ....F 856 470-2350
Haddonfield (G-4062)

Q Glass Company Inc ....G 973 335-5191
Towaco (G-10879)

▲ Qis Inc ....F 856 455-3736
Rosenhayn (G-9596)

Quark Enterprises Inc ....E 856 455-0376
Rosenhayn (G-9597)

▲ Radiant Communications Corp ....E 908 757-7444
South Plainfield (G-10323)

▲ Sensors Unlimited Inc ....D 609 333-8000
Princeton (G-9020)

Sterling Products Inc ....F 973 471-2858
Passaic (G-8109)

Technical Glass Products Inc ....G 973 989-5500
Dover (G-2107)

Thomas Clark Fiberglass LLC ....G 609 492-9257
Barnegat (G-163)

Triton Associated Industries ....E 856 697-3050
Buena (G-944)

▲ United Silica Products Inc ....F 973 209-8854
Franklin (G-3610)

3231 Glass Prdts Made Of Purchased Glass

A M K Glass Inc ....G 856 692-1488
Vineland (G-11183)

Above Rest Glass ....G 732 370-1616
Toms River (G-10738)

▲ Ace Fine Art Inc ....G 201 960-4447
Garfield (G-3724)

AGC Products Inc ....G 973 248-5039
Vineland (G-11184)

Amcor Phrm Packg USA LLC ....C 856 825-1100
Millville (G-6229)

Artistic Glass & Doors Inc ....G 856 768-1414
West Berlin (G-11577)

Ascalon Studios Inc ....F 856 768-3779
West Berlin (G-11578)

Atlantic International Tech ....F 973 625-0053
Rockaway (G-9444)

Avant Industries Ltd Inc ....G 973 242-1700
Newark (G-7060)

Bellco Glass Inc ....D 800 257-7043
Vineland (G-11192)

▲ Century Bathworks Inc ....D 973 785-4290
Woodland Park (G-12074)

Century Bathworks Inc ....E 201 785-1414
Woodland Park (G-12075)

◆ Comar Inc ....E 856 692-6100
Voorhees (G-11282)

Comar LLC ....C 856 507-5483
Vineland (G-11200)

Comfort Zone ....G 732 869-9990
Ocean Grove (G-7699)

County of Somerset ....C 732 469-3363
Bridgewater (G-814)

CR Laurence Co Inc ....F 201 770-1077
Secaucus (G-9758)

Crown Glass Co Inc ....G 908 642-1764
Branchburg (G-633)

Cumberland Rcycl Corp S Jersey ....E 856 825-4153
Millville (G-6245)

Demco Scientific Glassware Inc ....G 856 327-7898
Millville (G-6247)

▲ Eastern Glass Resources Inc ....E 973 483-8411
Harrison (G-4171)

Edward W Hiemer & Co ....F 973 772-5081
Clifton (G-1611)

▲ Fbn New Jersey Mfg Inc ....E 973 402-1443
Mountain Lakes (G-6825)

Femenella & Associates Inc ....G 908 722-6526
Branchburg (G-640)

Folio Art Glass Inc ....G 732 431-0044
Colts Neck (G-1783)

▲ Friedrich and Dimmock Inc ....E 856 825-0305
Millville (G-6249)

Gbw Manufacturing Inc ....E 973 279-0077
Totowa (G-10828)

◆ General Glass Intl Corp ....C 201 553-1850
Secaucus (G-9772)

Gerresheimer Glass Inc ....B 856 507-5852
Vineland (G-11224)

▲ Glass Dynamics LLC ....G...... 856 205-1503
Vineland (G-11225)

Glastron Inc ....E...... 856 692-0500
Vineland (G-11226)

H S Martin Company Inc ....F...... 856 692-8700
Vineland (G-11230)

▲ Hanson & Zollinger Inc ....F...... 856 626-3440
Berlin (G-422)

▲ Icup Inc ....E...... 856 751-2045
Cherry Hill (G-1373)

Insulite Inc ....F...... 732 255-1700
Toms River (G-10770)

Interior Specialties LLC ....F...... 856 663-1700
Pennsauken (G-8438)

▲ JE Berkowitz LP ....C...... 856 456-7800
Pedricktown (G-8349)

Jersey Tempered Glass Inc ....E...... 856 273-8700
Mount Laurel (G-6773)

▲ Klein Usa Inc ....F...... 973 246-8181
East Rutherford (G-2294)

◆ Kubik Maltbie Inc ....E...... 856 234-0052
Mount Laurel (G-6774)

Linda Spolitino ....G...... 609 345-3126
Atlantic City (G-96)

▲ McGrory Glass Inc ....D...... 856 579-3200
Paulsboro (G-8335)

Miric Industries Inc ....F...... 201 864-0233
North Bergen (G-7422)

Nds Technologies Inc ....E...... 856 691-0330
Vineland (G-11246)

Newman Glass Works Inc ....F...... 215 925-3565
Camden (G-1079)

Oldcastle Buildingenvelope Inc......D...... 856 234-9222
Moorestown (G-6549)

Penta Glass Industries Inc ....G...... 973 478-2110
Garfield (G-3755)

▲ Personlzed Exprssons By Audrey....F...... 973 478-5115
Garfield (G-3756)

Pike Machine Products Inc ....D...... 973 379-9128
Short Hills (G-9874)

Potters Industries LLC ....E...... 201 507-4169
Carlstadt (G-1205)

▲ Precision Electronic Glass Inc ......D...... 856 691-2234
Vineland (G-11254)

Proco Inc ....G...... 609 265-8777
Lumberton (G-5634)

Quality Glass Inc ....F...... 908 754-2652
South Plainfield (G-10320)

Quark Enterprises Inc ....E...... 856 455-0376
Rosenhayn (G-9597)

R A O Contract Sales NY Inc ....G...... 201 652-1500
Paterson (G-8285)

▲ Rambusch Decorating Company ....E...... 201 333-2525
Jersey City (G-4797)

S P Industries Inc ....D...... 856 691-3200
Vineland (G-11262)

▲ St Thomas Creations ....E...... 800 536-2284
Monroe Township (G-6345)

◆ Thermoseal Industries LLC ....D...... 856 456-3109
Gloucester City (G-3852)

Triton Associated Industries ....E...... 856 697-3050
Buena (G-944)

Union City Mirror & Table Co ....E...... 201 867-0050
Union City (G-11131)

V M Glass Co ....G...... 856 794-9333
Vineland (G-11274)

William Duling ....G...... 856 365-6323
Camden (G-1090)

3241 Cement, Hydraulic

▼ Anti Hydro International Inc ....F...... 908 284-9000
Flemington (G-3430)

Lafarge North America Inc ....G...... 201 437-2575
Bayonne (G-227)

Lehigh Cement Company ....G...... 973 579-2111
Sparta (G-10395)

Local Concrete Sup & Eqp Corp ......G...... 201 797-7979
Elmwood Park (G-2838)

Pavestone LLC ....E...... 973 948-7193
Branchville (G-709)

Tanis Concrete ....E...... 201 796-1556
Fair Lawn (G-3126)

3251 Brick & Structural Clay Tile

Glen-Gery Corporation ....E...... 908 359-5111
Hillsborough (G-4320)

▲ Magpie Marketing Inc ....G...... 201 507-9155
Rutherford (G-9627)

Morgan Advanced Ceramics Inc ......E...... 973 808-1621
Fairfield (G-3273)

3253 Ceramic Tile

Andrevin Inc ....G...... 732 270-2794
Toms River (G-10743)

Congoleum Corporation ....D...... 609 584-3601
Trenton (G-10922)

▲ Industrie Bitossi Inc ....E...... 201 796-0722
Elmwood Park (G-2831)

▲ L S P Industrial Ceramics Inc........G...... 609 397-8330
Lambertville (G-5193)

◆ Mannington Mills Inc ....A...... 856 935-3000
Salem (G-9694)

Maya Trading Corporation ....G...... 201 533-1400
Jersey City (G-4763)

◆ Nasco Stone and Tile LLC ....E...... 732 634-0589
Port Reading (G-8894)

▲ Standard Tile Watchung Corp........G...... 908 754-4200
Watchung (G-11458)

Stonework Dsign Consulting Inc.......E...... 973 575-0835
Fairfield (G-3318)

▼ Terra Designs Inc ....F...... 973 328-1135
Dover (G-2108)

3255 Clay Refractories

▲ Bartley Crucible Refractories ....F...... 609 393-0066
Trenton (G-10902)

Harbisonwalker Intl Inc ....G...... 732 388-8686
Rahway (G-9099)

3259 Structural Clay Prdts, NEC

R & R Irrigation Co Inc ....F...... 732 271-7070
Middlesex (G-6142)

3261 China Plumbing Fixtures & Fittings

▲ As America Inc ....C...... 732 980-3000
Piscataway (G-8637)

Benco Inc ....F...... 973 575-4440
Fairfield (G-3154)

▲ Ecom Group Inc ....E...... 718 504-7355
Edison (G-2498)

▲ Ginsey Industries Inc ....D...... 856 933-1300
Swedesboro (G-10586)

Hitrons Solutions Inc ....E...... 201 244-0300
Bergenfield (G-377)

▲ Hitrons Solutions Inc ....F...... 201 244-0300
Bergenfield (G-378)

◆ Lenape Products Inc ....E...... 609 394-5376
Trenton (G-10951)

◆ New Jersey Porcelain Co Inc ....F...... 609 394-5376
Trenton (G-10963)

Sap-Seal Products Inc ....G...... 201 385-5553
Bergenfield (G-384)

▲ Toilettree Products Inc ....G...... 845 358-5316
Ramsey (G-9157)

3262 China, Table & Kitchen Articles

▲ Nikko Ceramics Inc ....F...... 201 840-5200
Fairview (G-3364)

3263 Earthenware, Whiteware, Table & Kitchen Articles

Art Plaque Creations Inc ....F...... 973 482-2536
Kearny (G-4845)

3264 Porcelain Electrical Splys

Curran-Pfeiff Corp ....F...... 732 225-0555
Edison (G-2489)

Electro-Ceramic Industries ....E...... 201 342-2630
Hackensack (G-3911)

Escadaus Inc ....G...... 973 335-8888
Boonton (G-552)

▲ Fermag Technologies Inc ....G...... 732 985-7300
Toms River (G-10756)

House of Prill Inc ....E...... 732 442-2400
Lincroft (G-5311)

Isolantite Manufacturing Co ....E...... 908 647-3333
Stirling (G-10492)

▲ Merrimac Industries Inc ....D...... 973 575-1300
West Caldwell (G-11665)

Mitronics Products Inc ....G...... 908 647-5006
Gillette (G-3802)

Morgan Advanced Ceramics Inc ......E...... 973 808-1621
Fairfield (G-3273)

◆ New Jersey Porcelain Co Inc ....F...... 609 394-5376
Trenton (G-10963)

◆ Oxford Instrs Holdings Inc ....E...... 732 541-1300
Carteret (G-1263)

Pekay Industries Inc ....F...... 732 938-2722
Farmingdale (G-3390)

▲ Top Knobs Usa Inc ....E...... 908 359-6174
Somerville (G-10126)

3269 Pottery Prdts, NEC

Cameo China Inc ....G...... 201 865-7650
Secaucus (G-9755)

▲ Durand Glass Mfg Co Inc ....A...... 856 327-1850
Millville (G-6248)

◆ Franklin Mint LLC ....E...... 800 843-6468
Fort Lee (G-3559)

◆ Larose Industries LLC ....D...... 973 543-2037
Randolph (G-9189)

3271 Concrete Block & Brick

◆ Anchor Concrete Products Inc ....E...... 732 842-5010
Red Bank (G-9220)

Anchor Concrete Products Inc ....D...... 732 458-9440
Brick (G-711)

B&F and Son Masonry Company ......E...... 201 791-7630
Elmwood Park (G-2811)

Bell Supply Co ....G...... 856 663-3900
Pennsauken (G-8396)

Blades Landscaping Inc ....F...... 856 779-7665
Mount Laurel (G-6742)

Clayton Block Co ....D...... 201 955-6292
North Arlington (G-7371)

Clayton Block Company Inc ....G...... 732 751-7600
Trenton (G-10918)

Clayton Block Company Inc ....G...... 732 462-1860
Freehold (G-3658)

Clayton Block Company Inc ....E...... 732 681-0186
Wall Township (G-11326)

Clayton Block Company Inc ....F...... 609 693-9600
Forked River (G-3537)

Clayton Block Company Inc ....F...... 732 905-3234
Tinton Falls (G-10707)

Clayton Block Company Inc ....F...... 609 695-0767
Trenton (G-10919)

Clayton Block Company Inc ....G...... 609 693-3000
Waretown (G-11393)

Clayton Block Company Inc ....F...... 609 597-8128
West Creek (G-11685)

Clayton Block Company Inc ....F...... 732 751-1631
Wall Township (G-11327)

Clayton Block Company Inc ....E...... 732 549-1234
Edison (G-2478)

Clayton Block Company Inc ....F...... 732 349-3700
Toms River (G-10753)

Clayton Block Company LLC ....E...... 201 339-8585
Bayonne (G-210)

Creative Pavers ....G...... 201 782-1661
Montvale (G-6406)

Crh Americas ....E...... 732 292-2500
Red Bank (G-9224)

Dunbar Concrete Products Inc ....F...... 973 697-2525
Oak Ridge (G-7600)

▲ EP Henry Corporation ....D...... 856 845-6200
Woodbury (G-12028)

▲ GAF Elk Materials Corporation ......C...... 973 628-4083
Wayne (G-11508)

Greenrock Recycling LLC ....G...... 908 713-0008
Clinton (G-1745)

▼ Hycrete Inc ....E...... 201 386-8110
Fairfield (G-3233)

Josantos Cnstr & Dev LLC ....G...... 732 202-7389
Brick (G-724)

Paverart LLC ....G...... 856 783-7000
Lindenwold (G-5446)

▼ Phillips Companies Inc ....D...... 973 483-4124
Clinton (G-1748)

Procrete LLC ....G...... 609 365-2922
Linwood (G-5450)

R P Smith & Son Inc ....F...... 973 584-4063
Succasunna (G-10517)

Reuther Contracting Co Inc ....E...... 201 863-3550
North Bergen (G-7434)

Vogel Precast Inc ....G...... 732 552-8837
Lakewood (G-5178)

3272 Concrete Prdts

A & A Concrete Products Inc ....G...... 973 835-2239
Riverdale (G-9369)

Advanced Pavement Technologies .....F...... 973 366-8044
Rockaway (G-9438)

Associate Fireplace Builders ....G...... 908 273-5900
Summit (G-10526)

▲ Boccella Precast LLC ....F...... 856 767-3861
Berlin (G-416)

▲ Bradbury Burial Vault Co Inc ....E...... 856 227-2555
Blackwood (G-461)

Brent Material Company ... G ... 908 686-3832
Kenilworth *(G-4931)*
Brewster Vaults & Monuments ... F ... 856 785-1412
Millville *(G-6239)*
◆ **Ceresist Inc** ... F ... 973 345-3231
Paterson *(G-8156)*
Clayton Block Co ... D ... 201 955-6292
North Arlington *(G-7371)*
Clayton Block Company Inc ... E ... 732 681-0186
Wall Township *(G-11326)*
Clayton Block Company LLC ... E ... 201 339-8585
Bayonne *(G-210)*
▲ **Concrete Stone & Tile Corp** ... E ... 973 948-7193
Branchville *(G-705)*
▲ **Construction Specialties Inc** ... E ... 908 236-0800
Lebanon *(G-5257)*
Cooper Burial Vaults Co ... G ... 856 547-8405
Barrington *(G-169)*
Cooper-Wilbert Vault Co Inc ... E ... 856 547-8405
Barrington *(G-170)*
Creter Vault Corp ... E ... 908 782-7771
Flemington *(G-3435)*
Crossfield Products Corp ... D ... 908 245-2801
Roselle Park *(G-9580)*
CST Pavers ... F ... 856 299-5339
Pedricktown *(G-8347)*
▲ **CST Products LLC** ... E ... 856 299-5339
Penns Grove *(G-8377)*
Cumberland Marble & Monument ... G ... 856 691-3334
Vineland *(G-11207)*
Delaware Valley Vault Co Inc ... G ... 856 227-2555
Blackwood *(G-463)*
Di-Ferraro Inc ... E ... 973 694-7200
Wayne *(G-11493)*
Diamond Chip Realty LLC ... E ... 973 383-4651
Sparta *(G-10386)*
Double Twenties Inc ... F ... 973 827-7563
Franklin *(G-3602)*
Dunbar Concrete Products Inc ... F ... 973 697-2525
Oak Ridge *(G-7600)*
Duraamen Engineered Pdts Inc ... G ... 973 230-1301
Newark *(G-7106)*
▼ **Empire Blended Products Inc** ... E ... 732 269-4949
Bayville *(G-244)*
European Stone Art LLC ... F ... 201 441-9116
South Hackensack *(G-10160)*
Flemington Precast & Sup LLC ... F ... 908 782-3246
Flemington *(G-3443)*
Flexco Bldg Pdts Ltd Lblty Co ... F ... 732 780-1700
Marlboro *(G-5898)*
▲ **GAF Elk Materials Corporation** ... C ... 973 628-4083
Wayne *(G-11508)*
Garden State Precast Inc ... D ... 732 938-4436
Wall Township *(G-11343)*
Granville Concrete Products ... G ... 973 584-6653
Randolph *(G-9182)*
Gravity Vault LLC ... G ... 732 856-9599
Middletown *(G-6164)*
H T Hall Inc ... F ... 732 449-3441
Spring Lake *(G-10422)*
Hanson Aggregates Wrp Inc ... E ... 972 653-5500
Wall Township *(G-11345)*
Interntnal Dmnsional Stone LLC ... G ... 973 729-0359
Haskell *(G-4197)*
◆ **J B & Sons Concrete Products** ... F ... 856 767-4140
Berlin *(G-423)*
J F Gillespie Inc ... E ... 856 692-2233
Vineland *(G-11237)*
J L Erectors Inc ... E ... 856 232-9400
Blackwood *(G-470)*
▲ **Jarco U S Casting Corp** ... E ... 201 271-0003
Union City *(G-11115)*
Jersey Cast Stone Ltd Lblty Co ... F ... 856 333-6900
Pennsauken *(G-8445)*
▲ **Jersey Precast Corporation Inc** ... C ... 609 689-3700
Trenton *(G-10946)*
JM Ahle Co Inc ... G ... 732 388-5507
Rahway *(G-9108)*
Jpc Merger Sub LLC ... C ... 609 890-4343
Trenton *(G-10948)*
Kelken-Gold Inc ... G ... 732 416-6730
Sayreville *(G-9713)*
Kuiken Brothers Company ... E ... 201 796-2082
Fair Lawn *(G-3109)*
Liedl ... G ... 908 359-8335
Hillsborough *(G-4339)*
▲ **Massarellis Lawn Ornaments Inc** ... E ... 609 567-9700
Hammonton *(G-4139)*
Maund Enterprises Inc ... G ... 609 628-2475
Tuckahoe *(G-11012)*
Mershon Concrete LLC ... E ... 609 298-2150
Bordentown *(G-588)*
▲ **Midstate Filigree Systems Inc** ... D ... 609 448-8700
Cranbury *(G-1864)*
Northeast Con Pdts & Sup Inc ... G ... 973 728-1667
Hewitt *(G-4277)*
Northeast Concrete Pdts LLC ... G ... 973 728-1667
Hewitt *(G-4278)*
Oldcastle Infrastructure Inc ... E ... 609 561-3400
Williamstown *(G-11966)*
P J Gillespie Inc ... E ... 856 327-2993
Vineland *(G-11248)*
Paul Bros Inc ... E ... 856 697-5895
Newfield *(G-7326)*
Peerless Concrete Products Co ... E ... 973 838-3060
Butler *(G-1011)*
Precast Manufacturing Co LLC ... E ... 908 454-2122
Phillipsburg *(G-8569)*
Precast Systems Inc ... E ... 609 208-0569
Allentown *(G-29)*
Russell Cast Stone Inc ... D ... 856 753-4000
West Berlin *(G-11620)*
◆ **Sika Corporation** ... B ... 201 933-8800
Lyndhurst *(G-5678)*
Solid Cast Stone ... G ... 856 694-5245
Newfield *(G-7328)*
Strongwall Industries Inc ... G ... 201 445-4633
Ridgewood *(G-9330)*
Suburban Monument & Vault ... G ... 973 242-7007
Newark *(G-7289)*
Trap Rock Industries Inc ... B ... 609 924-0300
Kingston *(G-5012)*
Trap-Zap Environmental Systems ... E ... 201 251-9970
Wyckoff *(G-12122)*
Tri-State Quikrete ... E ... 973 347-4569
Flanders *(G-3423)*
▲ **Ulma Form-Works Inc** ... D ... 201 882-1122
Hawthorne *(G-4247)*
Van Brill Pool & Spa Center ... G ... 856 424-4333
Marlton *(G-5955)*

3273 Ready-Mixed Concrete

Abi Inc ... E ... 609 588-8225
Lawrenceville *(G-5222)*
Ace-Crete Products Inc ... F ... 732 269-1400
Bayville *(G-238)*
Action Supply Inc ... F ... 609 390-0663
Ocean View *(G-7701)*
Allied Concrete Co Inc ... G ... 973 627-6150
Rockaway *(G-9440)*
Allied Concrete Co Inc ... G ... 973 627-6150
Rockaway *(G-9441)*
Atlantic Masonry Supply Inc ... F ... 609 909-9292
Egg Harbor Township *(G-2678)*
◆ **Clayton Block Company Inc** ... E ... 888 763-8665
Wall Township *(G-11325)*
Clayton Block Company Inc ... F ... 732 349-3700
Toms River *(G-10753)*
Clayton Block Company Inc ... F ... 732 364-2404
Jackson *(G-4643)*
Clayton Block Company Inc ... E ... 732 549-1234
Edison *(G-2478)*
Concrete On Demand Inc ... F ... 201 337-0005
Oakland *(G-7620)*
County Concrete Corporation ... F ... 973 538-3113
Morristown *(G-6656)*
County Concrete Corporation ... D ... 973 744-2188
Kenvil *(G-4992)*
Diamond Chip Realty LLC ... E ... 973 383-4651
Sparta *(G-10386)*
Eastern Concrete Materials Inc ... G ... 609 698-2800
Barnegat *(G-159)*
Eastern Concrete Materials Inc ... C ... 201 797-7979
Saddle Brook *(G-9650)*
Eastern Concrete Materials Inc ... G ... 908 537-2135
Glen Gardner *(G-3821)*
Erial Concrete Inc ... F ... 856 784-8884
Erial *(G-3011)*
Ernest R Miles Construction Co ... F ... 856 697-2311
Newfield *(G-7321)*
Hanson Aggregates Bmc Inc ... G ... 856 447-4294
Newport *(G-7333)*
Herbert J Hinchman & Son Inc ... E ... 973 942-2063
Wayne *(G-11516)*
Holtec Government Services LLC ... G ... 856 291-0600
Camden *(G-1068)*
Joseph and William Stavola ... E ... 609 924-0300
Kingston *(G-5009)*
Kennedy Concrete Inc ... E ... 856 692-8650
Vineland *(G-11240)*
L & L Redi-Mix Inc ... D ... 609 859-2271
Southampton *(G-10367)*
Le-Ed Construction Inc ... E ... 732 341-4546
Toms River *(G-10775)*
Mershon Concrete LLC ... E ... 609 298-2150
Bordentown *(G-588)*
Miles Concrete Company Inc ... F ... 856 697-2311
Newfield *(G-7323)*
New Jersey Pulverizing Co Inc ... F ... 732 269-1400
Bayville *(G-249)*
Penn-Jersey Bldg Mtls Co Inc ... G ... 609 641-6994
Egg Harbor Township *(G-2692)*
▼ **Phillips Companies Inc** ... D ... 973 483-4124
Clinton *(G-1748)*
Ralph Clayton & Sons LLC ... E ... 800 662-3044
Cookstown *(G-1805)*
Ralph Clayton & Sons LLC ... E ... 732 462-1552
Freehold *(G-3697)*
Ralph Clayton & Sons LLC ... E ... 609 383-1818
Egg Harbor Township *(G-2694)*
Ralph Clayton & Sons LLC ... E ... 609 695-0767
Trenton *(G-10986)*
Reuther Material Co Inc ... E ... 201 863-3550
North Bergen *(G-7435)*
Salomone Redi-Mix LLC ... E ... 973 305-0022
Wayne *(G-11552)*
SCC Concrete Inc ... F ... 908 859-2172
Phillipsburg *(G-8574)*
Short Load Concrete LLC ... G ... 732 469-4420
Bridgewater *(G-889)*
STA-Seal Inc ... G ... 609 924-0300
Kingston *(G-5011)*
Suffolk County Contractors ... E ... 732 349-7726
Toms River *(G-10796)*
Tanis Concrete ... E ... 201 796-1556
Fair Lawn *(G-3126)*
Trap Rock Industries Inc ... B ... 609 924-0300
Kingston *(G-5012)*
Weldon Asphalt Corp ... E ... 908 322-7840
Watchung *(G-11461)*
Weldon Concrete Corp ... G ... 973 228-7473
Roseland *(G-9544)*
Weldon Materials Inc ... E ... 908 233-4444
Westfield *(G-11806)*
Weldon Quarry Co LLC ... E ... 908 233-4444
Westfield *(G-11807)*
Wjv Materials LLC ... E ... 856 299-8244
Pedricktown *(G-8356)*
Yogo Mix ... G ... 609 897-1379
Princeton Junction *(G-9071)*

3274 Lime

Lime Energy Co ... G ... 908 415-9469
South Plainfield *(G-10294)*
Lime Energy Co ... G ... 732 791-5380
Newark *(G-7180)*
Luxfer Magtech Inc ... E ... 803 610-9898
Manchester *(G-5846)*
Smith Lime Flour Co Inc ... F ... 973 344-1700
Kearny *(G-4898)*

3275 Gypsum Prdts

Art Plaque Creations Inc ... F ... 973 482-2536
Kearny *(G-4845)*
Baruffi Bros Inc ... F ... 856 692-6400
Vineland *(G-11191)*
▲ **Durabond Division US Gypsum** ... F ... 732 636-7900
Port Reading *(G-8893)*
Georgia-Pacific LLC ... D ... 856 966-7600
Camden *(G-1066)*
Proform Acoustic Surfaces LLC ... G ... 201 553-9614
Secaucus *(G-9800)*
United States Gypsum Company ... D ... 732 636-7900
Port Reading *(G-8896)*

3281 Cut Stone Prdts

A C D Custom Granite Inc ... F ... 732 695-2400
Ocean *(G-7651)*
Albert H Hopper Inc ... G ... 201 991-2266
North Arlington *(G-7367)*
Alps Technologies Inc ... E ... 732 764-0777
Somerset *(G-9949)*
American Stone Inc ... E ... 973 318-7707
Hillside *(G-4373)*
American Stone Inc ... F ... 973 318-7707
Hillside *(G-4374)*
▲ **Bcg Marble & Granite South LLC** ... G ... 732 367-3788
Jackson *(G-4641)*
◆ **Bcg Marble Gran Fabricators Co** ... F ... 201 343-8487
Hackensack *(G-3882)*

Bedrock Granite Inc............................E...... 732 741-0010
Shrewsbury (G-9883)

◆ Cambridge Pavers Inc......................C...... 201 933-5000
Lyndhurst (G-5644)

▲ Caputo International Inc..................G...... 732 225-5777
Edison (G-2474)

Charles Deluca....................................G...... 973 778-5621
Lodi (G-5556)

Cole Brothers Marble & Granite..........G...... 856 455-7989
Elmer (G-2795)

▲ Counter-Fit Inc...............................C...... 609 871-8888
Willingboro (G-11990)

▲ Elana Tile Contractors Inc..............G...... 973 386-0991
East Hanover (G-2208)

▲ Elite Stone Importers LLC................G...... 732 542-7900
Tinton Falls (G-10716)

▲ EP Henry Corporation.....................D...... 856 845-6200
Woodbury (G-12028)

EZ General Construction Corp............G...... 201 223-1101
Wayne (G-11500)

◆ Formia Marble & Stone Inc..............E...... 908 259-0606
Roselle (G-9558)

Gr Stone LLC......................................G...... 908 925-7290
Kenilworth (G-4943)

▲ Gran All Mrble Tile Imprts Inc.........G...... 856 354-4747
Cherry Hill (G-1369)

▲ Granite and Marble Assoc Inc..........G...... 908 416-1100
North Plainfield (G-7505)

H T Hall Inc...F...... 732 449-3441
Spring Lake (G-10422)

Hanson Aggregates Wrp Inc...............E...... 972 653-5500
Wall Township (G-11345)

Ilkem Granite & Marble 2 Corp...........F...... 732 613-1457
Old Bridge (G-7716)

Ilkem Marble and Granite Inc.............G...... 856 433-8714
Cherry Hill (G-1374)

▲ Industrial Consulting Mktg Inc........E...... 973 427-2474
Fair Lawn (G-3105)

Industrial Consulting Mktg Inc............E...... 877 405-5200
Fair Lawn (G-3106)

Innovative Cutng Concepts LLC...........G...... 609 484-9960
Egg Harbor Township (G-2684)

Interntnal Dmnsional Stone LLC..........G...... 973 729-0359
Haskell (G-4197)

▲ Marble Online Corporation...............G...... 201 998-9100
Kearny (G-4882)

Marmo Enterprises Inc.......................G...... 732 649-3011
Somerset (G-10023)

Marvic Corp..E...... 908 686-4340
Union (G-11074)

Murray Paving & Concrete LLC............E...... 201 670-0030
Hackensack (G-3950)

Natures Beauty Marble & Gran...........F...... 908 233-5300
Scotch Plains (G-9737)

▲ Phillipsburg Marble Co Inc..............E...... 908 859-3435
Phillipsburg (G-8568)

Premier Marble and Gran 2 Inc...........G...... 732 294-7891
Freehold (G-3691)

◆ Robert Young & Sons Inc................G...... 973 483-0451
Newark (G-7252)

Sanford & Birdsall Inc........................G...... 732 223-6966
Manasquan (G-5838)

Sculptured Stone Inc..........................F...... 973 557-1482
Boonton (G-568)

Solidsurface Designs Inc.....................E...... 856 910-7720
Pennsauken (G-8487)

▲ Sr International Rock Inc.................F...... 908 864-4700
Bound Brook (G-606)

Statewide Granite and Marble.............F...... 201 653-1700
Jersey City (G-4815)

Stavola Construction Mtls Inc.............E...... 732 542-2328
Tinton Falls (G-10729)

Stavola Construction Mtls Inc.............E...... 732 356-5700
Bound Brook (G-608)

▲ Stone Mar Natural Stone Co LLC.....G...... 856 988-1802
Marlton (G-5952)

Stone Systems New Jersey LLC...........F...... 973 778-5525
Fairfield (G-3316)

▲ Stone Truss Systems Inc................E...... 973 882-7377
Fairfield (G-3317)

Stoneworld At Redbank Inc.................G...... 732 383-5110
Red Bank (G-9245)

▲ Thin Stone Systems LLC.................G...... 973 882-7377
Fairfield (G-3327)

3291 Abrasive Prdts

3M Company.......................................B...... 973 884-2500
Whippany (G-11875)

▲ Advanced Abrasives Corporation......F...... 856 665-9300
Pennsauken (G-8383)

Agsco Corporation..............................E...... 973 244-0005
Pine Brook (G-8584)

▲ Alpex Wheel Co Inc........................F...... 201 871-1700
Tenafly (G-10659)

▲ Beacut Abrasives Corp....................F...... 973 249-1420
East Rutherford (G-2275)

Chessco Industries Inc........................E...... 609 882-0400
Ewing (G-3020)

East Coast Diamond TI Pdts Inc...........G...... 212 686-1034
Englewood (G-2899)

▲ Garfield Industries Inc....................E...... 973 575-3322
Fairfield (G-3212)

▲ Japan Steel Works America Inc........G...... 212 490-2630
Edison (G-2538)

▲ Mercury Floor Machines Inc.............E...... 201 568-4606
Englewood (G-2924)

New Jersey Diamond Products Co........F...... 973 684-0949
Paterson (G-8267)

▲ Robinson Tech Intl Corp..................G...... 973 287-6458
Fairfield (G-3303)

Steel Riser Corp.................................G...... 732 341-7031
Toms River (G-10795)

▲ Supply Plus NY Inc.........................E...... 973 481-4800
Paterson (G-8308)

William R Hall Co................................E...... 856 784-6700
Lindenwold (G-5447)

3292 Asbestos products

▲ Allied Tile Mfg Corp.......................G...... 718 647-2200
South Plainfield (G-10213)

Blavor Inc..G...... 973 265-4165
Montville (G-6438)

Hup & Sons..G...... 908 832-7878
Glen Gardner (G-3823)

▲ Hydro-Mechanical Systems Inc.......F...... 856 848-8888
Westville (G-11816)

◆ Stuart Steel Protection Corp...........E...... 732 469-5544
Somerset (G-10075)

Wick It LLC...G...... 973 249-2970
Passaic (G-8116)

3295 Minerals & Earths: Ground Or Treated

▼ Anthracite Industries Inc................G...... 908 537-2155
Asbury (G-59)

◆ Asbury Carbons Inc........................G...... 908 537-2155
Asbury (G-60)

◆ Asbury Graphite Mills Inc................E...... 908 537-2155
Asbury (G-61)

Asbury Graphite Mills Inc....................D...... 908 537-2157
Asbury (G-62)

Corp American Mica............................G...... 908 587-5237
Linden (G-5336)

Dicalite Minerals Corp.........................G...... 856 320-2919
Pennsauken (G-8413)

▲ Fine Minerals Intl Inc.....................G...... 732 318-6760
Edison (G-2512)

◆ G Holdings LLC...............................F...... 973 628-3000
Parsippany (G-7953)

◆ G-I Holdings Inc..............................G...... 973 628-3000
Wayne (G-11507)

◆ Isp Global Technologies Inc.............G...... 973 628-4000
Wayne (G-11524)

Isp Global Technologies LLC................G...... 973 628-4000
Wayne (G-11525)

▲ Mel Chemicals Inc..........................C...... 908 782-5800
Flemington (G-3455)

◆ Minmetals Inc................................F...... 201 809-1898
Leonia (G-5290)

3296 Mineral Wool

Advantage Fiberglass Inc....................G...... 609 926-4606
Egg Harbor Township (G-2675)

Fbm Galaxy Inc..................................E...... 856 966-1105
Camden (G-1064)

Insulation Materials Distrs..................G...... 908 925-2323
Linden (G-5360)

Johns Manville Corporation.................G...... 856 768-7000
Berlin (G-424)

Owens Corning Sales LLC....................C...... 201 998-5666
Kearny (G-4888)

▲ Pacor Inc.......................................E...... 609 324-1100
Bordentown (G-592)

Passaic Metal & Bldg Sups Co.............D...... 973 546-9000
Clifton (G-1685)

Pekay Industries Inc...........................F...... 732 938-2722
Farmingdale (G-3390)

◆ United States Mineral Pdts Co.........D...... 973 347-1200
Stanhope (G-10480)

3297 Nonclay Refractories

Curran-Pfeiff Corp..............................F...... 732 225-0555
Edison (G-2489)

Morgan Advanced Ceramics Inc...........E...... 973 808-1621
Fairfield (G-3273)

▲ P & R Castings LLC.........................E...... 732 302-3600
Somerset (G-10049)

Strongwall Industries Inc....................G...... 201 445-4633
Ridgewood (G-9330)

3299 Nonmetallic Mineral Prdts, NEC

Advanced Cerametrics Inc...................G...... 609 397-2900
Lambertville (G-5186)

Art Plaque Creations Inc.....................F...... 973 482-2536
Kearny (G-4845)

▲ Barrett Bronze Inc..........................E...... 914 699-6060
Wyckoff (G-12103)

Brambila Jorge Stucco & Stone...........G...... 856 451-2039
Bridgeton (G-753)

California Stucco Products...................G...... 201 457-1900
Hackensack (G-3892)

▲ Ceramic Products Inc......................G...... 201 342-8200
Hackensack (G-3896)

▲ Ceramsource Inc............................E...... 732 257-5002
East Brunswick (G-2131)

Crystex Composites LLC......................E...... 973 779-8866
Clifton (G-1593)

Digital Atelier LLC..............................G...... 609 890-6666
Trenton (G-10931)

▲ Environmolds LLC...........................F...... 908 273-5401
Summit (G-10531)

Georgia-Pacific LLC.............................D...... 856 966-7600
Camden (G-1066)

▲ Intersource USA Inc........................E...... 732 257-5002
East Brunswick (G-2152)

Kingston Nurseries LLC.......................F...... 609 430-0366
Kingston (G-5010)

Mediterranean Stucco Corp.................F...... 973 491-0160
Newark (G-7199)

Perfect Shapes Inc..............................G...... 856 783-3844
Elmer (G-2801)

Whibco Inc...E...... 856 825-5200
Port Elizabeth (G-8877)

33 PRIMARY METAL INDUSTRIES

3312 Blast Furnaces, Coke Ovens, Steel & Rolling Mills

A & A Ironwork Co Inc........................F...... 973 728-4300
Hewitt (G-4273)

Aibens Imort......................................G...... 609 902-9953
Princeton Junction (G-9049)

Air Technology Inc..............................G...... 973 334-4980
Boonton (G-538)

◆ Albea Americas Inc.........................C...... 908 689-3000
Washington (G-11437)

Alloy Stainless Products Co.................D...... 973 256-1616
Totowa (G-10810)

Amrod Corp..D...... 973 344-3806
Newark (G-7046)

◆ Aperam Stnlss Svc & Solutns..........E...... 908 988-0625
New Providence (G-6994)

Archer Day Inc....................................E...... 732 396-0600
Avenel (G-120)

▲ Atco Products Inc...........................E...... 973 379-3171
Springfield (G-10428)

Atlas Copco North America LLC............G...... 973 397-3400
Parsippany (G-7888)

Benedict-Miller LLC.............................F...... 908 497-1477
Kenilworth (G-4929)

Bilt Rite Tool & Die Co Inc...................G...... 973 227-2882
Fairfield (G-3158)

Bloomfield Iron Co Inc.........................G...... 973 748-7040
Belleville (G-291)

Bushwick Metals LLC...........................E...... 908 754-8700
South Plainfield (G-10231)

Camden Iron & Metal Inc.....................F...... 856 365-7500
Camden (G-1043)

◆ Camden Iron & Metal LLC................D...... 856 969-7065
Camden (G-1044)

CB&i LLC..C...... 856 482-3000
Trenton (G-10913)

▲ Century Tube Corp.........................E...... 908 534-2001
Somerville (G-10105)

CMI-Promex Inc..................................F...... 856 351-1000
Pedricktown (G-8346)

DAngelo Metal Products Inc.................F...... 908 862-8220
Linden (G-5341)

▲ Dso Fluid Handling Co Inc ....E 732 225-9100
  Edison **(G-2495)**

▲ Dynamic Defense Materials LLC ......G 856 552-4150
  Marlton **(G-5930)**

E C Electroplating Inc ....E 973 340-0227
  Garfield **(G-3740)**

▲ Easyflex East Inc ....G 201 853-9005
  Little Ferry **(G-5484)**

Electro Parts Inc ....G 856 767-5923
  West Berlin **(G-11593)**

Equipment Distributing Corp ....G 201 641-8414
  Ridgefield Park **(G-9305)**

▲ Ford Fasteners Inc ....G 201 487-3151
  Hackensack **(G-3916)**

Fox Steel Products LLC ....G 856 778-4661
  Mount Laurel **(G-6762)**

G M Stainless Inc ....F 908 575-1834
  Branchburg **(G-643)**

Hands On Wheels ....G 609 892-4693
  Atlantic City **(G-93)**

◆ Hoeganaes Corporation ....B 856 303-0366
  Cinnaminson **(G-1464)**

Interstate Welding & Mfg Co ....F 800 676-4666
  Beverly **(G-452)**

McAlister Welding & Fabg ....F 856 740-3890
  Glassboro **(G-3815)**

▲ Robinson Tech Intl Corp ....G 973 287-6458
  Fairfield **(G-3303)**

▲ Stainless Metal Source Intl ....G 973 977-2200
  Clifton **(G-1724)**

Tms International LLC ....G 732 721-7477
  Sayreville **(G-9725)**

Unity Steel Rule Die Co ....E 201 569-6400
  Englewood **(G-2951)**

US Pipe Fabrication LLC ....F 856 461-3000
  Riverside **(G-9404)**

Welded Products Co Inc ....E 973 589-0180
  Newark **(G-7313)**

Yarde Metals Inc ....E 973 463-1166
  East Hanover **(G-2248)**

3313 Electrometallurgical Prdts

Alpha Assembly Solutions Inc ....E 908 561-5170
  South Plainfield **(G-10214)**

◆ Alpha Assembly Solutions Inc ....E 908 791-3000
  Somerset **(G-9948)**

Hoyt Corporation ....E 201 894-0707
  Englewood **(G-2912)**

Thyssenkrupp Materials NA Inc ....F 212 972-8800
  Maywood **(G-6017)**

3315 Steel Wire Drawing & Nails & Spikes

Amark Industries Inc ....G 973 992-8900
  Livingston **(G-5505)**

Amark Wire LLC ....G 973 882-7818
  Fairfield **(G-3141)**

◆ Arca Industrial Inc ....G 732 339-0450
  East Windsor **(G-2336)**

◆ Arrow Fastener Co LLC ....B 201 843-6900
  Saddle Brook **(G-9640)**

Barrette Outdoor Living Inc ....F 609 965-5450
  Egg Harbor City **(G-2653)**

Belmont Whl Fence Mfg Inc ....E 973 472-5121
  Garfield **(G-3732)**

▲ Bergen Cable Technology LLC ....E 973 276-9596
  Fairfield **(G-3155)**

▲ Blue Gauntlet Fencing Gear Inc ......F 201 797-3332
  Saddle Brook **(G-9642)**

Boyle Tool & Die Co Inc ....F 856 853-1819
  West Deptford **(G-11694)**

Bushwick Metals LLC ....G 908 604-1450
  South Plainfield **(G-10230)**

▲ C D E Inc ....D 732 297-2540
  North Brunswick **(G-7459)**

▲ Dearborn A Belden Cdt Company ...D 908 925-8000
  Elizabeth **(G-2726)**

Evergard Steel Corp ....F 908 925-6800
  South Plainfield **(G-10253)**

Fence America New Jersey Inc ....G 973 472-5121
  Hackensack **(G-3912)**

Fisk Alloy Inc ....E 973 427-7550
  Hawthorne **(G-4219)**

◆ Fisk Alloy Wire Incorporated ....C 973 949-4491
  Hawthorne **(G-4220)**

Global Wire & Cable Inc ....E 973 471-1000
  Passaic **(G-8070)**

▲ Iwc ....F 732 968-8122
  Green Brook **(G-3862)**

▲ Jersey Specialty Co Inc ....E 413 525-2292
  Pennsauken **(G-8471)**

Kabel N Elettrotek Amer Inc ....G 973 265-0850
  Parsippany **(G-7969)**

◆ Metallia USA LLC ....G 212 536-8002
  Fort Lee **(G-3572)**

Ninsa LLC ....G 609 561-7103
  Hammonton **(G-4140)**

◆ Okonite Company Inc ....C 201 825-0300
  Ramsey **(G-9154)**

Phillips Enterprises Inc ....G 732 493-3191
  Ocean **(G-7674)**

◆ Plasma Powders & Systems Inc ......G 732 431-0992
  Marlboro **(G-5909)**

▲ Railing Dynamics Inc ....F 609 601-1300
  Ocean City **(G-7692)**

Roll Tech Industries ....F 609 730-9500
  Pennington **(G-8373)**

◆ Sandvik Inc ....C 201 794-5000
  Fair Lawn **(G-3120)**

▲ Screentek Manufacturing Co LLC .....F 973 328-2121
  Randolph **(G-9198)**

Security Fabricators Inc ....F 908 272-9171
  Kenilworth **(G-4977)**

Skyline Stl Fbrcatrs & Erctrs ....G 973 957-0234
  Rockaway **(G-9499)**

▲ United Wire Hanger Corp ....C 201 288-3212
  Hasbrouck Heights **(G-4193)**

◆ US Wire & Cable Corporation ....B 973 824-5530
  Newark **(G-7310)**

Wire Fabricators & Insulators ....E 973 768-2839
  Livingston **(G-5549)**

Wytech Industries Inc ....E 732 396-3900
  Rahway **(G-9132)**

3316 Cold Rolled Steel Sheet, Strip & Bars

American Strip Steel Inc ....F 800 526-1216
  South Plainfield **(G-10216)**

American Strip Steel Inc ....G 856 461-8300
  Delanco **(G-2002)**

Bigelow Components Corp ....E 973 467-1200
  Springfield **(G-10431)**

Fox Steel Products LLC ....G 856 778-4661
  Mount Laurel **(G-6762)**

◆ General Sullivan Group Inc ....E 609 745-5004
  Pennington **(G-8365)**

Leibrock Metal Products Inc ....G 732 695-0326
  Ocean **(G-7669)**

◆ Sandvik Inc ....C 201 794-5000
  Fair Lawn **(G-3120)**

3317 Steel Pipe & Tubes

Amer-RAC LLC ....F 856 488-6210
  Pennsauken **(G-8388)**

▲ Century Tube Corp ....E 908 534-2001
  Somerville **(G-10105)**

Delsea Pipe Inc ....G 856 589-9374
  Sewell **(G-9839)**

▲ Dodson Global Inc ....G 732 238-7001
  East Brunswick **(G-2134)**

◆ Fluorotherm Polymers Inc ....G 973 575-0760
  Parsippany **(G-7948)**

Fox Steel Products LLC ....G 856 778-4661
  Mount Laurel **(G-6762)**

Long Island Pipe of NJ ....E 201 939-1100
  Lyndhurst **(G-5658)**

▲ M & M International ....F 908 412-8300
  South Plainfield **(G-10295)**

▲ Morris Industries Inc ....D 973 835-6600
  Pompton Plains **(G-8868)**

New World Stainless LLC ....E 732 412-7137
  Somerset **(G-10040)**

Nippon Benkan Kagyo ....E 732 435-0777
  New Brunswick **(G-6954)**

▲ Rathgibson North Branch LLC ....C 908 253-3260
  Branchburg **(G-675)**

◆ Sandvik Inc ....C 201 794-5000
  Fair Lawn **(G-3120)**

◆ Silbo Industries Inc ....F 201 307-0900
  Montvale **(G-6434)**

Zekelman Industries Inc ....D 724 342-6851
  Westwood **(G-11849)**

3321 Gray Iron Foundries

Bierman-Everett Foundry Co ....G 973 373-8800
  South Orange **(G-10192)**

Bridgestate Foundry Corp ....G 856 767-0400
  Berlin **(G-417)**

▲ Campbell Foundry Company ....E 973 483-5480
  Harrison **(G-4166)**

Campbell Foundry Company ....E 201 998-3765
  Kearny **(G-4850)**

Emporia Foundry Inc ....E 973 483-5480
  Harrison **(G-4172)**

En Tech Corp ....F 201 784-1034
  Closter **(G-1753)**

En Tech Corp ....F 718 389-2058
  Closter **(G-1754)**

▲ General Foundries Inc ....E 732 951-9001
  North Brunswick **(G-7468)**

McWane Inc ....B 908 454-1161
  Phillipsburg **(G-8562)**

United States Pipe Fndry LLC ....C 609 387-6000
  Burlington **(G-991)**

▲ Universal Valve Company Inc ....F 908 351-0606
  Elizabeth **(G-2784)**

Water Works Supply Company ....E 973 835-2153
  Pompton Plains **(G-8874)**

3322 Malleable Iron Foundries

▲ Hafco Foundry & Machine Co ....F 201 447-0433
  Midland Park **(G-6176)**

3324 Steel Investment Foundries

Advance Process Systems Lim ....G 201 400-9190
  Branchville **(G-701)**

AJ Oster LLC ....G 973 673-5700
  Parsippany **(G-7876)**

Alcoa Power Generating Inc ....G 973 361-0300
  Dover **(G-2073)**

Atlantic Eqp Engineers Inc ....F 201 828-9400
  Upper Saddle River **(G-11134)**

Engineered Precision Cast Co ....D 732 671-2424
  Middletown **(G-6163)**

▼ Fortune Rvrside Auto Parts Inc ....E 732 381-3355
  Rahway **(G-9094)**

Howmet Castings & Services Inc ....A 973 361-0300
  Dover **(G-2087)**

Howmet Castings & Services Inc ....B 973 361-0300
  Dover **(G-2088)**

Howmet Castings & Services Inc ....B 973 361-2310
  Dover **(G-2089)**

Mark I Industries Inc ....F 609 884-0051
  Cape May **(G-1100)**

R W Wheaton Co ....G 908 241-4955
  Roselle Park **(G-9590)**

Rbc Dain Rauscher ....F 973 778-7300
  Woodland Park **(G-12089)**

3325 Steel Foundries, NEC

▲ Accurate Bushing Company Inc ....E 908 789-1121
  Garwood **(G-3779)**

D S Jh LLC ....E 973 782-4086
  Lincoln Park **(G-5298)**

Double O Manufacturing Inc ....G 732 752-9423
  Middlesex **(G-6113)**

H & R Welding LLC ....G 732 920-4881
  Brick **(G-720)**

Interstate Welding & Mfg Co ....F 800 676-4666
  Beverly **(G-452)**

T Wiker Enterprises Inc ....G 609 261-9494
  Hainesport **(G-4079)**

3331 Primary Smelting & Refining Of Copper

Amrod Corp ....D 973 344-3806
  Newark **(G-7046)**

3334 Primary Production Of Aluminum

◆ Helidex LLC ....G 201 636-2546
  East Rutherford **(G-2291)**

Ivey Katrina Owner ....G 973 951-8328
  Newark **(G-7163)**

Quick Fab Aluminum Mfg Co ....E 732 367-7200
  Lakewood **(G-5150)**

3339 Primary Nonferrous Metals, NEC

Alpha Assembly Solutions Inc ....E 908 561-5170
  South Plainfield **(G-10214)**

◆ Alpha Assembly Solutions Inc ....E 908 791-3000
  Somerset **(G-9948)**

Ames Advanced Materials Corp ....C 908 226-2038
  South Plainfield **(G-10218)**

◆ BASF Catalysts LLC ....D 732 205-5000
  Iselin **(G-4599)**

◆ Dallas Group of America Inc ....E 908 534-7800
  Whitehouse **(G-11915)**

◆ Electrum Inc ....F 732 396-1616
  Rahway **(G-9090)**

Ewing Recovery Corp ....G 609 883-0318
  Ewing **(G-3030)**

Fisk Alloy Inc...............................E......973 427-7550
Hawthorne (G-4219)

◆ Fisk Alloy Wire Incorporated............C......973 949-4491
Hawthorne (G-4220)

L D L Technology Inc.....................G......973 345-9111
Paterson (G-8235)

Luxfer Magtech Inc.......................E......803 610-9898
Manchester (G-5846)

Matthey Johnson Inc......................C......856 384-7132
West Deptford (G-11710)

▲ Mel Chemicals Inc......................C......908 782-5800
Flemington (G-3455)

Metallix Direct Gold LLC.................G......732 544-0891
Shrewsbury (G-9894)

▲ Metallix Refining Inc..................F......732 936-0050
Shrewsbury (G-9895)

▲ National Electronic Alloys Inc.........E......201 337-9400
Oakland (G-7638)

▼ Omg Electronic Chemicals Inc..........C......908 222-5800
South Plainfield (G-10311)

▲ Path Silicones Inc.....................F......201 796-0833
Elmwood Park (G-2847)

Perl Pigments LLC........................E......201 836-1212
East Brunswick (G-2164)

Premesco Inc.............................B......908 686-0513
Union (G-11084)

Starfuels Inc............................G......201 685-0400
Englewood (G-2944)

▼ Tower Systems Inc......................G......732 237-8800
Bayville (G-251)

▲ Umicore Precious Metals NJ LLC.........E......908 222-5006
South Plainfield (G-10333)

Umicore USA Inc..........................F......908 226-2053
South Plainfield (G-10334)

Victors Three-D Inc......................D......201 845-4433
Maywood (G-6018)

3341 Secondary Smelting & Refining Of Non-ferrous Metals

Aleris Rolled Products Inc...............C......856 881-3600
Clayton (G-1523)

Alpha Assembly Solutions Inc.............E......908 561-5170
South Plainfield (G-10214)

◆ Alpha Assembly Solutions Inc...........E......908 791-3000
Somerset (G-9948)

County of Somerset.......................C......732 469-3363
Bridgewater (G-814)

Cumberland Rcycl Corp S Jersey...........E......856 825-4153
Millville (G-6245)

Emil A Schroth Inc.......................E......732 938-5015
Howell (G-4538)

Federal Metals & Alloys Co...............E......908 756-0900
South Plainfield (G-10257)

Johnson Matthey Inc......................C......856 384-7000
West Deptford (G-11708)

Kearny Smelting & Ref Corp...............E......201 991-7276
Kearny (G-4874)

Matthey Johnson Inc......................C......856 384-7022
Paulsboro (G-8334)

Matthey Johnson Inc......................C......856 384-7132
West Deptford (G-11710)

▼ Metal MGT Pittsburgh Inc...............E......201 333-2902
Jersey City (G-4765)

◆ Minmetals Inc..........................F......201 809-1898
Leonia (G-5290)

▲ National Electronic Alloys Inc.........E......201 337-9400
Oakland (G-7638)

Nedohon Inc..............................G......302 533-5512
Wildwood Crest (G-11948)

Park Steel & Iron Co.....................F......732 775-7500
Neptune (G-6894)

◆ Recycling N Hensel Amer Inc............E......856 753-7614
West Berlin (G-11618)

Reldan Metals Inc........................E......732 238-8550
South River (G-10355)

Reldan Metals Inc........................C......732 238-8550
South River (G-10356)

Semi Conductor Manufacturing.............E......973 478-2880
Clifton (G-1714)

◆ Stainless Surplus LLC..................G......914 661-3800
Green Brook (G-3867)

▲ State Metal Industries Inc.............D......856 964-1510
Camden (G-1088)

3351 Rolling, Drawing & Extruding Of Copper

Amrod Corp...............................D......973 344-3806
Newark (G-7046)

▲ Amrod NA Corporation...................D......973 344-2978
Newark (G-7047)

▼ AT&T Technologies Inc..................A......201 771-2000
Berkeley Heights (G-389)

Belden Inc...............................F......908 925-8000
Elizabeth (G-2714)

Fisk Alloy Inc...........................E......973 427-7550
Hawthorne (G-4219)

◆ Fisk Alloy Wire Incorporated...........C......973 949-4491
Hawthorne (G-4220)

Freeport Minerals Corporation............D......908 351-3200
Elizabeth (G-2737)

Gulf Cable LLC...........................E......201 242-9906
Hasbrouck Heights (G-4183)

H Cross Company..........................E......201 964-9380
Moonachie (G-6468)

Handytube Corporation....................E......732 469-7420
Middlesex (G-6120)

Heyco Products Corp......................G......732 286-1800
Toms River (G-10766)

Hoyt Corporation.........................E......201 894-0707
Englewood (G-2912)

▲ Industrial Tube Corporation............E......908 369-3737
Hillsborough (G-4328)

Kearny Smelting & Ref Corp...............E......201 991-7276
Kearny (G-4874)

▲ Little Falls Alloys Inc................E......973 278-1666
Paterson (G-8243)

▲ National Electric Wire Co Inc..........E......609 758-3600
Cream Ridge (G-1938)

3353 Aluminum Sheet, Plate & Foil

AJ Oster LLC.............................G......973 673-5700
Parsippany (G-7876)

Amcor Flexibles Inc......................E......609 267-5900
Mount Holly (G-6723)

CMC Composites LLC.......................E......732 505-9400
Whiting (G-11938)

▲ Elkom North America Inc................G......732 786-0490
Manalapan (G-5807)

◆ Global Prtners In Shelding Inc.........E......973 574-9077
Fairfield (G-3215)

H Cross Company..........................E......201 964-9380
Moonachie (G-6468)

Yarde Metals Inc.........................E......973 463-1166
East Hanover (G-2248)

3354 Aluminum Extruded Prdts

Alcon Products Inc.......................F......609 267-3898
Westampton (G-11783)

▲ Aluminum Shapes Inc....................E......856 662-5500
Pennsauken (G-8387)

Aluminum Shapes LLC......................B......888 488-7427
Delair (G-1999)

▲ Aluseal LLC............................G......856 692-3355
Vineland (G-11186)

▲ Ango Electronics Corporation...........F......201 955-0800
North Arlington (G-7368)

▲ Coltwell Industries Inc................F......908 276-7600
Cranford (G-1905)

▲ Construction Specialties Inc...........E......908 236-0800
Lebanon (G-5257)

Construction Specialties Inc.............E......908 272-2771
Cranford (G-1906)

E-TEC Marine Products Inc................G......732 269-0442
Bayville (G-243)

◆ Frameware Inc..........................G......800 582-5608
Fairfield (G-3207)

Goetz & Ruschmann Inc....................E......973 383-9270
Newton (G-7345)

Kwg Industries LLC.......................E......908 218-8900
Hillsborough (G-4338)

Medicraft Inc............................F......201 421-3055
Elmwood Park (G-2841)

Medicraft Inc............................E......201 797-8820
Elmwood Park (G-2842)

Minalex Corporation......................E......908 534-4044
Whitehouse Station (G-11929)

Security Fabricators Inc.................F......908 272-9171
Kenilworth (G-4977)

▲ Shapes/Arch Holdings LLC...............B......856 662-5500
Delair (G-2001)

Unique Amrcn Alum Extrsion LLC...........E......732 271-0006
Middlesex (G-6157)

3355 Aluminum Rolling & Drawing, NEC

American Custom Fabricators..............G......732 237-0037
Bayville (G-239)

Domel Inc................................E......973 614-1800
Clifton (G-1602)

Gentek Building Products Inc.............E......732 381-0900
Avenel (G-130)

H Cross Company..........................E......201 964-9380
Moonachie (G-6468)

▲ Lapp Holding NA Inc....................E......973 660-9700
Florham Park (G-3515)

◆ Okonite Company Inc....................C......201 825-0300
Ramsey (G-9154)

3356 Rolling, Drawing-Extruding Of Nonferrous Metals

Advance Process Systems Lim..............G......201 400-9190
Branchville (G-701)

Alpha Assembly Solutions Inc.............E......908 561-5170
South Plainfield (G-10214)

◆ Alpha Assembly Solutions Inc...........E......908 791-3000
Somerset (G-9948)

American Aluminum Company.................D......908 233-3500
Mountainside (G-6834)

Construction Specialties Inc.............E......908 272-2771
Cranford (G-1906)

Fisk Alloy Inc...........................E......973 427-7550
Hawthorne (G-4219)

◆ Fisk Alloy Wire Incorporated...........C......973 949-4491
Hawthorne (G-4220)

H Cross Company..........................E......201 964-9380
Moonachie (G-6468)

Holistic Solar Usa Inc...................G......732 757-5500
Newark (G-7151)

▲ Industrial Tube Corporation............E......908 369-3737
Hillsborough (G-4328)

International Rollforms Inc...............E......856 228-7100
Deptford (G-2064)

Kearny Smelting & Ref Corp...............E......201 991-7276
Kearny (G-4874)

Komline-Sanderson Engrg Corp.............G......973 579-0090
Sparta (G-10394)

Matthey Johnson Inc......................C......856 384-7132
West Deptford (G-11710)

New Jersey Gold Buyers Corp..............G......732 765-4653
Marlboro (G-5906)

Nickel Savers............................G......201 405-1153
Oakland (G-7639)

Nickels Carpet Cleaning..................G......609 892-5783
Mays Landing (G-5995)

▲ Precision Roll Products Inc............F......973 822-9100
Florham Park (G-3520)

◆ Sandvik Inc............................C......201 794-5000
Fair Lawn (G-3120)

Swepco Tube LLC..........................C......973 778-3000
Clifton (G-1728)

Times Tin Cup............................G......973 983-1095
Mountain Lakes (G-6828)

Tin Panda Inc............................G......973 916-0707
Clifton (G-1732)

Tin Sigh Stop............................G......973 691-2712
Byram Township (G-1019)

Titanium Industries Inc..................G......973 428-1900
East Hanover (G-2242)

Titanium Smoking Kings LLC...............G......908 339-8876
Phillipsburg (G-8577)

Titanium Technical Services..............G......908 323-9899
Flemington (G-3472)

Union City Filament Corp.................E......201 945-3366
Ridgefield (G-9294)

3357 Nonferrous Wire Drawing

AFL Telecommunications Inc...............E......908 707-9500
Bridgewater (G-782)

AFL Telecommunications LLC...............D......864 486-7303
Jersey City (G-4687)

Alpha Wire Corporation...................C......908 925-8000
Elizabeth (G-2709)

Arose Inc................................E......856 481-4351
Blackwood (G-459)

Associated Plastics Inc..................F......732 574-2800
Rahway (G-9079)

▼ AT&T Technologies Inc..................A......201 771-2000
Berkeley Heights (G-389)

▼ Aw Machinery LLC.......................F......973 882-3223
Fairfield (G-3149)

Brim Electronics Inc.....................F......201 796-2886
Lodi (G-5555)

Bruker Ost LLC...........................C......732 541-1300
Carteret (G-1251)

CDM Electronics Inc......................C......856 740-1200
Turnersville (G-11016)

Colonial Wire & Cable Co Inc.............G......732 287-1557
Edison (G-2480)

Communications Supply Corp...............E......732 346-1864
Edison (G-2481)

▲ Computer Crafts Inc ....C ...973 423-3500
Hawthorne *(G-4214)*

▲ Daburn Wire & Cable Corp ....G ...973 328-3200
Dover *(G-2081)*

▲ Dearborn A Belden Cdt Company ...D 908 925-8000
Elizabeth *(G-2726)*

Esi ....E ...856 629-2492
Sicklerville *(G-9909)*

▲ Flexco Microwave Inc ....E ...908 835-1720
Port Murray *(G-8883)*

Francis Metals Company Inc ....F ...732 761-0500
Lakewood *(G-5101)*

Global Wire & Cable Inc ....E ...973 471-1000
Passaic *(G-8070)*

Harris Driver Co ....G ...973 267-8100
Morristown *(G-6668)*

Harrison Electro Mechanical ....F ...732 382-6008
Rahway *(G-9100)*

▲ Iboco Corp ....G ...732 417-0066
Lakewood *(G-5111)*

▲ Lapp Cable Works Inc ....E ...973 660-9632
Florham Park *(G-3514)*

M Parker Autoworks Inc ....E ...856 933-0801
Bellmawr *(G-337)*

▲ Micro-Tek Corporation ....G ...856 829-3855
Cinnaminson *(G-1473)*

Molecu-Wire Corporation ....F ...908 429-0300
Manville *(G-5857)*

National Communications Inc ....E ...973 325-3151
West Orange *(G-11774)*

Newtech Group Corp ....G ...732 355-0392
Kendall Park *(G-4919)*

Ofs Fitel LLC ....E ...732 748-7409
Somerset *(G-10043)*

Okonite Company ....D ...201 825-0300
Paterson *(G-8273)*

◆ Okonite Company Inc ....C ...201 825-0300
Ramsey *(G-9154)*

▲ Paramount Wire Co Inc ....E ...973 672-0500
East Orange *(G-2258)*

Prysmian Cbles Systems USA LLC ...F 732 469-5902
Bridgewater *(G-870)*

Seminole Wire & Cable Co Inc ....F ...856 324-2929
Pennsauken *(G-8483)*

▲ Sensors Unlimited Inc ....D ...609 333-8000
Princeton *(G-9020)*

Service Tech ....G ...908 788-0072
Flemington *(G-3466)*

◆ Te Wire & Cable LLC ....C ...201 845-9400
Saddle Brook *(G-9683)*

Tru Temp Sensors Inc ....G ...215 396-1550
Ocean City *(G-7698)*

Vytran LLC ....E ...732 972-2880
Morganville *(G-6599)*

Wire Fabricators & Insulators ....E ...973 768-2839
Livingston *(G-5549)*

Wireworks Corporation ....E ...908 686-7400
Hillside *(G-4437)*

3363 Aluminum Die Castings

American Aluminum Casting Co ....E ...973 372-3200
Irvington *(G-4556)*

Bierman-Everett Foundry Co ....G ...973 373-8800
South Orange *(G-10192)*

3364 Nonferrous Die Castings, Exc Aluminum

▲ Abco Die Casters Inc ....D ...973 624-7030
Newark *(G-7033)*

▲ Carteret Die-Casting Corp ....E ...732 246-0070
Somerset *(G-9967)*

▲ Certech Inc ....C ...201 842-6800
Wood Ridge *(G-12002)*

Flemington Aluminium & Brass ....G 908 782-6333
Flemington *(G-3441)*

◆ Maranatha Now Inc ....E ...609 599-1402
Trenton *(G-10955)*

Medalco Metals Inc ....G ...908 238-0513
Lebanon *(G-5271)*

▲ Microcast Technologies Corp ....D ...908 523-9503
Linden *(G-5385)*

Union Casting Industries Inc ....F ...908 686-8888
Union *(G-11096)*

W & E Baum Bronze Tablet Corp ....E ...732 866-1881
Freehold *(G-3704)*

Worldcast Network Inc ....G ...201 767-2040
Old Tappan *(G-7737)*

3365 Aluminum Foundries

Aluminum Shapes LLC ....B ...888 488-7427
Delair *(G-1999)*

▲ Atlantic Casting & Engineering ....C ...973 779-2450
Clifton *(G-1566)*

Bierman-Everett Foundry Co ....G ...973 373-8800
South Orange *(G-10192)*

◆ Bon Chef Inc ....D ...973 383-8848
Lafayette *(G-5026)*

Rosco Inc ....G ...908 789-1020
Garwood *(G-3792)*

▲ Shapes/Arch Holdings LLC ....B ...856 662-5500
Delair *(G-2001)*

TEC Cast Inc ....E ...201 935-3885
Carlstadt *(G-1226)*

TEC Cast Inc ....E ...201 935-3885
Moonachie *(G-6494)*

Union Casting Industries Inc ....F ...908 686-8888
Union *(G-11096)*

3366 Copper Foundries

▲ Accurate Bushing Company Inc ....E ...908 789-1121
Garwood *(G-3779)*

Amrod Corp ....D ...973 344-3806
Newark *(G-7046)*

Bierman-Everett Foundry Co ....G ...973 373-8800
South Orange *(G-10192)*

▲ Federal Bronze Cast Inds Inc ....G ...973 589-7575
Newark *(G-7123)*

▲ Industrial Tube Corporation ....E ...908 369-3737
Hillsborough *(G-4328)*

Ivey Katrina Owner ....G ...973 951-8328
Newark *(G-7163)*

◆ Maranatha Now Inc ....E ...609 599-1402
Trenton *(G-10955)*

Oavco Ltd Liability Company ....F ...609 454-5340
Hamilton *(G-4119)*

Richmond Industries Inc ....E ...732 355-1616
Dayton *(G-1987)*

Union Casting Industries Inc ....F ...908 686-8888
Union *(G-11096)*

3369 Nonferrous Foundries: Castings, NEC

Alloy Cast Products Inc ....F ...908 245-2255
Kenilworth *(G-4920)*

Arde Inc ....D ...201 784-9880
Carlstadt *(G-1126)*

Engineered Precision Cast Co ....D ...732 671-2424
Middletown *(G-6163)*

Howmet Castings & Services Inc ......A ...973 361-0300
Dover *(G-2087)*

IBC Inc ....G ...856 533-2806
Voorhees *(G-11289)*

▲ Jarco U S Casting Corp ....E ...201 271-0003
Union City *(G-11115)*

M D Carbide Tool Corp ....E ...973 263-0104
Towaco *(G-10874)*

Microcast Technologies Corp ....G ...732 943-7356
Avenel *(G-136)*

▲ Microcast Technologies Corp ....D ...908 523-9503
Linden *(G-5385)*

▲ S Jarco-U Castings Corporation ....G ...201 271-0003
Union City *(G-11127)*

Tusa Products Inc ....E ...609 448-8333
Ewing *(G-3072)*

Ultimate Trading Corp ....D ...973 228-7700
Rockaway *(G-9509)*

3398 Metal Heat Treating

Analytic Stress Relieving Inc ....D ...732 629-7232
Middlesex *(G-6097)*

Bennett Heat Trting Brzing Inc ....E ...973 589-0590
Newark *(G-7066)*

▲ Blue Blade Corp ....E ...908 272-2620
Kenilworth *(G-4930)*

Bodycote Thermal Proc Inc ....E ...908 245-0717
Roselle *(G-9550)*

Bodycote Thermal Processing ....E ...908 245-0717
Roselle *(G-9551)*

Braddock Heat Treating Company ....E ...732 356-2906
Bridgewater *(G-806)*

Curtiss-Wright Surfc Tech LLC ....F ...201 843-7800
Paramus *(G-7797)*

▲ E F Britten & Co Inc ....F ...908 276-4800
Cranford *(G-1908)*

Energy Beams Inc ....E ...973 291-6555
Bloomingdale *(G-528)*

Heinzelman Heat Treating LLC ....E ...201 933-4800
Carlstadt *(G-1165)*

Kenney Steel Treating Corp ....F ...201 998-4420
Kearny *(G-4875)*

Metal Improvement Co Inc ....G ...253 677-8604
Paramus *(G-7818)*

▲ Metal Improvement Company LLC ..E ...201 843-7800
Paramus *(G-7819)*

3399 Primary Metal Prdts, NEC

Acupowder International LLC ....G ...908 851-4500
Union *(G-11019)*

Atlantic Eqp Engineers Inc ....F ...201 828-9400
Upper Saddle River *(G-11134)*

Bozak Inc ....G ...732 282-1556
Spring Lake *(G-10420)*

Bway Corporation ....F ...609 883-4300
Trenton *(G-10908)*

Czar Industries Inc ....G ...609 392-1515
Trenton *(G-10928)*

◆ FW Winter Inc ....E ...856 963-7490
Camden *(G-1065)*

◆ Hoeganaes Corporation ....B ...856 303-0366
Cinnaminson *(G-1464)*

Hugo Neu Recycling LLC ....E ...914 530-2350
Kearny *(G-4866)*

Matthey Johnson Inc ....C ...856 384-7132
West Deptford *(G-11710)*

McW Precision ....F ...609 859-4400
Southampton *(G-10368)*

Mv Laboratories Inc ....G ...908 788-6906
Frenchtown *(G-3716)*

Performance Alloys & Materials ....G ...201 865-5268
Secaucus *(G-9797)*

▲ Robinson Tech Intl Corp ....G ...973 287-6458
Fairfield *(G-3303)*

Scientific Alloys Corp ....E ...973 478-8323
Clifton *(G-1712)*

Sentry Mfg LLC ....G ...856 642-0480
Moorestown *(G-6566)*

34 FABRICATED METAL PRODUCTS, EXCEPT MACHINERY AND TRANSPORTATION EQUIPMENT

3411 Metal Cans

▲ Allstate Can Corporation ....D ...973 560-9030
Parsippany *(G-7878)*

Bway Corporation ....C ...732 997-4100
Dayton *(G-1956)*

▲ Elemental Container Inc ....G ...908 687-7720
Union *(G-11051)*

▲ Innovation Foods LLC ....F ...856 455-2209
Bridgeton *(G-759)*

▲ JI Packaging Group Corp ....G ...609 610-0286
Pennington *(G-8368)*

▲ Medin Technologies Inc ....C ...973 779-2400
Totowa *(G-10836)*

▲ Penny Plate LLC ....D ...856 429-7583
Mount Laurel *(G-6789)*

▲ Phoenix Container Inc ....C ...732 247-3931
Trenton *(G-10973)*

Silgan Containers Mfg Corp ....D ...732 287-0300
Edison *(G-2609)*

Sonoco Products Company ....D ...609 655-0300
Dayton *(G-1989)*

Tin Can Lids LLC ....G ...201 503-0677
Tenafly *(G-10666)*

3412 Metal Barrels, Drums, Kegs & Pails

Andrew B Duffy Inc ....F ...856 845-4900
West Deptford *(G-11691)*

Cutler Bros Box & Lumber Co ....E ...201 943-2535
Fairview *(G-3359)*

◆ Granco Group LLC ....G ...973 515-4721
Roseland *(G-9539)*

◆ Joseph Oat Holdings Inc ....D ...856 541-2900
Camden *(G-1072)*

▲ Kraftware Corporation ....E ...732 345-7091
Roselle *(G-9562)*

Mauser Usa LLC ....C ...732 634-6000
Woodbridge *(G-12019)*

▲ Mauser Usa LLC ....G ...732 353-7100
East Brunswick *(G-2155)*

Patrick J Kelly Drums Inc ....G ...856 963-1795
Camden *(G-1082)*

▲ Pmm Inc ....E ...908 692-1465
Colts Neck *(G-1786)*

Rahway Steel Drum Co Inc ....E ...732 382-0113
Cranbury *(G-1877)*

Recycle Inc East ....D...... 908 756-2200
  South Plainfield (G-10325)
Romaco North America Inc ....G...... 609 584-2500
  Hamilton (G-4123)
Williams Scotsman Inc 856 429-0315
  Kearny (G-4906)

3421 Cutlery

Art of Shaving - Fl LLC ....G...... 732 410-2520
  Freehold (G-3648)
Ben Venuti ....G...... 908 389-9999
  Garwood (G-3781)
▲ Du-Mor Blade Co Inc ....E...... 856 829-9384
  Cinnaminson (G-1453)
Hobby Blade Specialty Inc ....G...... 908 317-9306
  Scotch Plains (G-9734)
▲ IDL Techni-Edge LLC ....C...... 908 497-9818
  Kenilworth (G-4945)
Kikuichi New York Inc ....G...... 201 567-8388
  Englewood Cliffs (G-2980)
Port A ....F...... 732 776-6511
  Asbury Park (G-81)
Revlon Inc ....F...... 732 287-1400
  Edison (G-2598)
▲ US Blade Mfg Co Inc ....E...... 908 272-2898
  Cranford (G-1930)

3423 Hand & Edge Tools

▲ Acon Watch Crown Company ....F...... 973 546-8585
  Garfield (G-3725)
American Logistics Network LLC ....G...... 201 391-1054
  Woodcliff Lake (G-12046)
Apex Saw & Tool Co Inc ....G...... 201 438-8777
  Lyndhurst (G-5641)
▲ Baumer of America Inc ....F...... 973 263-1569
  Towaco (G-10865)
Brasscraft Manufacturing Co ....G...... 856 241-7700
  Swedesboro (G-10574)
▲ C T A Manufacturing Corp ....E...... 201 896-1000
  Carlstadt (G-1135)
▲ Cementex Products Inc ....E...... 609 387-1040
  Burlington (G-957)
▲ Chicago Pneumatic Tool ....F...... 973 928-5222
  Clifton (G-1583)
▲ CS Osborne & Co ....D...... 973 483-3232
  Harrison (G-4168)
DAKA Manufacturing LLC ....G...... 908 782-0360
  Flemington (G-3436)
▲ Danielle Die Cut Products Inc ....E...... 973 278-3000
  Paterson (G-8167)
Dicar Diamond Tool Corp ....F...... 973 684-0949
  Paterson (G-8173)
▼ Dreyco Inc ....F...... 201 896-9000
  Carlstadt (G-1154)
Du-Matt Corporation ....G...... 201 861-4271
  West New York (G-11738)
▲ Excel Hobby Blades Corp ....E...... 973 278-4000
  Paterson (G-8187)
▲ General Tools & Instrs Co LLC ....E...... 212 431-6100
  Secaucus (G-9773)
Grobet File Company Amer LLC ....D...... 201 939-6700
  Carlstadt (G-1161)
Grommet Mart Inc ....F...... 973 278-4100
  Paterson (G-8205)
◆ Hayward Industries Inc ....B...... 908 351-5400
  Elizabeth (G-2746)
Hexacon Electric Company Inc ....E...... 908 245-6200
  Roselle Park (G-9586)
▲ IDL Techni-Edge LLC ....C...... 908 497-9818
  Kenilworth (G-4945)
Indo-US Mim TEC Private Ltd ....G...... 734 327-9842
  Princeton (G-8962)
J R S Tool & Metal Finishing ....G...... 908 753-2050
  South Plainfield (G-10282)
▲ Jdv Products Inc ....F...... 201 794-6467
  Fair Lawn (G-3108)
Jesco Iron Crafts Inc ....F...... 201 488-4545
  Bogota (G-533)
Jetyd Corporation ....F...... 201 512-9500
  Mahwah (G-5750)
▲ Legend Stone Products ....G...... 973 473-7088
  Clifton (G-1657)
◆ Mastercool USA Inc ....E...... 973 252-9119
  Randolph (G-9190)
▲ National Steel Rule Company ....D...... 908 862-3366
  Linden (G-5392)
National Steel Rule Company ....F...... 800 922-0885
  Linden (G-5393)
National Steel Rule Company ....D...... 908 862-3366
  Linden (G-5394)

▲ Ohaus Corporation ....D...... 973 377-9000
  Parsippany (G-7980)
Phoenix Industrial LLC ....G...... 908 955-0114
  Whitehouse Station (G-11932)
◆ Power Hawk Technologies Inc ....F...... 973 627-4646
  Rockaway (G-9489)
▲ S & G Tool Aid Corporation ....D...... 973 824-7730
  Newark (G-7257)
Sine Tru Tool Company Inc 732 591-1100
  Marlboro (G-5915)
Stanley Black & Decker Inc ....F...... 860 225-5111
  Jersey City (G-4813)
Swarovski North America Ltd ....G...... 908 253-7057
  Bridgewater (G-895)
▲ Thirty-Three Queen Realty Inc ....F...... 973 824-5527
  Newark (G-7297)
Yunta USA Inc ....G...... 614 835-6588
  Cranbury (G-1896)

3425 Hand Saws & Saw Blades

▲ IDL Techni-Edge LLC ....C...... 908 497-9818
  Kenilworth (G-4945)
▲ National Steel Rule Company ....D...... 908 862-3366
  Linden (G-5392)
Rf360 Technologies Inc ....E...... 848 999-3582
  Bridgewater (G-876)
▲ Tooling Etc LLC ....G...... 732 752-8080
  Middlesex (G-6156)

3429 Hardware, NEC

4 Way Lock LLC ....G...... 908 359-2002
  Hillsborough (G-4299)
Airborne Systems N Amer Inc ....F...... 856 663-1275
  Pennsauken (G-8385)
Allfasteners Usa LLC ....E...... 201 783-8836
  Carlstadt (G-1121)
▼ American Van Equipment Inc ....C...... 732 905-5900
  Lakewood (G-5050)
Andrex Inc ....F...... 908 852-2400
  Hackettstown (G-3998)
▲ Art Materials Service Inc ....D...... 732 545-8888
  New Brunswick (G-6913)
Artistic Hardware ....G...... 609 383-1909
  Northfield (G-7510)
◆ Ashley Norton Inc ....F...... 973 835-4027
  Pompton Plains (G-8859)
▲ Atco Products Inc ....G...... 973 379-3171
  Springfield (G-10428)
Bildisco Mfg Inc ....F...... 973 673-2400
  West Orange (G-11762)
Brim Electronics Inc ....F...... 201 796-2886
  Lodi (G-5555)
Carpenter & Paterson Inc ....E...... 973 772-1800
  Saddle Brook (G-9644)
▲ Celus Fasteners Mfg Inc ....E...... 800 289-7483
  Northvale (G-7520)
▲ Charles E Green & Son Inc ....F...... 973 485-3630
  Newark (G-7082)
CMF Ltd Inc ....E...... 609 695-3600
  Ewing (G-3022)
Commeatus LLC ....F...... 847 772-5314
  Plainsboro (G-8782)
◆ Component Hardware Group Inc ....D...... 800 526-3694
  Lakewood (G-5072)
Confires Fire Prtction Svc LLC ....F...... 908 822-2700
  South Plainfield (G-10241)
◆ Delta Procurement Inc ....G...... 201 623-9353
  Carlstadt (G-1149)
Firefighter One Ltd Lblty Co ....G...... 973 940-3061
  Sparta (G-10387)
G & S Precision Prototype ....G...... 732 370-3010
  Lakewood (G-5102)
General Sullivan Group Inc ....F...... 609 745-5000
  Pennington (G-8366)
Hanger Central LLC ....G...... 732 750-1161
  Edison (G-2526)
Ho-Ho-Kus Inc ....F...... 973 278-2274
  Paterson (G-8210)
Imperial Weld Ring Corp Inc ....F...... 908 354-0011
  Elizabeth (G-2749)
Ingersoll-Rand Company ....E...... 856 793-7000
  Mount Laurel (G-6766)
J Blanco Associates Inc ....F...... 973 427-0619
  Hawthorne (G-4228)
◆ JC Macelroy Co Inc ....D...... 732 572-7100
  Piscataway (G-8681)
Ka-Lor Cubicle and Sup Co Inc ....G...... 201 891-8077
  Franklin Lakes (G-3626)
▲ La Milagrosa 1 LLC ....F...... 973 928-1799
  Passaic (G-8081)

Mariner Sales and Power Inc ....G...... 732 477-7484
  Brick (G-725)
▲ Modern Sportswear Corporation ......F...... 201 804-2700
  Moonachie (G-6481)
▲ Mul-T-Lock Usa Inc ....E...... 973 778-3320
  Hackensack (G-3948)
Oceanview Marine Welding LLC ....G...... 609 624-9669
  Ocean View (G-7704)
Pekay Industries Inc ....F...... 732 938-2722
  Farmingdale (G-3390)
Penn Elcom Inc ....F...... 973 839-7777
  Pompton Plains (G-8869)
▲ Polytech Designs Inc ....F...... 973 340-1390
  Clifton (G-1696)
Ramsay David Cabinetmakers ....F...... 856 234-7776
  Moorestown (G-6562)
▲ Reich USA Corporation ....F...... 201 684-9400
  Mahwah (G-5767)
◆ Revere Survival Products Inc ....F...... 973 575-8811
  West Caldwell (G-11678)
▲ Rotor Clip Company Inc ....B...... 732 469-7707
  Somerset (G-10067)
Rsl LLC ....E...... 609 645-9777
  Egg Harbor Township (G-2696)
Saint-Gobain Prfmce Plas Corp ....D...... 732 652-0910
  Somerset (G-10070)
Shade Powers Co Inc ....F...... 201 767-3727
  Northvale (G-7549)
Steelstran Industries Inc ....G...... 732 566-5040
  Matawan (G-5989)
Taurus Precision Inc ....F...... 973 785-9254
  Little Falls (G-5470)
Tiburon Lockers Inc ....G...... 201 750-4960
  Rockleigh (G-9523)
▲ Unicorp ....C...... 973 674-1700
  Orange (G-7765)
Unified Door & Hdwr Group LLC ....C...... 215 364-8834
  Pennsauken (G-8495)
▲ Versabar Corporation ....F...... 973 279-8400
  Totowa (G-10857)
▼ Viking Marine Products Inc ....G...... 732 826-4552
  Edison (G-2642)
World and Main LLC ....C...... 609 860-9990
  Cranbury (G-1893)

3431 Enameled Iron & Metal Sanitary Ware

▲ Aero Manufacturing Co ....D...... 973 473-5300
  Clifton (G-1558)
Asd Holding Corp ....G...... 800 442-1902
  Piscataway (G-8638)
▲ Houzer Inc ....F...... 609 584-1900
  Hamilton (G-4107)
▲ Interlink Products Intl Inc ....E...... 908 862-8090
  Linden (G-5361)
Sapphire Bath Inc ....G...... 718 215-1262
  Paterson (G-8295)
Trano Bruce Plumbing & Heating ....G...... 908 654-3685
  Mountainside (G-6853)

3432 Plumbing Fixture Fittings & Trim, Brass

▲ As America Inc ....C...... 732 980-3000
  Piscataway (G-8637)
Bruce Supply Corp ....F...... 732 661-0500
  Keasbey (G-4909)
Carpenter & Paterson Inc ....E...... 609 227-2750
  Bordentown (G-578)
▲ Chatham Brass Co Inc ....G...... 908 668-0500
  South Plainfield (G-10237)
DAngelo Metal Products Inc ....E...... 908 862-8220
  Linden (G-5341)
◆ Durst Corporation Inc ....E...... 800 852-3906
  Cranford (G-1907)
▲ El Batal Corporation ....F...... 908 964-3427
  Union (G-11050)
Grove Supply Inc ....E...... 856 205-0687
  Vineland (G-11228)
Kessler Industries ....G...... 973 279-1417
  Paterson (G-8229)
◆ Kissler & Co Inc ....E...... 201 896-9600
  Carlstadt (G-1175)
Knickerbocker Machine Shop Inc ....D...... 973 256-1616
  Totowa (G-10834)
Majewski Plumbing & Htg LLC ....G...... 609 374-6001
  Villas (G-11179)
Msg Fire & Safety Inc ....G...... 732 833-8500
  Wall Township (G-11356)
Plumbing Supply Now LLC ....F...... 732 228-8852
  New Brunswick (G-6958)
Specialty Products Plus ....G...... 732 380-1188
  West Long Branch (G-11723)

Employee Codes: A=Over 500 employees, B=251-500
C=101-250, D=51-100, E=20-50, F=10-19, G=4-9   2019 Harris New Jersey
Manufacturers Directory   537

SIC

W C Davis Inc ....F...... 856 547-4750
Haddon Heights *(G-4050)*

Wm Steinen Mfg Co ....D...... 973 887-6400
Parsippany *(G-8042)*

3433 Heating Eqpt

◆ Amec Fster Wheeler N Amer Corp ...D...... 936 448-6323
Hampton *(G-4147)*

Ampericon Inc ....F...... 609 945-2591
Monmouth Junction *(G-6278)*

Applied Thermal Solutions Inc ....G...... 856 818-8194
Williamstown *(G-11951)*

C & F Burner Co ....E...... 201 998-8080
North Arlington *(G-7370)*

Carlisle Machine Works Inc ....E...... 856 825-0627
Millville *(G-6241)*

Energy Company Inc ....E...... 856 742-1916
Westville *(G-11814)*

▲ Ewc Controls Inc ....E...... 732 446-3110
Manalapan *(G-5809)*

▲ Heat-Timer Corporation ....E...... 973 575-4004
Fairfield *(G-3224)*

Holistic Solar Usa Inc ....G...... 732 757-5500
Newark *(G-7151)*

Inenergy Inc ....E...... 609 466-2512
Ringoes *(G-9337)*

▲ NM Knight Co Inc ....E...... 856 327-4855
Millville *(G-6263)*

▲ Panatech Corporation ....G...... 732 331-5692
Manalapan *(G-5823)*

Stafford Park Solar 1 LLC ....G...... 609 607-9500
Barnegat *(G-162)*

Stamm International Corp ....G...... 201 947-1700
Fort Lee *(G-3589)*

▲ Sun Pacific Power Corp ....F...... 888 845-0242
Manalapan *(G-5826)*

◆ Triangle Tube/Phase III Co Inc ....D...... 856 228-9940
Paulsboro *(G-8340)*

▲ Trinity Heating & Air Inc ....D...... 732 780-3779
Wall Township *(G-11376)*

Waage Electric Inc ....G...... 908 245-9363
Kenilworth *(G-4986)*

3441 Fabricated Structural Steel

Able Fab Co ....E...... 732 396-0600
Avenel *(G-118)*

◆ Acrow Corporation of America ....E...... 973 244-0080
Parsippany *(G-7871)*

Air & Specialties Sheet Metal ....F...... 908 233-8306
Mountainside *(G-6832)*

Airmet Inc ....G...... 973 481-5550
Newark *(G-7037)*

Ajay Metal Fabricators Inc ....G...... 908 523-0557
Linden *(G-5318)*

All American Metal Fabricators ....G...... 201 567-2898
Tenafly *(G-10658)*

Allied Metal Industries Inc ....E...... 973 824-7347
Newark *(G-7039)*

Alloy Welding Co ....F...... 908 218-1551
Branchburg *(G-613)*

American Mllwright Rigging LLC ....E...... 856 457-9574
Audubon *(G-111)*

American Strip Steel Inc ....F...... 800 526-1216
South Plainfield *(G-10216)*

American Strip Steel Inc ....G...... 856 461-8300
Delanco *(G-2002)*

Andrew B Duffy Inc ....F...... 856 845-4900
West Deptford *(G-11691)*

Anvil Iron Works Inc ....G...... 856 783-5959
Sicklerville *(G-9907)*

◆ Arca Industrial Inc ....G...... 732 339-0450
East Windsor *(G-2336)*

Archer Day Inc ....E...... 732 396-0600
Avenel *(G-120)*

Architectural Metals Inc ....G...... 718 765-0722
Carteret *(G-1247)*

Arnold Steel Co Inc ....D...... 732 363-1079
Howell *(G-4531)*

Atlantic Precision Tech LLC ....G...... 732 658-3060
North Brunswick *(G-7455)*

Atlas Enterprise ....F...... 908 561-1144
South Plainfield *(G-10222)*

B & B Iron Works ....E...... 862 238-7203
Clifton *(G-1570)*

B L White Welding & Steel Co ....G...... 973 684-4111
Paterson *(G-8144)*

Badger Blades LLC ....G...... 908 325-6587
Cranford *(G-1902)*

Banker Steel Nj LLC ....D...... 732 968-6061
South Plainfield *(G-10223)*

Bouras Industries Inc ....A...... 908 918-9400
Summit *(G-10527)*

Brayco Inc ....F...... 609 758-5235
Creamridge *(G-1940)*

Brunnquell Iron Works Inc ....E...... 609 409-6101
Cranbury *(G-1817)*

Burgess Steel Holding LLC ....G...... 201 871-3500
Englewood *(G-2887)*

Bushwick Metals LLC ....C...... 610 495-9100
Englewood *(G-2888)*

C M C Steel Fabricators Inc ....C...... 908 561-3484
South Plainfield *(G-10232)*

C W Grimmer & Sons Inc ....F...... 732 741-2189
Tinton Falls *(G-10706)*

▲ Capital Steel Service LLC ....E...... 609 882-6983
Ewing *(G-3017)*

Capitol Steel Inc ....F...... 609 538-9313
Trenton *(G-10909)*

Central Metals Inc ....D...... 215 462-7464
Camden *(G-1051)*

Com-Fab Inc ....G...... 973 296-0433
Hewitt *(G-4274)*

▲ Coordinated Metals Inc ....D...... 201 460-7280
Carlstadt *(G-1145)*

▼ Coronis Building Systems Inc ....E...... 609 261-2200
Columbus *(G-1798)*

Cs Industrial Services LLC ....G...... 609 381-4380
Newfield *(G-7320)*

D S Jh LLC ....E...... 973 782-4086
Lincoln Park *(G-5298)*

Ddm Steel Cnstr Ltd Lblty Co ....F...... 856 794-9400
Vineland *(G-11211)*

De Jong Iron Works Inc ....G...... 973 684-1633
Paterson *(G-8169)*

DMJ Industrial Services LLC ....G...... 973 692-8406
Wayne *(G-11494)*

Eagle Steel & Iron LLC ....G...... 908 587-1025
Stewartsville *(G-10483)*

Equipment Distributing Corp ....G...... 201 641-8414
Ridgefield Park *(G-9305)*

Falstrom Company ....F...... 973 777-0013
Passaic *(G-8066)*

Flame Cut Steel Inc ....F...... 973 373-9300
Irvington *(G-4569)*

▲ FMB Systems Inc ....D...... 973 485-5544
Harrison *(G-4175)*

Francis Metals Company Inc ....F...... 732 761-0500
Lakewood *(G-5101)*

▼ Frazier Industrial Company ....C...... 908 876-3001
Long Valley *(G-5610)*

▲ G J Oliver Inc ....D...... 908 454-9743
Phillipsburg *(G-8552)*

Gavan Graham Elec Pdts Corp ....E...... 908 729-9000
Union *(G-11058)*

Giant Stl Fabricators Erectors ....G...... 908 241-6766
Roselle *(G-9559)*

Glentech Inc ....F...... 908 685-2205
Somerville *(G-10113)*

Grimbilas Enterprises Corp ....G...... 973 686-5999
Wayne *(G-11514)*

H Barron Iron Works Inc ....F...... 856 456-9092
Gloucester City *(G-3843)*

Hackensack Steel Corp ....D...... 201 935-0090
Carlstadt *(G-1163)*

▲ Harold R Henrich Inc ....D...... 732 370-4455
Lakewood *(G-5107)*

Harris Structural Steel Co Inc ....E...... 732 752-6070
South Plainfield *(G-10272)*

Harris Structural Steel Co Inc ....G...... 732 752-6070
South Plainfield *(G-10273)*

◆ Helidex LLC ....E...... 201 636-2546
East Rutherford *(G-2291)*

Holler Metal Fabricators Inc ....G...... 732 635-9050
Metuchen *(G-6061)*

I K Construction Inc ....E...... 908 925-5200
East Orange *(G-2252)*

Imperial Metal Products Inc ....G...... 908 647-8181
Bound Brook *(G-602)*

▲ Industrial Metal Inc ....G...... 908 362-0084
Blairstown *(G-486)*

▼ Infinite Mfg Group Inc ....F...... 973 649-9950
Kearny *(G-4868)*

Innovative Metal Solutions LLC..........G...... 609 784-8406
Mount Holly *(G-6731)*

Inox Steel Corp ....G...... 609 268-2334
Shamong *(G-9858)*

Integrity Ironworks Corp ....G...... 732 254-2200
Sayreville *(G-9711)*

Iron Asylum Incorporated ....F...... 856 352-4283
Sewell *(G-9847)*

J & M Cstm Shtmtl Ltd Lblty Co ....G...... 856 627-6252
Sicklerville *(G-9911)*

J G Schmidt Steel ....F...... 973 473-4822
Passaic *(G-8075)*

◆ JC Macelroy Co Inc ....D...... 732 572-7100
Piscataway *(G-8681)*

Jersey Metal Works LLC ....G...... 732 565-1313
Somerset *(G-10009)*

John Cooper Company Inc ....F...... 201 487-4018
Hackensack *(G-3934)*

John F Pearce ....G...... 201 440-8765
Moonachie *(G-6474)*

John Maltese Iron Works Inc ....E...... 732 249-4350
North Brunswick *(G-7472)*

◆ Joseph Oat Holdings Inc ....E...... 856 541-2900
Camden *(G-1072)*

JP Technology Inc ....F...... 856 241-0111
Swedesboro *(G-10591)*

Leets Steel Inc ....G...... 917 416-7977
Sayreville *(G-9715)*

Lehigh Utility Associates Inc ....E...... 908 561-5252
South Plainfield *(G-10292)*

Lesli Katchen Steel Cnstr Inc ....G...... 732 521-2600
Jamesburg *(G-4673)*

Lingo Inc ....F...... 856 273-6594
Mount Laurel *(G-6775)*

Liquid Metalworks Ltd Lblty Co ....G...... 973 224-9710
Hackettstown *(G-4017)*

Lummus Technology Ventures LLC ......G...... 973 893-1515
Bloomfield *(G-509)*

M K Enterprises Inc ....G...... 201 891-4199
Wyckoff *(G-12115)*

Main Robert A & Sons Holdg Co ....E...... 201 447-3700
Wyckoff *(G-12116)*

Marino International Corp ....G...... 732 752-5100
South Plainfield *(G-10299)*

Max Gurtman & Sons Inc ....G...... 973 478-7000
Clifton *(G-1666)*

Metals Plus ....E...... 908 862-7677
Linden *(G-5384)*

Metals USA Plates & Shapes Inc ....E...... 973 242-1000
Newark *(G-7201)*

Metalwest LLC ....E...... 609 395-7007
Monroe Township *(G-6335)*

Metfab Steel Works LLC ....F...... 973 675-7676
Orange *(G-7756)*

Mk Metals Inc ....G...... 856 245-7033
Glendora *(G-3837)*

Morgan Towers Inc ....G...... 856 786-7200
Moorestown *(G-6546)*

Napco Separation Equipment Inc ....G...... 908 862-7677
Linden *(G-5391)*

Newark Ironworks Inc ....F...... 973 424-9790
Newark *(G-7214)*

Next Level Fabrication LLC ....G...... 609 703-0682
Egg Harbor Township *(G-2691)*

Oeg Building Materials Inc ....E...... 732 667-3636
Sayreville *(G-9720)*

Pabst Enterprises Equipment Co ....E...... 908 353-2880
Elizabeth *(G-2766)*

▲ Park Plus Inc ....E...... 201 917-5778
Fairview *(G-3366)*

Park Steel & Iron Co ....F...... 732 775-7500
Neptune *(G-6894)*

Passaic County Welders Inc ....F...... 973 696-1200
Wayne *(G-11539)*

Peter Garafano & Son Inc ....E...... 973 278-0350
Paterson *(G-8282)*

Polmar Iron Work Inc ....F...... 732 882-0900
Rahway *(G-9121)*

Precision Metalcrafters Inc ....E...... 856 629-1020
Williamstown *(G-11972)*

Prime Rebar LLC ....E...... 908 707-1234
Bridgewater *(G-869)*

Priore Construction Svcs LLC ....G...... 973 785-2262
Little Falls *(G-5465)*

R Way Tooling & Met Works LLC ....F...... 856 692-2218
Vineland *(G-11255)*

Rcc Fabricators Inc ....E...... 609 859-9350
Southampton *(G-10370)*

Riverside Marina Yacht Sls LLC ....F...... 856 461-1077
Riverside *(G-9403)*

RS Phillips Steel LLC ....E...... 973 827-6464
Sussex *(G-10565)*

Runding LLC ....G...... 973 277-8775
Oak Ridge *(G-7606)*

Samna Cnstrctn & Steel Fabrctn ....F...... 973 977-8400
Paterson *(G-8292)*

Sea Harbor Marine Inc ....G...... 732 477-8577
Brick *(G-731)*

Senco Metals LLC ....G.... 973 342-1742
Passaic *(G-8106)*
Southern New Jersey Stl Co Inc ....E.... 856 696-1612
Vineland *(G-11268)*
Springfield Metal Pdts Co Inc ....F.... 973 379-4600
Springfield *(G-10467)*
Squillace Stl Fabricators LLC ....G.... 908 241-6424
Roselle Park *(G-9591)*
Stateline Fabricators LLC ....E.... 908 387-8800
Phillipsburg *(G-8576)*
▲ Stirrup Metal Products Corp ....F.... 973 824-7086
Newark *(G-7287)*
Studio Dellarte ....G.... 718 599-3715
Jersey City *(G-4817)*
Susan R Bauer Inc ....G.... 973 657-1590
Ringwood *(G-9353)*
Theodore E Mozer Inc ....E.... 856 829-1432
Palmyra *(G-7786)*
Thomas Russo & Sons Inc ....G.... 201 332-4159
Jersey City *(G-4821)*
Tri-Steel Fabricators Inc ....E.... 609 392-8660
Trenton *(G-11004)*
United Steel Products Co Inc ....G.... 609 518-9230
Lumberton *(G-5637)*
Victory Iron Works Inc ....G.... 201 485-7181
Wyckoff *(G-12124)*
Vision Railings Ltd Lblty Co ....F.... 908 310-8926
Glen Gardner *(G-3824)*
W W Manufacturing Co Inc ....F.... 856 451-5700
Bridgeton *(G-777)*
Weir Welding Company Inc ....E.... 201 939-2284
Carlstadt *(G-1239)*
Westfield Shtmtl Works Inc ....E.... 908 276-5500
Kenilworth *(G-4989)*

3442 Metal Doors, Sash, Frames, Molding & Trim

4 Way Lock LLC ....G.... 908 359-2002
Hillsborough *(G-4299)*
Acme & Dorf Door Corp ....G.... 973 772-6774
Clifton *(G-1555)*
Alliance Vinyl Windows Co Inc ....E.... 856 456-4954
Oaklyn *(G-7650)*
▲ Allmark Door Company LLC ....F.... 610 358-9800
Springfield *(G-10425)*
Architectural Window Mfg Corp ....C.... 201 933-5094
Rutherford *(G-9614)*
Assa Abloy Entrance Sys US Inc ....E.... 609 443-5800
Trenton *(G-10897)*
Assa Abloy Entrance Systems US ....E.... 609 528-2580
Hamilton *(G-4103)*
Belleville Corporation ....F.... 201 991-6222
Kearny *(G-4846)*
Beta Industries Corp ....G.... 201 939-2400
Carlstadt *(G-1128)*
Bildisco Mfg Inc ....F.... 973 673-2400
West Orange *(G-11762)*
Century Bathworks Inc ....E.... 201 785-1414
Woodland Park *(G-12075)*
▲ Century Bathworks Inc ....D.... 973 785-4290
Woodland Park *(G-12074)*
Champion Opco LLC ....F.... 856 662-3400
West Berlin *(G-11580)*
Cronos-Prim Colorado LLC ....G.... 303 369-7477
Lodi *(G-5557)*
Dor-Win Manufacturing Co ....E.... 201 796-4300
Elmwood Park *(G-2821)*
Dorwin Manufacturing Co ....E.... 201 796-4300
Elmwood Park *(G-2822)*
Dry Bilge Systems Inc ....E.... 862 257-1800
Wallington *(G-11385)*
Elevator Entrance Inc ....E.... 973 790-9100
Paterson *(G-8181)*
Fast Doors LLC ....G.... 856 966-3278
Camden *(G-1063)*
Five Star Aluminum Products ....F.... 201 869-4181
North Bergen *(G-7405)*
Galaxy Metal Products LLC ....E.... 908 668-5200
Edison *(G-2517)*
Gray Overhead Door Co ....F.... 908 355-3889
Elizabeth *(G-2744)*
▲ Guardrite Steel Door Corp ....G.... 973 481-4424
Newark *(G-7142)*
Handi-Hut Inc ....E.... 973 614-1800
Clifton *(G-1632)*
Jersey Steel Door Inc ....G.... 973 482-4020
Newark *(G-7169)*
Lebanon Door LLC ....G.... 908 236-2620
Lebanon *(G-5269)*
▲ LMC-HB Corp ....F.... 862 239-9814
Paterson *(G-8244)*
Miric Industries Inc ....F.... 201 864-0233
North Bergen *(G-7422)*
▲ Northern Architectural Systems ....D.... 201 943-6400
Teterboro *(G-10688)*
Northern Architectural Systems ....E.... 201 943-6400
Carlstadt *(G-1192)*
Portaseal LLC ....G.... 973 539-0100
Morristown *(G-6695)*
Power Home Rmdlg Group LLC ....A.... 610 874-5000
Iselin *(G-4623)*
Quick Fab Aluminum Mfg Co ....E.... 732 367-7200
Lakewood *(G-5150)*
▲ Randall Mfg Co Inc ....E.... 973 482-8603
Newark *(G-7245)*
Remo Security Doors LLC ....G.... 213 983-1010
Englewood Cliffs *(G-2989)*
Revival Sash & Door LLC ....G.... 973 500-4242
Springfield *(G-10465)*
▲ Royal Aluminum Co Inc ....D.... 973 589-8880
Newark *(G-7253)*
◆ Royal Prime Inc ....F.... 908 354-7600
Elizabeth *(G-2775)*
▲ Rsl LLC ....D.... 609 484-1600
Egg Harbor Township *(G-2695)*
Security Holdings LLC ....D.... 201 457-0286
Carlstadt *(G-1215)*
Shutter DLight LLC ....G.... 908 956-4206
Plainfield *(G-8778)*
Silver Line Building Pdts LLC ....C.... 732 752-8704
Middlesex *(G-6148)*
Skyline Windows LLC ....E.... 201 531-9600
Wood Ridge *(G-12005)*
Starlite Window Mfg Co Inc ....F.... 973 278-9366
Paterson *(G-8300)*
Surburban Building Pdts Inc ....E.... 732 901-8900
Howell *(G-4551)*
Taylor Windows Inc ....F.... 973 672-3000
East Orange *(G-2264)*
◆ Thermwell Products Co Inc ....B.... 201 684-4400
Mahwah *(G-5781)*
Thomas Erectors Inc ....G.... 908 810-0030
Hillside *(G-4430)*
▲ Thomas Manufacturing Inc ....E.... 908 810-0030
Hillside *(G-4431)*
Total Installations ....G.... 908 943-3211
Elizabeth *(G-2782)*
Tricomp Inc ....C.... 973 835-1110
Pompton Plains *(G-8872)*
Tuckahoe Manufacturing Inc ....G.... 856 696-4100
Vineland *(G-11271)*
Verona Aluminum Products Inc ....G.... 973 857-4809
Verona *(G-11177)*
Warren Capital Inc ....G.... 732 910-8134
Warren *(G-11436)*
Weathercraft Manufacturing Co ....F.... 201 262-0055
Emerson *(G-2870)*
Window Factory Inc ....E.... 856 546-5050
Mount Ephraim *(G-6722)*
▲ Window Shapes Inc ....D.... 732 549-0708
Metuchen *(G-6081)*
Winstar Windows LLC ....G.... 973 403-0574
Essex Fells *(G-3012)*
Zulu Fire Doors Ltd Lblty Co ....G.... 973 569-9858
Paterson *(G-8326)*

3443 Fabricated Plate Work

Able Fab Co ....E.... 732 396-0600
Avenel *(G-118)*
◆ Acrison Inc ....D.... 201 440-8300
Moonachie *(G-6451)*
Aerojet Rocketdyne De Inc ....G.... 201 440-1453
Norwood *(G-7557)*
Airmet Inc ....G.... 973 481-5550
Newark *(G-7037)*
Airzone Systems ....G.... 201 207-6593
Montville *(G-6437)*
Akw Inc ....G.... 732 493-1883
Ocean *(G-7654)*
▲ Akw Inc ....G.... 732 530-9186
Shrewsbury *(G-9880)*
Amec Foster Wheeler USA Corp ....E.... 713 929-5000
Hampton *(G-4146)*
◆ Amec Fster Wheeler N Amer Corp ....D.... 936 448-6323
Hampton *(G-4147)*
American Auto Carriers Inc ....G.... 201 573-0371
Woodcliff Lake *(G-12045)*
Andrew B Duffy Inc ....F.... 856 845-4900
West Deptford *(G-11691)*
Arde Inc ....D.... 201 784-9880
Carlstadt *(G-1125)*
Arrow Shed LLC ....E.... 973 835-3200
Haskell *(G-4195)*
▲ Asa Hydraulik of America Inc ....G.... 908 541-1500
Branchburg *(G-623)*
Asco LP ....E.... 973 386-9000
Parsippany *(G-7886)*
▲ Atlas Industrial Mfg Co ....E.... 973 779-3970
Clifton *(G-1567)*
▲ Bartell Morrison (usa) LLC ....F.... 732 566-5400
Freehold *(G-3652)*
Billy D Dumpster Service LLC ....G.... 609 465-5990
Cape May Court House *(G-1107)*
Brennan Penrod Contractors LLC ....F.... 856 933-1100
Bellmawr *(G-329)*
Bulkhaul (usa) Limited ....F.... 908 272-3100
Iselin *(G-4602)*
Casale Industries Inc ....E.... 908 789-0040
Garwood *(G-3782)*
CB&i LLC ....C.... 856 482-3000
Trenton *(G-10913)*
Central Metal Fabricators Inc ....F.... 732 938-6900
Farmingdale *(G-3379)*
▲ Construction Specialties Inc ....E.... 908 236-0800
Lebanon *(G-5257)*
▲ Corban Energy Group Corp ....F.... 201 509-8555
Elmwood Park *(G-2818)*
▲ Cospack America Corp ....E.... 732 548-5858
Edison *(G-2484)*
▲ Crown Engineering Corp ....E.... 800 631-2153
Farmingdale *(G-3382)*
DC Fabricators Inc ....C.... 609 499-3000
Florence *(G-3474)*
De Ditrich Process Systems Inc ....E.... 908 317-2585
Mountainside *(G-6841)*
Deb Maintenance Inc ....E.... 856 786-0440
Cinnaminson *(G-1448)*
▼ Delta Cooling Towers Inc ....E.... 973 586-2201
Flanders *(G-3405)*
DR Technology Inc ....G.... 732 780-4664
Freehold *(G-3661)*
Dusenbery Engineering Co Inc ....G.... 973 539-2200
Morristown *(G-6661)*
▲ E F Britten & Co Inc ....F.... 908 276-4800
Cranford *(G-1908)*
▲ Edwards Coils Corp ....F.... 973 835-2800
Pompton Plains *(G-8863)*
Eks Parts Inc ....G.... 856 227-8811
Sewell *(G-9842)*
Enviro Pak Inc ....E.... 732 248-1600
Edison *(G-2504)*
Foster Wheeler Arabia Ltd ....G.... 908 730-4000
Hampton *(G-4151)*
Foster Wheeler Intl Corp ....F.... 908 730-4000
Hampton *(G-4152)*
Foster Whler Intl Holdings Inc ....G.... 908 730-4000
Hampton *(G-4154)*
▲ G J Oliver Inc ....D.... 908 454-9743
Phillipsburg *(G-8552)*
▲ Gate Technologies Inc ....G.... 973 300-0090
Sparta *(G-10388)*
Harsco Corporation ....E.... 856 779-7795
Cherry Hill *(G-1371)*
▲ Hiller Separation Process LLC ....G.... 512 556-5707
Fort Lee *(G-3561)*
Huber International Corp ....G.... 732 549-8600
Edison *(G-2532)*
▼ I S Parts International Inc ....E.... 856 691-2203
Vineland *(G-11234)*
Jaeger Thomas & Melissa DDS ....F.... 908 735-2722
Lebanon *(G-5266)*
▲ Jersey Tank Fabricators Inc ....E.... 609 758-7670
South Plainfield *(G-10283)*
◆ Joseph Oat Holdings Inc ....D.... 856 541-2900
Camden *(G-1072)*
JW Parr Leadburing Co ....G.... 973 256-8093
Little Falls *(G-5458)*
▲ Kooltronic Inc ....C.... 609 466-3400
Pennington *(G-8369)*
L & L Welding Contractors ....F.... 609 395-1600
Dayton *(G-1976)*
◆ Leland Limited Inc ....F.... 908 561-2000
South Plainfield *(G-10293)*
Linden Well Drilling ....E.... 908 862-6633
Linden *(G-5376)*
Lobster Life Systems Inc ....F.... 201 398-0303
Lodi *(G-5568)*
Maarky Thermal Systems Inc ....G.... 856 470-1504
Cherry Hill *(G-1386)*

SIC

Main Robert A & Sons Holdg Co ...E... 201 447-3700
Wyckoff *(G-12116)*

▲ Manning & Lewis Engrg Co Inc ...D... 908 687-2400
Union *(G-11073)*

▼ Meese Inc ...F... 201 796-4490
Saddle Brook *(G-9661)*

Modine Manufacturing Company ...G... 856 467-9710
Bridgeport *(G-741)*

Mystic Timber LLC ...G... 908 223-7878
Washington *(G-11449)*

Nova Flex Group ...F... 856 768-2275
West Berlin *(G-11611)*

▲ Perry Products Corporation ...E... 609 267-1600
Hainesport *(G-4076)*

Plate Concepts Inc ...G... 908 236-9570
Lebanon *(G-5273)*

▼ Polaris Plate Heat Exchngers L ...G... 732 345-7188
Shrewsbury *(G-9899)*

Power Products and Engrg LLC ...E... 855 769-3751
Trenton *(G-10979)*

Prospect Transportation Inc ...D... 201 933-9999
Carlstadt *(G-1209)*

Pulsonics Inc ...F... 800 999-6785
Belleville *(G-309)*

Ras Process Equipment ...E... 609 371-1000
Robbinsville *(G-9416)*

Roben Manufacturing Co Inc ...E... 732 364-6000
Lakewood *(G-5158)*

Rosenwach Tank Co LLC ...E... 732 563-4900
Somerset *(G-10066)*

Rudco Products Inc ...D... 856 691-0800
Vineland *(G-11261)*

Russell W Anderson Inc ...G... 201 825-2092
Mahwah *(G-5769)*

Scientific Alloys Corp ...F... 973 478-8323
Clifton *(G-1712)*

▲ Sheet Metal Products Inc ...D... 973 482-0450
Newark *(G-7269)*

▲ Shell Packaging Corporation ...E... 908 871-7000
Berkeley Heights *(G-412)*

Springfield Metal Pdts Co Inc ...F... 973 379-4600
Springfield *(G-10467)*

SPX Cooling Technologies Inc ...E... 908 450-8027
Bridgewater *(G-892)*

Stacks Envmtl Ltd Lblty Co ...G... 973 885-2036
Lake Hopatcong *(G-5037)*

▲ Stirrup Metal Products Corp ...F... 973 824-7086
Newark *(G-7287)*

Temptrol Corp ...E... 856 461-7977
Voorhees *(G-11295)*

Theodore E Mozer Inc ...E... 856 829-1432
Palmyra *(G-7786)*

◆ Titanium Fabrication Corp ...D... 973 227-5300
Fairfield *(G-3329)*

Tolan Machinery Company Inc ...E... 973 983-7212
Rockaway *(G-9506)*

Tolan Machinery Polishing Co ...E... 973 983-7212
Rockaway *(G-9507)*

◆ Triangle Tube/Phase III Co Inc ...D... 856 228-9940
Paulsboro *(G-8340)*

◆ Trs Inc ...E... 732 636-3300
Avenel *(G-151)*

▲ Ulma Form-Works Inc ...D... 201 882-1122
Hawthorne *(G-4247)*

Waage Electric Inc ...G... 908 245-9363
Kenilworth *(G-4986)*

Wastequip Manufacturing Co ...D... 856 784-5500
Sicklerville *(G-9917)*

Wastequip Manufacturing Co LLC ...E... 856 629-9222
Williamstown *(G-11986)*

Welded Products Co Inc ...E... 973 589-0180
Newark *(G-7313)*

Wind Tunnel Inc ...G... 201 485-7793
Mahwah *(G-5786)*

3444 Sheet Metal Work

67 Pollock Ave Corp ...G... 201 432-1156
Jersey City *(G-4679)*

A B Scantlebury Co Inc ...F... 973 770-3000
Newton *(G-7335)*

A R J Custom Fabrication Inc ...F... 609 695-6227
Trenton *(G-10887)*

A&B Heating & Cooling ...G... 908 289-2231
Elizabeth *(G-2705)*

Abco Metal LLC ...F... 973 772-8160
Paterson *(G-8122)*

Able Fab Co ...E... 732 396-0600
Avenel *(G-118)*

Aerosmith ...G... 973 614-9392
South Hackensack *(G-10147)*

Air & Specialties Sheet Metal ...F... 908 233-8306
Mountainside *(G-6832)*

Air Distribution Systems Inc ...D... 856 874-1100
Cherry Hill *(G-1336)*

Air Power Inc ...E... 973 882-5418
Fairfield *(G-3136)*

Airfiltronix Corp ...G... 973 779-5577
Clifton *(G-1560)*

Airmet Inc ...G... 973 481-5550
Newark *(G-7037)*

Airtec Inc ...G... 732 382-3700
Rahway *(G-9075)*

Ajay Metal Fabricators Inc ...G... 908 523-0557
Linden *(G-5318)*

◆ Allentown Inc ...B... 609 259-7951
Allentown *(G-24)*

Allied Metal Industries Inc ...E... 973 824-7347
Newark *(G-7039)*

Allmike Metal Technology Inc ...F... 201 935-2306
Moonachie *(G-6452)*

Altona Blower & Shtmtl Work ...G... 201 641-3520
Little Ferry *(G-5474)*

Aluma Systems Con Cnstr LLC ...G... 908 418-5073
Linden *(G-5322)*

Amerifab Corp ...G... 973 777-2120
Lodi *(G-5553)*

Andrew B Duffy Inc ...F... 856 845-4900
West Deptford *(G-11691)*

▲ Ango Electronics Corporation ...F... 201 955-0800
North Arlington *(G-7368)*

Architctural Metal Designs Inc ...E... 856 765-3000
Millville *(G-6234)*

▲ Argyle Industries Inc ...F... 908 725-8800
Branchburg *(G-620)*

Artus Corp ...E... 201 568-1000
Englewood *(G-2878)*

Asbury Awng Mfg & Installation ...G... 732 775-4881
Asbury Park *(G-71)*

Atco Rubber Products Inc ...E... 856 794-3393
Vineland *(G-11188)*

Atlantic Air Enterprises Inc ...F... 732 381-4000
Rahway *(G-9081)*

Atlantic Coastal Welding Inc ...F... 732 269-1088
Bayville *(G-240)*

B & S Sheet Metal Co Inc ...F... 973 427-3739
Hawthorne *(G-4205)*

Babbitt Mfg Co Inc ...F... 856 692-3245
Vineland *(G-11190)*

Banicki Sheet Metal Inc ...G... 201 385-5938
Bergenfield *(G-372)*

BCsmachine & Mfg Corp ...G... 908 561-1656
South Plainfield *(G-10224)*

Belden Inc ...F... 908 925-8000
Elizabeth *(G-2714)*

Benco Inc ...F... 973 575-4440
Fairfield *(G-3154)*

Bergen Homestate Corp ...G... 201 372-9740
Moonachie *(G-6456)*

Bill Chambers Sheet Metal ...G... 856 848-4774
Woodbury Heights *(G-12041)*

Blackhawk Cre Corporation ...F... 856 887-0162
Salem *(G-9692)*

Bloomfield Manufacturing Co ...F... 973 575-8900
Oakland *(G-7616)*

Bonland Industries Inc ...D... 973 694-3211
Wayne *(G-11481)*

Bouras Industries Inc ...A... 908 918-9400
Summit *(G-10527)*

BR Welding Inc ...F... 732 363-8253
Howell *(G-4532)*

Breure Sheet Metal Co Inc ...G... 973 772-6423
Clifton *(G-1578)*

Broadhurst Sheet Metal Works ...G... 973 304-4001
Hawthorne *(G-4210)*

▲ Brook Metal Products Inc ...F... 908 355-1601
Lawrence Township *(G-5215)*

Brothers Sheet Metal Inc ...F... 973 228-3221
Roseland *(G-9536)*

Burns Link Manufacturing Co ...F... 856 429-6844
Voorhees *(G-11281)*

Bushwick Metals LLC ...C... 610 495-9100
Englewood *(G-2888)*

C A Spalding Company ...E... 267 550-9000
Moorestown *(G-6511)*

C M C Steel Fabricators Inc ...C... 908 561-3484
South Plainfield *(G-10232)*

◆ Cain Machine Inc ...F... 856 825-7225
Millville *(G-6240)*

Casale Industries Inc ...E... 908 789-0040
Garwood *(G-3782)*

Central Metal Fabricators Inc ...F... 732 938-6900
Farmingdale *(G-3379)*

Classic Industries Inc ...G... 973 227-1366
Parsippany *(G-7906)*

Clifton Metal Products Co Inc ...F... 973 777-6100
Clifton *(G-1584)*

Coronation Sheet Metal Co ...G... 908 686-0930
Union *(G-11038)*

CPS Metals Inc ...F... 856 779-0846
Maple Shade *(G-5861)*

Crett Construction Inc ...F... 973 663-1184
Lake Hopatcong *(G-5035)*

Custom Fabricators Inc ...G... 908 862-4244
Linden *(G-5339)*

Cutmark Inc ...G... 856 234-3428
Mount Laurel *(G-6750)*

D&N Machine Manufacturing Inc ...E... 856 456-1366
Gloucester City *(G-3840)*

Danson Sheet Metal Inc ...E... 201 343-4876
Hackensack *(G-3905)*

Dasco Supply LLC ...F... 973 884-1390
Whippany *(G-11888)*

◆ Delair LLC ...D... 856 663-2900
Pennsauken *(G-8412)*

Delaware Valley Sign Corp ...D... 609 386-0100
Burlington *(G-962)*

Demand LLC ...F... 908 526-2020
Somerville *(G-10107)*

Diversified Fab Pdts Ltd Lblty ...G... 973 773-3189
Clifton *(G-1601)*

Dos Industrial Sales LLC ...G... 973 887-7800
East Hanover *(G-2205)*

Duct Mate Inc ...G... 201 488-8002
Hackensack *(G-3909)*

Ducts Inc ...G... 973 267-8482
Morris Plains *(G-6604)*

Ductworks Inc ...F... 908 754-8190
Plainfield *(G-8762)*

▲ Durex Inc ...D... 908 688-0800
Union *(G-11045)*

Dutra Sheet Metal Co ...G... 856 692-8058
Vineland *(G-11215)*

E P Homiek Shtmtl Sups Inc ...E... 732 364-7644
Lakewood *(G-5087)*

Edker Industries Inc ...E... 856 786-1971
Cinnaminson *(G-1455)*

Efco Corp ...F... 732 308-1010
Marlboro *(G-5896)*

Elgee Manufacturing Company ...G... 908 647-4100
Warren *(G-11408)*

Elmco Two Inc ...G... 856 365-2244
Camden *(G-1060)*

◆ Englert Inc ...C... 800 364-5378
Perth Amboy *(G-8517)*

Evs Interactive Inc ...F... 718 784-3690
Riverdale *(G-9377)*

▲ Ewc Controls Inc ...E... 732 446-3110
Manalapan *(G-5809)*

Excel Die Sharpening Corp ...G... 908 587-2606
Linden *(G-5345)*

▼ Fabulous Fabricators LLC ...E... 973 779-2400
Totowa *(G-10826)*

Fairfield Metal Ltd Lblty Co ...F... 973 276-8440
Fairfield *(G-3200)*

Falcon Industries Inc ...D... 732 563-9889
Somerset *(G-9992)*

Fiore Skylights Inc ...F... 856 346-0118
Somerdale *(G-9931)*

Fitts Sheet Metal Inc ...G... 201 923-9239
North Arlington *(G-7373)*

Franklen Sheet Metal Co Inc ...F... 732 988-0808
Ocean Grove *(G-7700)*

Frc Electrical Industries Inc ...E... 908 464-3200
New Providence *(G-7000)*

▲ GAF Elk Materials Corporation ...C... 973 628-4083
Wayne *(G-11508)*

◆ Garvey Corporation ...D... 609 561-2450
Hammonton *(G-4134)*

Gauer Metal Products Co Inc ...E... 908 241-4080
Kenilworth *(G-4942)*

Gaw Associates Inc ...F... 856 608-1428
Cherry Hill *(G-1367)*

General Aviation & Elec Mfg Co ...E... 201 487-1700
Hackensack *(G-3921)*

Giant Stl Fabricators Erectors ...G... 908 241-6766
Roselle *(G-9559)*

Globe Engineering Corp ...G... 609 898-0349
Cape May *(G-1099)*

Golden Metal Products Corp ...E... 973 399-1157
Hillside *(G-4394)*

Great Railing Inc ....F 856 875-0050
Williamstown (G-11960)

H & H Industries Inc ....E 856 663-4444
Pennsauken (G-8429)

H & H Production Machining ....G 973 383-6880
Sparta (G-10389)

Haenssler Shtmtl Works Inc .....F 973 373-6360
Newark (G-7143)

Handi-Hut Inc ....E 973 614-1800
Clifton (G-1632)

▲ Harold R Henrich Inc ....D 732 370-4455
Lakewood (G-5107)

Hays Sheet Metal Inc ....E 856 662-7722
Pennsauken (G-8430)

Hudson Awning Co Inc ....E 201 339-7171
Bayonne (G-223)

Hutchinson Industries Inc ....F 609 394-1010
Trenton (G-10940)

In-Line Shtmtl Fabricators ....G 201 339-8121
Bayonne (G-224)

Independent Metal Sales Inc ....F 609 261-8090
Hainesport (G-4074)

Independent Sheet Metal Co Inc ..D 973 423-1150
Riverdale (G-9379)

Industrial Process & Eqp Inc ....F 973 702-0330
. Sussex (G-10562)

Inox Components ....F 856 256-0800
Pitman (G-8745)

Intercoastal Fabricators Inc .....G 856 629-4105
Williamstown (G-11961)

International Shtmtl Plate Mfg ...E 908 722-6614
Somerville (G-10117)

▲ International Swimming Pools ..E 732 565-9229
New Brunswick (G-6935)

Internet-Sales USA Corporation ..G 775 468-8379
Rockaway (G-9467)

J & E Metal Fabricators Inc ......E 732 548-9650
Metuchen (G-6064)

J & M Air Inc ....E 908 707-4040
Somerville (G-10118)

James A Stanlick Jr ....G 973 366-7316
Wharton (G-11860)

Jason Metal Products Corp ....E 732 396-1132
Rahway (G-9107)

Jersey Sheet Metal & Machine ..E 973 366-8628
Dover (G-2093)

Jesco Iron Crafts Inc ....F 201 488-4545
Bogota (G-533)

▲ Jet Precision Metal Inc ....E 973 423-4350
Hawthorne (G-4229)

John E Herbst Heating & Coolg ..G 732 721-0088
Parlin (G-7866)

Joseph Bbinec Shtmtl Works Inc ..E .. 732 388-0155
Rahway (G-9109)

Kinetron Inc ....F 732 918-7777
Ocean (G-7667)

Klm Mechanical Contractors .....F 201 385-6965
Dumont (G-2115)

Lectro Products Inc ....G 732 462-2463
Freehold (G-3675)

Legrand AV Inc ....B 973 839-1011
Fairfield (G-3260)

Leibrock Metal Products Inc .....G 732 695-0326
Ocean (G-7669)

Lentine Sheet Metal Inc ....F 908 486-8974
Linden (G-5375)

Lynn Mechanical Contractors ....F 856 829-1717
Cinnaminson (G-1470)

M C Custom Shtmtl Fabrication ..G 856 767-9509
West Berlin (G-11606)

Madhu B Goyal MD ....G 908 769-0307
South Plainfield (G-10296)

Marino International Corp ....G 732 752-5100
South Plainfield (G-10299)

Marlyn Sheet Metal Inc ....F 856 863-6900
Clayton (G-1527)

Marx NJ Group LLC ....E 732 901-3880
Bound Brook (G-603)

Max Gurtman & Sons Inc ....E 973 478-7000
Clifton (G-1666)

▲ Medlaurel Inc ....E 856 461-6600
Delanco (G-2006)

Metal Dynamix LLC ....G 856 235-4559
Cherry Hill (G-1394)

Metal Specialties New Jersey ....G 609 261-9277
Mount Holly (G-6732)

▼ Metalfab Inc ....E 973 764-2000
Vernon (G-11160)

Metalix Inc ....G 973 546-2500
Little Falls (G-5461)

Michael Anthony Sign Dsign Inc ..E .. 732 453-6120
Piscataway (G-8690)

◆ Middle Atlantic Products Inc ..B 973 839-1011
Fairfield (G-3271)

Millar Sheet Metal ....G 201 997-1990
Kearny (G-4884)

Moreng Metal Products Inc ....D 973 256-2001
Totowa (G-10837)

Neumann Sheet Metal Inc ....G 908 756-0415
Plainfield (G-8771)

New Age Metal Fabg Co Inc ......D 973 227-9107
Fairfield (G-3277)

Nordic Metal LLC ....G 908 245-8900
Kenilworth (G-4964)

Oeg Building Materials Inc ....E 732 667-3636
Sayreville (G-9720)

P L M Manufacturing Company ..E 201 342-3636
Hackensack (G-3961)

Pabst Enterprises Equipment Co ..E .. 908 353-2880
Elizabeth (G-2766)

Par Sheet Metal Inc ....F 908 241-2477
Roselle (G-9570)

Par Troy Sheet Metal & AC LLC ..G .. 973 227-1150
Fairfield (G-3288)

Park Steel & Iron Co ....E 732 775-7500
Neptune (G-6894)

Passaic Metal & Bldg Sups Co ..D 973 546-9000
Clifton (G-1685)

Pcr Technologies Inc ....G 973 882-0017
Pine Brook (G-8613)

◆ Pemberton Fabricators Inc .....A 609 267-0922
Rancocas (G-9163)

Pepco Manufacturing Co ....D 856 783-3700
Somerdale (G-9933)

Pl Metal Products Inc ....G 201 955-0800
Linden (G-5408)

Pioneer Machine & Tool Co Inc ..E 856 779-8800
Maple Shade (G-5868)

Postage Bin ....G 732 333-0915
Freehold (G-3689)

Precision Metalcrafters Inc ....E 856 629-1020
Williamstown (G-11972)

Prism Sheet Metal Inc ....G 973 673-0213
Orange (G-7758)

Pro-Deck Supply ....G 609 771-1100
Trenton (G-10984)

Professional Envmtl Systems .....E 201 991-3000
Kearny (G-4895)

PTL Sheet Metal Inc ....G 201 501-8700
Dumont (G-2117)

Quality Sheet Metal & Wldg Inc ..F .. 732 469-7111
Piscataway (G-8703)

R M F Associates Inc ....C 908 687-9355
Union (G-11086)

Radiation Systems Inc ....G 201 891-7515
Wyckoff (G-12118)

▼ Rails Company Inc ....E 973 763-4320
Maplewood (G-5883)

Rainbow Metal Units Corp ....E 718 784-3690
Riverdale (G-9381)

Ranco Precision Sheet Metal .....G 973 472-8808
Clifton (G-1705)

Rangecraft Manufacturing Inc ....F 201 791-0440
Fair Lawn (G-3116)

Rhoads Metal Works Inc ....F 856 486-1551
Pennsauken (G-8478)

Ricklyn Co Inc ....G 908 689-6770
Columbia (G-1797)

Roof Deck Inc ....F 609 448-6666
East Windsor (G-2358)

Schrader & Company Inc ....F 973 579-1160
Newton (G-7357)

Seal-Spout Corp ....F 908 647-0648
Liberty Corner (G-5296)

◆ Service Metal Fabricating Inc ..D 973 625-8882
Rockaway (G-9498)

Service Metal Fabricating Inc .....G 973 989-7199
Dover (G-2106)

Shamong Manufacturing Company ..E .. 609 654-2549
Shamong (G-9859)

▲ Sheet Metal Products Inc ....D 973 482-0450
Newark (G-7269)

Sonrise Metal Inc ....F 973 423-4717
Hopatcong (G-4522)

South Jersey Metal Inc ....E 856 228-0642
Deptford (G-2066)

Sperro Metal Products LLC ....G 973 335-2000
Montville (G-6447)

Springfield Heating & AC Co ......F 908 233-8400
Mountainside (G-6852)

Springfield Metal Pdts Co Inc ....F 973 379-4600
Springfield (G-10467)

Star Metal Products ....E 908 474-9860
Linden (G-5429)

▲ Stirrup Metal Products Corp ...F 973 824-7086
Newark (G-7287)

▲ Strong Man Safety Pdts Corp ..G .. 973 831-1555
Pompton Plains (G-8871)

▲ Super Stud Building Pdts Inc ..D .. 732 662-6200
Edison (G-2626)

T J Eckardt Associates Inc ....F 856 767-4111
Berlin (G-430)

Tam Metal Products Inc ....E 201 848-7800
Mahwah (G-5779)

Theodore E Mozer Inc ....E 856 829-1432
Palmyra (G-7786)

Totowa Metal Fabricators Inc ....F 973 423-1943
North Haledon (G-7501)

Trenton Sheet Metal Inc ....E 609 695-6328
Trenton (G-11003)

▲ Ulma Form-Works Inc ....D 201 882-1122
Hawthorne (G-4247)

Unique Metal Products ....F 732 388-1888
Rahway (G-9130)

United Gutter Supply Inc ....E 201 933-6316
East Rutherford (G-2328)

Vfi Fabricators Inc ....E 856 629-8786
Williamstown (G-11985)

Vinch Recycling Inc ....F 609 393-0200
Lawrenceville (G-5246)

◆ Ware Industries Inc ....D 908 757-9000
South Plainfield (G-10345)

Weathercraft Manufacturing Co ..F .. 201 262-0055
Emerson (G-2870)

Wecom Inc ....E 856 863-8400
Glassboro (G-3820)

Welded Products Co Inc ....E 973 589-0180
Newark (G-7313)

Westfield Shtmtl Works Inc ....E 908 276-5500
Kenilworth (G-4989)

3446 Architectural & Ornamental Metal Work

67 Pollock Ave Corp ....G 201 432-1156
Jersey City (G-4679)

A & A Ironwork Co Inc ....F 973 728-4300
Hewitt (G-4273)

Abba Metal Works Inc ....G 973 684-0808
Paterson (G-8121)

Advanced Products LLC ....E 800 724-5464
Lakewood (G-5046)

Airmet Inc ....G 973 481-5550
Newark (G-7037)

Alberona Welding & Iron Works ..G .. 973 674-3375
Orange (G-7749)

Alessandra Miscellaneous Metal ..F .. 973 786-6805
Newton (G-7336)

All American Metal Fabricators ..G .. 201 567-2898
Tenafly (G-10658)

Architctural Metal Fabricators ....G 718 765-0722
Carteret (G-1246)

▲ Architectural Iron Designs .....G 908 757-2323
Plainfield (G-8758)

Armetec Corp ....G 973 485-2525
Newark (G-7052)

Artistic Railings Inc ....G 973 772-8540
Garfield (G-3730)

B L White Welding & Steel Co ....G 973 684-4111
Paterson (G-8144)

▲ Bamco Inc ....D 732 302-0889
Middlesex (G-6100)

Bedlam Corp ....F 973 774-8770
Montclair (G-6360)

Bolt Welding & Iron Works ....G 609 393-3993
Trenton (G-10906)

C & S Fencing Inc ....E 201 797-5440
Elmwood Park (G-2813)

C W Grimmer & Sons Inc ....F 732 741-2189
Tinton Falls (G-10706)

▲ Cacciola Iron Works Inc ....G 973 595-0854
Paterson (G-8153)

Carfaro Inc ....E 609 890-6600
Trenton (G-10910)

Ciccone Inc ....G 732 349-7071
Toms River (G-10752)

▼ Clems Ornamental Iron Works ..D .. 732 968-7200
Piscataway (G-8647)

Columbian Orna Ir Works Inc .....G 973 697-0927
Paterson (G-8160)

▲ Construction Specialties Inc ....E 908 236-0800
Lebanon (G-5257)

Creative Metal Works Inc ....F 973 579-3717
Sparta *(G-10385)*

Cusumano Perma-Rail Co ....G 908 245-9281
Roselle Park *(G-9581)*

◆ Delair LLC ....D 856 663-2900
Pennsauken *(G-8412)*

Doortec Archtctural Met GL LLC ....G 201 497-5056
River Vale *(G-9365)*

Empire Lumber & Millwork Co ....E 973 242-2700
Newark *(G-7115)*

F & C Prof Alum Railings Corp ....G 908 753-8886
Plainfield *(G-8765)*

Fairway Building Products LLC ....E 609 890-6600
Trenton *(G-10935)*

▲ FMB Systems Inc ....D 973 485-5544
Harrison *(G-4175)*

G & H Sheet Metal Works Inc ....G 973 923-1100
Hillside *(G-4393)*

▲ G-Tech Elevator Associates LLC ....F 866 658-9296
Linden *(G-5350)*

Garden State Iron Inc ....F 732 918-0760
Ocean *(G-7664)*

George Ciocher Inc ....G 732 818-3495
Toms River *(G-10761)*

Gervens Enterprises Inc ....F 973 838-1600
Bloomingdale *(G-529)*

Harsco Corporation ....E 908 454-7169
Plainfield *(G-8768)*

▲ International Design & Mfg LLC ....G 908 587-2884
Linden *(G-5363)*

▲ Interntnal Archtctral Irnworks ....E 973 741-0749
Irvington *(G-4577)*

Interstate Architectural & Ir ....G 201 941-0393
Cliffside Park *(G-1540)*

Interstate Panel LLC ....F 609 586-4411
Hamilton *(G-4108)*

J G Schmidt Steel ....F 973 473-4822
Passaic *(G-8075)*

J Kaufman Iron Works Inc ....F 973 925-9972
Paterson *(G-8216)*

James A Stanlick Jr ....G 973 366-7316
Wharton *(G-11860)*

James Zylstra Enterprises Inc ....G 973 383-6768
Lafayette *(G-5028)*

Joseph Monga Jr ....G 973 595-8517
Paterson *(G-8226)*

K & A Architectural Met GL LLC ....F 908 687-0247
Hillside *(G-4408)*

Kaufman Stairs Inc ....E 908 862-3579
Rahway *(G-9111)*

La Forge De Style LLC ....G 201 488-1955
South Hackensack *(G-10168)*

Leets Steel Inc ....G 917 416-7977
Sayreville *(G-9715)*

Lingo Inc ....F 856 273-6594
Mount Laurel *(G-6775)*

▲ LMC-HB Corp ....F 862 239-9814
Paterson *(G-8244)*

◆ Lmt Mercer Group Inc ....E 888 570-5252
Lawrenceville *(G-5236)*

Majka Railing Inc ....G 973 247-7603
Paterson *(G-8248)*

Marchione Industries Inc ....E 718 317-4900
Lyndhurst *(G-5661)*

McNichols Company ....F 877 884-4653
New Brunswick *(G-6945)*

◆ Merchant & Evans Inc ....E 609 387-3033
Burlington *(G-979)*

Mershon Concrete LLC ....E 609 298-2150
Bordentown *(G-588)*

Michael Anthony Sign Dsign Inc ....E 732 453-6120
Piscataway *(G-8690)*

Morsemere Iron Works Inc ....F 201 941-1133
Ridgefield *(G-9278)*

New Jersey Stair and Rail Inc ....G 732 583-8400
Matawan *(G-5981)*

Newman Ornamental Iron Works ....F 732 223-9042
Brielle *(G-908)*

North Jersey Metal Fabricators ....G 973 305-9830
Wayne *(G-11536)*

▲ Omnia Industries Inc ....E 973 239-7272
Cedar Grove *(G-1286)*

Papp Iron Works Inc ....D 908 731-1000
Plainfield *(G-8775)*

Par Troy Sheet Metal & AC LLC ....G 973 227-1150
Fairfield *(G-3288)*

Permanore Archtctural Finishes ....G 908 797-4177
Milford *(G-6194)*

Pioneer Railing Inc ....G 609 387-0981
Beverly *(G-453)*

Post To Post LLC ....G 609 646-9300
Egg Harbor Township *(G-2693)*

▲ Rambusch Decorating Company .....E 201 333-2525
Jersey City *(G-4797)*

Robert J Donaldson Inc ....F 856 629-2737
Williamstown *(G-11976)*

S & S Socius Inc ....G 732 698-2400
Edison *(G-2602)*

Security Fabricators Inc ....F 908 272-9171
Kenilworth *(G-4977)*

Studio Dellarte ....G 718 599-3715
Jersey City *(G-4817)*

Wayside Fence Company Inc ....E 201 791-7979
Fair Lawn *(G-3129)*

Zone Defense Inc ....F 973 328-0436
Hackettstown *(G-4042)*

3448 Prefabricated Metal Buildings & Cmpnts

Arrow Shed LLC ....E 973 835-3200
Haskell *(G-4195)*

Diamond Scooters Inc ....G 609 646-0003
Absecon *(G-2)*

Edward T Brady ....G 732 928-0257
Allentown *(G-25)*

Everlast Associates Inc ....G 609 261-1888
Southampton *(G-10362)*

Handi-Hut Inc ....E 973 614-1800
Clifton *(G-1632)*

Marino Building Systems Corp ....C 732 968-0555
South Plainfield *(G-10298)*

Mtn Government Services Inc ....F 703 443-6738
Holmdel *(G-4509)*

P M C Diners Inc ....F 201 337-6146
Oakland *(G-7640)*

Pre-Fab Structures Inc ....G 856 768-4257
Atco *(G-87)*

Walpole Woodworkers Inc ....G 973 539-3555
Morris Plains *(G-6628)*

3449 Misc Structural Metal Work

Alberona Welding & Iron Works ....G 973 674-3375
Orange *(G-7749)*

Architectural Metal and Glass ....G 732 994-7575
Lakewood *(G-5054)*

Bolt Welding & Iron Works ....G 609 393-3993
Trenton *(G-10906)*

Camtec Industries Inc ....F 732 332-9800
Colts Neck *(G-1777)*

Eagle Steel & Iron LLC ....G 908 587-1025
Stewartsville *(G-10483)*

Handi-Hut Inc ....G 973 614-1800
Clifton *(G-1632)*

▲ Haydon Corporation ....D 973 904-0800
Wayne *(G-11515)*

◆ Helidex LLC ....G 201 636-2546
East Rutherford *(G-2291)*

Inductotherm Technologies Inc ....G 609 267-9000
Rancocas *(G-9162)*

Kenric Inc ....G 856 294-9161
Swedesboro *(G-10592)*

Luso Machine Nj LLC ....F 973 242-1717
Newark *(G-7188)*

Lusotech LLC ....G 973 332-3861
Newark *(G-7190)*

Mainland Plate Glass Company ....F 609 277-2938
Pleasantville *(G-8815)*

Morsemere Iron Works Inc ....F 201 941-1133
Ridgefield *(G-9278)*

N E R Associates Inc ....G 908 454-5955
Phillipsburg *(G-8565)*

New Jersey Steel Corporation ....F 856 337-0054
Haddon Township *(G-4051)*

Paragon Iron Inc ....G 201 528-7307
Carlstadt *(G-1197)*

Pipeline Eqp Resources Co LLC ....G 888 232-7372
Boonton *(G-564)*

RS Phillips Steel LLC ....E 973 827-6464
Sussex *(G-10565)*

Specialty Measures ....G 609 882-6071
Ewing *(G-3066)*

Stelfast Inc ....G 440 879-0077
Edison *(G-2620)*

United Eqp Fabricators LLC ....G 973 242-2737
Newark *(G-7308)*

W2f Inc ....G 609 735-0135
New Egypt *(G-6987)*

Wired Products LLC ....F 551 231-5800
Paramus *(G-7844)*

3451 Screw Machine Prdts

Accurate Screw Machine Corp ....D 973 276-0379
Fairfield *(G-3133)*

Amark Industries Inc ....G 973 992-8900
Livingston *(G-5505)*

Automatic Machine Product ....G 973 383-9929
Newton *(G-7337)*

Bmb Machining LLC ....G 973 256-4010
Woodland Park *(G-12071)*

C & K Punch & Screw Mch Pdts ....G 201 343-6750
Hackensack *(G-3888)*

Champion Fasteners Inc ....E 609 267-5222
Lumberton *(G-5627)*

Chicago Pneumatic Tool ....G 973 276-1377
Fairfield *(G-3167)*

Congruent Machine Co Inc ....G 973 764-6767
Vernon *(G-11158)*

▲ Duro Manufacturing Company ....G 908 810-9588
Union *(G-11046)*

Eastern Machining Corporation ....G 856 694-3303
Franklinville *(G-3637)*

Edston Manufacturing Company ....G 908 647-0116
Fairfield *(G-3189)*

▲ Esco Precision Inc ....E 908 722-0800
Hillsborough *(G-4315)*

F P Schmidt Manufacturing Co ....F 201 343-4241
South Hackensack *(G-10161)*

Ferrum Industries Inc ....F 201 935-1220
Carlstadt *(G-1156)*

Form Cut Industries Inc ....G 973 483-5154
Newark *(G-7127)*

▲ Gadren Machine Co Inc ....F 856 456-4329
Collingswood *(G-1767)*

H & H Swiss Screw Machine PR ....E 908 688-6390
Hillside *(G-4395)*

Hi-Grade Products Mfg Co ....F 908 245-4133
Kenilworth *(G-4944)*

▲ International Tool & Mch LLC ....G 908 687-5580
Hillside *(G-4404)*

◆ J & S Precision Products Co ....E 609 654-0900
Medford *(G-6025)*

Karl Neuweiler Inc ....G 908 464-6532
Berkeley Heights *(G-404)*

Labern Machine Products LLC ....G 908 722-1970
Branchburg *(G-654)*

Main Robert A & Sons Holdg Co ....E 201 447-3700
Wyckoff *(G-12116)*

Meltom Manufacturing Inc ....G 973 546-0058
Clifton *(G-1667)*

Mw Industries Inc ....D 973 244-9200
Fairfield *(G-3274)*

Nova Precision Products Inc ....C 973 625-1586
Rockaway *(G-9480)*

O E M Manufacturers Ltd Inc ....G 201 475-8585
Elmwood Park *(G-2845)*

Orion Precision Industries ....G 732 247-9704
Somerset *(G-10046)*

Oroszlany Laszlo ....G 201 666-2101
Hillsdale *(G-4369)*

Peter Yaged ....G 973 427-4219
Hawthorne *(G-4238)*

S J Screw Company Inc ....E 908 475-2155
Belvidere *(G-366)*

Salem Manufacturing Corp ....F 973 751-6331
Belleville *(G-314)*

Sumatic Co Inc ....G 973 772-1288
Garfield *(G-3771)*

Supermatic Corp ....F 973 627-4433
Rockaway *(G-9502)*

Telemark Cnc LLC ....G 973 794-4857
Boonton *(G-571)*

Tool Shop Inc ....G 856 767-8077
West Berlin *(G-11630)*

Triangle Automatic Inc ....G 973 625-3830
Wharton *(G-11873)*

Ultimate Spinning Turning Corp ....G 201 372-9740
Moonachie *(G-6495)*

Welton V Johnson Engineering ....F 908 241-3100
Kenilworth *(G-4988)*

Zago Manufacturing Company ....E 973 643-6700
Newark *(G-7318)*

3452 Bolts, Nuts, Screws, Rivets & Washers

Accurate Prscsion Fstener Corp ....E 201 567-9700
Englewood *(G-2873)*

▲ Amerifast Corp ....F 908 668-1959
South Plainfield *(G-10217)*

◆ Arrow Fastener Co LLC ....B 201 843-6900
Saddle Brook *(G-9640)*

Bigelow Components Corp ....E 973 467-1200
  Springfield *(G-10431)*

▲ Celus Fasteners Mfg Inc ....E 800 289-7483
  Northvale *(G-7520)*

▲ Chicago Pneumatic Tool ....F 973 928-5222
  Clifton *(G-1583)*

Cold Headed Fasteners Inc ....G 856 461-3244
  Delanco *(G-2004)*

Edwin Leonel Ramirez ....G 732 648-5587
  Plainfield *(G-8764)*

F & R Grinding Inc ....F 908 996-0440
  Frenchtown *(G-3712)*

▲ Ford Atlantic Fastener Corp ....E 973 882-1191
  Pine Brook *(G-8601)*

General Sullivan Group Inc ....F 609 745-5000
  Pennington *(G-8366)*

▲ H K Metal Craft Mfg Corp ....E 973 471-7770
  Lodi *(G-5563)*

▲ Industrial Rivet & Fastener Co ....D 201 750-1040
  Northvale *(G-7528)*

◆ JC Macelroy Co Inc ....D 732 572-7100
  Piscataway *(G-8681)*

Kt Mt Corp ....F 877 791-4426
  Cinnaminson *(G-1469)*

Mechanitron Corporation Inc ....G 908 620-1001
  Roselle *(G-9565)*

Mrl Manufacturing Corp ....F 973 790-1744
  Haledon *(G-4084)*

◆ New Jersey Rivet Co LLC ....F 856 963-2237
  Camden *(G-1078)*

Nylok Corporation ....F 201 427-8555
  Hawthorne *(G-4235)*

Oroszlany Laszlo ....G 201 666-2101
  Hillsdale *(G-4369)*

◆ P & R Fasteners Inc ....E 732 302-3600
  Somerset *(G-10050)*

Pin Cancer Campaign ....G 973 600-4170
  Newton *(G-7353)*

▲ Scheinert & Sons Inc ....E 201 791-4600
  Saddle Brook *(G-9677)*

Shallcross Bolt & Specialties ....E 908 925-4700
  Linden *(G-5422)*

▲ Universal Metalcraft Inc ....E 973 345-3284
  Wayne *(G-11560)*

Wm H Brewster Jr Incorporated ....G 973 227-1050
  Fairfield *(G-3354)*

Zago Manufacturing Company ....E 973 643-6700
  Newark *(G-7318)*

3462 Iron & Steel Forgings

Able Gear & Machine Co ....G 973 983-8055
  Rockaway *(G-9434)*

◆ All Mtals Frge Group Ltd Lblty ....E 973 276-5000
  Fairfield *(G-3138)*

Atlantic Steel Solutions LLC ....F 973 978-0026
  Paterson *(G-8143)*

Bloomfield Iron Co Inc ....G 973 748-7040
  Belleville *(G-291)*

▲ Hafco Foundry & Machine Co ....F 201 447-0433
  Midland Park *(G-6176)*

JDM Engineering Inc ....G 732 780-0770
  Freehold *(G-3673)*

▲ Kumar & Kumar Inc ....G 732 322-0435
  Edison *(G-2546)*

▲ McWilliams Forge Company ....D 973 627-0200
  Rockaway *(G-9476)*

Pennsylvania Machine Works Inc ....E 856 467-0500
  Swedesboro *(G-10600)*

▲ Piping Supplies Inc ....G 609 561-9323
  Williamstown *(G-11968)*

▲ PSEG Nuclear LLC ....A 973 430-5191
  Newark *(G-7239)*

▲ Razer Scandinavia Inc ....G 732 441-1250
  Matawan *(G-5986)*

Sigma Engineering & Consulting ....F 732 356-3046
  Middlesex *(G-6147)*

State Tool Gear Co Inc ....F 973 642-6181
  Newark *(G-7286)*

Supply Technologies LLC ....E 201 641-7600
  Moonachie *(G-6492)*

▲ Taurus International Corp ....E 201 825-2420
  Ramsey *(G-9156)*

▲ Titanium Industries Inc ....E 973 983-1185
  Rockaway *(G-9504)*

Wyman-Gordon Forgings Inc ....G 973 627-0200
  Rockaway *(G-9514)*

3463 Nonferrous Forgings

▲ McWilliams Forge Company ....D 973 627-0200
  Rockaway *(G-9476)*

▲ Piping Supplies Inc ....G 609 561-9323
  Williamstown *(G-11968)*

Ramco Manufacturing Co Inc ....E 908 245-4500
  Kenilworth *(G-4973)*

3465 Automotive Stampings

▼ Engine Combo LLC ....F 201 290-4399
  Irvington *(G-4567)*

Robert Freeman ....G 973 751-0082
  Belleville *(G-312)*

▲ Taurus International Corp ....E 201 825-2420
  Ramsey *(G-9156)*

Tonys Auto Entp Ltd Lblty Co ....G 203 223-5776
  Edison *(G-2633)*

3466 Crowns & Closures

Amcor Flexibles LLC ....C 856 825-1400
  Millville *(G-6224)*

3469 Metal Stampings, NEC

▲ A K Stamping Co Inc ....E 908 232-7300
  Mountainside *(G-6831)*

◆ A Plus Products Incorporated ....E 732 866-9111
  Marlboro *(G-5892)*

◆ Accurate Forming LLC ....G 973 827-7155
  Hamburg *(G-4087)*

▲ Accurate Tool & Die Co Inc ....G 201 476-9348
  Montvale *(G-6394)*

▼ Acme Cosmetic Components LLC ..E 718 335-3000
  Secaucus *(G-9750)*

Artistic Hardware ....G 609 383-1909
  Northfield *(G-7510)*

Aspe Inc ....E 973 808-1155
  Fairfield *(G-3148)*

▲ Aspen Manufacturing Co Inc ....G 609 871-6400
  Beverly *(G-447)*

B E C Mfg Corp ....E 201 414-0000
  Glen Rock *(G-3828)*

Be CU Manufacturing Co Inc ....E 908 233-3342
  Scotch Plains *(G-9731)*

Bel-Tech Stamping Inc ....F 973 728-8229
  West Milford *(G-11726)*

Bernardaud Na Inc ....G 973 274-3555
  Kearny *(G-4847)*

Bigelow Components Corp ....E 973 467-1200
  Springfield *(G-10431)*

Bilt Rite Tool & Die Co Inc ....G 973 227-2882
  Fairfield *(G-3158)*

Boyle Tool & Die Co Inc ....F 856 853-1819
  West Deptford *(G-11694)*

Camptown Tool & Die Co Inc ....G 908 688-8406
  Kenilworth *(G-4932)*

▲ Carter Manufacturing Co Inc ....E 201 935-0770
  Moonachie *(G-6461)*

▲ Case Medical Inc ....C 201 313-1999
  South Hackensack *(G-10152)*

▲ Charles E Green & Son Inc ....E 973 485-3630
  Newark *(G-7082)*

Cincinnati Thermal Spray Inc ....E 973 379-0003
  Springfield *(G-10435)*

Clover Stamping Inc ....G 973 278-4888
  Paterson *(G-8158)*

▲ Coda Resources Ltd ....C 718 649-1666
  Matawan *(G-5971)*

▲ Coining Inc ....C 201 791-4020
  Montvale *(G-6403)*

▲ Coining Holding Company ....E 201 791-4020
  Montvale *(G-6404)*

Coining Manufacturing LLC ....E 973 253-0500
  Colts Neck *(G-1778)*

Coining Mfg ....G 973 253-0500
  Clifton *(G-1585)*

▲ Coining Technologies Inc ....D 866 897-2304
  Demarest *(G-2025)*

Deborah Sales & Mfg Co ....G 973 344-8466
  Newark *(G-7100)*

▲ Durex Inc ....D 908 688-0800
  Union *(G-11045)*

Duron Co Inc ....F 973 242-5704
  Newark *(G-7107)*

Eclipse Manufacturing LLC ....G 973 340-9939
  Garfield *(G-3741)*

Electronic Parts Specialty Co ....G 609 267-0055
  Mount Holly *(G-6726)*

Elray Manufacturing Company ....E 856 881-1935
  Glassboro *(G-3810)*

Epi Group Ltd Liability Co ....G 917 710-6607
  Lakewood *(G-5092)*

Extruders International Inc ....G 908 241-7750
  Roselle Park *(G-9584)*

F & G Tool & Die Inc ....G 908 241-5880
  Kenilworth *(G-4938)*

F & M Machine Co Inc ....F 908 245-8830
  Kenilworth *(G-4939)*

F G Clover Company Inc ....G 973 627-1160
  Rockaway *(G-9457)*

▲ Feldware Inc ....E 718 372-0486
  Rahway *(G-9093)*

◆ Frameware Inc ....F 800 582-5608
  Fairfield *(G-3207)*

G Big Corp ....G 973 242-6521
  Newark *(G-7129)*

General Stamping Co Inc ....F 973 627-9500
  Columbia *(G-1793)*

General Wire & Stamping Co ....F 973 366-8080
  Randolph *(G-9179)*

▲ Global Marketing Corp ....F 973 426-1088
  Randolph *(G-9181)*

Golden Metal Products Corp ....E 973 399-1157
  Hillside *(G-4394)*

H & T Tool Co Inc ....G 973 227-4858
  Fairfield *(G-3219)*

▲ H K Metal Craft Mfg Corp ....E 973 471-7770
  Lodi *(G-5563)*

▲ Hafco Foundry & Machine Co ....F 201 447-0433
  Midland Park *(G-6176)*

◆ Heyco Molded Products Inc ....F 732 286-4336
  Toms River *(G-10765)*

Heyco Stamped Products ....G 732 286-4336
  Toms River *(G-10767)*

Hnt Industries Inc ....G 908 322-0414
  Scotch Plains *(G-9733)*

House of Gold Inc ....E 856 665-0020
  Pennsauken *(G-8433)*

Ht Stamping Co LLC ....G 973 227-4858
  Fairfield *(G-3230)*

▼ Infor Metal & Tooling Mfg ....F 973 571-9520
  Cedar Grove *(G-1279)*

International Rollforms Inc ....E 856 228-7100
  Deptford *(G-2064)*

▲ J G Schmidt Co Inc ....D 732 563-9500
  Green Brook *(G-3863)*

J J Orly Inc ....F 908 276-9212
  Clark *(G-1498)*

J R M Products Inc ....G 732 203-0200
  Union Beach *(G-11103)*

Jmk Tool Die and Mfg Co Inc ....G 201 845-4710
  Rochelle Park *(G-9425)*

Jordan Manufacturing LLC ....G 973 383-8363
  Lafayette *(G-5029)*

Joy-Rei Enterprises Inc ....G 732 727-0742
  Parlin *(G-7867)*

K H Machine Works ....G 201 867-2338
  North Bergen *(G-7412)*

Laeger Metal Spinning Co Inc ....G 908 925-5530
  Linden *(G-5372)*

Leibrock Metal Products Inc ....G 732 695-0326
  Ocean *(G-7669)*

LMC Precision Inc ....F 973 522-0005
  Newark *(G-7183)*

Luso Machine Nj LLC ....F 973 242-1717
  Newark *(G-7188)*

Magic Metal Works Inc ....G 201 384-8457
  Bergenfield *(G-379)*

Main Robert A & Sons Holdg Co ....E 201 447-3700
  Wyckoff *(G-12116)*

Manttra Inc ....G 877 962-6887
  New Brunswick *(G-6944)*

Manutech Inc ....G 856 358-6136
  Elmer *(G-2800)*

Mechanical Components Corp ....G 732 938-3737
  Toms River *(G-10778)*

▲ Medlaurel Inc ....E 856 461-6600
  Delanco *(G-2006)*

▲ Metal Cutting Corporation ....D 973 239-1100
  Cedar Grove *(G-1282)*

▲ Metalis USA Inc ....F 973 625-3500
  Denville *(G-2047)*

▲ Micro Stamping Corporation ....C 732 302-0800
  Somerset *(G-10030)*

Minitec Corporation ....G 973 989-1426
  Dover *(G-2097)*

Mjse LLC ....F 201 791-9888
  Saddle Brook *(G-9663)*

Molnar Tools Inc ....F 908 580-0671
  Warren *(G-11423)*

Monroe Tool & Die Inc ....G 856 629-5164
  Williamstown *(G-11964)*

▲ National Manufacturing Co Inc ....C 973 635-8846
  Chatham *(G-1329)*

SIC

Employee Codes: A=Over 500 employees, B=251-500
C=101-250, D=51-100, E=20-50, F=10-19, G=4-9   2019 Harris New Jersey
Manufacturers Directory   543

▲ Newell Brands Inc ....B...... 201 610-6600
Hoboken *(G-4468)*

Par Metal Products Inc ....F...... 201 955-0800
North Arlington *(G-7376)*

Paramount Products Co Inc ....F...... 732 458-9200
Brick *(G-728)*

Pcr Technologies Inc ....G...... 973 882-0017
Pine Brook *(G-8613)*

Pepco Manufacturing Co ....D...... 856 783-3700
Somerdale *(G-9933)*

Peterson Brothers Mfg Co ....E...... 732 271-8240
Middlesex *(G-6136)*

Peterson Stamping & Mfg Co ....F...... 908 241-0900
Kenilworth *(G-4968)*

Philip Creter Inc ....G...... 908 686-2910
Union *(G-11083)*

Phillips Enterprises Inc ....G...... 732 493-3191
Ocean *(G-7674)*

Quality Swiss Screw Machine Co..........G...... 908 289-4334
Elizabeth *(G-2772)*

R M F Associates Inc ....C...... 908 687-9355
Union *(G-11086)*

▼ Rails Company Inc ....E...... 973 763-4320
Maplewood *(G-5883)*

Rapid Manufacturing Co Inc ....E...... 732 279-1252
Toms River *(G-10787)*

Rebuth Metal Services ....F...... 908 889-6400
Fanwood *(G-3373)*

Roseville Tool & Manufacturing ....E...... 973 992-5405
Livingston *(G-5538)*

S & W Precision Tool Corp ....F...... 908 526-6097
Bridgewater *(G-878)*

▲ S H P C Inc ....E...... 973 589-5242
Newark *(G-7258)*

Safeguard Coinbox Inc ....F...... 973 575-0040
Fairfield *(G-3306)*

Sandik Manufacturing Inc ....G...... 973 779-0707
Passaic *(G-8104)*

Short Run Stamping Company Inc........E...... 908 862-1070
Linden *(G-5423)*

Small Quantities NJ Inc ....D...... 732 248-9009
Edison *(G-2614)*

Sofield Manufacturing Co Inc ....G...... 201 931-1530
Ridgefield Park *(G-9316)*

Sowa Corp ....G...... 973 297-0008
Newark *(G-7279)*

Stampex Corp ....F...... 973 839-4040
Haskell *(G-4202)*

Stamping Com Inc ....G...... 732 493-4697
Ocean *(G-7685)*

Stamplus Manufacturing Inc ....F...... 908 241-8844
Roselle *(G-9573)*

▲ Stirrup Metal Products Corp ....F...... 973 824-7086
Newark *(G-7287)*

Superior Stamping Products LLC ....E...... 201 945-5874
Ridgefield *(G-9290)*

TMU Inc ....F...... 609 884-7656
Cape May *(G-1103)*

Triform Products Inc ....E...... 973 278-2042
Pompton Plains *(G-8873)*

Tryco Tool & Mfg Co Inc ....E...... 973 674-6867
Orange *(G-7764)*

Turul Bookbindery Inc ....G...... 973 361-2810
Wharton *(G-11874)*

Umetal LLC ....G...... 862 257-3032
Paterson *(G-8319)*

Unilite Incorporated ....G...... 973 667-1674
Nutley *(G-7596)*

United Spport Sltons - Lmt Inc ....G...... 973 857-2298
Cedar Grove *(G-1295)*

▲ Universal Tools & Mfg Co ....E...... 973 379-4193
Springfield *(G-10471)*

V H Exacta Corp ....G...... 856 235-7379
Moorestown *(G-6574)*

▲ Weiss-Aug Co Inc ....C...... 973 887-7600
East Hanover *(G-2246)*

Well Bilt Industries Inc ....F...... 908 486-6002
Linden *(G-5441)*

Wgjf Manufacturing Corp ....E...... 908 862-1730
Linden *(G-5442)*

3471 Electroplating, Plating, Polishing, Anodizing & Coloring

A & F Electroplating Inc ....G...... 973 983-2459
West Orange *(G-11757)*

A & L Industries Inc ....E...... 973 589-8070
Newark *(G-7028)*

A&A Company Inc ....E...... 908 561-2378
South Fabricated *(G-10205)*

Accu-Cote Inc ....G...... 856 845-7323
Thorofare *(G-10698)*

Acme Engraving Co Inc ....E...... 973 778-0885
Passaic *(G-8050)*

▲ Advanced Metal Processing ....G...... 856 327-0048
Millville *(G-6223)*

Aerotech Proc Solutions LLC ....G...... 973 782-4485
Paterson *(G-8126)*

Alcaro & Alcaro Plating Co ....E...... 973 746-1200
Montclair *(G-6357)*

All Metal Polishing Co Inc ....E...... 973 589-8070
Newark *(G-7038)*

Andarn Electro Service Inc ....E...... 973 523-2220
Paterson *(G-8139)*

Anodizing Corporation ....E...... 973 694-6449
Wayne *(G-11470)*

Art Metalcraft Plating Co Inc ....F...... 215 923-6625
Camden *(G-1040)*

Art Mold & Polishing Co Inc ....E...... 908 518-9191
Roselle *(G-9548)*

▲ B & M Finishers Inc ....E...... 908 241-5640
Kenilworth *(G-4925)*

Boyko Metal Finishing Co Inc ....G...... 973 623-4254
Newark *(G-7072)*

Boyko Metal Finishing Co Inc ....D...... 973 623-4254
Newark *(G-7071)*

Cameo Metal Products Inc ....F...... 732 388-4000
Rahway *(G-9084)*

Carlton Coke Met Fnishings LLC ....G...... 732 774-2210
Asbury Park *(G-72)*

Cemp Inc ....F...... 732 933-1000
Shrewsbury *(G-9884)*

Cramer Plating Inc ....E...... 908 453-2887
Buttzville *(G-1016)*

DAngelo Metal Products Inc ....F...... 908 862-8220
Linden *(G-5341)*

Deptford Plating Co Inc ....G...... 856 227-1144
Deptford *(G-2063)*

▲ Durex Inc ....D...... 908 688-0800
Union *(G-11045)*

Dynasty Metals Inc ....E...... 973 453-6630
Rockaway *(G-9454)*

E C Electroplating Inc ....E...... 973 340-0227
Garfield *(G-3740)*

Elkem Inc ....G...... 732 566-1700
Cliffwood *(G-1546)*

FER Plating Inc ....E...... 201 438-1010
Lyndhurst *(G-5655)*

▲ Foremost Manufacturing Co Inc ....D...... 908 687-4646
Union *(G-11056)*

G & H Metal Finishers Inc ....G...... 201 909-9808
Paterson *(G-8196)*

General Magnaplate Corporation ....D...... 908 862-6200
Linden *(G-5351)*

Glasseal Products Inc ....C...... 732 370-9100
Lakewood *(G-5104)*

▲ Hard Crome Solutions ....G...... 732 500-2568
Metuchen *(G-6060)*

Hill Cross Co Inc ....G...... 201 864-3393
West New York *(G-11740)*

Ideal Plating & Polishing Co ....F...... 973 759-5559
Paterson *(G-8212)*

Independence Plating Corp ....E...... 973 523-1776
Paterson *(G-8213)*

Industrial Hard Chromium Co ....F...... 973 344-2265
Passaic *(G-7156)*

Intrepid Industries Inc ....G...... 908 534-5300
Lebanon *(G-5265)*

J R S Tool & Metal Finishing ....G...... 908 753-2050
South Plainfield *(G-10282)*

Kenilworth Anodizing Co ....E...... 908 241-5640
Kenilworth *(G-4952)*

Madan Plastics Inc ....D...... 908 276-8484
Cranford *(G-1915)*

Manco Plating Incorporated ....G...... 973 485-6800
Newark *(G-7195)*

Mara Polishing & Plating Corp ....G...... 973 242-0800
Newark *(G-7196)*

Master Metal Polishing Corp ....E...... 973 684-0119
Paterson *(G-8252)*

Mastercraft Metal Finishing ....G...... 908 354-4404
Elizabeth *(G-2757)*

Mercer Coating & Lining Co Inc ....E...... 908 925-5000
Linden *(G-5381)*

Metal Finishing Co LLC ....G...... 973 778-9550
Passaic *(G-8089)*

Miller & Son ....E...... 732 759-6445
Belleville *(G-301)*

Mold Polishing Company Inc ....G...... 908 518-9191
Garwood *(G-3785)*

▲ National Mtal Fnshngs Corp Inc ......F...... 732 752-7770
Middlesex *(G-6133)*

New Brunswick Plating Inc ....D...... 732 545-6522
New Brunswick *(G-6953)*

Paramount Metal Finishing Co ....C...... 908 862-0772
Linden *(G-5403)*

▲ Paramount Plating Co Inc ....E...... 908 862-0772
Linden *(G-5404)*

Patel Metal Plating Inc ....E...... 732 574-1770
Edison *(G-2588)*

Platinum Plating Specialists ....G...... 732 221-2575
Clark *(G-1513)*

Polaris Plating Inc ....G...... 973 278-0033
Parsippany *(G-7998)*

Prem-Khichi Enterprises Inc ....E...... 973 242-0300
East Brunswick *(G-2167)*

Productive Industrial Finshg ....G...... 856 427-9646
Voorhees *(G-11292)*

Programatic Platers Inc ....F...... 718 721-4330
Tenafly *(G-10665)*

Sar Industrial Finishing Inc ....F...... 609 567-2772
Berlin *(G-429)*

Stainless Stock ....E...... 732 564-1164
Middlesex *(G-6153)*

▲ Stirrup Metal Products Corp ....F...... 973 824-7086
Newark *(G-7287)*

Suffern Plating Corp ....E...... 973 473-4404
Lodi *(G-5578)*

Sun Metal Finishing Inc ....E...... 973 684-0119
North Haledon *(G-7500)*

Super Chrome Inc ....G...... 732 774-2210
Asbury Park *(G-83)*

Tomken Plating ....E...... 856 829-0607
Cinnaminson *(G-1491)*

Trb Electro Corp ....E...... 973 278-9014
Paterson *(G-8316)*

Vanguard Research Industries ....E...... 908 753-2770
South Plainfield *(G-10340)*

Vigilant Design ....G...... 201 432-3900
Jersey City *(G-4826)*

Vortex Supply LLC ....G...... 856 352-6681
Blackwood *(G-483)*

▼ Water Master Co ....G...... 732 247-1900
Highland Park *(G-4289)*

▲ Zsombor Antal Designs Inc ....F...... 201 225-1750
River Edge *(G-9364)*

3479 Coating & Engraving, NEC

A S A P Nameplate & Labeling ....F...... 973 773-3934
Passaic *(G-8048)*

A Smith & Son Inc ....G...... 609 747-0800
Burlington *(G-945)*

▲ Abco Die Casters Inc ....D...... 973 624-7030
Newark *(G-7033)*

Acme Engraving Co Inc ....E...... 973 778-0885
Passaic *(G-8050)*

All American Powdercoating LLC ....G...... 732 349-7001
Toms River *(G-10741)*

▲ Alpha Processing Co Inc ....E...... 973 777-1737
Clifton *(G-1562)*

American Galvanizing Co Inc ....D...... 609 567-2090
Hammonton *(G-4126)*

◆ Andek Corporation ....F...... 856 866-7600
Moorestown *(G-6505)*

Armadillo Metalworks Inc ....E...... 973 777-2105
Passaic *(G-8051)*

Atlantic Eqp Engineers Inc ....F...... 201 828-9400
Upper Saddle River *(G-11134)*

▲ Awards Trophy Company ....G...... 908 687-5775
Hillside *(G-4378)*

Bannister Company Inc ....F...... 732 828-1353
Milltown *(G-6214)*

◆ Bel-Art Products Inc ....E...... 973 694-0500
Wayne *(G-11477)*

Boyko Metal Finishing Co Inc ....D...... 973 623-4254
Newark *(G-7071)*

▲ Brodie System Inc ....F...... 908 862-8620
Linden *(G-5328)*

Ceronics Inc ....G...... 732 566-5600
Matawan *(G-5970)*

Chapter Enterprises Inc ....G...... 732 560-8500
Bridgewater *(G-811)*

Cincinnati Thermal Spray Inc ....E...... 973 379-0003
Springfield *(G-10435)*

Diamond Hut Jewelry Exchange ....G...... 201 332-5372
Jersey City *(G-4728)*

Dynamic Coatings LLC ....G...... 732 998-6625
Matawan *(G-5974)*

Ferro Corporation ....G...... 908 226-2148
South Plainfield *(G-10258)*

Flexcraft Industries Inc...................G...... 973 589-3403
  Newark (G-7125)
Foster Engraving Corporation..............G...... 201 489-5979
  Hackensack (G-3918)
Gary R Banks Industrial Group ....F...... 856 687-2227
  West Berlin (G-11597)
General Magnaplate Corporation ....D...... 908 862-6200
  Linden (G-5351)
General Magnaplate Wisconsin............F...... 800 441-6173
  Linden (G-5352)
Golf Coast Polymer Services ....G...... 856 498-3434
  Elmer (G-2798)
Heros Salute Awards Co ....G...... 973 696-5085
  Wayne (G-11517)
Hot Dip Galvanizing ....G...... 732 442-7555
  Perth Amboy (G-8522)
▲ I V Miller & Sons............................F...... 732 493-4040
  Ocean (G-7666)
▲ Innovative Powder Coatings LLC ....G...... 856 661-0086
  Pennsauken (G-8436)
Isometric Micro Finish Coating ....G...... 732 306-6339
  Edison (G-2535)
Jema-American Inc ....G...... 732 968-5333
  Middlesex (G-6123)
Koehler Industries Inc ....G...... 732 364-2700
  Howell (G-4544)
Lantier Construction Company ....E...... 856 780-6366
  Moorestown (G-6536)
Lordon Inc ....G...... 908 813-1143
  Hackettstown (G-4019)
Microsurfaces Inc ....G...... 201 408-5596
  Englewood (G-2925)
New Jrsy Glvnzng & Tnnng Wks ....D...... 973 242-3200
  Newark (G-7210)
Newark Industrial Spraying.................F...... 973 344-6855
  Newark (G-7213)
Nicholas Galvanizing Co Inc ....E...... 201 795-1010
  Jersey City (G-4770)
Paramount Metal Finishing Co ....C...... 908 862-0772
  Linden (G-5403)
Peerless Coatings LLC ....E...... 973 427-8771
  Hawthorne (G-4237)
Penn Metal Finishing Co Inc ....G...... 609 387-3400
  Burlington (G-981)
Phoenix Powder Coating LLC................G...... 973 907-7500
  Haskell (G-4200)
▲ Plastics Consulting & Mfg Co ....E...... 800 222-0317
  Camden (G-1083)
Powtek Powder Coating Inc ....G...... 609 394-1144
  Ewing (G-3053)
Productive Industrial Finshg ....G...... 856 427-9646
  Voorhees (G-11292)
S D L Powder Coating Inc ....G...... 732 473-0800
  Toms River (G-10788)
Shore Bet Painting and Cnstr ....G...... 732 996-3455
  Bay Head (G-200)
▲ Superior Powder Coating Inc..............C...... 908 351-8707
  Elizabeth (G-2780)
Technical Nameplate Corp ....E...... 973 773-4256
  Passaic (G-8111)
Tresky Corp ....G...... 732 536-8600
  Morganville (G-6596)
United Label Corp ....G...... 973 589-6500
  Newark (G-7309)
Voigt & Schweitzer LLC ....D...... 732 442-7555
  Perth Amboy (G-8539)
W & E Baum Bronze Tablet Corp ....E...... 732 866-1881
  Freehold (G-3704)
Weiler & Sons LLC...............................G...... 856 767-8842
  Berlin (G-433)
▲ Winters Stamp Mfg Co Inc ....F...... 908 352-3725
  Martinsville (G-5965)

3482 Small Arms Ammunition

▲ Lightfield Ammunition Corp...............G...... 732 462-9200
  Freehold (G-3676)

3483 Ammunition, Large

▲ Lightfield Ammunition Corp...............G...... 732 462-9200
  Freehold (G-3676)

3484 Small Arms

2a Holdings Inc ....F...... 973 378-8011
  Maplewood (G-5873)
▲ Henry RAC Holding Corp ....D...... 201 858-4400
  Bayonne (G-222)
Way It Was Sporting Svc Inc ....G...... 856 231-0111
  Moorestown (G-6576)

3489 Ordnance & Access, NEC

American Aluminum Company.............D...... 908 233-3500
  Mountainside (G-6834)
Cartridge Actuated Devices ....E...... 973 347-2281
  Byram Township (G-1017)
Eastern Regional Waterway ....F...... 732 684-0409
  Brick (G-717)
Kongsberg Protech ....G...... 973 770-0574
  Mount Arlington (G-6714)

3491 Industrial Valves

Admiral Technology LLC.....................E...... 973 698-5920
  Rockaway (G-9437)
American Products Company Inc ....D...... 908 687-4100
  Union (G-11025)
▲ Armadillo Automation Inc.................E...... 856 829-2888
  Cinnaminson (G-1442)
◆ Asco LP ....B...... 800 972-2726
  Florham Park (G-3481)
▲ Asco Investment Corp ....G...... 973 966-2000
  Florham Park (G-3482)
▲ Automatic Switch Company ....A...... 973 966-2000
  Florham Park (G-3485)
Automatic Switch Company ....A...... 209 941-4111
  Florham Park (G-3486)
Automatic Switch Company ....F...... 732 596-1731
  Woodbridge (G-12014)
Barworth Inc ....G...... 973 376-4883
  Springfield (G-10430)
▲ Bio-Chem Fluidics Inc ....D...... 973 263-3001
  Boonton (G-544)
▲ Carpathian Industries LLC ....F...... 201 386-5356
  Hoboken (G-4446)
▲ Cavagna North America Inc ....E...... 732 469-2100
  Somerset (G-9973)
Chase Machine Co ....F...... 201 438-2214
  Lyndhurst (G-5648)
Chemiquip Products Co Inc ....G...... 201 868-4445
  Linden (G-5333)
Emerson Automation Solutions ....F...... 856 542-5252
  Bridgeport (G-736)
▲ Farrell Eqp & Cntrls Inc ....F...... 732 770-4142
  Roselle (G-9557)
Firefighter One Ltd Lblty Co ....G...... 973 940-3061
  Sparta (G-10387)
Fisher Service Co................................G...... 609 386-5000
  Burlington (G-968)
Flodyne Controls Inc ....E...... 908 464-6200
  New Providence (G-6999)
▲ Gadren Machine Co Inc ....G...... 856 456-4329
  Collingswood (G-1767)
Gasflo Products Inc ....E...... 973 276-9011
  Fairfield (G-3213)
Gemco Valve Co LLC...........................E...... 732 752-7900
  Middlesex (G-6118)
◆ Hayward Industrial Products.............C...... 908 351-5400
  Elizabeth (G-2745)
▲ Heat-Timer Corporation ....E...... 973 575-4004
  Fairfield (G-3224)
▲ Industrial Habonim Valves & AC..........F...... 201 820-3184
  Wayne (G-11519)
Instrment Vlve Svcs Burlington ....G...... 609 386-5000
  Burlington (G-973)
Magnatrol Valve Corporation ....F...... 856 829-4580
  Roebling (G-9526)
Micromat Co ....G...... 201 529-3738
  Ringwood (G-9349)
Neptune Research & Development ....E...... 973 808-8811
  West Caldwell (G-11667)
Picut Industries Inc............................D...... 908 754-1333
  Warren (G-11425)
▲ Plast-O-Matic Valves Inc..................D...... 973 256-3000
  Cedar Grove (G-1287)
Purity Labs ....E...... 201 372-0236
  East Rutherford (G-2313)
◆ Simple Home Automation Inc............C...... 877 405-2397
  Edison (G-2610)
Triflow Corporation ....G...... 856 768-7159
  West Berlin (G-11631)
◆ Tyco International MGT Co LLC ....E...... 609 720-4200
  Princeton (G-9038)
Wm Steinen Mfg Co ....D...... 973 887-6400
  Parsippany (G-8042)

3492 Fluid Power Valves & Hose Fittings

A V Hydraulics Ltd Lblty Co ....G...... 973 621-6800
  Newark (G-7030)
Air & Hydraulic Power Inc ....G...... 201 447-1589
  Wyckoff (G-12101)

▲ American Hose Hydraulic Co Inc......E...... 973 684-3225
  Paterson (G-8136)
▲ Automatic Switch Company ....A...... 973 966-2000
  Florham Park (G-3485)
▲ Gadren Machine Co Inc ....E...... 856 456-4329
  Collingswood (G-1767)
◆ Hayward Industrial Products.............C...... 908 351-5400
  Elizabeth (G-2745)
Industrial Hydraulics & Rubber ....E...... 856 966-2600
  Camden (G-1070)
Novaflex Industries Inc........................F...... 856 768-2275
  West Berlin (G-11612)
Robert H Hoover & Sons Inc ....G...... 973 347-4210
  Flanders (G-3417)
▲ Universal Valve Company Inc ....F...... 908 351-0606
  Elizabeth (G-2784)
▲ Valcor Engineering Corporation ....C...... 973 467-8400
  Springfield (G-10472)
◆ Versa Products Company Inc ....C...... 201 291-0379
  Paramus (G-7843)
▲ Westlock Controls Corporation ....C...... 201 794-7650
  Saddle Brook (G-9687)

3493 Steel Springs, Except Wire

Matthew Warren Inc ....F...... 908 788-5800
  Ringoes (G-9339)
◆ Sealy Mattress Co N J Inc.................C...... 973 345-8800
  Paterson (G-8297)
Spring Eureka Co Inc...........................E...... 973 589-4960
  Newark (G-7283)

3494 Valves & Pipe Fittings, NEC

▲ Ammark Corporation ....G...... 973 616-2555
  Pompton Plains (G-8857)
▲ Ceodeux Incorporated......................E...... 724 696-4340
  Hackettstown (G-4001)
▲ CP Test & Valve Products Inc ....E...... 201 998-1500
  Kearny (G-4851)
DAngelo Metal Products Inc ....F...... 908 862-8220
  Linden (G-5341)
Dason Stainless Products Co ....F...... 732 382-7272
  Rahway (G-9087)
◆ Durst Corporation Inc ....G...... 800 852-3906
  Cranford (G-1907)
▲ Everflow Supplies Inc......................E...... 908 436-1100
  Carteret (G-1252)
▼ Everlasting Valve Company Inc ....E...... 908 769-0700
  South Plainfield (G-10254)
▲ Exclusive Materials LLC...................G...... 732 886-9956
  Lakewood (G-5095)
Fluidyne Corp.....................................E...... 856 663-1818
  Pennsauken (G-8420)
▲ Gadren Machine Co Inc ....F...... 856 456-4329
  Collingswood (G-1767)
Gasflo Products Inc ....E...... 973 276-9011
  Fairfield (G-3213)
Gorton Heating Corp ....G...... 908 276-1323
  Cranford (G-1912)
◆ Hayward Industrial Products.............C...... 908 351-5400
  Elizabeth (G-2745)
◆ Hayward Industries Inc ....B...... 908 351-5400
  Elizabeth (G-2746)
Imperial Weld Ring Corp Inc ....E...... 908 354-0011
  Elizabeth (G-2749)
Knickerbocker Machine Shop Inc ....D...... 973 256-1616
  Totowa (G-10834)
Kraissl Company Inc ....E...... 201 342-0008
  Hackensack (G-3937)
Lindstrom & King Co Inc......................G...... 973 279-2511
  Paterson (G-8241)
▲ Marotta Controls Inc ....C...... 973 334-7800
  Montville (G-6444)
Newco Valves LLC ....E...... 732 257-0300
  East Brunswick (G-2159)
Nippon Benkan Kagyo ....E...... 732 435-0777
  New Brunswick (G-6954)
Pennsylvania Machine Works Inc ....E...... 856 467-0500
  Swedesboro (G-10600)
▲ Piping Supplies Inc..........................G...... 609 561-9323
  Williamstown (G-11968)
Primak Plumbing & Heating Inc............G...... 732 270-6282
  Toms River (G-10785)
Ramco Manufacturing Co Inc ....E...... 908 245-4500
  Kenilworth (G-4973)
RGI Inc ....F...... 973 697-2624
  Newfoundland (G-7332)
Scientific Machine and Sup Co ....E...... 732 356-1553
  Middlesex (G-6145)
Sims Pump Valve Company Inc ....E...... 201 792-0600
  Hoboken (G-4480)

Employee Codes: A=Over 500 employees, B=251-500
C=101-250, D=51-100, E=20-50, F=10-19, G=4-9   2019 Harris New Jersey
Manufacturers Directory   545

Symcon Inc ....G 973 728-8661
West Milford (G-11732)

Syntiro Dynamics LLC ....G 732 377-3307
Wall Township (G-11374)

Taylor Forge Stainless Inc ....D 908 722-1313
Branchburg (G-687)

Tkl Specialty Piping Inc ....G 908 454-0030
Phillipsburg (G-8578)

◆ Vac-U-Max ....E 973 759-4600
Belleville (G-319)

▲ Wire Cloth Manufacturers Inc ......E 973 328-1000
Mine Hill (G-6275)

Wm Steinen Mfg Co ....D 973 887-6400
Parsippany (G-8042)

▲ World Wide Metric Inc ....F 732 247-2300
Branchburg (G-696)

3495 Wire Springs

Matthew Warren Inc ....F 908 788-5800
Ringoes (G-9339)

Spring Eureka Co Inc ....E 973 589-4960
Newark (G-7283)

Window 25 LLC ....G 973 817-9464
Newark (G-7316)

3496 Misc Fabricated Wire Prdts

Accent Fence Inc ....E 609 965-6400
Egg Harbor City (G-2651)

Ace Electronics Inc ....D 732 603-9800
Metuchen (G-6045)

Acme Wire Forming LLC ....F 201 218-2912
Kinnelon (G-5014)

◆ Allentown Inc ....B 609 259-7951
Allentown (G-24)

Alpine Group Inc ....B 201 549-4400
East Rutherford (G-2269)

▼ Aw Machinery LLC ....F 973 882-3223
Fairfield (G-3149)

▲ Bamboo & Rattan Works Inc ....G 732 255-4239
Toms River (G-10746)

Belden Inc ....F 908 925-8000
Elizabeth (G-2714)

▲ Belleville Wire Cloth Co Inc ....E 973 239-0074
Cedar Grove (G-1269)

Belmont Whl Fence Mfg Inc ....E 973 472-5121
Garfield (G-3732)

▲ Better Sleep Inc ....F 908 464-2200
Branchburg (G-625)

Blue Claw Mfg & Supply Company ...G 856 696-4366
Richland (G-9249)

Boyle Tool & Die Co Inc ....F 856 853-1819
West Deptford (G-11694)

▲ Brown and Perkins Inc ....F 609 655-1150
Cranbury (G-1816)

▲ Carl Stahl Sava Industries Inc ....D 973 835-0882
Riverdale (G-9373)

Cerbaco Ltd ....E 908 996-1333
Frenchtown (G-3711)

◆ Clements Industries Inc ....E 201 440-5500
South Hackensack (G-10153)

Compass Wire Cloth & ....E 856 853-7616
Vineland (G-11202)

▲ Compass Wire Cloth Corp ....E 856 853-7616
Vineland (G-11203)

▲ Dearborn A Belden Cdt Company ...D 908 925-8000
Elizabeth (G-2726)

Deborah Sales & Mfg Co ....G 973 344-8466
Newark (G-7100)

◆ Delair LLC ....D 856 663-2900
Pennsauken (G-8412)

Doran Sling and Assembly Corp ....G 908 355-1101
Hillside (G-4390)

▲ Ecocom Inc ....G 201 393-0786
Montvale (G-6409)

Edwin R Burger & Son Inc ....E 856 468-2300
Sewell (G-9841)

Evergard Steel Corp ....F 908 925-6800
South Plainfield (G-10253)

▲ Fisk Alloy Conductors Inc ....C 973 825-8500
Hawthorne (G-4218)

Fisk Alloy Inc ....E 973 427-7550
Hawthorne (G-4219)

◆ Fisk Alloy Wire Incorporated ....C 973 949-4491
Hawthorne (G-4220)

Form Cut Industries Inc ....E 973 483-5154
Newark (G-7127)

Gabhen Inc ....G 973 256-0666
Totowa (G-10827)

▲ General Metal Manufacturing Co ...E 973 386-1818
East Hanover (G-2211)

General Wire & Stamping Co ....F 973 366-8080
Randolph (G-9179)

◆ Gentek Inc ....C 973 515-0900
Parsippany (G-7956)

▲ High Energy Group Ltd Lblty Co .....G 732 741-9099
Eatontown (G-2397)

▲ Jcc Military Supply LLC ....G 973 341-1314
Paterson (G-8221)

▲ Jersey Strand & Cable Inc ....D 908 213-9350
Phillipsburg (G-8557)

Main Robert A & Sons Holdg Co ....E 201 447-3700
Wyckoff (G-12116)

▲ Metal Textiles Corporation ....D 732 287-0800
Edison (G-2563)

Mpm Display Inc ....G 973 374-3477
Hillside (G-4416)

New Jersey Wire Cloth Co Inc ....G 973 340-0101
Clifton (G-1675)

▲ Newark Wire Cloth Company ....E 973 778-4478
Clifton (G-1677)

Newark Wire Works Inc ....E 732 661-2001
Edison (G-2573)

Parker-Hannifin Corporation ....D 908 458-8101
Cranford (G-1921)

Phillips Enterprises Inc ....G 732 493-3191
Ocean (G-7674)

Precision Ball Specialties ....F 856 881-5646
Williamstown (G-11971)

Robert J Donaldson Inc ....F 856 629-2737
Williamstown (G-11976)

Robert Main Sons Inc ....E 201 447-3700
Fair Lawn (G-3118)

Security Fabricators Inc ....F 908 272-9171
Kenilworth (G-4977)

Seminole Wire & Cable Co Inc ....E 856 324-2929
Pennsauken (G-8483)

▲ Skorr Products LLC ....F 973 523-2606
Paterson (G-8299)

▲ Unique Wire Weaving Co Inc ....E 908 688-4600
Hillside (G-4433)

▲ Vibration Muntings Contrls Inc ....D 800 569-8423
Bloomingdale (G-531)

▲ Vis USA LLC ....F 908 575-0606
Branchburg (G-693)

▼ William Kenyon & Sons Inc ....E 732 985-8980
Piscataway (G-8738)

▲ Wire Cloth Manufacturers Inc ....E 973 328-1000
Mine Hill (G-6275)

Wire Displays Inc ....F 973 537-0090
Dover (G-2110)

Wire Fabricators & Insulators ....E 973 768-2839
Livingston (G-5549)

Wytech Industries Inc ....D 732 396-3900
Rahway (G-9132)

3497 Metal Foil & Leaf

Amcor Flexibles Inc ....E 609 267-5900
Mount Holly (G-6723)

API Americas Inc ....D 732 382-6800
Rahway (G-9077)

Constantia Blythewood LLC ....D 732 974-4100
Belmar (G-347)

▲ Crown Roll Leaf Inc ....C 973 742-4000
Paterson (G-8164)

◆ Glitterex Corp ....D 908 272-9121
Cranford (G-1911)

▲ Hueck Foils Holding Co ....G 732 974-4100
Wall Township (G-11347)

▲ Materials Technology Inc ....G 732 246-1000
Somerset (G-10024)

◆ Revere Industries LLC ....C 856 881-3600
Clayton (G-1528)

Spectrum Foils Inc ....G 973 481-0808
Newark (G-7281)

3498 Fabricated Pipe & Pipe Fittings

A&M Industrial Inc ....F 908 862-1800
Avenel (G-117)

Belden Inc ....F 908 925-8000
Elizabeth (G-2714)

Bemis Company Inc ....B 908 689-3000
Washington (G-11441)

▲ Century Tube Corp ....E 908 534-2001
Somerville (G-10105)

Coolenheat Inc ....E 908 925-4473
Kendall Park (G-4918)

▲ Custom Alloy Corporation ....C 908 638-0257
High Bridge (G-4281)

▲ Esco Industries Corp ....F 973 478-5888
Woodcliff Lake (G-12056)

Euro Mechanical Inc ....F 201 313-8050
Fairview (G-3360)

▲ Fluorotherm Polymers Inc ....G 973 575-0760
Parsippany (G-7948)

◆ Foodline Piping Products Co ....G 856 767-1177
West Berlin (G-11594)

Fox Steel Products LLC ....G 856 778-4661
Mount Laurel (G-6762)

▲ G & J Steel & Tubing Inc ....D 908 526-4445
Hillsborough (G-4318)

Handytube Corporation ....G 732 469-7420
Middlesex (G-6120)

Imperial Weld Ring Corp Inc ....E 908 354-0011
Elizabeth (G-2749)

Jettron Products Inc ....G 973 887-0571
East Hanover (G-2220)

M P Tube Works Inc ....G 908 317-2500
Mountainside (G-6848)

Piping Solutions Inc ....G 732 537-1009
Bridgewater (G-867)

Precision Mfg Group LLC ....D 973 785-4630
Cedar Grove (G-1288)

Royal Seamless Corporation ....F 732 901-9595
Lakewood (G-5160)

S&W Fabricators Inc ....G 856 881-7418
Glassboro (G-3818)

Samstubend Inc ....F 973 278-2555
Paterson (G-8293)

Selling Precision Inc ....E 973 728-1214
West Milford (G-11731)

Symcon Inc ....G 973 728-8661
West Milford (G-11732)

Tube Craft of America Inc ....G 856 629-5626
Williamstown (G-11982)

▲ U V International LLC ....G 973 993-9454
Morristown (G-6705)

3499 Fabricated Metal Prdts, NEC

A Kessler Kreation Inc ....G 732 431-2468
Colts Neck (G-1776)

Advanced Precision Systems LLC ....G 908 730-8892
High Bridge (G-4280)

All State Medal Co Inc ....G 973 458-1458
Lodi (G-5552)

Apogee Technologies LLC ....F 973 575-8448
Towaco (G-10864)

▲ Awards Trophy Company ....G 908 687-5775
Hillside (G-4378)

Cargille-Sacher Labs Inc ....F 973 267-8888
Cedar Knolls (G-1300)

Cold Headed Fasteners Inc ....G 856 461-3244
Delanco (G-2004)

◆ Crestron Electronics Inc ....C 201 767-3400
Rockleigh (G-9516)

▲ D K Trading Inc ....G 856 225-1130
Camden (G-1057)

Escadaus Inc ....G 973 335-8888
Boonton (G-552)

Fan of Word ....G 201 341-5474
South Orange (G-10195)

▲ Faps Inc ....C 973 589-5656
Newark (G-7122)

Garden State Highway Pdts Inc ....E 856 692-7572
Millville (G-6250)

Gbw Manufacturing Inc ....G 973 279-0077
Totowa (G-10828)

Go R Design LLC ....E 609 286-2146
New Egypt (G-6983)

◆ Hamon Corporation ....D 908 333-2000
Somerville (G-10114)

Hickok Matthews Co Inc ....G 973 335-3400
Montville (G-6443)

Hookway Enterprises Inc ....F 973 691-0382
Netcong (G-6907)

Hurricane Hutch ....G 908 256-5912
Chester (G-1434)

▲ Icup Inc ....E 856 751-2045
Cherry Hill (G-1373)

▲ Ill Eagle Enterprises Ltd ....F 973 237-1111
Ringwood (G-9346)

Intermark Inc ....G 908 474-1311
Linden (G-5362)

Ironbound Metal ....G 973 242-5704
Newark (G-7161)

▲ Julius E Holland-Moritz Co Inc ....G 609 397-1231
Lambertville (G-5191)

▲ Kraftware Corporation ....E 732 345-7091
Roselle (G-9562)

Lacka Safe Corp ....F 201 896-9200
Carlstadt (G-1180)

Lighthouse Express Inc ....G 732 776-9555
Asbury Park *(G-79)*

NJ Logo Wear LLC ....G 609 597-9400
Manahawkin *(G-5794)*

▲ Norco Inc ....E 908 789-1550
Garwood *(G-3787)*

▲ Permadur Industries Inc ....D 908 359-9767
Hillsborough *(G-4344)*

Pipe Dreams Marine LLC ....G 609 628-9353
Tuckahoe *(G-11013)*

R A O Contract Sales NY Inc ....G 201 652-1500
Paterson *(G-8285)*

Raceweld Co Inc ....G 908 236-6533
Lebanon *(G-5274)*

Research and Pvd Materials ....G 973 575-4245
Fairfield *(G-3301)*

RISE Corporation ....E 973 575-7480
West Caldwell *(G-11679)*

Safe Man LLC ....G 800 320-2589
Alpha *(G-41)*

▲ Tassel Toppers LLC ....G 855 827-7357
Midland Park *(G-6187)*

Thyssenkrupp Materials NA Inc ......F 212 972-8800
Maywood *(G-6017)*

Tricomp Inc ....C 973 835-1110
Pompton Plains *(G-8872)*

Uac Packaging LLC ....G 908 595-6890
Hillsborough *(G-4361)*

▼ United Hospital Supply Corp ....C 609 387-7580
Burlington *(G-990)*

▲ Versabar Corporation ....F 973 279-8400
Totowa *(G-10857)*

Whimsy Diddles LLC ....G 609 560-1323
Chesilhurst *(G-1428)*

Williams Scotsman Inc ....G 856 429-0315
Kearny *(G-4906)*

Wm H Brewster Jr Incorporated .....G 973 227-1050
Fairfield *(G-3354)*

Zodiac Paintball Inc ....G 973 616-7230
Pompton Plains *(G-8876)*

35 INDUSTRIAL AND COMMERCIAL MACHINERY AND COMPUTER EQUIPMENT

3511 Steam, Gas & Hydraulic Turbines & Engines

Babcock & Wilcox Company ....G 609 261-2424
Cinnaminson *(G-1443)*

Babcock & Wilcox Powr Generatn ....F 973 227-7008
Fairfield *(G-3150)*

▲ Boc Group Inc ....A 908 665-2400
New Providence *(G-6995)*

▲ Hydro-Mechanical Systems Inc ....F 856 848-8888
Westville *(G-11816)*

I4 Sustainability LLC ....G 732 618-3310
Springfield *(G-10445)*

Linde North America Inc ....D 908 464-8100
New Providence *(G-7007)*

Lummus Overseas Corporation ....E 973 893-3000
Bloomfield *(G-508)*

Messer LLC ....E 973 579-2065
Sparta *(G-10398)*

◆ Messer North America Inc ....B 908 464-8100
Bridgewater *(G-851)*

Micheller & Son Hydraulics Inc ......F 908 687-1545
Roselle *(G-9566)*

Ocean Energy Industries Inc ....F 954 828-2177
Oakhurst *(G-7611)*

Polaris America Ltd Lblty Co ....E 614 540-1710
Lakewood *(G-5148)*

Solar Turbines Incorporated ....F 201 825-8200
Parsippany *(G-8017)*

3519 Internal Combustion Engines, NEC

Arrow Machine Company Inc ....G 973 642-2430
Newark *(G-7054)*

Barbs Harley-Davidson ....E 856 456-4141
Mount Ephraim *(G-6720)*

Cast Technology Inc ....G 908 753-5155
South Plainfield *(G-10235)*

Coates International Ltd ....G 732 449-7717
Wall Township *(G-11329)*

Cummins - Allison Corp ....G 201 791-2394
Elmwood Park *(G-2819)*

Cummins Inc ....D 973 491-0100
Kearny *(G-4853)*

Davis Hyundai ....F 609 883-3500
Ewing *(G-3026)*

Grobet File Company Amer LLC ....D 201 939-6700
Carlstadt *(G-1161)*

Henry Jackson Racing Engines ....G 609 758-7476
Cream Ridge *(G-1936)*

Melton Sales & Service ....E 609 699-4800
Bordentown *(G-587)*

Melton Sales & Service ....E 609 699-4800
Columbus *(G-1802)*

◆ Ocean Power & Equipment Co .....G 973 575-5775
West Caldwell *(G-11668)*

Penn Power Group LLC ....F 732 441-1489
Matawan *(G-5984)*

Penske Truck Leasing Co LP ....E 973 575-0169
Parsippany *(G-7987)*

Roy Anania ....G 201 498-1555
Hackensack *(G-3967)*

3523 Farm Machinery & Eqpt

3 IS Technologies Inc ....G 609 238-8213
Hainesport *(G-4067)*

◆ AFA Polytek North America Inc ....F 862 260-9450
Cedar Knolls *(G-1297)*

Edward Brown ....G 973 887-5255
East Hanover *(G-2207)*

Kinnery Precision LLC ....G 973 473-4664
Passaic *(G-8080)*

▼ Plant Food Company Inc ....E 609 448-0935
Cranbury *(G-1872)*

South Jersey Farmers Exchange ......G 856 769-0062
Woodstown *(G-12096)*

Steve Green Enterprises ....G 732 938-5572
Farmingdale *(G-3393)*

3524 Garden, Lawn Tractors & Eqpt

Creative Products Inc ....D 732 614-9035
Long Branch *(G-5596)*

D & S Companies LLC ....G 973 832-4959
Wayne *(G-11492)*

Lawn Medic Inc ....G 856 742-1111
Westville *(G-11818)*

McQuade Enterprises LLC ....G 609 501-2437
Millville *(G-6260)*

Robert Colaneri ....G 201 939-4405
East Rutherford *(G-2314)*

W W Manufacturing Co Inc ....F 856 451-5700
Bridgeton *(G-777)*

3531 Construction Machinery & Eqpt

▲ Breeze-Eastern LLC ....G 973 602-1001
Whippany *(G-11883)*

Breeze-Eastern LLC ....D 973 602-1001
Whippany *(G-11884)*

Clark Equipment Company ....A 973 618-2500
Pine Brook *(G-8593)*

Cornell Crane Mfg Ltd ....F 609 742-1900
Westville *(G-11811)*

Corrview International LLC ....G 973 770-0571
Hopatcong *(G-4519)*

County of Warren ....D 908 475-7975
Belvidere *(G-359)*

Dougherty Foundation Products ....G 201 337-5748
Franklin Lakes *(G-3621)*

Dragon Asphalt Equipment LLC ......F 732 922-9290
Lakewood *(G-5085)*

Elite Landscaping & Pavers ....G 732 252-6152
Freehold *(G-3663)*

F and M Equipment Ltd ....D 215 822-0145
South Plainfield *(G-10256)*

Fred McDowell Inc ....G 732 681-5000
Wall Township *(G-11342)*

G & A Pavers Llc ....G 201 562-5947
Englewood *(G-2908)*

Georgia-Pacific LLC ....D 856 966-7600
Camden *(G-1066)*

Hackettstown Public Works ....G 908 852-2320
Hackettstown *(G-4010)*

Hart Construction Service ....G 908 537-2060
Asbury *(G-64)*

Ingersoll-Rand Company ....E 856 793-7000
Mount Laurel *(G-6766)*

Ingersoll-Rand Intl Inc ....D 559 271-4625
Piscataway *(G-8677)*

Karla Landscaping Pavers ....G 732 333-5852
Howell *(G-4543)*

L Arden Corp ....G 973 523-6400
Paterson *(G-8234)*

Mapei Corporation ....G 732 254-4830
South River *(G-10352)*

Maritime Solutions Inc ....G 732 752-3831
Middlesex *(G-6129)*

Multi-Pak Corporation ....E 201 342-7474
Hackensack *(G-3949)*

▲ Neu Inc ....G 281 648-9751
Hamilton *(G-4118)*

NJ Paver Restorations LLC ....G 732 558-6011
Hillsborough *(G-4341)*

R & H Spring & Truck Repair ....F 732 681-9000
Wall Township *(G-11362)*

◆ Ransome Equipment Sales LLC ....G 856 797-8100
Lumberton *(G-5635)*

▼ Reinco Inc ....F 908 755-0921
Plainfield *(G-8777)*

Robert Young and Son Inc ....G 973 728-8133
Hewitt *(G-4279)*

▲ Solidia Technologies Inc ....E 908 315-5901
Piscataway *(G-8714)*

Trilenium Salvage Co ....G 732 462-2909
Morganville *(G-6597)*

Triple D Enterprises Inc ....G 609 859-3000
Southampton *(G-10373)*

Tuff Mfg Co Inc ....G 201 796-5319
Elmwood Park *(G-2858)*

▲ US Outworkers LLC ....G 973 362-1458
Sussex *(G-10569)*

W A Building Movers & Contrs ....F 908 654-8227
Garwood *(G-3793)*

3532 Mining Machinery & Eqpt

◆ Amec Fster Wheeler N Amer Corp ...D 936 448-6323
Hampton *(G-4147)*

▲ Enviro-Clear Company Inc ....F 908 638-5507
High Bridge *(G-4282)*

▲ Foremost Machine Builders Inc ....D 973 227-0700
Fairfield *(G-3206)*

Hosokawa Micron International ....C 908 273-6360
Summit *(G-10534)*

International Process Eqp Co ....G 856 665-4007
Pennsauken *(G-8439)*

◆ K-Tron International Inc ....D 856 589-0500
Sewell *(G-9851)*

Pallmann Pulverizers Co Inc ....E 973 471-1450
Clifton *(G-1682)*

3533 Oil Field Machinery & Eqpt

◆ Sandvik Inc ....C 201 794-5000
Fair Lawn *(G-3120)*

3534 Elevators & Moving Stairways

▲ Ahe Manufacturing Inc ....F 609 660-8000
Barnegat *(G-154)*

▲ Amerivator Systems Corporation ...G 973 471-1200
Clifton *(G-1565)*

Archi-Tread Inc ....G 973 725-5738
Kinnelon *(G-5015)*

Diamond Scooters Inc ....G 609 646-0003
Absecon *(G-2)*

Elevator Cabs of NY Inc ....D 973 790-9100
Paterson *(G-8178)*

Elevator Doors Inc ....E 973 790-9100
Paterson *(G-8179)*

Elevator Enterances NY Inc ....E 973 790-9100
Paterson *(G-8180)*

Elevator Entrance Inc ....E 973 790-9100
Paterson *(G-8181)*

Flor Lift of N J Inc ....E 973 429-2200
Fairfield *(G-3203)*

▲ G-Tech Elevator Associates LLC ...F 866 658-9296
Linden *(G-5350)*

Otis Elevator Company ....E 856 235-5200
Moorestown *(G-6552)*

Otis Elevator Intl Inc ....C 973 575-7030
Fairfield *(G-3285)*

◆ Schindler Elevator Corporation ....B 973 397-6500
Morristown *(G-6698)*

Schindler Elevator Corporation ....E 856 234-2220
Moorestown *(G-6565)*

◆ Schindler Enterprises Inc ....F 973 397-6500
Morristown *(G-6699)*

TEC Elevator Inc ....F 609 938-0647
Marmora *(G-5960)*

3535 Conveyors & Eqpt

Aerocon Inc ....D 800 405-2376
Belleville *(G-290)*

Allstate Conveyor Service ....E 856 768-6566
Voorhees *(G-11280)*

Employee Codes: A=Over 500 employees, B=251-500
C=101-250, D=51-100, E=20-50, F=10-19, G=4-9   2019 Harris New Jersey
Manufacturers Directory   547

SIC

Alpha Associates Inc ....E 732 730-1800
Lakewood *(G-5047)*

Automated Flexible Conveyors ....F 973 340-1695
Clifton *(G-1568)*

Boomerang Systems Inc ....E 973 538-1194
Florham Park *(G-3494)*

Buhler Inc ....E 201 847-0600
Mahwah *(G-5719)*

Carlisle Machine Works Inc ....E 856 825-0627
Millville *(G-6241)*

Century Conveyor Systems Inc ....E 908 205-0625
South Plainfield *(G-10236)*

▲ Coesia Health & Beauty Inc ....F 908 707-8008
Branchburg *(G-630)*

Conveyer Installers America ....G 908 453-4729
Belvidere *(G-358)*

Conveyors By North American ....G 973 777-6600
Clifton *(G-1589)*

▲ Coperion Corporation ....C 201 327-6300
Sewell *(G-9835)*

▲ Coperion K-Tron Pitman Inc ....F 856 589-0500
Sewell *(G-9836)*

Das Installations Inc ....F 973 473-6858
Garfield *(G-3737)*

Dyna Veyor Inc ....G 908 276-5384
Newark *(G-7108)*

Equipment Erectors Inc ....E 732 846-1212
Somerset *(G-9989)*

Essex Rise Conveyor Corp ....G 973 575-7483
West Caldwell *(G-11648)*

Flexlink Systems Inc ....E 973 983-2700
Branchburg *(G-641)*

Flexlink Systems Inc ....G 908 947-2140
Branchburg *(G-642)*

Flor Lift of N J Inc ....E 973 429-2200
Fairfield *(G-3203)*

Flow-Turn Inc ....E 908 687-3225
Union *(G-11055)*

▲ Foremost Machine Builders Inc........D 973 227-0700
Fairfield *(G-3206)*

◆ Garvey Corporation ....D 609 561-2450
Hammonton *(G-4134)*

Gauer Metal Products Co Inc ....E 908 241-4080
Kenilworth *(G-4942)*

Hy-Tek Material Handling Inc ....E 732 490-6282
Morganville *(G-6587)*

◆ Ipco US LLC ....E 973 720-7000
Totowa *(G-10833)*

J G Machine Works Inc......................G 732 203-2077
Edison *(G-2536)*

◆ K-Tron International Inc ....D 856 589-0500
Sewell *(G-9851)*

Keneco Inc ....G 908 241-3700
Kenilworth *(G-4951)*

Key Handling Systems Inc ....E 201 933-9333
Moonachie *(G-6476)*

Knotts Company Inc ....E 908 464-4800
Berkeley Heights *(G-405)*

Lynn Mechanical Contractors.............F 856 829-1717
Cinnaminson *(G-1470)*

Main Robert A & Sons Holdg Co ....E 201 447-3700
Wyckoff *(G-12116)*

▼ Metalfab Inc ....E 973 764-2000
Vernon *(G-11160)*

Metalfab Mtl Hdlg Systems LLC ....E 973 764-2000
Vernon *(G-11161)*

Pulsonics Inc ....F 800 999-6785
Belleville *(G-309)*

Reliabotics LLC ....G 732 791-5500
New Brunswick *(G-6967)*

▲ Robotunits Inc ....G 732 438-0500
Cranbury *(G-1879)*

Sparks Belting Company Inc ....G 973 227-4100
Fairfield *(G-3313)*

T O Najarian Associates ....D 732 389-0220
Eatontown *(G-2423)*

Tarlton C & T Co Inc ....E 908 964-9400
Union *(G-11093)*

TEC Installations Inc.........................F 973 684-0503
Paterson *(G-8312)*

Track Systems Inc.............................F 201 462-0095
Hasbrouck Heights *(G-4191)*

Traycon Manufacturing Co Inc ....F 201 939-5555
Hackensack *(G-3984)*

▲ Unex Manufacturing Inc ....D 732 928-2800
Lakewood *(G-5174)*

◆ Vac-U-Max ....E 973 759-4600
Belleville *(G-319)*

Vibra Screw Inc ....E 973 256-7410
Totowa *(G-10858)*

▲ Volta Belting USA Inc ....F 973 276-7905
Pine Brook *(G-8619)*

3536 Hoists, Cranes & Monorails

Bombardier Transportation..................B 973 624-9300
Newark *(G-7070)*

Breeze-Eastern LLC ....D 973 602-1001
Whippany *(G-11884)*

Courtney Boatlifts Inc ....G 732 892-8900
Point Pleasant Boro *(G-8841)*

Electro Lift Inc ....E 973 471-0204
Clifton *(G-1612)*

Holtec Government Services LLC ....G 856 291-0600
Camden *(G-1068)*

Maximum Material Handling LLC ....G 973 227-1227
Parsippany *(G-7976)*

◆ Palfinger North America ....D 609 588-5400
Trenton *(G-10971)*

Pcs Crane Services Inc ....F 201 366-4250
Fairview *(G-3367)*

Rudco Products Inc ....D 856 691-0800
Vineland *(G-11261)*

▲ Saturn Overhead Equipment LLC .....F 732 560-7210
Somerset *(G-10071)*

▼ Teledynamics LLC ....E 973 248-3360
Towaco *(G-10881)*

3537 Indl Trucks, Tractors, Trailers & Stackers

▲ Caravan Inc ....F 732 590-0210
Avenel *(G-124)*

Christensen Manufacturing ....F 609 466-9700
Pennington *(G-8361)*

Crown Equipment Corporation ....D 201 337-1211
Oakland *(G-7621)*

▲ Excalibur Miretti Group LLC ....F 973 808-8399
Fairfield *(G-3195)*

F and M Equipment Ltd ....D 215 822-0145
South Plainfield *(G-10256)*

Global Express Freight Inc ....G 201 376-6613
Bergenfield *(G-375)*

▲ Hanson & Zollinger Inc ....F 856 626-3440
Berlin *(G-422)*

◆ Hilman Incorporated ....D 732 462-6277
Marlboro *(G-5900)*

Intech Powercore Corporation ....G 201 767-8066
Closter *(G-1758)*

Morse Metal Products Co Inc ....G 732 422-3676
Princeton *(G-8981)*

◆ Palfinger North America ....D 609 588-5400
Trenton *(G-10971)*

▲ Permadur Industries Inc ....G 908 359-9767
Hillsborough *(G-4344)*

Prestige Forklift Maint Svc ....G 732 297-1001
New Brunswick *(G-6960)*

Rentalift Inc ....F 973 684-6111
Paterson *(G-8286)*

RISE Corporation ....E 973 575-7480
West Caldwell *(G-11679)*

▲ Saturn Overhead Equipment LLC .....F 732 560-7210
Somerset *(G-10071)*

Showtime Express ....G 732 238-2701
East Brunswick *(G-2176)*

Trucktech Parts & Services.................G 973 799-0500
Newark *(G-7303)*

Vanco USA LLC (de) ....C 609 499-4141
Bordentown *(G-599)*

Vehicle Technologies Inc ....G 609 406-9626
Ewing *(G-3076)*

3541 Machine Tools: Cutting

Alben Metal Products Inc ....G 973 279-8891
Paterson *(G-8130)*

American Mch Tool RPR Rbldg Co ....G 973 927-0820
Randolph *(G-9171)*

Armstrong & Sons ....G 732 223-1555
Manasquan *(G-5829)*

Array Solders Ltd Liability Co ....G 201 432-0095
Jersey City *(G-4696)*

▲ Autodrill LLC ....G 908 542-0244
Lebanon *(G-5251)*

Automated Tapping Systems Inc ....F 732 899-2282
Beachwood *(G-257)*

Camden Tool Inc ....E 856 966-6800
Camden *(G-1045)*

Charles F Kilian ....G 732 458-3554
Brick *(G-712)*

Chase Machine Co ....F 201 438-2214
Lyndhurst *(G-5648)*

Cutter Drill & Machine Inc ....G 732 206-1112
Howell *(G-4535)*

Eastern Machining Corporation ....G 856 694-3303
Franklinville *(G-3637)*

▲ Everite Machine Products Co ....E 856 330-6700
Pennsauken *(G-8419)*

▲ Fecken-Kirfel America Inc ....F 201 891-5530
Mahwah *(G-5736)*

Gary R Marzili ....G 856 782-1546
Sicklerville *(G-9910)*

Gauer Metal Products Co Inc ....E 908 241-4080
Kenilworth *(G-4942)*

General Electric Company ....B 973 887-6635
Parsippany *(G-7955)*

▼ Glebar Operating LLC ....D 201 337-1500
Ramsey *(G-9146)*

High Point Precision Products ....E 973 875-6229
Sussex *(G-10561)*

Hone-A-Matic Tool & Cutter Co ....G 732 382-6000
Rahway *(G-9102)*

Innovative Manufacturing Inc ....F 908 904-1884
Hillsborough *(G-4329)*

J & S Tool ....G 973 383-5059
Newton *(G-7347)*

▲ Jet Pulverizer Co Inc ....E 856 235-5554
Moorestown *(G-6531)*

Joe Mike Precision Fabrication ....F 609 953-1144
Medford *(G-6026)*

▲ Komo Machine Inc ....D 732 719-6222
Lakewood *(G-5117)*

L & M Machine & Tool Co Inc ....G 973 523-5288
Paterson *(G-8233)*

▲ Lever Manufacturing Corp ....E 201 684-4400
Mahwah *(G-5752)*

McGonegal Manufacturing Co ....G 201 438-2313
East Rutherford *(G-2301)*

Metaport Manufacturing LLC ....G 973 383-8363
Lafayette *(G-5031)*

▲ NASA Machine Tools Inc ....E 973 633-5200
Lincoln Park *(G-5302)*

Nova Precision Products Inc ....C 973 625-1586
Rockaway *(G-9480)*

Oroszlany Laszlo ....G 201 666-2101
Hillsdale *(G-4369)*

▲ Rowan Technologies Inc ....D 609 267-9000
Rancocas *(G-9165)*

▲ Royal Master Grinders Inc ....D 201 337-8500
Oakland *(G-7645)*

▼ TAC Technical Instrument Corp........F 609 882-2894
Trenton *(G-10995)*

Tool Shop Inc ....G 856 767-8077
West Berlin *(G-11630)*

▲ Tooling Etc LLC ....G 732 752-8080
Middlesex *(G-6156)*

Triple-T Cutting Tools Inc ....F 856 768-0800
West Berlin *(G-11632)*

▲ Uhlmann Packaging Systems LP .....D 973 402-8855
Towaco *(G-10883)*

Unique Precision Co Inc ....G 732 382-8699
Rahway *(G-9131)*

Web Industries Inc ....F 973 335-1200
Montville *(G-6449)*

3542 Machine Tools: Forming

▲ Action Packaging Automation ....G 609 448-9210
Roosevelt *(G-9527)*

American Made Fabricators Inc...........G 732 356-4306
Middlesex *(G-6096)*

◆ Arrow Fastener Co LLC ....B 201 843-6900
Saddle Brook *(G-9640)*

Benton Graphics Inc..........................E 609 587-4000
Trenton *(G-10903)*

▲ Bergen Cable Technology LLC ....E 973 276-9596
Fairfield *(G-3155)*

◆ Bruderer Machinery Inc ....E 201 941-2121
Ridgefield *(G-9252)*

Buhler Inc ....E 201 847-0600
Mahwah *(G-5719)*

C & S Machinery Rebuilding ....G 973 742-7302
Paterson *(G-8152)*

▲ Cozzoli Machine Company ....D 732 564-0400
Somerset *(G-9978)*

Doran LLC ....G 908 289-9200
Union *(G-11043)*

Edston Manufacturing Company ....G 908 647-0116
Fairfield *(G-3189)*

▼ Grimco Pneumatic Corp ....G 973 345-0660
Paterson *(G-8204)*

H & W Tool Co Inc ....F 973 366-0131
Dover *(G-2085)*

High-Technology Corporation F 201 488-0010
Hackensack *(G-3927)*
Hone-A-Matic Tool & Cutter Co G 732 382-6000
Rahway *(G-9102)*
Joy-Rei Enterprises Inc G 732 727-0742
Parlin *(G-7867)*
▲ **Magnetic Metals Corporation** C 856 964-7842
Camden *(G-1077)*
Mastercraft Iron Inc F 732 988-3113
Neptune *(G-6891)*
Rotech Tool & Mold Co Inc G 908 241-9669
Kenilworth *(G-4975)*
▲ **Royle Systems Group LLC** E 201 644-0345
Teterboro *(G-10690)*
▲ **Titanium Industries Inc** E 973 983-1185
Rockaway *(G-9504)*
Trumpf Inc E 609 925-8200
Cranbury *(G-1888)*
▲ **Trumpf Photonics Inc** C 609 925-8200
Cranbury *(G-1889)*
Ultimate Spinning Turning Corp G 201 372-9740
Moonachie *(G-6495)*
Vantage Tool & Mfg Inc G 908 647-1010
Warren *(G-11435)*
Williams Scotsman Inc G 856 429-0315
Kearny *(G-4906)*

3543 Industrial Patterns

Creative Patterns & Mfg G 973 589-1391
Rockaway *(G-9451)*
▲ **Method Assoc Inc** F 732 888-0444
Keyport *(G-5001)*
▲ **Motif Industries Inc** F 973 575-1800
East Hanover *(G-2223)*
West Pattern Works Inc F 609 443-6241
Cranbury *(G-1892)*

3544 Dies, Tools, Jigs, Fixtures & Indl Molds

21st Century Finishing Inc E 201 797-0212
Clifton *(G-1550)*
A Frieri Machine Tool Inc G 908 753-7555
South Plainfield *(G-10204)*
▲ **A K Stamping Co Inc** D 908 232-7300
Mountainside *(G-6831)*
Accurate Machine & Tool Co G 908 245-5545
Roselle Park *(G-9577)*
Accurate Mold Inc E 856 784-8484
Somerdale *(G-9929)*
▲ **Accurate Tool & Die Co Inc** G 201 476-9348
Montvale *(G-6394)*
Algene Marking Equipment Co G 973 478-9041
Garfield *(G-3727)*
Alloy Cast Products Inc F 908 245-2255
Kenilworth *(G-4920)*
Almark Tool & Manufacturing Co F 908 789-2440
Garwood *(G-3780)*
Amerimold Tech Inc E 732 462-7577
Jackson *(G-4638)*
Art Mold & Polishing Co Inc F 908 518-9191
Roselle *(G-9548)*
Art Mold & Tool Corporation G 201 935-3377
East Rutherford *(G-2272)*
B E C Mfg Corp E 201 414-0000
Glen Rock *(G-3828)*
Bach Tool Precision Inc G 973 962-6224
Ringwood *(G-9343)*
Barlics Manufacturing Co Inc G 732 381-6229
Rahway *(G-9082)*
▲ **Bihler of America Inc** C 908 213-9001
Phillipsburg *(G-8546)*
Bodine Tool and Machine Co Inc E 856 234-7800
Moorestown *(G-6509)*
Bonney-Vehslage Tool Co F 973 589-6975
Springfield *(G-10432)*
Boyle Tool & Die Co Inc F 856 853-1819
West Deptford *(G-11694)*
▲ **Brisar Industries Inc** D 973 278-2500
Paterson *(G-8150)*
▲ **C & C Metal Products Corp** D 201 569-7300
Englewood *(G-2889)*
C & K Punch & Screw Mch Pdts G 201 343-6750
Hackensack *(G-3888)*
C & S Tool Co F 973 887-6865
East Hanover *(G-2196)*
C A Spalding Company E 267 550-9000
Moorestown *(G-6511)*
C and C Tool Co LLC G 908 431-0330
Hillsborough *(G-4309)*
Camptown Tool & Die Co Inc G 908 688-8406
Kenilworth *(G-4932)*

▲ **Cavalla Inc** E 201 343-3338
Hackensack *(G-3895)*
▲ **Charles E Green & Son Inc** E 973 485-3630
Newark *(G-7082)*
City Diecutting Inc F 973 270-0370
Morristown *(G-6653)*
▲ **CK Manufacturing Inc** E 973 808-3500
Fairfield *(G-3168)*
Clover Stamping Inc G 973 278-4888
Paterson *(G-8158)*
▲ **Colwood Electronics Inc** G 732 938-5556
Farmingdale *(G-3380)*
Container Graphics Corp E 732 922-1180
Neptune *(G-6870)*
▲ **Continental Precision Corp** C 908 754-3030
Piscataway *(G-8650)*
Custom Extrusion Tech Inc F 732 367-5511
Lakewood *(G-5078)*
D & D Technology Inc G 908 688-5154
Union *(G-11040)*
Die Tech LLC G 201 343-8324
Hackensack *(G-3907)*
▲ **Duerr Tool & Die Co Inc** C 908 810-9035
Union *(G-11044)*
Dura-Carb Inc G 973 697-6665
Oak Ridge *(G-7601)*
Dynamic Die Cutting & Finshg F 973 589-8338
Newark *(G-7109)*
Eb Machine Corp G 973 442-7729
Wharton *(G-11857)*
Edgar C Barcus Co Inc F 856 456-0204
Westville *(G-11813)*
Electro Magnetic Products Inc E 856 235-3011
Moorestown *(G-6521)*
Elray Manufacturing Company E 856 881-1935
Glassboro *(G-3810)*
F & G Tool & Die Inc G 908 241-5880
Kenilworth *(G-4938)*
▲ **Fancort Industries Inc** F 973 575-0610
West Caldwell *(G-11650)*
Garden State Precision Inc G 201 945-6410
Ridgefield *(G-9262)*
Garden State Tool & Mold Corp G 908 245-2041
South Amboy *(G-10133)*
Gaum Inc E 609 586-0132
Robbinsville *(G-9412)*
General Tool Specialties Inc F 908 874-3040
Hillsborough *(G-4319)*
▲ **Globe Die-Cutting Products Inc** C 732 494-7744
Metuchen *(G-6057)*
▲ **Globe Industries Corp** F 973 992-8990
Clifton *(G-1626)*
Golden Rule Inc G 856 663-3074
Pennsauken *(G-8425)*
H & W Tool Co Inc F 973 366-0131
Dover *(G-2085)*
H-E Tool & Mfg Co Inc E 856 303-8787
Cinnaminson *(G-1461)*
Hanrahan Tool Co Inc G 732 919-7300
Farmingdale *(G-3386)*
Hartmann Tool Co Inc G 201 343-8700
Hackensack *(G-3926)*
▲ **Heinz Glas USA Inc** F 908 474-0300
Linden *(G-5355)*
Hofmann Tool & Die Corporation G 201 327-0226
Upper Saddle River *(G-11140)*
Hudson Manufacturing Corp F 973 376-7070
Millburn *(G-6199)*
Indo-US Mim TEC Private Ltd G 734 327-9842
Princeton *(G-8962)*
▼ **Infor Metal & Tooling Mfg** F 973 571-9520
Cedar Grove *(G-1279)*
Inventors Shop LLC E 856 303-8787
Cinnaminson *(G-1466)*
Ipsco Apollo Punch & Die Corp G 973 884-0900
East Hanover *(G-2218)*
J & J Marine Inc F 856 228-4744
Sewell *(G-9848)*
J P Rotella Co Inc F 973 942-2559
Haledon *(G-4083)*
J V Q Inc F 973 523-8806
Paterson *(G-8217)*
J-Mac Plastics Inc E 908 709-1111
Kenilworth *(G-4949)*
Jmk Tool Die and Mfg Co Inc G 201 845-4710
Rochelle Park *(G-9425)*
Jordan Manufacturing LLC G 973 383-8363
Lafayette *(G-5029)*
Kessler Steel Rule Die Inc G 856 767-0231
West Berlin *(G-11602)*

Koba Corp D 732 469-0110
Middlesex *(G-6124)*
L & Z Tool and Engineering Inc E 908 322-2220
Watchung *(G-11456)*
▲ **Lasercam LLc** E 201 941-1262
Ridgefield *(G-9273)*
◆ **Lawrence Mold and Tool Corp** E 609 392-5422
Lawrenceville *(G-5234)*
Lincoln Mold & Die Corp D 908 241-3344
Warren *(G-11420)*
▲ **Linden Mold and Tool Corp** E 732 381-1411
Rahway *(G-9114)*
Mold Polishing Company Inc G 908 518-9191
Garwood *(G-3785)*
Monroe Tool & Die Inc G 856 629-5164
Williamstown *(G-11964)*
▲ **Newton Tool & Mfg Inc** D 856 241-1500
Pennsauken *(G-8461)*
Olympic EDM Services Inc G 973 492-0664
Kinnelon *(G-5020)*
Omega Tool Die G 856 228-7100
Sewell *(G-9852)*
Orycon Control Technology Inc E 732 922-2400
Ocean *(G-7670)*
Pahco Machine Inc G 609 587-1188
Trenton *(G-10970)*
Peterson Steel Rule Die Corp F 201 935-6180
Carlstadt *(G-1200)*
Philip Creter Inc G 908 686-2910
Union *(G-11083)*
Pin Point Container Corp G 856 848-2115
Deptford *(G-2065)*
Precision Ball Specialties F 856 881-5646
Williamstown *(G-11971)*
Printco G 908 687-9518
Flemington *(G-3464)*
Progressive Tool & Mfg Corp G 908 245-7010
Kenilworth *(G-4972)*
Quality Die Shop Inc G 732 787-0041
North Middletown *(G-7504)*
R G Smith Tool & Mfg Co F 973 344-1395
Newark *(G-7243)*
Rebuth Metal Services F 908 889-6400
Fanwood *(G-3373)*
▲ **Redkeys Dies Inc** G 856 456-7890
Gloucester City *(G-3850)*
▲ **Resolv Corporation** F 973 220-5141
Orange *(G-7759)*
Rex Tool & Manufacturing Inc G 908 925-2727
Linden *(G-5415)*
Romar Machine & Tool Company E 201 337-7111
Franklin Lakes *(G-3631)*
Roseville Tool & Manufacturing E 973 992-5405
Livingston *(G-5538)*
Rotech Tool & Mold Co Inc G 908 241-9669
Kenilworth *(G-4975)*
Schneider & Marquard Inc E 973 383-2200
Newton *(G-7356)*
Seajay Manufacturing Corp F 732 774-0900
Neptune *(G-6897)*
Sigco Tool & Mfg Co Inc E 856 753-6565
West Berlin *(G-11621)*
▲ **Spec Steel Rule Dies Inc** E 609 443-4435
Windsor *(G-11999)*
Stampex Corp F 973 839-4040
Haskell *(G-4202)*
STS Technologies LLC F 973 277-5416
Mahwah *(G-5778)*
TEC Cast Inc E 201 935-3885
Carlstadt *(G-1226)*
Thal Precision Industries LLC G 732 381-6106
Clark *(G-1517)*
▲ **Thomson Lamination Co Inc** D 856 779-8521
Maple Shade *(G-5872)*
Tryco Tool & Mfg Co Inc E 973 674-6867
Orange *(G-7764)*
Turul Bookbindery Inc G 973 361-2810
Wharton *(G-11874)*
▲ **Union Tool & Mold Co Inc** E 973 763-6611
Maplewood *(G-5888)*
United Die Company Inc E 201 997-0250
Kearny *(G-4902)*
Unity Steel Rule Die Co E 201 569-6400
Englewood *(G-2951)*
Universal Mold & Tool Inc F 856 563-0488
Vineland *(G-11272)*
▲ **Universal Tools & Mfg Co** E 973 379-4193
Springfield *(G-10471)*
Valley Die Cutting Inc G 973 731-8884
Randolph *(G-9207)*

Vantage Tool & Mfg Inc ....G...... 908 647-1010
   Warren (G-11435)

Victory Tool & Mfg Co ....G...... 973 759-8733
   Belleville (G-322)

Viking Mold & Tool Corp ....G...... 609 476-9333
   Dorothy (G-2072)

Viz Mold & Die Ltd ....F...... 201 784-8383
   Northvale (G-7553)

Vmc Die Cutting Corp ....F...... 973 450-4655
   Belleville (G-323)

Well Bilt Industries Inc ....F...... 908 486-6002
   Linden (G-5441)

West Machine Works Inc ....G...... 732 549-2183
   Metuchen (G-6080)

West Pattern Works Inc ....F...... 609 443-6241
   Cranbury (G-1892)

Zin-Tech Inc ....E...... 856 661-0900
   Pennsauken (G-8499)

3545 Machine Tool Access

Accurate Diamond Tool Corp ....E... 201 265-8868
   Emerson (G-2861)

▼ Accuratus Ceramic Corp ....E... 908 213-7070
   Phillipsburg (G-8540)

◆ Acrison Inc ....D... 201 440-8300
   Moonachie (G-6451)

Advanced Cutting Services LLC ....G... 908 241-5332
   Roselle (G-9546)

Airbrasive Jet Tech LLC ....E... 201 725-7340
   South Plainfield (G-10209)

Alloy Cast Products Inc ....F... 908 245-2255
   Kenilworth (G-4920)

Almark Tool & Manufacturing Co ....F... 908 789-2440
   Garwood (G-3780)

Aloris Tool Technology Co Inc ....E... 973 772-1201
   Clifton (G-1561)

▲ Alpex Wheel Co Inc ....E... 201 871-1700
   Tenafly (G-10659)

American Aeronautic Mfg Co ....G... 973 442-8138
   Pine Brook (G-8585)

Automated Tapping Systems Inc ....F... 732 899-2282
   Beachwood (G-257)

B & S Tool and Cutter Service ....G... 201 488-3545
   Hackensack (G-3880)

B B Supply Corp ....F... 201 313-9021
   Cliffside Park (G-1536)

Bach Tool Precision Inc ....G... 973 962-6224
   Ringwood (G-9343)

▲ Bar-Lo Carbon Products Inc ....E... 973 227-2717
   Fairfield (G-3151)

▲ Belleville Scale & Balance LLC ....G... 973 759-4487
   Orange (G-7751)

Camden Tool Inc ....E... 856 966-6800
   Camden (G-1045)

Congruent Machine Co Inc ....G... 973 764-6767
   Vernon (G-11158)

Cutter Drill & Machine Inc ....G... 732 206-1112
   Howell (G-4535)

Daven Industries Inc ....E... 973 808-8848
   Fairfield (G-3180)

Defined Pro Machining LLC ....G... 973 891-1038
   Wharton (G-11855)

◆ Dessau International ....E... 201 791-2005
   Fair Lawn (G-3096)

▲ Dewitt Bros Tool Co Inc ....G... 908 298-3700
   Kenilworth (G-4935)

Digivac Company ....F... 732 765-0900
   Matawan (G-5972)

Dmg Mori Usa Inc ....G... 973 257-9620
   Rockaway (G-9453)

◆ Doosan Machine Tools Amer Corp ...D... 973 618-2500
   Pine Brook (G-8599)

E P Heller Company ....E... 973 377-2878
   Madison (G-5691)

Energy Beams Inc ....F... 973 291-6555
   Bloomingdale (G-528)

▲ Engineered Components Inc ....F... 908 788-8393
   Three Bridges (G-10704)

F & R Grinding Inc ....F... 908 996-0440
   Frenchtown (G-3712)

▲ Fulcrum Inc ....G... 973 473-6900
   Oradell (G-7744)

Grobet File Company Amer LLC ....D... 201 939-6700
   Carlstadt (G-1161)

H & W Tool Co Inc ....F... 973 366-0131
   Dover (G-2085)

Hainesport Tool & Machine Co ....F... 609 261-0016
   Mount Holly (G-6729)

▲ Handler Manufacturing Company .....E... 908 233-7796
   Westfield (G-11799)

Indo-US Mim TEC Private Ltd ....G...... 734 327-9842
   Princeton (G-8962)

▲ Industrial Brush Co Inc ....E...... 800 241-9860
   Fairfield (G-3236)

International Tool and Mfg ....G...... 973 227-6767
   Fairfield (G-3241)

J A Machine & Tool Co Inc ....F...... 201 767-1308
   Closter (G-1759)

J and J Contractors ....F...... 856 765-7521
   Millville (G-6256)

▲ Jdv Products Inc ....F...... 201 794-6467
   Fair Lawn (G-3108)

Jnt Technical Services Inc ....E...... 201 641-2130
   Little Ferry (G-5491)

Kennametal Inc ....C...... 412 248-8200
   Jersey City (G-4753)

KG Systems Inc ....G...... 973 515-4664
   Springfield (G-10451)

M D Carbide Tool Corp ....G...... 973 263-0104
   Towaco (G-10874)

Martin Tool Company Inc ....E...... 973 361-9212
   Wharton (G-11862)

New Jersey Diamond Products Co ....F...... 973 684-0949
   Paterson (G-8267)

Niko Trade Ltd-USA Inc ....G...... 973 575-4353
   Fairfield (G-3280)

Precision Ball Specialties ....F...... 856 881-5646
   Williamstown (G-11971)

▲ Ram Products Inc ....G...... 732 651-5500
   Dayton (G-1985)

Ramco Manufacturing Co Inc ....G...... 908 245-4500
   Kenilworth (G-4973)

▲ Ringfeder Pwr Transm USA Corp .....E...... 201 666-3320
   Westwood (G-11843)

Sandvik Inc ....C...... 281 275-4800
   Fair Lawn (G-3121)

◆ Sandvik Inc ....C...... 201 794-5000
   Fair Lawn (G-3120)

Sine Tru Tool Company Inc ....G...... 732 591-1100
   Marlboro (G-5915)

Sk & P Industries Inc ....G...... 973 482-1864
   Newark (G-7276)

Ss Tool & Manufacturing Co ....G...... 908 486-5497
   Linden (G-5428)

Technodiamant USA Inc ....E...... 908 850-8505
   Tranquility (G-10884)

▲ Teknics Industries Inc ....D...... 973 633-7575
   Lincoln Park (G-5306)

Tool Shop Inc ....G...... 856 767-8077
   West Berlin (G-11630)

Troy-Onic Inc ....E...... 973 584-6830
   Kenvil (G-4996)

▲ United Instrument Company LLC ...G...... 201 767-6000
   Northvale (G-7552)

▲ Universal Metalcraft Inc ....E...... 973 345-3284
   Wayne (G-11560)

William T Hutchinson Company ....F...... 908 688-0533
   Union (G-11100)

Wrightworks Engineering LLC ....G...... 609 882-8840
   Lawrenceville (G-5247)

Zenith Precision Inc ....F...... 201 933-8640
   East Rutherford (G-2331)

3546 Power Hand Tools

Black & Decker (us) Inc ....G...... 201 475-3524
   Elmwood Park (G-2812)

Chatham Lawn Mowler ....G...... 973 635-8855
   Chatham (G-1320)

▲ Colwood Electronics Inc ....G...... 732 938-5556
   Farmingdale (G-3380)

Congruent Machine Co Inc ....G...... 973 764-6767
   Vernon (G-11158)

Dcm Clean Air Products Inc ....G...... 732 363-2100
   Lakewood (G-5082)

Ingersoll-Rand Company ....G...... 908 238-7000
   Annandale (G-54)

Ingersoll-Rand Company ....G...... 856 793-7000
   Mount Laurel (G-6766)

J Paul Allen Inc ....G...... 973 702-1174
   Sussex (G-10563)

▲ Jdv Products Inc ....F...... 201 794-6467
   Fair Lawn (G-3108)

Mendham Garden Center ....G...... 973 543-4178
   Mendham (G-6041)

▲ National Steel Rule Company ....D...... 908 862-3366
   Linden (G-5392)

▲ Newell Brands Inc ....B...... 201 610-6600
   Hoboken (G-4468)

Precision Saw & Tool Corp ....F...... 973 773-7302
   Clifton (G-1698)

▲ Rennsteig Tools Inc ....G...... 330 315-3044
   Hackensack (G-3966)

▲ S & G Tool Aid Corporation ....D...... 973 824-7730
   Newark (G-7257)

▲ Singe Corporation ....G...... 908 289-7900
   Hillside (G-4426)

▲ Tdk Electronics Inc ....D...... 732 906-4300
   Iselin (G-4631)

Tdk Electronics Inc ....F...... 732 603-5941
   Lumberton (G-5636)

Toydriver LLC ....G...... 678 637-8500
   Garfield (G-3774)

William T Hutchinson Company ....F...... 908 688-0533
   Union (G-11100)

Winslow Rental & Supply Inc ....G...... 856 767-5554
   Berlin (G-434)

3547 Rolling Mill Machinery & Eqpt

Indemax Inc ....G...... 973 209-2424
   Vernon (G-11159)

3548 Welding Apparatus

Cerbaco Ltd ....E...... 908 996-1333
   Frenchtown (G-3711)

Cni Ceramic Nozzles Inc ....G...... 973 276-1535
   Fairfield (G-3170)

Cotterman Inc ....E...... 856 415-0800
   Wenonah (G-11574)

Frank Zotynia & Son Inc ....G...... 973 247-2800
   Paterson (G-8194)

Hexacon Electric Company Inc ....E...... 908 245-6200
   Roselle Park (G-9586)

▲ Orgo-Thermit Inc ....E...... 732 657-5781
   Manchester (G-5847)

◆ Rowan Technologies Inc ....D...... 609 267-9000
   Rancocas (G-9165)

◆ Stulz-Sickles Steel Company ....E...... 609 531-2172
   Burlington (G-986)

Waage Electric Inc ....G...... 908 245-9363
   Kenilworth (G-4986)

3549 Metalworking Machinery, NEC

A D J Group LLC ....G...... 609 743-2099
   Bordentown (G-573)

Air & Specialties Sheet Metal ....F...... 908 233-8306
   Mountainside (G-6832)

▼ Applied Resources Corp ....E...... 973 328-3882
   Wharton (G-11852)

Boomerang Systems Inc ....E...... 973 538-1194
   Florham Park (G-3494)

▲ K & S Industries Inc ....F...... 908 862-3030
   Linden (G-5368)

▲ Lever Manufacturing Corp ....E...... 201 684-4400
   Mahwah (G-5752)

◆ Mac Products Inc ....D...... 973 344-5149
   Kearny (G-4880)

Precious Metal Processing Cons ....G...... 201 944-8053
   Palisades Park (G-7777)

▲ Progressive Ruesch Inc ....E...... 973 962-7700
   Ringwood (G-9351)

Seal-Spout Corp ....F...... 908 647-0648
   Liberty Corner (G-5296)

TMU Inc ....F...... 609 884-7656
   Cape May (G-1103)

Tri-Power Consulting Svcs LLC ....E...... 973 227-7100
   Denville (G-2060)

▲ Weber and Scher Mfg Co Inc ....E...... 908 236-8484
   Lebanon (G-5275)

Werko Machine Co ....F...... 856 662-0669
   Pennsauken (G-8496)

3552 Textile Machinery

Baxter Corporation ....D...... 201 337-1212
   Franklin Lakes (G-3613)

▲ Benjamin Booth Company ....F...... 609 859-1995
   Southampton (G-10360)

Burlington Textile Machinery ....F...... 973 279-5900
   Paterson (G-8151)

C & S Machine Inc ....F...... 973 882-1097
   Fairfield (G-3161)

Cire Technologies Inc ....G...... 973 402-8301
   Mountain Lakes (G-6821)

◆ Clements Industries Inc ....E...... 201 440-5500
   South Hackensack (G-10153)

D R Kenyon & Son Inc ....F...... 908 722-0001
   Bridgewater (G-816)

▲ Daf Products Inc ....F...... 201 251-1222
   Wyckoff (G-12108)

Excel Industrial Co Inc ....G...... 609 275-1748
  Princeton Junction **(G-9057)**

I F Associates Inc ....F...... 732 223-2900
  Allenwood **(G-33)**

▲ Lever Manufacturing Corp ....E...... 201 684-4400
  Mahwah **(G-5752)**

M & S Machine & Tool Corp ....F...... 973 345-5847
  Paterson **(G-8247)**

◆ Pecata Enterprises Inc ....E...... 973 523-9498
  Paterson **(G-8280)**

▲ Snapco Manufacturing Corp ......G...... 973 282-0300
  Hillside **(G-4427)**

▼ Wizard Technology Inc ....F...... 732 730-0800
  Toms River **(G-10804)**

3553 Woodworking Machinery

Andys Custom Cabinets ....G...... 732 752-6443
  Green Brook **(G-3859)**

Atlas Woodworking Inc ....G...... 201 784-1949
  Closter **(G-1751)**

▲ Design of Tomorrow Inc ....F...... 973 227-1000
  Fairfield **(G-3185)**

Fix It Guy ....G...... 732 278-9000
  Toms River **(G-10759)**

Logpowercom LLC ....G...... 732 350-9663
  Whiting **(G-11940)**

▲ Samuelson Furniture Inc ....F...... 973 278-4372
  Paterson **(G-8294)**

Stapling Machines Inc ....E...... 973 627-4400
  Rockaway **(G-9500)**

3554 Paper Inds Machinery

175 Derousse LLC..........................G...... 856 662-0100
  Pennsauken **(G-8380)**

▼ Alpine Corrugated McHy Inc .....G...... 201 440-3030
  Ridgefield Park **(G-9299)**

◆ Colter & Peterson Inc ....E...... 973 684-0901
  West Caldwell **(G-11644)**

▲ Creative Laminating Inc ....E...... 201 939-1999
  Carlstadt **(G-1147)**

▲ Dietech Services LLC ....G...... 973 667-0798
  Nutley **(G-7585)**

Enser Corporation ....D...... 856 829-5522
  Cinnaminson **(G-1456)**

Holographic Finishing Inc ....F...... 201 941-4651
  Ridgefield **(G-9266)**

▼ Khanna Paper Inc ....G...... 201 850-1707
  North Bergen **(G-7415)**

Microfold Inc................................G...... 201 641-5052
  Teterboro **(G-10687)**

Retrievex....................................G...... 732 247-3200
  New Brunswick **(G-6968)**

Rotary Die Systems Inc ....G...... 856 234-3994
  Moorestown **(G-6563)**

Tri-State Knife Grinding Corp ....E...... 609 890-4989
  Robbinsville **(G-9418)**

▲ Woodward Jogger Aerators Inc ......F...... 201 933-6800
  East Rutherford **(G-2330)**

3555 Printing Trades Machinery & Eqpt

▼ Ackley Machine Corporation..........E...... 856 234-3626
  Moorestown **(G-6500)**

Acme Engraving Co Inc..................E...... 973 778-0885
  Passaic **(G-8050)**

Algene Marking Equipment Co ....G...... 973 478-9041
  Garfield **(G-3727)**

▲ Allison Systems Corporation .....F...... 856 461-9111
  Riverside **(G-9389)**

▲ Ancraft Press Corp ....F...... 201 792-9200
  Jersey City **(G-4691)**

◆ Anderson & Vreeland Inc ....E...... 973 227-2270
  Fairfield **(G-3143)**

AT Information Products Inc...........G...... 201 529-0202
  Mahwah **(G-5715)**

▲ Bell-Mark Sales Co Inc ....E...... 973 882-0202
  Pine Brook **(G-8588)**

Benton Graphics Inc......................E...... 609 587-4000
  Trenton **(G-10903)**

▲ Blankets Inc ....G...... 973 589-7800
  Newark **(G-7067)**

Charles M Jessup Inc ....G...... 732 324-0430
  Keasbey **(G-4910)**

City Envelope Inc ....G...... 201 792-9292
  Jersey City **(G-4712)**

Clarity Imaging Tech Inc ....E...... 877 272-4362
  Saddle Brook **(G-9647)**

Clarity Imaging Tech Inc ....E...... 413 693-1234
  Pennsauken **(G-8404)**

▲ Clarity Imaging Tech Inc ....G...... 877 272-4362
  Pennsauken **(G-8405)**

▲ Convertech Inc ....E...... 973 328-1850
  Wharton **(G-11854)**

▲ Cronite Co Inc ....E...... 973 887-7900
  Parsippany **(G-7910)**

Custom Roller Corp.......................G...... 908 298-7797
  Roselle **(G-9556)**

Deneka Printing Systems Inc...........G...... 609 752-0964
  Cream Ridge **(G-1934)**

Digital Design Inc..........................E...... 973 857-9500
  Cedar Grove **(G-1274)**

Domino Printing ....G...... 973 857-0900
  Cedar Grove **(G-1276)**

Ernest Schaefer Inc ....G...... 908 964-1280
  Union **(G-11052)**

Galvanic Prtg & Plate Co Inc ....E...... 201 939-3600
  Moonachie **(G-6466)**

Graphic Equipment Corporation ....E...... 732 494-5350
  Metuchen **(G-6058)**

▲ Interchange Equipment Inc ......E...... 973 473-5005
  Passaic **(G-8074)**

J Nelson Press Inc ....G...... 732 747-0330
  Englishtown **(G-3005)**

Kirkwood NJ Globe Acqstion LLC ....G...... 201 440-0800
  Ridgefield Park **(G-9310)**

Kohl & Madden Prtg Ink Corp ....E...... 201 935-8666
  Carlstadt **(G-1177)**

Mark/Trece Inc ....E...... 973 884-1005
  Whippany **(G-11897)**

Marko Engraving & Art Corp ....F...... 201 864-6500
  Weehawken **(G-11569)**

Marko Engraving & Art Corp ....F...... 201 945-6555
  Fairview **(G-3363)**

Mosstype Corporation ....G...... 201 444-8000
  Waldwick **(G-11306)**

Mosstype Holding Corp..................G...... 201 444-8000
  Waldwick **(G-11307)**

N B C Engraving Co Inc..................G...... 201 387-8011
  Bergenfield **(G-380)**

On Demand Machinery ....F...... 908 351-7137
  Elizabeth **(G-2765)**

Packaging Graphics Inc ....E...... 856 767-9000
  West Berlin **(G-11613)**

◆ Pamarco Global Graphics Inc ....E...... 908 241-1200
  Roselle **(G-9568)**

Pamarco Global Graphics Inc ....F...... 856 829-4585
  Palmyra **(G-7785)**

▲ Pamarco Technologies LLC ......E...... 908 241-1200
  Roselle **(G-9569)**

◆ Panpac LLC..............................F...... 856 376-3576
  Cherry Hill **(G-1405)**

◆ Polytype America Corp.............F...... 201 995-1000
  Lincoln Park **(G-5304)**

▼ Printers Service Florida Inc ....G...... 973 589-7800
  Newark **(G-7236)**

Verico Technology LLC ....C...... 201 842-0222
  East Rutherford **(G-2329)**

W R Chesnut Engineering Inc..........F...... 973 227-6995
  Fairfield **(G-3349)**

Wilenta Carting Inc ....F...... 201 325-0044
  Secaucus **(G-9828)**

▲ Zeiser Inc ....F...... 973 228-0800
  West Caldwell **(G-11682)**

3556 Food Prdts Machinery

Absecon Island Beverage Co ....G...... 609 653-8123
  Egg Harbor Township **(G-2674)**

◆ AGA Foodservice Inc ....D...... 856 428-4200
  Cherry Hill **(G-1333)**

Allen Steel Co...............................G...... 856 785-1171
  Leesburg **(G-5286)**

▲ Am-Mac Incorporated ....F...... 973 575-7567
  Fairfield **(G-3140)**

Arm & Hammer Animal Ntrtn LLC ......F...... 800 526-3563
  Princeton **(G-8910)**

Basha USA LLC.............................G...... 201 339-9770
  Bayonne **(G-204)**

Buhler Inc ....E...... 201 847-0600
  Mahwah **(G-5719)**

Caddy Corporation of America ....D...... 856 467-4222
  Swedesboro **(G-10575)**

Cornell Machine Co Inc ....G...... 973 379-6860
  Springfield **(G-10437)**

D&N Machine Manufacturing Inc ....E...... 856 456-1366
  Gloucester City **(G-3840)**

▲ Dantco Corp ....F...... 973 278-8776
  Paterson **(G-8168)**

◆ Erika-Record LLC ....G...... 973 614-8500
  Clifton **(G-1616)**

▲ Excalibur Bagel Bky Equip Inc ....E...... 201 797-2788
  Fair Lawn **(G-3099)**

▲ Excellent Bakery Equipment Co ......E...... 973 244-1664
  Fairfield **(G-3196)**

Expert Process Systems LLC ....G...... 570 424-0581
  Hackettstown **(G-4007)**

▲ FBM Baking Machines Inc ....G...... 609 860-0577
  Cranbury **(G-1834)**

◆ Gericke USA Inc ....G...... 855 888-0088
  Somerset **(G-9997)**

▲ Gram Equipment ....E...... 201 750-6500
  Hamilton **(G-4106)**

HCH Incorporated ....G...... 973 300-4551
  Sparta **(G-10391)**

Hill Machine Inc............................G...... 973 684-2808
  Paterson **(G-8209)**

Industl Envrnmntl Pollutn ....G...... 908 241-3830
  Roselle Park **(G-9587)**

J Hebrank Inc ....F...... 973 983-0001
  Rockaway **(G-9470)**

Joe Mike Precision Fabrication ....F...... 609 953-1144
  Medford **(G-6026)**

◆ Kuhl Corp ....D...... 908 782-5696
  Flemington **(G-3454)**

M B C Food Machinery Corp ....G...... 201 489-7000
  Hackensack **(G-3941)**

Machine Control Systems Inc..........E...... 732 529-6888
  Jackson **(G-4658)**

▲ Magna Industries Inc ....E...... 732 905-0957
  Lakewood **(G-5127)**

◆ Megas Yeeros LLC ....E...... 212 777-6342
  Lyndhurst **(G-5663)**

Nowak Inc ....F...... 973 366-7208
  Wharton **(G-11864)**

Patty-O-Matic Inc..........................F...... 732 938-2757
  Farmingdale **(G-3389)**

Rajbhog Foods Inc.........................G...... 551 222-4700
  Jersey City **(G-4794)**

▲ Rajbhog Foods Inc....................G...... 201 395-9400
  Jersey City **(G-4795)**

◆ Revent Incorporated ....E...... 732 777-5187
  Somerset **(G-10065)**

Solbern LLC ....E...... 973 227-3030
  Fairfield **(G-3312)**

Surfside Foods LLC ....G...... 856 785-2115
  Port Norris **(G-8889)**

Techno Design Inc ....G...... 973 478-0930
  Garfield **(G-3772)**

▼ Terriss Consolidated Inds ....G...... 732 988-0909
  Asbury Park **(G-84)**

TMU Inc ....F...... 609 884-7656
  Cape May **(G-1103)**

◆ Wilenta Feed Inc ....F...... 201 325-0044
  Secaucus **(G-9829)**

Willow Technology Inc ....G...... 732 671-1554
  Holmdel **(G-4515)**

▲ Wyssmont Company Inc ....E...... 201 947-4600
  Fort Lee **(G-3596)**

Zvonko Stulic & Son Inc.................G...... 973 589-3773
  Newark **(G-7319)**

3559 Special Ind Machinery, NEC

3 H Technology Institute LLC ....E...... 866 624-3484
  Mount Laurel **(G-6736)**

A S M Technical.............................G...... 973 225-0111
  Paterson **(G-8120)**

▼ Ackley Machine Corporation......E...... 856 234-3626
  Moorestown **(G-6500)**

Advance Machine Planning Inc ....F...... 732 356-4438
  Middlesex **(G-6094)**

Advance Process Systems Lim ....G...... 201 400-9190
  Branchville **(G-701)**

▲ Alaqua Inc ....F...... 201 758-1580
  Guttenberg **(G-3870)**

Allied Waste Products Inc ....G...... 973 473-7638
  Wallington **(G-11381)**

AM Cruz International LLC................G...... 732 340-0066
  Colonia **(G-1774)**

◆ Amano Cincinnati Incorporated ....D...... 973 403-1900
  Roseland **(G-9530)**

◆ Amano USA Holdings Inc ....G...... 973 403-1900
  Roseland **(G-9531)**

Amcor Phrm Packg USA LLC ....E...... 856 825-1400
  Millville **(G-6230)**

◆ American International Cont ....F...... 973 917-3331
  Boonton **(G-541)**

American Leistritz Extruder ....F...... 908 685-2333
  Branchburg **(G-616)**

Autoplast Systems Inc ....G...... 973 785-8333
  Woodland Park **(G-12070)**

Azego Technology Svcs US Inc.........G...... 201 327-7500
  Oakland **(G-7615)**

▲ Boc Group Inc .... A 908 665-2400
New Providence (G-6995)

◆ Brother International Corp .... B 908 704-1700
Bridgewater (G-808)

◆ Cain Machine Inc .... F 856 825-7225
Millville (G-6240)

▼ Carl Buck Corporation .... G 973 300-5575
Sparta (G-10381)

Clean Air Group .... G 908 232-4200
Parsippany (G-7907)

▲ Clinton Industries Inc .... E 201 440-0400
Little Ferry (G-5478)

▲ Clordisys Solutions Inc .... E 908 236-4100
Branchburg (G-629)

Comfortfit Labs Inc .... E 908 259-9100
Roselle (G-9554)

Concrete Cutting Partners Inc .... G 201 440-2233
Hackensack (G-3899)

▲ Coperion Corporation .... C 201 327-6300
Sewell (G-9835)

County Conservation Co Inc .... F 856 227-6900
Sewell (G-9837)

◆ Cryovation LLC .... G 609 914-4792
Hainesport (G-4071)

▲ Dantco Corp .... F 973 278-8776
Paterson (G-8168)

Dayton Grey Corp .... F 732 869-0060
Asbury Park (G-75)

Deitz Co Inc .... F 732 295-8212
Belmar (G-348)

Eagle Racing Inc .... G 732 367-8487
Lakewood (G-5088)

▼ Eco-Plug-System LLC .... G 855 326-7584
Hewitt (G-4275)

Energy Recycling Co LLC .... G 732 545-6619
New Brunswick (G-6924)

◆ Exim Incorporated .... G 908 561-8200
Piscataway (G-8664)

Expert Process Systems LLC .... G 570 424-0581
Hackettstown (G-4007)

F P Developments Inc .... E 856 875-7100
Williamstown (G-11957)

▲ Fette Compacting America Inc ..... E 973 586-8722
Rockaway (G-9459)

◆ Foremost Machine Builders Inc .... D 973 227-0700
Fairfield (G-3206)

◆ Franklin Miller Inc .... E 973 535-9200
Livingston (G-5512)

G & S Design & Manufacturing ...... F 908 862-2444
Linden (G-5349)

Glass Cycle Systems Inc .... G 973 838-0034
Riverdale (G-9378)

◆ Globepharma Inc .... F 732 296-9700
New Brunswick (G-6930)

▲ Gluefast Company Inc .... F 732 918-4600
Neptune (G-6881)

Grease N Go .... G 856 784-6555
Magnolia (G-5707)

Green Power Chemical LLC .... F 973 770-5600
Hopatcong (G-4520)

Henry Dudley .... G 732 240-6895
Toms River (G-10764)

◆ Hockmeyer Equipment Corp .... D 973 482-0225
Harrison (G-4176)

Hosokawa Micron International ...... D 908 273-6360
Summit (G-10535)

Hosokawa Micron International ...... D 908 273-6360
Summit (G-10536)

Hosokawa Micron International ...... F 866 507-4974
Pennsauken (G-8432)

◆ Hosokawa Micron Intl Inc .... D 908 273-6360
Summit (G-10537)

▲ Htp Connectivity LLC .... G 973 586-2286
Rockaway (G-9465)

◆ Hugo Neu Corporation .... F 646 467-6700
Kearny (G-4865)

▲ Ileos of America Inc .... C 908 753-7300
South Plainfield (G-10276)

Imperial Sewing Machine Co .... G 973 374-3405
Irvington (G-4574)

Imwoth LLC .... F 732 244-0950
Toms River (G-10769)

Indoor Entertainment of NJ .... E 609 522-6700
Wildwood (G-11945)

Inter Rep Associates Inc .... G 609 465-0077
Cape May Court House (G-1111)

Jason Equipment Corp .... E 973 983-7212
Rockaway (G-9471)

◆ Jaygo Incorporated .... G 908 688-3600
Randolph (G-9187)

▲ Jet Pulverizer Co Inc .... E 856 235-5554
Moorestown (G-6531)

John N Fehlinger Co Inc .... G 973 633-0699
Fairfield (G-3246)

John W Kennedy Company .... G 973 256-5525
Little Falls (G-5457)

▲ Jomar Corp .... E 609 646-8000
Egg Harbor Township (G-2686)

Jrz Enterprises LLC .... G 973 962-6330
Wayne (G-11526)

Kahle Automation .... G 973 993-1850
Morristown (G-6676)

▲ Kansai Special Amercn Mch Corp .. G 973 470-8321
East Rutherford (G-2293)

◆ Koch Mdlar Process Systems LLC .. D 201 368-2929
Paramus (G-7814)

▲ Kooltronic Inc .... C 609 466-3400
Pennington (G-8369)

Kyosis LLC .... G 908 202-8894
South River (G-10351)

Linde North America Inc .... D 908 464-8100
New Providence (G-7007)

Lmt Usa Inc .... G 973 586-8722
Rockaway (G-9475)

◆ Logan Instruments Corporation ..... F 732 302-9888
Somerset (G-10017)

M C Technologies Inc .... E 973 839-2779
Pompton Plains (G-8866)

▲ Manning & Lewis Engrg Co Inc ..... D 908 687-2400
Union (G-11073)

Mastercraft Electroplating .... G 908 354-4404
Elizabeth (G-2756)

◆ Messer North America Inc .... B 908 464-8100
Bridgewater (G-851)

Metal Finishing Co LLC .... G 973 778-9550
Passaic (G-8089)

Miracle Mile Automotive Inc .... G 732 886-6315
Lakewood (G-5136)

◆ N C Carpet Binding & Equipment ... F 973 481-3500
Newark (G-7207)

▲ Nicos Group Inc .... G 201 768-9501
Norwood (G-7571)

▲ Park Plus Inc .... G 201 651-8590
Oakland (G-7641)

Pharma Systems Inc .... G 973 636-9007
Hawthorne (G-4239)

▲ Ramco Equipment Corp .... E 908 687-6700
Hillside (G-4423)

◆ Recycle-Tech Corp .... E 201 475-5000
Elmwood Park (G-2853)

◆ Reliable Welding & Mch Work ...... E 201 865-1073
North Bergen (G-7432)

Ridge Manufacturing Corp .... D 973 586-2717
Rockaway (G-9494)

Safegaurd Document Destruction .... G 609 448-6695
Millstone Township (G-6212)

Safety-Kleen Systems Inc .... F 609 859-2049
Southampton (G-10371)

Science Pump Corporation .... E 856 963-7700
Camden (G-1086)

Seajay Manufacturing Corp .... F 732 774-0900
Neptune (G-6897)

Sony Corporation of America .... F 201 930-1000
Woodcliff Lake (G-12065)

▲ Spadix Technologies Inc .... G 732 356-6906
Middlesex (G-6150)

Starlight Electro-Optics Inc .... E 908 859-1362
Phillipsburg (G-8575)

Suez Treatment Solutions Inc .... E 201 676-2525
Leonia (G-5292)

Thanks For Being Green LLC .... E 856 333-0991
Pennsauken (G-8491)

Thompson Stone .... G 973 293-7237
Montague (G-6355)

Tilton Rack & Basket Co .... E 973 226-6010
Fairfield (G-3328)

Veeco .... E 732 560-5300
Somerset (G-10092)

Veeco Instruments Inc .... E 732 560-5300
Somerset (G-10093)

Vibra Screw Inc .... E 973 256-7410
Totowa (G-10858)

Victor International Marketing .... E 973 267-8900
Morristown (G-6707)

▲ Witte Co Inc .... E 908 689-6500
Washington (G-11454)

▲ Wyssmont Company Inc .... E 201 947-4600
Fort Lee (G-3596)

3561 Pumps & Pumping Eqpt

▲ Apple Air Compressor Corp .... F 888 222-9940
Rutherford (G-9613)

◆ Bio Compression Systems Inc ...... E 201 939-0716
Moonachie (G-6457)

▲ Boc Group Inc .... A 908 665-2400
New Providence (G-6995)

C & L Machining Company Inc .... G 856 456-1932
Brooklawn (G-914)

Callaghan Pump Controls Inc .... G 201 621-0505
Hackensack (G-3893)

Carter Pump Inc .... E 201 568-9798
Waldwick (G-11298)

Cooper Alloy Corporation .... F 908 688-4120
Hillside (G-4387)

Davis-Standard LLC .... E 908 722-6000
Somerset (G-9981)

Delta Sales Company Inc .... F 973 838-0371
Butler (G-999)

Dynaflow Engineering Inc .... G 732 356-9790
Middlesex (G-6114)

E Wortmann Machine Works Inc ..... F 201 288-1654
Teterboro (G-10672)

Energy Beams Inc .... F 973 291-6555
Bloomingdale (G-528)

Evey Vacuum Service .... G 856 692-4779
Vineland (G-11217)

Flowserve Corporation .... C 908 859-7000
Phillipsburg (G-8551)

Flowserve Corporation .... D 856 241-7800
Bridgeport (G-739)

Flowserve Corporation .... G 973 334-9444
Parsippany (G-7947)

Flowserve Corporation .... D 973 227-4565
Fairfield (G-3204)

◆ Hayward Industries Inc .... B 908 351-5400
Elizabeth (G-2746)

Hhh Machine Co .... G 908 276-1220
Cranford (G-1913)

Ingersoll-Rand Company .... E 856 793-7000
Mount Laurel (G-6766)

Interntional Cnsld Chemex Corp ..... E 732 828-7676
New Brunswick (G-6936)

Kraissl Company Inc .... E 201 342-0008
Hackensack (G-3937)

▲ Leistritz Advanced Tech Corp ...... E 201 934-8262
Allendale (G-11)

Linde North America Inc .... D 908 464-8100
New Providence (G-7007)

Magnatrol Valve Corporation .... F 856 829-4580
Roebling (G-9526)

Melville Industries Inc .... G 856 461-0091
Riverside (G-9400)

◆ Messer LLC .... C 908 464-8100
Bridgewater (G-849)

Messer LLC .... G 973 579-2065
Sparta (G-10398)

◆ Messer North America Inc .... B 908 464-8100
Bridgewater (G-851)

▲ Orion Machinery Co Ltd .... E 201 569-3220
Rutherford (G-9630)

Science Pump Corporation .... E 856 963-7700
Camden (G-1086)

Shoreway Industry .... G 856 307-2020
Clayton (G-1529)

▲ Valcor Engineering Corporation .... C 973 467-8400
Springfield (G-10472)

Valley Tech Inc .... G 908 534-5565
Whitehouse Station (G-11936)

▲ Vanton Pump & Equipment Corp ... E 908 688-4120
Hillside (G-4436)

◆ Xylem Dewatering Solutions Inc .... C 856 467-3636
Bridgeport (G-748)

3562 Ball & Roller Bearings

▲ Accurate Bushing Company Inc ..... E 908 789-1121
Garwood (G-3779)

C & L Machining Company Inc .... G 856 456-1932
Brooklawn (G-914)

Emmco Development Corp .... F 732 469-6464
Somerset (G-9985)

Federal Casters Corp .... D 973 483-6700
Harrison (G-4173)

General Dynamics Mission .... E 973 335-2230
Parsippany (G-7954)

Ingersoll-Rand Company .... E 856 793-7000
Mount Laurel (G-6766)

J C W Inc .... E 732 560-8061
Bridgewater (G-838)

Rbc Bearings Incorporated .... F 843 332-2691
   Ewing *(G-3058)*
▲ Rollon Corporation .... E 973 300-5492
   Hackettstown *(G-4032)*

3563 Air & Gas Compressors

Aavolyn Corp .... E 856 327-8040
   Millville *(G-6221)*
Aer X Dust Corporation .... G 732 946-9462
   Holmdel *(G-4493)*
Argus International Inc .... E 609 466-1677
   Ringoes *(G-9334)*
▲ Armco Compressor Products .... G 201 866-6766
   North Bergen *(G-7386)*
◆ Atlas Copco Hurricane LLC .... D 800 754-7408
   Parsippany *(G-7887)*
▲ Breeze-Eastern LLC .... G 973 602-1001
   Whippany *(G-11883)*
Busch LLC .... G 908 561-3233
   South Plainfield *(G-10229)*
Campbell Hausfeld LLC .... C 856 661-1800
   Pennsauken *(G-8399)*
◆ Croll-Reynolds Co Inc .... E 908 232-4200
   Parsippany *(G-7909)*
Eagletre-Pump Acquisition Corp ...... D 201 569-1173
   Rutherford *(G-9618)*
◆ Emse Corp .... F 973 227-9221
   Fairfield *(G-3191)*
Energy Beams Inc .... F 973 291-6555
   Bloomingdale *(G-528)*
▲ Falcon Safety Products Inc .... D 908 707-4900
   Branchburg *(G-639)*
Fleet Equipment Corporation .... F 201 337-3294
   Franklin Lakes *(G-3623)*
Gas Drying Inc .... F 973 361-2212
   Wharton *(G-11859)*
Ingersoll-Rand Company .... E 856 793-7000
   Mount Laurel *(G-6766)*
Jetstream of Houston LLP .... G 732 448-7830
   New Brunswick *(G-6938)*
Knf Neuberger Inc .... D 609 890-8889
   Trenton *(G-10950)*
Kraissl Company Inc .... G 201 342-0008
   Hackensack *(G-3937)*
▲ Metropolitan Vacuum Clr Co Inc ...... D 201 405-2225
   Oakland *(G-7636)*
▲ Orion Machinery Co Ltd .... E 201 569-3220
   Rutherford *(G-9630)*
Polvac Inc .... G 732 828-1662
   New Brunswick *(G-6959)*
▲ Trillium US .... G 973 827-1661
   Hamburg *(G-4096)*
▲ United Vacuum LLC .... F 973 827-1661
   Hamburg *(G-4097)*
◆ Vac-U-Max .... E 973 759-4600
   Belleville *(G-319)*
Vairtec Corporation .... G 201 445-6965
   Midland Park *(G-6189)*

3564 Blowers & Fans

Aer X Dust Corporation .... G 732 946-9462
   Holmdel *(G-4493)*
Air Clean Co Inc .... E 908 355-1515
   Elizabeth *(G-2708)*
Automated Flexible Conveyors .... F 973 340-1695
   Clifton *(G-1568)*
Bioclimatic Air Systems LLC .... E 856 764-4300
   Delran *(G-2010)*
Bioclimatic Inc .... E 856 764-4300
   Delran *(G-2011)*
Bionomic Industries Inc .... F 201 529-1094
   Mahwah *(G-5717)*
Bios International Corp .... E 973 492-8400
   Butler *(G-996)*
Brookaire Company LLC .... F 973 473-7527
   Carlstadt *(G-1132)*
Buhler Inc .... E 201 847-0600
   Mahwah *(G-5719)*
Building Performance Eqp Inc .... F 201 722-1414
   Hillsdale *(G-4364)*
◆ Camfil Usa Inc .... C 973 616-7300
   Riverdale *(G-9372)*
Cleanzones LLC .... F 732 534-5590
   Jackson *(G-4644)*
Creative Industrial Kitchens .... G 973 633-0420
   Wayne *(G-11490)*
◆ Croll-Reynolds Co Inc .... E 908 232-4200
   Parsippany *(G-7909)*
Cross Rip Ocean Engrg LLC .... G 973 455-0005
   Parsippany *(G-7911)*

CSM Environmental Systems LLC ...... F 908 789-5431
   Mountainside *(G-6838)*
▲ CSM Worldwide Inc .... E 908 233-2882
   Bridgewater *(G-815)*
▲ Csonka Worldwide .... E 609 514-2766
   Plainsboro *(G-8783)*
DR Technology Inc .... G 732 780-4664
   Freehold *(G-3661)*
Encur Inc .... G 732 264-2098
   Keyport *(G-4998)*
Envirnmntal Dynamics Group Inc ...... F 609 924-4489
   Rocky Hill *(G-9525)*
Filter Holdings Inc .... E 908 687-3500
   Union *(G-11054)*
Fmdk Technologies Inc .... E 201 828-9822
   Mahwah *(G-5740)*
Gpt Inc .... F 732 446-2400
   Manalapan *(G-5812)*
◆ Hamon Corporation .... D 908 333-2000
   Somerville *(G-10114)*
▲ Handler Manufacturing Company ...... E 908 233-7796
   Westfield *(G-11799)*
◆ Hayward Industrial Products .... C 908 351-5400
   Elizabeth *(G-2745)*
Indoor Environmental Tech .... E 973 709-1122
   Lincoln Park *(G-5299)*
◆ JC Macelroy Co Inc .... E 732 572-7100
   Piscataway *(G-8681)*
Klm Mechanical Contractors .... F 201 385-6965
   Dumont *(G-2115)*
▲ Kooltronic Inc .... C 609 466-3400
   Pennington *(G-8369)*
Lm Air Technology Inc .... E 732 381-8200
   Rahway *(G-9115)*
Mer Made Filter .... G 201 236-0217
   Ramsey *(G-9151)*
▲ Metropolitan Vacuum Clr Co Inc ...... D 201 405-2225
   Oakland *(G-7636)*
▲ Microelettrica-Usa LLC .... E 973 598-0806
   Budd Lake *(G-930)*
Naava Inc .... G 844 666-2282
   Hazlet *(G-4266)*
Palude Enterprises Inc .... G 732 241-5478
   Howell *(G-4548)*
Respironics Inc .... E 973 581-6000
   Parsippany *(G-8007)*
Safety Power Inc .... G 908 277-1826
   Summit *(G-10544)*
Science Pump Corporation .... E 856 963-7700
   Camden *(G-1086)*
Stamm International Corp .... G 201 947-1700
   Fort Lee *(G-3589)*
Sternvent Co Inc .... E 908 688-0807
   Union *(G-11092)*
Tri-Dim Filter Corporation .... F 856 786-2447
   Cinnaminson *(G-1493)*
Tri-Dim Filter Corporation .... F 973 709-1122
   Lincoln Park *(G-5308)*
▲ Wire Cloth Manufacturers Inc ...... E 973 328-1000
   Mine Hill *(G-6275)*

3565 Packaging Machinery

▲ Action Packaging Automation .... G 609 448-9210
   Roosevelt *(G-9527)*
Ajg Packaging LLC .... G 908 528-6052
   Pittstown *(G-8751)*
Alliance Food Equipment .... F 201 784-1101
   Trenton *(G-10891)*
AT Information Products Inc .... G 201 529-0202
   Mahwah *(G-5715)*
Banarez Enterprises Inc .... G 201 222-7515
   Jersey City *(G-4698)*
▲ Beauty-Fill LLC .... E 908 353-1600
   Hillside *(G-4381)*
▲ Campak Inc .... G 973 994-4888
   Livingston *(G-5508)*
◆ Clements Industries Inc .... E 201 440-5500
   South Hackensack *(G-10153)*
Copack International Inc .... G 973 405-5151
   Clifton *(G-1590)*
▲ Cozzoli Machine Company .... D 732 564-0400
   Somerset *(G-9978)*
Dalemark Industries Inc .... F 732 367-3100
   Lakewood *(G-5081)*
Deitz Co Inc .... F 732 295-8212
   Belmar *(G-348)*
▲ Elite Packaging Corp .... F 732 651-9955
   East Brunswick *(G-2140)*
F P Developments Inc .... E 856 875-7100
   Williamstown *(G-11957)*

Ganz Brothers Inc .... F 201 820-1975
   Paramus *(G-7801)*
Gloucester City Box Works LLC ...... F 856 456-9032
   Gloucester City *(G-3842)*
▲ Gram Equipment .... E 201 750-6500
   Hamilton *(G-4106)*
Greener Corp .... E 732 341-3880
   Bayville *(G-245)*
Groniger USA LLC .... G 704 588-3873
   Basking Ridge *(G-185)*
▲ Hair Systems Inc .... D 732 446-2202
   Englishtown *(G-3004)*
◆ Heisler Machine & Tool Co .... E 973 227-6300
   Fairfield *(G-3226)*
Herma US Inc .... E 973 521-7254
   Fairfield *(G-3227)*
▼ I S Parts International Inc .... E 856 691-2203
   Vineland *(G-11234)*
ID Technology LLC .... E 201 405-0767
   Oakland *(G-7632)*
J F C Machine Works LLC .... F 732 203-2077
   Holmdel *(G-4503)*
J G Machine Works Inc .... G 732 203-2077
   Edison *(G-2536)*
▲ K & S Industries Inc .... E 908 862-3030
   Linden *(G-5368)*
Kohl & Madden Prtg Ink Corp .... E 201 935-8666
   Carlstadt *(G-1177)*
▲ Kompac Technologies LLC .... E 908 534-8411
   Somerville *(G-10120)*
Labeling Systems LLC .... E 201 405-0767
   Oakland *(G-7634)*
Luciano Packaging Tech Inc .... G 908 722-3222
   Branchburg *(G-657)*
Mactec Packaging Tech LLC .... G 732 343-1607
   Sayreville *(G-9718)*
▲ Njrls Enterprises Inc .... F 732 846-6010
   Branchburg *(G-661)*
Norden Inc .... G 908 252-9483
   Branchburg *(G-662)*
Pabin Associates Inc .... G 201 288-7216
   Hasbrouck Heights *(G-4187)*
◆ Pace Packaging LLC .... D 973 227-1040
   Fairfield *(G-3287)*
Packaging Machinery & Eqp Co ...... G 973 325-2418
   West Orange *(G-11776)*
◆ Per-Fil Industries Inc .... E 856 461-5700
   Riverside *(G-9401)*
PMC Industries Inc .... E 201 342-3684
   Hackensack *(G-3964)*
Potdevin Machine Co .... F 973 227-8828
   West Caldwell *(G-11673)*
▲ Pro Pack Inc .... F 973 665-8333
   Wharton *(G-11868)*
▲ Pro-Motion Industries LLC .... F 856 809-0040
   Sicklerville *(G-9914)*
▲ Pro-Pac Service Inc .... F 973 962-8080
   Ringwood *(G-9350)*
Prodo-Pak Corp .... G 973 772-4500
   Garfield *(G-3760)*
▲ Prodo-Pak Corporation .... E 973 777-7770
   Garfield *(G-3761)*
Quality Carton Inc .... G 201 529-6900
   Mahwah *(G-5765)*
▲ Romaco Inc .... E 973 709-0691
   Lincoln Park *(G-5305)*
▲ Scandia Packaging Machinery Co ...... E 973 473-6100
   Mahwah *(G-5770)*
Signode Industrial Group LLC .... D 201 741-2791
   Newark *(G-7272)*
Sjd Direct Midwest LLC .... C 732 985-8405
   Edison *(G-2612)*
Sjd Direct Midwest LLC .... C 732 287-2525
   Edison *(G-2613)*
Specialty Tube Filling LLC .... G 908 262-2219
   Hillsborough *(G-4355)*
▲ Supplyone New York Inc .... E 718 392-7400
   Paterson *(G-8309)*
Techline Extrusion Systems .... G 973 831-0317
   Haskell *(G-4203)*
Vacuum Solutions Group Inc .... G 781 762-0414
   Teaneck *(G-10654)*
▼ Wagner Industries Inc .... F 973 347-0800
   Stanhope *(G-10481)*
◆ Weiler Labeling Systems LLC .... D 856 273-3377
   Moorestown *(G-6577)*
Wrap-Ade Machine Co Inc .... F 973 773-6150
   Clifton *(G-1740)*
▲ Wrapade Packaging Systems LLC ...... F 973 787-1788
   Fairfield *(G-3355)*

SIC

3566 Speed Changers, Drives & Gears

431 Converters Inc ....G....... 856 848-8949
Woodbury Heights (G-12040)
Able Gear & Machine Co ....G....... 973 983-8055
Rockaway (G-9434)
▲ Acme Gear Co Inc ....D....... 201 568-2245
Englewood (G-2874)
Drive Technology Inc ....G....... 732 422-6500
Monmouth Junction (G-6289)
Gears IV LLC ....G....... 201 401-3035
Bridgewater (G-826)
Jetyd Corporation ....F....... 201 512-9500
Mahwah (G-5750)
▲ Koellmann Gear Corporation ....C....... 201 447-0200
Waldwick (G-11303)
Martin Sprocket & Gear Inc ....F....... 973 633-5700
Wayne (G-11534)
Numeritool Manufacturing Corp ....G....... 973 827-7714
Franklin (G-3607)
Sew-Eurodrive Inc ....E....... 856 467-2277
Bridgeport (G-744)
Sew-Eurodrive Inc ....D....... 856 467-2277
Bridgeport (G-745)
State Tool Gear Co Inc ....F....... 973 642-6181
Newark (G-7286)
◆ Walter Machine Co Inc ....E....... 201 656-5654
Jersey City (G-4829)

3567 Indl Process Furnaces & Ovens

Abp Induction LLC ....F....... 732 932-6400
North Brunswick (G-7448)
Albapalant USA Inc ....G....... 201 831-9200
Boonton (G-539)
Argus International Inc ....E....... 609 466-1677
Ringoes (G-9334)
◆ C M Furnaces Inc ....E....... 973 338-6500
Bloomfield (G-493)
Cire Technologies Inc ....G....... 973 402-8301
Mountain Lakes (G-6821)
◆ Consarc Corporation ....E....... 609 267-8000
Rancocas (G-9159)
Corbett Industries Inc ....F....... 201 445-6311
Waldwick (G-11299)
Curran-Pfeiff Corp ....F....... 732 225-0555
Edison (G-2489)
▲ Electroheat Induction Inc ....G....... 908 494-0726
Jersey City (G-4731)
▲ Elnik Systems LLC ....E....... 973 239-6066
Cedar Grove (G-1277)
Energy Beams Inc ....F....... 973 291-6555
Bloomingdale (G-528)
Essex Products International ....E....... 973 226-2424
Caldwell (G-1024)
Gia-Tek LLC ....G....... 973 228-0875
West Caldwell (G-11652)
◆ Glenro Inc ....F....... 973 279-5900
Paterson (G-8199)
Hankin Acquisitions Inc ....F....... 908 722-9595
Hillsborough (G-4321)
Hankin Envmtl Systems Inc ....F....... 908 722-9595
Hillsborough (G-4322)
Hary Manufacturing Inc ....F....... 908 722-7100
Woodbridge (G-12018)
▲ Haydon Corporation ....D....... 973 904-0800
Wayne (G-11515)
Hed International Inc ....F....... 609 466-1900
Ringoes (G-9336)
◆ Inductotherm Corp ....C....... 609 267-9000
Rancocas (G-9161)
▲ L & L Kiln Mfg Inc ....E....... 856 294-0077
Swedesboro (G-10593)
Lydon Bros Corp ....E....... 201 343-4334
South Hackensack (G-10169)
Marsden Inc ....E....... 856 663-2227
Pennsauken (G-8452)
Pennington Furnace Supply Inc ....G....... 609 737-2500
Pennington (G-8371)
Procedyne Corp ....E....... 732 249-8347
New Brunswick (G-6962)
Pv/T Inc ....G....... 609 267-3933
Rancocas (G-9164)
▲ Radiant Energy Systems Inc ....E....... 973 423-5220
Hawthorne (G-4241)
Radiation Systems Inc ....G....... 201 891-7515
Wyckoff (G-12118)
◆ Rowan Technologies Inc ....D....... 609 267-9000
Rancocas (G-9165)
Saber Associates ....E....... 973 777-3800
Clifton (G-1708)

▲ Solar Products Inc ....E....... 973 248-9370
Pompton Lakes (G-8852)
▼ T-M Vacuum Products Inc ....E....... 856 829-2000
Cinnaminson (G-1487)
Therma-Tech Corporation ....F....... 973 345-0076
Paterson (G-8315)
Thermal Conduction Engineering ....G....... 201 865-1084
Secaucus (G-9820)
Waage Electric Inc ....G....... 908 245-9363
Kenilworth (G-4986)
▲ Wyssmont Company Inc ....E....... 201 947-4600
Fort Lee (G-3596)

3568 Mechanical Power Transmission Eqpt, NEC

A M Gatti Inc ....F....... 609 396-1577
Trenton (G-10886)
Accurate Bronze Bearing Co ....G....... 973 345-2304
Paterson (G-8124)
▲ Accurate Bushing Company Inc ....E....... 908 789-1121
Garwood (G-3779)
Amscot Structural Pdts Corp ....E....... 973 989-9800
Dover (G-2074)
▲ Andantex U S A Inc ....G....... 732 493-2812
Ocean (G-7655)
▲ Bcc (USA) Inc ....G....... 732 572-5450
Piscataway (G-8639)
Brilliant Light Power Inc ....E....... 609 490-0427
East Windsor (G-2365)
Daven Industries Inc ....G....... 973 808-8848
Fairfield (G-3180)
Emmco Development Corp ....F....... 732 469-6464
Somerset (G-9985)
▲ Gate Technologies Inc ....G....... 973 300-0090
Sparta (G-10388)
▲ Ggb LLC ....C....... 856 848-3200
Thorofare (G-10700)
Ggb LLC ....G....... 856 848-3200
Thorofare (G-10701)
Ggb LLC ....G....... 856 686-2675
Thorofare (G-10702)
▲ Hydro-Mechanical Systems Inc ....F....... 856 848-8888
Westville (G-11816)
Martin Sprocket & Gear Inc ....F....... 973 633-5700
Wayne (G-11534)
Moser Jewel Company ....G....... 908 454-1155
Phillipsburg (G-8564)
▲ Reich USA Corporation ....F....... 201 684-9400
Mahwah (G-5767)
Spadone Alfa Self Lbrcted Pdts ....G....... 203 972-8848
Brick (G-732)
Valcor Engineering Corporation ....E....... 973 467-8100
Springfield (G-10473)
Woyshner Service Company Inc ....G....... 856 461-9196
Delran (G-2022)

3569 Indl Machinery & Eqpt, NEC

Absolute Protective Systems ....E....... 732 287-4500
Piscataway (G-8624)
Admiral Filter Company LLC ....F....... 973 664-0400
Rockaway (G-9436)
▲ Adsorptech Inc ....G....... 732 356-1000
Middlesex (G-6092)
◆ Amec Fster Wheeler N Amer Corp ....D....... 936 448-6323
Hampton (G-4147)
▼ Amerilubes LLC ....G....... 704 399-7701
Waretown (G-11392)
◆ Boc Group Inc ....A....... 908 665-2400
New Providence (G-6995)
◆ Camfil Usa Inc ....C....... 973 616-7300
Riverdale (G-9372)
Carol Products Co Inc ....G....... 732 918-0800
Ocean (G-7658)
Celestech Inc ....G....... 856 986-2221
Haddonfield (G-4054)
▲ Clayton Associates Inc ....F....... 732 363-2100
Lakewood (G-5071)
Clayton Manufacturing Company ....F....... 609 409-9400
Cranbury (G-1824)
Coilhose Pneumatics Inc ....G....... 732 432-7177
East Brunswick (G-2133)
Complete Filter ....G....... 732 441-0321
South Amboy (G-10132)
Confires Fire Prtction Svc LLC ....F....... 908 822-2700
South Plainfield (G-10241)
Devco Corporation ....G....... 201 337-1600
Basking Ridge (G-181)
Eagle Fire & Safety Corp ....G....... 732 982-7388
Wall Township (G-11335)

▲ Eaton Filtration LLC ....B....... 732 767-4200
Tinton Falls (G-10714)
▲ Enviro-Clear Company Inc ....F....... 908 638-5507
High Bridge (G-4282)
Eurodia Industrie SA ....G....... 732 805-4001
Somerset (G-9990)
◆ Exim Incorporated ....G....... 908 561-8200
Piscataway (G-8664)
Filter Holdings Inc ....E....... 908 687-3500
Union (G-11054)
Foster Wheeler Zack Inc ....D....... 908 730-4000
Hampton (G-4153)
◆ Hayward Industries Inc ....B....... 908 351-5400
Elizabeth (G-2746)
◆ Hayward Pool Products Inc ....A....... 908 351-5400
Elizabeth (G-2748)
▲ Heinkel Filtering Systems Inc ....F....... 856 467-3399
Swedesboro (G-10588)
▲ Heller Industries Inc ....D....... 973 377-6800
Florham Park (G-3509)
▲ I & J Fisnar Inc ....F....... 973 646-5044
Pine Brook (G-8603)
Industrial Filters Company ....G....... 973 575-0533
Fairfield (G-3237)
Intech Powercore Corporation ....G....... 201 767-8066
Closter (G-1758)
▲ Integrated Packg Systems Inc ....G....... 973 664-0020
Denville (G-2040)
◆ Kason Corporation ....D....... 973 467-8140
Millburn (G-6201)
▼ Kavon Filter Products Co ....F....... 732 938-3135
Wall Township (G-11351)
Life Liners Inc ....G....... 973 635-9234
Chatham (G-1326)
Linde North America Inc ....D....... 908 464-8100
New Providence (G-7007)
Liquid-Solids Separation Corp ....E....... 201 236-4833
Ramsey (G-9149)
Madison Park Volunteer Fire Co ....E....... 732 727-1143
Parlin (G-7868)
Membranes International Inc ....G....... 973 998-5530
Ringwood (G-9348)
◆ Messer LLC ....C....... 908 464-8100
Bridgewater (G-849)
Messer LLC ....G....... 973 579-2065
Sparta (G-10398)
◆ Messer North America Inc ....B....... 908 464-8100
Bridgewater (G-851)
Microdysis Inc ....G....... 609 642-1184
Bordentown (G-589)
▲ Newton Tool & Mfg Inc ....D....... 856 241-1500
Pennsauken (G-8461)
▲ Nichem Co ....G....... 973 399-9810
Newark (G-7218)
NJ Service Testing & Insptn ....G....... 732 221-6357
Lincroft (G-5313)
▲ Palmer Electronics Inc ....F....... 973 772-5900
Garfield (G-3752)
Pulsonics Inc ....F....... 800 999-6785
Belleville (G-309)
◆ Smartpool LLC ....E....... 732 730-9880
Lakewood (G-5164)
◆ Specified Technologies Inc ....C....... 908 526-8000
Branchburg (G-684)
▲ Stauff Corporation ....E....... 201 444-7800
Waldwick (G-11309)
▲ Steamist Inc ....E....... 201 933-0700
East Rutherford (G-2320)
T M Industries Inc ....G....... 908 730-7674
Belvidere (G-367)
Teneyck Inc ....D....... 201 939-1100
Lyndhurst (G-5681)
Township of Carneys Point ....F....... 856 299-4973
Carneys Point (G-1244)
▲ Universal Filters Inc ....E....... 732 774-8555
Asbury Park (G-85)
Wab US Corp ....G....... 973 873-9155
Allendale (G-19)

3571 Electronic Computers

▲ Aaeon Electronics Inc ....E....... 732 203-9300
Hazlet (G-4254)
Aicumen Technologies Inc ....G....... 732 668-4204
Princeton (G-8903)
Andlogic Computers ....G....... 609 610-5752
Hamilton (G-4102)
Asi Computer Technologies Inc ....F....... 732 343-7100
Edison (G-2462)
▲ B2x Corporation ....G....... 201 714-2373
Jersey City (G-4697)

▲ **Carpenter LLC** ....F 609 689-3090
Trenton *(G-10911)*
◆ **Crestron Electronics Inc** ....C 201 767-3400
Rockleigh *(G-9516)*
▲ **Datapro International Inc** ....E 732 868-0588
Piscataway *(G-8652)*
▲ **DFI America LLC** ....E 732 562-0693
Piscataway *(G-8655)*
Dxl Enterprises Inc ....F 201 891-8718
Mahwah *(G-5733)*
Eom Worldwide Sales Corp ....G 732 994-7352
Lakewood *(G-5091)*
Esaw Industries Inc ....G 732 613-1400
East Brunswick *(G-2144)*
Fillimerica Inc ....G 800 435-7257
Montville *(G-6442)*
Five Elements Robotics LLC ....G 800 681-8514
Wall Township *(G-11340)*
◆ **Franklin Electronic Publs Inc** ....D 609 386-2500
Burlington *(G-969)*
Global Business Dimensions Inc ....E 973 831-5866
Pompton Plains *(G-8865)*
▲ **Hitechone Inc** ....G 201 500-8864
Englewood Cliffs *(G-2975)*
Ideal Data Inc ....F 201 998-9440
North Arlington *(G-7374)*
La Duca Technical Services LLC ....G 570 309-4009
West Milford *(G-11728)*
Lavitsky Computer Laboratories ....G 908 725-6206
Bridgewater *(G-840)*
Maingear Inc ....E 888 624-6432
Kenilworth *(G-4955)*
Mikros Systems Corporation ....G 609 987-1513
Princeton *(G-8978)*
Niksun Inc ....C 609 936-9999
Princeton *(G-8985)*
▼ **Novasom Industries Inc** ....G 732 994-5652
Lakewood *(G-5142)*
Oti America Inc ....G 732 429-1900
Iselin *(G-4621)*
Pascack Data Services Inc ....F 973 304-4858
Hawthorne *(G-4236)*
▲ **Pcs Revenue Ctrl Systems Inc** ....E 201 568-8300
Englewood Cliffs *(G-2987)*
▲ **Planitroi Inc** ....D 973 664-0700
Denville *(G-2049)*
Princeton Identity Inc ....E 609 256-6994
Hamilton *(G-4122)*
▲ **Reliance Electronics Inc** ....E 973 237-0400
Totowa *(G-10849)*
Rt Com USA Inc ....G 973 862-4210
Lafayette *(G-5032)*
S G A Business Systems Inc ....G 908 359-4626
Hillsborough *(G-4353)*
Spacetouch Inc ....G 609 712-6572
Princeton *(G-9027)*
Strahan Consulting Group LLC ....G 908 790-0873
Scotch Plains *(G-9742)*
Technical Advantage Inc ....G 973 402-5500
Boonton *(G-570)*
Techno City Inc ....G 862 414-3282
East Rutherford *(G-2323)*
▲ **Touch Dynamic Inc** ....D 732 382-5701
South Plainfield *(G-10331)*
Xceedium Inc ....D 201 536-1000
Jersey City *(G-4834)*

3572 Computer Storage Devices

150 Development Group LLC ....G 732 546-3812
Middlesex *(G-6089)*
Aurora Research Company Inc ....G 973 827-8055
Franklin *(G-3599)*
B-Hive Ltd Liability Company ....G 302 438-2769
Hightstown *(G-4294)*
Blueclone Networks LLC ....G 609 944-8433
Princeton *(G-8917)*
Creative Cmpt Concepts LLC ....G 877 919-7988
Williamstown *(G-11956)*
Dataram Memory ....E 609 799-0071
Princeton *(G-8929)*
Eclearview Technologies Inc ....G 732 695-6999
Ocean *(G-7662)*
EMC Corporation ....D 732 922-6353
Ocean *(G-7663)*
EMC Corporation ....F 908 226-0100
South Plainfield *(G-10249)*
EMC Corporation ....A 732 549-8500
East Brunswick *(G-2142)*
EMC Paving LLC ....G 908 636-1054
Piscataway *(G-8661)*
EMC Squared LLC ....G 973 586-8854
Rockaway *(G-9455)*
Gaw Associates Inc ....F 856 608-1428
Cherry Hill *(G-1367)*
Micronet Enertec Tech Inc ....D 201 225-0190
Montvale *(G-6420)*
▲ **Ner Data Products Inc** ....E 888 637-3282
Glassboro *(G-3817)*
Pascack Data Services Inc ....F 973 304-4858
Hawthorne *(G-4236)*
▲ **Plastic Reel Corp of America** ....E 201 933-5100
Carlstadt *(G-1202)*
Quantum Integrators Group LLC ....D 609 632-0621
Plainsboro *(G-8800)*
Sony Corporation of America ....B 201 930-1000
Paramus *(G-7834)*
Veeco Instruments Inc ....E 732 560-5300
Somerset *(G-10093)*
Western Digital Corporation ....G 609 734-7479
Princeton *(G-9042)*
Whiptail Technologies LLC ....D 973 585-6375
Whippany *(G-11914)*

3575 Computer Terminals

▲ **American Gaming & Elec Inc** ....E 609 704-3000
Hammonton *(G-4127)*
Computer Company North America ....F 909 265-3390
Bedminster *(G-262)*
Information Technolgy Corp ....G 201 556-1999
Paramus *(G-7807)*
▲ **Linden Group Corporation** ....F 973 983-8809
Cedar Knolls *(G-1308)*
Maingear Inc ....E 888 624-6432
Kenilworth *(G-4955)*
Metrofuser LLC ....D 908 245-2100
Elizabeth *(G-2758)*
Mimo Display LLC ....G 855 937-6466
Princeton *(G-8980)*
▲ **Touch Dynamic Inc** ....D 732 382-5701
South Plainfield *(G-10331)*

3577 Computer Peripheral Eqpt, NEC

Advancing Opportunities Inc ....G 201 907-0200
Teaneck *(G-10621)*
Alpha Tech Services ....G 973 283-2011
Boonton *(G-540)*
Amedia Networks Inc ....F 732 440-1992
Eatontown *(G-2376)*
American Fibertek Inc ....E 732 302-0660
Somerset *(G-9951)*
Antron Technologies Inc ....G 732 205-0415
Edison *(G-2457)*
Audio Dynamix Inc ....F 201 567-5488
Englewood *(G-2879)*
Automated Control Concepts Inc ....E 732 922-6611
Neptune *(G-6867)*
Beall Technologies Inc ....E 201 689-2130
Wyckoff *(G-12104)*
Behr Technology Inc ....G 908 537-9960
Hampton *(G-4148)*
Berkeley Varitronics Systems ....E 732 548-3737
Metuchen *(G-6047)*
▲ **Chiral Photonics Inc** ....F 973 732-0030
Pine Brook *(G-8590)*
Cisco Systems Inc ....C 732 635-4200
Iselin *(G-4604)*
Cisco Systems Inc ....G 856 642-7000
Moorestown *(G-6513)*
Cisco Systems Inc ....E 201 782-0842
Montvale *(G-6402)*
Conduent State Healthcare LLC ....G 973 824-3250
Newark *(G-7087)*
Conduent State Healthcare LLC ....G 973 754-6134
Paterson *(G-8163)*
Corporate Computer Systems ....F 732 739-5600
Newark *(G-7088)*
Data Base Access Systems Inc ....F 973 335-0800
Mountain Lakes *(G-6822)*
Dew Associates Inc ....E 973 702-0545
Sussex *(G-10557)*
Dialogic Inc ....C 973 967-6000
Parsippany *(G-7916)*
Diversified Display Pdts LLC ....E 908 686-2200
Hillside *(G-4389)*
Ems Aviation Inc ....C 856 234-5020
Moorestown *(G-6522)*
Envirosight LLC ....E 973 970-9284
Randolph *(G-9176)*
Epiq Systems Inc ....G 973 622-6111
Newark *(G-7117)*
EVs Broadcast Equipment Inc ....F 973 575-7811
Fairfield *(G-3194)*
Fotobridge ....G 856 809-9400
West Berlin *(G-11595)*
Fyth Labs Inc ....G 856 313-7362
Beverly *(G-451)*
Gulton Incorporated ....E 908 791-4622
South Plainfield *(G-10271)*
Humanscale Corporation ....C 732 537-2944
Piscataway *(G-8676)*
Jetty Life LLC ....G 800 900-6435
Manahawkin *(G-5793)*
Lexmark International Inc ....F 201 307-4600
Park Ridge *(G-7855)*
Link Computer Graphics Inc ....G 973 808-8990
Fairfield *(G-3263)*
Lucent Technologies World Svcs ....C 908 582-3000
New Providence *(G-7008)*
Maingear Inc ....E 888 624-6432
Kenilworth *(G-4955)*
▲ **Metrologic Instruments Inc** ....C 856 228-8100
Mount Laurel *(G-6782)*
Micro Innovations Corp ....D 732 346-9333
Edison *(G-2565)*
MRC Precision Metal Optics Inc ....E 941 753-8707
Northvale *(G-7538)*
MTS Systems Corporation ....A 856 875-4478
Williamstown *(G-11965)*
Ncs Pearson Inc ....D 201 896-1011
Lyndhurst *(G-5666)*
▲ **Ner Data Products Inc** ....E 888 637-3282
Glassboro *(G-3817)*
Netscout Systems Inc ....G 609 518-4100
Marlton *(G-5943)*
Omniplanar Inc ....G 800 782-4263
Blackwood *(G-476)*
Oxberry LLC ....G 201 935-3000
Carlstadt *(G-1194)*
Paradise Barxon Corp ....G 908 707-9141
Branchburg *(G-664)*
Parker-Hannifin Corporation ....F 856 825-8900
Millville *(G-6266)*
▲ **Pcs Revenue Ctrl Systems Inc** ....E 201 568-8300
Englewood Cliffs *(G-2987)*
Pim LLC ....E 646 225-6666
Ridgefield *(G-9283)*
▲ **PNC Electronics Inc** ....E 973 237-0400
Totowa *(G-10845)*
R T I Inc ....E 201 261-5852
Oradell *(G-7746)*
Radcom Equipment Inc ....G 201 518-0033
Paramus *(G-7828)*
▲ **Raritan Inc** ....E 732 764-8886
Somerset *(G-10061)*
▲ **Raritan Americas Inc** ....C 732 764-8886
Somerset *(G-10062)*
Ricoh Prtg Systems Amer Inc ....G 973 316-6051
Mountain Lakes *(G-6827)*
▲ **RSR Electronics Inc** ....E 732 381-8777
Rahway *(G-9126)*
▲ **S W Electronics & Mfg** ....C 856 222-9900
Moorestown *(G-6564)*
Salescaster Displays Corp ....G 908 322-3046
Scotch Plains *(G-9739)*
Scantron Corporation ....G 201 666-7009
Westwood *(G-11844)*
Sony Corporation of America ....B 201 930-1000
Paramus *(G-7834)*
Source Micro LLC ....F 973 328-1749
Randolph *(G-9200)*
Sqn Peripherals Inc ....E 609 261-5500
Rancocas *(G-9166)*
Symbology Enterprises Inc ....F 908 725-1699
Somerville *(G-10125)*
Technobox Inc ....G 856 809-2306
West Berlin *(G-11627)*
Telegenix Inc ....F 609 265-3910
Rancocas *(G-9167)*
Thomas Instrumentation Inc ....F 609 624-7777
Cape May Court House *(G-1115)*
Total Technology Inc ....E 856 617-0502
Cherry Hill *(G-1423)*
Western Scientific Computers ....F 973 263-9311
Mountain Lakes *(G-6830)*
Zaller Studios Inc ....G 973 743-5175
Bloomfield *(G-523)*
Zebra Technologies Corporation ....B 609 383-8743
Northfield *(G-7512)*

S I C

3578 Calculating & Accounting Eqpt

Bps Worldwide Inc ....E 856 874-0822
Cherry Hill *(G-1348)*
Business Control Systems Corp ....F 732 283-1301
Iselin *(G-4603)*
▲ Comtrex Systems Corporation ....E 856 778-0090
Moorestown *(G-6515)*
Longport Shields Inc ....G 856 727-0227
Moorestown *(G-6542)*
◆ Swintec Corp ....F 201 935-0115
Moonachie *(G-6493)*
United Pos Solutions Inc ....G 800 303-2567
Palisades Park *(G-7780)*
Worldwide Pt SL Ltd Lblty Co ....F 201 928-0222
Teaneck *(G-10655)*
▲ Zeiser Inc ....F 973 228-0800
West Caldwell *(G-11682)*

3579 Office Machines, NEC

Acedepotcom ....F 800 844-0962
Northvale *(G-7515)*
◆ Amano Cincinnati Incorporated ....D 973 403-1900
Roseland *(G-9530)*
▲ Amano USA Holdings Inc ....G 973 403-1900
Roseland *(G-9531)*
◆ Arrow Fastener Co LLC ....B 201 843-6900
Saddle Brook *(G-9640)*
Avante International Tech Inc ....E 609 799-9388
Princeton Junction *(G-9052)*
◆ Brother International Corp ....B 908 704-1700
Bridgewater *(G-808)*
Esg LLC ....F 973 347-2969
Budd Lake *(G-922)*
Hoarders Express LLC ....D 856 963-8471
Camden *(G-1067)*
J K Office Machine Inc ....G 908 273-8811
Berkeley Heights *(G-402)*
Opex Corporation ....F 856 727-1100
Moorestown *(G-6551)*
Pitney Bowes Inc ....F 908 903-2870
Warren *(G-11427)*
Pitney Bowes Inc ....C 800 521-0080
Newark *(G-7230)*
Pitney Bowes Inc ....C 856 764-2240
Delran *(G-2019)*
◆ Swintec Corp ....F 201 935-0115
Moonachie *(G-6493)*
Time Systems International Co ....E 201 871-1200
Englewood *(G-2947)*

3581 Automatic Vending Machines

Universal Vending MGT LLC ....F 908 233-4373
Westfield *(G-11804)*

3582 Commercial Laundry, Dry Clean & Pressing Mchs

▲ Air World Inc ....E 201 831-0700
Mahwah *(G-5711)*
Airworld Inc ....F 973 720-1008
Paterson *(G-8129)*
Fairfield Laundry McHy Corp ....E 973 575-4330
Fairfield *(G-3199)*
▲ Hoffman/New Yorker Inc ....G 201 488-1800
Hackensack *(G-3930)*
▲ Multimatic LLC ....G 201 767-9660
Northvale *(G-7539)*
One Click Cleaners ....G 732 804-9802
Manalapan *(G-5821)*
Professional Laundry Solutions ....G 973 392-0837
Newark *(G-7238)*
Sadwith Industries Corp ....G 732 531-3856
Ocean *(G-7680)*
▲ Utax USA Inc ....G 201 433-1200
Jersey City *(G-4825)*

3585 Air Conditioning & Heating Eqpt

Ade Inc ....F 609 693-6050
Forked River *(G-3535)*
▼ Atomizing Systems Inc ....F 201 447-1222
Ho Ho Kus *(G-4439)*
Ats Mechanical Inc ....G 609 298-2323
Bordentown *(G-576)*
Banicki Sheet Metal Inc ....G 201 385-5938
Bergenfield *(G-372)*
Bfhj Holdings Inc ....G 908 730-6280
Montvale *(G-6401)*
Bgs Inc ....F 732 442-5000
Lakewood *(G-5061)*

Bolttech Mannings Inc ....D 973 537-1576
Wharton *(G-11853)*
Calmac Manufacturing Corp ....E 201 797-1511
Fair Lawn *(G-3092)*
Chiller Solutions LLC ....G 973 835-2800
Pompton Plains *(G-8861)*
Comfortaire Ltd Liability Co ....G 856 692-5000
Vineland *(G-11201)*
▲ Construction Specialties Inc ....E 908 236-0800
Lebanon *(G-5257)*
Coolenheat Inc ....G 908 925-4473
Kendall Park *(G-4918)*
▲ Csonka Worldwide ....E 609 514-2766
Plainsboro *(G-8783)*
Daicel Chemtech Inc ....G 201 461-4466
Fort Lee *(G-3553)*
◆ Diversified Heat Transfer Inc ....D 800 221-1522
Towaco *(G-10869)*
Dolan Assoc Inc ....G 973 875-6408
Sussex *(G-10558)*
▲ Drytech Inc ....E 609 758-1794
Cookstown *(G-1803)*
Duct Mate Inc ....G 201 488-8002
Hackensack *(G-3909)*
Dukers Appliance Co USA Ltd ....G 917 378-8866
South Plainfield *(G-10248)*
Electro Impulse Laboratory Inc ....E 732 776-5800
Neptune *(G-6876)*
▲ Ener-G Rudox Inc ....E 201 438-0111
East Rutherford *(G-2286)*
▲ Ewc Controls Inc ....G 732 446-3110
Manalapan *(G-5809)*
◆ Fujitsu General America Inc ....D 973 575-0380
Fairfield *(G-3209)*
Harsco Corporation ....E 856 779-7795
Cherry Hill *(G-1371)*
Heritage Service Solutions LLC ....F 856 845-7311
Westville *(G-11815)*
Hussmann Corporation ....E 800 320-3510
West Deptford *(G-11703)*
Iceboxx LLC ....G 201 857-0404
Wyckoff *(G-12113)*
▲ Icy Cools Inc ....G 609 448-0172
Roosevelt *(G-9529)*
◆ Ingersoll-Rand US Trane ....D 732 652-7100
Piscataway *(G-8678)*
Kohlder Manufacturing Inc ....E 856 963-1801
Pennsauken *(G-8448)*
▲ Kooltronic Inc ....G 609 466-3400
Pennington *(G-8369)*
▲ Krowne Metal Corp ....E 973 305-3300
Wayne *(G-11530)*
▲ Lauda-Brinkmann LP ....E 856 764-7300
Delran *(G-2017)*
Lauda-Brinkmann Management Inc ......F 856 764-7300
Delran *(G-2018)*
Maco Appliance Parts & Sup Co ....G 609 272-8222
Absecon *(G-3)*
Mainstream Fluid & Air LLC ....F 908 931-1010
Berkeley Heights *(G-408)*
Mechanical Technologies LLC ....E 973 616-3800
Pine Brook *(G-8609)*
ML Mettler Corp ....G 201 869-0170
North Bergen *(G-7423)*
On Site Manufacturing Inc ....G 812 794-6040
Flemington *(G-3458)*
Piper Services LLC ....F 844 567-3900
Midland Park *(G-6183)*
▼ Ryder Technology ....G 215 817-7868
Villas *(G-11180)*
Sander Mechanical Service Inc ....E 732 560-0600
Branchburg *(G-679)*
◆ Sealed Unit Parts Co Inc ....C 732 223-1201
Allenwood *(G-34)*
▲ Sodastream USA Inc ....D 856 755-3400
Mount Laurel *(G-6808)*
Specialty Fabricators LLC ....E 609 758-6995
Wrightstown *(G-12100)*
SPX Dry Cooling Usa LLC ....F 908 450-8027
Bridgewater *(G-893)*
Stamm International Corp ....G 201 947-1700
Fort Lee *(G-3589)*
▲ Task International (usa) Inc ....F 732 739-0377
Keyport *(G-5005)*
Tecogen Inc ....G 732 356-5601
Piscataway *(G-8723)*
▲ Trane Inc ....B 732 652-7100
Piscataway *(G-8730)*
Trane Parts Center of NJ ....G 201 489-9001
Teterboro *(G-10695)*

Trane US Inc ....C 732 652-7100
Piscataway *(G-8731)*
Trane US Inc ....D 609 587-3400
Trenton *(G-11000)*
Trane US Inc ....G 973 882-3220
Pine Brook *(G-8618)*
◆ Walter Machine Co Inc ....E 201 656-5654
Jersey City *(G-4829)*
York International Corporation ....F 732 346-0606
Edison *(G-2649)*
Zanotti Transblock USA Corp ....G 917 584-9357
Delran *(G-2023)*

3586 Measuring & Dispensing Pumps

▲ Newton Tool & Mfg Inc ....D 856 241-1500
Pennsauken *(G-8461)*

3589 Service Ind Machines, NEC

A Plus Powerwashing ....G 732 245-3816
Neptune *(G-6863)*
▲ Aero Manufacturing Co ....D 973 473-5300
Clifton *(G-1558)*
◆ Amano USA Holdings Inc ....G 973 403-1900
Roseland *(G-9531)*
▲ Aqua Products Inc ....C 973 857-2700
Cedar Grove *(G-1268)*
Aries Filterworks Inc ....E 856 626-1550
Berlin *(G-414)*
Arrow Steel Inc ....F 973 523-1122
Paterson *(G-8142)*
Autoshred LLC ....G 732 244-0950
Toms River *(G-10745)*
Bishop Ascendant Inc ....F 201 572-7436
West Caldwell *(G-11642)*
◆ Cantel Medical Corp ....G 973 890-7220
Little Falls *(G-5454)*
Car Wash Parts Inc ....G 215 633-9250
Ventnor City *(G-11152)*
Chem-Aqua Inc ....F 972 438-0211
Monmouth Junction *(G-6281)*
Chen Brothers Machinery Co ....G 973 328-0086
Randolph *(G-9174)*
▲ Clayton Associates Inc ....F 732 363-2100
Lakewood *(G-5071)*
Clearwater Well Drilling Co ....G 609 698-1800
Manahawkin *(G-5791)*
CP Equipment Sales Co ....F 908 687-9621
Union *(G-11039)*
Custom Blends Inc ....G 215 934-7080
Ewing *(G-3025)*
Dcm Clean Air Products Inc ....G 732 363-2100
Lakewood *(G-5082)*
▼ Delta Cooling Towers Inc ....E 973 586-2201
Flanders *(G-3405)*
Detrex Corporation ....G 856 786-8686
Cinnaminson *(G-1452)*
▲ Dynatec Systems Inc ....F 609 387-0330
Burlington *(G-965)*
EAC Water Filters Inc ....F 888 524-8088
Allenwood *(G-32)*
East Brunswick Sewerage Auth ....F 732 257-8313
East Brunswick *(G-2138)*
Elgee Manufacturing Company ....G 908 647-4100
Warren *(G-11408)*
Energy Beams Inc ....F 973 291-6555
Bloomingdale *(G-528)*
Enpro Inc ....E 908 236-2137
Lebanon *(G-5260)*
Envirnmntal Mgt Chem Wste Svcs ......G 201 848-7676
Mahwah *(G-5735)*
Es Industrial ....D 732 842-5600
Red Bank *(G-9228)*
Evoqua Water Technologies LLC ....D 908 851-4250
Union *(G-11053)*
Evoqua Water Technologies LLC ....F 201 531-9338
East Rutherford *(G-2287)*
Favs Corp ....G 856 358-1515
Elmer *(G-2797)*
Filter Technologies Inc ....G 732 329-2500
Monmouth Junction *(G-6291)*
Filtrex Inc ....F 973 595-0400
Wayne *(G-11502)*
Fin-Tek Corporation ....G 973 628-2988
Wayne *(G-11503)*
◆ Franklin Miller Inc ....E 973 535-9200
Livingston *(G-5512)*
Glasco Uv LLC ....F 201 934-3348
Mahwah *(G-5741)*
Global Ecology Corporation ....G 973 655-9001
Roseland *(G-9538)*

GP Jager Inc .... G 973 750-1180
Boonton (G-555)
▼ Graver Water Systems LLC .... G 908 516-1400
New Providence (G-7003)
Graver Water Systems LLC .... F 973 465-2380
Newark (G-7138)
◆ Hayward Industries Inc .... B 908 351-5400
Elizabeth (G-2746)
Hayward Industries Inc .... G 908 351-0899
Elizabeth (G-2747)
Hickory Industries Inc .... E 201 223-4382
North Bergen (G-7409)
Hobart Sales and Service Inc .... E 973 227-9265
Fairfield (G-3229)
▼ Hungerford & Terry Inc .... E 856 881-3200
Clayton (G-1525)
Innovative Pressure Clg LLC .... G 609 738-3100
Cream Ridge (G-1937)
Interntional Cnsld Chemex Corp .... E 732 828-7676
New Brunswick (G-6936)
J & M Air Inc .... E 908 707-4040
Somerville (G-10118)
◆ Janico Inc .... F 732 370-2223
Freehold (G-3672)
▲ JDV Equipment Corp .... G 973 366-6556
Dover (G-2092)
Karcher North America Inc .... F 856 228-1800
Blackwood (G-474)
◆ Lanxess Sybron Chemicals Inc .... C 609 893-1100
Birmingham (G-457)
Margaritaville Inc .... G 973 728-7562
West Milford (G-11729)
▲ Mercury Floor Machines Inc .... E 201 568-4606
Englewood (G-2924)
Metawater Usa Inc .... G 201 935-3436
Rutherford (G-9628)
Metropolitan Compactors Svc .... G 908 653-0168
Cranford (G-1917)
▲ Metropolitan Vacuum Clr Co Inc .... D 201 405-2225
Oakland (G-7636)
Middlesex Water Company .... C 732 579-0290
Edison (G-2566)
Multi-Pak Corporation .... E 201 342-7474
Hackensack (G-3949)
Nitto Inc .... F 732 901-7905
Lakewood (G-5141)
Nitto Inc .... F 201 645-4950
Teaneck (G-10641)
NMP Water Systems LLC .... G 201 252-8333
Mahwah (G-5758)
Organica Water Inc .... F 609 651-8885
West Windsor (G-11782)
Pinto of Montville Inc .... G 973 584-2002
Kenvil (G-4994)
◆ Power Container Corp .... E 732 560-3655
Somerset (G-10054)
Powerwash Plus .... G 732 671-6767
Middletown (G-6166)
Premier Compaction Systems .... F 718 328-5990
Woodland Park (G-12087)
Pure H2o Technologies Inc .... F 973 622-0440
Newark (G-7240)
Quality Plus One Catering Inc .... G 732 967-1525
Old Bridge (G-7726)
Randall Manufacturing Co Inc .... E 973 746-2111
Hillside (G-4424)
Rlct Industries LLC .... G 609 712-1318
Pennington (G-8372)
▲ Seaboard Paper and Twine LLC .... E 973 413-8100
Paterson (G-8296)
Sitaras Toasters Equipment LLC .... G 732 910-2678
Cinnaminson (G-1485)
Site Drainer LLC .... G 862 225-9940
Clifton (G-1721)
South Jersey Water Cond Svc .... E 856 451-0620
Bridgeton (G-773)
Spiral Water Technologies Inc .... F 415 259-4929
Middlesex (G-6151)
Suez North America Inc .... F 201 767-9300
Paramus (G-7837)
◆ Suez Treatment Solutions Inc .... C 201 767-9300
Paramus (G-7838)
T & E Sales of Marlboro Inc .... G 732 549-7551
Metuchen (G-6076)
▲ U V International LLC .... G 973 993-9454
Morristown (G-6705)
▲ Unique Systems Inc .... F 973 455-0440
Cedar Knolls (G-1315)
Vac-U-Max .... F 973 759-4600
Belleville (G-320)
Vivreau Advanced Water Systems .... F 212 502-3749
Fairfield (G-3347)
Water Resources New Jersey LLC .... G 609 268-7965
Tabernacle (G-10620)

3592 Carburetors, Pistons, Rings & Valves

Fujikin of America Inc .... G 201 641-1119
Hasbrouck Heights (G-4182)
▲ Rotarex Inc North America .... D 724 696-3345
Hackettstown (G-4033)
Straval Machine Co Inc .... E 973 340-9955
Elmwood Park (G-2857)
Triflow Corporation .... G 856 768-7159
West Berlin (G-11631)

3593 Fluid Power Cylinders & Actuators

Excel Hydraulics LLC .... E 856 241-1145
Clarksboro (G-1519)
GE Aviation Systems LLC .... C 973 428-9898
Whippany (G-11892)
▲ Industrial Habonim Valves & AC .... F 201 820-3184
Wayne (G-11519)
▼ Motion Systems Corp .... D 732 389-1600
Eatontown (G-2411)
Van Hydraulics Inc .... E 732 442-5500
South Plainfield (G-10338)

3594 Fluid Power Pumps & Motors

Industrial Combustion Assn .... F 732 271-0300
Somerset (G-10004)
Mainstream LLC .... G 908 931-1010
Cranford (G-1916)
Neptune Products Inc .... F 973 366-8200
Dover (G-2100)
▲ PMC Liquiflo Equipment Co Inc .... E 908 518-0666
Garwood (G-3791)
Technol Inc .... F 856 848-5480
Westville (G-11821)

3596 Scales & Balances, Exc Laboratory

Advance Scale Company Inc .... E 856 784-4916
Lindenwold (G-5444)
American Garvens Corporation .... G 973 276-1093
Pine Brook (G-8586)
▲ Coperion K-Tron Pitman Inc .... F 856 589-0500
Sewell (G-9836)
Empire Scale & Balance .... G 856 299-1651
Penns Grove (G-8378)
▲ Ohaus Corporation .... D 973 377-9000
Parsippany (G-7980)
Technidyne Corporation .... G 732 363-1055
Toms River (G-10799)
W T Winter Associates Inc .... E 888 808-3611
Fairfield (G-3350)

3599 Machinery & Eqpt, Indl & Commercial, NEC

21st Century Mch Tls Co Inc .... G 973 808-2220
West Caldwell (G-11635)
A B Scantlebury Co Inc .... F 973 770-3000
Newton (G-7335)
A Frieri Machine Tool Inc .... G 908 753-7555
South Plainfield (G-10204)
Abco Tool & Machine Corp .... G 973 772-8160
Garfield (G-3723)
Able Gear & Machine Co .... G 973 983-8055
Rockaway (G-9434)
Accelerated Cnc LLC .... G 908 561-8875
South Plainfield (G-10206)
Ace Metal Kraft Co Inc .... E 973 278-6605
Woodland Park (G-12068)
Advance Machine Inc .... F 908 486-7244
Linden (G-5316)
▲ Aero Products Co Inc .... F 973 759-0959
Belleville (G-289)
Afk Machine Inc .... G 973 539-1329
Randolph (G-9170)
Alben Metal Products Inc .... G 973 279-8891
Paterson (G-8130)
All Mechanical Services Inc .... F 732 442-8292
Perth Amboy (G-8511)
All Tool Company Inc .... F 908 687-3636
Union (G-11021)
Alpha Lehigh Tool & Mch Co Inc .... E 908 454-6481
Alpha (G-35)
Altech Machine & Tool Inc .... G 201 652-4409
Midland Park (G-6169)
American Machine Spc NJ LLC .... E 201 664-0006
Westwood (G-11826)
American Pipe Benders & Fabric .... G 732 287-1122
Edison (G-2454)
Amex Tool Co .... F 908 735-5176
Asbury (G-58)
Andrex Inc .... F 908 852-2400
Hackettstown (G-3998)
◆ Ansun Protective Metals Inc .... G 732 302-0616
Middlesex (G-6098)
▲ Argyle Industries Inc .... F 908 725-8800
Branchburg (G-620)
Aries Precision Tool Inc .... G 201 252-8550
Ramsey (G-9139)
Astro Tool & Machine Co Inc .... E 732 382-2454
Rahway (G-9080)
▲ Atlantic Casting & Engineering .... C 973 779-2450
Clifton (G-1566)
Atlantic Coastal Welding Inc .... F 732 269-1088
Bayville (G-240)
Atlas Recording Machines Corp .... G 732 295-3663
Point Pleasant Boro (G-8837)
Avony Enterprises Inc .... E 212 242-8144
Trenton (G-10899)
Aztech Mfg Inc .... F 609 726-1212
Pemberton (G-8357)
B & C Machine Co Inc .... G 973 823-1120
Franklin (G-3600)
▲ Barnett Machine Tools Inc .... F 973 482-6222
Harrison (G-4164)
BCsmachine & Mfg Corp .... G 908 561-1656
South Plainfield (G-10224)
Berezin Nilolai .... G 856 692-6191
Vineland (G-11193)
Bertot Industries Inc .... G 973 267-0006
Morristown (G-6650)
Bisaga Inc .... F 856 784-7966
Somerdale (G-9930)
Biwal Manufacturing Co Inc .... E 973 778-0105
Clifton (G-1575)
Bk Machine Shop .... G 856 457-7150
Vineland (G-11196)
Blue Chip Industries Inc .... G 908 704-1466
Somerville (G-10104)
BP Machine Co Inc .... G 732 251-0449
Spotswood (G-10414)
Brenner Metal Products .... E 973 778-2466
Wallington (G-11383)
▲ Brodie System Inc .... F 908 862-8620
Linden (G-5328)
Brusso Hardware LLC .... F 212 337-8510
Belleville (G-292)
C & C Tool and Machine Co LLC .... G 856 764-0911
Riverside (G-9391)
C & N Tooling & Grinding Inc .... F 973 598-8411
Succasunna (G-10509)
C & S Tool Co .... F 973 887-6865
East Hanover (G-2196)
Cerbaco Ltd .... E 908 996-1333
Frenchtown (G-3711)
Chacko John .... G 732 494-1088
Edison (G-2475)
Chalmers & Kubeck Inc .... G 732 993-1251
New Brunswick (G-6915)
Charles F Kilian .... G 732 458-3554
Brick (G-712)
Charter Machine Company .... F 732 494-5350
Metuchen (G-6051)
◆ Clements Industries Inc .... E 201 440-5500
South Hackensack (G-10153)
Coates Precision Engineering .... G 732 449-9382
Wall Township (G-11330)
▲ Coesia Health & Beauty Inc .... F 908 707-8008
Branchburg (G-630)
Colinear Machine & Design Inc .... F 973 300-1681
Sparta (G-10382)
Computa-Base-Machining Inc .... F 856 767-9517
Berlin (G-421)
Concept Group LLC .... E 856 767-5506
West Berlin (G-11586)
Congruent Machine Co Inc .... G 973 764-6767
Vernon (G-11158)
▲ Connecting Products Inc .... G 609 688-1808
Skillman (G-9919)
Creative Machining Systems .... F 609 586-3932
Trenton (G-10925)
Crown Precision Corp .... G 973 470-0097
Passaic (G-8057)
Cutmark Inc .... G 856 234-3428
Mount Laurel (G-6750)
▲ Cutting Edge Casting Inc .... E 908 925-7500
Linden (G-5340)

SIC

D & H Cutoff Co............G....... 908 454-4961
Stewartsville *(G-10482)*
D N D Corp............G....... 908 637-4343
Great Meadows *(G-3854)*
Daven Industries Inc............E....... 973 808-8848
Fairfield *(G-3180)*
Delva Tool & Machine Corp............D....... 856 786-8700
Cinnaminson *(G-1450)*
Delva Tool & Machine Corp............D....... 856 829-0109
Cinnaminson *(G-1451)*
Dependable Precision Products............G....... 973 887-3304
Parsippany *(G-7915)*
Dewalt Manufacturing Co Inc............G....... 856 423-1207
Clarksboro *(G-1518)*
Diamond Machine Co Inc............G....... 609 490-8940
Roosevelt *(G-9528)*
Dihco Inc............G....... 201 327-0518
Upper Saddle River *(G-11139)*
Diversatech Inc............G....... 609 730-9668
Pennington *(G-8363)*
Diversitech Inc............E....... 973 835-2900
Riverdale *(G-9375)*
Drew-Wal Machine & Tool Corp............G....... 201 641-3887
Little Ferry *(G-5483)*
Dynametric Tool Inc............G....... 973 471-8009
Clifton *(G-1607)*
Dynamic Machining Inc............F....... 856 273-9830
Cinnaminson *(G-1454)*
Eastern Machining Corporation............G....... 856 694-3303
Franklinville *(G-3637)*
▲ Edgewater Manufacturing Co Inc.....E....... 201 664-0022
Fair Lawn *(G-3098)*
Edhard Corp............E....... 908 850-8444
Hackettstown *(G-4004)*
Edmund Kiss............G....... 973 810-2312
Landing *(G-5200)*
Elmi Machine Tool Corp............G....... 973 882-1277
Fairfield *(G-3190)*
Eugene Kozak............G....... 973 442-1001
Randolph *(G-9177)*
▲ Evans Machine & Tool Co............G....... 732 442-1144
Perth Amboy *(G-8518)*
▲ Everite Machine Products Co............E....... 856 330-6700
Pennsauken *(G-8419)*
Exactal Tool Ltd Inc............G....... 908 561-1177
South Plainfield *(G-10255)*
F & M Machine Co Inc............F....... 908 245-8830
Kenilworth *(G-4939)*
◆ F & R Machine Corp............E....... 973 684-8139
Paterson *(G-8188)*
F and L Machinery............G....... 973 218-6216
Springfield *(G-10442)*
Faber Precision Inc............G....... 973 983-1844
Rockaway *(G-9458)*
Fazzio Machine & Steel Inc............G....... 609 653-1098
Glassboro *(G-3811)*
Ferry Machine Corp............E....... 201 641-9191
Little Ferry *(G-5485)*
▲ Fgh Systems Inc............F....... 973 625-8114
Denville *(G-2037)*
Fims Manufacturing Corporation............E....... 201 845-7088
Oakland *(G-7628)*
Fischl Machine & Tool............G....... 908 829-5621
Hillsborough *(G-4316)*
▲ Flexline Inc............F....... 908 486-3322
Kenilworth *(G-4940)*
Fluets Corp............E....... 908 353-5229
Hillside *(G-4391)*
Fluid Filtration Corp............F....... 973 253-7070
Garfield *(G-3743)*
◆ Fortune International Inc............G....... 732 214-0700
Somerset *(G-9995)*
Frank E Ganter Inc............G....... 856 692-2218
Vineland *(G-11219)*
Fredericks Machine Inc............G....... 609 397-4991
Rosemont *(G-9592)*
G & B Machine Inc............G....... 908 707-1181
Somerville *(G-10110)*
G Catalano Inc............G....... 908 241-6333
Roselle Park *(G-9585)*
G P R Company Inc............E....... 973 227-6160
Fairfield *(G-3210)*
Gale Newson Inc............E....... 732 961-7610
Jackson *(G-4656)*
Gamma Machine & Tool Co Inc............G....... 973 398-8821
Landing *(G-5201)*
Gaum Inc............E....... 609 586-0132
Robbinsville *(G-9412)*
Gb Industries II Inc............G....... 973 728-5900
Ringwood *(G-9345)*
Geiger Tool & Mfg Co Inc............F....... 973 777-2136
Passaic *(G-8068)*
Geiger Tool Co Inc............F....... 973 777-5094
Passaic *(G-8069)*
General Electric Company............B....... 973 887-6635
Parsippany *(G-7955)*
General Mch Experimental Works............G....... 201 843-9035
Paramus *(G-7803)*
General Polygon Systems Inc............F....... 800 825-1655
Millville *(G-6251)*
Globe Engineering Corp............G....... 609 898-0349
Cape May *(G-1099)*
▲ Globe Industries Corp............F....... 973 992-8990
Clifton *(G-1626)*
Graphic Equipment Corporation............E....... 732 494-5350
Metuchen *(G-6058)*
Graphic Equipment Corporation............E....... 732 548-4400
Metuchen *(G-6059)*
Great Notch Industries Inc............G....... 201 343-8110
Hackensack *(G-3924)*
Grimaldi Development Corp............G....... 973 345-0660
Paterson *(G-8203)*
Grimes Manufacturing Inc............G....... 732 442-4572
Perth Amboy *(G-8520)*
H P Machine Shop Inc............G....... 856 692-1192
Vineland *(G-11229)*
Hanrahan Tool Co Inc............G....... 732 919-7300
Farmingdale *(G-3386)*
Harley Tool & Machine Inc............G....... 201 244-8899
Bergenfield *(G-376)*
Harrison Machine and Tool Inc............G....... 609 883-0800
Ewing *(G-3032)*
Henry Olsen Machine............G....... 856 662-2121
Cinnaminson *(G-1463)*
Hercules Welding & Machine Co............G....... 856 829-1820
Palmyra *(G-7783)*
Hhh Machine Co............G....... 908 276-1220
Cranford *(G-1913)*
Hunter Manufacturing Svcs Inc............F....... 973 287-6701
Fairfield *(G-3232)*
Hydracore Inc............G....... 732 548-5500
Metuchen *(G-6062)*
Hydratight Operations Inc............F....... 732 271-4100
Somerset *(G-10003)*
I I Galaxy Inc............G....... 732 828-2686
New Brunswick *(G-6933)*
▼ Imperial Machine & Tool Co............F....... 908 496-8100
Columbia *(G-1794)*
Independent Machine Company............E....... 973 882-0060
Fairfield *(G-3235)*
Indoor Entertainment of NJ............E....... 609 522-6700
Wildwood *(G-11945)*
Industrial Machine & Engrg Co............F....... 908 862-8874
Linden *(G-5358)*
Industrial Machine Corp............G....... 973 345-1800
Paterson *(G-8214)*
International Tool and Mfg............G....... 973 227-6767
Fairfield *(G-3241)*
J & M Manufacturing Inc............G....... 908 638-4298
High Bridge *(G-4283)*
J A W Products Inc............F....... 856 829-3210
Cinnaminson *(G-1467)*
J and M Precision Inc............G....... 856 661-9595
Pennsauken *(G-8442)*
J D Machine Parts Inc............F....... 856 691-8430
Vineland *(G-11236)*
J M C Tool & Mfg Co............G....... 908 241-8950
Kenilworth *(G-4948)*
J P Rotella Co Inc............F....... 973 942-2559
Haledon *(G-4083)*
J R Engineering & Machine............F....... 908 810-6300
Hillside *(G-4405)*
J R S Tool & Metal Finishing............G....... 908 753-2050
South Plainfield *(G-10282)*
Jamco Machine Products............G....... 856 461-2664
Riverside *(G-9397)*
Jaymar Precision Inc............G....... 856 365-8779
Camden *(G-1071)*
JBAT Inc............E....... 856 667-7307
Cherry Hill *(G-1378)*
Jordan Tooling & Manufacturing............G....... 609 261-2636
Hainesport *(G-4075)*
Jsm Co............G....... 732 695-9577
Tinton Falls *(G-10720)*
K-D Industries Inc............D....... 973 594-4800
Passaic *(G-8079)*
▼ Kavon Filter Products Co............F....... 732 938-3135
Wall Township *(G-11351)*
▲ Kelles Incorporated............F....... 908 241-9300
Kenilworth *(G-4950)*
Kern & Szalai Co............F....... 856 802-1500
Moorestown *(G-6533)*
Kimber Mfg Inc............D....... 201 840-5812
Ridgefield *(G-9271)*
Knudsen Precision Mfg............F....... 609 538-1100
Ewing *(G-3042)*
Kwg Industries LLC............E....... 908 218-8900
Hillsborough *(G-4338)*
L & M Machine & Tool Co Inc............G....... 973 523-5288
Paterson *(G-8233)*
▼ Lazar Technologies Inc............F....... 732 739-9622
Hazlet *(G-4263)*
Legend Machine & Grinding............F....... 908 685-1100
Bridgewater *(G-841)*
Luso Machine Nj LLC............F....... 973 242-1717
Newark *(G-7188)*
M & D Prcsion Cntrless Grnding............G....... 856 764-1616
Riverside *(G-9398)*
M & M Welding & Steel Fabg............G....... 908 647-6060
Stirling *(G-10493)*
M & RS Miller Auto Gear & Prt............F....... 201 339-2270
Bayonne *(G-228)*
M & S Holes Corp............G....... 908 298-6900
Kenilworth *(G-4954)*
M & S Machine & Tool Corp............F....... 973 345-5847
Paterson *(G-8247)*
M and D Precision Grinding............G....... 856 764-1616
Riverside *(G-9399)*
M D Carbide Tool Corp............E....... 973 263-0104
Towaco *(G-10874)*
M4 Machine LLC............G....... 718 928-9695
Livingston *(G-5522)*
Machine Parts Inc............F....... 973 491-5444
Newark *(G-7194)*
Machine Plus Inc............G....... 973 839-8884
Haskell *(G-4199)*
Machine Tech............F....... 732 738-6810
Edison *(G-2557)*
Manco Industries............G....... 973 971-3131
Irvington *(G-4580)*
Marlo Manufacturing Co Inc............E....... 973 423-0226
Boonton *(G-560)*
Marlton Pike Precision LLC............F....... 856 665-1900
Cherry Hill *(G-1389)*
Marshall Maintenance............C....... 609 394-7153
Trenton *(G-10956)*
Mas Machine Shop LLC............G....... 201 768-9110
Northvale *(G-7535)*
Mdi Manufacturing Inc............F....... 732 994-5599
Lakewood *(G-5133)*
Mechanitron Corporation Inc............G....... 908 620-1001
Roselle *(G-9565)*
Mediscope Manufacturing Inc............E....... 908 756-2411
Watchung *(G-11457)*
Mercer Machine & Tool Products............G....... 609 587-1106
Trenton *(G-10957)*
Metal Components Inc............E....... 973 247-1204
Paterson *(G-8256)*
Metal Hose Fabricators Inc............G....... 908 925-7345
Linden *(G-5383)*
Metronic Engineering Co Inc............F....... 201 337-1266
Oakland *(G-7635)*
Micheller & Son Hydraulics Inc............F....... 908 687-1545
Roselle *(G-9566)*
Mid-Lantic Precision Inc............F....... 856 456-3810
Gloucester City *(G-3845)*
Midway Machine Product Corp............G....... 609 499-4377
Florence *(G-3476)*
Miemie Design Services Inc............E....... 609 857-3688
Ltl Egg Hbr *(G-5617)*
Millson Precision Machining............G....... 732 424-1700
Piscataway *(G-8691)*
Milo Runtak Welding Machinery............G....... 201 391-0380
Park Ridge *(G-7856)*
Mjs Precision Inc............G....... 973 209-1300
Franklin *(G-3605)*
Modern Metric Machine Company............G....... 856 547-4044
Audubon *(G-113)*
Modern Precision Tech Inc............F....... 856 335-9303
West Berlin *(G-11609)*
Modular Packaging Systems Inc............F....... 973 970-9393
Rockaway *(G-9477)*
Monmouth Truck Ram Div LLC............G....... 732 741-5001
Shrewsbury *(G-9898)*
Monroe Machine & Design Inc............F....... 732 521-3434
Jamesburg *(G-4675)*
N & J Machine Products Corp............G....... 973 589-0031
Newark *(G-7206)*
N B & Sons LLC............G....... 856 692-6191
Vineland *(G-11244)*

▲ National Mtal Fnshngs Corp Inc ......F 732 752-7770
  Middlesex (G-6133)
National Precision Tool Co ....E 973 227-5005
  Fairfield (G-3275)
▲ New ERA Converting McHy Inc ....E 201 670-4848
  Paterson (G-8265)
New Jersey Balancing Svc Inc ....G 973 278-5106
  Paterson (G-8266)
NJ Precision Tech Inc ....E 800 409-3000
  Mountainside (G-6850)
Norms Auto Parts Inc ....G 908 852-5080
  Hackettstown (G-4029)
Northeast Precast Ltd Lblty Co ....D 856 765-9088
  Millville (G-6264)
Northland Tooling Technologies ....G 908 850-0023
  Hackettstown (G-4030)
▲ Norwalt Design Inc ....D 973 927-3200
  Randolph (G-9193)
Nowak Inc ....F 973 366-7208
  Wharton (G-11864)
Numerical Control Program Svc ....G 856 665-8737
  Cherry Hill (G-1402)
Nymar Manufacturing Company...........F 973 366-7265
  Randolph (G-9194)
▲ O K Tool Corporation ....G 908 561-9920
  Plainfield (G-8774)
Olympic EDM Services Inc ....G 973 492-0664
  Kinnelon (G-5020)
Omp Technologies Inc ....F 973 808-8500
  Fairfield (G-3284)
Optimum Precision Inc ....G 908 259-9017
  Kenilworth (G-4967)
P K Precision Machining Inc ....G 973 925-2020
  Riverdale (G-9380)
P L M Manufacturing Company ....E 201 342-3636
  Hackensack (G-3961)
P M Z Tool Inc ....G 908 647-2125
  Stirling (G-10494)
Pabst Enterprises Equipment Co ....E 908 353-2880
  Elizabeth (G-2766)
Pahco Machine Inc.............................G 609 587-1188
  Trenton (G-10970)
Parkway-Kew Corporation ....F 732 398-2100
  North Brunswick (G-7482)
Pedrick Tool & Machine Co.................G 856 829-8900
  Cinnaminson (G-1480)
Philip Creter Inc ....G 908 686-2910
  Union (G-11083)
Phoenix Machine Rebuilders Inc ....F 973 691-8029
  Roxbury Township (G-9600)
Phoenix Precision Co ....F 973 208-8877
  Newfoundland (G-7331)
Phoenix Tool & Machine Inc ....G 856 753-5565
  West Berlin (G-11614)
▲ Picut Mfg Co Inc ....D 908 754-1333
  Warren (G-11426)
Polo Machine Inc................................G 973 340-9984
  Garfield (G-3757)
Precision Forms Inc ....E 973 838-3800
  Butler (G-1012)
Precision Metal Machining Inc.............E 201 843-7427
  Carlstadt (G-1206)
Precision Metalcrafters Inc ....E 856 629-1020
  Williamstown (G-11972)
Precision Mfg Group LLC.....................D 973 785-4630
  Cedar Grove (G-1288)
Precision-Tech LLC ....E 609 517-2718
  Hammonton (G-4143)
▲ Premier Die Casting Company ....D 732 634-3000
  Avenel (G-142)
Pyle Precision Machining LLC..............G 856 376-3720
  Pedricktown (G-8353)
Quality Industries Inc ....F 973 478-4425
  Clifton (G-1703)
R & H Co Inc ....G 610 258-3177
  Phillipsburg (G-8571)
R G Dunn Acquisitions Co Inc ....E 973 762-1300
  Maplewood (G-5882)
R G Smith Tool & Mfg Co ....F 973 344-1395
  Newark (G-7243)
R J D Machine Products Inc.................F 609 392-1515
  Trenton (G-10985)
R Way Tooling & Met Works LLC...........F 856 692-2218
  Vineland (G-11255)
Raceweld Co Inc ....G 908 236-6533
  Lebanon (G-5274)
Rako Machine Products Inc..................G 609 758-1200
  Cream Ridge (G-1939)
Ramsey Machine & Tool Co Inc............G 973 376-7404
  Springfield (G-10463)

Raue Screw Machine Products Co........G ... 973 697-7500
  Oak Ridge (G-7604)
Rawco LLC ....G 908 832-7700
  Califon (G-1034)
▲ Reliable Welding & Mch Work...........E 201 865-1073
  North Bergen (G-7432)
Rendas Tool & Die Inc ....E 732 469-4670
  Somerset (G-10064)
Reuther Engineering.............................F 973 485-5800
  Edison (G-2597)
Ridge Precision Products Inc ....G 973 361-3508
  Dover (G-2104)
Romar Machine & Tool Company ....E 201 337-7111
  Franklin Lakes (G-3631)
Rotary Die Systems Inc ....G 856 234-3994
  Moorestown (G-6563)
Ruoff & Sons Inc ....E 856 931-2064
  Runnemede (G-9609)
S & S Precision Company Inc ....G 856 662-0006
  Pennsauken (G-8481)
S&P Machine Company Inc....................F 973 365-2101
  Passaic (G-8103)
Saint-Gobain Prfmce Plas Corp............F 732 652-0910
  Somerset (G-10070)
Schall Manufacturing Inc ....G 732 918-8800
  Ocean (G-7681)
Select Machine Tool Inc ....G 856 933-2100
  Mount Ephraim (G-6721)
Sensor Products Inc ....E 973 884-1755
  Madison (G-5702)
Sermach Inc...G 732 356-9021
  Middlesex (G-6146)
Shore Precision Mfg Inc ....F 732 914-0949
  Toms River (G-10791)
Sigma Engineering & Consulting ....F 732 356-3046
  Middlesex (G-6147)
South Jersey Precision Tl Mold..............F 856 327-0500
  Vineland (G-11266)
South River Machinery Corp...................F 201 487-1736
  Hackensack (G-3976)
Spectrum Design LLC ....G 856 694-1870
  Franklinville (G-3639)
Spl Holdings LLC ....G 856 764-2400
  Delran (G-2021)
Stanton Precision Products LLC............G 973 838-6951
  Butler (G-1015)
Star Process Heat Systems LLC............G 732 282-1002
  Neptune (G-6899)
▲ Star-Glo Industries LLC....................E 201 939-6162
  East Rutherford (G-2319)
Steel Mountain Fabricators LLC............F 908 862-2800
  Linden (G-5431)
Steel Mountain Fabricators LLC............E 201 741-3019
  North Bergen (G-7438)
Steimling & Son Inc ....F 732 613-1550
  Sayreville (G-9724)
Stollen Machine & Tool Company ....G 908 241-0622
  Kenilworth (G-4979)
Straval Machine Co Inc ....E 973 340-9955
  Elmwood Park (G-2857)
STS Technologies LLC ....F 973 277-5416
  Mahwah (G-5778)
Stuart Mills Inc ....G 973 579-5717
  Newton (G-7359)
Stuart Mills Inc ....G 973 579-5717
  Newton (G-7360)
◆ Stuart Steel Protection Corp ....G 732 469-5544
  Somerset (G-10075)
Superior Tool & Mfg Co ....G 908 526-9011
  Branchburg (G-685)
T & P Machine Shop Inc ....G 732 424-9141
  Piscataway (G-8722)
T-M Vacuum Products Inc ....F 856 829-2000
  Cinnaminson (G-1488)
Tam Metal Products Inc........................E 201 848-7800
  Mahwah (G-5779)
Taurus Precision Inc ....F 973 785-9254
  Little Falls (G-5470)
Tech Products Co Inc ....F 201 444-7777
  Midland Park (G-6188)
◆ Testrite Instrument Co Inc ....C 201 543-0240
  Hackensack (G-3982)
Third River Manufacturing LLC ....G 201 935-2795
  Carlstadt (G-1228)
Tjk Machine LLC ....G 856 691-7811
  Vineland (G-11270)
Tomcel Machine Inc ....G 973 256-8257
  Woodland Park (G-12093)
Townsend Machine Inc ....E 609 723-2603
  Chesterfield (G-1438)

Tracer Tool & Machine Co Inc...............F 201 337-6184
  Oakland (G-7648)
Triad Tool & Die Co ....D 908 534-1784
  Branchburg (G-690)
Triangle Manufacturing Co Inc ....D 201 825-1212
  Upper Saddle River (G-11148)
Triple S Industries..............................G 908 862-0110
  Linden (G-5437)
Tru Mfg Corp.......................................E 201 768-4050
  Norwood (G-7576)
Unique Precision Co Inc.......................G 732 382-8699
  Rahway (G-9131)
United Machine Inc ....G 973 345-4505
  Paterson (G-8320)
United Ring & Seal Inc.........................G 610 253-3800
  Whitehouse Station (G-11935)
▲ Universal Metalcraft Inc....................E 973 345-3284
  Wayne (G-11560)
V & L Machine and Tool Co Inc.............G 973 439-7216
  Fairfield (G-3337)
Valle Precision Machine Co ....G 973 773-3037
  Passaic (G-8113)
Vector Precision Machining ....G 856 740-5131
  Williamstown (G-11984)
Vep Manufacturing...............................F 732 657-0666
  Jackson (G-4668)
▲ Vermes Machine Co Inc....................E 856 642-9300
  Moorestown (G-6575)
Vulcan Tool Company Inc ....F 908 686-0550
  Union (G-11098)
▼ Wagner Industries Inc.......................F 973 347-0800
  Stanhope (G-10481)
Werko Machine Co ....F 856 662-0669
  Pennsauken (G-8496)
West Machine Works Inc ....G 732 549-2183
  Metuchen (G-6080)
Whitehouse Machine & Mfg Co ....G 908 534-4722
  Somerville (G-10128)
▼ William Kenyon & Sons Inc...............E 732 985-8980
  Piscataway (G-8738)
▲ Win-Tech Precision Products ....G 973 887-8727
  East Hanover (G-2247)
Woodbridge Machine & Tool Co ....G 732 634-0179
  Woodbridge (G-12024)
Woods Industrial LLC ....F 973 208-0664
  West Milford (G-11734)
Zala Machine Co Inc ....F 908 431-9106
  Hillsborough (G-4363)
Zenex Precision Products Corp ....F 973 523-6910
  Paterson (G-8325)

36 ELECTRONIC AND OTHER ELECTRICAL EQUIPMENT AND COMPONENTS, EXCEPT COMPUTER

3612 Power, Distribution & Specialty Transformers

A C Transformer Corp ....G 973 589-8574
  Newark (G-7029)
AFP Transformers Corporation ....D 732 248-0305
  Edison (G-2450)
Amperite Co Inc ....E 201 864-9503
  North Bergen (G-7384)
Baltimore Transformer Company ....E 973 942-2222
  Paterson (G-8146)
Beverly Manufacturing Co Inc ....G 856 764-7898
  Riverside (G-9390)
Cooper Power Systems LLC...................C 732 481-4630
  Ocean (G-7659)
Cooper Power Systems LLC...................C 856 719-1100
  West Berlin (G-11587)
Edko Electronics ....E 973 942-2222
  Paterson (G-8176)
◆ G & S Motor Equipment Co Inc ....D 201 998-9244
  Kearny (G-4857)
▲ Galaxy Trans & Magnetics LLC ....F 856 753-4546
  West Berlin (G-11596)
Glen Magnetics Inc ....E 908 454-3717
  Alpha (G-37)
▲ Globtek Inc ....B 201 784-1000
  Northvale (G-7526)
Hbs Electronics Inc..............................G 973 439-1147
  Fairfield (G-3223)
▲ High Energy Group Ltd Lblty Co ....G 732 741-9099
  Eatontown (G-2397)
High Gate Corp....................................F 609 267-0680
  Mount Holly (G-6730)

S I C

▲ Hitran Corporation ....C 908 782-5525
Flemington *(G-3448)*

Hoyt Corporation ....E 201 894-0707
Englewood *(G-2912)*

▲ Hunterdon Transformer Co Inc ....D 908 454-2400
Alpha *(G-38)*

Ivey Katrina Owner ....G 973 951-8328
Newark *(G-7163)*

▲ Jerome Industries Corp ....E 908 353-5700
Hackettstown *(G-4013)*

▼ KG Squared LLC ....F 973 627-0643
Rockaway *(G-9473)*

Krydon Group Inc ....G 877 854-1342
Moorestown *(G-6535)*

Magnetika Inc ....E 908 454-2600
Phillipsburg *(G-8560)*

Magnetran Inc ....F 856 768-7787
Ocean View *(G-7703)*

▲ Megatran Industries ....D 609 227-4300
Bordentown *(G-586)*

Mesa Veterans Power LLC ....G 856 222-1000
Moorestown *(G-6545)*

Microsignals Inc ....E 800 225-4508
Palisades Park *(G-7774)*

▲ Model Rectifier Corporation ....E 732 225-2100
Matawan *(G-5980)*

Nilsson Electrical Laboratory ....G 201 521-4860
Jersey City *(G-4771)*

◆ Nwl Inc ....C 609 298-7300
Bordentown *(G-591)*

Pioneer Power Solutions Inc ....D 212 867-0700
Fort Lee *(G-3582)*

▲ Power Magne-Tech Corp ....E 732 826-4700
Perth Amboy *(G-8529)*

▲ Power Magnetics Inc ....E 609 695-1170
Trenton *(G-10977)*

Power Magnetics Inc ....E 800 747-0845
Trenton *(G-10978)*

▲ Raritan Inc ....E 732 764-8886
Somerset *(G-10061)*

Siemens Corporation ....D 732 590-6895
Iselin *(G-4628)*

Somerset Cpitl Mark Tr MGT Inc ....F 848 228-0842
Chesterfield *(G-1437)*

▲ Transistor Devices Inc ....C 908 850-5088
Hackettstown *(G-4039)*

Transistor Devices Inc ....C 908 850-5088
Hackettstown *(G-4040)*

Voltis LLC ....G 607 349-9411
Fairfield *(G-3348)*

Wolock & Lott Transmission Eqp ....F 908 218-9292
Branchburg *(G-695)*

◆ Zero Surge Inc ....F 908 996-7700
Frenchtown *(G-3718)*

3613 Switchgear & Switchboard Apparatus

Aeropanel Corporation ....D 973 335-9636
Boonton *(G-537)*

Apelio Innovative Inds LLC ....F 973 777-8899
Kearny *(G-4844)*

▲ Astrodyne Corporation ....D 908 850-5088
Hackettstown *(G-3999)*

▲ Automatic Switch Company ....A 973 966-2000
Florham Park *(G-3485)*

Automation & Control Inc ....E 856 234-2300
Moorestown *(G-6507)*

Bel Fuse Inc ....C 201 432-0463
Jersey City *(G-4700)*

Blackhawk Cre Corporation ....F 856 887-0162
Salem *(G-9692)*

▲ Circonix Technologies LLC ....F 973 962-6160
Ringwood *(G-9344)*

▲ Comus International Inc ....C 973 777-6900
Clifton *(G-1587)*

Csl Services Inc ....F 856 755-9440
Pennsauken *(G-8409)*

▲ Cutting Board Company ....G 908 725-0187
Lebanon *(G-5258)*

Cutting Board Company ....G 908 725-0187
Branchburg *(G-636)*

▲ Dantco Corp ....F 973 278-8776
Paterson *(G-8168)*

Dos Industrial Sales LLC ....G 973 887-7800
East Hanover *(G-2205)*

Eagle Engineering & Automation ....G 732 899-2292
Point Pleasant Boro *(G-8844)*

Electronic Power Designs Inc ....F 973 838-7055
Bloomingdale *(G-527)*

▲ Everite Machine Products Co ....E 856 330-6700
Pennsauken *(G-8419)*

Galaxy Switchgear Inds LLC ....E 914 668-8200
Kearny *(G-4858)*

Hoyt Corporation ....E 201 894-0707
Englewood *(G-2912)*

Ivey Katrina Owner ....G 973 951-8328
Newark *(G-7163)*

Lincoln Electric Pdts Co Inc ....E 908 688-2900
Union *(G-11069)*

Machinery Electrics ....G 732 536-0600
Bayville *(G-247)*

Marine Electric Systems Inc ....E 201 531-8600
South Hackensack *(G-10171)*

▲ Precision Multiple Contrls Inc ....E 201 444-0600
Midland Park *(G-6184)*

Precision Multiple Contrls Inc ....D 201 444-0600
Midland Park *(G-6185)*

Primacy Engineering Inc ....F 201 731-3272
Englewood Cliffs *(G-2988)*

Sensigraphics Inc ....G 856 853-9100
Mount Laurel *(G-6804)*

◆ Sigma-Netics Inc ....E 973 227-6372
Riverdale *(G-9385)*

Symcon Inc ....G 973 728-8661
West Milford *(G-11732)*

Techniques Inc ....F 973 256-0947
Woodland Park *(G-12092)*

▲ Technology Dynamics Inc ....D 201 385-0500
Bergenfield *(G-385)*

Tsi Nomenclature Inc ....G 732 340-0646
Avenel *(G-152)*

3621 Motors & Generators

▲ ADI American Distributors LLC ....D 973 328-1181
Randolph *(G-9169)*

◆ Allu Group Inc ....F 201 288-2236
East Brunswick *(G-2125)*

Alstrom Energy Group LLC ....G 718 824-4901
Old Bridge *(G-7711)*

American Mdlar Pwr Sltions Inc ....G 973 588-4026
Boonton *(G-542)*

Ametek Inc ....G 732 417-0501
Edison *(G-2456)*

▲ Astrodyne Corporation ....D 908 850-5088
Hackettstown *(G-3999)*

Billows Electric Supply Co Inc ....C 856 751-2200
Delran *(G-2009)*

▲ Blutek Power Inc ....F 973 594-1800
Lodi *(G-5554)*

Boonton Electronics Corp ....G 973 386-9696
Parsippany *(G-7895)*

Cobra Power Systems Inc ....G 908 486-1800
Millstone Township *(G-6210)*

Dewey Electronics Corporation ....E 201 337-4700
Oakland *(G-7624)*

Eagle Engineering & Automation ....G 732 899-2292
Point Pleasant Boro *(G-8844)*

▼ Electro-Miniatures Corp ....D 201 460-0510
Moonachie *(G-6464)*

Electro-Steam Generator Corp ....E 609 288-9071
Rancocas *(G-9160)*

Energy Battery Group Inc ....E 404 255-7529
Flemington *(G-3440)*

◆ Ewc Controls Inc ....E 732 446-3110
Manalapan *(G-5809)*

Fishermens Energy NJ LLC ....F 609 286-9650
Cape May *(G-1098)*

H Power Corp ....G 973 249-5444
Clifton *(G-1631)*

▲ Hansome Energy Systems Inc ....E 908 862-9044
Linden *(G-5354)*

▲ Hitechone Inc ....G 201 500-8864
Englewood Cliffs *(G-2975)*

▲ Hydro-Mechanical Systems Inc ....F 856 848-8888
Westville *(G-11816)*

▲ Innovative Power Solutions LLC ....E 732 544-1075
Eatontown *(G-2404)*

▲ Multi-Tech Industries Inc ....F 732 431-0550
Marlboro *(G-5905)*

◆ Ocean Power Technologies Inc ....G 609 730-0400
Monroe Township *(G-6339)*

▲ Pht Aerospace LLC ....F 973 831-1230
Pompton Plains *(G-8870)*

▲ Power Magne-Tech Corp ....E 732 826-4700
Perth Amboy *(G-8529)*

▲ Power Magnetics Inc ....E 609 695-1170
Trenton *(G-10977)*

Power Magnetics Inc ....E 800 747-0845
Trenton *(G-10978)*

◆ Power Pool Plus Inc ....G 908 454-1124
Alpha *(G-40)*

Primacy Engineering Inc ....F 201 731-3272
Englewood Cliffs *(G-2988)*

Princeton Tech Group Intl Corp ....G 732 328-9308
Edison *(G-2591)*

Rajysan Incorporated ....E 800 433-1382
Swedesboro *(G-10605)*

Servo-Tek Products Company Inc ....E 973 427-4249
Hawthorne *(G-4243)*

Technology Dynamics Inc ....D 201 385-0500
Bergenfield *(G-386)*

Torque Gun Company LLC ....E 201 512-9800
South Hackensack *(G-10189)*

◆ Triangle Tube/Phase III Co Inc ....D 856 228-9940
Paulsboro *(G-8340)*

Universal Electric Mtr Svc Inc ....E 201 968-1000
Hackensack *(G-3988)*

Valcor Engineering Corporation ....E 973 467-8100
Springfield *(G-10473)*

3624 Carbon & Graphite Prdts

▲ Asbury Louisiana Inc ....E 908 537-2155
Asbury *(G-63)*

Bella Acqua Inc ....F 609 324-9024
Chesterfield *(G-1436)*

◆ F S R Inc ....D 973 785-4347
Woodland Park *(G-12078)*

◆ Mersen USA Ptt Corp ....C 973 334-0700
Boonton *(G-562)*

◆ Resintech Inc ....C 856 768-9600
West Berlin *(G-11619)*

3625 Relays & Indl Controls

Admartec Inc ....G 732 888-8248
Hazlet *(G-4255)*

Advanced Industrial Controls ....G 908 725-7575
Branchburg *(G-611)*

Alliance Technologies Group ....G 973 664-1151
East Hanover *(G-2193)*

American Teletimer Corp ....E 908 654-4200
Mountainside *(G-6835)*

Amperite Co Inc ....E 201 864-9503
North Bergen *(G-7384)*

Argus International Inc ....E 609 466-1677
Ringoes *(G-9334)*

Artisan Controls Corporation ....F 973 598-9400
Randolph *(G-9173)*

▲ Aso Safety Solutions Inc ....G 973 586-9600
Rockaway *(G-9443)*

▲ Astrodyne Corporation ....D 908 850-5088
Hackettstown *(G-3999)*

Atc Systems Inc ....G 732 560-0900
Middlesex *(G-6099)*

▲ Automatic Switch Company ....A 973 966-2000
Florham Park *(G-3485)*

Computer Control Corp ....F 973 492-8265
Butler *(G-998)*

▲ Comus International Inc ....C 973 777-6900
Clifton *(G-1587)*

▲ Control & Power Systems Inc ....E 973 439-0500
Fairfield *(G-3175)*

CSC ....G 973 412-6339
Parsippany *(G-7912)*

Deltronics Corporation ....F 856 825-8200
Millville *(G-6246)*

Electronic Power Designs Inc ....F 973 838-7055
Bloomingdale *(G-527)*

▲ Electronic Technology Inc ....C 973 371-5160
Irvington *(G-4566)*

General Electronic Engineering ....G 732 381-1144
Rahway *(G-9097)*

▲ Hansome Energy Systems Inc ....E 908 862-9044
Linden *(G-5354)*

Harrison Electro Mechanical ....F 732 382-6008
Rahway *(G-9100)*

Haz Laboratories ....F 908 453-3300
Washington *(G-11446)*

▲ Heat-Timer Corporation ....E 973 575-4004
Fairfield *(G-3224)*

Howman Associates Inc ....G 732 985-7474
Edison *(G-2531)*

Howman Electronics Inc ....F 908 534-2247
Lebanon *(G-5262)*

▲ Infinova Corporation ....E 732 355-9100
Monmouth Junction *(G-6293)*

Innolutions Inc ....G 609 490-9799
Princeton Junction *(G-9061)*

Instrumentation Technology Sls ....G 732 388-0866
Rahway *(G-9104)*

Intellicon Inc ....G 201 791-9499
Kearny *(G-4870)*

ITT Corporation ....D...... 973 284-0123
Clifton *(G-1644)*

Kapsch Trafficcom Usa Inc ....F....... 201 528-9814
Secaucus *(G-9784)*

L3harris Technologies Inc ....E....... 973 284-0123
Clifton *(G-1651)*

Lummus Overseas Corporation ....E...... 973 893-3000
Bloomfield *(G-508)*

M&L Power Systems Maint Inc ....E....... 732 679-1800
Old Bridge *(G-7718)*

▲ Megatran Industries ....D...... 609 227-4300
Bordentown *(G-586)*

Mid-State Controls Inc ....F....... 732 335-0500
Hazlet *(G-4265)*

Omega Engineering Inc ....C...... 856 467-4200
Bridgeport *(G-742)*

Panasonic Corp North America ....D...... 201 348-7000
Newark *(G-7220)*

Pkm Panel Systems Corp ....F....... 732 238-6760
Old Bridge *(G-7724)*

▲ Precision Multiple Contrls Inc ....E....... 201 444-0600
Midland Park *(G-6184)*

Precision Multiple Contrls Inc ....D...... 201 444-0600
Midland Park *(G-6185)*

Pressure Controls Inc ....G...... 973 751-5002
Belleville *(G-308)*

Quik-Flex Circuit Inc ....E...... 856 742-0550
Gloucester City *(G-3849)*

◆ Rab Lighting Inc ....C...... 201 784-8600
Northvale *(G-7544)*

Redkoh Industries Inc ....G...... 908 369-1590
Hillsborough *(G-4351)*

Relay Specialties Inc ....G...... 856 547-5000
Haddon Heights *(G-4048)*

Rockwell Automation Inc ....E...... 973 658-1500
Parsippany *(G-8008)*

Rockwell Automation Inc ....G...... 973 526-3901
Parsippany *(G-8009)*

◆ Sealed Unit Parts Co Inc ....C...... 732 223-1201
Allenwood *(G-34)*

Servo-Tek Products Company Inc.........E...... 973 427-4249
Hawthorne *(G-4243)*

◆ Sigma-Netics Inc ....E...... 973 227-6372
Riverdale *(G-9385)*

Special Technical Services ....G...... 609 259-2626
Flanders *(G-3420)*

Swatch Group Les Btques US Inc........G...... 201 271-1400
Weehawken *(G-11570)*

▲ Textol Systems Inc ....E...... 201 935-1220
Carlstadt *(G-1227)*

▲ Transistor Devices Inc ....C...... 908 850-5088
Hackettstown *(G-4039)*

Tsg Inc ....F....... 973 785-1118
Little Falls *(G-5471)*

Tusa Products Inc ....G...... 609 448-8333
Ewing *(G-3072)*

Valcor Engineering Corporation...........E...... 973 467-8400
Springfield *(G-10474)*

Walker Engineering Inc ....F....... 732 899-2550
Point Pleasant Boro *(G-8848)*

Whippany Actuation Systems LLC ....C...... 973 428-9898
Whippany *(G-11913)*

Wireless Telecom Group Inc ....D...... 973 386-9696
Parsippany *(G-8040)*

Xybion Corporation ....C...... 973 538-2067
Lawrenceville *(G-5248)*

3629 Electrical Indl Apparatus, NEC

Access Conrol Group LLC ....F....... 908 789-8700
Robbinsville *(G-9406)*

▲ Active Controls LLC ....G...... 856 669-0940
Paulsboro *(G-8328)*

Atm Aficionado LLC ....G...... 973 251-2115
Livingston *(G-5507)*

Avionic Instruments LLC ....C...... 732 388-3500
Avenel *(G-122)*

Cellular Empire Inc ....D...... 800 778-3513
Linden *(G-5331)*

Dengen Scientific Corporation ....E...... 201 687-2983
Union City *(G-11110)*

▲ Evapco-Blct Dry Cooling Inc............E...... 908 379-2665
Bridgewater *(G-821)*

Exide Technologies ....G...... 973 439-9612
West Caldwell *(G-11649)*

Industronic Inc ....G...... 908 393-5960
Bridgewater *(G-835)*

▲ Jsn Holdings LLC ....F....... 201 857-5900
Mahwah *(G-5751)*

▲ Mizco International Inc ....D...... 732 912-2000
Avenel *(G-137)*

◆ Ocean Power Technologies Inc........E...... 609 730-0400
Monroe Township *(G-6339)*

▲ Power Dynamics Inc ....E...... 973 560-0019
Whippany *(G-11906)*

Powerspec Inc ....E...... 732 494-9490
Somerville *(G-10123)*

▲ Princeton Power Systems Inc..........D...... 609 955-5390
Lawrenceville *(G-5242)*

Sparton Aydin LLC ....F....... 732 935-1320
Eatontown *(G-2421)*

Storis Inc ....G...... 888 478-6747
Mount Arlington *(G-6719)*

▲ Tdk-Lambda Americas Inc ....E...... 732 922-9300
Tinton Falls *(G-10731)*

Timothy P Bryan Elc Co Inc ....E...... 609 393-8325
Trenton *(G-10999)*

Weissco Power Ltd Liability Co............G...... 908 832-2173
Califon *(G-1037)*

3631 Household Cooking Eqpt

Chefman Direct Inc ....D...... 888 315-8407
Mahwah *(G-5722)*

Clean Bbq Inc ....G...... 732 299-8877
Edison *(G-2479)*

Haier America Trading LLC ....G...... 212 594-3330
Woodbridge *(G-12017)*

◆ Jarden LLC ....E...... 201 610-6600
Hoboken *(G-4458)*

◆ Sharp Electronics Corporation ....A...... 201 529-8200
Montvale *(G-6433)*

▲ Signature Marketing Group Ltd ....F....... 973 575-7785
Pine Brook *(G-8617)*

3632 Household Refrigerators & Freezers

▲ Bar-Maid Corporation ....C...... 973 478-7070
Garfield *(G-3731)*

▲ Troy Hills Manufacturing Inc ....G...... 973 263-1885
Towaco *(G-10882)*

3633 Household Laundry Eqpt

Artisan Gardens LLC ....G...... 201 857-2600
Ridgewood *(G-9322)*

3634 Electric Household Appliances

Aftek Inc ....G...... 609 588-0900
Hamilton *(G-4101)*

Argonautus LLC ....G...... 908 393-4379
Bridgewater *(G-792)*

▲ Brabantia USA Inc ....F....... 201 933-3192
East Rutherford *(G-2279)*

Conair Corporation ....D...... 239 673-2125
East Windsor *(G-2347)*

Conair Corporation ....C...... 609 426-1300
East Windsor *(G-2348)*

Edwards Creative Products Inc ....F....... 856 665-3200
Cherry Hill *(G-1358)*

Emerald Electronics Usa Inc ....G...... 718 872-5544
Passaic *(G-8063)*

Expert Appliance Center LLC ....E...... 732 946-0999
Marlboro *(G-5897)*

▲ Haydon Corporation ....D...... 973 904-0800
Wayne *(G-11515)*

◆ Homeco LLC ....E...... 732 802-7733
Piscataway *(G-8673)*

◆ Jarden LLC ....E...... 201 610-6600
Hoboken *(G-4458)*

▲ Maverick Industries Inc ....C...... 732 417-9666
Edison *(G-2559)*

◆ Rj Brands LLC ....C...... 888 315-8407
Mahwah *(G-5768)*

Rjticeco LLC ....G...... 973 697-0156
Stockholm *(G-10500)*

Technology General Corporation ....F....... 973 827-8209
Franklin *(G-3609)*

Vapor Lounge LLC ....G...... 973 627-1277
Rockaway *(G-9511)*

◆ Wanasavealotcom LLC ....F....... 732 286-6956
Toms River *(G-10802)*

◆ White Home Products Inc ....G...... 908 226-2501
Kenilworth *(G-4990)*

◆ Winiadaewoo Elec Amer Inc.............F....... 201 552-4950
Ridgefield Park *(G-9320)*

3635 Household Vacuum Cleaners

Hillsborough Vacuum LLC ....G...... 908 904-6600
Hillsborough *(G-4324)*

▲ Metropolitan Vacuum Clr Co Inc........D...... 201 405-2225
Oakland *(G-7636)*

3639 Household Appliances, NEC

Boutique USA Corp ....G...... 917 476-0472
Englewood *(G-2885)*

Groupe Seb USA ....F....... 856 825-6300
Millville *(G-6253)*

◆ Organize It-All Inc ....E...... 201 488-0808
Bogota *(G-534)*

▲ PC Marketing Inc ....E...... 201 943-6100
Ridgefield *(G-9282)*

◆ Royal Sovereign Intl Inc ....E...... 800 397-1025
Rockleigh *(G-9521)*

◆ Triangle Tube/Phase III Co Inc.........D...... 856 228-9940
Paulsboro *(G-8340)*

◆ Wanasavealotcom LLC ....F....... 732 286-6956
Toms River *(G-10802)*

3641 Electric Lamps

▲ Amati International LLC ....E...... 201 569-1000
Englewood Cliffs *(G-2957)*

▲ Bitro Group Inc ....E...... 201 641-1004
Hackensack *(G-3886)*

◆ E G L Company Inc ....C...... 908 508-1111
Berkeley Heights *(G-398)*

Ethan Allen Retail Inc ....C...... 973 473-1019
Passaic *(G-8065)*

Hamamatsu Corporation ....E...... 908 526-0941
Bridgewater *(G-829)*

▲ Hamamatsu Corporation ....D...... 908 231-0960
Bridgewater *(G-828)*

▲ Hanovia Specialty Lighting LLC ....F....... 973 651-5510
Fairfield *(G-3221)*

Hid Ultraviolet LLC ....F....... 973 383-8535
Sparta *(G-10392)*

Horiba Instruments Inc ....E...... 732 623-8335
Piscataway *(G-8674)*

Lumitron Corp ....F....... 908 508-9100
Berkeley Heights *(G-407)*

▲ Maxlite Inc ....D...... 973 244-7300
West Caldwell *(G-11663)*

Metal Textiles Corporation ....E...... 800 843-1215
Edison *(G-2564)*

Mks Inc ....E...... 856 451-5545
Bridgeton *(G-765)*

Natal Lamp & Shade Corp ....E...... 201 224-7844
Fort Lee *(G-3578)*

Oxberry LLC ....G...... 201 935-3000
Carlstadt *(G-1194)*

Oxford Lamp Inc ....F....... 732 462-3755
Freehold *(G-3686)*

Precision Filaments Inc ....F....... 732 462-3755
Freehold *(G-3690)*

Rhingo Pro LLC ....G...... 201 728-9099
Lodi *(G-5574)*

Union City Filament Corp ....E...... 201 945-3366
Ridgefield *(G-9294)*

3643 Current-Carrying Wiring Devices

ABB Installation Products Inc ....C...... 908 852-1122
Hackettstown *(G-3994)*

Ametek Inc ....G...... 732 370-9100
Lakewood *(G-5052)*

Amperite Co Inc ....E...... 201 864-9503
North Bergen *(G-7384)*

▲ Archtech Electronics Corp................E...... 732 355-1288
Dayton *(G-1951)*

Armel Electronics Inc ....E...... 201 869-4300
North Bergen *(G-7387)*

Asco Power Services Inc ....F....... 973 966-2000
Florham Park *(G-3483)*

Beall Technologies Inc ....E...... 201 689-2130
Wyckoff *(G-12104)*

Billows Electric Supply Co Inc ....C...... 856 751-2200
Delran *(G-2009)*

Bleema Manufacturing Corp ....E...... 973 371-1771
Irvington *(G-4563)*

Brim Electronics Inc ....F....... 201 796-2886
Lodi *(G-5555)*

◆ Cain Machine Inc ....F....... 856 825-7225
Millville *(G-6240)*

Calculagraph Co ....D...... 973 887-9400
East Hanover *(G-2198)*

Calculagraph Co ....G...... 973 887-9400
East Hanover *(G-2199)*

Connector Products Inc ....F....... 856 829-9190
Pennsauken *(G-8408)*

▲ Dearborn A Belden Cdt Company ...D...... 908 925-8000
Elizabeth *(G-2726)*

East Coast Electronics Inc ....G...... 908 431-7555
Hillsborough *(G-4313)*

S I C

Esi....E....856 629-2492
Sicklerville *(G-9909)*
Frc Electrical Industries Inc....E....908 464-3200
New Providence *(G-7000)*
G H Krauss Manufacturing Co....G....856 662-0815
Cherry Hill *(G-1365)*
Glasseal Products Inc....C....732 370-9100
Lakewood *(G-5104)*
Hofer Connectors Co Inc....E....973 427-1195
North Haledon *(G-7495)*
Hofer Machine & Tool Co Inc....F....973 427-1195
North Haledon *(G-7496)*
Howman Electronics Inc....F....908 534-2247
Lebanon *(G-5262)*
HPH Products Inc....G....609 883-0052
Ewing *(G-3037)*
Kraus & Naimer Inc....E....732 560-1240
Somerset *(G-10011)*
Lapp Usa Inc....G....973 660-9700
Florham Park *(G-3516)*
Lightning Prvntion Systems Inc....G....856 767-7806
West Berlin *(G-11603)*
▲ Lumenarc Inc....F....973 882-5918
West Caldwell *(G-11659)*
M&L Power Systems Maint Inc....E....732 679-1800
Old Bridge *(G-7718)*
◆ Mac Products Inc....D....973 344-5149
Kearny *(G-4880)*
Marine Electric Systems Inc....E....201 531-8600
South Hackensack *(G-10171)*
▲ Multi-Tech Industries Inc....F....732 431-0550
Marlboro *(G-5905)*
Newtech Group Corp....G....732 355-0392
Kendall Park *(G-4919)*
Pekay Industries Inc....F....732 938-2722
Farmingdale *(G-3390)*
Precision Mfg Group LLC....D....973 785-4630
Cedar Grove *(G-1288)*
Pressure Controls Inc....G....973 751-5002
Belleville *(G-308)*
◆ Richards Mfg A NJ Ltd Partnr....C....973 371-1771
Irvington *(G-4585)*
▲ Richards Mfg Co Sales Inc....E....973 371-1771
Irvington *(G-4586)*
▲ Roxboro Holdings Inc....D....732 919-3119
Wall Township *(G-11365)*
Rti Dge LLC....F....732 254-6389
Marlboro *(G-5912)*
Signal Systems International....G....732 793-4668
Lavallette *(G-5212)*
Simply Amazing LLC....F....732 249-4151
East Brunswick *(G-2177)*
Tycom Limited....C....973 753-3040
Morristown *(G-6704)*
▲ Unique Wire Weaving Co Inc....E....908 688-4600
Hillside *(G-4433)*
Vermont Cableworks Inc....G....802 674-6555
Edison *(G-2639)*
Volta Corporation....E....732 583-3300
Laurence Harbor *(G-5211)*

3644 Noncurrent-Carrying Wiring Devices

ABB Installation Products Inc....C....908 852-1122
Hackettstown *(G-3994)*
American Fittings Corp....G....201 664-0027
Fair Lawn *(G-3083)*
Armel Electronics Inc....E....201 869-4300
North Bergen *(G-7387)*
Billows Electric Supply Co Inc....C....856 751-2200
Delran *(G-2009)*
E & G Roman Corp....D....973 482-1123
Newark *(G-7110)*
◆ Heyco Molded Products Inc....F....732 286-4336
Toms River *(G-10765)*
Hope Electrical Products Co....G....973 882-7400
West Caldwell *(G-11653)*
Liberty Park Raceway LLC....F....201 333-7223
Jersey City *(G-4758)*
Moreng Metal Products Inc....D....973 256-2001
Totowa *(G-10837)*
Morgan Advanced Ceramics Inc....E....973 808-1621
Fairfield *(G-3273)*
Mulberry Metal Products Inc....D....908 688-8850
Union *(G-11078)*
▲ Multi-Tech Industries Inc....F....732 431-0550
Marlboro *(G-5905)*
Raceway Petroleum Inc....F....908 222-2999
North Plainfield *(G-7508)*
Raceway Petroleum Inc....G....732 729-7350
East Brunswick *(G-2171)*
Raceway Petroleum Inc....E....732 613-4404
East Brunswick *(G-2172)*
▲ Superflex Ltd....E....718 768-1400
Elizabeth *(G-2778)*

3645 Residential Lighting Fixtures

▲ Amati International LLC....E....201 569-1000
Englewood Cliffs *(G-2957)*
▲ American Brass and Crystal Inc....E....908 688-8611
Union *(G-11023)*
Apelio Innovative Inds LLC....F....973 777-8899
Kearny *(G-4844)*
Big Eye Lamp Inc....G....732 557-9400
Whiting *(G-11937)*
Cooper Lighting LLC....D....609 395-4277
Cranbury *(G-1828)*
▲ Cutting Edge Casting Inc....E....908 925-7500
Linden *(G-5340)*
Efficient Lighting Inc....F....973 846-8568
Parsippany *(G-7933)*
Encore Led Ltg Ltd Lblty Co....G....866 694-4533
Wayne *(G-11497)*
Estrin Calabrese Sales Agency....G....908 722-9980
Manville *(G-5855)*
Galaxy Switchgear Inds LLC....E....914 668-8200
Kearny *(G-4858)*
▲ Gemini Cut Glass Company Inc....G....201 568-7722
Englewood *(G-2909)*
▲ Generation Brands....G....856 764-0500
Burlington *(G-972)*
◆ Genie House Corp....E....609 859-0600
Southampton *(G-10363)*
Go R Design LLC....E....609 286-2146
New Egypt *(G-6983)*
Graybar Electric Company Inc....D....973 404-5555
Edison *(G-2522)*
▲ High Energy Group Ltd Lblty Co....G....732 741-9099
Eatontown *(G-2397)*
Infinlight Products Inc....G....888 665-7708
East Windsor *(G-2353)*
Jay-Bee Lamp & Shade Co Inc....G....201 265-0762
Paramus *(G-7809)*
▼ Kurt Versen Inc....F....201 664-5283
Montvale *(G-6418)*
◆ Lighting World Inc....E....732 919-1224
Farmingdale *(G-3387)*
M + 4 Inc....G....973 527-3262
Budd Lake *(G-927)*
▲ Pty Lighting LLC....G....855 303-4500
Hillside *(G-4421)*
▲ R B B Corp....E....973 770-1100
Ledgewood *(G-5279)*
Robert Wallace....G....609 649-0596
Stockton *(G-10502)*
▲ Starfire Lighting Inc....E....201 438-9540
Wood Ridge *(G-12006)*
▲ Superior Lighting Inc....F....908 759-0199
Elizabeth *(G-2779)*
T C S Technologies Inc....F....908 852-7555
Hackettstown *(G-4038)*
▼ William Spencer....G....856 235-1830
Mount Laurel *(G-6813)*

3646 Commercial, Indl & Institutional Lighting Fixtures

Absolume LLC....G....732 523-1231
Lakewood *(G-5043)*
▲ Amati International LLC....E....201 569-1000
Englewood Cliffs *(G-2957)*
▲ American Brass and Crystal Inc....E....908 688-8611
Union *(G-11023)*
▲ American Scientific Ltg Corp....E....718 369-1100
Trenton *(G-10892)*
◆ Amerlux LLC....C....973 882-5010
Oakland *(G-7614)*
Apelio Innovative Inds LLC....F....973 777-8899
Kearny *(G-4844)*
Articulight Inc....G....201 796-2690
Fair Lawn *(G-3085)*
Belfer....G....732 493-2666
Farmingdale *(G-3378)*
Bellemead Hot Glass....G....908 281-5516
Hillsborough *(G-4303)*
▲ Compact Fluorescent Systems....G....908 475-8991
Sparta *(G-10383)*
Cooper Lighting LLC....D....609 395-4277
Cranbury *(G-1828)*
▲ Coronet Inc....C....973 345-7660
Totowa *(G-10824)*
Durabrite Ltg Solutions LLC....G....201 915-0555
Jersey City *(G-4729)*
▲ Eluxnet USA Corporation....G....201 724-5986
Riverdale *(G-9376)*
Encore Led Ltg Ltd Lblty Co....G....866 694-4533
Wayne *(G-11497)*
▲ Former Circuit Inc....G....732 549-0056
Edison *(G-2513)*
▲ Genesis Lighting Mfg Inc....G....908 352-6720
Elizabethport *(G-2788)*
▲ Illuminating Experiences LLC....G....800 734-5858
New Brunswick *(G-6934)*
◆ Lighting World Inc....E....732 919-1224
Farmingdale *(G-3387)*
M + 4 Inc....G....973 527-3262
Budd Lake *(G-927)*
▲ Mercury Lighting Pdts Co Inc....C....973 244-9444
Fairfield *(G-3269)*
Mks Inc....E....856 451-5545
Bridgeton *(G-765)*
▲ North American Illumination....F....973 478-4700
Garfield *(G-3751)*
Picasso Lighting Inds LLC....E....201 246-8188
Kearny *(G-4893)*
Prg Group Inc....G....201 758-4000
Secaucus *(G-9798)*
▲ R B B Corp....E....973 770-1100
Ledgewood *(G-5279)*
◆ Rab Lighting Inc....C....201 784-8600
Northvale *(G-7544)*
▲ Rambusch Decorating Company....E....201 333-2525
Jersey City *(G-4797)*
▲ Reggiani Lighting Usa Inc....F....201 372-1717
Carlstadt *(G-1210)*
Robert Wallace....G....609 649-0596
Stockton *(G-10502)*
▲ Signify North America Corp....F....732 563-3000
Somerset *(G-10072)*
SMS Building Systems Ltd Lblty....F....856 520-8769
Cherry Hill *(G-1415)*
▲ Specialty Lighting Inds Inc....E....732 517-0800
Ocean *(G-7684)*
▲ Starfire Lighting Inc....E....201 438-9540
Wood Ridge *(G-12006)*
▲ Superior Lighting Inc....F....908 759-0199
Elizabeth *(G-2779)*
▲ Tektite Industries Inc....G....609 656-0600
Trenton *(G-10997)*
◆ Trinity Manufacturing LLC....C....732 549-2866
Metuchen *(G-6079)*
Vision Lighting Inc....G....973 720-1200
Paterson *(G-8323)*

3647 Vehicular Lighting Eqpt

Amperite Co Inc....E....201 864-9503
North Bergen *(G-7384)*
Elite Emrgncy Lights Ltd Lblty....F....732 534-2377
Lakewood *(G-5090)*
Spaghetti Engineering Corp....F....856 719-9989
West Berlin *(G-11623)*
Sun Display Systems LLC....E....973 226-4334
Fairfield *(G-3320)*
▲ Vehicle Safety Mfg LLC....E....973 643-3000
Newark *(G-7311)*

3648 Lighting Eqpt, NEC

A P M Hexseal Corporation....E....201 569-5700
Englewood *(G-2872)*
ABB Lighting Inc....G....866 222-8866
Toms River *(G-10737)*
Amperite Co Inc....E....201 864-9503
North Bergen *(G-7384)*
Archlit Inc....G....973 577-4400
Hopatcong *(G-4518)*
▲ Carpenter LLC....F....609 689-3090
Trenton *(G-10911)*
City of Jersey City....F....201 547-4470
Jersey City *(G-4713)*
▲ City Theatrical Inc....E....201 549-1160
Carlstadt *(G-1143)*
Cubalas Emergency Lighting LLC....G....908 514-0505
Roselle *(G-9555)*
◆ Eco Lighting USA Ltd Lblty Co....G....201 621-5661
South Hackensack *(G-10156)*
Encore Led Ltg Ltd Lblty Co....G....866 694-4533
Wayne *(G-11497)*
▲ Erco Lighting Inc....F....732 225-8856
Edison *(G-2506)*
▲ Galaxy Led Inc....G....201 541-5461
Englewood Cliffs *(G-2972)*

Garden State Irrigation .... F 201 848-1300
Wyckoff *(G-12112)*

▲ Gogreen Power Inc .... F 732 994-5901
Howell *(G-4540)*

▲ High Energy Group Ltd Lblty Co ...... G 732 741-9099
Eatontown *(G-2397)*

▲ I-Light Usa Inc .... G 908 317-0020
Mountainside *(G-6847)*

In The Spotlights .... G 973 361-7768
Rockaway *(G-9466)*

Innovtive Phtnics Slution Corp .... G 732 355-9300
Monmouth Junction *(G-6294)*

Izzo Enterprises Inc .... E 908 845-8200
Scotch Plains *(G-9735)*

▲ John G Papailias Co Inc .... G 201 767-4027
Northvale *(G-7532)*

Lightfox Inc .... E 973 209-9112
Morristown *(G-6679)*

Maxlite Inc .... F 800 555-5629
West Caldwell *(G-11662)*

Michele Maddalena .... G 973 244-0033
Fairfield *(G-3270)*

Musco Sports Lighting LLC .... G 732 751-9114
Wall Township *(G-11357)*

▲ Natale Machine & Tool Co Inc ...... F 201 933-5500
Carlstadt *(G-1189)*

◆ Pioneer & Co Inc .... E 856 866-9191
Moorestown *(G-6557)*

Princeton Tectonics .... E 609 298-9331
West Berlin *(G-11616)*

▲ Princeton Tectonics .... C 609 298-9331
Pennsauken *(G-8472)*

▼ Proactive Ltg Solutions LLC .... F 800 747-1209
North Arlington *(G-7377)*

◆ Rab Lighting Inc .... C 201 784-8600
Northvale *(G-7544)*

◆ Smartpool LLC .... E 732 730-9880
Lakewood *(G-5164)*

▲ Tektite Industries Inc .... G 609 656-0600
Trenton *(G-10997)*

This Is It Stageworks LLC .... G 201 653-2699
Jersey City *(G-4820)*

◆ Trinity Manufacturing LLC .... C 732 549-2866
Metuchen *(G-6079)*

▼ Unilux Inc .... E 201 712-1266
Saddle Brook *(G-9685)*

Wisely Products LLC .... G 929 329-9188
Jersey City *(G-4833)*

Zago Manufacturing Company ...... E 973 643-6700
Newark *(G-7318)*

3651 Household Audio & Video Eqpt

360 Media Innovations LLC .... G 201 228-0941
Union *(G-11018)*

▲ Apb-Dynasonics Inc .... G 973 785-1101
Totowa *(G-10813)*

Apogee Sound International LLC ...... E 201 934-8500
Ramsey *(G-9138)*

Audio Technologies and Codecs ...... F 973 624-1116
Newark *(G-7058)*

B and G Music LLC .... G 732 779-4555
Bayville *(G-241)*

▲ Bayview Entertainment LLC .... E 201 880-5331
Pompton Plains *(G-8860)*

◆ Bogen Communications Inc .... D 201 934-8500
Mahwah *(G-5718)*

Bogen Corporation .... G 201 934-8500
Ramsey *(G-9142)*

Broadway Empress Entrmt Inc ...... G 973 991-0009
Newark *(G-7078)*

Caregility Corporation .... E 732 413-6000
Eatontown *(G-2383)*

Celco .... F 201 327-1123
Mahwah *(G-5721)*

Concept Professional Systems .... G 732 938-5321
Wall Township *(G-11332)*

◆ Crestron Electronics Inc .... C 201 767-3400
Rockleigh *(G-9516)*

▲ CVE Inc .... D 201 770-0005
Riverdale *(G-9374)*

DMJ Technologies LLC .... G 201 261-5560
New Milford *(G-6989)*

Dtrovision LLC .... E 201 488-3232
Fair Lawn *(G-3097)*

◆ Emerson Radio Corp .... F 973 428-2000
Parsippany *(G-7936)*

Empirical Labs Inc .... F 973 541-9447
Lake Hiawatha *(G-5034)*

Excite View LLC .... E 201 227-7075
Tenafly *(G-10662)*

Ferro Industries Incorporated ...... E 732 246-3200
Colts Neck *(G-1782)*

▲ Fuchs Audio Tech Ltd Lblty Co ...... F 973 772-4420
Clifton *(G-1623)*

▲ Funai Corporation Inc .... E 201 806-7635
Rutherford *(G-9621)*

Gabriel Sound Ltd Liability Co ...... G 973 831-7800
Pompton Lakes *(G-8851)*

▲ GP Acoustics (us) Inc .... E 732 683-2356
Marlboro *(G-5899)*

Gzgn Inc .... F 201 842-7622
Rutherford *(G-9622)*

Innovative Concepts Design LLC ...... F 732 346-0061
Elizabeth *(G-2750)*

Itec Consultants LLC .... G 732 784-8322
Matawan *(G-5978)*

▼ Jvc Industrial America Inc .... E 800 247-3608
Wayne *(G-11527)*

Jvckenwood USA Corporation ...... E 973 317-5000
Wayne *(G-11528)*

▲ Kef America Inc .... E 732 414-2074
Marlboro *(G-5903)*

Kultur International Films Ltd ...... E 732 229-2343
Red Bank *(G-9233)*

◆ Lg Electronics USA Inc .... B 201 816-2000
Englewood Cliffs *(G-2982)*

▲ Lunar Audio Video LLC .... G 973 233-7700
Sayreville *(G-9717)*

▲ Mardee Company Inc .... E 908 753-4343
South Plainfield *(G-10297)*

▲ Mp Production .... F 973 729-9333
Sparta *(G-10400)*

Murray Electronics Inc .... G 201 405-1158
Oakland *(G-7637)*

▲ Oklahoma Sound Corp .... E 800 261-4112
Clifton *(G-1680)*

Peter-Lisand Machine Corp .... G 201 943-5600
New Milford *(G-6991)*

Philips Elec N Amer Corp .... D 973 804-2100
Ledgewood *(G-5278)*

Phoenix Systems .... G 201 788-5511
North Haledon *(G-7499)*

▲ Rcf USA Inc .... E 732 902-6100
Edison *(G-2595)*

Riotsound Inc .... E 917 273-5814
Newton *(G-7355)*

Rock Dreams Electronics LLC ...... E 609 890-0808
Trenton *(G-10988)*

Scj Group LLC .... G 201 289-5841
Teaneck *(G-10651)*

◆ Sdi Technologies Inc .... D 732 574-9000
Rahway *(G-9127)*

Sharkk LLC .... F 302 377-3974
Livingston *(G-5540)*

◆ Sharp Electronics Corporation ...... A 201 529-8200
Montvale *(G-6433)*

▲ Sierra Video Systems .... E 530 478-1000
Clinton *(G-1749)*

Signature Audio Video Systems ...... G 732 864-1039
Toms River *(G-10793)*

▲ Sondpex Corp America LLC ...... G 732 940-4430
Princeton *(G-9026)*

Sony Corporation of America ...... B 201 930-1000
Paramus *(G-7834)*

Sony Corporation of America ...... F 201 930-1000
Woodcliff Lake *(G-12065)*

Sony Electronics Inc .... A 201 930-1000
Paramus *(G-7835)*

Sound Chice Asstive Listening ...... E 908 647-2651
Gillette *(G-3803)*

Sound Professionals Inc .... G 609 267-4400
Hainesport *(G-4078)*

Sound United LLC .... E 201 762-6500
Mahwah *(G-5773)*

Stirling Audio Services LLC .... G 732 560-0707
Middlesex *(G-6154)*

Tech Giant LLC .... F 888 800-7745
Eatontown *(G-2425)*

▲ Techflex Inc .... F 973 300-9242
Sparta *(G-10409)*

Toshiba Amer Consmr Pdts Inc ...... C 973 628-8000
Wayne *(G-11558)*

Tusa Products Inc .... G 609 448-8333
Ewing *(G-3072)*

V P I Industries Inc .... G 732 583-6895
Cliffwood *(G-1548)*

Vanderbilt LLC .... G 973 316-3900
Parsippany *(G-8034)*

◆ Vcom Intl Multi-Media Corp .... D 201 814-0405
Fairfield *(G-3338)*

◆ Vcom Intl Multi-Media Corp .... D 201 296-0600
Fairfield *(G-3339)*

Wireworks Corporation .... E 908 686-7400
Hillside *(G-4437)*

Xbox Exclusive .... G 908 756-3731
South Plainfield *(G-10347)*

◆ York Telecom Corporation .... D 732 413-6000
Eatontown *(G-2430)*

Ytc Holdings Inc .... G 732 413-6000
Eatontown *(G-2431)*

Zenith Electronics Corporation ...... E 201 816-2071
Englewood Cliffs *(G-2998)*

3652 Phonograph Records & Magnetic Tape

Audio and Video Labs Inc .... E 856 661-5772
Delair *(G-2000)*

◆ Disc Makers Inc .... B 800 468-9353
Pennsauken *(G-8414)*

◆ Maxell Corporation of America ...... E 973 653-2400
Woodland Park *(G-12084)*

Metrolpolis Mastering LP .... E 212 604-9433
Edgewater *(G-2440)*

▲ PM Swapco Inc .... F 201 438-7700
Lyndhurst *(G-5672)*

Recorded Publications Labs .... E 856 963-3000
Camden *(G-1085)*

Simtronics Corporation .... F 732 747-0322
Little Silver *(G-5500)*

Sony Corporation of America ...... B 201 930-1000
Paramus *(G-7834)*

Sony Music Holdings Inc .... B 201 777-3933
Rutherford *(G-9634)*

Sun Plastics Co Inc .... F 908 490-0870
Watchung *(G-11459)*

United Sound Arts Inc .... F 732 229-4949
Eatontown *(G-2427)*

3661 Telephone & Telegraph Apparatus

Alcatel-Lucent USA Inc .... D 908 582-3275
New Providence *(G-6993)*

▼ AT&T Technologies Inc .... A 201 771-2000
Berkeley Heights *(G-389)*

Avaya Cala Inc .... G 866 462-8292
Morristown *(G-6642)*

Avaya Inc .... B 908 953-6000
Morristown *(G-6643)*

Avaya Inc .... C 732 852-2030
Lincroft *(G-5310)*

◆ Avaya World Services Inc .... E 908 953-6000
Morristown *(G-6644)*

◆ Bogen Communications Inc .... D 201 934-8500
Mahwah *(G-5718)*

Bogen Corporation .... G 201 934-8500
Ramsey *(G-9142)*

Centurum Information Tech Inc ...... G 856 751-1111
Marlton *(G-5924)*

▲ Chromis Fiberoptics Inc .... F 732 764-0900
Warren *(G-11405)*

Conair Corporation .... C 609 426-1300
East Windsor *(G-2348)*

▲ Dataprobe Inc .... E 201 934-9944
Allendale *(G-7)*

Dialogic Inc .... C 973 967-6000
Parsippany *(G-7916)*

DR Tielmann Inc .... G 732 332-1860
Colts Neck *(G-1781)*

Eagle Communications Inc .... G 973 366-6181
Denville *(G-2036)*

Eastern Instrumentation of .... G 856 231-0668
Moorestown *(G-6519)*

Faraday Photonics LLC .... G 973 239-2005
Verona *(G-11166)*

Fiber-Span Inc .... E 908 253-9080
Toms River *(G-10757)*

Foctek Photonics LLC .... G 732 828-8228
Milltown *(G-6215)*

▲ Infinova Corporation .... E 732 355-9100
Monmouth Junction *(G-6293)*

Iniven LLC .... G 908 722-3770
Branchburg *(G-649)*

Inlc Technology Corporation ...... F 908 834-8390
Warren *(G-11418)*

Innovance Inc .... G 732 529-2300
Piscataway *(G-8679)*

▲ Instock Wireless Components ...... F 973 335-6550
Boonton *(G-557)*

▲ IPC Systems Inc .... C 201 253-2000
Jersey City *(G-4750)*

J C Contracting Inc .... F 973 748-5600
Rahway *(G-9105)*

LAp Marketing MGT Svcs Inc ....F 609 654-9266
Cherry Hill *(G-1382)*
Lattice Incorporated ....F 856 910-1166
Pennsauken *(G-8450)*
Lcn Partners Inc ....F 215 755-1000
Berlin *(G-426)*
Lucent Technologies World Svcs ....C 908 582-3000
New Providence *(G-7008)*
Lyca Tel LLC ....E 973 286-0771
Newark *(G-7191)*
▲ Mizco International Inc ....D 732 912-2000
Avenel *(G-137)*
Nokia Inc ....F 908 582-3149
Murray Hill *(G-6860)*
Ntt Electronics America Inc ....F 201 556-1770
Saddle Brook *(G-9666)*
Oe Solutions America Inc ....F 201 568-1188
Ridgefield Park *(G-9313)*
Ofs Fitel LLC ....E 732 748-7409
Somerset *(G-10043)*
Ofs Specialty Photonics & Labs ....G 732 748-7401
Somerset *(G-10044)*
Packetstorm Communications Inc ....F 732 840-3871
Westwood *(G-11837)*
Parwan Electronics Corporation ....E 732 290-1900
Matawan *(G-5983)*
▲ Quintum Technologies Inc ....D 732 460-9000
Eatontown *(G-2419)*
Response Time Incorporated ....E 856 875-0025
Williamstown *(G-11974)*
Shore Microsystems Inc ....G 732 870-0800
Long Branch *(G-5606)*
Sierra Communication Intl LLC ....G 866 462-8292
Morristown *(G-6700)*
▲ Sonetronics Inc ....D 732 681-5016
Belmar *(G-354)*
Star Dynamic Corp ....D 732 257-7488
Garfield *(G-3769)*
▲ Subcom LLC ....B 732 578-7000
Eatontown *(G-2422)*
◆ Swintec Corp ....F 201 935-0115
Moonachie *(G-6493)*
Technology Corp America Inc ....G 866 462-8292
Morristown *(G-6703)*
Telcontel Corp ....F 732 441-0800
Laurence Harbor *(G-5210)*
Telecom Assistance Group Inc ....E 856 753-8585
West Berlin *(G-11628)*
▲ TMC Corporation ....G 609 860-1830
Metuchen *(G-6078)*
Tollgrade Communications Inc ....G 732 743-6720
Piscataway *(G-8729)*
Transcore LP ....F 201 329-9200
Teterboro *(G-10696)*
Vitex LLC ....G 201 296-0145
Englewood Cliffs *(G-2997)*
Vytran Corporation ....E 732 972-2880
Morganville *(G-6598)*
Vytran LLC ....E 732 972-2880
Morganville *(G-6599)*
Zzyzx LLC ....G 908 722-3770
Branchburg *(G-700)*

3663 Radio & T V Communications, Systs & Eqpt, Broadcast/Studio

Alcatel-Lucent USA Inc ....D 908 582-3275
New Providence *(G-6993)*
Anatech Microwave Company Inc ....G 973 772-7369
Garfield *(G-3728)*
▲ Antronix Inc ....E 609 860-0160
Cranbury *(G-1812)*
Aphelion Orbitals Inc ....G 321 289-0872
Union City *(G-11107)*
◆ Blitz Safe of America Inc ....F 201 569-5000
Englewood *(G-2884)*
▲ Blonder Tongue Labs Inc ....C 732 679-4000
Old Bridge *(G-7713)*
BNS Enterprises Inc ....G 908 285-6556
Hillsborough *(G-4306)*
◆ Bogen Communications Inc ....D 201 934-8500
Mahwah *(G-5718)*
Bogen Corporation ....G 201 934-8500
Ramsey *(G-9142)*
Cabletenna Corp ....G 609 395-9400
Cranbury *(G-1818)*
Cellebrite Inc ....D 973 206-7763
Parsippany *(G-7898)*
Cellgain Wireless LLC ....F 732 889-4671
Red Bank *(G-9223)*

Centurum Information Tech Inc ....G 856 751-1111
Marlton *(G-5924)*
◆ Checkpoint Systems Inc ....C 800 257-5540
West Deptford *(G-11697)*
Checkpoint Systems Inc ....C 856 848-1800
West Deptford *(G-11698)*
▲ Comm Port Technologies Inc ....G 732 738-8780
Cranbury *(G-1826)*
◆ Communication Devices Inc ....F 973 334-1980
Boonton *(G-546)*
Comodo Group Inc ....D 888 266-6361
Clifton *(G-1586)*
Computeradio ....G 973 220-0087
Montville *(G-6440)*
Comtron Inc ....F 732 446-7571
Springfield *(G-10436)*
◆ Cooper Wheelock Inc ....B 732 222-6880
Long Branch *(G-5595)*
◆ Crestron Electronics Inc ....C 201 767-3400
Rockleigh *(G-9516)*
Daysequerra Corporation ....F 856 719-9900
Pennsauken *(G-8411)*
Deckhouse Communications Inc ....G 201 961-5564
Fairfield *(G-3181)*
DMJ and Associates Inc ....E 732 613-7867
Sayreville *(G-9708)*
Draztic Designs LLC ....E 609 678-4200
Columbus *(G-1800)*
Eclearview Technologies Inc ....G 732 695-6999
Ocean *(G-7662)*
Eigent Technologies Inc ....G 732 673-0402
Holmdel *(G-4500)*
▼ Electromagnetic Tech Inds Inc ....D 973 394-1719
Boonton *(G-550)*
Engility LLC ....F 703 633-8300
Princeton Junction *(G-9055)*
Ensync Intrctive Solutions Inc ....G 732 542-4001
Freehold *(G-3664)*
EVs Broadcast Equipment Inc ....E 973 575-7811
Fairfield *(G-3193)*
◆ F S R Inc ....D 973 785-4347
Woodland Park *(G-12078)*
▲ Fei-Elcom Tech Inc ....E 201 767-8030
Northvale *(G-7524)*
Fiber-Span Inc ....E 908 253-9080
Toms River *(G-10757)*
Flir Security Inc ....G 201 368-9700
Ridgefield Park *(G-9306)*
Hbc Solutions Inc ....G 973 267-5990
Rockleigh *(G-9518)*
Homan Communications Inc ....G 609 654-9594
Medford *(G-6023)*
▲ ID Systems Inc ....C 201 996-9000
Woodcliff Lake *(G-12057)*
Imagine Communications Corp ....E 201 469-6740
Bridgewater *(G-832)*
In-Phase Technologies Inc ....E 609 298-9555
Bordentown *(G-584)*
▲ Infinova Corporation ....E 732 355-9100
Monmouth Junction *(G-6293)*
Iniven LLC ....G 908 722-3770
Branchburg *(G-649)*
Integrated Microwave Tech LLC ....G 908 852-3700
Hackettstown *(G-4012)*
Kaleidoscope Sound ....G 201 223-2868
Union City *(G-11117)*
▲ Kef America Inc ....E 732 414-2074
Marlboro *(G-5903)*
L3 Technologies Inc ....A 856 338-3000
Camden *(G-1074)*
Lcn Partners Inc ....F 215 755-1000
Berlin *(G-426)*
▲ Lg Elctrnics Mbilecomm USA Inc ....D 201 816-2000
Englewood Cliffs *(G-2981)*
Lightning Prvntion Systems Inc ....G 856 767-7806
West Berlin *(G-11603)*
Linearizer Technology Inc ....G 609 584-8424
Hamilton *(G-4111)*
Lockheed Martin Corporation ....B 856 787-3104
Mount Laurel *(G-6777)*
Lucent Technologies World Svcs ....C 908 582-3000
New Providence *(G-7008)*
Major Auto Installations Inc ....E 973 252-4262
Kenvil *(G-4993)*
▲ Martec Access Products Inc ....D 908 233-0101
Piscataway *(G-8688)*
Maxentric Technologies LLC ....E 201 242-9800
Fort Lee *(G-3570)*
Mediabridge Products LLC ....E 856 216-8222
Cherry Hill *(G-1392)*

▲ Merrimac Industries Inc ....D 973 575-1300
West Caldwell *(G-11665)*
Microsignals Inc ....E 800 225-4508
Palisades Park *(G-7774)*
Miranda MTI Inc ....F 973 376-4275
Springfield *(G-10454)*
▲ Mizco International Inc ....D 732 912-2000
Avenel *(G-137)*
Modulation Sciences Inc ....F 732 302-3090
Somerset *(G-10031)*
Mphase Technologies Inc ....F 973 256-3737
Clifton *(G-1671)*
▲ Myat Inc ....E 201 529-0145
Mahwah *(G-5756)*
▲ Natural Wireless LLC ....E 201 438-2865
East Rutherford *(G-2306)*
Network Communications Cons ....F 201 968-0684
Hackensack *(G-3953)*
On Site Communication ....E 201 488-4123
South Hackensack *(G-10177)*
Open Terra Inc ....G 732 765-9600
Matawan *(G-5982)*
Orbcomm LLC ....E 703 433-6300
Rochelle Park *(G-9427)*
OSI Laser Diode Inc ....E 732 549-9001
Edison *(G-2585)*
Panasonic Corp North America ....G 201 348-7000
Newark *(G-7221)*
Patchamp Inc ....G 201 457-1504
Hackensack *(G-3962)*
Peter-Lisand Machine Corp ....G 201 943-5600
New Milford *(G-6991)*
Philips Elec N Amer Corp ....D 973 471-9450
Clifton *(G-1690)*
Powertrunk Inc ....G 201 630-4520
Jersey City *(G-4787)*
Qualcomm Incorporated ....D 908 443-8000
Bridgewater *(G-874)*
R F Products Inc ....E 856 365-5500
Camden *(G-1084)*
R H A Audio Communications ....G 732 257-9180
East Brunswick *(G-2170)*
R P R Graphics Inc ....E 908 654-8080
Peapack *(G-8345)*
R&D Microwaves LLC ....E 908 212-1696
Boonton *(G-565)*
Radio Systems Design Inc ....E 856 467-8000
Swedesboro *(G-10604)*
Radwin Inc ....G 201 252-4224
Mahwah *(G-5766)*
Renae Telecom LLC ....D 908 362-8112
Elizabeth *(G-2774)*
Satellite Pros Inc ....G 908 823-9500
Whitehouse Station *(G-11933)*
Selway Partners LLC ....F 201 712-7974
Englewood *(G-2939)*
SES Engineering (us) Inc ....D 609 987-4000
Princeton *(G-9021)*
Siklu Inc ....F 201 267-9597
Fort Lee *(G-3588)*
▲ Techflex Inc ....F 973 300-9242
Sparta *(G-10409)*
Telcontel Corp ....F 732 441-0800
Laurence Harbor *(G-5210)*
▲ Telemetrics Inc ....E 201 848-9818
Allendale *(G-18)*
Telescript Inc ....G 201 767-6733
Norwood *(G-7575)*
Telvue Corporation ....E 800 885-8886
Mount Laurel *(G-6809)*
Turn-Key Technologies Inc ....F 732 553-9100
Sayreville *(G-9726)*
Turner Engineering Inc ....F 973 263-1000
Mountain Lakes *(G-6829)*
Ussecurenet LLC ....G 201 447-0130
Hawthorne *(G-4248)*
Videonet Comm Group LLC ....F 732 863-5310
Freehold *(G-3703)*
▲ Vitec Videocom Inc ....E 908 852-3700
Secaucus *(G-9827)*
▼ Wide Band Systems Inc ....F 973 586-6500
Rockaway *(G-9513)*
Wireless Communications Inc ....G 732 926-1000
Metuchen *(G-6082)*
Wireless Electronics Inc ....E 856 768-4310
West Berlin *(G-11634)*
Wireworks Corporation ....E 908 686-7400
Hillside *(G-4437)*
Zaxcom Inc ....F 973 835-5000
Pompton Plains *(G-8875)*

Zzyzx LLC ....G.... 908 722-3770
Branchburg (G-700)

3669 Communications Eqpt, NEC

A C L Equipment Corp ....G.... 973 740-9800
Livingston (G-5501)
Abris Distribution Inc ....E.... 732 252-9819
Manalapan (G-5799)
Ademco Inc ....G.... 732 505-6688
Toms River (G-10739)
Ademco Inc ....F.... 201 462-9570
Teterboro (G-10670)
Ademco Inc ....G.... 908 561-1888
South Plainfield (G-10207)
Ademco Inc ....G.... 856 985-9050
Marlton (G-5921)
Ademco Inc ....G.... 973 808-8233
Fairfield (G-3134)
AT&T Services Inc ....A.... 732 420-3131
Middletown (G-6159)
▲ Aurora Multimedia Corporation ....E.... 732 591-5800
Morganville (G-6583)
◆ Blitz Safe of America Inc ....F.... 201 569-5000
Englewood (G-2884)
◆ Bogen Communications Inc ....D.... 201 934-8500
Mahwah (G-5718)
Bogen Corporation ....G.... 201 934-8500
Ramsey (G-9142)
Caregility Corporation ....E.... 732 413-6000
Eatontown (G-2383)
Confires Fire Prtction Svc LLC ....F.... 908 822-2700
South Plainfield (G-10241)
◆ Cooper Wheelock Inc ....B.... 732 222-6880
Long Branch (G-5595)
◆ Crestron Electronics Inc ....C.... 201 767-3400
Rockleigh (G-9516)
Cricket Enterprises ....G.... 201 387-7978
Dumont (G-2112)
D2cf LLC ....G.... 973 699-4111
West Orange (G-11765)
Digitize Inc ....F.... 973 663-1011
Lake Hopatcong (G-5036)
Ea Pilot Supply ....G.... 201 934-8449
Bradley Beach (G-610)
▲ Electronic Marine Systems Inc ....F.... 732 680-4120
Rahway (G-9089)
Elymat Corp ....E.... 201 767-7105
Old Tappan (G-7733)
Elymat Industries Inc ....E.... 201 767-7105
Old Tappan (G-7734)
General Dynamics Mission ....C.... 973 261-1409
Florham Park (G-3507)
▲ Heat-Timer Corporation ....E.... 973 575-4004
Fairfield (G-3224)
Hope Center ....F.... 201 798-1234
Jersey City (G-4748)
Industronic Inc ....G.... 908 393-5960
Bridgewater (G-835)
Institute For Respnsble Online ....G.... 856 722-1048
Mount Laurel (G-6768)
Intellgent Trffic Sup Pdts LLC ....G.... 908 791-1200
South Plainfield (G-10278)
J C Contracting Inc ....F.... 973 748-5600
Rahway (G-9105)
Jen Electric Inc ....F.... 973 467-4901
Springfield (G-10448)
Kinly Inc ....E.... 973 585-3000
Cedar Knolls (G-1307)
L J Loeffler Systems Inc ....G.... 212 924-7597
Secaucus (G-9788)
Merchants Alarm Systems Inc ....E.... 973 779-1296
Wallington (G-11388)
▲ Moniteur Devices Inc ....F.... 973 857-1600
Cedar Grove (G-1283)
Netquest Corporation ....E.... 856 866-0505
Mount Laurel (G-6786)
Octopus Yachts Ltd Lblty Co ....F.... 732 698-8550
Belmar (G-352)
Pixell Creative Group LLC ....G.... 609 410-3024
Burlington (G-982)
Protection Industries Corp ....F.... 201 333-8050
Jersey City (G-4790)
▲ Sightlogix Inc ....E.... 609 951-0008
Princeton (G-9022)
Telegenix Inc ....F.... 609 265-3910
Rancocas (G-9167)
◆ Tyco International MGT Co LLC ....E.... 609 720-4200
Princeton (G-9038)
Work Zone Contractors LLC ....G.... 856 845-8201
Deptford (G-2068)
◆ York Telecom Corporation ....D.... 732 413-6000
Eatontown (G-2430)
Ytc Holdings Inc ....G.... 732 413-6000
Eatontown (G-2431)

3671 Radio & T V Receiving Electron Tubes

▲ Hamamatsu Corporation ....D.... 908 231-0960
Bridgewater (G-828)
Linear Photonics LLC ....G.... 609 584-5747
Hamilton (G-4109)
Linearizer Technology Inc ....D.... 609 584-5747
Hamilton (G-4110)
▲ Tdk Electronics Inc ....D.... 732 906-4300
Iselin (G-4631)
Troy-Onic Inc ....E.... 973 584-6830
Kenvil (G-4996)
Union City Filament Corp ....E.... 201 945-3366
Ridgefield (G-9294)
World Electronics Inc ....F.... 201 670-1177
Glen Rock (G-3835)

3672 Printed Circuit Boards

▲ ADI American Distributors LLC ....D.... 973 328-1181
Randolph (G-9169)
▲ Ai-Logix Inc ....E.... 732 469-0880
Somerset (G-9944)
▲ Altus Pcb LLC ....F.... 877 442-5887
Cresskill (G-1941)
▲ Applicad Inc ....E.... 732 751-2555
Wall Township (G-11318)
Argus International Inc ....E.... 609 466-1677
Ringoes (G-9334)
▼ AT&T Technologies Inc ....A.... 201 771-2000
Berkeley Heights (G-389)
▲ Cheringal Associates Inc ....D.... 201 784-8721
Norwood (G-7560)
Circuit Reproduction Co ....F.... 201 712-9292
Maywood (G-6002)
Circuit Tech Assembly LLC ....F.... 856 231-0777
West Berlin (G-11583)
Computer Control Corp ....F.... 973 492-8265
Butler (G-998)
Data Delay Devices ....E.... 973 202-3268
Clifton (G-1596)
▲ Delta Circuits Inc ....E.... 973 575-3000
Fairfield (G-3183)
Esi ....E.... 856 629-2492
Sicklerville (G-9909)
ESP Associates Inc ....F.... 973 208-9045
Newfoundland (G-7330)
GAb Electronic Services LLC ....E.... 856 786-0108
Cinnaminson (G-1459)
Garys Kids ....G.... 973 458-1818
Passaic (G-8067)
◆ Glenro Inc ....F.... 973 279-5900
Paterson (G-8199)
Harrison Electro Mechanical ....F.... 732 382-6008
Rahway (G-9100)
J R E Inc ....E.... 973 808-0055
West Caldwell (G-11655)
Jnbc Associates LLC ....G.... 973 560-5518
Parsippany (G-7967)
Mdj Inc ....E.... 201 457-9260
Hackensack (G-3945)
Medco West Electronics Inc ....G.... 201 457-9260
Hackensack (G-3946)
Mercury Systems Inc ....E.... 973 244-1040
West Caldwell (G-11664)
Modelware Inc ....F.... 732 264-3020
Holmdel (G-4508)
Omega Circuit and Engineering ....E.... 732 246-1661
New Brunswick (G-6957)
P W B Omni Inc ....G.... 856 384-1300
West Deptford (G-11713)
Pcr Technologies Inc ....G.... 973 882-0017
Pine Brook (G-8613)
▲ PNC Inc ....C.... 973 284-1600
Nutley (G-7592)
Ppi/Time Zero Inc ....C.... 973 278-6500
Fairfield (G-3293)
▲ Precision Graphics Inc ....D.... 908 707-8880
Branchburg (G-671)
Precision Products Co Inc ....E.... 201 712-5757
Maywood (G-6014)
Quik Flex Circuit Inc ....F.... 856 742-0550
Gloucester City (G-3848)
▲ R & D Circuits Inc ....C.... 732 549-4554
South Plainfield (G-10321)
▲ R R J Co Inc ....E.... 732 544-1514
Colts Neck (G-1787)
Redkoh Industries Inc ....G.... 908 369-1590
Hillsborough (G-4351)
Scl ....E.... 908 391-9882
Bridgewater (G-888)
▲ Shore Printed Circuits Inc ....E.... 732 380-0590
Eatontown (G-2420)
South Jersey Circuits ....G.... 609 479-3994
Burlington (G-985)
Spem Corporation ....E.... 732 356-3366
Piscataway (G-8717)
Sure Design ....F.... 732 919-3066
Wall Township (G-11372)
Swemco LLC ....C.... 856 222-9900
Moorestown (G-6570)
Syscom Technologies Corp ....D.... 856 642-7661
Moorestown (G-6572)
T V L Associates Inc ....G.... 973 790-6766
Wayne (G-11555)
Technical Aids To Independence ....F.... 973 674-1082
East Orange (G-2265)
Techniques Inc ....E.... 973 256-0947
Woodland Park (G-12092)
▲ Test Technology Inc ....D.... 856 596-1215
Marlton (G-5953)
Thomas Instrumentation Inc ....F.... 609 624-2630
Cape May Court House (G-1116)
Toby-Yanni Incorporated ....F.... 973 253-9800
Garfield (G-3773)
▲ Transistor Devices Inc ....C.... 908 850-5088
Hackettstown (G-4039)
Wireworks Corporation ....E.... 908 686-7400
Hillside (G-4437)

3674 Semiconductors

◆ Access Bio Inc ....F.... 732 873-4040
Somerset (G-9941)
▲ Ace Mountings Co Inc ....F.... 732 721-6200
South Amboy (G-10129)
Acolyte Technologies Corp ....G.... 212 629-3239
Perth Amboy (G-8510)
Advanced Micro Devices Inc ....C.... 732 787-2892
North Middletown (G-7502)
Aeon Corporation ....G.... 609 275-9003
Princeton Junction (G-9047)
Akela Laser Corporation ....F.... 732 305-7105
Monroe Township (G-6325)
Alcatel-Lucent USA Inc ....D.... 908 582-3275
New Providence (G-6993)
Altera Corporation ....G.... 732 649-3477
Somerset (G-9950)
American Microsemiconductor ....E.... 973 377-9566
Madison (G-5689)
Analog Devices Inc ....E.... 732 868-7100
Somerset (G-9953)
Ateksis USA Corp ....G.... 646 508-9074
East Rutherford (G-2274)
▲ Automatic Switch Company ....A.... 973 966-2000
Florham Park (G-3485)
Bel Fuse Inc ....C.... 201 432-0463
Jersey City (G-4700)
Cambridge Industries Group ....G.... 917 669-7337
Basking Ridge (G-178)
Candela Corporation ....F.... 908 753-6300
South Plainfield (G-10234)
Cast Inc ....G.... 201 391-8300
Woodcliff Lake (G-12051)
Compufab Sales Inc ....G.... 856 786-0175
Cinnaminson (G-1447)
Crystal Deltronic Industries ....E.... 973 328-6898
Dover (G-2079)
Crystal Deltronic Industries ....F.... 973 328-7000
Dover (G-2080)
Data Delay Devices ....E.... 973 202-3268
Clifton (G-1596)
▲ Dialight Corporation ....D.... 732 751-5809
Wall Township (G-11334)
Digitron Electronic Corp ....E.... 908 245-2012
Kenilworth (G-4936)
Discovery Semiconductors Inc ....E.... 609 434-1311
Ewing (G-3027)
Duet Microelectronics LLC ....F.... 908 854-3838
Raritan (G-9210)
Ecs Energy Ltd ....G.... 201 341-5044
Jackson (G-4655)
Elena Consultants & Elec ....E.... 908 654-8309
Mountainside (G-6845)
Enpirion Inc ....E.... 908 575-7550
Hampton (G-4150)
Frauscher Sensor Tech USA Inc ....F.... 609 285-5492
Princeton (G-8951)

Fuceltech Inc .... G 609 275-0070
　Princeton Junction *(G-9058)*

G T Associates .... G 973 694-6040
　Wayne *(G-11506)*

▲ Gce Market Inc .... G 856 401-8900
　Blackwood *(G-466)*

▲ Hamamatsu Corporation ...... D 908 231-0960
　Bridgewater *(G-828)*

Harrison Electro Mechanical ..... F 732 382-6008
　Rahway *(G-9100)*

Holistic Solar Usa Inc .... G 732 757-5500
　Newark *(G-7151)*

Hybrid-Tek LLC .... F 609 259-3355
　Clarksburg *(G-1521)*

Hydraulic Manifolds Usa LLC ..... G 973 728-1214
　West Milford *(G-11727)*

Ii-VI Incorporated .... F 973 227-1551
　Pine Brook *(G-8605)*

▲ Ii-VI Optoelectronic Dvcs Inc .... C 908 668-5000
　Warren *(G-11417)*

▲ Imperial Copy Products Inc .... E 973 927-5500
　Randolph *(G-9186)*

Infineon Tech Americas Corp ..... F 732 603-5914
　Iselin *(G-4612)*

Inphot Inc .... G 609 799-7172
　Plainsboro *(G-8791)*

Intense Inc .... E 732 249-2228
　North Brunswick *(G-7471)*

▲ Jerome Industries Corp .... E 908 353-5700
　Hackettstown *(G-4013)*

▲ Keyence Corporation America ... E 201 930-0100
　Elmwood Park *(G-2834)*

Kyocera International Inc .... D 856 691-7000
　Cherry Hill *(G-1381)*

Liberty Cnstr & Inv Group .... G 267 784-7931
　Cherry Hill *(G-1383)*

Lockheed Martin Corporation ..... E 732 321-4200
　Edison *(G-2552)*

Lucent Technologies World Svcs ... C 908 582-3000
　New Providence *(G-7008)*

M E C Technologies Inc .... E 732 505-0308
　Toms River *(G-10776)*

▲ Maxlite Inc .... D 973 244-7300
　West Caldwell *(G-11663)*

Mc Renewable Energy LLC .... F 732 369-9933
　Manasquan *(G-5833)*

Memory International Corp .... F 973 586-2653
　Denville *(G-2046)*

Micro-Tek Laboratories Inc ...... G 973 779-5577
　Clifton *(G-1669)*

Microsemi Stor Solutions Inc .... G 908 953-9400
　Basking Ridge *(G-191)*

Modelware Inc .... F 732 264-3020
　Holmdel *(G-4508)*

Moser Jewel Company .... G 908 454-1155
　Phillipsburg *(G-8564)*

▲ Multi-Tech Industries Inc ...... F 732 431-0550
　Marlboro *(G-5905)*

Multilink Technology Corp .... E 732 805-9355
　Somerset *(G-10036)*

Nanonex Corp .... F 732 355-1600
　Monmouth Junction *(G-6298)*

▲ Nanopv Corporation .... F 609 851-3666
　Ewing *(G-3047)*

◆ Nokia of America Corporation ... A 908 582-3275
　New Providence *(G-7014)*

▲ Nte Electronics Inc .... D 973 748-5089
　Bloomfield *(G-513)*

Pekay Industries Inc .... F 732 938-2722
　Farmingdale *(G-3390)*

▲ Pny Technologies Inc .... B 973 515-9700
　Parsippany *(G-7997)*

Princeton Lightwave Inc .... E 609 495-2600
　Cranbury *(G-1875)*

Renesas Electronics Amer Inc .... E 908 685-6000
　Bridgewater *(G-875)*

Reuge Management Group Inc ..... G 888 306-3253
　Hoboken *(G-4479)*

Richards Manufacturing Co Inc .... G 973 371-1711
　Irvington *(G-4584)*

▲ Roxboro Holdings Inc .... D 732 919-3119
　Wall Township *(G-11365)*

Rudolph Technologies Inc .... G 973 448-4307
　Ledgewood *(G-5280)*

Semi Conductor Manufacturing .... E 973 478-2880
　Clifton *(G-1714)*

◆ Sharp Electronics Corporation ... A 201 529-8200
　Montvale *(G-6433)*

Sunlight Aerospace Inc .... F 732 362-7501
　Edison *(G-2625)*

Tel-Instrument Elec Corp .... E 201 933-1600
　East Rutherford *(G-2325)*

Thinfilms Inc .... F 908 359-7014
　Hillsborough *(G-4360)*

United Silicon Carbide Inc .... F 732 355-0550
　Monmouth Junction *(G-6317)*

Universal Display Corporation .... C 609 671-0980
　Ewing *(G-3073)*

▼ William Kenyon & Sons Inc ..... E 732 985-8980
　Piscataway *(G-8738)*

Worldwide Solar Mfg LLC .... G 201 297-1177
　Closter *(G-1765)*

Xtreme Powertech LLC .... F 201 791-5050
　Upper Saddle River *(G-11150)*

Xybion Corporation .... C 973 538-2067
　Lawrenceville *(G-5248)*

3675 Electronic Capacitors

Electro-Ceramic Industries .... E 201 342-2630
　Hackensack *(G-3911)*

▲ Electronic Concepts Inc .... C 732 542-7880
　Eatontown *(G-2390)*

Energy Storage Corp .... D 732 542-7880
　Eatontown *(G-2392)*

▲ Megatran Industries .... D 609 227-4300
　Bordentown *(G-586)*

Metuchen Capacitors Inc .... E 800 899-6969
　Holmdel *(G-4506)*

▲ Nte Electronics Inc .... D 973 748-5089
　Bloomfield *(G-513)*

Tbt Group Inc .... G 856 753-4500
　Bellmawr *(G-344)*

3676 Electronic Resistors

▲ Nte Electronics Inc .... D 973 748-5089
　Bloomfield *(G-513)*

▼ State Electronics Parts Corp .... E 973 887-2550
　East Hanover *(G-2240)*

3677 Electronic Coils & Transformers

A C Transformer Corp .... G 973 589-8574
　Newark *(G-7029)*

AFP Transformers Corporation ..... D 732 248-0305
　Edison *(G-2450)*

Alecto Systems LLC .... G 973 875-6721
　Branchville *(G-702)*

▲ Automatic Switch Company ..... A 973 966-2000
　Florham Park *(G-3485)*

Baltimore Transformer Company ... E 973 942-2222
　Paterson *(G-8146)*

Behringer Fluid Systems Inc ...... G 973 948-0226
　Branchville *(G-703)*

Bel Fuse Inc .... C 201 432-0463
　Jersey City *(G-4700)*

Bel Hybrids & Magnetics Inc ..... F 201 432-0463
　Jersey City *(G-4701)*

Celco .... F 201 327-1123
　Mahwah *(G-5721)*

Edko Electronics .... E 973 942-2222
　Paterson *(G-8176)*

Electronic Transformer Corp ...... E 973 942-2222
　Paterson *(G-8177)*

Freed Transformer Company ...... F 973 942-2222
　Paterson *(G-8195)*

▲ Jerome Industries Corp .... E 908 353-5700
　Hackettstown *(G-4013)*

▲ Jinpan International USA Ltd ..... G 201 460-8778
　Carlstadt *(G-1170)*

▲ Jst Power Equipment Inc ...... G 201 460-8778
　Carlstadt *(G-1171)*

▲ Kef America Inc .... E 732 414-2074
　Marlboro *(G-5903)*

▼ KG Squared LLC .... F 973 627-0643
　Rockaway *(G-9473)*

Microsignals Inc .... E 800 225-4508
　Palisades Park *(G-7774)*

NMP Water Systems LLC .... G 201 252-8333
　Mahwah *(G-5758)*

SCI-Bore Inc .... G 973 414-9001
　East Orange *(G-2262)*

▲ Stonite Coil Corporation .... E 609 585-6600
　Trenton *(G-10993)*

Torelco Inc .... F 908 387-0814
　Alpha *(G-43)*

▲ Ultra Clean Technologies Corp ... E 856 451-2176
　Bridgeton *(G-776)*

3678 Electronic Connectors

ABB Installation Products Inc ..... C 908 852-1122
　Hackettstown *(G-3994)*

Adam Tech Asia Llc .... G 908 687-5000
　Union *(G-11020)*

AI Technology Inc .... E 609 799-9388
　Princeton Junction *(G-9048)*

Armel Electronics Inc .... E 201 869-4300
　North Bergen *(G-7387)*

Barantec Inc .... F 973 779-8774
　Clifton *(G-1571)*

Brim Electronics Inc .... F 201 796-2886
　Lodi *(G-5555)*

▲ Central Components Mfg LLC .... G 732 469-5720
　Middlesex *(G-6104)*

Components Corporation .... F 866 426-6726
　Denville *(G-2032)*

Da-Green Electronics Ltd .... F 732 254-2735
　Marlboro *(G-5894)*

◆ Fuji Electric Corp America ...... D 732 560-9410
　Edison *(G-2515)*

▲ Fujipoly America Corporation .... C 732 969-0100
　Carteret *(G-1255)*

Glasseal Products Inc .... C 732 370-9100
　Lakewood *(G-5104)*

▲ Heilind Electronics Inc .... E 888 881-5420
　Lumberton *(G-5629)*

▲ Heilind Mil-Aero LLC .... C 856 722-5535
　Lumberton *(G-5630)*

Huber+suhner Astrolab Inc ...... E 732 560-3800
　Warren *(G-11416)*

▲ I Trade Technology Ltd .... G 615 348-7233
　Mahwah *(G-5749)*

Kraus & Naimer Inc .... E 732 560-1240
　Somerset *(G-10011)*

◆ Lapp Usa LLC .... C 973 660-9700
　Florham Park *(G-3517)*

Newtech Group Corp .... G 732 355-0392
　Kendall Park *(G-4919)*

Princetel Inc .... E 609 588-8801
　Hamilton *(G-4121)*

▲ Richards Mfg Co Sales Inc ..... E 973 371-1771
　Irvington *(G-4586)*

Severna Operations Inc .... E 973 503-1600
　Parsippany *(G-8013)*

Te Connectivity Corporation ...... B 610 893-9800
　Eatontown *(G-2424)*

▲ Unicorp .... C 973 674-1700
　Orange *(G-7765)*

▲ Valconn Electronics Inc .... E 908 687-1600
　Union *(G-11097)*

◆ Wire-Pro Inc .... C 856 935-7560
　Salem *(G-9698)*

3679 Electronic Components, NEC

A P M Hexseal Corporation ...... E 201 569-5700
　Englewood *(G-2872)*

ABB Installation Products Inc ..... C 908 852-1122
　Hackettstown *(G-3994)*

Adcomm Inc .... C 201 342-3338
　South Hackensack *(G-10146)*

▲ ADI American Distributors LLC ... D 973 328-1181
　Randolph *(G-9169)*

Advanced Energy Voorhees Inc .... D 856 627-1287
　Voorhees *(G-11279)*

Advanced Technology Group Inc ... E 973 627-6955
　Rockaway *(G-9439)*

Aeon Engineering LLC .... G 518 253-7681
　Fort Lee *(G-3545)*

Algen Design Services Inc .... E 732 389-3630
　Eatontown *(G-2374)*

◆ Ameral International Inc .... F 856 456-9000
　Brooklawn *(G-913)*

American Fibertek Inc .... E 732 302-0660
　Somerset *(G-9951)*

Amperite Co Inc .... E 201 864-9503
　North Bergen *(G-7384)*

Andrex Inc .... F 908 852-2400
　Hackettstown *(G-3998)*

Andrex Systems Inc .... G 908 835-1720
　Port Murray *(G-8881)*

▲ Ango Electronics Corporation .... F 201 955-0800
　North Arlington *(G-7368)*

▼ Applied Resources Corp .... E 973 328-3882
　Wharton *(G-11852)*

Aspe Inc .... E 973 808-1155
　Fairfield *(G-3148)*

▲ Asti Corp .... F 201 501-8900
　Bergenfield *(G-371)*

▼ **AT&T Technologies Inc** ... A ... 201 771-2000
Berkeley Heights *(G-389)*

Autoremind Inc ... G ... 800 277-1299
Fair Lawn *(G-3087)*

◆ **Az-Em USA Branchburg NJ** ... G ... 908 429-0020
Branchburg *(G-624)*

Bel Fuse Inc ... C ... 201 432-0463
Jersey City *(G-4700)*

▲ **Bihler of America Inc** ... C ... 908 213-9001
Phillipsburg *(G-8546)*

Billows Electric Supply Co Inc ... C ... 856 751-2200
Delran *(G-2009)*

Bkh Electronics ... G ... 210 410-2757
Wanaque *(G-11391)*

Bomar Exo Ltd Liability Co ... F ... 732 356-7787
Middlesex *(G-6102)*

Ccard ... G ... 732 303-8264
Manalapan *(G-5803)*

▲ **Clantech Inc** ... G ... 908 281-7667
Hillsborough *(G-4310)*

▲ **Cobham New Jersey Inc** ... D ... 732 460-0212
Eatontown *(G-2384)*

Coherent Inc ... D ... 973 240-6851
East Hanover *(G-2200)*

Communication Products Co ... G ... 973 977-8490
Paterson *(G-8162)*

▲ **Compex Corporation** ... E ... 856 719-8657
West Berlin *(G-11585)*

▲ **Computer Crafts Inc** ... C ... 973 423-3500
Hawthorne *(G-4214)*

▲ **Creatone Inc** ... F ... 908 789-8700
Mountainside *(G-6837)*

▲ **Crestek Inc** ... E ... 609 883-4000
Ewing *(G-3024)*

Crystal Deltronic Industries ... E ... 973 328-6898
Dover *(G-2079)*

D&N Machine Manufacturing Inc ... E ... 856 456-1366
Gloucester City *(G-3840)*

Da-Green Electronics Ltd ... F ... 732 254-2735
Marlboro *(G-5894)*

▲ **Dantco Corp** ... F ... 973 278-8776
Paterson *(G-8168)*

Data Delay Devices ... E ... 973 202-3268
Clifton *(G-1596)*

▲ **Dialight Corporation** ... D ... 732 751-5809
Wall Township *(G-11334)*

Doralex Inc ... G ... 856 764-0694
Delran *(G-2016)*

▲ **Douglas Elec Components Inc** ... D ... 973 627-8230
Randolph *(G-9175)*

Dwill America LLC ... G ... 201 561-5737
Lodi *(G-5561)*

▼ **Electromagnetic Tech Inds Inc** ... D ... 973 394-1719
Boonton *(G-550)*

Electronic Connections Inc ... F ... 732 367-5588
Lakewood *(G-5089)*

Electronic Mfg Svcs Inc ... F ... 973 916-1001
Clifton *(G-1614)*

Empire Telecommunications Inc ... F ... 201 569-3339
Englewood Cliffs *(G-2968)*

Esi ... E ... 856 629-2492
Sicklerville *(G-9909)*

▲ **Ewc Controls Inc** ... E ... 732 446-3110
Manalapan *(G-5809)*

Excel Display Corp ... G ... 732 246-3724
New Brunswick *(G-6925)*

Famcam Inc ... E ... 973 503-1600
Parsippany *(G-7941)*

Foremost Corp ... G ... 973 839-3360
Wayne *(G-11504)*

Frc Electrical Industries Inc ... E ... 908 464-3200
New Providence *(G-7000)*

General Reliance Corporation ... E ... 973 361-1400
Denville *(G-2038)*

Glasseal Products Inc ... C ... 732 370-9100
Lakewood *(G-5104)*

Gold Enterprise Ltd ... C ... 954 614-1001
Point Pleasant Boro *(G-8845)*

GT Microwave Inc ... E ... 973 361-5700
Randolph *(G-9184)*

Gulton G I D ... G ... 908 791-4622
South Plainfield *(G-10270)*

Haz Laboratories ... F ... 908 453-3300
Washington *(G-11446)*

Herley Industries Inc ... D ... 973 884-2580
Whippany *(G-11895)*

Herley-Cti Inc ... F ... 973 884-2580
Whippany *(G-11896)*

Hermetic Solutions Group Inc ... F ... 732 722-8780
Tinton Falls *(G-10719)*

Heyco Products Corp ... G ... 732 286-1800
Toms River *(G-10766)*

Idt Energy Inc ... E ... 877 887-6866
Newark *(G-7154)*

Infiniti Components Inc ... G ... 908 537-9950
Hampton *(G-4156)*

▲ **Interplex Nas Inc** ... D ... 201 367-1300
Northvale *(G-7530)*

It Surplus Liquidators ... G ... 732 308-1935
Freehold *(G-3670)*

J A M I Enterprise Inc ... G ... 732 714-6811
Brick *(G-721)*

J P Rotella Co Inc ... F ... 973 942-2559
Haledon *(G-4083)*

JB Electronics ... F ... 609 497-2952
Princeton *(G-8965)*

▲ **Jerome Industries Corp** ... E ... 908 353-5700
Hackettstown *(G-4013)*

Jettron Products Inc ... E ... 973 887-0571
East Hanover *(G-2220)*

JFK Supplies Inc ... F ... 732 985-7800
Edison *(G-2539)*

Johanson Manufacturing Corp ... C ... 973 658-1051
Boonton *(G-559)*

K R Electronics Inc ... F ... 732 636-1900
Avenel *(G-133)*

▼ **KG Squared LLC** ... F ... 973 627-0643
Rockaway *(G-9473)*

Kinetics Industries Inc ... E ... 609 883-9700
Ewing *(G-3040)*

Lakeland Transformer Corp ... G ... 973 835-0818
Haskell *(G-4198)*

Lg Electronics USA Inc ... G ... 732 605-0385
Monroe Township *(G-6334)*

Magnetics & Controls Inc ... F ... 609 397-8203
Rosemont *(G-9593)*

◆ **Maxell Corporation of America** ... E ... 973 653-2400
Woodland Park *(G-12084)*

Meca Electronics Inc ... D ... 973 625-0661
Denville *(G-2045)*

◆ **Mechanical Ingenuity Corp** ... E ... 732 842-8889
Eatontown *(G-2410)*

Melstrom Manufacturing Corp ... D ... 732 938-7400
Wall Township *(G-11355)*

▲ **Mennekes Electronics Inc** ... E ... 973 882-8333
Fairfield *(G-3268)*

▲ **Merrimac Industries Inc** ... D ... 973 575-1300
West Caldwell *(G-11665)*

▲ **Metal Cutting Corporation** ... D ... 973 239-1100
Cedar Grove *(G-1282)*

Microwave Consulting Corp ... G ... 973 523-6700
Paterson *(G-8259)*

Model Electronics Inc ... D ... 201 961-9200
Ramsey *(G-9152)*

Model Electronics Inc ... E ... 201 961-1717
Ramsey *(G-9153)*

Mwt Materials Inc ... F ... 973 928-8300
Passaic *(G-8091)*

Noah LLC ... G ... 609 637-0039
Lawrenceville *(G-5240)*

Norsal Distribution Associates ... F ... 908 638-6430
High Bridge *(G-4284)*

◆ **Nwl Inc** ... C ... 609 298-7300
Bordentown *(G-591)*

Patriot American Solutions LLC ... D ... 862 209-4772
Rockaway *(G-9484)*

Pcr Technologies Inc ... G ... 973 882-0017
Pine Brook *(G-8613)*

Prima-TEC Electronics Corp ... G ... 201 947-4052
East Rutherford *(G-2312)*

Princeton Microwave Technology ... G ... 609 586-8140
Trenton *(G-10983)*

▲ **Quadrangle Products Inc** ... F ... 732 792-1234
Englishtown *(G-3008)*

Robert Wynn ... G ... 856 435-6398
Clementon *(G-1534)*

▲ **Roxboro Holdings Inc** ... D ... 732 919-3119
Wall Township *(G-11365)*

Rs Microwave Co Inc ... E ... 973 492-1207
Butler *(G-1014)*

Sensigraphics Inc ... G ... 856 853-9100
Mount Laurel *(G-6804)*

Seren Industrial Power Systems ... F ... 856 205-1131
Vineland *(G-11264)*

▲ **Silverstone Wireless LLC** ... G ... 845 458-5197
Lodi *(G-5575)*

▲ **Solar Products Inc** ... E ... 973 248-9370
Pompton Lakes *(G-8852)*

Spem Corporation ... E ... 732 356-3366
Piscataway *(G-8717)*

▲ **Spencer Industries Inc** ... E ... 973 751-2200
Belleville *(G-315)*

Spirent Communications Inc ... G ... 732 946-4018
Holmdel *(G-4514)*

▲ **Synergy Microwave Corp** ... D ... 973 881-8800
Paterson *(G-8311)*

▼ **T & E Industries Inc** ... E ... 973 672-5454
Orange *(G-7763)*

▲ **Tdk Electronics Inc** ... D ... 732 906-4300
Iselin *(G-4631)*

Tdk Electronics Inc ... F ... 732 603-5941
Lumberton *(G-5636)*

▲ **Technology Dynamics Inc** ... D ... 201 385-0500
Bergenfield *(G-385)*

Technology Dynamics Inc ... D ... 201 385-0500
Bergenfield *(G-386)*

Thomas Instrumentation Inc ... F ... 609 624-2630
Cape May Court House *(G-1116)*

▲ **Thomson Lamination Co Inc** ... D ... 856 779-8521
Maple Shade *(G-5872)*

Transistor Devices Inc ... C ... 908 850-5088
Hackettstown *(G-4040)*

Ttss Interactive Products Inc ... E ... 301 230-1464
Riverdale *(G-9388)*

Ute Microwave Inc ... E ... 732 922-1009
Ocean *(G-7686)*

Uthe Technology Inc ... G ... 609 883-4000
Trenton *(G-11007)*

Utz Technologies Inc ... E ... 973 339-1100
Little Falls *(G-5472)*

▲ **Valconn Electronics Inc** ... E ... 908 687-1600
Union *(G-11097)*

Value Added Vice Solutions LLC ... G ... 201 400-3247
Brielle *(G-910)*

▲ **VIP Industries Inc** ... E ... 973 472-7500
Clifton *(G-1735)*

▼ **Waveline Incorporated** ... E ... 973 226-9100
Fairfield *(G-3351)*

West Electronics Inc ... F ... 609 387-4300
Burlington *(G-993)*

Western Electronics Dist ... G ... 908 475-3303
Belvidere *(G-368)*

◆ **Wire-Pro Inc** ... C ... 856 935-7560
Salem *(G-9698)*

Wireworks Corporation ... E ... 908 686-7400
Hillside *(G-4437)*

▲ **YC Cable (east) Inc** ... E ... 732 868-0800
Piscataway *(G-8739)*

Zago Manufacturing Company ... E ... 973 643-6700
Newark *(G-7318)*

3691 Storage Batteries

E Group Inc ... G ... 856 320-9688
Mount Laurel *(G-6757)*

▲ **Energy Battery** ... G ... 908 751-5918
Flemington *(G-3439)*

Enersys ... D ... 800 719-7887
Somerset *(G-9986)*

▲ **Gogreen Power Inc** ... F ... 732 994-5901
Howell *(G-4540)*

▲ **Hoppecke Batteries Inc** ... E ... 856 616-0032
Hainesport *(G-4073)*

Krydon Group Inc ... G ... 877 854-1342
Moorestown *(G-6535)*

◆ **Maxell Corporation of America** ... E ... 973 653-2400
Woodland Park *(G-12084)*

▲ **Mizco International Inc** ... D ... 732 912-2000
Avenel *(G-137)*

Mphase Technologies Inc ... F ... 973 256-3737
Clifton *(G-1671)*

Orbit Energy & Power LLC ... E ... 800 836-3987
Mantua *(G-5853)*

Pacific Dnlop Holdings USA LLC ... G ... 732 345-5400
Red Bank *(G-9239)*

▲ **Skc Powertech Inc** ... F ... 973 347-7000
Budd Lake *(G-937)*

▲ **Tocad America Inc** ... E ... 973 627-9600
Rockaway *(G-9505)*

3692 Primary Batteries: Dry & Wet

Burlington Atlantic Corp ... G ... 732 888-7776
Hazlet *(G-4258)*

3694 Electrical Eqpt For Internal Combustion Engines

Auto Action Group Inc ... E ... 908 964-6290
Kenilworth *(G-4922)*

▲ **Dearborn A Belden Cdt Company** ... D ... 908 925-8000
Elizabeth *(G-2726)*

SIC

Dimilo Industries ....G...... 973 955-0460
  Passaic *(G-8059)*

Dmf Associated Engines LLC ....D...... 973 535-9773
  Livingston *(G-5510)*

Doolan Industries Incorporated ......G...... 856 985-1880
  Marlton *(G-5929)*

Engine Factory Inc ....G...... 908 236-9915
  Lebanon *(G-5259)*

▲ Fleetsource LLC ....E...... 732 566-4970
  Dayton *(G-1961)*

Incom (america) Inc ....G...... 908 464-3366
  Berkeley Heights *(G-401)*

J & R Rebuilders Inc ....G...... 856 627-1414
  Laurel Springs *(G-5207)*

Knite Inc ....G...... 609 258-9550
  Ewing *(G-3041)*

M Parker Autoworks Inc ....E...... 856 933-0801
  Bellmawr *(G-337)*

Mobile Power Inc ....G...... 908 852-3117
  Hackettstown *(G-4027)*

3695 Recording Media

Cabletime Ltd ....G...... 973 770-8070
  Mount Arlington *(G-6710)*

▲ Datacolor Inc ....D...... 609 924-2189
  Lawrenceville *(G-5229)*

Double Diamond Technologies ......G...... 609 624-1414
  Cape May *(G-1097)*

◆ Franklin Electronic Publs Inc ....D...... 609 386-2500
  Burlington *(G-969)*

Fujifilm North America Corp ....B...... 732 857-3000
  Edison *(G-2516)*

MD International Inc ....G...... 856 779-7633
  Cherry Hill *(G-1391)*

Network Access Systems Incorpr ....G...... 732 355-9770
  Dayton *(G-1981)*

Sony Corporation of America ....B...... 201 930-1000
  Paramus *(G-7834)*

▲ Synergem Inc ....E...... 732 692-6308
  Avenel *(G-148)*

3699 Electrical Machinery, Eqpt & Splys, NEC

AAS Technologies Inc ....G...... 201 342-7300
  Hackensack *(G-3874)*

Abacus Electric & Plumbing ....G...... 908 269-8057
  Chester *(G-1430)*

Ace Electric ....G...... 908 534-2404
  Somerville *(G-10100)*

◆ Advance International Inc ....E...... 212 213-2229
  Matawan *(G-5966)*

Almetek Industries Inc ....E...... 908 850-9700
  Hackettstown *(G-3997)*

Asco ....G...... 732 634-7017
  Woodbridge *(G-12012)*

Asco Power Technologies LP ....F...... 732 596-1733
  Woodbridge *(G-12013)*

◆ Asco Power Technologies LP ....B...... 973 966-2000
  Florham Park *(G-3484)*

Assa Abloy Entrance Sys US Inc ....E...... 609 443-5800
  Trenton *(G-10897)*

Assa Abloy Entrance Systems US ....E...... 609 528-2580
  Hamilton *(G-4103)*

Atlantex Instruments Inc ....G...... 201 391-5148
  Woodcliff Lake *(G-12047)*

Avida Incorporated ....G...... 201 802-0749
  Park Ridge *(G-7846)*

Bio-Key International Inc ....E...... 732 359-1100
  Wall Township *(G-11322)*

▲ Blonder Tongue Labs Inc ....C...... 732 679-4000
  Old Bridge *(G-7713)*

C J Electric ....G...... 201 891-0739
  Wyckoff *(G-12106)*

Candela Corporation ....F...... 908 753-6300
  South Plainfield *(G-10234)*

▲ Castle Industries Inc ....E...... 201 585-8400
  Englewood Cliffs *(G-2962)*

Celco ....F...... 201 327-1123
  Mahwah *(G-5721)*

Chamberlain Group Inc ....G...... 201 472-4200
  Whippany *(G-11885)*

◆ Checkpoint Systems Inc ....C...... 800 257-5540
  West Deptford *(G-11697)*

Checkpoint Systems Inc ....C...... 856 848-1800
  West Deptford *(G-11698)*

▲ Cleary Machinery Co Inc ....G...... 732 560-3200
  South Bound Brook *(G-10143)*

Commercial Pdts Svcs Group Inc ....G...... 609 730-4111
  Pennington *(G-8362)*

Connecting Products Inc ....F...... 609 512-1121
  Skillman *(G-9918)*

Crest Group Inc ....F...... 609 883-4000
  Trenton *(G-10926)*

▲ Crest Ultrasonics Corp ....G...... 609 883-4000
  Ewing *(G-3023)*

▲ Crestek Inc ....E...... 609 883-4000
  Ewing *(G-3024)*

Cuny and Guerber Inc ....E...... 201 617-5800
  Union City *(G-11109)*

▲ Daburn Wire & Cable Corp ....G...... 973 328-3200
  Dover *(G-2081)*

Daniel Maguire ....E...... 856 767-8443
  West Berlin *(G-11589)*

▼ Daq Electronics LLC ....E...... 732 981-0050
  Piscataway *(G-8651)*

▲ Dearborn A Belden Cdt Company ...D...... 908 925-8000
  Elizabeth *(G-2726)*

▼ Design Assistance Corporation ....F...... 856 241-9500
  Swedesboro *(G-10579)*

Dewey Electronics Corporation ......E...... 201 337-4700
  Oakland *(G-7624)*

Digitize Inc ....F...... 973 663-1011
  Lake Hopatcong *(G-5036)*

▲ Douglas Elec Components Inc .....D...... 973 627-8230
  Randolph *(G-9175)*

Dranetz Technologies Inc ....F...... 732 248-4358
  Edison *(G-2493)*

E-Beam Services Inc ....E...... 513 933-0031
  Cranbury *(G-1831)*

East Coast Panelboard Inc ....F...... 732 739-6400
  Tinton Falls *(G-10713)*

▲ East West Service Co Inc ....E...... 609 631-9000
  Trenton *(G-10933)*

Eaton Corporation ....E...... 732 767-9600
  Mountainside *(G-6844)*

Ecsi International Inc ....E...... 973 574-8555
  Clifton *(G-1610)*

Edmondmarks Technologies Inc ....E...... 732 643-0290
  Neptune *(G-6875)*

Electronic Control SEC Inc ....E...... 973 574-8555
  Clifton *(G-1613)*

▲ Ellenby Technologies Inc ....E...... 856 848-2020
  Woodbury Heights *(G-12042)*

Engineered Security Systems ....G...... 973 257-0555
  Towaco *(G-10871)*

Enterprisecc Ltd Liability Co ....G...... 201 266-0020
  Jersey City *(G-4732)*

Eos Energy Storage LLC ....E...... 732 225-8400
  Edison *(G-2505)*

Essex Products International ....G...... 973 226-2424
  Caldwell *(G-1024)*

Fastpulse Technology Inc ....F...... 973 478-5757
  Saddle Brook *(G-9652)*

Francis Metals Company Inc ....G...... 732 761-0500
  Lakewood *(G-5101)*

Frc Electrical Industries Inc ....E...... 908 464-3200
  New Providence *(G-7000)*

▲ Gogreen Power Inc ....F...... 732 994-5901
  Howell *(G-4540)*

Gsi ....G...... 908 608-1325
  Summit *(G-10533)*

H G Schaevitz LLC ....G...... 856 727-0250
  Moorestown *(G-6526)*

H I D Systems Inc ....G...... 973 383-8535
  Sparta *(G-10390)*

◆ Haas Laser Technologies Inc .....F...... 973 598-1150
  Flanders *(G-3412)*

Henry Bros Electronics Inc ....E...... 201 794-6500
  Fair Lawn *(G-3103)*

Hitrons Tech Inc ....G...... 201 941-0024
  Ridgefield *(G-9265)*

◆ I 2 R Corp ....G...... 732 919-1100
  Wall Township *(G-11348)*

Ifortress ....G...... 973 812-6400
  Woodland Park *(G-12082)*

▲ Infinova Corporation ....E...... 732 355-9100
  Monmouth Junction *(G-6293)*

Inrad Optics Inc ....D...... 201 767-1910
  Northvale *(G-7529)*

Inter World Highway LLC ....F...... 732 759-8235
  Long Branch *(G-5599)*

▲ International Cord Sets Inc ....F...... 973 227-2118
  Fairfield *(G-3240)*

Ironbound Metal ....G...... 973 242-5704
  Newark *(G-7161)*

Jvs Christmas Lighting ....G...... 201 664-4022
  Westwood *(G-11832)*

K & A Industries Inc ....G...... 908 226-7000
  South Plainfield *(G-10285)*

Ketec ....G...... 856 778-4343
  Moorestown *(G-6534)*

▲ Kft Fire Trainer LLC ....E...... 201 300-8100
  Montvale *(G-6417)*

L & R Manufacturing Co Inc ....C...... 201 991-5330
  Kearny *(G-4878)*

◆ L & R Manufacturing Co Inc ......D...... 201 991-5330
  Kearny *(G-4877)*

Laser Contractors LLC ....G...... 609 517-2407
  Medford *(G-6028)*

Lb Electric Co - North LLC ....G...... 973 366-2188
  Denville *(G-2044)*

LTS NJ Inc ....G...... 856 780-9888
  Mount Laurel *(G-6779)*

M & Z International Inc ....G...... 201 864-3331
  West New York *(G-11746)*

Max Flight Corp ....F...... 732 281-2007
  Toms River *(G-10777)*

▲ Maxlite Inc ....D...... 973 244-7300
  West Caldwell *(G-11663)*

▲ Metrologic Instruments Inc ....C...... 856 228-8100
  Mount Laurel *(G-6782)*

Mobile Intelligent Alerts Inc ....G...... 201 410-5324
  Holmdel *(G-4507)*

Mphase Technologies Inc ....F...... 973 256-3737
  Clifton *(G-1671)*

MTS Systems Corporation ....A...... 856 875-4478
  Williamstown *(G-11965)*

Multicomm Solutions Inc ....G...... 877 796-8480
  Toms River *(G-10780)*

New Skysonic Surveillance ....G...... 856 317-0600
  Cherry Hill *(G-1398)*

O S I Inc ....F...... 732 754-6271
  Metuchen *(G-6067)*

Ocean Energy Industries Inc ....F...... 954 828-2177
  Oakhurst *(G-7611)*

OHM Equipment LLC ....G...... 856 765-3011
  Millville *(G-6265)*

◆ Paige Electric Company LP ....E...... 908 687-7810
  Union *(G-11080)*

PCI Inc ....G...... 973 226-8007
  West Caldwell *(G-11671)*

Power Brooks Co LLC ....F...... 609 890-0100
  Hamilton *(G-4120)*

◆ PRC Laser Corporation ....G...... 973 347-0100
  Mount Arlington *(G-6718)*

Primary Systems Inc ....F...... 732 679-2200
  Old Bridge *(G-7725)*

Princeton Lightwave Inc ....E...... 609 495-2600
  Cranbury *(G-1875)*

Qsa Global National Corp ....G...... 865 888-6798
  Red Bank *(G-9241)*

Quantum Security Systems Inc .....G...... 609 252-0505
  Princeton *(G-9011)*

Radnet Inc ....F...... 908 709-1323
  Cranford *(G-1924)*

▲ Repco Inc ....F...... 856 762-0172
  Marlton *(G-5949)*

Resideo Funding Inc ....F...... 973 455-2000
  Morris Plains *(G-6625)*

Secure System Inc ....E...... 732 922-3609
  Stirling *(G-10496)*

Security 21 LLC ....G...... 856 384-7474
  Woodbury *(G-12036)*

Seminole Wire & Cable Co Inc ......F...... 856 324-2929
  Pennsauken *(G-8483)*

Seren Ips Inc ....D...... 856 205-1131
  Vineland *(G-11265)*

Signal Crafters Tech Inc ....G...... 973 781-0880
  East Hanover *(G-2239)*

Skycam Technologies LLC ....G...... 908 205-5548
  Perth Amboy *(G-8534)*

Specialized Fire & SEC Inc ....E...... 212 255-1010
  Riverdale *(G-9386)*

Starlight Electro-Optics Inc ....G...... 908 859-1362
  Phillipsburg *(G-8575)*

Stud Welding Co The Inc ....G...... 856 866-9300
  Moorestown *(G-6569)*

T F S Inc ....E...... 973 890-7651
  Totowa *(G-10854)*

Talon7 LLC ....F...... 908 595-2121
  Bridgewater *(G-896)*

▲ Techntime Bus Sltons Ltd Lblty ...F...... 973 246-8153
  East Rutherford *(G-2324)*

◆ Tiger Supplies Inc ....G...... 973 854-8635
  Irvington *(G-4588)*

Total Garage Solutions LLC ....E...... 732 749-3993
  Wall Township *(G-11375)*

U S Laser Corp ....E...... 201 848-9200
  Hillsdale *(G-4371)*

Vandermolen Corp ....G...... 973 992-8506
  Ledgewood *(G-5284)*

◆ Vicmarr Audio Inc ....E 732 289-9111
Edison *(G-2641)*

Vision Ten Inc ....F 201 935-3000
Carlstadt *(G-1236)*

Wickr Inc ....G 516 637-2882
Newark *(G-7315)*

Zenith Mfg & Chemical Corp ....F 201 767-1332
Norwood *(G-7577)*

37 TRANSPORTATION EQUIPMENT

3711 Motor Vehicles & Car Bodies

Autoaccess LLC ....F 908 240-5919
Sicklerville *(G-9908)*

◆ BMW of North America LLC ....A 201 307-4000
Woodcliff Lake *(G-12049)*

Bruce Kindberg ....G 973 664-0195
Rockaway *(G-9447)*

Cliffside Body Corporation ....E 201 945-3970
Fairview *(G-3358)*

Dejana Trck Utility Eqp Co LLC ....E 856 303-1315
Cinnaminson *(G-1449)*

Drive-Master Co Inc ....F 973 808-9709
Fairfield *(G-3188)*

Elite Emrgncy Lights Ltd Lblty ....F 732 534-2377
Lakewood *(G-5090)*

▲ Faps Inc ....C 973 589-5656
Newark *(G-7122)*

▼ First Priority Emergency Vhicl ....F 732 657-1104
Manchester *(G-5845)*

First Priority Global Ltd ....F 973 347-4321
Flanders *(G-3410)*

Garden St Chasis Remanuf ....E 732 283-1910
Woodbridge *(G-12016)*

Jontol Unlimited LLC ....G 858 652-1113
Blackwood *(G-473)*

Navistar Inc ....D 856 486-2300
Cherry Hill *(G-1397)*

▲ Odyssey Auto Specialty Inc ....F 973 328-2667
Wharton *(G-11865)*

▼ Orlando Systems Ltd Lblty Co ....G 908 400-5052
North Plainfield *(G-7507)*

P L Custom Body & Eqp Co Inc ....C 732 223-1411
Manasquan *(G-5836)*

Polar Truck Sales ....E 201 246-1010
Jersey City *(G-4784)*

R & H Spring & Truck Repair ....F 732 681-9000
Wall Township *(G-11362)*

◆ Rolls-Royce Motor Cars Na LLC ....A 201 307-4117
Woodcliff Lake *(G-12063)*

S L P Engineering Inc ....D 732 240-3696
Toms River *(G-10789)*

Teo Fabrications Inc ....G 973 764-5500
Vernon *(G-11163)*

Tesla Inc ....G 201 225-2544
Paramus *(G-7841)*

Toyota Motor Sales ....F 973 515-5012
Parsippany *(G-8030)*

Vending Trucks Inc ....E 732 969-5400
East Brunswick *(G-2190)*

W2f Inc ....G 609 735-0135
New Egypt *(G-6987)*

3713 Truck & Bus Bodies

Alexam Riverdale ....G 973 831-0065
Riverdale *(G-9370)*

American Bus & Coach LLC ....E 732 283-1982
Iselin *(G-4591)*

Barrier Enterprises Inc ....G 973 770-3983
Andover *(G-44)*

Bristol-Donald Company Inc ....E 973 589-2640
Newark *(G-7076)*

Christensen Manufacturing ....F 609 466-9700
Pennington *(G-8361)*

Cliffside Body Corporation ....E 201 945-3970
Fairview *(G-3358)*

▲ Columbia Industries Inc ....G 201 337-7332
Franklin Lakes *(G-3618)*

▼ Custom Sales & Service Inc ....E 609 561-6900
Hammonton *(G-4133)*

▼ Demountable Concepts Inc ....E 856 863-3081
Glassboro *(G-3809)*

Fleet Equipment Corporation ....F 201 337-3294
Franklin Lakes *(G-3623)*

Garden St Chasis Remanuf ....E 732 283-1910
Woodbridge *(G-12016)*

Jid Transportation LLC ....G 201 362-0841
West New York *(G-11744)*

Peter Garafano & Son Inc ....E 973 278-0350
Paterson *(G-8282)*

Summit Truck Body Inc ....E 908 277-4342
Summit *(G-10551)*

Transtar Truck Body & Wldg Co ....G 908 832-2688
Califon *(G-1036)*

Universal Parts ....G 908 601-6558
Linden *(G-5439)*

▼ Vacuum Sales Inc ....E 856 627-7790
Laurel Springs *(G-5209)*

Waldwick Volunteer ....E 201 445-8772
Waldwick *(G-11313)*

3714 Motor Vehicle Parts & Access

▲ Accurate Tool & Die Co Inc ....E 201 476-9348
Montvale *(G-6394)*

Allied-Signal China Ltd ....E 973 455-2000
Morristown *(G-6632)*

Alliedsignal Foreign Sls Corp ....G 973 455-2000
Morristown *(G-6633)*

◆ Allison Corp ....G 973 992-3800
Livingston *(G-5504)*

American Refuse Supply Inc ....F 973 684-3225
Paterson *(G-8137)*

Banks Bros Corporation ....D 973 680-4488
Bloomfield *(G-491)*

Bruce Kindberg ....G 973 664-0195
Rockaway *(G-9447)*

▲ C T A Manufacturing Corp ....E 201 896-1000
Carlstadt *(G-1135)*

▲ Carolina Fluid Handling Inc ....A 248 228-8900
West Berlin *(G-11579)*

▲ Cervinis Inc ....F 856 691-1744
Vineland *(G-11198)*

Chick Capoli Sales ....E 856 768-4500
West Berlin *(G-11581)*

▲ Clear Plus Windshield Wipers ....F 973 546-8800
Garfield *(G-3735)*

Custom Auto Radiator Inc ....F 609 242-9700
Forked River *(G-3539)*

Dana Automotive Inc ....F 973 667-1234
Nutley *(G-7584)*

Elite Emrgncy Lights Ltd Lblty ....F 732 534-2377
Lakewood *(G-5090)*

◆ Felco Products LLC ....G 973 890-7979
Paterson *(G-8192)*

▲ Fleetsource LLC ....E 732 566-4970
Dayton *(G-1961)*

Freehold Pntiac Bick GMC Trcks ....D 732 462-7093
Freehold *(G-3666)*

Garrett Motion Inc ....G 973 867-7016
Morristown *(G-6665)*

◆ Gentek Inc ....C 973 515-0900
Parsippany *(G-7956)*

Gorman Industries Inc ....E 973 345-5424
Paterson *(G-8201)*

Holman Enterprises Inc ....C 856 532-2410
Pennsauken *(G-8431)*

Holman Enterprises Inc ....E 609 383-6100
Mount Laurel *(G-6765)*

Honeywell International Inc ....G 973 455-2000
Morristown *(G-6672)*

Ida Automotive Inc ....G 732 591-1245
Morganville *(G-6588)*

J & R Rebuilders Inc ....F 856 627-1414
Laurel Springs *(G-5207)*

Jesel Inc ....D 732 901-1800
Lakewood *(G-5116)*

K & K Automotive Inc ....G 973 777-2235
Passaic *(G-8078)*

◆ Kinedyne LLC ....F 908 231-1800
Branchburg *(G-652)*

KRs Automotive Dev Group Inc ....F 732 667-7937
Middlesex *(G-6125)*

▲ Kumar Bros USA LLC ....G 732 266-3091
Englishtown *(G-3006)*

Level Ten Products Inc ....F 973 827-0900
Hamburg *(G-4094)*

Ls Rubber Industries Inc ....F 973 680-4488
Bloomfield *(G-507)*

▲ Manley Performance Pdts Inc ....D 732 905-3366
Lakewood *(G-5128)*

Matthey Johnson Inc ....C 856 384-7132
West Deptford *(G-11710)*

Maxzone Vehicle Lighting Corp ....F 732 393-9600
Edison *(G-2560)*

Momentum Usa Inc ....F 844 300-1553
Edison *(G-2569)*

MPT Racing Inc ....G 973 989-9220
Dover *(G-2099)*

▲ NAPA Concepts Ltd Liability Co ....G 201 673-2381
North Bergen *(G-7424)*

Newark Auto Top Co Inc ....F 973 677-9935
East Orange *(G-2256)*

Nitto Inc ....F 732 901-0035
Lakewood *(G-5140)*

▲ O T D Inc ....G 973 890-7979
Totowa *(G-10839)*

▲ Ogura Industrial Corp ....F 586 749-1900
Somerset *(G-10045)*

▲ Olde Grandad Industries Inc ....G 201 997-1899
Passaic *(G-8093)*

Overdrive Holdings Inc ....F 201 440-1911
South Hackensack *(G-10178)*

P & A Auto Parts Inc ....E 201 655-7117
Hackensack *(G-3960)*

Paintmaster Auto Body ....F 732 270-1700
Toms River *(G-10781)*

▲ Premier Products Inc ....D 856 231-1800
Marlton *(G-5948)*

Quality Remanufacturing Inc ....F 973 523-8800
Paterson *(G-8284)*

Ram Hydraulics Inc ....G 732 237-0904
Shrewsbury *(G-9900)*

Rebuilt Parts Co LLC ....E 856 662-3252
Pennsauken *(G-8476)*

▲ Research & Mfg Corp Amer ....F 908 862-6744
Linden *(G-5414)*

▼ Rony Inc ....G 201 891-2551
Wyckoff *(G-12120)*

▲ S & G Tool Aid Corporation ....G 973 824-7730
Newark *(G-7257)*

S L P Engineering Inc ....D 732 240-3696
Toms River *(G-10789)*

Shock Tech Inc ....E 845 368-8600
Mahwah *(G-5771)*

▲ Spalding Automotive Inc ....E 215 638-3334
Moorestown *(G-6567)*

Steed Perf6manc3 ....G 908 583-5580
Linden *(G-5430)*

◆ Tabco Technologies LLC ....G 201 438-0422
Carlstadt *(G-1225)*

Tekltd ....G 732 463-2100
Piscataway *(G-8724)*

Tesla Inc ....G 201 225-2544
Paramus *(G-7841)*

Top Rated Shopping Bargains ....F 800 556-5849
Hasbrouck Heights *(G-4190)*

Town Ford Inc ....D 609 298-4990
Bordentown *(G-597)*

▲ Transaxle LLC ....C 856 665-4445
Cinnaminson *(G-1492)*

Transmission Technology Co ....G 973 305-3600
Lincoln Park *(G-5307)*

Truckpro LLC ....E 201 229-0599
Teterboro *(G-10697)*

Turbine Tek Inc ....G 973 872-0903
Wayne *(G-11559)*

Turbo Solutions LLC ....F 856 209-6900
Pennsauken *(G-8494)*

Vahlco Racing Wheels LLC ....G 609 758-7013
New Egypt *(G-6986)*

Valcor Engineering Corporation ....E 973 467-8100
Springfield *(G-10473)*

◆ Volvo Car North America LLC ....B 201 768-7300
Rockleigh *(G-9524)*

VS Systematics Corp ....G 908 241-5110
Kenilworth *(G-4985)*

Wayne Motors Inc ....D 973 696-9710
Wayne *(G-11564)*

Well Manager LLC ....G 609 466-4347
Hopewell *(G-4529)*

◆ Wexco Industries Inc ....E 973 244-5777
Pine Brook *(G-8620)*

Z Squared Hg Inc ....G 908 315-3646
Hillsborough *(G-4362)*

3715 Truck Trailers

ASAP Containers NJ NY Corp ....F 732 659-4402
West Orange *(G-11759)*

◆ Automann Inc ....D 201 529-4996
Somerset *(G-9961)*

E Loc Total Logistics LLC ....G 609 685-6117
Mount Laurel *(G-6758)*

Fyx Fleet Roadside Assistance ....F 609 452-8900
Princeton *(G-8953)*

◆ Granco Group LLC ....G 973 515-4721
Roseland *(G-9539)*

▲ Hercules Enterprises LLC ....D 908 369-0000
Hillsborough *(G-4323)*

M W Trailer Repair Inc ....F 609 298-1113
Bordentown *(G-585)*

Richard Shafer ....G....... 856 358-3483
Elmer **(G-2802)**

Seacube Container Leasing Ltd ....G....... 201 391-0800
Park Ridge **(G-7859)**

Trac Intermodal LLC ....G....... 609 452-8900
Princeton **(G-9034)**

Universal Parts New Jersey LLC ....G....... 732 615-0626
Middletown **(G-6167)**

Vanco Usa LLC ....D....... 609 499-4141
Bordentown **(G-598)**

Vanco USA LLC (de) ....C....... 609 499-4141
Bordentown **(G-599)**

Wjm Trucking Inc ....G....... 856 381-3635
Mullica Hill **(G-6858)**

Wta Global LLC ....F....... 312 509-2559
Little Falls **(G-5473)**

3721 Aircraft

Abj LLC ....G....... 888 225-1931
Cranbury **(G-1806)**

Boeing Company ....A....... 314 232-1372
Mullica Hill **(G-6856)**

Boeing Company ....A....... 908 464-6959
Berkeley Heights **(G-390)**

Boeing Company ....A....... 610 591-1978
Swedesboro **(G-10573)**

Dassault Aircraft Svcs Corp ....F....... 201 440-6700
Little Ferry **(G-5481)**

▼ Defense Photonics Group Inc ....F....... 908 822-1075
South Plainfield **(G-10247)**

Defense Spport Svcs Intl 2 LLC ....F....... 856 866-2200
Marlton **(G-5927)**

Drone Go Home LLC ....G....... 732 991-3605
Holmdel **(G-4499)**

Drone Usa Inc ....F....... 203 220-2296
Pine Brook **(G-8600)**

Easy Aerial Inc ....G....... 646 639-4410
Edison **(G-2497)**

Enroute Computer Solutions Inc ....E....... 609 569-9255
Egg Harbor Township **(G-2683)**

Freestream Aircraft USA Ltd ....F....... 201 365-6080
Teterboro **(G-10706)**

Jet Aviation St Louis Inc ....E....... 201 462-4026
Teterboro **(G-10681)**

Lockheed Martin Corporation ....B....... 856 787-3104
Mount Laurel **(G-6777)**

Lockheed Martin Corporation ....D....... 856 722-7782
Moorestown **(G-6538)**

Pacific Microtronics Inc ....G....... 973 993-8665
Morris Plains **(G-6621)**

3724 Aircraft Engines & Engine Parts

Ademco I LLC ....G....... 973 455-2000
Morris Plains **(G-6601)**

Aerospace Industries LLC ....G....... 973 383-9307
Sparta **(G-10376)**

Allied-Signal China Ltd ....E....... 973 455-2000
Morristown **(G-6632)**

Alliedsignal Foreign Sls Corp ....G....... 973 455-2000
Morristown **(G-6633)**

Bright Lights Usa Inc ....E....... 856 546-5656
Camden **(G-1042)**

Capital Cooling Systems LLC ....G....... 973 773-8700
Lyndhurst **(G-5645)**

Dover Tool Connecticut LLC ....F....... 203 367-6376
Franklin Lakes **(G-3622)**

Hh Spinco Inc ....G....... 973 455-2000
Morris Plains **(G-6606)**

Honeywell International Inc ....C....... 800 601-3099
Morris Plains **(G-6609)**

Honeywell International Inc ....E....... 973 455-6633
Morristown **(G-6670)**

Honeywell International Inc ....E....... 973 285-5321
Morris Plains **(G-6610)**

Honeywell International Inc ....A....... 856 691-5111
Vineland **(G-11232)**

Honeywell International Inc ....A....... 856 234-5020
Moorestown **(G-6529)**

Honeywell International Inc ....D....... 973 455-2000
Morris Plains **(G-6611)**

Honeywell International Inc ....G....... 973 455-5168
Morristown **(G-6671)**

Honeywell International Inc ....C....... 877 841-2840
Morris Plains **(G-6612)**

Honeywell International Inc ....A....... 732 919-0010
Wall Township **(G-11346)**

Honeywell International Inc ....G....... 800 601-3099
Morris Plains **(G-6613)**

Honeywell Spain Holdings LLC ....G....... 973 455-2000
Morristown **(G-6673)**

Kreisler Manufacturing Corp ....G....... 201 791-0700
Elmwood Park **(G-2836)**

▲ Parts Life Inc ....D....... 856 786-8675
Moorestown **(G-6554)**

3728 Aircraft Parts & Eqpt, NEC

▲ Accurate Bushing Company Inc ....E....... 908 789-1121
Garwood **(G-3779)**

Aerospace Manufacturing Inc ....E....... 973 472-9888
Wallington **(G-11380)**

◆ Air Cruisers Company LLC ....B....... 732 681-3527
Wall Township **(G-11315)**

Alpine Machine & Tool Corp ....F....... 201 666-0959
Westwood **(G-11825)**

American Aluminum Company ....D....... 908 233-3500
Mountainside **(G-6834)**

▲ Arlington Prcsion Cmpnents LLC .....E....... 973 276-1377
Fairfield **(G-3145)**

Bar Fields Inc ....G....... 347 587-7795
Linden **(G-5325)**

Breeze-Eastern LLC ....D....... 973 602-1001
Whippany **(G-11884)**

▲ Breeze-Eastern LLC ....G....... 973 602-1001
Whippany **(G-11883)**

▲ Bright Lights Usa Inc ....D....... 856 546-5656
Mount Laurel **(G-6743)**

▼ Clearway LLC ....E....... 973 578-4578
Newark **(G-7084)**

Defense Support Svcs Intl LLC ....F....... 850 390-4737
Marlton **(G-5928)**

Doorsills LLC ....G....... 973 904-0270
Haledon **(G-4081)**

Drone Go Home LLC ....G....... 732 991-3605
Holmdel **(G-4499)**

▲ Drytech Inc ....E....... 609 758-1794
Cookstown **(G-1803)**

Enginred Arrsting Systems Corp ....E....... 856 241-8620
Logan Township **(G-5587)**

Exelis Inc/Northrop ....F....... 973 284-4212
Clifton **(G-1618)**

Export Management Consultants ....E....... 609 758-1166
Cookstown **(G-1804)**

Goodrich Corporation ....C....... 973 237-2700
Totowa **(G-10830)**

Ho-Ho-Kus Inc ....E....... 973 278-2274
Paterson **(G-8210)**

J A Machine & Tool Co Inc ....F....... 201 767-1308
Closter **(G-1759)**

Keeley Aerospace Ltd ....E....... 951 582-2113
Cranbury **(G-1849)**

Kreisler Industrial Corp ....D....... 201 289-5554
Elmwood Park **(G-2835)**

Kreisler Manufacturing Corp ....G....... 201 791-0700
Elmwood Park **(G-2836)**

Pacific Coast Systems LLC ....G....... 908 735-9955
Asbury **(G-68)**

Polytechnic Industries Inc ....F....... 856 235-6550
Mount Laurel **(G-6793)**

Rclc Inc ....F....... 732 877-1788
Woodbridge **(G-12020)**

Simtek Usa Inc ....G....... 862 757-8130
Little Falls **(G-5467)**

Terrestrial Imaging LLC ....G....... 800 359-0530
Brick **(G-733)**

▲ Thales Avionics Inc ....C....... 732 242-6300
Piscataway **(G-8725)**

Tolin Design Inc ....G....... 201 261-4455
Emerson **(G-2869)**

Vahl Inc ....E....... 732 249-4042
East Brunswick **(G-2188)**

Whippany Actuation Systems LLC ....C....... 973 428-9898
Whippany **(G-11913)**

▲ Zodiac US Corporation ....A....... 732 681-3527
Wall Township **(G-11379)**

3731 Shipbuilding & Repairing

Allen Steel Co ....G....... 856 785-1171
Leesburg **(G-5286)**

▼ American Rigging & Repair Inc ....F....... 866 478-7129
Roselle **(G-9547)**

▲ Bayonne Drydock & Repair Corp .....E....... 201 823-9295
Bayonne **(G-206)**

Bishop Ascendant Inc ....G....... 201 572-7436
West Caldwell **(G-11642)**

Conneaut Creek Ship Repr Inc ....G....... 212 863-9406
Jersey City **(G-4716)**

Dorchester Shipyard Inc ....F....... 856 785-8040
Dorchester **(G-2070)**

Kerney Service Group Inc ....E....... 908 486-2644
Linden **(G-5370)**

Maxwell McKenney Inc ....G....... 856 310-0700
Haddon Heights **(G-4046)**

Monmouth Marine Engines Inc ....F....... 732 528-9290
Brielle **(G-907)**

◆ Nvs International Inc ....E....... 908 523-0266
Linden **(G-5398)**

◆ Ocean Power & Equipment Co ....G....... 973 575-5775
West Caldwell **(G-11668)**

▲ Simplex Americas LLC ....E....... 908 237-9099
Flemington **(G-3467)**

Union Dry Dock & Repair Co ....G....... 201 792-9090
Hoboken **(G-4485)**

Union Dry Dock & Repair Co ....E....... 201 963-5833
Hoboken **(G-4486)**

Wittich Bros Marine Inc ....E....... 732 722-8656
Manasquan **(G-5844)**

3732 Boat Building & Repairing

A & D Indus & Mar Repr Inc ....G....... 732 541-1481
Port Reading **(G-8890)**

A PS Inlet Marina LLC ....G....... 732 681-3303
Belmar **(G-346)**

Barnegat Light Fibrgls Sup LLC ....G....... 609 294-8870
West Creek **(G-11684)**

Camp Marine Services Inc ....G....... 609 368-1777
Stone Harbor **(G-10503)**

Carver Boat Sales Inc ....G....... 732 892-0328
Point Pleasant Boro **(G-8839)**

Cherubini Yachts Ltd Lblty Co ....G....... 856 764-5319
Delran **(G-2014)**

▼ Commercial Water Sports Inc ....G....... 609 624-3404
Cape May Court House **(G-1110)**

Costa Mar Cnvas Enclosures LLC ....E....... 609 965-1538
Egg Harbor City **(G-2656)**

D&S Fisheries LLC ....G....... 914 438-3197
Colts Neck **(G-1780)**

Eh Yachts LLC ....D....... 609 965-2300
Egg Harbor City **(G-2660)**

Henriques Yachts Works ....G....... 732 269-1180
Bayville **(G-246)**

Jersey Cape Yachts Inc ....D....... 609 965-8650
Egg Harbor City **(G-2661)**

Lockwood Boat Works Inc ....E....... 732 721-1605
South Amboy **(G-10136)**

Marine Acquisition Inc ....D....... 609 965-2300
Egg Harbor City **(G-2664)**

Norma K Corporation ....G....... 732 477-6441
Point Pleasant Beach **(G-8829)**

▲ Steelstran Industries Inc ....E....... 732 574-0700
Avenel **(G-147)**

Sunsplash Marina LLC ....G....... 609 628-4445
Tuckahoe **(G-11014)**

Supply Technologies LLC ....E....... 201 641-7600
Moonachie **(G-6492)**

Tf Yachts LLC ....E....... 609 965-2300
Egg Harbor City **(G-2669)**

Tradewinds Marine Service ....G....... 848 448-6888
Toms River **(G-10800)**

Union Dry Dock & Repair Co ....E....... 201 963-5833
Hoboken **(G-4486)**

Van Duyne Bros Inc ....G....... 609 625-0299
Mays Landing **(G-5999)**

▲ Viking Yacht Company ....B....... 609 296-6000
New Gretna **(G-6988)**

Viking Yacht Company ....C....... 609 296-6000
Egg Harbor City **(G-2671)**

▲ Yank Marine Inc ....E....... 609 628-2928
Tuckahoe **(G-11015)**

3743 Railroad Eqpt

American Rail Company Inc ....F....... 732 785-1110
Brick **(G-710)**

Bombardier Transportation ....G....... 201 955-5874
Kearny **(G-4849)**

Hainesport Industrial Railroad ....F....... 609 261-8036
Hainesport **(G-4072)**

J M S Melgar Transport LLC ....G....... 908 834-1722
North Plainfield **(G-7506)**

Marmon Industrial LLC ....F....... 609 655-4287
Cranbury **(G-1863)**

▲ Multipower International Inc ....G....... 973 727-0327
Towaco **(G-10875)**

▼ Rails Company Inc ....E....... 973 763-4320
Maplewood **(G-5883)**

▲ Strato Inc ....D....... 732 981-1515
Piscataway **(G-8720)**

3751 Motorcycles, Bicycles & Parts

Barbs Harley-Davidson ....E....... 856 456-4141
Mount Ephraim **(G-6720)**

Bezerra Corporation ....G....... 973 595-7775
Totowa *(G-10819)*

◆ BMW of North America LLC ....A....... 201 307-4000
Woodcliff Lake *(G-12049)*

Electric Mobility Corporation ....C....... 856 468-1000
Sewell *(G-9844)*

▲ Hyper Bicycles Inc ....G....... 856 694-0352
Malaga *(G-5788)*

Morristown Cycle ....G....... 973 540-1244
Morristown *(G-6688)*

NJ Grass Choppers ....G....... 732 414-2850
Manalapan *(G-5819)*

Ross Bicycles LLC ....F....... 888 392-5628
Totowa *(G-10850)*

Wheels Motor Sports Inc ....G....... 732 606-9208
Bayville *(G-253)*

▲ Works Enduro Rider Inc ....G....... 908 637-6385
Great Meadows *(G-3858)*

3761 Guided Missiles & Space Vehicles

Lockheed Martin Corporation ....B....... 856 787-3104
Mount Laurel *(G-6777)*

Lockheed Martin Overseas LLC ....G....... 856 787-3105
Moorestown *(G-6541)*

Savit Corporation ....F....... 862 209-4516
Rockaway *(G-9497)*

3764 Guided Missile/Space Vehicle Propulsion Units & parts

Aphelion Orbitals Inc ....G....... 321 289-0872
Union City *(G-11107)*

Lockheed Martin Corporation ....B....... 856 787-3104
Mount Laurel *(G-6777)*

3769 Guided Missile/Space Vehicle Parts & Eqpt, NEC

Aeropanel Corporation ....D....... 973 335-9636
Boonton *(G-537)*

Breeze-Eastern LLC ....D....... 973 602-1001
Whippany *(G-11884)*

▲ Drytech Inc ....E....... 609 758-1794
Cookstown *(G-1803)*

H & W Tool Co Inc ....F....... 973 366-0131
Dover *(G-2085)*

▲ McWilliams Forge Company ....D....... 973 627-0200
Rockaway *(G-9476)*

Zenith Precision Inc ....F....... 201 933-8640
East Rutherford *(G-2331)*

3792 Travel Trailers & Campers

▼ Orlando Systems Ltd Lblty Co ....G....... 908 400-5052
North Plainfield *(G-7507)*

3795 Tanks & Tank Components

ALI Envmtl & Tank Svcs LLC ....F....... 908 755-2962
Scotch Plains *(G-9728)*

AST Construction Inc ....E....... 609 277-7101
Egg Harbor Township *(G-2677)*

Clogic LLC ....G....... 973 934-5223
Augusta *(G-115)*

Savit Corporation ....F....... 862 209-4516
Rockaway *(G-9497)*

3799 Transportation Eqpt, NEC

▲ Parts Life Inc ....D....... 856 786-8675
Moorestown *(G-6554)*

◆ Savino Del Bene USA Inc ....D....... 347 960-5568
Avenel *(G-145)*

Sealion Metal Fabricators Inc ....F....... 856 933-3914
Bellmawr *(G-342)*

Steve Green Enterprises ....F....... 732 938-5572
Farmingdale *(G-3393)*

38 MEASURING, ANALYZING AND CONTROLLING INSTRUMENTS; PHOTOGRAPHIC, MEDICAL AN

3812 Search, Detection, Navigation & Guidance Systs & Instrs

Aeronautical Instr & Rdo Co ....E....... 973 473-0034
Lodi *(G-5550)*

Aeropanel Corporation ....D....... 973 335-9636
Boonton *(G-537)*

Alk Technologies Inc ....C....... 609 683-0220
Princeton *(G-8906)*

Allied-Signal China Ltd ....E....... 973 455-2000
Morristown *(G-6632)*

Alliedsignal Foreign Sls Corp ....G....... 973 455-2000
Morristown *(G-6633)*

American Gas & Chemical Co Ltd ....E....... 201 767-7300
Northvale *(G-7518)*

▼ AT&T Technologies Inc ....A....... 201 771-2000
Berkeley Heights *(G-389)*

Atlantic Inertial Systems Inc ....B....... 973 237-2713
Totowa *(G-10816)*

Bae Systems Info & Elec Sys ....B....... 603 885-4321
Totowa *(G-10817)*

Bae Systems Info & Elec Sys ....E....... 973 633-6000
Wayne *(G-11473)*

Bae Systems Info & Elec Sys ....A....... 973 633-6000
Wayne *(G-11474)*

Bae Systems Tech Sol Srvc Inc ....E....... 856 638-1003
Mount Laurel *(G-6739)*

Check-It Electronics Corp ....E....... 973 520-8435
Elizabeth *(G-2720)*

◆ Checkpoint Systems Inc ....C....... 800 257-5540
West Deptford *(G-11697)*

Checkpoint Systems Inc ....E....... 856 848-1800
West Deptford *(G-11698)*

Dassault Procurement Svcs Inc ....E....... 201 261-4130
Little Ferry *(G-5482)*

Dengen Scientific Corporation ....E....... 201 687-2983
Union City *(G-11110)*

Dewey Electronics Corporation ....E....... 201 337-4700
Oakland *(G-7625)*

Drs Infrared Technologies LP ....G....... 973 898-1500
Parsippany *(G-7920)*

Drs Leonardo Inc ....E....... 973 775-4440
Newark *(G-7105)*

Drs Leonardo Inc ....E....... 973 898-1500
Parsippany *(G-7921)*

Drs Leonardo Inc ....E....... 973 898-1500
Florham Park *(G-3501)*

Drs Leonardo Inc ....E....... 201 337-3800
Oakland *(G-7626)*

▼ Electromagnetic Tech Inds Inc ....D....... 973 394-1719
Boonton *(G-550)*

Ferry Machine Corp ....E....... 201 641-9191
Little Ferry *(G-5485)*

GE Aviation Systems LLC ....C....... 973 428-9898
Whippany *(G-11892)*

General Dynamics Mission ....C....... 973 261-1409
Florham Park *(G-3507)*

Glasseal Products Inc ....C....... 732 370-9100
Lakewood *(G-5104)*

H Galow Co Inc ....E....... 201 768-0547
Norwood *(G-7564)*

Ho-Ho-Kus Inc ....E....... 973 278-2274
Paterson *(G-8210)*

Honeywell East Asia Inc ....G....... 973 455-2000
Morris Plains *(G-6608)*

Honeywell International Inc ....G....... 973 455-2000
Morristown *(G-6672)*

Innerspace Technology Inc ....E....... 201 933-1600
Carlstadt *(G-1168)*

Intertek Laboratories Inc ....E....... 908 903-1800
Stirling *(G-10491)*

Kearfott Corporation ....C....... 973 785-6000
Woodland Park *(G-12083)*

L3 Technologies Inc ....B....... 973 446-4000
Budd Lake *(G-925)*

L3harris Technologies Inc ....C....... 973 284-0123
Clifton *(G-1650)*

L3harris Technologies Inc ....E....... 973 284-0123
Clifton *(G-1652)*

L3harris Technologies Inc ....C....... 585 269-6600
Bloomfield *(G-505)*

Lcn Partners Inc ....F....... 215 755-1000
Berlin *(G-426)*

Lockheed Martin ....D....... 856 722-7782
Marlton *(G-5938)*

Lockheed Martin ....C....... 856 722-2418
Marlton *(G-5939)*

Lockheed Martin Corporation ....C....... 856 988-1085
Marlton *(G-5940)*

Lockheed Martin Corporation ....A....... 609 485-7601
Atlantic City *(G-97)*

Lockheed Martin Corporation ....A....... 856 234-1261
Mount Laurel *(G-6776)*

Lockheed Martin Corporation ....D....... 856 722-7782
Moorestown *(G-6538)*

Lockheed Martin Corporation ....C....... 856 792-9811
Cherry Hill *(G-1384)*

Lockheed Martin Corporation ....C....... 856 727-5800
Mount Laurel *(G-6778)*

Lockheed Martin Corporation ....A....... 856 722-4100
Moorestown *(G-6540)*

Lockheed Martin Corporation ....C....... 856 722-3336
Moorestown *(G-6539)*

Lockheed Martin Corporation ....B....... 856 787-3104
Mount Laurel *(G-6777)*

Lockheed Martin Integrtd Systm ....C....... 856 762-2222
Wall Township *(G-11353)*

Magos America Inc ....G....... 973 763-9597
Kearny *(G-4881)*

Mantech Systems Engrg Corp ....G....... 856 566-9155
Voorhees *(G-11291)*

Melton Sales & Service ....E....... 609 699-4800
Bordentown *(G-587)*

Melton Sales & Service ....E....... 609 699-4800
Columbus *(G-1802)*

▲ Milspray LLC ....E....... 732 886-2223
Lakewood *(G-5135)*

▲ Multi-Tech Industries Inc ....F....... 732 431-0550
Marlboro *(G-5905)*

Mwt Materials Inc ....F....... 973 928-8300
Passaic *(G-8091)*

National Prtective Systems Inc ....F....... 732 922-3609
Eatontown *(G-2412)*

Northrop Grumman Systems Corp ....C....... 609 272-9000
Pleasantville *(G-8816)*

Northrop Grumman Systems Corp ....G....... 908 276-6677
Cranford *(G-1919)*

Oavco Ltd Liability Company ....F....... 855 535-4227
Princeton *(G-8988)*

Oaviation Corporation ....E....... 609 619-3060
Princeton *(G-8989)*

Portable Defense LLC ....G....... 856 228-3010
Blackwood *(G-478)*

Premac Inc ....F....... 732 381-7550
Rahway *(G-9122)*

Primacy Engineering Inc ....F....... 201 731-3272
Englewood Cliffs *(G-2988)*

Sun Dial & Panel Corporation ....E....... 973 226-4334
Fairfield *(G-3319)*

Taurus Defense Solutions LLC ....G....... 617 916-6137
Medford *(G-6036)*

▲ Transistor Devices Inc ....C....... 908 850-5088
Hackettstown *(G-4039)*

Tru Temp Sensors Inc ....G....... 215 396-1550
Ocean City *(G-7698)*

3821 Laboratory Apparatus & Furniture

▲ 3d Biotek LLC ....G....... 908 801-6138
Bridgewater *(G-781)*

Abox Automation Corp ....G....... 973 659-9611
Pine Brook *(G-8583)*

Accuracy Devices ....G....... 973 427-8829
Hawthorne *(G-4204)*

Airfiltronix Corp ....G....... 973 779-5577
Clifton *(G-1560)*

Arrow Engineering Co Inc ....G....... 908 353-5229
Hillside *(G-4376)*

▼ Arthur H Thomas Company ....B....... 856 467-2000
Swedesboro *(G-10571)*

◆ Becton Dickinson and Company ....A....... 201 847-6800
Franklin Lakes *(G-3616)*

Bellco Glass Inc ....D....... 800 257-7043
Vineland *(G-11192)*

◆ Benchmark Scientific Inc ....E....... 908 769-5555
Sayreville *(G-9703)*

◆ Bsi Corp ....E....... 631 589-1118
Nutley *(G-7581)*

▲ C W Brabender Instrs Inc ....E....... 201 343-8425
South Hackensack *(G-10151)*

Cleanzones LLC ....F....... 732 534-5590
Jackson *(G-4644)*

Dek Tron International Corp ....E....... 908 226-1777
Plainfield *(G-8761)*

Delaware Technologies Inc ....F....... 856 234-7692
Mount Laurel *(G-6753)*

Denton Vacuum LLC ....G....... 856 439-9100
Moorestown *(G-6518)*

▲ Diagenode Inc ....G....... 862 209-4680
Denville *(G-2035)*

Difco Laboratories Inc ....G....... 410 316-4113
Franklin Lakes *(G-3619)*

◆ Emse Corp ....F....... 973 227-9221
Fairfield *(G-3191)*

Exodon LLC ....F....... 973 398-2900
Mount Arlington *(G-6712)*

Fluid Dynamics Inc ....G....... 908 200-5823
Flemington *(G-3444)*

Futurex Inc ....F....... 201 933-3943
Rochelle Park *(G-9423)*

G & H Sheet Metal Works Inc ....G 973 923-1100
Hillside (G-4393)

▲ Glen Mills Inc ....F 973 777-0777
Clifton (G-1625)

▲ Handler Manufacturing Company ....E 908 233-7796
Westfield (G-11799)

Hel Inc ....G 440 208-7360
Lawrenceville (G-5231)

Innovasystems Inc ....F 856 722-0410
Moorestown (G-6530)

Knf Neuberger Inc ....D 609 890-8889
Trenton (G-10950)

▲ Labnet International Inc ....E 732 417-0700
Iselin (G-4613)

Lm Air Technology Inc ....E 732 381-8200
Rahway (G-9115)

Micro-Tek Laboratories Inc ....G 973 779-5577
Clifton (G-1669)

Microdata Instrument Inc ....F 908 222-1717
South Plainfield (G-10300)

MSI Holdings LLC ....G 732 549-7144
Metuchen (G-6066)

▲ National Labnet Co ....E 732 417-0700
Iselin (G-4618)

▲ Ohaus Corporation ....D 973 377-9000
Parsippany (G-7980)

▲ Pacon Manufacturing Corp ....C 732 764-9070
Somerset (G-10051)

Randcastle Extrusion Systems ....G 973 239-1150
Cedar Grove (G-1290)

Rheometer Services ....G 732 922-8899
Wall Township (G-11364)

S P Industries Inc ....D 215 672-7800
Buena (G-941)

Scientific Machine and Sup Co ....E 732 356-1553
Middlesex (G-6145)

▲ Scientifix LLC ....G 856 780-5871
Mount Laurel (G-6803)

◆ Servolift LLC ....E 973 442-7878
Randolph (G-9199)

Spark Holland Inc ....G 609 799-7250
Franklinville (G-3638)

Specialty Pharmasource LLC ....F 973 784-4965
Denville (G-2059)

▲ Spex Certiprep Inc ....D 732 549-7144
Metuchen (G-6069)

Spex Certiprep Group LLC ....F 208 204-6656
Metuchen (G-6070)

Spex Sample Prep LLC ....F 732 549-7144
Metuchen (G-6072)

Spex Sample Prep LLC ....D 732 549-7144
Metuchen (G-6073)

Sphere Fluidics Incorporated ....G 888 258-0226
Monmouth Junction (G-6313)

▲ Thoma Inc ....F 856 608-6887
Moorestown (G-6573)

Thomas Scientific Inc ....B 800 345-2100
Swedesboro (G-10614)

Thomas Scientific Inc ....G 800 345-2100
Swedesboro (G-10615)

Tovatech LLC ....G 973 913-9734
Maplewood (G-5885)

Triad Scientific Inc ....G 732 292-1994
Manasquan (G-5841)

▼ United Hospital Supply Corp ....C 609 387-7580
Burlington (G-990)

Waage Electric Inc ....G 908 245-9363
Kenilworth (G-4986)

3822 Automatic Temperature Controls

A T C Companies Inc ....E 732 560-0900
Middlesex (G-6091)

Access Northern Security Inc ....F 732 462-2500
Freehold (G-3642)

Ademco Inc ....G 732 505-6688
Toms River (G-10739)

Ademco Inc ....F 201 462-9570
Teterboro (G-10670)

Ademco Inc ....G 908 561-1888
South Plainfield (G-10207)

Ademco Inc ....G 856 985-9050
Marlton (G-5921)

Aginova Inc ....G 732 804-3272
Freehold (G-3644)

Amega Scientific Corporation ....F 609 953-7295
Medford (G-6019)

▲ Ammark Corporation ....G 973 616-2555
Pompton Plains (G-8857)

▼ Atomizing Systems Inc ....F 201 447-1222
Ho Ho Kus (G-4439)

Brighton Air ....G 973 258-1500
Springfield (G-10433)

Building Performance Eqp Inc ....F 201 722-1414
Hillsdale (G-4364)

Burling Instruments Inc ....F 973 665-0601
Chatham (G-1319)

Calculagraph Co ....D 973 887-9400
East Hanover (G-2198)

Chatham Controls Corporation ....G 908 236-6019
Lebanon (G-5256)

Check-It Electronics Corp ....E 973 520-8435
Elizabeth (G-2720)

Comverge Giants Inc ....G 973 884-5970
Florham Park (G-3497)

Comverge Giants Inc ....G 973 884-5970
East Hanover (G-2202)

◆ Croll-Reynolds Co Inc ....E 908 232-4200
Parsippany (G-7909)

D & A Electronics Mfg ....F 732 938-7400
Wall Township (G-11333)

Energy Options Inc ....G 732 512-9100
Edison (G-2502)

Fluidsens International Inc ....G 914 338-3932
Twp Washinton (G-11017)

▲ Heat-Timer Corporation ....E 973 575-4004
Fairfield (G-3224)

Honeywell Asia Pacific Inc ....D 973 455-2000
Morris Plains (G-6607)

J & L Controls Inc ....G 732 460-0380
Lincroft (G-5312)

Johnson Controls Inc ....D 732 225-6700
Edison (G-2543)

▲ Megatran Industries ....G 609 227-4300
Bordentown (G-586)

Micro-Tek Laboratories Inc ....G 973 779-5577
Clifton (G-1669)

Msj Unlimited Services ....G 201 617-0764
Union City (G-11122)

National Refrigerants Inc ....G 856 455-4555
Bridgeton (G-766)

Niagara Conservation Corp ....F 973 829-0800
Cedar Knolls (G-1312)

NRG Bluewater Wind LLC ....G 201 748-5000
Hoboken (G-4469)

▲ Rees Scientific Corporation ....C 609 530-1055
Ewing (G-3060)

◆ Rowan Technologies Inc ....G 609 267-9000
Rancocas (G-9165)

Schneder Elc Bldngs Amrcas Inc ....E 201 348-9240
Secaucus (G-9808)

Siemens Industry Inc ....F 856 234-7666
Mount Laurel (G-6806)

◆ Sigma-Netics Inc ....E 973 227-6372
Riverdale (G-9385)

▲ Sisco Manufacturing Co Inc ....F 856 486-7550
Pennsauken (G-8486)

Sk & P Industries Inc ....G 973 482-1864
Newark (G-7275)

Sulzer Chemtech USA Inc ....E 856 768-2165
West Berlin (G-11624)

Tesa Rentals LLC ....F 973 300-0913
Sparta (G-10410)

Thermo Systems LLC ....D 609 371-3300
East Windsor (G-2362)

▲ Town & Country Plastics Inc ....F 732 780-5300
Marlboro (G-5917)

Trolex Corporation ....E 201 794-8004
Randolph (G-9204)

US Air Power Systems ....G 201 892-5235
Westwood (G-11846)

▲ Vu Sound Incorporated ....F 215 990-2864
Lumberton (G-5638)

3823 Indl Instruments For Meas, Display & Control

Accupac Inc ....C 215 256-7094
Lakewood (G-5044)

Accurate Thermal Systems LLC ....G 609 326-3190
Hainesport (G-4068)

▼ Accuratus Ceramic Corp ....E 908 213-7070
Phillipsburg (G-8540)

◆ Acrison Inc ....D 201 440-8300
Moonachie (G-6451)

ACS Quality Services Inc ....G 856 988-6550
Marlton (G-5920)

Aladdin Instruments Corp ....G 774 326-4919
Cherry Hill (G-1338)

▲ Align Sourcing Ltd Lblty Co ....G 609 375-8550
Trenton (G-10889)

American Compressed Gases Inc ....E 201 767-3200
Old Tappan (G-7732)

Amico Technologies Inc ....G 732 901-5900
Lakewood (G-5053)

Anvima Technologies LLC ....G 973 531-7077
Brookside (G-916)

Appleton Grp LLC ....C 973 285-3261
Morristown (G-6640)

Arcadia Equipment Inc ....F 201 342-3308
Hackensack (G-3877)

▲ Armadillo Automation Inc ....E 856 829-2888
Cinnaminson (G-1442)

ATI Trading Inc ....F 718 888-7918
Elizabeth (G-2712)

Audiocodes Inc ....G 732 469-0880
Somerset (G-9959)

▲ Audiocodes Inc ....F 732 469-0880
Somerset (G-9960)

Bishop Ascendant Inc ....G 201 572-7436
West Caldwell (G-11642)

▲ Boc Group Inc ....A 908 665-2400
New Providence (G-6995)

◆ Btech Inc ....E 973 983-1120
Rockaway (G-9448)

Burling Instruments Inc ....F 973 665-0601
Chatham (G-1319)

▲ Capintec Inc ....E 201 825-9500
Florham Park (G-3495)

Carlisle Machine Works Inc ....E 856 825-0627
Millville (G-6241)

Celco ....F 201 327-1123
Mahwah (G-5721)

▼ Cg Automation Solutions USA ....E 973 379-7400
Springfield (G-10434)

Check-It Electronics Corp ....E 973 520-8435
Elizabeth (G-2720)

▲ Circonix Technologies LLC ....F 973 962-6160
Ringwood (G-9344)

Control Instruments Corp ....E 973 575-9114
Fairfield (G-3176)

▲ Coperion K-Tron Pitman Inc ....F 856 589-0500
Sewell (G-9836)

Corporate Computer Systems ....F 732 739-5600
Newark (G-7088)

▼ Daq Electronics LLC ....E 732 981-0050
Piscataway (G-8651)

Delaware Technologies Inc ....F 856 234-7692
Mount Laurel (G-6753)

Delphian Corporation ....C 201 767-7300
Northvale (G-7521)

Difco Laboratories Inc ....G 410 316-4113
Franklin Lakes (G-3619)

Digital Binscom LLC ....G 908 867-7055
Long Valley (G-5609)

Digivac Company ....F 732 765-0900
Matawan (G-5972)

Dranetz Technologies Inc ....D 732 248-4358
Edison (G-2493)

Elaine Inc ....G 973 345-6200
Woodland Park (G-12076)

▲ Electronic Measuring Devices ....F 973 691-4755
Flanders (G-3407)

Emerson Process Management ....G 908 605-4551
Warren (G-11409)

F S Brainard & Co ....F 609 387-4300
Burlington (G-966)

▲ Gammon Technical Products Inc ....D 732 223-4600
Manasquan (G-5831)

Gerin Corporation Inc ....G 732 774-3256
Neptune (G-6880)

Global Power Technology Inc ....D 732 287-3680
Edison (G-2521)

Intertek Laboratories Inc ....E 908 903-1800
Stirling (G-10491)

▲ Intest Corporation ....G 856 505-8800
Mount Laurel (G-6770)

◆ Ipco US LLC ....E 973 720-7000
Totowa (G-10833)

▲ Istec Corporation ....F 973 383-9888
Sparta (G-10393)

J & W Servo Systems Company ....F 973 335-1007
Rockaway (G-9469)

▲ John G Papailias Co Inc ....G 201 767-4027
Northvale (G-7532)

▲ Kessler-Ellis Products Co ....D 732 935-1320
Eatontown (G-2407)

Linde North America Inc ....D 908 464-8100
New Providence (G-7007)

Malcam US ....G 973 218-2461
Short Hills (G-9872)

Marine Electric Systems Inc E 201 531-8600
South Hackensack *(G-10171)*

▲ **Marotta Controls Inc** C 973 334-7800
Montville *(G-6444)*

Matrix Controls Company Inc F 732 469-5551
Somerset *(G-10025)*

Mayfair Tech Ltd Lblty Co F 609 802-1262
Princeton *(G-8974)*

Measurement Control Corp G 800 504-9010
West Orange *(G-11773)*

Mesa Laboratories Inc E 973 492-8400
Butler *(G-1008)*

▲ **Meson Group Inc** E 201 767-7300
Northvale *(G-7536)*

◆ **Messer LLC** C 908 464-8100
Bridgewater *(G-849)*

Messer LLC G 973 579-2065
Sparta *(G-10398)*

◆ **Messer North America Inc** B 908 464-8100
Bridgewater *(G-851)*

Micro-Tek Laboratories Inc G 973 779-5577
Clifton *(G-1669)*

▼ **Multiforce Systems Corporation** F 609 683-4242
Princeton *(G-8982)*

Netquest Corporation E 856 866-0505
Mount Laurel *(G-6786)*

Newtek Sensor Solutions LLC G 856 406-6877
Pennsauken *(G-8460)*

▲ **NM Knight Co Inc** E 856 327-4855
Millville *(G-6263)*

Nordson Efd LLC C 609 259-9222
Robbinsville *(G-9414)*

Omega Engineering Inc F 856 467-4200
Swedesboro *(G-10599)*

Omega Engineering Inc C 856 467-4200
Bridgeport *(G-742)*

Orycon Control Technology Inc E 732 922-2400
Ocean *(G-7670)*

▲ **Palmer Electronics Inc** F 973 772-5900
Garfield *(G-3752)*

Pavan & Kievit Enterprises E 973 546-4615
Garfield *(G-3754)*

Pressure Controls Inc G 973 751-5002
Belleville *(G-308)*

Pyrometer LLC G 609 443-5522
Ewing *(G-3056)*

Pyrometer Instrument Co Inc E 609 443-5522
Windsor *(G-11997)*

▲ **Rees Scientific Corporation** C 609 530-1055
Ewing *(G-3060)*

Ribble Company Inc F 201 475-1812
Saddle Brook *(G-9672)*

Rosemount Inc F 973 257-2300
Parsippany *(G-8011)*

▲ **Roxboro Holdings Inc** D 732 919-3119
Wall Township *(G-11365)*

Schneder Elc Bldngs Amrcas Inc E 201 348-9240
Secaucus *(G-9808)*

Siemens Industry Inc G 732 302-1686
Warren *(G-11431)*

Signal Systems International G 732 793-4668
Lavallette *(G-5212)*

Sk & P Industries Inc G 973 482-1864
Newark *(G-7275)*

Spectro Analytical Instrs Inc F 201 642-3000
Mahwah *(G-5774)*

▼ **TAC Technical Instrument Corp** F 609 882-2894
Trenton *(G-10995)*

Theory Development Corp F 201 783-8770
Mahwah *(G-5780)*

Tru Temp Sensors Inc G 215 396-1550
Ocean City *(G-7698)*

▲ **TX Technology LLC** C 973 442-7500
Denville *(G-2061)*

V G Controls Inc G 973 764-6500
Oakland *(G-7649)*

Vertiv Corporation E 732 225-3741
Edison *(G-2640)*

Wra Manufacturing Company Inc G 908 416-2228
Hopatcong *(G-4523)*

3824 Fluid Meters & Counters

▲ **Action Packaging Automation** G 609 448-9210
Roosevelt *(G-9527)*

▲ **Chem Flowtronic Inc** G 973 785-0001
Little Falls *(G-5455)*

Chemiquip Products Co Inc G 201 868-4445
Linden *(G-5333)*

Ellis/Kuhnke Controls Inc G 732 291-3334
Eatontown *(G-2391)*

Heat-Timer Corporation E 212 481-2020
Fairfield *(G-3225)*

Instru-Met Corporation G 908 851-0700
Union *(G-11065)*

▲ **Kessler-Ellis Products Co** D 732 935-1320
Eatontown *(G-2407)*

▲ **Octal Corporation** E 201 862-1010
Teaneck *(G-10642)*

▲ **Parkeon Inc** E 856 234-8000
Moorestown *(G-6553)*

◆ **Pemberton Fabricators Inc** A 609 267-0922
Rancocas *(G-9163)*

Precision Dealer Services Inc E 908 237-1100
Flemington *(G-3461)*

Rio Supply G 856 719-0081
Sicklerville *(G-9915)*

3825 Instrs For Measuring & Testing Electricity

ABC Digital Electronics Inc G 201 666-6888
Old Tappan *(G-7731)*

Aeronautical Instr & Rdo Co E 973 473-0034
Lodi *(G-5550)*

Agilent Technologies Inc E 973 448-7129
Budd Lake *(G-917)*

▲ **Alltest Instruments Inc** F 732 919-3339
Farmingdale *(G-3376)*

▼ **Applied Resources Corp** E 973 328-3882
Wharton *(G-11852)*

Ballantine Laboratories Inc G 908 713-7742
Annandale *(G-53)*

Boonton Electronics Corp E 973 386-9696
Parsippany *(G-7895)*

◆ **Btech Inc** E 973 983-1120
Rockaway *(G-9448)*

▲ **Buttonwood Enterprises LLC** G 201 505-1901
Woodcliff Lake *(G-12050)*

Byram Laboratories Inc E 908 252-0852
Branchburg *(G-627)*

Celco F 201 327-1123
Mahwah *(G-5721)*

Cisco Systems Inc E 201 782-0842
Montvale *(G-6402)*

◆ **Communication Devices Inc** F 973 334-1980
Boonton *(G-546)*

Custom Metering Company Inc G 973 946-4195
Branchville *(G-706)*

Datalink Solutions Inc F 973 731-9373
West Orange *(G-11766)*

Dbmcorp Inc F 201 677-0008
Oakland *(G-7623)*

Dranetz Technologies Inc D 732 248-4358
Edison *(G-2493)*

Eastern Instrumentation of G 856 231-0668
Moorestown *(G-6519)*

Electro Impulse Laboratory Inc E 732 776-5800
Neptune *(G-6876)*

EMD Performance Materials Corp B 908 429-3500
Branchburg *(G-638)*

Energy Tracking LLC G 973 448-8660
Flanders *(G-3408)*

Energy Tracking Inc G 973 448-8660
Flanders *(G-3409)*

Global Power Technology Inc D 732 287-3680
Edison *(G-2521)*

Glow Tube Inc G 609 268-7707
Shamong *(G-9856)*

Hamamatsu Corporation E 908 526-0941
Bridgewater *(G-829)*

▼ **Imperial Machine & Tool Co** F 908 496-8100
Columbia *(G-1794)*

Instru-Met Corporation G 908 851-0700
Union *(G-11065)*

Intertek Laboratories Inc E 908 903-1800
Stirling *(G-10491)*

▲ **Intest Corporation** G 856 505-8800
Mount Laurel *(G-6770)*

Janke & Company Inc G 973 334-4477
Boonton *(G-558)*

▲ **Keyence Corporation America** E 201 930-0100
Elmwood Park *(G-2834)*

Link Computer Graphics Inc G 973 808-8990
Fairfield *(G-3263)*

Linseis Inc G 609 223-2070
Trenton *(G-10952)*

Marine Electric Systems Inc E 201 531-8600
South Hackensack *(G-10171)*

Microdysis Inc G 609 642-1184
Bordentown *(G-589)*

Mistras Group Inc C 609 716-4000
Princeton Junction *(G-9062)*

Mmtc Inc G 609 520-9699
Andover *(G-49)*

▲ **Multi-Tech Industries Inc** F 732 431-0550
Marlboro *(G-5905)*

Nanion Technologies Inc G 973 369-7960
Livingston *(G-5531)*

Nice Instrumentation F 732 851-4300
Manalapan *(G-5818)*

Omnitester Corp F 856 985-8960
Marlton *(G-5944)*

Panel Components & Systems F 973 448-9400
Stanhope *(G-10478)*

Photonics Management Corp G 908 231-0960
Bridgewater *(G-866)*

Powercomm Solutions LLC G 908 806-7025
Flemington *(G-3460)*

Pulsar Microwave Corp E 973 779-6262
Clifton *(G-1701)*

Quantem Corp E 609 883-9191
Ewing *(G-3057)*

Radcom Equipment Inc G 201 518-0033
Paramus *(G-7828)*

▲ **Rf Vii Inc** F 856 875-2121
Newfield *(G-7327)*

▲ **RSR Electronics Inc** E 732 381-8777
Rahway *(G-9126)*

▲ **Sadelco Inc** D 201 569-3323
Fort Lee *(G-3586)*

▲ **Satec Inc** E 908 258-0924
Union *(G-11088)*

Seaboard Instrument Co G 609 641-5300
Pleasantville *(G-8818)*

Seren Inc E 856 205-1131
Vineland *(G-11263)*

▲ **Sherry International Inc** F 908 279-7255
Warren *(G-11430)*

Signal Crafters Tech Inc G 973 781-0880
East Hanover *(G-2239)*

Spectro Analytical Instrs Inc F 201 642-3000
Mahwah *(G-5774)*

Spectrum Instrumentation Corp E 201 562-1999
Hackensack *(G-3978)*

▲ **Tcp Reliable Inc** G 848 229-2466
Edison *(G-2632)*

Tektronix Inc G 973 628-1363
Wayne *(G-11556)*

Thomas Instrumentation Inc F 609 624-2630
Cape May Court House *(G-1116)*

◆ **Tof Energy Corporation** D 908 691-2422
Bedminster *(G-280)*

▼ **Waveline Incorporated** E 973 226-9100
Fairfield *(G-3351)*

Wireless Telecom Group Inc D 973 386-9696
Parsippany *(G-8040)*

▲ **Zixel Ltd** G 732 972-3287
Morganville *(G-6600)*

3826 Analytical Instruments

Acustrip Co Inc G 973 299-8237
Mountain Lakes *(G-6819)*

Acustrip Company Inc F 973 299-8237
Denville *(G-2028)*

Advanced Imaging Assoc LLC G 973 823-8999
Franklin *(G-3597)*

Advanced Technical Support Inc D 609 298-2522
Bordentown *(G-574)*

Airscan Inc G 908 823-9425
Lebanon *(G-5249)*

◆ **Analytical Sales and Svcs Inc** F 973 616-0700
Flanders *(G-3400)*

Analyticon Instruments Corp G 973 379-6771
Springfield *(G-10426)*

Arrow Engineering Co Inc G 908 353-5229
Hillside *(G-4376)*

◆ **Becton Dickinson and Company** A 201 847-6800
Franklin Lakes *(G-3616)*

▲ **Belair Instrument Company LLC** E 973 912-8900
Pine Brook *(G-8587)*

Beta Industries Corp G 201 939-2400
Carlstadt *(G-1128)*

Biomedicon F 856 778-1880
Moorestown *(G-6508)*

Bios International Corp E 973 492-8400
Butler *(G-996)*

▲ **C W Brabender Instrs Inc** E 201 343-8425
South Hackensack *(G-10151)*

▲ **Cargille-Sacher Labs Inc** E 973 239-6633
Cedar Grove *(G-1271)*

▲ Chemglass Inc ....C 856 696-0014
Vineland (G-11199)

Chemspeed Technologies Inc ....F 732 329-1225
North Brunswick (G-7461)

Denville Diagnostics Imaging ....E 973 586-1212
Denville (G-2034)

Distek Inc ....D 732 422-7585
North Brunswick (G-7466)

Dolce Technologies LLC ....G 609 497-7319
Princeton (G-8932)

▲ Dynatec Systems Inc ....F 609 387-0330
Burlington (G-965)

E S Industries Inc ....G 856 753-8400
West Berlin (G-11591)

▲ Eci Technology Inc ....C 973 773-8686
Totowa (G-10825)

Edax Inc ....D 201 529-4880
Mahwah (G-5734)

Evex Analytical Instruments ....F 609 252-9192
Princeton (G-8944)

▲ Ezose Sciences Inc ....F 862 926-1950
Florham Park (G-3505)

▲ Fisher Scientific Chemical Div ....E 609 633-1422
Fair Lawn (G-3101)

Garden State Mgntic Imaging PC ....F 609 581-2727
Pennsauken (G-8423)

Horiba Instruments Inc ....G 732 494-8660
Piscataway (G-8675)

Hudson Robotics Inc ....E 973 376-7400
Springfield (G-10444)

◆ International Crystal Labs ....E 973 478-8944
Garfield (G-3748)

Isocolor Inc ....G 201 935-4494
Carlstadt (G-1169)

Lynred USA Inc ....E 973 882-0211
Fairfield (G-3266)

M D Laboratory Supplies Inc ....G 732 322-0773
Franklin Park (G-3635)

McKinley Scientific Llc ....F 973 579-4144
Sparta (G-10396)

Mesa Laboratories- Bgi Inc ....E 973 492-8400
Butler (G-1009)

Microdysis Inc ....G 609 642-1184
Bordentown (G-589)

▼ Mnemonics Inc ....G 856 234-0970
Mount Laurel (G-6784)

Moa Instrumentation Inc ....G 215 547-8308
Lawrenceville (G-5238)

▲ National Labnet Co ....E 732 417-0700
Iselin (G-4618)

New ERA Enterprises Inc ....G 856 794-2005
Newfield (G-7324)

Novartis Pharmaceuticals Corp ....G 862 778-8300
East Hanover (G-2230)

Packaged Gas Systems Inc ....G 908 755-2780
Springfield (G-10457)

Perma Pure LLC ....G 732 244-0010
Lakewood (G-5146)

▲ Princeton Biomeditech Corp ....D 732 274-1000
Monmouth Junction (G-6303)

Princeton Chromatography Inc ....G 609 860-1803
Cranbury (G-1874)

Princeton Research Instruments ....G 609 924-0570
Princeton (G-9004)

Princeton Separations Inc ....E 732 431-3338
Freehold (G-3694)

Pulsetor LLC ....G 609 303-0578
Lambertville (G-5196)

Rame-Hart Inc ....E 973 335-0560
Randolph (G-9197)

Rame-Hart Instrument Co LLC ....G 973 448-0305
Succasunna (G-10518)

Rudolph Instruments Inc ....G 973 227-0139
Denville (G-2056)

Setaram Inc ....G 908 262-7060
Cranbury (G-1881)

▲ Siemens Medical ....A 973 927-2828
Flanders (G-3419)

Spark Holland Inc ....G 609 799-7250
Franklinville (G-3638)

Sympatec Inc ....F 609 303-0066
Pennington (G-8374)

Symtera Analytics LLC ....F 718 696-9902
Wall Township (G-11373)

▲ Temptime Corporation ....D 973 984-6000
Morris Plains (G-6626)

Tess-Com Inc ....E 412 233-5782
Middlesex (G-6155)

Thermo Fisher Scientific Inc ....F 609 239-3185
Burlington (G-987)

Thermo Fisher Scientific Inc ....F 732 627-0220
Somerset (G-10087)

▲ Thorlabs Inc ....C 973 579-7227
Newton (G-7363)

▲ Topcon Medical Systems Inc ....D 201 599-5100
Oakland (G-7647)

Veeco Process Equipment Inc ....C 732 560-5300
Somerset (G-10094)

Waters Technologies Corp ....G 973 394-5660
Parsippany (G-8037)

Wra Manufacturing Company Inc ....G 908 416-2228
Hopatcong (G-4523)

3827 Optical Instruments

Anchor Optical Co ....C 856 546-1965
Barrington (G-166)

API Nanofabrication & RES Corp ....F 732 627-0808
Somerset (G-9954)

Argyle International Inc ....E 609 924-9484
Princeton (G-8909)

Artemis Optics and Coatings ....G 201 847-0887
Emerson (G-2863)

Avantier Inc ....G 732 491-8150
Metuchen (G-6046)

Cartiheal Inc ....G 917 703-6992
Closter (G-1752)

Cercis Inc ....E 609 737-5120
Pennington (G-8360)

Cgm Us Inc ....G 609 894-4420
Birmingham (G-456)

Chiral Photonics Inc ....F 973 732-0030
Pine Brook (G-8591)

Coherent Inc ....G 973 240-6851
East Hanover (G-2200)

▲ Datacolor Inc ....D 609 924-2189
Lawrenceville (G-5229)

▲ Dynasil Corporation America ....G 856 767-4600
West Berlin (G-11590)

Esco Products Inc ....E 973 697-3700
Oak Ridge (G-7602)

Hamamatsu Corporation ....E 908 231-0960
Middlesex (G-6119)

▲ High Vision Corporation ....G 862 238-7636
Clifton (G-1635)

Ii-VI Advanced Materials Inc ....G 973 227-1551
Pine Brook (G-8604)

Inlc Technology Corporation ....F 908 834-8390
Warren (G-11418)

Innovation Photonics LLC ....F 973 857-8380
Verona (G-11169)

Inrad Optics Inc ....D 201 767-1910
Northvale (G-7529)

▼ Integrated Photonics Inc ....G 908 281-8000
Hillsborough (G-4331)

Integrated Photonics Inc ....G 908 281-8000
Hillsborough (G-4332)

Katena Products Inc ....E 973 989-1600
Parsippany (G-7970)

Krell Technologies Inc ....E 732 775-7355
Neptune (G-6887)

Lithoptek LLC ....G 408 533-5847
Summit (G-10538)

▲ M H Optical Supplies Inc ....E 800 445-3090
South Hackensack (G-10170)

MRC Precision Metal Optics Inc ....E 941 753-8707
Northvale (G-7538)

Nanoopto Corporation ....E 732 627-0808
Somerset (G-10039)

Norland Products Inc ....E 609 395-1966
Cranbury (G-1865)

▲ O & S Research Inc ....E 856 829-2800
Cinnaminson (G-1477)

Opt-Sciences Corporation ....E 856 829-2800
Cinnaminson (G-1478)

Polarity LLC ....G 732 970-3855
Morganville (G-6595)

Quantum Coating Inc ....E 856 234-5444
Moorestown (G-6561)

Roper Scientific Inc ....E 941 556-2601
Trenton (G-10989)

Rudolph RES Analytical Corp ....D 973 584-1558
Hackettstown (G-4034)

Shanghai Optics Inc ....F 732 321-6915
Clark (G-1515)

Sirui USA LLC ....E 973 415-8082
Verona (G-11174)

Tag Optics Inc ....E 609 356-2142
Princeton (G-9031)

▲ Topcon Medical Systems Inc ....D 201 599-5100
Oakland (G-7647)

▲ US Vision Inc ....B 856 228-1000
Blackwood (G-482)

Veeco Instruments Inc ....E 732 560-5300
Somerset (G-10093)

3829 Measuring & Controlling Devices, NEC

Advanced Shore Imaging Associa ......F 732 678-0087
Northfield (G-7509)

AIG Industrial Group Inc ....F 201 767-7300
Northvale (G-7516)

Akers Biosciences Inc ....E 856 848-8698
West Deptford (G-11690)

Alison Control Inc ....E 973 575-7100
Fairfield (G-3137)

Amcor Phrm Packg USA LLC ....C 856 825-1100
Millville (G-6229)

American Gas & Chemical Co Ltd ....E 201 767-7300
Northvale (G-7518)

◆ American Sensor Tech Inc ....D 973 448-1901
Budd Lake (G-918)

Ballantine Laboratories Inc ....G 908 713-7742
Annandale (G-53)

◆ Becton Dickinson and Company ......A 201 847-6800
Franklin Lakes (G-3616)

Boonton Electronics Corp ....E 973 386-9696
Parsippany (G-7895)

▲ C W Brabender Instrs Inc ....E 201 343-8425
South Hackensack (G-10151)

▲ Capintec Inc ....E 201 825-9500
Florham Park (G-3495)

Checkpoint Security Systems Gr ....C 952 933-8858
West Deptford (G-11696)

Checkpoint Systems Inc ....C 952 933-8858
West Deptford (G-11699)

▲ Conistics Inc ....G 609 584-2600
Hamilton (G-4104)

Control Products Inc ....D 973 887-5000
East Hanover (G-2203)

▲ Coperion K-Tron Pitman Inc ....F 856 589-0500
Sewell (G-9836)

Core Laboratories LP ....F 609 896-2673
Lawrenceville (G-5228)

▲ Delmhorst Instrument Company ....E 973 334-2557
Towaco (G-10868)

Delphian Corporation ....C 201 767-7300
Northvale (G-7521)

Digital Binscom LLC ....G 908 867-7055
Long Valley (G-5609)

Digivac Company ....F 732 765-0900
Matawan (G-5972)

Dranetz Technologies Inc ....D 732 248-4358
Edison (G-2493)

▲ DRG International Inc ....E 973 564-7555
Springfield (G-10439)

Edax Inc ....D 201 529-4880
Mahwah (G-5734)

▲ Euroimmun US Inc ....E 973 656-1000
Mountain Lakes (G-6824)

Fluitec International LLC ....G 201 946-4584
Bayonne (G-217)

G E Inspection Technologies LP ....D 973 448-0077
Flanders (G-3411)

G R Bowler Inc ....G 973 525-7172
Andover (G-46)

H S Martin Company Inc ....F 856 692-8700
Vineland (G-11230)

Innerspace Technology Inc ....G 201 933-1600
Carlstadt (G-1168)

Instru-Met Corporation ....G 908 851-0700
Union (G-11065)

Instrument Sciences & Tech ....D 908 996-9920
Frenchtown (G-3714)

▲ Kanomax Usa Inc ....G 973 786-6386
Byram Township (G-1018)

Leak Detection Associates Inc ....G 609 415-2290
Egg Harbor Township (G-2687)

Life Recovery Systems Hd LLC ....G 973 283-2800
Kinnelon (G-5019)

▲ Lumiscope Co Inc ....D 678 291-3207
East Rutherford (G-2298)

Mab Enterprises Inc ....F 973 345-8282
Newark (G-7193)

Macro Sensors ....E 856 662-8000
Budd Lake (G-928)

Magnetic Products and Svcs Inc ....G 732 264-6651
Holmdel (G-4504)

Mallinckrodt LLC ....E 908 238-6600
Hampton (G-4158)

▲ Maquet Cardiovascular LLC ....D 973 709-7000
Wayne (G-11533)

Marine Cont Eqp Crtfction Corp	G	732 938-6622	Farmingdale (G-3388)
Mdr Diagnostics LLC	E	609 396-0021	Mount Laurel (G-6781)
▼ Medical Indicators Inc	F	609 737-1600	Hamilton (G-4113)
▲ Meson Group Inc	E	201 767-7300	Northvale (G-7536)
Micro-Tek Laboratories Inc	G	973 779-5577	Clifton (G-1669)
Mistras Group Inc	C	609 716-4000	Princeton Junction (G-9062)
Netquest Corporation	E	856 866-0505	Mount Laurel (G-6786)
▲ Northwest Instrument Inc	F	973 347-6830	Dover (G-2102)
▼ Orlando Systems Ltd Lblty Co	G	908 400-5052	North Plainfield (G-7507)
▲ Palmer Electronics Inc	F	973 772-5900	Garfield (G-3752)
Physical Acoustics Corporation	C	609 716-4000	Princeton Junction (G-9065)
Ptc Electronics Inc	G	201 847-0500	Mahwah (G-5764)
Radcom Equipment Inc	G	201 518-0033	Paramus (G-7828)
Reliability Maintenance Svcs	G	732 922-8878	Ocean (G-7679)
Roper Scientific Inc	E	941 556-2601	Trenton (G-10989)
Rudolph Technologies Inc	D	973 347-3891	Budd Lake (G-934)
▲ S & G Tool Aid Corporation	D	973 824-7730	Newark (G-7257)
Science Pump Corporation	E	856 963-7700	Camden (G-1086)
Scientific Machine and Sup Co	G	732 356-1553	Middlesex (G-6145)
◆ Scientific Sales Inc	F	609 844-0055	Lawrenceville (G-5243)
◆ Sensor Scientific Inc	G	973 227-7790	Fairfield (G-3310)
SGS UStesting Company	F	973 575-5252	Fairfield (G-3311)
Shock Tech Inc	E	845 368-8600	Mahwah (G-5771)
◆ Sigma-Netics Inc	G	973 227-6372	Riverdale (G-9385)
Sun Coast Precision Instrument	G	646 852-2331	Cresskill (G-1945)
▲ Superior Signal Company LLC	F	732 251-0800	Old Bridge (G-7728)
Tel-Instrument Elec Corp	E	201 933-1600	East Rutherford (G-2325)
Theory Development Corp	F	201 783-8770	Mahwah (G-5780)
Thwing-Albert Instrument Co	D	856 767-1000	West Berlin (G-11629)
▲ Topcon Medical Systems Inc	D	201 599-5100	Oakland (G-7647)
▲ Transistor Devices Inc	C	908 850-5088	Hackettstown (G-4039)
▲ United Instrument Company LLC	G	201 767-6000	Northvale (G-7552)
Venkateshwara Inc	F	908 964-4777	Somerset (G-10095)
▼ William Kenyon & Sons Inc	E	732 985-8980	Piscataway (G-8738)
Willrich Precision Instr Co	G	866 945-5742	Cresskill (G-1948)

3841 Surgical & Medical Instrs & Apparatus

3M Company	B	973 884-2500	Whippany (G-11875)
3M Company	C	908 788-4000	Flemington (G-3426)
▲ A D M Tronics Unlimited Inc	E	201 767-6040	Northvale (G-7513)
Aarisse Health Care Products	G	973 686-1811	Wayne (G-11464)
Abbott Point of Care Inc	B	609 454-9000	Princeton (G-8898)
Abbott Point of Care Inc	C	609 371-8923	East Windsor (G-2332)
◆ Acme International Inc	G	973 594-4866	Clifton (G-1556)
Adsorptech LLC	G	732 491-7727	Middlesex (G-6093)
Advanced Precision Inc	E	800 788-9473	Sparta (G-10375)

▲ Alfa Wassermann Inc	C	973 882-8630	West Caldwell (G-11637)
Alfa Wssrmann Dagnstc Tech LLC	F	800 220-4488	West Caldwell (G-11638)
▲ Allergan Inc	A	862 261-7000	Madison (G-5687)
Alto Development Corp	D	732 938-2266	Wall Township (G-11316)
▲ America Techma Inc	G	201 894-5887	Englewood Cliffs (G-2958)
American Diagnstc Imaging Inc	F	973 980-1724	Nutley (G-7578)
▲ Anderson Tool & Die Corp	E	908 862-5550	Linden (G-5324)
Antares Pharma Inc	C	609 359-3020	Ewing (G-3015)
Artegraft Inc	F	732 422-8333	North Brunswick (G-7453)
Ascensia Diabetes Care US Inc	C	973 560-6500	Parsippany (G-7885)
Augma Biomaterials USA Inc	G	201 509-4570	Monroe Township (G-6326)
Automated Medical Pdts Corp	G	732 602-7717	Sewaren (G-9831)
Baeta Corp	G	201 471-0988	Fort Lee (G-3548)
Bahadir USA LLC	G	856 517-3080	Carneys Point (G-1241)
▲ Bard Devices Inc	G	908 277-8000	Franklin Lakes (G-3611)
◆ Bausch & Lomb Incorporated	B	585 338-6000	Bridgewater (G-800)
Baxter Healthcare Corporation	D	856 489-2104	Cherry Hill (G-1342)
◆ Bayer Healthcare LLC	A	862 404-3000	Whippany (G-11878)
Bayer Hlthcare Phrmcticals Inc	E	973 709-3545	Wayne (G-11475)
▲ Bayer Hlthcare Phrmcticals Inc	A	862 404-3000	Whippany (G-11880)
Bbg Surgical Ltd Liability Co	G	888 575-6277	Lakewood (G-5059)
Bd Ventures LLC	E	201 847-6800	Franklin Lakes (G-3615)
◆ Becton Dickinson and Company	A	201 847-6800	Franklin Lakes (G-3616)
▲ Belair Instrument Company LLC	E	973 912-8900	Pine Brook (G-8587)
Beltor Manufacturing Corp	E	856 768-5570	Berlin (G-415)
Bernafon LLC	G	888 941-4203	Somerset (G-9962)
◆ Bio Compression Systems Inc	E	201 939-0716	Moonachie (G-6457)
Biodynamics LLC	B	201 227-9255	Englewood (G-2882)
Biomedicon	F	856 778-1880	Moorestown (G-6508)
Biosearch Medical Products Inc	D	908 252-0595	Branchburg (G-626)
Bipore Inc	F	201 767-1993	Northvale (G-7519)
Boston Scientific Corporation	E	973 709-7000	Wayne (G-11482)
Burpee Medsystems LLC	G	732 544-8900	Eatontown (G-2382)
▲ C R Bard Inc	C	908 277-8000	Franklin Lakes (G-3617)
C R Bard Inc	G	856 461-0946	Delran (G-2012)
▲ Canfield Property Group Inc	F	973 276-0300	Fairfield (G-3163)
◆ Cantel Medical Corp	B	973 890-7220	Little Falls (G-5454)
▲ Capintec Inc	E	201 825-9500	Florham Park (G-3495)
▲ Carnegie Surgical LLC	G	866 782-7144	East Windsor (G-2366)
◆ Catalent Pharma Solutions Inc	B	732 537-6200	Somerset (G-9971)
Cedge Industries Inc	F	201 641-3222	Barnegat (G-157)
Cenogenics Corporation	E	732 536-6457	Morganville (G-6584)
Ch Technologies USA Inc	G	201 666-2335	Westwood (G-11829)
Clinical Image Retrieval Syste	G	888 482-2362	Franklin (G-3601)
▲ Clordisys Solutions Inc	E	908 236-4100	Branchburg (G-629)

Collagen Matrix Inc	D	201 405-1477	Oakland (G-7619)
▲ Convatec Inc	B	908 231-2179	Bridgewater (G-813)
Cordis International Corp	A	732 524-0400	New Brunswick (G-6918)
Cranial Technologies Inc	E	201 265-3993	Paramus (G-7795)
▲ Crestek Inc	E	609 883-4000	Ewing (G-3024)
Cross Medical Specialties Inc	F	856 589-3288	Pitman (G-8744)
Cura Biomed Inc	G	609 647-1474	Princeton Junction (G-9054)
Cytosorbents Corporation	E	732 329-8885	Monmouth Junction (G-6285)
Cytosorbents Medical Inc	E	732 329-8885	Monmouth Junction (G-6286)
Data Medical Inc	F	800 790-9978	North Bergen (G-7399)
Datascope Corp	E	201 995-8000	Mahwah (G-5726)
Dexmed Inc	G	732 831-0507	Elizabeth (G-2728)
Dexmed LLC	G	732 831-0507	Elizabeth (G-2729)
Diabeto Inc	G	646 397-3175	Piscataway (G-8656)
▲ Diagnostix Plus Inc	E	201 530-5505	Teaneck (G-10627)
Difco Laboratories Inc	G	410 316-4113	Franklin Lakes (G-3619)
▼ Diopsys Inc	E	973 244-0622	Pine Brook (G-8598)
Edda Technology Inc	F	609 919-9889	Princeton (G-8938)
Ellis Instruments Inc	G	973 593-9222	Madison (G-5692)
◆ Emse Corp	F	973 227-9221	Fairfield (G-3191)
Endomedix Inc	G	848 248-1883	Montclair (G-6366)
Exalenz Bioscience Inc	E	732 232-4393	Wall Township (G-11338)
▲ Excelsior Medical LLC	C	732 776-7525	Neptune (G-6877)
Ferry Machine Corp	E	201 641-9191	Little Ferry (G-5485)
General Graphics Corporation	E	201 664-4083	Hillsdale (G-4367)
▲ Genesis Bps LLC	E	201 708-1400	Ramsey (G-9145)
Getinge Group Logistics Americ	E	973 709-6000	Wayne (G-11509)
▲ Getinge Usa Inc	C	800 475-9040	Wayne (G-11510)
Gibraltar Laboratories Inc	E	973 227-6882	Fairfield (G-3214)
Glastron Inc	E	856 692-0500	Vineland (G-11226)
◆ Globe Scientific Inc	E	201 599-1400	Mahwah (G-5744)
Glw Inc	G	845 492-0476	Kearny (G-4861)
Graydon Products Inc	E	856 234-9513	Moorestown (G-6524)
H & W Tool Co Inc	F	973 366-0131	Dover (G-2085)
H Galow Co Inc	E	201 768-0547	Norwood (G-7564)
Haldor USA Inc	E	856 254-2345	Cherry Hill (G-1370)
Haz Laboratories	F	908 453-3300	Washington (G-11446)
Health Care Alert LLC	F	732 676-2630	Middletown (G-6165)
Healthcare Cart	G	201 406-4797	Blairstown (G-485)
▲ IDL Techni-Edge LLC	C	908 497-9818	Kenilworth (G-4945)
Immunostics Inc	G	732 918-0770	Eatontown (G-2402)
▲ Immunostics Company Inc	G	732 918-0770	Eatontown (G-2403)
Indo-Mim Inc	G	734 327-9842	Princeton (G-8961)
▲ Instride Shoes LLC	E	908 874-6670	Hillsborough (G-4330)
▼ Integra Lfscnces Holdings Corp	C	609 275-0500	Plainsboro (G-8792)

SIC

Integra Lifesciences Corp	C	609 275-2700
Plainsboro (G-8793)		
Integra Lifesciences Corp	E	609 275-2700
Plainsboro (G-8795)		
Integra Lifesciences Corp	D	609 275-0500
Plainsboro (G-8794)		
Integra Lifesciences Sales LLC	B	609 275-0500
Plainsboro (G-8796)		
Intercure Inc	E	973 893-5653
Montclair (G-6372)		
Interpace Dagnostics Group Inc	E	412 224-6100
Parsippany (G-7965)		
Ivy Sports Medicine LLC	G	201 573-5423
Montvale (G-6416)		
Jaktool LLC	F	609 664-2451
Cranbury (G-1847)		
Jnj International Inv LLC	G	732 524-0400
New Brunswick (G-6939)		
Johnson & Johnson	G	908 722-9319
Raritan (G-9213)		
Johnson & Johnson	C	908 874-1000
Morris Plains (G-6618)		
Johnson & Johnson	C	732 524-0400
New Brunswick (G-6941)		
Johnson & Johnson	A	732 524-0400
New Brunswick (G-6940)		
Jrh Service & Sales LLC	G	908 832-9266
Lebanon (G-5267)		
Khan Zeshan	G	973 619-4736
Belleville (G-298)		
◆ L & R Manufacturing Co Inc	D	201 991-5330
Kearny (G-4877)		
Laboratory Diagnostics Co Inc	F	732 536-6300
Morganville (G-6591)		
Laboratory Diagnostics Co Inc	G	732 972-2145
Morganville (G-6592)		
Linkspine Inc	G	973 625-1333
Dover (G-2095)		
▲ Lumiscope Co Inc	D	678 291-3207
East Rutherford (G-2298)		
▲ Maddak Inc	G	973 628-7600
Wayne (G-11531)		
Mallinckrodt LLC	E	908 238-6600
Hampton (G-4158)		
Maxter Corporation	G	609 877-9700
Willingboro (G-11992)		
Medicraft Inc	F	201 421-3055
Elmwood Park (G-2841)		
Medicraft Inc	F	201 797-8820
Elmwood Park (G-2842)		
Medilogic Group LLC	G	201 794-2166
Hawthorne (G-4231)		
▲ Medin Technologies Inc	C	973 779-2400
Totowa (G-10836)		
Medtec Services LLC	G	201 722-9696
Westwood (G-11835)		
Medtronic Inc	C	908 289-5969
Swedesboro (G-10595)		
Medtronic Usa Inc	F	973 331-7914
Parsippany (G-7978)		
▲ Micro Stamping Corporation	C	732 302-0800
Somerset (G-10030)		
Microdose Therapeutx Inc	E	732 355-2100
Ewing (G-3046)		
◆ Mindray Ds Usa Inc	B	201 995-8000
Mahwah (G-5754)		
◆ Nephros Inc	F	201 343-5202
South Orange (G-10200)		
Newton Memorial Hospital Inc	G	973 726-0904
Sparta (G-10402)		
Next Medical Products LLC	F	908 722-4549
Branchburg (G-660)		
Nextgen Edge Inc	G	610 507-6904
West Milford (G-11730)		
Northeast Medical Systems Corp	G	856 910-8111
Cherry Hill (G-1400)		
Nu-Stent Technologies Inc	G	732 729-6270
Hillsborough (G-4342)		
Oncode-Med Inc	G	908 998-3647
Basking Ridge (G-194)		
Osteotech Inc	E	732 544-5942
Eatontown (G-2413)		
Osteotech Inc	C	732 542-2800
Eatontown (G-2414)		
Osteotech Inc	F	732 542-2800
Eatontown (G-2415)		
▲ P A K Manufacturing Inc	F	973 372-1090
Irvington (G-4581)		
Pausch LLC	G	732 747-6110
Tinton Falls (G-10724)		

Pentax of America Inc	E	973 628-6200
Montvale (G-6421)		
Pharmasource International LLC	G	732 985-6182
Piscataway (G-8700)		
Pharming Healthcare Inc	E	908 524-0888
Bridgewater (G-865)		
Phillips Precision Inc	C	201 797-8820
Elmwood Park (G-2849)		
Precise Cmpnents TI Design Inc	G	973 928-2928
Clifton (G-1697)		
Precision Spine Inc	F	601 420-4244
Parsippany (G-7999)		
Redfield Corporation	E	201 845-3990
Rochelle Park (G-9429)		
Regen Biologics Inc	F	201 651-5140
Glen Rock (G-3834)		
Respironics Inc	C	973 581-6000
Parsippany (G-8007)		
Rhein Medical Inc	F	727 209-2244
Denville (G-2053)		
▲ Schering Berlin Inc	G	862 404-3000
Whippany (G-11908)		
◆ Scimedx Corporation	E	800 221-5598
Dover (G-2105)		
Sensor Medical Technology LLC	G	425 358-7381
Denville (G-2057)		
Smartekg LLC	G	201 376-4556
Teaneck (G-10652)		
Somerset Outpatient Surgery	G	781 635-2807
Somerset (G-10073)		
State Technology Inc	G	856 467-8009
Bridgeport (G-746)		
Steris Instrument MGT Svcs Inc	G	908 904-1317
Hillsborough (G-4357)		
Stryker Corporation	D	201 760-8000
Allendale (G-17)		
Stryker Corporation	G	856 312-0046
Runnemede (G-9611)		
▲ Techtrade LLC	G	201 706-8130
Jersey City (G-4819)		
Teleflex Incorporated	D	856 349-7234
Gloucester City (G-3851)		
▲ Terumo Americas Holding Inc	D	732 302-4900
Somerset (G-10084)		
◆ Terumo Medical Corporation	C	732 302-4900
Somerset (G-10085)		
▲ Topcon Medical Systems Inc	D	201 599-5100
Oakland (G-7647)		
Total Tech Medical LLC	G	973 980-6458
Dover (G-2109)		
Tracer Tool & Machine Co Inc	F	201 337-6184
Oakland (G-7648)		
▲ Trimline Medical Products Corp	C	908 429-0590
Branchburg (G-691)		
Unionmed Tech Inc	G	917 714-3418
Bridgewater (G-899)		
United Medical PC	G	201 456-0222
Clifton (G-1733)		
United Medical PC	G	201 339-6111
Bayonne (G-236)		
▲ US China Allied Products Inc	G	201 461-9886
Fort Lee (G-3592)		
Vascular Therapies LLC	G	201 266-8310
Cresskill (G-1947)		
Vela Diagnostics USA Inc	G	973 852-3740
Fairfield (G-3341)		
Venarum Medical LLC	F	732 996-8513
Eatontown (G-2428)		
Vesag Health Inc	F	732 333-1876
North Brunswick (G-7492)		
◆ Viant Medical Inc	C	908 561-0717
South Plainfield (G-10341)		
Viatar Ctc Solutions Inc	G	617 299-6590
Short Hills (G-9879)		
◆ Viscot Medical LLC	E	973 887-9273
East Hanover (G-2245)		
Vitillo & Sons Inc	F	732 886-1393
Lakewood (G-5177)		
Vozeh Equipment Corp	G	201 337-3729
Franklin Lakes (G-3632)		
Westcon Orthopedics Inc	G	908 806-8981
Neshanic Station (G-6906)		
▲ Zeus Scientific Inc	D	908 526-3744
Branchburg (G-699)		
Zimmer Trabecular Met Tech Inc	C	973 576-0032
Parsippany (G-8044)		

3842 Orthopedic, Prosthetic & Surgical Appliances/Splys

3M Company	B	973 884-2500
Whippany (G-11875)		
Ace Box Landau Co Inc	G	201 871-4776
Englewood Cliffs (G-2956)		
Achilles Prosthetcs & Orthotcs	G	201 785-9944
Ramsey (G-9133)		
Acuitive Technologies Inc	F	973 617-7175
Allendale (G-5)		
Ahs Hospital Corp	E	908 522-2000
Summit (G-10523)		
▲ Alexander James Corp	D	908 362-9266
Blairstown (G-484)		
Alkaline Corporation	G	732 531-7830
Eatontown (G-2375)		
Alliance Hand & Physical	F	201 822-0100
Westwood (G-11824)		
◆ Ansell Healthcare Products LLC	C	732 345-5400
Iselin (G-4593)		
Ansell Limited	E	732 345-5400
Iselin (G-4595)		
◆ Ansell Protective Products LLC	A	732 345-5400
Iselin (G-4596)		
Araya Inc	G	201 445-7005
Ridgewood (G-9321)		
Armac Inc	F	973 457-0002
Florham Park (G-3480)		
Atlantic Prsthtic Orthotic Svc	G	609 927-6330
Linwood (G-5448)		
Banding Centers of America	G	973 805-9977
Florham Park (G-3487)		
Bard International Inc	D	908 277-8000
Franklin Lakes (G-3612)		
Bayside Orthopedics LLC	G	732 691-4898
Toms River (G-10751)		
◆ Becton Dickinson and Company	A	201 847-6800
Franklin Lakes (G-3616)		
▲ Belair Instrument Company LLC	E	973 912-8900
Pine Brook (G-8587)		
Biomed Innovative Cons LLC	G	732 599-7233
South Amboy (G-10131)		
Boston Scientific Corporation	G	973 709-7000
Wayne (G-11482)		
Brenner Metal Products	E	973 778-2466
Wallington (G-11382)		
Brick City Wheelchair RPS LLC	G	862 371-4311
Newark (G-7075)		
Burpee Medsystems LLC	G	732 544-8900
Eatontown (G-2382)		
▲ C R Bard Inc	C	908 277-8000
Franklin Lakes (G-3617)		
Cape Prosthetics-Orthotics	G	856 810-7900
Marlton (G-5923)		
▲ Capintec Inc	E	201 825-9500
Florham Park (G-3495)		
Carry Easy Inc	E	201 944-0042
Leonia (G-5287)		
Ces Imports LLC	G	610 299-7930
Stone Harbor (G-10504)		
Cocco Enterprises Inc	F	609 393-5939
Trenton (G-10920)		
Cranial Technologies Inc	C	908 754-0572
Edison (G-2485)		
Csus LLC	G	973 298-8599
Rockaway (G-9452)		
▲ Derma Sciences Inc	C	609 514-4744
Plainsboro (G-8784)		
Dexmed Inc	G	732 831-0507
Elizabeth (G-2728)		
Dynamic Safety Usa LLC	G	844 378-7200
Somerset (G-9983)		
Eastern Podiatry Labs Inc	G	609 882-4444
Ewing (G-3028)		
▲ Ebi LLC	A	800 526-2579
Parsippany (G-7929)		
Ebi LP	E	973 299-9022
Parsippany (G-7930)		
Ebi Medical Systems LLC	F	973 299-3330
Parsippany (G-7931)		
Edge Orthotics Inc	G	732 549-3343
Edison (G-2499)		
▲ Electric Mobility Corporation	C	856 468-1000
Sewell (G-9843)		
Endotec Inc	F	973 762-6100
South Orange (G-10194)		
◆ Ethicon Inc	A	732 524-0400
Somerville (G-10108)		
Ethicon Inc	C	908 306-0327
Bedminster (G-264)		

Ethicon Inc....C.... 908 218-0707
Bedminster *(G-265)*
Ethicon Inc....E.... 908 253-6464
Bridgewater *(G-820)*
Extremity Medical LLC....F.... 973 588-8980
Parsippany *(G-7940)*
Garden State Orthopedic Center....G.... 973 538-4948
Morristown *(G-6664)*
Garden State Prosthetics....G.... 732 922-6650
Ocean *(G-7665)*
▲ Gemtor Inc....E.... 732 583-6200
Matawan *(G-5976)*
Genzyme Corporation....G.... 973 256-2106
Totowa *(G-10829)*
▲ Getinge Usa Inc....C.... 800 475-9040
Wayne *(G-11510)*
Grateful Ped Inc....F.... 973 478-6511
Saddle Brook *(G-9654)*
Hanger Prsthetcs & Ortho Inc....G.... 973 736-0628
West Orange *(G-11769)*
Hanger Prsthetcs & Ortho Inc....G.... 732 919-7774
Wall Township *(G-11344)*
Hanger Prsthetcs & Ortho Inc....G.... 609 653-8323
Linwood *(G-5449)*
Hanger Prsthetcs & Ortho Inc....G.... 609 889-8447
Rio Grande *(G-9355)*
Harry J Lawall & Son Inc....G.... 856 691-7764
Vineland *(G-11231)*
Healqu LLC....G.... 844 443-2578
Jersey City *(G-4746)*
▲ Howmedica Osteonics Corp....C.... 201 831-5000
Mahwah *(G-5747)*
Icon Orthopedic Concepts LLC....G.... 973 794-6810
Boonton *(G-556)*
Independence Technology LLC....F.... 908 722-3767
Somerville *(G-10116)*
Infront Medical LLC....G.... 888 515-2532
Clifton *(G-1639)*
▼ Integra Lfscnces Holdings Corp....C.... 609 275-0500
Plainsboro *(G-8792)*
Isomedix Operations Inc....E.... 908 757-3727
South Plainfield *(G-10281)*
Ivy Capital Partners LLC....G.... 201 573-8400
Montvale *(G-6415)*
▲ J C Orthopedic Inc....G.... 732 458-7900
Brick *(G-722)*
J J L & W Inc....E.... 856 854-3100
Magnolia *(G-5708)*
J M M R Inc....G.... 201 612-5104
Fair Lawn *(G-3107)*
Jefferson Prosthetic Orthotic....G.... 973 762-0780
South Orange *(G-10197)*
Jentec Inc....G.... 201 784-1031
Northvale *(G-7531)*
▲ Jerome Group Inc....D.... 856 234-8600
West Deptford *(G-11707)*
Jjj Stretchers Inc....G.... 908 290-3505
Linden *(G-5364)*
Jnj International Inv LLC....G.... 732 524-0400
New Brunswick *(G-6939)*
Johnson & Johnson....G.... 908 722-9319
Raritan *(G-9213)*
Johnson & Johnson....C.... 908 874-1000
Morris Plains *(G-6618)*
Johnson & Johnson....C.... 732 524-0400
New Brunswick *(G-6941)*
Johnson & Johnson....A.... 732 524-0400
New Brunswick *(G-6940)*
Johnson & Johnson Medical Inc....A.... 908 218-0707
Somerville *(G-10119)*
Johnson Associates Systems Inc....F.... 856 228-2175
Blackwood *(G-471)*
K & S Drug & Surgical Inc....G.... 201 886-9191
Fort Lee *(G-3566)*
Kingwood Industrial Pdts Inc....G.... 908 852-8655
Hackettstown *(G-4015)*
Lightfield Llr Corporation....G.... 732 462-9200
Freehold *(G-3677)*
▲ Link Bio Inc....G.... 973 625-1333
Dover *(G-2094)*
▲ Lumiscope Co Inc....D.... 678 291-3207
East Rutherford *(G-2298)*
M B R Orthotics Inc....G.... 201 444-7750
Wyckoff *(G-12114)*
▲ Mar Machine Ken Manufacturing....E.... 973 278-5827
Paterson *(G-8250)*
Medical Device Bus Svcs Inc....G.... 732 524-0400
New Brunswick *(G-6946)*
Midlantic Medical Systems Inc....G.... 908 432-4599
Skillman *(G-9923)*

Nahallac LLC....G.... 908 635-0999
Whitehouse *(G-11917)*
North Jrsey Prsthtics Orthtics....G.... 201 943-4448
Palisades Park *(G-7775)*
Nouveau Prosthetics Ltd....F.... 732 739-0888
Hazlet *(G-4267)*
Nouveau Prosthetics Orthotics....F.... 732 739-0888
Hazlet *(G-4268)*
Onkos Surgical Inc....E.... 973 264-5400
Parsippany *(G-7981)*
Ortho-Dynamics Inc....G.... 973 742-4390
Paterson *(G-8274)*
▲ Orthofeet Inc....E.... 800 524-2845
Northvale *(G-7542)*
Ossur Americas Inc....G.... 856 345-6000
West Deptford *(G-11712)*
▲ Oticon Inc....C.... 732 560-1220
Somerset *(G-10047)*
▲ Oticon Medical LLC....E.... 732 560-0727
Somerset *(G-10048)*
◆ Pacific Dunlop Investments USA....F.... 732 345-5400
Red Bank *(G-9240)*
▲ Pacon Manufacturing Corp....C.... 732 764-9070
Somerset *(G-10051)*
▲ Peace Medical Inc....F.... 800 537-9564
Wharton *(G-11866)*
Precise Cmpnents Tl Design Inc....G.... 973 928-2928
Clifton *(G-1697)*
Precision Orthotic Lab of Nj....F.... 856 848-6226
West Deptford *(G-11714)*
▲ Preform Laboratories Inc....E.... 973 523-8610
Hackensack *(G-3965)*
Prescription Podiatry Labs....G.... 609 695-1221
Trenton *(G-10980)*
Priority Medical Inc....G.... 973 376-5077
Short Hills *(G-9875)*
Regen Biologics Inc....F.... 201 651-5140
Glen Rock *(G-3834)*
▲ Rep Trading Associates Inc....F.... 732 591-1140
Old Bridge *(G-7727)*
Respironics Inc....C.... 973 581-6000
Parsippany *(G-8007)*
Rinko Orthopedic Appliances....G.... 201 796-3121
Fair Lawn *(G-3117)*
▲ Sivantos Inc....B.... 732 562-6600
Piscataway *(G-8712)*
Songbird Hearing Inc....E.... 732 422-7203
North Brunswick *(G-7487)*
Sonic Innovations Inc....G.... 888 423-7834
Somerset *(G-10074)*
Spinal Kinetics LLC....G.... 908 687-2552
Union *(G-11091)*
Steris Corporation....G.... 908 904-1317
Hillsborough *(G-4356)*
▲ Superior Intl Srgical Sups LLC....F.... 609 695-6591
Ewing *(G-3067)*
Surgical Lser Sfety Cuncil Inc....G.... 216 272-0805
Cherry Hill *(G-1418)*
Swiss Orthopedic Inc....G.... 908 874-5522
Hillsborough *(G-4359)*
Switlik Parachute Company Inc....F.... 609 587-3300
Trenton *(G-10994)*
Teleflex Incorporated....D.... 856 349-7234
Gloucester City *(G-3851)*
Tgz Acquisition Company LLC....F.... 856 669-6600
Cinnaminson *(G-1489)*
Top Safety Products Company....F.... 908 707-8680
Branchburg *(G-689)*
Total Control Othotics Lab....G.... 609 499-2200
Florence *(G-3479)*
▲ Tronex International Inc....E.... 973 335-2888
Budd Lake *(G-938)*
▲ Universal Tape Supply Corp....F.... 609 653-3191
Somers Point *(G-9940)*
▲ Water-Jel Holding Company....D.... 201 507-8300
Carlstadt *(G-1237)*
▲ Water-Jel Technologies LLC....D.... 201 438-1598
Carlstadt *(G-1238)*
Zimmer Inc....G.... 856 778-8300
Mount Laurel *(G-6814)*
▲ Zimmer Biomet....C.... 201 797-7300
Fair Lawn *(G-3130)*
Zimmer Trabecular Met Tech Inc....C.... 973 576-0032
Parsippany *(G-8044)*
Zounds Inc....F.... 856 234-8844
Mount Laurel *(G-6815)*

3843 Dental Eqpt & Splys

American Medical & Dental Sups....F.... 877 545-6837
Montvale *(G-6396)*
Anna K Park....G.... 856 478-9500
Mullica Hill *(G-6855)*
Dental Models & Designs Inc....G.... 973 472-8009
Garfield *(G-3738)*
Dentalworx Lab Ltd Lblty Co....G.... 732 981-9096
Edison *(G-2491)*
Dentamach Inc....F.... 973 334-2220
Parsippany *(G-7914)*
▲ Dmg America LLC....D.... 201 894-5500
Ridgefield Park *(G-9304)*
E P R Industries Inc....F.... 856 488-1120
Pennsauken *(G-8416)*
Em Orthodontic Labs Inc....G.... 201 652-4411
Waldwick *(G-11302)*
▲ Essential Dental Systems Inc....E.... 201 487-9090
South Hackensack *(G-10159)*
▲ Floxite Company Inc....F.... 201 529-2019
Mahwah *(G-5739)*
Geistlich Pharma North America....E.... 609 779-6560
Princeton *(G-8954)*
▲ Handler Manufacturing Company....E.... 908 233-7796
Westfield *(G-11799)*
▲ Hiossen Inc....F.... 888 678-0001
Englewood Cliffs *(G-2974)*
Integrated Dental Systems LLC....E.... 201 676-2457
Englewood *(G-2914)*
Integrted Laminate Systems Inc....D.... 856 786-6500
Cinnaminson *(G-1465)*
▲ Ivoclar Vivadent Mfg Inc....D.... 732 563-4755
Somerset *(G-10006)*
J A W Products Inc....F.... 856 829-3210
Cinnaminson *(G-1467)*
Jacquet Jonpaul....G.... 856 825-4259
Millville *(G-6257)*
Keystone Europe LLC....G.... 856 663-4700
Cherry Hill *(G-1380)*
◆ L & R Manufacturing Co Inc....D.... 201 991-5330
Kearny *(G-4877)*
Milestone Education LLC....G.... 973 535-2717
Livingston *(G-5524)*
▲ Milestone Scientific Inc....F.... 973 535-2717
Livingston *(G-5525)*
▲ Mycone Dental Supply Co Inc....C.... 856 663-4700
Gibbstown *(G-3798)*
Palisades Dental LLc....F.... 201 569-0050
Englewood *(G-2929)*
Panthera Dental Inc....G.... 201 340-2766
East Rutherford *(G-2309)*
R Baron Associates Inc....G.... 215 396-3803
Mount Holly *(G-6734)*
R Yates Consumer Prd LLC....G.... 201 569-1030
Englewood *(G-2936)*
Raptor Resources Holdings Inc....G.... 732 252-5146
Freehold *(G-3698)*
Samuel H Fields Dental Labs....E.... 201 343-4626
Hackensack *(G-3971)*
South East Instruments LLC....G.... 201 569-0050
Englewood *(G-2943)*
▲ Spident USA Incorporated....G.... 201 944-0511
Little Ferry *(G-5497)*
Ss White Burs Inc....C.... 732 905-1100
Lakewood *(G-5167)*
▲ Takara Belmont Usa Inc....D.... 732 469-5000
Somerset *(G-10079)*
Takara Belmont Usa Inc....E.... 732 469-5000
Somerset *(G-10080)*
◆ Viscot Medical LLC....E.... 973 887-9273
East Hanover *(G-2245)*
William R Hall Co....E.... 856 784-6700
Lindenwold *(G-5447)*

3844 X-ray Apparatus & Tubes

G E Inspection Technologies LP....D.... 973 448-0077
Flanders *(G-3411)*
▼ Glenbrook Technologies Inc....F.... 973 361-8866
Randolph *(G-9180)*
Gray Star Inc....G.... 973 398-3331
Mount Arlington *(G-6713)*
Hamamatsu Corporation....E.... 908 231-0960
Middlesex *(G-6119)*
M T D Inc....G.... 908 362-6807
Hardwick *(G-4160)*
Security Defense Systems Corp....G.... 973 235-0606
Nutley *(G-7593)*
Spectro Analytical Instrs Inc....F.... 201 642-3000
Mahwah *(G-5774)*
▲ Swissray America Inc....E.... 908 353-0971
Elizabeth *(G-2781)*
Swissray International Inc....F.... 800 903-5543
Edison *(G-2629)*

▲ Vatech America Inc ....E 201 210-5028
   Fort Lee (G-3593)
▲ Villa Radiology Systems LLC ....G 203 262-8836
   Mount Laurel (G-6811)
Vision Ten Inc ....F 201 935-3000
   Carlstadt (G-1236)

3845 Electromedical & Electrotherapeutic Apparatus

3dimension Dgnstc Slution Corp .....G 201 780-4653
   Jersey City (G-4678)
3shape Inc ....F 908 867-0144
   Warren (G-11395)
Affil Endoscopy Services CL ....G 201 842-0020
   Clifton (G-1559)
Ahs Hospital Corp ....E 908 522-2000
   Summit (G-10523)
◆ Bayer Healthcare LLC ....A 862 404-3000
   Whippany (G-11878)
Burlington Cnty Endoscopy Ctr ....E 609 267-1555
   Lumberton (G-5624)
▲ C R Bard Inc ....C 908 277-8000
   Franklin Lakes (G-3617)
▲ Capintec Inc ....E 201 825-9500
   Florham Park (G-3495)
Cgm Us Inc ....E 609 894-4420
   Birmingham (G-456)
Circulite Inc ....F 201 478-7575
   Teaneck (G-10624)
Corentec America Inc ....G 949 379-6227
   Morristown (G-6655)
◆ Datascope Corp ....C 973 244-6100
   Fairfield (G-3178)
Datascope Corp ....G 201 995-8700
   Mahwah (G-5727)
Datascope Corp ....E 201 995-8000
   Mahwah (G-5726)
Davis Center Inc ....G 862 251-4637
   Succasunna (G-10512)
Diabeto Inc ....G 646 397-3175
   Piscataway (G-8656)
Dvx LLC ....G 609 924-3590
   Princeton (G-8934)
Echo Therapeutics Inc ....F 732 201-4189
   Edgewater (G-2437)
Electrocore Inc ....D 973 290-0097
   Basking Ridge (G-182)
▲ Enterix Inc ....E 732 429-1899
   Edison (G-2503)
Ethicon LLC ....D 908 218-3195
   Somerville (G-10109)
Fluent Diagnostics ....G 201 414-4516
   Pequannock (G-8504)
Getinge Group Logistics Americ ......E 973 709-6000
   Wayne (G-11509)
Highlands Acquisition Corp ....G 201 573-8400
   Montvale (G-6413)
Hilin Life Products Inc ....G 917 250-3575
   Newark (G-7150)
▲ Impact Instrumentation Inc ....C 973 882-1212
   West Caldwell (G-11654)
Medality Medical LLC ....G 215 990-0754
   Haddonfield (G-4060)
◆ Mindray Ds Usa Inc ....B 201 995-8000
   Mahwah (G-5754)
Morris County Imaging ....G 973 532-7900
   Morristown (G-6687)
Neurotron Medical Inc ....G 609 896-3444
   Ewing (G-3049)
Newcardio Inc ....F 877 332-4324
   Princeton (G-8984)
▲ Nextphase Medical Devices LLC ....E 201 968-9400
   Waldwick (G-11308)
▲ Nextron Medical Tech Inc ....D 973 575-0614
   Fairfield (G-3279)
Northeast Medical Systems Corp .....G 856 910-8111
   Cherry Hill (G-1400)
Princeton Trade and Technology .....F 609 683-0215
   Princeton (G-9006)
Radnet Inc ....F 908 709-1323
   Cranford (G-1925)
Refine Technology LLC ....F 973 952-0002
   Pine Brook (G-8615)
Respironics Inc ....C 973 581-6000
   Parsippany (G-8007)
▲ Rhythmedix LLC ....G 856 282-1080
   Mount Laurel (G-6800)
Simex Medical Imaging Inc ....G 201 490-0204
   Paramus (G-7832)

Sonotron Medical Systems Inc ....G 201 767-6040
   Northvale (G-7550)
St Jude Medical LLC ....E 800 645-5368
   Secaucus (G-9818)
Surgical Lser Sfety Cuncil Inc ....G 216 272-0805
   Cherry Hill (G-1418)
Syneron ....G 201 599-9451
   Paramus (G-7840)
▲ Topcon America Corporation ....B 201 599-5100
   Oakland (G-7646)
Total Tech Medical LLC ....G 973 980-6458
   Dover (G-2109)
Universal Medical Inc ....F 800 606-5511
   Ewing (G-3074)
V L V Associates ....G 973 428-2884
   Whippany (G-11911)
Vasculogic LLC ....G 908 278-3573
   Piscataway (G-8735)
Vectracor Incorporated ....F 973 904-0444
   Totowa (G-10856)
Zounds Inc ....F 856 234-8844
   Mount Laurel (G-6815)

3851 Ophthalmic Goods

◆ Bausch & Lomb Incorporated ......B 585 338-6000
   Bridgewater (G-800)
Bausch & Lomb Incorporated ....B 908 927-1400
   Bridgewater (G-801)
Complete Optical Laboratory ....G 973 338-8886
   Bloomfield (G-497)
Douglas Liva MD ....G 201 444-7770
   Ridgewood (G-9323)
Edison Ophthalmology Assoc LLC ....F 908 822-0070
   Edison (G-2501)
Essilor Laboratories Amer Inc ....F 732 563-9884
   Warren (G-11410)
Gafas Sales and Consulting Inc ....G 862 368-5428
   Secaucus (G-9771)
Hillcrest Opticians ....G 973 838-6666
   Kinnelon (G-5017)
I See Optical Laboratories ....F 856 227-9300
   Blackwood (G-469)
I See Optical Laboratories ....G 856 795-6435
   Voorhees (G-11288)
Khan Zeshan ....G 973 619-4736
   Belleville (G-298)
▲ Lab Tech Inc ....G 201 767-5613
   Northvale (G-7533)
Lens Depot Inc ....F 732 993-9766
   East Brunswick (G-2154)
Lens Lab Express ....G 201 861-0016
   West New York (G-11745)
Lens Mode Inc ....G 973 467-2000
   Millburn (G-6202)
▲ Liberty Sport Inc ....E 973 882-0986
   Fairfield (G-3262)
▲ Motif Industries Inc ....F 973 575-1800
   East Hanover (G-2223)
New Jersey Eye Center Inc ....F 201 384-7333
   Bergenfield (G-381)
Pam Optical Co ....G 973 744-8882
   Montclair (G-6382)
Pds Consultants Inc ....E 201 970-2313
   Sparta (G-10405)
▲ Phillips Safety Products Inc ....E 732 356-1493
   Middlesex (G-6138)
Sensor Medical Technology LLC ......G 425 358-7381
   Denville (G-2057)
Sheridan Optical Co Inc ....F 856 582-0963
   Pitman (G-8749)
Sho Eyeworks ....G 201 568-5500
   Paramus (G-7831)
Smith Optics Inc ....G 208 726-4477
   Secaucus (G-9815)
Special Optics Inc ....F 973 366-7289
   Denville (G-2058)
Spectacle Shoppe ....G 856 875-5046
   Williamstown (G-11980)
▲ Topcon Medical Systems Inc ....D 201 599-5100
   Oakland (G-7647)
Usv Optical Inc ....B 856 228-1000
   Glendora (G-3839)
Viva International Inc ....G 908 595-6200
   Branchburg (G-694)

3861 Photographic Eqpt & Splys

▲ AGFA Corporation ....B 800 540-2432
   Elmwood Park (G-2808)
AGFA Corporation ....E 201 440-0111
   Elmwood Park (G-2809)

AGFA Corporation ....E 201 440-0111
   Carlstadt (G-1119)
▲ AGFA Finance Corp ....C 201 796-0058
   Elmwood Park (G-2810)
▲ Agoura Hills Group ....E 818 888-0400
   Cherry Hill (G-1335)
▲ Ar2 Products LLC ....G 800 667-1263
   Pompton Plains (G-8858)
▲ Automatic Transfer Inc ....G 908 213-2830
   Alpha (G-36)
B&B Imaging LLC ....G 201 261-3131
   Paramus (G-7791)
Beta Industries Corp ....G 201 939-2400
   Carlstadt (G-1128)
Central Technology Inc ....F 732 431-3339
   Freehold (G-3656)
Clarity Imaging Tech Inc ....E 413 693-1234
   Pennsauken (G-8404)
Coda Inc ....E 201 825-7400
   Mahwah (G-5724)
Colex Imaging Inc ....G 201 414-5575
   Elmwood Park (G-2816)
Cytotherm LP ....F 609 396-1456
   Trenton (G-10927)
▲ Dyna-Lite Inc ....G 908 687-8800
   Union (G-11047)
Energy Storage Corp ....D 732 542-7880
   Eatontown (G-2392)
Enterprise Solution Products ....G 201 678-9200
   West New York (G-11739)
Facsimile Cmmncations Inds Inc .....G 201 672-0773
   Lyndhurst (G-5654)
Flir Systems Inc ....E 201 368-9700
   Ridgefield Park (G-9307)
Fujifilm Med Systems USA Inc ....F 973 686-2631
   Saddle River (G-9691)
Fujifilm North America Corp ....B 732 857-3000
   Edison (G-2516)
▲ Fujikura Graphics Inc ....G 201 420-5040
   Secaucus (G-9769)
▼ Fullview Inc ....G 732 275-6500
   Holmdel (G-4501)
▲ Hasselblad Inc ....E 800 456-0203
   Union (G-11061)
▲ Heights Usa Inc ....E 609 530-1300
   Ewing (G-3033)
Howard Packaging Corp ....G 973 904-0022
   Clifton (G-1636)
Hpi International Inc ....F 732 942-9900
   Lakewood (G-5110)
Image Remit Inc ....E 732 940-7900
   North Brunswick (G-7469)
Intertest Inc ....E 908 496-8008
   Columbia (G-1795)
▲ Iris ID Systems Inc ....E 609 819-4747
   Cranbury (G-1846)
James Colucci Enterprises LLC ....E 877 403-4900
   Short Hills (G-9870)
Liveu Inc ....D 201 742-5229
   Hackensack (G-3939)
Mri of West Morris PA ....F 973 927-1010
   Succasunna (G-10515)
▲ Ner Data Products Inc ....E 888 637-3282
   Glassboro (G-3817)
Oxberry LLC ....G 201 935-3000
   Carlstadt (G-1194)
Parker Acquisition Group Inc ....G 908 707-4900
   Branchburg (G-665)
Photographic Analysis Company ......G 973 696-1000
   Wayne (G-11542)
▼ Power Photo Corp ....D 732 200-1645
   Hillside (G-4420)
▼ Prestige Camera LLC ....E 718 257-5888
   Somerset (G-10056)
▲ Profoto US Inc ....F 973 822-1300
   Florham Park (G-3521)
▲ Quality Films Corp ....G 718 246-7150
   Hillside (G-4422)
Ricoh Prtg Systems Amer Inc ....G 973 316-6051
   Mountain Lakes (G-6827)
Roper Scientific Inc ....E 941 556-2601
   Trenton (G-10989)
◆ Rpl Supplies Inc ....F 973 767-0880
   Garfield (G-3766)
◆ Samsung Opt-Lctronics Amer Inc ...C 201 325-2612
   Teaneck (G-10650)
◆ Sharp Electronics Corporation ......A 201 529-8200
   Montvale (G-6433)
▲ Towne Technologies Inc ....F 908 722-9500
   Somerville (G-10127)

Vision Research Inc ....D 973 696-4500
  Wayne (G-11563)
West Essex Graphics Inc ....E 973 227-2400
  Fairfield (G-3352)
Xybion Corporation ....C 973 538-2067
  Lawrenceville (G-5248)
▲ Zeta Products Inc ....E 908 688-0440
  Annandale (G-56)
Zink Holdings LLC ....E 781 761-5400
  Edison (G-2650)

3873 Watch & Clock Devices & Parts

▲ Acon Watch Crown Company ....F 973 546-8585
  Garfield (G-3725)
▲ Belair Time Corporation ....D 732 905-0100
  Lakewood (G-5060)
◆ Clic Time LLC ....E 201 497-6743
  Woodcliff Lake (G-12053)
Dksh Luxury & Lifestyle N Amer ....G 609 750-8800
  Lawrence Township (G-5216)
Emdur Metal Products Inc ....F 856 541-1100
  Camden (G-1061)
Garrett Moore ....G 908 231-9231
  Bridgewater (G-825)
◆ Movado Group Inc ....B 201 267-8000
  Paramus (G-7822)
Quantum Vector Corp ....G 201 870-1782
  Westwood (G-11840)
Swatch Group Les Btques US Inc ....G 201 271-1400
  Weehawken (G-11570)
Watchitude LLC ....G 732 745-2626
  New Brunswick (G-6979)
Zeon US Inc ....G 516 532-7167
  North Bergen (G-7446)

39 MISCELLANEOUS MANUFACTURING INDUSTRIES

3911 Jewelry: Precious Metal

All State Medal Co Inc ....G 973 458-1458
  Lodi (G-5552)
Anna J Chung Ltd ....F 917 575-8100
  Edgewater (G-2433)
▲ Aubrey David Inc ....E 201 653-2200
  Bayonne (G-203)
Avanzato Jewelers LLC ....G 609 890-0500
  Trenton (G-10898)
Avigdor Ltd Liability Company ....E 973 898-4770
  Morristown (G-6645)
Aydin Jewelry Menufacturing ....G 201 818-1002
  Ramsey (G-9141)
Barrasso & Blasi Industries ....F 973 761-0595
  Maplewood (G-5874)
Bergio International Inc ....G 973 227-3230
  Fairfield (G-3156)
Bernard D Ascenzo ....G 856 795-0511
  Haddonfield (G-4053)
Bhamra Chain Manufacturing ....G 908 686-4555
  Union (G-11032)
Big Apple Jewelry Mfg ....G 201 531-1600
  East Rutherford (G-2277)
Brad Garman Designs ....G 732 229-6670
  Long Branch (G-5594)
Carol Dauplaise Ltd ....E 212 997-5290
  North Bergen (G-7393)
Christian Art ....G 201 867-8096
  West New York (G-11737)
Cinco Star LLC ....G 732 744-1617
  Edison (G-2477)
Creations By Sherry Lynn LLC ....G 800 742-3448
  Florham Park (G-3498)
Creations By Stefano Inc ....G 201 863-8337
  Secaucus (G-9759)
D Paglia & Sons Inc ....F 908 654-5999
  Mountainside (G-6839)
▲ DAmore Jewelers ....F 201 945-0530
  Cliffside Park (G-1537)
Danmola Lara ....G 973 762-7581
  South Orange (G-10193)
David E Connolly Inc ....F 908 654-4600
  Mountainside (G-6840)
DBC Inc ....D 212 819-1177
  Teaneck (G-10626)
▲ Devon Trading Corp ....E 973 812-9190
  Caldwell (G-1022)
Diamond Hut Jewelry Exchange ....G 201 332-5372
  Jersey City (G-4728)
◆ E Chabot Ltd ....E 212 575-1026
  Edison (G-2496)

Enamel Art Studio ....G 732 321-0774
  Metuchen (G-6055)
European Imports of LA Inc ....F 973 536-1823
  Paramus (G-7799)
Fehu Jewel LLC ....C 609 297-5491
  Plainsboro (G-8786)
◆ Franklin Mint LLC ....E 800 843-6468
  Fort Lee (G-3559)
Gem Vault Inc ....G 908 788-1770
  Flemington (G-3445)
▲ George Press Inc ....F 973 992-7797
  Livingston (G-5513)
Gold Buyers At Mall LLC ....G 201 512-5780
  Mahwah (G-5745)
Gold Signature Incorporated ....G 732 777-9170
  Piscataway (G-8667)
Goldstein Setting Co Inc ....F 908 964-1034
  Union (G-11060)
Grassman-Blake Inc ....E 973 379-6170
  Millburn (G-6198)
Guild & Facet LLC ....F 201 758-5368
  North Bergen (G-7408)
▲ H Ritani LLC ....E 888 974-8264
  Closter (G-1756)
Heights Jewelers LLC ....F 201 825-2381
  Allendale (G-9)
Hickok Matthews Co Inc ....G 973 335-3400
  Montville (G-6443)
Jct Design Enterprises Inc ....F 212 629-7412
  Union City (G-11116)
Jost Brothers Jewelry Mfg Corp ....F 908 453-2266
  Washington (G-11448)
Jostens Inc ....G 973 584-5843
  Succasunna (G-10514)
Joy Jewelery America Inc ....G 201 689-1150
  River Vale (G-9367)
K B Enterprises of New Jersey ....G 908 451-5282
  Hillsborough (G-4336)
Kole Design LLC ....G 732 409-0211
  Freehold (G-3674)
Krementz & Co ....F 973 621-8300
  Springfield (G-10452)
Labrada Inc ....G 201 461-2641
  Leonia (G-5289)
Lieberfarb Inc ....F 973 676-9090
  Rahway (G-9113)
▲ Littlegifts Inc ....F 212 868-2559
  Secaucus (G-9789)
◆ Lusterline Inc ....E 201 758-5148
  Union City (G-11120)
M S Brown Mfg Jewelers ....G 609 522-7604
  Wildwood (G-11946)
Mdviani Designs Inc ....G 201 840-5410
  Ridgefield (G-9275)
Midas Designs Ltd ....G 201 567-2700
  Maywood (G-6012)
Mj Gross Company - NJ ....G 212 542-3199
  Lakewood (G-5138)
Moonbabies LLC ....G 609 926-0201
  Somers Point (G-9938)
▲ Nadri Inc ....E 201 585-0088
  Fort Lee (G-3576)
NEi Gold Products of NJ ....G 201 488-5858
  Hackensack (G-3951)
Nei Jewelmasters of New Jersey ....F 201 488-5858
  Hackensack (G-3952)
Netfruits Inc ....G 732 249-2588
  New Brunswick (G-6951)
▲ Norco Inc ....E 908 789-1550
  Garwood (G-3787)
Novell Enterprises Inc ....D 732 428-8300
  Rahway (G-9120)
▼ Paul Winston Fine Jewelry Grou .....F 800 232-2728
  Englewood Cliffs (G-2986)
Pearl Baumell Company Inc ....G 415 421-2113
  Rutherford (G-9631)
Pin People LLC ....F 888 309-7467
  Montvale (G-6424)
Premesco Inc ....B 908 686-0513
  Union (G-11084)
Pretty Jewelry Co ....G 908 806-3377
  Flemington (G-3462)
Provost Square Associates Inc ....F 973 403-8755
  Caldwell (G-1028)
Robert Manse Designs LLC ....E 732 428-8305
  Rahway (G-9124)
Robertas Jewelers Inc ....G 973 875-5318
  Hamburg (G-4095)
Sara Emporium Inc ....G 201 792-7222
  Jersey City (G-4805)

Saud & Son Jewelry Inc ....G 201 866-4445
  West New York (G-11754)
Scott Kay Inc ....C 201 287-0100
  Secaucus (G-9811)
Scott Kay Sterling LLC ....G 201 287-0100
  Secaucus (G-9812)
Shopindia Inc ....G 732 409-0656
  Marlboro (G-5914)
Tapia Accessory Group Inc ....E 201 393-0028
  Teterboro (G-10694)
Tessler & Weiss/Premesco Inc ....C 800 535-3501
  Union (G-11094)
Top Rated Shopping Bargains ....F 800 556-5849
  Hasbrouck Heights (G-4190)
Trimarco Inc ....G 973 762-7380
  Maplewood (G-5886)
Ultimate Trading Corp ....D 973 228-7700
  Rockaway (G-9509)
Unistar Inc ....G 212 840-2100
  Princeton (G-9039)
United Diam Inc ....G 732 619-0950
  Matawan (G-5990)
W Kodak Jewelers Inc ....G 201 710-5491
  Hoboken (G-4487)
W W Jewelers Inc ....D 718 392-4500
  Jersey City (G-4828)
Weinman Bros Inc ....E 212 695-8116
  Jersey City (G-4830)
Wlxt LLC ....D 732 906-7979
  Metuchen (G-6083)
World Class Marketing Corp ....E 201 313-0022
  Fort Lee (G-3595)
▲ Zsombor Antal Designs Inc ....F 201 225-1750
  River Edge (G-9364)

3914 Silverware, Plated & Stainless Steel Ware

◆ AMG International Inc ....E 201 475-4800
  Parsippany (G-7880)
Dynamic Metals Inc ....E 908 769-0522
  Piscataway (G-8659)
◆ Freeman Products Inc ....F 201 475-4800
  Parsippany (G-7951)
◆ Hampton Forge Ltd ....G 732 389-5507
  Eatontown (G-2396)
▲ III Eagle Enterprises Ltd ....E 973 237-1111
  Ringwood (G-9346)
▲ Kraftware Corporation ....E 732 345-7091
  Roselle (G-9562)
▲ Medin Technologies Inc ....C 973 779-2400
  Totowa (G-10836)
Picture It Inc ....G 732 819-0420
  Edison (G-2589)
Trophy King Inc ....G 201 836-1482
  Teaneck (G-10653)

3915 Jewelers Findings & Lapidary Work

Corbo Jewelers Inc ....F 973 777-1635
  Clifton (G-1591)
▲ Diamond Universe LLC ....F 201 592-9500
  Fort Lee (G-3555)
Good As Gold Jewelers Inc ....G 732 286-1111
  Toms River (G-10762)
Grassman-Blake Inc ....E 973 379-6170
  Millburn (G-6198)
J Michaels Jewelers Inc ....G 908 771-9800
  Berkeley Heights (G-403)
Joseph Castings Inc ....F 201 712-0717
  Maywood (G-6010)
▲ Master Presentations Inc ....F 732 239-7093
  Lakewood (G-5131)
Mdviani Designs Inc ....G 201 840-5410
  Ridgefield (G-9275)
▲ Midas Chain Inc ....G 201 244-1150
  Northvale (G-7537)
Moser Jewel Company ....G 908 454-1155
  Phillipsburg (G-8564)
◆ Movado Group Inc ....B 201 267-8000
  Paramus (G-7822)
Rcdc Corporation ....G 212 382-0386
  Hoboken (G-4477)
▼ Smb International LLC ....G 732 222-4888
  West Long Branch (G-11722)
Solmor Manufacturing Co Inc ....G 973 824-7203
  Verona (G-11175)
Tessler & Weiss/Premesco Inc ....C 800 535-3501
  Union (G-11094)
Victors Three-D Inc ....D 201 845-4433
  Maywood (G-6018)

3931 Musical Instruments

AP Global Enterprises Inc .... G 732 919-6200
  Wall Township *(G-11317)*

▲ Malletech LLC .... F 732 774-0011
  Neptune *(G-6889)*

Master Strap LLC .... G 888 503-7779
  Marlboro *(G-5904)*

▲ Musikraft LLC .... G 856 697-8333
  Vineland *(G-11243)*

Peragallo Organ Company of NJ .... F 973 684-3414
  Paterson *(G-8281)*

Spem Corporation .... E 732 356-3366
  Piscataway *(G-8717)*

Trek II Products Inc .... G 732 214-9200
  New Brunswick *(G-6974)*

W E Wamsley Restorations Inc .... G 856 795-4001
  Haddonfield *(G-4066)*

3942 Dolls & Stuffed Toys

▲ Allure Pet Pdts Ltd Lblty Co .... F 973 339-9655
  Denville *(G-2029)*

Chic Btq Doll Design Co LLC .... G 201 784-7727
  Norwood *(G-7561)*

◆ De Zaio Productions Inc .... D 973 423-5000
  Fair Lawn *(G-3095)*

Dream Makers Inc .... G 201 248-5502
  Park Ridge *(G-7848)*

◆ Franklin Mint LLC .... E 800 843-6468
  Fort Lee *(G-3559)*

◆ Homeco LLC .... E 732 802-7733
  Piscataway *(G-8673)*

▲ Kids of America Corp .... E 973 808-8242
  Fairfield *(G-3250)*

Letts Play Inc .... G 856 297-2530
  Williamstown *(G-11963)*

▲ New Adventures LLC .... G 973 884-8887
  East Hanover *(G-2225)*

▲ Pretty Ugly LLC .... F 908 620-0931
  Bernardsville *(G-442)*

▲ Reeves International Inc .... E 973 694-5006
  Pequannock *(G-8506)*

▲ Ron Banafato Inc .... G 908 685-9447
  Phillipsburg *(G-8572)*

3944 Games, Toys & Children's Vehicles

▲ AG&e Holdings Inc .... E 609 704-3000
  Hammonton *(G-4124)*

▲ Ambo Consulting LLC .... G 732 663-0000
  Deal *(G-1997)*

▲ Amloid Corporation .... F 973 328-0654
  Cedar Knolls *(G-1298)*

Answers In Motion LLC .... G 732 267-7792
  Maple Shade *(G-5859)*

Atlas O LLC .... E 908 687-9590
  Hillside *(G-4377)*

Bally Technologies Inc .... F 609 641-7711
  Egg Harbor Township *(G-2679)*

Bucci Management Co Inc .... G 609 567-8808
  Hammonton *(G-4131)*

Classic Chess and Games Inc .... G 908 850-6553
  Hackettstown *(G-4002)*

Deluxe Innovations Inc .... G 201 857-5880
  Midland Park *(G-6174)*

Edison Nation Inc .... G 610 829-1039
  Phillipsburg *(G-8549)*

Electronics Boutique Amer Inc .... G 856 435-3900
  Clementon *(G-1532)*

◆ Epoch Everlasting Play LLC .... E 973 316-2500
  Parsippany *(G-7937)*

▲ Famosa North America Inc .... G 856 206-9844
  Mount Laurel *(G-6759)*

Froyo Skyview LLC .... G 718 607-5656
  Jersey City *(G-4741)*

Hirox - USA Inc .... G 201 342-2600
  Hackensack *(G-3929)*

◆ Horizon Group Usa Inc .... C 908 810-1111
  Warren *(G-11415)*

Horizon Group USA Inc .... G 908 810-1111
  Monroe Township *(G-6333)*

▲ Hygloss Products Inc .... E 973 458-1700
  Wallington *(G-11387)*

▲ Kiddesigns Inc .... E 732 574-9000
  Rahway *(G-9112)*

◆ Larose Industries LLC .... D 973 543-2037
  Randolph *(G-9189)*

▲ Majestic Industries Inc .... E 973 473-3434
  Passaic *(G-8084)*

▲ Morgan Cycle LLC .... G 973 218-9233
  Short Hills *(G-9873)*

Poof-Alex Holdings LLC .... G 734 454-9552
  Fairfield *(G-3292)*

Pride Products Mfg LLC .... F 908 353-1900
  Elizabeth *(G-2770)*

▲ Primetime Trading Corp .... E 646 580-8223
  Bayonne *(G-231)*

Proteus Designs LLC .... G 215 519-0135
  Moorestown *(G-6560)*

Reeves International Inc .... G 973 956-9555
  Wayne *(G-11547)*

Steico USA Inc .... F 732 364-6200
  Lakewood *(G-5168)*

Toysruscom Inc .... D 973 617-3500
  Parsippany *(G-8031)*

▲ Tucker International LLC .... F 856 216-1333
  Burlington *(G-988)*

Zimpli Kids Inc .... G 732 945-5995
  Neptune *(G-6903)*

3949 Sporting & Athletic Goods, NEC

AB Coaster LLC .... F 908 879-2713
  Chester *(G-1429)*

▲ Akadema Inc .... G 973 304-1470
  Bloomingdale *(G-525)*

Alden - Leeds Inc .... G 973 344-7986
  Kearny *(G-4841)*

Anglers Select LLC .... G 973 396-2959
  Boonton *(G-543)*

Aquasports Pools LLC .... F 732 247-6298
  New Brunswick *(G-6912)*

◆ Beachcarts USA .... G 201 319-0091
  Secaucus *(G-9752)*

Belleplain Supply Co Inc .... G 609 861-2345
  Woodbine *(G-12008)*

Bergen Manufacturing & Supply ..... E 201 854-3461
  North Bergen *(G-7389)*

Big Daddys Sports Haven .... G 856 453-9009
  Millville *(G-6237)*

Captain John Inc .... F 609 494-2094
  Barnegat Light *(G-164)*

CDK Industries LLC .... G 856 488-5456
  Cherry Hill *(G-1352)*

▲ Cover Co Inc .... G 908 707-9797
  Branchburg *(G-632)*

◆ Cressi Sub USA .... G 201 594-1450
  Saddle Brook *(G-9648)*

▲ Crown Products Inc .... E 732 493-0022
  Spring Lake *(G-10421)*

▲ De Zaio Productions Inc .... D 973 423-5000
  Fair Lawn *(G-3095)*

◆ Delair LLC .... D 856 663-2900
  Pennsauken *(G-8412)*

Elite Surf Snow Skateboard Sp ...... G 856 427-7873
  Cherry Hill *(G-1359)*

▲ Endurance Net Inc .... F 609 499-3450
  Florence *(G-3475)*

Fred S Burroughs North Jersey .... D 908 850-8773
  Hackettstown *(G-4008)*

G A D Inc .... G 973 383-3499
  Newton *(G-7344)*

Gamit Force Athc Ltd Lblty Co .... F 908 675-0733
  Long Branch *(G-5598)*

▲ Great Socks LLC .... G 856 964-9700
  Pennsauken *(G-8427)*

Greater ATL Cy Golf Assn LLC .... F 609 652-1800
  Galloway *(G-3722)*

Grill Creations .... G 908 264-8426
  Garwood *(G-3784)*

◆ Hayward Industrial Products .... C 908 351-5400
  Elizabeth *(G-2745)*

Holiday Bowl Inc .... E 201 337-6516
  Oakland *(G-7631)*

Impact Protective Eqp LLC .... G 973 377-0903
  Madison *(G-5695)*

Ingui Design LLC .... G 201 264-9126
  Ramsey *(G-9147)*

International Tech Lasers .... G 201 262-4580
  Emerson *(G-2864)*

▲ Interntnal Globl Solutions Inc .... G 201 791-1500
  Elmwood Park *(G-2832)*

▲ Interntonal Riding Helmets Inc ...... E 732 772-0165
  Marlboro *(G-5902)*

J & S Enterprises LLC .... F 973 696-9199
  Lincoln Park *(G-5300)*

J and S Sporting Apparel LLC .... G 732 787-5500
  Keansburg *(G-4838)*

JA Cissel Manufacturing Co .... G 732 901-0300
  Lakewood *(G-5113)*

Jersey Cover Corp .... F 732 286-6300
  Toms River *(G-10771)*

Julian Bait Company Inc .... G 732 291-0050
  Atlantic Highlands *(G-109)*

◆ Kayden Manufacturing Inc .... F 201 880-9898
  Hackensack *(G-3935)*

Lacrosse Republic .... G 856 853-8787
  West Deptford *(G-11709)*

◆ Landice Incorporated .... E 973 927-9010
  Randolph *(G-9188)*

Lob-Ster Inc .... G 818 764-6000
  Plainfield *(G-8770)*

Lure Lash Spa LLC .... F 973 783-5274
  Montclair *(G-6374)*

Mulbro Manufacturing & Svc Co ..... G 732 805-0290
  Middlesex *(G-6132)*

Nafs Paints Inc .... G 973 927-0729
  Flanders *(G-3415)*

Newbold Inc .... G 732 469-5654
  Middlesex *(G-6135)*

▲ Nomad Lcrosse Distrs Ltd Lblty ..... G 732 431-2255
  Freehold *(G-3683)*

Offshore Enterprises Inc .... G 609 345-9099
  Atlantic City *(G-100)*

Primal Surf .... G 609 264-1999
  Brigantine *(G-912)*

▲ Prince Sports Inc .... D 609 291-5800
  Bordentown *(G-593)*

◆ Pro Sports Inc .... E 732 294-5561
  Marlboro *(G-5910)*

Pure Soccer Academy Ltd Lblty ...... G 877 945-6423
  Pine Brook *(G-8614)*

Rags International Inc .... G 787 632-8447
  Springfield *(G-10462)*

RCM Ltd Inc .... G 201 337-3328
  Oakland *(G-7642)*

Reagent Chemical & RES Inc .... E 908 284-2800
  Ringoes *(G-9341)*

Richard Andrus .... G 856 825-1782
  Millville *(G-6269)*

Rke Atheltic Lettering .... G 732 280-1111
  Belmar *(G-353)*

Ron Jon Surf Shop Fla Inc .... F 609 494-8844
  Ship Bottom *(G-9862)*

Seaville Motorsports .... F 609 624-0040
  Somers Point *(G-9939)*

▲ Slendertone Distribution Inc .... G 732 660-1177
  Hoboken *(G-4481)*

South County Soccer League Inc .... G 908 310-9052
  Lambertville *(G-5197)*

Ss Equipment Holdings LLC .... E 732 627-0006
  Bridgewater *(G-894)*

Sterling Net & Twine Co Inc .... F 973 783-9800
  Montclair *(G-6390)*

Stingray Sport Pdts Ltd Lblty .... G 201 300-6482
  Fair Lawn *(G-3123)*

◆ Technogym USA Corp .... F 800 804-0952
  Fairfield *(G-3324)*

Tee-Rific Golf Center .... F 908 253-9300
  Branchburg *(G-688)*

Totowa Kickboxing Ltd Lblty Co ...... F 973 507-9106
  Totowa *(G-10855)*

◆ Ultimate Trining Munitions Inc .... E 908 725-9000
  Branchburg *(G-692)*

Um Equity Corp .... G 856 354-2200
  Haddonfield *(G-4065)*

Willowbrook Golf Center LLC .... F 973 256-6922
  Wayne *(G-11565)*

3951 Pens & Mechanical Pencils

Cameo Metal Forms Inc .... F 718 788-1106
  Woodland Park *(G-12073)*

▲ Cameo Novelty & Pen Corp .... E 973 923-1600
  Hillside *(G-4384)*

▲ Newell Brands Inc .... B 201 610-6600
  Hoboken *(G-4468)*

Pen Company of America LLC .... F 908 374-7949
  Garwood *(G-3790)*

Pen Company of America LLC .... E 908 374-7949
  Linden *(G-5406)*

◆ Rotuba Extruders Inc .... C 908 486-1000
  Linden *(G-5416)*

Touch of Class Promotions LLC ...... G 267 994-0860
  Voorhees *(G-11296)*

3952 Lead Pencils, Crayons & Artist's Mtrls

Algene Marking Equipment Co .... G 973 478-9041
  Garfield *(G-3727)*

◆ Asbury Carbons Inc .... G 908 537-2155
  Asbury *(G-60)*

▲ Case It Inc .... E 800 441-4710
  Lyndhurst *(G-5646)*

▲ Chavant Inc ....F 732 751-0003
Wall Township (G-11323)
Congruent Machine Co Inc ....G 973 764-6767
Vernon (G-11158)
Empty Walls Inc ....G 609 452-8488
Princeton (G-8940)
▲ Excel Hobby Blades Corp ....E 973 278-4000
Paterson (G-8187)
◆ General Pencil Company Inc ....G 201 653-5351
Jersey City (G-4742)
◆ Meadowbrook Inventions Inc ....E 908 766-0606
Bernardsville (G-439)
Norwood Industries Inc ....F 856 858-6195
Haddon Township (G-4052)
▲ Pertech Printing Inks Inc ....E 908 354-1700
Carlstadt (G-1199)
Rich Art Color Co Inc ....F 201 767-0009
Northvale (G-7547)
U J Ramelson Co Inc ....G 973 589-5422
Newark (G-7304)
◆ Utrecht Manufacturing Corp ....D 609 409-8001
Cranbury (G-1891)

3953 Marking Devices

A A A Stamp and Seal Mfg Co ....G 201 796-1500
Saddle Brook (G-9636)
A Quick Cut Stamping Embossing ......F 856 321-0050
Maple Shade (G-5858)
Adco Signs of NJ Inc ....E 908 965-2112
Elizabeth (G-2707)
▲ All-State International Inc ....C 908 272-0800
Cranford (G-1899)
American Marking Systems Inc ....E 973 478-5600
Clifton (G-1563)
American Stamp Mfg Co ....F 212 227-1877
Clifton (G-1564)
American Stencyl Inc ....G 201 251-6460
Mahwah (G-5714)
Blue Ring Stencils LLC ....E 866 763-3873
Lumberton (G-5623)
C Q Corporation ....F 201 935-8488
East Rutherford (G-2281)
Classic Marking Products Inc ....G 973 383-2223
Roxbury Township (G-9599)
Container Graphics Corp ....E 732 922-1180
Neptune (G-6870)
Dalemark Industries Inc ....F 732 367-3100
Lakewood (G-5081)
Digital Design Inc ....E 973 857-9500
Cedar Grove (G-1274)
Harrisburg Stamp & Stencil Co ....G 717 236-9000
Woodbury (G-12032)
Innovative Art Concepts LLC ....F 201 828-9146
Ramsey (G-9148)
J D Crew Inc ....G 856 665-3676
Pennsauken (G-8443)
L & F Graphics Ltd Lblty Co ....G 973 240-7033
Paterson (G-8232)
Lafarge Road Marking Inc ....C 973 884-0300
Parsippany (G-7972)
Max Pro Services LLC ....G 973 396-2373
Livingston (G-5523)
Newark Stamp & Die Works Inc ....G 973 485-7111
Newark (G-7217)
Oraton Custom Products ....G 908 235-9424
Columbia (G-1796)
▲ Pic Graphics ....E 201 420-5040
Jersey City (G-4783)
▲ Private Label Products Inc ....E 201 773-4230
Fair Lawn (G-3115)
▲ Ranger Industries Inc ....E 732 389-3535
Tinton Falls (G-10725)
Shachihata Inc (usa) ....F 732 905-7159
Lakewood (G-5162)
Time Log Industries Inc ....G 609 965-5017
Egg Harbor City (G-2670)
Trodat Usa Inc ....F 732 529-8500
Somerset (G-10089)
◆ Trodat USA LLC ....D 732 562-9500
Somerset (G-10090)
▲ Winters Stamp Mfg Co Inc ....F 908 352-3725
Martinsville (G-5965)

3955 Carbon Paper & Inked Ribbons

▲ Agoura Hills Group ....E 818 888-0400
Cherry Hill (G-1335)
Bergen Cnty Crtrdge Xchnge LLC ......G 201 493-8182
Midland Park (G-6171)
Clarity Imaging Solutions Inc ....G 866 684-2212
Cherry Hill (G-1353)

▲ Commander Imaging Products Inc ..E 973 742-9298
Paterson (G-8161)
▲ GSC Imaging LLC ....F 856 317-9301
Pennsauken (G-8428)
▲ Ner Data Products Inc ....E 888 637-3282
Glassboro (G-3817)
Ricoh Prtg Systems Amer Inc ....G 973 316-6051
Mountain Lakes (G-6827)
◆ Turbon International Inc ....G 800 282-6650
Cherry Hill (G-1424)
Turbon International Inc ....F 413 386-6739
Cherry Hill (G-1425)
Waste Not Computers & Supplies ......G 201 384-4444
Dumont (G-2118)

3961 Costume Jewelry & Novelties

▲ Alster Import Company Inc ....F 201 332-7245
Jersey City (G-4690)
▲ C & C Metal Products Corp ....D 201 569-7300
Englewood (G-2889)
Golden Treasure Imports Inc ....G 732 723-1830
Englishtown (G-3002)
▲ HMS Monaco Et Cie Ltd ....E 201 533-0007
Jersey City (G-4747)
▲ Infinite Classic Inc ....G 973 227-2790
Fairfield (G-3239)
▲ International Inspirations LLC ....G 201 868-2000
North Bergen (G-7411)
Jacmel Jewelry Inc ....D 201 223-0435
Secaucus (G-9782)
▲ Lesilu Productions Inc ....E 212 947-6419
West Orange (G-11771)
Lighthouse Express Inc ....G 732 776-9555
Asbury Park (G-79)
▲ Littlegifts Inc ....F 212 868-2559
Secaucus (G-9789)
Meeshaa Inc ....G 908 279-7985
Edison (G-2561)
Nes Jewelry Inc ....G 646 213-4094
Clifton (G-1674)
▲ Norco Inc ....E 908 789-1550
Garwood (G-3787)
▲ Q-Eximtrade Inc ....G 732 366-4667
Carteret (G-1265)
San Marel Designs Inc ....G 973 426-9554
Budd Lake (G-935)
▲ Scaasis Originals Inc ....E 732 775-7474
Neptune (G-6895)
▲ Superior Jewelry Co ....F 215 677-8100
Northfield (G-7511)
Swarovski North America Ltd ....G 732 632-1856
Edison (G-2627)
Swarovski North America Ltd ....G 856 686-1805
Deptford (G-2067)
Swarovski North America Ltd ....G 856 662-5453
Cherry Hill (G-1419)
Swarovski North America Ltd ....G 201 265-4888
Paramus (G-7839)
Swarovski North America Ltd ....G 609 344-1323
Atlantic City (G-103)
Swarovski North America Ltd ....G 973 812-7500
Wayne (G-11554)
Tapia Accessory Group Inc ....E 201 393-0028
Teterboro (G-10694)
Ultimate Trading Corp ....G 973 228-7700
Rockaway (G-9509)
Umbrella & Chairs LLC ....G 973 284-1240
Englewood (G-2949)

3965 Fasteners, Buttons, Needles & Pins

◆ Allary Corporation ....F 908 851-0077
Union (G-11022)
▲ Alpine Machine & Tool Corp ....F 201 666-0959
Westwood (G-11825)
Amershoe Corp ....G 201 569-7300
Englewood (G-2876)
Arlo Corporation ....G 973 618-0030
Roseland (G-9533)
▲ C & C Metal Products Corp ....D 201 569-7300
Englewood (G-2889)
▲ Captive Fasteners Corp ....B 201 337-6800
Oakland (G-7618)
▲ Case It Inc ....E 800 441-4710
Lyndhurst (G-5646)
Communique Inc ....G 973 751-7588
Belleville (G-293)
Fastenation Inc ....G 973 591-1277
Clifton (G-1619)
▲ Mona Slide Fasteners Inc ....E 718 325-7700
Belleville (G-303)

Nyltite Corp of America ....F 908 561-1300
South Plainfield (G-10310)
Omaha Standard Inc Tr NJ ....G 609 588-5400
Trenton (G-10969)
Primesource Building Pdts Inc ....E 732 296-0600
New Brunswick (G-6961)
▲ Quality Stays LLC ....G 800 868-8195
Clifton (G-1704)
▲ Royal Slide Sales Co Inc ....G 973 777-1177
Garfield (G-3764)
Royal Zipper Manufg Company ....F 973 777-1177
Garfield (G-3765)
▲ Snapco Manufacturing Corp ....E 973 282-0300
Hillside (G-4427)
Straps Manufacturing NJ Inc ....F 201 368-5201
Wyckoff (G-12121)
▲ Yale Hook & Eye Co Inc ....F 973 824-1440
Hillside (G-4438)
YKK (usa) Inc ....G 201 935-4200
Lyndhurst (G-5684)

3991 Brooms & Brushes

▲ Andon Brush Co Inc ....E 973 256-6611
Little Falls (G-5452)
Around Clock Sweeping LLC ....G 973 887-1144
Parsippany (G-7882)
▲ Benjamin Booth Company ....F 609 859-1995
Southampton (G-10360)
▲ Charles E Green & Son Inc ....E 973 485-3630
Newark (G-7082)
▲ Danline Inc ....E 973 376-1000
Springfield (G-10438)
◆ Delta Lambskin Products Inc ....E 201 871-9233
Englewood (G-2897)
▲ Fifty/Fifty Group Inc ....E 201 343-1243
Hackensack (G-3913)
Gordon Brush Mfg Co Inc ....G 973 827-4600
Franklin (G-3604)
▲ Industrial Brush Co Inc ....E 800 241-9860
Fairfield (G-3236)
◆ Keystone Plastics Inc ....D 908 561-1300
South Plainfield (G-10287)
Manufacturers Brush Corp ....G 973 882-6966
Roselle (G-9563)
Mw Jenkins Sons Incorporated ....F 973 239-5150
Cedar Grove (G-1284)
▲ Newark Brush Company LLC ....F 973 376-1000
Springfield (G-10456)
Rubigo Cosmetics ....G 973 636-6573
Little Falls (G-5466)
▲ Silver Brush Limited ....G 609 443-4900
Windsor (G-11998)
▲ Spectrum Paint Applicator ....E 973 732-9180
Newark (G-7282)

3993 Signs & Advertising Displays

A B S Sign Company Inc ....G 609 522-6833
Wildwood (G-11941)
A C Display Studios Inc ....G 609 345-0814
Atlantic City (G-88)
A C L Equipment Corp ....G 973 740-9800
Livingston (G-5501)
A Sign Company ....G 609 298-3388
Trenton (G-10888)
A Sign of Excellence Inc ....G 732 264-0404
Hazlet (G-4253)
ABC Sign Systems Inc ....F 856 665-0950
Pennsauken (G-8381)
Ace Sign Company Inc ....G 732 826-3858
Perth Amboy (G-8509)
Adco Signs of NJ Inc ....E 908 965-2112
Elizabeth (G-2707)
Adiant ....F 800 264-8303
Somerville (G-10101)
▲ Aesys Inc ....G 201 871-3223
Emerson (G-2862)
All Colors Screen Printing LLC ....G 732 777-6033
Highland Park (G-4286)
Alpha 1 Studio Inc ....G 609 859-2200
Southampton (G-10359)
Alu Inc ....E 201 935-2213
Moonachie (G-6453)
American Graphic Systems Inc ....G 201 796-0666
Fair Lawn (G-3084)
American Sign Instllations LLC ....G 856 506-0610
Millville (G-6231)
American Stencyl Inc ....G 201 251-6460
Mahwah (G-5714)
American Woodcarving LLC ....G 973 835-8510
Wayne (G-11469)

Arnold Furniture Mfrs Inc .... F 973 399-0505
  Irvington *(G-4558)*

Art Dmensions .... G 908 322-8488
  Scotch Plains *(G-9730)*

Artsign Studio .... G 856 546-4889
  Haddon Heights *(G-4043)*

Astro Outdoor Advertising Inc .... F 856 881-4300
  Glassboro *(G-3807)*

Atlas Flasher & Supply Co Inc .... E 856 423-3333
  Mickleton *(G-6086)*

▲ Aura Badge Co .... D 856 881-9026
  Clayton *(G-1524)*

Aura Signs Inc .... G 866 963-7446
  Hillsborough *(G-4302)*

▲ Azar International Inc .... E 845 624-8808
  Paramus *(G-7790)*

B & A Grafx Inc .... F 646 302-8849
  Harrison *(G-4163)*

B4inc Inc .... F 609 747-9600
  Burlington *(G-951)*

▲ Bamboo & Rattan Works Inc .... G 732 255-4239
  Toms River *(G-10746)*

Banner Design Inc .... E 908 687-5335
  Hillside *(G-4379)*

Bbk Technologies Inc .... G 908 231-0306
  Raritan *(G-9208)*

Bergen Digital Graphics LLC .... G 201 825-0011
  Upper Saddle River *(G-11135)*

Bergen Sign Company Inc .... E 973 742-7755
  Wayne *(G-11478)*

▲ Blanc Industries Inc .... E 973 537-0090
  Dover *(G-2075)*

Blazing Visuals .... G 732 781-1401
  Point Pleasant Boro *(G-8838)*

Brilliant Brdcstg Concept Inc .... F 732 287-9201
  Rahway *(G-9083)*

▲ Brinker Industries .... E 973 678-1200
  Dover *(G-2077)*

Bruce Kindberg .... G 973 664-0195
  Rockaway *(G-9447)*

Brunswick Signs & Exhibit .... G 732 246-2500
  North Brunswick *(G-7458)*

Cad Signs LLC .... G 201 267-0457
  Hackensack *(G-3889)*

Cad Signs Nyc Corp .... E 201 525-5415
  Hackensack *(G-3890)*

▲ Carpenter LLC .... F 609 689-3090
  Trenton *(G-10911)*

CDI Group Inc .... F 908 862-1493
  Linden *(G-5330)*

▼ Central Art & Enginering Inc .... G 609 758-5922
  Cream Ridge *(G-1932)*

Cnr Products Co .... G 201 384-7003
  Bergenfield *(G-374)*

Colorcraft Sign Co .... F 609 386-1115
  Beverly *(G-449)*

Craft Signs .... G 201 656-1991
  Jersey City *(G-4719)*

▲ Creoh Trading Corp .... F 718 821-0570
  Lakewood *(G-5074)*

Custom Graphics of Vineland .... E 856 691-7858
  Vineland *(G-11209)*

D & N Sporting Goods Inc .... F 856 778-0055
  Mount Laurel *(G-6751)*

D3 Led LLC .... G 201 583-9486
  North Bergen *(G-7398)*

Dale Behre .... G 908 850-4225
  Hackettstown *(G-4003)*

Davis Sign Systems Inc .... G 973 394-9909
  Boonton *(G-549)*

Daysol Inc .... D 908 272-5900
  Kenilworth *(G-4934)*

DCI Signs & Awnings Inc .... E 973 350-0400
  Newark *(G-7096)*

Delaware Valley Sign Corp .... D 609 386-0100
  Burlington *(G-962)*

▲ Design Display Group Inc .... C 201 438-6000
  Carlstadt *(G-1150)*

▲ Design Productions Inc .... G 201 447-5656
  Waldwick *(G-11300)*

Designer Sign Systems LLC .... F 212 939-5577
  Carlstadt *(G-1151)*

Designs By James .... G 856 692-1316
  Vineland *(G-11213)*

Digital Arts Imaging LLC .... F 908 237-4646
  Flemington *(G-3437)*

▲ Dimensional Communications Inc ...D 201 767-1500
  Mahwah *(G-5730)*

Dpj Inc .... F 732 499-8600
  Rahway *(G-9088)*

▲ Dublin Management Assoc of NJ ....C 609 387-1600
  Burlington *(G-964)*

▲ East Trading West Inv LLC .... G 973 678-0800
  Orange *(G-7753)*

Em Signs .... G 973 300-9703
  Newton *(G-7341)*

▲ Empro Products Co Inc .... G 973 302-4351
  Belleville *(G-295)*

Ervin Advertising Co Inc .... G 732 363-7645
  Howell *(G-4539)*

Essex Morris Sign Co .... G 973 386-1755
  Whippany *(G-11890)*

▲ Et Manufacturing & Sales Inc .... E 973 777-6662
  Passaic *(G-8064)*

▲ Exhibit Co Inc .... G 732 465-1070
  Piscataway *(G-8663)*

Exhibit Network Inc .... F 732 751-9600
  Oakhurst *(G-7608)*

F & A Signs Inc .... G 732 442-9399
  Hopelawn *(G-4525)*

F & S Awning and Blind Co Inc .... G 732 738-4110
  Edison *(G-2509)*

Fastsigns .... G 973 887-6700
  East Hanover *(G-2209)*

Fedex Office & Print Svcs Inc .... G 856 427-0099
  Cherry Hill *(G-1361)*

Fioplex .... G 856 689-7213
  Swedesboro *(G-10585)*

Four Way Enterprises Inc .... F 973 633-5757
  Wayne *(G-11505)*

Franbeth Inc .... G 856 488-1480
  Pennsboken *(G-8422)*

Future Image Sign & Awning .... G 201 440-1400
  Teterboro *(G-10677)*

G-Force River Signs LLC .... G 609 397-4467
  Lambertville *(G-5189)*

Garden State Highway Pdts Inc .... E 856 692-7572
  Millville *(G-6250)*

General Sign Co Inc .... G 856 753-3535
  West Berlin *(G-11598)*

Genesis Marketing Group Inc .... G 201 836-1392
  Teaneck *(G-10632)*

GF Supplies LLC .... G 336 539-1666
  Elmwood Park *(G-2827)*

Glasscare Inc .... F 201 943-1122
  Cliffside Park *(G-1539)*

Graphic Presentations Systems .... F 732 981-1120
  Piscataway *(G-8670)*

Graphic Solutions & Signs LLC .... G 201 343-7446
  Ridgefield Park *(G-9308)*

Griffin Signs Inc .... E 856 786-8517
  Cinnaminson *(G-1460)*

Heros Salute Awards Co .... G 973 696-5085
  Wayne *(G-11517)*

Hiresprint LLC .... F 201 488-1626
  Hackensack *(G-3928)*

Hub Sign Crane Corp .... G 732 252-9090
  Manalapan *(G-5813)*

I Associates LLC .... F 215 262-7754
  Pennsauken *(G-8434)*

Identity Depot Inc .... G 973 584-9301
  Ledgewood *(G-5276)*

◆ Impact Displays Inc .... E 201 804-6262
  Carlstadt *(G-1167)*

Impressions Signs and Prtg Inc .... G 973 653-3058
  Garfield *(G-3747)*

▼ Infinite Mfg Group Inc .... G 973 649-9950
  Kearny *(G-4868)*

Infinite Sign Industries Inc .... G 973 649-9950
  Kearny *(G-4869)*

Insign Inc .... E 856 424-1161
  West Deptford *(G-11705)*

Ionni Sign Inc .... G 973 625-3815
  Rockaway *(G-9468)*

J & G Diversified .... G 732 543-2537
  New Brunswick *(G-6937)*

J D Crew Inc .... G 856 665-3676
  Pennsauken *(G-8443)*

J H M Communications Inc .... F 908 859-6668
  Phillipsburg *(G-8556)*

J Vitale Sign Co Inc .... G 732 388-8401
  Rahway *(G-9106)*

J&E Business Services LLC .... G 973 984-8444
  Clifton *(G-1645)*

▲ Jarco U S Casting Corp .... E 201 271-0003
  Union City *(G-11115)*

Jaynes Signwork .... G 856 362-0503
  Bridgeton *(G-761)*

Jencks Signs Corp .... G 908 542-1400
  Warren *(G-11419)*

JKA Specialties Mfr Inc .... F 609 859-2090
  Southampton *(G-10366)*

Kar Industrial .... G 856 985-8730
  Marlton *(G-5935)*

Kdf Reprographics Inc .... F 201 784-9991
  South Hackensack *(G-10167)*

Kna Graphics Inc .... G 908 272-4232
  Kenilworth *(G-4953)*

◆ Kubik Maltbie Inc .... E 856 234-0052
  Mount Laurel *(G-6774)*

L & F Graphics Ltd Lblty Co .... G 973 240-7033
  Paterson *(G-8232)*

◆ L&M Architectural Graphics Inc .....F 973 575-7665
  Fairfield *(G-3254)*

Larue Manufacturing Corp .... G 908 534-2700
  Whitehouse *(G-11916)*

Lettering Plus Sign Company .... G 856 299-0404
  Pedricktown *(G-8350)*

Lincoln Signs & Awnings Inc .... G 732 442-3151
  Perth Amboy *(G-8525)*

M & W Franklin LLC .... G 609 927-0885
  Egg Harbor Township *(G-2689)*

M C Signs .... G 609 399-7446
  Ocean City *(G-7691)*

▲ Madhouz LLC .... G 609 206-8009
  Glassboro *(G-3814)*

Mag Signs .... F 609 747-9600
  Burlington *(G-978)*

Majestic Signs LLC .... G 201 837-8104
  Teaneck *(G-10639)*

Manhattan Neon Sign Corp .... F 212 714-0430
  Hoboken *(G-4465)*

Manhattan Signs & Designs Ltd .... E 973 278-3603
  Paterson *(G-8249)*

Mark-O-Lite Sign Co Inc .... G 732 462-8530
  Howell *(G-4546)*

Mason Display Innovations Inc .... F 609 860-0675
  Asbury *(G-67)*

Mc Does Inc .... G 856 985-8730
  Marlton *(G-5941)*

McLain Studios Inc .... G 732 775-0271
  Asbury Park *(G-80)*

▲ Mechtronics Corporation .... E 845 231-1400
  Franklin Lakes *(G-3628)*

▲ Medlaurel Inc .... E 856 461-6600
  Delanco *(G-2006)*

▼ Mega Media Concepts Ltd Lblty ......G 973 919-5661
  Sparta *(G-10397)*

Mej Signs Inc .... G 609 584-6881
  Hamilton *(G-4114)*

Merchandising Display Corp .... G 973 299-8400
  Boonton *(G-561)*

▲ Metaline Products Company Inc ......E 732 721-1373
  South Amboy *(G-10137)*

Michael Anthony Sign Dsign Inc .... E 732 453-6120
  Piscataway *(G-8690)*

Michele Maddalena .... G 973 244-0033
  Fairfield *(G-3270)*

Montana Electrical Decorating .... G 973 344-1815
  Newark *(G-7204)*

Mr Quick Sign .... G 201 670-1690
  Midland Park *(G-6181)*

▲ MS Signs Inc .... G 973 569-1111
  Saddle Brook *(G-9664)*

Nes Light Inc .... G 201 840-0400
  Ridgefield *(G-9279)*

New Dawn Inc .... G 732 774-1377
  Neptune *(G-6892)*

Nickel Artistic Services LLC .... G 973 627-0390
  Rockaway *(G-9479)*

Nickolaos Kappatos Entps Inc .... F 856 939-1099
  Glendora *(G-3838)*

Nomadic North America LLC .... G 703 866-9200
  Fairfield *(G-3282)*

North Star Signs Inc .... G 973 244-1144
  Highland Lakes *(G-4285)*

Northwind Enterprises Inc .... E 732 274-2000
  Dayton *(G-1982)*

NW Sign Industries Inc .... E 856 802-1677
  Moorestown *(G-6547)*

NW Sign Industries Inc .... D 856 802-1677
  Moorestown *(G-6548)*

Opdyke Awnings Inc .... F 732 449-5940
  Wall Township *(G-11360)*

Outfront Media LLC .... D 973 575-6900
  Fairfield *(G-3286)*

▲ Ovadia Corporation .... E 973 256-9200
  Little Falls *(G-5462)*

P & G Lighting & Sign Service .... G 908 925-3191
  Linden *(G-5400)*

Packet Media LLC ....G....... 856 779-3800
Englishtown (G-3007)
Parrish Sign Co Inc ....G....... 856 696-4040
Vineland (G-11250)
Pat Bry Advertising Spc ....G....... 732 591-0999
Morganville (G-6593)
▲ Permalith Plastics LLC ....D....... 215 925-5659
Pennsauken (G-8468)
Presentation Solutions Inc ....G....... 732 961-1960
Jackson (G-4662)
Princeton Packet Inc ....C....... 609 924-3244
Princeton (G-9001)
Printing & Signs Express Inc .....G....... 201 368-1255
Mahwah (G-5763)
Pro-Pack Corp ....G....... 908 725-5000
Branchburg (G-672)
Progress Displays Inc ....G....... 908 757-6650
Edison (G-2592)
Rand Diversified Companies LLC ...B.... 732 985-0800
Edison (G-2594)
▲ Resources Inc In Display ....E....... 908 272-5900
Kenilworth (G-4974)
Riccarr Displays Inc..................E....... 973 983-6701
Rockaway (G-9493)
Rich Designs ....G....... 908 369-5035
Hillsborough (G-4352)
Ricztone Inc..............................G....... 609 695-6263
Trenton (G-10987)
Riedel Sign Company Inc ....G....... 201 641-9121
Little Ferry (G-5495)
Robden Enterprises Inc ....G....... 973 273-1200
Newark (G-7251)
▲ Roxboro Holdings Inc ....D....... 732 919-3119
Wall Township (G-11365)
S S P Enterprises Inc ....G....... 732 602-7878
Iselin (G-4625)
▲ Sabrimax Corp ....F....... 201 871-0808
Englewood (G-2938)
Salmon Signs ....G....... 856 589-5600
Pitman (G-8748)
▼ Sama Plastics Corp ....E....... 973 239-7200
Cedar Grove (G-1292)
Sign A Rama ....G....... 609 702-1444
Hainesport (G-4077)
Sign A Rama ....G....... 201 489-6969
Hackensack (G-3974)
Sign A Rama ....G....... 973 471-5558
Clifton (G-1718)
Sign Engineers Inc ....G....... 732 382-4224
Colonia (G-1775)
Sign On Inc ....G....... 201 384-7714
Bloomingdale (G-530)
Sign Shoppe Inc ....G....... 856 384-2937
Woodbury (G-12037)
Sign Spec Inc ....D....... 856 663-2292
Elmer (G-2804)
Sign Up Inc ....G....... 201 902-8640
Secaucus (G-9814)
Signal Sign Company LLC ....F....... 973 535-9277
Livingston (G-5541)
Signarama ....G....... 609 465-9400
Cape May Court House (G-1114)
Signs & Custom Metal Inc ....F....... 201 200-0110
Jersey City (G-4809)
Signs of 2000 ....F....... 973 253-1333
Clifton (G-1719)
Signs of Security Inc ....E....... 973 340-8404
Garfield (G-3768)
Sjshore Marketing Ltd Lblty Co ...F.... 609 390-1400
Marmora (G-5959)
Smith Enterprises ....G....... 215 416-9881
Mount Laurel (G-6807)
South Shore Sign Co Inc ....F....... 718 984-5624
Matawan (G-5988)
Spectrum Neon Sign Group LLC ...G.... 856 317-9223
Pennsauken (G-8488)
Speedy Sign-A-Rama..................G....... 973 605-8313
Morristown (G-6701)
Spinningdesigns Inc ....F....... 732 775-7050
Farmingdale (G-3392)
Stephen Swinton Studio Inc ......G....... 908 537-9135
Washington (G-11452)
▲ Stone Graphics ....F....... 732 919-1111
Wall Township (G-11371)
Suburban Sign Co Inc ....E....... 908 862-7222
Linden (G-5433)
Sun Neon Sign and Electric Co ...G.... 856 667-6977
Cherry Hill (G-1417)
Sweet Sign Systems Inc ....G....... 732 521-9300
Jamesburg (G-4677)

T L C Specialties Inc ....F....... 732 244-4225
Toms River (G-10798)
Tally Display Corp......................G....... 973 777-7760
Fairfield (G-3323)
Tdk Associates Corp ....G....... 862 210-8085
Roseland (G-9542)
Tech-Pak Inc ....F....... 201 935-3800
Wood Ridge (G-12007)
Technical Nameplate Corp ....E....... 973 773-4256
Passaic (G-8111)
◆ Testrite Instrument Co Inc .....C....... 201 543-0240
Hackensack (G-3982)
Tlg Signs Inc.............................G....... 609 912-0500
Lawrenceville (G-5244)
Total Image and Sign ....G....... 201 941-2307
Ridgefield (G-9291)
Touch of Class Promotions LLC ...G.... 267 994-0860
Voorhees (G-11296)
Trademarksign ....F....... 848 223-4548
Jackson (G-4667)
Traffic Safety & Equipment Co ...F.... 201 327-6050
Mahwah (G-5783)
▲ Trans World Marketing Corp ...C.... 201 935-5565
East Rutherford (G-2327)
Trukmanns Inc ....E....... 973 538-7718
Cedar Knolls (G-1314)
Two Jays Bingo Supply Inc ....F....... 609 267-4542
Hainesport (G-4080)
Urban Sign & Crane Inc ....G....... 856 691-8388
Vineland (G-11273)
▲ US Propack Inc ....G....... 732 294-4500
Freehold (G-3702)
US Sign and Lighting Svc LLC ....G.... 973 305-8900
Wayne (G-11561)
Vital Signs Medcl Legl Consltn ...F.... 908 537-7857
Asbury (G-70)
Vitillo & Sons Inc ....F....... 732 886-1393
Lakewood (G-5177)
Winemiller Press Inc ....G....... 732 223-0100
Manasquan (G-5843)
Wurz Signsystems LLC ....G....... 856 461-4397
Pennsauken (G-8498)
Yasheel Inc ....G....... 856 275-6812
Sewell (G-9854)
Yates Sign Co Inc ....E....... 732 578-1818
Farmingdale (G-3397)

3995 Burial Caskets

Agoura Hills Group ....G....... 818 888-0400
Cherry Hill (G-1334)
Marchione Industries Inc............F....... 718 317-4900
Lyndhurst (G-5661)

3996 Linoleum & Hard Surface Floor Coverings, NEC

Congoleum Corporation..............D....... 609 584-3601
Trenton (G-10922)
▲ Dyerich Flooring Designs Ltd ...G.... 973 357-0600
Paterson (G-8175)
Evertile Flooring Co Inc ....G....... 973 242-7474
Newark (G-7119)
Locktile Industries Llc ....F....... 888 562-5845
Newark (G-7184)
◆ Mannington Mills Inc ....A....... 856 935-3000
Salem (G-9694)
S Geno Carpet and Flooring ....G....... 215 669-1400
Mount Royal (G-6818)
Takasago Intl Corp USA ....E....... 201 727-4200
Teterboro (G-10693)
Tbs Industrial Flooring Pdts ....G....... 732 899-1486
Point Pleasant Beach (G-8832)

3999 Manufacturing Industries, NEC

(gt) Global Tech Inc....................F....... 732 447-7083
Dayton (G-1950)
5 Star Industries Inc..................F....... 862 255-2040
Kearny (G-4839)
A-Wit Technologies Inc ....G....... 800 985-2948
Williamstown (G-11949)
Absolute Protective Systems ......E....... 732 287-4500
Piscataway (G-8624)
Acadia Scenic Inc ....E....... 201 653-8889
Jersey City (G-4684)
Accurate Screw Machine Corp ....D.... 973 276-0379
Fairfield (G-3133)
◆ Advance International Inc ....E....... 212 213-2229
Matawan (G-5966)
Almetek Industries Inc ....G....... 908 850-9700
Hackettstown (G-3997)

▲ Amaryllis Inc ....G....... 973 635-0500
Chatham (G-1318)
◆ American Consolidation Inc ....D....... 201 438-4351
Carlstadt (G-1123)
American National Red Cross .....E....... 973 797-3300
Fairfield (G-3142)
American Process Systems ....G....... 908 216-6781
Port Murray (G-8880)
Ameritex Industries Corp ....F....... 609 502-0123
Princeton Junction (G-9051)
Amneal Pharmaceuticals Inc .....A....... 908 409-6822
Bridgewater (G-786)
▲ Amneal Pharmaceuticals LLC ...E.... 908 947-3120
Bridgewater (G-788)
Ana Design Corp ....F....... 609 394-0300
Trenton (G-10893)
▲ Animals Etc Inc ....G....... 609 386-8442
Burlington (G-950)
Aqualink LLC ....F....... 201 849-9771
Fort Lee (G-3547)
Arafat Lafi ....G....... 201 854-7300
North Bergen (G-7385)
Artisan Model Mold ....G....... 908 453-3524
Belvidere (G-357)
Artline Heat Transfer Inc ....F....... 973 599-0104
Parsippany (G-7883)
▲ Aura Badge Co ....D....... 856 881-9026
Clayton (G-1524)
Authenticity Brewing LLC ....G....... 862 432-9622
Sparta (G-10379)
Berk Gold Stamping Corporation ...E.... 973 786-6052
Andover (G-45)
▲ Bigflysports Inc ....G....... 201 653-4414
Secaucus (G-9753)
Binex Line Corp ....F....... 201 662-7600
Fort Lee (G-3550)
Bio-Key International Inc............E....... 732 359-1100
Wall Township (G-11322)
Boruch Trading Ltd Lblty Co ......G.... 718 614-9575
Lakewood (G-5063)
BSD Industries Ltd Liability ....G....... 732 534-4341
Lakewood (G-5068)
C Bennett Scopes Inc ....G....... 856 464-6889
Mantua (G-5851)
Cambrdge Inds For Vslly Impred ...G.... 732 247-6668
Somerset (G-9965)
▲ Candle Artisans Incorporated ...E.... 908 689-2000
Washington (G-11443)
Carbone America Scp Division ....G.... 973 334-0700
Boonton (G-545)
◆ Cellunet Manufacturing Compnay ...F.... 609 386-3361
Burlington (G-956)
Cem Industries Inc ....G....... 908 244-8080
Harrison (G-4167)
Central Art & Engineering Inc ....G.... 609 758-5922
Cream Ridge (G-1931)
Cimquest Inc ....D....... 732 699-0400
Branchburg (G-628)
Clover Garden Ctr Ltd Lblty Co ...G.... 856 235-4625
Mount Laurel (G-6748)
Competech Smrtcard Sltions Inc ...G.... 201 256-4184
Englewood Cliffs (G-2963)
Conair Corporation ....C....... 609 426-1300
East Windsor (G-2348)
Connector Mfg Co ....G....... 513 860-4455
Jersey City (G-4717)
▲ Cover Co Inc ....E....... 908 707-9797
Branchburg (G-632)
▲ Creative Display Inc ....G....... 732 918-8010
Neptune (G-6873)
Custom Docks Inc.......................F....... 973 948-3732
Sandyston (G-9699)
▲ Cutting Edge Grower Supply LLC ...G.... 732 905-9220
Howell (G-4536)
Destiny Foundation ....G....... 732 987-9008
Lakewood (G-5083)
Digital Outdoor Advg LLC ....G....... 732 616-2232
Tinton Falls (G-10711)
Distek Inc ....D....... 732 422-7585
North Brunswick (G-7466)
▲ Dlite Products Inc ....G....... 201 444-0822
Wyckoff (G-12109)
Dnp Foods America Ltd Lblty Co ...G.... 201 654-5581
Waldwick (G-11301)
Doosan Heavy Inds Amer LLC ....G.... 201 944-4554
Englewood Cliffs (G-2967)
E-Vents Registration LLC ....F....... 201 722-9221
Westwood (G-11830)
Eaton Corporation ....E....... 609 835-4230
Mount Holly (G-6725)

Emdur Metal Products Inc ....F 856 541-1100
Camden *(G-1061)*

Esd Professional Inc ....G 212 300-7673
Palisades Park *(G-7773)*

F G Clover Company Inc ....G 973 627-1160
Rockaway *(G-9457)*

Fit Fabrication LLC ....G 973 685-7344
Clifton *(G-1621)*

Five Kids Group Inc ....G 732 774-5331
Neptune *(G-6878)*

Fluid Coating Systems Inc ....G 973 767-1028
Garfield *(G-3742)*

▲ Foldtex II Ltd ....E 908 928-0919
Westfield *(G-11797)*

◆ Folica Inc ....E 609 860-8430
Dayton *(G-1963)*

Force Industries LLC ....G 973 332-1532
Butler *(G-1000)*

Fragrance Factory Inc ....G 973 835-2002
Pompton Plains *(G-8864)*

◆ Franklin Mint LLC ....E 800 843-6468
Fort Lee *(G-3559)*

Freeman Technical Sales Inc ....G 908 464-4784
New Providence *(G-7001)*

◆ Fuji Electric Corp America ....D 732 560-9410
Edison *(G-2515)*

G G Tauber Company Inc ....E 800 638-6667
Neptune *(G-6879)*

▲ Galleria Enterprises Inc ....G 646 416-6683
Fairfield *(G-3211)*

▲ General Tools Mfg Co LLC ....G 201 770-1380
Secaucus *(G-9774)*

▲ Gramercy Products Incorporated .....E 212 868-2559
Secaucus *(G-9778)*

Green Globe USA LLC ....G 201 577-4468
Carteret *(G-1256)*

Griffith Electric Sup Co Inc ....D 609 695-6121
Trenton *(G-10937)*

Gwenstone Inc ....G 732 785-2600
Lakewood *(G-5106)*

Hair Depot Limited ....F 973 251-9924
Maplewood *(G-5878)*

Halfway Hounds ....G 201 970-6235
Park Ridge *(G-7852)*

▲ Han Hean U S A Corp ....G 732 494-3256
Edison *(G-2524)*

Harry Shaw Model Maker Inc ....G 609 268-0647
Shamong *(G-9857)*

◆ Hartz Mountain Corporation ....C 800 275-1414
Secaucus *(G-9780)*

Hudson Displays Co ....E 973 623-8255
Newark *(G-7153)*

Hutchinson Industries Inc ....G 609 394-1010
Trenton *(G-10943)*

▲ Hygloss Products Inc ....E 973 458-1700
Wallington *(G-11387)*

Immunogenetics Inc ....D 856 697-1441
Buena *(G-940)*

Industrial Water Institute ....G 609 585-4880
Trenton *(G-10944)*

Inman Mold and Mfg Co ....G 732 381-3033
Springfield *(G-10446)*

▲ Inopak Ltd ....F 973 962-1121
Ringwood *(G-9347)*

▲ Jersey Jack Pinball Inc ....E 732 364-9900
Lakewood *(G-5115)*

JKA Specialties Mfr Inc ....F 609 859-2090
Southampton *(G-10366)*

Joseph C Hansen Company Inc ....G 201 222-1677
Jersey City *(G-4752)*

Kanar Inc ....F 201 933-2800
Carlstadt *(G-1172)*

Klein Distributors Inc ....G 732 446-7632
Burlington *(G-977)*

Krohn Technical Products Inc ....F 201 933-9696
Carlstadt *(G-1179)*

Kudas Industries Inc ....F 412 751-0260
Denville *(G-2043)*

▼ Left-Handed Libra LLC ....F 973 623-1112
Newark *(G-7178)*

Lexi Industries ....F 201 297-7900
Northvale *(G-7534)*

Liquid Iron Industries Inc ....G 856 336-2639
West Berlin *(G-11604)*

Little House Candles Inc ....G 609 758-2996
New Egypt *(G-6985)*

▲ Littlegifts Inc ....F 212 868-2559
Secaucus *(G-9789)*

▲ Look of Love Wigs Inc ....F 908 687-9502
Edison *(G-2553)*

▲ Loving Pets Corporation ....E 609 655-3700
Cranbury *(G-1859)*

Lux Naturals LLC ....G 848 229-2950
Edison *(G-2554)*

Mar-Kal Products Corp ....E 973 783-7155
Carlstadt *(G-1185)*

Massage Chair Inc ....G 732 201-7777
Brick *(G-727)*

◆ McT Dairies Inc ....F 973 258-9600
Millburn *(G-6203)*

McT Manufacturing Inc ....G 877 258-9600
Millburn *(G-6204)*

▲ Merlin Industries Inc ....D 609 807-1000
Hamilton *(G-4116)*

▲ Mfv International Corporation ....G 973 993-1687
Morristown *(G-6686)*

▲ Microelettrica-Usa LLC ....E 973 598-0806
Budd Lake *(G-930)*

▼ Middle East Marketing Group ....G 201 503-0150
Englewood *(G-2926)*

Minniti J Hair Replacement Inc ....G 856 427-9600
Cherry Hill *(G-1395)*

Mountain LLC ....G 908 409-6823
Bridgewater *(G-853)*

My Magic ....G 201 703-1171
Fair Lawn *(G-3113)*

Naomi Pet International Inc ....G 201 660-7918
Northvale *(G-7540)*

Natal Lamp & Shade Corp ....E 201 224-7844
Fort Lee *(G-3578)*

◆ National Christmas Pdts Inc ....E 908 709-4141
Cranford *(G-1918)*

▲ Neilmax Industries Inc ....G 908 756-8800
Edison *(G-2571)*

◆ New Brunswick Lamp Shade Co ....E 732 545-0377
New Brunswick *(G-6952)*

New Jersey Air Products Inc ....F 908 964-9001
Kenilworth *(G-4963)*

▲ Newell Brands Inc ....B 201 610-6600
Hoboken *(G-4468)*

▲ Nova Distributors LLC ....F 908 222-1010
Edison *(G-2580)*

Novelty Hair Goods Co ....G 856 963-5876
Camden *(G-1080)*

Pacent Engineering ....G 914 390-9150
Ocean *(G-7671)*

Palumbo Associates Inc ....F 908 534-2142
Whitehouse Station *(G-11931)*

Peach Boutique LLC ....C 908 351-0739
Elizabeth *(G-2768)*

◆ Peerless Umbrella Co Inc ....C 973 578-4900
Newark *(G-7225)*

Pennock Company ....E 215 492-7900
Pennsauken *(G-8464)*

Pet Salon Inc ....F 609 350-6480
Margate City *(G-5890)*

▲ Pet Salon Inc ....F 609 350-6480
Margate City *(G-5891)*

Peters Laboratories ....F 856 767-4144
Berlin *(G-428)*

Pharmakon Corp ....F 856 829-3161
Cinnaminson *(G-1481)*

Polish Nail ....G 732 627-9799
Middlesex *(G-6139)*

Power Packaging Services Corp ....G 201 261-2566
Paramus *(G-7827)*

Prestige Industries LLC ....E 866 492-2244
Lyndhurst *(G-5673)*

◀ Q10 Products LLC ....F 201 567-9299
Clifton *(G-1702)*

Quallis Brands LLC ....G 862 252-0664
East Orange *(G-2261)*

▲ Rainmen USA Incorporated ....D 201 784-3244
Norwood *(G-7573)*

Rapid Models & Prototypes Inc ....G 856 933-2929
Runnemede *(G-9607)*

Rapsoco Inc ....G 908 977-7321
Elizabeth *(G-2773)*

Razac Products Inc ....G 973 622-3700
Newark *(G-7246)*

Rclc Inc ....F 732 877-1788
Woodbridge *(G-12020)*

◆ Rdo Induction Ltd Liability Co ....G 908 835-7222
Washington *(G-11450)*

Red Ray Manufacturing ....G 908 722-0040
Branchburg *(G-677)*

▲ Riverstone Industries Corp ....G 973 586-2564
Rockaway *(G-9495)*

▲ RSR Electronics Inc ....E 732 381-8777
Rahway *(G-9126)*

◆ S Frankford & Sons Inc ....F 856 222-4134
Mount Laurel *(G-6801)*

▲ Scientific Models Inc ....E 908 464-7070
Berkeley Heights *(G-411)*

Services Equipment Com LLC ....G 973 992-4404
Livingston *(G-5539)*

Shooting Star Inc ....G 908 789-2500
Scotch Plains *(G-9741)*

▲ Skaffles Group Ltd Lblty Co ....G 732 901-2100
Lakewood *(G-5163)*

▲ Sli Production Corp ....E 201 621-4260
Moonachie *(G-6489)*

▲ Smartplay International Inc ....E 609 880-1860
Beverly *(G-454)*

★ Star Soap/Star Candle/Prayer C ......C 201 690-9090
Ridgefield Park *(G-9318)*

Stephen L Feilinger ....E 609 294-1884
Ltl Egg Hbr *(G-5620)*

Steps To Literacy LLC ....E 732 560-8363
Bound Brook *(G-609)*

▼ Strategic Mktg Promotions Inc ....F 845 623-7777
Mahwah *(G-5777)*

◆ Sun Taiyang Co Ltd ....D 201 549-7100
Moonachie *(G-6491)*

▲ Sunshine Bouquet Company ....C 732 274-2900
Dayton *(G-1990)*

Surfs Up Candle & Charm ....G 848 404-9559
Belmar *(G-355)*

Suroma Ltd Liability Company ....G 908 735-7700
Annandale *(G-55)*

Synthetic Grass Surfaces Inc ....G 973 778-9594
Lodi *(G-5579)*

▲ Takara Belmont Usa Inc ....D 732 469-5000
Somerset *(G-10079)*

Tech Art Inc ....F 201 525-0044
Hackensack *(G-3981)*

Technology General Corporation ....F 973 827-8209
Franklin *(G-3609)*

◆ Teluca Inc ....G 973 232-0002
West Orange *(G-11779)*

Ten One Design Ltd Lblty Co ....G 201 474-8232
Montclair *(G-6391)*

This Is It Stageworks LLC ....E 201 653-2699
Jersey City *(G-4820)*

Tom Ponte Model Makers Inc ....G 973 627-5906
Rockaway *(G-9508)*

Tri-Met Industries Inc ....G 908 231-0004
Bridgewater *(G-897)*

Triangle Manufacturing Co ....G 201 962-7433
Upper Saddle River *(G-11147)*

Tropical Expressions Inc ....G 732 899-8680
Point Pleasant Boro *(G-8846)*

◆ Tyco International MGT Co LLC ....E 609 720-4200
Princeton *(G-9038)*

Ultimate Hair World Ltd Lblty ....F 973 622-6900
Bloomfield *(G-521)*

◆ USA Tealight Inc ....F 732 943-2408
Avenel *(G-153)*

Venture Stationers Inc ....E 212 288-7235
Closter *(G-1763)*

Vira Manufacturing Inc ....E 732 771-8269
Perth Amboy *(G-8538)*

▲ Vo-Toys Inc ....E 973 482-8915
Clifton *(G-1736)*

▲ Wg Products Inc ....G 973 256-5999
Totowa *(G-10862)*

Wolf Form Co Inc ....E 201 567-6556
Old Tappan *(G-7736)*

▲ Xpet LLC ....E 973 272-7502
Clifton *(G-1742)*

Zycal Bioceuticals Mfg LLC ....G 888 779-9225
Toms River *(G-10806)*

73 BUSINESS SERVICES

7372 Prepackaged Software

3i Infotech Financial Software ....G 732 710-4444
Edison *(G-2442)*

3i Infotech Inc ....G 732 710-4444
Edison *(G-2443)*

51maps Inc ....G 800 927-5181
Wenonah *(G-11572)*

Able Group Technologies Inc ....G 732 591-9299
Morganville *(G-6579)*

Accelerated Technologies Inc ....G 609 632-0350
Princeton *(G-8899)*

Accely Inc ....F 609 598-1882
Avenel *(G-119)*

Accession Data Systems ....G 973 992-7392
Livingston *(G-5502)*

Acclivity LLC .... E 973 586-2200
Rockaway *(G-9435)*

Ackk Studios LLC .... G 973 876-1327
Bloomfield *(G-489)*

Acqueon Technologies Inc .... G 609 945-3139
Princeton *(G-8900)*

Acrelic Interactive LLC .... G 908 222-2900
Warren *(G-11396)*

Adherence Solutions LLC .... G 800 521-2269
Fairfield *(G-3135)*

Advance Digital Inc .... C 201 459-2808
Jersey City *(G-4686)*

Aim Computer Associates Inc ... G 201 489-3100
Bergenfield *(G-369)*

Airchartercom LLC .... G 212 999-4926
West New York *(G-11735)*

Alaquest International Inc .... F 908 713-9399
Lebanon *(G-5250)*

Alcatel-Lucent USA Inc .... D 908 582-3275
New Providence *(G-6993)*

Aliron International Inc .... E 540 808-1615
South Plainfield *(G-10210)*

Alk Technologies Inc .... C 609 683-0220
Princeton *(G-8906)*

All Solutions Inc .... E 973 535-9100
Livingston *(G-5503)*

Alloy Software Inc .... F 973 661-9700
Bloomfield *(G-490)*

Almond Branch Inc .... E 973 728-3479
West Milford *(G-11724)*

Alt Shift Creative LLC .... G 609 619-0009
Flanders *(G-3399)*

Altibase Incorporated .... G 888 837-7333
Mahwah *(G-5713)*

Amber Road Inc .... C 201 935-8588
East Rutherford *(G-2270)*

American Soft Solutions Corp .... G 732 272-0052
Morganville *(G-6582)*

Amerindia Technologies Inc ...... E 609 664-2224
Cranbury *(G-1808)*

Anju Clinplus LLC .... F 732 764-6969
Bound Brook *(G-600)*

Antenna Software Inc .... E 201 217-3824
Jersey City *(G-4694)*

Aone Touch Inc .... G 732 261-6841
Bordentown *(G-575)*

Aplnow LLC .... G 732 223-5575
Manasquan *(G-5828)*

Appex Innovation Solutions LLC .... G 215 313-3332
Princeton *(G-8908)*

Apprentice Fs Inc .... E 973 960-0875
Jersey City *(G-4695)*

Aptimized LLC .... G 203 733-2868
Cedar Grove *(G-1267)*

Ariba Inc .... E 908 333-3400
Bridgewater *(G-793)*

Artezio LLC .... G 609 786-2435
Princeton *(G-8912)*

Astrix Software Technology ...... F 732 661-0400
Red Bank *(G-9221)*

Athletic Organizational Aids ..... E 201 652-1485
Midland Park *(G-6170)*

Auraplayer USA Inc .... F 617 879-9013
West Orange *(G-11760)*

Aurora Information Systems ...... G 856 596-4180
Cherry Hill *(G-1340)*

Automated Office Inc .... G 888 362-7638
Cherry Hill *(G-1341)*

Automated Resource Group Inc .... D 201 391-8357
Montvale *(G-6397)*

Avada Software LLC .... F 973 697-1043
Rockaway *(G-9445)*

Avaya Inc .... C 732 852-2030
Lincroft *(G-5310)*

◆ Avaya World Services Inc ..... E 908 953-6000
Morristown *(G-6644)*

Avyakta It Services LLC .... F 609 790-7517
East Windsor *(G-2345)*

Aztec Software Associates Inc ... E 973 258-0011
Springfield *(G-10429)*

Bandemar Networks LLC .... G 732 991-5112
East Brunswick *(G-2128)*

Basic Commerce & Industries ... G 609 482-3740
Hammonton *(G-4130)*

Basys Inc .... G 732 616-5276
Mount Laurel *(G-6740)*

Bavelle Tech Sltions Ltd Lblty ... F 973 992-8086
East Hanover *(G-2195)*

Bdiplus Inc .... G 347 597-2539
Basking Ridge *(G-176)*

Beseech Ltd Liability Company ... G 908 461-7888
Belford *(G-281)*

Bio-Key International Inc .... E 732 359-1100
Wall Township *(G-11322)*

Biostat Inc .... G 201 541-5688
Englewood *(G-2883)*

Blue Line Planning Inc .... G 609 577-0100
Crosswicks *(G-1949)*

Blue Marlin Systems Inc .... D 973 722-0816
Long Valley *(G-5608)*

Bluebird Auto Rentl Systems LP ... E 973 989-2423
Dover *(G-2076)*

BMC Software Inc .... G 703 761-0400
Woodcliff Lake *(G-12048)*

Brainstorm Software Corp .... G 856 234-4945
Moorestown *(G-6510)*

Brittingham Sftwr Design Inc ..... G 908 832-2691
Califon *(G-1031)*

Burgiss Group LLC .... D 201 427-9600
Hoboken *(G-4444)*

Business Dev Solutions Inc .... G 856 433-8005
Cherry Hill *(G-1350)*

Business Software Applications ... G 908 500-9980
Somerset *(G-9964)*

Buzzboard Inc .... G 415 906-6934
Lyndhurst *(G-5643)*

C Systems LLC .... F 732 338-9347
Edison *(G-2472)*

Cape Atlantic Software LLC ...... G 609 442-1331
Egg Harbor Township *(G-2682)*

Cardinal Health Systems Inc .... B 732 537-6544
Somerset *(G-9966)*

Catalogic Software Inc .... C 201 249-8980
Woodcliff Lake *(G-12052)*

Ce Tech LLC .... G 908 229-3803
Whitehouse Station *(G-11919)*

Channel Logistics LLC .... F 856 614-5441
Camden *(G-1052)*

Chisholm Technologies Inc .... G 732 859-5578
Shrewsbury *(G-9886)*

Circleblack Inc .... F 800 315-1241
Kingston *(G-5007)*

Clientsrver Tech Solutions LLC ... G 732 710-4495
Iselin *(G-4605)*

Cloudageit Ltd Liability Co .... G 888 205-4128
North Brunswick *(G-7463)*

Co-Co Collaborative LLC .... G 917 685-5547
Short Hills *(G-9867)*

Cognizant Tech Solutions Corp ... D 201 801-0233
Teaneck *(G-10625)*

Coles and Blenman Network LLC ... G 973 432-7041
Bloomfield *(G-496)*

Com Tek Wrkplace Solutions LLC ... F 973 927-6814
Lyndhurst *(G-5649)*

Commvault Americas Inc .... G 888 746-3849
Tinton Falls *(G-10708)*

Commvault Systems Inc .... C 732 870-4000
Tinton Falls *(G-10709)*

Compco Analytical Inc .... G 201 641-3936
Little Ferry *(G-5480)*

Comprehensive Healthcare Systm ... D 732 362-2000
Edison *(G-2482)*

Computech Applications LLC ..... G 201 261-5251
Oradell *(G-7742)*

Computer Doc Associates Inc ... D 908 647-4445
Martinsville *(G-5962)*

Computer Sources .... G 201 791-9443
Elmwood Park *(G-2817)*

Continuity Logic LLC .... D 866 321-5079
Fairfield *(G-3174)*

Corner Stone Software Inc .... G 732 938-5229
Howell *(G-4534)*

Criterion Software LLC .... F 908 754-1166
Freehold *(G-3659)*

Csf Corporation .... E 732 302-2222
Somerset *(G-9979)*

Custom Business Software LLC ... G 732 534-9557
Freehold *(G-3660)*

Custom Workflow Solutions LLC ... F 917 647-9222
Florham Park *(G-3499)*

Cybage Software Inc .... G 848 219-1221
Princeton *(G-8926)*

Cyberextrudercom Inc .... G 973 623-7900
Wayne *(G-11491)*

Cygate Sftwr & Consulting LLC ... G 732 452-1881
Edison *(G-2490)*

Cypher Insurance Software .... G 856 216-0575
Stratford *(G-10505)*

Daddy Donkey Labs LLC .... G 646 461-4677
Fair Haven *(G-3079)*

Datamotion Inc .... E 973 455-1245
Florham Park *(G-3500)*

Datayog Inc .... F 714 253-6558
Jersey City *(G-4721)*

Dcm Group Inc .... G 732 516-1173
Newark *(G-7097)*

Dell Software Inc .... E 201 556-4600
Rochelle Park *(G-9422)*

Determine Inc .... E 800 608-0809
Cherry Hill *(G-1356)*

Diacritech LLC .... A 732 238-1157
Jersey City *(G-4727)*

Direct Computer Resources Inc ... E 201 848-0018
Franklin Lakes *(G-3620)*

Dma Data Industries Inc .... G 201 444-5733
Wyckoff *(G-12110)*

Docbox Solutions Ltd Lblty Co ... G 201 650-0970
Montclair *(G-6363)*

Double Check .... G 973 984-2229
Morris Plains *(G-6603)*

Dun & Bradstreet Inc .... E 973 921-5500
Short Hills *(G-9868)*

Dymax Systems Inc .... F 732 918-2424
Neptune *(G-6874)*

Easy Analytic Software Inc .... G 856 931-5780
Bellmawr *(G-331)*

Easy Soft Inc .... F 732 398-1001
North Brunswick *(G-7467)*

Ebaotech Inc USA .... G 917 977-1145
Jersey City *(G-4730)*

Ebic Prparedness Solutions LLC ... G 719 244-6209
Leonia *(G-5288)*

Eclearview Technologies Inc .... G 732 695-6999
Ocean *(G-7662)*

Edison Design Group Inc .... G 732 993-3341
Monroe *(G-6321)*

Educhat Inc .... G 201 871-8649
Englewood *(G-2900)*

Educloud Inc .... E 201 944-0445
Cliffside Park *(G-1538)*

Effexoft Inc .... G 732 221-3642
Somerset *(G-9984)*

Elevate Hr Inc .... F 973 917-3230
Parsippany *(G-7934)*

Enertia LLC .... G 856 330-4767
Pennsauken *(G-8418)*

Enforsys Inc .... E 973 515-8126
Millburn *(G-6197)*

Enterprise Services LLC .... D 609 259-9400
Princeton *(G-8941)*

Eroomsystem Technologies Inc ... F 732 730-0116
Lakewood *(G-5093)*

Espertech Inc .... F 973 577-6406
Wayne *(G-11498)*

Ezcom Software Inc .... E 201 731-1800
Englewood *(G-2904)*

Ezrirx LLC .... G 718 502-6610
Lakewood *(G-5096)*

Factonomy Inc .... F 201 848-7812
Wyckoff *(G-12111)*

Fieldview Cfd Inc .... G 425 460-8284
Rutherford *(G-9620)*

First Internet Systems .... F 201 991-1889
North Arlington *(G-7372)*

First Mountain Consulting .... G 973 325-8480
West Orange *(G-11767)*

Fis Avantgard LLC .... G 732 530-9303
Tinton Falls *(G-10717)*

Fis Data Systems Inc .... E 201 945-1774
Ridgefield *(G-9261)*

Fis Financial Systems LLC .... D 856 784-7230
Voorhees *(G-11285)*

Flexicious LLC .... G 646 340-5066
Jersey City *(G-4735)*

Forge Ahead LLC .... G 908 346-4794
Skillman *(G-9920)*

Foundation Software Inc .... G 908 359-0588
Belle Mead *(G-286)*

Four Bros Ventures Inc .... G 732 890-9469
East Brunswick *(G-2146)*

Foursconsulting Ltd Lblty Co ..... G 732 599-4324
South Plainfield *(G-10261)*

Freyr Inc .... C 908 483-7958
Princeton *(G-8952)*

Frith Group .... G 732 281-8343
Brick *(G-718)*

Fusar Technologies Inc .... G 201 563-0189
Kearny *(G-4856)*

Genexosome Technologies Inc ... F 646 762-4517
Freehold *(G-3667)*

SIC

Genomesafe LLC	G	203 676-3752	West Orange (G-11768)
Gerbino Computer Systems Inc	G	201 342-8240	Hackensack (G-3922)
GL Consulting Inc	E	201 938-0200	Jersey City (G-4743)
Global IDS Inc	D	609 683-1066	Princeton (G-8955)
Gray Hair Software Inc	E	866 507-9999	Mount Laurel (G-6764)
Greycell Labs Inc	E	732 444-0123	Edison (G-2523)
Gwf Associates LLC	E	732 933-8780	Eatontown (G-2395)
Harms Software Inc	D	973 402-9500	Parsippany (G-7959)
Healthper Inc	G	888 257-1804	Princeton (G-8958)
Healthstar Communications Inc	E	201 560-5370	Mahwah (G-5746)
Hozric LLC	G	908 420-8821	Green Brook (G-3861)
HP Enterprise	F	908 898-4728	Berkeley Heights (G-400)
Hr Acuity LLC	F	888 598-0161	Florham Park (G-3511)
Hue Box LLC	G	908 904-9501	Bridgewater (G-831)
I Physician Hub	D	732 274-0155	Monmouth Junction (G-6292)
I-Exceed Tech Solutions Inc	G	917 693-3207	Princeton (G-8960)
▼ Image Access Corp	E	201 342-7878	Rockleigh (G-9519)
Immedis Inc	F	212 239-2625	Iselin (G-4611)
Incentx LLC	G	302 202-2894	Lakewood (G-5112)
Indotronix International Corp	G	609 750-0700	Plainsboro (G-8790)
Innovative Sftwr Solutions Inc	D	856 910-9190	Maple Shade (G-5864)
Innovi Mobile LLC	F	646 588-0165	Millburn (G-6200)
Inspire Works Inc	F	908 730-7447	Florham Park (G-3513)
Intangible Labs Inc	F	917 375-1301	Hoboken (G-4457)
Integrate Tech Inc	G	201 693-5625	Upper Saddle River (G-11141)
Integration International Inc	E	973 796-2300	Parsippany (G-7962)
Integration Partners-Ny Corp	B	973 871-2100	Parsippany (G-7963)
Intellect Design Arena Inc	F	732 769-1037	Piscataway (G-8680)
Interactive Advisory Software	E	770 951-2929	Egg Harbor Township (G-2685)
International Bus Mchs Corp	E	201 307-5136	Park Ridge (G-7853)
Interntnal Digital Systems Inc	F	201 983-7700	Fort Lee (G-3564)
Intrinsiq Spclty Solutions Inc	E	973 251-2039	Livingston (G-5516)
Invessence Inc	G	201 977-1955	Chatham (G-1322)
Ipjukebox Ltd Liability Co	G	201 286-4535	Newark (G-7158)
It Worqs LLC	E	732 494-0009	Metuchen (G-6063)
J-Tech Creations Inc	G	201 944-2968	Fort Lee (G-3565)
Junganew LLC	G	201 832-0892	Rutherford (G-9625)
Juniper Networks Inc	D	908 947-4436	Bridgewater (G-839)
Justice Laboratory Software	G	973 586-8551	Denville (G-2042)
Kaizen Technologies Inc	E	732 452-9555	Edison (G-2545)
Kingster LLC	G	310 951-5127	Paramus (G-7813)
Kittyhawk Digital LLC	G	269 767-8399	Emerson (G-2866)
Kronos Saashr Inc	E	978 250-9800	Branchburg (G-653)
Labvantage Solutions Inc	E	908 707-4100	Somerset (G-10013)
Lattice Incorporated	F	856 910-1166	Pennsauken (G-8450)

Limosys LLC	E	212 222-4433	Englewood Cliffs (G-2983)
Link2consult Inc	F	888 522-0902	Fort Lee (G-3568)
Liquid Holdings Group Inc	D	212 293-1836	Hoboken (G-4464)
Lm Matrix Solutions LLC	G	908 756-7952	Bridgewater (G-846)
Local Wisdom Inc	E	609 269-2320	Lambertville (G-5194)
Lumeta Corporation	E	732 357-3500	Somerset (G-10019)
M + P International Inc	E	973 239-3005	Verona (G-11170)
Machine Atomated Ctrl Tech LLC	E	732 921-8935	Piscataway (G-8685)
Majesco	G	973 461-5200	Morristown (G-6684)
Markov Processes International	E	908 608-1558	Summit (G-10539)
Marlabs Incorporated	D	732 694-1000	Piscataway (G-8687)
Maxisit Inc	C	732 494-2005	Metuchen (G-6065)
▲ Medical Transcription Billing	F	732 873-5133	Somerset (G-10027)
Megaplex Software Inc	G	908 647-3273	Warren (G-11421)
Melillo Consulting Inc	E	732 563-8400	Somerset (G-10028)
Mentor Graphics Corporation	C	908 604-0800	Bedminster (G-274)
Microsoft Corporation	G	732 476-5600	Iselin (G-4617)
Microsoft Corporation	G	908 809-7320	Bridgewater (G-852)
Microtelecom Ltd Liability Co	G	866 676-5679	Fort Lee (G-3573)
Microwize Technology Inc	F	800 955-0321	Paramus (G-7820)
Millennium Info Tech Inc	D	609 750-7120	Princeton (G-8979)
Mind-Alliance Systems LLC	G	212 920-1911	Livingston (G-5526)
Mistras Group Inc	C	609 716-4000	Princeton Junction (G-9062)
Moblty Inc	E	973 535-3600	Livingston (G-5527)
Modelware Inc	F	732 264-3020	Holmdel (G-4508)
Montgomery Investment Tech	G	610 688-8111	Cinnaminson (G-1475)
Mosaic Golf LLC	G	201 906-6136	Hoboken (G-4467)
Mplayer Entertainment LLC	E	302 229-3034	Cherry Hill (G-1396)
Ms Health Software Corp	G	908 850-5564	Hackettstown (G-4028)
MSI Technologies LLC	F	973 263-0080	Parsippany (G-7979)
Mtbc Acquisition Corp	G	732 873-5133	Somerset (G-10033)
Mtbc Health Inc	G	732 873-5133	Somerset (G-10034)
Mtbc Practice Management Corp	C	732 873-5133	Somerset (G-10035)
Munipol Systems	F	856 985-2929	Marlton (G-5942)
Museami Inc	F	609 917-3000	North Brunswick (G-7478)
Mvn Usa Inc	G	732 817-1400	Holmdel (G-4510)
Nb Ventures Inc	C	732 382-6565	Clark (G-1509)
Nconnex Inc	G	413 658-5582	New Brunswick (G-6950)
Netcom Systems Inc	E	732 393-6100	Edison (G-2572)
Netx Information Systems Inc	F	609 298-9118	Long Beach Township (G-5592)
New Venture Partners LLC	A	908 464-8131	New Providence (G-7013)
Ngenious Solutions Inc	G	732 873-3385	Piscataway (G-8696)
Nicomac Systems Inc	G	201 871-0916	Norwood (G-7570)
Nlyte Software Americas Ltd	G	650 561-8200	Edison (G-2576)
Nlyte Software Inc	E	732 395-6920	Edison (G-2577)

Nogpo Inc	F	908 642-3545	Basking Ridge (G-193)
◆ Nokia of America Corporation	A	908 582-3275	New Providence (G-7014)
Northwind Ventures Inc	G	917 509-1964	Vernon (G-11162)
Noshpeak LLC	F	978 631-7662	Bloomfield (G-512)
Novega Venture Partners Inc	G	732 528-2600	Holmdel (G-4511)
Nxlevel Inc	E	609 483-6900	Lambertville (G-5195)
OBagel Hoboken Ltd Lblty Co	G	201 683-8599	Hoboken (G-4470)
Objectif Lune LLC	G	973 780-0100	Bloomfield (G-514)
Objectif Lune LLC	G	203 878-7206	Bloomfield (G-515)
Objecutive Inc	F	201 242-1522	Fort Lee (G-3579)
Oli Systems Inc	E	973 539-4996	Cedar Knolls (G-1313)
Onco Inc	F	732 292-7460	Wall Township (G-11359)
One Source Solutions LLC	G	732 536-0578	Freehold (G-3685)
Ontimeworks LLC	F	800 689-3568	New Providence (G-7015)
Open Solutions Inc	G	856 424-0150	Cherry Hill (G-1403)
Optherium Labs Ou	G	516 253-1777	Holmdel (G-4512)
Oracle America Inc	D	732 623-4821	Edison (G-2584)
Oracle America Inc	D	609 750-0640	East Rutherford (G-2307)
Oracle Corporation	C	908 547-6200	Bridgewater (G-860)
Oracle Corporation	B	201 842-7000	East Rutherford (G-2308)
Orangehrm Inc	E	914 458-4254	Secaucus (G-9795)
Os33 Services Corp	G	866 796-0310	Iselin (G-4620)
Our Team Fitness LLC	G	848 208-5047	Oceanport (G-7705)
◆ Output Services Group Inc	E	201 871-1100	Ridgefield Park (G-9314)
Oxford Biochronometrics LLC	G	201 755-5932	Montclair (G-6380)
Pace Business Solutions Inc	E	908 451-0355	Manahawkin (G-5795)
Pai Services LLC	C	856 231-4667	Mount Laurel (G-6787)
Parabole LLC	G	609 917-8479	Monmouth Junction (G-6299)
Pario Group LLC	G	732 906-2302	Edison (G-2586)
Patientstar LLC	F	856 722-0808	Mount Laurel (G-6788)
Paylocity Holding Corporation	B	908 917-3027	Springfield (G-10458)
Pds Prclnical Data Systems Inc	F	973 398-2800	Mount Arlington (G-6717)
Picture Window Software LLC	G	908 362-4000	Blairstown (G-487)
Pinsonault Associates LLC	E	800 372-9009	Parsippany (G-7994)
Pjm Software Inc	E	973 330-0405	Clifton (G-1693)
Planet Associates Inc	E	201 693-8700	Park Ridge (G-7858)
Plescia & Company Inc	F	856 793-0137	Marlton (G-5947)
Polaris Consulting & Svcs Ltd	F	732 590-8151	Jersey City (G-4785)
Polysystems Inc	G	312 332-5670	Cherry Hill (G-1410)
Predictive Analytcs Dcision	G	973 541-7020	Parsippany (G-8000)
Primepoint LLC	E	609 298-7373	Westampton (G-11789)
Princeton Blue Inc	E	908 369-0961	Princeton (G-8998)
Priority-Software US LLC	G	973 586-2200	Rockaway (G-9490)
Promia Incorporated	G	609 252-1850	Princeton (G-9009)
Proscape Technologies Inc	E	215 441-0300	Hillsborough (G-4347)

Ptc Inc F 973 631-6195 Morristown *(G-6696)*

Qad Inc C 856 273-1717 Mount Laurel *(G-6797)*

Qcom Inc E 732 772-0990 Freehold *(G-3695)*

Qellus LLC G 856 761-6575 Mount Laurel *(G-6798)*

Quadramed Corporation E 732 751-0400 Eatontown *(G-2418)*

Quarterspot Inc F 917 647-9170 Wayne *(G-11545)*

Radix M I S G 973 707-2121 Bloomfield *(G-516)*

Ramco Systems Corporation E 609 620-4800 Princeton *(G-9012)*

Rbs Intrntonal Direct Mktg LLC G 856 663-2500 Cherry Hill *(G-1413)*

Re Systems Group Inc G 201 883-1572 Westwood *(G-11842)*

Real Soft Inc A 609 409-3636 Monmouth Junction *(G-6308)*

Red Dash Media LLC G 732 579-2396 Piscataway *(G-8704)*

Red Oak Software Inc F 973 316-6064 Mountain Lakes *(G-6826)*

Redi-Data Inc F 973 227-4380 Fairfield *(G-3299)*

▲ Redi-Direct Marketing Inc B 973 808-4500 Fairfield *(G-3300)*

Regenus Ctr Core Therapies LLC G 862 295-1620 Florham Park *(G-3522)*

Relational Architects Inc E 201 420-0400 Hoboken *(G-4478)*

Relational Security Corp E 201 875-3456 Secaucus *(G-9803)*

Relatnship Capitl Partners Inc F 908 962-4881 Short Hills *(G-9876)*

Relayware Inc F 201 433-3331 Jersey City *(G-4799)*

Relpro Inc G 908 962-4881 Short Hills *(G-9877)*

Remote Landlord Systems LLC G 732 534-4445 Lakewood *(G-5154)*

Rey Consulting Inc F 201 337-0051 Oakland *(G-7643)*

Rhodium Software Inc G 848 248-2906 Dayton *(G-1986)*

Robokiller LLC E 723 838-1901 South Amboy *(G-10140)*

RSD America Inc F 201 996-1000 Teaneck *(G-10649)*

Rx Trade Zone Inc G 833 933-6600 Edison *(G-2601)*

Sage Software Inc D 856 231-4667 Mount Laurel *(G-6802)*

Saksoft Inc C 201 451-4609 Jersey City *(G-4803)*

Samsung SDS Globl Scl Amer Inc E 201 229-4456 Ridgefield Park *(G-9315)*

Scalable Systems Inc E 732 993-4320 Piscataway *(G-8709)*

Scimar Technologies LLC G 609 208-1796 Allentown *(G-31)*

Scivantage Inc D 646 452-0001 Jersey City *(G-4806)*

Scottline LLC E 732 534-3123 Piscataway *(G-8710)*

Sensiple Inc F 732 283-0499 Iselin *(G-4626)*

Sfp Software Inc G 856 235-7778 Mount Laurel *(G-6805)*

Shiva Software Group Inc E 973 691-5475 Flanders *(G-3418)*

Sierra Communication Intl LLC G 866 462-8292 Morristown *(G-6700)*

Signify Fincl Solutions LLC E 862 930-4682 Parsippany *(G-8015)*

Simon & Schuster Inc E 973 656-6000 Parsippany *(G-8016)*

Simtronics Corporation F 732 747-0322 Little Silver *(G-5500)*

Sirma Group Inc B 646 357-3067 Jersey City *(G-4811)*

Sitetracker Inc F 551 486-2087 Montclair *(G-6389)*

Smartlinx Solutions LLC D 732 385-5507 Iselin *(G-4629)*

Software Developers LLC E 888 315-6652 Lakewood *(G-5165)*

Software Practices and Tech G 908 464-2923 Summit *(G-10548)*

Software Services & Solutions F 203 630-2000 Lawrence Township *(G-5220)*

Specialty Systems Inc E 732 341-1011 Toms River *(G-10794)*

Sphinx Software Inc G 609 275-5085 Plainsboro *(G-8803)*

SRS Software LLC E 201 802-1300 Montvale *(G-6435)*

▲ Ssam Sports Inc G 917 553-0596 Allendale *(G-15)*

Ssam Sports Inc G 917 553-0596 Allendale *(G-16)*

Stealthbits Technologies Inc D 201 301-9328 Hawthorne *(G-4245)*

Stellar Data Recovery G 877 778-6087 Metuchen *(G-6074)*

Storis Inc C 888 478-6747 Mount Arlington *(G-6719)*

Storm City Entertainment Inc F 856 885-6902 Sicklerville *(G-9916)*

Streamserve Inc E 781 863-1510 Asbury Park *(G-82)*

Strikeforce Technologies Inc G 732 661-9641 Edison *(G-2621)*

Strivr Inc G 973 216-7379 Livingston *(G-5542)*

Structured Healthcare MGT Inc E 201 569-3290 Englewood *(G-2945)*

Sunbird Software Inc D 732 993-4476 Somerset *(G-10077)*

Sunrise Intl Educatn Inc D 917 525-0272 North Brunswick *(G-7489)*

Supply Chain Technologies LLC G 856 206-9849 Shrewsbury *(G-9903)*

Surround Technologies LLC G 973 743-1277 Bloomfield *(G-520)*

Swapshub Company Inc G 732 529-4813 Piscataway *(G-8721)*

Swce Inc E 908 766-5695 Bernardsville *(G-444)*

Sybase Inc D 973 537-5700 Parsippany *(G-8023)*

T N T Information Systems G 609 799-9488 Plainsboro *(G-8804)*

Tab Networks G 201 746-0067 Woodcliff Lake *(G-12066)*

Taptask LLC G 201 294-2371 Clifton *(G-1730)*

Taxstream LLC D 201 610-0390 Hoboken *(G-4484)*

Tech Brains Solutions Inc E 732 952-0552 Somerset *(G-10083)*

Technovision Inc E 732 381-0200 Metuchen *(G-6077)*

Think Big Solutions Inc G 732 968-0211 Princeton Junction *(G-9068)*

Think Big Solutions Inc G 609 716-7343 Princeton *(G-9033)*

Third Wave Bus Systems LLC E 201 703-2100 Wayne *(G-11557)*

Thomson Reuters Corporation F 973 662-3070 Nutley *(G-7595)*

Total Cover It LLC G 973 342-4623 South Orange *(G-10202)*

Total Reliance LLC F 732 640-5079 Dayton *(G-1993)*

Transportation Tech Svcs Inc E 201 335-0238 Mahwah *(G-5784)*

Trendmark LLC G 551 226-7973 Princeton *(G-9035)*

Trisys Inc G 973 360-2300 Florham Park *(G-3523)*

Tropaion Inc G 908 654-3870 Springfield *(G-10469)*

True Influence LLC F 888 223-1586 Princeton *(G-9036)*

Truefort Inc E 201 766-2023 Weehawken *(G-11571)*

Tunnel Networks Inc G 609 414-9799 East Windsor *(G-2363)*

Turbot Hq Inc F 973 922-0297 Maplewood *(G-5887)*

Twinpod Inc G 908 758-5858 Princeton *(G-9037)*

U S Tech Solutions Inc D 201 524-9600 Jersey City *(G-4824)*

Ubertesters Inc F 201 203-7903 Ridgewood *(G-9333)*

Unicorn Group Inc D 973 360-5904 Fairfield *(G-3334)*

Unicorn Group Inc C 973 360-0688 Florham Park *(G-3525)*

Uniken Inc G 917 324-0399 Chatham *(G-1331)*

Uniphy Health Holdings LLC E 844 586-4749 Newark *(G-7307)*

Universal Business Automation G 973 575-3568 Montville *(G-6448)*

US Software Group Inc E 732 361-4636 South Plainfield *(G-10337)*

Utah Intermediate Holding Corp C 856 787-2700 Mount Laurel *(G-6810)*

Valuemomentum Inc D 908 755-0025 Piscataway *(G-8734)*

Vantage Business Systems Inc G 609 625-7020 Mays Landing *(G-6000)*

Varsity Software Inc G 609 309-9955 Lawrenceville *(G-5245)*

Venture App LLC G 908 644-3985 Summit *(G-10553)*

Vertican Technologies Inc G 800 435-7257 Fairfield *(G-3342)*

Vibgyor Solutions Inc G 609 750-9158 Princeton Junction *(G-9069)*

Visionware Systems Inc F 609 924-0800 Skillman *(G-9928)*

Vst Consulting Inc D 732 404-0025 Iselin *(G-4635)*

▲ Vu Sound Incorporated F 215 990-2864 Lumberton *(G-5638)*

Vyral Systems Inc G 201 321-2488 Hawthorne *(G-4251)*

Wizcom Corporation E 609 750-0601 Princeton Junction *(G-9070)*

Wizdata Systems Inc F 973 975-4113 Parsippany *(G-8041)*

Workwave LLC F 866 794-1658 Holmdel *(G-4516)*

World Software Corporation E 201 444-3228 Glen Rock *(G-3836)*

X-Factor Cmmnctons Hldings Inc G 877 741-3727 Northvale *(G-7554)*

Xanthus Inc G 973 643-0920 Newark *(G-7317)*

Xchange Software Inc G 732 444-4943 Iselin *(G-4636)*

Xchange Software Inc E 732 444-6666 Parlin *(G-7869)*

Yeghen Computer System F 732 996-5500 Ocean *(G-7687)*

Zoluu LLC G 862 686-1774 Fair Lawn *(G-3131)*

Zultner & Company F 609 452-0216 Princeton *(G-9045)*

Zwivel LLC E 844 499-4835 Paramus *(G-7845)*

Zycus Inc E 609 799-5664 Princeton *(G-9046)*

S I C

76 MISCELLANEOUS REPAIR SERVICES

7692 Welding Repair

34 Welding LLC G 973 440-0116 Landing *(G-5199)*

A 1 Fencing Inc F 908 527-1066 Elizabeth *(G-2704)*

Alba Translations CPA G 973 340-1130 Lodi *(G-5551)*

Atlas Enterprise F 908 561-1144 South Plainfield *(G-10222)*

Auto Tig Welding Fabricating G 973 839-8877 Pompton Lakes *(G-8850)*

B L White Welding & Steel Co G 973 684-4111 Paterson *(G-8144)*

Blue Light Welding & Fabg LLC G 856 629-5891 Williamstown *(G-11953)*

Bluewater Industries Inc F 609 427-1012 Dennisville *(G-2027)*

BR Welding Inc F 732 363-8253 Howell *(G-4532)*

Browns Welding Service G 732 988-9530 Neptune *(G-6868)*

C A Spalding Company E 267 550-9000 Moorestown *(G-6511)*

Chizzys Service Center G 201 641-7222 Little Ferry *(G-5476)*

CMI-Promex Inc ....F 856 351-1000
  Pedricktown *(G-8346)*

Creative Machining Systems ....F 609 586-3932
  Trenton *(G-10925)*

D J B Welding Inc ....G 732 657-7478
  Jackson *(G-4649)*

D K Tool & Die Welding Group ....E 908 241-7600
  Roselle Park *(G-9582)*

D N D Corp ....G 908 637-4343
  Great Meadows *(G-3854)*

Edward Kurth and Son Inc ....E 856 227-5252
  Sewell *(G-9840)*

Elmco Two Inc ....G 856 365-2244
  Camden *(G-1060)*

Eme Electrical Contractors ....G 973 228-6608
  Caldwell *(G-1023)*

Ferry Machine Corp ....E 201 641-9191
  Little Ferry *(G-5485)*

Folgore Mobil Welding Inc ....E 732 541-2974
  Carteret *(G-1254)*

Frank E Ganter Inc ....G 856 692-2218
  Vineland *(G-11219)*

Garden State Welding LLC ....G 973 857-0792
  Verona *(G-11168)*

Ironbound Welding Inc ....G 973 589-3128
  Newark *(G-7162)*

J D Machine Parts Inc ....F 856 691-8430
  Vineland *(G-11236)*

J P Rotella Co Inc ....F 973 942-2559
  Haledon *(G-4083)*

John B Horay Welding ....G 856 336-2154
  West Berlin *(G-11601)*

Js Welding LLC ....G 973 442-2202
  Hackettstown *(G-4014)*

K H Machine Works ....G 201 867-2338
  North Bergen *(G-7412)*

Kt Welding ....G 908 862-7370
  Linden *(G-5371)*

Laurelton Welding Service Inc ....G 732 899-6348
  Point Pleasant Beach *(G-8827)*

Lodi Welding Co Inc ....G 908 852-8367
  Hackettstown *(G-4018)*

Louis Iron Works Inc ....G 973 624-2700
  Newark *(G-7186)*

Lusotech LLC ....G 973 332-3861
  Newark *(G-7190)*

M & M Welding & Steel Fabg ....G 908 647-6060
  Stirling *(G-10493)*

Machine Plus Inc ....G 973 839-8884
  Haskell *(G-4199)*

McAlister Welding & Fabg ....F 856 740-3890
  Glassboro *(G-3815)*

Micheller & Son Hydraulics Inc ....F 908 687-1545
  Roselle *(G-9566)*

Oceanview Marine Welding LLC ....G 609 624-9669
  Ocean View *(G-7704)*

▲ Orgo-Thermit Inc ....E 732 657-5781
  Manchester *(G-5847)*

P K Welding LLC ....F 908 928-1002
  Garwood *(G-3789)*

Pabst Enterprises Equipment Co ....E 908 353-2880
  Elizabeth *(G-2766)*

Pennetta & Sons ....E 201 420-1693
  Jersey City *(G-4781)*

Peter Garafano & Son Inc ....E 973 278-0350
  Paterson *(G-8282)*

Pmje Welding LLC ....G 973 685-7344
  Clifton *(G-1694)*

Precision Welding Machine ....G 609 625-1465
  Mays Landing *(G-5998)*

Reuther Engineering ....F 973 485-5800
  Edison *(G-2597)*

Ricklyn Co Inc ....G 908 689-6770
  Columbia *(G-1797)*

Serious Welding & Mech LLC ....F 732 698-7478
  South River *(G-10357)*

Sine Tru Tool Company Inc ....G 732 591-1100
  Marlboro *(G-5915)*

Specialty Measures ....G 609 882-6071
  Ewing *(G-3066)*

Stecher Dave Welding & Fabg Sp ....G 856 467-3558
  Swedesboro *(G-10610)*

Sulzer Pump Services (us) Inc ....E 856 542-5046
  Bridgeport *(G-747)*

Union City Whirlpool Repair ....G 908 428-9146
  Union City *(G-11132)*

Vep Manufacturing ....F 732 657-0666
  Jackson *(G-4668)*

▲ Vermes Machine Co Inc ....E 856 642-9300
  Moorestown *(G-6575)*

W W Manufacturing Co Inc ....F 856 451-5700
  Bridgeton *(G-777)*

Wel-Fab Inc ....E 609 261-1393
  Rancocas *(G-9168)*

Weld Tech Fab ....G 732 919-2185
  Farmingdale *(G-3395)*

Welded Products Co Inc ....E 973 589-0180
  Newark *(G-7313)*

Welding & Radiator Supply Co ....G 609 965-0433
  Egg Harbor City *(G-2672)*

Willow Run Construction Inc ....F 201 659-7266
  Jersey City *(G-4832)*

7694 Armature Rewinding Shops

Absecon Electric Motor Works ....G 609 641-1523
  Absecon *(G-1)*

▲ Atlantic Kenmark Electric Inc ....F 201 991-2117
  North Arlington *(G-7369)*

Atlantic Switch Generator LLC ....F 609 518-1900
  Hainesport *(G-4069)*

D Electric Motors Inc ....G 856 696-5959
  Vineland *(G-11210)*

Electrical Motor Repr Co of NJ ....F 609 392-6149
  Trenton *(G-10934)*

General Electric Company ....C 201 866-2161
  North Bergen *(G-7406)*

George J Bender Inc ....E 908 687-0081
  Union *(G-11059)*

Hights Electric Motor Service ....G 609 448-2298
  Hightstown *(G-4296)*

Jarvis Electric Motors Inc ....G 856 662-7710
  Pennsauken *(G-8444)*

Johnnys Service Center ....G 732 738-0569
  Fords *(G-3532)*

Lakewood Elc Mtr Sls & Svc ....G 732 363-2865
  Howell *(G-4545)*

Lockwoods Electric Motor Svc ....E 609 587-2333
  Trenton *(G-10953)*

▲ Longo Elctrical-Mechanical Inc ....D 973 537-0400
  Wharton *(G-11861)*

Longo Elctrical-Mechanical Inc ....E 973 537-0400
  Linden *(G-5377)*

Lowder Electric and Cnstr ....G 732 764-6000
  Middlesex *(G-6128)*

▲ McIntosh Industries Inc ....E 908 688-7475
  Hillside *(G-4415)*

Motors and Drives Inc ....G 732 462-7683
  Freehold *(G-3681)*

Motors and Drives Inc ....G 609 344-8058
  Atlantic City *(G-98)*

Mt Salem Electric Co Inc ....F 908 735-6126
  Pittstown *(G-8754)*

New Jersey Electric Motors ....G 908 526-5225
  Somerville *(G-10121)*

Phil Desiere Electric Mtr Svc ....F 856 692-8442
  Vineland *(G-11251)*

Precision Devices Inc ....G 609 882-2230
  Ewing *(G-3054)*

RSI Company ....G 973 227-7800
  Fairfield *(G-3304)*

◆ SMS Electric Motor Car LLC ....F 215 428-2502
  Bridgewater *(G-890)*

Story Electric Mtr Repr Co Inc ....G 973 256-1636
  Little Falls *(G-5469)*

Universal Electric Mtr Svc Inc ....E 201 968-1000
  Hackensack *(G-3988)*

Willier Elc Mtr Repr Co Inc ....E 856 627-2262
  Gibbsboro *(G-3797)*

Willier Elc Mtr Repr Co Inc ....E 856 627-3535
  Gibbsboro *(G-3796)*

ALPHABETIC SECTION

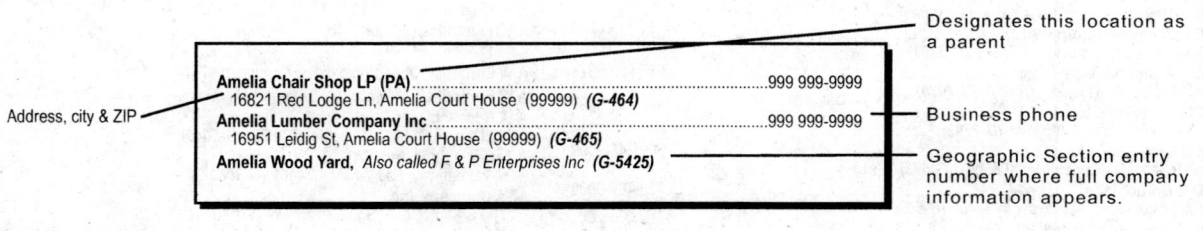

Designates this location as a parent

Address, city & ZIP

Amelia Chair Shop LP (PA) 999 999-9999
16821 Red Lodge Ln, Amelia Court House (99999) **(G-464)**
Amelia Lumber Company Inc 999 999-9999
16951 Leidig St, Amelia Court House (99999) **(G-465)**
Amelia Wood Yard, Also called F & P Enterprises Inc **(G-5425)**

Business phone

Geographic Section entry number where full company information appears.

See footnotes for symbols and codes identification.

* Companies listed alphabetically.

* Complete physical or mailing address.

(gt) Global Tech Inc 732 447-7083
32 Marc Dr Dayton (08810) **(G-1950)**
10-31 Incorporated 908 496-4946
2 W Crisman Rd Columbia (07832) **(G-1791)**
10x Daily LLC 732 276-6407
10 Blue Jay Way Lakewood (08701) **(G-5041)**
140 Main Street Corp 732 974-2929
2175 Highway 35 Ste 13 Sea Girt (08750) **(G-9744)**
150 Development Group LLC 732 546-3812
242 Lincoln Blvd Ste 2 Middlesex (08846) **(G-6089)**
175 Derousse LLC 856 662-0100
175 Derousse Ave Pennsauken (08110) **(G-8380)**
1800iprint, Lumberton Also called New Jersey Tech Group LLC **(G-5633)**
201 Food Packing Inc 973 463-0777
7 Great Meadow Ln East Hanover (07936) **(G-2192)**
202 Smoothie LLC 973 985-4973
11 Danielle Dr Wayne (07470) **(G-11463)**
21st Century Finishing Inc 201 797-0212
40 Webro Rd Clifton (07012) **(G-1550)**
21st Century Mch Tls Co Inc 973 808-2220
1140 Bloomfield Ave # 219 West Caldwell (07006) **(G-11635)**
21st Century Media Newsppr LLC (HQ) 215 504-4200
600 Perry St Trenton (08618) **(G-10885)**
224 Graphics Inc 973 433-9224
1275 Bloomfield Ave Fairfield (07004) **(G-3132)**
24 Horas Inc 973 817-7400
68 Madison St Ste A Newark (07105) **(G-7026)**
26 Flavors LLC 855 662-7299
29 Riverside Ave Bldg 2 Newark (07104) **(G-7027)**
2a Holdings Inc 973 378-8011
12 Hoffman St Maplewood (07040) **(G-5873)**
3 H Technology Institute LLC 866 624-3484
3000 Atrium Way Ste 296 Mount Laurel (08054) **(G-6736)**
3 Hti, Mount Laurel Also called 3 H Technology Institute LLC **(G-6736)**
3 IS Technologies Inc 609 238-8213
4 Colfax Ln Hainesport (08036) **(G-4067)**
34 Welding LLC 973 440-0116
95 Ford Rd Landing (07850) **(G-5199)**
35 Food Corp 732 442-1640
545 Us Highway 9 N Woodbridge (07095) **(G-12011)**
360 Media Innovations LLC 201 228-0941
1511a Stuyvesant Ave Union (07083) **(G-11018)**
39 Idea Factory Row LLC 908 244-8631
39 Bonetown Rd Flemington (08822) **(G-3425)**
3d Biotek LLC 908 801-6138
1031 Us 206 Ste 202 Bridgewater (08807) **(G-781)**
3dimension Dgnstc Slution Corp 201 780-4653
394 Union St Fl 1 Jersey City (07304) **(G-4678)**
3forty Group Inc 973 773-1806
90 Dayton Ave Ste 6a Passaic (07055) **(G-8047)**
3i Infotech Financial Software (HQ) 732 710-4444
450 Rritan Ctr Pkwy Ste B Edison (08837) **(G-2442)**
3i Infotech Inc 732 710-4444
450 Rritan Ctr Pkwy Ste B Edison (08837) **(G-2443)**
3lab Inc 201 227-4742
37 Smith St Englewood (07631) **(G-2871)**
3M Company 908 788-4000
500 Rte 202 Flemington (08822) **(G-3426)**
3M Company 973 884-2500
140 Algonquin Pkwy Whippany (07981) **(G-11875)**
3r Biopharma LLC 914 486-1898
324 Perry Dr North Brunswick (08902) **(G-7447)**
3shape Inc 908 867-0144
10 Independence Blvd # 150 Warren (07059) **(G-11395)**
4 D Motion, Allendale Also called Ssam Sports Inc **(G-16)**
4 Over Inc 201 440-1656
4 Empire Blvd Moonachie (07074) **(G-6450)**
4 Way Lock LLC 908 359-2002
5 Ilene Ct Ste 12 Hillsborough (08844) **(G-4299)**

42 Design Square LLC 888 272-5979
350 Parsippany Rd Apt 128 Parsippany (07054) **(G-7870)**
431 Converters Inc 856 848-8949
230 Glassboro Rd Woodbury Heights (08097) **(G-12040)**
5 Elements Robotics, Wall Township Also called Five Elements Robotics LLC **(G-11340)**
5 Kids Group Ltd Liability Co 732 774-5331
37 State Route 35 N Neptune (07753) **(G-6861)**
5 Star Industries Inc 862 255-2040
2 Fish House Rd Kearny (07032) **(G-4839)**
50 Plus Monthly Inc 973 584-7911
5 Clearfield Rd Succasunna (07876) **(G-10508)**
51maps Inc 800 927-5181
500 E Mantua Ave Wenonah (08090) **(G-11572)**
67 Pollock Ave Corp 201 432-1156
67 Pollock Ave Jersey City (07305) **(G-4679)**
7th Seventh Day Wellness Ctr 856 308-0991
6 Sherwick Ct Sicklerville (08081) **(G-9906)**
814 Americas, Elizabeth Also called Smithfield Packaged Meats Corp **(G-2776)**
9001 Corporation 201 963-2233
507 Summit Ave Ste 7 Jersey City (07306) **(G-4680)**
9002 Corporation 201 792-9595
318 Central Ave Jersey City (07307) **(G-4681)**
911 Tatical Direct, Toms River Also called Enailsupply Corporation **(G-10755)**
A & A Coating, South Plainfield Also called A&A Company Inc **(G-10205)**
A & A Concrete Products Inc 973 835-2239
2 S Corporate Dr Riverdale (07457) **(G-9369)**
A & A Ironwork Co Inc 973 728-4300
955 Burnt Meadow Rd Hewitt (07421) **(G-4273)**
A & A Soft Pretzel Company 856 338-0208
1100 N 32nd St Camden (08105) **(G-1038)**
A & D Indus & Mar Repr Inc 732 541-1481
900 Port Reading Ave B2 Port Reading (07064) **(G-8890)**
A & F Electroplating Inc 973 983-2459
106 Ashland Ave West Orange (07052) **(G-11757)**
A & J Carpets Inc 856 227-1753
4461 Route 42 Blackwood (08012) **(G-458)**
A & L Industries Inc 973 589-8070
23 George St Newark (07105) **(G-7028)**
A & R Sewing Company Inc 201 332-0622
451 Communipaw Ave Jersey City (07304) **(G-4682)**
A & S Frozen Inc 201 672-0510
96 E Union Ave East Rutherford (07073) **(G-2268)**
A & S Packaging & Display 201 531-1900
120 Kero Rd Carlstadt (07072) **(G-1117)**
A 1 Fencing Inc 908 527-1066
166 7th St Elizabeth (07201) **(G-2704)**
A A A Stamp and Seal Mfg Co 201 796-1500
361 N Midland Ave Saddle Brook (07663) **(G-9636)**
A A Sayia & Company Inc 201 659-1179
1 Newark St Ste 29 Hoboken (07030) **(G-4442)**
A A World Class Corp, Fort Lee Also called World Class Marketing Corp **(G-3595)**
A and P Pharmacy 908 850-7640
7 Naughright Rd Ste V Hackettstown (07840) **(G-3993)**
A Andersen Shtmtl Fabrication, Linden Also called Lentine Sheet Metal Inc **(G-5375)**
A B S Sign Company Inc 609 522-6833
3008 Park Blvd Wildwood (08260) **(G-11941)**
A B Scantlebury Co Inc 973 770-3000
108 Phil Hardin Rd Newton (07860) **(G-7335)**
A B T, Totowa Also called Advanced Biotech Overseas LLC **(G-10808)**
A B Tees LLC 201 239-0022
7 Sherman Ave Fl 3 Jersey City (07307) **(G-4683)**
A C Bakery Distributors Inc 973 977-2255
1 Industrial Plz Paterson (07503) **(G-8118)**
A C C, Neptune Also called Automated Control Concepts Inc **(G-6867)**
A C D, Burlington Also called American Custom Drying Co **(G-948)**
A C D Custom Granite Inc 732 695-2400
1304 Roller Rd Ocean (07712) **(G-7651)**

A **L** **P** **H** **A** **B** **E** **T** **I** **C**

A C Display Studios Inc 609 345-0814
2715 Arctic Ave Atlantic City (08401) *(G-88)*

A C F, Bayville *Also called American Custom Fabricators* *(G-239)*

A C L Equipment Corp (PA) 973 740-9800
Northfield Rd Livingston (07039) *(G-5501)*

A C Transformer Corp 973 589-8574
89 Madison St Newark (07105) *(G-7029)*

A Cheerful Giver Inc 856 358-4438
300 Front St Elmer (08318) *(G-2792)*

A D J Group LLC 609 743-2099
12 Trainor Cir Bordentown (08505) *(G-573)*

A D M Corporation 732 469-0900
100 Lincoln Blvd Middlesex (08846) *(G-6090)*

A D M Tronics Unlimited Inc (PA) 201 767-6040
224 Pegasus Ave Ste A Northvale (07647) *(G-7513)*

A Division NJ Bus Forms, Englewood *Also called Infoseal LLC* *(G-2913)*

A E Stone Inc (PA) 609 641-2781
1435 Doughty Rd Egg Harbor Township (08234) *(G-2673)*

A F C, Fair Lawn *Also called Associated Fabrics Corporation* *(G-3086)*

A Frieri Machine Tool Inc 908 753-7555
1112 Belmont Ave South Plainfield (07080) *(G-10204)*

A G S, Dayton *Also called Fleetsource LLC* *(G-1961)*

A Gimenez Trading LLC 973 697-2240
5 Wegmann Way Oak Ridge (07438) *(G-7599)*

A H Hoffmann LLC 732 988-6000
209 W Sylvania Ave Neptune (07753) *(G-6862)*

A I T, Princeton Junction *Also called Amerasia Intl Tech Inc* *(G-9050)*

A I T, Princeton Junction *Also called AI Technology Inc* *(G-9048)*

A J P Scientific Inc 973 472-7200
82 Industrial St E Clifton (07012) *(G-1551)*

A K Stamping Co Inc 908 232-7300
1159 Us Highway 22 Mountainside (07092) *(G-6831)*

A Kessler Kreation Inc 732 431-2468
31 Continental Ct Colts Neck (07722) *(G-1776)*

A L Don Co, Matawan *Also called Steelstran Industries Inc* *(G-5989)*

A L M, Wayne *Also called Polymeric Resources Corp* *(G-11543)*

A L Wilson Chemical Co 201 997-3300
1050 Harrison Ave Kearny (07032) *(G-4840)*

A M D, Millville *Also called Architctural Metal Designs Inc* *(G-6234)*

A M Gatti Inc 609 396-1577
524 Tindall Ave Trenton (08610) *(G-10886)*

A M Graphics Inc 201 767-5320
68 Schraalenburg Rd Ste 6 Harrington Park (07640) *(G-4161)*

A M K Glass Inc 856 692-1488
2880 Industrial Way Vineland (08360) *(G-11183)*

A M M, Belvidere *Also called Artisan Model Mold* *(G-357)*

A N Laggren Awngs Canvas Mfg 908 756-1948
1414 South Ave Plainfield (07062) *(G-8756)*

A O S, Eatontown *Also called American Oil & Supply Co* *(G-2377)*

A P A I, Roosevelt *Also called Action Packaging Automation* *(G-9527)*

A P M Hexseal Corporation 201 569-5700
44 Honeck St Englewood (07631) *(G-2872)*

A Plus Installation, Bloomfield *Also called A Plus Installs LLC* *(G-488)*

A Plus Installs LLC 201 255-4412
29 27 Curtis St Fl 1 Flr 1 Bloomfield (07003) *(G-488)*

A Plus Powerwashing 732 245-3816
503 Moore Rd Neptune (07753) *(G-6863)*

A Plus Products Incorporated 732 866-9111
8 Timber Ln Marlboro (07746) *(G-5892)*

A PS Inlet Marina LLC 732 681-3303
610 5th Ave Belmar (07719) *(G-346)*

A Quick Cut Stamping Embossing 856 321-0050
803 N Forklanding Rd Maple Shade (08052) *(G-5858)*

A R Bothers Woodworking Inc 908 725-2891
236 Dukes Pkwy E Somerville (08876) *(G-10099)*

A R C Plasmet Corp 201 867-8533
4131 Bergen Tpke North Bergen (07047) *(G-7379)*

A R J Custom Fabrication Inc 609 695-6227
151 Taylor St Trenton (08638) *(G-10887)*

A S 4 Plastic Inc 973 925-5223
116 Getty Ave Paterson (07503) *(G-8119)*

A S A P Nameplate & Labeling 973 773-3934
92 1st St Passaic (07055) *(G-8048)*

A S L, Trenton *Also called American Scientific Ltg Corp* *(G-10892)*

A S M, Fairfield *Also called Accurate Screw Machine Corp* *(G-3133)*

A S M Technical 973 225-0111
34 Waite St Paterson (07524) *(G-8120)*

A Sign Company 609 298-3388
258 Old York Rd Trenton (08620) *(G-10888)*

A Sign of Excellence Inc 732 264-0404
6 Surrey Dr Hazlet (07730) *(G-4253)*

A Smith & Son Inc 609 747-0800
300 W Broad St Burlington (08016) *(G-945)*

A Stitch Ahead 609 586-1068
1770 Front Lake Ave Lawrenceville (08648) *(G-5221)*

A T C Companies Inc 732 560-0900
207 Blackford Ave Middlesex (08846) *(G-6091)*

A T L, Ramsey *Also called Aero TEC Laboratories Inc* *(G-9135)*

A T S Rheosystems, Bordentown *Also called Advanced Technical Support Inc* *(G-574)*

A To Z Printing & Promotion 973 916-9995
1455 Main Ave Ste 2 Clifton (07011) *(G-1552)*

A V Hydraulics Ltd Lblty Co 973 621-6800
2 Avenue C Newark (07114) *(G-7030)*

A W Eurostile, Ocean *Also called Akw Inc* *(G-7654)*

A W Eurostile, Shrewsbury *Also called Akw Inc* *(G-9880)*

A W Ross Inc 973 471-5900
297 Monroe St Ste 1 Passaic (07055) *(G-8049)*

A Zeregas Sons Inc (PA) 201 797-1400
20-1 Broadway Fair Lawn (07410) *(G-3080)*

A&A Company Inc 908 561-2378
2700 S Clinton Ave South Plainfield (07080) *(G-10205)*

A&B Heating & Cooling 908 289-2231
107 Trumbull St Elizabeth (07206) *(G-2705)*

A&C Catalysts Inc 908 474-9393
1600 W Blancke St Linden (07036) *(G-5315)*

A&E Medical, Wall Township *Also called Alto Development Corp* *(G-11316)*

A&E Promotions LLC 732 382-2300
118 Woodlake Ct A Holmdel (07733) *(G-4491)*

A&J Flooring Outlet, Blackwood *Also called A & J Carpets Inc* *(G-458)*

A&M Industrial Inc 908 862-1800
22b Cragwood Rd Avenel (07001) *(G-117)*

A&M Petro Marine Division, Avenel *Also called A&M Industrial Inc* *(G-117)*

A&P, Hackettstown *Also called A and P Pharmacy* *(G-3993)*

A&R Printing Corporation 732 886-0505
421 W County Line Rd Lakewood (08701) *(G-5042)*

A-1 Fasteners, Camden *Also called Art Metalcraft Plating Co Inc* *(G-1040)*

A-1 Plastic Bags Inc 973 344-4441
136 Tichenor St Newark (07105) *(G-7031)*

A-1 Tablecloth Co Inc 201 727-4364
450 Huyler St Ste 102 South Hackensack (07606) *(G-10145)*

A-1 Thrifty Centers, Woodbridge *Also called Stone Mountain Printing Inc* *(G-12022)*

A-One Merchandising Corp 718 773-7500
170 Schuyler Ave North Arlington (07031) *(G-7366)*

A-Wit Technologies Inc 800 985-2948
656 Ironwood Dr Williamstown (08094) *(G-11949)*

A. L. Don Co., Avenel *Also called Steelstran Industries Inc* *(G-147)*

A1 Copying Center, Manasquan *Also called Ahern Blueprinting Inc* *(G-5827)*

A1 Custom Countertops Inc 856 200-3596
20 Old Salem Rd Woodstown (08098) *(G-12094)*

AA Graphics Inc 201 398-0710
431 N Midland Ave Saddle Brook (07663) *(G-9637)*

AAA Pharmaceutical 856 423-2700
157-160 W Jefferson St Paulsboro (08066) *(G-8327)*

AAA Pharmaceutical (PA) 609 288-6060
681 Main St Lumberton (08048) *(G-5621)*

AAA Umbrella Co, Norwood *Also called Rainmen USA Incorporated* *(G-7573)*

Aaeon Electronics Inc (HQ) 732 203-9300
11 Crown Plz Ste 208 Hazlet (07730) *(G-4254)*

Aak Foodservice, Hillside *Also called Oasis Trading Co Inc* *(G-4419)*

Aak USA Inc (HQ) 973 344-1300
499 Thornall St Ste 5 Edison (08837) *(G-2444)*

Aall American Fasteners, Cinnaminson *Also called Kt Mt Corp* *(G-1469)*

Aarc, Jersey City *Also called All Amrcan Recycl Corp Clifton* *(G-4688)*

Aarhuskarlshamn USA Inc (PA) 973 344-1300
131 Marsh St Newark (07114) *(G-7032)*

Aarisse Health Care Products 973 686-1811
11 Robin Hood Way Wayne (07470) *(G-11464)*

Aarubco Rubber Co Inc 973 772-8177
259 2nd St Saddle Brook (07663) *(G-9638)*

AAS Technologies Inc 201 342-7300
290 Lodi St Hackensack (07601) *(G-3874)*

Aavolyn Corp 856 327-8040
207 Bogden Blvd Ste M Millville (08332) *(G-6221)*

AB Aerospace, Linden *Also called Bar Fields Inc* *(G-5325)*

AB Coaster LLC 908 879-2713
360 State Route 24 Ste 4 Chester (07930) *(G-1429)*

AB Science Usa LLC (HQ) 973 218-2437
51 John F Kennedy Pkwy Short Hills (07078) *(G-9863)*

Abacus Electric & Plumbing 908 269-8057
95 W Main St Ste 252 Chester (07930) *(G-1430)*

Abatetech Inc 609 265-2107
30 Maple Ave Lumberton (08048) *(G-5622)*

ABB Installation Products Inc 908 852-1122
1 Esna Park Hackettstown (07840) *(G-3994)*

ABB Lighting Inc 866 222-8866
1501 Industrial Way Toms River (08755) *(G-10737)*

Abba Metal Works Inc 973 684-0808
337 River St Paterson (07524) *(G-8121)*

Abbey Commemoratives, Kenilworth *Also called Arbee Company Inc* *(G-4921)*

Abbott Artkives LLC 201 232-9477
187 Branch Brook Dr Belleville (07109) *(G-288)*

Abbott Laboratories 732 346-6649
18 Mayfield Ave Edison (08837) *(G-2445)*

Abbott Laboratories 609 443-9300
400 College Rd E Princeton (08540) *(G-8897)*

(G-0000) Company's Geographic Section entry number

Abbott Laboratories ... 856 988-5572
10000 Lincoln Dr E # 201 Marlton (08053) ***(G-5919)***

Abbott Laboratories Parsipanny ... 973 428-4000
30 N Jefferson Rd Whippany (07981) ***(G-11876)***

Abbott Point of Care Inc (HQ) ... 609 454-9000
400 College Rd E Princeton (08540) ***(G-8898)***

Abbott Point of Care Inc ... 609 371-8923
104 Windsor Center Dr East Windsor (08520) ***(G-2332)***

Abbott Screen Printing, Belleville *Also called Abbott Artkives LLC* ***(G-288)***

ABC Digital Electronics Inc ... 201 666-6888
44 Country Squire Rd Old Tappan (07675) ***(G-7731)***

ABC Holdings Inc ... 856 219-3444
1000 Delsea Dr Ste F3 Westville (08093) ***(G-11809)***

ABC Printing ... 973 664-1160
20 Wall St Ste C Rockaway (07866) ***(G-9433)***

ABC Sign Systems Inc ... 856 665-0950
7970 National Hwy Pennsauken (08110) ***(G-8381)***

Abco Die Casters Inc ... 973 624-7030
39 Tompkins Point Rd Newark (07114) ***(G-7033)***

Abco Metal LLC ... 973 772-8160
138 3rd Ave Paterson (07514) ***(G-8122)***

Abco Tool & Machine Corp ... 973 772-8160
2 Elm St Garfield (07026) ***(G-3723)***

ABG Accessories, Elizabeth *Also called Elegant Headwear Co Inc* ***(G-2732)***

ABG Lab LLC ... 973 559-5663
20-21 Wagaraw Rd Bldg 31b Fair Lawn (07410) ***(G-3081)***

Abi Inc ... 609 588-8225
227 Bakers Basin Rd Lawrenceville (08648) ***(G-5222)***

Ability2work A NJ Nnprfit Corp ... 908 782-3458
42 State Route 12 Flemington (08822) ***(G-3427)***

Abj Drone Services, Cranbury *Also called Abj LLC* ***(G-1806)***

Abj LLC (PA) ... 888 225-1931
2661 Us Highway 130 Cranbury (08512) ***(G-1806)***

Able Fab Co ... 732 396-0600
18 Mileed Way Avenel (07001) ***(G-118)***

Able Gear & Machine Co ... 973 983-8055
91 Stickle Ave Rockaway (07866) ***(G-9434)***

Able Group Technologies Inc ... 732 591-9299
281 State Route 79 N Morganville (07751) ***(G-6579)***

Abon Pharmaceuticals LLC ... 201 367-1702
140 Legrand Ave Northvale (07647) ***(G-7514)***

Aboudi Printing LLC ... 732 542-2929
132 Lewis St Ste B Eatontown (07724) ***(G-2373)***

About Our Town Inc ... 732 968-1615
2 Lakeview Ave Ste 312 Piscataway (08854) ***(G-8623)***

Above Environmental Services ... 973 702-7021
57 Vernon Crossing Rd Vernon (07462) ***(G-11156)***

Above Rest Glass ... 732 370-1616
2345 Route 9 Ste 31 Toms River (08755) ***(G-10738)***

Abox Automation Corp ... 973 659-9611
45 Us Highway 46 Ste 606 Pine Brook (07058) ***(G-8583)***

Abp Induction LLC ... 732 932-6400
1460 Livingston Ave 200-1 North Brunswick (08902) ***(G-7448)***

Abraxis Bioscience Inc (HQ) ... 908 673-9000
86 Morris Ave Summit (07901) ***(G-10520)***

Abraxis Bioscience Inc ... 908 673-9000
86 Morris Ave Summit (07901) ***(G-10521)***

Abrazil LLC ... 732 658-5191
1 Jacques Ave Kendall Park (08824) ***(G-4917)***

Abris Distribution Inc (PA) ... 732 252-9819
522 Us Highway 9 Ste 377 Manalapan (07726) ***(G-5799)***

ABS Company, The, Chester *Also called AB Coaster LLC* ***(G-1429)***

Absecon Electric Motor Works ... 609 641-1523
500 White Horse Pike Absecon (08201) ***(G-1)***

Absecon Island Beverage Co ... 609 653-8123
6754 Washington Ave B Egg Harbor Township (08234) ***(G-2674)***

Absecon Mills Inc ... 609 965-5373
901 W Aloe St Cologne (08213) ***(G-1773)***

Absolume LLC (PA) ... 732 523-1231
1153 Tiffany Ln Lakewood (08701) ***(G-5043)***

Absolute Business Services Inc ... 856 265-9447
325 Maurice St Millville (08332) ***(G-6222)***

Absolute Protective Systems ... 732 287-4500
51 Suttons Ln Piscataway (08854) ***(G-8624)***

Abuelito Cheese Inc ... 973 345-3503
607 Main St Paterson (07503) ***(G-8123)***

AC Bakery, Paterson *Also called A C Bakery Distributors Inc* ***(G-8118)***

AC Catalyts, Linden *Also called A&C Catalysts Inc* ***(G-5315)***

Academia Furniture LLC ... 973 472-0100
74 Passaic St Wood Ridge (07075) ***(G-12000)***

Academia Furniture Industries, Wood Ridge *Also called Academia Furniture LLC* ***(G-12000)***

Academy of Proplayers, Bloomingdale *Also called Akadema Inc* ***(G-525)***

Acadia Scenic Inc ... 201 653-8889
150 Pacific Ave Ste 6 Jersey City (07304) ***(G-4684)***

ACC Foods Ltd Liability Co ... 856 848-8877
280 Jessup Rd West Deptford (08086) ***(G-11689)***

Acceledev Chemical LLC (PA) ... 862 239-1524
18 Apple Ln Wayne (07470) ***(G-11465)***

Acceledev Chemical LLC ... 732 274-1451
11 Deerpark Dr Ste 119 Monmouth Junction (08852) ***(G-6276)***

Accelerated Cnc LLC ... 908 561-8875
2500 S Clinton Ave South Plainfield (07080) ***(G-10206)***

Accelerated Technologies Inc ... 609 632-0350
2 Research Way Fl 2 # 2 Princeton (08540) ***(G-8899)***

Accelis Pharma, Monroe Township *Also called Novotec Pharma LLC* ***(G-6338)***

Accelrx Labs LLC ... 609 301-6446
55 Lake Dr East Windsor (08520) ***(G-2333)***

Accely Inc ... 609 598-1882
381 Blair Rd Avenel (07001) ***(G-119)***

Accent Fence Inc ... 609 965-6400
1450 Bremen Ave Egg Harbor City (08215) ***(G-2651)***

Accent Press Inc ... 973 785-3127
132 Winifred Dr Totowa (07512) ***(G-10807)***

Accent Printing Solutions, New Providence *Also called Bowmar Enterprises Inc* ***(G-6996)***

Access Bio Inc (PA) ... 732 873-4040
65 Clyde Rd Ste A Somerset (08873) ***(G-9941)***

Access Conrol Group LLC ... 908 789-8700
1226 Us Highway 130 Robbinsville (08691) ***(G-9406)***

Access Controls International, Freehold *Also called Access Northern Security Inc* ***(G-3642)***

Access Northern Security Inc (PA) ... 732 462-2500
303 W Main St Ste 4 Freehold (07728) ***(G-3642)***

Access Publishing Co, Ocean *Also called Access Response Inc* ***(G-7652)***

Access Response Inc ... 732 660-0770
3321 Doris Ave Ocean (07712) ***(G-7652)***

Accession Data Systems ... 973 992-7392
25 Hickory Pl Livingston (07039) ***(G-5502)***

Accessories Plus, Ogdensburg *Also called AJ Siris Products Corp* ***(G-7708)***

Accessrec LLC ... 973 955-0514
55 Park Slope Clifton (07011) ***(G-1553)***

Acclivity LLC ... 973 586-2200
300 Round Hill Dr Ste 2 Rockaway (07866) ***(G-9435)***

Accu Seal Rubber Inc ... 732 246-4333
18f Home News Row New Brunswick (08901) ***(G-6908)***

Accu-Cote Inc ... 856 845-7323
3410 Jessup Rd Thorofare (08086) ***(G-10698)***

Accucolor LLC (PA) ... 732 870-1999
185 Broadway Long Branch (07740) ***(G-5593)***

Accumix Pharmaceuticals LLC ... 609 632-2225
42 Morris Dr Old Bridge (08857) ***(G-7710)***

Accupac Inc ... 215 256-7094
1700 Oak St Lakewood (08701) ***(G-5044)***

Accuracy Devices ... 973 427-8829
321 Central Ave Hawthorne (07506) ***(G-4204)***

Accurate Bronze Bearing Co ... 973 345-2304
64 Illinois Ave Paterson (07503) ***(G-8124)***

Accurate Bushing Company Inc ... 908 789-1121
443 North Ave Ste 1 Garwood (07027) ***(G-3779)***

Accurate Diamond Tool Corp ... 201 265-8868
1 Palisade Ave Emerson (07630) ***(G-2861)***

Accurate Forming LLC ... 973 827-7155
24 Ames Blvd Hamburg (07419) ***(G-4087)***

Accurate Machine & Tool Co ... 908 245-5545
135 W Clay Ave Roselle Park (07204) ***(G-9577)***

Accurate Mold Inc ... 856 784-8484
900 Chestnut Ave Ste G Somerdale (08083) ***(G-9929)***

Accurate Oil, Midland Park *Also called Accurate Tank Testing LLC* ***(G-6168)***

Accurate Plastic Printers LLC ... 973 591-0180
30 Colfax Ave Clifton (07013) ***(G-1554)***

Accurate Prscsion Fstener Corp ... 201 567-9700
20 Honeck St Englewood (07631) ***(G-2873)***

Accurate Screw Machine, Fairfield *Also called Mw Industries Inc* ***(G-3274)***

Accurate Screw Machine Corp ... 973 276-0379
10 Audrey Pl Fairfield (07004) ***(G-3133)***

Accurate Tank Testing LLC ... 201 848-8224
140 Greenwood Ave Midland Park (07432) ***(G-6168)***

Accurate Thermal Systems LLC ... 609 326-3190
4104 Sylon Blvd Hainesport (08036) ***(G-4068)***

Accurate Tool & Die Co Inc ... 201 476-9348
6 Westminster Ct Montvale (07645) ***(G-6394)***

Accurate Transmissions, Montvale *Also called Accurate Tool & Die Co Inc* ***(G-6394)***

Accuratus Ceramic Corp ... 908 213-7070
35 Howard St Phillipsburg (08865) ***(G-8540)***

Ace Bag & Burlap Company Inc ... 973 242-2200
166 Frelinghuysen Ave Newark (07114) ***(G-7034)***

Ace Box Co, Englewood Cliffs *Also called Ace Box Landau Co Inc* ***(G-2956)***

Ace Box Landau Co Inc ... 201 871-4776
600 E Palisade Ave Ste 21 Englewood Cliffs (07632) ***(G-2956)***

Ace Crete Product, Bayville *Also called New Jersey Pulverizing Co Inc* ***(G-249)***

Ace Electric ... 908 534-2404
3470 Us Highway 22 Somerville (08876) ***(G-10100)***

Ace Electronics Inc ... 732 603-9800
235 Liberty St Metuchen (08840) ***(G-6045)***

Ace Fine Art Inc ... 201 960-4447
141 Lanza Ave Bldg 3d Garfield (07026) ***(G-3724)***

Ace Metal Kraft Co Inc ... 973 278-6605
815 Mcbride Ave Woodland Park (07424) ***(G-12068)***

A L P H A B E T I C

Ace Mountings Co Inc (PA) 732 721-6200
11 Cross Ave South Amboy (08879) *(G-10129)*

Ace Powder Coating, Newark *Also called A & L Industries Inc (G-7028)*

Ace Reprographic Service Inc 973 684-5945
74 E 30th St Paterson (07514) *(G-8125)*

Ace Restoration 267 897-2384
24 Mariner Dr Sewell (08080) *(G-9833)*

Ace Sign Company Inc 732 826-3858
419 Summit Ave Perth Amboy (08861) *(G-8509)*

Ace-Crete Products Inc 732 269-1400
250 Hickory Ln Bayville (08721) *(G-238)*

Aceco Industrial Packaging Co, Newark *Also called Ace Bag & Burlap Company Inc (G-7034)*

Acedepotcom (PA) 800 844-0962
159 Paris Ave Northvale (07647) *(G-7515)*

Acetris Health LLC 201 961-9000
Park 80 West Plz 1 Saddle Brook (07663) *(G-9639)*

Acetylon Pharmaceuticals Inc (HQ) 908 673-9000
86 Morris Ave Summit (07901) *(G-10522)*

Acey Industries Inc 973 595-1222
9 Cranberry Ct North Haledon (07508) *(G-7494)*

Acg North America LLC 908 757-3425
262 Old New Brunswick Rd A Piscataway (08854) *(G-8625)*

Achievement Journal LLC 732 297-1570
5 Larson Ct North Brunswick (08902) *(G-7449)*

Achilles Prosthetcs & Orthotcs 201 785-9944
503 N Franklin Tpke # 12 Ramsey (07446) *(G-9133)*

Aci, Wall Township *Also called Applicad Inc (G-11318)*

Aci, Moorestown *Also called Automation & Control Inc (G-6507)*

Acino Products Ltd Lblty Co 609 695-4300
9b S Gold Dr Hamilton (08691) *(G-4100)*

Ackerson Drapery Decorator Svc 732 797-1967
500 James St Ste 14 Lakewood (08701) *(G-5045)*

Ackk Studios LLC 973 876-1327
411 E Passaic Ave Bloomfield (07003) *(G-489)*

Ackley Machine Corporation 856 234-3626
1273 N Church St Ste 106 Moorestown (08057) *(G-6500)*

Acme & Dorf Door Corp 973 772-6774
490 Getty Ave 500 Clifton (07011) *(G-1555)*

Acme Cosmetic Components LLC 718 335-3000
80 Seaview Dr Ste 1 Secaucus (07094) *(G-9750)*

Acme Drapemaster America Inc 732 512-0613
125 Clearview Rd Edison (08837) *(G-2446)*

Acme Engraving Co Inc (PA) 973 778-0885
19-37 Delaware Ave Passaic (07055) *(G-8050)*

Acme Flagpole Division, Mount Laurel *Also called Lingo Inc (G-6775)*

Acme Gear Co Inc 201 568-2245
130 W Forest Ave Englewood (07631) *(G-2874)*

Acme International Inc 973 594-4866
2a Monhegan St Clifton (07013) *(G-1556)*

Acme Manufacturing Co 732 541-2800
900 Port Reading Ave A2 Port Reading (07064) *(G-8891)*

Acme Markets Inc 609 884-7217
Lafayette & Ocean Sts Cape May (08204) *(G-1091)*

Acme Ring Div, Maplewood *Also called Barrasso & Blasi Industries (G-5874)*

Acme Wire Forming LLC 201 218-2912
18 Pepperidge Tree Ter Kinnelon (07405) *(G-5014)*

Acolyte Technologies Corp 212 629-3239
1000 Amboy Ave Perth Amboy (08861) *(G-8510)*

Acon Watch Crown Company 973 546-8585
260 Division Ave Garfield (07026) *(G-3725)*

Acorn Industry Inc 732 536-6256
6 Hoffer Ct Englishtown (07726) *(G-2999)*

Acqua Bella Mfg and Supply, Chesterfield *Also called Bella Acqua Inc (G-1436)*

Acqueon Technologies Inc 609 945-3139
100 Overlook Ctr Fl 2 Princeton (08540) *(G-8900)*

Acrelic Interactive LLC (PA) 908 222-2900
16 Mount Bethel Rd Warren (07059) *(G-11396)*

Acrilex Inc (PA) 201 333-1500
230 Culver Ave Jersey City (07305) *(G-4685)*

Acrison Inc (PA) 201 440-8300
20 Empire Blvd Moonachie (07074) *(G-6451)*

Acrison International, Moonachie *Also called Acrison Inc (G-6451)*

Acro Display Inc (PA) 215 229-1100
2250 Sherman Ave Unit A1 Pennsauken (08110) *(G-8382)*

Acrow Corporation of America (PA) 973 244-0080
181 New Rd Ste 202 Parsippany (07054) *(G-7871)*

Acrylics Unlimited 973 862-6014
11 Millpond Dr Unit 2 Lafayette (07848) *(G-5024)*

ACS Quality Services Inc 856 988-6550
20 Elmgate Rd Marlton (08053) *(G-5920)*

Actavis Inc 973 394-8925
400 Interpace Pkwy # 400 Parsippany (07054) *(G-7872)*

Actavis Elizabeth LLC (HQ) 908 527-9100
200 Elmora Ave Elizabeth (07202) *(G-2706)*

Actavis Elizabeth LLC 908 527-9100
1 Executive Dr Fort Lee (07024) *(G-3544)*

Actavis Elizabeth LLC 973 442-3200
5 Giralda Farms Madison (07940) *(G-5685)*

Actavis LLC 732 947-5300
47 Brunswick Ave Edison (08817) *(G-2447)*

Actavis LLC 800 272-5525
360 Mount Kemble Ave # 3 Morristown (07960) *(G-6630)*

Actavis LLC 732 843-4904
661 Us Highway 1 North Brunswick (08902) *(G-7450)*

Actavis LLC (HQ) 862 261-7000
5 Giralda Farms Madison (07940) *(G-5686)*

Actavis Pharma Inc (HQ) 862 261-7000
400 Interpace Pkwy Ste A1 Parsippany (07054) *(G-7873)*

Actavis US, Elizabeth *Also called Actavis Elizabeth LLC (G-2706)*

Actega North America Inc (HQ) 856 829-6300
950 S Chester Ave Ste B2 Delran (08075) *(G-2008)*

Actega North America Inc 856 829-6300
1450 Taylors Ln Cinnaminson (08077) *(G-1439)*

Action Copy Centers Inc 973 744-5520
590 Valley Rd Ste 2 Montclair (07043) *(G-6356)*

Action Graphics Inc (PA) 973 633-6500
600 Ryerson Rd Ste G Lincoln Park (07035) *(G-5297)*

Action Graphics Inc 856 783-1825
424 E Gibbsboro Rd Lindenwold (08021) *(G-5443)*

Action Instant Printing Center, Brielle *Also called Toms River Printing Corp (G-909)*

Action Packaging Automation 609 448-9210
15 Oscar Dr Roosevelt (08555) *(G-9527)*

Action Press Park Slope 718 624-3457
5 Rustic Ln Holmdel (07733) *(G-4492)*

Action Supply Inc 609 390-0663
1413 Stagecoach Rd Ocean View (08230) *(G-7701)*

Active Controls LLC 856 669-0940
1501 Grandview Ave # 400 Paulsboro (08066) *(G-8328)*

Active Imprints, Monmouth Junction *Also called Wally Enterprises Inc (G-6319)*

Active Learning Associates 908 284-0404
126 Main St Flemington (08822) *(G-3428)*

Activus Solutions LLC 973 713-0696
217 Bloomingdale Ave Cranford (07016) *(G-1897)*

Acton Mobile Industries Inc 610 485-5100
2013 Route 130 N Burlington (08016) *(G-946)*

Acuitive Technologies Inc 973 617-7175
50 Commerce Dr Allendale (07401) *(G-5)*

Acupac Packaging Inc 201 529-3434
55 Ramapo Valley Rd Mahwah (07430) *(G-5710)*

Acupowder International LLC (HQ) 908 851-4500
901 Lehigh Ave Union (07083) *(G-11019)*

Acustrip Co Inc 973 299-8237
10 Craven Rd Mountain Lakes (07046) *(G-6819)*

Acustrip Company Inc (PA) 973 299-8237
124 E Main St Apt 109b Denville (07834) *(G-2028)*

Ad Lines, Trenton *Also called Central Record Publications (G-10915)*

Adagio Teas Inc (PA) 973 253-7400
170 Kipp Ave Elmwood Park (07407) *(G-2807)*

Adam Gates & Company LLC 908 829-3386
249 Homestead Rd Ste 5 Hillsborough (08844) *(G-4300)*

Adam Metal Products Company, Ledgewood *Also called R B B Corp (G-5279)*

Adam Spence Vascular Tech, Wall Township *Also called Fermatex Vascular Tech LLC (G-11339)*

Adam Tech Asia Llc (HQ) 908 687-5000
909 Rahway Ave Union (07083) *(G-11020)*

Adams Bill Printing & Graphics 856 455-7177
300 Ramah Rd Bridgeton (08302) *(G-749)*

Adams Printing, Bridgeton *Also called Adams Bill Printing & Graphics (G-749)*

Adare Pharmaceuticals Inc 862 261-7000
400 Interpace Pkwy Parsippany (07054) *(G-7874)*

Adare Pharmaceuticals Inc (HQ) 877 731-5116
1200 Lenox Dr Ste 100 Lawrenceville (08648) *(G-5223)*

Adco Chemical Company Inc 973 589-0880
49 Rutherford St Newark (07105) *(G-7035)*

Adco Signs of NJ Inc 908 965-2112
57 Westfield Ave Elizabeth (07208) *(G-2707)*

Adcomm Government Systems, South Hackensack *Also called Adcomm Inc (G-10146)*

Adcomm Inc 201 342-3338
89 Leuning St Ste 9 South Hackensack (07606) *(G-10146)*

Add Rob Litho LLC 201 556-0700
11 W Passaic St Ste 1 Rochelle Park (07662) *(G-9420)*

Addressing Machine & Sup Div, Hillside *Also called Singe Corporation (G-4426)*

Ade Inc 609 693-6050
719 Old Shore Rd Forked River (08731) *(G-3535)*

Ademco I LLC 973 455-2000
115 Tabor Rd Morris Plains (07950) *(G-6601)*

Ademco Inc 732 505-6688
224 Route 37 E Toms River (08753) *(G-10739)*

Ademco Inc 201 462-9570
100 Hollister Rd Teterboro (07608) *(G-10670)*

Ademco Inc 908 561-1888
107 Corporate Blvd South Plainfield (07080) *(G-10207)*

Ademco Inc 856 985-9050
1000 Lincoln Dr E Marlton (08053) *(G-5921)*

Ademco Inc 973 808-8233
14 Madison Rd Unit A Fairfield (07004) *(G-3134)*

Adherence Solutions LLC 800 521-2269
75 Lane Rd Ste 404 Fairfield (07004) *(G-3135)*
Adhesves Sealants Coatings Div, Edison *Also called HB Fuller Company (G-2528)*
Adhisa Molding 862 324-5222
11 Patton Dr West Caldwell (07006) *(G-11636)*
ADI American Distributors LLC (PA) 973 328-1181
2 Emery Ave Ste 1 Randolph (07869) *(G-9169)*
ADI Global Distribution, Toms River *Also called Ademco Inc (G-10739)*
ADI Global Distribution, Teterboro *Also called Ademco Inc (G-10670)*
ADI Global Distribution, South Plainfield *Also called Ademco Inc (G-10207)*
ADI Global Distribution, Marlton *Also called Ademco Inc (G-5921)*
ADI Global Distribution, Fairfield *Also called Ademco Inc (G-3134)*
Adiant (PA) 800 264-8303
92 E Main St Ste 405 Somerville (08876) *(G-10101)*
Adidas North America Inc 201 843-4555
1 Garden State Plz Paramus (07652) *(G-7787)*
Adidas North America Inc 732 695-0085
1 Premium Outlet Blvd Tinton Falls (07753) *(G-10705)*
Adidas Outlet Store Tinton FLS, Tinton Falls *Also called Adidas North America Inc (G-10705)*
Adler International Ltd (PA) 201 843-4525
205 Maywood Ave Maywood (07607) *(G-6001)*
Adlers Pharmacy Ltc Inc 856 685-7440
100 Dobbs Ln Ste 205 Cherry Hill (08034) *(G-1332)*
ADM Tronics, Northvale *Also called Sonotron Medical Systems Inc (G-7550)*
Adma Biologics Inc (PA) 201 478-5552
465 State Rt 17 Ramsey (07446) *(G-9134)*
Admartec Inc 732 888-8248
12 Crown Plz Ste 204 Hazlet (07730) *(G-4255)*
Admera Health LLC 908 222-0533
126 Corporate Blvd South Plainfield (07080) *(G-10208)*
Admints & Zagabor, Bellmawr *Also called Hit Promo LLC (G-334)*
Admiral Filter Company LLC 973 664-0400
18 Green Pond Rd Ste 3 Rockaway (07866) *(G-9436)*
Admiral Technology LLC 973 698-5920
18 Green Pond Rd Ste 3 Rockaway (07866) *(G-9437)*
Adorage Inc 201 886-7000
1055 River Rd Apt Th10 Edgewater (07020) *(G-2432)*
Adotta America, Englewood *Also called Europrojects Intl Inc (G-2903)*
Adpro Imprints 732 531-2133
1206 State Route 35 Ocean (07712) *(G-7653)*
Adron Inc 973 334-1600
94 Fanny Rd Boonton (07005) *(G-536)*
ADS, Logan Township *Also called Advanced Drainage Systems Inc (G-5584)*
ADS, Cherry Hill *Also called Air Distribution Systems Inc (G-1336)*
ADS Sales Co Inc 732 591-0500
1010 Campus Dr Morganville (07751) *(G-6580)*
Adsorptech Inc (PA) 732 356-1000
452 Lincoln Blvd Middlesex (08846) *(G-6092)*
Adsorptech LLC 732 491-7727
452 Lincoln Blvd Middlesex (08846) *(G-6093)*
Adtranz, Kearny *Also called Bombardier Transportation (G-4849)*
Advance Digital Inc 201 459-2808
185 Hudson St Ste 3100 Jersey City (07311) *(G-4686)*
Advance International Inc (PA) 212 213-2229
8 Willow Ridge Ct Matawan (07747) *(G-5966)*
Advance Machine Inc 908 486-7244
531 Pennsylvania Ave Linden (07036) *(G-5316)*
Advance Machine Planning Inc 732 356-4438
200 Egel Ave Middlesex (08846) *(G-6094)*
Advance Printing Co, Garwood *Also called Ocsidot Inc (G-3788)*
Advance Process Systems Lim 201 400-9190
130 Gunn Rd Branchville (07826) *(G-701)*
Advance Scale Company Inc (PA) 856 784-4916
2400 Egg Harbor Rd Lindenwold (08021) *(G-5444)*
Advanced Abrasives Corporation 856 665-9300
7980 National Hwy Pennsauken (08110) *(G-8383)*
Advanced Biotech, Totowa *Also called Centrome Inc (G-10822)*
Advanced Biotech Overseas LLC (PA) 973 339-6242
10 Taft Rd Totowa (07512) *(G-10808)*
Advanced Brewing Sys LLC 973 633-1777
91 Savoy Pl Prospect Park (07508) *(G-9072)*
Advanced Cerametrics Inc (PA) 609 397-2900
245 N Main St Lambertville (08530) *(G-5186)*
Advanced Cutting Services LLC 908 241-5332
169 E Highland Pkwy Roselle (07203) *(G-9546)*
Advanced Drainage Systems Inc 856 467-4779
300 Progress Ct Logan Township (08085) *(G-5584)*
Advanced Energy Voorhees Inc 856 627-1287
1007 Laurel Oak Rd Voorhees (08043) *(G-11279)*
Advanced Food Systems Inc 732 873-6776
21 Roosevelt Ave Somerset (08873) *(G-9942)*
Advanced Formulations, Long Valley *Also called Millennium Research LLC (G-5612)*
Advanced Imaging Assoc LLC (PA) 973 823-8999
190 Munsonhurst Rd Ste 1 Franklin (07416) *(G-3597)*
Advanced Industrial Controls 908 725-7575
10 County Line Rd Ste 30 Branchburg (08876) *(G-611)*

Advanced Metal Processing 856 327-0048
326 S Wade Blvd Millville (08332) *(G-6223)*
Advanced Micro Devices Inc 732 787-2892
16 Snyder Dr North Middletown (07748) *(G-7502)*
Advanced Orthmolecular RES Inc 317 292-9013
30-38 Industrial St W Clifton (07012) *(G-1557)*
Advanced Orthmolecular RES LLC, Clifton *Also called Advanced Orthmolecular RES Inc (G-1557)*
Advanced Pavement Technologies 973 366-8044
195 Green Pond Rd Rockaway (07866) *(G-9438)*
Advanced Polymer Inc 201 964-3000
400 Paterson Plank Rd Carlstadt (07072) *(G-1118)*
Advanced Precision Inc 800 788-9473
15 Wilson Dr Ste B Sparta (07871) *(G-10375)*
Advanced Precision Systems LLC 908 730-8892
6 Sunset Dr High Bridge (08829) *(G-4280)*
Advanced Products LLC 800 724-5464
1915 Swarthmore Ave Lakewood (08701) *(G-5046)*
Advanced Protective Products 201 794-2000
17-10 River Rd Ste 4c Fair Lawn (07410) *(G-3082)*
Advanced Sewer 973 278-1948
10 Memorial Dr Woodland Park (07424) *(G-12069)*
Advanced Shore Imaging Associa 732 678-0087
2605 Shore Rd Northfield (08225) *(G-7509)*
Advanced Studies In Medicine, Somerville *Also called Galen Publishing LLC (G-10111)*
Advanced Technical Support Inc 609 298-2522
231 Crosswicks Rd Bordentown (08505) *(G-574)*
Advanced Technology Group Inc 973 627-6955
101 Round Hill Dr Ste 3 Rockaway (07866) *(G-9439)*
Advancing Opportunities Inc 201 907-0200
639 Teaneck Rd Teaneck (07666) *(G-10621)*
Advansix Inc (PA) 973 526-1800
300 Kimball Dr Ste 101 Parsippany (07054) *(G-7875)*
Advanstar Communications Inc 973 944-7777
5 Paragon Dr Montvale (07645) *(G-6395)*
Advanstar Communications Inc 732 596-0276
485 Us Highway 1 S # 200 Iselin (08830) *(G-4590)*
Advantage Asia, Garfield *Also called Clear Plus Windshield Wipers (G-3735)*
Advantage Ds LLC 856 307-9600
8 Deptford Rd Glassboro (08028) *(G-3806)*
Advantage Engineering Group, Boonton *Also called Technical Advantage Inc (G-570)*
Advantage Fiberglass Inc 609 926-4606
4 Prospect Ave Egg Harbor Township (08234) *(G-2675)*
Advantage Molding Products 732 303-8667
2106 Highway 35 Sea Girt (08750) *(G-9745)*
Advantage Molding Products 732 303-8667
865 Hwy 33 Freehold (07728) *(G-3643)*
Advantage Publications, Fort Lee *Also called N J W Magazine (G-3575)*
Advantice Health LLC 973 946-7550
7 E Frederick Pl Ste 100 Cedar Knolls (07927) *(G-1296)*
Advaxis Inc (PA) 609 452-9813
305 College Rd E Princeton (08540) *(G-8901)*
Adventure Industries LLC (PA) 609 426-1777
59 Lake Dr East Windsor (08520) *(G-2334)*
Advertisers Service Group Inc 201 440-5577
65 Railroad Ave Ridgefield Park (07660) *(G-9298)*
Advocate Publishing Corp 973 497-4200
171 Clifton Ave Newark (07104) *(G-7036)*
AE Litho Offset Printers Inc 609 239-0070
450 Broad St Beverly (08010) *(G-445)*
Aelitho Group, Beverly *Also called AE Litho Offset Printers Inc (G-445)*
Aeon Corporation 609 275-9003
186 Princeton Hightstown Princeton Junction (08550) *(G-9047)*
Aeon Engineering LLC 518 253-7681
442 Main St Ste 5 Fort Lee (07024) *(G-3545)*
Aeon Industries Inc 732 246-3224
76 Veronica Ave Somerset (08873) *(G-9943)*
Aer X Dust Corporation 732 946-9462
12 Windingbrook Way Holmdel (07733) *(G-4493)*
Aerie Pharmaceuticals Inc 908 470-4320
550 Hills Dr Ste 310 Bedminster (07921) *(G-258)*
Aero Manufacturing Co 973 473-5300
310 Allwood Rd Clifton (07012) *(G-1558)*
Aero Products Co Inc 973 759-0959
21 N 8th St Belleville (07109) *(G-289)*
Aero TEC Laboratories Inc (PA) 201 825-1400
45 Spear Rd Ramsey (07446) *(G-9135)*
Aerocon, Belleville *Also called Vac-U-Max (G-319)*
Aerocon Inc 800 405-2376
69 William St Belleville (07109) *(G-290)*
Aerodefense, Holmdel *Also called Drone Go Home LLC (G-4499)*
Aeroflex Ctrl Components Inc, Eatontown *Also called Cobham New Jersey Inc (G-2384)*
Aerogroup Retail Holdings Inc 732 819-9843
207 Meadow Rd Ste A Edison (08817) *(G-2448)*
Aerojet Rocketdyne De Inc 201 440-1453
500 Walnut St Norwood (07648) *(G-7557)*
Aeronautical Instr & Rdo Co (PA) 973 473-0034
234 Garibaldi Ave Lodi (07644) *(G-5550)*

Aeropanel Corporation 973 335-9636
661 Myrtle Ave Boonton (07005) *(G-537)*

Aeropres Corporation 908 292-1240
318 Valley Rd Hillsborough (08844) *(G-4301)*

Aerosmith 973 614-9392
176 Saddle River Ave B South Hackensack (07606) *(G-10147)*

Aerospace Industries LLC 973 383-9307
520 Lafayette Rd Sparta (07871) *(G-10376)*

Aerospace Manufacturing Inc 973 472-9888
80 Van Winkle Ave Wallington (07057) *(G-11380)*

Aerospace Nylok, Hawthorne *Also called Nylok Corporation* *(G-4235)*

Aerotech Proc Solutions LLC 973 782-4485
57 Wood St Paterson (07524) *(G-8126)*

Aesys Inc 201 871-3223
27 Bland St Emerson (07630) *(G-2862)*

Aeterna Zentaris Inc 908 626-5428
20 Independence Blvd # 401 Warren (07059) *(G-11397)*

AF Pharma LLC 908 769-7040
1500 Garden St Apt 2i Hoboken (07030) *(G-4443)*

AFA Polytek North America Inc 862 260-9450
240 Cedar Knolls Rd # 201 Cedar Knolls (07927) *(G-1297)*

Affil Endoscopy Services CL 201 842-0020
925 Clifton Ave Ste 100 Clifton (07013) *(G-1559)*

Affinity Chemical Woodbine LLC 973 873-4070
82 Crenshaw Dr Flanders (07836) *(G-3398)*

Affordable Lead Solutions LLC 856 207-1348
26 Blew Valley Ln Bridgeton (08302) *(G-750)*

Affordable Offset Printing Inc 856 661-0722
809 Hylton Rd Ste 11 Pennsauken (08110) *(G-8384)*

Affordable Roofing, Pennsauken *Also called Affordable Offset Printing Inc* *(G-8384)*

Afi, Somerset *Also called American Fibertek Inc* *(G-9951)*

Afina Corporation 973 684-7650
40 Warren St Paterson (07524) *(G-8127)*

Afk Machine Inc (PA) 973 539-1329
50 High Ridge Rd Randolph (07869) *(G-9170)*

AFL Telecommunications Inc 908 707-9500
745 Us Highway 202/206 Bridgewater (08807) *(G-782)*

AFL Telecommunications LLC 864 486-7303
123 Town Square Pl Jersey City (07310) *(G-4687)*

Aflag Pharmaceuticals LLC 732 609-4139
163 Jefferson Blvd Edison (08817) *(G-2449)*

Aflex Extrusion Technologies 732 752-0048
240b N Randolphville Rd Piscataway (08854) *(G-8626)*

AFP Transformers Corporation 732 248-0305
970 New Durham Rd Edison (08817) *(G-2450)*

Africa World Press 609 695-3200
541 W Ingham Ave Ste B Ewing (08638) *(G-3013)*

Africa World Red Sea Press, Ewing *Also called Red Sea Press Inc* *(G-3059)*

Aftek Inc 609 588-0900
2960 E State Street Ext Hamilton (08619) *(G-4101)*

AG&e Holdings Inc (PA) 609 704-3000
223 Pratt St Hammonton (08037) *(G-4124)*

AGA Foodservice Inc (PA) 856 428-4200
110 Woodcrest Rd Cherry Hill (08003) *(G-1333)*

Agape Child Care Center, West Milford *Also called Almond Branch Inc* *(G-11724)*

Agape Inc 973 923-7625
487 Chancellor Ave Irvington (07111) *(G-4553)*

Agate Lacquer Tri-Nat LLC 732 968-1080
824 South Ave Middlesex (08846) *(G-6095)*

Agau Inc 732 583-4343
1077 State Route 34 Ste M Matawan (07747) *(G-5967)*

AGC Products Inc 973 248-5039
3740 N West Blvd Vineland (08360) *(G-11184)*

AGFA Corporation (HQ) 800 540-2432
611 River Dr Ste 305 Elmwood Park (07407) *(G-2808)*

AGFA Corporation 201 440-0111
580 Gotham Pkwy Carlstadt (07072) *(G-1119)*

AGFA Corporation 908 231-5000
1318 State Hwy 31 Somerville (08876) *(G-10102)*

AGFA Corporation 201 440-0111
611 River Dr Ste 305 Elmwood Park (07407) *(G-2809)*

AGFA Corporation 201 288-4101
580 Gotham Pkwy Carlstadt (07072) *(G-1120)*

AGFA Corporation, Elmwood Park, Elmwood Park *Also called AGFA Finance Corp* *(G-2810)*

AGFA Finance Corp 201 796-0058
611 River Dr Elmwood Park (07407) *(G-2810)*

AGFA Graphics, Elmwood Park *Also called AGFA Corporation* *(G-2808)*

Agile Therapeutics Inc 609 683-1880
101 Poor Farm Rd Princeton (08540) *(G-8902)*

Agilent Technologies Inc 973 448-7129
550 Clark Dr Ste 2 Budd Lake (07828) *(G-917)*

Agilex Flavors Fragrances Inc (HQ) 732 885-0702
140 Centennial Ave Piscataway (08854) *(G-8627)*

Agilex Fragrances, Piscataway *Also called Aromatic Technologies Inc* *(G-8636)*

Agilis Chemicals Inc. 973 910-2424
830 Morris Tpke Fl 4 Short Hills (07078) *(G-9864)*

Aginova Inc (PA) 732 804-3272
3 Chambry Ct Freehold (07728) *(G-3644)*

Agno Pharma 609 223-0638
5 Wingate Ct Allentown (08501) *(G-23)*

Agoura Hills Group 818 888-0400
4 Executive Campus # 104 Cherry Hill (08002) *(G-1334)*

Agoura Hills Group (HQ) 818 888-0400
4 Executive Campus # 104 Cherry Hill (08002) *(G-1335)*

Agrilink Foods, Parsippany *Also called Birds Eye Foods Inc* *(G-7894)*

Agrium Advanced Tech US Inc 732 296-8448
1470 Jersey Ave North Brunswick (08902) *(G-7451)*

Agro Foods Inc 201 954-9152
441 Schooleys Mountain Rd Hackettstown (07840) *(G-3995)*

Agsco Corporation 973 244-0005
60 Chapin Rd Pine Brook (07058) *(G-8584)*

Agway, Burlington *Also called Klein Distributors Inc* *(G-977)*

Agway Energy Services LLC 973 887-5300
240 State Route 10 Whippany (07981) *(G-11877)*

Ahb Foods, Mount Laurel *Also called American Harvest Baking Co Inc* *(G-6737)*

Ahe Manufacturing Inc 609 660-8000
127 S Main St Barnegat (08005) *(G-154)*

Ahern Blueprinting Inc 732 223-1476
231 Parker Ave Manasquan (08736) *(G-5827)*

Ahs Hospital Corp 908 522-2000
99 Beauvoir Ave Summit (07901) *(G-10523)*

Ahzanis Castle LLC 973 874-3191
134 E Main St Paterson (07522) *(G-8128)*

Ai Container, Boonton *Also called American International Cont* *(G-541)*

AI Technology Inc 609 799-9388
70 Washington Rd Princeton Junction (08550) *(G-9048)*

Ai-Logix Inc 732 469-0880
27 Worlds Fair Dr Ste 2 Somerset (08873) *(G-9944)*

AIAC, Fairfield *Also called Titanium Fabrication Corp* *(G-3329)*

Aibens Imort 609 902-9953
7 York Rd Princeton Junction (08550) *(G-9049)*

Aic, Branchburg *Also called Advanced Industrial Controls* *(G-611)*

Aicumen Technologies Inc 732 668-4204
11 Nestlewood Way Princeton (08540) *(G-8903)*

AIG Industrial Group Inc (HQ) 201 767-7300
220 Pegasus Ave Northvale (07647) *(G-7516)*

Aim Computer Associates Inc 201 489-3100
19 Dover Ct Bergenfield (07621) *(G-369)*

Ainsworth Media 856 854-1400
732 Haddon Ave Collingswood (08108) *(G-1766)*

Air & Hydraulic Power Inc. 201 447-1589
555 Goffle Rd Wyckoff (07481) *(G-12101)*

Air & Specialties Sheet Metal 908 233-8306
276 Sheffield St Mountainside (07092) *(G-6832)*

Air BP, Linden *Also called BP Corporation North Amer Inc* *(G-5327)*

Air Clean Co Inc 908 355-1515
1135 Chestnut St Elizabeth (07201) *(G-2708)*

Air Cruisers Company LLC (HQ) 732 681-3527
1747 State Route 34 Wall Township (07727) *(G-11315)*

Air Distribution Systems Inc 856 874-1100
1000 Astoria Blvd Cherry Hill (08003) *(G-1336)*

Air Liquide Advanced Materials 908 231-9060
197 Meister Ave Bldg A Branchburg (08876) *(G-612)*

Air Power Inc 973 882-5418
25 Commerce Rd Ste N Fairfield (07004) *(G-3136)*

Air Products, Paulsboro *Also called Coim USA Inc* *(G-8331)*

Air Products and Chemicals Inc 732 446-5676
405 Route 33 Manalapan (07726) *(G-5800)*

Air Protection Packaging Corp 973 577-4343
1200 Fuller Rd Ste 2 Linden (07036) *(G-5317)*

Air Technology Inc 973 334-4980
429 Rockaway Valley Rd # 1100 Boonton (07005) *(G-538)*

Air World Inc 201 831-0700
126 Christie Ave Mahwah (07430) *(G-5711)*

Airborne Systems N Amer Inc (HQ) 856 663-1275
5800 Magnolia Ave Pennsauken (08109) *(G-8385)*

Airborne Systems N Amer NJ Inc 856 663-1275
5800 Magnolia Ave Pennsauken (08109) *(G-8386)*

Airborne Systems NA, Pennsauken *Also called Airborne Systems N Amer Inc* *(G-8385)*

Airbrasive Jet Tech LLC 201 725-7340
3461 S Clinton Ave South Plainfield (07080) *(G-10209)*

Airbrush Action Inc 732 223-7878
79 S Main St Ste 1 Barnegat (08005) *(G-155)*

Airchartercom LLC 212 999-4926
6515 Kennedy Blvd E West New York (07093) *(G-11735)*

Airdye Solutions LLC (PA) 540 433-9101
21 Glen Rock Rd Cedar Grove (07009) *(G-1266)*

Airfiltronix Corp (HQ) 973 779-5577
154 Huron Ave Clifton (07013) *(G-1560)*

Airgas Usa LLC 609 685-4241
1910 Old Cuthbert Rd Cherry Hill (08034) *(G-1337)*

Airgas Usa LLC 856 829-7878
600 Union Landing Rd Cinnaminson (08077) *(G-1440)*

Airmet Inc 973 481-5550
794 N 6th St Newark (07107) *(G-7037)*

Airmet Metal Works, Newark *Also called Airmet Inc* *(G-7037)*

Airoyal Division, Butler *Also called Delta Sales Company Inc* *(G-999)*

Airscan Inc 908 823-9425
  291 Rt 22 Ste 12 Lebanon (08833) *(G-5249)*
Airtec Inc 732 382-3700
  17 W Scott Ave Rahway (07065) *(G-9075)*
Airtec-Unique, Rahway *Also called Airtec Inc (G-9075)*
Airtech Vacuum, Rutherford *Also called Apple Air Compressor Corp (G-9613)*
Airworld Inc 973 720-1008
  70 Spruce St Paterson (07501) *(G-8129)*
Airzone Systems 201 207-6593
  28 Valhalla Rd Montville (07045) *(G-6437)*
AlSha&anna Nation of Trends 201 951-8197
  2 Park Sq Apt 2210 Rahway (07065) *(G-9076)*
AJ Oster LLC 973 673-5700
  150 Lackawanna Ave Parsippany (07054) *(G-7876)*
AJ Siris Products Corp 973 823-0050
  150 Main St Ogdensburg (07439) *(G-7708)*
Ajay Metal Fabricators Inc 908 523-0557
  355 Dalziel Rd Linden (07036) *(G-5318)*
Ajg Packaging LLC 908 528-6052
  10 Northwood Dr Pittstown (08867) *(G-8751)*
Ajj Powernutrition LLC 908 452-5164
  1930 State Route 57 Hackettstown (07840) *(G-3996)*
Akadema Inc 973 304-1470
  46 Star Lake Rd Ste B Bloomingdale (07403) *(G-525)*
Akay USA LLC 732 254-7177
  500 Hartle St Sayreville (08872) *(G-9700)*
Akcros Chemicals Inc 800 500-7890
  500 Jersey Ave New Brunswick (08901) *(G-6909)*
Akela Laser Corporation 732 305-7105
  1095 Cranbury S Riv 14 Monroe Township (08831) *(G-6325)*
Akers Biosciences Inc 856 848-8698
  201 Grove Rd West Deptford (08086) *(G-11690)*
Akila Holdings Inc 609 454-5034
  12 Hampstead Ct Princeton (08540) *(G-8904)*
Akorn Inc 609 662-9100
  5 Cedarbrook Dr Ste 7 Cranbury (08512) *(G-1807)*
Akorn Inc 732 532-1000
  275 Pierce St Somerset (08873) *(G-9945)*
Akorn Inc 732 448-7043
  69 Veronica Ave Ste 6b Somerset (08873) *(G-9946)*
Akorn Inc 732 846-8066
  72 Veronica Ave Ste 6 Somerset (08873) *(G-9947)*
Akrimax Pharmaceuticals LLC 908 372-0506
  11 Commerce Dr Ste 103 Cranford (07016) *(G-1898)*
Aks Pharma Inc 856 521-0710
  201 Front St Elmer (08318) *(G-2793)*
Akw Inc 732 493-1883
  1414 Roller Rd Rear Ocean (07712) *(G-7654)*
Akw Inc (PA) 732 530-9186
  41 Newman Springs Rd E Shrewsbury (07702) *(G-9880)*
Akzo Chemicals, Edison *Also called Nouryon Surface Chemistry (G-2579)*
Akzo Nobel Coatings Inc 732 617-7734
  300 Campus Dr Ste B Morganville (07751) *(G-6581)*
Al and John Inc 973 742-4990
  147 Clinton Rd Caldwell (07006) *(G-1020)*
Al Richrds Homemade Chocolates 201 436-0915
  851 Broadway Bayonne (07002) *(G-201)*
Aladdin Color Inc 609 518-9858
  19 E Main St Ste D Moorestown (08057) *(G-6501)*
Aladdin Instruments Corp 774 326-4919
  22 Cherrywood Ct Cherry Hill (08003) *(G-1338)*
Aladdin Manufacturing Corp 973 616-4600
  100 Alexander Ave Pompton Plains (07444) *(G-8856)*
Aladen Athletic Wear LLC 973 838-2425
  465 W Main St Ste 5 Wyckoff (07481) *(G-12102)*
Alan Chemical Corporation Inc 973 628-7777
  573 Valley Rd Ste 1 Wayne (07470) *(G-11466)*
Alan Paul Accessories Inc 609 924-4022
  66 Witherspoon St # 3300 Princeton (08542) *(G-8905)*
Alan Paul Neckware, Princeton *Also called Alan Paul Accessories Inc (G-8905)*
Alan Schatzberg & Associates 201 440-8855
  45 Ruta Ct South Hackensack (07606) *(G-10148)*
Alaqua Inc 201 758-1580
  7004 Boulevard E Apt 28a Guttenberg (07093) *(G-3870)*
Alaquest International Inc 908 713-9399
  28 Molasses Hill Rd Lebanon (08833) *(G-5250)*
Alba Translations CPA 973 340-1130
  436 Main St Lodi (07644) *(G-5551)*
Albapalant USA Inc 201 831-9200
  5 Cheryl Ln Boonton (07005) *(G-539)*
Albea Americas Inc (HQ) 908 689-3000
  191 State Route 31 N Washington (07882) *(G-11437)*
Alben Metal Products Inc 973 279-8891
  11 Iowa Ave Paterson (07503) *(G-8130)*
Alberona Welding & Iron Works 973 674-3375
  452 Scotland Rd Orange (07050) *(G-7749)*
Albert Forte Neckwear Co Inc 856 423-2342
  127 Fellowship Ln Mullica Hill (08062) *(G-6854)*
Albert H Hopper Inc 201 991-2266
  329 Ridge Rd North Arlington (07031) *(G-7367)*

Albert Paper Products Company 973 373-0330
  464 Coit St Irvington (07111) *(G-4554)*
Alboum W Hat Company Inc 201 399-4110
  1439 Springfield Ave Irvington (07111) *(G-4555)*
Alcami New Jersey Corporation 732 346-5100
  165 Fieldcrest Ave Edison (08837) *(G-2451)*
Alcan Baltek Corporation 201 767-1400
  108 Fairway Ct Northvale (07647) *(G-7517)*
Alcaro & Alcaro Plating Co 973 746-1200
  112 Pine St Montclair (07042) *(G-6357)*
Alcatel-Lucent USA Inc 908 582-3275
  600 Mountain Ave 700 New Providence (07974) *(G-6993)*
Alchem Pharmtech Inc 848 565-5694
  1 Deerpark Dr Ste H2 Monmouth Junction (08852) *(G-6277)*
Alchemy Billboards LLC 973 977-8828
  125 5th Ave Paterson (07524) *(G-8131)*
Alco Trimming 201 854-8608
  8608 Grand Ave Rear North Bergen (07047) *(G-7380)*
Alcoa Howmet, Dover, Dover *Also called Howmet Castings & Services Inc (G-2088)*
Alcoa Hwmet Dver Alloy Oprtons, Dover *Also called Howmet Castings & Services Inc (G-2089)*
Alcoa Power Generating Inc 973 361-0300
  9 Roy St Dover (07801) *(G-2073)*
Alcon Products Inc 609 267-3898
  161 Burrs Rd Westampton (08060) *(G-11783)*
Alcop Adhesive Label Co 609 871-4400
  826 Perkins Ln Beverly (08010) *(G-446)*
Alden - Leeds Inc 973 344-7986
  100 Hackensack Ave Kearny (07032) *(G-4841)*
Alden - Leeds Inc (PA) 973 589-3544
  55 Jacobus Ave Ste 1 Kearny (07032) *(G-4842)*
Alden Leeds, Kearny *Also called Alden - Leeds Inc (G-4842)*
Alecto Systems LLC 973 875-6721
  130 Gunn Rd Branchville (07826) *(G-702)*
Alembic Pharmaceuticals Inc (HQ) 908 393-9604
  750 Us Highway 202 # 100 Bridgewater (08807) *(G-783)*
Alere Distribution, Freehold *Also called Alere Inc (G-3646)*
Alere Inc 732 620-4244
  500 Halls Mill Rd Freehold (07728) *(G-3645)*
Alere Inc 732 358-5921
  569 Halls Mill Rd Freehold (07728) *(G-3646)*
Aleris Rolled Products Inc 856 881-3600
  838 N Delsea Dr Clayton (08312) *(G-1523)*
Alessandra Miscellaneous Metal 973 786-6805
  75 Mill St Ste B Newton (07860) *(G-7336)*
Alete Printing LLC 856 468-3536
  722 Dartmouth Ct Wenonah (08090) *(G-11573)*
Alex Brands, Fairfield *Also called Poof-Alex Holdings LLC (G-3292)*
Alex Real LLC 732 730-8770
  1876 Lakewood Rd Toms River (08755) *(G-10740)*
Alexam Riverdale 973 831-0065
  4000 Riverdale Rd Riverdale (07457) *(G-9370)*
Alexander Communications Group 973 265-2300
  36 Midvale Rd Ste 2e Mountain Lakes (07046) *(G-6820)*
Alexander James Corp 908 362-9266
  845 State Route 94 Blairstown (07825) *(G-484)*
Alexander Marketing Services, Mountain Lakes *Also called Alexander Communications Group (G-6820)*
Alfa Wassermann Inc (PA) 973 882-8630
  4 Henderson Dr West Caldwell (07006) *(G-11637)*
Alfa Wssrmann Dagnstc Tech LLC 800 220-4488
  4 Henderson Dr West Caldwell (07006) *(G-11638)*
Alfred Dunner Inc 212 944-6660
  200 Walsh Dr Parsippany (07054) *(G-7877)*
Algar/Display Connection Corp 201 438-1000
  70 Outwater Ln Ste 4 Garfield (07026) *(G-3726)*
Algen Design Services Inc 732 389-3630
  40 Industrial Way E Eatontown (07724) *(G-2374)*
Algene Marking Equipment Co 973 478-9041
  232 Palisade Ave Garfield (07026) *(G-3727)*
Align Pharmaceuticals LLC 908 834-0960
  200 Connell Dr Ste 1500 Berkeley Heights (07922) *(G-387)*
Align Sourcing Ltd Lblty Co 609 375-8550
  46 Doe Dr Trenton (08620) *(G-10889)*
Aliron International Inc (PA) 540 808-1615
  1 Cragwood Rd Ste 101 South Plainfield (07080) *(G-10210)*
Alisa, Englishtown *Also called Golden Treasure Imports Inc (G-3002)*
Alison Control Inc 973 575-7100
  35 Daniel Rd W Fairfield (07004) *(G-3137)*
Alk Technologies Inc (HQ) 609 683-0220
  1 Independence Way # 400 Princeton (08540) *(G-8906)*
Alkaline Corporation 732 531-7830
  38 Industrial Way E Ste 2 Eatontown (07724) *(G-2375)*
Alkaline Corporation 732 531-7830
  714 W Park Ave Oakhurst (07755) *(G-7607)*
Alkazone, Hackensack *Also called Better Healthlab Inc (G-3884)*
Alkazone Global Inc 201 880-7966
  200 S Newman St Hackensack (07601) *(G-3875)*

A L P H A B E T I C

Alkon Signature Inc 917 716-9137
333 Cantor Ave Linden (07036) *(G-5319)*

All American Extrusion Inc 973 881-9030
239 Lindbergh Pl Paterson (07503) *(G-8132)*

All American Metal Fabricators 201 567-2898
34 Harold St Tenafly (07670) *(G-10658)*

All American Oil Recovery Co 973 628-9278
1067 State Route 23 Wayne (07470) *(G-11467)*

All American Poly Corp (PA) 732 752-3200
40 Turner Pl Piscataway (08854) *(G-8628)*

All American Powdercoating LLC 732 349-7001
2002 Route 9 Toms River (08755) *(G-10741)*

All American Print & Copy Ctr 732 758-6200
500 State Route 35 Red Bank (07701) *(G-9219)*

All Amrcan Recycl Corp Clifton 201 656-3363
2 Hope St Jersey City (07307) *(G-4688)*

All Colors Screen Printing LLC 732 777-6033
176 Woodbridge Ave Highland Park (08904) *(G-4286)*

All County Recycling Inc 609 393-6445
391 Enterprise Ave Trenton (08638) *(G-10890)*

ALI Envmtl & Tank Svcs LLC 908 755-2962
2560 Us Highway 22 346 Scotch Plains (07076) *(G-9728)*

All In Color Inc 973 626-0987
132 Beckwith Ave Paterson (07503) *(G-8133)*

All In Icing 973 896-5990
24 Woods Edge Rd Stanhope (07874) *(G-10476)*

All Madina Inc 973 226-7772
592 Passaic Ave West Caldwell (07006) *(G-11639)*

All Mechanical Services Inc 732 442-8292
430 High St Perth Amboy (08861) *(G-8511)*

All Merchandise Display Corp 718 257-2221
7 W Shelton Ter Hillside (07205) *(G-4372)*

All Metal Polishing Co Inc 973 589-8070
23 George St Newark (07105) *(G-7038)*

All Mtals Frge Group Ltd Lblty (PA) 973 276-5000
75 Lane Rd Ste 303 Fairfield (07004) *(G-3138)*

All Natural Products 212 391-2870
4000 Bordentown Ave # 20 Sayreville (08872) *(G-9701)*

All Print Resources Group Inc 201 994-0600
256 Sheffield St Mountainside (07092) *(G-6833)*

All Racks Industries Inc 212 244-1069
101 Roselle St Linden (07036) *(G-5320)*

All Seasons Construction Inc 908 852-0955
43 Flocktown Rd Long Valley (07853) *(G-5607)*

All Seasons Door & Window Inc (PA) 732 238-7100
28 Edgeboro Rd East Brunswick (08816) *(G-2124)*

All Seasons Pool & Spa, Marlton *Also called Van Brill Pool & Spa Center (G-5955)*

All Size Polybags, New Brunswick *Also called R K S Plastics Inc (G-6965)*

All Smith Spinning and Turning, Moonachie *Also called Bergen Homestate Corp (G-6456)*

All Solutions Inc 973 535-9100
355 Eisenhower Pkwy # 210 Livingston (07039) *(G-5503)*

All Sports Stadium, Washington *Also called Armin Kososki (G-11439)*

All State Medal Co Inc 973 458-1458
16 Adams Pl Lodi (07644) *(G-5552)*

All State Plastics Inc 732 654-5054
237 Raritan St South Amboy (08879) *(G-10130)*

All Structures LLC 732 233-7071
21 Rumson Rd Little Silver (07739) *(G-5499)*

All Surface Asphalt Paving 732 295-3800
528 Hardenberg Ave Point Pleasant Boro (08742) *(G-8835)*

All Tool Company Inc 908 687-3636
899 Rahway Ave Union (07083) *(G-11021)*

All-Lace Processing Corp 201 867-1974
1109 Grand Ave Ste 4 North Bergen (07047) *(G-7381)*

All-State Fence Inc 732 431-4944
347 Mount Pleasant Ave # 300 West Orange (07052) *(G-11758)*

All-State International Inc (PA) 908 272-0800
1 Commerce Dr Cranford (07016) *(G-1899)*

All-State Legal, Cranford *Also called All-State International Inc (G-1899)*

Allary Corporation 908 851-0077
2204 Morris Ave Ste 209 Union (07083) *(G-11022)*

Allegra Marketing Print & Mail, Marmora *Also called Sjshore Marketing Ltd Lblty Co (G-5959)*

Allegro Creative, Hightstown *Also called Allegro Mfg (G-4293)*

Allegro Mfg 323 724-0101
150 Milford Rd Hightstown (08520) *(G-4293)*

Allegro Nutrition Inc 732 364-3777
1023 Waverly Ave Neptune (07753) *(G-6864)*

Allegro Printing Corporation 609 641-7060
408 S 4th Ave Galloway (08205) *(G-3719)*

Allen Cabinets and Millwork 973 694-0665
60 Newark Pompton Tpke Pequannock (07440) *(G-8503)*

Allen Flavors Inc (PA) 908 561-5995
230 Saint Nicholas Ave South Plainfield (07080) *(G-10211)*

Allen Flavors Inc 908 753-0544
220 Saint Nicholas Ave South Plainfield (07080) *(G-10212)*

Allen Steel Co 856 785-1171
202 High St Leesburg (08327) *(G-5286)*

Allentown Inc (PA) 609 259-7951
165 Route 526 Allentown (08501) *(G-24)*

Allergan Inc 908 306-0374
1 Crossroads Dr Bedminster (07921) *(G-259)*

Allergan Inc 862 261-7000
16 Airport Rd Morristown (07960) *(G-6631)*

Allergan Inc (HQ) 862 261-7000
5 Giralda Farms Madison (07940) *(G-5687)*

Allergan Finance, Madison *Also called Actavis LLC (G-5686)*

Allergan Pharmacy, Parsippany *Also called Watson Laboratories Inc (G-8038)*

Allergan Sales LLC 973 442-3200
5 Giralda Farms Madison (07940) *(G-5688)*

Allersearch Labs, Eatontown *Also called Alkaline Corporation (G-2375)*

Allfasteners Usa LLC 201 783-8836
480 Meadow Ln Carlstadt (07072) *(G-1121)*

Allgrind Plastics Inc 908 479-4400
6 Vliet Farm Rd Asbury (08802) *(G-57)*

Alliance Contract Mfg, Berlin *Also called Hanson & Zollinger Inc (G-422)*

Alliance Corrugated Box Inc 877 525-5269
10 E Saddle River Rd Saddle River (07458) *(G-9690)*

Alliance Design Group, Totowa *Also called Alliance Design Inc (G-10809)*

Alliance Design Inc 973 904-9450
434 Union Blvd Totowa (07512) *(G-10809)*

Alliance Food Equipment 201 784-1101
1 S Gold Dr Trenton (08691) *(G-10891)*

Alliance Hand & Physical 201 822-0100
24 Booker St Ste 3 Westwood (07675) *(G-11824)*

Alliance Sand Co Inc (PA) 908 534-4116
51 Tannery Rd Somerville (08876) *(G-10103)*

Alliance Sensors Group, Moorestown *Also called H G Schaevitz LLC (G-6526)*

Alliance Store Fixture, Moonachie *Also called Amko Displays Corporation (G-6454)*

Alliance Technologies Group 973 664-1151
57 Eagle Rock Ave East Hanover (07936) *(G-2193)*

Alliance Vinyl Windows Co Inc 856 456-4954
301 Crescent Blvd Oaklyn (08107) *(G-7650)*

Allied Asphalt Division, Piscataway *Also called Ziegler Chem & Mineral Corp (G-8741)*

Allied Concrete Co Inc (PA) 973 627-6150
205 Franklin Ave Rockaway (07866) *(G-9440)*

Allied Concrete Co Inc 973 627-6150
205 Franklin Ave Rockaway (07866) *(G-9441)*

Allied Embroidery, Englewood *Also called Sniderman John (G-2942)*

Allied Envelope Co Inc (PA) 201 440-2000
33 Commerce Rd Carlstadt (07072) *(G-1122)*

Allied Environmental Signage, Farmingdale *Also called Yates Sign Co Inc (G-3397)*

Allied Felt Group Div, Bloomingdale *Also called Central Shippee Inc (G-526)*

Allied Food Products Inc 908 357-2454
1600 W Elizabeth Ave Linden (07036) *(G-5321)*

Allied Group Inc 973 543-4994
5 Cold Hill Rd S Ste 19 Mendham (07945) *(G-6038)*

Allied Metal, North Bergen *Also called Allied Specialty Group Inc (G-7382)*

Allied Metal Industries Inc 973 824-7347
118 Harper St 144 Newark (07114) *(G-7039)*

Allied Old English Inc 732 636-2060
100 Markley St Port Reading (07064) *(G-8892)*

Allied Pharma Inc 732 738-3295
20 Corrielle St Fords (08863) *(G-3529)*

Allied Plastics Holdings LLC (PA) 718 729-5500
560 Ferry St Newark (07105) *(G-7040)*

Allied Plastics New Jersey LLC 973 956-9200
155 Sherman Ave Paterson (07502) *(G-8134)*

Allied Printing Resources, Carlstadt *Also called Allied Envelope Co Inc (G-1122)*

Allied Printing-Graphics Inc 973 227-0520
4 Madison Rd Fairfield (07004) *(G-3139)*

Allied Specialty Foods Inc 856 507-1100
1585 W Forest Grove Rd Vineland (08360) *(G-11185)*

Allied Specialty Group Inc (PA) 201 223-4600
3223 Dell Ave North Bergen (07047) *(G-7382)*

Allied Steaks, Vineland *Also called Allied Specialty Foods Inc (G-11185)*

Allied Steel Dist & Svc Ctr, Newark *Also called Allied Metal Industries Inc (G-7039)*

Allied Tile Mfg Corp 718 647-2200
631 Montrose Ave South Plainfield (07080) *(G-10213)*

Allied Waste Products Inc 973 473-7638
61 Midland Ave Ste 61-71 Wallington (07057) *(G-11381)*

Allied Wide, Fairfield *Also called 224 Graphics Inc (G-3132)*

Allied-Signal China Ltd 973 455-2000
101 Columbia Rd Morristown (07960) *(G-6632)*

Alliedsignal Foreign Sls Corp 973 455-2000
101 Columbia Rd Morristown (07960) *(G-6633)*

Allison Corp (PA) 973 992-3800
15-33 Okner Pkwy Livingston (07039) *(G-5504)*

Allison Systems Corporation 856 461-9111
220 Adams St Riverside (08075) *(G-9389)*

Allmark Door Company LLC (PA) 610 358-9800
15 Stern Ave Springfield (07081) *(G-10425)*

Allmike Metal Technology Inc 201 935-2306
65 Anderson Ave Moonachie (07074) *(G-6452)*

Allos Therapeutics Inc 609 936-3760
302 Carnegie Ctr Ste 200 Princeton (08540) *(G-8907)*

Alloy Cast Products Inc 908 245-2255
700 Swenson Dr Kenilworth (07033) *(G-4920)*

Alloy Software Inc 973 661-9700
  400 Broadacres Dr Ste 100 Bloomfield (07003) *(G-490)*

Alloy Stainless Products Co, Totowa *Also called Knickerbocker Machine Shop Inc* *(G-10834)*

Alloy Stainless Products Co 973 256-1616
  611 Union Blvd Totowa (07512) *(G-10810)*

Alloy Welding Co 908 218-1551
  6 Culnen Dr Ste A Branchburg (08876) *(G-613)*

Allstar Disposal 973 398-8808
  118 Hudson Ave Hopatcong (07843) *(G-4517)*

Allstate Can Corporation 973 560-9030
  1 Woodhollow Rd Parsippany (07054) *(G-7878)*

Allstate Conveyor Service 856 768-6566
  256 Terrace Blvd Voorhees (08043) *(G-11280)*

Allstate Paper Box Co Inc (PA) 973 589-2600
  223 Raymond Blvd Newark (07105) *(G-7041)*

Alltec Stores, Fairfield *Also called Vcom Intl Multi-Media Corp* *(G-3339)*

Alltest Instruments Inc 732 919-3339
  500 Central Ave Farmingdale (07727) *(G-3376)*

Alltite Gasket Co 732 254-2154
  323 William St South River (08882) *(G-10348)*

Allu Group Inc 201 288-2236
  25 Kimberly Rd Ste A East Brunswick (08816) *(G-2125)*

Allure Box & Display Co 212 807-7070
  216 Charles St Hackensack (07601) *(G-3876)*

Allure Pet Pdts Ltd Lblty Co 973 339-9655
  321 Palmer Rd Denville (07834) *(G-2029)*

Alm Media LLC 973 642-0075
  238 Mulberry St Fl 2 Newark (07102) *(G-7042)*

Alma Park Alpacas 732 620-1052
  2800 Monmouth Rd Jobstown (08041) *(G-4835)*

Almark Tool & Manufacturing Co 908 789-2440
  27 South Ave Garwood (07027) *(G-3780)*

Almatica Pharma Inc 877 447-7979
  44 Whippany Rd Ste 3 Morristown (07960) *(G-6634)*

Almetek Industries Inc 908 850-9700
  2 Joy Dr Hackettstown (07840) *(G-3997)*

Almike Metal Products, Moonachie *Also called Allmike Metal Technology Inc* *(G-6452)*

Almond Branch Inc 973 728-3479
  184 Marshall Hill Rd West Milford (07480) *(G-11724)*

Aln, Woodcliff Lake *Also called American Logistics Network LLC* *(G-12046)*

Aloe Creme Laboratories Div, Branchburg *Also called Aloe Science Inc* *(G-614)*

Aloe Science Inc 908 231-8888
  160 Meister Ave Ste 20 Branchburg (08876) *(G-614)*

Aloris Tool Technology Co Inc 973 772-1201
  407 Getty Ave Clifton (07011) *(G-1561)*

Alpex Wheel Co Inc (PA) 201 871-1700
  29 Atwood Ave Tenafly (07670) *(G-10659)*

Alpha 1 Studio Inc 609 859-2200
  3 Linda Ln Southampton (08088) *(G-10359)*

Alpha Advanced Materials, Somerset *Also called Alpha Assembly Solutions Inc* *(G-9948)*

Alpha Assembly Solutions Inc 908 561-5170
  109 Corporate Blvd South Plainfield (07080) *(G-10214)*

Alpha Assembly Solutions Inc (HQ) 908 791-3000
  300 Atrium Dr Fl 3 Somerset (08873) *(G-9948)*

Alpha Associates Inc 732 730-1800
  145 Lehigh Ave Lakewood (08701) *(G-5047)*

Alpha Engneered Composites LLC (PA) 732 634-5700
  145 Lehigh Ave Lakewood (08701) *(G-5048)*

Alpha Industries, Lyndhurst *Also called Epsilon Plastics Inc* *(G-5651)*

Alpha Industries MGT Inc (PA) 201 933-6000
  800 Page Ave Lyndhurst (07071) *(G-5639)*

Alpha Lehigh Tool & Mch Co Inc 908 454-6481
  41 Industrial Rd Alpha (08865) *(G-35)*

Alpha Plastics, Middlesex *Also called Fram Trak Industries Inc* *(G-6117)*

Alpha Processing Co Inc 973 777-1737
  210 Delawanna Ave Clifton (07014) *(G-1562)*

Alpha Tech Services 973 283-2011
  121 Hawkins Pl Ste 197 Boonton (07005) *(G-540)*

Alpha Wire, Elizabeth *Also called Belden Inc* *(G-2714)*

Alpha Wire Corporation (PA) 908 925-8000
  711 Lidgerwood Ave Elizabeth (07202) *(G-2709)*

AlphaGraphics, Cherry Hill *Also called C Jackson Associates Inc* *(G-1351)*

AlphaGraphics, Totowa *Also called Viskal Printing LLC* *(G-10860)*

AlphaGraphics, Midland Park *Also called Wilker Graphics LLC* *(G-6190)*

AlphaGraphics, Cranbury *Also called Your Printer V20 Ltd* *(G-1895)*

AlphaGraphics 201 327-2200
  1 Lethbridge Plz Ste 22 Mahwah (07430) *(G-5712)*

AlphaGraphics 856 761-8000
  2050 Springdale Rd # 700 Cherry Hill (08003) *(G-1339)*

AlphaGraphics 321, North Brunswick *Also called Carl A Venable Inc* *(G-7460)*

Alphagraphics Printshops of th, Parsippany *Also called Digital Print Solutions Inc* *(G-7917)*

AlphaGraphics Printshops of Th 973 984-0066
  60 Speedwell Ave Morristown (07960) *(G-6635)*

Alpharma US Inc 201 228-5090
  400 Crossing Blvd Ste 701 Bridgewater (08807) *(G-784)*

Alphawire, Elizabeth *Also called Alpha Wire Corporation* *(G-2709)*

Alpine Bakery Inc 201 902-0605
  521-523 30th St Union City (07087) *(G-11104)*

Alpine Corrugated McHy Inc 201 440-3030
  100 Challenger Rd Ste 304 Ridgefield Park (07660) *(G-9299)*

Alpine Creamery 973 726-0777
  14 White Deer Plz Sparta (07871) *(G-10377)*

Alpine Custom Floors 201 533-0100
  173 Sherman Ave Jersey City (07307) *(G-4689)*

Alpine Group Inc (PA) 201 549-4400
  1 Meadowlands Plz Ste 800 East Rutherford (07073) *(G-2269)*

Alpine Machine & Tool Corp 201 666-0959
  42 Bergenline Ave Westwood (07675) *(G-11825)*

Alpro Inc 201 342-4498
  50 Romanelli Ave South Hackensack (07606) *(G-10149)*

Alps Technologies Inc 732 764-0777
  500 Memorial Dr Ste 1 Somerset (08873) *(G-9949)*

Alster Import Company Inc 201 332-7245
  16 Burma Rd Jersey City (07305) *(G-4690)*

Alstrom Energy Group LLC 718 824-4901
  11 Jocama Blvd Ste 11a Old Bridge (08857) *(G-7711)*

Alt Shift Creative LLC 609 619-0009
  15 Mountain Ave Flanders (07836) *(G-3399)*

Altaflo LLC 973 300-3344
  23 Wilson Dr Ste 1 Sparta (07871) *(G-10378)*

Altantic Printing and Design 732 557-9600
  467 Lakehurst Rd Toms River (08755) *(G-10742)*

Altare Publishing Inc 727 237-1330
  100 Campus Town Cir # 103 Ewing (08638) *(G-3014)*

Altech Machine & Tool Inc 201 652-4409
  230 Bank St Midland Park (07432) *(G-6169)*

Alteon 201 934-1624
  170 Williams Dr Ramsey (07446) *(G-9136)*

Altera Corporation 732 649-3477
  106 Charles St Somerset (08873) *(G-9950)*

Alternate Side Street Suspende 201 291-7878
  16 Arcadian Way Ste C1 Paramus (07652) *(G-7788)*

Alternative Air Fixture, Willingboro *Also called Alternative Air LLC* *(G-11988)*

Alternative Air LLC (PA) 609 261-5870
  30 Echo Ln Willingboro (08046) *(G-11988)*

Altibase Incorporated 888 837-7333
  1 International Blvd Mahwah (07495) *(G-5713)*

Altima Innovations Inc 732 474-1500
  211 Evans Way Branchburg (08876) *(G-615)*

Altivity Packaging, Wayne *Also called Graphic Packaging Intl LLC* *(G-11513)*

Alto Development Corp (PA) 732 938-2266
  5206 Asbury Rd Wall Township (07727) *(G-11316)*

Altona Blower & Shtmtl Work 201 641-3520
  23 N Washington Ave Little Ferry (07643) *(G-5474)*

Altona Blower & Shtmtl Works, Little Ferry *Also called Altona Blower & Shtmtl Work* *(G-5474)*

Altria Group Distribution Co 804 274-2000
  9 Campus Dr Ste 3 Parsippany (07054) *(G-7879)*

Altus Pcb LLC 877 442-5887
  45 Legion Dr Cresskill (07626) *(G-1941)*

Alu Inc 201 935-2213
  240 Anderson Ave Moonachie (07074) *(G-6453)*

Aluma Systems Con Cnstr LLC 908 418-5073
  1800 Lower Rd Linden (07036) *(G-5322)*

Aluminum Shapes Inc 856 662-5500
  9000 River Rd Pennsauken (08110) *(G-8387)*

Aluminum Shapes LLC 888 488-7427
  9000 River Rd Delair (08110) *(G-1999)*

Aluseal LLC 856 692-3355
  1649 Castpa Pl Vineland (08360) *(G-11186)*

Alva-Tech Inc 609 747-1133
  1208 Columbus Rd Ste G Burlington Township (08016) *(G-995)*

Alvaro P Escandon Inc 973 274-1040
  528 Ferry St Newark (07105) *(G-7043)*

Alvaro Stairs LLC 201 864-6754
  4201 Tonnelle Ave Ste 12 North Bergen (07047) *(G-7383)*

Alvogen Group Inc (PA) 973 796-3400
  44 Whippany Rd Ste 300 Morristown (07960) *(G-6636)*

Alvogen Inc 973 796-3400
  44 Whippany Rd Ste 108 Morristown (07960) *(G-6637)*

Alvogen Pb Research & Dev LLC 973 796-3400
  44 Whippany Rd Ste 300 Morristown (07960) *(G-6638)*

Alvogen Pharma Us Inc (HQ) 973 796-3400
  44 Whippany Rd Ste 300 Morristown (07960) *(G-6639)*

Always Be Secure LLC 917 887-2286
  195 Route 9 Ste 109 Manalapan (07726) *(G-5801)*

Alyce Intimate, Lakewood *Also called Vaeg LLC* *(G-5175)*

Alzo International Inc 732 254-1901
  650 Jernee Mill Rd Sayreville (08872) *(G-9702)*

AM Best Company Inc (PA) 908 439-2200
  1 Ambest Rd Oldwick (08858) *(G-7738)*

AM Best Company Inc 908 439-2200
  Am Best Rd Oldwick (08858) *(G-7739)*

AM Cruz International LLC 732 340-0066
  13 New York Ave Colonia (07067) *(G-1774)*

AM Wood Inc 732 246-1506
  18 Kennedy Blvd East Brunswick (08816) *(G-2126)*

A
L
P
H
A
B
E
T
I
C

Am-Mac Incorporated................................973 575-7567
  311 Route 46 W Ste C Fairfield (07004) *(G-3140)*

Amalco, Mountainside *Also called American Aluminum Company (G-6834)*

Amalia Carrara Inc................................201 348-4500
  2111 Kerrigan Ave Union City (07087) *(G-11105)*

Amano Cincinnati Distributor, Roseland *Also called Amano Cincinnati Incorporated (G-9530)*

Amano Cincinnati Incorporated (HQ)................................973 403-1900
  140 Harrison Ave Roseland (07068) *(G-9530)*

Amano USA Holdings Inc (HQ)................................973 403-1900
  140 Harrison Ave Roseland (07068) *(G-9531)*

Amante International Ltd................................908 518-1688
  510 Codding Rd Westfield (07090) *(G-11793)*

Amarin Corporation PLC................................908 719-1315
  1430 Us Highway 206 # 100 Bedminster (07921) *(G-260)*

Amarin Pharma Inc................................908 719-1315
  440 Route 22 Bridgewater (08807) *(G-785)*

Amark Industries Inc (PA)................................973 992-8900
  293 Eisenhower Pkwy # 100 Livingston (07039) *(G-5505)*

Amark Wire LLC................................973 882-7818
  18 Passaic Ave Unit 6 Fairfield (07004) *(G-3141)*

Amaryllis Inc (PA)................................973 635-0500
  418 River Rd Chatham (07928) *(G-1318)*

Amas Pharmaceuticals LLC................................908 883-1129
  100 Connell Dr Ste 2300 Berkeley Heights (07922) *(G-388)*

Amati International LLC................................201 569-1000
  560 Sylvan Ave Ste 2053 Englewood Cliffs (07632) *(G-2957)*

Amb Enterprises LLC (PA)................................973 225-1070
  25 Lake St Paterson (07501) *(G-8135)*

Amber Road Inc (HQ)................................201 935-8588
  1 Meadowlands Plz # 1500 East Rutherford (07073) *(G-2270)*

Ambix Laboratories, Totowa *Also called Organics Corporation America (G-10841)*

Ambo Consulting LLC................................732 663-0000
  82 Norwood Ave Ste 2 Deal (07723) *(G-1997)*

Ambriola Company Inc................................973 228-3600
  7 Patton Dr West Caldwell (07006) *(G-11640)*

Ambro Manufacturing Inc................................908 806-8337
  6 Kings Ct Flemington (08822) *(G-3429)*

Amcor Flexibles Inc................................609 267-5900
  220 Shreve St Mount Holly (08060) *(G-6723)*

Amcor Flexibles LLC................................856 825-1400
  1633 Wheaton Ave Millville (08332) *(G-6224)*

Amcor Flexibles Mil, Millville *Also called Amcor Flexibles LLC (G-6224)*

Amcor Flexibles Mount Holly, Mount Holly *Also called Amcor Flexibles Inc (G-6723)*

Amcor Phrm Packg USA Inc................................856 825-3050
  1600 Malone St Millville (08332) *(G-6225)*

Amcor Phrm Packg USA Inc................................856 728-9300
  918 E Malaga Rd Williamstown (08094) *(G-11950)*

Amcor Phrm Packg USA LLC (HQ)................................856 327-1540
  625 Sharp St N Millville (08332) *(G-6226)*

Amcor Phrm Packg USA LLC................................856 825-1400
  1200 N 10th St Millville (08332) *(G-6227)*

Amcor Phrm Packg USA LLC................................856 825-1400
  1633 Wheaton Ave Millville (08332) *(G-6228)*

Amcor Phrm Packg USA LLC................................856 825-1100
  1501 N 10th St Millville (08332) *(G-6229)*

Amcor Phrm Packg USA LLC................................856 825-1400
  1101 Wheaton Ave Millville (08332) *(G-6230)*

Amcor Rigid Packaging Usa LLC................................856 327-1540
  625 Sharp St N Millville (08332) *(G-6231)*

AMD Fine Linens LLC................................201 568-5255
  471 S Dean St Englewood (07631) *(G-2875)*

Amec Foster Wheeler USA Corp................................713 929-5000
  53 Frontage Rd Hampton (08827) *(G-4146)*

Amec Fster Wheeler N Amer Corp (HQ)................................936 448-6323
  53 Frontage Rd Hampton (08827) *(G-4147)*

Amedia Networks Inc................................732 440-1992
  541 Industrial Way W B Eatontown (07724) *(G-2376)*

Amega Scientific Corporation................................609 953-7295
  617 Stokes Rd Medford (08055) *(G-6019)*

Amer-RAC LLC................................856 488-6210
  8128 River Rd Pennsauken (08110) *(G-8388)*

Ameral International Inc................................856 456-9000
  7 Railroad Ln Brooklawn (08030) *(G-913)*

Amerasia Intl Tech Inc................................609 799-9388
  70 Washington Rd Princeton Junction (08550) *(G-9050)*

Amerchol Corporation (HQ)................................732 248-6000
  136 Talmadge Rd Edison (08817) *(G-2452)*

America Oggi, Norwood *Also called Gruppo Editoriale Oggi Inc (G-7563)*

America Techma Inc................................201 894-5887
  385 Sylvan Ave Ste 28 Englewood Cliffs (07632) *(G-2958)*

American Aeronautic Mfg Co................................973 442-8138
  45 Us Highway 46 Ste 606 Pine Brook (07058) *(G-8585)*

American Aluminum Casting Co (PA)................................973 372-3200
  324 Coit St Irvington (07111) *(G-4556)*

American Aluminum Company................................908 233-3500
  230 Sheffield St Mountainside (07092) *(G-6834)*

American Architectual Stone, North Plainfield *Also called Granite and Marble Assoc Inc (G-7505)*

American Auto Carriers Inc................................201 573-0371
  188 Broadway Ste 1 Woodcliff Lake (07677) *(G-12045)*

American Baby Headwear Co Inc (PA)................................908 558-0017
  1000 Jefferson Ave Elizabeth (07201) *(G-2710)*

American Bank Note Holographic (HQ)................................609 208-0591
  2 Applegate Dr Robbinsville (08691) *(G-9407)*

American Beryllia Inc................................973 248-8080
  16 1st Ave Haskell (07420) *(G-4194)*

American Biltrite Inc................................856 778-0700
  105 Whittendale Dr Moorestown (08057) *(G-6502)*

American Bindery Depot Inc................................732 287-2370
  191 Talmadge Rd Edison (08817) *(G-2453)*

American Braiding & Mfg Corp................................732 938-6333
  247 Old Tavern Rd Howell (07731) *(G-4530)*

American Brass and Crystal Inc................................908 688-8611
  835 Lehigh Ave Union (07083) *(G-11023)*

American Bus & Coach LLC................................732 283-1982
  1020 Green St Iselin (08830) *(G-4591)*

American Business Paper Inc................................732 363-5788
  222 River Ave Lakewood (08701) *(G-5049)*

American Casein Company (PA)................................609 387-2988
  109 Elbow Ln Burlington (08016) *(G-947)*

American Chemical & Coating Co................................908 353-2260
  410 Division St Elizabeth (07201) *(G-2711)*

American Coding and Mkg Ink Co................................908 756-0373
  1220 North Ave Plainfield (07062) *(G-8757)*

American Compressed Gases Inc (PA)................................201 767-3200
  189 Central Ave Old Tappan (07675) *(G-7732)*

American Consolidation Inc................................201 438-4351
  500 Washington Ave Carlstadt (07072) *(G-1123)*

American Custom Drying Co................................609 387-3933
  109 Elbow Ln Burlington (08016) *(G-948)*

American Custom Fabricators................................732 237-0037
  215 Hickory Ln Ste A Bayville (08721) *(G-239)*

American Dawn Inc................................856 467-9211
  520 Pdricktown Rd Ste B Bridgeport (08014) *(G-734)*

American Diagnstc Imaging Inc................................973 980-1724
  410 Centre St 2 Nutley (07110) *(G-7578)*

American Directory Publishing................................609 494-4055
  1816 Long Beach Blvd Surf City (08008) *(G-10554)*

American Display, Whitehouse *Also called Larue Manufacturing Corp (G-11916)*

American Envelope................................908 241-9900
  612 E Elizabeth Ave Linden (07036) *(G-5323)*

American Estates Wines Inc................................908 273-5060
  19 Hillside Ave Summit (07901) *(G-10524)*

American Fibertek Inc................................732 302-0660
  120 Belmont Dr Somerset (08873) *(G-9951)*

American Fittings Corp (PA)................................201 664-0027
  17-10 Willow St Fair Lawn (07410) *(G-3083)*

American Flux & Metal LLC................................609 561-7500
  352 Fleming Pike Hammonton (08037) *(G-4125)*

American Flyer, Clifton *Also called Naluco Inc (G-1672)*

American Food & Bev Inds LLC................................347 241-9827
  50 S Center St Ste 20 Orange (07050) *(G-7750)*

American Foreclosures Inc................................201 501-0200
  15 W Main St Apt 1 Bergenfield (07621) *(G-370)*

American Fur Felt LLC................................973 344-3026
  53 Rome St Newark (07105) *(G-7044)*

American Galvanizing Co Inc................................609 567-2090
  1919 S 12th St Hammonton (08037) *(G-4126)*

American Gaming & Elec Inc (HQ)................................609 704-3000
  223 Pratt St Hammonton (08037) *(G-4127)*

American Garvens Corporation................................973 276-1093
  19a Chapin Rd Pine Brook (07058) *(G-8586)*

American Gas & Chemical Co Ltd................................201 767-7300
  220 Pegasus Ave Northvale (07647) *(G-7518)*

American Graphic Solutions, Lakewood *Also called American Business Paper Inc (G-5049)*

American Graphic Systems Inc................................201 796-0666
  39-26 Broadway Fair Lawn (07410) *(G-3084)*

American Graphix, Elizabeth *Also called On Demand Machinery (G-2765)*

American Harlequin Corporation................................856 234-5505
  1531 Glen Ave Moorestown (08057) *(G-6503)*

American Harvest Baking Co Inc (PA)................................856 642-9955
  823 E Gate Dr Ste 3 Mount Laurel (08054) *(G-6737)*

American Home Essentials Inc................................908 561-3200
  600 Mont Rose Ave South Plainfield (07080) *(G-10215)*

American Home Mfg LLC................................732 465-1530
  4 Corporate Pl Piscataway (08854) *(G-8629)*

American Hose Hydraulic Co Inc (PA)................................973 684-3225
  700 21st Ave Paterson (07513) *(G-8136)*

American Ingredients Inc................................714 630-6000
  265 Harrison Tpke Kearny (07032) *(G-4843)*

American International Cont................................973 917-3331
  3 Mars Ct Ste 4 Boonton (07005) *(G-541)*

American Intr Resources Inc................................908 851-0014
  1206 Francyne Way Union (07083) *(G-11024)*

American Jewel Window Systems, Livingston *Also called Versatile Distributors Inc (G-5546)*

American Leistritz Extruder................................908 685-2333
  169 Meister Ave Branchburg (08876) *(G-616)*

American Lighting, Garfield *Also called North American Illumination (G-3751)*

American Logistics Network LLC 201 391-1054
188 Broadway Ste 1 Woodcliff Lake (07677) *(G-12046)*

American Machine Spc NJ LLC 201 664-0006
51 Bergenline Ave Westwood (07675) *(G-11826)*

American Made Fabricators Inc 732 356-4306
84 Baekeland Ave Middlesex (08846) *(G-6096)*

American Marking Systems Inc (PA) 973 478-5600
1015 Paulison Ave Clifton (07011) *(G-1563)*

American Mch Tool RPR Rbldg Co 973 927-0820
12 Middlebury Blvd Randolph (07869) *(G-9171)*

American Mdlar Pwr Sltions Inc 973 588-4026
429 Rockaway Valley Rd Boonton (07005) *(G-542)*

American Medical & Dental Sups 877 545-6837
240 W Grand Ave Montvale (07645) *(G-6396)*

American Micro Technologies, Linden *Also called American Envelope (G-5323)*

American Microsemiconductor 973 377-9566
133 Kings Rd Madison (07940) *(G-5689)*

American Mllwright Rigging LLC 856 457-9574
119 Washington Ter Audubon (08106) *(G-111)*

American National Red Cross 973 797-3300
209 Fairfield Rd Fairfield (07004) *(G-3142)*

American Oil & Supply Co 732 389-5514
22 Meridian Rd Ste 6 Eatontown (07724) *(G-2377)*

American Panel TEC, South Plainfield *Also called Marino Building Systems Corp (G-10298)*

American Pharmaceutical LLC 732 645-3030
1 New England Ave Piscataway (08854) *(G-8630)*

American Pipe Benders & Fabric 732 287-1122
191 Vineyard Rd Ste 5 Edison (08817) *(G-2454)*

American Plastic Works Inc 800 494-7326
1270 Glen Ave Moorestown (08057) *(G-6504)*

American Plus Printers Inc 732 528-2170
2604 Atlantic Ave Ste 300 Wall (07719) *(G-11314)*

American Power Cord Corp 973 574-8301
4 Smalley Ave Somerset (08873) *(G-9952)*

American Process Systems 908 216-6781
131 Cherry Tree Bend Rd Port Murray (07865) *(G-8880)*

American Products Company Inc 908 687-4100
610 Rahway Ave Ste 1 Union (07083) *(G-11025)*

American Prvate Label Pdts LLC 845 733-8151
24b Munsonhurst Rd Franklin (07416) *(G-3598)*

American Rail Company Inc 732 785-1110
1133 Industrial Pkwy B Brick (08724) *(G-710)*

American Refuse Supply Inc (PA) 973 684-3225
700 21st Ave Paterson (07513) *(G-8137)*

American Renolit Corp La 856 241-4901
301 Berkeley Dr B Swedesboro (08085) *(G-10570)*

American Renolit Corporation 973 706-6912
1310 Hamburg Tpke Ste 5 Wayne (07470) *(G-11468)*

American Rigging & Repair Inc 866 478-7129
356 W 1st Ave Roselle (07203) *(G-9547)*

American Scientific Ltg Corp 718 369-1100
725 E State St Trenton (08609) *(G-10892)*

American Sensor Tech Inc (HQ) 973 448-1901
450 Clark Dr Ste 4 Budd Lake (07828) *(G-918)*

American Shale Oil LLC (HQ) 973 438-3500
520 Broad St Ste 1 Newark (07102) *(G-7045)*

American Sign Instllations LLC 856 506-0610
209 S 15th St Millville (08332) *(G-6232)*

American Soc of Mech Engineers 973 244-2282
150 Clove Rd Ste 6 Little Falls (07424) *(G-5451)*

American Soft Solutions Corp 732 272-0052
704 Ginesi Dr Ste 28a Morganville (07751) *(G-6582)*

American Spraytech LLC 908 725-6060
205 Meister Ave Branchburg (08876) *(G-617)*

American Stamp Mfg Co 212 227-1877
1015 Paulison Ave Clifton (07011) *(G-1564)*

American Standard, Piscataway *Also called Asd Holding Corp (G-8638)*

American Standard Brands, Piscataway *Also called As America Inc (G-8637)*

American Standard Intl Inc 732 652-7100
1 Centennial Ave Ste 101 Piscataway (08854) *(G-8631)*

American Sten-Cyl, Mahwah *Also called American Stencyl Inc (G-5714)*

American Stencyl Inc 201 251-6460
37 Hillside Ave Mahwah (07430) *(G-5714)*

American Stone Inc 973 318-7707
215 Us Highway 22 Hillside (07205) *(G-4373)*

American Stone Inc (PA) 973 318-7707
215 Us Highway 22 Hillside (07205) *(G-4374)*

American Strip Steel Inc (HQ) 800 526-1216
400 Metuchen Rd South Plainfield (07080) *(G-10216)*

American Strip Steel Inc 856 461-8300
901 Coopertown Rd Delanco (08075) *(G-2002)*

American Teletimer Corp 908 654-4200
1167 Globe Ave Mountainside (07092) *(G-6835)*

American Tire Distributors 973 646-5600
50 Us Highway 46 Totowa (07512) *(G-10811)*

American Traffic & St Sign Co, Orange *Also called East Trading West Inv LLC (G-7753)*

American Transparent Plastic 732 287-3000
180 National Rd Edison (08817) *(G-2455)*

American Van Equipment Inc (PA) 732 905-5900
149 Lehigh Ave Lakewood (08701) *(G-5050)*

American Water - Pridesa LLC (PA) 856 435-7711
1 Water St Camden (08102) *(G-1039)*

American Woodcarving LLC 973 835-8510
1123 State Route 23 Wayne (07470) *(G-11469)*

American Youth Enterprises Inc 609 909-1900
120 Marlin Ln Mays Landing (08330) *(G-5992)*

American/Krengel Stamp Mfg Co, Clifton *Also called American Stamp Mfg Co (G-1564)*

Americare Laboratories Ltd 973 279-5100
126 Pennsylvania Ave # 104 Paterson (07503) *(G-8138)*

Americhem Enterprises Inc 732 363-4840
6 Round Valley Ln Lakewood (08701) *(G-5051)*

Ameriderm Laboratories, Paterson *Also called Americare Laboratories Ltd (G-8138)*

Amerifab Corp 973 777-2120
196 Garibaldi Ave Ste 1 Lodi (07644) *(G-5553)*

Amerifast Corp 908 668-1959
104 Sylvania Pl South Plainfield (07080) *(G-10217)*

Amerigen Pharmaceuticals Inc 732 993-9826
9 Polito Ave Ste 900 Lyndhurst (07071) *(G-5640)*

Amerigen Pharmaceuticals Ltd (PA) 732 993-9826
197 State Route 18 East Brunswick (08816) *(G-2127)*

Amerilubes LLC 704 399-7701
5 Mantoloking Ln Waretown (08758) *(G-11392)*

Amerimold Tech Inc 732 462-7577
150 Park Ave Jackson (08527) *(G-4638)*

Amerindia Technologies Inc 609 664-2224
101 Interchange Plz # 201 Cranbury (08512) *(G-1808)*

Ameritex Industries Corp 609 502-0123
39 Everett Dr Ste 2 Princeton Junction (08550) *(G-9051)*

Amerivator Systems Corporation 973 471-1200
220 Scoles Ave Clifton (07012) *(G-1565)*

Amerlux Lighting Systems, Oakland *Also called Amerlux LLC (G-7614)*

Amerlux LLC (HQ) 973 882-5010
178 Bauer Dr Oakland (07436) *(G-7614)*

Amershoe Corp 201 569-7300
456 Nordhoff Pl Englewood (07631) *(G-2876)*

Amertech Towerservices Inc 732 389-2200
149 Avenue At The Cmn Shrewsbury (07702) *(G-9881)*

Ames Advanced Materials Corp 908 226-2038
3900 S Clinton Ave South Plainfield (07080) *(G-10218)*

Ames Rubber Corporation (PA) 973 827-9101
19 Ames Blvd Hamburg (07419) *(G-4088)*

Ametek Inc 732 417-0501
52 Mayfield Ave Edison (08837) *(G-2456)*

Ametek Inc 732 370-9100
485 Oberlin Ave S Lakewood (08701) *(G-5052)*

Ametek CTS, Edison *Also called Ametek Inc (G-2456)*

Amex Tool Co 908 735-5176
4 Fox Hill Ln Asbury (08802) *(G-58)*

Amfico, Fair Lawn *Also called American Fittings Corp (G-3083)*

Amfine Chemical Corporation (HQ) 201 818-0159
777 Perrace Ave Ste 602b Hasbrouck Heights (07604) *(G-4181)*

AMG International Inc (PA) 201 475-4800
71 Walsh Dr Ste 101 Parsippany (07054) *(G-7880)*

Amici Imports Inc 908 272-8300
335 Centennial Ave Unit 7 Cranford (07016) *(G-1900)*

Amico Technologies Inc 732 901-5900
1200 River Ave Ste 3a Lakewood (08701) *(G-5053)*

Amicus Therapeutics Inc (PA) 609 662-2000
1 Cedarbrook Dr Cranbury (08512) *(G-1809)*

Amicus Therapeutics Us Inc 609 662-2000
1 Cedarbrook Dr Cranbury (08512) *(G-1810)*

Amiee Lynn Accessories, Ridgefield *Also called Lynn Amiee Inc (G-9274)*

Amish Dairy Products LLC 973 256-7676
41 Vreeland Ave Ste 208 Totowa (07512) *(G-10812)*

Amko Displays Corporation 201 460-7199
7 Purcell Ct Moonachie (07074) *(G-6454)*

Amloid Corporation 973 328-0654
7 Ridgedale Ave Ste 1a Cedar Knolls (07927) *(G-1298)*

Ammark Corporation 973 616-2555
230 W Parkway Ste 12 Pompton Plains (07444) *(G-8857)*

Amneal Pharmaceuticals Inc 908 409-6822
400 Crossing Blvd Fl 3 Bridgewater (08807) *(G-786)*

Amneal Pharmaceuticals Inc (PA) 908 947-3120
400 Crossing Blvd Fl 3 Bridgewater (08807) *(G-787)*

Amneal Pharmaceuticals LLC 908 947-3120
1 New England Ave Bldg A Piscataway (08854) *(G-8632)*

Amneal Pharmaceuticals LLC 908 947-3120
47 Colonial Dr Bldg B Piscataway (08854) *(G-8633)*

Amneal Pharmaceuticals LLC 908 409-6823
65 Readington Rd Bldg B Branchburg (08876) *(G-618)*

Amneal Pharmaceuticals LLC (HQ) 908 947-3120
400 Crossing Blvd Fl 3 Bridgewater (08807) *(G-788)*

Amneal Pharmaceuticals LLC 908 231-1911
131 Chambers Brook Rd Branchburg (08876) *(G-619)*

Amneal-Agila LLC 908 947-3120
400 Crossing Blvd Fl 3 Bridgewater (08807) *(G-789)*

Amoco, Burlington *Also called American Casein Company (G-947)*

Amorosos Baking Co 215 471-4740
151 Benigno Blvd Bellmawr (08031) *(G-327)*

AMP Custom Rubber Inc 732 888-2714
3 Cass St Ste 8 Keyport (07735) ***(G-4997)***
Ampericon Inc 609 945-2591
1 Tamaron Ct Monmouth Junction (08852) ***(G-6278)***
Amperite Co Inc 201 864-9503
4201 Tonnelle Ave Ste 6 North Bergen (07047) ***(G-7384)***
Amps, Boonton *Also called American Mdlar Pwr Sltions Inc* ***(G-542)***
Amrod Corp 973 344-3806
305a Craneway St Newark (07114) ***(G-7046)***
Amrod NA Corporation (PA) 973 344-2978
305a Craneway St Newark (07114) ***(G-7047)***
AMS, New Brunswick *Also called Art Materials Service Inc* ***(G-6913)***
AMS Products LLC 973 442-5790
105 W Dewey Ave Ste 305 Wharton (07885) ***(G-11850)***
AMS Toy Intl Inc 973 442-5790
105 W Dewey Ave Wharton (07885) ***(G-11851)***
Amscan Inc 973 983-0888
25 Green Pond Rd Rockaway (07866) ***(G-9442)***
Amscot Structural Pdts Corp 973 989-8800
241 E Blackwell St Dover (07801) ***(G-2074)***
Amt Stitch Inc 732 376-0009
257 New Brunswick Ave Perth Amboy (08861) ***(G-8512)***
Amtopp Corporation 973 994-8074
9 Peach Tree Hill Rd Livingston (07039) ***(G-5506)***
Amy Publications LLC 973 235-1800
11 Robert St Nutley (07110) ***(G-7579)***
Amys Omelette Hse Burlington (PA) 609 386-4800
637 High St Burlington (08016) ***(G-949)***
Ana Design Corp 609 394-0300
1 Ott St Trenton (08638) ***(G-10893)***
Analog Devices Inc 732 868-7100
285 Davidson Ave Ste 402 Somerset (08873) ***(G-9953)***
Analytic Stress Relieving Inc 732 629-7232
190 Egel Ave Middlesex (08846) ***(G-6097)***
Analytical Measurements, Hopatcong *Also called Wra Manufacturing Company Inc* ***(G-4523)***
Analytical Sales and Svcs Inc 973 616-0700
179 Rte 206 Flanders (07836) ***(G-3400)***
Analytical Testing, Edison *Also called Alcami New Jersey Corporation* ***(G-2451)***
Analyticon Instruments Corp 973 379-6771
500 Morris Ave Springfield (07081) ***(G-10426)***
Anatech Microwave Company Inc 973 772-7369
70 Outwater Ln Ste 3 Garfield (07026) ***(G-3728)***
Anatolian Naturals Inc 201 893-0142
1 Bridge Plz N Ste 275 Fort Lee (07024) ***(G-3546)***
Anchor, Red Bank *Also called Crh Americas Inc* ***(G-9224)***
Anchor Concrete Products Inc (HQ) 732 842-5010
331 Newman Springs Rd # 236 Red Bank (07701) ***(G-9220)***
Anchor Concrete Products Inc 732 458-9440
975 Burnt Tavern Rd Brick (08724) ***(G-711)***
Anchor Home Products, West Milford *Also called Anchor Sales & Marketing Inc* ***(G-11725)***
Anchor Optical Co 856 546-1965
101 E Gloucester Pike Barrington (08007) ***(G-166)***
Anchor Sales & Marketing Inc 973 545-2277
755 Macopin Rd 1 West Milford (07480) ***(G-11725)***
Ancraft Press Corp 201 792-9200
234 16th St Fl 8 Jersey City (07310) ***(G-4691)***
Andantex U S A Inc 732 493-2812
1705 Valley Rd Ocean (07712) ***(G-7655)***
Andarn Electro Service Inc 973 523-2220
72 Michigan Ave Paterson (07503) ***(G-8139)***
Andek Corporation 856 866-7600
850 Glen Ave Moorestown (08057) ***(G-6505)***
Anderson & Vreeland Inc (PA) 973 227-2270
8 Evans St Fairfield (07004) ***(G-3143)***
Anderson Publishing Ltd 908 301-1995
180 Glenside Ave Scotch Plains (07076) ***(G-9729)***
Anderson Tool & Die Corp 908 862-5550
1430 W Blancke St Linden (07036) ***(G-5324)***
Andis Inc 973 627-0400
124 E Main St Denville (07834) ***(G-2030)***
Andlogic Computers 609 610-5752
866 Nj 33 6 Hamilton (08619) ***(G-4102)***
Andon Brush Co Inc 973 256-6611
1 Merrit Ave Little Falls (07424) ***(G-5452)***
Andrea Aromatics Inc 609 695-7710
150 Enterprise Ave Trenton (08638) ***(G-10894)***
Andrea Company, Orange *Also called Savignano Food Corp* ***(G-7760)***
Andrevin Inc 732 270-2794
792 Fischer Blvd Toms River (08753) ***(G-10743)***
Andrew B Duffy Inc 856 845-4900
322 Crown Point Rd West Deptford (08086) ***(G-11691)***
Andrew P Mc Hugh Inc 856 547-8953
124 Clements Bridge Rd # 2 Barrington (08007) ***(G-167)***
Andrews Glass, Vineland *Also called AGC Products Inc* ***(G-11184)***
Andrex Inc 908 852-2400
101 Bilby Rd Ste E Hackettstown (07840) ***(G-3998)***
Andrex Systems Inc 908 835-1720
17 Karrville Rd Port Murray (07865) ***(G-8881)***
Andrus Bait Company, Millville *Also called Richard Andrus* ***(G-6269)***
Andy Graphics Service Bureau 201 866-9407
3711 Park Ave Union City (07087) ***(G-11106)***
Andys Custom Cabinets 732 752-6443
143 Jefferson Ave Green Brook (08812) ***(G-3859)***
Angelos Italian Ices Icecream 201 962-7575
96 E Main St Ramsey (07446) ***(G-9137)***
Angelos Panetteria Inc 201 435-4659
14 Wales Ave Jersey City (07306) ***(G-4692)***
Angels Bakery USA LLC 718 389-1400
110 Raskulinecz Rd Carteret (07008) ***(G-1245)***
Anglers Select LLC 973 396-2959
311 Mechanic St Boonton (07005) ***(G-543)***
Ango Electronics Corporation 201 955-0800
29 Ewing Ave North Arlington (07031) ***(G-7368)***
Anheuser-Busch LLC 973 645-7700
30 Montgomery St Ste 700 Jersey City (07302) ***(G-4693)***
Anhydrides & Chemicals Inc 973 465-0077
2 Margaretta St Newark (07105) ***(G-7048)***
Anichem LLC 732 821-6500
195 Black Horse Ln North Brunswick (08902) ***(G-7452)***
Animals Etc Inc 609 386-8442
210 Mitchell Ave Burlington (08016) ***(G-950)***
Anisha Enterprises Inc 908 964-3380
2165 Morris Ave Ste 1 Union (07083) ***(G-11026)***
Anjoyx LLC 323 505-2002
7 Elana Dr Jackson (08527) ***(G-4639)***
Anju Clinplus LLC 732 764-6969
1661 Route 22 West Bound Brook (08805) ***(G-600)***
Ankur International Inc 609 409-6009
1206 Cranbury S River Rd Cranbury (08512) ***(G-1811)***
Anna J Chung Ltd 917 575-8100
5 Park St Edgewater (07020) ***(G-2433)***
Anna K Park 856 478-9500
50 N Main St Mullica Hill (08062) ***(G-6855)***
Anne Alanna Inc 609 465-3787
41 Pierces Point Rd Cape May Court House (08210) ***(G-1106)***
Annette & Jim Dizenzo Sls LLC (PA) 973 875-0895
6 Glenview Ln Sussex (07461) ***(G-10556)***
Annin & Co (PA) 973 228-9400
105 Eisenhower Pkwy # 203 Roseland (07068) ***(G-9532)***
Annin Flag Makers, Roseland *Also called Annin & Co* ***(G-9532)***
Annitti Enterprises Inc 973 345-1725
138 Grand St Paterson (07501) ***(G-8140)***
Anodizing Corporation 973 694-6449
10 Legrande Ter Wayne (07470) ***(G-11470)***
Ans Nutrition Inc 212 235-5205
700 Central Ave Farmingdale (07727) ***(G-3377)***
ANS Plastics Corporation 732 247-2776
625 Jersey Ave Ste 11a New Brunswick (08901) ***(G-6910)***
Anscott Chemical Inds Inc 973 696-7575
26 Hanes Dr Wayne (07470) ***(G-11471)***
Ansell Alabama, Iselin *Also called Ansell Inc* ***(G-4594)***
Ansell Hawkeye Inc (HQ) 662 258-3200
111 Wood Ave S Ste 210 Iselin (08830) ***(G-4592)***
Ansell Healthcare Products LLC (HQ) 732 345-5400
111 Wood Ave S Ste 210 Iselin (08830) ***(G-4593)***
Ansell Inc (HQ) 334 794-4231
111 Wood Ave S Ste 210 Iselin (08830) ***(G-4594)***
Ansell Limited 732 345-5400
111 Wood Ave S Ste 210 Iselin (08830) ***(G-4595)***
Ansell Protective Products LLC 732 345-5400
111 Wood Ave S Ste 210 Iselin (08830) ***(G-4596)***
Ansonia Bridal Veils, North Bergen *Also called Kathy Gibson Designs Inc* ***(G-7414)***
Ansun Protective Metals Inc 732 302-0616
130 Lincoln Blvd Middlesex (08846) ***(G-6098)***
Answers In Motion LLC 732 267-7792
204 S Lippincott Ave Maple Shade (08052) ***(G-5859)***
Ant Stores, Clifton *Also called Light Inc* ***(G-1659)***
Antares Pharma Inc (PA) 609 359-3020
100 Princeton S Ste 300 Ewing (08628) ***(G-3015)***
Antenna Software Inc (HQ) 201 217-3824
111 Town Square Pl # 520 Jersey City (07310) ***(G-4694)***
Anthem, Clifton *Also called Disposable Hygiene LLC* ***(G-1600)***
Anthony & Sons Bakery Itln Bky 973 625-2323
20 Luger Rd Denville (07834) ***(G-2031)***
Anthony Excavating & Dem 609 926-8804
22 English Ln Egg Harbor Township (08234) ***(G-2676)***
Anthracite Industries Inc (HQ) 908 537-2155
405 Old Main St Asbury (08802) ***(G-59)***
Anti Hydro International Inc 908 284-9000
45 River Rd Ste 200 Flemington (08822) ***(G-3430)***
Antonio Mozzarella Factory Inc (PA) 973 353-9411
631 Frelinghuysen Ave Newark (07114) ***(G-7049)***
Antonio Mozzarella Factory Inc 973 353-9411
631 Frelinghuysen Ave # 2 Newark (07114) ***(G-7050)***
Antonio's Pasta, Woodbridge *Also called 35 Food Corp* ***(G-12011)***
Antron Technologies Inc 732 205-0415
40 Brunswick Ave Ste 104 Edison (08817) ***(G-2457)***
Antronics, Cranbury *Also called Cabletenna Corp* ***(G-1818)***

Antronix Inc (PA) 609 860-0160
440 Forsgate Dr Cranbury (08512) *(G-1812)*

Anuco Inc 973 887-9465
911 Charles Dr Unit 3 East Hanover (07936) *(G-2194)*

Anvil Iron Works Inc 856 783-5959
Little Mill Rd Sicklerville (08081) *(G-9907)*

Anvima Technologies LLC 973 531-7077
68 Woodland Rd Brookside (07926) *(G-916)*

Aone Touch Inc 732 261-6841
35 E Burlington St Bordentown (08505) *(G-575)*

Aos Thermal Compounds LLC 732 389-5514
22 Meridian Rd Ste 6 Eatontown (07724) *(G-2378)*

AP Cultech, South Plainfield Also called Cultech Inc *(G-10244)*

AP Deauville LLC 732 545-0200
594 Jersey Ave Ste 1 New Brunswick (08901) *(G-6911)*

AP Global Enterprises Inc 732 919-6200
5044 Industrial Rd Wall Township (07727) *(G-11317)*

AP International, Wall Township Also called AP Global Enterprises Inc *(G-11317)*

AP Packaging, Linden Also called Air Protection Packaging Corp *(G-5317)*

AP&g Co Inc 718 492-3648
75 E 2nd St Bayonne (07002) *(G-202)*

Apb-Dynasonics Inc 973 785-1101
145 Shepherds Ln Totowa (07512) *(G-10813)*

Apco Extruders Inc 732 287-3000
180 National Rd Edison (08817) *(G-2458)*

Apelio Innovative Inds LLC 973 777-8899
46 Sellers St Kearny (07032) *(G-4844)*

Aperam Stnlss Svc & Solutns 908 988-0625
98 Floral Ave Ste 102 New Providence (07974) *(G-6994)*

Apex Saw & Tool Co Inc 201 438-8777
595 New York Ave Lyndhurst (07071) *(G-5641)*

Aphelion Orbitals Inc 321 289-0872
540 39th St Ste 40 Union City (07087) *(G-11107)*

Aphena Phrma Slutions - NJ LLC 973 947-5441
2 Cranberry Rd Unit A3 Parsippany (07054) *(G-7881)*

API, Sparta Also called Advanced Precision Inc *(G-10375)*

API Americas Inc 732 382-6800
329 New Brunswick Ave Rahway (07065) *(G-9077)*

API Inc 973 227-9335
10 Industrial Rd Fairfield (07004) *(G-3144)*

API Nanofabrication & RES Corp 732 627-0808
1600 Cottontail Ln Ste 1 Somerset (08873) *(G-9954)*

Apicore LLC (HQ) 646 884-3765
15 Corporate Pl S Ste 110 Piscataway (08854) *(G-8634)*

Apicore US LLC, Somerset Also called Mylan API US LLC *(G-10038)*

Apl2000, Manasquan Also called Aplnow LLC *(G-5828)*

Aplnow LLC (PA) 732 223-5575
2640 Highway 70 Ste 4 Manasquan (08736) *(G-5828)*

Apogee Sound International LLC 201 934-8500
50 Spring St Ste 1 Ramsey (07446) *(G-9138)*

Apogee Technologies LLC 973 575-8448
3 Cole Rd Towaco (07082) *(G-10864)*

Apollo East LLC 856 486-1882
7895 Airport Hwy Pennsauken (08109) *(G-8389)*

Apollo Graphics NJ, Cinnaminson Also called Samuel Elliott Inc *(G-1483)*

Apollo Machine Shop, Hillsdale Also called Oroszlany Laszlo *(G-4369)*

Apparel Strgc Alliances LLC 732 833-7771
41 Greenwich Dr Jackson (08527) *(G-4640)*

Appco Pharma LLC (PA) 732 271-8300
120 Belmont Dr Somerset (08873) *(G-9955)*

Appco Pharma LLC 732 271-8300
262 Old New Brunswick Rd Piscataway (08854) *(G-8635)*

Appco Pharma LLC 732 271-8300
120 Belmont Dr Somerset (08873) *(G-9956)*

Appco Pharmaceuticals Corp., Somerset Also called Appco Pharma LLC *(G-9955)*

Appetito Provisions Company 201 864-3410
406 Lafayette Rd Harrington Park (07640) *(G-4162)*

Appetizers Made Easy Inc 201 531-1212
25 Branca Rd Ste B East Rutherford (07073) *(G-2271)*

Appex Innovation Solutions LLC 215 313-3332
103 Carnegie Ctr Princeton (08540) *(G-8908)*

Applause Musical Products, Vineland Also called Musikraft LLC *(G-11243)*

Apple Air Compressor Corp (PA) 888 222-9940
301 Veterans Blvd Rutherford (07070) *(G-9613)*

Apple Corrugated Box Ltd 201 635-1269
1 Passaic St Unit 76 Wood Ridge (07075) *(G-12001)*

Applegate Farms LLC 908 725-2768
750 Rte 202 Ste 300 Bridgewater (08807) *(G-790)*

Applegate Frm Hmmade Ice Cream (PA) 973 744-5900
616 Grove St Montclair (07043) *(G-6358)*

Apples & Honey Press LLC 973 379-7200
11 Edison Pl Springfield (07081) *(G-10427)*

Appleton Grp LLC 973 285-3261
55 Madison Ave Morristown (07960) *(G-6640)*

Applicad Inc 732 751-2555
5029 Industrial Rd Wall Township (07727) *(G-11318)*

Applied Color Systems, Lawrenceville Also called Datacolor Inc *(G-5229)*

Applied Image Inc 732 410-2444
800 Business Park Dr Freehold (07728) *(G-3647)*

Applied Microphone Technology, Sparta Also called Mp Production *(G-10400)*

Applied Nutrition Corp 973 734-0023
10 Saddle Rd Cedar Knolls (07927) *(G-1299)*

Applied Optronics, South Plainfield Also called Candela Corporation *(G-10234)*

Applied Psychological Services, Princeton Also called Princeton Information Center *(G-8999)*

Applied Resources Corp (PA) 973 328-3882
105 W Dewey Ave Ste 311 Wharton (07885) *(G-11852)*

Applied Thermal Solutions Inc 856 818-8194
93 Eldridge Ave Williamstown (08094) *(G-11951)*

Apprentice Fs Inc 973 960-0875
190 Chrstpher Columbus Dr Jersey City (07302) *(G-4695)*

Aprecia Pharmaceuticals Inc 215 359-3300
89 Twin Rivers Dr East Windsor (08520) *(G-2335)*

Aptapharma Corporation 856 665-0025
1533 Union Ave Pennsauken (08110) *(G-8390)*

Aptimized LLC 203 733-2868
579 Pompton Ave Ste 104 Cedar Grove (07009) *(G-1267)*

Apw Company, Rockaway Also called KG Squared LLC *(G-9473)*

Aqua Controls, West Deptford Also called Aquatrols Corp of America *(G-11692)*

Aqua Products Inc 856 829-8444
2703 River Rd Cinnaminson (08077) *(G-1441)*

Aqua Products Inc (HQ) 973 857-2700
25 Rutgers Ave Cedar Grove (07009) *(G-1268)*

Aqualink LLC 201 849-9771
304 Main St Ste 2 Fort Lee (07024) *(G-3547)*

Aquamar, Carteret Also called Lm Foods LLC *(G-1259)*

Aquarius Biotechnologies Inc 908 443-1860
1545 Rte 206 S Ste 302 Bedminster (07921) *(G-261)*

Aquasports Pools LLC 732 247-6298
999 Jersey Ave New Brunswick (08901) *(G-6912)*

Aquatrols Corp of America 856 537-6003
1273 Imperial Way West Deptford (08066) *(G-11692)*

Aquestive Therapeutics Inc (PA) 908 941-1900
30 Technology Dr Ste 2a Warren (07059) *(G-11398)*

Ar2 Products LLC 800 667-1263
210 W Parkway Ste 9 Pompton Plains (07444) *(G-8858)*

Arab Voice Newspaper 973 523-7815
956 Main St Paterson (07503) *(G-8141)*

Arafat Lafi 201 854-7300
7329 Broadway North Bergen (07047) *(G-7385)*

Aramani Inc 201 945-1160
369 Henry St Fairview (07022) *(G-3356)*

Arawak Paving Co Inc (PA) 609 561-4100
7503 Weymouth Rd Hammonton (08037) *(G-4128)*

Araya Inc 201 445-7005
10 Garber Sq Ste A Ridgewood (07450) *(G-9321)*

Araya Rebirth, Ridgewood Also called Araya Inc *(G-9321)*

Arbee Company Inc 908 241-7717
16 N 26th St Kenilworth (07033) *(G-4921)*

ARC International N Amer LLC (HQ) 856 825-5620
601 S Wade Blvd Millville (08332) *(G-6233)*

Arca Industrial Inc 732 339-0450
31 Dennison Dr East Windsor (08520) *(G-2336)*

Arcadia Consmr Healthcare Inc 800 824-4894
440 Us Highway 22 Ste 210 Bridgewater (08807) *(G-791)*

Arcadia Equipment Inc 201 342-3308
140 Lawrence St Hackensack (07601) *(G-3877)*

Arch America, Delair Also called Shapes/Arch Holdings LLC *(G-2001)*

Arch Crown Inc 973 731-6300
460 Hillside Ave Ste 1 Hillside (07205) *(G-4375)*

Arch Parent Inc 732 621-2873
801 Us Highway 1 S Iselin (08830) *(G-4597)*

Arch Personal Care Products LP 908 226-9329
70 Tyler Pl South Plainfield (07080) *(G-10219)*

Archer Day Inc 732 396-0600
18 Mileed Way Avenel (07001) *(G-120)*

Archer Plastics Inc 856 692-0242
1510 Jesse Bridge Rd Elmer (08318) *(G-2794)*

Archer Seating Clearing House, Elmer Also called Archer Plastics Inc *(G-2794)*

Archi-Tread Inc 973 725-5738
191 Brook Valley Rd Kinnelon (07405) *(G-5015)*

Architctral Cbinetry Mllwk LLC 908 213-2001
1425 3rd Ave Phillipsburg (08865) *(G-8541)*

Architctral Metals Fabricaters, Carteret Also called Architectural Metals Inc *(G-1247)*

Architctural Metal Designs Inc 856 765-3000
1505 Pineland Ave Millville (08332) *(G-6234)*

Architctural Metal Fabricators 718 765-0722
66 Grant Ave Carteret (07008) *(G-1246)*

Architectural Acrylics, Pennsauken Also called Scott W Springman *(G-8482)*

Architectural Iron Designs 908 757-2323
950 S 2nd St Plainfield (07063) *(G-8758)*

Architectural Metal and Glass 732 994-7575
644 Cross St Unit 14 Lakewood (08701) *(G-5054)*

Architectural Metals Inc 718 765-0722
66 Grant Ave Carteret (07008) *(G-1247)*

Architectural Wdwkg Assoc 908 996-7866
4 7th St Frenchtown (08825) *(G-3708)*

Architectural Window Mfg Corp 201 933-5094
  359 Veterans Blvd Rutherford (07070) *(G-9614)*

Archlit Inc 973 577-4400
  42 Ithanell Rd Hopatcong (07843) *(G-4518)*

Archon Vitamin LLC (PA) 732 537-1220
  3775 Park Ave Unit 1 Edison (08820) *(G-2459)*

Archon Vitamin LLC 973 371-1700
  3775 Park Ave Unit 1 Edison (08820) *(G-2460)*

Archtech Electronics Corp 732 355-1288
  117 Docks Corner Rd Ste A Dayton (08810) *(G-1951)*

Arctic Foods Inc 908 689-0590
  251 E Washington Ave Washington (07882) *(G-11438)*

Arctic Glacier USA Inc 973 771-3391
  363 Bloomfield Ave Ste 3b Montclair (07042) *(G-6359)*

Arctic Ice Cream Co, Ewing Also called Arctic Products Co Inc *(G-3016)*

Arctic Products Co Inc 609 393-4264
  22 Arctic Pkwy Ewing (08638) *(G-3016)*

Arcy Manufacturing Co Inc 201 635-1910
  575 Industrial Rd Carlstadt (07072) *(G-1124)*

Ardagh Glass Inc 508 478-2500
  443 S East Ave Bridgeton (08302) *(G-751)*

Ardagh Glass Inc 732 969-0827
  50 Bryla St Carteret (07008) *(G-1248)*

Arde Barinco or Arde, Carlstadt Also called Arde Inc *(G-1125)*

Arde Inc (HQ) 201 784-9880
  875 Washington Ave Carlstadt (07072) *(G-1125)*

Arde Inc 201 784-9880
  875 Washington Ave Carlstadt (07072) *(G-1126)*

Ardmore Inc 973 481-2406
  29 Riverside Ave Bldg 14 Newark (07104) *(G-7051)*

Area Auto Racing News Inc 609 888-3618
  2831 S Broad St Trenton (08610) *(G-10895)*

Arglen Industries Inc 732 888-8100
  1 Bethany Rd Ste 44 Hazlet (07730) *(G-4256)*

Argonautus LLC 908 393-4379
  867 Country Club Rd Bridgewater (08807) *(G-792)*

Argus International Inc (PA) 609 466-1677
  424 Route 31 N Ringoes (08551) *(G-9334)*

Argyle Industries Inc 908 725-8800
  160 Meister Ave Ste 12 Branchburg (08876) *(G-620)*

Argyle International Inc 609 924-9484
  254 Wall St Princeton (08540) *(G-8909)*

Arias Mountain-Coffee LLC 973 927-9595
  42 Bartley Rd Flanders (07836) *(G-3401)*

Ariba Inc 908 333-3400
  1160 Us Highway 22 # 110 Bridgewater (08807) *(G-793)*

Ariel Laboratories LP 908 755-4080
  31 Davis St South Plainfield (07080) *(G-10220)*

Aries Filterworks Inc 856 626-1550
  117 Jackson Rd Berlin (08009) *(G-414)*

Aries Precision Tool Inc 201 252-8550
  37 Orchard St Ramsey (07446) *(G-9139)*

Arizona Iced Tea, Maplewood Also called Maplewood Beverage Packers LLC *(G-5880)*

Arla Foods Ingredients N Amer 908 604-8551
  106 Allen Rd Ste 401 Basking Ridge (07920) *(G-175)*

Arlington Machine & Tool Co, Fairfield Also called Arlington Prcsion Cmpnents LLC *(G-3145)*

Arlington Prcsion Cmpnents LLC 973 276-1377
  90 New Dutch Ln Fairfield (07004) *(G-3145)*

Arlo Corporation 973 618-0030
  119 Harrison Ave Roseland (07068) *(G-9533)*

Arm & Hammer Animal & Fd Prod, Princeton Also called Arm & Hammer Animal Ntrtn LLC *(G-8910)*

Arm & Hammer Animal Ntrtn LLC (HQ) 800 526-3563
  469 N Harrison St Princeton (08540) *(G-8910)*

Arm National Food Inc 609 695-4911
  539 Chestnut Ave Trenton (08611) *(G-10896)*

Armac Associates, Florham Park Also called Armac Inc *(G-3480)*

Armac Inc (PA) 973 457-0002
  71 Passaic Ave Florham Park (07932) *(G-3480)*

Armadillo Automation Inc 856 829-2888
  835 Industrial Hwy Ste 4 Cinnaminson (08077) *(G-1442)*

Armadillo Metalworks Inc 973 777-2105
  61 Willet St Ste 1 Passaic (07055) *(G-8051)*

Armco Compressor Products 201 866-6766
  2042 46th St North Bergen (07047) *(G-7386)*

Armco Machine, North Bergen Also called Armco Compressor Products *(G-7386)*

Armel Electronics Inc 201 869-4300
  1601 75th St North Bergen (07047) *(G-7387)*

Armetec Corp 973 485-2525
  166 Abington Ave Newark (07107) *(G-7052)*

Armin Kososki 908 689-0411
  297 State Route 31 S Washington (07882) *(G-11439)*

Armkel LLC 609 683-5900
  469 N Harrison St Princeton (08540) *(G-8911)*

Armorpoxy Inc 908 810-9613
  805 Lehigh Ave Union (07083) *(G-11027)*

Armotek Industries Inc 856 829-4585
  1 Roto Ave Palmyra (08065) *(G-7781)*

Armstrong & Sons 732 223-1555
  2335 Highway 34 Manasquan (08736) *(G-5829)*

Arna Marketing Group Inc 908 625-7395
  60 Readington Rd Branchburg (08876) *(G-621)*

Arna Marketing Inc 908 231-1100
  60 Readington Rd Branchburg (08876) *(G-622)*

Arnhem Inc 908 709-4045
  1 Elm St Ste 1 # 1 Westfield (07090) *(G-11794)*

Arnhem Group, The, Westfield Also called Arnhem Inc *(G-11794)*

Arno Therapeutics Inc 862 703-7170
  200 Route 31 Ste 104 Flemington (08822) *(G-3431)*

Arnold Desks Inc 908 686-5656
  120 Coit St Irvington (07111) *(G-4557)*

Arnold Furniture Mfrs Inc (PA) 973 399-0505
  400 Coit St Irvington (07111) *(G-4558)*

Arnold Gisler Furn Fabricators, Irvington Also called Arnold Kolax Furniture Inc *(G-4559)*

Arnold Kolax Furniture Inc 973 375-3344
  120 Coit St Irvington Irvington (07111) *(G-4559)*

Arnold Reception Desks Inc 973 375-8101
  120 Coit St Irvington (07111) *(G-4560)*

Arnold Steel Co Inc 732 363-1079
  79 Randolph Rd Howell (07731) *(G-4531)*

Arnolds Desk, Irvington Also called Arnold Desks Inc *(G-4557)*

Arnolds Yacht Basin Inc (PA) 732 892-3000
  1671 Beaver Dam Rd Ste 1 Point Pleasant Boro (08742) *(G-8836)*

Arol Chemical Products Co 973 344-1510
  649 Ferry St Newark (07105) *(G-7053)*

Aroma Chemicals, Monmouth Junction Also called Bwi Chemicals *(G-6280)*

Aromatic Technologies Inc (HQ) 732 393-7300
  140 Centennial Ave Piscataway (08854) *(G-8636)*

Arome America LLC 908 806-7003
  2 Van Fleet Rd Neshanic Station (08853) *(G-6904)*

Aromiens Inc 732 225-8689
  98 Mayfield Ave Edison (08837) *(G-2461)*

Arose Inc (PA) 856 481-4351
  1001 Lower Landing Rd # 412 Blackwood (08012) *(G-459)*

Around Clock Sweeping LLC 973 887-1144
  45 Essex Rd Parsippany (07054) *(G-7882)*

Arpac Technology 973 252-0012
  45 Park Ave Randolph (07869) *(G-9172)*

Arquest Inc (PA) 609 395-9500
  14 Scotto Farm Ln Millstone Township (08535) *(G-6209)*

Array Solders Ltd Liability Co 201 432-0095
  329 Mercer Loop Jersey City (07302) *(G-4696)*

Arrow Engineering Co Inc 908 353-5229
  260 Pennsylvania Ave Hillside (07205) *(G-4376)*

Arrow Fastener Co LLC 201 843-6900
  271 Mayhill St Saddle Brook (07663) *(G-9640)*

Arrow Information Packagig LLC 856 317-9000
  7100 Westfield Ave Pennsauken (08110) *(G-8391)*

Arrow Machine Company Inc 973 642-2430
  117 Norfolk St Newark (07103) *(G-7054)*

Arrow Paper Company Inc (PA) 908 756-1111
  633 North Ave Plainfield (07060) *(G-8759)*

Arrow Shed LLC 973 835-3200
  1 3rd Ave Haskell (07420) *(G-4195)*

Arrow Steel Inc 973 523-1122
  629 E 19th St Paterson (07514) *(G-8142)*

Arrow Thin Films, Emerson Also called Artemis Optics and Coatings *(G-2863)*

Art Craft, Florham Park Also called Washington Stamp Exchange Inc *(G-3526)*

ART DISPLAY ESSENTIALS, Columbia Also called 10-31 Incorporated *(G-1791)*

Art Dmensions 908 322-8488
  1998 Us Highway 22 Scotch Plains (07076) *(G-9730)*

Art Flag Co Inc 212 334-1890
  890 River Rd Fair Haven (07704) *(G-3078)*

Art Materials Service Inc 732 545-8888
  625 Joyce Kilmer Ave New Brunswick (08901) *(G-6913)*

Art Metalcraft Plating Co Inc 215 923-6625
  529 S 2nd St Camden (08103) *(G-1040)*

Art Mold & Polishing Co Inc 908 518-9191
  220 Columbus Ave Roselle (07203) *(G-9548)*

Art Mold & Tool Corporation 201 935-3377
  742 Paterson Ave East Rutherford (07073) *(G-2272)*

Art of Natural Solution Inc (PA) 973 812-0500
  45 Commerce Way Unit K Totowa (07512) *(G-10814)*

Art of Natural Solution Inc 917 745-7894
  140 Commerce Way Unit A Totowa (07512) *(G-10815)*

Art of Shaving - Fl LLC 732 410-2520
  3710 Us Highway 9 Freehold (07728) *(G-3648)*

Art Plaque Creations Inc 973 482-2536
  70 Arlington Ave Kearny (07032) *(G-4845)*

Art Press Printing, Barrington Also called Andrew P Mc Hugh Inc *(G-167)*

Art-Deco Division, Woodland Park Also called Pochet of America Inc *(G-12086)*

Artegraft Inc 732 422-8333
  206 N Center Dr North Brunswick (08902) *(G-7453)*

Artemis Optics and Coatings 201 847-0887
  9 Ackerman Ave Emerson (07630) *(G-2863)*

Artex Knitting Mills Inc 856 456-2800
  300 Harvard Ave Westville (08093) *(G-11810)*

Artezio LLC 609 786-2435
195 Nassau St Rear 32 Princeton (08542) *(G-8912)*

Artflag, Fair Haven Also called Art Flag Co Inc *(G-3078)*

Arthroglide, Fair Lawn Also called J M M R Inc *(G-3107)*

Arthur A Kaplan Co Inc 201 806-2100
30 Murray Hill Pkwy # 300 East Rutherford (07073) *(G-2273)*

Arthur A Topilow William Lrner 732 528-0760
19 Davis Ave 2 Neptune (07753) *(G-6865)*

Arthur Gordon Associates Inc 732 431-3361
6 Paragon Way Ste 109 Freehold (07728) *(G-3649)*

Arthur H Thomas Company (PA) 856 467-2000
1654 High Hill Rd Swedesboro (08085) *(G-10571)*

Arthur Schuman Inc (PA) 973 227-0030
40 New Dutch Ln Fairfield (07004) *(G-3146)*

Artic Ice Manufacturing Co 973 772-7000
158 Semel Ave Garfield (07026) *(G-3729)*

Articulight Inc 201 796-2690
15-06 Morlot Ave Fair Lawn (07410) *(G-3085)*

Artique Glass Studio Inc 201 444-3500
483 S Broad St Glen Rock (07452) *(G-3826)*

Artisan Controls Corporation (PA) 973 598-9400
111 Canfield Ave Ste B-18 Randolph (07869) *(G-9173)*

Artisan Gardens LLC 201 857-2600
76 N Maple Ave Ste 279 Ridgewood (07450) *(G-9322)*

Artisan Model Mold 908 453-3524
275 Buckhorn Dr Belvidere (07823) *(G-357)*

Artisan Oven Inc 201 488-6261
105 S State St Hackensack (07601) *(G-3878)*

Artistic Bias Products Co Inc 732 382-4141
1905 Elizabeth Ave Rahway (07065) *(G-9078)*

Artistic Creations, Westfield Also called Foldtex II Ltd *(G-11797)*

Artistic Doors and Windows Inc 732 726-9400
10 S Inman Ave Avenel (07001) *(G-121)*

Artistic Glass & Doors Inc 856 768-1414
154 Cooper Rd Ste 201 West Berlin (08091) *(G-11577)*

Artistic Hardware 609 383-1909
430 Tilton Rd Ste 2 Northfield (08225) *(G-7510)*

Artistic Railings Inc (PA) 973 772-8540
500 River Dr Garfield (07026) *(G-3730)*

Artistic Typography Corp 845 783-1990
161 Coolidge Ave Englewood (07631) *(G-2877)*

Artline Heat Transfer Inc 973 599-0104
2 Eastmans Rd Parsippany (07054) *(G-7883)*

Artmolds Journal LLC 908 273-5600
18 Bank St Ste 1 Summit (07901) *(G-10525)*

Arts Embroidery LLC 732 870-2400
175 Monmouth Rd West Long Branch (07764) *(G-11719)*

Arts Weekly Inc 973 812-6766
52 Sindle Ave Little Falls (07424) *(G-5453)*

Arts Windows Inc 732 905-9595
154537 W Unit 1 St 37 Toms River (08755) *(G-10744)*

Artsign Studio 856 546-4889
916 Kings Hwy Ste C Haddon Heights (08035) *(G-4043)*

Artus Corp 201 568-1000
201 S Dean St Englewood (07631) *(G-2878)*

Arysta LLC 856 417-8100
11 Technology Dr Logan Township (08085) *(G-5585)*

Arysta/ Labrea Bakery, Logan Township Also called Arysta LLC *(G-5585)*

As America Inc (HQ) 732 980-3000
1 Centennial Ave Ste 101 Piscataway (08854) *(G-8637)*

Asa Hydraulik of America Inc 908 541-1500
160 Meister Ave Ste 20a Branchburg (08876) *(G-623)*

ASAP Containers NJ NY Corp 732 659-4402
25 Mountain Dr West Orange (07052) *(G-11759)*

ASAP Nameplate and Label Co, Passaic Also called Technical Nameplate Corp *(G-8111)*

ASAP Postal Printing 609 597-7421
775 N Main St Manahawkin (08050) *(G-5790)*

ASAP Printed Products, Passaic Also called A S A P Nameplate & Labeling *(G-8048)*

Asbury Awng Mfg & Installation 732 775-4881
508 Main St Asbury Park (07712) *(G-71)*

Asbury Carbons (PA) 908 537-2155
405 Old Main St Asbury (08802) *(G-60)*

Asbury Graphite Mills Inc (HQ) 908 537-2155
405 Old Main St Asbury (08802) *(G-61)*

Asbury Graphite Mills Inc 908 537-2157
156 Asbury West Portal Rd Asbury (08802) *(G-62)*

Asbury Louisiana Inc (HQ) 908 537-2155
405 Old Main St Asbury (08802) *(G-63)*

Asbury Park Press Inc 732 922-6000
3600 Route 66 Neptune (07753) *(G-6866)*

Asbury Syrup Company Inc 732 774-5746
3504 Rose Ave Ste 3 Ocean (07712) *(G-7656)*

Ascalon Art Studios, West Berlin Also called Ascalon Studios Inc *(G-11578)*

Ascalon Studios Inc 856 768-3779
430 Cooper Rd West Berlin (08091) *(G-11578)*

Ascend Laboratories LLC 201 476-1977
339 Jefferson Rd Ste 101 Parsippany (07054) *(G-7884)*

Ascendia Pharmaceuticals LLC 732 640-0058
661 Us Highway 1 2 North Brunswick (08902) *(G-7454)*

Ascensia Diabetes Care US Inc (HQ) 973 560-6500
5 Woodhollow Rd Ste 3 Parsippany (07054) *(G-7885)*

Ascent Aromatics Inc 908 755-0120
120 Case Dr South Plainfield (07080) *(G-10221)*

Ascentta Inc 732 868-1766
370 Campus Dr Ste 105 Somerset (08873) *(G-9957)*

Asco 732 634-7017
475 Us Highway 9 S Woodbridge (07095) *(G-12012)*

Asco LP (HQ) 800 972-2726
160 Park Ave Florham Park (07932) *(G-3481)*

Asco LP 973 386-9000
7 Eastmans Rd Parsippany (07054) *(G-7886)*

Asco Investment Corp 973 966-2000
50-60 Hanover Rd Florham Park (07932) *(G-3482)*

Asco Power Services Inc (HQ) 973 966-2000
160 Park Ave Florham Park (07932) *(G-3483)*

Asco Power Technologies LP 732 596-1733
1460 Us Highway 9 N # 209 Woodbridge (07095) *(G-12013)*

Asco Power Technologies LP (HQ) 973 966-2000
160 Park Ave Florham Park (07932) *(G-3484)*

Asco Power Technology, Florham Park Also called Automatic Switch Company *(G-3486)*

Ascot Tag and Label Co Inc 973 482-0900
577 3rd St Newark (07107) *(G-7055)*

Asd Holding Corp 800 442-1902
1 Centennial Ave Piscataway (08854) *(G-8638)*

Ash Ingredients Inc 201 689-1322
65 Harristown Rd Ste 307 Glen Rock (07452) *(G-3827)*

Asha44 LLC 201 306-3600
175 Us Highway 46 Unit A Fairfield (07004) *(G-3147)*

Ashland, Wayne Also called Interntonal Specialty Pdts Inc *(G-11522)*

Ashland LLC 908 243-3500
1005 Route 202/206 Bridgewater (08807) *(G-794)*

Ashland LLC 732 353-7718
50 S Minnisink Ave Ste 2 Parlin (08859) *(G-7861)*

Ashland Spcalty Ingredients GP 908 243-3500
1005 Route 202/206 Bridgewater (08807) *(G-795)*

Ashland Spcalty Ingredients GP 732 353-7708
50 S Minnisink Ave Ste 1 Parlin (08859) *(G-7862)*

Ashley Norton Inc 973 835-4027
210 W Parkway Ste 1 Pompton Plains (07444) *(G-8859)*

Asi, Woodland Park Also called Autoplast Systems Inc *(G-12070)*

Asi Computer Technologies Inc 732 343-7100
131 Fieldcrest Ave Edison (08837) *(G-2462)*

Asiamerica Group Inc 201 497-5993
245 Old Hook Rd Westwood (07675) *(G-11827)*

Aslegacy Spirits LLC 609 784-8383
8 Adam Ct Eastampton (08060) *(G-2371)*

Asme, Little Falls Also called American Soc of Mech Engineers *(G-5451)*

Aso Safety Solutions Inc 973 586-9600
300 Round Hill Dr Ste 6 Rockaway (07866) *(G-9443)*

Aspe Inc 973 808-1155
9 Spielman Rd Fairfield (07004) *(G-3148)*

Aspen Appliance Parts, Beverly Also called Aspen Manufacturing Co Inc *(G-447)*

Aspen Manufacturing Co Inc 609 871-6400
703 Van Rossum Ave Unit 5 Beverly (08010) *(G-447)*

Asphalt Plant, Roseland Also called Weldon Concrete Corp *(G-9544)*

Aspire Pharmaceuticals Inc (PA) 732 447-1444
41 Veronica Ave Somerset (08873) *(G-9958)*

Assa Abloy Entrance Sys US Inc 609 443-5800
300 Horizon Center Blvd # 302 Trenton (08691) *(G-10897)*

Assa Abloy Entrance Systems US 609 528-2580
300 Horizon Center Blvd # 300 Hamilton (08691) *(G-4103)*

Assem - Pak Inc 856 692-3355
1649 Castpa Pl Vineland (08360) *(G-11187)*

Asset Backed Alert, Hoboken Also called Harrison Scott Pblications Inc *(G-4453)*

Associate Fireplace Builders 908 273-5900
331 Springfield Ave Summit (07901) *(G-10526)*

Associated Asphalt Mktg LLC 210 249-9988
400 Grove Rd West Deptford (08066) *(G-11693)*

Associated Cleaning Systems 201 530-9197
569 Oritani Pl Teaneck (07666) *(G-10622)*

Associated Fabrics Corporation 201 300-6053
15-01 Pollitt Dr Ste 7 Fair Lawn (07410) *(G-3086)*

Associated Marble Co, Lodi Also called Charles Deluca *(G-5556)*

Associated Plastics Inc 732 574-2800
179 E Inman Ave Rahway (07065) *(G-9079)*

Associated University Presses, Plainsboro Also called Rosemont Publishing & Printing *(G-8802)*

Assured Automtn Flow Solutions, Roselle Also called Farrell Eqp & Contrls Inc *(G-9557)*

AST Construction Inc 609 277-7101
5 Canale Dr Egg Harbor Township (08234) *(G-2677)*

Asti Corp 201 501-8900
45 W Broad St Bergenfield (07621) *(G-371)*

Asti Magnetics, Bergenfield Also called Asti Corp *(G-371)*

Astra Cleaners of Hazlet 732 264-4144
35 Hazlet Ave Hazlet (07730) *(G-4257)*

Astral Diagnostics Inc 856 224-0900
1224 Forest Pkwy Ste 200 Paulsboro (08066) *(G-8329)*

A
L
P
H
A
B
E
T
I
C

Astrazeneca Pharmaceuticals LP 973 975-0324
  Fl 2 Flr Morristown (07960) *(G-6641)*

Astrix Software Technology (PA) 732 661-0400
  125 Half Mile Rd Ste 200 Red Bank (07701) *(G-9221)*

Astrix Technology Group, Red Bank *Also called Astrix Software Technology* *(G-9221)*

Astro Outdoor Advertising Inc (PA) 856 881-4300
  230 E High St Glassboro (08028) *(G-3807)*

Astro Sign Co, Glassboro *Also called Astro Outdoor Advertising Inc* *(G-3807)*

Astro Tool & Machine Co Inc 732 382-2454
  810 Martin St Rahway (07065) *(G-9080)*

Astrodyne Corporation (PA) 908 850-5088
  36 Newburgh Rd Hackettstown (07840) *(G-3999)*

Astrodyne Tdi, Hackettstown *Also called Transistor Devices Inc* *(G-4039)*

Astrodyne Tdi, Hackettstown *Also called Transistor Devices Inc* *(G-4040)*

AT Information Products Inc (PA) 201 529-0202
  575 Corporate Dr Ste 401 Mahwah (07430) *(G-5715)*

AT&T Services Inc 732 420-3131
  200 S Laurel Ave Middletown (07748) *(G-6159)*

AT&T Technologies Inc 201 771-2000
  1 Oak Way Berkeley Heights (07922) *(G-389)*

Atara LLC 916 765-2217
  4315 Park Ave Apt 2i Union City (07087) *(G-11108)*

Atc Labs, Newark *Also called Audio Technologies and Codecs* *(G-7058)*

Atc Systems Inc 732 560-0900
  207 Blackford Ave Middlesex (08846) *(G-6099)*

Atco Pallet Company 856 461-8141
  1000 Creek Rd Delanco (08075) *(G-2003)*

Atco Products Inc 973 379-3171
  115 Victory Rd Springfield (07081) *(G-10428)*

Atco Rubber Products Inc 856 794-3393
  1480 N West Blvd Vineland (08360) *(G-11188)*

Ateksis USA Corp (HQ) 646 508-9074
  1 Meadowlands Plz Ste 200 East Rutherford (07073) *(G-2274)*

Atg, Rockaway *Also called Advanced Technology Group Inc* *(G-9439)*

Athletes Alley 732 842-1127
  483 Broad St Shrewsbury (07702) *(G-9882)*

Athletic Organizational Aids 201 652-1485
  54 Fairhaven Dr Midland Park (07432) *(G-6170)*

ATI Trading Inc 718 888-7918
  765 York St Elizabeth (07201) *(G-2712)*

ATL 201 825-1400
  45 Spear Rd Ramsey (07446) *(G-9140)*

Atlantank, Carlstadt *Also called Atlantic Coolg Tech & Svcs LLC* *(G-1127)*

Atlantex Instruments Inc 201 391-5148
  7 Reeds Ln Woodcliff Lake (07677) *(G-12047)*

Atlantic Air Enterprises Inc 732 381-4000
  856 Elston St Rahway (07065) *(G-9081)*

Atlantic Associates Intl Inc 856 662-1717
  7001 Westfield Ave Pennsauken (08110) *(G-8392)*

Atlantic Boatlifts, Point Pleasant Boro *Also called Courtney Boatlifts Inc* *(G-8841)*

Atlantic C&E, Clifton *Also called Atlantic Casting & Engineering* *(G-1566)*

Atlantic Can Company 609 518-9950
  1200 Highland Dr Westampton (08060) *(G-11784)*

Atlantic Casting & Engineering 973 779-2450
  810 Bloomfield Ave Clifton (07012) *(G-1566)*

Atlantic City News, Ventnor City *Also called Phildelphia-Newspapers-Llc* *(G-11154)*

Atlantic City Week 609 646-4848
  8025 Black Horse Pike # 350 Pleasantville (08232) *(G-8805)*

Atlantic Coast Woodwork Inc 609 294-2478
  160 Country Club Blvd Ltl Egg Hbr (08087) *(G-5613)*

Atlantic Coastal Welding Inc 732 269-1088
  16 Butler Blvd Bayville (08721) *(G-240)*

Atlantic Coolg Tech & Svcs LLC 201 939-0900
  80 Kero Rd Carlstadt (07072) *(G-1127)*

Atlantic Eqp Engineers Inc 201 828-9400
  24 Industrial Ave Upper Saddle River (07458) *(G-11134)*

Atlantic Exterior Wall Systems 973 646-8200
  25 Mansard Ct Wayne (07470) *(G-11472)*

Atlantic Flooring LLC 609 296-7700
  121 Middle Holly Ln Ltl Egg Hbr (08087) *(G-5614)*

Atlantic Hemotology & Oncology, Neptune *Also called Arthur A Topilow William Lrner* *(G-6865)*

Atlantic Indus WD Pdts LLC 609 965-4555
  411 S London Ave Egg Harbor City (08215) *(G-2652)*

Atlantic Inertial Systems Inc 973 237-2713
  20f Commerce Way Totowa (07512) *(G-10816)*

Atlantic International Tech 973 625-0053
  114 Beach St Ste 3 Rockaway (07866) *(G-9444)*

Atlantic Kenmark Electric Inc 201 991-2117
  11 Ewing Ave North Arlington (07031) *(G-7369)*

Atlantic Lining Co Inc 609 723-2400
  2206 Saylors Pond Rd 2 Jobstown (08041) *(G-4836)*

Atlantic Masonry Supply Inc 609 909-9292
  6422 Black Horse Pike Egg Harbor Township (08234) *(G-2678)*

Atlantic Mills Inc 973 344-2001
  1 Market St Ste 9 Passaic (07055) *(G-8052)*

Atlantic Precision Tech LLC 732 658-3060
  432 Quarry Ln North Brunswick (08902) *(G-7455)*

Atlantic Protective Pouches, Toms River *Also called Whe Research Inc* *(G-10803)*

Atlantic Prsthtic Orthotic Svc 609 927-6330
  199 New Rd Ste 56 Linwood (08221) *(G-5448)*

Atlantic Prtg & Graphics LLC 732 493-4222
  1301 N W Park Ave Ste D Ocean (07712) *(G-7657)*

Atlantic Rubber Enterprises 973 697-5900
  35 Union Valley Rd Newfoundland (07435) *(G-7329)*

Atlantic Spring, Ringoes *Also called Matthew Warren Inc* *(G-9339)*

Atlantic Steel Solutions LLC 973 978-0026
  74 Railroad Ave Bldg 102 Paterson (07501) *(G-8143)*

Atlantic Switch Generator LLC 609 518-1900
  4108 Sylon Blvd Hainesport (08036) *(G-4069)*

Atlantic Towers, Bayville *Also called Tower Systems Inc* *(G-251)*

Atlantic U S, Old Bridge *Also called Quality Plus One Catering Inc* *(G-7726)*

Atlantic Waste Services 201 368-0428
  28 North Dr Rochelle Park (07662) *(G-9421)*

Atlantic Wood Industries Inc 609 267-4700
  1517 Hwy 38 Hainesport (08036) *(G-4070)*

Atlantis Aromatics Inc 732 919-1112
  5047 Industrial Rd Ste 4 Wall Township (07727) *(G-11319)*

Atlas Auto Trim Inc 732 985-6800
  81 Us Highway 1 Edison (08817) *(G-2463)*

Atlas Bronze, Trenton *Also called Maranatha Now Inc* *(G-10955)*

Atlas Copco Hurricane LLC 800 754-7408
  6 Century Dr Ste 85 Parsippany (07054) *(G-7887)*

Atlas Copco North America LLC (HQ) 973 397-3400
  6 Century Dr Ste 85 Parsippany (07054) *(G-7888)*

Atlas Enterprise 908 561-1144
  2505 S Clinton Ave South Plainfield (07080) *(G-10222)*

Atlas Flasher & Supply Co Inc 856 423-3333
  430 Swedesboro Ave Mickleton (08056) *(G-6086)*

Atlas Industrial Mfg Co (PA) 973 779-3970
  81 Somerset Pl Clifton (07012) *(G-1567)*

Atlas O LLC 908 687-9590
  378 Florence Ave Hillside (07205) *(G-4377)*

Atlas Recording Machines Corp 732 295-3663
  2140 Bridge Ave Point Pleasant Boro (08742) *(G-8837)*

Atlas Refinery Inc 973 589-2002
  142 Lockwood St Newark (07105) *(G-7056)*

Atlas Welders & Fabricators, South Plainfield *Also called Atlas Enterprise* *(G-10222)*

Atlas Woodwork Inc 973 621-9595
  212 Wright St Newark (07114) *(G-7057)*

Atlas Woodworking Inc 201 784-1949
  15 Naugle St Closter (07624) *(G-1751)*

Atm Aficionado LLC 973 251-2115
  184 S Livingston Ave Livingston (07039) *(G-5507)*

Atomizing Systems Inc 201 447-1222
  1 Hollywood Ave Ste 1 # 1 Ho Ho Kus (07423) *(G-4439)*

Atrium Publishing, Springfield *Also called Wpi Communications Inc* *(G-10475)*

Ats Mechanical Inc 609 298-2323
  74 Crosswicks St Bordentown (08505) *(G-576)*

Attitudes In Dressing Inc (PA) 908 354-7218
  107 Trumbull St Bldg B8 Elizabeth (07206) *(G-2713)*

Aubrey David Inc 201 653-2200
  260 Broadway Ste 1 Bayonne (07002) *(G-203)*

Audio and Video Labs Inc 856 661-5772
  7905 N Crescent Blvd Delair (08110) *(G-2000)*

Audio Dynamix Inc 201 567-5488
  170 Coolidge Ave Englewood (07631) *(G-2879)*

Audio Technologies and Codecs (PA) 973 624-1116
  105 Lock St Ste 411 Newark (07103) *(G-7058)*

Audiocodes Inc 732 469-0880
  27 Worlds Fair Dr Ste 2 Somerset (08873) *(G-9959)*

Audiocodes Inc (HQ) 732 469-0880
  200 Cottontail Ln A101e Somerset (08873) *(G-9960)*

Audrey Hepburn Collection, Boonton *Also called Evh LLC* *(G-553)*

Augenbrauns Bridal Passaic LLC 845 425-3439
  200 Central Ave Lakewood (08701) *(G-5055)*

Augma Biomaterials USA Inc 201 509-4570
  1989 Englishtown Rd Ste 1 Monroe Township (08831) *(G-6326)*

Aunt Gussies Cookies Crackers, Garfield *Also called Direct Sales and Services Inc* *(G-3739)*

Aunt Kittys Foods Inc 856 691-2100
  270 N Mill Rd Vineland (08360) *(G-11189)*

Auntie Annes Soft Pretzels 856 845-3667
  1750 Deptford Center Rd # 2086 Woodbury (08096) *(G-12025)*

Auntie Annes Soft Pretzels 856 722-0433
  400 W Route 38 Moorestown (08057) *(G-6506)*

Aura Badge Co 856 881-9026
  264 W Clayton Ave Clayton (08312) *(G-1524)*

Aura Detergent LLC 718 824-2162
  649 Ferry St Newark (07105) *(G-7059)*

Aura Signs Inc 866 963-7446
  6 Ilene Ct Ste 9 Hillsborough (08844) *(G-4302)*

Auraplayer USA Inc 617 879-9013
  21 Dale Dr West Orange (07052) *(G-11760)*

Aurex Labs Ltd Lblty Co 609 308-2304
  10 Lake Dr East Windsor (08520) *(G-2337)*

Auro Health LLC (HQ) 732 839-9400
  2572 Brunswick Pike Lawrence Township (08648) *(G-5214)*

Auro Packaging LLC 732 839-9408
  203 Windsor Center Dr East Windsor (08520) *(G-2338)*

Aurobindo Pharma USA Inc 732 839-9402
  6 Wheeling Rd Dayton (08810) *(G-1952)*

Aurobindo Pharma USA Inc 732 839-9400
  279 Prncton Hightstown Rd East Windsor (08520) *(G-2339)*

Aurobindo Pharma USA Inc 732 839-9400
  2400 Us Highway 130 Dayton (08810) *(G-1953)*

Aurobindo Pharma USA Inc (HQ) 732 839-9400
  279 Prnctn Hightstown Rd East Windsor (08520) *(G-2340)*

Aurobindo Pharma USA Inc 609 409-6774
  102 Melrich Rd Cranbury (08512) *(G-1813)*

Aurobindo Pharma USA LLC 732 839-9400
  279 Prnceton Hightstown Rd East Windsor (08520) *(G-2341)*

Aurolife Pharma LLC 732 839-9746
  6 Wheeling Rd Dayton (08810) *(G-1954)*

Aurolife Pharma LLC 732 839-9408
  Unit Iii 203 Windsor East Windsor (08520) *(G-2342)*

Aurolife Pharma LLC (HQ) 732 839-4377
  2400 Us Highway 130 Dayton (08810) *(G-1955)*

Auromedics Pharma LLC 732 823-4122
  279 Prncton Hightstown Rd East Windsor (08520) *(G-2343)*

Auromedics Pharma LLC 732 839-9400
  279 Prncton Hightstown Rd East Windsor (08520) *(G-2344)*

Aurora Apparel Inc 201 646-4590
  1 Riverside Sq Mall # 146 Hackensack (07601) *(G-3879)*

Aurora Apparels, Hackensack *Also called Aurora Apparel Inc (G-3879)*

Aurora Information Systems 856 596-4180
  1873 Marlton Pike E # 220 Cherry Hill (08003) *(G-1340)*

Aurora Multimedia Corporation 732 591-5800
  205 Commercial Ct Morganville (07751) *(G-6583)*

Aurora Research Company Inc 973 827-8055
  200 Munsonhurst Rd # 201 Franklin (07416) *(G-3599)*

Aurorae, Ramsey *Also called Ingui Design LLC (G-9147)*

Aus Inc (PA) 856 234-9200
  155 Gaither Dr Ste A Mount Laurel (08054) *(G-6738)*

Ausome LLC 732 951-8818
  80 E State Rt 4 Ste 290 Paramus (07652) *(G-7789)*

Austarpharma LLC 732 225-2930
  18 Mayfield Ave Edison (08837) *(G-2464)*

Authenticity Brewing LLC 862 432-9622
  23 Kroghs Ln Sparta (07871) *(G-10379)*

Auto Action Group Inc 908 964-6290
  121 N Michigan Ave Ste A Kenilworth (07033) *(G-4922)*

Auto Shopper, Toms River *Also called Showcase Publications Inc (G-10792)*

Auto Tig Welding Fabricating 973 839-8877
  88 Cannonball Rd Ste B Pompton Lakes (07442) *(G-8850)*

Auto-Stak Systems Inc (PA) 201 358-9070
  49 Old Hook Rd Westwood (07675) *(G-11828)*

Autoaccess LLC 908 240-5919
  451 Church Rd Sicklerville (08081) *(G-9908)*

Autodrill LLC 908 542-0244
  1221 Us Highway 22 Ste 6 Lebanon (08833) *(G-5251)*

Automann Inc (PA) 201 529-4996
  850 Randolph Rd Somerset (08873) *(G-9961)*

Automann USA, Somerset *Also called Automann Inc (G-9961)*

Automated Control Concepts Inc (PA) 732 922-6611
  3535 State Route 66 # 14 Neptune (07753) *(G-6867)*

Automated Flexible Conveyors 973 340-1695
  55 Walman Ave Clifton (07011) *(G-1568)*

Automated Medical Pdts Corp 732 602-7717
  440 Cliff Rd Sewaren (07077) *(G-9831)*

Automated Office Inc 888 362-7638
  9 Executive Campus Cherry Hill (08002) *(G-1341)*

Automated Resource Group Inc 201 391-8357
  135 Chestnut Ridge Rd # 2 Montvale (07645) *(G-6397)*

Automated Tapping Systems Inc 732 899-2282
  1110 Beach Ave Beachwood (08722) *(G-257)*

Automatic Machine Product 973 383-9929
  56 Paterson Ave Newton (07860) *(G-7337)*

Automatic Plating-Accu-Cote, Thorofare *Also called Accu-Cote Inc (G-10698)*

Automatic Roll, Edison *Also called Northeast Foods Inc (G-2578)*

Automatic Switch Company (HQ) 973 966-2000
  50-60 Hanover Rd Florham Park (07932) *(G-3485)*

Automatic Switch Company 209 941-4111
  50 Hanover Rd Florham Park (07932) *(G-3486)*

Automatic Switch Company 732 596-1731
  1460 Us Highway 9 N # 209 Woodbridge (07095) *(G-12014)*

Automatic Transfer Inc 908 213-2830
  2 Industrial Rd Alpha (08865) *(G-36)*

Automation & Control Inc 856 234-2300
  1491 Lancer Dr Moorestown (08057) *(G-6507)*

Automation Dynamics Systems, Old Tappan *Also called ABC Digital Electronics Inc (G-7731)*

Autopartsource, Edison *Also called Momentum Usa Inc (G-2569)*

Autoplast Systems Inc 973 785-8333
  256 Bergen Blvd Woodland Park (07424) *(G-12070)*

Autoremind Inc 800 277-1299
  14-25 Plaza Rd Ste N35 Fair Lawn (07410) *(G-3087)*

Autoshred, Toms River *Also called Imwoth LLC (G-10769)*

Autoshred LLC 732 244-0950
  1358 Hooper Ave Toms River (08753) *(G-10745)*

Avacyn Pharmaceuticals Inc 201 836-2599
  719 Downing St Teaneck (07666) *(G-10623)*

Avada Software LLC 973 697-1043
  100 Enterprise Dr Ste 301 Rockaway (07866) *(G-9445)*

Avail Inc (PA) 732 560-2222
  564a Union Ave Bridgewater (08807) *(G-796)*

Avalon Globocare Corp (PA) 732 780-4400
  4400 Route 9 S Ste 3100 Freehold (07728) *(G-3650)*

Avant Industries Ltd Inc (PA) 973 242-1700
  780 Frelinghuysen Ave Newark (07114) *(G-7060)*

Avante International Tech Inc 609 799-9388
  70 Washington Rd Princeton Junction (08550) *(G-9052)*

Avantegarde Image LLC 732 363-8701
  535 E County Line Rd Lakewood (08701) *(G-5056)*

Avanti, Cranbury *Also called Kt America Corp (G-1853)*

Avanti Linens Inc (PA) 201 641-7766
  234 Moonachie Rd Ste 1 Moonachie (07074) *(G-6455)*

Avantier Inc (PA) 732 491-8150
  148 Main St Metuchen (08840) *(G-6046)*

Avantik, Pine Brook *Also called Belair Instrument Company LLC (G-8587)*

Avantor Performance Mtls LLC 610 573-2759
  1013 Route 202/206 Bridgewater (08807) *(G-797)*

Avantor Performance Mtls LLC 908 859-2151
  600 N Broad St Phillipsburg (08865) *(G-8542)*

Avanzato Jewelers LLC 609 890-0500
  2440 Whthrse Hmlton Sq Rd Trenton (08690) *(G-10898)*

Avaya Cala Inc 866 462-8292
  350 Mount Kemble Ave Morristown (07960) *(G-6642)*

Avaya Inc 908 953-6000
  350 Mount Kemble Ave # 2 Morristown (07960) *(G-6643)*

Avaya Inc 732 852-2030
  307 Mddletown Lincroft Rd Lincroft (07738) *(G-5310)*

Avaya World Services Inc 908 953-6000
  350 Mount Kemble Ave Morristown (07960) *(G-6644)*

Avenel Pallet Co Inc 732 752-0500
  1800 S 2nd St Dunellen (08812) *(G-2119)*

Aventis Inc 800 981-2491
  55 Corporate Dr Bridgewater (08807) *(G-798)*

Aventis Phrmcticals Foundation 908 981-5000
  55 Corporate Dr Bridgewater (08807) *(G-799)*

Aversas Italian Bakery Inc 856 227-8005
  801 Route 168 Blackwood (08012) *(G-460)*

Avery Dennison Corporation 201 956-6100
  16-00 Pollitt Dr Ste 3 Fair Lawn (07410) *(G-3088)*

Avet Pharmaceuticals Inc., East Brunswick *Also called Heritage Pharmaceuticals Inc (G-2151)*

Avet Pharmaceuticals Labs Inc., East Brunswick *Also called Heritage Pharma Labs Inc (G-2149)*

Avet Pharmaceuticals Labs Inc., East Brunswick *Also called Heritage Pharma Labs Inc (G-2150)*

Avet Phrmcuticals Holdings Inc, East Brunswick *Also called Heritage Pharma Holdings Inc (G-2148)*

Aviation International News, Midland Park *Also called Convention News Company Inc (G-6173)*

Avida Incorporated 201 802-0749
  174 Kinderkamack Rd Ste A Park Ridge (07656) *(G-7846)*

Avigdor Jewelry, Morristown *Also called Avigdor Ltd Liability Company (G-6645)*

Avigdor Ltd Liability Company 973 898-4770
  25 Tikvah Way Morristown (07960) *(G-6645)*

Avionic Instruments LLC 732 388-3500
  1414 Randolph Ave Avenel (07001) *(G-122)*

Avitex Co Inc (PA) 973 242-2410
  461 Frelinghuysen Ave Newark (07114) *(G-7061)*

Avitex Co Inc 973 242-2410
  32 Noble St Newark (07114) *(G-7062)*

Avon Products Inc 973 779-5590
  1166 Broad St Clifton (07013) *(G-1569)*

Avony Enterprises Inc 212 242-8144
  39 Meade St Ste 122 Trenton (08638) *(G-10899)*

Avstar Publishing Corp 908 236-6210
  3 Burlinghoff Ln Lebanon (08833) *(G-5252)*

Avyakta It Services LLC 609 790-7517
  37 Sussex Ln East Windsor (08520) *(G-2345)*

Aw Machinery LLC 973 882-3223
  7 Just Rd Fairfield (07004) *(G-3149)*

Awards Trophy Company 908 687-5775
  611 Us Highway 22 Hillside (07205) *(G-4378)*

Awning Design Inc 908 462-1131
  1014 Nj 33 Business Freehold (07728) *(G-3651)*

Awnings By Texas Canvas, Fairfield *Also called Texas Canvas Co Inc (G-3326)*

Awsm Industries, Paramus *Also called Royale Pigments & Chem Inc (G-7830)*

Axg Corporation 212 213-3313
  700 Plaza Dr Ste 204 Secaucus (07094) *(G-9751)*

Axiam Printing, Union *Also called Anisha Enterprises Inc (G-11026)*

Axiom Ingredients LLC 732 669-2458
  33 Wood Ave S Ste 600 Iselin (08830) *(G-4598)*

A L P H A B E T I C

Aydin Jewelry Menufecturing 201 818-1002
  119 E Main St Ramsey (07446) *(G-9141)*

Ayerspace Inc 212 582-8410
  25 Fairfield Ave West Caldwell (07006) *(G-11641)*

Ayr Composition Inc 908 241-8118
  320 Chestnut St Roselle Park (07204) *(G-9578)*

Ayr Graphics & Printing Inc 908 241-8118
  7 Mark Rd Ste A Kenilworth (07033) *(G-4923)*

Az-Em USA Branchburg NJ 908 429-0020
  70 Meister Ave Branchburg (08876) *(G-624)*

Azar Displays, Paramus *Also called Azar International Inc (G-7790)*

Azar International Inc (PA) 845 624-8808
  80 W Century Rd Ste 400 Paramus (07652) *(G-7790)*

Azco Steel Company, South Plainfield *Also called Bushwick Metals LLC (G-10231)*

Azego Technology Svcs US Inc (PA) 201 327-7500
  103 Bauer Dr Ste A Oakland (07436) *(G-7615)*

Azimuth Renewable Energy, Manasquan *Also called Mc Renewable Energy LLC (G-5833)*

Aztec Graphics Inc 609 587-1000
  420 Whitehead Rd Trenton (08619) *(G-10900)*

Aztec Software Associates Inc (PA) 973 258-0011
  51 Commerce St Springfield (07081) *(G-10429)*

Aztech Mfg Inc 609 726-1212
  147 W Hampton St Pemberton (08068) *(G-8357)*

Aztek Sand Grav Cmpny-Division, Hammonton *Also called Arawak Paving Co Inc (G-4128)*

B & A Grafx Inc 646 302-8849
  1 Cape May St Harrison (07029) *(G-4163)*

B & B Custom Cabinets, Matawan *Also called Kitchen Crafters Plus (G-5979)*

B & B Iron Works 862 238-7203
  1 Broad St Clifton (07013) *(G-1570)*

B & B Millwork & Doors Inc 973 249-0300
  327 Monroe Ave Kenilworth (07033) *(G-4924)*

B & B Poultry Co Inc 856 692-8893
  Almond Rd Norma (08347) *(G-7365)*

B & B Press Inc 908 840-4093
  24 Cokesbury Rd Ste 11 Lebanon (08833) *(G-5253)*

B & C Custom WD Handrail Corp 732 530-6640
  26 Sunset Ave Red Bank (07701) *(G-9222)*

B & C Machine Co Inc 973 823-1120
  22 Lasinski Rd Ste I Franklin (07416) *(G-3600)*

B & F Mason Contractors, Elmwood Park *Also called B&F and Son Masonry
Company (G-2811)*

B & G International, Union *Also called B & G Plastics Inc (G-11023)*

B & G Plastics Inc (PA) 973 824-9220
  1085 Morris Ave Ste 5d Union (07083) *(G-11028)*

B & H Printers Inc 908 688-6990
  470 Schooleys Mountain Rd # 1 Hackettstown (07840) *(G-4000)*

B & L Printing Co, Hillsborough *Also called Premium Service Printing (G-4345)*

B & M Finishers Inc 908 241-5640
  201 S 31st St Kenilworth (07033) *(G-4925)*

B & R Bindery Division, Trenton *Also called B & R Printing Inc (G-10901)*

B & R Printing Inc 609 448-3328
  84 Hummingbird Dr Trenton (08690) *(G-10901)*

B & S Sheet Metal Co Inc 973 427-3739
  60 5th Ave Hawthorne (07506) *(G-4205)*

B & S Tool and Cutter Service 201 488-3545
  99 John St Hackensack (07601) *(G-3880)*

B & W Plastics Inc 973 383-0020
  20 Wilson Dr Sparta (07871) *(G-10380)*

B and G Music LLC 732 779-4555
  2 Teal Pl Bayville (08721) *(G-241)*

B and W Printing Company Inc 908 241-3060
  730 Fairfield Ave Kenilworth (07033) *(G-4926)*

B B Supply Corp 201 313-9021
  421 Nelson Ave Cliffside Park (07010) *(G-1536)*

B C T, Upper Saddle River *Also called Business Cards Tomorrow (G-11136)*

B D, Franklin Lakes *Also called Becton Dickinson and Company (G-3616)*

B E C Mfg Corp 201 414-0000
  649 Lincoln Ave Glen Rock (07452) *(G-3828)*

B F Goodrich Performance Mtls, Pedricktown *Also called Lubrizol Advanced Mtls
Inc (G-8351)*

B L White Welding & Steel Co 973 684-4111
  527 E 33rd St Paterson (07504) *(G-8144)*

B P, Wayne *Also called BP Lubricants USA Inc (G-11484)*

B P Graphics Inc 732 942-2315
  315 4th St Lakewood (08701) *(G-5057)*

B Spinelli Farm Containers 732 616-7505
  3992 Highway 516 Matawan (07747) *(G-5968)*

B T O Industries Inc 973 243-0011
  11 Lenox Ter West Orange (07052) *(G-11761)*

B T Partners Inc 609 652-6511
  3 N New York Rd Ste 23 Galloway (08205) *(G-3720)*

B Tech, Rockaway *Also called Btech Inc (G-9448)*

B V S, Metuchen *Also called Berkeley Varitronics Systems (G-6047)*

B Witching Bath Company LLC (PA) 973 423-1820
  174 Lincoln Ave Hawthorne (07506) *(G-4206)*

B&B Imaging LLC 201 261-3131
  733 Bush Pl Paramus (07652) *(G-7791)*

B&F and Son Masonry Company 201 791-7630
  10 North St Elmwood Park (07407) *(G-2811)*

B&G Foods Inc (PA) 973 401-6500
  4 Gatehall Dr Ste 110 Parsippany (07054) *(G-7889)*

B&G Foods Inc 973 403-6795
  426 Eagle Rock Ave Roseland (07068) *(G-9534)*

B&G Foods Inc 973 401-6500
  4 Gatehall Dr Ste 110 Parsippany (07054) *(G-7890)*

B&G Foods North America Inc (HQ) 973 401-6500
  4 Gatehall Dr Ste 110 Parsippany (07054) *(G-7891)*

B&M Technologies Inc 201 291-8505
  109 5th St Ste 1 Saddle Brook (07663) *(G-9641)*

B-Hive Ltd Liability Company 302 438-2769
  10 Olivia Rd Hightstown (08520) *(G-4294)*

B-Tea Beverage LLC 201 512-8400
  12-17 River Rd Fair Lawn (07410) *(G-3089)*

B.I. Foods, Pennsauken *Also called Beef International Inc (G-8395)*

B2x Corporation 201 714-2373
  10 Exchange Pl Fl 25 Jersey City (07302) *(G-4697)*

B4inc Inc 609 747-9600
  1208 Columbus Rd Ste F Burlington (08016) *(G-951)*

Bab Printing Jan Service (PA) 908 272-6224
  945 Lincoln Ave E Cranford (07016) *(G-1901)*

Babbitt Mfg Co Inc 856 692-3245
  719 E Park Ave Vineland (08360) *(G-11190)*

Babcock & Wilcox Company 609 261-2424
  1000 Taylors Ln Ste 4 Cinnaminson (08077) *(G-1443)*

Babcock & Wilcox Powr Generatn 973 227-7008
  277 Fairfield Rd Ste 331a Fairfield (07004) *(G-3150)*

Baby Time International Inc 973 481-7400
  250 Passaic St Newark (07104) *(G-7063)*

Bach Tool Precision Inc 973 962-6224
  51 Executive Pkwy Ringwood (07456) *(G-9343)*

Backroads Inc 973 948-4176
  160 County Road 521 Newton (07860) *(G-7338)*

Badge Company of New Jersey, Annandale *Also called Suroma Ltd Liability Company (G-55)*

Badger Blades LLC 908 325-6587
  216 North Ave E Ste 2 Cranford (07016) *(G-1902)*

Bae Systems Info & Elec Sys 603 885-4321
  100 Campus Rd Ste 1 Totowa (07512) *(G-10817)*

Bae Systems Info & Elec Sys 973 633-6000
  150 Parish Dr Wayne (07470) *(G-11473)*

Bae Systems Info & Elec Sys 973 633-6000
  164 Totowa Rd Wayne (07470) *(G-11474)*

Bae Systems Tech Sol Srvc Inc 856 638-1003
  8000 Midlantic Dr 700n Mount Laurel (08054) *(G-6739)*

Baer Aggregates Inc 908 454-4412
  454 River Rd Phillipsburg (08865) *(G-8543)*

Baeta Corp 201 471-0988
  1 Bridge Plz N Ste 2 Fort Lee (07024) *(G-3548)*

Bagel Chateau, Westfield *Also called S M Z Enterprises Inc (G-11803)*

Bagel Chateau, Millburn *Also called Millburn Bagel Inc (G-6205)*

Bagel Club 908 806-6022
  20 Commerce St Ste 5 Flemington (08822) *(G-3432)*

Bagel Street 609 936-1755
  660 Plainsboro Rd Ste 18 Plainsboro (08536) *(G-8780)*

Bahadir USA LLC 856 517-3080
  431 S Pnnsville Auburn Rd Carneys Point (08069) *(G-1241)*

Bai Brands LLC 609 586-0500
  201 Elizabeth St Bordentown (08505) *(G-577)*

Bai Lar Interior Services Inc 732 738-0350
  554 New Brunswick Ave Fords (08863) *(G-3530)*

Baker Adhesives, Paterson *Also called Amb Enterprises LLC (G-8135)*

Baker/Titan Adhesives 973 225-1070
  25 Lake St Paterson (07501) *(G-8145)*

Bakers Perfection Inc 973 983-0700
  198 Green Pond Rd Ste 5 Rockaway (07866) *(G-9446)*

Bakers Puff Pastry, Paterson *Also called Mardon Associates Inc (G-8251)*

Bal Togs Inc 201 866-0201
  6605-09 Smith Ave North Bergen (07047) *(G-7388)*

Bal-Edge Corporation 973 895-8826
  151 Industrial Way E Eatontown (07724) *(G-2379)*

Bal-Togs, North Bergen *Also called Bal Togs Inc (G-7388)*

Bali Designs, Rahway *Also called Robert Manse Designs LLC (G-9124)*

Ballantine Laboratories Inc 908 713-7742
  312 Old Allerton Rd Annandale (08801) *(G-53)*

Ballard Collection Inc 908 604-0082
  221 Stirling Rd Warren (07059) *(G-11399)*

Ballet Makers Inc (PA) 973 595-9000
  1 Campus Rd Totowa (07512) *(G-10818)*

Bally Gaming, Egg Harbor Township *Also called Bally Technologies Inc (G-2679)*

Bally Technologies Inc 609 641-7711
  3133 Fire Rd Egg Harbor Township (08234) *(G-2679)*

Balthazar Bakery, Englewood *Also called Provence LLC (G-2935)*

Baltimore Transformer Company 973 942-2222
  460 Totowa Ave Paterson (07522) *(G-8146)*

Bamboo & Rattan Works Inc 732 255-4239
  1931 Silverton Rd Toms River (08753) *(G-10746)*

Bamco Inc (PA) 732 302-0889
  30 Baekeland Ave Middlesex (08846) *(G-6100)*

Banarez Enterprises Inc 201 222-7515
  175 Baldwin Ave Jersey City (07306) *(G-4698)*

Bandemar Networks LLC 732 991-5112
  3 New Dover Rd East Brunswick (08816) *(G-2128)*

Banding Centers of America 973 805-9977
  83 Hanover Ave Ste 160 Florham Park (07932) *(G-3487)*

Banicki Sheet Metal Inc 201 385-5938
  44 Garden St Bergenfield (07621) *(G-372)*

Banilivy Rug Corp 212 684-3629
  15 S Dean St Englewood (07631) *(G-2880)*

Banker Steel Nj LLC 732 968-6061
  1640 New Market Ave South Plainfield (07080) *(G-10223)*

Banks Bros Corporation (PA) 973 680-4488
  24 Federal Plz Bloomfield (07003) *(G-491)*

Banner Design Inc 908 687-5335
  600 N Union Ave Ste 11 Hillside (07205) *(G-4379)*

Bannister Company Inc 732 828-1353
  216 Brook Dr Milltown (08850) *(G-6214)*

Bannon Group Ltd 201 451-6500
  234 16th St Fl 8 Jersey City (07310) *(G-4699)*

Banquet Services International 732 270-1188
  2214 Route 37 E Ste 1 Toms River (08753) *(G-10747)*

Bar Fields Inc 347 587-7795
  1400 W Elizabeth Ave Linden (07036) *(G-5325)*

Bar Lan Inc 856 596-2330
  327 Gull Cv Brigantine (08203) *(G-911)*

Bar-Lo Carbon Products Inc 973 227-2717
  31 Daniel Rd Fairfield (07004) *(G-3151)*

Bar-Maid Corporation 973 478-7070
  362 Midland Ave Ste 2 Garfield (07026) *(G-3731)*

Barantec Inc 973 779-8774
  777 Passaic Ave Ste 345 Clifton (07012) *(G-1571)*

Barbeitos Inc 732 726-9543
  6 Pocahont Pl Avenel (07001) *(G-123)*

Barbieri, Anthony J, Carlstadt *Also called Designer Sign Systems LLC (G-1151)*

Barbs Harley-Davidson 856 456-4141
  926 Black Horse Pike Mount Ephraim (08059) *(G-6720)*

Bard Asia Pacific Division, Franklin Lakes *Also called Bard International Inc (G-3612)*

Bard Devices Inc (HQ) 908 277-8000
  1 Becton Dr Franklin Lakes (07417) *(G-3611)*

Bard International Inc (HQ) 908 277-8000
  1 Becton Dr Franklin Lakes (07417) *(G-3612)*

Barkercraft, Westville *Also called Intelco (G-11817)*

Barkin Expanding Envelope Co, Manchester *Also called Red Wallet Connection Inc (G-5849)*

Barlics Manufacturing Co Inc 732 381-6229
  815 Martin St Rahway (07065) *(G-9082)*

Barmensen Labs LLC 732 593-3515
  2685 Hwy 516 Old Bridge (08857) *(G-7712)*

Barnegat Light Fibrgls Sup LLC 609 294-8870
  304 Forge Rd Unit 12 West Creek (08092) *(G-11684)*

Barnes & Noble Booksellers Inc 201 272-3635
  125 Chubb Ave Fl 3 Lyndhurst (07071) *(G-5642)*

Barnes & Noble.com, Lyndhurst *Also called Barnes & Noble Booksellers Inc (G-5642)*

Barnet Products LLC 201 346-4620
  920 Sylvan Ave Ste 210 Englewood Cliffs (07632) *(G-2959)*

Barnett Machine Tools Inc 973 482-6222
  401 Supor Blvd Bldg 3n Harrison (07029) *(G-4164)*

Baron Herzog, Bayonne *Also called Royal Wine Corporation (G-233)*

Barrasso & Blasi Industries 973 761-0595
  1581 Springfield Ave Maplewood (07040) *(G-5874)*

Barrett Asphalt Inc 609 561-4100
  7503 Weymouth Rd Hammonton (08037) *(G-4129)*

Barrett Bronze Inc 914 699-6060
  540 Ravine Ct Wyckoff (07481) *(G-12103)*

Barrett Industries Corporation (HQ) 973 533-1001
  73 Headquarters Plz Morristown (07960) *(G-6646)*

Barrett Paving Materials Inc (HQ) 973 533-1001
  3 Becker Farm Rd Ste 307 Roseland (07068) *(G-9535)*

Barrette Outdoor Living Inc 609 965-5450
  545 Tilton Rd Ste 100 Egg Harbor City (08215) *(G-2653)*

Barrier Enterprises Inc 973 770-3983
  175 Stanhope Sparta Rd Andover (07821) *(G-44)*

Barrington Press Inc (PA) 201 843-6556
  37 Spring Valley Ave Paramus (07652) *(G-7792)*

Barry Callebaut USA LLC 856 663-2260
  1500 Suckle Hwy Pennsauken (08110) *(G-8393)*

Barry Callebaut USA LLC 856 663-2260
  1600 Suckle Hwy Pennsauken (08110) *(G-8394)*

Barry Urner Publications Inc 732 240-5330
  1001 Corporate Cir Toms River (08755) *(G-10748)*

Bart Foods Group LLC 973 650-8837
  1275 Bloomfield Ave Fairfield (07004) *(G-3152)*

Bartell Morrison (usa) LLC 732 566-5400
  200 Commerce Ave Freehold (07728) *(G-3652)*

Bartlett Printing & Graphic 609 386-1525
  4495 Route 130 S Burlington (08016) *(G-952)*

Bartley Crucible Refractories 609 393-0066
  15 Muirhead Ave Trenton (08638) *(G-10902)*

Barton & Cooney LLC (PA) 609 747-9300
  300 Richards Run Burlington (08016) *(G-953)*

Baruffi Bros Inc (PA) 856 692-6400
  907 N Main Rd Bldg D Vineland (08360) *(G-11191)*

Barworth Inc 973 376-4883
  673 Morris Tpke Springfield (07081) *(G-10430)*

BASF Americas Corporation (HQ) 973 245-6000
  100 Park Ave Florham Park (07932) *(G-3488)*

BASF California Inc (HQ) 973 245-6000
  100 Campus Dr Florham Park (07932) *(G-3489)*

BASF Catalysts Holdg China LLC (HQ) 973 245-6000
  100 Campus Dr Florham Park (07932) *(G-3490)*

BASF Catalysts LLC (HQ) 732 205-5000
  33 Wood Ave S Iselin (08830) *(G-4599)*

BASF Catalysts LLC 732 205-5000
  700 Blair Rd Carteret (07008) *(G-1249)*

BASF Corporation (HQ) 973 245-6000
  100 Park Ave Florham Park (07932) *(G-3491)*

BASF Corporation 908 689-7470
  2 Pleasant View Ave Washington (07882) *(G-11440)*

BASF Corporation 848 221-2786
  227 Oak Ridge Pkwy Toms River (08755) *(G-10749)*

BASF Corporation 732 205-5086
  25 Middlesex Tpke Iselin (08830) *(G-4600)*

BASF Corporation 732 205-5000
  33 Wood Ave S Fl 2 Iselin (08830) *(G-4601)*

BASF Corporation 732 205-2700
  2655 Route 22 W Union (07083) *(G-11029)*

BASF Corporation 973 426-5429
  450 Clark Dr Ste 3 Budd Lake (07828) *(G-919)*

BASF Corporation 973 245-6000
  175 Raritan Center Pkwy Edison (08837) *(G-2465)*

BASF Engineering Plastics, Budd Lake *Also called BASF Corporation (G-919)*

BASF Plant Science LP 973 245-3238
  100 Park Ave Florham Park (07932) *(G-3492)*

Basfin Corporation (HQ) 973 245-6000
  100 Park Ave Florham Park (07932) *(G-3493)*

Basha USA LLC 201 339-9770
  390 Broadway Bayonne (07002) *(G-204)*

Bashian Bros Inc (PA) 201 330-1001
  65 Railroad Ave Ste 8 Ridgefield (07657) *(G-9250)*

Bashian Rugs, Ridgefield *Also called Bashian Bros Inc (G-9250)*

Basic Commerce & Industries 609 482-3740
  856 S Route 30 Ste 5a Hammonton (08037) *(G-4130)*

Basic Ltd 718 871-6106
  575 Prospect St Ste 241 Lakewood (08701) *(G-5058)*

Basic Plastics Company Inc (PA) 973 977-8151
  318 Mclean Blvd Bldg 5 Paterson (07504) *(G-8147)*

Basic Solutions Ltd 201 978-7691
  330 Adams Ct Manalapan (07726) *(G-5802)*

Baskin-Robbins, Teaneck *Also called Dunkin Donuts Baskin Robbins (G-10628)*

Bassano Graphics, Hawthorne *Also called Bassano Prtrs & Lithographers (G-4207)*

Bassano Prtrs & Lithographers 973 423-1400
  67 Royal Ave Hawthorne (07506) *(G-4207)*

Bassil Bookbinding Company Inc 201 440-4925
  535 S River St Hackensack (07601) *(G-3881)*

Basu Group Inc 908 517-9138
  227 Us Hwy 1 162 North Brunswick (08902) *(G-7456)*

Basys Inc 732 616-5276
  1200 S Church St Ste 7 Mount Laurel (08054) *(G-6740)*

Batallure Beauty LLC (PA) 609 716-1200
  104 Carnegie Ctr Ste 202 Princeton (08540) *(G-8913)*

Bathware House Ltd Lblty Co 732 546-3220
  524 W Edgar Rd Linden (07036) *(G-5326)*

Battistini Foods 609 476-2184
  20 Brandywine Ct Egg Harbor Township (08234) *(G-2680)*

Bauer Enterprises, Ringwood *Also called Susan R Bauer Inc (G-9353)*

Bauer Publishing Company LP (HQ) 201 569-6699
  270 Sylvan Ave Ste 210 Englewood Cliffs (07632) *(G-2960)*

Bauer Sport Shop 201 384-6522
  48 Dumont Ave Dumont (07628) *(G-2111)*

Baum, W & E, Freehold *Also called W & E Baum Bronze Tablet Corp (G-3704)*

Baumar Industries Inc 973 667-5490
  29 E Centre St Nutley (07110) *(G-7580)*

Baumer of America Inc 973 263-1569
  425 Main Rd Towaco (07082) *(G-10865)*

Baumgartner Associates, Somerset *Also called Pacon Manufacturing Corp (G-10051)*

Bausch & Lomb Incorporated (HQ) 585 338-6000
  400 Somerset Corp Blvd Bridgewater (08807) *(G-800)*

Bausch & Lomb Incorporated 908 927-1400
  400 Somerset Corp Blvd Bridgewater (08807) *(G-801)*

Bausch Health Americas Inc (HQ) 908 927-1400
  400 Somerset Corp Blvd Bridgewater (08807) *(G-802)*

Bausch Health Us LLC (HQ) 908 927-1400
  400 Somerset Corp Blvd Bridgewater (08807) *(G-803)*

Bausch Health Us LLC 908 927-1400
  700 Rte 202 206n Bridgewater (08807) *(G-804)*

Bavelle Tech Sltions Ltd Lblty 973 992-8086
  100 Eagle Rock Ave # 301 East Hanover (07936) *(G-2195)*

A
L
P
H
A
B
E
T
I
C

Baxter Corporation (PA) 201 337-1212
  511 Commerce St Franklin Lakes (07417) *(G-3613)*

Baxter Healthcare Corporation 732 225-4700
  100 Raritan Center Pkwy # 120 Edison (08837) *(G-2466)*

Baxter Healthcare Corporation 856 489-2104
  2 Esterbrook Ln Cherry Hill (08003) *(G-1342)*

Bay Shore Press Inc 732 957-0070
  320 Kings Hwy E Middletown (07748) *(G-6160)*

Bay State Milling Company 973 772-3400
  404 Getty Ave Clifton (07011) *(G-1572)*

Bay Treasure Seafood LLC 732 240-3474
  2002 Route 9 Unit 4 Toms River (08755) *(G-10750)*

Bayard's Chocolate House, Atlantic City *Also called James Candy Company (G-95)*

Bayer Consumer Care Inc 973 267-6198
  36 Columbia Rd Morristown (07960) *(G-6647)*

Bayer Healthcare LLC 973 254-5000
  36 Columbia Rd Morristown (07960) *(G-6648)*

Bayer Healthcare LLC (HQ) 862 404-3000
  100 Bayer Blvd Whippany (07981) *(G-11878)*

Bayer Healthcare LLC 973 254-5000
  36 Columbia Rd Morristown (07960) *(G-6649)*

Bayer Hlthcare Phrmcticals Inc 862 404-3000
  100 Bayer Blvd Whippany (07981) *(G-11879)*

Bayer Hlthcare Phrmcticals Inc 973 709-3545
  6 Westbelt Wayne (07470) *(G-11475)*

Bayer Hlthcare Phrmcticals Inc (HQ) 862 404-3000
  100 Bayer Blvd Whippany (07981) *(G-11880)*

Bayer U S LLC 973 709-3545
  6 Westbelt Wayne (07470) *(G-11476)*

Bayonne Community News 201 437-2460
  447 Broadway Bayonne (07002) *(G-205)*

Bayonne Drydock & Repair Corp 201 823-9295
  100 Military Ocean Trml Bayonne (07002) *(G-206)*

Bayshore Recycling Corp 732 738-6000
  75 Crows Mill Rd Keasbey (08832) *(G-4908)*

Bayside Orthopedics LLC 732 691-4898
  780 Route 37 W Ste 330 Toms River (08755) *(G-10751)*

Bayview Entertainment LLC 201 880-5331
  210 W Parkway Ste 7 Pompton Plains (07444) *(G-8860)*

Bayway Refinery, Linden *Also called Phillips 66 Company (G-5407)*

Bbg Surgical Ltd Liability Co 888 575-6277
  1950 Rutgers Blvd D Lakewood (08701) *(G-5059)*

Bbk Technologies Inc 908 231-0306
  13 Rte 206 S Raritan (08869) *(G-9208)*

Bbm Fairway Inc 856 596-0999
  49 S Maple Ave Marlton (08053) *(G-5922)*

Bbm Group LLC 201 482-6500
  280 Broad Ave Fl 3 Palisades Park (07650) *(G-7767)*

Bcc (USA) Inc 732 572-5450
  143 Ethel Rd W Piscataway (08854) *(G-8639)*

Bcg Marble & Granite South LLC 732 367-3788
  150 Faraday Ave Jackson (08527) *(G-4641)*

Bcg Marble Gran Fabricators Co 201 343-8487
  167 Sussex St Hackensack (07601) *(G-3882)*

BCI, Hammonton *Also called Basic Commerce & Industries (G-4130)*

BCsmachine & Mfg Corp 908 561-1656
  3575 Kennedy Rd South Plainfield (07080) *(G-10224)*

BCT, Egg Harbor City *Also called Business Cards Tomorrow Inc (G-2654)*

Bd Biscnces Systems Rgents Inc (PA) 201 847-6800
  1 Becton Dr Franklin Lakes (07417) *(G-3614)*

Bd Ventures LLC 201 847-6800
  1 Becton Dr Franklin Lakes (07417) *(G-3615)*

Bdd, Bayonne *Also called Bayonne Drydock & Repair Corp (G-206)*

Bdiplus Inc 347 597-2539
  26 Liberty Ridge Rd Basking Ridge (07920) *(G-176)*

Be & K Plastics LLC 609 386-3200
  340 E Broad St Burlington (08016) *(G-954)*

Be CU Manufacturing Co Inc (PA) 908 233-3342
  2347 Beryllium Rd Scotch Plains (07076) *(G-9731)*

Bea's Brooklyn's Best, Old Bridge *Also called Deluxe Gourmet Spc Ltd Lblty (G-7714)*

Beach Nutts Media Inc 609 886-4113
  2503 Bayshore Rd Villas (08251) *(G-11178)*

Beachcarts USA 201 319-0091
  296 Julianne Ter Secaucus (07094) *(G-9752)*

Beachcomber, The, Surf City *Also called Jersey Shore News Mgazines Inc (G-10555)*

Beachwood Canvas Works LLC 732 929-1783
  39 Lake Ave Island Heights (08732) *(G-4637)*

Beacon C M P Corp 908 851-9393
  295 N Michigan Ave Ste G Kenilworth (07033) *(G-4927)*

Beacon Offset Printing LLC 201 488-4241
  204 Russell Pl Hackensack (07601) *(G-3883)*

Beacon, The, Clifton *Also called Diocese of Paterson (G-1599)*

Beacut Abrasives Corp 973 249-1420
  788 Paterson Ave East Rutherford (07073) *(G-2275)*

Beall Technologies Inc 201 689-2130
  210 Braen Ave Wyckoff (07481) *(G-12104)*

Bear USa Inc (PA) 201 943-4748
  460 Bergen Blvd Ste 370 Palisades Park (07650) *(G-7768)*

Bearhands Ltd 201 807-9898
  90 Dayton Ave Ste 9 Passaic (07055) *(G-8053)*

Bearing Castings USA, Piscataway *Also called Bcc (USA) Inc (G-8639)*

Beatrice Home Fashions Inc (PA) 908 561-7370
  151 Helen St South Plainfield (07080) *(G-10225)*

Beau Label 973 318-7800
  385 Hillside Ave Hillside (07205) *(G-4380)*

Beauty Wood Designs 908 687-9697
  284 Concord Ave Union (07083) *(G-11030)*

Beauty-Fill LLC 908 353-1600
  1319 N Broad St Hillside (07205) *(G-4381)*

Beauty-Pack LLC 732 802-8200
  170 Circle Dr N Piscataway (08854) *(G-8640)*

Beaver Run Farms (PA) 973 427-1000
  10 Wagaraw Rd Hawthorne (07506) *(G-4208)*

Beaver Run Farms 973 875-5555
  300 Beaver Run Rd Lafayette (07848) *(G-5025)*

Bebe Girdle, Harrison *Also called Dolce Vita Intimates LLC (G-4169)*

Bebus Cabinetry LLC 201 729-9300
  12 Ames Ave Rutherford (07070) *(G-9615)*

Becton Dickinson and Company (PA) 201 847-6800
  1 Becton Dr Franklin Lakes (07417) *(G-3616)*

Bedding Industries of America, North Brunswick *Also called Ther-A-Pedic Sleep Products (G-7490)*

Bedding Shoppe Inc 973 334-9000
  811 Route 46 Parsippany (07054) *(G-7892)*

Bedlam Corp 973 774-8770
  33 Church St Montclair (07042) *(G-6360)*

Bedrock Granite Inc 732 741-0010
  803 Shrewsbury Ave Shrewsbury (07702) *(G-9883)*

Beef International Inc 856 663-6763
  7010 Central Hwy Pennsauken (08109) *(G-8395)*

Beers Steel Erecting, Hackensack *Also called John Cooper Company Inc (G-3934)*

Behr Technology Inc 908 537-9960
  223 State Route 31 Hampton (08827) *(G-4148)*

Behringer Fluid Systems Inc 973 948-0226
  17 Ridge Rd Branchville (07826) *(G-703)*

Behrman House Inc 973 379-7200
  241 Millburn Ave B Millburn (07041) *(G-6195)*

Beilis Development LLC 862 203-3650
  20-21 Wagaraw Rd Bldg 31b Fair Lawn (07410) *(G-3090)*

Bel Fuse Inc (PA) 201 432-0463
  206 Van Vorst St Jersey City (07302) *(G-4700)*

Bel Hybrids & Magnetics Inc 201 432-0463
  206 Van Vorst St Jersey City (07302) *(G-4701)*

Bel-Art Products Inc (HQ) 973 694-0500
  661 Rte 23 Wayne (07470) *(G-11477)*

Bel-Capri, Hackensack *Also called Losurdo Foods Inc (G-3940)*

Bel-Ray Company Inc (HQ) 732 378-4000
  1201 Bowman Ave Wall Township (07727) *(G-11320)*

Bel-Tech Stamping Inc 973 728-8229
  26 Industrial Rd Ste A West Milford (07480) *(G-11726)*

Belair Instrument Company LLC (PA) 973 912-8900
  19 Chapin Rd Bldg C Pine Brook (07058) *(G-8587)*

Belair Time Corporation 732 905-0100
  1995 Swarthmore Ave Ste 3 Lakewood (08701) *(G-5060)*

Belden Inc 908 925-8000
  711 Lidgerwood Ave Elizabeth (07202) *(G-2714)*

Belfer 732 493-2666
  10 Ruckle Ave Farmingdale (07727) *(G-3378)*

Belfer Lighting Manufacturing, Farmingdale *Also called Lighting World Inc (G-3387)*

Bell arte Inc 908 355-1199
  10 W Mravlag Pl Elizabeth (07201) *(G-2715)*

Bell Container Corp 973 344-4400
  615 Ferry St Newark (07105) *(G-7064)*

Bell Supply Co (PA) 856 663-3900
  7221 N Crescent Blvd Pennsauken (08110) *(G-8396)*

Bell'arte, Elizabeth *Also called Bell arte Inc (G-2715)*

Bell-Mark Sales Co Inc (PA) 973 882-0202
  331 Changebridge Rd Ste 1 Pine Brook (07058) *(G-8588)*

Bella Acqua Inc 609 324-9024
  214 Sykesville Rd Ste 1a Chesterfield (08515) *(G-1436)*

Bella Palermo Pastry Shop 908 931-0298
  541 Boulevard Kenilworth (07033) *(G-4928)*

Bellco Glass Inc 800 257-7043
  340 Edrudo Rd Vineland (08360) *(G-11192)*

Belle Printing Group LLC (PA) 856 235-5151
  3838 Church Rd Mount Laurel (08054) *(G-6741)*

Bellemead Hot Glass 908 281-5516
  884 Route 206 Hillsborough (08844) *(G-4303)*

Belleplain Supply Co Inc 609 861-2345
  346 Hands Mill Rd Woodbine (08270) *(G-12008)*

Belleplain Supply Gun Center, Woodbine *Also called Belleplain Supply Co Inc (G-12008)*

Bellerophon Therapeutics Inc 908 574-4770
  184 Liberty Corner Rd # 302 Warren (07059) *(G-11400)*

Belleville Corporation 201 991-6222
  328 Belleville Tpke Kearny (07032) *(G-4846)*

Belleville Scale & Balance LLC 973 759-4487
  50 S Center St Ste 13 Orange (07050) *(G-7751)*

Belleville Wire Cloth Co Inc (PA).....973 239-0074
18 Rutgers Ave Cedar Grove (07009) ***(G-1269)***
Bellevue Parfums USA LLC.....908 262-7774
2 Jill Ct Bldg 21 Hillsborough (08844) ***(G-4304)***
Bellia & Sons.....856 845-2234
1047 N Broad St Woodbury (08096) ***(G-12026)***
Bellino, Englewood *Also called AMD Fine Linens LLC* ***(G-2875)***
Bellview Farms Inc.....856 697-7172
150 Atlantic St Landisville (08326) ***(G-5205)***
Bellview Winery, Landisville *Also called Bellview Farms Inc* ***(G-5205)***
Bellwood Aeromatics Inc.....201 670-4617
4 Spielman Rd Fairfield (07004) ***(G-3153)***
Belmont Bakery, North Haledon *Also called Mini Frost Foods Corporation* ***(G-7498)***
Belmont Whl Fence Mfg Inc.....973 472-5121
112 Monroe St Garfield (07026) ***(G-3732)***
Belting Industries Group LLC (HQ).....908 272-8591
1090 Lousons Rd Union (07083) ***(G-11031)***
Beltor Manufacturing Corp.....856 768-5570
50 Union Ave Ste 12 Berlin (08009) ***(G-415)***
Bemis Company Inc.....908 689-3000
31 State St Washington (07882) ***(G-11441)***
Ben Hamon Moore Co.....800 344-0400
51 Chestnut Ridge Rd Montvale (07645) ***(G-6398)***
Ben Venuti.....908 389-9999
512 North Ave Garwood (07027) ***(G-3781)***
Ben-Aharon & Son Inc.....201 541-2388
15 Smith St Englewood (07631) ***(G-2881)***
Benchmark Scientific Inc.....908 769-5555
2600a Main St Sayreville (08872) ***(G-9703)***
Benckiser N Reckitt Amer Inc.....973 404-2600
399 Interpace Pkwy # 101 Parsippany (07054) ***(G-7893)***
Benco Inc.....973 575-4440
10 Madison Rd Ste E Fairfield (07004) ***(G-3154)***
Benco Products New York, Fairfield *Also called Benco Inc* ***(G-3154)***
Bender Enterprises, Union *Also called George J Bender Inc* ***(G-11059)***
Benedict-Miller LLC.....908 497-1477
100 N 12th St 5 Kenilworth (07033) ***(G-4929)***
Beneduce Vineyard.....908 996-3823
1 Jeremiah Ln Pittstown (08867) ***(G-8752)***
Benjamin Booth Company.....609 859-1995
523 Meadowyck Ln Southampton (08088) ***(G-10360)***
Benjamin Moore, Flanders *Also called Technical Coatings Co* ***(G-3422)***
Benjamin Moore & Co (HQ).....201 573-9600
101 Paragon Dr Montvale (07645) ***(G-6399)***
Benjamin Moore & Co.....973 344-1200
134 Lister Ave Newark (07105) ***(G-7065)***
Benjamin Moore & Co.....973 569-5000
203 Kuller Rd Clifton (07011) ***(G-1573)***
Bennett Cabinets.....732 548-1616
1251 Us Highway 1 Edison (08837) ***(G-2467)***
Bennett Heat Trting Brzing Inc (PA).....973 589-0590
690 Ferry St Newark (07105) ***(G-7066)***
Bentley Laboratories LLC (PA).....732 512-0200
111 Fieldcrest Ave Edison (08837) ***(G-2468)***
Benton Bindery Inc.....732 431-9064
43 Sycamore Ave Freehold (07728) ***(G-3653)***
Benton Graphics Inc.....609 587-4000
3 Industrial Dr Trenton (08619) ***(G-10903)***
Ber Plastics Inc.....973 839-2100
5 Curtis St Riverdale (07457) ***(G-9371)***
Berat Corporation.....609 953-7700
208 Route 70 Medford (08055) ***(G-6020)***
Berennial International.....973 675-6266
355 Main St Orange (07050) ***(G-7752)***
Berezin Nilolai.....856 692-6191
402 E Wheat Rd Vineland (08360) ***(G-11193)***
Berg East Imports Inc.....908 354-5252
120 E Gloucester Pike Barrington (08007) ***(G-168)***
Berg Furniture USA, Barrington *Also called Berg East Imports Inc* ***(G-168)***
Bergen Cable Technology LLC (PA).....973 276-9596
343 Kaplan Dr Fairfield (07004) ***(G-3155)***
Bergen Cnty Crtrdge Xchnge LLC.....201 493-8182
268 Greenwood Ave Midland Park (07432) ***(G-6171)***
Bergen Digital Graphics LLC.....201 825-0011
346 State Rt 17 Upper Saddle River (07458) ***(G-11135)***
Bergen Homestate Corp.....201 372-9740
9 Willow St Moonachie (07074) ***(G-6456)***
Bergen Instant Printing Inc.....201 945-7303
14 State Rt 5 1 Palisades Park (07650) ***(G-7769)***
Bergen International LLC (PA).....201 299-4499
196 Paterson Ave Ste 202 East Rutherford (07073) ***(G-2276)***
Bergen Manufacturing & Supply.....201 854-3461
2025 85th St North Bergen (07047) ***(G-7389)***
Bergen Marzipan & Chocolate.....201 385-8343
205 S Washington Ave Bergenfield (07621) ***(G-373)***
Bergen Screen Printing, North Haledon *Also called Acey Industries Inc* ***(G-7494)***
Bergen Sign Company Inc (PA).....973 742-7755
90 Newark Pompton Tpke Wayne (07470) ***(G-11478)***
Bergenline Gelato LLC.....201 861-1100
7903 Bergenline Ave North Bergen (07047) ***(G-7390)***
Bergio International Inc (PA).....973 227-3230
12 Daniel Rd Fairfield (07004) ***(G-3156)***
Berje Incorporated (PA).....973 748-8980
700 Blair Rd Carteret (07008) ***(G-1250)***
Berk Gold Stamping Corporation (PA).....973 786-6052
196 Pequest Rd Andover (07821) ***(G-45)***
Berkeley Times, Lakehurst *Also called Micro Media Publications Inc* ***(G-5039)***
Berkeley Varitronics Systems.....732 548-3737
255 Liberty St Metuchen (08840) ***(G-6047)***
Berlitz Languages US Inc (HQ).....609 759-5371
7 Roszel Rd Fl 3 Princeton (08540) ***(G-8914)***
Bernafon LLC.....888 941-4203
2501 Cottontail Ln # 102 Somerset (08873) ***(G-9962)***
Bernard D Ascenzo.....856 795-0511
61 Centre St Haddonfield (08033) ***(G-4053)***
Bernard Miller Fabricators.....856 541-9499
1135 Mount Ephraim Ave Camden (08103) ***(G-1041)***
Bernardaud Na Inc.....973 274-3555
1 Jacobus Ave Kearny (07032) ***(G-4847)***
Bernardsville News.....908 766-3900
17 Morristown Rd Bernardsville (07924) ***(G-435)***
Bernardsville Print Center, Bernardsville *Also called R & B Printing Inc* ***(G-443)***
Bernie's Copy Center, Lakewood *Also called Penn Copy Center Inc* ***(G-5145)***
Berry Blast Smoothies LLC.....856 692-6174
1194 Sharp Rd Vineland (08360) ***(G-11194)***
Berry Business Forms, Cranford *Also called Berry Business Procedure Co* ***(G-1903)***
Berry Business Procedure Co.....908 272-6464
6 Park St Cranford (07016) ***(G-1903)***
Berry Global Inc.....732 356-2870
87 Lincoln Blvd Middlesex (08846) ***(G-6101)***
Berry Global Inc.....908 353-3850
100 Dowd Ave Elizabeth (07206) ***(G-2716)***
Berry Global Inc.....980 689-1660
190 Strykers Rd Phillipsburg (08865) ***(G-8544)***
Berry Global Inc.....908 454-0900
190 Strykers Rd Phillipsburg (08865) ***(G-8545)***
Berry Global Inc.....609 395-4199
4 Aurora Dr Ste 403 Cranbury (08512) ***(G-1814)***
Berry Global Inc.....718 205-3115
322 3rd St Elizabeth (07206) ***(G-2717)***
Berry Global Films LLC (HQ).....201 641-6600
95 Chestnut Ridge Rd Montvale (07645) ***(G-6400)***
Berry Global Group Inc.....732 469-2470
34 Engelhard Dr Monroe Township (08831) ***(G-6327)***
Bertolotti LLC.....201 941-3116
54 Industrial Ave Fairview (07022) ***(G-3357)***
Bertone Aromatics.....201 444-9821
26 Dora Ave Waldwick (07463) ***(G-11297)***
Bertot Industries Inc.....973 267-0006
23 Malcolm St Ste 1 Morristown (07960) ***(G-6650)***
Besam Entrance Solutions, Hamilton *Also called Assa Abloy Entrance Systems US* ***(G-4103)***
Beseech Ltd Liability Company.....908 461-7888
259 East Rd Belford (07718) ***(G-281)***
Best American Hands.....203 247-2028
475 Bloy St Hillside (07205) ***(G-4382)***
Best Cast, River Edge *Also called Zsombor Antal Designs Inc* ***(G-9364)***
Best Draperies Inc.....856 429-5453
1 Kresson Rd Cherry Hill (08034) ***(G-1343)***
Best Drapery & Blind Mfg Co, Cherry Hill *Also called Best Draperies Inc* ***(G-1343)***
Best Drapery and Design, Cherry Hill *Also called Best Drapery Inc* ***(G-1344)***
Best Drapery Inc.....856 429-2242
1 Crescent Way Cherry Hill (08002) ***(G-1344)***
Best Electric Motor Co, Freehold *Also called Motors and Drives Inc* ***(G-3681)***
Best of Farms LLC.....201 512-8400
12-17 River Rd Fair Lawn (07410) ***(G-3091)***
Best Value Rugs & Carpets Inc.....732 752-3528
215 Rt 22 E Dunellen (08812) ***(G-2120)***
Bestar, Manalapan *Also called Onwards Inc* ***(G-5822)***
Bestmark National LLC.....862 772-4863
171 Coit St Irvington (07111) ***(G-4561)***
Bestwork Inds For The Blind.....856 424-2510
1940 Olney Ave 200 Cherry Hill (08003) ***(G-1345)***
Beta Industries Corp.....201 939-2400
707 Commercial Ave Carlstadt (07072) ***(G-1128)***
Beta Pharma Inc.....609 436-4100
5 Vaughn Dr Ste 106 Princeton (08540) ***(G-8915)***
Beta Plastics.....201 933-1400
120 Amor Ave Carlstadt (07072) ***(G-1129)***
Beta Tech, Carlstadt *Also called Beta Industries Corp* ***(G-1128)***
Betco Glass Inc.....856 327-4301
824 Columbia Ave Millville (08332) ***(G-6235)***
Beterrific Corp (PA).....201 735-7711
900 Palisade Ave Apt 1d Fort Lee (07024) ***(G-3549)***
Bethel Bindery.....609 296-5043
1500 Route 539 Ltl Egg Hbr (08087) ***(G-5615)***
Bethel Industries Inc.....201 656-8222
3423 John F Kennedy Blvd Jersey City (07307) ***(G-4702)***

ALPHABETIC

Betsy & Adam Ltd...212 302-3750
  90 Dayton Ave Ste 36 Passaic (07055) *(G-8054)*

Better Healthlab Inc...201 880-7966
  200 S Newman St Unit 1 Hackensack (07601) *(G-3884)*

Better Image Graphics Inc......................................856 262-0735
  1041 Glassboro Rd Ste E6 Williamstown (08094) *(G-11952)*

Better Sleep Inc...908 464-2200
  100 Readington Rd Branchburg (08876) *(G-625)*

Better Team USA Corporation...................................973 365-0947
  95b Industrial St E Clifton (07012) *(G-1574)*

Beverage Works Nj Inc...973 439-5700
  10 Dwight Pl Fairfield (07004) *(G-3157)*

Beverage Works Ny Inc (PA)....................................732 938-7600
  1800 State Route 34 # 203 Wall Township (07719) *(G-11321)*

Beverly Manufacturing Co Inc..................................856 764-7898
  63 Webster St Riverside (08075) *(G-9390)*

Beverly Transformers, Riverside *Also called Beverly Manufacturing Co Inc (G-9390)*

Bezerra Corporation...973 595-7775
  232 Union Blvd Totowa (07512) *(G-10819)*

Bezwada Biomedical LLC...908 281-7529
  15 Ilene Ct Ste 1 Hillsborough (08844) *(G-4305)*

Bfhj Holdings Inc (PA)...908 730-6280
  26 Chestnut Ridge Rd Montvale (07645) *(G-6401)*

Bga Construction Inc (PA)......................................973 809-9745
  321 Changebridge Rd Pine Brook (07058) *(G-8589)*

Bgs Inc...732 442-5000
  910 E County Line Rd # 101 Lakewood (08701) *(G-5061)*

Bhamra Chain Manufacturing...................................908 686-4555
  1020 Springfield Rd Union (07083) *(G-11032)*

Biach, Somerset *Also called Hydratight Operations Inc (G-10003)*

Biazzo Dairy Products Inc......................................201 941-6800
  1145 Edgewater Ave Ridgefield (07657) *(G-9251)*

Bib and Tucker Inc...201 489-9600
  51 Main St Hackensack (07601) *(G-3885)*

Bie Real Estate Holdings LLC..................................856 691-9765
  3539 Reilly Ct Vineland (08360) *(G-11195)*

Bierman-Everett Foundry Co....................................973 373-8800
  7 Speir Dr South Orange (07079) *(G-10192)*

Big 3 Precision Products Inc...................................856 293-1400
  30 Gorton Rd Millville (08332) *(G-6236)*

Big Apple Jewelry Mfg..201 531-1600
  62 Railroad Ave East Rutherford (07073) *(G-2277)*

Big Bucks Enterprises Inc.......................................908 320-7009
  55 Willow St Washington (07882) *(G-11442)*

Big Color System Inc...201 236-0404
  681 Lawlins Rd Unit 30 Wyckoff (07481) *(G-12105)*

Big Daddys Sports Haven..856 453-9009
  595 Sherman Ave Millville (08332) *(G-6237)*

Big Dog Natural, Lakewood *Also called Gwenstone Inc (G-5106)*

Big Eye Lamp Inc...732 557-9400
  870 Route 530 Ste 2 Whiting (08759) *(G-11937)*

Big Red Pin LLC..732 993-9765
  28 May St Apt 1 Edison (08837) *(G-2469)*

Bigelow Components Corp.......................................973 467-1200
  74 Diamond Rd Springfield (07081) *(G-10431)*

Bigflysports Inc...201 653-4414
  60 Metro Way Ste 2 Secaucus (07094) *(G-9753)*

Bigflysports Com, Secaucus *Also called Bigflysports Inc (G-9753)*

Bihler of America Inc..908 213-9001
  85 Industrial Rd Bldg B Phillipsburg (08865) *(G-8546)*

Bildisco Door Mfg, West Orange *Also called Bildisco Mfg Inc (G-11762)*

Bildisco Mfg Inc..973 673-2400
  21 Central Ave West Orange (07052) *(G-11762)*

Bill Chambers Sheet Metal......................................856 848-4774
  371 Glassboro Rd Ste 5 Woodbury Heights (08097) *(G-12041)*

Bill's Canvas Shop, Woodbine *Also called G & J Solutions Inc (G-12009)*

Billows Electric Supply Co Inc (PA)............................856 751-2200
  1813 Underwood Blvd Delran (08075) *(G-2009)*

Bills Printing Service Inc.......................................609 888-1841
  2829 S Broad St Trenton (08610) *(G-10904)*

Billy D Dumpster Service LLC..................................609 465-5990
  1 Kimbles Beach Rd Cape May Court House (08210) *(G-1107)*

Billykirk (PA)...201 222-9092
  150 Bay St Fl 3 Jersey City (07302) *(G-4703)*

Bilt Rite Tool & Die Co Inc......................................973 227-2882
  29 Montesano Rd Fairfield (07004) *(G-3158)*

Bimbo Bakeries Usa Inc...732 886-1881
  160 Airport Rd Ste 4 Lakewood (08701) *(G-5062)*

Bimbo Bakeries Usa Inc...732 390-7715
  5 Alvin Ct East Brunswick (08816) *(G-2129)*

Bimbo Bakeries Usa Inc...856 435-0500
  1340 Blckwood Clemtons Rd Clementon (08021) *(G-1531)*

Bimbo Bakeries Usa Inc...973 872-6167
  100 Riverview Dr Wayne (07470) *(G-11479)*

Bimbo Bakeries USA Inc...973 256-8200
  930 Riverview Dr Ste 100 Totowa (07512) *(G-10820)*

Bimini Bay Outfitters Ltd.......................................201 529-3550
  43 Mckee Dr Ste 1 Mahwah (07430) *(G-5716)*

Bind-Rite Graphics Inc..201 863-8100
  100 Castle Rd Secaucus (07094) *(G-9754)*

Bind-Rite Robbinsville LLC......................................609 208-1917
  1 Applegate Dr Robbinsville (08691) *(G-9408)*

Bind-Rite Services Inc...201 440-5585
  16 Horizon Blvd South Hackensack (07606) *(G-10150)*

Bindgraphics Inc...908 245-1110
  490 W 1st Ave Roselle (07203) *(G-9549)*

Bindi Dessert, Kearny *Also called Bindi North America Inc (G-4848)*

Bindi North America Inc (PA)...................................973 812-8118
  630 Belleville Tpke Kearny (07032) *(G-4848)*

Binding Products Inc...212 947-1192
  430 Communipaw Ave Ste 1 Jersey City (07304) *(G-4704)*

Binex Line Corp...201 662-7600
  2 Executive Dr Ste 755 Fort Lee (07024) *(G-3550)*

Bio Compression Systems Inc..................................201 939-0716
  120 W Commercial Ave Moonachie (07074) *(G-6457)*

Bio-Chem Fluidics Inc..973 263-3001
  85 Fulton St Unit 12 Boonton (07005) *(G-544)*

Bio-Chem Valve, Boonton *Also called Bio-Chem Fluidics Inc (G-544)*

Bio-Key International Inc (PA)..................................732 359-1100
  3349 Hwy 138 Ste E Wall Township (07719) *(G-11322)*

Bio-Nature Labs Ltd Lblty Co...................................732 738-5550
  195 Campus Dr Edison (08837) *(G-2470)*

Bioactive Resources LLC..908 561-3114
  138 Sylvania Pl South Plainfield (07080) *(G-10226)*

Bioalert Technologies LLC.......................................551 655-2939
  114 Hollywood Ave Englewood Cliffs (07632) *(G-2961)*

Biochemical Sciences Inc..856 467-1813
  200 Commodore Dr Swedesboro (08085) *(G-10572)*

Bioclimatic Air Systems Inc.....................................856 764-4300
  600 Delran Pkwy Ste D Delran (08075) *(G-2010)*

Bioclimatic Inc (PA)...856 764-4300
  600 Delran Pkwy Ste D Delran (08075) *(G-2011)*

Biodynamics LLC (HQ)...201 227-9255
  84 Honeck St Englewood (07631) *(G-2882)*

Biofarma Us LLC...609 301-6446
  55 Lake Dr East Windsor (08520) *(G-2346)*

Biogenesis Inc...201 678-1992
  444 Marshall St Paterson (07503) *(G-8148)*

Biogenesis-Labs, Paterson *Also called Biogenesis Inc (G-8148)*

Biomed Innovative Cons LLC....................................732 599-7233
  104 N Broadway Apt D South Amboy (08879) *(G-10131)*

Biomedicon...856 778-1880
  30 E Central Ave Moorestown (08057) *(G-6508)*

Biomedtrix LLC...973 331-7800
  9 Whippany Rd Bldg B2-7 Whippany (07981) *(G-11881)*

Biomet Bone Healing Tech, Parsippany *Also called Ebi LLC (G-7929)*

Biomet Fair Lawn, L.P., Fair Lawn *Also called Zimmer Biomet (G-3130)*

Biomet Spine and Biomet Trauma, Parsippany *Also called Ebi LP (G-7930)*

Bionomic Industries Inc..201 529-1094
  777 Corporate Dr Mahwah (07430) *(G-5717)*

Bionpharma Inc..609 380-3313
  600 Alexander Rd Ste 2-4b Princeton (08540) *(G-8916)*

Biopharm International, Iselin *Also called Advanstar Communications Inc (G-4590)*

Biophore LLC...609 275-3713
  4510 Quail Ridge Dr Plainsboro (08536) *(G-8781)*

Bios International Corp...973 492-8400
  10 Park Pl Ste 3 Butler (07405) *(G-996)*

Biosearch Medical Products Inc.................................908 252-0595
  35 Industrial Pkwy Branchburg (08876) *(G-626)*

Biostat Inc..201 541-5688
  14 N Dean St Englewood (07631) *(G-2883)*

Biotech Atlantic Inc..732 389-4789
  6 Industrial Way W Ste E1 Eatontown (07724) *(G-2380)*

Biotech Support Group LLC......................................732 613-1967
  29 Hershey Rd East Brunswick (08816) *(G-2130)*

Biovail Distribution Company....................................908 927-1400
  700 Us Highway 202/206 Bridgewater (08807) *(G-805)*

Bipore Inc..201 767-1993
  31 Industrial Pkwy Northvale (07647) *(G-7519)*

Birds Beware Corporation.......................................732 671-6377
  50 Townsend Dr Middletown (07748) *(G-6161)*

Birds Eye Foods Inc (HQ)..585 383-1850
  121 Woodcrest Rd Cherry Hill (08003) *(G-1346)*

Birds Eye Foods Inc..920 435-5300
  399 Jefferson Rd Parsippany (07054) *(G-7894)*

Birnn Chocolates Inc...732 214-8680
  314 Cleveland Ave Highland Park (08904) *(G-4287)*

Bisaga Inc..856 784-7966
  212 Ashland Ave Somerdale (08083) *(G-9930)*

Bishop Ascendant Inc...201 572-7436
  1083 Bloomfield Ave West Caldwell (07006) *(G-11642)*

Bistis Press Printing Co..973 373-8033
  1310 Clinton Ave Irvington (07111) *(G-4562)*

Bitro Group Inc...201 641-1004
  300 Lodi St Hackensack (07601) *(G-3886)*

Bittner Industries Inc..856 817-8400
  2060 Springdale Rd # 700 Cherry Hill (08003) *(G-1347)*

Bitwine Inc..888 866-9435
  4 Thatcher Rd Tenafly (07670) *(G-10660)*

Bivalve Packing Inc (HQ) 856 785-0270
6957 Miller Ave Port Norris (08349) ***(G-8885)***
Biwal Manufacturing Co Inc 973 778-0105
48 Industrial St W Clifton (07012) ***(G-1575)***
Bk Machine Shop 856 457-7150
586 N West Blvd Vineland (08360) ***(G-11196)***
Bkh Electronics 210 410-2757
9j Brookside Hts Wanaque (07465) ***(G-11391)***
Bkt Exim Us Inc (HQ) 732 817-1400
960 Holmdel Rd Ste 2-02 Holmdel (07733) ***(G-4494)***
Bkt Tires Inc 844 258-8473
960 Holmdel Rd Ste 2 Holmdel (07733) ***(G-4495)***
Blacher Canvas Products Inc 732 968-3666
604 Bound Brook Rd Dunellen (08812) ***(G-2121)***
Black & Decker (us) Inc 201 475-3524
213 Us Highway 46 Elmwood Park (07407) ***(G-2812)***
Black Lagoon Inc 609 815-1654
78 Orourke Dr Trenton (08691) ***(G-10905)***
Black Prince, Clifton *Also called Prince Black Distillery Inc* ***(G-1699)***
Black Sea Fisheries 973 553-1580
306 Whiteman St Apt 6 Fort Lee (07024) ***(G-3551)***
Blackhawk Cre Corporation (PA) 856 887-0162
25 New Market St Salem (08079) ***(G-9692)***
Blades Landscaping Inc 856 779-7665
2028 Briggs Rd Mount Laurel (08054) ***(G-6742)***
Blades Ldscpg Lawn Maint & Ir, Mount Laurel *Also called Blades Landscaping Inc* ***(G-6742)***
Blanc Industries Inc (PA) 973 537-0090
88 King St Ste 1 Dover (07801) ***(G-2075)***
Blankets Inc 973 589-7800
26 Blanchard St Newark (07105) ***(G-7067)***
Blaustein M Furs, Short Hills *Also called M Blaustein Inc* ***(G-9871)***
Blavor Inc 973 265-4165
1 Mountain Ave Montville (07045) ***(G-6438)***
Blazing Visuals 732 781-1401
2138 Bridge Ave Point Pleasant Boro (08742) ***(G-8838)***
Bleema Manufacturing Corp 973 371-1771
517 Lyons Ave Irvington (07111) ***(G-4563)***
Blispak Acquisition Corp 973 884-4141
1 Apollo Dr Ste 3 Whippany (07981) ***(G-11882)***
Blissful Bites 973 670-6928
36 Butternut Dr Vernon (07462) ***(G-11157)***
Blitz Safe of America Inc 201 569-5000
33 Honeck St Englewood (07631) ***(G-2884)***
Blizzard Parts & Service, Paterson *Also called P & S Blizzard Corporation* ***(G-8275)***
Blonder Tongue Labs Inc (PA) 732 679-4000
1 Jake Brown Rd Old Bridge (08857) ***(G-7713)***
Bloomfield Drapery Co Inc 973 777-3566
948 Paterson Ave Ste A East Rutherford (07073) ***(G-2278)***
Bloomfield Iron Co Inc 973 748-7040
21 Florence Ave Belleville (07109) ***(G-291)***
Bloomfield Life Inc 973 233-5001
632 Pompton Ave Cedar Grove (07009) ***(G-1270)***
Bloomfield Manufacturing Co (PA) 973 575-8900
29 Crosby Ln Oakland (07436) ***(G-7616)***
Bloomfield News LLC 973 226-2127
172 Orton Rd West Caldwell (07006) ***(G-11643)***
Blu-J2 LLC 201 750-1407
91 Alpine Ct Demarest (07627) ***(G-2024)***
Blue Blade Corp 908 272-2620
123 N 8th St A Kenilworth (07033) ***(G-4930)***
Blue Blade Steel, Kenilworth *Also called Blue Blade Corp* ***(G-4930)***
Blue Chip Industries Inc 908 704-1466
50 Old Camplain Rd Somerville (08876) ***(G-10104)***
Blue Claw Mfg & Supply Company 856 696-4366
118 Clover Ln Richland (08350) ***(G-9249)***
Blue Dog Graphics, Hackensack *Also called Typestyle Inc* ***(G-3986)***
Blue Dome Inc 646 415-9331
335 Clifton Ave Clifton (07011) ***(G-1576)***
Blue Dome Press, Clifton *Also called Blue Dome Inc* ***(G-1576)***
Blue Fish Clothing Inc 908 996-3720
62 Trenton Ave Frnt Frnt Frenchtown (08825) ***(G-3709)***
Blue Gauntlet Fencing Co, Saddle Brook *Also called Blue Gauntlet Fencing Gear Inc* ***(G-9642)***
Blue Gauntlet Fencing Gear Inc 201 797-3332
280 N Midland Ave Ste 138 Saddle Brook (07663) ***(G-9642)***
Blue Light Welding & Fabg LLC 856 629-5891
2164 Grant Ave Williamstown (08094) ***(G-11953)***
Blue Line Planning Inc 609 577-0100
153 Crsswcks Chstrfeld Rd Crosswicks (08515) ***(G-1949)***
Blue Marlin Systems Inc 973 722-0816
2 Ranney Rd Long Valley (07853) ***(G-5608)***
Blue Monkey Inc 201 805-0055
456b Sylvan St Saddle Brook (07663) ***(G-9643)***
Blue Parachute LLC 732 767-1320
263 Amboy Ave Ste 1 Metuchen (08840) ***(G-6048)***
Blue Ribbon Awards Inc 732 560-0046
12 Worlds Fair Dr Ste J Somerset (08873) ***(G-9963)***
Blue Ring Stencils LLC (PA) 866 763-3873
140 Mount Holly By Pass # 10 Lumberton (08048) ***(G-5623)***
Bluebird Auto Rentl Systems LP (PA) 973 989-2423
200 Mineral Springs Rd Dover (07801) ***(G-2076)***
Blueclone Networks LLC 609 944-8433
103 Carnegie Ctr Ste 300 Princeton (08540) ***(G-8917)***
Bluewater Inc 973 532-1225
50 Division Ave Ste 42 Millington (07946) ***(G-6207)***
Bluewater Industries Inc 609 427-1012
1089 Rt 47 Dennisville (08214) ***(G-2027)***
Bluewater Wldg & Fabrication, Dennisville *Also called Bluewater Industries Inc* ***(G-2027)***
Blusa Defense Manufacturing, Mount Laurel *Also called Bright Lights Usa Inc* ***(G-6743)***
Blutek Power Inc 973 594-1800
300 1 State Rte 17 Ste B2 Lodi (07644) ***(G-5554)***
Bm USA Incorporated (HQ) 800 624-5499
75 Triangle Blvd Carlstadt (07072) ***(G-1130)***
Bmb Machining LLC 973 256-4010
86 Lackawanna Ave 208b Woodland Park (07424) ***(G-12071)***
BMC Software Inc 703 761-0400
50 Tice Blvd Woodcliff Lake (07677) ***(G-12048)***
Bmca Holdings Corporation 973 628-3000
1361 Alps Rd Wayne (07470) ***(G-11480)***
Bmg Entertainment, Rutherford *Also called Sony Music Holdings Inc* ***(G-9634)***
Bmk Enterprises, Rockaway *Also called Bruce Kindberg* ***(G-9447)***
BMW Group, Woodcliff Lake *Also called BMW of North America LLC* ***(G-12049)***
BMW of North America LLC (HQ) 201 307-4000
300 Chestnut Ridge Rd Woodcliff Lake (07677) ***(G-12049)***
Bng Industries LLC 862 229-2414
1 Cape May St Ste 2 Harrison (07029) ***(G-4165)***
BNP Media Inc 201 291-9001
210 E Rte 4 Ste 203 Paramus (07652) ***(G-7793)***
BNS Enterprises Inc 908 285-6556
186 Wildflower Ln Hillsborough (08844) ***(G-4306)***
BO&nic, Wall Township *Also called Nicholas Oliver LLC* ***(G-11358)***
Bob's Custom Docks, Sandyston *Also called Custom Docks Inc* ***(G-9699)***
Bobs Poly Tape Printers Inc 973 824-3005
124 Orchard St Newark (07102) ***(G-7068)***
Boc Gases, Sparta *Also called Messer LLC* ***(G-10398)***
Boc Group Inc 908 665-2400
575 Mountain Ave New Providence (07974) ***(G-6995)***
Boccella Precast LLC 856 767-3861
324 New Brooklyn Rd Berlin (08009) ***(G-416)***
Bodine Tool and Machine Co Inc 856 234-7800
1273 N Church St Ste 104 Moorestown (08057) ***(G-6509)***
Body Wrappers, Elizabeth *Also called Garylin Togs* ***(G-2741)***
Body Wrappers, Elizabeth *Also called Attitudes In Dressing Inc* ***(G-2713)***
Bodybio Inc (PA) 856 825-8338
45 Reese Rd Millville (08332) ***(G-6238)***
Bodycote Thermal Proc Inc 908 245-0717
304 Cox St Roselle (07203) ***(G-9550)***
Bodycote Thermal Processing 908 245-0717
304 Cox St Roselle (07203) ***(G-9551)***
Boehringer Ingelheim Animal 732 729-5700
631 Us Highway 1 North Brunswick (08902) ***(G-7457)***
Boeing Company 314 232-1372
203 Churchill Way Mullica Hill (08062) ***(G-6856)***
Boeing Company 908 464-6959
400 Connell Dr Ste 6200 Berkeley Heights (07922) ***(G-390)***
Boeing Company 610 591-1978
800 Arlington Blvd Swedesboro (08085) ***(G-10573)***
Bogen Communications Inc 201 934-8500
1200 Macarthur Blvd # 303 Mahwah (07430) ***(G-5718)***
Bogen Corporation (PA) 201 934-8500
50 Spring St Ste 1 Ramsey (07446) ***(G-9142)***
Boiron America Inc 862 229-6770
1 Gateway Ctr Ste 2540114 Newark (07102) ***(G-7069)***
Bold Hat Makers, Newark *Also called Headwear Creations Inc* ***(G-7149)***
Bolt Welding & Iron Works 609 393-3993
78 Wall St Trenton (08609) ***(G-10906)***
Bolttech Mannings Inc 973 537-1576
321 Richard Mine Rd Ste 1 Wharton (07885) ***(G-11853)***
Bolttech-Mannings, Wharton *Also called Bolttech Mannings Inc* ***(G-11853)***
Bomar Crystal Company, Middlesex *Also called Bomar Exo Ltd Liability Co* ***(G-6102)***
Bomar Exo Ltd Liability Co 732 356-7787
200b Wood Ave Middlesex (08846) ***(G-6102)***
Bombardier Transportation 201 955-5874
1148 Newark Tpke Kearny (07032) ***(G-4849)***
Bombardier Transportation 973 624-9300
60 Earhart Dr Newark (07114) ***(G-7070)***
Bon Architectual Mill Work LLC 856 320-2872
9120 Pennsauken Hwy Pennsauken (08110) ***(G-8397)***
Bon Chef Inc (PA) 973 383-8848
205 State Route 94 Lafayette (07848) ***(G-5026)***
Bon Jour, Norwood *Also called Mt Embroidery & Promotions LLC* ***(G-7569)***
Bon Jour Promotions, Norwood *Also called Bon-Jour Group LLC* ***(G-7558)***
Bon Venture Services LLC 973 584-5699
34 Ironia Rd Flanders (07836) ***(G-3402)***
Bon-Jour Group LLC 201 646-1070
1100 Blanch Ave Norwood (07648) ***(G-7558)***
Bon-Ton Instant Blnds Intriors, Egg Harbor Township *Also called SF Lutz LLC* ***(G-2697)***

ALPHABETIC

Bondi Digital Publishing LLC 212 405-1655
　33 Hilliard Ave　Edgewater (07020) *(G-2434)*

Bonland Industries Inc (PA) 973 694-3211
　50 Newark Pompton Tpke　Wayne (07470) *(G-11481)*

Bonney-Vehslage Tool Co 973 589-6975
　3 Dundar Rd　Springfield (07081) *(G-10432)*

Bono USA Inc 973 978-7361
　19 Gardner Rd Ste E　Fairfield (07004) *(G-3159)*

Bookazine Co Inc (PA) 201 339-7777
　75 Hook Rd　Bayonne (07002) *(G-207)*

Bookcode Corp 732 742-0481
　2312 Plaza Dr　Woodbridge (07095) *(G-12015)*

Boomerang Systems Inc (PA) 973 538-1194
　30a Vreeland Rd　Florham Park (07932) *(G-3494)*

Boonton Electronics Corp 973 386-9696
　25 Eastmans Rd　Parsippany (07054) *(G-7895)*

Boonton Plastic Molding Co, Boonton *Also called Valley Plastic Molding Co* *(G-572)*

Boost Company, The, Riverside *Also called Drink A Toast Company Inc* *(G-9394)*

Bopp Films, Livingston *Also called Inteplast Group Corporation* *(G-5515)*

Borak Group Inc 718 665-8500
　255 Us Highway 1 And 9　Jersey City (07306) *(G-4705)*

Borealis Compounds Inc (HQ) 908 850-6200
　176 Thomas Rd　Port Murray (07865) *(G-8882)*

Boro Printing Inc 732 229-1899
　813 Broadway　West Long Branch (07764) *(G-11720)*

Borton Enterprises 856 453-9221
　178 Woodruff Rd　Bridgeton (08302) *(G-752)*

Boruch Trading Ltd Lblty Co 718 614-9575
　69 Gudz Rd　Lakewood (08701) *(G-5063)*

Bosco Products Inc 973 334-7534
　441 Main Rd　Towaco (07082) *(G-10866)*

Bossen Architectural Millwork 856 786-1100
　1818 Bannard St　Cinnaminson (08077) *(G-1444)*

Bossett Sailmakers, Sea Girt *Also called North Sales* *(G-9746)*

Bostik Inc 856 848-8669
　2000 Nolte Dr　Paulsboro (08066) *(G-8330)*

Boston Scientific Corporation 973 709-7000
　45 Barbour Pond Dr　Wayne (07470) *(G-11482)*

Bot Beverages, Lawrenceville *Also called Bot LLC* *(G-5224)*

Bot LLC 609 439-1537
　12 Clementon Way　Lawrenceville (08648) *(G-5224)*

Bottos Gnine Itln Style Susage, Mount Royal *Also called CW Brown Foods Inc* *(G-6816)*

Boulevard Lunch Service Inc 732 381-5772
　251 Willow Way　Clark (07066) *(G-1495)*

Bouras Industries Inc 908 918-9400
　25 Deforest Ave Ste 100　Summit (07901) *(G-10527)*

Boutique USA Corp 917 476-0472
　1 William St　Englewood (07631) *(G-2885)*

Bowmar Enterprises Inc 908 277-3000
　558 Cent Ave　New Providence (07974) *(G-6996)*

Boxworks Inc 856 456-9030
　1100 Market St　Bellmawr (08031) *(G-328)*

Boyds Pharmacy Inc 609 499-0100
　306 Broad St　Florence (08518) *(G-3473)*

Boyko Metal Finishing Co Inc (PA) 973 623-4254
　100 Poinier St　Newark (07114) *(G-7071)*

Boyko Metal Finishing Co Inc 973 623-4254
　100 Poinier St　Newark (07114) *(G-7072)*

Boyle Tool & Die Co Inc 856 853-1819
　135 Crown Point Rd　West Deptford (08086) *(G-11694)*

Bozak Inc 732 282-1556
　204 State Route 71 Ste B1　Spring Lake (07762) *(G-10420)*

Bozzone Custom Woodwork Inc 973 334-5598
　4 Taylortown Rd　Montville (07045) *(G-6439)*

BP Corporation North Amer Inc 973 633-2200
　1500 Valley Rd　Wayne (07470) *(G-11483)*

BP Corporation North Amer Inc 908 474-5000
　Park And Brunswick Ave　Linden (07036) *(G-5327)*

BP Lubricants USA Inc (HQ) 973 633-2200
　1500 Valley Rd　Wayne (07470) *(G-11484)*

BP Machine Co Inc 732 251-0449
　10 American Way Ste 3　Spotswood (08884) *(G-10414)*

BP Print Group Inc 732 905-9830
　315 4th St　Lakewood (08701) *(G-5064)*

Bps Worldwide Inc 856 874-0822
　1860 Greentree Rd　Cherry Hill (08003) *(G-1348)*

BR Welding Inc 732 363-8253
　3 Brook Rd　Howell (07731) *(G-4532)*

Brabantia USA Inc 201 933-3192
　20 Murray Hill Pkwy # 260　East Rutherford (07073) *(G-2279)*

Bracco Diagnostics Inc (HQ) 609 514-2200
　259 Prospect Plains Rd　Monroe Township (08831) *(G-6328)*

Bracco Research USA Inc 609 514-2517
　4c Cedarbrook Dr　Cranbury (08512) *(G-1815)*

Bracco USA Inc (HQ) 609 514-2200
　259 Prospect Plains Rd　Monroe Township (08831) *(G-6329)*

Braco Manufacturing Inc 732 752-7777
　4031b New Brunswick Ave　South Plainfield (07080) *(G-10227)*

Brad Garman Designs 732 229-6670
　30 Ava Ct　Long Branch (07740) *(G-5594)*

Bradbury Burial Vault Co Inc 856 227-2555
　761 Lower Landing Rd　Blackwood (08012) *(G-461)*

Braddock Heat Treating Company 732 356-2906
　123 Chimney Rock Rd　Bridgewater (08807) *(G-806)*

Brady Manufacturing Co, Allentown *Also called Edward T Brady* *(G-25)*

Braen Stone Company, Haledon *Also called Stone Industries Inc* *(G-4085)*

Brainstorm Cell Thrpeutics Inc (PA) 201 488-0460
　3 University Plaza Dr　Hackensack (07601) *(G-3887)*

Brainstorm Software Corp 856 234-4945
　16 Apple Orchard Rd　Moorestown (08057) *(G-6510)*

Brambila Jorge Stucco & Stone 856 451-2039
　148 S Giles St　Bridgeton (08302) *(G-753)*

Branchville Bagels Inc 973 948-7077
　332 Us Highway 206 N　Branchville (07826) *(G-704)*

Brand Aromatics Intl Inc 732 363-1204
　1600 Oak St　Lakewood (08701) *(G-5065)*

Branded Screen Printing 908 879-7411
　45 Warren St Ste A　Chester (07930) *(G-1431)*

Brandmuscle Inc 973 685-0022
　200 Clifton Blvd Ste 6　Clifton (07011) *(G-1577)*

Brasscraft Manufacturing Co 856 241-7700
　1 Warner Ct　Swedesboro (08085) *(G-10574)*

Bravo Pack Inc 856 872-2937
　90 Twinbridge Dr　Pennsauken (08110) *(G-8398)*

Bravo Print & Mail Inc 201 806-3750
　491a Washington Ave　Carlstadt (07072) *(G-1131)*

Brawer Bros Inc (PA) 973 238-0163
　375 Diamond Bridge Ave　Hawthorne (07506) *(G-4209)*

Brayco Inc 609 758-5235
　951 County Hwy 537　Creamridge (08514) *(G-1940)*

Brazilian Press & Advertising 973 344-4555
　78 Fillmore St Ste 1　Newark (07105) *(G-7073)*

Brazilian Voice 973 491-6200
　412 Chestnut St　Newark (07105) *(G-7074)*

Bread & Bagels 856 667-2333
　1600 Church Rd　Cherry Hill (08002) *(G-1349)*

Bread Guy Inc 973 881-9002
　840 E 28th St　Paterson (07513) *(G-8149)*

Brecoflex Co LLC 732 460-9500
　222 Industrial Way W　Eatontown (07724) *(G-2381)*

Breen Color Concentrates LLC 609 397-8200
　11 Kari Dr　Lambertville (08530) *(G-5187)*

Breeze-Eastern LLC (HQ) 973 602-1001
　35 Melanie Ln　Whippany (07981) *(G-11883)*

Breeze-Eastern LLC 973 602-1001
　35 Melanie Ln　Whippany (07981) *(G-11884)*

Brennan Penrod Contractors LLC 856 933-1100
　420 Benigno Blvd Unit B　Bellmawr (08031) *(G-329)*

Brenner Metal Products (PA) 973 778-2466
　16 Main Ave　Wallington (07057) *(G-11382)*

Brenner Metal Products 973 778-2466
　51 Paterson Ave　Wallington (07057) *(G-11383)*

Brenntag Specialties Inc (HQ) 908 561-6100
　1 Cragwood Rd Ste 302　South Plainfield (07080) *(G-10228)*

Brent Material Company 908 686-3832
　308 N 14th St　Kenilworth (07033) *(G-4931)*

Brent River Corp (HQ) 908 722-6021
　208 Cougar Ct　Hillsborough (08844) *(G-4307)*

Brent River Corp 908 722-6021
　208 Cougar Ct　Hillsborough (08844) *(G-4308)*

Breure Sheet Metal Co Inc 973 772-6423
　46 Walman Ave　Clifton (07011) *(G-1578)*

Brewers Apprentice The Inc 732 863-9411
　865 State Route 33 Ste 4　Freehold (07728) *(G-3654)*

Brewster Vaults & Monuments 856 785-1412
　1017 Steep Run Rd　Millville (08332) *(G-6239)*

Breyer Manufacturing, Wayne *Also called Reeves International Inc* *(G-11547)*

Brian Lenhart Interactive LLC 610 737-5314
　2 Ridge Dr E　Berkeley Heights (07922) *(G-391)*

Brian's Embroidery, Kenvil *Also called Pro Image Promotions Inc* *(G-4995)*

Briars Usa 732 821-7600
　891 Georges Rd　Monmouth Junction (08852) *(G-6279)*

Brick City Wheelchair RPS LLC 862 371-4311
　92 Hansbury Ave　Newark (07112) *(G-7075)*

Brick-Wall Corp (PA) 732 787-0226
　25 1st Ave Ste 200　Atlantic Highlands (07716) *(G-104)*

Brick-Wall Corp 609 693-6223
　2215 Lacey Rd　Forked River (08731) *(G-3536)*

Bridgestate Foundry Corp 856 767-0400
　175 Jackson Rd　Berlin (08009) *(G-417)*

Bright Ideas Usa LLC 732 886-8865
　890 Morris Ave　Lakewood (08701) *(G-5066)*

Bright Lights Usa Inc 856 546-5656
　9th & Liberty　Camden (08104) *(G-1042)*

Bright Lights Usa Inc (PA) 856 546-5656
　11000 Midlantic Dr　Mount Laurel (08054) *(G-6743)*

Brighton Air 973 258-1500
　21 Springfield Ave　Springfield (07081) *(G-10433)*

Brilliant Brdcstg Concept Inc 732 287-9201
　800 New Brunswick Ave # 1　Rahway (07065) *(G-9083)*

(G-0000) Company's Geographic Section entry number

Brilliant Light Power Inc 609 490-0427
493 Old Trenton Rd East Windsor (08512) ***(G-2365)***
Brim Electronics Inc 201 796-2886
120 Home Pl Lodi (07644) ***(G-5555)***
Brim Technologies, Eatontown *Also called Bal-Edge Corporation* ***(G-2379)***
Brimar Industries Inc 973 340-7889
64 Outwater Ln Garfield (07026) ***(G-3733)***
Bringhurst Bros Inc 856 767-0110
38 W Taunton Rd Berlin (08009) ***(G-418)***
Bringhurst Meats, Berlin *Also called Bringhurst Bros Inc* ***(G-418)***
Brinker Displays, Dover *Also called Brinker Industries* ***(G-2077)***
Brinker Industries 973 678-1200
88 King St Ste 1 Dover (07801) ***(G-2077)***
Brisar Delvco, Paterson *Also called Delvco Pharma Packg Svcs Inc* ***(G-8172)***
Brisar Delvco Packaging Svcs, Paterson *Also called Brisar Industries Inc* ***(G-8150)***
Brisar Industries Inc 973 278-2500
76 Wood St Paterson (07524) ***(G-8150)***
Brisco Apparel Co Inc 718 715-7110
575 Prospect St Ste 230 Lakewood (08701) ***(G-5067)***
Bristol-Donald Company Inc 973 589-2640
50 Roanoke Ave Newark (07105) ***(G-7076)***
Bristol-Myers Squibb, Trenton *Also called E R Squibb & Sons Inter-AM* ***(G-10932)***
Bristol-Myers Squibb, Princeton *Also called E R Squibb & Sons Inter-AM* ***(G-8936)***
Bristol-Myers Squibb Company 609 419-5000
100 Nassau Park Blvd # 200 Princeton (08540) ***(G-8918)***
Bristol-Myers Squibb Company 212 546-4000
311 Pnnington Rocky Hl Rd Pennington (08534) ***(G-8359)***
Bristol-Myers Squibb Company 609 252-4875
Province Line Rd Rr 206 Princeton (08540) ***(G-8919)***
Bristol-Myers Squibb Company 908 218-3700
685 Us Highway 202/206 Bridgewater (08807) ***(G-807)***
Bristol-Myers Squibb Company 212 546-4000
171 Long Ave Hillside (07205) ***(G-4383)***
Bristol-Myers Squibb Company 609 302-3000
3401 Princeton Pike Lawrenceville (08648) ***(G-5225)***
Brite Concepts Inc 201 270-8544
90 W Palisade Ave Englewood (07631) ***(G-2886)***
Brittingham Sftwr Design Inc 908 832-2691
440 Hwy 513 Califon (07830) ***(G-1031)***
Brix City Brewing 201 440-0865
4 Alsan Way Little Ferry (07643) ***(G-5475)***
Broadhurst Sheet Metal Works 973 304-4001
230 Warburton Ave Hawthorne (07506) ***(G-4210)***
Broadview Technologies Inc 973 465-0077
7-33 Amsterdam St Newark (07105) ***(G-7077)***
Broadway Empress Entrmt Inc 973 991-0009
15-21 Oraton St Newark (07104) ***(G-7078)***
Broadway Kleer-Guard Corp 609 662-3970
1 S Middlesex Ave Monroe Township (08831) ***(G-6330)***
Brodie System Inc 908 862-8620
1539 W Elizabeth Ave Linden (07036) ***(G-5328)***
Bromilows Candy Co (PA) 973 684-1496
350 Rifle Camp Rd Woodland Park (07424) ***(G-12072)***
Brook Hollow Winery LLC 908 496-8200
594 State Hwy 94 Columbia (07832) ***(G-1792)***
Brook Metal Products Inc 908 355-1601
16 Sunset Rd Lawrence Township (08648) ***(G-5215)***
Brook Saddle Ridge Equest 609 953-1600
10 Saddle Brook Ct Shamong (08088) ***(G-9855)***
Brookaire Company LLC 973 473-7527
329 Veterans Blvd Carlstadt (07072) ***(G-1132)***
Brookline Chemical Corp 301 767-1177
26 Hanes Dr Wayne (07470) ***(G-11485)***
Brooklyn Bean Roastery, South Plainfield *Also called Two Rivers Coffee LLC* ***(G-10332)***
Brooks Power Systems, Hamilton *Also called Power Brooks Co LLC* ***(G-4120)***
Brother International Corp (HQ) 908 704-1700
200 Crossing Blvd Fl 1 Bridgewater (08807) ***(G-808)***
Brothers Sheet Metal Inc 973 228-3221
15 Grand Roseland (07068) ***(G-9536)***
Brown and Perkins Inc 609 655-1150
1193 Cranbury S River Rd Cranbury (08512) ***(G-1816)***
Brown Chemical Co Inc (PA) 201 337-0900
302 W Oakland Ave Oakland (07436) ***(G-7617)***
Browns Awning Co, Ocean City *Also called Robert Brown* ***(G-7694)***
Browns Welding Service 732 988-9530
105 Oxonia Ave Neptune (07753) ***(G-6868)***
Bruce Kindberg 973 664-0195
305 Us Highway 46 Rockaway (07866) ***(G-9447)***
Bruce McCoy Sr 609 217-6153
5402 Tall Pnes Pine Hill (08021) ***(G-8621)***
Bruce Supply Corp 732 661-0500
300 Smith St Keasbey (08832) ***(G-4909)***
Bruce Teleky Inc 718 965-9694
430 Communipaw Ave Ste 2 Jersey City (07304) ***(G-4706)***
Bruderer Machinery Inc (PA) 201 941-2121
1200 Hendricks Cswy Ridgefield (07657) ***(G-9252)***
Bruere Heating & AC, Clifton *Also called Breure Sheet Metal Co Inc* ***(G-1578)***
Bruker Ost LLC 732 541-1300
600 Milik St Carteret (07008) ***(G-1251)***

Brummer's Chocolates, Westfield *Also called George Brummer* ***(G-11798)***
Brunnquell Iron Works Inc 609 409-6101
2557 Us Highway 130 Ste 3 Cranbury (08512) ***(G-1817)***
Brunswick Hot Mix Corp 908 233-4444
141 Central Ave Westfield (07090) ***(G-11795)***
Brunswick Signs & Exhibit 732 246-2500
1510 Jersey Ave North Brunswick (08902) ***(G-7458)***
Brusso Hardware LLC 212 337-8510
67-69 Greylock Ave Belleville (07109) ***(G-292)***
Bsa Consulting, Somerset *Also called Business Software Applications* ***(G-9964)***
BSC USA LLC 908 487-4437
111 Grand Ave Ste 220 Palisades Park (07650) ***(G-7770)***
BSD Industries Ltd Liability 732 534-4341
110 Columbus Ave S Lakewood (08701) ***(G-5068)***
Bsdi, Califon *Also called Brittingham Sftwr Design Inc* ***(G-1031)***
Bsi Corp 631 589-1118
52 E Centre St Ste 2 Nutley (07110) ***(G-7581)***
Bsrm Inc 888 509-0668
691 Cornwallis Dr Mount Laurel (08054) ***(G-6744)***
Bta Pharmaceuticals Inc 908 927-1400
700 Us Highway 202/206 Bridgewater (08807) ***(G-809)***
Btech Inc 973 983-1120
10 Astro Pl Ste A Rockaway (07866) ***(G-9448)***
Btm, Paterson *Also called Burlington Textile Machinery* ***(G-8151)***
Bucati Leather Inc 732 254-0480
427 Whitehead Ave Ste 2 South River (08882) ***(G-10349)***
Bucci Management Co Inc 609 567-8808
603 N 1st Rd Hammonton (08037) ***(G-4131)***
Buckets Plus Inc 732 545-0420
345 Sandford St New Brunswick (08901) ***(G-6914)***
Buckhead Beef N E, Edison *Also called Buckhead Meat Company* ***(G-2471)***
Buckhead Meat Company 732 661-4900
220 Raritan Center Pkwy Edison (08837) ***(G-2471)***
Bucks County Brewing Co Inc 609 929-0148
80 Lambert Ln Ste 120 Lambertville (08530) ***(G-5188)***
Budget Banners, Ocean *Also called Adpro Imprints* ***(G-7653)***
Budget Instant Printing, Clark *Also called Phillip Balderose* ***(G-1512)***
Budget Print Center 973 743-0073
332 Broad St Bloomfield (07003) ***(G-492)***
Buhler Inc 201 847-0600
40 Whitney Rd Mahwah (07430) ***(G-5719)***
Builders Firstsource Inc 856 767-3153
210 Williamstown Rd Berlin (08009) ***(G-419)***
Buildgreen Solutions, Lakewood *Also called Bgs Inc* ***(G-5061)***
Building Materials Corp Amer, Wayne *Also called Bmca Holdings Corporation* ***(G-11480)***
Building Materials Mfg Corp (HQ) 973 628-3000
1 Campus Dr Parsippany (07054) ***(G-7896)***
Building Performance Eqp Inc 201 722-1414
80 Broadway Ste 101 Hillsdale (07642) ***(G-4364)***
Bulbrite Industries Inc 201 531-5900
145 W Commercial Ave Moonachie (07074) ***(G-6458)***
Bulkhaul (usa) Limited (HQ) 908 272-3100
485 Us Highway 1 S E230b Iselin (08830) ***(G-4602)***
Bumper Specialties Inc 856 345-7650
1607 Imperial Way West Deptford (08066) ***(G-11695)***
Bunn Industries Incorporated (PA) 609 890-2900
2651 E State Street Ext Trenton (08619) ***(G-10907)***
Buona Vita Inc 856 453-7972
1 S Industrial Blvd Bridgeton (08302) ***(G-754)***
Buonaventura Bag and Cases LLC 212 960-3442
95 Main Ave Ste 1 Clifton (07014) ***(G-1579)***
Buono Bagel-To The Max, Ramsey *Also called Frell Corp* ***(G-9144)***
Burdol Inc 856 453-0336
1791 S Burlington Rd Bridgeton (08302) ***(G-755)***
Burger Maker Inc (PA) 201 939-4747
666 16th St Carlstadt (07072) ***(G-1133)***
Burgess Steel Holding LLC 201 871-3500
200 W Forest Ave Englewood (07631) ***(G-2887)***
Burgiss Group LLC 201 427-9600
111 River St Fl 10th Hoboken (07030) ***(G-4444)***
Burkley Case, Clifton *Also called Buonaventura Bag and Cases LLC* ***(G-1579)***
Burling Instruments Inc 973 665-0601
16 River Rd Chatham (07928) ***(G-1319)***
Burlington Atlantic Corp 732 888-7776
1 Crown Plz Hazlet (07730) ***(G-4258)***
Burlington Cnty Endoscopy Ctr 609 267-1555
140 Mount Holly By Pass # 5 Lumberton (08048) ***(G-5624)***
Burlington Coat Factory 908 994-9562
651 Kapkowski Rd Ste 30 Elizabeth (07201) ***(G-2718)***
Burlington County Times, Willingboro *Also called Burlington Times Inc* ***(G-11989)***
Burlington Design Center Inc 856 778-7772
3019 Marne Hwy Mount Laurel (08054) ***(G-6745)***
Burlington Press Corporation 609 387-0030
328 High St Ste C Burlington (08016) ***(G-955)***
Burlington Textile Machinery 973 279-5900
39 Mcbride Ave Paterson (07501) ***(G-8151)***
Burlington Times Inc (HQ) 609 871-8000
4284 Route 130 Willingboro (08046) ***(G-11989)***

A L P H A B E T I C

Burns Link Manufacturing Co 856 429-6844
253 American Way Voorhees (08043) *(G-11281)*
Burpee Medsystems LLC 732 544-8900
15 Christopher Way Eatontown (07724) *(G-2382)*
Busch LLC 908 561-3233
39 Davis St South Plainfield (07080) *(G-10229)*
Busch Vacuum, South Plainfield *Also called Busch LLC (G-10229)*
Bush Refrigeration, Pennsauken *Also called Kohlder Manufacturing Inc (G-8448)*
Bushwick Metals LLC 908 604-1450
1641 New Market Ave South Plainfield (07080) *(G-10230)*
Bushwick Metals LLC 908 754-8700
1641 New Market Ave South Plainfield (07080) *(G-10231)*
Bushwick Metals LLC 610 495-9100
25 Rockwood Pl Englewood (07631) *(G-2888)*
Business Card Express, Marlton *Also called Five Macs Inc (G-5931)*
Business Cards Tomorrow 201 236-0088
11 Industrial Ave Upper Saddle River (07458) *(G-11136)*
Business Cards Tomorrow Inc 609 965-0808
129 Cincinnati Ave Egg Harbor City (08215) *(G-2654)*
Business Control Systems Corp 732 283-1301
1173 Green St Iselin (08830) *(G-4603)*
Business Dev Solutions Inc 856 433-8005
311 Hadleigh Dr Cherry Hill (08003) *(G-1350)*
Business Software Applications 908 500-9980
6 Sunny Ct Somerset (08873) *(G-9964)*
BUSINESS TODAY, Princeton *Also called Foundation For Student Comm (G-8950)*
Butler Prtg & Laminating Inc 973 838-8550
250 Hamburg Tpke Butler (07405) *(G-997)*
Butler Sign Co., Wayne *Also called Four Way Enterprises Inc (G-11505)*
Butterfly Bow Ties LLC 973 626-2536
911 Garden St Union (07083) *(G-11033)*
Buttonwood Enterprises LLC 201 505-1901
52 Winding Way Woodcliff Lake (07677) *(G-12050)*
Buy Buy Baby Inc (HQ) 908 688-0888
650 Liberty Ave Union (07083) *(G-11034)*
Buyers Laboratory, LLC, Fairfield *Also called Keypoint Intelligence LLC (G-3249)*
Buzzboard Inc (PA) 415 906-6934
1050 Wall St W Ste 630 Lyndhurst (07071) *(G-5643)*
Bway Corporation 732 997-4100
7 Wheeling Rd Dayton (08810) *(G-1956)*
Bway Corporation 609 883-4300
6 Litho Rd Trenton (08648) *(G-10908)*
Bwi Chemicals 732 689-0913
6 Libby Dr Monmouth Junction (08852) *(G-6280)*
Bylada Foods LLC (PA) 201 933-7474
140 W Commercial Ave Moonachie (07074) *(G-6459)*
Bylada Foods LLC 201 933-7474
1 Branca Rd East Rutherford (07073) *(G-2280)*
Byram Laboratories Inc (PA) 908 252-0852
1 Columbia Rd Branchburg (08876) *(G-627)*
Byram Labs, Branchburg *Also called Byram Laboratories Inc (G-627)*
C & C Metal Products Corp (PA) 201 569-7300
456 Nordhoff Pl Englewood (07631) *(G-2889)*
C & C Tool and Machine Co LLC 856 764-0911
38 W Scott St Riverside (08075) *(G-9391)*
C & D Sales 609 383-9292
73 E West Jersey Ave Pleasantville (08232) *(G-8806)*
C & E Canners Inc 609 561-1078
1249 Mays Landing Rd Hammonton (08037) *(G-4132)*
C & F Burner Co 201 998-8080
39 River Rd North Arlington (07031) *(G-7370)*
C & K Plastics Inc 732 549-0011
159 Liberty St Metuchen (08840) *(G-6049)*
C & K Punch & Screw Mch Pdts 201 343-6750
160 Hobart St Hackensack (07601) *(G-3888)*
C & L Machining Company Inc 856 456-1932
110 S New Broadway Brooklawn (08030) *(G-914)*
C & M Shade Corp 201 807-1200
53 Dwight Pl Fairfield (07004) *(G-3160)*
C & N Packaging Inc 631 491-1400
155 Us Highway 46 Ste 200 Wayne (07470) *(G-11486)*
C & N Tooling & Grinding Inc 973 598-8411
19 State Route 10 E # 14 Succasunna (07876) *(G-10509)*
C & S Fencing Inc 201 797-5440
75 Midland Ave 77 Elmwood Park (07407) *(G-2813)*
C & S Machine Inc 973 882-1097
22 Commerce Rd Ste Q Fairfield (07004) *(G-3161)*
C & S Machinery Rebuilding 973 742-7302
636 E 19th St Ste 642 Paterson (07514) *(G-8152)*
C & S Specialty Inc 201 750-7740
121 Piermont Rd Norwood (07648) *(G-7559)*
C & S Tool Co 973 887-6865
304 Ridgedale Ave East Hanover (07936) *(G-2196)*
C & Y Group East Coast Inc 973 732-4816
150 Saint Charles St Newark (07105) *(G-7079)*
C A D, Fairfield *Also called Cartridge Actuated Devices (G-3166)*
C A P S, Englewood *Also called Central Admxture Phrm Svcs Inc (G-2892)*
C A R, Forked River *Also called Custom Auto Radiator Inc (G-3539)*
C A Spalding Company 267 550-9000
355 Crider Ave Moorestown (08057) *(G-6511)*
C and C Tool Co LLC 908 431-0330
198 Us Highway 206 Ste 1 Hillsborough (08844) *(G-4309)*
C and R Printing Corporation 201 528-8912
400 Gotham Pkwy Ste 4 Carlstadt (07072) *(G-1134)*
C Bennett Scopes Inc 856 464-6889
550 Bridgeton Pike Mantua (08051) *(G-5851)*
C C S, Newark *Also called Corporate Computer Systems (G-7088)*
C D E Inc 732 297-2540
950 Schweitzer Pl North Brunswick (08902) *(G-7459)*
C E I, Ridgefield *Also called Cosmetic Essence LLC (G-9257)*
C E S, Upper Saddle River *Also called Componding Engrg Solutions Inc (G-11137)*
C G Automation Group, Union City *Also called Cuny and Guerber Inc (G-11109)*
C G I Cstm Fiberglas & Decking 609 646-5302
48 S Main St Pleasantville (08232) *(G-8807)*
C Harry Marean Printing 609 965-4708
1717 Philadelphia Ave Egg Harbor City (08215) *(G-2655)*
C J Electric 201 891-0739
327 Franklin Ave Wyckoff (07481) *(G-12106)*
C Jackson Associates Inc 856 761-8000
2050 Springdale Rd # 700 Cherry Hill (08003) *(G-1351)*
C M C Steel Fabricators Inc 908 561-3484
14 Harmich Rd South Plainfield (07080) *(G-10232)*
C M Furnaces Inc 973 338-6500
103 Dewey St Bloomfield (07003) *(G-493)*
C M H Hele-Shaw Inc 201 974-0570
1714 Willow Ave Hoboken (07030) *(G-4445)*
C M M Rentals, Vineland *Also called Cumberland Marble & Monument (G-11207)*
C Q Corporation 201 935-8488
480 Paterson Ave East Rutherford (07073) *(G-2281)*
C R Bard Inc (HQ) 908 277-8000
1 Becton Dr Franklin Lakes (07417) *(G-3617)*
C R Bard Inc 856 461-0946
1822 Underwood Blvd Delran (08075) *(G-2012)*
C S Hot Stamping 201 840-4004
20 Edgewater Pl Edgewater (07020) *(G-2435)*
C S L Water Quality, Warren *Also called C S L Water Treatment Inc (G-11401)*
C S L Water Treatment Inc 908 647-1400
156 Mount Bethel Rd Warren (07059) *(G-11401)*
C S T Pavers, Branchville *Also called Concrete Stone & Tile Corp (G-705)*
C Systems LLC 732 338-9347
510 Thornall St Ste 310 Edison (08837) *(G-2472)*
C T A Manufacturing Corp 201 896-1000
263 Veterans Blvd Carlstadt (07072) *(G-1135)*
C Technologies Inc 908 707-1009
685 Us Highway 202/206 # 102 Bridgewater (08807) *(G-810)*
C W Brabender Instrs Inc 201 343-8425
50 E Wesley St South Hackensack (07606) *(G-10151)*
C W Brown & Company, Mount Royal *Also called CW Brown Foods Inc (G-6817)*
C W Grimmer & Sons Inc 732 741-2189
75 W Gilbert St Tinton Falls (07701) *(G-10706)*
C.B.M. Co., Randolph *Also called Chen Brothers Machinery Co (G-9174)*
C.E.S. Towing & Recovery, Roselle *Also called Cubalas Emergency Lighting LLC (G-9555)*
C/S Corporate, Lebanon *Also called Construction Specialties Inc (G-5257)*
C2 Imaging LLC (HQ) 646 557-6300
201 Plaza Two Jersey City (07311) *(G-4707)*
C3 Concepts Inc 212 840-1116
1435 51st St Ste 2d North Bergen (07047) *(G-7391)*
Cabinet Tronics Inc 609 267-2625
100 Birmingham Rd Birmingham (08011) *(G-455)*
Cabio Newspaper 201 902-0811
604 56th St West New York (07093) *(G-11736)*
Cabletenna Corp 609 395-9400
440 Forsgate Dr Cranbury (08512) *(G-1818)*
Cabletime Ltd 973 770-8070
100 Valley Rd Ste 203 Mount Arlington (07856) *(G-6710)*
Cabletime USA, Mount Arlington *Also called Cabletime Ltd (G-6710)*
Caboki LLC 609 642-2108
3 Corporate Dr Cranbury (08512) *(G-1819)*
Cacciola Iron Works Inc 973 595-0854
65 N 9th St Paterson (07522) *(G-8153)*
Cad Signs LLC 201 267-0457
169 Lodi St Hackensack (07601) *(G-3889)*
Cad Signs Nyc Corp 201 525-5415
169 Lodi St Hackensack (07601) *(G-3890)*
Cadbury Adams USA LLC (HQ) 973 503-2000
100 Deforest Ave East Hanover (07936) *(G-2197)*
Caddy Corporation of America 856 467-4222
509 Sharptown Rd Swedesboro (08085) *(G-10575)*
Cadence Distributors LLC 646 808-3031
200 S Newman St Unit 8 Hackensack (07601) *(G-3891)*
Caesars Pasta LLC 856 227-2585
1001 Lower Landing Rd Blackwood (08012) *(G-462)*
Cain Machine Inc 856 825-7225
2248 E Main St Millville (08332) *(G-6240)*
Cake Specialty Inc 973 238-0500
255 Goffle Rd Hawthorne (07506) *(G-4211)*

Caladrius Biosciences Inc (PA) 908 842-0100
110 Allen Rd Ste 2 Basking Ridge (07920) *(G-177)*

Calandra Italian & French Bky 973 484-5598
204 1st Ave W Newark (07107) *(G-7080)*

Calandra's Bakery, Newark *Also called Calandra Italian & French Bky (G-7080)*

Calculagraph Co (PA) 973 887-9400
280 Ridgedale Ave East Hanover (07936) *(G-2198)*

Calculagraph Co 973 887-9400
272 Ridgedale Ave 280 East Hanover (07936) *(G-2199)*

Caldwell Progress, Bernardsville *Also called Parker Publications Inc (G-441)*

Caled Chemical, Wayne *Also called Anscott Chemical Inds Inc (G-11471)*

Calgonate, Branchburg *Also called Top Safety Products Company (G-689)*

California Closet Co, Fairfield *Also called Rainbow Closets Inc (G-3297)*

California Stucco Products 201 457-1900
85 Zabriskie St Ste 1 Hackensack (07601) *(G-3892)*

Caliz - Malko LLC 973 207-5200
66 Clinton Rd Fairfield (07004) *(G-3162)*

Callaghan Pump Controls Inc 201 621-0505
106 Hobart St Hackensack (07601) *(G-3893)*

Calmac Manufacturing Corp 201 797-1511
3-00 Banta Pl Fair Lawn (07410) *(G-3092)*

Caloric Color Co Inc 973 471-4748
176 Saddle River Rd A Garfield (07026) *(G-3734)*

Calyptus Pharmaceuticals Inc 908 720-6049
174 Nassau St Ste 364 Princeton (08542) *(G-8920)*

Camber Pharmaceuticals Inc 732 529-0430
1031 Centennial Ave Piscataway (08854) *(G-8641)*

Cambrdge Inds For Vslly Impred 732 247-6668
1230 Hamilton St Somerset (08873) *(G-9965)*

Cambrex Corporation (PA) 201 804-3000
1 Meadowlands Plz # 1510 East Rutherford (07073) *(G-2282)*

Cambridge Bagel Factory, Bloomfield *Also called Cambridge Bagels Inc (G-494)*

Cambridge Bagels Inc 973 743-5683
648 Bloomfield Ave Bloomfield (07003) *(G-494)*

Cambridge Industries Co Inc 973 465-4565
7 Amsterdam St 33 Newark (07105) *(G-7081)*

Cambridge Industries Group 917 669-7337
4 Raritan Pl Basking Ridge (07920) *(G-178)*

Cambridge Pavers Inc 201 933-5000
1 Jerome Ave Lyndhurst (07071) *(G-5644)*

Cambridge Pavingstones, Lyndhurst *Also called Cambridge Pavers Inc (G-5644)*

Cambridge Resources, Matawan *Also called Coda Resources Ltd (G-5971)*

Cambridge Therapeutic Tech LLC 914 420-5555
90 Main St Ste 107 Hackensack (07601) *(G-3894)*

Camden Iron & Metal Inc (HQ) 856 365-7500
1500 S 6th St Camden (08104) *(G-1043)*

Camden Iron & Metal LLC (HQ) 856 969-7065
201 N Front St Camden (08102) *(G-1044)*

Camden Tool Inc 856 966-6800
129 York St Camden (08102) *(G-1045)*

Cameco Inc 973 239-2845
100 Pine St Verona (07044) *(G-11164)*

Cameo China Inc 201 865-7650
501 Penhorn Ave Ste 12 Secaucus (07094) *(G-9755)*

Cameo China East, Secaucus *Also called Cameo China Inc (G-9755)*

Cameo Metal Forms, Rahway *Also called Cameo Metal Products Inc (G-9084)*

Cameo Metal Forms Inc 718 788-1106
12 Andrews Dr Woodland Park (07424) *(G-12073)*

Cameo Metal Products Inc 732 388-4000
1745 Elizabeth Ave Rahway (07065) *(G-9084)*

Cameo Novelty & Pen Corp 973 923-1600
400 Hillside Ave Hillside (07205) *(G-4384)*

Camfil Usa Inc (HQ) 973 616-7300
1 N Corporate Dr Riverdale (07457) *(G-9372)*

Camp Marine Services Inc 609 368-1777
1000 Stone Harbor Blvd Stone Harbor (08247) *(G-10503)*

Campak Inc 973 994-4888
119 Naylon Ave Livingston (07039) *(G-5508)*

Campbell Company of Canada 856 342-4800
1 Campbell Pl Camden (08103) *(G-1046)*

Campbell Converting Corp 609 835-2720
703 Van Rossum Ave Unit 2 Beverly (08010) *(G-448)*

Campbell Foundry Company (PA) 973 483-5480
800 Bergen St Harrison (07029) *(G-4166)*

Campbell Foundry Company 201 998-3765
1235 Harrison Tpke Kearny (07032) *(G-4850)*

Campbell Group, Harrison *Also called Campbell Foundry Company (G-4166)*

Campbell Hausfeld LLC 856 661-1800
8550 Remington Ave Pennsauken (08110) *(G-8399)*

Campbell Soup Company (PA) 856 342-4800
1 Campbell Pl Camden (08103) *(G-1047)*

Campbell Soup Company 856 342-4759
827 Memorial Ave Bldg 80 Camden (08103) *(G-1048)*

Campbell Soup Supply Co LLC (HQ) 856 342-4800
1 Campbell Pl Camden (08103) *(G-1049)*

Campbell's Pharmacy, Sea Girt *Also called 140 Main Street Corp (G-9744)*

Campbell-Soup Company, Camden *Also called Campbell Soup Supply Co LLC (G-1049)*

Camptown Tool & Die Co Inc 908 688-8406
25 Sidney Cir Kenilworth (07033) *(G-4932)*

Campus Coordinates LLC 732 866-6060
1711 Ginesi Dr Ste 1 Freehold (07728) *(G-3655)*

Camtec Industries Inc 732 332-9800
28 Saddle Ridge Rd Colts Neck (07722) *(G-1777)*

Canac Kitchens of NJ Inc 201 567-9585
99 N Dean St Englewood (07631) *(G-2890)*

Canada Bread, Wayne *Also called Bimbo Bakeries Usa Inc (G-11479)*

Canada Dry Bottling Co NY LP 732 572-1660
1760 New Durham Rd South Plainfield (07080) *(G-10233)*

Canada Dry Del Vly Btlg Co 856 662-6767
8275 Us Hwy 130 Pennsauken (08110) *(G-8400)*

Canada Dry Dstrg Wilmington De 609 645-7070
11 Canale Dr Egg Harbor Township (08234) *(G-2681)*

Canada Dry of Delaware Valley, Pennsauken *Also called Canada Dry Del Vly Btlg Co (G-8400)*

Canada Dry of Delaware Valley, Pennsauken *Also called Foulkrod Associates (G-8421)*

Canada Dry Potomac Corporation 856 665-6200
8275 Us Hwy 130 Pennsauken (08110) *(G-8401)*

Canary' Closets & Cabinetry, Union *Also called John Canary Custom Wdwkg Inc (G-11067)*

Candela Corporation 908 753-6300
111 Corporate Blvd Ste I South Plainfield (07080) *(G-10234)*

Candle Artisans Incorporated 908 689-2000
253 E Washington Ave Washington (07882) *(G-11443)*

Candy Treasure LLC 201 830-3600
66 Welsh Rd Lebanon (08833) *(G-5254)*

Canfield Clinic Systems, Fairfield *Also called Canfield Property Group Inc (G-3163)*

Canfield Property Group Inc 973 276-0300
253 Passaic Ave Ste 1 Fairfield (07004) *(G-3163)*

Cantel Medical Corp (PA) 973 890-7220
150 Clove Rd Ste 36 Little Falls (07424) *(G-5454)*

Cantol Inc (HQ) 609 846-7912
4701 Mediterranean Ave Wildwood (08260) *(G-11942)*

Cantone Press Inc 201 569-3435
161 Coolidge Ave Englewood (07631) *(G-2891)*

Canvas Creations 609 465-8428
14 Swainton Goshen Rd Cape May Court House (08210) *(G-1108)*

Caolion BNC Co Ltd 201 641-4709
65 Challenger Rd Ste 44 Ridgefield Park (07660) *(G-9300)*

Cape Atlantic Software LLC 609 442-1331
6523 Mill Rd Egg Harbor Township (08234) *(G-2682)*

Cape May Brewing Company, Cape May *Also called Cape May Brewing Ltd Lblty Co (G-1092)*

Cape May Brewing Company, Cape May *Also called Cape May Brewing Ltd Lblty Co (G-1093)*

Cape May Brewing Ltd Lblty Co 609 849-9933
1288 Hornet Rd Cape May (08204) *(G-1092)*

Cape May Brewing Ltd Lblty Co (PA) 609 849-9933
409 Breakwater Rd Cape May (08204) *(G-1093)*

Cape May County Herald, Rio Grande *Also called Seawave Corp (G-9358)*

Cape May Foods, Millville *Also called Lamonica Fine Foods LLC (G-6258)*

Cape May Star & Wave, Cape May *Also called Sample Media Inc (G-1101)*

Cape May Winery & Vineyard, Cape May *Also called W J R B Inc (G-1104)*

Cape Prosthetics-Orthotics 856 810-7900
100 Brick Rd Ste 315 Marlton (08053) *(G-5923)*

Cape Publishing Inc 609 898-4500
513 Washington St Fl 2 Cape May (08204) *(G-1094)*

Capezio, Totowa *Also called Ballet Makers Inc (G-10818)*

Capintec Inc (HQ) 201 825-9500
7 Vreeland Rd Ste 101 Florham Park (07932) *(G-3495)*

Capital Contracting & Design (PA) 908 561-8411
640 North Ave Plainfield (07060) *(G-8760)*

Capital Cooling Systems LLC 973 773-8700
1050 Wall St W Ste 202 Lyndhurst (07071) *(G-5645)*

Capital Foods Inc 908 587-9050
1701 E Elizabeth Ave Linden (07036) *(G-5329)*

Capital Gasket and Rubber Inc 856 939-3670
325 E Clements Bridge Rd Runnemede (08078) *(G-9604)*

Capital Label and Affixing Co 856 786-1700
1100 Taylors Ln Ste 5 Cinnaminson (08077) *(G-1445)*

Capital Printing Corporation 732 560-1515
420 South Ave Middlesex (08846) *(G-6103)*

Capital Soap Products LLC 973 333-6100
62 Kearney St Paterson (07522) *(G-8154)*

Capital Steel Service LLC 609 882-6983
82 Stokes Ave Ewing (08638) *(G-3017)*

Capitol Bindery Inc 609 883-5971
312 Stokes Ave Ewing (08638) *(G-3018)*

Capitol Box Corp (PA) 201 867-6018
1300 6th St North Bergen (07047) *(G-7392)*

Capitol Foam Products Inc 201 933-5277
75 E Union Ave East Rutherford (07073) *(G-2283)*

Capitol Steel Inc 609 538-9313
10 Escher St Trenton (08609) *(G-10909)*

Capitol Steel Products, Trenton *Also called Capitol Steel Inc (G-10909)*

Capra Custom Cabinetry 908 797-9848
259 E Washington Ave Washington (07882) *(G-11444)*

A
L
P
H
A
B
E
T
I
C

Caps Padel, Cherry Hill *Also called Daman International Inc (G-1355)*
Capsugel Inc (HQ) 862 242-1700
  412 Mount Kemble Ave 200c Morristown (07960) *(G-6651)*
Capsugel Holdings Us Inc (HQ) 862 242-1700
  412 Mount Kemble Ave 200c Morristown (07960) *(G-6652)*
Capsugel US, Morristown *Also called Capsugel Inc (G-6651)*
Captain John Inc 609 494-2094
  16 E 12th St Barnegat Light (08006) *(G-164)*
Captivate Internationalllc 732 734-0403
  28 May St Apt 1 Edison (08837) *(G-2473)*
Captive Fasteners Corp 201 337-6800
  19 Thornton Rd Oakland (07436) *(G-7618)*
Captive Plastics LLC 812 424-2904
  190 Strykers Rd Phillipsburg (08865) *(G-8547)*
Captive Plastics LLC 732 469-7900
  251 Circle Dr N Piscataway (08854) *(G-8642)*
Caputo International Inc 732 225-5777
  112 Northfield Ave Edison (08837) *(G-2474)*
Car Boline, Rahway *Also called Carboline Company (G-9085)*
Car Wash Parts Inc 215 633-9250
  6927 Atlantic Ave Ventnor City (08406) *(G-11152)*
Caraco Pharmaceutical Labs 609 819-8200
  270 Prospect Plains Rd Cranbury (08512) *(G-1820)*
Caraustar Clifton Primary Pack 973 472-4900
  43 Samworth Rd Clifton (07012) *(G-1580)*
Caraustar Industries Inc 908 782-0505
  869 State Route 12 Frenchtown (08825) *(G-3710)*
Caravan Inc 732 590-0210
  160 Essex Ave E Avenel (07001) *(G-124)*
Caravan Ingredients Inc 973 256-8886
  100 Adams Dr Totowa (07512) *(G-10821)*
Caravan Ingredients Inc 201 672-0510
  96 E Union Ave East Rutherford (07073) *(G-2284)*
Caravan Products, East Rutherford *Also called A & S Frozen Inc (G-2268)*
Carboline Company 908 233-3150
  449 South Ave E Westfield (07090) *(G-11796)*
Carboline Company 732 388-2912
  842 Elston St Rahway (07065) *(G-9085)*
Carbon Fiber Element LLC 973 809-9432
  690 New Durham Rd Metuchen (08840) *(G-6050)*
Carbone America Scp Division 973 334-0700
  400 Myrtle Ave 1 Boonton (07005) *(G-545)*
Cardinal Fibreglass Industries 718 625-4350
  1050 State St Perth Amboy (08861) *(G-8513)*
Cardinal Health Systems Inc (HQ) 732 537-6544
  14 Schoolhouse Rd Somerset (08873) *(G-9966)*
Cardinal International Inc 973 628-0900
  30 Corporate Dr Wayne (07470) *(G-11487)*
Cardinal Millville DC ARC Intl, Millville *Also called ARC International N Amer LLC (G-6233)*
Carecam International Inc 973 227-0720
  10 Plog Rd Fairfield (07004) *(G-3164)*
Caregility Corporation 732 413-6000
  81 Corbett Way Eatontown (07724) *(G-2383)*
Caret Corporation (PA) 973 423-6098
  180 Passaic Ave Ste 3 Fairfield (07004) *(G-3165)*
Carfaro, Trenton *Also called Fairway Building Products LLC (G-10935)*
Carfaro Inc 609 890-6600
  2075 E State Street Ext Trenton (08619) *(G-10910)*
Cargill Incorporated 908 820-9800
  132 Corbin St Elizabeth (07201) *(G-2719)*
Cargille Laboratories, Cedar Grove *Also called Cargille-Sacher Labs Inc (G-1271)*
Cargille-Sacher Labs Inc (PA) 973 239-6633
  55 Commerce Rd Cedar Grove (07009) *(G-1271)*
Cargille-Sacher Labs Inc 973 267-8888
  4 E Frederick Pl Cedar Knolls (07927) *(G-1300)*
Carib Chemical Co Inc 201 791-6700
  103 Main Ave Elmwood Park (07407) *(G-2814)*
Carib Chemical Co Inc (PA) 201 791-6700
  125 Main Ave Elmwood Park (07407) *(G-2815)*
Carib International, Elmwood Park *Also called Carib Chemical Co Inc (G-2814)*
Carib-Display Co (PA) 732 583-1648
  18 Northland Ln Matawan (07747) *(G-5969)*
Cariletha Company Inc 609 222-3055
  2206 Sedgefield Dr Mount Laurel (08054) *(G-6746)*
Carl A Venable Inc 732 985-6677
  65 Hidden Lake Dr North Brunswick (08902) *(G-7460)*
Carl Buck Corporation 973 300-5575
  14 Park Lake Rd Ste 3 Sparta (07871) *(G-10381)*
Carl Stahl Sava Industries Inc (HQ) 973 835-0882
  4 N Corporate Dr Riverdale (07457) *(G-9373)*
Carl Streit & Son Co 732 775-0803
  703 Atkins Ave Neptune (07753) *(G-6869)*
Carlascio Custom & Orthopedic (PA) 201 333-8716
  283 Grove St Apt 1 Jersey City (07302) *(G-4708)*
Carlee Corporation 201 768-6800
  28 Piermont Rd Rockleigh (07647) *(G-9515)*
Carlisle Machine Works Inc 856 825-0627
  412 S Wade Blvd Ste 5 Millville (08332) *(G-6241)*

Carlton Coke Met Fnishings LLC 732 774-2210
  1004 1st Ave Asbury Park (07712) *(G-72)*
Carlyle Custom Convertibles (PA) 973 546-4502
  6 Empire Blvd Moonachie (07074) *(G-6460)*
Carnegie Deli Products Inc 201 507-5557
  605 Washington Ave Carlstadt (07072) *(G-1136)*
Carnegie Pharmaceuticals LLC 732 783-7013
  600 Delran Pkwy Ste C Delran (08075) *(G-2013)*
Carnegie Surgical LLC (PA) 866 782-7144
  151 One Mile Rd East Windsor (08512) *(G-2366)*
Carner Bros, Roseland *Also called Zc Utility Services LLC (G-9545)*
Carneys Point Fire Company Aux, Carneys Point *Also called Township of Carneys Point (G-1244)*
Carol Dauplaise Ltd 212 997-5290
  5901 W Side Ave North Bergen (07047) *(G-7393)*
Carol Products Co Inc 732 918-0800
  1750 Brielle Ave Ste A1 Ocean (07712) *(G-7658)*
Carol S Miller Corporation 201 406-4578
  98 Saddlewood Dr Hillsdale (07642) *(G-4365)*
Carolace Embroidery Co Inc (PA) 201 945-2151
  65 Railroad Ave Ste 3 Ridgefield (07657) *(G-9253)*
Carole Hchman Design Group Inc (HQ) 866 267-3945
  90 Hudson St Fl 9 Jersey City (07302) *(G-4709)*
Carolina Fluid Handling Inc 248 228-8900
  140 Bradford Dr West Berlin (08091) *(G-11579)*
Carpathian Industries LLC 201 386-5356
  51 Newark St Ste 508 Hoboken (07030) *(G-4446)*
Carpenter & Paterson Inc 973 772-1800
  369 Jefferson St Saddle Brook (07663) *(G-9644)*
Carpenter & Paterson Inc 609 227-2750
  2 Altran Ct Ste 2 # 2 Bordentown (08505) *(G-578)*
Carpenter Emergency Lighting, Trenton *Also called Carpenter LLC (G-10911)*
Carpenter LLC 609 689-3090
  2 Marlen Dr Trenton (08691) *(G-10911)*
Carpet Hardware Systems, Montclair *Also called Bedlam Corp (G-6360)*
Carrier Transicold of NJ, Matawan *Also called Penn Power Group LLC (G-5984)*
Carry Cases Plus, Paterson *Also called Century Service Affiliates Inc (G-8155)*
Carry Easy Inc 201 944-0042
  131 Fort Lee Rd Fl 2 Leonia (07605) *(G-5287)*
Carson & Gebel Ribbon Co LLC 973 627-4200
  17 Green Pond Rd Rockaway (07866) *(G-9449)*
Carstens Publications Inc 973 383-3355
  108 Phil Hardin Rd Newton (07860) *(G-7339)*
Carter Manufacturing Co Inc 201 935-0770
  55 Anderson Ave Moonachie (07074) *(G-6461)*
Carter Pump Inc 201 568-9798
  152d Franklin Tpke Waldwick (07463) *(G-11298)*
Carteret Die-Casting Corp 732 246-0070
  74 Veronica Ave Somerset (08873) *(G-9967)*
Cartiheal Inc 917 703-6992
  3 Reuten Dr Closter (07624) *(G-1752)*
Cartolith Group 908 624-9833
  28 Sager Pl Hillside (07205) *(G-4385)*
Carton Brewing Company LLC 732 654-2337
  6 E Washington Ave Atlantic Highlands (07716) *(G-105)*
Cartridge Actuated Devices (HQ) 973 575-8760
  51 Dwight Pl Fairfield (07004) *(G-3166)*
Cartridge Actuated Devices 973 347-2281
  40 Old Indian Spring Rd Byram Township (07821) *(G-1017)*
Cartridge World Paramus, Paramus *Also called B&B Imaging LLC (G-7791)*
Carver Boat Sales Inc 732 892-0328
  714 Canal St Point Pleasant Boro (08742) *(G-8839)*
Cary Compounds LLC 732 274-2626
  5 Nicholas Ct Dayton (08810) *(G-1957)*
Casa Di Bertacchi Corporation 856 696-5600
  1910 Gallagher Dr Vineland (08360) *(G-11197)*
Casale Industries Inc 908 789-0040
  50 Center St Garwood (07027) *(G-3782)*
Casas News Publishing Co 908 245-6767
  325 E Westfield Ave Roselle Park (07204) *(G-9579)*
Case It Inc 800 441-4710
  1050 Valley Brook Ave B Lyndhurst (07071) *(G-5646)*
Case Medical Inc 201 313-1999
  19 Empire Blvd South Hackensack (07606) *(G-10152)*
Case Pork Roll Co Inc 609 396-8171
  644 Washington St Trenton (08611) *(G-10912)*
Case Princeton Co Inc 908 687-1750
  615 Sherwood Pkwy Ste 5 Mountainside (07092) *(G-6836)*
Cases By Source Inc 201 831-0005
  215 Island Rd Mahwah (07430) *(G-5720)*
Casino Player Publishing LLC 609 404-0600
  333 E Jimmie Leeds Rd # 7 Galloway (08205) *(G-3721)*
Cassies Restaurant, Englewood *Also called Lbd Corp (G-2917)*
Cast Inc 201 391-8300
  11 Stonewall Ct Woodcliff Lake (07677) *(G-12051)*
Cast Technology Inc 908 753-5155
  161 West St South Plainfield (07080) *(G-10235)*
Castellane Manufacturing Co 609 625-3427
  1405 Cantillon Blvd Mays Landing (08330) *(G-5993)*

(G-0000) Company's Geographic Section entry number

Castle Creek Phrmceuticals LLC 862 286-0400
  6 Century Dr Ste 2 Parsippany (07054) *(G-7897)*

Castle Foods, Union *Also called Kalustyan Corporation (G-11068)*

Castle Industries Inc 201 585-8400
  120 Sylvan Ave Ste 3 Englewood Cliffs (07632) *(G-2962)*

Castle Printing, Ledgewood *Also called Steb Inc (G-5282)*

Castle Printing Center, Ledgewood *Also called Steb Inc (G-5281)*

Castle Woodcraft Assoc LLC 732 349-1519
  161 Atlantic City Blvd Pine Beach (08741) *(G-8582)*

Casual Classics Inc 916 294-9880
  11 Dori Ln Barnegat (08005) *(G-156)*

Catalent Inc (PA) 732 537-6200
  14 Schoolhouse Rd Somerset (08873) *(G-9968)*

Catalent Cts LLC 201 785-0275
  75 Commerce Dr Allendale (07401) *(G-6)*

Catalent CTS Kansas City LLC 732 537-6200
  14 Schoolhouse Rd Somerset (08873) *(G-9969)*

Catalent Pharma Solutions LLC (HQ) 732 537-6200
  14 Schoolhouse Rd Somerset (08873) *(G-9970)*

Catalent Pharma Solutions Inc (HQ) 732 537-6200
  14 Schoolhouse Rd Somerset (08873) *(G-9971)*

Catalent US Holding I LLC 877 587-1835
  14 Schoolhouse Rd Somerset (08873) *(G-9972)*

Catalogic Software Inc 201 249-8980
  50 Tice Blvd Ste 110 Woodcliff Lake (07677) *(G-12052)*

Catalogue Publishers Inc 973 423-3600
  20-10 Maple Ave 35f-2 Fair Lawn (07410) *(G-3093)*

Catalyst Chemicals and Ref Div, West Deptford *Also called Johnson Matthey Inc (G-11708)*

Catalyst Chemicals and Ref Div, West Deptford *Also called Matthey Johnson Inc (G-11710)*

Catamaran Media, Pleasantville *Also called Current Newspaper LLC (G-8809)*

Catching Zzz LLC 888 339-1604
  91 New England Ave Piscataway (08854) *(G-8643)*

Catchmaster, Bayonne *Also called AP&g Co Inc (G-202)*

Catering By Maddalenas Inc 609 466-7510
  415 Route 31 N Ringoes (08551) *(G-9335)*

Catholic Star Herald 856 583-6142
  15 N 7th St Camden (08102) *(G-1050)*

Caudalie Usa Inc 201 939-4969
  30 Commerce Rd Carlstadt (07072) *(G-1137)*

Cavagna North America Inc 732 469-2100
  50 Napoleon Ct Somerset (08873) *(G-9973)*

Cavalier Chemical Co Inc 908 558-0110
  42 Colonial Way Short Hills (07078) *(G-9865)*

Cavalla Inc 201 343-3338
  111 Union St Hackensack (07601) *(G-3895)*

Caw LLC 973 429-7004
  248 Montgomery St Bloomfield (07003) *(G-495)*

CB&i LLC 856 482-3000
  200 Horizon Center Blvd Trenton (08691) *(G-10913)*

Cbt Supply Inc 800 770-7042
  83 Jacobs Rd Rockaway (07866) *(G-9450)*

CC Packaging LLC (PA) 732 213-9008
  93 Storm Jib Ct Bayville (08721) *(G-242)*

CCA Industries Inc 201 935-3232
  1099 Wall St W Ste 275 Lyndhurst (07071) *(G-5647)*

CCA/Custom Change Aprons, Toms River *Also called Philip Papalia (G-10783)*

Ccard 732 303-8264
  17 Belle Terre Dr Manalapan (07726) *(G-5803)*

Ccbcc Operations LLC 609 324-7424
  948 Farnsworth Ave Bordentown (08505) *(G-579)*

CCC, Kenvil *Also called County Concrete Corporation (G-4992)*

Ccg Marketing Solutions, West Caldwell *Also called Corporate Mailings Inc (G-11645)*

CCL Label Inc 609 443-3700
  120 Stockton St Hightstown (08520) *(G-4295)*

CCL Label Inc 609 586-1332
  104 N Gold Dr Robbinsville (08691) *(G-9409)*

CCL Label Inc 856 273-0700
  92 Ark Rd Lumberton (08048) *(G-5625)*

CCL Label (delaware) Inc 609 259-1055
  104 N Gold Dr Trenton (08691) *(G-10914)*

CCL Label Tubedec, Lumberton *Also called CCL Label Inc (G-5625)*

CDI, Boonton *Also called Communication Devices Inc (G-546)*

CDI Group Inc 908 862-1493
  1135 W Elizabeth Ave Linden (07036) *(G-5330)*

CDK Industries LLC 856 488-5456
  900 Haddonfield Rd Ste 6 Cherry Hill (08002) *(G-1352)*

CDM Electronics Inc (PA) 856 740-1200
  130 American Blvd Turnersville (08012) *(G-11016)*

Cds., Sparta *Also called Gate Technologies Inc (G-10388)*

Cdss, Princeton *Also called Chryslis Data Sltons Svcs Corp (G-8922)*

Ce De Candy Inc (PA) 908 964-0660
  1091 Lousons Rd Union (07083) *(G-11035)*

Ce Tech LLC 908 229-3803
  8 Fairway Dr Whitehouse Station (08889) *(G-11919)*

Cedar Hill Landscaping 732 469-1400
  127 Cedar Grove Ln Somerset (08873) *(G-9974)*

Cedar Hill Topsoil, Somerset *Also called Cedar Hill Landscaping (G-9974)*

Cedge Industries Inc 201 641-3222
  237 Rahway Rd Barnegat (08005) *(G-157)*

Cei Holdings Inc (PA) 732 888-7788
  2182 State Route 35 Holmdel (07733) *(G-4496)*

Cejon Inc 201 437-8780
  53 Hook Rd Bayonne (07002) *(G-208)*

Celator Pharmaceuticals Inc (HQ) 609 243-0123
  200 Princeton S Ewing (08628) *(G-3019)*

Celco, Berkeley Heights *Also called Connell Mining Products LLC (G-395)*

Celco 201 327-1123
  14 Industrial Ave Ste 2 Mahwah (07430) *(G-5721)*

Celebration (us) Inc 609 261-5200
  681 Main St Lumberton (08048) *(G-5626)*

Celestech Inc 856 986-2221
  221 Kngs Hwy W Hddonfield Haddonfield (08033) *(G-4054)*

Celgene Cellular Therapeutics, Warren *Also called Celgene Corporation (G-11403)*

Celgene Cellular Therapeutics 908 673-9000
  33 Technology Dr Warren (07059) *(G-11402)*

Celgene Corporation 908 464-8101
  300 Connell Dr Ste 6000 Berkeley Heights (07922) *(G-392)*

Celgene Corporation 732 271-1001
  7 Powderhorn Dr Warren (07059) *(G-11403)*

Celgene Corporation 908 967-1432
  400 Connell Dr Ste 4000 Berkeley Heights (07922) *(G-393)*

Celgene Corporation 908 897-4603
  556 Morris Ave Summit (07901) *(G-10528)*

Celgene Corporation (PA) 908 673-9000
  86 Morris Ave Summit (07901) *(G-10529)*

Celgene Corporation 908 673-9000
  45 Horsehill Rd Ste 107 Cedar Knolls (07927) *(G-1301)*

Celgene Corporation 908 673-9000
  106 Allen Rd Basking Ridge (07920) *(G-179)*

Celimmune 908 399-2954
  110 Old Driftway Ln Lebanon (08833) *(G-5255)*

Cell Distributors Inc (PA) 718 473-0162
  319 Ridge Rd Dayton (08810) *(G-1958)*

Celldex Therapeutics Inc (PA) 908 200-7500
  53 Frontage Rd Ste 220 Hampton (08827) *(G-4149)*

Cellebrite Inc 973 206-7763
  7 Campus Dr Ste 201 Parsippany (07054) *(G-7898)*

Cellectar Biosciences Inc (PA) 608 441-8120
  100 Campus Dr Ste 207 Florham Park (07932) *(G-3496)*

Cellgain Wireless LLC 732 889-4671
  68 White St Ste 265 Red Bank (07701) *(G-9223)*

Cellular Empire Inc 800 778-3513
  1400 W Elizabeth Ave Linden (07036) *(G-5331)*

Cellular Innovations, Avenel *Also called Mizco International Inc (G-137)*

Cellular Sciences Inc 908 237-1561
  84 Park Ave Flemington (08822) *(G-3433)*

Cellunet Manufacturing Compnay 609 386-3361
  460 Veterans Dr Burlington (08016) *(G-956)*

Celsion Corporation (PA) 609 896-9100
  997 Lenox Dr Ste 100 Lawrenceville (08648) *(G-5226)*

Celtic Passions LLC 973 865-7046
  35 Park Dr Nutley (07110) *(G-7582)*

Celus Fasteners Mfg Inc (PA) 800 289-7483
  200 Paris Ave Northvale (07647) *(G-7520)*

Cem Industries Inc 908 244-8080
  300 Somerset St Apt 217 Harrison (07029) *(G-4167)*

Cementex Insulated Tools, Burlington *Also called Cementex Products Inc (G-957)*

Cementex Products Inc 609 387-1040
  650 Jacksonville Rd Burlington (08016) *(G-957)*

Cemp Inc 732 933-1000
  479 Broad St Shrewsbury (07702) *(G-9884)*

Cenogenics Corporation (PA) 732 536-6457
  100 County Road 520 Morganville (07751) *(G-6584)*

Center Stage Productions, Fair Lawn *Also called De Zaio Productions Inc (G-3095)*

Central Admxture Phrm Svcs Inc 201 541-0080
  160 W Forest Ave Englewood (07631) *(G-2892)*

Central Art & Engineering Inc 609 758-5922
  500 Goldman Dr Cream Ridge (08514) *(G-1931)*

Central Art & Enginering Inc 609 758-5922
  500 Goldman Dr Cream Ridge (08514) *(G-1932)*

Central Bakery, Hackensack *Also called Artisan Oven Inc (G-3878)*

Central Components Mfg LLC 732 469-5720
  440 Lincoln Blvd Middlesex (08846) *(G-6104)*

Central Concrete Aggregates, Forked River *Also called Pioneer Concrete Corp (G-3542)*

Central Ink Corporation 856 467-5562
  2085 Center Square Rd A Swedesboro (08085) *(G-10576)*

Central Jersey Hot Mix Asp LLC 732 323-0226
  577 S Hope Chapel Rd Jackson (08527) *(G-4642)*

Central Metal Fabricators Inc 732 938-6900
  300 Central Ave Farmingdale (07727) *(G-3379)*

Central Metals Inc 215 462-7464
  1054 S 2nd St Camden (08103) *(G-1051)*

Central Mills Inc 732 329-2009
  473 Ridge Rd Dayton (08810) *(G-1959)*

Central Mills Inc (PA) 732 329-2009
  473 Ridge Rd Dayton (08810) *(G-1960)*

Central Plastics Incorporated..........................973 808-0990
  333 New Rd Ste 3 Parsippany (07054) *(G-7899)*
Central Poly-Bag Corp.....................................908 862-7570
  2400 Bedle Pl Linden (07036) *(G-5332)*
Central Record Publications.............................609 654-5000
  600 Perry St Trenton (08618) *(G-10915)*
Central Safety Equipment Co (PA)....................609 386-6448
  300 W Broad St Burlington (08016) *(G-958)*
Central Shippee Inc...973 838-1100
  46 Star Lake Rd Bloomingdale (07403) *(G-526)*
Central Technology Inc....................................732 431-3339
  843 State Route 33 Ste 11 Freehold (07728) *(G-3656)*
Centro Alternativo De......................................973 365-0995
  21 Howe Ave Passaic (07055) *(G-8055)*
Centrome Inc..973 339-6242
  10 Taft Rd Totowa (07512) *(G-10822)*
Centryco, Burlington *Also called Central Safety Equipment Co (G-958)*
Centurum Information Tech Inc (HQ)..................856 751-1111
  651 Route 73 N Ste 107 Marlton (08053) *(G-5924)*
Century Bathworks Inc (PA).............................973 785-4290
  250 Lackawanna Ave Ste 2 Woodland Park (07424) *(G-12074)*
Century Bathworks Inc....................................201 785-1414
  250 Lackawanna Ave Ste 1 Woodland Park (07424) *(G-12075)*
Century Conveyor Systems Inc.........................908 205-0625
  4301 S Clinton Ave South Plainfield (07080) *(G-10236)*
Century Metals, Ewing *Also called Ewing Recovery Corp (G-3030)*
Century Printing Corp......................................732 981-0544
  10 New England Ave Piscataway (08854) *(G-8644)*
Century Service Affiliates Inc (PA)....................973 742-3516
  510 E 31st St Paterson (07504) *(G-8155)*
Century Shower Door, Woodland Park *Also called Century Bathworks Inc (G-12074)*
Century Tube Corp..908 534-2001
  22 Tannery Rd Somerville (08876) *(G-10105)*
Cenveo Worldwide Limited...............................201 434-2100
  25 Linden Ave E Jersey City (07305) *(G-4710)*
Ceodeux Incorporated.....................................724 696-4340
  101 Bilby Rd Ste B Hackettstown (07840) *(G-4001)*
Cerami Wood Products Inc...............................732 968-7222
  154 12th St Piscataway (08854) *(G-8645)*
Ceramic Products Inc......................................201 342-8200
  221 Park St Hackensack (07601) *(G-3896)*
Ceramsource Inc...732 257-5002
  26 Kennedy Blvd Ste B East Brunswick (08816) *(G-2131)*
Cerbaco Ltd..908 996-1333
  809 Harrison St Frenchtown (08825) *(G-3711)*
Cercis Inc..609 737-5120
  25 Route 31 S Ste C2030 Pennington (08534) *(G-8360)*
Ceresist Inc...973 345-3231
  176 E 7th St Ste 2 Paterson (07524) *(G-8156)*
Cerexa Inc...510 285-9200
  400 Interpace Pkwy Ste A1 Parsippany (07054) *(G-7900)*
Ceronics Inc...732 566-5600
  5 Dock St Matawan (07747) *(G-5970)*
Certech Inc (HQ)...201 842-6800
  1 Park Pl W Wood Ridge (07075) *(G-12002)*
Certified Cabinet Corp.....................................732 741-0755
  9 S Main St Marlboro (07746) *(G-5893)*
Certified Clam Corp...732 872-6650
  190 Bay Ave Ste 1 Highlands (07732) *(G-4291)*
Certified Labeling Solutions, Hillsborough *Also called Distributor Label Products (G-4312)*
Certified Processing Corp.................................973 923-5200
  184 Us Highway 22 Hillside (07205) *(G-4386)*
Cervini's Auto Design, Vineland *Also called Cervinis Inc (G-11198)*
Cervinis Inc..856 691-1744
  3656 N Mill Rd Vineland (08360) *(G-11198)*
Ces Fence, East Hanover *Also called Comprelli Equipment and Svc (G-2201)*
Ces Imports LLC...610 299-7930
  252 93rd St Stone Harbor (08247) *(G-10504)*
CET Films, Lakewood *Also called Custom Extrusion Tech Inc (G-5078)*
Cetylite Industries Inc......................................856 665-6111
  9051 River Rd Pennsauken (08110) *(G-8402)*
CFS, Sparta *Also called Compact Fluorescent Systems (G-10383)*
Cg Automation Solutions USA (PA)....................973 379-7400
  60 Fadem Rd Springfield (07081) *(G-10434)*
Cgi North America, Jersey City *Also called Dg3 Group America Inc (G-4724)*
Cgm Us Inc (PA)...609 894-4420
  300 Birmingham Rd Birmingham (08011) *(G-456)*
Cgs Sales and Service LLC..............................856 665-6154
  6950 River Rd Pennsauken (08110) *(G-8403)*
Cgw News LLC..973 473-3972
  107 Mount Prospect Ave Clifton (07013) *(G-1581)*
Ch Technologies USA Inc.................................201 666-2335
  778 Carver Ave Westwood (07675) *(G-11829)*
Chabot Jewelry, Edison *Also called E Chabot Ltd (G-2496)*
Chacko John...732 494-1088
  21 Remington Dr Edison (08820) *(G-2475)*
Chain Store Age Magazine, Newark *Also called Ensembleiq Inc (G-7116)*
Challenge Printing Co Inc (PA)..........................973 471-4700
  2 Bridewell Pl Clifton (07014) *(G-1582)*

Challenge Printing Company The, Clifton *Also called Challenge Printing Co Inc (G-1582)*
Chalmers & Kubeck Inc....................................732 993-1251
  8 Jules Ln New Brunswick (08901) *(G-6915)*
Chamberlain Group Inc....................................201 472-4200
  35 Melanie Ln Whippany (07981) *(G-11885)*
Chambord Prints Inc..201 795-2007
  38 Jackson St Hoboken (07030) *(G-4447)*
Champion Fasteners Inc (PA)............................609 267-5222
  707 Smithville Rd Lumberton (08048) *(G-5627)*
Champion Ink Co Inc.......................................201 868-4100
  2045 88th St North Bergen (07047) *(G-7394)*
Champion Opco LLC..856 662-3400
  414 Bloomfield Dr Ste 1 West Berlin (08091) *(G-11580)*
Champion Plastics Div, Clifton *Also called X-L Plastics Inc (G-1741)*
Champion Sports Products Co, Marlboro *Also called Pro Sports Inc (G-5910)*
Champion Window Delaware Vly, West Berlin *Also called Champion Opco LLC (G-11580)*
Champions Oncology Inc (PA)...........................201 808-8400
  1 University Plz Ste 307 Hackensack (07601) *(G-3897)*
Chandler Pharmacy & Surgicals, New Brunswick *Also called Chandler Pharmacy LLC (G-6916)*
Chandler Pharmacy LLC..................................732 543-1568
  272 George St New Brunswick (08901) *(G-6916)*
Chanks USA LLC...856 265-0203
  2516 Mays Landing Rd Millville (08332) *(G-6242)*
Channel Logistics LLC.....................................856 614-5441
  121 Market St Ste 2 Camden (08102) *(G-1052)*
Chapter Enterprises Inc...................................732 560-8500
  8w Chimney Rock Rd Bridgewater (08807) *(G-811)*
Charabot & Co Inc..201 812-2762
  400 International Dr Budd Lake (07828) *(G-920)*
Charcole Products, Belleville *Also called William R Tatz Industries (G-325)*
Chariot Courier & Trans Svcs...........................888 532-9125
  7 Parr Dr Sayreville (08872) *(G-9704)*
Charles Deluca...973 778-5621
  239 Garibaldi Ave Lodi (07644) *(G-5556)*
Charles E Green & Son Inc...............................973 485-3630
  625 3rd St Newark (07107) *(G-7082)*
Charles F Kilian..732 458-3554
  682 Rolling Hills Ct Brick (08724) *(G-712)*
Charles Kerr Enterprises Inc............................732 738-6500
  1090 King Georges Post Rd # 802 Edison (08837) *(G-2476)*
Charles Komar & Sons Inc (PA)........................212 725-1500
  90 Hudson St Fl 9 Jersey City (07302) *(G-4711)*
Charles M Jessup Inc......................................732 324-0430
  177 Smith St Keasbey (08832) *(G-4910)*
Charter Fincl Pubg Netwrk Inc.........................732 450-8866
  499 Broad St Shrewsbury (07702) *(G-9885)*
Charter Machine, Metuchen *Also called Graphic Equipment Corporation (G-6059)*
Charter Machine Company...............................732 494-5350
  55 Wester Ave Metuchen (08840) *(G-6051)*
Chartwell Promotions Ltd Inc...........................732 780-6900
  1 Chartwell Ct Freehold (07728) *(G-3657)*
Chase Machine Co...201 438-2214
  127 Park Ave Lyndhurst (07071) *(G-5648)*
Chatham Bookseller Inc...................................973 822-1361
  8 Green Village Rd Madison (07940) *(G-5690)*
Chatham Brass Co Inc.....................................908 668-0500
  1253 New Market Ave Ste D South Plainfield (07080) *(G-10237)*
Chatham Controls Corporation..........................908 236-6019
  6 Corral Cir Lebanon (08833) *(G-5256)*
Chatham Lawn Mowler.....................................973 635-8855
  14 Commerce St Chatham (07928) *(G-1320)*
Chatham Lawnmower Service, Chatham *Also called Chatham Lawn Mowler (G-1320)*
Chatham Print & Design, Chatham *Also called Thewal Inc (G-1330)*
Chatlos Systems, Denville *Also called TX Technology LLC (G-2061)*
Chavant Inc..732 751-0003
  5043 Industrial Rd Wall Township (07727) *(G-11323)*
Check-It Electronics Corp.................................973 520-8435
  560 Trumbull St Elizabeth (07206) *(G-2720)*
Checkpoint Security Systems Gr......................952 933-8858
  101 Wolf Dr West Deptford (08086) *(G-11696)*
Checkpoint Systems Inc (HQ)...........................800 257-5540
  101 Wolf Dr West Deptford (08086) *(G-11697)*
Checkpoint Systems Inc...................................856 848-1800
  201 Wolf Dr West Deptford (08086) *(G-11698)*
Checkpoint Systems Inc...................................952 933-8858
  101 Wolf Dr West Deptford (08086) *(G-11699)*
Cheesecake Factory Inc...................................973 921-0930
  1200 Morris Tpke Ste D103 Short Hills (07078) *(G-9866)*
Cheesecake Factory, The, Short Hills *Also called Cheesecake Factory Inc (G-9866)*
Chefler Foods LLC..201 596-3710
  400 Lyster Ave Saddle Brook (07663) *(G-9645)*
Chefman, Mahwah *Also called Rj Brands LLC (G-5768)*
Chefman Direct Inc..888 315-8407
  200 Performance Dr # 207 Mahwah (07495) *(G-5722)*
Chelten House Products Inc (PA).......................856 467-1600
  607 Heron Dr Bridgeport (08014) *(G-735)*

(G-0000) Company's Geographic Section entry number

Chem Flowtronic Inc 973 785-0001
195 Paterson Ave Ste 4 Little Falls (07424) ***(G-5455)***
Chem Power Mfg Div, Cedar Knolls *Also called Foster and Company Inc* ***(G-1305)***
Chem-Aqua Inc 972 438-0211
34 Stouts Ln Monmouth Junction (08852) ***(G-6281)***
Chem-Fleur Inc 973 589-4266
150 Firmench Way Newark (07114) ***(G-7083)***
Chem-Is-Try Inc 732 372-7311
160 Liberty St Ste 4 Metuchen (08840) ***(G-6052)***
Chemaid Laboratories Inc (HQ) 201 843-3300
100 Mayhill St Saddle Brook (07663) ***(G-9646)***
Chembiopower Inc 908 209-5595
211 Warren St Ste 503 Warren (07059) ***(G-11404)***
Chemetall Americas, New Providence *Also called Chemetall US Inc* ***(G-6997)***
Chemetall US Inc (HQ) 908 464-6900
675 Central Ave New Providence (07974) ***(G-6997)***
Chemglass Inc 856 696-0014
3800 N Mill Rd Vineland (08360) ***(G-11199)***
Chemical Resources Inc (PA) 609 520-0000
103 Carnegie Ctr Ste 100 Princeton (08540) ***(G-8921)***
Chemicals Services, Linden *Also called Just In Time Chemical Sales &* ***(G-5366)***
Chemique Inc 856 235-4161
315 N Washington Ave Moorestown (08057) ***(G-6512)***
Chemiquip Products Co Inc 201 868-4445
109 Bradford Ave Linden (07036) ***(G-5333)***
Chemmark Development Inc 908 561-0923
70 Tyler Pl South Plainfield (07080) ***(G-10238)***
Chemo Dynamics Inc 732 721-4700
3 Crossman Rd S Sayreville (08872) ***(G-9705)***
Chemours Company 856 540-3398
Bldg 603 Rr 130 Deepwater (08023) ***(G-1998)***
Chemres, Princeton *Also called Chemical Resources Inc* ***(G-8921)***
Chemspeed Technologies Inc 732 329-1225
113 N Center Dr North Brunswick (08902) ***(G-7461)***
Chemtract LLC 732 820-0427
2144 Gilbride Rd Martinsville (08836) ***(G-5961)***
Chemtrade Chemicals Corp (HQ) 973 515-0900
90 E Halsey Rd Ste 301 Parsippany (07054) ***(G-7901)***
Chemtrade Chemicals US LLC (HQ) 973 515-0900
90 E Halsey Rd Parsippany (07054) ***(G-7902)***
Chemtrade Gcc Holding Company (HQ) 973 515-0900
90 E Halsey Rd Ste 301 Parsippany (07054) ***(G-7903)***
Chemtrade Solutions LLC (HQ) 973 515-0900
90 E Halsey Rd Ste 301 Parsippany (07054) ***(G-7904)***
Chemtrade Solutions LLC 908 464-1500
235 Snyder Ave Berkeley Heights (07922) ***(G-394)***
Chemtrade Water Chemical Inc (HQ) 973 515-0900
90 E Halsey Rd Ste 301 Parsippany (07054) ***(G-7905)***
Chemtreat Inc 609 654-9522
520 Stokes Rd Ste B11 Medford (08055) ***(G-6021)***
Chen Brothers Machinery Co 973 328-0086
503 State Route 10 Randolph (07869) ***(G-9174)***
Chenille Products Inc 201 703-1917
30 Henry Ave Palisades Park (07650) ***(G-7771)***
Cheringal Associates Inc 201 784-8721
500 Walnut St Norwood (07648) ***(G-7560)***
Cherishmet Inc 201 842-7612
301 State Rt 17 Ste 800 Rutherford (07070) ***(G-9616)***
Cherokee Pharma Llc 732 422-7800
1085 Cranbury S Riv 1 Jamesburg (08831) ***(G-4671)***
Cherokee Rubber Company, Flanders *Also called Targa Industries Inc* ***(G-3421)***
Cherri Stone Interactive LLC 844 843-7765
182 N Crest Pl Lakewood (08701) ***(G-5069)***
Cherry Hill Pharmacy, Cherry Hill *Also called Nuclear Diagnostic Products of* ***(G-1401)***
Cherry Hill Precision Co, Cherry Hill *Also called JBAT Inc* ***(G-1378)***
Cherubini Yachts Ltd Lblty Co 856 764-5319
51 Norman Ave Delran (08075) ***(G-2014)***
Chessco Industries Inc 609 882-0400
1013 Whitehead Road Ext Ewing (08638) ***(G-3020)***
Cheveux Cosmetics Corporation 732 446-7516
30 Park Ave Englishtown (07726) ***(G-3000)***
Chevron Phillips Chem Co LP 732 738-2000
1200 State St Perth Amboy (08861) ***(G-8514)***
Chevron USA Inc 732 738-2000
1200 State St Perth Amboy (08861) ***(G-8515)***
Chic Bebe Inc 201 941-5414
53 Howard Park Dr Tenafly (07670) ***(G-10661)***
Chic Btq Doll Design Co LLC 201 784-7727
331 Piermont Rd Ste 8 Norwood (07648) ***(G-7561)***
Chic LLC 732 354-0035
200 State Route 18 Ste 1 East Brunswick (08816) ***(G-2132)***
Chicago Pneumatic Tool 973 276-1377
90 New Dutch Ln Fairfield (07004) ***(G-3167)***
Chicago Pneumatic Tool (HQ) 973 928-5222
222 Getty Ave Clifton (07011) ***(G-1583)***
Chick Capoli Sales 856 768-4500
420 Commerce Ln Ste 7 West Berlin (08091) ***(G-11581)***
Chiha Inc 201 861-2000
5711 Kennedy Blvd North Bergen (07047) ***(G-7395)***
Chiha Sales, North Bergen *Also called Chiha Inc* ***(G-7395)***
Children's Tecnology Review, Flemington *Also called Active Learning Associates* ***(G-3428)***
Childrens Research & Dev Co 856 546-8814
216 9th Ave Haddon Heights (08035) ***(G-4044)***
Chiller Solutions LLC 973 835-2800
101 Alexander Ave Unit 3 Pompton Plains (07444) ***(G-8861)***
Chips Ice Cream LLC 732 840-6332
149 Newtons Corner Rd Howell (07731) ***(G-4533)***
Chiral Photonics Inc 973 732-0030
26 Chapin Rd Ste 1104 Pine Brook (07058) ***(G-8590)***
Chiral Photonics Inc 973 732-0030
26 Chapin Rd Ste 1104 Pine Brook (07058) ***(G-8591)***
Chirgotis, Wm G, Chatham *Also called National Home Planning Service* ***(G-1328)***
Chisholm Technologies Inc 732 859-5578
450 Shrewsbury Plz # 301 Shrewsbury (07702) ***(G-9886)***
Chizzy's Truck & Auto Repair, Little Ferry *Also called Chizzys Service Center* ***(G-5476)***
Chizzys Service Center 201 641-7222
44 Bergen Tpke Little Ferry (07643) ***(G-5476)***
Chocmod USA Inc 201 585-8730
2200 Fletcher Ave Ste 3 Fort Lee (07024) ***(G-3552)***
Chocolate Face Cupcake 609 624-2253
1963 Route 9 N Cape May Court House (08210) ***(G-1109)***
Choice Cabinetry LLC 908 707-8801
61 5th St Somerville (08876) ***(G-10106)***
CHR International Inc 201 262-8186
296 Kinderkamack Rd # 220 Oradell (07649) ***(G-7741)***
Chris's Cookies, Teterboro *Also called Food & Beverage Inc* ***(G-10674)***
Christensen Manufacturing 609 466-9700
11 Moores Mill Mt Rose Rd Pennington (08534) ***(G-8361)***
Christian Art 201 867-8096
567 52nd St Ste 15 West New York (07093) ***(G-11737)***
Christian Dior Perfumes LLC 609 409-3628
283 Prospect Plains Rd A Cranbury (08512) ***(G-1821)***
Christian Mssons In Many Lands 732 449-8880
2751 18th Ave Wall Township (07719) ***(G-11324)***
Christine Valmy Inc (PA) 973 575-1050
285 Changebridge Rd Ste 1 Pine Brook (07058) ***(G-8592)***
Christopher F Maier 908 459-5100
352 Great Meadows Rd Hope (07844) ***(G-4524)***
Christopher Fischer, North Bergen *Also called C3 Concepts Inc* ***(G-7391)***
Christopher Szuco 732 684-7643
1061 Windsor Rd Millstone Twp (08535) ***(G-6213)***
Chroma Inks USA, Morganville *Also called Chroma Trading Usa Inc* ***(G-6585)***
Chroma Trading Usa Inc 732 956-4431
18 Guest Dr Morganville (07751) ***(G-6585)***
Chromcraft Revington Inc (HQ) 662 562-8203
140 Bradford Dr Ste A West Berlin (08091) ***(G-11582)***
Chromis Fiberoptics Inc 732 764-0900
6 Powderhorn Dr Warren (07059) ***(G-11405)***
Chromocell Corporation (PA) 732 565-1113
685 Us Highway 1 North Brunswick (08902) ***(G-7462)***
Chryslis Data Sltons Svcs Corp (PA) 609 375-2000
100 Overlook Ctr Fl 2 Princeton (08540) ***(G-8922)***
Church & Dwight Co Inc (PA) 609 806-1200
500 Charles Ewing Blvd Ewing (08628) ***(G-3021)***
Church & Dwight Co Inc 732 730-3100
800 Airport Rd Lakewood (08701) ***(G-5070)***
Church & Dwight Co Inc 609 655-6101
326 Cranbury Half Acre Rd Cranbury (08512) ***(G-1822)***
Church & Dwight Co Inc 609 683-8021
101 Thanet Cir Ste 1 Princeton (08540) ***(G-8923)***
Church Vestment Mfg Co Inc 973 942-2833
41 Paterson Ave Ste 1 Paterson (07522) ***(G-8157)***
Ciao Cupcake 609 964-6167
7 Wycklow Dr Trenton (08691) ***(G-10916)***
Ciao Milano, Englewood Cliffs *Also called Fyi Marketing Inc* ***(G-2971)***
Cibo Vita Inc 862 238-8020
12 Vreeland Ave Totowa (07512) ***(G-10823)***
CIC Letter Service Inc 201 896-1900
111 Commerce Rd Carlstadt (07072) ***(G-1138)***
Ciccone Inc 732 349-7071
2002 Route 9 Toms River (08755) ***(G-10752)***
Ciccone Brothers, Toms River *Also called Ciccone Inc* ***(G-10752)***
Cielito Lindo 580 286-1127
224 French St New Brunswick (08901) ***(G-6917)***
Cimquest Inc 732 699-0400
3434 Rte 22 Ste 130 Branchburg (08876) ***(G-628)***
Cinchseal Associates Inc 856 662-5162
23b Roland Ave Mount Laurel (08054) ***(G-6747)***
Cincinnati Thermal Spray Inc 973 379-0003
80 Fadem Rd Springfield (07081) ***(G-10435)***
Cinco Star LLC 732 744-1617
2 Karnell Ct Edison (08820) ***(G-2477)***
Cinderella Cheese Cake, Riverside *Also called Cinderella Cheesecake Co Inc* ***(G-9392)***
Cinderella Cheesecake Co Inc 856 461-6302
208 N Fairview St Riverside (08075) ***(G-9392)***
Cipla USA Inc (HQ) 908 356-8900
10 Independence Blvd # 300 Warren (07059) ***(G-11406)***
Cir Systems, Franklin *Also called Clinical Image Retrieval Syste* ***(G-3601)***

ALPHABETIC

Circa Promotions Inc 732 264-1200
58 Village Ct Hazlet (07730) **(G-4259)**
Circle D Light, Carlstadt *Also called Natale Machine & Tool Co Inc* **(G-1189)**
Circle Fabrics, Carlstadt *Also called Circle Visual Inc* **(G-1139)**
Circle Visual Inc 212 719-5153
340 13th St Carlstadt (07072) **(G-1139)**
Circleblack Inc 800 315-1241
4428 Route 27 Bldg C Kingston (08528) **(G-5007)**
Circonix Technologies LLC (HQ) 973 962-6160
29 Executive Pkwy Ringwood (07456) **(G-9344)**
Circuit Reproduction Co 201 712-9292
219 Hergesell Ave Maywood (07607) **(G-6002)**
Circuit Tech Assembly LLC 856 231-0777
154 Cooper Rd Ste 101 West Berlin (08091) **(G-11583)**
Circulite Inc 201 478-7575
500 F W Burr Blvd Ste 40 Teaneck (07666) **(G-10624)**
Cire Technologies Inc 973 402-8301
251 Boulevard Mountain Lakes (07046) **(G-6821)**
Cisco Systems Inc 732 635-4200
111 Wood Ave S Ste 2 Iselin (08830) **(G-4604)**
Cisco Systems Inc 856 642-7000
308 Harper Dr Ste 100 Moorestown (08057) **(G-6513)**
Cisco Systems Inc 201 782-0842
1 Paragon Dr Ste 275 Montvale (07645) **(G-6402)**
Cispharma Inc 609 235-9807
1212 Cranbury S River Rd Cranbury (08512) **(G-1823)**
Citgo, Clifton *Also called Masouleh Corp* **(G-1664)**
Citi-Chem Inc 609 231-6655
122 E Kings Hwy Ste 503 Maple Shade (08052) **(G-5860)**
Citius Pharmaceuticals Inc (PA) 978 938-0338
11 Commerce Dr Ste 100 Cranford (07016) **(G-1904)**
Citizen of Morris County, The, Denville *Also called Andis Inc* **(G-2030)**
Citroil Aromatic, Carlstadt *Also called Citroil Enterprises Inc* **(G-1140)**
Citroil Enterprises Inc 201 933-8405
444 Washington Ave Carlstadt (07072) **(G-1140)**
Citromax Flavors Inc 201 933-8405
444 Washington Ave Carlstadt (07072) **(G-1141)**
Citromax Usa Inc 201 933-8405
444 Washington Ave Carlstadt (07072) **(G-1142)**
City Design Group Inc 201 329-7711
201 Gates Rd Ste C Little Ferry (07643) **(G-5477)**
City Diecutting Inc 973 270-0370
1 Cory Rd Ste C Morristown (07960) **(G-6653)**
City Envelope Inc 201 792-9292
235 Orient Ave Apt 1 Jersey City (07305) **(G-4712)**
City of Jersey City 201 547-4470
575 State Rt 440 Jersey City (07305) **(G-4713)**
City Theatrical Inc (PA) 201 549-1160
475 Barell Ave Carlstadt (07072) **(G-1143)**
City Window Fashions, Hoboken *Also called Matiss Inc* **(G-4466)**
Civic Research Institute Inc (PA) 609 683-4450
4478 Route 27 Ste 202 Kingston (08528) **(G-5008)**
CJ TMI Manufacturing Amer LLC 609 669-0100
2 Applegate Dr Robbinsville (08691) **(G-9410)**
CJS Hesse, Forked River *Also called Brick-Wall Corp* **(G-3536)**
CK, Metuchen *Also called C & K Plastics Inc* **(G-6049)**
CK Manufacturing Inc 973 808-3500
8 Gardner Rd Fairfield (07004) **(G-3168)**
Cko Kickboxing, Totowa *Also called Totowa Kickboxing Ltd Lblty Co* **(G-10855)**
Clantech Inc 908 281-7667
198 Us Highway 206 Ste 10 Hillsborough (08844) **(G-4310)**
Claremont Distilled Spirits 973 227-7027
25 Commerce Rd Fairfield (07004) **(G-3169)**
Clarici Graphics Inc 609 587-7204
88 Youngs Rd Trenton (08619) **(G-10917)**
Clarity Imaging Solutions Inc 866 684-2212
4 Executive Campus # 104 Cherry Hill (08002) **(G-1353)**
Clarity Imaging Tech Inc 877 272-4362
250 Pehle Ave Ste 402 Saddle Brook (07663) **(G-9647)**
Clarity Imaging Tech Inc 413 693-1234
4350 Haddonfield Rd # 300 Pennsauken (08109) **(G-8404)**
Clarity Imaging Tech Inc (HQ) 877 272-4362
4350 Haddonfield Rd # 300 Pennsauken (08109) **(G-8405)**
Clark Cooper, Roebling *Also called Magnatrol Valve Corporation* **(G-9526)**
Clark Equipment Company 973 618-2500
19a Chapin Rd Pine Brook (07058) **(G-8593)**
Clark Stek-O Corp 201 437-0770
148 E 5th St Bayonne (07002) **(G-209)**
Classic Chess and Games Inc 908 850-6553
52 Main St Hackettstown (07840) **(G-4002)**
Classic Cooking LLC 718 439-0200
1600 St Grges Ave Ste 301 Rahway (07065) **(G-9086)**
Classic Coves, Budd Lake *Also called M + 4 Inc* **(G-927)**
Classic Designer Woodwork Inc 201 280-3711
60 Hazelhurst Ave Glen Rock (07452) **(G-3829)**
Classic Graphic Inc 856 753-0055
35 W White Horse Pike Berlin (08009) **(G-420)**
Classic Impressions 908 689-3137
2 Witte Ln Great Meadows (07838) **(G-3853)**
Classic Industries Inc 973 227-1366
50 Us Highway 46 Ste 100 Parsippany (07054) **(G-7906)**
Classic Marking Products Inc 973 383-2223
3 Gold Mine Rd Ste 104 Roxbury Township (07836) **(G-9599)**
Classic Printers & Converters 732 985-1100
140 Ethel Rd W Ste K Piscataway (08854) **(G-8646)**
Classic Silks Com I 908 204-0940
131 Roundtop Rd Bernardsville (07924) **(G-436)**
Clausen Company Inc 732 738-1165
1055 King George Rd Fords (08863) **(G-3531)**
Clawson Machine Division, Franklin *Also called Technology General Corporation* **(G-3609)**
Clayton Associates Inc 732 363-2100
1650 Oak St Lakewood (08701) **(G-5071)**
Clayton Block, Trenton *Also called Ralph Clayton & Sons LLC* **(G-10986)**
Clayton Block, Freehold *Also called Ralph Clayton & Sons LLC* **(G-3697)**
Clayton Block Co 201 955-6292
2 Porete Ave North Arlington (07031) **(G-7371)**
Clayton Block Company Inc 732 751-7600
11111 Martins Ln Trenton (08620) **(G-10918)**
Clayton Block Company Inc (PA) 888 763-8665
1355 Campus Pkwy Ste 200 Wall Township (07753) **(G-11325)**
Clayton Block Company Inc 732 462-1860
225 Throckmorton St Freehold (07728) **(G-3658)**
Clayton Block Company Inc 732 681-0186
1601 18th Ave Wall Township (07719) **(G-11326)**
Clayton Block Company Inc 732 549-1234
1025 Route 1 Edison (08837) **(G-2478)**
Clayton Block Company Inc 732 349-3700
194 Chestnut St Toms River (08753) **(G-10753)**
Clayton Block Company Inc 732 364-2404
1215 E Veterans Hwy Jackson (08527) **(G-4643)**
Clayton Block Company Inc 609 693-9600
2011 Lacey Rd Forked River (08731) **(G-3537)**
Clayton Block Company Inc 732 905-3234
100 Commerce Dr Tinton Falls (07753) **(G-10707)**
Clayton Block Company Inc 609 695-0767
1200 New York Ave Trenton (08608) **(G-10919)**
Clayton Block Company Inc 609 693-3000
Rr 9 Waretown (08758) **(G-11393)**
Clayton Block Company Inc 609 597-8128
Us Hwy 9 West Creek (08092) **(G-11685)**
Clayton Block Company Inc 732 751-1631
1355 Campus Pkwy Ste 200 Wall Township (07753) **(G-11327)**
Clayton Block Company LLC (HQ) 201 339-8585
440 Hook Rd Bayonne (07002) **(G-210)**
Clayton Concrete, Cookstown *Also called Ralph Clayton & Sons LLC* **(G-1805)**
Clayton Concrete, Jackson *Also called Clayton Block Company Inc* **(G-4643)**
Clayton Industries, Cranbury *Also called Clayton Manufacturing Company* **(G-1824)**
Clayton Manufacturing Company 609 409-9400
10 S River Rd Ste 6 Cranbury (08512) **(G-1824)**
Clayton Rolling Mill, Clayton *Also called Aleris Rolled Products Inc* **(G-1523)**
Clayton Sand Company 732 751-7600
1355 Campus Pkwy Wall Township (07753) **(G-11328)**
Clean Air Group 908 232-4200
6 Campus Dr Ste 2 Parsippany (07054) **(G-7907)**
Clean Bbq Inc 732 299-8877
47 Langstaff Ave Edison (08817) **(G-2479)**
Clean-Tex Services Inc (PA) 908 912-2700
1420 E Linden Ave Linden (07036) **(G-5334)**
Cleanzones LLC 732 534-5590
640 Herman Rd Ste 2 Jackson (08527) **(G-4644)**
Clear Control LLC 973 823-8200
93 Main St Ogdensburg (07439) **(G-7709)**
Clear Cut Window Distrs of NJ 201 512-1804
127 Tam O Shanter Dr Mahwah (07430) **(G-5723)**
Clear Plus Windshield Wipers 973 546-8800
100 Outwater Ln Garfield (07026) **(G-3735)**
Cleardrain, Riverside *Also called Melville Industries Inc* **(G-9400)**
Clearwater Well Drilling Co 609 698-1800
1073 Prospect Ave Manahawkin (08050) **(G-5791)**
Clearway LLC 973 578-4578
414 Wilson Ave Newark (07105) **(G-7084)**
Cleary Machinery Co Inc 732 560-3200
24 Cedar St South Bound Brook (08880) **(G-10143)**
Clem's, Piscataway *Also called Clems Ornemental Iron Works* **(G-8647)**
Clements Industries Inc 201 440-5500
50 Ruta Ct South Hackensack (07606) **(G-10153)**
Clems Ornemental Iron Works 732 968-7200
110 11th St Piscataway (08854) **(G-8647)**
Clench, Lodi *Also called Tony Jones Apparel Inc* **(G-5580)**
Clenesco Products Corp 908 245-5255
298 Cox St Roselle (07203) **(G-9552)**
Cleve Shirtmakers Inc 201 825-6122
200 Meadowlands Pkwy # 2 Secaucus (07094) **(G-9756)**
Cli Group, The, Paterson *Also called Custom Laminations Inc* **(G-8166)**
Clic Time LLC 201 497-6743
50 Tice Blvd Ste 340 Woodcliff Lake (07677) **(G-12053)**
Clientsrver Tech Solutions LLC 732 710-4495
2 Austin Ave Fl 2 # 2 Iselin (08830) **(G-4605)**

Cliffside Body Corporation 201 945-3970
  130 Broad Ave Fairview (07022) *(G-3358)*

Clifton Adhesive Inc 973 694-0845
  48 Burgess Pl Wayne (07470) *(G-11488)*

Clifton Adhesives, Wayne *Also called Royal Adhesives & Sealants LLC (G-11549)*

Clifton Metal Products Co Inc 973 777-6100
  41 Clifton Blvd Clifton (07011) *(G-1584)*

Clincial Genomics, Edison *Also called Enterix Inc (G-2503)*

Clinical Image Retrieval Syste 888 482-2362
  12 Cork Hill Rd Ste 2 Franklin (07416) *(G-3601)*

Clinton Envelope, Pennsauken *Also called Tpg Graphics LLC (G-8493)*

Clinton Industries Inc 201 440-0400
  207 Redneck Ave Little Ferry (07643) *(G-5478)*

Clio Foods & Provisions LLC 908 505-2546
  145 E Highland Pkwy Roselle (07203) *(G-9553)*

Clip Strip Corp 201 342-9155
  241 Main St Fl 5 Hackensack (07601) *(G-3898)*

Clogic LLC 973 934-5223
  4 Sunset Ln Augusta (07822) *(G-115)*

Clogic Defense, Augusta *Also called Clogic LLC (G-115)*

Clordisys Solutions Inc. 908 236-4100
  50 Tannery Rd Ste 1 Branchburg (08876) *(G-629)*

Closets By Dsign - Cntl Jersey, Hamilton *Also called Denmatt Industries LLC (G-4105)*

Clothes Horse International 856 829-8460
  2200 Wallace Blvd Ste A Cinnaminson (08077) *(G-1446)*

Cloudageit Ltd Liability Co 888 205-4128
  1308 Plymouth Rd North Brunswick (08902) *(G-7463)*

Clover Bags & Paper LLC 917 721-6783
  120 Industrial Ave Little Ferry (07643) *(G-5479)*

Clover Garden Ctr Ltd Lblty Co 856 235-4625
  1017 S Church St Mount Laurel (08054) *(G-6748)*

Clover Hill Coffee Co, Colts Neck *Also called Colt Media Inc (G-1779)*

Clover Stamping Inc 973 278-4888
  60 Spruce St Paterson (07501) *(G-8158)*

Clyde Otis Music Group 845 425-8198
  494 N Woodland St Englewood (07631) *(G-2893)*

CMC Composites LLC 732 505-9400
  870 Route 530 Ste 12 Whiting (08759) *(G-11938)*

CMC Joist & Deck, South Plainfield *Also called C M C Steel Fabricators Inc (G-10232)*

CMF Ltd Inc 609 695-3600
  599 W Ingham Ave Ewing (08638) *(G-3022)*

Cmg, Branchburg *Also called Custom Molders Group LLC (G-635)*

Cmg Plastics, Branchburg *Also called Custom Molders Corp (G-634)*

CMI-Promex Inc 856 351-1000
  7 Benjamin Green Rd Pedricktown (08067) *(G-8346)*

Cmic Cmo USA Corporation 609 395-9700
  Cedar Brook Corporate Ctr Cranbury (08512) *(G-1825)*

Cmml, Wall Township *Also called Christian Mssons In Many Lands (G-11324)*

CMS Technology Inc 512 913-1898
  10 Finderne Ave Ste A Bridgewater (08807) *(G-812)*

Cmyk Printing Inc 201 458-1300
  651 Garden St Carlstadt (07072) *(G-1144)*

CNG Publishing Company 973 768-0978
  43 Manchester Way Burlington (08016) *(G-959)*

Cni Ceramic Nozzles Inc 973 276-1535
  23 Commerce Rd Ste L Fairfield (07004) *(G-3170)*

Cno Corporation 732 785-5799
  611 Yellowbrick Rd Brick (08724) *(G-713)*

Cnr Products Co 201 384-7003
  74 Portland Ave Bergenfield (07621) *(G-374)*

Cns Confectionery Products LLC 201 823-1400
  33 Hook Rd Bayonne (07002) *(G-211)*

Co-Co Collaborative LLC 917 685-5547
  61 Taylor Rd Short Hills (07078) *(G-9867)*

Coast Rubber and Gasket Inc 609 747-0110
  1208 Columbus Rd Ste G Burlington (08016) *(G-960)*

Coast Star 732 223-0076
  13 Broad St Manasquan (08736) *(G-5830)*

Coast To Coast Lea & Vinyl Inc (PA) 732 525-8877
  1 Crossman Rd S Sayreville (08872) *(G-9706)*

Coastal Creations, Lavallette *Also called Signal Systems International (G-5212)*

Coastal Metal Recycling Corp 732 738-6000
  75 Crows Mill Rd Keasbey (08832) *(G-4911)*

Coaster Inc 732 775-3010
  1011 Main St Ste B Asbury Park (07712) *(G-73)*

Coaster, The, Asbury Park *Also called Coaster Inc (G-73)*

Coates International Ltd (PA) 732 449-7717
  2100 Highway 34 Wall Township (07719) *(G-11329)*

Coates Precision Engineering 732 449-9382
  2100 State Route 34 Wall Township (07719) *(G-11330)*

Cobham New Jersey Inc 732 460-0212
  40 Industrial Way E Eatontown (07724) *(G-2384)*

Cobon Plastics Corp 973 344-6330
  90 South St Newark (07114) *(G-7085)*

Cobra Power Systems Inc (PA) 908 486-1800
  304 Monmouth Rd Millstone Township (08510) *(G-6210)*

Cobra Products Inc 856 241-7700
  1 Warner Ct Swedesboro (08085) *(G-10577)*

Cobyco Inc 732 446-4448
  65 Wilson Ave Manalapan (07726) *(G-5804)*

Coca Cola Bottling Co Mid Amer 732 398-4800
  60 Deans Rhode Hall Rd Monmouth Junction (08852) *(G-6282)*

Coca-Cola Refreshments USA Inc 732 398-4800
  60 Deans Rhode Hall Rd Monmouth Junction (08852) *(G-6283)*

Coca-Cola Refreshments USA Inc 201 635-6300
  60 Deans Rhode Hall Rd Monmouth Junction (08852) *(G-6284)*

Cocco Enterprises Inc (PA) 609 393-5939
  3575 Quakerbridge Rd # 204 Trenton (08619) *(G-10920)*

Cockpit Usa Inc 212 575-1616
  725 New Point Rd Elizabeth (07201) *(G-2721)*

Coco International Inc 973 694-1200
  6 Highpoint Dr Wayne (07470) *(G-11489)*

Cocoa Services Inc 856 234-1700
  905 N Lenola Rd Moorestown (08057) *(G-6514)*

Cococare Products Inc 973 989-8880
  85 Franklin Rd Ste 3a Dover (07801) *(G-2078)*

Coda Inc (PA) 201 825-7400
  30 Industrial Ave Ste 1 Mahwah (07430) *(G-5724)*

Coda Resources Ltd (PA) 718 649-1666
  100 Matawan Rd Ste 300 Matawan (07747) *(G-5971)*

Codenoll, Mountain Lakes *Also called Data Base Access Systems Inc (G-6822)*

Coesia Health & Beauty Inc (PA) 908 707-8008
  335 Chambers Brook Rd Branchburg (08876) *(G-630)*

Coffee Associates Inc (PA) 201 945-1060
  178 Old River Rd Edgewater (07020) *(G-2436)*

Coffee Company LLC (PA) 609 399-5533
  928 Boardwalk Ocean City (08226) *(G-7688)*

Coffee Company LLC 609 398-2326
  917 Asbury Ave Unit A Ocean City (08226) *(G-7689)*

Cognizant Tech Solutions Corp (PA) 201 801-0233
  500 Frank W Burr Blvd Teaneck (07666) *(G-10625)*

Cohansey Cove 609 884-7726
  705 Jonathan Hoffman Rd Cape May (08204) *(G-1095)*

Coherent Inc 973 240-6851
  31 Farinella Dr East Hanover (07936) *(G-2200)*

Coherent Advnced Crystal Group, East Hanover *Also called Coherent Inc (G-2200)*

Coilhose Pneumatics Inc 732 432-7177
  19 Kimberly Rd East Brunswick (08816) *(G-2133)*

Coim USA Inc 856 224-1668
  675 Billingsport Rd Paulsboro (08066) *(G-8331)*

Coim USA Inc (HQ) 856 224-8560
  286 Mantua Grove Rd # 1 West Deptford (08066) *(G-11700)*

Coining Inc 201 791-4020
  15 Mercedes Dr Montvale (07645) *(G-6403)*

Coining Holding Company (HQ) 201 791-4020
  15 Mercedes Dr Montvale (07645) *(G-6404)*

Coining Manufactures, Montvale *Also called Coining Holding Company (G-6404)*

Coining Manufacturing LLC 973 253-0500
  11 Lafayette Ky Colts Neck (07722) *(G-1778)*

Coining Mfg 973 253-0500
  35 Monhegan St Ste 4 Clifton (07013) *(G-1585)*

Coining Technologies Inc 866 897-2304
  35 Monhegan St Demarest (07627) *(G-2025)*

Colaneri Brothers, East Rutherford *Also called Robert Colaneri (G-2314)*

Colas Inc (HQ) 973 290-9082
  73 Headquarters Plz 10t Morristown (07960) *(G-6654)*

Cold Headed Fasteners Inc 856 461-3244
  401 Creek Rd Ste D Delanco (08075) *(G-2004)*

Cold Spring Ice Inc 609 884-3405
  906 Schellenger St Cape May (08204) *(G-1096)*

Cole Brothers Marble & Granite 856 455-7989
  892 Parvin Mill Rd Elmer (08318) *(G-2795)*

Colemax Group LLC (PA) 201 489-1080
  41 Grand Ave Ste 103 River Edge (07661) *(G-9359)*

Coles and Blenman Network LLC 973 432-7041
  117 Orange St Bloomfield (07003) *(G-496)*

Colex Imaging Inc 201 414-5575
  55-57 Bushes Ln Elmwood Park (07407) *(G-2816)*

Colfajas Inc 973 727-4813
  5 West St Succasunna (07876) *(G-10510)*

Colgate-Palmolive Company 732 878-6062
  251 S 8th Ave Highland Park (08904) *(G-4288)*

Colgate-Palmolive Company 732 878-7500
  909 River Rd Piscataway (08854) *(G-8648)*

Colgate-Palmolive Company 609 239-6001
  400 Elbow Ln Burlington (08016) *(G-961)*

Colibri Scentique Ltd Lblty Co 201 445-5715
  68 Chadwick Pl Glen Rock (07452) *(G-3830)*

Colie Sail Makers Inc 732 892-4344
  1649 Bay Ave Point Pleasant Boro (08742) *(G-8840)*

Colinear Machine & Design Inc 973 300-1681
  7 Wilson Dr Sparta (07871) *(G-10382)*

Collagen Matrix Inc (PA) 201 405-1477
  15 Thornton Rd Oakland (07436) *(G-7619)*

Collection Xiix Ltd 201 854-7740
  7001 Anpesil Dr Ste 2 North Bergen (07047) *(G-7396)*

College Spun Media Inc 973 945-5040
  95 River St Ste 408 Hoboken (07030) *(G-4448)*

**A
L
P
H
A
B
E
T
I
C**

Collins and Company LLC......973 427-4068
121 Wagaraw Rd Hawthorne (07506) *(G-4212)*
Colonial - Bende Ribbons Inc......973 777-8700
180 Autumn St Passaic (07055) *(G-8056)*
Colonial Uphl & Win Treatments......609 641-3124
425 S Main St Pleasantville (08232) *(G-8808)*
Colonial Wire & Cable Co Inc......732 287-1557
85 National Rd Edison (08817) *(G-2480)*
Colonna Brothers Inc (PA)......800 626-8384
4102 Bergen Tpke North Bergen (07047) *(G-7397)*
Color Coded LLC......718 482-1063
249 Thomas Mcgovern Dr # 3 Jersey City (07305) *(G-4714)*
Color Comp Inc......856 262-3040
1041 Glassboro Rd Ste E5 Williamstown (08094) *(G-11954)*
Color Company, Linden *Also called Colorflo Inc (G-5335)*
Color Decor Ltd Liability Co......973 689-2699
518 E 36th St Paterson (07504) *(G-8159)*
Color Kinetics, Somerset *Also called Signify North America Corp (G-10072)*
Color Screen Pros Inc......973 268-5080
100 Verona Ave Newark (07104) *(G-7086)*
Color Techniques Inc......908 412-9292
260 Ryan St South Plainfield (07080) *(G-10239)*
Colorcraft Sign Co......609 386-1115
400 Magnolia St Beverly (08010) *(G-449)*
Colorflo Inc......908 862-3010
1261 W Elizabeth Ave Linden (07036) *(G-5335)*
Colorful Story Books Inc......908 561-3333
4301 New Brunswick Ave South Plainfield (07080) *(G-10240)*
Colorite Plastics Company (HQ)......201 941-2900
101 Railroad Ave Ridgefield (07657) *(G-9254)*
Colorite Polymers......800 631-1577
101 Railroad Ave Ridgefield (07657) *(G-9255)*
Coloron Plastics Corporation......908 685-1210
169 Meister Ave Branchburg (08876) *(G-631)*
Colorsource Inc......856 488-8100
7025 Central Hwy Pennsauken (08109) *(G-8406)*
Colortec Printing and Mailing......856 767-0108
424 Kelley Dr Ste A West Berlin (08091) *(G-11584)*
Colortec Printing Ink, Parsippany *Also called Prismacolor Corp (G-8002)*
Colt Media Inc......732 946-3276
4 Wedgewood Ave Colts Neck (07722) *(G-1779)*
Colter & Peterson Inc (PA)......973 684-0901
19 Fairfield Pl West Caldwell (07006) *(G-11644)*
Colton Industries Inc......908 277-2040
117 Colt Rd Summit (07901) *(G-10530)*
Coltwell Industries Inc......908 276-7600
55 Winans Ave Cranford (07016) *(G-1905)*
Columbia Fuel Services Inc......732 751-0044
1717 Highway 34 Wall Township (07727) *(G-11331)*
Columbia Industries Inc (PA)......201 337-7332
567 Commerce St Franklin Lakes (07417) *(G-3618)*
Columbia Paint Lab Inc......201 435-4884
452 Communipaw Ave Jersey City (07304) *(G-4715)*
Columbia Press Inc......973 575-6535
12 Industrial Rd Fairfield (07004) *(G-3171)*
Columbian Orna Ir Works Inc......973 697-0927
332 Vreeland Ave Paterson (07513) *(G-8160)*
Colwood Electronics Inc......732 938-5556
44 Main St Farmingdale (07727) *(G-3380)*
Com Tek Wrkplace Solutions LLC......973 927-6814
1099 Wall St W Ste 269 Lyndhurst (07071) *(G-5649)*
Com-Fab Inc......973 296-0433
921 Burnt Meadow Rd B Hewitt (07421) *(G-4274)*
Comar Inc (PA)......856 692-6100
201 Laurel Rd Fl 2 Voorhees (08043) *(G-11282)*
Comar Inc......856 507-5461
201 Laurel Rd Fl 2 Voorhees (08043) *(G-11283)*
Comar LLC......856 507-5483
3100 N Mill Rd Vineland (08360) *(G-11200)*
Comar Glass, Voorhees *Also called Comar Inc (G-11282)*
Comarco Products Inc......856 342-7557
501 Jackson St Camden (08104) *(G-1053)*
Comarco Quality Pork Products, Camden *Also called Comarco Products Inc (G-1053)*
Combocap Inc......646 722-2743
125 Algonquin Pkwy Whippany (07981) *(G-11886)*
Comet Tool Company Inc......856 256-1070
651 Lambs Rd Pitman (08071) *(G-8743)*
Comex Systems Inc......800 543-6959
101 Pleasant Hill Rd Chester (07930) *(G-1432)*
Comfort Concepts Inc......201 941-6700
501 Broad Ave Ste 7 Ridgefield (07657) *(G-9256)*
Comfort Rvolution Holdings LLC......732 272-9111
442 Highway 35 Fl 1 Eatontown (07724) *(G-2385)*
Comfort Zone......732 869-9990
44 Main Ave Ocean Grove (07756) *(G-7699)*
Comfortaire Htg & A Conditio, Vineland *Also called Comfortaire Ltd Liability Co (G-11201)*
Comfortaire Ltd Liability Co......856 692-5000
1435 E Sherman Ave Vineland (08361) *(G-11201)*
Comfortfit Labs Inc......908 259-9100
246 Columbus Ave Roselle (07203) *(G-9554)*
Comm Port Technologies Inc......732 738-8780
1 Corporate Dr Ste F Cranbury (08512) *(G-1826)*
Command Nutritionals LLC......973 227-8210
10 Washington Ave Ste 1 Fairfield (07004) *(G-3172)*
Command Web Offset Company Inc (PA)......201 863-8100
100 Castle Rd Secaucus (07094) *(G-9757)*
Commander Imaging Products Inc......973 742-9298
70 Spruce St Ste 8 Paterson (07501) *(G-8161)*
Commeatus LLC......847 772-5314
5216 Fox Run Dr Plainsboro (08536) *(G-8782)*
Commerce Enterprises Inc......201 368-2100
61 S Paramus Rd Ste 135 Paramus (07652) *(G-7794)*
Commerce Register Inc......201 445-3000
190 Godwin Ave Midland Park (07432) *(G-6172)*
Commercial Business Forms Inc......973 682-9000
240 Cedar Knolls Rd # 203 Cedar Knolls (07927) *(G-1302)*
Commercial Composition & Prtg......856 662-0557
1601 Sherman Ave Ste B Pennsauken (08110) *(G-8407)*
Commercial Pdts Svcs Group Inc (PA)......609 730-4111
1580 Reed Rd Pennington (08534) *(G-8362)*
Commercial Products Co Inc......973 427-6887
117 Ethel Ave Ste 143 Hawthorne (07506) *(G-4213)*
Commercial Water Sports Inc......609 624-3404
28 Clermont Dr Cape May Court House (08210) *(G-1110)*
Communication Devices Inc (PA)......973 334-1980
85 Fulton St Unit 2 Boonton (07005) *(G-546)*
Communication Products Co......973 977-8490
201 Mclean Blvd Paterson (07504) *(G-8162)*
Communications Supply Corp......732 346-1864
104 Sunfield Ave Edison (08837) *(G-2481)*
Communique Inc......973 751-7588
120 Greylock Ave Belleville (07109) *(G-293)*
Community News Network Inc......856 428-3399
6 S Haddon Ave Ste 1 Haddonfield (08033) *(G-4055)*
Community News Service LLC......609 396-1511
15 Princess Rd K Lawrenceville (08648) *(G-5227)*
Community Pride Publications......609 921-8760
55 Prnceton Hightstown Rd Princeton Junction (08550) *(G-9053)*
Commvault Americas Inc......888 746-3849
1 Commvault Way Tinton Falls (07724) *(G-10708)*
Commvault Systems Inc (PA)......732 870-4000
1 Commvault Way Tinton Falls (07724) *(G-10709)*
Comodo Group Inc (PA)......888 266-6361
1255 Broad St Clifton (07013) *(G-1586)*
Compact Fluorescent Systems......908 475-8991
463 Stanhope Rd Sparta (07871) *(G-10383)*
Compass Wire Cloth &......856 853-7616
1942 N Mill Rd Vineland (08360) *(G-11202)*
Compass Wire Cloth Corp......856 853-7616
1942 N Mill Rd Vineland (08360) *(G-11203)*
Compco Analytical Inc......201 641-3936
215 Gates Rd Ste U Little Ferry (07643) *(G-5480)*
Competech Smrtcard Sltions Inc......201 256-4184
440 Sylvan Ave Ste 250 Englewood Cliffs (07632) *(G-2963)*
Compex Corporation......856 719-8657
439 Commerce Ln Ste 1 West Berlin (08091) *(G-11585)*
Complementary Coatings Corp (HQ)......845 786-5000
101 Paragon Dr Montvale (07645) *(G-6405)*
Complete Filter......732 441-0321
3 Donamar Ln South Amboy (08879) *(G-10132)*
Complete Optical Laboratory......973 338-8886
1255 Broad St Ste 202 Bloomfield (07003) *(G-497)*
Compliance Educational Systems, Marlton *Also called Plescia & Company Inc (G-5947)*
Componding Engrg Solutions Inc......973 340-4000
72 Danebury Downs Upper Saddle River (07458) *(G-11137)*
Component Hardware Group Inc (PA)......800 526-3694
1890 Swarthmore Ave Lakewood (08701) *(G-5072)*
Components Corporation......866 426-6726
6 Kinsey Pl Denville (07834) *(G-2032)*
Composecure LLC......908 518-0500
309 Pierce St Somerset (08873) *(G-9975)*
Composecure LLC (PA)......908 518-0500
500 Memorial Dr Ste 4 Somerset (08873) *(G-9976)*
Composition Printing, Jersey City *Also called Logomania Inc (G-4760)*
Compounders Inc......732 938-5007
15 Marl Rd Farmingdale (07727) *(G-3381)*
Comprehensive Connectivity Com, Fairfield *Also called Vcom Intl Multi-Media Corp (G-3338)*
Comprehensive Healthcare Systm......732 362-2000
2025 Lincoln Hwy Edison (08817) *(G-2482)*
Comprehensive Mktg Systems, Union *Also called Comprehensive Mktg Systems (G-11036)*
Comprehensive Mktg Systems......908 810-9778
850 Springfield Rd # 353 Union (07083) *(G-11036)*
Comprelli Equipment and Svc......973 428-8687
9 Brace Dr East Hanover (07936) *(G-2201)*
Comptime Inc......201 760-2400
385 N Franklin Tpke Ste 6 Ramsey (07446) *(G-9143)*
Comptime Print & Copy Center, Ramsey *Also called Comptime Inc (G-9143)*
Compufab Sales Inc......856 786-0175
2303 Garry Rd Ste 1 Cinnaminson (08077) *(G-1447)*

Compupharma Inc 973 227-6003
242 Old New Brunswick Rd Piscataway (08854) *(G-8649)*

Computa-Base-Machining Inc 856 767-9517
411 N Grove St Berlin (08009) *(G-421)*

Computech Applications LLC 201 261-5251
768 Howard Ct E Oradell (07649) *(G-7742)*

Computer Aided Software Tech, Woodcliff Lake *Also called Cast Inc (G-12051)*

Computer Company North America 909 265-3390
356 Wren Ln Bedminster (07921) *(G-262)*

Computer Control Corp 973 492-8265
10 Park Pl Ste 1 Butler (07405) *(G-998)*

Computer Crafts Inc 973 423-3500
57 Thomas Rd N Hawthorne (07506) *(G-4214)*

Computer Doc Associates Inc 908 647-4445
2007 Washington Valley Rd Martinsville (08836) *(G-5962)*

Computer Sources 201 791-9443
37 Leliarts Ln Elmwood Park (07407) *(G-2817)*

Computeradio 973 220-0087
7 Brittany Rd Montville (07045) *(G-6440)*

Comtrex Systems Corporation (PA) 856 778-0090
101 Foster Rd B Moorestown (08057) *(G-6515)*

Comtron Inc 732 446-7571
12 Commerce St Springfield (07081) *(G-10436)*

Comus International Inc (PA) 973 777-6900
454 Allwood Rd Clifton (07012) *(G-1587)*

Comverge Giants Inc 973 884-5970
25a Vreeland Rd Ste 300 Florham Park (07932) *(G-3497)*

Comverge Giants Inc (HQ) 973 884-5970
120 Eagle Rock Ave # 190 East Hanover (07936) *(G-2202)*

Conagraphics Inc 973 331-1113
1180 Us Highway 46 Ste 2 Parsippany (07054) *(G-7908)*

Conair Corporation 239 673-2125
150 Milford Rd East Windsor (08520) *(G-2347)*

Conair Corporation 609 426-1300
150 Milford Rd East Windsor (08520) *(G-2348)*

Concept Group LLC (HQ) 856 767-5506
380 Cooper Rd West Berlin (08091) *(G-11586)*

Concept Professional Systems 732 938-5321
5005 Belmar Blvd Ste B1 Wall Township (07727) *(G-11332)*

Concord Products Company Inc 856 933-3000
317 Salina Rd Sewell (08080) *(G-9834)*

Concord Truss Co, Woodbury Heights *Also called Woodbury Roof Truss Inc (G-12044)*

Concorde Specialty Gases Inc 732 544-9899
36 Eaton Rd Eatontown (07724) *(G-2386)*

Concrete Cutting Partners Inc 201 440-2233
508 Hudson St Hackensack (07601) *(G-3899)*

Concrete On Demand Inc 201 337-0005
45 Edison Ave Ste 1 Oakland (07436) *(G-7620)*

Concrete Stone & Tile Corp (PA) 973 948-7193
17 Ridge Rd Branchville (07826) *(G-705)*

Conduent State Healthcare LLC 973 824-3250
60 Park Pl Ste 605 Newark (07102) *(G-7087)*

Conduent State Healthcare LLC 973 754-6134
100 Hamilton Plz Ste 400 Paterson (07505) *(G-8163)*

Conexion Printing, Hawthorne *Also called Tekno Inc (G-4246)*

Confectionately Yours LLC 732 821-6863
3391 State Route 27 # 121 Franklin Park (08823) *(G-3633)*

Confires Fire Prtction Svc LLC 908 822-2700
910 Oak Tree Ave South Plainfield (07080) *(G-10241)*

Congoleum Corporation (PA) 609 584-3000
3500 Quakerbridge Rd Trenton (08619) *(G-10921)*

Congoleum Corporation 609 584-3601
3705 Quakerbridge Rd # 211 Trenton (08619) *(G-10922)*

Congoleum Corporation 609 584-3000
1945 E State Street Ext Trenton (08619) *(G-10923)*

Congruent Machine Co Inc 973 764-6767
107 Maple Grange Rd Vernon (07462) *(G-11158)*

Conistics Inc 609 584-2600
1800 E State St Ste 148 Hamilton (08609) *(G-4104)*

Conjupro Biotherapuetics Inc 609 356-0210
302 Carnegie Ctr Ste 100 Princeton (08540) *(G-8924)*

Conkur Printing Co Inc 212 541-5980
161 Coolidge Ave Englewood (07631) *(G-2894)*

Conneaut Creek Ship Repr Inc 212 863-9406
333 Washington St Ste 201 Jersey City (07302) *(G-4716)*

Connecting Products Inc 609 512-1121
186 Tamarack Cir Skillman (08558) *(G-9918)*

Connecting Products Inc 609 688-1808
194 Tamarack Cir Ste 1 Skillman (08558) *(G-9919)*

Connector Mfg Co 513 860-4455
123 Town Square Pl Jersey City (07310) *(G-4717)*

Connector Products Inc 856 829-9190
1300 John Tipton Blvd Pennsauken (08110) *(G-8408)*

Connell Mining Products LLC 908 673-3700
200 Connell Dr Berkeley Heights (07922) *(G-395)*

Conopco Inc 201 894-7760
940 Sylvan Ave Englewood Cliffs (07632) *(G-2964)*

Conopco Inc 856 722-1664
305 Fellowship Rd Ste 114 Mount Laurel (08054) *(G-6749)*

Conopco Inc 920 499-2509
800 Sylvan Ave Englewood Cliffs (07632) *(G-2965)*

Consarc Corporation (HQ) 609 267-8000
100 Indel Ave Rancocas (08073) *(G-9159)*

Consoldate Cntiner Holdings NJ, Cranbury *Also called Consolidated Cont Holdings LLC (G-1827)*

Consolidated Cont Holdings LLC 609 655-0855
4 Pleasant Hill Rd Cranbury (08512) *(G-1827)*

Consolidated Container Co LP 908 289-5862
28-36 Slater Dr Elizabeth (07206) *(G-2722)*

Consolidated Packg Group Inc 201 440-4240
30 Bergen Tpke Ridgefield Park (07660) *(G-9301)*

Constant Services Inc 973 227-2990
17 Commerce Rd Ste 2 Fairfield (07004) *(G-3173)*

Constantia Blythewood LLC 732 974-4100
1111 N Point Blvd Belmar (07719) *(G-347)*

Constantine Engrg Labs Co, Mahwah *Also called Celco (G-5721)*

Constitution Arms, Maplewood *Also called 2a Holdings Inc (G-5873)*

Constitution Co, Woodbury *Also called Dewechter Inc (G-12027)*

Construction Services, Wayne *Also called Orsillo & Company (G-11537)*

Construction Specialties (PA) 908 236-0800
3 Werner Way Ste 100 Lebanon (08833) *(G-5257)*

Construction Specialties Inc 908 272-2771
49 Meeker Ave Cranford (07016) *(G-1906)*

Consumer Graphics Inc 732 469-4699
18 Fordham Rd Somerset (08873) *(G-9977)*

Contact Len Lab, Millburn *Also called Lens Mode Inc (G-6202)*

Container Graphics Corp 732 922-1180
3535 Highway 66 Ste 2 Neptune (07753) *(G-6870)*

Container Manufacturing, Middlesex *Also called Container Mfg Inc (G-6105)*

Container Mfg Inc 732 563-0100
50 Baekeland Ave Middlesex (08846) *(G-6105)*

Conte Farms 609 268-0513
299 Flyatt Rd Tabernacle (08088) *(G-10618)*

Contech, Elizabeth *Also called Consolidated Container Co LP (G-2722)*

Contempocork LLC 201 262-7738
175 Dorchester Rd River Edge (07661) *(G-9360)*

Contemporary Cabling Company 732 382-5064
90 Brookside Ter Clark (07066) *(G-1496)*

Contemprary Grphics Bndery Inc 856 663-7277
1200 Ferry Ave Camden (08104) *(G-1054)*

Contes Pasta Company Inc 856 697-3400
310 Wheat Rd Vineland (08360) *(G-11204)*

Conti-Robert and Co JV 732 520-5000
2045 Lincoln Hwy Edison (08817) *(G-2483)*

Continental Aromatics 973 238-9300
1 Thomas Rd S Hawthorne (07506) *(G-4215)*

Continental Cast Stone East, West Berlin *Also called Russell Cast Stone Inc (G-11620)*

Continental Cookies Inc 201 498-1966
185 S Newman St Hackensack (07601) *(G-3900)*

Continental Cup Company LLC 602 803-4666
90 Boulderwood Dr Bernardsville (07924) *(G-437)*

Continental Food & Bev Inc 973 815-1600
495 River Rd Clifton (07014) *(G-1588)*

Continental Precision Corp (PA) 908 754-3030
25 Howard St Piscataway (08854) *(G-8650)*

Continntal Concession Sups Inc 516 629-4906
1135 Springfield Rd Union (07083) *(G-11037)*

Continuity Logic LLC 866 321-5079
55 Lane Rd Ste 303 Fairfield (07004) *(G-3174)*

Contour Next, Parsippany *Also called Ascensia Diabetes Care US Inc (G-7885)*

Contract Coatings Inc 201 343-3131
161 Beech St Hackensack (07601) *(G-3901)*

Contract Filling Inc 973 433-0053
10 Cliffside Dr Cedar Grove (07009) *(G-1272)*

Control & Power Systems Inc 973 439-0500
17 Spielman Rd Fairfield (07004) *(G-3175)*

Control Demolition, Bayonne *Also called Control Industries Inc (G-212)*

Control Group, Norwood *Also called Norwood Printing Inc (G-7572)*

Control Group, Norwood *Also called Cheringal Associates Inc (G-7560)*

Control Industries Inc (PA) 201 437-3826
197 E 22nd St Ste 4 Bayonne (07002) *(G-212)*

Control Instruments Corp 973 575-9114
25 Law Dr Fairfield (07004) *(G-3176)*

Control Products, East Hanover *Also called Calculagraph Co (G-2198)*

Control Products Inc 973 887-5000
272 Ridgedale Ave 280 East Hanover (07936) *(G-2203)*

Convatec Healthcare A, S.A.R., Bridgewater *Also called Convatec Inc (G-813)*

Convatec Inc (HQ) 908 231-2179
1160 Rte 22 Ste 201 Bridgewater (08807) *(G-813)*

Convenience Works, West Deptford *Also called Hussmann Corporation (G-11703)*

Convention News Company Inc (PA) 201 444-5075
214 Franklin Ave Midland Park (07432) *(G-6173)*

Conversion Technology Co Inc 732 752-5660
4301 New Brunswick Ave A South Plainfield (07080) *(G-10242)*

Convertech Inc 973 328-1850
353 Richard Mine Rd Ste 4 Wharton (07885) *(G-11854)*

Converter Company, The, Woodbury Heights *Also called 431 Converters Inc* ***(G-12040)***
Converting Resources, Paterson *Also called Stonebridge Paper LLC* ***(G-8303)***
Conveyer Installers America 908 453-4729
5 Tamarack Rd Belvidere (07823) ***(G-358)***
Conveyors By North American 973 777-6600
156 Huron Ave Clifton (07013) ***(G-1589)***
Cookie Cupboard, Cedar Grove *Also called Fairfield Gourmet Food Corp* ***(G-1278)***
Cookman Creamery LLC 732 361-5215
1 Mariners Bnd Brielle (08730) ***(G-906)***
Coolenheat Inc 908 925-4473
11 Clinton Ct Kendall Park (08824) ***(G-4918)***
Cooper Alloy Corporation 908 688-4120
201 Sweetland Ave Ste 1 Hillside (07205) ***(G-4387)***
Cooper Burial Vaults Co 856 547-8405
621 Atlantic Ave Barrington (08007) ***(G-169)***
Cooper Lighting LLC 609 395-4277
1 Broadway Rd Cranbury (08512) ***(G-1828)***
Cooper Notification, Long Branch *Also called Cooper Wheelock Inc* ***(G-5595)***
Cooper Power Systems LLC 732 481-4630
42 Cindy Ln Ocean (07712) ***(G-7659)***
Cooper Power Systems LLC 856 719-1100
402 Bloomfield Dr Ste 1 West Berlin (08091) ***(G-11587)***
Cooper Wheelock Inc 732 222-6880
273 Branchport Ave Long Branch (07740) ***(G-5595)***
Cooper-Wilbert Vault Co Inc (PA) 856 547-8405
621 Atlantic Ave Barrington (08007) ***(G-170)***
Coordinated Metals Inc 201 460-7280
626 16th St Carlstadt (07072) ***(G-1145)***
Copack International Inc 973 405-5151
23 Carol St Clifton (07014) ***(G-1590)***
Coperion Corporation (HQ) 201 327-6300
590 Woodbury Glassboro Rd Sewell (08080) ***(G-9835)***
Coperion K-Tron Pitman Inc (HQ) 856 589-0500
590 Woodbury Glassboro Rd Sewell (08080) ***(G-9836)***
Copy Depot, The, Randolph *Also called Graphics Depot Inc* ***(G-9183)***
Copy-Rite Printing 609 597-9182
378 N Main St Ste A Manahawkin (08050) ***(G-5792)***
Cor Products Inc 973 731-4952
20 Standish Ave West Orange (07052) ***(G-11763)***
Corban Energy Group Corp 201 509-8555
418 Falmouth Ave Elmwood Park (07407) ***(G-2818)***
Corbco Inc 609 549-6299
40 Canterbury Dr Forked River (08731) ***(G-3538)***
Corbett Industries Inc 201 445-6311
39 Hewson Ave Ste B Waldwick (07463) ***(G-11299)***
Corbi Printing Co Inc 856 547-2444
106 W Atlantic Ave Audubon (08106) ***(G-112)***
Corbo Jewelers Inc 973 777-1635
1055 Bloomfield Ave Clifton (07012) ***(G-1591)***
Corbo Jewelers of Styertowne, Clifton *Also called Corbo Jewelers Inc* ***(G-1591)***
Cordes Printing Inc 201 652-7272
460 Braen Ave Wyckoff (07481) ***(G-12107)***
Cordis International Corp 732 524-0400
1 Johnson And Johnson Plz New Brunswick (08933) ***(G-6918)***
Core 3 Brewery Ltd Lblty Co 856 562-0386
3171 Coles Mill Rd Franklinville (08322) ***(G-3636)***
Core Acquisition LLC (PA) 732 983-6025
215 Wood Ave Ste 215 # 215 Middlesex (08846) ***(G-6106)***
Core Care America, Lyndhurst *Also called CCA Industries Inc* ***(G-5647)***
Core Laboratories LP 609 896-2673
11 Princess Rd Ste H Lawrenceville (08648) ***(G-5228)***
Corentec America Inc 949 379-6227
60 Washington St Ste 202 Morristown (07960) ***(G-6655)***
Corepharma LLC 732 983-6025
215 Wood Ave Ste 215 # 215 Middlesex (08846) ***(G-6107)***
Corgi Spirits LLC 862 219-3114
150 Pacific Ave Bldg P Jersey City (07304) ***(G-4718)***
Corim Industries, Brick *Also called Corim International Coffee Imp* ***(G-714)***
Corim International Coffee Imp (PA) 800 942-4201
1112 Industrial Pkwy Brick (08724) ***(G-714)***
Cormedix Inc (PA) 908 517-9500
400 Connell Dr Ste 5000 Berkeley Heights (07922) ***(G-396)***
Corn Products International, Bridgewater *Also called Ingredion Incorporated* ***(G-836)***
Cornell Crane Mfg Ltd 609 742-1900
224 Llenroc Ln Westville (08093) ***(G-11811)***
Cornell Machine Co Inc 973 379-6860
45 Brown Ave Springfield (07081) ***(G-10437)***
Corner Stone Software Inc 732 938-5229
1246 Hwy 33 Howell (07731) ***(G-4534)***
Cornerstone Imaging, Flemington *Also called Cornerstone Prints Imaging LLC* ***(G-3434)***
Cornerstone Prints Imaging LLC 908 782-7966
179 State Route 31 Ste 8 Flemington (08822) ***(G-3434)***
Corning Pharmaceutical GL LLC 856 794-7100
563 Crystal Ave Vineland (08360) ***(G-11205)***
Coronation Sheet Metal Co 908 686-0930
2198 Stanley Ter Union (07083) ***(G-11038)***
Coronet Inc 973 345-7660
55 Shepherds Ln Totowa (07512) ***(G-10824)***
Coronet Led, Totowa *Also called Coronet Inc* ***(G-10824)***
Coronis Building Systems Inc 609 261-2200
92 Columbus Jobstown Rd Columbus (08022) ***(G-1798)***
Corp American Mica 908 587-5237
1015 Pennsylvania Ave Linden (07036) ***(G-5336)***
Corporate Computer Systems 732 739-5600
33 Washington St Ste 1002 Newark (07102) ***(G-7088)***
Corporate Envelope & Prtg Co 732 752-4333
299r Us Highway 22 Green Brook (08812) ***(G-3860)***
Corporate Mailings Inc (PA) 973 439-1168
14 Henderson Dr West Caldwell (07006) ***(G-11645)***
Corporate Mailings Inc 973 808-0009
26 Parsippany Rd Whippany (07981) ***(G-11887)***
Corrigan Center For Integrativ 973 239-0700
67 Haller Dr Cedar Grove (07009) ***(G-1273)***
Corrview International LLC 973 770-0571
9 Pahaquarry Rd Hopatcong (07843) ***(G-4519)***
Corte Provisions, Newark *Also called Seabrite Corp* ***(G-7265)***
Cosette Pharmaceuticals Inc 314 283-4776
111 Coolidge St South Plainfield (07080) ***(G-10243)***
Cosmetic Coatings Inc 201 438-7150
219 Broad St Carlstadt (07072) ***(G-1146)***
Cosmetic Concepts Inc 973 546-1234
20 Chestnut St Garfield (07026) ***(G-3736)***
Cosmetic Essence LLC (HQ) 732 888-7788
2182 Hwy 35 Holmdel (07733) ***(G-4497)***
Cosmetic Essence LLC 201 941-9800
1135 Pleasantview Ter Ridgefield (07657) ***(G-9257)***
Cosmetic Essence Inc 732 888-7788
2182 State Route 35 Holmdel (07733) ***(G-4498)***
Cosmic Custom Screen Prtg LLC (PA) 856 629-8337
935 S Black Horse Pike Williamstown (08094) ***(G-11955)***
Cosmopolitan Food Group Inc 908 998-1818
50 Harrison St Ste 208 Hoboken (07030) ***(G-4449)***
Cospack America Corp 732 548-5858
3856 Park Ave Edison (08820) ***(G-2484)***
Cosrich Group Inc (HQ) 866 771-7473
51 La France Ave 55 Bloomfield (07003) ***(G-498)***
Costa Custom Cabinets Inc 973 429-7004
248 Montgomery St Bloomfield (07003) ***(G-499)***
Costa Mar Cnvas Enclosures LLC 609 965-1538
1324 Moss Mill Rd Egg Harbor City (08215) ***(G-2656)***
Costa's Cabinets, Bloomfield *Also called Costa Custom Cabinets Inc* ***(G-499)***
Costume Gallery Inc 609 386-6601
700 Creek Rd Delanco (08075) ***(G-2005)***
Cottage Lace and Ribbon Co Inc (PA) 732 776-9353
210 3rd Ave Ste 21 Neptune (07753) ***(G-6871)***
Cotterman Inc 856 415-0800
100 Hayes Ave Wenonah (08090) ***(G-11574)***
Cottrell Graphics & Advg Spc 732 349-7430
2121 Route 9 Toms River (08755) ***(G-10754)***
Coty Research and Development, Morris Plains *Also called Coty US LLC* ***(G-6602)***
Coty US LLC 973 490-8700
410 American Rd Morris Plains (07950) ***(G-6602)***
Coughlan Products LLC 973 845-6440
37 Ironia Rd Ste 5 Flanders (07836) ***(G-3403)***
Counter Efx Inc 908 203-0155
301 Roycefield Rd Bldg 5 Hillsborough (08844) ***(G-4311)***
Counter-Fit Inc 609 871-8888
1 Ironside Ct Willingboro (08046) ***(G-11990)***
Counting Sheep Coffee Inc 973 589-4104
41 Malvern St Newark (07105) ***(G-7089)***
Country Club Ice Cream 973 729-5570
4 Tyler St Sparta (07871) ***(G-10384)***
Country Club Products Inc 908 352-5400
706 Trumbull St Elizabeth (07201) ***(G-2723)***
Country Oven 732 494-4838
1585 Oak Tree Rd Ste 207 Iselin (08830) ***(G-4606)***
County Concrete Corporation 973 538-3113
Ridgedale Ave Morristown (07960) ***(G-6656)***
County Concrete Corporation (PA) 973 744-2188
50 Railroad Ave Kenvil (07847) ***(G-4992)***
County Conservation Co Inc 856 227-6900
212 Blckwood Barnsboro Rd Sewell (08080) ***(G-9837)***
County Graphics Forms MGT LLC 908 474-9797
2 Stercho Rd Linden (07036) ***(G-5337)***
County Line Phrmaceuticals LLC 262 439-8109
10 Bloomfield Ave Ste 3 Pine Brook (07058) ***(G-8594)***
County of Somerset 732 469-3363
40 Polhemus Ln Bridgewater (08807) ***(G-814)***
County of Warren 908 475-7975
519 S 185 County Rd Belvidere (07823) ***(G-359)***
Courier News, Somerville *Also called Gannett Co Inc* ***(G-10112)***
Courier Newspaper, The, Middletown *Also called Bay Shore Press Inc* ***(G-6160)***
Courtney Boatlifts Inc 732 892-8900
1209 Bay Ave Point Pleasant Boro (08742) ***(G-8841)***
Couse & Bolten Co 973 344-6330
90 S St Dock 5 Newark (07114) ***(G-7090)***
Couture Exchange 732 933-1123
703 Broad St Ste 1 Shrewsbury (07702) ***(G-9887)***

Covalnce Spcalty Adhesives LLC.................................732 356-2870
  87 Lincoln Blvd Middlesex (08846) *(G-6108)*

Covalnce Spcialty Coatings LLC................................732 356-2870
  87 Lincoln Blvd Middlesex (08846) *(G-6109)*

Coventry of New Jersey Inc..856 988-5521
  10000 Lincoln Dr E # 201 Marlton (08053) *(G-5925)*

Cover Co Inc...908 707-9797
  19 Readington Rd Branchburg (08876) *(G-632)*

Covia Holdings Corporation......................................856 785-2700
  1100 Whitehead Rd Dividing Creek (08315) *(G-2069)*

Covia Holdings Corporation......................................856 451-6400
  1660 S Burlington Rd Bridgeton (08302) *(G-756)*

Cox Stationers and Printers......................................908 928-1010
  1634 E Elizabeth Ave Linden (07036) *(G-5338)*

Cozy Formal Wear (PA)..973 661-9781
  695 Passaic Ave Nutley (07110) *(G-7583)*

Cozy Home Fashions, Secaucus *Also called Sander Sales Enterprises Ltd (G-9806)*

Cozzoli Machine Company (PA)...................................732 564-0400
  50 Schoolhouse Rd Somerset (08873) *(G-9978)*

Cozzolino Furniture Design Inc..................................973 731-9292
  20 Standish Ave West Orange (07052) *(G-11764)*

Cozzolino Inc., West Orange *Also called Cozzolino Furniture Design Inc (G-11764)*

CP Equipment Sales Co...908 687-9621
  1504 Oakland Ave Union (07083) *(G-11039)*

CP Test & Valve Products Inc....................................201 998-1500
  234 Sanford Ave Kearny (07032) *(G-4851)*

CPB Inc...856 697-2700
  701 S Harding Hwy Buena (08310) *(G-939)*

CPS Metals Inc..856 779-0846
  450 S Fellowship Rd Maple Shade (08052) *(G-5861)*

CR Laurence Co Inc..856 727-1022
  1511 Lancer Dr Moorestown (08057) *(G-6516)*

CR Laurence Co Inc..201 770-1077
  70 Seaview Dr Secaucus (07094) *(G-9758)*

Cr Ocean Engineering, LLC, Parsippany *Also called Cross Rip Ocean Engrg LLC (G-7911)*

CRA-Z Works Co Inc..732 390-8238
  242 Main St Sayreville (08872) *(G-9707)*

Craft Signs..201 656-1991
  136 Franklin St Jersey City (07307) *(G-4719)*

Craft-Pak Inc..718 763-0700
  1 Ashley Pl Towaco (07082) *(G-10867)*

Craftmaster Printing Inc (PA)....................................732 775-0011
  2024 State Route 33 Neptune (07753) *(G-6872)*

Craftsmen Photo Lithographers................................973 316-5791
  38 Beach St East Hanover (07936) *(G-2204)*

Craig Robertson..973 293-8666
  19 State Route 23 Montague (07827) *(G-6354)*

Cramer Plating Inc..908 453-2887
  4 Hoyt Ln Buttzville (07829) *(G-1016)*

Cranford Diagnostic Imaging, Cranford *Also called Radnet Inc (G-1924)*

Cranial Technologies Inc...908 754-0572
  2163 Oak Tree Rd Edison (08820) *(G-2485)*

Cranial Technologies Inc...201 265-3993
  115 W Century Rd Ste 280 Paramus (07652) *(G-7795)*

Crave Foods LLC..973 233-1220
  19 Club Rd Montclair (07043) *(G-6361)*

Cravings..732 531-7122
  310 Main St Allenhurst (07711) *(G-21)*

Cravings Gourmet Desserts, Allenhurst *Also called Cravings (G-21)*

Crazy Cups, Newark *Also called 26 Flavors LLC (G-7027)*

Crazy Steve's Pickles & Salsa, Trenton *Also called Crazy Steves Concoctions LLC (G-10924)*

Crazy Steves Concoctions LLC..................................908 787-2089
  38 Herbert Rd Trenton (08691) *(G-10924)*

Cream Ridge Winery...609 259-9797
  145 Route 539 Cream Ridge (08514) *(G-1933)*

Creamer Glass LLC...856 327-2023
  2201 Quince Ln Millville (08332) *(G-6243)*

Creamer Glass LLC...856 327-2023
  411 N 10th St Millville (08332) *(G-6244)*

Creamy Creation LLC (HQ)...585 344-3300
  61 S Paramus Rd Ste 535 Paramus (07652) *(G-7796)*

Creations By Sherry Lynn LLC...................................800 742-3448
  90 Park Ave Ste 414 Florham Park (07932) *(G-3498)*

Creations By Stefano Inc...201 863-8337
  1261 Paterson Plank Rd Secaucus (07094) *(G-9759)*

Creationsrewards Net LLC...908 526-3127
  116 S 19th Ave Manville (08835) *(G-5854)*

Creative Cabinet Designs Inc.....................................973 402-5886
  301 Main St Boonton (07005) *(G-547)*

Creative Cmpt Concepts LLC......................................877 919-7988
  2030 N Black Horse Pike Williamstown (08094) *(G-11956)*

Creative Color Lithographers....................................908 789-2295
  611 South Ave Garwood (07027) *(G-3783)*

Creative Competitions Inc...856 256-2797
  406 Ganttown Rd Sewell (08080) *(G-9838)*

Creative Concepts Corporation.................................201 750-1234
  70 Oak St Ste 202 Norwood (07648) *(G-7562)*

Creative Concepts of NJ LLC......................................732 833-1776
  580 N County Line Rd Jackson (08527) *(G-4645)*

Creative Desserts...732 477-0808
  42 Capri Dr Brick (08723) *(G-715)*

Creative Display Inc..732 918-8010
  349 Essex Rd Neptune (07753) *(G-6873)*

Creative Embroidery Corp...973 497-5700
  305 3rd Ave W Ste 3 Newark (07107) *(G-7091)*

Creative Film Corp..732 367-2166
  700 Vassar Ave Ste 2 Lakewood (08701) *(G-5073)*

Creative Industrial Kitchens......................................973 633-0420
  8 Leo Pl Wayne (07470) *(G-11490)*

Creative Innovations Inc..973 636-9060
  20-21 Wagaraw Rd Bldg 31b Fair Lawn (07410) *(G-3094)*

Creative Laminating Inc...201 939-1999
  179 Commerce Rd Carlstadt (07072) *(G-1147)*

Creative Machining Systems......................................609 586-3932
  124 Youngs Rd Trenton (08619) *(G-10925)*

Creative Metal Works Inc..973 579-3717
  22b Gail Ct Sparta (07871) *(G-10385)*

Creative Organization, Clifton *Also called Q10 Products LLC (G-1702)*

Creative Patterns & Mfg...973 589-1391
  114 Beach St Ste 4 Rockaway (07866) *(G-9451)*

Creative Pavers..201 782-1661
  45 Akers Ave Montvale (07645) *(G-6406)*

Creative Products Inc...732 614-9035
  92 Shrewsbury Dr Long Branch (07740) *(G-5596)*

Creative Safety Products, South Hackensack *Also called Encore Enterprises Inc (G-10158)*

Creative Serving, Union *Also called Durex Inc (G-11045)*

Creative Wood Products Inc.......................................732 370-0051
  370 Whitesville Rd Ste 8 Jackson (08527) *(G-4646)*

Creatone Inc..908 789-8700
  1011 Us Highway 22 Ste 1 Mountainside (07092) *(G-6837)*

Creoh Packaging, Lakewood *Also called Creoh Trading Corp (G-5074)*

Creoh Trading Corp..718 821-0570
  910 E County Line Rd Lakewood (08701) *(G-5074)*

Creoh Usa LLC...718 821-0570
  1771 Madison Ave Ste 7 Lakewood (08701) *(G-5075)*

Crescent Bottling Co Inc...856 964-2268
  1001 N 25th St Camden (08105) *(G-1055)*

Crescent Uniforms LLC...732 398-1866
  33 Hasbrouck Dr Franklin Park (08823) *(G-3634)*

Cressi Sub USA..201 594-1450
  3 Rosol Ln Saddle Brook (07663) *(G-9648)*

Crest Foam Industries, Moonachie *Also called Inoac Usa Inc (G-6471)*

Crest Foam Industries Inc, Moonachie *Also called Woodbridge Inoac Technical (G-6498)*

Crest Group Inc (HQ)...609 883-4000
  Scotch Trenton Mercer Air Trenton (08628) *(G-10926)*

Crest Ultrasonics Corp (HQ)......................................609 883-4000
  18 Graphics Dr Ewing (08628) *(G-3023)*

Crest Wood Fence, Andover *Also called New Jersey Fence & Guardrail (G-50)*

Crestek Inc (PA)...609 883-4000
  18 Graphics Dr Ewing (08628) *(G-3024)*

Creston Electronics Inc (PA)......................................201 767-3400
  15 Volvo Dr Rockleigh (07647) *(G-9516)*

Cresttek, Trenton *Also called Crest Group Inc (G-10926)*

Creter Vault Corp (PA)..908 782-7771
  417 Route 202 Flemington (08822) *(G-3435)*

Crett Construction Inc..973 663-1184
  18 Cella St Lake Hopatcong (07849) *(G-5035)*

Crh Americas Inc...732 292-2500
  331 Newman Springs Rd Red Bank (07701) *(G-9224)*

Cricket Enterprises...201 387-7978
  60 Hillcrest Dr Dumont (07628) *(G-2112)*

Crijuodama Baking Corp T...732 451-1250
  1900 Highway 70 Ste 209 Lakewood (08701) *(G-5076)*

Crincoli Woodwork Co Inc...908 352-9332
  160 Spring St Elizabeth (07201) *(G-2724)*

Criterion Publishing Co...732 548-8300
  87 Forrest St Metuchen (08840) *(G-6053)*

Criterion Software LLC..908 754-1166
  205 Us Highway 9 30 Freehold (07728) *(G-3659)*

Croce & Longo Associates, Cherry Hill *Also called Croces Pasta Poducts (G-1354)*

Croces Pasta Poducts...856 795-6000
  811 Marlton Pike W Cherry Hill (08002) *(G-1354)*

Croda Inc (HQ)...732 417-0800
  300 Columbus Cir Ste A Edison (08837) *(G-2486)*

Croda Investments Inc (HQ).......................................732 417-0800
  300 Columbus Cir Ste A Edison (08837) *(G-2487)*

Croll-Reynolds Co Inc (PA)...908 232-4200
  6 Campus Dr Ste 2 Parsippany (07054) *(G-7909)*

Crompton Corp..732 826-6600
  1000 Convery Blvd Perth Amboy (08861) *(G-8516)*

Cronite Co Inc (PA)...973 887-7900
  120 E Halsey Rd Parsippany (07054) *(G-7910)*

Cronos Design, Lodi *Also called Cronos-Prim Colorado LLC (G-5557)*

Cronos-Prim Colorado LLC..303 369-7477
  300-2 State Rt 17 S Ste C Lodi (07644) *(G-5557)*

Cross Counter Inc (PA)..973 677-0600
  200 Freeway Dr E East Orange (07018) *(G-2251)*

A L P H A B E T I C

Cross Country Box Co Inc 973 673-8349
474 Getty Ave Clifton (07011) *(G-1592)*

Cross H Co, Moonachie *Also called H Cross Company (G-6468)*

Cross Medical Specialties Inc 856 589-3288
450 Andbro Dr Unit 7 Pitman (08071) *(G-8744)*

Cross Rip Ocean Engrg LLC 973 455-0005
6 Campus Dr Parsippany (07054) *(G-7911)*

Crossfield Products Corp 908 245-2801
140 Valley Rd Roselle Park (07204) *(G-9580)*

Crossfire Publications 516 352-9087
551 Bloomfield Ave C14 Caldwell (07006) *(G-1021)*

Crowfoot Asphalt, West Berlin *Also called Crowfoot Associates Inc (G-11588)*

Crowfoot Associates Inc 609 561-0107
Winslow Township West Berlin (08091) *(G-11588)*

Crown Clothing Co 856 691-0343
609 Paul St Vineland (08360) *(G-11206)*

Crown Engineering Corp 800 631-2153
550 Sqnkum Yellowbrook Rd Farmingdale (07727) *(G-3382)*

Crown Equipment Corporation 201 337-1211
104 Bauer Dr Oakland (07436) *(G-7621)*

Crown Glass Co Inc 908 642-1764
990 Evergreen Dr Branchburg (08876) *(G-633)*

Crown Lift Trucks, Oakland *Also called Crown Equipment Corporation (G-7621)*

Crown Precision Corp 973 470-0097
61 Willet St Ste 6 Passaic (07055) *(G-8057)*

Crown Products Inc 732 493-0022
102 Pitney Ave Spring Lake (07762) *(G-10421)*

Crown Roll Leaf Inc (PA) 973 742-4000
91 Illinois Ave Paterson (07503) *(G-8164)*

Crown Roll Leaf Inc 973 684-2600
12 Columbia Ave Paterson (07503) *(G-8165)*

Crown Trophy 973 808-8400
101 Us Highway 46 Ste 136 Pine Brook (07058) *(G-8595)*

Crt International Inc 973 887-7737
260 Wagner St Middlesex (08846) *(G-6110)*

Crush Rite, Stockholm *Also called Rjticeco LLC (G-10500)*

Crust and Crumb Bakery 609 492-4966
800 N Bay Ave Ste 9 Beach Haven (08008) *(G-255)*

Cryopak Verification Tech Inc (PA) 732 346-9200
551 Raritan Center Pkwy Edison (08837) *(G-2488)*

Cryovation LLC (PA) 609 914-4792
9b Mary Way Hainesport (08036) *(G-4071)*

Crystal Beverage Corporation (PA) 201 991-2342
174 Sanford Ave Kearny (07032) *(G-4852)*

Crystal Deltronic Industries (PA) 973 328-6898
60 Harding Ave Dover (07801) *(G-2079)*

Crystal Deltronic Industries 973 328-7000
60 Harding Ave Dover (07801) *(G-2080)*

Crystal Ware, Lakewood *Also called Cw International Sales LLC (G-5079)*

Crystal World Inc 201 488-0909
283 Veterans Blvd Carlstadt (07072) *(G-1148)*

Crystex Composites LLC 973 779-8866
125 Clifton Blvd Clifton (07011) *(G-1593)*

Cs Industrial Services LLC 609 381-4380
303 Catawba Ave Newfield (08344) *(G-7320)*

CS Osborne & Co (PA) 973 483-3232
125 Jersey St Harrison (07029) *(G-4168)*

CSC 973 412-6339
168 Emily Pl Parsippany (07054) *(G-7912)*

CSC Brands LP 800 257-8443
1 Campbell Pl Camden (08103) *(G-1056)*

Csf Corporation (PA) 732 302-2222
285 Davidson Ave Ste 103 Somerset (08873) *(G-9979)*

Csg Systems Inc 973 337-4400
1455 Broad St Ste 110 Bloomfield (07003) *(G-500)*

Csi, Fairfield *Also called Constant Services Inc (G-3173)*

Csi Services Inc 856 755-9440
7905 Browning Rd Ste 316 Pennsauken (08109) *(G-8409)*

CSM Environmental Systems LLC 908 789-5431
269 Sheffield St Ste 1 Mountainside (07092) *(G-6838)*

CSM Worldwide Inc (PA) 908 233-2882
36 S Adamsville Rd 7 Bridgewater (08807) *(G-815)*

Csonka Worldwide 609 514-2766
501 Plainsboro Rd Ph Plainsboro (08536) *(G-8783)*

CSS, Englewood Cliffs *Also called Competech Smrtcard Sltions Inc (G-2963)*

CST Pavers 856 299-5339
345 Route 130 Pedricktown (08067) *(G-8347)*

CST Products LLC 856 299-5339
345 Route 130 Penns Grove (08069) *(G-8377)*

Csus LLC 973 298-8599
300 Forge Way Ste 3 Rockaway (07866) *(G-9452)*

Ctechnologiesinc.com, Bridgewater *Also called C Technologies Inc (G-810)*

Cubalas Emergency Lighting LLC (PA) 908 514-0505
340 Cox St Roselle (07203) *(G-9555)*

Cubist Pharmaceuticals LLC (HQ) 908 740-4000
2000 Galloping Hill Rd Kenilworth (07033) *(G-4933)*

Cuisinarts Division, East Windsor *Also called Conair Corporation (G-2348)*

Cuisine Innvtons Unlimited LLC 732 730-9310
180 Lehigh Ave Lakewood (08701) *(G-5077)*

Cultech Inc 732 225-2722
3500 Hadley Rd South Plainfield (07080) *(G-10244)*

Cumberland & Salem Guide, Bridgeton *Also called James Kinkade (G-760)*

Cumberland Dairy Inc (PA) 800 257-8484
899 Landis Ave Rosenhayn (08352) *(G-9594)*

Cumberland Dairy Inc 856 451-1300
80 Edward Ave Bridgeton (08302) *(G-757)*

Cumberland Marble & Monument 856 691-3334
2858 S West Blvd Vineland (08360) *(G-11207)*

Cumberland News Inc 856 691-2244
603 E Landis Ave Vineland (08360) *(G-11208)*

Cumberland Rcycl Corp S Jersey 856 825-4153
N Delsea Dr Millville (08332) *(G-6245)*

Cummins - Allison Corp 201 791-2394
495 Boulevard Ste 6 Elmwood Park (07407) *(G-2819)*

Cummins Inc 973 491-0100
435 Bergen Ave Kearny (07032) *(G-4853)*

Cummins-Allison, Elmwood Park *Also called Cummins - Allison Corp (G-2819)*

Cunningham Marine Hydraulics, Hoboken *Also called C M H Hele-Shaw Inc (G-4445)*

Cuny and Guerber Inc 201 617-5800
2100 Kerrigan Ave Union City (07087) *(G-11109)*

Cupcake Celebrations 973 885-0826
107 Paddock Dr Columbus (08022) *(G-1799)*

Cupcake Kitschen 862 221-8872
1042 Ash Dr Mahwah (07430) *(G-5725)*

Cura Biomed Inc 609 647-1474
103 S Longfellow Dr Princeton Junction (08550) *(G-9054)*

Curran & Connors Inc 609 514-0104
5 Independence Way # 300 Princeton (08540) *(G-8925)*

Curran-Pfeiff Corp 732 225-0555
Liddle Ave Edison (08837) *(G-2489)*

Current Newspaper LLC 609 383-8994
1000 W Washington Ave Pleasantville (08232) *(G-8809)*

Curtain Care Plus Inc 800 845-6155
17 Industrial St W Clifton (07012) *(G-1594)*

Curtiss-Wright Surface Tech, Paramus *Also called Metal Improvement Company LLC (G-7819)*

Curtiss-Wright Surfc Tech LLC (HQ) 201 843-7800
80 E Rte 4 Ste 310 Paramus (07652) *(G-7797)*

Curvon Corporation 732 747-3832
34 Apple St Tinton Falls (07724) *(G-10710)*

Custom Alloy Corporation (PA) 908 638-0257
3 Washington Ave Ste 5 High Bridge (08829) *(G-4281)*

Custom Auto Radiator Inc 609 242-9700
441 S Main St Forked River (08731) *(G-3539)*

Custom Barres LLC 848 245-9464
436 W Commodore Blvd # 28 Jackson (08527) *(G-4647)*

Custom Bedding Co 973 761-1100
1677 Springfield Ave Maplewood (07040) *(G-5875)*

Custom Blends Inc 215 934-7080
18 Graphics Dr Ewing (08628) *(G-3025)*

Custom Book Bindery Inc 973 815-1400
9 Sheridan Ave Clifton (07011) *(G-1595)*

Custom Building Products Inc 856 467-9226
2115 High Hill Rd Logan Township (08085) *(G-5586)*

Custom Business Software LLC 732 534-9557
87 Broad St Freehold (07728) *(G-3660)*

Custom Cabinets By Jim Bucko 609 522-6646
135 W Burk Ave Wildwood (08260) *(G-11943)*

Custom Chemicals Corp 201 791-5100
30 Paul Kohner Pl Elmwood Park (07407) *(G-2820)*

Custom Converters Inc 973 994-9000
115 Naylon Ave Livingston (07039) *(G-5509)*

Custom Counters By Precision 973 773-0111
11-17 Linden St Passaic (07055) *(G-8058)*

Custom Creations (PA) 201 651-9676
294 W Oakland Ave Oakland (07436) *(G-7622)*

Custom Decorators Service 973 625-0516
415 E Main St Ste 3 Denville (07834) *(G-2033)*

Custom Docks Inc 973 948-3732
234 Us Highway 206 N Sandyston (07826) *(G-9699)*

Custom Essence 732 249-6405
53 Veronica Ave Somerset (08873) *(G-9980)*

Custom Extrusion Tech Inc 732 367-5511
1650 Corporate Rd W Lakewood (08701) *(G-5078)*

Custom Fabricators Inc 908 862-4244
400 Commerce Rd Linden (07036) *(G-5339)*

Custom Gasket Mfg LLC 201 331-6363
640 E Palisade Ave # 201 Englewood Cliffs (07632) *(G-2966)*

Custom Golf, Oakland *Also called RCM Ltd Inc (G-7642)*

Custom Graphics of Vineland 856 691-7858
71 W Landis Ave Vineland (08360) *(G-11209)*

Custom Kitchen By Lubrich, Manasquan *Also called Michael Lubrich (G-5834)*

Custom Labels Inc 973 473-1934
345 Kaplan Dr Fairfield (07004) *(G-3177)*

Custom Laminations Inc 973 279-9174
932 Market St Paterson (07513) *(G-8166)*

Custom Liners Inc 732 940-0084
345 State Rt 17 Upper Saddle River (07458) *(G-11138)*

(G-0000) Company's Geographic Section entry number

Custom Metering Company Inc....973 946-4195
36 Mattison Ave Branchville (07826) *(G-706)*
Custom Mobile Food Equipment, Hammonton *Also called Custom Sales & Service Inc (G-4133)*
Custom Molders Corp....908 218-7997
160 Meister Ave Ste 1 Branchburg (08876) *(G-634)*
Custom Molders Group LLC (PA)....908 218-7997
160 Meister Ave Ste 1 Branchburg (08876) *(G-635)*
Custom Quick Label Inc....856 596-7555
300 Greentree Rd # 207 Marlton (08053) *(G-5926)*
Custom Roller Inc (PA)....908 298-7797
240b Columbus Ave Roselle (07203) *(G-9556)*
Custom Sales & Service Inc....609 561-6900
275 S 2nd Rd Hammonton (08037) *(G-4133)*
Custom Wood Furniture Inc....973 579-4880
37 E Clinton St Ste 1 Newton (07860) *(G-7340)*
Custom Woodwork, Red Bank *Also called F T Millwork Inc (G-9229)*
Custom Workflow Solutions LLC (PA)....917 647-9222
17 Broadway Fl 2 Florham Park (07932) *(G-3499)*
Customer Complaint Dept, Monmouth Junction *Also called Tris Pharma Inc (G-6315)*
Cusumano Perma-Rail Co....908 245-9281
213 W Westfield Ave Roselle Park (07204) *(G-9581)*
Cutler Bros Box & Lumber Co (PA)....201 943-2535
711 W Prospect Ave Fairview (07022) *(G-3359)*
Cutmark Inc....856 234-3428
102 Gaither Dr Ste 2 Mount Laurel (08054) *(G-6750)*
Cutter Drill & Machine Inc....732 206-1112
175 Ramtown Greenville Rd # 7 Howell (07731) *(G-4535)*
Cutting Board Company (PA)....908 725-0187
291 Route 22 E Bldg 6 Lebanon (08833) *(G-5258)*
Cutting Board Company....908 725-0187
2 Dreahook Rd Branchburg (08876) *(G-636)*
Cutting Edge Casting Inc....908 925-7500
1233 W Saint Georges Ave Linden (07036) *(G-5340)*
Cutting Edge Grower Supply LLC....732 905-9220
97 Glen Arden Dr Howell (07731) *(G-4536)*
Cutting Edge Industries, Linden *Also called Cutting Edge Casting Inc (G-5340)*
Cutting Edge Stencils, Ramsey *Also called Innovative Art Concepts LLC (G-9148)*
Cutting Records Inc....201 488-8444
190 Main St Ste 403 Hackensack (07601) *(G-3902)*
Cvc Specialty Chemicals Inc (HQ)....856 533-3000
844 N Lenola Rd V Moorestown (08057) *(G-6517)*
Cvc Thermoset Specialities, Maple Shade *Also called Emerald Performance Mtls LLC (G-5862)*
Cvc Thermoset Specialties, Moorestown *Also called Cvc Specialty Chemicals Inc (G-6517)*
CVE Inc....201 770-0005
5 N Corporate Dr Riverdale (07457) *(G-9374)*
CW Brown Foods Inc (PA)....856 423-3700
161 Kings Hwy Mount Royal (08061) *(G-6816)*
CW Brown Foods Inc....856 423-3700
161 Kings Hwy Mount Royal (08061) *(G-6817)*
Cw International Sales LLC....732 367-4444
600 James St Lakewood (08701) *(G-5079)*
Cwi Architectural Millwork LLC....856 307-7900
8 Deptford Rd Dept D Glassboro (08028) *(G-3808)*
Cws Software, Florham Park *Also called Custom Workflow Solutions LLC (G-3499)*
Cyalume Specialty Products Inc....732 469-7760
100 W Main St Ste A10 Bound Brook (08805) *(G-601)*
Cybage Software Inc....848 219-1221
500 College Rd E Ste 203 Princeton (08540) *(G-8926)*
Cyberextrudercom Inc....973 623-7900
1401 Valley Rd Ste 208 Wayne (07470) *(G-11491)*
Cyclacel Pharmaceuticals Inc (PA)....908 517-7330
200 Connell Dr Ste 1500 Berkeley Heights (07922) *(G-397)*
Cyclase Dynamics Inc....973 420-3259
16 E 27th St Barnegat Light (08006) *(G-165)*
Cygate Sftwr & Consulting LLC....732 452-1881
22 Meridian Rd Unit 9 Edison (08820) *(G-2490)*
Cypher Insurance Software....856 216-0575
32 Sunnybrook Rd Stratford (08084) *(G-10505)*
Cypress Pharmaceuticals Inc....601 856-4393
10 N Park Pl Ste 201 Morristown (07960) *(G-6657)*
Cytec Industries Inc....973 357-3100
504 Carnegie Ctr Princeton (08540) *(G-8927)*
Cytosorbents Corporation (PA)....732 329-8885
7 Deerpark Dr Ste K Monmouth Junction (08852) *(G-6285)*
Cytosorbents Medical Inc (HQ)....732 329-8885
7 Deerpark Dr Ste K Monmouth Junction (08852) *(G-6286)*
Cytotherm LP....609 396-1456
110 Sewell Ave Trenton (08610) *(G-10927)*
Czar Industries Inc....609 392-1515
1424-1426 Heath Ave Trenton (08638) *(G-10928)*
D & A Electronics Mfg....732 938-7400
5303 Asbury Rd Wall Township (07727) *(G-11333)*
D & A Granulation LLC....732 994-7480
1970 Rutgers Univ Blvd Lakewood (08701) *(G-5080)*
D & D Technology Inc....908 688-5154
254 Elmwood Ave Union (07083) *(G-11040)*
D & F Wicker Import Co Inc (PA)....973 736-5861
295 State Route 10 E Succasunna (07876) *(G-10511)*
D & G LLC....201 289-5750
29 1st St Apt 605 Hackensack (07601) *(G-3903)*
D & H Cutoff Co....908 454-4961
2600 State Route 57 Stewartsville (08886) *(G-10482)*
D & H Pallets LLC....973 481-2981
45 Verona Ave Newark (07104) *(G-7092)*
D & I Printing Co Inc....201 871-3620
23 Chestnut St Englewood (07631) *(G-2895)*
D & N Machine Co, Gloucester City *Also called D&N Machine Manufacturing Inc (G-3840)*
D & N Sporting Goods Inc....856 778-0055
109 W Park Dr Mount Laurel (08054) *(G-6751)*
D & S Companies LLC....973 832-4959
10 Myrtle Ave Wayne (07470) *(G-11492)*
D A F, Wyckoff *Also called Daf Products Inc (G-12108)*
D A K Office Services Inc....609 586-8222
3100 Quakerbridge Rd Trenton (08619) *(G-10929)*
D and M Discount Fuels....856 935-0919
383 E Broadway Salem (08079) *(G-9693)*
D C Herring Co, Eatontown *Also called Daniel C Herring Co Inc (G-2387)*
D D P, Hillside *Also called Diversified Display Pdts LLC (G-4389)*
D Depasquale Paving LLC....301 674-9775
1 Reagan Dr Jackson (08527) *(G-4648)*
D Electric Motors Inc....856 696-5959
94 W Sherman Ave Vineland (08360) *(G-11210)*
D J B Welding Inc....732 657-7478
1461 Toms River Rd Jackson (08527) *(G-4649)*
D K Tool & Die Welding Group (PA)....908 241-7600
181 W Clay Ave Roselle Park (07204) *(G-9582)*
D K Trading Inc....856 225-1130
941 S 2nd St Camden (08103) *(G-1057)*
D Kwitman & Son Inc (PA)....201 798-5511
1015 Adams St Hoboken (07030) *(G-4450)*
D L Imprints....732 493-8555
1701 Valley Rd Ste E Ocean (07712) *(G-7660)*
D L Printing Co Inc....732 750-1917
283 Prospect Ave Avenel (07001) *(G-125)*
D L V Lounge Inc....973 783-6988
300 Bloomfield Ave Montclair (07042) *(G-6362)*
D N D Corp....908 637-4343
13 Cemetery Rd Great Meadows (07838) *(G-3854)*
D P I, West Caldwell *Also called Direct Prtg Impressions Inc (G-11646)*
D P X, Parsippany *Also called Dpi Newco LLC (G-7919)*
D Paglia & Sons Inc....908 654-5999
280 Sheffield St Mountainside (07092) *(G-6839)*
D R Kenyon & Son Inc....908 722-0001
400 Us Highway 22 Bridgewater (08807) *(G-816)*
D R Printing, Parsippany *Also called Printing Industries LLC (G-8001)*
D S F Inc....908 218-5153
401 Us Highway 202 Raritan (08869) *(G-9209)*
D S F Millwork, Raritan *Also called D S F Inc (G-9209)*
D S Jh LLC....973 782-4086
107 Beaverbrook Rd Ste 3 Lincoln Park (07035) *(G-5298)*
D S M, Parsippany *Also called DSM Nutritional Products LLC (G-7922)*
D&B, Short Hills *Also called Dun & Bradstreet Inc (G-9868)*
D&E Nutraceuticals Inc....212 235-5200
700 Central Ave Farmingdale (07727) *(G-3383)*
D&N Machine Manufacturing Inc....856 456-1366
334 Nicholson Rd Gloucester City (08030) *(G-3840)*
D&S Fisheries LLC....914 438-3197
6 Birch Ln Colts Neck (07722) *(G-1780)*
D'Orazio Frozen Foods, Bellmawr *Also called DOrazio Foods Inc (G-330)*
D-K Tool & Die Welding, Roselle Park *Also called D K Tool & Die Welding Group (G-9582)*
D2cf LLC (PA)....973 699-4111
108 Coccio Dr West Orange (07052) *(G-11765)*
D3 Led LLC....201 583-9486
1609 54th St North Bergen (07047) *(G-7398)*
Da-Green Electronics Ltd....732 254-2735
4 Timber Ln Ste B Marlboro (07746) *(G-5894)*
Dab Design Inc....732 224-8686
331 Newman Springs Rd # 143 Red Bank (07701) *(G-9225)*
Daburn Electronics & Cable, Dover *Also called Daburn Wire & Cable Corp (G-2081)*
Daburn Wire & Cable Corp (PA)....973 328-3200
44 Richboynton Rd Dover (07801) *(G-2081)*
Daco Limited Partnership (PA)....973 263-1100
100 Fulton St Boonton (07005) *(G-548)*
Daddy Donkey Labs LLC....646 461-4677
115 Park Rd Fair Haven (07704) *(G-3079)*
Daf Products Inc....201 251-1222
420 Braen Ave Wyckoff (07481) *(G-12108)*
Daicel Chemtech Inc....201 461-4466
1 Parker Plz Fort Lee (07024) *(G-3553)*
Daiichi Sankyo Inc....908 992-6400
211 Mount Airy Rd Basking Ridge (07920) *(G-180)*
Daily Dollar LLC....732 236-9709
48 E Sedgwick St Monroe Township (08831) *(G-6331)*

ALPHABETIC

Daily News LP 212 210-2100
  125 Theodore Conrad Dr Jersey City (07305) *(G-4720)*

Daily Plan It Executive Center 609 514-9494
  707 Alexander Rd Ste 208 Princeton (08540) *(G-8928)*

Daily Targum, New Brunswick Also called Targum Publishing Company *(G-6973)*

Dainippon Sumitomo Pharma Amer (HQ) 201 592-2050
  1 Bridge Plz N Ste 510 Fort Lee (07024) *(G-3554)*

Dairy Delight LLC 201 939-7878
  1 Industrial Dr Rutherford (07070) *(G-9617)*

Dairy Deluxe Corp 845 549-0665
  153 Lawrence St Hackensack (07601) *(G-3904)*

Dairy Maid Confectionery Co 609 399-0100
  852 Boardwalk Ocean City (08226) *(G-7690)*

Dairy Queen, Clarksburg Also called Millstone Dq Inc *(G-1522)*

Dairy Queen 732 892-5700
  2506 Bridge Ave Point Pleasant Boro (08742) *(G-8842)*

Dairyland, Irvington Also called Agape Inc *(G-4553)*

DAKA Manufacturing LLC 908 782-0360
  19 Floral Rd Flemington (08822) *(G-3436)*

Dala Beauty LLC 732 380-7354
  1129 Broad St Ste 105 Shrewsbury (07702) *(G-9888)*

Dale Behre 908 850-4225
  108 East Ave Ste 6 Hackettstown (07840) *(G-4003)*

Dalemark Industries Inc 732 367-3100
  575 Prospect St Ste 211 Lakewood (08701) *(G-5081)*

Dales's Custom Auto & Sign, Hackettstown Also called Dale Behre *(G-4003)*

Dallas Group of America Inc (PA) 908 534-7800
  374 Rte 22 Whitehouse (08888) *(G-11915)*

Daman International Inc 917 945-9708
  105 Rye Rd Cherry Hill (08003) *(G-1355)*

Damascus Bakery Inc 718 855-1456
  60 Mcclellan St Newark (07114) *(G-7093)*

Damascus Bakery NJ LLC 718 855-1456
  60 Mcclellan St Newark (07114) *(G-7094)*

Damask Candies, Swedesboro Also called Damask Kandies *(G-10578)*

Damask Kandies 856 467-1661
  2255 Route 322 Swedesboro (08085) *(G-10578)*

Damco, Princeton Also called Accelerated Technologies Inc *(G-8899)*

DAmore Jewelers 201 945-0530
  731 Anderson Ave Cliffside Park (07010) *(G-1537)*

Dan Maguire Electrical Contr, West Berlin Also called Daniel Maguire *(G-11589)*

Dan Mar Jewelers, Union Also called Goldstein Setting Co Inc *(G-11060)*

Dana Automotive Inc 973 667-1234
  217 Darling Ave Nutley (07110) *(G-7584)*

Dana Poly Corp 800 474-1020
  85 Harrison St Dover Dover (07801) *(G-2082)*

DAngelo Metal Products Inc 908 862-8220
  360 Dalziel Rd Linden (07036) *(G-5341)*

Dani Leather USA Inc 973 598-0890
  37 Ironia Rd Ste 2 Flanders (07836) *(G-3404)*

Daniel & Ellissa, Carlstadt Also called New Top Inc *(G-1191)*

Daniel C Herring Co Inc 732 530-6557
  20 Meridian Rd Ste 6 Eatontown (07724) *(G-2387)*

Daniel Maguire 856 767-8443
  140 Collings Ave West Berlin (08091) *(G-11589)*

Danielle Die Cut Products Inc 973 278-3000
  238 Lindbergh Pl Ste 3 Paterson (07503) *(G-8167)*

Danline Inc 973 376-1000
  1 Silver Ct Springfield (07081) *(G-10438)*

Danline Quality Brushes, Springfield Also called Danline Inc *(G-10438)*

Danmar Press Inc 201 487-4400
  24 E Wesley St South Hackensack (07606) *(G-10154)*

Danmark Enterprises Inc 732 321-3366
  692 Oak Tree Ave South Plainfield (07080) *(G-10245)*

Danmola Lara 973 762-7581
  524 N Wyoming Ave South Orange (07079) *(G-10193)*

Danson Sheet Metal Inc 201 343-4876
  140 Atlantic St Hackensack (07601) *(G-3905)*

Dantco Corp 973 278-8776
  9 Oak St Paterson (07501) *(G-8168)*

Dantco Mixers, Paterson Also called Dantco Corp *(G-8168)*

Daq Electronics LLC 732 981-0050
  262 Old New Brunswick Rd B Piscataway (08854) *(G-8651)*

Dark City Brewery LLC 917 273-4995
  1001 Main St Asbury Park (07712) *(G-74)*

Darling Ingredients Inc 973 465-1900
  825 Wilson Ave Newark (07105) *(G-7095)*

DArtagnan Inc (PA) 973 344-0565
  600 Green Ln Union (07083) *(G-11041)*

Das Installations Inc 973 473-6858
  176 Saddle River Rd D Garfield (07026) *(G-3737)*

Dasco Supply LLC 973 884-1390
  150 Algonquin Pkwy Whippany (07981) *(G-11888)*

Dason Stainless Products Co 732 382-7272
  1773 Elizabeth Ave Rahway (07065) *(G-9087)*

Dassault Aircraft Svcs Corp (HQ) 201 440-6700
  200 Riser Rd Little Ferry (07643) *(G-5481)*

Dassault Procurement Svcs Inc (HQ) 201 261-4130
  200 Riser Rd Little Ferry (07643) *(G-5482)*

Data Base Access Systems Inc 973 335-0800
  60 Midvale Rd Ste 206 Mountain Lakes (07046) *(G-6822)*

Data Cntrum Communications Inc 201 391-1911
  135 Chestnut Ridge Rd # 2 Montvale (07645) *(G-6407)*

Data Communique Inc 201 508-6000
  65 Challenger Rd Fl 4 Ridgefield Park (07660) *(G-9302)*

Data Communique Intl Inc (HQ) 201 508-6000
  65 Challenger Rd Ste 400 Ridgefield Park (07660) *(G-9303)*

Data Delay Devices (PA) 973 202-3268
  3 Mount Prospect Ave Clifton (07013) *(G-1596)*

Data Medical Inc 800 790-9978
  2075 91st St North Bergen (07047) *(G-7399)*

Datacolor Inc (HQ) 609 924-2189
  5 Princess Rd Lawrenceville (08648) *(G-5229)*

Datalink Solutions Inc 973 731-9373
  27 Fundus Rd West Orange (07052) *(G-11766)*

Datamotion Inc (PA) 973 455-1245
  200 Park Ave Ste 302 Florham Park (07932) *(G-3500)*

Datapro International Inc 732 868-0588
  201 Circle Dr N Ste 101 Piscataway (08854) *(G-8652)*

Dataprobe Inc (PA) 201 934-9944
  1 Pearl Ct B Allendale (07401) *(G-7)*

Dataram Memory 609 799-0071
  777 Alexander Rd Ste 100 Princeton (08540) *(G-8929)*

Datascan Graphics Inc 973 543-4803
  55 Madison Ave Ste 400 Morristown (07960) *(G-6658)*

Datascope Corp (HQ) 973 244-6100
  15 Law Dr Fairfield (07004) *(G-3178)*

Datascope Corp 201 995-8000
  800 Macarthur Blvd Mahwah (07430) *(G-5726)*

Datascope Corp 201 995-8700
  1300 Macarthur Blvd Mahwah (07430) *(G-5727)*

Datascope Patient Monitoring, Mahwah Also called Datascope Corp *(G-5726)*

Datayog Inc 714 253-6558
  155 Morgan St Jersey City (07302) *(G-4721)*

Dato Company Inc (PA) 732 225-2272
  8 Plainsboro Rd Cranbury (08512) *(G-1829)*

Datwyler Pharma Packaging 856 663-2202
  9012 Pennsauken Hwy Pennsauken (08110) *(G-8410)*

Daum Inc (HQ) 862 210-8522
  368 Passaic Ave Ste 300 Fairfield (07004) *(G-3179)*

Dauphin North America, Boonton Also called Daco Limited Partnership *(G-548)*

Dauson Corrugated Container 973 827-1494
  3627 State Rt 23 Hamburg (07419) *(G-4089)*

Daven Industries Inc 973 808-8848
  55 Dwight Pl Fairfield (07004) *(G-3180)*

Daves Salad House Inc 908 965-0773
  577 Pennsylvania Ave Elizabeth (07201) *(G-2725)*

David Bradley Chocolatier Inc (PA) 609 443-4747
  92 N Main St Bldg 19 Windsor (08561) *(G-11995)*

David Bradley Chocolatier Inc. 732 536-7719
  520 Us Highway 9 Englishtown (07726) *(G-3001)*

David E Connolly Inc 908 654-4600
  1091 Bristol Rd Mountainside (07092) *(G-6840)*

David Gross Group, Lakewood Also called Mj Gross Company - NJ *(G-5138)*

David Leiz Custom Woodwork 908 486-1533
  2301 E Edgar Rd Bldg 5a Linden (07036) *(G-5342)*

David Mitchell Inc 856 429-2610
  3037 5th St Voorhees (08043) *(G-11284)*

David Ramsay, Moorestown Also called Ramsay David Cabinetmakers *(G-6562)*

David Sisco Jr 908 454-0880
  1223 S Main St Phillipsburg (08865) *(G-8548)*

Davidmark LLC 609 277-7361
  711 N Main St Ste 7 Pleasantville (08232) *(G-8810)*

Davion Inc (PA) 973 485-0793
  2 Progress Rd North Brunswick (08902) *(G-7464)*

Davis Center Inc 862 251-4637
  19 State Route 10 E # 25 Succasunna (07876) *(G-10512)*

Davis Hyundai 609 883-3500
  1655 N Olden Avenue Ext Ewing (08638) *(G-3026)*

Davis Hyundai & Mitsubishi, Ewing Also called Davis Hyundai *(G-3026)*

Davis Sign Systems Inc 973 394-9909
  65 Harrison St Boonton (07005) *(G-549)*

Davis-Standard LLC 908 722-6000
  220 Davidson Ave Ste 401 Somerset (08873) *(G-9981)*

Davlyn Industries Inc 609 655-5974
  366 Prncton Hightstown Rd East Windsor (08520) *(G-2349)*

Davy Jnes Swmming Pool Pnt Div, Trenton Also called Performance Industries Inc *(G-10972)*

Dawn Bible Students Assn 201 438-6421
  199 Railroad Ave East Rutherford (07073) *(G-2285)*

Dawnex Industries, Riverdale Also called Rainbow Metal Units Corp *(G-9381)*

Dax Haircare, Fairfield Also called Imperial Dax Co Inc *(G-3234)*

Daybrook Holdings Inc 973 538-6766
  161 Madison Ave Ste 200 Morristown (07960) *(G-6659)*

Daysequerra Corporation (PA) 856 719-9900
  7209 Browning Rd Pennsauken (08109) *(G-8411)*

Daysol Inc 908 272-5900
  40 Boright Ave Kenilworth (07033) *(G-4934)*

Dayton Grey Corp 732 869-0060
1008 1st Ave Asbury Park (07712) *(G-75)*

Db Designs Inc 732 616-5018
10 Damascus Dr Marlboro (07746) *(G-5895)*

DBC Inc 212 819-1177
300 Frank W Burr Blvd # 56 Teaneck (07666) *(G-10626)*

Dbmcorp Inc 201 677-0008
32a Spruce St Oakland (07436) *(G-7623)*

DC Fabricators Inc 609 499-3000
801 W Front St Florence (08518) *(G-3474)*

Dcg Printing Inc 732 530-4441
661 State Rte 35 Shrewsbury (07702) *(G-9889)*

DCI Signs & Awnings Inc 973 350-0400
110 Riverside Ave Newark (07104) *(G-7096)*

Dcm Clean Air Products Inc 732 363-2100
1650 Oak St Lakewood (08701) *(G-5082)*

Dcm Group Inc 732 516-1173
563 Broad St Newark (07102) *(G-7097)*

Ddm Steel Cnstr Ltd Lblty Co 856 794-9400
3659 N Delsea Dr Vineland (08360) *(G-11211)*

De Ditrich Process Systems Inc (PA) 908 317-2585
244 Sheffield St Mountainside (07092) *(G-6841)*

De Jong Iron Works Inc 973 684-1633
223 Godwin Ave 231 Paterson (07501) *(G-8169)*

De Leon Plastics Corp 973 653-3480
473 Getty Ave Paterson (07503) *(G-8170)*

De Rossi & Son Co Inc 856 691-0061
411 S 6th St Vineland (08360) *(G-11212)*

De Saussure Equipment Co Inc 201 845-6517
23 W Howcroft Rd Maywood (07607) *(G-6003)*

De Zaio Productions Inc 973 423-5000
20-10 Maple Ave Bldg 31c Fair Lawn (07410) *(G-3095)*

Dealaman Enterprises Inc 908 647-5533
214 Mountainview Rd Warren (07059) *(G-11407)*

Deans Graphics 609 261-8817
16 Mill St Ste D Mount Holly (08060) *(G-6724)*

Dearborn A Belden Cdt Company (HQ) 908 925-8000
711 Lidgerwood Ave Elizabeth (07202) *(G-2726)*

Deb El Food Products LLC 908 409-0010
2 Papetti Plz Elizabeth (07206) *(G-2727)*

Deb El Food Products LLC (PA) 908 351-0330
520 Broad St Fl 6 Newark (07102) *(G-7098)*

Deb El Foods, Newark *Also called Deb El Food Products LLC* *(G-7098)*

Deb Maintenance Inc 856 786-0440
1000 Union Landing Rd Cinnaminson (08077) *(G-1448)*

Deb-El Foods Corporation 908 351-0330
520 Broad St Newark (07102) *(G-7099)*

Deborah Sales & Mfg Co 973 344-8466
109 Meeker Ave Newark (07114) *(G-7100)*

Deckhouse Communications Inc 201 961-5564
1275 Bloomfield Ave Ste 7 Fairfield (07004) *(G-3181)*

Decorating With Fabric Inc 845 352-5064
1 Broadway Park Ridge (07656) *(G-7847)*

Decoration Operations, Williamstown *Also called Piramal Glass - Usa Inc (G-11970)*

Decorative Iron Works, Paterson *Also called Joseph Monga Jr (G-8226)*

Dee & L LLC 201 858-0138
67 Lefante Dr Bayonne (07002) *(G-213)*

Dee Jay Printing Inc 973 227-7787
16 Passaic Ave Unit 3 Fairfield (07004) *(G-3182)*

Deep Foods Inc (PA) 908 810-7500
1090 Springfield Rd Ste 1 Union (07083) *(G-11042)*

Deer Out Animal Repellant LLC 908 769-4242
3651 S Clinton Ave South Plainfield (07080) *(G-10246)*

Deerbrook Fabrics, Guttenberg *Also called O Stitch Matic Inc (G-3871)*

Defense Photonics Group Inc 908 822-1075
126 Corporate Blvd Ste A South Plainfield (07080) *(G-10247)*

Defense Spport Svcs Intl 2 LLC 856 866-2200
901 Lincoln Dr W Ste 200 Marlton (08053) *(G-5927)*

Defense Support Svcs Intl LLC (HQ) 850 390-4737
901 Lincoln Dr W Ste 200 Marlton (08053) *(G-5928)*

Defined Pro Machining LLC 973 891-1038
105 W Dewey Ave Ste 419 Wharton (07885) *(G-11855)*

Degussa, Parsippany *Also called Evonik Corporation (G-7938)*

Deitz Co Inc 732 295-8212
1750 Hwy 34 Belmar (07719) *(G-348)*

Deitz, Michael & Sons, Hillside *Also called M Deitz & Sons Inc (G-4412)*

Dejana Trck Grter Philadelphia, Cinnaminson *Also called Dejana Trck Utility Eqp Co LLC (G-1449)*

Dejana Trck Utility Eqp Co LLC 856 303-1315
2502 Route 130 N Cinnaminson (07077) *(G-1449)*

Dek Tron International Corp 908 226-1777
244 E 3rd St Plainfield (07060) *(G-8761)*

Del Bakers Inc 856 461-0089
412 Kossuth St Riverside (08075) *(G-9393)*

Del Buono Bakery Inc 856 546-9585
319 Black Horse Pike Haddon Heights (08035) *(G-4045)*

Del-Val Food Ingredients Inc 856 778-6623
3001 Irwin Rd Ste A Mount Laurel (08054) *(G-6752)*

Delair LLC 856 663-2900
9000 River Rd Pennsauken (08110) *(G-8412)*

Delaware Pipeline Company LLC 973 455-7500
1 Sylvan Way Ste 2 Parsippany (07054) *(G-7913)*

Delaware Technologies Inc 856 234-7692
641 Mount Laurel Rd Mount Laurel (08054) *(G-6753)*

Delaware Valley Box & Lbr Co, Trenton *Also called Bunn Industries Incorporated (G-10907)*

Delaware Valley Installation 856 546-0097
200 Evergreen Rd Runnemede (08078) *(G-9605)*

Delaware Valley News, Frenchtown *Also called Hunterdon County Democrat Inc (G-3713)*

Delaware Valley Sign Corp (PA) 609 386-0100
112 Connecticut Dr Burlington (08016) *(G-962)*

Delaware Valley Vault, Blackwood *Also called Bradbury Burial Vault Co Inc (G-461)*

Delaware Valley Vault Co Inc 856 227-2555
761 Lower Landing Rd Blackwood (08012) *(G-463)*

Deleet Merchandising Corp (PA) 212 962-6565
26 Blanchard St Newark (07105) *(G-7101)*

Delgard Premier Alum Fencing, Pennsauken *Also called Delair LLC (G-8412)*

Delgen Press Inc 973 472-2266
250 Delawanna Ave Clifton (07014) *(G-1597)*

Delicious Bagels Inc (PA) 732 892-9265
2259 Bridge Ave Point Pleasant Boro (08742) *(G-8843)*

Delicious Fresh Pierogi Inc 908 245-0550
594 Chestnut St Roselle Park (07204) *(G-9583)*

Delight Foods USA LLC 201 369-1199
438 Saint Pauls Ave Jersey City (07306) *(G-4722)*

Delisa Pallet Corp 732 667-7070
116 South Ave Middlesex (08846) *(G-6111)*

Dell Aquila Baking Company 201 886-0613
308 W Hudson Ave Englewood (07631) *(G-2896)*

Dell Software Inc 201 556-4600
80 Parkway Rochelle Park (07662) *(G-9422)*

Delmhorst Instrument Company 973 334-2557
51 Indian Ln E Towaco (07082) *(G-10868)*

Delphian Corporation 201 767-7300
220 Pegasus Ave Northvale (07647) *(G-7521)*

Delsea Pipe Inc 856 589-9374
445 Delsea Dr Sewell (08080) *(G-9839)*

Delta Circuits Inc 973 575-3000
26 Spielman Rd Fairfield (07004) *(G-3183)*

Delta Cooling Towers Inc (PA) 973 586-2201
185 Us Highway 206 Flanders (07836) *(G-3405)*

Delta Corrugated Ppr Pdts Corp 201 941-1910
199 W Ruby Ave Palisades Park (07650) *(G-7772)*

Delta Galil USA Inc (HQ) 201 902-0055
1 Harmon Plz Fl 5 Secaucus (07094) *(G-9760)*

Delta Lambskin Products Inc 201 871-9233
595 Ridge Rd Englewood (07631) *(G-2897)*

Delta Paper Corporation 856 532-0333
122 Kissel Rd Burlington (08016) *(G-963)*

Delta Procurement Inc 201 623-9353
400 Gotham Pkwy Carlstadt (07072) *(G-1149)*

Delta Sales Company Inc 973 838-0371
1355 State Rt 23 Butler (07405) *(G-999)*

Deltech Resins Co (PA) 973 589-0880
49 Rutherford St Newark (07105) *(G-7102)*

Deltronics Corporation 856 825-8200
22 Easterwood St Millville (08332) *(G-6246)*

Delucca's Bakery, Riverside *Also called Del Bakers Inc (G-9393)*

Deluxe Check Printers, Mountain Lakes *Also called Deluxe Corporation (G-6823)*

Deluxe Corporation 973 334-8000
105 Route 46 W Mountain Lakes (07046) *(G-6823)*

Deluxe Foods International 862 257-1909
29 E 25th St Paterson (07514) *(G-8171)*

Deluxe Gourmet Spc Ltd Lblty 732 485-7519
85 Corona Ct Old Bridge (08857) *(G-7714)*

Deluxe Innovations Inc 201 857-5880
140 Greenwood Ave Ste 2a Midland Park (07432) *(G-6174)*

Delva Tool & Machine Corp (PA) 856 786-8700
1603 Industrial Hwy Cinnaminson (08077) *(G-1450)*

Delva Tool & Machine Corp 856 829-0109
1911 Rowland St Cinnaminson (08077) *(G-1451)*

Delvco Pharma Packg Svcs Inc 973 278-2500
150 E 7th St Paterson (07524) *(G-8172)*

Demaio Inc 609 965-4094
543 Columbia Rd Egg Harbor City (08215) *(G-2657)*

Demand LLC 908 526-2020
36 S Adamsville Rd 1 Somerville (08876) *(G-10107)*

Demco Scientific Glassware Inc 856 327-7898
25 N 6th St Millville (08332) *(G-6247)*

Demountable Concepts Inc 856 863-3081
200 Acorn Rd Glassboro (08028) *(G-3809)*

Denali Company LLC (PA) 732 219-7771
211 Broad St Red Bank (07701) *(G-9226)*

Denby USA Limited 800 374-6479
1065 Rte 22 Ste 3b Bridgewater (08807) *(G-817)*

Deneka Printing Systems Inc (PA) 609 752-0964
100c Goldman Dr Cream Ridge (08514) *(G-1934)*

Dengen Scientific Corporation 201 687-2983
315 4th St Union City (07087) *(G-11110)*

Denmatt Industries LLC 609 689-0099
2080 E State Street Ext Hamilton (08619) ***(G-4105)***
Dennis Kessler Steel Rule Die, West Berlin *Also called Kessler Steel Rule Die Inc* ***(G-11602)***
Dental Designs, Garfield *Also called Dental Models & Designs Inc* ***(G-3738)***
Dental Manufacturing, Pennsauken *Also called E P R Industries Inc* ***(G-8416)***
Dental Models & Designs Inc 973 472-8009
20 Passaic St Ste 3 Garfield (07026) ***(G-3738)***
Dentalworx Lab Ltd Lblty Co 732 981-9096
1000 New Durham Rd Edison (08817) ***(G-2491)***
Dentamach Inc 973 334-2220
14 Walsh Dr Ste 102 Parsippany (07054) ***(G-7914)***
Dentistry Today Inc 973 882-4700
100 Passaic Ave Ste 220 Fairfield (07004) ***(G-3184)***
Denton Vacuum LLC 856 439-9100
1259 N Church St Moorestown (08057) ***(G-6518)***
Denville Dairy, Denville *Also called Rolo Systems* ***(G-2055)***
Denville Diagnostic Imaging, Denville *Also called Denville Diagnostics Imaging* ***(G-2034)***
Denville Diagnostics Imaging 973 586-1212
161 E Main St Ste 101 Denville (07834) ***(G-2034)***
Deosen Usa Inc 908 382-6518
1140 Stelton Rd Ste 205 Piscataway (08854) ***(G-8653)***
Dependable Precision Products 973 887-3304
42 Schindler Ct Parsippany (07054) ***(G-7915)***
Deptford Plating Co Inc 856 227-1144
Dein Ave Rr 41 Deptford (08096) ***(G-2063)***
Derma Sciences Inc (HQ) 609 514-4744
311 Enterprise Dr Plainsboro (08536) ***(G-8784)***
Dermarite Industries LLC 973 247-3491
7777 W Side Ave North Bergen (07047) ***(G-7400)***
Dermatological Soc of NJ Inc 856 546-5600
208 White Horse Pike Barrington (08007) ***(G-171)***
Deroche Canvas, Belvidere *Also called Pv Deroche LLC* ***(G-365)***
Derv2000 ....503 470-9158
420 Belgrove Dr Kearny (07032) ***(G-4854)***
Desi Talk LLC (PA) 212 675-7515
35 Journal Sq Ste 204 Jersey City (07306) ***(G-4723)***
Desiere Electric Motor Service, Vineland *Also called Phil Desiere Electric Mtr Svc* ***(G-11251)***
Design & Molding Services Inc 732 752-0300
25 Howard St Piscataway (08854) ***(G-8654)***
Design Assistance Corporation 856 241-9500
3 Killdeer Ct Ste 301 Swedesboro (08085) ***(G-10579)***
Design Display Group Inc (PA) 201 438-6000
105 Amor Ave Carlstadt (07072) ***(G-1150)***
Design Factory Nj Inc 908 964-8833
1210 Liberty Ave Hillside (07205) ***(G-4388)***
Design N Stitch Inc 201 488-1314
107 Pink St Hackensack (07601) ***(G-3906)***
Design of Tomorrow Inc 973 227-1000
24 Sherwood Ln Fairfield (07004) ***(G-3185)***
Design Productions Inc 201 447-5656
9 Industrial Park Waldwick (07463) ***(G-11300)***
Designcore Ltd 718 499-0337
585 Windsor Dr Ste 1 Secaucus (07094) ***(G-9761)***
Designer, Garfield *Also called US Magic Box Inc* ***(G-3775)***
Designer Bagel, South Plainfield *Also called Danmark Enterprises Inc* ***(G-10245)***
Designer Kitchens 732 370-5500
250 Faraday Ave Jackson (08527) ***(G-4650)***
Designer Sign Systems LLC 212 939-5577
50 Broad St Carlstadt (07072) ***(G-1151)***
Designs By James 856 692-1316
892 N Delsea Dr Vineland (08360) ***(G-11213)***
Desisti Lighting, Mountainside *Also called I-Light Usa Inc* ***(G-6847)***
Dessau Company, Fair Lawn *Also called Dessau International* ***(G-3096)***
Dessau International 201 791-2005
15-01 Pollitt Dr Ste 10 Fair Lawn (07410) ***(G-3096)***
Destiny Foundation 732 987-9008
564 Marc Dr Lakewood (08701) ***(G-5083)***
Detail Doctor, Shrewsbury *Also called Cemp Inc* ***(G-9884)***
Detailed Designs, Plainfield *Also called Injectron Corporation* ***(G-8769)***
Details, Englewood *Also called Sabrimax Corp* ***(G-2938)***
Detergent 20 LLC 732 545-0200
594 Jersey Ave New Brunswick (08901) ***(G-6919)***
Determine Inc 800 608-0809
200 Lake Dr E Cherry Hill (08002) ***(G-1356)***
Detrex Corporation 856 786-8686
835 Industrial Hwy Ste 1 Cinnaminson (08077) ***(G-1452)***
Devatal Inc 609 586-1575
644 Newkirk Ave Trenton (08610) ***(G-10930)***
Devco Corporation 201 337-1600
131 Morristown Rd Bldg B Basking Ridge (07920) ***(G-181)***
Devece & Shaffer Inc 856 829-7282
400 Legion Ave Palmyra (08065) ***(G-7782)***
Devon Products 732 438-3855
230 W Parkway Ste 3 Pompton Plains (07444) ***(G-8862)***
Devon Trading Corp 973 812-9190
5 Fairfield Rd Caldwell (07006) ***(G-1022)***
Dew Associates Inc 973 702-0545
7 Armstrong Rd Sussex (07461) ***(G-10557)***
Dewalt Industrial Tools, Elmwood Park *Also called Black & Decker (us) Inc* ***(G-2812)***
Dewalt Manufacturing Co Inc 856 423-1207
88 W Cohawkin Rd Clarksboro (08020) ***(G-1518)***
Dewechter Inc 856 845-0225
58 S Broad St Woodbury (08096) ***(G-12027)***
Dewey Electronics Corporation (PA) 201 337-4700
27 Muller Rd Oakland (07436) ***(G-7624)***
Dewey Electronics Corporation 201 337-4700
27 Muller Rd Oakland (07436) ***(G-7625)***
Dewitt Bros Tool Co Inc 908 298-3700
140 Market St Kenilworth (07033) ***(G-4935)***
Dewy Meadow Farms Inc (PA) 908 218-5655
1018 Rector Rd Bridgewater (08807) ***(G-818)***
Dewy Meadow Foods, Inc., Bridgewater *Also called Dewy Meadow Farms Inc* ***(G-818)***
Dex-O-Tex Floor Coverings, Roselle Park *Also called Crossfield Products Corp* ***(G-9580)***
Dexmed Inc 732 831-0507
433 N Broad St Fl 1 Elizabeth (07208) ***(G-2728)***
Dexmed LLC 732 831-0507
433 N Broad St Fl 1 Elizabeth (07208) ***(G-2729)***
Dezine Line Inc 973 989-1009
17 Robert St Ste B2 Wharton (07885) ***(G-11856)***
DFI America LLC 732 562-0693
15 Corporate Pl S Ste 201 Piscataway (08854) ***(G-8655)***
Dg3 Group America Inc (HQ) 201 793-5000
100 Burma Rd Jersey City (07305) ***(G-4724)***
Dg3 Holdings LLC (HQ) 201 793-5000
100 Burma Rd Jersey City (07305) ***(G-4725)***
Dg3 North America Inc 201 793-5000
100 Burma Rd Jersey City (07305) ***(G-4726)***
Di-Ferraro Inc 973 694-7200
28 Burgess Pl Wayne (07470) ***(G-11493)***
Diabeto Inc 646 397-3175
200 Centennial Ave # 200 Piscataway (08854) ***(G-8656)***
Diacritech LLC 732 238-1157
201 Marin Blvd Apt 1112 Jersey City (07302) ***(G-4727)***
Diagenode Inc 862 209-4680
400 Morris Ave Ste 101 Denville (07834) ***(G-2035)***
Diagnostix Plus Inc 201 530-5505
811 Queen Anne Rd Teaneck (07666) ***(G-10627)***
Dialight Corporation (HQ) 732 751-5809
1501 Hwy 34 Wall Township (07727) ***(G-11334)***
Dialogic Inc (HQ) 973 967-6000
4 Gatehall Dr Ste 9 Parsippany (07054) ***(G-7916)***
Diamex International Corp (PA) 973 838-8844
23 Birch Rd Kinnelon (07405) ***(G-5016)***
Diamond Bright Metal Proc, Middlesex *Also called Stainless Stock* ***(G-6153)***
Diamond Chip Realty LLC 973 383-4651
33 Demarest Rd Sparta (07871) ***(G-10386)***
Diamond Essence, Edison *Also called Meeshaa Inc* ***(G-2561)***
Diamond Foods USA Inc 732 543-2186
599 Nassau St North Brunswick (08902) ***(G-7465)***
Diamond Hut Jewelry Exchange 201 332-5372
Hudson Mall Rr 440 Jersey City (07304) ***(G-4728)***
Diamond Machine Co Inc 609 490-8940
30 N Valley Rd Roosevelt (08555) ***(G-9528)***
Diamond Sand & Gravel, Sparta *Also called Diamond Chip Realty LLC* ***(G-10386)***
Diamond Scooters Inc 609 646-0003
645 S Mill Rd Ste 1 Absecon (08201) ***(G-2)***
Diamond Sg Intl Ltd Lblty Co 732 861-9850
20 Meridian Rd Ste 9 Eatontown (07724) ***(G-2388)***
Diamond Universe LLC 201 592-9500
2460 Lemoine Ave Ste 302 Fort Lee (07024) ***(G-3555)***
Diamond Wholesale Co 201 727-9595
30 Congress Dr Moonachie (07074) ***(G-6462)***
Diane Matson Inc 609 288-6833
49 Brighton Rd Westampton (08060) ***(G-11785)***
Diaz Wholesale & Mfg Co Inc 404 629-3616
4 Rosol Ln Saddle Brook (07663) ***(G-9649)***
Dicalite Minerals Corp 856 320-2919
9111 River Rd Pennsauken (08110) ***(G-8413)***
Dicar Inc (HQ) 973 575-1377
30 Chapin Rd Ste 1212 Pine Brook (07058) ***(G-8596)***
Dicar Inc 973 575-4220
5 Bader Rd Pine Brook (07058) ***(G-8597)***
Dicar Diamond Tool Corp 973 684-0949
108 Kentucky Ave Paterson (07503) ***(G-8173)***
Die Tech LLC 201 343-8324
58 Mckinley St Hackensack (07601) ***(G-3907)***
Dietech Services LLC 973 667-0798
40 Holmes St Nutley (07110) ***(G-7585)***
Difco Laboratories Inc (HQ) 410 316-4113
1 Becton Dr Franklin Lakes (07417) ***(G-3619)***
Digipol Technologies, Denville *Also called Rudolph Instruments Inc* ***(G-2056)***
Digitails, West Berlin *Also called Spaghetti Engineering Corp* ***(G-11623)***
Digital Arts Imaging LLC 908 237-4646
105 State Route 31 Ste 10 Flemington (08822) ***(G-3437)***
Digital Atelier LLC 609 890-6666
60 Sculptors Way Ste A Trenton (08619) ***(G-10931)***

Digital Binscom LLC 908 867-7055
59 E Mill Rd Ste 1-103 Long Valley (07853) *(G-5609)*

Digital Color Concepts Inc 908 264-0504
256 Sheffield St Mountainside (07092) *(G-6842)*

Digital Design Inc 973 857-9500
67 Sand Park Rd Cedar Grove (07009) *(G-1274)*

Digital Documents Inc 609 520-0094
101 Main St Princeton (08540) *(G-8930)*

Digital Lizard LLC 201 684-0900
500 Corporate Dr Mahwah (07430) *(G-5728)*

Digital Outdoor Advg LLC 732 616-2232
788 Shrewsbury Ave Ste 22 Tinton Falls (07724) *(G-10711)*

Digital Print Solutions Inc 973 263-1890
5 Eastmans Rd Parsippany (07054) *(G-7917)*

Digital Printed Communications, Morristown *Also called Pica Printings Inc* *(G-6693)*

Digital Productions Inc 856 224-1111
100 Berkeley Dr Ste B Swedesboro (08085) *(G-10580)*

Digitize Inc 973 663-1011
158 Edison Rd Lake Hopatcong (07849) *(G-5036)*

Digitron Electronic Corp 908 245-2012
144 Market St Kenilworth (07033) *(G-4936)*

Digivac Company 732 765-0900
105 B Church St Ste 4 Matawan (07747) *(G-5972)*

Dihco Inc 201 327-0518
612 E Crescent Ave Ste A Upper Saddle River (07458) *(G-11139)*

Dijon Enterprises LLC 201 876-9463
21 Curie Ave Wallington (07057) *(G-11384)*

Dikeman Laminating Corporation 973 473-5696
181 Sargeant Ave Clifton (07013) *(G-1598)*

Diligaf Enterprises Inc (HQ) 201 684-0900
500 Corporate Dr Mahwah (07430) *(G-5729)*

Dim Inc 908 925-2043
10 Grant St Linden (07036) *(G-5343)*

Dimensional Communications Inc 201 767-1500
1595 Macarthur Blvd Mahwah (07430) *(G-5730)*

Dimilo Industries 973 955-0460
90 Dayton Ave Ste 38 Passaic (07055) *(G-8059)*

Dina Hernandez 973 772-8883
236 Harrison Ave Ste A Lodi (07644) *(G-5558)*

Ding Moo LLC 973 881-8622
18 Alabama Ave Paterson (07503) *(G-8174)*

Dingmans Dairy, Paterson *Also called Ding Moo LLC* *(G-8174)*

Diocesan Media Center, The, Camden *Also called Diocese of Camden New Jersey* *(G-1058)*

Diocese of Camden New Jersey (PA) 856 756-7900
631 Market St Camden (08102) *(G-1058)*

Diocese of Paterson 973 279-8845
597 Valley Rd Clifton (07013) *(G-1599)*

Diopsys Inc 973 244-0622
16 Chapin Rd Ste 912 Pine Brook (07058) *(G-8598)*

Dippin Chips, Montclair *Also called Thats How We Roll LLC* *(G-6392)*

Direct Computer Resources Inc (PA) 201 848-0018
120 Birch Rd Franklin Lakes (07417) *(G-3620)*

Direct Development LLC 732 739-8890
97 Apple St 2 Tinton Falls (07724) *(G-10712)*

Direct Prtg Impressions Inc 973 227-6111
33 Fairfield Pl West Caldwell (07006) *(G-11646)*

Direct Sales and Services Inc 973 340-4480
141 Lanza Ave Bldg 8 Garfield (07026) *(G-3739)*

Directory & Almanac, Newark *Also called Advocate Publishing Corp* *(G-7036)*

Disc Makers Inc 800 468-9353
7905 N Crescent Blvd Pennsauken (08110) *(G-8414)*

Discount Digital Print LLC 201 659-9600
422 11th St Union City (07087) *(G-11111)*

Discount Pillow Factory LLC 973 444-1617
90 Dayton Ave Passaic (07055) *(G-8060)*

Discovery Map 973 868-4552
19 Wetmore Ave Morristown (07960) *(G-6660)*

Discovery Semiconductors Inc 609 434-1311
119 Silvia St Ewing (08628) *(G-3027)*

Dishman Usa Inc 732 560-4300
476 Union Ave Ste 2 Middlesex (08846) *(G-6112)*

Dispersion Technology Inc 732 364-4488
1885 Swarthmore Ave Lakewood (08701) *(G-5084)*

Display Equation LLC 201 343-4135
135 Spring Valley Ave Hackensack (07601) *(G-3908)*

Display Impressions 856 488-1777
8400a Remington Ave Pennsauken (08110) *(G-8415)*

Display Pro Manufacturing, Kenilworth *Also called Daysol Inc* *(G-4934)*

Disposable Hygiene LLC (PA) 973 779-1982
60 Page Rd Clifton (07012) *(G-1600)*

Distek Inc 732 422-7585
121 N Center Dr North Brunswick (08902) *(G-7466)*

Distinctive Wdwrk By Rob Hoffm 609 877-8122
703 Van Rossum Ave Unit 1 Beverly (08010) *(G-450)*

Distinctive Woodwork Inc 609 714-8505
70 Stacy Haines Rd Ste D Lumberton (08048) *(G-5628)*

Distributor Label Products 908 704-9997
51 Old Camplain Rd Hillsborough (08844) *(G-4312)*

Disys Commerce Inc 201 567-0457
100 W Forest Ave Ste H Englewood (07631) *(G-2898)*

Diversatech Inc 609 730-9668
1584 Reed Rd Pennington (08534) *(G-8363)*

Diversfied Globl Grphics Group, Jersey City *Also called Dg3 Holdings LLC* *(G-4725)*

Diversfied Globl Grphics Group, Jersey City *Also called Dg3 North America Inc* *(G-4726)*

Diversfield Impressions, Irvington *Also called Diversified Impressions Inc* *(G-4564)*

Diversified Display Pdts LLC 908 686-2200
777 Ramsey Ave Hillside (07205) *(G-4389)*

Diversified Fab Pdts Ltd Lblty 973 773-3189
158 River Rd Clifton (07014) *(G-1601)*

Diversified Fixtures, Lakewood *Also called Vitillo & Sons Inc* *(G-5177)*

Diversified Foam Products Inc 856 662-1981
121 High Hill Rd Swedesboro (08085) *(G-10581)*

Diversified Heat Transfer Inc 800 221-1522
439 Main Rd Towaco (07082) *(G-10869)*

Diversified Impressions Inc 973 399-9041
119 Coit St Irvington (07111) *(G-4564)*

Diversified Industries, Swedesboro *Also called Diversified Foam Products Inc* *(G-10581)*

Diversitech Inc 973 835-2900
18 Hamburg Tpke Riverdale (07457) *(G-9375)*

Diversity Direct, Monmouth Junction *Also called Real Soft Inc* *(G-6308)*

Diversity In Action, Roseland *Also called Know America Media LLC* *(G-9540)*

Diversity/Careers In Enginrng, Springfield *Also called Renard Commumnications Inc* *(G-10464)*

Divine Printing 732 632-8800
131 Liberty St Metuchen (08840) *(G-6054)*

Division Name Process Systems, Mickleton *Also called Saint-Gobain Prfmce Plas Corp* *(G-6088)*

DJeet 732 224-8887
637 Broad St Shrewsbury (07702) *(G-9890)*

Dksh Luxury & Lifestyle N Amer 609 750-8800
9 Princess Rd Ste D Lawrence Township (08648) *(G-5216)*

Dlite Products Inc 201 444-0822
540 Ravine Ct Wyckoff (07481) *(G-12109)*

Dm Graphic Center LLC 973 882-8990
26 Commerce Rd Ste L Fairfield (07004) *(G-3186)*

Dma Data Industries Inc 201 444-5733
479 Goffle Rd Wyckoff (07481) *(G-12110)*

DMC, Edison *Also called Dollfus Mieg Company Inc* *(G-2492)*

DMC Soft, Cherry Hill *Also called Automated Office Inc* *(G-1341)*

DMD Stairs & Rails LLC 732 901-0102
370 Whitesville Rd Ste 8 Jackson (08527) *(G-4651)*

Dmf Associated Engines LLC 973 535-9773
W Hobart Gap Rd Livingston (07039) *(G-5510)*

Dmg, Edison *Also called Aerogroup Retail Holdings Inc* *(G-2448)*

Dmg America LLC 201 894-5500
65 Challenger Rd Ste 340 Ridgefield Park (07660) *(G-9304)*

Dmg Mori Seiki, Rockaway *Also called Dmg Mori Usa Inc* *(G-9453)*

Dmg Mori Usa Inc 973 257-9620
400 Commons Way Ste A Rockaway (07866) *(G-9453)*

DMJ and Associates Inc 732 613-7867
27 William St Sayreville (08872) *(G-9708)*

DMJ Industrial Services LLC 973 692-8406
1 Hilltop Ter Wayne (07470) *(G-11494)*

DMJ Technologies LLC 201 261-5560
775 Maple St New Milford (07646) *(G-6989)*

Dmr Sign Systems, Dover *Also called Envirnmntal Dsign Grphic Entps* *(G-2083)*

DMS Inc 973 928-3040
218 Little Falls Rd 7-8 Cedar Grove (07009) *(G-1275)*

DMS Laboratories Inc 908 782-3353
2 Darts Mill Rd Flemington (08822) *(G-3438)*

Dmv-Fnterra Excipients USA LLC 609 858-2111
61 S Paramus Rd Ste 535 Paramus (07652) *(G-7798)*

Dmz Industries, Fairfield *Also called Control & Power Systems Inc* *(G-3175)*

Dnp Foods America Ltd Lblty Co 201 654-5581
2 Dipippo Ct Waldwick (07463) *(G-11301)*

DO Productions LLC 856 866-3566
11 Gregg St Lodi (07644) *(G-5559)*

Docbox Solutions Ltd Lblty Co 201 650-0970
140 Upper Mountain Ave Montclair (07042) *(G-6363)*

Dock Resins Corporation 908 862-2351
76 Porcupine Rd Pedricktown (08067) *(G-8348)*

Doctor Tee Shirt, Manasquan *Also called J & G Graphics Inc* *(G-5832)*

Document Concepts Inc 856 251-1975
1040 Mantua Pike Wenonah (08090) *(G-11575)*

Document Depot, Princeton *Also called Digital Documents Inc* *(G-8930)*

Doddle & Co LLC 917 836-1299
41 Watchung Plz Ste 354 Montclair (07042) *(G-6364)*

Dodson Global Inc 732 238-7001
27 Cotters Ln East Brunswick (08816) *(G-2134)*

Doerre Fence Co LLC 732 751-9700
392 Adelphia Rd Farmingdale (07727) *(G-3384)*

Dohrman Printing Co Inc 201 933-0346
445 Industrial Rd Carlstadt (07072) *(G-1152)*

DOING BUSINESS AS, Bordentown *Also called Microdysis Inc* *(G-589)*

Dolan & Traynor Inc 973 696-8700
32 Riverview Dr Wayne (07470) *(G-11495)*

Dolan Assoc Inc 973 875-6408
71 Holland Rd A Sussex (07461) *(G-10558)*

Dolan LLC 800 451-9998
421 Executive Dr Princeton (08540) *(G-8931)*

Dolce Brothers Printing Inc (PA) 201 843-0400
29 Brook Ave Maywood (07607) *(G-6004)*

Dolce Printing 201 843-0400
29 Brook Ave Maywood (07607) *(G-6005)*

Dolce Technologies LLC 609 497-7319
90 Nassau St Fl 4 Princeton (08542) *(G-8932)*

Dolce Vita Intimates LLC (PA) 973 482-8400
1000 1st St Harrison (07029) *(G-4169)*

Dolco Packaging Corp (HQ) 201 941-2900
101 Railroad Ave Ridgefield (07657) *(G-9258)*

Dollfus Mieg Company Inc 732 662-1005
86 Northfield Ave Edison (08837) *(G-2492)*

Domel Inc 973 614-1800
3 Grunwald St Clifton (07013) *(G-1602)*

Dominion Colour Corp USA 973 279-9591
881 Allwood Rd Ste 2 Clifton (07012) *(G-1603)*

Domino Foods Inc (HQ) 732 590-1173
99 Wood Ave S Ste 901 Iselin (08830) *(G-4607)*

Domino Printing 973 857-0900
67 Sand Park Rd Cedar Grove (07009) *(G-1276)*

Domino Sugar, Iselin *Also called Domino Foods Inc (G-4607)*

Domtar 201 942-2077
2900 Cindel Dr Delran (08075) *(G-2015)*

Don Schreiber Co, Asbury *Also called Johnthan Leasing Corp (G-66)*

Don Shrts Pcture Frmes Molding 732 363-1323
294 Lanes Mill Rd Howell (07731) *(G-4537)*

Don Shurts Frames & Molding, Howell *Also called Don Shrts Pcture Frmes Molding (G-4537)*

Donna Karan International Inc 609 345-3402
1931 Atlantic Ave Atlantic City (08401) *(G-89)*

Donnelley Financial LLC 973 882-7000
5 Henderson Dr West Caldwell (07006) *(G-11647)*

DONNELLY CONSTRUCTION, Wayne *Also called Donnelly Industries Inc (G-11496)*

Donnelly Industries Inc 973 672-1800
557 Rte 23 Wayne (07470) *(G-11496)*

Donray Printing Inc 973 515-8100
2 Eastmans Rd Parsippany (07054) *(G-7918)*

Dons Collection, Secaucus *Also called Golden Season Fashion USA Inc (G-9775)*

Doolan Industries Incorporated (PA) 856 985-1880
5 Blue Anchor St Marlton (08053) *(G-5929)*

Door Center Enterprises Inc 609 333-1233
105 Crusher Rd Hopewell (08525) *(G-4526)*

Door Stop LLC 718 599-5112
109 Kero Rd Carlstadt (07072) *(G-1153)*

Doorsills LLC 973 904-0270
302 Legion Pl Haledon (07508) *(G-4081)*

Doorstop, Carlstadt *Also called Door Stop LLC (G-1153)*

Doortec Archtctural Met GL LLC (PA) 201 497-5056
303 Martin St River Vale (07675) *(G-9365)*

Doosan Heavy Inds Amer LLC 201 944-4554
140 Sylvan Ave Englewood Cliffs (07632) *(G-2967)*

Doosan Machine Tools, Pine Brook *Also called Clark Equipment Company (G-8593)*

Doosan Machine Tools Amer Corp (HQ) 973 618-2500
19a Chapin Rd Pine Brook (07058) *(G-8599)*

Dor-Win Manufacturing Co 201 796-4300
109 Midland Ave Elmwood Park (07407) *(G-2821)*

Dorado Systems LLC 856 354-0048
8 Kings Hwy E Haddonfield (08033) *(G-4056)*

Doralex Inc 856 764-0694
403 Saint Mihiel Dr Delran (08075) *(G-2016)*

Doran Company, Union *Also called Doran LLC (G-11043)*

Doran LLC 908 289-9200
599 Green Ln Union (07083) *(G-11043)*

Doran Sling and Assembly Corp 908 355-1101
1285 Central Ave Ste 2 Hillside (07205) *(G-4390)*

DOrazio Foods Inc 856 931-1900
960 Creek Rd Bellmawr (08031) *(G-330)*

Dorchester Shipyard Inc 856 785-8040
13 Front St Dorchester (08316) *(G-2070)*

Dorf Feature Service Inc 908 518-1802
187 Mill Ln Ste 3 Mountainside (07092) *(G-6843)*

Dorwin Manufacturing Co 201 796-4300
109 Midland Ave Elmwood Park (07407) *(G-2822)*

Dorzar Corporation 973 589-6363
50 Avenue L Ste 5 Newark (07105) *(G-7103)*

Dos Industrial Sales LLC 973 887-7800
7d Great Meadow Ln East Hanover (07936) *(G-2205)*

Dosch-King Company Inc (PA) 973 887-0145
16 Troy Hills Rd Whippany (07981) *(G-11889)*

Dosch-King Emulsions, Whippany *Also called Dosch-King Company Inc (G-11889)*

Dosis Fragrance LLC 718 874-0074
250 Passaic St Newark (07104) *(G-7104)*

DOT Graphix Inc 609 994-3416
79 S Main St Ste 13 Barnegat (08005) *(G-158)*

Double Check 973 984-2229
101 Gibraltar Dr Ste 1e Morris Plains (07950) *(G-6603)*

Double Diamond Technologies 609 624-1414
705 Route 9 Cape May (08204) *(G-1097)*

Double O Manufacturing Inc 732 752-9423
2b Smalley Ave Middlesex (08846) *(G-6113)*

Double Twenties Inc 973 827-7563
20 Park Dr Franklin (07416) *(G-3602)*

Dougherty Foundation Products 201 337-5748
851 Meadow Ln Franklin Lakes (07417) *(G-3621)*

Douglas Elec Components Inc 973 627-8230
5 Middlebury Blvd Randolph (07869) *(G-9175)*

Douglas Liva MD 201 444-7770
625 Franklin Tpke Ridgewood (07450) *(G-9323)*

Douglas Maybury Assoc 908 879-5878
385 State Route 24 Ste 3e Chester (07930) *(G-1433)*

Douglass Industries Inc 609 804-6040
412 Boston Ave Egg Harbor City (08215) *(G-2658)*

Douglass Weave Appeal, Egg Harbor City *Also called Douglass Industries Inc (G-2658)*

Dove Chocolate Discoveries LLC 866 922-3683
400 Valley Rd Ste 200 Mount Arlington (07856) *(G-6711)*

Dover Tool Connecticut LLC (PA) 203 367-6376
620 Franklin Lake Rd Franklin Lakes (07417) *(G-3622)*

Dow Chemical Company 800 258-2436
1 Riverview Dr Somerset (08873) *(G-9982)*

Dow Jones & Company Inc 609 520-4000
4300 Us Highway 1 Monmouth Junction (08852) *(G-6287)*

Dow Jones & Company Inc 609 520-4000
4300 N Rt 1 & Ridge Rd Cranbury (08512) *(G-1830)*

Dow Jones & Company Inc 609 520-5730
5 Schalks Crossing Rd Plainsboro (08536) *(G-8785)*

Dow Jones & Company Inc 609 520-5238
4300 Us Highway 1 Monmouth Junction (08852) *(G-6288)*

Dowden Health Media Inc (HQ) 201 740-6100
110 Summit Ave Ste 1 Montvale (07645) *(G-6408)*

Down Shore Publishing Corp 609 978-1233
638 Teal St West Creek (08092) *(G-11686)*

Downtown Printing Center Inc 732 246-7990
46 Paterson St Ste 1 New Brunswick (08901) *(G-6920)*

Dpc Cirrus 973 927-2828
62 Flanders Bartley Rd Flanders (07836) *(G-3406)*

Dpc Instrument Systems, Flanders *Also called Siemens Medical (G-3419)*

Dpi Copies Prtg & Graphics Inc 856 874-1355
2070 Marlton Pike E Ste 3 Cherry Hill (08003) *(G-1357)*

Dpi Newco LLC 973 257-8113
45 Waterview Blvd Parsippany (07054) *(G-7919)*

Dpj Inc 732 499-8600
245 E Inman Ave Rahway (07065) *(G-9088)*

Dpj Signs, Rahway *Also called Dpj Inc (G-9088)*

Dpk Consulting LLC 732 764-0100
220 Old New Brunswick Rd # 201 Piscataway (08854) *(G-8657)*

Dpsg, Avenel *Also called Snapple Distributors Inc (G-146)*

Dr Pregers Sensible Foods Inc 201 703-1300
9 Boumar Pl Elmwood Park (07407) *(G-2823)*

Dr Reddys Laboratories Inc (HQ) 609 375-9900
107 College Rd E Ste 100 Princeton (08540) *(G-8933)*

Dr Schar Usa Inc 856 803-5100
305 Heron Dr Swedesboro (08085) *(G-10582)*

Dr Sofa, Guttenberg *Also called Sofa Doctor Inc (G-3872)*

DR Technology Inc 732 780-4664
73 South St Freehold (07728) *(G-3661)*

DR Tielmann Inc 732 332-1860
4 Hialeah Dr Colts Neck (07722) *(G-1781)*

Dragon Asphalt Equipment LLC 732 922-9290
845 Towbin Ave Lakewood (08701) *(G-5085)*

Drake Corp 732 254-1530
110 Tices Ln East Brunswick (08816) *(G-2135)*

Dranetz Technologies Inc (HQ) 732 248-4358
1000 New Durham Rd Edison (08817) *(G-2493)*

Drapekings, North Bergen *Also called Dru Whitacre Media Svcs Ltd (G-7402)*

Drapery & More Inc 201 271-9661
2321 Kennedy Blvd Ste 1 North Bergen (07047) *(G-7401)*

Drawbase Software, Lyndhurst *Also called Com Tek Wrkplace Solutions LLC (G-5649)*

Draztic Designs LLC 609 678-4200
205 Petticoat Bridge Rd Columbus (08022) *(G-1800)*

Dream Cabinetry 732 806-8444
212 2nd St Unit 2 Lakewood (08701) *(G-5086)*

Dream Makers Inc 201 248-5502
53 Glendale Rd Park Ridge (07656) *(G-7848)*

Dream On ME Industries Inc (PA) 732 752-7220
1532 S Washington Ave # 1 Piscataway (08854) *(G-8658)*

Dream Well Collection Inc 732 545-5900
633 Nassau St New Brunswick (08902) *(G-6921)*

Dreamstar Construction LLC 732 393-2572
248 Clubhouse Dr Middletown (07748) *(G-6162)*

Dreamwell, New Brunswick *Also called Dream Well Collection Inc (G-6921)*

Drew & Rogers Inc (PA) 973 575-6210
30 Plymouth St Ste 2 Fairfield (07004) *(G-3187)*

Drew-Wal Machine & Tool Corp 201 641-3887
76 Monroe St Little Ferry (07643) *(G-5483)*

(G-0000) Company's Geographic Section entry number

Dreyco Inc (PA) 201 896-9000
263 Veterans Blvd Carlstadt (07072) *(G-1154)*

DRG International Inc (PA) 973 564-7555
841 Mountain Ave Springfield (07081) *(G-10439)*

Drifire LLC 866 266-4035
28 Kennedy Blvd Ste 300 East Brunswick (08816) *(G-2136)*

Drink A Toast Company Inc 856 461-1000
603 Harrison St Riverside (08075) *(G-9394)*

Driscoll Foods, Clifton Also called Metropolitan Foods Inc *(G-1668)*

Driscoll Label Company Inc 973 585-7291
19 West St East Hanover (07936) *(G-2206)*

Dritac Flooring Products LLC 973 614-9000
60 Webro Rd Clifton (07012) *(G-1604)*

Dritac Flooring Products LLC (PA) 973 614-9000
60 Webro Rd Clifton (07012) *(G-1605)*

Drive Technology Inc 732 422-6500
2031 Us Highway 130 1l Monmouth Junction (08852) *(G-6289)*

Drive-Master Co Inc 973 808-9709
37 Daniel Rd Fairfield (07004) *(G-3188)*

Drom Fragrances, Towaco Also called Drom International Inc *(G-10870)*

Drom International Inc (HQ) 973 316-8400
5 Jacksonville Rd Towaco (07082) *(G-10870)*

Drone Go Home LLC 732 991-3605
101 Crawfords Corner Rd 4101r Holmdel (07733) *(G-4499)*

Drone Usa Inc (PA) 203 220-2296
330 Changebridge Rd # 101 Pine Brook (07058) *(G-8600)*

Drs Data & Imaging Systems, Oakland Also called Drs Leonardo Inc *(G-7626)*

Drs Infrared Technologies LP 973 898-1500
5 Sylvan Way Ste 305 Parsippany (07054) *(G-7920)*

Drs Leonardo Inc 973 775-4440
95 William St Newark (07102) *(G-7105)*

Drs Leonardo Inc 973 898-1500
5 Sylvan Way Ste 305 Parsippany (07054) *(G-7921)*

Drs Leonardo Inc 973 898-1500
200 Campus Dr Ste 410 Florham Park (07932) *(G-3501)*

Drs Leonardo Inc 201 337-3800
133 Bauer Dr Oakland (07436) *(G-7626)*

Drs Srvillance Support Systems, Florham Park Also called Drs Leonardo Inc *(G-3501)*

Dru Whitacre Media Svcs Ltd (PA) 201 770-9950
3200 Liberty Ave Ste 2c North Bergen (07047) *(G-7402)*

Drug Delivery Technology LLC 973 299-1200
219 Changebridge Rd Montville (07045) *(G-6441)*

Dry Bilge Systems Inc 862 257-1800
460 Main Ave Ste C Wallington (07057) *(G-11385)*

Drytech Inc 609 758-1794
54 Wrghtstown Cokstown Rd Cookstown (08511) *(G-1803)*

Dse Healthcare Solutions LLC 732 417-1870
105 Fieldcrest Ave 502a Edison (08837) *(G-2494)*

DSM Nutritional Products LLC 908 475-7093
206 Macks Island Dr Belvidere (07823) *(G-360)*

DSM Nutritional Products LLC 908 475-0150
253 260 Macks Island Dr Belvidere (07823) *(G-361)*

DSM Nutritional Products LLC 908 475-5300
200 Roche Dr Belvidere (07823) *(G-362)*

DSM Nutritional Products LLC 908 475-5300
218 Roche Dr Belvidere (07823) *(G-363)*

DSM Nutritional Products LLC (HQ) 800 526-0189
45 Waterview Blvd Parsippany (07054) *(G-7922)*

DSM Sight & Life Inc 973 257-8208
45 Waterview Blvd Parsippany (07054) *(G-7923)*

Dso Fluid Handling Co Inc 732 225-9100
300 Mcgaw Dr Ste 2 Edison (08837) *(G-2495)*

Dso Sanitary Supply, Edison Also called Dso Fluid Handling Co Inc *(G-2495)*

Dsrv Inc 973 631-1200
330 Waterloo Valley Rd # 2 Budd Lake (07828) *(G-921)*

Dtrovision LLC 201 488-3232
22-10 States Rte 208 Fair Lawn (07410) *(G-3097)*

Du Technologies Inc 201 729-0070
300 W Commercial Ave Moonachie (07074) *(G-6463)*

Du-Matt Corporation 201 861-4271
12 65th St West New York (07093) *(G-11738)*

Du-Mor Blade Co Inc 856 829-9384
1002 Union Landing Rd Cinnaminson (08077) *(G-1453)*

Dublin Management Assoc of NJ 609 387-1600
321 High St Burlington (08016) *(G-964)*

Dubon Corp 212 812-2171
1356 Stanley Ter Elizabeth (07208) *(G-2730)*

Duct Mate Inc 201 488-8002
190 Lexington Ave Hackensack (07601) *(G-3909)*

Ducts Inc 973 267-8482
8 Moraine Rd Morris Plains (07950) *(G-6604)*

Ductworks Inc 908 754-8190
434 W Front St Plainfield (07060) *(G-8762)*

Dudley Lab, Toms River Also called Henry Dudley *(G-10764)*

Duerr Tool & Die Co Inc 908 810-9035
1135 Springfield Rd Union (07083) *(G-11044)*

Duet Microelectronics LLC 908 854-3838
575 Route 28 Ste 100 Raritan (08869) *(G-9210)*

Dukers Appliance Co USA Ltd 917 378-8866
4475 S Clinton Ave # 115 South Plainfield (07080) *(G-10248)*

Dulce A Dessert Bar LLC 908 461-2418
609 S Atlantic Ave Matawan (07747) *(G-5973)*

Dun & Bradstreet Inc 973 921-5500
103 John F Kennedy Pkwy Short Hills (07078) *(G-9868)*

Dun-Rite Communications Inc 201 444-0080
31 Industrial Ave Mahwah (07430) *(G-5731)*

Dun-Rite Sand & Gravel Co (PA) 856 692-2520
573 E Grant Ave Vineland (08360) *(G-11214)*

Dunbar Concrete Products Inc 973 697-2525
173 Oak Ridge Rd Oak Ridge (07438) *(G-7600)*

Dunbar Sales Company Inc 201 437-6500
39 Avenue C Ste 1 Bayonne (07002) *(G-214)*

Dune Grass Publishing LLC 609 774-6562
39 Indiana Ave Blackwood (08012) *(G-464)*

Dunkin Donuts Baskin Robbins 201 692-1900
332 Cedar Ln Teaneck (07666) *(G-10628)*

Dunkin' Donuts, Ringoes Also called Jay Jariwala *(G-9338)*

Dunkin' Donuts, Rockaway Also called O O M Inc *(G-9482)*

Dunkin' Donuts, Jersey City Also called 9001 Corporation *(G-4680)*

Dunkin' Donuts, Jersey City Also called 9002 Corporation *(G-4681)*

Dunkin' Donuts, Cinnaminson Also called G N J Inc *(G-1458)*

Dunkin' Donuts, West Caldwell Also called All Madina Inc *(G-11639)*

Dunkin' Donuts, Mount Laurel Also called J K P Donuts Inc *(G-6772)*

Dunkin' Donuts, Gibbstown Also called Ram Donuts Corp *(G-3799)*

Dunn Meadow Pharmacy, Fort Lee Also called LLC Dunn Meadow *(G-3569)*

Dupont, Parlin Also called E I Du Pont De Nemours & Co *(G-7863)*

Dura-Carb Inc 973 697-6665
204 Chamberlain Rd Oak Ridge (07438) *(G-7601)*

Duraamen Engineered Pdts Inc (PA) 973 230-1301
457 Frelinghuysen Ave Newark (07114) *(G-7106)*

Durabak Depot, Teaneck Also called Worldwide Safety Systems LLC *(G-10656)*

Durabond Division US Gypsum 732 636-7900
300 Markley St Port Reading (07064) *(G-8893)*

Durabrite Ltg Solutions LLC 201 915-0555
4 Beacon Way Apt 2003 Jersey City (07304) *(G-4729)*

Duragates, Plainfield Also called Architectural Iron Designs *(G-8758)*

Duran Cutting Corp 973 916-0006
90 Dayton Ave Ste 6 Passaic (07055) *(G-8061)*

Durand Glass Mfg Co Inc 856 327-1850
901 S Wade Blvd Millville (08332) *(G-6248)*

Duratape International, Union Also called Wet-N-Stick LLC *(G-11099)*

Durex Inc (PA) 908 688-0800
5 Stahuber Ave Union (07083) *(G-11045)*

Durisan, Passaic Also called Sanit Technologies LLC *(G-8105)*

Duro Bag Manufacturing Company 908 351-2400
750 Dowd Ave Elizabeth (07201) *(G-2731)*

Duro Manufacturing Company 908 810-9588
5 Stahuber Ave Union (07083) *(G-11046)*

Duron Co Inc 973 242-5704
238 Emmet St Newark (07114) *(G-7107)*

Durst Corporation Inc (PA) 800 852-3906
129 Dermody St Cranford (07016) *(G-1907)*

Dusenbery Engineering Co Inc 973 539-2200
309 E Hanover Ave Morristown (07960) *(G-6661)*

Dutra Sheet Metal Co 856 692-8058
1940 S West Blvd Ste E Vineland (08360) *(G-11215)*

Dux Paint LLC 973 473-2376
18 Mill St Lodi (07644) *(G-5560)*

Dvash Foods USA Inc 929 360-0758
300 Corporate Dr Mahwah (07430) *(G-5732)*

Dvs Industries, Burlington Also called Delaware Valley Sign Corp *(G-962)*

Dvx LLC 609 924-3590
2 Carter Brook Ln Princeton (08540) *(G-8934)*

Dwill America LLC 201 561-5737
174 Terrace Ave Lodi (07644) *(G-5561)*

Dxl Enterprises Inc 201 891-8718
575 Corporate Dr Ste 420 Mahwah (07430) *(G-5733)*

Dye Into Print Inc 973 772-8019
167 Fornelius Ave Clifton (07013) *(G-1606)*

Dyer Communications Inc 732 219-5788
75 W Front St Ste 2 Red Bank (07701) *(G-9227)*

Dyerich Flooring Designs Ltd 973 357-0600
35 Dale Ave Paterson (07505) *(G-8175)*

Dymax Systems Inc 732 918-2424
3455 State Route 66 Ste 6 Neptune (07753) *(G-6874)*

Dyna Veyor Inc 908 276-5384
10 Hudson St Newark (07103) *(G-7108)*

Dyna-Lite Inc 908 687-8800
1050 Commerce Ave Ste 2 Union (07083) *(G-11047)*

Dyna-Sea Group Inc 201 928-0133
765 Carroll Pl Teaneck (07666) *(G-10629)*

Dynaclear Packaging, Wharton Also called Pro Pack Inc *(G-11868)*

Dynaflow Engineering Inc 732 356-9790
106 Egel Ave Middlesex (08846) *(G-6114)*

Dynametric Tool Inc 973 471-8009
27 Somerset Pl Clifton (07012) *(G-1607)*

Dynamic Blending Company Inc 856 541-6626
1475 S 6th St Camden (08104) *(G-1059)*

A L P H A B E T I C

Dynamic Coatings LLC 732 998-6625
253 Main St Ste 120 Matawan (07747) ***(G-5974)***
Dynamic Defense Materials LLC 856 552-4150
100 Sharp Rd Marlton (08053) ***(G-5930)***
Dynamic Die Cutting & Finshg 973 589-8338
104-110 South St Newark (07114) ***(G-7109)***
Dynamic Machining Inc 856 273-9830
1920 Bannard St Cinnaminson (08077) ***(G-1454)***
Dynamic Metals Inc 908 769-0522
1713 S 2nd St Piscataway (08854) ***(G-8659)***
Dynamic Printing & Graphics 973 473-7177
250 Delawanna Ave Clifton (07014) ***(G-1608)***
Dynamic Safety International, Somerset *Also called Dynamic Safety Usa LLC* ***(G-9983)***
Dynamic Safety Usa LLC 844 378-7200
400 Apgar Dr Ste H Somerset (08873) ***(G-9983)***
Dynasil Corporation America 856 767-4600
385 Cooper Rd West Berlin (08091) ***(G-11590)***
Dynasty Metals Inc 973 453-6630
164 Franklin Ave Rockaway (07866) ***(G-9454)***
Dynatec Systems Inc (PA) 609 387-0330
360 Connecticut Dr Burlington (08016) ***(G-965)***
E & E Group Corp 201 814-0414
7 Maple Ave 2 South Hackensack (07606) ***(G-10155)***
E & G Roman Corp 973 482-1123
14 Ogden St Newark (07104) ***(G-7110)***
E & H Laminating & Slitting Co, Paterson *Also called Annitti Enterprises Inc* ***(G-8140)***
E & M Bindery Inc 973 777-9300
11 Peekay Dr Clifton (07014) ***(G-1609)***
E & T Plastic Mfg Co Inc 201 596-5017
200 Green St Teterboro (07608) ***(G-10671)***
E & T Plastic Mfg Co Inc 856 787-0900
824 E Gate Dr Ste E Mount Laurel (08054) ***(G-6754)***
E & T Sales Co Inc 856 787-0900
824 E Gate Dr Ste E Mount Laurel (08054) ***(G-6755)***
E & W Piece Dye Works 973 942-8718
293 Morrissee Ave Haledon (07508) ***(G-4082)***
E and E USA, Passaic *Also called Emerald Electronics Usa Inc* ***(G-8063)***
E B R Manufacturing Inc 973 263-8810
10 Woodhaven Rd Parsippany (07054) ***(G-7924)***
E Berkowitz & Co Inc 856 608-1118
520 Fellowship Rd B202 Mount Laurel (08054) ***(G-6756)***
E C D Ventures Inc 856 875-1100
3501 Route 42 Ste 130 Blackwood (08012) ***(G-465)***
E C Electroplating Inc 973 340-0227
125 Clark St Garfield (07026) ***(G-3740)***
E C S, Pennington *Also called Electrochemical Society Inc* ***(G-8364)***
E C S, Egg Harbor Township *Also called Enroute Computer Solutions Inc* ***(G-2683)***
E C S I, Clifton *Also called Ecsi International Inc* ***(G-1610)***
E Chabot Ltd 212 575-1026
195 Carter Dr Ste 2 Edison (08817) ***(G-2496)***
E F Britten & Co Inc 908 276-4800
22 South Ave W Cranford (07016) ***(G-1908)***
E G L, Berkeley Heights *Also called E G L Company Inc* ***(G-398)***
E G L Company Inc 908 508-1111
100 Industrial Rd Berkeley Heights (07922) ***(G-398)***
E Group Inc 856 320-9688
129 Gaither Dr Ste M Mount Laurel (08054) ***(G-6757)***
E I Du Pont De Nemours & Co 732 257-1579
250 Cheesequake Rd Parlin (08859) ***(G-7863)***
E J M Store Fixtures Inc 973 372-7907
460 Coit St Irvington (07111) ***(G-4565)***
E L Baxter Co Inc 732 229-8219
1227 Deal Rd Ocean (07712) ***(G-7661)***
E Loc Total Logistics LLC 609 685-6117
144 Canterbury Rd Mount Laurel (08054) ***(G-6758)***
E M D, Flanders *Also called Electronic Measuring Devices* ***(G-3407)***
E M R Photoelectric Div, Princeton Junction *Also called Schlumberger Technology Corp* ***(G-9066)***
E P Heller Company 973 377-2878
21 Samson Ave 25 Madison (07940) ***(G-5691)***
E P Homiek Shtmtl Sups Inc 732 364-7644
1352 River Ave Ste 4 Lakewood (08701) ***(G-5087)***
E P R Industries Inc 856 488-1120
4576 S Crescent Blvd Pennsauken (08109) ***(G-8416)***
E R Squibb & Sons LLC (HQ) 732 246-3195
25 Kennedy Blvd East Brunswick (08816) ***(G-2137)***
E R Squibb & Sons Inter-AM 609 252-5144
3551 Lawrenceville Rd Princeton (08540) ***(G-8935)***
E R Squibb & Sons Inter-AM 609 818-3715
3 Hamilton Health Pl Trenton (08690) ***(G-10932)***
E R Squibb & Sons Inter-AM (HQ) 609 252-4111
3551 Lawrenceville Rd Princeton (08540) ***(G-8936)***
E S Industries Inc 856 753-8400
701 S Route 73 A West Berlin (08091) ***(G-11591)***
E S S, Towaco *Also called Engineered Security Systems* ***(G-10871)***
E W Williams Publications (HQ) 201 592-7007
2125 Center Ave Ste 305 Fort Lee (07024) ***(G-3556)***
E Wortmann Machine Works Inc 201 288-1654
50 Hollister Rd Teterboro (07608) ***(G-10672)***

E-Beam Services Inc 513 933-0031
118 Melrich Rd Cranbury (08512) ***(G-1831)***
E-Lo Sportswear LLC 862 902-5220
1 Cape May St Harrison (07029) ***(G-4170)***
E-TEC Marine Products Inc 732 269-0442
245 Hickory Ln Bayville (08721) ***(G-243)***
E-Vents Registration LLC 201 722-9221
40 Tillman St Westwood (07675) ***(G-11830)***
E5 Usa Inc 973 773-0750
61 Willet St Ste 24 Passaic (07055) ***(G-8062)***
Ea Pilot Supply 201 934-8449
603 Fletcher Lake Ave Bradley Beach (07720) ***(G-610)***
EAC Water Filters Inc 888 524-8088
2215 Allenwood Rd Allenwood (08720) ***(G-32)***
Eagle Communications Inc 973 366-6181
2902 Vantage Ct Denville (07834) ***(G-2036)***
Eagle Drives & Controls, Point Pleasant Boro *Also called Eagle Engineering & Automation* ***(G-8844)***
Eagle Engineering & Automation 732 899-2292
2111 Herbertsville Rd Point Pleasant Boro (08742) ***(G-8844)***
Eagle Fabrication Inc 732 739-5300
63 Ohio Dr Ltl Egg Hbr (08087) ***(G-5616)***
Eagle Fire & Safety Corp 732 982-7388
1604 Westminster Ln Wall Township (07719) ***(G-11335)***
Eagle Fire Protection, Wall Township *Also called Eagle Fire & Safety Corp* ***(G-11335)***
Eagle Gutter Supply, East Rutherford *Also called United Gutter Supply Inc* ***(G-2328)***
Eagle Pharmaceuticals Inc (PA) 201 326-5300
50 Tice Blvd Ste 315 Woodcliff Lake (07677) ***(G-12054)***
Eagle Products Div, Paterson *Also called Gorman Industries Inc* ***(G-8201)***
Eagle Racing Inc 732 367-8487
810 Cross St Ste 4 Lakewood (08701) ***(G-5088)***
Eagle Steel & Iron LLC 908 587-1025
102 Willever Way Stewartsville (08886) ***(G-10483)***
Eagle Work Clothes Inc (PA) 908 964-8888
20 Quail Run Florham Park (07932) ***(G-3502)***
Eagleburgmann Industries LP 856 241-7300
614 Heron Dr Ste 8 Swedesboro (08085) ***(G-10583)***
Eagletre-Pump Acquisition Corp 201 569-1173
301 Veterans Blvd Rutherford (07070) ***(G-9618)***
Eaglevision Usa LLC 908 322-1892
150 North Ave Fanwood (07023) ***(G-3372)***
Earle The Walter R Corp (PA) 732 308-1113
1800 State Route 34 # 205 Wall Township (07719) ***(G-11336)***
Earle The Walter R Corp 732 657-8551
655 S Hope Chapel Rd Jackson (08527) ***(G-4652)***
Earle Asphalt Company 732 657-8551
655 S Hope Chapel Rd Jackson (08527) ***(G-4653)***
Earle Asphalt Company (PA) 732 308-1113
1800 State Route 34 # 205 Wall Township (07719) ***(G-11337)***
Earle Companies, The, Wall Township *Also called Earle Asphalt Company* ***(G-11337)***
Earth Color New York Inc (HQ) 973 884-1300
249 Pomeroy Rd Parsippany (07054) ***(G-7925)***
Earth Digital, Parsippany *Also called Earthcolor Inc* ***(G-7928)***
Earth Thebault Inc (HQ) 973 884-1300
249 Pomeroy Rd Parsippany (07054) ***(G-7926)***
Earthcolor Inc 973 952-8360
249 Pomeroy Rd Parsippany (07054) ***(G-7927)***
Earthcolor Inc (HQ) 973 884-1300
249 Pomeroy Rd Parsippany (07054) ***(G-7928)***
Earthwork Associates Inc 609 624-9395
477 Corsons Tavern Rd Ocean View (08230) ***(G-7702)***
East Brunswick Sewerage Auth 732 257-8313
25 Harts Ln East Brunswick (08816) ***(G-2138)***
East Coast Brewing Co LLC 732 202-7782
528 Arnold Ave Point Pleasant Beach (08742) ***(G-8823)***
East Coast Cabinets Inc 856 488-9710
2250 Sherman Ave Unit A1 Pennsauken (08110) ***(G-8417)***
East Coast Custom, Sayreville *Also called CRA-Z Works Co Inc* ***(G-9707)***
East Coast Diamond Tl Pdts Inc 212 686-1034
1 W Forest Ave Ste 1i Englewood (07631) ***(G-2899)***
East Coast Distributors Inc 732 223-5995
1 Industrial Way W E Eatontown (07724) ***(G-2389)***
East Coast Electronics Inc 908 431-7555
216 Us Highway 206 20a Hillsborough (08844) ***(G-4313)***
East Coast Media LLC 908 575-9700
14 Park Ave Hillsborough (08844) ***(G-4314)***
East Coast Pallets LLC 732 308-3616
17 Sweetmans Ln Manalapan (07726) ***(G-5805)***
East Coast Panelboard Inc 732 739-6400
101 Tornillo Way Tinton Falls (07712) ***(G-10713)***
East Coast Plastics Inc 856 768-8700
427 Commerce Ln Ste 7 West Berlin (08091) ***(G-11592)***
East Coast Power Systems, Tinton Falls *Also called East Coast Panelboard Inc* ***(G-10713)***
East Coast Rubber Products 856 384-2747
1000 Delsea Dr Ste D2 Westville (08093) ***(G-11812)***
East Coast Salt Dist Inc 732 833-2973
621 Wright Debow Rd Jackson (08527) ***(G-4654)***
East Coast Storage Eqp Co Inc (PA) 732 451-1316
620 Burtis St Brick (08723) ***(G-716)***

East Trading West Inv LLC 973 678-0800
200 S Jefferson St Orange (07050) *(G-7753)*

East West Service Co Inc 609 631-9000
2 Marlen Dr Trenton (08691) *(G-10933)*

Eastern Cold Drawn, North Brunswick Also called C D E Inc *(G-7459)*

Eastern Concrete Materials Inc 609 698-2800
201 Route 539 Barnegat (08005) *(G-159)*

Eastern Concrete Materials Inc (HQ) 201 797-7979
250 Pehle Ave Ste 503 Saddle Brook (07663) *(G-9650)*

Eastern Concrete Materials Inc 973 702-7866
80 Estate Dr 23n Sussex (07461) *(G-10559)*

Eastern Concrete Materials Inc 973 827-7625
3620 State Rt 23 N Hamburg (07419) *(G-4090)*

Eastern Concrete Materials Inc 908 537-2135
1 Railroad Ave Glen Gardner (08826) *(G-3821)*

Eastern Glass Resources Inc (PA) 973 483-8411
770 Supor Blvd Harrison (07029) *(G-4171)*

Eastern Impressions, West Caldwell Also called Fortress Graphics LLC *(G-11651)*

Eastern Instrumentation of 856 231-0668
710 E Main St Ste 1a Moorestown (08057) *(G-6519)*

Eastern Machining Corporation 856 694-3303
1197 Fries Mill Rd Franklinville (08322) *(G-3637)*

Eastern Molding Co Inc 973 759-0220
597 Main St Belleville (07109) *(G-294)*

Eastern Podiatry Labs Inc 609 882-4444
1702 5th St Ewing (08638) *(G-3028)*

Eastern Regional Waterway 732 684-0409
2316 2nd Ave Brick (08723) *(G-717)*

Eastern Sign Company, Egg Harbor Township Also called M & W Franklin LLC *(G-2689)*

Eastside Express Corporation 908 486-3300
2025 E Linden Ave Linden (07036) *(G-5344)*

Easy Aerial Inc 646 639-4410
198 Pear Blossom Dr Edison (08837) *(G-2497)*

Easy Analytic Software Inc 856 931-5780
101 Haag Ave Bellmawr (08031) *(G-331)*

Easy Soft Inc 732 398-1001
212 N Center Dr North Brunswick (08902) *(G-7467)*

Easy Stop Food & Fuel Corp 973 517-0478
19 Exeter Ln Hamburg (07419) *(G-4091)*

Easy Street Publications Inc 917 699-7820
1473 Ridgeway St Union (07083) *(G-11048)*

Easy Undies LLC 201 715-4909
23 Springfield Ave Springfield (07081) *(G-10440)*

Easydook Midatlantic, Somers Point Also called Seaville Motorsports *(G-9939)*

Easyflex East Inc 201 853-9005
101 Industrial Ave Little Ferry (07643) *(G-5484)*

Easylving Brand, The, Springfield Also called Easy Undies LLC *(G-10440)*

Eatem Corporation 856 692-1663
1829 Gallagher Dr Vineland (08360) *(G-11216)*

Eatem Foods, Vineland Also called Eatem Corporation *(G-11216)*

Eaton Corporation 732 767-9600
1115 Globe Ave A Mountainside (07092) *(G-6844)*

Eaton Corporation 609 835-4230
96 Stemmers Ln Mount Holly (08060) *(G-6725)*

Eaton Filtration LLC 732 767-4200
44 Apple St Ste 3 Tinton Falls (07724) *(G-10714)*

Eb Machine Corp 973 442-7729
320 Richard Mine Rd Wharton (07885) *(G-11857)*

Ebaotech Inc USA 917 977-1145
101 Hudson St Ste 2100 Jersey City (07302) *(G-4730)*

Ebco Tool, East Hanover Also called Edward Brown *(G-2207)*

Ebelle Debelle Phrm Inc 973 823-0665
5 Witherwood Dr Hamburg (07419) *(G-4092)*

Ebi LLC 800 526-2579
399 Jefferson Rd Parsippany (07054) *(G-7929)*

Ebi LP 973 299-9022
399 Jefferson Rd Parsippany (07054) *(G-7930)*

Ebi Medical Systems LLC 973 299-3330
100 Interpace Pkwy Ste 1 Parsippany (07054) *(G-7931)*

Ebic Prparedness Solutions LLC 719 244-6209
236 Overlook Ave Leonia (07605) *(G-5288)*

Ebin New York Inc 201 288-8887
506 Us Highway 46 Teterboro (07608) *(G-10673)*

Ebmachine, Wharton Also called Eb Machine Corp *(G-11857)*

Ebocent, Paramus Also called European Imports of LA Inc *(G-7799)*

Ebsco Industries Inc 201 933-1800
201 Highway 17 Ste 300 Rutherford (07070) *(G-9619)*

Ebsco Industries Inc 732 542-8600
1151 Broad St Ste 212 Shrewsbury (07702) *(G-9891)*

Ebsco Industries Inc 201 569-2500
30 Park Rd Ste 2 Tinton Falls (07724) *(G-10715)*

Ebsco Information Services, Shrewsbury Also called Ebsco Industries Inc *(G-9891)*

Ebsco Publishing Inc 201 968-9899
2 University Plz Ste 310 Hackensack (07601) *(G-3910)*

Ecca, Bloomfield Also called Complete Optical Laboratory *(G-497)*

Ecce Panis Inc 877 706-0510
447 Gotham Pkwy Carlstadt (07072) *(G-1155)*

Echo Molding Inc 908 688-0099
911 Springfield Rd Ste 1 Union (07083) *(G-11049)*

Echo Therapeutics Inc (PA) 732 201-4189
1809 Hudson Park Edgewater (07020) *(G-2437)*

Eci, Hackensack Also called Electro-Ceramic Industries *(G-3911)*

Eci, Lakewood Also called Electronic Connections Inc *(G-5089)*

Eci Technology Inc 973 773-8686
60 Gordon Dr Totowa (07512) *(G-10825)*

Eclearview Technologies Inc 732 695-6999
60 Barberry Dr Ocean (07712) *(G-7662)*

Eclecticism Publishing LLC 212 714-4714
33 Stanwyck Ct Robbinsville (08691) *(G-9411)*

Eclipse International, North Brunswick Also called Mattress Dev Co Del LLC *(G-7476)*

Eclipse Manufacturing LLC 973 340-9939
438 Lanza Ave Garfield (07026) *(G-3741)*

Eclipse Sleep Products LLC 732 628-0002
1375 Jersey Ave Ste 1 New Brunswick (08902) *(G-6922)*

Eco Lighting USA Ltd Lblty Co 201 621-5661
217 Huyler St South Hackensack (07606) *(G-10156)*

Eco LLC 609 683-9030
344 Nassau St Ste F Princeton (08540) *(G-8937)*

Eco Pro Tungsten, Boonton Also called Anglers Select LLC *(G-543)*

Eco-Plug-System LLC 855 326-7584
1946 Union Valley Rd Hewitt (07421) *(G-4275)*

Ecocom Inc 201 393-0786
221 W Grand Ave Ste 168 Montvale (07645) *(G-6409)*

Ecolab Inc 856 596-4845
110 Marter Ave Ste 411 Moorestown (08057) *(G-6520)*

Ecom Group Inc (PA) 718 504-7355
3775 Park Ave Unit 3 Edison (08820) *(G-2498)*

Ecomelectronics, Edison Also called Ecom Group Inc *(G-2498)*

Econ Forms, Marlboro Also called Efco Corp *(G-5896)*

Ecp, Cherry Hill Also called Edwards Creative Products Inc *(G-1358)*

Ecs Energy Ltd 201 341-5044
16 Meadow Run Ct Jackson (08527) *(G-4655)*

Ecseco, Brick Also called East Coast Storage Eqp Co Inc *(G-716)*

Ecsi International Inc (HQ) 973 574-8555
790 Bloomfield Ave Ste C1 Clifton (07012) *(G-1610)*

Edax Inc (HQ) 201 529-4880
91 Mckee Dr Mahwah (07430) *(G-5734)*

Edda Technology Inc 609 919-9889
5 Independence Way # 210 Princeton (08540) *(G-8938)*

Eddie Domani Inc 908 469-8863
20 Butler St Elizabethport (07206) *(G-2787)*

Ede Pharmaceutical, Hamburg Also called Ebelle Debelle Phrm Inc *(G-4092)*

Edenbridge Pharmaceuticals LLC 201 292-1292
169 Lackawanna Ave # 110 Parsippany (07054) *(G-7932)*

Edesia Oil LLC 732 851-7979
225 County Road 522 B Manalapan (07726) *(G-5806)*

Edgar C Barcus Co Inc 856 456-0204
416 Gateway Blvd Westville (08093) *(G-11813)*

Edge Orthopedics, Boonton Also called Icon Orthopedic Concepts LLC *(G-556)*

Edge Orthotics Inc 732 549-3343
209 Pierson Ave Edison (08837) *(G-2499)*

Edgeco, Barnegat Also called Cedge Industries Inc *(G-157)*

Edgemont Pharmaceuticals LLC 908 375-8039
92 Roxiticus Rd Far Hills (07931) *(G-3374)*

Edgewater Manufacturing Co Inc (PA) 201 664-0022
17-10 Willow St Fair Lawn (07410) *(G-3098)*

Edgewell Personal Care LLC 973 753-3000
240 Cedar Knolls Rd Cedar Knolls (07927) *(G-1303)*

Edgewell Personal Care LLC 201 785-8000
75 Commerce Dr Allendale (07401) *(G-8)*

Edhard Corp 908 850-8444
279 Blau Rd Hackettstown (07840) *(G-4004)*

Edison Design Group Inc (PA) 732 993-3341
95 Cobblestone Blvd Monroe (08831) *(G-6321)*

Edison Finishing 732 287-6660
191 Vineyard Rd Ste 3 Edison (08817) *(G-2500)*

Edison Lithog & Prtg Corp (PA) 201 902-9191
3725 Tonnelle Ave North Bergen (07047) *(G-7403)*

Edison Nation Inc (PA) 610 829-1039
909 New Brunswick Ave Phillipsburg (08865) *(G-8549)*

Edison Ophthalmology Assoc LLC 908 822-0070
2177 Oak Tree Rd Ste 203t Edison (08820) *(G-2501)*

Edker Industries Inc 856 786-1971
1401 Union Landing Rd Cinnaminson (08077) *(G-1455)*

Edko Electronics 973 942-2222
460 Totowa Ave Paterson (07522) *(G-8176)*

Edmondmarks Technologies Inc 732 643-0290
3535 State Route 66 Ste 3 Neptune (07753) *(G-6875)*

Edmund Kiss 973 810-2312
12 Orben Dr Unit 1 Landing (07850) *(G-5200)*

Edmund Optics Inc (PA) 856 547-3488
101 E Gloucester Pike Barrington (08007) *(G-172)*

Edmund Scientific Co, Barrington Also called Edmund Optics Inc *(G-172)*

EDS, South Hackensack Also called Essential Dental Systems Inc *(G-10159)*

Edston Manufacturing Company 908 647-0116
125 Clinton Rd Unit 2 Fairfield (07004) *(G-3189)*

Educational & Lab Systems, Fairfield Also called Design of Tomorrow Inc *(G-3185)*

A
L
P
H
A
B
E
T
I
C

Educhat Inc 201 871-8649
17 Lane Dr Englewood (07631) *(G-2900)*

Educloud Inc 201 944-0445
206 Grant Ave Cliffside Park (07010) *(G-1538)*

Edward Brown 973 887-5255
8 Great Meadow Ln B East Hanover (07936) *(G-2207)*

Edward Kurth and Son Inc 856 227-5252
220 Blckwood Barnsboro Rd Sewell (08080) *(G-9840)*

Edward P Paul & Co Inc (PA) 908 757-4212
525 South Ave Plainfield (07060) *(G-8763)*

Edward T Brady 732 928-0257
12 Waldron Rd Allentown (08501) *(G-25)*

Edward W Hiemer & Co 973 772-5081
141 Wabash Ave Clifton (07011) *(G-1611)*

Edwards Brothers Inc 856 848-6900
1301 Metropolitan Ave # 300 West Deptford (08066) *(G-11701)*

Edwards Coils Corp 973 835-2800
101 Alexander Ave Unit 3 Pompton Plains (07444) *(G-8863)*

Edwards Creative Products Inc 856 665-3200
910 Beechwood Ave Cherry Hill (08002) *(G-1358)*

Edwards Engineering, Pompton Plains Also called Chiller Solutions LLC *(G-8861)*

Edwin Leonel Ramirez 732 648-5587
918 Putnam Ave Plainfield (07060) *(G-8764)*

Edwin R Burger & Son Inc 856 468-2300
732 Main St Sewell (08080) *(G-9841)*

Efco Corp 732 308-1010
77 Vanderburg Rd Marlboro (07746) *(G-5896)*

Effexoft Inc 732 221-3642
1553 State Route 27 # 1100 Somerset (08873) *(G-9984)*

Efficient Lighting Inc 973 846-8568
2 Cranberry Rd Ste 5b Parsippany (07054) *(G-7933)*

Egg Harbor Boats, Egg Harbor City Also called Eh Yachts LLC *(G-2660)*

Egg Harbor Rope Products Inc 609 965-2435
5105 White Horse Pike Egg Harbor City (08215) *(G-2659)*

Egg Harbor Yacht-Div, Egg Harbor City Also called Marine Acquisition Inc *(G-2664)*

Eh Yachts LLC 609 965-2300
801 Philadelphia Ave Egg Harbor City (08215) *(G-2660)*

Eick-Rbert A Qulty Bookbinding, Madison Also called Robert A Eick Qlty
Bookbinding *(G-5701)*

Eigent Technologies Inc 732 673-0402
10 Cindy Ln Holmdel (07733) *(G-4500)*

Eight OClock Coffee Company (HQ) 201 571-9214
155 Chestnut Ridge Rd # 2 Montvale (07645) *(G-6410)*

Eisai Inc (HQ) 201 692-1100
100 Tice Blvd Woodcliff Lake (07677) *(G-12055)*

Ej Machine & Tool Co, Landing Also called Edmund Kiss *(G-5200)*

Ejz Foods LLC 201 229-0500
21 Empire Blvd South Hackensack (07606) *(G-10157)*

Ekr Therapeutics Incorporated 877 435-2524
1545 Us Highway 206 # 300 Bedminster (07921) *(G-263)*

Eks Parts Inc 856 227-8811
220 Blckwood Barnsboro Rd Sewell (08080) *(G-9842)*

Ektelon, Viking Athletics, Bordentown Also called Prince Sports Inc *(G-593)*

El Batal Corporation 908 964-3427
1060 Commerce Ave Union (07083) *(G-11050)*

El Estelcil, Union City Also called U S A Distributors Inc *(G-11130)*

Elaine Inc 973 345-6200
1 Hazel St Woodland Park (07424) *(G-12076)*

Elaine K Josephson Inc 609 259-2256
7f Jules Ln New Brunswick (08901) *(G-6923)*

Elan Food Laboratories Inc 973 344-8014
268 Doremus Ave Newark (07105) *(G-7111)*

Elan Inc (PA) 973 344-8014
268 Doremus Ave Newark (07105) *(G-7112)*

Elan Vanilla, Newark Also called Elan Food Laboratories Inc *(G-7111)*

Elana Tile Contractors Inc 973 386-0991
8 Merry Ln Ste B East Hanover (07936) *(G-2208)*

Elastograf Inc 973 209-3161
19 Ames Blvd Hamburg (07419) *(G-4093)*

Elbee Litho Inc 732 698-7738
292 Dunhams Corner Rd East Brunswick (08816) *(G-2139)*

Elco Glass Industries Co Inc 732 363-6550
16 Tree Line Dr Freehold (07728) *(G-3662)*

Elder & Jenks Co Div, Bayonne Also called Muralo Company Inc *(G-229)*

Eldon Glass & Mirror Co 973 589-2099
58 Stockton St 76 Newark (07105) *(G-7113)*

Electedface LLC 609 924-3636
26 Snowden Ln Princeton (08540) *(G-8939)*

Election Graphics Inc 201 758-9966
15 Rockland Ter Verona (07044) *(G-11165)*

Electric Catalytic Pdts Group, Union Also called Evoqua Water Technologies LLC *(G-11053)*

Electric Mobility Corporation (PA) 856 468-1000
591 Mantua Blvd Sewell (08080) *(G-9843)*

Electric Mobility Corporation 856 468-1000
599 Mantua Blvd Sewell (08080) *(G-9844)*

Electrical Motor Repr Co of NJ 609 392-6149
809 E State St Trenton (08609) *(G-10934)*

Electro Impulse Laboratory Inc 732 776-5800
1805 State Route 33 Neptune (07753) *(G-6876)*

Electro Lift Inc 973 471-0204
204 Sargeant Ave Clifton (07013) *(G-1612)*

Electro Magnetic Products Inc 856 235-3011
355 Crider Ave Moorestown (08057) *(G-6521)*

Electro Mechanical Tech, Hillside Also called McIntosh Industries Inc *(G-4415)*

Electro Parts Inc 856 767-5923
465 E Taunton Ave Ste 201 West Berlin (08091) *(G-11593)*

Electro Plated Wire, Hawthorne Also called Fisk Alloy Wire Incorporated *(G-4220)*

Electro-Ceramic Industries 201 342-2630
75 Kennedy St Hackensack (07601) *(G-3911)*

Electro-Miniatures Corp (PA) 201 460-0510
68 W Commercial Ave Moonachie (07074) *(G-6464)*

Electro-Steam Generator Corp 609 288-9071
50 Indel Ave Rancocas (08073) *(G-9160)*

Electrochemical Society Inc 609 737-1902
65 S Main St Pennington (08534) *(G-8364)*

Electrocore Inc 973 290-0097
150 Allen Rd Ste 201 Basking Ridge (07920) *(G-182)*

Electroheat Induction Inc 908 494-0726
81 Oakland Ave 3 Jersey City (07306) *(G-4731)*

Electroid Co Div, Springfield Also called Valcor Engineering Corporation *(G-10473)*

Electromagnetic Tech Inds Inc 973 394-1719
50 Intervale Rd Ste 11 Boonton (07005) *(G-550)*

Electronic Assemblies, Inc Esi, Sicklerville Also called Esi *(G-9909)*

Electronic Brazing Co Div, Boonton Also called Janke & Company Inc *(G-558)*

Electronic Concepts Inc (HQ) 732 542-7880
526 Industrial Way W Eatontown (07724) *(G-2390)*

Electronic Connections Inc (PA) 732 367-5588
195 Lehigh Ave Ste 3 Lakewood (08701) *(G-5089)*

Electronic Control SEC Inc (PA) 973 574-8555
790 Bloomfield Ave Ste C1 Clifton (07012) *(G-1613)*

Electronic Manufacturing Co, Maplewood Also called R G Dunn Acquisitions Co
Inc *(G-5882)*

Electronic Marine Systems Inc (PA) 732 680-4120
800 Ferndale Pl Rahway (07065) *(G-9089)*

Electronic Measuring Devices 973 691-4755
15 Mill Rd Flanders (07836) *(G-3407)*

Electronic Mfg Svcs Inc 973 916-1001
48 Industrial St W Clifton (07012) *(G-1614)*

Electronic Parts Specialty Co 609 267-0055
10 Eagle Ave Ste 1100 Mount Holly (08060) *(G-6726)*

Electronic Power Designs Inc 973 838-7055
132 Union Ave Bloomingdale (07403) *(G-527)*

Electronic Specialty Products, Newfoundland Also called ESP Associates Inc *(G-7330)*

Electronic Technology Inc 973 371-5160
511 Lyons Ave Irvington (07111) *(G-4566)*

Electronic Transformer Corp 973 942-2222
460 Totowa Ave Paterson (07522) *(G-8177)*

Electronics Boutique Amer Inc 856 435-3900
1468 Blckwood Clmenton Rd Clementon (08021) *(G-1532)*

Electronix Express, Rahway Also called RSR Electronics Inc *(G-9126)*

Electrophysics, Fairfield Also called Lynred USA Inc *(G-3266)*

Electrum Inc 732 396-1616
827 Martin St Rahway (07065) *(G-9090)*

Electrum Recovery Works, Rahway Also called Electrum Inc *(G-9090)*

Elegant Desserts Inc 201 933-7309
275 Warren St Lyndhurst (07071) *(G-5650)*

Elegant Headwear Co Inc (PA) 908 558-1200
1000 Jefferson Ave Elizabeth (07201) *(G-2732)*

Eleison Pharmaceuticals Inc 215 416-7620
311 Farnsworth Ave Ste 1 Bordentown (08505) *(G-580)*

Elektromek Inc 973 614-9000
60 Webro Rd Clifton (07012) *(G-1615)*

Elemental Container Inc 908 687-7720
860 Springfield Rd Union (07083) *(G-11051)*

Elemental Interiors 646 861-3596
204 Bellevue Ave Montclair (07043) *(G-6365)*

Elementis Chromium Inc (HQ) 609 443-2000
469 Old Trenton Rd East Windsor (08512) *(G-2367)*

Elementis Global LLC (HQ) 609 443-2000
469 Old Trenton Rd East Windsor (08512) *(G-2368)*

Elementis Specialties, East Windsor Also called Elementis Global LLC *(G-2368)*

Elementis Specialties Inc (HQ) 609 443-2000
469 Old Trenton Rd East Windsor (08512) *(G-2369)*

Elementis Specialties Inc 201 432-0800
469 Old Trenton Rd East Windsor (08512) *(G-2370)*

Elements Accessories Inc 646 801-5187
16 Essex Rd Maplewood (07040) *(G-5876)*

Elements Global Group LLC 908 468-8407
527 Meyersville Rd Gillette (07933) *(G-3801)*

Elena Consultants & Elec 908 654-8309
1175 Globe Ave Mountainside (07092) *(G-6845)*

Elevate Hr Inc (PA) 973 917-3230
1055 Parsippany Blvd # 511 Parsippany (07054) *(G-7934)*

Elevator Cabs of NY Inc 973 790-9100
15 Jane St Paterson (07522) *(G-8178)*

Elevator Doors Inc 973 790-9100
15 Jane St Paterson (07522) *(G-8179)*

Elevator Doors-Elevator Cabs, Paterson *Also called Elevator Cabs of NY Inc (G-8178)*

Elevator Enterances NY Inc 973 790-9100
15 Jane St Paterson (07522) *(G-8180)*

Elevator Entrance Inc 973 790-9100
15 Jane St Paterson (07522) *(G-8181)*

Elgee Manufacturing Company 908 647-4100
225 Stirling Rd Warren (07059) *(G-11408)*

Elgee Power Vac Sweeper, Warren *Also called Elgee Manufacturing Company (G-11408)*

Eli Lillybranchburg 908 541-8000
33 Imclone Dr Branchburg (08876) *(G-637)*

Elie Tahari Ltd (PA) 973 671-6300
16 Bleeker St Millburn (07041) *(G-6196)*

Elis Hot Bagels Inc 732 566-4523
1055 Hwy 34 Ste C Matawan (07747) *(G-5975)*

Elite Cabinetry Corp 973 583-0194
97 Main St Newark (07105) *(G-7114)*

Elite Emrgncy Lights Ltd Lblty 732 534-2377
1000 Bennett Blvd Ste 6 Lakewood (08701) *(G-5090)*

Elite Graphix LLC 732 274-2356
45 Stouts Ln Ste 2 Monmouth Junction (08852) *(G-6290)*

Elite Laboratories Inc 201 750-2646
165 Ludlow Ave Northvale (07647) *(G-7522)*

Elite Landscaping & Pavers 732 252-6152
3102 Kapalua Ct Freehold (07728) *(G-3663)*

Elite Packaging Corp 732 651-9955
40 Cotters Ln Ste E East Brunswick (08816) *(G-2140)*

Elite Pharmaceuticals Inc (PA) 201 750-2646
165 Ludlow Ave Northvale (07647) *(G-7523)*

Elite Stone Importers LLC 732 542-7900
45 Park Rd Tinton Falls (07724) *(G-10716)*

Elite Surf Snow Skateboard Sp 856 427-7873
259 Marlton Pike E Cherry Hill (08034) *(G-1359)*

Elixens America Inc 732 388-3555
1443 Pinewood St Bldg 4u Rahway (07065) *(G-9091)*

Elkay Products Co Inc 973 376-7550
35 Brown Ave Springfield (07081) *(G-10441)*

Elkem Inc 732 566-1700
443 County Rd Cliffwood (07721) *(G-1546)*

Elkem Silicones USA Corp (HQ) 732 227-2060
2 Tower Center Blvd # 1601 East Brunswick (08816) *(G-2141)*

Elkom North America Inc 732 786-0490
680 Madison Ave Manalapan (07726) *(G-5807)*

Ellenby Technologies Inc 856 848-2020
412 Grandview Ave Woodbury Heights (08097) *(G-12042)*

Ellis Controls, Eatontown *Also called Ellis/Kuhnke Controls Inc (G-2391)*

Ellis Instruments Inc 973 593-9222
4 Elmer St Ste 1 Madison (07940) *(G-5692)*

Ellis/Kuhnke Controls Inc 732 291-3334
132 Lewis St Ste A2 Eatontown (07724) *(G-2391)*

Elmco Two Inc 856 365-2244
1045 Cambridge Ave Camden (08105) *(G-1060)*

Elmer Times Co Inc 856 358-6171
21 State St Elmer (08318) *(G-2796)*

Elmi Machine Tool Corp 973 882-1277
15 Spielman Rd 2 Fairfield (07004) *(G-3190)*

Elmwood Press Inc 201 794-6273
85 Main Ave Elmwood Park (07407) *(G-2824)*

Elnik Systems LLC 973 239-6066
107 Commerce Rd Cedar Grove (07009) *(G-1277)*

Eloa - New Jersey, Warren *Also called Essilor Laboratories Amer Inc (G-11410)*

Elray Manufacturing Company 856 881-1935
17 Liberty St Glassboro (08028) *(G-3810)*

Elusys Therapeutics Inc 973 808-0222
4 Century Dr Ste 260 Parsippany (07054) *(G-7935)*

Eluxnet USA Corporation 201 724-5986
3 S Corporate Dr Ste 2c Riverdale (07457) *(G-9376)*

Elvi Pharma LLC 732 640-2707
60 Ethel Rd W Ste 1 Piscataway (08854) *(G-8660)*

Elymat Corp 201 767-7105
180 Old Tappan Rd Ste 11 Old Tappan (07675) *(G-7733)*

Elymat Industries Inc 201 767-7105
180 Old Tappan Rd Ste 3 Old Tappan (07675) *(G-7734)*

Em Orthodontic Labs Inc 201 652-4411
6 Lafayette Pl Waldwick (07463) *(G-11302)*

Em Signs 973 300-9703
80 Merriam Ave Newton (07860) *(G-7341)*

Embroideries Unlimited Inc 201 692-1560
532 Wyndham Rd Teaneck (07666) *(G-10630)*

Embroidery Concepts 973 942-8555
41 Paterson Ave 43 Paterson (07522) *(G-8182)*

Embroidery In Stitches Inc 732 460-2660
1020 Campus Dr Morganville (07751) *(G-6586)*

EMC Aviation, Cookstown *Also called Export Management Consultants (G-1804)*

EMC Corporation 732 922-6353
8 The Fellsway Ocean (07712) *(G-7663)*

EMC Corporation 908 226-0100
4041 Hadley Rd Ste F South Plainfield (07080) *(G-10249)*

EMC Corporation 732 549-8500
1 Tower Center Blvd Fl 23 East Brunswick (08816) *(G-2142)*

EMC Paving LLC 908 636-1054
57 Justice St Piscataway (08854) *(G-8661)*

EMC Squared LLC 973 586-8854
30 Rolling Ridge Dr Rockaway (07866) *(G-9455)*

EMC Technologists, Wall Township *Also called I 2 R Corp (G-11348)*

EMC Toy, Ocean *Also called EMC Corporation (G-7663)*

Emc3, Marlton *Also called Doolan Industries Incorporated (G-5929)*

EMD Performance Materials Corp 908 429-3500
70 Meister Ave Branchburg (08876) *(G-638)*

Emdeon Corporation 201 703-3400
669 River Dr Ste 240 Elmwood Park (07407) *(G-2825)*

Emdur Art Products, Camden *Also called Emdur Metal Products Inc (G-1061)*

Emdur Metal Products Inc 856 541-1100
1115 Mount Vernon St Camden (08103) *(G-1061)*

Eme Electrical Contractors 973 228-6608
35 Roseland Ave Caldwell (07006) *(G-1023)*

Emerald Electronics Usa Inc 718 872-5544
90 Dayton Ave Ste 50 Passaic (07055) *(G-8063)*

Emerald Performance Mtls LLC 856 533-3000
2980 Route 73 N Maple Shade (08052) *(G-5862)*

Emerging Technologies, Bridgeton *Also called Mks Inc (G-765)*

Emerson Automation Solutions 856 542-5252
4 Killdeer Ct Ste 200 Bridgeport (08014) *(G-736)*

Emerson Process Management 908 605-4551
20 Independence Blvd Warren (07059) *(G-11409)*

Emerson Radio Corp (PA) 973 428-2000
35 Waterview Blvd Ste 140 Parsippany (07054) *(G-7936)*

Emerson Speed Printing Inc 201 265-7977
379 Kinderkamack Rd Oradell (07649) *(G-7743)*

Emil A Schroth Inc 732 938-5015
Copper Av Yellow Brook Rd Howell (07731) *(G-4538)*

Emil Dipalma Inc 973 477-2766
182 Stephens State Pk Rd Hackettstown (07840) *(G-4005)*

Emisphere Technologies Inc 973 532-8000
4 Becker Farm Rd Ste 103 Roseland (07068) *(G-9537)*

Emmco Development Corp 732 469-6464
243 Belmont Dr Somerset (08873) *(G-9985)*

Empanada King, Clifton *Also called Nijama Corporation (G-1678)*

Empire Architectural Millwork, Newark *Also called Empire Lumber & Millwork Co (G-7115)*

Empire Blended Distributors, Bayville *Also called Empire Blended Products Inc (G-244)*

Empire Blended Products Inc 732 269-4949
250 Hickory Ln Bayville (08721) *(G-244)*

Empire Industries Inc 973 279-2050
40 Warren St Paterson (07524) *(G-8183)*

Empire Lumber & Millwork Co 973 242-2700
377 Frelinghuysen Ave Newark (07114) *(G-7115)*

Empire Scale & Balance 856 299-1651
35 S Broad St Ste D Penns Grove (08069) *(G-8378)*

Empire Specialty Foods Inc 646 773-2630
6 Brookdale Rd East Brunswick (08816) *(G-2143)*

Empire Telecommunications Inc 201 569-3339
239 Fairview Ave Englewood Cliffs (07632) *(G-2968)*

Empirical Group LLC 201 571-0300
155 Chestnut Ridge Rd Montvale (07645) *(G-6411)*

Empirical Labs Inc 973 541-9447
41 N Beverwyck Rd Lake Hiawatha (07034) *(G-5034)*

Employment Horizons Inc 973 538-8822
10 Ridgedale Ave Cedar Knolls (07927) *(G-1304)*

Emporia Foundry Inc 973 483-5480
800 Bergen St Harrison (07029) *(G-4172)*

Emporium Leather Company Inc 201 330-7720
501 Penhorn Ave Ste 9 Secaucus (07094) *(G-9762)*

Empro Products Co Inc 973 302-4351
47 Montgomery St Belleville (07109) *(G-295)*

Empty Walls Inc 609 452-8488
3495 Us Highway 1 Ste 21 Princeton (08540) *(G-8940)*

EMR, Camden *Also called Camden Iron & Metal LLC (G-1044)*

Ems Aviation Inc 856 234-5020
121 Whittendale Dr Moorestown (08057) *(G-6522)*

Emse Corp 973 227-9221
10 Plog Rd Fairfield (07004) *(G-3191)*

Emseco, Fairfield *Also called Emse Corp (G-3191)*

En Tech Corp 201 784-1034
91 Ruckman Rd Ste 1 Closter (07624) *(G-1753)*

En Tech Corp (PA) 718 389-2058
91 Ruckman Rd Closter (07624) *(G-1754)*

Ena Meat Packing Inc (PA) 973 742-4790
240 E 5th St Paterson (07524) *(G-8184)*

Enailsupply Corporation 909 725-1698
2161 Whitesville Rd Ste C Toms River (08755) *(G-10755)*

Enaltec Labs Inc 908 864-8000
991 Route 22 Ste 200 Bridgewater (08807) *(G-819)*

Enamel Art Studio 732 321-0774
120 Liberty St Metuchen (08840) *(G-6055)*

Encore Enterprises Inc (PA) 201 489-5044
57 Leuning St South Hackensack (07606) *(G-10158)*

Encore International LLC 973 423-3880
270 Lafayette Ave Hawthorne (07506) *(G-4216)*

A
L
P
H
A
B
E
T
I
C

Encore Led Ltg Ltd Lblty Co 866 694-4533
155 Us Highway 46 Wayne (07470) *(G-11497)*
Encore Pharmaceutical Inc 973 267-9331
49 Moraine Rd Morris Plains (07950) *(G-6605)*
Encur Inc 732 264-2098
200 Division St Keyport (07735) *(G-4998)*
Endo Phrmaceuticals Valera Inc 609 235-3230
8 Clarke Dr Cranbury (08512) *(G-1832)*
Endomedix Inc 848 248-1883
1 Normal Ave Cels404 Montclair (07043) *(G-6366)*
Endot Industries Inc (PA) 973 625-8500
60 Green Pond Rd Rockaway (07866) *(G-9456)*
Endotec Inc (PA) 973 762-6100
20 Valley St Ste 210 South Orange (07079) *(G-10194)*
Endurance Net Inc 609 499-3450
763 B Railroad Ave Florence (08518) *(G-3475)*
Ener-G Rudox Inc 201 438-0111
180 E Union Ave East Rutherford (07073) *(G-2286)*
Energy Battery 908 751-5918
1200 County Road 523 Flemington (08822) *(G-3439)*
Energy Battery Group Inc 404 255-7529
1200 County Road 523 Flemington (08822) *(G-3440)*
Energy Beams Inc 973 291-6555
185 Hamburg Tpke Bloomingdale (07403) *(G-528)*
Energy Chem America Inc 201 816-2307
920 Sylvan Ave Englewood Cliffs (07632) *(G-2969)*
Energy Combustion Systems, Westville *Also called Energy Company Inc (G-11814)*
Energy Company Inc 856 742-1916
50 Cutler Ave Ste 6 Westville (08093) *(G-11814)*
Energy Options Inc 732 512-9100
3 Ethel Rd Ste 300 Edison (08817) *(G-2502)*
Energy Recycling Co LLC 732 545-6619
100 Jersey Ave Ste C8 New Brunswick (08901) *(G-6924)*
Energy Storage Corp (PA) 732 542-7880
526 Industrial Way W Eatontown (07724) *(G-2392)*
Energy Tracking LLC 973 448-8660
16 Southwind Dr Flanders (07836) *(G-3408)*
Energy Tracking Inc 973 448-8660
16 Southwind Dr Flanders (07836) *(G-3409)*
Enersys 800 719-7887
80 Veronica Ave Ste 1 Somerset (08873) *(G-9986)*
Enertia LLC 856 330-4767
10471049 Thomas Busch Pennsauken (08110) *(G-8418)*
Enforsys Inc (PA) 973 515-8126
27 Bleeker St 222 Millburn (07041) *(G-6197)*
Enforsys Systems, Millburn *Also called Enforsys Inc (G-6197)*
ENG SCIENTIFIC, Clifton *Also called A J P Scientific Inc (G-1551)*
Engelhard, Iselin *Also called BASF Catalysts LLC (G-4599)*
Engelhard Corporation 732 205-5000
101 Wood Ave S Iselin (08830) *(G-4608)*
Engility LLC 703 633-8300
15 Roszel Rd Princeton Junction (08550) *(G-9055)*
Engine Combo LLC 201 290-4399
300 Nye Ave Irvington (07111) *(G-4567)*
Engine Efficiency Associates, Rahway *Also called Electronic Marine Systems Inc (G-9089)*
Engine Factory Inc 908 236-9915
24 Cokesbury Rd Ste 15 Lebanon (08833) *(G-5259)*
Engineered Components Inc 908 788-8393
546 Old York Rd Three Bridges (08887) *(G-10704)*
Engineered Mtl Arresting Sys, Logan Township *Also called Enginred Arrsting Systems Corp (G-5587)*
Engineered Plastic Pdts Inc (PA) 908 647-3500
269 Mercer St Stirling (07980) *(G-10489)*
Engineered Precision Cast Co 732 671-2424
952 Palmer Ave Middletown (07748) *(G-6163)*
Engineered Security Systems (PA) 973 257-0555
1 Indian Ln E Towaco (07082) *(G-10871)*
Engineered Silicone Pdts LLC 973 300-5120
75 Mill St Ste 2 Newton (07860) *(G-7342)*
Engineering Laboratories Inc 201 337-8116
360 W Oakland Ave Oakland (07436) *(G-7627)*
Enginred Arrsting Systems Corp 856 241-8620
2239 High Hill Rd Logan Township (08085) *(G-5587)*
Englert Inc (PA) 800 364-5378
1200 Amboy Ave Perth Amboy (08861) *(G-8517)*
Englewood Lab LLC (PA) 201 567-2267
88 W Sheffield Ave Englewood (07631) *(G-2901)*
Engo Co 908 754-6600
128 Case Dr South Plainfield (07080) *(G-10250)*
Engraved Images Ltd 908 234-0323
Demunn Pl Rr 202 Far Hills (07931) *(G-3375)*
Enjou Chocolat Morristown Inc 973 993-9090
8 Dehart St Ste 1 Morristown (07960) *(G-6662)*
Enor Corporation 201 750-1680
246 S Dean St Englewood (07631) *(G-2902)*
Enpirion Inc 908 575-7550
53 Frontage Rd Ste 210 Hampton (08827) *(G-4150)*
Enpro Inc 908 236-2137
1401 Us Highway 22 Lebanon (08833) *(G-5260)*
Enroute Computer Solutions Inc (PA) 609 569-9255
2511 Fire Rd Ste A4 Egg Harbor Township (08234) *(G-2683)*
Ensembleiq Inc 201 855-7600
1 Gateway Ctr 11-43 Newark (07102) *(G-7116)*
Enser Corporation (PA) 856 829-5522
1902 Taylors Ln Cinnaminson (08077) *(G-1456)*
Ensinger Grenloch Inc (HQ) 856 227-0500
1 Main St Grenloch (08032) *(G-3869)*
Ensinger Hyde, Grenloch *Also called Ensinger Grenloch Inc (G-3869)*
Enspharma, Morris Plains *Also called Encore Pharmaceutical Inc (G-6605)*
Ensync Intrctive Solutions Inc 732 542-4001
83 South St Ste 202 Freehold (07728) *(G-3664)*
Enteris Biopharma Inc 973 453-3518
83 Fulton St Boonton (07005) *(G-551)*
Enterix Inc 732 429-1899
236 Fernwood Ave Edison (08837) *(G-2503)*
Enterprise Container LLC (PA) 201 797-7200
575 N Midland Ave Saddle Brook (07663) *(G-9651)*
Enterprise Services LLC 609 259-9400
989 Lenox Dr Princeton (08544) *(G-8941)*
Enterprise Solution Products 201 678-9200
28 Av At Pt Imperial 23 West New York (07093) *(G-11739)*
Enterprisecc Ltd Liability Co 201 266-0020
521 Palisade Ave Jersey City (07307) *(G-4732)*
Entourage Imaging Inc 888 926-6571
39 Everett Dr Ste 1-2 Princeton Junction (08550) *(G-9056)*
Entourage Yearbooks, Princeton Junction *Also called Entourage Imaging Inc (G-9056)*
Envelope Freedom Holdings LLC (PA) 201 699-5800
65 Railroad Ave Ridgefield (07657) *(G-9259)*
Envelopes & Printed Pdts Inc 973 942-1232
135 Fairview Ave Prospect Park (07508) *(G-9073)*
Envigo Crs Inc (PA) 732 873-2550
100 Mettlers Rd Somerset (08873) *(G-9987)*
Envirnmntal Dsign Grphic Entps 973 361-1829
215 State Route 10 Dover (07869) *(G-2083)*
Envirnmntal Dynamics Group Inc (PA) 609 924-4489
5 Crscent Ave Rocky Hill (08553) *(G-9525)*
Envirnmntal Mgt Chem Wste Svcs (PA) 201 848-7676
45 Whitney Rd Bldg B Mahwah (07430) *(G-5735)*
Enviro Pak Inc 732 248-1600
125 National Rd Edison (08817) *(G-2504)*
Enviro Safe Wtr Trtmnt Systems, Elmer *Also called Favs Corp (G-2797)*
Enviro-Clear Company Inc 908 638-5507
152 Cregar Rd High Bridge (08829) *(G-4282)*
Envirochem Inc 732 238-6700
425 Whitehead Ave South River (08882) *(G-10350)*
Environmental Technical Drlg, Farmingdale *Also called Environmental Technical Drlg (G-3385)*
Environmental Technical Drlg 732 938-3222
408 Cranberry Rd Farmingdale (07727) *(G-3385)*
Environmolds LLC 908 273-5401
18 Bank St Ste 1 Summit (07901) *(G-10531)*
Envirosight LLC (PA) 973 970-9284
111 Canfield Ave Ste B-3 Randolph (07869) *(G-9176)*
Enzon Pharmaceuticals Inc (PA) 732 980-4500
20 Commerce Dr Ste 135 Cranford (07016) *(G-1909)*
Enzon Pharmaceuticals Inc 732 980-4500
300 Corporate Ct Ste C South Plainfield (07080) *(G-10251)*
Eom Worldwide Sales Corp 732 994-7352
39 Harmony Dr Lakewood (08701) *(G-5091)*
Eon Labs Inc 609 627-8600
506 Carnegie Ctr Ste 400 Princeton (08540) *(G-8942)*
Eos Energy Storage LLC 732 225-8400
214 Fernwood Ave Bldg B Edison (08837) *(G-2505)*
EP Henry Corporation (PA) 856 845-6200
201 Park Ave Woodbury (08096) *(G-12028)*
Ep Systems Inc 570 424-0581
470 Schooleys Mountain Rd Hackettstown (07840) *(G-4006)*
Epco, Middletown *Also called Engineered Precision Cast Co (G-6163)*
Epcos, Lumberton *Also called Tdk Electronics Inc (G-5636)*
Epd, Bloomingdale *Also called Electronic Power Designs Inc (G-527)*
Epi, Caldwell *Also called Essex Products International (G-1024)*
Epi Group Ltd Liability Co 917 710-6607
410 Monmouth Ave Lakewood (08701) *(G-5092)*
Epic Holding Inc 732 249-6867
15 Footes Ln Morristown (07960) *(G-6663)*
Epic Industries, Morristown *Also called Epic Holding Inc (G-6663)*
Epic Millwork LLC 732 296-0273
1022 Hamilton St Ste J Somerset (08873) *(G-9988)*
Epicore Networks USA Inc 609 267-9118
4 Lina Ln Mount Holly (08060) *(G-6727)*
Epiq Systems Inc 973 622-6111
50 Park Pl Ste 701 Newark (07102) *(G-7117)*
Epoch Everlasting Play LLC 973 316-2500
75d Lackawanna Ave Parsippany (07054) *(G-7937)*
Epoch Times 908 548-8026
50 Cragwood Rd Ste 305 South Plainfield (07080) *(G-10252)*
Epolin Chemical LLC (HQ) 973 465-9495
358-364 Adams St Newark (07105) *(G-7118)*

Eppley Building & Design Inc	973 636-9499
220 Goffle Rd Ste B Hawthorne (07506) *(G-4217)*	
Epsilon Plastics Inc (HQ)	201 933-6000
Page & Schuyler Ave 8 Lyndhurst (07071) *(G-5651)*	
Equipment Distributing Corp (PA)	201 641-8414
3 Eucker St Ridgefield Park (07660) *(G-9305)*	
Equipment Erectors Inc	732 846-1212
15 Veronica Ave Somerset (08873) *(G-9989)*	
Equistar Chemicals, Newark *Also called Lyondell Chemical Company* *(G-7192)*	
Erco Ceilings Somers Point Inc	609 517-2531
5 Chestnut St Somers Point (08244) *(G-9936)*	
Erco Lighting Inc (PA)	732 225-8856
160 Rrtan Ctr Pkwy Ste 10 Edison (08837) *(G-2506)*	
Erial Concrete Inc	856 784-8884
965 Hickstown Rd Erial (08081) *(G-3011)*	
Erika-Record LLC	973 614-8500
37 Atlantic Way Clifton (07012) *(G-1616)*	
Erj Baking LLC	201 906-1300
235 N Pleasant Ave Ridgewood (07450) *(G-9324)*	
Ernest R Miles Construction Co	856 697-2311
1445 Catawba Ave Newfield (08344) *(G-7321)*	
Ernest Schaefer Inc	908 964-1280
731 Lehigh Ave Union (07083) *(G-11052)*	
Eroomsystem Technologies Inc (PA)	732 730-0116
150 Airport Rd Ste 1200 Lakewood (08701) *(G-5093)*	
Ervin Advertising Co Inc (PA)	732 363-7645
4880 Us Hwy Rte 9 S Howell (07731) *(G-4539)*	
Es Industrial	732 842-5600
10 Mechanic St Ste 200 Red Bank (07701) *(G-9228)*	
Esaw Industries Inc	732 613-1400
5 Litchfield Rd East Brunswick (08816) *(G-2144)*	
Escada US Subco LLC	201 865-5200
55 Hartz Way Ste 17 Secaucus (07094) *(G-9763)*	
Escadaus Inc	973 335-8888
2 Wood Glen Way Boonton (07005) *(G-552)*	
Esco Industries Corp	973 478-5888
30 Stonewall Ct Woodcliff Lake (07677) *(G-12056)*	
Esco Optics, Oak Ridge *Also called Esco Products Inc* *(G-7602)*	
Esco Precision Inc	908 722-0800
71 Old Camplain Rd Hillsborough (08844) *(G-4315)*	
Esco Products Inc	973 697-3700
95 Chamberlain Rd Oak Ridge (07438) *(G-7602)*	
Esd Professional Inc	212 300-7673
468a Commercial Ave Palisades Park (07650) *(G-7773)*	
Esg LLC	973 347-2969
21 Tall Oaks Ln Budd Lake (07828) *(G-922)*	
Esi	856 629-2492
1541 New Broklyn Erial Rd Sicklerville (08081) *(G-9909)*	
Esjay Pharma LLC	609 469-5920
70 Lake Dr East Windsor (08520) *(G-2350)*	
Esjay Pharma LLC (PA)	732 438-1816
27 Ridgeview Way Allentown (08501) *(G-26)*	
ESP, Newton *Also called Engineered Silicone Pdts LLC* *(G-7342)*	
ESP Associates Inc	973 208-9045
2713 State Rt 23 Ste 8a Newfoundland (07435) *(G-7330)*	
Espertech Inc	973 577-6406
26 Hamilton Ave Wayne (07470) *(G-11498)*	
Esquire Business Forms	609 883-1155
1668 N Olden Avenue Ext Ewing (08638) *(G-3029)*	
Esquire Graphics & Bus Forms, Ewing *Also called Esquire Business Forms* *(G-3029)*	
Ess, South Hackensack *Also called On Site Communication* *(G-10177)*	
Ess Group Inc	609 755-3139
129 Eayrestown Rd Southampton (08088) *(G-10361)*	
Essential Dental Systems Inc	201 487-9090
89 Leuning St Ste 8 South Hackensack (07606) *(G-10159)*	
Essential Machining, Brick *Also called Charles F Kilian* *(G-712)*	
Essentra Packaging US Inc	856 439-1700
1224 N Church St Moorestown (08057) *(G-6523)*	
Essentra Plastics LLC	518 437-5138
95 Campus Dr Edison (08837) *(G-2507)*	
Essex Coatings LLC	732 855-9400
135 Essex Ave E Avenel (07001) *(G-126)*	
Essex Morris Sign Co	973 386-1755
30 Troy Rd Ste 2 Whippany (07981) *(G-11890)*	
Essex Products International	973 226-2424
494 Mountain Ave Caldwell (07006) *(G-1024)*	
Essex Rise Conveyor Corp	973 575-7483
4 Fairfield Cres West Caldwell (07006) *(G-11648)*	
Essex West Graphics Inc (PA)	973 227-2400
305 Fairfield Ave Fairfield (07004) *(G-3192)*	
Essilor Laboratories Amer Inc	732 563-9884
5 Powderhorn Dr Warren (07059) *(G-11410)*	
Estrin Calabrese Sales Agency	908 722-9980
17 S Main St Ste 3 Manville (08835) *(G-5855)*	
ET Browne Drug Co Inc (PA)	201 894-9020
440 Sylvan Ave Englewood Cliffs (07632) *(G-2970)*	
Et Manufacturing & Sales Inc	973 777-6662
90 Dayton Ave Ste C5 Passaic (07055) *(G-8064)*	
Ethan Allen Retail Inc	973 473-1019
1 Market St Ste 1 # 1 Passaic (07055) *(G-8065)*	

Ethel M Chocolates, Mount Arlington *Also called Mars Retail Group Inc* *(G-6715)*	
Ethicon Endo - Surgery, Bridgewater *Also called Ethicon Inc* *(G-820)*	
Ethicon Endo-Surgery, Bedminster *Also called Ethicon Inc* *(G-265)*	
Ethicon Inc (HQ)	732 524-0400
Us Route 22 Somerville (08876) *(G-10108)*	
Ethicon Inc	908 306-0327
135 Us Highway 202 206 # 4 Bedminster (07921) *(G-264)*	
Ethicon Inc	908 218-0707
135 Us Highway 202 206 # 4 Bedminster (07921) *(G-265)*	
Ethicon Inc	908 253-6464
520 Us Highway 22 Ste 1 Bridgewater (08807) *(G-820)*	
Ethicon LLC (HQ)	908 218-3195
Rr 22 Box W Somerville (08876) *(G-10109)*	
Ethylene Atlantic Corp	856 467-0010
136 Church St Swedesboro (08085) *(G-10584)*	
Eti, Irvington *Also called Electronic Technology Inc* *(G-4566)*	
Euclid Chemical Company	732 390-9770
77 Milltown Rd Ste B7 East Brunswick (08816) *(G-2145)*	
Eugene Kozak	973 442-1001
193 Franklin Rd Randolph (07869) *(G-9177)*	
Euro American Foods Group, Bayonne *Also called European Amrcn Foods Group Inc* *(G-215)*	
Euro Mechanical Inc	201 313-8050
16 Industrial Ave Fairview (07022) *(G-3360)*	
Eurodia Industrie SA	732 805-4001
20 Worlds Fair Dr Ste F Somerset (08873) *(G-9990)*	
Euroimmun US Inc	973 656-1000
1 Bloomfield Ave 1 # 1 Mountain Lakes (07046) *(G-6824)*	
European Amrcn Foods Group Inc (PA)	201 436-6106
698 Kennedy Blvd Bayonne (07002) *(G-215)*	
European Amrcn Foods Group Inc	201 583-1101
425 Route 3 Secaucus (07094) *(G-9764)*	
European Coffee Classics Inc	856 428-7202
1401 Berlin Rd Ste A Cherry Hill (08034) *(G-1360)*	
European Imports of LA Inc	973 536-1823
25 Columbine Rd Paramus (07652) *(G-7799)*	
European Pretzel One LLC	201 867-6117
1619 54th St North Bergen (07047) *(G-7404)*	
European Stone Art LLC	201 441-9116
208 Huyler St South Hackensack (07606) *(G-10160)*	
Europrojects Intl Inc (PA)	201 408-5215
500 Nordhoff Pl Ste 5 Englewood (07631) *(G-2903)*	
Eva Maria Wolfe	412 777-2000
6 Westbelt Wayne (07470) *(G-11499)*	
Evans Chemetics LP (HQ)	201 992-3100
Glenpointe Center West 4 Teaneck (07666) *(G-10631)*	
Evans Machine & Tool Co	732 442-1144
410 Summit Ave Perth Amboy (08861) *(G-8518)*	
Evapco-Blct Dry Cooling Inc	908 379-2665
685 Route 202/206 Ste 300 Bridgewater (08807) *(G-821)*	
Evening Journal Association (HQ)	201 653-1000
1 Harmon Plz Ste 1000 Secaucus (07094) *(G-9765)*	
Evening News, The, Salem *Also called Medianews Group Inc* *(G-9695)*	
Evenus Pharmaceutical Labs Inc	609 395-8625
506 Carnegie Ctr Ste 100 Princeton (08540) *(G-8943)*	
Everbind Marco, Lodi *Also called Marco Book Co Inc* *(G-5570)*	
Evereast Trading Inc	201 944-6484
2125 Center Ave Ste 401 Fort Lee (07024) *(G-3557)*	
Everflow Supplies Inc (PA)	908 436-1100
100 Middlesex Ave Carteret (07008) *(G-1252)*	
Evergard Steel Corp	908 925-6800
3313 Revere Rd South Plainfield (07080) *(G-10253)*	
Evergreen Information Svcs Inc	973 339-9672
8 Cedarwood Ter Woodland Park (07424) *(G-12077)*	
Evergreen Kosher LLC	732 370-4500
945 River Ave Lakewood (08701) *(G-5094)*	
Evergreen Lakewood, Lakewood *Also called Evergreen Kosher LLC* *(G-5094)*	
Evergreen Printing Company, Bellmawr *Also called Green Horse Media LLC* *(G-333)*	
Everite Machine Products Co	856 330-6700
1555 Route 73 Pennsauken (08110) *(G-8419)*	
Everlast Associates Inc	609 261-1888
203 Route 530 Southampton (08088) *(G-10362)*	
Everlast Sheds, Southampton *Also called Everlast Associates Inc* *(G-10362)*	
Everlasting Valve Company Inc	908 769-0700
108 Somogyi Ct South Plainfield (07080) *(G-10254)*	
Evertile Flooring Co Inc	973 242-7474
127 Frelinghuysen Ave Newark (07114) *(G-7119)*	
Evertlast Interiors	732 252-9965
52 Main St Ste 6 Manalapan (07726) *(G-5808)*	
Everythingbenefits, New Providence *Also called Ontimeworks LLC* *(G-7015)*	
Evex Analytical Instruments	609 252-9192
857 State Rd Princeton (08540) *(G-8944)*	
Evex Instruments, Princeton *Also called Evex Analytical Instruments* *(G-8944)*	
Evey Vacuum Service	856 692-4779
158 W Weymouth Rd Vineland (08360) *(G-11217)*	
Evh LLC	973 257-0076
6 Mars Ct Unit F5 Boonton (07005) *(G-553)*	

Eviva LLC (PA)..973 925-4028
  30 Wood St Paterson (07524) *(G-8185)*

Evonik Corporation...732 981-5000
  2 Turner Pl Piscataway (08854) *(G-8662)*

Evonik Corporation (HQ).....................................973 929-8000
  299 Jefferson Rd Parsippany (07054) *(G-7938)*

Evonik Foams Inc (HQ)......................................973 929-8000
  299 Jefferson Rd Parsippany (07054) *(G-7939)*

Evoqua Water Technologies LLC...........................908 851-4250
  2 Milltown Ct Union (07083) *(G-11053)*

Evoqua Water Technologies LLC...........................908 353-7400
  624 Evans St Elizabeth (07201) *(G-2733)*

Evoqua Water Technologies LLC...........................201 531-9338
  20 Murray Hill Pkwy # 140 East Rutherford (07073) *(G-2287)*

Evotec (us) Inc (HQ)..650 228-1400
  303b College Rd E Princeton (08540) *(G-8945)*

Evs, Fairfield *Also called EVs Broadcast Equipment Inc (G-3194)*

EVs Broadcast Equipment Inc (HQ).....................973 575-7811
  9 Law Dr Ste 4 Fairfield (07004) *(G-3193)*

EVs Broadcast Equipment Inc.............................973 575-7811
  700 Route 46 E Ste 300 Fairfield (07004) *(G-3194)*

Evs Interactive Inc..718 784-3690
  100 Riverdale Rd Riverdale (07457) *(G-9377)*

Ewc Controls Inc..732 446-3110
  385 State Route 33 Manalapan (07726) *(G-5809)*

Ewing Recovery Corp..609 883-0318
  1565 6th St Ewing (08638) *(G-3030)*

Ex-Press Printing, Linden *Also called Noble Metals Corp (G-5397)*

Exactal Tool & Die, South Plainfield *Also called Exactal Tool Ltd Inc (G-10255)*

Exactal Tool Ltd Inc..908 561-1177
  3586 Kennedy Rd Ste 3 South Plainfield (07080) *(G-10255)*

Exalent Packaging Inc..973 742-9600
  55 1st Ave Paterson (07514) *(G-8186)*

Exalenz Bioscience Inc......................................732 232-4393
  1712 M St Wall Township (07719) *(G-11338)*

Excalibur Bagel Bky Equip Inc............................201 797-2788
  4-1 Banta Pl Fair Lawn (07410) *(G-3099)*

Excalibur Miretti Group LLC................................973 808-8399
  285 Eldridge Rd Fairfield (07004) *(G-3195)*

Excel Blades, Paterson *Also called Excel Hobby Blades Corp (G-8187)*

Excel Color Graphics Inc....................................856 848-3345
  207 W Jersey Ave Woodbury Heights (08097) *(G-12043)*

Excel Die Sharpening Corp.................................908 587-2606
  19 Grant St Linden (07036) *(G-5345)*

Excel Display Corp..732 246-3724
  100 Jersey Ave Ste A6 New Brunswick (08901) *(G-6925)*

Excel Hobby Blades Corp...................................973 278-4000
  481 Getty Ave Paterson (07503) *(G-8187)*

Excel Hydraulics LLC...856 241-1145
  152 Berkley Rd Clarksboro (08020) *(G-1519)*

Excel Industrial Co Inc.......................................609 275-1748
  17 Huntington Dr Princeton Junction (08550) *(G-9057)*

Excell Brands Ltd Liability Co..............................908 561-1130
  3 Independence Way # 114 Princeton (08540) *(G-8946)*

Excellence In Baking Inc....................................732 287-1313
  2062 State Route 27 Edison (08817) *(G-2508)*

Excellent Bakery Equipment Co...........................973 244-1664
  19 Spielman Rd Fairfield (07004) *(G-3196)*

Excellent Prtg & Graphics LLC............................973 773-6661
  333 Hazel St Clifton (07011) *(G-1617)*

Excelsior Medical LLC (HQ)...............................732 776-7525
  1933 Heck Ave Neptune (07753) *(G-6877)*

Excerpta Medica Inc (HQ)..................................908 547-2100
  685 Us Highway 202/206 Bridgewater (08807) *(G-822)*

Excite View LLC...201 227-7075
  4 Thatcher Rd Ste 2001 Tenafly (07670) *(G-10662)*

Exclusive Materials LLC.....................................732 886-9956
  1385 Pasadena St Lakewood (08701) *(G-5095)*

Executive Clothiers, Shrewsbury *Also called Michael Duru Clothiers LLC (G-9896)*

Exelis Geospatial Systems, Bloomfield *Also called L3harris Technologies Inc (G-505)*

Exelis Inc/Northrop..973 284-4212
  77 River Rd Clifton (07014) *(G-1618)*

Exeltis Usa Inc (HQ)..973 324-0200
  180 Park Ave Ste 101 Florham Park (07932) *(G-3503)*

Exeltis USA Dermatology LLC............................973 805-4060
  180 Park Ave Ste 101 Florham Park (07932) *(G-3504)*

Exemplify Biopharma Inc...................................732 500-3208
  3000 Eastpark Blvd Cranbury (08512) *(G-1833)*

Exhibit Co Inc...732 465-1070
  239 Old New Brunswick Rd Piscataway (08854) *(G-8663)*

Exhibit Network Inc..732 751-9600
  434 Brookside Ave Oakhurst (07755) *(G-7608)*

Exide Battery, West Caldwell *Also called Exide Technologies (G-11649)*

Exide Technologies...973 439-9612
  1 Dodge Dr West Caldwell (07006) *(G-11649)*

Exim Incorporated (PA).....................................908 561-8200
  30 Thames Ave Piscataway (08854) *(G-8664)*

Exma Industries, Lakewood *Also called Exclusive Materials LLC (G-5095)*

Exodon LLC..973 398-2900
  111 Howard Blvd Ste 204 Mount Arlington (07856) *(G-6712)*

Exothermic Molding Inc......................................908 272-2299
  50 Lafayette Pl Kenilworth (07033) *(G-4937)*

Expert Appliance Center LLC...............................732 946-0999
  460 County Road 520 Marlboro (07746) *(G-5897)*

Expert Process Systems LLC.............................570 424-0581
  470 Schooleys Mountain Rd A Hackettstown (07840) *(G-4007)*

Export Management Consultants...........................609 758-1166
  54 Wrghtstown Cokstown Rd Cookstown (08511) *(G-1804)*

Express Press, Galloway *Also called Allegro Printing Corporation (G-3719)*

Express Printing Inc..908 925-6300
  209 W Saint Georges Ave Linden (07036) *(G-5346)*

Express Printing Services Inc..............................973 585-7355
  26 Commerce Rd Ste L Fairfield (07004) *(G-3197)*

Exquisities, Clifton *Also called International Delights LLC (G-1642)*

Extra Office Inc...732 381-9774
  580 Leesville Ave Rahway (07065) *(G-9092)*

Extracts and Ingredients, Union *Also called Morre-TEC Industries Inc (G-11076)*

Extreme Digital Graphics Inc...............................973 227-5599
  7 Kingsbridge Rd Ste 1 Fairfield (07004) *(G-3198)*

Extreme Pallet Inc...973 286-1717
  315 Astor St Newark (07114) *(G-7120)*

Extremity Medical LLC......................................973 588-8980
  300 Interpace Pkwy # 410 Parsippany (07054) *(G-7940)*

Extruders International Inc...................................908 241-7750
  181 W Clay Ave Roselle Park (07204) *(G-9584)*

Extrusion Technik USA Inc..................................732 354-0177
  67 Veronica Ave Ste 15-16 Somerset (08873) *(G-9991)*

Eyelet Embroideries Inc.....................................201 945-2151
  65 Railroad Ave Ste 3 Ridgefield (07657) *(G-9260)*

Eyetech Inc..646 454-1779
  700 Us Highway 202/206 Bridgewater (08807) *(G-823)*

Eywa Pharma Inc..609 751-9600
  2 Research Way Fl 3 Princeton (08540) *(G-8947)*

EZ General Construction Corp.............................201 223-1101
  155 Webster Dr Wayne (07470) *(G-11500)*

Ez-Dumpster LLC...908 752-2787
  829 Madison Ave Bridgewater (08807) *(G-824)*

Ezcom Software Inc..201 731-1800
  25 Rockwood Pl Ste 420 Englewood (07631) *(G-2904)*

Ezose Sciences Inc..862 926-1950
  300 Campus Dr Ste 300 Florham Park (07932) *(G-3505)*

Ezrirx LLC (PA)...718 502-6610
  1525 Prospect St Ste 203 Lakewood (08701) *(G-5096)*

F & A Signs Inc...732 442-9399
  49 W Pond Rd Hopelawn (08861) *(G-4525)*

F & C Prof Alum Railings Corp.............................908 753-8886
  1149 W Front St Plainfield (07063) *(G-8765)*

F & D, Millville *Also called Friedrich and Dimmock Inc (G-6249)*

F & G Tool & Die Inc...908 241-5880
  195 Sumner Ave Kenilworth (07033) *(G-4938)*

F & M Expressions Unlimited, Mahwah *Also called Flanagan Holdings Inc (G-5737)*

F & M Machine Co Inc..908 245-8830
  751 Lexington Ave Kenilworth (07033) *(G-4939)*

F & R Grinding Inc..908 996-0440
  138 County Road 513 Frenchtown (08825) *(G-3712)*

F & R Machine Corp..973 684-8139
  41 Bleeker St Paterson (07524) *(G-8188)*

F & R Pallets Inc..856 964-8516
  201 Erie St Camden (08102) *(G-1062)*

F & S Awning and Blind Co Inc............................732 738-4110
  13 Coral St Edison (08837) *(G-2509)*

F and L Machinery..973 218-6216
  48 Commerce St Springfield (07081) *(G-10442)*

F and M Equipment Ltd.....................................215 822-0145
  2820 Hamilton Blvd South Plainfield (07080) *(G-10256)*

F G Clover Company Inc.....................................973 627-1160
  40 Stickle Ave Rockaway (07866) *(G-9457)*

F I Companies, Old Bridge *Also called Forman Industries Inc (G-7715)*

F L Feldman Associates......................................732 776-8544
  811 Memorial Dr Asbury Park (07712) *(G-76)*

F M B Systems, Harrison *Also called FMB Systems Inc (G-4175)*

F M C Research and Dev Div, Ewing *Also called FMC Corporation (G-3031)*

F M T, Hillsborough *Also called Fischl Machine & Tool (G-4316)*

F M W Piping Contractors, Carteret *Also called Folgore Mobil Welding Inc (G-1254)*

F P Developments Inc..856 875-7100
  402 S Main St Williamstown (08094) *(G-11957)*

F P Schmidt Manufacturing Co............................201 343-4241
  143 Leuning St South Hackensack (07606) *(G-10161)*

F S Brainard & Co..609 387-4300
  5 Terri Ln Ste 15 Burlington (08016) *(G-966)*

F S R Inc...973 785-4347
  244 Bergen Blvd Woodland Park (07424) *(G-12078)*

F S T Printing Inc...732 560-3749
  1324 Bound Brook Rd Middlesex (08846) *(G-6115)*

F T Millwork Inc...732 741-1216
  9 Catherine St Red Bank (07701) *(G-9229)*

F W Bennett & Son Inc 973 383-4050
403 Sparta Rd Lafayette (07848) *(G-5027)*

F&S Awning & Sign, Edison *Also called F & S Awning and Blind Co Inc* *(G-2509)*

F&S Produce Company Inc 856 453-0316
730 Lebanon Rd Rosenhayn (08352) *(G-9595)*

F&S Produce Company Inc (PA) 856 453-0316
500 W Elmer Rd Vineland (08360) *(G-11218)*

Faber Precision Inc 973 983-1844
198 Green Pond Rd Ste 6 Rockaway (07866) *(G-9458)*

Fabian Couture Group LLC 800 367-6251
205 Chubb Ave Bldg C Lyndhurst (07071) *(G-5652)*

Fabian Formals Inc 201 460-7776
205 Chubb Ave Ste 2 Lyndhurst (07071) *(G-5653)*

Fablok Mills Inc 908 464-1950
140 Spring St New Providence (07974) *(G-6998)*

Fabric Bee, South Hackensack *Also called Pioneer Embroidery Co* *(G-10181)*

Fabric Chemical Corporation 201 432-0440
61 Cornelison Ave Jersey City (07304) *(G-4733)*

Fabricolor Holding Intl LLC 973 742-5800
24 1/2 Van Houten St Paterson (07505) *(G-8189)*

Fabrictex LLC 732 225-3990
278 Raritan Center Pkwy Edison (08837) *(G-2510)*

Fabulous Fabricators LLC 973 779-2400
11 Jackson Rd Totowa (07512) *(G-10826)*

Fabuwood Cabinetry Corp 201 432-6555
69-95 Blanchard St Newark (07105) *(G-7121)*

Facsimile Cmmncations Inds Inc 201 672-0773
230 Clay Ave Lyndhurst (07071) *(G-5654)*

Factonomy Inc 201 848-7812
459 Oldwoods Rd Wyckoff (07481) *(G-12111)*

Factory Fit, Bellmawr *Also called M Parker Autoworks Inc* *(G-337)*

FAEEC, Basking Ridge *Also called Foundation For Embryonic* *(G-183)*

Fairfield Gourmet Food Corp (PA) 973 575-4365
11 Cliffside Dr Cedar Grove (07009) *(G-1278)*

Fairfield Laundry McHy Corp 973 575-4330
5 Montesano Rd Ste 1 Fairfield (07004) *(G-3199)*

Fairfield Metal Ltd Lblty Co 973 276-8440
9 Audrey Pl Fairfield (07004) *(G-3200)*

Fairfield Stamping, Saddle Brook *Also called Mjse LLC* *(G-9663)*

Fairfield Textiles Corp (PA) 973 227-1656
34 Waite St Paterson (07524) *(G-8190)*

Fairway Building Products LLC 609 890-6600
2075 E State Street Ext Trenton (08619) *(G-10935)*

Falcon Graphics Inc 908 232-1991
70 Westfield Ave Clark (07066) *(G-1497)*

Falcon Industries Inc 732 563-9889
371 Campus Dr Somerset (08873) *(G-9992)*

Falcon Papers & Plastics, Avenel *Also called G R Impex Ltd Liability Co* *(G-129)*

Falcon Printing, Clark *Also called Falcon Graphics Inc* *(G-1497)*

Falcon Printing & Graphics 732 462-6862
339 W Main St Freehold (07728) *(G-3665)*

Falcon Safety Products Inc (HQ) 908 707-4900
25 Imclone Dr Branchburg (08876) *(G-639)*

Falstrom Company 973 777-0013
1 Falstrom Ct Passaic (07055) *(G-8066)*

Famcam Inc 973 503-1600
3 Eastmans Rd Parsippany (07054) *(G-7941)*

Family Screen Printing Inc 856 933-2780
124 Harding Ave Ste 124 # 124 Bellmawr (08031) *(G-332)*

Famosa North America Inc 856 206-9844
3000 Atrium Way Ste 101 Mount Laurel (08054) *(G-6759)*

Fan of Word 201 341-5474
249 Waverly Pl South Orange (07079) *(G-10195)*

Fancort Industries Inc 973 575-0610
31 Fairfield Pl West Caldwell (07006) *(G-11650)*

Fancyheat Corporation 973 589-1450
40 Veronica Ave Somerset (08873) *(G-9993)*

Fantasia Industries Corp 201 261-7070
20 Park Pl Paramus (07652) *(G-7800)*

Fanwood Crushed Stone Company 908 322-7840
1 New Providence Rd Watchung (07069) *(G-11455)*

Faps Inc (PA) 973 589-5656
371 Craneway St Newark (07114) *(G-7122)*

Faraday Photonics LLC 973 239-2005
62 Depot St Verona (07044) *(G-11166)*

Faraj Inc 201 313-4480
107 Pennsylvania Ave Paterson (07503) *(G-8191)*

Farbest Brands, Park Ridge *Also called Farbest-Tallman Foods Corp* *(G-7849)*

Farbest-Tallman Foods Corp (PA) 714 897-7199
1 Maynard Dr Ste 3101 Park Ridge (07656) *(G-7849)*

Farmplast LLC 973 287-6070
125 E Halsey Rd Parsippany (07054) *(G-7942)*

Farrell Eqp & Contrls Inc 732 770-4142
263 Cox St Roselle (07203) *(G-9557)*

Fashion Central LLC 732 887-7683
556 Warren Ave Lakewood (08701) *(G-5097)*

Fashion Institute of Ncc, Newark *Also called New Community Corp* *(G-7208)*

Fashion Windows Etc, Paterson *Also called Metro Mills Inc* *(G-8257)*

Fast Copy Printing Center 732 739-4646
81 Broad St Keyport (07735) *(G-4999)*

Fast Doors LLC 856 966-3278
1661 Davis St Camden (08103) *(G-1063)*

Fast T'S, Keyport *Also called Fast Copy Printing Center* *(G-4999)*

Fast-Pak Trading Inc 201 293-4757
375 County Ave Ste 2 Secaucus (07094) *(G-9766)*

Fastenation Inc 973 591-1277
120 Brighton Rd Ste 2 Clifton (07012) *(G-1619)*

Fastpulse Technology Inc 973 478-5757
220 Midland Ave Saddle Brook (07663) *(G-9652)*

Fastsigns, Lawrenceville *Also called Tlg Signs Inc* *(G-5244)*

Fastsigns, Newark *Also called Robden Enterprises Inc* *(G-7251)*

Fastsigns, Upper Saddle River *Also called Bergen Digital Graphics LLC* *(G-11135)*

Fastsigns, Marlton *Also called Mc Does Inc* *(G-5941)*

Fastsigns, Secaucus *Also called Sign Up Inc* *(G-9814)*

Fastsigns, Raritan *Also called Bbk Technologies Inc* *(G-9208)*

Fastsigns 973 887-6700
50 State Route 10 Ste 2 East Hanover (07936) *(G-2209)*

Faubel Pharma Services 908 730-7563
3 3rd St Ste 102 Bordentown (08505) *(G-581)*

Faulding Holdings Inc 908 527-9100
200 Elmora Ave Elizabeth (07202) *(G-2734)*

Faulkner Information Svcs LLC 856 662-2070
143 Old Marlton Pike Medford (08055) *(G-6022)*

Faust Thermographic Supply 908 474-0555
325 Cantor Ave Linden (07036) *(G-5347)*

Favs Corp 856 358-1515
331 Husted Station Rd Elmer (08318) *(G-2797)*

Fazzio Machine & Steel Inc 609 653-1098
3278 Glassboro Crs Kys Rd Glassboro (08028) *(G-3811)*

FBM Baking Machines Inc 609 860-0577
1 Corporate Dr Ste D Cranbury (08512) *(G-1834)*

Fbm Galaxy Inc 856 966-1105
2201 Mount Ephraim Ave Camden (08104) *(G-1064)*

Fbn New Jersey Mfg Inc 973 402-1443
8 Morris Ave Mountain Lakes (07046) *(G-6825)*

FEC, Franklin Lakes *Also called Fleet Equipment Corporation* *(G-3623)*

Fecken-Kirfel America Inc 201 891-5530
6 Leighton Pl Ste 1 Mahwah (07430) *(G-5736)*

Federal Bronze Cast Inds Inc (PA) 973 589-7575
9 Backus St Newark (07105) *(G-7123)*

Federal Casters Corp (PA) 973 483-6700
785 Harrison Ave Harrison (07029) *(G-4173)*

Federal Equipment & Mfg Co Inc 973 340-7600
194 Westervelt Pl Lodi (07644) *(G-5562)*

Federal Lorco Petroleum LLC 908 352-0542
450 S Front St Elizabeth (07202) *(G-2735)*

Federal Metals & Alloys Co 908 756-0900
4216 S Clinton Ave South Plainfield (07080) *(G-10257)*

Federal Petroleum, Elizabeth *Also called Federal Lorco Petroleum LLC* *(G-2735)*

Federal Plastics Corporation 908 272-5800
570 South Ave E Bldg F1 Cranford (07016) *(G-1910)*

Federal Pretzel Baking Co (PA) 215 467-0505
300 Eagle Ct Bridgeport (08014) *(G-737)*

Fedex Office & Print Svcs Inc 201 525-5070
1071 Main St River Edge (07661) *(G-9361)*

Fedex Office & Print Svcs Inc 856 427-0099
1160 Route 70 E Cherry Hill (08034) *(G-1361)*

Fedex Office & Print Svcs Inc 732 636-3580
1 Quality Way Iselin (08830) *(G-4609)*

Fedex Office & Print Svcs Inc 732 249-9222
212 Rte 18 New Brunswick (08901) *(G-6926)*

Fedex Office & Print Svcs Inc 856 273-5959
1211 Route 73 Ste E Mount Laurel (08054) *(G-6760)*

Fedex Office & Print Svcs Inc 201 672-0508
120 Route 17 East Rutherford (07073) *(G-2288)*

Fedex Office & Print Svcs Inc 973 376-3966
55 Route 22 Springfield (07081) *(G-10443)*

Fedex Office Commercial Press, Roselle *Also called Howard Press Inc* *(G-9561)*

Fedex Office Print & Ship Ctr, New Brunswick *Also called Fedex Office & Print Svcs Inc* *(G-6926)*

Fedplast Inc 732 901-1153
1174 Buckwald Ct Lakewood (08701) *(G-5098)*

Feed Your Soul Ltd Lblty Co 201 204-0720
78 John Miller Way # 100 Kearny (07032) *(G-4855)*

Fehlberg Mfg Inc 973 399-1905
10 Renee Pl 16 Irvington (07111) *(G-4568)*

Fehu Jewel LLC 609 297-5491
2912 Quail Ridge Dr Plainsboro (08536) *(G-8786)*

Fei-Elcom Tech Inc 201 767-8030
260 Union St Northvale (07647) *(G-7524)*

Felco Products LLC 973 890-7979
18 Furler St Totowa (07512) *(G-8192)*

Feldware Inc 718 372-0486
900 Hart St Rahway (07065) *(G-9093)*

Fellowship In Prayer Inc 609 924-6863
291 Witherspoon St Princeton (08542) *(G-8948)*

Femco, Lodi *Also called Federal Equipment & Mfg Co Inc* ***(G-5562)***
Femenella & Associates Inc 908 722-6526
10 County Line Rd Ste 24 Branchburg (08876) ***(G-640)***
Femto Calibrations, Somerset *Also called Venkateshwara Inc* ***(G-10095)***
Fence America New Jersey Inc 973 472-5121
210 S Newman St Ste 1 Hackensack (07601) ***(G-3912)***
Fencemax 609 646-2265
1624 Harding Hwy Newfield (08344) ***(G-7322)***
FER Plating Inc 201 438-1010
52 Park Ave Lyndhurst (07071) ***(G-5655)***
Ferber Plastics, Passaic *Also called Et Manufacturing & Sales Inc* ***(G-8064)***
Ferguson Containers Co Inc 908 454-9755
16 Industrial Rd Phillipsburg (08865) ***(G-8550)***
Fermag Technologies Inc 732 985-7300
146 Village Rd Toms River (08755) ***(G-10756)***
Fermatex Vascular Tech LLC 732 681-7070
1746 Rte 34 Wall Township (07727) ***(G-11339)***
Fernandes Custom Cabinets 732 446-2829
233 Pease Rd Manalapan (07726) ***(G-5810)***
Ferrante Press Inc 609 239-4257
516 Bloomfield Ave Verona (07044) ***(G-11167)***
Ferrero U S A Inc (HQ) 732 764-9300
7 Sylvan Way Fl 4 Parsippany (07054) ***(G-7943)***
Ferrett Printing Inc 856 686-4896
468 Warwick Rd Woodbury (08096) ***(G-12029)***
Ferring Pharmaceuticals Inc (HQ) 973 796-1600
100 Interpace Pkwy Parsippany (07054) ***(G-7944)***
Ferring Production Inc 973 796-1600
100 Interpace Pkwy Parsippany (07054) ***(G-7945)***
Ferro Corporation 856 467-3000
170 Route 130 S Bridgeport (08014) ***(G-738)***
Ferro Corporation 732 287-4925
54 Kellogg Ct Edison (08817) ***(G-2511)***
Ferro Corporation 908 226-2148
2501 S Clinton Ave South Plainfield (07080) ***(G-10258)***
Ferro Industries Incorporated 732 246-3200
14 Evergreen Ln Colts Neck (07722) ***(G-1782)***
Ferrum Industries Inc 201 935-1220
735 Commercial Ave Carlstadt (07072) ***(G-1156)***
Ferry Machine Corp 201 641-9191
75 Industrial Ave Little Ferry (07643) ***(G-5485)***
Fette Compacting America Inc 973 586-8722
400 Forge Way Rockaway (07866) ***(G-9459)***
Fette-America, Rockaway *Also called Lmt Usa Inc* ***(G-9475)***
Ff1 Professional Safety Svcs, Sparta *Also called Firefighter One Ltd Lblty Co* ***(G-10387)***
Fgh Systems Inc 973 625-8114
10 Prospect Pl Denville (07834) ***(G-2037)***
Fh Group International Inc 201 210-2426
265 Secaucus Rd Secaucus (07094) ***(G-9767)***
Fiabila USA Inc 973 659-9510
114 Iron Mountain Rd Mine Hill (07803) ***(G-6272)***
Fiber-Span Inc 908 253-9080
670 Commons Way Toms River (08755) ***(G-10757)***
Fibercontrol, Colts Neck *Also called DR Tielmann Inc* ***(G-1781)***
Fiberguide Industries Inc (HQ) 908 647-6601
1 Bay St Ste 1 # 1 Stirling (07980) ***(G-10490)***
Fibertech Group Inc (HQ) 856 697-1600
450 N East Blvd Landisville (08326) ***(G-5206)***
Fidelity Chemical Products Div, South Plainfield *Also called Omg Electronic Chemicals Inc* ***(G-10311)***
Fidelity Industries Inc (PA) 973 696-9120
559 Rte 23 Wayne (07470) ***(G-11501)***
Fidelity Industries Inc 973 777-2592
750 Bloomfield Ave Ste 1 Clifton (07012) ***(G-1620)***
Fidelity Wallcoverings, Wayne *Also called Fidelity Industries Inc* ***(G-11501)***
Fields Samuel H Dental Labs, Hackensack *Also called Samuel H Fields Dental Labs* ***(G-3971)***
Fieldsboro Plant, Bordentown *Also called Stepan Company* ***(G-595)***
Fieldview Cfd Inc 425 460-8284
301 Route 17 Fl 7 Rutherford (07070) ***(G-9620)***
Fifty/Fifty Group Inc 201 343-1243
241 Main St Fl 5 Hackensack (07601) ***(G-3913)***
Fillimerica Inc 800 435-7257
170 Chngbrdge Rd Bldg A42 Montville (07045) ***(G-6442)***
Fillo Factory Inc 201 439-1036
10 Fairway Ct Northvale (07647) ***(G-7525)***
Filter Holdings Inc 908 687-3500
20 Milltown Rd Union (07083) ***(G-11054)***
Filter Process & Supply, Monmouth Junction *Also called Filter Technologies Inc* ***(G-6291)***
Filter Technologies Inc 732 329-2500
45 Stouts Ln Ste 3 Monmouth Junction (08852) ***(G-6291)***
Filtrex Inc 973 595-0400
450 Hamburg Tpke Ste 2 Wayne (07470) ***(G-11502)***
Fims Manufacturing Corporation 201 845-7088
8 Allerman Rd Oakland (07436) ***(G-7628)***
Fin-Tek Corporation (PA) 973 628-2988
6 Leo Pl Wayne (07470) ***(G-11503)***
Fin-Tek Ozone, Wayne *Also called Fin-Tek Corporation* ***(G-11503)***
Financial Advisor Magazine, Shrewsbury *Also called Charter Fincl Pubg Netwrk Inc* ***(G-9885)***
Financial Information Inc 908 222-5300
1 Cragwood Rd Ste 2 South Plainfield (07080) ***(G-10259)***
Fine Linen Inc 908 469-3634
107 Trumbull St Elizabeth (07206) ***(G-2736)***
Fine Minerals Intl Inc 732 318-6760
11 Progress St Edison (08820) ***(G-2512)***
Fine Wear U S A 201 313-3777
22 E Columbia Ave Fort Lee (07024) ***(G-3558)***
Finex Trade 609 921-2747
315 Riverside Dr Princeton (08540) ***(G-8949)***
Finlandia Cheese Inc (HQ) 973 316-6699
2001 Us Highway 46 # 303 Parsippany (07054) ***(G-7946)***
Finn & Emma LLC 973 227-7770
1275 Bloomfield Ave Ste 5 Fairfield (07004) ***(G-3201)***
Finn Emma, Fairfield *Also called Finn & Emma LLC* ***(G-3201)***
Fioplex 856 689-7213
49 Fredrick Blvd Swedesboro (08085) ***(G-10585)***
Fiore Skylights Inc 856 346-0118
700 Grace St Somerdale (08083) ***(G-9931)***
Firefighter One Ltd Lblty Co 973 940-3061
34 Wilson Dr Sparta (07871) ***(G-10387)***
Firefreeze Worldwide Inc 973 627-0722
272 Us Highway 46 Rockaway (07866) ***(G-9460)***
Fireplace Place Summit, The, Summit *Also called Associate Fireplace Builders* ***(G-10526)***
Firetrainer Symtron 201 794-0200
17-01 Pollitt Dr Fair Lawn (07410) ***(G-3100)***
Firma Foods USA Corporation 201 794-1181
25 Rockwood Pl Ste 220 Englewood (07631) ***(G-2905)***
Firmenich, Newark *Also called Chem-Fleur Inc* ***(G-7083)***
First For Women Magazine, Englewood Cliffs *Also called Bauer Publishing Company LP* ***(G-2960)***
First Friday Global Inc 201 776-6709
130 Mount Pleasant Ave Newark (07104) ***(G-7124)***
First Internet Systems 201 991-1889
16 Geraldine Rd North Arlington (07031) ***(G-7372)***
First Juice Inc 973 895-3085
19 Tulip Ln Randolph (07869) ***(G-9178)***
First Mountain Consulting 973 325-8480
3 Colony Ct West Orange (07052) ***(G-11767)***
First National Servicing & Dev 732 341-5409
102 Starc Rd Toms River (08755) ***(G-10758)***
First Nighter Formals, Lyndhurst *Also called Fabian Formals Inc* ***(G-5653)***
First Priority Emergency Vhicl (HQ) 732 657-1104
2444 Ridgeway Blvd # 500 Manchester (08759) ***(G-5845)***
First Priority Global Ltd (PA) 973 347-4321
160 Gold Mine Rd Flanders (07836) ***(G-3410)***
First Priority Specialty Pdts, Manchester *Also called First Priority Emergency Vhicl* ***(G-5845)***
Fis Avantgard LLC 732 530-9303
106 Apple St Ste 110 Tinton Falls (07724) ***(G-10717)***
Fis Data Systems Inc 201 945-1774
1008 Virgil Ave Ridgefield (07657) ***(G-9261)***
Fis Financial Systems LLC 856 784-7230
600 Laurel Oak Rd Voorhees (08043) ***(G-11285)***
Fischl Machine & Tool 908 829-5621
5 Ilene Ct Ste 7 Hillsborough (08844) ***(G-4316)***
Fischlers Dawnpoint 856 428-2092
212 Walt Whitman Blvd Cherry Hill (08003) ***(G-1362)***
Fisher Canvas Products Inc 609 239-2733
415 Saint Mary St Burlington (08016) ***(G-967)***
Fisher Scientific Chemical Div 609 633-1422
1 Reagent Ln Fair Lawn (07410) ***(G-3101)***
Fisher Scientific Company LLC 201 796-7100
1 Reagent Ln Fair Lawn (07410) ***(G-3102)***
Fisher Service Co 609 386-5000
120 Kissel Rd Burlington (08016) ***(G-968)***
Fisher, Harold & Sons, Cinnaminson *Also called Harold F Fisher & Sons Inc* ***(G-1462)***
Fisherman's Pride, Newark *Also called Ruggiero Sea Food Inc* ***(G-7254)***
Fishermens Energy NJ LLC 609 286-9650
985 Ocean Dr Cape May (08204) ***(G-1098)***
Fisk Alloy Conductors Inc (HQ) 973 825-8500
10 Thomas Rd N Hawthorne (07506) ***(G-4218)***
Fisk Alloy Inc (PA) 973 427-7550
10 Thomas Rd N Hawthorne (07506) ***(G-4219)***
Fisk Alloy Wire Incorporated 973 949-4491
10 Thomas Rd N Hawthorne (07506) ***(G-4220)***
Fit Fabrication LLC 973 685-7344
310 Colfax Ave Clifton (07013) ***(G-1621)***
Fit Graphix (PA) 201 488-4670
390 Maple Hill Dr Hackensack (07601) ***(G-3914)***
Fitts Sheet Metal Inc 201 923-9239
44 Inman Pl North Arlington (07031) ***(G-7373)***
Five Elements Robotics LLC 800 681-8514
1333 Campus Pkwy Wall Township (07753) ***(G-11340)***
Five Kids Group Inc 732 774-5331
37 Highway 35 N Fl 2 Neptune (07753) ***(G-6878)***
Five Macs Inc 856 596-3150
8 E Stow Rd Ste 140 Marlton (08053) ***(G-5931)***

642 2019 Harris New Jersey Manufacturers Directory (G-0000) Company's Geographic Section entry number

Five Star Aluminum Products 201 869-4181
  2012 86th St North Bergen (07047) *(G-7405)*

Five Star Building Products, North Bergen *Also called Five Star Aluminum Products (G-7405)*

Five Star Supplies NJ Corp 908 862-8801
  1301 W Elizabeth Ave A Linden (07036) *(G-5348)*

Fix It Guy 732 278-9000
  2562 Balfrey Dr Toms River (08753) *(G-10759)*

Fixture It Inc 201 445-0939
  397 Rock Rd Glen Rock (07452) *(G-3831)*

Fixturecraft, Ewing *Also called S L Enterprises Inc (G-3064)*

Fizzics Group LLC 917 545-4533
  1775 State Route 34 D14 Wall Township (07727) *(G-11341)*

Fizzy Lizzy LLC 212 966-3232
  64 Wayne St Jersey City (07302) *(G-4734)*

Fka West-Ward Pharmaceuticals, Eatontown *Also called Hikma Pharmaceuticals USA Inc (G-2399)*

Flame Cut Steel Inc 973 373-9300
  300 Coit St Irvington (07111) *(G-4569)*

Flanagan Holdings Inc (PA) 201 512-3338
  211 Island Rd Mahwah (07430) *(G-5737)*

Flavor & Fragrance Spc Inc (PA) 201 828-9400
  3 Industrial Ave Mahwah (07430) *(G-5738)*

Flavor and Fd Ingredients Inc 201 298-6964
  256 Lackland Dr Middlesex (08846) *(G-6116)*

Flavor and Fd Ingredients Inc (PA) 732 805-0335
  21 Worlds Fair Dr Somerset (08873) *(G-9994)*

Flavor and Fragrance Division, Teterboro *Also called Mastertaste Inc (G-10686)*

Flavor Associates Inc 973 238-9300
  1 Thomas Rd N Hawthorne (07506) *(G-4221)*

Flavor Development Corp 201 784-8188
  10 Reuten Dr Closter (07624) *(G-1755)*

Flavor Dynamics Inc 888 271-8424
  640 Montrose Ave South Plainfield (07080) *(G-10260)*

Flavor Materials International, Carlstadt *Also called Flavors of Origin Inc (G-1157)*

Flavor Materials International, Avenel *Also called Flavors of Origin Inc (G-127)*

Flavor Solutions Inc 732 354-1931
  120 New England Ave Piscataway (08854) *(G-8665)*

Flavors of Origin Inc 201 460-8306
  700 Gotham Pkwy Carlstadt (07072) *(G-1157)*

Flavors of Origin Inc (PA) 732 499-9700
  10 Engelhard Ave Avenel (07001) *(G-127)*

Flavour Tee International LLC 201 440-3281
  66 Industrial Ave Little Ferry (07643) *(G-5486)*

Flech Paper Products Inc 973 357-8111
  55 1st Ave Ste 1 Paterson (07514) *(G-8193)*

Fleck Knitwear Co Inc 908 754-8888
  400 Leland Ave Plainfield (07062) *(G-8766)*

Fleet Equipment Corporation (PA) 201 337-3294
  567 Commerce St Franklin Lakes (07417) *(G-3623)*

Fleet Packaging Inc 866 302-0340
  75 S Orange Ave Ste 216 South Orange (07079) *(G-10196)*

Fleetsource LLC 732 566-4970
  2382 Us Highway 130 Dayton (08810) *(G-1961)*

Flemington Alumininum & Brass 908 782-6333
  24 Junction Rd Flemington (08822) *(G-3441)*

Flemington Bituminous Corp 908 782-2722
  356 State Route 31 Flemington (08822) *(G-3442)*

Flemington Knitting Mills 908 995-9590
  123 Dawn Rd Milford (08848) *(G-6192)*

Flemington Precast & Sup LLC 908 782-3246
  18 Allen St Flemington (08822) *(G-3443)*

Flex Moulding Inc 201 487-8080
  22 E Lafayette St Hackensack (07601) *(G-3915)*

Flex Products LLC 201 440-1570
  640 Dell Rd Ste 1 Carlstadt (07072) *(G-1158)*

Flexabar Corporation (PA) 732 901-6500
  1969 Rutgers Blvd Lakewood (08701) *(G-5099)*

Flexbiosys Inc 908 300-3244
  291 Us Highway 22 Ste 32 Lebanon (08833) *(G-5261)*

Flexco Bldg Pdts Ltd Lblty Co 732 780-1700
  15 Timber Ln Marlboro (07746) *(G-5898)*

Flexco Microwave Inc 908 835-1720
  17 Karrville Rd Port Murray (07865) *(G-8883)*

Flexcon Container, Berkeley Heights *Also called Shell Packaging Corporation (G-412)*

Flexcraft Company, Neptune *Also called Holocraft Corporation (G-6885)*

Flexcraft Industries Inc 973 589-3403
  390 Adams St Newark (07114) *(G-7125)*

Flexdell Corp 732 901-7771
  1969 Rutgers Blvd Lakewood (08701) *(G-5100)*

Flexi Printing Plate Co Inc 201 939-3600
  50 Commercial Ave Moonachie (07074) *(G-6465)*

Flexible Components, Somerset *Also called Saint-Gobain Prfmce Plas Corp (G-10070)*

Flexible Foam, Red Bank *Also called Innocor Foam Tech - Acp Inc (G-9231)*

Flexicious LLC 646 340-5066
  57 Sip Ave Apt 4b Jersey City (07306) *(G-4735)*

Flexline Inc 908 486-3322
  11 Columbus Ave Kenilworth (07033) *(G-4940)*

Flexlink Systems Inc 973 983-2700
  335 Chambers Brook Rd Branchburg (08876) *(G-641)*

Flexlink Systems Inc 908 947-2140
  335 Chambers Brook Rd Branchburg (08876) *(G-642)*

Flexo-Craft Prints Inc 973 482-7200
  1000 1st St Harrison (07029) *(G-4174)*

Flexon Inds Div US Wire Cable, Newark *Also called US Wire & Cable Corporation (G-7310)*

Flexon Industries, Newark *Also called Thirty-Three Queen Realty Inc (G-7297)*

Flexpaq, South Plainfield *Also called Ileos of America Inc (G-10276)*

Flextron Systems, Gloucester City *Also called Quik Flex Circuit Inc (G-3848)*

Flint Group North America, Dayton *Also called Flint Group US LLC (G-1962)*

Flint Group US LLC 732 329-4627
  6 Corn Rd Dayton (08810) *(G-1962)*

Flir Security Inc 201 368-9700
  65 Challenger Rd Ridgefield Park (07660) *(G-9306)*

Flir Systems Inc 201 368-9700
  65 Challenger Rd Ridgefield Park (07660) *(G-9307)*

FLM Graphics Corporation (PA) 973 575-9450
  123 Lehigh Dr Fairfield (07004) *(G-3202)*

Flodyne Controls Inc 908 464-6200
  48 Commerce Dr New Providence (07974) *(G-6999)*

Flooring Concepts Nj LLC 732 409-7600
  289 Highway 33 Ste 2c Manalapan (07726) *(G-5811)*

Floors At Home, Brick *Also called Cno Corporation (G-713)*

Flor Lift of N J Inc 973 429-2200
  19 Gardner Rd Ste M Fairfield (07004) *(G-3203)*

Floral Glass Industries Inc 201 939-4600
  99 Murray Hill Pkwy # 10 East Rutherford (07073) *(G-2289)*

Florentine Press Inc 201 386-9200
  234 16th St Fl 4 Jersey City (07310) *(G-4736)*

Florlift of NJ, Fairfield *Also called Flor Lift of N J Inc (G-3203)*

Flortek Corporation 201 436-7700
  39 W 55th St Bayonne (07002) *(G-216)*

Flottec LLC (PA) 973 588-4717
  5 Hillcrest Rd Boonton (07005) *(G-554)*

Flow-Turn Inc 908 687-3225
  1050 Commerce Ave Union (07083) *(G-11055)*

Flowserve Corporation 908 859-7000
  222 Cameron Dr Ste 200 Phillipsburg (08865) *(G-8551)*

Flowserve Corporation 856 241-7800
  401 Heron Dr Bridgeport (08014) *(G-739)*

Flowserve Corporation 973 334-9444
  333 Littleton Rd Ste 303 Parsippany (07054) *(G-7947)*

Flowserve Corporation 973 227-4565
  142 Clinton Rd Fairfield (07004) *(G-3204)*

Floxite Company Inc 201 529-2019
  31 Industrial Ave Ste 2 Mahwah (07430) *(G-5739)*

Fluent Diagnostics 201 414-4516
  22 W Parkway Pequannock (07440) *(G-8504)*

Fluets Corp 908 353-5229
  260 Pennsylvania Ave Hillside (07205) *(G-4391)*

Fluid Coating Systems Inc 973 767-1028
  13 Barthold St Garfield (07026) *(G-3742)*

Fluid Dynamics Inc 908 200-5823
  18 Commerce St Ste 1819 Flemington (08822) *(G-3444)*

Fluid Filtration Corp 973 253-7070
  102 Van Winkle Ave Garfield (07026) *(G-3743)*

Fluidsens International Inc 914 338-3932
  703 Beechwood Dr Twp Washinton (07676) *(G-11017)*

Fluidyne Corp 856 663-1818
  9100 Collins Ave Pennsauken (08110) *(G-8420)*

Fluitec International LLC 201 946-4584
  179 W 5th St Bayonne (07002) *(G-217)*

Fluoropharma Medical Inc 973 744-1565
  8 Hillside Ave Ste 108 Montclair (07042) *(G-6367)*

Fluorotherm Polymers Inc 973 575-0760
  333 New Rd Ste 1 Parsippany (07054) *(G-7948)*

Flying Fish Studio 609 884-2760
  130 Park Blvd West Cape May (08204) *(G-11683)*

Flying Models, Newton *Also called Carstens Publications Inc (G-7339)*

FMB Systems Inc 973 485-5544
  70 Supor Blvd Harrison (07029) *(G-4175)*

FMC Corporation 973 256-0768
  1130 Mcbride Ave Woodland Park (07424) *(G-12079)*

FMC Corporation 732 541-3000
  500 Roosevelt Ave Carteret (07008) *(G-1253)*

FMC Corporation 609 963-6200
  801-701 Princeton S Ewing (08628) *(G-3031)*

Fmdk Technologies Inc 201 828-9822
  63 Ramapo Valley Rd 63w Mahwah (07430) *(G-5740)*

Fmw Drilling, Cinnaminson *Also called Foundation Monitoring (G-1457)*

Foam Rubber Fabricators Inc 973 751-1445
  740 Washington Ave Belleville (07109) *(G-296)*

Foamex, East Rutherford *Also called Fxi Inc (G-2290)*

Foctek Photonics LLC 732 828-8228
  15 Birch St Milltown (08850) *(G-6215)*

Foil-On, Moonachie *Also called Screen-Trans Development Corp (G-6488)*

Folditure, Hoboken *Also called Gendell Assoicates PA (G-4452)*

A
L
P
H
A
B
E
T
I
C

Foldtex II Ltd 908 928-0919
  705 E Broad St Westfield (07090) *(G-11797)*

Folex Imaging, Fairfield *Also called H S Folex Schleussner Inc (G-3220)*

Foley-Waite Associates Inc 908 298-0700
  746 Colfax Ave Kenilworth (07033) *(G-4941)*

Folgore Mobil Welding Inc 732 541-2974
  526 Roosevelt Ave Carteret (07008) *(G-1254)*

Folica Inc (PA) 609 860-8430
  11 Corn Rd Ste B Dayton (08810) *(G-1963)*

Folica.com, Dayton *Also called Folica Inc (G-1963)*

Folio Art Glass Inc 732 431-0044
  73 State Route 34 S Colts Neck (07722) *(G-1783)*

Food & Beverage Inc 201 288-8881
  100 Hollister Rd Unit C-1 Teterboro (07608) *(G-10674)*

Food Circus Super Markets Inc 732 291-4079
  9 East Ave 36 Atlantic Highlands (07716) *(G-106)*

Food Ingredient Solutions LLC (PA) 201 440-4377
  10 Malcolm Ave Ste 1 Teterboro (07608) *(G-10675)*

Food Mfg 973 920-7000
  100 Enterprise Dr Rockaway (07866) *(G-9461)*

Food Sciences Corp (PA) 856 778-4192
  821 E Gate Dr Mount Laurel (08054) *(G-6761)*

Foodline Piping Products Co 856 767-1177
  225 Edgewood Ave West Berlin (08091) *(G-11594)*

Foodtek Inc (PA) 973 257-4000
  9 Whippany Rd Bldg C-2 Whippany (07981) *(G-11891)*

Foozys, Edison *Also called Sock Drawer and More LLC (G-2615)*

Forbes Magazine, Jersey City *Also called Nsgv Inc (G-4774)*

Forbes Magazine, Jersey City *Also called Forbes Media LLC (G-4737)*

Forbes Media LLC 212 620-2200
  499 Washington Blvd Jersey City (07310) *(G-4737)*

Forbo Siegling LLC 201 567-6100
  130 Coolidge Ave Englewood (07631) *(G-2906)*

Force Industries LLC 973 332-1532
  32 Boonton Ave 1 Butler (07405) *(G-1000)*

Ford Atlanic, Pine Brook *Also called Ford Atlantic Fastener Corp (G-8601)*

Ford Atlantic Fastener Corp 973 882-1191
  341 Changebridge Rd Pine Brook (07058) *(G-8601)*

Ford Fasteners Inc 201 487-3151
  110 S Newman St Hackensack (07601) *(G-3916)*

Fordham Inc 973 575-7840
  20 Gloria Ln Fairfield (07004) *(G-3205)*

Fordion Packaging Ltd 201 692-1344
  185 Linden St Ste 3 Hackensack (07601) *(G-3917)*

Fordoz Pharma Corp 609 469-5949
  69 Prnceton Hightstown Rd East Windsor (08520) *(G-2351)*

Forem Packaging Inc 973 589-0402
  2 Joseph St Newark (07105) *(G-7126)*

Foremost Corp 973 839-3360
  2025 Hamburg Tpke Ste A Wayne (07470) *(G-11504)*

Foremost Machine Builders Inc 973 227-0700
  23 Spielman Rd Fairfield (07004) *(G-3206)*

Foremost Manufacturing Co Inc 908 687-4646
  941 Ball Ave Union (07083) *(G-11056)*

Foresight Enviroprobe Inc 609 259-1244
  19 Trenton Lakewood Rd Clarksburg (08510) *(G-1520)*

Foresight Group LLC 888 992-8880
  100 Ims Dr Parsippany (07054) *(G-7949)*

Forest Laboratories LLC 631 436-4534
  185 Hudson St Jersey City (07311) *(G-4738)*

Forest Laboratories LLC 631 501-5399
  1900 Plaza Five Jersey City (07311) *(G-4739)*

Forest Pharmaceuticals Inc (HQ) 862 261-7000
  400 Interpace Pkwy Ste A1 Parsippany (07054) *(G-7950)*

Forge Ahead LLC 908 346-4794
  1800 Route 206 Skillman (08558) *(G-9920)*

Forget ME Not Chocolates By NA 856 753-8916
  121 Lakeside Dr Atco (08004) *(G-86)*

Forino Kitchen Cabinets Inc 201 573-0990
  33 S Maple Ave Park Ridge (07656) *(G-7850)*

Form Cut Industries Inc 973 483-5154
  195 Mount Pleasant Ave Newark (07104) *(G-7127)*

Form Tops Lminators of Trenton 609 409-4357
  37 Merlot Ct Jamesburg (08831) *(G-4672)*

Forman Industries Inc 732 727-8100
  3150 Bordentown Ave Old Bridge (08857) *(G-7715)*

Former Circuit Inc 732 549-0056
  5 Sutton Pl Edison (08817) *(G-2513)*

Formia Marble & Stone Inc 908 259-0606
  219 E 11th Ave Roselle (07203) *(G-9558)*

Formosa Plastics Corp USA (PA) 973 992-2090
  9 Peach Tree Hill Rd Livingston (07039) *(G-5511)*

Forms & Flyers of New Jersey 856 629-0718
  102 Sicklerville Rd Williamstown (08094) *(G-11958)*

Fornazor International Inc (PA) 201 664-4000
  455 Hillsdale Ave Hillsdale (07642) *(G-4366)*

Forsters Cleaning & Tailoring 201 659-4411
  248 Central Ave Jersey City (07307) *(G-4740)*

Fort Nassau Graphics, West Deptford *Also called Publishers Inc (G-11715)*

Fortress Graphics LLC 973 276-0100
  33 Fairfield Pl West Caldwell (07006) *(G-11651)*

Fortune International Inc 732 214-0700
  56 Veronica Ave Somerset (08873) *(G-9995)*

Fortune Metal Recycling, Rahway *Also called Fortune Rvrside Auto Parts Inc (G-9094)*

Fortune Rvrside Auto Parts Inc (PA) 732 381-3355
  900 Leesville Ave Rahway (07065) *(G-9094)*

Fossil Fuel 973 366-9111
  105 W Dewey Ave Wharton (07885) *(G-11858)*

Foster and Company Inc (PA) 973 267-4100
  15 Wing Dr Cedar Knolls (07927) *(G-1305)*

Foster Engraving Corporation 201 489-5979
  174 S Main St Ste B Hackensack (07601) *(G-3918)*

Foster Wheeler, Hampton *Also called Foster Whler Intl Holdings Inc (G-4154)*

Foster Wheeler, Hampton *Also called Foster Wheeler Intl Corp (G-4152)*

Foster Wheeler Arabia Ltd 908 730-4000
  53 Frontage Rd Hampton (08827) *(G-4151)*

Foster Wheeler Intl Corp (HQ) 908 730-4000
  Perryville Corporate Pk 5 Hampton (08827) *(G-4152)*

Foster Wheeler Zack Inc (HQ) 908 730-4000
  53 Frontage Rd Hampton (08827) *(G-4153)*

Foster Whler Intl Holdings Inc (HQ) 908 730-4000
  Perryville Corporate Pk 5 Hampton (08827) *(G-4154)*

Foto Fantasy 732 548-8446
  2850 Woodbridge Ave Edison (08837) *(G-2514)*

Fotobridge 856 809-9400
  154 Cooper Rd Ste 203 West Berlin (08091) *(G-11595)*

Fougera Pharmaceuticals Inc 973 514-4241
  1 Health Plz East Hanover (07936) *(G-2210)*

Foulkrod Associates 856 662-6767
  8275 N Crescent Blvd Pennsauken (08110) *(G-8421)*

Foundation For Embryonic 973 656-2847
  140 Allen Rd Basking Ridge (07920) *(G-183)*

Foundation For Student Comm 609 258-1111
  48 University Pl Ste 305 Princeton (08540) *(G-8950)*

Foundation Monitoring 856 829-0410
  515 Wellfleet Rd Cinnaminson (08077) *(G-1457)*

Foundation Software Inc 908 359-0588
  58 Livingston Dr Belle Mead (08502) *(G-286)*

Four Bros Ventures Inc 732 890-9469
  15 Timothy Ln East Brunswick (08816) *(G-2146)*

Four Star Color, Newton *Also called Red Oak Packaging Inc (G-7354)*

Four Way Enterprises Inc 973 633-5757
  582 Fairfield Rd Wayne (07470) *(G-11505)*

Fourconsulting Ltd Lblty Co 732 599-4324
  295 Durham Ave Ste 206 South Plainfield (07080) *(G-10261)*

Fox Steel Products LLC 856 778-4661
  8 Fox Run Dr Mount Laurel (08054) *(G-6762)*

Fpc USA, Livingston *Also called Formosa Plastics Corp USA (G-5511)*

Fractal Solutions Corp 201 608-6828
  725 River Rd Unit 32135 Edgewater (07020) *(G-2438)*

Fragales Bakery Inc 973 546-0327
  6874 Gaston Ave Garfield (07026) *(G-3744)*

Fragrance Exchange Inc 732 641-2210
  1075 Cranbury Rd Ste 7 Monroe Township (08831) *(G-6332)*

Fragrance Factory, Northvale *Also called Takasago Intl Corp USA (G-7551)*

Fragrance Factory Inc 973 835-2002
  12 Peck Ave Pompton Plains (07444) *(G-8864)*

Fragrance Solutions Corp 732 832-7800
  3357 S Clinton Ave South Plainfield (07080) *(G-10262)*

Fralinger's Org Salt Wtr Taffy, Atlantic City *Also called Fralingers Inc (G-90)*

Fralingers Inc (PA) 609 345-2177
  1325 Boardwalk Ste 1 Atlantic City (08401) *(G-90)*

Fralingers Inc 609 345-2177
  1519 Boardwalk Atlantic City (08401) *(G-91)*

Fram Trak Industries Inc 732 424-8400
  205 Hallock Ave Middlesex (08846) *(G-6117)*

Frameco Inc 973 989-1424
  158 W Clinton St Ste B Dover (07801) *(G-2084)*

Framesmith Gallery, The, Princeton *Also called Empty Walls Inc (G-8940)*

Frameware Inc 800 582-5608
  8 Audrey Pl Fairfield (07004) *(G-3207)*

Franbeth Inc 856 488-1480
  5505 N Crescent Blvd Pennsauken (08110) *(G-8422)*

Francis Cable Systems, Lakewood *Also called Francis Metals Company Inc (G-5101)*

Francis Metals Company Inc 732 761-0500
  687 Prospect St Ste 430 Lakewood (08701) *(G-5101)*

Franco Manufacturing Co Inc (PA) 732 494-0500
  555 Prospect St Metuchen (08840) *(G-6056)*

Frank & Jims Inc 609 646-1655
  711 N Main St Ste 3 Pleasantville (08232) *(G-8811)*

Frank B Ross Co Inc (PA) 732 669-0810
  970 New Brunswick Ave H Rahway (07065) *(G-9095)*

Frank Burton & Sons Inc 856 455-1202
  333 W Broad St Bridgeton (08302) *(G-758)*

Frank E Ganter Inc 856 692-2218
  224 S Lincoln Ave Vineland (08361) *(G-11219)*

Frank J Zechman 732 495-0077
  515 Highway 36 Belford (07718) *(G-282)*

Frank Jims Storm Windows Doors, Pleasantville *Also called Frank & Jims Inc* ***(G-8811)***
Frank Zotynia & Son Inc 973 247-2800
38 Governor St Paterson (07501) ***(G-8194)***
Frankford Umbrellas, Mount Laurel *Also called S Frankford & Sons Inc* ***(G-6801)***
Franklen Sheet Metal Co Inc 732 988-0808
122 S Main St Ocean Grove (07756) ***(G-7700)***
Franklin Electronic Publs Inc (PA) 609 386-2500
3 Terri Ln Ste 6 Burlington (08016) ***(G-969)***
Franklin Graphics Inc 201 935-5900
60 Brickell Ave Westwood (07675) ***(G-11831)***
Franklin Miller Inc 973 535-9200
60 Okner Pkwy Livingston (07039) ***(G-5512)***
Franklin Mint LLC 800 843-6468
400 Kelby St Ste 15 Fort Lee (07024) ***(G-3559)***
Franklin Mint Trading, Fort Lee *Also called Franklin Mint LLC* ***(G-3559)***
Franklin Precast Tanks, Franklin *Also called Double Twenties Inc* ***(G-3602)***
Franklin Press, Westwood *Also called Franklin Graphics Inc* ***(G-11831)***
Franks Cabinet Shop Inc 908 658-4396
1992 Burnt Mills Rd Pluckemin (07978) ***(G-8822)***
Franks Upholstery & Draperies 856 779-8585
621 S Forklanding Rd Maple Shade (08052) ***(G-5863)***
Fratelli Beretta Usa Inc 201 438-0723
750 Clark Dr Budd Lake (07828) ***(G-923)***
Frauscher Sensor Tech USA Inc 609 285-5492
300 Carnegie Ctr Ste 320 Princeton (08540) ***(G-8951)***
Frazier Industrial Company (PA) 908 876-3001
91 Fairview Ave Long Valley (07853) ***(G-5610)***
Frc Electrical Industries Inc 908 464-3200
705 Central Ave Ste 3 New Providence (07974) ***(G-7000)***
Fred McDowell Inc 732 681-5000
34 St Hwy Wall Township (07753) ***(G-11342)***
Fred S Burroughs North Jersey 908 850-8773
6 Rushmore Ln Hackettstown (07840) ***(G-4008)***
Fredericks Machine Inc 609 397-4991
99 Kingwood Stockton Rd Rosemont (08556) ***(G-9592)***
Fredon Development Inds LLC 973 383-7576
393 State Route 94 S Newton (07860) ***(G-7343)***
Fredon Welding & Iron Works, Lafayette *Also called James Zylstra Enterprises Inc* ***(G-5028)***
Freed Foods Inc 512 829-5535
225 Long Ave Ste 15 Hillside (07205) ***(G-4392)***
Freed Transformer Company 973 942-2222
460 Totowa Ave Paterson (07522) ***(G-8195)***
Freedom Plastics LLC 201 337-9450
37 Edison Ave Oakland (07436) ***(G-7629)***
Freedom Vinyl Systems Inc 973 692-0332
67 2nd St Pequannock (07440) ***(G-8505)***
Freehold Buick, Freehold *Also called Freehold Pntiac Bick GMC Trcks* ***(G-3666)***
Freehold Pntiac Bick GMC Trcks 732 462-7093
4404 Us Highway 9 Freehold (07728) ***(G-3666)***
Freeman Products Inc (PA) 201 475-4800
71 Walsh Dr Ste 101 Parsippany (07054) ***(G-7951)***
Freeman Products Worldwide, Parsippany *Also called AMG International Inc* ***(G-7880)***
Freeman Technical Sales Inc 908 464-4784
148 Maple St New Providence (07974) ***(G-7001)***
Freeport Minerals Corporation 908 351-3200
48 94 Bayway Ave Elizabeth (07202) ***(G-2737)***
Freeport-Mcmoran Inc 908 558-4361
48-94 Bayway Ave Elizabeth (07202) ***(G-2738)***
Freestream Aircraft USA Ltd 201 365-6080
200 Fred Wehran Dr Ste 1 Teterboro (07608) ***(G-10676)***
Freeze, Dayton *Also called Central Mills Inc* ***(G-1960)***
Frell Corp 201 825-2500
885 State Rt 17 Ste 5 Ramsey (07446) ***(G-9144)***
French Color Fragrance Co Inc (PA) 201 567-6883
488 Grand Ave Englewood (07631) ***(G-2907)***
French Textile Co Inc 973 471-5000
835 Bloomfield Ave Ste 1 Clifton (07012) ***(G-1622)***
French Toast, Dayton *Also called Frenchtoastcom LLC* ***(G-1964)***
French Toast, Dayton *Also called Lollytogs Ltd* ***(G-1979)***
Frenchtoastcom LLC 732 438-5500
321 Herrod Blvd Dayton (08810) ***(G-1964)***
Frenchtown Partition Plant, Frenchtown *Also called Caraustar Industries Inc* ***(G-3710)***
Freshpet Inc (PA) 201 520-4000
400 Plaza Dr Fl 1 Secaucus (07094) ***(G-9768)***
Frewitt USA Inc 908 829-5245
249 Homestead Rd Hillsborough (08844) ***(G-4317)***
Freyr Inc 908 483-7958
150 College Rd W Ste 102 Princeton (08540) ***(G-8952)***
Friday Morning Quarterback 856 424-6873
1930 Marlton Pike E F36 Cherry Hill (08003) ***(G-1363)***
Friedrich and Dimmock Inc 856 825-0305
2127 Wheaton Ave Millville (08332) ***(G-6249)***
Friends Hardwood Floors Inc 732 859-4019
60 Monmouth Rd Oakhurst (07755) ***(G-7609)***
Frimpeks Inc 201 266-0116
30 Sherwood Ln Ste 6 Fairfield (07004) ***(G-3208)***
Frisch Plastics Corp 973 685-5936
81 Windsor Dr Pine Brook (07058) ***(G-8602)***
Frith Group (PA) 732 281-8343
445 Brick Blvd Ste 103 Brick (08723) ***(G-718)***
Fritnationalsupply, Newark *Also called Ivey Katrina Owner* ***(G-7163)***
Frontend Graphics Inc 856 547-1600
1951 Old Cuthbert Rd # 414 Cherry Hill (08034) ***(G-1364)***
Frontline Industries Inc 973 373-7211
990 Chancellor Ave Irvington (07111) ***(G-4570)***
Frontline Med Cmmnications Inc (HQ) 973 206-3434
7 Century Dr Ste 302 Parsippany (07054) ***(G-7952)***
Frontline Med Communications, Parsippany *Also called Frontline Med Cmmnications Inc* ***(G-7952)***
Frost King, Mahwah *Also called Thermwell Products Co Inc* ***(G-5781)***
Frost Tech Inc 732 396-0071
830 Elston St Rahway (07065) ***(G-9096)***
Froyo Skyview LLC 718 607-5656
42 Dales Ave Jersey City (07306) ***(G-4741)***
Frozen Desserts LLC 508 872-3573
39 Friends Ave Haddonfield (08033) ***(G-4057)***
Frozen Falls LLC 908 350-3939
413 King Gorge Rd Ste 202 Basking Ridge (07920) ***(G-184)***
Fruta Loca LLC 732 642-8233
547 Broadway Fl 1 Long Branch (07740) ***(G-5597)***
Fs Solutions, New Brunswick *Also called Jetstream of Houston LLP* ***(G-6938)***
Fti Inc 973 443-0004
8 Vreeland Rd Florham Park (07932) ***(G-3506)***
Fu WEI Inc 732 937-8388
40 Cotters Ln Bldg B East Brunswick (08816) ***(G-2147)***
Fu WEI International, East Brunswick *Also called Fu WEI Inc* ***(G-2147)***
Fuceltech Inc 609 275-0070
11 Glengarry Way Princeton Junction (08550) ***(G-9058)***
Fuchs Audio Tech Ltd Lblty Co 973 772-4420
407 Getty Ave Clifton (07011) ***(G-1623)***
Fuel Bio Holdings Ltd Lblty Co 908 344-6875
534 S Front St Elizabeth (07202) ***(G-2739)***
Fuel Management Services Inc 732 929-1964
13 Main Bayway Toms River (08753) ***(G-10760)***
Fuel One Inc 732 726-9500
869 Us Highway 1 Avenel (07001) ***(G-128)***
Fuel Ox LLC 908 747-4375
117 Buffalo Hollow Rd Glen Gardner (08826) ***(G-3822)***
Fuel Stop Inc 201 697-3319
2570 Us Highway 22 E Union (07083) ***(G-11057)***
Fuji Electric Corp America (HQ) 732 560-9410
50 Northfield Ave Edison (08837) ***(G-2515)***
Fujifilm Med Systems USA Inc 973 686-2631
155 Clearwater Rd Saddle River (07458) ***(G-9691)***
Fujifilm North America Corp 732 857-3000
1100 King Georges Post Rd Edison (08837) ***(G-2516)***
Fujikin of America Inc 201 641-1119
777 Terrace Ave Ste 110 Hasbrouck Heights (07604) ***(G-4182)***
Fujikura Graphics Inc 201 420-5040
700 Penhorn Ave Ste 2 Secaucus (07094) ***(G-9769)***
Fujipoly America Corporation 732 969-0100
900 Milik St Carteret (07008) ***(G-1255)***
Fujitsu General America Inc 973 575-0380
353 Rte 46 W Fairfield (07004) ***(G-3209)***
Fulcrum Inc 973 473-6900
660 Kinderkamack Rd # 203 Oradell (07649) ***(G-7744)***
Fulfillment Printing and Mail 609 953-9500
77 Oswego Trl Medford Lakes (08055) ***(G-6037)***
Full Circle Mfg Group 908 353-8933
534 S Front St Elizabeth (07202) ***(G-2740)***
Full House Printing Inc 201 798-7073
303 1st St Hoboken (07030) ***(G-4451)***
Full Service Mailers Inc 973 478-8813
123 S Newman St Hackensack (07601) ***(G-3919)***
Fullview Inc 732 275-6500
3 Fieldpoint Dr Holmdel (07733) ***(G-4501)***
Funai Corporation Inc (HQ) 201 806-7635
201 Route 17 Ste 903 Rutherford (07070) ***(G-9621)***
Funnibonz LLC 609 915-3685
3 Lake View Ct Princeton Junction (08550) ***(G-9059)***
Furniture of America NJ 201 605-8200
50 Enterprise Ave N Secaucus (07094) ***(G-9770)***
Furs By Severyn, Linden *Also called S & H R Inc* ***(G-5417)***
Fusar Technologies Inc 201 563-0189
78 John Miller Way # 310 Kearny (07032) ***(G-4856)***
Future Image Sign & Awning 201 440-1400
270 North St Teterboro (07608) ***(G-10677)***
Future Image Signs, Teterboro *Also called Future Image Sign & Awning* ***(G-10677)***
Future Signs, Trenton *Also called Ricztone Inc* ***(G-10987)***
Futurex Inc 201 933-3943
114 Essex St Ste 100 Rochelle Park (07662) ***(G-9423)***
Futurrex Inc 973 209-1563
24 Munsonhurst Rd Ste F Franklin (07416) ***(G-3603)***
FW Winter Inc 856 963-7490
550 Delaware Ave Camden (08102) ***(G-1065)***
Fxi Inc 201 933-8540
13 Manor Rd East Rutherford (07073) ***(G-2290)***

ALPHABETIC

Fyi Marketing Inc 646 546-5226
22 Laurie Dr Englewood Cliffs (07632) *(G-2971)*

Fyth Labs Inc 856 313-7362
455 Warren St E Beverly (08010) *(G-451)*

Fyx Fleet Roadside Assistance (HQ) 609 452-8900
750 College Rd E Princeton (08540) *(G-8953)*

G & A Coml Seating Pdts Corp 908 233-8000
152 Glen Rd Mountainside (07092) *(G-6846)*

G & A Pavers Llc 201 562-5947
2123 Sterling Blvd Englewood (07631) *(G-2908)*

G & B Machine Inc 908 707-1181
35 N Middaugh St Ste B Somerville (08876) *(G-10110)*

G & F Graphic Services, Pennsauken *Also called Inserts East Incorporated (G-8437)*

G & H Metal Finishers Inc 201 909-9808
282 Dakota St Paterson (07503) *(G-8196)*

G & H Metal Product, Hillside *Also called G & H Sheet Metal Works Inc (G-4393)*

G & H Sheet Metal Works Inc 973 923-1100
1423 Chestnut Ave Hillside (07205) *(G-4393)*

G & H Soho Inc 201 216-9400
413 Market St Elmwood Park (07407) *(G-2826)*

G & J Solutions Inc 609 861-9838
419 Madison Ave Woodbine (08270) *(G-12009)*

G & J Steel & Tubing Inc 908 526-4445
406 Roycefield Rd Hillsborough (08844) *(G-4318)*

G & M Custom Formica Work 732 888-0360
120 Francis St Ste 5 Keyport (07735) *(G-5000)*

G & M Printwear 856 742-5551
549 S Broadway Ste 2 Gloucester City (08030) *(G-3841)*

G & R Fuel Corp 973 732-0530
822 Clinton Ave Newark (07108) *(G-7128)*

G & S Design & Manufacturing 908 862-2444
330 Dalziel Rd Linden (07036) *(G-5349)*

G & S Motor Equipment Co Inc 201 998-9244
1800 Harrison Ave Kearny (07032) *(G-4857)*

G & S Precision Prototype 732 370-3010
115 Somerset Ave Lakewood (08701) *(G-5102)*

G & S Technologies, Kearny *Also called G & S Motor Equipment Co Inc (G-4857)*

G & W Laboratories Inc (PA) 908 753-2000
301 Helen St South Plainfield (07080) *(G-10263)*

G & W Laboratories Inc 732 474-0729
1551 S Washington Ave Piscataway (08854) *(G-8666)*

G & W Laboratories Inc 908 753-2000
101 Coolidge St South Plainfield (07080) *(G-10264)*

G & Y Specialty Foods LLC 956 821-9652
2 Andrews Dr Ste 5 Woodland Park (07424) *(G-12080)*

G A D Inc 973 383-3499
914 Cedar Ridge Rd Newton (07860) *(G-7344)*

G A F, Wayne *Also called G-I Holdings Inc (G-11507)*

G Big Corp 973 242-6521
189 Frelinghuysen Ave Newark (07114) *(G-7129)*

G Catalano Inc 908 241-6333
222 Valley Rd Roselle Park (07204) *(G-9585)*

G E C, Metuchen *Also called Graphic Equipment Corporation (G-6058)*

G E Inspection Technologies LP 973 448-0077
199 Us Highway 206 Flanders (07836) *(G-3411)*

G G Tauber Company Inc 800 638-6667
3535 State Route 66 Ste 1 Neptune (07753) *(G-6879)*

G H Krauss Manufacturing Co 856 662-0815
1209 Route 38 Cherry Hill (08002) *(G-1365)*

G Holdings LLC (PA) 973 628-3000
1 Campus Dr Parsippany (07054) *(G-7953)*

G I Trade Copy, Riverside *Also called Good Impressions Inc (G-9395)*

G J Chemical Co (PA) 973 589-1450
40 Veronica Ave Somerset (08873) *(G-9996)*

G J Haerer Co Inc (PA) 973 614-8090
372 Ridgewood Ave Glen Ridge (07028) *(G-3825)*

G J Oliver Inc 908 454-9743
50 Industrial Rd Phillipsburg (08865) *(G-8552)*

G M Fence Co, East Hanover *Also called General Metal Manufacturing Co (G-2211)*

G M Stainless Inc (PA) 908 575-1834
41 Imclone Dr Branchburg (08876) *(G-643)*

G N J Inc (PA) 856 786-1127
N Riderton Rd Rr 130 Cinnaminson (08077) *(G-1458)*

G P R Company Inc 973 227-6160
8 Spielman Rd Fairfield (07004) *(G-3210)*

G R Bowler Inc 973 525-7172
511 Maxim Dr Andover (07821) *(G-46)*

G R Impex Ltd Liability Co (PA) 301 873-5333
2 Terminal Way Bldg A Avenel (07001) *(G-129)*

G R P Signs, Newark *Also called Silver Edmar (G-7273)*

G S Babu & Co 732 939-5190
57 Woodland Dr Plainsboro (08536) *(G-8787)*

G T Associates 973 694-6040
440 Indian Rd Wayne (07470) *(G-11506)*

G W Laboratories, Piscataway *Also called G & W Laboratories Inc (G-8666)*

G&W PA Laboratories LLC 908 753-2000
111 Coolidge St South Plainfield (07080) *(G-10265)*

G-Force River Signs LLC 609 397-4467
9 S Main St Lambertville (08530) *(G-5189)*

G-I Holdings Inc (HQ) 973 628-3000
1361 Alps Rd Wayne (07470) *(G-11507)*

G-III Apparel Group Ltd 732 438-0209
308 Herrod Blvd Dayton (08810) *(G-1965)*

G-III Leather Fashions Inc 212 403-0500
308 Herrod Blvd Dayton (08810) *(G-1966)*

G-Tech Elevator Associates LLC 866 658-9296
12 Sherman St Linden (07036) *(G-5350)*

GAb Electronic Services LLC 856 786-0108
1703 Industrial Hwy Ste 8 Cinnaminson (08077) *(G-1459)*

Gabhen Inc 973 256-0666
1 Maltese Dr Totowa (07512) *(G-10827)*

Gabriel Sound Ltd Liability Co 973 831-7800
138 Cannonball Rd Pompton Lakes (07442) *(G-8851)*

Gadde Pharma LLC 609 651-7772
41 Madison Dr Plainsboro (08536) *(G-8788)*

Gade Float Valves, Collingswood *Also called Gadren Machine Co Inc (G-1767)*

Gadren Machine Co Inc (PA) 856 456-4329
590 N Atl Ave Apt 305 Collingswood (08108) *(G-1767)*

GAF, Parsippany *Also called Standard Industries Inc (G-8021)*

GAF Elk Materials Corporation 973 628-4083
1361 Alps Rd Wayne (07470) *(G-11508)*

Gafas Sales and Consulting Inc 862 368-5428
114 Sandpiper Ky Secaucus (07094) *(G-9771)*

Gail Gersons Wine & Dine Resta 732 758-0888
812 Broad St Shrewsbury (07702) *(G-9892)*

Galaxy Led Inc 201 541-5461
600 Sylvan Ave Ste 106 Englewood Cliffs (07632) *(G-2972)*

Galaxy Metal Products LLC 908 668-5200
2960 Woodbridge Ave Edison (08837) *(G-2517)*

Galaxy of Graphics, East Rutherford *Also called Arthur A Kaplan Co Inc (G-2273)*

Galaxy Switchgear Inds LLC 914 668-8200
46 Sellers St Kearny (07032) *(G-4858)*

Galaxy Trans & Magnetics LLC 856 753-4546
386 Cooper Rd West Berlin (08091) *(G-11596)*

Gale Newson Inc (PA) 732 961-7610
460 Faraday Ave Ste 7 Jackson (08527) *(G-4656)*

Galen Publishing LLC 908 253-9001
166 W Main St Somerville (08876) *(G-10111)*

Gallant Laboratories Inc 609 654-4146
2407 Delancey Way Marlton (08053) *(G-5932)*

Galleria Enterprises Inc 646 416-6683
26 Commerce Rd Ste I Fairfield (07004) *(G-3211)*

Gallery of Rugs Inc 908 934-0040
447 Springfield Ave Summit (07901) *(G-10532)*

Galvanic Prtg & Plate Co Inc 201 939-3600
50 Commercial Ave Moonachie (07074) *(G-6466)*

Galvanotech, Linden *Also called G & S Design & Manufacturing (G-5349)*

Galves Auto Price List Inc 201 393-0051
430 Industrial Ave Ste 3 Teterboro (07608) *(G-10678)*

Gambert Custom Shirts, Newark *Also called Gambert Shirt Corp (G-7130)*

Gambert Shirt Corp 973 424-9105
436 Ferry St Ste 2 Newark (07105) *(G-7130)*

Gamit Force Athc Ltd Llty Co 908 675-0733
459 Atlantic Ave Long Branch (07740) *(G-5598)*

Gamka Sales Co Inc 732 248-1400
983 New Durham Rd Edison (08817) *(G-2518)*

Gamma Machine & Tool Co Inc 973 398-8821
32 Oneida Ave Landing (07850) *(G-5201)*

Gammon Technical Products Inc (PA) 732 223-4600
2300 Highway 34 Manasquan (08736) *(G-5831)*

Gangi Graphics Inc 732 840-8680
1669 Route 88 Brick (08724) *(G-719)*

Gann Law Books Inc 973 268-1200
1 Washington Park # 1300 Newark (07102) *(G-7131)*

Gannett Co Inc 908 243-6953
92 E Main St Ste 202 Somerville (08876) *(G-10112)*

Gannett Stllite Info Ntwrk Inc 856 691-5000
891 E Oak Rd Vineland (08360) *(G-11220)*

Gannett Stllite Info Ntwrk LLC 973 428-6200
100 Commons Way Rockaway (07866) *(G-9462)*

Gannett Stllite Info Ntwrk LLC 609 561-2300
891 E Oak Rd Unit A Vineland (08360) *(G-11221)*

Gannett Stllite Info Ntwrk LLC 856 663-6000
301 Cuthbert Blvd Cherry Hill (08002) *(G-1366)*

Ganter Distillers Liabilit 609 344-7867
807 Baltic Ave Atlantic City (08401) *(G-92)*

Ganz Brothers Inc 201 820-1975
12 Mulberry Ct Paramus (07652) *(G-7801)*

Garafano Tank Service, Paterson *Also called Peter Garafano & Son Inc (G-8282)*

Gardellas Rvioli Itln Deli LLC 856 697-3509
527 S Brewster Rd Vineland (08360) *(G-11222)*

Garden St Chasis Remanuf 732 283-1910
1 Pennville Rd Woodbridge (07095) *(G-12016)*

Garden State Alnce Orthopaedic, Morristown *Also called Garden State Orthopedic Center (G-6664)*

Garden State Btlg Ltd Llty Co 201 991-2342
174 Sanford Ave Kearny (07032) *(G-4859)*

Garden State Fabricators...732 928-5006
575 Monmouth Rd Cream Ridge (08514) ***(G-1935)***
Garden State Fuel...856 442-0061
600 Buck Rd Monroeville (08343) ***(G-6351)***
Garden State Highway Pdts Inc (PA)...856 692-7572
301 Riverside Dr D Millville (08332) ***(G-6250)***
Garden State Iron Inc...732 918-0760
3418 Sunset Ave Ocean (07712) ***(G-7664)***
Garden State Irrigation...201 848-1300
500 W Main St Ste 5 Wyckoff (07481) ***(G-12112)***
Garden State Mgntic Imaging PC...609 581-2727
6027 S Crescent Blvd Pennsauken (08110) ***(G-8423)***
Garden State Orthopedic Center...973 538-4948
95 Mount Kemble Ave Morristown (07960) ***(G-6664)***
Garden State Precast Inc...732 938-4436
1630 Wyckoff Rd Wall Township (07727) ***(G-11343)***
Garden State Precision Inc...201 945-6410
510 Church St Ridgefield (07657) ***(G-9262)***
Garden State Prosthetics...732 922-6650
3500 Sunset Ave Ocean (07712) ***(G-7665)***
Garden State Recycl Edison LLC...732 393-0200
355 Meadow Rd Edison (08837) ***(G-2519)***
Garden State Sign, Howell *Also called Ervin Advertising Co Inc* ***(G-4539)***
Garden State Tool & Mold Corp...908 245-2041
501 Bordentown Ave South Amboy (08879) ***(G-10133)***
Garden State Welding LLC...973 857-0792
89 Claremont Ave Verona (07044) ***(G-11168)***
Garden State Woman Mag LLC...908 879-7143
210 Parker Rd Long Valley (07853) ***(G-5611)***
Gardner Resources Inc...732 872-0755
188 Bay Ave Highlands (07732) ***(G-4292)***
Garelick Farms LLC...609 499-2600
Cumberland Blvd Rr 130 Burlington (08016) ***(G-970)***
Garfield Industries Inc...973 575-3322
62 Clinton Rd Ste 1 Fairfield (07004) ***(G-3212)***
Garfield Molding Co Inc...973 777-5700
10 Midland Ave Wallington (07057) ***(G-11386)***
Garley Inc...215 788-5756
46 Tall Timber Ln Burlington (08016) ***(G-971)***
Garment Bar, Deptford *Also called International Rollforms Inc* ***(G-2064)***
Garratt-Callahan Company...732 287-2200
306 Talmadge Rd Edison (08817) ***(G-2520)***
Garrett Moore...908 231-9231
1048 Hoffman Rd Bridgewater (08807) ***(G-825)***
Garrett Motion Inc (PA)...973 867-7016
89 Headquarters Plz Morristown (07960) ***(G-6665)***
Garrison Printing Company Inc...856 488-1900
7155 Airport Hwy Pennsauken (08109) ***(G-8424)***
Garvey Corporation (PA)...609 561-2450
208 S Route 73 Hammonton (08037) ***(G-4134)***
Gary Ell Photography, Burlington *Also called Pixell Creative Group LLC* ***(G-982)***
Gary R Banks Industrial Group...856 687-2227
575 N Route 73 Ste C6 West Berlin (08091) ***(G-11597)***
Gary R Marzili...856 782-1546
840 Jarvis Rd Sicklerville (08081) ***(G-9910)***
Garylin Togs...908 354-7218
107 Trumbull St Elizabeth (07206) ***(G-2741)***
Garys Kids...973 458-1818
314 Monroe St Passaic (07055) ***(G-8067)***
Gas Drying Inc...973 361-2212
355 W Dewey Ave Wharton (07885) ***(G-11859)***
Gasflo Products Inc...973 276-9011
19 Industrial Rd Fairfield (07004) ***(G-3213)***
Gaspari Nutrition, Neptune *Also called Allegro Nutrition Inc* ***(G-6864)***
Gass Custom Woodworking...201 493-9282
169 Birchwood Rd Paramus (07652) ***(G-7802)***
Gate Technologies Inc...973 300-0090
27 Wilson Dr Unit C Sparta (07871) ***(G-10388)***
Gatehuse Media PA Holdings Inc...732 246-7677
104 Church St New Brunswick (08901) ***(G-6927)***
Gateway Property Solutions Ltd...732 901-9700
730 Airport Rd Unit 1 Lakewood (08701) ***(G-5103)***
Gauer Metal Products Co Inc...908 241-4080
175 N Michigan Ave Kenilworth (07033) ***(G-4942)***
Gaum Inc (PA)...609 586-0132
1080 Us Highway 130 Robbinsville (08691) ***(G-9412)***
Gavan Graham Elec Pdts Corp (PA)...908 729-9000
751 Rahway Ave Union (07083) ***(G-11058)***
Gaw Associates Inc...856 608-1428
670 Deer Rd Bldg A Cherry Hill (08034) ***(G-1367)***
Gaw Technology, Cherry Hill *Also called Gaw Associates Inc* ***(G-1367)***
Gb Industries II Inc...973 728-5900
341 Margaret King Ave Ringwood (07456) ***(G-9345)***
Gbd Cabinet Shop, Pluckemin *Also called Franks Cabinet Shop Inc* ***(G-8822)***
Gbw Manufacturing Inc...973 279-0077
20 W End Rd Totowa (07512) ***(G-10828)***
Gcah, Madison *Also called General Commis Archives & Hstr* ***(G-5693)***
Gce Market Inc (PA)...856 401-8900
1001 Lower Landing Rd # 307 Blackwood (08012) ***(G-466)***
GCI, Secaucus *Also called General Glass Intl Corp* ***(G-9772)***
Gdb International Inc (PA)...732 246-3001
1 Home News Row New Brunswick (08901) ***(G-6928)***
GE Aviation Systems LLC...973 428-9898
110 Algonquin Pkwy Whippany (07981) ***(G-11892)***
GE Healthcare Inc...908 757-0500
900 Durham Ave South Plainfield (07080) ***(G-10266)***
Gears IV LLC...201 401-3035
11 Jeffrey Ln Bridgewater (08807) ***(G-826)***
Geiger Tool & Mfg Co Inc...973 777-2136
50 Liberty St Passaic (07055) ***(G-8068)***
Geiger Tool Co Inc...973 777-5094
50 Liberty St Passaic (07055) ***(G-8069)***
Geislers Liquor Store...856 845-0482
195 Crown Point Rd Thorofare (08086) ***(G-10699)***
Geistlich Pharma North America...609 779-6560
202 Carnegie Ctr Ste 103 Princeton (08540) ***(G-8954)***
Gel Concepts LLC...973 884-8995
30 Leslie Ct Whippany (07981) ***(G-11893)***
Gel Spice Co Inc (PA)...201 339-0700
48 Hook Rd Bayonne (07002) ***(G-218)***
Gel Spice Co LLC...201 339-0700
48 Hook Rd Bayonne (07002) ***(G-219)***
Gel United Ltd Liability Co...855 435-8683
635 N Midland Ave 3184 Saddle Brook (07663) ***(G-9653)***
Gelbsteins Bakery, Lakewood *Also called Y & J Bakers Inc* ***(G-5184)***
Gelotti Confections LLC...973 403-9968
194 Bloomfield Ave Caldwell (07006) ***(G-1025)***
Gem Vault Inc...908 788-1770
23 Turntable Jct Flemington (08822) ***(G-3445)***
Gemco Valve Co LLC...732 752-7900
301 Smalley Ave Middlesex (08846) ***(G-6118)***
Gemcraft Inc...732 449-8944
1921 State Route 71 Belmar (07719) ***(G-349)***
Gemini Cut Glass Company Inc...201 568-7722
4 E Forest Ave Englewood (07631) ***(G-2909)***
Gemini Plastic Films Corp...973 340-0700
535 Midland Ave Garfield (07026) ***(G-3745)***
Gemini Sound, Elizabeth *Also called Innovative Concepts Design LLC* ***(G-2750)***
Gemtor Inc...732 583-6200
1 Johnson Ave Matawan (07747) ***(G-5976)***
Genavite LLC...201 343-3131
171 Beech St Hackensack (07601) ***(G-3920)***
Gendell Assoicates PA...201 656-4498
1031 Bloomfield St Hoboken (07030) ***(G-4452)***
Gene Mignola Inc...732 775-9291
704 Cookman Ave Asbury Park (07712) ***(G-77)***
General A & E, Hackensack *Also called General Aviation & Elec Mfg Co* ***(G-3921)***
General Aviation & Elec Mfg Co...201 487-1700
30 Jersey Pl Hackensack (07601) ***(G-3921)***
General Carbon Corporation...973 523-2223
33 Paterson St Paterson (07501) ***(G-8197)***
General Chemical, Parsippany *Also called Chemtrade Solutions LLC* ***(G-7904)***
General Chemical, Berkeley Heights *Also called Chemtrade Solutions LLC* ***(G-394)***
General Chemical Prfmce Pdts, Parsippany *Also called Chemtrade Chemicals US LLC* ***(G-7902)***
General Commis Archives & Hstr...973 408-3189
36 Madison Ave Madison (07940) ***(G-5693)***
General Dynamics Mission...973 261-1409
7 9 Vreeland Rd Florham Park (07932) ***(G-3507)***
General Dynamics Mission...973 335-2230
222 New Rd Ste 1 Parsippany (07054) ***(G-7954)***
General Electric Company...973 887-6635
700 Parsippany Rd Parsippany (07054) ***(G-7955)***
General Electric Company...201 866-2161
6001 Tonnelle Ave North Bergen (07047) ***(G-7406)***
General Electronic Engineering (PA)...732 381-1144
132 W Main St Rahway (07065) ***(G-9097)***
General Film Products Inc...908 351-0454
107 Trumbull St Ste 302 Elizabeth (07206) ***(G-2742)***
General Foam, East Rutherford *Also called Pmc Inc* ***(G-2310)***
General Foundries Inc (PA)...732 951-9001
1 Progress Rd North Brunswick (08902) ***(G-7468)***
General Glass Intl Corp...201 553-1850
101 Venture Way Secaucus (07094) ***(G-9772)***
General Graphics Corporation (PA)...201 664-4083
63 Briarcliff Rd Hillsdale (07642) ***(G-4367)***
General Hydraulics, Springfield *Also called Barworth Inc* ***(G-10430)***
General Machine Kraft, Phillipsburg *Also called N E R Associates Inc* ***(G-8565)***
General Magnaplate Corporation (PA)...908 862-6200
1331 W Edgar Rd Linden (07036) ***(G-5351)***
General Magnaplate Wisconsin...800 441-6173
1331 W Edgar Rd Linden (07036) ***(G-5352)***
General Mch Experimental Works...201 843-9035
117 Gertrude Ave Ste 1 Paramus (07652) ***(G-7803)***
General Metal & Glass Co, Camden *Also called William Duling* ***(G-1090)***
General Metal Manufacturing Co...973 386-1818
170 State Route 10 East Hanover (07936) ***(G-2211)***

ALPHABETIC

General Pallet LLC..732 549-1000
  97 River Rd Flemington (08822) *(G-3446)*

General Pencil Company Inc (PA)..........................201 653-5351
  67 Fleet St Jersey City (07306) *(G-4742)*

General Performance Products, Parsippany *Also called Chemtrade Chemicals Corp (G-7901)*

General Polygon Systems Inc...............................800 825-1655
  203 Peterson St Millville (08332) *(G-6251)*

General Reliance Corporation...............................973 361-1400
  88 Ford Rd Ste 20 Denville (07834) *(G-2038)*

General Sign Co Inc...856 753-3535
  105 Chestnut Ave West Berlin (08091) *(G-11598)*

General Stamping Co Inc.....................................973 627-9500
  309 Sr 94 Columbia (07832) *(G-1793)*

General Sullivan Group Inc (PA)...........................609 745-5004
  85 Route 31 N Pennington (08534) *(G-8365)*

General Sullivan Group Inc.................................609 745-5000
  85 Route 31 N Pennington (08534) *(G-8366)*

General Tool Specialties Inc.................................908 874-3040
  284 Sunnymeade Rd Hillsborough (08844) *(G-4319)*

General Tools & Instrs Co LLC (PA).......................212 431-6100
  75 Seaview Dr Secaucus (07094) *(G-9773)*

General Tools Mfg Co LLC...................................201 770-1380
  75 Seaview Dr Secaucus (07094) *(G-9774)*

General Wire & Stamping Co................................973 366-8080
  1 Emery Ave Ste 3 Randolph (07869) *(G-9179)*

Generation Brands...856 764-0500
  6 Campus Dr Burlington (08016) *(G-972)*

Generon Biomed Inc...908 203-4701
  1200 Us Highway 22 # 2000 Bridgewater (08807) *(G-827)*

Genesis Bps LLC...201 708-1400
  465 Route 17 S Ramsey (07446) *(G-9145)*

Genesis Lighting Mfg Inc.....................................908 352-6720
  107 Trumbull St Ste 104 Elizabethport (07206) *(G-2788)*

Genesis Marketing Group Inc..............................201 836-1392
  269 Edgemont Ter Teaneck (07666) *(G-10632)*

Genevieves Home Made Candy Sp, Garfield *Also called Genevieves Inc (G-3746)*

Genevieves Inc..973 772-8816
  174 Ray St Garfield (07026) *(G-3746)*

Genexosome Technologies Inc..............................646 762-4517
  4400 Route 9 N Freehold (07728) *(G-3667)*

Genie House Corp (PA)......................................609 859-0600
  139 Red Lion Rd Southampton (08088) *(G-10363)*

Genomesafe LLC..203 676-3752
  4 Linden Ave West Orange (07052) *(G-11768)*

Gentek Inc (HQ)...973 515-0900
  90 E Halsey Rd Ste 301 Parsippany (07054) *(G-7956)*

Gentek Building Products Inc...............................732 381-0900
  11 Cragwood Rd Avenel (07001) *(G-130)*

Genua & Mulligan Printing...................................973 894-1500
  1 Trenton Ave Clifton (07011) *(G-1624)*

Genzyme Biosurgery, Ridgefield *Also called Genzyme Corporation (G-9263)*

Genzyme Corporation...973 256-2106
  25 Madison Rd Totowa (07512) *(G-10829)*

Genzyme Corporation...201 313-9660
  1125 Pleasantview Ter Ridgefield (07657) *(G-9263)*

Geolytics Inc..908 707-1505
  3322 Us Highway 22 # 806 Branchburg (08876) *(G-644)*

George Brummer..908 232-1904
  125 E Broad St Westfield (07090) *(G-11798)*

George Ciocher Inc..732 818-3495
  1241 Birmingham Ave Toms River (08757) *(G-10761)*

George J Bender Inc..908 687-0081
  1 Milltown Ct Union (07083) *(G-11059)*

George Pnterman Kitchens Baths, Manasquan *Also called Sanford & Birdsall Inc (G-5838)*

George Press Inc..973 992-7797
  74 S Livingston Ave Livingston (07039) *(G-5513)*

George Scher Engineering, Lebanon *Also called Weber and Scher Mfg Co Inc (G-5275)*

Georges Wine and Spirits Galle.............................973 948-9950
  7 Main St Branchville (07826) *(G-707)*

Georgia-Pacific LLC..908 995-2228
  623 Riegelsville Rd Milford (08848) *(G-6193)*

Georgia-Pacific LLC..856 966-7600
  1101 S Front St Camden (08103) *(G-1066)*

Gep, Clark *Also called Nb Ventures Inc (G-1509)*

Gerardi Press Inc...973 627-2600
  3 Luger Rd Ste 3 # 3 Denville (07834) *(G-2039)*

Gerber Products Company (HQ)............................973 593-7500
  12 Vreeland Rd Fl 2 Florham Park (07932) *(G-3508)*

Gerbino Computer Systems Inc............................201 342-8240
  200 Passaic St Ste 100 Hackensack (07601) *(G-3922)*

Gericke USA Inc..855 888-0088
  14 Worlds Fair Dr Ste C Somerset (08873) *(G-9997)*

Gerin Corporation Inc...732 774-3256
  1109 7th Ave Neptune (07753) *(G-6880)*

Gerresheimer Glass Inc (HQ)...............................856 692-3600
  537 Crystal Ave Vineland (08360) *(G-11223)*

Gerresheimer Glass Inc.......................................856 507-5852
  91 W Forest Grove Rd Vineland (08360) *(G-11224)*

Gervens Enterprises Inc.......................................973 838-1600
  122 Hamburg Tpke Ste D Bloomingdale (07403) *(G-529)*

Getinge Group Logistics Americ............................973 709-6000
  45 Barbour Pond Dr Wayne (07470) *(G-11509)*

Getinge Usa Inc (HQ)...800 475-9040
  45 Barbour Pond Dr Wayne (07470) *(G-11510)*

GF Supplies LLC (PA)..336 539-1666
  319 E 54th St Elmwood Park (07407) *(G-2827)*

Ggb Bearing Technology, Thorofare *Also called Ggb LLC (G-10701)*

Ggb LLC (HQ)..856 848-3200
  1451 Metropolitan Thorofare (08086) *(G-10700)*

Ggb LLC..856 848-3200
  700 Mid Atlantic Pkwy Thorofare (08086) *(G-10701)*

Ggb LLC..856 686-2675
  1414 Metropolitan Ave Thorofare (08086) *(G-10702)*

Ggb N.A., Thorofare *Also called Ggb LLC (G-10702)*

Gia-Tek LLC...973 228-0875
  66 Westover Ave West Caldwell (07006) *(G-11652)*

Giambri's Candy, Clementon *Also called Giambris Quality Sweets Inc (G-1533)*

Giambris Quality Sweets Inc.................................856 783-1099
  26 Brand Ave Clementon (08021) *(G-1533)*

Giannella Bakery, Paterson *Also called Lo Presti & Sons LLC (G-8245)*

Giant Stl Fabricators Erectors...............................908 241-6766
  197 E Highland Pkwy Roselle (07203) *(G-9559)*

Gibbons Company Ltd...441 294-5047
  614 Progress St Elizabeth (07201) *(G-2743)*

Gibraltar Laboratories Inc (HQ)............................973 227-6882
  122 Fairfield Rd Fairfield (07004) *(G-3214)*

Gifford Group Inc..212 569-8500
  35 Obrien St Kearny (07032) *(G-4860)*

Gilbert Storms Jr...973 835-5729
  1456 Ringwood Ave Apt 1 Haskell (07420) *(G-4196)*

Gilbys, Haskell *Also called Gilbert Storms Jr (G-4196)*

Gild-N-Son Manufacturing, Kearny *Also called Belleville Corporation (G-4846)*

Gill Assoc Idntfcation Systems, Wayne *Also called Gill Associates LLC (G-11511)*

Gill Associates LLC..973 835-5456
  2025 Hamburg Tpke Ste M Wayne (07470) *(G-11511)*

Gillespie Industries, Vineland *Also called P J Gillespie Inc (G-11248)*

Gingko Tree Inc (PA)..973 652-9380
  601 W Linden Ave Linden (07036) *(G-5353)*

Ginseng Up Corporation......................................800 446-7364
  24 Link Dr Rockleigh (07647) *(G-9517)*

Ginsey Home Solutions, Swedesboro *Also called Ginsey Industries Inc (G-10586)*

Ginsey Industries Inc...856 933-1300
  2078 Center Square Rd Swedesboro (08085) *(G-10586)*

Gio Vali Handbag Corp..973 279-3032
  463 Grand St Paterson (07505) *(G-8198)*

Giovali Handbag, Paterson *Also called Gio Vali Handbag Corp (G-8198)*

Givaudan East, East Hanover *Also called Givaudan Fragrances Corp (G-2214)*

Givaudan Flavors, East Hanover *Also called Givaudan Fragrances Corp (G-2213)*

Givaudan Flavors Corporation...............................973 463-8192
  6 Santa Fe Way Cranbury (08512) *(G-1835)*

Givaudan Flavors Corporation...............................609 409-6200
  6 Santa Fe Way Cranbury (08512) *(G-1836)*

Givaudan Flavors Corporation...............................973 386-9800
  245 Merry Ln East Hanover (07936) *(G-2212)*

Givaudan Fragrances Corp...................................973 386-9800
  245 Merry Ln East Hanover (07936) *(G-2213)*

Givaudan Fragrances Corp...................................973 576-9500
  717 Ridgedale Ave East Hanover (07936) *(G-2214)*

Givaudan Fragrances Corp...................................973 560-1939
  717 Ridgedale Ave East Hanover (07936) *(G-2215)*

Givaudan Fragrances Corp...................................973 448-6500
  300 Waterloo Valley Rd Budd Lake (07828) *(G-924)*

GL Associates, Jersey City *Also called GL Consulting Inc (G-4743)*

GL Consulting Inc (PA).......................................201 938-0200
  210 Hudson St Ste 1000 Jersey City (07311) *(G-4743)*

Glamorous Glo..732 361-3235
  42 Carolyn Ct Eatontown (07724) *(G-2393)*

Glasco Uv LLC...201 934-3348
  126 Christie Ave Mahwah (07430) *(G-5741)*

Glasplex LLC..973 940-8940
  8 Estate Dr Sussex (07461) *(G-10560)*

Glass Cycle Systems Inc......................................973 838-0034
  5 Mathews Ave Riverdale (07457) *(G-9378)*

Glass Dynamics LLC...856 205-1503
  2662 Hance Bridge Rd Vineland (08361) *(G-11225)*

Glass House, The, Lumberton *Also called Proco Inc (G-5634)*

Glass Warehouse...856 825-1400
  1101 Wheaton Ave Millville (08332) *(G-6252)*

Glassblowerscom LLC (PA)..................................856 232-7898
  234 Bells Lake Rd Blackwood (08012) *(G-467)*

Glassboro News & Food Store...............................856 881-1181
  255 E High St Glassboro (08028) *(G-3812)*

Glasscare Inc...201 943-1122
  666 Anderson Ave Cliffside Park (07010) *(G-1539)*

Glasseal Products Inc...732 370-9100
  485 Oberlin Ave S Lakewood (08701) *(G-5104)*

2019 Harris New Jersey
Manufacturers Directory

(G-0000) Company's Geographic Section entry number

Glassroots Inc 973 353-9555
  10 Bleeker St Newark (07102) *(G-7132)*
Glassworks Studio Inc 973 656-0800
  151 South St Ste B103 Morristown (07960) *(G-6666)*
Glastron Inc. 856 692-0500
  510 N West Blvd Vineland (08360) *(G-11226)*
Glaxosmithkline Consumer (HQ) 251 591-4188
  184 Libery Corner Rd Warren (07059) *(G-11411)*
Glaxosmithkline Consumer Hlth (HQ) 215 751-5046
  184 Liberty Corner Rd Warren (07059) *(G-11412)*
Glaxosmithkline LLC 856 952-6023
  505 S Vineyard Blvd Collingswood (08108) *(G-1768)*
Glaxosmithkline LLC 609 472-8175
  24 Cohasset Ln Cherry Hill (08003) *(G-1368)*
Glebar Company, Ramsey *Also called Glebar Operating LLC* *(G-9146)*
Glebar Operating LLC 201 337-1500
  565 E Crescent Ave Ramsey (07446) *(G-9146)*
Gleeson Agency, East Rutherford *Also called Dawn Bible Students Assn* *(G-2285)*
Gleicher Manufacturing Corp 908 233-2211
  851 Jerusalem Rd Scotch Plains (07076) *(G-9732)*
Glen Magnetics Inc 908 454-3717
  1165 3rd Ave Alpha (08865) *(G-37)*
Glen Mills Inc 973 777-0777
  220 Delawanna Ave Clifton (07014) *(G-1625)*
Glen Rock Ham, Caldwell *Also called Al and John Inc* *(G-1020)*
Glen Rock Stair Corp 201 337-9595
  551 Commerce St Franklin Lakes (07417) *(G-3624)*
Glen-Gery Brick, Hillsborough *Also called Glen-Gery Corporation* *(G-4320)*
Glen-Gery Corporation 908 359-5111
  75 Hamilton Rd Hillsborough (08844) *(G-4320)*
Glenbrook Technologies Inc 973 361-8866
  11 Emery Ave Randolph (07869) *(G-9180)*
Glenburnie Feed & Grain 856 986-8128
  87 Chapel Hill Rd Mount Laurel (08054) *(G-6763)*
Glenmark Phrmceuticals Inc USA (HQ) 201 684-8000
  750 Corporate Dr Mahwah (07430) *(G-5742)*
Glenmark Therapeutics Inc USA 201 684-8000
  750 Corporate Dr Mahwah (07430) *(G-5743)*
Glenro Inc (PA) 973 279-5900
  39 Mcbride Ave Paterson (07501) *(G-8199)*
Glentech Inc 908 685-2205
  46 4th St Somerville (08876) *(G-10113)*
Glenwood LLC 201 569-0050
  111 Cedar Ln Englewood (07631) *(G-2910)*
Glenwood-Palisades, Englewood *Also called Glenwood LLC* *(G-2910)*
Glitterex Corp 908 272-9121
  7 Commerce Dr Cranford (07016) *(G-1911)*
Glitterwrap Inc (HQ) 800 745-4883
  701 Ford Rd Ste 1 Rockaway (07866) *(G-9463)*
Global Business Dimensions Inc (PA) 973 831-5866
  220 W Parkway Ste 8 Pompton Plains (07444) *(G-8865)*
Global Commodities Exportacao 201 613-1532
  126 Jackson St Newark (07105) *(G-7133)*
Global Direct Marketing Group 856 427-6116
  229 Kings Hwy E Haddonfield (08033) *(G-4058)*
Global Ecology Corporation (PA) 973 655-9001
  101 Eisenhower Pkwy # 300 Roseland (07068) *(G-9538)*
Global Express Freight Inc 201 376-6613
  136 W Central Ave Bergenfield (07621) *(G-375)*
Global Force and Artic Bloc, Newark *Also called Global Manufacturing LLC* *(G-7134)*
Global Furniture Group, Marlton *Also called Global Industries Inc* *(G-5933)*
Global Graphics Intergration 973 334-9653
  14 Willard Ln Towaco (07082) *(G-10872)*
Global IDS Inc 609 683-1066
  182 Nassau St Ste 202 Princeton (08542) *(G-8955)*
Global Industries Inc (PA) 856 596-3390
  17 W Stow Rd Marlton (08053) *(G-5933)*
Global Ingredients Inc 973 278-6677
  317 9th Ave Paterson (07514) *(G-8200)*
Global Manufacturing LLC 973 494-5413
  35 William St Fl 2 Newark (07102) *(G-7134)*
Global Marketing Corp 973 426-1088
  155 Canfield Ave Randolph (07869) *(G-9181)*
Global Power Technology Inc (PA) 732 287-3680
  1000 New Durham Rd Edison (08817) *(G-2521)*
Global Prtners In Shelding Inc 973 574-9077
  5 Just Rd Fairfield (07004) *(G-3215)*
Global Seven Inc 973 209-7474
  198 Green Pond Rd Ste 4 Rockaway (07866) *(G-9464)*
Global Spclty Products-Usa Inc 609 518-7577
  10 Eagle Ave Ste 500 Mount Holly (08060) *(G-6728)*
Global Strategy Institute A 973 615-7447
  55 Park Ave Unit 35 Bloomfield (07003) *(G-501)*
Global Weavers Corp 973 824-5500
  9-13 Dey St Newark (07103) *(G-7135)*
Global Wire & Cable Inc 973 471-1000
  61 Willet St Ste 4b Passaic (07055) *(G-8070)*
Globe Casing Co, Carlstadt *Also called Globe Packaging Co Inc* *(G-1159)*

Globe Die-Cutting Products Inc 732 494-7744
  76 Liberty St Metuchen (08840) *(G-6057)*
Globe Engineering Corp 609 898-0349
  1213 Delaware Ave Cape May (08204) *(G-1099)*
Globe Industries Corp 973 992-8990
  48 Industrial St W Clifton (07012) *(G-1626)*
Globe Manufacturing Sales Co, Mountainside *Also called A K Stamping Co Inc* *(G-6831)*
Globe Packaging Co Inc 201 896-1144
  368 Paterson Plank Rd Carlstadt (07072) *(G-1159)*
Globe Pharma Inc 732 296-9700
  2b Janine Pl New Brunswick (08901) *(G-6929)*
Globe Photo Engraving Co LLC 201 489-2300
  19 N Washington Ave Ste 1 Little Ferry (07643) *(G-5487)*
Globe Photo Engraving Corp 201 489-2300
  19 N Washington Ave Little Ferry (07643) *(G-5488)*
Globe Scientific Inc 201 599-1400
  400 Corporate Dr Mahwah (07430) *(G-5744)*
Globela Pharma LLC 888 588-8511
  62 Hauxhurst Ave Weehawken (07086) *(G-11567)*
Globepharma Inc 732 296-9700
  2b Janine Pl New Brunswick (08901) *(G-6930)*
Globtek Inc (PA) 201 784-1000
  186 Veterans Dr Northvale (07647) *(G-7526)*
Glocal Expertise Llc 718 928-3839
  185 Zabriskie St Jersey City (07307) *(G-4744)*
Glopak Corp 908 753-8735
  132 Case Dr South Plainfield (07080) *(G-10267)*
Gloucester City Box Works LLC 856 456-9032
  775 Charles St Gloucester City (08030) *(G-3842)*
Gloucester County Times 856 845-7484
  309 S Broad St Woodbury (08096) *(G-12030)*
Glow Tube Inc 609 268-7707
  83 Springers Brook Rd Shamong (08088) *(G-9856)*
Glue Fold Inc 973 575-8400
  40 Webro Rd Clifton (07012) *(G-1627)*
Gluefast Company Inc 732 918-4600
  3535 State Route 66 Ste 1 Neptune (07753) *(G-6881)*
Glw Inc 845 492-0476
  78 John Miller Way # 447 Kearny (07032) *(G-4861)*
Glysortia LLC 715 426-5358
  281 Hampshire Dr Plainsboro (08536) *(G-8789)*
GM Construction, Fairfield *Also called Michele Maddalena* *(G-3270)*
GM Precision Machine, Sicklerville *Also called Gary R Marzili* *(G-9910)*
GMC-I New Wrld Btiligungs GMBH, Edison *Also called Global Power Technology Inc* *(G-2521)*
Gmp Publications Inc 609 859-3400
  4 Linda Ln Ste B Southampton (08088) *(G-10364)*
Gmpc Printing 973 546-6060
  1 Trenton Ave Clifton (07011) *(G-1628)*
Gms Litho Corp 973 575-9400
  16 Passaic Ave Unit 3 Fairfield (07004) *(G-3216)*
Go Foton Corporation (PA) 732 412-7375
  28 Worlds Fair Dr Somerset (08873) *(G-9998)*
Go R Design LLC 609 286-2146
  74 Hemlock Dr New Egypt (08533) *(G-6983)*
Go Waddle Inc 301 452-5084
  23 Baldwin Dr Berkeley Heights (07922) *(G-399)*
Goetz & Ruschmann Inc 973 383-9270
  1 Brooks Plz Newton (07860) *(G-7345)*
Goffco Industries LLC 973 492-0150
  10 Park Pl Ste 300 Butler (07405) *(G-1001)*
Gogreen Power Inc 732 994-5901
  4675 Us Highway 9 Howell (07731) *(G-4540)*
Gold Buyers At Mall LLC (PA) 201 512-5780
  1 International Blvd # 200 Mahwah (07495) *(G-5745)*
Gold Enterprise Ltd 954 614-1001
  1671 Beaver Dam Rd Ste 11 Point Pleasant Boro (08742) *(G-8845)*
Gold Signature Incorporated 732 777-9170
  1260 Stelton Rd Piscataway (08854) *(G-8667)*
Gold Star Distribution LLC 973 882-5300
  120 Eagle Rock Ave # 326 East Hanover (07936) *(G-2216)*
Golden Fluff Inc 732 367-5448
  118 Monmouth Ave Lakewood (08701) *(G-5105)*
Golden Metal Products Corp 973 399-1157
  100 Hoffman Pl Ste 1 Hillside (07205) *(G-4394)*
Golden Platter Foods Inc 973 344-8770
  37 Tompkins Point Rd Newark (07114) *(G-7136)*
Golden Rule Creations Inc 201 337-4050
  250 Terrace Rd Franklin Lakes (07417) *(G-3625)*
Golden Rule Inc 856 663-3074
  7150 N Park Dr Ste 620 Pennsauken (08109) *(G-8425)*
Golden Season Fashion USA Inc 201 552-2088
  555 Secacus Rd Ste 1 Secaucus (07094) *(G-9775)*
Golden Treasure Imports Inc 732 723-1830
  522 Us Highway 9 Englishtown (07726) *(G-3002)*
Golden Tropics Ltd 973 484-0202
  1489-1495 Mccarter Hwy Newark (07104) *(G-7137)*
Golden W Ppr Converting Corp 908 412-8889
  121 Helen St South Plainfield (07080) *(G-10268)*

A
L
P
H
A
B
E
T
I
C

Goldens Inc 215 850-2512
9 Kings Hwy W Haddonfield (08033) *(G-4059)*

Goldsmith & Revere, Ridgefield Park *Also called Dmg America LLC (G-9304)*

Goldstar Performance Products, East Hanover *Also called Gold Star Distribution LLC (G-2216)*

Goldstein & Burton Inc 201 440-0065
20 Potash Rd Oakland (07436) *(G-7630)*

Goldstein Setting Co Inc 908 964-1034
2464 Morris Ave Union (07083) *(G-11060)*

Golf Coast Polymer Services 856 498-3434
107 Madison Rd Elmer (08318) *(G-2798)*

Golf Odyssey LLC 973 564-6223
60 Woodcrest Ave Short Hills (07078) *(G-9869)*

Good As Gold Jewelers Inc 732 286-1111
226 Route 37 W Ste 9 Toms River (08755) *(G-10762)*

Good Earth Teas Inc 831 423-7913
155 Chestnut Ridge Rd Montvale (07645) *(G-6412)*

Good Humor/Breyers, Englewood Cliffs *Also called Conopco Inc (G-2965)*

Good Impressions Inc 856 461-3232
28 E Scott St Riverside (08075) *(G-9395)*

Good Impressions Inc (PA) 908 689-3071
325 W Washington Ave Washington (07882) *(G-11445)*

Good Neighbor Pharmacy, Florence *Also called Boyds Pharmacy Inc (G-3473)*

Good To Go Inc 856 429-2005
310 S Burnt Mill Rd Voorhees (08043) *(G-11286)*

Goodlite Products Inc 718 697-7502
500 Division St Perth Amboy (08861) *(G-8519)*

Goodrich Corporation 973 237-2700
20 Commerce Way Totowa (07512) *(G-10830)*

Goose Country LLC 646 860-8815
10 Bramble Ln Matawan (07747) *(G-5977)*

Gopole, Pompton Plains *Also called Ar2 Products LLC (G-8858)*

Goralski Embroidery, Park Ridge *Also called Goralski Inc (G-7851)*

Goralski Inc 201 573-1529
4 Marti Rd Park Ridge (07656) *(G-7851)*

Gordon Brush Mfg Co Inc 973 827-4600
15 Park Dr Franklin (07416) *(G-3604)*

Gordon Fergusson Intr Dctg Ser, Maplewood *Also called Gordon Frgson Intr Dsigns Svcs (G-5877)*

Gordon Frgson Intr Dsigns Svcs 973 378-2330
205 Rutgers St Maplewood (07040) *(G-5877)*

Gordon Terminal Service Co PA 201 437-8300
2 Hook Rd Bayonne (07002) *(G-220)*

Gordon Terminal Service Co. NJ, Bayonne *Also called Gordon Terminal Service Co PA (G-220)*

Gorgias Press 732 699-0343
46 Orris Ave Piscataway (08854) *(G-8668)*

Gorgias Press LLC 732 885-8900
954 River Rd Piscataway (08854) *(G-8669)*

Gorgo Pallet Company, Vineland *Also called Lt Chini Inc (G-11242)*

Gorman Industries Inc 973 345-5424
700 21st Ave Paterson (07513) *(G-8201)*

Gorton Heating Corp 908 276-1323
546 South Ave E Cranford (07016) *(G-1912)*

Gotham Group, The, Egg Harbor Township *Also called Winsome Digital Inc (G-2702)*

Gotham Ink of New England Inc (HQ) 201 478-5600
100 North St Teterboro (07608) *(G-10679)*

Gotham Project, Bayonne *Also called GP Wine Works LLC (G-221)*

Gottscho Printing Systems, Branchburg *Also called Flexlink Systems Inc (G-642)*

Gourmet Basics, Piscataway *Also called Snack Innovations Inc (G-8713)*

Gourmet Kitchen LLC 732 775-5222
1238 Corlies Ave Neptune (07753) *(G-6882)*

Gowasabi, Palisades Park *Also called Sushi House Inc (G-7779)*

Goya Foods Inc 201 348-4900
100 Seaview Dr Secaucus (07094) *(G-9776)*

Goya Foods Inc 201 865-3470
650 New County Rd Secaucus (07094) *(G-9777)*

GP Acoustics (us) Inc 732 683-2356
10 Timber Ln Marlboro (07746) *(G-5899)*

GP Jager Inc 973 750-1180
328 W Main St Boonton (07005) *(G-555)*

GP Wine Works LLC 201 997-6055
82 E 3rd St Bayonne (07002) *(G-221)*

Gps Specialty Doors, Fairfield *Also called Global Prtners In Shelding Inc (G-3215)*

Gpschartscom 609 226-8842
5021 Winchester Ave Ventnor City (08406) *(G-11153)*

Gpt Inc 732 446-2400
227 State Route 33 Manalapan (07726) *(G-5812)*

Gr Stone LLC 908 925-7290
91 Market St Kenilworth (07033) *(G-4943)*

Graduation Outlet, Fairfield *Also called Trim and Tassels LLC (G-3333)*

Grafwed Internet Media Studios 201 632-1771
37 Millington Dr Midland Park (07432) *(G-6175)*

Graham Packaging Company LP 717 849-8500
201 Elizabeth St Bordentown (08505) *(G-582)*

Gram Equipment, Trenton *Also called Alliance Food Equipment (G-10891)*

Gram Equipment (PA) 201 750-6500
1 S Gold Dr Hamilton (08691) *(G-4106)*

Gramercy Products Incorporated 212 868-2559
600 Mdwlands Pkwy Ste 131 Secaucus (07094) *(G-9778)*

Gran All Mrble Tile Imprts Inc (PA) 856 354-4747
932 Marlton Pike W Cherry Hill (08002) *(G-1369)*

Granco Group LLC 973 515-4721
101 Eisenhower Pkwy # 300 Roseland (07068) *(G-9539)*

Grand Displays Inc 201 994-1500
3725 Tonnelle Ave North Bergen (07047) *(G-7407)*

Grand Displays Inc (PA) 201 994-1500
1700 Suckle Hwy Pennsauken (08110) *(G-8426)*

Grand Life Inc 201 556-8975
40 Broad St Carlstadt (07072) *(G-1160)*

Grandi Pastai Italiani Inc 201 786-5050
250 Moonachie Rd Ste 201 Moonachie (07074) *(G-6467)*

Grandpa Po's Nutra Nuts, Ridgewood *Also called Nutra Nuts Inc (G-9325)*

Grandview Printing Co Inc 973 890-0006
33 W End Rd Totowa (07512) *(G-10831)*

Granite and Marble Assoc Inc 908 416-1100
310 Tremont Ave North Plainfield (07063) *(G-7505)*

Grant Industries, Elmwood Park *Also called Carib Chemical Co Inc (G-2815)*

Grant Industries Inc 201 791-8700
103 Main Ave Elmwood Park (07407) *(G-2828)*

Grant Industries Inc (PA) 201 791-6700
125 Main Ave Elmwood Park (07407) *(G-2829)*

Grant Industries Inc 201 791-6700
125 Main Ave Elmwood Park (07407) *(G-2830)*

Granulation Technology Inc 973 276-0740
12 Industrial Rd Fairfield (07004) *(G-3217)*

Granville Concrete Products 973 584-6653
1076 State Route 10 Randolph (07869) *(G-9182)*

Grape Bginnings Handson Winery 732 380-7356
151 Industrial Way E B Eatontown (07724) *(G-2394)*

Graph Tech Sales & Service 201 218-1749
6 Farmstead Ln Fairfield (07004) *(G-3218)*

Graphcorr LLC 732 355-0088
4 Corn Rd Dayton (08810) *(G-1967)*

Graphic Action Inc 908 213-0055
296 S Main St Phillipsburg (08865) *(G-8553)*

Graphic Arts Printing 201 343-6554
170 Parmelee Ave Hawthorne (07506) *(G-4222)*

Graphic Concepts, Bound Brook *Also called Star Promotions Inc (G-607)*

Graphic Equipment Corporation (PA) 732 494-5350
55 Wester Ave Metuchen (08840) *(G-6058)*

Graphic Equipment Corporation 732 548-4400
19 Wester Ave Metuchen (08840) *(G-6059)*

Graphic Express Menu Co Inc 973 685-0022
200 Clifton Blvd Ste 6 Clifton (07011) *(G-1629)*

Graphic Image 856 262-8900
1401 N Blck Horse Pike A Williamstown (08094) *(G-11959)*

Graphic Imagery Inc 908 755-2882
556 Central Ave Ste 1 New Providence (07974) *(G-7002)*

Graphic Impressions, Middlesex *Also called Promo Graphic Inc (G-6141)*

Graphic Impressions Inc 201 487-8788
316 Prospect Ave Apt 10f Hackensack (07601) *(G-3923)*

Graphic Impressions Prtg Co 856 728-2266
4391 Route 42 Blackwood (08012) *(G-468)*

Graphic Management 908 654-8400
21 Lafayette Pl Kearny (07032) *(G-4862)*

Graphic Packaging Intl LLC 973 709-9100
5 Haul Rd Wayne (07470) *(G-11512)*

Graphic Packaging Intl LLC 732 424-2100
5 Haul Rd Wayne (07470) *(G-11513)*

Graphic Presentations Systems 732 981-1120
262 Old New Brnswk Rd F Piscataway (08854) *(G-8670)*

Graphic Solutions & Signs LLC 201 343-7446
200 Brinkerhoff St Ridgefield Park (07660) *(G-9308)*

Graphic Systems, Piscataway *Also called Graphic Presentations Systems (G-8670)*

Graphicolor Corporation 856 691-2507
1370 S Main Rd Vineland (08360) *(G-11227)*

Graphics Depot Inc 973 927-8200
11 Middlebury Blvd Ste 4 Randolph (07869) *(G-9183)*

Grassman-Blake Inc 973 379-6170
58 E Willow St Millburn (07041) *(G-6198)*

Grasso Foods Inc 856 467-2223
9 Ogden Rd Woolwich Township (08085) *(G-12097)*

Grateful Ped Inc 973 478-6511
339 10th St Saddle Brook (07663) *(G-9654)*

Graver Chemical Products, Newark *Also called Graver Water Systems LLC (G-7138)*

Graver Water Division, New Providence *Also called Graver Water Systems LLC (G-7003)*

Graver Water Systems LLC (HQ) 908 516-1400
675 Central Ave Ste 3 New Providence (07974) *(G-7003)*

Graver Water Systems LLC 973 465-2380
72 Lockwood St Newark (07105) *(G-7138)*

Gravity Vault LLC 732 856-9599
37 Kanes Ln Middletown (07748) *(G-6164)*

Gray Hair Software Inc 866 507-9999
124 Gaither Dr Ste 160 Mount Laurel (08054) *(G-6764)*

(G-0000) Company's Geographic Section entry number

Gray Overhead Door Co 908 355-3889
439 3rd Ave Elizabeth (07206) *(G-2744)*

Gray Star Inc 973 398-3331
200 Valley Rd Ste 103 Mount Arlington (07856) *(G-6713)*

Graybar Electric Company Inc 973 404-5555
105 Feldcrest Ave Ste 207 Edison (08837) *(G-2522)*

Graydon Products Inc 856 234-9513
800 Glen Ave Moorestown (08057) *(G-6524)*

Graytor Printing Company Inc 201 933-0100
149 Park Ave Lyndhurst (07071) *(G-5656)*

Grease N Go 856 784-6555
334 S White Horse Pike Magnolia (08049) *(G-5707)*

Great Eastern Color Lith 201 843-5656
210 E State Rt 4 Ste 211 Paramus (07652) *(G-7804)*

Great Northern Commercial Svcs 908 475-8855
401 Greenwich St Belvidere (07823) *(G-364)*

Great Northern Corporation 856 241-0080
500a Pedricktown Rd Swedesboro (08085) *(G-10587)*

Great Notch Industries Inc 201 343-8110
140 Liberty St Hackensack (07601) *(G-3924)*

Great Railing Inc 856 875-0050
1086 N Black Horse Pike Williamstown (08094) *(G-11960)*

Great Socks LLC (PA) 856 964-9700
7001 N Park Dr Pennsauken (08109) *(G-8427)*

Greater ATL Cy Golf Assn LLC 609 652-1800
401 S New York Rd Galloway (08205) *(G-3722)*

Greater Media Newspapers (HQ) 732 358-5200
198 Us Highway 9 Ste 100 Englishtown (07726) *(G-3003)*

Greater Media Newspapers 732 254-7004
201 Hartle St Ste B Sayreville (08872) *(G-9709)*

Greater New York Box Co Inc 609 631-7900
1400 E State St Trenton (08609) *(G-10936)*

Greco Industries LLC 732 919-6200
7 Colts Gait Ln Colts Neck (07722) *(G-1784)*

Green Building Solutions, Pennington *Also called Commercial Pdts Svcs Group Inc (G-8362)*

Green Distribution LLC 201 293-4381
565 Windsor Dr Secaucus (07094) *(G-9779)*

Green Fresh Fruit Salad, Pleasantville *Also called Salad Chef Inc (G-8817)*

Green Globe USA LLC 201 577-4468
21 Louis St Carteret (07008) *(G-1256)*

Green Horse Media LLC 856 933-0222
101 Haag Ave Bellmawr (08031) *(G-333)*

Green Labs LLC 862 220-4845
211 Warren St Ste 206 Newark (07103) *(G-7139)*

Green Land & Logging LLC 908 894-2361
328 Rosemont Ringoes Rd Stockton (08559) *(G-10501)*

Green Life America, Elmwood Park *Also called Interntnal Globl Solutions Inc (G-2832)*

Green Line Botanicals LLC 609 759-0221
8 Crown Plz Ste 103 Hazlet (07730) *(G-4260)*

Green Power Chemical LLC 973 770-5600
151 Sparta Stanhope Rd Hopatcong (07843) *(G-4520)*

Green Power Chemical Sciences, Hopatcong *Also called Green Power Chemical LLC (G-4520)*

Green Village Packing Co, Green Village *Also called Kleemeyer & Merkel Inc (G-3868)*

Greenbaum Interiors LLC (PA) 973 279-3000
101 Washington St Paterson (07505) *(G-8202)*

Greenbrook Stairs Inc 908 221-9145
14 Dayton St Bernardsville (07924) *(G-438)*

Greenbuilt Intl Bldg Co 609 300-9091
1081 Pndleton Ct Voorhees (08043) *(G-11287)*

Greene Bros Spclty Cof Rasters (PA) 908 979-0022
313 High St Hackettstown (07840) *(G-4009)*

Greene's Beans Cafe, Hackettstown *Also called Greene Bros Spclty Cof Rasters (G-4009)*

Greener Corners Ltd Lblty Co 201 638-2218
1178 W Laurelton Pkwy Teaneck (07666) *(G-10633)*

Greener Corp (PA) 732 341-3880
4 Helmly St Bayville (08721) *(G-245)*

Greenproducts.info, Rockaway *Also called Internet-Sales USA Corporation (G-9467)*

Greenrock Recycling LLC 908 713-0008
3 Frontage Rd Clinton (08809) *(G-1745)*

Greentree Packing Inc 212 675-2868
65 Central Ave Passaic (07055) *(G-8071)*

Greenville Colorants LLC (PA) 201 595-0200
90 Paterson St New Brunswick (08901) *(G-6931)*

Greenway Products & Svcs LLC (PA) 732 442-0200
14 Home News Row New Brunswick (08901) *(G-6932)*

Greetingtap 347 731-4263
832 Spicer Ave South Plainfield (07080) *(G-10269)*

Gregory Associates, Hasbrouck Heights *Also called Pabin Associates Inc (G-4187)*

Greif Inc 609 448-5300
200 Rike Dr Millstone Township (08535) *(G-6211)*

Grewe Plastics Inc 973 485-7602
119 S 15th St Newark (07107) *(G-7140)*

Grey House Publishing Inc 201 968-0500
2 University Plz Hackensack (07601) *(G-3925)*

Greycell Labs Inc 732 444-0123
190 State Route 27 # 102 Edison (08820) *(G-2523)*

Griff Decorative Film, Lakewood *Also called Creative Film Corp (G-5073)*

Griffen LLC 973 723-5344
44 Prospect St Apt 531 Morristown (07960) *(G-6667)*

Griffin Signs Inc 856 786-8517
484 N Randolph Ave Cinnaminson (08077) *(G-1460)*

Griffith Electric Sup Co Inc (PA) 609 695-6121
5 2nd St Trenton (08611) *(G-10937)*

Griffith Shade Company Inc 973 667-1474
308 Washington Ave Ste 1 Nutley (07110) *(G-7586)*

Grignard Company LLC 732 340-1111
505 Capobianco Plz Rahway (07065) *(G-9098)*

Grill Creations 908 264-8426
100 North Ave Ste 8 Garwood (07027) *(G-3784)*

Grimaldi Development Corp 973 345-0660
65 1st Ave Paterson (07514) *(G-8203)*

Grimbilas Enterprises Corp 973 686-5999
29 Hanes Dr Wayne (07470) *(G-11514)*

Grimco Pneumatic Corp 973 345-0660
65 1st Ave Paterson (07514) *(G-8204)*

Grimes Manufacturing Inc 732 442-4572
599 State St Perth Amboy (08861) *(G-8520)*

Grip Tight Tools, Union *Also called El Batal Corporation (G-11050)*

Grobet File Company Amer LLC (PA) 201 939-6700
750 Washington Ave Carlstadt (07072) *(G-1161)*

Grobet USA, Carlstadt *Also called Grobet File Company Amer LLC (G-1161)*

Groezinger Provisions Inc 732 775-3220
1200 7th Ave Neptune (07753) *(G-6883)*

Grommet Mart Inc 973 278-4100
85-99 Hazel St Paterson (07503) *(G-8205)*

Groniger USA LLC 704 588-3873
180 Mount Airy Rd Basking Ridge (07920) *(G-185)*

Groomershelper.com, Margate City *Also called Pet Salon Inc (G-5891)*

Gross Printing Associates Inc 718 832-1110
180 Brighton Rd Clifton (07012) *(G-1630)*

Group Martin LLC Jj 862 240-1813
90 South St Newark (07114) *(G-7141)*

Groupe Seb USA 856 825-6300
2121 Eden Rd Millville (08332) *(G-6253)*

Grove Supply Inc 856 205-0687
144 W Forest Grove Rd Vineland (08360) *(G-11228)*

Grow Company Inc 201 941-8777
55 Railroad Ave Ridgefield (07657) *(G-9264)*

Growmark Fs LLC 609 267-7054
2545 Route 206 Eastampton (08060) *(G-2372)*

Growtech LLC 732 993-8683
2 Corporate Dr Ste E Cranbury (08512) *(G-1837)*

Gruppo Editoriale Oggi Inc 201 358-6582
55 Walnut St Ste 209 Norwood (07648) *(G-7563)*

GSC, Columbia *Also called General Stamping Co Inc (G-1793)*

GSC Imaging LLC 856 317-9301
7150 N Park Dr Ste 540 Pennsauken (08109) *(G-8428)*

Gsds, Mahwah *Also called Diligaf Enterprises Inc (G-5729)*

Gsi 908 608-1325
12 Princeton St Summit (07901) *(G-10533)*

Gsk Consumer Health Inc (HQ) 919 269-5000
184 Liberty Corner Rd # 78 Warren (07059) *(G-11413)*

Gsk Consumer Healthcare 973 539-0645
2 Sylvan Way Parsippany (07054) *(G-7957)*

GT Microwave Inc 973 361-5700
2 Emery Ave Ste 2 # 2 Randolph (07869) *(G-9184)*

GTM Marketing Inc 856 227-2333
1960 Harris Dr Woodbury (08096) *(G-12031)*

Guardian Drug Company Inc 609 860-2600
2 Charles Ct Dayton (08810) *(G-1968)*

Guardrite Steel Door Corp 973 481-4424
81-87 Springdale Ave Newark (07107) *(G-7142)*

Guerbet LLC 812 333-0059
821 Alexander Rd Ste 204 Princeton (08540) *(G-8956)*

Guernsey Crest Ice Cream Co 973 742-4620
134 19th Ave Paterson (07513) *(G-8206)*

Guess Inc 201 941-3683
39 The Promenade Bldg 300 Edgewater (07020) *(G-2439)*

Guild & Facet LLC 201 758-5368
3114 Tonnelle Ave North Bergen (07047) *(G-7408)*

Guild Facet, North Bergen *Also called Guild & Facet LLC (G-7408)*

Gulbrandsen Chemicals, Clinton *Also called Gulbrandsen Technologies Inc (G-1746)*

Gulbrandsen Technologies Inc (PA) 908 735-5458
2 Main St Clinton (08809) *(G-1746)*

Gulco Inc 908 238-2030
1 Riverside Way Phillipsburg (08865) *(G-8554)*

Gulf Cable LLC (PA) 201 242-9906
777 Terrace Ave Ste 101 Hasbrouck Heights (07604) *(G-4183)*

Gulton G I D 908 791-4622
116 Corporate Blvd Ste A South Plainfield (07080) *(G-10270)*

Gulton Incorporated 908 791-4622
116 Corporate Blvd Ste A South Plainfield (07080) *(G-10271)*

Gum Runners LLC 201 333-0756
333 Washington St 2 Jersey City (07302) *(G-4745)*

Guttenplans Frozen Dough Inc 732 495-9480
100 State Route 36 E North Middletown (07748) *(G-7503)*

A
L
P
H
A
B
E
T
I
C

Gwenstone Inc 732 785-2600
1790 Swarthmore Ave Lakewood (08701) *(G-5106)*

Gwf Associates LLC 732 933-8780
1 Sheila Dr Ste 8 Eatontown (07724) *(G-2395)*

Gwynn-E Co 215 423-6400
222 Cedar St Moorestown (08057) *(G-6525)*

Gzgn Inc 201 842-7622
301 Nj 17 Ste 800 Rutherford (07070) *(G-9622)*

H & H Graphic Printing Inc 201 369-9700
400 Gotham Pkwy Ste 1 Carlstadt (07072) *(G-1162)*

H & H Industries Inc 856 663-4444
7612 N Crescent Blvd Pennsauken (08110) *(G-8429)*

H & H Production Machining 973 383-6880
30 White Lake Rd Sparta (07871) *(G-10389)*

H & H Sheet Metal & Machining, Sparta Also called H & H Production Machining *(G-10389)*

H & H Swiss Screw Machine PR 908 688-6390
1478 Chestnut Ave Hillside (07205) *(G-4395)*

H & L Printing Co 201 288-0877
343 Boulevard Ste A Hasbrouck Heights (07604) *(G-4184)*

H & R Welding LLC 732 920-4881
307 Drum Point Rd Brick (08723) *(G-720)*

H & S Fuel Inc 908 769-1362
1100 South Ave Plainfield (07062) *(G-8767)*

H & T, Clayton Also called Hungerford & Terry Inc *(G-1525)*

H & T Tool Co Inc 973 227-4858
19 Gardner Rd Ste C Fairfield (07004) *(G-3219)*

H & W Tool Co Inc (PA) 973 366-0131
22 Lee Ave Dover (07801) *(G-2085)*

H Barron Iron Works Inc 856 456-9092
316 Water St Gloucester City (08030) *(G-3843)*

H C Graphics Screenprinting 973 247-0544
238 Lindbergh Pl Ste 3 Paterson (07503) *(G-8207)*

H Cross Company 201 964-9380
150 W Commercial Ave Moonachie (07074) *(G-6468)*

H G Schaevitz LLC 856 727-0250
102 Commerce Dr Ste 8 Moorestown (08057) *(G-6526)*

H Galow Co Inc 201 768-0547
15 Maple St Norwood (07648) *(G-7564)*

H I D Systems Inc 973 383-8535
520 Lafayette Rd Sparta (07871) *(G-10390)*

H K Metal Craft Mfg Corp 973 471-7770
35 Industrial Rd Lodi (07644) *(G-5563)*

H Lauzon Furniture Co Inc 201 837-7598
1098 Decatur Ave Teaneck (07666) *(G-10634)*

H M Hays Sheet Metal Co, Pennsauken Also called Hays Sheet Metal Inc *(G-8430)*

H P Machine Shop Inc 856 692-1192
415 Oxford St Vineland (08360) *(G-11229)*

H Power Corp 973 249-5444
1373 Broad St Clifton (07013) *(G-1631)*

H Ritani LLC 888 974-8264
101 Carlson Ct Closter (07624) *(G-1756)*

H S Folex Schleussner Inc 973 575-7626
24 Just Rd Fairfield (07004) *(G-3220)*

H S Martin Company Inc 856 692-8700
1149 S East Blvd Vineland (08360) *(G-11230)*

H T Hall Inc (PA) 732 449-3441
1716 State Route 71 Ste 1 Spring Lake (07762) *(G-10422)*

H&H Swiss, Hillside Also called H & H Swiss Screw Machine PR *(G-4395)*

H-E Tool & Mfg Co Inc 856 303-8787
800 Industrial Hwy Unit A Cinnaminson (08077) *(G-1461)*

H.N. Lucas & Son, Delran Also called Spl Holdings LLC *(G-2021)*

Haas Laser Technologies Inc (PA) 973 598-1150
37 Ironia Rd Flanders (07836) *(G-3412)*

Hackensack Steel Corp 201 935-0090
645 Industrial Rd Carlstadt (07072) *(G-1163)*

Hackettstown Public Works 908 852-2320
309 E Plane St Hackettstown (07840) *(G-4010)*

Haddad Bros Inc 718 377-5505
118 John F Kennedy Dr N Bloomfield (07003) *(G-502)*

Haenssler Shtmtl Works Inc 973 373-6360
592 Hawthorne Ave Newark (07112) *(G-7143)*

Hafco Foundry & Machine Co 201 447-0433
301 Greenwood Ave Ste 2 Midland Park (07432) *(G-6176)*

Hahns Woodworking 908 722-2742
181 Meister Ave Branchburg (08876) *(G-645)*

Hai Tai Boutique, Hackensack Also called D & G LLC *(G-3903)*

Haier America Trading LLC 212 594-3330
581 Main St 6 Woodbridge (07095) *(G-12017)*

Haights Cross Cmmnications Inc (PA) 212 209-0500
295 Prncton Hightstown Rd Princeton Junction (08550) *(G-9060)*

Hain Celestial Group Inc 201 935-4500
50 Knickerbocker Rd Moonachie (07074) *(G-6469)*

Haineport Tools & Maintenance, Mount Holly Also called Hainesport Tool & Machine Co *(G-6729)*

Hainesport Industrial Railroad 609 261-8036
5900 Delaware Ave Hainesport (08036) *(G-4072)*

Hainesport Tool & Machine Co 609 261-0016
1924 Ark Rd Mount Holly (08060) *(G-6729)*

Hair Depot Limited 973 251-9924
53 Peachtree Rd Maplewood (07040) *(G-5878)*

Hair Systems Inc 732 446-2202
30 Park Ave Englishtown (07726) *(G-3004)*

Hakakian Behzad 973 267-2506
52 Horsehill Rd Cedar Knolls (07927) *(G-1306)*

Hal Leonard LLC 973 337-5034
33 Plymouth St Ste 302 Montclair (07042) *(G-6368)*

Haldor USA Inc 856 254-2345
100 Springdale Rd 83-206 Cherry Hill (08003) *(G-1370)*

Halfway Hounds 201 970-6235
108 E Main St Park Ridge (07656) *(G-7852)*

Hallco Inc 609 729-0161
5914 New Jersey Ave Wildwood (08260) *(G-11944)*

Halo Farm Inc 609 695-3311
970 Spruce St Lawrenceville (08648) *(G-5230)*

Halo Mark, Bound Brook Also called Marx NJ Group LLC *(G-603)*

Halo Pharmaceutical Inc (HQ) 973 428-4000
30 N Jefferson Rd Whippany (07981) *(G-11894)*

Halo Pub Ice Cream 609 921-1710
9 Hulfish St Princeton (08542) *(G-8957)*

Halo Pub Inc 609 586-1811
4617 Nottingham Way Trenton (08690) *(G-10938)*

Halsey News 973 645-0017
2 Prudential Dr Newark (07102) *(G-7144)*

Halsted Bag, Cranbury Also called Halsted Corporation *(G-1838)*

Halsted Corporation 201 333-0670
51 Commerce Dr Ste 3 Cranbury (08512) *(G-1838)*

Hamamatsu Corporation (HQ) 908 231-0960
360 Foothill Rd Bridgewater (08807) *(G-828)*

Hamamatsu Corporation 908 231-0960
250 Wood Ave Middlesex (08846) *(G-6119)*

Hamamatsu Corporation 908 526-0941
360 Foothill Rd Bridgewater (08807) *(G-829)*

Hamilton Embroidery Co Inc 201 867-4084
907 21st St Union City (07087) *(G-11112)*

Hammer Bedding Corp 973 589-2400
1 Mott St Newark (07105) *(G-7145)*

Hammer Manufacturing, Linden Also called Wgjf Manufacturing Corp *(G-5442)*

Hammer Press Printers Inc 973 334-4500
2 Cranberry Rd Ste 2 # 2 Parsippany (07054) *(G-7958)*

Hammonton Gazette Inc 609 704-1939
14 Tilton St Hammonton (08037) *(G-4135)*

Hammonton News, The, Vineland Also called Gannett Stllite Info Ntwrk LLC *(G-11221)*

Hamon Corporation (HQ) 908 333-2000
46 E Main St 300 Somerville (08876) *(G-10114)*

Hampton Forge Ltd (PA) 732 389-5507
446 Highway 35 Ste 3 Eatontown (07724) *(G-2396)*

Hampton Industries Inc 973 574-8900
1 Market St Ste 13 Passaic (07055) *(G-8072)*

Han Hean U S A Corp 732 494-3256
3856 Park Ave Edison (08820) *(G-2524)*

Hand Craft Mfg, Newark Also called Personality Handkerchiefs Inc *(G-7227)*

Handcraft Manufacturing Corp 973 565-0077
640 Frelinghuysen Ave # 1 Newark (07114) *(G-7146)*

Handi-Hut Inc 973 614-1800
3 Grunwald St Clifton (07013) *(G-1632)*

Handler Manufacturing Company 908 233-7796
612 North Ave E Westfield (07090) *(G-11799)*

Handmade Furniture, West Creek Also called Woodward Wood Products Design *(G-11688)*

Hands On Wheels 609 892-4693
509 Atlantic Ave Atlantic City (08401) *(G-93)*

Handy Store Fixtures Inc 973 242-1600
337 Sherman Ave Newark (07114) *(G-7147)*

Handytube Corporation 732 469-7420
250 Lackland Dr Ste 1 Middlesex (08846) *(G-6120)*

Hanes Companies - NJ LLC 201 729-9100
104 Sunfield Ave Edison (08837) *(G-2525)*

Hanger Central LLC 732 750-1161
12 Parkway Pl Edison (08837) *(G-2526)*

Hanger Prsthetcs & Ortho Inc 973 736-0628
59 Main St Ste 111 West Orange (07052) *(G-11769)*

Hanger Prsthetcs & Ortho Inc 732 919-7774
5100 Belmar Blvd Wall Township (07727) *(G-11344)*

Hanger Prsthetcs & Ortho Inc 609 653-8323
210 New Rd Ste 7 Linwood (08221) *(G-5449)*

Hanger Prsthetcs & Ortho Inc 609 889-8447
1 Secluded Ln Rio Grande (08242) *(G-9355)*

Hangsterfers Laboratories 856 468-0216
175 Ogden Rd West Deptford (08051) *(G-11702)*

Hankin Acquisitions Inc 908 722-9595
1 Harvard Way Ste 6 Hillsborough (08844) *(G-4321)*

Hankin Envmtl Systems Inc 908 722-9595
1 Harvard Way Ste 6 Hillsborough (08844) *(G-4322)*

Hanover Direct Inc (PA) 201 863-7300
1500 Harbor Blvd Ste 3 Weehawken (07086) *(G-11568)*

Hanover Direct Operating Group, Weehawken Also called Hanover Direct Inc *(G-11568)*

Hanovia Colight, Fairfield Also called Hanovia Specialty Lighting LLC *(G-3221)*

Hanovia Specialty Lighting LLC..............................973 651-5510
  6 Evans St Fairfield (07004) *(G-3221)*

Hanrahan Tool Co Inc..732 919-7300
  415 Cranberry Rd Farmingdale (07727) *(G-3386)*

Hansen Lithography Ltd..732 270-1188
  2214 Route 37 E Ste 1 Toms River (08753) *(G-10763)*

Hansome Energy Systems Inc (PA)........................908 862-9044
  365 Dalziel Rd Linden (07036) *(G-5354)*

Hanson & Zollinger Inc...856 626-3440
  117 Jackson Rd Berlin (08009) *(G-422)*

Hanson Aggregates Bmc Inc...................................856 447-4294
  1191 Railroad Ave Newport (08345) *(G-7333)*

Hanson Aggregates Wrp Inc (HQ)..........................972 653-5500
  1333 Campus Pkwy Wall Township (07753) *(G-11345)*

Hanssem...732 425-7695
  50 Idlewild Rd Edison (08817) *(G-2527)*

Hanwha Techwin America, Teaneck *Also called Samsung Opt-Lctronics Amer Inc (G-10650)*

Hapa, Branchburg *Also called Flexlink Systems Inc (G-641)*

Happle Printing...609 476-0100
  81 Cape May Ave Dorothy (08317) *(G-2071)*

Happy Chef Inc...973 492-2525
  22 Park Pl Ste 2 Butler (07405) *(G-1002)*

Harbisonwalker Intl Inc...732 388-8686
  868 Elston St Rahway (07065) *(G-9099)*

Hard Crome Solutions...732 500-2568
  195 Central Ave Metuchen (08840) *(G-6060)*

Harlequin Floors, Moorestown *Also called American Harlequin Corporation (G-6503)*

Harley Davidson Camden County, Mount Ephraim *Also called Barbs Harley-Davidson (G-6720)*

Harley Tool & Machine Inc......................................201 244-8899
  24 Mcdermott Pl Bergenfield (07621) *(G-376)*

Harmony Elastomers LLC..973 340-4000
  34 Trenton Ave Paterson (07513) *(G-8208)*

Harmony Sand & Gravel Inc...................................908 475-4690
  County Rd 519 Phillipsburg (08865) *(G-8555)*

Harms Software Inc..973 402-9500
  28 Eastmans Rd Parsippany (07054) *(G-7959)*

Harold F Fisher & Sons Inc....................................800 624-2868
  875 Industrial Hwy Ste 8 Cinnaminson (08077) *(G-1462)*

Harold R Henrich Inc..732 370-4455
  300 Syracuse Ct Lakewood (08701) *(G-5107)*

Harris Broadcast, Rockleigh *Also called Hbc Solutions Inc (G-9518)*

Harris Broadcast, Bridgewater *Also called Imagine Communications Corp (G-832)*

Harris Corporation, Clifton *Also called L3harris Technologies Inc (G-1650)*

Harris Corporation, Clifton *Also called L3harris Technologies Inc (G-1652)*

Harris Driver Co (PA)..973 267-8100
  200 Madison Ave Ste 2 Morristown (07960) *(G-6668)*

Harris Freeman & Co Inc..856 787-9026
  344 New Albany Rd Moorestown (08057) *(G-6527)*

Harris Structural Steel Co Inc (PA)........................732 752-6070
  1640 New Market Ave South Plainfield (07080) *(G-10272)*

Harris Structural Steel Co Inc................................732 752-6070
  1640 New Market Ave South Plainfield (07080) *(G-10273)*

Harris Tea Company, Moorestown *Also called Harris Freeman & Co Inc (G-6527)*

Harrisburg Stamp & Stencil Co...............................717 236-9000
  10 Greenwood Ave Ste C Woodbury (08096) *(G-12032)*

Harrison Electro Mechanical...................................732 382-6008
  1607 Coach St Rahway (07065) *(G-9100)*

Harrison Hose and Tubing Inc................................609 631-8804
  2705 Kuser Rd Robbinsville (08691) *(G-9413)*

Harrison Machine and Tool Inc..............................609 883-0800
  21 Lexington Ave Ewing (08618) *(G-3032)*

Harrison Press, Trenton *Also called North Eastern Business Forms (G-10967)*

Harrison Scott Pblications Inc................................201 659-1700
  5 Marine View Plz Ste 400 Hoboken (07030) *(G-4453)*

Harry J Lawall & Son Inc.......................................856 691-7764
  3071 E Chestnut Ave C9 Vineland (08361) *(G-11231)*

Harry Shaw Model Maker Inc.................................609 268-0647
  401 Stokes Rd Shamong (08088) *(G-9857)*

Harsco Corporation...856 779-7795
  1960 Old Cuthbert Rd # 100 Cherry Hill (08034) *(G-1371)*

Harsco Corporation...908 454-7169
  709 Loretta Ter Plainfield (07062) *(G-8768)*

Hart Construction Service.......................................908 537-2060
  466 Mine Rd Asbury (08802) *(G-64)*

Hartin Paint & Filler Corp.......................................201 438-3300
  219 Broad St Carlstadt (07072) *(G-1164)*

Hartmann Tool Co Inc..201 343-8700
  147 Lodi St Hackensack (07601) *(G-3926)*

Hartz Mountain Corporation (HQ)..........................800 275-1414
  400 Plaza Dr Ste 400 # 400 Secaucus (07094) *(G-9780)*

Harvard Printing Group...973 672-0800
  175 Us Highway 46 Fairfield (07004) *(G-3222)*

Harvester Inc..201 445-1122
  31 Cordier St Irvington (07111) *(G-4571)*

Harvester Chemical, Irvington *Also called Harvester Inc (G-4571)*

Harwill Corporation...609 895-1955
  92 N Main St Windsor (08561) *(G-11996)*

Harwill Express Press, Windsor *Also called Harwill Corporation (G-11996)*

Hary Manufacturing Inc..908 722-7100
  210 Grove Ave Woodbridge (07095) *(G-12018)*

Hasselblad Bron Incorporated, Union *Also called Hasselblad Inc (G-11061)*

Hasselblad Inc..800 456-0203
  1080a Garden State Rd Union (07083) *(G-11061)*

Hat Box...732 961-2262
  605 E County Line Rd # 1 Lakewood (08701) *(G-5108)*

Hathaway Plastic...908 688-9494
  911 Springfield Rd Ste 1 Union (07083) *(G-11062)*

Hatteras Press Inc..732 935-9800
  56 Park Rd Tinton Falls (07724) *(G-10718)*

Hausmann Enterprises LLC.....................................201 767-0255
  130 Union St Northvale (07647) *(G-7527)*

Hausmann Industries, Northvale *Also called Hausmann Enterprises LLC (G-7527)*

Hawk Dairy Inc...973 466-9030
  30 Jabez St Newark (07105) *(G-7148)*

Hawk Graphics Inc...973 895-5569
  1248 Sussex Tpke Randolph (07869) *(G-9185)*

Hawks and Co, Westville *Also called Heritage Service Solutions LLC (G-11815)*

Hawthorne Kitchens Inc..973 427-9010
  120 5th Ave Hawthorne (07506) *(G-4223)*

Hawthorne Machine Products, Hawthorne *Also called Peter Yaged (G-4238)*

Hawthorne Paint Company Inc................................973 423-2335
  18 Mill St Lodi (07644) *(G-5564)*

Hawthorne Press...973 427-3330
  463 Lafayette Ave Hawthorne (07506) *(G-4224)*

Hawthorne Rubber Mfg Corp...................................973 427-3337
  35 4th Ave Hawthorne (07506) *(G-4225)*

Haydon Corporation (PA)...973 904-0800
  415 Hamburg Tpke Ste 1 Wayne (07470) *(G-11515)*

Hayes Mindish Inc..609 641-9880
  1401 N Main St Ste 7 Pleasantville (08232) *(G-8812)*

Haymarket Media Inc..201 799-4800
  140 E Ridgewood Ave 370s Paramus (07652) *(G-7805)*

Hays Sheet Metal Inc...856 662-7722
  7070 Bldg B Kaighns Ave Pennsauken (08109) *(G-8430)*

Hayward Flow Control, Elizabeth *Also called Hayward Pool Products Inc (G-2748)*

Hayward Industrial Products (HQ)...........................908 351-5400
  620 Division St Elizabeth (07201) *(G-2745)*

Hayward Industries Inc (PA)...................................908 351-5400
  620 Division St Elizabeth (07201) *(G-2746)*

Hayward Industries Inc..908 351-0899
  628 Henry St Bldg 6 Elizabeth (07201) *(G-2747)*

Hayward Plastic Products Div, Elizabeth *Also called Hayward Industrial Products (G-2745)*

Hayward Pool Products Inc.....................................908 351-5400
  620 Division St Elizabeth (07201) *(G-2748)*

Haywood Pool Products, Elizabeth *Also called Hayward Industries Inc (G-2746)*

Haz Laboratories..908 453-3300
  39 Hartmans Corner Rd Washington (07882) *(G-11446)*

HB Fuller Company...732 287-8330
  59 Brunswick Ave Edison (08817) *(G-2528)*

HB Technik USA Ltd Lblty Prtnr..............................973 875-8688
  99 George Hill Rd Branchville (07826) *(G-708)*

Hb-Technik-Usa LLC, Branchville *Also called HB Technik USA Ltd Lblty Prtnr (G-708)*

Hbc Solutions Inc...973 267-5990
  22 Paris Ave Ste 110 Rockleigh (07647) *(G-9518)*

Hbs Electronics Inc..973 439-1147
  1275 Bloomfield Ave # 17 Fairfield (07004) *(G-3223)*

HCH Incorporated...973 300-4551
  99 Demarest Rd Ste 4 Sparta (07871) *(G-10391)*

Hd Microsystems, Parlin *Also called Hitachi Chem Dupont Microsyst (G-7864)*

Head Piece Heaven...201 262-0788
  449 2nd St Oradell (07649) *(G-7745)*

Headquarters Pub LLC..609 347-2579
  2 Convention Blvd Atlantic City (08401) *(G-94)*

Headwear Creations Inc...973 622-1144
  200 Wright St Newark (07114) *(G-7149)*

Healios Inc..908 731-5061
  56 Main St Ste 1d Flemington (08822) *(G-3447)*

Healqu LLC...844 443-2578
  210 Fairmount Ave Jersey City (07306) *(G-4746)*

Health & Natural Beauty, Piscataway *Also called Health and Natural Beauty USA (G-8671)*

Health and Natural Beauty USA..............................732 640-1830
  140 Ethel Rd W Ste W Piscataway (08854) *(G-8671)*

Health Care Alert LLC...732 676-2630
  1715 State Route 35 # 208 Middletown (07748) *(G-6165)*

Health Monitor Network, Montvale *Also called Data Cntrum Communications Inc (G-6407)*

Health Pharma USA LLC...732 540-8421
  1600 Hart St Rahway (07065) *(G-9101)*

Health Science Funding LLC...................................973 984-6159
  55 Madison Ave Morristown (07960) *(G-6669)*

Healthcare Cart..201 406-4797
  71 Auble Rd Blairstown (07825) *(G-485)*

Healthper Inc (PA)..888 257-1804
  124 Brookstone Dr Princeton (08540) *(G-8958)*

Healthstar Communications Inc (PA).......................201 560-5370
  1000 Wyckoff Ave Ste 202 Mahwah (07430) *(G-5746)*

A
L
P
H
A
B
E
T
I
C

Healthy Italia Retail LLC 973 966-5200
  55 Main St Apt 1 Madison (07940) *(G-5694)*

Heard Woodworking LLC 908 232-3978
  31 Normandy Dr Westfield (07090) *(G-11800)*

Heat-Timer Corporation (PA) 973 575-4004
  20 New Dutch Ln Fairfield (07004) *(G-3224)*

Heat-Timer Corporation 212 481-2020
  20 New Dutch Ln Fairfield (07004) *(G-3225)*

Heat-Timer Service, Fairfield Also called Heat-Timer Corporation *(G-3225)*

Heavenly Havens Creamery LLC 609 259-6600
  33 S Main St Allentown (08501) *(G-27)*

Heavenly Souffle, Millington Also called Rw Delights Inc *(G-6208)*

Hed International Inc 609 466-1900
  449 Route 31 N Ringoes (08551) *(G-9336)*

Heidelberg Press, Westampton Also called Diane Matson Inc *(G-11785)*

Heidi's European Pretzel, North Bergen Also called European Pretzel One LLC *(G-7404)*

Heights Jewelers LLC 201 825-2381
  11 Ceely Ct Allendale (07401) *(G-9)*

Heights Usa Inc 609 530-1300
  1445 Lower Ferry Rd Ewing (08618) *(G-3033)*

Heilind Electronics Inc 888 881-5420
  120 Mount Holly Byp Lumberton (08048) *(G-5629)*

Heilind Electronics Inc, Lumberton Also called Heilind Electronics Inc *(G-5629)*

Heilind Mil-Aero LLC (HQ) 856 722-5535
  100c Mount Holly Byp Lumberton (08048) *(G-5630)*

Heinkel Filtering Systems Inc 856 467-3399
  520 Sharptown Rd Swedesboro (08085) *(G-10588)*

Heinrich Bauer Publishing LP 201 569-6699
  270 Sylvan Ave Ste 100 Englewood (07632) *(G-2911)*

Heinrich Bauer Verlag (HQ) 201 569-0006
  270 Sylvan Ave Ste 100 Englewood Cliffs (07632) *(G-2973)*

Heinz Glas USA Inc 908 474-0300
  360 Hurst St Linden (07036) *(G-5355)*

Heinzelman Heat Treating LLC 201 933-4800
  790 Washington Ave Carlstadt (07072) *(G-1165)*

Heisler Industries, Fairfield Also called Heisler Machine & Tool Co *(G-3226)*

Heisler Machine & Tool Co 973 227-6300
  224 Passaic Ave Fairfield (07004) *(G-3226)*

Hel Inc 440 208-7360
  4 Princess Rd Ste 208 Lawrenceville (08648) *(G-5231)*

Helen Morley LLC 201 348-6459
  35 Buckingham Rd Cresskill (07626) *(G-1942)*

Helidex LLC 201 636-2546
  186 Paterson Ave Ste 303 East Rutherford (07073) *(G-2291)*

Helidex Offshore, East Rutherford Also called Helidex LLC *(G-2291)*

Heliolite, Cranbury Also called Lumiko USA Inc *(G-1860)*

Heller Industries Inc (PA) 973 377-6800
  4 Vreeland Rd Ste 1 Florham Park (07932) *(G-3509)*

Helsinn Therapeutics US Inc 908 231-1435
  170 Wood Ave S Fl 1 Iselin (08830) *(G-4610)*

Hempel (usa) Inc 201 939-2801
  127 Kingsland Ave Clifton (07014) *(G-1633)*

Henderson Aquatic Inc (PA) 856 825-4771
  1 Whitall Ave Millville (08332) *(G-6254)*

Hengrui Therapeutics Inc 609 423-2155
  506 Carnegie Ctr Ste 102 Princeton (08540) *(G-8959)*

Henkel US Operations Corp 908 685-7000
  10 Finderne Ave Ste B Bridgewater (08807) *(G-830)*

Henriques Yachts Works 732 269-1180
  198 Hilton Ave Bayville (08721) *(G-246)*

Henry Bros Electronics Inc (HQ) 201 794-6500
  17-01 Pollitt Dr Ste 5 Fair Lawn (07410) *(G-3103)*

Henry Dudley 732 240-6895
  1508 Wellington Ave Toms River (08757) *(G-10764)*

Henry Jackson Racing Engines 609 758-7476
  787 Monmouth Rd Cream Ridge (08514) *(G-1936)*

Henry Olsen Machine 856 662-2121
  2504 Route 73 Cinnaminson (08077) *(G-1463)*

Henry RAC Holding Corp 201 858-4400
  59 E 1st St Bayonne (07002) *(G-222)*

Henry Repeating Arms Company, Bayonne Also called Henry RAC Holding Corp *(G-222)*

Hepion Pharmaceuticals Inc (PA) 732 902-4000
  399 Thornall St Ste 1 Edison (08837) *(G-2529)*

Herald News, Woodland Park Also called North Jersey Media Group Inc *(G-12085)*

Herald News (PA) 973 569-7000
  1 Garret Mountain Plz # 201 Woodland Park (07424) *(G-12081)*

Herbakraft Incorporated 732 463-1000
  121 Ethel Rd W Ste 6 Piscataway (08854) *(G-8672)*

Herbalist & Alchemist Inc 908 689-9020
  51 S Wandling Ave Washington (07882) *(G-11447)*

Herbert J Hinchman & Son Inc 973 942-2063
  26 Pike Dr Wayne (07470) *(G-11516)*

Herborium Group Inc (PA) 201 849-4431
  1 Bridge Plz N Ste 275 Fort Lee (07024) *(G-3560)*

Herbst John E Heating & Coolg, Parlin Also called John E Herbst Heating & Coolg *(G-7866)*

Hercules Enterprises LLC 908 369-0000
  321 Valley Rd Hillsborough (08844) *(G-4323)*

Hercules LLC 732 777-4697
  20 Lee St Edison (08817) *(G-2530)*

Hercules Welding & Machine Co 856 829-1820
  618 W 5th St Palmyra (08065) *(G-7783)*

Hercules World Industries, Newfoundland Also called Atlantic Rubber Enterprises *(G-7329)*

Heritage Bag Company 856 467-2247
  2123 High Hill Rd Swedesboro (08085) *(G-10589)*

Heritage Inc 201 447-2600
  225 Franklin Ave Ste 4 Midland Park (07432) *(G-6177)*

Heritage Pharma Holdings Inc (HQ) 732 429-1000
  1 Tower Center Blvd # 1700 East Brunswick (08816) *(G-2148)*

Heritage Pharma Labs Inc 732 238-7880
  8 Elkins Rd East Brunswick (08816) *(G-2149)*

Heritage Pharma Labs Inc (HQ) 732 238-7880
  21 Cotters Ln Ste B East Brunswick (08816) *(G-2150)*

Heritage Pharmaceuticals Inc (HQ) 732 429-1000
  1 Tower Center Blvd # 1700 East Brunswick (08816) *(G-2151)*

Heritage Publishing 732 747-7770
  440 State Route 34 Ste 2 Colts Neck (07722) *(G-1785)*

Heritage Service Solutions LLC 856 845-7311
  1000 Delsea Dr Ste A1 Westville (08093) *(G-11815)*

Herley Industries Inc 973 884-2580
  9 Whippany Rd Whippany (07981) *(G-11895)*

Herley-Cti Inc (HQ) 973 884-2580
  9 Whippany Rd Whippany (07981) *(G-11896)*

Herma US Inc 973 521-7254
  39 Plymouth St Unit 300 Fairfield (07004) *(G-3227)*

Herman Eickhoff 609 871-1809
  400 John F Kennedy Way Willingboro (08046) *(G-11991)*

Hermetic Solutions Group Inc (PA) 732 722-8780
  4000 State Route 66 # 310 Tinton Falls (07753) *(G-10719)*

Hermitage Press of New Jersey (PA) 609 882-3600
  1595 5th St Ewing (08638) *(G-3034)*

Heros Salute Awards Co 973 696-5085
  1875 State Route 23 Ste 1 Wayne (07470) *(G-11517)*

Herr Foods Incorporated 732 356-1295
  790 New Brunswick Rd Somerset (08873) *(G-9999)*

Herr Foods Incorporated 732 905-1600
  100 Kenyon Dr Lakewood (08701) *(G-5109)*

Hershey Industries Inc 908 353-3344
  1209 Central Ave Hillside (07205) *(G-4396)*

Heschel Some, Hackensack Also called Somes Uniforms Inc *(G-3975)*

Hess Corporation 609 882-8477
  601 Jack Stephan Way Ewing (08628) *(G-3035)*

Hexacon Electric Company Inc 908 245-6200
  161 W Clay Ave Roselle Park (07204) *(G-9586)*

Hey Doll, West Orange Also called Lesilu Productions Inc *(G-11771)*

Heyco Molded Products Inc (HQ) 732 286-4336
  1800 Industrial Way Toms River (08755) *(G-10765)*

Heyco Products Corp (HQ) 732 286-1800
  1800 Industrial Way Toms River (08755) *(G-10766)*

Heyco Stamped Products 732 286-4336
  1800 Industrial Way Toms River (08755) *(G-10767)*

Hh Spinco Inc 973 455-2000
  115 Tabor Rd Morris Plains (07950) *(G-6606)*

Hhh Machine Co 908 276-1220
  20 Quine St Cranford (07016) *(G-1913)*

Hi-Grade Products Mfg Co 908 245-4133
  752 Jefferson Ave Kenilworth (07033) *(G-4944)*

Hibrett Puratex, Pennsauken Also called Atlantic Associates Intl Inc *(G-8392)*

Hickok Matthews Co Inc 973 335-3400
  337 Main Rd Montville (07045) *(G-6443)*

Hickory Industries Inc 201 223-4382
  4900 W Side Ave North Bergen (07047) *(G-7409)*

Hicube Coating LLC 973 883-7404
  200 Circle Ave Clifton (07011) *(G-1634)*

Hid Ultraviolet LLC 973 383-8535
  520 Lafayette Rd Sparta (07871) *(G-10392)*

High Energy Group Ltd Lblty Co 732 741-9099
  331 Newman Spg Rd Eatontown (07724) *(G-2397)*

High Gate Corp 609 267-0680
  100 Campus Dr Mount Holly (08060) *(G-6730)*

High Point Brewing Co Inc 973 838-7400
  22 Park Pl Butler (07405) *(G-1003)*

High Point Precision Products 973 875-6229
  1 First St Sussex (07461) *(G-10561)*

High Point Wheat Beer Company, Butler Also called High Point Brewing Co Inc *(G-1003)*

High Tech Manufacturing Inc 973 372-7907
  460 Coit St Bldg D Irvington (07111) *(G-4572)*

High Vision Corporation 862 238-7636
  211 River Rd Clifton (07014) *(G-1635)*

High-Technology Corporation (PA) 201 488-0010
  144 South St Hackensack (07601) *(G-3927)*

Highland Products Inc 973 366-0156
  River St Dover (07801) *(G-2086)*

Highlands Acquisition Corp 201 573-8400
  1 Paragon Dr Ste 125 Montvale (07645) *(G-6413)*

Highpoint Corporation 201 460-1364
  63 E Pierrepont Ave Rutherford (07070) *(G-9623)*

Highroad Press LLC 201 708-6900
  220 Anderson Ave Moonachie (07074) *(G-6470)*

Hights Electric Motor Service................................609 448-2298
156 Stockton St Hightstown (08520) *(G-4296)*

Hikma Injectables USA Inc................................732 542-1191
200 Industrial Way W Eatontown (07724) *(G-2398)*

Hikma Pharmaceuticals USA Inc (HQ)................732 542-1191
246 Industrial Way W # 7 Eatontown (07724) *(G-2399)*

Hikma Pharmaceuticals USA Inc.......................732 542-1191
465 Industrial Way W Eatontown (07724) *(G-2400)*

Hikma Pharmaceuticals USA Inc.......................856 424-3700
2 Esterbrook Ln Cherry Hill (08003) *(G-1372)*

Hilin Life Products Inc....................................917 250-3575
211 Warren St Ste 211 # 211 Newark (07103) *(G-7150)*

Hill Cross Co Inc..201 864-3393
543 56th St West New York (07093) *(G-11740)*

Hill Machine Inc (PA)......................................973 684-2808
295 Governor St Paterson (07501) *(G-8209)*

Hill Mixers Machine, Paterson *Also called Hill Machine Inc (G-8209)*

Hill Pharma Inc...973 521-7400
6 Madison Rd Fairfield (07004) *(G-3228)*

Hill-Rom Holdings Inc....................................856 486-2117
202 Commerce Dr Ste 2 Moorestown (08057) *(G-6528)*

Hillard Bloom Packing Co Inc..........................856 785-0120
2601 Ogden Ave Port Norris (08349) *(G-8886)*

Hillary's Fashions, Warren *Also called Hillarys Fashion Boutique LLC (G-11414)*

Hillarys Fashion Boutique LLC.........................732 667-7733
177 Washington Valley Rd Warren (07059) *(G-11414)*

Hillcrest Opticians.......................................973 838-6666
11 Kiel Ave Ste D-1 Kinnelon (07405) *(G-5017)*

Hiller Separation Process LLC.........................512 556-5707
2125 Center Ave Ste 507 Fort Lee (07024) *(G-3561)*

Hillman Rollers, Marlboro *Also called Hilman Incorporated (G-5900)*

Hillsborough Vacuum LLC...............................908 904-6600
54 Buckland Dr Hillsborough (08844) *(G-4324)*

Hillside Beverage Packing LLC........................908 353-6773
5 Evans Terminal Hillside (07205) *(G-4397)*

Hillside Candy LLC (PA)..................................973 926-2300
35 Hillside Ave Hillside (07205) *(G-4398)*

Hillside Candy LLC.......................................908 241-4747
1112 Walnut St Roselle (07203) *(G-9560)*

Hillside Plastics Corporation..........................973 923-2700
125 Long Ave Hillside (07205) *(G-4399)*

Hilman Incorporated (PA)...............................732 462-6277
12 Timber Ln Marlboro (07746) *(G-5900)*

Hinck Turkey Farm Inc..................................732 681-0508
3930 Belmar Blvd Neptune (07753) *(G-6884)*

Hiossen Inc (HQ)...888 678-0001
270 Sylvan Ave Ste 1130 Englewood Cliffs (07632) *(G-2974)*

Hiresprint LLC..201 488-1626
225 Park St Hackensack (07601) *(G-3928)*

Hirox - USA Inc (HQ).....................................201 342-2600
100 Commerce Way Ste 4 Hackensack (07601) *(G-3929)*

Hisamitsu Phrm Co Inc..................................973 765-0122
100 Campus Dr Ste 117 Florham Park (07932) *(G-3510)*

Hispanic Outlook In Higher.............................201 587-8800
299 Market St Ste 140 Saddle Brook (07663) *(G-9655)*

Hispanic Outlook-12 Mag Inc..........................201 587-8800
42-32 Debruin Dr Fair Lawn (07410) *(G-3104)*

Hit Promo LLC..800 237-6305
440 Benigno Blvd Unit D Bellmawr (08031) *(G-334)*

Hitachi Chem Dupont Microsyst (PA)................732 613-2175
Cheesequake Rd Bldg 424 Parlin (08859) *(G-7864)*

Hitechone Inc...201 500-8864
440 Sylvan Ave Ste 2508 Englewood Cliffs (07632) *(G-2975)*

Hitran Corporation.......................................908 782-5525
362 Highway 31 Flemington (08822) *(G-3448)*

Hitrons Solutions Inc....................................201 244-0300
88 Portland Ave Ste M Bergenfield (07621) *(G-377)*

Hitrons Solutions Inc....................................201 244-0300
88 Portland Ave Ste M Bergenfield (07621) *(G-378)*

Hitrons Tech Inc..201 941-0024
1 Remsen Pl Ste 107 Ridgefield (07657) *(G-9265)*

Hks Marketing, Bayonne *Also called Royal Wine Corporation (G-234)*

HMS Monaco Et Cie Ltd.................................201 533-0007
629 Grove St Fl 5 Jersey City (07310) *(G-4747)*

Hnt Industries Inc..908 322-0414
233 Union Ave Scotch Plains (07076) *(G-9733)*

Ho-Ho-Kus Inc..973 278-2274
189 Lyon St 201 Paterson (07524) *(G-8210)*

Ho-Ho-Kus Smked Delicacies LLC....................201 445-1677
320 Enos Pl Ho Ho Kus (07423) *(G-4440)*

Hoarders Express LLC...................................856 963-8471
529 Market St Camden (08102) *(G-1067)*

Hobart Feg Service Center, Fairfield *Also called Hobart Sales and Service Inc (G-3229)*

Hobart Group Holdings LLC............................908 470-1780
240 Main St Gladstone (07934) *(G-3804)*

Hobart Sales and Service Inc..........................973 227-9265
4 Gloria Ln Fairfield (07004) *(G-3229)*

Hobby Blade Specialty Inc..............................908 317-9306
725 Jerusalem Rd Scotch Plains (07076) *(G-9734)*

Hobby Publications Inc..................................732 536-5160
83 South St Ste 307 Freehold (07728) *(G-3668)*

Hoboken Executive Art Inc.............................201 420-8262
320 Washington St Ste A Hoboken (07030) *(G-4454)*

Hoboken Mary Ltd Liability Co.........................201 234-9910
1109 Washington St Apt 2 Hoboken (07030) *(G-4455)*

Hock & Mandel, Lodi *Also called All State Medal Co Inc (G-5552)*

Hockmeyer Equipment Corp (PA).....................973 482-0225
610 Supor Blvd Harrison (07029) *(G-4176)*

Hoda Inc...609 695-3000
532 Mulberry St Trenton (08638) *(G-10939)*

Hoeganaes Corporation (HQ)..........................856 303-0366
1001 Taylors Ln Cinnaminson (08077) *(G-1464)*

Hofer Connectors Co Inc...............................973 427-1195
126 Linda Vista Ave North Haledon (07508) *(G-7495)*

Hofer Machine & Tool Co Inc..........................973 427-1195
126 Linda Vista Ave North Haledon (07508) *(G-7496)*

Hoffman/New Yorker Inc (PA)..........................201 488-1800
46 Clinton Pl Hackensack (07601) *(G-3930)*

Hoffmann-La Roche Inc (HQ)..........................973 890-2268
150 Clove Rd Ste 88th Little Falls (07424) *(G-5456)*

Hoffmann-La Roche Inc.................................973 235-8216
701 Union Blvd Totowa (07512) *(G-10832)*

Hoffmann-La Roche Inc.................................973 235-3092
340 Kingsland St Nutley (07110) *(G-7587)*

Hoffmann-La Roche Inc.................................973 235-1016
500 Kingsland St Nutley (07110) *(G-7588)*

Hofmann Tool & Die Corporation.....................201 327-0226
356 State Rt 17 Upper Saddle River (07458) *(G-11140)*

Hojiblanca USA Inc......................................201 384-3007
175 Washington Ave Ste 18 Dumont (07628) *(G-2113)*

Holiday Bowl Inc..201 337-6516
29 Spruce St Oakland (07436) *(G-7631)*

Holistic Solar Usa Inc...................................732 757-5500
105 Lock St Ste 407 Newark (07103) *(G-7151)*

Holland Manufacturing Co Inc (PA)..................973 584-8141
15 Main St Succasunna (07876) *(G-10513)*

Holler Metal Fabricators Inc...........................732 635-9050
215 Liberty St Metuchen (08840) *(G-6061)*

Holly Packaging Inc......................................856 327-8281
1101 N 10th St Millville (08332) *(G-6255)*

Holman Enterprises Inc.................................856 532-2410
9040 Burrough Dover Ln Pennsauken (08110) *(G-8431)*

Holman Enterprises Inc.................................609 383-6100
1311 Route 73 Mount Laurel (08054) *(G-6765)*

Holman Jaguar and Infinite, Mount Laurel *Also called Holman Enterprises Inc (G-6765)*

Holmdel Acpnctr & Ntrl Med Ctr......................732 888-4910
721 N Beers St Ste Suite Holmdel (07733) *(G-4502)*

Holocraft Corporation (PA).............................732 502-9500
50 Flexcraft Dr Neptune (07753) *(G-6885)*

Holographic Finishing Inc..............................201 941-4651
501 Hendricks Cswy Ridgefield (07657) *(G-9266)*

Holtec Government Services LLC......................856 291-0600
1 Holtec Blvd Camden (08104) *(G-1068)*

Holtec International......................................856 797-0900
1 Holtec Blvd Camden (08104) *(G-1069)*

Homan Communications Inc............................609 654-9594
194 Route 70 Ste 9 Medford (08055) *(G-6023)*

Homasote Company......................................609 883-3300
932 Lower Ferry Rd Ewing (08628) *(G-3036)*

Home News & Tribune, Neptune *Also called Asbury Park Press Inc (G-6866)*

Home News Tribune......................................908 243-6600
92 E Main St Ste 202 Somerville (08876) *(G-10115)*

Home Organization LLC.................................201 351-2121
570 Piermont Rd Ste 136 Closter (07624) *(G-1757)*

Home Warehouse Outlet, Jersey City *Also called Orient Originals Inc (G-4778)*

Homeco LLC...732 802-7733
739 South Ave Piscataway (08854) *(G-8673)*

Homespun Global LLC...................................917 674-9684
4000 Bordentown Ave # 18 Sayreville (08872) *(G-9710)*

Homestyle Kitchens & Baths LLC.....................908 979-9000
453 Route 46 E Hackettstown (07840) *(G-4011)*

Hometown Office Sups & Prtg Co, Bordentown *Also called Hometown Office Sups & Prtg Co (G-583)*

Hometown Office Sups & Prtg Co.....................609 298-9020
192 Us Highway 130 Bordentown (08505) *(G-583)*

Hone-A-Matic Tool & Cutter Co.......................732 382-6000
187 Wescott Dr Rahway (07065) *(G-9102)*

Honeyware Inc (PA)......................................201 997-5900
244 Dukes St Kearny (07032) *(G-4863)*

Honeywell, Freehold *Also called Prestone Products Corporation (G-3692)*

Honeywell, Mount Laurel *Also called Metrologic Instruments Inc (G-6782)*

Honeywell Asia Pacific Inc.............................973 455-2000
115 Tabor Rd Morris Plains (07950) *(G-6607)*

Honeywell Authorized Dealer, Branchburg *Also called Sander Mechanical Service Inc (G-679)*

Honeywell Authorized Dealer, Pennsauken *Also called McAllister Service Company (G-8453)*

Honeywell Authorized Dealer, Berlin *Also called T J Eckardt Associates Inc (G-430)*

Honeywell Authorized Dealer, Bordentown *Also called Ats Mechanical Inc* **(G-576)**
Honeywell East Asia Inc (HQ)....................................973 455-2000
115 Tabor Rd Morris Plains (07950) **(G-6608)**
Honeywell International Inc.......................................800 601-3099
115 Tabor Rd Morris Plains (07950) **(G-6609)**
Honeywell International Inc.......................................973 455-6633
20 Airport Rd Morristown (07960) **(G-6670)**
Honeywell International Inc.......................................973 285-5321
8 Waterloo Dr Morris Plains (07950) **(G-6610)**
Honeywell International Inc.......................................856 691-5111
2658 N West Blvd Vineland (08360) **(G-11232)**
Honeywell International Inc.......................................856 234-5020
121 Whittendale Dr Moorestown (08057) **(G-6529)**
Honeywell International Inc.......................................973 455-2000
115 Tabor Rd Morris Plains (07950) **(G-6611)**
Honeywell International Inc.......................................973 455-5168
101 Columbia Rd Morristown (07960) **(G-6671)**
Honeywell International Inc.......................................877 841-2840
115 Tabor Rd Morris Plains (07950) **(G-6612)**
Honeywell International Inc.......................................732 919-0010
5047 Industrial Rd Ste 2 Wall Township (07727) **(G-11346)**
Honeywell International Inc.......................................973 455-2000
Columbia Tpke Morristown (07962) **(G-6672)**
Honeywell International Inc.......................................800 601-3099
115 Tabor Rd Morris Plains (07950) **(G-6613)**
Honeywell International Inc.......................................973 455-2000
115 Tabor Rd Morris Plains (07950) **(G-6614)**
Honeywell Scanning & Mobility, Blackwood *Also called Omniplanar Inc* **(G-476)**
Honeywell Spain Holdings LLC (HQ)...........................973 455-2000
101 Columbia Rd Morristown (07960) **(G-6673)**
Honeywell Speclty Wax & Additv (HQ).........................973 455-2000
101 Columbia Rd Morristown (07960) **(G-6674)**
Honig Chemical & Proc Corp.....................................973 344-0881
414 Wilson Ave Newark (07105) **(G-7152)**
Hoof Fe Dye Works, Paterson *Also called North Jersey Skein Dyeing Co* **(G-8270)**
Hookway Enterprises Inc..973 691-0382
130 Allen St Netcong (07857) **(G-6907)**
Hopatcong Fuel On You LLC......................................973 770-0854
107 Tulsa Trl Hopatcong (07843) **(G-4521)**
Hope Center...201 798-1234
43 Charles St Jersey City (07307) **(G-4748)**
Hope Electrical Products Co......................................973 882-7400
3 Fairfield Cres West Caldwell (07006) **(G-11653)**
Hopewell Valley Vineyards LLC...................................609 737-4465
46 Yard Rd Pennington (08534) **(G-8367)**
Hoppecke Batteries Inc..856 616-0032
2 Berry Dr Hainesport (08036) **(G-4073)**
Horiba Instruments Inc..732 623-8335
20 Knightsbridge Rd Piscataway (08854) **(G-8674)**
Horiba Instruments Inc..732 494-8660
20 Knightsbridge Rd Piscataway (08854) **(G-8675)**
Horizon Group Usa Inc (PA).....................................908 810-1111
45 Technology Dr Warren (07059) **(G-11415)**
Horizon Group USA Inc..908 810-1111
773 Cranbury S Rvr Rd 200 Monroe Township (08831) **(G-6333)**
Horizon Label LLC...856 767-0777
1049 Industrial Dr West Berlin (08091) **(G-11599)**
Horizon Printing, Clark *Also called Tanter Inc* **(G-1516)**
Horowitz, Newark *Also called RAB Food Group LLC* **(G-7244)**
Horphag Research (usa) Inc......................................201 459-0300
5 Marine View Plz Ste 403 Hoboken (07030) **(G-4456)**
Horsetracs..732 228-7646
99 Oak Ave West Creek (08092) **(G-11687)**
Hosepharm Ltd Liability Co.......................................732 376-0044
351 Smith St Perth Amboy (08861) **(G-8521)**
Hosokawa Micron International...................................908 273-6360
10 Chatham Rd Summit (07901) **(G-10534)**
Hosokawa Micron International...................................908 273-6360
10 Chatham Rd Summit (07901) **(G-10535)**
Hosokawa Micron International...................................908 273-6360
10 Chatham Rd Summit (07901) **(G-10536)**
Hosokawa Micron International...................................866 507-4974
751 Hylton Rd Pennsauken (08110) **(G-8432)**
Hosokawa Micron Intl Inc (HQ)..................................908 273-6360
10 Chatham Rd Summit (07901) **(G-10537)**
Hosokawa Micron Powder Systems, Summit *Also called Hosokawa Micron International* **(G-10535)**
Hosokawa Micron Powder Systems, Summit *Also called Hosokawa Micron Intl Inc* **(G-10537)**
Hosokawa Tech, Summit *Also called Hosokawa Micron International* **(G-10534)**
Hospital & Health Care Compen, Oakland *Also called John R Zabka Associates Inc* **(G-7633)**
Hospitality GL Brands USA Inc...................................800 869-5258
185 Industrial Ave Ridgefield Park (07660) **(G-9309)**
Hospitality Glass Brands LLC.....................................800 869-8258
52 Forest Ave Paramus (07652) **(G-7806)**
Hot Dip Galvanizing...732 442-7555
1190 Amboy Ave Perth Amboy (08861) **(G-8522)**
Hot Runner Technology...908 431-5711
216 Us Highway 206 Hillsborough (08844) **(G-4325)**
Hotpack, Buena *Also called S P Industries Inc* **(G-941)**

Houghton Chemical Corporation.................................201 460-8071
30 Amor Ave Carlstadt (07072) **(G-1166)**
House Foods America Corp.......................................732 537-9500
801 Randolph Rd Somerset (08873) **(G-10000)**
House of Cupcakes LLC...908 413-3076
51 Suydam Rd Somerset (08873) **(G-10001)**
House of Gold Inc..856 665-0020
1505 Suckle Hwy Pennsauken (08110) **(G-8433)**
House of Herbs I LLC..973 779-2422
38 Ann St Passaic (07055) **(G-8073)**
House of Prill Inc...732 442-2400
716 Newman Springs Rd # 303 Lincroft (07738) **(G-5311)**
House Pearl Fashions (us) Ltd (HQ).............................973 778-7551
300-2 D&E Rr 17 Lodi (07644) **(G-5565)**
Household and Per Pdts Indust, Montvale *Also called Rodman Media Corp* **(G-6432)**
Houses Magazine Inc..973 605-1877
173 Morris St Morris Plains (07950) **(G-6615)**
Houzer Inc (HQ)..609 584-1900
2605 Kuser Rd Hamilton (08691) **(G-4107)**
Hovione LLC..609 918-2600
40 Lake Dr East Windsor (08520) **(G-2352)**
Howard Lippincott...856 764-8282
74 Norman Ave Riverside (08075) **(G-9396)**
Howard Packaging Corp...973 904-0022
86 Cobble St Clifton (07013) **(G-1636)**
Howard Press Inc...908 245-4400
450 W 1st Ave Roselle (07203) **(G-9561)**
Howell Precision Tool Co, Farmingdale *Also called Hanrahan Tool Co Inc* **(G-3386)**
HOWELL TOWNSHIP PAL, Howell *Also called Howell Township Police* **(G-4541)**
Howell Township Police...732 919-2805
115 Kent Rd Howell (07731) **(G-4541)**
Howes Standard Publishing Co...................................856 691-2000
1980 S West Blvd Vineland (08360) **(G-11233)**
Howman Associates Inc...732 985-7474
12 Garden St Edison (08817) **(G-2531)**
Howman Controls, Edison *Also called Howman Associates Inc* **(G-2531)**
Howman Electronics Inc..908 534-2247
291 Us Highway 22 Ste 40 Lebanon (08833) **(G-5262)**
Howman Engineering, Lebanon *Also called Howman Electronics Inc* **(G-5262)**
Howmedica Osteonics Corp (HQ)................................201 831-5000
325 Corporate Dr Mahwah (07430) **(G-5747)**
Howmet Castings & Services Inc.................................973 361-0300
9 Roy St Dover (07801) **(G-2087)**
Howmet Castings & Services Inc.................................973 361-0300
9 Roy St Dover (07801) **(G-2088)**
Howmet Castings & Services Inc.................................973 361-2310
10 Roy St Dover (07801) **(G-2089)**
Howmet Corporation-Dover Cast, Dover *Also called Alcoa Power Generating Inc* **(G-2073)**
Hoyt Corporation..201 894-0707
520 S Dean St Englewood (07631) **(G-2912)**
Hozric LLC..908 420-8821
11 Ridge Rd Green Brook (08812) **(G-3861)**
HP Enterprise..908 898-4728
200 Connell Dr Ste 5000 Berkeley Heights (07922) **(G-400)**
Hpfs, Berkeley Heights *Also called HP Enterprise* **(G-400)**
HPH Products Inc...609 883-0052
182 Carlton Ave Ewing (08618) **(G-3037)**
Hpi International Inc..732 942-9900
301 1st St Lakewood (08701) **(G-5110)**
Hr Acuity LLC...888 598-0161
25a Vreeland Rd Ste 101 Florham Park (07932) **(G-3511)**
HR Industries Inc...201 941-8000
605 Broad Ave Ste 102 Ridgefield (07657) **(G-9267)**
HRA International Inc (PA)...609 395-0939
489 Hillrose Way Monroe (08831) **(G-6322)**
HRP Capital Inc (PA)...201 242-4938
173 Bridge Plz N Fort Lee (07024) **(G-3562)**
Hsh Assoc Financial Publishers..................................973 838-3330
1200 State Rt 23 Butler (07405) **(G-1004)**
Ht Stamping Co LLC...973 227-4858
19 Gardner Rd Ste C Fairfield (07004) **(G-3230)**
Htp Connectivity LLC..973 586-2286
300 Round Hill Dr Ste 4 Rockaway (07866) **(G-9465)**
Huahai US Inc..609 655-1688
700 Atrium Dr Somerset (08873) **(G-10002)**
Hub Print & Copy Center LLC....................................201 585-7887
2037 Lemoine Ave Fort Lee (07024) **(G-3563)**
Hub Sign Crane Corp..732 252-9090
67 Wood Ave Manalapan (07726) **(G-5813)**
Hub, The, Fort Lee *Also called Hub Print & Copy Center LLC* **(G-3563)**
Huber International Corp..732 549-8600
499 Thornall St Ste 8 Edison (08837) **(G-2532)**
Huber+suhner Astrolab Inc.......................................732 560-3800
4 Powderhorn Dr Warren (07059) **(G-11416)**
Hudson Awning & Sign Co, Bayonne *Also called Hudson Awning Co Inc* **(G-223)**
Hudson Awning Co Inc..201 339-7171
27 Cottage St Bayonne (07002) **(G-223)**
Hudson Bread, North Bergen *Also called Prestige Bread Jersey Cy Inc* **(G-7430)**

Hudson Cosmetic Mfg Corp 973 472-2323
93 Entin Rd Ste 4 Clifton (07014) *(G-1637)*
Hudson Displays Co 973 623-8255
687 Frelinghuysen Ave # 1 Newark (07114) *(G-7153)*
Hudson Drapery Service, Jersey City *Also called Forsters Cleaning & Tailoring (G-4740)*
Hudson Group (hg) Inc (HQ) 201 939-5050
1 Meadowlands Plz East Rutherford (07073) *(G-2292)*
Hudson Industries Corporation (HQ) 973 402-0100
271 Us Highway 46 F207 Fairfield (07004) *(G-3231)*
Hudson Manufacturing Corp 973 376-7070
12 E Willow St Millburn (07041) *(G-6199)*
Hudson Reporter, Califon *Also called Newspaper Media Group LLC (G-1032)*
Hudson Robotics Inc 973 376-7400
10 Stern Ave Springfield (07081) *(G-10444)*
Hudson Valley Enviromental Inc 732 967-0060
2063 Basswood Ct Toms River (08755) *(G-10768)*
Hudson West Publishing Co 201 991-1600
39 Seeley Ave Kearny (07032) *(G-4864)*
Hue Box LLC 908 904-9501
9 Sally Ct Bridgewater (08807) *(G-831)*
Hueck Foils Holding Co (HQ) 732 974-4100
1955 State Route 34 3c Wall Township (07719) *(G-11347)*
Huggle Hounds, Denville *Also called Allure Pet Pdts Ltd Lblty Co (G-2029)*
Hugo Neu Corporation (PA) 646 467-6700
78 John Miller Way Ste 1 Kearny (07032) *(G-4865)*
Hugo Neu Recycling LLC 914 530-2350
78 John Miller Way Ste 1 Kearny (07032) *(G-4866)*
Humanscale Corporation 732 537-2944
220 Circle Dr N Piscataway (08854) *(G-8676)*
Hummel Chemical, South Plainfield *Also called Hummel Croton Inc (G-10274)*
Hummel Croton Inc 908 754-1800
10 Harmich Rd South Plainfield (07080) *(G-10274)*
Hummel Distributing Corp (PA) 908 688-5300
850 Springfield Rd Union (07083) *(G-11063)*
Hummel Printing Inc 908 688-5300
850 Springfield Rd Union (07083) *(G-11064)*
Hungerford & Terry Inc (PA) 856 881-3200
226 N Atlantic Ave Clayton (08312) *(G-1525)*
Hunter Manufacturing Svcs Inc 973 287-6701
19 Just Rd Fairfield (07004) *(G-3232)*
Hunterdon Brewing Company LLC 908 454-7445
12 Coddington Rd Whitehouse Station (08889) *(G-11920)*
Hunterdon County Democrat Inc (PA) 908 782-4747
200 State Route 31 # 202 Flemington (08822) *(G-3449)*
Hunterdon County Democrat Inc 908 996-4047
207 Harrison St Frenchtown (08825) *(G-3713)*
Hunterdon Observer, Flemington *Also called Hunterdon County Democrat Inc (G-3449)*
Hunterdon Transformer Co Inc (PA) 908 454-2400
75 Industrial Rd Alpha (08865) *(G-38)*
Hup & Sons 908 832-7878
10 White Tail Ln Glen Gardner (08826) *(G-3823)*
Hurricane Hutch 908 256-5912
190 Lamerson Rd Chester (07930) *(G-1434)*
Hussmann Corporation 800 320-3510
875 Kings Hwy Ste 205 West Deptford (08096) *(G-11703)*
Hutcheon and Simon, Hackensack *Also called Danson Sheet Metal Inc (G-3905)*
Hutchinson Cabinets 856 468-5500
244 Bark Bridge Rd Sewell (08080) *(G-9845)*
Hutchinson Industries Inc 609 394-1010
251 Southard St Trenton (08609) *(G-10940)*
Hutchinson Industries Inc (HQ) 609 394-1010
460 Southard St Trenton (08638) *(G-10941)*
Hutchinson Industries Inc 609 394-1010
84 Parker Ave Ste 86 Trenton (08609) *(G-10942)*
Hutchinson Industries Inc 609 394-1010
106 108 Mulberry St Trenton (08609) *(G-10943)*
Hutchison Medipharma (us) Inc 973 567-3254
25a Vreeland Rd Ste 304 Florham Park (07932) *(G-3512)*
Hve, Toms River *Also called Hudson Valley Enviromental Inc (G-10768)*
Hy-Tek Material Handling Inc 732 490-6282
704 Ginesi Dr Ste 25 Morganville (07751) *(G-6587)*
Hy-Test Packaging Corp 973 754-7000
515 E 41st St Paterson (07504) *(G-8211)*
Hybrid-Tek LLC 609 259-3355
9 Trenton Lakewood Rd # 2 Clarksburg (08510) *(G-1521)*
Hychem Corporation 732 280-8803
611 Main St Ste B-2 Belmar (07719) *(G-350)*
Hycrete Inc 201 386-8110
14 Spielman Rd Fairfield (07004) *(G-3233)*
Hydracore Inc 732 548-5500
60 Liberty St Metuchen (08840) *(G-6062)*
Hydratight Operations Inc 732 271-4100
12 Worlds Fair Dr Ste A Somerset (08873) *(G-10003)*
Hydraulic Manifolds Usa LLC 973 728-1214
264 Marshall Hill Rd West Milford (07480) *(G-11727)*
Hydro-Mechanical Systems Inc 856 848-8888
1030 Delsea Dr Unit 8 Westville (08093) *(G-11816)*
Hydrocrbon Tech Innovation LLC 609 394-3102
1501 New York Ave Lawrenceville (08648) *(G-5232)*
Hydromer Inc (PA) 908 526-2828
35 Indtl Pkwy Branchburg (08876) *(G-646)*
Hygloss Products Inc 973 458-1700
45 Hathaway St Wallington (07057) *(G-11387)*
Hygrade Business Group Inc (PA) 800 836-7714
30 Seaview Dr Secaucus (07094) *(G-9781)*
Hyman W Fisher Inc 973 992-9155
121 E Northfield Rd Livingston (07039) *(G-5514)*
Hyp Hair Inc 201 843-4004
372 Orange Rd Montclair (07042) *(G-6369)*
Hyper Bicycles Inc (PA) 856 694-0352
177 Malaga Park Dr Malaga (08328) *(G-5788)*
I & J Fisnar Inc 973 646-5044
19 Chapin Rd Bldg C Pine Brook (07058) *(G-8603)*
I 2 R Corp (PA) 732 919-1100
5033 Industrial Rd Ste 6 Wall Township (07727) *(G-11348)*
I Associates LLC 215 262-7754
9255 Commerce Hwy Pennsauken (08110) *(G-8434)*
I C S, Fairfield *Also called International Cord Sets Inc (G-3240)*
I F A, Allenwood *Also called I F Associates Inc (G-33)*
I F Associates Inc 732 223-2900
3303 Atlantic Ave Allenwood (08720) *(G-33)*
I F F, Dayton *Also called Interntnal Flvors Frgrnces Inc (G-1972)*
I Fcb Holdings Inc (HQ) 201 934-2000
933 Macarthur Blvd Mahwah (07430) *(G-5748)*
I I Galaxy Inc 732 828-2686
235 Jersey Ave Ste 3 New Brunswick (08901) *(G-6933)*
I K Construction Inc 908 925-5200
174 Evergreen Pl 805 East Orange (07018) *(G-2252)*
I M N G, Parsippany *Also called Interntonal Med News Group LLC (G-7964)*
I Physician Hub 732 274-0155
462 New Rd Monmouth Junction (08852) *(G-6292)*
I Print Nb 201 662-1133
9252 Kennedy Blvd North Bergen (07047) *(G-7410)*
I S Parts International Inc 856 691-2203
3603 N Mill Rd Vineland (08360) *(G-11234)*
I See Optical Laboratories (PA) 856 227-9300
44 W Church St Blackwood (08012) *(G-469)*
I See Optical Laboratories 856 795-6435
312 W Somerdale Rd Voorhees (08043) *(G-11288)*
I T S Products, South Plainfield *Also called Intellgent Trffic Sup Pdts LLC (G-10278)*
I T W Covid, Cranbury *Also called Illinois Tool Works Inc (G-1839)*
I Trade Technology Ltd (PA) 615 348-7233
115 Franklin Tpke Ste 144 Mahwah (07430) *(G-5749)*
I V Miller & Sons 732 493-4040
15 Cindy Ln Ocean (07712) *(G-7666)*
I W Tremont Co, Hawthorne *Also called IW Tremont Co Inc (G-4227)*
I-Exceed Tech Solutions Inc 917 693-3207
103 Carnegie Ctr Ste 300 Princeton (08540) *(G-8960)*
I-Light Usa Inc 908 317-0020
1011 Us Highway 22 Ste 3 Mountainside (07092) *(G-6847)*
I-Yell-O Foods Inc 732 525-2201
603 Washington Ave South Amboy (08879) *(G-10134)*
I.S.t, Parlin *Also called Industrial Summit Tech Corp (G-7865)*
I3 Software, Newark *Also called Dcm Group Inc (G-7097)*
I4 Sustainability LLC 732 618-3310
140 Mountain Ave Ste 303 Springfield (07081) *(G-10445)*
Iacobucci USA Inc 732 935-6633
151 Industrial Way E A2 Eatontown (07724) *(G-2401)*
Iacovelli Stairs Incorporated 609 693-3476
707 Challenger Way Forked River (08731) *(G-3540)*
Iam International Inc 908 713-9651
4 Saddle Ridge Dr Lebanon (08833) *(G-5263)*
IBC Inc 856 533-2806
1000 Main St Ste 309 Voorhees (08043) *(G-11289)*
IBC Pharmaceuticals Inc 973 540-9595
300 The American Rd Morris Plains (07950) *(G-6616)*
IBM, Park Ridge *Also called International Bus Mchs Corp (G-7853)*
Iboco Corp 732 417-0066
1205 Paco Way Ste B Lakewood (08701) *(G-5111)*
Icb Enterprises, Trenton *Also called Power Magnetics Inc (G-10978)*
Ice Cold Novelty Products Inc 732 751-0011
5005 Belmar Blvd Ste B2 Wall Township (07727) *(G-11349)*
Iceberg Coffee LLC 908 675-6972
865 Rte 33 Ste 4 Freehold (07728) *(G-3669)*
Iceboxx LLC 201 857-0404
600 Braen Ave Wyckoff (07481) *(G-12113)*
ICEE Company 856 939-1540
155 E 9th Ave Runnemede (08078) *(G-9606)*
Icelandirect Inc (PA) 800 763-4690
127 Kingsland Ave Ste 101 Clifton (07014) *(G-1638)*
Ichrom Solutions, Franklinville *Also called Spark Holland Inc (G-3638)*
ICM, Fair Lawn *Also called Industrial Consulting Mktg Inc (G-3105)*
Icon Orthopedic Concepts LLC 973 794-6810
6 Mars Ct Ste 3 Boonton (07005) *(G-556)*
Icote USA Inc (PA) 908 359-7575
465 Amwell Rd Hillsborough (08844) *(G-4326)*

ALPHABETIC

Ics Corporation..215 427-3355
  100 Friars Blvd West Deptford (08086) *(G-11704)*

Icup Inc...856 751-2045
  1152 Marlkress Rd Ste 200 Cherry Hill (08003) *(G-1373)*

Icy Cools Inc..609 448-0172
  15 Oscar Dr Roosevelt (08555) *(G-9529)*

Icykidz...973 342-9665
  539 Union Ave Irvington (07111) *(G-4573)*

ID Systems Inc (PA).......................................201 996-9000
  123 Tice Blvd Woodcliff Lake (07677) *(G-12057)*

ID Technology LLC...201 405-0767
  48 Spruce St Oakland (07436) *(G-7632)*

Ida Automotive Inc...732 591-1245
  600 Texas Rd Morganville (07751) *(G-6588)*

Ideal Data Inc...201 998-9440
  420 River Rd North Arlington (07031) *(G-7374)*

Ideal Jacobs Corporation..................................973 275-5100
  515 Valley St Bsmt 1 Maplewood (07040) *(G-5879)*

Ideal Kitchens Inc...732 295-2780
  407 Route 35 Point Pleasant Beach (08742) *(G-8824)*

Ideal Plating, Paterson *Also called Independence Plating Corp (G-8213)*

Ideal Plating & Polishing Co..............................973 759-5559
  107 Alabama Ave Paterson (07503) *(G-8212)*

Ideal Tile Company Toms River, Toms River *Also called Andrevin Inc (G-10743)*

Identity Depot Inc..973 584-9301
  244 Main St Ledgewood (07852) *(G-5276)*

Ideon LLC..908 431-3126
  249 Homestead Rd Ste 1 Hillsborough (08844) *(G-4327)*

IDL Techni-Edge LLC.......................................908 497-9818
  30 Boright Ave Kenilworth (07033) *(G-4945)*

IDS, Fort Lee *Also called Interntnal Digital Systems Inc (G-3564)*

IDS, Englewood *Also called Integrated Dental Systems LLC (G-2914)*

Idt Energy Inc (HQ).......................................877 887-6866
  520 Broad St Fl 9 Newark (07102) *(G-7154)*

Ifc Products Inc..908 587-1221
  568 E Elizabeth Ave Linden (07036) *(G-5356)*

Ifc Solutions Inc..908 862-8810
  1601 E Linden Ave Linden (07036) *(G-5357)*

Ifortress..973 812-6400
  228 Lackawanna Ave Woodland Park (07424) *(G-12082)*

Igi Corp...908 753-5570
  6 Ingersoll Rd South Plainfield (07080) *(G-10275)*

Ii-VI Advanced Materials Inc..............................973 227-1551
  20 Chapin Rd Ste 1007 Pine Brook (07058) *(G-8604)*

Ii-VI Advanced Materials Sic S, Pine Brook *Also called Ii-VI Incorporated (G-8605)*

Ii-VI Incorporated...973 227-1551
  20 Chapin Rd Ste 1007 Pine Brook (07058) *(G-8605)*

Ii-VI Optoelectronic Dvcs Inc (HQ).........................908 668-5000
  141 Mount Bethel Rd Warren (07059) *(G-11417)*

Ii-VI Wide Band Gap, Inc., Pine Brook *Also called Ii-VI Advanced Materials Inc (G-8604)*

Ikaria Therapeutics LLC....................................908 238-6600
  Perryvle 3 Corp Park Fl 3 Hampton (08827) *(G-4155)*

Ileos of America Inc.......................................908 753-7300
  550 Hadley Rd South Plainfield (07080) *(G-10276)*

Ilg, Cherry Hill *Also called Agoura Hills Group (G-1335)*

Ilkem Granite & Marble 2 Corp..............................732 613-1457
  4420 Bordentown Ave Old Bridge (08857) *(G-7716)*

Ilkem Marble & Granite, Cherry Hill *Also called Ilkem Marble and Granite Inc (G-1374)*

Ilkem Marble and Granite Inc...............................856 433-8714
  2010 Springdale Rd # 300 Cherry Hill (08003) *(G-1374)*

Ill Eagle Enterprises Ltd..................................973 237-1111
  101 Miller Ln Ringwood (07456) *(G-9346)*

Ill-Eagle Enterprises, Ringwood *Also called Ill Eagle Enterprises Ltd (G-9346)*

Illinois Tool Works Inc....................................609 395-5600
  32 Commerce Dr Ste 1 Cranbury (08512) *(G-1839)*

Illinois Tool Works Inc....................................732 968-5300
  6 Ringwood Dr Parsippany (07054) *(G-7960)*

Illinois Tools, Passaic *Also called Atlantic Mills Inc (G-8052)*

Illuminating Experiences LLC...............................800 734-5858
  625 Jersey Ave Ste 7 New Brunswick (08901) *(G-6934)*

Ilsi, Fairfield *Also called Industrial Lbeling Systems Inc (G-3238)*

Imaan Trading Inc..201 779-2062
  286 Bergen Ave Jersey City (07305) *(G-4749)*

Image Access Corp (PA).....................................201 342-7878
  22 Paris Ave Ste 210 Rockleigh (07647) *(G-9519)*

Image Builder Appliques, Woodcliff Lake *Also called Uniport Industries Corporation (G-12067)*

Image Makers Instant Printing..............................973 633-1771
  1581 State Route 23 Wayne (07470) *(G-11518)*

Image Point..908 684-1768
  69 Water St Newton (07860) *(G-7346)*

Image Remit Inc..732 940-7900
  205 N Center Dr North Brunswick (08902) *(G-7469)*

Image Screen Printing Inc..................................732 560-1817
  532 Lincoln Blvd Middlesex (08846) *(G-6121)*

Imagery Embroidery Corporation.............................201 343-9333
  2907 Jeannette St 2911 Union City (07087) *(G-11113)*

Images Costume Productions.................................609 859-7372
  881 Westminster Dr N Southampton (08088) *(G-10365)*

Imagine Audio LLC...856 488-1466
  304 Haddonfield Rd Cherry Hill (08002) *(G-1375)*

Imagine Communications Corp................................201 469-6740
  1160 Us Highway 22 Bridgewater (08807) *(G-832)*

Imagine Gold LLC...201 488-5988
  60 Romanelli Ave South Hackensack (07606) *(G-10162)*

Imagine Screen Printing, Dayton *Also called Central Mills Inc (G-1959)*

Imagine Screen Prtg & Prod LLC.............................732 329-2009
  473 Ridge Rd Dayton (08810) *(G-1969)*

Imclone Systems LLC (HQ)...................................908 541-8000
  440 Us Highway 22 Bridgewater (08807) *(G-833)*

Imclone Systems LLC..908 218-0147
  33 Imclone Dr Branchburg (08876) *(G-647)*

Imclone Systems LLC..908 541-8100
  50 Imclone Dr Branchburg (08876) *(G-648)*

Immedis Inc...212 239-2625
  485 Route 1 S Ste 330 Iselin (08830) *(G-4611)*

Immtech Pharmaceuticals Inc................................212 791-2911
  93 Prospect Ave Montclair (07042) *(G-6370)*

Immunogenetics Inc...856 697-1441
  Lincoln Ave & Wheat Rd Buena (08310) *(G-940)*

Immunomedics Inc (PA).....................................973 605-8200
  300 The American Rd Morris Plains (07950) *(G-6617)*

Immunostics Inc...732 918-0770
  38 Industrial Way E Ste 5 Eatontown (07724) *(G-2402)*

Immunostics Company Inc...................................732 918-0770
  38 Industrial Way E Ste 1 Eatontown (07724) *(G-2403)*

Impact Air 45, Englewood *Also called Palisades Dental LLc (G-2929)*

Impact Design Inc..908 289-2900
  248 3rd St Elizabethport (07206) *(G-2789)*

Impact Displays Inc..201 804-6262
  310 13th St Carlstadt (07072) *(G-1167)*

Impact Instrumentation Inc.................................973 882-1212
  27 Fairfield Pl West Caldwell (07006) *(G-11654)*

Impact Medical, West Caldwell *Also called Impact Instrumentation Inc (G-11654)*

Impact Printing..862 225-9167
  15 Vogt Ln 1 Little Ferry (07643) *(G-5489)*

Impact Protective Eqp LLC..................................973 377-0903
  8 Westerly Ave Madison (07940) *(G-5695)*

Impact Unlimited Inc (PA).................................732 274-2000
  250 Ridge Rd Dayton (08810) *(G-1970)*

Impact Visal Systems, Cream Ridge *Also called Central Art & Enginering Inc (G-1932)*

Impact Xm, Dayton *Also called Impact Unlimited Inc (G-1970)*

Impact Xm, Dayton *Also called Northwind Enterprises Inc (G-1982)*

Impax Laboratories LLC....................................732 595-4600
  100 Somerset Corp Blvd # 3000 Bridgewater (08807) *(G-834)*

Impax Labs, Bridgewater *Also called Impax Laboratories LLC (G-834)*

Imperial Copy Products Inc.................................973 927-5500
  961 State Route 10 1ee Randolph (07869) *(G-9186)*

Imperial Dax Co Inc..973 227-6105
  120 New Dutch Ln Fairfield (07004) *(G-3234)*

Imperial Design..856 742-8480
  729 Charles St Gloucester City (08030) *(G-3844)*

Imperial Drug & Spice Corp.................................201 348-1551
  5620 Kennedy Blvd W West New York (07093) *(G-11741)*

Imperial Electro-Plating, Lyndhurst *Also called FER Plating Inc (G-5655)*

Imperial Machine & Tool Co (HQ)............................908 496-8100
  8 W Crisman Rd Columbia (07832) *(G-1794)*

Imperial Metal Products Inc................................908 647-8181
  8 W Chimney Rock Rd Bound Brook (08805) *(G-602)*

Imperial Sewing Machine Co.................................973 374-3405
  584 S 21st St Irvington (07111) *(G-4574)*

Imperial Weld Ring Corp Inc................................908 354-0011
  80 Front St 88 Elizabeth (07206) *(G-2749)*

Impex, Jersey City *Also called Delight Foods USA LLC (G-4722)*

Important Papers Inc......................................856 751-4544
  12 Downing St Cherry Hill (08003) *(G-1376)*

Important Papers & Printing, Cherry Hill *Also called Important Papers Inc (G-1376)*

Importers Service Corp.....................................732 248-1946
  65 Brunswick Ave Edison (08817) *(G-2533)*

Impressions Signs and Prtg Inc.............................973 653-3058
  396 Midland Ave Ste 2 Garfield (07026) *(G-3747)*

Impressions Unlimited Prtg LLC.............................856 256-0200
  638 Delsea Dr Sewell (08080) *(G-9846)*

Imprint Ink, Shrewsbury *Also called Athletes Alley (G-9882)*

Imprintz Cstm Printed Graphics.............................609 386-5673
  691 Main St Lumberton (08048) *(G-5631)*

IMS, Princeton *Also called Intelligent Mtl Solutions Inc (G-8963)*

Imwoth LLC...732 244-0950
  52 Hyers St Ste A-5 Toms River (08753) *(G-10769)*

In Mocean Group LLC.......................................732 960-2415
  2400 Rte 1 North Brunswick (08902) *(G-7470)*

In The Spotlights..973 361-7768
  301 Mount Hope Ave # 2091 Rockaway (07866) *(G-9466)*

In-Line Shtmtl Fabricators.................................201 339-8121
  85 E 21st St Bayonne (07002) *(G-224)*

In-Phase Technologies Inc 609 298-9555
401 Bordentown Hedding Rd Bordentown (08505) *(G-584)*
INB Manhattan Drug Company Inc (HQ) 973 926-0816
225 Long Ave Ste 15 Hillside (07205) *(G-4400)*
INB Manhattan Drug Company Inc 973 926-0816
210 Route 22 Hillside (07205) *(G-4401)*
INB Manhattan Drug Company Inc 973 926-0816
225 Long Ave Ste 6 Hillside (07205) *(G-4402)*
Inca Kola, Clifton *Also called Continental Food & Bev Inc (G-1588)*
INCAST, Montvale *Also called Investment Casting Institute (G-6414)*
Incentx LLC 302 202-2894
209 2nd St Ste 6 Lakewood (08701) *(G-5112)*
Incom (america) Inc 908 464-3366
330 Snyder Ave Berkeley Heights (07922) *(G-401)*
Increase Beverage Intl Inc 609 303-3117
7250 Westfield Ave Ste M Pennsauken (08110) *(G-8435)*
Indemax Inc 973 209-2424
1 Industrial Dr Vernon (07462) *(G-11159)*
Independence Plating Corp (PA) 973 523-1776
107 Alabama Ave Paterson (07503) *(G-8213)*
Independence Technology LLC 908 722-3767
W Ethicon Bldg Rr 22 Somerville (08876) *(G-10116)*
Independent Converting Eqp, Fairfield *Also called Independent Machine Company (G-3235)*
Independent Machine Company 973 882-0060
20 Industrial Rd Fairfield (07004) *(G-3235)*
Independent Metal Sales Inc 609 261-8090
1900 Park Ave W Hainesport (08036) *(G-4074)*
Independent Press, The, Bloomfield *Also called Worrall Community Newspapers (G-522)*
Independent Prj Cons Ltd Lblty 973 780-8002
374 Chestnut St Ste C Newark (07105) *(G-7155)*
Independent Sheet Metal Co Inc 973 423-1150
2 N Corporate Dr 2 # 2 Riverdale (07457) *(G-9379)*
India Cafe, South Plainfield *Also called Sukhadias Sweets & Snacks (G-10328)*
Indo-Mim Inc (PA) 734 327-9842
214 Carnegie Ctr Ste 104 Princeton (08540) *(G-8961)*
Indo-US Mim TEC Private Ltd 734 327-9842
214 Carnegie Ctr Ste 104 Princeton (08540) *(G-8962)*
Indoor Entertainment of NJ 609 522-6700
5301 Ocean Ave Wildwood (08260) *(G-11945)*
Indoor Environmental Tech 973 709-1122
600 Ryerson Rd Ste F Lincoln Park (07035) *(G-5299)*
Indotronix International Corp 609 750-0700
101 Morgan Ln Ste 210 Plainsboro (08536) *(G-8790)*
Inductotherm Corp (HQ) 609 267-9000
10 Indel Ave Rancocas (08073) *(G-9161)*
Inductotherm Group, Rancocas *Also called Inductotherm Technologies Inc (G-9162)*
Inductotherm Technologies Inc (HQ) 609 267-9000
10 Indel Ave Rancocas (08073) *(G-9162)*
Indusco, Fairfield *Also called Industrial Brush Co Inc (G-3236)*
Industl Envrnmntl Pollutn 908 241-3830
176 W Westfield Ave Roselle Park (07204) *(G-9587)*
Industrial Brush Co Inc 800 241-9860
105 Clinton Rd Ste 1 Fairfield (07004) *(G-3236)*
Industrial Combustion Assn 732 271-0300
20 Worlds Fair Dr Ste C Somerset (08873) *(G-10004)*
Industrial Consulting & MGT, Fair Lawn *Also called Industrial Consulting Mktg Inc (G-3106)*
Industrial Consulting Mktg Inc 973 427-2474
20-21 Wagaraw Rd Bldg 39 Fair Lawn (07410) *(G-3105)*
Industrial Consulting Mktg Inc 877 405-5200
20-21 Wagaraw Rd Bldg 38 Fair Lawn (07410) *(G-3106)*
Industrial Ferguson Foundry, Union *Also called Union Casting Industries Inc (G-11096)*
Industrial Filters Company 973 575-0533
9 Industrial Rd Fairfield (07004) *(G-3237)*
Industrial Habonim Valves & AC 201 820-3184
22 Riverview Dr Ste 103 Wayne (07470) *(G-11519)*
Industrial Hard Chromium Co 973 344-2265
7 Rome St Newark (07105) *(G-7156)*
Industrial Hydraulics & Rubber 856 966-2600
458 Atlantic Ave Camden (08104) *(G-1070)*
Industrial Lbeling Systems Inc 973 808-8188
50 Kulick Rd Fairfield (07004) *(G-3238)*
Industrial Machine & Engrg Co, Linden *Also called Industrial Machine & Engrg Co (G-5358)*
Industrial Machine & Engrg Co 908 862-8874
1807 W Elizabeth Ave Linden (07036) *(G-5358)*
Industrial Machine Corp 973 345-1800
44 Lehigh Ave Paterson (07503) *(G-8214)*
Industrial Metal Inc 908 362-0084
169 Cedar Lake Rd Blairstown (07825) *(G-486)*
Industrial Process & Eqp Inc (PA) 973 702-0330
803 State Rt 23 Sussex (07461) *(G-10562)*
Industrial Rivet & Fastener Co (PA) 201 750-1040
200 Paris Ave Northvale (07647) *(G-7528)*
Industrial Stl & Fastener Corp 610 667-2220
167 Old Blmont Ave Fl 2 Flr 2 Cherry Hill (08034) *(G-1377)*
Industrial Summit Tech Corp (HQ) 732 238-2211
250 Cheesequake Rd Parlin (08859) *(G-7865)*
Industrial Tube Corporation 908 369-3737
297 Valley Rd Hillsborough (08844) *(G-4328)*
Industrial Water Institute 609 585-4880
33 Maitland Rd Trenton (08620) *(G-10944)*
Industrial Water Tech Inc 732 888-1233
6 Village Ct Hazlet (07730) *(G-4261)*
Industrie Bitossi Inc (HQ) 201 796-0722
410 Market St Elmwood Park (07407) *(G-2831)*
Industronic Inc 908 393-5960
1170 Us Highway 22 # 108 Bridgewater (08807) *(G-835)*
Industry Publications Inc 973 331-9545
140 Littleton Rd Ste 320 Parsippany (07054) *(G-7961)*
Inenergy Inc 609 466-2512
293 Wertsville Rd Ringoes (08551) *(G-9337)*
Infineon Tech Americas Corp 732 603-5914
186 Wood Ave S Iselin (08830) *(G-4612)*
Infineum USA LP (HQ) 800 441-1074
1900 E Linden Ave Linden (07036) *(G-5359)*
Infinite Classic Inc 973 227-2790
30 Sherwood Ln Ste 8 Fairfield (07004) *(G-3239)*
Infinite Mfg Group Inc 973 649-9950
35 Obrien St Kearny (07032) *(G-4867)*
Infinite Mfg Group Inc (PA) 973 649-9950
35 Obrien St Kearny (07032) *(G-4868)*
Infinite Sign, Kearny *Also called Infinite Mfg Group Inc (G-4868)*
Infinite Sign Industries Inc 973 649-9950
35 Obrien St Kearny (07032) *(G-4869)*
Infiniti Components Inc (PA) 908 537-9950
223 State Route 31 Hampton (08827) *(G-4156)*
Infinity Compounding LLC 856 467-3030
2079 Center Square Rd Logan Township (08085) *(G-5588)*
Infinity Ltl Engnred Compounds, Logan Township *Also called Infinity Compounding LLC (G-5588)*
Infinity Sourcing Services LLC 212 868-2900
560 Sylvan Ave Ste 3155 Englewood Cliffs (07632) *(G-2976)*
Infinlight Products Inc (PA) 888 665-7708
859130 N 126e East Windsor (08520) *(G-2353)*
Infinova Corporation 732 355-9100
51 Stouts Ln Ste 1 Monmouth Junction (08852) *(G-6293)*
Infinova Networks, Monmouth Junction *Also called Infinova Corporation (G-6293)*
Infor Metal & Tooling Mfg 973 571-9520
16 Commerce Rd Cedar Grove (07009) *(G-1279)*
Information Services Intl, Budd Lake *Also called Mars Incorporated (G-929)*
Information Technolgy Corp 201 556-1999
121 Gertrude Ave Paramus (07652) *(G-7807)*
Information Today Inc 908 219-0279
630 Central Ave Fl 2 New Providence (07974) *(G-7004)*
Information Today Inc (PA) 609 654-6266
143 Old Marlton Pike Medford (08055) *(G-6024)*
Infoseal LLC 201 569-4500
55 W Sheffield Ave Englewood (07631) *(G-2913)*
Infront Medical LLC 888 515-2532
1033 Us Highway 46 A202 Clifton (07013) *(G-1639)*
Ingersoll-Rand Company 908 238-7000
1467 Route 31 S Annandale (08801) *(G-54)*
Ingersoll-Rand Company 973 882-0924
26 Chapin Rd Ste 1107 Pine Brook (07058) *(G-8606)*
Ingersoll-Rand Company 856 793-7000
3001 Irwin Rd Mount Laurel (08054) *(G-6766)*
Ingersoll-Rand Intl Inc 559 271-4625
1 Centennial Ave Ste 101 Piscataway (08854) *(G-8677)*
Ingersoll-Rand US Trane (HQ) 732 652-7100
1 Centennial Ave Ste 101 Piscataway (08854) *(G-8678)*
Ingrasselino Products LLC 800 960-1316
63 Dewey St Clifton (07013) *(G-1640)*
Ingredient House LLC 609 285-5987
24 Vreeland Dr Ste 1 Skillman (08558) *(G-9921)*
Ingredion Incorporated 908 685-5000
10 Finderne Ave Ste A Bridgewater (08807) *(G-836)*
Ingui Design LLC 201 264-9126
46 N Central Ave Ramsey (07446) *(G-9147)*
Iniven, Branchburg *Also called Zzyzx LLC (G-700)*
Iniven LLC 908 722-3770
5 Columbia Rd Branchburg (08876) *(G-649)*
Injectable Mfg Fcilty, Cherry Hill *Also called Hikma Pharmaceuticals USA Inc (G-1372)*
Injection Works Inc 856 802-6444
104 Gaither Dr Mount Laurel (08054) *(G-6767)*
Injectron Corporation 908 753-1990
1000 S 2nd St Plainfield (07063) *(G-8769)*
Ink On Paper Communications (PA) 732 758-6280
450 Shrewsbury Plz # 372 Shrewsbury (07702) *(G-9893)*
Ink Well Printers LLC 908 272-8090
38 S 21st St Kenilworth (07033) *(G-4946)*
Inkworkx Custom Screen Prtg 609 898-5198
289 State Route 33 Manalapan (07726) *(G-5814)*
Inlc Technology Corporation 908 834-8390
30 Technology Dr Ste 1d Warren (07059) *(G-11418)*
Inman Mold and Mfg Co (PA) 732 381-3033
4 Commerce St Springfield (07081) *(G-10446)*
Inman Mold and Mfg Co 732 381-3033
273 E Inman Ave Rahway (07065) *(G-9103)*

ALPHABETIC

Innan Molding, Rahway *Also called Barlics Manufacturing Co Inc* *(G-9082)*

Innerspace Technology Inc 201 933-1600
728 Garden St Carlstadt (07072) *(G-1168)*

Innocor Inc (HQ) 732 945-6222
200 Schulz Dr Ste 2 Red Bank (07701) *(G-9230)*

Innocor Foam Tech - Acp Inc (HQ) 732 945-6222
200 Schulz Dr Ste 2 Red Bank (07701) *(G-9231)*

Innocor Foam Technologies LLC (HQ) 844 824-9348
200 Schulz Dr Ste 2 Red Bank (07701) *(G-9232)*

Innolutions Inc 609 490-9799
4 Wellesley Ct Princeton Junction (08550) *(G-9061)*

Innophos Inc 973 587-8735
259 Prospect Plains Rd A Cranbury (08512) *(G-1840)*

Innophos LLC (HQ) 609 495-2495
259 Prospect Plains Rd A Cranbury (08512) *(G-1841)*

Innophos LLC 973 808-5900
43 West St East Hanover (07936) *(G-2217)*

Innophos Holdings Inc (PA) 609 495-2495
259 Prospect Plains Rd A Cranbury (08512) *(G-1842)*

Innophos Inc (HQ) 609 495-2495
259 Prospect Plains Rd A Cranbury (08512) *(G-1843)*

Innophos Investments II Inc (HQ) 609 495-2495
259 Prospect Plains Rd Cranbury (08512) *(G-1844)*

Innophos Invstmnts Hldings Inc (HQ) 609 495-2495
259 Prospect Plains Rd Cranbury (08512) *(G-1845)*

Innova Group Inc 856 696-1053
327 Tuckahoe Rd Vineland (08360) *(G-11235)*

Innovance Inc 732 529-2300
15 Corporate Pl S Ste 101 Piscataway (08854) *(G-8679)*

Innovance Networks, Piscataway *Also called Innovance Inc* *(G-8679)*

Innovasystems Inc 856 722-0410
1245 N Church St Ste 6 Moorestown (08057) *(G-6530)*

Innovation Design Center, Voorhees *Also called Comar Inc* *(G-11283)*

Innovation Foods LLC 856 455-2209
71 Bridgeton Ave Bridgeton (08302) *(G-759)*

Innovation In Medtech LLC 888 202-5939
5 Rolling Hill Dr Chatham (07928) *(G-1321)*

Innovation Photonics LLC 973 857-8380
62 Depot St Verona (07044) *(G-11169)*

Innovative Art Concepts LLC 201 828-9146
630 Swan St Ramsey (07446) *(G-9148)*

Innovative Awards Inc 609 888-1400
634 Arena Dr Ste 102 Trenton (08610) *(G-10945)*

Innovative Computer Systems, Hackensack *Also called Gerbino Computer Systems Inc* *(G-3922)*

Innovative Concepts Design LLC 732 346-0061
107 Trumbull St Ste 203 Elizabeth (07206) *(G-2750)*

Innovative Cosmtc Concepts LLC (PA) 212 391-8110
399 Thornall St Ste 26 Edison (08837) *(G-2534)*

Innovative Cosmtc Concepts LLC 973 225-0264
61 Kuller Rd Clifton (07011) *(G-1641)*

Innovative Cutng Concepts LLC 609 484-9960
203 Cates Rd Egg Harbor Township (08234) *(G-2684)*

Innovative Design, Edison *Also called Innovative Cosmtc Concepts LLC* *(G-2534)*

Innovative Design Inc 201 227-2555
80 Broadway Cresskill (07626) *(G-1943)*

Innovative Disposables LLC 908 222-7111
3611 Kennedy Rd South Plainfield (07080) *(G-10277)*

Innovative Manufacturing Inc 908 904-1884
198 Us Highway 206 Ste 4 Hillsborough (08844) *(G-4329)*

Innovative Metal Solutions LLC 609 784-8406
10 Eagle Ave Ste 400b Mount Holly (08060) *(G-6731)*

Innovative Photonic Solutions, Monmouth Junction *Also called Innovtive Phtnics Slution Corp* *(G-6294)*

Innovative Powder Coatings LLC 856 661-0086
9105 Burrough Dover Ln Pennsauken (08110) *(G-8436)*

Innovative Power Solutions LLC 732 544-1075
373 South St Eatontown (07724) *(G-2404)*

Innovative Pressure Clg LLC 609 738-3100
10 Arnytown Hrnerstown Rd Cream Ridge (08514) *(G-1937)*

Innovative Resin Systems Inc 973 465-6887
257 Wilson Ave Newark (07105) *(G-7157)*

Innovative Resin Systems Inc (PA) 973 465-6887
70 Verkade Dr Wayne (07470) *(G-11520)*

Innovative Resin Systems Inc 973 633-5342
70 Verkade Dr Wayne (07470) *(G-11521)*

Innovative Sftwr Solutions Inc 856 910-9190
3000 S Lenola Rd Maple Shade (08052) *(G-5864)*

Innovi Mobile LLC 646 588-0165
45 Essex St Ste 201 Millburn (07041) *(G-6200)*

Innovtive Phtnics Slution Corp 732 355-9300
4250 Us Highway 1 Ste 1 Monmouth Junction (08852) *(G-6294)*

Ino Therapeutics LLC (HQ) 908 238-6600
1425 Us Route 206 Bedminster (07921) *(G-266)*

Inoac Usa Inc 201 807-0809
100 Carol Pl Moonachie (07074) *(G-6471)*

Inopak Ltd 973 962-1121
24 Executive Pkwy Ringwood (07456) *(G-9347)*

Inox Components 856 256-0800
And 553 Rr 55 Pitman (08071) *(G-8745)*

Inox Steel Corp 609 268-2334
48 Meetinghouse Ct Shamong (08088) *(G-9858)*

Inphot Inc 609 799-7172
13 Blossom Hill Dr Plainsboro (08536) *(G-8791)*

Inrad Optics, Northvale *Also called MRC Precision Metal Optics Inc* *(G-7538)*

Inrad Optics Inc (PA) 201 767-1910
181 Legrand Ave Northvale (07647) *(G-7529)*

Inserch By Merc U.S.a, Hackensack *Also called Merc USA Inc* *(G-3947)*

Inserts East Incorporated 856 663-8181
7045 Central Hwy Pennsauken (08109) *(G-8437)*

Insign Inc 856 424-1161
1709 Imperial Way West Deptford (08066) *(G-11705)*

Insl-X, Montvale *Also called Complementary Coatings Corp* *(G-6405)*

Insmed Incorporated (PA) 908 977-9900
10 Finderne Ave Bldg 10 # 10 Bridgewater (08807) *(G-837)*

Inspire Pharmaceuticals Inc 908 423-1000
1 Merck Dr Whitehouse Station (08889) *(G-11921)*

Inspire Works Inc 908 730-7447
24 Midwood Dr Florham Park (07932) *(G-3513)*

Installations Unlimited, Kenilworth *Also called Auto Action Group Inc* *(G-4922)*

Instant Business Cards, Belmar *Also called Watonka Printing Inc* *(G-356)*

Instant Imprints 973 252-9500
286 Us Highway 206 119b Flanders (07836) *(G-3413)*

Instant Printing, Orange *Also called Berennial International* *(G-7752)*

Instant Printing of Dover Inc 973 366-6855
241 E Blackwell St Dover (07801) *(G-2090)*

Instapak Corp Sealed Air 201 791-7600
80 Parker Ave Fl 2 Rochelle Park (07662) *(G-9424)*

Institutational Edge LLC 201 944-5447
120 Van Nostrand Ave # 201 Englewood Cliffs (07632) *(G-2977)*

Institute For Respnsble Online 856 722-1048
82 Hillside Ln Mount Laurel (08054) *(G-6768)*

Instock Wireless Components 973 335-6550
50 Intervale Rd Ste 1 Boonton (07005) *(G-557)*

Instore Magazine, Montclair *Also called Retail Management Pubg Inc* *(G-6388)*

Instrctnal Cmpt Based Training, Bridgewater *Also called Excerpta Medica Inc* *(G-822)*

Instride Shoes LLC 908 874-6670
29 Polhemus Dr Hillsborough (08844) *(G-4330)*

Instrment Vlve Svcs Burlington 609 386-5000
120 Kissel Rd Burlington (08016) *(G-973)*

Instru-Met Corporation 908 851-0700
931 Lehigh Ave Union (07083) *(G-11065)*

Instrument Sciences & Tech 908 996-9920
1131 State Route 12 Frenchtown (08825) *(G-3714)*

Instrumentation Technology Sls 732 388-0866
205 E Inman Ave Rahway (07065) *(G-9104)*

Insul-Stop Inc 732 706-1978
240 Boundary Rd Marlboro (07746) *(G-5901)*

Insulation Material Distrs, Linden *Also called Insulation Materials Distrs* *(G-5360)*

Insulation Materials Distrs 908 925-2323
501 S Park Ave Linden (07036) *(G-5360)*

Insulite Inc 732 255-1700
1890 Church Rd Toms River (08753) *(G-10770)*

Int'l Purchasing Exchange, Somerset *Also called Sysco Guest Supply LLC* *(G-10078)*

Intangible Labs Inc 917 375-1301
333 River St Apt 1144 Hoboken (07030) *(G-4457)*

Intarome Fragrance Corporation (PA) 201 767-8700
370 Chestnut St Norwood (07648) *(G-7565)*

Intech Powercore Corporation 201 767-8066
250 Herbert Ave Closter (07624) *(G-1758)*

Integra, Plainsboro *Also called Derma Sciences Inc* *(G-8784)*

Integra Lfscnces Holdings Corp (PA) 609 275-0500
311 Enterprise Dr Plainsboro (08536) *(G-8792)*

Integra Lifesciences Corp (HQ) 609 275-2700
311 Enterprise Dr Plainsboro (08536) *(G-8793)*

Integra Lifesciences Corp 609 275-0500
311 Enterprise Dr Plainsboro (08536) *(G-8794)*

Integra Lifesciences Corp 609 275-2700
105 Morgan Ln Plainsboro (08536) *(G-8795)*

Integra Lifesciences Sales LLC 609 275-0500
311 Enterprise Dr Plainsboro (08536) *(G-8796)*

Integrate Tech Inc 201 693-5625
19 Barnfield Ct Upper Saddle River (07458) *(G-11141)*

Integrated Biopharma Inc (PA) 888 319-6962
225 Long Ave Ste 13 Hillside (07205) *(G-4403)*

Integrated Dental Systems LLC 201 676-2457
145 Cedar Ln Ste 205 Englewood (07631) *(G-2914)*

Integrated Microwave Tech LLC (HQ) 908 852-3700
101 Bilby Rd Ste 15 Hackettstown (07840) *(G-4012)*

Integrated Packaging Inds Inc (PA) 973 839-0500
45 Carey Ave Ste 210 Butler (07405) *(G-1005)*

Integrated Packg Systems Inc 973 664-0020
3 Luger Rd Ste 5 Denville (07834) *(G-2040)*

Integrated Photonics Inc (HQ) 908 281-8000
132 Stryker Ln Ste 1 Hillsborough (08844) *(G-4331)*

Integrated Photonics Inc 908 281-8000
132 Stryker Ln Ste 1 Hillsborough (08844) *(G-4332)*

Integration International Inc (PA) 973 796-2300
160 Littleton Rd Ste 106 Parsippany (07054) *(G-7962)*

Integration Partners-Ny Corp 973 871-2100
1719 State Rt 10 Ste 114 Parsippany (07054) *(G-7963)*

Integrity Ironworks Corp 732 254-2200
33 Brookside Ave Sayreville (08872) *(G-9711)*

Integrity Medical Devices Del 609 567-8175
360 Fairview Ave Hammonton (08037) *(G-4136)*

Integrted Laminate Systems Inc 856 786-6500
1301 Industrial Hwy Cinnaminson (08077) *(G-1465)*

Intek Plastics Inc 973 427-7331
150 5th Ave Hawthorne (07506) *(G-4226)*

Intelco (PA) 856 456-6755
250 Harvard Ave Westville (08093) *(G-11817)*

Intelco 856 384-8562
1927 Nolte Dr Paulsboro (08066) *(G-8332)*

Intellect Design Arena Inc (HQ) 732 769-1037
20 Corporate Pl S Piscataway (08854) *(G-8680)*

Intellect Neurosciences Inc 201 608-5101
550 Sylvan Ave Ste 101 Englewood Cliffs (07632) *(G-2978)*

INTELLECT SEEC, Piscataway Also called Intellect Design Arena Inc *(G-8680)*

Intellgent Trffic Sup Pdts LLC 908 791-1200
3005 Hadley Rd Ste 5 South Plainfield (07080) *(G-10278)*

Intellicon Inc 201 791-9499
46 Sellers St Kearny (07032) *(G-4870)*

Intelligent Mtl Solutions Inc 609 514-4031
201 Washington Rd Princeton (08540) *(G-8963)*

Intelligentproject LLC 732 928-3421
15 Walter Dr Ste 4 Jackson (08527) *(G-4657)*

Intellisphere LLC (HQ) 609 716-7777
666 Plainsboro Rd Ste 300 Plainsboro (08536) *(G-8797)*

Intense Inc 732 249-2228
1200 Airport Rd Ste A North Brunswick (08902) *(G-7471)*

Inteplast Group Corporation (PA) 973 994-8000
9 Peach Tree Hill Rd Livingston (07039) *(G-5515)*

Inter City Press Inc 908 236-9911
143 Petticoat Ln Lebanon (08833) *(G-5264)*

Inter Parfums Inc 609 860-1967
60 Stults Rd Dayton (08810) *(G-1971)*

Inter Rep Associates Inc (PA) 609 465-0077
131 Kimbles Beach Rd Cape May Court House (08210) *(G-1111)*

Inter Trend, Union Also called Deep Foods Inc *(G-11042)*

Inter World Highway LLC 732 759-8235
205 Westwood Ave Long Branch (07740) *(G-5599)*

Interactive Advisory Software 770 951-2929
3393 Bargaintown Rd # 200 Egg Harbor Township (08234) *(G-2685)*

Interbahm International Inc 732 499-9700
10 Engelhard Ave Avenel (07001) *(G-131)*

Interchange Equipment Inc 973 473-5005
90 Dayton Ave Ste 120 Passaic (07055) *(G-8074)*

Interchange Group Inc 973 783-7032
52 Watchung Ave Montclair (07043) *(G-6371)*

Intercoastal Fabricators Inc 856 629-4105
300 Thomas Ave Ste 301 Williamstown (08094) *(G-11961)*

Intercure Inc 973 893-5653
356 Bloomfield Ave Ste 5 Montclair (07042) *(G-6372)*

Intercure Limited and Resperat, Montclair Also called Intercure Inc *(G-6372)*

Interfashion Cosmetics Corp 201 288-5858
32 Henry St Teterboro (07608) *(G-10680)*

Interfoam, Paterson Also called Kohler Industries Inc *(G-8231)*

Interganic Fzco LLC 224 436-0372
125 Stryker Ln Ste 3 Hillsborough (08844) *(G-4333)*

Intergrated Media Solutions, Manalapan Also called Lead Conversion Plus *(G-5816)*

Intergrated Scales Systems, Fairfield Also called Lizard Label Co *(G-3265)*

Interior Art & Design Inc 201 488-8855
59 Oak St Hackensack (07601) *(G-3931)*

Interior Specialties LLC 856 663-1700
6006 S Crescent Blvd Pennsauken (08109) *(G-8438)*

Interlink Products Intl Inc 908 862-8090
1315 E Elizabeth Ave Linden (07036) *(G-5361)*

Intermark Inc 908 474-1311
601 E Linden Ave Linden (07036) *(G-5362)*

International Aromatics Inc (PA) 201 964-0900
200 Anderson Ave Moonachie (07074) *(G-6472)*

International Beauty Products 973 575-6400
39 Us Highway 46 Ste 804 Pine Brook (07058) *(G-8607)*

International Bus Mchs Corp 201 307-5136
225 Brae Blvd Park Ridge (07656) *(G-7853)*

International Chefs Inc 917 645-2900
33 Bella Vista Ave Saddle Brook (07663) *(G-9656)*

International Coconut Corp 908 289-1555
225 W Grand St Elizabeth (07202) *(G-2751)*

International Container Co 201 440-1600
409 S River St Hackensack (07601) *(G-3932)*

International Cord Sets Inc 973 227-2118
6 Spielman Rd Fairfield (07004) *(G-3240)*

International Crystal Labs (PA) 973 478-8944
11 Erie St Ste 2 Garfield (07026) *(G-3748)*

International Data Group Inc 732 460-9404
6 Windsor Dr Eatontown (07724) *(G-2405)*

International Delights LLC 973 928-5431
230 Brighton Rd Clifton (07012) *(G-1642)*

International Design & Mfg LLC 908 587-2884
1217 Pennsylvania Ave Linden (07036) *(G-5363)*

International Graphics Inc 908 753-5570
6 Ingersoll Rd South Plainfield (07080) *(G-10279)*

International Inspirations LLC 201 868-2000
8101 Tonnelle Ave North Bergen (07047) *(G-7411)*

International Molasses Corp 201 368-8036
121 E Hunter Ave Maywood (07607) *(G-6006)*

International Molasses Corp 201 368-8036
88 Market St Fl 2 Saddle Brook (07663) *(G-9657)*

International Paper Company 856 853-7000
33 Phoenix Dr West Deptford (08086) *(G-11706)*

International Paper Company 732 828-1700
101 Ford Ave Milltown (08850) *(G-6216)*

International Paper Company 856 931-8000
370 Benigno Blvd Bellmawr (08031) *(G-335)*

International Paper Company 732 251-2000
140 Summerhill Rd Spotswood (08884) *(G-10415)*

International Paper Company 856 546-7000
100 E Gloucester Pike Barrington (08007) *(G-173)*

International Paper Company 973 405-2400
261 River Rd Clifton (07014) *(G-1643)*

International Playthings, Parsippany Also called Epoch Everlasting Play LLC *(G-7937)*

International Point of Sale, Teaneck Also called Worldwide Pt SL Ltd Lblty Co *(G-10655)*

International Process Eqp Co 856 665-4007
9300 N Crescent Blvd Pennsauken (08110) *(G-8439)*

International Processing Corp 732 826-4240
1250 Amboy Ave Perth Amboy (08861) *(G-8523)*

International Products Corp (PA) 609 386-8770
201 Connecticut Dr Burlington (08016) *(G-974)*

International Roll Forms, Sewell Also called Omega Tool Die *(G-9852)*

International Rollforms Inc (PA) 856 228-7100
8 International Ave Deptford (08096) *(G-2064)*

International Shtmtl Plate Mfg 908 722-6614
112 Veterans Mem Dr E Somerville (08876) *(G-10117)*

International Swimming Pools 732 565-9229
14c Van Dyke Ave New Brunswick (08901) *(G-6935)*

International Tape Co, Somers Point Also called Interntnal Adhsive Coating Inc *(G-9937)*

International Tech Lasers (PA) 201 262-4580
70 Kinderkamack Rd Ste 7 Emerson (07630) *(G-2864)*

International Tool & Mch LLC 908 687-5580
446 Hillside Ave Hillside (07205) *(G-4404)*

International Tool and Mfg 973 227-6767
30 Sherwood Ln Ste 10 Fairfield (07004) *(G-3241)*

International Vitamin Corp 973 371-4400
209 40th St Irvington (07111) *(G-4575)*

International Vitamin Corp 973 416-2000
191 40th St Irvington (07111) *(G-4576)*

Internet-Sales USA Corporation 775 468-8379
65 Fleetwood Dr Rockaway (07866) *(G-9467)*

Interntional Cnsld Chemex Corp 732 828-7676
235 Jersey Ave New Brunswick (08901) *(G-6936)*

Interntnal Adhsive Coating Inc 603 893-1894
110 W New Jersey Ave Somers Point (08244) *(G-9937)*

Interntnal Archtctral Irnworks 973 741-0749
181 Coit St Irvington (07111) *(G-4577)*

Interntnal Bscits Cnfctons Inc 856 813-1008
10000 Lincoln Dr E # 102 Marlton (08053) *(G-5934)*

Interntnal Digital Systems Inc 201 983-7700
400 Kelby St Ste 6 Fort Lee (07024) *(G-3564)*

Interntnal Dmnsional Stone LLC 973 729-0359
14 Doty Rd Unit B Haskell (07420) *(G-4197)*

Interntnal Flvors Frgrnces Inc 732 264-4500
800 Rose Ln Union Beach (07735) *(G-11101)*

Interntnal Flvors Frgrnces Inc 732 264-4500
800 Rose Ln Union Beach (07735) *(G-11102)*

Interntnal Flvors Frgrnces Inc 732 329-4600
150 Docks Corner Rd Dayton (08810) *(G-1972)*

Interntnal Flvors Frgrnces Inc 732 264-4500
600 Highway 36 Hazlet (07730) *(G-4262)*

Interntnal Folding Ppr Box Sls 201 941-3100
1039 Hoyt Ave Ridgefield (07657) *(G-9268)*

Interntnal Globl Solutions Inc 201 791-1500
130 Kipp Ave Elmwood Park (07407) *(G-2832)*

Interntnal Ingrdent Sltons Inc 856 778-6623
3001 Irwin Rd Ste A Mount Laurel (08054) *(G-6769)*

Interntnal Pharma Remedies Inc 201 417-3891
244 Dixon Ave Paterson (07501) *(G-8215)*

Interntonal Flavors Fragrances, Hazlet Also called Interntnal Flvors Frgrnces Inc *(G-4262)*

Interntonal Med News Group LLC (HQ) 973 290-8237
7 Century Dr Ste 302 Parsippany (07054) *(G-7964)*

Interntonal Riding Helmets Inc 732 772-0165
15 Timber Ln Marlboro (07746) *(G-5902)*

Interntonal Specialty Pdts Inc (HQ) 859 815-3333
1361 Alps Rd Wayne (07470) *(G-11522)*

Interpace Dagnostics Group Inc (PA) 412 224-6100
300 Interpace Pkwy # 382 Parsippany (07054) *(G-7965)*

A L P H A B E T I C

Interplast Inc 609 386-4990
  100 Connecticut Dr Burlington (08016) *(G-975)*

Interplex Nas Inc 201 367-1300
  232 Pegasus Ave Northvale (07647) *(G-7530)*

Intersil Design Center, Bridgewater *Also called Renesas Electronics Amer Inc (G-875)*

Intersource USA Inc 732 257-5002
  25 Kimberly Rd Ste A East Brunswick (08816) *(G-2152)*

Interstate Architectural & Ir 201 941-0393
  243 Laird Ave Cliffside Park (07010) *(G-1540)*

Interstate Cnncting Components, Lumberton *Also called Heiling Mil-Aero LLC (G-5630)*

Interstate Panel LLC (PA) 609 586-4411
  67 Benson Ave Hamilton (08610) *(G-4108)*

Interstate Welding & Mfg Co 800 676-4666
  1510 Village Ct Beverly (08010) *(G-452)*

Intertape Polymer Corp 201 391-3315
  648 Athlone Ter River Vale (07675) *(G-9366)*

Intertek Caleb Brett, Carteret *Also called Intertek USA Inc (G-1257)*

Intertek Laboratories Inc 908 903-1800
  340 Union St Stirling (07980) *(G-10491)*

Intertek USA Inc 732 969-5200
  1000 Port Carteret Dr C Carteret (07008) *(G-1257)*

Intertest Inc (PA) 908 496-8008
  303 State Route 94 Ste 1 Columbia (07832) *(G-1795)*

Intervet Inc. 908 740-1182
  2000 Galloping Hill Rd Kenilworth (07033) *(G-4947)*

Intest Corporation (PA) 856 505-8800
  804 E Gate Dr Ste 200 Mount Laurel (08054) *(G-6770)*

Intex Millwork Solutions LLC 856 293-4100
  45 Mill St Mays Landing (08330) *(G-5994)*

Intrepid Industries Inc 908 534-5300
  291 Us Highway 22 Ste 3 Lebanon (08833) *(G-5265)*

Intrinsiq Spclty Solutions Inc 973 251-2039
  354 Eisenhower Pkwy # 2025 Livingston (07039) *(G-5516)*

Invaderm Corporation 732 307-7926
  25 Worlds Fair Dr Somerset (08873) *(G-10005)*

Inventek Colloidal Clrs LLC 856 206-0058
  106 Gaither Dr Mount Laurel (08054) *(G-6771)*

Inventiv Health Clinical LLC (HQ) 973 348-1000
  131 Morristown Rd Basking Ridge (07920) *(G-186)*

Inventors Shop LLC 856 303-8787
  800 Industrial Hwy Unit A Cinnaminson (08077) *(G-1466)*

Inverness Med Ntrtionals Group, Freehold *Also called Ivc Industries Inc (G-3671)*

Inversand Company Inc (HQ) 856 881-2345
  226 N Atlantic Ave Clayton (08312) *(G-1526)*

Invessence Inc 201 977-1955
  1 Main St Ste 202 Chatham (07928) *(G-1322)*

Investment Casting Institute 201 573-9770
  1 Paragon Dr Ste 110 Montvale (07645) *(G-6414)*

Invitation Studio 732 740-5558
  12 Hemingway Ct Morganville (07751) *(G-6589)*

Ionni Sign Inc (PA) 973 625-3815
  14 White Meadow Ave Rockaway (07866) *(G-9468)*

Iop Communications, Shrewsbury *Also called Ink On Paper Communications (G-9893)*

IPC Information Systems, Jersey City *Also called IPC Systems Inc (G-4750)*

IPC Systems Inc (PA) 201 253-2000
  3 2nd St Fl Plz10 Jersey City (07311) *(G-4750)*

Ipca Pharmaceuticals Inc (HQ) 908 412-6561
  51 Cragwood Rd Ste 307 South Plainfield (07080) *(G-10280)*

Ipco US LLC 973 720-7000
  21 Campus Rd Totowa (07512) *(G-10833)*

Ipe, Sussex *Also called Industrial Process & Eqp Inc (G-10562)*

Ipec, Pennsauken *Also called International Process Eqp Co (G-8439)*

Iphysicianhub, Monmouth Junction *Also called I Physician Hub (G-6292)*

Ipjukebox Ltd Liability Co 201 286-4535
  211 Wrren St Ste 1022nwa Newark (07103) *(G-7158)*

Ipp/Pressworks, Cherry Hill *Also called Pressworks (G-1411)*

Ips, Eatontown *Also called Innovative Power Solutions LLC (G-2404)*

Ips, Denville *Also called Integrated Packg Systems Inc (G-2040)*

Ipsco Apollo Punch & Die Corp 973 884-0900
  10 Great Meadow Ln East Hanover (07936) *(G-2218)*

Iris ID Systems Inc 609 819-4747
  8 Clarke Dr Ste 1 Cranbury (08512) *(G-1846)*

Iron Asylum Incorporated 856 352-4283
  233 Delsea Dr Sewell (08080) *(G-9847)*

Iron Chef, Passaic *Also called Mirrotek International LLC (G-8090)*

Iron Mountain Plastics Inc 201 445-0063
  112 Greenwood Ave Midland Park (07432) *(G-6178)*

Iron4u Inc 609 514-5163
  5 Independence Way # 300 Princeton (08540) *(G-8964)*

Ironbound Express Inc 973 491-5151
  65 Jabez St Newark (07105) *(G-7159)*

Ironbound Intermodal Inds Inc 973 491-5151
  65 Jabez St Newark (07105) *(G-7160)*

Ironbound Metal 973 242-5704
  238 Emmet St Newark (07114) *(G-7161)*

Ironbound Welding Inc 973 589-3128
  156 Walnut St Newark (07105) *(G-7162)*

ISC, Edison *Also called Importers Service Corp (G-2533)*

Isco 856 672-9182
  1 Commerce Dr Bldg 3 Barrington (08007) *(G-174)*

Isdin Corp 862 242-8129
  36 Cattano Ave Morristown (07960) *(G-6675)*

Island Beach Distillery 609 242-5054
  713 Old Shore Rd Forked River (08731) *(G-3541)*

Isocolor Inc 201 935-4494
  631 Central Ave Carlstadt (07072) *(G-1169)*

Isolantite Manufacturing Co 908 647-3333
  337 Warren Ave Stirling (07980) *(G-10492)*

Isomedix Operations Inc 908 757-3727
  3459 S Clinton Ave South Plainfield (07080) *(G-10281)*

Isometric Micro Finish Coating 732 306-6339
  477 Plainfield Rd Edison (08820) *(G-2535)*

Isowave Division, Dover *Also called Crystal Deltronic Industries (G-2079)*

Isowave Division, Dover *Also called Crystal Deltronic Industries (G-2080)*

Isp Chemco LLC (PA) 973 628-4000
  1361 Alps Rd Wayne (07470) *(G-11523)*

Isp Chemicals LLC 973 635-1551
  116 Summit Ave Chatham (07928) *(G-1323)*

Isp Global Technologies Inc (HQ) 973 628-4000
  1361 Alps Rd Wayne (07470) *(G-11524)*

Isp Global Technologies LLC (HQ) 973 628-4000
  1361 Alps Rd Wayne (07470) *(G-11525)*

Isp Sutton Laboratories, Chatham *Also called Isp Chemicals LLC (G-1323)*

Istec Corporation 973 383-9888
  5 Park Lake Rd Ste 6 Sparta (07871) *(G-10393)*

Istec Flow Measurement & Ctrl, Sparta *Also called Istec Corporation (G-10393)*

It Cosmetics, Jersey City *Also called LOreal USA Products Inc (G-4761)*

It Surplus Liquidators 732 308-1935
  179 South St Ste 1 Freehold (07728) *(G-3670)*

It Talent, Somerset *Also called Tech Brains Solutions Inc (G-10083)*

It Worqs LLC 732 494-0009
  16 Pearl St Ste 102 Metuchen (07840) *(G-6063)*

Italian Tile Decor, Elmwood Park *Also called Industrie Bitossi Inc (G-2831)*

Italian Treasures 856 770-9188
  1020 Voorhees Town Ctr Voorhees (08043) *(G-11290)*

Itec Consultants LLC 732 784-8322
  38 Hyer Ct Matawan (07747) *(G-5978)*

Itg Brands LLC 973 386-9087
  50 Williams Pkwy Ste B East Hanover (07936) *(G-2219)*

Itl, Emerson *Also called International Tech Lasers (G-2864)*

ITM, Hillside *Also called International Tool & Mch LLC (G-4404)*

Its A Wig, Moonachie *Also called Sli Production Corp (G-6489)*

Its The Pitts Inc 609 645-7319
  619 Church St Pleasantville (08232) *(G-8813)*

ITT Corporation 973 284-0123
  100 Kingsland Rd Clifton (07014) *(G-1644)*

ITT Defense Electronics & Svcs, Clifton *Also called ITT Corporation (G-1644)*

Iultrasonic, Maplewood *Also called Tovatech LLC (G-5885)*

Ivax Pharmaceuticals LLC 201 767-1700
  400 Chestnut Ridge Rd Woodcliff Lake (07677) *(G-12058)*

Ivc Industries Inc 732 308-3000
  500 Halls Mill Rd Freehold (07728) *(G-3671)*

Ivey Katrina Owner 973 951-8328
  95 Montrose St Newark (07106) *(G-7163)*

Ivoclar Vivadent Mfg Inc 732 563-4755
  500 Memorial Dr Somerset (08873) *(G-10006)*

Ivy Capital Partners LLC 201 573-8400
  102 Chestnut Ridge Rd # 1 Montvale (07645) *(G-6415)*

Ivy Pharama Inc 201 221-4179
  140 E Ridgewood Ave # 415 Paramus (07652) *(G-7808)*

Ivy Sports Medicine LLC 201 573-5423
  102 Chestnut Ridge Rd # 1 Montvale (07645) *(G-6416)*

Ivy-Dry Inc 973 575-1992
  299b Fairfield Ave Fairfield (07004) *(G-3242)*

IW Tremont Co Inc 973 427-3800
  18 Utter Ave Hawthorne (07506) *(G-4227)*

Iwc 732 968-8122
  12 Red Bud Ln Green Brook (08812) *(G-3862)*

Iweddingband.com, New Brunswick *Also called Netfruits Inc (G-6951)*

Iweiss, Fairview *Also called Tankleff Inc (G-3369)*

Iws License Corp 732 872-0014
  29 4th Ave Atlantic Highlands (07716) *(G-107)*

Iza and Vanessa Music, Englewood *Also called Clyde Otis Music Group (G-2893)*

Izunami, Palisades Park *Also called Esd Professional Inc (G-7773)*

Izzo Enterprises Inc 908 845-8200
  2006 Route 22 Scotch Plains (07076) *(G-9735)*

J & E Metal Fabricators Inc 732 548-9650
  1 Coan Pl Metuchen (08840) *(G-6064)*

J & G Diversified 732 543-2537
  235 Jersey Ave Ste 5 New Brunswick (08901) *(G-6937)*

J & G Graphics Inc 732 223-6660
  221 Parker Ave Manasquan (08736) *(G-5832)*

J & J Marine Inc 856 228-4744
  1596 Hurffville Rd Sewell (08080) *(G-9848)*

J & J Snack Foods Corp (PA) 856 665-9533
  6000 Central Hwy Pennsauken (08109) *(G-8440)*

J & J Snack Foods Corp 856 467-9552
300 Eagle Ct Bridgeport (08014) *(G-740)*

J & J Snack Foods Corp 856 933-3597
361 Benigno Blvd Ste A Bellmawr (08031) *(G-336)*

J & J Snack Foods Corp PA (HQ) 856 665-9533
6000 Central Hwy Pennsauken (08109) *(G-8441)*

J & J Tool & Die, Sewell *Also called J & J Marine Inc (G-9848)*

J & L Controls Inc 732 460-0380
15 Leland Ter Lincroft (07738) *(G-5312)*

J & M Air Inc 908 707-4040
189 S Bridge St Somerville (08876) *(G-10118)*

J & M Cstm Shtmtl Ltd Lblty Co 856 627-6252
1331 New Broklyn Erial Rd Sicklerville (08081) *(G-9911)*

J & M Manufacturing Inc 908 638-4298
54 Main St High Bridge (08829) *(G-4283)*

J & R Custom Woodworking Inc 973 625-4114
449 E Main St Denville (07834) *(G-2041)*

J & R Foods Inc 732 229-4020
309 Morris Ave Ste 5 Long Branch (07740) *(G-5600)*

J & R Pallets, Camden *Also called F & R Pallets Inc (G-1062)*

J & R Rebuilders Inc 856 627-1414
330 Washington Ave Laurel Springs (08021) *(G-5207)*

J & S Enterprises LLC 973 696-9199
175 Beaverbrook Rd Lincoln Park (07035) *(G-5300)*

J & S Finishing Inc 201 854-0338
443 62nd St Fl 1 West New York (07093) *(G-11742)*

J & S Housewares, Newark *Also called Global Weavers Corp (G-7135)*

J & S Precision Products Co 609 654-0900
16 Medford Evesboro Rd Medford (08055) *(G-6025)*

J & S Tool 973 383-5059
56 Paterson Ave Ste 4 Newton (07860) *(G-7347)*

J & T Embroidery Inc 201 867-4897
646 36th St Union City (07087) *(G-11114)*

J & W Servo Systems Company 973 335-1007
53 Green Pond Rd Ste 2 Rockaway (07866) *(G-9469)*

J A M I Enterprise Inc 732 714-6811
1129 Industrial Pkwy A Brick (08724) *(G-721)*

J A Machine & Tool Co Inc 201 767-1308
84 Herbert Ave Closter (07624) *(G-1759)*

J A Visual Group, Hackensack *Also called Njiw Limited Liability Company (G-3954)*

J A W Products Inc 856 829-3210
835 Industrial Hwy # 125 Cinnaminson (08077) *(G-1467)*

J and J Contractors 856 765-7521
604 5th St N Millville (08332) *(G-6256)*

J and M Precision Inc 856 661-9595
8103 River Rd Pennsauken (08110) *(G-8442)*

J and S Sporting Apparel LLC 732 787-5500
224 Main St Keansburg (07734) *(G-4838)*

J B & Sons Concrete Products (PA) 856 767-4140
358 New Brooklyn Rd Berlin (08009) *(G-423)*

J B Offset Printing Corp 201 264-4400
55 Walnut St Ste 209 Norwood (07648) *(G-7566)*

J Blanco Associates Inc 973 427-0619
280 9th Ave 1 Hawthorne (07506) *(G-4228)*

J C Contracting Inc 973 748-5600
681 Mill St Rahway (07065) *(G-9105)*

J C Hansen, Jersey City *Also called Joseph C Hansen Company Inc (G-4752)*

J C Orthopedic Inc (PA) 732 458-7900
1680 Route 88 Brick (08724) *(G-722)*

J C Penney Optical, Blackwood *Also called US Vision Inc (G-482)*

J C Penney Optical, Glendora *Also called Usv Optical Inc (G-3839)*

J C W Inc 732 560-8061
795 E Main St Bridgewater (08807) *(G-838)*

J D Crew Inc 856 665-3676
1426 Union Ave Pennsauken (08110) *(G-8443)*

J D M Associates Inc 973 773-8699
127 Kipp Ave Lodi (07644) *(G-5566)*

J D Machine Parts Inc 856 691-8430
158 W Weymouth Rd Vineland (08360) *(G-11236)*

J E B Urban Renewal Associates, Wayne *Also called Anodizing Corporation (G-11470)*

J E I, Brick *Also called J A M I Enterprise Inc (G-721)*

J F C Machine Works LLC 732 203-2077
2182 State Route 35 Holmdel (07733) *(G-4503)*

J F Gillespie Inc 856 692-2233
2547 Brunetta Dr Vineland (08360) *(G-11237)*

J F I Printing 973 759-3444
357 Cortlandt St Belleville (07109) *(G-297)*

J G Carpenter Contractor 732 271-8991
300 Lincoln Blvd Middlesex (08846) *(G-6122)*

J G Machine Works Inc 732 203-2077
2147 State Route 27 Ste D Edison (08817) *(G-2536)*

J G Papailias, Northvale *Also called John G Papailias Co Inc (G-7532)*

J G Schmidt Co Inc 732 563-9500
354 U S Rt 22 Green Brook (08812) *(G-3863)*

J G Schmidt Iron Works, Passaic *Also called J G Schmidt Steel (G-8075)*

J G Schmidt Steel 973 473-4822
211 Central Ave Passaic (07055) *(G-8075)*

J Gennaro Trucking 973 773-0805
13 Garfield Pl Garfield (07026) *(G-3749)*

J H M Communications Inc 908 859-6668
1593 Springtown Rd Phillipsburg (08865) *(G-8556)*

J Harris Company 917 731-5080
57 Barnsdale Rd Madison (07940) *(G-5696)*

J Hebrank Inc 973 983-0001
20 Pine St Rockaway (07866) *(G-9470)*

J J L & W Inc 856 854-3100
424 N White Horse Pike Magnolia (08049) *(G-5708)*

J J Orly Inc 908 276-9212
67 Walnut Ave Ste 307 Clark (07066) *(G-1498)*

J Josephson Inc (HQ) 201 440-7000
35 Horizon Blvd South Hackensack (07606) *(G-10163)*

J Josephson Inc 201 440-7000
35 Empire Blvd South Hackensack (07606) *(G-10164)*

J Josephson Inc 201 426-2646
14 Central Blvd South Hackensack (07606) *(G-10165)*

J K A Specialties, Southampton *Also called JKA Specialties Mfr Inc (G-10366)*

J K Design Inc 908 428-4700
465 Amwell Rd Hillsborough (08844) *(G-4334)*

J K Office Machine Inc 908 273-8811
33 Debbie Pl Berkeley Heights (07922) *(G-402)*

J K P Donuts Inc 856 234-9844
807 Route 73 Mount Laurel (08054) *(G-6772)*

J K Print Management, Hillsborough *Also called J K Design Inc (G-4334)*

J Kaufman Iron Works Inc 973 925-9972
217 Godwin Ave Paterson (07501) *(G-8216)*

J L Erectors Inc 856 232-9400
835 Camden Ave Blackwood (08012) *(G-470)*

J M C Tool & Mfg Co 908 241-8950
845 Fairfield Ave Kenilworth (07033) *(G-4948)*

J M M R Inc 201 612-5104
25-9 Broadway Fair Lawn (07410) *(G-3107)*

J M S Melgar Transport LLC 908 834-1722
15 Pearl St North Plainfield (07060) *(G-7506)*

J Media LLC (PA) 201 600-4573
55 Walnut St Ste 105a Norwood (07648) *(G-7567)*

J Michaels Jewelers Inc 908 771-9800
370 Springfield Ave Berkeley Heights (07922) *(G-403)*

J Nelson Press Inc 732 747-0330
362 Us Highway 9 Unit 120 Englishtown (07726) *(G-3005)*

J OBrien Co Inc 973 379-8844
40 Commerce St Springfield (07081) *(G-10447)*

J P Egan Industries Inc 973 642-1500
676 S 14th St Newark (07103) *(G-7164)*

J P Rotella Co Inc 973 942-2559
20 E Barbour St Haledon (07508) *(G-4083)*

J Paul Allen Inc 973 702-1174
127 Sally Harden Rd Sussex (07461) *(G-10563)*

J R E Inc 973 808-0055
22 Fairfield Pl West Caldwell (07006) *(G-11655)*

J R Engineering & Machine 908 810-6300
663 Ramsey Ave Hillside (07205) *(G-4405)*

J R M Products Inc 732 203-0200
701 Locust St Union Beach (07735) *(G-11103)*

J R S Mch & Tl Sls Corp Ameri, South Plainfield *Also called J R S Tool & Metal Finishing (G-10282)*

J R S Tool & Metal Finishing 908 753-2050
107 Borman Rd South Plainfield (07080) *(G-10282)*

J S Manufacturing, Edison *Also called Chacko John (G-2475)*

J S Paluch Co Inc 732 516-1900
510 Thornall St Ste 140 Edison (08837) *(G-2537)*

J S Paluch Co Inc 732 238-2412
6 Alvin Ct Ste 1 East Brunswick (08816) *(G-2153)*

J S R, Hillside *Also called Jomel Seams Reasonable LLC (G-4407)*

J S W, Edison *Also called Japan Steel Works America Inc (G-2538)*

J Spinelli & Sons Excavating, Elmer *Also called J Spinelli & Sons Inc (G-2799)*

J Spinelli & Sons Inc 856 691-3133
615 Gershal Ave Elmer (08318) *(G-2799)*

J T Baker Chemical Co, Phillipsburg *Also called Avantor Performance Mtls LLC (G-8542)*

J T Murdoch Shoes 973 748-6484
623 Bloomfield Ave Bloomfield (07003) *(G-503)*

J V Q Inc 973 523-8806
245 E 17th St Paterson (07524) *(G-8217)*

J Vitale Sign Co Inc 732 388-8401
2204 Elizabeth Ave Ste 1 Rahway (07065) *(G-9106)*

J&E Business Services LLC 973 984-8444
1 Trenton Ave Clifton (07011) *(G-1645)*

J&K Ingredients, Paterson *Also called Jk Ingredients Inc (G-8224)*

J&S Houseware Corp 973 824-5500
9 Dey St Ste 13 Newark (07103) *(G-7165)*

J-M Eagle, Livingston *Also called J-M Manufacturing Company Inc (G-5517)*

J-M Manufacturing Company Inc 800 621-4404
9 Peach Tree Hill Rd Livingston (07039) *(G-5517)*

J-Mac Plastics Inc (PA) 908 709-1111
40 Lafayette Pl Kenilworth (07033) *(G-4949)*

J-Tech Creations Inc 201 944-2968
1 Bridge Plz N Ste 275 Fort Lee (07024) *(G-3565)*

J.E. Holland-Moritz Co., Inc., Lambertville *Also called Julius E Holland-Moritz Co Inc* ***(G-5191)***
JA Cissel Manufacturing Co..........732 901-0300
1995 Rutgers Blvd Lakewood (08701) ***(G-5113)***
JA Heilferty LLC..........201 836-5060
133 Cedar Ln Teaneck (07666) ***(G-10635)***
Ja-Bar Silicone Corp..........973 786-5000
252 Brighton Rd Andover (07821) ***(G-47)***
Jace Systems, Cinnaminson *Also called Tgz Acquisition Company LLC* ***(G-1489)***
Jachts - Columbia Can LLC..........973 925-8020
90 6th Ave Paterson (07524) ***(G-8218)***
Jackie Evans Fashions, Passaic *Also called Jackie Evans Inc* ***(G-8076)***
Jackie Evans Inc..........973 471-6991
18 3rd St 26 Passaic (07055) ***(G-8076)***
Jaclo Industries, Cranford *Also called Durst Corporation Inc* ***(G-1907)***
Jaclyn Holdings Parent LLC (PA)..........201 909-6000
197 W Spring Valley Ave Maywood (07607) ***(G-6007)***
Jaclyn LLC..........201 909-6000
197 W Spring Valley Ave # 101 Maywood (07607) ***(G-6008)***
Jacmel Jewelry Inc..........201 223-0435
401 Penhorn Ave Ste 1 Secaucus (07094) ***(G-9782)***
Jacquar Fuel..........732 441-0700
107 Hawkins Rd Manalapan (07726) ***(G-5815)***
Jacquard Fabrics Inc..........732 905-4545
1965 Swarthmore Ave Lakewood (08701) ***(G-5114)***
Jacquard Fabrics Co, Lakewood *Also called Jacquard Fabrics Inc* ***(G-5114)***
Jacqueline Embroidery Co..........732 278-8121
445 Thompson St Apt G Hackensack (07601) ***(G-3933)***
Jacquet Jonpaul..........856 825-4259
25 E Main St Ste D Millville (08332) ***(G-6257)***
Jad Bagels LLC..........201 567-4500
52 E Palisade Ave Englewood (07631) ***(G-2915)***
Jade Apparel Group, Newark *Also called Sinai Manufacturing Corp* ***(G-7274)***
Jade Eastern Trading Inc (PA)..........201 440-8500
13 Division St Ste A Moonachie (07074) ***(G-6473)***
Jaeger Thomas & Melissa DDS..........908 735-2722
1128 State Rd 31 Lebanon (08833) ***(G-5266)***
Jag Footwear ACC & Ret Corp..........609 845-1700
32 Springside Rd Westampton (08060) ***(G-11786)***
Jai Ganesh Fuel LLC..........201 246-8995
815 Kearny Ave Kearny (07032) ***(G-4871)***
Jak Diversified II Inc..........973 439-1182
241 Clinton Rd West Caldwell (07006) ***(G-11656)***
Jaktool LLC..........609 664-2451
259 Prospect Plains Rd Cranbury (08512) ***(G-1847)***
Jamco Machine Products..........856 461-2664
209 Adams St Ste 1 Riverside (08075) ***(G-9397)***
James A Stanlick Jr..........973 366-7316
845 Berkshire Valley Rd Wharton (07885) ***(G-11860)***
James Candy Company (PA)..........609 344-1519
1519 Boardwalk Atlantic City (08401) ***(G-95)***
James Colucci Enterprises LLC..........877 403-4900
150 Jfk Pkwy Short Hills (07078) ***(G-9870)***
James D Morrissey Inc..........609 859-2860
223 Sooy Place Rd Vincentown (08088) ***(G-11182)***
James Kinkade..........856 451-1177
9 Oak Dr Bridgeton (08302) ***(G-760)***
James R Macauley Inc..........856 767-3474
1 Industrial Dr Waterford Works (08089) ***(G-11462)***
James Zylstra Enterprises Inc..........973 383-6768
52 State Route 15 Lafayette (07848) ***(G-5028)***
Jamm Litho, Long Branch *Also called Accucolor LLC* ***(G-5593)***
Jamol Laboratories Inc..........201 262-6363
13 Ackerman Ave Emerson (07630) ***(G-2865)***
Jan Packaging Inc..........973 361-7200
100 Harrison St Dover (07801) ***(G-2091)***
Janas LLC..........732 536-6719
3 Oxford Ct Morganville (07751) ***(G-6590)***
Jane Carter Solution, Newark *Also called Left-Handed Libra LLC* ***(G-7178)***
Janet Shops Inc..........973 748-4992
550 Bloomfield Ave Bloomfield (07003) ***(G-504)***
Janico Inc..........732 370-2223
88 Industrial Ct Freehold (07728) ***(G-3672)***
Janke & Company Inc..........973 334-4477
283 Myrtle Ave Boonton (07005) ***(G-558)***
Jannetti Publications..........856 256-2300
200 E Holly Ave Sewell (08080) ***(G-9849)***
Janssen Global Services LLC..........908 704-4000
700 Route 202 Raritan (08869) ***(G-9211)***
Janssen Pharmaceuticals Inc (HQ)..........609 730-2000
1125 Trnton Harbourton Rd Titusville (08560) ***(G-10735)***
Janssen Pharmaceuticals Inc..........908 218-6908
1 Campus Dr Somerset (08873) ***(G-10007)***
Janssen Pharmaceuticals Inc..........908 218-7701
1 Cottontail Ln Somerset (08873) ***(G-10008)***
Janssen Pharmaceuticals Inc..........908 735-4844
Km 0 Hm 5 Rr 362 Pittstown (08867) ***(G-8753)***
Janssen Research & Dev LLC (HQ)..........908 704-4000
920 Us Highway 202 Raritan (08869) ***(G-9212)***
Japan Steel Works America Inc (HQ)..........212 490-2630
379 Thornall St Ste 5 Edison (08837) ***(G-2538)***
Japanese-American Society NJ, Fort Lee *Also called Aqualink LLC* ***(G-3547)***
Jarahian Millwork Inc..........732 240-5151
870 Route 530 Ste 4 Whiting (08759) ***(G-11939)***
Jarchem Industries Inc..........973 344-0600
414 Wilson Ave Newark (07105) ***(G-7166)***
Jarco U S Casting Corp..........201 271-0003
4407 Park Ave Union City (07087) ***(G-11115)***
Jarden LLC (HQ)..........201 610-6600
221 River St Hoboken (07030) ***(G-4458)***
Jarit, Plainsboro *Also called Integra Lifesciences Corp* ***(G-8793)***
Jarvis Electric Motors Inc..........856 662-7710
6001 S Crescent Blvd Pennsauken (08110) ***(G-8444)***
Jasco Printing, Tabernacle *Also called Jasco Specialties and Forms* ***(G-10619)***
Jasco Specialties and Forms..........856 627-5511
86 Patty Bowker Rd Tabernacle (08088) ***(G-10619)***
Jason Equipment Corp..........973 983-7212
164 Franklin Ave Rockaway (07866) ***(G-9471)***
Jason Industrial Inc (HQ)..........973 227-4904
340 Kaplan Dr Fairfield (07004) ***(G-3243)***
Jason Metal Products Corp..........732 396-1132
1072 Randolph Ave Rahway (07065) ***(G-9107)***
Jason Mills LLC..........732 651-7200
440 S Main St Ste 7 Milltown (08850) ***(G-6217)***
Jasper Fashion Ltd Lblty Co..........917 561-4533
336 Murray St Elizabeth (07202) ***(G-2752)***
Jassmine Corp..........848 565-0515
489 Getty Ave Clifton (07011) ***(G-1646)***
Jav Latin America Express..........201 868-5004
6321 Bergenline Ave West New York (07093) ***(G-11743)***
Jay Bee Oil & Gas Company, Clark *Also called Jay-Bee Oil & Gas Inc* ***(G-1499)***
Jay Franco & Sons Inc..........732 721-0022
115 Kennedy Dr Sayreville (08872) ***(G-9712)***
Jay Gerish Company..........973 403-0655
2 York Ave West Caldwell (07006) ***(G-11657)***
Jay Jariwala..........908 806-8266
1019 Us Highway 202 Ringoes (08551) ***(G-9338)***
Jay-Bee Lamp & Shade Co Inc..........201 265-0762
540 Salem St Paramus (07652) ***(G-7809)***
Jay-Bee Oil & Gas Inc (PA)..........908 686-1493
60 Walnut Ave Ste 190 Clark (07066) ***(G-1499)***
Jaygo Incorporated..........908 688-3600
7 Emery Ave Randolph (07869) ***(G-9187)***
Jaymar Precision Inc..........856 365-8779
1169 Cooper St Camden (08102) ***(G-1071)***
Jaynes Signwork..........856 362-0503
143 Pcks Crnr Cohansey Rd Bridgeton (08302) ***(G-761)***
JB Electronics..........609 497-2952
101 Wall St Princeton (08540) ***(G-8965)***
JBAT Inc..........856 667-7307
28 Coles Ave Cherry Hill (08002) ***(G-1378)***
Jbq Printing & Marketing, Hackettstown *Also called B & H Printers Inc* ***(G-4000)***
JC Macelroy Co Inc (PA)..........732 572-7100
91 Ethel Rd W Piscataway (08854) ***(G-8681)***
JC Pallets Inc..........973 345-1102
354 Marshall St Paterson (07503) ***(G-8219)***
JC Printing & Advertising Inc..........973 881-8612
168 8th Ave Paterson (07514) ***(G-8220)***
Jcc Military Supply LLC..........973 341-1314
125 5th Ave Paterson (07524) ***(G-8221)***
Jcdecaux Mallscape LLC..........201 288-2024
440 State Rt 17 Ste 9 Hasbrouck Heights (07604) ***(G-4185)***
Jch Partners & Co LLC..........732 664-6440
8 Man O War Ln Howell (07731) ***(G-4542)***
Jct Design Enterprises Inc..........212 629-7412
1701 Summit Ave Union City (07087) ***(G-11116)***
JDM Engineering Inc..........732 780-0770
60 Jerseyville Ave Freehold (07728) ***(G-3673)***
JDV Equipment Corp..........973 366-6556
1 Princeton Ave Ste 2 Dover (07801) ***(G-2092)***
Jdv Products Inc..........201 794-6467
22-01 Raphael St Fair Lawn (07410) ***(G-3108)***
JE Berkowitz LP..........856 456-7800
1 Gateway Blvd Pedricktown (08067) ***(G-8349)***
Je Sozio, Piscataway *Also called Sozio Inc* ***(G-8715)***
Je TAime Shoes..........201 845-7463
Garden State Plz Mall Paramus (07652) ***(G-7810)***
Jean's Canvas Products, Belford *Also called Kerry Wilkens Inc* ***(G-283)***
Jed Display LLC..........201 340-2329
254-262 Wright St Newark (07114) ***(G-7167)***
Jefferson Printing Serivce..........973 491-0019
184 Jefferson St Newark (07105) ***(G-7168)***
Jefferson Prosthetic Orthotic..........973 762-0780
120 Prospect St Ste B South Orange (07079) ***(G-10197)***
Jeffrey Klein Ribbon Designs, Paterson *Also called Klein Ribbon Corp* ***(G-8230)***
Jeiven Phrm Consulting Inc..........908 233-4508
6 Jacobs Ln Scotch Plains (07076) ***(G-9736)***

Jem Printing Inc..908 782-9986
  35 Main St Flemington (08822) *(G-3450)*

Jema-American Inc...732 968-5333
  824 South Ave Middlesex (08846) *(G-6123)*

Jems Pharma LLC..609 386-0141
  301 High St Burlington (08016) *(G-976)*

Jen Electric Inc...973 467-4901
  631 Morris Ave Springfield (07081) *(G-10448)*

Jencks Signs Corp..908 542-1400
  16 Geiger Ln Warren (07059) *(G-11419)*

Jenisse Leisure Products Inc..............................973 331-1177
  5 Van Duyne Ct Towaco (07082) *(G-10873)*

Jenkins Brush Comp, Cedar Grove *Also called Mw Jenkins Sons Incorporated (G-1284)*

Jenny Jump Farm, Hope *Also called Christopher F Maier (G-4524)*

Jentec Inc...201 784-1031
  20 Charles St Ste C Northvale (07647) *(G-7531)*

Jerhel Plastics Inc...201 436-6662
  63 Hook Rd Bayonne (07002) *(G-225)*

Jerome Group Inc...856 234-8600
  1414 Metropolitan Ave West Deptford (08066) *(G-11707)*

Jerome Industries Corp (HQ)...............................908 353-5700
  36 Newburgh Rd Hackettstown (07840) *(G-4013)*

Jerome Medical, West Deptford *Also called Jerome Group Inc (G-11707)*

Jersey Boring & Drlg Co Inc...............................973 242-3800
  36 Pier Ln W Fairfield (07004) *(G-3244)*

Jersey Bound Latino LLC...................................908 591-2830
  841 Hueston St Union (07083) *(G-11066)*

Jersey Bound Latino Magazine, Union *Also called Jersey Bound Latino LLC (G-11066)*

Jersey Cape Yachts Inc.....................................609 965-8650
  2143 River Rd Egg Harbor City (08215) *(G-2661)*

Jersey Cast Stone Ltd Lblty Co............................856 333-6900
  6845 Westfield Ave Pennsauken (08110) *(G-8445)*

Jersey Cider Works LLC (PA)..............................917 604-0067
  42 Erwin Park Rd Montclair (07042) *(G-6373)*

Jersey Cider Works LLC....................................908 940-4115
  360 County Road 579 Asbury (08802) *(G-65)*

Jersey Concrete, Toms River *Also called Clayton Block Company Inc (G-10753)*

Jersey Cover Corp...732 286-6300
  1746 Route 9 Toms River (08755) *(G-10771)*

Jersey Jack Pinball Inc.....................................732 364-9900
  1645 Oak St Lakewood (08701) *(G-5115)*

Jersey Job Guide Inc..732 263-9675
  422 Morris Ave Ste 5 Long Branch (07740) *(G-5601)*

Jersey Journal, Secaucus *Also called Evening Journal Association (G-9765)*

Jersey Lift Truck, Paterson *Also called Rentalift Inc (G-8286)*

Jersey Metal Works LLC.....................................732 565-1313
  1022 Hamilton St Untid Somerset (08873) *(G-10009)*

Jersey Ordnance Inc...609 267-2112
  600 Highland Dr Ste 602 Westampton (08060) *(G-11787)*

Jersey Plastic Molders Inc.................................973 926-1800
  149 Shaw Ave Irvington (07111) *(G-4578)*

Jersey Precast, Trenton *Also called Jpc Merger Sub LLC (G-10948)*

Jersey Precast Corporation Inc............................609 689-3700
  853 Nottingham Way Trenton (08638) *(G-10946)*

Jersey Printing Associates Inc.............................732 872-9654
  153 1st Ave Ste 1 Atlantic Highlands (07716) *(G-108)*

Jersey Sheet Metal & Machine.............................973 366-8628
  90 E Dickerson St Dover (07801) *(G-2093)*

Jersey Shore Cosmetics LLC...............................908 500-9954
  23 Pleasant View Way Flemington (08822) *(G-3451)*

Jersey Shore News Mgazines Inc (PA)....................609 494-5900
  1816 Long Beach Blvd Surf City (08008) *(G-10555)*

Jersey Shore Publications..................................732 892-1276
  749 Bay Ave Brick (08724) *(G-723)*

Jersey Shore Vacation Magazine, Brick *Also called Jersey Shore Publications (G-723)*

Jersey Specialty Co Inc.....................................413 525-2292
  7861 Airport Hwy Pennsauken (08109) *(G-8446)*

Jersey Steel Door Inc.......................................973 482-4020
  95 N 11th St Newark (07107) *(G-7169)*

Jersey Strand & Cable Inc..................................908 213-9350
  259 Center St Ste 3 Phillipsburg (08865) *(G-8557)*

Jersey Tank Fabricators Inc................................609 758-7670
  1271 New Market Ave Ste D South Plainfield (07080) *(G-10283)*

Jersey Tempered Glass Inc.................................856 273-8700
  2035 Briggs Rd Mount Laurel (08054) *(G-6773)*

Jesco Iron Crafts Inc..201 488-4545
  201 W Fort Lee Rd Bogota (07603) *(G-533)*

Jescraft, Bogota *Also called Jesco Iron Crafts Inc (G-533)*

Jese Apparel LLC (PA)......................................732 969-3200
  8 Nicholas Ct B Dayton (08810) *(G-1973)*

Jesel Inc...732 901-1800
  1985 Cedarbridge Ave # 2 Lakewood (08701) *(G-5116)*

Jet Aviation Aircraft Maint, Teterboro *Also called Jet Aviation St Louis Inc (G-10681)*

Jet Aviation St Louis Inc...................................201 462-4026
  113 Chrles A Lindbergh Dr Teterboro (07608) *(G-10681)*

Jet Precision Metal Inc......................................973 423-4350
  7 Schoon Ave Hawthorne (07506) *(G-4229)*

Jet Pulverizer Co Inc..856 235-5554
  1255 N Church St Moorestown (08057) *(G-6531)*

Jetstream of Houston LLP...................................732 448-7830
  17 Jules Ln New Brunswick (08901) *(G-6938)*

Jettron Products Inc...973 887-0571
  56 State Route 10 East Hanover (07936) *(G-2220)*

Jetty Life LLC..800 900-6435
  509 N Main St 3 Manahawkin (08050) *(G-5793)*

Jetyd Corporation...201 512-9500
  218 Island Rd Mahwah (07430) *(G-5750)*

Jevek Solutions, Cranbury *Also called Jaktool LLC (G-1847)*

Jewish Media Group, River Edge *Also called Jewish Standard Inc (G-9362)*

Jewish Standard Inc...201 837-8818
  70 Grand Ave Ste 104 River Edge (07661) *(G-9362)*

Jewish Times of South Jersey..............................609 646-2063
  21 W Delilah Rd Pleasantville (08232) *(G-8814)*

Jewm Inc..973 942-1555
  514 Totowa Ave Paterson (07522) *(G-8222)*

Jfc Technologies, Bound Brook *Also called Cyalume Specialty Products Inc (G-601)*

JFK Supplies Inc...732 985-7800
  85 Lexington Ave Edison (08817) *(G-2539)*

JG Tire, Middlesex *Also called J G Carpenter Contractor (G-6122)*

Jgs, Green Brook *Also called J G Schmidt Co Inc (G-3863)*

JHM Signs, Phillipsburg *Also called J H M Communications Inc (G-8556)*

Jhp Group Holdings Inc.....................................973 658-3569
  1 Upper Pond Rd Ste 4 Parsippany (07054) *(G-7966)*

Jiaherb Inc (HQ)...973 439-6869
  1 Chapin Rd Ste 1 # 1 Pine Brook (07058) *(G-8608)*

Jiangsu Hengrui Medicine Co..............................609 395-8625
  506 Carnegie Ctr Princeton (08540) *(G-8966)*

Jid Transportation LLC......................................201 362-0841
  158 61st St Apt 2 West New York (07093) *(G-11744)*

Jig Grinding Specialists, Pennsauken *Also called J and M Precision Inc (G-8442)*

Jigsaw Publishing LLC......................................973 838-4838
  8 Hemlock Ct Butler (07405) *(G-1006)*

Jimcam Publishing Inc.......................................201 843-5700
  19 W Pleasant Ave Fl 1 Maywood (07607) *(G-6009)*

Jimenez Pallets LLC...862 267-3900
  244 Dukes St Kearny (07032) *(G-4872)*

Jimmys Cookies LLC..973 779-8500
  125 Entin Rd Clifton (07014) *(G-1647)*

Jing, Carlstadt *Also called Jinpan International USA Ltd (G-1170)*

Jinpan International USA Ltd...............................201 460-8778
  390 Veterans Blvd Carlstadt (07072) *(G-1170)*

JIT Manufacturing Inc.......................................973 247-7300
  50 Peel St Paterson (07524) *(G-8223)*

Jjj Stretchers Inc..908 290-3505
  1628 E Elizabeth Ave Linden (07036) *(G-5364)*

Jjs Own Ltd Liability Company.............................551 486-8510
  71 Pickens St Little Ferry (07643) *(G-5490)*

Jk Ingredients Inc...973 340-8700
  160 E 5th St Paterson (07524) *(G-8224)*

JKA Specialties Mfr Inc.....................................609 859-2090
  157 Eayrestown Rd Southampton (08088) *(G-10366)*

Jl Packaging Group Corp (PA).............................609 610-0286
  2 Birch St Pennington (08534) *(G-8368)*

Jlb Hauling Ltd Liability Co................................856 514-2771
  90 Dolbow Ave Pennsville (08070) *(G-8500)*

Jli Marketing & Printing Corp..............................732 828-8877
  6 Corporate Dr Ste 1 Cranbury (08512) *(G-1848)*

JM Ahle Co Inc..732 388-5507
  625 Leesville Ave Rahway (07065) *(G-9108)*

JM Huber Corporation (PA)................................732 603-3630
  499 Thornall St Ste 8 Edison (08837) *(G-2540)*

Jmc Design & Graphics Inc.................................973 276-9033
  144 Fairfield Rd Fairfield (07004) *(G-3245)*

Jmd Printing, Newton *Also called Skylands Press (G-7358)*

Jmee Financial Division, Washington *Also called Arctic Foods Inc (G-11438)*

JMJ Profile Inc..856 767-3930
  154 Cooper Rd Ste 1303 West Berlin (08091) *(G-11600)*

Jmk Tool Die and Mfg Co Inc (PA).......................201 845-4710
  19 W Passaic St Rochelle Park (07662) *(G-9425)*

Jmm Studios..609 861-3094
  1524 Dehirsch Ave Woodbine (08270) *(G-12010)*

Jmp Press Inc..201 444-0236
  19 Sheridan Ave Ho Ho Kus (07423) *(G-4441)*

Jnbc Associates LLC..973 560-5518
  100 Jefferson Rd Parsippany (07054) *(G-7967)*

Jnj International Inv LLC....................................732 524-0400
  One Johnson/Johnson Plaza New Brunswick (08933) *(G-6939)*

Jnt Technical Services Inc..................................201 641-2130
  85 Industrial Ave Little Ferry (07643) *(G-5491)*

Jobe Industries Inc..908 862-0400
  1600 W Elizabeth Ave Linden (07036) *(G-5365)*

Jodhpuri Inc (PA)..973 299-7009
  260a Walsh Dr Parsippany (07054) *(G-7968)*

Joe Mike Precision Fabrication.............................609 953-1144
  6 Tidswell Ave Medford (08055) *(G-6026)*

Joey's Fine Foods, Newark *Also called Luna Foods LLC (G-7187)*

Joffe Lumber & Supply Co Inc.............................856 825-9550
  18 Burns Ave Vineland (08360) *(G-11238)*

Joffe Millwork & Supply, Vineland *Also called Joffe Lumber & Supply Co Inc* **(G-11238)**

Johanna Foods Inc (PA) 908 788-2200
20 Johanna Farms Rd Flemington (08822) **(G-3452)**

Johanson Manufacturing Corp 973 658-1051
301 Rockaway Valley Rd Boonton (07005) **(G-559)**

John Anthony Bread Distributor 973 523-9258
298 21st Ave Paterson (07501) **(G-8225)**

John B Horay Welding 856 336-2154
399 Blaine Ave West Berlin (08091) **(G-11601)**

John B Stetson Company 212 563-1848
86 Hudson St Hoboken (07030) **(G-4459)**

John Canary Custom Wdwkg Inc 908 851-2894
697 Rahway Ave Union (07083) **(G-11067)**

John Cooper Company Inc 201 487-4018
250 Maywood Ave Ste C Hackensack (07601) **(G-3934)**

John Crane Inc 856 467-6185
301 Berkeley Dr Ste B Swedesboro (08085) **(G-10590)**

John E Herbst Heating & Coolg 732 721-0088
3143 Bordentown Ave 2b Parlin (08859) **(G-7866)**

John F Pearce 201 440-8765
76 Frederick St Moonachie (07074) **(G-6474)**

John G Papailias Co Inc 201 767-4027
245 Pegasus Ave Northvale (07647) **(G-7532)**

John H Abbott Inc 609 561-0303
4 Mullica Way Egg Harbor City (08215) **(G-2662)**

John J Chando Jr Inc (PA) 732 793-2122
209 Downer Ave Mantoloking (08738) **(G-5850)**

John M Sniderman Inc (PA) 201 450-4291
405 Henry St Fairview (07022) **(G-3361)**

John Maltese Iron Works Inc 732 249-4350
1453 Jersey Ave North Brunswick (08902) **(G-7472)**

John N Fehlinger Co Inc 973 633-0699
16 Passaic Ave Unit 8 Fairfield (07004) **(G-3246)**

John Patrick Publishing LLC 609 883-2700
1707 4th St Ewing (08638) **(G-3038)**

John R Zabka Associates Inc (PA) 201 405-0075
3 Post Rd Ste 3 # 3 Oakland (07436) **(G-7633)**

John S Swift Co, Teterboro *Also called John S Swift Print of NJ Inc* **(G-10683)**

John S Swift Company Inc 201 935-2002
375 North St Ste N Teterboro (07608) **(G-10682)**

John S Swift Print of NJ Inc 201 678-3232
375 North St Ste N Teterboro (07608) **(G-10683)**

John W Kennedy Company 973 256-5525
60 Sindle Ave Little Falls (07424) **(G-5457)**

John Wiley & Sons Inc (PA) 201 748-6000
111 River St Ste 2000 Hoboken (07030) **(G-4460)**

John Wiley & Sons Inc 732 302-2265
41 Saw Mill Pond Rd Edison (08817) **(G-2541)**

John Wiley & Sons Inc 201 748-6000
111 River St Ste 4 Hoboken (07030) **(G-4461)**

John Wiley and Sons, Hoboken *Also called Wiley Publishing LLC* **(G-4488)**

John Wm Macy Cheesesticks Inc 201 791-8036
80 Kipp Ave Elmwood Park (07407) **(G-2833)**

John Wm. Macy's Cheesesticks, Elmwood Park *Also called John Wm Macy Cheesesticks Inc* **(G-2833)**

Johnnys Service Center 732 738-0569
53 Lawrence St Fords (08863) **(G-3532)**

Johns Manville Corporation 856 768-7000
437 N Grove St Berlin (08009) **(G-424)**

Johns Manville Corporation 732 225-9190
Liddle Ave Edison (08837) **(G-2542)**

Johnson & Johnson (PA) 732 524-0400
1 Johnson And Johnson Plz New Brunswick (08933) **(G-6940)**

Johnson & Johnson 732 524-0400
35 Azalea Pl Piscataway (08854) **(G-8682)**

Johnson & Johnson 732 524-0400
51 Pettit Pl Princeton (08540) **(G-8967)**

Johnson & Johnson 917 573-8007
472 Chestnut St Ridgefield (07657) **(G-9269)**

Johnson & Johnson 732 524-0400
10 Stymiest Rd Lambertville (08530) **(G-5190)**

Johnson & Johnson 732 524-0400
6 Greenwood Ct Branchburg (08876) **(G-650)**

Johnson & Johnson 732 524-0400
205 Waverly Ct Trenton (08691) **(G-10947)**

Johnson & Johnson 908 722-9319
1000 Rte 202 Raritan (08869) **(G-9213)**

Johnson & Johnson 908 704-6809
1101 Us Highway 202 Raritan (08869) **(G-9214)**

Johnson & Johnson 908 526-5425
1003 Us Highway 202 P Raritan (08869) **(G-9215)**

Johnson & Johnson 908 874-1000
201 Tabor Rd Morris Plains (07950) **(G-6618)**

Johnson & Johnson 732 524-0400
100 Albany St Ste 100 # 100 New Brunswick (08901) **(G-6941)**

Johnson & Johnson 732 422-5000
691 Rte 1 North Brunswick (08902) **(G-7473)**

Johnson & Johnson Consumer Inc (HQ) 908 874-1000
199 Grandview Rd Skillman (08558) **(G-9922)**

Johnson & Johnson Medical Inc (HQ) 908 218-0707
Us Rt 22 Somerville (08876) **(G-10119)**

Johnson Associates Systems Inc 856 228-2175
. 900 Route 168 Ste F4 Blackwood (08012) **(G-471)**

Johnson Controls Inc 856 245-9977
1001 Lower Landing Rd # 409 Blackwood (08012) **(G-472)**

Johnson Controls Inc 732 225-6700
264 Fernwood Ave Edison (08837) **(G-2543)**

Johnson Matthey Inc 856 384-7000
2001 Nolte Dr West Deptford (08066) **(G-11708)**

Johnson Matthey Phrm Mtls, West Deptford *Also called Matthey Johnson Inc* **(G-11711)**

Johnston Letter Co Inc 973 482-7535
209 Pleasant Hill Rd Flanders (07836) **(G-3414)**

Johnthan Leasing Corp 908 226-3434
630 Fox Farm Rd Asbury (08802) **(G-66)**

Jolt Company Inc (PA) 201 288-0535
100 Hollister Rd Unit 1 Teterboro (07608) **(G-10684)**

Jolt Energy Gum, Jersey City *Also called Gum Runners LLC* **(G-4745)**

Jomar Corp 609 646-8000
115 E Parkway Dr Egg Harbor Township (08234) **(G-2686)**

Jomel Industries Inc 973 282-0300
140 Central Ave Ste 1 Hillside (07205) **(G-4406)**

Jomel Seams Reasonable LLC (PA) 973 282-0300
140 Cent Ave Hillside (07205) **(G-4407)**

Jon-Da Printing Co Inc 201 653-6200
234 16th St Fl 6 Jersey City (07310) **(G-4751)**

Jonas Media Group Inc 973 438-1900
520 Broad St Ste 400 Newark (07102) **(G-7170)**

Jontol Unlimited LLC (PA) 858 652-1113
1134 S Black Horse Pike Blackwood (08012) **(G-473)**

Jordache Ltd 908 226-4930
200 Helen St South Plainfield (07080) **(G-10284)**

Jordan Manufacturing LLC 973 383-8363
28 Randazzo Rd Lafayette (07848) **(G-5029)**

Jordan Tooling & Manufacturing 609 261-2636
1307 Maine Ave Hainesport (08036) **(G-4075)**

Jorgensen Carr Ltd 201 792-2278
45 Glenwood Pl East Orange (07017) **(G-2253)**

Jory Engravers Inc 201 939-1546
23 W Erie Ave Rutherford (07070) **(G-9624)**

Josantos Cnstr & Dev LLC 732 202-7389
13 Riverview Dr Brick (08723) **(G-724)**

Jose Moreira 201 991-9001
712 Kearny Ave Kearny (07032) **(G-4873)**

Josemi Inc 917 710-2110
1201 Hudson St Apt 216s Hoboken (07030) **(G-4462)**

Joseph and William Stavola (PA) 609 924-0300
460 River Rd Kingston (08528) **(G-5009)**

Joseph Bbinec Shtmtl Works Inc 732 388-0155
774 Martin St Rahway (07065) **(G-9109)**

Joseph C Hansen Company Inc 201 222-1677
234 16th St Fl 8 Jersey City (07310) **(G-4752)**

Joseph Castings Inc 201 712-0717
25 Brook Ave Maywood (07607) **(G-6010)**

Joseph Epstein Food Entps, East Rutherford *Also called Appetizers Made Easy Inc* **(G-2271)**

Joseph Mnniti Hair Replacement, Cherry Hill *Also called Minniti J Hair Replacement Inc* **(G-1395)**

Joseph Monga Jr 973 595-8517
7383 Belmont Ave Paterson (07522) **(G-8226)**

Joseph Naticchia 609 882-7709
1597 5th St Ewing (08638) **(G-3039)**

Joseph Oat Holdings Inc 856 541-2900
2500 S Broadway Camden (08104) **(G-1072)**

Joseph Titone & Sons', Burlington *Also called Cellunet Manufacturing Compnay* **(G-956)**

Jost Brothers Jewelry Mfg Corp 908 453-2266
295 Jost Dr Washington (07882) **(G-11448)**

Jostens Inc 973 584-5843
86 Roseville Rd Succasunna (07876) **(G-10514)**

Journal News V Inc 201 986-1458
424 Acorn Dr Paramus (07652) **(G-7811)**

Journal Register Company, Trenton *Also called 21st Century Media Newsppr LLC* **(G-10885)**

Joy Jewelery America Inc 201 689-1150
228 Rivervale Rd Ste A River Vale (07675) **(G-9367)**

Joy Snacks LLC 732 272-0707
365 Blair Rd Ste A Avenel (07001) **(G-132)**

Joy-Rei Enterprises Inc 732 727-0742
3143 Bordentown Ave 5b Parlin (08859) **(G-7867)**

Joyce Food LLC (PA) 973 491-9696
80 Avenue K Newark (07105) **(G-7171)**

Joyce Leslie Inc (PA) 201 804-7800
401 Towne Centre Dr Hillsborough (08844) **(G-4335)**

Joyrei Enterprises, Parlin *Also called Joy-Rei Enterprises Inc* **(G-7867)**

JP Group International LLC 201 820-1444
525 Palmer Ave Maywood (07607) **(G-6011)**

JP Technology Inc 856 241-0111
2150 High Hill Rd Swedesboro (08085) **(G-10591)**

Jpc Merger Sub Llc 609 890-4343
853 Nottingham Way Trenton (08638) **(G-10948)**

Jppc, Ewing *Also called John Patrick Publishing LLC* **(G-3038)**
JRC Web Accessories 973 625-3888
46 Passaic Ave Fairfield (07004) **(G-3247)**
Jrh Service & Sales LLC 908 832-9266
30 Boulder Hill Rd Lebanon (08833) **(G-5267)**
Jrm Industries Inc (PA) 973 779-9340
1 Mattimore St Passaic (07055) **(G-8077)**
Jrz Enterprises LLC 973 962-6330
15 Corporate Dr Ste 5 Wayne (07470) **(G-11526)**
Js Welding LLC (PA) 973 442-2202
34 Brookside Ave Hackettstown (07840) **(G-4014)**
Jsc Wire & Cable, Pennsauken *Also called Jersey Specialty Co Inc* **(G-8446)**
Jsm Co 732 695-9577
1052 Wayside Rd Tinton Falls (07712) **(G-10720)**
Jsn Holdings LLC 201 857-5900
1 International Blvd Mahwah (07495) **(G-5751)**
Jst Power Equipment Inc 201 460-8778
390 Veterans Blvd Carlstadt (07072) **(G-1171)**
Jt Fuels LLC 973 527-4470
1470 Us Highway 46 Ledgewood (07852) **(G-5277)**
Jtp Romark Logistics, Westfield *Also called Romark Logistics CES LLC* **(G-11802)**
Jtwo Inc 201 410-1616
4 Birch Rd Kinnelon (07405) **(G-5018)**
Jubili Bead & Yarn Shoppe 856 858-7844
713 Haddon Ave Collingswood (08108) **(G-1769)**
Judith Roth Studio Collection 973 543-4455
3 Stone House Rd Mendham (07945) **(G-6039)**
Juice Hub LLP 732 784-8265
1555 Main St Ste A Rahway (07065) **(G-9110)**
Julia Clemente 201 488-2161
120 Leuning St South Hackensack (07606) **(G-10166)**
Julian Bait Company Inc 732 291-0050
990 State Route 36 Atlantic Highlands (07716) **(G-109)**
Julian Enterprises, Atlantic Highlands *Also called Julian Bait Company Inc* **(G-109)**
Julius E Holland-Moritz Co Inc 609 397-1231
599 Brunswick Pike Lambertville (08530) **(G-5191)**
Jump Design Group Inc 201 558-9191
350 Old Secaucus Rd Secaucus (07094) **(G-9783)**
Jump Start Press 732 892-4994
802 Cedar Ave Point Pleasant Beach (08742) **(G-8825)**
Junction Drugs, Fort Lee *Also called K & S Drug & Surgical Inc* **(G-3566)**
June Jacobs Labs LLC (PA) 201 329-9100
46 Graphic Pl Moonachie (07074) **(G-6475)**
Junganew LLC 201 832-0892
1 Orient Way Ste F104 Rutherford (07070) **(G-9625)**
Juniper Networks Inc 908 947-4436
200 Somerset Corp Blvd Bridgewater (08807) **(G-839)**
Jury Vrdict Rview Publications 973 376-9002
45 Springfield Ave Ste 2 Springfield (07081) **(G-10449)**
Just A Touch of Baking LLC 732 679-5123
3141 Us Highway 9 Old Bridge (08857) **(G-7717)**
Just Glass & Mirror Inc 856 728-8383
1250 N Black Horse Pike Williamstown (08094) **(G-11962)**
Just In Time Chemical Sales & 908 862-7726
1711 W Elizabeth Ave Linden (07036) **(G-5366)**
Just Plastics, Kearny *Also called Gifford Group Inc* **(G-4860)**
Just US Books Inc 973 672-7701
356 Glenwood Ave Ste 7a East Orange (07017) **(G-2254)**
Justice Laboratory Software 973 586-8551
1 Indian Rd Ste 2 Denville (07834) **(G-2042)**
Juvenile Planet, Lakewood *Also called Steico USA Inc* **(G-5168)**
Juventio LLC 973 908-8097
466 Southern Blvd Ste 2 Chatham (07928) **(G-1324)**
Jvc Industrial America Inc (HQ) 800 247-3608
1700 Valley Rd Ste 1 Wayne (07470) **(G-11527)**
Jvckenwood USA Corporation 973 317-5000
500 Valley Rd Ste 202 Wayne (07470) **(G-11528)**
Jvm Sales Corp 908 862-4866
3401a Tremley Point Rd Linden (07036) **(G-5367)**
Jvs Christmas Lighting 201 664-4022
15 Charles St Ste 4 Westwood (07675) **(G-11832)**
Jvs Copy Services Inc 856 415-9090
460 Main St Sewell (08080) **(G-9850)**
JW Parr Leadburing Co (PA) 973 256-8093
87 Parkway Little Falls (07424) **(G-5458)**
K & A Architectural Met GL LLC 908 687-0247
766b Ramsey Ave Hillside (07205) **(G-4408)**
K & A Industries Inc 908 226-7000
51 Cragwood Rd Ste 204 South Plainfield (07080) **(G-10285)**
K & C Fundraising, Clayton *Also called William Cromley* **(G-1530)**
K & E Components, Riverdale *Also called Diversitech Inc* **(G-9375)**
K & K Automotive Inc 973 777-2235
979 Main Ave Passaic (07055) **(G-8078)**
K & S Drug & Surgical Inc 201 886-9191
266 Columbia Ave Fort Lee (07024) **(G-3566)**
K & S Industries Inc 908 862-3030
333 Dalziel Rd Linden (07036) **(G-5368)**
K & Z Pickle Co, Camden *Also called Kaplan & Zubrin* **(G-1073)**
K 2 Mill Work, Columbus *Also called K2 Millwork Ltd Liability Co* **(G-1801)**
K B Enterprises of New Jersey 908 451-5282
15 Ilene Ct Ste 1211 Hillsborough (08844) **(G-4336)**
K H Machine Works 201 867-2338
4322 Grand Ave North Bergen (07047) **(G-7412)**
K Jabat Inc 732 469-8177
342 Us Highway 22 Green Brook (08812) **(G-3864)**
K K S Criterion Chocolates 732 542-7847
125 Lewis St Eatontown (07724) **(G-2406)**
K M Media Group LLC 973 330-3000
220 Entin Rd Clifton (07014) **(G-1648)**
K R B Printing For Business 856 751-5200
1165 Marlkress Rd Ste G Cherry Hill (08003) **(G-1379)**
K R Electronics Inc 732 636-1900
91 Avenel St Avenel (07001) **(G-133)**
K Ron Art & Mirrors Inc 201 313-7080
395 Broad Ave Ridgefield (07657) **(G-9270)**
K-D Industries Inc 973 594-4800
18 Falstrom Ct Passaic (07055) **(G-8079)**
K-Deer, Westwood *Also called Kristine Deer Inc* **(G-11833)**
K-Tron International Inc (HQ) 856 589-0500
590 Woodbury Glassboro Rd Sewell (08080) **(G-9851)**
K2 Millwork Ltd Liability Co 609 379-6411
2180 Hedding Rd Columbus (08022) **(G-1801)**
Ka-Lor Cubicle and Sup Co Inc 201 891-8077
483 Bowers Ln Franklin Lakes (07417) **(G-3626)**
Kabab & Curry Express 732 416-6560
4 Brunswick Ave Edison (08817) **(G-2544)**
Kabel N Elettrotek Amer Inc 973 265-0850
2 Cranberry Rd Ste 5a Parsippany (07054) **(G-7969)**
Kadakia International Group, South Plainfield *Also called Kadakia International Inc* **(G-10286)**
Kadakia International Inc 908 754-4445
669 Montrose Ave South Plainfield (07080) **(G-10286)**
Kahle Automation 973 993-1850
89 Headquarters Plz S Morristown (07960) **(G-6676)**
Kairos Enterprises LLC 201 731-3181
210 Sylvan Ave Ste 22 Englewood Cliffs (07632) **(G-2979)**
Kaizen Technologies Inc (PA) 732 452-9555
1 State Route 27 Ste 10 Edison (08820) **(G-2545)**
Kaleidoscope Sound 201 223-2868
514 Monastery Pl Union City (07087) **(G-11117)**
Kalustyan Corporation (PA) 908 688-6111
855 Rahway Ave Union (07083) **(G-11068)**
Kamat Pharmatech LLC 732 406-6421
675 Us Highway 1 North Brunswick (08902) **(G-7474)**
Kampack Inc 973 589-7400
100 Frontage Rd Newark (07114) **(G-7172)**
Kanar Inc 201 933-2800
1 Kero Rd Carlstadt (07072) **(G-1172)**
Kane Wood Fuel 856 589-3292
512 Cedar Ave Pitman (08071) **(G-8746)**
Kanomax Usa Inc 973 786-6386
219 Us Highway 206 Byram Township (07821) **(G-1018)**
Kansai Special Amercn Mch Corp 973 470-8321
1 Madison St Ste F11 East Rutherford (07073) **(G-2293)**
Kansai Special USA, East Rutherford *Also called Kansai Special Amercn Mch Corp* **(G-2293)**
Kansas City Design Inc 609 460-4629
201 S Main St Lambertville (08530) **(G-5192)**
Kaplan & Zubrin (PA) 856 964-1083
Second Kaighns Ave Camden (08103) **(G-1073)**
Kappus Plastic Company Inc 908 537-2288
61 State Route 31 65 Hampton (08827) **(G-4157)**
Kapsch Trafficcom Usa Inc 201 528-9814
300 Lighting Way Ste 302 Secaucus (07094) **(G-9784)**
Kar Industrial 856 985-8730
906 Route 73 N Marlton (08053) **(G-5935)**
Karcher North America Inc 856 228-1800
500 University Ct Blackwood (08012) **(G-474)**
Karebay Biochem Inc 732 823-1545
11 Deerpark Dr Ste 102a Monmouth Junction (08852) **(G-6295)**
Karen Lee Ballard, Warren *Also called Ballard Collection Inc* **(G-11399)**
Karl Neuweiler Inc 908 464-6532
23 Russo Pl Berkeley Heights (07922) **(G-404)**
Karla Landscaping Pavers 732 333-5852
11 Woodland Dr Howell (07731) **(G-4543)**
Karnak Corporation (PA) 732 388-0300
330 Central Ave Clark (07066) **(G-1500)**
Karnak Midwest LLC (HQ) 732 388-0300
330 Central Ave Clark (07066) **(G-1501)**
Kas Oriental Rugs Inc (PA) 732 545-1900
62 Veronica Ave Ste A Somerset (08873) **(G-10010)**
Kasanova Inc 201 368-8400
175 State Rt 17 Wood Ridge (07075) **(G-12003)**
Kashee & Sons Inc (PA) 201 867-6900
600 Meadowlands Pkwy 21b Secaucus (07094) **(G-9785)**
Kashiv Biosciences LLC 732 475-0500
20 New England Ave Piscataway (08854) **(G-8683)**
Kashmir 856 691-8969
3926 N Delsea Dr Vineland (08360) **(G-11239)**

ALPHABETIC

Kashmir Crown Baking LLC (PA) 908 474-1470
710 W Linden Ave Linden (07036) *(G-5369)*

Kason Corporation (PA) 973 467-8140
6771 E Willow St Millburn (07041) *(G-6201)*

Kasper, Elizabeth *Also called Nine West Holdings Inc (G-2760)*

Kasper, Englewood *Also called Nine West Holdings Inc (G-2928)*

Katadin Inc 908 526-0166
53 Dreahook Rd Branchburg (08876) *(G-651)*

Kate Spade & Company 201 295-7569
5901 W Side Ave North Bergen (07047) *(G-7413)*

Kate Spade & Company 609 395-3109
120 Herrod Blvd Ste 8 Dayton (08810) *(G-1974)*

Katena Products Inc (PA) 973 989-1600
6 Campus Dr Ste 310 Parsippany (07054) *(G-7970)*

Kates-Bylston Publications Inc 732 746-0211
3349 State Route 138 D Wall Township (07719) *(G-11350)*

Kathy Gibson Designs Inc (PA) 201 420-0088
1435 51st St Ste 2 North Bergen (07047) *(G-7414)*

Kathy Jeanne Inc 973 575-9898
7 Industrial Rd Fairfield (07004) *(G-3248)*

Katies Closets 973 300-4007
3 Lower Hill Rd Newton (07860) *(G-7348)*

Katis Kupcakes 609 332-2172
233 Hedgeman Rd Moorestown (08057) *(G-6532)*

Katzs Delicatessen Mfg 212 254-2246
100 Industrial Rd Carlstadt (07072) *(G-1173)*

Kaufman Stairs Inc (PA) 908 862-3579
150 E Inman Ave Rahway (07065) *(G-9111)*

Kavon Filter Products Co 732 938-3135
5022 Industrial Rd Wall Township (07727) *(G-11351)*

Kay Printing & Envelope Co Inc 973 330-3000
220 Entin Rd Clifton (07014) *(G-1649)*

Kay Window Fashions Inc 862 591-1554
271 2nd St Saddle Brook (07663) *(G-9658)*

Kayden Manufacturing Inc. 201 880-9898
83a Burlews Ct Ste A Hackensack (07601) *(G-3935)*

Kayline Processing Inc (PA) 609 695-1449
31 Coates St Trenton (08611) *(G-10949)*

KB Food Enterprises Inc 973 278-2800
19 E 5th St Paterson (07524) *(G-8227)*

Kdf Reprographics Inc 201 784-9991
65 Worth St South Hackensack (07606) *(G-10167)*

Kearfott Corporation (HQ) 973 785-6000
1150 Mcbride Ave Ste 1 Woodland Park (07424) *(G-12083)*

Kearny Recycle, Kearny *Also called Tilcon New York Inc (G-4901)*

Kearny Smelting & Ref Corp 201 991-7276
936 Harrison Ave Ste 5 Kearny (07032) *(G-4874)*

Keco Engineered Controls, Lakewood *Also called Amico Technologies Inc (G-5053)*

Kedrion Biopharma Inc (HQ) 201 242-8900
400 Kelby St Ste 11 Fort Lee (07024) *(G-3567)*

Keefe Printing Inc 732 295-2099
501 Atlantic Ave Point Pleasant Beach (08742) *(G-8826)*

Keeley Aerospace Ltd 951 582-2113
2559 Us Highway 130 Cranbury (08512) *(G-1849)*

Kef America, Marlboro *Also called GP Acoustics (us) Inc (G-5899)*

Kef America Inc 732 414-2074
10 Timber Ln Marlboro (07746) *(G-5903)*

Kelken Construction Systems, Sayreville *Also called Kelken-Gold Inc (G-9713)*

Kelken-Gold Inc 732 416-6730
550 Hartle St Ste C Sayreville (08872) *(G-9713)*

Kelles Incorporated 908 241-9300
20 Hoiles Dr Ste D Kenilworth (07033) *(G-4950)*

Kelles Machining Center, Kenilworth *Also called Kelles Incorporated (G-4950)*

Kellogg Company 201 634-9140
164 Monroe Ave River Edge (07661) *(G-9363)*

Kellogg Company 609 567-1688
322 S Egg Harbor Rd Hammonton (08037) *(G-4137)*

Kellogg's Eggo, Hammonton *Also called Kellogg Company (G-4137)*

Kelsey Humus, Great Meadows *Also called Partac Peat Corporation (G-3856)*

Kelun Pharmaceutical, Cranbury *Also called Klus Pharma Inc (G-1850)*

Kempak Industries 908 687-4188
33 Fernhill Rd Springfield (07081) *(G-10450)*

Kempton Wood Products 732 449-8673
2800 Ridgewood Rd Ste 2 Wall Township (07719) *(G-11352)*

Ken Bauer & Sons, Hillsdale *Also called Ken Bauer Inc (G-4368)*

Ken Bauer Inc 201 664-6881
277 Broadway Ste A Hillsdale (07642) *(G-4368)*

Keneco Inc 908 241-3700
123 N 8th St Kenilworth (07033) *(G-4951)*

Kenilworth Anodizing Co 908 241-5640
201 S 31st St Ste A Kenilworth (07033) *(G-4952)*

Kenlen Wire Products Division, Livingston *Also called Amark Industries Inc (G-5505)*

Kennametal Inc 412 248-8200
123 Town Square Pl Jersey City (07310) *(G-4753)*

Kennedy Concrete Inc 856 692-8650
1969 S East Ave Vineland (08360) *(G-11240)*

Kennedy Shop N Bag, Willingboro *Also called Herman Eickhoff (G-11991)*

Kennetex Inc 610 444-0600
53 E 34th St Paterson (07514) *(G-8228)*

Kenneth Asmar Custom Interiors 732 544-6137
548 Shrewsbury Ave Tinton Falls (07701) *(G-10721)*

Kenney Steel Treating Corp. 201 998-4420
100 Quincy Pl Kearny (07032) *(G-4875)*

Kenric Inc 856 294-9161
110 Richardson Ave Swedesboro (08085) *(G-10592)*

Kenrich Petrochemicals Inc (PA) 201 823-9000
570 Broadway Bayonne (07002) *(G-226)*

Kep Marine, Eatontown *Also called Sparton Aydin LLC (G-2421)*

Kerk Cabinetry LLC 856 881-4213
45 Dogwood Ave Glassboro (08028) *(G-3813)*

Kern & Szalai Co 856 802-1500
351 Crider Ave Moorestown (08057) *(G-6533)*

Kern & Szalai Machine Company, Moorestown *Also called Kern & Szalai Co (G-6533)*

Kerney Service Group Inc (PA) 908 486-2644
1700 E Elizabeth Ave Linden (07036) *(G-5370)*

Kerney Ship Repair, Linden *Also called Kerney Service Group Inc (G-5370)*

Kerrigan Lewis Wire/Cdt, Elizabeth *Also called Dearborn A Belden Cdt Company (G-2726)*

Kerry Flavor Systems Us LLC 513 771-4682
160 Terminal Ave Clark (07066) *(G-1502)*

Kerry Inc 845 584-3081
222 Terminal Ave Clark (07066) *(G-1503)*

Kerry Inc 201 373-1111
546 Us Highway 46 Teterboro (07608) *(G-10685)*

Kerry Inc 908 237-1595
26 Minneakoning Rd Flemington (08822) *(G-3453)*

Kerry Ingredients, Flemington *Also called Kerry Inc (G-3453)*

Kerry Ingredients & Flavours, Clark *Also called Kerry Flavor Systems Us LLC (G-1502)*

Kerry Ingredients and Flavours, Clark *Also called Mastertaste Inc (G-1508)*

Kerry Ingredients and Flavours, Teterboro *Also called Kerry Inc (G-10685)*

Kerry Wilkens Inc 732 787-0070
780 State Route 36 Belford (07718) *(G-283)*

Keskes Printing LLC 856 767-4733
5 W Taunton Ave Berlin (08009) *(G-425)*

Kessler Industries 973 279-1417
40 Warren St Paterson (07524) *(G-8229)*

Kessler Steel Rule Die Inc 856 767-0231
1004 Industrial Dr Ste 10 West Berlin (08091) *(G-11602)*

Kessler-Ellis Products Co (PA) 732 935-1320
10 Industrial Way E Ste 6 Eatontown (07724) *(G-2407)*

Kestrel Closets LLC 973 586-1144
29 Hillside Rd Rockaway (07866) *(G-9472)*

Ket, Eatontown *Also called Kessler-Ellis Products Co (G-2407)*

Ketec 856 778-4343
1256 N Church St Ste A Moorestown (08057) *(G-6534)*

Keurig Dr Pepper Inc 908 684-4400
562 Ervey Rd Andover (07821) *(G-48)*

Keurig Dr Pepper Inc 732 969-1600
1200 Milik St Carteret (07008) *(G-1258)*

Keurig Dr Pepper Inc 201 933-0070
600 Commercial Ave Carlstadt (07072) *(G-1174)*

Keurig Dr Pepper Inc 201 832-0695
100 Electric Ave Secaucus (07094) *(G-9786)*

Keurig Dr Pepper Inc 732 388-5545
433 Blair Rd Avenel (07001) *(G-134)*

Key Handling Systems Inc 201 933-9333
137 W Commercial Ave Moonachie (07074) *(G-6476)*

Keydata International, Piscataway *Also called Datapro International Inc (G-8652)*

Keyence Corporation America (HQ) 201 930-0100
669 River Dr Ste 403 Elmwood Park (07407) *(G-2834)*

Keypoint Intelligence LLC 201 489-6439
108 John St Hackensack (07601) *(G-3936)*

Keypoint Intelligence LLC (HQ) 973 797-2100
80 Little Falls Rd Fairfield (07004) *(G-3249)*

Keysight Technologies, Budd Lake *Also called Agilent Technologies (G-917)*

Keystone Adjustable Cap Co Inc 856 356-2809
1591 Hylton Rd Ste B Pennsauken (08110) *(G-8447)*

Keystone Dyeing and Finishing (PA) 718 482-7780
10 Pine Hill Ct Dayton (08810) *(G-1975)*

Keystone Europe LLC 856 663-4700
616 Hollywood Ave Cherry Hill (08002) *(G-1380)*

Keystone Folding Box Company 973 483-1054
367 Verona Ave Newark (07104) *(G-7173)*

Keystone Industries, Gibbstown *Also called Mycone Dental Supply Co Inc (G-3798)*

Keystone Packaging Service 908 454-8567
555 Warren St Phillipsburg (08865) *(G-8558)*

Keystone Plastics Inc 908 561-1300
3451 S Clinton Ave South Plainfield (07080) *(G-10287)*

Keystone Printing Inc 201 387-7252
21c E Madison Ave Dumont (07628) *(G-2114)*

Kft Fire Trainer LLC 201 300-8100
17 Philips Pkwy Montvale (07645) *(G-6417)*

KG Squared LLC 973 627-0643
5 Astro Pl Ste B Rockaway (07866) *(G-9473)*

KG Systems Inc 973 515-4664
765 Mountain Ave Ste 120 Springfield (07081) *(G-10451)*

(G-0000) Company's Geographic Section entry number

Khan Zeshan 973 619-4736
55 Salter Pl Belleville (07109) *(G-298)*

Khanna Paper Inc 201 850-1707
3135 Kennedy Blvd Ste 349 North Bergen (07047) *(G-7415)*

Kicksonfirecom LLC 718 753-4248
28 Lighthouse Dr South Amboy (08879) *(G-10135)*

Kidcuteture LLC 609 532-0149
5 Rosalind Dr Lawrenceville (08648) *(G-5233)*

Kidde Fire Trainers, Montvale *Also called Kft Fire Trainer LLC (G-6417)*

Kiddesigns Inc 732 574-9000
1299 Main St Rahway (07065) *(G-9112)*

Kids of America Corp 973 808-8242
103 Route 46 W Fairfield (07004) *(G-3250)*

Kiehls Since 1851 Inc 201 843-1125
355 N Highway 17 Paramus (07652) *(G-7812)*

Kik Custom Products, Freehold *Also called Prestone Products Corporation (G-3693)*

Kikuichi New York Inc 201 567-8388
560 Sylvan Ave Ste 3110 Englewood Cliffs (07632) *(G-2980)*

Killian Graphics 973 635-5844
142 Southern Blvd Chatham (07928) *(G-1325)*

Kimber Mfg Inc 201 840-5812
161 Railroad Ave Ridgefield (07657) *(G-9271)*

Kimbo Educational, Eatontown *Also called United Sound Arts Inc (G-2427)*

Kinect Auto Parts Corporation 862 702-8252
75 Lane Rd Ste 201 Fairfield (07004) *(G-3251)*

Kinedyne LLC (HQ) 908 231-1800
3040 Us Highway 22 # 150 Branchburg (08876) *(G-652)*

Kinetics Control Systems, Ewing *Also called Kinetics Industries Inc (G-3040)*

Kinetics Industries Inc 609 883-9700
140 Stokes Ave Ewing (08638) *(G-3040)*

Kinetron Inc 732 918-7777
1416 Roller Rd Ocean (07712) *(G-7667)*

Kingchem Life Science LLC (PA) 201 825-9988
5 Pearl Ct Allendale (07401) *(G-10)*

Kingster LLC 310 951-5127
618 Mazur Ave Paramus (07652) *(G-7813)*

Kingston Nurseries LLC 609 430-0366
140 Mapleton Rd Kingston (08528) *(G-5010)*

Kingwood Industrial Pdts Inc 908 852-8655
261 Main St Unit 12 Hackettstown (07840) *(G-4015)*

Kini Products Inc 732 299-5555
7 Forest Hill Dr New Egypt (08533) *(G-6984)*

Kinly Inc 973 585-3000
2 Ridgedale Ave Ste 100 Cedar Knolls (07927) *(G-1307)*

Kinnarney Rubber Co Inc 856 468-1320
450 Main St Mantua (08051) *(G-5852)*

Kinnery Metal, Passaic *Also called Kinnery Precision LLC (G-8080)*

Kinnery Precision LLC 973 473-4664
11 Exchange Pl Passaic (07055) *(G-8080)*

Kinzee Industries Inc 201 408-4301
80 Brayton St Englewood (07631) *(G-2916)*

Kirkwood NJ Globe Acqstion LLC 201 440-0800
1 Teaneck Rd Ridgefield Park (07660) *(G-9310)*

Kirms Printing Co Inc 732 774-8000
1520 Washington Ave Neptune (07753) *(G-6886)*

Kissler & Co Inc 201 896-9600
770 Central Blvd Carlstadt (07072) *(G-1175)*

Kitchen and More Inc 908 272-3388
542 South Ave E Cranford (07016) *(G-1914)*

Kitchen Crafters Plus 732 566-7995
1 Suydam Pl Matawan (07747) *(G-5979)*

Kitchen Direct Inc 908 359-1188
739 Rte 206 Hillsborough (08844) *(G-4337)*

Kitchen King Inc (PA) 732 341-9660
1561 Route 9 Ste 9 Toms River (08755) *(G-10772)*

Kitchen Table Bakers Inc 516 931-5113
100 Passaic Ave Ste 155 Fairfield (07004) *(G-3252)*

Kitchenexpo, Toms River *Also called Universal Interlock Corp (G-10801)*

Kitchens By Frank Inc 732 364-1343
2345 Route 9 Ste 5 Toms River (08755) *(G-10773)*

Kittyhawk Digital LLC 269 767-8399
35 Linwood Ave Emerson (07630) *(G-2866)*

Klabin Fragrances Inc 973 857-3600
71 Village Park Rd Cedar Grove (07009) *(G-1280)*

Kleemeyer & Merkel Inc 973 377-0875
68 Britten Rd Green Village (07935) *(G-3868)*

Klein Distributors Inc 732 446-7632
600 E Route 130 Burlington (08016) *(G-977)*

Klein Ribbon Corp 973 684-4671
176 E 7th St Ste 2 Paterson (07524) *(G-8230)*

Klein Usa Inc 973 246-8181
1 Madison St Ste F East Rutherford (07073) *(G-2294)*

Klm Mechanical Contractors 201 385-6965
109 W Shore Ave Dumont (07628) *(G-2115)*

Klus Pharma Inc 609 662-1913
8 Clarke Dr Ste 4 Cranbury (08512) *(G-1850)*

Kmba Fashions Inc 973 789-1652
272 Elmwood Ave Bldg 3 East Orange (07018) *(G-2255)*

Kmsco Inc 732 238-8666
42a Cindy Ln Ocean (07712) *(G-7668)*

Kna Graphics Inc 908 272-4232
303 N 14th St Kenilworth (07033) *(G-4953)*

Knf Neuberger Inc (HQ) 609 890-8889
2 Black Forest Rd Trenton (08691) *(G-10950)*

Kng Textile Inc 704 564-0390
478 Walnut St Fl 2 Ridgefield (07657) *(G-9272)*

Knickerbocker Bed Company 201 933-3100
770 Commercial Ave Carlstadt (07072) *(G-1176)*

Knickerbocker Machine Shop Inc (PA) 973 256-1616
611 Union Blvd Totowa (07512) *(G-10834)*

Knight Gas Burner Co, Millville *Also called NM Knight Co Inc (G-6263)*

Knite Inc 609 258-9550
18 W Piper Ave Ste 201 Ewing (08628) *(G-3041)*

Knobware, Englewood *Also called C & C Metal Products Corp (G-2889)*

Knock Knock Give A Sock Inc 917 885-6983
60 Stanford Ave West Orange (07052) *(G-11770)*

Knock Out Graphics Inc 732 774-3331
522 Cookman Ave Ste 3n Asbury Park (07712) *(G-78)*

Knotts Company Inc 908 464-4800
350 Snyder Ave Berkeley Heights (07922) *(G-405)*

Know America Media LLC (PA) 770 650-1102
157 Eagle Rock Ave Roseland (07068) *(G-9540)*

Knudsen Precision Mfg 609 538-1100
113 Walters Ave Ewing (08638) *(G-3042)*

Koadings Inc 732 517-0784
540 N Edgemere Dr Allenhurst (07711) *(G-22)*

Koba Corp 732 469-0110
60 Baekeland Ave Middlesex (08846) *(G-6124)*

Kobo Products Inc (PA) 908 757-0033
3474 S Clinton Ave South Plainfield (07080) *(G-10288)*

Kobo Products Inc 908 941-3406
690 Montrose Ave South Plainfield (07080) *(G-10289)*

Kobo Products Inc 908 757-0033
234 Saint Nicholas Ave South Plainfield (07080) *(G-10290)*

Kobolak & Son Inc 856 829-6106
1818 Bannard St Cinnaminson (08077) *(G-1468)*

Koch Mdlar Process Systems LLC (PA) 201 368-2929
45 Eisenhower Dr Ste 350 Paramus (07652) *(G-7814)*

Kodak W Jewelers of Bayonne, Hoboken *Also called W Kodak Jewelers Inc (G-4487)*

Koday Press Inc 201 387-0001
69 Armour Pl Dumont (07628) *(G-2116)*

Koehler Industries Inc 732 364-2700
25 Arnold Blvd Howell (07731) *(G-4544)*

Koellmann Gear Corporation 201 447-0200
8 Industrial Park Waldwick (07463) *(G-11303)*

Kohl & Madden Prtg Ink Corp (HQ) 201 935-8666
651 Garden St Carlstadt (07072) *(G-1177)*

Kohlder Manufacturing Inc 856 963-1801
1700 Admiral Wilson Blvd Pennsauken (08109) *(G-8448)*

Kohler Industries Inc 336 545-3289
155 Mcbride Ave Ste 1 Paterson (07501) *(G-8231)*

Kohouts Bakery 973 772-7270
75 Jewell St Fl 1 Garfield (07026) *(G-3750)*

Kole Design LLC 732 409-0021
35 Cedar Ct Freehold (07728) *(G-3674)*

Kolon USA Incorporated 201 641-5800
65 Challenger Rd Ridgefield Park (07660) *(G-9311)*

Komar Company, The, Jersey City *Also called Charles Komar & Sons Inc (G-4711)*

Komar Intimates LLC (HQ) 212 725-1500
90 Hudson St Jersey City (07302) *(G-4754)*

Komar Kids LLC (HQ) 212 725-1500
90 Hudson St Jersey City (07302) *(G-4755)*

Komatsu Northeast, South Plainfield *Also called F and M Equipment Ltd (G-10256)*

Komfort & Kare, Magnolia *Also called J J L & W Inc (G-5708)*

Komline-Sanderson Engrg Corp 973 579-0090
34 White Lake Rd Ste C Sparta (07871) *(G-10394)*

Komo Innovative Cnc Solutions, Lakewood *Also called Komo Machine Inc (G-5117)*

Komo Machine Inc 732 719-6222
1 Komo Dr Lakewood (08701) *(G-5117)*

Kompac Technologies LLC 908 534-8411
7 Commerce St Somerville (08876) *(G-10120)*

Kongsberg Protech 973 770-0574
200 Valley Rd Ste 204 Mount Arlington (07856) *(G-6714)*

Kooltronic Inc (PA) 609 466-3400
30 Pennington Hopewell Rd Pennington (08534) *(G-8369)*

Koons Steel, Englewood *Also called Bushwick Metals LLC (G-2888)*

Kop Marble Granite Inc 973 283-8000
155 Lions Head Dr W Wayne (07470) *(G-11529)*

Kop-Coat Inc 800 221-4466
36 Pine St Rockaway (07866) *(G-9474)*

Koppers Chocolate LLC 212 243-0220
10 Exchange Pl Ste 2800 Jersey City (07302) *(G-4756)*

Korfund Dynamics, Bloomingdale *Also called Vibration Muntings Contrls Inc (G-531)*

Kos Pharmaceuticals Inc (HQ) 609 495-0500
1 Cedarbrook Dr Cranbury (08512) *(G-1851)*

Kozak Precision Products, Randolph *Also called Eugene Kozak (G-9177)*

Kp Excavation LLC 201 933-4200
570 Commerce Blvd Unit B Carlstadt (07072) *(G-1178)*

Kp Fuel Corporation 973 350-1202
  864 Mount Prospect Ave Newark (07104) *(G-7174)*

Kraemer Koating, Lakewood *Also called Miracle Mile Automotive Inc (G-5136)*

Kraemer Properties Inc (PA) 732 886-6557
  1925 Swarthmore Ave Ste 1 Lakewood (08701) *(G-5118)*

Kraft Tape Printers Inc 973 824-3005
  124 Orchard St Newark (07102) *(G-7175)*

Kraftware Corporation (PA) 732 345-7091
  270 Cox St Roselle (07203) *(G-9562)*

Kraftwork Custom Design 609 883-8444
  182 Homecrest Ave Ewing (08638) *(G-3043)*

Kraissl Company Inc 201 342-0008
  299 Williams Ave Hackensack (07601) *(G-3937)*

Kramer Consumer Healthcare, Bridgewater *Also called Arcadia Consmr Healthcare Inc (G-791)*

Kramme Consolidated Inc (PA) 856 358-8151
  Main St Monroeville (08343) *(G-6352)*

Kraus & Naimer Inc (PA) 732 560-1240
  760 New Brunswick Rd Somerset (08873) *(G-10011)*

Krauses Homemade Candy Inc 201 943-4790
  461 Fairview Ave 465 Fairview (07022) *(G-3362)*

Kreisler Industrial, Elmwood Park *Also called Kreisler Manufacturing Corp (G-2836)*

Kreisler Industrial Corp (HQ) 201 289-5554
  180 Van Riper Ave Elmwood Park (07407) *(G-2835)*

Kreisler Manufacturing Corp (PA) 201 791-0700
  180 Van Riper Ave Elmwood Park (07407) *(G-2836)*

Krell Technologies Inc 732 775-7355
  11 Evergreen Ave Neptune (07753) *(G-6887)*

Krementz & Co (PA) 973 621-8300
  51 Commerce St Springfield (07081) *(G-10452)*

Krementz Gemstones, Springfield *Also called Krementz & Co (G-10452)*

Krfc Custom Woodworking Inc 732 363-0522
  1328 River Ave Ste 25 Lakewood (08701) *(G-5119)*

Krfc Design Center, Lakewood *Also called Krfc Custom Woodworking Inc (G-5119)*

Krimstock Enterprises, Pennsauken *Also called J D Crew Inc (G-8443)*

Kristine Deer Inc 201 497-3333
  174 Westwood Ave Westwood (07675) *(G-11833)*

Kristino Handbags & ACC, Sussex *Also called Annette & Jim Dizenzo Sls LLC (G-10556)*

Krogh's Restaurant, Sparta *Also called Summerlands Inc (G-10408)*

Krohn Industries, Carlstadt *Also called Krohn Technical Products Inc (G-1179)*

Krohn Technical Products Inc 201 933-9696
  303 Veterans Blvd Carlstadt (07072) *(G-1179)*

Kronos Saashr Inc 978 250-9800
  3040 Rte 22 Branchburg (08876) *(G-653)*

Kronos Worldwide Inc 609 860-6200
  5 Cedarbrook Dr Ste 2 Cranbury (08512) *(G-1852)*

Krowne Metal Corp 973 305-3300
  100 Haul Rd Wayne (07470) *(G-11530)*

KRs Automotive Dev Group Inc 732 667-7937
  278 Lincoln Blvd Ste 2 Middlesex (08846) *(G-6125)*

Krydon Group Inc 877 854-1342
  365 New Albany Rd Ste C Moorestown (08057) *(G-6535)*

Kt America Corp 609 655-5333
  2650 Us Highway 130 Ste I Cranbury (08512) *(G-1853)*

Kt Mt Corp (PA) 877 791-4426
  2303 Garry Rd Unit 12 Cinnaminson (08077) *(G-1469)*

Kt Welding 908 862-7370
  328 Spruce St Linden (07036) *(G-5371)*

Ktb Acquisition Sub Inc, Fairfield *Also called Ktb Foods Inc (G-3253)*

Ktb Foods Inc (HQ) 973 240-0200
  100 Passaic Ave Ste 155 Fairfield (07004) *(G-3253)*

Kubik Maltbie Inc 856 234-0052
  7000 Commerce Pkwy Ste C Mount Laurel (08054) *(G-6774)*

Kudas Industries Inc 412 751-0260
  6 Dorchester Dr Denville (07834) *(G-2043)*

Kuehne Chemical Company Inc (PA) 973 589-0700
  86 N Hackensack Ave Kearny (07032) *(G-4876)*

Kufall Printing 732 505-9847
  4 Oak Ridge Pkwy Toms River (08755) *(G-10774)*

Kuhl Corp 908 782-5696
  39 Kuhl Rd Flemington (08822) *(G-3454)*

Kuiken Brothers Company (PA) 201 796-2082
  6-02 Fair Lawn Ave Fair Lawn (07410) *(G-3109)*

Kultur International Films Ltd 732 229-2343
  2 Bridge Ave Ste 633 Red Bank (07701) *(G-9233)*

Kultur Video, Red Bank *Also called Kultur International Films Ltd (G-9233)*

Kumar & Kumar Inc 732 322-0435
  57 Denise Dr Edison (08820) *(G-2546)*

Kumar Bros USA LLC (PA) 732 266-3091
  74 Oxford Ct Englishtown (07726) *(G-3006)*

Kupelian Foods Inc 201 440-8055
  146 Bergen Tpke Ridgefield Park (07660) *(G-9312)*

Kurt Versen Inc 201 664-5283
  1 Paragon Dr Ste 157 Montvale (07645) *(G-6418)*

Kushner Draperies Mfg LLC 856 317-9696
  5305 Marlton Pike Pennsauken (08109) *(G-8449)*

Kvk Usa Inc 732 846-2355
  19 Home News Row Bldg A New Brunswick (08901) *(G-6942)*

Kwality Foods Ltd Liability Co 732 906-1941
  1734 Oak Tree Rd Edison (08820) *(G-2547)*

Kwg Industries LLC 908 218-8900
  330 Roycefield Rd Unit B Hillsborough (08844) *(G-4338)*

Kwik Enterprises LLC 732 663-1559
  1806 Bellmore St Oakhurst (07755) *(G-7610)*

Kwik Kopy Printing, Brigantine *Also called Bar Lan Inc (G-911)*

Kync Design LLC 201 552-2067
  701 Penhorn Ave Ste 1 Secaucus (07094) *(G-9787)*

Kyocera International Inc 856 691-7000
  1515 Burnt Mill Rd Cherry Hill (08003) *(G-1381)*

Kyosis LLC 908 202-8894
  148 Whitehead Ave Ste 1 South River (08882) *(G-10351)*

Kyowa Hakko Kirin Cal Inc 609 580-7400
  212 Carnegie Ctr Ste 101 Princeton (08540) *(G-8968)*

Kyowa Kirin Inc 908 234-1096
  135 Rte 202 206 Ste 6 Bedminster (07921) *(G-267)*

L & F Graphics Ltd Lblty Co 973 240-7033
  207 E 15th St Paterson (07524) *(G-8232)*

L & L Kiln Mfg Inc 856 294-0077
  505 Sharptown Rd Swedesboro (08085) *(G-10593)*

L & L Redi-Mix Inc (PA) 609 859-2271
  1939 Route 206 Southampton (08088) *(G-10367)*

L & L Welding Contractors 609 395-1600
  3 Wheeling Rd Dayton (08810) *(G-1976)*

L & M Machine & Tool Co Inc 973 523-5288
  105 Lehigh Ave Paterson (07503) *(G-8233)*

L & R Manufacturing Co Inc (PA) 201 991-5330
  577 Elm St Kearny (07032) *(G-4877)*

L & R Manufacturing Co Inc 201 991-5330
  John Hay Ave Kearny (07032) *(G-4878)*

L & S Contracting Inc 609 397-1281
  259 Route 31 N Hopewell (08525) *(G-4527)*

L & T, Closter *Also called Luxury and Trash Ltd Lblty Co (G-1760)*

L & Z Tool and Engineering Inc 908 322-2220
  1691 Us Highway 22 Watchung (07069) *(G-11456)*

L A Dreyfus Co 732 549-1600
  3775 Park Ave Edison (08820) *(G-2548)*

L A S Printing Co 201 991-5362
  3035 John F Kennedy Blvd Jersey City (07306) *(G-4757)*

L and Ds Sapore Ravioli Cheese 732 563-9190
  429b Lincoln Blvd Middlesex (08846) *(G-6126)*

L Arden Corp 973 523-6400
  72 Putnam St Paterson (07524) *(G-8234)*

L D L Technology Inc 973 345-9111
  137 Pennsylvania Ave Paterson (07503) *(G-8235)*

L E Rosellis Food Specialties 609 654-4816
  155 Church Rd Medford (08055) *(G-6027)*

L Gambert LLC 973 344-3440
  61 Freeman St Ste 4 Newark (07105) *(G-7176)*

L Gambert Shirts, Newark *Also called L Gambert LLC (G-7176)*

L J Loeffler Systems Inc 212 924-7597
  95 Centre Ave Secaucus (07094) *(G-9788)*

L N S Industries, Egg Harbor Township *Also called LNS Inc (G-2688)*

L S P Industrial Ceramics Inc 609 397-8330
  34 Mount Airy Village Rd Lambertville (08530) *(G-5193)*

L V M H Perfumes & Cosmetics, Cranbury *Also called Christian Dior Perfumes LLC (G-1821)*

L&M Architectural Graphics Inc 973 575-7665
  20 Montesano Rd Fairfield (07004) *(G-3254)*

L&M Signs, Fairfield *Also called L&M Architectural Graphics Inc (G-3254)*

L&W Audio/Video Inc 212 980-2862
  1034 Clinton St Apt 101 Hoboken (07030) *(G-4463)*

L-E-M Plastics and Supplies 201 933-9150
  255 Highland Cross Ste 4 Rutherford (07070) *(G-9626)*

L3 Technologies Inc 856 338-3000
  1 Federal St Camden (08103) *(G-1074)*

L3 Technologies Inc 973 446-4000
  450 Clark Dr Ste 1 Budd Lake (07828) *(G-925)*

L3harris Technologies Inc 973 284-0123
  77 River Rd Clifton (07014) *(G-1650)*

L3harris Technologies Inc 973 284-0123
  77 River Rd Clifton (07014) *(G-1651)*

L3harris Technologies Inc 973 284-0123
  77 River Rd Clifton (07014) *(G-1652)*

L3harris Technologies Inc 585 269-6600
  1515 Broad St Bloomfield (07003) *(G-505)*

La Bella Mozzarella 201 997-1737
  15 Arlington Ave Kearny (07032) *(G-4879)*

La Bonbonniere, Edison *Also called Excellence In Baking Inc (G-2508)*

La Casa De Tortilla 732 398-0660
  2017 State Route 27 Somerset (08873) *(G-10012)*

La Cour Inc (PA) 973 227-3300
  36 Kulick Rd Fairfield (07004) *(G-3255)*

La Duca Technical Services LLC 570 309-4009
  51 Shadowglyn Ln West Milford (07480) *(G-11728)*

La Favorite Industries Inc 973 279-1266
  33 Shady St Paterson (07524) *(G-8236)*

La Forchetta 973 304-4797
  27 Utter Ave Hawthorne (07506) *(G-4230)*

La Forge De Style LLC 201 488-1955
57 Romanelli Ave South Hackensack (07606) *(G-10168)*

La Marca Industries, Watchung *Also called L & Z Tool and Engineering Inc (G-11456)*

La Mart Manufacturing Corp 718 384-6917
1465 Palisade Ave Teaneck (07666) *(G-10636)*

La Milagrosa 1 LLC 973 928-1799
100 8th St Bldg 400b Passaic (07055) *(G-8081)*

La Pace Imports Inc 973 895-5420
3 Ascot Ln Morristown (07960) *(G-6677)*

La Tribuna Publication Inc 201 617-1360
300 36th St Apt 1 Union City (07087) *(G-11118)*

Lab Express Inc 973 227-1700
10 Madison Rd Ste A Fairfield (07004) *(G-3256)*

Lab Express International, Fairfield *Also called Lab Express Inc (G-3256)*

Lab Tech Inc (PA) 201 767-5613
170 Legrand Ave Northvale (07647) *(G-7533)*

Label Graphics II, Fairfield *Also called Label Graphics Mfg Inc (G-3257)*

Label Graphics Mfg Inc (PA) 973 890-5665
175 Paterson Ave Little Falls (07424) *(G-5459)*

Label Graphics Mfg Inc 973 276-1555
315 Fairfield Rd Fairfield (07004) *(G-3257)*

Label Master Inc 973 546-3110
89 Dell Glen Ave Lodi (07644) *(G-5567)*

Label Solutions Inc 201 599-0909
151 W Passaic St 2 Rochelle Park (07662) *(G-9426)*

Labeling Systems LLC 201 405-0767
48 Spruce St Oakland (07436) *(G-7634)*

Labern Machine Products LLC 908 722-1970
3388 Us Highway 22 Branchburg (08876) *(G-654)*

Labern Realty, Branchburg *Also called Labern Machine Products LLC (G-654)*

Labnet International Inc 732 417-0700
33 Wood Ave S Ste 600 Iselin (08830) *(G-4613)*

Laboratory Diagnostics Co Inc (HQ) 732 536-6300
100 County Road 520 Morganville (07751) *(G-6591)*

Laboratory Diagnostics Co Inc 732 972-2145
712 Ginesi Dr Morganville (07751) *(G-6592)*

Labrada Inc 201 461-2641
41 Palmer Pl Leonia (07605) *(G-5289)*

Labvantage Solutions Inc (HQ) 908 707-4100
265 Davidson Ave Ste 220 Somerset (08873) *(G-10013)*

Lacka Safe Corp 201 896-9200
400 Meadow Ln Carlstadt (07072) *(G-1180)*

Lacoa Inc 973 754-1000
21 Wallace St Elmwood Park (07407) *(G-2837)*

Lacrosse Republic 856 853-8787
711 Mantua Pike Ste 2 West Deptford (08096) *(G-11709)*

Laeger Metal Spinning Co Inc 908 925-5530
1514 E Elizabeth Ave Linden (07036) *(G-5372)*

Laennec Publishing Inc 973 882-9500
4 Woodhollow Rd Ste 1 Parsippany (07054) *(G-7971)*

Lafarge North America Inc 201 437-2575
6 Commerce St Bayonne (07002) *(G-227)*

Lafarge Road Marking Inc 973 884-0300
400 Lanidex Plz Parsippany (07054) *(G-7972)*

Laird & Company (PA) 732 542-0312
1 Laird Rd Eatontown (07724) *(G-2408)*

Lakeland Transformer Corp 973 835-0818
6 Paul Pl Haskell (07420) *(G-4198)*

Lakewood Elc Mtr Sls & Svc 732 363-2865
6850 Us Highway 9 Howell (07731) *(G-4545)*

Lally-Pak Inc 908 351-4141
1209 Central Ave Hillside (07205) *(G-4409)*

Lamart Corp 973 772-6262
37 Chestnut St Clifton (07011) *(G-1653)*

Lamart Corporation (PA) 973 772-6262
16 Richmond St Clifton (07011) *(G-1654)*

Lamart Corporation 973 772-6262
162 Circle Ave Clifton (07011) *(G-1655)*

Lamart Manufacturing Co, Teaneck *Also called La Mart Manufacturing Corp (G-10636)*

Lamatek Inc (PA) 856 599-6000
1226 Forest Pkwy Paulsboro (08066) *(G-8333)*

Lamb Printing Inc 908 852-0837
700 Grand Ave Hackettstown (07840) *(G-4016)*

Laminated Industries Inc (PA) 908 862-5995
2000 Brunswick Ave Linden (07036) *(G-5373)*

Laminated Paperboard Corp 908 862-5995
2000 Brunswick Ave Linden (07036) *(G-5374)*

Laminetics Inc 732 367-1116
1151 River Ave Lakewood (08701) *(G-5120)*

Lamitech Inc (HQ) 609 860-8037
322 Half Acre Rd Cranbury (08512) *(G-1854)*

Lamonica Fine Foods LLC 856 776-2126
48 Gorton Rd Millville (08332) *(G-6258)*

Lanco Container, Paterson *Also called Lanco-York Inc (G-8237)*

Lanco-York Inc (PA) 973 278-7400
864 E 25th St Paterson (07513) *(G-8237)*

Landew Sawdust Co Inc 973 344-5255
21 Poinier St Newark (07114) *(G-7177)*

Landice Incorporated 973 927-9010
111 Canfield Ave Ste A-1 Randolph (07869) *(G-9188)*

Landice Treadmills, Randolph *Also called Landice Incorporated (G-9188)*

Landsberg New Jersey Div 1088, Cranbury *Also called Orora Packaging Solutions (G-1866)*

Langan Engineering Environmen (PA) 973 560-4900
300 Kimball Dr Ste 4 Parsippany (07054) *(G-7973)*

Lantier Construction Company 856 780-6366
214 W Main St Ste 200 Moorestown (08057) *(G-6536)*

Lanxess Solutions US Inc 732 826-1018
1000 Coventry Blvd Perth Amboy (08861) *(G-8524)*

Lanxess Solutions US Inc 973 235-1800
10 Kingsland St Nutley (07110) *(G-7589)*

Lanxess Solutions US Inc 973 887-7411
215 Merry Ln East Hanover (07936) *(G-2221)*

Lanxess Solutions US Inc 732 738-1000
1020 King George Post Rd Fords (08863) *(G-3533)*

Lanxess Sybron Chemicals Inc (HQ) 609 893-1100
200 Birmingham Rd Birmingham (08011) *(G-457)*

LAp Marketing MGT Svcs Inc 609 654-9266
104 Old Carriage Rd Cherry Hill (08034) *(G-1382)*

Lapp Cable Works Inc 973 660-9632
29 Hanover Rd Florham Park (07932) *(G-3514)*

Lapp Holding NA Inc (HQ) 973 660-9700
29 Hanover Rd Florham Park (07932) *(G-3515)*

Lapp Usa Inc 973 660-9700
29 Hanover Rd Florham Park (07932) *(G-3516)*

Lapp Usa LLC 973 660-9700
29 Hanover Rd Florham Park (07932) *(G-3517)*

Laraccas Manufacturing Inc 973 571-1452
29 Manor Rd Livingston (07039) *(G-5518)*

Laras Designs, South Orange *Also called Danmola Lara (G-10193)*

Lardieri Custom Woodworking 732 905-6334
1830 Swarthmore Ave Ste 6 Lakewood (08701) *(G-5121)*

Larose Industries LLC (PA) 973 543-2037
1578 Sussex Tpke Randolph (07869) *(G-9189)*

Larsen Marine Services LLC 609 408-3564
333 45th Pl Sea Isle City (08243) *(G-9748)*

Larson-Juhl US LLC 973 439-1801
165 Clinton Rd Caldwell (07006) *(G-1026)*

Larue Manufacturing Corp 908 534-2700
291 Rte 22 E Whitehouse (08888) *(G-11916)*

Laser Contractors LLC 609 517-2407
433 Mckendimen Rd Medford (08055) *(G-6028)*

Laser Save, Freehold *Also called Central Technology Inc (G-3656)*

Lasercam LLc (PA) 201 941-1262
1039 Hoyt Ave Ridgefield (07657) *(G-9273)*

Lasermetrics Division, Saddle Brook *Also called Fastpulse Technology Inc (G-9652)*

Laserwave Graphics Inc 732 745-7764
24a Joyce Kilmer Ave N New Brunswick (08901) *(G-6943)*

Lassonde Pappas and Co Inc (HQ) 856 455-1000
1 Collins Dr Ste 200 Carneys Point (08069) *(G-1242)*

Lassonde Pappas and Co Inc 856 455-1001
1019 Parsonage Rd Bridgeton (08302) *(G-762)*

Latex Products Division, Bloomfield *Also called Mid-State Enterprises Inc (G-510)*

Latino U S A 732 870-1475
647 Broadway Long Branch (07740) *(G-5602)*

Latino USA Newspaper, Long Branch *Also called Latino U S A (G-5602)*

Latta Graphics Inc 201 440-4040
651 Garden St Carlstadt (07072) *(G-1181)*

Lattice Incorporated (PA) 856 910-1166
7150 N Park Dr Ste 500 Pennsauken (08109) *(G-8450)*

Lattimer, Vineland *Also called I S Parts International Inc (G-11234)*

Lauda-Brinkmann LP 856 764-7300
1819 Underwood Blvd Ste 2 Delran (08075) *(G-2017)*

Lauda-Brinkmann Management Inc 856 764-7300
1819 Underwood Blvd Ste 2 Delran (08075) *(G-2018)*

Lauderdale Millwork Inc 908 508-9550
77 Industrial Rd Berkeley Heights (07922) *(G-406)*

Laureate Press 609 646-1545
1336 W Central Ave Egg Harbor City (08215) *(G-2663)*

Laurel Manufacturers, Delanco *Also called Medlaurel Inc (G-2006)*

Laurelton Welding Service Inc 732 899-6348
117 Channel Dr Point Pleasant Beach (08742) *(G-8827)*

Lava Lunch, Maplewood *Also called Elements Accessories Inc (G-5876)*

Lavanila, Shrewsbury *Also called Dala Beauty LLC (G-9888)*

Lavitsky Computer Laboratories 908 725-6206
865 Sherwood Rd Bridgewater (08807) *(G-840)*

Lawless Jerky LLC 310 869-5733
37 N Maple Ave Apt 30 Marlton (08053) *(G-5936)*

Lawn Doctor of Mercer County, New Brunswick *Also called Elaine K Josephson Inc (G-6923)*

Lawn Medic Inc 856 742-1111
512 River Dr Westville (08093) *(G-11818)*

Lawn Medic of Delaware Valley, Westville *Also called Lawn Medic Inc (G-11818)*

Lawrence M Gichan Incorporated 201 330-3222
900 Dell Ave North Bergen (07047) *(G-7416)*

Lawrence Mold and Tool Corp (PA) 609 392-5422
1412 Ohio Ave Lawrenceville (08648) *(G-5234)*

Lawrence Packaging, Moonachie *Also called Lps Industries Inc (G-6477)*

Lawyers Diary & Manual, New Providence *Also called Skinder-Strauss LLC (G-7018)*

Lawyers Diary and Manual LLC 973 642-1440
  890 Mountain Ave Ste 300 New Providence (07974) **(G-7005)**
LAZAR CAPPER, Hazlet Also called Lazar Technologies Inc **(G-4263)**
Lazar Technologies Inc 732 739-9622
  39 Evergreen St Hazlet (07730) **(G-4263)**
Lb Book Bindery LLC 973 244-0442
  19 Gardner Rd Ste I Fairfield (07004) **(G-3258)**
Lb Electric Co - North LLC 973 366-2188
  12 Knoll Top Ct Denville (07834) **(G-2044)**
Lbd Corp 201 541-6760
  18 S Dean St Englewood (07631) **(G-2917)**
Lbu Inc 973 773-4800
  7 4th Ave 33 Paterson (07524) **(G-8238)**
LCI Graphics Inc 973 893-2913
  2400 Main St Ste 8 Sayreville (08872) **(G-9714)**
Lcn Partners Inc 215 755-1000
  115 Cross Keys Rd Berlin (08009) **(G-426)**
Lcn Solutions, Berlin Also called Lcn Partners Inc **(G-426)**
Le BEC Fin Fine Foods, Linden Also called Dim Inc **(G-5343)**
Le Bon Magot Ltd Liability Co 609 895-0211
  69 Lawrncvlle Pnnngton Rd Lawrenceville (08648) **(G-5235)**
Le Papillon Ltd 908 753-7300
  500 Hadley Rd South Plainfield (07080) **(G-10291)**
Le Papillon of New Jersey, South Plainfield Also called Le Papillon Ltd **(G-10291)**
Le-Ed Concrete & Supply Co, Toms River Also called Le-Ed Construction Inc **(G-10775)**
Le-Ed Construction Inc 732 341-4546
  1609 Route 9 Toms River (08755) **(G-10775)**
Lead Bead Publishing Company 732 246-0410
  46 Shelly Dr Somerset (08873) **(G-10014)**
Lead Conversion Plus 802 497-1557
  500 Craig Rd Ste 101 Manalapan (07726) **(G-5816)**
Leader Printers, Wildwood Also called Hallco Inc **(G-11944)**
Leading Pharma LLC (PA) 201 746-9160
  3 Oak Rd Fairfield (07004) **(G-3259)**
Leading Pharma LLC 201 746-9160
  155 Chestnut Ridge Rd # 100 Montvale (07645) **(G-6419)**
Leak Detection Associates Inc 609 415-2290
  6638 Delilah Rd Egg Harbor Township (08234) **(G-2687)**
Learning Links-Usa Inc 516 437-9071
  26 Haypress Rd Cranbury (08512) **(G-1855)**
Leather Works NJ Ltd Lblty Co 732 452-1100
  55 Parsonage Rd Ste 2100a Edison (08837) **(G-2549)**
Lebanon Cheese Company Inc 908 236-2611
  3 Railroad Ave Lebanon (08833) **(G-5268)**
Lebanon Door Company, Lebanon Also called Lebanon Door LLC **(G-5269)**
Lebanon Door LLC 908 236-2620
  119 Main St Lebanon (08833) **(G-5269)**
Leco Plastics Inc 201 343-3330
  130 Gameville St Hackensack (07601) **(G-3938)**
Lectro Products Inc 732 462-2463
  22 Francis Mills Rd Freehold (07728) **(G-3675)**
Ledonne Leather Co Inc 201 531-2100
  730 5th St Lyndhurst (07071) **(G-5657)**
Lee Sims Chocolates, Jersey City Also called Sims Lee Inc **(G-4810)**
Lees Woodworking Inc 732 681-1002
  24 W Jumping Brook Rd Neptune (07753) **(G-6888)**
Leets Steel Inc 917 416-7977
  495 Raritan St Sayreville (08872) **(G-9715)**
Leeward International Inc 201 836-8830
  400 Frank W Burr Blvd # 68 Teaneck (07666) **(G-10637)**
Left-Handed Libra LLC 973 623-1112
  50 Park Pl Ste 1001 Newark (07102) **(G-7178)**
Legacy Converting Inc (PA) 609 642-7020
  3 Security Dr Ste 301 Cranbury (08512) **(G-1856)**
Legacy Vulcan LLC 973 253-8828
  208 Piaget Ave Clifton (07011) **(G-1656)**
Legend Machine & Grinding 908 685-1100
  36 S Adamsville Rd Bridgewater (08807) **(G-841)**
Legend Stone Products 973 473-7088
  185 River Rd Clifton (07014) **(G-1657)**
Leggett & Platt Incorporated 732 225-2440
  521 Sunfield Ave Edison (08837) **(G-2550)**
Leggett & Platt 2502, Edison Also called Leggett & Platt Incorporated **(G-2550)**
Leggs Hns Bli Plytx Fctry Outl 908 289-7262
  651 Kapkowski Rd Ste 1008 Elizabeth (07201) **(G-2753)**
Legrand AV Inc 973 839-1011
  300 Fairfield Rd Fairfield (07004) **(G-3260)**
Lehigh Cement Company 973 579-2111
  66 Demarest Rd Sparta (07871) **(G-10395)**
Lehigh Phoenis, Rockaway Also called Phoenix Color Corp **(G-9485)**
Lehigh Utility Associates Inc 908 561-5252
  1300 New Market Ave South Plainfield (07080) **(G-10292)**
Lehigh Valley Dairy Farms, Burlington Also called Tuscan/Lehigh Dairies Inc **(G-989)**
Leibrock Metal Products Inc 732 695-0326
  1800 Brielle Ave Ocean (07712) **(G-7669)**
Leistritz Advanced Tech Corp (HQ) 201 934-8262
  165 Chestnut St Ste 1 Allendale (07401) **(G-11)**
Leistritz Pump, Allendale Also called Leistritz Advanced Tech Corp **(G-11)**

Leiz Custom Woodworking, Linden Also called David Leiz Custom Woodwork **(G-5342)**
Leland Limited Inc 908 561-2000
  2614 S Clinton Ave South Plainfield (07080) **(G-10293)**
Lemon Inc 201 417-5412
  72 Mohawk Ave Norwood (07648) **(G-7568)**
Lenape Products Inc 609 394-5376
  610 Plum St Trenton (08638) **(G-10951)**
Leng-Dor USA Inc (HQ) 732 254-4300
  11 Commerce Dr Cranbury (08512) **(G-1857)**
Lens Depot Inc 732 993-9766
  40c Cotters Ln Ste D East Brunswick (08816) **(G-2154)**
Lens Lab Express 201 861-0016
  5917 Bergenline Ave West New York (07093) **(G-11745)**
Lens Mode Inc 973 467-2000
  150 Main St Ste 1 Millburn (07041) **(G-6202)**
Lens Savers Division, Garfield Also called International Crystal Labs **(G-3748)**
Lentine Sheet Metal Inc 908 486-8974
  1210 E Elizabeth Ave Linden (07036) **(G-5375)**
Leo Pharma Inc 973 637-1690
  7 Giralda Farms Ste 2 Madison (07940) **(G-5697)**
Leo Prager Inc 201 266-8888
  2322 Sterling Blvd Englewood (07631) **(G-2918)**
Leo's Famous Yum Yum, Medford Also called Leos Ice Cream Company **(G-6029)**
Leon Levin, East Brunswick Also called Chic LLC **(G-2132)**
Leonard's Novelty Bakery, Moonachie Also called Royal Baking Co Inc **(G-6487)**
Leone Industries Inc 856 455-2000
  443 S East Ave Bridgeton (08302) **(G-763)**
Leopard Inc 908 964-3600
  1 Montgomery St Hillside (07205) **(G-4410)**
Leos Ice Cream Company 856 797-8771
  7 Tomlinson Mill Rd Ste 5 Medford (08055) **(G-6029)**
Les Metalliers Champenois, Paterson Also called LMC-HB Corp **(G-8244)**
Les Tout Petite Inc 201 941-8675
  24 W Railroad Ave Tenafly (07670) **(G-10663)**
Lesilu Productions Inc 212 947-6419
  70 Winding Way West Orange (07052) **(G-11771)**
Lesli Katchen Steel Cnstr Inc 732 521-2600
  300 Buckelew Ave Ste 109 Jamesburg (08831) **(G-4673)**
Lettering Plus Sign Company 856 299-0404
  438 Perkintown Rd Pedricktown (08067) **(G-8350)**
Lettie Press Inc 201 391-6388
  1 Evelyn St Park Ridge (07656) **(G-7854)**
Letts Play Inc 856 297-2530
  1400 Sunset Ave Williamstown (08094) **(G-11963)**
Level Designs Group LLC 973 761-1675
  495 W South Orange Ave South Orange (07079) **(G-10198)**
Level Ten Products Inc 973 827-0900
  3670 State Rt 94 Hamburg (07419) **(G-4094)**
Lever Manufacturing Corp 201 684-4400
  420 State Rt 17 Mahwah (07430) **(G-5752)**
Levi Strauss & Co 732 493-4595
  1 Premium Outlet Blvd Tinton Falls (07753) **(G-10722)**
Levine Industries Inc (PA) 973 742-1000
  70 Levine St Paterson (07503) **(G-8239)**
Levine Packaging Co, Paterson Also called Levine Industries Inc **(G-8239)**
Levine Packaging Supply Corp 973 575-3456
  400 Us Highway 46 Fairfield (07004) **(G-3261)**
Levomed Inc 908 359-4804
  2 Rue Matisse Somerset (08873) **(G-10015)**
Levy & Rappel, Saddle Brook Also called Grateful Ped Inc **(G-9654)**
Levy Innovation 908 303-4492
  3 Brigade Hill Rd Morristown (07960) **(G-6678)**
Lewis Scheller Printing Corp 732 843-5050
  1723 Hwy 27 Somerset (08873) **(G-10016)**
Lexi Industries 201 297-7900
  252 Livingston St Northvale (07647) **(G-7534)**
Lexicon Pharmaceuticals Inc 609 466-5500
  110 Allen Rd Ste 3 Basking Ridge (07920) **(G-187)**
Lexington Graphics Corp 973 345-2493
  161 Elmwood Dr Clifton (07013) **(G-1658)**
Lexisnexis Matthew Bender, Newark Also called Matthew Bender & Company Inc **(G-7197)**
Lexmark International Inc 201 307-4600
  1 Maynard Dr Ste 3 Park Ridge (07656) **(G-7855)**
Lexora Home, Newark Also called Lexora Inc **(G-7179)**
Lexora Inc 855 453-9672
  425 Ferry St Newark (07105) **(G-7179)**
Lf Graphics, Paterson Also called L & F Graphics Ltd Lblty Co **(G-8232)**
Lg Elctrnics Mbilecomm USA Inc (HQ) 201 816-2000
  1000 Sylvan Ave Englewood Cliffs (07632) **(G-2981)**
Lg Electronics USA Inc (HQ) 201 816-2000
  1000 Sylvan Ave Englewood Cliffs (07632) **(G-2982)**
Lg Electronics USA Inc 732 605-0385
  380 Deans Rhode Hall Rd Monroe Township (08831) **(G-6334)**
Lg Group Aic, Englewood Cliffs Also called Lg Electronics USA Inc **(G-2982)**
Lg Infocomm U.S.A., Englewood Cliffs Also called Lg Elctrnics Mbilecomm USA Inc **(G-2981)**
LG&p In-Store Agency, Paramus Also called Lloyd Gerstner & Partners LLC **(G-7815)**
Liberty Cnstr & Inv Group 267 784-7931
  1878 Marlton Pike E Ste 7 Cherry Hill (08003) **(G-1383)**

(G-0000) Company's Geographic Section entry number

Liberty Coca-Cola Bevs LLC 215 427-4500
1250 Glen Ave Moorestown (08057) *(G-6537)*

Liberty Coca-Cola Bevs LLC 609 390-5002
519 Route Us 9 S Marmora (08223) *(G-5958)*

Liberty Coca-Cola Bevs LLC 856 988-3844
5 E Stow Rd Ste G Marlton (08053) *(G-5937)*

Liberty Envelope Inc 973 546-5600
45 E 5th St Paterson (07524) *(G-8240)*

Liberty Lamp & Shade, Paramus *Also called Jay-Bee Lamp & Shade Co Inc* *(G-7809)*

Liberty Park Raceway LLC 201 333-7223
99 Caven Point Rd Jersey City (07305) *(G-4758)*

Liberty Sport Inc 973 882-0986
107 Fairfield Rd Fairfield (07004) *(G-3262)*

Licensee Services Inc 609 465-2003
502 S Main St Cape May Court House (08210) *(G-1112)*

Licini Bros Provision, Union City *Also called Licini Brothers Inc* *(G-11119)*

Licini Brothers Inc 201 865-1130
907 West St Union City (07087) *(G-11119)*

Lidestri Foods Inc 856 661-3218
1550 John Tipton Blvd Pennsauken (08110) *(G-8451)*

Lidestri Foods of New Jersey, Pennsauken *Also called Lidestri Foods Inc* *(G-8451)*

Lieberfarb Inc 973 676-9090
2100 Felver Ct Rahway (07065) *(G-9113)*

Liedl 908 359-8335
462 Long Hill Rd Hillsborough (08844) *(G-4339)*

Lieth Holdings LLC (PA) 201 358-8282
30 Westwood Ave Ste A Westwood (07675) *(G-11834)*

Life Liners Inc (PA) 973 635-9234
6 Essex Rd Chatham (07928) *(G-1326)*

Life of Party LLC 732 828-0886
832 Ridgewood Ave Ste 4 North Brunswick (08902) *(G-7475)*

Life Recovery Systems Hd LLC (PA) 973 283-2800
170 Kinnelon Rd Rm 5 Kinnelon (07405) *(G-5019)*

Life Science Laboratories LLC 732 367-1900
170 Oberlin Ave N Ste 26 Lakewood (08701) *(G-5122)*

Life Science Labs Mfg LLC 732 367-9937
170 Oberlin Ave N Ste 26 Lakewood (08701) *(G-5123)*

Life Scnce Labs Spplements LLC 732 367-1749
216 River Ave Lakewood (08701) *(G-5124)*

Life Skills Education Inc 507 645-2994
51 Commerce St Springfield (07081) *(G-10453)*

Lifecell Corporation 908 947-1100
95 Corporate Dr Bridgewater (08807) *(G-842)*

Lifecell Corporation 908 947-1100
220 Evans Way Ste 3 Branchburg (08876) *(G-655)*

Lifecell Corporation (HQ) 908 947-1100
1 Millennium Way Branchburg (08876) *(G-656)*

Lifegas, Dayton *Also called Linde Gas North America LLC* *(G-1977)*

Light Inc 973 777-2704
345 Clifton Ave Clifton (07011) *(G-1659)*

Lightfield Ammunition Corp 732 462-9200
912 State Route 33 Freehold (07728) *(G-3676)*

Lightfield Llr Corporation 732 462-9200
912 State Route 33 Freehold (07728) *(G-3677)*

Lightfox Inc 973 209-9112
67 E Park Pl Ste 750 Morristown (07960) *(G-6679)*

Lighthouse Express Inc 732 776-9555
809 Memorial Dr Asbury Park (07712) *(G-79)*

Lighting World Inc 732 919-1224
10 Ruckle Ave Farmingdale (07727) *(G-3387)*

Lightingindustries Picasso, Kearny *Also called Picasso Lighting Inds LLC* *(G-4893)*

Lightning Press Inc 973 890-4422
140 Furler St Totowa (07512) *(G-10835)*

Lightning Prvntion Systems Inc 856 767-7806
154 Cooper Rd Ste 1201 West Berlin (08091) *(G-11603)*

Lightscape Materials Inc 609 734-2224
201 Washington Rd Princeton (08540) *(G-8969)*

Ligno Tech USA Inc 908 429-6660
721 Us Highway 202 Bridgewater (08807) *(G-843)*

Lignotech U S A, Bridgewater *Also called Ligno Tech USA Inc* *(G-843)*

Lilly, Bridgewater *Also called Imclone Systems LLC* *(G-833)*

Lime Energy Co 908 415-9469
2100 S Clinton Ave South Plainfield (07080) *(G-10294)*

Lime Energy Co 732 791-5380
100 Mulberry St 4 Newark (07102) *(G-7180)*

Limecrest Quarry Developer LLC 973 383-7100
217 Limecrest Rd Lafayette (07848) *(G-5030)*

Limosys LLC 212 222-4433
550 Sylvan Ave Ste 100 Englewood Cliffs (07632) *(G-2983)*

Limpert Brothers Inc 856 691-1353
200 N West Blvd Vineland (08360) *(G-11241)*

Lincoln Electric Pdts Co Inc 908 688-2900
947 Lehigh Ave Union (07083) *(G-11069)*

Lincoln Mercury of Wayne, Wayne *Also called Wayne Motors Inc* *(G-11564)*

Lincoln Mold & Die Corp 908 241-3344
13 Deerwood Trl Warren (07059) *(G-11420)*

Lincoln Signs & Awnings Inc 732 442-3151
895 State St Perth Amboy (08861) *(G-8525)*

Linda Spolitino 609 345-3126
1917 Kuehnle Ave Atlantic City (08401) *(G-96)*

Linde Elec & Specialty Gasses, Alpha *Also called Linde North America Inc* *(G-39)*

Linde Elec & Specialty Gasses, Stewartsville *Also called Linde North America Inc* *(G-10485)*

Linde Gas North America LLC 908 329-9300
1 Greenwich St Stewartsville (08886) *(G-10484)*

Linde Gas North America LLC 908 777-9125
225 Strykers Rd Phillipsburg (08865) *(G-8559)*

Linde Gas North America LLC 732 438-9977
174 Ridge Rd Ste A Dayton (08810) *(G-1977)*

Linde Gas North America LLC (HQ) 908 508-3000
200 Somerset Corp Blvd # 7000 Bridgewater (08807) *(G-844)*

Linde Gas USA LLC (HQ) 908 464-8100
200 Somset Corp B 7000 Bridgewater (08807) *(G-845)*

Linde Global Helium Inc 908 464-8100
575 Mountain Ave New Providence (07974) *(G-7006)*

Linde Merchant Production, LLC, New Providence *Also called Messer Merchant Production LLC* *(G-7011)*

Linde North America Inc 908 464-8100
575 Mountain Ave New Providence (07974) *(G-7007)*

Linde North America Inc 908 454-7455
80 Industrial Rd Alpha (08865) *(G-39)*

Linde North America Inc 908 329-9700
1 Greenwich St Ste 100 Stewartsville (08886) *(G-10485)*

Linden Group Corporation 973 983-8809
2b Wing Dr Cedar Knolls (07927) *(G-1308)*

Linden Mold and Tool Corp. 732 381-1411
155 Wescott Dr Rahway (07065) *(G-9114)*

Linden Well Drilling 908 862-6633
2020 Clinton St Linden (07036) *(G-5376)*

Linder & Company Inc 201 386-8788
1183 W Side Ave Jersey City (07306) *(G-4759)*

Linder Graphics, Jersey City *Also called Linder & Company Inc* *(G-4759)*

Lindstrom & King Co Inc 973 279-2511
108 Mclean Blvd Paterson (07514) *(G-8241)*

Linear Photonics LLC 609 584-5747
3 Nami Ln Ste 7c Hamilton (08619) *(G-4109)*

Linearizer Technology Inc (PA) 609 584-5747
3 Nami Ln Unit C9 Hamilton (08619) *(G-4110)*

Linearizer Technology Inc 609 584-8424
3 Nami Ln Unit C9 Hamilton (08619) *(G-4111)*

Linen Enterprises, Moorestown *Also called Star Linen Inc* *(G-6568)*

Linen For Tables 973 345-8472
407 20th Ave Paterson (07513) *(G-8242)*

Lingo Inc 856 273-6594
10 Opal Ct Mount Laurel (08054) *(G-6775)*

Link Bio Inc 973 625-1333
69 King St Ste 2 Dover (07801) *(G-2094)*

Link Color NA Inc 201 438-8222
23c Poplar St East Rutherford (07073) *(G-2295)*

Link Computer Graphics Inc 973 808-8990
17a Daniel Rd Fairfield (07004) *(G-3263)*

Link Instruments, Fairfield *Also called Link Computer Graphics Inc* *(G-3263)*

Link News 732 222-4300
176 Broadway Long Branch (07740) *(G-5603)*

Link2consult Inc 888 522-0902
1 Bridge Plz N Ste 275 Fort Lee (07024) *(G-3568)*

Linker Machines, Rockaway *Also called J Hebrank Inc* *(G-9470)*

Linkspine Inc 973 625-1333
69 King St Ste 2 Dover (07801) *(G-2095)*

Linoleum Sales Company Inc 201 438-1844
135 Park Ave East Rutherford (07073) *(G-2296)*

Linseis Inc 609 223-2070
109 N Gold Dr Trenton (08691) *(G-10952)*

Linthicum Sails 856 783-4288
607 Grace St Somerdale (08083) *(G-9932)*

Lion Extruding Corp 973 344-4648
106 Rutherford St Newark (07105) *(G-7181)*

Lion Sales Corp 732 417-9363
125 Jackson Ave Ste 5 Edison (08837) *(G-2551)*

Lion Visual Ltd Liability Co 973 278-3802
1275 Bloomfield Ave 54b Fairfield (07004) *(G-3264)*

Lioni Latticini Inc (PA) 908 686-6061
555 Lehigh Ave Union (07083) *(G-11070)*

Lioni Mozzarella & Spclty 908 624-9450
555 Lehigh Ave Union (07083) *(G-11071)*

Lioni Specialty Foods, Union *Also called Lioni Mozzarella & Spclty* *(G-11071)*

Lipoid LLC 973 735-2692
744 Broad St Ste 1801 Newark (07102) *(G-7182)*

Lippincott Marine, Riverside *Also called Howard Lippincott* *(G-9396)*

Liquid Elements 856 321-7646
1000 E Park Ave Maple Shade (08052) *(G-5865)*

Liquid Holdings Group Inc 212 293-1836
111 River St Ste 1204 Hoboken (07030) *(G-4464)*

Liquid Iron Industries Inc 856 336-2639
150 Cooper Rd Ste B4 West Berlin (08091) *(G-11604)*

Liquid Metalworks Ltd Lblty Co 973 224-9710
700 Grand Ave Ste B Hackettstown (07840) *(G-4017)*

Liquid-Solids Separation Corp (HQ) 201 236-4833
25 Arrow Rd Ramsey (07446) **(G-9149)**
Lisabelle, Maywood *Also called JP Group International LLC* **(G-6011)**
Lithoptek LLC (PA) 408 533-5847
26 Ridge Rd Summit (07901) **(G-10538)**
Lithos Estiatorio Ltd Lblty Co 973 758-1111
405 Eisenhower Pkwy Livingston (07039) **(G-5519)**
Lithuanian Bakery T J Inc 908 354-0970
131 Inslee Pl Elizabeth (07206) **(G-2754)**
Little Falls Alloys Inc (PA) 973 278-1666
171-191 Caldwell Ave Paterson (07501) **(G-8243)**
Little Falls Shop Rite Super 973 256-0909
171 Browertown Rd Ste 2 Little Falls (07424) **(G-5460)**
Little Fox Inc 609 919-9691
720 E Palisade Ave # 104 Englewood Cliffs (07632) **(G-2984)**
Little House Candles Inc 609 758-2996
20 Province Line Rd New Egypt (08533) **(G-6985)**
Little Jimmy's, Iselin *Also called Magliones Italian Ices LLC* **(G-4614)**
Little Miss Cupcake LLC 732 370-3083
200 Tudor Ct Lakewood (08701) **(G-5125)**
Little Prints Day Care II LLC 973 396-8989
235 Lexington Ave Passaic (07055) **(G-8082)**
Littlegifts Inc 212 868-2559
600 Mdwlands Pkwy Ste 131 Secaucus (07094) **(G-9789)**
Liva Eye Center, Ridgewood *Also called Douglas Liva MD* **(G-9323)**
Liveu Inc 201 742-5229
2 University Plz Ste 505 Hackensack (07601) **(G-3939)**
Living Fashions Llc 732 626-5200
602 Hartle St Sayreville (08872) **(G-9716)**
Livingston Bagel Warren Inc 973 994-1915
37 E Northfield Rd Livingston (07039) **(G-5520)**
Liz Claiborne, North Bergen *Also called Kate Spade & Company* **(G-7413)**
Liz Claiborne, Dayton *Also called Kate Spade & Company* **(G-1974)**
Liz Fields Llc 201 408-5640
41 Smith St Englewood (07631) **(G-2919)**
Lizard Label Co (PA) 973 808-3322
20 Kulick Rd Ste A Fairfield (07004) **(G-3265)**
LLC Dunn Meadow 201 297-4603
1555 Center Ave Ste 1 Fort Lee (07024) **(G-3569)**
Llc, Incoco Products, Clifton *Also called Innovative Cosmtc Concepts LLC* **(G-1641)**
Lloyd Gerstner & Partners LLC 201 634-9099
650 From Rd Ste 552 Paramus (07652) **(G-7815)**
Lloyd's Awnings, Millville *Also called Lloyds of Millville Inc* **(G-6259)**
Lloyds of Millville Inc 856 825-0345
208 S Wade Blvd Millville (08332) **(G-6259)**
Lm Air Technology Inc 732 381-8200
1467 Pinewood St Rahway (07065) **(G-9115)**
Lm Foods LLC 732 855-9500
100 Raskulinecz Rd Carteret (07008) **(G-1259)**
Lm Matrix Solutions LLC 908 756-7952
991 Us Highway 22 Ste 200 Bridgewater (08807) **(G-846)**
Lm PC Products, Beverly *Also called Fyth Labs Inc* **(G-451)**
LMC Precision Inc 973 522-0005
91 Rome St Newark (07105) **(G-7183)**
LMC-HB Corp 862 239-9814
23 27 East 23rd St Paterson (07514) **(G-8244)**
Lmp Printing Corp 973 428-1987
1 Trenton Ave Clifton (07011) **(G-1660)**
Lmt Mercer Group Inc 888 570-5252
690 Puritan Ave Lawrenceville (08648) **(G-5236)**
Lmt Usa Inc 973 586-8722
400 Forge Way Rockaway (07866) **(G-9475)**
LNS Inc 609 927-6656
24 Buckingham Dr Egg Harbor Township (08234) **(G-2688)**
Lo Gatto Bookbinding 201 438-4344
390 Paterson Ave East Rutherford (07073) **(G-2297)**
Lo Presti & Sons LLC 973 523-9258
298 21st Ave Paterson (07501) **(G-8245)**
Lob-Ster Inc 818 764-6000
1118 North Ave Plainfield (07062) **(G-8770)**
Lobster House, Cape May *Also called Cold Spring Ice Inc* **(G-1096)**
Lobster Life Systems Inc 201 398-0303
10 Dell Glen Ave Ste 5a Lodi (07644) **(G-5568)**
Lobster Sports, Plainfield *Also called Lob-Ster Inc* **(G-8770)**
Local Concrete Sup & Eqp Corp 201 797-7979
475 Market St Ste 3fl Elmwood Park (07407) **(G-2838)**
Local Wisdom Inc 609 269-2320
287 S Main St Ste 2 Lambertville (08530) **(G-5194)**
Locker Lady, The, Union *Also called American Intr Resources Inc* **(G-11024)**
Lockheed Martin 856 722-7782
3000 Lincoln Dr E Ste E Marlton (08053) **(G-5938)**
Lockheed Martin 856 722-2418
3000 Lincoln Dr E Ste E Marlton (08053) **(G-5939)**
Lockheed Martin Adv, Cherry Hill *Also called Lockheed Martin Corporation* **(G-1384)**
Lockheed Martin Corporation 856 988-1085
10000 Sagemore Dr # 10203 Marlton (08053) **(G-5940)**
Lockheed Martin Corporation 609 485-7601
Aasl Bldg 316 Atlantic City (08405) **(G-97)**
Lockheed Martin Corporation 856 234-1261
750 Centerton Rd Mount Laurel (08054) **(G-6776)**
Lockheed Martin Corporation 856 722-7782
199 Bortons Landing Rd Moorestown (08057) **(G-6538)**
Lockheed Martin Corporation 856 792-9811
3 Executive Campus # 600 Cherry Hill (08002) **(G-1384)**
Lockheed Martin Corporation 856 787-3104
532 Fellowship Rd Mount Laurel (08054) **(G-6777)**
Lockheed Martin Corporation 732 321-4200
2890 Woodbridge Ave Ste 3 Edison (08837) **(G-2552)**
Lockheed Martin Corporation 856 722-3336
199 Bortons Landing Rd Moorestown (08057) **(G-6539)**
Lockheed Martin Corporation 856 727-5800
700 E Gate Dr Ste 200 Mount Laurel (08054) **(G-6778)**
Lockheed Martin Corporation 856 722-4100
199 Bortons Landing Rd Moorestown (08057) **(G-6540)**
Lockheed Martin Integrtd Systm 856 762-2222
1800 State Route 34 Wall Township (07719) **(G-11353)**
Lockheed Martin Overseas LLC 856 787-3105
199 Bortons Landing Rd Moorestown (08057) **(G-6541)**
Locktile Industries Llc 888 562-5845
127 Frelinghuysen Ave Newark (07114) **(G-7184)**
Lockwood Boat Works Inc 732 721-1605
1825 State Route 35 South Amboy (08879) **(G-10136)**
Lockwoods Electric Motor Svc 609 587-2333
2239 Nottingham Way Trenton (08619) **(G-10953)**
Lodi Cml Cooperative LLC 201 820-2380
170 Gregg St Ste 5 Lodi (07644) **(G-5569)**
Lodi Welding Co Inc 908 852-8367
133 Willow Grove St Hackettstown (07840) **(G-4018)**
Lodor Offset Corporation 201 935-7100
111 Amor Ave Carlstadt (07072) **(G-1182)**
Logan Instruments Corporation 732 302-9888
19c Schoolhouse Rd Ste C Somerset (08873) **(G-10017)**
Logomania Inc 201 798-0531
110 1/2 Erie St Jersey City (07302) **(G-4760)**
Logomatcentral.com, Cedar Grove *Also called Mat Logo Central LLC* **(G-1281)**
Logpowercom LLC 732 350-9663
47 Lacey Rd Whiting (08759) **(G-11940)**
Lola Products, Hackensack *Also called Fifty/Fifty Group Inc* **(G-3913)**
Lollytogs Ltd 732 438-5500
321 Herrod Blvd Dayton (08810) **(G-1978)**
Lollytogs Ltd 732 438-5500
321 Herrod Blvd Dayton (08810) **(G-1979)**
London Nite, Passaic *Also called Betsy & Adam Ltd* **(G-8054)**
Long Island Pipe of NJ 201 939-1100
700 Schuyler Ave Lyndhurst (07071) **(G-5658)**
Longo Associates Inc 201 825-1500
100 Hilltop Rd Ramsey (07446) **(G-9150)**
Longo Elctrical-Mechanical Inc 973 537-0400
1625 Pennsylvania Ave Linden (07036) **(G-5377)**
Longo Elctrical-Mechanical Inc (PA) 973 537-0400
1 Harry Shupe Blvd Wharton (07885) **(G-11861)**
Longo Industries, Wharton *Also called Longo Elctrical-Mechanical Inc* **(G-11861)**
Longport Shields Inc 856 727-0227
5 Twosome Dr Moorestown (08057) **(G-6542)**
Longrun Press Inc 856 719-9202
1002 Industrial Dr West Berlin (08091) **(G-11605)**
Longview Coffee Co NJ Inc 908 788-4186
843 State Route 12 B10 Frenchtown (08825) **(G-3715)**
Longview Coffee Company, Frenchtown *Also called Longview Coffee Co NJ Inc* **(G-3715)**
Lonza Biologics Inc 603 610-4809
412 Mount Kemble Ave # 200 Morristown (07960) **(G-6680)**
Lonza Inc (HQ) 201 316-9200
412 Mount Kemble Ave # 200 Morristown (07960) **(G-6681)**
Lonza Walkersville Inc 201 316-9259
412 Mount Kemble Ave 200s Morristown (07960) **(G-6682)**
Look of Love Wigs Inc (PA) 908 687-9502
1795b State Route 27 Edison (08817) **(G-2553)**
Lopes Sausage Co 973 344-3063
304 Walnut St Newark (07105) **(G-7185)**
Lordon Inc 908 813-1143
453 Us Highway 46 E Ste 1 Hackettstown (07840) **(G-4019)**
LOreal Usa Inc 732 499-6617
30 Terminal Ave Clark (07066) **(G-1504)**
LOreal Usa Inc 212 818-1500
100 Terminal Ave Clark (07066) **(G-1505)**
LOreal Usa Inc 732 499-6690
159 Terminal Ave Clark (07066) **(G-1506)**
LOreal Usa Inc 732 499-2809
175 Terminal Ave Clark (07066) **(G-1507)**
LOreal Usa Inc 609 860-7500
35 Broadway Rd Cranbury (08512) **(G-1858)**
LOreal USA Products Inc 732 873-3520
111 Town Square Pl # 317 Jersey City (07310) **(G-4761)**
LOreal USA Products Inc 732 873-3520
100 Commerce Dr Somerset (08873) **(G-10018)**
Loree Jon Pool Tables Plus, Green Brook *Also called Pool Tables Plus Inc* **(G-3866)**
Lorenzo & Sons Provisions, Englewood *Also called Lorenzo Food Group Inc* **(G-2920)**

674 2019 Harris New Jersey Manufacturers Directory (G-0000) Company's Geographic Section entry number

Lorenzo Food Group Inc..201 868-9088
196 Coolidge Ave Englewood (07631) *(G-2920)*

Lornan Litho Inc..609 818-1198
130 Route 31 N Ste E Pennington (08534) *(G-8370)*

Losurdo Foods Inc (PA)..201 343-6680
20 Owens Rd Hackensack (07601) *(G-3940)*

Lotito Foods Inc...973 684-2900
510 E 35th St Paterson (07504) *(G-8246)*

Louis A Nelson Inc..973 743-7404
224 Glenwood Ave Bloomfield (07003) *(G-506)*

Louis Iron Works Inc...973 624-2700
218 Lackawanna Ave Newark (07103) *(G-7186)*

Louis N Rothberg & Son Inc..................................732 356-9505
550 Cedar Ave Middlesex (08846) *(G-6127)*

Love Pallet LLC..908 964-3385
460 Mundet Pl Hillside (07205) *(G-4411)*

Loveline Industries Inc..973 928-3427
90 Dayton Ave Ste 33 Passaic (07055) *(G-8083)*

Loving Pets Corporation.......................................609 655-3700
110 Melrich Rd Ste 1 Cranbury (08512) *(G-1859)*

Lowder Electric and Cnstr....................................732 764-6000
250 Hallock Ave Ste B Middlesex (08846) *(G-6128)*

Lowell / Edwards, Hoboken Also called L&W Audio/Video Inc *(G-4463)*

Lowell Electronics, Glen Rock Also called World Electronics Inc *(G-3835)*

LP Thebault Co...973 884-1300
249 Pomeroy Rd Parsippany (07054) *(G-7974)*

LPI, Passaic Also called Geiger Tool Co Inc *(G-8069)*

Lps Industries Inc (PA)...201 438-3515
10 Caesar Pl Moonachie (07074) *(G-6477)*

Lrk Inc...609 924-6881
830 State Rd Ste 3 Princeton (08540) *(G-8970)*

Lrk Seating Products LLC......................................973 462-2743
15 Melrose Dr Livingston (07039) *(G-5521)*

Lrp and P Graphics, Cherry Hill Also called Pad and Publ Assembly Corp *(G-1404)*

Lrp and P Graphics...856 424-0158
1165 Marlkress Rd Ste M Cherry Hill (08003) *(G-1385)*

Lrp and Profit, Cherry Hill Also called Lrp and P Graphics *(G-1385)*

Ls Rubber Industries Inc (HQ)...............................973 680-4488
24 Federal Plz Bloomfield (07003) *(G-507)*

Lsl Supplements, Lakewood Also called Life Scnce Labs Spplements LLC *(G-5124)*

Lt Apparel Group, Dayton Also called Lollytogs Ltd *(G-1978)*

Lt Chini Inc..856 692-0303
646 S Delsea Dr Vineland (08360) *(G-11242)*

LTS Lhmann Thrapy Systems Corp..........................973 575-5170
21 Henderson Dr West Caldwell (07006) *(G-11658)*

LTS NJ Inc..856 780-9888
109 W Park Dr Unit C Mount Laurel (08054) *(G-6779)*

Lubrizol Advanced Mtls Inc...................................856 299-3764
76 Porcupine Rd Pedricktown (08067) *(G-8351)*

Lubrizol Corporation...732 981-0149
377 Hoes Ln Ste 210 Piscataway (08854) *(G-8684)*

Lubrizol Global Management.................................973 471-1300
1 Industrial St W Clifton (07012) *(G-1661)*

Lucas World Inc...832 293-3770
100 International Dr Budd Lake (07828) *(G-926)*

Luccas Bakery Inc..609 561-5558
631 Egg Harbor Rd Hammonton (08037) *(G-4138)*

Lucent, New Providence Also called Nokia of America Corporation *(G-7014)*

Lucent Technologies World Svcs.............................908 582-3000
600 Mountain Ave New Providence (07974) *(G-7008)*

Luciano Brothers, Millville Also called Cumberland Rcycl Corp S Jersey *(G-6245)*

Luciano Packaging Tech Inc..................................908 722-3222
29 County Line Rd Branchburg (08876) *(G-657)*

Lucid Lighting, Stockton Also called Robert Wallace *(G-10502)*

Lucky Dog Custom Apparel, Pleasantville Also called Its The Pitts Inc *(G-8813)*

Lucy's Ravioli Kitchen, Princeton Also called Lrk Inc *(G-8970)*

Ludovicos, Haddonfield Also called Goldens Inc *(G-4059)*

Luis Network, Norwood Also called J Media LLC *(G-7567)*

Lukach Interiors Inc...973 777-1499
208 River Rd Clifton (07014) *(G-1662)*

Lukoil N Arlington Ltd Lblty..................................856 722-6425
302 Harper Dr Ste 303 Moorestown (08057) *(G-6543)*

Lumber Super Mart...732 739-1428
State Hwy No 36 Hazlet (07730) *(G-4264)*

Lumenarc Inc..973 882-5918
37 Fairfield Pl West Caldwell (07006) *(G-11659)*

Lumeta Corporation (PA)......................................732 357-3500
300 Atrium Dr Ste 300 # 300 Somerset (08873) *(G-10019)*

Lumiko USA Inc...609 409-6900
47 Commerce Dr 3 Cranbury (08512) *(G-1860)*

Luminer Converting Group, Lakewood Also called Kraemer Properties Inc *(G-5118)*

Lumiscope Co Inc...678 291-3207
33 Whelan Rd East Rutherford (07073) *(G-2298)*

Lumitron Arospc Ltg Components, Berkeley Heights Also called Lumitron Corp *(G-407)*

Lumitron Corp..908 508-9100
35 Russo Pl Berkeley Heights (07922) *(G-407)*

Lummus Overseas Corporation..............................973 893-3000
1515 Broad St Bloomfield (07003) *(G-508)*

Lummus Technology Ventures LLC...........................973 893-1515
1515 Broad St Ste A110 Bloomfield (07003) *(G-509)*

Luna Foods LLC...973 482-1400
135 Manchester Pl Newark (07104) *(G-7187)*

Lunar Audio Video LLC (PA)..................................973 233-7700
701 Hartle St Unit 703 Sayreville (08872) *(G-9717)*

Lunet Inc...201 261-3883
300 N State Rt 17 Ste 3 Paramus (07652) *(G-7816)*

Lupin Pharmaceuticals Inc...................................908 603-6075
390 Campus Dr Somerset (08873) *(G-10020)*

Lupin Pharmaceuticals Inc...................................908 603-6000
400 Campus Dr Somerset (08873) *(G-10021)*

Lure Lash, Montclair Also called Lure Lash Spa LLC *(G-6374)*

Lure Lash Spa LLC..973 783-5274
416 Bloomfield Ave Montclair (07042) *(G-6374)*

Lush Decor, East Brunswick Also called Triangle Home Fashions LLC *(G-2187)*

Luso Glass, Newark Also called Eldon Glass & Mirror Co Inc *(G-7113)*

Luso Machine Nj LLC..973 242-1717
29 Avenue C Newark (07114) *(G-7188)*

Luso-Americano Co Inc..973 344-3200
66 Union St Newark (07105) *(G-7189)*

Lusotech LLC...973 332-3861
82-84 Vanderpool St Newark (07114) *(G-7190)*

Lust For Life Footwear LLC (PA)............................646 732-9742
1086 Teaneck Rd Ste 3d Teaneck (07666) *(G-10638)*

Lusterline Inc..201 758-5148
501 30th St Ste 1a Union City (07087) *(G-11120)*

Lux Home Inc..845 623-2821
483 N Rte 17 Paramus (07652) *(G-7817)*

Lux Naturals LLC...848 229-2950
9 Coral St Edison (08837) *(G-2554)*

Luxfer Magtech Inc..803 610-9898
2590 Ridgeway Blvd Manchester (08759) *(G-5846)*

Luxury and Trash Ltd Lblty Co...............................201 315-4018
1 Closter Cmns 258 Closter (07624) *(G-1760)*

Luye Pharma USA Ltd..609 799-7600
502 Carnegie Ctr Ste 100 Princeton (08540) *(G-8971)*

LV Adhesive Inc...201 507-0080
341 Michele Pl Carlstadt (07072) *(G-1183)*

Lvmh Fragrance Brands US LLC..............................212 931-2668
208 Fernwood Ave Edison (08837) *(G-2555)*

Lyca Tel LLC (PA)...973 286-0771
24 Commerce St Ste 100 Newark (07102) *(G-7191)*

Lycatel, Newark Also called Lyca Tel LLC *(G-7191)*

Lyciret Corp..973 882-0322
377 Crane St Orange (07050) *(G-7754)*

Lycored Corp...201 601-0060
300 Harmon Meadow Blvd # 440 Secaucus (07094) *(G-9790)*

Lycored Corp (HQ)..973 882-0322
377 Crane St Orange (07050) *(G-7755)*

Lycored USA, Orange Also called Lycored Corp *(G-7755)*

Lydem LLC..856 566-1419
1 E Broad St Palmyra (08065) *(G-7784)*

Lydon Bros Corp...201 343-4334
254 Green St South Hackensack (07606) *(G-10169)*

Lyle/Carlstrom Associates Inc...............................908 526-2270
131 Chambers Brook Rd Branchburg (08876) *(G-658)*

Lympha Press USA..732 792-9677
265 Willow Brook Rd # 4 Freehold (07728) *(G-3678)*

Lynch Industries, Burlington Also called Dublin Management Assoc of NJ *(G-964)*

Lynn Amiee Inc..201 840-6766
65 Railroad Ave Ste 209 Ridgefield (07657) *(G-9274)*

Lynn Mechanical Contractors.................................856 829-1717
1810 Rowland St Cinnaminson (08077) *(G-1470)*

Lynred USA Inc..973 882-0211
373 Us Highway 46 Fairfield (07004) *(G-3266)*

Lyondell Chemical Company..................................973 578-2200
300 Doremus Ave Newark (07105) *(G-7192)*

Lyondell Chemical Company..................................732 985-6262
340 Meadow Rd Edison (08837) *(G-2556)*

M & D Prcsion Cntrless Grnding.............................856 764-1616
120 Kossuth St Riverside (08075) *(G-9398)*

M & E Packaging Corp...201 635-1381
900 Page Ave Fl 2 Lyndhurst (07071) *(G-5659)*

M & M International...908 412-8300
3619 Kennedy Rd Ste A South Plainfield (07080) *(G-10295)*

M & M Mars, Hackettstown Also called Mars Incorporated *(G-4021)*

M & M Printing Corp..201 288-7787
216 Boulevard Hasbrouck Heights (07604) *(G-4186)*

M & M Welding & Machine, Stirling Also called M & M Welding & Steel Fabg *(G-10493)*

M & M Welding & Steel Fabg..................................908 647-6060
344 Essex St Stirling (07980) *(G-10493)*

M & RS Miller Auto Gear & Prt...............................201 339-2270
699 Kennedy Blvd Bayonne (07002) *(G-228)*

M & S Holes Corp...908 298-6900
20 Hoiles Dr Ste A1 Kenilworth (07033) *(G-4954)*

M & S Machine & Tool Corp...................................973 345-5847
108 Maryland Ave Paterson (07503) *(G-8247)*

ALPHABETIC

M & W Franklin LLC...609 927-0885
3011 Ocean Heights Ave B Egg Harbor Township (08234) *(G-2689)*
M & Z International Inc...201 864-3331
358 Oswego Ct West New York (07093) *(G-11746)*
M + 4 Inc...973 527-3262
98 Crease Rd Budd Lake (07828) *(G-927)*
M + P International Inc...973 239-3005
271 Grove Ave Ste G Verona (07044) *(G-11170)*
M and D Precision Grinding...856 764-1616
120 Kossuth St Riverside (08075) *(G-9399)*
M and R Manufacturing...732 905-1061
575 Prospect St Ste 202 Lakewood (08701) *(G-5126)*
M B C Food Machinery Corp...201 489-7000
78 Mckinley St Hackensack (07601) *(G-3941)*
M B R Orthotics Inc...201 444-7750
579 Goffle Rd Wyckoff (07481) *(G-12114)*
M Blaustein Inc (PA)...973 379-1080
516 Millburn Ave Short Hills (07078) *(G-9871)*
M C Custom Shtmtl Fabrication...856 767-9509
215 Old Egg Harbor Rd C West Berlin (08091) *(G-11606)*
M C M Custom Furniture Inc...908 523-1666
817 E Linden Ave Linden (07036) *(G-5378)*
M C Signs...609 399-7446
323 Ocean Ave Ocean City (08226) *(G-7691)*
M C Technologies Inc...973 839-2779
4 Kinney Pl Pompton Plains (07444) *(G-8866)*
M Chasen & Son Inc...973 374-8956
123 S 20th St Irvington (07111) *(G-4579)*
M D Carbide Tool Corp...973 263-0104
19 Old Jacksonville Rd Towaco (07082) *(G-10874)*
M D I, Asbury *Also called Mason Display Innovations Inc (G-67)*
M D Laboratory Supplies Inc...732 322-0773
4 Minebrook Ln Franklin Park (08823) *(G-3635)*
M Deitz & Sons Inc...908 686-8800
490 Hillside Ave Hillside (07205) *(G-4412)*
M E C Technologies Inc...732 505-0308
2200 Industrial Way S Toms River (08755) *(G-10776)*
M E I, Flemington *Also called Mel Chemicals Inc (G-3455)*
M G S...609 698-7000
309 Route 72 Barnegat (08005) *(G-160)*
M G X Inc...732 329-0088
45 Stouts Ln Monmouth Junction (08852) *(G-6296)*
M H Optical Supplies Inc...800 445-3090
128 Leuning St South Hackensack (07606) *(G-10170)*
M J Powers & Co Publishers...973 898-1200
65 Madison Ave Ste 220 Morristown (07960) *(G-6683)*
M K Enterprises Inc...201 891-4199
430 W Main St Wyckoff (07481) *(G-12115)*
M K Woodworking Inc...609 771-1350
1476 Prospect St Ewing (08638) *(G-3044)*
M London Inc (PA)...201 459-6460
629 Grove St Fl 8 Jersey City (07310) *(G-4762)*
M P I, Newark *Also called Machine Parts Inc (G-7194)*
M P S, Holmdel *Also called Magnetic Products and Svcs Inc (G-4504)*
M P Tube Works Inc...908 317-2500
237 Sheffield St Mountainside (07092) *(G-6848)*
M Parker Autoworks Inc...856 933-0801
150 Heller Pl 17w Bellmawr (08031) *(G-337)*
M R, Bloomfield *Also called Minor Rubber Co Inc (G-511)*
M R C Millwork & Trim Inc...201 954-2176
319 Hobar Ct Franklin Lakes (07417) *(G-3627)*
M Rafi Sons Garment Industries...732 381-7660
1463 Pinewood St Rahway (07065) *(G-9116)*
M S Brown Jewelers, Wildwood *Also called M S Brown Mfg Jewelers (G-11946)*
M S Brown Mfg Jewelers (PA)...609 522-7604
3304 Pacific Ave Wildwood (08260) *(G-11946)*
M S C Paper Products Corp...908 686-2200
777 Ramsey Ave Hillside (07205) *(G-4413)*
M S Plastics and Packg Co...973 492-2400
10 Park Pl Ste 100 Butler (07405) *(G-1007)*
M T D Inc...908 362-6807
24 Slabtown Creek Rd Hardwick (07825) *(G-4160)*
M W Trailer Repair Inc...609 298-1113
400 Rising Sun Rd Bordentown (08505) *(G-585)*
M&L Power Systems Maint Inc...732 679-1800
109 White Oak Ln Ste 82 Old Bridge (08857) *(G-7718)*
M/C Communications LLC...908 766-0402
180 Mount Airy Rd Ste 205 Basking Ridge (07920) *(G-188)*
M2 Electric LLC...973 770-4596
3 Iron Mountain Rd Mine Hill (07803) *(G-6273)*
M2 Enterprises, Mine Hill *Also called M2 Electric LLC (G-6273)*
M4 Machine LLC...718 928-9695
7 Industrial Pkwy Ste 18 Livingston (07039) *(G-5522)*
Maarky Thermal Systems Inc...856 470-1504
1415 Marlton Pike E # 604 Cherry Hill (08034) *(G-1386)*
Mab Enterprises Inc...973 345-8282
123 S 15th St Newark (07107) *(G-7193)*
MAC Cosmetics Inc...856 661-9024
2000 Route 38 Ste 200 Cherry Hill (08002) *(G-1387)*
Mac Power, Kearny *Also called Mac Products Inc (G-4880)*
Mac Products Inc...973 344-5149
60 Pennsylvania Ave Kearny (07032) *(G-4880)*
Machine Atomated Ctrl Tech LLC...732 921-8935
1308 Centennial Ave # 109 Piscataway (08854) *(G-8685)*
Machine Control Systems Inc...732 529-6888
47 Portchester Dr Jackson (08527) *(G-4658)*
Machine Parts Inc...973 491-5444
17 Ferdon St Newark (07105) *(G-7194)*
Machine Plus Inc...973 839-8884
97 4th Ave Haskell (07420) *(G-4199)*
Machine Tech...732 738-6810
3125 Woodbridge Ave Ste 4 Edison (08837) *(G-2557)*
Machinery Electrics...732 536-0600
904 Main St Bayville (08721) *(G-247)*
Macie Publishing Company...973 983-8700
13 E Main St Ste 3 Mendham (07945) *(G-6040)*
Mack Trading LLC...973 794-4904
486 Lake Shore Dr Hewitt (07421) *(G-4276)*
Maclearie Printing LLC...732 681-2772
917 18th Ave Wall Township (07719) *(G-11354)*
Macleods Pharma Usa Inc...609 269-5250
103 College Rd E Ste 200 Princeton (08540) *(G-8972)*
Maco Appliance Parts & Sup Co...609 272-8222
1101 N New Rd Absecon (08201) *(G-3)*
Macro Sensors...856 662-8000
450 Clark Dr Ste 4 Budd Lake (07828) *(G-928)*
Macromedia Incorporated (PA)...201 646-4000
150 River St Hackensack (07601) *(G-3942)*
Mactec Packaging Tech LLC...732 343-1607
550 Hartle St Ste A Sayreville (08872) *(G-9718)*
Madan Plastics Inc...908 276-8484
370 North Ave E Cranford (07016) *(G-1915)*
Maddak Inc (HQ)...973 628-7600
661 State Route 23 Wayne (07470) *(G-11531)*
Maddalenas Cheese Cake Catrg, Ringoes *Also called Catering By Maddalenas Inc (G-9335)*
Made Solutions LLC...201 254-3693
18-01 River Rd Fair Lawn (07410) *(G-3110)*
Madhouz LLC...609 206-8009
8 Deptford Rd Dept A Glassboro (08028) *(G-3814)*
Madhu B Goyal MD...908 769-0307
908 Oak Tree Ave Ste C South Plainfield (07080) *(G-10296)*
Madison Eagle, Madison *Also called Parker Publications (G-5699)*
Madison Industries Inc...732 727-2225
554 Water Works Rd Old Bridge (08857) *(G-7719)*
Madison Park Volunteer Fire Co...732 727-1143
3011 Cheesequake Rd Parlin (08859) *(G-7868)*
Madison Shoe Company, Carlstadt *Also called Bm USA Incorporated (G-1130)*
Mafco Magnasweet, Camden *Also called Mafco Worldwide Corporation (G-1075)*
Mafco Worldwide Corporation (HQ)...856 964-8840
300 Jefferson St Camden (08104) *(G-1075)*
Mafco Worldwide LLC...856 964-8840
300 Jefferson St Camden (08104) *(G-1076)*
Mag Signs...609 747-9600
1208 Columbus Rd Ste F Burlington (08016) *(G-978)*
Magazinexperts LLC...973 383-0888
103 Spring St Newton (07860) *(G-7349)*
Maggio Fine, Bellmawr *Also called Maggio Printing LLC (G-338)*
Maggio Printing LLC...856 931-7805
171 Heller Pl Bellmawr (08031) *(G-338)*
Magic Metal Works Inc...201 384-8457
40 W Englewood Ave Bergenfield (07621) *(G-379)*
Magic Printing Corp...732 726-0620
386 Avenel St Avenel (07001) *(G-135)*
Magliones Italian Ices LLC...732 283-0705
111 Madison St Iselin (08830) *(G-4614)*
Magna Industries Inc...732 905-0957
1825 Swarthmore Ave Ste 1 Lakewood (08701) *(G-5127)*
Magna Publishing, Montclair *Also called Hyp Hair Inc (G-6369)*
Magnalube Inc...718 729-1000
1331 W Edgar Rd Linden (07036) *(G-5379)*
Magnatrol Valve Corporation...856 829-4580
941 Hamilton Ave Roebling (08554) *(G-9526)*
Magnesium Elektron Powders NJ, Manchester *Also called Reade Manufacturing Company (G-5848)*
Magnetic Metals Corporation (HQ)...856 964-7842
1900 Hayes Ave Camden (08105) *(G-1077)*
Magnetic Products and Svcs Inc...732 264-6651
2135 State Route 35 Ste 1 Holmdel (07733) *(G-4504)*
Magnetic Ticket & Label Corp...973 759-6500
151 Cortlandt St Belleville (07109) *(G-299)*
Magnetics & Controls Inc...609 397-8203
99 Kingwood Stockton Rd Rosemont (08556) *(G-9593)*
Magnetika Inc...908 454-2600
300 Red School Ln Phillipsburg (08865) *(G-8560)*
Magnetran Inc...856 768-7787
24 Elizabeth Ln Ocean View (08230) *(G-7703)*
Magnifica Inc...323 202-0386
5 Cedarbrook Dr Cranbury (08512) *(G-1861)*

Magnum Computer Recycling, Pennsauken *Also called Thanks For Being Green LLC (G-8491)*

Magnuson Products 973 472-9292
6 Chelsea Rd Clifton (07012) *(G-1663)*

Magos America Inc 973 763-9597
78 John Miller Way # 309 Kearny (07032) *(G-4881)*

Magpie Marketing Inc 201 507-9155
194 Woodland Ave Rutherford (07070) *(G-9627)*

Magruder Color Company Inc 817 837-3293
14 Takolusa Dr Holmdel (07733) *(G-4505)*

Maidenform 732 621-2216
485 Us Highway 1 S Iselin (08830) *(G-4615)*

Maidenform Brands Inc (HQ) 888 573-0299
485 Us Highway 1 S Iselin (08830) *(G-4616)*

Maier's Sunbeam Bakery, East Brunswick *Also called Bimbo Bakeries Usa Inc (G-2129)*

Mail Direct Paper Company LLC 201 933-2782
515 Vly Brook Ave Ste A Lyndhurst (07071) *(G-5660)*

Mail Time Inc 908 859-5500
224 Stockton St Phillipsburg (08865) *(G-8561)*

Main Attractions, South Plainfield *Also called Sconda Canvas Products (G-10326)*

Main Fuel LLC 201 941-2707
73 Palisade Ave Cliffside Park (07010) *(G-1541)*

Main Robert A & Sons Holdg Co (PA) 201 447-3700
555 Goffle Rd Wyckoff (07481) *(G-12116)*

Main Street Auto & Fuel LLC 732 238-0044
227 Main St Sayreville (08872) *(G-9719)*

Main Street Graphics Inc 856 755-3523
30 W Main St Maple Shade (08052) *(G-5866)*

Main Tape Company Inc (PA) 609 395-1704
1 Capital Dr Ste 101 Cranbury (08512) *(G-1862)*

Mainetti Americas Inc (PA) 201 215-2900
115 Enterprise Ave S Secaucus (07094) *(G-9791)*

Mainetti USA Inc (HQ) 201 215-2900
300 Mac Ln Keasbey (08832) *(G-4912)*

Maingear Inc 888 624-6432
206 Market St Kenilworth (07033) *(G-4955)*

Mainland Plate Glass Company 609 277-2938
53 E West Jersey Ave Pleasantville (08232) *(G-8815)*

Mainstream LLC 908 931-1010
230 Cristiani St Cranford (07016) *(G-1916)*

Mainstream Fluid & Air LLC (PA) 908 931-1010
47 Russo Pl Berkeley Heights (07922) *(G-408)*

Majer Design, Ewing *Also called M K Woodworking Inc (G-3044)*

Majesco (HQ) 973 461-5200
412 Mount Kemble Ave 110c Morristown (07960) *(G-6684)*

Majestic Industries Inc 973 473-3434
2 Canal St Passaic (07055) *(G-8084)*

Majestic Signs LLC 201 837-8104
951 Teaneck Rd Teaneck (07666) *(G-10639)*

Majewski Plumbing & Htg LLC 609 374-6001
14 E Miami Ave Villas (08251) *(G-11179)*

Majka Railing Inc 973 247-7603
125 Mcbride Ave Paterson (07501) *(G-8248)*

Major Auto Installations Inc 973 252-4262
47 N Dell Ave Ste 10 Kenvil (07847) *(G-4993)*

Major Printing Co Inc 908 686-7296
934 Savitt Pl Union (07083) *(G-11072)*

Major Products Co Inc (HQ) 201 641-5555
66 Industrial Ave Little Ferry (07643) *(G-5492)*

Make Wine With US, Wallington *Also called Dijon Enterprises LLC (G-11384)*

Malcam US 973 218-2461
51 John F Kennedy Pkwy Short Hills (07078) *(G-9872)*

Malletech LLC 732 774-0011
1107 11th Ave Neptune (07753) *(G-6889)*

Mallinckrodt Ard Inc 510 400-0700
1425 Us Highway 206 Bedminster (07921) *(G-268)*

Mallinckrodt Ard LLC (HQ) 908 238-6600
1425 Us Highway 206 Bedminster (07921) *(G-269)*

Mallinckrodt Hospital Pdts Inc 908 238-6600
1425 Us Route 206 Bedminster (07921) *(G-270)*

Mallinckrodt Hospital Pdts Inc (HQ) 314 654-2000
1425 Us Route 206 Bedminster (07921) *(G-271)*

Mallinckrodt LLC 908 238-6600
53 Frontage Rd Hampton (08827) *(G-4158)*

Mallinckrodt Parmaceuticals, Hampton *Also called Mallinckrodt LLC (G-4158)*

Mallinckrodt Pharmaceuticals, Bedminster *Also called Mallinckrodt Ard Inc (G-268)*

Malt Products Corporation (PA) 201 845-4420
88 Market St Saddle Brook (07663) *(G-9659)*

Malt Products Corporation 201 845-9106
88 Market St Saddle Brook (07663) *(G-9660)*

Mamamancinis Holdings Inc (PA) 201 532-1212
25 Branca Rd East Rutherford (07073) *(G-2299)*

Mamrout Paper Group Corp 718 510-5484
55 Talmadge Rd Edison (08817) *(G-2558)*

Man-How Inc 609 392-4895
1150 Southard St Ste 3 Trenton (08638) *(G-10954)*

Manco Industries 973 971-3131
673 S 21st St Irvington (07111) *(G-4580)*

Manco Plating Incorporated 973 485-6800
390 Park Ave Newark (07107) *(G-7195)*

Mane USA Inc (HQ) 973 633-5533
60 Demarest Dr Wayne (07470) *(G-11532)*

Mango Custom Cabinets Inc 908 813-3077
216 W Stiger St Hackettstown (07840) *(G-4020)*

Manhattan Door Corp 718 963-1111
109 Kero Rd Carlstadt (07072) *(G-1184)*

Manhattan Gunite, Closter *Also called En Tech Corp (G-1754)*

Manhattan Neon Sign Corp 212 714-0430
650 Newark St Hoboken (07030) *(G-4465)*

Manhattan Signs & Designs Ltd 973 278-3603
130 Beckwith Ave Ste 2b Paterson (07503) *(G-8249)*

Manley Performance Pdts Inc (PA) 732 905-3366
1960 Swarthmore Ave Lakewood (08701) *(G-5128)*

Manna Group LLC 856 881-7650
137 Gaither Dr Ste F Mount Laurel (08054) *(G-6780)*

Manner Textile Processing Inc 973 942-8718
41 Oakdale Ct North Haledon (07508) *(G-7497)*

Manning & Lewis Engrg Co Inc 908 687-2400
675 Rahway Ave Ste 1 Union (07083) *(G-11073)*

Manning Publication Co. 856 375-2597
1233 Heartwood Dr Cherry Hill (08003) *(G-1388)*

Mannington Mills Inc (PA) 856 935-3000
75 Mannington Mills Rd Salem (08079) *(G-9694)*

Mannington Rsilient Floors Div, Salem *Also called Mannington Mills Inc (G-9694)*

Mantech Systems Engrg Corp 856 566-9155
1000 Haddonfield Berlin R Voorhees (08043) *(G-11291)*

Manttra Inc 877 962-6887
1130 Somerset St New Brunswick (08901) *(G-6944)*

Manufacturers Brush Corp 973 882-6966
310 W 1st Ave Roselle (07203) *(G-9563)*

Manufacturing / Consultants, Manalapan *Also called Ccard (G-5803)*

Manufacturing Branch, Phillipsburg *Also called Magnetika Inc (G-8560)*

Manufacturing Chem Dyestuff, Cranford *Also called Orient Corporation of America (G-1920)*

Manutech Inc 856 358-6136
29 State St Elmer (08318) *(G-2800)*

Manva Industries Inc 973 667-2606
48 Franklin Ave Nutley (07110) *(G-7590)*

Manville Rubber Products Inc 908 526-9111
1009 Kennedy Blvd Manville (08835) *(G-5856)*

Manzi Printing 732 542-1927
132 Lewis St Ste B2 Eatontown (07724) *(G-2409)*

Mapei Corporation 732 254-4830
O Off South River (08882) *(G-10352)*

Mapei Corporation 732 254-4830
Whitehead South River (08882) *(G-10353)*

Mapleton Nurseries, Kingston *Also called Kingston Nurseries LLC (G-5010)*

Maplewood Beverage Packers LLC 973 416-4582
45 Camptown Rd Maplewood (07040) *(G-5880)*

Maquet, Fairfield *Also called Datascope Corp (G-3178)*

Maquet Cardiac Assist, Mahwah *Also called Datascope Corp (G-5727)*

Maquet Cardiovascular LLC 973 709-7000
45 Barbour Pond Dr Wayne (07470) *(G-11533)*

Mar Machine Ken Manufacturing 973 278-5827
477 E 30th St Paterson (07504) *(G-8250)*

Mar-Kal Products Corp 973 783-7155
145 Commerce Rd Carlstadt (07072) *(G-1185)*

Mara Polishing & Plating Corp 973 242-0800
105 W Peddie St Newark (07112) *(G-7196)*

Maranatha Ceramic Tile & Marbl 609 758-1168
253 Cokstown New Egypt Rd Wrightstown (08562) *(G-12099)*

Maranatha Now Inc 609 599-1402
445 Bunting Ave Trenton (08611) *(G-10955)*

Maranatha Stairs, Wrightstown *Also called Maranatha Ceramic Tile & Marbl (G-12099)*

Marathon Enterprises Inc (PA) 201 935-3330
9 Smith St Englewood (07631) *(G-2921)*

Marble and Granite, Wayne *Also called EZ General Construction Corp (G-11500)*

Marble and Granite Design Ctr, Cranbury *Also called Ankur International Inc (G-1811)*

Marble Online Corporation 201 998-9100
260 Schuyler Ave Fl 1 Kearny (07032) *(G-4882)*

Marbleworld Manufacturing, Hammonton *Also called Bucci Management Co Inc (G-4131)*

Marcal Manufacturing LLC (HQ) 201 796-4000
1 Market St Elmwood Park (07407) *(G-2839)*

Marcal Paper Mills LLC 800 631-8451
1 Market St Elmwood Park (07407) *(G-2840)*

Marchione Industries Inc 718 317-4900
136 Park Ave Lyndhurst (07071) *(G-5661)*

Marco Book Co Inc 973 458-0485
60 Industrial Rd Lodi (07644) *(G-5570)*

Marcotex International Inc 201 991-8200
69 Sellers St Kearny (07032) *(G-4883)*

Mardee Company Inc 908 753-4343
242 Saint Nicholas Ave South Plainfield (07080) *(G-10297)*

Mardee Video Company, South Plainfield *Also called Mardee Company Inc (G-10297)*

Mardon Associates Inc 973 977-2251
1 Industrial Plz Paterson (07503) *(G-8251)*

Margaritaville Inc 973 728-7562
129 Lincoln Ave West Milford (07480) ***(G-11729)***
Maria, Paterson *Also called Mar Machine Ken Manufacturing* ***(G-8250)***
Marian, Glen Rock *Also called Melissa Spice Trading Corp* ***(G-3832)***
Mariano Press LLC 732 247-3659
14 Veronica Ave Somerset (08873) ***(G-10022)***
Mariell, Budd Lake *Also called San Marel Designs Inc* ***(G-935)***
Marijon Dyeing & Finishing Co 201 933-9770
219 Murray Hill Pkwy East Rutherford (07073) ***(G-2300)***
Marine Acquisition Inc 609 965-2300
801 Philadelphia Ave Egg Harbor City (08215) ***(G-2664)***
Marine Cont Eqp Crtfction Corp 732 938-6622
160 Sqnkum Yellowbrook Rd Farmingdale (07727) ***(G-3388)***
Marine East, Brick *Also called Mariner Sales and Power Inc* ***(G-725)***
Marine Electric Systems Inc 201 531-8600
80 Wesley St South Hackensack (07606) ***(G-10171)***
Marine Oil Service Inc 908 282-6440
450 S Front St Elizabeth (07202) ***(G-2755)***
Mariner Sales and Power Inc (PA) 732 477-7484
834 Mantoloking Rd Brick (08723) ***(G-725)***
Mariners Annual, Edison *Also called Charles Kerr Enterprises Inc* ***(G-2476)***
Marino Building Systems Corp 732 968-0555
1640 New Market Ave 1a South Plainfield (07080) ***(G-10298)***
Marino International Corp 732 752-5100
1640 New Market Ave South Plainfield (07080) ***(G-10299)***
Marino Ware Division, South Plainfield *Also called Ware Industries Inc* ***(G-10345)***
Maritime Solutions Inc 732 752-3831
200 Pond Ave Middlesex (08846) ***(G-6129)***
Mark Alan Printing & Graphics 732 981-9011
1032 Stelton Rd Ste 2 Piscataway (08854) ***(G-8686)***
Mark I Industries Inc 609 884-0051
910 Shunpike Rd Cape May (08204) ***(G-1100)***
Mark I Interiors, Plainfield *Also called A N Laggren Awngs Canvas Mfg* ***(G-8756)***
Mark Lithographers, Cedar Knolls *Also called Mark Lithography Inc* ***(G-1309)***
Mark Lithography Inc 973 538-5557
4 Saddle Rd Cedar Knolls (07927) ***(G-1309)***
Mark Ronald Associates Inc (PA) 908 558-0011
1227 Central Ave Hillside (07205) ***(G-4414)***
Mark's Hmmade Ice Cream Dlghts, North Bergen *Also called Marks Ice Cream* ***(G-7417)***
Mark-O-Lite Sign Co Inc 732 462-8530
1420 Us Highway 9 Howell (07731) ***(G-4546)***
Mark/Trece Inc 973 884-1005
160 Algonquin Pkwy Ste 1 Whippany (07981) ***(G-11897)***
Markbilt Inc 201 891-7842
308 Canterbury Ln Wyckoff (07481) ***(G-12117)***
Marketing Administration Assoc 732 840-3021
1101 Industrial Pkwy Brick (08724) ***(G-726)***
Marko Engraving & Art Corp (PA) 201 864-6500
19 Baldwin Ave Weehawken (07086) ***(G-11569)***
Marko Engraving & Art Corp 201 945-6555
439 Fairview Ave Fairview (07022) ***(G-3363)***
Markov Processes International 908 608-1558
475 Sprngfeld Ave Ste 401 Summit (07901) ***(G-10539)***
Marks Ice Cream 201 861-5099
8205 Bergenline Ave North Bergen (07047) ***(G-7417)***
Marks Management Systems Inc 856 866-0588
590 E Kings Hwy Maple Shade (08052) ***(G-5867)***
Markus Wiener Publishers Inc 609 921-1141
231 Nassau St Princeton (08542) ***(G-8973)***
Marlabs Incorporated (PA) 732 694-1000
1 Corporate Pl S Fl 3 Piscataway (08854) ***(G-8687)***
Marlene Embroidery Inc 201 868-1682
6805 Madison St West New York (07093) ***(G-11747)***
Marlene Lace, North Bergen *Also called Marlene Trimmings LLC* ***(G-7418)***
Marlene Trimmings LLC 201 926-3108
407 77th St North Bergen (07047) ***(G-7418)***
Marlin Candle Co, Ltl Egg Hbr *Also called Stephen L Feilinger* ***(G-5620)***
Marlo Manufacturing Co Inc 973 423-0226
301 Division St Boonton (07005) ***(G-560)***
Marlo Plastic Products Inc 732 792-1988
3535 State Route 66 Ste 1 Neptune (07753) ***(G-6890)***
Marlow Candy & Nut Co Inc 201 569-7606
65 Honeck St Englewood (07631) ***(G-2922)***
Marlton Creative Design Center, Marlton *Also called Packaging Corporation America* ***(G-5945)***
Marlton Pike Precision LLC 856 665-1900
728 Beechwood Ave Cherry Hill (08002) ***(G-1389)***
Marlyn Sheet Metal Inc 856 863-6900
606 N Delsea Dr Clayton (08312) ***(G-1527)***
Marmaxx Operating Corp 973 575-7910
901 Bloomfield Ave West Caldwell (07006) ***(G-11660)***
Marmo Enterprises Inc 732 649-3011
468 Elizabeth Ave Somerset (08873) ***(G-10023)***
Marmon Industrial LLC 609 655-4287
101 Interchange Plz # 106 Cranbury (08512) ***(G-1863)***
Marotta Controls Inc (PA) 973 334-7800
78 Boonton Ave Montville (07045) ***(G-6444)***
Marquis, Moonachie *Also called Jade Eastern Trading Inc* ***(G-6473)***
Marquis - Whos Who Inc 908 673-1006
430 Mountain Ave Ste 403 New Providence (07974) ***(G-7009)***
Mars Incorporated 908 852-1000
700 High St Hackettstown (07840) ***(G-4021)***
Mars Incorporated 908 850-2420
800 High St Hackettstown (07840) ***(G-4022)***
Mars Incorporated 973 691-3500
100 International Dr Budd Lake (07828) ***(G-929)***
Mars Chocolate North Amer LLC (HQ) 908 852-1000
800 High St Hackettstown (07840) ***(G-4023)***
Mars Chocolate North Amer LLC 908 979-5070
700 High St Hackettstown (07840) ***(G-4024)***
Mars Food Us LLC 908 852-1000
800 High St Hackettstown (07840) ***(G-4025)***
Mars Retail Group Inc 973 398-2078
400 Valley Rd Ste 204 Mount Arlington (07856) ***(G-6715)***
Mars Wrigley Conf US LLC (HQ) 908 852-1000
800 High St Hackettstown (07840) ***(G-4026)***
Marsden Inc 856 663-2227
6800 Westfield Ave Pennsauken (08110) ***(G-8452)***
Marshall Industrial Tech, Trenton *Also called Marshall Maintenance* ***(G-10956)***
Marshall Maintenance (PA) 609 394-7153
529 S Clinton Ave Trenton (08611) ***(G-10956)***
Marshalls, West Caldwell *Also called Marmaxx Operating Corp* ***(G-11660)***
Marte Cabinets Countertops LLC 973 525-9502
48 Palmer St Apt 1 Passaic (07055) ***(G-8085)***
Martec Access Products Inc 908 233-0101
60 Kingsbridge Rd Piscataway (08854) ***(G-8688)***
Martin Corporation 856 451-0900
171 N Pearl St Bridgeton (08302) ***(G-764)***
Martin Sprocket & Gear Inc 973 633-5700
7 Highpoint Dr Wayne (07470) ***(G-11534)***
Martin Tool Company Inc 973 361-9212
60 State Route 15 S Wharton (07885) ***(G-11862)***
Martins Specialty Sausage Co (PA) 856 423-4000
150 Harmony Rd Mickleton (08056) ***(G-6087)***
Marty Anderson & Assoc Inc 201 798-0507
4200 Grand Ave North Bergen (07047) ***(G-7419)***
Marvic Corp 908 686-4340
2450 Iorio Ct Union (07083) ***(G-11074)***
Marvic Formica In Design, Union *Also called Marvic Corp* ***(G-11074)***
Marx NJ Group LLC 732 901-3880
14 Easy St Ste 14e4 Bound Brook (08805) ***(G-603)***
Mary Bridget Enterprises 609 267-4830
2305 Garry Rd Ste B Cinnaminson (08077) ***(G-1471)***
Mas Epoxies, Cinnaminson *Also called Phoenix Resins Inc* ***(G-1482)***
Mas Machine Shop LLC 201 768-9110
267 Livingston St Northvale (07647) ***(G-7535)***
Masco Cabinetry LLC 732 363-3797
450 Oberlin Ave S Lakewood (08701) ***(G-5129)***
Masco Cabinetry LLC 732 942-5138
440-450 Oberlin Ave S Lakewood (08701) ***(G-5130)***
Mason Display Innovations Inc 609 860-0675
1 Deer Hill Rd Asbury (08802) ***(G-67)***
Masouleh Corp (PA) 973 470-8900
301 River Rd Clifton (07014) ***(G-1664)***
Massage Chair Inc 732 201-7777
1692 Route 88 Ste 1 Brick (08724) ***(G-727)***
Massarellis Lawn Ornaments Inc 609 567-9700
500 S Egg Harbor Rd Hammonton (08037) ***(G-4139)***
Massimo Zanetti Beverage USA 201 440-1700
10 Empire Blvd Moonachie (07074) ***(G-6478)***
Massina Wildlife Management, Washington *Also called Big Bucks Enterprises Inc* ***(G-11442)***
Master Bond Inc 201 343-8983
154 Hobart St Hackensack (07601) ***(G-3943)***
Master Craft Interiors, Saddle Brook *Also called RFS Commercial Inc* ***(G-9671)***
Master Drapery Workroom Inc 908 272-4404
220 N 14th St Kenilworth (07033) ***(G-4956)***
Master Metal Finishers, Paterson *Also called Master Metal Polishing Corp* ***(G-8252)***
Master Metal Polishing Corp 973 684-0119
57 Wood St Paterson (07524) ***(G-8252)***
Master Presentations Inc 732 239-7093
182 Hadassah Ln Lakewood (08701) ***(G-5131)***
Master Printing Inc 201 842-9100
445 Industrial Rd Carlstadt (07072) ***(G-1186)***
Master Repro Inc 201 447-4800
95 Greenwood Ave Midland Park (07432) ***(G-6179)***
Master Shoe Products, Belleville *Also called Petronio Shoe Products Corp* ***(G-307)***
Master Strap LLC 888 503-7779
20 Hastings Rd Ste B Marlboro (07746) ***(G-5904)***
Mastercool USA Inc 973 252-9119
1 Aspen Dr Ste 1 # 1 Randolph (07869) ***(G-9190)***
Mastercraft Electroplating 908 354-4404
801 Magnolia Ave Ste 4 Elizabeth (07201) ***(G-2756)***
Mastercraft Iron Inc 732 988-3113
1111 10th Ave Neptune (07753) ***(G-6891)***
Mastercraft Metal Finishing 908 354-4404
801 Magnolia Ave Elizabeth (07201) ***(G-2757)***
Mastercrafts, South Hackensack *Also called Robert J Smith* ***(G-10184)***

678 2019 Harris New Jersey Manufacturers Directory (G-0000) Company's Geographic Section entry number

Mastergraphx, Monmouth Junction Also called M G X Inc (G-6296)

Masterpiece Kitchens Inc 609 518-7887
2060 Springdale Rd # 800 Cherry Hill (08003) (G-1390)

Masters Interiors Inc 973 253-0784
1500 Main Ave Ste 23 Clifton (07011) (G-1665)

Mastertaste Inc (HQ) 732 882-0202
160 Terminal Ave Clark (07066) (G-1508)

Mastertaste Inc 201 373-1111
546 Us Highway 46 Teterboro (07608) (G-10686)

Mastery Education, Montvale Also called Peoples Eductl Holdings Inc (G-6423)

Mat Logo Central LLC 973 433-0311
216 Little Falls Rd Cedar Grove (07009) (G-1281)

Matchless United Companies (HQ) 908 862-7300
801 E Linden Ave Ste 1 Linden (07036) (G-5380)

Material Imports 201 229-1180
10 Oxford Dr Moonachie (07074) (G-6479)

Materials Research Group Inc 908 245-3301
244 W 1st Ave Roselle (07203) (G-9564)

Materials Technology Inc 732 246-1000
220 Churchill Ave Somerset (08873) (G-10024)

Mateson Chemical Corporation 215 423-3200
510 Whitmore St Cinnaminson (08077) (G-1472)

Math League Press, Tenafly Also called Mathematics League Inc (G-10664)

Mathcloud, Cliffside Park Also called Educloud Inc (G-1538)

Mathematics League Inc 201 568-6328
17 Lancaster Rd Tenafly (07670) (G-10664)

Matheson Gas Products, Basking Ridge Also called Matheson Tri-Gas Inc (G-190)

Matheson Gas Products Inc 201 867-4101
959 Us Highway 46 Parsippany (07054) (G-7975)

Matheson Tri-Gas Inc (HQ) 908 991-9200
150 Allen Rd Ste 302 Basking Ridge (07920) (G-189)

Matheson Tri-Gas Inc 908 991-9200
150 Allen Rd Ste 301 Basking Ridge (07920) (G-190)

Matinas Biopharma Inc 908 443-1860
1545 Route 206 Ste 302 Bedminster (07921) (G-272)

Matinas Biopharma Holdings Inc (PA) 908 443-1860
1545 Route 206 Ste 302 Bedminster (07921) (G-273)

Matiss Inc (PA) 201 648-0002
51 Harrison St Fl 5 Hoboken (07030) (G-4466)

Matisse Chocolatier Inc (PA) 201 568-2288
260 Grand Ave Ste 6 Englewood (07631) (G-2923)

Matrix Apparel, Spring Lake Also called Matrix Sales Group LLC (G-10423)

Matrix Controls Company Inc 732 469-5551
330 Elizabeth Ave Somerset (08873) (G-10025)

Matrix Sales Group LLC 908 461-4148
309 Morris Ave Ste E Spring Lake (07762) (G-10423)

Matrixx Initiatives Inc (PA) 877 942-2626
1 Grand Blvd Bridgewater (08807) (G-847)

Matter Magazine, Maplewood Also called Visual Impact Advertising Inc (G-5889)

Matthew Bender & Company Inc (HQ) 518 487-3000
744 Broad St Fl 8 Newark (07102) (G-7197)

Matthew Warren Inc 908 788-5800
137 Us Highway 202 Ringoes (08551) (G-9339)

Matthey Johnson Inc 856 384-7022
2003 Nolte Dr Paulsboro (08066) (G-8334)

Matthey Johnson Inc 856 384-7132
2001 Nolte Dr West Deptford (08066) (G-11710)

Matthey Johnson Inc 856 384-7001
2003 Nolte Dr West Deptford (08066) (G-11711)

Matthias Paper Corporation (PA) 856 467-6970
301 Arlington Blvd Swedesboro (08085) (G-10594)

Mattress Dev Co Del LLC 732 628-0800
1375 Jersey Ave North Brunswick (08902) (G-7476)

Mauden International, Pine Brook Also called International Beauty Products (G-8607)

Maund Enterprises Inc 609 628-2475
112 Buckhill Rd Tuckahoe (08250) (G-11012)

Mauser Usa LLC 732 634-6000
14 Convery Blvd Woodbridge (07095) (G-12019)

Mauser Usa LLC (HQ) 732 353-7100
35 Cotters Ln Ste C East Brunswick (08816) (G-2155)

Maverick Caterers LLC 718 433-3776
20 Railroad Ave Hackensack (07601) (G-3944)

Maverick Housewares, Edison Also called Maverick Industries Inc (G-2559)

Maverick Industries Inc 732 417-9666
94 Mayfield Ave Edison (08837) (G-2559)

Maverick Oil Co 732 747-8637
9 Central Ave Red Bank (07701) (G-9234)

Max Flight Corp 732 281-2007
7 Executive Dr Toms River (08755) (G-10777)

Max Gurtman & Sons Inc 973 478-7000
622 Lexington Ave Clifton (07011) (G-1666)

Max Pro Services LLC 973 396-2373
184 S Livingston Ave Livingston (07039) (G-5523)

Maxell Corporation of America (HQ) 973 653-2400
3 Garret Mountain Plz # 300 Woodland Park (07424) (G-12084)

Maxentric Technologies LLC (PA) 201 242-9800
2071 Lemoine Ave Ste 302 Fort Lee (07024) (G-3570)

Maximum Humn Prfmce Hldngs LLC (PA) 973 785-9055
165 Clinton Rd West Caldwell (07006) (G-11661)

Maximum Material Handling LLC 973 227-1227
750 Edwards Rd Parsippany (07054) (G-7976)

Maxisit Inc 732 494-2005
203 Main St Metuchen (08840) (G-6065)

Maxlite Inc 800 555-5629
10 York Ave West Caldwell (07006) (G-11662)

Maxlite Inc (PA) 973 244-7300
12 York Ave West Caldwell (07006) (G-11663)

Maxsyl Leather Co LLC 201 864-0579
131 35th St Union City (07087) (G-11121)

Maxter Corporation 609 877-9700
18 Chalford Ln Willingboro (08046) (G-11992)

Maxwell McKenney Inc 856 310-0700
116 White Horse Pike # 6 Haddon Heights (08035) (G-4046)

Maxzone Vehicle Lighting Corp 732 393-9600
24 Kilmer Rd Edison (08817) (G-2560)

May National Associates NJ Inc 973 473-3330
995 Towbin Ave Lakewood (08701) (G-5132)

Maya Liquidation, Jersey City Also called Maya Trading Corporation (G-4763)

Maya Trading Corporation 201 533-1400
746-748 Tonnelle Ave Jersey City (07307) (G-4763)

Mayab Happy Tacos Inc 732 293-0400
450 Florida Grove Rd Perth Amboy (08861) (G-8526)

Mayabeque Products Inc 201 869-0531
7424 Bergenline Ave Ste 1 North Bergen (07047) (G-7420)

Mayfair Tech Ltd Lblty Co 609 802-1262
66 Witherspoon St Princeton (08542) (G-8974)

Mays Landing Sand & Gravel Co (HQ) 856 447-4294
1101 Railroad Ave Newport (08345) (G-7334)

Maywood Furniture, Maywood Also called De Saussure Equipment Co Inc (G-6003)

Mbs Installations Inc 888 446-9135
29 Summerhill Ave Jackson (08527) (G-4659)

Mc, Cedar Grove Also called Metal Cutting Corporation (G-1282)

Mc Does Inc 856 985-8730
906 Route 73 N Marlton (08053) (G-5941)

Mc Ginley Packaging Methods 201 493-9330
80 Greenwood Ave Midland Park (07432) (G-6180)

Mc Lain Screen Printing, Asbury Park Also called McLain Studios Inc (G-80)

Mc Lean Corrugated Containers, Pennsauken Also called McLean Packaging Corporation (G-8456)

Mc Renewable Energy LLC 732 369-9933
50 Fletcher Ave Manasquan (08736) (G-5833)

McAlister Welding & Fabg 856 740-3890
112 Maple Leaf Ct Glassboro (08028) (G-3815)

McAllister Service Company (PA) 856 665-4545
7116 Park Ave Pennsauken (08109) (G-8453)

McBride Awning Co 732 892-6256
304 Richmond Ave Point Pleasant Beach (08742) (G-8828)

McC Norsal, Paterson Also called Microwave Consulting Corp (G-8259)

McCain Ellios Foods Inc 201 368-0600
11 Gregg St Lodi (07644) (G-5571)

McCormicks Bindery Inc 856 663-8035
5815 Magnolia Ave Pennsauken (08109) (G-8454)

McGinnis Printing 732 758-0060
20 Monmouth St Red Bank (07701) (G-9235)

McGonegal Manufacturing Co 201 438-2313
405 Railroad Ave East Rutherford (07073) (G-2301)

McGraw-Hill Glbl Edctn Hldngs 609 371-8301
104 Windsor Center Dr East Windsor (08520) (G-2354)

McGrory Glass Inc 856 579-3200
1400 Grandview Ave Paulsboro (08066) (G-8335)

MCI Service Parts 732 967-9081
35 Cotters Ln East Brunswick (08816) (G-2156)

McIntosh Industries Inc 908 688-7475
676 Ramsey Ave Hillside (07205) (G-4415)

McKella 2-8-0 Inc 856 813-1153
7025 Central Hwy Pennsauken (08109) (G-8455)

McKella 280, Pennsauken Also called McKella 2-8-0 Inc (G-8455)

McKinley Scientific Llc (PA) 973 579-4144
33 Wilson Dr Ste C Sparta (07871) (G-10396)

McLain Studios Inc 732 775-0271
1203 Main St Asbury Park (07712) (G-80)

McLean Packaging Corporation (PA) 856 359-2600
1504 Glen Ave Moorestown (08057) (G-6544)

McLean Packaging Corporation 856 359-2600
1000 Thomas Busch Mem Hwy Pennsauken (08110) (G-8456)

McM Products USA Inc 646 756-4090
500 Plaza Dr Ste 101 Secaucus (07094) (G-9792)

McMunn Associates 856 858-3440
900 Haddon Ave Ste 302 Collingswood (08108) (G-1770)

McNichols Company 877 884-4653
2 Home News Row New Brunswick (08901) (G-6945)

McQuade Enterprises LLC 609 501-2437
511 N 6th St Millville (08332) (G-6260)

McT Dairies Inc (HQ) 973 258-9600
15 Bleeker St Ste 103 Millburn (07041) (G-6203)

McT Manufacturing Inc 877 258-9600
15 Bleeker St Ste 101 Millburn (07041) (G-6204)

McW Precision...609 859-4400
  137 Eayrestown Rd Southampton (08088) *(G-10368)*

McWane Inc...908 454-1161
  183 Sitgreaves St Phillipsburg (08865) *(G-8562)*

McWilliams Forge Company (HQ).....................973 627-0200
  387 Franklin Ave Rockaway (07866) *(G-9476)*

MD International Inc...................................856 779-7633
  383 Kings Hwy N Ste B1 Cherry Hill (08034) *(G-1391)*

Mdb Construction.......................................908 628-8010
  236 Cokesbury Rd Lebanon (08833) *(G-5270)*

Mdc, Boonton Also called Merchandising Display Corp *(G-561)*

Mdi Manufacturing Inc.................................732 994-5599
  100 Syracuse Ct Lakewood (08701) *(G-5133)*

Mdj Inc...201 457-9260
  25 Dicarolis Ct 21 Hackensack (07601) *(G-3945)*

Mdr Diagnostics LLC.................................609 396-0021
  199 6th Ave Ste C Mount Laurel (08054) *(G-6781)*

Mdr LLC...973 731-7100
  401 Pleasant Valley Way # 2 West Orange (07052) *(G-11772)*

Mdviani Designs Inc...................................201 840-5410
  724 Bergen Blvd Ste 2 Ridgefield (07657) *(G-9275)*

Mead Wilbert, Wayne Also called Di-Ferraro Inc *(G-11493)*

Meadowbrook Inventions Inc........................908 766-0606
  260 Mine Brook Rd Bernardsville (07924) *(G-439)*

Meadowfarmalpacas Aolcom, Lawrenceville Also called Meadowgate Farm
Alpacas *(G-5237)*

Meadowgate Farm Alpacas..........................609 219-0529
  3071 Lawrenceville Rd Lawrenceville (08648) *(G-5237)*

Meadowlands Bindery Inc............................201 935-6161
  146 W Commercial Ave Moonachie (07074) *(G-6480)*

Meadowlands Castle, Lyndhurst Also called Medieval Times USA Inc *(G-5662)*

Meadows Knitting Corp...............................973 482-6400
  1875 Mccarter Hwy Newark (07104) *(G-7198)*

Meal Quik, Piscataway Also called Red Dash Media LLC *(G-8704)*

Measurement & Computing Co, West Orange Also called Measurement Control
Corp *(G-11773)*

Measurement Control Corp...........................800 504-9010
  9 Cummings Cir West Orange (07052) *(G-11773)*

Meca Electronics Inc................................973 625-0661
  459 E Main St Denville (07834) *(G-2045)*

Mech-Tronics, Mount Holly Also called High Gate Corp *(G-6730)*

Mechanical Components Corp........................732 938-3737
  1 Executive Dr Unit B Toms River (08755) *(G-10778)*

Mechanical Ingenuity Corp..........................732 842-8889
  28 Eaton Rd Ste 3 Eatontown (07724) *(G-2410)*

Mechanical Technologies LLC.......................973 616-3800
  10 Bloomfield Ave Ste 6 Pine Brook (07058) *(G-8609)*

Mechanictron, Roselle Also called Mechanitron Corporation Inc *(G-9565)*

Mechanitron Corporation Inc........................908 620-1001
  310 W 1st Ave Roselle (07203) *(G-9565)*

Mechtronics Corporation.............................845 231-1400
  939 Huron Rd Franklin Lakes (07417) *(G-3628)*

Med Connection LLC..................................908 213-7012
  65 Howard St Phillipsburg (08865) *(G-8563)*

Med-Con Tech Ltd Lblty Co...........................888 654-0856
  24 E Main St Unit 5033 Clinton (08809) *(G-1747)*

Meda Pharmaceuticals Inc...........................732 564-2200
  265 Davidson Ave Ste 300 Somerset (08873) *(G-10026)*

Medalco Metals Inc..................................908 238-0513
  5 Chrystal Dr Lebanon (08833) *(G-5271)*

Medality Medical LLC................................215 990-0754
  3 S Haddon Ave Ste 3 # 3 Haddonfield (08033) *(G-4060)*

Medallion International Inc...........................973 616-3401
  233 W Parkway Pompton Plains (07444) *(G-8867)*

Medavante-Prophase Inc (HQ).....................609 528-9400
  100 American Metro Blvd Hamilton (08619) *(G-4112)*

Medchem Express LLC................................732 783-7915
  11 Deerpark Dr Monmouth Junction (08852) *(G-6297)*

Medco West Electronics Inc.........................201 457-9260
  25 Dicarolis Ct 21 Hackensack (07601) *(G-3946)*

Medford Cedar Products Inc.........................609 859-1400
  59 Old Red Lion Rd Southampton (08088) *(G-10369)*

Medi-Physics, South Plainfield Also called GE Healthcare Inc *(G-10266)*

Media Vista Inc...732 747-8060
  60 Broad St Ste 100 Red Bank (07701) *(G-9236)*

Mediabridge Products LLC...........................856 216-8222
  1951 Old Cuthbert Rd Cherry Hill (08034) *(G-1392)*

Medianews Group Inc................................856 451-1000
  93 5th St Salem (08079) *(G-9695)*

Mediavista News, Red Bank Also called Media Vista Inc *(G-9236)*

Medica...760 634-5440
  53 Richboynton Rd Dover (07801) *(G-2096)*

Medical Device Bus Svcs Inc.......................732 524-0400
  1 Johnson And Johnson Plz New Brunswick (08933) *(G-6946)*

Medical Indicators Inc (PA).........................609 737-1600
  16 Thmas J Rhdes Indus Dr Hamilton (08619) *(G-4113)*

Medical Manager, Elmwood Park Also called Emdeon Corporation *(G-2825)*

Medical Scrubs Collectn NJ LLC (HQ).............732 719-8600
  1655 Corporate Rd W Lakewood (08701) *(G-5134)*

Medical Transcription Billing (PA)..................732 873-5133
  7 Clyde Rd Somerset (08873) *(G-10027)*

Medici International Inc...............................973 684-6084
  85 5th Ave Build18 Paterson (07524) *(G-8253)*

Medicines Company (PA).............................973 290-6000
  8 Sylvan Way Parsippany (07054) *(G-7977)*

Medicis Pharmaceutical Corp (HQ).................866 246-8245
  700 Us Highway 202/206 Bridgewater (08807) *(G-848)*

Medico Graphics Services Inc.......................201 216-1660
  683 Garfield Ave Jersey City (07305) *(G-4764)*

Medicon Inc...201 669-7456
  17 Beechwood Rd Allendale (07401) *(G-12)*

Medicraft Inc..201 421-3055
  50 Bushes Ln Elmwood Park (07407) *(G-2841)*

Medicraft Inc (PA)....................................201 797-8820
  7 Paul Kohner Pl Elmwood Park (07407) *(G-2842)*

Medicure Pharma Inc.................................888 435-2220
  116 Village Blvd Ste 200 Princeton (08540) *(G-8975)*

Medieval Times USA Inc.............................201 933-2220
  149 Polito Ave Lyndhurst (07071) *(G-5662)*

Medilogic Group LLC................................201 794-2166
  275 Goffle Rd Hawthorne (07506) *(G-4231)*

Medimtriks Pharmaceuticals Inc....................973 882-7512
  383 Us Highway 46 Fairfield (07004) *(G-3267)*

Medin Technologies Inc.............................973 779-2400
  11 Jackson Rd Totowa (07512) *(G-10836)*

Mediscope Manufacturing Inc (PA).................908 756-2411
  744 Mountain Blvd Fl 2w Watchung (07069) *(G-11457)*

Medison Pharmaceuticals Inc........................856 304-8516
  201 Circle Dr N Ste 101 Piscataway (08854) *(G-8689)*

Mediterranean Chef Inc..............................855 628-0903
  3 Borinski Dr Lincoln Park (07035) *(G-5301)*

Mediterranean Stucco Corp..........................973 491-0160
  111 Main St Newark (07105) *(G-7199)*

Meditron Devices, Waldwick Also called Nextphase Medical Devices LLC *(G-11308)*

Medlaurel Inc...856 461-6600
  620 Cooper St Delanco (08075) *(G-2006)*

Medplast West Berlin Inc (HQ).....................856 753-7600
  225 Old Egg Harbor Rd West Berlin (08091) *(G-11607)*

Medtec Services LLC..................................201 722-9696
  67 Woodland Ave Westwood (07675) *(G-11835)*

Medtronic Inc...908 289-5969
  1130 Commerce Blvd # 100 Swedesboro (08085) *(G-10595)*

Medtronic Usa Inc...................................973 331-7914
  300 Interpace Pkwy # 340 Parsippany (07054) *(G-7978)*

Meese Inc (HQ).......................................201 796-4490
  535 N Midland Ave Saddle Brook (07663) *(G-9661)*

Meeshaa Inc...908 279-7985
  18 Tingley Ln Edison (08820) *(G-2561)*

Mega Brands America Inc...........................973 535-1313
  68 Passaic St Wood Ridge (07075) *(G-12004)*

Mega Industries LLC..................................973 779-8772
  79 South St Passaic (07055) *(G-8086)*

Mega Media Concepts Ltd Lblty.....................973 919-5661
  26 Gail Ct Ste 1 Sparta (07871) *(G-10397)*

Megalith Pharmaceuticals Inc........................877 436-7220
  302 Carnegie Ctr Princeton (08540) *(G-8976)*

Megaplex Software Inc...............................908 647-3273
  21 Broadway Rd Warren (07059) *(G-11421)*

Megas Yeeros LLC...................................212 777-6342
  165 Chubb Ave Lyndhurst (07071) *(G-5663)*

Megasafe, Netcong Also called Hookway Enterprises Inc *(G-6907)*

Megatran Industries (PA).............................609 227-4300
  312 Rising Sun Rd Bordentown (08505) *(G-586)*

MEI, East Brunswick Also called Mon-Eco Industries Inc *(G-2157)*

Mej Signs Inc..609 584-6881
  3100 Quakerbridge Rd # 5 Hamilton (08619) *(G-4114)*

Mek International Inc..................................215 712-2490
  3 Stonewall Ct Woodcliff Lake (07677) *(G-12059)*

Mel Chemicals Inc (HQ)..............................908 782-5800
  500 Brbrtown Pt Breeze Rd Flemington (08822) *(G-3455)*

Melicks Town Farm Inc (PA).........................908 439-2318
  Old Turn Pike Rd Oldwick (08858) *(G-7740)*

Melillo Consulting Inc (PA)...........................732 563-8400
  285 Davidson Ave Ste 202 Somerset (08873) *(G-10028)*

Melissa Spice Trading Corp..........................862 262-7773
  123 Glen Ave Glen Rock (07452) *(G-3832)*

Melita USA, Cherry Hill Also called European Coffee Classics Inc *(G-1360)*

Melitta Usa Inc..856 428-7202
  1401 Berlin Rd Ste A Cherry Hill (08034) *(G-1393)*

Mellon D P M L L C (HQ)............................732 563-0030
  2 Worlds Fair Dr Ste 310 Somerset (08873) *(G-10029)*

Melovino Meadery....................................855 635-6846
  2933 Vauxhall Rd Vauxhall (07088) *(G-11151)*

Melstrom Manufacturing Corp.......................732 938-7400
  5303 Asbury Rd Wall Township (07727) *(G-11355)*

Meltdown..609 207-0527
  13302 Long Beach Blvd Long Beach Township (08008) *(G-5591)*

Meltom Manufacturing Inc 973 546-0058
22 Franklin Ave Clifton (07011) *(G-1667)*

Melton Industries, Bordentown *Also called Melton Sales & Service* *(G-587)*

Melton Industries, Columbus *Also called Melton Sales & Service* *(G-1802)*

Melton Sales & Service 609 699-4800
1723 Burlington Bordentown (08505) *(G-587)*

Melton Sales & Service (PA) 609 699-4800
13 Petticoat Bridge Rd Columbus (08022) *(G-1802)*

Melville Industries Inc 856 461-0091
219 Saint Mihiel Dr Ste 2 Riverside (08075) *(G-9400)*

Mem Group, Englewood *Also called Middle East Marketing Group* *(G-2926)*

Membranes International Inc 973 998-5530
219 Margaret King Ave # 2 Ringwood (07456) *(G-9348)*

Memco, Roselle *Also called Pamarco Global Graphics Inc* *(G-9568)*

Memomind Pharma Inc 201 302-9020
2125 Center Ave Fort Lee (07024) *(G-3571)*

Memory International Corp 973 586-2653
25 Redwood Rd Denville (07834) *(G-2046)*

Menardi-Criswell, Pennsauken *Also called Hosokawa Micron International* *(G-8432)*

Menasha Packaging Company LLC 973 893-1300
160 Chubb Ave Ste 101 Lyndhurst (07071) *(G-5664)*

Menasha Packaging Company LLC 732 985-0800
112 Truman Dr Edison (08817) *(G-2562)*

Mendels Muffins and Stuff Inc 973 881-9900
53 Jersey St Paterson (07501) *(G-8254)*

Mendez Dairy Co Inc 732 442-6337
450 Fayette St Perth Amboy (08861) *(G-8527)*

Mendham Garden Center 973 543-4178
11 W Main St Mendham (07945) *(G-6041)*

Mendles Just Bread Inc 973 881-9900
53 Jersey St Paterson (07501) *(G-8255)*

Mennekes Electronics Inc 973 882-8333
277 Fairfield Rd Ste 111 Fairfield (07004) *(G-3268)*

Mennen Company (HQ) 973 630-1500
191 E Hanover Ave Morristown (07960) *(G-6685)*

Menshen Packaging USA Inc 201 445-7436
21 Industrial Park Waldwick (07463) *(G-11304)*

Mentor Graphics Corporation 908 604-0800
550 Hills Dr Ste 100 Bedminster (07921) *(G-274)*

Menu Express 856 216-7777
1053 Thomas Busch Mem Hwy Pennsauken (08110) *(G-8457)*

Menu Solutions Inc 718 575-5160
233 Cortlandt St Belleville (07109) *(G-300)*

Mer Made Filter 201 236-0217
25 Arrow Rd Ramsey (07446) *(G-9151)*

Merc USA Inc 201 489-3527
41 Newman St Hackensack (07601) *(G-3947)*

Mercer C AlphaGraphics 609 921-0959
100 Youngs Rd Hamilton (08619) *(G-4115)*

Mercer Coating & Lining Co Inc 908 925-5000
1410 E Linden Ave Linden (07036) *(G-5381)*

Mercer Gasket and Shim, Bellmawr *Also called Mercer Rubber Company* *(G-339)*

Mercer Machine & Tool Products 609 587-1106
332 Darcy Ave Trenton (08629) *(G-10957)*

Mercer Rubber Company 856 931-5000
110 Benigno Blvd Bellmawr (08031) *(G-339)*

Merchandising Display Corp 973 299-8400
14 Deer Trl Boonton (07005) *(G-561)*

Merchant & Evans Inc (PA) 609 387-3033
308 Connecticut Dr Burlington (08016) *(G-979)*

Merchants Alarm Systems Inc 973 779-1296
203 Paterson Ave Ste 5 Wallington (07057) *(G-11388)*

Merck & Co Inc (PA) 908 740-4000
2000 Galloping Hill Rd Kenilworth (07033) *(G-4957)*

Merck & Co Inc 908 740-4000
251 S 31st St Kenilworth (07033) *(G-4958)*

Merck & Co Inc 800 224-5318
2 Giralda Farms Madison (07940) *(G-5698)*

Merck & Co Inc 908 298-4000
2000 Galloping Hill Rd Kenilworth (07033) *(G-4959)*

Merck & Co Inc 908 298-4000
566 Morris Ave Summit (07901) *(G-10540)*

Merck & Co Inc 908 740-4000
126 E Lincoln Ave Rahway (07065) *(G-9117)*

Merck & Co Inc 908 423-1000
1 Merck Dr Whitehouse Station (08889) *(G-11922)*

Merck & Co Inc 609 771-8790
100 Sam Weinroth Rd Ewing (08628) *(G-3045)*

Merck Animal Health, Whitehouse Station *Also called Merck Sharp & Dohme Corp* *(G-11926)*

Merck Holdings LLC (HQ) 908 423-1000
1 Merck Dr Whitehouse Station (08889) *(G-11923)*

Merck Resource Management Inc 908 423-1000
1 Merck Dr Whitehouse Station (08889) *(G-11924)*

Merck Sharp & Dohme (ia) LLC (HQ) 908 423-1000
1 Merck Dr Whitehouse Station (08889) *(G-11925)*

Merck Sharp & Dohme Corp (HQ) 908 740-4000
2000 Galloping Hill Rd Kenilworth (07033) *(G-4960)*

Merck Sharp & Dohme Corp 908 423-1000
2000 Galloping Hill Rd Kenilworth (07033) *(G-4961)*

Merck Sharp & Dohme Corp 908 423-3000
2 Merck Dr Whitehouse Station (08889) *(G-11926)*

Merck Sharp & Dohme Corp 732 594-4000
126 E Lincoln Ave Rahway (07065) *(G-9118)*

Merck Sharp & Dohme Corp 908 685-3892
203 River Rd Branchburg (08876) *(G-659)*

Merck Sharp Dhme Argentina Inc (HQ) 908 423-1000
1 Merck Dr Whitehouse Station (08889) *(G-11927)*

Merck Sharpe & Dohme De PR Inc 908 423-1000
1 Merck Dr Whitehouse Station (08889) *(G-11928)*

Mercury Adhesives Inc 973 472-3307
140 Dayton Ave Passaic (07055) *(G-8087)*

Mercury Floor Machines Inc 201 568-4606
110 S Van Brunt St Englewood (07631) *(G-2924)*

Mercury Lighting Pdts Co Inc 973 244-9444
20 Audrey Pl Fairfield (07004) *(G-3269)*

Mercury Plastic Bag Co Inc (PA) 973 778-7200
168 7th St Passaic (07055) *(G-8088)*

Mercury Systems Inc 973 244-1040
2 Henderson Dr Ste B West Caldwell (07006) *(G-11664)*

Merlin Controls, Mahwah *Also called Fmdk Technologies Inc* *(G-5740)*

Merlin Industries Inc (PA) 609 807-1000
2904 E State Street Ext Hamilton (08619) *(G-4116)*

Merlyn Cabinetry LLC 908 583-6950
1801 W Edgar Rd Unit 2 Linden (07036) *(G-5382)*

Merrill Corporation 973 643-4403
60 Park Pl Ste 400 Newark (07102) *(G-7200)*

Merrill Corporation 908 810-3740
649 Rahway Ave Union (07083) *(G-11075)*

Merrimac Industries Inc (HQ) 973 575-1300
41 Fairfield Pl West Caldwell (07006) *(G-11665)*

Mersen USA Ptt Corp (HQ) 973 334-0700
400 Myrtle Ave Boonton (07005) *(G-562)*

Mershon Concrete LLC 609 298-2150
5251 Us Highway 130 Bordentown (08505) *(G-588)*

Mesa Laboratories Inc 973 492-8400
10 Park Pl Butler (07405) *(G-1008)*

Mesa Laboratories- Bgi Inc 973 492-8400
10 Park Pl Butler (07405) *(G-1009)*

Mesa Veterans Power LLC 856 222-1000
365 New Albany Rd Ste C Moorestown (08057) *(G-6545)*

Meson Group Inc (PA) 201 767-7300
220 Pegasus Ave Northvale (07647) *(G-7536)*

Messer LLC (HQ) 908 464-8100
200 Somerset Corp Blvd # 7000 Bridgewater (08807) *(G-849)*

Messer LLC 908 329-9619
1 Greenwich St Ste 200 Stewartsville (08886) *(G-10486)*

Messer LLC 512 330-0153
200 Somerset Corp Blvd Bridgewater (08807) *(G-850)*

Messer LLC 908 464-8100
100 Mountain Ave New Providence (07974) *(G-7010)*

Messer LLC 973 579-2065
20 Demarest Rd Sparta (07871) *(G-10398)*

Messer Merchant Production LLC (HQ) 908 464-8100
575 Mountain Ave New Providence (07974) *(G-7011)*

Messer North America, Bridgewater *Also called Messer LLC* *(G-849)*

Messer North America Inc (HQ) 908 464-8100
200 Somerset Corporate Bl Bridgewater (08807) *(G-851)*

Mesys, South Hackensack *Also called Marine Electric Systems Inc* *(G-10171)*

Metal Components Inc 973 247-1204
92 Maryland Ave Paterson Paterson (07503) *(G-8256)*

Metal Cutting Corporation 973 239-1100
89 Commerce Rd Cedar Grove (07009) *(G-1282)*

Metal Dynamix LLC 856 235-4559
670 Deer Rd Ste 201 Cherry Hill (08034) *(G-1394)*

Metal Fabrication, Newark *Also called Ironbound Metal* *(G-7161)*

Metal Fabricators, Phillipsburg *Also called R & H Co Inc* *(G-8571)*

Metal Finishing Co LLC 973 778-9550
25 Prospect St Passaic (07055) *(G-8089)*

Metal Hose Fabricators Inc 908 925-7345
1122 Fedirko Ct Linden (07036) *(G-5383)*

Metal Improvement Co Inc 253 677-8604
80 E Rte 4 Ste 310 Paramus (07652) *(G-7818)*

Metal Improvement Company LLC (HQ) 201 843-7800
80 E Rte 4 Ste 310 Paramus (07652) *(G-7819)*

Metal MGT Pittsburgh Inc 201 333-2902
1 Linden Ave E Jersey City (07305) *(G-4765)*

Metal Powder Inds Federation 609 452-7700
105 College Rd E Ste 101 Princeton (08540) *(G-8977)*

Metal Specialties New Jersey 609 261-9277
1 Compass Ln Mount Holly (08060) *(G-6732)*

Metal Textiles Corporation (HQ) 732 287-0800
970 New Durham Rd Edison (08817) *(G-2563)*

Metal Textiles Corporation 800 843-1215
206 Talmadge Rd Edison (08817) *(G-2564)*

Metalfab Inc 973 764-2000
Prices Switch Rd Vernon (07462) *(G-11160)*

Metalfab Mtl Hdlg Systems LLC 973 764-2000
11 Prices Switch Rd Vernon (07462) *(G-11161)*

Metalgraphics, East Brunswick *Also called Prem-Khichi Enterprises Inc* *(G-2167)*

Metaline Products Company Inc 732 721-1373
101 N Feltus St South Amboy (08879) *(G-10137)*

Metalis USA Inc 973 625-3500
88 Ford Rd Denville (07834) *(G-2047)*

Metalix Inc 973 546-2500
9 Villa Rd Little Falls (07424) *(G-5461)*

Metallia USA LLC 212 536-8002
2200 Fletcher Ave Ste 7 Fort Lee (07024) *(G-3572)*

Metallix Direct Gold LLC 732 544-0891
59 Avenue At The Cmn # 201 Shrewsbury (07702) *(G-9894)*

Metallix Refining Inc (PA) 732 936-0050
59 Avenue At The Cmn # 201 Shrewsbury (07702) *(G-9895)*

Metallo Gasket Company Inc 732 545-7223
16 Bethany St New Brunswick (08901) *(G-6947)*

Metals Plus 908 862-7677
200 Marion Ave Linden (07036) *(G-5384)*

Metals USA Plates & Shapes Inc 973 242-1000
178-204 Frelinghuyen Ave Newark (07114) *(G-7201)*

Metalwest LLC 609 395-7007
1 Fitzgerald Ave Monroe Township (08831) *(G-6335)*

Metaport Manufacturing LLC 973 383-8363
28 Randazzo Rd Lafayette (07848) *(G-5031)*

Metawater Usa Inc (PA) 201 935-3436
301 State Rt 17 Ste 504 Rutherford (07070) *(G-9628)*

Metfab Steel Works LLC 973 675-7676
560 Freeman St Orange (07050) *(G-7756)*

Method Assoc Inc 732 888-0444
120 Francis St Ste 2 Keyport (07735) *(G-5001)*

Metrie Inc 973 584-0040
1578 Sussex Tpke Ste 300 Randolph (07869) *(G-9191)*

Metro Bindery of New Jersey 973 667-4190
187 Washington Ave Nutley (07110) *(G-7591)*

METRO ELECTRIC DUSTER, Oakland *Also called Metropolitan Vacuum Clr Co Inc* *(G-7636)*

Metro Features, New Milford *Also called Metro Publishing Group Inc* *(G-6990)*

Metro Flag Co, Wharton *Also called National Flag & Display Co Inc* *(G-11863)*

Metro Industrial Supply, Roselle *Also called American Rigging & Repair Inc* *(G-9547)*

Metro Mills Inc 973 942-6034
151 Linwood Ave Paterson (07502) *(G-8257)*

Metro Optics LLC 908 413-0004
38 Winding Way Flemington (08822) *(G-3456)*

Metro Prtg & Promotions LLC 973 316-1600
311 Mechanic St 2 Boonton (07005) *(G-563)*

Metro Publishing Group Inc 201 385-2000
626 Mccarthy Dr New Milford (07646) *(G-6990)*

Metro Railings LLC 877 504-8300
2 Technology Dr Unit 4569 Warren (07059) *(G-11422)*

Metro Seliger Industries Inc 201 438-4530
330 Washington Ave Carlstadt (07072) *(G-1187)*

Metro Sport Inc 973 879-3831
271 Hilltop Rd Mendham (07945) *(G-6042)*

Metro Web Corp 201 553-0700
5901 Tonnelle Ave North Bergen (07047) *(G-7421)*

Metrofuser LLC (PA) 908 245-2100
475 Division St Bldg 1 Elizabeth (07201) *(G-2758)*

Metrolab Div, Newark *Also called Sk & P Industries Inc* *(G-7276)*

Metrolab Division, Newark *Also called Sk & P Industries Inc* *(G-7275)*

Metrologic Instruments Inc (HQ) 856 228-8100
534 Fellowship Rd Mount Laurel (08054) *(G-6782)*

Metrolpolis Mastering LP 212 604-9433
33 Hilliard Ave Edgewater (07020) *(G-2440)*

Metronic Engineering Co Inc 201 337-1266
32 Iron Horse Rd Oakland (07436) *(G-7635)*

Metroplex Products Company Inc 732 249-0653
377 Deans Rhode Hall Rd Monroe Township (08831) *(G-6336)*

Metropolitan Cabinet Works, Fair Lawn *Also called Creative Innovations Inc* *(G-3094)*

Metropolitan Compactors Svc 908 653-0168
21 Quine St Cranford (07016) *(G-1917)*

Metropolitan Foods Inc (PA) 973 672-9400
174 Delawanna Ave Clifton (07014) *(G-1668)*

Metropolitan Manufacturing Inc 201 933-8111
450 Murray Hill Pkwy East Rutherford (07073) *(G-2302)*

Metropolitan Vacuum Clr Co Inc 201 405-2225
5 Raritan Rd Oakland (07436) *(G-7636)*

Metrowest Jewish News, Whippany *Also called New Jersey Jewish News* *(G-11898)*

Mettler Mechanical, North Bergen *Also called ML Mettler Corp* *(G-7423)*

Metuchen Capacitors Inc 800 899-6969
2139 Highway 35 Ste 2 Holmdel (07733) *(G-4506)*

Mfb Soft Pretzels Inc 609 953-6773
617 Stokes Rd Medford (08055) *(G-6030)*

Mfv International Corporation 973 993-1687
89 Headquarters Plz Morristown (07960) *(G-6686)*

Mg Decor LLC 201 923-5493
100 Schindler Ct Apt 308 East Rutherford (07073) *(G-2303)*

Mgl Forms, New Providence *Also called Mgl Printing Solution LLC* *(G-7012)*

Mgl Printing Solution LLC 908 665-1999
154 South St Ste 1 New Providence (07974) *(G-7012)*

Michael, Cherry Hill *Also called Serene House USA Inc* *(G-1414)*

Michael Anthony Sign & Awng Co, Piscataway *Also called Michael Anthony Sign Dsign Inc* *(G-8690)*

Michael Anthony Sign Dsign Inc 732 453-6120
250 Stelton Rd Ste 1 Piscataway (08854) *(G-8690)*

Michael Duru Clothiers LLC 732 741-1999
801 Broad St Shrewsbury (07702) *(G-9896)*

Michael Foods, Elizabethport *Also called Papettis Hygrade Egg Pdts Inc* *(G-2790)*

Michael Lubrich 732 223-4235
5 Mount Ln Manasquan (08736) *(G-5834)*

Michael's Quick Printing, Hightstown *Also called National Certified Printing* *(G-4297)*

Michaels Cabinet Connection 609 889-6611
1054 Route 47 S Rio Grande (08242) *(G-9356)*

Michele Maddalena 973 244-0033
1275 Bloomfield Ave Fairfield (07004) *(G-3270)*

Michelex Corporation (PA) 201 977-1177
204 Haledon Ave Prospect Park (07508) *(G-9074)*

Michelle Ste Wine Estates Ltd 973 770-8100
200 Valley Rd Ste 200 # 200 Mount Arlington (07856) *(G-6716)*

Micheller & Son Hydraulics Inc 908 687-1545
534 W 1st Ave Ste 540 Roselle (07203) *(G-9566)*

Micro Innovations Corp 732 346-9333
1090 King Georges Post Rd Edison (08837) *(G-2565)*

Micro Logic Inc (PA) 201 962-7510
31 Industrial Ave Ste 7 Mahwah (07430) *(G-5753)*

Micro Media Publications Inc 732 657-7344
15 Union Ave Lakehurst (08733) *(G-5039)*

Micro Medical Technologies, Somerset *Also called Micro Stamping Corporation* *(G-10030)*

Micro Stamping Corporation (PA) 732 302-0800
140 Belmont Dr Somerset (08873) *(G-10030)*

Micro-Mark, Berkeley Heights *Also called Scientific Models Inc* *(G-411)*

Micro-Tek Corporation 856 829-3855
1600 Taylors Ln Cinnaminson (08077) *(G-1473)*

Micro-Tek Laboratories Inc (PA) 973 779-5577
154 Huron Ave Clifton (07013) *(G-1669)*

Microcast Technologies Corp 732 943-7356
17 Mileed Way Avenel (07001) *(G-136)*

Microcast Technologies Corp (PA) 908 523-9503
1611 W Elizabeth Ave Linden (07036) *(G-5385)*

Microdata Instrument Inc 908 222-1717
1207 Hogan Dr South Plainfield (07080) *(G-10300)*

Microdose Defense Products, Ewing *Also called Microdose Therapeutx Inc* *(G-3046)*

Microdose Therapeutx Inc 732 355-2100
7 Graphics Dr Ewing (08628) *(G-3046)*

Microdysis Inc 609 642-1184
1200 Florence Columbus Rd # 21 Bordentown (08505) *(G-589)*

Microelettrica-Usa LLC 973 598-0806
300 International Dr # 2 Budd Lake (07828) *(G-930)*

Microfold Inc 201 641-5052
375 North St Ste C Teterboro (07608) *(G-10687)*

Microgen Inc 973 575-9025
33 Clinton Rd Ste 102 West Caldwell (07006) *(G-11666)*

Micromat Co 201 529-3738
1165 Greenwood Lake Tpke E Ringwood (07456) *(G-9349)*

Micron Powder Systems, Summit *Also called Hosokawa Micron International* *(G-10536)*

Micronet Enertec Tech Inc 201 225-0190
28 W Grand Ave Ste 3 Montvale (07645) *(G-6420)*

Microseal Industries Inc 973 523-0704
610 E 36th St Paterson (07513) *(G-8258)*

Microsemi Stor Solutions Inc 908 953-9400
180 Mount Airy Rd Basking Ridge (07920) *(G-191)*

Microsignals Inc 800 225-4508
29 Fairview St Ste 1a Palisades Park (07650) *(G-7774)*

Microsoft Corporation 732 476-5600
101 Wood Ave S Ste 900 Iselin (08830) *(G-4617)*

Microsoft Corporation 908 809-7320
400 Commons Way Ste 279 Bridgewater (08807) *(G-852)*

Microsurfaces Inc 201 408-5596
1 W Forest Ave Ste 2b Englewood (07631) *(G-2925)*

Microtelecom Ltd Liability Co (PA) 866 676-5679
1 Bridge Plz N Ste 275 Fort Lee (07024) *(G-3573)*

Microwave Consulting Corp 973 523-6700
150 Railroad Ave Paterson (07501) *(G-8259)*

Microwize Technology Inc (PA) 800 955-0321
1 Kalisa Way Ste 104 Paramus (07652) *(G-7820)*

Mid Atlantic Graphix Inc 609 569-9990
2558 Tilton Rd Egg Harbor Township (08234) *(G-2690)*

Mid State Bindery 908 755-9388
262 Lackland Dr Middlesex (08846) *(G-6130)*

Mid-Lantic Precision Inc 856 456-3810
940 Market St Gloucester City (08030) *(G-3845)*

Mid-State Controls Inc 732 335-0500
8 Crown Plz Ste 102 Hazlet (07730) *(G-4265)*

Mid-State Enterprises Inc 973 427-6040
49 Ackerman St Bloomfield (07003) *(G-510)*

Midas Chain Inc 201 244-1150
151 Veterans Dr Northvale (07647) *(G-7537)*

Midas Designs Ltd 201 567-2700
124 Lafayette Ave Maywood (07607) *(G-6012)*

Middle Atlantic Products, Fairfield *Also called Legrand AV Inc* *(G-3260)*

Middle Atlantic Products Inc..............................973 839-1011
  300 Fairfield Rd Fairfield (07004) *(G-3271)*

Middle East Marketing Group (PA)....................201 503-0150
  266 S Dean St Englewood (07631) *(G-2926)*

Middleburg Yarn Processing Co (PA)................973 238-1800
  375 Diamond Bridge Ave Hawthorne (07506) *(G-4232)*

Middlesex Publications.......................................732 435-0005
  850 Us Highway 1 Fl 4 Flr 4 North Brunswick (08902) *(G-7477)*

Middlesex Water Company..................................732 579-0290
  100 Fairview Ave Edison (08817) *(G-2566)*

Midhattan Woodworking Corp.............................732 727-3020
  3130 Bordentown Ave Old Bridge (08857) *(G-7720)*

Midland Farms Inc...800 749-6455
  845 E 25th St Paterson (07513) *(G-8260)*

Midland Screen Printing Inc...............................201 703-0066
  280 N Midland Ave Ste 218 Saddle Brook (07663) *(G-9662)*

Midlantic Color Graphics LLC............................856 786-3113
  2303 Garry Rd Ste 9 Cinnaminson (08077) *(G-1474)*

Midlantic Medical Systems Inc...........................908 432-4599
  61 Fieldstone Rd Skillman (08558) *(G-9923)*

Midlantic Shutter & Milwork...............................908 806-3400
  108 Church St Flemington (08822) *(G-3457)*

Midstate Filigree Systems Inc............................609 448-8700
  22 Brick Yard Rd Cranbury (08512) *(G-1864)*

Midway Machine Product Corp............................609 499-4377
  763a Railroad Ave Florence (08518) *(G-3476)*

Miemie Design Services Inc...............................609 857-3688
  1341 Radio Rd Ltl Egg Hbr (08087) *(G-5617)*

Mighty Mug Incorporated...................................732 382-3911
  665 Martin St Rahway (07065) *(G-9119)*

MII Organics, Hillsborough *Also called Interganic Fzco LLC (G-4333)*

Mike Dolly Screen Printing................................732 294-8979
  17 Elm St Freehold (07728) *(G-3679)*

Mikros Systems Corporation (PA).......................609 987-1513
  707 Alexander Rd Princeton (08540) *(G-8978)*

Mil-Comm Products Company Inc.......................201 935-8561
  2 Carlton Ave Ste C East Rutherford (07073) *(G-2304)*

Miles Concrete Co, Newfield *Also called Ernest R Miles Construction Co (G-7321)*

Miles Concrete Company Inc..............................856 697-2311
  1445 Catawba Ave Newfield (08344) *(G-7323)*

Milestone Education LLC....................................973 535-2717
  220 S Orange Ave Livingston (07039) *(G-5524)*

Milestone Scientific Inc (PA).............................973 535-2717
  220 S Orange Ave Ste 102 Livingston (07039) *(G-5525)*

Milk Farm, Lawrenceville *Also called Halo Farm Inc (G-5230)*

Millar Sheet Metal...201 997-1990
  39 Rizzolo Rd Ste 2 Kearny (07032) *(G-4884)*

Millburn Bagel Inc...973 258-1334
  321 Millburn Ave Ste 14 Millburn (07041) *(G-6205)*

Millenium Graphics, Marlboro *Also called SAM Graphics Inc (G-5913)*

Millenium Worldwide, Newton *Also called Riotsound Inc (G-7355)*

Millennium Brokerage Svcs LLC.........................732 928-0900
  156 E Commodore Blvd A Jackson (08527) *(G-4660)*

Millennium Info Tech Inc....................................609 750-7120
  4390 Us Highway 1 Ste 121 Princeton (08540) *(G-8979)*

Millennium Research LLC...................................908 867-7646
  99 W Mill Rd Long Valley (07853) *(G-5612)*

Millennium Systems Intl, Parsippany *Also called Harms Software Inc (G-7959)*

Miller & Son..973 759-6445
  24 Belleville Ave Belleville (07109) *(G-301)*

Miller Auto Parts, Bayonne *Also called M & RS Miller Auto Gear & Prt (G-228)*

Miller Berry & Sons Inc......................................856 785-1420
  2615 Robinstown Rd Port Norris (08349) *(G-8887)*

Milligan & Higgins Div, Fairfield *Also called Hudson Industries Corporation (G-3231)*

Millington Quarry Inc...908 542-0055
  135 Stonehouse Rd Basking Ridge (07920) *(G-192)*

Millner Kitchens Inc..609 890-7300
  200b Whitehead Rd Ste 108 Hamilton (08619) *(G-4117)*

Millner Kitchens Inc..609 890-7300
  200 Whitehead Rd Ste 108 Trenton (08619) *(G-10958)*

Millner Lumber Co, Trenton *Also called Millner Kitchens Inc (G-10958)*

Millson Precision Machining...............................732 424-1700
  145 11th St Piscataway (08854) *(G-8691)*

Millstone Dq Inc..609 259-6733
  40 Trenton Lakewood Rd Clarksburg (08510) *(G-1522)*

Milltex Manufacturing, Brick *Also called Marketing Administration Assoc (G-726)*

Millville Vials, Millville *Also called Nipro Phrmpckging Amricas Corp (G-6262)*

Millwood Inc..732 967-8818
  7 Brick Plant Rd Ste C South River (08882) *(G-10354)*

Milo Runtak Welding Machinery..........................201 391-0380
  174 Kinderkamack Rd Ste A Park Ridge (07656) *(G-7856)*

Milspray LLC (HQ)...732 886-2223
  845 Towbin Ave Lakewood (08701) *(G-5135)*

Milspray Military Technologies, Lakewood *Also called Milspray LLC (G-5135)*

Mimeocom Inc...973 286-2901
  158 Mount Olivet Ave Newark (07114) *(G-7202)*

Mimo Display LLC (PA)......................................855 937-6466
  743 Alexander Rd Ste 15 Princeton (08540) *(G-8980)*

Mimo Monitors, Princeton *Also called Mimo Display LLC (G-8980)*

Minalex Corporation..908 534-4044
  25 Coddington Rd Whitehouse Station (08889) *(G-11929)*

Minardi Baking Co Inc.......................................973 742-1107
  20 Luger Rd Denville (07834) *(G-2048)*

Mincing Overseas Spice Company, Dayton *Also called Mincing Trading Corporation (G-1980)*

Mincing Trading Corporation...............................732 355-9944
  10 Tower Rd Dayton (08810) *(G-1980)*

Mind-Alliance Systems LLC...............................212 920-1911
  21 Herbert Ter Livingston (07039) *(G-5526)*

Mindray Ds Usa Inc (HQ)...................................201 995-8000
  800 Macarthur Blvd Mahwah (07430) *(G-5754)*

Mindray North America, Mahwah *Also called Mindray Ds Usa Inc (G-5754)*

Mindwise Media LLC..973 701-0685
  26 Floral St Chatham (07928) *(G-1327)*

Mine Hill Spartan...973 442-2280
  274 Us Highway 46 Mine Hill (07803) *(G-6274)*

Minerva Custom Products LLC...........................201 447-4731
  49 Lockwood Dr Waldwick (07463) *(G-11305)*

Minhura Inc...862 763-4078
  24 William St North Arlington (07031) *(G-7375)*

Mini Frost Foods Corporation.............................973 427-4258
  23 Willow Brook Ct North Haledon (07508) *(G-7498)*

Miniature Folding Inc...201 773-6477
  14 Wenzel St Elmwood Park (07407) *(G-2843)*

Minitec Corporation...973 989-1426
  158 W Clinton St Ste V Dover (07801) *(G-2097)*

Minmetals Inc (PA)..201 809-1898
  120 Schor Ave Leonia (07605) *(G-5290)*

Minniti J Hair Replacement Inc...........................856 427-9600
  905 Marlton Pike W Cherry Hill (08002) *(G-1395)*

Minor Rubber Co Inc (PA)..................................973 338-6800
  49 Ackerman St Bloomfield (07003) *(G-511)*

Mint Printing LLC..973 546-2060
  475 Westminster Pl Lodi (07644) *(G-5572)*

Minuteman Press, Ho Ho Kus *Also called Jmp Press Inc (G-4441)*

Minuteman Press, Northvale *Also called Palm Press Inc (G-7543)*

Minuteman Press, Clifton *Also called Lmp Printing Corp (G-1660)*

Minuteman Press, Somerville *Also called Roan Printing Inc (G-10124)*

Minuteman Press, Secaucus *Also called Sonata Graphics Inc (G-9816)*

Minuteman Press, Hasbrouck Heights *Also called M & M Printing Corp (G-4186)*

Minuteman Press, Middlesex *Also called Scarlet Printing (G-6143)*

Minuteman Press, Ewing *Also called Tedco Inc (G-3069)*

Minuteman Press, Clifton *Also called Genua & Mulligan Printing (G-1624)*

Minuteman Press, Berlin *Also called Classic Graphic Inc (G-420)*

Minuteman Press, Wall Township *Also called Verni Vito (G-11377)*

Minuteman Press, Cherry Hill *Also called Bittner Industries Inc (G-1347)*

Minuteman Press...973 403-0146
  359 Bloomfield Ave Caldwell (07006) *(G-1027)*

Minuteman Press...732 536-8788
  349 Us Highway 9 Ste 5 Manalapan (07726) *(G-5817)*

Minwax Group (inc)...201 818-7500
  10 Montinview Rd Ste N300 Upper Saddle River (07458) *(G-11142)*

Miracle Mile Automotive Inc...............................732 886-6315
  1925 Swarthmore Ave Ste 1 Lakewood (08701) *(G-5136)*

Miracle Verde Group LLC...................................201 399-2222
  47 Sellers St Kearny (07032) *(G-4885)*

Mirage Wholesale Group LLC.............................718 757-6590
  107 Trumbull St Unit A44 Elizabeth (07206) *(G-2759)*

Miranda MTI Inc..973 376-4275
  195 Mountain Ave Springfield (07081) *(G-10454)*

Mire Enterprises LLC...732 882-1010
  1501 W Blancke St Ste 3 Linden (07036) *(G-5386)*

Miric Industries Inc..201 864-0233
  1516 Union Tpke North Bergen (07047) *(G-7422)*

Miric Revolving Swinging Doors, North Bergen *Also called Miric Industries Inc (G-7422)*

Miroad Rubber USA LLC....................................480 280-2543
  182 Whitman Ave Edison (08817) *(G-2567)*

Mironova Labs, Fairfield *Also called Pharmatech International Inc (G-3291)*

Mirrotek International LLC.................................973 472-1400
  90 Dayton Ave Passaic (07055) *(G-8090)*

Mischief International Inc....................................201 840-6888
  501 Broad Ave Ste 12 Ridgefield (07657) *(G-9276)*

Misco Toys, Edison *Also called Missry Associates Inc (G-2568)*

MISS Sportswear Inc...212 391-2535
  745 Joyce Kilmer Ave New Brunswick (08901) *(G-6948)*

Missa Bay Citrus Company................................856 241-0900
  101 Arlington Blvd Swedesboro (08085) *(G-10596)*

Missa Bay LLC (HQ)..856 241-0900
  101 Arlington Blvd Swedesboro (08085) *(G-10597)*

Mission Systems & Training, Marlton *Also called Lockheed Martin (G-5938)*

Missionary Society of St Paul.............................201 825-7300
  997 Macarthur Blvd Mahwah (07430) *(G-5755)*

Missry Associates Inc..732 752-7500
  250 Carter Dr Ste 3 Edison (08817) *(G-2568)*

Mister Boardwalk, Lakewood *Also called Wardale Corp (G-5180)*

Mister Boardwalk, Lakewood *Also called M and R Manufacturing (G-5126)*

A L P H A B E T I C

Mister Cookie Face Inc...732 370-5533
1989 Rutgers Blvd Lakewood (08701) *(G-5137)*

Mister Good Lube Inc..732 842-3266
473 Broad St Shrewsbury (07702) *(G-9897)*

Mistras Group Inc (PA)..609 716-4000
195 Clarksville Rd Ste 2 Princeton Junction (08550) *(G-9062)*

Mitronics Products Inc..908 647-5006
239 Morristown Rd Ste 1 Gillette (07933) *(G-3802)*

Mitsubishi Tanabe Pharma (HQ)...............................908 607-1950
525 Wshngton Blvd Fl 1400 Flr 1400 Jersey City (07310) *(G-4766)*

Mitzi Intl Handbag & ACC Ltd..................................973 483-5015
250 Passaic St Newark (07104) *(G-7203)*

Mizco International Inc..732 912-2000
80 Essex Ave E Avenel (07001) *(G-137)*

Mj Corporate Sales Inc..856 778-0055
109 W Park Dr Unit A Mount Laurel (08054) *(G-6783)*

Mj Family Care, Paterson Also called Conduent State Healthcare LLC *(G-8163)*

Mj Gross Company - NJ...212 542-3199
2 Commonwealth Dr Lakewood (08701) *(G-5138)*

Mjg Technologies Incorporated................................856 228-6118
832 Camden Ave Blackwood (08012) *(G-475)*

Mjs of Spotswood LLC..732 251-7400
19 Summerhill Rd Spotswood (08884) *(G-10416)*

Mjs Pizza Bar & Grill, Spotswood Also called Mjs of Spotswood LLC *(G-10416)*

Mjs Precision Inc..973 209-1300
12 Cork Hill Rd Ste 3 Franklin (07416) *(G-3605)*

Mjse LLC...201 791-9888
374 N Midland Ave Saddle Brook (07663) *(G-9663)*

Mk Metals Inc..856 245-7033
293 Lower Landing Rd Glendora (08029) *(G-3837)*

Mk Wood Inc..973 450-5110
681 Main St Belleville (07109) *(G-302)*

Mks Inc...856 451-5545
7 N Industrial Blvd Bridgeton (08302) *(G-765)*

ML Mettler Corp..201 869-0170
8905 Bergenwood Ave North Bergen (07047) *(G-7423)*

ML Woodwork Inc...201 953-2175
348 Bullard Ave Paramus (07652) *(G-7821)*

Mm Packaging Group LLC..908 759-0101
2401 E Linden Ave Linden (07036) *(G-5387)*

Mmp Ergonomics Co, Hasbrouck Heights Also called Track Systems Inc *(G-4191)*

Mmtc Inc..609 520-9699
5 Stonypoint Rd Andover (07821) *(G-49)*

Mnemonics Inc..856 234-0970
102 Gaither Dr Ste 4 Mount Laurel (08054) *(G-6784)*

Mnw LLC...908 591-7277
301 Dalziel Rd Linden (07036) *(G-5388)*

Moa Instrumentation Inc.......................................215 547-8308
20 Carla Way Lawrenceville (08648) *(G-5238)*

Mobile Intelligent Alerts Inc.................................201 410-5324
72 Middletown Rd Holmdel (07733) *(G-4507)*

Mobile Power Inc...908 852-3117
392 Watters Rd Hackettstown (07840) *(G-4027)*

Mobility123, Absecon Also called Diamond Scooters Inc *(G-2)*

Moblty Inc..973 535-3600
651 W Mount Pleasant Ave # 270 Livingston (07039) *(G-5527)*

Mococo Partners Corp..347 768-3344
439 E 22nd St Paterson (07514) *(G-8261)*

Mocvd Systems, Somerset Also called Veeco *(G-10092)*

Mod Hatter..609 492-0999
1103 N Bay Ave Beach Haven (08008) *(G-256)*

Mod-Tek Converting LLC...856 662-6884
2550 Haddonfield Rd Ste E Pennsauken (08110) *(G-8458)*

Mod-U-Kraf Homes LLC (HQ)....................................540 482-0273
140 Bradford Dr Ste A West Berlin (08091) *(G-11608)*

Model Electronics Inc (PA)....................................201 961-9200
615 E Crescent Ave Ramsey (07446) *(G-9152)*

Model Electronics Inc..201 961-1717
526 State Rt 17 Ramsey (07446) *(G-9153)*

Model Rectifier Corporation....................................732 225-2100
360 Main St Ste 2 Matawan (07747) *(G-5980)*

Modelware Inc..732 264-3020
28 Red Coach Ln Holmdel (07733) *(G-4508)*

Modern Drummer Publications...................................973 239-4140
271 Us Highway 46 H212 Fairfield (07004) *(G-3272)*

Modern Fuel Inc..973 471-1501
158 Colfax Ave Clifton (07013) *(G-1670)*

Modern Graphic Arts, Clifton Also called Sandy Alexander Inc *(G-1710)*

Modern Metric Machine Company................................856 547-4044
101 W Nicholson Rd Audubon (08106) *(G-113)*

Modern Precision Tech Inc......................................856 335-9303
225 Old Egg Harbor Rd West Berlin (08091) *(G-11609)*

Modern Showcase Inc..201 935-2929
610 Commercial Ave Carlstadt (07072) *(G-1188)*

Modern Sportswear Corporation................................201 804-2700
102 W Commercial Ave Moonachie (07074) *(G-6481)*

Modern Store Equipment...609 241-7438
2045 Route 130 N Burlington (08016) *(G-980)*

Modernlinefurniture Inc...908 486-0200
531 N Stiles St Linden (07036) *(G-5389)*

Modine Manufacturing Company................................856 467-9710
244 High Hills Rd Bridgeport (08014) *(G-741)*

Modroto, Saddle Brook Also called Meese Inc *(G-9661)*

Modtek, Pennsauken Also called Mod-Tek Converting LLC *(G-8458)*

Modular Packaging Systems Inc................................973 970-9393
385 Franklin Ave Ste C Rockaway (07866) *(G-9477)*

Modulation Sciences Inc..732 302-3090
12 Worlds Fair Dr Ste A Somerset (08873) *(G-10031)*

Mojo Organics Inc..201 633-6519
185 Hudson St Ste 2500 Jersey City (07311) *(G-4767)*

Mold Polishing Company Inc.....................................908 518-9191
45 North Ave Ste 3 Garwood (07027) *(G-3785)*

Molders Fishing Preserve..732 446-2850
318 John Wall Rd Jamesburg (08831) *(G-4674)*

Moldworks Worldwide LLC.......................................908 474-8082
985 E Linden Ave Linden (07036) *(G-5390)*

Molecu-Wire Corporation..908 429-0300
1215 Kennedy Blvd Manville (08835) *(G-5857)*

Molnar Tool and Dye, Ocean Also called Stamping Com Inc *(G-7685)*

Molnar Tools Inc...908 580-0671
3 Stoningham Dr Warren (07059) *(G-11423)*

Momentum Usa Inc (PA)...844 300-1553
120 Fieldcrest Ave Edison (08837) *(G-2569)*

Mon-Eco Industries Inc...732 257-7942
5 Joanna Ct Ste G East Brunswick (08816) *(G-2157)*

Mona Belts, Belleville Also called Mona Slide Fasteners Inc *(G-303)*

Mona Slide Fasteners Inc (PA).................................718 325-7700
233 Cortlandt St Belleville (07109) *(G-303)*

Monarch Art Plastics Co LLC....................................856 235-5151
3838 Church Rd Mount Laurel (08054) *(G-6785)*

Monarch Plastics, Mount Laurel Also called Monarch Art Plastics Co LLC *(G-6785)*

Monarch Robe and Towel Company, South Plainfield Also called Monarch Towel Company Inc *(G-10301)*

Monarch Towel Company Inc (PA).............................800 729-7623
301 Hollywood Ave South Plainfield (07080) *(G-10301)*

Mondelez Global LLC...201 794-4000
22-11 State Rt 208 Fair Lawn (07410) *(G-3111)*

Mondelez Global LLC...201 794-4080
21-05 Route 208 Fair Lawn (07410) *(G-3112)*

Mondelez International Inc.....................................973 503-2000
200 Deforest Ave East Hanover (07936) *(G-2222)*

Moniteur Devices Inc..973 857-1600
36 Commerce Rd Cedar Grove (07009) *(G-1283)*

Monitor Newspaper, Tinton Falls Also called Direct Development LLC *(G-10712)*

Monmouth and Ocean County Awng, Asbury Park Also called Asbury Awng Mfg & Installation *(G-71)*

Monmouth Bioproducts LLC....................................732 863-0300
918 State Route 33 Ste 3 Freehold (07728) *(G-3680)*

Monmouth Hose & Hydraulics, Shrewsbury Also called Monmouth Truck Ram Div LLC *(G-9898)*

Monmouth Journal..732 747-7007
212 Maple Ave Ste 1 Red Bank (07701) *(G-9237)*

Monmouth Marine Engines Inc.................................732 528-9290
536 Union Ln Brielle (08730) *(G-907)*

Monmouth Rubber & Plastics, Long Branch Also called Monmouth Rubber Corp *(G-5604)*

Monmouth Rubber Corp...732 229-3444
75 Long Branch Ave Long Branch (07740) *(G-5604)*

Monmouth Truck Ram Div LLC...................................732 741-5001
799 Shrewsbury Ave Shrewsbury (07702) *(G-9898)*

Monogram Center Inc...732 442-1800
437 Amboy Ave Perth Amboy (08861) *(G-8528)*

Monroe Machine & Design Inc..................................732 521-3434
566 Buckelew Ave Jamesburg (08831) *(G-4675)*

Monroe Tool & Die Inc...856 629-5164
197 Sharp Rd Williamstown (08094) *(G-11964)*

Monroeville Vineyard & Winery.................................856 521-0523
314 Richwood Rd Monroeville (08343) *(G-6353)*

Monster Coatings Inc..973 983-7662
12 Midway Ct Rockaway (07866) *(G-9478)*

Montana Electrical Decorating..................................973 344-1815
62 Mcwhorter St Newark (07105) *(G-7204)*

Montclair Dispatch LLC..973 509-8861
423 Bloomfield Ave Montclair (07042) *(G-6375)*

Montclair Fuel LLC...973 744-4300
651 Bloomfield Ave Montclair (07042) *(G-6376)*

Montclair Times Editorial, Montclair Also called North Jersey Media Group Inc *(G-6379)*

Monte Printing & Graphics Inc..................................908 241-6600
540 W Westfield Ave Roselle Park (07204) *(G-9588)*

Montego Bay, Ridgefield Also called PC Marketing Inc *(G-9282)*

Montana Taranto Foods Inc.....................................201 943-8484
400 Victoria Ter Ridgefield (07657) *(G-9277)*

Montgomery Investment Tech (PA)..............................610 688-8111
700 Route 130 N Ste 105 Cinnaminson (08077) *(G-1475)*

Montgomery News...908 874-0020
88 Orchard Rd Ste 10 Skillman (08558) *(G-9924)*

Montrose Molders, Piscataway Also called Continental Precision Corp *(G-8650)*

Montrose Molders Corporation..................................908 754-3030
25 Howard St Piscataway (08854) *(G-8692)*

Montrose Molders Corporation 908 754-3030
  230 Saint Nicholas Ave South Plainfield (07080) *(G-10302)*

Moon, Ridgefield Park *Also called Oe Solutions America Inc (G-9313)*

Moonbabies LLC 609 926-0201
  505 New Rd Ste 7 Somers Point (08244) *(G-9938)*

Moonlight Imaging LLC 973 300-1001
  286 Houses Corner Rd C Sparta (07871) *(G-10399)*

Moosavi Oriental Rugs, Secaucus *Also called Moosavi Rugs Inc (G-9793)*

Moosavi Rugs Inc 201 617-9500
  100 Park Plaza Dr 208n Secaucus (07094) *(G-9793)*

More Copy Printing Service 201 327-1106
  302 State Rt 17 Upper Saddle River (07458) *(G-11143)*

Moreira, Jose B, Attorney, Kearny *Also called Jose Moreira (G-4873)*

Morelli Contracting LLC 732 356-8800
  201 Egel Ave Ste B Middlesex (08846) *(G-6131)*

Moreng Metal Products Inc 973 256-2001
  100 W End Rd Totowa (07512) *(G-10837)*

Morgan Advanced Ceramics Inc 973 808-1621
  26 Madison Rd Fairfield (07004) *(G-3273)*

Morgan Cycle LLC 973 218-9233
  227 Old Short Hills Rd Short Hills (07078) *(G-9873)*

Morgan Printing Service Inc 732 721-2959
  333 S Pine Ave South Amboy (08879) *(G-10138)*

Morgan Technical Ceramics, Wood Ridge *Also called Certech Inc (G-12002)*

Morgan Towers Inc 856 786-7200
  212 W Route 38 Ste 300 Moorestown (08057) *(G-6546)*

Morre-TEC Industries Inc 908 688-9009
  1 Gary Rd Union (07083) *(G-11076)*

Morris County Duplicating 973 993-8484
  8 Farview Ave Cedar Knolls (07927) *(G-1310)*

Morris County Imaging 973 532-7900
  310 Madison Ave Ste 110 Morristown (07960) *(G-6687)*

Morris Industries Inc (PA) 973 835-6600
  777 State Rt 23 Pompton Plains (07444) *(G-8868)*

Morris Plains Pip Inc 973 533-9330
  465 W Mount Pleasant Ave Livingston (07039) *(G-5528)*

Morrison Press Inc 201 488-4848
  10 Mckinley St Ste 3 Closter (07624) *(G-1761)*

Morristown Cycle 973 540-1244
  103 Washington St Morristown (07960) *(G-6688)*

Morse Metal Products Co Inc (PA) 732 422-3676
  1 Hunters Run Princeton (08540) *(G-8981)*

Morsemere Iron Works Inc 201 941-1133
  1085 Linden Ave Ste 2 Ridgefield (07657) *(G-9278)*

Mosaic Golf LLC 201 906-6136
  900 Monroe St Apt 312 Hoboken (07030) *(G-4467)*

Moscova Enterprises Inc 848 628-4873
  101 Hudson St Jersey City (07302) *(G-4768)*

Moser Jewel Company 908 454-1155
  518 State Route 57 Phillipsburg (08865) *(G-8564)*

Mosse Beverage Industries LLC 732 977-5558
  15 Osprey Ln Bayville (08721) *(G-248)*

Mosstype Corporation 201 444-8000
  150 Franklin Tpke Waldwick (07463) *(G-11306)*

Mosstype Holding Corp (PA) 201 444-8000
  150 Franklin Tpke Waldwick (07463) *(G-11307)*

Mostly Software Development, West Orange *Also called First Mountain Consulting (G-11767)*

Motif Industries Inc 973 575-1800
  299 Ridgedale Ave Ste 5 East Hanover (07936) *(G-2223)*

Motion Control Tech Inc 973 361-2226
  158 W Clinton St Ste Ff Dover (07801) *(G-2098)*

Motion Systems Corp 732 389-1600
  600 Industrial Way W Eatontown (07724) *(G-2411)*

Motion Systems LLC (HQ) 212 686-4666
  250 Passaic St Newark (07104) *(G-7205)*

Motiva Enterprises LLC 732 855-3266
  111 State St Sewaren (07077) *(G-9832)*

Motiva Sales Terminal, Sewaren *Also called Motiva Enterprises LLC (G-9832)*

Motomco, Woodland Park *Also called Elaine Inc (G-12076)*

Motor Sport Industry, East Brunswick *Also called MCI Service Parts (G-2156)*

Motors and Drives Inc (PA) 732 462-7683
  5 Asbury Ave Freehold (07728) *(G-3681)*

Motors and Drives Inc 609 344-8058
  1413 Marmora Ave Atlantic City (08401) *(G-98)*

Mount Hope Quarry, Parsippany *Also called Tilcon New York Inc (G-8029)*

Mountain LLC 908 409-6823
  400 Crossing Blvd Fl 5 Bridgewater (08807) *(G-853)*

Mountain Millwork 908 647-1100
  142 Mountain Ave Warren (07059) *(G-11424)*

Mountain Printing Company Inc 856 767-7600
  27 N Atlantic Ave Berlin (08009) *(G-427)*

Mountain Top Logging LLC 908 413-2982
  99 Main St Lebanon (08833) *(G-5272)*

Movado Group Inc (PA) 201 267-8000
  650 From Rd Ste 375 Paramus (07652) *(G-7822)*

Mp Custom FL LLC 973 417-2288
  624 Alps Rd Wayne (07470) *(G-11535)*

Mp Millwork, Wayne *Also called Mp Custom FL LLC (G-11535)*

Mp Production 973 729-9333
  104 Hillside Rd Sparta (07871) *(G-10400)*

Mphase Technologies Inc (PA) 973 256-3737
  777 Passaic Ave Ste 385 Clifton (07012) *(G-1671)*

Mplayer Entertainment LLC 302 229-3034
  329 Greenleigh Ct Cherry Hill (08002) *(G-1396)*

Mpm Display Inc 973 374-3477
  1 Us Hwy Rt 22 W Hillside (07205) *(G-4416)*

Mpt Delivery Systems Inc 973 278-0283
  95 Prince St Paterson (07501) *(G-8262)*

Mpt Delivery Systems Inc 973 279-4132
  95 Prince St Paterson (07501) *(G-8263)*

Mpt Industries, Dover *Also called MPT Racing Inc (G-2099)*

MPT Racing Inc 973 989-9220
  85 Franklin Rd Ste 6b Dover (07801) *(G-2099)*

Mr Good Lube, Shrewsbury *Also called Mister Good Lube Inc (G-9897)*

Mr Green Tea Ice Cream Corp 732 446-9800
  25 Church St Unit 104 Keyport (07735) *(G-5002)*

Mr Green Tea Ice Cream Corp 732 446-9800
  42 E Front St Keyport (07735) *(G-5003)*

Mr Ice Buckets, New Brunswick *Also called Buckets Plus Inc (G-6914)*

Mr Pauls Custom Cabinets 732 528-9427
  2416 Highway 35 Ste E Manasquan (08736) *(G-5835)*

Mr Quick Sign 201 670-1690
  30 Dairy St Midland Park (07432) *(G-6181)*

Mr Quickly Inc 908 687-6000
  1965 Morris Ave Union (07083) *(G-11077)*

MRC Global (us) Inc 856 881-0345
  70 Sewell St Ste J Glassboro (08028) *(G-3816)*

MRC Global (us) Inc 732 225-4005
  28 Kennedy Blvd Ste 100 East Brunswick (08816) *(G-2158)*

MRC Precision Metal Optics Inc 941 753-8707
  181 Legrand Ave Northvale (07647) *(G-7538)*

Mri International 973 383-3645
  44 Clinton St Newton (07860) *(G-7350)*

Mri of West Morris PA 973 927-1010
  66 Sunset Strip Ste 105 Succasunna (07876) *(G-10515)*

Mrl Manufacturing Corp 973 790-1744
  59 Lee Ave Haledon (07508) *(G-4084)*

Mrp New Jersey LLC 732 873-7148
  17 Veronica Ave Somerset (08873) *(G-10032)*

Mrs Fieldbrook Food, Lakewood *Also called Mister Cookie Face Inc (G-5137)*

Mrs Mazzulas Food Products 732 248-0555
  240 Carter Dr Edison (08817) *(G-2570)*

Mrs Sullivans Inc (PA) 908 246-8937
  1990 Washington Valley Rd Martinsville (08836) *(G-5963)*

Mrs. Sullivan's Pies, Martinsville *Also called Mrs Sullivans Inc (G-5963)*

Ms Health Software Corp 908 850-5564
  128 Willow Grove St Hackettstown (07840) *(G-4028)*

MS Signs Inc 973 569-1111
  280 N Midland Ave Ste 128 Saddle Brook (07663) *(G-9664)*

MSC Marketing & Technology 201 507-9100
  808 Page Ave 8 Lyndhurst (07071) *(G-5665)*

Msg Fire & Safety Inc 732 833-8500
  5142 W Hurley Pond Rd # 1 Wall Township (07727) *(G-11356)*

MSI, Middlesex *Also called Maritime Solutions Inc (G-6129)*

MSI, Palisades Park *Also called Microsignals Inc (G-7774)*

MSI Holdings LLC 732 549-7144
  203 Norcross Ave Metuchen (08840) *(G-6066)*

MSI Technologies LLC (PA) 973 263-0080
  1055 Parsippany Blvd 205a Parsippany (07054) *(G-7979)*

Msj Unlimited Services 201 617-0764
  519 35th St Union City (07087) *(G-11122)*

Msn Pharmaceuticals Inc. 732 356-9900
  20 Duke Rd Piscataway (08854) *(G-8693)*

Mt Embroidery & Promotions LLC 201 646-1070
  70 Oak St Ste 103 Norwood (07648) *(G-7569)*

Mt Holly Pharmacy 609 914-4890
  1613 Rd 38th Unit 5 10 Lumberton (08048) *(G-5632)*

Mt Salem Electric Co Inc 908 735-6126
  79 Mount Salem Rd Pittstown (08867) *(G-8754)*

Mtbc, Somerset *Also called Medical Transcription Billing (G-10027)*

Mtbc Acquisition Corp (HQ) 732 873-5133
  7 Clyde Rd Somerset (08873) *(G-10033)*

Mtbc Health Inc (HQ) 732 873-5133
  7 Clyde Rd Somerset (08873) *(G-10034)*

Mtbc Practice Management Corp 732 873-5133
  7 Clyde Rd Somerset (08873) *(G-10035)*

Mteixeira Soapstone VA LLC 201 757-8608
  1100 Palisade Ave Fort Lee (07024) *(G-3574)*

MTI Solar, Somerset *Also called Materials Technology Inc (G-10024)*

Mtn Government Services Inc (HQ) 703 443-6738
  200 Telegraph Rd Holmdel (07733) *(G-4509)*

MTS Systems Corporation 856 875-4478
  745 Debra Dr Williamstown (08094) *(G-11965)*

Mualema LLC 609 820-6098
  2214 Town Ct N Lawrence Township (08648) *(G-5217)*

Mueller Die Cut Solutions Inc 201 791-5000
  150 N Midland Ave Saddle Brook (07663) *(G-9665)*

Muirhead Ringoes NJ Inc 609 695-7803
1040 Pennsylvania Ave Trenton (08638) *(G-10959)*

Mul-T-Lock Usa Inc 973 778-3320
100 Commerce Way Ste 2 Hackensack (07601) *(G-3948)*

Mulberry Metal Products Inc (PA) 908 688-8850
2199 Stanley Ter Union (07083) *(G-11078)*

Mulbro Manufacturing & Svc Co 732 805-0290
488 Lincoln Blvd Middlesex (08846) *(G-6132)*

Mule Road Pharmacy 732 244-3737
600 Mule Rd Toms River (08757) *(G-10779)*

Multalloy 9070, Howell Also called Multalloy LLC *(G-4547)*

Multalloy LLC 732 961-1520
507 Oak Glen Rd Howell (07731) *(G-4547)*

Multi Packaging Solutions Inc 908 757-6000
901 Durham Ave South Plainfield (07080) *(G-10303)*

Multi-Pak Corporation 201 342-7474
180 Atlantic St Hackensack (07601) *(G-3949)*

Multi-Pak Packaging, West Caldwell Also called Jak Diversified II Inc *(G-11656)*

Multi-Plastics Inc 856 241-9014
210 Commodore Dr Swedesboro (08085) *(G-10598)*

Multi-Plastics Extrusions Inc 732 388-2300
30 Production Way Avenel (07001) *(G-138)*

Multi-Tech Industries Inc 732 431-0550
64 S Main St Marlboro (07746) *(G-5905)*

Multi-Tex Products Corp 201 991-7262
54 2nd Ave Kearny (07032) *(G-4886)*

Multicomm Solutions Inc 877 796-8480
1285 Rolls Ct Toms River (08755) *(G-10780)*

Multiforce Systems Corporation 609 683-4242
101 Wall St Princeton (08540) *(G-8982)*

Multilink Technology Corp 732 805-9355
300 Atrium Dr Fl 2 Somerset (08873) *(G-10036)*

Multimatic Dry Cleaning Mch, Northvale Also called Multimatic LLC *(G-7539)*

Multimatic LLC (PA) 201 767-9660
162 Veterans Dr Northvale (07647) *(G-7539)*

Multipower International Inc 973 727-0327
7 Woodshire Ter Towaco (07082) *(G-10875)*

Municipal Record Service, Audubon Also called Corbi Printing Co Inc *(G-112)*

Munipol Systems 856 985-2929
1 Eves Dr Ste 111 Marlton (08053) *(G-5942)*

Muralo Company Inc (PA) 201 437-0770
148 E 5th St Bayonne (07002) *(G-229)*

Murdoch, J T Shoes, Bloomfield Also called J T Murdoch Shoes *(G-503)*

Murray Electronics Inc 201 405-1158
12 Fox Ct Oakland (07436) *(G-7637)*

Murray Paving & Concrete LLC 201 670-0030
210 S Newman St Ste 1 Hackensack (07601) *(G-3950)*

Musco Lighting, Wall Township Also called Musco Sports Lighting LLC *(G-11357)*

Musco Sports Lighting LLC 732 751-9114
5146 W Hurley Pond Rd # 1 Wall Township (07727) *(G-11357)*

Muse Monthly LLC 609 443-3509
192 Dorchester Dr East Windsor (08520) *(G-2355)*

Museami Inc 609 917-3000
2 King Arthur Ct Ste A North Brunswick (08902) *(G-7478)*

Mushroom Wisdom Inc 973 470-0010
1 Madison St Ste F6 East Rutherford (07073) *(G-2305)*

Music Trades Corp 201 871-1965
80 West St Ste 200 Englewood (07631) *(G-2927)*

Music Trades Magazine, Englewood Also called Music Trades Corp *(G-2927)*

Musikraft LLC (PA) 856 697-8333
528b N Harding Hwy Vineland (08360) *(G-11243)*

Mv Laboratories Inc (PA) 908 788-6906
843 State Route 12 B17 Frenchtown (08825) *(G-3716)*

Mvn Usa Inc 732 817-1400
960 Holmdel Rd Holmdel (07733) *(G-4510)*

Mw Industries Inc 973 244-9200
10 Audrey Pl Fairfield (07004) *(G-3274)*

Mw Jenkins Sons Incorporated 973 239-5150
444 Pompton Ave Cedar Grove (07009) *(G-1284)*

Mwt Materials Inc 973 928-8300
90 Dayton Ave Ste 6e Passaic (07055) *(G-8091)*

My House Kitchen Inc 201 262-9000
492 N Rte 17 Paramus (07652) *(G-7823)*

My Magic 201 703-1171
0 Plaza Rd Fair Lawn (07410) *(G-3113)*

My Way Prints Inc 973 492-1212
1376 State Rt 23 Ste E Butler (07405) *(G-1010)*

Myat Inc (PA) 201 529-0145
360 Franklin Tpke Mahwah (07430) *(G-5756)*

Mycone Dental Supply Co Inc (PA) 856 663-4700
480 S Democrat Rd Gibbstown (08027) *(G-3798)*

Myers Group LLC 973 761-6414
74 Blanchard Rd South Orange (07079) *(G-10199)*

Mylan API Inc (HQ) 732 748-8882
49 Napoleon Ct Somerset (08873) *(G-10037)*

Mylan API US LLC 732 748-8882
49 Napoleon Ct Somerset (08873) *(G-10038)*

Myos Rens Technology Inc 973 509-0444
45 Horsehill Rd Ste 106 Cedar Knolls (07927) *(G-1311)*

Myriams Dream Book Bindery 609 345-5555
1102 Atlantic Ave Atlantic City (08401) *(G-99)*

Mystic Timber LLC 908 223-7878
95 Youmans Ave Washington (07882) *(G-11449)*

Mysuperfoods Ltd Liability Co 646 283-7455
371 Springfield Ave Ste 2 Summit (07901) *(G-10541)*

N & J Machine Products Corp 973 589-0031
222 Thomas St Newark (07114) *(G-7206)*

N B & Sons LLC 856 692-6191
402 E Wheat Rd Vineland (08360) *(G-11244)*

N B C Engraving Co Inc 201 387-8011
160 Woodbine St Bergenfield (07621) *(G-380)*

N C Carpet Binding & Equipment 973 481-3500
858 Summer Ave Newark (07104) *(G-7207)*

N E A Products Co, Belleville Also called Robert Freeman *(G-312)*

N E R Associates Inc 908 454-5955
45 Howard St Phillipsburg (08865) *(G-8565)*

N G C, Kendall Park Also called Newtech Group Corp *(G-4919)*

N J S, Flanders Also called North Jersey Specialists Inc *(G-3416)*

N J W Magazine 201 886-2185
177 Main St Ste 232 Fort Lee (07024) *(G-3575)*

N Research, West Caldwell Also called Neptune Research & Development *(G-11667)*

N V E Pharmaceuticals, Andover Also called V E N Inc *(G-52)*

N W Sign Industries, Moorestown Also called NW Sign Industries Inc *(G-6547)*

Naava Inc (PA) 844 666-2282
32 Appleton Dr Hazlet (07730) *(G-4266)*

Nabisco, Fair Lawn Also called Mondelez Global LLC *(G-3111)*

Nabisco, Fair Lawn Also called Mondelez Global LLC *(G-3112)*

Nabisco Royal Argentina Inc (HQ) 973 503-2000
200 Deforest Ave East Hanover (07936) *(G-2224)*

Nablus Pastry & Sweets 973 881-8003
1050 Main St Fl 1 Paterson (07503) *(G-8264)*

Nadri Inc 201 585-0088
2 Executive Dr Ste 500 Fort Lee (07024) *(G-3576)*

Nafs Paints Inc 973 927-0729
5 Laurel Dr Unit 4 Flanders (07836) *(G-3415)*

Nahallac LLC 908 635-0999
6 Carman Ln Whitehouse (08888) *(G-11917)*

Nalco Company LLC 609 617-2246
66 Riverside Ave Red Bank (07701) *(G-9238)*

Naluco Inc 800 601-8198
23 Carol St Clifton (07014) *(G-1672)*

Namf, Fairfield Also called New Age Metal Fabg Co Inc *(G-3277)*

Nan Bread Distribution 201 475-9311
41 Leliarts Ln Elmwood Park (07407) *(G-2844)*

Nan Ya Plastics Corp America (PA) 973 992-1775
9 Peach Tree Hill Rd Livingston (07039) *(G-5529)*

Nan Ya Plastics Corp USA (HQ) 973 992-1775
9 Peach Tree Hill Rd Livingston (07039) *(G-5530)*

Nana Creations Inc 201 263-1112
329 Lincoln Ave Fort Lee (07024) *(G-3577)*

Nanasi Enterprises, Hackensack Also called Nei Jewelmasters of New Jersey *(G-3952)*

Nanion Technologies Inc 973 369-7960
1 Naylon Pl Ste 3 Livingston (07039) *(G-5531)*

Nanodesal, Pennington Also called Rlct Industries LLC *(G-8372)*

Nanonex Corp 732 355-1600
1 Deerpark Dr Ste O Monmouth Junction (08852) *(G-6298)*

Nanoopto, Somerset Also called API Nanofabrication & RES Corp *(G-9954)*

Nanoopto Corporation 732 627-0808
1600 Cottontail Ln Ste 1 Somerset (08873) *(G-10039)*

Nanopv Corporation (PA) 609 851-3666
122 Mountainview Rd Ewing (08560) *(G-3047)*

Nanopv Technology, Ewing Also called Nanopv Corporation *(G-3047)*

Naomi Pet International Inc 201 660-7918
20 Charles St Ste D Northvale (07647) *(G-7540)*

NAPA Auto Parts, Hackettstown Also called Norms Auto Parts Inc *(G-4029)*

NAPA Concepts Ltd Liability Co 201 673-2381
36-3 Bergen Ridge Rd North Bergen (07047) *(G-7424)*

Napco Separation Equipment Inc 908 862-7677
200 Marion Ave Linden (07036) *(G-5391)*

Narva Inc 973 218-1200
101 Victory Rd Springfield (07081) *(G-10455)*

NASA Machine Tools Inc 973 633-5200
1 Frassetto Way Ste B Lincoln Park (07035) *(G-5302)*

Nasco Stone and Tile LLC 732 634-0589
200 Markley St Port Reading (07064) *(G-8894)*

Nassau Communications Inc 609 208-9099
650 Whitehead Rd Lawrence Township (08648) *(G-5218)*

Nassau Printers, Lawrence Township Also called Nassau Communications Inc *(G-5218)*

Nassaus Window Fashions Inc 201 689-6030
799 N State Rt 17 Paramus (07652) *(G-7824)*

Natal Lamp & Shade Corp 201 224-7844
5 Horizon Rd Apt 2601 Fort Lee (07024) *(G-3578)*

Natale Machine & Tool Co Inc 201 933-5500
339 13th St Carlstadt (07072) *(G-1189)*

Natali Vineyards LLC 609 465-0075
221 Route 47 N Cape May Court House (08210) *(G-1113)*

Natalie Lamp & Shade, Fort Lee Also called Natal Lamp & Shade Corp *(G-3578)*

2019 Harris New Jersey
Manufacturers Directory

(G-0000) Company's Geographic Section entry number

Nathji Plus Inc 609 877-7600
1 Rose St Willingboro (08046) *(G-11993)*

Naticchia's Custom Woodworking, Ewing *Also called Joseph Naticchia* *(G-3039)*

National Auto Detailing Netwrk 856 931-5529
111 Harding Ave Bellmawr (08031) *(G-340)*

National Casein New Jersey Inc 856 829-1880
401 Marthas Ln Cinnaminson (08077) *(G-1476)*

National Certified Printing 609 443-6323
387 Mercer St A Hightstown (08520) *(G-4297)*

National Christmas Pdts Inc 908 709-4141
2 Commerce Dr Cranford (07016) *(G-1918)*

National Color Graphics 856 435-6800
1755 Williamstwn Erl Rd Sicklerville (08081) *(G-9912)*

National Communications Inc 973 325-3151
69 Washington St West Orange (07052) *(G-11774)*

National Display Group Inc 856 661-1212
6850 River Rd Pennsauken (08110) *(G-8459)*

National Diversified Sales Inc 559 562-9888
401 Bordentown Hedding Rd Bordentown (08505) *(G-590)*

National Electric Wire Co Inc 609 758-3600
100 Goldman Dr Cream Ridge (08514) *(G-1938)*

National Electronic Alloys Inc (PA) 201 337-9400
3 Fir Ct Oakland (07436) *(G-7638)*

National Fence Systems Inc 732 636-5600
1033 Rte One Avenel Avenel (07001) *(G-139)*

National Flag & Display Co Inc 973 366-1776
353 Richard Mine Rd Ste 5 Wharton (07885) *(G-11863)*

National Fuel LLC 973 227-4549
287 Changebridge Rd Pine Brook (07058) *(G-8610)*

National Home Planning Service 973 376-3200
79 Thornley Dr Chatham (07928) *(G-1328)*

National Housing Institute 973 509-1600
60 S Fullerton Ave # 206 Montclair (07042) *(G-6377)*

National Labnet Co 732 417-0700
33 Wood Ave S Ste 600 Iselin (08830) *(G-4618)*

National Lecithim Inc (PA) 973 940-8920
93 Spring St Ste 303 Newton (07860) *(G-7351)*

National Manufacturing Co Inc 973 635-8846
12 River Rd Chatham (07928) *(G-1329)*

National Metals, Middlesex *Also called National Mtal Fnshngs Corp Inc* *(G-6133)*

National Mtal Fnshngs Corp Inc (PA) 732 752-7770
897 South Ave Middlesex (08846) *(G-6133)*

National Paint Supply, North Brunswick *Also called Nautical Marine Paint Corp* *(G-7479)*

National Plastic Printing 973 785-1460
130 Furler St Totowa (07512) *(G-10838)*

National Precision Tool Co 973 227-5005
24 Sherwood Ln Fairfield (07004) *(G-3275)*

National Prtective Systems Inc 732 922-3609
1 Meridian Rd Eatontown (07724) *(G-2412)*

National Public Seating, Clifton *Also called NPS Public Furniture Corp* *(G-1679)*

National Refrigerants Inc 856 455-4555
661 Kenyon Ave Bridgeton (08302) *(G-766)*

National Register Publishing, New Providence *Also called Marquis - Whos Who Inc* *(G-7009)*

National Reprographics Inc 609 896-4100
3175 Princeton Pike Lawrenceville (08648) *(G-5239)*

National Sports Sales, Belleville *Also called Red Diamond Co - Athc Letering* *(G-310)*

National Steel Rule Company (PA) 908 862-3366
750 Commerce Rd Linden (07036) *(G-5392)*

National Steel Rule Company 800 922-0885
620 Commerce Rd Linden (07036) *(G-5393)*

National Steel Rule Company 908 862-3366
712 Commerce Rd Linden (07036) *(G-5394)*

National Strch Chem Holdg Corp (HQ) 908 685-5000
10 Finderne Ave Bridgewater (08807) *(G-854)*

National Tax Training School, Mahwah *Also called Union Institute Inc* *(G-5785)*

National Tree Company, Cranford *Also called National Christmas Pdts Inc* *(G-1918)*

National Woodworking Co 908 851-9316
985 Tinkettle Turn Union (07083) *(G-11079)*

Natl Adhesies Div of Henke 908 685-7000
10 Finderne Ave Bridgewater (08807) *(G-855)*

Natural Green, Bridgewater *Also called J C W Inc* *(G-838)*

Natural Wireless LLC 201 438-2865
23a Poplar St East Rutherford (07073) *(G-2306)*

Naturally Scientific Inc 201 585-7055
600 Willow Tree Rd Leonia (07605) *(G-5291)*

Naturalvert LLC 848 229-4600
150 Florence Ave Ste D Hawthorne (07506) *(G-4233)*

Nature Labs LLC 856 839-0400
46 N West Ave Ste B Vineland (08360) *(G-11245)*

Naturee Nuts Inc 732 786-4663
636 N Michigan Ave Kenilworth (07033) *(G-4962)*

Natures Beauty Marble & Gran 908 233-5300
2476 Plainfield Ave Scotch Plains (07076) *(G-9737)*

Natures Choice Corporation (PA) 973 969-3299
482 Houses Corner Rd Sparta (07871) *(G-10401)*

Natures Rule LLC 888 819-4220
1319 N Broad St Hillside (07205) *(G-4417)*

Naturex Holdings Inc (HQ) 201 440-5000
375 Huyler St South Hackensack (07606) *(G-10172)*

Naturex Inc 201 440-5000
125 Phillips Ave South Hackensack (07606) *(G-10173)*

Naturex Inc (HQ) 201 440-5000
375 Huyler St South Hackensack (07606) *(G-10174)*

Nautical Marine Paint Corp (PA) 732 821-3200
1999 Elizabeth St North Brunswick (08902) *(G-7479)*

Nautilus Neurosciences Inc 908 437-1320
135 Rte 202 Bedminster (07921) *(G-275)*

Navinta LLC 609 883-1135
1499 Lower Ferry Rd Ewing (08618) *(G-3048)*

Navistar Inc 856 486-2300
535 Route 38 Ste 300 Cherry Hill (08002) *(G-1397)*

Nb Bookbinding Inc 973 247-1200
356 Getty Ave Bldg 2 Clifton (07011) *(G-1673)*

Nb Ventures Inc (PA) 732 382-6565
100 Walnut Ave Ste 304 Clark (07066) *(G-1509)*

Nbs Group Sup Med Pdts Div LLC 732 745-9292
257 Livingston Ave Fl 3 New Brunswick (08901) *(G-6949)*

Nbs Medical, New Brunswick *Also called Nbs Group Sup Med Pdts Div LLC* *(G-6949)*

NC Carpet, Newark *Also called N C Carpet Binding & Equipment* *(G-7207)*

Nconnex Inc 413 658-5582
1 Richmond St Apt 3079 New Brunswick (08901) *(G-6950)*

Ncs Pearson Inc 201 896-1011
1099 Wall St W Lyndhurst (07071) *(G-5666)*

Nds, Bordentown *Also called National Diversified Sales Inc* *(G-590)*

Nds Technologies Inc 856 691-0330
891 E Oak Rd Unit B Vineland (08360) *(G-11246)*

Nedco Conveyor Technology, Union *Also called Tarlton C & T Co Inc* *(G-11093)*

Nedohon Inc (PA) 302 533-5512
302 E Newark Ave Wildwood Crest (08260) *(G-11948)*

NEi Gold Products of NJ 201 488-5858
44 Burlews Ct Hackensack (07601) *(G-3951)*

Nei House of Chains, Hackensack *Also called NEi Gold Products of NJ* *(G-3951)*

Nei Jewelmasters of New Jersey (PA) 201 488-5858
44 Burlews Ct Hackensack (07601) *(G-3952)*

Neill Supply Co, Lyndhurst *Also called Long Island Pipe of NJ* *(G-5658)*

Neill Supply Co., Inc., Lyndhurst *Also called Teneyck Inc* *(G-5681)*

Neilmax Industries Inc 908 756-8800
15a Progress St Edison (08820) *(G-2571)*

Nekoosa Coated Products LLC 800 440-1250
6 Ingersoll Rd South Plainfield (07080) *(G-10304)*

Nellsam Group Inc 201 951-9459
36 Washington Ave Fl 1 Cliffside Park (07010) *(G-1542)*

Nema Associates Inc 973 274-0052
408 E Elizabeth Ave Linden (07036) *(G-5395)*

Nema Food Distribution Inc 973 256-4415
18 Commerce Rd Ste D Fairfield (07004) *(G-3276)*

Neopharma Inc (HQ) 609 201-2185
211 College Rd E Ste 101 Princeton (08540) *(G-8983)*

Nephros Inc (PA) 201 343-5202
380 Lackawanna Pl South Orange (07079) *(G-10200)*

Neptune Products Inc 973 366-8200
353 E Blackwell St Dover (07801) *(G-2100)*

Neptune Research & Development 973 808-8811
267 Fairfield Ave West Caldwell (07006) *(G-11667)*

Ner Data Products Inc (HQ) 888 637-3282
307 Delsea Dr S Glassboro (08028) *(G-3817)*

Nes Enterprises Inc 201 964-1400
513 Washington Ave Carlstadt (07072) *(G-1190)*

Nes Jewelry Inc 646 213-4094
43 Samworth Rd Clifton (07012) *(G-1674)*

Nes Light Inc 201 840-0400
1179 Edgewater Ave Ridgefield (07657) *(G-9279)*

Ness Plastics Inc 201 854-4072
6040 Kennedy Blvd E 22f West New York (07093) *(G-11748)*

Nestle Beverage Division, Freehold *Also called Nestle Usa Inc* *(G-3682)*

Nestle Health Science, Bridgewater *Also called Nestle Healthcare Ntrtn Inc* *(G-856)*

Nestle Healthcare Ntrtn Inc (HQ) 800 422-2752
1007 Us Highway 202/206 Bridgewater (08807) *(G-856)*

Nestle Infant Nutrition, Florham Park *Also called Gerber Products Company* *(G-3508)*

Nestle Usa Inc 732 462-1300
61 Jerseyville Ave Freehold (07728) *(G-3682)*

Nestle Inc 973 390-9555
326 Smith St Keasbey (08832) *(G-4913)*

Nestle Waters North Amer Inc 201 451-4000
111 Thomas Mcgovern Dr Jersey City (07305) *(G-4769)*

Netcom, Hackensack *Also called Network Communications Cons* *(G-3953)*

Netcom Systems Inc (PA) 732 393-6100
200 Metroplex Dr Edison (08817) *(G-2572)*

Netfruits Inc 732 249-2588
100 Jersey Ave New Brunswick (08901) *(G-6951)*

Netquest Corporation 856 866-0505
523 Fellowship Rd Ste 205 Mount Laurel (08054) *(G-6786)*

Netscout Systems Inc 609 518-4100
2000 Lincoln Dr E Marlton (08053) *(G-5943)*

Network Access Systems Incorpr 732 355-9770
19 Issac Dr Dayton (08810) *(G-1981)*

Network Communications Cons 201 968-0684
20 E Kennedy St Hackensack (07601) *(G-3953)*

Network Typesetting Inc 732 819-0949
1637 Stelton Rd Ste B4 Piscataway (08854) *(G-8694)*

Netx Information Systems Inc (PA) 609 298-9118
76 Auburn Rd Long Beach Township (08008) *(G-5592)*

Neu Inc 281 648-9751
1 N Johnston Ave Ste 2 Hamilton (08609) *(G-4118)*

Neumann Sheet Metal Inc 908 756-0415
759 North Ave Plainfield (07062) *(G-8771)*

Neurotron Medical Inc 609 896-3444
800 Silvia St Ewing (08628) *(G-3049)*

Neuweiler, K H, Berkeley Heights *Also called Karl Neuweiler Inc* *(G-404)*

New Adventures LLC 973 884-8887
6 Deforest Ave Ste 7 East Hanover (07936) *(G-2225)*

New Age Metal Fabg Co Inc 973 227-9107
26 Daniel Rd W Fairfield (07004) *(G-3277)*

New Art Ring Co, Maplewood *Also called Trimarco Inc* *(G-5886)*

New Brunswick Lamp Shade Co 732 545-0377
7 Terminal Rd New Brunswick (08901) *(G-6952)*

New Brunswick Plating Inc (PA) 732 545-6522
596 Jersey Ave New Brunswick (08901) *(G-6953)*

New Century Millwork Inc 973 882-0222
131 Lincoln Blvd Middlesex (08846) *(G-6134)*

New Community Corp 973 643-5300
200 S Orange Ave Newark (07103) *(G-7208)*

New Dawn Inc 732 774-1377
60 Steiner Ave Neptune (07753) *(G-6892)*

New Dimensions Industries LLC 201 531-1010
151 Cooper Rd West Berlin (08091) *(G-11610)*

New England Bedding Trnspt Inc 631 484-0147
102 3rd Ave Kearny (07032) *(G-4887)*

New ERA Converting McHy Inc 201 670-4848
235 Mclean Blvd Paterson (07504) *(G-8265)*

New ERA Enterprises Inc 856 794-2005
208 N West Blvd Newfield (08344) *(G-7324)*

New Great American Veal, Newark *Also called Dorzar Corporation* *(G-7103)*

New Heaven Chemicals Iowa LLC 201 506-9109
18 Jenny Ln Sussex (07461) *(G-10564)*

New Horizon Graphics Inc 609 584-1301
2 Christine Ave Trenton (08619) *(G-10960)*

New Horizon Press Publishers 908 604-6311
34 Church St Liberty Corner (07938) *(G-5295)*

New Industrial Foam Corp 908 561-4010
1355 W Front St Ste 3 Plainfield (07063) *(G-8772)*

New Jersey 50 Plus, Toms River *Also called Pentacle Publishing Corp* *(G-10782)*

New Jersey Air Products Inc 908 964-9001
4 Mark Rd Ste D Kenilworth (07033) *(G-4963)*

New Jersey Automotive Mag, Nutley *Also called Thomas Greco Publishing Inc* *(G-7594)*

New Jersey Balancing Svc Inc 973 278-5106
138 Michigan Ave Ste 40 Paterson (07503) *(G-8266)*

New Jersey Bindery Svcs LLC 732 200-8024
4301 New Brunswick Ave South Plainfield (07080) *(G-10305)*

New Jersey Bus & Indust Assn (PA) 609 393-7707
10 W Lafayette St Trenton (08608) *(G-10961)*

New Jersey Business Magazine 973 882-5004
310 Passaic Ave Ste 201 Fairfield (07004) *(G-3278)*

New Jersey Department Treasury 609 292-5133
101 Carroll St Trenton (08609) *(G-10962)*

New Jersey Diamond Products Co 973 684-0949
108 Kentucky Ave Paterson (07503) *(G-8267)*

New Jersey Drapery Service, Verona *Also called Proclean Services Inc* *(G-11172)*

New Jersey Electric Motors 908 526-5225
84 Somerset St Ste A Somerville (08876) *(G-10121)*

New Jersey Eye Center Inc 201 384-7333
1 N Washington Ave Bergenfield (07621) *(G-381)*

New Jersey Fence & Guardrail 973 786-5400
32 Main St Andover (07821) *(G-50)*

New Jersey Gold Buyers Corp (PA) 732 765-4653
460 County Road 520 Marlboro (07746) *(G-5906)*

New Jersey Hardwoods Inc 908 754-0990
1340 W Front St Plainfield (07063) *(G-8773)*

New Jersey Headwear Corp 973 497-0102
305 3rd Ave W Ste 5 Newark (07107) *(G-7209)*

New Jersey Herald (HQ) 973 383-1500
2 Spring St Newton (07860) *(G-7352)*

New Jersey Jewish News (PA) 973 887-3900
901 State Route 10 Whippany (07981) *(G-11898)*

New Jersey Jury, Springfield *Also called Jury Vrdict Rview Publications* *(G-10449)*

New Jersey Label LLC 201 880-5102
30 Wesley St Unit 7 South Hackensack (07606) *(G-10175)*

New Jersey Line X, Bridgewater *Also called Chapter Enterprises Inc* *(G-811)*

New Jersey Monthly LLC 973 539-8230
55 S Park Pl Morristown (07960) *(G-6689)*

New Jersey National Guard, Woodbury *Also called NJ Dept Military Vtrans* *(G-12033)*

New Jersey Polverizing, Bayville *Also called Ace-Crete Products Inc* *(G-238)*

New Jersey Porcelain Co Inc (PA) 609 394-5376
600 Plum St Trenton (08638) *(G-10963)*

New Jersey Pulverizing Co Inc 732 269-1400
250 Hickory Ln Bayville (08721) *(G-249)*

New Jersey Reprographics Inc 908 789-1616
110 Center St Garwood (07027) *(G-3786)*

New Jersey Rivet Co LLC 856 963-2237
1785 Haddon Ave Camden (08103) *(G-1078)*

New Jersey Stair and Rail Inc 732 583-8400
746 Lloyd Rd Matawan (07747) *(G-5981)*

New Jersey Steel Corporation 856 337-0054
2840 Mount Ephraim Ave Haddon Township (08104) *(G-4051)*

New Jersey Tech Group LLC 609 301-6405
1632 Route 38 Lumberton (08048) *(G-5633)*

New Jersey Wire Cloth Co Inc 973 340-0101
55 Park Slope Clifton (07011) *(G-1675)*

New Jrsey Sfood Mktg Group LLC 609 296-7026
143 Leektown Rd Egg Harbor City (08215) *(G-2665)*

New Jrsey State Leag Mncplitie, Trenton *Also called New Jrsey State Leag
Mncplties* *(G-10964)*

New Jrsey State Leag Mncplties 609 695-3481
222 W State St Trenton (08608) *(G-10964)*

New Jrsy Glvnzng & Tnnng Wks 973 242-3200
139 Haynes Ave Newark (07114) *(G-7210)*

New Life Color Reproductions 201 943-7005
610 Broad Ave Ridgefield (07657) *(G-9280)*

New Line Prtg & Tech Solutions 973 405-6133
790 Bloomfield Ave Ste 3 Clifton (07012) *(G-1676)*

New Satellite Network LLC 908 922-0967
1942 Sunset Pl Scotch Plains (07076) *(G-9738)*

New Skysonic Surveillance 856 317-0600
7905 Browning Rd Ste 200 Cherry Hill (08002) *(G-1398)*

New Standard Printing Corp 973 366-0006
118 Lincoln Ave Dover (07801) *(G-2101)*

New Top Inc 201 438-3990
40 Broad St Carlstadt (07072) *(G-1191)*

New Venture Partners LLC 908 464-8131
430 Mountain Ave Ste 404 New Providence (07974) *(G-7013)*

New View Media 973 691-3002
1 Old Wolfe Rd Ste 203 Budd Lake (07828) *(G-931)*

New World International Inc 973 881-8100
46 Lewis St Paterson (07501) *(G-8268)*

New World Leather, South Orange *Also called Myers Group LLC* *(G-10199)*

New World Stainless LLC 732 412-7137
100 Randolph Rd Ste 5 Somerset (08873) *(G-10040)*

New York Blackboard of NJ Inc 973 926-1600
83 Us Highway 22 Hillside (07205) *(G-4418)*

New York Botany Inc 201 564-7444
20 Charles St Ste B Northvale (07647) *(G-7541)*

New York Daily News, Jersey City *Also called Daily News LP* *(G-4720)*

New York Folding Box Co Inc 973 347-6932
20 Continental Dr Stanhope (07874) *(G-10477)*

New York Fur, Fairview *Also called Prime Fur & Leather Inc* *(G-3368)*

New York Kitchen Specialist, Springfield *Also called Narva Inc* *(G-10455)*

New York Popular Inc 718 499-2020
400 Federal Blvd Carteret (07008) *(G-1260)*

New York Poultry Co 908 523-1600
3351 Tremley Point Rd # 2 Linden (07036) *(G-5396)*

New York-NJ Trail Conference (PA) 201 512-9348
600 Ramapo Valley Rd Mahwah (07430) *(G-5757)*

Newage Painting Corporation 908 547-4734
78 Fillmore St Ste 7 Newark (07105) *(G-7211)*

Newark Asphalt Corp 973 482-3503
1500 Mccarter Hwy Newark (07104) *(G-7212)*

Newark Auto Products, East Orange *Also called Newark Auto Top Co Inc* *(G-2256)*

Newark Auto Top Co Inc 973 677-9935
23 Centerway East Orange (07017) *(G-2256)*

Newark Brush Company LLC 973 376-1000
1 Silver Ct Springfield (07081) *(G-10456)*

Newark Fibers Inc (PA) 201 768-6800
28 Piermont Rd Rockleigh (07647) *(G-9520)*

Newark Industrial Spraying 973 344-6855
12 Amsterdam St Newark (07105) *(G-7213)*

Newark Ironworks Inc 973 424-9790
41 Frelinghuysen Ave # 43 Newark (07114) *(G-7214)*

Newark Liner & Washer Inc 973 482-5400
819 Broadway Newark (07104) *(G-7215)*

Newark Morning Ledger Co (PA) 973 392-4141
1 Gateway Ctr Ste 1100 Newark (07102) *(G-7216)*

Newark Morning Ledger Co 732 560-1560
20 Duke Rd Piscataway (08854) *(G-8695)*

Newark Morning Ledger Co 973 882-6120
26 Riverside Dr Pine Brook (07058) *(G-8611)*

Newark Nut Company, Jersey City *Also called Nutscom Inc* *(G-4776)*

Newark Stamp & Die Works Inc 973 485-7111
35 Verona Ave Newark (07104) *(G-7217)*

Newark Steel & Orna Sup Co, Newark *Also called Newark Ironworks Inc* *(G-7214)*

Newark Trade Digital Graphics, Orange *Also called Newark Trade Typographers* *(G-7757)*

Newark Trade Typographers 973 674-3727
177 Oakwood Ave Orange (07050) *(G-7757)*

Newark Wire Cloth Company 973 778-4478
160 Fornelius Ave Clifton (07013) *(G-1677)*

Newark Wire Works Inc 732 661-2001
1059 King Georges Rd 10 # 103 Edison (08837) *(G-2573)*

Newbold Inc 732 469-5654
200 Egel Ave Middlesex (08846) *(G-6135)*

Newbold Target, Middlesex *Also called Newbold Inc (G-6135)*

Newcardio Inc 877 332-4324
103 Carnegie Ctr Ste 300 Princeton (08540) *(G-8984)*

Newco Valves LLC 732 257-0300
19a Cotters Ln East Brunswick (08816) *(G-2159)*

Newell Brands, Hoboken *Also called Jarden LLC (G-4458)*

Newell Brands Inc (PA) 201 610-6600
221 River St Ste 13 Hoboken (07030) *(G-4468)*

Newfuturevest Two LLC (PA) 609 586-8004
17a Marlen Dr Trenton (08691) *(G-10965)*

Newline Prtg & Tech Solutions 973 405-6133
1011 Us Highway 22 Ste 1 Mountainside (07092) *(G-6849)*

Newman Glass Works Inc 215 925-3565
1515 Haddon Ave Camden (08103) *(G-1079)*

Newman Ornamental Iron Works 732 223-9042
207 Union Ave Brielle (08730) *(G-908)*

Newmans, East Brunswick *Also called Newco Valves LLC (G-2159)*

News Inc Gloucester City 856 456-1199
34 S Broadway Gloucester City (08030) *(G-3846)*

Newspaper Media Group LLC (PA) 856 779-3800
2 Executive Campus # 400 Cherry Hill (08002) *(G-1399)*

Newspaper Media Group LLC 201 798-7800
19 Winchester Dr Califon (07830) *(G-1032)*

Newtech Group Corp 732 355-0392
54 Inverness Dr Kendall Park (08824) *(G-4919)*

Newtek Sensor Solutions LLC 856 406-6877
7300 N Route 130 Unit 7 Pennsauken (08110) *(G-8460)*

Newton Biopharma Solutions LLC 908 874-7145
8 Fine Rd Hillsborough (08844) *(G-4340)*

Newton Memorial Hospital Inc 973 726-0904
89 Sparta Ave Ste 210 Sparta (07871) *(G-10402)*

Newton Screen Printing Co 973 827-0486
75 Main St Franklin (07416) *(G-3606)*

Newton Screenprinting, Franklin *Also called Newton Screen Printing Co (G-3606)*

Newton Tool, Newton *Also called T & M Newton Corporation (G-7361)*

Newton Tool & Mfg Inc 856 241-1500
7249b Browning Rd Pennsauken (08109) *(G-8461)*

Newtype Inc 973 361-6000
447 State Route 10 Ste 14 Randolph (07869) *(G-9192)*

Nexira Inc 908 704-7480
15 Somerset St Somerville (08876) *(G-10122)*

Next Level Fabrication LLC 609 703-0682
205 Zion Rd Egg Harbor Township (08234) *(G-2691)*

Next Medical Products LLC 908 722-4549
45 Columbia Rd Branchburg (08876) *(G-660)*

Nextgen Edge Inc 610 507-6904
50 Beacon Hill Rd Apt A West Milford (07480) *(G-11730)*

Nextphase Medical Devices LLC (PA) 201 968-9400
150 Hopper Ave Waldwick (07463) *(G-11308)*

Nextron Infusion Services, Fairfield *Also called Nextron Medical Tech Inc (G-3279)*

Nextron Medical Tech Inc 973 575-0614
45 Kulick Rd Fairfield (07004) *(G-3279)*

Nextwave Web LLC 973 742-4339
229 Marshall St Paterson (07503) *(G-8269)*

Nexus Plastics Incorporated 973 427-3311
1 Loretto Ave Hawthorne (07506) *(G-4234)*

Nexxbrands, West Long Branch *Also called Shrem Consulting Ltd Lblty Co (G-11721)*

Nfs, Avenel *Also called National Fence Systems Inc (G-139)*

Ngenious Solutions Inc 732 873-3385
30 Knightsbridge Rd # 525 Piscataway (08854) *(G-8696)*

Niaflex Corporation 407 851-6620
9 Peach Tree Hill Rd Livingston (07039) *(G-5532)*

Niagara Conservation Corp 973 829-0800
45 Horsehill Rd Ste 105 Cedar Knolls (07927) *(G-1312)*

Nice Instrumentation 732 851-4300
205 Park Ave Manalapan (07726) *(G-5818)*

Nichem Co 973 399-9810
750 Frelinghuysen Ave Newark (07114) *(G-7218)*

Nicholas Galvanizing Co Inc 201 795-1010
120 Duffield Ave Jersey City (07306) *(G-4770)*

Nicholas Oliver LLC 732 690-7144
1933 State Route 35 Wall Township (07719) *(G-11358)*

Nickel Artistic Services LLC 973 627-0390
39 Us Highway 46 Rockaway (07866) *(G-9479)*

Nickel Savers 201 405-1153
90 Andrew Ave Oakland (07436) *(G-7639)*

Nickels Carpet Cleaning 609 892-5783
957 Morningside Dr Mays Landing (08330) *(G-5995)*

Nickolaos Kappatos Entps Inc 856 939-1099
1215 Black Horse Pike Glendora (08029) *(G-3838)*

Nickos Construction Inc 267 240-3997
17 Arcadian Dr Sicklerville (08081) *(G-9913)*

Nicks Workshop Inc 856 784-6097
171 Clementon Rd W Gibbsboro (08026) *(G-3794)*

Nicolosi Foods Inc 201 624-1702
2214 Summit Ave Union City (07087) *(G-11123)*

Nicomac Systems Inc 201 871-0916
54 Summit St Norwood (07648) *(G-7570)*

Nicos Group Inc 201 768-9501
80 Oak St Ste 201 Norwood (07648) *(G-7571)*

Nifty Packaging, Old Bridge *Also called Rep Trading Associates Inc (G-7727)*

Nighthawk Interactive LLC 732 243-9922
1090 King Georges Post Rd # 402 Edison (08837) *(G-2574)*

Nijama Corporation 973 272-3223
132 Getty Ave Clifton (07011) *(G-1678)*

Nike Inc 732 695-0108
1 Premium Outlet Blvd # 699 Tinton Falls (07753) *(G-10723)*

Nikko Ceramics Inc (HQ) 201 840-5200
815 Fairview Ave Ste 9 Fairview (07022) *(G-3364)*

Niko Trade Ltd-USA Inc 973 575-4353
271 Us Highway 46 D107 Fairfield (07004) *(G-3280)*

Niksun Inc (PA) 609 936-9999
457 N Harrison St Princeton (08540) *(G-8985)*

Nilsson Electrical Laboratory 201 521-4860
333 W Side Ave Jersey City (07305) *(G-4771)*

Nine West Holdings Inc 908 354-8895
651 Kapkowski Rd Ste 2032 Elizabeth (07201) *(G-2760)*

Nine West Holdings Inc 201 541-7004
33 E Palisade Ave Englewood (07631) *(G-2928)*

Nini Disposal 609 587-2411
410 Whitehead Rd Trenton (08619) *(G-10966)*

Ninsa LLC 609 561-7103
125 Lincoln St Hammonton (08037) *(G-4140)*

Nippon Benkan Kagyo 732 435-0777
475 Jersey Ave New Brunswick (08901) *(G-6954)*

Nippon Paint (usa) Inc (HQ) 201 692-1111
400 Frank W Burr Blvd # 10 Teaneck (07666) *(G-10640)*

Nippon Paint America, Teaneck *Also called Nippon Paint (usa) Inc (G-10640)*

Nipro Glass Americas Corp 856 825-1400
1633 Wheaton Ave Millville (08332) *(G-6261)*

Nipro Phrmpckging Amricas Corp (HQ) 856 825-1400
1200 N 10th St Millville (08332) *(G-6262)*

Nirwana Foods LLC 201 659-2200
778 Newark Ave Jersey City (07306) *(G-4772)*

Nitka Graphics Inc 201 797-3000
13-63 Henrietta Ct Fair Lawn (07410) *(G-3114)*

Nitta Casings Inc 800 526-3970
141 Southside Ave Bridgewater (08807) *(G-857)*

Nitto Inc (HQ) 732 901-7905
1990 Rutgers Blvd Lakewood (08701) *(G-5139)*

Nitto Inc 732 901-0035
1975 Swarthmore Ave Lakewood (08701) *(G-5140)*

Nitto Inc 732 901-7905
1990 Rutgers Blvd Lakewood (08701) *(G-5141)*

Nitto Inc 201 645-4950
400 Frank W Burr Blvd # 66 Teaneck (07666) *(G-10641)*

Nitto Denko Automotive, Lakewood *Also called Nitto Inc (G-5139)*

NJ Advance Media LLC 732 902-4300
2015 State Route 27 # 300 Edison (08817) *(G-2575)*

NJ Copy Center LLC 973 788-1600
10 Madison Rd Ste C Fairfield (07004) *(G-3281)*

NJ Dept Military Vtrans 856 384-8831
658 N Evergreen Ave Woodbury (08096) *(G-12033)*

NJ Fuel Haulers Inc 732 740-3681
3617 Us Highway 9 Old Bridge (08857) *(G-7721)*

NJ Grass Choppers 732 414-2850
254 Monmouth Rd Manalapan (07726) *(G-5819)*

NJ Logo Wear LLC 609 597-9400
100 Mckinley Ave Ste 6 Manahawkin (08050) *(G-5794)*

NJ Memorial Art, Verona *Also called Ferrante Press Inc (G-11167)*

NJ Paver Restorations LLC 732 558-6011
857 Amwell Rd Hillsborough (08844) *(G-4341)*

NJ Precision Tech Inc 800 409-3000
1081 Bristol Rd Mountainside (07092) *(G-6850)*

NJ Press Media 732 643-3604
3601 State Route 66 Neptune (07753) *(G-6893)*

NJ Service Testing & Insptn 732 221-6357
26 Oak St Lincroft (07738) *(G-5313)*

Njbia, Trenton *Also called New Jersey Bus & Indust Assn (G-10961)*

Njiw Limited Liability Company 201 355-2955
87 Burlews Ct Hackensack (07601) *(G-3954)*

Njr Clean Energy Ventures Corp (HQ) 732 938-1000
1415 Wyckoff Rd Belmar (07719) *(G-351)*

Njrls Enterprises Inc 732 846-6010
3380 Us Highway 22 3a Branchburg (08876) *(G-661)*

Njs Associates Company 973 960-8688
1170 Route 22 Ste 209 Bridgewater (08807) *(G-858)*

Nlyte Software Americas Ltd (HQ) 650 561-8200
275 Raritan Center Pkwy Edison (08837) *(G-2576)*

Nlyte Software Inc 732 395-6920
275 Raritan Center Pkwy Edison (08837) *(G-2577)*

A L P H A B E T I C

NM Knight Co Inc 856 327-4855
  1001 S 2nd St Millville (08332) *(G-6263)*

NMP Water Systems LLC 201 252-8333
  63 Ramapo Valley Rd # 103 Mahwah (07430) *(G-5758)*

Nmr Manufacturing LLC 908 769-3234
  25 Davis St South Plainfield (07080) *(G-10306)*

No Fire Technologies Inc 201 818-1616
  5 James St South Hackensack (07606) *(G-10176)*

Noah LLC 609 637-0039
  610 Lawrenceville Rd Lawrenceville (08648) *(G-5240)*

Nobel Biocare Procera LLC 201 529-7100
  800 Corporate Dr Mahwah (07430) *(G-5759)*

Nobelus LLC 800 895-2747
  1665 Jersey Ave North Brunswick (08902) *(G-7480)*

Noble Metals, Linden *Also called Express Printing Inc (G-5346)*

Noble Metals Corp 908 925-6300
  209 W Saint Georges Ave Linden (07036) *(G-5397)*

Nobleworks Inc 201 420-0095
  500 Paterson Plank Rd Union City (07087) *(G-11124)*

Nogpo Inc 908 642-3545
  4 Patriot Hill Dr Basking Ridge (07920) *(G-193)*

Nokia Inc 908 582-3149
  600-700 Mountain Ave Murray Hill (07974) *(G-6860)*

Nokia of America Corporation (HQ) 908 582-3275
  600 Mountain Ave Ste 700 New Providence (07974) *(G-7014)*

Nomad Lcrosse Distrs Ltd Lblty 732 431-2255
  62 Jackson St Ste 2 Freehold (07728) *(G-3683)*

Nomadic North America LLC 703 866-9200
  46 Just Rd Fairfield (07004) *(G-3282)*

Non Profit Times, Morris Plains *Also called Npt Publishing Group Inc (G-6620)*

Nonzero Foundation Inc 609 688-0793
  321 Prospect Ave Princeton (08540) *(G-8986)*

Noodle Fan 732 446-2820
  557 Englishtown Rd Monroe Township (08831) *(G-6337)*

Noodle Gogo 908 222-8898
  4811 Stelton Rd South Plainfield (07080) *(G-10307)*

Noopys Research Inc 856 358-6001
  108 Harding Hwy Newfield (08344) *(G-7325)*

Norco Inc 908 789-1550
  237 South Ave Garwood (07027) *(G-3787)*

Norco Manufacturing Inc 201 854-3461
  2025 85th St North Bergen (07047) *(G-7425)*

Norden Inc (HQ) 908 252-9483
  230 Industrial Pkwy Ste A Branchburg (08876) *(G-662)*

Norden Packaging, Branchburg *Also called Norden Inc (G-662)*

Nordic Metal LLC 908 245-8900
  500 S 31st St Kenilworth (07033) *(G-4964)*

Nordson Efd LLC 609 259-9222
  8 Applegate Dr Robbinsville (08691) *(G-9414)*

Norland Products Inc 609 395-1966
  2540 Us Highway 130 # 100 Cranbury (08512) *(G-1865)*

Norlo of New Jersey LLC 646 492-3293
  105 Alexander Ave Montclair (07043) *(G-6378)*

Norma K Corporation 732 477-6441
  30 Broadway Point Pleasant Beach (08742) *(G-8829)*

Norman Weil Inc 201 940-7345
  140 E Ridgewood Ave # 415 Paramus (07652) *(G-7825)*

Norman Weil Textile, Paramus *Also called Norman Weil Inc (G-7825)*

Norms Auto Parts Inc 908 852-5080
  135 Willow Grove St Hackettstown (07840) *(G-4029)*

Norpak Corporation (PA) 973 589-4200
  70 Blanchard St Newark (07105) *(G-7219)*

Norsal Distribution Associates 908 638-6430
  150 Cregar Rd High Bridge (08829) *(G-4284)*

North America Printing 973 726-7713
  156 Woodport Rd Sparta (07871) *(G-10403)*

North American Composites Co 609 625-8101
  5450 Atlantic Ave Mays Landing (08330) *(G-5996)*

North American Frontier Corp 201 222-1931
  195 New York Ave Jersey City (07307) *(G-4773)*

North American Illumination...................................973 478-4700
  79 Commerce St Ste 2 Garfield (07026) *(G-3751)*

North Bergen Asphalt, North Bergen *Also called Tilcon New York Inc (G-7440)*

North Bergen Marble & Granite 201 945-9988
  217 Palisade Ave Cliffside Park (07010) *(G-1543)*

North Church Gravel Inc 201 796-1556
  173 Oak Ridge Rd Oak Ridge (07438) *(G-7603)*

North Eastern Business Forms 609 392-1161
  1111 Chestnut Ave Trenton (08611) *(G-10967)*

North Eastern Pallet Exchange 908 289-0018
  725 Spring St Ste 2 Elizabeth (07201) *(G-2761)*

North Jersey Com. Newspaper, Woodland Park *Also called Herald News (G-12081)*

North Jersey Media Group Inc (HQ) 201 646-4000
  150 River St Hackensack (07601) *(G-3955)*

North Jersey Media Group Inc 201 933-1166
  9 Lincoln Ave Rutherford (07070) *(G-9629)*

North Jersey Media Group Inc 973 233-5000
  130 Valley Rd Ste D Montclair (07042) *(G-6379)*

North Jersey Media Group Inc 973 569-7100
  1 Garret Mountain Plz # 201 Woodland Park (07424) *(G-12085)*

North Jersey Media Group Inc 201 485-7800
  6 Leighton Pl Mahwah (07430) *(G-5760)*

North Jersey Metal Fabricators 973 305-9830
  130 Ryerson Ave Ste 107 Wayne (07470) *(G-11536)*

North Jersey Skein Dyeing Co 201 247-4202
  152 Putnam St Paterson (07524) *(G-8270)*

North Jersey Specialists Inc 973 927-1616
  5 Laurel Dr Unit 6 Flanders (07836) *(G-3416)*

North Jrsey Mdia Group Fndtion, Hackensack *Also called North Jersey Media Group Inc (G-3955)*

North Jrsey Prsthtics Orthtics 201 943-4448
  39 Broad Ave Palisades Park (07650) *(G-7775)*

North Sales 732 528-8899
  11 Chicago Blvd Sea Girt (08750) *(G-9746)*

North Star Signs Inc 973 244-1144
  3 Callan Ct Highland Lakes (07422) *(G-4285)*

Northcott Silk USA Inc 201 672-9600
  1099 Wall St W Ste 250 Lyndhurst (07071) *(G-5667)*

Northeast Bindery Inc 908 436-3737
  419 Trumbull St Elizabeth (07206) *(G-2762)*

Northeast Chemicals Inc (PA) 508 634-6900
  2 Tower Center Blvd East Brunswick (08816) *(G-2160)*

Northeast Chemicals Inc (PA) 732 227-0100
  2 Tower Center Blvd Fl 12 East Brunswick (08816) *(G-2161)*

Northeast Chemicals Inc. 732 673-6966
  7 Elkins Rd East Brunswick (08816) *(G-2162)*

Northeast Con Pdts & Sup Inc 973 728-1667
  937 Burnt Meadow Rd Hewitt (07421) *(G-4277)*

Northeast Concrete Pdts LLC 973 728-1667
  937 Burnt Meadow Rd Hewitt (07421) *(G-4278)*

Northeast Foods Inc 732 549-2243
  1 Gourmet Ln Ste 1 # 1 Edison (08837) *(G-2578)*

Northeast Medical Systems Corp 856 910-8111
  901 Beechwood Ave Cherry Hill (08002) *(G-1400)*

Northeast Precast Ltd Lblty Co 856 765-9088
  92 Reese Rd Millville (08332) *(G-6264)*

Northeast Pro-Tech Inc (PA) 973 777-5654
  61 Willet St Bldg L Passaic (07055) *(G-8092)*

Northeast Tomato Company Inc 973 684-4890
  4 22 Erie St Paterson (07524) *(G-8271)*

Northern Architectural Systems (PA) 201 943-6400
  111 Central Ave Teterboro (07608) *(G-10688)*

Northern Architectural Systems 201 943-6400
  599 Gotham Pkwy Carlstadt (07072) *(G-1192)*

Northern State Periodicals LLC 973 782-6100
  251 Vreeland Ave Ste B Paterson (07504) *(G-8272)*

Northland Tooling Technologies 908 850-0023
  999 Willow Grove St Ste 2 Hackettstown (07840) *(G-4030)*

Northrop Grumman Systems Corp 609 272-9000
  8025 Black Horse Pike Pleasantville (08232) *(G-8816)*

Northrop Grumman Systems Corp 908 276-6677
  12 Park St Cranford (07016) *(G-1919)*

Northstar Travel Media LLC (PA) 201 902-2000
  100 Lighting Way Ste 200 Secaucus (07094) *(G-9794)*

Northwest Instrument Inc 973 347-6830
  69 King St Dover (07801) *(G-2102)*

Northwind Enterprises Inc 732 274-2000
  250 Ridge Rd Dayton (08810) *(G-1982)*

Northwind Ventures Inc 917 509-1964
  39 Woodland Dr Vernon (07462) *(G-11162)*

Norwalt Design Inc 973 927-3200
  961 Route 10 E Ste 2a Randolph (07869) *(G-9193)*

Norwood Industries Inc 856 858-6195
  107 Norwood Ave Haddon Township (08108) *(G-4052)*

Norwood Printing Inc 201 784-8721
  530 Walnut St Norwood (07648) *(G-7572)*

Noshpeak LLC 978 631-7662
  38 Patton Dr Bloomfield (07003) *(G-512)*

Notie Corp 609 259-3477
  177 Route 526 Allentown (08501) *(G-28)*

Nourhan Trading Group Inc 732 381-8110
  62 Minue St Carteret (07008) *(G-1261)*

Nouryon Surface Chemistry 732 985-6262
  340 Meadow Rd Edison (08837) *(G-2579)*

Nouryon Surface Chemistry 312 544-7000
  500 Jersey Ave New Brunswick (08901) *(G-6955)*

Nouveau Prosthetics Ltd 732 739-0888
  984 State Route 36 Hazlet (07730) *(G-4267)*

Nouveau Prosthetics Orthotics 732 739-0888
  984 State Route 36 Hazlet (07730) *(G-4268)*

Nouveautes Inc 973 882-8850
  70 Clinton Rd Ste 1 Fairfield (07004) *(G-3283)*

Nova Chemicals Inc 973 726-0056
  56 Castlewood Trl Sparta (07871) *(G-10404)*

Nova Distributors LLC 908 222-1010
  184 Whitman Ave Edison (08817) *(G-2580)*

Nova Flex Group 856 768-2275
  1024 Industrial Dr West Berlin (08091) *(G-11611)*

Nova Precision Products Inc 973 625-1586
  160 Franklin Ave Rockaway (07866) *(G-9480)*

Novacote Flexpack, West Deptford *Also called Coim USA Inc* ***(G-11700)***
Novacyl Inc.......609 259-0444
1 Union St Ste 108 Robbinsville (08691) ***(G-9415)***
Novaera Solutions Inc.......732 452-3605
33 Wood Ave S Ste 600 Iselin (08830) ***(G-4619)***
Novaflex Industries Inc.......856 768-2275
1024 Industrial Dr West Berlin (08091) ***(G-11612)***
Novapac Laboratories Inc.......973 414-8800
510 Ryerson Rd Ste 1 Lincoln Park (07035) ***(G-5303)***
Novartis Corporation (HQ).......212 307-1122
1 S Ridgedale Ave East Hanover (07936) ***(G-2226)***
Novartis Corporation.......862 778-8300
1 Health Plz East Hanover (07936) ***(G-2227)***
Novartis Corporation.......973 503-7488
59 State Route 10 East Hanover (07936) ***(G-2228)***
Novartis Pharmaceuticals, East Hanover *Also called Novartis Corporation* ***(G-2227)***
Novartis Pharmaceuticals Corp (HQ).......862 778-8300
1 Health Plz East Hanover (07936) ***(G-2229)***
Novartis Pharmaceuticals Corp.......862 778-8300
1 Health Plz East Hanover (07936) ***(G-2230)***
Novartis Pharmaceuticals Corp.......973 538-1296
220 E Hanover Ave Morris Plains (07950) ***(G-6619)***
Novartis Pharmaceuticals Corp.......862 778-8300
1 S Ridgedale Ave East Hanover (07936) ***(G-2231)***
Novasom Industries Inc.......732 994-5652
15 Enclave Blvd Lakewood (08701) ***(G-5142)***
Novega Venture Partners Inc.......732 528-2600
23 Main St Holmdel (07733) ***(G-4511)***
Novel Ingrdent Inv Hldings Inc.......973 808-5900
72 Deforest Ave East Hanover (07936) ***(G-2232)***
Novel Ingredient Holdings Inc.......973 808-5900
72 Deforest Ave East Hanover (07936) ***(G-2233)***
Novel Ingredient Services, LLC, Cranbury *Also called Innophos LLC* ***(G-1841)***
Novel Laboratories Inc.......908 603-6000
400 Campus Dr Somerset (08873) ***(G-10041)***
Novel Technology Labs, Kearny *Also called A L Wilson Chemical Co* ***(G-4840)***
Novell Design Studio, Rahway *Also called Novell Enterprises Inc* ***(G-9120)***
Novell Enterprises Inc.......732 428-8300
2100 Felver Ct Rahway (07065) ***(G-9120)***
Novelty Cone Co Inc.......856 665-9525
807 Sherman Ave Pennsauken (08110) ***(G-8462)***
Novelty Hair Goods Co.......856 963-5876
1138 S Broadway 40 Camden (08103) ***(G-1080)***
Novembal USA Inc.......732 947-3030
3 Greek Ln Edison (08817) ***(G-2581)***
Novitium Pharma LLC.......609 469-5920
70 Lake Dr East Windsor (08520) ***(G-2356)***
Novo Nordisk Inc (HQ).......609 987-5800
800 Scudders Mill Rd Plainsboro (08536) ***(G-8798)***
Novo Nordisk Inc.......609 987-5800
1100 Camput Rd Princeton (08540) ***(G-8987)***
Novotec Pharma LLC.......609 632-2239
20 Spruce Meadows Dr Monroe Township (08831) ***(G-6338)***
Nowak Inc.......973 366-7208
17 Robert St Wharton (07885) ***(G-11864)***
NPS, East Hanover *Also called Novartis Pharmaceuticals Corp* ***(G-2229)***
NPS Public Furniture Corp.......973 594-1100
149 Entin Rd Clifton (07014) ***(G-1679)***
Npt Publishing Group Inc.......973 401-0202
201 Littleton Rd Ste 2 Morris Plains (07950) ***(G-6620)***
NRG Bluewater Wind LLC.......201 748-5000
22 Hudson Pl Ste 3 Hoboken (07030) ***(G-4469)***
Nsgv Inc (HQ).......212 620-2200
499 Washington Blvd Fl 9 Jersey City (07310) ***(G-4774)***
Nte Electronics Inc.......973 748-5089
44 Farrand St Bloomfield (07003) ***(G-513)***
Ntt Electronics America Inc.......201 556-1770
250 Pehle Ave Ste 706 Saddle Brook (07663) ***(G-9666)***
Nu Grafix Inc.......201 413-1776
430 Communipaw Ave Jersey City (07304) ***(G-4775)***
Nu Products Seasonings, Oakland *Also called Goldstein & Burton Inc* ***(G-7630)***
Nu Steel, Avenel *Also called Tatara Group Inc* ***(G-149)***
Nu Tech, Franklin Lakes *Also called Nutech Corp* ***(G-3629)***
Nu World, Carteret *Also called Nu-World Corporation* ***(G-1262)***
Nu-EZ Custom Bindery LLC.......201 488-4140
111 Essex St Ste 1 Hackensack (07601) ***(G-3956)***
Nu-Meat Technology Inc.......908 754-3400
601 Hadley Rd South Plainfield (07080) ***(G-10308)***
Nu-Plan Business Systems Inc.......732 231-6944
64 Washington St Clark (07066) ***(G-1510)***
Nu-Stent Technologies Inc.......732 729-6270
1 Ilene Ct Hillsborough (08844) ***(G-4342)***
Nu-World Corporation (HQ).......732 541-6300
300 Milik St Carteret (07008) ***(G-1262)***
Nu-World Corporation.......732 541-6300
340 Mill Rd Edison (08817) ***(G-2582)***
Nuchas Tsq LLC.......212 913-9682
5905 Kennedy Blvd North Bergen (07047) ***(G-7426)***
Nuclear Diagnostic Pdts Inc.......973 664-9696
101 Round Hill Dr Ste 4 Rockaway (07866) ***(G-9481)***
Nuclear Diagnostic Products of.......856 489-5733
2 Keystone Ave Ste 200 Cherry Hill (08003) ***(G-1401)***
Numerical Control Program Svc.......856 665-8737
917 Northwood Ave Cherry Hill (08002) ***(G-1402)***
Numeritool Manufacturing Corp.......973 827-7714
58 Woodland Rd Franklin (07416) ***(G-3607)***
Nurturme, Hillside *Also called Freed Foods Inc* ***(G-4392)***
Nutech Corp.......908 707-2097
322 Freemans Ln Franklin Lakes (07417) ***(G-3629)***
Nutra Nuts Inc (PA).......323 260-7457
247 Emmett Pl Ridgewood (07450) ***(G-9325)***
Nutra-Med Packaging Inc.......973 625-2274
118 Algonquin Pkwy Whippany (07981) ***(G-11899)***
Nutri Sport Pharmacal Inc.......973 827-9287
200 N Church Rd Franklin (07416) ***(G-3608)***
Nutri-Force Nutrition, North Bergen *Also called Vs Hercules LLC* ***(G-7442)***
Nutri-Pet Research Inc.......732 786-8822
227 State Route 33 Ste 10 Manalapan (07726) ***(G-5820)***
Nutrition Zone, Hackettstown *Also called Ajj Powernutrition LLC* ***(G-3996)***
Nutro Laboratories Inc.......908 755-7984
650 Hadley Rd Ste C South Plainfield (07080) ***(G-10309)***
Nutsco Inc.......856 966-6400
1115 S 2nd St Camden (08103) ***(G-1081)***
Nutscom Inc.......800 558-6887
10 Exchange Pl Ste 2800 Jersey City (07302) ***(G-4776)***
Nvs International Inc.......908 523-0266
1600 Lower Rd Linden (07036) ***(G-5398)***
NW Sign Industries Inc.......856 802-1677
360 Crider Ave Moorestown (08057) ***(G-6547)***
NW Sign Industries Inc (PA).......856 802-1677
360 Crider Ave Moorestown (08057) ***(G-6548)***
Nwl Inc (HQ).......609 298-7300
312 Rising Sun Rd Bordentown (08505) ***(G-591)***
Nwl Capacitors, Bordentown *Also called Nwl Inc* ***(G-591)***
Nwl Transformers, Bordentown *Also called Megatran Industries* ***(G-586)***
Nxlevel Inc.......609 483-6900
201 S Main St Ste 5 Lambertville (08530) ***(G-5195)***
NXLEVEL SOLUTIONS, Lambertville *Also called Nxlevel Inc* ***(G-5195)***
Nyc Concrete Materials, Saddle Brook *Also called Eastern Concrete Materials Inc* ***(G-9650)***
Nyc Concrete Materials, Elmwood Park *Also called Local Concrete Sup & Eqp Corp* ***(G-2838)***
Nyc Rugs, Englewood *Also called Ben-Aharon & Son Inc* ***(G-2881)***
Nyc Woodworking Inc.......718 222-1221
39 Kingfisher Ct Marlboro (07746) ***(G-5907)***
Nylok Corporation.......201 427-8555
S11 Thomas Rd S Hawthorne (07506) ***(G-4235)***
Nyltite Corp of America.......908 561-1300
3451 S Clinton Ave South Plainfield (07080) ***(G-10310)***
Nymar Manufacturing Company.......973 366-7265
215 State Route 10 2-4 Randolph (07869) ***(G-9194)***
Nyp Corp (frmr Ny-Pters Corp) (PA).......908 351-6550
805 E Grand St Elizabeth (07201) ***(G-2763)***
O & S Research Inc.......856 829-2800
1912 Bannard St Cinnaminson (08077) ***(G-1477)***
O Berk Company LLC.......201 941-1610
215 Bergen Blvd Fairview (07022) ***(G-3365)***
O E M Manufacturers Ltd Inc.......201 475-8585
65 Leliarts Ln Elmwood Park (07407) ***(G-2845)***
O I A, Bogota *Also called Organize It-All Inc* ***(G-534)***
O K Tool Corporation.......908 561-9920
1233 North Ave Plainfield (07062) ***(G-8774)***
O O M Inc.......973 328-9408
387 Us Highway 46 Rockaway (07866) ***(G-9482)***
O S C, Clifton *Also called Oklahoma Sound Corp* ***(G-1680)***
O S I Inc.......732 754-6271
101 Hillside Ave Metuchen (08840) ***(G-6067)***
O Stitch Matic Inc.......201 861-3045
427 69th St Guttenberg (07093) ***(G-3871)***
O T D Inc.......973 890-7979
18 Furler St Totowa (07512) ***(G-10839)***
O'Dowd Advertising, Pine Brook *Also called Odowd Enterprises Inc* ***(G-8612)***
O'Neil Color Compounding Corp, Garfield *Also called Primex Color Compounding* ***(G-3758)***
O'Shea's Printing Services, Hackensack *Also called OShea Services Inc* ***(G-3958)***
Oasis CD Manufacturing, Delair *Also called Audio and Video Labs Inc* ***(G-2000)***
Oasis Entertainment Group.......973 256-7077
17 Frederick Ct Cedar Grove (07009) ***(G-1285)***
Oasis Trading Co Inc (HQ).......908 964-0477
635 Ramsey Ave Hillside (07205) ***(G-4419)***
Oav Air Bearing, Princeton *Also called Oavco Ltd Liability Company* ***(G-8988)***
Oav Air Bearings, Hamilton *Also called Oavco Ltd Liability Company* ***(G-4119)***
Oavco Ltd Liability Company (PA).......855 535-4227
103 Carnegie Ctr Princeton (08540) ***(G-8988)***
Oavco Ltd Liability Company.......609 454-5340
1800 E State St Ste 130 Hamilton (08609) ***(G-4119)***
Oaviation Corporation.......609 619-3060
103 Carnegie Ctr Ste 212 Princeton (08540) ***(G-8989)***

ALPHABETIC

OBagel Hoboken Ltd Lblty Co.................................201 683-8599
  600 Washington St Hoboken (07030) *(G-4470)*

Obare Services Ltd Lblty Co.................................908 456-1887
  593 Meadow St Elizabeth (07201) *(G-2764)*

Oberg & Lindquist Corp (PA).................................201 664-1300
  671 Broadway Westwood (07675) *(G-11836)*

Object Design, Wharton *Also called AMS Products LLC (G-11850)*

Objectif Lune LLC (HQ).................................973 780-0100
  300 Broadacres Dr Ste 410 Bloomfield (07003) *(G-514)*

Objectif Lune LLC.................................203 878-7206
  300 Broadacres Dr Ste 410 Bloomfield (07003) *(G-515)*

Objecutive Inc.................................201 242-1522
  2125 Center Ave Ste 411 Fort Lee (07024) *(G-3579)*

Observer Park.................................201 798-7007
  51 Garden St Hoboken (07030) *(G-4471)*

Observer, The, Kearny *Also called Hudson West Publishing Co (G-4864)*

Ocd Pharmaceuticals.................................610 366-2314
  1001 Us Highway 202 Raritan (08869) *(G-9216)*

Ocean City Coffee Company, Ocean City *Also called Coffee Company LLC (G-7688)*

Ocean City Coffee Company, Ocean City *Also called Coffee Company LLC (G-7689)*

Ocean City Sentinel The, Ocean City *Also called Sample Media Inc (G-7695)*

Ocean Drive Clothing Co., Kenilworth *Also called Ocean Drive Inc (G-4965)*

Ocean Drive Inc.................................908 964-2591
  530 N Michigan Ave Kenilworth (07033) *(G-4965)*

Ocean Energy Industries Inc.................................954 828-2177
  715 W Park Ave Unit 1073 Oakhurst (07755) *(G-7611)*

Ocean Foam Fabricators LLC.................................973 745-1445
  740 Washington Ave Belleville (07109) *(G-304)*

Ocean Power & Equipment Co.................................973 575-5775
  1140 Bloomfield Ave # 107 West Caldwell (07006) *(G-11668)*

Ocean Power Technologies Inc (PA).................................609 730-0400
  28 Engelhard Dr Ste B Monroe Township (08831) *(G-6339)*

Ocean Star.................................732 899-7606
  421 River Ave Point Pleasant Beach (08742) *(G-8830)*

Ocean-Craft International, Northfield *Also called Superior Jewelry Co (G-7511)*

Oceanic Graphic Intl Inc.................................201 883-1816
  105 Main St Ste 1 Hackensack (07601) *(G-3957)*

Oceanic Graphic Printing, Hackensack *Also called Oceanic Graphic Intl Inc (G-3957)*

Oceanic Trading, Neptune *Also called Scaasis Originals Inc (G-6895)*

Oceanview Marine Welding LLC.................................609 624-9669
  414 Woodbine Ocean View R Ocean View (08230) *(G-7704)*

Ocsidot Inc.................................908 789-3300
  116 South Ave Garwood (07027) *(G-3788)*

Octal Corporation.................................201 862-1010
  125 Galway Pl Ste B Teaneck (07666) *(G-10642)*

Octopus Yachts Ltd Lblty Co.................................732 698-8550
  2400 Belmar Blvd Ste C-1 Belmar (07719) *(G-352)*

Odin Pharmaceuticals LLC.................................732 554-1100
  300 Franklin Square Dr Somerset (08873) *(G-10042)*

Odowd Enterprises Inc.................................973 227-4607
  48 Us Highway 46 Ste 2 Pine Brook (07058) *(G-8612)*

Odyssey Auto Specialty Inc.................................973 328-2667
  317 Richard Mine Rd Wharton (07885) *(G-11865)*

Odyssey of The Mind, Sewell *Also called Creative Competitions Inc (G-9838)*

Oe Solutions America Inc.................................201 568-1188
  65 Challenger Rd Ste 240 Ridgefield Park (07660) *(G-9313)*

Oeg Building Materials Inc.................................732 667-3636
  6001 Bordentown Ave Sayreville (08872) *(G-9720)*

Office Needs Inc.................................732 381-7770
  1120 Raritan Rd Ste 2 Clark (07066) *(G-1511)*

Officeclocks.com, Bridgewater *Also called Garrett Moore (G-825)*

Officemate International Corp (PA).................................732 225-7422
  90 Newfeld Ave Rritan Ctr Raritan Ctr Edison (08837) *(G-2583)*

Offshore Enterprises Inc.................................609 345-9099
  433 N Maryland Ave Atlantic City (08401) *(G-100)*

Ofs Fitel LLC.................................732 748-7409
  25 Schoolhouse Rd Somerset (08873) *(G-10043)*

Ofs Specialty Photonics & Labs.................................732 748-7401
  25 Schoolhouse Rd Somerset (08873) *(G-10044)*

Ogura Industrial Corp (HQ).................................586 749-1900
  100 Randolph Rd Somerset (08873) *(G-10045)*

Ohaus Corporation (HQ).................................973 377-9000
  7 Campus Dr Ste 310 Parsippany (07054) *(G-7980)*

OHM Equimpent LLC.................................856 765-3011
  2525 S 2nd St Millville (08332) *(G-6265)*

OHM Laboratories Inc (HQ).................................732 418-2235
  1385 Livingston Ave North Brunswick (08902) *(G-7481)*

OHM Laboratories Inc.................................609 720-9200
  2 Independence Way Princeton (08540) *(G-8990)*

OHM Laboratories Inc.................................732 514-1072
  14 Terminal Rd New Brunswick (08901) *(G-6956)*

Oil Technologies Services Inc (PA).................................856 845-4142
  1501 Grandview Ave Ste 1 Paulsboro (08066) *(G-8336)*

Oil Technologies Services Inc.................................856 845-4142
  1501 Grandview Ave Ste 1 Paulsboro (08066) *(G-8337)*

Oil Technologies Services Inc.................................856 845-4142
  1177 W Elizabeth Ave Linden (07036) *(G-5399)*

Oiltest Inc.................................908 245-9330
  109 Aldene Rd Ste 4 Roselle (07203) *(G-9567)*

Oklahoma Sound Corp (PA).................................800 261-4112
  149 Entin Rd Clifton (07014) *(G-1680)*

Okonite Company.................................201 825-0300
  959 Market St Paterson (07513) *(G-8273)*

Okonite Company Inc (PA).................................201 825-0300
  102 Hilltop Rd Ramsey (07446) *(G-9154)*

Old Barracks Association Inc.................................609 396-1776
  101 Barrack St Trenton (08608) *(G-10968)*

OLD BARRACKS MUSEUM, Trenton *Also called Old Barracks Association Inc (G-10968)*

Old Bridge Chemicals Inc.................................732 727-2225
  554 Water Works Rd Old Bridge (08857) *(G-7722)*

Old Fashion Kitchen Inc (PA).................................732 364-4100
  1045 Towbin Ave Lakewood (08701) *(G-5143)*

Old Fashioned Kitchen, Lakewood *Also called Old Fashion Kitchen Inc (G-5143)*

Old Hights Print Shop Inc.................................609 443-4700
  16 Nancy Ct Jackson (08527) *(G-4661)*

Old Monmouth Candy Co, Freehold *Also called Old Monmouth Peanut Brittle Co (G-3684)*

Old Monmouth Peanut Brittle Co.................................732 462-1311
  627 Park Ave Freehold (07728) *(G-3684)*

Old Ue LLC.................................800 752-4012
  65 Railroad Ave Ridgefield (07657) *(G-9281)*

Old York Cellars.................................908 284-9463
  80 Old York Rd Ringoes (08551) *(G-9340)*

Oldcastle Buildingenvelope Inc.................................856 234-9222
  1500 Glen Ave Moorestown (08057) *(G-6549)*

Oldcastle Infrastructure Inc.................................609 561-3400
  1920 12th St Rt 54 Williamstown (08094) *(G-11966)*

Olde Grandad Industries Inc.................................201 997-1899
  1 Market St Ste 15 Passaic (07055) *(G-8093)*

Oli Systems Inc.................................973 539-4996
  240 Cedar Knolls Rd # 301 Cedar Knolls (07927) *(G-1313)*

Olivos USA Inc (HQ).................................201 893-0142
  1 Bridge Plz N Ste 275 Fort Lee (07024) *(G-3580)*

Olon USA Inc.................................973 577-6038
  100 Campus Dr Ste 105 Florham Park (07932) *(G-3518)*

Olsen, H Machine, Cinnaminson *Also called Henry Olsen Machine (G-1463)*

Olympic Custom Tools, Kinnelon *Also called Olympic EDM Services Inc (G-5020)*

Olympic EDM Services Inc.................................973 492-0664
  20 Kiel Ave Kinnelon (07405) *(G-5020)*

Omaha Standard Inc Tr NJ.................................609 588-5400
  572 Whitehead Rd Trenton (08619) *(G-10969)*

Omaha Standards, Trenton *Also called Palfinger North America (G-10971)*

Omega Circuit and Engineering.................................732 246-1661
  8 Terminal Rd New Brunswick (08901) *(G-6957)*

Omega Engineering Inc.................................856 467-4200
  1 Killdeer Ct Swedesboro (08085) *(G-10599)*

Omega Engineering Inc.................................856 467-4200
  1 Omega Cir Bridgeport (08014) *(G-742)*

Omega Graphics, Shrewsbury *Also called Dcg Printing Inc (G-9889)*

Omega Heat Transfer Co Inc.................................732 340-0023
  36 Rock Spring Ave West Orange (07052) *(G-11775)*

Omega Packaging Corp.................................973 890-9505
  55 Kings Rd Totowa (07512) *(G-10840)*

Omega Plastics Corp (HQ).................................201 507-9100
  Page & Schuyler Ave Ste 5 Lyndhurst (07071) *(G-5668)*

Omega Process Controls, Bridgeport *Also called Omega Engineering Inc (G-742)*

Omega Shielding Products Inc.................................973 366-0080
  9 Emery Ave Randolph (07869) *(G-9195)*

Omega Tool Die.................................856 228-7100
  8 International Ave Sewell (08080) *(G-9852)*

Omg Electronic Chemicals Inc.................................908 222-5800
  400 Corporate Ct Ste A South Plainfield (07080) *(G-10311)*

Omni Baking Company LLC.................................856 205-1485
  2621 Freddy Ln Bldg 7 Vineland (08360) *(G-11247)*

Omni Wall Coverings, Edison *Also called W C Omni Incorporated (G-2643)*

Omnia Industries Inc.................................973 239-7272
  5 Cliffside Dr Cedar Grove (07009) *(G-1286)*

Omniactive Hlth Tchnlogies Inc (HQ).................................866 588-3629
  67 E Park Pl Ste 500 Morristown (07960) *(G-6690)*

Omniflow USA, Springfield *Also called I4 Sustainability LLC (G-10445)*

Omniplanar Inc.................................800 782-4263
  90 Coles Rd Blackwood (08012) *(G-476)*

Omnitester Corp (PA).................................856 985-8960
  101 Flintlock Ln Marlton (08053) *(G-5944)*

Omp Technologies Inc.................................973 808-8500
  24 Commerce Rd Ste H Fairfield (07004) *(G-3284)*

Omthera Pharmaceuticals Inc.................................908 741-4399
  707 State Rd Ste 206 Princeton (08540) *(G-8991)*

On Demand Machinery.................................908 351-7137
  150 Broadway Elizabeth (07206) *(G-2765)*

On Demand Print Group.................................201 636-2270
  442 Valley Brook Ave Lyndhurst (07071) *(G-5669)*

On Site Communication.................................201 488-4123
  15 Worth St South Hackensack (07606) *(G-10177)*

On Site Manufacturing Inc.................................812 794-6040
  1042 County Road 523 Flemington (08822) *(G-3458)*

Onco Inc.................................732 292-7460
  1551 Hwy 138 Wall Township (07719) *(G-11359)*

Oncode-Med Inc 908 998-3647
11 Georgetown Ct Basking Ridge (07920) *(G-194)*
One Two Three Inc 856 251-1238
537 Mantua Pike Ste B Woodbury (08096) *(G-12034)*
One Click Cleaners 732 804-9802
43 Kipling Way Manalapan (07726) *(G-5821)*
One Source Solutions LLC 732 536-0578
3 Industrial Ct Ste 3 # 3 Freehold (07728) *(G-3685)*
Onguard Fence Systems Ltd 908 429-5522
355 New Albany Rd Moorestown (08057) *(G-6550)*
Onguard Fence Systems Ltd 908 429-5522
18 Culnen Dr Branchburg (08876) *(G-663)*
Onkos Surgical Inc 973 264-5400
77 E Halsey Rd Parsippany (07054) *(G-7981)*
Ono Pharma USA Inc 609 219-1010
2000 Lenox Dr Ste 101 Lawrenceville (08648) *(G-5241)*
Onpharma Inc 408 335-6850
400 Somerset Corporate Bl Bridgewater (08807) *(G-859)*
Ont Sutter 201 265-0262
17c Palisade Ave Emerson (07630) *(G-2867)*
Ontimeworks LLC 800 689-3568
1253 Springfield Ave New Providence (07974) *(G-7015)*
Onwards Inc 732 309-7348
10 Connor Dr Manalapan (07726) *(G-5822)*
Onyx Graphics LLC 908 281-0038
115 Stryker Ln Ste 4 Hillsborough (08844) *(G-4343)*
Onyx Valve, Cinnaminson *Also called Armadillo Automation Inc (G-1442)*
Opalsoft Consulting, Cherry Hill *Also called MD International Inc (G-1391)*
Opdyke Awnings Inc 732 449-5940
2036 State Route 35 Wall Township (07719) *(G-11360)*
Open Solutions Inc 856 424-0150
2091 Springdale Rd Ste 7 Cherry Hill (08003) *(G-1403)*
Open Terra Inc 732 765-9600
20 Reddington Dr Matawan (07747) *(G-5982)*
Opex Corporation 856 727-1100
835 Lancer Dr Moorestown (08057) *(G-6551)*
Opici Import Co Inc 201 689-3256
25 De Boer Dr Glen Rock (07452) *(G-3833)*
Oppenheim Plastics Co Inc 201 391-3811
27 Sherwood Downs Park Ridge (07656) *(G-7857)*
Opt, Monroe Township *Also called Ocean Power Technologies Inc (G-6339)*
Opt-Sciences Corporation (PA) 856 829-2800
1912 Bannard St Cinnaminson (08077) *(G-1478)*
Optherium Labs Ou 516 253-1777
21 Riverside Ln Holmdel (07733) *(G-4512)*
Optics Plastics 201 939-3344
537 New York Ave Lyndhurst (07071) *(G-5670)*
Optimer Pharmaceuticals LLC 858 909-0736
2000 Galloping Hill Rd Kenilworth (07033) *(G-4966)*
Optimum Precision Inc 908 259-9017
147 N Michigan Ave Kenilworth (07033) *(G-4967)*
Optimum Precision Machine & TI, Kenilworth *Also called Optimum Precision Inc (G-4967)*
Options Edge LLC 973 701-0051
53 Division Ave Apt 12 Summit (07901) *(G-10542)*
Oracle America Inc 732 623-4821
399 Thornall St Ste 39 Edison (08837) *(G-2584)*
Oracle America Inc 609 750-0640
1 Meadowlands Plz Ste 700 East Rutherford (07073) *(G-2307)*
Oracle Corporation 908 547-6200
400 Crossing Blvd Fl 6 Bridgewater (08807) *(G-860)*
Oracle Corporation 201 842-7000
1 Meadowlands Plz # 1400 East Rutherford (07073) *(G-2308)*
Oral Fixation LLC 609 937-9972
53 Railroad Pl A Hopewell (08525) *(G-4528)*
Oral Manufacturing, Eatontown *Also called Hikma Pharmaceuticals USA Inc (G-2400)*
Orange Mattress, Maplewood *Also called Custom Bedding Co (G-5875)*
Orange Sanitary, Orange *Also called Serranis Bakery (G-7761)*
Orangehrm Inc 914 458-4254
538 Teal Plz Secaucus (07094) *(G-9795)*
Oraton Custom Products 908 235-9424
407 State Route 94 Columbia (07832) *(G-1796)*
Orbcomm LLC (HQ) 703 433-6300
395 W Passaic St Ste 3 Rochelle Park (07662) *(G-9427)*
Orbit Energy & Power LLC 800 836-3987
106 Mantua Blvd Mantua (08051) *(G-5853)*
Orcas International Inc 973 448-2801
9 Lenel Rd Landing (07850) *(G-5202)*
Orcas Naturals, Landing *Also called Unique Encapsulation Tech LLC (G-5204)*
Orcas Naturals, Landing *Also called Orcas International Inc (G-5202)*
Orchid Chemicals, Princeton *Also called Orchid Pharmaceuticals Inc (G-8992)*
Orchid Pharmaceuticals Inc 609 951-2209
116 Village Blvd Ste 200 Princeton (08540) *(G-8992)*
Orens Daily Roast Inc 201 432-2008
430 Communipaw Ave Ste 13 Jersey City (07304) *(G-4777)*
Organica Aromatics Corp 609 443-3333
20 Lake D East Windsor (08520) *(G-2357)*
Organica Water Inc (PA) 609 651-8885
61 Prnceton Hightstown Rd West Windsor (08550) *(G-11782)*

Organics Corporation America 973 890-9002
55 W End Rd Totowa (07512) *(G-10841)*
Organize It-All Inc (PA) 201 488-0808
24 River Rd Ste 201 Bogota (07603) *(G-534)*
Organon USA Inc 908 423-1000
1 Merck Dr Whitehouse Station (08889) *(G-11930)*
Orgo-Thermit Inc (PA) 732 657-5781
3500 Colonial Dr Manchester (08759) *(G-5847)*
Orient Corporation of America (HQ) 908 298-0990
6 Commerce Dr Ste 301 Cranford (07016) *(G-1920)*
Orient Originals Inc 201 332-5005
55 Edward Hart Dr Jersey City (07305) *(G-4778)*
Origin Almond Corporation 609 576-5695
6 Grant Dr Laurel Springs (08021) *(G-5208)*
Original Bagel & Bialy Co Inc 973 227-5777
2 Fairfield Cres West Caldwell (07006) *(G-11669)*
Original Toy Company, The, Piscataway *Also called Homeco LLC (G-8673)*
Orion Machinery Co Ltd 201 569-3220
301 Veterans Blvd Rutherford (07070) *(G-9630)*
Orion Precision Industries 732 247-9704
8 Veronica Ave Somerset (08873) *(G-10046)*
Orlando Systems Ltd Lblty Co 908 400-5052
375 North Dr Apt A10 North Plainfield (07060) *(G-7507)*
Orlando's Italian Bakery, Lodi *Also called Dina Hernandez (G-5558)*
Ornate Millwork LLC 866 464-5596
15 Hazelwood Ln Lakewood (08701) *(G-5144)*
Orora Packaging Solutions 609 249-5200
1 Capital Dr Ste 102 Cranbury (08512) *(G-1866)*
Orora Visual LLC 973 916-2804
1155 Bloomfield Ave Clifton (07012) *(G-1681)*
Oroszlany Laszlo 201 666-2101
121 Patterson St Hillsdale (07642) *(G-4369)*
Orsillo & Company 973 248-1833
189 Berdan Ave Wayne (07470) *(G-11537)*
Ortho Biotech Products LP 908 541-4000
430 Route 22 Bridgewater (08807) *(G-861)*
Ortho-Clinical Diagnostics Inc (PA) 908 218-8000
1001 Route 202 Raritan (08869) *(G-9217)*
Ortho-Dynamics Inc 973 742-4390
210 E 16th St Paterson (07524) *(G-8274)*
Orthodox Baking Co Inc 973 844-9393
555 Cortlandt St Belleville (07109) *(G-305)*
Orthoessentials, Mount Holly *Also called R Baron Associates Inc (G-6734)*
Orthofeet Inc 800 524-2845
152 Veterans Dr Ste A Northvale (07647) *(G-7542)*
Orycon Control Technology Inc 732 922-2400
3407 Rose Ave Ocean (07712) *(G-7670)*
Os33 Services Corp (PA) 866 796-0310
120 Wood Ave S Ste 505 Iselin (08830) *(G-4620)*
Osem USA Inc 201 871-4433
333 Sylvan Ave Ste 302 Englewood Cliffs (07632) *(G-2985)*
OSG Billing Services, Carlstadt *Also called Output Services Group Inc (G-1193)*
OSG Billing Services, Ridgefield Park *Also called Output Services Group Inc (G-9314)*
OShea Services Inc 201 343-8668
483 Main St Hackensack (07601) *(G-3958)*
OSI Laser Diode Inc 732 549-9001
4 Olsen Ave Edison (08820) *(G-2585)*
Osmotica, Bridgewater *Also called Vertical/Trigen Holdings LLC (G-904)*
Osmotica Pharmaceutical Corp 908 809-1300
400 Crossing Blvd Bridgewater (08807) *(G-862)*
Osmotica Pharmaceuticals PLC (PA) 908 809-1300
400 Crossing Blvd Bridgewater (08807) *(G-863)*
Ossb and L Pharma LLC 732 940-8701
6 Bel Air Ct Milltown (08850) *(G-6218)*
Osstem, Englewood Cliffs *Also called Hiossen Inc (G-2974)*
Ossur Americas Inc 856 345-6000
680 Grove Rd West Deptford (08066) *(G-11712)*
Osteotech Inc 732 544-5942
51 James Way Eatontown (07724) *(G-2413)*
Osteotech Inc (HQ) 732 542-2800
51 James Way Eatontown (07724) *(G-2414)*
Osteotech Inc 732 542-2800
201 Industrial Way W Eatontown (07724) *(G-2415)*
OSullivan Communications Corp (PA) 973 227-5112
1 Fairfield Cres West Caldwell (07006) *(G-11670)*
Otex Specialty Narrow Fabrics (PA) 908 879-3636
4 Essex Ave Ste 403 Bernardsville (07924) *(G-440)*
Oti America Inc 732 429-1900
517 Us Highway 1 S # 2150 Iselin (08830) *(G-4621)*
Oticon Inc (HQ) 732 560-1220
580 Howard Ave Ste B Somerset (08873) *(G-10047)*
Oticon Medical Inc 732 560-0727
580 Howard Ave Somerset (08873) *(G-10048)*
Otis Elevator Company 856 235-5200
30 Twosome Dr Ste 4 Moorestown (08057) *(G-6552)*
Otis Elevator Intl Inc 973 575-7030
105 Fairfield Rd Fairfield (07004) *(G-3285)*
Otis Graphics Inc 201 438-7120
290 Grant Ave Lyndhurst (07071) *(G-5671)*

A L P H A B E T I C

Our Team Fitness LLC 848 208-5047
117 E Main St Oceanport (07757) *(G-7705)*

Our Town, Maywood Also called Jimcam Publishing Inc *(G-6009)*

Outfront Media LLC 973 575-6900
185 Us Highway 46 Fairfield (07004) *(G-3286)*

Outlook Therapeutics Inc 609 619-3990
7 Clarke Dr Cranbury (08512) *(G-1867)*

Output Services Group Inc 201 871-1100
775 Washington Ave Carlstadt (07072) *(G-1193)*

Output Services Group Inc (HQ) 201 871-1100
100 Challenger Rd Ste 303 Ridgefield Park (07660) *(G-9314)*

Outwater Plastics Industries, Bogota Also called Outwater Plstcs/Industries Inc *(G-535)*

Outwater Plstcs/Industries Inc (PA) 201 498-8750
24 River Rd Ste 108 Bogota (07603) *(G-535)*

Ovadia Corporation 973 256-9200
101 E Main St Ste 501 Little Falls (07424) *(G-5462)*

Oven Art LLC 973 910-2266
200 S Newman St Unit 7 Hackensack (07601) *(G-3959)*

Oven Arts, Hackensack Also called Oven Art LLC *(G-3959)*

Over The Rainbow Bridge Crysta, Sicklerville Also called 7th Seventh Day Wellness Ctr *(G-9906)*

Overdrive Holdings Inc 201 440-1911
540 Huyler St South Hackensack (07606) *(G-10178)*

Overlook Hospital, Summit Mri, Summit Also called Ahs Hospital Corp *(G-10523)*

Owens Corning Sales LLC 201 998-5666
1249 Newark Tpke Kearny (07032) *(G-4888)*

Owens Plastic Products Inc 856 447-3500
393 Main St Cedarville (08311) *(G-1317)*

Oxberry LLC 201 935-3000
427 9th St Carlstadt (07072) *(G-1194)*

Oxford Biochronometrics LLC 201 755-5932
153 Pine St Montclair (07042) *(G-6380)*

Oxford Instrs Holdings Inc (HQ) 732 541-1300
600 Milik St Carteret (07008) *(G-1263)*

Oxford Lamp Inc 732 462-3755
17 Bannard St Ste 30 Freehold (07728) *(G-3686)*

Oxford Lighting Co, Freehold Also called Oxford Lamp Inc *(G-3686)*

Oxford Quarry, Oxford Also called Tilcon New York Inc *(G-7766)*

Ozone Confectioners Bakers Sup 201 791-4444
27 W Lincoln St Verona (07044) *(G-11171)*

P & A Auto Parts Inc (PA) 201 655-7117
530 River St Hackensack (07601) *(G-3960)*

P & G Lighting & Sign Service 908 925-3191
633 E Elizabeth Ave Linden (07036) *(G-5400)*

P & R Castings LLC 732 302-3600
325 Pierce St Somerset (08873) *(G-10049)*

P & R Fasteners Inc (PA) 732 302-3600
325 Pierce St Somerset (08873) *(G-10050)*

P & R Publishing, Phillipsburg Also called Presbyterian Reformed Pubg Co *(G-8570)*

P & S Blizzard Corporation 973 523-1700
722 Madison Ave Paterson (07501) *(G-8275)*

P A K Manufacturing Inc 973 372-1090
704 S 21st St Irvington (07111) *(G-4581)*

P B M, Monmouth Junction Also called Princeton Biomeditech Corp *(G-6303)*

P C C, Totowa Also called Precision Textiles LLC *(G-10846)*

P C G, Fairfield Also called Print Communications Group Inc *(G-3295)*

P C M, Camden Also called Plastics Consulting & Mfg Co *(G-1083)*

P D Q Digital, Englewood Also called PDQ Print & Copy Inc *(G-2931)*

P D Q Plastics Inc 201 823-0270
7 Hook Rd Bayonne (07002) *(G-230)*

P D Salco Inc 973 716-0517
61 Shrewsbury Dr Livingston (07039) *(G-5533)*

P E G, Vineland Also called Precision Electronic Glass Inc *(G-11254)*

P J Gillespie Inc 856 327-2993
2565 Brunetta Dr Vineland (08360) *(G-11248)*

P J Murphy Forest Pdts Corp (PA) 973 316-0800
150 River Rd Ste L1 Montville (07045) *(G-6445)*

P K Precision Machining Inc 973 925-2020
7 Mathews Ave Riverdale (07457) *(G-9380)*

P K Welding LLC 908 928-1002
520 South Ave Garwood (07027) *(G-3789)*

P L Custom Body & Eqp Co Inc 732 223-1411
2201 Atlantic Ave Manasquan (08736) *(G-5836)*

P L M Manufacturing Company 201 342-3636
293 Hudson St Hackensack (07601) *(G-3961)*

P M C Diners Inc 201 337-6146
56 Spruce St Oakland (07436) *(G-7640)*

P M Construction Co, Phillipsburg Also called Philip Mamrak *(G-8567)*

P M M I, Carlstadt Also called Precision Metal Machining Inc *(G-1206)*

P M Z Tool Inc 908 647-2125
321 Warren Ave Stirling (07980) *(G-10494)*

P O V Incorporated (PA) 914 258-4361
29 Park St Montclair (07042) *(G-6381)*

P R I, Princeton Also called Princeton Research Instruments *(G-9004)*

P S I Cement Inc 609 716-1515
12 Robert Dr Princeton Junction (08550) *(G-9063)*

P W B Omni Inc 856 384-1300
1319 Vallee Dr West Deptford (08096) *(G-11713)*

P W Perkins Co Inc 856 769-3525
221 Commissioners Pike Woodstown (08098) *(G-12095)*

P-Americas LLC 973 739-4900
15 Melanie Ln Whippany (07981) *(G-11900)*

Pabin Associates Inc (PA) 201 288-7216
281 Springfield Ave Hasbrouck Heights (07604) *(G-4187)*

Pabst Enterprises Equipment Co 908 353-2880
676 Pennsylvania Ave Elizabeth (07201) *(G-2766)*

Pac Team America Inc (PA) 201 599-5000
205 Robin Rd Ste 200 Paramus (07652) *(G-7826)*

Pace Business Solutions Inc 908 451-0355
297 Route 72 W Manahawkin (08050) *(G-5795)*

Pace Packaging LLC 973 227-1040
3 Sperry Rd Fairfield (07004) *(G-3287)*

Pace Press Incorporated 201 935-7711
1 Caesar Pl Moonachie (07074) *(G-6482)*

Pace Target Brokerage Inc 856 629-2551
716 Clayton Rd Williamstown (08094) *(G-11967)*

Pacent Engineering 914 390-9150
3430 Sunset Ave Ste 18 Ocean (07712) *(G-7671)*

Pacific Coast Systems LLC 908 735-9955
4 Fox Hill Ln Asbury (08802) *(G-68)*

Pacific Dnlop Holdings USA LLC (HQ) 732 345-5400
200 Schulz Dr Red Bank (07701) *(G-9239)*

Pacific Dunlop Investments USA (HQ) 732 345-5400
200 Schulz Dr Red Bank (07701) *(G-9240)*

Pacific Microtronics Inc 973 993-8665
8 Laurel Ln Morris Plains (07950) *(G-6621)*

Pacifichealth Laboratories Inc (PA) 732 739-2900
800 Lanidex Plz Ste 220 Parsippany (07054) *(G-7982)*

Pacira Pharmaceuticals Inc (PA) 973 254-3560
5 Sylvan Way Ste 300 Parsippany (07054) *(G-7983)*

Package Development Co Inc 973 983-8500
100 Round Hill Dr Ste 8 Rockaway (07866) *(G-9483)*

Packaged Gas Systems Inc (PA) 908 755-2780
18 Stern Ave Springfield (07081) *(G-10457)*

Packageman 201 898-1922
331 Main St Belleville (07109) *(G-306)*

Packaging Corporation America 856 596-5020
8 E Stow Rd Ste 100 Marlton (08053) *(G-5945)*

Packaging Corporation America 908 452-9271
101 Bilby Rd Bldg 1 Hackettstown (07840) *(G-4031)*

Packaging Corporation America 856 696-0114
46 N West Ave Ste A Vineland (08360) *(G-11249)*

Packaging Graphics Inc 856 767-9000
435 Commerce Ln West Berlin (08091) *(G-11613)*

Packaging Machinery & Eqp Co 973 325-2418
181 Watson Ave West Orange (07052) *(G-11776)*

Packet Media LLC (PA) 856 779-3800
198 Us Highway 9 Ste 100 Englishtown (07726) *(G-3007)*

Packet Publications, Princeton Also called Princeton Packet Inc *(G-9001)*

Packetstorm Communications Inc 732 840-3871
6 Sullivan St Westwood (07675) *(G-11837)*

Packom LLC 201 378-8382
385 Main St Little Falls (07424) *(G-5463)*

Pacon Manufacturing Corp 732 764-9070
400 Pierce St Somerset (08873) *(G-10051)*

Pacor Inc (PA) 609 324-1100
333 Rising Sun Rd Bordentown (08505) *(G-592)*

Pad and Publ Assembly Corp 856 424-0158
1165 Marlkress Rd Ste M Cherry Hill (08003) *(G-1404)*

Page 2 LLC 862 239-9830
508 Hamburg Tpke Ste 108 Wayne (07470) *(G-11538)*

Page Stamp LLC 732 390-1700
110 Kings Mill Rd Monroe Township (08831) *(G-6340)*

Pahco Machine Inc (PA) 609 587-1188
572 Whitehead Rd Ste 101 Trenton (08619) *(G-10970)*

Pai Services LLC 856 231-4667
305 Fellowship Rd Ste 300 Mount Laurel (08054) *(G-6787)*

Paige Company Containers Inc (PA) 201 461-7800
1 Paul Kohner Pl Elmwood Park (07407) *(G-2846)*

Paige Electric Company LP (PA) 908 687-7810
1160 Springfield Rd Union (07083) *(G-11080)*

Painting Inc 201 489-6565
60 Leuning St South Hackensack (07606) *(G-10179)*

Paintmaster Auto Body 732 270-1700
1920 Route 37 E Ste 1 Toms River (08753) *(G-10781)*

Painton Studios Inc 732 302-0200
299 Us Highway 22 Ste 21 Green Brook (08812) *(G-3865)*

Palatin Technologies Inc 609 495-2200
4b Cedarbrook Dr Cranbury (08512) *(G-1868)*

Palenque Meat Provisions LLC 908 718-1557
23 Grant St Linden (07036) *(G-5401)*

Palfinger North America 609 588-5400
572 Whitehead Rd Ste 301 Trenton (08619) *(G-10971)*

Palisades Dental LLc 201 569-0050
111 Cedar Ln Englewood (07631) *(G-2929)*

Palisades Magnolia Prpts LLC 201 424-7180
169 Roosevelt Pl Unit B Palisades Park (07650) *(G-7776)*

Pallet Services Inc......856 514-3908
66 Pennsgrve Pedrcktwn Rd Pedricktown (08067) *(G-8352)*
Pallmann Industries, Clifton *Also called Pallmann Pulverizers Co Inc (G-1682)*
Pallmann Pulverizers Co Inc......973 471-1450
820 Bloomfield Ave Clifton (07012) *(G-1682)*
Palm Press Inc......201 767-6504
202 Livingston St Northvale (07647) *(G-7543)*
Palma Inc......973 429-1490
628 State Route 10 Ste 2 Whippany (07981) *(G-11901)*
Palmarozzo Bindery......908 688-5300
850 Springfield Rd Union (07083) *(G-11081)*
Palmer Electronics Inc......973 772-5900
156 Belmont Ave Garfield (07026) *(G-3752)*
Palmer Industries Div, Garfield *Also called Palmer Electronics Inc (G-3752)*
Palmer's Cocoa Butter Formula, Englewood Cliffs *Also called ET Browne Drug Co Inc (G-2970)*
Palmetto Adhesives Company......856 451-0400
1785 S Burlington Rd Bridgeton (08302) *(G-767)*
Palnet, Williamstown *Also called Premier Asset Logistics Networ (G-11973)*
Palsgaard Incorporated......973 998-7951
101 Gibraltar Dr Ste 2b Morris Plains (07950) *(G-6622)*
Palude Enterprises Inc......732 241-5478
1933 Hwy 35 Ste 105-144 Howell (07731) *(G-4548)*
Palumbo Associates Inc......908 534-2142
27 Ridge Rd Whitehouse Station (08889) *(G-11931)*
Palumbo Millwork Inc......732 938-3266
5033 Industrial Rd Ste 8 Wall Township (07727) *(G-11361)*
Pam International Co Inc (PA)......201 291-1200
45 Mayhill St Saddle Brook (07663) *(G-9667)*
Pam Optical Co......973 744-8882
107 Park St Montclair (07042) *(G-6382)*
Pamarco Global Graphics Inc (HQ)......908 241-1200
235 E 11th Ave Roselle (07203) *(G-9568)*
Pamarco Global Graphics Inc......856 829-4585
1 Roto Ave Palmyra (08065) *(G-7785)*
Pamarco Technologies LLC (PA)......908 241-1200
235 E 11th Ave Roselle (07203) *(G-9569)*
Pan American Coffee Company (PA)......201 963-2329
500 16th St Hoboken (07030) *(G-4472)*
Pan Graphics Inc......973 478-2100
45 Hartmann Ave Garfield (07026) *(G-3753)*
Pan Technology Inc......201 438-7878
117 Moonachie Ave Carlstadt (07072) *(G-1195)*
Panasonic Corp North America......201 348-7000
2 Riverfront Plz Ste 200 Newark (07102) *(G-7220)*
Panasonic Corp North America......201 348-7000
2 Riverfront Plz Ste 200 Newark (07102) *(G-7221)*
Panatech Corporation......732 331-5692
5 Elkridge Way Manalapan (07726) *(G-5823)*
Panda Plates Inc......917 848-8777
266 Audubon Rd Englewood (07631) *(G-2930)*
Panel Components & Systems (PA)......973 448-9400
149 Main St Stanhope (07874) *(G-10478)*
Panos Brands LLC......800 229-1706
1209 W Saint Georges Ave Linden (07036) *(G-5402)*
Panos Holding Company (HQ)......201 843-8900
395 W Passaic St Ste 2 Rochelle Park (07662) *(G-9428)*
Panova Inc......973 263-1700
33 Jacksonville Rd Ste 2 Towaco (07082) *(G-10876)*
Panpac LLC......856 376-3576
1971 Old Cuthbert Rd Cherry Hill (08034) *(G-1405)*
Panther Printing Inc......239 542-1050
29 Northfield Ave West Orange (07052) *(G-11777)*
Panthera Dental Inc......201 340-2766
1 Meadowlands Plz Ste 200 East Rutherford (07073) *(G-2309)*
Pantina Cosmetics Inc......201 288-7767
30 Henry St Teterboro (07608) *(G-10689)*
Pantone LLC......201 935-5500
590 Commerce Blvd Carlstadt (07072) *(G-1196)*
Pao Ba Avo LLC......908 962-9090
545 Edgar Rd Elizabeth (07202) *(G-2767)*
Papa Johns New Jersey......609 395-0045
1267 S River Rd Ste 400 Cranbury (08512) *(G-1869)*
Paper Board Products, Hackensack *Also called International Container Co (G-3932)*
Paper Clip Communication Inc......973 256-1333
125 Paterson Ave Ste 4 Little Falls (07424) *(G-5464)*
Paper Dove Press LLC......201 641-7938
16 Monnett St Little Ferry (07643) *(G-5493)*
Paper Tube and Core, Paterson *Also called Paper Tubes Cores & Boxes Inc (G-8276)*
Paper Tubes Cores & Boxes Inc......973 977-8823
239 Lindbergh Pl Paterson (07503) *(G-8276)*
Papertec, Garfield *Also called Wjj and Company LLC (G-3778)*
Papery of Marlton LLC......856 985-1776
300 Route 73 S Ste B Marlton (08053) *(G-5946)*
Papettis Hygrade Egg Pdts Inc (HQ)......908 282-7900
1 Papetti Plz Elizabethport (07206) *(G-2790)*
Papillon Ribbon & Bow Inc......973 928-6128
35 Monhegan St Clifton (07013) *(G-1683)*
Papp Iron Works Inc......908 731-1000
950 S 2nd St Plainfield (07063) *(G-8775)*
Pappas Lassonde Holdings Inc (HQ)......856 455-1000
1 Collins Dr Ste 200 Carneys Point (08069) *(G-1243)*
Papyrus, Marlton *Also called Schurman Fine Papers (G-5950)*
Par Code Symbology Inc......973 918-0550
119 Harrison Ave Roseland (07068) *(G-9541)*
Par Metal Products, North Arlington *Also called Ango Electronics Corporation (G-7368)*
Par Metal Products Inc......201 955-0800
21 Ewing Ave North Arlington (07031) *(G-7376)*
Par Sheet Metal Inc......908 241-2477
220 W 1st Ave Roselle (07203) *(G-9570)*
Par Troy Sheet Metal & AC LLC......973 227-1150
122 Clinton Rd Fairfield (07004) *(G-3288)*
Parabole LLC......609 917-8479
1100 Cornwall Rd Monmouth Junction (08852) *(G-6299)*
Paradigm Packaging East LLC (HQ)......201 909-3400
141 5th St Saddle Brook (07663) *(G-9668)*
Paradise......973 425-0505
1098 Mount Kemble Ave # 2 Morristown (07960) *(G-6691)*
Paradise Barxon Corp......908 707-9141
185 Industrial Pkwy Ste H Branchburg (08876) *(G-664)*
Paradise Publishing Group LLC......609 227-7642
25 Middlebury Ln Ste 3b Willingboro (08046) *(G-11994)*
Paragon Iron Inc......201 528-7307
550 Industrial Rd Ste 3 Carlstadt (07072) *(G-1197)*
Paramount Bakeries Inc (PA)......973 482-6638
61 Davenport Ave Newark (07107) *(G-7222)*
Paramount Bakeries Inc......973 482-6638
18-28 Springdale Ave East Orange (07019) *(G-2257)*
Paramount Cosmetics, Clifton *Also called Hudson Cosmetic Mfg Corp (G-1637)*
Paramount Cosmetics Inc......973 472-2323
93 Entin Rd Ste 4 Clifton (07014) *(G-1684)*
Paramount Fixture Corporation......973 485-1585
175 Mount Pleasant Ave Newark (07104) *(G-7223)*
Paramount Fixture Sales, Newark *Also called Paramount Fixture Corporation (G-7223)*
Paramount Metal Finishing Co......908 862-0772
1515 W Elizabeth Ave Linden (07036) *(G-5403)*
Paramount Modular Concepts, Oakland *Also called P M C Diners Inc (G-7640)*
Paramount Packaging, Haddonfield *Also called Global Direct Marketing Group (G-4058)*
Paramount Plating, Linden *Also called Paramount Metal Finishing Co (G-5403)*
Paramount Plating Co Inc......908 862-0772
1515 W Elizabeth Ave Linden (07036) *(G-5404)*
Paramount Products Co Inc......732 458-9200
1104 Industrial Pkwy Brick (08724) *(G-728)*
Paramount Wire Co Inc......973 672-0500
2-8 Central Ave East Orange (07018) *(G-2258)*
Paravista Inc......732 752-1222
123 Lehigh Dr Fairfield (07004) *(G-3289)*
Paravista Imaging and Printing, Fairfield *Also called Paravista Inc (G-3289)*
Parikh Worldwide Media, Jersey City *Also called Desi Talk LLC (G-4723)*
Pario Group LLC......732 906-2302
70 Stephenville Pkwy Edison (08820) *(G-2586)*
Paris Corporation New Jersey (PA)......609 265-9200
800 Highland Dr Westampton (08060) *(G-11788)*
Pariser Industries Inc (PA)......973 569-9090
91 Michigan Ave Paterson (07503) *(G-8277)*
Park Ave Printing, Trenton *Also called Steven Madola (G-10992)*
Park Avenue Meats Inc......718 731-4196
194 Albion Ave Paterson (07502) *(G-8278)*
Park Electric Motor Co, Atlantic City *Also called Motors and Drives Inc (G-98)*
Park Plus Inc......201 917-5778
83 Broad Ave Fairview (07022) *(G-3366)*
Park Plus Inc (PA)......201 651-8590
31 Iron Horse Rd Ste 1 Oakland (07436) *(G-7641)*
Park Printing Services Inc......856 675-1600
7300 N Crescent Blvd # 21 Pennsauken (08110) *(G-8463)*
Park Steel & Iron Co (PA)......732 775-7500
9 Evergreen Ave Neptune (07753) *(G-6894)*
Parkeon Inc......856 234-8000
40 Twosome Dr Ste 7 Moorestown (08057) *(G-6553)*
Parker Acquisition Group Inc (PA)......908 707-4900
25 Imclone Dr Branchburg (08876) *(G-665)*
Parker Labs......973 276-9500
286 Eldridge Rd Fairfield (07004) *(G-3290)*
Parker Publications......908 766-3900
155 Main St Madison (07940) *(G-5699)*
Parker Publications Corporated, Whippany *Also called Recorder Publishing Co Inc (G-11907)*
Parker Publications Inc......908 766-3900
17 Morristown Rd 19 Bernardsville (07924) *(G-441)*
Parker-Hannifin Corporation......856 825-8900
525 Orange St Millville (08332) *(G-6266)*
Parker-Hannifin Corporation......908 458-8101
135 Bryant Ave Cranford (07016) *(G-1921)*
Parking Survival Experts, Paramus *Also called Alternate Side Street Suspende (G-7788)*
Parkway Plastics Inc......800 881-4996
561 Stelton Rd Piscataway (08854) *(G-8697)*

ALPHABETIC

Parkway Printing Inc ...732 308-0300
52 N Main St Ste 11 Marlboro (07746) *(G-5908)*
Parkway-Kew Corporation ...732 398-2100
2095 Excelsior Ave North Brunswick (08902) *(G-7482)*
Parmelee Wrench, Harrison *Also called CS Osborne & Co (G-4168)*
Parr, J W Leadburing Co, Little Falls *Also called JW Parr Leadburing Co (G-5458)*
Parrish Sign Co Inc ...856 696-4040
2242 S Delsea Dr Vineland (08360) *(G-11250)*
Parsells Printing Inc ...973 473-2700
938 Spring Valley Rd # 1 Maywood (07607) *(G-6013)*
Parsons Cabinets Inc ...973 279-4954
79 Beverly Rd Montclair (07043) *(G-6383)*
Partac Peat Corp ...908 637-4191
95 Shades Of Death Rd Great Meadows (07838) *(G-3855)*
Partac Peat Corporation ...908 637-4631
95 Kelsey Park Great Meadows (07838) *(G-3856)*
Partake Foods, Jersey City *Also called Vivis Life LLC (G-4827)*
Parth Enterprises Inc ...732 404-0665
665 State Route 27 Iselin (08830) *(G-4622)*
Partners In Vision Inc ...888 748-1112
1090 King Georges Post Rd # 103 Edison (08837) *(G-2587)*
Parts Life Inc (PA) ...856 786-8675
30 Twosome Dr Ste 1 Moorestown (08057) *(G-6554)*
Party City Corporation ...973 537-1707
477 State Route 10 # 102 Randolph (07869) *(G-9196)*
Party City of North Bergen ...201 865-0040
3111 Kennedy Blvd North Bergen (07047) *(G-7427)*
Parwan Electronics Corporation (PA) ...732 290-1900
1230 Hwy 34 Matawan (07747) *(G-5983)*
Pascack Data Services Inc ...973 304-4858
200 Central Ave Ste 100 Hawthorne (07506) *(G-4236)*
Pascack Press ...201 664-2105
69 Woodland Ave Westwood (07675) *(G-11838)*
Pascack Valley Copy Center ...201 664-1917
41 Bergenline Ave Ste 1 Westwood (07675) *(G-11839)*
Passaic Color & Chemical, Paterson *Also called Royce Associates A Ltd Partnr (G-8289)*
Passaic County Welders Inc ...973 696-1200
100 Parish Dr Wayne (07470) *(G-11539)*
Passaic Metal & Bldg Sups Co (PA) ...973 546-9000
5 Central Ave Ste 1 Clifton (07011) *(G-1685)*
Passaic Rubber Co (PA) ...973 696-9500
45 Demarest Dr Wayne (07470) *(G-11540)*
Pastarama Distributors Inc ...609 847-0378
164 Center St Sewell (08080) *(G-9853)*
Pat Bry Advertising Spc ...732 591-0999
Tennant Rd Rr 79 Morganville (07751) *(G-6593)*
Pata Pal, Denville *Also called Qualserv Imports Inc (G-2050)*
Patagonia Pharmaceuticals LLC ...201 264-7866
50 Tice Blvd Ste A26 Woodcliff Lake (07677) *(G-12060)*
Patchamp Inc ...201 457-1504
20 E Kennedy St Hackensack (07601) *(G-3962)*
Patchworks Co Inc ...973 627-2002
18 N Salem St Dover (07801) *(G-2103)*
Patel Metal Plating Inc ...732 574-1770
6 Emerson St Edison (08820) *(G-2588)*
Patel Printing Plus Corp ...908 964-6422
1036 Commerce Ave Union (07083) *(G-11082)*
Patella Construction Corp ...973 916-0100
99 South St Passaic (07055) *(G-8094)*
Patella Woodworking, Passaic *Also called Patella Construction Corp (G-8094)*
Paterson Bleachery Inc (PA) ...973 684-1034
207 E 15th St 219 Paterson (07524) *(G-8279)*
Paterson Laundry & Die Div, Paterson *Also called Fairfield Textiles Corp (G-8190)*
Paterson Stamp Works, Clifton *Also called American Marking Systems Inc (G-1563)*
Path Silicones Inc (PA) ...201 796-0833
21 Wallace St Elmwood Park (07407) *(G-2847)*
Patheon Biologics LLC ...609 919-3300
201 College Rd E Princeton (08540) *(G-8993)*
Patientstar LLC ...856 722-0808
1000 Bishops Gate Blvd # 200 Mount Laurel (08054) *(G-6788)*
Patrick J Kelly Drums Inc ...856 963-1795
1810 River Ave Camden (08105) *(G-1082)*
Patriot American Solutions LLC ...862 209-4772
5 Astro Pl Rockaway (07866) *(G-9484)*
Patriot Pickle Inc ...973 709-9487
20 Edison Dr Wayne (07470) *(G-11541)*
Patterson Smith Publishing ...973 744-3291
23 Prospect Ter Montclair (07042) *(G-6384)*
Patty-O-Matic Inc ...732 938-2757
183 County Rte 547 Farmingdale (07727) *(G-3389)*
Patwin Plastics Inc ...908 486-6600
2300 E Linden Ave Linden (07036) *(G-5405)*
Paul Bros Inc ...856 697-5895
113 Church St Newfield (08344) *(G-7326)*
Paul Burkhardt & Sons Inc ...856 435-2020
648 7th Ave Lindenwold (08021) *(G-5445)*
Paul Dyeing Company ...973 484-1121
626 Orange St Newark (07107) *(G-7224)*
Paul Englehardt ...908 637-4556
Island Rd Great Meadows (07838) *(G-3857)*
Paul Fago Cabinet Making Inc ...856 384-0496
425 S Columbia St Woodbury (08096) *(G-12035)*
Paul Scammacca, Ceo, Middletown *Also called Birds Beware Corporation (G-6161)*
Paul Winston Fine Jewelry Grou (PA) ...800 232-2728
619 E Palisade Ave Ste 1 Englewood Cliffs (07632) *(G-2986)*
Paulaur Corporation ...609 395-8844
105 Melrich Rd Cranbury (08512) *(G-1870)*
Paulist Press Inc ...201 825-7300
997 Macarthur Blvd Mahwah (07430) *(G-5761)*
Paulsboro Refining Company LLC ...973 455-7500
800 Billingsport Rd Paulsboro (08066) *(G-8338)*
Pausch LLC ...732 747-6110
808 Shrewsbury Ave Tinton Falls (07724) *(G-10724)*
Pavan & Kievit Enterprises ...973 546-4615
113 Dewitt St Ste 210 Garfield (07026) *(G-3754)*
Paverart LLC ...856 783-7000
2512 Egg Harbor Rd Ste C Lindenwold (08021) *(G-5446)*
Pavestone LLC ...973 948-7193
183 Ridge Rd Branchville (07826) *(G-709)*
Pavexpress ...201 330-8300
499 River Rd Clifton (07014) *(G-1686)*
Paw Bioscience Products LLC ...732 460-0088
38 Industrial Way E Ste 5 Eatontown (07724) *(G-2416)*
Paylocity Holding Corporation ...908 917-3027
21 Fadem Rd Ste 10 Springfield (07081) *(G-10458)*
Pba of West Windsor ...609 799-6535
376 N Post Rd Princeton Junction (08550) *(G-9064)*
Pbf Energy, Paulsboro *Also called Paulsboro Refining Company LLC (G-8338)*
Pbf Energy Company LLC (HQ) ...973 455-7500
1 Sylvan Way Ste 2 Parsippany (07054) *(G-7984)*
Pbf Energy Inc (PA) ...973 455-7500
1 Sylvan Way Ste 2 Parsippany (07054) *(G-7985)*
Pbf Holding Company LLC (HQ) ...973 455-7500
1 Sylvan Way Ste 2 Parsippany (07054) *(G-7986)*
PBL Biomedical Laboratories, Piscataway *Also called Pestka Biomedical Labs Inc (G-8699)*
PC & S, Stanhope *Also called Panel Components & Systems (G-10478)*
PC Marketing Inc (PA) ...201 943-6100
1040 Wilt Ave Ridgefield (07657) *(G-9282)*
PC Science Training Center, Denville *Also called Justice Laboratory Software (G-2042)*
PCA, Hackettstown *Also called Packaging Corporation America (G-4031)*
PCA/Supply Services 302a, Vineland *Also called Packaging Corporation America (G-11249)*
PCC, Somerset *Also called Power Container Corp (G-10054)*
PCC Asia LLC (PA) ...973 890-3873
200 Maltese Dr Totowa (07512) *(G-10842)*
PCI, Lebanon *Also called Plate Concepts Inc (G-5273)*
PCI Inc ...973 226-8007
185 Fairfield Ave Ste 4c West Caldwell (07006) *(G-11671)*
Pcr Technologies Inc ...973 882-0017
26 Chapin Rd Ste 1111 Pine Brook (07058) *(G-8613)*
Pcs Crane Services Inc ...201 366-4250
83 Broad Ave Fairview (07022) *(G-3367)*
Pcs Revenue Ctrl Systems Inc ...201 568-8300
560 Sylvan Ave Ste 2050 Englewood Cliffs (07632) *(G-2987)*
Pdec, Eatontown *Also called East Coast Distributors Inc (G-2389)*
PDM Litho Inc ...718 301-1740
220 Entin Rd Clifton (07014) *(G-1687)*
PDM Packaging Inc ...201 864-1115
4102 Bergen Tpke North Bergen (07047) *(G-7428)*
PDQ Print & Copy Inc ...201 569-2288
161 Coolidge Ave Englewood (07631) *(G-2931)*
Pdr Equity LLC (PA) ...201 358-7200
200 Jefferson Park Whippany (07981) *(G-11902)*
Pdr Network, Whippany *Also called Pdr Equity LLC (G-11902)*
Pds Biotechnology Corporation (PA) ...800 208-3343
300 Connell Dr Ste 4000 Berkeley Heights (07922) *(G-409)*
Pds Consultants Inc ...201 970-2313
22 Rainbow Trl Sparta (07871) *(G-10405)*
Pds Prclnical Data Systems Inc ...973 398-2800
100 Valley Rd Ste 204 Mount Arlington (07856) *(G-6717)*
Pe Burkhardt & Sons, Lindenwold *Also called Paul Burkhardt & Sons Inc (G-5445)*
Peace Medical Inc ...800 537-9564
105 W Dewey Ave Unit 1-2 Wharton (07885) *(G-11866)*
Peach Boutique LLC (PA) ...908 351-0739
1139 E Jersey St Ste 319 Elizabeth (07201) *(G-2768)*
Peachtree Kay, Clifton *Also called K M Media Group LLC (G-1648)*
Peacock Communications Inc (PA) ...973 763-3311
215 Rutgers St Maplewood (07040) *(G-5881)*
Peacock Products Inc ...201 385-5585
48 Woodbine St Bergenfield (07621) *(G-382)*
Peak Finance Holdings LLC (HQ) ...856 969-7100
121 Woodcrest Rd Cherry Hill (08003) *(G-1406)*
Pearl Baumell Company Inc ...415 421-2113
201 State Rt 17 Ste 302 Rutherford (07070) *(G-9631)*
Pearson Business Services, Old Tappan *Also called Pearson Technology Centre Inc (G-7735)*

Pearson Education Inc (HQ) 201 236-7000
221 River St Hoboken (07030) *(G-4473)*

Pearson Education Inc 914 287-8000
221 River St Hoboken (07030) *(G-4474)*

Pearson Education Inc 609 395-6000
258 Prospect Plains Rd Cranbury (08512) *(G-1871)*

Pearson Education Inc 201 785-2721
221 River St Ste 200 Hoboken (07030) *(G-4475)*

Pearson Inc 201 236-7000
1 Lake St Upper Saddle River (07458) *(G-11144)*

Pearson Longman, Hoboken *Also called Pearson Education Inc (G-4474)*

Pearson Technology Centre Inc (HQ) 201 767-5000
200 Old Tappan Rd Ste 1 Old Tappan (07675) *(G-7735)*

PEC, Matawan *Also called Parwan Electronics Corporation (G-5983)*

Pecata Enterprises Inc 973 523-9498
18 Market St Paterson (07501) *(G-8280)*

Pechter's, Harrison *Also called R P Baking LLC (G-4179)*

Pechters Southern NJ LLC 856 786-8000
2 Surrey Ln Cinnaminson (08077) *(G-1479)*

Pedestal Pallet Inc 732 968-7488
777 N Avenue Ext Dunellen (08812) *(G-2122)*

Pedibrush LLC 856 796-2963
211 7th Ave Haddon Heights (08035) *(G-4047)*

Pedrick Tool & Machine Co 856 829-8900
1515 River Rd Cinnaminson (08077) *(G-1480)*

Peel Away Labs Inc 516 603-3116
304 Newark Ave Jersey City (07302) *(G-4779)*

Peel Away Labs Inc 201 420-0051
304 Newark Ave Jersey City (07302) *(G-4780)*

Peeq Imaging 212 490-3850
480 Gotham Pkwy Carlstadt (07072) *(G-1198)*

Peeq Media, Somerset *Also called Toppan Printing Co Amer Inc (G-10088)*

Peerless Coating Services, Hawthorne *Also called Peerless Coatings LLC (G-4237)*

Peerless Coatings LLC 973 427-8771
220a Goffle Rd Hawthorne (07506) *(G-4237)*

Peerless Concrete Products Co 973 838-3060
246 Main St Butler (07405) *(G-1011)*

Peerless Umbrella Co Inc (PA) 973 578-4900
427 Ferry St Newark (07105) *(G-7225)*

Pegasus Group Publishing Inc 973 884-9100
188 State Route 10 Fl 2 East Hanover (07936) *(G-2234)*

Pegasus Home Fashions Inc 908 965-1919
107 Trumbull St G1s13 Elizabeth (07206) *(G-2769)*

Pegasus Products Inc 908 707-1122
19 Readington Rd Branchburg (08876) *(G-666)*

Pekay Industries Inc 732 938-2722
452 Sqnkum Yellowbrook Rd Farmingdale (07727) *(G-3390)*

Pelco Packaging Corporation 973 675-4994
545 N Arlington Ave Ste 7 East Orange (07017) *(G-2259)*

Pella Window Store, Paramus *Also called Lux Home Inc (G-7817)*

Pemberton Fabricators Inc 609 267-0922
30 Indel Ave Rancocas (08073) *(G-9163)*

Pemco Dental Corporation 800 526-4170
35 Stern Ave Springfield (07081) *(G-10459)*

Pemfab, Rancocas *Also called Pemberton Fabricators Inc (G-9163)*

Pen Company of America LLC 908 374-7949
502 South Ave Garwood (07027) *(G-3790)*

Pen Company of America LLC (HQ) 908 374-7949
1401 S Park Ave Linden (07036) *(G-5406)*

Pen Master, Randolph *Also called Larose Industries LLC (G-9189)*

Pendotech, Princeton *Also called Mayfair Tech Ltd Lblty Co (G-8974)*

Penetone Corporation (PA) 201 567-3000
125 Kingsland Ave Ste 205 Clifton (07014) *(G-1688)*

Penetone Corporation 609 921-0501
1000 Herrontown Rd Princeton (08540) *(G-8994)*

Penick Corporation 856 678-3601
33 Industrial Park Rd Newark (07114) *(G-7226)*

Penn Color Inc 201 791-5100
30 Kohner Dr Elmwood Park (07407) *(G-2848)*

Penn Copy Center Inc 646 251-0313
5 Morning Glory Ln Lakewood (08701) *(G-5145)*

Penn Elcom Inc 973 839-7777
232 W Parkway Pompton Plains (07444) *(G-8869)*

Penn Jersey Advance Centl Svcs, Secaucus *Also called Penn Jersey Advance Inc (G-9796)*

Penn Jersey Advance Inc 201 775-6610
1 Harmon Plz Fl 9 Secaucus (07094) *(G-9796)*

Penn Jersey Press Inc 856 627-2200
10 United States Ave E Gibbsboro (08026) *(G-3795)*

Penn Metal Finishing Co Inc 609 387-3400
700 Jacksonville Rd Burlington (08016) *(G-981)*

Penn Power Group LLC 732 441-1489
4118 Hiway 34 Matawan (07747) *(G-5984)*

Penn Rillton Div, The, Bridgeton *Also called Whibco Inc (G-779)*

Penn-Jersey Bldg Mtls Co Inc (PA) 609 641-6994
2819 Fire Rd Egg Harbor Township (08234) *(G-2692)*

Pennant Ingredients Inc 856 428-4300
1941 Old Cuthbert Rd Cherry Hill (08034) *(G-1407)*

Pennetta & Sons 201 420-1693
428 Hoboken Ave Jersey City (07306) *(G-4781)*

Pennington Furnace Supply Inc 609 737-2500
6 Brookside Ave Pennington (08534) *(G-8371)*

Pennock Company 215 492-7900
7135 Colonial Ln Pennsauken (08109) *(G-8464)*

Pennock Floral Co, Pennsauken *Also called Pennock Company (G-8464)*

Pennsylvania Crusher, Sewell *Also called K-Tron International Inc (G-9851)*

Pennsylvania Machine Works Inc 856 467-0500
Rr 551 Swedesboro (08085) *(G-10600)*

Penny Plate LLC (HQ) 856 429-7583
1400 Horizon Way Ste 300 Mount Laurel (08054) *(G-6789)*

Penny Press 856 547-1991
908 N White Horse Pike Stratford (08084) *(G-10506)*

Pennzoil-Quaker State Company 856 423-1388
1224 Forest Pkwy Ste 100 Paulsboro (08066) *(G-8339)*

Penske Truck Leasing Co LP 973 575-0169
600 Edwards Rd Parsippany (07054) *(G-7987)*

Penta Digital Incorporated 201 839-5392
234 16th St Fl 8 Jersey City (07310) *(G-4782)*

Penta Glass Industries Inc 973 478-2110
71 Hepworth Pl Garfield (07026) *(G-3755)*

Penta International Corp 973 740-2300
50 Okner Pkwy Livingston (07039) *(G-5534)*

Penta Manufacturing Company, Livingston *Also called Penta International Corp (G-5534)*

Pentacle Publishing Corp 732 240-3000
1830 Route 9 Ste 1 Toms River (08755) *(G-10782)*

Pentax of America Inc 973 628-6200
3 Paragon Dr Montvale (07645) *(G-6421)*

Peoples Education Inc 201 712-0090
25 Philips Pkwy 105 Montvale (07645) *(G-6422)*

Peoples Eductl Holdings Inc (PA) 201 712-0090
25 Philips Pkwy 105 Montvale (07645) *(G-6423)*

Pepco Manufacturing Co (PA) 856 783-3700
210 E Evergreen Ave Somerdale (08083) *(G-9933)*

Pepsi 732 238-1598
5 Lexington Ave East Brunswick (08816) *(G-2163)*

Pepsi Cola Btlg Co Pennsauken 856 665-6616
8191 N Crescent Blvd Pennsauken (08110) *(G-8465)*

Pepsi Cola Co 609 476-5001
1440 Pinewood Blvd Mays Landing (08330) *(G-5997)*

Pepsi-Cola Metro Btlg Co Inc 201 955-2691
680 Belleville Tpke Kearny (07032) *(G-4889)*

Pepsi-Cola Metro Btlg Co Inc 732 922-9000
3411 Sunset Ave Ocean (07712) *(G-7672)*

Pepsi-Cola Metro Btlg Co Inc 732 424-3000
2200 New Brunswick Ave Piscataway (08854) *(G-8698)*

Pepsi-Cola Nat Brnd Bevs Ltd (PA) 856 665-6200
8275 N Crescent Blvd Pennsauken (08110) *(G-8466)*

Pepsico, East Brunswick *Also called Pepsi (G-2163)*

Pepsico, Piscataway *Also called Pepsi-Cola Metro Btlg Co Inc (G-8698)*

Pepsico, Whippany *Also called P-Americas LLC (G-11900)*

Pepsico Inc 856 661-4604
8275 N Route 130 Pennsauken (08110) *(G-8467)*

Pequod Communications, Princeton *Also called Wong Robinson & Co Inc (G-9044)*

Per-Fil Industries Inc 856 461-5700
407 Adams St Riverside (08075) *(G-9401)*

Peragallo Organ Company of NJ 973 684-3414
306 Buffalo Ave Paterson (07503) *(G-8281)*

Peragallo Pipe Organ, Paterson *Also called Peragallo Organ Company of NJ (G-8281)*

Perc, Boonton *Also called Pipeline Eqp Resources Co LLC (G-564)*

Perceptions Inc 973 344-5333
280 Central Ave Kearny (07032) *(G-4890)*

Perco Inc 908 464-3000
620 Springfield Ave Berkeley Heights (07922) *(G-410)*

Perdue Farms Inc 609 298-4100
73 Silver Lake Rd Bridgeton (08302) *(G-768)*

Pereg Gourmet Natural Foods, Clifton *Also called Pereg Gourmet Spices Ltd (G-1689)*

Pereg Gourmet Spices Ltd 718 261-6767
25 Styertowne Rd Clifton (07012) *(G-1689)*

Perfect Clicks LLC 845 323-6116
172 Broadway Rear Bldg Woodcliff Lake (07677) *(G-12061)*

Perfect Printing Inc 856 787-1877
1533 Glen Ave Moorestown (08057) *(G-6555)*

Perfect Shapes Inc 856 783-3844
110 Salem St Elmer (08318) *(G-2801)*

Perfecto Foods LLC 201 889-5328
79 Stuyvesant Ave Kearny (07032) *(G-4891)*

Performance Alloys & Materials 201 865-5268
462 Dunlin Plz Secaucus (07094) *(G-9797)*

Performance Chemicals, Florham Park *Also called BASF Plant Science LP (G-3492)*

Performance Industries Inc 609 392-1450
51 Tucker St Trenton (08618) *(G-10972)*

Performance Laboratories Inc, Hackensack *Also called Preform Laboratories Inc (G-3965)*

Peribu Collections LLC, Skillman *Also called Peribu Global Sourcing (G-9925)*

Peribu Global Sourcing 704 560-2035
5 Brookside Dr Skillman (08558) *(G-9925)*

Perimeter Solutions LP 732 541-3000
500 Roosevelt Ave Carteret (07008) *(G-1264)*

Perk & Pantry 856 451-4333
97 Trench Rd Ste 4 Bridgeton (08302) *(G-769)*

Perkins Plumbing & Heating 201 327-2736
89 Fawnhill Rd Upper Saddle River (07458) *(G-11145)*

Perl Pigments LLC 201 836-1212
400 Cotters Ln East Brunswick (08816) *(G-2164)*

Perlen Packaging, Whippany *Also called Perlin Converting LLC* *(G-11903)*

Perlin Converting LLC 973 887-0257
135 Algonquin Pkwy Whippany (07981) *(G-11903)*

Perma Pure LLC (HQ) 732 244-0010
1001 New Hampshire Ave Lakewood (08701) *(G-5146)*

Permabond LLC (PA) 610 323-5003
223 Churchill Ave Somerset (08873) *(G-10052)*

Permadur Industries Inc 908 359-9767
186 Route 206 Hillsborough (08844) *(G-4344)*

Permagraphics Inc 201 814-1200
25 Graphic Pl Moonachie (07074) *(G-6483)*

Permalith Plastics LLC 215 925-5659
6901 N Crescent Blvd Pennsauken (08110) *(G-8468)*

Permanore Archtctural Finishes 908 797-4177
3 Parkland Dr Milford (08848) *(G-6194)*

Pernix Therapeutics LLC 800 793-2145
10 N Park Pl Ste 201 Morristown (07960) *(G-6692)*

Perry Products Corporation 609 267-1600
25 Mount Laurel Rd Hainesport (08036) *(G-4076)*

Personal Secure, Stirling *Also called Secure System Inc* *(G-10496)*

Personality Handkerchiefs Inc 973 565-0077
640 Frelinghuysen Ave Newark (07114) *(G-7227)*

Personlzed Exprssons By Audrey 973 478-5115
63 Harrison Ave Garfield (07026) *(G-3756)*

Pertech Corp K & E Printing, Carlstadt *Also called Pertech Printing Inks Inc* *(G-1199)*

Pertech Printing Inks Inc 908 354-1700
140 Grand St Carlstadt (07072) *(G-1199)*

Pestka Biomedical Labs Inc 732 777-9123
131 Ethel Rd W Ste 6 Piscataway (08854) *(G-8699)*

Pet Devices LLC 929 244-0012
184 S Livingston Ave Livingston (07039) *(G-5535)*

Pet Salon Inc 609 350-6480
8510 Ventnor Ave Margate City (08402) *(G-5890)*

Pet Salon Inc (PA) 609 350-6480
3 S Franklin Ave Margate City (08402) *(G-5891)*

Peter Garafano & Son Inc 973 278-0350
500 Marshall St Paterson (07503) *(G-8282)*

Peter L Demaree 732 531-2133
1206 State Route 35 Ocean (07712) *(G-7673)*

Peter Morley LLC 732 264-0010
21 Village Ct Hazlet (07730) *(G-4269)*

Peter Thomas Roth Labs LLC 201 329-9100
45 Mayhill St Saddle Brook (07663) *(G-9669)*

Peter Yaged 973 427-4219
58 Braen Ave Hawthorne (07506) *(G-4238)*

Peter-Lisand Machine Corp 201 943-5600
262 Voorhis Ave New Milford (07646) *(G-6991)*

Peters Laboratories 856 767-4144
1 Hillside Ln Berlin (08009) *(G-428)*

Peterson Brothers Mfg Co 732 271-8240
10 Baekeland Ave Middlesex (08846) *(G-6136)*

Peterson Stamping & Mfg Co 908 241-0900
75 N Michigan Ave Kenilworth (07033) *(G-4968)*

Peterson Steel Rule Die Corp 201 935-6180
35 Broad St Carlstadt (07072) *(G-1200)*

Petit Pois Corp 856 608-9644
50 Twosome Dr Ste 3 Moorestown (08057) *(G-6556)*

Petnet Solutions Inc 865 218-2000
86-110 Orchard St Ste 2 Hackensack (07601) *(G-3963)*

Petro Extrusion Tech Inc 908 789-3338
205 Hallock Ave Ste B Middlesex (08846) *(G-6137)*

Petro Extrusion Technology, Middlesex *Also called Petro Extrusion Tech Inc* *(G-6137)*

Petro Packaging Co Inc 908 272-4054
16 Quine St Cranford (07016) *(G-1922)*

Petro Pallet LLC 732 230-3287
575 Ridge Rd Monmouth Junction (08852) *(G-6300)*

Petro Plastics Company Inc 908 789-1200
500 Hoiles Dr Kenilworth (07033) *(G-4969)*

Petronio Shoe Products Corp 973 751-7579
305 Cortlandt St Belleville (07109) *(G-307)*

Pets First Inc 908 289-2900
248 3rd St Elizabethport (07206) *(G-2791)*

Pfizer, Peapack *Also called Pharmacia & Upjohn Company LLC* *(G-8344)*

Pfizer Inc 732 591-2106
11 Erin Ln Old Bridge (08857) *(G-7723)*

Pfizer Inc 973 993-0977
182 Tabor Rd Morris Plains (07950) *(G-6623)*

Pfizer Inc 201 294-8060
8810 Durham Ave North Bergen (07047) *(G-7429)*

Pfizer Inc 908 251-5685
43 Spruce Hollow Rd Dunellen (08812) *(G-2123)*

Pfizer Inc 973 660-5000
1 Giralda Farms Madison (07940) *(G-5700)*

Pfizer Inc 609 434-4920
1001 Jack Stephan Way Ewing (08628) *(G-3050)*

Pfizer Inc 908 901-8000
100 Rte 206 N Peapack (07977) *(G-8342)*

Pfizer Inc 212 733-2323
400 Crossing Blvd Fl 7 Bridgewater (08807) *(G-864)*

Pfizer Inc 973 739-0430
400 Webro Rd Parsippany (07054) *(G-7988)*

Pfk Coach Phyllis Flood Knerr 856 429-5425
119 Walnut St Haddonfield (08033) *(G-4061)*

Pflaumer Brothers Inc (PA) 609 883-4610
1008 Whitehead Road Ext Ewing (08638) *(G-3051)*

Pg Marble, Freehold *Also called Premier Marble and Gran 2 Inc* *(G-3691)*

Pgi Nonwovens, Landisville *Also called Fibertech Group Inc* *(G-5206)*

Pharm Ops Inc 908 454-7733
101 Broad St Phillipsburg (08865) *(G-8566)*

Pharma Chem, Kearny *Also called Pharmachem Laboratories LLC* *(G-4892)*

Pharma Synergy LLC 856 241-2316
103 Somerfield Rd Swedesboro (08085) *(G-10601)*

Pharma Systems Inc 973 636-9007
662 Goffle Rd Ste 3 Hawthorne (07506) *(G-4239)*

Pharmaceutical Litho Label Inc (PA) 336 785-4000
450 North Ave E Cranford (07016) *(G-1923)*

Pharmaceutical Innovations 973 242-2900
897 Frelinghuysen Ave Newark (07114) *(G-7228)*

Pharmachem Laboratories, Paterson *Also called Mpt Delivery Systems Inc* *(G-8262)*

Pharmachem Laboratories Inc 973 256-1340
15 Adams Dr Totowa (07512) *(G-10843)*

Pharmachem Laboratories Inc 201 343-3611
130 Wesley St South Hackensack (07606) *(G-10180)*

Pharmachem Laboratories LLC (HQ) 201 246-1000
265 Harrison Tpke Kearny (07032) *(G-4892)*

Pharmacia & Upjohn Inc (HQ) 908 901-8000
100 Route 206 N Peapack (07977) *(G-8343)*

Pharmacia & Upjohn Company LLC (HQ) 908 901-8000
100 Rte 206 N Peapack (07977) *(G-8344)*

Pharmaderm, East Hanover *Also called Fougera Pharmaceuticals Inc* *(G-2210)*

Pharmakon Corp 856 829-3161
2200 Wallace Blvd Ste C Cinnaminson (08077) *(G-1481)*

Pharmaseq Inc 732 355-0100
11 Deerpark Dr Ste 104 Monmouth Junction (08852) *(G-6301)*

Pharmasource International LLC 732 985-6182
1090 Stelton Rd Piscataway (08854) *(G-8700)*

Pharmatech International Inc 973 244-0393
21 Just Rd Fairfield (07004) *(G-3291)*

Pharmctclprscrptnsrvcllc Lcnda 973 491-9000
155 Jefferson St Newark (07105) *(G-7229)*

Pharmedium Services LLC 847 457-2362
36 Stults Rd Dayton (08810) *(G-1983)*

Pharmetic Mfg Company LLC 732 254-1901
650 Jernee Mill Rd Sayreville (08872) *(G-9721)*

Pharming Healthcare Inc 908 524-0888
685 Us Highway 202/206 Bridgewater (08807) *(G-865)*

Pharmion Corporation (HQ) 908 673-9000
86 Morris Ave Summit (07901) *(G-10543)*

Phelps Dodge, Elizabeth *Also called Freeport Minerals Corporation* *(G-2737)*

Phibro Animal Health Corp (HQ) 201 329-7300
300 Frank W Burr Blvd Teaneck (07666) *(G-10643)*

Phibro Animal Health Holdings, Teaneck *Also called Phibro-Tech Inc* *(G-10645)*

Phibro Anmal Hlth Holdings Inc (HQ) 201 329-7300
300 Frank W Burr Blvd Teaneck (07666) *(G-10644)*

Phibro-Tech Inc (HQ) 201 329-7300
300 Frank W Burr Blvd # 21 Teaneck (07666) *(G-10645)*

Phibrochem Inc 201 329-7300
300 Frank W Burr Blvd # 21 Teaneck (07666) *(G-10646)*

Phil Desiere Electric Mtr Svc 856 692-8442
1338 Almond Rd Vineland (08360) *(G-11251)*

Philadelphia Inquirer 856 779-3840
53 Haddonfield Rd Ste 300 Cherry Hill (08002) *(G-1408)*

Philcorr LLC 856 205-0557
2317 Almond Rd Vineland (08360) *(G-11252)*

Phildelphia-Newspapers-Llc 609 823-0453
109 S Dorset Ave Ventnor City (08406) *(G-11154)*

Philip Creter Inc 908 686-2910
20 Monroe St Union (07083) *(G-11083)*

Philip Holzer and Assoc LLC 212 691-9500
350 Michele Pl Carlstadt (07072) *(G-1201)*

Philip Lief Group Inc 609 430-1000
371 Sayre Dr Princeton (08540) *(G-8995)*

Philip Mamrak 908 454-6089
531 Victory Ave Phillipsburg (08865) *(G-8567)*

Philip Morris USA Inc 908 781-6400
2 Crossroads Dr Ste 200b Bedminster (07921) *(G-276)*

Philip Papalia 732 349-5530
21 Dugan Ln Toms River (08755) *(G-10783)*

Philips Elec N Amer Corp 973 804-2100
1 Samsung Pl Ledgewood (07852) *(G-5278)*

Philips Elec N Amer Corp 973 471-9450
215 Entin Rd Clifton (07014) *(G-1690)*

Phillip Balderose 732 574-1330
70 Westfield Ave Clark (07066) *(G-1512)*
Phillips 66 Company 908 296-0709
1400 S Park Ave Linden (07036) *(G-5407)*
Phillips Companies Inc (PA) 973 483-4124
7 Frontage Rd Clinton (08809) *(G-1748)*
Phillips Enterprises Inc 732 493-3191
3600 Sunset Ave Ocean (07712) *(G-7674)*
Phillips Precision Inc 201 797-8820
7 Paul Kohner Pl Elmwood Park (07407) *(G-2849)*
Phillips Precision Medicraft, Elmwood Park *Also called Phillips Precision Inc (G-2849)*
Phillips Safety Products Inc 732 356-1493
123 Lincoln Blvd Ste 2 Middlesex (08846) *(G-6138)*
Phillips Scientific Co, Mahwah *Also called Theory Development Corp (G-5780)*
Phillipsburg Marble Co Inc 908 859-3435
1 Marble Hill Rd Phillipsburg (08865) *(G-8568)*
Phoenix Alliance Group LLC 732 495-4800
337 State Route 36 Port Monmouth (07758) *(G-8879)*
Phoenix Business Forms Inc 856 691-2266
2231 N East Blvd Vineland (08360) *(G-11253)*
Phoenix Chemical Inc 908 707-0232
151 Industrial Pkwy Branchburg (08876) *(G-667)*
Phoenix Color Corp 800 632-4111
40 Green Pond Rd Rockaway (07866) *(G-9485)*
Phoenix Container Inc 732 247-3931
6 Litho Rd Trenton (08648) *(G-10973)*
Phoenix Down Corporation 973 812-8100
85 Route 46 Totowa (07512) *(G-10844)*
Phoenix Friction Products, Middlesex *Also called KRs Automotive Dev Group Inc (G-6125)*
Phoenix Glass LLC 856 692-0100
615 Alvine Rd Pittsgrove (08318) *(G-8750)*
Phoenix Industrial LLC 908 955-0114
531 Route 22 E 194 Whitehouse Station (08889) *(G-11932)*
Phoenix Industries LLC 973 366-4199
105 W Dewey Ave Ste 204 Wharton (07885) *(G-11867)*
Phoenix Machine Rebuilders Inc 973 691-8029
4 Gold Mine Rd Roxbury Township (07836) *(G-9600)*
Phoenix Manufactoring Inc 732 380-1666
1306 Brielle Ave Ocean (07712) *(G-7675)*
Phoenix Packing & Gasket Co 732 938-7377
247 Old Tavern Rd Howell (07731) *(G-4549)*
Phoenix Pkg & Gasket Mfg Co, Howell *Also called Phoenix Packing & Gasket Co (G-4549)*
Phoenix Powder Coating LLC 973 907-7500
400 Union Ave Ste 2 Haskell (07420) *(G-4200)*
Phoenix Precision Co 973 208-8877
2963 State Rt 23 Newfoundland (07435) *(G-7331)*
Phoenix Resins Inc 888 627-3769
602 Union Landing Rd Cinnaminson (08077) *(G-1482)*
Phoenix Systems 201 788-5511
39 Morningside Ave North Haledon (07508) *(G-7499)*
Phoenix Tool & Machine Inc 856 753-5565
1044 Industrial Dr Ste 5 West Berlin (08091) *(G-11614)*
Photo Offset Prtg & Pubg Co 609 587-4900
536 Highway 33 Trenton (08619) *(G-10974)*
Photo Screen of N J, Carlstadt *Also called Screen Reproductions Co Inc (G-1214)*
Photographic Analysis Company (PA) 973 696-1000
190 Parish Dr Wayne (07470) *(G-11542)*
Photographic Tech Intl, Newton *Also called Mri International (G-7350)*
Photon Technology Intl, Birmingham *Also called Cgm Us Inc (G-456)*
Photonics Management Corp (HQ) 908 231-0960
360 Foothill Rd Bridgewater (08807) *(G-866)*
Photoscribe, Teaneck *Also called DBC Inc (G-10626)*
Pht Aerospace LLC (PA) 973 831-1230
230 W Parkway Ste 2 Pompton Plains (07444) *(G-8870)*
Physical Acoustics Corporation 609 716-4000
195 Clarksville Rd Princeton Junction (08550) *(G-9065)*
Physicans Educatn Resource LLC 609 378-3701
666 Plainsboro Rd Ste 300 Plainsboro (08536) *(G-8799)*
Physician's Weekly, Basking Ridge *Also called M/C Communications LLC (G-188)*
Physicians Weekly LLC (HQ) 908 766-0421
180 Mount Airy Rd Ste 205 Basking Ridge (07920) *(G-195)*
Physitemp Instruments, Clifton *Also called Micro-Tek Laboratories Inc (G-1669)*
Phytobologic Pharmaceutics LLC 856 975-0444
154 Cooper Rd Ste 202 West Berlin (08091) *(G-11615)*
Phytoceuticals Inc 201 791-2255
37 Midland Ave Ste 1 Elmwood Park (07407) *(G-2850)*
PI Metal Products Inc 201 955-0800
1717 Pennsylvania Ave Linden (07036) *(G-5408)*
Pic Corporation 908 862-7977
1101 W Elizabeth Ave Linden (07036) *(G-5409)*
Pic Graphics 201 420-5040
926 Newark Ave Ste 400 Jersey City (07306) *(G-4783)*
Pica Printings Inc 973 540-0420
103 Ridgedale Ave Ste 4 Morristown (07960) *(G-6693)*
Picasso Lighting Inds LLC 201 246-8188
46 Sellers St Kearny (07032) *(G-4893)*
Picture Framing Magazine, Freehold *Also called Hobby Publications Inc (G-3668)*
Picture It Awards, Edison *Also called Picture It Inc (G-2589)*

Picture It Inc 732 819-0420
1703 State Route 27 Ste 2 Edison (08817) *(G-2589)*
Picture Knits Inc 973 340-3131
489 Getty Ave Clifton (07011) *(G-1691)*
Picture Window Software LLC 908 362-4000
47 Cook Rd Blairstown (07825) *(G-487)*
Picut Industries Inc (PA) 908 754-1333
140 Mount Bethel Rd Warren (07059) *(G-11425)*
Picut Mfg Co Inc 908 754-1333
140 Mount Bethel Rd Warren (07059) *(G-11426)*
Piemonte & Liebhauser LLC 973 937-6200
25b Vreeland Rd Ste 104 Florham Park (07932) *(G-3519)*
Pierangeli Group Inc 856 582-4060
221 Jersey Ave Gloucester City (08030) *(G-3847)*
Pierce-Roberts Rubber Company 609 394-5245
1450 Heath Ave Ewing (08638) *(G-3052)*
Pierre Fbre Phrmaceuticals Inc 973 898-1042
8 Campus Dr Ste 2 Parsippany (07054) *(G-7989)*
Pierrepont & Co, Rutherford *Also called Highpont Corporation (G-9623)*
Pierson Industries Inc 973 627-7945
7 Astro Pl Rockaway (07866) *(G-9486)*
Pike Machine Products Inc 973 379-9128
17 Clive Hills Rd Short Hills (07078) *(G-9874)*
Pilkington North America Inc 973 470-5703
125 Kingsland Ave Clifton (07014) *(G-1692)*
Pilot Chemical Company Ohio 732 634-6613
267 Homestead Ave Avenel (07001) *(G-140)*
Pim Brands LLC 732 560-8300
500 Pierce St Somerset (08873) *(G-10053)*
Pim LLC 646 225-6666
742 Bergen Blvd Ridgefield (07657) *(G-9283)*
Pin Cancer Campaign 973 600-4170
34 County Road 519 Newton (07860) *(G-7353)*
Pin Express, Plainfield *Also called Edwin Leonel Ramirez (G-8764)*
Pin People LLC 888 309-7467
1 Paragon Dr Ste 150 Montvale (07645) *(G-6424)*
Pin Point Container Corp 856 848-2115
669 Tanyard Rd Deptford (08096) *(G-2065)*
Pine Hill Printing Inc 856 346-2915
200 Erial Rd Pine Hill (08021) *(G-8622)*
Pinelands Brewing Ltd Lblty Co 609 296-6169
140 7th Ave Unit 15 Ltl Egg Hbr (08087) *(G-5618)*
Pinnacle Cosmetic Packg LLC 908 241-7777
80 Market St Kenilworth (07033) *(G-4970)*
Pinnacle Cosmetics Packaging, Kenilworth *Also called Pinnacle Cosmetic Packg LLC (G-4970)*
Pinnacle Food Group Inc 856 969-7100
399 Jefferson Rd Parsippany (07054) *(G-7990)*
Pinnacle Foods Finance LLC (HQ) 973 541-6620
399 Jefferson Rd Parsippany (07054) *(G-7991)*
Pinnacle Foods Group LLC 856 969-7100
121 Woodcrest Rd Cherry Hill (08003) *(G-1409)*
Pinnacle Foods Group LLC (HQ) 856 969-8238
399 Jefferson Rd Parsippany (07054) *(G-7992)*
Pinnacle Foods Inc (HQ) 973 541-6620
399 Jefferson Rd Parsippany (07054) *(G-7993)*
Pinnacle Grphic Communications, Clifton *Also called J&E Business Services LLC (G-1645)*
Pinnacle Materials Inc (PA) 732 254-7676
39 Edgeboro Rd East Brunswick (08816) *(G-2165)*
Pinnacle Press Inc 201 652-0500
41 Prospect St Midland Park (07432) *(G-6182)*
Pinsonault Associates LLC 800 372-9009
5 Woodhollow Rd Ste 2 Parsippany (07054) *(G-7994)*
Pinto of Montville Inc 973 584-2002
25 Pine St Kenvil (07847) *(G-4994)*
Pinto Printing 856 232-2550
12 Sycamore Dr Blackwood (08012) *(G-477)*
Pioneer & Co Inc 856 866-9191
97 Foster Rd Ste 5 Moorestown (08057) *(G-6557)*
Pioneer Associates Inc (PA) 201 592-7007
2125 Center Ave Ste 305 Fort Lee (07024) *(G-3581)*
Pioneer Concrete Corp 609 693-6151
2011 Lacey Rd Forked River (08731) *(G-3542)*
Pioneer Embroidery Co 973 777-6418
31 Saddle River Ave South Hackensack (07606) *(G-10181)*
Pioneer Industries, Carlstadt *Also called Security Holdings LLC (G-1215)*
Pioneer Machine & Tool Co Inc 856 779-8800
425 E Broadway Maple Shade (08052) *(G-5868)*
Pioneer Power Solutions Inc (PA) 212 867-0700
400 Kelby St Ste 12 Fort Lee (07024) *(G-3582)*
Pioneer Railing Inc 609 387-0981
401 Railroad Ave Beverly (08010) *(G-453)*
PIP Printing, Butler *Also called My Way Prints Inc (G-1010)*
PIP Printing, Parsippany *Also called Conagraphics Inc (G-7908)*
PIP Printing, Paramus *Also called Barrington Press Inc (G-7792)*
PIP Printing, Livingston *Also called Morris Plains Pip Inc (G-5528)*
Pipe Dreams Marine LLC 609 628-9353
251 Mill Rd Tuckahoe (08250) *(G-11013)*

Pipeline Eqp Resources Co LLC.............................888 232-7372
9 Mars Ct Ste 4 Boonton (07005) *(G-564)*

Pipeline Renewal Technologies, Randolph Also called Envirosight LLC *(G-9176)*

Piper Heating and Cooling, Midland Park Also called Piper Services LLC *(G-6183)*

Piper Services LLC.............................844 567-3900
268 Greenwood Ave Midland Park (07432) *(G-6183)*

Piping Solutions Inc.............................732 537-1009
81 Chimney Rock Rd Ste 4 Bridgewater (08807) *(G-867)*

Piping Supplies Inc.............................609 561-9323
18 E Black Horse Pike Williamstown (08094) *(G-11968)*

Piramal Glass - Usa Inc (HQ).............................856 293-6400
329 Herrod Blvd Dayton (08810) *(G-1984)*

Piramal Glass - Usa Inc.............................856 728-9300
918 E Malaga Rd Williamstown (08094) *(G-11969)*

Piramal Glass - Usa Inc.............................856 293-6400
918 E Malaga Rd Williamstown (08094) *(G-11970)*

Pirate Brands LLC.............................973 401-6500
4 Gatehall Dr Ste 110 Parsippany (07054) *(G-7995)*

Pirates Booty, Parsippany Also called Pirate Brands LLC *(G-7995)*

Pirolli Printing Co Inc.............................856 933-1285
860 W Browning Rd Bellmawr (08031) *(G-341)*

Pitney Bowes Inc.............................908 903-2870
15 Mountainview Rd Warren (07059) *(G-11427)*

Pitney Bowes Inc.............................800 521-0080
158 Mount Olivet Ave Newark (07114) *(G-7230)*

Pitney Bowes Inc.............................856 764-2240
1835 Underwood Blvd Ste 1 Delran (08075) *(G-2019)*

Pixell Creative Group LLC.............................609 410-3024
302 Wood St Burlington (08016) *(G-982)*

Pj Food Service, Cranbury Also called Papa Johns New Jersey *(G-1869)*

Pjm Software Inc.............................973 330-0405
33 Mayer Dr Clifton (07012) *(G-1693)*

Pkc Finewoodworking LLC.............................201 951-8880
836 Main Rd Towaco (07082) *(G-10877)*

Pkm Panel Systems Corp.............................732 238-6760
4420 Bordentown Ave Old Bridge (08857) *(G-7724)*

Pl A Kadmonpharmaceuticals.............................732 230-3092
1 Deerpark Dr Monmouth Junction (08852) *(G-6302)*

Pl Custom Emergency Vehicles, Manasquan Also called P L Custom Body & Eqp Co Inc *(G-5836)*

Plagidos Winery LLC.............................609 567-4633
570 N 1st Rd Hammonton (08037) *(G-4141)*

Plan It Roi, Denville Also called Planitroi Inc *(G-2049)*

Planet Associates Inc.............................201 693-8700
24 Wampum Rd Park Ridge (07656) *(G-7858)*

Planet Popcorn LLC.............................732 294-8680
Freehold Mall Freehold (07728) *(G-3687)*

Planitroi Inc (PA).............................973 664-0700
100-10 Ford Rd Ste 10 Denville (07834) *(G-2049)*

Plant Food Company Inc.............................609 448-0935
38 Hightstwn Crnbry Sta Cranbury (08512) *(G-1872)*

Plantfusion.............................732 537-1220
3775 Park Ave Edison (08820) *(G-2590)*

Plaskolite New Jersey LLC.............................908 486-1000
1401 S Park Ave Linden (07036) *(G-5410)*

Plasma Powders & Systems Inc.............................732 431-0992
228 Boundary Rd Ste 2 Marlboro (07746) *(G-5909)*

Plast-O-Matic Valves Inc.............................973 256-3000
1384 Pompton Ave Ste 1 Cedar Grove (07009) *(G-1287)*

Plastasonics Inc.............................732 998-8361
235 Hickory Ln Ste B Bayville (08721) *(G-250)*

Plasti Foam.............................908 722-5254
68 County Line Rd Branchburg (08876) *(G-668)*

Plastic By All LLC.............................732 785-5900
1127 Industrial Pkwy B Brick (08724) *(G-729)*

Plastic Plus Group LLC.............................862 701-6981
7 Eastmans Rd Parsippany (07054) *(G-7996)*

Plastic Plus Inc.............................973 614-0271
184 Willet St Passaic (07055) *(G-8095)*

Plastic Profiles Co Div, Parsippany Also called Central Plastics Incorporated *(G-7899)*

Plastic Reel Corp of America (PA).............................201 933-5100
40 Triangle Blvd Carlstadt (07072) *(G-1202)*

Plastic Specialties & Tech Inc (HQ).............................201 941-2900
101 Railroad Ave Ridgefield (07657) *(G-9284)*

Plastico Products LLC.............................973 923-1944
34 Loretto St Irvington (07111) *(G-4582)*

Plastics Consulting & Mfg Co.............................800 222-0317
1435 Ferry Ave Camden (08104) *(G-1083)*

Plastics For Chemicals Inc (PA).............................609 242-9100
710 Old Shore Rd Forked River (08731) *(G-3543)*

Plastics Galore LLC.............................732 363-8447
1970 Swarthmore Ave Ste 8 Lakewood (08701) *(G-5147)*

Plastiform Packaging Inc.............................973 983-8900
114 Beach St Ste 6 Rockaway (07866) *(G-9487)*

Plastinetics Inc.............................818 364-1611
439 Main Rd Towaco (07082) *(G-10878)*

Plastinetics Inc.............................973 618-9090
195 Fairfield Ave West Caldwell (07006) *(G-11672)*

Plastpac Inc (PA).............................908 272-7200
30 Boright Ave Kenilworth (07033) *(G-4971)*

Plastpro 2000 Inc.............................973 992-2090
9 Peach Tree Hill Rd Livingston (07039) *(G-5536)*

Plastpro Doors, Livingston Also called Plastpro 2000 Inc *(G-5536)*

Plate Concepts Inc.............................908 236-9570
1221 Us Highway 22 Ste 3 Lebanon (08833) *(G-5273)*

Platinum Designs LLC.............................908 782-4010
93 Rake Rd Flemington (08822) *(G-3459)*

Platinum Plating Specialists.............................732 221-2575
11 Blake Dr Clark (07066) *(G-1513)*

Platon Interiors.............................201 567-5533
180 S Van Brunt St Englewood (07631) *(G-2932)*

Platypus Print Productions LLC.............................732 772-1212
253 State Route 79 N Morganville (07751) *(G-6594)*

Plcs LLC.............................856 722-1333
102 Gaither Dr Ste 1 Mount Laurel (08054) *(G-6790)*

Pleasant, Point Pleasant Beach Also called Norma K Corporation *(G-8829)*

Plescia & Company Inc.............................856 793-0137
205 Shady Ln Marlton (08053) *(G-5947)*

Plextone, Kenilworth Also called Seagrave Coatings Corp *(G-4976)*

Plexus Publishing Inc.............................609 654-6500
143 Old Marlton Pike Medford (08055) *(G-6031)*

Plumbing Supply Now LLC.............................732 228-8852
167 Black Horse Ln New Brunswick (08902) *(G-6958)*

Plus Packaging Inc.............................973 538-2216
10 Mount Pleasant Rd Morristown (07960) *(G-6694)*

Plx Pharma Inc.............................973 409-6541
9 Fishers Ln Ste E Sparta (07871) *(G-10406)*

PM Pool Service, Scotch Plains Also called Izzo Enterprises Inc *(G-9735)*

PM Swapco Inc.............................201 438-7700
1099 Wall St W Ste 390 Lyndhurst (07071) *(G-5672)*

PMC, Midland Park Also called Precision Multiple Contrls Inc *(G-6185)*

Pmc Inc.............................201 933-8540
13 Manor Rd East Rutherford (07073) *(G-2310)*

PMC Group Inc (PA).............................856 533-1866
1288 Route 73 Ste 401 Mount Laurel (08054) *(G-6791)*

PMC Group Polymer Products, Mount Laurel Also called Polymer Products Company Inc *(G-6792)*

PMC Industries Inc.............................201 342-3684
275 Hudson St Hackensack (07601) *(G-3964)*

PMC Liquiflo Equipment Co Inc.............................908 518-0666
443 North Ave Garwood (07027) *(G-3791)*

PMC Thermocouple Division, Saddle Brook Also called Te Wire & Cable LLC *(G-9683)*

Pmje Welding LLC.............................973 685-7344
310 Colfax Ave Unit A Clifton (07013) *(G-1694)*

Pmm Inc.............................908 692-1465
11 Lafayette Ky Colts Neck (07722) *(G-1786)*

Pmp Composites Corporation.............................609 587-1188
572 Whitehead Rd Ste 101 Trenton (08619) *(G-10975)*

Pmv Pharmaceuticals Inc.............................650 241-2822
8 Clarke Dr Ste 3 Cranbury (08512) *(G-1873)*

PNC Electronics Inc.............................973 237-0400
20 W End Rd Totowa (07512) *(G-10845)*

PNC Inc.............................973 284-1600
115 E Centre St Nutley (07110) *(G-7592)*

Pny Technologies Inc (PA).............................973 515-9700
100 Jefferson Rd Parsippany (07054) *(G-7997)*

Pochet of America Inc.............................973 942-4923
1 Garret Mountain Plz # 502 Woodland Park (07424) *(G-12086)*

Point Lobster Company Inc.............................732 892-1718
1 Saint Louis Ave Point Pleasant Beach (08742) *(G-8831)*

Poland Spring, Jersey City Also called Nestle Waters North Amer Inc *(G-4769)*

Polar Truck Sales.............................201 246-1010
350 Sip Ave Jersey City (07306) *(G-4784)*

Polaris America Ltd Lblty Co.............................614 540-1710
1985 Rutgers Blvd Lakewood (08701) *(G-5148)*

Polaris Consulting & Svcs Ltd.............................732 590-8151
111 Town Square Pl # 340 Jersey City (07310) *(G-4785)*

Polaris Plate Heat Exchngers L.............................732 345-7188
1151 Broad St Ste 218 Shrewsbury (07702) *(G-9899)*

Polaris Plating Inc.............................973 278-0033
36 Teaneck Rd Parsippany (07054) *(G-7998)*

Polaris Thermal, Shrewsbury Also called Polaris Plate Heat Exchngers L *(G-9899)*

Polarity LLC.............................732 970-3855
330 Mockingbird Ln Morganville (07751) *(G-6595)*

Polish Nail.............................732 627-9799
570 Union Ave Middlesex (08846) *(G-6139)*

Polish Press, Mahwah Also called Missionary Society of St Paul *(G-5755)*

Polmar Iron Work Inc.............................732 882-0900
673 New Brunswick Ave Rahway (07065) *(G-9121)*

Polo Machine Inc (PA).............................973 340-9984
223 Banta Ave Garfield (07026) *(G-3757)*

Polvac Inc.............................732 828-1662
235 Jersey Ave Ste 1 New Brunswick (08901) *(G-6959)*

Poly Bag Division, Hamburg Also called Dauson Corrugated Container *(G-4089)*

Poly Molding LLC.............................973 835-7161
96 4th Ave Haskell (07420) *(G-4201)*

Poly Source Enterprises LLC 732 580-5409
  17 Duchess Ct Freehold (07728) *(G-3688)*

Poly-Dyn International, South Plainfield *Also called Polymer Dynamix LLC* *(G-10312)*

Poly-Gel LLC 973 884-3300
  30 Leslie Ct Whippany (07981) *(G-11904)*

Poly-Smith Ptfe LLC 732 287-0610
  21 Industrial Dr Keyport (07735) *(G-5004)*

Poly-Version Inc 201 451-7600
  49 Fisk St Jersey City (07305) *(G-4786)*

Polyair Inter Pack Inc 201 804-1725
  495 Meadow Ln Carlstadt (07072) *(G-1203)*

Polyair Inter Pack Inc 201 804-1700
  495 Meadow Ln Carlstadt (07072) *(G-1204)*

Polycast, Hackensack *Also called Spartech LLC* *(G-3977)*

Polycel Structural Foam Inc 908 722-5254
  60 Readington Rd Branchburg (08876) *(G-669)*

Polycel Structural Foam Inc 908 722-5254
  68 County Line Rd Branchburg (08876) *(G-670)*

Polyfil Corporation 973 627-4070
  74 Green Pond Rd Rockaway (07866) *(G-9488)*

Polygel, Whippany *Also called Poly-Gel LLC* *(G-11904)*

Polymathes Holdings I LLC (PA) 609 945-1690
  20 Nassau St Ste M Princeton (08542) *(G-8996)*

Polymer Additives Inc 856 467-8247
  170 Us Route 130 S Bridgeport (08014) *(G-743)*

Polymer Additives Inc 856 467-8220
  170 Us 130 Swedesboro (08085) *(G-10602)*

Polymer Dynamix LLC 732 381-1600
  1000 Coolidge St South Plainfield (07080) *(G-10312)*

Polymer Molded Products 732 907-1990
  10 Easy St Bound Brook (08805) *(G-604)*

Polymer Products Company Inc 856 533-1866
  1288 Route 73 Ste 401 Mount Laurel (08054) *(G-6792)*

Polymer Technologies Inc 973 778-9100
  10 Clifton Blvd Ste 3 Clifton (07011) *(G-1695)*

Polymeric Resources Corp (PA) 973 694-4141
  55 Haul Rd Ste A Wayne (07470) *(G-11543)*

Polymite, Allenhurst *Also called Koadings Inc* *(G-22)*

Polyorganic Technoligies Corp 609 288-8233
  26 Kennedy Blvd Ste C East Brunswick (08816) *(G-2166)*

Polysystems Inc 312 332-5670
  2 Executive Campus # 320 Cherry Hill (08002) *(G-1410)*

Polytech Designs Inc 973 340-1390
  26 W 1st St Clifton (07011) *(G-1696)*

Polytechnic Industries Inc 856 235-6550
  14 Roland Ave Mount Laurel (08054) *(G-6793)*

Polytype America Corp 201 995-1000
  600 Ryerson Rd Ste M Lincoln Park (07035) *(G-5304)*

Polyvel Inc 609 567-0080
  100 9th St Hammonton (08037) *(G-4142)*

Pom Gear, Linden *Also called Cellular Empire Inc* *(G-5331)*

Pomi USA Inc 732 541-4115
  253 Main St Ste 380 Matawan (07747) *(G-5985)*

Pompton Lakes Quarry, Pompton Lakes *Also called Tilcon New York Inc* *(G-8855)*

Poof-Alex Holdings LLC 734 454-9552
  40 Lane Rd Fairfield (07004) *(G-3292)*

Pool Ladder, Hackensack *Also called Kayden Manufacturing Inc* *(G-3935)*

Pool Tables Plus Inc (PA) 732 968-8228
  299 Us Highway 22 Ste 24 Green Brook (08812) *(G-3866)*

Poor Boy Pallet LLC 856 451-3771
  45 Finley Rd Bridgeton (08302) *(G-770)*

Poplar Bindery Inc 856 727-8030
  300 Mill St Moorestown (08057) *(G-6558)*

Popularity Products, Carteret *Also called New York Popular Inc* *(G-1260)*

Por-15 Inc 973 887-1999
  64 S Jefferson Rd Ste 2 Whippany (07981) *(G-11905)*

Porfirio Foods Inc 609 393-4116
  320 Anderson St Trenton (08611) *(G-10976)*

Port A (PA) 732 776-6511
  911 Kingsley St Asbury Park (07712) *(G-81)*

Portable Container Services, Roseland *Also called Granco Group LLC* *(G-9539)*

Portable Defense LLC 856 228-3010
  54 Gravers Ln Blackwood (08012) *(G-478)*

Portaseal LLC 973 539-0100
  1 John St Morristown (07960) *(G-6695)*

Porton Usa LLC (HQ) 908 791-9100
  3001 Hadley Rd Ste 1-4 South Plainfield (07080) *(G-10313)*

Portuguese Baking Company Inc 973 466-0118
  221 Malvern St Newark (07105) *(G-7231)*

Post To Post LLC 609 646-9300
  2545 Fire Rd Ste 1 Egg Harbor Township (08234) *(G-2693)*

Postage Bin 732 333-0915
  31 E Main St Ste 4 Freehold (07728) *(G-3689)*

Potdevin Machine Co 973 227-8828
  26 Fairfield Pl West Caldwell (07006) *(G-11673)*

Potters Industries LLC 201 507-4169
  600 Industrial Rd Carlstadt (07072) *(G-1205)*

Potti-Bags Inc 201 796-5555
  120 Ackerman Ave Elmwood Park (07407) *(G-2851)*

Pov Reports, Montclair *Also called P O V Incorporated* *(G-6381)*

Power Apparel LLC 516 442-1333
  40 Chestnut St Ste 13 Lakewood (08701) *(G-5149)*

Power Bag and Film LLC 908 832-6648
  189 W Valley Brook Rd Califon (07830) *(G-1033)*

Power Brooks Co LLC 609 890-0100
  2 Marlen Dr Hamilton (08691) *(G-4120)*

Power By Gogreen, Howell *Also called Gogreen Power Inc* *(G-4540)*

Power Container Corp 732 560-3655
  33 Schoolhouse Rd Ste 2 Somerset (08873) *(G-10054)*

Power Dynamics Inc 973 560-0019
  145 Algonquin Pkwy Ste 2 Whippany (07981) *(G-11906)*

Power Hawk Technologies Inc 973 627-4646
  300 Forge Way Ste 2 Rockaway (07866) *(G-9489)*

Power Home Rmdlg Group LLC 610 874-5000
  485 Us Highway 1 S C Iselin (08830) *(G-4623)*

Power Magne-Tech Corp 732 826-4700
  653 Sayre Ave Perth Amboy (08861) *(G-8529)*

Power Magnetic, Perth Amboy *Also called Power Magne-Tech Corp* *(G-8529)*

Power Magnetics Inc (PA) 609 695-1170
  377 Reservoir St Trenton (08618) *(G-10977)*

Power Magnetics Inc 800 747-0845
  377 Reservoir St Trenton (08618) *(G-10978)*

Power Packaging Services Corp 201 261-2566
  20 Park Pl Paramus (07652) *(G-7827)*

Power Photo Corp (PA) 732 200-1645
  40 Montgomery St Hillside (07205) *(G-4420)*

Power Pool Plus Inc 908 454-1124
  7 Edge Rd Alpha (08865) *(G-40)*

Power Products and Engrg LLC 855 769-3751
  324 Meadowbrook Rd Trenton (08691) *(G-10979)*

Powercomm Solutions LLC 908 806-7025
  15 Minneakoning Rd # 311 Flemington (08822) *(G-3460)*

Powerhuse Frmltons Ltd Labilit 888 666-7715
  150 Maple Ave Ste 216 South Plainfield (07080) *(G-10314)*

Powers Powershot Photo, Hillside *Also called Power Photo Corp* *(G-4420)*

Powerspec Inc 732 494-9490
  25 4th St Somerville (08876) *(G-10123)*

Powertrunk Inc (HQ) 201 630-4520
  66 York St Ste 4 Jersey City (07302) *(G-4787)*

Powerwash Plus 732 671-6767
  25 Oriole Rd Middletown (07748) *(G-6166)*

Powtek Powder Coating Inc 609 394-1144
  233 Dickinson St Ewing (08638) *(G-3053)*

Ppe, Trenton *Also called Power Products and Engrg LLC* *(G-10979)*

PPG Auto Glass, Pennsauken *Also called PPG Industries Inc* *(G-8469)*

PPG Industries Inc 856 273-7870
  823 E Gate Dr Ste 4 Mount Laurel (08054) *(G-6794)*

PPG Industries Inc 856 662-9323
  75 Twinbridge Dr Ste C Pennsauken (08110) *(G-8469)*

Ppi/Time Zero Inc (HQ) 973 278-6500
  11 Madison Rd Fairfield (07004) *(G-3293)*

PQ Corporation 732 750-9040
  2 Paddock St Avenel (07001) *(G-141)*

PR Products Distributors Inc 973 928-1120
  189 Berdan Ave Ste 281 Wayne (07470) *(G-11544)*

Prads, Parsippany *Also called Predictive Analytcs Dcision* *(G-8000)*

Pratt Displays, Allendale *Also called Pratt Industries USA Inc* *(G-13)*

Pratt Industries USA Inc 201 934-1900
  3 Pearl Ct Unit 3f Allendale (07401) *(G-13)*

Praxair Inc 732 738-4150
  60 Crows Mill Rd Keasbey (08832) *(G-4914)*

Praxair Cryomag Services Inc 732 738-4000
  Industrial Ave Keasbey (08832) *(G-4915)*

Praxair Distribution Inc 908 862-7200
  515 E Edgar Rd Linden (07036) *(G-5411)*

Praxair Distribution Inc 973 589-7895
  425 Avenue P Newark (07105) *(G-7232)*

PRC Laser Corporation 973 347-0100
  111 Howard Blvd Ste 170 Mount Arlington (07856) *(G-6718)*

PRC of America, Carlstadt *Also called Plastic Reel Corp of America* *(G-1202)*

Pre-Fab Structures Inc (PA) 856 768-4257
  907 Wedgewood Way Atco (08004) *(G-87)*

Preachers Illustration Service, Ventnor City *Also called Voicings Publication Inc* *(G-11155)*

Precast Manufacturing Co LLC 908 454-2122
  187 Strykers Rd Phillipsburg (08865) *(G-8569)*

Precast Systems Inc 609 208-0569
  57 Sharon Station Rd Allentown (08501) *(G-29)*

Precious Cosmetics Packaging 973 478-4633
  40 Meta Ln Lodi (07644) *(G-5573)*

Precious Metal Processing Cons 201 944-8053
  430 Bergen Blvd Palisades Park (07650) *(G-7777)*

Precise Cmpnents TI Design Inc 973 928-2928
  10 Clifton Blvd Unit A4 Clifton (07011) *(G-1697)*

Precise Continental, Harrison *Also called Precise Corporate Printing Inc* *(G-4177)*

Precise Corporate Printing Inc 973 350-0330
  1 Cape May St Ste 250 Harrison (07029) *(G-4177)*

Precise Technology Inc 856 241-1760
  406 Heron Dr Ste A Swedesboro (08085) *(G-10603)*

Precision, Wayne *Also called Jrz Enterprises LLC* ***(G-11526)***
Precision Ball Specialties......856 881-5646
1451 Glassboro Rd Williamstown (08094) ***(G-11971)***
Precision Dealer Services Inc......908 237-1100
4 Ryerson Rd Flemington (08822) ***(G-3461)***
Precision Devices Inc......609 882-2230
20 Lexington Ave Ste 3 Ewing (08618) ***(G-3054)***
Precision Electronic Glass Inc......856 691-2234
1013 Hendee Rd Vineland (08360) ***(G-11254)***
Precision Filaments Inc......732 462-3755
17 Bannard St Ste 30 Freehold (07728) ***(G-3690)***
Precision Forms Inc......973 838-3800
97 Decker Rd Butler (07405) ***(G-1012)***
Precision Graphics Inc......908 707-8880
21 County Line Rd Branchburg (08876) ***(G-671)***
Precision Metal Machining Inc......201 843-7427
800 Central Blvd Ste C Carlstadt (07072) ***(G-1206)***
Precision Metalcrafters Inc......856 629-1020
17 Filbert St Williamstown (08094) ***(G-11972)***
Precision Mfg Group LLC (HQ)......973 785-4630
501 Little Falls Rd Cedar Grove (07009) ***(G-1288)***
Precision Multiple Contrls Inc (PA)......201 444-0600
33 Greenwood Ave Midland Park (07432) ***(G-6184)***
Precision Multiple Contrls Inc......201 444-0600
33 Greenwood Ave Midland Park (07432) ***(G-6185)***
Precision Optical Lab, Williamstown *Also called Spectacle Shoppe* ***(G-11980)***
Precision Orthotic Lab of Nj......856 848-6226
1595 Imperial Way Ste 103 West Deptford (08066) ***(G-11714)***
Precision Press, Garwood *Also called New Jersey Reprographics Inc* ***(G-3786)***
Precision Printing Group Inc......856 753-0900
606 Stamford Dr # 606 Mount Laurel (08054) ***(G-6795)***
Precision Products Co Inc......201 712-5757
219 Hergesell Ave Maywood (07607) ***(G-6014)***
Precision Roll Products Inc......973 822-9100
306 Columbia Tpke Florham Park (07932) ***(G-3520)***
Precision Saw & Tool Corp......973 773-7302
56 Colfax Ave Clifton (07013) ***(G-1698)***
Precision Shape Solutions, Dover *Also called Service Metal Fabricating Inc* ***(G-2106)***
Precision Specialties, Belleville *Also called Communique Inc* ***(G-293)***
Precision Spine Inc (PA)......601 420-4244
5 Sylvan Way Ste 2 Parsippany (07054) ***(G-7999)***
Precision Textiles LLC (PA)......973 890-3873
200 Maltese Dr Totowa (07512) ***(G-10846)***
Precision Welding, Wharton *Also called James A Stanlick Jr* ***(G-11860)***
Precision Welding Machine......609 625-1465
13th St Mays Landing (08330) ***(G-5998)***
Precision-Tech LLC......609 517-2718
931 8th St Hammonton (08037) ***(G-4143)***
Predictive Analytcs Dcision......973 541-7020
2001 Route 46 Ste 310 Parsippany (07054) ***(G-8000)***
Preferred Plastics Inc......856 662-6250
6512 Park Ave Pennsauken (08109) ***(G-8470)***
Preform Laboratories Inc......973 523-8610
34 George St Hackensack (07601) ***(G-3965)***
Prem-Khichi Enterprises Inc......973 242-0300
9 Colburn Rd East Brunswick (08816) ***(G-2167)***
Premac Inc......732 381-7550
167 Wescott Dr Rahway (07065) ***(G-9122)***
Premesco Inc......908 686-0513
2389 Vauxhall Rd Union (07083) ***(G-11084)***
Premesco Seamless Ring Co Div, Union *Also called Premesco Inc* ***(G-11084)***
Premier Asset Logistics Networ (PA)......877 725-6381
100 N Black Horse Pike # 100 Williamstown (08094) ***(G-11973)***
Premier Compaction Systems......718 328-5990
264 Lackawanna Ave Ste 1 Woodland Park (07424) ***(G-12087)***
Premier Die Casting Company......732 634-3000
1177 Rahway Ave Avenel (07001) ***(G-142)***
Premier Graphics Inc......732 872-9933
165 1st Ave C Atlantic Highlands (07716) ***(G-110)***
Premier Marble and Gran 2 Inc......732 294-7891
200 Commerce Ave Ste 200 # 200 Freehold (07728) ***(G-3691)***
Premier Press Inc......856 665-0722
7120 Airport Hwy Pennsauken (08109) ***(G-8471)***
Premier Printing Solutions LLC......732 525-0740
513 S Pine Ave South Amboy (08879) ***(G-10139)***
Premier Products Inc......856 231-1800
1002 Lincoln Dr W Ste B Marlton (08053) ***(G-5948)***
Premier Ribbon Company......973 589-2600
223 Raymond Blvd Newark (07105) ***(G-7233)***
Premier Specialties Inc......732 469-6615
201 Egel Ave Ste 3a Middlesex (08846) ***(G-6140)***
Premier Supplies, Secaucus *Also called Print By Premier LLC* ***(G-9799)***
Premiere Raceway Sys LLC......732 629-7715
230 Saint Nicholas Ave Piscataway (08854) ***(G-8701)***
Premio Foods Inc (PA)......800 864-7622
50 Utter Ave Hawthorne (07506) ***(G-4240)***
Premium Clor Graphics Handpack, Carlstadt *Also called Premium Color Group LLC* ***(G-1207)***
Premium Color Group LLC......973 472-7007
651 Garden St Carlstadt (07072) ***(G-1207)***
Premium Imports Inc......718 486-7125
90 Dayton Ave Ste 98 Passaic (07055) ***(G-8096)***
Premium Service Printing......908 707-1311
46 Old Camplain Rd Hillsborough (08844) ***(G-4345)***
Prentco, Flemington *Also called Printco* ***(G-3464)***
Presbyterian Reformed Pubg Co......908 454-0505
1102 Marble Hill Rd Phillipsburg (08865) ***(G-8570)***
Prescription Dynamics Inc......201 746-6262
310 Ridge Rd Mahwah (07430) ***(G-5762)***
Prescription Podiatry Labs......609 695-1221
826 S Broad St Trenton (08611) ***(G-10980)***
Presentation Solutions Inc......732 961-1960
432 Clearstream Rd Jackson (08527) ***(G-4662)***
President Cont Group II LLC (PA)......201 933-7500
200 W Commercial Ave Moonachie (07074) ***(G-6484)***
Presperse Corporation (PA)......732 356-5200
19 Schoolhouse Rd Somerset (08873) ***(G-10055)***
Press of Atlantic City, Vineland *Also called South Jersey Publishing Co* ***(G-11267)***
Press of Atlantic City, The, Pleasantville *Also called South Jersey Publishing Co* ***(G-8819)***
Press of Atlantic City, The, Pleasantville *Also called Wilmington Trust Sp Services* ***(G-8821)***
Press Room Inc......609 689-3817
100 Youngs Rd Ste 2 Trenton (08619) ***(G-10981)***
Pressto Graphics......732 286-9300
109 Foxwood Ter Toms River (08755) ***(G-10784)***
Pressure Controls Inc......973 751-5002
406 Cortlandt St Belleville (07109) ***(G-308)***
Pressure Pipe Division, Burlington *Also called United States Pipe Fndry LLC* ***(G-991)***
Pressure Wash, West Milford *Also called Margaritaville Inc* ***(G-11729)***
Pressworks......856 427-9001
1879 Old Cuthbert Rd # 28 Cherry Hill (08034) ***(G-1411)***
Prestige Associates Inc......609 393-1509
39 Meade St Trenton (08638) ***(G-10982)***
Prestige Bread Jersey Cy Inc......201 422-7900
5601-5711 Tonnelle Ave North Bergen (07047) ***(G-7430)***
Prestige Camera LLC......718 257-5888
245 Belmont Dr Somerset (08873) ***(G-10056)***
Prestige Forklift Maint Svc......732 297-1001
31 Timber Ridge Rd New Brunswick (08902) ***(G-6960)***
Prestige Industries LLC......866 492-2244
1099 Wall St W Ste 353 Lyndhurst (07071) ***(G-5673)***
Prestige Laboratories Inc......973 772-8922
100 Oak St East Rutherford (07073) ***(G-2311)***
Prestige Millwork LLC......908 526-5100
27e Kearney St Ste B Bridgewater (08807) ***(G-868)***
Presto Printing Service Inc......908 756-5337
19 S Plainfield Ave South Plainfield (07080) ***(G-10315)***
Prestone Press LLC......347 468-7900
29 Brook Ave 1 Maywood (07607) ***(G-6015)***
Prestone Printing Company, Maywood *Also called Prestone Press LLC* ***(G-6015)***
Prestone Products Corporation......732 431-8200
Halls Mill Rd Freehold (07728) ***(G-3692)***
Prestone Products Corporation......732 577-7800
250 Halls Mill Rd Freehold (07728) ***(G-3693)***
Pretium Packaging LLC......314 727-8200
208 Cougar Ct Hillsborough (08844) ***(G-4346)***
Pretty Jewelry Co......908 806-3377
80 Main St 82 Flemington (08822) ***(G-3462)***
Pretty Lil Cupcakes......201 256-1205
317 Essex St Harrison (07029) ***(G-4178)***
Pretty Ugly LLC......908 620-0931
20 Olcott Sq Bernardsville (07924) ***(G-442)***
Prg Group Inc......201 758-4000
915 Secaucus Rd Secaucus (07094) ***(G-9798)***
Priamo Designs Ltd......201 861-8808
6614 Broadway West New York (07093) ***(G-11749)***
Pride Products Mfg LLC......908 353-1900
5 Slater Dr Elizabeth (07206) ***(G-2770)***
Prima-TEC Electronics Corp......201 947-4052
316 Main St East Rutherford (07073) ***(G-2312)***
Primacy Engineering Inc (PA)......201 731-3272
560 Sylvan Ave Ste 1212 Englewood Cliffs (07632) ***(G-2988)***
Primak Plumbing & Heating Inc......732 270-6282
904 Dorset Psge Toms River (08753) ***(G-10785)***
Primal Surf......609 264-1999
3106 Revere Blvd Brigantine (08203) ***(G-912)***
Primary Systems Inc......732 679-2200
30 State Route 18 Old Bridge (08857) ***(G-7725)***
Prime Choice Foods, Passaic *Also called House of Herbs I LLC* ***(G-8073)***
Prime Coding Services LLC......732 254-3036
58 Frost Ave East Brunswick (08816) ***(G-2168)***
Prime Fur & Leather Inc......201 941-9600
29 Industrial Ave 31 Fairview (07022) ***(G-3368)***
Prime Ingredients Inc......201 791-6655
280 N Midland Ave Ste 340 Saddle Brook (07663) ***(G-9670)***
Prime Rebar LLC......908 707-1234
36 Adamsville Rd Bridgewater (08807) ***(G-869)***

Prime Time International Co (PA) 623 780-8600	
500 Frank W Burr Blvd # 24 Teaneck (07666) *(G-10647)*	
Primepak Company, Teaneck *Also called JA Heilferty LLC* *(G-10635)*	
Primepoint LLC 609 298-7373	
2 Springside Rd Westampton (08060) *(G-11789)*	
Primesource Building Pdts Inc 732 296-0600	
20 Van Dyke Ave New Brunswick (08901) *(G-6961)*	
Primetime Trading Corp 646 580-8223	
148 E 5th St Bayonne (07002) *(G-231)*	
Primex Color Compounding (HQ) 800 282-7933	
61 River Dr Garfield (07026) *(G-3758)*	
Primex Plastics Corporation 973 470-8000	
65 River Dr Garfield (07026) *(G-3759)*	
Primo Division, Irvington *Also called Jersey Plastic Molders Inc* *(G-4578)*	
Prince Agri Products Inc (HQ) 201 329-7300	
300 Frank W Burr Blvd Teaneck (07666) *(G-10648)*	
Prince Black Distillery Inc 212 695-6187	
691 Clifton Ave Clifton (07011) *(G-1699)*	
Prince Chikovani Inc 347 622-2789	
363 Avenue A Fl 1 Bayonne (07002) *(G-232)*	
Prince Sports Inc 609 291-5800	
334 Rising Sun Rd Bordentown (08505) *(G-593)*	
Prince Sterilization Svcs LLC 973 227-6882	
122 Fairfield Rd Fairfield (07004) *(G-3294)*	
Prince-Chikovani, Bayonne *Also called Prince Chikovani Inc* *(G-232)*	
Princetel Inc (PA) 609 588-8801	
2560 E State Street Ext Hamilton (08619) *(G-4121)*	
Princeton Alumni Weekly, Princeton *Also called Princton Almni Pblications Inc* *(G-9008)*	
Princeton Biomeditech Corp 908 281-0112	
75 Orchard Rd Skillman (08558) *(G-9926)*	
Princeton Biomeditech Corp (PA) 732 274-1000	
4242 Us Highway 1 Monmouth Junction (08852) *(G-6303)*	
Princeton Biopharma Strategies 609 203-5303	
660 Pretty Brook Rd Princeton (08540) *(G-8997)*	
Princeton Blue Inc 908 369-0961	
5 Independence Way # 300 Princeton (08540) *(G-8998)*	
Princeton Chromatography Inc 609 860-1803	
1206 S River Rd Ste 1 Cranbury (08512) *(G-1874)*	
Princeton Enduring Biotech Inc 732 406-3041	
190 Major Rd Monmouth Junction (08852) *(G-6304)*	
Princeton Enduring Biotech Inc 732 406-3041	
190 Major Rd Monmouth Junction (08852) *(G-6305)*	
Princeton Hosted Solutions LLC 856 470-2350	
30 Washington Ave Ste D2 Haddonfield (08033) *(G-4062)*	
Princeton Identity Inc 609 256-6994	
300 Horizon Center Blvd # 304 Hamilton (08691) *(G-4122)*	
Princeton Information Center 609 924-7019	
330 N Harrison St Ste 6 Princeton (08540) *(G-8999)*	
Princeton Keynes Group Inc (PA) 609 951-2239	
116 Village Blvd Ste 200 Princeton (08540) *(G-9000)*	
Princeton Keynes Group Inc 609 208-1777	
470 Mulberry St Newark (07114) *(G-7234)*	
Princeton Lightwave Inc 609 495-2600	
2555 Route 130 Ste 1 Cranbury (08512) *(G-1875)*	
Princeton Microwave Technology 609 586-8140	
5 Nami Ln Ste 1 Trenton (08619) *(G-10983)*	
Princeton Packet Inc (HQ) 609 924-3244	
300 Witherspoon St Princeton (08542) *(G-9001)*	
Princeton Power Systems Inc 609 955-5390	
3175 Princeton Pike Lawrenceville (08648) *(G-5242)*	
Princeton Publishing Group 609 577-0693	
650 Rosedale Rd Princeton (08540) *(G-9002)*	
Princeton Quadrangle Club 609 258-0376	
33 Prospect Ave Princeton (08540) *(G-9003)*	
Princeton Research Instruments 609 924-0570	
42 Cherry Valley Rd Princeton (08540) *(G-9004)*	
Princeton Separations Inc 732 431-3338	
100 Commerce Ave Freehold (07728) *(G-3694)*	
Princeton Supply Corp 609 683-9100	
301 N Harrison St Ste 473 Princeton (08540) *(G-9005)*	
Princeton Tech Group Intl Corp 732 328-9308	
182 Whitman Ave Edison (08817) *(G-2591)*	
Princeton Tectonics 609 298-9331	
110 Collings Ave West Berlin (08091) *(G-11616)*	
Princeton Tectonics (PA) 609 298-9331	
1777 Hylton Rd Pennsauken (08110) *(G-8472)*	
Princeton Trade and Technology 609 683-0215	
1 Wall St Princeton (08540) *(G-9006)*	
Princeton University Press (PA) 609 258-4900	
41 William St Ste 1 Princeton (08540) *(G-9007)*	
Princetonian Graphics Inc 732 329-8282	
45 Stouts Ln Ste 4 Monmouth Junction (08852) *(G-6306)*	
Princton Almni Pblications Inc 609 258-4885	
194 Nassau St Ste 38 Princeton (08542) *(G-9008)*	
Print By Premier LLC 212 947-1365	
525 Windsor Dr Secaucus (07094) *(G-9799)*	
Print Cbf, Cedar Knolls *Also called Commercial Business Forms Inc* *(G-1302)*	
Print Communications Group Inc 973 882-9444	
175 Us Highway 46 Unit A Fairfield (07004) *(G-3295)*	

Print Factory Ltd Liability Co 973 866-5230	
730 Clifton Ave Clifton (07013) *(G-1700)*	
Print Factory Nyc, Clifton *Also called Print Factory Ltd Liability Co* *(G-1700)*	
Print Group Inc 201 487-4400	
24 E Wesley St South Hackensack (07606) *(G-10182)*	
Print Group The, South Hackensack *Also called Print Group Inc* *(G-10182)*	
Print Mail Communications LLC 856 488-0345	
7025 Colonial Hwy Ste 2 Pennsauken (08109) *(G-8473)*	
Print Media LLC 973 467-0007	
232 Morris Ave Springfield (07081) *(G-10460)*	
Print Peel 201 507-0080	
341 Michele Pl Carlstadt (07072) *(G-1208)*	
Print Post 973 732-0950	
274 Chestnut St Newark (07105) *(G-7235)*	
Print Shop, Trenton *Also called New Jersey Department Treasury* *(G-10962)*	
Print Shop, The, Matawan *Also called Agau Inc* *(G-5967)*	
Print Shoppe Inc 908 782-9213	
15 Minneakoning Rd # 305 Flemington (08822) *(G-3463)*	
Print Signs and Designs, Bridgeton *Also called Burdol Inc* *(G-755)*	
Print Solutions LLC 201 567-9622	
320 S Dean St Englewood (07631) *(G-2933)*	
Print Tech LLC (PA) 908 232-2287	
49 Fadem Rd Springfield (07081) *(G-10461)*	
Print Tech LLC 908 232-0767	
349 South Ave E Westfield (07090) *(G-11801)*	
Printco 908 687-9518	
12 Minneakoning Rd 103b Flemington (08822) *(G-3464)*	
Printech, Flemington *Also called Jem Printing Inc* *(G-3450)*	
Printers of Salem County LLC 856 935-5032	
38 Market St Salem (08079) *(G-9696)*	
Printers Place Inc (PA) 973 744-8889	
8 S Fullerton Ave Montclair (07042) *(G-6385)*	
Printers Plus, Lakewood *Also called A&R Printing Corporation* *(G-5042)*	
Printers Service Florida Inc (PA) 973 589-7800	
26 Blanchard St Newark (07105) *(G-7236)*	
Printing & Signs Express Inc 201 368-1255	
634 Wyckoff Ave Mahwah (07430) *(G-5763)*	
Printing Center Inc 973 383-6362	
1 White Lake Rd Sparta (07871) *(G-10407)*	
Printing Delite Inc 973 676-3033	
279 To 281 Sanford St East Orange (07018) *(G-2260)*	
Printing Industries LLC 973 334-9775	
1543 Us Hwy Rte 46 E Parsippany (07054) *(G-8001)*	
Printing Lab LLC 201 305-0404	
609 55th St West New York (07093) *(G-11750)*	
Printing Plus of South Jersey 856 767-3941	
406 N Route 73 West Berlin (08091) *(G-11617)*	
Printing Services 908 269-8349	
185 Old Turnpike Rd Port Murray (07865) *(G-8884)*	
Printing Techniques, Nutley *Also called Manva Industries Inc* *(G-7590)*	
Printmaker International Ltd (HQ) 212 629-9260	
503 Chancellor Ave Irvington (07111) *(G-4583)*	
Printology 201 345-4632	
229 Godwin Ave Midland Park (07432) *(G-6186)*	
Printpluscom Inc 908 859-4774	
452a County Road 519 Stewartsville (08886) *(G-10487)*	
Printsmith 908 245-3000	
253 W Westfield Ave Roselle Park (07204) *(G-9589)*	
Printwrap Corporation 973 239-1144	
95 Sand Park Rd Cedar Grove (07009) *(G-1289)*	
Priore Construction Svcs LLC 973 785-2262	
5 Peckman Rd Little Falls (07424) *(G-5465)*	
Priority Medical Inc 973 376-5077	
748 Morris Tpke Ste 203 Short Hills (07078) *(G-9875)*	
Priority-Software US LLC (HQ) 973 586-2200	
300 Round Hill Dr Ste 2 Rockaway (07866) *(G-9490)*	
Prisco Digital Ltd Lblty Co (PA) 973 589-7800	
26 Blanchard St Newark (07105) *(G-7237)*	
Prisco Printers Service, Newark *Also called Deleet Merchandising Corp* *(G-7101)*	
Prism Color Corporation 856 234-7515	
31 Twosome Dr Ste 1 Moorestown (08057) *(G-6559)*	
Prism Dgtal Communications LLC 973 232-5038	
1011 Us Highway 22 Ste A Mountainside (07092) *(G-6851)*	
Prism Sheet Metal Inc 973 673-0213	
50 S Center St Ste 9 Orange (07050) *(G-7758)*	
Prismacolor Corp 973 887-6040	
120 E Halsey Rd Parsippany (07054) *(G-8002)*	
Private Label Products Inc 201 773-4230	
20-21 Wagaraw Rd Bldg 34 Fair Lawn (07410) *(G-3115)*	
Pro Academy, East Rutherford *Also called Techntime Bus Sltons Ltd Lblty* *(G-2324)*	
Pro Gad Sales, Newton *Also called G A D Inc* *(G-7344)*	
Pro Image Promotions Inc 973 252-8000	
480 Us Highway 46 Kenvil (07847) *(G-4995)*	
Pro Pack Inc 973 665-8333	
321 Richard Mine Rd Ste 1 Wharton (07885) *(G-11868)*	
Pro Plastics Inc 908 925-5555	
1190 Sylvan St Linden (07036) *(G-5412)*	
Pro Screen Printing Inc 201 246-7600	
590 Belleville Tpke # 24 Kearny (07032) *(G-4894)*	

A
L
P
H
A
B
E
T
I
C

Pro Sports Inc 732 294-5561
  1 Champion Way Marlboro (07746) *(G-5910)*

Pro Tapes & Specialties Inc 732 346-0900
  621 Us Highway 1 Unit A North Brunswick (08902) *(G-7483)*

Pro World 856 406-1020
  961 Bethel Ave Pennsauken (08110) *(G-8474)*

Pro-Deck Supply 609 771-1100
  3 Pembroke Ct Trenton (08648) *(G-10984)*

Pro-Motion Industries LLC 856 809-0040
  102 Allied Pkwy Sicklerville (08081) *(G-9914)*

Pro-Pac Service Inc 973 962-8080
  15 Van Natta Dr Ringwood (07456) *(G-9350)*

Pro-Pack Corp 908 725-5000
  160 Meister Ave Ste 18 Branchburg (08876) *(G-672)*

Proactive Ltg Solutions LLC 800 747-1209
  21 Ewing Ave North Arlington (07031) *(G-7377)*

Procedyne Corp (PA) 732 249-8347
  11 Industrial Dr New Brunswick (08901) *(G-6962)*

Proclean Services Inc 973 857-5408
  150 Linden Ave Verona (07044) *(G-11172)*

Proco Inc 609 265-8777
  15 Queen St Lumberton (08048) *(G-5634)*

Procrete LLC 609 365-2922
  4 Evergreen Rd Linwood (08221) *(G-5450)*

Procter & Gamble Mfg Co 732 602-4500
  100 Essex Ave E Avenel (07001) *(G-143)*

Prodo-Pak Corp 973 772-4500
  130 Monroe St Garfield (07026) *(G-3760)*

Prodo-Pak Corporation 973 777-7770
  77 Commerce St Garfield (07026) *(G-3761)*

Product Club Corp 973 664-0565
  41 Pine St Ste 15 Rockaway (07866) *(G-9491)*

Product Identification Co Inc 973 227-7770
  141 Lanza Ave Bldg 19 Garfield (07026) *(G-3762)*

Productive Industrial Finshg 856 427-9646
  103 American Way Voorhees (08043) *(G-11292)*

Productive Plastics Inc (PA) 856 778-4300
  103 W Park Dr Mount Laurel (08054) *(G-6796)*

Professional Disposables Inc 845 365-1700
  400 Chestnut Ridge Rd Woodcliff Lake (07677) *(G-12062)*

Professional Envmtl Systems 201 991-3000
  1806 Harrison Ave Kearny (07032) *(G-4895)*

Professional Laundry Solutions 973 392-0837
  443 Orange St Newark (07107) *(G-7238)*

Professional Printing Services 856 428-6300
  116 N Haddon Ave Ste G Haddonfield (08033) *(G-4063)*

Professional Reproductions Inc 212 268-1222
  75 Vanderburg Rd Marlboro (07746) *(G-5911)*

Profiles of Frameware, Fairfield *Also called Frameware Inc (G-3207)*

Proform Acoustic Surfaces LLC 201 553-9614
  307 Julianne Ter Secaucus (07094) *(G-9800)*

Proforma, Cedar Grove *Also called Repromatic Printing Inc (G-1291)*

Proforma Ayr Graphics & Prtg, Kenilworth *Also called Ayr Graphics & Printing Inc (G-4923)*

Profoto US Inc 973 822-1300
  220 Park Ave Ste 120 Florham Park (07932) *(G-3521)*

Progard, Englewood *Also called Enor Corporation (G-2902)*

Progenics Pharmaceuticals Inc 646 975-2500
  110 Clyde Rd Ste 4 Somerset (08873) *(G-10057)*

Programatic Platers Inc 718 721-4330
  32 Laurel Ave Tenafly (07670) *(G-10665)*

Progress Displays Inc 908 757-6650
  39 Progress St Edison (08820) *(G-2592)*

Progress Printing Co 201 433-3133
  338 Montgomery St Jersey City (07302) *(G-4788)*

Progress Woodwork 732 906-8680
  225 Pierson Ave Edison (08837) *(G-2593)*

Progressive 4 Color Ltd Lblty 973 736-5800
  24 Park Ave West Orange (07052) *(G-11778)*

Progressive Machine Company, Hackensack *Also called P L M Manufacturing Company (G-3961)*

Progressive Offset Inc 201 569-3900
  161 Coolidge Ave Englewood (07631) *(G-2934)*

Progressive Ruesch Inc 973 962-7700
  21 Van Natta Dr Ringwood (07456) *(G-9351)*

Progressive Tool & Mfg Corp 908 245-7010
  708 Fairfield Ave Kenilworth (07033) *(G-4972)*

Prohaska & Co Inc 732 238-3420
  34 Allwood Rd East Brunswick (08816) *(G-2169)*

Project Feed Usa Inc 201 443-7143
  127a Dwight St Jersey City (07305) *(G-4789)*

Prolong Pharmaceuticals LLC 908 444-4660
  300 Corporate Ct Ste B South Plainfield (07080) *(G-10316)*

Promeko Inc 201 861-9446
  543 59th St West New York (07093) *(G-11751)*

Promia Incorporated 609 252-1850
  322 Commons Way Princeton (08540) *(G-9009)*

Promius Pharma LLC 609 282-1400
  107 College Rd E Ste 100 Princeton (08540) *(G-9010)*

Promo Graphic Inc 732 629-7300
  112 Wood Ave Middlesex (08846) *(G-6141)*

Promotion In Motion Inc (PA) 201 962-8530
  25 Commerce Dr Allendale (07401) *(G-14)*

Promotion In Motion Inc 732 560-8300
  500 Pierce St Somerset (08873) *(G-10058)*

Promotion In Motion Companies, Allendale *Also called Promotion In Motion Inc (G-14)*

Promotional Graphics Inc 973 423-3900
  81 E 26th St Paterson (07514) *(G-8283)*

Pronto Printing & Copying Ctr 201 426-0009
  630 Swan St Ramsey (07446) *(G-9155)*

Proscape Technologies Inc 215 441-0300
  14 Dogwood Dr Hillsborough (08844) *(G-4347)*

Prospect Group LLC 718 635-4007
  260 Centennial Ave Piscataway (08854) *(G-8702)*

Prospect Transportation Inc (PA) 201 933-9999
  630 Industrial Rd Carlstadt (07072) *(G-1209)*

Prosthetic Orthotic Solutions, Marlton *Also called Cape Prosthetics-Orthotics (G-5923)*

Protameen Chemicals Inc (PA) 973 256-4374
  375 Minnisink Rd Totowa (07512) *(G-10847)*

Protec Secure Card Ltd Lblty 732 542-0700
  80 Corbett Way Eatontown (07724) *(G-2417)*

Protech Oxyplast, Fairfield *Also called Protech Powder Coatings Inc (G-3296)*

Protech Powder Coatings Inc (PA) 973 276-1292
  21 Audrey Pl Fairfield (07004) *(G-3296)*

Protection Industries Corp 201 333-8050
  107 York St Jersey City (07302) *(G-4790)*

Proteus Designs LLC 215 519-0135
  900 N Lenola Rd Bldg 9 Moorestown (08057) *(G-6560)*

Protoform Inc 609 261-6920
  112 Burrs Rd Westampton (08060) *(G-11790)*

Provence LLC 201 503-9717
  214 S Dean St Englewood (07631) *(G-2935)*

Provid Pharmaceuticals Inc 732 565-1101
  7 Deerpark Dr Ste M11 Monmouth Junction (08852) *(G-6307)*

Provost Square Associates Inc 973 403-8755
  6 Provost Sq Caldwell (07006) *(G-1028)*

Proximo Distillers LLC 201 204-1718
  333 Washington St Fl 4 Jersey City (07302) *(G-4791)*

Prudent Publishing Co Inc 973 347-4554
  400 N Frontage Rd Landing (07850) *(G-5203)*

Prysmian Cbles Systems USA LLC 732 469-5902
  111 Chimney Rock Rd Bridgewater (08807) *(G-870)*

PSC, Eatontown *Also called Protec Secure Card Ltd Lblty (G-2417)*

PSEG Nuclear LLC 973 430-5191
  80 Park Plz Ste 3 Newark (07102) *(G-7239)*

Psnj, Cinnaminson *Also called Pechters Southern NJ LLC (G-1479)*

Ptc Electronics Inc 201 847-0500
  45 Whitney Rd Ste B9 Mahwah (07430) *(G-5764)*

Ptc Inc 973 631-6195
  89 Headquarters Plz Morristown (07960) *(G-6696)*

Ptc Therapeutics Inc (PA) 908 222-7000
  100 Corporate Ct South Plainfield (07080) *(G-10317)*

Ptic, Teaneck *Also called Prime Time International Co (G-10647)*

PTL Sheet Metal Inc 201 501-8700
  70 Davies Ave Dumont (07628) *(G-2117)*

Pts Intermediate Holdings LLC 732 537-6200
  14 Schoolhouse Rd Somerset (08873) *(G-10059)*

Pty Lighting LLC (PA) 855 303-4500
  100 Hoffman Pl Hillside (07205) *(G-4421)*

Publishers Inc 856 853-2800
  1757 Imperial Way West Deptford (08066) *(G-11715)*

Publishers Partnership Co 201 689-1613
  23 N Pleasant Ave Ridgewood (07450) *(G-9326)*

Publishing Technology Inc 732 563-9292
  317 George St Ste 320 New Brunswick (08901) *(G-6963)*

Puebla Foods Inc (PA) 973 246-6311
  26 Jefferson St Passaic (07055) *(G-8097)*

Puebla Foods Inc 973 473-4494
  26 Jefferson St Passaic (07055) *(G-8098)*

Pueblo Latino Laundry LLC 201 864-1666
  1717 Bergenline Ave Union City (07087) *(G-11125)*

Puent-Romer Communications Inc 973 509-7591
  423 Bloomfield Ave Montclair (07042) *(G-6386)*

Pulaski Meat Products Co 908 925-5380
  123 N Wood Ave Linden (07036) *(G-5413)*

Pulasky Meat Products Co, Linden *Also called Pulaski Meat Products Co (G-5413)*

Pulsar Microwave Corp 973 779-6262
  48 Industrial St W Clifton (07012) *(G-1701)*

Pulsetor LLC 609 303-0578
  243 N Union St Ste 207 Lambertville (08530) *(G-5196)*

Pulsonics Inc 800 999-6785
  69 William St Belleville (07109) *(G-309)*

Puratos Corporation (HQ) 856 428-4300
  1705 Suckle Hwy Pennsauken (08110) *(G-8475)*

Purdue Pharma LP 203 588-8000
  100 Prnctn S Corpt Ctr # 250 Ewing (08628) *(G-3055)*

Pure H2o Technologies Inc 973 622-0440
  211 Warren St Ste 19 Newark (07103) *(G-7240)*

Pure Rubber Products Co. 973 784-3690
  300 Round Hill Dr Ste 5 Rockaway (07866) *(G-9492)*

Pure Soccer Academy Ltd Lblty................................877 945-6423
  330 Changebridge Rd # 101 Pine Brook (07058) *(G-8614)*
Pure TEC Corporation (HQ)................................201 941-2900
  101 Railroad Ave Ridgefield (07657) *(G-9285)*
Pure Tech International Inc................................908 722-4968
  3040 Us Highway 22 # 130 Branchburg (08876) *(G-673)*
Pure Tech International Inc (HQ)................................908 722-4800
  201 Industrial Pkwy Branchburg (08876) *(G-674)*
Purelink, Fair Lawn *Also called Dtrovision LLC (G-3097)*
Purely Organic SA LLC................................201 942-0400
  142 Liberty Ave Jersey City (07306) *(G-4792)*
Purevolution................................973 919-4047
  62 Fayson Lake Rd Kinnelon (07405) *(G-5021)*
Purity Labs................................201 372-0236
  1 Maple St East Rutherford (07073) *(G-2313)*
Push Beverages LLC................................973 766-2663
  7 Longfellow Dr Succasunna (07876) *(G-10516)*
Putterwheel, Allendale *Also called Ssam Sports Inc (G-15)*
Pv Deroche LLC................................908 475-2266
  283 County Route 519 Belvidere (07823) *(G-365)*
Pv/T Inc................................609 267-3933
  100 Indel Ave Rancocas (08073) *(G-9164)*
Pvh Corp................................908 685-0050
  651 Kapkowski Rd Ste 1416 Elizabeth (07201) *(G-2771)*
Pvh Corp................................609 344-6273
  32 N Michigan Ave Atlantic City (08401) *(G-101)*
Pvh Corp................................908 685-0050
  1001 Frontier Rd Ste 100 Bridgewater (08807) *(G-871)*
Pvh Corp................................732 833-9602
  537 Monmouth Rd Ste 332 Jackson (08527) *(G-4663)*
Pvh Corp................................908 685-0050
  1001 Frontier Rd Ste 100 Bridgewater (08807) *(G-872)*
Pvh Corp................................908 685-0148
  1001 Frontier Rd 100 Bridgewater (08807) *(G-873)*
Pvh Corp................................908 788-5880
  41 Liberty Vlg Flemington (08822) *(G-3465)*
Pwg Lighting, Hillside *Also called Pty Lighting LLC (G-4421)*
Pyle Precision Machining LLC................................856 376-3720
  175 Route 130 Pedricktown (08067) *(G-8353)*
Pyramid Food Services Corp................................973 900-6513
  93-105 Albert Ave Newark (07105) *(G-7241)*
Pyrometer LLC................................609 443-5522
  70 Weber Ave Ewing (08638) *(G-3056)*
Pyrometer Instrument Co Inc................................609 443-5522
  92 N Main St Bldg 18d Windsor (08561) *(G-11997)*
Pyrometer Instrument Company, Ewing *Also called Pyrometer LLC (G-3056)*
Q Glass Company Inc................................973 335-5191
  624 Rte 202 Towaco (07082) *(G-10879)*
Q P 195 Inc................................732 531-8860
  827 W Park Ave Ocean (07712) *(G-7676)*
Q P 500 Inc................................732 531-8860
  827 W Park Ave Ocean (07712) *(G-7677)*
Q&Q Pharma Research Company................................973 267-0160
  19 Meadow Bluff Rd Morris Plains (07950) *(G-6624)*
Q-Eximtrade Inc (PA)................................732 366-4667
  1336 Roosevelt Ave Carteret (07008) *(G-1265)*
Q-Pak Corporation................................973 483-4404
  2145 Mccarter Hwy Newark (07104) *(G-7242)*
Q10 Products LLC................................201 567-9299
  1 Entin Rd Ste 7a Clifton (07014) *(G-1702)*
Qad Inc................................856 273-1717
  10000 Midlantic Dr 100w Mount Laurel (08054) *(G-6797)*
Qcom Inc................................732 772-0990
  4400 Route 9 S Ste 1000 Freehold (07728) *(G-3695)*
Qellus LLC................................856 761-6575
  309 Fellowship Rd Mount Laurel (08054) *(G-6798)*
Qis Inc................................856 455-3736
  778 Vineland Ave Rosenhayn (08352) *(G-9596)*
Qrx Pharma Incorporated................................908 506-2900
  1430 Us Highway 206 # 230 Bedminster (07921) *(G-277)*
Qsa Global National Corp................................865 888-6798
  331 Newman Springs Rd Red Bank (07701) *(G-9241)*
Qsa National, Red Bank *Also called Qsa Global National Corp (G-9241)*
Quad/Graphics Inc................................609 534-7308
  80 Stemmers Ln Westampton (08060) *(G-11791)*
Quad/Graphics Inc................................732 469-0189
  13 Jensen Dr Ste 100 Somerset (08873) *(G-10060)*
Quadelle Textile Corp................................201 865-1112
  573 56th St West New York (07093) *(G-11752)*
Quadramed Corporation................................732 751-0400
  23 Christopher Way # 303 Eatontown (07724) *(G-2418)*
Quadrangle Products Inc................................732 792-1234
  28 Harrison Ave Unit D Englishtown (07726) *(G-3008)*
Quadrant Media Corp Inc................................973 701-8900
  7 Century Dr Ste 302 Parsippany (07054) *(G-8003)*
Quagen Pharmaceuticals LLC (PA)................................973 228-9600
  11 Patton Dr West Caldwell (07006) *(G-11674)*
Quagen Pharmaceuticals LLC................................973 228-9600
  34 Fairfield Pl West Caldwell (07006) *(G-11675)*
Quaker Soap Div, Newark *Also called Darling Ingredients Inc (G-7095)*

Qualco Inc................................973 473-1222
  225 Passaic St Passaic (07055) *(G-8099)*
Qualcomm Incorporated................................908 443-8000
  500 Smrst Corp Blvd Fl 4 Bridgewater (08807) *(G-874)*
Qualipac America Corp................................973 754-9920
  1 Garret Mountain Plz # 502 Woodland Park (07424) *(G-12088)*
Qualis Packaging Inc (PA)................................908 782-0305
  550 Hadley Rd South Plainfield (07080) *(G-10318)*
Quality Bath, Lakewood *Also called Tlw Bath Ltd Liability Company (G-5172)*
Quality Carton Inc (PA)................................201 529-6900
  1 International Blvd # 610 Mahwah (07495) *(G-5765)*
Quality Cosmetics Mfg................................908 755-9588
  4455 S Clinton Ave South Plainfield (07080) *(G-10319)*
Quality Die Shop Inc................................732 787-0041
  17 Argonne Pl North Middletown (07748) *(G-7504)*
Quality Eyework, South Hackensack *Also called M H Optical Supplies Inc (G-10170)*
Quality Films Corp................................718 246-7150
  500 Hillside Ave Hillside (07205) *(G-4422)*
Quality Glass Inc................................908 754-2652
  2300 S Clinton Ave Ste C South Plainfield (07080) *(G-10320)*
Quality Indexing LLC................................908 810-0200
  939 Lehigh Ave Union (07083) *(G-11085)*
Quality Industries Inc................................973 478-4425
  204 Getty Ave Clifton (07011) *(G-1703)*
Quality Medical Supplies, Leonia *Also called Carry Easy Inc (G-5287)*
Quality Plus One Catering Inc (PA)................................732 967-1525
  10 Kerry Ct Old Bridge (08857) *(G-7726)*
Quality Print Solutions................................888 679-7237
  589 Franklin Tpke Ridgewood (07450) *(G-9327)*
Quality Remanufacturing Inc................................973 523-8800
  565 E 37th St Paterson (07504) *(G-8284)*
Quality Sheet Metal & Wldg Inc................................732 469-7111
  23 Clawson St Piscataway (08854) *(G-8703)*
Quality Stays LLC (PA)................................800 868-8195
  10 Underwood Pl Ste 2 Clifton (07013) *(G-1704)*
Quality Sweets................................732 283-3799
  1396 Oak Tree Rd Iselin (08830) *(G-4624)*
Quality Swiss Screw Machine Co................................908 289-4334
  849 4th Ave Elizabeth (07202) *(G-2772)*
Quallis Brands LLC................................862 252-0664
  211 Glenwood Ave East Orange (07017) *(G-2261)*
Qualserv Imports Inc................................973 620-9234
  3125 State Route 10 Denville (07834) *(G-2050)*
Quantem Corp................................609 883-9191
  1457 Lower Ferry Rd Ste 1 Ewing (08618) *(G-3057)*
Quantum Coating Inc................................856 234-5444
  1259 N Church St Bldg 1 Moorestown (08057) *(G-6561)*
Quantum Integrators Group LLC................................609 632-0621
  8 Madison Dr Plainsboro (08536) *(G-8800)*
Quantum Security Systems Inc................................609 252-0505
  124 Fairfield Rd Princeton (08540) *(G-9011)*
Quantum Vector Corp................................201 870-1782
  700 Broadway Westwood (07675) *(G-11840)*
Quark Enterprises Inc................................856 455-0376
  320 Morton Ave Rosenhayn (08352) *(G-9597)*
Quarterspot Inc................................917 647-9170
  145 Us Highway 46 Fl 3 Wayne (07470) *(G-11545)*
Ques Aprv A R Knitwear Inc................................201 869-1333
  2201 74th St North Bergen (07047) *(G-7431)*
Quest Diagnostics Incorporated (PA)................................973 520-2700
  500 Plaza Dr Ste G Secaucus (07094) *(G-9801)*
Quest Intl Flavors Fragrances................................973 576-9500
  717 Ridgedale Ave East Hanover (07936) *(G-2235)*
Qugen Inc................................609 716-6300
  666 Plainsboro Rd Ste 215 Plainsboro (08536) *(G-8801)*
Quick Bias Bnding Trmming Inds................................732 422-0123
  9 Creekside Ct North Brunswick (08902) *(G-7484)*
Quick Fab Aluminum Mfg Co................................732 367-7200
  1830 Swarthmore Ave Ste 1 Lakewood (08701) *(G-5150)*
Quick Frozen Foods Intl................................201 592-7007
  2125 Center Ave Ste 305 Fort Lee (07024) *(G-3583)*
Quickie Print & Copy Shop, Ocean *Also called Q P 500 Inc (G-7677)*
Quickly Printing, Union *Also called Mr Quickly Inc (G-11077)*
Quiet Tone Inc................................732 431-2826
  12 Vine St Freehold (07728) *(G-3696)*
Quik Flex Circuit Inc................................856 742-0550
  85 Nicholson Rd Gloucester City (08030) *(G-3848)*
Quik-Fab Aluminum Mfg, Lakewood *Also called Quick Fab Aluminum Mfg Co (G-5150)*
Quik-Flex Circuit Inc................................856 742-0550
  85 Nicholson Rd Gloucester City (08030) *(G-3849)*
Quik-Sab, Lakewood *Also called Vinylast Inc (G-5176)*
Quikie Print & Copy Shop, Ocean *Also called Q P 195 Inc (G-7676)*
Quintum Technologies Inc (HQ)................................732 460-9000
  71 James Way Eatontown (07724) *(G-2419)*
Qwik Pack & Ship, Blackwood *Also called E C D Ventures Inc (G-465)*
R & B Printing Inc................................908 766-4073
  19-21 Mine Brook Rd Fl 1 Bernardsville (07924) *(G-443)*
R & D Circuits Inc (PA)................................732 549-4554
  3601 S Clinton Ave South Plainfield (07080) *(G-10321)*

A L P H A B E T I C

R & H Co Inc..610 258-3177
  1286 Strykers Rd Phillipsburg (08865) *(G-8571)*

R & H Spring & Truck Repair......................732 681-9000
  4806 W Hurley Pond Rd Wall Township (07719) *(G-11362)*

R & K Industries Inc.................................732 531-1123
  259 Overbrook Ave Oakhurst (07755) *(G-7612)*

R & M Chemical Technologies...................908 537-9516
  7 Imlaydale Rd Hampton (08827) *(G-4159)*

R & M Manufacturing Inc..........................609 495-8032
  20 Abeel Rd Monroe Township (08831) *(G-6341)*

R & R Fuel Inc..201 223-0786
  3205 Hudson Ave Union City (07087) *(G-11126)*

R & R Irrigation Co Inc.............................732 271-7070
  283 Lincoln Blvd Middlesex (08846) *(G-6142)*

R & R Printing & Copy Center....................732 249-9450
  46 Old Camplain Rd Hillsborough (08844) *(G-4348)*

R A O Contract Sales, Paterson *Also called R A O Contract Sales NY Inc (G-8285)*

R A O Contract Sales NY Inc......................201 652-1500
  94 Fulton St Ste 4 Paterson (07501) *(G-8285)*

R B B Corp...973 770-1100
  7 Orben Dr Ledgewood (07852) *(G-5279)*

R B Badat Landscaping Inc........................609 877-7138
  507 Woodlane Rd Mount Holly (08060) *(G-6733)*

R Baron Associates Inc.............................215 396-3803
  10 Lippincott Ln Ste 6 Mount Holly (08060) *(G-6734)*

R C Fine Foods Inc.................................908 359-5500
  139 Stryker Ln Hillsborough (08844) *(G-4349)*

R D I, Ocean City *Also called Railing Dynamics Inc (G-7692)*

R E Pierson Materials, Williamstown *Also called Richard E Pierson Mtls Corp (G-11975)*

R E Pierson Materials, Vineland *Also called Richard E Pierson Mtls Corp (G-11260)*

R E Pierson Materials, Pilesgrove *Also called Richard E Pierson Mtls Corp (G-8580)*

R F Products Inc (PA).............................856 365-5500
  1500 Davis St Camden (08103) *(G-1084)*

R G Dunn Acquisitions Co Inc....................973 762-1300
  71 Newark Way Maplewood (07040) *(G-5882)*

R G Smith Tool & Mfg Co..........................973 344-1395
  245 South St Newark (07114) *(G-7243)*

R H A Audio Communications, East Brunswick *Also called R H A Audio Communications (G-2170)*

R H A Audio Communications.....................732 257-9180
  725 State Route 18 East Brunswick (08816) *(G-2170)*

R H Vassallo Inc.....................................856 358-8841
  Us Rte 40 & State 47 Malaga (08328) *(G-5789)*

R J Blen Grphic Arts Cnverting..................732 545-3501
  6 Jules Ln New Brunswick (08901) *(G-6964)*

R J D Machine Products Inc.......................609 392-1515
  1424-1428 Heath Ave Trenton (08638) *(G-10985)*

R K S Plastics Inc...................................732 435-8517
  100 Jersey Ave Ste B6 New Brunswick (08901) *(G-6965)*

R L Plastics Inc......................................732 340-1100
  20 Production Way Avenel (07001) *(G-144)*

R L R Foil Stamping LLC...........................973 778-9464
  245 4th St Ste 4 Passaic (07055) *(G-8100)*

R L S Enterprises, Branchburg *Also called Njrls Enterprises Inc (G-661)*

R M A, Hillside *Also called Mark Ronald Associates Inc (G-4414)*

R M F Associates Inc...............................908 687-9355
  202 Carolyn Rd Union (07083) *(G-11086)*

R Neumann & Co.....................................201 659-3400
  300 Observer Hwy Ste 1 Hoboken (07030) *(G-4476)*

R P Baking LLC.......................................973 483-3374
  840 Jersey St Harrison (07029) *(G-4179)*

R P I, Asbury *Also called Reed Presentations Inc (G-69)*

R P L, Garfield *Also called Rpl Supplies Inc (G-3766)*

R P R Graphics Inc..................................908 654-8080
  87 Main St Peapack (07977) *(G-8345)*

R P Smith & Son Inc................................973 584-4063
  199 Main St Succasunna (07876) *(G-10517)*

R R Donnelley & Sons Company..................973 439-8321
  5 Henderson Dr West Caldwell (07006) *(G-11676)*

R R J Co Inc...732 544-1514
  13 Provincial Pl Colts Neck (07722) *(G-1787)*

R S Rubber Corp.....................................973 777-2200
  55 Paterson Ave Wallington (07057) *(G-11389)*

R Squared Sls & Logistics LLC...................201 329-9745
  30 Congress Dr Moonachie (07074) *(G-6485)*

R T I Inc..201 261-5852
  401 Hasbrouck Blvd Oradell (07649) *(G-7746)*

R Tape Corporation (HQ)..........................908 753-5570
  6 Ingersoll Rd South Plainfield (07080) *(G-10322)*

R V Livolsi Incorporated (PA).....................732 286-2200
  20 E Water St Toms River (08753) *(G-10786)*

R W Wheaton Co.....................................908 241-4955
  215 W Clay Ave Roselle Park (07204) *(G-9590)*

R Way Tooling & Met Works LLC.................856 692-2218
  224 S Lincoln Ave Vineland (08361) *(G-11255)*

R World Enterprises.................................201 795-2428
  197 Congress St Jersey City (07307) *(G-4793)*

R Yates Consumer Prd LLC........................201 569-1030
  204 Green St Englewood (07631) *(G-2936)*

R& D Consulting, Brookside *Also called Anvima Technologies LLC (G-916)*

R&D Altanova, South Plainfield *Also called R & D Circuits Inc (G-10321)*

R&D Microwaves LLC...............................908 212-1696
  301 Rockaway Valley Rd # 3 Boonton (07005) *(G-565)*

R&L Sheet Metal, Towaco *Also called Apogee Technologies LLC (G-10864)*

R&R Cosmetics LLC.................................732 340-1000
  1140 Randolph Ave Rahway (07065) *(G-9123)*

R-Way Machine and Fabrication, Vineland *Also called R Way Tooling & Met Works LLC (G-11255)*

R-Way Tooling Co, Vineland *Also called Frank E Ganter Inc (G-11219)*

Ra Liquidating, Woodbridge *Also called Rclc Inc (G-12020)*

Raason Cabinetry, Englishtown *Also called Acorn Industry Inc (G-2999)*

RAB Food Group LLC (HQ).........................201 553-1100
  80 Avenue K Newark (07105) *(G-7244)*

Rab Lighting Inc (PA)...............................201 784-8600
  170 Ludlow Ave Northvale (07647) *(G-7544)*

Raceway Petroleum Inc.............................908 222-2999
  643 Us Highway 22 North Plainfield (07060) *(G-7508)*

Raceway Petroleum Inc.............................732 729-7350
  114 Ryders Ln East Brunswick (08816) *(G-2171)*

Raceway Petroleum Inc.............................732 613-4404
  523 State Route 18 East Brunswick (08816) *(G-2172)*

Raceweld Co Inc......................................908 236-6533
  1120 Us Highway 22 Lebanon (08833) *(G-5274)*

Radcom Equipment Inc.............................201 518-0033
  10 Forest Ave Paramus (07652) *(G-7828)*

Radha Beauty Products LLC.......................732 993-6242
  220 Kinderkamack Rd Ste C Westwood (07675) *(G-11841)*

Radiant Communications Corp (PA).............908 757-7444
  5001 Hadley Rd South Plainfield (07080) *(G-10323)*

Radiant Cut Diamond, Hoboken *Also called Rcdc Corporation (G-4477)*

Radiant Energy Systems Inc.....................973 423-5220
  175 N Ethel Ave Hawthorne (07506) *(G-4241)*

Radiation Systems Inc..............................201 891-7515
  455 W Main St Wyckoff (07481) *(G-12118)*

Radio Systems Design Inc.........................856 467-8000
  601 Heron Dr Swedesboro (08085) *(G-10604)*

Radix Computer Carrers, Bloomfield *Also called Radix M I S (G-516)*

Radix M I S..973 707-2121
  50 Hazelwood Rd Bloomfield (07003) *(G-516)*

Radnet Inc..908 709-1323
  25 S Union Ave Cranford (07016) *(G-1924)*

Radnet Inc..908 709-1323
  25 S Union Ave Cranford (07016) *(G-1925)*

Radwin Inc...201 252-4224
  900 Corporate Dr Mahwah (07430) *(G-5766)*

Rafael Pharmaceuticals Inc (PA)...............609 409-7050
  1 Duncan Dr Cranbury (08512) *(G-1876)*

Raffettos Corp..201 372-1222
  62 W Commercial Ave Moonachie (07074) *(G-6486)*

Ragar Co Inc..732 493-1416
  2106 Kings Hwy Ocean (07712) *(G-7678)*

Rags International Inc..............................787 632-8447
  15 Tooker Ave Springfield (07081) *(G-10462)*

Rahway Steel Drum Co Inc.......................732 382-0113
  26 Brick Yard Rd Cranbury (08512) *(G-1877)*

Railing Designs Unlimited, Belleville *Also called Bloomfield Iron Co Inc (G-291)*

Railing Dynamics Inc................................609 593-5400
  1201 N 10th St Millville (08332) *(G-6267)*

Railing Dynamics Inc (HQ)........................609 601-1300
  3814 Waterview Blvd Ocean City (08226) *(G-7692)*

Railpace Co Inc.......................................732 388-4984
  257 Oak Ridge Rd Clark (07066) *(G-1514)*

Rails Company Inc (PA)...........................973 763-4320
  101 Newark Way Maplewood (07040) *(G-5883)*

Rainbow Closets Inc (PA).........................973 882-3800
  4 Gardner Rd Ste 5 Fairfield (07004) *(G-3297)*

Rainbow Metal Units Corp.........................718 784-3690
  1 Kenner Ct Riverdale (07457) *(G-9381)*

Rainmen USA Incorporated (PA).................201 784-3244
  10 Maple St Norwood (07648) *(G-7573)*

Rajbhog Foods Inc...................................551 222-4700
  60 Amity St Jersey City (07304) *(G-4794)*

Rajbhog Foods Inc (PA)............................201 395-9400
  812 Newark Ave Jersey City (07306) *(G-4795)*

Rajbhog Foods(nj) Inc.............................551 222-4700
  60 Amity St Jersey City (07304) *(G-4796)*

Rajysan Incorporated..............................800 433-1382
  3 Hawk Ct Swedesboro (08085) *(G-10605)*

Rak Foam Sales Inc.................................908 668-1122
  1355 W Front St Ste 2 Plainfield (07063) *(G-8776)*

Rako Machine Products Inc........................609 758-1200
  845 Monmouth Rd Cream Ridge (08514) *(G-1939)*

Ralph Clayton & Sons LLC........................800 662-3044
  58 Goldman Dr Cookstown (08511) *(G-1805)*

Ralph Clayton & Sons LLC........................609 695-0767
  1144 New York Ave Trenton (08638) *(G-10986)*

Ralph Clayton & Sons LLC........................732 462-1552
  64 Institute St Freehold (07728) *(G-3697)*

Ralph Clayton & Sons LLC 609 383-1818
103 Chestnut Ave Egg Harbor Township (08234) *(G-2694)*

Ralph Lauren Corporation 201 531-6000
9 Polito Ave Fl 5 Lyndhurst (07071) *(G-5674)*

Ram Donuts Corp 856 599-0015
431 Harmony Rd Gibbstown (08027) *(G-3799)*

Ram Hydraulics Inc 732 237-0904
745 Shrewsbury Ave Shrewsbury (07702) *(G-9900)*

Ram Products Inc 732 651-5500
182 Ridge Rd Ste D Dayton (08810) *(G-1985)*

Ramblewood Cleaners Inc (PA) 856 235-6051
1155 Route 73 Ste B Mount Laurel (08054) *(G-6799)*

Rambusch Decorating Company 201 333-2525
160 Cornelison Ave Jersey City (07304) *(G-4797)*

Rambusch Lighting, Jersey City *Also called Rambusch Decorating Company (G-4797)*

Ramco, Hillside *Also called Randall Manufacturing Co Inc (G-4424)*

Ramco Equipment Corp 908 687-6700
32 Montgomery St Hillside (07205) *(G-4423)*

Ramco Manufacturing Co Inc (PA) 908 245-4500
365 Carnegie Ave Kenilworth (07033) *(G-4973)*

Ramco Systems Corporation (HQ) 609 620-4800
136 Main St Ste 305 Princeton (08540) *(G-9012)*

Rame Hart Instrument, Succasunna *Also called Rame-Hart Instrument Co LLC (G-10518)*

Rame-Hart Inc 973 335-0560
5 Emery Ave Ste 1 Randolph (07869) *(G-9197)*

Rame-Hart Instrument Co LLC 973 448-0305
19 State Route 10 E # 11 Succasunna (07876) *(G-10518)*

Ramsay David Cabinetmakers 856 234-7776
310 Mill St Moorestown (08057) *(G-6562)*

Ramsey Building Supply, Midland Park *Also called Precision Multiple Contrls Inc (G-6184)*

Ramsey Graphics and Printing 201 300-2912
262 Market St Ste 1 Elmwood Park (07407) *(G-2852)*

Ramsey Machine & Tool Co Inc 973 376-7404
60 Tooker Ave Springfield (07081) *(G-10463)*

Ranbaxy Pharmaceuticals, Princeton *Also called OHM Laboratories Inc (G-8990)*

Ranbaxy USA Inc 609 720-9200
2 Independence Way Princeton (08540) *(G-9013)*

Ranco Precision Sheet Metal 973 472-8808
40 Colorado St Clifton (07014) *(G-1705)*

Rand Diversified Companies LLC 732 985-0800
112 Truman Dr Edison (08817) *(G-2594)*

Randall Manufacturing Co, Hillside *Also called Ramco Equipment Corp (G-4423)*

Randall Manufacturing Co Inc 973 746-2111
32 Montgomery St Hillside (07205) *(G-4424)*

Randall Mfg Co Inc 973 482-8603
200 Sylvan Ave Newark (07104) *(G-7245)*

Randcastle Extrusion Systems 973 239-1150
220 Little Falls Rd # 6 Cedar Grove (07009) *(G-1290)*

Randells Cstm Fniture Kitchens 856 216-9400
1864 Marlton Pike E Cherry Hill (08003) *(G-1412)*

Random 8 Woodworks LLC (PA) 856 417-3329
459 Clems Run Mullica Hill (08062) *(G-6857)*

Random 8 Woodworks LLC 856 364-7627
32 W Mill St Pedricktown (08067) *(G-8354)*

Randy Hangers LLC 201 215-2900
115 Enterprise Ave S Secaucus (07094) *(G-9802)*

Rangecraft Manufacturing Inc 201 791-0440
4-40 Banta Pl Fair Lawn (07410) *(G-3116)*

Ranger Industries Inc (PA) 732 389-3535
15 Park Rd Tinton Falls (07724) *(G-10725)*

Ransome Equipment Sales LLC 856 797-8100
106 Ark Rd Lumberton (08048) *(G-5635)*

Ranx Pharmaceuticals Inc 571 214-8989
1085 Cranbury S River Rd Jamesburg (08831) *(G-4676)*

Raos Specialty Foods Inc (HQ) 212 269-0151
441 Bloomfield Ave Montclair (07042) *(G-6387)*

Raphel Marketing Inc 609 348-6646
118 S Newton Pl Atlantic City (08401) *(G-102)*

Rapid Manufacturing Co Inc 732 279-1252
25 Bay Point Dr Toms River (08753) *(G-10787)*

Rapid Models & Prototypes Inc 856 933-2929
101 C Rose Ave Runnemede (08078) *(G-9607)*

Rapsoco Inc 908 977-7321
648 Newark Ave Elizabeth (07208) *(G-2773)*

Raptor Resources Holdings Inc (PA) 732 252-5146
41 Howe Ln Freehold (07728) *(G-3698)*

Raritan Inc (HQ) 732 764-8886
400 Cottontail Ln Somerset (08873) *(G-10061)*

Raritan Americas Inc (HQ) 732 764-8886
400 Cottontail Ln Somerset (08873) *(G-10062)*

Raritan Computer, Somerset *Also called Raritan Americas Inc (G-10062)*

Raritan Container, New Brunswick *Also called Raritan Packaging Industries (G-6966)*

Raritan Packaging Industries 732 246-7200
570 Jersey Ave New Brunswick (08901) *(G-6966)*

Raritan Phrmctcals Incoporated 732 238-1685
8 Joanna Ct East Brunswick (08816) *(G-2173)*

Ras Process Equipment 609 371-1000
324 Meadowbrook Rd Robbinsville (08691) *(G-9416)*

Rascal Company, The, Sewell *Also called Electric Mobility Corporation (G-9843)*

Rascal Company, The, Sewell *Also called Electric Mobility Corporation (G-9844)*

Rasi Laboratories Inc 732 873-8500
320 Half Acre Rd Cranbury (08512) *(G-1878)*

Rasi Labs, Cranbury *Also called Rasi Laboratories Inc (G-1878)*

Rasta Imposta, Runnemede *Also called Silvertop Associates Inc (G-9610)*

Rastelli Brothers Inc (PA) 856 803-1100
300 Heron Dr Swedesboro (08085) *(G-10606)*

Rastelli Foods, Swedesboro *Also called Rastelli Brothers Inc (G-10606)*

Rathgibson North Branch LLC 908 253-3260
100 Aspen Hill Rd Branchburg (08876) *(G-675)*

Raue Screw Machine Products Co 973 697-7500
173 Oak Ridge Rd Oak Ridge (07438) *(G-7604)*

Rauhauser's Own Make Candies, Ocean City *Also called Rauhausers Inc (G-7693)*

Rauhausers Inc 609 399-1465
721 Asbury Ave Unit A Ocean City (08226) *(G-7693)*

Rawco LLC 908 832-7700
452 County Road 513 Califon (07830) *(G-1034)*

Rawco Precision Manufacturing, Califon *Also called Rawco LLC (G-1034)*

Raybeam Manufacturing Corp 201 941-4529
700 Grand Ave Ste 5 Ridgefield (07657) *(G-9286)*

Rays Reproduction Inc 201 666-5650
39 Bland St Emerson (07630) *(G-2868)*

Razac Products Inc 973 622-3700
25 Brenner St Newark (07108) *(G-7246)*

Razer Scandinavia Inc 732 441-1250
432 State Route 34 Ste 1a Matawan (07747) *(G-5986)*

RB, Parsippany *Also called Benckiser N Reckitt Amer Inc (G-7893)*

RB Manufacturing LLC 908 533-2000
799 Us Highway 206 Hillsborough (08844) *(G-4350)*

RB Manufacturing LLC (HQ) 973 404-2600
399 Interpace Pkwy Parsippany (07054) *(G-8004)*

Rbc Bearings Incorporated 843 332-2691
400 Sullivan Way Ste 1 Ewing (08628) *(G-3058)*

Rbc Bearings-Houston, Ewing *Also called Rbc Bearings Incorporated (G-3058)*

Rbc Dain Rauscher 973 778-7300
3 Garret Mountain Plz # 201 Woodland Park (07424) *(G-12089)*

Rbdel Inc 609 324-0040
272 Dunns Mill Rd Bordentown (08505) *(G-594)*

Rbi Toys, Phillipsburg *Also called Ron Banafato Inc (G-8572)*

Rbs Intrntonal Direct Mktg LLC (PA) 856 663-2500
2 Executive Campus # 200 Cherry Hill (08002) *(G-1413)*

Rcc Fabricators Inc 609 859-9350
2035 Route 206 Southampton (08088) *(G-10370)*

Rcdc Corporation 212 382-0386
59 Madison St 2 Hoboken (07030) *(G-4477)*

Rcf USA Inc 732 902-6100
110 Talmadge Rd Edison (08817) *(G-2595)*

Rclc Inc (PA) 732 877-1788
1480 Us Highway 9 N # 301 Woodbridge (07095) *(G-12020)*

RCM Ltd Inc 201 337-3328
25 Cardinal Dr Oakland (07436) *(G-7642)*

Rdi, East Windsor *Also called Roof Deck Inc (G-2358)*

Rdl Marketing Group LLC 732 446-0817
352a Sweetmans Ln Perrineville (08535) *(G-8507)*

Rdo Induction Ltd Liability Co 908 835-7222
2170 State Route 57 W Washington (07882) *(G-11450)*

Re Systems Group Inc 201 883-1572
700 Broadway Ste 204 Westwood (07675) *(G-11842)*

Reade Manufacturing Company (HQ) 732 657-6451
2590 Ridgeway Blvd Manchester (08759) *(G-5848)*

Readington Farms Inc 908 534-2121
12 Mill Rd Whitehouse (08888) *(G-11918)*

Ready Pac Produce Inc 609 499-1900
700 Railroad Ave Florence (08518) *(G-3477)*

Ready-Pac Club Chef, Florence *Also called Ready Pac Produce Inc (G-3477)*

Reagent Chemical & RES Inc 908 284-2800
115 Us Highway 202 Ste E Ringoes (08551) *(G-9341)*

Real Kosher LLC 973 690-5394
146 Christie St Newark (07105) *(G-7247)*

Real Soft Inc 609 409-3636
68 Culver Rd Ste 100 Monmouth Junction (08852) *(G-6308)*

Rebtex Inc 908 722-3549
40 Industrial Pkwy Branchburg (08876) *(G-676)*

Rebuilt Parts Co LLC 856 662-3252
7929 River Rd Pennsauken (08110) *(G-8476)*

Rebuth Metal Services (PA) 908 889-6400
130 Farley Ave Fanwood (07023) *(G-3373)*

Reckitt Benckiser LLC (HQ) 973 404-2600
399 Interpace Pkwy # 101 Parsippany (07054) *(G-8005)*

Reckitt Benckiser LLC 973 404-2600
1 Philips Pkwy Montvale (07645) *(G-6425)*

Recombine LLC 646 470-7422
3 Regent St Ste 301 Livingston (07039) *(G-5537)*

Reconserve Inc 732 826-4240
1250 Amboy Ave Perth Amboy (08861) *(G-8530)*

Recorded Publications Labs 856 963-3000
1100 E State St Camden (08105) *(G-1085)*

Recorder Newspaper, Stirling *Also called Recorder Publishing Co (G-10495)*

Recorder Newspaper...973 226-4000
  6 Brookside Ave Caldwell (07006) *(G-1029)*

Recorder Publishing Co...908 647-1180
  254 Mercer St Stirling (07980) *(G-10495)*

Recorder Publishing Co Inc (PA)............................908 766-3900
  100 S Jefferson Rd # 104 Whippany (07981) *(G-11907)*

Recruit Co Ltd...201 216-0600
  111 Pavonia Ave Jersey City (07310) *(G-4798)*

Recruit USA, Jersey City *Also called Recruit Co Ltd (G-4798)*

Rectico Inc..973 575-0009
  12 Gloria Ln Ste 1 Fairfield (07004) *(G-3298)*

Recycle Inc...908 756-2200
  20a Harmich Rd South Plainfield (07080) *(G-10324)*

Recycle Inc East..908 756-2200
  20a Harmich Rd South Plainfield (07080) *(G-10325)*

Recycle-Tech Corp..201 475-5000
  418 Falmouth Ave Elmwood Park (07407) *(G-2853)*

Recycled Pprbd Inc Clifton....................................201 768-7468
  1 Ackerman Ave Clifton (07011) *(G-1706)*

Recycling, Bridgewater *Also called County of Somerset (G-814)*

Recycling N Hensel Amer Inc.................................856 753-7614
  1003 Industrial Dr West Berlin (08091) *(G-11618)*

Red Bank Cabinet, Tinton Falls *Also called Kenneth Asmar Custom Interiors (G-10721)*

Red Bank Gstrntrology Assoc PA...........................732 842-4294
  365 Broad St Ste 2e Red Bank (07701) *(G-9242)*

Red Dash Media LLC...732 579-2396
  30 Knightsbridge Rd # 525 Piscataway (08854) *(G-8704)*

Red Diamond Co - Athc Letering.............................973 759-2005
  368 Cortlandt St Belleville (07109) *(G-310)*

Red Letter Press Inc...609 597-5257
  16 Deerhorn Trl Upper Saddle River (07458) *(G-11146)*

Red Oak Packaging Inc...862 268-8200
  52 Paterson Ave Ste 2 Newton (07860) *(G-7354)*

Red Oak Software Inc (PA).....................................973 316-6064
  115 Us Highway 46 F1000 Mountain Lakes (07046) *(G-6826)*

Red Ray Manufacturing...908 722-0040
  10 County Line Rd Ste 3 Branchburg (08876) *(G-677)*

Red Sea Press Inc...609 695-3200
  541 W Ingham Ave Ste B Ewing (08638) *(G-3059)*

Red Square Foods Inc...732 846-0190
  62 Berry St Somerset (08873) *(G-10063)*

Red Wallet Connection Inc.....................................201 223-2644
  106 Cardigan Ct Manchester (08759) *(G-5849)*

Reda Furniture LLC...732 948-1703
  25 Ocean Ave Manasquan (08736) *(G-5837)*

Reddaway Manufacturing Co Inc.............................973 589-1410
  32 Euclid Ave Newark (07105) *(G-7248)*

Redfield Corporation...201 845-3990
  336 W Passaic St Ste 3 Rochelle Park (07662) *(G-9429)*

Redhawk Distribution Inc......................................516 884-9911
  6835 Westfield Ave Pennsauken (08110) *(G-8477)*

Redhedink LLC..973 890-2320
  135 Minnisink Rd Totowa (07512) *(G-10848)*

Redi-Data Inc (PA)..973 227-4380
  5 Audrey Pl Fairfield (07004) *(G-3299)*

Redi-Direct Marketing Inc (PA)..............................973 808-4500
  107 Little Falls Rd Fairfield (07004) *(G-3300)*

Redkeys Dies Inc..856 456-7890
  1307 Market St Gloucester City (08030) *(G-3850)*

Redkoh Datatest Industries, Hillsborough *Also called Redkoh Industries Inc (G-4351)*

Redkoh Industries Inc (PA)...................................908 369-1590
  300 Valley Rd Hillsborough (08844) *(G-4351)*

Redmond Bcms Inc...973 664-2000
  103 Pocono Rd Denville (07834) *(G-2051)*

Redpuro Import, Warren *Also called Redpuro LLC (G-11428)*

Redpuro LLC...908 370-4460
  106 Mount Horeb Rd Apt 8b Warren (07059) *(G-11428)*

Redyref, Riverdale *Also called Evs Interactive Inc (G-9377)*

Reed & Perrine Inc...732 446-6363
  396 Main St Tennent (07763) *(G-10668)*

Reed & Perrine Sales Inc......................................732 446-6363
  396 Main St Tennent (07763) *(G-10669)*

Reed Presentations Inc (PA).................................908 832-0007
  630 Fox Farm Rd Asbury (08802) *(G-69)*

Reed-Lane Inc..973 709-1090
  359 Newark Pompton Tpke Wayne (07470) *(G-11546)*

Rees Scientific Corporation....................................609 530-1055
  1007 Whitehead Road Ext # 1 Ewing (08638) *(G-3060)*

Reeves Enterprises Inc..800 883-6752
  562 Central Ave New Providence (07974) *(G-7016)*

Reeves International Inc (PA)..................................973 694-5006
  14 Industrial Rd Pequannock (07440) *(G-8506)*

Reeves International Inc...973 956-9555
  34 Owens Dr Wayne (07470) *(G-11547)*

Refferals Only Inc...609 921-1033
  3321 Lawrenceville Rd Princeton (08540) *(G-9014)*

Refine Technology LLC...973 952-0002
  26 Chapin Rd Ste 1107 Pine Brook (07058) *(G-8615)*

Refresco Us Inc..973 361-9794
  92 N Main St Wharton (07885) *(G-11869)*

Refrig-It Warehouse..973 344-4545
  77 Hackensack Ave Kearny (07032) *(G-4896)*

Refuel Inc...917 645-2974
  150 Wesley St South Hackensack (07606) *(G-10183)*

Regado Biosciences Inc...908 580-2109
  106 Allen Rd Ste 401 Basking Ridge (07920) *(G-196)*

Regal Crown Fd Svc Specialist...............................508 752-2679
  20 Edison Dr Wayne (07470) *(G-11548)*

Regal Litho Prtrs Ltd Lblty Co................................732 901-1500
  1725 Oak St Lakewood (08701) *(G-5151)*

Regen Biologics Inc (PA).......................................201 651-5140
  233 Rock Rd Glen Rock (07452) *(G-3834)*

Regency Cabinetry LLC..732 363-5630
  525 Oberlin Ave S Lakewood (08701) *(G-5152)*

Regency Cabinetry LLC (PA)...................................732 363-5630
  525 Oberlin Ave S Lakewood (08701) *(G-5153)*

Regent, Lakewood *Also called Regency Cabinetry LLC (G-5153)*

Regent Cabinets LLC (PA)......................................732 363-5630
  1719 State Rt 10 Ste 220 Parsippany (07054) *(G-8006)*

Regentree LLC...609 734-4328
  116 Village Blvd Ste 200 Princeton (08540) *(G-9015)*

Regenus Ctr Core Therapies LLC............................862 295-1620
  17 Hanover Rd Florham Park (07932) *(G-3522)*

Reggiani Lighting Usa Inc......................................201 372-1717
  372 Starke Rd Carlstadt (07072) *(G-1210)*

Reggie's Roast Coffees, Linden *Also called Mire Enterprises LLC (G-5386)*

Regi US Inc..862 702-3901
  8 Fairfield Cres Unit 1 West Caldwell (07006) *(G-11677)*

Regina Wine Co...973 589-6911
  828 Raymond Blvd Newark (07105) *(G-7249)*

Regional Directory, Surf City *Also called American Directory Publishing (G-10554)*

Register Lithographers Ltd....................................973 916-2804
  1155 Bloomfield Ave Clifton (07012) *(G-1707)*

Rehtek Machine Co., Passaic *Also called S&P Machine Company Inc (G-8103)*

Reich USA Corporation...201 684-9400
  300 Rte 17 Ste H Mahwah (07430) *(G-5767)*

Reilys Candy Inc...609 953-0040
  719 Stokes Rd 721 Medford (08055) *(G-6032)*

Reinco Inc..908 755-0921
  520 North Ave Plainfield (07060) *(G-8777)*

Reiss Corporation (PA)..732 446-6100
  36 Bingham Ave Rumson (07760) *(G-9601)*

Reiss Manufacturing, Rumson *Also called Reiss Corporation (G-9601)*

Reiss Manufacturing Inc (HQ)...............................732 446-6100
  36 Bingham Ave Rumson (07760) *(G-9602)*

Relational Architects Inc.......................................201 420-0400
  33 Newark St Ste 3a Hoboken (07030) *(G-4478)*

Relational Security Corp...201 875-3456
  1 Harmon Plz Ste 700 Secaucus (07094) *(G-9803)*

Relatnship Capitl Partners Inc................................908 962-4881
  51 Jfk Pkwy Fl 1 Short Hills (07078) *(G-9876)*

Relaxzen Inc...732 936-1500
  621 Shrewsbury Ave Shrewsbury (07702) *(G-9901)*

Relay Specialties Inc..856 547-5000
  1810 Prospect Ridge Blvd Haddon Heights (08035) *(G-4048)*

Relayware Inc...201 433-3331
  30 Montgomery St Ste 1210 Jersey City (07302) *(G-4799)*

Reldan Metals Inc (PA)..732 238-8550
  396 Whitehead Ave 402 South River (08882) *(G-10355)*

Reldan Metals Inc...732 238-8550
  396 Whitehead Ave 402 South River (08882) *(G-10356)*

Reliability Maintenance Svcs..................................732 922-8878
  823 W Park Ave Pmb 245 Ocean (07712) *(G-7679)*

Reliable Envelope and Graphics.............................201 794-7756
  85 Main Ave Elmwood Park (07407) *(G-2854)*

Reliable Pallet Services LLC (PA)............................973 900-2260
  460 Hillside Ave Ste 1 Hillside (07205) *(G-4425)*

Reliable Pallet Services LLC...................................732 243-9642
  74 Liberty St Metuchen (08840) *(G-6068)*

Reliable Paper Recycling Inc..................................201 333-5244
  1 Caven Point Ave Jersey City (07305) *(G-4800)*

Reliable Rbr Plastic McHy Div, North Bergen *Also called Reliable Welding & Mch Work (G-7432)*

Reliable Welding & Mch Work..................................201 865-1073
  2008 Union Tpke North Bergen (07047) *(G-7432)*

Reliable Wood Products LLC..................................856 456-6300
  145 Broadway Westville (08093) *(G-11819)*

Reliabotics LLC...732 791-5500
  24 Van Dyke Ave New Brunswick (08901) *(G-6967)*

Reliance Electronics Inc...973 237-0400
  145 Shepherds Ln Totowa (07512) *(G-10849)*

Reliance Graphics Inc (PA).....................................973 239-5411
  80 Pompton Ave Ste 1 Verona (07044) *(G-11173)*

Reliance Vitamin LLC..732 537-1220
  3775 Park Ave Unit 1 Edison (08820) *(G-2596)*

Reliant Vitamins, Edison *Also called Plantfusion (G-2590)*

Relpro Inc..908 962-4881
  51 Jfk Pkwy Fl 1w Short Hills (07078) *(G-9877)*

Relsec, Secaucus *Also called Relational Security Corp (G-9803)*

Relx Inc 973 812-1900
1167 Mcbride Ave Ste 3 Woodland Park (07424) *(G-12090)*
Rema Corrosion Control 201 256-8400
240 Pegasus Ave Northvale (07647) *(G-7545)*
Rema Tip Top/North America Inc (HQ) 201 768-8100
240 Pegasus Ave Unit 2 Northvale (07647) *(G-7546)*
Remco Press Inc 201 751-5703
4201 Tonnelle Ave Ste 4 North Bergen (07047) *(G-7433)*
Reminder Newspaper 856 825-8811
2 W Vine St Millville (08332) *(G-6268)*
Remo Security Doors LLC 213 983-1010
560 Sylvan Ave Ste 2048 Englewood Cliffs (07632) *(G-2989)*
Remote Landlord Systems LLC 732 534-4445
525 E County Line Rd Lakewood (08701) *(G-5154)*
Rempac Foam Corp 973 881-8880
370 W Passaic St Rochelle Park (07662) *(G-9430)*
Rempac LLC (PA) 201 843-4585
370 W Passaic St Rochelle Park (07662) *(G-9431)*
Renae Telecom LLC 908 362-8112
745 Thomas St Elizabeth (07202) *(G-2774)*
Renaissance Creations LLC 551 206-1878
95 8th St Fl 2 Passaic (07055) *(G-8101)*
Renaissance House 201 408-4048
465 Westview Ave Englewood (07631) *(G-2937)*
Renaissance Lakewood LLC (HQ) 732 901-2052
1200 Paco Way Lakewood (08701) *(G-5155)*
Renaissance Lakewood LLC 732 367-9000
1720 Oak St Lakewood (08701) *(G-5156)*
Renaissance Pharmaceuticals, Lakewood *Also called Renaissance Lakewood LLC (G-5155)*
Renaissance Pharmaceuticals, Lakewood *Also called Renaissance Lakewood LLC (G-5156)*
Renard Commmunications Inc 973 912-8550
197 Mountain Ave Springfield (07081) *(G-10464)*
Renault Winery Inc 609 965-2111
72 N Bremen Ave Egg Harbor City (08215) *(G-2666)*
Renault Winery Restaurant, Egg Harbor City *Also called Renault Winery Inc (G-2666)*
Rendas Tool & Die Inc 732 469-4670
417 Elizabeth Ave Somerset (08873) *(G-10064)*
Renell Label Print Inc 201 652-6544
15 Sunflower Ave Paramus (07652) *(G-7829)*
Renesas Electronics Amer Inc 908 685-6000
440 Us Highway 22 Ste 100 Bridgewater (08807) *(G-875)*
Rennoc Corporation 856 327-5400
1450 E Chestnut Ave Ste B Vineland (08361) *(G-11256)*
Rennsteig Tools Inc (HQ) 330 315-3044
411 Hackensack Ave # 200 Hackensack (07601) *(G-3966)*
Rentalift Inc 973 684-6111
48 Alabama Ave Paterson (07503) *(G-8286)*
Rep Trading Associates Inc 732 591-1140
4 Jocama Blvd Old Bridge (08857) *(G-7727)*
Repco Inc 856 762-0172
6 Eves Dr Unit 1 Marlton (08053) *(G-5949)*
Reporte Hispano 609 933-1400
42 Dorann Ave Princeton (08540) *(G-9016)*
Repro Tronics Inc 201 722-1880
348 Golf View Dr Ltl Egg Hbr (08087) *(G-5619)*
Repromatic Printing Inc 973 239-7610
216 Little Falls Rd # 3 Cedar Grove (07009) *(G-1291)*
Resdel Corporation (PA) 609 886-1111
Industrial Park Rio Grande (08242) *(G-9357)*
Research & Education Assn 732 819-8880
61 Ethel Rd W Piscataway (08854) *(G-8705)*
Research & Mfg Corp Amer (PA) 908 862-6744
1130 W Elizabeth Ave Linden (07036) *(G-5414)*
Research and Pvd Materials 973 575-4245
373 Us Highway 46 Bldg E Fairfield (07004) *(G-3301)*
Research Dev & Manufacture, Dayton *Also called (gt) Global Tech Inc (G-1950)*
Research Institute of America, Newark *Also called Thomson Reuters Corporation (G-7299)*
Research Manufacturing, Linden *Also called Research & Mfg Corp Amer (G-5414)*
Resideo Funding Inc (HQ) 973 455-2000
115 Tabor Rd Morris Plains (07950) *(G-6625)*
Residex LLC 856 232-0880
1001 Lower Landing Rd # 412 Blackwood (08012) *(G-479)*
Resintech Inc (PA) 856 768-9600
160 Cooper Rd West Berlin (08091) *(G-11619)*
Resolv Corporation 973 220-5141
164 Elmwynd Dr Orange (07050) *(G-7759)*
Resources Inc In Display (PA) 908 272-5900
40 Boright Ave Kenilworth (07033) *(G-4974)*
Respironics Inc 973 581-6000
5 Woodhollow Rd Ste 1 Parsippany (07054) *(G-8007)*
Respironics Healthscan, Parsippany *Also called Respironics Inc (G-8007)*
Response Time Incorporated 856 875-0025
1 Fiber Optic Ln Williamstown (08094) *(G-11974)*
Restomotive Laboratories, Whippany *Also called Por-15 Inc (G-11905)*
Restortions By Peter Schichtel 973 605-8818
10 New St Morristown (07960) *(G-6697)*
Retail Management Pubg Inc 212 981-0217
28 Valley Rd Montclair (07042) *(G-6388)*
Retawa, Hoboken *Also called Reuge Management Group Inc (G-4479)*
Retrievex 732 247-3200
5 Home News Row New Brunswick (08901) *(G-6968)*
Retrographics Publishing Inc 201 501-0505
3 Reuten Dr Closter (07624) *(G-1762)*
Retrospect The For Local News, Collingswood *Also called Ainsworth Media (G-1766)*
Reuge Management Group Inc 888 306-3253
89 River St Unit 1002 Hoboken (07030) *(G-4479)*
Reuther Contracting Co Inc 201 863-3550
5303 Tonnelle Ave 5311 North Bergen (07047) *(G-7434)*
Reuther Engineering 973 485-5800
154 Silver Lake Ave Edison (08817) *(G-2597)*
Reuther Material, North Bergen *Also called Reuther Contracting Co Inc (G-7434)*
Reuther Material Co Inc 201 863-3550
5303 Tonnelle Ave North Bergen (07047) *(G-7435)*
Revel Nail LLC 855 738-3501
90 Coles Rd Blackwood (08012) *(G-480)*
Revelation Art Gallery, Denville *Also called Revelation Gallery Inc (G-2052)*
Revelation Gallery Inc 973 627-6558
22 Broadway Denville (07834) *(G-2052)*
Revent Incorporated 732 777-5187
22 Roosevelt Ave Somerset (08873) *(G-10065)*
Revere Industries LLC (PA) 856 881-3600
838 N Delsea Dr Clayton (08312) *(G-1528)*
Revere Packaging, Clayton *Also called Revere Industries LLC (G-1528)*
Revere Plastics Inc 201 641-0777
16 Industrial Ave Little Ferry (07643) *(G-5494)*
Revere Survival Products Inc 973 575-8811
3 Fairfield Cres West Caldwell (07006) *(G-11678)*
Review and Judge LLC 732 987-3905
910 E County Line Rd 202c Lakewood (08701) *(G-5157)*
Review Printing Inc 856 589-7200
53 E Holly Ave 55 Pitman (08071) *(G-8747)*
Reviva Labs Inc 856 428-3885
705 Hopkins Rd Haddonfield (08033) *(G-4064)*
Revival Sash & Door LLC 973 500-4242
78 Diamond Rd Springfield (07081) *(G-10465)*
Revlon Inc 732 287-1400
2147 State Route 27 Fl 3 Edison (08817) *(G-2598)*
Revlon Consumer Products Corp 732 287-1400
2121 State Route 27 Edison (08817) *(G-2599)*
Rex Lumber Company 732 446-4200
1 Station St Manalapan (07726) *(G-5824)*
Rex Sign, Neptune *Also called New Dawn Inc (G-6892)*
Rex Tool & Manufacturing Inc 908 925-2727
544 E Elizabeth Ave Linden (07036) *(G-5415)*
Rex Vinegar Co, Newark *Also called Regina Wine Co (G-7249)*
Rex Wine Vinegar Company 973 589-6911
828 Raymond Blvd Ste 830 Newark (07105) *(G-7250)*
Rey Consulting Inc 201 337-0051
350 Ramapo Valley Rd Oakland (07436) *(G-7643)*
Rf Vii Inc 856 875-2121
104 Church St Newfield (08344) *(G-7327)*
Rf360 Technologies Inc 848 999-3582
500 Somerset Corp Blvd Bridgewater (08807) *(G-876)*
Rfc Container LLC (PA) 856 692-0404
2066 S East Ave Vineland (08360) *(G-11257)*
Rfc Container Company, Vineland *Also called Rfc Container LLC (G-11257)*
Rff Services LLC 201 564-0040
40 Edison Ave Ste C Oakland (07436) *(G-7644)*
Rfm Printing Inc 732 938-4400
1715 Hwy 34 Wall Township (07727) *(G-11363)*
RFS Commercial Inc 201 796-0006
280 N Midland Ave Bldg M Saddle Brook (07663) *(G-9671)*
Rga Graphics, Clifton *Also called Kay Printing & Envelope Co Inc (G-1649)*
RGI Inc 973 697-2624
27 Union Valley Rd Newfoundland (07435) *(G-7332)*
Rhein Manufacturing, Denville *Also called Rhein Medical Inc (G-2053)*
Rhein Medical Inc (HQ) 727 209-2244
4 Stewart Ct Denville (07834) *(G-2053)*
Rheometer Services 732 922-8899
1933 Hwy 35 Ste 105283 Wall Township (07719) *(G-11364)*
Rhingo Pro LLC 201 728-9099
32 Us Highway 46 E Lodi (07644) *(G-5574)*
Rhoads Metal Works Inc 856 486-1551
1551 John Tipton Blvd Pennsauken (08110) *(G-8478)*
Rhoads OHara Architectural 856 692-4100
3690 N West Blvd Vineland (08360) *(G-11258)*
Rhodia, Princeton *Also called Solvay Holding Inc (G-9024)*
Rhodium Software Inc 848 248-2906
10 Scotto Pl Dayton (08810) *(G-1986)*
Rhythmedix LLC 856 282-1080
5000 Atrium Way Ste 1 Mount Laurel (08054) *(G-6800)*
Ribble Company Inc 201 475-1812
280 N Midland Ave Ste 380 Saddle Brook (07663) *(G-9672)*
Ribbon Bazaar, Neptune *Also called Cottage Lace and Ribbon Co Inc (G-6871)*

Riccarr Displays Inc 973 983-6701
  52 Green Pond Rd Rockaway (07866) *(G-9493)*

Ricci Bros Sand Company Inc 856 785-0166
  2099 Dragston Rd Port Norris (08349) *(G-8888)*

Ricci Brothers Sand, Port Norris *Also called Ricci Bros Sand Company Inc* *(G-8888)*

Rich Art Color Co Inc 201 767-0009
  202 Pegasus Ave Northvale (07647) *(G-7547)*

Rich Designs 908 369-5035
  867 Amwell Rd Hillsborough (08844) *(G-4352)*

Rich Products Corporation 856 696-5600
  1910 Gallagher Dr Vineland (08360) *(G-11259)*

Rich Products Corporation 800 356-7094
  100 American Legion Dr Riverside (08075) *(G-9402)*

Richard Andrus 856 825-1782
  708 E Main St Millville (08332) *(G-6269)*

Richard E Pierson Mtls Corp 856 740-2400
  151 Industrial Dr Williamstown (08094) *(G-11975)*

Richard E Pierson Mtls Corp 856 691-0083
  184 W Sherman Ave Vineland (08360) *(G-11260)*

Richard E Pierson Mtls Corp (PA) 856 467-4199
  426 Swedesboro Rd Pilesgrove (08098) *(G-8580)*

Richard J Bell Co Inc 201 847-0887
  465 W Main St Wyckoff (07481) *(G-12119)*

Richard Rein 609 452-7000
  15 Princess Rd K Lawrence Township (08648) *(G-5219)*

Richard Shafer 856 358-3483
  38 Martin Ave Elmer (08318) *(G-2802)*

Richards Industries, West Caldwell *Also called RISE Corporation* *(G-11679)*

Richards Manufacturing Co Inc 973 371-1771
  517 Lyons Ave Irvington (07111) *(G-4584)*

Richards Mfg A NJ Ltd Partnr 973 371-1771
  517 Lyons Ave Irvington (07111) *(G-4585)*

Richards Mfg Co Sales Inc 973 371-1771
  517 Lyons Ave Irvington (07111) *(G-4586)*

Richmond Industries Inc. 732 355-1616
  1 Chris Ct Dayton (08810) *(G-1987)*

Ricklyn Co Inc 908 689-6770
  43 Centerville Rd Columbia (07832) *(G-1797)*

Ricks Cleanouts Inc 973 340-7454
  654 River Dr Garfield (07026) *(G-3763)*

Rico Foods Inc 973 278-0589
  527 E 18th St Paterson (07514) *(G-8287)*

Rico Products, Paterson *Also called Rico Foods Inc* *(G-8287)*

Ricoh Prtg Systems Amer Inc 973 316-6051
  115 Route 46 Bldg F Mountain Lakes (07046) *(G-6827)*

Ricoh Systems, Mountain Lakes *Also called Ricoh Prtg Systems Amer Inc* *(G-6827)*

Riconpharma LLC (HQ) 973 627-4685
  100 Ford Rd Ste 9 Denville (07834) *(G-2054)*

Ricztone Inc 609 695-6263
  19 Bow Hill Ave Trenton (08610) *(G-10987)*

Ridge Manufacturing Corp 973 586-2717
  5 Astro Pl Ste A Rockaway (07866) *(G-9494)*

Ridge Precision Products Inc. 973 361-3508
  288 Us Highway 46 Ste D Dover (07801) *(G-2104)*

Ridgewood Energy O Fund LLC 201 447-9000
  14 Philips Pkwy Montvale (07645) *(G-6426)*

Ridgewood Energy S Fund LLC 201 307-0470
  14 Philips Pkwy Montvale (07645) *(G-6427)*

Ridgewood Energy T Fund LLC 800 942-5550
  14 Philips Pkwy Montvale (07645) *(G-6428)*

Ridgewood Energy U Fund LLC 201 447-9000
  14 Philips Pkwy Montvale (07645) *(G-6429)*

Ridgewood Energy V Fund LLC 800 942-5550
  14 Philips Pkwy Montvale (07645) *(G-6430)*

Ridgewood Energy Y Fund LLC 201 447-9000
  14 Philips Pkwy Montvale (07645) *(G-6431)*

Ridgewood Press Inc 201 670-9797
  609 Franklin Tpke Ridgewood (07450) *(G-9328)*

Riedel Sign Company Inc 201 641-9121
  15 Warren St Little Ferry (07643) *(G-5495)*

Riegel Cmmunications Group Inc 609 771-0555
  1 Graphics Dr Ewing (08628) *(G-3061)*

Riegel Holding Company Inc 609 771-0361
  1 Graphics Dr Ewing (08628) *(G-3062)*

Riegel Printing Company, Ewing *Also called Riegel Holding Company Inc* *(G-3062)*

Riephoff Saw Mill Inc 609 259-7265
  763 Route 524 Allentown (08501) *(G-30)*

Right Angle, Hoboken *Also called Hoboken Executive Art Inc* *(G-4454)*

Rigo Industries Inc 973 881-1780
  50 California Ave Paterson (07503) *(G-8288)*

Rimtec Manufacturing Corp 609 387-0011
  1702 Beverly Rd Burlington (08016) *(G-983)*

Ring Container Tech LLC 973 258-0707
  50 Fadem Rd Springfield (07081) *(G-10466)*

Ringfeder Pwr Transm USA Corp 201 666-3320
  165 Carver Ave Westwood (07675) *(G-11843)*

Rinko Orthopedic Appliances 201 796-3121
  25-09 Broadway Ste 1 Fair Lawn (07410) *(G-3117)*

Rio Supply 856 719-0081
  100 Allied Pkwy Sicklerville (08081) *(G-9915)*

Riogen Inc 609 529-0503
  1 Deerpark Dr Ste L3 Monmouth Junction (08852) *(G-6309)*

Riotsound Inc 917 273-5814
  17 Hampton House Rd # 15 Newton (07860) *(G-7355)*

Ripe Life Wines LLC 201 560-3233
  253 Indian Trail Dr Franklin Lakes (07417) *(G-3630)*

RISE Corporation 973 575-7480
  4 Fairfield Cres West Caldwell (07006) *(G-11679)*

Rising Health LLC 201 961-9000
  Park 80 W Plz Saddle Brook (07663) *(G-9673)*

Rising Pharma Holdings Inc (PA) 201 961-9000
  250 Pehle Ave Ste 601 Saddle Brook (07663) *(G-9674)*

Rising Pharmaceuticals Inc (HQ) 201 961-9000
  250 Pehle Ave Ste 601 Saddle Brook (07663) *(G-9675)*

Risse & Risse Graphics Inc 856 751-7671
  901 E Clements Bridge Rd # 3 Runnemede (08078) *(G-9608)*

River Horse Brewery Co Inc 609 883-0890
  2 Graphics Dr Ewing (08628) *(G-3063)*

Riverdale Color Mfg Inc (PA) 732 376-9300
  1 Walnut St Perth Amboy (08861) *(G-8531)*

Riverdale Quarry, Riverdale *Also called Tilcon New York Inc* *(G-9387)*

Riverdale Quarry LLC 973 835-0028
  125 Hamburg Tpke Riverdale (07457) *(G-9382)*

Riverside Graphics Inc 201 876-9000
  243 Cortlandt St Belleville (07109) *(G-311)*

Riverside Marina Yacht Sls LLC 856 461-1077
  74 Norman Ave Ste 1 Riverside (08075) *(G-9403)*

Riverstone Industries Corp 973 586-2564
  65 Fleetwood Dr Ste 200 Rockaway (07866) *(G-9495)*

Rj Bielan Graphic Arts, New Brunswick *Also called R J Blen Grphic Arts Cnverting* *(G-6964)*

Rj Brands LLC (PA) 888 315-8407
  200 Performance Dr # 207 Mahwah (07495) *(G-5768)*

Rjb Design Group Co., Wyckoff *Also called Richard J Bell Co Inc* *(G-12119)*

Rjd Machine Products, Trenton *Also called Czar Industries Inc* *(G-10928)*

Rjticeco LLC 973 697-0156
  4 Northwoods Trl Stockholm (07460) *(G-10500)*

Rke Atheltic Lettering 732 280-1111
  1901 State Route 71 1c Belmar (07719) *(G-353)*

Rlct Industries LLC 609 712-1318
  2 E Acres Dr Pennington (08534) *(G-8372)*

Rmx, Mount Laurel *Also called Rhythmedix LLC* *(G-6800)*

Road Dept, Belvidere *Also called County of Warren* *(G-359)*

Roan Printing Inc 908 526-5990
  4 E Main St Somerville (08876) *(G-10124)*

Robard, Mount Laurel *Also called Food Sciences Corp* *(G-6761)*

Robden Enterprises Inc 973 273-1200
  210 Market St Newark (07102) *(G-7251)*

Roben Manufacturing Co Inc. 732 364-6000
  760 Vassar Ave Lakewood (08701) *(G-5158)*

Robert A Eick Qlty Bookbinding 973 822-2100
  34 Central Ave Madison (07940) *(G-5701)*

Robert Brown 609 398-6262
  1125 West Ave 1 Ocean City (08226) *(G-7694)*

Robert Colaneri 201 939-4405
  236 Park Ave 238 East Rutherford (07073) *(G-2314)*

Robert F Gaiser Inc 973 838-9254
  292 Main St Butler (07405) *(G-1013)*

Robert Freeman 973 751-0082
  320 Washington Ave Belleville (07109) *(G-312)*

Robert H Hoover & Sons Inc 973 347-4210
  149 Gold Mine Rd Flanders (07836) *(G-3417)*

Robert J Donaldson Inc 856 629-2737
  1287 Glassboro Rd Williamstown (08094) *(G-11976)*

Robert J Smith 201 641-6555
  152 Louis St South Hackensack (07606) *(G-10184)*

Robert Main Sons Inc 201 447-3700
  20-21 Wagaraw Rd Fair Lawn (07410) *(G-3118)*

Robert Manse Designs LLC 732 428-8305
  2100 Felver Ct Rahway (07065) *(G-9124)*

Robert Nichols Contracting 973 902-2632
  407 Conklintown Rd Ringwood (07456) *(G-9352)*

Robert Stewart Inc (PA) 973 751-5151
  120 Little St Belleville (07109) *(G-313)*

Robert Technologies, Marlboro *Also called Rti Dge LLC* *(G-5912)*

Robert Wallace 609 649-0596
  811 Rosemont Ringoes Rd Stockton (08559) *(G-10502)*

Robert Weidener 201 703-5700
  9 12th St Fair Lawn (07410) *(G-3119)*

Robert Wynn 856 435-6398
  36 Windmill Dr Clementon (08021) *(G-1534)*

Robert Young & Sons Inc. 973 483-0451
  25 Grafton Ave Newark (07104) *(G-7252)*

Robert Young and Son Inc 973 728-8133
  830 Burnt Meadow Rd Hewitt (07421) *(G-4279)*

Roberta's Hut, Hamburg *Also called Robertas Jewelers Inc* *(G-4095)*

Robertas Jewelers Inc 973 875-5318
  175 State Rt 23 S Ste D Hamburg (07419) *(G-4095)*

Robertet Inc (HQ) 201 405-1000
  400 International Dr Budd Lake (07828) *(G-932)*

Robertet Flavors Inc 732 271-1804
10 Colonial Dr Piscataway (08854) *(G-8706)*
Robertet Flavors & Fragrances, Piscataway *Also called Robertet Flavors Inc (G-8706)*
Robertet Fragrances Inc (HQ) 201 405-1000
400 International Dr Budd Lake (07828) *(G-933)*
Robertet Fragrances Inc 973 575-4550
30 Stewart Pl Fairfield (07004) *(G-3302)*
Robertson Industries, Montague *Also called Craig Robertson (G-6354)*
Robinson Tech Intl Corp 973 287-6458
310 Fairfield Rd Fairfield (07004) *(G-3303)*
Robokiller LLC 723 838-1901
101 S Broadway South Amboy (08879) *(G-10140)*
Robotunits Inc 732 438-0500
8 Corporate Dr Ste 1 Cranbury (08512) *(G-1879)*
Roche Diagnostics Corporation 908 253-0707
1080 Us Highway 202 S Branchburg (08876) *(G-678)*
Rock Dreams Electronics LLC 609 890-0808
362 State Highway 33 Trenton (08619) *(G-10988)*
Rock of Ages Monuments, Spring Lake *Also called H T Hall Inc (G-10422)*
Rock Solid Woodworking LLC 732 974-1261
508 Washington Blvd Apt A Sea Girt (08750) *(G-9747)*
Rock Team Alliance, Marlton *Also called Westrock Rkt LLC (G-5956)*
Rockline Industries Inc 973 257-2884
1 Kramer Way Montville (07045) *(G-6446)*
Rockwell Automation Inc 973 658-1500
299 Cherry Hill Rd # 200 Parsippany (07054) *(G-8008)*
Rockwell Automation Inc 973 526-3901
700 Lanidex Plz Ste 101 Parsippany (07054) *(G-8009)*
Rockwood Corporation 908 355-8600
869a State Route 12 Frenchtown (08825) *(G-3717)*
Rockwood Holdings Inc (HQ) 609 514-0300
100 Overlook Ctr Ste 101 Princeton (08540) *(G-9017)*
Rockwood Specialties Group Inc (HQ) 609 514-0300
100 Overlook Ctr Ste 101 Princeton (08540) *(G-9018)*
Rodman Media Corp 201 825-2552
25 Philips Pkwy Fl 2 Montvale (07645) *(G-6432)*
Roelynn Litho Inc 732 942-9650
687 Prospect St Ste 410 Lakewood (08701) *(G-5159)*
Roger Software Distribution, Teaneck *Also called RSD America Inc (G-10649)*
Rohm America LLC (PA) 973 929-8000
299 Jefferson Rd Parsippany (07054) *(G-8010)*
Roi Rnovations, Princeton *Also called Refferals Only Inc (G-9014)*
Rolferrys Specialties Inc 856 456-2999
601 New Broadway Brooklawn (08030) *(G-915)*
Roll Tech Industries 609 730-9500
55 Route 31 S Ste A Pennington (08534) *(G-8373)*
Rollon Corporation 973 300-5492
101 Bilby Rd Ste B Hackettstown (07840) *(G-4032)*
Rolls Offset Group Inc (PA) 201 727-1110
264 Castle Ter Lyndhurst (07071) *(G-5675)*
Rolls-Royce Motor Cars Na LLC 201 307-4117
300 Chestnut Ridge Rd Woodcliff Lake (07677) *(G-12063)*
Rolo Systems 973 627-4214
34a Broadway Denville (07834) *(G-2055)*
Roma Moulding Inc 732 346-0999
115 Northfield Ave Edison (08837) *(G-2600)*
Roma Vinegar, Newark *Also called Rex Wine Vinegar Company (G-7250)*
Romaco Inc 973 709-0691
6 Frassetto Way Ste D Lincoln Park (07035) *(G-5305)*
Romaco North America Inc 609 584-2500
8 Commerce Way Ste 115 Hamilton (08691) *(G-4123)*
Romar Machine & Tool Company 201 337-7111
521 Commerce St Franklin Lakes (07417) *(G-3631)*
Romark Logistics CES LLC (PA) 908 789-2800
822 South Ave W Westfield (07090) *(G-11802)*
Romax Parking Solutions, Oakland *Also called Park Plus Inc (G-7641)*
Rombiolo LLC 973 680-0405
168 Broughton Ave Bloomfield (07003) *(G-517)*
Romulus Emprises Inc 609 683-4549
60 Woodside Ave Hightstown (08520) *(G-4298)*
Ron Banafato Inc 908 685-9447
1161 3rd Ave Phillipsburg (08865) *(G-8572)*
Ron Jon Surf Shop Fla Inc 609 494-8844
201 W 9th St Ship Bottom (08008) *(G-9862)*
Ronald Perry 201 702-2407
14 Westervelt Pl 1 Jersey City (07304) *(G-4801)*
Roned Printing & Reproduction 973 386-1848
6 Deforest Ave Ste 2 East Hanover (07936) *(G-2236)*
Ronell Industries Inc (PA) 908 245-5255
298 Cox St Roselle (07203) *(G-9571)*
Ronsil Silicone Rubber Div, Rumson *Also called Reiss Manufacturing Inc (G-9602)*
Rony Inc 201 891-2551
393 Crescent Ave Ste 12 Wyckoff (07481) *(G-12120)*
Roof Deck Inc 609 448-6666
80 Twin Rivers Dr East Windsor (08520) *(G-2358)*
Room Service Amenities, Morganville *Also called ADS Sales Co Inc (G-6580)*
Roper Scientific Inc (HQ) 941 556-2601
3660 Quakerbridge Rd Trenton (08619) *(G-10989)*
Rosalindas Discount Furniture 973 928-2838
76 Lexington Ave Passaic (07055) *(G-8102)*
Rosano Asphalt LLC 732 620-8400
Asbury Rd Ste 360 Farmingdale (07727) *(G-3391)*
Rosco Inc 908 789-1020
55 South Ave Garwood (07027) *(G-3792)*
Rose Brand East, Secaucus *Also called Rose Brand Wipers Inc (G-9804)*
Rose Brand Wipers Inc (PA) 201 809-1730
4 Emerson Ln Secaucus (07094) *(G-9804)*
Rose Brand Wipers Inc 201 770-1441
4 Emerson Ln Secaucus (07094) *(G-9805)*
Roseland Manufacturing, Roseland *Also called B&G Foods Inc (G-9534)*
Roselli, L E, Medford *Also called L E Rosellis Food Specialties (G-6027)*
Rosemont Publishing & Printing 609 269-8094
10 Schalks Crossing Rd Plainsboro (08536) *(G-8802)*
Rosemount Inc 973 257-2300
1160 Parsippany Blvd # 102 Parsippany (07054) *(G-8011)*
Rosenwach Group, Somerset *Also called Rosenwach Tank Co LLC (G-10066)*
Rosenwach Tank Co LLC 732 563-4900
1100 Randolph Rd Somerset (08873) *(G-10066)*
Roseville Tool & Manufacturing 973 992-5405
22 Okner Pkwy Livingston (07039) *(G-5538)*
Ross Bicycles LLC 888 392-5628
205 Us Highway 46 Ste 10 Totowa (07512) *(G-10850)*
Rossow Cosmetiques - Usa Inc 732 872-1464
100 Matawan Rd Ste 350 Matawan (07747) *(G-5987)*
Rossow USA, Matawan *Also called Rossow Cosmetiques - Usa Inc (G-5987)*
Rotarex Inc North America 724 696-3345
101 Bilby Rd Ste B Hackettstown (07840) *(G-4033)*
Rotarex Trade, Hackettstown *Also called Rotarex Inc North America (G-4033)*
Rotary Die Systems Inc 856 234-3994
876 N Lenola Rd Ste 9a Moorestown (08057) *(G-6563)*
Rotech Tool & Mold Co Inc 908 241-9669
824 Fairfield Ave Kenilworth (07033) *(G-4975)*
Rotor Clamp, Somerset *Also called Rotor Clip Company Inc (G-10067)*
Rotor Clip Company Inc (PA) 732 469-7707
187 Davidson Ave Somerset (08873) *(G-10067)*
Rotuba Extruders Inc 908 486-1000
1401 S Park Ave Linden (07036) *(G-5416)*
Rouses Pt Pharmaceuticals LLC 239 390-1495
11 Commerce Dr Ste 101 Cranford (07016) *(G-1926)*
Route 22 Fuel LLC 908 526-5270
1240 Us Highway 22 Bridgewater (08807) *(G-877)*
Rowan Technologies Inc (PA) 609 267-9000
10 Indel Ave Rancocas (08073) *(G-9165)*
Roxboro Holdings Inc (HQ) 732 919-3119
1501 State Route 34 Wall Township (07727) *(G-11365)*
Roy Anania 201 498-1555
149 S State St Hackensack (07601) *(G-3967)*
Roy D Smith Inc 201 384-4163
20 Foster St Bergenfield (07621) *(G-383)*
Roy Press Inc 732 922-9460
57 Bridgewaters Dr Apt 17 Oceanport (07757) *(G-7706)*
Roy Press Printers, Oceanport *Also called Roy Press Inc (G-7706)*
Royal Adhesives & Sealants LLC 973 694-0845
48 Burgess Pl Wayne (07470) *(G-11549)*
Royal Aluminum Co Inc 973 589-8880
620 Market St Ste 1 Newark (07105) *(G-7253)*
Royal Baking Co Inc 201 296-0888
8 Empire Blvd Moonachie (07074) *(G-6487)*
Royal Cabinet Company Inc 908 203-8000
15 Easy St Bound Brook (08805) *(G-605)*
Royal Cosmetics Corporation 732 246-7275
4 Jules Ln A New Brunswick (08901) *(G-6969)*
Royal Crest Home Fashions Inc 201 461-4600
170 Fair St Palisades Park (07650) *(G-7778)*
Royal Ingredients LLC 856 241-2004
510 Sharptown Rd Swedesboro (08085) *(G-10607)*
Royal Lace Co Inc 718 495-9327
902 E Hazelwood Ave Rahway (07065) *(G-9125)*
Royal Master Grinders Inc 201 337-8500
143 Bauer Dr Oakland (07436) *(G-7645)*
Royal Oak Railings LLC 973 208-8900
3 Field Ct Oak Ridge (07438) *(G-7605)*
Royal Pallet Inc 973 299-0445
771 Knoll Rd Boonton (07005) *(G-566)*
Royal Pharmaceuticals LLC 732 292-2661
1967 Highway 34 Ste 103 Wall Township (07719) *(G-11366)*
Royal Prime Inc (PA) 908 354-7600
1027 Newark Ave Ste 1 Elizabeth (07208) *(G-2775)*
Royal Printing Service 201 863-3131
441 51st St West New York (07093) *(G-11753)*
Royal Seamless Corporation 732 901-9595
1000 Airport Rd Ste 203 Lakewood (08701) *(G-5160)*
Royal Slide Sales, Garfield *Also called Royal Zipper Manufg Company (G-3765)*
Royal Slide Sales Co Inc (PA) 973 777-1177
42 Hepworth Pl Garfield (07026) *(G-3764)*
Royal Sovereign Intl Inc (PA) 800 397-1025
2 Volvo Dr Rockleigh (07647) *(G-9521)*

A L P H A B E T I C

Royal Wine Corporation (PA) 718 384-2400
  63 Lefante Dr Bayonne (07002) *(G-233)*

Royal Wine Corporation 201 535-9006
  63 Lefante Dr Bayonne (07002) *(G-234)*

Royal Zipper Manufg Company 973 777-1177
  42 Hepworth Pl Garfield (07026) *(G-3765)*

Royale Cosmetics, New Brunswick Also called Royal Cosmetics Corporation *(G-6969)*

Royale Pigments & Chem Inc 201 845-4666
  12 N State Rt 17 Ste 203 Paramus (07652) *(G-7830)*

Royalty Press Inc 856 663-2288
  165 Broadway Westville (08093) *(G-11820)*

Royalty Press Group, Westville Also called Royalty Press Inc *(G-11820)*

Royce Associates A Ltd Partnr (PA) 201 438-5200
  35 Carlton Ave East Rutherford (07073) *(G-2315)*

Royce Associates A Ltd Partnr 973 279-0400
  28 Paterson St Paterson (07501) *(G-8289)*

Royce International Corp 201 438-5200
  35 Carlton Ave East Rutherford (07073) *(G-2316)*

Royce Leather, Secaucus Also called Emporium Leather Company Inc *(G-9762)*

Royer Comm Graphics, Pennsauken Also called Royercomm Corporation *(G-8480)*

Royer Graphics Inc 856 344-7935
  101 Lincoln Dr Clementon (08021) *(G-1535)*

Royer Group Inc 856 324-0171
  7120 Airport Hwy Pennsauken (08109) *(G-8479)*

Royercomm Corporation 856 665-6400
  7120 Airport Hwy Pennsauken (08109) *(G-8480)*

Royle Systems Group LLC 201 644-0345
  375 North St Ste M Teterboro (07608) *(G-10690)*

Roysons Corporation 973 625-5570
  40 Vanderhoof Ave Rockaway (07866) *(G-9496)*

Roysons Wall Covering, Rockaway Also called Roysons Corporation *(G-9496)*

Rp Products LLC 732 254-4222
  646 State Route 18 East Brunswick (08816) *(G-2174)*

RPC Driveline Service, Pennsauken Also called Rebuilt Parts Co LLC *(G-8476)*

RPI Industries Inc 609 714-2330
  220 Route 70 Medford (08055) *(G-6033)*

Rpl, Camden Also called Recorded Publications Labs *(G-1085)*

Rpl Supplies Inc 973 767-0880
  141 Lanza Ave Bldg 3a Garfield (07026) *(G-3766)*

RPM Prfrmnce Catings Group Inc (HQ) 888 788-4323
  280 West Ave Long Branch (07740) *(G-5605)*

Rq Floors Corp (PA) 201 654-3587
  425 Victoria Ter Ridgefield (07657) *(G-9287)*

Rq Floors Corp 201 654-3587
  550 Huyler St South Hackensack (07606) *(G-10185)*

RR Bowker LLC (HQ) 908 286-1090
  630 Central Ave New Providence (07974) *(G-7017)*

Rs Microwave Co Inc 973 492-1207
  22 Park Pl Butler (07405) *(G-1014)*

RS Phillips Steel LLC 973 827-6464
  128 Lake Pochung Rd Sussex (07461) *(G-10565)*

RSD America Inc 201 996-1000
  300 Frank W Burr Blvd # 54 Teaneck (07666) *(G-10649)*

RSI Company 973 227-7800
  333 Us Highway 46 Fairfield (07004) *(G-3304)*

Rsi-Fairfield Division, Fairfield Also called RSI Company *(G-3304)*

Rsl LLC (PA) 609 484-1600
  3092 English Creek Ave Egg Harbor Township (08234) *(G-2695)*

Rsl LLC 609 645-9777
  3049 Fernwood Ave Egg Harbor Township (08234) *(G-2696)*

RSR Electronics Inc 732 381-8777
  900 Hart St Rahway (07065) *(G-9126)*

RSR Enterprises LLC 732 369-6053
  1480 Long Rd Martinsville (08836) *(G-5964)*

Rt Com USA Inc 973 862-4210
  10 Millpond Dr Unit 2 Lafayette (07848) *(G-5032)*

Rti, Fairfield Also called Robinson Tech Intl Corp *(G-3303)*

Rti Computer Services, Oradell Also called R T I Inc *(G-7746)*

Rti Dge LLC 732 254-6389
  4 Timber Ln Ste B Marlboro (07746) *(G-5912)*

Rubber & Silicone Products Co 973 227-2300
  17 Montesano Rd Fairfield (07004) *(G-3305)*

Rubber Fab & Molding Inc 908 852-7725
  1100 Rte 519 Johnsonburg (07846) *(G-4837)*

Rubigo Cosmetics 973 636-6573
  101 E Main St Bldg 12 Little Falls (07424) *(G-5466)*

Rudco Products Inc (PA) 856 691-0800
  114 E Oak Rd Vineland (08360) *(G-11261)*

Rudolph Instruments Inc 973 227-0139
  400 Morris Ave Ste 120 Denville (07834) *(G-2056)*

Rudolph RES Analytical Corp (PA) 973 584-1558
  55 Newburgh Rd Hackettstown (07840) *(G-4034)*

Rudolph Technologies Inc 973 448-4307
  1705 Us Highway 46 Ste 3 Ledgewood (07852) *(G-5280)*

Rudolph Technologies Inc 973 347-3891
  550 Clark Dr Ste 1 Budd Lake (07828) *(G-934)*

Ruffino Packaging Co, Hackensack Also called Ruffino Paper Box Mfg Co *(G-3968)*

Ruffino Paper Box Mfg Co 201 487-1260
  63 Green St Hackensack (07601) *(G-3968)*

Ruggiero Sea Food Inc (PA) 973 589-0524
  474 Wilson Ave Newark (07105) *(G-7254)*

Ruggiero Sea Food Inc 973 589-0524
  117 Avenue L Newark (07105) *(G-7255)*

Ruichem Usa Inc 978 992-1811
  2050 Center Ave Ste 365 Fort Lee (07024) *(G-3584)*

Rumblewood Cleaners, Mount Laurel Also called Ramblewood Cleaners Inc *(G-6799)*

Rumsons Kitchens Inc 732 842-1810
  103 E River Rd Rumson (07760) *(G-9603)*

Runding LLC 973 277-8775
  90 Greendale Dr Oak Ridge (07438) *(G-7606)*

Ruoff & Sons Inc 856 931-2064
  1030 Rose Ave Runnemede (08078) *(G-9609)*

Rush Graphics Inc 973 427-9393
  1122 Goffle Rd 32 Hawthorne (07506) *(G-4242)*

Rush Index Tabs Inc 800 914-3036
  60 Willow St East Rutherford (07073) *(G-2317)*

Rush Printing and Binding Svcs, East Rutherford Also called Rush Index Tabs Inc *(G-2317)*

Russell Cast Stone Inc 856 753-4000
  400 Cooper Rd West Berlin (08091) *(G-11620)*

Russell W Anderson Inc 201 825-2092
  1 Fyke Rd Mahwah (07430) *(G-5769)*

Russo Seamless Gutter LLC 732 836-0151
  45 Cherie Dr Brick (08724) *(G-730)*

Rust-Oleum Corporation 847 367-7700
  173 Belmont Dr Somerset (08873) *(G-10068)*

Rust-Oleum Corporation 732 652-2378
  480 Frelinghuysen Ave Newark (07114) *(G-7256)*

Rust-Oleum Corporation 732 469-8100
  323 Campus Dr Somerset (08873) *(G-10069)*

Rutgers Food Innovation Center 856 459-1900
  450 E Broad St Bridgeton (08302) *(G-771)*

Rutler Screen Printing Inc 908 859-3327
  169 Belview Rd Phillipsburg (08865) *(G-8573)*

Rw Delights Inc 718 683-1038
  50 Division Ave Ste 44 Millington (07946) *(G-6208)*

Rx Trade Zone Inc 833 933-6600
  22 Meridian Rd Unit 15 Edison (08820) *(G-2601)*

Ryder Global, Villas Also called Ryder Technology *(G-11180)*

Ryder Technology 215 817-7868
  36 E Drumbed Rd Villas (08251) *(G-11180)*

S & G Tool Aid Corporation 973 824-7730
  43 E Alpine St Newark (07114) *(G-7257)*

S & H R Inc 908 925-3797
  401 N Wood Ave Ste 1 Linden (07036) *(G-5417)*

S & J Villari Livestock LLC (HQ) 856 468-0807
  1481 Glassboro Rd Wenonah (08090) *(G-11576)*

S & M Retaining Rings, Newton Also called Schneider & Marquard Inc *(G-7356)*

S & S Manufacturing, Edison Also called S & S Socius Inc *(G-2602)*

S & S Precision Company Inc 856 662-0006
  2205 Sherman Ave Pennsauken (08110) *(G-8481)*

S & S Printing, Somerdale Also called Staines Inc *(G-9935)*

S & S Socius Inc 732 698-2400
  115 Fieldcrest Ave Edison (08837) *(G-2602)*

S & W Precision Tool Corp 908 526-6097
  3 Holly Ct Bridgewater (08807) *(G-878)*

S and D Fuel LLC 908 248-8188
  1351 Magie Ave Union (07083) *(G-11087)*

S C T, Franklin Lakes Also called Vozeh Equipment Corp *(G-3632)*

S D L Powder Coating Inc 732 473-0800
  1591 Route 37 W Ste E4 Toms River (08755) *(G-10788)*

S Frankford & Sons Inc 856 222-4134
  110 Gaither Dr Ste A Mount Laurel (08054) *(G-6801)*

S G A Business Systems Inc 908 359-4626
  83 Haverford Ct Hillsborough (08844) *(G-4353)*

S G A Custom Shirtmakers, Newark Also called Skip Gambert & Associates Inc *(G-7277)*

S Geno Carpet and Flooring 215 669-1400
  153 Sunset Dr Mount Royal (08061) *(G-6818)*

S Goldberg & Co Inc (PA) 201 342-1200
  3 University Plz Ste 400 Hackensack (07601) *(G-3969)*

S H P C Inc 973 589-5242
  187 Christie St Newark (07105) *(G-7258)*

S J Quarry Materials Inc 856 691-3133
  615 Gershal Ave Elmer (08318) *(G-2803)*

S J Screw Company Inc 908 475-2155
  Front & Hardwick St Belvidere (07823) *(G-366)*

S J T Imaging Inc 201 262-7744
  475 Kinderkamack Rd Ste 2 Oradell (07649) *(G-7747)*

S Jarco-U Castings Corporation 201 271-0003
  109 45th St Union City (07087) *(G-11127)*

S Johnson & Son, Belvidere Also called S J Screw Company Inc *(G-366)*

S K, Totowa Also called Sk Custom Creations Inc *(G-10852)*

S L Enterprises Inc (PA) 908 272-8145
  1603 N Olden Ave Ewing (08638) *(G-3064)*

S L P Engineering Inc 732 240-3696
  1501 Industrial Way Toms River (08755) *(G-10789)*

S M P, Mahwah Also called Strategic Mktg Promotions Inc *(G-5777)*

S M Z Enterprises Inc 908 232-1921
  223 South Ave E Westfield (07090) *(G-11803)*

S O S Gases Inc (PA)....201 998-7800
1100 Harrison Ave Kearny (07032) ***(G-4897)***
S P Industries Inc....856 691-3200
1172 N West Blvd Vineland (08360) ***(G-11262)***
S P Industries Inc....215 672-7800
1002 Harding Hwy Buena (08310) ***(G-941)***
S S P Enterprises Inc....732 602-7878
825 Us Highway 1 S Iselin (08830) ***(G-4625)***
S Swanson LLC....201 750-5050
157 Veterans Dr Ste B Northvale (07647) ***(G-7548)***
S V O Inc....973 983-8380
28 State Route 10 W Succasunna (07876) ***(G-10519)***
S V Pharma Inc....201 433-1512
227 Ocean Ave Jersey City (07305) ***(G-4802)***
S W Electronics & Mfg (PA)....856 222-9900
1215 N Church St Moorestown (08057) ***(G-6564)***
S W I International Inc....973 334-2525
487 Division St Boonton (07005) ***(G-567)***
S&A Molders Inc....732 851-7770
75 Mount Vernon Rd Manalapan (07726) ***(G-5825)***
S&P Machine Company Inc....973 365-2101
135 Monroe St Passaic (07055) ***(G-8103)***
S&S Precision, Pennsauken *Also called S & S Precision Company Inc* ***(G-8481)***
S&W Fabricators Inc....856 881-7418
100 Delsea Dr S Glassboro (08028) ***(G-3818)***
SA Bendheim Ltd (PA)....973 471-1733
82 Totowa Rd Ste 1 Wayne (07470) ***(G-11550)***
SA Richards Inc....201 947-3850
1600 Parker Ave Apt 23a Fort Lee (07024) ***(G-3585)***
Saad Collection Inc....732 763-4015
160 Rrtan Ctr Pkwy Unit 5 Edison (08837) ***(G-2603)***
Saas.com, Branchburg *Also called Kronos Saashr Inc* ***(G-653)***
Saber Associates....973 777-3800
1111 Paulison Ave Clifton (07011) ***(G-1708)***
Sabert Corporation (PA)....800 722-3781
2288 Main St Sayreville (08872) ***(G-9722)***
Sabert Corporation....732 721-5544
879 Main St Ste 899 Sayreville (08872) ***(G-9723)***
Sabinsa Corporation (PA)....732 777-1111
20 Lake Dr East Windsor (08520) ***(G-2359)***
Sabre Die Cutting Co Inc....973 357-9800
68 Mill St Paterson (07501) ***(G-8290)***
Sabrett Hot Dog, Englewood *Also called Marathon Enterprises Inc* ***(G-2921)***
Sabrimax Corp....201 871-0808
50 E Palisade Ave Ste 413 Englewood (07631) ***(G-2938)***
Saddle Brook Controls, Saddle Brook *Also called Ribble Company Inc* ***(G-9672)***
Saddlebrook Ridge Equest Ctr, Shamong *Also called Brook Saddle Ridge Equest* ***(G-9855)***
Sadelco Inc....201 569-3323
96 Linwood Plz Fort Lee (07024) ***(G-3586)***
Sadwith Industries Corp....732 531-3856
1015 Berkeley Ave Ocean (07712) ***(G-7680)***
Safas Corporation (PA)....973 772-5252
2 Ackerman Ave Clifton (07011) ***(G-1709)***
Safe Man LLC....800 320-2589
801 Vulcanite Ave Alpha (08865) ***(G-41)***
Safe-Strap Company Inc....973 442-4623
105 W Dewey Ave Ste 410 Wharton (07885) ***(G-11870)***
Safegaurd Document Destruction....609 448-6695
800 Rike Dr Millstone Township (08535) ***(G-6212)***
Safeguard Business Systems, Hazlet *Also called Peter Morley LLC* ***(G-4269)***
Safeguard Coinbox Inc....973 575-0040
101 Clinton Rd Fairfield (07004) ***(G-3306)***
Safer Holding Corp....973 485-1458
1875 Mccarter Hwy Newark (07104) ***(G-7259)***
Safer Textile, Newark *Also called Safer Holding Corp* ***(G-7259)***
Safer Textile Processing Corp....973 482-6400
1875 Mccarter Hwy Newark (07104) ***(G-7260)***
Safer Textiles, Newark *Also called Meadows Knitting Corp* ***(G-7198)***
Safety Power Inc....908 277-1826
55 Union Pl Ste 178 Summit (07901) ***(G-10544)***
Safety-Kleen Systems Inc....609 859-2049
123 Red Lion Rd Southampton (08088) ***(G-10371)***
Safetysign.com, Garfield *Also called Brimar Industries Inc* ***(G-3733)***
Safire Silk Inc....201 636-4061
135 Grand St Carlstadt (07072) ***(G-1211)***
Safran Aerosystems Evacuation, Wall Township *Also called Air Cruisers Company LLC* ***(G-11315)***
Sage Chemical Inc....201 489-5172
2 University Plz Ste 204 Hackensack (07601) ***(G-3970)***
Sage Payroll Services, Mount Laurel *Also called Pai Services LLC* ***(G-6787)***
Sage Software Inc....856 231-4667
305 Fellowship Rd Ste 300 Mount Laurel (08054) ***(G-6802)***
Sahara Textile Inc....973 247-9900
52 Courtland St Paterson (07503) ***(G-8291)***
Saint La Salle Auxiliary Inc....732 842-4359
850 Newman Springs Rd Lincroft (07738) ***(G-5314)***
Saint-Gobain Prfmce Plas Corp....973 696-4700
150 Dey Rd Wayne (07470) ***(G-11551)***
Saint-Gobain Prfmce Plas Corp....856 423-6630
210 Harmony Rd Mickleton (08056) ***(G-6088)***
Saint-Gobain Prfmce Plas Corp....732 652-0910
1600 Cottontail Ln Somerset (08873) ***(G-10070)***
Saker Shoprites Inc....908 925-1550
1911 Pennsylvania Ave Linden (07036) ***(G-5418)***
Saksoft Inc (HQ)....201 451-4609
30 Montgomery St Ste 1240 Jersey City (07302) ***(G-4803)***
Salad Chef Inc....609 641-5455
125 Shadeland Ave Pleasantville (08232) ***(G-8817)***
Salem Manufacturing Corp....973 751-6331
115 Roosevelt Ave Belleville (07109) ***(G-314)***
Salem Oak Vineyards Ltd Lblty....856 889-2121
62 N Railroad Ave Pedricktown (08067) ***(G-8355)***
Salem Packing Co....856 878-0002
705 Salem Quinton Rd Salem (08079) ***(G-9697)***
Salem Press, Hackensack *Also called Ebsco Publishing Inc* ***(G-3910)***
Salem Publishing, Hackensack *Also called Grey House Publishing Inc* ***(G-3925)***
Salerno's Custom Cabinetry, Saddle Brook *Also called Salernos Kitchen Cabinets* ***(G-9676)***
Salernos Kitchen Cabinets....201 794-1990
599 N Midland Ave Saddle Brook (07663) ***(G-9676)***
Salescaster Displays Corp....908 322-3046
2095 Portland Ave Scotch Plains (07076) ***(G-9739)***
Salix Pharmaceuticals Ltd (HQ)....866 246-8245
400 Somerset Corp Blvd Bridgewater (08807) ***(G-879)***
Sally Miller LLC....732 729-4840
30 N Main St Milltown (08850) ***(G-6219)***
Salmon Signs....856 589-5600
478 W Holly Ave Pitman (08071) ***(G-8748)***
Salomone Redi-Mix LLC....973 305-0022
17 Demarest Dr Wayne (07470) ***(G-11552)***
Salon Interiors Inc....201 488-7888
62 Leuning St South Hackensack (07606) ***(G-10186)***
Saltopia Infused Sea Salt LLC....908 850-1926
9 Reservoir Rd Hackettstown (07840) ***(G-4035)***
Salus Pharma LLC....732 329-8089
11 Deerpark Dr Ste 118 Monmouth Junction (08852) ***(G-6310)***
SAM Graphics Inc....732 431-0440
35 Vanderburg Rd Marlboro (07746) ***(G-5913)***
Sama Plastics Corp....973 239-7200
20 Sand Park Rd Cedar Grove (07009) ***(G-1292)***
Samad Brothers Inc....201 372-0909
419 Murray Hill Pkwy East Rutherford (07073) ***(G-2318)***
Samax Enterprise Inc....973 350-9400
29-75 Riverside Ave Ste 2 Newark (07104) ***(G-7261)***
Samna Cnstrctn & Steel Fabrctn....973 977-8400
75 Dale Ave Paterson (07501) ***(G-8292)***
Sample Media Inc (PA)....609 399-5411
112 E 8th St Ocean City (08226) ***(G-7695)***
Sample Media Inc....609 884-2021
600 Park Blvd Ste 5 Cape May (08204) ***(G-1101)***
Samseng Tissue Co....609 479-3997
122 Kissel Rd Ste C Burlington (08016) ***(G-984)***
Samson Sign Company, Waldwick *Also called Superior Trademark Inc* ***(G-11310)***
Samstubend Inc....973 278-2555
31 Maryland Ave Paterson (07503) ***(G-8293)***
Samsung Opt-Lctronics Amer Inc....201 325-2612
500 Frank W Burr Blvd # 43 Teaneck (07666) ***(G-10650)***
Samsung SDS Globl Scl Amer Inc (HQ)....201 229-4456
100 Challenger Rd Ste 601 Ridgefield Park (07660) ***(G-9315)***
Samuel Elliott Inc....856 773-6000
1818 Bannard St Cinnaminson (08077) ***(G-1483)***
Samuel H Fields Dental Labs....201 343-4626
197 Union St Hackensack (07601) ***(G-3971)***
Samuelson Furniture Inc....973 278-4372
11-13 Maryland Ave Paterson (07503) ***(G-8294)***
San Marel Designs Inc....973 426-9554
98 Us Highway 46 Ste 10 Budd Lake (07828) ***(G-935)***
Sancon Dumpster Rental Svcs, Newark *Also called Sancon Services Inc* ***(G-7262)***
Sancon Services Inc....973 344-2500
50 E Peddie St Newark (07114) ***(G-7262)***
Sander Mechanical Service Inc....732 560-0600
55 Columbia Rd Branchburg (08876) ***(G-679)***
Sander Sales Enterprises Ltd....201 808-6705
200 Seaview Dr Fl 2 Secaucus (07094) ***(G-9806)***
Sandik Manufacturing Inc....973 779-0707
100 8th St Ste 8 Passaic (07055) ***(G-8104)***
Sandkamp Woodworks LLC....201 200-0101
430 Communipaw Ave Ste 1 Jersey City (07304) ***(G-4804)***
Sandoval Graphic Co, Somerdale *Also called Sandoval Graphics & Printing* ***(G-9934)***
Sandoval Graphics & Printing....856 435-7320
9 Minnetonka Rd Somerdale (08083) ***(G-9934)***
Sandoz Inc (HQ)....609 627-8500
100 College Rd W Princeton (08540) ***(G-9019)***
Sandoz Inc....862 778-8300
1 Health Plz East Hanover (07936) ***(G-2237)***
Sandvik Inc (HQ)....201 794-5000
17-02 Nevins Rd Fair Lawn (07410) ***(G-3120)***
Sandvik Inc....281 275-4800
17-2 Nevins Rd Fair Lawn (07410) ***(G-3121)***

Sandvik & Coromant, Fair Lawn *Also called Sandvik Inc (G-3120)*

Sandvik Coromant, Fair Lawn *Also called Sandvik Inc (G-3121)*

Sandy Alexander Inc (PA).................................973 470-8100
200 Entin Rd Clifton (07014) *(G-1710)*

Sanford & Birdsall Inc.................................732 223-6966
1704 Atlantic Ave Manasquan (08736) *(G-5838)*

Sanherb Biotech Inc.................................347 946-5896
4 Mccullough Close Belle Mead (08502) *(G-287)*

Sanit Technologies LLC.................................862 238-7555
90 Dayton Ave Ste 11 Passaic (07055) *(G-8105)*

Sanket Corporation.................................732 287-0201
15 Wood Acres Dr Edison (08820) *(G-2604)*

Sankyo U S A, Basking Ridge *Also called Daiichi Sankyo Inc (G-180)*

Sanofi Avntis Phrmctcals Group, Bridgewater *Also called Sanofi US Services Inc (G-883)*

Sanofi US Services Inc (HQ).................................336 407-4994
55 Corporate Dr Bridgewater (08807) *(G-880)*

Sanofi US Services Inc.................................336 407-4994
55 Corporate Dr Bridgewater (08807) *(G-881)*

Sanofi US Services Inc.................................908 231-4000
200 Cronjing Blvd Fl 2 Flr 2 Bridgewater (08807) *(G-882)*

Sanofi US Services Inc.................................908 231-4000
1041 Rte 202/206 Bridgewater (08807) *(G-883)*

Sanofi-Aventis US LLC (HQ).................................908 981-5000
55 Corporate Dr Bridgewater (08807) *(G-884)*

Sanofi-Synthelabo Inc.................................908 231-2000
55 Corporate Dr Bridgewater (08807) *(G-885)*

Sanofi-Synthelabo Inc (HQ).................................908 981-5000
55 Corporate Dr Bridgewater (08807) *(G-886)*

Santon Inc.................................201 444-9080
128 Grand View Dr Toms River (08753) *(G-10790)*

Sap-Seal Products Inc.................................201 385-5553
52 Woodbine St Ste 2 Bergenfield (07621) *(G-384)*

Sapore Ravioli & Cheese, Middlesex *Also called L and Ds Sapore Ravioli Cheese (G-6126)*

Saporito Inc.................................201 265-8212
959 Edgewater Ave Ridgefield (07657) *(G-9288)*

Sapphire Bath Inc.................................718 215-1262
93 Harrison St Ste 5 Paterson (07501) *(G-8295)*

Sapphire Envelope & Graphics.................................856 782-2227
214 Davis Rd Magnolia (08049) *(G-5709)*

Sapphire Flvors Fragrances LLC.................................973 200-8849
6 Commerce Rd Fairfield (07004) *(G-3307)*

Saputo Cheese USA Inc.................................201 508-6400
861 Washington Ave Carlstadt (07072) *(G-1212)*

Sar Industrial Finishing Inc.................................609 567-2772
104 N Route 73 Berlin (08009) *(G-429)*

Sara Beth Division, Jersey City *Also called Carole Hchman Design Group Inc (G-4709)*

Sara Emporium Inc.................................201 792-7222
833 Newark Ave Jersey City (07306) *(G-4805)*

Sarkli-Repechage Ltd.................................201 549-4200
300 Castle Rd Secaucus (07094) *(G-9807)*

Satec Inc.................................908 258-0924
10 Milltown Ct Union (07083) *(G-11088)*

Satellite Pros Inc.................................908 823-9500
148 Main St Whitehouse Station (08889) *(G-11933)*

Satex Fabrics Ltd.................................212 221-5555
704 76th St North Bergen (07047) *(G-7436)*

Sato Lbling Solutions Amer Inc.................................973 287-3641
30 Chapin Rd Ste 1201 Pine Brook (07058) *(G-8616)*

Saturn Beauty Group LLC.................................908 561-5000
140 Ethel Rd W Ste G Piscataway (08854) *(G-8707)*

Saturn Overhead Equipment LLC.................................732 560-7210
100 Apgar Dr Somerset (08873) *(G-10071)*

Sau-Sea Swimming Pool Products.................................609 859-8500
1855 Route 206 Southampton (08088) *(G-10372)*

Saud & Son Jewelry Inc.................................201 866-4445
441 60th St West New York (07093) *(G-11754)*

Saud Jewelry, West New York *Also called Saud & Son Jewelry Inc (G-11754)*

Sausea Swimming Pool Enamels, Southampton *Also called Sau-Sea Swimming Pool Products (G-10372)*

Savient Pharmaceuticals Inc (HQ).................................732 418-9300
400 Crossing Blvd Fl 3 Bridgewater (08807) *(G-887)*

Savignano Food Corp.................................973 673-3355
107 S Jefferson St Orange (07050) *(G-7760)*

Savino Del Bene USA Inc (HQ).................................347 960-5568
34 Engelhard Ave Avenel (07001) *(G-145)*

Savit Corporation.................................862 209-4516
400 Commons Way Ste D Rockaway (07866) *(G-9497)*

Savita Naturals Ltd.................................856 467-4949
617 Heron Dr Swedesboro (08085) *(G-10608)*

Savorx Flavors LLC.................................908 265-3033
120 New England Ave Piscataway (08854) *(G-8708)*

Savoury Systems Intl LLC.................................908 526-2524
230 Industrial Pkwy Ste C Branchburg (08876) *(G-680)*

Sawdust Depot LLC.................................973 344-5255
704 Hulses Corner Rd Howell (07731) *(G-4550)*

Sawitz Store Fixture, Carlstadt *Also called Sawitz Studios Inc (G-1213)*

Sawitz Studios Inc.................................201 842-9444
130 Grand St Carlstadt (07072) *(G-1213)*

Saxa Pharmaceuticals LLC.................................862 571-7630
22 Candlelight Dr Holmdel (07733) *(G-4513)*

Saxton Falls Sand & Gravel Co.................................908 852-0121
Waterloo Valley Rd Budd Lake (07828) *(G-936)*

Saybolt LP.................................908 523-2000
1026 W Elizabeth Ave # 5 Linden (07036) *(G-5419)*

Scaasis Originals Inc.................................732 775-7474
1006 11th Ave Neptune (07753) *(G-6895)*

Scafa Modern Art Group, The, Lyndhurst *Also called Scafa-Tornabene Art Pubg Co (G-5676)*

Scafa-Tornabene Art Pubg Co.................................201 842-8500
165 Chubb Ave Ste 4 Lyndhurst (07071) *(G-5676)*

Scala Pastry.................................732 398-9808
1896 Us Highway 130 North Brunswick (08902) *(G-7485)*

Scalable Systems Inc.................................732 993-4320
15 Corporate Pl S Ste 222 Piscataway (08854) *(G-8709)*

Scandia Packaging Machinery Co.................................973 473-6100
30 Herlihy Dr Mahwah (07430) *(G-5770)*

Scantron Corporation.................................201 666-7009
99 Kinderkamack Rd # 211 Westwood (07675) *(G-11844)*

Scarlet Printing.................................732 560-1415
253 Beechwood Ave Middlesex (08846) *(G-6143)*

SCC Concrete Inc.................................908 859-2172
1051 River Rd Phillipsburg (08865) *(G-8574)*

Scen'a Video Tape, Ridgefield Park *Also called Kolon USA Incorporated (G-9311)*

Schairer Brothers.................................609 965-0996
254 S Bremen Ave Egg Harbor City (08215) *(G-2667)*

Schall Manufacturing Inc.................................732 918-8800
3501 Rose Ave Ocean (07712) *(G-7681)*

Scheinert & Sons Inc.................................201 791-4600
404 N Midland Ave 2 Saddle Brook (07663) *(G-9677)*

Scheller, Lewis Printing, Somerset *Also called Lewis Scheller Printing Corp (G-10016)*

Schellmark Inc.................................732 345-7143
7 Thistledown St Tinton Falls (07753) *(G-10726)*

Schellmark Interactive, Tinton Falls *Also called Schellmark Inc (G-10726)*

Scher Chemicals Inc.................................973 471-1300
Industrial West Clifton (07012) *(G-1711)*

Scher Fabrics Inc.................................212 382-2266
18 Duncan Way Freehold (07728) *(G-3699)*

Schering Berlin Inc (HQ).................................862 404-3000
100 Bayer Blvd Whippany (07981) *(G-11908)*

Schering-Plough Corp.................................908 595-3638
3070 Us Highway 22 Branchburg (08876) *(G-681)*

Scherng-Plough Pdts Caribe Inc.................................908 423-1000
1 Merck Dr Whitehouse Station (08889) *(G-11934)*

Schiapparelli Biosystems, West Caldwell *Also called Alfa Wassermann Inc (G-11637)*

Schifano Construction Corp..................................732 752-3450
1 Smalley Ave Middlesex (08846) *(G-6144)*

Schiffenhaus Industries Inc (HQ).................................973 484-5000
2013 Mccarter Hwy Newark (07104) *(G-7263)*

Schindler Elevator Corporation (HQ).................................973 397-6500
20 Whippany Rd Morristown (07960) *(G-6698)*

Schindler Elevator Corporation.................................856 234-2220
840 N Lenola Rd Ste 4 Moorestown (08057) *(G-6565)*

Schindler Enterprises Inc (HQ).................................973 397-6500
20 Whippany Rd Morristown (07960) *(G-6699)*

Schlumberger Technology Corp.................................609 275-3815
20 Wallace Rd Princeton Junction (08550) *(G-9066)*

Schmutzerland, Englewood *Also called Umbrella & Chairs LLC (G-2949)*

Schneder Elc Bldngs Amrcas Inc.................................201 348-9240
210 Meadowlands Pkwy Secaucus (07094) *(G-9808)*

Schneider & Marquard Inc.................................973 383-2200
112 Phil Hardin Rd Newton (07860) *(G-7356)*

Schneiders Kitchens Inc.................................908 689-5649
252 State Route 31 N Washington (07882) *(G-11451)*

Scholastic Book Fairs Inc.................................609 578-4142
2540 Us Highway 130 # 105 Cranbury (08512) *(G-1880)*

Scholastic Inc.................................201 633-2400
100 Plaza Dr Fl 4 Secaucus (07094) *(G-9809)*

Scholastic National Field Off, Secaucus *Also called Scholastic Uk Group LLC (G-9810)*

Scholastic Uk Group LLC.................................201 633-2400
100 Plaza Dr Fl 4 Secaucus (07094) *(G-9810)*

Schon J Tool & Machine Co.................................732 928-6665
150 Park Ave Jackson (08527) *(G-4664)*

Schon Tool, Jackson *Also called Schon J Tool & Machine Co (G-4664)*

School Publications Co Inc.................................732 988-1100
1520 Washington Ave Neptune (07753) *(G-6896)*

School Spirit Promotions.................................609 588-6902
3 Ely Ct Trenton (08690) *(G-10990)*

Schott Nyc Corp.................................800 631-5407
735 Rahway Ave Union (07083) *(G-11089)*

Schrader & Company Inc.................................973 579-1160
188 Halsey Rd Newton (07860) *(G-7357)*

Schroth's Gold & Silversmiths, Montville *Also called Hickok Matthews Co Inc (G-6443)*

Schulke Inc.................................973 521-7163
30 Two Bridges Rd Ste 225 Fairfield (07004) *(G-3308)*

Schuman Cheese, Fairfield *Also called Arthur Schuman Inc (G-3146)*

Schurman Fine Papers.................................856 985-1776
300 State Hwy Rte 73 Marlton (08053) *(G-5950)*

Schusters Shoes Inc 856 885-4551
  1122 Rembrandt Way 1 Williamstown (08094) *(G-11977)*
Schutz Container Systems Inc (HQ) 908 429-1637
  200 Aspen Hill Rd Branchburg (08876) *(G-682)*
Schutz Corp (HQ) 908 526-6161
  200 Aspen Hill Rd Branchburg (08876) *(G-683)*
Schweid & Sons, Carlstadt *Also called Burger Maker Inc (G-1133)*
Schweitzer-Mauduit Intl Inc 732 723-6100
  85 Main St Spotswood (08884) *(G-10417)*
SCI, Wall Township *Also called Selective Coatings & Inks (G-11368)*
SCI, Ocean *Also called Selective Coatings & Inks (G-7682)*
SCI-Bore Inc 973 414-9001
  364 Glenwood Ave Ste 8c East Orange (07017) *(G-2262)*
Sciecure Pharma Inc 732 329-8089
  11 Deerpark Dr Ste 120 Monmouth Junction (08852) *(G-6311)*
Science Pump Corporation 856 963-7700
  1431 Ferry Ave Camden (08104) *(G-1086)*
Scientific Alloys Corp 973 478-8323
  5 Troast Ct Clifton (07011) *(G-1712)*
Scientific Design Company (PA) 201 641-0500
  49 Industrial Ave Little Ferry (07643) *(G-5496)*
Scientific Machine and Sup Co 732 356-1553
  700 Cedar Ave Middlesex (08846) *(G-6145)*
Scientific Models Inc 908 464-7070
  340 Snyder Ave Berkeley Heights (07922) *(G-411)*
Scientific Sales Inc 609 844-0055
  3 Glenbrook Ct Lawrenceville (08648) *(G-5243)*
Scientifix LLC 856 780-5871
  520 Fellowship Rd E508 Mount Laurel (08054) *(G-6803)*
Scimar Technologies LLC 609 208-1796
  32 Cliffwood Dr Allentown (08501) *(G-31)*
Scimedx Corporation 800 221-5598
  53 Richboynton Rd Dover (07801) *(G-2105)*
Scivantage Inc (PA) 646 452-0001
  499 Washington Blvd Fl 11 Jersey City (07310) *(G-4806)*
Scj Group LLC 201 289-5841
  492 Cedar Ln Ste 102c Teaneck (07666) *(G-10651)*
Scl 908 391-9882
  7 Emmons Ct Bridgewater (08807) *(G-888)*
Scodix Inc 855 726-3491
  250 Pehle Ave Ste 101 Saddle Brook (07663) *(G-9678)*
Sconda Canvas Products 732 225-3500
  20 Harmich Rd South Plainfield (07080) *(G-10326)*
Scories Inc 973 923-1372
  28 Vassar Ave Newark (07112) *(G-7264)*
Scott Graphics Printing Co Inc 201 262-0473
  690 River Rd Ste D New Milford (07646) *(G-6992)*
Scott Kay Inc 201 287-0100
  55 Hartz Way Ste 1 Secaucus (07094) *(G-9811)*
Scott Kay Sterling LLC 201 287-0100
  55 Hartz Way Ste 1 Secaucus (07094) *(G-9812)*
Scott W Springman 856 751-2411
  7026 Camden Ave C Pennsauken (08110) *(G-8482)*
Scottline LLC 732 534-3123
  15 Corporate Pl S Ste 402 Piscataway (08854) *(G-8710)*
Scotts Company LLC 201 246-0180
  125 Baler Blvd North Arlington (07031) *(G-7378)*
Screen Play Inc 973 227-9014
  1275 Bloomfield Ave Ste 5 Fairfield (07004) *(G-3309)*
Screen Printing & Embroidery, Pleasantville *Also called C & D Sales (G-8806)*
Screen Printing & Embroidery 732 256-9610
  5005 Belmar Blvd Ste B6 Wall Township (07727) *(G-11367)*
Screen Reproductions Co Inc 201 935-0830
  850 Washington Ave Carlstadt (07072) *(G-1214)*
Screen Tech Inc of New Jersey 908 862-8000
  1800 W Blancke St Linden (07036) *(G-5420)*
Screen-Trans Development Corp 201 933-7800
  100 Grand St Moonachie (07074) *(G-6488)*
Screened Images Inc 732 651-8181
  7 Joanna Ct Ste H East Brunswick (08816) *(G-2175)*
Screens & Fabricated Metals, Woodland Park *Also called Century Bathworks Inc (G-12075)*
Screens Incorporated 973 633-8558
  130 Ryerson Ave Ste 219 Wayne (07470) *(G-11553)*
Screentek Manufacturing Co LLC 973 328-2121
  220 Franklin Rd B Randolph (07869) *(G-9198)*
Sct Software, Shrewsbury *Also called Supply Chain Technologies LLC (G-9903)*
Sculptured Stone Inc 973 557-1482
  501b Division St Boonton (07005) *(G-568)*
Scunci Division, East Windsor *Also called Conair Corporation (G-2347)*
Scynexis Inc 201 884-5485
  1 Evertrust Plz Fl 13 Jersey City (07302) *(G-4807)*
Sdi Technologies Inc (PA) 732 574-9000
  1299 Main St Rahway (07065) *(G-9127)*
SE Tylos USA 973 837-8001
  140 Commerce Way Totowa (07512) *(G-10851)*
Sea Breeze Fruit Flavors Inc 973 334-7777
  441 Main Rd Towaco (07082) *(G-10880)*
Sea Habor Marine Inc 732 477-8577
  310 Firehouse Rd Brick (08723) *(G-731)*

Sea Harvest Inc 609 884-3000
  985 Ocean Dr Cape May (08204) *(G-1102)*
Sea Isle Ice Co Inc (PA) 609 263-8748
  230 42nd St Sea Isle City (08243) *(G-9749)*
Seaboard Industries 732 901-5700
  1957 Rutgers University B Lakewood (08701) *(G-5161)*
Seaboard Instrument Co 609 641-5300
  4 N 1st St Pleasantville (08232) *(G-8818)*
Seaboard Paper and Twine LLC 973 413-8100
  37 E 6th St Paterson (07524) *(G-8296)*
Seabrite Corp 973 491-0399
  574 Ferry St Newark (07105) *(G-7265)*
Seabrook Brothers & Sons Inc 856 455-8080
  85 Finley Rd Bridgeton (08302) *(G-772)*
Seacube Container Leasing Ltd 201 391-0800
  1 Maynard Dr Park Ridge (07656) *(G-7859)*
Seagrave Coatings Corp 201 933-1000
  209 N Michigan Ave Kenilworth (07033) *(G-4976)*
Seagull Stain Glass, Atlantic City *Also called Linda Spolitino (G-96)*
Seahawk Services, Paulsboro *Also called Oil Technologies Services Inc (G-8336)*
Seahawk Services, Paulsboro *Also called Oil Technologies Services Inc (G-8337)*
Seahawk Services, Linden *Also called Oil Technologies Services Inc (G-5399)*
Seajay Manufacturing Corp 732 774-0900
  9 Memorial Dr Ste 1 Neptune (07753) *(G-6897)*
Seal-Spout Corp 908 647-0648
  50 Allen Rd Liberty Corner (07938) *(G-5296)*
Sealed Air Corporation 201 712-7000
  301 Mayhill St Saddle Brook (07663) *(G-9679)*
Sealed Air Corporation 973 890-4735
  301 Mayhill St Saddle Brook (07663) *(G-9680)*
Sealed Air Holdings 201 791-7600
  200 Riverfront Blvd # 301 Elmwood Park (07407) *(G-2855)*
Sealed Unit Parts Co Inc 732 223-1201
  2230 Landmark Pl Allenwood (08720) *(G-34)*
Sealion Metal Fabricators Inc 856 933-3914
  776 Creek Rd Bellmawr (08031) *(G-342)*
Seals-Eastern Incorporated 732 747-9200
  134 Pearl St Red Bank (07701) *(G-9243)*
Sealy Mattress Co N J Inc 973 345-8800
  697 River St Paterson (07524) *(G-8297)*
Sealy Paterson, Paterson *Also called Sealy Mattress Co N J Inc (G-8297)*
Seating Expert, Livingston *Also called Lrk Seating Products LLC (G-5521)*
Seaview Golf Resort, Galloway *Also called Greater ATL Cy Golf Assn LLC (G-3722)*
Seaville Motorsports 609 624-0040
  65 Dockside Dr Somers Point (08244) *(G-9939)*
Seawave Corp 609 886-8600
  1508 Route 47 Rio Grande (08242) *(G-9358)*
Sebastian & King Ltd Lblty Co 908 874-6953
  816 Robin Rd Hillsborough (08844) *(G-4354)*
Secord Inc 908 754-2147
  1812 Front St Scotch Plains (07076) *(G-9740)*
Secure System Inc 732 922-3609
  320 Essex St Ste 3 Stirling (07980) *(G-10496)*
Security 21 LLC 856 384-7474
  119 Steeplechase Ct Woodbury (08096) *(G-12036)*
Security Defense Systems Corp 973 235-0606
  160 Park Ave Ste 1 Nutley (07110) *(G-7593)*
Security Fabricators Inc 908 272-9171
  321 Lafayette Ave Kenilworth (07033) *(G-4977)*
Security Holdings LLC (PA) 201 457-0286
  111 Kero Rd Carlstadt (07072) *(G-1215)*
Security Systems Unlimited, Mount Laurel *Also called E Berkowitz & Co Inc (G-6756)*
Sekisui America Corporation (HQ) 201 423-7960
  333 Meadowlands Pkwy Secaucus (07094) *(G-9813)*
Seldom Seen Designs LLC (PA) 973 535-8805
  9 Summit Dr Caldwell (07006) *(G-1030)*
Select Enterprises Inc 732 287-8622
  71 Executive Ave Edison (08817) *(G-2605)*
Select Machine Tool Inc 856 933-2100
  19 Thompson Ave Mount Ephraim (08059) *(G-6721)*
Select Records, Lyndhurst *Also called PM Swapco Inc (G-5672)*
Selective Coatings & Inks (PA) 732 938-7677
  5008 Industrial Rd Wall Township (07727) *(G-11368)*
Selective Coatings & Inks 732 493-0707
  1750 Brielle Ave Ste B4 Ocean (07712) *(G-7682)*
Selfmade Boutique, Jersey City *Also called Selfmade LLC (G-4808)*
Selfmade LLC 201 792-8968
  290 Hoboken Ave Jersey City (07306) *(G-4808)*
Sell All Properties LLC 856 963-8800
  301 Market St Ste 1 Camden (08102) *(G-1087)*
Sellercloud, Lakewood *Also called Software Developers LLC (G-5165)*
Selling Precision, West Milford *Also called Hydraulic Manifolds Usa LLC (G-11727)*
Selling Precision Inc 973 728-1214
  264 Marshall Hill Rd West Milford (07480) *(G-11731)*
Selway Partners LLC (PA) 201 712-7974
  74 Grand Ave B Englewood (07631) *(G-2939)*
Semels Embroidery Inc 973 473-6868
  1078 Route 46 Clifton (07013) *(G-1713)*

Semi Conductor Manufacturing....................973 478-2880
5 Troast Ct Clifton (07011) *(G-1714)*

Semi-Hex, Jersey City *Also called General Pencil Company Inc (G-4742)*

Semiconductor Manufacturing, Clifton *Also called Semi Conductor Manufacturing (G-1714)*

Seminole Wire & Cable Co Inc....................856 324-2929
7861 Airport Hwy Pennsauken (08109) *(G-8483)*

Seminole Wire Products, Pennsauken *Also called Seminole Wire & Cable Co Inc (G-8483)*

Senat Poultry LLC....................973 742-9316
28 Warren St Paterson (07524) *(G-8298)*

Senco Metals LLC....................973 342-1742
90 Dayton Ave Ste 100 Passaic (07055) *(G-8106)*

Senor Lopez (PA)....................732 229-7622
15 Spring Ct Tinton Falls (07724) *(G-10727)*

Sensbl Inc....................862 225-3803
615 Barnett Pl Ridgewood (07450) *(G-9329)*

Sensient Cosmetics Technology, South Plainfield *Also called Sensient Technologies Corp (G-10327)*

Sensient Technologies Corp....................908 757-4500
107 Wade Ave South Plainfield (07080) *(G-10327)*

Sensigraphics Inc....................856 853-9100
105 W Park Dr Mount Laurel (08054) *(G-6804)*

Sensiple Inc (PA)....................732 283-0499
555 Us Highway 1 S # 330 Iselin (08830) *(G-4626)*

Sensonics Inc....................856 547-7702
411 Black Horse Pike # 1 Haddon Heights (08035) *(G-4049)*

Sensonics International, Haddon Heights *Also called Sensonics Inc (G-4049)*

Sensor Medical Technology LLC....................425 358-7381
4 Stewart Ct Denville (07834) *(G-2057)*

Sensor Products Inc....................973 884-1755
300 Madison Ave Ste 200 Madison (07940) *(G-5702)*

Sensor Scientific Inc (PA)....................973 227-7790
6 Kingsbridge Rd Ste 4 Fairfield (07004) *(G-3310)*

Sensoredge Inc....................973 975-4163
140 Littleton Rd Ste 220 Parsippany (07054) *(G-8012)*

Sensors Unlimited Inc....................609 333-8000
330 Carter Rd Ste 100 Princeton (08540) *(G-9020)*

Sensory Solutions LLC....................973 615-7600
1 Ledgewood Ct Warren (07059) *(G-11429)*

Sentrex Ingredients LLC....................908 862-4440
350 Cantor Ave Linden (07036) *(G-5421)*

Sentrimed Ltd Liability Co....................914 582-8631
49 Holly Oak Dr Voorhees (08043) *(G-11293)*

Sentry Mfg LLC....................856 642-0480
351 Crider Ave Moorestown (08057) *(G-6566)*

Sentry Water Management....................973 616-9000
35 Newark Pompton Tpke Riverdale (07457) *(G-9383)*

Seqirus Inc....................919 577-5000
1 Health Plz Ste 310 East Hanover (07936) *(G-2238)*

Seqirus USA Inc....................908 739-0200
25 Deforest Ave Summit (07901) *(G-10545)*

Sequin City, North Bergen *Also called Sequins of Distinction Inc (G-7437)*

Sequins of Distinction Inc....................201 348-8111
1302 13th St North Bergen (07047) *(G-7437)*

Seren Inc....................856 205-1131
1670 Gallagher Dr Vineland (08360) *(G-11263)*

Seren Industrial Power Systems, Vineland *Also called Seren Inc (G-11263)*

Seren Industrial Power Systems....................856 205-1131
1670 Gallagher Dr Vineland (08360) *(G-11264)*

Seren Ips Inc....................856 205-1131
1670 Gallagher Dr Vineland (08360) *(G-11265)*

Serene House USA Inc....................609 980-1214
1814 Marlton Pike E # 350 Cherry Hill (08003) *(G-1414)*

Seri-Arts, Carlstadt *Also called Vernon Display Graphics Inc (G-1235)*

Serious Welding & Mech LLC....................732 698-7478
427 Whitehead Ave Ste 3 South River (08882) *(G-10357)*

Sermach Inc....................732 356-9021
311 Lincoln Blvd Ste C Middlesex (08846) *(G-6146)*

Serranis Bakery....................973 678-1777
114 S Essex Ave Orange (07050) *(G-7761)*

Serratelli Hat Company Inc....................973 623-4133
418 Central Ave Newark (07107) *(G-7266)*

Service Apex, Bridgewater *Also called Avail Inc (G-796)*

Service Data Corp Inc....................908 522-0020
265 Oak Ridge Ave Summit (07901) *(G-10546)*

Service Data Forms, Summit *Also called Service Data Corp Inc (G-10546)*

Service Machine Co, Middlesex *Also called Sermach Inc (G-6146)*

Service Metal Fabricating Inc (PA)....................973 625-8882
10 Stickle Ave Rockaway (07866) *(G-9498)*

Service Metal Fabricating Inc....................973 989-7199
243 E Blackwell St Dover (07801) *(G-2106)*

Service Seal Div, Kenilworth *Also called Flexline Inc (G-4940)*

Service Tech....................908 788-0072
109 Rake Factory Rd Flemington (08822) *(G-3466)*

Services Equipment Com LLC....................973 992-4404
4 Tamarack Dr Livingston (07039) *(G-5539)*

Servo-Tek Products Company Inc....................973 427-4249
1096 Goffle Rd Hawthorne (07506) *(G-4243)*

Servolift LLC....................973 442-7878
35 Righter Rd Ste A Randolph (07869) *(G-9199)*

Servometer, Cedar Grove *Also called Precision Mfg Group LLC (G-1288)*

SES Engineering (us) Inc....................609 987-4000
4 Research Way Princeton (08540) *(G-9021)*

Setaram Inc (HQ)....................908 262-7060
2555 Us Highway 130 Ste 2 Cranbury (08512) *(G-1881)*

Setco LLC....................610 321-9760
34 Engelhard Dr Monroe Township (08831) *(G-6342)*

Setcon Industries Inc....................973 283-0500
5 Mathews Ave Ste 7 Riverdale (07457) *(G-9384)*

Seven Mile Pubg & Creative....................609 967-7707
355 24th St Avalon (08202) *(G-116)*

Seven Up Bottle Co, South Plainfield *Also called Canada Dry Bottling Co NY LP (G-10233)*

Severino Pasta Mfg Co Inc....................856 854-3716
110 Haddon Ave Collingswood (08108) *(G-1771)*

Severna Operations Inc....................973 503-1600
3 Eastmans Rd Parsippany (07054) *(G-8013)*

Seviroli Foods Inc....................856 931-1900
960 Creek Rd Bellmawr (08031) *(G-343)*

Sew-Eurodrive Inc....................856 467-2277
200 High Hill Rd Bridgeport (08014) *(G-744)*

Sew-Eurodrive Inc....................856 467-2277
2107 High Hill Rd Bridgeport (08014) *(G-745)*

SF Lutz LLC....................609 646-9490
3143 Fire Rd Ste F Egg Harbor Township (08234) *(G-2697)*

Sfp Software Inc....................856 235-7778
162 Knotty Oak Dr Mount Laurel (08054) *(G-6805)*

Sfx Installations, Mount Laurel *Also called Scientifix LLC (G-6803)*

SGB Packaging Group Inc....................201 488-3030
401 Hackensack Ave Fl 7 Hackensack (07601) *(G-3972)*

Sgfootwear Company, Hackensack *Also called S Goldberg & Co Inc (G-3969)*

Sgh Inc....................609 698-8868
79 S Main St Ste 2 Barnegat (08005) *(G-161)*

Sgi Apparel Ltd....................201 342-1200
3 University Plz Ste 400 Hackensack (07601) *(G-3973)*

SGS International Inc....................718 836-1000
185 Sumner Ave Ste A Kenilworth (07033) *(G-4978)*

SGS UStesting Company (HQ)....................973 575-5252
291 Fairfield Ave Fairfield (07004) *(G-3311)*

Sgw Fuel Delivery....................609 209-8773
353 Churchill Ave Trenton (08610) *(G-10991)*

Shabazz Fruit Cola Company LLC....................973 230-4641
24 Wyndmoor Ave Newark (07112) *(G-7267)*

Shachihata Inc (usa)....................732 905-7159
525 Oberlin Ave S Lakewood (08701) *(G-5162)*

Shade Powers Co Inc....................201 767-3727
112 Paris Ave Ste C Northvale (07647) *(G-7549)*

Shafer Brothers Trailers, Elmer *Also called Richard Shafer (G-2802)*

Shaffer Products Inc....................908 206-1980
20 Milltown Rd Union (07083) *(G-11090)*

Shahnawaz Food LLC....................908 413-4206
19 Ten Eyck Pl Edison (08820) *(G-2606)*

Shallcross Bolt & Specialties....................908 925-4700
1 Mccandless St Linden (07036) *(G-5422)*

Shamong Manufacturing Company....................609 654-2549
33 Bunker Hill Rd Shamong (08088) *(G-9859)*

Shamrock Technologies Inc (PA)....................973 242-2999
Foot Of Pacific St Newark (07114) *(G-7268)*

Shanghai Freemen Americas LLC (HQ)....................732 981-1288
2035 Route 27 Ste 3005 Edison (08817) *(G-2607)*

Shanghai Optics Inc (PA)....................732 321-6915
17 Brant Ave Ste 6 Clark (07066) *(G-1515)*

Shani Auto Fuel Corp....................856 241-9767
541 Kings Hwy Woolwich Township (08085) *(G-12098)*

Shapes/Arch Holdings LLC (PA)....................856 662-5500
9000 River Rd Delair (08110) *(G-2001)*

Sharagano, Harrison *Also called E-Lo Sportswear LLC (G-4170)*

Sharkk LLC....................302 377-3974
70 S Orange Ave Ste 105 Livingston (07039) *(G-5540)*

Sharmatek Inc....................908 852-5087
999 Willow Grove St Hackettstown (07840) *(G-4036)*

Sharp Electronics Corporation (HQ)....................201 529-8200
100 Paragon Dr Ste 100 # 100 Montvale (07645) *(G-6433)*

Sharp Impressions Inc....................201 573-4943
163 Belmont Ave Ste 1 Garfield (07026) *(G-3767)*

Sharp Manufacturing Co Amer, Montvale *Also called Sharp Electronics Corporation (G-6433)*

Sharrott Wine....................609 567-9463
370 S Egg Harbor Rd Hammonton (08037) *(G-4144)*

Shasun USA Inc....................732 465-0700
15 Corporate Pl S Ste 222 Piscataway (08854) *(G-8711)*

Shaw Industries Inc....................609 655-8300
1267 S River Rd Ste 100 Cranbury (08512) *(G-1882)*

Shearman Cabinets....................973 677-0071
195 N Munn Ave East Orange (07017) *(G-2263)*

Sheet Metal Products Inc....................973 482-0450
794 N 6th St Newark (07107) *(G-7269)*

Sheex Inc....................856 334-3021
10000 Lincoln Dr E # 303 Marlton (08053) *(G-5951)*

Sheex Performance Sleep, Marlton *Also called Sheex Inc (G-5951)*
Shekia Group LLC 732 372-7668
  1130 King Georges Post Rd Edison (08837) *(G-2608)*
Shelan Chemical Company Inc 732 796-1003
  174 Tournament Dr Monroe Township (08831) *(G-6343)*
Shelby Mechanical Inc 856 665-4540
  1009 Broad St Cinnaminson (08077) *(G-1484)*
Shell Packaging Corporation (PA) 908 871-7000
  200 Connell Dr Ste 1200 Berkeley Heights (07922) *(G-412)*
Shelterforce Magazine, Montclair *Also called National Housing Institute (G-6377)*
Sheridan Communications, Alpha *Also called Sheridan Printing Company Inc (G-42)*
Sheridan Optical Co Inc 856 582-0963
  108 Clinton Ave Pitman (08071) *(G-8749)*
Sheridan Optical Lab, Pitman *Also called Sheridan Optical Co Inc (G-8749)*
Sheridan Printing Company Inc 908 454-0700
  1425 3rd Ave Alpha (08865) *(G-42)*
Sheris Cookery Inc 973 589-2060
  33 Delancey St Newark (07105) *(G-7270)*
Sherman Group Holdings 201 735-9000
  2200 Fletcher Ave Office Fort Lee (07024) *(G-3587)*
Sherman Nat Inc (HQ) 201 735-9000
  10 Sterling Blvd Ste 302 Englewood (07631) *(G-2940)*
Sherman Printing Co Inc 973 345-2493
  161 Elmwood Dr Clifton (07013) *(G-1715)*
Shermans 1400 Brdway N Y C Ltd 201 735-9000
  10 Sterling Blvd Englewood (07631) *(G-2941)*
Sheroy Printing Inc 973 242-4040
  40 Commerce St Newark (07102) *(G-7271)*
Sherry International Inc 908 279-7255
  31 Mountain Blvd Bldg M Warren (07059) *(G-11430)*
Sherwood Brands Corporation 973 249-8200
  120 Jersey Ave New Brunswick (08901) *(G-6970)*
Shields Business Solutions, Moorestown *Also called Longport Shields Inc (G-6542)*
Shifman Mattress Company, Newark *Also called Hammer Bedding Corp (G-7145)*
Shindo International Inc 973 470-8100
  200 Entin Rd Clifton (07014) *(G-1716)*
Shipmaster, Monroe Township *Also called Broadway Kleer-Guard Corp (G-6330)*
Shiseido America Inc (HQ) 609 371-5800
  366 Prncton Hightstown Rd East Windsor (08520) *(G-2360)*
Shiseido Americas Corporation 609 371-5800
  366 Prncton Hightstown Rd East Windsor (08520) *(G-2361)*
Shiseido Amrcas Innovation Ctr, East Windsor *Also called Shiseido Americas Corporation (G-2361)*
Shiva Fuel Inc 732 826-3228
  737 New Brunswick Ave Perth Amboy (08861) *(G-8532)*
Shiva Software Group Inc 973 691-5475
  2 Fennimore Ct Flanders (07836) *(G-3418)*
Shm, Englewood *Also called Structured Healthcare MGT Inc (G-2945)*
Sho Eyeworks 201 568-5500
  240 Frisch Ct Ste 104 Paramus (07652) *(G-7831)*
Shock Tech Inc (PA) 845 368-8600
  211 Island Rd Mahwah (07430) *(G-5771)*
Shooting Star Inc 908 789-2500
  2500 Plainfield Ave Scotch Plains (07076) *(G-9741)*
Shop Rite 299, Neptune *Also called Shop Rite Supermarkets Inc (G-6898)*
Shop Rite 633, Absecon *Also called Shop-Rite Supermarkets Inc (G-4)*
Shop Rite of Medford, Medford *Also called Berat Corporation (G-6020)*
Shop Rite Supermarkets Inc 732 775-4250
  2200 Highway 66 Neptune (07753) *(G-6898)*
Shop Rite Supermarkets Inc 732 442-1717
  Convery Blvd Fayette Perth Amboy (08861) *(G-8533)*
Shop-Rite Supermarkets Inc 609 646-2448
  616 White Horse Pike Absecon (08201) *(G-4)*
Shopindia Inc 732 409-0656
  3 Topaz Ct Marlboro (07746) *(G-5914)*
Shoppe, Villas *Also called Beach Nutts Media Inc (G-11178)*
Shoppe CMC Shoppers Guide (PA) 609 886-4112
  2503 Bayshore Rd Villas (08251) *(G-11181)*
Shoprite, Perth Amboy *Also called Shop Rite Supermarkets Inc (G-8533)*
Shore Awning Co 732 775-3351
  1933 State Route 35 # 126 Wall Township (07719) *(G-11369)*
Shore Bet Painting and Cnstr. 732 996-3455
  102 Osborne Ave Bay Head (08742) *(G-200)*
Shore Drilling Inc 732 935-1776
  23 Branch Ave Oceanport (07757) *(G-7707)*
Shore Microsystems Inc (PA) 732 870-0800
  45 Memorial Pkwy Long Branch (07740) *(G-5606)*
Shore Point Distrg Co Inc 732 308-3334
  100 Shore Point Dr Freehold (07728) *(G-3700)*
Shore Precision Mfg Inc 732 914-0949
  1000 Industrial Way Ste D Toms River (08755) *(G-10791)*
Shore Printed Circuits Inc 732 380-0590
  3 Meridian Rd Eatontown (07724) *(G-2420)*
Shoreway Industry 856 307-2020
  260 W Clayton Ave Clayton (08312) *(G-1529)*
Short Load Concrete LLC 732 469-4420
  81 Chimney Rock Rd Ste 1 Bridgewater (08807) *(G-889)*

Short Run Stamping Company Inc (PA) 908 862-1070
  925 E Linden Ave Linden (07036) *(G-5423)*
Shotmeyer Bros, Lafayette *Also called Beaver Run Farms (G-5025)*
Showcase Printing of Iselin 732 283-0438
  181 E James Pl Iselin (08830) *(G-4627)*
Showcase Publications Inc 732 349-1134
  90 Irons St Toms River (08753) *(G-10792)*
Showtech 973 249-6336
  40 Entin Rd Clifton (07014) *(G-1717)*
Showtime Express 732 238-2701
  5 Lexington Ave East Brunswick (08816) *(G-2176)*
Shree Ji Printing Corporation 201 842-9500
  55 Veterans Blvd Carlstadt (07072) *(G-1216)*
Shree Meldi Krupa LLC 732 407-5295
  71 Walsh Dr Ste B Parsippany (07054) *(G-8014)*
Shrem Consulting Ltd Lblty Co 917 371-0581
  457 Monmouth Rd West Long Branch (07764) *(G-11721)*
Shriji Polymers LLC 609 906-2355
  1 Graphics Dr Ewing (08628) *(G-3065)*
Shrivers Salt Wtr Taffy Fudge 609 399-0100
  852 Boardwalk Ocean City (08226) *(G-7696)*
Shure-Pak Corporation 856 825-0808
  1500 N Ten St Millville (08332) *(G-6270)*
Shutter DLight LLC 908 956-4206
  970 Madison Ave Plainfield (07060) *(G-8778)*
Si Packaging LLC 973 869-9920
  1 Orient Way Ste F191 Rutherford (07070) *(G-9632)*
Sibi Distributors 908 658-4448
  1370 Meiners Dr Basking Ridge (07920) *(G-197)*
Sic-Naics LLC 929 344-2633
  331 Newman Springs Rd Red Bank (07701) *(G-9244)*
Siccode, Red Bank *Also called Sic-Naics LLC (G-9244)*
Siding Depot, Clifton *Also called Passaic Metal & Bldg Sups Co (G-1685)*
Sidney Scheinert & Son, Saddle Brook *Also called Scheinert & Sons Inc (G-9677)*
Siegfried Usa LLC (HQ) 856 678-3601
  33 Industrial Park Rd Pennsville (08070) *(G-8501)*
Siegfried USA Holding Inc (HQ) 856 678-3601
  33 Industrial Park Rd Pennsville (08070) *(G-8502)*
Siemens Corporation 732 590-6895
  170 Wood Ave S Fl 1 Iselin (08830) *(G-4628)*
Siemens Fire Safety, Mount Laurel *Also called Siemens Industry Inc (G-6806)*
Siemens Industry Inc 856 234-7666
  2000 Crawford Pl Ste 300 Mount Laurel (08054) *(G-6806)*
Siemens Industry Inc 732 302-1686
  163 Washington Valley Rd Warren (07059) *(G-11431)*
Siemens Medical 973 927-2828
  62 Flanders Bartley Rd Flanders (07836) *(G-3419)*
Sierra Communication Intl LLC (HQ) 866 462-8292
  350 Mount Kemble Ave Morristown (07960) *(G-6700)*
Sierra Packaging Inc 732 571-2900
  2106 Kings Hwy Ocean (07712) *(G-7683)*
Sierra Video Systems 530 478-1000
  6 State Route 173 Clinton (08809) *(G-1749)*
Sigco Tool & Mfg Co Inc 856 753-6565
  110 Collings Ave West Berlin (08091) *(G-11621)*
Sight2site Media LLC 856 637-2479
  269 W White Horse Pike Pomona (08240) *(G-8849)*
Sightlogix Inc 609 951-0008
  745 Alexander Rd Ste 5 Princeton (08540) *(G-9022)*
Sigma Engineering & Consulting 732 356-3046
  220 Lincoln Blvd Ste A Middlesex (08846) *(G-6147)*
Sigma Extruding Corp (HQ) 201 933-5353
  Page & Schuyler Ave Lyndhurst (07071) *(G-5677)*
Sigma Plastics Group, Lyndhurst *Also called Omega Plastics Corp (G-5668)*
Sigma Plastics Group, The, Lyndhurst *Also called Alpha Industries MGT Inc (G-5639)*
Sigma Stretch Film, Lyndhurst *Also called Sigma Extruding Corp (G-5677)*
Sigma-Netics Inc 973 227-6372
  2 N Corporate Dr Riverdale (07457) *(G-9385)*
Sign A Rama 609 702-1444
  1413 Rte 38 Hainesport (08036) *(G-4077)*
Sign A Rama 201 489-6969
  379 Main St Hackensack (07601) *(G-3974)*
Sign A Rama 973 471-5558
  681 Van Houten Ave Clifton (07013) *(G-1718)*
Sign Engineers Inc 732 382-4224
  13 New York Ave Colonia (07067) *(G-1775)*
Sign On Inc 201 384-7714
  4 Maple Lake Rd Bloomingdale (07403) *(G-530)*
Sign Shoppe Inc 856 384-2937
  370 Glassboro Rd Woodbury (08097) *(G-12037)*
Sign Spec Inc 856 663-2292
  602 Centerton Rd Elmer (08318) *(G-2804)*
Sign Tech, Westfield *Also called Print Tech LLC (G-11801)*
Sign Up Inc 201 902-8640
  255 State Rt 3 Ste 104a Secaucus (07094) *(G-9814)*
Sign-A-Rama, Hainesport *Also called Sign A Rama (G-4077)*
Sign-A-Rama, Cape May Court House *Also called Signarama (G-1114)*
Sign-A-Rama, Hackensack *Also called Sign A Rama (G-3974)*

A L P H A B E T I C

Sign-A-Rama, Kenilworth *Also called Kna Graphics Inc* ***(G-4953)***
Sign-A-Rama, Ledgewood *Also called Identity Depot Inc* ***(G-5276)***
Sign-A-Rama, Hamilton *Also called Mej Signs Inc* ***(G-4114)***
Sign-A-Rama, Clifton *Also called Sign A Rama* ***(G-1718)***
Signal Crafters Tech Inc....973 781-0880
57 Eagle Rock Ave East Hanover (07936) ***(G-2239)***
Signal Graphics, Egg Harbor Township *Also called Mid Atlantic Graphix Inc* ***(G-2690)***
Signal Sign Company LLC....973 535-9277
105 Dorsa Ave Livingston (07039) ***(G-5541)***
Signal Systems International (PA)....732 793-4668
1700 Grand Central Ave Lavallette (08735) ***(G-5212)***
Signarama....609 465-9400
315 S Main St Cape May Court House (08210) ***(G-1114)***
Signarama Roseland, Roseland *Also called Tdk Associates Corp* ***(G-9542)***
Signature Audio Video Systems....732 864-1039
164 Kettle Creek Rd Toms River (08753) ***(G-10793)***
Signature Crafts, Hawthorne *Also called Signature Marketing & Mfg* ***(G-4244)***
Signature Marketing & Mfg....973 427-3700
301 Wagaraw Rd Hawthorne (07506) ***(G-4244)***
Signature Marketing Group Ltd (PA)....973 575-7785
25 Riverside Dr Ste 4 Pine Brook (07058) ***(G-8617)***
Signify Fincl Solutions LLC....862 930-4682
300 Interpace Pkwy Ste A Parsippany (07054) ***(G-8015)***
Signify North America Corp (HQ)....732 563-3000
200 Franklin Square Dr Somerset (08873) ***(G-10072)***
Signmasters Inc....973 614-8300
217 Brook Ave Ste 2 Passaic (07055) ***(G-8107)***
Signode Industrial Group LLC....201 741-2791
151-161 Buffington St Newark (07112) ***(G-7272)***
Signpros, Glendora *Also called Nickolaos Kappatos Entps Inc* ***(G-3838)***
Signs & Custom Metal Inc....201 200-0110
62 Monitor St Jersey City (07304) ***(G-4809)***
Signs By Tomorrow, Iselin *Also called S S P Enterprises Inc* ***(G-4625)***
Signs of 2000....973 253-1333
421 Broad St Clifton (07013) ***(G-1719)***
Signs of Security Inc....973 340-8404
64 Outwater Ln Ste 2 Garfield (07026) ***(G-3768)***
Sigo Signs, Elmwood Park *Also called GF Supplies LLC* ***(G-2827)***
Sika, Lakewood *Also called May National Associates NJ Inc* ***(G-5132)***
Sika Corporation (HQ)....201 933-8800
201 Polito Ave Lyndhurst (07071) ***(G-5678)***
Sika Corporation....201 933-8800
875 Valley Brook Ave Lyndhurst (07071) ***(G-5679)***
Sika Corporation....856 298-2313
251 S White Horse Pike Audubon (08106) ***(G-114)***
Sika Fibers LLC....201 933-8800
201 Polito Ave Lyndhurst (07071) ***(G-5680)***
Sika Liquid Plasics Division, Audubon *Also called Sika Corporation* ***(G-114)***
Siklu Inc (HQ)....201 267-9597
2037 Lemoine Ave Fort Lee (07024) ***(G-3588)***
Silab Inc....732 335-1030
1301 State Route 36 Ste 8 Hazlet (07730) ***(G-4270)***
Silbo Industries Inc....201 307-0900
50 Chestnut Ridge Rd # 204 Montvale (07645) ***(G-6434)***
Silgan Containers Mfg Corp....732 287-0300
135 National Rd Edison (08817) ***(G-2609)***
Silicon Press Inc....908 273-8919
25 Beverly Rd Summit (07901) ***(G-10547)***
Silk City Snacks LLC....973 928-3161
200 Clifton Blvd Clifton (07011) ***(G-1720)***
Siloa Inc....908 234-9040
2493c Lamington Rd Bedminster (07921) ***(G-278)***
Silver Brush Limited....609 443-4900
92 N Main St Ste 19-I Windsor (08561) ***(G-11998)***
Silver Edmar....973 817-7483
186 Van Buren St Newark (07105) ***(G-7273)***
Silver Line Building Pdts LLC....732 752-8704
207 Pond Ave Middlesex (08846) ***(G-6148)***
Silver Palate Kitchens Inc....201 568-0110
211 Knickerbocker Rd Cresskill (07626) ***(G-1944)***
Silver Silk, Carlstadt *Also called Safire Silk Inc* ***(G-1211)***
Silverstone Wireless LLC (PA)....845 458-5197
6 9 Park Pl Lodi (07644) ***(G-5575)***
Silverton Packaging Corp....732 341-0986
75 Fairway Blvd Monroe Township (08831) ***(G-6344)***
Silvertop Associates Inc (PA)....856 939-9599
600 E Clements Bridge Rd Runnemede (08078) ***(G-9610)***
Silverwear, Dayton *Also called Jese Apparel LLC* ***(G-1973)***
Sima Enterprises, Wall Township *Also called Sima S Enterprises LLC* ***(G-11370)***
Sima S Enterprises LLC....877 223-7639
1298 Evans Rd Wall Township (07719) ***(G-11370)***
Simex Medical Imaging Inc....201 490-0204
68 Alden Rd Paramus (07652) ***(G-7832)***
Simi Granola LLC....848 459-5619
10 S New Prospect Rd Jackson (08527) ***(G-4665)***
Simmons Pet Food Inc....856 662-7412
9130 Griffith Morgan Ln Pennsauken (08110) ***(G-8484)***
Simmons Pet Food Nj Inc....856 662-7412
9130 Griffith Morgan Ln Pennsauken (08110) ***(G-8485)***
Simon & Schuster Inc....856 461-6500
100 Front St Delran (08075) ***(G-2020)***
Simon & Schuster Inc....973 656-6000
1639 State Rt 10 Ste 200 Parsippany (07054) ***(G-8016)***
Simple Home Automation Inc....877 405-2397
32 Brunswick Ave Edison (08817) ***(G-2610)***
Simplex Americas LLC....908 237-9099
20 Bartles Corner Rd Flemington (08822) ***(G-3467)***
Simply Amazing LLC....732 249-4151
233 State Route 18 Ste 22 East Brunswick (08816) ***(G-2177)***
Sims Lee Inc (PA)....201 433-1308
743 Bergen Ave Jersey City (07306) ***(G-4810)***
Sims Metal Management, Jersey City *Also called Metal MGT Pittsburgh Inc* ***(G-4765)***
Sims Pump Valve Company Inc....201 792-0600
1314 Park Ave Hoboken (07030) ***(G-4480)***
Simtek Usa Inc....862 757-8130
13 Fairfield Ave Little Falls (07424) ***(G-5467)***
Simtronics Corporation....732 747-0322
50 Birch Ave Ste 100 Little Silver (07739) ***(G-5500)***
Sinai Manufacturing Corp....973 522-1003
133 Kossuth St Newark (07105) ***(G-7274)***
Sinclair and Rush Inc....862 262-8189
640 Dell Rd Carlstadt (07072) ***(G-1217)***
Sine Tru Tool Company Inc....732 591-1100
238 Boundary Rd Ste 2 Marlboro (07746) ***(G-5915)***
Singe Corporation....908 289-7900
1290 Central Ave Hillside (07205) ***(G-4426)***
Single Vender Outsource, Succasunna *Also called S V O Inc* ***(G-10519)***
Sino Monthly Jersey, Edison *Also called Sino Monthly New Jersey Inc* ***(G-2611)***
Sino Monthly New Jersey Inc....732 650-0688
18 Sheppard Pl Edison (08817) ***(G-2611)***
Sir Speedy, Montclair *Also called Action Copy Centers Inc* ***(G-6356)***
Sir Speedy, Cranbury *Also called Dato Company Inc* ***(G-1829)***
Sir Speedy, Clifton *Also called Tanzola Printing Inc* ***(G-1729)***
Sir Speedy, Pennsauken *Also called Franbeth Inc* ***(G-8422)***
Sir Speedy, Newark *Also called Sheroy Printing Inc* ***(G-7271)***
Sir Speedy, Piscataway *Also called Mark Alan Printing & Graphics* ***(G-8686)***
Sir Speedy, Trenton *Also called D A K Office Services Inc* ***(G-10929)***
Sir Speedy, Maple Shade *Also called Marks Management Systems Inc* ***(G-5867)***
Sir Speedy, Paramus *Also called Lunet Inc* ***(G-7816)***
Sir Speedy, Sewell *Also called Yasheel Inc* ***(G-9854)***
Sirma Group Inc....646 357-3067
1 Evertrust Plz Ste 1103 Jersey City (07302) ***(G-4811)***
Sirui USA LLC....973 415-8082
29 Commerce Ct Verona (07044) ***(G-11174)***
Sisco Manufacturing Co Inc....856 486-7550
7930 National Hwy Pennsauken (08110) ***(G-8486)***
SISSCO DIVISION, Hillsborough *Also called Permadur Industries Inc* ***(G-4344)***
Sitaras Toasters Equipment LLC....732 910-2678
602 Union Landing Rd Cinnaminson (08077) ***(G-1485)***
Site Drainer LLC....862 225-9940
18 Sebago St Clifton (07013) ***(G-1721)***
Sitetracker Inc (PA)....551 486-2087
491 Bloomfield Ave # 301 Montclair (07042) ***(G-6389)***
Sivantos Inc (HQ)....732 562-6600
10 Constitution Ave Piscataway (08854) ***(G-8712)***
Six Thirteen Originals LLC....201 316-1900
18 Industrial Ave Ste C Mahwah (07430) ***(G-5772)***
Sj Magazine....856 722-9300
1000 S Lenola Rd Ste 102 Maple Shade (08052) ***(G-5869)***
Sjd Direct Midwest LLC....732 985-8405
112 Truman Dr Edison (08817) ***(G-2612)***
Sjd Direct Midwest LLC....732 287-2525
3 Ethel Rd Ste 301 Edison (08817) ***(G-2613)***
Sjshore Marketing Ltd Lblty Co....609 390-1400
533 S Shore Rd Ste 1 Marmora (08223) ***(G-5959)***
Sk & P Industries Inc (PA)....973 482-1864
73 Norfolk St Newark (07103) ***(G-7275)***
Sk & P Industries Inc....973 482-1864
73 Norfolk St Newark (07103) ***(G-7276)***
Sk Custom Creations Inc....973 754-9261
50 Furler St Totowa (07512) ***(G-10852)***
Sk Life Science Inc....201 421-3800
461 From Rd Ste 100 Paramus (07652) ***(G-7833)***
Skaffles Group Ltd Lblty Co (PA)....732 901-2100
139 Ocean Ave Lakewood (08701) ***(G-5163)***
Skc Powertech Inc....973 347-7000
850 Clark Dr Ste 2 Budd Lake (07828) ***(G-937)***
Skinder-Strauss LLC (PA)....973 642-1440
890 Mountain Ave Ste 300 New Providence (07974) ***(G-7018)***
Skip Gambert & Associates Inc....973 344-3373
436 Ferry St Ste 2 Newark (07105) ***(G-7277)***
Sklsi, Paramus *Also called Sk Life Science Inc* ***(G-7833)***
Skorr Products LLC....973 523-2606
90 George St Paterson (07503) ***(G-8299)***

Sks Fuel Inc 973 200-0796
941 Mcbride Ave Woodland Park (07424) *(G-12091)*

Skunktown Distillery LLC 908 824-7754
12 Minneakoning Rd 110b Flemington (08822) *(G-3468)*

Skusky Inc 732 912-7220
143 Vanderburgh Ave Rutherford (07070) *(G-9633)*

SKW Quab Chemicals Inc 201 556-0300
250 Pehle Ave Ste 403 Saddle Brook (07663) *(G-9681)*

Sky Growth Intermediate 201 802-4000
300 Tice Blvd Woodcliff Lake (07677) *(G-12064)*

Skycam Technologies LLC 908 205-5548
235 Kearny Ave Perth Amboy (08861) *(G-8534)*

Skylands Press 973 383-5006
57 Trinity St Newton (07860) *(G-7358)*

Skyline Stl Fbrcatrs & Erctrs 973 957-0234
419 Franklin Ave Ste 3 Rockaway (07866) *(G-9499)*

Skyline Windows LLC 201 531-9600
210 Park Pl E Wood Ridge (07075) *(G-12005)*

Slack Incorporated 856 848-1000
6900 Grove Rd Thorofare (08086) *(G-10703)*

Sleep Innovations, Red Bank *Also called Innocor Inc (G-9230)*

Slendertone Distribution Inc 732 660-1177
221 River St Ste 9 Hoboken (07030) *(G-4481)*

Sli Production Corp 201 621-4260
7 Capital Dr Moonachie (07074) *(G-6489)*

Slp Performance, Toms River *Also called S L P Engineering Inc (G-10789)*

Slt Foods Inc 732 661-1030
303 Ridge Rd Dayton (08810) *(G-1988)*

Slt Imports, Dayton *Also called Slt Foods Inc (G-1988)*

Slys Express LLC 908 787-7516
518 Lindegar St Linden (07036) *(G-5424)*

Small Molecules Inc 201 918-4664
38 Jackson St Hoboken (07030) *(G-4482)*

Small Quantities NJ Inc 732 248-9009
66 Ethel Rd Edison (08817) *(G-2614)*

Smart Desks, Rockaway *Also called Cbt Supply Inc (G-9450)*

Smart Gear Toys, Deal *Also called Ambo Consulting LLC (G-1997)*

Smartekg LLC 201 376-4556
287 Rutland Ave Teaneck (07666) *(G-10652)*

Smarties, Union *Also called Ce De Candy Inc (G-11035)*

Smartlinx Solutions LLC (PA) 732 385-5507
111 Wood Ave S Ste 400 Iselin (08830) *(G-4629)*

Smartplay International Inc 609 880-1860
1550 Bridgeboro Rd Beverly (08010) *(G-454)*

Smartpool LLC 732 730-9880
1940 Rutgers Blvd Lakewood (08701) *(G-5164)*

Smb International LLC 732 222-4888
121 State Route 36 # 180 West Long Branch (07764) *(G-11722)*

Smf, Linden *Also called Steel Mountain Fabricators LLC (G-5431)*

Smith Bearing, Garwood *Also called Accurate Bushing Company Inc (G-3779)*

Smith Enterprises 215 416-9881
100 Hillside Ln Mount Laurel (08054) *(G-6807)*

Smith Lime Flour Co Inc 973 344-1700
60 Central Ave Kearny (07032) *(G-4898)*

Smith Optics Inc 208 726-4477
300 Lighting Way Ste 400 Secaucus (07094) *(G-9815)*

Smithfield Packaged Meats Corp 908 354-2674
814 2nd Ave Elizabeth (07202) *(G-2776)*

Smiths Group North America, Swedesboro *Also called John Crane Inc (G-10590)*

Smitteez Sportswear, Keansburg *Also called J and S Sporting Apparel LLC (G-4838)*

Smittys Door Service Inc 908 284-0506
170 Oak Grove Rd Pittstown (08867) *(G-8755)*

SMK Nutra Makers, Parsippany *Also called Shree Meldi Krupa LLC (G-8014)*

Smock, Thomas Woodworking, Eatontown *Also called Thomas Smock Woodworking (G-2426)*

SMR Research Corporation 908 852-7677
300 Valentine St Ste A Hackettstown (07840) *(G-4037)*

SMS Building Systems Ltd Lblty 856 520-8769
5 N Olney Ave Ste 100a Cherry Hill (08003) *(G-1415)*

SMS Electric Motor Car LLC 215 428-2502
18 Totten Dr Bridgewater (08807) *(G-890)*

SMS International, Clifton *Also called Stainless Metal Source Intl (G-1724)*

Snack Innovations Inc (PA) 718 509-9366
41 Ethel Rd W Piscataway (08854) *(G-8713)*

Snap Set Specialists Inc 856 629-9552
300 Thomas Ave Bldg 6 Williamstown (08094) *(G-11978)*

Snapco Manufacturing Corp 973 282-0300
140 Central Ave Ste 1 Hillside (07205) *(G-4427)*

Snapple Beverage Corp 201 933-0070
600 Commercial Ave Carlstadt (07072) *(G-1218)*

Snapple Distributors Inc (HQ) 732 815-2800
433 Blair Rd Ste 1 Avenel (07001) *(G-146)*

Sneaker Swarm LLC 908 693-9262
581 Main St Ste 640 Woodbridge (07095) *(G-12021)*

Sniderman John 201 569-5482
133 E Palisade Ave Apt H Englewood (07631) *(G-2942)*

Sno Skins Inc 973 884-8801
622 State Route 10 Ste 19 Whippany (07981) *(G-11909)*

Snotex USA Inc 973 762-0358
116 Irvington Ave Apt 2f South Orange (07079) *(G-10201)*

SNS Oriental Rugs LLC 201 355-8786
455 Barell Ave Carlstadt (07072) *(G-1219)*

So Many Waves, Newark *Also called Razac Products Inc (G-7246)*

So Nikki, Lakewood *Also called Power Apparel LLC (G-5149)*

Socafe LLC 973 589-4104
41-43 Malvern St Newark (07105) *(G-7278)*

Society Trnsaction Periodicals, Piscataway *Also called Transaction Publishers Inc (G-8732)*

Sock Company Inc (PA) 201 307-0675
40 Carver Ave Westwood (07675) *(G-11845)*

Sock Drawer and More LLC 888 637-3399
95 Mayfield Ave Edison (08837) *(G-2615)*

Socks 47 Ltd Liability Company 201 866-2222
4620 Bergenline Ave Union City (07087) *(G-11128)*

Sodastream USA Inc 856 755-3400
136 Gaither Dr Ste 200 Mount Laurel (08054) *(G-6808)*

Sofa Doctor Inc 718 292-6300
148 71st St Guttenberg (07093) *(G-3872)*

Sofield Manufacturing Co Inc 201 931-1530
2 Main St Ridgefield Park (07660) *(G-9316)*

Software Developers LLC 888 315-6652
410 Monmouth Ave Apt 502 Lakewood (08701) *(G-5165)*

Software Practices and Tech 908 464-2923
73 Stone Ridge Rd Summit (07901) *(G-10548)*

Software Services & Solutions 203 630-2000
15 Laurel Wood Dr Lawrence Township (08648) *(G-5220)*

Soh LLC 646 943-4066
150 Bay St Apt 715 Jersey City (07302) *(G-4812)*

Sohha Savory Yogurt, Lawrence Township *Also called Mualema LLC (G-5217)*

Solar Compounds Corporation 908 862-2813
1201 W Blancke St Linden (07036) *(G-5425)*

Solar Products Inc 973 248-9370
228 Wanaque Ave Pompton Lakes (07442) *(G-8852)*

Solar Turbines Incorporated 201 825-8200
300 Kimball Dr Ste 4 Parsippany (07054) *(G-8017)*

Solaris Pharma Corporation 908 864-0404
1031 Rte 202/206 200 Bridgewater (08807) *(G-891)*

Solbern LLC 973 227-3030
8 Kulick Rd Fairfield (07004) *(G-3312)*

Solenis LLC 201 767-7400
49 Walnut St Norwood (07648) *(G-7574)*

Solgen Pharmaceuticals Inc 732 983-6025
1514 Edison Glen Ter Edison (08837) *(G-2616)*

Solid Cast Stone 856 694-5245
470 Grubb Rd Newfield (08344) *(G-7328)*

Solid Color Inc 212 239-3930
78 John Miller Way # 420 Kearny (07032) *(G-4899)*

Solidia Technologies Inc 908 315-5901
11 Colonial Dr Piscataway (08854) *(G-8714)*

Solidsurface Designs Inc 856 910-7720
1651 Sherman Ave Pennsauken (08110) *(G-8487)*

Soligenix Inc (PA) 609 538-8200
29 Emmons Dr Ste B10 Princeton (08540) *(G-9023)*

Solmor Manufacturing Co Inc 973 824-7203
3 Stonewood Pkwy Verona (07044) *(G-11175)*

Solutia Inc 908 862-0278
2000 Brunswick Ave Linden (07036) *(G-5426)*

Solv-TEC Incorporated 609 261-4242
75 N Main St Medford (08055) *(G-6034)*

Solvay Holding Inc 609 860-4000
504 Carnegie Ctr Princeton (08540) *(G-9024)*

Solvay Spclty Polymers USA LLC 856 853-8119
10 Leonard Ln West Deptford (08086) *(G-11716)*

Solvay USA Inc (HQ) 609 860-4000
504 Carnegie Ctr Princeton (08540) *(G-9025)*

Solvay USA Inc 732 297-0100
219 Black Horse Ln North Brunswick (08902) *(G-7486)*

Solvay USA Inc 609 860-4000
Cn 1120 Cranbury (08512) *(G-1883)*

Solvent & Envmtl Svcs Div, Cinnaminson *Also called Detrex Corporation (G-1452)*

Soma Labs Inc 732 271-3444
248 Wagner St 252 Middlesex (08846) *(G-6149)*

Somerset Cpitl Mark Tr MGT Inc 848 228-0842
1 Donlonton Cir Chesterfield (08515) *(G-1437)*

Somerset Outpatient Surgery 781 635-2807
100 Franklin Square Dr # 100 Somerset (08873) *(G-10073)*

Somerset Wood Products Co 908 526-0030
1 Johnson Dr Raritan (08869) *(G-9218)*

Somerville Acquisitions Co Inc (PA) 908 782-9500
45 River Rd Ste 300 Flemington (08822) *(G-3469)*

Somes Uniforms Inc (PA) 201 843-1199
314 Main St Hackensack (07601) *(G-3975)*

Something Different Linen Inc 973 272-0601
167 Fornelius Ave Clifton (07013) *(G-1722)*

Sonata Graphics Inc 201 866-0186
1247 Paterson Plank Rd # 65 Secaucus (07094) *(G-9816)*

Sondpex Corp America LLC 732 940-4430
4185 Route 27 Princeton (08540) *(G-9026)*

Sondpex Electronics, Princeton *Also called Sondpex Corp America LLC (G-9026)*

Sondra Roberts Inc 212 684-3344
3 Empire Blvd South Hackensack (07606) *(G-10187)*

Sonetronics Inc (PA) 732 681-5016
1718 H St Belmar (07719) *(G-354)*

Songbird Hearing Inc 732 422-7203
210 N Center Dr North Brunswick (08902) *(G-7487)*

Sonia Fashion Inc 201 864-3483
422 11th St Union City (07087) *(G-11129)*

Sonic Innovations Inc 888 423-7834
2501 Cottontail Ln Somerset (08873) *(G-10074)*

Sonneborn LLC (HQ) 201 760-2940
600 Parsippany Rd Ste 100 Parsippany (07054) *(G-8018)*

Sonneborn Holding LLC 201 760-2940
600 Parsippany Rd Ste 100 Parsippany (07054) *(G-8019)*

Sonneborn US Holdings LLC (HQ) 201 760-2940
600 Parsippany Rd Ste 100 Parsippany (07054) *(G-8020)*

Sonoco Corrflex, Ridgefield Park *Also called Sonoco Display & Packaging LLC (G-9317)*

Sonoco Display & Packaging LLC 201 612-4008
55 Challenger Rd Ste 500 Ridgefield Park (07660) *(G-9317)*

Sonoco Products Company 609 655-0300
5 Stults Rd Dayton (08810) *(G-1989)*

Sonotron Medical Systems Inc 201 767-6040
224 Pegasus Ave Northvale (07647) *(G-7550)*

Sonrise Metal Inc 973 423-4717
32 Shore Rd Hopatcong (07843) *(G-4522)*

Sony Corporation of America 201 930-1000
115 W Century Rd Ste 250 Paramus (07652) *(G-7834)*

Sony Corporation of America 201 930-1000
123 Tice Blvd Woodcliff Lake (07677) *(G-12065)*

Sony Electronics Inc 201 930-1000
115 W Century Rd Ste 250 Paramus (07652) *(G-7835)*

Sony Music Holdings Inc 201 777-3933
301 State Rte Hwy Rutherford (07070) *(G-9634)*

Sound Chice Assstive Listening 908 647-2651
498 Long Hill Rd Gillette (07933) *(G-3803)*

Sound Professionals Inc 609 267-4400
3444 Sylon Blvd Hainesport (08036) *(G-4078)*

Sound United LLC 201 762-6500
100 Corporate Dr Mahwah (07430) *(G-5773)*

Soundview Paper Company, Elmwood Park *Also called Marcal Manufacturing LLC (G-2839)*

Soundview Paper Holdings LLC (HQ) 201 796-4000
1 Market St Elmwood Park (07407) *(G-2856)*

Source Direct Inc 856 768-7445
2200 Garry Rd Ste 3 Cinnaminson (08077) *(G-1486)*

Source Direct Plastics Div, Cinnaminson *Also called Source Direct Inc (G-1486)*

Source Micro LLC 973 328-1749
5 Rolling Ridge Rd Randolph (07869) *(G-9200)*

Source One, Totowa *Also called Fabulous Fabricators LLC (G-10826)*

Source Packaging, Mahwah *Also called Cases By Source Inc (G-5720)*

Sourland Mountain Wdwkg LLC T 908 806-7661
17 Higginsville Rd Neshanic Station (08853) *(G-6905)*

South Amboy Designer T Shirt L 732 456-2594
603 Washington Ave Ste 5b South Amboy (08879) *(G-10141)*

South American Imports Corp 201 941-2020
7 Cecelia Ave Cliffside Park (07010) *(G-1544)*

South Bergenite Editorial, Rutherford *Also called North Jersey Media Group Inc (G-9629)*

South Brunswick Furniture Inc 732 658-8850
1015 Edward St Linden (07036) *(G-5427)*

South County Soccer League Inc 908 310-9052
3 Ferry St Lambertville (08530) *(G-5197)*

South East Instruments LLC 201 569-0050
111 Cedar Ln Englewood (07631) *(G-2943)*

South Jersey Circuits 609 479-3994
340 E Broad St Unit 1c Burlington (08016) *(G-985)*

South Jersey Countertop Co 856 768-7960
1044 Industrial Dr Ste 12 West Berlin (08091) *(G-11622)*

South Jersey Farmers Exchange 856 769-0062
101 East Ave Woodstown (08098) *(G-12096)*

South Jersey Metal Inc 856 228-0642
1651 Hurffville Rd Deptford (08096) *(G-2066)*

South Jersey Precision TI Mold 856 327-0500
4375 S Lincoln Ave Vineland (08361) *(G-11266)*

South Jersey Pretzel Inc 856 435-5055
912 N White Horse Pike A Stratford (08084) *(G-10507)*

South Jersey Publishing Co (HQ) 609 272-7000
1000 W Washington Ave Pleasantville (08232) *(G-8819)*

South Jersey Publishing Co 856 692-0455
22 W Landis Ave Vineland (08360) *(G-11267)*

South Jersey Water Cond Svc 856 451-0620
760 Shiloh Pike Bridgeton (08302) *(G-773)*

South River Food Machinery, Hackensack *Also called South River Machinery Corp (G-3976)*

South River Machinery Corp 201 487-1736
115 S River St Hackensack (07601) *(G-3976)*

South Shore Sign Co Inc 718 984-5624
550 Morristown Rd Matawan (07747) *(G-5988)*

South Shore Signs, Matawan *Also called South Shore Sign Co Inc (G-5988)*

South State Inc 856 881-6030
1340 Glassboro Rd Williamstown (08094) *(G-11979)*

South State Speed Shop, Hackensack *Also called Roy Anania (G-3967)*

Southern New Jersey Stl Co Inc (PA) 856 696-1612
2591 N East Blvd Vineland (08360) *(G-11268)*

Southern NJ Steel, Vineland *Also called Southern New Jersey Stl Co Inc (G-11268)*

Southern Ocean Mar Sportswear, Barnegat *Also called Sgh Inc (G-161)*

Southwind Equestrian 856 364-9690
385 Lebanon Rd Millville (08332) *(G-6271)*

Sowa Corp 973 297-0008
223 Murray St Newark (07114) *(G-7279)*

Soyka-Smith Design Research, Montclair *Also called Interchange Group Inc (G-6371)*

Sozio Inc 732 572-5600
51 Ethel Rd W Piscataway (08854) *(G-8715)*

Space and Navigation, Budd Lake *Also called L3 Technologies Inc (G-925)*

Space-Eyes, Camden *Also called Channel Logistics LLC (G-1052)*

Spacetouch Inc 609 712-6572
34 Chambers St Princeton (08542) *(G-9027)*

Spadix Technologies Inc 732 356-6906
110 Egel Ave Middlesex (08846) *(G-6150)*

Spadone Alfa Self Lbrcted Pdts 203 972-8848
532 Vincent Dr Brick (08723) *(G-732)*

Spadone Bearings, Brick *Also called Spadone Alfa Self Lbrcted Pdts (G-732)*

Spaghetti Engineering Corp 856 719-9989
150 Cooper Rd Ste C7 West Berlin (08091) *(G-11623)*

Spalding Automotive Inc (PA) 215 638-3334
355 Crider Ave Moorestown (08057) *(G-6567)*

Spark Holland Inc 609 799-7250
118 Karenlynn Dr Franklinville (08322) *(G-3638)*

Spark Wire Products Co Inc 973 773-6945
158 River Rd Clifton (07014) *(G-1723)*

Sparks Belting Company Inc 973 227-4100
5 Spielman Rd Fairfield (07004) *(G-3313)*

Spartech LLC 201 489-4000
215 S Newman St Hackensack (07601) *(G-3977)*

Spartech LLC 973 344-2700
297 Ferry St Newark (07105) *(G-7280)*

Sparton Aydin LLC 732 935-1320
10 Industrial Way E Eatontown (07724) *(G-2421)*

Spc Publication, Neptune *Also called School Publications Co Inc (G-6896)*

Spct, Elizabeth *Also called Superior Powder Coating Inc (G-2780)*

Spec Steel Rule Dies Inc 609 443-4435
92 N Main St Bldg 1b Windsor (08561) *(G-11999)*

Special Optics Inc 973 366-7289
3 Stewart Ct Denville (07834) *(G-2058)*

Special T S Screen Prtg & EMB, Flemington *Also called Ambro Manufacturing Inc (G-3429)*

Special Technical Services 609 259-2626
11 Carlton Rd Flanders (07836) *(G-3420)*

Speciality Pharma Mfg LLC 201 675-3411
609 Industrial Rd Carlstadt (07072) *(G-1220)*

Specialized Fire & SEC Inc 212 255-1010
20 Cotluss Rd Ste 9 Riverdale (07457) *(G-9386)*

Specialized Metal Stamping, Glen Rock *Also called B E C Mfg Corp (G-3828)*

Specialty Casting Inc 856 845-3105
42 Curtis Ave Woodbury (08096) *(G-12038)*

Specialty Fabricators LLC 609 758-6995
118 Meany Rd Wrightstown (08562) *(G-12100)*

Specialty Kraft Converters LLC 732 225-2080
150 Fieldcrest Ave Edison (08837) *(G-2617)*

Specialty Lighting Inds Inc 732 517-0800
1306 Doris Ave Ocean (07712) *(G-7684)*

Specialty Measures 609 882-6071
15 Dawes Ave Ewing (08638) *(G-3066)*

Specialty Pharmasource LLC 973 784-4965
400 Morris Ave Ste 121 Denville (07834) *(G-2059)*

Specialty Products & Insul Co, Camden *Also called Fbm Galaxy Inc (G-1064)*

Specialty Products Plus 732 380-1188
215 Locust Ave West Long Branch (07764) *(G-11723)*

Specialty Rubber Inc 609 704-2555
4500 White Horse Pike Elwood (08217) *(G-2860)*

Specialty Systems Inc (PA) 732 341-1011
1451 Route 37 W Ste 1 Toms River (08755) *(G-10794)*

Specialty Tube Filling LLC 908 262-2219
1 Ilene Ct Bldg 8u6 Hillsborough (08844) *(G-4355)*

Specified Technologies Inc 908 526-8000
210 Evans Way Branchburg (08876) *(G-684)*

Spectacle Shoppe 856 875-5046
202 Dickens Ct Williamstown (08094) *(G-11980)*

Spectra Mattress Inc 732 545-5900
633 Nassau St North Brunswick (08902) *(G-7488)*

Spectraform, Linden *Also called Thomas H Cox & Son Inc (G-5435)*

Spectro Analytical Instrs Inc (PA) 201 642-3000
91 Mckee Dr Mahwah (07430) *(G-5774)*

Spectrum Chemicals & Lab Pdts, New Brunswick *Also called Spectrum Laboratory Pdts Inc (G-6971)*

Spectrum Communications, Kenvil *Also called Major Auto Installations Inc (G-4993)*

Spectrum Design LLC 856 694-1870
1106 Grant Ave Franklinville (08322) *(G-3639)*

Spectrum Foils Inc 973 481-0808
29 Riverside Ave Bldg 1 Newark (07104) *(G-7281)*

Spectrum Instrumentation Corp 201 562-1999
  401 Hackensack Ave Fl 4 Hackensack (07601) *(G-3978)*
Spectrum International LLC 908 998-9338
  109 Aldene Rd Ste 1 Roselle (07203) *(G-9572)*
Spectrum Laboratory Pdts Inc (PA) 732 214-1300
  769 Jersey Ave New Brunswick (08901) *(G-6971)*
Spectrum Laboratory Pdts Inc 732 214-1300
  755 769 & 777 Jersey Ave New Brunswick (08901) *(G-6972)*
Spectrum Neon Sign Group LLC 856 317-9223
  9130 Pennsauken Hwy Ste B Pennsauken (08110) *(G-8488)*
Spectrum Paint Applicator 973 732-9180
  425 Ferry St Fl 2 Newark (07105) *(G-7282)*
Spectrum Plastics 732 564-1899
  250 Circle Dr N Piscataway (08854) *(G-8716)*
Spectrum Quality Products, New Brunswick *Also called Spectrum Laboratory Pdts Inc (G-6972)*
Speed Center USA, Saddle Brook *Also called Blue Monkey Inc (G-9643)*
Speedway, Swedesboro *Also called Cobra Products Inc (G-10577)*
Speedway LLC 732 750-7800
  750 Cliff Rd Port Reading (07064) *(G-8895)*
Speedwell Targets, Frenchtown *Also called Rockwood Corporation (G-3717)*
Speedy Sign-A-Rama 973 605-8313
  166 Ridgedale Ave Ste 4 Morristown (07960) *(G-6701)*
Spem Corporation 732 356-3366
  403 Bell St Piscataway (08854) *(G-8717)*
Spencer Industries Inc (PA) 973 751-2200
  80 Holmes St Belleville (07109) *(G-315)*
Spencer's, Mount Laurel *Also called William Spencer (G-6813)*
Spendylove Home Care LLC 732 430-5789
  878 Georges Rd Monmouth Junction (08852) *(G-6312)*
Sperro Metal Products LLC 973 335-2000
  2 Skyline Dr Montville (07045) *(G-6447)*
Sperry Marine Division, Cranford *Also called Northrop Grumman Systems Corp (G-1919)*
Spex Certiprep Inc (PA) 732 549-7144
  203 Norcross Ave Metuchen (08840) *(G-6069)*
Spex Certiprep Group LLC 208 204-6656
  203 Norcross Ave Metuchen (08840) *(G-6070)*
Spex Certprep Group LLC 732 549-7144
  203 Norcross Ave Metuchen (08840) *(G-6071)*
Spex Sample Prep LLC 732 549-7144
  65 Liberty St Metuchen (08840) *(G-6072)*
Spex Sample Prep (PA) 732 549-7144
  203 Norcross Ave Metuchen (08840) *(G-6073)*
Sphere Fluidics Incorporated 888 258-0226
  11 Deerpark Dr Ste 210 Monmouth Junction (08852) *(G-6313)*
Sphinx Software Inc 609 275-5085
  2 Red Oak Dr Plainsboro (08536) *(G-8803)*
SPI, Summit *Also called Safety Power Inc (G-10544)*
Spice Chain Corporation 800 584-0422
  35 Kimberly Rd East Brunswick (08816) *(G-2178)*
Spident USA Incorporated 201 944-0511
  205 Redneck Ave Little Ferry (07643) *(G-5497)*
Spinal Kinetics LLC (PA) 908 687-2552
  950 W Chestnut St Union (07083) *(G-11091)*
Spindlers Bake Shop 201 288-1345
  247 Boulevard Hasbrouck Heights (07604) *(G-4188)*
Spinningdesigns Inc 732 775-7050
  5106 Rte 34 Farmingdale (07727) *(G-3392)*
Spiral Binding LLC (PA) 973 256-0666
  1 Maltese Dr Totowa (07512) *(G-10853)*
Spiral Water Technologies Inc 415 259-4929
  200 Pond Ave Middlesex (08846) *(G-6151)*
Spiralseal, Cliffwood *Also called Sprialseal Inc (G-1547)*
Spirent Communications Inc 732 946-4018
  101 Crawfords Corner Rd Holmdel (07733) *(G-4514)*
Spirit Tex LLC 201 440-1113
  201 Gates Rd Ste E Little Ferry (07643) *(G-5498)*
Spl Holdings LLC 856 764-2400
  211 Carriage Ln Delran (08075) *(G-2021)*
Sports Factory, Lincoln Park *Also called J & S Enterprises LLC (G-5300)*
Sports Impact Inc 732 257-1451
  52 Yorktown Rd East Brunswick (08816) *(G-2179)*
Sports Stop Inc 856 881-2763
  31 Delsea Dr N Glassboro (08028) *(G-3819)*
Sportstar World Wide Inc 732 254-9214
  19 Thomas St South River (08882) *(G-10358)*
Spotless Shade, Edison *Also called Spotless Venetian Blind Servic (G-2618)*
Spotless Venetian Blind Servic 732 548-1711
  1217 Us Highway 1 Edison (08837) *(G-2618)*
Spray Tech & Marketing, Parsippany *Also called Industry Publications Inc (G-7961)*
Spray-Tek Inc (PA) 732 469-0050
  344 Cedar Ave Middlesex (08846) *(G-6152)*
Sprialseal Inc 732 738-6113
  284 Cliffwood Ave Cliffwood (07721) *(G-1547)*
Spring Aire, Mountainside *Also called Springfield Heating & AC Co (G-6852)*
Spring Eureka Co Inc 973 589-4960
  9 Manufacturers Pl Newark (07105) *(G-7283)*

Spring Time Mattress Mfg Corp (PA) 973 473-5400
  25 Saddle River Ave South Hackensack (07606) *(G-10188)*
Springdale Farm Market Inc 856 424-8674
  1638 Springdale Rd Cherry Hill (08003) *(G-1416)*
Springer Scnce + Bus Media LLC 201 348-4033
  333 Mdwlands Pkwy Fl 2 Secaucus (07094) *(G-9817)*
Springfield Heating & AC Co 908 233-8400
  217 Sheffield St Mountainside (07092) *(G-6852)*
Springfield Metal Pdts Co Inc 973 379-4600
  8 Commerce St Springfield (07081) *(G-10467)*
Springtime Bedding, South Hackensack *Also called Spring Time Mattress Mfg Corp (G-10188)*
Sprint Screening, Mount Laurel *Also called D & N Sporting Goods Inc (G-6751)*
SPS Alfachem Inc (PA) 973 676-5141
  164 Elmwynd Dr Orange (07050) *(G-7762)*
SPX Cooling Technologies Inc 908 450-8027
  1200 Us Highway 22 Ste 14 Bridgewater (08807) *(G-892)*
SPX Dry Cooling Usa LLC 908 450-8027
  1200 Rte 22 Ste 1 Bridgewater (08807) *(G-893)*
Sqn Banking Systems, Rancocas *Also called Sqn Peripherals Inc (G-9166)*
Sqn Peripherals Inc (HQ) 609 261-5500
  65 Indel Ave Rancocas (08073) *(G-9166)*
Squash Beef LLC 917 577-8723
  12 Downing Hill Ln Colts Neck (07722) *(G-1788)*
Squillace Stl Fabricators LLC 908 241-6424
  240 W Westfield Ave Roselle Park (07204) *(G-9591)*
Squire Corrugated Cont Corp 908 862-9111
  110 Allen Rd Ste 3 Basking Ridge (07920) *(G-198)*
Sr Custom Woodcraft Ltd Lblty 732 942-7601
  1980 Swarthmore Ave Lakewood (08701) *(G-5166)*
Sr International Rock Inc 908 864-4700
  7 Easy St Ste E Bound Brook (08805) *(G-606)*
Sre Ventures LLC 973 785-0099
  163 E Main St Little Falls (07424) *(G-5468)*
SRS Health Software, Montvale *Also called SRS Software LLC (G-6435)*
SRS Software LLC 201 802-1300
  155 Chestnut Ridge Rd Montvale (07645) *(G-6435)*
Ss Equipment Holdings LLC 732 627-0006
  1425 Frontier Rd Bridgewater (08807) *(G-894)*
Ss Tool & Manufacturing Co 908 486-5497
  1 Garfield St Linden (07036) *(G-5428)*
Ss White Burs Inc 732 905-1100
  1145 Towbin Ave Lakewood (08701) *(G-5167)*
Ssam Sports Inc (PA) 917 553-0596
  234 Macintyre Ln Allendale (07401) *(G-15)*
Ssam Sports Inc 917 553-0596
  2 Myrtle Ave Unit 599 Allendale (07401) *(G-16)*
Ssi, Branchburg *Also called Savoury Systems Intl LLC (G-680)*
Ssi North America, Randolph *Also called Surface Source Intl Inc (G-9202)*
Ssi North America Inc 973 598-0152
  961 State Route 10 Ste 2i Randolph (07869) *(G-9201)*
St Jude Medical LLC 800 645-5368
  333 Mdwlands Pkwy Ste 502 Secaucus (07094) *(G-9818)*
St Louis Trimming Div, Englewood Cliffs *Also called Trimtex Company Inc (G-2994)*
St Martin Cabinetry Inc 732 902-6020
  100 Newfield Ave Ste B Edison (08837) *(G-2619)*
St Thomas Creations (HQ) 800 536-2284
  3a S Middlesex Ave Monroe Township (08831) *(G-6345)*
STA-Seal Inc (PA) 609 924-0300
  Promenade Blvd Rr 27 Kingston (08528) *(G-5011)*
Stacks Envmtl Ltd Lblty Co 973 885-2036
  5 Crescent Dr Lake Hopatcong (07849) *(G-5037)*
Stafford Park Solar 1 LLC 609 607-9500
  500 Barnegat Blvd N Barnegat (08005) *(G-162)*
Stained Glass Overlay, West Berlin *Also called Artistic Glass & Doors Inc (G-11577)*
Staines Inc 856 784-2718
  610 S White Horse Pike Somerdale (08083) *(G-9935)*
Stainless Metal Source Intl 973 977-2200
  207 Piaget Ave Clifton (07011) *(G-1724)*
Stainless Stock 732 564-1164
  333 Cedar Ave Ste 1 Middlesex (08846) *(G-6153)*
Stainless Surplus LLC 914 661-3800
  6 Pheasant Run Green Brook (08812) *(G-3867)*
Stairshop, Red Bank *Also called B & C Custom WD Handrail Corp (G-9222)*
Stairworks Inc 908 276-2829
  335 Centennial Ave Unit 8 Cranford (07016) *(G-1927)*
Stamm International Corp (PA) 201 947-1700
  1530 Palisade Ave Ste Phd Fort Lee (07024) *(G-3589)*
Stampex Corp 973 839-4040
  75 4th Ave Haskell (07420) *(G-4202)*
Stamping Com Inc 732 493-4697
  3600 Sunset Ave Ocean (07712) *(G-7685)*
Stamplus Manufacturing Inc 908 241-8844
  654 W 1st Ave Roselle (07203) *(G-9573)*
Stanbee Company Inc (PA) 201 933-9666
  70 Broad St Carlstadt (07072) *(G-1221)*
Stand Out Signs, Hopelawn *Also called F & A Signs Inc (G-4525)*
Standard Coating Corporation 201 945-5058
  461 Broad Ave Ridgefield (07657) *(G-9289)*

A L P H A B E T I C

Standard Embossing Plate Mfg 973 344-6670
  129 Pulaski St Newark (07105) *(G-7284)*

Standard Industries Inc 856 241-0241
  700 2nd St Ste C&D Swedesboro (08085) *(G-10609)*

Standard Industries Inc (HQ) 973 628-3000
  1 Campus Dr Parsippany (07054) *(G-8021)*

Standard Merchandising, Pennsauken *Also called Great Socks LLC (G-8427)*

Standard Prtg & Mail Svcs Inc 973 790-3333
  30 Plymouth St Ste A Fairfield (07004) *(G-3314)*

Standard Tile Watchung Corp 908 754-4200
  1515 Us Highway 22 Ste 24 Watchung (07069) *(G-11458)*

Stanger Robert A & Co LP 732 389-3600
  1129 Broad St Fl 2 Shrewsbury (07702) *(G-9902)*

Stanlar Enterprises Inc 973 680-4488
  24 Federal Plz Bloomfield (07003) *(G-518)*

Stanley Black & Decker Inc 860 225-5111
  123 Town Square Pl Jersey City (07310) *(G-4813)*

Stanley Black Dcker Tchni-Edge, Kenilworth *Also called IDL Techni-Edge LLC (G-4945)*

Stanley Tools, Jersey City *Also called Stanley Black & Decker Inc (G-4813)*

Stanson Corporation (PA) 973 344-8666
  2 N Hackensack Ave Kearny (07032) *(G-4900)*

Stanton Precision Products LLC 973 838-6951
  10 Park Pl Bldg 4 Butler (07405) *(G-1015)*

Staple Sewing Aids Corporation 973 249-0022
  90 Dayton Ave Bldg 6c Passaic (07055) *(G-8108)*

Staples, Iselin *Also called Arch Parent Inc (G-4597)*

Stapling Machines Inc (PA) 973 627-4400
  41 Pine St Ste 101 Rockaway (07866) *(G-9500)*

Star Bindery Inc 609 519-5732
  963 Lincoln Ave Franklinville (08322) *(G-3640)*

Star Candle Company, Ridgefield Park *Also called Star Soap/Star Candle/Prayer C (G-9318)*

Star Creations Inc (PA) 212 221-3570
  1506 Stelton Rd Piscataway (08854) *(G-8718)*

Star Dynamic Corp 732 257-7488
  100 Outwater Ln Garfield (07026) *(G-3769)*

Star Embroidery Corp 973 481-4300
  305 3rd Ave W Ste 7 Newark (07107) *(G-7285)*

Star Group, The, Lodi *Also called Star Narrow Fabrics Inc (G-5576)*

Star Ledger, Piscataway *Also called Newark Morning Ledger Co (G-8695)*

Star Ledger, Pine Brook *Also called Newark Morning Ledger Co (G-8611)*

Star Linen Inc (PA) 800 782-7999
  1501 Lancer Dr Moorestown (08057) *(G-6568)*

Star Litho Inc 973 641-1603
  175 Us Highway 46 Unit C Fairfield (07004) *(G-3315)*

Star Metal Products 908 474-9860
  1125 W Elizabeth Ave Linden (07036) *(G-5429)*

Star Narrow Fabrics Inc 973 778-8600
  80a Industrial Rd Lodi (07644) *(G-5576)*

Star National, Newark *Also called S H P C Inc (G-7258)*

Star News Group 732 223-0076
  13 Broad St Manasquan (08736) *(G-5839)*

Star Pharma Inc 718 466-1790
  42 Devon Dr East Brunswick (08816) *(G-2180)*

Star Process Heat Systems LLC 732 282-1002
  208 Iris Dr Neptune (07753) *(G-6899)*

Star Promotions Inc 732 356-5959
  11 Maiden Ln Bound Brook (08805) *(G-607)*

Star Snacks Co LLC 201 200-9820
  111 Port Jersey Blvd Jersey City (07305) *(G-4814)*

Star Soap/Star Candle/Prayer C 201 690-9090
  300 Industrial Ave Ridgefield Park (07660) *(G-9318)*

Star-Glo Industries LLC (PA) 201 939-6162
  2 Carlton Ave East Rutherford (07073) *(G-2319)*

Starfire Lighting Inc 201 438-9540
  7 Donna Dr Wood Ridge (07075) *(G-12006)*

Starfuels Inc 201 685-0400
  285 Grand Ave Englewood (07631) *(G-2944)*

Stark Pharma Technology Inc 848 217-4059
  15 Corporate Pl S Ste 350 Piscataway (08854) *(G-8719)*

Starlight Electro-Optics Inc 908 859-1362
  660 Hrmony Brass Cstle Rd Phillipsburg (08865) *(G-8575)*

Starlight One Corp 862 684-0561
  10 Van Orden Pl Clifton (07011) *(G-1725)*

Starlite Window Mfg Co, Paterson *Also called Starlite Window Mfg Co Inc (G-8300)*

Starlite Window Mfg Co Inc 973 278-9366
  50 E 25th St Paterson (07514) *(G-8300)*

Starnet Business Solutions 201 252-2863
  46 Industrial Ave Ste 2 Mahwah (07430) *(G-5775)*

Starnet Printing Inc 201 760-2600
  46 Industrial Ave Ste 2 Mahwah (07430) *(G-5776)*

Starphil Inc 908 353-8943
  107 Trumbull St R12 Elizabeth (07206) *(G-2777)*

State Electronics Parts Corp 973 887-2550
  36 State Route 10 Ste 6 East Hanover (07936) *(G-2240)*

State Metal Industries Inc (PA) 856 964-1510
  941 S 2nd St Camden (08103) *(G-1088)*

State Metal Trading, Camden *Also called D K Trading Inc (G-1057)*

State Technology Inc 856 467-8009
  610 Pedricktown Rd Bridgeport (08014) *(G-746)*

State Tool Gear Co Inc 973 642-6181
  211 Camden St Newark (07103) *(G-7286)*

Stateline Fabricators LLC 908 387-8800
  100 Foul Rift Rd Phillipsburg (08865) *(G-8576)*

Statewide Granite & Marble, Jersey City *Also called Statewide Granite and Marble (G-4815)*

Statewide Granite and Marble 201 653-1700
  109 Carlton Ave Jersey City (07306) *(G-4815)*

Stauff Corporation (HQ) 201 444-7800
  7 William Demarest Pl Waldwick (07463) *(G-11309)*

Stauts Printing & Graphics 609 654-5382
  12 Maine Trl Medford (08055) *(G-6035)*

Stavola Asphalt Company Inc (PA) 732 542-2328
  175 Drift Rd Tinton Falls (07724) *(G-10728)*

Stavola Construction Mtls Inc (PA) 732 542-2328
  175 Drift Rd Tinton Falls (07724) *(G-10729)*

Stavola Construction Mtls Inc 732 356-5700
  810 Thompson Ave Bound Brook (08805) *(G-608)*

Stavola Contracting, Bound Brook *Also called Stavola Construction Mtls Inc (G-608)*

Stavola Contracting Co Inc 732 935-0156
  120 Old Bergen Mill Rd Englishtown (07726) *(G-3009)*

Stavola Holding Corporation 732 542-2328
  175 Drift Rd Tinton Falls (07724) *(G-10730)*

Stavola Paving Company, Tinton Falls *Also called Stavola Asphalt Company Inc (G-10728)*

Stealthbits Technologies Inc (PA) 201 301-9328
  200 Central Ave Hawthorne (07506) *(G-4245)*

Steamist Inc 201 933-0700
  25 E Union Ave Ste 1 East Rutherford (07073) *(G-2320)*

Steb Inc (PA) 973 584-0990
  1501 Us Highway 46 Ledgewood (07852) *(G-5281)*

Steb Inc 973 584-0990
  1501 Us Highway 46 Ledgewood (07852) *(G-5282)*

Stecher Dave Welding & Fabg Sp 856 467-3558
  1040 Township Line Rd Swedesboro (08085) *(G-10610)*

Steed Perf6manc3 ....908 583-5580
  1034 E Elizabeth Ave Linden (07036) *(G-5430)*

Steel Mountain Fabricators LLC (PA) 908 862-2800
  1312 W Elizabeth Ave Linden (07036) *(G-5431)*

Steel Mountain Fabricators LLC 201 741-3019
  2712 Secaucus Rd North Bergen (07047) *(G-7438)*

Steel Riser Corp 732 341-7031
  402 Marc Dr Toms River (08753) *(G-10795)*

Steelstran Industries Inc 732 566-5040
  Foot Of Dock St Matawan (07747) *(G-5989)*

Steelstran Industries Inc (PA) 732 574-0700
  35 Mileed Way Avenel (07001) *(G-147)*

Stefan Enterprises Inc 973 253-6005
  141 Lanza Ave Bldg 16e Garfield (07026) *(G-3770)*

Steico USA Inc 732 364-6200
  250 Carey St Lakewood (08701) *(G-5168)*

Steimling & Son Inc 732 613-1550
  7 Nickel Ave Sayreville (08872) *(G-9724)*

Stelfast Inc 440 879-0077
  104 Sunfield Ave Edison (08837) *(G-2620)*

Stellar Data Recovery (PA) 877 778-6087
  48 Bridge St Metuchen (08840) *(G-6074)*

Stepan Company 201 845-3030
  100 W Hunter Ave Maywood (07607) *(G-6016)*

Stepan Company 609 298-1222
  4th St Fieldsboro Bordentown (08505) *(G-595)*

Stephan L Green Trailers, Farmingdale *Also called Steve Green Enterprises (G-3393)*

Stephco Sales Inc 973 278-5454
  238 Lindbergh Pl Ste 3 Paterson (07503) *(G-8301)*

Stephen Douglas Plastics Inc 973 523-3030
  22 Green St 36 Paterson (07501) *(G-8302)*

Stephen Gould Corporation (PA) 973 428-1500
  35 S Jefferson Rd Whippany (07981) *(G-11910)*

Stephen L Feilinger 609 294-1884
  655 Route 9 N Ltl Egg Hbr (08087) *(G-5620)*

Stephen Swinton Studio Inc 908 537-9135
  49 New Hampton Rd Washington (07882) *(G-11452)*

Steppin Out Magazine 201 703-0911
  21-07 Maple Ave Fair Lawn (07410) *(G-3122)*

Steps Clothing Inc 201 420-1496
  30 Mall Dr W Unit B59a Jersey City (07310) *(G-4816)*

Steps To Literacy LLC 732 560-8363
  4 Easy St Bound Brook (08805) *(G-609)*

Steri-Pharma LLC (PA) 201 857-8210
  120 N State Rt 17 Paramus (07652) *(G-7836)*

Sterigenics US LLC 856 241-8880
  303 Heron Dr Swedesboro (08085) *(G-10611)*

Steris Corporation 908 904-1317
  10 Ilene Ct Hillsborough (08844) *(G-4356)*

Steris Instrument MGT Svcs Inc 908 904-1317
  10 Ilene Ct Hillsborough (08844) *(G-4357)*

Sterling Marine Products, Montclair *Also called Sterling Net & Twine Co Inc (G-6390)*

Sterling Net & Twine Co Inc (PA) 973 783-9800
  18 Label St Montclair (07042) *(G-6390)*

Sterling Products Inc 973 471-2858
  90 Dayton Ave Ste 77 Passaic (07055) *(G-8109)*

Sterling Publishing Co Inc 732 248-6563
1 Barnes And Noble Way Monroe Township (08831) ***(G-6346)***
Sterling Publishing Warehouse, Monroe Township *Also called Sterling Publishing Co Inc* ***(G-6346)***
Sterling Sound, Edgewater *Also called Metrolpolis Mastering LP* ***(G-2440)***
Sterling System, Edison *Also called Cygate Sftwr & Consulting LLC* ***(G-2490)***
Stern Knit Inc 732 364-8055
3 Fillmore Ave Lakewood (08701) ***(G-5169)***
Sternvent Co Inc 908 688-0807
No5 Stahuber Ave Union (07083) ***(G-11092)***
Stessl & Neugebauer Inc 908 277-3340
9 Industrial Pl Summit (07901) ***(G-10549)***
Steve Green Enterprises 732 938-5572
74 Sqankum Yellowbrook Rd Farmingdale (07727) ***(G-3393)***
Steven Industries Inc 201 437-6500
39 Avenue C Ste 1 Bayonne (07002) ***(G-235)***
Steven Madola 609 989-8022
2001 S Broad St Trenton (08610) ***(G-10992)***
Steven Orros 732 972-1104
106 Timber Hill Dr Monroe Township (08831) ***(G-6347)***
Steven's Dunbar Companies, Bayonne *Also called Dunbar Sales Company Inc* ***(G-214)***
Steward LLC 609 816-8825
345 Witherspoon St Princeton (08542) ***(G-9028)***
Steward Mag, Princeton *Also called Steward LLC* ***(G-9028)***
Stewart Business Forms Inc 856 768-2011
138 Frankford Ave Blackwood (08012) ***(G-481)***
Stewart-Morris Inc 973 822-2777
71 Kings Rd Ste 1 Madison (07940) ***(G-5703)***
STI, Ewing *Also called Surface Technology Inc* ***(G-3068)***
STI, Branchburg *Also called Specified Technologies Inc* ***(G-684)***
Stiles Enterprises Inc 973 625-9660
114 Beach St Rockaway (07866) ***(G-9501)***
Stimson Lane Wine & Spirit, Mount Arlington *Also called Michelle Ste Wine Estates Ltd* ***(G-6716)***
Stingray Sport Pdts Ltd Lblty 201 300-6482
20-10 Maple Ave Bldg 35e Fair Lawn (07410) ***(G-3123)***
Stirling Audio Services LLC 732 560-0707
201 Wood Ave Middlesex (08846) ***(G-6154)***
Stirrup Metal Products Corp 973 824-7086
215 Emmet St Newark (07114) ***(G-7287)***
Stobbs Printing Co Inc 973 748-4441
18 Washington St Bloomfield (07003) ***(G-519)***
Stollen Machine & Tool Company 908 241-0622
761 Lexington Ave Kenilworth (07033) ***(G-4979)***
Stoncor Group Inc (HQ) 800 257-7953
1000 E Park Ave Maple Shade (08052) ***(G-5870)***
Stone Graphics 732 919-1111
5020 Industrial Rd Wall Township (07727) ***(G-11371)***
Stone Industries Inc (PA) 973 595-6250
400 Central Ave 402 Haledon (07508) ***(G-4085)***
Stone Mar Natural Stone Co LLC (PA) 856 988-1802
8 E Stow Rd Ste 200 Marlton (08053) ***(G-5952)***
Stone Mountain Printing Inc 732 636-8450
74 Main St Fl 1 Woodbridge (07095) ***(G-12022)***
Stone Surfaces Inc 201 935-8803
890 Paterson Plank Rd East Rutherford (07073) ***(G-2321)***
Stone Systems New Jersey LLC 973 778-5525
5 Washington Ave Fairfield (07004) ***(G-3316)***
Stone Truss Systems Inc (PA) 973 882-7377
23 Commerce Rd Ste O Fairfield (07004) ***(G-3317)***
Stone World Magazine, Paramus *Also called BNP Media Inc* ***(G-7793)***
Stonebridge Paper LLC 973 413-8100
37 E 6th St Paterson (07524) ***(G-8303)***
Stonework Dsign Consulting Inc (PA) 973 575-0835
25 Pier Ln W Fairfield (07004) ***(G-3318)***
Stoneworld At Redbank Inc 732 383-5110
247 Cooper Rd Red Bank (07701) ***(G-9245)***
Stonhard, Maple Shade *Also called Stoncor Group Inc* ***(G-5870)***
Stonhard Manufacturing Co Inc (HQ) 856 779-7500
1000 E Park Ave Maple Shade (08052) ***(G-5871)***
Stonite Coil Corporation 609 585-6600
476 Route 156 Trenton (08620) ***(G-10993)***
Store 266, Atlantic Highlands *Also called Food Circus Super Markets Inc* ***(G-106)***
Storemaxx Inc 201 440-8800
343 S River St Hackensack (07601) ***(G-3979)***
Storis Inc (PA) 888 478-6747
400 Valley Rd Ste 302 Mount Arlington (07856) ***(G-6719)***
Storis Management Systems, Mount Arlington *Also called Storis Inc* ***(G-6719)***
Storm City Entertainment Inc 856 885-6902
700 Liberty Pl Sicklerville (08081) ***(G-9916)***
Story Electric Mtr Repr Co Inc 973 256-1636
20 Francisco Ave Little Falls (07424) ***(G-5469)***
Storybook Knits, Kinnelon *Also called Jtwo Inc* ***(G-5018)***
Str8line Publishing Company 919 717-6740
511 Frelinghuysen Ave Newark (07114) ***(G-7288)***
Strahan Consulting Group LLC 908 790-0873
1290 Martine Ave Scotch Plains (07076) ***(G-9742)***
Strap-Its, Demarest *Also called Blu-J2 LLC* ***(G-2024)***
Straps Manufacturing NJ Inc 201 368-5201
480 Braen Ave Wyckoff (07481) ***(G-12121)***
Strategic Content Imaging 201 863-8100
100 Castle Rd Secaucus (07094) ***(G-9819)***
Strategic Mktg Promotions Inc (PA) 845 623-7777
1200 Macarthur Blvd # 251 Mahwah (07430) ***(G-5777)***
Strato Inc 732 981-1515
100 New England Ave Ste 1 Piscataway (08854) ***(G-8720)***
Straval Machine Co Inc 973 340-9955
20 Bushes Ln Elmwood Park (07407) ***(G-2857)***
Streamserve Inc (HQ) 781 863-1510
100 Tormee Dr Asbury Park (07712) ***(G-82)***
Street Lights Dept, Jersey City *Also called City of Jersey City* ***(G-4713)***
Strides Pharma Inc 609 773-5000
2 Tower Center Blvd # 1102 East Brunswick (08816) ***(G-2181)***
Strikeforce Technologies Inc 732 661-9641
1090 King Georges Post Rd Edison (08837) ***(G-2621)***
Strive Pharmaceuticals Inc (PA) 609 269-2001
19 Lexington Ave East Brunswick (08816) ***(G-2182)***
Strivr Inc 973 216-7379
20 Downing Pl Livingston (07039) ***(G-5542)***
Strong Man Safety Pdts Corp 973 831-1555
240 W Parkway Pompton Plains (07444) ***(G-8871)***
Strongwall Industries Inc 201 445-4633
107 Chestnut St Ridgewood (07450) ***(G-9330)***
Structural Foam Plastics, Branchburg *Also called Plasti Foam* ***(G-668)***
Structural Steel Fabricators, Lincoln Park *Also called D S Jh LLC* ***(G-5298)***
Structured Healthcare MGT Inc 201 569-3290
456 Nordhoff Pl Englewood (07631) ***(G-2945)***
Stryker Corporation 201 760-8000
2 Pearl Ct Allendale (07401) ***(G-17)***
Stryker Corporation 856 312-0046
165 E 9th Ave Unit F Runnemede (08078) ***(G-9611)***
Stryker Orthopaedics, Mahwah *Also called Howmedica Osteonics Corp* ***(G-5747)***
STS Technologies LLC 973 277-5416
282 Franklin Tpke Mahwah (07430) ***(G-5778)***
Stuart Mills Inc (PA) 973 579-5717
25 Stillwater Rd Newton (07860) ***(G-7359)***
Stuart Mills Inc 973 579-5717
25 Stillwater Rd Newton (07860) ***(G-7360)***
Stuart Steel Protection Corp 732 469-5544
411 Elizabeth Ave Somerset (08873) ***(G-10075)***
Stud Welding Co The Inc 856 866-9300
750 Glen Ave Moorestown (08057) ***(G-6569)***
Studio Dellarte 718 599-3715
234 16th St Fl 1 Jersey City (07310) ***(G-4817)***
Studio L Contracting LLC 201 837-1650
18 Dicarolis Ct Hackensack (07601) ***(G-3980)***
Studio042, Montclair *Also called Puent-Romer Communications Inc* ***(G-6386)***
Stull Technologies LLC 732 873-5000
17 Veronica Ave Somerset (08873) ***(G-10076)***
Stulz-Sickles Steel Company (PA) 609 531-2172
2 Campus Dr Burlington (08016) ***(G-986)***
Stuyvesant Press Inc 973 399-3880
119 Coit St Irvington (07111) ***(G-4587)***
Style Plus, Trenton *Also called Man-How Inc* ***(G-10954)***
Stylex Inc 856 461-5600
740 Coopertown Rd Delanco (08075) ***(G-2007)***
Stylus Custom Apparel Inc 908 587-0800
729 E Elizabeth Ave Linden (07036) ***(G-5432)***
Subcom LLC (HQ) 732 578-7000
250 Industrial Way W Eatontown (07724) ***(G-2422)***
Subito Music Service Inc 973 857-3440
60 Depot St Verona (07044) ***(G-11176)***
Subsidariry of Vac-U-Max, Belleville *Also called Aerocon Inc* ***(G-290)***
Suburban Aluminum Mfg, Howell *Also called Surburban Building Pdts Inc* ***(G-4551)***
Suburban Auto Seat Co Inc (PA) 973 778-9227
35 Industrial Rd Lodi (07644) ***(G-5577)***
Suburban Essex Magazine, Fairfield *Also called Vicinity Publications Inc* ***(G-3344)***
Suburban Fence Company, Trenton *Also called Hoda Inc* ***(G-10939)***
Suburban Guides Inc 201 452-4989
97 Spring Lake Blvd Waretown (08758) ***(G-11394)***
Suburban Monument & Vault 973 242-7007
203 Sherman Ave Newark (07114) ***(G-7289)***
Suburban Parent Magazine, North Brunswick *Also called Middlesex Publications* ***(G-7477)***
Suburban Sign Co Inc 908 862-7222
210 Marion Ave Linden (07036) ***(G-5433)***
Success Publishers LLC 609 443-0792
29 Hampton Hollow Dr Perrineville (08535) ***(G-8508)***
Success Sewing Inc 973 622-0328
50 Columbia St Ste 2 Newark (07102) ***(G-7290)***
Sudarshan North America Inc 201 652-2046
76 N Walnut St Ridgewood (07450) ***(G-9331)***
Sueta Music Ed Publications 888 725-2333
13 E Main St Ste 3 Mendham (07945) ***(G-6043)***
Suez North America Inc 201 767-9300
461 From Rd Ste 400 Paramus (07652) ***(G-7837)***
Suez Treatment Solutions Inc (HQ) 201 767-9300
461 From Rd Ste 400 Paramus (07652) ***(G-7838)***

ALPHABETIC

(PA)=Parent Co (HQ)=Headquarters (DH)=Div Headquarters

Suez Treatment Solutions Inc 201 676-2525
600 Willow Tree Rd Leonia (07605) *(G-5292)*

Suffern Plating Corp 973 473-4404
210 Garibaldi Ave Lodi (07644) *(G-5578)*

Suffolk County Contractors 732 349-7726
242 Dover Rd Unit 2 Toms River (08757) *(G-10796)*

Suffolk Molds, Wayne *Also called C & N Packaging Inc (G-11486)*

Suffolk Recycling, Toms River *Also called Suffolk County Contractors (G-10796)*

Sugar and Plumm LLC 201 334-1600
146 Redneck Ave Moonachie (07074) *(G-6490)*

Suite K Value Added Svcs LLC 732 590-0647
31 Executive Ave Ste A Edison (08817) *(G-2622)*

Suite K Value Added Svcs LLC 609 655-6890
31 Executive Ave Ste A Edison (08817) *(G-2623)*

Suite K Value Added Svcs LLC (PA) 609 655-6890
31 Executive Ave Ste A Edison (08817) *(G-2624)*

Suite-K, Edison *Also called Suite K Value Added Svcs LLC (G-2623)*

Suite-K, Edison *Also called Suite K Value Added Svcs LLC (G-2624)*

Sukhadias Sweets & Snacks (PA) 908 222-0069
124 Case Dr South Plainfield (07080) *(G-10328)*

Sullivan Steel Service, Pennington *Also called General Sullivan Group Inc (G-8365)*

Sullivan-Carson Inc (PA) 856 566-1400
1010 Hddonfield Berlin Rd Voorhees (08043) *(G-11294)*

Sultan Foods Inc 908 874-6953
115 Stryker Ln Ste 13 Hillsborough (08844) *(G-4358)*

Sulzer Bingham Pumps, Bridgeport *Also called Sulzer Pump Services (us) Inc (G-747)*

Sulzer Chemtech USA Inc 856 768-2165
1008 Industrial Dr Ste F West Berlin (08091) *(G-11624)*

Sulzer Pump Services (us) Inc 856 542-5046
621 Heron Dr Bridgeport (08014) *(G-747)*

Suman Realty LLC 908 350-8039
103 Saint Josephs Dr Stirling (07980) *(G-10497)*

Sumangel Jewellers, Piscataway *Also called Star Creations Inc (G-8718)*

Sumatic Co Inc 973 772-1288
102 Dewitt St Garfield (07026) *(G-3771)*

Summer Sweets LLC 732 240-9376
3071 Rt 35 N Toms River (08755) *(G-10797)*

Summerlands Inc 973 729-8428
23 White Deer Plz Sparta (07871) *(G-10408)*

Summit Filter Corp, Union *Also called Filter Holdings Inc (G-11054)*

Summit Hill Flavors, Somerset *Also called Flavor and Fd Ingredients Inc (G-9994)*

Summit Millwork & Supply Inc 908 273-1486
235 Morris Ave Summit (07901) *(G-10550)*

Summit Professional Networks 201 526-1230
33 41 Newark St Fl 2 Hoboken (07030) *(G-4483)*

Summit Truck Body Inc (PA) 908 277-4342
50 Franklin Pl Summit (07901) *(G-10551)*

Summus Inc 215 820-3918
521 Irish Hill Rd Ste A Runnemede (08078) *(G-9612)*

Sun Basket Inc 408 669-4418
600 Highland Dr Ste 614 Westampton (08060) *(G-11792)*

Sun Chemical Corporation 201 933-4500
631 Central Ave Carlstadt (07072) *(G-1222)*

Sun Chemical Corporation (HQ) 973 404-6000
35 Waterview Blvd Ste 100 Parsippany (07054) *(G-8022)*

Sun Chemical Corporation 201 438-4831
390 Central Ave East Rutherford (07073) *(G-2322)*

Sun Chemical Corporation 201 935-8666
651 Garden St Carlstadt (07072) *(G-1223)*

Sun Coast Precision Instrument 646 852-2331
80 Broadway Fl 1 Cresskill (07626) *(G-1945)*

Sun Dial & Panel Corporation 973 226-4334
2 Daniel Rd Ste 102 Fairfield (07004) *(G-3319)*

Sun Display Systems, Fairfield *Also called Sun Dial & Panel Corporation (G-3319)*

Sun Display Systems LLC 973 226-4334
2 Daniel Rd Fairfield (07004) *(G-3320)*

Sun Metal Finishing Inc 973 684-0119
5 Sicomac Rd 105 North Haledon (07508) *(G-7500)*

Sun Neon Sign and Electric Co 856 667-6977
4 Saddle Ln Cherry Hill (08002) *(G-1417)*

Sun Noodle New Jersey LLC 201 530-1100
40 Kero Rd Carlstadt (07072) *(G-1224)*

Sun Pacific Power Corp 888 845-0242
215 Gordons Corner Rd 1a Manalapan (07726) *(G-5826)*

Sun Pharmaceutical Inds Inc 313 871-8400
2 Independence Way Princeton (08540) *(G-9029)*

Sun Pharmaceutical Inds Inc 609 495-2800
1 Commerce Dr Cranbury (08512) *(G-1884)*

Sun Pharmaceutical Inds Inc (HQ) 609 495-2800
270 Prospect Plains Rd Cranbury (08512) *(G-1885)*

Sun Plastics Co Inc 908 490-0870
35 Blue Wolf Trl Watchung (07069) *(G-11459)*

Sun Taiyang Co Ltd 201 549-7100
85 Oxford Dr Moonachie (07074) *(G-6491)*

Sun Trading, Moonachie *Also called Sun Taiyang Co Ltd (G-6491)*

Sunbird Software Inc 732 993-4476
200 Cottontail Ln B106e Somerset (08873) *(G-10077)*

Sunbrite Dye Co Inc (PA) 973 777-9830
35 8th St Ste 6 Passaic (07055) *(G-8110)*

Sunco & Frenchie Ltd Lblty Co 973 478-1011
489 Getty Ave Door2 Clifton (07011) *(G-1726)*

Sunday Star Ledger, Newark *Also called Newark Morning Ledger Co (G-7216)*

Sunflower Seed 908 735-3822
38 Old Highway 22 Clinton (08809) *(G-1750)*

Sungard, Voorhees *Also called Fis Financial Systems LLC (G-11285)*

Sunglo Fabrics Inc 201 935-0830
50 California Ave Paterson (07503) *(G-8304)*

Sungood, Kenilworth *Also called Naturee Nuts Inc (G-4962)*

Sunham Home Fashions LLC 908 363-1100
700 Central Park Ave New Providence (07974) *(G-7019)*

Sunlight Aerospace Inc 732 362-7501
2045 State Route 27 1w Edison (08817) *(G-2625)*

Sunovion Pharmaceuticals Inc 201 592-2050
1 Bridge Plz N Ste 510 Fort Lee (07024) *(G-3590)*

Sunpak Division, Rockaway *Also called Tocad America Inc (G-9505)*

Sunrise Food Trading Inc 718 305-4388
163 Washington Valley Rd # 103 Warren (07059) *(G-11432)*

Sunrise Intl Educatn Inc 917 525-0272
1542 Edly Cove Ct North Brunswick (08902) *(G-7489)*

Sunrise Pharmaceutical Inc (PA) 732 382-6085
665 E Lincoln Ave Rahway (07065) *(G-9128)*

Sunrise Snacks Rockland Inc 845 352-2676
787 E 27th St Paterson (07504) *(G-8305)*

Sunset Printing and Engrv Corp 973 537-9600
10 Kice Ave Wharton (07885) *(G-11871)*

Sunset Stationers, Wharton *Also called Sunset Printing and Engrv Corp (G-11871)*

Sunshine Bouquet Company (PA) 732 274-2900
3 Chris Ct Ste A Dayton (08810) *(G-1990)*

Sunshine Container, Milltown *Also called Sunshine Metal & Sign Inc (G-6220)*

Sunshine Lane Mixed Media, Mendham *Also called Surviving Life Corp (G-6044)*

Sunshine Metal & Sign Inc 973 676-4432
14 Louise Dr Milltown (08850) *(G-6220)*

Sunsplash Marina LLC 609 628-4445
5 Mosquito Landing Rd Tuckahoe (08250) *(G-11014)*

Supco, Allenwood *Also called Sealed Unit Parts Co Inc (G-34)*

Super Chrome Inc 732 774-2210
1004 1st Ave Asbury Park (07712) *(G-83)*

Super Stud Building Pdts Inc 732 662-6200
2960 Woodbridge Ave Edison (08837) *(G-2626)*

Super Wash, Boonton *Also called S W I International Inc (G-567)*

Superfine Online Inc 212 827-0063
205 E 11th Ave Roselle (07203) *(G-9574)*

Superflex Ltd 718 768-1400
400 S 2nd St Elizabeth (07206) *(G-2778)*

Superior Custom Kitchens LLC 908 753-6005
126 Mount Bethel Rd Warren (07059) *(G-11433)*

Superior Intl Srgical Sups LLC 609 695-6591
46 Oak Ln Ewing (08618) *(G-3067)*

Superior Jewelry Co 215 677-8100
430 Tilton Rd Ste 1 Northfield (08225) *(G-7511)*

Superior Lighting Inc 908 759-0199
1245 Virginia St Elizabeth (07208) *(G-2779)*

Superior Marine Canvas 856 241-1724
75 Belfiore Dr Swedesboro (08085) *(G-10612)*

Superior Powder Coating Inc (PA) 908 351-8707
600 Progress St Elizabeth (07201) *(G-2780)*

Superior Printing Ink Co Inc (PA) 201 478-5600
100 North St Teterboro (07608) *(G-10691)*

Superior Printing Ink Co Inc 973 242-5868
252 Wright St Newark (07114) *(G-7291)*

Superior Promotional Bags, Toms River *Also called Alex Real LLC (G-10740)*

Superior Signal Company LLC 732 251-0800
178 W Greystone Rd Old Bridge (08857) *(G-7728)*

Superior Smoke, Old Bridge *Also called Superior Signal Company LLC (G-7728)*

Superior Stamping Products LLC 201 945-5874
1200 Hendricks Cswy Ridgefield (07657) *(G-9290)*

Superior Tool & Mfg Co 908 526-9011
42 Columbia Rd Ste 2 Branchburg (08876) *(G-685)*

Superior Trademark Inc 201 652-1900
45 Zazzetti St Waldwick (07463) *(G-11310)*

Supermatic Corp 973 627-4433
27 Old Beach Glen Rd Rockaway (07866) *(G-9502)*

Supermedia LLC 973 649-9900
50 Burnett Ave Maplewood (07040) *(G-5884)*

Superseal Manufacturing Co Inc (HQ) 908 561-5910
125 Helen St South Plainfield (07080) *(G-10329)*

Supertex Inc 973 345-1000
860 Market St Paterson (07513) *(G-8306)*

Supplies-Supplies Inc 908 272-5100
85 Maple St Watchung (07069) *(G-11460)*

Supply Chain Technologies LLC 856 206-9849
1161 Broad St Ste 312 Shrewsbury (07702) *(G-9903)*

Supply Plus NJ Inc 973 782-5930
3 E 26th St Paterson (07514) *(G-8307)*

Supply Plus NY Inc 973 481-4800
3 E 26th St Paterson (07514) *(G-8308)*

Supply Technologies LLC 201 641-7600
50 Graphic Pl Moonachie (07074) *(G-6492)*

Supplyone New York Inc 718 392-7400
143 Getty Ave Paterson (07503) ***(G-8309)***
Supreme Graphics and Prtg Inc 718 989-9817
1027 State St Perth Amboy (08861) ***(G-8535)***
Supreme Ink Corp 973 344-2922
65 Mcwhorter St Newark (07105) ***(G-7292)***
Supreme Manufacturing Co Inc 732 254-0087
5 Connerty Ct East Brunswick (08816) ***(G-2183)***
Surati NJ LLC 732 251-3404
15 American Way Spotswood (08884) ***(G-10418)***
Surburban Building Pdts Inc (PA) 732 901-8900
1178 Lkwood Frmingdale Rd Howell (07731) ***(G-4551)***
Sure Design 732 919-3066
5027 Industrial Rd Ste 3 Wall Township (07727) ***(G-11372)***
Sureway Prtg & Graphics LLC 609 430-4333
338 Wall St Princeton (08540) ***(G-9030)***
Surf's Up Candle, Belmar *Also called Surfs Up Candle & Charm* ***(G-355)***
Surface Source Intl Inc 973 598-0152
961 State Route 10 Ste 2i Randolph (07869) ***(G-9202)***
Surface Technology Inc 609 259-0099
1405 Lower Ferry Rd Ewing (08618) ***(G-3068)***
Surfs Up Candle & Charm 848 404-9559
1703 Main St 3 Belmar (07719) ***(G-355)***
Surfside Foods LLC 856 785-2115
1733 Main St Port Norris (08349) ***(G-8889)***
Surfside Products, Port Norris *Also called Surfside Foods LLC* ***(G-8889)***
Surgical Lser Sfety Cuncil Inc 216 272-0805
405 Hialeah Dr Cherry Hill (08002) ***(G-1418)***
Suroma Ltd Liability Company 908 735-7700
223 Hamden Rd Annandale (08801) ***(G-55)***
Surround Technologies LLC (PA) 973 743-1277
650 Bloomfield Ave # 102 Bloomfield (07003) ***(G-520)***
Suruchi Foods LLC 201 432-2201
114 Baldwin Ave Ste A Jersey City (07306) ***(G-4818)***
Survirvor Windows II, Hillside *Also called Survivor II Inc* ***(G-4428)***
Surviving Life Corp 973 543-3370
3 Muirfield Ln Mendham (07945) ***(G-6044)***
Survivor II Inc 908 353-1155
1239 Central Ave Hillside (07205) ***(G-4428)***
Susan Mills Inc (PA) 908 355-1400
1285 Central Ave Hillside (07205) ***(G-4429)***
Susan R Bauer Inc 973 657-1590
427 Margaret King Ave Ringwood (07456) ***(G-9353)***
Sushi House Inc 201 482-0609
225 Commercial Ave Palisades Park (07650) ***(G-7779)***
Sussex Humus & Supply Inc 973 779-8812
29 Kenyon St Clifton (07013) ***(G-1727)***
Sussex Wine Merchants, Moorestown *Also called Petit Pois Corp* ***(G-6556)***
Sustainable Gardening Inst Inc 973 383-0497
85 Lawrence Rd Lafayette (07848) ***(G-5033)***
Sustanble Bldg Innovations Inc 800 560-4143
2435 Highway 34 Ste 204 Manasquan (08736) ***(G-5840)***
Sutherland Packaging Inc 973 786-5141
254 Brighton Rd Andover (07821) ***(G-51)***
Suuchi Inc 201 284-0789
2321 Kennedy Blvd Ste S4 North Bergen (07047) ***(G-7439)***
Suven Life Sciences Ltd 732 274-0037
1100 Cornwall Rd Ste 5 Monmouth Junction (08852) ***(G-6314)***
Suzie Mac Specialties Inc 732 238-3500
3 Joanna Ct Ste C East Brunswick (08816) ***(G-2184)***
Sv Pharma Inc 732 651-1336
9 Autumn Ln East Brunswick (08816) ***(G-2185)***
Svtc Pharma Inc 201 652-0013
60 E Ridgewood Ave Ridgewood (07450) ***(G-9332)***
Swapshub Company Inc 732 529-4813
15 Corporate Pl S Ste 130 Piscataway (08854) ***(G-8721)***
Swarovski North America Ltd 732 632-1856
55 Parsonage Rd Unit 333 Edison (08837) ***(G-2627)***
Swarovski North America Ltd 856 686-1805
1750 Deptford Center Rd Deptford (08096) ***(G-2067)***
Swarovski North America Ltd 856 662-5453
2000 Route 38 Cherry Hill (08002) ***(G-1419)***
Swarovski North America Ltd 201 265-4888
700 Paramus Park Paramus (07652) ***(G-7839)***
Swarovski North America Ltd 609 344-1323
2801 Pacific Ave Atlantic City (08401) ***(G-103)***
Swarovski North America Ltd 973 812-7500
1400 Willowbrook Mall Wayne (07470) ***(G-11554)***
Swarovski North America Ltd 908 253-7057
400 Commons Way Bridgewater (08807) ***(G-895)***
Swatch Group Les Btques US Inc 201 271-1400
1200 Harbor Blvd Weehawken (07086) ***(G-11570)***
Swce Group, The, Bernardsville *Also called Swce Inc* ***(G-444)***
Swce Inc (PA) 908 766-5695
360 Mount Harmony Rd Bernardsville (07924) ***(G-444)***
Sweet Delight 732 263-9100
65 Monmouth Rd Oakhurst (07755) ***(G-7613)***
Sweet Eats Bakery, Voorhees *Also called Good To Go Inc* ***(G-11286)***
Sweet Orange LLC 908 522-0011
545 Morris Ave Summit (07901) ***(G-10552)***
Sweet Potato Pie Inc 973 279-3405
140 Auburn St Paterson (07501) ***(G-8310)***
Sweet Sign Systems Inc 732 521-9300
9 Davison Ave Ste 5 Jamesburg (08831) ***(G-4677)***
Sweet Solutions Inc 732 512-0777
117 Fieldcrest Ave Edison (08837) ***(G-2628)***
Sweetly Spirited Cupcakes Ltd 917 846-4238
10 Newport Dr Princeton Junction (08550) ***(G-9067)***
Swemco, Moorestown *Also called S W Electronics & Mfg* ***(G-6564)***
Swemco LLC (HQ) 856 222-9900
121 Whittendale Dr Ste A Moorestown (08057) ***(G-6570)***
Swepco Tube LLC 973 778-3000
1 Clifton Blvd Clifton (07011) ***(G-1728)***
Swintec Corp (PA) 201 935-0115
320 W Coml Ave Ste 1 Moonachie (07074) ***(G-6493)***
Swiss Madison LLC 434 623-4766
19 Stults Rd Dayton (08810) ***(G-1991)***
Swiss Orthopedic Inc 908 874-5522
188 Us Highway 206 Hillsborough (08844) ***(G-4359)***
Swissray America Inc 908 353-0971
1180 Mclester St Ste 2 Elizabeth (07201) ***(G-2781)***
Swissray International Inc (HQ) 800 903-5543
1090 King Georges Rd 1203 Edison (08837) ***(G-2629)***
Swissray Medical Systems, Elizabeth *Also called Swissray America Inc* ***(G-2781)***
Swisstex Company 201 861-8000
220 61st St Ste 2 West New York (07093) ***(G-11755)***
Switlik Parachute Company Inc 609 587-3300
Lalor & Hancock Sts Trenton (08609) ***(G-10994)***
Swm Spotswood Mill 732 723-6102
85 Main St Spotswood (08884) ***(G-10419)***
Sxwell USA LLC 732 345-5400
111 Wood Ave S Ste 210 Iselin (08830) ***(G-4630)***
Sybase Inc 973 537-5700
400 Interpace Pkwy Ste D1 Parsippany (07054) ***(G-8023)***
Sylvan Chemical Corporation 201 934-4224
7 Prescott Pl Fair Lawn (07410) ***(G-3124)***
Symbiomix Therapeutics LLC (HQ) 609 722-7250
105 Lock St Ste 409 Newark (07103) ***(G-7293)***
Symbology Enterprises Inc (PA) 908 725-1699
50 Division St Ste 203 Somerville (08876) ***(G-10125)***
Symcon Controls, West Milford *Also called Symcon Inc* ***(G-11732)***
Symcon Inc 973 728-8661
47 Cedar Ln West Milford (07480) ***(G-11732)***
Sympatec Inc (HQ) 609 303-0066
1600 Reed Rd C Pennington (08534) ***(G-8374)***
Symphony Inc 856 727-9596
1263 Glen Ave Ste 220 Moorestown (08057) ***(G-6571)***
Symphony Pastries, Moorestown *Also called Symphony Inc* ***(G-6571)***
Symrise Inc (HQ) 201 288-3200
300 North St Teterboro (07608) ***(G-10692)***
Symrise Inc 201 288-3200
250 Pehle Ave Ste 207 Saddle Brook (07663) ***(G-9682)***
Symrise Inc 908 429-6824
180 Industrial Pkwy Branchburg (08876) ***(G-686)***
Symtech Enterprise Intl, Branchburg *Also called Paradise Barxon Corp* ***(G-664)***
Symtera Analytics LLC 718 696-9902
1806 State Route 35 Wall Township (07719) ***(G-11373)***
Synasia Inc 732 205-9880
240 Amboy Ave Metuchen (08840) ***(G-6075)***
Syncom Pharmaceuticals Inc (PA) 973 787-2405
125 Clinton Rd Unit 5 Fairfield (07004) ***(G-3321)***
Synergem Inc 732 692-6308
2323 Randolph Ave Ste 2 Avenel (07001) ***(G-148)***
Synergetica International Inc 732 780-5865
9 Inverness Dr Marlboro (07746) ***(G-5916)***
Synergy Microwave Corp (PA) 973 881-8800
201 Mclean Blvd Paterson (07504) ***(G-8311)***
Syneron 201 599-9451
707 Reeder Rd Paramus (07652) ***(G-7840)***
Synray Corporation 908 245-2600
209 N Michigan Ave Kenilworth (07033) ***(G-4980)***
Synthetic Grass Surfaces Inc 973 778-9594
6 Robert Ct Lodi (07644) ***(G-5579)***
Synthetic Grass Surfaces NJ, Lodi *Also called Synthetic Grass Surfaces Inc* ***(G-5579)***
Synthetic Surfaces Inc (PA) 908 233-6803
2450 Plainfield Ave Scotch Plains (07076) ***(G-9743)***
Syntiro Dynamics LLC 732 377-3307
1606 Cammar Dr Wall Township (07719) ***(G-11374)***
Sysco Guest Supply LLC (HQ) 732 537-2297
300 Davidson Ave Somerset (08873) ***(G-10078)***
Syscom Technologies Corp 856 642-7661
1537 Glen Ave Moorestown (08057) ***(G-6572)***
Sytheon Ltd 973 988-1075
315 Wootton St Ste N Boonton (07005) ***(G-569)***
T & B Specialties Inc 732 928-4500
479 Wright Debow Rd Jackson (08527) ***(G-4666)***
T & C, Marlboro *Also called Town & Country Plastics Inc* ***(G-5917)***
T & E Industries Inc 973 672-5454
215 Watchung Ave Orange (07050) ***(G-7763)***

T & E Sales of Marlboro Inc 732 549-7551
913 Middlesex Ave Metuchen (08840) *(G-6076)*

T & M Newton Corporation 973 383-1232
119 Fredon Springdale Rd Newton (07860) *(G-7361)*

T & M Pallet Co Inc 908 454-3042
116 Edison Rd Stewartsville (08886) *(G-10488)*

T & M Terminal Company 419 902-2810
1 Sylvan Way Parsippany (07054) *(G-8024)*

T & P Machine Shop Inc 732 424-9141
600 Prospect Ave Ste E Piscataway (08854) *(G-8722)*

T A G, West Berlin *Also called Telecom Assistance Group Inc (G-11628)*

T C E, Secaucus *Also called Thermal Conduction Engineering (G-9820)*

T C P Reliable Manufacturing 732 346-9200
551 Raritan Center Pkwy Edison (08837) *(G-2630)*

T C S Technologies Inc 908 852-7555
430 Sand Shore Rd Ste 1 Hackettstown (07840) *(G-4038)*

T F S Inc 973 890-7651
40 Vreeland Ave Ste 101 Totowa (07512) *(G-10854)*

T G Type-O-Graphics Inc 973 253-3333
19-03 Maple Ave Ste 3 Fair Lawn (07410) *(G-3125)*

T J Eckardt Associates Inc 856 767-4111
230 Williamstown Rd Berlin (08009) *(G-430)*

T J'S Ice Cream Plus, Ocean City *Also called Tjs Ice Cream (G-7697)*

T L C Specialties Inc 732 244-4225
188 Walnut St Toms River (08753) *(G-10798)*

T M Baxter Services LLC 908 500-9065
1307 Washington Gdns Washington (07882) *(G-11453)*

T M Industries Inc 908 730-7674
2013 Brookfield Glen Dr Belvidere (07823) *(G-367)*

T N T Information Systems 609 799-9488
666 Plainsboro Rd Ste 100 Plainsboro (08536) *(G-8804)*

T O Najarian Associates 732 389-0220
1 Industrial Way W Ste D5 Eatontown (07724) *(G-2423)*

T V L Associates Inc 973 790-6766
3 Donna Ln Wayne (07470) *(G-11555)*

T Wiker Enterprises Inc 609 261-9494
5900 Delaware Ave Hainesport (08036) *(G-4079)*

T-M Vacuum Products Inc (PA) 856 829-2000
630 S Warrington Ave Cinnaminson (08077) *(G-1487)*

T-M Vacuum Products Inc 856 829-2000
630 S Warrington Ave Cinnaminson (08077) *(G-1488)*

T3i Group LLC 856 424-1100
1111 Marlkress Rd Ste 101 Cherry Hill (08003) *(G-1420)*

Tab Networks 201 746-0067
50 Tice Blvd Ste 365 Woodcliff Lake (07677) *(G-12066)*

Tabco Technologies LLC (PA) 201 438-0422
400 Gotham Pkwy Carlstadt (07072) *(G-1225)*

Tablecloth Co, Paterson *Also called Jewm Inc (G-8222)*

Tabloid Graphic Services Inc 856 486-0410
7101 Westfield Ave Pennsauken (08110) *(G-8489)*

TAC Technical Instrument Corp 609 882-2894
21 W Piper Ave Trenton (08628) *(G-10995)*

Tach-It, South Hackensack *Also called Clements Industries Inc (G-10153)*

Tactic, Trenton *Also called TAC Technical Instrument Corp (G-10995)*

Tadbik NJ Inc 973 882-9595
17 Madison Rd Fairfield (07004) *(G-3322)*

Tag, Teterboro *Also called Tapia Accessory Group Inc (G-10694)*

Tag Minerals Inc 732 252-5146
41 Howe Ln Freehold (07728) *(G-3701)*

Tag Optics Inc 609 356-2142
200 N Harrison St Princeton (08540) *(G-9031)*

Tahari Arthur S Levine, Millburn *Also called Tahari ASL LLC (G-6206)*

Tahari ASL LLC (PA) 888 734-7459
16 Bleeker St Millburn (07041) *(G-6206)*

Taisho Pharmaceutical R&D Inc 973 285-0870
350 Mount Kemble Ave # 4 Morristown (07960) *(G-6702)*

Takara Belmont Usa Inc (HQ) 732 469-5000
101 Belmont Dr Somerset (08873) *(G-10079)*

Takara Belmont Usa Inc 732 469-5000
101 Belmont Dr Somerset (08873) *(G-10080)*

TAKASAGO INTERNATIONAL CORPORATION (U.S.A.), Teterboro *Also called Takasago Intl Corp USA (G-10693)*

Takasago Intl Corp USA (HQ) 201 767-9001
4 Volvo Dr Rockleigh (07647) *(G-9522)*

Takasago Intl Corp USA 201 767-9001
267 Union St Northvale (07647) *(G-7551)*

Takasago Intl Corp USA 201 727-4200
100 Green St Teterboro (07608) *(G-10693)*

Talent Investment LLC 732 931-0088
12 Crown Plz Hazlet (07730) *(G-4271)*

Talent Technology Center, Hazlet *Also called Talent Investment LLC (G-4271)*

Talenti Gelato LLC (HQ) 800 298-4020
800 Sylvan Ave Englewood Cliffs (07632) *(G-2990)*

Tally Display Corp 973 777-7760
19 Gardner Rd Ste A Fairfield (07004) *(G-3323)*

Talon7 LLC 908 595-2121
991 Us Highway 22 Ste 200 Bridgewater (08807) *(G-896)*

Tam Metal Products Inc 201 848-7800
55 Whitney Rd Mahwah (07430) *(G-5779)*

Tamaras European American Deli 973 875-5461
13 Essex Rd Sussex (07461) *(G-10566)*

Tamir Biotechnology Inc 800 419-5061
51 Jfk Pkwy Fl 1w Short Hills (07078) *(G-9878)*

Tanda Sleep, Piscataway *Also called Catching Zzz LLC (G-8643)*

Tandem Color Imaging Graphics (PA) 973 513-9779
207 Wanaque Ave Pompton Lakes (07442) *(G-8853)*

Tandem Color Imaging Graphics 973 513-9779
207 Wanaque Ave Pompton Lakes (07442) *(G-8854)*

Tandem Graphics, Pompton Lakes *Also called Tandem Color Imaging Graphics (G-8853)*

Tandem Graphics, Pompton Lakes *Also called Tandem Color Imaging Graphics (G-8854)*

Tandem Technologies, Mahwah *Also called Transportation Tech Svcs Inc (G-5784)*

Tangent Graphics Inc 201 488-2840
23 Chestnut St Englewood (07631) *(G-2946)*

Tanis Concrete 201 796-1556
17-68 River Rd Fair Lawn (07410) *(G-3126)*

Tankleff Inc 201 402-6500
815 Fairview Ave Ste 10 Fairview (07022) *(G-3369)*

Tanter Inc 732 382-3555
151 Westfield Ave Ste 3 Clark (07066) *(G-1516)*

Tanzola Printing Inc 973 779-0858
270 Colfax Ave Clifton (07013) *(G-1729)*

Tap For Message, South Plainfield *Also called Greetingtap (G-10269)*

Tap Into LLC 908 370-1158
66 W 4th St New Providence (07974) *(G-7020)*

Tap Pharmaceutical Products 908 470-9700
500 Hills Dr Ste 125 Bedminster (07921) *(G-279)*

Tape Graphics 201 393-9500
208 Boulevard Ste A Hasbrouck Heights (07604) *(G-4189)*

Tapes and Coatings, Middlesex *Also called Covalnce Spcialty Coatings LLC (G-6109)*

Tapestry Inc 856 488-2220
2000 Route 38 Ste 1720 Cherry Hill (08002) *(G-1421)*

Tapia Accessory Group Inc 201 393-0028
370 North St Teterboro (07608) *(G-10694)*

Tapintonet 908 279-0303
598 Central Ave Ste 7 New Providence (07974) *(G-7021)*

Taptask LLC 201 294-2371
83 Rolling Hills Rd Clifton (07013) *(G-1730)*

Taree Pharma LLC 609 252-9596
342 Herrontown Rd Princeton (08540) *(G-9032)*

Targa Industries Inc 973 584-3733
5 Laurel Dr Unit 13 Flanders (07836) *(G-3421)*

Targanta Therapeutics Corp (HQ) 973 290-6000
8 Sylvan Way Parsippany (07054) *(G-8025)*

Target Coatings Inc 800 752-9922
17-12 River Rd Fair Lawn (07410) *(G-3127)*

Targeted Healthcare, Plainsboro *Also called Intellisphere LLC (G-8797)*

Targum Publishing Company 732 247-1286
126 College Ave Ste 431 New Brunswick (08901) *(G-6973)*

Tarlton C & T Co Inc (PA) 908 964-9400
967 Lehigh Ave Union (07083) *(G-11093)*

Taro Pharmaceuticals USA Inc 609 655-9002
1 Commerce Dr Cranbury (08512) *(G-1886)*

Taryag Legacy Foundation Inc 732 569-2467
1136 Somerset Ave Lakewood (08701) *(G-5170)*

Task International (usa) Inc 732 739-0377
3 Cass St Keyport (07735) *(G-5005)*

Tassel Toppers LLC 855 827-7357
445 Godwin Ave Ste 8 Midland Park (07432) *(G-6187)*

Taste It Presents Inc 908 241-9191
200 Sumner Ave Kenilworth (07033) *(G-4981)*

Taste Italy Manufacturing LLC 856 223-0707
1301 Bremen Ave Egg Harbor City (08215) *(G-2668)*

Tasty Bake Distributing Center, Egg Harbor Township *Also called Tasty Baking Company (G-2698)*

Tasty Baking Company 609 641-8588
203 Cates Rd Egg Harbor Township (08234) *(G-2698)*

Tasty Cake South Jersey 856 428-8414
1871 Old Cuthbert Rd B Cherry Hill (08034) *(G-1422)*

Tatara Group Inc 732 231-6031
381 Blair Rd Avenel (07001) *(G-149)*

Taunton Graphics Inc 856 719-8084
1049 Industrial Dr West Berlin (08091) *(G-11625)*

Taurus Defense Solutions LLC 617 916-6137
13 Butler Ct Medford (08055) *(G-6036)*

Taurus International Corp 201 825-2420
275 N Franklin Tpke Ste 3 Ramsey (07446) *(G-9156)*

Taurus Precision Inc 973 785-9254
129 Paterson Ave Little Falls (07424) *(G-5470)*

Taxstream LLC 201 610-0390
95 River St Ste 5c Hoboken (07030) *(G-4484)*

Taylor Communications Inc 732 560-3410
625 Pierce St Ste A Somerset (08873) *(G-10081)*

Taylor Communications Inc 732 561-8210
7 Costco Dr Monroe Township (08831) *(G-6348)*

Taylor Communications Inc 973 467-8259
899 Mountain Ave Ste 2f Springfield (07081) *(G-10468)*

Taylor Farms New Jersey Inc 856 241-0097
406 Heron Dr Ste A Swedesboro (08085) *(G-10613)*

Taylor Forge Stainless Inc.....908 722-1313
22 Readington Rd Branchburg (08876) ***(G-687)***
Taylor Made Cabinets Inc.....609 978-6900
516 E Bay Ave Manahawkin (08050) ***(G-5796)***
Taylor Made Custom Cabinetry.....856 786-5433
7035 Central Hwy 200 Pennsauken (08109) ***(G-8490)***
Taylor Products Inc.....732 225-4620
255 Raritan Center Pkwy Edison (08837) ***(G-2631)***
Taylor Provisions Company.....609 392-1113
63 Perrine Ave Trenton (08638) ***(G-10996)***
Taylor Window Factory, East Orange *Also called Taylor Windows Inc* ***(G-2264)***
Taylor Windows Inc.....973 672-3000
61 Central Ave East Orange (07018) ***(G-2264)***
Tbb Inc (PA).....973 589-8875
115-129 Kossuth St Newark (07105) ***(G-7294)***
Tbc Color Imaging Inc.....973 470-8100
200 Entin Rd Clifton (07014) ***(G-1731)***
Tbc Digital, Clifton *Also called Tbc Color Imaging Inc* ***(G-1731)***
Tbl Licencing, Elizabeth *Also called Vf Outdoor LLC* ***(G-2785)***
Tbl Performance Plastics, Sparta *Also called Thermoplastics Bio-Logics LLC* ***(G-10411)***
Tbs Industrial Flooring Pdts.....732 899-1486
300 New Jersey Ave Point Pleasant Beach (08742) ***(G-8832)***
Tbt Group Inc.....856 753-4500
191 Heller Pl Bellmawr (08031) ***(G-344)***
Tcp Reliable Inc (PA).....848 229-2466
551 Raritan Center Pkwy Edison (08837) ***(G-2632)***
Tcp/Reliable, Edison *Also called T C P Reliable Manufacturing* ***(G-2630)***
Tdk Associates Corp.....862 210-8085
12 Eisenhower Pkwy Ste 9 Roseland (07068) ***(G-9542)***
Tdk Electronics Inc (HQ).....732 906-4300
485b Us Highway 1 S # 200 Iselin (08830) ***(G-4631)***
Tdk Electronics Inc.....732 603-5941
120 Munt Holly Byp Unit 2 Lumberton (08048) ***(G-5636)***
Tdk-Lambda Americas Inc (HQ).....732 922-9300
405 Essex Rd Tinton Falls (07753) ***(G-10731)***
Tdk-Lmbda Amricas High Pwr Div, Tinton Falls *Also called Tdk-Lambda Americas Inc* ***(G-10731)***
Te Connectivity Corporation.....610 893-9800
250 Industrial Way W Eatontown (07724) ***(G-2424)***
Te Wire & Cable LLC.....201 845-9400
107 5th St Saddle Brook (07663) ***(G-9683)***
Tea Elle Woodworks.....732 938-9660
53 Main St Farmingdale (07727) ***(G-3394)***
Team Nisca.....732 271-7367
100 Randolph Rd Somerset (08873) ***(G-10082)***
TEC, Irvington *Also called Engine Combo LLC* ***(G-4567)***
TEC Cast Inc (PA).....201 935-3885
440 Meadow Ln Carlstadt (07072) ***(G-1226)***
TEC Cast Inc.....201 935-3885
2 W Commercial Ave Moonachie (07074) ***(G-6494)***
TEC Elevator Inc.....609 938-0647
510 Route Us 9 S Marmora (08223) ***(G-5960)***
TEC Installations Inc.....973 684-0503
375 E 22nd St Paterson (07514) ***(G-8312)***
Tech Art Inc.....201 525-0044
25 Green St Hackensack (07601) ***(G-3981)***
Tech Brains Solutions Inc.....732 952-0552
220 Davidson Ave Ste 303 Somerset (08873) ***(G-10083)***
Tech Giant LLC.....888 800-7745
556 Industrial Way W Eatontown (07724) ***(G-2425)***
Tech Products Co Inc.....201 444-7777
300 Greenwood Ave Midland Park (07432) ***(G-6188)***
Tech-Pak Inc.....201 935-3800
3 Ethel Blvd Wood Ridge (07075) ***(G-12007)***
Techart, Hackensack *Also called Tech Art Inc* ***(G-3981)***
Techenzyme Inc.....732 632-8600
75 State Route 27 Ste 300 Iselin (08830) ***(G-4632)***
Techflex Inc (HQ).....973 300-9242
104 Demarest Rd Ste 1 Sparta (07871) ***(G-10409)***
Techline Extrusion Systems.....973 831-0317
89 4th Ave Haskell (07420) ***(G-4203)***
Technical Advantage Inc (PA).....973 402-5500
34 Farber Hill Rd Boonton (07005) ***(G-570)***
Technical Aids To Independence.....973 674-1082
219 S 18th St Unit 2 East Orange (07018) ***(G-2265)***
Technical Coatings Co (HQ).....973 927-8600
360 Us Highway 206 Flanders (07836) ***(G-3422)***
Technical Glass Products Inc.....973 989-5500
243 E Blackwell St Dover (07801) ***(G-2107)***
Technical Nameplate Corp.....973 773-4256
92 1st St Passaic (07055) ***(G-8111)***
Technical Oil Products Co Inc (PA).....973 940-8920
93 Spring St Ste 303 Newton (07860) ***(G-7362)***
Technical Systems Group, Little Falls *Also called Tsg Inc* ***(G-5471)***
Technick Products Inc.....908 791-0400
1000 Coolidge St South Plainfield (07080) ***(G-10330)***
Technidyne Corporation.....732 363-1055
2190 Route 9 Ste 9 Toms River (08755) ***(G-10799)***
Technimold Inc.....908 232-8331
112 Pine Bank Rd Flemington (08822) ***(G-3470)***
Technique Precision, Somerdale *Also called Bisaga Inc* ***(G-9930)***
Techniques Inc.....973 256-0947
14 Alexandria Ct Woodland Park (07424) ***(G-12092)***
Technitool Inc.....856 768-2707
1028 Industrial Dr West Berlin (08091) ***(G-11626)***
Techno City Inc.....862 414-3282
1 Meadowlands Plz Ste 200 East Rutherford (07073) ***(G-2323)***
Techno Design Inc.....973 478-0930
11 Erie St Ste 1 Garfield (07026) ***(G-3772)***
Technobox Inc.....856 809-2306
154 Cooper Rd Ste 901 West Berlin (08091) ***(G-11627)***
Technodiamant USA Inc.....908 850-8505
35a Kennedy Rd Tranquility (07879) ***(G-10884)***
Technogym USA Corp (HQ).....800 804-0952
700 Us Highway 46 Fairfield (07004) ***(G-3324)***
Technol Inc.....856 848-5480
1030 Delsea Dr Unit 8e Westville (08093) ***(G-11821)***
Technology Corp America Inc.....866 462-8292
350 Mount Kemble Ave Morristown (07960) ***(G-6703)***
Technology Dynamics Inc (PA).....201 385-0500
100 School St Ste 1 Bergenfield (07621) ***(G-385)***
Technology Dynamics Inc.....201 385-0500
100 School St Bergenfield (07621) ***(G-386)***
Technology General Corporation (PA).....973 827-8209
12 Cork Hill Rd Franklin (07416) ***(G-3609)***
Technology Reviews Inc.....973 537-9511
14 Red Barn Ln Randolph (07869) ***(G-9203)***
Technology Solutions Sector, Mount Laurel *Also called Bae Systems Tech Sol Srvc Inc* ***(G-6739)***
Technovations, Randolph *Also called Technology Reviews Inc* ***(G-9203)***
Technovision Inc.....732 381-0200
42 Bridge St Metuchen (08840) ***(G-6077)***
Techntime Bus Sltons Ltd Lblty.....973 246-8153
1 Madison St Ste B4 East Rutherford (07073) ***(G-2324)***
Techsetters Inc.....856 240-7905
900 Haddon Ave Ste 300 Collingswood (08108) ***(G-1772)***
Techtrade LLC.....201 706-8130
30 Montgomery St Ste 690 Jersey City (07302) ***(G-4819)***
Teckchek (PA).....919 497-0136
77 Milltown Rd Ste C4 East Brunswick (08816) ***(G-2186)***
Tecnicam, Livingston *Also called Campak Inc* ***(G-5508)***
Tecogen Inc.....732 356-5601
417 Bell St Piscataway (08854) ***(G-8723)***
Tectubes USA Inc.....856 589-1250
1299 W Forest Grove Rd Vineland (08360) ***(G-11269)***
Ted-Steel Indstries, Linden *Also called Ted-Steel Industries Ltd* ***(G-5434)***
Ted-Steel Industries Ltd.....212 279-3878
101 Roselle St Linden (07036) ***(G-5434)***
Tedco Inc.....609 883-0799
35 Scotch Rd Ewing (08628) ***(G-3069)***
Tee-Rific Golf Center.....908 253-9300
3091 Us Highway 22 Branchburg (08876) ***(G-688)***
Teefx Screen Printing LLC.....973 942-6800
250 Belmont Ave Haledon (07508) ***(G-4086)***
Teixeira's Bakery, Newark *Also called Portuguese Baking Company Inc* ***(G-7231)***
Teixeira's Bakery, Newark *Also called Tbb Inc* ***(G-7294)***
Tek Molding.....973 702-0450
1440 County Rd 565 Sussex (07461) ***(G-10567)***
Tek-Pak Div, Rochelle Park *Also called Rempac LLC* ***(G-9431)***
Tekkote Corporation.....201 585-1708
580 Willow Tree Rd Leonia (07605) ***(G-5293)***
Tekltd (PA).....732 463-2100
95 Mitchell Ave Piscataway (08854) ***(G-8724)***
Teknics Industries Inc.....973 633-7575
170 Beaverbrook Rd Ste 1 Lincoln Park (07035) ***(G-5306)***
Teknics Sales, Lincoln Park *Also called Teknics Industries Inc* ***(G-5306)***
Tekno Inc.....973 423-2004
86 5th Ave Hawthorne (07506) ***(G-4246)***
Tektite Industries Inc.....609 656-0600
309 N Clinton Ave Trenton (08638) ***(G-10997)***
Tektite Mfg Division, Trenton *Also called Tektite Industries Inc* ***(G-10997)***
Tektronix Inc.....973 628-1363
1133 State Route 23 Ste 4 Wayne (07470) ***(G-11556)***
Tel-Instrument Elec Corp (PA).....201 933-1600
1 Branca Rd East Rutherford (07073) ***(G-2325)***
Telcontel Corp.....732 441-0800
11 Industrial Dr Laurence Harbor (08879) ***(G-5210)***
Telecom Assistance Group Inc.....856 753-8585
150 Cooper Rd Ste F15 West Berlin (08091) ***(G-11628)***
Teledynamics LLC.....973 248-3360
45 Indian Ln E Ste 1 Towaco (07082) ***(G-10881)***
Teleflex Incorporated.....856 349-7234
860 Charles St Gloucester City (08030) ***(G-3851)***
Telegenix Inc.....609 265-3910
71 Indel Ave Rancocas (08073) ***(G-9167)***
Telemark Cnc LLC.....973 794-4857
429 Rockaway Valley Rd Boonton (07005) ***(G-571)***

ALPHABETIC

Telemetrics Inc 201 848-9818	**Tfi OEM Commercial Group, Lakewood** *Also called Masco Cabinetry LLC* **(G-5130)**
75 Commerce Dr Allendale (07401) **(G-18)**	**Tgz Acquisition Company LLC** 856 669-6600
Telescript Inc (PA) 201 767-6733	855 Industrial Hwy Ste 4 Cinnaminson (08077) **(G-1489)**
445 Livingston St Norwood (07648) **(G-7575)**	**Thal Precision Industries LLC** 732 381-6106
Teligent Inc (PA) 856 697-1441	33 Terminal Ave Clark (07066) **(G-1517)**
105 Lincoln Ave Buena (08310) **(G-942)**	**Thales Avionics Inc (HQ)** 732 242-6300
Teligent Inc 856 697-1441	140 Centennial Ave Piscataway (08854) **(G-8725)**
711 S Harding Hwy Buena (08310) **(G-943)**	**Thanks For Being Green LLC** 856 333-0991
Tellas Ltd 201 399-8888	5070b Central Hwy Pennsauken (08109) **(G-8491)**
600 Sylvan Ave Ste 4 Englewood Cliffs (07632) **(G-2991)**	**Thats How We Roll LLC (PA)** 973 240-0200
Teluca Inc 973 232-0002	214 Glenridge Ave Montclair (07042) **(G-6392)**
414 Eagle Rock Ave West Orange (07052) **(G-11779)**	**The Aquarian Weekly, Little Falls** *Also called Arts Weekly Inc* **(G-5453)**
Telvue Corporation (PA) 800 885-8886	**The Creative Print Group Inc** 856 486-1700
16000 Horizon Way Ste 100 Mount Laurel (08054) **(G-6809)**	7905 Browning Rd Ste 112 Pennsauken (08109) **(G-8492)**
Templar Food Products, New Providence *Also called Reeves Enterprises Inc* **(G-7016)**	**The Door Center Publishing, Hopewell** *Also called Door Center Enterprises Inc* **(G-4526)**
Temptime Corporation (HQ) 973 984-6000	**The Vine, Princeton** *Also called Venture Info Network* **(G-9041)**
116 The American Rd Morris Plains (07950) **(G-6626)**	**The Westfield Leader, Westfield** *Also called Watthung Communications Inc* **(G-11805)**
Temptrol Corp 856 461-7977	**Theberge Cabinets Inc** 201 941-1141
242 Terrace Blvd Ste E Voorhees (08043) **(G-11295)**	202 Broad Ave Fairview (07022) **(G-3370)**
Ten One Design Ltd Lblty Co 201 474-8232	**Thebgb Inc (PA)** 917 749-5309
149 Chestnut St Montclair (07042) **(G-6391)**	840 E 28th St Paterson (07513) **(G-8314)**
Tenax Finishing Products Co 973 589-9000	**Themac, East Rutherford** *Also called McGonegal Manufacturing Co* **(G-2301)**
390 Adams St Newark (07114) **(G-7295)**	**Theodore E Mozer Inc** 856 829-1432
Teneyck Inc 201 939-1100	14 E 4th St Palmyra (08065) **(G-7786)**
700 Schuyler Ave Lyndhurst (07071) **(G-5681)**	**Theory Development Corp** 201 783-8770
Teo Fabrications Inc 973 764-5500	31 Industrial Ave Ste 1 Mahwah (07430) **(G-5780)**
95 Maple Grange Rd Vernon (07462) **(G-11163)**	**Thepositive Press** 856 266-8765
Terhune Bros Woodworking 973 962-6686	2020 Bannard St Cinnaminson (08077) **(G-1490)**
58 Bearfort Ter Ringwood (07456) **(G-9354)**	**Ther-A-Pedic Sleep Products (PA)** 732 628-0800
Terminal Printing Co 201 659-5924	1375 Jersey Ave North Brunswick (08902) **(G-7490)**
85 Washington Ave Belleville (07109) **(G-316)**	**Therapeutic Proteins Inc** 312 620-1500
Terra Chips, Moonachie *Also called Hain Celestial Group Inc* **(G-6469)**	20 New England Ave Piscataway (08854) **(G-8726)**
Terra Designs Inc (PA) 973 328-1135	**Therma-Tech Corporation** 973 345-0076
241 E Blackwell St Rear Dover (07801) **(G-2108)**	300 Dakota St Ste 1 Paterson (07503) **(G-8315)**
Terrestrial Imaging LLC 800 359-0530	**Thermal Chek Inc** 856 742-1200
375 Herbertsville Rd Brick (08724) **(G-733)**	912 Broadway Westville (08093) **(G-11822)**
Terrignos Bakery 856 451-6368	**Thermal Conduction Engineering** 201 865-1084
632 N Pearl St Bridgeton (08302) **(G-774)**	865 Roosevelt Ave Secaucus (07094) **(G-9820)**
Terriss Consolidated Inds 732 988-0909	**Thermo Cote Inc** 973 464-3575
807 Summerfield Ave Asbury Park (07712) **(G-84)**	198 Green Pond Rd Ste 5 Rockaway (07866) **(G-9503)**
Terumo Americas Holding Inc (HQ) 732 302-4900	**Thermo Fisher Scientific Inc** 609 239-3185
265 Davidson Ave Ste 320 Somerset (08873) **(G-10084)**	19 London Rd Burlington (08016) **(G-987)**
Terumo Medical Corporation (HQ) 732 302-4900	**Thermo Fisher Scientific Inc** 732 627-0220
265 Davidson Ave Ste 320 Somerset (08873) **(G-10085)**	265 Davidson Ave Ste 101 Somerset (08873) **(G-10087)**
Tesa Rentals LLC 973 300-0913	**Thermo Plastic Tech Inc** 908 687-4833
286 Houses Corner Rd Sparta (07871) **(G-10410)**	1119 Morris Ave Union (07083) **(G-11095)**
Tesla Inc 201 225-2544	**Thermo Systems LLC** 609 371-3300
530 N Rte 17 Paramus (07652) **(G-7841)**	84 Twin Rivers Dr East Windsor (08520) **(G-2362)**
Tesla Motors, Paramus *Also called Tesla Inc* **(G-7841)**	**Thermo X-Press Printing LLC** 973 585-6505
Tess-Com Inc (PA) 412 233-5782	12d Great Meadow Ln East Hanover (07936) **(G-2241)**
400 South Ave Ste 11 Middlesex (08846) **(G-6155)**	**Thermo-Graphics Inc** 908 486-0100
Tessler & Weiss/Premesco Inc 800 535-3501	386 Avenel St Avenel (07001) **(G-150)**
2389 Vauxhall Rd Union (07083) **(G-11094)**	**Thermoplastic Processes, Stirling** *Also called Tpi Partners Inc* **(G-10498)**
Test Technology Inc (HQ) 856 596-1215	**Thermoplastics Bio-Logics LLC** 973 383-2834
5 E Stow Rd Marlton (08053) **(G-5953)**	18 White Lake Rd Sparta (07871) **(G-10411)**
Testrite Instrument Co Inc 201 543-0240	**Thermoseal Industries LLC (HQ)** 856 456-3109
216 S Newman St Hackensack (07601) **(G-3982)**	600 Jersey Ave Gloucester City (08030) **(G-3852)**
Testrite Visual Products, Hackensack *Also called Testrite Instrument Co Inc* **(G-3982)**	**Thermwell Products Co Inc (PA)** 201 684-4400
Tetley USA Inc (HQ) 800 728-0084	420 Rte 17 Mahwah (07430) **(G-5781)**
890 Mountain Ave Ste 105 New Providence (07974) **(G-7022)**	**Thermwell Products Co Inc** 201 684-4400
Tetra Lubricants, Florham Park *Also called Fti Inc* **(G-3506)**	420 State Rt 17 Mahwah (07430) **(G-5782)**
Teva Api Inc 201 307-6900	**Thewal Inc** 973 635-1880
400 Interpace Pkwy Ste A1 Parsippany (07054) **(G-8026)**	12 Center St Chatham (07928) **(G-1330)**
Teva Pharmaceuticals 888 838-2872	**Thibaut & Walker Co Inc** 973 589-3331
400 Interpace Pkwy Ste A1 Parsippany (07054) **(G-8027)**	49 Rutherford St Newark (07105) **(G-7296)**
Teva Pharmaceuticals Usa Inc 973 575-2775	**Thiladel Phia, Moorestown** *Also called CR Laurence Co Inc* **(G-6516)**
8 Gloria Ln Ste 10 Fairfield (07004) **(G-3325)**	**Thin Stone Systems LLC** 973 882-7377
Teva Womens Health Inc 201 930-3300	23 Commerce Rd Ste O Fairfield (07004) **(G-3327)**
400 Campus Dr Somerset (08873) **(G-10086)**	**Thinfilms Inc** 908 359-7014
Tevco Enterprises Inc 908 754-7306	15 Ilene Ct Ste 6 Hillsborough (08844) **(G-4360)**
55 E 6th St Paterson (07524) **(G-8313)**	**Things 2 B, Elmer** *Also called Perfect Shapes Inc* **(G-2801)**
Tex Gul Inc 973 857-3200	**Think Big Solutions Inc (PA)** 732 968-0211
874 Pompton Ave Ste A2 Cedar Grove (07009) **(G-1293)**	5 Jacob Dr Princeton Junction (08550) **(G-9068)**
Tex-Net Inc 609 499-9111	**Think Big Solutions Inc** 609 716-7343
763 Railroad Ave B Florence (08518) **(G-3478)**	14 Farber Rd Princeton (08540) **(G-9033)**
Texas Canvas, Fairfield *Also called Lion Visual Ltd Liability Co* **(G-3264)**	**Think Tin, Parsippany** *Also called Allstate Can Corporation* **(G-7878)**
Texas Canvas Co Inc (PA) 973 278-3802	**Third Ave Chocolate Shoppe** 732 449-7535
1275 Bloomfield Ave 54b Fairfield (07004) **(G-3326)**	1118 3rd Ave Spring Lake (07762) **(G-10424)**
Textol Systems Inc 201 935-1220	**Third River Manufacturing LLC** 201 935-2795
735 Commercial Ave Carlstadt (07072) **(G-1227)**	503 Washington Ave Carlstadt (07072) **(G-1228)**
Textron Inc 201 945-1500	**Third Wave Bus Systems LLC** 201 703-2100
143 River Rd Edgewater (07020) **(G-2441)**	1680 State Route 23 # 320 Wayne (07470) **(G-11557)**
Texx Team LLC 201 289-1039	**Thirty-Three Queen Realty Inc (PA)** 973 824-5527
589 Hillsdale Ave Hillsdale (07642) **(G-4370)**	1 Flexon Plz Newark (07114) **(G-7297)**
Tf Yachts LLC 609 965-2300	**This Is It Stageworks LLC** 201 653-2699
801 Philadelphia Ave Egg Harbor City (08215) **(G-2669)**	345 18th Street Jersey Cy Jersey City (07310) **(G-4820)**
TFH Publications Inc 732 897-6860	**Thoma Inc (PA)** 856 608-6887
85 W Sylvania Ave Neptune (07753) **(G-6900)**	1640 Nixon Dr 323 Moorestown (08057) **(G-6573)**
TFH Publications Inc 732 988-8400	
211 W Sylvania Ave Neptune (07753) **(G-6901)**	

(G-0000) Company's Geographic Section entry number

Thomas A Caserta Inc ... 609 586-2807
11 S Gold Dr Ste E Robbinsville (08691) ***(G-9417)***
Thomas Clark Fiberglass LLC ... 609 492-9257
145 Old Halfway Rd Barnegat (08005) ***(G-163)***
Thomas Cobb & Sons ... 856 451-0671
146 Cobbs Mill Rd Bridgeton (08302) ***(G-775)***
Thomas Erectors Inc ... 908 810-0030
630 Ramsey Ave Hillside (07205) ***(G-4430)***
Thomas Greco Publishing Inc (PA) ... 973 667-6965
244 Chestnut St Ste 4 Nutley (07110) ***(G-7594)***
Thomas H Cox & Son Inc ... 908 928-1010
1634 E Elizabeth Ave Linden (07036) ***(G-5435)***
Thomas Instrumentation Inc ... 609 624-7777
118 Kings Hwy Cape May Court House (08210) ***(G-1115)***
Thomas Instrumentation Inc (PA) ... 609 624-2630
133 Landing Rd Cape May Court House (08210) ***(G-1116)***
Thomas Manufacturing Inc ... 908 810-0030
630 Ramsey Ave Ste 1 Hillside (07205) ***(G-4431)***
Thomas Publishing Company LLC ... 973 543-4994
95 W Main St Ste 8 Chester (07930) ***(G-1435)***
Thomas Register, Chester *Also called Thomas Publishing Company LLC* ***(G-1435)***
Thomas Russo & Sons Inc ... 201 332-4159
854 Communipaw Ave Jersey City (07304) ***(G-4821)***
Thomas Scientific, Swedesboro *Also called Arthur H Thomas Company* ***(G-10571)***
Thomas Scientific Inc ... 800 345-2100
1654 High Hill Rd Swedesboro (08085) ***(G-10614)***
Thomas Scientific LLC (HQ) ... 800 345-2100
1654 High Hill Rd Swedesboro (08085) ***(G-10615)***
Thomas Smock Woodworking ... 732 542-9167
306 Broad St Eatontown (07724) ***(G-2426)***
Thompson Stone ... 973 293-7237
3 Myrtle Dr Montague (07827) ***(G-6355)***
Thomsom Health Care Inc ... 201 358-7300
5 Paragon Dr Montvale (07645) ***(G-6436)***
Thomson Financial, Newark *Also called Thomson Reuters (markets) LLC* ***(G-7298)***
Thomson Lamination Co Inc ... 856 779-8521
504 E Linwood Ave Maple Shade (08052) ***(G-5872)***
Thomson Reuters (markets) LLC ... 973 286-7200
2 Gateway Ctr Fl 11 Newark (07102) ***(G-7298)***
Thomson Reuters Corporation ... 973 662-3070
492 River Rd Nutley (07110) ***(G-7595)***
Thomson Reuters Corporation ... 212 337-4281
2 Gateway Ctr Fl 11 Newark (07102) ***(G-7299)***
Thorlabs Inc (PA) ... 973 579-7227
56 Sparta Ave Newton (07860) ***(G-7363)***
Thrombogenics Inc ... 732 590-2900
101 Wood Ave S Ste 610 Iselin (08830) ***(G-4633)***
Thryv Inc ... 908 237-0956
27 Minneakoning Rd # 204 Flemington (08822) ***(G-3471)***
Thryv Inc ... 856 988-2700
401 Route 73 N Bldg 20 Marlton (08053) ***(G-5954)***
Thumann Incorporated (PA) ... 201 935-3636
670 Dell Rd Ste 1 Carlstadt (07072) ***(G-1229)***
Thumanns, Carlstadt *Also called Thumann Incorporated* ***(G-1229)***
Thwing-Albert Instrument Co ... 856 767-1000
14 W Collings Ave West Berlin (08091) ***(G-11629)***
Thyssenkrupp Materials NA Inc ... 212 972-8800
25 E Spring Valley Ave Maywood (07607) ***(G-6017)***
Tiburon Lockers Inc ... 201 750-4960
22 Paris Ave Ste 106 Rockleigh (07647) ***(G-9523)***
TIC, East Rutherford *Also called Tel-Instrument Elec Corp* ***(G-2325)***
Tiffany Packaging ... 973 726-8130
270 Sparta Ave Sparta (07871) ***(G-10412)***
Tiger Supplies Inc ... 973 854-8635
27 Selvage St Irvington (07111) ***(G-4588)***
Tilcon New York Inc (HQ) ... 973 366-7741
9 Entin Rd Parsippany (07054) ***(G-8028)***
Tilcon New York Inc ... 973 835-0028
125 Hamburg Tpke Riverdale (07457) ***(G-9387)***
Tilcon New York Inc ... 800 789-7625
2414 95th St North Bergen (07047) ***(G-7440)***
Tilcon New York Inc ... 800 789-7625
Foot Of Broad St Pompton Lakes (07442) ***(G-8855)***
Tilcon New York Inc ... 800 789-7625
411 Bergen Ave Kearny (07032) ***(G-4901)***
Tilcon New York Inc ... 800 789-7625
9 Entin Rd Ste 12 Parsippany (07054) ***(G-8029)***
Tilcon New York Inc ... 800 789-7625
Mount Pisgah Ave Oxford (07863) ***(G-7766)***
Tilcon New York Inc ... 973 347-2405
11 Lackawanna Dr Stanhope (07874) ***(G-10479)***
Tilton Rack & Basket Co ... 973 226-6010
66 Passaic Ave Fairfield (07004) ***(G-3328)***
Time Log Industries Inc ... 609 965-5017
312 N Leipzig Ave Egg Harbor City (08215) ***(G-2670)***
Time Systems International Co ... 201 871-1200
142 S Van Brunt St Englewood (07631) ***(G-2947)***
Timeline Promotions Inc ... 973 226-1512
19 Aldrin Dr West Caldwell (07006) ***(G-11680)***
Times of Trenton Pubg Corp ... 609 989-5454
413 River View Plz Trenton (08611) ***(G-10998)***
Times Tin Cup ... 973 983-1095
35 Rainbow Trl Mountain Lakes (07046) ***(G-6828)***
Timothy P Bryan Elc Co Inc ... 609 393-8325
1926 Chestnut Ave Trenton (08611) ***(G-10999)***
Timplex Corp ... 973 875-5500
1370 State Rt 23 Sussex (07461) ***(G-10568)***
Tin Can Lids LLC ... 201 503-0677
48 Lylewood Dr Tenafly (07670) ***(G-10666)***
Tin Man Snacks LLC ... 732 329-9100
351 Herrod Blvd Dayton (08810) ***(G-1992)***
Tin Panda Inc ... 973 916-0707
875 Bloomfield Ave Clifton (07012) ***(G-1732)***
Tin Sigh Stop ... 973 691-2712
5 Meteor Trl Byram Township (07821) ***(G-1019)***
Tingley Rubber Corporation (PA) ... 800 631-5498
1551 S Washington Ave # 403 Piscataway (08854) ***(G-8727)***
Tinton Falls Systems, Tinton Falls *Also called Commvault Americas Inc* ***(G-10708)***
Tipico Products Co Inc ... 732 942-8820
490 Oberlin Ave S Lakewood (08701) ***(G-5171)***
Titan, Clifton *Also called Chicago Pneumatic Tool* ***(G-1583)***
Titan America LLC ... 973 690-5896
178 Marsh St Newark (07114) ***(G-7300)***
Titan Trading Co, Wyckoff *Also called Straps Manufacturing NJ Inc* ***(G-12121)***
Titanium Fabrication Corp (HQ) ... 973 227-5300
110 Lehigh Dr Fairfield (07004) ***(G-3329)***
Titanium Industries Inc (PA) ... 973 983-1185
18 Green Pond Rd Ste 1 Rockaway (07866) ***(G-9504)***
Titanium Industries Inc ... 973 428-1900
64 State Route 10 East Hanover (07936) ***(G-2242)***
Titanium Smoking Kings LLC ... 908 339-8876
509 March Blvd Phillipsburg (08865) ***(G-8577)***
Titanium Technical Services ... 908 323-9899
21 New York Ave Flemington (08822) ***(G-3472)***
Tjk Machine LLC ... 856 691-7811
870 E Elmer Rd Vineland (08360) ***(G-11270)***
Tjs Ice Cream ... 609 398-5055
100 E Atlantic Blvd Ocean City (08226) ***(G-7697)***
Tkl Specialty Piping Inc ... 908 454-0030
175 Broad St Phillipsburg (08865) ***(G-8578)***
TLC Signs & Banners, Toms River *Also called T L C Specialties Inc* ***(G-10798)***
Tlg Signs Inc ... 609 912-0500
2901 Us Highway 1 Ste 3 Lawrenceville (08648) ***(G-5244)***
Tlw Bath Ltd Liability Company ... 732 942-7117
1144 E Cnty Ln Rd Lakewood (08701) ***(G-5172)***
TMC Corporation ... 609 860-1830
335 High St Bldg B1 Metuchen (08840) ***(G-6078)***
Tmg Enterprises Inc (PA) ... 732 469-2900
200 Circle Dr N Piscataway (08854) ***(G-8728)***
Tms International LLC ... 732 721-7477
1 Crossman Rd N Sayreville (08872) ***(G-9725)***
TMU Inc ... 609 884-7656
910 Shunpike Rd Ste A Cape May (08204) ***(G-1103)***
Tnss Enterprises, Bloomfield *Also called Ultimate Hair World Ltd Lblty* ***(G-521)***
Toadhall Promotions, Manasquan *Also called Winemiller Press Inc* ***(G-5843)***
Toby-Yanni Incorporated ... 973 253-9800
62 Plauderville Ave Garfield (07026) ***(G-3773)***
Tocad America Inc (HQ) ... 973 627-9600
53 Green Pond Rd Ste 4 Rockaway (07866) ***(G-9505)***
Todd Shelton LLC ... 844 626-6355
450 Murray Hill Pkwy C2 East Rutherford (07073) ***(G-2326)***
Tof Energy Corporation ... 908 691-2422
90 Washington Valley Rd Bedminster (07921) ***(G-280)***
Tofutti Brands Inc ... 908 272-2400
50 Jackson Dr Cranford (07016) ***(G-1928)***
Toilettree Products Inc ... 845 358-5316
41 Orchard St Ste 1 Ramsey (07446) ***(G-9157)***
Token Torch Ltd Liability Co ... 973 629-1805
3 Hudson Ave East Orange (07018) ***(G-2266)***
Tolan Machinery Company Inc ... 973 983-7212
164 Franklin Ave Rockaway (07866) ***(G-9506)***
Tolan Machinery Polishing Co ... 973 983-7212
164 Franklin Ave Rockaway (07866) ***(G-9507)***
Tolin Design Inc ... 201 261-4455
16 Bland St Emerson (07630) ***(G-2869)***
Toll Compaction Group, Neptune *Also called Toll Compaction Service Inc* ***(G-6902)***
Toll Compaction Service Inc (PA) ... 732 776-8225
14 Memorial Dr Neptune (07753) ***(G-6902)***
Tollgrade Communications Inc ... 732 743-6720
30 Knightsbridge Rd # 602 Piscataway (08854) ***(G-8729)***
Toltec Products LLC ... 908 832-2131
68 Beavers Rd Califon (07830) ***(G-1035)***
Tom James Company ... 732 826-8400
581 Cortlandt St Perth Amboy (08861) ***(G-8536)***
Tom James of Perth Amboy 2, Perth Amboy *Also called Tom James Company* ***(G-8536)***
Tom Ponte Model Makers Inc ... 973 627-5906
25 Pine St Ste 2 Rockaway (07866) ***(G-9508)***

Tomasello Winery Inc (PA) 609 561-0567
225 N White Horse Pike Hammonton (08037) ***(G-4145)***
Tomcel Machine Inc 973 256-8257
86 Lackawanna Ave Ste 301 Woodland Park (07424) ***(G-12093)***
Tomken Plating 856 829-0607
625 Pear St Cinnaminson (08077) ***(G-1491)***
Tommax Inc 732 224-1046
65 Mechanic St Ste 205 Red Bank (07701) ***(G-9246)***
Tommys Pallet Yard LLC 609 424-3996
2499 Old York Rd Bordentown (08505) ***(G-596)***
Toms River Printing Corp 732 240-2033
11 S Tamarack Dr Brielle (08730) ***(G-909)***
Tomwar Corp 856 740-0111
413 Paradise Rd Williamstown (08094) ***(G-11981)***
Tone Embroidery Corp 201 943-1082
333 Bergen Blvd Fairview (07022) ***(G-3371)***
Toni Embroidery 201 664-6909
185 W Leach Ave Park Ridge (07656) ***(G-7860)***
Tony Jones Apparel Inc 973 773-6200
300-1 State Rt 17 S 1c Lodi (07644) ***(G-5580)***
Tonymacx86 LLC 973 584-5273
23 Lookout Dr Ledgewood (07852) ***(G-5283)***
Tonys Auto Entp Ltd Lblty Co 203 223-5776
98 Loring Ave Edison (08817) ***(G-2633)***
Too Cool of Ocean City 908 810-6363
530 N Michigan Ave Kenilworth (07033) ***(G-4982)***
Tool Shop Inc 856 767-8077
335 Chestnut Ave West Berlin (08091) ***(G-11630)***
Tooling & Mfg Unlimited, Cape May *Also called TMU Inc* ***(G-1103)***
Tooling Etc LLC 732 752-8080
250 Hallock Ave Middlesex (08846) ***(G-6156)***
Top Knobs Usa Inc (HQ) 908 359-6174
3 Millennium Way Somerville (08876) ***(G-10126)***
Top Line Seating Inc 908 241-9051
540 S 31st St Kenilworth (07033) ***(G-4983)***
Top Rated Shopping Bargains 800 556-5849
92 Railroad Ave Ste 105 Hasbrouck Heights (07604) ***(G-4190)***
Top Safety Products Company 908 707-8680
160 Meister Ave Ste 16 Branchburg (08876) ***(G-689)***
Topcon America Corporation (HQ) 201 599-5100
111 Bauer Dr Oakland (07436) ***(G-7646)***
Topcon Medical Systems Inc (HQ) 201 599-5100
111 Bauer Dr Oakland (07436) ***(G-7647)***
Topifram Laboratories Inc 201 894-9020
440 Sylvan Ave Ste 100 Englewood Cliffs (07632) ***(G-2992)***
Toppan Printing Co Amer Inc 732 469-8400
1100 Randolph Rd Somerset (08873) ***(G-10088)***
Toppan Vintage Inc 201 226-9220
109 5th St Saddle Brook (07663) ***(G-9684)***
Torelco Inc 908 387-0814
55 Industrial Rd Alpha (08865) ***(G-43)***
Tornqvist Div, Wayne *Also called Grimbilas Enterprises Corp* ***(G-11514)***
Torpac Capsules, Fairfield *Also called Torpac Inc* ***(G-3330)***
Torpac Inc (PA) 973 244-1125
333 Us Highway 46 Fairfield (07004) ***(G-3330)***
Torque Gun Co, The, South Hackensack *Also called Torque Gun Company LLC* ***(G-10189)***
Torque Gun Company LLC 201 512-9800
120 Wesley St South Hackensack (07606) ***(G-10189)***
Torrent Pharma Inc (HQ) 269 544-2299
150 Allen Rd Ste 102 Basking Ridge (07920) ***(G-199)***
Toscana Cheese Company Inc 201 617-1500
575 Windsor Dr Secaucus (07094) ***(G-9821)***
Toshiba Amer Consmr Pdts Inc 973 628-8000
82 Totowa Rd Wayne (07470) ***(G-11558)***
Total American Services Inc (HQ) 206 626-3500
100 Town Square Pl # 401 Jersey City (07310) ***(G-4822)***
Total Control Othotics Lab 609 499-2200
14 W Front St Florence (08518) ***(G-3479)***
Total Cover It LLC 973 342-4623
223 Waverly Pl South Orange (07079) ***(G-10202)***
Total Garage Solutions LLC 732 749-3993
1709 State Route 34 Ste 2 Wall Township (07727) ***(G-11375)***
Total Image and Sign 201 941-2307
719 Grand Ave Ste 1 Ridgefield (07657) ***(G-9291)***
Total Ink Solutions LLC 201 487-9600
200 S Newman St Unit 4 Hackensack (07601) ***(G-3983)***
Total Installations 908 943-3211
941 Olive St Elizabeth (07201) ***(G-2782)***
Total Logistics, Hainesport *Also called T Wiker Enterprises Inc* ***(G-4079)***
Total Lubricants USA, Linden *Also called Total Specialties Usa Inc* ***(G-5436)***
Total Reliance LLC 732 640-5079
11b Corn Rd Dayton (08810) ***(G-1993)***
Total Relief Services, Livingston *Also called Max Pro Services LLC* ***(G-5523)***
Total Remodeling, Elizabeth *Also called Total Installations* ***(G-2782)***
Total Specialties Usa Inc 908 862-9300
5 N Stiles St Linden (07036) ***(G-5436)***
Total Tech Medical LLC 973 980-6458
289 Munt Hope Ave Apt J14 Dover (07801) ***(G-2109)***
Total Technology Inc 856 617-0502
950 Kings Hwy N Ste 105 Cherry Hill (08034) ***(G-1423)***
Totalcat Group Inc (HQ) 908 497-9610
135 Dermody St Cranford (07016) ***(G-1929)***
Totally T Shirts & More Inc 609 894-0011
201 W Hampton St Pemberton (08068) ***(G-8358)***
Totowa Asphalt, Parsippany *Also called Tilcon New York Inc* ***(G-8028)***
Totowa Kickboxing Ltd Lblty Co 973 507-9106
1 Us Highway 46 Totowa (07512) ***(G-10855)***
Totowa Metal Fabricators Inc 973 423-1943
40 Lee Dr North Haledon (07508) ***(G-7501)***
Touch Dynamic Inc (PA) 732 382-5701
121 Corporate Blvd South Plainfield (07080) ***(G-10331)***
Touch of Class Promotions LLC 267 994-0860
19 Festival Dr Voorhees (08043) ***(G-11296)***
Touch of Lace, Fairview *Also called Tone Embroidery Corp* ***(G-3371)***
Touchboards, Long Branch *Also called Inter World Highway LLC* ***(G-5599)***
Toufayan Bakeries, Ridgefield *Also called Toufayan Bakery Inc* ***(G-9292)***
Toufayan Bakery Inc (PA) 201 941-2000
175 Railroad Ave Ridgefield (07657) ***(G-9292)***
Tovatech LLC 973 913-9734
205 Rutgers St Maplewood (07040) ***(G-5885)***
Tovli Inc 718 417-6677
49 Hunter St Newark (07114) ***(G-7301)***
Tower Systems Inc 732 237-8800
235 Hickory Ln Bayville (08721) ***(G-251)***
Town & Country Plastics Inc 732 780-5300
10b Timber Ln Marlboro (07746) ***(G-5917)***
Town Ford Inc 609 298-4990
860 Us Highway 206 Bordentown (08505) ***(G-597)***
Town of Hackettstown, The, Hackettstown *Also called Hackettstown Public Works* ***(G-4010)***
Towne Technologies Inc 908 722-9500
6-10 Bell Ave Somerville (08876) ***(G-10127)***
Townsend Machine Inc 609 723-2603
246 Sykesville Rd Chesterfield (08515) ***(G-1438)***
Township of Carneys Point 856 299-4973
Walker Ave & D St Carneys Point (08069) ***(G-1244)***
Toydriver LLC 678 637-8500
100 Outwater Ln Garfield (07026) ***(G-3774)***
Toyo Ink America LLC 201 804-0620
350 Starke Rd Ste 400 Carlstadt (07072) ***(G-1230)***
Toyota Motor Sales 973 515-5012
300 Webro Rd Parsippany (07054) ***(G-8030)***
Toys "R" Us, Parsippany *Also called Toysruscom Inc* ***(G-8031)***
Toysruscom Inc 973 617-3500
5 Woodhollow Rd Ste 1 Parsippany (07054) ***(G-8031)***
Tpg Graphics LLC 856 314-0117
9130 Pennsauken Hwy Ste C Pennsauken (08110) ***(G-8493)***
Tpi Partners Inc 908 561-3000
1268 Valley Rd Stirling (07980) ***(G-10498)***
Tq3 north America Inc (PA) 973 882-7900
23 Commerce Rd Ste I Fairfield (07004) ***(G-3331)***
Trac Intermodal LLC (HQ) 609 452-8900
750 College Rd E Princeton (08540) ***(G-9034)***
Trac Interstar LLC, Princeton *Also called Fyx Fleet Roadside Assistance* ***(G-8953)***
Tracer Tool & Machine Co Inc (PA) 201 337-6184
32 Iron Horse Rd Oakland (07436) ***(G-7648)***
Track Systems Inc 201 462-0095
174 Boulevard Ste 6 Hasbrouck Heights (07604) ***(G-4191)***
Trade Images, Buena *Also called CPB Inc* ***(G-939)***
Trade Thermographers Inc 201 489-2060
82 Chestnut Ave Rochelle Park (07662) ***(G-9432)***
Trademark Plastics Corporation 908 925-5900
494 Broad St Rm 202 Newark (07102) ***(G-7302)***
Trademarksign 848 223-4548
631 Herman Rd Jackson (08527) ***(G-4667)***
Tradewinds Marine Service 848 448-6888
122 Eton Ct Toms River (08757) ***(G-10800)***
Traffic Safety & Equipment Co 201 327-6050
457 State Rt 17 Mahwah (07430) ***(G-5783)***
Trane Inc (HQ) 732 652-7100
1 Centennial Ave Ste 101 Piscataway (08854) ***(G-8730)***
Trane Parts Center of NJ 201 489-9001
375 North St Ste J Teterboro (07608) ***(G-10695)***
Trane US Inc 732 652-7100
1 Centennial Ave Ste 101 Piscataway (08854) ***(G-8731)***
Trane US Inc 609 587-3400
2231 E State Street Ext Trenton (08619) ***(G-11000)***
Trane US Inc 973 882-3220
26 Chapin Rd Ste 1103 Pine Brook (07058) ***(G-8618)***
Trano Bruce Plumbing & Heating 908 654-3685
872 Woodland Ave Mountainside (07092) ***(G-6853)***
Trans World Marketing Corp (PA) 201 935-5565
360 Murray Hill Pkwy East Rutherford (07073) ***(G-2327)***
Transaction Publishers Inc (PA) 732 445-2280
10 Corporate Pl S Ste 102 Piscataway (08854) ***(G-8732)***
Transaxle LLC (PA) 856 665-4445
2501 Route 73 Cinnaminson (08077) ***(G-1492)***

Transcore LP 201 329-9200
  25 Central Ave Teterboro (07608) *(G-10696)*

Transfer Truck & Equipment, Flanders *Also called Robert H Hoover & Sons Inc (G-3417)*

Transglobe Usa Inc 973 465-1998
  175 Broad St Carlstadt (07072) *(G-1231)*

Transistor Devices Inc (PA) 908 850-5088
  36 Newburgh Rd Hackettstown (07840) *(G-4039)*

Transistor Devices Inc 908 850-5088
  36 Newburgh Rd Hackettstown (07840) *(G-4040)*

Transmission Technology Co 973 305-3600
  1 High Mountain Trl Lincoln Park (07035) *(G-5307)*

Transport Products Inc 973 857-6090
  20 Village Park Rd Cedar Grove (07009) *(G-1294)*

Transportation Tech Svcs Inc 201 335-0238
  90 Mckee Dr Mahwah (07430) *(G-5784)*

Transtar Truck Body & Wldg Co 908 832-2688
  514 County Road 513 Califon (07830) *(G-1036)*

Trap Rock Industries Inc (PA) 609 924-0300
  460 River Rd Kingston (08528) *(G-5012)*

Trap Rock Industries Inc 609 924-0300
  Pennington Hwy Rr 31 Pennington (08534) *(G-8375)*

Trap Rock Industries Inc 609 924-0300
  Rr 29 Titusville (08560) *(G-10736)*

Trap Rock Industries LLC 609 924-0300
  460 River Rd Kingston (08528) *(G-5013)*

Trap-Zap Environmental Systems 201 251-9970
  255 Braen Ave Wyckoff (07481) *(G-12122)*

Travel Weekly 201 902-1931
  100 Lighting Way Ste 200 Secaucus (07094) *(G-9822)*

Traycon Manufacturing Co Inc 201 939-5555
  235 Main St Ste 204 Hackensack (07601) *(G-3984)*

Trb Electro Corp 973 278-9014
  6 Morris St Paterson (07501) *(G-8316)*

Treasure Chest Corp 973 328-7747
  10 N Main St Ste 1 Wharton (07885) *(G-11872)*

Treasure Hunt, Phillipsburg *Also called David Sisco Jr (G-8548)*

Tree-Ripe Products, East Hanover *Also called 201 Food Packing Inc (G-2192)*

Trek Inc 732 269-6300
  43 Cranmer Rd Bayville (08721) *(G-252)*

Trek II Products Inc 732 214-9200
  400 Jersey Ave Ste 1 New Brunswick (08901) *(G-6974)*

Tremont Printing Co 973 227-0742
  72 Deer Park Rd Fairfield (07004) *(G-3332)*

Trend Printing/Intl Label 201 941-6611
  1183 Edgewater Ave Ridgefield (07657) *(G-9293)*

Trendmark LLC 551 226-7973
  465 Meadow Rd Apt 10207 Princeton (08540) *(G-9035)*

Trent Box Manufacturing Co 609 587-7515
  1384 Yardville Ham Rd Trenton (08691) *(G-11001)*

Trenton Corrugated Products 609 695-0808
  17 Shelton Ave Ewing (08618) *(G-3070)*

Trenton Printing LLC 609 695-6485
  1150 Southard St Ste 2 Trenton (08638) *(G-11002)*

Trenton Sheet Metal Inc 609 695-6328
  30 Adam Ave Trenton (08618) *(G-11003)*

Trentypo Inc 609 883-5971
  304 Stokes Ave Ewing (08638) *(G-3071)*

Tresky Corp 732 536-8600
  704 Ginesi Dr Ste 11 Morganville (07751) *(G-6596)*

Tretina Printing Inc 732 264-2324
  1301 Concord Hwy 36 101 Hazlet (07730) *(G-4272)*

Trf Music Inc 201 335-0005
  106 Apple St Ste 302 Tinton Falls (07724) *(G-10732)*

Trf Production Music Libraries, Tinton Falls *Also called Trf Music Inc (G-10732)*

Tri Dim Filter, Cinnaminson *Also called Tri-Dim Filter Corporation (G-1493)*

Tri G Manufacturing LLC 732 460-1881
  8 Iroquois Ct Colts Neck (07722) *(G-1789)*

Tri Tech Telecom, Columbus *Also called Draztic Designs LLC (G-1800)*

Tri Tech Tool & Design Co Inc 732 469-5433
  30 Cherry St South Bound Brook (08880) *(G-10144)*

Tri-Chem Inc 973 751-9200
  681 Main St Ste 24 Belleville (07109) *(G-317)*

Tri-Cor Flexible Packaging Inc 973 940-1500
  27 Brookfield Dr Sparta (07871) *(G-10413)*

Tri-Delta Plastics, Hillsborough *Also called Brent River Corp (G-4307)*

Tri-Dim Filter, Lincoln Park *Also called Indoor Environmental Tech (G-5299)*

Tri-Dim Filter Corporation 856 786-2447
  1306 Sylvania Ave Cinnaminson (08077) *(G-1493)*

Tri-Dim Filter Corporation 973 709-1122
  600 Ryerson Rd Ste F Lincoln Park (07035) *(G-5308)*

Tri-G Manufacturing, Colts Neck *Also called Tri G Manufacturing LLC (G-1789)*

Tri-Met Industries Inc 908 231-0004
  36 Adamsville Rd Bridgewater (08807) *(G-897)*

Tri-Power Consulting Svcs LLC 973 227-7100
  2 Richwood Pl Denville (07834) *(G-2060)*

Tri-State Buns LLC 973 418-8323
  808 Warren St 810 Harrison (07029) *(G-4180)*

Tri-State Glass & Mirror Inc (PA) 732 591-5545
  11a Jocama Blvd Old Bridge (08857) *(G-7729)*

Tri-State Knife Grinding Corp 609 890-4989
  3 S Gold Dr Robbinsville (08691) *(G-9418)*

Tri-State Orthopedic, Mount Laurel *Also called Zimmer Inc (G-6814)*

Tri-State Quikrete 973 347-4569
  150 Gold Mine Rd Flanders (07836) *(G-3423)*

Tri-Steel Fabricators Inc 609 392-8660
  501 Prospect St Trenton (08618) *(G-11004)*

Triad Scientific Inc 732 292-1994
  6 Stockton Lake Blvd Manasquan (08736) *(G-5841)*

Triad Tool & Die Co 908 534-1784
  9 Commerce St Branchburg (08876) *(G-690)*

Triaddisplay, Hillsborough *Also called Aura Signs Inc (G-4302)*

Triangle Automatic Inc 973 625-3830
  105 W Dewey Ave Ste 305 Wharton (07885) *(G-11873)*

Triangle Home Fashions LLC 732 355-9800
  120 Tices Ln East Brunswick (08816) *(G-2187)*

Triangle Ink Co Inc (PA) 201 935-2777
  53-57 Van Dyke St Wallington (07057) *(G-11390)*

Triangle Manufacturing Co 201 962-7433
  116 Pleasant Ave Upper Saddle River (07458) *(G-11147)*

Triangle Manufacturing Co Inc 201 825-1212
  120 Pleasant Ave Upper Saddle River (07458) *(G-11148)*

Triangle Reprocenter, Toms River *Also called R V Livolsi Incorporated (G-10786)*

Triangle Tube/Phase III Co Inc 856 228-9940
  1240 Forest Pkwy Ste 100 Paulsboro (08066) *(G-8340)*

Triarco Industries LLC 973 942-5100
  259 Prospect Plains Rd A Cranbury (08512) *(G-1887)*

Tribuna Hispana 609 646-9167
  1614 Dolphin Ave Pleasantville (08232) *(G-8820)*

Trico Web LLC 201 438-3860
  75 Broad St Carlstadt (07072) *(G-1232)*

Tricomp Inc 973 835-1110
  230 W Parkway Ste 14 Pompton Plains (07444) *(G-8872)*

Tricorbraun Inc 732 353-7104
  111 Interstate Blvd Monroe Township (08831) *(G-6349)*

Triefeldt Studios Inc 609 656-2380
  1115 Hamilton Ave Trenton (08629) *(G-11005)*

Triflow Corporation 856 768-7159
  150 Cooper Rd Ste A1 West Berlin (08091) *(G-11631)*

Triflow Specialties, West Berlin *Also called Triflow Corporation (G-11631)*

Trifluent Pharma LLC 210 552-2057
  10-16 Aquarium Dr Secaucus (07094) *(G-9823)*

Triform Products Inc 973 278-2042
  164 W Parkway Pompton Plains (07444) *(G-8873)*

Trigen Laboratories LLC 732 721-0070
  400 Crossing Blvd Bridgewater (08807) *(G-898)*

Trilenium Salvage Co 732 462-2909
  147 Tennent Rd Morganville (07751) *(G-6597)*

Trillium US 973 827-1661
  3627 State Rt 23 Hamburg (07419) *(G-4096)*

Trilogy Publications LLC 201 816-1211
  560 Sylvan Ave Ste 1240 Englewood Cliffs (07632) *(G-2993)*

Trim and Tassels LLC 973 808-1566
  333 Us Highway 46 B Fairfield (07004) *(G-3333)*

Trim Brush Company Inc 973 887-2525
  22 Littell Rd Bldg 1 East Hanover (07936) *(G-2243)*

Trim Factory Inc 856 769-8546
  1210 Route 40 Pilesgrove (08098) *(G-8581)*

Trimarco Inc 973 762-7380
  1847 Springfield Ave # 1849 Maplewood (07040) *(G-5886)*

Trimline Medical Products Corp 908 429-0590
  34 Columbia Rd Branchburg (08876) *(G-691)*

Trimtex Company Inc 201 945-2151
  325 Sylvan Ave Ste 102 Englewood Cliffs (07632) *(G-2994)*

Trinity Heating & Air Inc (PA) 732 780-3779
  2211 Allenwood Rd Wall Township (07719) *(G-11376)*

Trinity Manufacturing LLC 732 549-2866
  60 Leonard St Metuchen (08840) *(G-6079)*

Trinity Plastics Inc (HQ) 973 994-8018
  9 Peach Tree Hill Rd Livingston (07039) *(G-5543)*

Trinity Press Inc 973 881-0690
  655 Market St Paterson (07513) *(G-8317)*

Trinity Solar Systems, Wall Township *Also called Trinity Heating & Air Inc (G-11376)*

Triple D Enterprises Inc 609 859-3000
  135 Eayrestown Rd Southampton (08088) *(G-10373)*

Triple S Industries 908 862-0110
  1108 E Linden Ave Linden (07036) *(G-5437)*

Triple-T Cutting Tools Inc 856 768-0800
  135 Edgewood Ave Ste A West Berlin (08091) *(G-11632)*

Tripp Nyc Inc 201 520-0420
  5200 W Side Ave North Bergen (07047) *(G-7441)*

Tris Pharma Inc 732 940-0358
  2031 Us Highway 130 Ste H Monmouth Junction (08852) *(G-6315)*

Tris Pharma Inc (PA) 732 940-2800
  2033 Rte 130 Ste D Monmouth Junction (08852) *(G-6316)*

Tristate Crating Pallet Co Inc 973 357-8293
  85 Fulton St Paterson (07501) *(G-8318)*

Trisys Inc 973 360-2300
  215 Ridgedale Ave Ste 2 Florham Park (07932) *(G-3523)*

A L P H A B E T I C

Triton Associated Industries 856 697-3050
  N Brewster Rd Buena (08310) *(G-944)*

Triumph Brewing of Princeton 609 773-0111
  287 S Main St Ste 16 Lambertville (08530) *(G-5198)*

Triumph Knitting Machine Svc (PA) 201 646-0022
  238 Main St Ste 102 Hackensack (07601) *(G-3985)*

Triumph Plastics LLC 973 584-5500
  99 Bartley Flanders Rd Flanders (07836) *(G-3424)*

Trodat Usa Inc (HQ) 732 529-8500
  48 Heller Park Ln Somerset (08873) *(G-10089)*

Trodat USA LLC 732 562-9500
  48 Heller Park Ln Somerset (08873) *(G-10090)*

Trolex Corporation 201 794-8004
  6 Aspen Dr Randolph (07869) *(G-9204)*

Tronex International Inc (PA) 973 335-2888
  300 International Dr Budd Lake (07828) *(G-938)*

Tropaion Inc 908 654-3870
  955 S Springfield Ave C302 Springfield (07081) *(G-10469)*

Trophy King Inc 201 836-1482
  309 Queen Anne Rd Teaneck (07666) *(G-10653)*

Tropical Cheese Industries (PA) 732 442-4898
  452 Fayette St Perth Amboy (08861) *(G-8537)*

Tropical Expressions Inc 732 899-8680
  2127 Bridge Ave Point Pleasant Boro (08742) *(G-8846)*

Troy Corporation (PA) 973 443-4200
  8 Vreeland Rd Florham Park (07932) *(G-3524)*

Troy Hills Manufacturing Inc 973 263-1885
  2 Como Ct Towaco (07082) *(G-10882)*

Troy-Onic Inc 973 584-6830
  90 N Dell Ave Kenvil (07847) *(G-4996)*

Trs Containers, Avenel Also called Trs Inc *(G-151)*

Trs Inc 732 636-3300
  301 Essex Ave E Avenel (07001) *(G-151)*

Tru Mfg Corp 201 768-4050
  40 Oak St Ste 2 Norwood (07648) *(G-7576)*

Tru Temp Sensors Inc 215 396-1550
  113 Breton Ct Ocean City (08226) *(G-7698)*

Truckeros News LLC 732 340-1043
  1720 Lawrence St Rahway (07065) *(G-9129)*

Truckpro LLC 201 229-0599
  150 Central Ave Teterboro (07608) *(G-10697)*

Truckpro 192, Teterboro Also called Truckpro LLC *(G-10697)*

Trucktech Parts & Services 973 799-0500
  13 Avenue C Newark (07114) *(G-7303)*

True Influence LLC (PA) 888 223-1586
  103 Carnegie Ctr Ste 300 Princeton (08540) *(G-9036)*

True Romance, Englewood Cliffs Also called Paul Winston Fine Jewelry Grou *(G-2986)*

Truefort Inc 201 766-2023
  3 W 18th St Weehawken (07086) *(G-11571)*

Trugman-Nash, Millburn Also called McT Dairies Inc *(G-6203)*

Truimph Knitting Mills, Hackensack Also called Triumph Knitting Machine Svc *(G-3985)*

Trukmann's Reprographics, Cedar Knolls Also called Trukmanns Inc *(G-1314)*

Trukmanns Inc 973 538-7718
  4 Wing Dr Cedar Knolls (07927) *(G-1314)*

Trumpf Inc 609 925-8200
  2601 Route 130 Cranbury (08512) *(G-1888)*

Trumpf Photonics Inc 609 925-8200
  2601 Us Highway 130 Cranbury (08512) *(G-1889)*

Truss Engineering 201 871-4800
  120 Charlotte Pl Ste 206 Englewood (07632) *(G-2948)*

Tryco Tool & Mfg Co Inc 973 674-6867
  363 S Jefferson St Orange (07050) *(G-7764)*

Trylon, Lyndhurst Also called Marchione Industries Inc *(G-5661)*

Tsb, Harrison Also called Tri-State Buns LLC *(G-4180)*

Tsg LLC 732 372-7668
  1130 King Georges Post Rd Edison (08837) *(G-2634)*

Tsg Cabinets, Edison Also called Shekia Group LLC *(G-2608)*

Tsg Inc 973 785-1118
  28 Muller Pl Little Falls (07424) *(G-5471)*

Tsi Nomenclature Inc 732 340-0646
  1400 Rahway Ave Avenel (07001) *(G-152)*

Ttss Interactive Products Inc 301 230-1464
  100 Riverdale Rd Riverdale (07457) *(G-9388)*

Tube Craft of America Inc 856 629-5626
  667 Lebanon Ave Williamstown (08094) *(G-11982)*

Tube Line, New Brunswick Also called Nippon Benkan Kagyo *(G-6954)*

Tuckahoe Brewing Company LLC 609 645-2739
  3092 English Creek Ave Egg Harbor Twp (08234) *(G-2703)*

Tuckahoe Manufacturing Inc 856 696-4100
  327 Tuckahoe Rd Vineland (08360) *(G-11271)*

Tuckahoe Sand & Gravel Co Inc 609 861-2082
  2819 Fire Rd Egg Harbor Township (08234) *(G-2699)*

Tucker International LLC 856 216-1333
  460 Veterans Dr B Burlington (08016) *(G-988)*

Tuerff Sziber Capitol Copy Svc 609 989-8776
  116 W State St Trenton (08608) *(G-11006)*

Tuff Mfg Co Inc 201 796-5319
  4 Midland Ave Elmwood Park (07407) *(G-2858)*

Tuff Mutters LLC 973 291-6679
  2 Kiel Ave Unit 155 Kinnelon (07405) *(G-5022)*

Tulex Pharmaceuticals Inc 609 619-3098
  5 Cedarbrook Dr Cranbury (08512) *(G-1890)*

Tumi Holdings Inc (HQ) 908 756-4400
  499 Thornall St Ste 10 Edison (08837) *(G-2635)*

Tun Tavern Brewery & Rest, Atlantic City Also called Headquarters Pub LLC *(G-94)*

Tunnel Barrel & Drum Co Inc 201 933-1444
  329 Veterans Blvd Carlstadt (07072) *(G-1233)*

Tunnel Networks Inc 609 414-9799
  53 Winchester Dr East Windsor (08520) *(G-2363)*

Turbine Tek Inc 973 872-0903
  130 Ryerson Ave Ste 303 Wayne (07470) *(G-11559)*

Turbo Solutions LLC (PA) 856 209-6900
  8500 Remington Ave Unit 1 Pennsauken (08110) *(G-8494)*

Turbon International Inc (HQ) 800 282-6650
  4 Executive Campus # 104 Cherry Hill (08002) *(G-1424)*

Turbon International Inc 413 386-6739
  4 Executive Campus # 104 Cherry Hill (08002) *(G-1425)*

Turbon USA, Cherry Hill Also called Turbon International Inc *(G-1424)*

Turbot Hq Inc (PA) 973 922-0297
  105 Oakview Ave Maplewood (07040) *(G-5887)*

Turn-Key Technologies Inc 732 553-9100
  2400 Main St Ste 11 Sayreville (08872) *(G-9726)*

Turner Engineering Inc 973 263-1000
  14 Morris Ave Mountain Lakes (07046) *(G-6829)*

Turning Star Inc 201 881-7077
  600 Willow Tree Rd Leonia (07605) *(G-5294)*

Turnkey Solutions, Mahwah Also called Envirnmntal Mgt Chem Wste Svcs *(G-5735)*

Turquoise Chemistry Inc 908 561-0002
  537 New Durham Rd Piscataway (08854) *(G-8733)*

Turul Bookbindery Inc 973 361-2810
  60 State Route 15 S Wharton (07885) *(G-11874)*

Tusa Products Inc 609 448-8333
  1515 Parkway Ave Ewing (08628) *(G-3072)*

Tuscan/Lehigh Dairies Inc (HQ) 570 385-1884
  117 Cumberland Blvd Burlington (08016) *(G-989)*

Tuscany Especially Itln Foods 732 308-1118
  13a S Main St Store 5 Marlboro (07746) *(G-5918)*

TWI Pharmaceuticals Usa Inc 201 762-1410
  115 W Century Rd Ste 180 Paramus (07652) *(G-7842)*

Twill Inc 908 665-1700
  22 Russo Pl Berkeley Heights (07922) *(G-413)*

Twinpod Inc 908 758-5858
  252 Nassau St Princeton (08542) *(G-9037)*

Twisted Networking, Freehold Also called Custom Business Software LLC *(G-3660)*

Two 12 Fashion LLC 848 222-1562
  1525 Prospect St Ste 205 Lakewood (08701) *(G-5173)*

Two Jays Bingo Supply Inc (PA) 609 267-4542
  709 Park Ave E Hainesport (08036) *(G-4080)*

Two Jays Specialties, Hainesport Also called Two Jays Bingo Supply Inc *(G-4080)*

Two Little Guys Co 973 744-7502
  107 Trumbull St Ste 102 Elizabeth (07206) *(G-2783)*

Two Little Guys Lemonade Co, Elizabeth Also called Two Little Guys Co *(G-2783)*

Two River Times, Red Bank Also called Dyer Communications Inc *(G-9227)*

Two Rivers Coffee LLC 908 205-0018
  101 Kentile Rd Unit 13 South Plainfield (07080) *(G-10332)*

Two Vic's Sports Stop, Glassboro Also called Sports Stop Inc *(G-3819)*

TX Technology LLC 973 442-7500
  100 Ford Rd Ste 18 Denville (07834) *(G-2061)*

Tyco International MGT Co LLC (HQ) 609 720-4200
  9 Roszel Rd Ste 2 Princeton (08540) *(G-9038)*

Tycom Limited (HQ) 973 753-3040
  10 Park Ave Morristown (07960) *(G-6704)*

Typecom LLC (PA) 201 969-1901
  1275 15th St Apt 19a Fort Lee (07024) *(G-3591)*

Typeline 201 251-2201
  506 Spencer Dr Wyckoff (07481) *(G-12123)*

Typen Graphics Inc 973 838-6544
  170 Kinnelon Rd Rm 12 Kinnelon (07405) *(G-5023)*

Typestyle Inc 201 343-3343
  222 River St Hackensack (07601) *(G-3986)*

Tyson Fresh Meats Inc 605 235-2061
  5 Becker Farm Rd Ste 408 Roseland (07068) *(G-9543)*

Tyz-All Plastics LLC 201 343-1200
  130 Gamewell St Hackensack (07601) *(G-3987)*

U I S Industries Inc (PA) 201 946-2600
  15 Exchange Pl Ste 1120 Jersey City (07302) *(G-4823)*

U J Ramelson Co Inc 973 589-5422
  165 Thomas St Newark (07114) *(G-7304)*

U P N Pallet Co Inc 856 299-1192
  305 N Virginia Ave Penns Grove (08069) *(G-8379)*

U S 1 Publishing Co, Lawrence Township Also called Richard Rein *(G-5219)*

U S A Distributors Inc 201 348-1959
  3510 Bergenline Ave Ste 4 Union City (07087) *(G-11130)*

U S Box, Fairfield Also called United States Box Corp *(G-3336)*

U S Ink Division, East Rutherford Also called Sun Chemical Corporation *(G-2322)*

U S Laser Corp 201 848-9200
  41 Crest Rd Hillsdale (07642) *(G-4371)*

U S Screening Corp...............................973 242-1110
  780 Frelinghuysen Ave Newark (07114) *(G-7305)*

U S Silica Company...............................856 785-0720
  9035 Noble St Mauricetown (08329) *(G-5991)*

U S Tech Solutions Inc (PA)....................201 524-9600
  10 Exchange Pl Ste 1710 Jersey City (07302) *(G-4824)*

U T C, Rockaway *Also called Ultimate Trading Corp (G-9509)*

U V International, Morristown *Also called U V International LLC (G-6705)*

U V International LLC (PA).....................973 993-9454
  360 Mount Kemble Ave # 2 Morristown (07960) *(G-6705)*

Uac Packaging LLC..............................908 595-6890
  330 Roycefield Rd Unit C Hillsborough (08844) *(G-4361)*

Ubertesters Inc..................................201 203-7903
  72 S Maple Ave Ridgewood (07450) *(G-9333)*

Ubi, Plainfield *Also called United Bedding Industries LLC (G-8779)*

Udico, Kearny *Also called United Die Company Inc (G-4902)*

Uehling Instrument Company, Garfield *Also called Pavan & Kievit Enterprises (G-3754)*

Uff, Hillside *Also called United Forms Finishing Corp (G-4434)*

Ufp Berlin LLC...................................856 767-0596
  159 Jackson Rd Berlin (08009) *(G-431)*

Uhlmann Packaging Systems LP...............973 402-8855
  44 Indian Ln E Towaco (07082) *(G-10883)*

Ukrainian National Association (PA)..........973 292-9800
  2200 State Rt 10 Ste 201 Parsippany (07054) *(G-8032)*

Ulma Form-Works Inc (HQ)....................201 882-1122
  58 5th Ave Hawthorne (07506) *(G-4247)*

Ultimate Hair World Ltd Lblty.................973 622-6900
  16 Molter Pl Bloomfield (07003) *(G-521)*

Ultimate Home Products Div, Kearny *Also called Marcotex International Inc (G-4883)*

Ultimate Outdoors, Glen Gardner *Also called Vision Railings Ltd Lblty Co (G-3824)*

Ultimate Spinning Turning Corp..............201 372-9740
  9 Willow St Moonachie (07074) *(G-6495)*

Ultimate Textile, Paterson *Also called Pecata Enterprises Inc (G-8280)*

Ultimate Trading Corp..........................973 228-7700
  385 Franklin Ave Ste A Rockaway (07866) *(G-9509)*

Ultimate Trining Munitions Inc (PA)..........908 725-9000
  55 Readington Rd Branchburg (08876) *(G-692)*

Ultra Chemical Inc (PA)........................732 224-0200
  2 Bridge Ave Ste 631 Red Bank (07701) *(G-9247)*

Ultra Clean Technologies Corp................856 451-2176
  1274 Highway 77 Bridgeton (08302) *(G-776)*

Ultra Electronics Herley, Whippany *Also called Herley-Cti Inc (G-11896)*

Ultraflex Systems Florida Inc.................973 627-8608
  1578 Sussex Tpke Ste 400 Randolph (07869) *(G-9205)*

Um Equity Corp (HQ)...........................856 354-2200
  56 N Haddon Ave Ste 300 Haddonfield (08033) *(G-4065)*

Umbrella & Chairs LLC.........................973 284-1240
  8 Old Quarry Rd Englewood (07631) *(G-2949)*

Umbrella Publishing, Butler *Also called Jigsaw Publishing LLC (G-1006)*

Umbrellas Unlimited............................201 476-1011
  808 Rivervale Rd River Vale (07675) *(G-9368)*

Umc Inc...973 325-0031
  24 Burnett Ter West Orange (07052) *(G-11780)*

Umetal LLC.......................................862 257-3032
  219 Lafayette St Paterson (07524) *(G-8319)*

Umicore Precious Metals NJ LLC..............908 222-5006
  3950 S Clinton Ave South Plainfield (07080) *(G-10333)*

Umicore USA Inc................................908 226-2053
  3900 S Clinton Ave South Plainfield (07080) *(G-10334)*

Unalext, Middlesex *Also called Unique Amrcn Alum Extrsion LLC (G-6157)*

Uncle Eds Creamery............................609 818-0100
  155 W Delaware Ave Pennington (08534) *(G-8376)*

Uncle Jimmys Cheesecakes...................201 248-1820
  420 Palisade Ave Cliffside Park (07010) *(G-1545)*

Undercover Chocolate Co LLC................973 668-5000
  50 Williams Pkwy Ste B2 East Hanover (07936) *(G-2244)*

Unette Corporation..............................973 328-6800
  1578 Sussex Tpke Ste 5 Randolph (07869) *(G-9206)*

Unex Manufacturing Inc (PA)..................732 928-2800
  691 New Hampshire Ave Lakewood (08701) *(G-5174)*

Ungerer & Company............................973 628-0600
  4 Ungerer Way Lincoln Park (07035) *(G-5309)*

UNI-Tech Drilling Company Inc................856 694-4200
  61 Grays Ferry Rd Franklinville (08322) *(G-3641)*

UNI-Vac, Hamburg *Also called United Vacuum LLC (G-4097)*

Unicorn Group Inc (PA).........................973 360-0688
  25b Hanover Rd Florham Park (07932) *(G-3525)*

Unicorn Group Inc..............................973 360-5904
  23 Daniel Rd Fairfield (07004) *(G-3334)*

Unicorp..973 674-1700
  291 Cleveland St Orange (07050) *(G-7765)*

Unified Door & Hdwr Group LLC..............215 364-8834
  1650 Suckle Hwy Pennsauken (08110) *(G-8495)*

Unified Resources, Kenilworth *Also called Resources Inc In Display (G-4974)*

Unifoil Corporation..............................973 244-9900
  12 Daniel Rd Fairfield (07004) *(G-3335)*

Uniforms By Cozy, Nutley *Also called Cozy Formal Wear Inc (G-7583)*

Uniken Inc..917 324-0399
  466 Southern Blvd Ste 2 Chatham (07928) *(G-1331)*

Unilever Hpc-USA, Englewood Cliffs *Also called Unilever United States Inc (G-2995)*

Unilever United States Inc (HQ)...............201 735-9661
  700 Sylvan Ave Englewood Cliffs (07632) *(G-2995)*

Unilever United States Inc.....................800 298-5018
  800 Sylvan Ave Englewood Cliffs (07632) *(G-2996)*

Unilite Incorporated............................973 667-1674
  151 River Rd Nutley (07110) *(G-7596)*

Unilux Inc (HQ)..................................201 712-1266
  59 5th St Saddle Brook (07663) *(G-9685)*

Unimac Graphics LLC..........................201 372-1000
  350 Michele Pl Carlstadt (07072) *(G-1234)*

Union Beverage Packers LLC.................908 206-9111
  600 N Union Ave Ste 7 Hillside (07205) *(G-4432)*

Union Casting Industries Inc (PA)............908 686-8888
  2365 Us Highway 22 W Union (07083) *(G-11096)*

Union City Filament Corp......................201 945-3366
  1039 Hoyt Ave A Ridgefield (07657) *(G-9294)*

Union City Mirror & Table Co..................201 867-0050
  129 34th St Union City (07087) *(G-11131)*

Union City Whirlpool Repair...................908 428-9146
  507 43rd St Union City (07087) *(G-11132)*

Union Container Corp...........................973 242-3600
  439 Frelinghuysen Ave Newark (07114) *(G-7306)*

Union County Seating & Sup Co..............908 241-4949
  135 N Michigan Ave Kenilworth (07033) *(G-4984)*

Union Dry Dock & Repair Co (PA)............201 792-9090
  51 Newark St Ste 504 Hoboken (07030) *(G-4485)*

Union Dry Dock & Repair Co..................201 963-5833
  901 Sinatra Dr Hoboken (07030) *(G-4486)*

Union Hill Corp..................................732 786-9422
  29 Park Ave Englishtown (07726) *(G-3010)*

Union Institute Inc..............................800 914-8138
  67 Ramapo Valley Rd # 102 Mahwah (07430) *(G-5785)*

Union Tool & Mold Co Inc......................973 763-6611
  220 Rutgers St Maplewood (07040) *(G-5888)*

Unionmed Tech Inc.............................917 714-3418
  1031 Us Highway 202/206 # 101 Bridgewater (08807) *(G-899)*

Unionville Vineyards LLC......................908 788-0400
  9 Rocktown Rd Ringoes (08551) *(G-9342)*

Unionwear, Newark *Also called New Jersey Headwear Corp (G-7209)*

Unipack Inc......................................973 450-9880
  681 Main St Ste 27 Belleville (07109) *(G-318)*

UNIPACK,INC., Belleville *Also called Unipack Inc (G-318)*

Uniphy Health Holdings LLC..................844 586-4749
  211 Warren St Ste 507 Newark (07103) *(G-7307)*

Uniplast Industries Inc.........................201 288-4672
  1-5 Plant Rd Hasbrouck Heights (07604) *(G-4192)*

Uniport Industries Corporation................201 391-6422
  23 Campbell Ave Woodcliff Lake (07677) *(G-12067)*

Unipro, Totowa *Also called O T D Inc (G-10839)*

Unique Amrcn Alum Extrsion LLC............732 271-0006
  333 Cedar Ave Unit A Middlesex (08846) *(G-6157)*

Unique Embroidery Inc.........................201 943-9191
  64 Bushes Ln Elmwood Park (07407) *(G-2859)*

Unique Encapsulation Tech LLC..............973 448-2801
  9 Lenel Rd Landing (07850) *(G-5204)*

Unique Impressions Ltd Lblty.................201 751-4088
  718 25th St Union City (07087) *(G-11133)*

Unique Metal Products.........................732 388-1888
  17 W Scott Ave Rahway (07065) *(G-9130)*

Unique Precision Co Inc........................732 382-8699
  2095 Elizabeth Ave Rahway (07065) *(G-9131)*

Unique Screen Printing Corp..................908 925-3773
  10 Mckinley St 16 Linden (07036) *(G-5438)*

Unique Systems Inc............................973 455-0440
  4 Saddle Rd Cedar Knolls (07927) *(G-1315)*

Unique Wire Weaving Co Inc..................908 688-4600
  762 Ramsey Ave Hillside (07205) *(G-4433)*

Unique/Pereny, Ringoes *Also called Hed International Inc (G-9336)*

Uniquiwa's, Jersey City *Also called Ronald Perry (G-4801)*

Unisphere Media LLC..........................908 795-3701
  630 Central Ave New Providence (07974) *(G-7023)*

Unistar Creations, Princeton *Also called Unistar Inc (G-9039)*

Unistar Inc.......................................212 840-2100
  61 Castleton Rd Princeton (08540) *(G-9039)*

Unitao Nutraceuticals LLC.....................973 983-1121
  6 Reservoir Pl Rockaway (07866) *(G-9510)*

United Asphalt Company.......................856 753-9811
  237 N Grove St Berlin (08009) *(G-432)*

United Bedding Industries LLC................908 668-0220
  300 W 4th St Plainfield (07060) *(G-8779)*

United Cabinet Works LLC.....................917 686-3395
  550 County Ave Secaucus (07094) *(G-9824)*

United City Ice Cube Co Inc...................201 945-8387
  695 Elm Ave Ridgefield (07657) *(G-9295)*

United Crbral Plsy Bldg Blocks, Teaneck *Also called Advancing Opportunities Inc (G-10621)*

A
L
P
H
A
B
E
T
I
C

United Diam Inc 732 619-0950
  12 Grenoble Ct Matawan (07747) *(G-5990)*

United Die Company Inc 201 997-0250
  199 Devon Ter Kearny (07032) *(G-4902)*

United Energy Corp (PA) 732 994-5225
  3598 Us Highway 9 Ste 303 Howell (07731) *(G-4552)*

United Envelope, Ridgefield Also called Old Ue LLC *(G-9281)*

United Envelope LLC (HQ) 201 699-5800
  65 Railroad Ave Ridgefield (07657) *(G-9296)*

United Eqp Fabricators LLC 973 242-2737
  175 Orange St Newark (07103) *(G-7308)*

United Farm Processing Corp 856 451-4612
  458 Garrison Rd Rosenhayn (08352) *(G-9598)*

United Federated Systems, Totowa Also called T F S Inc *(G-10854)*

United Forms Finishing Corp 908 687-0494
  1413 Chestnut Ave Ste 2 Hillside (07205) *(G-4434)*

United Fuel Distributors LLC 908 906-9053
  103 Spisso Ct South Plainfield (07080) *(G-10335)*

United Gutter Supply Inc 201 933-6316
  1 Maple St Ste 1 # 1 East Rutherford (07073) *(G-2328)*

United Hospital Supply Corp 609 387-7580
  4422 Route 130 S Burlington (08016) *(G-990)*

United Instrument Company LLC 201 767-6000
  207 Washington St Ste A Northvale (07647) *(G-7552)*

United Label Corp 973 589-6500
  65 Chambers St Newark (07105) *(G-7309)*

United Machine Inc 973 345-4505
  239 Lindbergh Pl Ste 2a Paterson (07503) *(G-8320)*

United Medical PC 201 456-0222
  535 Lexington Ave Clifton (07011) *(G-1733)*

United Medical PC (PA) 201 339-6111
  988 Broadway Bayonne (07002) *(G-236)*

United Mijovi Amer Ltd Lblty 732 718-1001
  21 Roseland Pl New Brunswick (08902) *(G-6975)*

United Natural Trading Co 732 650-9905
  96 Executive Ave Edison (08817) *(G-2636)*

United Plastics Group Inc 732 873-8777
  30 Commerce Dr Somerset (08873) *(G-10091)*

United Pos Solutions Inc 800 303-2567
  535 Broad Ave Palisades Park (07650) *(G-7780)*

United Premium Foods LLC 732 510-5600
  1 Amboy Ave Woodbridge (07095) *(G-12023)*

United Resin Inc 856 358-2574
  321 Willow Grove Rd Elmer (08318) *(G-2805)*

United Ring & Seal Inc 610 253-3800
  7 Blackberry Ln Whitehouse Station (08889) *(G-11935)*

United Shippers Associates, Whippany Also called Corporate Mailings Inc *(G-11887)*

United Silica Products Inc 973 209-8854
  3 Park Dr Franklin (07416) *(G-3610)*

United Silicon Carbide Inc 732 355-0550
  7 Deerpark Dr Ste E Monmouth Junction (08852) *(G-6317)*

United Silicon Carbide Inc 732 565-9500
  100 Jersey Ave Bldg A New Brunswick (08901) *(G-6976)*

United Sound Arts Inc 732 229-4949
  1 Industrial Way W D-E Eatontown (07724) *(G-2427)*

United Spport Sltons - Lmt Inc (PA) 973 857-2298
  134 Sand Park Rd Cedar Grove (07009) *(G-1295)*

United State Annuities, Monroe Also called Webannuitiescom Inc *(G-6324)*

United States Box Corp 973 481-2000
  14 Madison Rd Ste E Fairfield (07004) *(G-3336)*

United States Cold Storage Inc (HQ) 856 354-8181
  2 Aquarium Dr Ste 400 Camden (08103) *(G-1089)*

United States Gypsum Company 732 636-7900
  300 Markley St Port Reading (07064) *(G-8896)*

United States Mineral Pdts Co (PA) 973 347-1200
  41 Furnace St Stanhope (07874) *(G-10480)*

United States Pipe Fndry LLC 609 387-6000
  1101 E Pearl St Ste 1 Burlington (08016) *(G-991)*

United Steel Products Co Inc 609 518-9230
  130 Mount Holly By Pass # 5 Lumberton (08048) *(G-5637)*

United Vacuum LLC 973 827-1661
  3627 State Rt 23 Bldg 3 Hamburg (07419) *(G-4097)*

United Window & Door Mfg Inc (PA) 973 912-0600
  24 Fadem Rd 36 Springfield (07081) *(G-10470)*

United Wire Hanger Corp 201 288-3212
  1-5 Plant Rd Hasbrouck Heights (07604) *(G-4193)*

Unitex International Inc 856 786-5000
  2702 Cindel Dr Ste 3 Cinnaminson (08077) *(G-1494)*

Unity Engraving Company, Englewood Also called Unity Graphics & Engraving Co *(G-2950)*

Unity Graphics & Engraving Co 201 541-5462
  210 S Van Brunt St Englewood (07631) *(G-2950)*

Unity Steel Rule Die Co 201 569-6400
  210 S Van Brunt St Englewood (07631) *(G-2951)*

Univeg Logistics America Inc 856 241-0097
  100 Dartmouth Dr Ste 400 Swedesboro (08085) *(G-10616)*

Universal Business Automation 973 575-3568
  170 Changebridge Rd D3 Montville (07045) *(G-6448)*

Universal Company, Bloomfield Also called Zwier Corp *(G-524)*

Universal Display Corporation (PA) 609 671-0980
  375 Phillips Blvd Ste 1 Ewing (08618) *(G-3073)*

Universal Electric Mtr Svc Inc 201 968-1000
  131 S Newman St Hackensack (07601) *(G-3988)*

Universal Filters Inc 732 774-8555
  1207 Main St Ste A Asbury Park (07712) *(G-85)*

Universal Forest Products, Berlin Also called Ufp Berlin LLC *(G-431)*

Universal Interlock Corp 732 818-8484
  910 Hooper Ave Toms River (08753) *(G-10801)*

Universal Labs, New Brunswick Also called Universal Prtein Spplmnts Corp *(G-6977)*

Universal Medical Inc 800 606-5511
  275 Phillips Blvd Ewing (08618) *(G-3074)*

Universal Metalcraft Inc 973 345-3284
  24 Burgess Pl Wayne (07470) *(G-11560)*

Universal Mold & Tool Inc 856 563-0488
  1200 S West Blvd Ste 4e Vineland (08360) *(G-11272)*

Universal Pallet Inc 732 356-2624
  118 Smoke Rise Dr Warren (07059) *(G-11434)*

Universal Parts 908 601-6558
  1057 Pennsylvania Ave Linden (07036) *(G-5439)*

Universal Parts New Jersey LLC 732 615-0626
  3 Chanowich Ct Middletown (07748) *(G-6167)*

Universal Prtein Spplmnts Corp (PA) 732 545-3130
  3 Terminal Rd New Brunswick (08901) *(G-6977)*

Universal Systems Installers 732 656-9002
  10 Red Oak Ct Monroe (08831) *(G-6323)*

Universal Tape Supply Corp (PA) 609 653-3191
  110 W New Jersey Ave Somers Point (08244) *(G-9940)*

Universal Thd & Scallop Cutng, North Bergen Also called Walker Eight Corp *(G-7443)*

Universal Tools & Mfg Co 973 379-4193
  115 Victory Rd Springfield (07081) *(G-10471)*

Universal Valve Company Inc 908 351-0606
  478 Schiller St Elizabeth (07206) *(G-2784)*

Universal Vending MGT LLC 908 233-4373
  425 North Ave E Ste 2 Westfield (07090) *(G-11804)*

University Fashions By Janet 856 228-1615
  1888 Winslow Rd Bldg B Williamstown (08094) *(G-11983)*

University Publications Inc 212 268-4222
  562 Morley Ct Belford (07718) *(G-284)*

Unlimited Print Products Inc 609 882-0653
  41 Lexington Ave Ewing (08618) *(G-3075)*

Unlimited Silk Screen Products, Ewing Also called Unlimited Print Products Inc *(G-3075)*

UOP LLC 973 455-2096
  115 Tabor Rd Morris Plains (07950) *(G-6627)*

Up Solution, Palisades Park Also called United Pos Solutions Inc *(G-7780)*

Up United LLC 718 383-5700
  495 N Bridge St Bridgewater (08807) *(G-900)*

Upfield US Inc 201 894-2540
  433 Hackensack Ave # 401 Hackensack (07601) *(G-3989)*

UPS Store 5952, Bordentown Also called Rbdel Inc *(G-594)*

UPS Store, The, Little Falls Also called Sre Ventures LLC *(G-5468)*

Uptown Bagels, Logan Township Also called Uptown Bakeries *(G-5589)*

Uptown Bakeries, Bridgeport Also called J & J Snack Foods Corp *(G-740)*

Uptown Bakeries 856 467-9552
  300 Eagle Ct Logan Township (08085) *(G-5589)*

Urban Millwork & Supply Corp 973 278-7072
  90 2nd Ave Paterson (07514) *(G-8321)*

Urban Sign & Crane Inc 856 691-8388
  527 E Chestnut Ave Vineland (08360) *(G-11273)*

Urban State 646 836-4311
  209 Hollywood Ave Hillside (07205) *(G-4435)*

Urigen Pharmaceuticals Inc 732 640-0160
  675 Us Highway 1 Ste 206b North Brunswick (08902) *(G-7491)*

Urso Fuel Corp 973 325-3324
  10 Rollinson St West Orange (07052) *(G-11781)*

US Advanced Materials Division, Parsippany Also called Sun Chemical Corporation *(G-8022)*

US Air Power Systems 201 892-5235
  56 Otoole St Westwood (07675) *(G-11846)*

US Blade Mfg Co Inc 908 272-2898
  90 Myrtle St Cranford (07016) *(G-1930)*

US China Allied Products Inc 201 461-9886
  555 North Ave Apt 12h Fort Lee (07024) *(G-3592)*

US Display Group Inc 931 455-9585
  100 Electric Ave Secaucus (07094) *(G-9825)*

US Frontline News Inc 646 284-6233
  139 Anderson Ave Demarest (07627) *(G-2026)*

US Gov Turamco, Carlstadt Also called Delta Procurement Inc *(G-1149)*

US Led Installation Group, Cherry Hill Also called Liberty Cnstr & Inv Group *(G-1383)*

US Magic Box Inc 973 772-2070
  221 Macarthur Ave Garfield (07026) *(G-3775)*

US Minerals, Stanhope Also called United States Mineral Pdts Co *(G-10480)*

US New Jersey Summit West, Summit Also called Celgene Corporation *(G-10528)*

US News & World Report Inc 212 716-6800
  99 Wood Ave S Ste 304 Iselin (08830) *(G-4634)*

US Outworkers LLC 973 362-1458
  6 Hunter Ridge Rd Sussex (07461) *(G-10569)*

US Pharma Lab Inc (PA) 888 296-8775
  22 Van Dyke Ave New Brunswick (08901) *(G-6978)*

US Pipe Fabrication LLC.............................856 461-3000
  200 Rhawn St Riverside (08075) *(G-9404)*

US Plastic Sales LLC................................908 754-9404
  651 Metuchen Rd South Plainfield (07080) *(G-10336)*

US Propack Inc......................................732 294-4500
  341 Fairfield Rd Freehold (07728) *(G-3702)*

US Sign and Lighting Svc LLC.......................973 305-8900
  105 Dorsa Ave Wayne (07470) *(G-11561)*

US Software Group Inc..............................732 361-4636
  1550 Park Ave Ste 202 South Plainfield (07080) *(G-10337)*

US Vision Inc (HQ).................................856 228-1000
  1 Harmon Dr Blackwood (08012) *(G-482)*

US Wire & Cable Corporation (PA)...................973 824-5530
  366 Frelinghuysen Ave Newark (07114) *(G-7310)*

USA Head Office & Warehouse, South Hackensack *Also called Youniversal Labortories (G-10191)*

USA Tealight Inc...................................732 943-2408
  4 Cragwood Rd Avenel (07001) *(G-153)*

USA Wood Door Inc..................................856 384-9663
  1475 Imperial Way West Deptford (08066) *(G-11717)*

Uscap, Fort Lee *Also called US China Allied Products Inc (G-3592)*

Ussecurenet LLC....................................201 447-0130
  1086 Goffle Rd Ste 101 Hawthorne (07506) *(G-4248)*

Ussg, South Plainfield *Also called US Software Group Inc (G-10337)*

Usv Optical Inc (HQ)...............................856 228-1000
  1 Harmon Dr Glen Oaks Par Glendora (08029) *(G-3839)*

Utah Intermediate Holding Corp.....................856 787-2700
  1020 Briggs Rd Mount Laurel (08054) *(G-6810)*

Utax USA Inc.......................................201 433-1200
  30 Montgomery St Ste 1320 Jersey City (07302) *(G-4825)*

Ute Microwave Inc..................................732 922-1009
  3500 Sunset Ave Ste D1 Ocean (07712) *(G-7686)*

Uthe Technology Inc (HQ)...........................609 883-4000
  Scotch Rd Trenton (08628) *(G-11007)*

Utility Development Corp...........................973 994-4334
  112 Naylon Ave Livingston (07039) *(G-5544)*

Utrecht Art Supply, Cranbury *Also called Utrecht Manufacturing Corp (G-1891)*

Utrecht Manufacturing Corp (HQ)....................609 409-8001
  6 Corp Dr Ste 1 Cranbury (08512) *(G-1891)*

Utz Technologies Inc (PA)..........................973 339-1100
  4 Peckman Rd Little Falls (07424) *(G-5472)*

Uvitec Printing Ink Co Inc.........................973 778-0737
  14 Mill St Lodi (07644) *(G-5581)*

V & L Machine and Tool Co Inc......................973 439-7216
  30 Sherwood Ln Ste 11 Fairfield (07004) *(G-3337)*

V & S Perth Amboy, Perth Amboy *Also called Voigt & Schweitzer LLC (G-8539)*

V A Design, South Plainfield *Also called Visual Architectural Designs (G-10342)*

V A Metal Products, Paterson *Also called Alben Metal Products Inc (G-8130)*

V and S Woodworks Inc..............................201 568-0659
  105 Piermont Rd Tenafly (07670) *(G-10667)*

V Custom Millwork Inc..............................732 469-9600
  1480 Us Highway 22 Bridgewater (08807) *(G-901)*

V E N Inc..973 786-7862
  15 Whitehall Rd Andover (07821) *(G-52)*

V F I Fabricators, Williamstown *Also called Vfi Fabricators Inc (G-11985)*

V G Controls Inc...................................973 764-6500
  17 Raritan Rd Ste 2 Oakland (07436) *(G-7649)*

V H Exacta Corp....................................856 235-7379
  107 Whittendale Dr Moorestown (08057) *(G-6574)*

V I P, Clifton *Also called Vo-Toys Inc (G-1736)*

V L V Associates...................................973 428-2884
  34 Troy Rd Whippany (07981) *(G-11911)*

V M Display.......................................973 365-8027
  90 Dayton Ave Ste 1g Passaic (07055) *(G-8112)*

V M Glass Co.......................................856 794-9333
  3231 N Mill Rd Vineland (08360) *(G-11274)*

V P I Industries Inc...............................732 583-6895
  77 Cliffwood Ave Ste 3b Cliffwood (07721) *(G-1548)*

V S M, Newark *Also called Vehicle Safety Mfg LLC (G-7311)*

Vac-U-Max (PA).....................................973 759-4600
  69 William St Belleville (07109) *(G-319)*

Vac-U-Max..973 759-4600
  69 William St Belleville (07109) *(G-320)*

Vacs Bandage Company Inc...........................973 345-3355
  163 Pennsylvania Ave Paterson (07503) *(G-8322)*

Vacumet Corp.......................................973 628-0405
  22 Riverview Dr Ste 101 Wayne (07470) *(G-11562)*

Vacuum Sales Inc...................................856 627-7790
  51 Stone Rd Laurel Springs (08021) *(G-5209)*

Vacuum Solutions Group Inc.........................781 762-0414
  555 Cedar Ln Ste 1 Teaneck (07666) *(G-10654)*

Vaeg LLC...917 533-0138
  1776 Avenue Of The States #3 Lakewood (08701) *(G-5175)*

Vahl Inc...732 249-4042
  34 Kennedy Blvd Ste 2 East Brunswick (08816) *(G-2188)*

Vahlco Racing Wheels LLC...........................609 758-7013
  849 Route 539 New Egypt (08533) *(G-6986)*

Vairtec Corporation................................201 445-6965
  265 Greenwood Ave Midland Park (07432) *(G-6189)*

Valconn Electronics Inc............................908 687-1600
  909 Rahway Ave Union (07083) *(G-11097)*

Valcor Engineering Corporation (PA)................973 467-8400
  2 Lawrence Rd Springfield (07081) *(G-10472)*

Valcor Engineering Corporation.....................973 467-8100
  45 Fadem Rd Springfield (07081) *(G-10473)*

Valcor Engineering Corporation.....................973 467-8400
  2 Lawrence Rd Springfield (07081) *(G-10474)*

Valdez Creek Min Ltd Lblty Co......................732 704-1427
  73 Broad St Ste 2 Red Bank (07701) *(G-9248)*

Valeant Pharmaceuticals Intl, Bridgewater *Also called Bausch Health Americas Inc (G-802)*

Valenzano Winery...................................856 701-7871
  1090 Route 206 Shamong (08088) *(G-9860)*

Valenzano Winery LLC...............................609 268-6731
  340 Forked Neck Rd Shamong (08088) *(G-9861)*

Valeritas Holdings Inc.............................908 927-9920
  750 Route 202 Ste 600 Bridgewater (08807) *(G-902)*

Valero Ref Company-New Jersey......................856 224-6000
  800 Billingsport Rd Paulsboro (08066) *(G-8341)*

Validus Pharmaceuticals LLC (PA)...................973 265-2777
  119 Cherry Hill Rd #310 Parsippany (07054) *(G-8033)*

Valle Precision Machine Co.........................973 773-3037
  58 Myrtle Ave Passaic (07055) *(G-8113)*

Valley Die Cutting Inc.............................973 731-8884
  100 Washington St Randolph (07869) *(G-9207)*

Valley Plastic Molding Co..........................973 334-2100
  30 Plane St Ste 4 Boonton (07005) *(G-572)*

Valley Prtg & Graphic Design, Westwood *Also called Pascack Valley Copy Center (G-11839)*

Valley Tech Inc....................................908 534-5565
  295 Us Highway 22 E 201w Whitehouse Station (08889) *(G-11936)*

Valtris Specialty Chemicals, Bridgeport *Also called Polymer Additives Inc (G-743)*

Valtris Specialty Chemicals, Swedesboro *Also called Polymer Additives Inc (G-10602)*

Valuation Services Group, Mount Laurel *Also called Aus Inc (G-6738)*

Value Added Vice Solutions LLC.....................201 400-3247
  1111 Shore Dr Brielle (08730) *(G-910)*

Valuemomentum Inc (HQ).............................908 755-0025
  220 Old New Brunswick Rd #100 Piscataway (08854) *(G-8734)*

Valuewalk LLC......................................973 767-2181
  381 Terhune Ave Passaic (07055) *(G-8114)*

Van Brill Pool & Spa Center........................856 424-4333
  850 Route 70 W Marlton (08053) *(G-5955)*

Van Duyne Bros Inc.................................609 625-0299
  5112 Oakwood Blvd Mays Landing (08330) *(G-5999)*

Van Grouw Welding & Fabg, Wyckoff *Also called M K Enterprises Inc (G-12115)*

Van Heusen, Elizabeth *Also called Pvh Corp (G-2771)*

Van Heusen, Atlantic City *Also called Pvh Corp (G-101)*

Van Heusen, Bridgewater *Also called Pvh Corp (G-871)*

Van Heusen, Jackson *Also called Pvh Corp (G-4663)*

Van Heusen, Bridgewater *Also called Pvh Corp (G-872)*

Van Heusen, Bridgewater *Also called Pvh Corp (G-873)*

Van Heusen, Flemington *Also called Pvh Corp (G-3465)*

Van Hydraulics Inc.................................732 442-5500
  110 Snyder Rd South Plainfield (07080) *(G-10338)*

Van Ness Plastic Molding Co........................973 778-9500
  400 Brighton Rd Clifton (07012) *(G-1734)*

Van-Nick Pallet Inc................................908 753-1800
  104 Snyder Rd South Plainfield (07080) *(G-10339)*

Vanco Millwork Inc.................................973 992-3061
  18 Microlab Rd Livingston (07039) *(G-5545)*

Vanco Usa LLC......................................609 499-4141
  1170 Florence Columbus Rd Bordentown (08505) *(G-598)*

Vanco USA LLC (de).................................609 499-4141
  1170 Florence Columbus Rd Bordentown (08505) *(G-599)*

Vanderbilt LLC.....................................973 316-3900
  2 Cranberry Rd Ste 3b Parsippany (07054) *(G-8034)*

Vanderbilt Industries, Parsippany *Also called Vanderbilt LLC (G-8034)*

Vandereems Manufacturing Co........................973 427-2355
  40 Schoon Ave Hawthorne (07506) *(G-4249)*

Vandermolen Corp...................................973 992-8506
  106 Hillcrest Ave Ledgewood (07852) *(G-5284)*

Vanguard Container Corp............................732 651-9717
  35 Cotters Ln Ste 1 East Brunswick (08816) *(G-2189)*

Vanguard Printing..................................856 358-2665
  531 Garden Rd Elmer (08318) *(G-2806)*

Vanguard Research Industries.......................908 753-2770
  239 Saint Nicholas Ave South Plainfield (07080) *(G-10340)*

Vans Inc...732 493-1516
  1 Premium Outlet Blvd #815 Tinton Falls (07753) *(G-10733)*

Vantage Brands, West Long Branch *Also called Smb International LLC (G-11722)*

Vantage Business Systems Inc.......................609 625-7020
  6019 Main St Mays Landing (08330) *(G-6000)*

Vantage Tool & Mfg Inc.............................908 647-1010
  223 Stirling Rd Warren (07059) *(G-11435)*

Vanton Pump & Equipment Corp.......................908 688-4120
  201 Sweetland Ave Ste 1 Hillside (07205) *(G-4436)*

Vapor Lounge LLC...................................973 627-1277
  15 Van Duyne Ave Rockaway (07866) *(G-9511)*

Varsity Software Inc 609 309-9955
  124 Lwrncvlle Pnnngton Rd Lawrenceville (08648) *(G-5245)*

Vascular Therapies Inc 201 266-8310
  105 Union Ave Cresskill (07626) *(G-1946)*

Vascular Therapies LLC 201 266-8310
  105 Union Ave Ste 2 Cresskill (07626) *(G-1947)*

Vasculogic LLC 908 278-3573
  37 E Burgess Dr Piscataway (08854) *(G-8735)*

Vascure Natural LLC 732 528-6492
  3828 River Rd Point Pleasant Boro (08742) *(G-8847)*

Vaswani Inc (PA) 877 376-4425
  75 Carter Dr Ste 1 Edison (08817) *(G-2637)*

Vaswani Inc 877 376-4425
  75 Carter Dr Ste 1 Edison (08817) *(G-2638)*

Vaswani Inc 732 377-9794
  201 Circle Dr N Ste 114 Piscataway (08854) *(G-8736)*

Vatech America Inc 201 210-5028
  2200 Fletcher Ave 705a Fort Lee (07024) *(G-3593)*

Vcom Intl Multi-Media Corp (PA) 201 814-0405
  80 Little Falls Rd Fairfield (07004) *(G-3338)*

Vcom Intl Multi-Media Corp 201 296-0600
  80 Little Falls Rd Fairfield (07004) *(G-3339)*

Vector Foiltec LLC 862 702-8909
  55 Lane Rd Ste 110 Fairfield (07004) *(G-3340)*

Vector Precision Machining 856 740-5131
  1558 Janvier Rd Williamstown (08094) *(G-11984)*

Vectracor Incorporated 973 904-0444
  785 Totowa Rd Ste 100 Totowa (07512) *(G-10856)*

Veeco 732 560-5300
  394 Elizabeth Ave Somerset (08873) *(G-10092)*

Veeco Instruments Inc 732 560-5300
  394 Elizabeth Ave Somerset (08873) *(G-10093)*

Veeco Process Equipment Inc 732 560-5300
  394 Elizabeth Ave Somerset (08873) *(G-10094)*

Vehicle Safety Mfg LLC (HQ) 973 643-3000
  408 Central Ave Newark (07107) *(G-7311)*

Vehicle Technologies Inc 609 406-9626
  17 Decou Ave Ewing (08628) *(G-3076)*

Vela Diagnostics USA Inc 973 852-3740
  353c Rte 46 W Ste 250 Fairfield (07004) *(G-3341)*

Veloso Industries Inc 908 925-0999
  1020 E Elizabeth Ave Linden (07036) *(G-5440)*

Venarum Medical LLC 732 996-8513
  20 Meridian Rd Ste 9 Eatontown (07724) *(G-2428)*

Vending Trucks Inc 732 969-5400
  5 Litchfield Rd East Brunswick (08816) *(G-2190)*

Venetian Caterers, The, Garfield *Also called Venetian Corp (G-3776)*

Venetian Corp 973 546-2250
  546 River Dr Garfield (07026) *(G-3776)*

Venkateshwara Inc 908 964-4777
  285 Davidson Ave Ste 100 Somerset (08873) *(G-10095)*

Vensun Pharmaceuticals Inc 908 278-8386
  103 Carnegie Ctr Ste 300 Princeton (08540) *(G-9040)*

Venture App LLC 908 644-3985
  12 Aubrey St Summit (07901) *(G-10553)*

Venture Info Network 609 279-0777
  226 Linden Ln Princeton (08540) *(G-9041)*

Venture Shuffleboard, Lawrence Township *Also called Brook Metal Products Inc (G-5215)*

Venture Stationers Inc 212 288-7235
  570 Piermont Rd Ste A17 Closter (07624) *(G-1763)*

Venus Laboratories Inc 973 257-8983
  50 Lackawanna Ave Parsippany (07054) *(G-8035)*

Veolia Es 732 469-5100
  125 Factory Ln Middlesex (08846) *(G-6158)*

Vep Manufacturing 732 657-0666
  575 S Hope Chapel Rd Jackson (08527) *(G-4668)*

Verallia North America, Bridgeton *Also called Ardagh Glass Inc (G-751)*

Verico Technology LLC 201 842-0222
  405 Murray Hill Pkwy East Rutherford (07073) *(G-2329)*

Verizon, Maplewood *Also called Supermedia LLC (G-5884)*

Verizon Communications Inc 201 666-9934
  285 Old Hook Rd Westwood (07675) *(G-11847)*

Verizon Communications Inc 609 646-9939
  2546 Fire Rd Egg Harbor Township (08234) *(G-2700)*

Vermeer Pharma LLC 973 270-0073
  36 Canfield Rd Morristown (07960) *(G-6706)*

Vermes Machine Co Inc 856 642-9300
  351 Crider Ave Moorestown (08057) *(G-6575)*

Vermont Cableworks Inc 802 674-6555
  31 National Rd Edison (08817) *(G-2639)*

Verna Printing, Belleville *Also called Vernw Printing Company (G-321)*

Verni Vito 732 449-1760
  1818 State Route 35 Ste 8 Wall Township (07719) *(G-11377)*

Vernon Display Graphics Inc 201 935-7117
  145 Commerce Rd Carlstadt (07072) *(G-1235)*

Vernw Printing Company 973 751-6462
  85 Washington Ave Belleville (07109) *(G-321)*

Verona Aluminum Products Inc 973 857-4809
  320 Bloomfield Ave Verona (07044) *(G-11177)*

Veroni Usa Inc 609 970-0320
  1110 Commerce Blvd # 200 Logan Township (08085) *(G-5590)*

Versa Products Company Inc 201 291-0379
  22 Spring Valley Rd Paramus (07652) *(G-7843)*

Versabar Corporation 973 279-8400
  100 Maltese Dr Totowa (07512) *(G-10857)*

Versatile Distributors Inc 973 773-0550
  293 Eisenhower Pkwy # 100 Livingston (07039) *(G-5546)*

Vertellus LLC 973 440-4400
  1705 Us Highway 46 Ledgewood (07852) *(G-5285)*

Vertical Pharmaceuticals LLC 732 721-0070
  400 Crossing Blvd Bridgewater (08807) *(G-903)*

Vertical Protective AP LLC 203 904-6099
  830 Broad St Ste 3 Shrewsbury (07702) *(G-9904)*

Vertical/Trigen Holdings LLC (HQ) 732 721-0070
  400 Crossing Blvd Bridgewater (08807) *(G-904)*

Vertican Technologies Inc 800 435-7257
  55 Lane Rd Ste 210 Fairfield (07004) *(G-3342)*

Vertice Pharma LLC (PA) 877 530-1633
  630 Central Ave New Providence (07974) *(G-7024)*

Vertis Inc 215 781-1668
  80 Stemmers Ln Mount Holly (08060) *(G-6735)*

Vertiv Corporation 732 225-3741
  3a Fernwood Ave Edison (08837) *(G-2640)*

Vesag Health Inc 732 333-1876
  675 Us Highway 1 B202c North Brunswick (08902) *(G-7492)*

Vestal Printing, Cliffwood *Also called Vestal Publishing Co Inc (G-1549)*

Vestal Publishing Co Inc 732 583-3232
  280 Cliffwood Ave Ste A Cliffwood (07721) *(G-1549)*

Vet Construction Inc 732 987-4922
  29 N County Line Rd # 218 Jackson (08527) *(G-4669)*

Vetex, Ewing *Also called Vehicle Technologies Inc (G-3076)*

Vf Outdoor LLC 908 352-5390
  651 Kapkowski Rd Ste 2034 Elizabeth (07201) *(G-2785)*

Vfi Fabricators Inc 856 629-8786
  300 Thomas Ave Ste 101 Williamstown (08094) *(G-11985)*

Vgyaan Pharmaceuticals LLC 609 452-2770
  23 Orchard Rd Unit 180 Skillman (08558) *(G-9927)*

Viant Medical Inc (HQ) 908 561-0717
  6 Century Ln South Plainfield (07080) *(G-10341)*

Viatar Ctc Solutions Inc 617 299-6590
  29 Clive Hills Rd Short Hills (07078) *(G-9879)*

Vibgyor Solutions Inc 609 750-9158
  14 Washington Rd Ste 623 Princeton Junction (08550) *(G-9069)*

Vibra Screw Inc 973 256-7410
  755 Union Blvd Totowa (07512) *(G-10858)*

Vibra-Metrics, Princeton Junction *Also called Physical Acoustics Corporation (G-9065)*

Vibration Isolation Co, Newark *Also called Mab Enterprises Inc (G-7193)*

Vibration Muntings Contrls Inc (PA) 800 569-8423
  113 Main St Bloomingdale (07403) *(G-531)*

Vicinity Media Group Inc 973 276-1688
  165 Passaic Ave Fairfield (07004) *(G-3343)*

Vicinity Publications Inc 973 276-1688
  165 Passaic Ave Ste 107 Fairfield (07004) *(G-3344)*

Vicmarr Audio Inc 732 289-9111
  9 Kilmer Ct Edison (08817) *(G-2641)*

Victor International Marketing 973 267-8900
  35 Airport Rd Ste Ll25 Morristown (07960) *(G-6707)*

Victor Securities Inc 646 481-4835
  285 Grand Ave Bldg No3 Englewood (07631) *(G-2952)*

Victoria Offset, Carlstadt *Also called Lodor Offset Corporation (G-1182)*

Victors Settings, Maywood *Also called Victors Three-D Inc (G-6018)*

Victors Three-D Inc 201 845-4433
  25 Brook Ave Maywood (07607) *(G-6018)*

Victory Box Corp 908 245-5100
  645 W 1st Ave Roselle (07203) *(G-9575)*

Victory International USA LLC 732 417-5900
  40 Christopher Way Eatontown (07724) *(G-2429)*

Victory Iron Works Inc 201 485-7181
  780 Mountain Ave Wyckoff (07481) *(G-12124)*

Victory Press 201 729-1007
  1 Caesar Pl Moonachie (07074) *(G-6496)*

Victory Tool & Mfg Co 973 759-8733
  231 Valley St 233 Belleville (07109) *(G-322)*

Videonet Comm Group LLC 732 863-5310
  7 Seaman Rd Freehold (07728) *(G-3703)*

Vieiras Bakery Inc 973 589-7719
  34-48 Ave K Newark (07105) *(G-7312)*

Vigilant Design 201 432-3900
  535 Communipaw Ave Jersey City (07304) *(G-4826)*

Vigor Inc 973 851-9539
  45 Frances St Totowa (07512) *(G-10859)*

Viking Fender Company, Edison *Also called Viking Marine Products Inc (G-2642)*

Viking Marine Products Inc 732 826-4552
  977 New Durham Rd Edison (08817) *(G-2642)*

Viking Mold & Tool Corp 609 476-9333
  64 Tuckahoe Rd Dorothy (08317) *(G-2072)*

Viking Yacht Company (PA) 609 296-6000
  On The Bass Riv Rr 9 New Gretna (08224) *(G-6988)*

Viking Yacht Company....609 296-6000
2713 Green Bank Rd Egg Harbor City (08215) *(G-2671)*
Villa Milagro Vineyards LLC....908 995-2072
33 Warren Glen Rd Phillipsburg (08865) *(G-8579)*
Villa Radiology Systems LLC....203 262-8836
124 Gaither Dr Ste 140 Mount Laurel (08054) *(G-6811)*
Villari's, Wenonah *Also called S & J Villari Livestock LLC (G-11576)*
Vinch Recycling Inc....609 393-0200
1 Vinch Ave Lawrenceville (08648) *(G-5246)*
Vine Hill Farm....973 383-0100
100 Parsons Rd Newton (07860) *(G-7364)*
Vineland Kosher Poultry Inc (PA)....856 692-1871
1050 S Mill Rd Vineland (08360) *(G-11275)*
Vineland Packaging Corp....856 794-3300
3602 N Mill Rd Vineland (08360) *(G-11276)*
Vineland Specialty Foods L L C....856 742-5001
201 Harvard Ave Westville (08093) *(G-11823)*
Vineland Syrup Inc....856 691-5772
723 S East Blvd Vineland (08360) *(G-11277)*
Vintage Print Gallery....201 501-0505
3 Reuten Dr Closter (07624) *(G-1764)*
Vinylast Inc....732 367-7200
1830 Swarthmore Ave Ste 1 Lakewood (08701) *(G-5176)*
VIP Industries Inc....973 472-7500
90 Brighton Rd Clifton (07012) *(G-1735)*
Vira Insight LLC....732 442-6756
100 Ethel Rd W Piscataway (08854) *(G-8737)*
Vira Manufacturing Inc....732 771-8269
1 Buckingham Ave Perth Amboy (08861) *(G-8538)*
Virginia Lawyers Weekly, Princeton *Also called Dolan LLC (G-8931)*
Virid Biosciences Limited....732 410-9573
246 Sandringham Rd Cherry Hill (08003) *(G-1426)*
Viridbio Solutions, Cherry Hill *Also called Virid Biosciences Limited (G-1426)*
Vis USA LLC....908 575-0606
210 Meister Ave Branchburg (08876) *(G-693)*
Viscot Medical LLC (PA)....973 887-9273
32 West St East Hanover (07936) *(G-2245)*
Vish Group, North Brunswick *Also called Vish LLC (G-7493)*
Vish LLC....201 529-2900
1605 Jersey Ave North Brunswick (08902) *(G-7493)*
Vision Lighting Inc....973 720-1200
48 N 2nd St Paterson (07522) *(G-8323)*
Vision Railings Ltd Lblty Co....908 310-8926
213 Dee Dee Dr Glen Gardner (08826) *(G-3824)*
Vision Research Inc (HQ)....973 696-4500
100 Dey Rd Wayne (07470) *(G-11563)*
Vision Ten Inc....201 935-3000
180 Broad St Carlstadt (07072) *(G-1236)*
Visionware Systems Inc....609 924-0800
174 Tamarack Cir Skillman (08558) *(G-9928)*
Viskal Printing LLC....973 812-6600
40e Commerce Way Totowa (07512) *(G-10860)*
Vislink, Hackettstown *Also called Integrated Microwave Tech LLC (G-4012)*
Vistapharm Inc (HQ)....908 376-1622
630 Central Ave New Providence (07974) *(G-7025)*
Visual Architectural Designs....908 754-3000
15 Harmich Rd South Plainfield (07080) *(G-10342)*
Visual Impact Advertising Inc....973 763-4900
9 Highland Pl Apt 3 Maplewood (07040) *(G-5889)*
Vita-Pure Inc (PA)....908 245-1212
410 W 1st Ave Roselle (07203) *(G-9576)*
Vitacare Pharma LLC....908 754-1792
111 Skyline Dr South Plainfield (07080) *(G-10343)*
Vital Signs Medcl Legl Consltn....908 537-7857
10 Magnolia Ln Asbury (08802) *(G-70)*
Vitamia & Sons, Lodi *Also called Vitamia Pasta Boy Inc (G-5582)*
Vitamia Pasta Boy Inc....973 546-1140
206 Harrison Ave Ste 214 Lodi (07644) *(G-5582)*
Vitamin Retailer Magazine Inc....732 432-9600
431 Cranbury Rd Ste C East Brunswick (08816) *(G-2191)*
Vitamin Shoppe Industries Inc (HQ)....201 868-5959
300 Harmon Meadow Blvd Secaucus (07094) *(G-9826)*
Vitamin Shoppe, The, Secaucus *Also called Vitamin Shoppe Industries Inc (G-9826)*
Vitamins For Life, Oakhurst *Also called Kwik Enterprises LLC (G-7610)*
Vitaquest International LLC....973 787-9900
100 Lehigh Dr Fairfield (07004) *(G-3345)*
Vitaquest International LLC....973 575-9200
21 Dwight Pl Fairfield (07004) *(G-3346)*
Vitaquest International LLC (PA)....973 575-9200
8 Henderson Dr West Caldwell (07006) *(G-11681)*
Vitec Videocom Inc....908 852-3700
700 Penhorn Ave Ste 1 Secaucus (07094) *(G-9827)*
Vitex LLC....201 296-0145
210 Sylvan Ave Ste 25 Englewood Cliffs (07632) *(G-2997)*
Vitillo & Sons Inc....732 886-1393
1930 Swarthmore Ave Lakewood (08701) *(G-5177)*
Viva Chemical Corporation....201 461-5281
1512 Palisade Ave Apt 5m Fort Lee (07024) *(G-3594)*
Viva International Group, Branchburg *Also called Viva International Inc (G-694)*
Viva International Inc....908 595-6200
3140 Rte 22 Branchburg (08876) *(G-694)*
Vivis Life LLC....201 798-1938
25 Park Ln S Apt 709 Jersey City (07310) *(G-4827)*
Vivitone Inc (PA)....973 427-8114
111 Ethel Ave Hawthorne (07506) *(G-4250)*
Vivreau Advanced Water Systems....212 502-3749
14 Madison Rd Ste 30 Fairfield (07004) *(G-3347)*
Viz Mold & Die Ltd....201 784-8383
210 Industrial Pkwy Northvale (07647) *(G-7553)*
Viziflex Seels Inc....201 488-3446
406 N Midland Ave Saddle Brook (07663) *(G-9686)*
Vmc Die Cutting Corp....973 450-4655
357 Cortlandt St Belleville (07109) *(G-323)*
Vo-Toys Inc (PA)....973 482-8915
179 Entin Rd Clifton (07014) *(G-1736)*
Vogel Precast Inc....732 552-8837
1509 Prospect St Lakewood (08701) *(G-5178)*
Voicings Publication Inc....609 822-9401
3 S Weymouth Ave Ste 2 Ventnor City (08406) *(G-11155)*
Voigt & Schweitzer LLC....732 442-7555
1190 Amboy Ave Perth Amboy (08861) *(G-8539)*
Vol Employees Beneficiary Assn, Ridgefield *Also called Grow Company Inc (G-9264)*
Volta Belting USA Inc....973 276-7905
60 Chapin Rd Ste 3 Pine Brook (07058) *(G-8619)*
Volta Corporation (PA)....732 583-3300
11 Industrial Dr Laurence Harbor (08879) *(G-5211)*
Voltek Division, Secaucus *Also called Sekisui America Corporation (G-9813)*
Voltis LLC....607 349-9411
55 Dwight Pl Unit A Fairfield (07004) *(G-3348)*
Volvo Car North America LLC (HQ)....201 768-7300
1 Volvo Dr Rockleigh (07647) *(G-9524)*
Vonage, Holmdel *Also called Novega Venture Partners Inc (G-4511)*
Vortex Supply LLC....856 352-6681
1001 Lower Landing Rd # 205 Blackwood (08012) *(G-483)*
Vozeh Equipment Corp....201 337-3729
509 Commerce St Ste 1 Franklin Lakes (07417) *(G-3632)*
Vrpark, Rutherford *Also called Gzgn Inc (G-9622)*
Vs Hercules LLC (HQ)....201 868-5959
2101 91st St North Bergen (07047) *(G-7442)*
VS Systematics Corp....908 241-5110
300 S Michigan Ave Kenilworth (07033) *(G-4985)*
Vsar Resources LLC....973 233-6000
30 Engelhard Dr Monroe Township (08831) *(G-6350)*
Vst Consulting Inc....732 404-0025
200 Middlesex Tpke # 102 Iselin (08830) *(G-4635)*
Vu Sound Incorporated....215 990-2864
1 Cameron Ln Lumberton (08048) *(G-5638)*
Vu World, Lumberton *Also called Vu Sound Incorporated (G-5638)*
Vulcan Information Packaging, Rutherford *Also called Ebsco Industries Inc (G-9619)*
Vulcan Tool Company Inc....908 686-0550
1080 Garden State Rd # 1 Union (07083) *(G-11098)*
Vyral Entertainment, Hawthorne *Also called Vyral Systems Inc (G-4251)*
Vyral Systems Inc....201 321-2488
300 Mountain Ave Hawthorne (07506) *(G-4251)*
Vytran Corporation....732 972-2880
1400 Campus Dr Morganville (07751) *(G-6598)*
Vytran LLC....732 972-2880
1400 Campus Dr Morganville (07751) *(G-6599)*
W & E Baum Bronze Tablet Corp....732 866-1881
89 Bannard St Freehold (07728) *(G-3704)*
W & S Steel Products, Berlin *Also called Weiler & Sons LLC (G-433)*
W A Building Movers & Contrs....908 654-8227
246 North Ave Apt 1 Garwood (07027) *(G-3793)*
W A Cleary Corporation (PA)....732 247-8000
1049 Rte 27 Somerset (08873) *(G-10096)*
W A Cleary Products Inc....732 246-2829
1049 Somerset St Somerset (08873) *(G-10097)*
W B Mason Co Inc....888 926-2766
151 Heller Pl Bellmawr (08031) *(G-345)*
W B Mason Co Inc....888 926-2766
350 Commerce Dr Egg Harbor Township (08234) *(G-2701)*
W C Davis Inc....856 547-4750
126 W Atlantic Ave Haddon Heights (08035) *(G-4050)*
W C Omni Incorporated....732 248-0999
166 National Rd Edison (08817) *(G-2643)*
W E Wamsley Restorations Inc....856 795-4001
26 Tanner St Haddonfield (08033) *(G-4066)*
W F Sherman & Son Inc....732 223-1505
84 Broad St Manasquan (08736) *(G-5842)*
W G I Corp....732 370-2900
1875 Swarthmore Ave Lakewood (08701) *(G-5179)*
W Gerriets International Inc....609 771-8111
130 Winterwood Ave Ewing (08638) *(G-3077)*
W J R B Inc....609 884-1169
711 Town Bank Rd Cape May (08204) *(G-1104)*
W Kodak Jewelers Inc (PA)....201 710-5491
60 Newark St Hoboken (07030) *(G-4487)*

ALPHABETIC

W R Chesnut Engineering Inc 973 227-6995
2 Industrial Rd 101 Fairfield (07004) *(G-3349)*

W R Grace & Co-Conn 732 868-6914
8 Heller Park Ln Somerset (08873) *(G-10098)*

W R Grace & Co-Conn 732 777-4877
340 Meadow Rd Edison (08837) *(G-2644)*

W T Winter Associates Inc 888 808-3611
20a Kulick Rd Fairfield (07004) *(G-3350)*

W W Jewelers Inc 718 392-4500
35 Journal Sq Ste 231 Jersey City (07306) *(G-4828)*

W W Manufacturing Co Inc 856 451-5700
60 Rosenhayn Ave Bridgeton (08302) *(G-777)*

W W Manufacturing Jewelers, Jersey City Also called W W Jewelers Inc *(G-4828)*

W Y Industries, North Bergen Also called WY Industries Inc *(G-7444)*

W.A. Cleary Products, Somerset Also called W A Cleary Products Inc *(G-10097)*

W2f Inc (PA) 609 735-0135
167 Archertown Rd New Egypt (08533) *(G-6987)*

Waage Electric Inc 908 245-9363
720 Colfax Ave Kenilworth (07033) *(G-4986)*

Wab US Corp 973 873-9155
3 Pearl Ct Ste E Allendale (07401) *(G-19)*

Wacoal America Inc (HQ) 201 933-8400
1 Wacoal Plz Lyndhurst (07071) *(G-5682)*

Wacoal International Corp (HQ) 201 933-8400
1 Wacoal Plz Lyndhurst (07071) *(G-5683)*

Waffle Waffle LLC (PA) 201 559-1286
43 River Rd Nutley (07110) *(G-7597)*

Wagner Carbide Saw Division, Middlesex Also called Tooling Etc LLC *(G-6156)*

Wagner Foto Screen Process 908 624-0800
4 Mark Rd Kenilworth (07033) *(G-4987)*

Wagner Industries Inc 973 347-0800
51 Sparta Rd Stanhope (07874) *(G-10481)*

Wagner Provision Co Inc 856 423-1630
54 E Broad St Gibbstown (08027) *(G-3800)*

Wagner Rack Inc 973 278-6966
2 Broad St Clifton (07013) *(G-1737)*

Wagonhouse Winery LLC 609 780-8019
1401 State Highway 45 Swedesboro (08085) *(G-10617)*

Wakefern Food Corp (PA) 908 527-3300
5000 Riverside Dr Keasbey (08832) *(G-4916)*

Wakefern Food Corp 732 819-0140
Old Post Rd Rr 1 Edison (08837) *(G-2645)*

Wakefern General Merchandise, Keasbey Also called Wakefern Food Corp *(G-4916)*

Wakefern Personnel, Edison Also called Wakefern Food Corp *(G-2645)*

Walden Farms, Linden Also called Panos Brands LLC *(G-5402)*

Walden Lang In-Pak Service 973 595-5250
474 Getty Ave 2 Clifton (07011) *(G-1738)*

Walden Mott Corp 201 962-3704
225 N Franklin Tpke Ste 1 Ramsey (07446) *(G-9158)*

Waldwick Plastics Corp 201 445-7436
21 Industrial Park Waldwick (07463) *(G-11311)*

Waldwick Printing Co 201 652-5848
1 Harrison Ave Waldwick (07463) *(G-11312)*

Waldwick Volunteer 201 445-8772
20 Whites Ln Waldwick (07463) *(G-11313)*

Walgreen Eastern Co Inc 973 728-3172
1502 Union Valley Rd West Milford (07480) *(G-11733)*

Walgreen Eastern Co Inc 609 522-1291
5000 Park Blvd Wildwood (08260) *(G-11947)*

Walgreens, West Milford Also called Walgreen Eastern Co Inc *(G-11733)*

Walgreens, Wildwood Also called Walgreen Eastern Co Inc *(G-11947)*

Walker Eight Corp 201 861-4208
510 73rd St North Bergen (07047) *(G-7443)*

Walker Engineering Inc 732 899-2550
2111 Herbertsville Rd Point Pleasant Boro (08742) *(G-8848)*

Wall Street Group Inc 201 333-4784
2 Hollywood Ct B South Plainfield (07080) *(G-10344)*

Wall Street Journal, Monmouth Junction Also called Dow Jones & Company Inc *(G-6287)*

Wall Street Journal 609 520-4000
4300 Us Highway 1 Monmouth Junction (08852) *(G-6318)*

Wallscape, East Brunswick Also called Rp Products LLC *(G-2174)*

Wally Enterprises Inc 732 329-2613
4266 Us Route 1 Monmouth Junction (08852) *(G-6319)*

Walpole Woodworkers Inc 973 539-3555
540 Tabor Rd Morris Plains (07950) *(G-6628)*

Walter Machine Co Inc 201 656-5654
84 Cambridge Ave 98 Jersey City (07307) *(G-4829)*

Wanasavealotcom LLC 732 286-6956
524 Fielders Ln Toms River (08755) *(G-10802)*

Ward Sand & Material, Vincentown Also called James D Morrissey Inc *(G-11182)*

Wardale Corp 800 813-4050
575 Prospect St Ste 202 Lakewood (08701) *(G-5180)*

Ware Industries Inc (PA) 908 757-9000
400 Metuchen Rd South Plainfield (07080) *(G-10345)*

Warehouse, Clifton Also called Fidelity Industries Inc *(G-1620)*

Warehouse Solutions Inc 201 880-1110
3-29 27th St Fl 4 Fair Lawn (07410) *(G-3128)*

Warner Chilcott (us) LLC 973 442-3200
17 Airport Rd Ste 2 Morristown (07960) *(G-6708)*

Warner Chilcott (us) LLC (HQ) 862 261-7000
400 Interpace Pkwy Parsippany (07054) *(G-8036)*

Warner Chilcott Laboratories, Parsippany Also called Warner Chilcott (us) LLC *(G-8036)*

Warp Processing Inc (PA) 973 238-1800
375 Diamond Bridge Ave Hawthorne (07506) *(G-4252)*

Warren Capital Inc 732 910-8134
6 Westwood Ct Warren (07059) *(G-11436)*

Warren Pallet Company Inc 908 995-7172
601 County Road 627 Bloomsbury (08804) *(G-532)*

Wasak Inc 973 605-8122
45 S Park Pl Ste 224 Morristown (07960) *(G-6709)*

Washington Stamp Exchange Inc 973 966-0001
2 Vreeland Rd Florham Park (07932) *(G-3526)*

Wasmund Bindery, Toms River Also called Santon Inc *(G-10790)*

Waste Not Computers & Supplies 201 384-4444
94 Washington Ave Dumont (07628) *(G-2118)*

Wastequip Manufacturing Co 856 784-5500
1031 Hickstown Rd Sicklerville (08081) *(G-9917)*

Wastequip Manufacturing Co LLC 856 629-9222
New Brooklyn & Filbert St Williamstown (08094) *(G-11986)*

Watchitude LLC 732 745-2626
24a Joyce Kilmer Ave N New Brunswick (08901) *(G-6979)*

Water Dynamics Incorporated 973 428-8330
9 Valley Forge Dr Whippany (07981) *(G-11912)*

Water Mark Technologies Inc 973 663-3438
762 State Route 15 S 2d Lake Hopatcong (07849) *(G-5038)*

Water Master Co 732 247-1900
13 S 3rd Ave Highland Park (08904) *(G-4289)*

Water On Time Bottled 862 252-9798
59 N 14th St East Orange (07017) *(G-2267)*

Water Resources New Jersey LLC 609 268-7965
1609 Route 206 Tabernacle (08088) *(G-10620)*

Water Resources of New Jersey, Tabernacle Also called Water Resources New Jersey LLC *(G-10620)*

Water Works Supply Company (PA) 973 835-2153
660 State Rt 23 Pompton Plains (07444) *(G-8874)*

Water-Jel Holding Company 201 507-8300
50 Brd St Carlstadt (07072) *(G-1237)*

Water-Jel Technologies LLC 201 438-1598
50 Broad St Carlstadt (07072) *(G-1238)*

Waterloov, Oakhurst Also called R & K Industries Inc *(G-7612)*

Waters Technologies Corp 973 394-5660
1259 Route 46 Ste 3 Parsippany (07054) *(G-8037)*

Watonka Printing Inc 732 974-8878
1608 State Route 71 Belmar (07719) *(G-356)*

Watson Laboratories Inc (HQ) 951 493-5300
400 Interpace Pkwy Parsippany (07054) *(G-8038)*

Watthung Communications Inc 908 232-4407
251 North Ave W Ste 7 Westfield (07090) *(G-11805)*

Waveline Incorporated 973 226-9100
160 Passaic Ave Fairfield (07004) *(G-3351)*

Way It Was Sporting Svc Inc 856 231-0111
620 Chestnut St Moorestown (08057) *(G-6576)*

Wayne County Foods Inc 973 399-0101
360 Coit St Irvington (07111) *(G-4589)*

Wayne Motors Inc 973 696-9710
1910 State Route 23 Wayne (07470) *(G-11564)*

Wayside Fence Company Inc 201 791-7979
38-06 Broadway Fair Lawn (07410) *(G-3129)*

Wcd Enterprises Inc 732 888-4422
1 Main St Keyport (07735) *(G-5006)*

Wearbest Sil-Tex Mills Ltd (PA) 973 340-8844
325 Midland Ave Garfield (07026) *(G-3777)*

Weatherbeeta USA Inc 732 287-1182
201 Mill Rd Edison (08837) *(G-2646)*

Weathercraft Manufacturing Co 201 262-0055
13 Emerson Plz E Emerson (07630) *(G-2870)*

Weaver Associates Printing, Cranford Also called Bab Printing Jan Service *(G-1901)*

Weavers Fiberglass 609 597-4324
19 Parker St Manahawkin (08050) *(G-5797)*

Web Industries Inc 973 335-1200
5 Mars Ct Montville (07045) *(G-6449)*

Web-Cote Ltd 973 827-2299
141 Wheatsworth Rd Hamburg (07419) *(G-4098)*

Web-Cote Industries, Hamburg Also called Web-Cote Ltd *(G-4098)*

Webannuitiescom Inc (PA) 732 521-5110
8 Talmadge Dr Monroe (08831) *(G-6324)*

Webb Press 609 386-0100
340 E Broad St Burlington (08016) *(G-992)*

Webb-Mason Inc 732 747-6585
628 Shrewsbury Ave Ste G Tinton Falls (07701) *(G-10734)*

Webco Graphics, Lakewood Also called W G I Corp *(G-5179)*

Weber & Doebrich Inc 201 868-6122
119 61st St West New York (07093) *(G-11756)*

Weber and Scher Mfg Co Inc 908 236-8484
1231 Us Highway 22 Lebanon (08833) *(G-5275)*

Weber Packaging Inc 201 262-6022
494 Demarest Ave Oradell (07649) *(G-7748)*

Webers Candy Store 856 455-8277
111 Old Cohansey Rd Bridgeton (08302) *(G-778)*

Webtech Inc 609 259-2800
108 N Gold Dr Robbinsville (08691) *(G-9419)*

Wecom Inc 856 863-8400
20 Warrick Ave Glassboro (08028) *(G-3820)*

Wedo, West New York *Also called Weber & Doebrich Inc (G-11756)*

Weekly News, The, Budd Lake *Also called New View Media (G-931)*

Wees Beyond Products Corp 862 238-8800
1 Market St Ste 6 Passaic (07055) *(G-8115)*

Weidener Construction, Fair Lawn *Also called Robert Weidener (G-3119)*

Weiler & Sons LLC 856 767-8842
170 Jackson Rd Berlin (08009) *(G-433)*

Weiler Labeling Systems LLC 856 273-3377
1256 N Church St Moorestown (08057) *(G-6577)*

Weiling Yang 201 440-5329
65 Challenger Rd Ridgefield Park (07660) *(G-9319)*

Weinman Bros Inc 212 695-8116
111 Town Square Pl # 434 Jersey City (07310) *(G-4830)*

Weir Welding Company Inc (PA) 201 939-2284
316 12th St Carlstadt (07072) *(G-1239)*

Weiss-Aug Co Inc (PA) 973 887-7600
220 Merry Ln East Hanover (07936) *(G-2246)*

Weissco Power Ltd Liability Co 908 832-2173
516 County Road 513 Califon (07830) *(G-1037)*

Wel-Fab Inc 609 261-1393
50 Indel Ave Rancocas (08073) *(G-9168)*

Weld Tech Fab 732 919-2185
282 Lemon Rd Farmingdale (07727) *(G-3395)*

Welded Products Co Inc 973 589-0180
330 Raymond Blvd Ste 336 Newark (07105) *(G-7313)*

Welding & Radiator Supply Co 609 965-0433
1144 W White Horse Pike Egg Harbor City (08215) *(G-2672)*

Welding Materials, Watchung *Also called Fanwood Crushed Stone Company (G-11455)*

Weldon Asphalt Corp 973 627-7500
311 W Main St Ste 1 Rockaway (07866) *(G-9512)*

Weldon Asphalt Corp 908 322-7840
1 New Providence Rd Watchung (07069) *(G-11461)*

Weldon Asphalt Division, Westfield *Also called Brunswick Hot Mix Corp (G-11795)*

Weldon Concrete Co., Westfield *Also called Weldon Materials Inc (G-11806)*

Weldon Concrete Corp 973 228-7473
1 Eisenhower Pkwy Roseland (07068) *(G-9544)*

Weldon Materials Inc (PA) 908 233-4444
141 Central Ave Westfield (07090) *(G-11806)*

Weldon Materials Inc 201 991-3200
1100 Harrison Ave Kearny (07032) *(G-4903)*

Weldon Quarry Co LLC 908 233-4444
141 Central Ave Westfield (07090) *(G-11807)*

Well Bilt Industries Inc 908 486-6002
2 Maple Ave Linden (07036) *(G-5441)*

Well Manager LLC 609 466-4347
371 Route 31 N Hopewell (08525) *(G-4529)*

Wells Trading LLC 201 552-9909
7000 Kennedy Blvd E M-9 Guttenberg (07093) *(G-3873)*

Wells-Gardner, Hammonton *Also called American Gaming & Elec Inc (G-4127)*

Wellspring Info Inc 800 268-3682
41 Watchung Plz Ste 506 Montclair (07042) *(G-6393)*

Welter & Kreutz Printing Co 201 489-9098
51 Worth St South Hackensack (07606) *(G-10190)*

Welton V Johnson Engineering 908 241-3100
22 N 26th St Kenilworth (07033) *(G-4988)*

Wenner Bread Products Inc 631 563-6262
571 Jersey Ave New Brunswick (08901) *(G-6980)*

Werko Machine Co 856 662-0669
9200 Collins Ave Pennsauken (08110) *(G-8496)*

West Dry Industries Inc. 908 757-4400
755 W Broad St Westfield (07090) *(G-11808)*

West Electronics, Burlington *Also called F S Brainard & Co (G-966)*

West Electronics Inc 609 387-4300
5 Terri Ln Burlington (08016) *(G-993)*

West Essex Graphics Inc 973 227-2400
305 Fairfield Ave Fairfield (07004) *(G-3352)*

West Essex Tribune Inc 973 992-1771
495 S Livingston Ave Livingston (07039) *(G-5547)*

West Hudson Lumber & Mllwk Co 201 991-7191
60 Arlington Ave Kearny (07032) *(G-4904)*

West Machine Works Inc 732 549-2183
101 Liberty St Metuchen (08840) *(G-6080)*

West Pattern Works Inc 609 443-6241
124 S Main St Cranbury (08512) *(G-1892)*

West Penetone, Clifton *Also called Penetone Corporation (G-1688)*

West Phrm Svcs Lakewood Inc 732 730-3295
1200 Paco Way Lakewood (08701) *(G-5181)*

West-Ward Injectables, Inc., Eatontown *Also called Hikma Injectables USA Inc (G-2398)*

Westar Tool LLC 856 507-8852
427 Commerce Ln Ste 7 West Berlin (08091) *(G-11633)*

Westbrook Industries, Scotch Plains *Also called Hnt Industries Inc (G-9733)*

Westbury Press Inc 201 894-0444
1 W Forest Ave Englewood (07631) *(G-2953)*

Westchester Denim Brothers Inc 203 260-1629
736 Slocum Ave Ridgefield (07657) *(G-9297)*

Westchester Lace & Textiles 201 864-2150
70 S Orange Ave Ste 220 Livingston (07039) *(G-5548)*

Westcon Orthopedics Inc 908 806-8981
4 Craig Rd Neshanic Station (08853) *(G-6906)*

Westerleigh Concepts Inc 908 205-8888
2 Hollywood Ct South Plainfield (07080) *(G-10346)*

Western Digital Corporation 609 734-7479
116 Village Blvd Ste 200 Princeton (08540) *(G-9042)*

Western Electronics Dist 908 475-3303
300 5th St Belvidere (07823) *(G-368)*

Western Pacific Foods Inc 908 838-0186
650 Belleville Tpke Ste 2 Kearny (07032) *(G-4905)*

Western Rock Products, Wall Township *Also called Hanson Aggregates Wrp Inc (G-11345)*

Western Scientific Computers 973 263-9311
28 W Shore Rd Mountain Lakes (07046) *(G-6830)*

Westfield Shtmtl Works Inc 908 276-5500
261 Monroe Ave Kenilworth (07033) *(G-4989)*

Westlock Controls Corporation (HQ) 201 794-7650
280 N Midland Ave Ste 232 Saddle Brook (07663) *(G-9687)*

Westrock Cp LLC 732 866-1890
21 Millpond Ln Colts Neck (07722) *(G-1790)*

Westrock Cp LLC 973 594-6000
1401 Broad St Ste 1 Clifton (07013) *(G-1739)*

Westrock Rkt LLC 973 594-6000
29g Commerce Way Totowa (07512) *(G-10861)*

Westrock Rkt LLC 856 596-8604
5000 Lincoln Dr E Marlton (08053) *(G-5956)*

Westrock Rkt Company 732 274-2500
1 Corn Rd Dayton (08810) *(G-1994)*

Westrock Rkt Company 973 484-5000
2013 Mccarter Hwy Newark (07104) *(G-7314)*

Westwood Construction, Millstone Twp *Also called Christopher Szuco (G-6213)*

Westwood Sleep Centers, Westwood *Also called Lieth Holdings LLC (G-11834)*

Wet Planet Beverages, Teterboro *Also called Jolt Company Inc (G-10684)*

Wet-N-Stick LLC 908 687-8273
2816 Morris Ave Ste 21 Union (07083) *(G-11099)*

Wexco Industries Inc 973 244-5777
3 Barnet Rd Pine Brook (07058) *(G-8620)*

Wexford International Inc 908 781-7200
190 Main St Ste 102 Gladstone (07934) *(G-3805)*

Wg Products Inc 973 256-5999
70 Maltese Dr Totowa (07512) *(G-10862)*

Wgjf Manufacturing Corp 908 862-1730
417 Commerce Rd Linden (07036) *(G-5442)*

What A Tee 2 Inc 201 457-0060
82 Sussex St Hackensack (07601) *(G-3990)*

What's On In Haddonfield, Haddonfield *Also called Community News Network Inc (G-4055)*

Whe Research Inc 732 240-3871
1545 Route 37 W Ste 6 Toms River (08755) *(G-10803)*

Wheal-Grace Corp 973 450-8100
300 Ralph St Belleville (07109) *(G-324)*

Wheatland Tube Co, Westwood *Also called Zekelman Industries Inc (G-11849)*

Wheaton Sands Products, Millville *Also called Glass Warehouse (G-6252)*

Wheaton Science Products, Millville *Also called Amcor Phrm Packg USA LLC (G-6229)*

Wheels Motor Sports Inc 732 606-9208
13 Penny Ln Bayville (08721) *(G-253)*

Whibco Inc (PA) 856 455-9200
87 E Commerce St Bridgeton (08302) *(G-779)*

Whibco Inc 856 825-5200
377 Port Commerland Rd Port Elizabeth (08348) *(G-8877)*

Whibco of New Jersey Inc 856 455-9200
377 Port Cumberland Rd Port Elizabeth (08348) *(G-8878)*

Whimsy Diddles LLC 609 560-1323
59 Briarhill Dr Chesilhurst (08089) *(G-1428)*

Whippany Actuation Systems LLC 973 428-9898
110 Algonquin Pkwy Whippany (07981) *(G-11913)*

Whips International, Cherry Hill *Also called CDK Industries LLC (G-1352)*

Whiptail Technologies Inc., Whippany *Also called Whiptail Technologies LLC (G-11914)*

Whiptail Technologies LLC 973 585-6375
9 Whippany Rd Ste 67 Whippany (07981) *(G-11914)*

White Castle 732 721-3565
987 Us Highway 9 South Amboy (08879) *(G-10142)*

White Eagle Printing Co Inc 609 586-2032
2550 Kuser Rd Trenton (08691) *(G-11008)*

White Home Products Inc 908 226-2501
30 Boright Ave 4 Kenilworth (07033) *(G-4990)*

White Lotus Home Ltd Lblty Co 732 828-2111
745 Joyce Kilmer Ave New Brunswick (08901) *(G-6981)*

Whitehouse Machine & Mfg Co 908 534-4722
3585 Us Highway 22 Somerville (08876) *(G-10128)*

Whitehouse Prtg & Labeling LLC 973 521-7648
50 Kulick Rd Fairfield (07004) *(G-3353)*

Whitewave Foods, Bridgeton *Also called Wwf Operating Company (G-780)*

Whittle & Mutch Inc 856 235-1165
712 Fellowship Rd Mount Laurel (08054) *(G-6812)*

Whole Year Trading Co Inc 732 238-1196
117 Docks Corner Rd Ste B Dayton (08810) *(G-1995)*

Whoot Newspaper, Pleasantville *Also called Atlantic City Week* *(G-8805)*

Wick It LLC 973 249-2970
1 Gregory Ave Passaic (07055) *(G-8116)*

Wickr Inc 516 637-2882
211 Warren St Ste 34 Newark (07103) *(G-7315)*

Wide Band Systems Inc 973 586-6500
389 Franklin Ave Rockaway (07866) *(G-9513)*

Wilcox Press 973 827-7474
6 Main St Hamburg (07419) *(G-4099)*

Wilcoy Press, Pine Hill *Also called Bruce McCoy Sr* *(G-8621)*

Wild Bills Olde Fashioned Soda, Millington *Also called Bluewater Inc* *(G-6207)*

Wild Flavors Inc 908 820-9800
132 Corbin St Bldg 1200 Elizabeth (07201) *(G-2786)*

Wild Juice US, Elizabeth *Also called Wild Flavors Inc* *(G-2786)*

Wilenta Carting Inc 201 325-0044
46 Henry St Secaucus (07094) *(G-9828)*

Wilenta Feed Inc 201 325-0044
46 Henry St Secaucus (07094) *(G-9829)*

Wiley Publishing LLC (HQ) 201 748-6000
111 River St Hoboken (07030) *(G-4488)*

Wiley Subscription Services 201 748-6000
111 River St Hoboken (07030) *(G-4489)*

Wiley-Interscience, Hoboken *Also called Wiley Subscription Services* *(G-4489)*

Wilker Graphics LLC 201 447-4800
95 Greenwood Ave Midland Park (07432) *(G-6190)*

William Cromley 856 881-6019
101 S Delsea Dr Clayton (08312) *(G-1530)*

William Duling 856 365-6323
613 Kaighn Ave 15 Camden (08103) *(G-1090)*

William Kenyon & Sons Inc (HQ) 732 985-8980
90 Ethel Rd W Piscataway (08854) *(G-8738)*

William Opdyke Awnings Inc (PA) 732 449-5940
2036 State Route 35 Wall Township (07719) *(G-11378)*

William R Hall Co 856 784-6700
901 E Gibbsboro Rd Lindenwold (08021) *(G-5447)*

William R Tatz Industries 973 751-0720
11 Railroad Pl Belleville (07109) *(G-325)*

William Robert Graphics Inc 201 239-7400
234 16th St Fl 7 Jersey City (07310) *(G-4831)*

William Spencer (PA) 856 235-1830
20 Lake Dr Mount Laurel (08054) *(G-6813)*

William T Hutchinson Company 908 688-0533
453 Lehigh Ave Union (07083) *(G-11100)*

Williams Scotsman Inc 856 429-0315
150 Western Rd Kearny (07032) *(G-4906)*

Williams Scotsman - NY Cy, Kearny *Also called Williams Scotsman Inc* *(G-4906)*

Willier Elc Mtr Repr Co Inc (PA) 856 627-3535
1 Linden Ave Gibbsboro (08026) *(G-3796)*

Willier Elc Mtr Repr Co Inc 856 627-2262
3 Democrat Rd Ste Td Gibbsboro (08026) *(G-3797)*

Willier Technical Services, Gibbsboro *Also called Willier Elc Mtr Repr Co Inc* *(G-3797)*

Willings Nutraceutical Corp 856 424-9088
1936 Olney Ave Ste A Cherry Hill (08003) *(G-1427)*

Willow Creek Winery Inc 609 770-8782
160 Stevens St 168 Cape May (08204) *(G-1105)*

Willow Iron Works, Jersey City *Also called 67 Pollock Ave Corp* *(G-4679)*

Willow Run Construction Inc 201 659-7266
67 Pollock Ave Jersey City (07305) *(G-4832)*

Willow Technology Inc 732 671-1554
12 Valley Point Dr Holmdel (07733) *(G-4515)*

Willowbrook Golf Center LLC 973 256-6922
366 Us Highway 46 Wayne (07470) *(G-11565)*

Willrich Precision Instr Co 866 945-5742
80 Broadway Ste 105 Cresskill (07626) *(G-1948)*

Wilmington Trust Sp Services 609 272-7000
1000 W Washington Ave Pleasantville (08232) *(G-8821)*

Wilpak Industries Inc 201 997-7600
244 Dukes St Kearny (07032) *(G-4907)*

Wilshire Technologies Inc 609 683-1117
243 Wall St Princeton (08540) *(G-9043)*

Wilsonart LLC 800 822-7613
11 Twosome Dr Moorestown (08057) *(G-6578)*

Win-Tech Precision Products 973 887-8727
5a Littell Rd East Hanover (07936) *(G-2247)*

Wind Tunnel Inc 201 485-7793
60 Whitney Rd Ste 13 Mahwah (07430) *(G-5786)*

Windmill Health Products, Fairfield *Also called Vitaquest International LLC* *(G-3346)*

Windmill Press Inc 856 663-8990
1051 Thomas Busch Mem Hwy Pennsauken (08110) *(G-8497)*

Window 25 LLC 973 817-9464
103 Van Buren St Newark (07105) *(G-7316)*

Window Designs By Powers, Northvale *Also called Shade Powers Co Inc* *(G-7549)*

Window Factory Inc 856 546-5050
603 N Black Horse Pike Mount Ephraim (08059) *(G-6722)*

Window Plus Home Improvement 973 591-9993
207 Monroe St Passaic (07055) *(G-8117)*

Window Repairs & Restoration, Gloucester City *Also called Pierangeli Group Inc* *(G-3847)*

Window Shapes Inc 732 549-0708
225 Liberty St Metuchen (08840) *(G-6081)*

Window Trends 973 887-6676
194 Fieldcrest Rd Parsippany (07054) *(G-8039)*

Windsor Labs LLC 609 301-6446
55 Lake Dr East Windsor (08520) *(G-2364)*

Windtree Therapeutics Inc 973 339-2889
710 Union Blvd Totowa (07512) *(G-10863)*

Winemiller Press Inc 732 223-0100
2411 Atlantic Ave Ste 6 Manasquan (08736) *(G-5843)*

Winery Pak LLC 800 434-4599
3 Wing Dr Ste 101 Cedar Knolls (07927) *(G-1316)*

Winetree Publishing, Monroe Township *Also called Steven Orros* *(G-6347)*

Wingold Embroidery LLC 732 845-9802
5 Monarch Ln Freehold (07728) *(G-3705)*

Winiadaewoo Elec Amer Inc (PA) 201 552-4950
65 Challenger Rd Ste 360 Ridgefield Park (07660) *(G-9320)*

Winslow Rental & Supply Inc 856 767-5554
204 Williamstown Rd Berlin (08009) *(G-434)*

Winsome Digital Inc 609 645-2211
202 W Parkway Dr Egg Harbor Township (08234) *(G-2702)*

Winstar Windows LLC 973 403-0574
217 Roseland Ave Essex Fells (07021) *(G-3012)*

Winter Scale & Equipment, Fairfield *Also called W T Winter Associates Inc* *(G-3350)*

Winters Bank Signs, Martinsville *Also called Winters Stamp Mfg Co Inc* *(G-5965)*

Winters Stamp Mfg Co Inc 908 352-3725
1024 Mayflower Ct Martinsville (08836) *(G-5965)*

Winthrop, Bridgewater *Also called Sanofi-Aventis US LLC* *(G-884)*

Wire Cloth Manufacturers Inc (PA) 973 328-1000
110 Iron Mountain Rd Mine Hill (07803) *(G-6275)*

Wire Displays Inc 973 537-0090
88 King St Ste 1 Dover (07801) *(G-2110)*

Wire Fabricators & Insulators 973 768-2839
20 Harding Pl Livingston (07039) *(G-5549)*

Wire-Pro Inc (HQ) 856 935-7560
90 W Broadway Salem (08079) *(G-9698)*

Wired Products LLC 551 231-5800
49 E Midland Ave Ste 6 Paramus (07652) *(G-7844)*

Wireless Communications Inc 732 926-1000
55 Liberty St Metuchen (08840) *(G-6082)*

Wireless Communications & Elec, West Berlin *Also called Wireless Electronics Inc (G-11634)*

Wireless Electronics Inc 856 768-4310
153 Cooper Rd West Berlin (08091) *(G-11634)*

Wireless Experience of PA Inc (PA) 732 552-0050
509 N Main St Manahawkin (08050) *(G-5798)*

Wireless Experience, The, Manahawkin *Also called Wireless Experience of PA Inc (G-5798)*

Wireless Telecom Group Inc (PA) 973 386-9696
25 Eastmans Rd Parsippany (07054) *(G-8040)*

Wireworks Corporation 908 686-7400
380 Hillside Ave Hillside (07205) *(G-4437)*

Wisco Promo & Uniform Inc 973 767-2022
160 Us Highway 46 Saddle Brook (07663) *(G-9688)*

Wisdom USA Inc 201 933-1998
175 Broad St Carlstadt (07072) *(G-1240)*

Wise Foods Inc 201 440-2876
150 Carol Pl Moonachie (07074) *(G-6497)*

Wisely Products LLC 929 329-9188
77 Hudson St Apt 2406 Jersey City (07302) *(G-4833)*

Wisesorbent Technology LLC 856 872-7713
11 E Stow Rd Marlton (08053) *(G-5957)*

Witte Co Inc 908 689-6500
507 Rte 31 S Washington (07882) *(G-11454)*

Wittich Bros Marine Inc 732 722-8656
25a Abe Voorhees Dr Manasquan (08736) *(G-5844)*

Wizard Technology Inc 732 730-0800
2165 Route 9 Toms River (08755) *(G-10804)*

Wizcom Corporation 609 750-0601
19 Washington Rd Ste D Princeton Junction (08550) *(G-9070)*

Wizdata Systems Inc 973 975-4113
140 Littleton Rd Ste 220 Parsippany (07054) *(G-8041)*

Wjj and Company LLC 973 246-7480
141 Lanza Ave Bldg 29 Garfield (07026) *(G-3778)*

Wjm Trucking Inc 856 381-3635
515 Macintosh Dr Mullica Hill (08062) *(G-6858)*

Wjv Materials LLC 856 299-8244
93 Pennsgrve Pedrcktwn Pedricktown (08067) *(G-8356)*

Wl Ring, Metuchen *Also called Wlxt LLC* *(G-6083)*

Wlxt LLC 732 906-7979
16 Wernik Pl Metuchen (08840) *(G-6083)*

Wm H Brewster Jr Incorporated 973 227-1050
16 Kulick Rd Fairfield (07004) *(G-3354)*

Wm Leiber Inc 732 938-2080
190 Georgia Tavern Rd Farmingdale (07727) *(G-3396)*

Wm Steinen Mfg Co (PA) 973 887-6400
29 E Halsey Rd Parsippany (07054) *(G-8042)*

Wm.h. Brewster Jr, Fairfield *Also called Wm H Brewster Jr Incorporated* *(G-3354)*

Wohners (PA) 201 568-7307
29 Bergen St Englewood (07631) *(G-2954)*

Wolf Form Co Inc 201 567-6556
  289 Orangeburgh Rd Old Tappan (07675) *(G-7736)*

Wolock & Lott Transmission Eqp 908 218-9292
  25 Chambers Brook Rd Branchburg (08876) *(G-695)*

Woman's World Magazine, Englewood Cliffs *Also called Heinrich Bauer Verlag* *(G-2973)*

Wong Robinson & Co Inc (PA) 609 951-0300
  743 Alexander Rd Ste 15 Princeton (08540) *(G-9044)*

Wood & Laminates Inc 973 773-7475
  102 Us Highway 46 E Lodi (07644) *(G-5583)*

Wood Products Inc 609 859-0303
  34 Allentown Rd Southampton (08088) *(G-10374)*

Wood Textures 732 230-5005
  251 Herrod Blvd Dayton (08810) *(G-1996)*

Wood Works 856 728-4520
  1111 N Black Horse Pike Williamstown (08094) *(G-11987)*

Wood's Industrial Services, West Milford *Also called Woods Industrial LLC* *(G-11734)*

Woodbridge Inoac Technical 201 807-0809
  100 Carol Pl Moonachie (07074) *(G-6498)*

Woodbridge Inoac Technical Pro 201 807-0809
  100 Carol Pl Moonachie (07074) *(G-6499)*

Woodbridge Machine & Tool Co 732 634-0179
  259 Bergen St Woodbridge (07095) *(G-12024)*

Woodbury Roof Truss Inc 856 845-3848
  692 S Evergreen Ave Woodbury Heights (08097) *(G-12044)*

Woodhaven Lumber & Millwork (PA) 732 901-0030
  200 James St Lakewood (08701) *(G-5182)*

Woodhaven Lumber & Millwork 732 295-8800
  1303 Richmond Ave Point Pleasant Beach (08742) *(G-8833)*

Woodhut LLC 732 414-6440
  210 Jerseyville Ave Freehold (07728) *(G-3706)*

Woodland Manufacturing Company 609 587-4180
  1936 E State Street Ext Trenton (08619) *(G-11009)*

Woodline Works Corporation 732 828-9100
  625 Jersey Ave Ste 9 New Brunswick (08901) *(G-6982)*

Woodpeckers, Belleville *Also called Woodpeckers Inc* *(G-326)*

Woodpeckers Inc 973 751-4744
  323 Cortlandt St Belleville (07109) *(G-326)*

Woods Industrial LLC 973 208-0664
  81 Hudson Dr West Milford (07480) *(G-11734)*

Woodshop Inc 732 349-8006
  58 Flint Rd Toms River (08757) *(G-10805)*

Woodstock Farms, Edison *Also called United Natural Trading Co* *(G-2636)*

Woodtec Inc 908 979-0180
  300 W Stiger St Hackettstown (07840) *(G-4041)*

Woodward Jogger Aerators Inc (PA) 201 933-6800
  45 Carlton Ave East Rutherford (07073) *(G-2330)*

Woodward Wood Products Design 609 597-2708
  612 Main St West Creek (08092) *(G-11688)*

Word Center Printing 609 586-5825
  1905 Highway 33 Ste 10 Trenton (08690) *(G-11010)*

Wordmasters 201 327-4201
  213 E Allendale Ave Allendale (07401) *(G-20)*

Work n Gear LLC 856 848-7676
  1692 Clements Bridge Rd H Woodbury (08096) *(G-12039)*

Work Zone Contractors LLC 856 845-8201
  664 Oak Ave Deptford (08096) *(G-2068)*

Work'n Gear 8047, Woodbury *Also called Work n Gear LLC* *(G-12039)*

Works Enduro Rider Inc 908 637-6385
  1 Jenny Jump Ave Great Meadows (07838) *(G-3858)*

Workwave LLC (HQ) 866 794-1658
  101 Crawfords Corner Rd Holmdel (07733) *(G-4516)*

World and Main LLC (HQ) 609 860-9990
  324a Half Acre Rd Cranbury (08512) *(G-1893)*

World Class Intl Kit 712, Linden *Also called Saker Shoprites Inc* *(G-5418)*

World Class Marketing Corp (HQ) 201 313-0022
  2147 Hudson Ter Fort Lee (07024) *(G-3595)*

World Confections Inc 718 768-8100
  14 S Orange Ave Ste A South Orange (07079) *(G-10203)*

World Electronics Inc 201 670-1177
  37 Hanover Pl Glen Rock (07452) *(G-3835)*

World Impro, Palisades Park *Also called BSC USA LLC* *(G-7770)*

World Journal LLC 732 632-8890
  41a Bridge St Metuchen (08840) *(G-6084)*

World of Coffee Inc 908 647-1218
  328 Essex St Stirling (07980) *(G-10499)*

World of Tea, Stirling *Also called World of Coffee Inc* *(G-10499)*

World Pac Paper LLC 877 837-2737
  600 E Crescent Ave # 301 Upper Saddle River (07458) *(G-11149)*

World Plastic Extruders Inc 201 933-2915
  41 Park Ave Rutherford (07070) *(G-9635)*

World Scientific Publishing Co 201 487-9655
  27 Warren St Ph 401 Hackensack (07601) *(G-3991)*

World Software Corporation 201 444-3228
  266 Harristown Rd Ste 201 Glen Rock (07452) *(G-3836)*

World Wide Metric Inc (PA) 732 247-2300
  37 Readington Rd Branchburg (08876) *(G-696)*

World Wide Packaging LLC (PA) 973 805-6500
  15 Vreeland Rd Ste 4 Florham Park (07932) *(G-3527)*

Worldcast Network Inc 201 767-2040
  20 Foxwood Sq S Old Tappan (07675) *(G-7737)*

Worldox, Glen Rock *Also called World Software Corporation* *(G-3836)*

Worldwide Glass Resources Inc 856 205-1508
  1022 Spruce St Vineland (08360) *(G-11278)*

Worldwide Pt SL Ltd Lblty Co 201 928-0222
  555 Cedar Ln Ste 7 Teaneck (07666) *(G-10655)*

Worldwide Safety Systems LLC 888 613-4501
  1297 Sussex Rd Teaneck (07666) *(G-10656)*

Worldwide Solar Mfg LLC 201 297-1177
  39 Walker Ave Closter (07624) *(G-1765)*

Worldwide Whl Flr Cvg Inc (PA) 732 906-1400
  1055 Us Highway 1 Edison (08837) *(G-2647)*

Worrall Community Newspapers 973 743-4040
  266 Liberty St Bloomfield (07003) *(G-522)*

Worthington Biochemical Corp (PA) 732 942-1660
  730 Vassar Ave Lakewood (08701) *(G-5183)*

Wostbrock Embroidery Inc 201 445-3074
  11 Paterson Ave Ste 1 Midland Park (07432) *(G-6191)*

Woyshner Service Company Inc 856 461-9196
  813 Edgewood Ave Delran (08075) *(G-2022)*

Wpi Communications Inc 973 467-8700
  55 Morris Ave Ste 312 Springfield (07081) *(G-10475)*

Wpi-Salem Division, Salem *Also called Wire-Pro Inc* *(G-9698)*

Wra Manufacturing Company Inc 908 416-2228
  17 Portside Rd Hopatcong (07843) *(G-4523)*

Wrap-Ade Machine Co Inc 973 773-6150
  180 Brighton Rd Ste B Clifton (07012) *(G-1740)*

Wrapade, Clifton *Also called Wrap-Ade Machine Co Inc* *(G-1740)*

Wrapade Packaging Systems LLC 973 787-1788
  15 Gardner Rd Ste 200 Fairfield (07004) *(G-3355)*

Wrightworks Engineering LLC 609 882-8840
  12 Rosetree Ln Lawrenceville (08648) *(G-5247)*

Wsc International, Delran *Also called Woyshner Service Company Inc* *(G-2022)*

Wt Media LLC 609 921-3490
  4 Applegate Dr Trenton (08691) *(G-11011)*

Wta Global LLC 312 509-2559
  125 Long Hill Rd Apt 3c Little Falls (07424) *(G-5473)*

Wurz Signsystems LLC 856 461-4397
  2600 Haddonfield Rd Pennsauken (08110) *(G-8498)*

Wwf Operating Company 856 459-3890
  70 Rosenhayn Ave Bridgeton (08302) *(G-780)*

Wwp, Florham Park *Also called World Wide Packaging LLC* *(G-3527)*

Www.vandlmachinetool.com, Fairfield *Also called V & L Machine and Tool Co Inc* *(G-3337)*

WY Industries Inc 201 617-8000
  2500 Secaucus Rd North Bergen (07047) *(G-7444)*

Wyeth Holdings Corporation, Madison *Also called Wyeth Holdings LLC* *(G-5704)*

Wyeth Holdings LLC (HQ) 973 660-5000
  5 Giralda Farms Madison (07940) *(G-5704)*

Wyeth LLC 973 660-5000
  5 Giralda Farms Madison (07940) *(G-5705)*

Wyeth-Ayerst (asia) Ltd (HQ) 973 660-5500
  5 Giralda Farms Madison (07940) *(G-5706)*

Wyeth-Ayerst Pharmaceutical 732 274-4221
  865 Ridge Rd Monmouth Junction (08852) *(G-6320)*

Wyman-Gordon Forgings Inc 973 627-0200
  387 Franklin Ave Rockaway (07866) *(G-9514)*

Wynnpharm Inc 732 409-1005
  86 W Main St Freehold (07728) *(G-3707)*

Wyssmont Company Inc 201 947-4600
  1470 Bergen Blvd Fort Lee (07024) *(G-3596)*

Wytech Industries Inc (PA) 732 396-3900
  960 E Hazelwood Ave Rahway (07065) *(G-9132)*

X Hockey Pro Shops, Bridgewater *Also called Ss Equipment Holdings LLC* *(G-894)*

X-Factor Cmmnctons Hldings Inc (PA) 877 741-3727
  100 Stonehurst Ct Northvale (07647) *(G-7554)*

X-L Plastics Inc 973 777-9400
  220 Clifton Blvd Clifton (07011) *(G-1741)*

Xanthus Inc 973 643-0920
  105 Lock St Ste 215 Newark (07103) *(G-7317)*

Xbox Exclusive 908 756-3731
  111 Eleanor St South Plainfield (07080) *(G-10347)*

Xceedium Inc 201 536-1000
  30 Montgomery St Ste 1020 Jersey City (07302) *(G-4834)*

Xceptional Instruments LLC 315 750-4345
  1200 Grand St Apt 423 Hoboken (07030) *(G-4490)*

Xcessory LLC 917 647-7523
  5901 W Side Ave Fl 7n North Bergen (07047) *(G-7445)*

Xchange Software Inc (PA) 732 444-4943
  10 Austin Ave Fl 2 Iselin (08830) *(G-4636)*

Xchange Software Inc 732 444-6666
  499 Ernston Rd Ste A7 Parlin (08859) *(G-7869)*

Xenon-Vr, Belleville *Also called Khan Zeshan* *(G-298)*

Xpet LLC 973 272-7502
  179 Entin Rd Clifton (07014) *(G-1742)*

Xstatic Pro Inc 718 237-2299
  55 Hook Rd 46 Bayonne (07002) *(G-237)*

Xtreme Powertech LLC 201 791-5050
  123 Pleasant Ave Upper Saddle River (07458) *(G-11150)*

Xybion Corporation (PA) 973 538-2067
  2000 Lenox Dr Ste 101 Lawrenceville (08648) **(G-5248)**

Xylem Dewatering Solutions Inc (HQ) 856 467-3636
  84 Floodgate Rd Bridgeport (08014) **(G-748)**

Y & J Bakers Inc 732 363-3636
  415 Clifton Ave Lakewood (08701) **(G-5184)**

Y C S, Ocean *Also called Yeghen Computer System* **(G-7687)**

Yale Hook & Eye Co Inc 973 824-1440
  33 Race St Hillside (07205) **(G-4438)**

Yamate Chocolatier Inc 732 249-4847
  320 Cleveland Ave Highland Park (08904) **(G-4290)**

Yank Marine Inc 609 628-2928
  7 Mosquito Landing Rd Tuckahoe (08250) **(G-11015)**

Yankee Tool Inc 973 664-0878
  17 Edgewater Dr Denville (07834) **(G-2062)**

Yard, Hoboken *Also called Union Dry Dock & Repair Co* **(G-4486)**

Yarde Metals Inc 973 463-1166
  603 Murray Rd East Hanover (07936) **(G-2248)**

Yardworks, Little Silver *Also called All Structures LLC* **(G-5499)**

Yasheel Inc 856 275-6812
  11 Samantha Ct Sewell (08080) **(G-9854)**

Yated Neeman Inc 845 369-1600
  110 Shady Lane Dr Lakewood (08701) **(G-5185)**

Yates Sign Co Inc 732 578-1818
  69 Megill Rd Farmingdale (07727) **(G-3397)**

YC Cable (east) Inc 732 868-0800
  240 Circle Dr N Piscataway (08854) **(G-8739)**

Yeghen Computer System 732 996-5500
  5 Brook Dr Ste 101 Ocean (07712) **(G-7687)**

Yerg Accounting Supplies, Lakehurst *Also called Yerg Inc* **(G-5040)**

Yerg Inc 973 759-4041
  7 Fawnhollow Ln Lakehurst (08759) **(G-5040)**

Yes Pac, Piscataway *Also called Prospect Group LLC* **(G-8702)**

Yes Press, Carlstadt *Also called Latta Graphics Inc* **(G-1181)**

Yesco Sign & Lighting, Burlington *Also called B4inc Inc* **(G-951)**

Yi Pin Food Prods, Edison *Also called Yipin Food Products Inc* **(G-2648)**

Yinlink International Inc 973 818-4664
  2 Corporate Dr Ste A Cranbury (08512) **(G-1894)**

Yipin Food Products Inc 718 788-3059
  29 Mack Dr Edison (08817) **(G-2648)**

YKK (usa) Inc 201 935-4200
  1099 Wall St W Ste 244 Lyndhurst (07071) **(G-5684)**

Yo Got It 732 475-7913
  606 Arnold Ave Point Pleasant Beach (08742) **(G-8834)**

Yogo Mix 609 897-1379
  44 Normandy Dr Princeton Junction (08550) **(G-9071)**

Yogurt Paradise LLC 732 534-6395
  10 S New Prospect Rd Jackson (08527) **(G-4670)**

Yoland Corporation 862 257-9036
  924 E 25th St Paterson (07513) **(G-8324)**

Yolo Candy LLC 201 252-8765
  1 International Blvd # 208 Mahwah (07495) **(G-5787)**

Yonkers Plywood Manufacturing 732 727-1200
  3130 Bordentown Ave Old Bridge (08857) **(G-7730)**

York International Corporation 732 346-0606
  160 Rritan Ctr Pkwy Ste 6 Edison (08837) **(G-2649)**

York Street Caterers Inc 201 868-9088
  196 Coolidge Ave Englewood (07631) **(G-2955)**

York Telecom Corporation (HQ) 732 413-6000
  81 Corbett Way Eatontown (07724) **(G-2430)**

Yorktel, Eatontown *Also called York Telecom Corporation* **(G-2430)**

Youniversal Labortories (PA) 201 807-9000
  100 Louis St South Hackensack (07606) **(G-10191)**

Your Printer V20 Ltd 609 771-4000
  6 Corporate Dr Ste 1 Cranbury (08512) **(G-1895)**

Youre So Invited LLC 201 664-8600
  260 Westwood Ave Westwood (07675) **(G-11848)**

Ytc Holdings Inc (PA) 732 413-6000
  81 Corbett Way Eatontown (07724) **(G-2431)**

Yuhl Products Inc 908 276-5180
  15 N 7th St Kenilworth (07033) **(G-4991)**

Yukon Graphics Inc 973 575-5700
  239 New Rd Ste B110 Parsippany (07054) **(G-8043)**

Yumble, Englewood *Also called Panda Plates Inc* **(G-2930)**

Yunta USA Inc 614 835-6588
  2553 Us Highway 130 Ste 3 Cranbury (08512) **(G-1896)**

Z Fab LLC 973 248-0686
  24 Bodie Rd Wayne (07470) **(G-11566)**

Z Line Beachwear 732 793-1234
  3263 Route 35 N Lavallette (08735) **(G-5213)**

Z Squared Hg Inc 908 315-3646
  1 Jill Ct Ste 7 Hillsborough (08844) **(G-4362)**

Z-Line, Lavallette *Also called Z Line Beachwear* **(G-5213)**

Z-Tech, Pennsauken *Also called Zin-Tech Inc* **(G-8499)**

Zack Painting Co Inc 732 738-7900
  900 King George Rd Fords (08863) **(G-3534)**

Zacs International LLC 609 368-3482
  2107 Route 130 N Unit 2 Burlington (08016) **(G-994)**

Zaffre, Lakewood *Also called Cherri Stone Interactive LLC* **(G-5069)**

Zago Manufacturing Company 973 643-6700
  21 E Runyon St Newark (07114) **(G-7318)**

Zahk Sales Inc 516 633-9179
  1405 Boxwood Dr Branchburg (08876) **(G-697)**

Zaiya Inc 201 343-3988
  185 Kenneth St Hackensack (07601) **(G-3992)**

Zala Machine Co Inc 908 431-9106
  109 Stryker Ln Ste 11 Hillsborough (08844) **(G-4363)**

Zala Machine Shop, Hillsborough *Also called Zala Machine Co Inc* **(G-4363)**

Zaller Studios Inc 973 743-5175
  265 Watsessing Ave Bloomfield (07003) **(G-523)**

Zanotti Transblock USA Corp 917 584-9357
  1810 Underwood Blvd Ste 1 Delran (08075) **(G-2023)**

Zaxcom Inc 973 835-5000
  230 W Parkway Ste 9 Pompton Plains (07444) **(G-8875)**

Zaxcom Video, Pompton Plains *Also called Zaxcom Inc* **(G-8875)**

Zc Utility Services LLC 973 226-1840
  10 Steel Ct Roseland (07068) **(G-9545)**

Zebra Technologies Corporation 609 383-8743
  1501 Tilton Rd Northfield (08225) **(G-7512)**

Zeeks Tees, Belford *Also called Frank J Zechman* **(G-282)**

Zeeks Tees 732 291-2700
  515 State Route 36 Belford (07718) **(G-285)**

Zeiser Inc 973 228-0800
  15 Patton Dr West Caldwell (07006) **(G-11682)**

Zekelman Industries Inc 724 342-6851
  90 Hurlbut St Westwood (07675) **(G-11849)**

Zenas Patisserie 856 303-8700
  308 Broad St Riverton (08077) **(G-9405)**

Zenex Precision Products Corp 973 523-6910
  69 George St Paterson (07503) **(G-8325)**

Zenia Pharma LLC 973 246-9718
  575 Grove St Unit F1 Clifton (07013) **(G-1743)**

Zenith Electronics Corporation 201 816-2071
  1000 Sylvan Ave Fl 1 Englewood Cliffs (07632) **(G-2998)**

Zenith Energy US LP (PA) 732 515-7410
  1 Highland Ave Metuchen (08840) **(G-6085)**

Zenith Laboratories Inc 201 767-1700
  140 Legrand Ave Northvale (07647) **(G-7555)**

Zenith Laboratories Inc (HQ) 201 767-1700
  140 Legrand Ave Northvale (07647) **(G-7556)**

Zenith Mfg & Chemical Corp 201 767-1332
  85 Oak St Norwood (07648) **(G-7577)**

Zenith Precision Inc 201 933-8640
  536 Paterson Ave East Rutherford (07073) **(G-2331)**

Zenith Ultrasonic, Norwood *Also called Zenith Mfg & Chemical Corp* **(G-7577)**

Zeon US Inc 516 532-7167
  5903 W Side Ave North Bergen (07047) **(G-7446)**

Zerega Pasta, Fair Lawn *Also called A Zeregas Sons Inc* **(G-3080)**

Zero Surge Inc 908 996-7700
  889 State Route 12 Ste 2 Frenchtown (08825) **(G-3718)**

Zestos Foods LLC 888 407-5852
  1297 Sussex Rd Teaneck (07666) **(G-10657)**

Zeta Products Inc 908 688-0440
  18 Westgate Dr Annandale (08801) **(G-56)**

Zeus Industrial Products Inc 908 292-6500
  134 Chubb Way Branchburg (08876) **(G-698)**

Zeus Scientific Inc 908 526-3744
  200 Evans Way Branchburg (08876) **(G-699)**

Zicam, Bridgewater *Also called Matrixx Initiatives Inc* **(G-847)**

Ziegler Chem & Mineral Corp (PA) 732 752-4111
  600 Prospect Ave Ste A Piscataway (08854) **(G-8740)**

Ziegler Chem & Mineral Corp 732 752-4111
  600 Prospect Ave Ste 1 Piscataway (08854) **(G-8741)**

Ziggy Snack Foods LLC 917 662-6038
  200 Clifton Blvd Ste 1 Clifton (07011) **(G-1744)**

Zimmer Inc 856 778-8300
  1001 Briggs Rd Ste 275 Mount Laurel (08054) **(G-6814)**

Zimmer Biomet 201 797-7300
  20-01 Pollitt Dr Fair Lawn (07410) **(G-3130)**

Zimmer Trabecular Met Tech Inc 973 576-0032
  10 Pomeroy Rd Parsippany (07054) **(G-8044)**

Zimpli Kids Inc 732 945-5995
  3301 Route 66 Ste 130 Neptune (07753) **(G-6903)**

Zin-Tech Inc (PA) 856 661-0900
  1416 Union Ave Pennsauken (08110) **(G-8499)**

Zinas Salads Inc 973 428-0660
  11 Great Meadow Ln East Hanover (07936) **(G-2249)**

Zinicola Baking Co 973 667-1306
  127 King St Nutley (07110) **(G-7598)**

Zink Holdings LLC (PA) 781 761-5400
  114 Tived Ln E Edison (08837) **(G-2650)**

Zion Industries Inc 973 998-0162
  39 E Hanover Ave Ste G Morris Plains (07950) **(G-6629)**

Zip Rib, Burlington *Also called Merchant & Evans Inc* **(G-979)**

Zippityprint LLC 216 438-0001
  182 Harrisonville Rd Mullica Hill (08062) **(G-6859)**

Zippityprint.com, Mullica Hill *Also called Zippityprint LLC* **(G-6859)**

Zirti LLC..201 509-8404
  296 Midland Ave Ste A Saddle Brook (07663) *(G-9689)*

Zixel Ltd..732 972-3287
  4 Pegasus Ct Morganville (07751) *(G-6600)*

Zodiac Aerosystems, Wall Township *Also called Zodiac US Corporation* *(G-11379)*

Zodiac Paintball Inc..973 616-7230
  4 Sage Way Pompton Plains (07444) *(G-8876)*

Zodiac US Corporation (HQ)................................732 681-3527
  1747 State Route 34 Wall Township (07727) *(G-11379)*

Zoetis Inc (PA)..973 822-7000
  10 Sylvan Way Ste 105 Parsippany (07054) *(G-8045)*

Zoetis LLC (HQ)..973 822-7000
  10 Sylvan Way Ste 105 Parsippany (07054) *(G-8046)*

Zoetis Products LLC (HQ)....................................973 660-5000
  100 Campus Dr Ste 3 Florham Park (07932) *(G-3528)*

Zoetis Products LLC..973 660-5000
  440 Rte 22 Bridgewater (08807) *(G-905)*

Zollanvari Ltd..201 330-3344
  600 Mdwlands Pkwy Ste 130 Secaucus (07094) *(G-9830)*

Zoluu LLC..862 686-1774
  0-74 Saddle River Rd Fair Lawn (07410) *(G-3131)*

Zone Defense Inc..973 328-0436
  428 Sand Shore Rd 7 Hackettstown (07840) *(G-4042)*

Zone First, Randolph *Also called Trolex Corporation* *(G-9204)*

Zone Two Inc..732 237-0766
  245 Hickory Ln Ste 2 Bayville (08721) *(G-254)*

Zoo Printing Inc..856 686-0800
  551 Mid Atlantic Pkwy West Deptford (08066) *(G-11718)*

Zoomessence Inc..732 416-6638
  550 Hartle St Ste B Sayreville (08872) *(G-9727)*

Zoono USA Ltd Liability Co..................................732 722-8757
  1151 Broad St Ste 115 Shrewsbury (07702) *(G-9905)*

Zounds Inc..856 234-8844
  3131 Route 38 Ste 19 Mount Laurel (08054) *(G-6815)*

Zounds Hearing, Mount Laurel *Also called Zounds Inc* *(G-6815)*

Zrike Brands, Moonachie *Also called R Squared Sls & Logistics LLC* *(G-6485)*

Zsombor Antal Designs Inc................................201 225-1750
  822 Kinderkamack Rd River Edge (07661) *(G-9364)*

Zultner & Company..609 452-0216
  12 Wallingford Dr Princeton (08540) *(G-9045)*

Zulu Fire Doors Ltd Lblty Co................................973 569-9858
  923 Market St Paterson (07513) *(G-8326)*

Zvonko Stulic & Son Inc......................................973 589-3773
  21 Main St Newark (07105) *(G-7319)*

Zwier Corp..973 748-4009
  497 Bloomfield Ave Bloomfield (07003) *(G-524)*

Zwivel LLC..844 499-4835
  45 Eisenhower Dr Ste 220 Paramus (07652) *(G-7845)*

Zxchem USA Inc..732 529-6352
  255 Old New Brunswick Rd Piscataway (08854) *(G-8742)*

Zycal Bioceuticals Mfg LLC (PA)..........................888 779-9225
  5a Executive Dr Toms River (08755) *(G-10806)*

Zycus Inc (HQ)..609 799-5664
  103 Carnegie Ctr Ste 321 Princeton (08540) *(G-9046)*

Zymet Inc..973 428-5245
  7 Great Meadow Ln East Hanover (07936) *(G-2250)*

Zzyzx LLC..908 722-3770
  5 Columbia Rd Branchburg (08876) *(G-700)*

**A
L
P
H
A
B
E
T
I
C**

PRODUCT INDEX

• Product categories are listed in alphabetical order.

A

ABRASIVES
ABRASIVES: Polishing Rouge
ACADEMIC TUTORING SVCS
ACCELERATORS, RUBBER PROCESSING: Cyclic or Acyclic
ACCELEROMETERS
ACCOUNTING MACHINES & CASH REGISTERS
ACETONE: Natural
ACID RESIST: Etching
ACIDS
ACIDS: Boric
ACIDS: Hydrochloric
ACRYLIC RESINS
ACTUATORS: Indl, NEC
ACUPUNCTURISTS' OFFICES
ADDITIVE BASED PLASTIC MATERIALS: Plasticizers
ADHESIVES
ADHESIVES & SEALANTS
ADHESIVES: Adhesives, paste
ADHESIVES: Adhesives, plastic
ADHESIVES: Epoxy
ADVERTISING AGENCIES
ADVERTISING AGENCIES: Consultants
ADVERTISING CURTAINS
ADVERTISING DISPLAY PRDTS
ADVERTISING MATERIAL DISTRIBUTION
ADVERTISING REPRESENTATIVES: Electronic Media
ADVERTISING REPRESENTATIVES: Media
ADVERTISING REPRESENTATIVES: Newspaper
ADVERTISING REPRESENTATIVES: Printed Media
ADVERTISING SPECIALTIES, WHOLESALE
ADVERTISING SVCS: Bus Card
ADVERTISING SVCS: Direct Mail
ADVERTISING SVCS: Display
ADVERTISING SVCS: Outdoor
ADVERTISING SVCS: Poster, Outdoor
ADVERTISING SVCS: Sample Distribution
ADVERTISING SVCS: Transit
AEROSOLS
AGENTS, BROKERS & BUREAUS: Personal Service
AGENTS: Loan, Farm Or Business
AGRICULTURAL CHEMICALS: Trace Elements
AGRICULTURAL EQPT: BARN, SILO, POULTRY,
   DAIRY/LIVESTOCK MACH
AGRICULTURAL EQPT: Fertilizing Machinery
AGRICULTURAL EQPT: Trailers & Wagons, Farm
AGRICULTURAL EQPT: Turf Eqpt, Commercial
AIR CLEANING SYSTEMS
AIR CONDITIONING & VENTILATION EQPT & SPLYS:
   Wholesales
AIR CONDITIONING EQPT
AIR CONDITIONING UNITS: Complete, Domestic Or Indl
AIR COOLERS: Metal Plate
AIR MATTRESSES: Plastic
AIR POLLUTION MEASURING SVCS
AIR PURIFICATION EQPT
AIRCRAFT & AEROSPACE FLIGHT INSTRUMENTS & GUID-
   ANCE SYSTEMS
AIRCRAFT & HEAVY EQPT REPAIR SVCS
AIRCRAFT ASSEMBLY PLANTS
AIRCRAFT CONTROL SYSTEMS: Electronic Totalizing Coun-
   ters
AIRCRAFT ENGINES & ENGINE PARTS: Cooling Systems
AIRCRAFT ENGINES & PARTS
AIRCRAFT EQPT & SPLYS WHOLESALERS
AIRCRAFT FLIGHT INSTRUMENTS
AIRCRAFT MAINTENANCE & REPAIR SVCS
AIRCRAFT PARTS & AUXILIARY EQPT: Aircraft Training Eqpt
AIRCRAFT PARTS & AUXILIARY EQPT: Armament, Exc
   Guns
AIRCRAFT PARTS & AUXILIARY EQPT: Assys, Subassem-
   blies/Parts
AIRCRAFT PARTS & AUXILIARY EQPT: Body & Wing Assys
   & Parts
AIRCRAFT PARTS & AUXILIARY EQPT: Body Assemblies &
   Parts
AIRCRAFT PARTS & AUXILIARY EQPT: Deicing Eqpt

AIRCRAFT PARTS & AUXILIARY EQPT: Landing Assemblies
   & Brakes
AIRCRAFT PARTS & AUXILIARY EQPT: Military Eqpt & Arma-
   ment
AIRCRAFT PARTS & AUXILIARY EQPT: Tanks, Fuel
AIRCRAFT PARTS & EQPT, NEC
AIRCRAFT PARTS WHOLESALERS
AIRCRAFT PARTS/AUX EQPT: Airframe Assy, Exc Guided
   Missiles
AIRCRAFT SEATS
AIRCRAFT SERVICING & REPAIRING
AIRCRAFT TURBINES
AIRCRAFT: Airplanes, Fixed Or Rotary Wing
AIRCRAFT: Autogiros
AIRCRAFT: Motorized
AIRCRAFT: Research & Development, Manufacturer
AIRPORTS, FLYING FIELDS & SVCS
ALARM SYSTEMS WHOLESALERS
ALARMS: Burglar
ALARMS: Fire
ALCOHOL, ETHYL: For Beverage Purposes
ALCOHOL: Ethyl & Ethanol
ALKALIES & CHLORINE
ALLOYS: Additive, Exc Copper Or Made In Blast Furnaces
ALTERNATORS: Automotive
ALUMINUM
ALUMINUM PRDTS
ALUMINUM: Coil & Sheet
ALUMINUM: Rolling & Drawing
AMMUNITION
AMMUNITION: Small Arms
AMPLIFIERS
AMPLIFIERS: RF & IF Power
AMUSEMENT & RECREATION SVCS, NEC
AMUSEMENT & RECREATION SVCS: Physical Fitness In-
   struction
AMUSEMENT & RECREATION SVCS: Tourist Attraction,
   Commercial
AMUSEMENT & RECREATION SVCS: Video Game Arcades
AMUSEMENT & RECREATION SVCS: Yoga Instruction
AMUSEMENT ARCADES
AMUSEMENT MACHINES: Coin Operated
AMUSEMENT PARK DEVICES & RIDES
AMUSEMENT PARK DEVICES & RIDES Carousels Or Merry-
   Go-Rounds
ANALYZERS: Electrical Testing
ANALYZERS: Network
ANALYZERS: Respiratory
ANESTHESIA EQPT
ANESTHETICS: Bulk Form
ANIMAL FEED & SUPPLEMENTS: Livestock & Poultry
ANIMAL FEED: Wholesalers
ANIMAL FOOD & SUPPLEMENTS: Bird Food, Prepared
ANIMAL FOOD & SUPPLEMENTS: Cat
ANIMAL FOOD & SUPPLEMENTS: Dog
ANIMAL FOOD & SUPPLEMENTS: Dog & Cat
ANIMAL FOOD & SUPPLEMENTS: Feed Supplements
ANIMAL FOOD & SUPPLEMENTS: Livestock
ANIMAL FOOD & SUPPLEMENTS: Poultry
ANIMAL FOOD & SUPPLEMENTS: Slaughtering of nonfood
   animals
ANODIZING SVC
ANTENNAS: Radar Or Communications
ANTENNAS: Receiving
ANTIBIOTICS
ANTIBIOTICS, PACKAGED
ANTIFREEZE
ANTIHISTAMINE PREPARATIONS
ANTIQUE FURNITURE RESTORATION & REPAIR
APPAREL DESIGNERS: Commercial
APPAREL: Hand Woven
APPLIANCE PARTS: Porcelain Enameled
APPLIANCES, HOUSEHOLD: Drycleaning Machines, Incl
   Coin-Op
APPLIANCES, HOUSEHOLD: Kitchen, Major, Exc Refrigs &
   Stoves
APPLIANCES: Household, NEC
APPLIANCES: Household, Refrigerators & Freezers

APPLIANCES: Major, Cooking
APPLIANCES: Small, Electric
APPLICATIONS SOFTWARE PROGRAMMING
AQUARIUM ACCESS, METAL
ARCHITECTURAL SVCS
ARCHITECTURAL SVCS: House Designer
ARMATURE REPAIRING & REWINDING SVC
ARMOR PLATES
AROMATIC CHEMICAL PRDTS
ART DEALERS & GALLERIES
ART DESIGN SVCS
ART GOODS, WHOLESALE
ART MARBLE: Concrete
ART RESTORATION SVC
ART SPLY STORES
ARTIFICIAL FLOWERS & TREES
ARTIST'S MATERIALS & SPLYS
ARTISTS' MATERIALS, WHOLESALE
ARTISTS' MATERIALS: Clay, Modeling
ARTISTS' MATERIALS: Frames, Artists' Canvases
ARTISTS' MATERIALS: Ink, Drawing, Black & Colored
ARTISTS' MATERIALS: Palettes
ARTISTS' MATERIALS: Pencil Holders
ASBESTOS PRDTS: Clutch Facings
ASBESTOS PRDTS: Pipe Covering, Heat Insulatng Matl, Exc
   Felt
ASBESTOS PRDTS: Wick
ASBESTOS PRODUCTS
ASH TRAYS: Stamped Metal
ASPHALT & ASPHALT PRDTS
ASPHALT COATINGS & SEALERS
ASPHALT MINING & BITUMINOUS STONE QUARRYING
   SVCS
ASPHALT MINING SVCS
ASPHALT MIXTURES WHOLESALERS
ASPHALT PLANTS INCLUDING GRAVEL MIX TYPE
ASSEMBLING & PACKAGING SVCS: Cosmetic Kits
ASSEMBLING SVC: Clocks
ASSEMBLING SVC: Plumbing Fixture Fittings, Plastic
ASSOCIATIONS: Business
ASSOCIATIONS: Real Estate Management
ASSOCIATIONS: Scientists'
ASSOCIATIONS: Trade
ATHLETIC ORGANIZATION
ATOMIZERS
AUCTION SVCS: Motor Vehicle
AUDIO & VIDEO EQPT, EXC COMMERCIAL
AUDIO COMPONENTS
AUDIO ELECTRONIC SYSTEMS
AUDIO-VISUAL PROGRAM PRODUCTION SVCS
AUDIOLOGICAL EQPT: Electronic
AUDIOLOGISTS' OFFICES
AUDITING SVCS
AUTHOR
AUTO & HOME SUPPLY STORES: Auto & Truck Eqpt & Parts
AUTO & HOME SUPPLY STORES: Automotive Access
AUTO & HOME SUPPLY STORES: Automotive parts
AUTO & HOME SUPPLY STORES: Speed Shops, Incl Race
   Car Splys
AUTO & HOME SUPPLY STORES: Truck Eqpt & Parts
AUTOCLAVES: Laboratory
AUTOMATED TELLER MACHINE OR ATM REPAIR SVCS
AUTOMATIC REGULATING CONTROL: Building Svcs Moni-
   toring, Auto
AUTOMATIC REGULATING CONTROLS: AC & Refrigeration
AUTOMATIC REGULATING CONTROLS: Appliance, Exc Air-
   Cond/Refr
AUTOMATIC REGULATING CONTROLS: Elect Air Cleaner,
   Automatic
AUTOMATIC REGULATING CONTROLS: Electric Heat
AUTOMATIC REGULATING CONTROLS: Energy Cutoff,
   Residtl/Comm
AUTOMATIC REGULATING CONTROLS: Hardware, Environ-
   mental Reg
AUTOMATIC REGULATING CONTROLS: Hydronic Pressure
   Or Temp
AUTOMATIC REGULATING CONTROLS: Pressure, Air-Cond
   Sys

AUTOMATIC TELLER MACHINES
AUTOMOBILE FINANCE LEASING
AUTOMOBILE RECOVERY SVCS
AUTOMOBILE STORAGE GARAGE
AUTOMOBILES & OTHER MOTOR VEHICLES WHOLE-
  SALERS
AUTOMOBILES: Wholesalers
AUTOMOTIVE & TRUCK GENERAL REPAIR SVC
AUTOMOTIVE BODY SHOP
AUTOMOTIVE BODY, PAINT & INTERIOR REPAIR & MAIN-
  TENANCE SVC
AUTOMOTIVE EMISSIONS TESTING SVCS
AUTOMOTIVE GLASS REPLACEMENT SHOPS
AUTOMOTIVE LETTERING & PAINTING SVCS
AUTOMOTIVE PARTS, ACCESS & SPLYS
AUTOMOTIVE PARTS: Plastic
AUTOMOTIVE PRDTS: Rubber
AUTOMOTIVE REPAIR SHOPS: Electrical Svcs
AUTOMOTIVE REPAIR SHOPS: Engine Repair
AUTOMOTIVE REPAIR SHOPS: Machine Shop
AUTOMOTIVE REPAIR SHOPS: Trailer Repair
AUTOMOTIVE REPAIR SHOPS: Truck Engine Repair, Exc
  Indl
AUTOMOTIVE REPAIR SHOPS: Wheel Alignment
AUTOMOTIVE REPAIR SVC
AUTOMOTIVE SPLYS & PARTS, NEW, WHOL: Auto Servic-
  ing Eqpt
AUTOMOTIVE SPLYS & PARTS, NEW, WHOLESALE: Radia-
  tors
AUTOMOTIVE SPLYS & PARTS, NEW, WHOLESALE: Splys
AUTOMOTIVE SPLYS & PARTS, NEW, WHOLESALE: Trailer
  Parts
AUTOMOTIVE SPLYS & PARTS, NEW, WHOLESALE: Trim
AUTOMOTIVE SPLYS & PARTS, USED, WHOLESALE
AUTOMOTIVE SPLYS & PARTS, WHOLESALE, NEC
AUTOMOTIVE SPLYS/PART, NEW, WHOL: Spring, Shock
  Absorb/Strut
AUTOMOTIVE SVCS, EXC REPAIR & CARWASHES: Glass
  Tinting
AUTOMOTIVE SVCS, EXC REPAIR & CARWASHES: Lubri-
  cation
AUTOMOTIVE SVCS, EXC REPAIR & CARWASHES: Trailer
  Maintenance
AUTOMOTIVE SVCS, EXC REPAIR: Washing & Polishing
AUTOMOTIVE TOWING & WRECKING SVC
AUTOMOTIVE WELDING SVCS
AUTOMOTIVE: Seating
AUTOTRANSFORMERS: Electric
AVIATION SCHOOL
AWNINGS & CANOPIES
AWNINGS & CANOPIES: Awnings, Fabric, From Purchased
  Matls
AWNINGS & CANOPIES: Canopies, Fabric, From Purchased
  Matls
AWNINGS: Fiberglass
AWNINGS: Metal
AXLES

B

BABY FORMULA
BABY PACIFIERS: Rubber
BADGES, WHOLESALE
BADGES: Identification & Insignia
BAGS & CONTAINERS: Textile, Exc Sleeping
BAGS & SACKS: Shipping & Shopping
BAGS: Canvas
BAGS: Cement, Made From Purchased Materials
BAGS: Food Storage & Frozen Food, Plastic
BAGS: Food Storage & Trash, Plastic
BAGS: Garment & Wardrobe, Plastic Film
BAGS: Garment, Plastic Film, Made From Purchased Materi-
  als
BAGS: Knapsacks, Canvas, Made From Purchased Materials
BAGS: Laundry, From Purchased Materials
BAGS: Paper
BAGS: Plastic
BAGS: Plastic & Pliofilm
BAGS: Plastic, Made From Purchased Materials
BAGS: Rubber Or Rubberized Fabric
BAGS: Shipping
BAGS: Textile
BAGS: Wardrobe, Closet Access, Made From Purchased Ma-
  terials
BAKERIES, COMMERCIAL: On Premises Baking Only
BAKERIES: On Premises Baking & Consumption

BAKERY MACHINERY
BAKERY PRDTS, FROZEN: Wholesalers
BAKERY PRDTS: Bagels, Fresh Or Frozen
BAKERY PRDTS: Biscuits, Baked, Baking Powder & Raised
BAKERY PRDTS: Biscuits, Dry
BAKERY PRDTS: Bread, All Types, Fresh Or Frozen
BAKERY PRDTS: Cakes, Bakery, Exc Frozen
BAKERY PRDTS: Cakes, Bakery, Frozen
BAKERY PRDTS: Cones, Ice Cream
BAKERY PRDTS: Cookies
BAKERY PRDTS: Cookies & crackers
BAKERY PRDTS: Doughnuts, Exc Frozen
BAKERY PRDTS: Doughnuts, Frozen
BAKERY PRDTS: Dry
BAKERY PRDTS: Frozen
BAKERY PRDTS: Matzoth
BAKERY PRDTS: Pastries, Danish, Frozen
BAKERY PRDTS: Pastries, Exc Frozen
BAKERY PRDTS: Pies, Exc Frozen
BAKERY PRDTS: Pretzels
BAKERY PRDTS: Wholesalers
BAKERY: Wholesale Or Wholesale & Retail Combined
BALLASTS: Lamp
BALLASTS: Lighting
BALLOONS: Toy & Advertising, Rubber
BANKING SCHOOLS, TRAINING
BAR FIXTURES: Wood
BARBECUE EQPT
BARGES BUILDING & REPAIR
BARRELS: Shipping, Metal
BARRETTES
BARRICADES: Metal
BARS: Concrete Reinforcing, Fabricated Steel
BARS: Extruded, Aluminum
BASES, BEVERAGE
BASKETS, GIFT, WHOLESALE
BATH SHOPS
BATHING SUIT STORES
BATHMATS: Rubber
BATHROOM ACCESS & FITTINGS: Vitreous China & Earth-
  enware
BATTERIES, EXC AUTOMOTIVE: Wholesalers
BATTERIES: Alkaline, Cell Storage
BATTERIES: Rechargeable
BATTERIES: Storage
BATTERIES: Wet
BATTERY CHARGERS
BATTERY CHARGERS: Storage, Motor & Engine Generator
  Type
BEARINGS
BEARINGS & PARTS Ball
BEARINGS: Ball & Roller
BEARINGS: Roller & Parts
BEAUTY & BARBER SHOP EQPT
BEAUTY & BARBER SHOP EQPT & SPLYS WHOLESALERS
BEAUTY SALONS
BED SHEETING, COTTON
BEDDING & BEDSPRINGS STORES
BEDDING, BEDSPREADS, BLANKETS & SHEETS
BEDDING, BEDSPREADS, BLANKETS & SHEETS: Com-
  forters & Quilts
BEDDING, FROM SILK OR MANMADE FIBER
BEDS & ACCESS STORES
BEDSPREADS & BED SETS, FROM PURCHASED MATERI-
  ALS
BEDSPREADS, COTTON
BEER, WINE & LIQUOR STORES
BEER, WINE & LIQUOR STORES: Beer, Packaged
BEER, WINE & LIQUOR STORES: Hard Liquor
BEER, WINE & LIQUOR STORES: Wine
BEESWAX PROCESSING
BELLOWS
BELTING: Fabric
BELTING: Plastic
BELTING: Rubber
BELTING: Transmission, Rubber
BELTS: Conveyor, Made From Purchased Wire
BENCHES: Seating
BEVERAGE BASES & SYRUPS
BEVERAGE PRDTS: Malt, By-Prdts
BEVERAGE STORES
BEVERAGE, NONALCOHOLIC: Iced Tea/Fruit Drink, Bot-
  tled/Canned
BEVERAGES, ALCOHOLIC: Ale

BEVERAGES, ALCOHOLIC: Beer
BEVERAGES, ALCOHOLIC: Beer & Ale
BEVERAGES, ALCOHOLIC: Brandy
BEVERAGES, ALCOHOLIC: Cocktails
BEVERAGES, ALCOHOLIC: Distilled Liquors
BEVERAGES, ALCOHOLIC: Neutral Spirits, Fruit
BEVERAGES, ALCOHOLIC: Vodka
BEVERAGES, ALCOHOLIC: Wines
BEVERAGES, MALT
BEVERAGES, MILK BASED
BEVERAGES, NONALCOHOLIC: Bottled & canned soft
  drinks
BEVERAGES, NONALCOHOLIC: Carbonated
BEVERAGES, NONALCOHOLIC: Carbonated, Canned & Bot-
  tled, Etc
BEVERAGES, NONALCOHOLIC: Cider
BEVERAGES, NONALCOHOLIC: Flavoring extracts & syrups,
  nec
BEVERAGES, NONALCOHOLIC: Fruit Drnks, Under 100%
  Juice, Can
BEVERAGES, NONALCOHOLIC: Fruits, Crushed, For Foun-
  tain Use
BEVERAGES, NONALCOHOLIC: Soft Drinks, Canned & Bot-
  tled, Etc
BEVERAGES, NONALCOHOLIC: Tea, Iced, Bottled &
  Canned, Etc
BEVERAGES, WINE & DISTILLED ALCOHOLIC, WHOLE-
  SALE: Liquor
BEVERAGES, WINE & DISTILLED ALCOHOLIC, WHOLE-
  SALE: Wine
BEVERAGES, WINE/DISTILLED ALCOH, WHOL:
  Brandy/Brandy Spirits
BEVERAGES, WINE/DISTILLED ALCOHOLIC, WHOL: Cock-
  tls, Premixed
BICYCLES, PARTS & ACCESS
BIDETS: Vitreous China
BILLIARD EQPT & SPLYS WHOLESALERS
BILLING & BOOKKEEPING SVCS
BINDING SVC: Books & Manuals
BINDING SVC: Pamphlets
BINDING SVC: Trade
BINDINGS: Bias, Made From Purchased Materials
BIOLOGICAL PRDTS: Bacteriological Media
BIOLOGICAL PRDTS: Exc Diagnostic
BIOLOGICAL PRDTS: Extracts
BIOLOGICAL PRDTS: Vaccines
BIOLOGICAL PRDTS: Vaccines & Immunizing
BIRTH CONTROL DEVICES: Rubber
BLADES: Knife
BLADES: Saw, Hand Or Power
BLANKBOOKS & LOOSELEAF BINDERS
BLANKBOOKS: Albums, Record
BLANKBOOKS: Ledgers & Ledger Sheets
BLANKETS: Horse
BLASTING SVC: Sand, Metal Parts
BLINDS & SHADES: Vertical
BLINDS : Window
BLOCKS & BRICKS: Concrete
BLOCKS: Acoustical, Concrete
BLOCKS: Landscape Or Retaining Wall, Concrete
BLOCKS: Paving, Asphalt, Not From Refineries
BLOCKS: Paving, Concrete
BLOCKS: Paving, Cut Stone
BLOCKS: Roof Ballast, Concrete
BLOCKS: Sewer & Manhole, Concrete
BLOCKS: Standard, Concrete Or Cinder
BLOOD RELATED HEALTH SVCS
BLOWERS & FANS
BLOWERS & FANS
BLUEPRINTING SVCS
BOAT & BARGE COMPONENTS: Metal, Prefabricated
BOAT BUILDING & REPAIR
BOAT BUILDING & REPAIRING: Fiberglass
BOAT BUILDING & REPAIRING: Lifeboats
BOAT BUILDING & REPAIRING: Yachts
BOAT BUILDING & RPRG: Fishing, Small, Lobster, Crab,
  Oyster
BOAT DEALERS
BOAT DEALERS: Marine Splys & Eqpt
BOAT DEALERS: Motor
BOAT DEALERS: Sailboats & Eqpt
BOAT DEALERS: Sails & Eqpt
BOAT LIFTS
BOAT REPAIR SVCS
BOAT YARD: Boat yards, storage & incidental repair

BOATS & OTHER MARINE EQPT: Plastic
BODIES: Truck & Bus
BODY PARTS: Automobile, Stamped Metal
BOILER REPAIR SHOP
BOLT CAPS: Vitreous China & Earthenware
BOLTS: Metal
BONDERIZING: Bonderizing, Metal Or Metal Prdts
BOOK STORES
BOOK STORES: Children's
BOOKS, WHOLESALE
BOTTLE CAPS & RESEALERS: Plastic
BOTTLED GAS DEALERS: Liquefied Petro, Dlvrd To Customers
BOTTLED WATER DELIVERY
BOTTLES: Plastic
BOULDER: Crushed & Broken
BOUTIQUE STORES
BOWLING EQPT & SPLY STORES
BOWLING PIN REFINISH OR REPAIR SVCS
BOXES & CRATES: Rectangular, Wood
BOXES & SHOOK: Nailed Wood
BOXES: Corrugated
BOXES: Fuse, Electric
BOXES: Mail Or Post Office, Collection/Storage, Sheet Metal
BOXES: Paperboard, Folding
BOXES: Paperboard, Set-Up
BOXES: Plastic
BOXES: Solid Fiber
BOXES: Stamped Metal
BOXES: Wirebound, Wood
BOXES: Wooden
BRASS & BRONZE PRDTS: Die-casted
BRASS FOUNDRY, NEC
BRASS GOODS, WHOLESALE
BRASS ROLLING & DRAWING
BRASSWORK: Ornamental, Structural
BRAZING: Metal
BRIC-A-BRAC
BRICK, STONE & RELATED PRDTS WHOLESALERS
BRICKS : Ceramic Glazed, Clay
BROADCASTING & COMMS EQPT: Antennas, Transmitting/Comms
BROADCASTING & COMMUNICATION EQPT: Transmit-Receiver, Radio
BROADCASTING & COMMUNICATIONS EQPT: Cellular Radio Telephone
BROADCASTING & COMMUNICATIONS EQPT: Studio Eqpt, Radio & TV
BROADCASTING & COMMUNICATIONS EQPT: Transmitting, Radio/TV
BROKERS & DEALERS: Securities
BROKERS: Food
BROKERS: Printing
BROOMS & BRUSHES
BROOMS & BRUSHES: Household Or Indl
BROOMS & BRUSHES: Paint Rollers
BROOMS & BRUSHES: Paintbrushes
BROOMS & BRUSHES: Street Sweeping, Hand Or Machine
BRUSHES
BRUSHES & BRUSH STOCK CONTACTS: Electric
BUCKLES & PARTS
BUILDING & OFFICE CLEANING SVCS
BUILDING & STRUCTURAL WOOD MEMBERS
BUILDING COMPONENTS: Structural Steel
BUILDING PRDTS & MATERIALS DEALERS
BUILDING PRDTS: Concrete
BUILDING PRDTS: Stone
BUILDING STONE, ARTIFICIAL: Concrete
BUILDINGS & COMPONENTS: Prefabricated Metal
BUILDINGS, PREFABRICATED: Wholesalers
BUILDINGS: Portable
BUILDINGS: Prefabricated, Metal
BUILDINGS: Prefabricated, Wood
BUILDINGS: Prefabricated, Wood
BULLETIN BOARDS: Cork
BULLION, PRECIOUS METAL, WHOLESALE
BURGLAR ALARM MAINTENANCE & MONITORING SVCS
BURGLARY PROTECTION SVCS
BURIAL VAULTS: Concrete Or Precast Terrazzo
BURLAP & BURLAP PRDTS
BURLAP WHOLESALERS
BURNERS: Gas, Domestic
BURS: Dental
BUS BARS: Electrical
BUSHINGS & BEARINGS

BUSHINGS & BEARINGS: Copper, Exc Machined
BUSINESS ACTIVITIES: Non-Commercial Site
BUSINESS FORMS WHOLESALERS
BUSINESS FORMS: Printed, Manifold
BUSINESS MACHINE REPAIR, ELECTRIC
BUSINESS SUPPORT SVCS
BUTTONS

C

CABINETS & CASES: Show, Display & Storage, Exc Wood
CABINETS: Bathroom Vanities, Wood
CABINETS: Entertainment
CABINETS: Entertainment Units, Household, Wood
CABINETS: Factory
CABINETS: Kitchen, Metal
CABINETS: Kitchen, Wood
CABINETS: Office, Wood
CABINETS: Show, Display, Etc, Wood, Exc Refrigerated
CABLE & OTHER PAY TELEVISION DISTRIBUTION
CABLE & PAY TELEVISION SVCS: Closed Circuit
CABLE & PAY TELEVISION SVCS: Direct Broadcast Satellite
CABLE TELEVISION PRDTS
CABLE: Coaxial
CABLE: Fiber
CABLE: Fiber Optic
CABLE: Nonferrous, Shipboard
CABLE: Noninsulated
CABLE: Ropes & Fiber
CABLE: Steel, Insulated Or Armored
CAFFEINE & DERIVATIVES
CAGES: Wire
CALCULATING & ACCOUNTING EQPT
CALENDARS, WHOLESALE
CALIBRATING SVCS, NEC
CAMERA & PHOTOGRAPHIC SPLYS STORES: Cameras
CAMERA & PHOTOGRAPHIC SPLYS STORES: Photographic Splys
CAMERAS & RELATED EQPT: Photographic
CANDLE SHOPS
CANDLES
CANDLES: Wholesalers
CANDY & CONFECTIONS: Candy Bars, Including Chocolate Covered
CANDY & CONFECTIONS: Chocolate Candy, Exc Solid Chocolate
CANDY & CONFECTIONS: Fruit & Fruit Peel
CANDY & CONFECTIONS: Licorice
CANDY & CONFECTIONS: Marzipan
CANDY & CONFECTIONS: Nuts, Candy Covered
CANDY & CONFECTIONS: Nuts, Glace
CANDY & CONFECTIONS: Popcorn Balls/Other Trtd Popcorn Prdts
CANDY, NUT & CONFECTIONERY STORES: Candy
CANDY, NUT & CONFECTIONERY STORES: Confectionery
CANDY, NUT & CONFECTIONERY STORES: Produced For Direct Sale
CANDY: Chocolate From Cacao Beans
CANDY: Hard
CANDY: Soft
CANNED SPECIALTIES
CANS & TUBES: Ammunition, Board Laminated With Metal Foil
CANS: Composite Foil-Fiber, Made From Purchased Materials
CANS: Metal
CANS: Tin
CANVAS PRDTS
CANVAS PRDTS, WHOLESALE
CANVAS PRDTS: Boat Seats
CANVAS PRDTS: Convertible Tops, Car/Boat, Fm Purchased Mtrl
CAPACITORS: NEC
CAPS: Plastic
CAR WASH EQPT
CAR WASH EQPT & SPLYS WHOLESALERS
CARBIDES
CARBON & GRAPHITE PRDTS, NEC
CARBON BLACK
CARBON PAPER & INKED RIBBONS
CARBON SPECIALTIES Electrical Use
CARBONS: Electric
CARDBOARD PRDTS, EXC DIE-CUT
CARDIOVASCULAR SYSTEM DRUGS, EXC DIAGNOSTIC
CARDS: Color
CARDS: Greeting
CARDS: Identification

CARPETS, RUGS & FLOOR COVERING
CARPETS: Hand & Machine Made
CARPETS: Textile Fiber
CARRIER EQPT: Telephone Or Telegraph
CARRYING CASES, WHOLESALE
CASES, WOOD
CASES: Carrying
CASES: Carrying, Clothing & Apparel
CASES: Plastic
CASES: Shipping, Wood, Wirebound
CASH REGISTERS & PARTS
CASINGS: Sheet Metal
CASKET LININGS
CAST STONE: Concrete
CASTERS
CASTINGS GRINDING: For The Trade
CASTINGS: Aerospace Investment, Ferrous
CASTINGS: Aerospace, Aluminum
CASTINGS: Aluminum
CASTINGS: Bronze, NEC, Exc Die
CASTINGS: Commercial Investment, Ferrous
CASTINGS: Copper & Copper-Base Alloy, NEC, Exc Die
CASTINGS: Die, Aluminum
CASTINGS: Die, Copper & Copper Alloy
CASTINGS: Die, Nonferrous
CASTINGS: Die, Zinc
CASTINGS: Gray Iron
CASTINGS: Machinery, Nonferrous, Exc Die or Aluminum Copper
CASTINGS: Precision
CASTINGS: Steel
CASTINGS: Zinc
CATALOG & MAIL-ORDER HOUSES
CATALOG SALES
CATALYSTS: Chemical
CATERERS
CAULKING COMPOUNDS
CEILING SYSTEMS: Luminous, Commercial
CELLULOSE DERIVATIVE MATERIALS
CEMENT: Hydraulic
CEMENT: Masonry
CEMETERY MEMORIAL DEALERS
CERAMIC FIBER
CHAINS: Power Transmission
CHANDELIERS: Commercial
CHANDELIERS: Residential
CHARCOAL: Activated
CHART & GRAPH DESIGN SVCS
CHASING SVC: Metal
CHASSIS: Automobile House Trailer
CHASSIS: Motor Vehicle
CHEESE WHOLESALERS
CHEMICAL ELEMENTS
CHEMICAL PROCESSING MACHINERY & EQPT
CHEMICAL SPLYS FOR FOUNDRIES
CHEMICAL: Sodm Compnds/Salts, Inorg, Exc Rfnd Sodm Chloride
CHEMICALS & ALLIED PRDTS WHOLESALERS, NEC
CHEMICALS & ALLIED PRDTS, WHOL: Chemical, Organic, Synthetic
CHEMICALS & ALLIED PRDTS, WHOL: Food Additives/Preservatives
CHEMICALS & ALLIED PRDTS, WHOLESALE: Aerosols
CHEMICALS & ALLIED PRDTS, WHOLESALE: Alkalines & Chlorine
CHEMICALS & ALLIED PRDTS, WHOLESALE: Aromatic
CHEMICALS & ALLIED PRDTS, WHOLESALE: Chemical Additives
CHEMICALS & ALLIED PRDTS, WHOLESALE: Chemicals, Indl
CHEMICALS & ALLIED PRDTS, WHOLESALE: Chemicals, Indl & Heavy
CHEMICALS & ALLIED PRDTS, WHOLESALE: Chemicals, Rustproofing
CHEMICALS & ALLIED PRDTS, WHOLESALE: Compressed Gas
CHEMICALS & ALLIED PRDTS, WHOLESALE: Detergents
CHEMICALS & ALLIED PRDTS, WHOLESALE: Dry Ice
CHEMICALS & ALLIED PRDTS, WHOLESALE: Essential Oils
CHEMICALS & ALLIED PRDTS, WHOLESALE: Indl Gases
CHEMICALS & ALLIED PRDTS, WHOLESALE: Metal Polishes
CHEMICALS & ALLIED PRDTS, WHOLESALE: Plastics Film
CHEMICALS & ALLIED PRDTS, WHOLESALE: Plastics Materials, NEC

CHEMICALS & ALLIED PRDTS, WHOLESALE: Plastics Prdts, NEC
CHEMICALS & ALLIED PRDTS, WHOLESALE: Plastics Sheets & Rods
CHEMICALS & ALLIED PRDTS, WHOLESALE: Polyurethane Prdts
CHEMICALS & ALLIED PRDTS, WHOLESALE: Resins
CHEMICALS & ALLIED PRDTS, WHOLESALE: Resins, Plastics
CHEMICALS & ALLIED PRDTS, WHOLESALE: Silicon Lubricants
CHEMICALS & ALLIED PRDTS, WHOLESALE: Spec Clean/Sanitation
CHEMICALS & ALLIED PRDTS, WHOLESALE: Waxes, Exc Petroleum
CHEMICALS: Agricultural
CHEMICALS: Aluminum Chloride
CHEMICALS: Aluminum Compounds
CHEMICALS: Aluminum Sulfate
CHEMICALS: Ammonium Compounds, Exc Fertilizers, NEC
CHEMICALS: Barium & Barium Compounds
CHEMICALS: Brine
CHEMICALS: Caustic Soda
CHEMICALS: Copper Compounds Or Salts, Inorganic
CHEMICALS: Fire Retardant
CHEMICALS: High Purity Grade, Organic
CHEMICALS: High Purity, Refined From Technical Grade
CHEMICALS: Inorganic, NEC
CHEMICALS: Magnesium Compounds Or Salts, Inorganic
CHEMICALS: Medicinal
CHEMICALS: Medicinal, Organic, Uncompounded, Bulk
CHEMICALS: NEC
CHEMICALS: Nickel Compounds Or Salts, Inorganic
CHEMICALS: Nonmetallic Compounds
CHEMICALS: Organic, NEC
CHEMICALS: Phenol
CHEMICALS: Phosphates, Defluorinated/Ammoniated, Exc Fertlr
CHEMICALS: Reagent Grade, Refined From Technical Grade
CHEMICALS: Soda Ash
CHEMICALS: Sodium Bicarbonate
CHEMICALS: Sodium/Potassium Cmpnds,Exc Bleach,Alkalies/Alum
CHEMICALS: Sulfur, Incl Rcvrd/Refined, Fm Sour Natural Gas
CHEMICALS: Water Treatment
CHEMICALS: Zinc Chloride
CHEWING GUM
CHILDREN'S & INFANTS' CLOTHING STORES
CHILDREN'S WEAR STORES
CHINA & GLASS REPAIR SVCS
CHINAWARE WHOLESALERS
CHIROPRACTORS' OFFICES
CHOCOLATE, EXC CANDY FROM BEANS: Chips, Powder, Block, Syrup
CHOCOLATE, EXC CANDY FROM PURCH CHOC: Chips, Powder, Block
CHRISTMAS NOVELTIES, WHOLESALE
CHRISTMAS TREE LIGHTING SETS: Electric
CHRISTMAS TREES: Artificial
CHROMATOGRAPHY EQPT
CIGARETTE LIGHTER FLINTS
CIGARETTE LIGHTERS
CIGARETTE STORES
CIRCUIT BOARDS, PRINTED: Television & Radio
CIRCUIT BOARDS: Wiring
CIRCUITS, INTEGRATED: Hybrid
CIRCUITS: Electronic
CLAY MINING, COMMON
CLAYS, EXC KAOLIN & BALL
CLEANING EQPT: Commercial
CLEANING EQPT: Dirt Sweeping Units, Indl
CLEANING EQPT: Floor Washing & Polishing, Commercial
CLEANING EQPT: High Pressure
CLEANING EQPT: Janitors' Carts
CLEANING OR POLISHING PREPARATIONS, NEC
CLEANING PRDTS: Ammonia, Household
CLEANING PRDTS: Bleaches, Household, Dry Or Liquid
CLEANING PRDTS: Degreasing Solvent
CLEANING PRDTS: Deodorants, Nonpersonal
CLEANING PRDTS: Disinfectants, Household Or Indl Plant
CLEANING PRDTS: Drain Pipe Solvents Or Cleaners
CLEANING PRDTS: Drycleaning Preparations
CLEANING PRDTS: Floor Waxes
CLEANING PRDTS: Indl Plant Disinfectants Or Deodorants
CLEANING PRDTS: Metal Polish

CLEANING PRDTS: Polishing Preparations & Related Prdts
CLEANING PRDTS: Sanitation Preparations
CLEANING PRDTS: Sanitation Preps, Disinfectants/Deodorants
CLEANING PRDTS: Specialty
CLEANING PRDTS: Stain Removers
CLEANING SVCS
CLIPPERS: Fingernail & Toenail
CLOCK REPAIR SVCS
CLOSURES: Closures, Stamped Metal
CLOSURES: Plastic
CLOTHING & ACCESS, WOMEN, CHILD & INFANT, WHOL: Blouses
CLOTHING & ACCESS, WOMEN, CHILD & INFANT, WHSLE: Sportswear
CLOTHING & ACCESS, WOMEN, CHILDREN & INFANT, WHOL: Uniforms
CLOTHING & ACCESS, WOMEN, CHILDREN/INFANT, WHOL: Baby Goods
CLOTHING & ACCESS, WOMEN, CHILDREN/INFANT, WHOL: Nightwear
CLOTHING & ACCESS, WOMEN, CHILDREN/INFANT, WHOL: Outerwear
CLOTHING & ACCESS, WOMENS, CHILDREN & INFANTS, WHOL: Hats
CLOTHING & ACCESS: Costumes, Masquerade
CLOTHING & ACCESS: Costumes, Theatrical
CLOTHING & ACCESS: Handicapped
CLOTHING & ACCESS: Handkerchiefs, Exc Paper
CLOTHING & ACCESS: Men's Miscellaneous Access
CLOTHING & APPAREL STORES: Custom
CLOTHING & FURNISHINGS, MEN'S & BOYS', WHOLESALE: Outerwear
CLOTHING & FURNISHINGS, MEN'S & BOYS', WHOLESALE: Scarves
CLOTHING & FURNISHINGS, MEN'S & BOYS', WHOLESALE: Shirts
CLOTHING & FURNISHINGS, MEN'S & BOYS', WHOLESALE: Trousers
CLOTHING & FURNISHINGS, MEN'S & BOYS', WHOLESALE: Umbrellas
CLOTHING & FURNISHINGS, MEN'S & BOYS', WHOLESALE: Uniforms
CLOTHING ACCESS STORES: Belts, Custom
CLOTHING STORES, NEC
CLOTHING STORES: Dancewear
CLOTHING STORES: T-Shirts, Printed, Custom
CLOTHING STORES: Uniforms & Work
CLOTHING STORES: Unisex
CLOTHING: Access
CLOTHING: Access, Women's & Misses'
CLOTHING: Aprons, Exc Rubber/Plastic, Women, Misses, Junior
CLOTHING: Aprons, Work, Exc Rubberized & Plastic, Men's
CLOTHING: Athletic & Sportswear, Men's & Boys'
CLOTHING: Athletic & Sportswear, Women's & Girls'
CLOTHING: Baker, Barber, Lab/Svc Ind Apparel, Washable, Men
CLOTHING: Bathing Suits & Swimwear, Girls, Children & Infant
CLOTHING: Bathing Suits & Swimwear, Knit
CLOTHING: Bathrobes, Mens & Womens, From Purchased Materials
CLOTHING: Belts
CLOTHING: Blouses, Women's & Girls'
CLOTHING: Blouses, Womens & Juniors, From Purchased Mtrls
CLOTHING: Brassieres
CLOTHING: Bridal Gowns
CLOTHING: Capes & Jackets, Women's & Misses'
CLOTHING: Caps, Baseball
CLOTHING: Children & Infants'
CLOTHING: Children's, Girls'
CLOTHING: Clergy Vestments
CLOTHING: Coats & Jackets, Leather & Sheep-Lined
CLOTHING: Coats & Suits, Men's & Boys'
CLOTHING: Coats, Leatherette, Oiled Fabric, Etc, Mens & Boys
CLOTHING: Coats, Overcoats & Vests
CLOTHING: Costumes
CLOTHING: Disposable
CLOTHING: Down-Filled, Men's & Boys'
CLOTHING: Dresses
CLOTHING: Dressing Gowns, Mens/Womens, From Purchased Matls

CLOTHING: Formal Jackets, Mens & Youth, From Purchased Matls
CLOTHING: Furs
CLOTHING: Garments, Indl, Men's & Boys
CLOTHING: Girdles & Panty Girdles
CLOTHING: Gowns & Dresses, Wedding
CLOTHING: Gowns, Formal
CLOTHING: Hats & Caps, NEC
CLOTHING: Hats & Caps, Uniform
CLOTHING: Hats & Headwear, Knit
CLOTHING: Hosiery, Men's & Boys'
CLOTHING: Hosiery, Pantyhose & Knee Length, Sheer
CLOTHING: Hospital, Men's
CLOTHING: Jackets, Field, Military
CLOTHING: Jackets, Overall & Work
CLOTHING: Jeans, Men's & Boys'
CLOTHING: Jerseys, Knit
CLOTHING: Leather
CLOTHING: Leather & sheep-lined clothing
CLOTHING: Lounge, Bed & Leisurewear
CLOTHING: Men's & boy's underwear & nightwear
CLOTHING: Millinery
CLOTHING: Neckwear
CLOTHING: Outerwear, Knit
CLOTHING: Outerwear, Lthr, Wool/Down-Filled, Men, Youth/Boy
CLOTHING: Outerwear, Women's & Misses' NEC
CLOTHING: Raincoats, Exc Vulcanized Rubber, Purchased Matls
CLOTHING: Robes & Dressing Gowns
CLOTHING: Service Apparel, Women's
CLOTHING: Shirts
CLOTHING: Shirts, Dress, Men's & Boys'
CLOTHING: Shirts, Knit
CLOTHING: Shirts, Sports & Polo, Men's & Boys'
CLOTHING: Skirts
CLOTHING: Sleeping Garments, Women's & Children's
CLOTHING: Socks
CLOTHING: Sportswear, Women's
CLOTHING: Suits & Skirts, Women's & Misses'
CLOTHING: Suits, Men's & Boys', From Purchased Materials
CLOTHING: Sweaters & Sweater Coats, Knit
CLOTHING: T-Shirts & Tops, Knit
CLOTHING: T-Shirts & Tops, Women's & Girls'
CLOTHING: Tailored Dress/Sport Coats, Mens & Boys
CLOTHING: Tailored Suits & Formal Jackets
CLOTHING: Ties, Neck, Men's & Boys', From Purchased Material
CLOTHING: Trousers & Slacks, Men's & Boys'
CLOTHING: Underwear, Men's & Boys'
CLOTHING: Underwear, Women's & Children's
CLOTHING: Uniforms & Vestments
CLOTHING: Uniforms, Ex Athletic, Women's, Misses' & Juniors'
CLOTHING: Uniforms, Firemen's, From Purchased Materials
CLOTHING: Uniforms, Military, Men/Youth, Purchased Materials
CLOTHING: Uniforms, Policemen's, From Purchased Materials
CLOTHING: Uniforms, Team Athletic
CLOTHING: Uniforms, Work
CLOTHING: WarmUp, Jogging & Sweat Suits, Girls' & Children's
CLOTHING: Waterproof Outerwear
CLOTHING: Womens/Misses Coats, Jackets & Vests, Down-Filled
CLOTHING: Work Apparel, Exc Uniforms
CLOTHING: Work, Men's
CLOTHING: Work, Waterproof, Exc Raincoats
COAL MINING SERVICES
COAL MINING SVCS: Anthracite, Contract Basis
COAL, MINERALS & ORES, WHOLESALE: Coal
COATING COMPOUNDS: Tar
COATING SVC
COATING SVC: Metals & Formed Prdts
COATING SVC: Metals, With Plastic Or Resins
COATING SVC: Rust Preventative
COATING SVC: Silicon
COATINGS: Air Curing
COATINGS: Epoxy
COATINGS: Polyurethane
CODEINE & DERIVATIVES
COFFEE MAKERS: Electric
COFFEE SVCS
COILS & TRANSFORMERS

COILS, WIRE: Aluminum, Made In Rolling Mills
COIN-OPERATED LAUNDRY
COLLECTION AGENCY, EXC REAL ESTATE
COLOR LAKES OR TONERS
COLOR PIGMENTS
COLOR SEPARATION: Photographic & Movie Film
COLORS: Pigments, Inorganic
COLORS: Pigments, Organic
COLUMNS, FRACTIONING: Metal Plate
COMFORTERS & QUILTS, FROM MANMADE FIBER OR
   SILK
COMMERCIAL & INDL SHELVING WHOLESALERS
COMMERCIAL & OFFICE BUILDINGS RENOVATION & RE-
   PAIR
COMMERCIAL ART & GRAPHIC DESIGN SVCS
COMMERCIAL ART & ILLUSTRATION SVCS
COMMERCIAL CONTAINERS WHOLESALERS
COMMERCIAL EQPT & SPLYS, WHOLESALE: Hotel
COMMERCIAL EQPT WHOLESALERS, NEC
COMMERCIAL EQPT, WHOLESALE: Bakery Eqpt & Splys
COMMERCIAL EQPT, WHOLESALE: Coffee Brewing Eqpt &
   Splys
COMMERCIAL EQPT, WHOLESALE: Comm Cooking & Food
   Svc Eqpt
COMMERCIAL EQPT, WHOLESALE: Display Eqpt, Exc Re-
   frigerated
COMMERCIAL EQPT, WHOLESALE: Restaurant, NEC
COMMERCIAL EQPT, WHOLESALE: Scales, Exc Laboratory
COMMERCIAL EQPT, WHOLESALE: Store Fixtures & Display
   Eqpt
COMMERCIAL LAUNDRY EQPT
COMMERCIAL PRINTING & NEWSPAPER PUBLISHING
   COMBINED
COMMERCIAL REFRIGERATORS WHOLESALERS
COMMODITY CONTRACTS BROKERS, DEALERS
COMMON SAND MINING
COMMUNICATION HEADGEAR: Telephone
COMMUNICATIONS EQPT & SYSTEMS, NEC
COMMUNICATIONS EQPT REPAIR & MAINTENANCE
COMMUNICATIONS EQPT WHOLESALERS
COMMUNICATIONS EQPT: Microwave
COMMUNICATIONS SVCS
COMMUNICATIONS SVCS: Cellular
COMMUNICATIONS SVCS: Data
COMMUNICATIONS SVCS: Facsimile Transmission
COMMUNICATIONS SVCS: Internet Connectivity Svcs
COMMUNICATIONS SVCS: Internet Host Svcs
COMMUNICATIONS SVCS: Online Svc Providers
COMMUNICATIONS SVCS: Satellite Earth Stations
COMMUNICATIONS SVCS: Telephone Or Video
COMMUNICATIONS SVCS: Telephone, Data
COMMUNICATIONS SVCS: Telephone, Local
COMMUNICATIONS SVCS: Telephone, Local & Long Dis-
   tance
COMMUNICATIONS SVCS: Telephone, Voice
COMMUTATORS: Electric Motors
COMMUTATORS: Electronic
COMPACT LASER DISCS: Prerecorded
COMPOST
COMPRESSORS: Air & Gas
COMPRESSORS: Air & Gas, Including Vacuum Pumps
COMPUTER & COMPUTER SOFTWARE STORES
COMPUTER & COMPUTER SOFTWARE STORES: Periph-
   eral Eqpt
COMPUTER & COMPUTER SOFTWARE STORES: Printers
   & Plotters
COMPUTER & COMPUTER SOFTWARE STORES: Software
   & Access
COMPUTER & COMPUTER SOFTWARE STORES: Soft-
   ware, Bus/Non-Game
COMPUTER & COMPUTER SOFTWARE STORES: Soft-
   ware, Computer Game
COMPUTER & DATA PROCESSING EQPT REPAIR & MAIN-
   TENANCE
COMPUTER & OFFICE MACHINE MAINTENANCE & RE-
   PAIR
COMPUTER & SFTWR STORE: Modem, Monitor,
   Terminal/Disk Drive
COMPUTER CALCULATING SVCS
COMPUTER DISKETTES WHOLESALERS
COMPUTER FACILITIES MANAGEMENT SVCS
COMPUTER FORMS
COMPUTER GRAPHICS SVCS
COMPUTER INTERFACE EQPT: Indl Process
COMPUTER PAPER WHOLESALERS

COMPUTER PERIPHERAL EQPT REPAIR & MAINTE-
   NANCE
COMPUTER PERIPHERAL EQPT, NEC
COMPUTER PERIPHERAL EQPT, WHOLESALE
COMPUTER PERIPHERAL EQPT: Decoders
COMPUTER PERIPHERAL EQPT: Graphic Displays, Exc Ter-
   minals
COMPUTER PERIPHERAL EQPT: Input Or Output
COMPUTER PROCESSING SVCS
COMPUTER PROGRAMMING SVCS
COMPUTER PROGRAMMING SVCS: Custom
COMPUTER RELATED MAINTENANCE SVCS
COMPUTER RELATED SVCS, NEC
COMPUTER SERVICE BUREAU
COMPUTER SOFTWARE DEVELOPMENT
COMPUTER SOFTWARE DEVELOPMENT & APPLICA-
   TIONS
COMPUTER SOFTWARE SYSTEMS ANALYSIS & DESIGN:
   Custom
COMPUTER SOFTWARE WRITERS
COMPUTER STORAGE DEVICES, NEC
COMPUTER STORAGE UNITS: Auxiliary
COMPUTER SYSTEM SELLING SVCS
COMPUTER SYSTEMS ANALYSIS & DESIGN
COMPUTER TERMINALS
COMPUTER TRAINING SCHOOLS
COMPUTER-AIDED DESIGN SYSTEMS SVCS
COMPUTER-AIDED ENGINEERING SYSTEMS SVCS
COMPUTER-AIDED MANUFACTURING SYSTEMS SVCS
COMPUTERS, NEC
COMPUTERS, NEC, WHOLESALE
COMPUTERS, PERIPH & SOFTWARE, WHLSE: Acctg
   Machs, Readable
COMPUTERS, PERIPH & SOFTWARE, WHLSE: Personal &
   Home Entrtn
COMPUTERS, PERIPHERALS & SOFTWARE, WHOLE-
   SALE: Printers
COMPUTERS, PERIPHERALS & SOFTWARE, WHOLE-
   SALE: Software
COMPUTERS, PERIPHERALS & SOFTWARE, WHOLE-
   SALE: Terminals
COMPUTERS: Indl, Process, Gas Flow
COMPUTERS: Mini
COMPUTERS: Personal
CONCENTRATES, DRINK
CONCENTRATES, FLAVORING, EXC DRINK
CONCRETE CURING & HARDENING COMPOUNDS
CONCRETE PRDTS
CONCRETE PRDTS, PRECAST, NEC
CONCRETE: Bituminous
CONCRETE: Dry Mixture
CONCRETE: Ready-Mixed
CONDENSERS: Heat Transfer Eqpt, Evaporative
CONDENSERS: Motors Or Generators
CONDENSERS: Steam
CONDUITS & FITTINGS: Electric
CONFECTIONERY PRDTS WHOLESALERS
CONFECTIONS & CANDY
CONFINEMENT SURVEILLANCE SYS MAINTENANCE &
   MONITORING SVCS
CONNECTORS & TERMINALS: Electrical Device Uses
CONNECTORS: Cord, Electric
CONNECTORS: Electrical
CONNECTORS: Electronic
CONNECTORS: Power, Electric
CONSTRUCTION & MINING MACHINERY WHOLESALERS
CONSTRUCTION EQPT REPAIR SVCS
CONSTRUCTION EQPT: Blade, Grader, Scraper, Dozer/Snow
   Plow
CONSTRUCTION EQPT: Cranes
CONSTRUCTION EQPT: Dozers, Tractor Mounted, Material
   Moving
CONSTRUCTION EQPT: Subgraders
CONSTRUCTION EQPT: Wrecker Hoists, Automobile
CONSTRUCTION MATERIALS, WHOLESALE: Architectural
   Metalwork
CONSTRUCTION MATERIALS, WHOLESALE: Awnings
CONSTRUCTION MATERIALS, WHOLESALE: Block, Con-
   crete & Cinder
CONSTRUCTION MATERIALS, WHOLESALE: Brick, Exc Re-
   fractory
CONSTRUCTION MATERIALS, WHOLESALE: Building
   Stone
CONSTRUCTION MATERIALS, WHOLESALE: Building
   Stone, Granite

CONSTRUCTION MATERIALS, WHOLESALE: Building
   Stone, Marble
CONSTRUCTION MATERIALS, WHOLESALE: Building, Ex-
   terior
CONSTRUCTION MATERIALS, WHOLESALE: Cement
CONSTRUCTION MATERIALS, WHOLESALE: Concrete Mix-
   tures
CONSTRUCTION MATERIALS, WHOLESALE: Glass
CONSTRUCTION MATERIALS, WHOLESALE: Gravel
CONSTRUCTION MATERIALS, WHOLESALE: Masons' Ma-
   terials
CONSTRUCTION MATERIALS, WHOLESALE: Metal Build-
   ings
CONSTRUCTION MATERIALS, WHOLESALE: Millwork
CONSTRUCTION MATERIALS, WHOLESALE: Pallets, Wood
CONSTRUCTION MATERIALS, WHOLESALE: Paving Mate-
   rials
CONSTRUCTION MATERIALS, WHOLESALE: Prefabricated
   Structures
CONSTRUCTION MATERIALS, WHOLESALE: Roof, As-
   phalt/Sheet Metal
CONSTRUCTION MATERIALS, WHOLESALE: Roofing &
   Siding Material
CONSTRUCTION MATERIALS, WHOLESALE: Sand
CONSTRUCTION MATERIALS, WHOLESALE: Septic Tanks
CONSTRUCTION MATERIALS, WHOLESALE: Siding, Exc
   Wood
CONSTRUCTION MATERIALS, WHOLESALE: Skylights, All
   Materials
CONSTRUCTION MATERIALS, WHOLESALE: Stone,
   Crushed Or Broken
CONSTRUCTION MATERIALS, WHOLESALE: Stucco
CONSTRUCTION MATERIALS, WHOLESALE: Tile & Clay
   Prdts
CONSTRUCTION MATERIALS, WHOLESALE: Window
   Frames
CONSTRUCTION MATERIALS, WHOLESALE: Windows
CONSTRUCTION MATLS, WHOL: Lumber, Rough,
   Dressed/Finished
CONSTRUCTION MTRLS, WHOL: Exterior Flat Glass,
   Plate/Window
CONSTRUCTION SAND MINING
CONSTRUCTION: Apartment Building
CONSTRUCTION: Athletic & Recreation Facilities
CONSTRUCTION: Bridge
CONSTRUCTION: Chemical Facility
CONSTRUCTION: Commercial & Institutional Building
CONSTRUCTION: Commercial & Office Building, New
CONSTRUCTION: Dam
CONSTRUCTION: Dams, Waterways, Docks & Other Marine
CONSTRUCTION: Electric Power Line
CONSTRUCTION: Food Prdts Manufacturing or Packing Plant
CONSTRUCTION: Foundation & Retaining Wall
CONSTRUCTION: Gas Main
CONSTRUCTION: Greenhouse
CONSTRUCTION: Heavy Highway & Street
CONSTRUCTION: Hospital
CONSTRUCTION: Indl Building & Warehouse
CONSTRUCTION: Indl Buildings, New, NEC
CONSTRUCTION: Indl Plant
CONSTRUCTION: Marine
CONSTRUCTION: Natural Gas Compressor Station
CONSTRUCTION: Nonresidential Buildings, Custom
CONSTRUCTION: Power & Communication Transmission
   Tower
CONSTRUCTION: Refineries
CONSTRUCTION: Religious Building
CONSTRUCTION: Residential, Nec
CONSTRUCTION: Sewer Line
CONSTRUCTION: Single-Family Housing
CONSTRUCTION: Single-family Housing, New
CONSTRUCTION: Steel Buildings
CONSTRUCTION: Street Surfacing & Paving
CONSTRUCTION: Swimming Pools
CONSTRUCTION: Transmitting Tower, Telecommunication
CONSTRUCTION: Warehouse
CONSTRUCTION: Waste Water & Sewage Treatment Plant
CONSTRUCTION: Water & Sewer Line
CONSULTING SVC: Actuarial
CONSULTING SVC: Business, NEC
CONSULTING SVC: Chemical
CONSULTING SVC: Computer
CONSULTING SVC: Data Processing
CONSULTING SVC: Engineering
CONSULTING SVC: Human Resource

CONSULTING SVC: Management
CONSULTING SVC: Marketing Management
CONSULTING SVC: Online Technology
CONSULTING SVC: Sales Management
CONSULTING SVC: Telecommunications
CONSULTING SVCS, BUSINESS: Agricultural
CONSULTING SVCS, BUSINESS: Communications
CONSULTING SVCS, BUSINESS: Energy Conservation
CONSULTING SVCS, BUSINESS: Environmental
CONSULTING SVCS, BUSINESS: Publishing
CONSULTING SVCS, BUSINESS: Sys Engnrg, Exc Computer/Prof
CONSULTING SVCS, BUSINESS: Systems Analysis & Engineering
CONSULTING SVCS, BUSINESS: Systems Analysis Or Design
CONSULTING SVCS, BUSINESS: Test Development & Evaluation
CONSULTING SVCS, BUSINESS: Traffic
CONSULTING SVCS: Oil
CONSULTING SVCS: Psychological
CONSULTING SVCS: Scientific
CONTACTS: Electrical
CONTAINERS, GLASS: Cosmetic Jars
CONTAINERS, GLASS: Medicine Bottles
CONTAINERS: Cargo, Wood & Wood With Metal
CONTAINERS: Corrugated
CONTAINERS: Foil, Bakery Goods & Frozen Foods
CONTAINERS: Food & Beverage
CONTAINERS: Food, Metal
CONTAINERS: Frozen Food & Ice Cream
CONTAINERS: Glass
CONTAINERS: Metal
CONTAINERS: Plastic
CONTAINERS: Plywood & Veneer, Wood
CONTAINERS: Sanitary, Food
CONTAINERS: Shipping & Mailing, Fiber
CONTAINERS: Shipping, Bombs, Metal Plate
CONTAINERS: Shipping, Metal, Milk, Fluid
CONTAINERS: Shipping, Wood
CONTAINERS: Wood
CONTAINMENT VESSELS: Reactor, Metal Plate
CONTRACTOR: Dredging
CONTRACTORS: Access Control System Eqpt
CONTRACTORS: Antenna Installation
CONTRACTORS: Asbestos Removal & Encapsulation
CONTRACTORS: Asphalt
CONTRACTORS: Awning Installation
CONTRACTORS: Boiler Maintenance Contractor
CONTRACTORS: Boring, Building Construction
CONTRACTORS: Bridge Painting
CONTRACTORS: Building Eqpt & Machinery Installation
CONTRACTORS: Building Movers
CONTRACTORS: Building Sign Installation & Mntnce
CONTRACTORS: Building Site Preparation
CONTRACTORS: Cable Laying
CONTRACTORS: Carpentry Work
CONTRACTORS: Carpentry, Cabinet & Finish Work
CONTRACTORS: Carpentry, Cabinet Building & Installation
CONTRACTORS: Carpentry, Finish & Trim Work
CONTRACTORS: Carpet Laying
CONTRACTORS: Ceramic Floor Tile Installation
CONTRACTORS: Closet Organizers, Installation & Design
CONTRACTORS: Commercial & Office Building
CONTRACTORS: Communications Svcs
CONTRACTORS: Computer Installation
CONTRACTORS: Concrete
CONTRACTORS: Concrete Breaking, Street & Highway
CONTRACTORS: Concrete Repair
CONTRACTORS: Construction Site Cleanup
CONTRACTORS: Core Drilling & Cutting
CONTRACTORS: Countertop Installation
CONTRACTORS: Demolition, Building & Other Structures
CONTRACTORS: Directional Oil & Gas Well Drilling Svc
CONTRACTORS: Drywall
CONTRACTORS: Electric Power Systems
CONTRACTORS: Electrical
CONTRACTORS: Electronic Controls Installation
CONTRACTORS: Energy Management Control
CONTRACTORS: Epoxy Application
CONTRACTORS: Excavating
CONTRACTORS: Excavating Slush Pits & Cellars Svcs
CONTRACTORS: Exterior Painting
CONTRACTORS: Exterior Wall System Installation
CONTRACTORS: Fence Construction

CONTRACTORS: Fiber Optic Cable Installation
CONTRACTORS: Fiberglass Work
CONTRACTORS: Fire Detection & Burglar Alarm Systems
CONTRACTORS: Fire Sprinkler System Installation Svcs
CONTRACTORS: Floor Laying & Other Floor Work
CONTRACTORS: Flooring
CONTRACTORS: Garage Doors
CONTRACTORS: Gas Field Svcs, NEC
CONTRACTORS: General Electric
CONTRACTORS: Glass Tinting, Architectural & Automotive
CONTRACTORS: Glass, Glazing & Tinting
CONTRACTORS: Heating & Air Conditioning
CONTRACTORS: Heating Systems Repair & Maintenance Svc
CONTRACTORS: Highway & Street Construction, General
CONTRACTORS: Highway & Street Paving
CONTRACTORS: Home & Office Intrs Finish, Furnish/Remodel
CONTRACTORS: Hydraulic Eqpt Installation & Svcs
CONTRACTORS: Indl Building Renovation, Remodeling & Repair
CONTRACTORS: Kitchen & Bathroom Remodeling
CONTRACTORS: Lighting Syst
CONTRACTORS: Machine Rigging & Moving
CONTRACTORS: Machinery Installation
CONTRACTORS: Maintenance, Parking Facility Eqpt
CONTRACTORS: Marble Installation, Interior
CONTRACTORS: Masonry & Stonework
CONTRACTORS: Mechanical
CONTRACTORS: Office Furniture Installation
CONTRACTORS: Oil & Gas Building, Repairing & Dismantling Svc
CONTRACTORS: Oil & Gas Field Geological Exploration Svcs
CONTRACTORS: Oil & Gas Well Drilling Svc
CONTRACTORS: Oil & Gas Wells Pumping Svcs
CONTRACTORS: Oil Field Lease Tanks: Erectg, Clng/Rprg Svcs
CONTRACTORS: Oil/Gas Field Casing,Tube/Rod Running,Cut/Pull
CONTRACTORS: Oil/Gas Well Construction, Rpr/Dismantling Svcs
CONTRACTORS: On-Site Welding
CONTRACTORS: Ornamental Metal Work
CONTRACTORS: Painting & Wall Covering
CONTRACTORS: Painting, Commercial
CONTRACTORS: Painting, Commercial, Interior
CONTRACTORS: Parking Lot Maintenance
CONTRACTORS: Plumbing
CONTRACTORS: Prefabricated Window & Door Installation
CONTRACTORS: Process Piping
CONTRACTORS: Protective Lining Install, Underground Sewage
CONTRACTORS: Refrigeration
CONTRACTORS: Resilient Floor Laying
CONTRACTORS: Roofing
CONTRACTORS: Safety & Security Eqpt
CONTRACTORS: Sandblasting Svc, Building Exteriors
CONTRACTORS: Septic System
CONTRACTORS: Sheet Metal Work, NEC
CONTRACTORS: Shoring & Underpinning
CONTRACTORS: Siding
CONTRACTORS: Single-family Home General Remodeling
CONTRACTORS: Solar Energy Eqpt
CONTRACTORS: Sound Eqpt Installation
CONTRACTORS: Spraying, Nonagricultural
CONTRACTORS: Standby Or Emergency Power Specialization
CONTRACTORS: Stone Masonry
CONTRACTORS: Storage Tank Erection, Metal
CONTRACTORS: Store Front Construction
CONTRACTORS: Structural Steel Erection
CONTRACTORS: Svc Well Drilling Svcs
CONTRACTORS: Tile Installation, Ceramic
CONTRACTORS: Timber Removal
CONTRACTORS: Ventilation & Duct Work
CONTRACTORS: Warm Air Heating & Air Conditioning
CONTRACTORS: Water Intake Well Drilling Svc
CONTRACTORS: Water Well Drilling
CONTRACTORS: Water Well Servicing
CONTRACTORS: Waterproofing
CONTRACTORS: Weather Stripping
CONTRACTORS: Well Bailing, Cleaning, Swabbing & Treating Svc
CONTRACTORS: Window Treatment Installation

CONTRACTORS: Windows & Doors
CONTRACTORS: Wood Floor Installation & Refinishing
CONTRACTORS: Wrecking & Demolition
CONTROL CIRCUIT DEVICES
CONTROL EQPT: Buses Or Trucks, Electric
CONTROL EQPT: Electric
CONTROL EQPT: Noise
CONTROL PANELS: Electrical
CONTROLS & ACCESS: Indl, Electric
CONTROLS & ACCESS: Motor
CONTROLS: Air Flow, Refrigeration
CONTROLS: Automatic Temperature
CONTROLS: Environmental
CONTROLS: Relay & Ind
CONTROLS: Thermostats
CONTROLS: Thermostats, Exc Built-in
CONTROLS: Voice
CONTROLS: Water Heater
CONVENIENCE STORES
CONVENTION & TRADE SHOW SVCS
CONVERTERS: Data
CONVERTERS: Frequency
CONVERTERS: Phase Or Rotary, Electrical
CONVERTERS: Power, AC to DC
CONVERTERS: Torque, Exc Auto
CONVEYOR SYSTEMS
CONVEYOR SYSTEMS: Belt, General Indl Use
CONVEYOR SYSTEMS: Bucket Type
CONVEYOR SYSTEMS: Bulk Handling
CONVEYOR SYSTEMS: Pneumatic Tube
CONVEYOR SYSTEMS: Robotic
CONVEYORS & CONVEYING EQPT
CONVEYORS: Overhead
COOKING & FOOD WARMING EQPT: Commercial
COOKING & FOODWARMING EQPT: Commercial
COOKING EQPT, HOUSEHOLD: Indoor
COOKING SCHOOL
COOLING TOWERS: Metal
COOLING TOWERS: Wood
COPPER ORES
COPPER: Rolling & Drawing
CORES: Fiber, Made From Purchased Materials
CORES: Magnetic
CORK & CORK PRDTS
CORK & CORK PRDTS: Tiles
CORRUGATED PRDTS: Boxes, Partition, Display Items, Sheet/Pad
CORRUGATING MACHINES
COSMETIC PREPARATIONS
COSMETICS & TOILETRIES
COSMETICS WHOLESALERS
COSMETOLOGY & PERSONAL HYGIENE SALONS
COSMETOLOGY SCHOOL
COSTUME JEWELRY & NOVELTIES: Apparel, Exc Precious Metals
COSTUME JEWELRY & NOVELTIES: Exc Semi & Precious
COUGH MEDICINES
COUNTER & SINK TOPS
COUNTERS & COUNTING DEVICES
COUNTERS OR COUNTER DISPLAY CASES, EXC WOOD
COUNTERS OR COUNTER DISPLAY CASES, WOOD
COUNTING DEVICES: Controls, Revolution & Timing
COUNTING DEVICES: Gauges, Press Temp Corrections Computing
COUPLINGS: Hose & Tube, Hydraulic Or Pneumatic
COUPLINGS: Pipe
COUPON REDEMPTION SVCS
COURIER OR MESSENGER SVCS
COURIER SVCS, AIR: Letter Delivery, Private
COURIER SVCS: Ground
COURIER SVCS: Package By Vehicle
COVERS & PADS Chair, Made From Purchased Materials
COVERS: Automobile Seat
COVERS: Canvas
COVERS: Hot Tub & Spa
CRANES: Indl Plant
CRANKSHAFTS & CAMSHAFTS: Machining
CREDIT BUREAUS
CRUDE PETROLEUM & NATURAL GAS PRODUCTION
CRUDE PETROLEUM & NATURAL GAS PRODUCTION
CRUDE PETROLEUM PRODUCTION
CRYSTALS
CULTURE MEDIA
CUPS & PLATES: Foamed Plastics
CUPS: Paper, Made From Purchased Materials

INDEX

ELECTRICAL GOODS, WHOLESALE: Modems, Computer
ELECTRICAL GOODS, WHOLESALE: Motor Ctrls, Starters & Relays
ELECTRICAL GOODS, WHOLESALE: Motors
ELECTRICAL GOODS, WHOLESALE: Paging & Signaling Eqpt
ELECTRICAL GOODS, WHOLESALE: Panelboards
ELECTRICAL GOODS, WHOLESALE: Radio & TV Or TV Eqpt & Parts
ELECTRICAL GOODS, WHOLESALE: Radio Parts & Access, NEC
ELECTRICAL GOODS, WHOLESALE: Semiconductor Devices
ELECTRICAL GOODS, WHOLESALE: Signaling, Eqpt
ELECTRICAL GOODS, WHOLESALE: Telephone & Telegraphic Eqpt
ELECTRICAL GOODS, WHOLESALE: Telephone Eqpt
ELECTRICAL GOODS, WHOLESALE: Transformer & Transmission Eqpt
ELECTRICAL GOODS, WHOLESALE: Tubes, Rcvg & Txmtg Or Indl
ELECTRICAL GOODS, WHOLESALE: Video Eqpt
ELECTRICAL GOODS, WHOLESALE: Wire & Cable
ELECTRICAL GOODS, WHOLESALE: Wire & Cable, Ctrl & Sig
ELECTRICAL GOODS, WHOLESALE: Wire & Cable, Electronic
ELECTRICAL GOODS, WHOLESALE: Wire & Cable, Power
ELECTRICAL INDL APPARATUS, NEC
ELECTRICAL MEASURING INSTRUMENT REPAIR & CALIBRATION SVCS
ELECTRICAL SPLYS
ELECTRICAL SUPPLIES: Porcelain
ELECTROCARS: Golfer Transportation
ELECTRODES: Fluorescent Lamps
ELECTRODES: Indl Process
ELECTROMEDICAL EQPT
ELECTROMEDICAL EQPT WHOLESALERS
ELECTROMETALLURGICAL PRDTS
ELECTRON TUBES
ELECTRON TUBES: Parts
ELECTRONIC COMPONENTS
ELECTRONIC DEVICES: Solid State, NEC
ELECTRONIC EQPT REPAIR SVCS
ELECTRONIC LOADS & POWER SPLYS
ELECTRONIC PARTS & EQPT WHOLESALERS
ELECTRONIC TRAINING DEVICES
ELECTROPLATING & PLATING SVC
ELEVATORS & EQPT
ELEVATORS WHOLESALERS
ELEVATORS: Installation & Conversion
ELEVATORS: Stair, Motor Powered
EMBLEMS: Embroidered
EMBOSSING SVC: Paper
EMBROIDERING & ART NEEDLEWORK FOR THE TRADE
EMBROIDERING SVC
EMBROIDERING SVC: Schiffli Machine
EMBROIDERY ADVERTISING SVCS
EMBROIDERY KITS
EMERGENCY ALARMS
EMPLOYMENT AGENCY SVCS
EMPLOYMENT SVCS: Labor Contractors
ENAMELS
ENCLOSURES: Electronic
ENCODERS: Digital
ENERGY MEASUREMENT EQPT
ENGINE PARTS & ACCESS: Internal Combustion
ENGINE REBUILDING: Diesel
ENGINE REBUILDING: Gas
ENGINEERING SVCS
ENGINEERING SVCS: Aviation Or Aeronautical
ENGINEERING SVCS: Building Construction
ENGINEERING SVCS: Chemical
ENGINEERING SVCS: Construction & Civil
ENGINEERING SVCS: Electrical Or Electronic
ENGINEERING SVCS: Industrial
ENGINEERING SVCS: Machine Tool Design
ENGINEERING SVCS: Mechanical
ENGINEERING SVCS: Structural
ENGINES & ENGINE PARTS: Guided Missile, Research & Develpt
ENGINES: Diesel & Semi-Diesel Or Duel Fuel
ENGINES: Gasoline, NEC
ENGINES: Internal Combustion, NEC
ENGRAVING SVC, NEC

ENGRAVING SVC: Jewelry & Personal Goods
ENGRAVING SVCS
ENGRAVING: Bank Note
ENGRAVINGS: Plastic
ENTERTAINERS
ENTERTAINERS & ENTERTAINMENT GROUPS
ENTERTAINMENT PROMOTION SVCS
ENTERTAINMENT SVCS
ENVELOPES
ENVELOPES WHOLESALERS
ENZYMES
EPOXY RESINS
EQUIPMENT: Rental & Leasing, NEC
ERASERS: Rubber Or Rubber & Abrasive Combined
ESTER GUM
ETCHING & ENGRAVING SVC
ETHYLENE-PROPYLENE RUBBERS: EPDM Polymers
EXHAUST SYSTEMS: Eqpt & Parts
EXPANSION JOINTS: Rubber
EXPLORATION, METAL MINING
EXPLOSIVES
EXPLOSIVES, EXC AMMO & FIREWORKS WHOLESALERS
EXTENSION CORDS
EXTERMINATING PRDTS: Household Or Indl Use
EXTRACTS, FLAVORING
EXTRUDED SHAPES, NEC: Copper & Copper Alloy
EYEGLASS CASES
EYEGLASSES
EYES: Artificial
Ethylene Glycols

F

FABRIC STORES
FABRICATED METAL PRODUCTS, NEC
FABRICS & CLOTHING: Rubber Coated
FABRICS: Alpacas, Cotton
FABRICS: Alpacas, Mohair, Woven
FABRICS: Animal Fiber, Narrow Woven
FABRICS: Apparel & Outerwear, Broadwoven
FABRICS: Apparel & Outerwear, Cotton
FABRICS: Automotive, Cotton
FABRICS: Automotive, From Manmade Fiber
FABRICS: Bandage Cloth, Cotton
FABRICS: Basket Weave, Cotton
FABRICS: Broadwoven, Cotton
FABRICS: Broadwoven, Synthetic Manmade Fiber & Silk
FABRICS: Broadwoven, Wool
FABRICS: Coated Or Treated
FABRICS: Decorative Trim & Specialty, Including Twist Weave
FABRICS: Denims
FABRICS: Fiberglass, Broadwoven
FABRICS: Hat Band
FABRICS: Jacquard Woven, Cotton
FABRICS: Lace & Decorative Trim, Narrow
FABRICS: Lace & Lace Prdts
FABRICS: Lace, Knit, NEC
FABRICS: Laminated
FABRICS: Laundry, Cotton
FABRICS: Manmade Fiber, Narrow
FABRICS: Nonwoven
FABRICS: Paper, Broadwoven
FABRICS: Pile, Circular Knit
FABRICS: Polypropylene, Broadwoven
FABRICS: Print, Cotton
FABRICS: Resin Or Plastic Coated
FABRICS: Rubberized
FABRICS: Scrub Cloths
FABRICS: Seat Cover, Automobile, Cotton
FABRICS: Shirting, Cotton
FABRICS: Shoe
FABRICS: Spunbonded
FABRICS: Trimmings
FABRICS: Trimmings, Textile
FABRICS: Umbrella Cloth, Cotton
FABRICS: Underwear, Cotton
FABRICS: Upholstery, Cotton
FABRICS: Wall Covering, From Manmade Fiber Or Silk
FABRICS: Warp & Flat Knit Prdts
FABRICS: Warp Knit, Lace & Netting
FABRICS: Weft Or Circular Knit
FABRICS: Woven Wire, Made From Purchased Wire
FABRICS: Woven, Narrow Cotton, Wool, Silk
FACE PLATES
FACILITIES SUPPORT SVCS
FACSIMILE COMMUNICATION EQPT

FAMILY CLOTHING STORES
FANS, VENTILATING: Indl Or Commercial
FARM PRDTS, RAW MATERIALS, WHOLESALE: Nuts & Nut By-Prdts
FARM SPLY STORES
FARM SPLYS WHOLESALERS
FARM SPLYS, WHOLESALE: Feed
FARM SPLYS, WHOLESALE: Fertilizers & Agricultural Chemicals
FARM SPLYS, WHOLESALE: Greenhouse Eqpt & Splys
FARM SPLYS, WHOLESALE: Insecticides
FARM SPLYS, WHOLESALE: Soil, Potting & Planting
FASTENERS WHOLESALERS
FASTENERS: Metal
FASTENERS: Metal
FASTENERS: Notions, NEC
FASTENERS: Notions, Zippers
FATTY ACID ESTERS & AMINOS
FELT, WHOLESALE
FENCE POSTS: Iron & Steel
FENCES & FENCING MATERIALS
FENCING DEALERS
FENCING MADE IN WIREDRAWING PLANTS
FENCING MATERIALS: Docks & Other Outdoor Prdts, Wood
FENCING MATERIALS: Plastic
FENCING MATERIALS: Snow Fence, Wood
FENCING MATERIALS: Wood
FENCING: Chain Link
FERRITES
FERROALLOYS
FERTILIZER, AGRICULTURAL: Wholesalers
FERTILIZERS: NEC
FERTILIZERS: Nitrogenous
FERTILIZERS: Phosphatic
FIBER & FIBER PRDTS: Acrylic
FIBER & FIBER PRDTS: Organic, Noncellulose
FIBER & FIBER PRDTS: Polyester
FIBER & FIBER PRDTS: Synthetic Cellulosic
FIBER & FIBER PRDTS: Vinyl
FIBER OPTICS
FILE FOLDERS
FILM & SHEET: Unsuppported Plastic
FILM BASE: Cellulose Acetate Or Nitrocellulose Plastics
FILTERS
FILTERS & SOFTENERS: Water, Household
FILTERS & STRAINERS: Pipeline
FILTERS: Air
FILTERS: Air Intake, Internal Combustion Engine, Exc Auto
FILTERS: Gasoline, Internal Combustion Engine, Exc Auto
FILTERS: General Line, Indl
FILTERS: Motor Vehicle
FILTERS: Paper
FILTRATION DEVICES: Electronic
FILTRATION SAND MINING
FINANCIAL SVCS
FINDINGS & TRIMMINGS Fabric, NEC
FINDINGS & TRIMMINGS: Apparel
FINDINGS & TRIMMINGS: Fabric
FINDINGS & TRIMMINGS: Furniture, Fabric
FINGERNAILS, ARTIFICIAL
FINGERPRINT EQPT
FINISHING AGENTS: Textile
FIRE ALARM MAINTENANCE & MONITORING SVCS
FIRE ARMS, SMALL: Guns Or Gun Parts, 30 mm & Below
FIRE ARMS, SMALL: Rifles Or Rifle Parts, 30 mm & below
FIRE DETECTION SYSTEMS
FIRE ESCAPES
FIRE EXTINGUISHER CHARGES
FIRE EXTINGUISHER SVC
FIRE EXTINGUISHERS: Portable
FIRE OR BURGLARY RESISTIVE PRDTS
FIRE PROTECTION EQPT
FIRE PROTECTION, GOVERNMENT: Local
FIREPLACE & CHIMNEY MATERIAL: Concrete
FIREWOOD, WHOLESALE
FISH & SEAFOOD PROCESSORS: Canned Or Cured
FISH & SEAFOOD PROCESSORS: Fresh Or Frozen
FISH FOOD
FISH LIVER OILS: For Medicinal Use, Refined Or Concentrated
FISHING EQPT: Lures
FISHING EQPT: Nets & Seines
FITTINGS & ASSEMBLIES: Hose & Tube, Hydraulic Or Pneumatic
FITTINGS: Pipe

FITTINGS: Pipe, Fabricated
FIXTURES & EQPT: Kitchen, Metal, Exc Cast Aluminum
FIXTURES & EQPT: Kitchen, Porcelain Enameled
FIXTURES: Bank, Metal, Ornamental
FIXTURES: Cut Stone
FLAGPOLES
FLAGS: Fabric
FLAT GLASS: Antique
FLAT GLASS: Construction
FLAT GLASS: Laminated
FLAT GLASS: Tempered
FLAT GLASS: Window, Clear & Colored
FLAVORS OR FLAVORING MATERIALS: Synthetic
FLOOR CLEANING & MAINTENANCE EQPT: Household
FLOOR COVERING STORES
FLOOR COVERING STORES: Carpets
FLOOR COVERING STORES: Rugs
FLOOR COVERING: Plastic
FLOOR COVERINGS WHOLESALERS
FLOOR COVERINGS: Aircraft & Automobile
FLOOR COVERINGS: Rubber
FLOOR COVERINGS: Tile, Support Plastic
FLOORING: Hard Surface
FLOORING: Hardwood
FLOORING: Rubber
FLOORING: Tile
FLORIST: Flowers, Fresh
FLORISTS
FLOWER ARRANGEMENTS: Artificial
FLOWERS, ARTIFICIAL, WHOLESALE
FLOWERS, FRESH, WHOLESALE
FLOWERS: Artificial & Preserved
FLUID METERS & COUNTING DEVICES
FLUID POWER PUMPS & MOTORS
FLUID POWER VALVES & HOSE FITTINGS
FLUXES
FLY TRAPS: Electrical
FOAM CHARGE MIXTURES
FOAM RUBBER
FOAM RUBBER, WHOLESALE
FOAMS & RUBBER, WHOLESALE
FOIL & LEAF: Metal
FOIL BOARD: Made From Purchased Materials
FOIL: Aluminum
FOIL: Copper
FOIL: Zinc
FOOD CASINGS: Plastic
FOOD COLORINGS
FOOD PRDTS & SEAFOOD: Shellfish, Fresh, Shucked
FOOD PRDTS, BREAKFAST: Cereal, Granola & Muesli
FOOD PRDTS, BREAKFAST: Cereal, Oats, Rolled
FOOD PRDTS, CANNED OR FRESH PACK: Fruit Juices
FOOD PRDTS, CANNED: Baby Food
FOOD PRDTS, CANNED: Barbecue Sauce
FOOD PRDTS, CANNED: Beans & Bean Sprouts
FOOD PRDTS, CANNED: Chili Sauce, Tomato
FOOD PRDTS, CANNED: Ethnic
FOOD PRDTS, CANNED: Fruit Juices, Fresh
FOOD PRDTS, CANNED: Fruits
FOOD PRDTS, CANNED: Fruits & Fruit Prdts
FOOD PRDTS, CANNED: Italian
FOOD PRDTS, CANNED: Jams, Including Imitation
FOOD PRDTS, CANNED: Mexican, NEC
FOOD PRDTS, CANNED: Seasonings, Tomato
FOOD PRDTS, CANNED: Soups
FOOD PRDTS, CANNED: Soups, Exc Seafood
FOOD PRDTS, CANNED: Spaghetti & Other Pasta Sauce
FOOD PRDTS, CANNED: Tomato Sauce.
FOOD PRDTS, CANNED: Vegetable Pastes
FOOD PRDTS, CONFECTIONERY, WHOLESALE: Candy
FOOD PRDTS, CONFECTIONERY, WHOLESALE: Nuts, Salted/Roasted
FOOD PRDTS, CONFECTIONERY, WHOLESALE: Pretzels
FOOD PRDTS, CONFECTIONERY, WHOLESALE: Snack Foods
FOOD PRDTS, CONFECTIONERY, WHOLESALE: Syrups, Fountain
FOOD PRDTS, DAIRY, WHOLESALE: Frozen Dairy Desserts
FOOD PRDTS, DAIRY, WHOLESALE: Milk, Canned Or Dried
FOOD PRDTS, FISH & SEAFOOD, WHOLESALE: Seafood
FOOD PRDTS, FISH & SEAFOOD: Clams, Canned, Jarred, Etc
FOOD PRDTS, FISH & SEAFOOD: Fish, Canned, Jarred, Etc
FOOD PRDTS, FISH & SEAFOOD: Fish, Frozen, Prepared
FOOD PRDTS, FISH & SEAFOOD: Fish, Smoked

FOOD PRDTS, FISH & SEAFOOD: Fresh, Prepared
FOOD PRDTS, FISH & SEAFOOD: Oysters, Canned, Jarred, Etc
FOOD PRDTS, FISH & SEAFOOD: Prepared Cakes & Sticks
FOOD PRDTS, FISH & SEAFOOD: Seafood, Frozen, Prepared
FOOD PRDTS, FROZEN: Breakfasts, Packaged
FOOD PRDTS, FROZEN: Dinners, Packaged
FOOD PRDTS, FROZEN: Ethnic Foods, NEC
FOOD PRDTS, FROZEN: Fruits & Vegetables
FOOD PRDTS, FROZEN: Fruits, Juices & Vegetables
FOOD PRDTS, FROZEN: NEC
FOOD PRDTS, FROZEN: Pizza
FOOD PRDTS, FROZEN: Snack Items
FOOD PRDTS, FROZEN: Soups
FOOD PRDTS, FROZEN: Vegetables, Exc Potato Prdts
FOOD PRDTS, FROZEN: Whipped Topping
FOOD PRDTS, FRUITS & VEGETABLES, FRESH, WHOLESALE: Vegetable
FOOD PRDTS, MEAT & MEAT PRDTS, WHOLESALE: Fresh
FOOD PRDTS, POULTRY, WHOLESALE: Poultry Prdts, NEC
FOOD PRDTS, WHOL: Canned Goods, Fruit, Veg, Seafood/Meats
FOOD PRDTS, WHOLESALE: Beans, Dry, Bulk
FOOD PRDTS, WHOLESALE: Breakfast Cereals
FOOD PRDTS, WHOLESALE: Chocolate
FOOD PRDTS, WHOLESALE: Coffee & Tea
FOOD PRDTS, WHOLESALE: Coffee, Green Or Roasted
FOOD PRDTS, WHOLESALE: Cookies
FOOD PRDTS, WHOLESALE: Cooking Oils
FOOD PRDTS, WHOLESALE: Dried or Canned Foods
FOOD PRDTS, WHOLESALE: Flavorings & Fragrances
FOOD PRDTS, WHOLESALE: Health
FOOD PRDTS, WHOLESALE: Juices
FOOD PRDTS, WHOLESALE: Molasses, Indl
FOOD PRDTS, WHOLESALE: Natural & Organic
FOOD PRDTS, WHOLESALE: Pasta & Rice
FOOD PRDTS, WHOLESALE: Salad Dressing
FOOD PRDTS, WHOLESALE: Salt, Edible
FOOD PRDTS, WHOLESALE: Sauces
FOOD PRDTS, WHOLESALE: Sausage Casings
FOOD PRDTS, WHOLESALE: Specialty
FOOD PRDTS, WHOLESALE: Spices & Seasonings
FOOD PRDTS, WHOLESALE: Tea
FOOD PRDTS, WHOLESALE: Water, Mineral Or Spring, Bottled
FOOD PRDTS: Almond Pastes
FOOD PRDTS: Animal & marine fats & oils
FOOD PRDTS: Blackstrap Molasses, Purchd Raw Sugar/Syrup
FOOD PRDTS: Breakfast Bars
FOOD PRDTS: Cereals
FOOD PRDTS: Chewing Gum Base
FOOD PRDTS: Cocoa, Butter
FOOD PRDTS: Cocoa, Powdered
FOOD PRDTS: Coconut, Desiccated & Shredded
FOOD PRDTS: Coffee
FOOD PRDTS: Coffee Extracts
FOOD PRDTS: Coffee Roasting, Exc Wholesale Grocers
FOOD PRDTS: Cooking Oils, Refined Vegetable, Exc Corn
FOOD PRDTS: Corn Chips & Other Corn-Based Snacks
FOOD PRDTS: Dessert Mixes & Fillings
FOOD PRDTS: Desserts, Ready-To-Mix
FOOD PRDTS: Doughs, Frozen Or Refrig From Purchased Flour
FOOD PRDTS: Dressings, Salad, Raw & Cooked Exc Dry Mixes
FOOD PRDTS: Dried & Dehydrated Fruits, Vegetables & Soup Mix
FOOD PRDTS: Edible Oil Prdts, Exc Corn Oil
FOOD PRDTS: Edible fats & oils
FOOD PRDTS: Eggs, Processed
FOOD PRDTS: Eggs, Processed, Dehydrated
FOOD PRDTS: Emulsifiers
FOOD PRDTS: Flavored Ices, Frozen
FOOD PRDTS: Flour & Other Grain Mill Products
FOOD PRDTS: Flour Mixes & Doughs
FOOD PRDTS: Flour, Cake From Purchased Flour
FOOD PRDTS: Flours & Flour Mixes, From Purchased Flour
FOOD PRDTS: Fresh Vegetables, Peeled Or Processed
FOOD PRDTS: Fruit Juices
FOOD PRDTS: Fruit Pops, Frozen
FOOD PRDTS: Fruits & Vegetables, Pickled
FOOD PRDTS: Fruits, Dehydrated Or Dried
FOOD PRDTS: Gelatin Dessert Preparations

FOOD PRDTS: Glucose
FOOD PRDTS: Granola & Energy Bars, Nonchocolate
FOOD PRDTS: Granulated Cane Sugar
FOOD PRDTS: Ice, Blocks
FOOD PRDTS: Ice, Cubes
FOOD PRDTS: Instant Coffee
FOOD PRDTS: Luncheon Meat, Poultry
FOOD PRDTS: Macaroni Prdts, Dry, Alphabet, Rings Or Shells
FOOD PRDTS: Macaroni, Noodles, Spaghetti, Pasta, Etc
FOOD PRDTS: Malt
FOOD PRDTS: Margarine & Vegetable Oils
FOOD PRDTS: Margarine, Including Imitation
FOOD PRDTS: Margarine-Butter Blends
FOOD PRDTS: Mayonnaise & Dressings, Exc Tomato Based
FOOD PRDTS: Menhaden Oil
FOOD PRDTS: Mixes, Bread & Roll From Purchased Flour
FOOD PRDTS: Mixes, Cake, From Purchased Flour
FOOD PRDTS: Mixes, Doughnut From Purchased Flour
FOOD PRDTS: Mixes, Pancake From Purchased Flour
FOOD PRDTS: Mixes, Pizza From Purchased Flour
FOOD PRDTS: Mixes, Salad Dressings, Dry
FOOD PRDTS: Mixes, Seasonings, Dry
FOOD PRDTS: Mustard, Prepared
FOOD PRDTS: Nuts & Seeds
FOOD PRDTS: Olive Oil
FOOD PRDTS: Oriental Noodles
FOOD PRDTS: Pasta, Uncooked, Packaged With Other Ingredients
FOOD PRDTS: Peanut Butter
FOOD PRDTS: Pickles, Vinegar
FOOD PRDTS: Pizza Doughs From Purchased Flour
FOOD PRDTS: Pizza, Refrigerated
FOOD PRDTS: Popcorn, Popped
FOOD PRDTS: Popcorn, Unpopped
FOOD PRDTS: Potato & Corn Chips & Similar Prdts
FOOD PRDTS: Potato Chips & Other Potato-Based Snacks
FOOD PRDTS: Poultry, Processed, Frozen
FOOD PRDTS: Poultry, Slaughtered & Dressed
FOOD PRDTS: Preparations
FOOD PRDTS: Prepared Sauces, Exc Tomato Based
FOOD PRDTS: Raw cane sugar
FOOD PRDTS: Rice, Milled
FOOD PRDTS: Salads
FOOD PRDTS: Seasonings & Spices
FOOD PRDTS: Shortening & Solid Edible Fats
FOOD PRDTS: Soup Mixes
FOOD PRDTS: Spices, Including Ground
FOOD PRDTS: Sugar
FOOD PRDTS: Sugar, Refined Cane, Purchased Raw Sugar/Syrup
FOOD PRDTS: Syrup, Maple
FOOD PRDTS: Syrup, Pancake, Blended & Mixed
FOOD PRDTS: Syrup, Sorghum, For Sweetening
FOOD PRDTS: Syrups
FOOD PRDTS: Tea
FOOD PRDTS: Tofu Desserts, Frozen
FOOD PRDTS: Tofu, Exc Frozen Desserts
FOOD PRDTS: Tortillas
FOOD PRDTS: Turkey, Processed, Frozen
FOOD PRDTS: Vegetable Oil Mills, NEC
FOOD PRDTS: Vegetables, Dried or Dehydrated Exc Freeze-Dried
FOOD PRDTS: Vegetables, Pickled
FOOD PRDTS: Vinegar
FOOD PRDTS: Yeast
FOOD PRODUCTS MACHINERY
FOOD STORES: Convenience, Independent
FOOD STORES: Cooperative
FOOD STORES: Delicatessen
FOOD STORES: Frozen Food &Freezer Plans, Exc Meat
FOOD STORES: Grocery, Chain
FOOD STORES: Grocery, Independent
FOOD STORES: Supermarkets
FOOD STORES: Supermarkets, Chain
FOOTWEAR, WHOLESALE: Athletic
FOOTWEAR, WHOLESALE: Shoe Access
FORGINGS
FORGINGS: Automotive & Internal Combustion Engine
FORGINGS: Gear & Chain
FORGINGS: Metal , Ornamental, Ferrous
FORGINGS: Missile, Ferrous
FORGINGS: Nonferrous
FORGINGS: Nuclear Power Plant, Ferrous
FORMS: Concrete, Sheet Metal

FOUNDRIES: Aluminum
FOUNDRIES: Brass, Bronze & Copper
FOUNDRIES: Gray & Ductile Iron
FOUNDRIES: Iron
FOUNDRIES: Nonferrous
FOUNDRIES: Steel
FOUNDRIES: Steel Investment
FOUNDRY MATERIALS: Insulsleeves
FOUNDRY SAND MINING
FRAMES & FRAMING WHOLESALE
FRANCHISES, SELLING OR LICENSING
FREEZERS: Household
FREIGHT FORWARDING ARRANGEMENTS
FREIGHT TRANSPORTATION ARRANGEMENTS
FRICTION MATERIAL, MADE FROM POWDERED METAL
FRUIT & VEGETABLE MARKETS
FRUITS & VEGETABLES WHOLESALERS: Fresh
FRUITS: Artificial & Preserved
FUEL ADDITIVES
FUEL CELLS: Solid State
FUEL OIL DEALERS
FUELS: Diesel
FUELS: Ethanol
FUELS: Jet
FUELS: Oil
FUND RAISING ORGANIZATION, NON-FEE BASIS
FUNGICIDES OR HERBICIDES
FUR: Coats
FURNACES & OVENS: Indl
FURNACES & OVENS: Vacuum
FURNACES: Indl, Electric
FURNACES: Indl, Fuel-Fired, Metal Melting
FURNITURE & CABINET STORES: Cabinets, Custom Work
FURNITURE & CABINET STORES: Custom
FURNITURE & FIXTURES Factory
FURNITURE REPAIR & MAINTENANCE SVCS
FURNITURE STORES
FURNITURE STORES: Cabinets, Kitchen, Exc Custom Made
FURNITURE STORES: Custom Made, Exc Cabinets
FURNITURE STORES: Office
FURNITURE STORES: Outdoor & Garden
FURNITURE UPHOLSTERY REPAIR SVCS
FURNITURE WHOLESALERS
FURNITURE, HOUSEHOLD: Wholesalers
FURNITURE, OFFICE: Wholesalers
FURNITURE, OUTDOOR & LAWN: Wholesalers
FURNITURE, WHOLESALE: Bar
FURNITURE, WHOLESALE: Chairs
FURNITURE, WHOLESALE: Juvenile
FURNITURE, WHOLESALE: Lockers
FURNITURE, WHOLESALE: Shelving
FURNITURE, WHOLESALE: Sofas & Couches
FURNITURE: Bar furniture
FURNITURE: Benches, Office, Wood
FURNITURE: Box Springs, Assembled
FURNITURE: Cafeteria
FURNITURE: Chair Beds
FURNITURE: Chairs & Couches, Wood, Upholstered
FURNITURE: Chairs, Dental
FURNITURE: Chairs, Household Upholstered
FURNITURE: Chairs, Household, Metal
FURNITURE: Chairs, Office Exc Wood
FURNITURE: Chairs, Office Wood
FURNITURE: Chests, Cedar
FURNITURE: Church
FURNITURE: Desks & Tables, Office, Wood
FURNITURE: Frames, Box Springs Or Bedsprings, Metal
FURNITURE: Hospital
FURNITURE: Hotel
FURNITURE: Household, Metal
FURNITURE: Household, Upholstered, Exc Wood Or Metal
FURNITURE: Household, Wood
FURNITURE: Hydraulic Barber & Beauty Shop Chairs
FURNITURE: Institutional, Exc Wood
FURNITURE: Juvenile, Wood
FURNITURE: Juvenile, Wood
FURNITURE: Kitchen & Dining Room
FURNITURE: Kitchen & Dining Room, Metal
FURNITURE: Laboratory
FURNITURE: Lawn & Garden, Except Wood & Metal
FURNITURE: Lawn, Wood
FURNITURE: Library
FURNITURE: Mattresses & Foundations
FURNITURE: Mattresses, Box & Bedsprings
FURNITURE: Mattresses, Innerspring Or Box Spring

FURNITURE: NEC
FURNITURE: Novelty, Wood
FURNITURE: Office Panel Systems, Wood
FURNITURE: Office, Exc Wood
FURNITURE: Office, Wood
FURNITURE: School
FURNITURE: Sleep
FURNITURE: Sofa Beds Or Convertible Sofas)
FURNITURE: Spring Cushions
FURNITURE: Table Tops, Marble
FURNITURE: Tables & Table Tops, Wood
FURNITURE: Tables, Household, Metal
FURNITURE: Upholstered
FURNITURE: Vehicle
FURNITURE: Wall Cases, Office, Exc Wood
FURNITURE: Wardrobes, Household, Wood
FURNITURE: Wicker & Rattan
FURRIERS
FUSES: Electric

G

GAMES & TOYS: Baby Carriages & Restraint Seats
GAMES & TOYS: Blocks
GAMES & TOYS: Board Games, Children's & Adults'
GAMES & TOYS: Craft & Hobby Kits & Sets
GAMES & TOYS: Dolls & Doll Clothing
GAMES & TOYS: Dolls, Exc Stuffed Toy Animals
GAMES & TOYS: Kits, Science, Incl Microscopes/Chemistry Sets
GAMES & TOYS: Marbles
GAMES & TOYS: Models, Railroad, Toy & Hobby
GAMES & TOYS: Wagons, Coaster, Express & Play, Children's
GARBAGE CONTAINERS: Plastic
GARBAGE DISPOSERS & COMPACTORS: Commercial
GAS & OIL FIELD EXPLORATION SVCS
GAS & OIL FIELD SVCS, NEC
GAS & OTHER COMBINED SVCS
GAS STATIONS
GAS: Refinery
GASES: Argon
GASES: Flourinated Hydrocarbon
GASES: Helium
GASES: Indl
GASES: Nitrogen
GASES: Oxygen
GASKET MATERIALS
GASKETS
GASKETS & SEALING DEVICES
GASOLINE FILLING STATIONS
GASTROINTESTINAL OR GENITOURINARY SYSTEM DRUGS
GATES: Ornamental Metal
GAUGES
GEARS
GEARS: Power Transmission, Exc Auto
GELATIN CAPSULES
GEM STONES MINING, NEC: Natural
GEMSTONE & INDL DIAMOND MINING SVCS
GENERAL COUNSELING SVCS
GENERAL MERCHANDISE, NONDURABLE, WHOLESALE
GENERATING APPARATUS & PARTS: Electrical
GENERATION EQPT: Electronic
GENERATOR REPAIR SVCS
GENERATORS SETS: Motor, Automotive
GENERATORS: Electric
GENERATORS: Storage Battery Chargers
GENERATORS: Ultrasonic
GIFT SHOP
GIFT WRAP: Paper, Made From Purchased Materials
GIFT, NOVELTY & SOUVENIR STORES: Gifts & Novelties
GIFTS & NOVELTIES: Wholesalers
GIFTWARE: Brass
GILSONITE MINING SVCS
GLASS & GLASS CERAMIC PRDTS, PRESSED OR BLOWN: Tableware
GLASS FABRICATORS
GLASS PRDTS, FROM PURCHASED GLASS: Art
GLASS PRDTS, FROM PURCHASED GLASS: Glass Beads, Reflecting
GLASS PRDTS, FROM PURCHASED GLASS: Insulating
GLASS PRDTS, FROM PURCHASED GLASS: Mirrored
GLASS PRDTS, FROM PURCHASED GLASS: Novelties, Fruit, Etc
GLASS PRDTS, PRESSED OR BLOWN: Barware

GLASS PRDTS, PRESSED OR BLOWN: Bulbs, Electric Lights
GLASS PRDTS, PRESSED OR BLOWN: Furnishings & Access
GLASS PRDTS, PRESSED OR BLOWN: Glassware, Art Or Decorative
GLASS PRDTS, PRESSED OR BLOWN: Glassware, Novelty
GLASS PRDTS, PRESSED OR BLOWN: Lighting Eqpt Parts
GLASS PRDTS, PRESSED OR BLOWN: Optical
GLASS PRDTS, PRESSED OR BLOWN: Ornaments, Christmas Tree
GLASS PRDTS, PRESSED OR BLOWN: Scientific Glassware
GLASS PRDTS, PRESSED OR BLOWN: Tubing
GLASS PRDTS, PURCHASED GLASS: Glassware, Scientific/Tech
GLASS STORE: Leaded Or Stained
GLASS STORES
GLASS, AUTOMOTIVE: Wholesalers
GLASS: Fiber
GLASS: Flat
GLASS: Indl Prdts
GLASS: Insulating
GLASS: Plate
GLASS: Pressed & Blown, NEC
GLASS: Stained
GLASS: Structural
GLASSWARE STORES
GLASSWARE WHOLESALERS
GLASSWARE: Indl
GLASSWARE: Laboratory & Medical
GLOBAL POSITIONING SYSTEMS & EQPT
GLOVES: Fabric
GLOVES: Leather, Work
GLOVES: Plastic
GLOVES: Safety
GLUE
GOLD ORES
GOLD STAMPING, EXC BOOKS
GOLF EQPT
GOLF GOODS & EQPT
GOURMET FOOD STORES
GOVERNMENT, EXECUTIVE OFFICES: County Supervisor/Exec Office
GRAIN & FIELD BEANS WHOLESALERS
GRANITE: Crushed & Broken
GRANITE: Cut & Shaped
GRANITE: Dimension
GRANITE: Dimension
GRAPHIC ARTS & RELATED DESIGN SVCS
GRAPHITE MINING SVCS
GRASSES: Artificial & Preserved
GRATINGS: Tread, Fabricated Metal
GRAVE VAULTS, METAL
GRAVEL & PEBBLE MINING
GRAVEL MINING
GREASE TRAPS: Concrete
GREASES: Lubricating
GREENSAND MINING SVCS
GREETING CARD SHOPS
GREETING CARDS WHOLESALERS
GRINDING SVC: Precision, Commercial Or Indl
GRINDING SVCS: Ophthalmic Lens, Exc Prescription
GRIT: Steel
GRITS: Crushed & Broken
GROCERIES WHOLESALERS, NEC
GROCERIES, GENERAL LINE WHOLESALERS
GROUTING EQPT: Concrete
GUIDANCE SYSTEMS & EQPT: Space Vehicle
GUIDED MISSILES & SPACE VEHICLES
GUIDED MISSILES & SPACE VEHICLES: Research & Development
GUM & WOOD CHEMICALS
GUTTERS
GUTTERS: Sheet Metal
GYPSUM & CALCITE MINING SVCS
GYPSUM PRDTS
GYROSCOPES

H

HAIR & HAIR BASED PRDTS
HAIR CARE PRDTS
HAIR CARE PRDTS: Bleaches
HAIR CARE PRDTS: Hair Coloring Preparations
HAIR DRESSING, FOR THE TRADE
HAIRBRUSHES, WHOLESALE

HAND TOOLS, NEC: Wholesalers
HANDBAGS
HANDBAGS: Women's
HANDLES: Brush Or Tool, Plastic
HANGERS: Garment, Plastic
HANGERS: Garment, Wire
HANGERS: Garment, Wire
HARD RUBBER PRDTS, NEC
HARDWARE
HARDWARE & BUILDING PRDTS: Plastic
HARDWARE & EQPT: Stage, Exc Lighting
HARDWARE STORES
HARDWARE STORES: Builders'
HARDWARE STORES: Door Locks & Lock Sets
HARDWARE STORES: Tools
HARDWARE STORES: Tools, Power
HARDWARE WHOLESALERS
HARDWARE, WHOLESALE: Bolts
HARDWARE, WHOLESALE: Builders', NEC
HARDWARE, WHOLESALE: Power Tools & Access
HARDWARE, WHOLESALE: Screws
HARDWARE, WHOLESALE: Security Devices, Locks
HARDWARE, WHOLESALE: Washers
HARDWARE: Aircraft & Marine, Incl Pulleys & Similar Items
HARDWARE: Builders'
HARDWARE: Cabinet
HARDWARE: Furniture, Builders' & Other Household
HARDWARE: Hangers, Wall
HARDWARE: Luggage
HARDWARE: Parachute
HARNESS ASSEMBLIES: Cable & Wire
HARNESS WIRING SETS: Internal Combustion Engines
HARNESSES, HALTERS, SADDLERY & STRAPS
HEADPHONES: Radio
HEALTH AIDS: Exercise Eqpt
HEALTH FOOD & SUPPLEMENT STORES
HEALTH SCREENING SVCS
HEARING AIDS
HEAT EXCHANGERS
HEAT EXCHANGERS: After Or Inter Coolers Or Condensers, Etc
HEAT TREATING: Metal
HEATERS: Swimming Pool, Electric
HEATING & AIR CONDITIONING EQPT & SPLYS WHOLE-SALERS
HEATING & AIR CONDITIONING UNITS, COMBINATION
HEATING APPARATUS: Steam
HEATING EQPT & SPLYS
HEATING EQPT: Complete
HEATING EQPT: Induction
HEATING PADS: Nonelectric
HEATING UNITS & DEVICES: Indl, Electric
HEAVY DISTILLATES
HELMETS: Athletic
HIGH ENERGY PARTICLE PHYSICS EQPT
HOBBY GOODS, WHOLESALE
HOBBY SUPPLIES, WHOLESALE
HOBBY, TOY & GAME STORES: Arts & Crafts & Splys
HOISTS
HOLDERS, PAPER TOWEL, GROCERY BAG, ETC: Plastic
HOLDING COMPANIES: Banks
HOLDING COMPANIES: Investment, Exc Banks
HOLDING COMPANIES: Personal, Exc Banks
HOME ENTERTAINMENT EQPT: Electronic, NEC
HOME ENTERTAINMENT REPAIR SVCS
HOME FURNISHINGS WHOLESALERS
HOME HEALTH CARE SVCS
HOME IMPROVEMENT & RENOVATION CONTRACTOR AGENCY
HOMEFURNISHING STORE: Bedding, Sheet, Blanket,Spread/Pillow
HOMEFURNISHING STORES: Beddings & Linens
HOMEFURNISHING STORES: Closet organizers & shelving units
HOMEFURNISHING STORES: Fireplaces & Wood Burning Stoves
HOMEFURNISHING STORES: Lighting Fixtures
HOMEFURNISHING STORES: Metalware
HOMEFURNISHING STORES: Mirrors
HOMEFURNISHING STORES: Venetian Blinds
HOMEFURNISHING STORES: Vertical Blinds
HOMEFURNISHING STORES: Window Furnishings
HOMEFURNISHING STORES: Window Shades, NEC
HOMEFURNISHINGS & SPLYS, WHOLESALE: Decorative
HOMEFURNISHINGS, WHOLESALE: Blankets

HOMEFURNISHINGS, WHOLESALE: Blinds, Vertical
HOMEFURNISHINGS, WHOLESALE: Carpets
HOMEFURNISHINGS, WHOLESALE: Curtains
HOMEFURNISHINGS, WHOLESALE: Draperies
HOMEFURNISHINGS, WHOLESALE: Fireplace Eqpt & Access
HOMEFURNISHINGS, WHOLESALE: Kitchenware
HOMEFURNISHINGS, WHOLESALE: Linens, Table
HOMEFURNISHINGS, WHOLESALE: Rugs
HOMEFURNISHINGS, WHOLESALE: Sheets, Textile
HOMEFURNISHINGS, WHOLESALE: Towels
HOMEFURNISHINGS, WHOLESALE: Wood Flooring
HOMES, MODULAR: Wooden
HOODS: Range, Sheet Metal
HOPPERS: Metal Plate
HORNS: Marine, Compressed Air Or Steam
HORSE & PET ACCESSORIES: Textile
HORSE ACCESS: Harnesses & Riding Crops, Etc, Exc Leather
HORSESHOES
HOSE: Fire, Rubber
HOSE: Flexible Metal
HOSE: Garden, Plastic
HOSE: Plastic
HOSE: Pneumatic, Rubber Or Rubberized Fabric, NEC
HOSES & BELTING: Rubber & Plastic
HOSPITAL EQPT REPAIR SVCS
HOSPITALS: Medical & Surgical
HOTELS & MOTELS
HOUSEHOLD APPLIANCE REPAIR SVCS
HOUSEHOLD APPLIANCE STORES
HOUSEHOLD APPLIANCE STORES: Appliance Parts
HOUSEHOLD APPLIANCE STORES: Electric
HOUSEHOLD ARTICLES: Metal
HOUSEHOLD FURNISHINGS, NEC
HOUSEHOLD SEWING MACHINES WHOLESALERS: Electric
HOUSEWARE STORES
HOUSEWARES, ELECTRIC, EXC COOKING APPLIANCES & UTENSILS
HOUSEWARES, ELECTRIC: Cooking Appliances
HOUSEWARES, ELECTRIC: Dryers, Hand & Face
HOUSEWARES, ELECTRIC: Heaters, Sauna
HOUSEWARES, ELECTRIC: Heating, Bsbrd/Wall, Radiant Heat
HOUSEWARES, ELECTRIC: Ice Crushers
HOUSEWARES, ELECTRIC: Lighters, Cigar
HOUSEWARES: Dishes, China
HOUSEWARES: Dishes, Earthenware
HOUSEWARES: Dishes, Plastic
HUMIDIFIERS & DEHUMIDIFIERS
HYDRAULIC EQPT REPAIR SVC
HYDRAULIC FLUIDS: Synthetic Based
Hard Rubber & Molded Rubber Prdts

I

ICE
ICE CREAM & ICES WHOLESALERS
IGNEOUS ROCK: Crushed & Broken
IGNITION SYSTEMS: Internal Combustion Engine
INCINERATORS
INDL & PERSONAL SVC PAPER WHOLESALERS
INDL & PERSONAL SVC PAPER, WHOL: Bags, Paper/Disp Plastic
INDL & PERSONAL SVC PAPER, WHOL: Boxes, Corrugtd/Solid Fiber
INDL & PERSONAL SVC PAPER, WHOL: Boxes, Setup Paperboard
INDL & PERSONAL SVC PAPER, WHOL: Closures, Paper/Disp Plastc
INDL & PERSONAL SVC PAPER, WHOL: Cups, Disp, Plastic/Paper
INDL & PERSONAL SVC PAPER, WHOL: Paper, Wrap/Coarse/Prdts
INDL & PERSONAL SVC PAPER, WHOLESALE: Boxes & Containers
INDL & PERSONAL SVC PAPER, WHOLESALE: Boxes, Fldng Pprboard
INDL & PERSONAL SVC PAPER, WHOLESALE: Disposable
INDL & PERSONAL SVC PAPER, WHOLESALE: Paperboard & Prdts
INDL & PERSONAL SVC PAPER, WHOLESALE: Press Sensitive Tape
INDL & PERSONAL SVC PAPER, WHOLESALE: Shipping Splys

INDL CONTRACTORS: Exhibit Construction
INDL EQPT CLEANING SVCS
INDL EQPT SVCS
INDL GASES WHOLESALERS
INDL HELP SVCS
INDL MACHINERY & EQPT WHOLESALERS
INDL MACHINERY REPAIR & MAINTENANCE
INDL PATTERNS: Foundry Cores
INDL PROCESS INSTR: Transmit, Process Variables
INDL PROCESS INSTRUMENTS: Analyzers
INDL PROCESS INSTRUMENTS: Control
INDL PROCESS INSTRUMENTS: Controllers, Process Variables
INDL PROCESS INSTRUMENTS: Indl Flow & Measuring
INDL PROCESS INSTRUMENTS: Manometers
INDL PROCESS INSTRUMENTS: Moisture Meters
INDL PROCESS INSTRUMENTS: On-Stream Gas Or Liquid Analysis
INDL PROCESS INSTRUMENTS: PH Instruments
INDL PROCESS INSTRUMENTS: Temperature
INDL PROCESS INSTRUMENTS: Water Quality Monitoring/Cntrl Sys
INDL SPLYS WHOLESALERS
INDL SPLYS, WHOL: Fasteners, Incl Nuts, Bolts, Screws, Etc
INDL SPLYS, WHOLESALE: Abrasives
INDL SPLYS, WHOLESALE: Bearings
INDL SPLYS, WHOLESALE: Bottler Splys
INDL SPLYS, WHOLESALE: Brushes, Indl
INDL SPLYS, WHOLESALE: Clean Room Splys
INDL SPLYS, WHOLESALE: Drums, New Or Reconditioned
INDL SPLYS, WHOLESALE: Fasteners & Fastening Eqpt
INDL SPLYS, WHOLESALE: Filters, Indl
INDL SPLYS, WHOLESALE: Gaskets
INDL SPLYS, WHOLESALE: Gaskets & Seals
INDL SPLYS, WHOLESALE: Gears
INDL SPLYS, WHOLESALE: Plastic Bottles
INDL SPLYS, WHOLESALE: Power Transmission, Eqpt & Apparatus
INDL SPLYS, WHOLESALE: Rubber Goods, Mechanical
INDL SPLYS, WHOLESALE: Tanks, Pressurized
INDL SPLYS, WHOLESALE: Tools
INDL SPLYS, WHOLESALE: Twine
INDL SPLYS, WHOLESALE: Valves & Fittings
INDUCTORS
INFANTS' WEAR STORES
INFORMATION RETRIEVAL SERVICES
INK OR WRITING FLUIDS
INK: Duplicating
INK: Gravure
INK: Letterpress Or Offset
INK: Lithographic
INK: Printing
INK: Screen process
INSECTICIDES
INSECTICIDES & PESTICIDES
INSPECTION & TESTING SVCS
INSTRUMENT LANDING SYSTEMS OR ILS: Airborne Or Ground
INSTRUMENTS & ACCESSORIES: Surveying
INSTRUMENTS & METERS: Measuring, Electric
INSTRUMENTS, LABORATORY: Amino Acid Analyzers
INSTRUMENTS, LABORATORY: Analyzers, Automatic Chemical
INSTRUMENTS, LABORATORY: Blood Testing
INSTRUMENTS, LABORATORY: Gas Analyzing
INSTRUMENTS, LABORATORY: Liquid Chromatographic
INSTRUMENTS, LABORATORY: Mass Spectroscopy
INSTRUMENTS, LABORATORY: Nephelometers, Exc Meteorological
INSTRUMENTS, LABORATORY: Spectrographs
INSTRUMENTS, LABORATORY: Spectrometers
INSTRUMENTS, MEASURING & CNTRL: Geophysical & Meteorological
INSTRUMENTS, MEASURING & CNTRL: Radiation & Testing, Nuclear
INSTRUMENTS, MEASURING & CNTRL: Testing, Abrasion, Etc
INSTRUMENTS, MEASURING & CNTRL: Whole Body Counters, Nuclear
INSTRUMENTS, MEASURING & CNTRLG: Aircraft & Motor Vehicle
INSTRUMENTS, MEASURING & CNTRLG: Thermometers/Temp Sensors
INSTRUMENTS, MEASURING & CNTRLNG: Press & Vac Ind, Acft Eng

INSTRUMENTS, MEASURING & CONTROLLING: Dosimetry, Personnel
INSTRUMENTS, MEASURING & CONTROLLING: Gas Detectors
INSTRUMENTS, MEASURING & CONTROLLING: Surveying & Drafting
INSTRUMENTS, MEASURING & CONTROLLING: Ultrasonic Testing
INSTRUMENTS, MEASURING/CNTRLG: Fire Detect Sys, Non-Electric
INSTRUMENTS, MEASURING/CNTRLNG: Med Diagnostic Sys, Nuclear
INSTRUMENTS, OPTICAL: Coating & Grinding, Lens
INSTRUMENTS, OPTICAL: Elements & Assemblies, Exc Ophthalmic
INSTRUMENTS, OPTICAL: Lenses, All Types Exc Ophthalmic
INSTRUMENTS, OPTICAL: Light Sources, Standard
INSTRUMENTS, OPTICAL: Magnifying, NEC
INSTRUMENTS, OPTICAL: Polarizers
INSTRUMENTS, OPTICAL: Test & Inspection
INSTRUMENTS, SURGICAL & MED: Cleaning Eqpt, Ultrasonic Med
INSTRUMENTS, SURGICAL & MED: Needles & Syringes, Hypodermic
INSTRUMENTS, SURGICAL & MEDI: Knife Blades/Handles, Surgical
INSTRUMENTS, SURGICAL & MEDICAL: Blood & Bone Work
INSTRUMENTS, SURGICAL & MEDICAL: Blood Pressure
INSTRUMENTS, SURGICAL & MEDICAL: Catheters
INSTRUMENTS, SURGICAL & MEDICAL: Inhalation Therapy
INSTRUMENTS, SURGICAL & MEDICAL: Lasers, Surgical
INSTRUMENTS, SURGICAL & MEDICAL: Needles, Suture
INSTRUMENTS, SURGICAL & MEDICAL: Ophthalmic
INSTRUMENTS, SURGICAL & MEDICAL: Oxygen Tents
INSTRUMENTS, SURGICAL/MED: Microsurgical, Exc Electromedical
INSTRUMENTS: Analytical
INSTRUMENTS: Analyzers, Internal Combustion Eng, Electronic
INSTRUMENTS: Combustion Control, Indl
INSTRUMENTS: Electronic, Analog-Digital Converters
INSTRUMENTS: Endoscopic Eqpt, Electromedical
INSTRUMENTS: Flow, Indl Process
INSTRUMENTS: Frequency Meters, Electrical, Mech & Electronic
INSTRUMENTS: Indl Process Control
INSTRUMENTS: Laser, Scientific & Engineering
INSTRUMENTS: Liquid Analysis, Indl Process
INSTRUMENTS: Liquid Level, Indl Process
INSTRUMENTS: Measurement, Indl Process
INSTRUMENTS: Measuring & Controlling
INSTRUMENTS: Measuring Electricity
INSTRUMENTS: Measuring, Electrical Energy
INSTRUMENTS: Measuring, Electrical Power
INSTRUMENTS: Medical & Surgical
INSTRUMENTS: Microwave Test
INSTRUMENTS: Nautical
INSTRUMENTS: Optical, Analytical
INSTRUMENTS: Oscillographs & Oscilloscopes
INSTRUMENTS: Photographic, Electronic
INSTRUMENTS: Power Measuring, Electrical
INSTRUMENTS: Pressure Measurement, Indl
INSTRUMENTS: Radio Frequency Measuring
INSTRUMENTS: Telemetering, Indl Process
INSTRUMENTS: Temperature Measurement, Indl
INSTRUMENTS: Test, Digital, Electronic & Electrical Circuits
INSTRUMENTS: Test, Electronic & Electrical Measurement
INSTRUMENTS: Test, Electronic & Electrical Circuits
INSTRUMENTS: Testing, Semiconductor
INSTRUMENTS: Thermal Conductive, Indl
INSTRUMENTS: Thermal Property Measurement
INSTRUMENTS: Vibration
INSTRUMENTS: Viscometer, Indl Process
INSULATING BOARD, CELLULAR FIBER
INSULATING COMPOUNDS
INSULATION & CUSHIONING FOAM: Polystyrene
INSULATION & ROOFING MATERIALS: Wood, Reconstituted
INSULATION MATERIALS WHOLESALERS
INSULATION: Fiberglass
INSULATORS, PORCELAIN: Electrical
INSURANCE BROKERS, NEC
INTEGRATED CIRCUITS, SEMICONDUCTOR NETWORKS, ETC
INTERCOMMUNICATIONS SYSTEMS: Electric

INTERIOR DECORATING SVCS
INTERIOR DESIGN SVCS, NEC
INTERIOR DESIGNING SVCS
INTERIOR REPAIR SVCS
INTRAVENOUS SOLUTIONS
INVENTOR
INVERTERS: Nonrotating Electrical
INVERTERS: Rotating Electrical
INVESTMENT FUNDS, NEC
INVESTORS, NEC
IRON & STEEL: Corrugating, Cold-Rolled
IRON OXIDES
IRRADIATION EQPT

J

JANITORIAL & CUSTODIAL SVCS
JANITORIAL EQPT & SPLYS WHOLESALERS
JARS: Plastic
JEWELERS' FINDINGS & MATERIALS
JEWELERS' FINDINGS & MATERIALS: Bearings, Synthetic
JEWELERS' FINDINGS & MATERIALS: Castings
JEWELERS' FINDINGS & MTLS: Jewel Prep, Instr, Tools, Watches
JEWELERS' FINDINGS/MTRLS: Gem Prep, Settings, Real/Imitation
JEWELRY & PRECIOUS STONES WHOLESALERS
JEWELRY APPAREL
JEWELRY FINDINGS & LAPIDARY WORK
JEWELRY REPAIR SVCS
JEWELRY STORES
JEWELRY STORES: Precious Stones & Precious Metals
JEWELRY, PRECIOUS METAL: Bracelets
JEWELRY, PRECIOUS METAL: Medals, Precious Or Semi-precious
JEWELRY, PRECIOUS METAL: Mountings & Trimmings
JEWELRY, PRECIOUS METAL: Necklaces
JEWELRY, PRECIOUS METAL: Pearl, Natural Or Cultured
JEWELRY, PRECIOUS METAL: Pins
JEWELRY, PRECIOUS METAL: Rings, Finger
JEWELRY, PRECIOUS METAL: Rosaries/Other Sm Religious Article
JEWELRY, PRECIOUS METAL: Settings & Mountings
JEWELRY, WHOLESALE
JEWELRY: Decorative, Fashion & Costume
JEWELRY: Precious Metal
JOB PRINTING & NEWSPAPER PUBLISHING COMBINED
JOB TRAINING & VOCATIONAL REHABILITATION SVCS

K

KAOLIN MINING
KITCHEN ARTICLES: Coarse Earthenware
KITCHEN CABINET STORES, EXC CUSTOM
KITCHEN CABINETS WHOLESALERS
KITCHEN TOOLS & UTENSILS WHOLESALERS
KITCHEN UTENSILS: Bakers' Eqpt, Wood
KITCHEN UTENSILS: Wooden
KITCHENWARE STORES
KITS: Plastic
KNIVES: Agricultural Or indl

L

LABELS: Cotton, Printed
LABELS: Paper, Made From Purchased Materials
LABELS: Woven
LABOR RESOURCE SVCS
LABORATORIES, TESTING: Food
LABORATORIES, TESTING: Hazardous Waste
LABORATORIES, TESTING: Product Testing
LABORATORIES, TESTING: Product Testing, Safety/Performance
LABORATORIES: Biological
LABORATORIES: Biological Research
LABORATORIES: Biotechnology
LABORATORIES: Commercial Nonphysical Research
LABORATORIES: Dental Orthodontic Appliance Production
LABORATORIES: Dental, Crown & Bridge Production
LABORATORIES: Electronic Research
LABORATORIES: Environmental Research
LABORATORIES: Medical
LABORATORIES: Medical Pathology
LABORATORIES: Noncommercial Research
LABORATORIES: Physical Research, Commercial
LABORATORIES: Testing
LABORATORIES: Testing

LABORATORY APPARATUS & FURNITURE
LABORATORY APPARATUS, EXC HEATING & MEASURING
LABORATORY APPARATUS: Sample Preparation Apparatus
LABORATORY APPARATUS: Shakers & Stirrers
LABORATORY CHEMICALS: Organic
LABORATORY EQPT, EXC MEDICAL: Wholesalers
LABORATORY EQPT: Chemical
LABORATORY EQPT: Clinical Instruments Exc Medical
LABORATORY EQPT: Incubators
LABORATORY EQPT: Measuring
LACE GOODS & WARP KNIT FABRIC DYEING & FINISHING
LAMINATED PLASTICS: Plate, Sheet, Rod & Tubes
LAMINATING MATERIALS
LAMINATING SVCS
LAMP & LIGHT BULBS & TUBES
LAMP BULBS & TUBES, ELECTRIC: Filaments
LAMP BULBS & TUBES, ELECTRIC: For Specialized Applications
LAMP BULBS & TUBES, ELECTRIC: Parts
LAMP BULBS & TUBES/PARTS, ELECTRIC: Generalized Applications
LAMP STORES
LAMPS: Boudoir, Residential
LAMPS: Incandescent, Filament
LAMPS: Ultraviolet
LAMPS: Wall, Residential
LANDING MATS: Aircraft, Metal
LANGUAGE SCHOOLS
LAPIDARY WORK & DIAMOND CUTTING & POLISHING
LAPIDARY WORK: Contract Or Other
LAPIDARY WORK: Jewel Cut, Drill, Polish, Recut/Setting
LARD: From Slaughtering Plants
LASER SYSTEMS & EQPT
LASERS: Welding, Drilling & Cutting Eqpt
LAUNDRIES, EXC POWER & COIN-OPERATED
LAUNDRY & DRYCLEANING SVCS, EXC COIN-OPERATED: Pickup
LAUNDRY & GARMENT SVCS, NEC: Hand Laundries
LAUNDRY & GARMENT SVCS: Tailor Shop, Exc Custom/Merchant
LAUNDRY EQPT: Commercial
LAUNDRY SVCS: Indl
LAWN & GARDEN EQPT
LAWN MOWER REPAIR SHOP
LEAD
LEAD PENCILS & ART GOODS
LEAD-IN WIRES: Electric Lamp
LEASING & RENTAL SVCS: Earth Moving Eqpt
LEASING & RENTAL: Construction & Mining Eqpt
LEASING & RENTAL: Medical Machinery & Eqpt
LEASING & RENTAL: Other Real Estate Property
LEASING & RENTAL: Trucks, Without Drivers
LEASING: Passenger Car
LEATHER & CANVAS GOODS: Leggings Or Chaps, NEC
LEATHER GOODS: Belt Laces
LEATHER GOODS: Card Cases
LEATHER GOODS: Cases
LEATHER GOODS: Cosmetic Bags
LEATHER GOODS: Garments
LEATHER GOODS: Personal
LEATHER GOODS: Safety Belts
LEATHER GOODS: Wallets
LEATHER TANNING & FINISHING
LEATHER, LEATHER GOODS & FURS, WHOLESALE
LEATHER: Accessory Prdts
LEATHER: Bag
LEATHER: Handbag
LEATHER: Mechanical
LEATHER: Processed
LEGAL & TAX SVCS
LEGAL OFFICES & SVCS
LEGAL SVCS: General Practice Attorney or Lawyer
LEGAL SVCS: Malpractice & Negligence Law
LENS COATING: Ophthalmic
LETTER WRITING SVCS
LIFE INSURANCE: Fraternal Organizations
LIGHTER FLUID
LIGHTING EQPT: Flashlights
LIGHTING EQPT: Floodlights
LIGHTING EQPT: Motor Vehicle, Flasher Lights
LIGHTING EQPT: Motor Vehicle, NEC
LIGHTING EQPT: Outdoor
LIGHTING EQPT: Spotlights
LIGHTING FIXTURES WHOLESALERS
LIGHTING FIXTURES, NEC

LIGHTING FIXTURES: Arc
LIGHTING FIXTURES: Decorative Area
LIGHTING FIXTURES: Fluorescent, Commercial
LIGHTING FIXTURES: Indl & Commercial
LIGHTING FIXTURES: Motor Vehicle
LIGHTING FIXTURES: Ornamental, Commercial
LIGHTING FIXTURES: Public
LIGHTING FIXTURES: Residential
LIGHTING FIXTURES: Street
LIGHTING FIXTURES: Swimming Pool
LIGHTING FIXTURES: Underwater
LIGHTING MAINTENANCE SVC
LIME
LIMESTONE: Crushed & Broken
LINEN SPLY SVC: Non-Clothing
LINENS & TOWELS WHOLESALERS
LINENS: Napkins, Fabric & Nonwoven, From Purchased Materials
LINENS: Tablecloths, From Purchased Materials
LINER STRIPS: Rubber
LINERS & COVERS: Fabric
LINERS & LINING
LIQUEFIED PETROLEUM GAS DEALERS
LIQUID CRYSTAL DISPLAYS
LITHOGRAPHIC PLATES
LOCKS
LOCKS: Safe & Vault, Metal
LOGGING
LOGGING CAMPS & CONTRACTORS
LOOSELEAF BINDERS
LOOSELEAF BINDERS: Library
LOTIONS OR CREAMS: Face
LOUDSPEAKERS
LUBRICATING EQPT: Indl
LUBRICATION SYSTEMS & EQPT
LUGGAGE & BRIEFCASES
LUGGAGE & LEATHER GOODS STORES
LUGGAGE WHOLESALERS
LUGGAGE: Traveling Bags
LUMBER & BLDG MATLS DEALER, RET: Garage Doors, Sell/Install
LUMBER & BLDG MATRLS DEALERS, RET: Bath Fixtures, Eqpt/Sply
LUMBER & BLDG MTRLS DEALERS, RET: Doors, Storm, Wood/Metal
LUMBER & BLDG MTRLS DEALERS, RET: Planing Mill Prdts/Lumber
LUMBER & BUILDING MATERIALS DEALER, RET: Door & Window Prdts
LUMBER & BUILDING MATERIALS DEALER, RET: Masonry Matls/Splys
LUMBER & BUILDING MATERIALS DEALERS, RET: Solar Heating Eqpt
LUMBER & BUILDING MATERIALS DEALERS, RETAIL: Countertops
LUMBER & BUILDING MATERIALS DEALERS, RETAIL: Paving Stones
LUMBER & BUILDING MATERIALS DEALERS, RETAIL: Tile, Ceramic
LUMBER & BUILDING MATERIALS RET DEALERS: Millwork & Lumber
LUMBER & BUILDING MATLS DEALERS, RET: Concrete/Cinder Block
LUMBER: Hardwood Dimension & Flooring Mills
LUMBER: Plywood, Hardwood
LUMBER: Plywood, Prefinished, Hardwood
LUMBER: Rails, Fence, Round Or Split
LUMBER: Siding, Dressed
LUMBER: Veneer, Hardwood

M

MACHINE PARTS: Stamped Or Pressed Metal
MACHINE SHOPS
MACHINE TOOL ACCESS: Cutting
MACHINE TOOL ACCESS: Diamond Cutting, For Turning, Etc
MACHINE TOOL ACCESS: Dresser, Abrasive Wheel Or Other
MACHINE TOOL ACCESS: Drill Bushings, Drilling Jig
MACHINE TOOL ACCESS: Drills
MACHINE TOOL ACCESS: Files
MACHINE TOOL ACCESS: Hopper Feed Devices
MACHINE TOOL ACCESS: Machine Attachments & Access, Drilling
MACHINE TOOL ACCESS: Tool Holders
MACHINE TOOL ACCESS: Tools & Access
MACHINE TOOL ATTACHMENTS & ACCESS

MACHINE TOOLS & ACCESS
MACHINE TOOLS, METAL CUTTING: Cutoff
MACHINE TOOLS, METAL CUTTING: Drilling
MACHINE TOOLS, METAL CUTTING: Exotic, Including Explosive
MACHINE TOOLS, METAL CUTTING: Grind, Polish, Buff, Lapp
MACHINE TOOLS, METAL CUTTING: Tool Replacement & Rpr Parts
MACHINE TOOLS, METAL FORMING: Container, Metal Incl Cans
MACHINE TOOLS, METAL FORMING: Crimping, Metal
MACHINE TOOLS, METAL FORMING: Forming, Metal Deposit
MACHINE TOOLS, METAL FORMING: Magnetic Forming
MACHINE TOOLS, METAL FORMING: Marking
MACHINE TOOLS, METAL FORMING: Mechanical, Pneumatic Or Hyd
MACHINE TOOLS, METAL FORMING: Punching & Shearing
MACHINE TOOLS, METAL FORMING: Rebuilt
MACHINE TOOLS, METAL FORMING: Spinning, Metal
MACHINE TOOLS: Metal Cutting
MACHINE TOOLS: Metal Forming
MACHINERY & EQPT, AGRICULTURAL, WHOL: Farm Eqpt Parts/Splys
MACHINERY & EQPT, AGRICULTURAL, WHOLESALE: Lawn & Garden
MACHINERY & EQPT, INDL, WHOL: Controlling Instruments/Access
MACHINERY & EQPT, INDL, WHOL: Environ Pollution Cntrl, Air
MACHINERY & EQPT, INDL, WHOLESALE: Cement Making
MACHINERY & EQPT, INDL, WHOLESALE: Chemical Process
MACHINERY & EQPT, INDL, WHOLESALE: Compaction
MACHINERY & EQPT, INDL, WHOLESALE: Conveyor Systems
MACHINERY & EQPT, INDL, WHOLESALE: Dairy Prdts Manufacturing
MACHINERY & EQPT, INDL, WHOLESALE: Drilling, Exc Bits
MACHINERY & EQPT, INDL, WHOLESALE: Engines & Parts, Diesel
MACHINERY & EQPT, INDL, WHOLESALE: Engines, Gasoline
MACHINERY & EQPT, INDL, WHOLESALE: Food Manufacturing
MACHINERY & EQPT, INDL, WHOLESALE: Food Product Manufacturng
MACHINERY & EQPT, INDL, WHOLESALE: Hydraulic Systems
MACHINERY & EQPT, INDL, WHOLESALE: Indl Machine Parts
MACHINERY & EQPT, INDL, WHOLESALE: Instruments & Cntrl Eqpt
MACHINERY & EQPT, INDL, WHOLESALE: Machine Tools & Access
MACHINERY & EQPT, INDL, WHOLESALE: Machine Tools & Metalwork
MACHINERY & EQPT, INDL, WHOLESALE: Measure/Test, Electric
MACHINERY & EQPT, INDL, WHOLESALE: Packaging
MACHINERY & EQPT, INDL, WHOLESALE: Plastic Prdts Machinery
MACHINERY & EQPT, INDL, WHOLESALE: Processing & Packaging
MACHINERY & EQPT, INDL, WHOLESALE: Pulverizing
MACHINERY & EQPT, INDL, WHOLESALE: Recycling
MACHINERY & EQPT, INDL, WHOLESALE: Screening
MACHINERY & EQPT, INDL, WHOLESALE: Sewing
MACHINERY & EQPT, INDL, WHOLESALE: Textile
MACHINERY & EQPT, INDL, WHOLESALE: Textile & Leather
MACHINERY & EQPT, WHOLESALE: Concrete Processing
MACHINERY & EQPT, WHOLESALE: Construction & Mining, Ladders
MACHINERY & EQPT, WHOLESALE: Construction, General
MACHINERY & EQPT: Electroplating
MACHINERY & EQPT: Farm
MACHINERY & EQPT: Gas Producers, Generators/Other Rltd Eqpt
MACHINERY & EQPT: Liquid Automation
MACHINERY & EQPT: Metal Finishing, Plating Etc
MACHINERY & EQPT: Petroleum Refinery
MACHINERY & EQPT: Vibratory Parts Handling Eqpt
MACHINERY BASES
MACHINERY, CALCULATING: Calculators & Adding

MACHINERY, COMMERCIAL LAUNDRY & Drycleaning: Pressing
MACHINERY, COMMERCIAL LAUNDRY: Washing, Incl Coin-Operated
MACHINERY, EQPT & SUPPLIES: Parking Facility
MACHINERY, FOOD PRDTS: Beverage
MACHINERY, FOOD PRDTS: Cutting, Chopping, Grinding, Mixing
MACHINERY, FOOD PRDTS: Dairy & Milk
MACHINERY, FOOD PRDTS: Food Processing, Smokers
MACHINERY, FOOD PRDTS: Homogenizing, Dairy, Fruit/Vegetable
MACHINERY, FOOD PRDTS: Mixers, Commercial
MACHINERY, FOOD PRDTS: Ovens, Bakery
MACHINERY, FOOD PRDTS: Processing, Poultry
MACHINERY, MAILING: Address Labeling
MACHINERY, MAILING: Postage Meters
MACHINERY, METALWORKING: Assembly, Including Robotic
MACHINERY, METALWORKING: Coil Winding, For Springs
MACHINERY, METALWORKING: Rotary Slitters, Metalworking
MACHINERY, OFFICE: Sorters, Filing
MACHINERY, OFFICE: Stapling, Hand Or Power
MACHINERY, OFFICE: Time Clocks &Time Recording Devices
MACHINERY, OFFICE: Typing & Word Processing
MACHINERY, PACKAGING: Carton Packing
MACHINERY, PACKAGING: Packing & Wrapping
MACHINERY, PACKAGING: Vacuum
MACHINERY, PAPER INDUSTRY: Converting, Die Cutting & Stampng
MACHINERY, PAPER INDUSTRY: Cutting
MACHINERY, PAPER INDUSTRY: Fourdrinier
MACHINERY, PRINTING TRADES: Bookbinding Machinery
MACHINERY, PRINTING TRADES: Bronzing Or Dusting
MACHINERY, PRINTING TRADES: Plates
MACHINERY, PRINTING TRADES: Plates, Engravers' Metal
MACHINERY, PRINTING TRADES: Presses, Envelope
MACHINERY, PRINTING TRADES: Presses, Gravure
MACHINERY, PRINTING TRADES: Printing Trade Parts & Attchts
MACHINERY, PRINTING TRADES: Type, Foundry
MACHINERY, SEWING: Sewing & Hat & Zipper Making
MACHINERY, TEXTILE: Card Clothing
MACHINERY, TEXTILE: Fiber & Yarn Preparation
MACHINERY, TEXTILE: Finishing
MACHINERY, TEXTILE: Loom Parts &Attachments, Jacquard
MACHINERY, TEXTILE: Winders
MACHINERY, WOODWORKING: Box Making, For Wooden Boxes
MACHINERY, WOODWORKING: Cabinet Makers'
MACHINERY, WOODWORKING: Furniture Makers
MACHINERY, WOODWORKING: Scarfing
MACHINERY: Assembly, Exc Metalworking
MACHINERY: Automotive Related
MACHINERY: Bottle Washing & Sterilzing
MACHINERY: Brake Burnishing Or Washing
MACHINERY: Centrifugal
MACHINERY: Concrete Prdts
MACHINERY: Construction
MACHINERY: Cryogenic, Industrial
MACHINERY: Custom
MACHINERY: Die Casting
MACHINERY: Electronic Component Making
MACHINERY: Engraving
MACHINERY: Extruding, Synthetic Filament
MACHINERY: Folding
MACHINERY: Gas Separators
MACHINERY: Gear Cutting & Finishing
MACHINERY: General, Industrial, NEC
MACHINERY: Glass Cutting
MACHINERY: Glassmaking
MACHINERY: Grinding
MACHINERY: Ice Cream
MACHINERY: Ice Making
MACHINERY: Industrial, NEC
MACHINERY: Labeling
MACHINERY: Lapping
MACHINERY: Marking, Metalworking
MACHINERY: Metalworking
MACHINERY: Milling
MACHINERY: Mining
MACHINERY: Ozone
MACHINERY: Packaging
MACHINERY: Paper Industry Miscellaneous

INDEX

MACHINERY: Pharmaciutical
MACHINERY: Plastic Working
MACHINERY: Printing Presses
MACHINERY: Recycling
MACHINERY: Riveting
MACHINERY: Road Construction & Maintenance
MACHINERY: Rubber Working
MACHINERY: Saw & Sawing
MACHINERY: Semiconductor Manufacturing
MACHINERY: Sheet Metal Working
MACHINERY: Sifting & Screening
MACHINERY: Specialty
MACHINERY: Stone Working
MACHINERY: Textile
MACHINERY: Thread Rolling
MACHINERY: Tire Shredding
MACHINERY: Voting
MACHINERY: Woodworking
MACHINES: Forming, Sheet Metal
MACHINISTS' TOOLS & MACHINES: Measuring, Metalworking Type
MACHINISTS' TOOLS: Precision
MACHINISTS' TOOLS: Scales, Measuring, Precision
MAGNETIC INK & OPTICAL SCANNING EQPT
MAGNETIC RESONANCE IMAGING DEVICES: Nonmedical
MAGNETS: Ceramic
MAGNETS: Permanent
MAIL PRESORTING SVCS
MAIL-ORDER BOOK CLUBS
MAIL-ORDER HOUSES: Arts & Crafts Eqpt & Splys
MAIL-ORDER HOUSES: Clothing, Exc Women's
MAIL-ORDER HOUSES: Computer Eqpt & Electronics
MAIL-ORDER HOUSES: Computers & Peripheral Eqpt
MAIL-ORDER HOUSES: Food
MAIL-ORDER HOUSES: General Merchandise
MAIL-ORDER HOUSES: Order Taking Office Only
MAILBOX RENTAL & RELATED SVCS
MAILING MACHINES WHOLESALERS
MAILING SVCS, NEC
MANAGEMENT CONSULTING SVCS: Automation & Robotics
MANAGEMENT CONSULTING SVCS: Banking & Finance
MANAGEMENT CONSULTING SVCS: Business
MANAGEMENT CONSULTING SVCS: Construction Project
MANAGEMENT CONSULTING SVCS: Food & Beverage
MANAGEMENT CONSULTING SVCS: General
MANAGEMENT CONSULTING SVCS: Hospital & Health
MANAGEMENT CONSULTING SVCS: Incentive Or Award Program
MANAGEMENT CONSULTING SVCS: Industrial
MANAGEMENT CONSULTING SVCS: Industry Specialist
MANAGEMENT CONSULTING SVCS: Information Systems
MANAGEMENT CONSULTING SVCS: Maintenance
MANAGEMENT CONSULTING SVCS: Manufacturing
MANAGEMENT CONSULTING SVCS: Merchandising
MANAGEMENT CONSULTING SVCS: New Products & Svcs
MANAGEMENT CONSULTING SVCS: Training & Development
MANAGEMENT CONSULTING SVCS: Transportation
MANAGEMENT SERVICES
MANAGEMENT SVCS, FACILITIES SUPPORT: Environ Remediation
MANAGEMENT SVCS: Administrative
MANAGEMENT SVCS: Business
MANAGEMENT SVCS: Construction
MANAGEMENT SVCS: Hotel Or Motel
MANHOLES & COVERS: Metal
MANICURE PREPARATIONS
MANIFOLDS: Pipe, Fabricated From Purchased Pipe
MANUFACTURED & MOBILE HOME DEALERS
MANUFACTURING INDUSTRIES, NEC
MAPS
MARBLE BOARD
MARBLE, BUILDING: Cut & Shaped
MARBLE: Crushed & Broken
MARINAS
MARINE APPAREL STORES
MARINE CARGO HANDLING SVCS
MARINE CARGO HANDLING SVCS: Marine Terminal
MARINE ENGINE REPAIR SVCS
MARINE HARDWARE
MARINE RELATED EQPT
MARINE SPLY DEALERS
MARINE SPLYS WHOLESALERS
MARINE SVC STATIONS
MARKETS: Meat & fish

MARKING DEVICES
MARKING DEVICES: Embossing Seals & Hand Stamps
MARKING DEVICES: Embossing Seals, Corporate & Official
MARKING DEVICES: Pads, Inking & Stamping
MARKING DEVICES: Screens, Textile Printing
MARKING DEVICES: Seal Presses, Notary & Hand
MARKING DEVICES: Time Stamps, Hand, Rubber Or Metal
MATERIALS HANDLING EQPT WHOLESALERS
MATS OR MATTING, NEC: Rubber
MATS, MATTING & PADS: Auto, Floor, Exc Rubber Or Plastic
MATS: Table, Plastic & Textile
MATTRESS PROTECTORS, EXC RUBBER
MATTRESS STORES
MEAL DELIVERY PROGRAMS
MEAT & MEAT PRDTS WHOLESALERS
MEAT CUTTING & PACKING
MEAT MARKETS
MEAT PRDTS: Canned
MEAT PRDTS: Canned Exc Baby Food, From Slaughtered Meat
MEAT PRDTS: Cured, From Slaughtered Meat
MEAT PRDTS: Frankfurters, From Purchased Meat
MEAT PRDTS: Frozen
MEAT PRDTS: Ham, Boiled, From Purchased Meat
MEAT PRDTS: Head Cheese, From Purchased Meat
MEAT PRDTS: Meat By-Prdts, From Slaughtered Meat
MEAT PRDTS: Pork, Cured, From Purchased Meat
MEAT PRDTS: Pork, From Slaughtered Meat
MEAT PRDTS: Sausage Casings, Natural
MEAT PRDTS: Sausages & Related Prdts, From Purchased Meat
MEAT PRDTS: Sausages, From Purchased Meat
MEAT PRDTS: Snack Sticks, Incl Jerky, From Purchased Meat
MEAT.PRDTS: Spiced Meats, From Purchased Meat
MEAT PRDTS: Veal, From Slaughtered Meat
MEAT PROCESSED FROM PURCHASED CARCASSES
MEAT PROCESSING MACHINERY
MEATS, PACKAGED FROZEN: Wholesalers
MECHANICAL INSTRUMENT REPAIR SVCS
MED, DENTAL & HOSPITAL EQPT, WHOL: Incontinent Prdts/Splys
MEDIA: Magnetic & Optical Recording
MEDICAL & HOSPITAL EQPT WHOLESALERS
MEDICAL & SURGICAL SPLYS: Bandages & Dressings
MEDICAL & SURGICAL SPLYS: Clothing, Fire Resistant & Protect
MEDICAL & SURGICAL SPLYS: Cosmetic Restorations
MEDICAL & SURGICAL SPLYS: Cotton, Incl Cotton Balls
MEDICAL & SURGICAL SPLYS: Foot Appliances, Orthopedic
MEDICAL & SURGICAL SPLYS: Ligatures
MEDICAL & SURGICAL SPLYS: Limbs, Artificial
MEDICAL & SURGICAL SPLYS: Orthopedic Appliances
MEDICAL & SURGICAL SPLYS: Personal Safety Eqpt
MEDICAL & SURGICAL SPLYS: Prosthetic Appliances
MEDICAL & SURGICAL SPLYS: Space Helmets
MEDICAL & SURGICAL SPLYS: Splints, Pneumatic & Wood
MEDICAL & SURGICAL SPLYS: Sponges
MEDICAL & SURGICAL SPLYS: Stretchers
MEDICAL & SURGICAL SPLYS: Supports, Abdominal, Ankle, Etc
MEDICAL & SURGICAL SPLYS: Sutures, Non & Absorbable
MEDICAL & SURGICAL SPLYS: Trusses, Orthopedic & Surgical
MEDICAL EQPT REPAIR SVCS, NON-ELECTRIC
MEDICAL EQPT: CAT Scanner Or Computerized Axial Tomography
MEDICAL EQPT: Diagnostic
MEDICAL EQPT: Electromedical Apparatus
MEDICAL EQPT: Electrotherapeutic Apparatus
MEDICAL EQPT: Laser Systems
MEDICAL EQPT: MRI/Magnetic Resonance Imaging Devs, Nuclear
MEDICAL EQPT: Pacemakers
MEDICAL EQPT: Patient Monitoring
MEDICAL EQPT: Sterilizers
MEDICAL EQPT: Ultrasonic Scanning Devices
MEDICAL EQPT: Ultrasonic, Exc Cleaning
MEDICAL EQPT: X-Ray Apparatus & Tubes, Fluoroscopic
MEDICAL EQPT: X-Ray Apparatus & Tubes, Radiographic
MEDICAL EQPT: X-ray Generators
MEDICAL SVCS ORGANIZATION
MEDICAL, DENTAL & HOSPITAL EQPT, WHOL: Hosptl Eqpt/Furniture

MEDICAL, DENTAL & HOSPITAL EQPT, WHOL: Surgical Eqpt & Splys
MEDICAL, DENTAL & HOSPITAL EQPT, WHOLESALE: Baths, Whirlpool
MEDICAL, DENTAL & HOSPITAL EQPT, WHOLESALE: Diagnostic, Med
MEDICAL, DENTAL & HOSPITAL EQPT, WHOLESALE: Hearing Aids
MEDICAL, DENTAL & HOSPITAL EQPT, WHOLESALE: Med Eqpt & Splys
MEDICAL, DENTAL & HOSPITAL EQPT, WHOLESALE: Medical Lab
MEDICAL, DENTAL & HOSPITAL EQPT, WHOLESALE: Orthopedic
MEDICAL, DENTAL/HOSPITAL EQPT, WHOL: Veterinarian Eqpt/Sply
MEMBERSHIP ORGANIZATIONS, NEC: Charitable
MEMBERSHIP ORGANIZATIONS, NEC: Literary, Film Or Cultural
MEMBERSHIP ORGANIZATIONS, PROF: Education/Teacher Assoc
MEMBERSHIP ORGANIZATIONS, RELIGIOUS: Assembly Of God Church
MEMBERSHIP ORGANIZATIONS, RELIGIOUS: Catholic Church
MEMBERSHIP ORGANIZATIONS, RELIGIOUS: Nonchurch
MEN'S & BOYS' CLOTHING ACCESS STORES
MEN'S & BOYS' CLOTHING STORES
MEN'S & BOYS' CLOTHING WHOLESALERS, NEC
MEN'S & BOYS' SPORTSWEAR CLOTHING STORES
MEN'S & BOYS' SPORTSWEAR WHOLESALERS
MEN'S CLOTHING STORES: Everyday, Exc Suits & Sportswear
METAL & STEEL PRDTS: Abrasive
METAL CUTTING SVCS
METAL FABRICATORS: Architechtural
METAL FABRICATORS: Plate
METAL FABRICATORS: Sheet
METAL FABRICATORS: Structural, Ship
METAL FABRICATORS: Structural, Ship
METAL FINISHING SVCS
METAL MINING SVCS
METAL SERVICE CENTERS & OFFICES
METAL SPINNING FOR THE TRADE
METAL STAMPING, FOR THE TRADE
METAL STAMPINGS: Ornamental
METAL STAMPINGS: Patterned
METAL STAMPINGS: Perforated
METAL TREATING COMPOUNDS
METAL: Battery
METALS SVC CENTERS & WHOL: Structural Shapes, Iron Or Steel
METALS SVC CENTERS & WHOLESALERS: Bars, Metal
METALS SVC CENTERS & WHOLESALERS: Cable, Wire
METALS SVC CENTERS & WHOLESALERS: Ferroalloys
METALS SVC CENTERS & WHOLESALERS: Foundry Prdts
METALS SVC CENTERS & WHOLESALERS: Iron & Steel Prdt, Ferrous
METALS SVC CENTERS & WHOLESALERS: Nonferrous Sheets, Etc
METALS SVC CENTERS & WHOLESALERS: Pipe & Tubing, Steel
METALS SVC CENTERS & WHOLESALERS: Rope, Wire, Exc Insulated
METALS SVC CENTERS & WHOLESALERS: Sheets, Metal
METALS SVC CENTERS & WHOLESALERS: Stampings, Metal
METALS SVC CENTERS & WHOLESALERS: Steel
METALS SVC CENTERS & WHOLESALERS: Steel Decking
METALS SVC CNTRS & WHOL: Metal Wires, Ties, Cables/Screening
METALS SVC CTRS & WHOL: Aluminum Bars, Rods, Etc
METALS: Precious NEC
METALS: Primary Nonferrous, NEC
METALWORK: Miscellaneous
METALWORK: Ornamental
METALWORKING MACHINERY WHOLESALERS
METERS: Power Factor & Phase Angle
METERS: Pyrometers, Indl Process
MGMT CONSULTING SVCS: Matls, Incl Purch, Handle & Invntry
MICA
MICROCIRCUITS, INTEGRATED: Semiconductor
MICROFILM EQPT

MICROFILM EQPT WHOLESALERS
MICROFILM SVCS
MICROPHONES
MICROWAVE COMPONENTS
MICROWAVE OVENS: Household
MILITARY INSIGNIA
MILITARY INSIGNIA, TEXTILE
MILL PRDTS: Structural & Rail
MILLINERY SUPPLIES: Veils & Veiling, Bridal, Funeral, Etc
MILLING: Feed, Wheat
MILLING: Grain Cereals, Cracked
MILLWORK
MINE & QUARRY SVCS: Nonmetallic Minerals
MINE DEVELOPMENT, METAL
MINE EXPLORATION SVCS: Nonmetallic Minerals
MINERAL PIGMENT MINING
MINERAL WOOL
MINERAL WOOL INSULATION PRDTS
MINERALS: Ground Or Otherwise Treated
MINERALS: Ground or Treated
MINING MACHINES & EQPT: Clarifying, Mineral
MINING MACHINES & EQPT: Feeders, Ore & Aggregate
MINING MACHINES & EQPT: Pulverizers, Stone, Stationary
MIXERS: Hot Metal
MIXTURES & BLOCKS: Asphalt Paving
MOBILE COMMUNICATIONS EQPT
MOBILE HOMES
MODELS
MODELS: General, Exc Toy
MODELS: Railroad, Exc Toy
MODULES: Solid State
MOLDED RUBBER PRDTS
MOLDING COMPOUNDS
MOLDINGS & TRIM: Metal, Exc Automobile
MOLDINGS & TRIM: Wood
MOLDINGS: Picture Frame
MOLDS: Indl
MOLDS: Plastic Working & Foundry
MOLECULAR DEVICES: Solid State
MONORAIL SYSTEMS
MONUMENTS & GRAVE MARKERS, EXC TERRAZZO
MONUMENTS: Concrete
MONUMENTS: Cut Stone, Exc Finishing Or Lettering Only
MOPS: Floor & Dust
MORTAR: High Temperature, Nonclay
MOTION PICTURE & VIDEO PRODUCTION SVCS
MOTION PICTURE & VIDEO PRODUCTION SVCS: Educational, TV
MOTION PICTURE PRODUCTION & DISTRIBUTION
MOTION PICTURE PRODUCTION & DISTRIBUTION: Television
MOTOR & GENERATOR PARTS: Electric
MOTOR REPAIR SVCS
MOTOR SCOOTERS & PARTS
MOTOR VEHICLE ASSEMBLY, COMPLETE: Ambulances
MOTOR VEHICLE ASSEMBLY, COMPLETE: Autos, Incl Specialty
MOTOR VEHICLE ASSEMBLY, COMPLETE: Military Motor Vehicle
MOTOR VEHICLE ASSEMBLY, COMPLETE: Snow Plows
MOTOR VEHICLE ASSEMBLY, COMPLETE: Truck & Tractor Trucks
MOTOR VEHICLE DEALERS: Automobiles, New & Used
MOTOR VEHICLE DEALERS: Pickups & Vans, Used
MOTOR VEHICLE DEALERS: Trucks, Tractors/Trailers, New & Used
MOTOR VEHICLE PARTS & ACCESS: Air Conditioner Parts
MOTOR VEHICLE PARTS & ACCESS: Body Components & Frames
MOTOR VEHICLE PARTS & ACCESS: Clutches
MOTOR VEHICLE PARTS & ACCESS: Cylinder Heads
MOTOR VEHICLE PARTS & ACCESS: Engines & Parts
MOTOR VEHICLE PARTS & ACCESS: Fuel Pumps
MOTOR VEHICLE PARTS & ACCESS: Fuel Systems & Parts
MOTOR VEHICLE PARTS & ACCESS: Transmission Housings Or Parts
MOTOR VEHICLE PARTS & ACCESS: Transmissions
MOTOR VEHICLE PARTS & ACCESS: Water Pumps
MOTOR VEHICLE PARTS & ACCESS: Wheel rims
MOTOR VEHICLE PARTS & ACCESS: Windshield Frames
MOTOR VEHICLE PARTS & ACCESS: Wipers, Windshield
MOTOR VEHICLE SPLYS & PARTS WHOLESALERS: New
MOTOR VEHICLE SPLYS & PARTS WHOLESALERS: Used
MOTOR VEHICLE: Hardware
MOTOR VEHICLE: Radiators

MOTOR VEHICLES & CAR BODIES
MOTOR VEHICLES, WHOLESALE: Trailers for passenger vehicles
MOTOR VEHICLES, WHOLESALE: Trailers, Truck, New & Used
MOTOR VEHICLES, WHOLESALE: Truck bodies
MOTORCYCLE ACCESS
MOTORCYCLE DEALERS
MOTORCYCLE PARTS & ACCESS DEALERS
MOTORCYCLE REPAIR SHOPS
MOTORCYCLES & RELATED PARTS
MOTORS: Electric
MOTORS: Generators
MOTORS: Torque
MOUNTING MERCHANDISE ON CARDS
MOUTHWASHES
MOVIE THEATERS, EXC DRIVE-IN
MOVING SVC: Local
MOWERS & ACCESSORIES
MULTIPLEX EQPT: Radio, Television & Broadcast
MUSEUMS
MUSEUMS & ART GALLERIES
MUSIC ARRANGING & COMPOSING SVCS
MUSIC DISTRIBUTION APPARATUS
MUSICAL INSTRUMENT LESSONS
MUSICAL INSTRUMENT PARTS & ACCESS, WHOLESALE
MUSICAL INSTRUMENT REPAIR
MUSICAL INSTRUMENTS & ACCESS: Carrying Cases
MUSICAL INSTRUMENTS & ACCESS: NEC
MUSICAL INSTRUMENTS & SPLYS STORES
MUSICAL INSTRUMENTS: Guitars & Parts, Electric & Acoustic
MUSICAL INSTRUMENTS: Organs
MUSICAL INSTRUMENTS: Synthesizers, Music
MUSICAL INSTRUMENTS: Violins & Parts

N

NAME PLATES: Engraved Or Etched
NATIONAL SECURITY, GOVERNMENT: National Guard
NATURAL GAS LIQUIDS PRODUCTION
NATURAL GAS PRODUCTION
NATURAL LIQUEFIED PETROLEUM GAS PRODUCTION
NAVIGATIONAL SYSTEMS & INSTRUMENTS
NET & NETTING PRDTS
NETTING: Rope
NEW & USED CAR DEALERS
NEWS SYNDICATES
NEWSPAPERS & PERIODICALS NEWS REPORTING SVCS
NICKEL ALLOY
NONCURRENT CARRYING WIRING DEVICES
NONDAIRY BASED FROZEN DESSERTS
NONFERROUS: Rolling & Drawing, NEC
NOTIONS: Fasteners, Slide Zippers
NOTIONS: Hooks, Crochet
NOVELTIES
NOVELTIES & SPECIALTIES: Metal
NOVELTIES, DURABLE, WHOLESALE
NOVELTIES: Leather
NOVELTIES: Paper, Made From Purchased Materials
NOVELTIES: Plastic
NOVELTY SHOPS
NOZZLES & SPRINKLERS Lawn Hose
NOZZLES: Fire Fighting
NOZZLES: Spray, Aerosol, Paint Or Insecticide
NUCLEAR FUELS SCRAP REPROCESSING
NURSERIES & LAWN & GARDEN SPLY STORE, RET: Lawn/Garden Splys
NURSERIES & LAWN & GARDEN SPLY STORES, RETAIL: Top Soil
NURSERIES & LAWN/GARDEN SPLY STORE, RET: Lawnmowers/Tractors
NURSERY & GARDEN CENTERS
NUTS: Metal

O

OFFICE EQPT WHOLESALERS
OFFICE EQPT, WHOLESALE: Calculating Machines
OFFICE EQPT, WHOLESALE: Calculators, Electronic
OFFICE EQPT, WHOLESALE: Duplicating Machines
OFFICE FIXTURES: Exc Wood
OFFICE FURNITURE REPAIR & MAINTENANCE SVCS
OFFICE SPLY & STATIONERY STORES
OFFICE SPLY & STATIONERY STORES: Office Forms & Splys
OFFICE SPLYS, NEC, WHOLESALE

OFFICES & CLINICS DOCTORS OF MED: Intrnl Med Practitioners
OFFICES & CLINICS OF DENTISTS: Dental Clinics & Offices
OFFICES & CLINICS OF DENTISTS: Specialist, Practitioners
OFFICES & CLINICS OF DOCTORS OF MEDICINE: Gastronomist
OFFICES & CLINICS OF DOCTORS OF MEDICINE: Group Health Assoc
OFFICES & CLINICS OF DOCTORS OF MEDICINE: Neurosurgeon
OFFICES & CLINICS OF DOCTORS OF MEDICINE: Oncologist
OFFICES & CLINICS OF DOCTORS OF MEDICINE: Ophthalmologist
OFFICES & CLINICS OF DOCTORS OF MEDICINE: Radiologist
OFFICES & CLINICS OF DRS OF MEDICINE: Geriatric
OFFICES & CLINICS OF DRS OF MEDICINE: Physician, Orthopedic
OFFICES & CLINICS OF HEALTH PRACTITIONERS: Physical Therapy
OIL FIELD SVCS, NEC
OIL TREATING COMPOUNDS
OILS & ESSENTIAL OILS
OILS & GREASES: Blended & Compounded
OILS & GREASES: Lubricating
OILS: Essential
OILS: Lubricating
OILS: Peppermint
OILS: Vegetable Oils, Vulcanized Or Sulfurized
OLEFINS
OMNIBEARING INDICATORS
OPERATOR: Apartment Buildings
OPERATOR: Nonresidential Buildings
OPHTHALMIC GOODS
OPHTHALMIC GOODS WHOLESALERS
OPHTHALMIC GOODS, NEC, WHOLESALE: Frames
OPHTHALMIC GOODS, NEC, WHOLESALE: Lenses
OPHTHALMIC GOODS: Frames & Parts, Eyeglass & Spectacle
OPHTHALMIC GOODS: Lenses, Ophthalmic
OPHTHALMIC GOODS: Protectors, Eye
OPTICAL GOODS STORES
OPTICAL GOODS STORES: Contact Lenses, Prescription
OPTICAL GOODS STORES: Eyeglasses, Prescription
OPTICAL GOODS STORES: Opticians
OPTICAL INSTRUMENTS & APPARATUS
OPTICAL INSTRUMENTS & LENSES
OPTICAL ISOLATORS
OPTOMETRISTS' OFFICES
ORAL PREPARATIONS
ORDNANCE
ORGAN TUNING & REPAIR SVCS
ORGANIZATIONS: Biotechnical Research, Noncommercial
ORGANIZATIONS: Civic & Social
ORGANIZATIONS: Medical Research
ORGANIZATIONS: Noncommercial Social Research
ORGANIZATIONS: Religious
ORGANIZATIONS: Research Institute
ORGANIZATIONS: Scientific Research Agency
ORGANIZERS, CLOSET & DRAWER Plastic
ORIENTED STRANDBOARD
ORNAMENTS: Lawn
ORTHODONTIST
OUTLETS: Electric, Convenience
OVENS: Infrared
OXALIC ACID & METALLIC SALTS

P

PACKAGE DESIGN SVCS
PACKAGED FROZEN FOODS WHOLESALERS, NEC
PACKAGING & LABELING SVCS
PACKAGING MATERIALS, INDL: Wholesalers
PACKAGING MATERIALS, WHOLESALE
PACKAGING MATERIALS: Paper
PACKAGING MATERIALS: Paper, Coated Or Laminated
PACKAGING MATERIALS: Plastic Film, Coated Or Laminated
PACKAGING MATERIALS: Polystyrene Foam
PACKAGING: Blister Or Bubble Formed, Plastic
PACKING & CRATING SVC
PACKING & CRATING SVCS: Containerized Goods For Shipping
PACKING MATERIALS: Mechanical
PACKING SVCS: Shipping
PADS, SCOURING: Soap Impregnated

INDEX

PADS: Athletic, Protective
PADS: Mattress
PAGERS: One-way
PAILS: Meta, Exc Shipping
PAINT & PAINTING SPLYS STORE
PAINT STORE
PAINTING SVC: Metal Prdts
PAINTS & ADDITIVES
PAINTS & ALLIED PRODUCTS
PAINTS, VARNISHES & SPLYS WHOLESALERS
PAINTS, VARNISHES & SPLYS, WHOLESALE: Colors & Pigments
PAINTS, VARNISHES & SPLYS, WHOLESALE: Paints
PAINTS: Marine
PAINTS: Oil Or Alkyd Vehicle Or Water Thinned
PAINTS: Waterproof
PALLET REPAIR SVCS
PALLETS
PALLETS & SKIDS: Wood
PALLETS: Metal
PALLETS: Plastic
PALLETS: Wooden
PANEL & DISTRIBUTION BOARDS & OTHER RELATED APPARATUS
PANEL & DISTRIBUTION BOARDS: Electric
PANELS, CORRUGATED: Plastic
PANELS: Building, Wood
PANELS: Electric Metering
PANELS: Wood
PAPER & BOARD: Die-cut
PAPER & ENVELOPES: Writing, Made From Purchased Materials
PAPER CONVERTING
PAPER MANUFACTURERS: Exc Newsprint
PAPER PRDTS: Feminine Hygiene Prdts
PAPER PRDTS: Infant & Baby Prdts
PAPER PRDTS: Sanitary
PAPER PRDTS: Towels, Napkins/Tissue Paper, From Purchd Mtrls
PAPER, WHOLESALE: Fine
PAPER, WHOLESALE: Printing
PAPER: Adhesive
PAPER: Bag
PAPER: Cardboard
PAPER: Chart & Graph, Ruled
PAPER: Coated & Laminated, NEC
PAPER: Corrugated
PAPER: Envelope
PAPER: Gift Wrap
PAPER: Metallic Covered, Made From Purchased Materials
PAPER: Newsprint
PAPER: Packaging
PAPER: Poster & Art
PAPER: Printer
PAPER: Specialty Or Chemically Treated
PAPER: Wallpaper
PAPER: Wrapping & Packaging
PAPER: Wrapping, Waterproof Or Coated
PAPERBOARD
PAPERBOARD CONVERTING
PAPERBOARD PRDTS: Binders' Board
PAPERBOARD PRDTS: Coated & Treated Board
PAPERBOARD PRDTS: Folding Boxboard
PAPERBOARD PRDTS: Milk Carton Board
PAPERBOARD PRDTS: Packaging Board
PAPERBOARD PRDTS: Specialty Board
PAPERBOARD PRDTS: Strawboard
PAPERBOARD: Coated
PAPERBOARD: Corrugated
PARACHUTES
PARKING GARAGE
PARKING METERS
PARTITIONS & FIXTURES: Except Wood
PARTITIONS WHOLESALERS
PARTITIONS: Wood & Fixtures
PARTS: Metal
PATTERNS: Indl
PAVERS
PAVING MATERIALS: Prefabricated, Concrete
PAVING MIXTURES
PAYROLL SVCS
PEARLS, WHOLESALE
PEAT MINING & PROCESSING SVCS
PEAT MINING SVCS
PENS & PARTS: Ball Point

PENS & PENCILS: Mechanical, NEC
PERFUME: Concentrated
PERFUME: Perfumes, Natural Or Synthetic
PERFUMES
PERSONAL CREDIT INSTITUTIONS: Auto/Consumer Finance Co's
PESTICIDES
PESTICIDES WHOLESALERS
PET SPLYS
PET SPLYS WHOLESALERS
PETROLEUM & PETROLEUM PRDTS, WHOLESALE Butane Gas
PETROLEUM PRDTS WHOLESALERS
PETS & PET SPLYS, WHOLESALE
PHARMACEUTICAL PREPARATIONS: Adrenal
PHARMACEUTICAL PREPARATIONS: Druggists' Preparations
PHARMACEUTICAL PREPARATIONS: Medicines, Capsule Or Ampule
PHARMACEUTICAL PREPARATIONS: Pills
PHARMACEUTICAL PREPARATIONS: Powders
PHARMACEUTICAL PREPARATIONS: Proprietary Drug PRDTS
PHARMACEUTICAL PREPARATIONS: Solutions
PHARMACEUTICAL PREPARATIONS: Tablets
PHARMACEUTICALS
PHARMACEUTICALS: Mail-Order Svc
PHARMACEUTICALS: Medicinal & Botanical Prdts
PHARMACIES & DRUG STORES
PHOSPHATES
PHOTOCOPY MACHINE REPAIR SVCS
PHOTOCOPY MACHINES
PHOTOCOPY SPLYS WHOLESALERS
PHOTOCOPYING & DUPLICATING SVCS
PHOTOENGRAVING SVC
PHOTOFINISHING LABORATORIES
PHOTOGRAPH DEVELOPING & RETOUCHING SVCS
PHOTOGRAPHIC & OPTICAL GOODS EQPT REPAIR SVCS
PHOTOGRAPHIC CONTROL SYSTEMS: Electronic
PHOTOGRAPHIC EQPT & SPLYS
PHOTOGRAPHIC EQPT & SPLYS WHOLESALERS
PHOTOGRAPHIC EQPT & SPLYS, WHOLESALE: Identity Recorders
PHOTOGRAPHIC EQPT & SPLYS, WHOLESALE: Motion Picture Camera
PHOTOGRAPHIC EQPT & SPLYS, WHOLESALE: Printing Apparatus
PHOTOGRAPHIC EQPT & SPLYS, WHOLESALE: Processing
PHOTOGRAPHIC EQPT & SPLYS: Cameras, Still & Motion Pictures
PHOTOGRAPHIC EQPT & SPLYS: Developers, Not Chemical Plants
PHOTOGRAPHIC EQPT & SPLYS: Film, Sensitized
PHOTOGRAPHIC EQPT & SPLYS: Flashlight Apparatus, Exc Bulbs
PHOTOGRAPHIC EQPT & SPLYS: Plates, Sensitized
PHOTOGRAPHIC EQPT & SPLYS: Printing Eqpt
PHOTOGRAPHIC EQPT & SPLYS: Processing Eqpt
PHOTOGRAPHIC EQPT & SPLYS: Toners, Prprd, Not Chem Plnts
PHOTOGRAPHIC EQPT & SPLYS: Trays, Printing & Processing
PHOTOGRAPHIC EQPT & SPLYS: X-Ray Film
PHOTOGRAPHIC EQPT REPAIR SVCS
PHOTOGRAPHIC EQPT/SPLYS, WHOL: Cameras/Projectors/Eqpt/Splys
PHOTOGRAPHIC SVCS
PHOTOGRAPHY SVCS: Commercial
PHOTOTYPESETTING SVC
PHOTOVOLTAIC Solid State
PHYSICAL EXAMINATION SVCS, INSURANCE
PHYSICAL FITNESS CENTERS
PHYSICIANS' OFFICES & CLINICS: Medical doctors
PICTURE FRAMES: Metal
PICTURE FRAMES: Wood
PICTURE PROJECTION EQPT
PIECE GOODS & NOTIONS WHOLESALERS
PIECE GOODS, NOTIONS & DRY GOODS, WHOL: Textile Converters
PIECE GOODS, NOTIONS & DRY GOODS, WHOL: Textiles, Woven
PIECE GOODS, NOTIONS & DRY GOODS, WHOL: Trimmings, Apparel

PIECE GOODS, NOTIONS & DRY GOODS, WHOL: Yard Goods, Woven
PIECE GOODS, NOTIONS & DRY GOODS, WHOLESALE: Fabrics
PIECE GOODS, NOTIONS & DRY GOODS, WHOLESALE: Fabrics, Lace
PIECE GOODS, NOTIONS & DRY GOODS, WHOLESALE: Sewing Access
PIECE GOODS, NOTIONS & OTHER DRY GOODS, WHOL: Flags/Banners
PIECE GOODS, NOTIONS & OTHER DRY GOODS, WHOL: Millinery Sply
PIECE GOODS, NOTIONS & OTHER DRY GOODS, WHOLESALE: Fabrics
PIECE GOODS, NOTIONS & OTHER DRY GOODS, WHOLESALE: Ribbons
PIECE GOODS, NOTIONS & OTHER DRY GOODS, WHOLESALE: Zippers
PIECE GOODS, NOTIONS/DRY GOODS, WHOL: Linen Piece, Woven
PILE DRIVING EQPT
PILLOW FILLING MTRLS: Curled Hair, Cotton Waste, Moss
PILLOW TUBING
PILLOWCASES
PILOT SVCS: Aviation
PINS
PIPE & FITTING: Fabrication
PIPE & FITTINGS: Cast Iron
PIPE & FITTINGS: Pressure, Cast Iron
PIPE JOINT COMPOUNDS
PIPE SECTIONS, FABRICATED FROM PURCHASED PIPE
PIPE, CAST IRON: Wholesalers
PIPE, IRRIGATION: Concrete
PIPE, SEWER: Concrete
PIPE: Concrete
PIPE: Plastic
PIPE: Sewer, Cast Iron
PIPE: Sheet Metal
PIPELINE & POWER LINE INSPECTION SVCS
PIPELINE TERMINAL FACILITIES: Independent
PIPELINES: Crude Petroleum
PIPES & TUBES
PIPES & TUBES: Steel
PIPES: Steel & Iron
PIVOTS: Power Transmission
PLACEMATS: Plastic Or Textile
PLANING MILLS: Millwork
PLANTERS: Plastic
PLANTS: Artificial & Preserved
PLAQUES: Picture, Laminated
PLASMAS
PLASTER WORK: Ornamental & Architectural
PLASTER, ACOUSTICAL: Gypsum
PLASTIC PRDTS
PLASTICIZERS, ORGANIC: Cyclic & Acyclic
PLASTICS FILM & SHEET
PLASTICS FILM & SHEET: Polyethylene
PLASTICS FILM & SHEET: Polypropylene
PLASTICS FILM & SHEET: Polyvinyl
PLASTICS FILM & SHEET: Vinyl
PLASTICS FINISHED PRDTS: Laminated
PLASTICS MATERIAL & RESINS
PLASTICS MATERIALS, BASIC FORMS & SHAPES WHOLESALERS
PLASTICS PROCESSING
PLASTICS SHEET: Packing Materials
PLASTICS: Blow Molded
PLASTICS: Extruded
PLASTICS: Finished Injection Molded
PLASTICS: Injection Molded
PLASTICS: Molded
PLASTICS: Polystyrene Foam
PLASTICS: Thermoformed
PLATE WORK: Metalworking Trade
PLATEMAKING SVC: Color Separations, For The Printing Trade
PLATEMAKING SVC: Embossing, For The Printing Trade
PLATEMAKING SVC: Gravure, Plates Or Cylinders
PLATEMAKING SVC: Letterpress
PLATES
PLATES: Sheet & Strip, Exc Coated Prdts
PLATES: Steel
PLATING & FINISHING SVC: Decorative, Formed Prdts
PLATING & POLISHING SVC
PLATING COMPOUNDS

INDEX

RADIO, TELEVISION/CONSUMER ELEC STORES: Video Cameras/Access
RADIO, TV & CONSUMER ELEC STORES: Automotive Sound Eqpt
RADIO, TV & CONSUMER ELECTRONICS: VCR & Access
RADIOS WHOLESALERS
RAILINGS: Prefabricated, Metal
RAILROAD CARGO LOADING & UNLOADING SVCS
RAILROAD EQPT
RAILROAD EQPT: Cars & Eqpt, Dining
RAILROAD EQPT: Cars & Eqpt, Train, Freight Or Passenger
RAILROAD EQPT: Cars, Motor
RAILROAD EQPT: Engines, Locomotive, Steam
RAILROAD EQPT: Locomotives & Parts, Electric Or Nonelectric
RAILROAD MAINTENANCE & REPAIR SVCS
RAILROAD RELATED EQPT
RAILROAD SWITCHING & TERMINAL SVCS
RAILS: Elevator, Guide
RAILS: Rails, rolled & drawn, aluminum
RAMPS: Prefabricated Metal
RAZORS, RAZOR BLADES
REAL ESTATE AGENCIES: Rental
REAL ESTATE AGENCIES: Selling
REAL ESTATE AGENTS & MANAGERS
REAL ESTATE INVESTMENT TRUSTS
REAL ESTATE OPERATORS, EXC DEVELOPERS: Apartment Hotel
REAL ESTATE OPERATORS, EXC DEVELOPERS: Commercial/Indl Bldg
RECLAIMED RUBBER: Reworked By Manufacturing Process
RECORD BLANKS: Phonographic
RECORDERS: Sound
RECORDING & PLAYBACK HEADS: Magnetic
RECORDING HEADS: Speech & Musical Eqpt
RECORDING TAPE: Video, Blank
RECORDS & TAPES: Prerecorded
RECORDS OR TAPES: Masters
RECOVERY SVCS: Metal
RECOVERY SVCS: Solvents
RECREATIONAL SPORTING EQPT REPAIR SVCS
RECTIFIERS: Electronic, Exc Semiconductor
RECYCLABLE SCRAP & WASTE MATERIALS WHOLESALERS
RECYCLING: Paper
REELS: Fiber, Textile, Made From Purchased Materials
REFINERS & SMELTERS: Aluminum
REFINERS & SMELTERS: Brass, Secondary
REFINERS & SMELTERS: Copper
REFINERS & SMELTERS: Gold, Secondary
REFINERS & SMELTERS: Lead, Secondary
REFINERS & SMELTERS: Nonferrous Metal
REFINERS & SMELTERS: Platinum Group Metal Refining, Primary
REFINERS & SMELTERS: Platinum Group Metals, Secondary
REFINERS & SMELTERS: Silicon, Primary, Over 99% Pure
REFINERS & SMELTERS: Silver
REFINERS & SMELTERS: Zinc, Primary, Including Slabs & Dust
REFINERS & SMELTERS: Zinc, Primary, Including Zinc Residue
REFINING LUBRICATING OILS & GREASES, NEC
REFINING: Petroleum
REFRACTORIES: Clay
REFRACTORIES: Nonclay
REFRACTORY CASTABLES
REFRIGERATION & HEATING EQUIPMENT
REFRIGERATION EQPT & SPLYS WHOLESALERS
REFRIGERATION EQPT: Complete
REFRIGERATION SVC & REPAIR
REFUSE SYSTEMS
REGULATORS: Transmission & Distribution Voltage
REGULATORS: Transmission & Distribution Voltage
RELAYS & SWITCHES: Indl, Electric
RELAYS: Electric Power
RELAYS: Electronic Usage
RELIGIOUS SPLYS WHOLESALERS
REMOVERS & CLEANERS
REMOVERS: Paint
RENTAL CENTERS: Furniture
RENTAL CENTERS: Party & Banquet Eqpt & Splys
RENTAL SVCS: Business Machine & Electronic Eqpt
RENTAL SVCS: Costume
RENTAL SVCS: Eqpt, Theatrical
RENTAL SVCS: Stores & Yards Eqpt

RENTAL SVCS: Tuxedo
RENTAL: Passenger Car
RENTAL: Trucks, With Drivers
REPRODUCTION SVCS: Video Tape Or Disk
RESEARCH & DEVELOPMENT SVCS, COMMERCIAL: Engineering Lab
RESEARCH, DEV & TESTING SVCS, COMM: Chem Lab, Exc Testing
RESEARCH, DEVELOPMENT & TEST SVCS, COMM: Business Analysis
RESEARCH, DEVELOPMENT & TEST SVCS, COMM: Cmptr Hardware Dev
RESEARCH, DEVELOPMENT & TEST SVCS, COMM: Research, Exc Lab
RESEARCH, DEVELOPMENT & TESTING SVCS, COMM: Research Lab
RESEARCH, DEVELOPMENT & TESTING SVCS, COMMERCIAL: Business
RESEARCH, DEVELOPMENT & TESTING SVCS, COMMERCIAL: Energy
RESEARCH, DEVELOPMENT & TESTING SVCS, COMMERCIAL: Medical
RESEARCH, DEVELOPMENT & TESTING SVCS, COMMERCIAL: Physical
RESEARCH, DVLPMT & TESTING SVCS, COMM: Merger, Acq & Reorg
RESEARCH, DVLPT & TEST SVCS, COMM: Mkt Analysis or Research
RESEARCH, DVLPT & TESTING SVCS, COMM: Survey, Mktg
RESIDENTIAL REMODELERS
RESIDUES
RESINS: Custom Compound Purchased
RESISTORS
RESPIRATORY SYSTEM DRUGS
RESTAURANT EQPT REPAIR SVCS
RESTAURANT EQPT: Carts
RESTAURANT EQPT: Food Wagons
RESTAURANTS: Delicatessen
RESTAURANTS:Full Svc, American
RESTAURANTS:Full Svc, Diner
RESTAURANTS:Full Svc, Family, Independent
RESTAURANTS:Full Svc, Italian
RESTAURANTS:Limited Svc, Coffee Shop
RESTAURANTS:Limited Svc, Ice Cream Stands Or Dairy Bars
RESTAURANTS:Ltd Svc, Ice Cream, Soft Drink/Fountain Stands
RETAIL BAKERY: Bagels
RETAIL BAKERY: Bread
RETAIL BAKERY: Cakes
RETAIL BAKERY: Cookies
RETAIL BAKERY: Doughnuts
RETAIL BAKERY: Pastries
RETAIL BAKERY: Pretzels
RETAIL LUMBER YARDS
RETAIL STORES, NEC
RETAIL STORES: Alcoholic Beverage Making Eqpt & Splys
RETAIL STORES: Artificial Limbs
RETAIL STORES: Awnings
RETAIL STORES: Baby Carriages & Strollers
RETAIL STORES: Batteries, Non-Automotive
RETAIL STORES: Binoculars & Telescopes
RETAIL STORES: Communication Eqpt
RETAIL STORES: Cosmetics
RETAIL STORES: Decals
RETAIL STORES: Electronic Parts & Eqpt
RETAIL STORES: Fire Extinguishers
RETAIL STORES: Hair Care Prdts
RETAIL STORES: Hearing Aids
RETAIL STORES: Hospital Eqpt & Splys
RETAIL STORES: Infant Furnishings & Eqpt
RETAIL STORES: Medical Apparatus & Splys
RETAIL STORES: Monuments, Finished To Custom Order
RETAIL STORES: Motors, Electric
RETAIL STORES: Orthopedic & Prosthesis Applications
RETAIL STORES: Perfumes & Colognes
RETAIL STORES: Pet Food
RETAIL STORES: Pet Splys
RETAIL STORES: Pets
RETAIL STORES: Photocopy Machines
RETAIL STORES: Plumbing & Heating Splys
RETAIL STORES: Police Splys
RETAIL STORES: Rock & Stone Specimens
RETAIL STORES: Rubber Stamps

RETAIL STORES: Safety Splys & Eqpt
RETAIL STORES: Spas & Hot Tubs
RETAIL STORES: Telephone Eqpt & Systems
RETAIL STORES: Water Purification Eqpt
REUPHOLSTERY & FURNITURE REPAIR
REUPHOLSTERY SVCS
RHEOSTATS: Electronic
RIBBONS & BOWS
RIBBONS, NEC
RIBBONS: Machine, Inked Or Carbon
RIDING APPAREL STORES
RIVETS: Metal
ROAD CONSTRUCTION EQUIPMENT WHOLESALERS
ROAD MATERIALS: Bituminous, Not From Refineries
ROBOTS, SERVICES OR NOVELTY, WHOLESALE
ROLL FORMED SHAPES: Custom
ROLLERS & FITTINGS: Window Shade
ROLLING MILL EQPT: Finishing
ROLLS & ROLL COVERINGS: Rubber
ROLLS: Rubber, Solid Or Covered
ROOF DECKS
ROOFING GRANULES
ROOFING MATERIALS: Asphalt
ROOFING MATERIALS: Sheet Metal
ROOM COOLERS: Portable
ROPE
RUBBER
RUBBER PRDTS: Appliance, Mechanical
RUBBER PRDTS: Mechanical
RUBBER PRDTS: Medical & Surgical Tubing, Extrudd & Lathe-Cut
RUBBER PRDTS: Oil & Gas Field Machinery, Mechanical
RUBBER PRDTS: Sheeting
RUBBER PRDTS: Silicone
RUBBER PRDTS: Sponge
RUBBER PRDTS: Wet Suits
RUBBER STAMP, WHOLESALE
RUBBER STRUCTURES: Air-Supported
RUGS : Tufted
RULERS: Metal
RUST RESISTING

S

SAFES & VAULTS: Metal
SAFETY EQPT & SPLYS WHOLESALERS
SAFETY INSPECTION SVCS
SAILS
SALT
SAMPLE BOOKS
SAND & GRAVEL
SAND MINING
SAND: Hygrade
SANITARY SVC, NEC
SANITARY SVCS: Chemical Detoxification
SANITARY SVCS: Environmental Cleanup
SANITARY SVCS: Radioactive Waste Materials, Disposal
SANITARY SVCS: Refuse Collection & Disposal Svcs
SANITARY SVCS: Sewage Treatment Facility
SANITARY SVCS: Waste Materials, Recycling
SANITARY WARE: Metal
SANITATION CHEMICALS & CLEANING AGENTS
SASHES: Door Or Window, Metal
SATELLITE COMMUNICATIONS EQPT
SATELLITES: Communications
SAW BLADES
SAWDUST & SHAVINGS
SAWING & PLANING MILLS
SAWING & PLANING MILLS: Custom
SAWS & SAWING EQPT
SCALES & BALANCES, EXC LABORATORY
SCALES: Indl
SCANNING DEVICES: Optical
SCHOOL BUS SVC
SCHOOLS: Vocational, NEC
SCIENTIFIC INSTRUMENTS WHOLESALERS
SCRAP & WASTE MATERIALS, WHOLESALE: Metal
SCRAP & WASTE MATERIALS, WHOLESALE: Nonferrous Metals Scrap
SCRAP & WASTE MATERIALS, WHOLESALE: Paper
SCRAP & WASTE MATERIALS, WHOLESALE: Plastics Scrap
SCREENS: Window, Metal
SCREENS: Window, Wood Framed
SCREENS: Woven Wire
SCREW MACHINE PRDTS

SCREW MACHINES
SCREWS: Metal
SEALANTS
SEALING COMPOUNDS: Sealing, synthetic rubber or plastic
SEALS: Hermetic
SEALS: Oil, Rubber
SEARCH & DETECTION SYSTEMS, EXC RADAR
SEARCH & NAVIGATION SYSTEMS
SEARCH & RESCUE SVCS
SEATING: Stadium
SECRETARIAL SVCS
SECURITY CONTROL EQPT & SYSTEMS
SECURITY DEVICES
SECURITY DISTRIBUTORS
SECURITY EQPT STORES
SECURITY PROTECTIVE DEVICES MAINTENANCE & MONITORING SVCS
SECURITY SYSTEMS SERVICES
SEMICONDUCTOR CIRCUIT NETWORKS
SEMICONDUCTORS & RELATED DEVICES
SENSORS: Radiation
SENSORS: Temperature For Motor Windings
SENSORS: Temperature, Exc Indl Process
SEPARATORS: Metal Plate
SEPTIC TANKS: Concrete
SEWAGE & WATER TREATMENT EQPT
SEWAGE TREATMENT SYSTEMS & EQPT
SEWING CONTRACTORS
SEWING MACHINES & PARTS: Indl
SHADES: Lamp & Light, Residential
SHADES: Lamp Or Candle
SHADES: Window
SHAPES & PILINGS, STRUCTURAL: Steel
SHAPES: Extruded, Aluminum, NEC
SHAVING PREPARATIONS
SHEET METAL SPECIALTIES, EXC STAMPED
SHEETING: Laminated Plastic
SHEETS & SHEETINGS, COTTON
SHEETS: Fabric, From Purchased Materials
SHELLAC
SHELTERED WORKSHOPS
SHELVES & SHELVING: Wood
SHERARDIZING SVC: Metals Or Metal Prdts
SHIMS: Metal
SHIP BLDG/RPRG: Submersible Marine Robots, Manned/Unmanned
SHIP BUILDING & REPAIRING: Cargo, Commercial
SHIP BUILDING & REPAIRING: Dredges
SHIP BUILDING & REPAIRING: Fishing Vessels, Large
SHIP BUILDING & REPAIRING: Rigging, Marine
SHIPBUILDING & REPAIR
SHIPPING AGENTS
SHOE MATERIALS: Counters
SHOE MATERIALS: Rands
SHOE MATERIALS: Rubber
SHOE STORES
SHOE STORES: Athletic
SHOE STORES: Children's
SHOE STORES: Orthopedic
SHOES & BOOTS WHOLESALERS
SHOES: Athletic, Exc Rubber Or Plastic
SHOES: Ballet Slippers
SHOES: Canvas, Rubber Soled
SHOES: Children's, Sandals, Exc Rubber Or Plastic
SHOES: Men's
SHOES: Orthopedic, Children's
SHOES: Orthopedic, Men's
SHOES: Orthopedic, Women's
SHOES: Plastic Or Rubber
SHOES: Plastic Or Rubber Soles With Fabric Uppers
SHOES: Women's, Dress
SHOT PEENING SVC
SHOWCASES & DISPLAY FIXTURES: Office & Store
SHOWER STALLS: Metal
SHREDDERS: Indl & Commercial
SHUTTERS, DOOR & WINDOW: Metal
SIDING & STRUCTURAL MATERIALS: Wood
SIDING: Sheet Metal
SIGN LETTERING & PAINTING SVCS
SIGN PAINTING & LETTERING SHOP
SIGNALING APPARATUS: Electric
SIGNALS: Traffic Control, Electric
SIGNALS: Transportation
SIGNS & ADVERTISING SPECIALTIES
SIGNS & ADVERTISING SPECIALTIES: Artwork, Advertising

SIGNS & ADVERTISING SPECIALTIES: Displays, Paint Process
SIGNS & ADVERTISING SPECIALTIES: Novelties
SIGNS & ADVERTISING SPECIALTIES: Signs
SIGNS & ADVERTSG SPECIALTIES: Displays/Cutouts Window/Lobby
SIGNS, ELECTRICAL: Wholesalers
SIGNS, EXC ELECTRIC, WHOLESALE
SIGNS: Electrical
SIGNS: Neon
SILICA MINING
SILICON WAFERS: Chemically Doped
SILICONES
SILK SCREEN DESIGN SVCS
SILVER ORES
SILVERWARE & PLATED WARE
SIMULATORS: Flight
SINK TOPS, PLASTIC LAMINATED
SIRENS: Vehicle, Marine, Indl & Warning
SKIN CARE PRDTS: Suntan Lotions & Oils
SKYLIGHTS
SLAB & TILE, ROOFING: Concrete
SLAB & TILE: Precast Concrete, Floor
SLAB, CROSSING: Concrete
SLAUGHTERING & MEAT PACKING
SLIDES & EXHIBITS: Prepared
SLINGS: Lifting, Made From Purchased Wire
SLIP RINGS
SLIPPERS: House
SMOKE DETECTORS
SMOKERS' SPLYS, WHOLESALE
SNOW PLOWING SVCS
SOAPS & DETERGENTS
SOAPS & DETERGENTS: Dishwashing Compounds
SOAPSTONE MINING
SOCIAL SVCS: Individual & Family
SOFT DRINKS WHOLESALERS
SOFTWARE PUBLISHERS: Application
SOFTWARE PUBLISHERS: Business & Professional
SOFTWARE PUBLISHERS: Computer Utilities
SOFTWARE PUBLISHERS: Education
SOFTWARE PUBLISHERS: Home Entertainment
SOFTWARE PUBLISHERS: NEC
SOFTWARE PUBLISHERS: Operating Systems
SOFTWARE PUBLISHERS: Publisher's
SOFTWARE TRAINING, COMPUTER
SOLAR CELLS
SOLAR HEATING EQPT
SOLDERING EQPT: Electrical, Exc Handheld
SOLDERING EQPT: Electrical, Handheld
SOLDERS
SOLVENTS
SOLVENTS: Organic
SONAR SYSTEMS & EQPT
SOUND REPRODUCING EQPT
SOUVENIR SHOPS
SOUVENIRS, WHOLESALE
SPACE VEHICLE EQPT
SPACE VEHICLES
SPEAKER MONITORS
SPEAKER SYSTEMS
SPECIAL EVENTS DECORATION SVCS
SPECIALTY FOOD STORES: Coffee
SPECIALTY FOOD STORES: Health & Dietetic Food
SPECIALTY FOOD STORES: Juices, Fruit Or Vegetable
SPECIALTY FOOD STORES: Tea
SPECIALTY FOOD STORES: Vitamin
SPECIALTY OUTPATIENT CLINICS, NEC
SPICE & HERB STORES
SPONGES: Bleached & Dyed
SPOOLS: Fiber, Made From Purchased Materials
SPORTING & ATHLETIC GOODS: Bowling Alleys & Access
SPORTING & ATHLETIC GOODS: Cases, Gun & Rod
SPORTING & ATHLETIC GOODS: Driving Ranges, Golf, Electronic
SPORTING & ATHLETIC GOODS: Fishing Eqpt
SPORTING & ATHLETIC GOODS: Fishing Tackle, General
SPORTING & ATHLETIC GOODS: Guards, Football, Soccer, Etc
SPORTING & ATHLETIC GOODS: Hockey Eqpt & Splys, NEC
SPORTING & ATHLETIC GOODS: Hunting Eqpt
SPORTING & ATHLETIC GOODS: Pools, Swimming, Exc Plastic
SPORTING & ATHLETIC GOODS: Pools, Swimming, Plastic

SPORTING & ATHLETIC GOODS: Rackets/Frames, Tennis, Etc
SPORTING & ATHLETIC GOODS: Rods & Rod Parts, Fishing
SPORTING & ATHLETIC GOODS: Shafts, Golf Club
SPORTING & ATHLETIC GOODS: Shooting Eqpt & Splys, General
SPORTING & ATHLETIC GOODS: Skateboards
SPORTING & ATHLETIC GOODS: Target Shooting Eqpt
SPORTING & ATHLETIC GOODS: Targets, Archery & Rifle Shooting
SPORTING & ATHLETIC GOODS: Team Sports Eqpt
SPORTING & ATHLETIC GOODS: Tennis Eqpt & Splys
SPORTING & ATHLETIC GOODS: Treadmills
SPORTING & ATHLETIC GOODS: Water Sports Eqpt
SPORTING & ATHLETIC GOODS: Winter Sports
SPORTING & RECREATIONAL GOODS & SPLYS WHOLESALERS
SPORTING & RECREATIONAL GOODS, WHOLESALE: Athletic Goods
SPORTING & RECREATIONAL GOODS, WHOLESALE: Boat Access & Part
SPORTING & RECREATIONAL GOODS, WHOLESALE: Fishing
SPORTING & RECREATIONAL GOODS, WHOLESALE: Fishing Tackle
SPORTING & RECREATIONAL GOODS, WHOLESALE: Golf
SPORTING & RECREATIONAL GOODS, WHOLESALE: Surfing
SPORTING GOODS
SPORTING GOODS STORES, NEC
SPORTING GOODS STORES: Ammunition
SPORTING GOODS STORES: Baseball Eqpt
SPORTING GOODS STORES: Camping Eqpt
SPORTING GOODS STORES: Firearms
SPORTING GOODS STORES: Hockey Eqpt, Exc Skates
SPORTING GOODS STORES: Pool & Billiard Tables
SPORTING GOODS STORES: Specialty Sport Splys, NEC
SPORTING GOODS STORES: Surfing Eqpt & Splys
SPORTING GOODS STORES: Team sports Eqpt
SPORTING GOODS: Fishing Nets
SPORTING GOODS: Surfboards
SPORTING/ATHLETIC GOODS: Gloves, Boxing, Handball, Etc
SPORTS APPAREL STORES
SPORTS CLUBS, MANAGERS & PROMOTERS
SPOUTING: Plastic & Fiberglass Reinforced
SPOUTS: Sheet Metal
SPRAYING & DUSTING EQPT
SPRAYING EQPT: Agricultural
SPRAYS: Artificial & Preserved
SPRINGS: Coiled Flat
SPRINGS: Steel
SPRINGS: Upholstery, Unassembled
SPRINGS: Wire
SPRINKLING SYSTEMS: Fire Control
SQUIBS: Electric
STAFFING, EMPLOYMENT PLACEMENT
STAGE LIGHTING SYSTEMS
STAINLESS STEEL
STAINLESS STEEL WARE
STAIRCASES & STAIRS, WOOD
STAMPINGS: Automotive
STAMPINGS: Metal
STAPLES
STAPLES: Steel, Wire Or Cut
STATIONARY & OFFICE SPLYS, WHOL: Computer/Photocopying Splys
STATIONARY & OFFICE SPLYS, WHOLESALE: Blank Books
STATIONARY & OFFICE SPLYS, WHOLESALE: Inked Ribbons
STATIONARY & OFFICE SPLYS, WHOLESALE: Marking Devices
STATIONARY/OFFICE SPLYS, WHOL: Soc Stationery/Greeting Cards
STATIONERY & OFFICE SPLYS WHOLESALERS
STATIONERY ARTICLES: Pottery
STATIONERY PRDTS
STATIONERY: Made From Purchased Materials
STATUES: Nonmetal
STEEL & ALLOYS: Tool & Die
STEEL FABRICATORS
STEEL MILLS
STEEL, COLD-ROLLED: Strip NEC, From Purchased Hot-Rolled
STEEL, HOT-ROLLED: Sheet Or Strip

INDEX

STEEL: Cold-Rolled
STEEL: Laminated
STENCILS
STONE: Cast Concrete
STONE: Dimension, NEC
STONE: Quarrying & Processing, Own Stone Prdts
STORE FIXTURES: Exc Wood
STORE FIXTURES: Wood
STORES: Auto & Home Supply
STRAINERS: Line, Piping Systems
STRAPPING
STRAPS: Apparel Webbing
STRAPS: Braids, Textile
STRIPS: Copper & Copper Alloy
STRUCTURAL SUPPORT & BUILDING MATERIAL: Concrete
STUCCO
STUDIOS: Artists & Artists' Studios
STUDS & JOISTS: Sheet Metal
SUBSCRIPTION FULFILLMENT SVCS: Magazine, Newspaper, Etc
SUGAR SUBSTITUTES: Organic
SUGAR SUBSTITUTES: Sorbitol
SUNDRIES & RELATED PRDTS: Medical & Laboratory, Rubber
SUPERMARKETS & OTHER GROCERY STORES
SUPPOSITORIES
SURFACE ACTIVE AGENTS
SURFACE ACTIVE AGENTS: Penetrants
SURFACE ACTIVE AGENTS: Softeners, Textile Assisting
SURFACE ACTIVE AGENTS: Textile Processing Assistants
SURGICAL & MEDICAL INSTRUMENTS WHOLESALERS
SURGICAL APPLIANCES & SPLYS
SURGICAL APPLIANCES & SPLYS
SURGICAL EQPT: See Also Instruments
SURGICAL IMPLANTS
SURVEYING & MAPPING: Land Parcels
SURVEYING SVCS: Photogrammetric Engineering
SVC ESTABLISH EQPT, WHOLESALE: Carpet/Rug Clean Eqpt & Sply
SVC ESTABLISHMENT EQPT & SPLYS WHOLESALERS
SVC ESTABLISHMENT EQPT, WHOL: Cleaning & Maint Eqpt & Splys
SVC ESTABLISHMENT EQPT, WHOL: Concrete Burial Vaults & Boxes
SVC ESTABLISHMENT EQPT, WHOLESALE: Beauty Parlor Eqpt & Sply
SVC ESTABLISHMENT EQPT, WHOLESALE: Floor Machinery, Maint
SVC ESTABLISHMENT EQPT, WHOLESALE: Vacuum Cleaning Systems
SWEEPING COMPOUNDS
SWIMMING POOL & HOT TUB CLEANING & MAINTENANCE SVCS
SWIMMING POOL ACCESS: Leaf Skimmers Or Pool Rakes
SWIMMING POOL EQPT: Filters & Water Conditioning Systems
SWIMMING POOL SPLY STORES
SWIMMING POOLS, EQPT & SPLYS: Wholesalers
SWITCHES
SWITCHES: Electric Power
SWITCHES: Electric Power, Exc Snap, Push Button, Etc
SWITCHES: Electronic
SWITCHES: Electronic Applications
SWITCHES: Time, Electrical Switchgear Apparatus
SWITCHGEAR & SWITCHBOARD APPARATUS
SWITCHGEAR & SWITCHGEAR ACCESS, NEC
SWITCHING EQPT: Radio & Television Communications
SYRUPS, DRINK
SYRUPS: Pharmaceutical
SYSTEMS ENGINEERING: Computer Related
SYSTEMS INTEGRATION SVCS
SYSTEMS INTEGRATION SVCS: Office Computer Automation
SYSTEMS SOFTWARE DEVELOPMENT SVCS

T

TABLE OR COUNTERTOPS, PLASTIC LAMINATED
TABLE TOPS: Porcelain Enameled
TABLECLOTHS & SETTINGS
TABLES: Lift, Hydraulic
TABLETS: Bronze Or Other Metal
TAGS & LABELS: Paper
TAGS: Paper, Blank, Made From Purchased Paper
TANK COMPONENTS: Military, Specialized
TANK REPAIR SVCS

TANKS & OTHER TRACKED VEHICLE CMPNTS
TANKS: Concrete
TANKS: Cryogenic, Metal
TANKS: For Tank Trucks, Metal Plate
TANKS: Fuel, Including Oil & Gas, Metal Plate
TANKS: Lined, Metal
TANKS: Plastic & Fiberglass
TANKS: Standard Or Custom Fabricated, Metal Plate
TANKS: Water, Metal Plate
TANNERIES: Leather
TANNING AGENTS: Synthetic Organic
TANNING SALON EQPT & SPLYS, WHOLESALE
TAPE DRIVES
TAPE STORAGE UNITS: Computer
TAPES, ADHESIVE: MedicaL
TAPES: Fabric
TAPES: Gummed, Cloth Or Paper Based, From Purchased Matls
TAPES: Pressure Sensitive
TARGET DRONES
TELECOMMUNICATION EQPT REPAIR SVCS, EXC TELEPHONES
TELECOMMUNICATION SYSTEMS & EQPT
TELECOMMUNICATIONS CARRIERS & SVCS: Wired
TELECOMMUNICATIONS CARRIERS & SVCS: Wireless
TELEGRAPHS & RELATED APPARATUS
TELEMARKETING BUREAUS
TELEMETERING EQPT
TELEPHONE ANSWERING MACHINES
TELEPHONE CENTRAL OFFICE EQPT: Dial Or Manual
TELEPHONE EQPT INSTALLATION
TELEPHONE EQPT: NEC
TELEPHONE STATION EQPT & PARTS: Wire
TELEPHONE SWITCHING EQPT
TELEPHONE SWITCHING EQPT: Toll Switching
TELEPHONE: Automatic Dialers
TELEPHONE: Fiber Optic Systems
TELEPHONE: Switchboards
TELEVISION BROADCASTING & COMMUNICATIONS EQPT
TELEVISION SETS
TELEVISION SETS WHOLESALERS
TELEVISION: Closed Circuit Eqpt
TEMPORARY HELP SVCS
TEN PIN CENTERS
TERMINAL BOARDS
TEST BORING SVCS: Nonmetallic Minerals
TEST KITS: Pregnancy
TESTERS: Battery
TESTERS: Environmental
TESTERS: Gas, Exc Indl Process
TESTERS: Integrated Circuit
TESTERS: Liquid, Exc Indl Process
TESTERS: Physical Property
TEXTILE & APPAREL SVCS
TEXTILE BAGS WHOLESALERS
TEXTILE CONVERTERS: Knit Goods
TEXTILE FABRICATORS
TEXTILE FINISH: Chem Coat/Treat, Fire Resist, Manmade
TEXTILE FINISHING: Calendering, Cotton
TEXTILE FINISHING: Chem Coating/Treating, Broadwoven, Cotton
TEXTILE FINISHING: Decorative, Cotton, Broadwoven
TEXTILE FINISHING: Dyeing, Broadwoven, Cotton
TEXTILE FINISHING: Dyeing, Manmade Fiber & Silk, Broadwoven
TEXTILE FINISHING: Embossing, Cotton, Broadwoven
TEXTILE MACHINERY ACCESS, HARDWOOD
TEXTILE: Finishing, Cotton Broadwoven
TEXTILE: Finishing, Raw Stock NEC
TEXTILE: Goods, NEC
TEXTILES
TEXTILES: Crash, Linen
TEXTILES: Linen Fabrics
TEXTILES: Mill Waste & Remnant
TEXTILES: Padding & Wadding
THEATRICAL SCENERY
THERMOMETERS: Medical, Digital
THERMOPLASTIC MATERIALS
THERMOPLASTICS
THERMOSETTING MATERIALS
THIN FILM CIRCUITS
THREAD: Embroidery
THYROID PREPARATIONS
TIES, FORM: Metal
TILE: Asphalt, Floor

TILE: Brick & Structural, Clay
TILE: Clay, Drain & Structural
TILE: Mosaic, Ceramic
TILE: Vinyl, Asbestos
TILE: Wall & Floor, Ceramic
TILE: Wall, Ceramic
TIMING DEVICES: Electronic
TIN
TIRE & INNER TUBE MATERIALS & RELATED PRDTS
TIRE & TUBE REPAIR MATERIALS, WHOLESALE
TIRE CORD & FABRIC
TIRE DEALERS
TIRES & INNER TUBES
TIRES & TUBES, WHOLESALE: Automotive
TIRES: Truck
TITANIUM MILL PRDTS
TOBACCO & PRDTS, WHOLESALE: Cigarettes
TOBACCO & PRDTS, WHOLESALE: Cigars
TOBACCO & TOBACCO PRDTS WHOLESALERS
TOBACCO LEAF PROCESSING
TOBACCO: Cigarettes
TOBACCO: Cigars
TOILET PREPARATIONS
TOILET SEATS: Wood
TOILETRIES, COSMETICS & PERFUME STORES
TOILETRIES, WHOLESALE: Perfumes
TOILETRIES, WHOLESALE: Razor Blades
TOILETRIES, WHOLESALE: Toilet Soap
TOILETRIES, WHOLESALE: Toiletries
TOILETS: Portable Chemical, Plastics
TOOL & DIE STEEL
TOOLS: Hand
TOOLS: Hand, Hammers
TOOLS: Hand, Jewelers'
TOOLS: Hand, Mechanics
TOOLS: Hand, Power
TOOLS: Hand, Stonecutters'
TOOTHPASTES, GELS & TOOTHPOWDERS
TOWELS: Fabric & Nonwoven, Made From Purchased Materials
TOWELS: Indl
TOWELS: Paper
TOWERS, SECTIONS: Transmission, Radio & Television
TOWING & TUGBOAT SVC
TOYS
TOYS & HOBBY GOODS & SPLYS, WHOLESALE: Amusement Goods
TOYS & HOBBY GOODS & SPLYS, WHOLESALE: Arts/Crafts Eqpt/Sply
TOYS & HOBBY GOODS & SPLYS, WHOLESALE: Dolls
TOYS & HOBBY GOODS & SPLYS, WHOLESALE: Toys & Games
TOYS, HOBBY GOODS & SPLYS WHOLESALERS
TOYS: Dolls, Stuffed Animals & Parts
TOYS: Electronic
TOYS: Rubber
TOYS: Video Game Machines
TRADE SHOW ARRANGEMENT SVCS
TRADING STAMP PROMOTION & REDEMPTION
TRAILERS & PARTS: Truck & Semi's
TRAILERS & TRAILER EQPT
TRAILERS: Bodies
TRAILERS: Demountable Cargo Containers
TRAILERS: Semitrailers, Truck Tractors
TRAILERS: Truck, Chassis
TRANSDUCERS: Pressure
TRANSFORMERS: Control
TRANSFORMERS: Distribution
TRANSFORMERS: Distribution, Electric
TRANSFORMERS: Electric
TRANSFORMERS: Electronic
TRANSFORMERS: Machine Tool
TRANSFORMERS: Meters, Electronic
TRANSFORMERS: Power Related
TRANSFORMERS: Rectifier
TRANSFORMERS: Specialty
TRANSFORMERS: Tripping
TRANSISTORS
TRANSLATION & INTERPRETATION SVCS
TRANSMISSIONS: Motor Vehicle
TRANSPORTATION EPQT & SPLYS, WHOLESALE: Marine Crafts/Splys
TRANSPORTATION EPQT/SPLYS, WHOL: Guided Missiles/Space Veh

TRANSPORTATION EPQT/SPLYS, WHOL: Marine Propulsn Mach/Eqpt
TRANSPORTATION EQPT & SPLYS WHOLESALERS, NEC
TRANSPORTATION SVCS, WATER: Boat Cleaning
TRANSPORTATION SVCS, WATER: Intracoastal, Freight
TRANSPORTATION SVCS, WATER: Salvaging & Surveying, Marine
TRANSPORTATION SVCS: Railroads, Belt line
TRANSPORTATION: Deep Sea Domestic Freight
TRANSPORTATION: Deep Sea Foreign Freight
TRANSPORTATION: Local Passenger, NEC
TRANSPORTATION: Monorail Transit Systems
TRAP ROCK: Crushed & Broken
TRAPS: Animal & Fish, Wire
TRAPS: Stem
TRAVEL AGENCIES
TRAYS: Plastic
TRIM: Window, Wood
TROPHIES, NEC
TROPHIES, PLATED, ALL METALS
TROPHIES: Metal, Exc Silver
TROPHY & PLAQUE STORES
TRUCK & BUS BODIES: Ambulance
TRUCK & BUS BODIES: Automobile Wrecker Truck
TRUCK & BUS BODIES: Bus Bodies
TRUCK & BUS BODIES: Dump Truck
TRUCK & BUS BODIES: Tank Truck
TRUCK & BUS BODIES: Truck Cabs, Motor Vehicles
TRUCK & BUS BODIES: Truck, Motor Vehicle
TRUCK BODIES: Body Parts
TRUCK BODY SHOP
TRUCK DRIVER SVCS
TRUCK GENERAL REPAIR SVC
TRUCK PAINTING & LETTERING SVCS
TRUCK PARTS & ACCESSORIES: Wholesalers
TRUCKING & HAULING SVCS: Building Materials
TRUCKING & HAULING SVCS: Contract Basis
TRUCKING & HAULING SVCS: Haulage & Cartage, Light, Local
TRUCKING & HAULING SVCS: Hazardous Waste
TRUCKING & HAULING SVCS: Machinery, Heavy
TRUCKING & HAULING SVCS: Mail Carriers, Contract
TRUCKING & HAULING SVCS: Petroleum, Local
TRUCKING, AUTOMOBILE CARRIER
TRUCKING, DUMP
TRUCKING, REFRIGERATED: Long-Distance
TRUCKING: Except Local
TRUCKING: Local, With Storage
TRUCKING: Local, Without Storage
TRUCKS & TRACTORS: Industrial
TRUCKS, INDL: Wholesalers
TRUCKS: Forklift
TRUCKS: Indl
TRUSSES & FRAMING: Prefabricated Metal
TRUSSES: Wood, Floor
TRUSSES: Wood, Roof
TUB CONTAINERS: Plastic
TUBE & TUBING FABRICATORS
TUBES: Electron, NEC
TUBES: Photomultiplier
TUBES: Steel & Iron
TUBING, COLD-DRAWN: Mech Or Hypodermic Sizes, Stainless
TUBING: Copper
TUBING: Flexible, Metallic
TUBING: Glass
TUBING: Plastic
TUBING: Seamless
TUNGSTEN MILL PRDTS
TURBINES & TURBINE GENERATOR SET UNITS, COMPLETE
TURBINES & TURBINE GENERATOR SET UNITS: Gas, Complete
TURBINES & TURBINE GENERATOR SETS
TURBINES: Hydraulic, Complete
TURBINES: Steam
TURKEY PROCESSING & SLAUGHTERING
TURNKEY VENDORS: Computer Systems
TWINE
TWINE PRDTS
TYPESETTING SVC
TYPESETTING SVC: Computer
TYPESETTING SVC: Hand Composition
TYPEWRITERS & PARTS
TYPOGRAPHY

U

ULTRASONIC EQPT: Cleaning, Exc Med & Dental
ULTRASONIC EQPT: Dental
UMBRELLAS & CANES
UMBRELLAS: Garden Or Wagon
UNDERCOATINGS: Paint
UNDERGROUND GOLD MINING
UNIFORM STORES
UNSUPPORTED PLASTICS: Floor Or Wall Covering
UPHOLSTERY WORK SVCS
USED BOOK STORES
USED CAR DEALERS
USED MERCHANDISE STORES
USED MERCHANDISE STORES: Building Materials
USED MERCHANDISE STORES: Musical Instruments
UTENSILS: Household, Cooking & Kitchen, Metal
UTENSILS: Household, Cooking & Kitchen, Porcelain Enameled

V

VACUUM CLEANER STORES
VACUUM CLEANERS: Household
VACUUM CLEANERS: Indl Type
VACUUM PUMPS & EQPT: Laboratory
VACUUM SYSTEMS: Air Extraction, Indl
VALUE-ADDED RESELLERS: Computer Systems
VALVE REPAIR SVCS, INDL
VALVES
VALVES & PARTS: Gas, Indl
VALVES & PIPE FITTINGS
VALVES & REGULATORS: Pressure, Indl
VALVES Solenoid
VALVES: Aerosol, Metal
VALVES: Aircraft, Control, Hydraulic & Pneumatic
VALVES: Aircraft, Hydraulic
VALVES: Control, Automatic
VALVES: Fire Hydrant
VALVES: Fluid Power, Control, Hydraulic & pneumatic
VALVES: Indl
VALVES: Plumbing & Heating
VALVES: Regulating & Control, Automatic
VALVES: Regulating, Process Control
VALVES: Water Works
VANILLIN: Synthetic
VARNISHES, NEC
VARNISHING SVC: Metal Prdts
VAULTS & SAFES WHOLESALERS
VEGETABLE OILS: Medicinal Grade, Refined Or Concentrated
VEGETABLES, FROZEN: Wholesaler
VEHICLES: All Terrain
VENDING MACHINES & PARTS
VENETIAN BLIND REPAIR SHOP
VENETIAN BLINDS & SHADES
VENTILATING EQPT: Metal
VENTILATING EQPT: Sheet Metal
VERIFIERS: Punch Card
VESSELS: Process, Indl, Metal Plate
VETERINARY PHARMACEUTICAL PREPARATIONS
VETERINARY PRDTS: Instruments & Apparatus
VIALS: Glass
VIDEO & AUDIO EQPT, WHOLESALE
VIDEO EQPT
VIDEO REPAIR SVCS
VIDEO TAPE PRODUCTION SVCS
VISUAL COMMUNICATIONS SYSTEMS
VISUAL EFFECTS PRODUCTION SVCS
VITAMINS: Natural Or Synthetic, Uncompounded, Bulk
VITAMINS: Pharmaceutical Preparations
VOCATIONAL REHABILITATION AGENCY

W

WALL COVERINGS: Rubber
WALLBOARD: Gypsum
WALLPAPER & WALL COVERINGS
WALLPAPER: Embossed Plastic, Textile Backed
WALLS: Curtain, Metal
WAREHOUSING & STORAGE FACILITIES, NEC
WAREHOUSING & STORAGE, REFRIGERATED: Cold Storage Or Refrig
WAREHOUSING & STORAGE: Fur
WAREHOUSING & STORAGE: General
WAREHOUSING & STORAGE: General
WAREHOUSING & STORAGE: Household Goods

WAREHOUSING & STORAGE: Miniwarehouse
WARFARE COUNTER-MEASURE EQPT
WARM AIR HEATING & AC EQPT & SPLYS, WHOLESALE Air Filters
WARM AIR HEATING & AC EQPT & SPLYS, WHOLESALE Furnaces
WARM AIR HEATING/AC EQPT/SPLYS, WHOL Dehumidifiers, Exc Port
WARM AIR HEATING/AC EQPT/SPLYS, WHOL Warm Air Htg Eqpt/Splys
WARP KNIT FABRIC FINISHING
WASHCLOTHS & BATH MITTS, FROM PURCHASED MATERIALS
WASHERS
WASHERS: Metal
WASHERS: Rubber
WATCH & CLOCK STORES
WATCH REPAIR SVCS
WATCHES
WATER HEATERS
WATER PURIFICATION EQPT: Household
WATER PURIFICATION PRDTS: Chlorination Tablets & Kits
WATER SOFTENER SVCS
WATER SPLY: Irrigation
WATER SUPPLY
WATER TREATMENT EQPT: Indl
WATER: Mineral, Carbonated, Canned & Bottled, Etc
WATER: Pasteurized & Mineral, Bottled & Canned
WATER: Pasteurized, Canned & Bottled, Etc
WAXES: Petroleum, Not Produced In Petroleum Refineries
WEATHER STRIP: Sponge Rubber
WEATHER STRIPS: Metal
WEDDING CONSULTING SVCS
WEIGHING MACHINERY & APPARATUS
WEIGHING SVCS: Food & Commodity
WELDING & CUTTING APPARATUS & ACCESS, NEC
WELDING EQPT
WELDING EQPT & SPLYS WHOLESALERS
WELDING EQPT & SPLYS: Electrodes
WELDING EQPT & SPLYS: Resistance, Electric
WELDING EQPT REPAIR SVCS
WELDING EQPT: Electrical
WELDING REPAIR SVC
WELDING SPLYS, EXC GASES: Wholesalers
WELDING TIPS: Heat Resistant, Metal
WELDMENTS
WET CORN MILLING
WHEELCHAIRS
WHEELS
WHEELS & PARTS
WHEELS: Abrasive
WHEELS: Buffing & Polishing
WHEELS: Water
WHIRLPOOL BATHS: Hydrotherapy
WIG & HAIRPIECE STORES
WIGS & HAIRPIECES
WIGS, DOLL: Hair
WIGS, WHOLESALE
WINCHES
WIND TUNNELS
WINDINGS: Coil, Electronic
WINDMILLS: Electric Power Generation
WINDOW & DOOR FRAMES
WINDOW BLIND CLEANING SVCS
WINDOW FRAMES & SASHES: Plastic
WINDOW FRAMES, MOLDING & TRIM: Vinyl
WINDOWS: Frames, Wood
WINE CELLARS, BONDED: Wine, Blended
WIRE
WIRE & CABLE: Aluminum
WIRE & CABLE: Nonferrous, Aircraft
WIRE & CABLE: Nonferrous, Automotive, Exc Ignition Sets
WIRE & CABLE: Nonferrous, Building
WIRE & WIRE PRDTS
WIRE CLOTH & WOVEN WIRE PRDTS, MADE FROM PURCHASED WIRE
WIRE FENCING & ACCESS WHOLESALERS
WIRE MATERIALS: Copper
WIRE MATERIALS: Steel
WIRE PRDTS: Ferrous Or Iron, Made In Wiredrawing Plants
WIRE PRDTS: Steel & Iron
WIRE: Communication
WIRE: Mesh
WIRE: Nonferrous
WIRE: Nonferrous, Appliance Fixture

INDEX

WIRE: Steel, Insulated Or Armored
WIRING DEVICES WHOLESALERS
WOMEN'S & CHILDREN'S CLOTHING WHOLESALERS,
   NEC
WOMEN'S & GIRLS' SPORTSWEAR WHOLESALERS
WOMEN'S CLOTHING STORES
WOMEN'S CLOTHING STORES: Ready-To-Wear
WOMEN'S SPECIALTY CLOTHING STORES
WOMEN'S SPORTSWEAR STORES
WOOD FENCING WHOLESALERS
WOOD PRDTS: Brackets
WOOD PRDTS: Door Trim
WOOD PRDTS: Moldings, Unfinished & Prefinished
WOOD PRDTS: Mulch Or Sawdust
WOOD PRDTS: Mulch, Wood & Bark
WOOD PRDTS: Poles

WOOD PRDTS: Policemen's Clubs
WOOD PRDTS: Trophy Bases
WOOD PRDTS: Veneer Work, Inlaid
WOOD PRDTS: Yard Sticks
WOOD PRODUCTS: Reconstituted
WOOD TREATING: Creosoting
WOOD TREATING: Flooring, Block
WOOD TREATING: Millwork
WOODWORK & TRIM: Exterior & Ornamental
WOODWORK & TRIM: Interior & Ornamental
WOODWORK: Interior & Ornamental, NEC
WOOL: Glass
WORD PROCESSING SVCS
WOVEN WIRE PRDTS, NEC
WRENCHES

X

X-RAY EQPT & TUBES

Y

YACHT BASIN OPERATIONS
YARN & YARN SPINNING
YARN : Crochet, Spun
YARN MILLS: Texturizing
YARN MILLS: Texturizing, Throwing & Twisting
YARN MILLS: Throwing
YARN MILLS: Winding
YARN WHOLESALERS
YARN: Manmade & Synthetic Fiber, Spun
YARN: Manmade & Synthetic Fiber, Twisting Or Winding
YARN: Specialty & Novelty

PRODUCT SECTION

BOXES: Folding

Edgar & Son Paperboard .... G 999 999-9999
Yourtown (G-11480)

Ready Box Co .... E 999 999-9999
Anytown (G-7097)

Product category

City

Indicates approximate employment figure
A = Over 500 employees, B = 251-500
C = 101-250, D = 51-100, E = 20-50
F = 10-19, G = 4-9

Business phone

Geographic Section entry number where full
company information appears.

See footnotes for symbols and codes identification.

• Refer to the Industrial Product Index preceding this section to locate product headings.

ABRASIVES

3M Company .... B 973 884-2500
Whippany (G-11875)

Advanced Abrasives Corporation .... F 856 665-9300
Pennsauken (G-8383)

Beacut Abrasives Corp .... F 973 249-1420
East Rutherford (G-2275)

Chessco Industries Inc .... E 609 882-0400
Ewing (G-3020)

East Coast Diamond TI Pdts Inc .... G 212 686-1034
Englewood (G-2899)

Mercury Floor Machines Inc .... E 201 568-4606
Englewood (G-2924)

New Jersey Diamond Products Co .... F 973 684-0949
Paterson (G-8267)

Robinson Tech Intl Corp .... G 973 287-6458
Fairfield (G-3303)

William R Hall Co .... E 856 784-6700
Lindenwold (G-5447)

ABRASIVES: Polishing Rouge

Agsco Corporation .... E 973 244-0005
Pine Brook (G-8584)

ACADEMIC TUTORING SVCS

Davis Center Inc .... G 862 251-4637
Succasunna (G-10512)

ACCELERATORS, RUBBER PROCESSING: Cyclic or Acyclic

Brown Chemical Co Inc .... E 201 337-0900
Oakland (G-7617)

ACCELEROMETERS

Core Laboratories LP .... F 609 896-2673
Lawrenceville (G-5228)

ACCOUNTING MACHINES & CASH REGISTERS

Worldwide Pt SL Ltd Lblty Co .... F 201 928-0222
Teaneck (G-10655)

ACETONE: Natural

Gingko Tree Inc .... G 973 652-9380
Linden (G-5353)

ACID RESIST: Etching

Advanced Polymer Inc .... F 201 964-3000
Carlstadt (G-1118)

ACIDS

Anichem LLC .... G 732 821-6500
North Brunswick (G-7452)

Evans Chemetics LP .... G 201 992-3100
Teaneck (G-10631)

ACIDS: Boric

Solvay Holding Inc .... A 609 860-4000
Princeton (G-9024)

Solvay USA Inc .... C 732 297-0100
North Brunswick (G-7486)

ACIDS: Hydrochloric

Gingko Tree Inc .... G 973 652-9380
Linden (G-5353)

ACRYLIC RESINS

Rohm America LLC .... D 973 929-8000
Parsippany (G-8010)

United Resin Inc .... F 856 358-2574
Elmer (G-2805)

ACTUATORS: Indl, NEC

Textol Systems Inc .... E 201 935-1220
Carlstadt (G-1227)

Valcor Engineering Corporation .... E 973 467-8400
Springfield (G-10474)

Whippany Actuation Systems LLC .... C 973 428-9898
Whippany (G-11913)

ACUPUNCTURISTS' OFFICES

Holmdel Acpnctr & Ntrl Med Ctr .... G 732 888-4910
Holmdel (G-4502)

ADDITIVE BASED PLASTIC MATERIALS: Plasticizers

Composecure LLC .... C 908 518-0500
Somerset (G-9975)

Composecure LLC .... C 908 518-0500
Somerset (G-9976)

Technology Reviews Inc .... G 973 537-9511
Randolph (G-9203)

ADHESIVES

Amb Enterprises LLC .... E 973 225-1070
Paterson (G-8135)

Amerasia Intl Tech Inc .... E 609 799-9388
Princeton Junction (G-9050)

American Chemical & Coating Co .... G 908 353-2260
Elizabeth (G-2711)

Annitti Enterprises Inc .... E 973 345-1725
Paterson (G-8140)

Baker/Titan Adhesives .... E 973 225-1070
Paterson (G-8145)

Bostik Inc .... D 856 848-8669
Paulsboro (G-8330)

Coim USA Inc .... D 856 224-8560
West Deptford (G-11700)

Compounders Inc .... G 732 938-5007
Farmingdale (G-3381)

Dritac Flooring Products LLC .... F 973 614-9000
Clifton (G-1604)

Elektromek Inc .... F 973 614-9000
Clifton (G-1615)

Frimpeks Inc .... F 201 266-0116
Fairfield (G-3208)

HB Fuller Company .... E 732 287-8330
Edison (G-2528)

Henkel US Operations Corp .... E 908 685-7000
Bridgewater (G-830)

Hercules LLC .... G 732 777-4697
Edison (G-2530)

Master Bond Inc .... E 201 343-8983
Hackensack (G-3943)

Mc Ginley Packaging Methods .... G 201 493-9330
Midland Park (G-6180)

Mercury Adhesives Inc .... G 973 472-3307
Passaic (G-8087)

Mon-Eco Industries Inc .... F 732 257-7942
East Brunswick (G-2157)

National Casein New Jersey Inc .... E 856 829-1880
Cinnaminson (G-1476)

Natl Adhesies Div of Henke .... G 908 685-7000
Bridgewater (G-855)

Norland Products Inc .... E 609 395-1966
Cranbury (G-1865)

Palmetto Adhesives Company .... F 856 451-0400
Bridgeton (G-767)

Petronio Shoe Products Corp .... F 973 751-7579
Belleville (G-307)

Solar Compounds Corporation .... E 908 862-2813
Linden (G-5425)

Steven Industries Inc .... E 201 437-6500
Bayonne (G-235)

Synthetic Surfaces Inc .... G 908 233-6803
Scotch Plains (G-9743)

Zymet Inc .... F 973 428-5245
East Hanover (G-2250)

ADHESIVES & SEALANTS

A D M Tronics Unlimited Inc .... E 201 767-6040
Northvale (G-7513)

Alan Chemical Corporation Inc .... G 973 628-7777
Wayne (G-11466)

Alva-Tech Inc .... F 609 747-1133
Burlington Township (G-995)

American Casein Company .... E 609 387-2988
Burlington (G-947)

Andek Corporation .... F 856 866-7600
Moorestown (G-6505)

API Americas Inc .... D 732 382-6800
Rahway (G-9077)

Artistic Bias Products Co Inc .... E 732 382-4141
Rahway (G-9078)

Clark Stek-O Corp .... D 201 437-0770
Bayonne (G-209)

Covalnce Spcalty Adhesives LLC .... A 732 356-2870
Middlesex (G-6108)

Custom Building Products Inc .... D 856 467-9226
Logan Township (G-5586)

Dritac Flooring Products LLC .... D 973 614-9000
Clifton (G-1605)

Essentra Plastics LLC .... G 518 437-5138
Edison (G-2507)

Flexcraft Industries Inc .... G 973 589-3403
Newark (G-7125)

Kop-Coat Inc .... E 800 221-4466
Rockaway (G-9474)

Mapei Corporation .... F 732 254-4830
South River (G-10353)

Mapei Corporation .... E 732 254-4830
South River (G-10352)

National Strch Chem Holdg Corp .... A 908 685-5000
Bridgewater (G-854)

Permabond LLC .... G 610 323-5003
Somerset (G-10052)

Princeton Keynes Group Inc .... F 609 951-2239
Princeton (G-9000)

Princeton Keynes Group Inc .... F 609 208-1777
Newark (G-7234)

Rust-Oleum Corporation .... F 732 652-2378
Newark (G-7256)

Saint-Gobain Prfmce Plas Corp .... D 732 652-0910
Somerset (G-10070)

Sap-Seal Products Inc .... G 201 385-5553
Bergenfield (G-384)

Spiral Binding LLC .... C 973 256-0666
Totowa (G-10853)

Universal Tape Supply Corp .... F 609 653-3191
Somers Point (G-9940)

ADHESIVES: Adhesives, paste

Aos Thermal Compounds LLC .... F 732 389-5514
Eatontown (G-2378)

P R O D U C T

ADHESIVES: Adhesives, plastic

Clifton Adhesive Inc ....E 973 694-0845
Wayne **(G-11488)**

ADHESIVES: Epoxy

Sika Corporation ....B 201 933-8800
Lyndhurst **(G-5678)**

ADVERTISING AGENCIES

Access Response Inc ....G 732 660-0770
Ocean **(G-7652)**
Advertisers Service Group Inc ....F 201 440-5577
Ridgefield Park **(G-9298)**
B T O Industries Inc ....G 973 243-0011
West Orange **(G-11761)**
Corporate Mailings Inc ....C 973 439-1168
West Caldwell **(G-11645)**
Corporate Mailings Inc ....D 973 808-0009
Whippany **(G-11887)**
Gail Gersons Wine & Dine Resta ....G 732 758-0888
Shrewsbury **(G-9892)**
Global Graphics Intergration ....F 973 334-9653
Towaco **(G-10872)**
Healthstar Communications Inc ....E 201 560-5370
Mahwah **(G-5746)**
Killian Graphics ....G 973 635-5844
Chatham **(G-1325)**
Moonlight Imaging LLC ....G 973 300-1001
Sparta **(G-10399)**
Pro-Pack Corp ....G 908 725-5000
Branchburg **(G-672)**
Prohaska & Co Inc ....G 732 238-3420
East Brunswick **(G-2169)**
Schellmark Inc ....G 732 345-7143
Tinton Falls **(G-10726)**
Slendertone Distribution Inc ....G 732 660-1177
Hoboken **(G-4481)**
Typecom LLC ....G 201 969-1901
Fort Lee **(G-3591)**
Wt Media LLC ....F 609 921-3490
Trenton **(G-11011)**

ADVERTISING AGENCIES: Consultants

Cherri Stone Interactive LLC ....G 844 843-7765
Lakewood **(G-5069)**
Digital Outdoor Advg LLC ....G 732 616-2232
Tinton Falls **(G-10711)**
Moscova Enterprises Inc ....F 848 628-4873
Jersey City **(G-4768)**
Nema Associates Inc ....F 973 274-0052
Linden **(G-5395)**
Suzie Mac Specialties Inc ....E 732 238-3500
East Brunswick **(G-2184)**
Tap Into LLC ....G 908 370-1158
New Providence **(G-7020)**

ADVERTISING CURTAINS

Prestige Industries LLC ....E 866 492-2244
Lyndhurst **(G-5673)**

ADVERTISING DISPLAY PRDTS

Digital Outdoor Advg LLC ....G 732 616-2232
Tinton Falls **(G-10711)**
Hudson Displays Co ....E 973 623-8255
Newark **(G-7153)**
Pharmakon Corp ....F 856 829-3161
Cinnaminson **(G-1481)**
Power Packaging Services Corp ....G 201 261-2566
Paramus **(G-7827)**
Strategic Mktg Promotions Inc ....F 845 623-7777
Mahwah **(G-5777)**

ADVERTISING MATERIAL DISTRIBUTION

Enertia LLC ....G 856 330-4767
Pennsauken **(G-8418)**
Riverside Graphics Inc ....F 201 876-9000
Belleville **(G-311)**

ADVERTISING REPRESENTATIVES: Electronic Media

Retail Management Pubg Inc ....F 212 981-0217
Montclair **(G-6388)**

ADVERTISING REPRESENTATIVES: Media

Diacritech LLC ....A 732 238-1157
Jersey City **(G-4727)**

ADVERTISING REPRESENTATIVES: Newspaper

David Sisco Jr ....G 908 454-0880
Phillipsburg **(G-8548)**
Times of Trenton Pubg Corp ....A 609 989-5454
Trenton **(G-10998)**

ADVERTISING REPRESENTATIVES: Printed Media

Data Communique Inc ....E 201 508-6000
Ridgefield Park **(G-9302)**
J D M Associates Inc ....G 973 773-8699
Lodi **(G-5566)**
Progress Displays Inc ....G 908 757-6650
Edison **(G-2592)**

ADVERTISING SPECIALTIES, WHOLESALE

A&E Promotions LLC ....G 732 382-2300
Holmdel **(G-4491)**
ADS Sales Co Inc ....G 732 591-0500
Morganville **(G-6580)**
All Colors Screen Printing LLC ....G 732 777-6033
Highland Park **(G-4286)**
Circa Promotions Inc ....G 732 264-1200
Hazlet **(G-4259)**
Digital Outdoor Advg LLC ....G 732 616-2232
Tinton Falls **(G-10711)**
Drew & Rogers Inc ....E 973 575-6210
Fairfield **(G-3187)**
G G Tauber Company Inc ....E 800 638-6667
Neptune **(G-6879)**
Genesis Marketing Group Inc ....G 201 836-1392
Teaneck **(G-10632)**
Imprintz Cstm Printed Graphics ....G 609 386-5673
Lumberton **(G-5631)**
J&E Business Services LLC ....G 973 984-8444
Clifton **(G-1645)**
Newton Screen Printing Co ....G 973 827-0486
Franklin **(G-3606)**
One Two Three Inc ....F 856 251-1238
Woodbury **(G-12034)**
Penny Press ....G 856 547-1991
Stratford **(G-10506)**
Pro-Pack Corp ....G 908 725-5000
Branchburg **(G-672)**
Wally Enterprises Inc ....F 732 329-2613
Monmouth Junction **(G-6319)**

ADVERTISING SVCS: Bus Card

Silver Edmar ....G 973 817-7483
Newark **(G-7273)**

ADVERTISING SVCS: Direct Mail

About Our Town Inc ....G 732 968-1615
Piscataway **(G-8623)**
Access Response Inc ....G 732 660-0770
Ocean **(G-7652)**
Arna Marketing Group Inc ....D 908 625-7395
Branchburg **(G-621)**
Brisar Industries Inc ....D 973 278-2500
Paterson **(G-8150)**
C and R Printing Corporation ....F 201 528-8912
Carlstadt **(G-1134)**
Comprehensive Mktg Systems ....G 908 810-9778
Union **(G-11036)**
Ics Corporation ....G 215 427-3355
West Deptford **(G-11704)**
Ideal Data Inc ....F 201 998-9440
North Arlington **(G-7374)**
Johnston Letter Co Inc ....G 973 482-7535
Flanders **(G-3414)**
Madhouz LLC ....G 609 206-8009
Glassboro **(G-3814)**
Metro Seliger Industries Inc ....G 201 438-4530
Carlstadt **(G-1187)**
Redi-Direct Marketing Inc ....B 973 808-4500
Fairfield **(G-3300)**
Total Reliance LLC ....F 732 640-5079
Dayton **(G-1993)**
Verizon Communications Inc ....D 609 646-9939
Egg Harbor Township **(G-2700)**

Zippityprint LLC ....F 216 438-0001
Mullica Hill **(G-6859)**

ADVERTISING SVCS: Display

Dublin Management Assoc of NJ ....C 609 387-1600
Burlington **(G-964)**
Larue Manufacturing Corp ....G 908 534-2700
Whitehouse **(G-11916)**
Madhouz LLC ....G 609 206-8009
Glassboro **(G-3814)**
Northwind Enterprises Inc ....E 732 274-2000
Dayton **(G-1982)**

ADVERTISING SVCS: Outdoor

Fedex Office & Print Svcs Inc ....E 856 427-0099
Cherry Hill **(G-1361)**
Kar Industrial ....G 856 985-8730
Marlton **(G-5935)**
Outfront Media LLC ....D 973 575-6900
Fairfield **(G-3286)**

ADVERTISING SVCS: Poster, Outdoor

Stephen Swinton Studio Inc ....G 908 537-9135
Washington **(G-11452)**

ADVERTISING SVCS: Sample Distribution

Redi-Direct Marketing Inc ....B 973 808-4500
Fairfield **(G-3300)**

ADVERTISING SVCS: Transit

David Sisco Jr ....G 908 454-0880
Phillipsburg **(G-8548)**
Grafwed Internet Media Studios ....G 201 632-1771
Midland Park **(G-6175)**

AEROSOLS

American Spraytech LLC ....E 908 725-6060
Branchburg **(G-617)**

AGENTS, BROKERS & BUREAUS: Personal Service

Gold Enterprise Ltd ....C 954 614-1001
Point Pleasant Boro **(G-8845)**
Patty-O-Matic Inc ....F 732 938-2757
Farmingdale **(G-3389)**

AGENTS: Loan, Farm Or Business

Max Pro Services LLC ....G 973 396-2373
Livingston **(G-5523)**

AGRICULTURAL CHEMICALS: Trace Elements

Avantor Performance Mtls LLC ....B 908 859-2151
Phillipsburg **(G-8542)**
Flottec LLC ....G 973 588-4717
Boonton **(G-554)**

AGRICULTURAL EQPT: BARN, SILO, POULTRY, DAIRY/LIVESTOCK MACH

Edward Brown ....G 973 887-5255
East Hanover **(G-2207)**

AGRICULTURAL EQPT: Fertilizing Machinery

Plant Food Company Inc ....E 609 448-0935
Cranbury **(G-1872)**

AGRICULTURAL EQPT: Trailers & Wagons, Farm

Steve Green Enterprises ....F 732 938-5572
Farmingdale **(G-3393)**

AGRICULTURAL EQPT: Turf Eqpt, Commercial

South Jersey Farmers Exchange ....G 856 769-0062
Woodstown **(G-12096)**

AIR CLEANING SYSTEMS

Croll-Reynolds Co Inc ....E 908 232-4200
Parsippany **(G-7909)**

Palude Enterprises Inc ....G....... 732 241-5478
Howell **(G-4548)**

AIR CONDITIONING & VENTILATION EQPT & SPLYS: Wholesales

ML Mettler Corp ....G....... 201 869-0170
North Bergen **(G-7423)**
Passaic Metal & Bldg Sups Co ....D....... 973 546-9000
Clifton **(G-1685)**

AIR CONDITIONING EQPT

Ats Mechanical Inc.........................G....... 609 298-2323
Bordentown **(G-576)**
Kooltronic Inc...............................C....... 609 466-3400
Pennington **(G-8369)**
Mainstream Fluid & Air LLC..................F....... 908 931-1010
Berkeley Heights **(G-408)**
Mechanical Technologies LLC...............E....... 973 616-3800
Pine Brook **(G-8609)**
Task International (usa) Inc.................F....... 732 739-0377
Keyport **(G-5005)**

AIR CONDITIONING UNITS: Complete, Domestic Or Indl

Construction Specialties Inc ....E....... 908 236-0800
Lebanon **(G-5257)**
Daicel Chemtech Inc........................G....... 201 461-4466
Fort Lee **(G-3553)**
SPX Dry Cooling Usa LLC..................E....... 908 450-8027
Bridgewater **(G-893)**
Tecogen Inc.................................E....... 732 356-5601
Piscataway **(G-8723)**

AIR COOLERS: Metal Plate

Airzone Systems ....G....... 201 207-6593
Montville **(G-6437)**

AIR MATTRESSES: Plastic

Glasplex LLC ....G....... 973 940-8940
Sussex **(G-10560)**
L-E-M Plastics and Supplies ....G....... 201 933-9150
Rutherford **(G-9626)**
Mamrout Paper Group Corp..................G....... 718 510-5484
Edison **(G-2558)**
Plastics Galore LLC.........................G....... 732 363-8447
Lakewood **(G-5147)**

AIR POLLUTION MEASURING SVCS

Valley Tech Inc ....G....... 908 534-5565
Whitehouse Station **(G-11936)**

AIR PURIFICATION EQPT

Air Clean Co Inc.............................G....... 908 355-1515
Elizabeth **(G-2708)**
Bioclimatic Air Systems LLC ....E....... 856 764-4300
Delran **(G-2010)**
Bioclimatic Inc...............................E....... 856 764-4300
Delran **(G-2011)**
Bionomic Industries Inc ....F....... 201 529-1094
Mahwah **(G-5717)**
CSM Environmental Systems LLC ....F....... 908 789-5431
Mountainside **(G-6838)**
CSM Worldwide Inc..........................E....... 908 233-2882
Bridgewater **(G-815)**
Csonka Worldwide...........................E....... 609 514-2766
Plainsboro **(G-8783)**
DR Technology Inc ....G....... 732 780-4664
Freehold **(G-3661)**
Encur Inc....................................G....... 732 264-2098
Keyport **(G-4998)**
Lm Air Technology Inc.......................E....... 732 381-8200
Rahway **(G-9115)**
Naava Inc ....G....... 844 666-2282
Hazlet **(G-4266)**
Safety Power Inc ....G....... 908 277-1826
Summit **(G-10544)**

AIRCRAFT & AEROSPACE FLIGHT INSTRUMENTS & GUIDANCE SYSTEMS

Bae Systems Info & Elec Sys...............A....... 973 633-6000
Wayne **(G-11474)**
Honeywell International Inc ....C....... 973 455-2000
Morristown **(G-6672)**

Lockheed Martin Corporation................A....... 856 234-1261
Mount Laurel **(G-6776)**

AIRCRAFT & HEAVY EQPT REPAIR SVCS

Thales Avionics Inc...........................C....... 732 242-6300
Piscataway **(G-8725)**

AIRCRAFT ASSEMBLY PLANTS

Boeing Company ....A....... 314 232-1372
Mullica Hill **(G-6856)**
Boeing Company ....A....... 908 464-6959
Berkeley Heights **(G-390)**
Dassault Aircraft Svcs Corp ....F....... 201 440-6700
Little Ferry **(G-5481)**
Defense Photonics Group Inc ....F....... 908 822-1075
South Plainfield **(G-10247)**
Easy Aerial Inc ....G....... 646 639-4410
Edison **(G-2497)**
Jet Aviation St Louis Inc ....E....... 201 462-4026
Teterboro **(G-10681)**
Lockheed Martin Corporation................D....... 856 722-7782
Moorestown **(G-6538)**
Pacific Microtronics Inc......................G....... 973 993-8665
Morris Plains **(G-6621)**

AIRCRAFT CONTROL SYSTEMS: Electronic Totalizing Counters

Honeywell East Asia Inc ....G....... 973 455-2000
Morris Plains **(G-6608)**

AIRCRAFT ENGINES & ENGINE PARTS: Cooling Systems

Capital Cooling Systems LLC................G....... 973 773-8700
Lyndhurst **(G-5645)**

AIRCRAFT ENGINES & PARTS

Aerospace Industries LLC ....G....... 973 383-9307
Sparta **(G-10376)**
Allied-Signal China Ltd.......................E....... 973 455-2000
Morristown **(G-6632)**
Alliedsignal Foreign Sls Corp ....E....... 973 455-2000
Morristown **(G-6633)**
Bright Lights Usa Inc ....E....... 856 546-5656
Camden **(G-1042)**
Dover Tool Connecticut LLC.................F....... 203 367-6376
Franklin Lakes **(G-3622)**
Honeywell International Inc ....C....... 800 601-3099
Morris Plains **(G-6609)**
Honeywell International Inc ....E....... 973 455-6633
Morristown **(G-6670)**
Honeywell International Inc ....E....... 973 285-5321
Morris Plains **(G-6610)**
Honeywell International Inc ....A....... 856 691-5111
Vineland **(G-11232)**
Honeywell International Inc ....A....... 856 234-5020
Moorestown **(G-6529)**
Honeywell International Inc ....D....... 973 455-2000
Morris Plains **(G-6611)**
Honeywell International Inc ....G....... 973 455-5168
Morristown **(G-6671)**
Honeywell International Inc ....C....... 877 841-2840
Morris Plains **(G-6612)**
Honeywell International Inc ....A....... 732 919-0010
Wall Township **(G-11346)**
Honeywell International Inc ....G....... 800 601-3099
Morris Plains **(G-6613)**
Honeywell Spain Holdings LLC ....G....... 973 455-2000
Morristown **(G-6673)**
Parts Life Inc ....D....... 856 786-8675
Moorestown **(G-6554)**

AIRCRAFT EQPT & SPLYS WHOLESALERS

Aeropanel Corporation ....D....... 973 335-9636
Boonton **(G-537)**
Dassault Procurement Svcs Inc ....F....... 201 261-4130
Little Ferry **(G-5482)**

AIRCRAFT FLIGHT INSTRUMENTS

Dassault Procurement Svcs Inc ....F....... 201 261-4130
Little Ferry **(G-5482)**
H Galow Co Inc..............................E....... 201 768-0547
Norwood **(G-7564)**

AIRCRAFT MAINTENANCE & REPAIR SVCS

GE Aviation Systems LLC ....C....... 973 428-9898
Whippany **(G-11892)**
Jet Aviation St Louis Inc ....E....... 201 462-4026
Teterboro **(G-10681)**

AIRCRAFT PARTS & AUXILIARY EQPT: Aircraft Training Eqpt

Pacific Coast Systems LLC...................G....... 908 735-9955
Asbury **(G-68)**

AIRCRAFT PARTS & AUXILIARY EQPT: Armament, Exc Guns

Breeze-Eastern LLC..........................G....... 973 602-1001
Whippany **(G-11883)**

AIRCRAFT PARTS & AUXILIARY EQPT: Assys, Subassemblies/Parts

Doorsills LLC ....G....... 973 904-0270
Haledon **(G-4081)**
Export Management Consultants...........E....... 609 758-1166
Cookstown **(G-1804)**

AIRCRAFT PARTS & AUXILIARY EQPT: Body & Wing Assys & Parts

Keeley Aerospace Ltd ....E....... 951 582-2113
Cranbury **(G-1849)**

AIRCRAFT PARTS & AUXILIARY EQPT: Body Assemblies & Parts

Arlington Prcsion Cmpnents LLC ....E....... 973 276-1377
Fairfield **(G-3145)**
Kreisler Manufacturing Corp ....G....... 201 791-0700
Elmwood Park **(G-2836)**
Vahl Inc ....E....... 732 249-4042
East Brunswick **(G-2188)**

AIRCRAFT PARTS & AUXILIARY EQPT: Deicing Eqpt

Clearway LLC ....G....... 973 578-4578
Newark **(G-7084)**

AIRCRAFT PARTS & AUXILIARY EQPT: Landing Assemblies & Brakes

Enginred Arrsting Systems Corp ....E....... 856 241-8620
Logan Township **(G-5587)**
Zodiac US Corporation ....A....... 732 681-3527
Wall Township **(G-11379)**

AIRCRAFT PARTS & AUXILIARY EQPT: Military Eqpt & Armament

Polytechnic Industries Inc ....F....... 856 235-6550
Mount Laurel **(G-6793)**

AIRCRAFT PARTS & AUXILIARY EQPT: Tanks, Fuel

Air Cruisers Company LLC...................B....... 732 681-3527
Wall Township **(G-11315)**

AIRCRAFT PARTS & EQPT, NEC

Accurate Bushing Company Inc...........E....... 908 789-1121
Garwood **(G-3779)**
Aerospace Manufacturing Inc...............E....... 973 472-9888
Wallington **(G-11380)**
American Aluminum Company.............D....... 908 233-3500
Mountainside **(G-6834)**
Bar Fields Inc ....F....... 347 587-7795
Linden **(G-5325)**
Breeze-Eastern LLC..........................D....... 973 602-1001
Whippany **(G-11884)**
Bright Lights Usa Inc ....D....... 856 546-5656
Mount Laurel **(G-6743)**
Defense Support Svcs Intl LLC ....F....... 850 390-4737
Marlton **(G-5928)**
Drytech Inc ....E....... 609 758-1794
Cookstown **(G-1803)**
Exelis Inc/Northrop ....F....... 973 284-4212
Clifton **(G-1618)**
Goodrich Corporation ....C....... 973 237-2700
Totowa **(G-10830)**

PRODUCT

Ho-Ho-Kus Inc ....E 973 278-2274
Paterson (G-8210)

J A Machine & Tool Co Inc ....F 201 767-1308
Closter (G-1759)

Kreisler Industrial Corp ....D 201 289-5554
Elmwood Park (G-2835)

Rclc Inc ....F 732 877-1788
Woodbridge (G-12020)

Terrestrial Imaging LLC ....G 800 359-0530
Brick (G-733)

Thales Avionics Inc ....C 732 242-6300
Piscataway (G-8725)

Tolin Design Inc ....G 201 261-4455
Emerson (G-2869)

Whippany Actuation Systems LLC .....C 973 428-9898
Whippany (G-11913)

AIRCRAFT PARTS WHOLESALERS

Aerospace Industries LLC ....G 973 383-9307
Sparta (G-10376)

AIRCRAFT PARTS/AUX EQPT: Airframe Assy, Exc Guided Missiles

Alpine Machine & Tool Corp ....F 201 666-0959
Westwood (G-11825)

AIRCRAFT SEATS

Air Cruisers Company LLC ....B 732 681-3527
Wall Township (G-11315)

AIRCRAFT SERVICING & REPAIRING

Defense Spport Svcs Intl 2 LLC ......F 856 866-2200
Marlton (G-5927)

AIRCRAFT TURBINES

Ademco I LLC ....G 973 455-2000
Morris Plains (G-6601)

Hh Spinco Inc ....G 973 455-2000
Morris Plains (G-6606)

Kreisler Manufacturing Corp ....G 201 791-0700
Elmwood Park (G-2836)

AIRCRAFT: Airplanes, Fixed Or Rotary Wing

Boeing Company ....A 610 591-1978
Swedesboro (G-10573)

Defense Spport Svcs Intl 2 LLC ......F 856 866-2200
Marlton (G-5927)

AIRCRAFT: Autogiros

Drone Go Home LLC ....G 732 991-3605
Holmdel (G-4499)

AIRCRAFT: Motorized

Abj LLC ....G 888 225-1931
Cranbury (G-1806)

Drone Usa Inc ....F 203 220-2296
Pine Brook (G-8600)

Freestream Aircraft USA Ltd ....F 201 365-6080
Teterboro (G-10676)

AIRCRAFT: Research & Development, Manufacturer

Enroute Computer Solutions Inc ......E 609 569-9255
Egg Harbor Township (G-2683)

Lockheed Martin Corporation ....B 856 787-3104
Mount Laurel (G-6777)

AIRPORTS, FLYING FIELDS & SVCS

Bombardier Transportation ....B 973 624-9300
Newark (G-7070)

Defense Support Svcs Intl LLC ....F 850 390-4737
Marlton (G-5928)

ALARM SYSTEMS WHOLESALERS

Absolute Protective Systems ....E 732 287-4500
Piscataway (G-8624)

ALARMS: Burglar

Merchants Alarm Systems Inc ....E 973 779-1296
Wallington (G-11388)

ALARMS: Fire

Digitize Inc ....F 973 663-1011
Lake Hopatcong (G-5036)

ALCOHOL, ETHYL: For Beverage Purposes

Creamy Creation LLC ....G 585 344-3300
Paramus (G-7796)

ALCOHOL: Ethyl & Ethanol

Gingko Tree Inc ....G 973 652-9380
Linden (G-5353)

ALKALIES & CHLORINE

Kuehne Chemical Company Inc ....E 973 589-0700
Kearny (G-4876)

PMC Group Inc ....F 856 533-1866
Mount Laurel (G-6791)

Qualco Inc ....E 973 473-1222
Passaic (G-8099)

ALLOYS: Additive, Exc Copper Or Made In Blast Furnaces

Alpha Assembly Solutions Inc ....E 908 561-5170
South Plainfield (G-10214)

Alpha Assembly Solutions Inc ....E 908 791-3000
Somerset (G-9948)

ALTERNATORS: Automotive

Mobile Power Inc ....G 908 852-3117
Hackettstown (G-4027)

ALUMINUM

Helidex LLC ....G 201 636-2546
East Rutherford (G-2291)

Ivey Katrina Owner ....G 973 951-8328
Newark (G-7163)

Quick Fab Aluminum Mfg Co ....E 732 367-7200
Lakewood (G-5150)

ALUMINUM PRDTS

Alcon Products Inc ....F 609 267-3898
Westampton (G-11783)

Aluminum Shapes Inc ....E 856 662-5500
Pennsauken (G-8387)

Aluminum Shapes LLC ....B 888 488-7427
Delair (G-1999)

Ango Electronics Corporation ....F 201 955-0800
North Arlington (G-7368)

Coltwell Industries Inc ....E 908 276-7600
Cranford (G-1905)

Construction Specialties Inc ....E 908 236-0800
Lebanon (G-5257)

Construction Specialties Inc ....E 908 272-2771
Cranford (G-1906)

E-TEC Marine Products Inc ....G 732 269-0442
Bayville (G-243)

Goetz & Ruschmann Inc ....G 973 383-9270
Newton (G-7345)

Kwg Industries LLC ....E 908 218-8900
Hillsborough (G-4338)

Medicraft Inc ....F 201 421-3055
Elmwood Park (G-2841)

Medicraft Inc ....F 201 797-8820
Elmwood Park (G-2842)

Minalex Corporation ....E 908 534-4044
Whitehouse Station (G-11929)

Security Fabricators Inc ....F 908 272-9171
Kenilworth (G-4977)

Shapes/Arch Holdings LLC ....B 856 662-5500
Delair (G-2001)

Unique Amrcn Alum Extrsion LLC ....E 732 271-0006
Middlesex (G-6157)

ALUMINUM: Coil & Sheet

H Cross Company ....E 201 964-9380
Moonachie (G-6468)

ALUMINUM: Rolling & Drawing

Gentek Building Products Inc ....E 732 381-0900
Avenel (G-130)

AMMUNITION

Lightfield Ammunition Corp ....G 732 462-9200
Freehold (G-3676)

AMMUNITION: Small Arms

Lightfield Ammunition Corp ....G 732 462-9200
Freehold (G-3676)

AMPLIFIERS

Bogen Communications Inc ....D 201 934-8500
Mahwah (G-5718)

Bogen Corporation ....G 201 934-8500
Ramsey (G-9142)

Celco ....F 201 327-1123
Mahwah (G-5721)

Fuchs Audio Tech Ltd Lblty Co ....F 973 772-4420
Clifton (G-1623)

Sound Chice Assstive Listening ......G 908 647-2651
Gillette (G-3803)

AMPLIFIERS: RF & IF Power

Fiber-Span Inc ....E 908 253-9080
Toms River (G-10757)

AMUSEMENT & RECREATION SVCS, NEC

Indoor Entertainment of NJ ....E 609 522-6700
Wildwood (G-11945)

AMUSEMENT & RECREATION SVCS: Physical Fitness Instruction

Our Team Fitness LLC ....G 848 208-5047
Oceanport (G-7705)

AMUSEMENT & RECREATION SVCS: Tourist Attraction, Commercial

Christopher F Maier ....F 908 459-5100
Hope (G-4524)

AMUSEMENT & RECREATION SVCS: Video Game Arcades

Xbox Exclusive ....G 908 756-3731
South Plainfield (G-10347)

AMUSEMENT & RECREATION SVCS: Yoga Instruction

Kristine Deer Inc ....G 201 497-3333
Westwood (G-11833)

AMUSEMENT ARCADES

AG&e Holdings Inc ....E 609 704-3000
Hammonton (G-4124)

AMUSEMENT MACHINES: Coin Operated

Jersey Jack Pinball Inc ....E 732 364-9900
Lakewood (G-5115)

Shooting Star Inc ....G 908 789-2500
Scotch Plains (G-9741)

Smartplay International Inc ....E 609 880-1860
Beverly (G-454)

AMUSEMENT PARK DEVICES & RIDES

Able Gear & Machine Co ....G 973 983-8055
Rockaway (G-9434)

Modular Packaging Systems Inc ......F 973 970-9393
Rockaway (G-9477)

Precision Forms Inc ....E 973 838-3800
Butler (G-1012)

AMUSEMENT PARK DEVICES & RIDES Carousels Or Merry-Go-Rounds

Indoor Entertainment of NJ ....E 609 522-6700
Wildwood (G-11945)

ANALYZERS: Electrical Testing

Celco ....F 201 327-1123
Mahwah (G-5721)

Linseis Inc ....G 609 223-2070
Trenton (G-10952)

(G-0000) Company's Geographic Section entry number

ANALYZERS: Network

Cisco Systems Inc ....E 201 782-0842
Montvale (G-6402)

Datalink Solutions Inc ....F 973 731-9373
West Orange (G-11766)

ANALYZERS: Respiratory

Impact Instrumentation Inc ....C 973 882-1212
West Caldwell (G-11654)

ANESTHESIA EQPT

Precision Spine Inc ....F 601 420-4244
Parsippany (G-7999)

ANESTHETICS: Bulk Form

Janssen Pharmaceuticals Inc ....A 609 730-2000
Titusville (G-10735)

Messer LLC ....G 973 579-2065
Sparta (G-10398)

ANIMAL FEED & SUPPLEMENTS: Livestock & Poultry

Darling Ingredients Inc ....C 973 465-1900
Newark (G-7095)

Glenburnie Feed & Grain ....G 856 986-8128
Mount Laurel (G-6763)

ANIMAL FEED: Wholesalers

Phibro Anmal Hlth Holdings Inc ....G 201 329-7300
Teaneck (G-10644)

Wilenta Carting Inc ....F 201 325-0044
Secaucus (G-9828)

Wilenta Feed Inc ....F 201 325-0044
Secaucus (G-9829)

ANIMAL FOOD & SUPPLEMENTS: Bird Food, Prepared

R World Enterprises ....G 201 795-2428
Jersey City (G-4793)

ANIMAL FOOD & SUPPLEMENTS: Cat

Mars Incorporated ....F 973 691-3500
Budd Lake (G-929)

ANIMAL FOOD & SUPPLEMENTS: Dog

Gwenstone Inc ....G 732 785-2600
Lakewood (G-5106)

Simmons Pet Food Nj Inc ....B 856 662-7412
Pennsauken (G-8485)

Xceptional Instruments LLC ....G 315 750-4345
Hoboken (G-4490)

ANIMAL FOOD & SUPPLEMENTS: Dog & Cat

Freshpet Inc ....E 201 520-4000
Secaucus (G-9768)

Mars Food Us LLC ....F 908 852-1000
Hackettstown (G-4025)

Phibro Anmal Hlth Holdings Inc ....G 201 329-7300
Teaneck (G-10644)

Simmons Pet Food Inc ....C 856 662-7412
Pennsauken (G-8484)

ANIMAL FOOD & SUPPLEMENTS: Feed Supplements

Penetone Corporation ....G 609 921-0501
Princeton (G-8994)

Pet Devices LLC ....G 929 244-0012
Livingston (G-5535)

Pharmacia & Upjohn Company LLC .....B 908 901-8000
Peapack (G-8344)

Prince Agri Products Inc ....D 201 329-7300
Teaneck (G-10648)

ANIMAL FOOD & SUPPLEMENTS: Livestock

International Processing Corp ....F 732 826-4240
Perth Amboy (G-8523)

Reconserve Inc ....G 732 826-4240
Perth Amboy (G-8530)

ANIMAL FOOD & SUPPLEMENTS: Poultry

New York Poultry Co ....F 908 523-1600
Linden (G-5396)

ANIMAL FOOD & SUPPLEMENTS: Slaughtering of nonfood animals

Buckhead Meat Company ....C 732 661-4900
Edison (G-2471)

ANODIZING SVC

Aerotech Proc Solutions LLC ....G 973 782-4485
Paterson (G-8126)

Andarn Electro Service Inc ....E 973 523-2220
Paterson (G-8139)

Anodizing Corporation ....G 973 694-6449
Wayne (G-11470)

B & M Finishers Inc ....E 908 241-5640
Kenilworth (G-4925)

Independence Plating Corp ....E 973 523-1776
Paterson (G-8213)

Kenilworth Anodizing Co ....E 908 241-5640
Kenilworth (G-4952)

Master Metal Polishing Corp ....E 973 684-0119
Paterson (G-8252)

Super Chrome Inc ....G 732 774-2210
Asbury Park (G-83)

Trb Electro Corp ....E 973 278-9014
Paterson (G-8316)

ANTENNAS: Radar Or Communications

Electromagnetic Tech Inds Inc ....D 973 394-1719
Boonton (G-550)

Lcn Partners Inc ....F 215 755-1000
Berlin (G-426)

Magos America Inc ....G 973 763-9597
Kearny (G-4881)

ANTENNAS: Receiving

Dwill America LLC ....G 201 561-5737
Lodi (G-5561)

Gulton G I D ....G 908 791-4622
South Plainfield (G-10270)

It Surplus Liquidators ....G 732 308-1935
Freehold (G-3670)

Lg Electronics USA Inc ....G 732 605-0385
Monroe Township (G-6334)

Patriot American Solutions LLC ....D 862 209-4772
Rockaway (G-9484)

ANTIBIOTICS

Pfizer Inc ....F 973 660-5000
Madison (G-5700)

ANTIBIOTICS, PACKAGED

Capsugel Inc ....D 862 242-1700
Morristown (G-6651)

Pfizer Inc ....C 908 901-8000
Peapack (G-8342)

ANTIFREEZE

BASF Corporation ....B 973 245-6000
Florham Park (G-3491)

Basfin Corporation ....A 973 245-6000
Florham Park (G-3493)

Full Circle Mfg Group ....F 908 353-8933
Elizabeth (G-2740)

Prestone Products Corporation ....E 732 577-7800
Freehold (G-3693)

ANTIHISTAMINE PREPARATIONS

Janssen Pharmaceuticals Inc ....A 609 730-2000
Titusville (G-10735)

ANTIQUE FURNITURE RESTORATION & REPAIR

Restortions By Peter Schichtel ....G 973 605-8818
Morristown (G-6697)

APPAREL DESIGNERS: Commercial

Suuchi Inc ....C 201 284-0789
North Bergen (G-7439)

Two 12 Fashion LLC ....G 848 222-1562
Lakewood (G-5173)

APPAREL: Hand Woven

Bearhands Ltd ....G 201 807-9898
Passaic (G-8053)

APPLIANCE PARTS: Porcelain Enameled

Aspen Manufacturing Co Inc ....G 609 871-6400
Beverly (G-447)

APPLIANCES, HOUSEHOLD: Drycleaning Machines, Incl Coin-Op

Artisan Gardens LLC ....G 201 857-2600
Ridgewood (G-9322)

APPLIANCES, HOUSEHOLD: Kitchen, Major, Exc Refrigs & Stoves

Organize It-All Inc ....E 201 488-0808
Bogota (G-534)

PC Marketing Inc ....E 201 943-6100
Ridgefield (G-9282)

Royal Sovereign Intl Inc ....E 800 397-1025
Rockleigh (G-9521)

Wanasavealotcom LLC ....F 732 286-6956
Toms River (G-10802)

APPLIANCES: Household, NEC

Boutique USA Corp ....G 917 476-0472
Englewood (G-2885)

APPLIANCES: Household, Refrigerators & Freezers

Bar-Maid Corporation ....C 973 478-7070
Garfield (G-3731)

APPLIANCES: Major, Cooking

Haier America Trading LLC ....G 212 594-3330
Woodbridge (G-12017)

Signature Marketing Group Ltd ....F 973 575-7785
Pine Brook (G-8617)

APPLIANCES: Small, Electric

Conair Corporation ....D 239 673-2125
East Windsor (G-2347)

Edwards Creative Products Inc ....F 856 665-3200
Cherry Hill (G-1358)

Jarden LLC ....E 201 610-6600
Hoboken (G-4458)

White Home Products Inc ....G 908 226-2501
Kenilworth (G-4990)

Winiadaewoo Elec Amer Inc ....F 201 552-4950
Ridgefield Park (G-9320)

APPLICATIONS SOFTWARE PROGRAMMING

Alloy Software Inc ....F 973 661-9700
Bloomfield (G-490)

Channel Logistics LLC ....F 856 614-5441
Camden (G-1052)

James Colucci Enterprises LLC ....E 877 403-4900
Short Hills (G-9870)

Mobile Intelligent Alerts Inc ....G 201 410-5324
Holmdel (G-4507)

Utah Intermediate Holding Corp ....C 856 787-2700
Mount Laurel (G-6810)

AQUARIUM ACCESS, METAL

Julius E Holland-Moritz Co Inc ....G 609 397-1231
Lambertville (G-5191)

ARCHITECTURAL SVCS

LMC-HB Corp ....F 862 239-9814
Paterson (G-8244)

National Home Planning Service ....G 973 376-3200
Chatham (G-1328)

Zacs International LLC ....G 609 368-3482
Burlington (G-994)

ARCHITECTURAL SVCS: House Designer

Marlene Trimmings LLC ....G 201 926-3108
North Bergen (G-7418)

Employee Codes: A=Over 500 employees, B=251-500
C=101-250, D=51-100, E=20-50, F=10-19, G=4-9

2019 Harris New jersey
Manufacturers Directory

771

PRODUCT

ARMATURE REPAIRING & REWINDING SVC

Longo Elctrical-Mechanical Inc ....D 973 537-0400
Wharton *(G-11861)*

ARMOR PLATES

Dynamic Defense Materials LLC ....G 856 552-4150
Marlton *(G-5930)*

AROMATIC CHEMICAL PRDTS

Bertone Aromatics ....G 201 444-9821
Waldwick *(G-11297)*
Bwi Chemicals ....G 732 689-0913
Monmouth Junction *(G-6280)*

ART DEALERS & GALLERIES

Empty Walls Inc ....G 609 452-8488
Princeton *(G-8940)*
Environmolds LLC ....F 908 273-5401
Summit *(G-10531)*
Revelation Gallery Inc ....G 973 627-6558
Denville *(G-2052)*

ART DESIGN SVCS

Digital Atelier LLC ....G 609 890-6666
Trenton *(G-10931)*
J D M Associates Inc ....G 973 773-8699
Lodi *(G-5566)*
Minerva Custom Products LLC ....G 201 447-4731
Waldwick *(G-11305)*

ART GOODS, WHOLESALE

Printers Service Florida Inc ....G 973 589-7800
Newark *(G-7236)*
Scafa-Tornabene Art Pubg Co ....E 201 842-8500
Lyndhurst *(G-5676)*

ART MARBLE: Concrete

Cumberland Marble & Monument.........G 856 691-3334
Vineland *(G-11207)*

ART RESTORATION SVC

Revelation Gallery Inc ....G 973 627-6558
Denville *(G-2052)*

ART SPLY STORES

Utrecht Manufacturing Corp ....D 609 409-8001
Cranbury *(G-1891)*

ARTIFICIAL FLOWERS & TREES

Pennock Company ....E 215 492-7900
Pennsauken *(G-8464)*

ARTIST'S MATERIALS & SPLYS

Meadowbrook Inventions Inc ....E 908 766-0606
Bernardsville *(G-439)*
Rich Art Color Co Inc ....F 201 767-0009
Northvale *(G-7547)*
U J Ramelson Co Inc ....G 973 589-5422
Newark *(G-7304)*
Utrecht Manufacturing Corp ....D 609 409-8001
Cranbury *(G-1891)*

ARTISTS' MATERIALS, WHOLESALE

Silver Brush Limited ....G 609 443-4900
Windsor *(G-11998)*

ARTISTS' MATERIALS: Clay, Modeling

Chavant Inc.....................................F 732 751-0003
Wall Township *(G-11323)*

ARTISTS' MATERIALS: Frames, Artists' Canvases

Empty Walls Inc ....G 609 452-8488
Princeton *(G-8940)*

ARTISTS' MATERIALS: Ink, Drawing, Black & Colored

Algene Marking Equipment Co.............G 973 478-9041
Garfield *(G-3727)*

Pertech Printing Inks Inc ....E 908 354-1700
Carlstadt *(G-1199)*

ARTISTS' MATERIALS: Palettes

Norwood Industries Inc ....F 856 858-6195
Haddon Township *(G-4052)*

ARTISTS' MATERIALS: Pencil Holders

Case It Inc ....E 800 441-4710
Lyndhurst *(G-5646)*

ASBESTOS PRDTS: Clutch Facings

Hydro-Mechanical Systems Inc ....F 856 848-8888
Westville *(G-11816)*

ASBESTOS PRDTS: Pipe Covering, Heat Insulatng Matl, Exc Felt

Stuart Steel Protection Corp ....E 732 469-5544
Somerset *(G-10075)*

ASBESTOS PRDTS: Wick

Wick It LLC ....G 973 249-2970
Passaic *(G-8116)*

ASBESTOS PRODUCTS

Blavor Inc..G 973 265-4165
Montville *(G-6438)*

ASH TRAYS: Stamped Metal

House of Gold Inc ....E 856 665-0020
Pennsauken *(G-8433)*

ASPHALT & ASPHALT PRDTS

A E Stone Inc ....E 609 641-2781
Egg Harbor Township *(G-2673)*
Arawak Paving Co Inc ....E 609 561-4100
Hammonton *(G-4128)*
Beaver Run Farms ....G 973 427-1000
Hawthorne *(G-4208)*
Beaver Run Farms ....G 973 875-5555
Lafayette *(G-5025)*
Dosch-King Company Inc ....F 973 887-0145
Whippany *(G-11889)*
Earle Asphalt Company ....D 732 657-8551
Jackson *(G-4653)*
Eastern Concrete Materials Inc ....E 973 827-7625
Hamburg *(G-4090)*
Newark Asphalt Corp ....G 973 482-3503
Newark *(G-7212)*
Riverdale Quarry LLC ....E 973 835-0028
Riverdale *(G-9382)*
South State Inc ....E 856 881-6030
Williamstown *(G-11979)*

ASPHALT COATINGS & SEALERS

Lodor Offset Corporation ....F 201 935-7100
Carlstadt *(G-1182)*
Newark Asphalt Corp ....G 973 482-3503
Newark *(G-7212)*

ASPHALT MINING & BITUMINOUS STONE QUARRYING SVCS

Eastern Concrete Materials Inc ....G 973 702-7866
Sussex *(G-10559)*

ASPHALT MINING SVCS

Ziegler Chem & Mineral Corp...............E 732 752-4111
Piscataway *(G-8741)*

ASPHALT MIXTURES WHOLESALERS

Central Jersey Hot Mix Asp LLC ....G 732 323-0226
Jackson *(G-4642)*
Stone Industries Inc..........................D 973 595-6250
Haledon *(G-4085)*

ASPHALT PLANTS INCLUDING GRAVEL MIX TYPE

Dragon Asphalt Equipment LLC...........F 732 922-9290
Lakewood *(G-5085)*
Fred McDowell Inc ....G 732 681-5000
Wall Township *(G-11342)*

Robert Young and Son Inc ....G 973 728-8133
Hewitt *(G-4279)*

ASSEMBLING & PACKAGING SVCS: Cosmetic Kits

Beauty-Pack LLC ....F 732 802-8200
Piscataway *(G-8640)*
Cei Holdings Inc ....E 732 888-7788
Holmdel *(G-4496)*
Cosmetic Essence LLC ....C 732 888-7788
Holmdel *(G-4497)*
Cosmetic Essence Inc ....E 732 888-7788
Holmdel *(G-4498)*
SGB Packaging Group Inc ....G 201 488-3030
Hackensack *(G-3972)*

ASSEMBLING SVC: Clocks

Emdur Metal Products Inc ....F 856 541-1100
Camden *(G-1061)*
Garrett Moore ....G 908 231-9231
Bridgewater *(G-825)*

ASSEMBLING SVC: Plumbing Fixture Fittings, Plastic

Majewski Plumbing & Htg LLC ....G 609 374-6001
Villas *(G-11179)*
Plumbing Supply Now LLC ....F 732 228-8852
New Brunswick *(G-6958)*
W C Davis Inc ....F 856 547-4750
Haddon Heights *(G-4050)*

ASSOCIATIONS: Business

Seawave Corp ....E 609 886-8600
Rio Grande *(G-9358)*

ASSOCIATIONS: Real Estate Management

McQuade Enterprises LLC ....G 609 501-2437
Millville *(G-6260)*

ASSOCIATIONS: Scientists'

Electrochemical Society Inc ....E 609 737-1902
Pennington *(G-8364)*

ASSOCIATIONS: Trade

Metal Powder Inds Federation ....F 609 452-7700
Princeton *(G-8977)*
New Jersey Bus & Indust Assn ....D 609 393-7707
Trenton *(G-10961)*

ATHLETIC ORGANIZATION

New York-NJ Trail Conference..............F 201 512-9348
Mahwah *(G-5757)*

ATOMIZERS

Accurate Screw Machine Corp ....D 973 276-0379
Fairfield *(G-3133)*
American Consolidation Inc ....D 201 438-4351
Carlstadt *(G-1123)*
Amneal Pharmaceuticals Inc ....A 908 409-6822
Bridgewater *(G-786)*
Amneal Pharmaceuticals LLC ....E 908 947-3120
Bridgewater *(G-788)*
Cutting Edge Grower Supply LLC ....G 732 905-9220
Howell *(G-4536)*
Distek Inc ....D 732 422-7585
North Brunswick *(G-7466)*
Griffith Electric Sup Co Inc ....D 609 695-6121
Trenton *(G-10937)*
Industrial Water Institute ....G 609 585-4880
Trenton *(G-10944)*
Mfv International Corporation ....G 973 993-1687
Morristown *(G-6686)*
Mountain LLC ....G 908 409-6823
Bridgewater *(G-853)*
New Jersey Air Products Inc ....F 908 964-9001
Kenilworth *(G-4963)*
Riverstone Industries Corp..................G 973 586-2564
Rockaway *(G-9495)*
Tri-Met Industries Inc ....G 908 231-0004
Bridgewater *(G-897)*

AUCTION SVCS: Motor Vehicle

Toyota Motor Sales ....F 973 515-5012
Parsippany *(G-8030)*

AUDIO & VIDEO EQPT, EXC COMMERCIAL

Bayview Entertainment LLC ....E...... 201 880-5331
Pompton Plains (G-8860)
Broadway Empress Entrmt Inc ....G...... 973 991-0009
Newark (G-7078)
Crestron Electronics Inc ....C...... 201 767-3400
Rockleigh (G-9516)
CVE Inc ....D...... 201 770-0005
Riverdale (G-9374)
Emerson Radio Corp ....F...... 973 428-2000
Parsippany (G-7936)
Funai Corporation Inc ....E...... 201 806-7635
Rutherford (G-9621)
Itec Consultants LLC ....G...... 732 784-8322
Matawan (G-5978)
Kef America Inc ....E...... 732 414-2074
Marlboro (G-5903)
Lg Electronics USA Inc ....B...... 201 816-2000
Englewood Cliffs (G-2982)
Lunar Audio Video LLC ....G...... 973 233-7700
Sayreville (G-9717)
Mardee Company Inc ....E...... 908 753-4343
South Plainfield (G-10297)
Philips Elec N Amer Corp ....D...... 973 804-2100
Ledgewood (G-5278)
Sierra Video Systems ....E...... 530 478-1000
Clinton (G-1749)
Signature Audio Video Systems ....G...... 732 864-1039
Toms River (G-10793)
Sony Corporation of America ....B...... 201 930-1000
Paramus (G-7834)
Sony Electronics Inc ....A...... 201 930-1000
Paramus (G-7835)
Stirling Audio Services LLC ....G...... 732 560-0707
Middlesex (G-6154)
Techflex Inc ....F...... 973 300-9242
Sparta (G-10409)
Vcom Intl Multi-Media Corp ....D...... 201 296-0600
Fairfield (G-3339)
Wireworks Corporation ....E...... 908 686-7400
Hillside (G-4437)
Xbox Exclusive ....G...... 908 756-3731
South Plainfield (G-10347)
Zenith Electronics Corporation ....E...... 201 816-2071
Englewood Cliffs (G-2998)

AUDIO COMPONENTS

Sony Corporation of America ....F...... 201 930-1000
Woodcliff Lake (G-12065)

AUDIO ELECTRONIC SYSTEMS

360 Media Innovations LLC ....G...... 201 228-0941
Union (G-11018)
Apb-Dynasonics Inc ....G...... 973 785-1101
Totowa (G-10813)
Audio Technologies and Codecs ....F...... 973 624-1116
Newark (G-7058)
Concept Professional Systems ....G...... 732 938-5321
Wall Township (G-11332)
DMJ Technologies LLC ....G...... 201 261-5560
New Milford (G-6989)
Dtrovision LLC ....E...... 201 488-3232
Fair Lawn (G-3097)
Empirical Labs Inc ....F...... 973 541-9447
Lake Hiawatha (G-5034)
Ferro Industries Incorporated ....E...... 732 246-3200
Colts Neck (G-1782)
Innovative Concepts Design LLC ....F...... 732 346-0061
Elizabeth (G-2750)
Phoenix Systems ....G...... 201 788-5511
North Haledon (G-7499)
Riotsound Inc ....E...... 917 273-5814
Newton (G-7355)
Scj Group LLC ....G...... 201 289-5841
Teaneck (G-10651)
Sondpex Corp America LLC ....G...... 732 940-4430
Princeton (G-9026)
V P I Industries Inc ....G...... 732 583-6895
Cliffwood (G-1548)
Vanderbilt LLC ....E...... 973 316-3900
Parsippany (G-8034)

AUDIO-VISUAL PROGRAM PRODUCTION SVCS

Vu Sound Incorporated ....F...... 215 990-2864
Lumberton (G-5638)

AUDIOLOGICAL EQPT: Electronic

Davis Center Inc ....G...... 862 251-4637
Succasunna (G-10512)

AUDIOLOGISTS' OFFICES

Davis Center Inc ....G...... 862 251-4637
Succasunna (G-10512)

AUDITING SVCS

Sony Music Holdings Inc ....B...... 201 777-3933
Rutherford (G-9634)

AUTHOR

Letts Play Inc ....G...... 856 297-2530
Williamstown (G-11963)

AUTO & HOME SUPPLY STORES: Auto & Truck Eqpt & Parts

Chapter Enterprises Inc ....G...... 732 560-8500
Bridgewater (G-811)
Norms Auto Parts Inc ....G...... 908 852-5080
Hackettstown (G-4029)

AUTO & HOME SUPPLY STORES: Automotive Access

American Van Equipment Inc ....C...... 732 905-5900
Lakewood (G-5050)
M & RS Miller Auto Gear & Prt ....F...... 201 339-2270
Bayonne (G-228)
Rebuilt Parts Co LLC ....F...... 856 662-3252
Pennsauken (G-8476)

AUTO & HOME SUPPLY STORES: Automotive parts

Custom Auto Radiator Inc ....F...... 609 242-9700
Forked River (G-3539)
P & A Auto Parts Inc ....E...... 201 655-7117
Hackensack (G-3960)

AUTO & HOME SUPPLY STORES: Speed Shops, Incl Race Car Splys

Bruce Kindberg ....G...... 973 664-0195
Rockaway (G-9447)

AUTO & HOME SUPPLY STORES: Truck Eqpt & Parts

Robert H Hoover & Sons Inc ....G...... 973 347-4210
Flanders (G-3417)

AUTOCLAVES: Laboratory

Benchmark Scientific Inc ....E...... 908 769-5555
Sayreville (G-9703)

AUTOMATED TELLER MACHINE OR ATM REPAIR SVCS

Longport Shields Inc ....G...... 856 727-0227
Moorestown (G-6542)

AUTOMATIC REGULATING CONTROL: Building Svcs Monitoring, Auto

J & L Controls Inc ....G...... 732 460-0380
Lincroft (G-5312)

AUTOMATIC REGULATING CONTROLS: AC & Refrigeration

Atomizing Systems Inc ....F...... 201 447-1222
Ho Ho Kus (G-4439)
Msj Unlimited Services ....G...... 201 617-0764
Union City (G-11122)
National Refrigerants Inc ....E...... 856 455-4555
Bridgeton (G-766)
Siemens Industry Inc ....E...... 856 234-7666
Mount Laurel (G-6806)

AUTOMATIC REGULATING CONTROLS: Appliance, Exc Air-Cond/Refr

Vu Sound Incorporated ....F...... 215 990-2864
Lumberton (G-5638)

AUTOMATIC REGULATING CONTROLS: Elect Air Cleaner, Automatic

Sulzer Chemtech USA Inc ....C...... 856 768-2165
West Berlin (G-11624)

AUTOMATIC REGULATING CONTROLS: Electric Heat

Heat-Timer Corporation ....E...... 973 575-4004
Fairfield (G-3224)

AUTOMATIC REGULATING CONTROLS: Energy Cutoff, Residtl/Comm

Building Performance Eqp Inc ....F...... 201 722-1414
Hillsdale (G-4364)

AUTOMATIC REGULATING CONTROLS: Hardware, Environmental Reg

Comverge Giants Inc ....G...... 973 884-5970
Florham Park (G-3497)
Comverge Giants Inc ....G...... 973 884-5970
East Hanover (G-2202)

AUTOMATIC REGULATING CONTROLS: Hydronic Pressure Or Temp

A T C Companies Inc ....E...... 732 560-0900
Middlesex (G-6091)
Sisco Manufacturing Co Inc ....F...... 856 486-7550
Pennsauken (G-8486)

AUTOMATIC REGULATING CONTROLS: Pressure, Air-Cond Sys

US Air Power Systems ....G...... 201 892-5235
Westwood (G-11846)

AUTOMATIC TELLER MACHINES

Bps Worldwide Inc ....E...... 856 874-0822
Cherry Hill (G-1348)
Longport Shields Inc ....G...... 856 727-0227
Moorestown (G-6542)

AUTOMOBILE FINANCE LEASING

Volvo Car North America LLC ....B...... 201 768-7300
Rockleigh (G-9524)

AUTOMOBILE RECOVERY SVCS

Zc Utility Services LLC ....G...... 973 226-1840
Roseland (G-9545)

AUTOMOBILE STORAGE GARAGE

Boomerang Systems Inc ....E...... 973 538-1194
Florham Park (G-3494)

AUTOMOBILES & OTHER MOTOR VEHICLES WHOLESALERS

Autoaccess LLC ....F...... 908 240-5919
Sicklerville (G-9908)
P L Custom Body & Eqp Co Inc ....C...... 732 223-1411
Manasquan (G-5836)

AUTOMOBILES: Wholesalers

BMW of North America LLC ....A...... 201 307-4000
Woodcliff Lake (G-12049)
Shock Tech Inc ....E...... 845 368-8600
Mahwah (G-5771)

AUTOMOTIVE & TRUCK GENERAL REPAIR SVC

Bombardier Transportation ....B...... 973 624-9300
Newark (G-7070)
Faps Inc ....C...... 973 589-5656
Newark (G-7122)
Freehold Pntiac Bick GMC Trcks ....D...... 732 462-7093
Freehold (G-3666)
Holman Enterprises Inc ....E...... 609 383-6100
Mount Laurel (G-6765)
Liquid Iron Industries Inc ....G...... 856 336-2639
West Berlin (G-11604)
P & S Blizzard Corporation ....G...... 973 523-1700
Paterson (G-8275)

PRODUCT

Town Ford Inc..........................D......609 298-4990
  Bordentown (G-597)
Wayne Motors Inc...................D......973 696-9710
  Wayne (G-11564)

AUTOMOTIVE BODY SHOP

Dale Behre................................G......908 850-4225
  Hackettstown (G-4003)
Freehold Pntiac Bick GMC Trcks.....D......732 462-7093
  Freehold (G-3666)
Wayne Motors Inc...................D......973 696-9710
  Wayne (G-11564)

AUTOMOTIVE BODY, PAINT & INTERIOR REPAIR & MAINTENANCE SVC

Drive-Master Co Inc................F......973 808-9709
  Fairfield (G-3188)
Holman Enterprises Inc............E......609 383-6100
  Mount Laurel (G-6765)
Summit Truck Body Inc.............E......908 277-4342
  Summit (G-10551)
Town Ford Inc.........................D......609 298-4990
  Bordentown (G-597)

AUTOMOTIVE EMISSIONS TESTING SVCS

Superior Signal Company LLC............F......732 251-0800
  Old Bridge (G-7728)

AUTOMOTIVE GLASS REPLACEMENT SHOPS

Quality Glass Inc....................F......908 754-2652
  South Plainfield (G-10320)

AUTOMOTIVE LETTERING & PAINTING SVCS

Painting Inc............................F......201 489-6565
  South Hackensack (G-10179)

AUTOMOTIVE PARTS, ACCESS & SPLYS

Accurate Tool & Die Co Inc........G......201 476-9348
  Montvale (G-6394)
Allied-Signal China Ltd.............E......973 455-2000
  Morristown (G-6632)
Alliedsignal Foreign Sls Corp.....G......973 455-2000
  Morristown (G-6633)
Allison Corp............................G......973 992-3800
  Livingston (G-5504)
American Refuse Supply Inc.......F......973 684-3225
  Paterson (G-8137)
Banks Bros Corporation...........D......973 680-4488
  Bloomfield (G-491)
Bruce Kindberg.......................G......973 664-0195
  Rockaway (G-9447)
C T A Manufacturing Corp.........E......201 896-1000
  Carlstadt (G-1135)
Chick Capoli Sales...................E......856 768-4500
  West Berlin (G-11581)
Dana Automotive Inc...............F......973 667-1234
  Nutley (G-7584)
Elite Emrgncy Lights Ltd Lblty.....F......732 534-2377
  Lakewood (G-5090)
Fleetsource LLC......................E......732 566-4970
  Dayton (G-1961)
Freehold Pntiac Bick GMC Trcks.....D......732 462-7093
  Freehold (G-3666)
Garrett Motion Inc..................F......973 867-7016
  Morristown (G-6665)
Gentek Inc.............................C......973 515-0900
  Parsippany (G-7956)
Gorman Industries Inc.............E......973 345-5424
  Paterson (G-8201)
Holman Enterprises Inc............E......609 383-6100
  Mount Laurel (G-6765)
Honeywell International Inc.......C......973 455-2000
  Morristown (G-6672)
Ida Automotive Inc..................G......732 591-1245
  Morganville (G-6588)
J & R Rebuilders Inc.................G......856 627-1414
  Laurel Springs (G-5207)
Jesel Inc................................D......732 901-1800
  Lakewood (G-5116)
Kinedyne LLC..........................F......908 231-1800
  Branchburg (G-652)
Kumar Bros USA LLC...............G......732 266-3091
  Englishtown (G-3006)

Ls Rubber Industries Inc...........F......973 680-4488
  Bloomfield (G-507)
Maxzone Vehicle Lighting Corp...F......732 393-9600
  Edison (G-2560)
MPT Racing Inc.......................G......973 989-9220
  Dover (G-2099)
Newark Auto Top Co Inc...........F......973 677-9935
  East Orange (G-2256)
Nitto Inc................................F......732 901-0035
  Lakewood (G-5140)
Ogura Industrial Corp..............F......586 749-1900
  Somerset (G-10045)
Olde Grandad Industries Inc.....G......201 997-1899
  Passaic (G-8093)
P & A Auto Parts Inc................E......201 655-7117
  Hackensack (G-3960)
Paintmaster Auto Body.............F......732 270-1700
  Toms River (G-10781)
Rebuilt Parts Co LLC................F......856 662-3252
  Pennsauken (G-8476)
Research & Mfg Corp Amer........F......908 862-6744
  Linden (G-5414)
Rony Inc.................................F......201 891-2551
  Wyckoff (G-12120)
S & G Tool Aid Corporation.......D......973 824-7730
  Newark (G-7257)
S L P Engineering Inc...............D......732 240-3696
  Toms River (G-10789)
Shock Tech Inc.......................E......845 368-8600
  Mahwah (G-5771)
Spalding Automotive Inc...........E......215 638-3334
  Moorestown (G-6567)
Steed Perf6manc3..................G......908 583-5580
  Linden (G-5430)
Tabco Technologies LLC...........G......201 438-0422
  Carlstadt (G-1225)
Tekltd...................................G......732 463-2100
  Piscataway (G-8724)
Tesla Inc...............................G......201 225-2544
  Paramus (G-7841)
Town Ford Inc.........................D......609 298-4990
  Bordentown (G-597)
Turbine Tek Inc......................G......973 872-0903
  Wayne (G-11559)
Valcor Engineering Corporation....E......973 467-8100
  Springfield (G-10473)
Volvo Car North America LLC.....B......201 768-7300
  Rockleigh (G-9524)
VS Systematics Corp...............G......908 241-5110
  Kenilworth (G-4985)
Wayne Motors Inc..................D......973 696-9710
  Wayne (G-11564)
Z Squared Hg Inc...................G......908 315-3646
  Hillsborough (G-4362)

AUTOMOTIVE PARTS: Plastic

Kinect Auto Parts Corporation.......G......862 702-8252
  Fairfield (G-3251)

AUTOMOTIVE PRDTS: Rubber

Aero TEC Laboratories Inc........E......201 825-1400
  Ramsey (G-9135)
Hutchinson Industries Inc.........F......609 394-1010
  Trenton (G-10940)
Hutchinson Industries Inc.........C......609 394-1010
  Trenton (G-10941)
Hutchinson Industries Inc.........F......609 394-1010
  Trenton (G-10942)

AUTOMOTIVE REPAIR SHOPS: Electrical Svcs

Cellgain Wireless LLC...............F......732 889-4671
  Red Bank (G-9223)

AUTOMOTIVE REPAIR SHOPS: Engine Repair

Gamka Sales Co Inc................E......732 248-1400
  Edison (G-2518)

AUTOMOTIVE REPAIR SHOPS: Machine Shop

Metal Specialties New Jersey.......G......609 261-9277
  Mount Holly (G-6732)

AUTOMOTIVE REPAIR SHOPS: Trailer Repair

Richard Shafer.......................G......856 358-3483
  Elmer (G-2802)

AUTOMOTIVE REPAIR SHOPS: Truck Engine Repair, Exc Indl

Robert H Hoover & Sons Inc......G......973 347-4210
  Flanders (G-3417)
Trucktech Parts & Services.......G......973 799-0500
  Newark (G-7303)

AUTOMOTIVE REPAIR SHOPS: Wheel Alignment

Trucktech Parts & Services.......G......973 799-0500
  Newark (G-7303)

AUTOMOTIVE REPAIR SVC

Bruce Kindberg.......................G......973 664-0195
  Rockaway (G-9447)
J & R Rebuilders Inc.................G......856 627-1414
  Laurel Springs (G-5207)
Johnnys Service Center............G......732 738-0569
  Fords (G-3532)

AUTOMOTIVE SPLYS & PARTS, NEW, WHOL: Auto Servicing Eqpt

Blackhawk Cre Corporation.......F......856 887-0162
  Salem (G-9692)

AUTOMOTIVE SPLYS & PARTS, NEW, WHOLESALE: Radiators

Bruce Kindberg.......................G......973 664-0195
  Rockaway (G-9447)
Modine Manufacturing Company.........G......856 467-9710
  Bridgeport (G-741)

AUTOMOTIVE SPLYS & PARTS, NEW, WHOLESALE: Splys

Tabco Technologies LLC...........G......201 438-0422
  Carlstadt (G-1225)

AUTOMOTIVE SPLYS & PARTS, NEW, WHOLESALE: Trailer Parts

M W Trailer Repair Inc.............F......609 298-1113
  Bordentown (G-585)
Overdrive Holdings Inc.............F......201 440-1911
  South Hackensack (G-10178)

AUTOMOTIVE SPLYS & PARTS, NEW, WHOLESALE: Trim

Newark Auto Top Co Inc...........F......973 677-9935
  East Orange (G-2256)

AUTOMOTIVE SPLYS & PARTS, USED, WHOLESALE

Rebuilt Parts Co LLC................F......856 662-3252
  Pennsauken (G-8476)

AUTOMOTIVE SPLYS & PARTS, WHOLESALE, NEC

BMW of North America LLC.......A......201 307-4000
  Woodcliff Lake (G-12049)
Dreyco Inc.............................F......201 896-9000
  Carlstadt (G-1154)
Jrz Enterprises LLC.................G......973 962-6330
  Wayne (G-11526)
M & RS Miller Auto Gear & Prt....F......201 339-2270
  Bayonne (G-228)
P & A Auto Parts Inc................E......201 655-7117
  Hackensack (G-3960)
Volvo Car North America LLC.....B......201 768-7300
  Rockleigh (G-9524)
Wexco Industries Inc..............E......973 244-5777
  Pine Brook (G-8620)

AUTOMOTIVE SPLYS/PART, NEW, WHOL: Spring, Shock Absorb/Strut

Shock Tech Inc.......................E......845 368-8600
  Mahwah (G-5771)

AUTOMOTIVE SVCS, EXC REPAIR & CARWASHES: Glass Tinting

Glasscare Inc...........................F....... 201 943-1122
Cliffside Park *(G-1539)*

AUTOMOTIVE SVCS, EXC REPAIR & CARWASHES: Lubrication

Grease N Go.............................G....... 856 784-6555
Magnolia *(G-5707)*

AUTOMOTIVE SVCS, EXC REPAIR & CARWASHES: Trailer Maintenance

Ashland LLC...........................G....... 908 243-3500
Bridgewater *(G-794)*
Steve Green Enterprises ....F....... 732 938-5572
Farmingdale *(G-3393)*

AUTOMOTIVE SVCS, EXC REPAIR: Washing & Polishing

National Auto Detailing Netwrk ....E....... 856 931-5529
Bellmawr *(G-340)*
T & E Sales of Marlboro Inc ....G....... 732 549-7551
Metuchen *(G-6076)*

AUTOMOTIVE TOWING & WRECKING SVC

Cubalas Emergency Lighting LLC ....G....... 908 514-0505
Roselle *(G-9555)*
J Spinelli & Sons Inc ....E....... 856 691-3133
Elmer *(G-2799)*

AUTOMOTIVE WELDING SVCS

Specialty Measures...................G....... 609 882-6071
Ewing *(G-3066)*

AUTOMOTIVE: Seating

Johnson Controls Inc...................E....... 856 245-9977
Blackwood *(G-472)*
Union County Seating & Sup Co ....E....... 908 241-4949
Kenilworth *(G-4984)*

AUTOTRANSFORMERS: Electric

A C Transformer Corp ....G....... 973 589-8574
Newark *(G-7029)*

AVIATION SCHOOL

Aus Inc ....G....... 856 234-9200
Mount Laurel *(G-6738)*

AWNINGS & CANOPIES

Michael Anthony Sign Dsign Inc ....E....... 732 453-6120
Piscataway *(G-8690)*

AWNINGS & CANOPIES: Awnings, Fabric, From Purchased Matls

Awning Design Inc...................G....... 908 462-1131
Freehold *(G-3651)*
Blacher Canvas Products Inc ....G....... 732 968-3666
Dunellen *(G-2121)*
G & J Solutions Inc...................F....... 609 861-9838
Woodbine *(G-12009)*
Lion Visual Ltd Liability Co...........G....... 973 278-3802
Fairfield *(G-3264)*
Opdyke Awnings Inc...................F....... 732 449-5940
Wall Township *(G-11360)*
Sconda Canvas Products...........E....... 732 225-3500
South Plainfield *(G-10326)*
Shore Awning Co...................G....... 732 775-3351
Wall Township *(G-11369)*
Texas Canvas Co Inc...................G....... 973 278-3802
Fairfield *(G-3326)*

AWNINGS & CANOPIES: Canopies, Fabric, From Purchased Matls

Hudson Awning Co Inc...................E....... 201 339-7171
Bayonne *(G-223)*

AWNINGS: Fiberglass

McBride Awning Co...................G....... 732 892-6256
Point Pleasant Beach *(G-8828)*

AWNINGS: Metal

Asbury Awng Mfg & Installation ....G....... 732 775-4881
Asbury Park *(G-71)*
Hudson Awning Co Inc...................E....... 201 339-7171
Bayonne *(G-223)*
Weathercraft Manufacturing Co ....F....... 201 262-0055
Emerson *(G-2870)*

AXLES

Turbo Solutions LLC...................F....... 856 209-6900
Pennsauken *(G-8494)*

BABY FORMULA

Buy Buy Baby Inc...................F....... 908 688-0888
Union *(G-11034)*
Gerber Products Company ....C....... 973 593-7500
Florham Park *(G-3508)*

BABY PACIFIERS: Rubber

Baby Time International Inc...............G....... 973 481-7400
Newark *(G-7063)*
Doddle & Co LLC...................G....... 917 836-1299
Montclair *(G-6364)*

BADGES, WHOLESALE

Colorcraft Sign Co...................F....... 609 386-1115
Beverly *(G-449)*
Touch of Class Promotions LLC ....G....... 267 994-0860
Voorhees *(G-11296)*

BADGES: Identification & Insignia

Almetek Industries Inc...................E....... 908 850-9700
Hackettstown *(G-3997)*
Aura Badge Co...................D....... 856 881-9026
Clayton *(G-1524)*
Competech Smrtcard Sltions Inc ....G....... 201 256-4184
Englewood Cliffs *(G-2963)*
E-Vents Registration LLC...................F....... 201 722-9221
Westwood *(G-11830)*
G G Tauber Company Inc...................E....... 800 638-6667
Neptune *(G-6879)*

BAGS & CONTAINERS: Textile, Exc Sleeping

A D M Corporation...................D....... 732 469-0900
Middlesex *(G-6090)*
Elements Accessories Inc...................G....... 646 801-5187
Maplewood *(G-5876)*
Philip Papalia...................F....... 732 349-5530
Toms River *(G-10783)*
Shaffer Products Inc...................E....... 908 206-1980
Union *(G-11090)*

BAGS & SACKS: Shipping & Shopping

Fleet Packaging Inc...................G....... 866 302-0340
South Orange *(G-10196)*

BAGS: Canvas

Halsted Corporation...................E....... 201 333-0670
Cranbury *(G-1838)*

BAGS: Cement, Made From Purchased Materials

P S I Cement Inc...................G....... 609 716-1515
Princeton Junction *(G-9063)*

BAGS: Food Storage & Frozen Food, Plastic

Refrig-It Warehouse...................D....... 973 344-4545
Kearny *(G-4896)*

BAGS: Food Storage & Trash, Plastic

Harris Freeman & Co Inc...................D....... 856 787-9026
Moorestown *(G-6527)*
Nova Distributors LLC...................F....... 908 222-1010
Edison *(G-2580)*

BAGS: Garment & Wardrobe, Plastic Film

Basic Ltd...................E....... 718 871-6106
Lakewood *(G-5058)*

BAGS: Garment, Plastic Film, Made From Purchased Materials

Sigma Extruding Corp...................D....... 201 933-5353
Lyndhurst *(G-5677)*

BAGS: Knapsacks, Canvas, Made From Purchased Materials

Lbu Inc...................E....... 973 773-4800
Paterson *(G-8238)*

BAGS: Laundry, From Purchased Materials

Lbu Inc...................E....... 973 773-4800
Paterson *(G-8238)*

BAGS: Paper

Filter Holdings Inc...................E....... 908 687-3500
Union *(G-11054)*

BAGS: Plastic

Allied Plastics New Jersey LLC...........D....... 973 956-9200
Paterson *(G-8134)*
American Transparent Plastic ....E....... 732 287-3000
Edison *(G-2455)*
Apco Extruders Inc...................E....... 732 287-3000
Edison *(G-2458)*
CCL Label Inc...................D....... 609 443-3700
Hightstown *(G-4295)*
Duro Bag Manufacturing Company ....C....... 908 351-2400
Elizabeth *(G-2731)*
Epsilon Plastics Inc...................D....... 201 933-6000
Lyndhurst *(G-5651)*
Ez-Dumpster LLC...................G....... 908 752-2787
Bridgewater *(G-824)*
Freedom Plastics LLC...................F....... 201 337-9450
Oakland *(G-7629)*
Gemini Plastic Films Corp...................E....... 973 340-0700
Garfield *(G-3745)*
Global Direct Marketing Group...........G....... 856 427-6116
Haddonfield *(G-4058)*
Goetz & Ruschmann Inc...................E....... 973 383-9270
Newton *(G-7345)*
Inteplast Group Corporation...........B....... 973 994-8000
Livingston *(G-5515)*
Keystone Packaging Service ....G....... 908 454-8567
Phillipsburg *(G-8558)*
M S Plastics and Packg Co...........F....... 973 492-2400
Butler *(G-1007)*
Trinity Plastics Inc...................C....... 973 994-8018
Livingston *(G-5543)*

BAGS: Plastic & Pliofilm

Ace Box Landau Co Inc...................G....... 201 871-4776
Englewood Cliffs *(G-2956)*
Alpha Industries MGT Inc...................C....... 201 933-6000
Lyndhurst *(G-5639)*
General Film Products Inc...................E....... 908 351-0454
Elizabeth *(G-2742)*
Tiffany Packaging...................G....... 973 726-8130
Sparta *(G-10412)*

BAGS: Plastic, Made From Purchased Materials

A-1 Plastic Bags Inc...................D....... 973 344-4441
Newark *(G-7031)*
All American Poly Corp...................C....... 732 752-3200
Piscataway *(G-8628)*
ANS Plastics Corporation...................F....... 732 247-2776
New Brunswick *(G-6910)*
Basic Plastics Company Inc...........E....... 973 977-8151
Paterson *(G-8147)*
Beta Plastics...................C....... 201 933-1400
Carlstadt *(G-1129)*
Central Poly-Bag Corp...................F....... 908 862-7570
Linden *(G-5332)*
Consolidated Packg Group Inc...........C....... 201 440-4240
Ridgefield Park *(G-9301)*
Craft-Pak Inc...................F....... 718 763-0700
Towaco *(G-10867)*
Dana Poly Corp...................E....... 800 474-1020
Dover *(G-2082)*
Essentra Packaging US Inc...................G....... 856 439-1700
Moorestown *(G-6523)*
Flexbiosys Inc...................F....... 908 300-3244
Lebanon *(G-5261)*

Employee Codes: A=Over 500 employees, B=251-500
C=101-250, D=51-100, E=20-50, F=10-19, G=4-9

2019 Harris New Jersey
Manufacturers Directory

775

PRODUCT

BAGS: Plastic, Made From Purchased Materials

Halsted Corporation ....E 201 333-0670
　Cranbury (G-1838)
Heritage Bag Company ....D 856 467-2247
　Swedesboro (G-10589)
Hershey Industries Inc ....F 908 353-3344
　Hillside (G-4396)
Lps Industries Inc ....C 201 438-3515
　Moonachie (G-6477)
M & E Packaging Corp ....G 201 635-1381
　Lyndhurst (G-5659)
Mercury Plastic Bag Co Inc ....E 973 778-7200
　Passaic (G-8088)
Nexus Plastics Incorporated ....D 973 427-3311
　Hawthorne (G-4234)
Omega Plastics Corp ....D 201 507-9100
　Lyndhurst (G-5668)
Plus Packaging Inc ....G 973 538-2216
　Morristown (G-6694)
Potti-Bags Inc ....G 201 796-5555
　Elmwood Park (G-2851)
Power Bag and Film LLC ....G 908 832-6648
　Califon (G-1033)
R K S Plastics Inc ....G 732 435-8517
　New Brunswick (G-6965)
Source Direct Inc ....F 856 768-7445
　Cinnaminson (G-1486)
Spectrum Plastics ....G 732 564-1899
　Piscataway (G-8716)
X-L Plastics Inc ....C 973 777-9400
　Clifton (G-1741)

BAGS: Rubber Or Rubberized Fabric

Glopak Corp ....E 908 753-8735
　South Plainfield (G-10267)
Mfv International Corporation ....G 973 993-1687
　Morristown (G-6686)

BAGS: Shipping

Flexo-Craft Prints Inc ....E 973 482-7200
　Harrison (G-4174)

BAGS: Textile

Ace Bag & Burlap Company Inc ....F 973 242-2200
　Newark (G-7034)
AMS Products LLC ....F 973 442-5790
　Wharton (G-11850)
Kt America Corp ....F 609 655-5333
　Cranbury (G-1853)
Nyp Corp (frmr Ny-Pters Corp) ....D 908 351-6550
　Elizabeth (G-2763)

BAGS: Wardrobe, Closet Access, Made From Purchased Materials

Katies Closets ....G 973 300-4007
　Newton (G-7348)
Kestrel Closets LLC ....G 973 586-1144
　Rockaway (G-9472)

BAKERIES, COMMERCIAL: On Premises Baking Only

A C Bakery Distributors Inc ....F 973 977-2255
　Paterson (G-8118)
Acme Markets Inc ....E 609 884-7217
　Cape May (G-1091)
All In Icing ....G 973 896-5990
　Stanhope (G-10476)
All Natural Products ....F 212 391-2870
　Sayreville (G-9701)
Alpine Bakery Inc ....G 201 902-0605
　Union City (G-11104)
Auntie Annes Soft Pretzels ....E 856 722-0433
　Moorestown (G-6506)
Aversas Italian Bakery Inc ....E 856 227-8005
　Blackwood (G-460)
Bagel Street ....E 609 936-1755
　Plainsboro (G-8780)
Berat Corporation ....C 609 953-7700
　Medford (G-6020)
Bimbo Bakeries Usa Inc ....D 856 435-0500
　Clementon (G-1531)
Blissful Bites ....G 973 670-6928
　Vernon (G-11157)
Bread Guy Inc ....F 973 881-9002
　Paterson (G-8149)
Calandra Italian & French Bky ....D 973 484-5598
　Newark (G-7080)

Campbell Soup Company ....A 856 342-4800
　Camden (G-1047)
Campbell Soup Company ....G 856 342-4759
　Camden (G-1048)
Carnegie Deli Products Inc ....D 201 507-5557
　Carlstadt (G-1136)
Chocolate Face Cupcake ....G 609 624-2253
　Cape May Court House (G-1109)
Ciao Cupcake ....G 609 964-6167
　Trenton (G-10916)
Cinderella Cheesecake Co Inc ....F 856 461-6302
　Riverside (G-9392)
Conte Farms ....F 609 268-0513
　Tabernacle (G-10618)
Crijuodama Baking Corp T ....G 732 451-1250
　Lakewood (G-5076)
Cupcake Celebrations ....G 973 885-0826
　Columbus (G-1799)
Cupcake Kitschen ....G 862 221-8872
　Mahwah (G-5725)
Del Bakers Inc ....E 856 461-0089
　Riverside (G-9393)
Dell Aquila Baking Company ....G 201 886-0613
　Englewood (G-2896)
Erj Baking LLC ....G 201 906-1300
　Ridgewood (G-9324)
Excellence In Baking Inc ....G 732 287-1313
　Edison (G-2508)
Food Circus Super Markets Inc ....G 732 291-4079
　Atlantic Highlands (G-106)
Herman Eickhoff ....C 609 871-1809
　Willingboro (G-11991)
House of Cupcakes LLC ....G 908 413-3076
　Somerset (G-10001)
International Delights LLC ....C 973 928-5431
　Clifton (G-1642)
J & J Snack Foods Corp ....C 856 933-3597
　Bellmawr (G-336)
J & J Snack Foods Corp ....B 856 665-9533
　Pennsauken (G-8440)
J & J Snack Foods Corp ....C 856 467-9552
　Bridgeport (G-740)
John Anthony Bread Distributor ....G 973 523-9258
　Paterson (G-8225)
Julia Clemente ....G 201 488-2161
　South Hackensack (G-10166)
Just A Touch of Baking LLC ....G 732 679-5123
　Old Bridge (G-7717)
Kashmir Crown Baking LLC ....E 908 474-1470
　Linden (G-5369)
KB Food Enterprises Inc ....F 973 278-2800
　Paterson (G-8227)
Little Falls Shop Rite Super ....B 973 256-0909
　Little Falls (G-5460)
Little Miss Cupcake LLC ....G 732 370-3083
　Lakewood (G-5125)
Livingston Bagel Warren Inc ....E 973 994-1915
　Livingston (G-5520)
Lo Presti & Sons LLC ....E 973 523-9258
　Paterson (G-8245)
Luccas Bakery Inc ....E 609 561-5558
　Hammonton (G-4138)
Mendels Muffins and Stuff Inc ....G 973 881-9900
　Paterson (G-8254)
Minardi Baking Co Inc ....E 973 742-1107
　Denville (G-2048)
Mini Frost Foods Corporation ....E 973 427-4258
　North Haledon (G-7498)
Nan Bread Distribution ....G 201 475-9311
　Elmwood Park (G-2844)
Orthodox Baking Co Inc ....E 973 844-9393
　Belleville (G-305)
Paramount Bakeries Inc ....G 973 482-6638
　East Orange (G-2257)
Pechters Southern NJ LLC ....E 856 786-8000
　Cinnaminson (G-1479)
Portuguese Baking Company Inc ....G 973 466-0118
　Newark (G-7231)
Pretty Lil Cupcakes ....E 201 256-1205
　Harrison (G-4178)
R P Baking LLC ....E 973 483-3374
　Harrison (G-4179)
Rombiolo LLC ....G 973 680-0405
　Bloomfield (G-517)
Scala Pastry ....G 732 398-9808
　North Brunswick (G-7485)
Serranis Bakery ....F 973 678-1777
　Orange (G-7761)
Shop Rite Supermarkets Inc ....C 732 442-1717
　Perth Amboy (G-8533)

Shop Rite Supermarkets Inc ....C 732 775-4250
　Neptune (G-6898)
Shop-Rite Supermarkets Inc ....C 609 646-2448
　Absecon (G-4)
Sibi Distributors ....G 908 658-4448
　Basking Ridge (G-197)
Springdale Farm Market Inc ....E 856 424-8674
　Cherry Hill (G-1416)
Sweetly Spirited Cupcakes Ltd ....G 917 846-4238
　Princeton Junction (G-9067)
Terrignos Bakery ....E 856 451-6368
　Bridgeton (G-774)
Thebgb Inc ....G 917 749-5309
　Paterson (G-8314)
Tri-State Buns LLC ....E 973 418-8323
　Harrison (G-4180)
Y & J Bakers Inc ....E 732 363-3636
　Lakewood (G-5184)
Zenas Patisserie ....G 856 303-8700
　Riverton (G-9405)

BAKERIES: On Premises Baking & Consumption

Aversas Italian Bakery Inc ....E 856 227-8005
　Blackwood (G-460)
Cake Specialty Inc ....F 973 238-0500
　Hawthorne (G-4211)
Campbell Soup Company ....G 856 342-4759
　Camden (G-1048)
Campbell Soup Supply Co LLC ....G 856 342-4800
　Camden (G-1049)
Catering By Maddalenas Inc ....G 609 466-7510
　Ringoes (G-9335)
Del Buono Bakery Inc ....E 856 546-9585
　Haddon Heights (G-4045)
Dina Hernandez ....G 973 772-8883
　Lodi (G-5558)
Dunkin Donuts Baskin Robbins ....G 201 692-1900
　Teaneck (G-10628)
Elis Hot Bagels Inc ....E 732 566-4523
　Matawan (G-5975)
Millburn Bagel Inc ....E 973 258-1334
　Millburn (G-6205)
Minardi Baking Co Inc ....E 973 742-1107
　Denville (G-2048)
Mini Frost Foods Corporation ....E 973 427-4258
　North Haledon (G-7498)
Terrignos Bakery ....E 856 451-6368
　Bridgeton (G-774)
Wenner Bread Products Inc ....C 631 563-6262
　New Brunswick (G-6980)
Y & J Bakers Inc ....E 732 363-3636
　Lakewood (G-5184)

BAKERY MACHINERY

Erika-Record LLC ....G 973 614-8500
　Clifton (G-1616)
Machine Control Systems Inc ....G 732 529-6888
　Jackson (G-4658)
Magna Industries Inc ....E 732 905-0957
　Lakewood (G-5127)
Wilenta Feed Inc ....F 201 325-0044
　Secaucus (G-9829)

BAKERY PRDTS, FROZEN: Wholesalers

Chanks USA LLC ....G 856 265-0203
　Millville (G-6242)
Mini Frost Foods Corporation ....E 973 427-4258
　North Haledon (G-7498)

BAKERY PRDTS: Bagels, Fresh Or Frozen

Bagel Club ....F 908 806-6022
　Flemington (G-3432)
Branchville Bagels Inc ....G 973 948-7077
　Branchville (G-704)
Cambridge Bagels Inc ....F 973 743-5683
　Bloomfield (G-494)
Danmark Enterprises Inc ....G 732 321-3366
　South Plainfield (G-10245)
Delicious Bagels Inc ....G 732 892-9265
　Point Pleasant Boro (G-8843)
Elis Hot Bagels Inc ....E 732 566-4523
　Matawan (G-5975)
Frell Corp ....F 201 825-2500
　Ramsey (G-9144)
Jad Bagels LLC ....G 201 567-4500
　Englewood (G-2915)

Millburn Bagel Inc ....E 973 258-1334
  Millburn (G-6205)
Original Bagel & Bialy Co Inc ....E 973 227-5777
  West Caldwell (G-11669)
S M Z Enterprises Inc ....F 908 232-1921
  Westfield (G-11803)
Uptown Bakeries ....C 856 467-9552
  Logan Township (G-5589)

BAKERY PRDTS: Biscuits, Baked, Baking Powder & Raised

Ecce Panis Inc ....G 877 706-0510
  Carlstadt (G-1155)
Katis Kupcakes ....G 609 332-2172
  Moorestown (G-6532)

BAKERY PRDTS: Biscuits, Dry

Interntnal Bscits Cnfctons Inc ....G 856 813-1008
  Marlton (G-5934)
Mondelez Global LLC ....A 201 794-4000
  Fair Lawn (G-3111)
Nabisco Royal Argentina Inc ....G 973 503-2000
  East Hanover (G-2224)

BAKERY PRDTS: Bread, All Types, Fresh Or Frozen

Angelos Panetteria Inc ....G 201 435-4659
  Jersey City (G-4692)
Del Buono Bakery Inc ....E 856 546-9585
  Haddon Heights (G-4045)
Fragales Bakery Inc ....F 973 546-0327
  Garfield (G-3744)
Prestige Bread Jersey Cy Inc ....D 201 422-7900
  North Bergen (G-7430)
Vieiras Bakery Inc ....D 973 589-7719
  Newark (G-7312)
Wenner Bread Products Inc ....C 631 563-6262
  New Brunswick (G-6980)
Zinicola Baking Co ....G 973 667-1306
  Nutley (G-7598)

BAKERY PRDTS: Cakes, Bakery, Exc Frozen

Ability2work A NJ Nnprfit Corp ....F 908 782-3458
  Flemington (G-3427)
Ahzanis Castle LLC ....G 973 874-3191
  Paterson (G-8128)
Cheesecake Factory Inc ....G 973 921-0930
  Short Hills (G-9866)
Pao Ba Avo LLC ....G 908 962-9090
  Elizabeth (G-2767)

BAKERY PRDTS: Cakes, Bakery, Frozen

Cinderella Cheesecake Co Inc ....F 856 461-6302
  Riverside (G-9392)
Country Oven ....G 732 494-4838
  Iselin (G-4606)

BAKERY PRDTS: Cones, Ice Cream

Chips Ice Cream LLC ....G 732 840-6332
  Howell (G-4533)
Meltdown ....G 609 207-0527
  Long Beach Township (G-5591)
Millstone Dq Inc ....G 609 259-6733
  Clarksburg (G-1522)
Novelty Cone Co Inc ....E 856 665-9525
  Pennsauken (G-8462)

BAKERY PRDTS: Cookies

Caliz - Malko LLC ....G 973 207-5200
  Fairfield (G-3162)
Continental Cookies Inc ....F 201 498-1966
  Hackensack (G-3900)
Fairfield Gourmet Food Corp ....G 973 575-4365
  Cedar Grove (G-1278)
Food & Beverage Inc ....D 201 288-8881
  Teterboro (G-10674)
J & J Snack Foods Corp ....B 856 665-9533
  Pennsauken (G-8440)
J & J Snack Foods Corp ....C 856 467-9552
  Bridgeport (G-740)
Jassmine Corp ....G 848 565-0515
  Clifton (G-1646)
Jimmys Cookies LLC ....C 973 779-8500
  Clifton (G-1647)

Joyce Food LLC ....C 973 491-9696
  Newark (G-7171)
Royal Baking Co Inc ....E 201 296-0888
  Moonachie (G-6487)
Vivis Life LLC ....G 201 798-1938
  Jersey City (G-4827)

BAKERY PRDTS: Cookies & crackers

Bakers Perfection Inc ....E 973 983-0700
  Rockaway (G-9446)
Birds Eye Foods Inc ....C 585 383-1850
  Cherry Hill (G-1346)
Campbell Soup Company ....A 856 342-4800
  Camden (G-1047)
Campbell Soup Company ....G 856 342-4759
  Camden (G-1048)
Direct Sales and Services Inc ....E 973 340-4480
  Garfield (G-3739)
Gerber Products Company ....C 973 593-7500
  Florham Park (G-3508)
John Wm Macy Cheesesticks Inc ....D 201 791-8036
  Elmwood Park (G-2833)
Kitchen Table Bakers Inc ....E 516 931-5113
  Fairfield (G-3252)
Little Falls Shop Rite Super ....B 973 256-0909
  Little Falls (G-5460)
Lo Presti & Sons LLC ....G 973 523-9258
  Paterson (G-8245)
Luna Foods LLC ....G 973 482-1400
  Newark (G-7187)
Mini Frost Foods Corporation ....E 973 427-4258
  North Haledon (G-7498)
Mondelez Global LLC ....A 201 794-4080
  Fair Lawn (G-3112)
Oven Art LLC ....E 973 910-2266
  Hackensack (G-3959)
Silk City Snacks LLC ....E 973 928-3161
  Clifton (G-1720)

BAKERY PRDTS: Doughnuts, Exc Frozen

9001 Corporation ....E 201 963-2233
  Jersey City (G-4680)
9002 Corporation ....E 201 792-9595
  Jersey City (G-4681)
G N J Inc ....F 856 786-1127
  Cinnaminson (G-1458)
J K P Donuts Inc ....G 856 234-9844
  Mount Laurel (G-6772)
Jay Jariwala ....F 908 806-8266
  Ringoes (G-9338)
Lodi Cml Cooperative LLC ....G 201 820-2380
  Lodi (G-5569)
O O M Inc ....G 973 328-9408
  Rockaway (G-9482)
Ram Donuts Corp ....G 856 599-0015
  Gibbstown (G-3799)

BAKERY PRDTS: Doughnuts, Frozen

J & J Snack Foods Corp ....B 856 665-9533
  Pennsauken (G-8440)

BAKERY PRDTS: Dry

Arysta LLC ....G 856 417-8100
  Logan Township (G-5585)
Deep Foods Inc ....C 908 810-7500
  Union (G-11042)
Pace Target Brokerage Inc ....E 856 629-2551
  Williamstown (G-11967)

BAKERY PRDTS: Frozen

A & S Frozen Inc ....E 201 672-0510
  East Rutherford (G-2268)
I-Yell-O Foods Inc ....G 732 525-2201
  South Amboy (G-10134)
J & J Snack Foods Corp ....C 856 467-9552
  Bridgeport (G-740)
J & J Snack Foods Corp ....C 856 933-3597
  Bellmawr (G-336)
Mnw LLC ....E 908 591-7277
  Linden (G-5388)
Nema Food Distribution Inc ....C 973 256-4415
  Fairfield (G-3276)
Rich Products Corporation ....A 800 356-7094
  Riverside (G-9402)
Sugar and Plumm LLC ....G 201 334-1600
  Moonachie (G-6490)
Wenner Bread Products Inc ....C 631 563-6262
  New Brunswick (G-6980)

BAKERY PRDTS: Matzoth

RAB Food Group LLC ....D 201 553-1100
  Newark (G-7244)

BAKERY PRDTS: Pastries, Danish, Frozen

Mardon Associates Inc ....F 973 977-2251
  Paterson (G-8251)
Royal Baking Co Inc ....E 201 296-0888
  Moonachie (G-6487)

BAKERY PRDTS: Pastries, Exc Frozen

Nuchas Tsq LLC ....F 212 913-9682
  North Bergen (G-7426)

BAKERY PRDTS: Pies, Exc Frozen

Mendles Just Bread Inc ....G 973 881-9900
  Paterson (G-8255)
Sweet Potato Pie Inc ....E 973 279-3405
  Paterson (G-8310)

BAKERY PRDTS: Pretzels

A & A Soft Pretzel Company ....G 856 338-0208
  Camden (G-1038)
Auntie Annes Soft Pretzels ....E 856 845-3667
  Woodbury (G-12025)
European Pretzel One LLC ....F 201 867-6117
  North Bergen (G-7404)
Federal Pretzel Baking Co ....E 215 467-0505
  Bridgeport (G-737)
J & J Snack Foods Corp ....C 856 933-3597
  Bellmawr (G-336)
J & J Snack Foods Corp PA ....G 856 665-9533
  Pennsauken (G-8441)
South Jersey Pretzel Inc ....F 856 435-5055
  Stratford (G-10507)

BAKERY PRDTS: Wholesalers

Aversas Italian Bakery Inc ....E 856 227-8005
  Blackwood (G-460)
Bread Guy Inc ....F 973 881-9002
  Paterson (G-8149)
Catering By Maddalenas Inc ....G 609 466-7510
  Ringoes (G-9335)
Damascus Bakery Inc ....E 718 855-1456
  Newark (G-7093)
Del Bakers Inc ....E 856 461-0089
  Riverside (G-9393)
Livingston Bagel Warren Inc ....E 973 994-1915
  Livingston (G-5520)
Lo Presti & Sons LLC ....E 973 523-9258
  Paterson (G-8245)
Luccas Bakery Inc ....E 609 561-5558
  Hammonton (G-4138)
Minardi Baking Co Inc ....E 973 742-1107
  Denville (G-2048)
Portuguese Baking Company Inc ....G 973 466-0118
  Newark (G-7231)
Serranis Bakery ....F 973 678-1777
  Orange (G-7761)
Uptown Bakeries ....C 856 467-9552
  Logan Township (G-5589)
Y & J Bakers Inc ....E 732 363-3636
  Lakewood (G-5184)

BAKERY: Wholesale Or Wholesale & Retail Combined

American Harvest Baking Co Inc ....E 856 642-9955
  Mount Laurel (G-6737)
Amorosos Baking Co ....B 215 471-4740
  Bellmawr (G-327)
Angels Bakery USA LLC ....E 718 389-1400
  Carteret (G-1245)
Anthony & Sons Bakery Itln Bky ....D 973 625-2323
  Denville (G-2031)
Artisan Oven Inc ....G 201 488-6261
  Hackensack (G-3878)
Bimbo Bakeries Usa Inc ....D 732 886-1881
  Lakewood (G-5062)
Bimbo Bakeries Usa Inc ....D 732 390-7715
  East Brunswick (G-2129)
Bimbo Bakeries Usa Inc ....E 973 872-6167
  Wayne (G-11479)
Cake Specialty Inc ....F 973 238-0500
  Hawthorne (G-4211)
Celtic Passions LLC ....F 973 865-7046
  Nutley (G-7582)

P R O D U C T

Cravings ...... F 732 531-7122
Allenhurst *(G-21)*

Creative Desserts ...... G 732 477-0808
Brick *(G-715)*

Crust and Crumb Bakery ...... G 609 492-4966
Beach Haven *(G-255)*

Damascus Bakery Inc ...... E 718 855-1456
Newark *(G-7093)*

Damascus Bakery NJ LLC ...... D 718 855-1456
Newark *(G-7094)*

Dr Schar Usa Inc ...... E 856 803-5100
Swedesboro *(G-10582)*

Feed Your Soul Ltd Lblty Co ...... G 201 204-0720
Kearny *(G-4855)*

Good To Go Inc ...... E 856 429-2005
Voorhees *(G-11286)*

Kohouts Bakery ...... G 973 772-7270
Garfield *(G-3750)*

Mfb Soft Pretzels Inc ...... G 609 953-6773
Medford *(G-6030)*

Mondelez Global LLC ...... A 201 794-4000
Fair Lawn *(G-3111)*

Nablus Pastry & Sweets ...... G 973 881-8003
Paterson *(G-8264)*

Nexira Inc ...... F 908 704-7480
Somerville *(G-10122)*

Northeast Foods Inc ...... D 732 549-2243
Edison *(G-2578)*

Omni Baking Company LLC ...... B 856 205-1485
Vineland *(G-11247)*

Paramount Bakeries Inc ...... G 973 482-6638
Newark *(G-7222)*

Perk & Pantry ...... G 856 451-4333
Bridgeton *(G-769)*

Provence LLC ...... C 201 503-9717
Englewood *(G-2935)*

Spindlers Bake Shop ...... G 201 288-1345
Hasbrouck Heights *(G-4188)*

Tasty Baking Company ...... G 609 641-8588
Egg Harbor Township *(G-2698)*

Tasty Cake South Jersey ...... G 856 428-8414
Cherry Hill *(G-1422)*

Toufayan Bakery Inc ...... C 201 941-2000
Ridgefield *(G-9292)*

Vitamia Pasta Boy Inc ...... F 973 546-1140
Lodi *(G-5582)*

Zaiya Inc ...... E 201 343-3988
Hackensack *(G-3992)*

BALLASTS: Lamp

Amperite Co Inc ...... E 201 864-9503
North Bergen *(G-7384)*

BALLASTS: Lighting

Magnetika Inc ...... E 908 454-2600
Phillipsburg *(G-8560)*

BALLOONS: Toy & Advertising, Rubber

Ansell Healthcare Products LLC ...... C 732 345-5400
Iselin *(G-4593)*

Pacific Dnlop Holdings USA LLC ...... G 732 345-5400
Red Bank *(G-9239)*

BANKING SCHOOLS, TRAINING

Ipjukebox Ltd Liability Co ...... G 201 286-4535
Newark *(G-7158)*

BANQUET HALL FACILITIES

Renault Winery Inc ...... E 609 965-2111
Egg Harbor City *(G-2666)*

BAR FIXTURES: Wood

Pool Tables Plus Inc ...... G 732 968-8228
Green Brook *(G-3866)*

BARBECUE EQPT

Clean Bbq Inc ...... G 732 299-8877
Edison *(G-2479)*

Jarden LLC ...... E 201 610-6600
Hoboken *(G-4458)*

BARGES BUILDING & REPAIR

Monmouth Marine Engines Inc ...... F 732 528-9290
Brielle *(G-907)*

Union Dry Dock & Repair Co ...... G 201 792-9090
Hoboken *(G-4485)*

BARRELS: Shipping, Metal

Joseph Oat Holdings Inc ...... D 856 541-2900
Camden *(G-1072)*

Mauser Usa LLC ...... E 732 353-7100
East Brunswick *(G-2155)*

Williams Scotsman Inc 856 429-0315
Kearny *(G-4906)*

BARRETTES

Bigflysports Inc ...... G 201 653-4414
Secaucus *(G-9753)*

BARRICADES: Metal

Garden State Highway Pdts Inc ...... E 856 692-7572
Millville *(G-6250)*

BARS: Concrete Reinforcing, Fabricated Steel

Eagle Steel & Iron LLC ...... G 908 587-1025
Stewartsville *(G-10483)*

Inductotherm Technologies Inc ...... G 609 267-9000
Rancocas *(G-9162)*

Kenric Inc 856 294-9161
Swedesboro *(G-10592)*

Lusotech LLC ...... G 973 332-3861
Newark *(G-7190)*

New Jersey Steel Corporation ...... F 856 337-0054
Haddon Township *(G-4051)*

Paragon Iron Inc ...... F 201 528-7307
Carlstadt *(G-1197)*

BARS: Extruded, Aluminum

Aluseal LLC ...... E 856 692-3355
Vineland *(G-11186)*

BASES, BEVERAGE

Bluewater Inc ...... E 973 532-1225
Millington *(G-6207)*

Reeves Enterprises Inc ...... G 800 883-6752
New Providence *(G-7016)*

Sensient Technologies Corp ...... E 908 757-4500
South Plainfield *(G-10327)*

BASKETS, GIFT, WHOLESALE

Reeves International Inc ...... E 973 694-5006
Pequannock *(G-8506)*

BATH SHOPS

Hawthorne Kitchens Inc ...... F 973 427-9010
Hawthorne *(G-4223)*

BATHING SUIT STORES

Signal Systems International ...... G 732 793-4668
Lavallette *(G-5212)*

BATHMATS: Rubber

Innocor Inc ...... C 732 945-6222
Red Bank *(G-9230)*

Innocor Foam Tech - Acp Inc ...... D 732 945-6222
Red Bank *(G-9231)*

BATHROOM ACCESS & FITTINGS: Vitreous China & Earthenware

Ginsey Industries Inc ...... D 856 933-1300
Swedesboro *(G-10586)*

Hitrons Solutions Inc ...... F 201 244-0300
Bergenfield *(G-377)*

Lenape Products Inc ...... E 609 394-5376
Trenton *(G-10951)*

Toiletree Products Inc ...... G 845 358-5316
Ramsey *(G-9157)*

BATTERIES, EXC AUTOMOTIVE: Wholesalers

BNS Enterprises Inc ...... G 908 285-6556
Hillsborough *(G-4306)*

Btech Inc ...... E 973 983-1120
Rockaway *(G-9448)*

Enersys ...... D 800 719-7887
Somerset *(G-9986)*

Exide Technologies ...... G 973 439-9612
West Caldwell *(G-11649)*

BATTERIES, EXC AUTOMOTIVE:

Paris Corporation New Jersey ...... D 609 265-9200
Westampton *(G-11788)*

Tocad America Inc ...... E 973 627-9600
Rockaway *(G-9505)*

BATTERIES: Alkaline, Cell Storage

Gogreen Power Inc ...... F 732 994-5901
Howell *(G-4540)*

BATTERIES: Rechargeable

Mizco International Inc ...... D 732 912-2000
Avenel *(G-137)*

Skc Powertech Inc ...... F 973 347-7000
Budd Lake *(G-937)*

BATTERIES: Storage

E Group Inc ...... G 856 320-9688
Mount Laurel *(G-6757)*

Energy Battery ...... G 908 751-5918
Flemington *(G-3439)*

Enersys ...... D 800 719-7887
Somerset *(G-9986)*

Hoppecke Batteries Inc ...... E 856 616-0032
Hainesport *(G-4073)*

Krydon Group Inc ...... G 877 854-1342
Moorestown *(G-6535)*

Maxell Corporation of America ...... E 973 653-2400
Woodland Park *(G-12084)*

Mphase Technologies Inc ...... F 973 256-3737
Clifton *(G-1671)*

Orbit Energy & Power LLC ...... E 800 836-3987
Mantua *(G-5853)*

Pacific Dnlop Holdings USA LLC ...... G 732 345-5400
Red Bank *(G-9239)*

Tocad America Inc ...... E 973 627-9600
Rockaway *(G-9505)*

BATTERIES: Wet

Burlington Atlantic Corp ...... G 732 888-7776
Hazlet *(G-4258)*

BATTERY CHARGERS

Dengen Scientific Corporation ...... E 201 687-2983
Union City *(G-11110)*

Exide Technologies ...... G 973 439-9612
West Caldwell *(G-11649)*

Jsn Holdings LLC ...... F 201 857-5900
Mahwah *(G-5751)*

Mizco International Inc ...... D 732 912-2000
Avenel *(G-137)*

Storis Inc ...... C 888 478-6747
Mount Arlington *(G-6719)*

Timothy P Bryan Elc Co Inc ...... G 609 393-8325
Trenton *(G-10999)*

BATTERY CHARGERS: Storage, Motor & Engine Generator Type

Energy Battery Group Inc ...... G 404 255-7529
Flemington *(G-3440)*

BEARINGS

Bcc (USA) Inc ...... G 732 572-5450
Piscataway *(G-8639)*

BEARINGS & PARTS Ball

C & L Machining Company Inc ...... G 856 456-1932
Brooklawn *(G-914)*

Emmco Development Corp ...... F 732 469-6464
Somerset *(G-9985)*

BEARINGS: Ball & Roller

Accurate Bushing Company Inc ...... E 908 789-1121
Garwood *(G-3779)*

General Dynamics Mission ...... E 973 335-2230
Parsippany *(G-7954)*

Rbc Bearings Incorporated ...... F 843 332-2691
Ewing *(G-3058)*

Rollon Corporation ...... E 973 300-5492
Hackettstown *(G-4032)*

BEARINGS: Roller & Parts

Ingersoll-Rand Company ...... E 856 793-7000
Mount Laurel *(G-6766)*

BEAUTY & BARBER SHOP EQPT

5 Star Industries Inc ....F 862 255-2040
Kearny *(G-4839)*

Ameritex Industries Corp ....F 609 502-0123
Princeton Junction *(G-9051)*

Binex Line Corp ....F 201 662-7600
Fort Lee *(G-3550)*

Boruch Trading Ltd Lblty Co ....G 718 614-9575
Lakewood *(G-5063)*

Cimquest Inc ....D 732 699-0400
Branchburg *(G-628)*

Conair Corporation ....C 609 426-1300
East Windsor *(G-2348)*

Doosan Heavy Inds Amer LLC ....G 201 944-4554
Englewood Cliffs *(G-2967)*

Eaton Corporation ....E 609 835-4230
Mount Holly *(G-6725)*

Esd Professional Inc ....G 212 300-7673
Palisades Park *(G-7773)*

Freeman Technical Sales Inc ....G 908 464-4784
New Providence *(G-7001)*

Hutchinson Industries Inc ....G 609 394-1010
Trenton *(G-10943)*

Kanar Inc ....F 201 933-2800
Carlstadt *(G-1172)*

Krohn Technical Products Inc ....F 201 933-9696
Carlstadt *(G-1179)*

McT Dairies Inc ....F 973 258-9600
Millburn *(G-6203)*

Neilmax Industries Inc ....G 908 756-8800
Edison *(G-2571)*

Quallis Brands LLC ....G 862 252-0664
East Orange *(G-2261)*

Sun Taiyang Co Ltd ....D 201 549-7100
Moonachie *(G-6491)*

Takara Belmont Usa Inc ....D 732 469-5000
Somerset *(G-10079)*

Zycal Bioceuticals Mfg LLC ....G 888 779-9225
Toms River *(G-10806)*

BEAUTY & BARBER SHOP EQPT & SPLYS WHOLESALERS

Lure Lash Spa LLC ....F 973 783-5274
Montclair *(G-6374)*

BEAUTY SALONS

Protameen Chemicals Inc ....E 973 256-4374
Totowa *(G-10847)*

Scories Inc ....F 973 923-1372
Newark *(G-7264)*

BED SHEETING, COTTON

Peel Away Labs Inc ....G 201 420-0051
Jersey City *(G-4780)*

Skusky Inc ....E 732 912-7220
Rutherford *(G-9633)*

BEDDING & BEDSPRINGS STORES

Bedding Shoppe Inc ....G 973 334-9000
Parsippany *(G-7892)*

Hanover Direct Inc ....B 201 863-7300
Weehawken *(G-11568)*

BEDDING, BEDSPREADS, BLANKETS & SHEETS

Chic Bebe Inc ....G 201 941-5414
Tenafly *(G-10661)*

Colonial Uphl & Win Treatments ....G 609 641-3124
Pleasantville *(G-8808)*

Marketing Administration Assoc ....G 732 840-3021
Brick *(G-726)*

Star Linen Inc ....E 800 782-7999
Moorestown *(G-6568)*

Starlight One Corp ....G 862 684-0561
Clifton *(G-1725)*

Sunham Home Fashions LLC ....D 908 363-1100
New Providence *(G-7019)*

United Bedding Industries LLC ....E 908 668-0220
Plainfield *(G-8779)*

White Lotus Home Ltd Lblty Co ....F 732 828-2111
New Brunswick *(G-6981)*

BEDDING, BEDSPREADS, BLANKETS & SHEETS: Comforters & Quilts

Global Weavers Corp ....G 973 824-5500
Newark *(G-7135)*

J&S Houseware Corp ....G 973 824-5500
Newark *(G-7165)*

Sahara Textile Inc ....E 973 247-9900
Paterson *(G-8291)*

BEDDING, FROM SILK OR MANMADE FIBER

Chic Bebe Inc ....G 201 941-5414
Tenafly *(G-10661)*

BEDS & ACCESS STORES

Global Weavers Corp ....G 973 824-5500
Newark *(G-7135)*

BEDSPREADS & BED SETS, FROM PURCHASED MATERIALS

Ackerson Drapery Decorator Svc ....G 732 797-1967
Lakewood *(G-5045)*

Beatrice Home Fashions Inc ....E 908 561-7370
South Plainfield *(G-10225)*

D Kwitman & Son Inc ....F 201 798-5511
Hoboken *(G-4450)*

BEDSPREADS, COTTON

Metro Mills Inc ....E 973 942-6034
Paterson *(G-8257)*

BEER, WINE & LIQUOR STORES

Geislers Liquor Store ....F 856 845-0482
Thorofare *(G-10699)*

K & S Drug & Surgical Inc ....G 201 886-9191
Fort Lee *(G-3566)*

BEER, WINE & LIQUOR STORES: Beer, Packaged

Carton Brewing Company LLC ....G 732 654-2337
Atlantic Highlands *(G-105)*

Headquarters Pub LLC ....E 609 347-2579
Atlantic City *(G-94)*

BEER, WINE & LIQUOR STORES: Hard Liquor

Crescent Bottling Co Inc ....G 856 964-2268
Camden *(G-1055)*

BEER, WINE & LIQUOR STORES: Wine

Cream Ridge Winery ....G 609 259-9797
Cream Ridge *(G-1933)*

Georges Wine and Spirits Galle ....G 973 948-9950
Branchville *(G-707)*

Natali Vineyards LLC ....G 609 465-0075
Cape May Court House *(G-1113)*

W J R B Inc ....G 609 884-1169
Cape May *(G-1104)*

BEESWAX PROCESSING

Frank B Ross Co Inc ....F 732 669-0810
Rahway *(G-9095)*

BELLOWS

Precision Mfg Group LLC ....D 973 785-4630
Cedar Grove *(G-1288)*

BELTING: Fabric

Belting Industries Group LLC ....E 908 272-8591
Union *(G-11031)*

BELTING: Plastic

Brecoflex Co LLC ....D 732 460-9500
Eatontown *(G-2381)*

Dyna Veyor Inc ....G 908 276-5384
Newark *(G-7108)*

BELTING: Rubber

Aarubco Rubber Co Inc ....E 973 772-8177
Saddle Brook *(G-9638)*

Belting Industries Group LLC ....E 908 272-8591
Union *(G-11031)*

Passaic Rubber Co ....D 973 696-9500
Wayne *(G-11540)*

T & B Specialties Inc ....G 732 928-4500
Jackson *(G-4666)*

BELTING: Transmission, Rubber

Polytech Designs Inc ....F 973 340-1390
Clifton *(G-1696)*

BELTS: Conveyor, Made From Purchased Wire

Vis USA LLC ....F 908 575-0606
Branchburg *(G-693)*

BENCHES: Seating

Jcdecaux Mallscape LLC ....G 201 288-2024
Hasbrouck Heights *(G-4185)*

BEVERAGE BASES & SYRUPS

Citromax Flavors Inc ....G 201 933-8405
Carlstadt *(G-1141)*

Origin Almond Corporation ....G 609 576-5695
Laurel Springs *(G-5208)*

Savorx Flavors LLC ....G 908 265-3033
Piscataway *(G-8708)*

BEVERAGE PRDTS: Malt, By-Prdts

Malt Products Corporation ....E 201 845-4420
Saddle Brook *(G-9659)*

Malt Products Corporation ....E 201 845-9106
Saddle Brook *(G-9660)*

BEVERAGE STORES

Greene Bros Spclty Cof Rasters ....F 908 979-0022
Hackettstown *(G-4009)*

BEVERAGE, NONALCOHOLIC: Iced Tea/Fruit Drink, Bottled/Canned

Nirwana Foods LLC ....F 201 659-2200
Jersey City *(G-4772)*

BEVERAGES, ALCOHOLIC: Ale

Geislers Liquor Store ....F 856 845-0482
Thorofare *(G-10699)*

Group Martin LLC Jj ....F 862 240-1813
Newark *(G-7141)*

BEVERAGES, ALCOHOLIC: Beer

Anheuser-Busch LLC ....C 973 645-7700
Jersey City *(G-4693)*

Brix City Brewing ....G 201 440-0865
Little Ferry *(G-5475)*

Bucks County Brewing Co Inc ....G 609 929-0148
Lambertville *(G-5188)*

Cape May Brewing Ltd Lblty Co ....F 609 849-9933
Cape May *(G-1092)*

Cape May Brewing Ltd Lblty Co ....E 609 849-9933
Cape May *(G-1093)*

Carton Brewing Company LLC ....G 732 654-2337
Atlantic Highlands *(G-105)*

Dark City Brewery LLC ....G 917 273-4995
Asbury Park *(G-74)*

East Coast Brewing Co LLC ....G 732 202-7782
Point Pleasant Beach *(G-8823)*

Fizzics Group LLC ....G 917 545-4533
Wall Township *(G-11341)*

Headquarters Pub LLC ....E 609 347-2579
Atlantic City *(G-94)*

High Point Brewing Co Inc ....G 973 838-7400
Butler *(G-1003)*

Hunterdon Brewing Company LLC ....D 908 454-7445
Whitehouse Station *(G-11920)*

Pinelands Brewing Ltd Lblty Co ....F 609 296-6169
Ltl Egg Hbr *(G-5618)*

River Horse Brewery Co Inc ....F 609 883-0890
Ewing *(G-3063)*

Shore Point Distrg Co Inc ....C 732 308-3334
Freehold *(G-3700)*

Tuckahoe Brewing Company LLC ....F 609 645-2739
Egg Harbor Twp *(G-2703)*

PRODUCT

BEVERAGES, ALCOHOLIC: Beer & Ale

Advanced Brewing Sys LLC ....G....... 973 633-1777
Prospect Park *(G-9072)*
Brewers Apprentice The Inc ....G....... 732 863-9411
Freehold *(G-3654)*
Core 3 Brewery Ltd Lbity Co..........G....... 856 562-0386
Franklinville *(G-3636)*
ICEE Company ....G....... 856 939-1540
Runnemede *(G-9606)*
Proximo Distillers LLC ....D....... 201 204-1718
Jersey City *(G-4791)*
Summerlands Inc ....E....... 973 729-8428
Sparta *(G-10408)*
Triumph Brewing of Princeton .....G....... 609 773-0111
Lambertville *(G-5198)*

BEVERAGES, ALCOHOLIC: Brandy

Laird & Company ....E....... 732 542-0312
Eatontown *(G-2408)*

BEVERAGES, ALCOHOLIC: Cocktails

Hoboken Mary Ltd Liability Co .....G....... 201 234-9910
Hoboken *(G-4455)*
Shrem Consulting Ltd Lbity Co..........G....... 917 371-0581
West Long Branch *(G-11721)*

BEVERAGES, ALCOHOLIC: Distilled Liquors

Claremont Distilled Spirits ....F....... 973 227-7027
Fairfield *(G-3169)*
Corgi Spirits LLC ....G....... 862 219-3114
Jersey City *(G-4718)*
Custom Blends Inc ....G....... 215 934-7080
Ewing *(G-3025)*
Ganter Distillers Liabilit ....G....... 609 344-7867
Atlantic City *(G-92)*
Island Beach Distillery...................G....... 609 242-5054
Forked River *(G-3541)*
Prince Black Distillery Inc ....E....... 212 695-6187
Clifton *(G-1699)*
Skunktown Distillery LLC ....G....... 908 824-7754
Flemington *(G-3468)*
White Castle ....E....... 732 721-3565
South Amboy *(G-10142)*

BEVERAGES, ALCOHOLIC: Neutral Spirits, Fruit

Aslegacy Spirits LLC.....................G....... 609 784-8383
Eastampton *(G-2371)*

BEVERAGES, ALCOHOLIC: Vodka

Aslegacy Spirits LLC.....................G....... 609 784-8383
Eastampton *(G-2371)*

BEVERAGES, ALCOHOLIC: Wines

American Estates Wines Inc ....G....... 908 273-5060
Summit *(G-10524)*
Bellview Farms Inc.........................G....... 856 697-7172
Landisville *(G-5205)*
Beneduce Vineyard ....G....... 908 996-3823
Pittstown *(G-8752)*
Brook Hollow Winery LLC ....G....... 908 496-8200
Columbia *(G-1792)*
Cream Ridge Winery ....G....... 609 259-9797
Cream Ridge *(G-1933)*
Dijon Enterprises LLC ....G....... 201 876-9463
Wallington *(G-11384)*
GP Wine Works LLC ....G....... 201 997-6055
Bayonne *(G-221)*
Grape Bginnings Handson Winery.......G....... 732 380-7356
Eatontown *(G-2394)*
Hojiblanca USA Inc ....G....... 201 384-3007
Dumont *(G-2113)*
Hopewell Valley Vineyards LLC .....E....... 609 737-4465
Pennington *(G-8367)*
Hunterdon Brewing Company LLC...D....... 908 454-7445
Whitehouse Station *(G-11920)*
Jersey Cider Works LLC ....G....... 917 604-0067
Montclair *(G-6373)*
Jersey Cider Works LLC ....G....... 908 940-4115
Asbury *(G-65)*
Melovino Meadery ....G....... 855 635-6846
Vauxhall *(G-11151)*
Michelle Ste Wine Estates Ltd .....G....... 973 770-8100
Mount Arlington *(G-6716)*
Monroeville Vineyard & Winery ......F....... 856 521-0523
Monroeville *(G-6353)*

Natali Vineyards LLC ....G....... 609 465-0075
Cape May Court House *(G-1113)*
Old York Cellars ....G....... 908 284-9463
Ringoes *(G-9340)*
Opici Import Co Inc ....E....... 201 689-3256
Glen Rock *(G-3833)*
Petit Pois Inc ....G....... 856 608-9644
Moorestown *(G-6556)*
Plagidos Winery LLC ....G....... 609 567-4633
Hammonton *(G-4141)*
Redpuro LLC ....G....... 908 370-4460
Warren *(G-11428)*
Ripe Life Wines LLC ....G....... 201 560-3233
Franklin Lakes *(G-3630)*
Royal Wine Corporation ....G....... 718 384-2400
Bayonne *(G-233)*
Royal Wine Corporation ....C....... 201 535-9006
Bayonne *(G-234)*
Salem Oak Vineyards Ltd Lbity ....G....... 856 889-2121
Pedricktown *(G-8355)*
Sharrott Wine ....G....... 609 567-9463
Hammonton *(G-4144)*
Southwind Equestrian ....G....... 856 364-9690
Millville *(G-6271)*
Unionville Vineyards LLC ....G....... 908 788-0400
Ringoes *(G-9342)*
Valenzano Winery ....G....... 856 701-7871
Shamong *(G-9860)*
Valenzano Winery LLC ....F....... 609 268-6731
Shamong *(G-9861)*
Villa Milagro Vineyards LLC ....G....... 908 995-2072
Phillipsburg *(G-8579)*
W J R B Inc ....G....... 609 884-1169
Cape May *(G-1104)*
Wagonhouse Winery LLC ....G....... 609 780-8019
Swedesboro *(G-10617)*
Willow Creek Winery Inc ....G....... 609 770-8782
Cape May *(G-1105)*
Winery Pak LLC ....G....... 800 434-4599
Cedar Knolls *(G-1316)*

BEVERAGES, MALT

Sunco & Frenchie Ltd Lbity Co .....G....... 973 478-1011
Clifton *(G-1726)*

BEVERAGES, MILK BASED

Cumberland Dairy Inc...................D....... 800 257-8484
Rosenhayn *(G-9594)*

BEVERAGES, NONALCOHOLIC: Bottled & canned soft drinks

Alkazone Global Inc ....G....... 201 880-7966
Hackensack *(G-3875)*
Beverage Works Nj Inc ....F....... 973 439-5700
Fairfield *(G-3157)*
Beverage Works Ny Inc ....F....... 732 938-7600
Wall Township *(G-11321)*
Bot LLC ....G....... 609 439-1537
Lawrenceville *(G-5224)*
Canada Dry Bottling Co NY LP ......D....... 732 572-1660
South Plainfield *(G-10233)*
Canada Dry Del Vly Btlg Co ....E....... 856 662-6767
Pennsauken *(G-8400)*
Canada Dry Dstrg Wilmington De ....E....... 609 645-7070
Egg Harbor Township *(G-2681)*
Canada Dry Potomac Corporation ....G....... 856 665-6200
Pennsauken *(G-8401)*
Coca Cola Bottling Co Mid Amer ....F....... 732 398-4800
Monmouth Junction *(G-6282)*
Coca-Cola Refreshments USA Inc ....F....... 732 398-4800
Monmouth Junction *(G-6283)*
Coca-Cola Refreshments USA Inc ....B....... 201 635-6300
Monmouth Junction *(G-6284)*
Crescent Bottling Co Inc ....G....... 856 964-2268
Camden *(G-1055)*
Evereast Trading Inc ....G....... 201 944-6484
Fort Lee *(G-3557)*
Foulkrod Associates ....A....... 856 662-6767
Pennsauken *(G-8421)*
Ginseng Up Corporation ....F....... 800 446-7364
Rockleigh *(G-9517)*
Iceberg Coffee LLC ....G....... 908 675-6972
Freehold *(G-3669)*
Increase Beverage Intl Inc ....F....... 609 303-3117
Pennsauken *(G-8435)*
Liberty Coca-Cola Bevs LLC ....D....... 215 427-4500
Moorestown *(G-6537)*
Liberty Coca-Cola Bevs LLC ....D....... 609 390-5002
Marmora *(G-5958)*

Liberty Coca-Cola Bevs LLC ....E....... 856 988-3844
Marlton *(G-5937)*
Mococo Partners Corp ....G....... 347 768-3344
Paterson *(G-8261)*
Push Beverages LLC ....G....... 973 766-2663
Succasunna *(G-10516)*
Snapple Beverage Corp ....D....... 201 933-0070
Carlstadt *(G-1218)*
Two Little Guys Co ....G....... 973 744-7502
Elizabeth *(G-2783)*
Unilever United States Inc.............A....... 201 735-9661
Englewood Cliffs *(G-2995)*

BEVERAGES, NONALCOHOLIC: Carbonated

P-Americas LLC ....C....... 973 739-4900
Whippany *(G-11900)*
Pepsi ....G....... 732 238-1598
East Brunswick *(G-2163)*
Pepsi Cola Btlg Co Pennsauken........G....... 856 665-6616
Pennsauken *(G-8465)*
Pepsi Cola Co ....F....... 609 476-5001
Mays Landing *(G-5997)*
Pepsi-Cola Metro Btlg Co Inc ....F....... 201 955-2691
Kearny *(G-4889)*
Pepsi-Cola Metro Btlg Co Inc ....C....... 732 922-9000
Ocean *(G-7672)*
Pepsi-Cola Metro Btlg Co Inc ....B....... 732 424-3000
Piscataway *(G-8698)*
Pepsico Inc ....E....... 856 661-4604
Pennsauken *(G-8467)*
V E N Inc ....C....... 973 786-7862
Andover *(G-52)*

BEVERAGES, NONALCOHOLIC: Carbonated, Canned & Bottled, Etc

Crystal Beverage Corporation ....G....... 201 991-2342
Kearny *(G-4852)*
Fizzy Lizzy LLC ....G....... 212 966-3232
Jersey City *(G-4734)*
Garden State Btlg Ltd Lbity Co ....F....... 201 991-2342
Kearny *(G-4859)*
Jolt Company Inc..........................E....... 201 288-0535
Teterboro *(G-10684)*
Maplewood Beverage Packers LLC .....C....... 973 416-4582
Maplewood *(G-5880)*
Relaxzen Inc ....F....... 732 936-1500
Shrewsbury *(G-9901)*
Sensbl Inc ....F....... 862 225-3803
Ridgewood *(G-9329)*

BEVERAGES, NONALCOHOLIC: Cider

Melicks Town Farm Inc ....F....... 908 439-2318
Oldwick *(G-7740)*

BEVERAGES, NONALCOHOLIC: Flavoring extracts & syrups, nec

Adron Inc ....E....... 973 334-1600
Boonton *(G-536)*
Advanced Food Systems Inc ....E....... 732 873-6776
Somerset *(G-9942)*
Arnhem Inc ....G....... 908 709-4045
Westfield *(G-11794)*
Asbury Syrup Company Inc............F....... 732 774-5746
Ocean *(G-7656)*
Cargill Incorporated ....G....... 908 820-9800
Elizabeth *(G-2719)*
Centrome Inc ....E....... 973 339-6242
Totowa *(G-10822)*
Citromax Usa Inc..........................E....... 201 933-8405
Carlstadt *(G-1142)*
Farbest-Tallman Foods Corp ....D....... 714 897-7199
Park Ridge *(G-7849)*
Flavor and Fd Ingredients Inc ....E....... 201 298-6964
Middlesex *(G-6116)*
Flavor and Fd Ingredients Inc ....E....... 732 805-0335
Somerset *(G-9994)*
Flavors of Origin Inc ....E....... 732 499-9700
Avenel *(G-127)*
Givaudan Flavors Corporation ....D....... 609 409-6200
Cranbury *(G-1836)*
Givaudan Fragrances Corp ....C....... 973 386-9800
East Hanover *(G-2213)*
Innophos LLC ....G....... 973 808-5900
East Hanover *(G-2217)*
Interbahm International Inc ....E....... 732 499-9700
Avenel *(G-131)*

Kerry Flavor Systems Us LLC ....C...... 513 771-4682
   Clark *(G-1502)*

Kerry Inc ....D...... 908 237-1595
   Flemington *(G-3453)*

Malt Products Corporation.....................E...... 201 845-4420
   Saddle Brook *(G-9659)*

Malt Products Corporation.....................E...... 201 845-9106
   Saddle Brook *(G-9660)*

Mane USA Inc ....C...... 973 633-5533
   Wayne *(G-11532)*

Mastertaste Inc ....C...... 732 882-0202
   Clark *(G-1508)*

Premier Specialties Inc ....F...... 732 469-6615
   Middlesex *(G-6140)*

R C Fine Foods Inc ....D...... 908 359-5500
   Hillsborough *(G-4349)*

Robertet Inc ....E...... 201 405-1000
   Budd Lake *(G-932)*

Savoury Systems Intl LLC ....E...... 908 526-2524
   Branchburg *(G-680)*

Solvay USA Inc ....B...... 609 860-4000
   Princeton *(G-9025)*

Solvay USA Inc ....C...... 732 297-0100
   North Brunswick *(G-7486)*

Takasago Intl Corp USA ....E...... 201 727-4200
   Teterboro *(G-10693)*

Vineland Syrup Inc ....E...... 856 691-5772
   Vineland *(G-11277)*

Wild Flavors Inc ....F...... 908 820-9800
   Elizabeth *(G-2786)*

BEVERAGES, NONALCOHOLIC: Fruit Drnks, Under 100% Juice, Can

First Juice Inc ....G...... 973 895-3085
   Randolph *(G-9178)*

Mosse Beverage Industries LLC ....G...... 732 977-5558
   Bayville *(G-248)*

Tuscan/Lehigh Dairies Inc......................D...... 570 385-1884
   Burlington *(G-989)*

BEVERAGES, NONALCOHOLIC: Fruits, Crushed, For Fountain Use

Limpert Brothers Inc................................E...... 856 691-1353
   Vineland *(G-11241)*

BEVERAGES, NONALCOHOLIC: Soft Drinks, Canned & Bottled, Etc

Bai Brands LLC ....G...... 609 586-0500
   Bordentown *(G-577)*

Briars Usa ....G...... 732 821-7600
   Monmouth Junction *(G-6279)*

Ccbcc Operations LLC ....D...... 609 324-7424
   Bordentown *(G-579)*

Continental Food & Bev Inc ....F...... 973 815-1600
   Clifton *(G-1588)*

Hillside Beverage Packing LLC ....G...... 908 353-6773
   Hillside *(G-4397)*

Keurig Dr Pepper Inc ....D...... 908 684-4400
   Andover *(G-48)*

Keurig Dr Pepper Inc ....F...... 732 969-1600
   Carteret *(G-1258)*

Keurig Dr Pepper Inc ....D...... 201 933-0070
   Carlstadt *(G-1174)*

Keurig Dr Pepper Inc ....D...... 201 832-0695
   Secaucus *(G-9786)*

Keurig Dr Pepper Inc ....D...... 732 388-5545
   Avenel *(G-134)*

Pepsi-Cola Nat Brnd Bevs Ltd ....B...... 856 665-6200
   Pennsauken *(G-8466)*

Shabazz Fruit Cola Company LLC ....G...... 973 230-4641
   Newark *(G-7267)*

Snapple Distributors Inc ....E...... 732 815-2800
   Avenel *(G-146)*

Supreme Manufacturing Co Inc.............F...... 732 254-0087
   East Brunswick *(G-2183)*

Union Beverage Packers LLC.................C...... 908 206-9111
   Hillside *(G-4432)*

BEVERAGES, NONALCOHOLIC: Tea, Iced, Bottled & Canned, Etc

B-Tea Beverage LLC ....E...... 201 512-8400
   Fair Lawn *(G-3089)*

Continntal Concession Sups Inc............E...... 516 629-4906
   Union *(G-11037)*

BEVERAGES, WINE & DISTILLED ALCOHOLIC, WHOLESALE: Liquor

Aslegacy Spirits LLC...............................G...... 609 784-8383
   Eastampton *(G-2371)*

BEVERAGES, WINE & DISTILLED ALCOHOLIC, WHOLESALE: Wine

Petit Pois Corp ....G...... 856 608-9644
   Moorestown *(G-6556)*

Royal Wine Corporation ....C...... 718 384-2400
   Bayonne *(G-233)*

Royal Wine Corporation ....C...... 201 535-9006
   Bayonne *(G-234)*

BEVERAGES, WINE/DISTILLED ALCOH, WHOL: Brandy/Brandy Spirits

Laird & Company ....E...... 732 542-0312
   Eatontown *(G-2408)*

BEVERAGES, WINE/DISTILLED ALCOHOLIC, WHOL: Cocktls, Premixed

Hoboken Mary Ltd Liability Co ....G...... 201 234-9910
   Hoboken *(G-4455)*

Shrem Consulting Ltd Lblty Co ....G...... 917 371-0581
   West Long Branch *(G-11721)*

BICYCLES, PARTS & ACCESS

Hyper Bicycles Inc ....G...... 856 694-0352
   Malaga *(G-5788)*

BIDETS: Vitreous China

Hitrons Solutions Inc ....F...... 201 244-0300
   Bergenfield *(G-378)*

BILLIARD EQPT & SPLYS WHOLESALERS

Pool Tables Plus Inc ....G...... 732 968-8228
   Green Brook *(G-3866)*

BILLING & BOOKKEEPING SVCS

Verizon Communications Inc..................E...... 201 666-9934
   Westwood *(G-11847)*

BINDING SVC: Books & Manuals

A S A P Nameplate & Labeling...............F...... 973 773-3934
   Passaic *(G-8048)*

Action Copy Centers Inc ....G...... 973 744-5520
   Montclair *(G-6356)*

Allegro Printing Corporation ....G...... 609 641-7060
   Galloway *(G-3719)*

American Graphic Systems Inc...............G...... 201 796-0666
   Fair Lawn *(G-3084)*

Ancraft Press Corp ....F...... 201 792-9200
   Jersey City *(G-4691)*

Bar Lan Inc ....G...... 856 596-2330
   Brigantine *(G-911)*

Berk Gold Stamping Corporation.........E...... 973 786-6052
   Andover *(G-45)*

Binding Products Inc ....E...... 212 947-1192
   Jersey City *(G-4704)*

Budget Print Center ....G...... 973 743-0073
   Bloomfield *(G-492)*

C Jackson Associates Inc ....E...... 856 761-8000
   Cherry Hill *(G-1351)*

Cornerstone Prints Imaging LLC...........G...... 908 782-7966
   Flemington *(G-3434)*

Craftsmen Photo Lithographers ....E...... 973 316-5791
   East Hanover *(G-2204)*

Creative Color Lithographers ....F...... 908 789-2295
   Garwood *(G-3783)*

Custom Book Bindery Inc ....F...... 973 815-1400
   Clifton *(G-1595)*

D & I Printing Co Inc ....F...... 201 871-3620
   Englewood *(G-2895)*

D A K Office Services Inc ....G...... 609 586-8222
   Trenton *(G-10929)*

Devece & Shaffer Inc ....G...... 856 829-7282
   Palmyra *(G-7782)*

Fedex Office & Print Svcs Inc ....F...... 732 249-9222
   New Brunswick *(G-6926)*

Fedex Office & Print Svcs Inc ....F...... 856 273-5959
   Mount Laurel *(G-6760)*

Fedex Office & Print Svcs Inc ....F...... 856 427-0099
   Cherry Hill *(G-1361)*

Grandview Printing Co Inc......................F...... 973 890-0006
   Totowa *(G-10831)*

Holographic Finishing Inc.......................F...... 201 941-4651
   Ridgefield *(G-9266)*

Hub Print & Copy Center LLC ....G...... 201 585-7887
   Fort Lee *(G-3563)*

Instant Printing of Dover Inc..................G...... 973 366-6855
   Dover *(G-2090)*

Jersey Printing Associates Inc ....E...... 732 872-9654
   Atlantic Highlands *(G-108)*

Jmp Press Inc ....G...... 201 444-0236
   Ho Ho Kus *(G-4441)*

John S Swift Company Inc ....G...... 201 935-2002
   Teterboro *(G-10682)*

Johnston Letter Co Inc ....G...... 973 482-7535
   Flanders *(G-3414)*

Latta Graphics Inc...................................E...... 201 440-4040
   Carlstadt *(G-1181)*

Lunet Inc ....G...... 201 261-3883
   Paramus *(G-7816)*

Marco Book Co Inc ....E...... 973 458-0485
   Lodi *(G-5570)*

Mariano Press LLC ....F...... 732 247-3659
   Somerset *(G-10022)*

Marks Management Systems Inc...........G...... 856 866-0588
   Maple Shade *(G-5867)*

Metro Bindery of New Jersey ....F...... 973 667-4190
   Nutley *(G-7591)*

Mid State Bindery ....G...... 908 755-9388
   Middlesex *(G-6130)*

Morris Plains Pip Inc ....G...... 973 533-9330
   Livingston *(G-5528)*

Myriams Dream Book Bindery ....G...... 609 345-5555
   Atlantic City *(G-99)*

New Jersey Bindery Svcs LLC ....G...... 732 200-8024
   South Plainfield *(G-10305)*

OShea Services Inc ....G...... 201 343-8668
   Hackensack *(G-3958)*

Pad and Publ Assembly Corp ....E...... 856 424-0158
   Cherry Hill *(G-1404)*

Palm Press Inc ....G...... 201 767-6504
   Northvale *(G-7543)*

Palmarozzo Bindery ....G...... 908 688-5300
   Union *(G-11081)*

Permagraphics Inc ....F...... 201 814-1200
   Moonachie *(G-6483)*

Philip Holzer and Assoc LLC ....E...... 212 691-9500
   Carlstadt *(G-1201)*

Premier Printing Solutions LLC..............G...... 732 525-0740
   South Amboy *(G-10139)*

Puent-Romer Communications Inc ....G...... 973 509-7591
   Montclair *(G-6386)*

R & B Printing Inc ....G...... 908 766-4073
   Bernardsville *(G-443)*

Redmond Bcms Inc ....D...... 973 664-2000
   Denville *(G-2051)*

Roan Printing Inc ....F...... 908 526-5990
   Somerville *(G-10124)*

Royer Group Inc.......................................E...... 856 324-0171
   Pennsauken *(G-8479)*

Scarlet Printing ....G...... 732 560-1415
   Middlesex *(G-6143)*

Scott Graphics Printing Co Inc...............G...... 201 262-0473
   New Milford *(G-6992)*

Sheroy Printing Inc..................................F...... 973 242-4040
   Newark *(G-7271)*

Sonata Graphics Inc ....G...... 201 866-0186
   Secaucus *(G-9816)*

Standard Prtg & Mail Svcs Inc ....F...... 973 790-3333
   Fairfield *(G-3314)*

Star Promotions Inc.................................F...... 732 356-5959
   Bound Brook *(G-607)*

Steb Inc ....G...... 973 584-0990
   Ledgewood *(G-5281)*

Tanter Inc ....G...... 732 382-3555
   Clark *(G-1516)*

Tanzola Printing Inc ....G...... 973 779-0858
   Clifton *(G-1729)*

Tech-Pak Inc ....F...... 201 935-3800
   Wood Ridge *(G-12007)*

Tedco Inc ....G...... 609 883-0799
   Ewing *(G-3069)*

Thewal Inc..G...... 973 635-1880
   Chatham *(G-1330)*

Toppan Printing Co Amer Inc..................C...... 732 469-8400
   Somerset *(G-10088)*

Verni Vito ....G...... 732 449-1760
   Wall Township *(G-11377)*

Westbury Press Inc..................................D...... 201 894-0444
   Englewood *(G-2953)*

P R O D U C T

Employee Codes: A=Over 500 employees, B=251-500
C=101-250, D=51-100, E=20-50, F=10-19, G=4-9   2019 Harris New jersey
Manufacturers Directory   781

BINDING SVC: Books & Manuals (cont'd)

Wilker Graphics LLC ....G....... 201 447-4800
Midland Park **(G-6190)**

Windmill Press Inc ....G....... 856 663-8990
Pennsauken **(G-8497)**

Yasheel Inc ....G....... 856 275-6812
Sewell **(G-9854)**

BINDING SVC: Pamphlets

McCormicks Bindery Inc ....E....... 856 663-8035
Pennsauken **(G-8454)**

BINDING SVC: Trade

Miniature Folding Inc ....F....... 201 773-6477
Elmwood Park **(G-2843)**

BINDINGS: Bias, Made From Purchased Materials

Quick Bias Bnding Trmming Inds ....F....... 732 422-0123
North Brunswick **(G-7484)**

BIOLOGICAL PRDTS: Bacteriological Media

Monmouth Bioproducts LLC ....G....... 732 863-0300
Freehold **(G-3680)**

BIOLOGICAL PRDTS: Exc Diagnostic

A J P Scientific Inc ....G....... 973 472-7200
Clifton **(G-1551)**

Adma Biologics Inc ....D....... 201 478-5552
Ramsey **(G-9134)**

Brainstorm Cell Thrpeutics Inc ....F....... 201 488-0460
Hackensack **(G-3887)**

Devatal Inc ....G....... 609 586-1575
Trenton **(G-10930)**

DSM Nutritional Products LLC ....C....... 908 475-7093
Belvidere **(G-360)**

DSM Nutritional Products LLC ....B....... 800 526-0189
Parsippany **(G-7922)**

Epicore Networks USA Inc ....E....... 609 267-9118
Mount Holly **(G-6727)**

Evotec (us) Inc ....E....... 650 228-1400
Princeton **(G-8945)**

Genzyme Corporation ....G....... 973 256-2106
Totowa **(G-10829)**

Imclone Systems LLC ....C....... 908 541-8000
Bridgewater **(G-833)**

Imclone Systems LLC ....D....... 908 218-0147
Branchburg **(G-647)**

Integra Lfscnces Holdings Corp ....C....... 609 275-0500
Plainsboro **(G-8792)**

Integra Lifesciences Corp ....D....... 609 275-0500
Plainsboro **(G-8794)**

Intervet Inc ....G....... 908 740-1182
Kenilworth **(G-4947)**

Lonza Walkersville Inc ....G....... 201 316-9259
Morristown **(G-6682)**

Medchem Express LLC ....G....... 732 783-7915
Monmouth Junction **(G-6297)**

Novaera Solutions Inc ....D....... 732 452-3605
Iselin **(G-4619)**

Pestka Biomedical Labs Inc ....E....... 732 777-9123
Piscataway **(G-8699)**

Pharming Healthcare Inc ....E....... 908 524-0888
Bridgewater **(G-865)**

Princeton Enduring Biotech Inc ....G....... 732 406-3041
Monmouth Junction **(G-6305)**

Princeton Enduring Biotech Inc ....G....... 732 406-3041
Monmouth Junction **(G-6304)**

Seqirus USA Inc ....F....... 908 739-0200
Summit **(G-10545)**

Soligenix Inc ....F....... 609 538-8200
Princeton **(G-9023)**

Teligent Inc ....F....... 856 697-1441
Buena **(G-943)**

Worthington Biochemical Corp ....E....... 732 942-1660
Lakewood **(G-5183)**

Wyeth Holdings LLC ....E....... 973 660-5000
Madison **(G-5704)**

BIOLOGICAL PRDTS: Extracts

Weiling Yang ....G....... 201 440-5329
Ridgefield Park **(G-9319)**

BIOLOGICAL PRDTS: Vaccines

Merck & Co Inc ....B....... 908 740-4000
Kenilworth **(G-4957)**

Merck & Co Inc ....D....... 908 740-4000
Rahway **(G-9117)**

Organon USA Inc ....G....... 908 423-1000
Whitehouse Station **(G-11930)**

BIOLOGICAL PRDTS: Vaccines & Immunizing

Nathji Plus Inc ....G....... 609 877-7600
Willingboro **(G-11993)**

Seqirus Inc ....G....... 919 577-5000
East Hanover **(G-2238)**

BIRTH CONTROL DEVICES: Rubber

Ansell Inc ....D....... 334 794-4231
Iselin **(G-4594)**

BLADES: Knife

Du-Mor Blade Co Inc ....E....... 856 829-9384
Cinnaminson **(G-1453)**

US Blade Mfg Co Inc ....E....... 908 272-2898
Cranford **(G-1930)**

BLADES: Saw, Hand Or Power

Tooling Etc LLC ....G....... 732 752-8080
Middlesex **(G-6156)**

BLANKBOOKS & LOOSELEAF BINDERS

Black Lagoon Inc ....G....... 609 815-1654
Trenton **(G-10905)**

BLANKBOOKS: Albums, Record

Cutting Records Inc ....G....... 201 488-8444
Hackensack **(G-3902)**

BLANKBOOKS: Ledgers & Ledger Sheets

Newark Morning Ledger Co ....G....... 973 882-6120
Pine Brook **(G-8611)**

BLANKETS: Horse

Clothes Horse International ....F....... 856 829-8460
Cinnaminson **(G-1446)**

Curvon Corporation ....E....... 732 747-3832
Tinton Falls **(G-10710)**

BLASTING SVC: Sand, Metal Parts

Mercer Coating & Lining Co Inc ....F....... 908 925-5000
Linden **(G-5381)**

BLINDS & SHADES: Vertical

Metro Mills Inc ....E....... 973 942-6034
Paterson **(G-8257)**

BLINDS : Window

Uncle Jimmys Cheesecakes ....G....... 201 248-1820
Cliffside Park **(G-1545)**

Worldwide Whl Flr Cvg Inc ....E....... 732 906-1400
Edison **(G-2647)**

BLOCKS & BRICKS: Concrete

Clayton Block Co ....D....... 201 955-6292
North Arlington **(G-7371)**

Clayton Block Company Inc ....F....... 732 751-7600
Trenton **(G-10918)**

Clayton Block Company Inc ....F....... 732 751-1631
Wall Township **(G-11327)**

Clayton Block Company Inc ....E....... 732 549-1234
Edison **(G-2478)**

Clayton Block Company Inc ....F....... 732 349-3700
Toms River **(G-10753)**

Clayton Block Company LLC ....E....... 201 339-8585
Bayonne **(G-210)**

Crh Americas Inc ....E....... 732 292-2500
Red Bank **(G-9224)**

Greenrock Recycling LLC ....E....... 908 713-0008
Clinton **(G-1745)**

Hycrete Inc ....E....... 201 386-8110
Fairfield **(G-3233)**

Paverart LLC ....F....... 856 783-7000
Lindenwold **(G-5446)**

Phillips Companies Inc ....D....... 973 483-4124
Clinton **(G-1748)**

Procrete LLC ....G....... 609 365-2922
Linwood **(G-5450)**

BLOCKS: Acoustical, Concrete

B&F and Son Masonry Company ....E....... 201 791-7630
Elmwood Park **(G-2811)**

BLOCKS: Landscape Or Retaining Wall, Concrete

Blades Landscaping Inc ....F....... 856 779-7665
Mount Laurel **(G-6742)**

Josantos Cnstr & Dev LLC ....G....... 732 202-7389
Brick **(G-724)**

BLOCKS: Paving, Asphalt, Not From Refineries

D Depasquale Paving LLC ....G....... 301 674-9775
Jackson **(G-4648)**

BLOCKS: Paving, Concrete

Creative Pavers ....G....... 201 782-1661
Montvale **(G-6406)**

BLOCKS: Paving, Cut Stone

Cambridge Pavers Inc ....C....... 201 933-5000
Lyndhurst **(G-5644)**

EP Henry Corporation ....D....... 856 845-6200
Woodbury **(G-12028)**

BLOCKS: Roof Ballast, Concrete

GAF Elk Materials Corporation ....C....... 973 628-4083
Wayne **(G-11508)**

BLOCKS: Sewer & Manhole, Concrete

Dunbar Concrete Products Inc ....F....... 973 697-2525
Oak Ridge **(G-7600)**

Vogel Precast Inc ....G....... 732 552-8837
Lakewood **(G-5178)**

BLOCKS: Standard, Concrete Or Cinder

Anchor Concrete Products Inc ....E....... 732 842-5010
Red Bank **(G-9220)**

Anchor Concrete Products Inc ....D....... 732 458-9440
Brick **(G-711)**

Bell Supply Co. ....E....... 856 663-3900
Pennsauken **(G-8396)**

Clayton Block Company Inc ....G....... 732 462-1860
Freehold **(G-3658)**

Clayton Block Company Inc ....E....... 732 681-0186
Wall Township **(G-11326)**

Clayton Block Company Inc ....F....... 609 693-9600
Forked River **(G-3537)**

Clayton Block Company Inc ....F....... 732 905-3234
Tinton Falls **(G-10707)**

Clayton Block Company Inc ....F....... 609 695-0767
Trenton **(G-10919)**

Clayton Block Company Inc ....F....... 609 693-3000
Waretown **(G-11393)**

Clayton Block Company Inc ....F....... 609 597-8128
West Creek **(G-11685)**

EP Henry Corporation ....D....... 856 845-6200
Woodbury **(G-12028)**

R P Smith & Son Inc ....F....... 973 584-4063
Succasunna **(G-10517)**

Reuther Contracting Co Inc ....E....... 201 863-3550
North Bergen **(G-7434)**

BLOOD RELATED HEALTH SVCS

Conduent State Healthcare LLC ....G....... 973 824-3250
Newark **(G-7087)**

BLOWERS & FANS

Aer X Dust Corporation ....G....... 732 946-9462
Holmdel **(G-4493)**

Automated Flexible Conveyors ....F....... 973 340-1695
Clifton **(G-1568)**

Bios International Corp ....E....... 973 492-8400
Butler **(G-996)**

Filter Holdings Inc ....E....... 908 687-3500
Union **(G-11054)**

Fmdk Technologies Inc ....G....... 201 828-9822
Mahwah **(G-5740)**

Hamon Corporation ....D....... 908 333-2000
Somerville **(G-10114)**

Hayward Industrial Products ....C....... 908 351-5400
Elizabeth **(G-2745)**

Indoor Environmental Tech.................E 973 709-1122
Lincoln Park **(G-5299)**

JC Macelroy Co Inc.........................D 732 572-7100
Piscataway **(G-8681)**

Klm Mechanical Contractors...........F 201 385-6965
Dumont **(G-2115)**

Kooltronic Inc...................................C 609 466-3400
Pennington **(G-8369)**

Mer Made Filter................................G 201 236-0217
Ramsey **(G-9151)**

Metropolitan Vacuum Clr Co Inc......D 201 405-2225
Oakland **(G-7636)**

Microelettrica-Usa LLC...................E 973 598-0806
Budd Lake **(G-930)**

Respironics Inc................................C 973 581-6000
Parsippany **(G-8007)**

Science Pump Corporation...............E 856 963-7700
Camden **(G-1086)**

Stamm International Corp.................G 201 947-1700
Fort Lee **(G-3589)**

Tri-Dim Filter Corporation................F 973 709-1122
Lincoln Park **(G-5308)**

Wire Cloth Manufacturers Inc.........E 973 328-1000
Mine Hill **(G-6275)**

BLOWERS & FANS

Creative Industrial Kitchens ....G 973 633-0420
Wayne **(G-11490)**

BLUEPRINTING SVCS

Ahern Blueprinting Inc....................F 732 223-1476
Manasquan **(G-5827)**

All American Print & Copy Ctr ....G 732 758-6200
Red Bank **(G-9219)**

Bellia & Sons..................................E 856 845-2234
Woodbury **(G-12026)**

Comptime Inc...................................G 201 760-2400
Ramsey **(G-9143)**

Professional Reproductions Inc.........F 212 268-1222
Marlboro **(G-5911)**

R V Livolsi Incorporated..................G 732 286-2200
Toms River **(G-10786)**

BOAT & BARGE COMPONENTS: Metal, Prefabricated

Riverside Marina Yacht Sls LLC ....F 856 461-1077
Riverside **(G-9403)**

BOAT BUILDING & REPAIR

A & D Indus & Mar Repr Inc ....E 732 541-1481
Port Reading **(G-8890)**

A PS Inlet Marina LLC......................G 732 681-3303
Belmar **(G-346)**

Barnegat Light Fibrgls Sup LLC........G 609 294-8870
West Creek **(G-11684)**

Carver Boat Sales Inc......................G 732 892-0328
Point Pleasant Boro **(G-8839)**

Commercial Water Sports Inc...........G 609 624-3404
Cape May Court House **(G-1110)**

Costa Mar Cnvas Enclosures LLC.....E 609 965-1538
Egg Harbor City **(G-2656)**

Jersey Cape Yachts Inc....................D 609 965-8650
Egg Harbor City **(G-2661)**

Lockwood Boat Works Inc.................E 732 721-1605
South Amboy **(G-10136)**

Marine Acquisition Inc......................D 609 965-2300
Egg Harbor City **(G-2664)**

Steelstran Industries Inc.................E 732 574-0700
Avenel **(G-147)**

Sunsplash Marina LLC ....G 609 628-4445
Tuckahoe **(G-11014)**

Supply Technologies LLC..................E 201 641-7600
Moonachie **(G-6492)**

Tradewinds Marine Service...............G 848 448-6888
Toms River **(G-10800)**

Union Dry Dock & Repair Co ....E 201 963-5833
Hoboken **(G-4486)**

Yank Marine Inc..............................G 609 628-2928
Tuckahoe **(G-11015)**

BOAT BUILDING & REPAIRING: Fiberglass

Henriques Yachts Works ....G 732 269-1180
Bayville **(G-246)**

BOAT BUILDING & REPAIRING: Lifeboats

Van Duyne Bros Inc.........................G 609 625-0299
Mays Landing **(G-5999)**

BOAT BUILDING & REPAIRING: Yachts

Camp Marine Services Inc ....G 609 368-1777
Stone Harbor **(G-10503)**

Cherubini Yachts Ltd Lblty Co...........G 856 764-5319
Delran **(G-2014)**

Eh Yachts LLC.................................D 609 965-2300
Egg Harbor City **(G-2660)**

Tf Yachts LLC..................................D 609 965-2300
Egg Harbor City **(G-2669)**

Viking Yacht Company......................B 609 296-6000
New Gretna **(G-6988)**

Viking Yacht Company......................C 609 296-6000
Egg Harbor City **(G-2671)**

BOAT BUILDING & RPRG: Fishing, Small, Lobster, Crab, Oyster

D&S Fisheries LLC...........................G 914 438-3197
Colts Neck **(G-1780)**

Norma K Corporation ....G 732 477-6441
Point Pleasant Beach **(G-8829)**

BOAT DEALERS

Carver Boat Sales Inc......................G 732 892-0328
Point Pleasant Boro **(G-8839)**

Custom Docks Inc............................F 973 948-3732
Sandyston **(G-9699)**

Marine Acquisition Inc......................D 609 965-2300
Egg Harbor City **(G-2664)**

BOAT DEALERS: Marine Splys & Eqpt

Fisher Canvas Products Inc..............G 609 239-2733
Burlington **(G-967)**

Oil Technologies Services Inc...........G 856 845-4142
Paulsboro **(G-8336)**

Oil Technologies Services Inc...........G 856 845-4142
Paulsboro **(G-8337)**

Oil Technologies Services Inc...........G 856 845-4142
Linden **(G-5399)**

BOAT DEALERS: Motor

Arnolds Yacht Basin Inc...................G 732 892-3000
Point Pleasant Boro **(G-8836)**

BOAT DEALERS: Sailboats & Eqpt

Colie Sail Makers Inc.......................G 732 892-4344
Point Pleasant Boro **(G-8840)**

BOAT DEALERS: Sails & Eqpt

A PS Inlet Marina LLC......................G 732 681-3303
Belmar **(G-346)**

BOAT LIFTS

Courtney Boatlifts Inc.......................G 732 892-8900
Point Pleasant Boro **(G-8841)**

BOAT REPAIR SVCS

Riverside Marina Yacht Sls LLC ....F 856 461-1077
Riverside **(G-9403)**

BOAT YARD: Boat yards, storage & incidental repair

A PS Inlet Marina LLC......................G 732 681-3303
Belmar **(G-346)**

Riverside Marina Yacht Sls LLC ....F 856 461-1077
Riverside **(G-9403)**

BOATS & OTHER MARINE EQPT: Plastic

A & D Indus & Mar Repr Inc ....E 732 541-1481
Port Reading **(G-8890)**

BODIES: Truck & Bus

Bristol-Donald Company Inc..............E 973 589-2640
Newark **(G-7076)**

Christensen Manufacturing ....F 609 466-9700
Pennington **(G-8361)**

Cliffside Body Corporation ....E 201 945-3970
Fairview **(G-3358)**

Fleet Equipment Corporation ....F 201 337-3294
Franklin Lakes **(G-3623)**

BODY PARTS: Automobile, Stamped Metal

Engine Combo LLC...........................F 201 290-4399
Irvington **(G-4567)**

Tonys Auto Entp Ltd Lblty Co...........G 203 223-5776
Edison **(G-2633)**

BOILER REPAIR SHOP

Edward Kurth and Son Inc................E 856 227-5252
Sewell **(G-9840)**

BOLT CAPS: Vitreous China & Earthenware

Sap-Seal Products Inc......................G 201 385-5553
Bergenfield **(G-384)**

BOLTS: Metal

General Sullivan Group Inc..............F 609 745-5000
Pennington **(G-8366)**

JC Macelroy Co Inc.........................D 732 572-7100
Piscataway **(G-8681)**

BONDERIZING: Bonderizing, Metal Or Metal Prdts

Tresky Corp.....................................G 732 536-8600
Morganville **(G-6596)**

BOOK STORES

Barnes & Noble Booksellers Inc........E 201 272-3635
Lyndhurst **(G-5642)**

Light Inc...G 973 777-2704
Clifton **(G-1659)**

New Horizon Press Publishers ....G 908 604-6311
Liberty Corner **(G-5295)**

Publishers Partnership Co................D 201 689-1613
Ridgewood **(G-9326)**

BOOK STORES: Children's

Apples & Honey Press LLC..............F 973 379-7200
Springfield **(G-10427)**

Letts Play Inc.................................G 856 297-2530
Williamstown **(G-11963)**

BOOKS, WHOLESALE

Behrman House Inc.........................F 973 379-7200
Millburn **(G-6195)**

Bookazine Co Inc............................D 201 339-7777
Bayonne **(G-207)**

Marco Book Co Inc..........................E 973 458-0485
Lodi **(G-5570)**

Sterling Publishing Co Inc...............F 732 248-6563
Monroe Township **(G-6346)**

BOTTLE CAPS & RESEALERS: Plastic

Berry Global Inc..............................C 732 356-2870
Middlesex **(G-6101)**

Berry Global Inc..............................C 908 353-3850
Elizabeth **(G-2716)**

Berry Global Inc..............................E 908 454-0900
Phillipsburg **(G-8545)**

Berry Global Inc..............................C 718 205-3115
Elizabeth **(G-2717)**

Captive Plastics LLC.......................C 812 424-2904
Phillipsburg **(G-8547)**

Newark Liner & Washer Inc...............F 973 482-5400
Newark **(G-7215)**

BOTTLED GAS DEALERS: Liquefied Petro, Dlvrd To Customers

Welding & Radiator Supply Co ....G 609 965-0433
Egg Harbor City **(G-2672)**

BOTTLED WATER DELIVERY

Nestle Waters North Amer Inc ....D 201 451-4000
Jersey City **(G-4769)**

Vivreau Advanced Water Systems .....F 212 502-3749
Fairfield **(G-3347)**

BOTTLES: Plastic

Amcor Phrm Packg USA LLC ....C 856 327-1540
Millville **(G-6226)**

Amcor Rigid Packaging Usa LLC.......D 856 327-1540
Millville **(G-6231)**

Brent River Corp ....G....... 908 722-6021
   Hillsborough *(G-4308)*
Flexbiosys Inc ....F..... 908 300-3244
   Lebanon *(G-5261)*
Imagine Gold LLC 201 488-5988
   South Hackensack *(G-10162)*
Q-Pak Corporation ....E..... 973 483-4404
   Newark *(G-7242)*
Qualipac America Corp ....F..... 973 754-9920
   Woodland Park *(G-12088)*
Setco LLC 610 321-9760
   Monroe Township *(G-6342)*
Shriji Polymers LLC ....E..... 609 906-2355
   Ewing *(G-3065)*
Unette Corporation ....D..... 973 328-6800
   Randolph *(G-9206)*

BOULDER: *Crushed & Broken*

Tilcon New York Inc ....D..... 973 835-0028
   Riverdale *(G-9387)*

BOUTIQUE STORES

Hillarys Fashion Boutique LLC..............F..... 732 667-7733
   Warren *(G-11414)*
Peach Boutique LLC ....G..... 908 351-0739
   Elizabeth *(G-2768)*
Selfmade LLC ....G..... 201 792-8968
   Jersey City *(G-4808)*

BOWLING EQPT & SPLY STORES

Mulbro Manufacturing & Svc Co ....G..... 732 805-0290
   Middlesex *(G-6132)*

BOWLING PIN REFINISH OR REPAIR SVCS

Mulbro Manufacturing & Svc Co ....G..... 732 805-0290
   Middlesex *(G-6132)*

BOXES & CRATES: *Rectangular, Wood*

Arrow Information Packagig LLC ....G..... 856 317-9000
   Pennsauken *(G-8391)*
Boxworks Inc..G..... 856 456-9030
   Bellmawr *(G-328)*

BOXES & SHOOK: *Nailed Wood*

Boxworks Inc..G..... 856 456-9030
   Bellmawr *(G-328)*
T & M Pallet Co Inc.............................E..... 908 454-3042
   Stewartsville *(G-10488)*

BOXES: Corrugated

Ace Box Landau Co Inc ....G....... 201 871-4776
   Englewood Cliffs *(G-2956)*
Albert Paper Products Company..........E..... 973 373-0330
   Irvington *(G-4554)*
Alliance Corrugated Box Inc.................E..... 877 525-5269
   Saddle River *(G-9690)*
Allstate Paper Box Co Inc ....D..... 973 589-2600
   Newark *(G-7041)*
B Spinelli Farm Containers ....G..... 732 616-7505
   Matawan *(G-5968)*
Bell Container Corp ....C..... 973 344-4400
   Newark *(G-7064)*
Bunn Industries Incorporated.............F..... 609 890-2900
   Trenton *(G-10907)*
Dauson Corrugated Container.............F..... 973 827-1494
   Hamburg *(G-4089)*
Delta Corrugated Ppr Pdts Corp ....C..... 201 941-1910
   Palisades Park *(G-7772)*
Delvco Pharma Packg Svcs Inc............D..... 973 278-2500
   Paterson *(G-8172)*
E L Baxter Co Inc ....F..... 732 229-8219
   Ocean *(G-7661)*
Enterprise Container LLC ....F..... 201 797-7200
   Saddle Brook *(G-9651)*
Ferguson Containers Co Inc.................E..... 908 454-9755
   Phillipsburg *(G-8550)*
Georgia-Pacific LLC............................C..... 908 995-2228
   Milford *(G-6193)*
Great Northern Corporation.................G..... 856 241-0080
   Swedesboro *(G-10587)*
HR Industries Inc ....F..... 201 941-8000
   Ridgefield *(G-9267)*
International Container Co ....E..... 201 440-1600
   Hackensack *(G-3932)*
Lanco-York Inc ....E..... 973 278-7400
   Paterson *(G-8237)*

Levine Industries Inc ....E..... 973 742-1000
   Paterson *(G-8239)*
Levine Packaging Supply Corp ....E..... 973 575-3456
   Fairfield *(G-3261)*
McLean Packaging Corporation............D..... 856 359-2600
   Moorestown *(G-6544)*
McLean Packaging Corporation............D..... 856 359-2600
   Pennsauken *(G-8456)*
Menasha Packaging Company LLC ....C..... 732 985-0800
   Edison *(G-2562)*
Orora Packaging Solutions ....E..... 609 249-5200
   Cranbury *(G-1866)*
Packaging Corporation America ....G..... 856 596-5020
   Marlton *(G-5945)*
Packaging Corporation America ....G..... 908 452-9271
   Hackettstown *(G-4031)*
Paige Company Containers Inc ....E..... 201 461-7800
   Elmwood Park *(G-2846)*
Pin Point Container Corp ....G..... 856 848-2115
   Deptford *(G-2065)*
President Cont Group II LLC.................B..... 201 933-7500
   Moonachie *(G-6484)*
Raritan Packaging Industries ....E..... 732 246-7200
   New Brunswick *(G-6966)*
Rfc Container LLC ....D..... 856 692-0404
   Vineland *(G-11257)*
Schiffenhaus Industries Inc.................C..... 973 484-5000
   Newark *(G-7263)*
Squire Corrugated Cont Corp...............D..... 908 862-9111
   Basking Ridge *(G-198)*
Sutherland Packaging Inc ....D..... 973 786-5141
   Andover *(G-51)*
Trent Box Manufacturing Co ....E..... 609 587-7515
   Trenton *(G-11001)*
Trenton Corrugated Products................G..... 609 695-0808
   Ewing *(G-3070)*
US Display Group Inc ....F..... 931 455-9585
   Secaucus *(G-9825)*
Victory Box Corp.................................G..... 908 245-5100
   Roselle *(G-9575)*
Vineland Packaging Corp.....................E..... 856 794-3300
   Vineland *(G-11276)*
Weber Packaging Inc ....G..... 201 262-6022
   Oradell *(G-7748)*
Westrock Rkt Company ....D..... 732 274-2500
   Dayton *(G-1994)*
Woodland Manufacturing Company .....F..... 609 587-4180
   Trenton *(G-11009)*

BOXES: *Fuse, Electric*

Hope Electrical Products Co.................G..... 973 882-7400
   West Caldwell *(G-11653)*

BOXES: *Mail Or Post Office, Collection/Storage, Sheet Metal*

Postage Bin ....G..... 732 333-0915
   Freehold *(G-3689)*

BOXES: *Paperboard, Folding*

Albert Paper Products Company...........E..... 973 373-0330
   Irvington *(G-4554)*
Contemprary Grphics Bndery Inc ....C..... 856 663-7277
   Camden *(G-1054)*
Cultech Inc ....C..... 732 225-2722
   South Plainfield *(G-10244)*
Global Direct Marketing Group.............G..... 856 427-6116
   Haddonfield *(G-4058)*
International Container Co ....E..... 201 440-1600
   Hackensack *(G-3932)*
Interntnal Folding Ppr Box Sls ....E..... 201 941-3100
   Ridgefield *(G-9268)*
Keystone Folding Box Company ....D..... 973 483-1054
   Newark *(G-7173)*
McLean Packaging Corporation............D..... 856 359-2600
   Moorestown *(G-6544)*
Multi Packaging Solutions Inc ....C..... 908 757-6000
   South Plainfield *(G-10303)*
New York Folding Box Co Inc ....E..... 973 347-6932
   Stanhope *(G-10477)*
R J Blen Grphc Arts Cnverting ....E..... 732 545-3501
   New Brunswick *(G-6964)*

BOXES: *Paperboard, Set-Up*

Capitol Box Corp.................................E..... 201 867-6018
   North Bergen *(G-7392)*
Exalent Packaging Inc ....E..... 973 742-9600
   Paterson *(G-8186)*

Global Direct Marketing Group.............G..... 856 427-6116
   Haddonfield *(G-4058)*
McLean Packaging Corporation............D..... 856 359-2600
   Moorestown *(G-6544)*
McLean Packaging Corporation............D..... 856 359-2600
   Pennsauken *(G-8456)*
Ruffino Paper Box Mfg Co ....F..... 201 487-1260
   Hackensack *(G-3968)*
Shure-Pak Corporation ....G..... 856 825-0808
   Millville *(G-6270)*
United States Box Corp ....E..... 973 481-2000
   Fairfield *(G-3336)*

BOXES: *Plastic*

McLean Packaging Corporation............D..... 856 359-2600
   Moorestown *(G-6544)*
United States Box Corp ....E..... 973 481-2000
   Fairfield *(G-3336)*

BOXES: *Solid Fiber*

SA Richards Inc ....G..... 201 947-3850
   Fort Lee *(G-3585)*

BOXES: *Stamped Metal*

Case Medical Inc ....C..... 201 313-1999
   South Hackensack *(G-10152)*

BOXES: *Wirebound, Wood*

B Spinelli Farm Containers ....G..... 732 616-7505
   Matawan *(G-5968)*

BOXES: *Wooden*

Bunn Industries Incorporated.............F..... 609 890-2900
   Trenton *(G-10907)*
Cutler Bros Box & Lumber Co ....E..... 201 943-2535
   Fairview *(G-3359)*
E L Baxter Co Inc ....F..... 732 229-8219
   Ocean *(G-7661)*

BRASS & BRONZE PRDTS: *Die-casted*

Flemington Alumininum & Brass ....G..... 908 782-6333
   Flemington *(G-3441)*
Union Casting Industries Inc ....F..... 908 686-8888
   Union *(G-11096)*
W & E Baum Bronze Tablet Corp.........E..... 732 866-1881
   Freehold *(G-3704)*

BRASS FOUNDRY, NEC

Industrial Tube Corporation ....E..... 908 369-3737
   Hillsborough *(G-4328)*

BRASS GOODS, WHOLESALE

Fortress Graphics LLC ....E..... 973 276-0100
   West Caldwell *(G-11651)*

BRASS ROLLING & DRAWING

Kearny Smelting & Ref Corp.................E..... 201 991-7276
   Kearny *(G-4874)*

BRASSWORK: *Ornamental, Structural*

Bedlam Corp.......................................F..... 973 774-8770
   Montclair *(G-6360)*

BRAZING: *Metal*

Bennett Heat Trting Brzing Inc ....E..... 973 589-0590
   Newark *(G-7066)*
E F Britten & Co Inc ....F..... 908 276-4800
   Cranford *(G-1908)*

BRIC-A-BRAC

Middle East Marketing Group ....G..... 201 503-0150
   Englewood *(G-2926)*

BRICK, STONE & RELATED PRDTS WHOLESALERS

Aladdin Manufacturing Corp.................B..... 973 616-4600
   Pompton Plains *(G-8856)*

BRICKS : *Ceramic Glazed, Clay*

Magpie Marketing Inc ....G..... 201 507-9155
   Rutherford *(G-9627)*

BROADCASTING & COMMS EQPT: Antennas, Transmitting/Comms

Electromagnetic Tech Inds Inc ....D....... 973 394-1719
Boonton (G-550)
Lcn Partners Inc ....F....... 215 755-1000
Berlin (G-426)
Lightning Prvntion Systems Inc ....G....... 856 767-7806
West Berlin (G-11603)
Philips Elec N Amer Corp ....D....... 973 471-9450
Clifton (G-1690)

BROADCASTING & COMMUNICATION EQPT: Transmit-Receiver, Radio

Martec Access Products Inc ....D....... 908 233-0101
Piscataway (G-8688)

BROADCASTING & COMMUNICATIONS EQPT: Cellular Radio Telephone

Cellebrite Inc ....D....... 973 206-7763
Parsippany (G-7898)

BROADCASTING & COMMUNICATIONS EQPT: Studio Eqpt, Radio & TV

EVs Broadcast Equipment Inc ....E....... 973 575-7811
Fairfield (G-3193)
Kaleidoscope Sound ....G....... 201 223-2868
Union City (G-11117)

BROADCASTING & COMMUNICATIONS EQPT: Transmitting, Radio/TV

Myat Inc. ....E....... 201 529-0145
Mahwah (G-5756)

BROKERS & DEALERS: Securities

Stanger Robert A & Co LP ....E....... 732 389-3600
Shrewsbury (G-9902)

BROKERS: Food

BSC USA LLC ....F....... 908 487-4437
Palisades Park (G-7770)
Dvash Foods USA Inc ....G....... 929 360-0758
Mahwah (G-5732)
Ingrasselino Products LLC ....G....... 800 960-1316
Clifton (G-1640)
Lioni Mozzarella & Spclty ....E....... 908 624-9450
Union (G-11071)
Losurdo Foods Inc ....E....... 201 343-6680
Hackensack (G-3940)
Metropolitan Foods Inc ....C....... 973 672-9400
Clifton (G-1668)

BROKERS: Printing

Budget Print Center ....G....... 973 743-0073
Bloomfield (G-492)
Elbee Litho Inc ....G....... 732 698-7738
East Brunswick (G-2139)
Fortress Graphics LLC ....E....... 973 276-0100
West Caldwell (G-11651)
Longrun Press Inc ....F....... 856 719-9202
West Berlin (G-11605)

BROOMS & BRUSHES

Andon Brush Co Inc ....E....... 973 256-6611
Little Falls (G-5452)
Fifty/Fifty Group Inc ....E....... 201 343-1243
Hackensack (G-3913)
Gordon Brush Mfg Co Inc ....G....... 973 827-4600
Franklin (G-3604)
Industrial Brush Co Inc ....E....... 800 241-9860
Fairfield (G-3236)
Keystone Plastics Inc ....D....... 908 561-1300
South Plainfield (G-10287)
Rubigo Cosmetics ....G....... 973 636-6573
Little Falls (G-5466)

BROOMS & BRUSHES: Household Or Indl

Benjamin Booth Company ....F....... 609 859-1995
Southampton (G-10360)
Danline Inc ....E....... 973 376-1000
Springfield (G-10438)
Mw Jenkins Sons Incorporated ....F....... 973 239-5150
Cedar Grove (G-1284)

BROOMS & BRUSHES: Paint Rollers

Charles E Green & Son Inc ....E....... 973 485-3630
Newark (G-7082)
Delta Lambskin Products Inc ....E....... 201 871-9233
Englewood (G-2897)

BROOMS & BRUSHES: Paintbrushes

Silver Brush Limited ....G....... 609 443-4900
Windsor (G-11998)
Spectrum Paint Applicator ....E....... 973 732-9180
Newark (G-7282)

BROOMS & BRUSHES: Street Sweeping, Hand Or Machine

Around Clock Sweeping LLC ....G....... 973 887-1144
Parsippany (G-7882)
Newark Brush Company LLC ....F....... 973 376-1000
Springfield (G-10456)

BRUSHES

Manufacturers Brush Corp ....G....... 973 882-6966
Roselle (G-9563)

BRUSHES & BRUSH STOCK CONTACTS: Electric

Mersen USA Ptt Corp ....C....... 973 334-0700
Boonton (G-562)

BUCKLES & PARTS

Allary Corporation ....F....... 908 851-0077
Union (G-11022)

BUILDING & OFFICE CLEANING SVCS

Professional Laundry Solutions ....G....... 973 392-0837
Newark (G-7238)

BUILDING & STRUCTURAL WOOD MEMBERS

Arnold Steel Co Inc ....D....... 732 363-1079
Howell (G-4531)
Marino International Corp ....G....... 732 752-5100
South Plainfield (G-10299)
Timplex Corp ....F....... 973 875-5500
Sussex (G-10568)

BUILDING COMPONENTS: Structural Steel

Arnold Steel Co Inc ....D....... 732 363-1079
Howell (G-4531)
Badger Blades LLC ....E....... 908 325-6587
Cranford (G-1902)
Burgess Steel Holding LLC ....G....... 201 871-3500
Englewood (G-2887)
Capitol Steel Inc ....F....... 609 538-9313
Trenton (G-10909)
Central Metals Inc ....D....... 215 462-7464
Camden (G-1051)
Com-Fab Inc ....G....... 973 296-0433
Hewitt (G-4274)
Coordinated Metals Inc ....D....... 201 460-7280
Carlstadt (G-1145)
Coronis Building Systems Inc ....E....... 609 261-2200
Columbus (G-1798)
Ddm Steel Cnstr Ltd Lblty Co ....F....... 856 794-9400
Vineland (G-11211)
H Barron Iron Works Inc ....F....... 856 456-9092
Gloucester City (G-3843)
J G Schmidt Steel ....F....... 973 473-4822
Passaic (G-8075)
John Maltese Iron Works Inc ....E....... 732 249-4350
North Brunswick (G-7472)
Park Plus Inc ....E....... 201 917-5778
Fairview (G-3366)
Passaic County Welders Inc ....E....... 973 696-1200
Wayne (G-11539)
Rcc Fabricators Inc. ....E....... 609 859-9350
Southampton (G-10370)
Stateline Fabricators LLC ....E....... 908 387-8800
Phillipsburg (G-8576)
Tri-Steel Fabricators Inc ....E....... 609 392-8660
Trenton (G-11004)

BUILDING PRDTS & MATERIALS DEALERS

Cusumano Perma-Rail Co ....G....... 908 245-9281
Roselle Park (G-9581)
Ironbound Welding Inc ....G....... 973 589-3128
Newark (G-7162)
Newark Ironworks Inc ....F....... 973 424-9790
Newark (G-7214)
Portaseal LLC ....G....... 973 539-0100
Morristown (G-6695)
Precision Multiple Contrls Inc ....E....... 201 444-0600
Midland Park (G-6184)
Precision Multiple Contrls Inc ....D....... 201 444-0600
Midland Park (G-6185)
Superior Custom Kitchens LLC ....E....... 908 753-6005
Warren (G-11433)
Timplex Corp ....F....... 973 875-5500
Sussex (G-10568)

BUILDING PRDTS: Concrete

Flexco Bldg Pdts Ltd Lblty Co ....F....... 732 780-1700
Marlboro (G-5898)
JM Ahle Co Inc ....G....... 732 388-5507
Rahway (G-9108)

BUILDING PRDTS: Stone

Ilkem Granite & Marble 2 Corp ....F....... 732 613-1457
Old Bridge (G-7716)
Interntnal Dmnsional Stone LLC ....G....... 973 729-0359
Haskell (G-4197)

BUILDING STONE, ARTIFICIAL: Concrete

Diamond Chip Realty LLC ....E....... 973 383-4651
Sparta (G-10386)
Interntnal Dmnsional Stone LLC ....G....... 973 729-0359
Haskell (G-4197)

BUILDINGS & COMPONENTS: Prefabricated Metal

Mtn Government Services Inc ....F....... 703 443-6738
Holmdel (G-4509)
Pre-Fab Structures Inc ....G....... 856 768-4257
Atco (G-87)
Walpole Woodworkers Inc ....E....... 973 539-3555
Morris Plains (G-6628)

BUILDINGS, PREFABRICATED: Wholesalers

Benco Inc. ....F....... 973 575-4440
Fairfield (G-3154)

BUILDINGS: Portable

Arrow Shed LLC ....E....... 973 835-3200
Haskell (G-4195)
Edward T Brady ....G....... 732 928-0257
Allentown (G-25)
Everlast Associates Inc ....G....... 609 261-1888
Southampton (G-10362)
Handi-Hut Inc ....E....... 973 614-1800
Clifton (G-1632)

BUILDINGS: Prefabricated, Metal

P M C Diners Inc ....F....... 201 337-6146
Oakland (G-7640)

BUILDINGS: Prefabricated, Wood

Laraccas Manufacturing Inc ....E....... 973 571-1452
Livingston (G-5518)
Marino International Corp ....G....... 732 752-5100
South Plainfield (G-10299)
Sustanble Bldg Innovations Inc ....G....... 800 560-4143
Manasquan (G-5840)
Walpole Woodworkers Inc ....E....... 973 539-3555
Morris Plains (G-6628)

BUILDINGS: Prefabricated, Wood

R H Vassallo Inc ....G....... 856 358-8841
Malaga (G-5789)

BULLETIN BOARDS: Cork

New York Blackboard of NJ Inc ....G....... 973 926-1600
Hillside (G-4418)
R A O Contract Sales NY Inc ....G....... 201 652-1500
Paterson (G-8285)

P
R
O
D
U
C
T

BULLION, PRECIOUS METAL, WHOLESALE

BASF Catalysts LLC ....D...... 732 205-5000
Iselin *(G-4599)*

BURGLAR ALARM MAINTENANCE & MONITORING SVCS

Engineered Security Systems ....E 973 257-0555
Towaco *(G-10871)*

BURGLARY PROTECTION SVCS

Merchants Alarm Systems Inc ....E 973 779-1296
Wallington *(G-11388)*

BURIAL VAULTS: Concrete Or Precast Terrazzo

Bradbury Burial Vault Co Inc ....E 856 227-2555
Blackwood *(G-461)*
Brewster Vaults & Monuments ....F 856 785-1412
Millville *(G-6239)*
Cooper Burial Vaults Co ....G 856 547-8405
Barrington *(G-169)*
Cooper-Wilbert Vault Co Inc ....E 856 547-8405
Barrington *(G-170)*
Creter Vault Corp ....E 908 782-7771
Flemington *(G-3435)*
Delaware Valley Vault Co Inc ....G 856 227-2555
Blackwood *(G-463)*
Di-Ferraro Inc ....E 973 694-7200
Wayne *(G-11493)*
Gravity Vault LLC ....G 732 856-9599
Middletown *(G-6164)*
Maund Enterprises Inc ....G 609 628-2475
Tuckahoe *(G-11012)*

BURLAP & BURLAP PRDTS

Halsted Corporation ....E 201 333-0670
Cranbury *(G-1838)*

BURLAP WHOLESALERS

Nyp Corp (frmr Ny-Pters Corp) ....D 908 351-6550
Elizabeth *(G-2763)*

BURNERS: Gas, Domestic

Carlisle Machine Works Inc ....E 856 825-0627
Millville *(G-6241)*

BURS: Dental

Ss White Burs Inc ....C 732 905-1100
Lakewood *(G-5167)*

BUS BARS: Electrical

M&L Power Systems Maint Inc ....E 732 679-1800
Old Bridge *(G-7718)*

BUSHINGS & BEARINGS

Ivey Katrina Owner ....G 973 951-8328
Newark *(G-7163)*
Oavco Ltd Liability Company ....F 609 454-5340
Hamilton *(G-4119)*

BUSHINGS & BEARINGS: Copper, Exc Machined

Maranatha Now Inc ....E 609 599-1402
Trenton *(G-10955)*

BUSINESS ACTIVITIES: Non-Commercial Site

39 Idea Factory Row LLC ....G 908 244-8631
Flemington *(G-3425)*
Ajg Packaging LLC ....G 908 528-6052
Pittstown *(G-8751)*
Align Sourcing Ltd Lblty Co ....G 609 375-8550
Trenton *(G-10889)*
Atara LLC ....G 916 765-2217
Union City *(G-11108)*
Avyakta It Services LLC ....F 609 790-7517
East Windsor *(G-2345)*
Beseech Ltd Liability Company ....G 908 461-7888
Belford *(G-281)*
Bioalert Technologies LLC ....G 551 655-2939
Englewood Cliffs *(G-2961)*

Buttonwood Enterprises LLC ....G 201 505-1901
Woodcliff Lake *(G-12050)*
Chariot Courier & Trans Svcs ....F 888 532-9125
Sayreville *(G-9704)*
Cherri Stone Interactive LLC ....G 844 843-7765
Lakewood *(G-5069)*
Cloudageit Ltd Liability Co ....G 888 205-4128
North Brunswick *(G-7463)*
Commeatus LLC ....F 847 772-5314
Plainsboro *(G-8782)*
Creative Products Inc ....D 732 614-9035
Long Branch *(G-5596)*
Defined Pro Machining LLC ....G 973 891-1038
Wharton *(G-11855)*
Dengen Scientific Corporation ....E 201 687-2983
Union City *(G-11110)*
Docbox Solutions Ltd Lblty Co ....G 201 650-0970
Montclair *(G-6363)*
Durabrite Ltg Solutions LLC ....G 201 915-0555
Jersey City *(G-4729)*
Eagle Steel & Iron LLC ....G 908 587-1025
Stewartsville *(G-10483)*
East Coast Salt Dist Inc ....G 732 833-2973
Jackson *(G-4654)*
Effexoft Inc ....G 732 221-3642
Somerset *(G-9984)*
Energy Tracking LLC ....G 973 448-8660
Flanders *(G-3408)*
Fan of Word ....G 201 341-5474
South Orange *(G-10195)*
Fioplex ....G 856 689-7213
Swedesboro *(G-10585)*
Frameware Inc ....F 800 582-5608
Fairfield *(G-3207)*
Fred S Burroughs North Jersey ....D 908 850-8773
Hackettstown *(G-4008)*
Froyo Skyview LLC ....G 718 607-5656
Jersey City *(G-4741)*
Goldens Inc ....G 215 850-2512
Haddonfield *(G-4059)*
Gpschartscom ....G 609 226-8842
Ventnor City *(G-11153)*
Hangsterfers Laboratories ....E 856 468-0216
West Deptford *(G-11702)*
Inter Rep Associates Inc ....G 609 465-0077
Cape May Court House *(G-1111)*
Internet-Sales USA Corporation ....G 775 468-8379
Rockaway *(G-9467)*
JI Packaging Group Corp ....G 609 610-0286
Pennington *(G-8368)*
Levomed Inc ....G 908 359-4804
Somerset *(G-10015)*
M D Laboratory Supplies Inc ....G 732 322-0773
Franklin Park *(G-3635)*
M2 Electric LLC ....F 973 770-4596
Mine Hill *(G-6273)*
Master Strap LLC ....G 888 503-7779
Marlboro *(G-5904)*
Mobile Intelligent Alerts Inc ....G 201 410-5324
Holmdel *(G-4507)*
Mplayer Entertainment LLC ....G 302 229-3034
Cherry Hill *(G-1396)*
Nickos Construction Inc ....F 267 240-3997
Sicklerville *(G-9913)*
Njiw Limited Liability Company ....G 201 355-2955
Hackensack *(G-3954)*
Noshpeak LLC ....F 978 631-7662
Bloomfield *(G-512)*
Oncode-Med Inc ....G 908 998-3647
Basking Ridge *(G-194)*
Procrete LLC ....G 609 365-2922
Linwood *(G-5450)*
Quallis Brands LLC ....G 862 252-0664
East Orange *(G-2261)*
Scimar Technologies LLC ....G 609 208-1796
Allentown *(G-31)*
Shrem Consulting Ltd Lblty Co ....G 917 371-0581
West Long Branch *(G-11721)*
Sight2site Media LLC ....G 856 637-2479
Pomona *(G-8849)*
Sima S Enterprises LLC ....G 877 223-7639
Wall Township *(G-11370)*
Ssam Sports Inc ....G 917 553-0596
Allendale *(G-15)*
Strivr Inc ....G 973 216-7379
Livingston *(G-5542)*
Tap Into LLC ....G 908 370-1158
New Providence *(G-7020)*
Tonymacx86 LLC ....G 973 584-5273
Ledgewood *(G-5283)*

Trim and Tassels LLC ....G 973 808-1566
Fairfield *(G-3333)*
Ultimate Spinning Turning Corp ....G 201 372-9740
Moonachie *(G-6495)*
Umbrella & Chairs LLC ....G 973 284-1240
Englewood *(G-2949)*
United Cabinet Works LLC ....G 917 686-3395
Secaucus *(G-9824)*
Urban State ....G 646 836-4311
Hillside *(G-4435)*
Venture App LLC ....G 908 644-3985
Summit *(G-10553)*
Vu Sound Incorporated ....F 215 990-2864
Lumberton *(G-5638)*
Wittich Bros Marine Inc ....E 732 722-8656
Manasquan *(G-5844)*
Zestos Foods LLC ....G 888 407-5852
Teaneck *(G-10657)*
Zoluu LLC ....G 862 686-1774
Fair Lawn *(G-3131)*

BUSINESS FORMS WHOLESALERS

Berry Business Procedure Co ....G 908 272-6464
Cranford *(G-1903)*
Drew & Rogers Inc ....E 973 575-6210
Fairfield *(G-3187)*
Important Papers Inc ....G 856 751-4544
Cherry Hill *(G-1376)*
Peter Morley LLC ....G 732 264-0010
Hazlet *(G-4269)*
Service Data Corp Inc ....G 908 522-0020
Summit *(G-10546)*
Stewart Business Forms Inc ....F 856 768-2011
Blackwood *(G-481)*

BUSINESS FORMS: Printed, Manifold

Drew & Rogers Inc ....E 973 575-6210
Fairfield *(G-3187)*
Hygrade Business Group Inc ....E 800 836-7714
Secaucus *(G-9781)*
Infoseal LLC ....D 201 569-4500
Englewood *(G-2913)*
North Eastern Business Forms ....G 609 392-1161
Trenton *(G-10967)*
Snap Set Specialists Inc ....G 856 629-9552
Williamstown *(G-11978)*
Stewart Business Forms Inc ....F 856 768-2011
Blackwood *(G-481)*
Taylor Communications Inc ....D 732 560-3410
Somerset *(G-10081)*
Watonka Printing Inc ....G 732 974-8878
Belmar *(G-356)*
Webb Press ....G 609 386-0100
Burlington *(G-992)*

BUSINESS MACHINE REPAIR, ELECTRIC

Cummins - Allison Corp ....G 201 791-2394
Elmwood Park *(G-2819)*
J K Office Machine Inc ....G 908 273-8811
Berkeley Heights *(G-402)*

BUSINESS SUPPORT SVCS

Co-Co Collaborative LLC ....G 917 685-5547
Short Hills *(G-9867)*
SA Bendheim Ltd ....E 973 471-1733
Wayne *(G-11550)*

BUTTONS

Mona Slide Fasteners Inc ....E 718 325-7700
Belleville *(G-303)*

CABINETS & CASES: Show, Display & Storage, Exc Wood

Atlantic Coast Woodwork Inc ....G 609 294-2478
Ltl Egg Hbr *(G-5613)*
Custom Creations ....G 201 651-9676
Oakland *(G-7622)*

CABINETS: Bathroom Vanities, Wood

A R Bothers Woodworking Inc ....E 908 725-2891
Somerville *(G-10099)*
Frank Burton & Sons Inc ....G 856 455-1202
Bridgeton *(G-758)*
Intelco ....E 856 384-8562
Paulsboro *(G-8332)*

Kinzee Industries Inc ....F 201 408-4301
  Englewood *(G-2916)*
Lexora Inc ....G 855 453-9672
  Newark *(G-7179)*

CABINETS: Entertainment

Bernard Miller Fabricators ....G 856 541-9499
  Camden *(G-1041)*
L&W Audio/Video Inc ....G 212 980-2862
  Hoboken *(G-4463)*
Parsons Cabinets Inc ....G 973 279-4954
  Montclair *(G-6383)*

CABINETS: Entertainment Units, Household, Wood

Imagine Audio LLC ....G 856 488-1466
  Cherry Hill *(G-1375)*

CABINETS: Factory

Acorn Industry Inc ....F 732 536-6256
  Englishtown *(G-2999)*
Modernlinefurniture Inc ....E 908 486-0200
  Linden *(G-5389)*
Universal Interlock Corp ....G 732 818-8484
  Toms River *(G-10801)*
West Hudson Lumber & Mllwk Co ....G 201 991-7191
  Kearny *(G-4904)*

CABINETS: Kitchen, Metal

Rumsons Kitchens Inc ....G 732 842-1810
  Rumson *(G-9603)*

CABINETS: Kitchen, Wood

10-31 Incorporated ....E 908 496-4946
  Columbia *(G-1791)*
A & J Carpets Inc ....G 856 227-1753
  Blackwood *(G-458)*
A W Ross Inc ....F 973 471-5900
  Passaic *(G-8049)*
Alkon Signature Inc ....G 917 716-9137
  Linden *(G-5319)*
Allen Cabinets and Millwork ....G 973 694-0665
  Pequannock *(G-8503)*
Bcg Marble Gran Fabricators Co ....F 201 343-8487
  Hackensack *(G-3882)*
Bebus Cabinetry LLC ....G 201 729-9300
  Rutherford *(G-9615)*
Bennett Cabinets ....G 732 548-1616
  Edison *(G-2467)*
Bernard Miller Fabricators ....G 856 541-9499
  Camden *(G-1041)*
Capra Custom Cabinetry ....G 908 797-9848
  Washington *(G-11444)*
Castle Woodcraft Assoc LLC ....F 732 349-1519
  Pine Beach *(G-8582)*
Certified Cabinet Corp ....G 732 741-0755
  Marlboro *(G-5893)*
Choice Cabinetry LLC ....E 908 707-8801
  Somerville *(G-10106)*
CPB Inc ....E 856 697-2700
  Buena *(G-939)*
Custom Cabinets By Jim Bucko ....G 609 522-6646
  Wildwood *(G-11943)*
Custom Wood Furniture Inc ....F 973 579-4880
  Newton *(G-7340)*
David Leiz Custom Woodwork ....G 908 486-1533
  Linden *(G-5342)*
Designer Kitchens ....F 732 370-5500
  Jackson *(G-4650)*
Dream Cabinetry ....G 732 806-8444
  Lakewood *(G-5086)*
Elite Cabinetry Corp ....G 973 583-0194
  Newark *(G-7114)*
Empire Industries Inc ....D 973 279-2050
  Paterson *(G-8183)*
Eppley Building & Design Inc ....E 973 636-9499
  Hawthorne *(G-4217)*
F L Feldman Associates ....F 732 776-8544
  Asbury Park *(G-76)*
Fabuwood Cabinetry Corp ....A 201 432-6555
  Newark *(G-7121)*
Fernandes Custom Cabinets ....G 732 446-2829
  Manalapan *(G-5810)*
Foley-Waite Associates Inc ....F 908 298-0700
  Kenilworth *(G-4941)*
Forman Industries Inc ....D 732 727-8100
  Old Bridge *(G-7715)*

Franks Cabinet Shop Inc ....G 908 658-4396
  Pluckemin *(G-8822)*
G & M Custom Formica Work ....G 732 888-0360
  Keyport *(G-5000)*
Gemcraft Inc ....G 732 449-8944
  Belmar *(G-349)*
Hanssem ....G 732 425-7695
  Edison *(G-2527)*
Hutchinson Cabinets ....E 856 468-5500
  Sewell *(G-9845)*
Ideal Kitchens Inc ....F 732 295-2780
  Point Pleasant Beach *(G-8824)*
J & R Custom Woodworking Inc ....G 973 625-4114
  Denville *(G-2041)*
John Canary Custom Wdwkg Inc ....F 908 851-2894
  Union *(G-11067)*
Kasanova Inc ....G 201 368-8400
  Wood Ridge *(G-12003)*
Ken Bauer Inc ....E 201 664-6881
  Hillsdale *(G-4368)*
Kenneth Asmar Custom Interiors ....G 732 544-6137
  Tinton Falls *(G-10721)*
Kerk Cabinetry LLC ....G 856 881-4213
  Glassboro *(G-3813)*
Kitchen and More Inc ....F 908 272-3388
  Cranford *(G-1914)*
Kitchen Crafters Plus ....G 732 566-7995
  Matawan *(G-5979)*
Kitchen Direct Inc ....G 908 359-1188
  Hillsborough *(G-4337)*
Kitchen King Inc ....F 732 341-9660
  Toms River *(G-10772)*
Kobolak & Son Inc ....G 856 829-6106
  Cinnaminson *(G-1468)*
L&W Audio/Video Inc ....G 212 980-2862
  Hoboken *(G-4463)*
M C M Custom Furniture Inc ....G 908 523-1666
  Linden *(G-5378)*
M K Woodworking Inc ....G 609 771-1350
  Ewing *(G-3044)*
Marte Cabinets Countertops LLC ....G 973 525-9502
  Passaic *(G-8085)*
Masterpiece Kitchens Inc ....G 609 518-7887
  Cherry Hill *(G-1390)*
Merlyn Cabinetry LLC ....G 908 583-6950
  Linden *(G-5382)*
Michael Lubrich ....G 732 223-4235
  Manasquan *(G-5834)*
Michaels Cabinet Connection ....G 609 889-6611
  Rio Grande *(G-9356)*
Millner Kitchens Inc ....G 609 890-7300
  Hamilton *(G-4117)*
Mk Wood Inc ....G 973 450-5110
  Belleville *(G-302)*
Mp Custom FL LLC ....F 973 417-2288
  Wayne *(G-11535)*
Mr Pauls Custom Cabinets ....G 732 528-9427
  Manasquan *(G-5835)*
Oberg & Lindquist Corp ....E 201 664-1300
  Westwood *(G-11836)*
Palumbo Millwork Inc ....G 732 938-3266
  Wall Township *(G-11361)*
Parsons Cabinets Inc ....G 973 279-4954
  Montclair *(G-6383)*
Paul Burkhardt & Sons Inc ....G 856 435-2020
  Lindenwold *(G-5445)*
Paul Fago Cabinet Making Inc ....G 856 384-0496
  Woodbury *(G-12035)*
Platinum Designs LLC ....G 908 782-4010
  Flemington *(G-3459)*
Platon Interiors ....G 201 567-5533
  Englewood *(G-2932)*
R & M Manufacturing Inc ....G 609 495-8032
  Monroe Township *(G-6341)*
Regency Cabinetry LLC ....G 732 363-5630
  Lakewood *(G-5152)*
Regency Cabinetry LLC ....F 732 363-5630
  Lakewood *(G-5153)*
Regent Cabinets LLC ....E 732 363-5630
  Parsippany *(G-8006)*
Royal Cabinet Company Inc ....G 908 203-8000
  Bound Brook *(G-605)*
Salernos Kitchen Cabinets ....E 201 794-1990
  Saddle Brook *(G-9676)*
Sandkamp Woodworks LLC ....G 201 200-0101
  Jersey City *(G-4804)*
Shearman Cabinets ....G 973 677-0071
  East Orange *(G-2263)*
Shekia Group LLC ....G 732 372-7668
  Edison *(G-2608)*

St Martin Cabinetry Inc ....G 732 902-6020
  Edison *(G-2619)*
Studio L Contracting LLC ....G 201 837-1650
  Hackensack *(G-3980)*
Superior Custom Kitchens LLC ....E 908 753-6005
  Warren *(G-11433)*
Theberge Cabinets Inc ....G 201 941-1141
  Fairview *(G-3370)*
Tsg LLC ....G 732 372-7668
  Edison *(G-2634)*
United Cabinet Works LLC ....G 917 686-3395
  Secaucus *(G-9824)*
Visual Architectural Designs ....F 908 754-3000
  South Plainfield *(G-10342)*
Vitillo & Sons Inc ....F 732 886-1393
  Lakewood *(G-5177)*

CABINETS: Office, Wood

Arnold Desks Inc ....E 908 686-5656
  Irvington *(G-4557)*
Atlantic Coast Woodwork Inc ....G 609 294-2478
  Ltl Egg Hbr *(G-5613)*
Kitchens By Frank Inc ....G 732 364-1343
  Toms River *(G-10773)*
Pemco Dental Corporation ....E 800 526-4170
  Springfield *(G-10459)*

CABINETS: Show, Display, Etc, Wood, Exc Refrigerated

10-31 Incorporated ....E 908 496-4946
  Columbia *(G-1791)*
Afina Corporation ....E 973 684-7650
  Paterson *(G-8127)*
Costa Custom Cabinets Inc ....F 973 429-7004
  Bloomfield *(G-499)*
CPB Inc ....E 856 697-2700
  Buena *(G-939)*
Showtech Inc ....G 973 249-6336
  Clifton *(G-1717)*

CABLE & OTHER PAY TELEVISION DISTRIBUTION

T V L Associates Inc ....G 973 790-6766
  Wayne *(G-11555)*

CABLE & PAY TELEVISION SVCS: Closed Circuit

Absolute Protective Systems ....E 732 287-4500
  Piscataway *(G-8624)*

CABLE & PAY TELEVISION SVCS: Direct Broadcast Satellite

DMJ and Associates Inc ....E 732 613-7867
  Sayreville *(G-9708)*

CABLE TELEVISION PRDTS

Antronix Inc ....E 609 860-0160
  Cranbury *(G-1812)*
Cabletenna Corp ....G 609 395-9400
  Cranbury *(G-1818)*
Mediabridge Products LLC ....E 856 216-8222
  Cherry Hill *(G-1392)*

CABLE: Coaxial

Flexco Microwave Inc ....E 908 835-1720
  Port Murray *(G-8883)*
Harris Driver Co ....G 973 267-8100
  Morristown *(G-6668)*
Wire Fabricators & Insulators ....E 973 768-2839
  Livingston *(G-5549)*

CABLE: Fiber

Contemporary Cabling Company ....G 732 382-5064
  Clark *(G-1496)*
Dun-Rite Communications Inc ....G 201 444-0080
  Mahwah *(G-5731)*
Huber+suhner Astrolab Inc ....E 732 560-3800
  Warren *(G-11416)*
Motion Control Tech Inc ....F 973 361-2226
  Dover *(G-2098)*
Newtech Group Corp ....G 732 355-0392
  Kendall Park *(G-4919)*

PRODUCT

CABLE: Fiber Optic

AFL Telecommunications Inc ....E 908 707-9500
  Bridgewater *(G-782)*
AT&T Technologies Inc ....A 201 771-2000
  Berkeley Heights *(G-389)*
Aw Machinery LLC ....F 973 882-3223
  Fairfield *(G-3149)*
Computer Crafts Inc ....C 973 423-3500
  Hawthorne *(G-4214)*
Ofs Fitel LLC ....E 732 748-7409
  Somerset *(G-10043)*
Sensors Unlimited Inc ....D 609 333-8000
  Princeton *(G-9020)*
Vytran LLC ....E 732 972-2880
  Morganville *(G-6599)*

CABLE: Nonferrous, Shipboard

Alpha Wire Corporation.......................C 908 925-8000
  Elizabeth *(G-2709)*

CABLE: Noninsulated

Alpine Group Inc ....B 201 549-4400
  East Rutherford *(G-2269)*
Gentek Inc..C 973 515-0900
  Parsippany *(G-7956)*
Jersey Strand & Cable Inc..................D 908 213-9350
  Phillipsburg *(G-8557)*

CABLE: Ropes & Fiber

Steelstran Industries Inc ....E 732 574-0700
  Avenel *(G-147)*

CABLE: Steel, Insulated Or Armored

Arca Industrial Inc...............................G 732 339-0450
  East Windsor *(G-2336)*
Bergen Cable Technology LLC............E 973 276-9596
  Fairfield *(G-3155)*
Kabel N Elettrotek Amer Inc...............G 973 265-0850
  Parsippany *(G-7969)*
Okonite Company Inc ....C 201 825-0300
  Ramsey *(G-9154)*
US Wire & Cable Corporation ....B 973 824-5530
  Newark *(G-7310)*
Wire Fabricators & Insulators.............E 973 768-2839
  Livingston *(G-5549)*

CAFFEINE & DERIVATIVES

Certified Processing Corp....................G 973 923-5200
  Hillside *(G-4386)*

CAGES: Wire

Allentown Inc..B 609 259-7951
  Allentown *(G-24)*

CALCULATING & ACCOUNTING EQPT

Zeiser Inc ....F 973 228-0800
  West Caldwell *(G-11682)*

CALENDARS, WHOLESALE

Judith Roth Studio Collection ....G 973 543-4455
  Mendham *(G-6039)*

CALIBRATING SVCS, NEC

State Technology Inc ....G 856 467-8009
  Bridgeport *(G-746)*

CAMERA & PHOTOGRAPHIC SPLYS STORES: Cameras

AAS Technologies Inc ....G 201 342-7300
  Hackensack *(G-3874)*
Eom Worldwide Sales Corp ....G 732 994-7352
  Lakewood *(G-5091)*

CAMERA & PHOTOGRAPHIC SPLYS STORES: Photographic Splys

Gill Associates LLC ....G 973 835-5456
  Wayne *(G-11511)*

CAMERAS & RELATED EQPT: Photographic

Ar2 Products LLC ....G 800 667-1263
  Pompton Plains *(G-8858)*

Fullview Inc..G 732 275-6500
  Holmdel *(G-4501)*
Intertest Inc...E 908 496-8008
  Columbia *(G-1795)*
Liveu Inc ....D 201 742-5229
  Hackensack *(G-3939)*
Oxberry LLC ....G 201 935-3000
  Carlstadt *(G-1194)*
Photographic Analysis Company.........G 973 696-1000
  Wayne *(G-11542)*
Prestige Camera LLC ....E 718 257-5888
  Somerset *(G-10056)*
Quality Films Corp ....G 718 246-7150
  Hillside *(G-4422)*
Roper Scientific Inc ....E 941 556-2601
  Trenton *(G-10989)*

CANDLE SHOPS

A Cheerful Giver Inc ....F 856 358-4438
  Elmer *(G-2792)*
Surfs Up Candle & Charm ....G 848 404-9559
  Belmar *(G-355)*

CANDLES

Ana Design Corp...................................F 609 394-0300
  Trenton *(G-10893)*
Candle Artisans Incorporated.............E 908 689-2000
  Washington *(G-11443)*
Fragrance Factory Inc ....G 973 835-2002
  Pompton Plains *(G-8864)*
Little House Candles Inc ....G 609 758-2996
  New Egypt *(G-6985)*
Lux Naturals LLC ....G 848 229-2950
  Edison *(G-2554)*
Star Soap/Star Candle/Prayer C ....C 201 690-9090
  Ridgefield Park *(G-9318)*
Stephen L Feilinger...............................G 609 294-1884
  Ltl Egg Hbr *(G-5620)*
Surfs Up Candle & Charm ....G 848 404-9559
  Belmar *(G-355)*
USA Tealight Inc ....F 732 943-2408
  Avenel *(G-153)*

CANDLES: Wholesalers

A Cheerful Giver Inc ....F 856 358-4438
  Elmer *(G-2792)*
Lux Naturals LLC ....G 848 229-2950
  Edison *(G-2554)*

CANDY & CONFECTIONS: Candy Bars, Including Chocolate Covered

Mars Wrigley Conf US LLC ....C 908 852-1000
  Hackettstown *(G-4026)*
Minhura Inc..G 862 763-4078
  North Arlington *(G-7375)*
Sherwood Brands Corporation.............F 973 249-8200
  New Brunswick *(G-6970)*

CANDY & CONFECTIONS: Chocolate Candy, Exc Solid Chocolate

Al Richrds Homemade Chocolates ....F 201 436-0915
  Bayonne *(G-201)*
Bromilows Candy Co ....G 973 684-1496
  Woodland Park *(G-12072)*
Enjou Chocolat Morristown Inc ....G 973 993-9090
  Morristown *(G-6662)*
Genevieves Inc......................................F 973 772-8816
  Garfield *(G-3746)*
Sims Lee Inc ....F 201 433-1308
  Jersey City *(G-4810)*

CANDY & CONFECTIONS: Fruit & Fruit Peel

Cns Confectionery Products LLC ....F 201 823-1400
  Bayonne *(G-211)*

CANDY & CONFECTIONS: Licorice

Mafco Worldwide Corporation..............C 856 964-8840
  Camden *(G-1075)*

CANDY & CONFECTIONS: Marzipan

Bergen Marzipan & Chocolate ....G 201 385-8343
  Bergenfield *(G-373)*

CANDY & CONFECTIONS: Nuts, Candy Covered

Nutscom Inc ....G 800 558-6887
  Jersey City *(G-4776)*

CANDY & CONFECTIONS: Nuts, Glace

Naturee Nuts Inc ....F 732 786-4663
  Kenilworth *(G-4962)*

CANDY & CONFECTIONS: Popcorn Balls/Other Trtd Popcorn Prdts

Nutra Nuts Inc ....G 323 260-7457
  Ridgewood *(G-9325)*

CANDY, NUT & CONFECTIONERY STORES: Candy

Birnn Chocolates Inc ....G 732 214-8680
  Highland Park *(G-4287)*
Bromilows Candy Co ....G 973 684-1496
  Woodland Park *(G-12072)*
Damask Kandies ....G 856 467-1661
  Swedesboro *(G-10578)*
Enjou Chocolat Morristown Inc ....G 973 993-9090
  Morristown *(G-6662)*
Genevieves Inc......................................F 973 772-8816
  Garfield *(G-3746)*
Giambris Quality Sweets Inc................G 856 783-1099
  Clementon *(G-1533)*
Hillside Candy LLC ....E 908 241-4747
  Roselle *(G-9560)*
K K S Criterion Chocolates ....E 732 542-7847
  Eatontown *(G-2406)*
Krauses Homemade Candy Inc ....F 201 943-4790
  Fairview *(G-3362)*
Matisse Chocolatier Inc.......................G 201 568-2288
  Englewood *(G-2923)*
Nutscom Inc ....G 800 558-6887
  Jersey City *(G-4776)*
Rauhausers Inc ....F 609 399-1465
  Ocean City *(G-7693)*
Reilys Candy Inc ....F 609 953-0040
  Medford *(G-6032)*
Shrivers Salt Wtr Taffy Fudge ....E 609 399-0100
  Ocean City *(G-7696)*
Sims Lee Inc ....F 201 433-1308
  Jersey City *(G-4810)*
Webers Candy Store..............................G 856 455-8277
  Bridgeton *(G-778)*

CANDY, NUT & CONFECTIONERY STORES: Confectionery

Fralingers Inc ....E 609 345-2177
  Atlantic City *(G-90)*
James Candy Company ....E 609 344-1519
  Atlantic City *(G-95)*
Old Monmouth Peanut Brittle Co ....G 732 462-1311
  Freehold *(G-3684)*

CANDY, NUT & CONFECTIONERY STORES: Produced For Direct Sale

George Brummer ....G 908 232-1904
  Westfield *(G-11798)*

CANDY: Chocolate From Cacao Beans

Genevieves Inc......................................F 973 772-8816
  Garfield *(G-3746)*
George Brummer ....G 908 232-1904
  Westfield *(G-11798)*
Mars Incorporated................................F 973 691-3500
  Budd Lake *(G-929)*

CANDY: Hard

Lucas World Inc ....G 832 293-3770
  Budd Lake *(G-926)*

CANDY: Soft

Shrivers Salt Wtr Taffy Fudge ....E 609 399-0100
  Ocean City *(G-7696)*
Yolo Candy LLC ....G 201 252-8765
  Mahwah *(G-5787)*

CANNED SPECIALTIES

Bakers Perfection Inc ....E 973 983-0700
Rockaway *(G-9446)*

CSC Brands LP ....F 800 257-8443
Camden *(G-1056)*

F&S Produce Company Inc ....C 856 453-0316
Rosenhayn *(G-9595)*

F&S Produce Company Inc ....C 856 453-0316
Vineland *(G-11218)*

Goya Foods Inc ....B 201 348-4900
Secaucus *(G-9776)*

Mushroom Wisdom Inc ....F 973 470-0010
East Rutherford *(G-2305)*

Nestle Healthcare Ntrtn Inc ....C 800 422-2752
Bridgewater *(G-856)*

Novartis Corporation ....E 212 307-1122
East Hanover *(G-2226)*

Project Feed Usa Inc ....F 201 443-7143
Jersey City *(G-4789)*

Universal Prtein Spplmnts Corp ......D 732 545-3130
New Brunswick *(G-6977)*

CANS & TUBES: Ammunition, Board Laminated With Metal Foil

Hicube Coating LLC ....G 973 883-7404
Clifton *(G-1634)*

CANS: Composite Foil-Fiber, Made From Purchased Materials

Sonoco Products Company ....D 609 655-0300
Dayton *(G-1989)*

CANS: Metal

Bway Corporation ....C 732 997-4100
Dayton *(G-1956)*

Elemental Container Inc ....G 908 687-7720
Union *(G-11051)*

Medin Technologies Inc ....C 973 779-2400
Totowa *(G-10836)*

Silgan Containers Mfg Corp ....D 732 287-0300
Edison *(G-2609)*

Sonoco Products Company ....D 609 655-0300
Dayton *(G-1989)*

CANS: Tin

JI Packaging Group Corp ....G 609 610-0286
Pennington *(G-8368)*

Tin Can Lids LLC ....G 201 503-0677
Tenafly *(G-10666)*

CANVAS PRDTS

Beachwood Canvas Works LLC ....F 732 929-1783
Island Heights *(G-4637)*

Colie Sail Makers Inc ....G 732 892-4344
Point Pleasant Boro *(G-8840)*

Costa Mar Cnvas Enclosures LLC .....E 609 965-1538
Egg Harbor City *(G-2656)*

Howard Lippincott ....G 856 764-8282
Riverside *(G-9396)*

Lloyds of Millville Inc ....G 856 825-0345
Millville *(G-6259)*

Meese Inc ....F 201 796-4490
Saddle Brook *(G-9661)*

Revere Plastics Inc ....G 201 641-0777
Little Ferry *(G-5494)*

Robert Brown ....G 609 398-6262
Ocean City *(G-7694)*

Superior Marine Canvas ....G 856 241-1724
Swedesboro *(G-10612)*

William Opdyke Awnings Inc ....G 732 449-5940
Wall Township *(G-11378)*

CANVAS PRDTS, WHOLESALE

Howard Lippincott ....G 856 764-8282
Riverside *(G-9396)*

CANVAS PRDTS: Boat Seats

Canvas Creations ....G 609 465-8428
Cape May Court House *(G-1108)*

Fisher Canvas Products Inc ....G 609 239-2733
Burlington *(G-967)*

CANVAS PRDTS: Convertible Tops, Car/Boat, Fm Purchased Mtrl

Pv Deroche LLC ....E 908 475-2266
Belvidere *(G-365)*

CAPACITORS: NEC

Electro-Ceramic Industries ....E 201 342-2630
Hackensack *(G-3911)*

Electronic Concepts Inc ....C 732 542-7880
Eatontown *(G-2390)*

Energy Storage Corp ....D 732 542-7880
Eatontown *(G-2392)*

Megatran Industries ....D 609 227-4300
Bordentown *(G-586)*

Metuchen Capacitors Inc ....E 800 899-6969
Holmdel *(G-4506)*

Nte Electronics Inc ....D 973 748-5089
Bloomfield *(G-513)*

Tbt Group Inc ....G 856 753-4500
Bellmawr *(G-344)*

CAPS: Plastic

AJ Siris Products Corp ....E 973 823-0050
Ogdensburg *(G-7708)*

CAR WASH EQPT

Car Wash Parts Inc ....G 215 633-9250
Ventnor City *(G-11152)*

Chen Brothers Machinery Co ....G 973 328-0086
Randolph *(G-9174)*

Interntional Cnsld Chemex Corp ......E 732 828-7676
New Brunswick *(G-6936)*

T & E Sales of Marlboro ....G 732 549-7551
Metuchen *(G-6076)*

CAR WASH EQPT & SPLYS WHOLESALERS

Car Wash Parts Inc ....G 215 633-9250
Ventnor City *(G-11152)*

Chen Brothers Machinery Co ....G 973 328-0086
Randolph *(G-9174)*

Interntional Cnsld Chemex Corp ......E 732 828-7676
New Brunswick *(G-6936)*

Jrz Enterprises LLC ....G 973 962-6330
Wayne *(G-11526)*

CARBIDES

United Silicon Carbide Inc ....G 732 565-9500
New Brunswick *(G-6976)*

CARBON & GRAPHITE PRDTS, NEC

Asbury Louisiana Inc ....E 908 537-2155
Asbury *(G-63)*

Resintech Inc ....C 856 768-9600
West Berlin *(G-11619)*

CARBON BLACK

Total American Services Inc ....F 206 626-3500
Jersey City *(G-4822)*

CARBON PAPER & INKED RIBBONS

Ner Data Products Inc ....E 888 637-3282
Glassboro *(G-3817)*

CARBON SPECIALTIES Electrical Use

Bella Acqua Inc ....F 609 324-9024
Chesterfield *(G-1436)*

CARBONS: Electric

F S R Inc ....D 973 785-4347
Woodland Park *(G-12078)*

CARDBOARD PRDTS, EXC DIE-CUT

Laminated Paperboard Corp ....G 908 862-5995
Linden *(G-5374)*

CARDIOVASCULAR SYSTEM DRUGS, EXC DIAGNOSTIC

Bristol-Myers Squibb Company ....E 212 546-4000
Hillside *(G-4383)*

Ebelle Debelle Phrm Inc ....F 973 823-0665
Hamburg *(G-4092)*

I Fcb Holdings Inc ....E 201 934-2000
Mahwah *(G-5748)*

Novartis Corporation ....E 212 307-1122
East Hanover *(G-2226)*

Pfizer Inc ....F 973 660-5000
Madison *(G-5700)*

Sanofi US Services Inc ....A 336 407-4994
Bridgewater *(G-880)*

Vascular Therapies Inc ....G 201 266-8310
Cresskill *(G-1946)*

Zenith Laboratories Inc ....C 201 767-1700
Northvale *(G-7556)*

CARDS: Color

Flortek Corporation ....E 201 436-7700
Bayonne *(G-216)*

CARDS: Greeting

Amaryllis Inc ....G 973 635-0500
Chatham *(G-1318)*

Easy Street Publications Inc ....G 917 699-7820
Union *(G-11048)*

Greetingtap ....G 347 731-4263
South Plainfield *(G-10269)*

Magnetic Ticket & Label Corp ....E 973 759-6500
Belleville *(G-299)*

Nobleworks Inc ....F 201 420-0095
Union City *(G-11124)*

Prudent Publishing Co Inc ....E 973 347-4554
Landing *(G-5203)*

Saint La Salle Auxiliary Inc ....G 732 842-4359
Lincroft *(G-5314)*

Schurman Fine Papers ....E 856 985-1776
Marlton *(G-5950)*

CARDS: Identification

Competech Smrtcard Sltions Inc ......G 201 256-4184
Englewood Cliffs *(G-2963)*

Protec Secure Card Ltd Lblty ....E 732 542-0700
Eatontown *(G-2417)*

Team Nisca ....G 732 271-7367
Somerset *(G-10082)*

CARPETS, RUGS & FLOOR COVERING

A & J Carpets Inc ....G 856 227-1753
Blackwood *(G-458)*

Amici Imports Inc ....F 908 272-8300
Cranford *(G-1900)*

Bamboo & Rattan Works Inc ....G 732 255-4239
Toms River *(G-10746)*

Banilivy Rug Corp ....G 212 684-3629
Englewood *(G-2880)*

Bashian Bros Inc ....E 201 330-1001
Ridgefield *(G-9250)*

Cno Corporation ....G 732 785-5799
Brick *(G-713)*

Gallery of Rugs Inc ....G 908 934-0040
Summit *(G-10532)*

Hakakian Behzad ....E 973 267-2506
Cedar Knolls *(G-1306)*

Kas Oriental Rugs Inc ....E 732 545-1900
Somerset *(G-10010)*

Kashee & Sons Inc ....F 201 867-6900
Secaucus *(G-9785)*

La Forchetta ....G 973 304-4797
Hawthorne *(G-4230)*

Moosavi Rugs Inc ....G 201 617-9500
Secaucus *(G-9793)*

Samad Brothers Inc ....F 201 372-0909
East Rutherford *(G-2318)*

Seldom Seen Designs LLC ....G 973 535-8805
Caldwell *(G-1030)*

Shaw Industries Inc ....B 609 655-8300
Cranbury *(G-1882)*

SNS Oriental Rugs LLC ....G 201 355-8786
Carlstadt *(G-1219)*

Stiles Enterprises Inc ....F 973 625-9660
Rockaway *(G-9501)*

Worldwide Whl Flr Cvg Inc ....E 732 906-1400
Edison *(G-2647)*

Zollanvari Ltd ....F 201 330-3344
Secaucus *(G-9830)*

CARPETS: Hand & Machine Made

Ben-Aharon & Son Inc ....G 201 541-2388
Englewood *(G-2881)*

Kync Design LLC ....G 201 552-2067
Secaucus *(G-9787)*

Employee Codes: A=Over 500 employees, B=251-500
C=101-250, D=51-100, E=20-50, F=10-19, G=4-9

2019 Harris New Jersey
Manufacturers Directory

789

PRODUCT

CARPETS: Textile Fiber

Aladdin Manufacturing Corp.................B...... 973 616-4600
Pompton Plains (G-8856)

CARRIER EQPT: Telephone Or Telegraph

Instock Wireless Components.............F...... 973 335-6550
Boonton (G-557)
Parwan Electronics Corporation ....E...... 732 290-1900
Matawan (G-5983)

CARRYING CASES, WHOLESALE

Kini Products Inc ....G...... 732 299-5555
New Egypt (G-6984)

CASES, WOOD

Minerva Custom Products LLC ....G...... 201 447-4731
Waldwick (G-11305)

CASES: Carrying

Motion Systems LLC ....F...... 212 686-4666
Newark (G-7205)

CASES: Carrying, Clothing & Apparel

Gibbons Company Ltd ....E...... 441 294-5047
Elizabeth (G-2743)
Selfmade LLC ....G...... 201 792-8968
Jersey City (G-4808)

CASES: Plastic

Case It Inc...........................E...... 800 441-4710
Lyndhurst (G-5646)
Case Princeton Co Inc.................E...... 908 687-1750
Mountainside (G-6836)
Dr Reddys Laboratories Inc ....E...... 609 375-9900
Princeton (G-8933)
Garden State Fabricators ....G...... 732 928-5006
Cream Ridge (G-1935)
Qualipac America Corp ....F...... 973 754-9920
Woodland Park (G-12088)
Sealed Air Holdings ....G...... 201 791-7600
Elmwood Park (G-2855)

CASES: Shipping, Wood, Wirebound

Caudalie Usa Inc ....G...... 201 939-4969
Carlstadt (G-1137)
Minerva Custom Products LLC ....G...... 201 447-4731
Waldwick (G-11305)

CASH REGISTERS & PARTS

United Pos Solutions Inc..............G...... 800 303-2567
Palisades Park (G-7780)

CASINGS: Sheet Metal

Legrand AV Inc ....B...... 973 839-1011
Fairfield (G-3260)
Middle Atlantic Products Inc..........B...... 973 839-1011
Fairfield (G-3271)

CASKET LININGS

Agoura Hills Group ....G...... 818 888-0400
Cherry Hill (G-1334)

CAST STONE: Concrete

Jarco U S Casting Corp................E...... 201 271-0003
Union City (G-11115)

CASTERS

Federal Casters Corp..................D...... 973 483-6700
Harrison (G-4173)
J C W Inc.............................E...... 732 560-8061
Bridgewater (G-838)

CASTINGS GRINDING: For The Trade

Legend Machine & Grinding.............F...... 908 685-1100
Bridgewater (G-841)
M and D Precision Grinding............G...... 856 764-1616
Riverside (G-9399)
Unique Precision Co Inc...............G...... 732 382-8699
Rahway (G-9131)

CASTINGS: Aerospace Investment, Ferrous

Advance Process Systems Lim ....G...... 201 400-9190
Branchville (G-701)
AJ Oster LLC ....G...... 973 673-5700
Parsippany (G-7876)
Atlantic Eqp Engineers Inc ....F...... 201 828-9400
Upper Saddle River (G-11134)

CASTINGS: Aerospace, Aluminum

Atlantic Casting & Engineering ....C...... 973 779-2450
Clifton (G-1566)
TEC Cast Inc ....E...... 201 935-3885
Carlstadt (G-1226)

CASTINGS: Aluminum

Rosco Inc ....G...... 908 789-1020
Garwood (G-3792)
Union Casting Industries Inc ....F...... 908 686-8888
Union (G-11096)

CASTINGS: Bronze, NEC, Exc Die

Federal Bronze Cast Inds Inc..........E...... 973 589-7575
Newark (G-7123)

CASTINGS: Commercial Investment, Ferrous

Engineered Precision Cast Co..........D...... 732 671-2424
Middletown (G-6163)
Howmet Castings & Services Inc ....A...... 973 361-0300
Dover (G-2087)
Howmet Castings & Services Inc ....B...... 973 361-0300
Dover (G-2088)
Howmet Castings & Services Inc ....B...... 973 361-2310
Dover (G-2089)
R W Wheaton Co ....G...... 908 241-4955
Roselle Park (G-9590)

CASTINGS: Copper & Copper-Base Alloy, NEC, Exc Die

Union Casting Industries Inc ....F...... 908 686-8888
Union (G-11096)

CASTINGS: Die, Aluminum

American Aluminum Casting Co ....E...... 973 372-3200
Irvington (G-4556)
Bierman-Everett Foundry Co ....E...... 973 373-8800
South Orange (G-10192)

CASTINGS: Die, Copper & Copper Alloy

Maranatha Now Inc ....E...... 609 599-1402
Trenton (G-10955)

CASTINGS: Die, Nonferrous

Certech Inc ....C...... 201 842-6800
Wood Ridge (G-12002)
Medalco Metals Inc ....G...... 908 238-0513
Lebanon (G-5271)
Worldcast Network Inc ....G...... 201 767-2040
Old Tappan (G-7737)

CASTINGS: Die, Zinc

Abco Die Casters Inc ....D...... 973 624-7030
Newark (G-7033)
Carteret Die-Casting Corp.............E...... 732 246-0070
Somerset (G-9967)
Microcast Technologies Corp...........D...... 908 523-9503
Linden (G-5385)

CASTINGS: Gray Iron

Bierman-Everett Foundry Co ....G...... 973 373-8800
South Orange (G-10192)
Bridgestate Foundry Corp ....G...... 856 767-0400
Berlin (G-417)
General Foundries Inc ....E...... 732 951-9001
North Brunswick (G-7468)

CASTINGS: Machinery, Nonferrous, Exc Die or Aluminum Copper

Arde Inc..............................D...... 201 784-9880
Carlstadt (G-1126)
Tusa Products Inc ....G...... 609 448-8333
Ewing (G-3072)

CASTINGS: Precision

Alloy Cast Products Inc...............F...... 908 245-2255
Kenilworth (G-4920)
Jarco U S Casting Corp................E...... 201 271-0003
Union City (G-11115)

CASTINGS: Steel

Interstate Welding & Mfg Co ....F...... 800 676-4666
Beverly (G-452)

CASTINGS: Zinc

Microcast Technologies Corp...........D...... 908 523-9503
Linden (G-5385)

CATALOG & MAIL-ORDER HOUSES

10-31 Incorporated....................E...... 908 496-4946
Columbia (G-1791)
Barnes & Noble Booksellers Inc........E...... 201 272-3635
Lyndhurst (G-5642)
Hanover Direct Inc ....B...... 201 863-7300
Weehawken (G-11568)
Ivc Industries Inc ....B...... 732 308-3000
Freehold (G-3671)
Work n Gear LLC ....G...... 856 848-7676
Woodbury (G-12039)

CATALOG SALES

Edmund Optics Inc ....C...... 856 547-3488
Barrington (G-172)

CATALYSTS: Chemical

A&C Catalysts Inc ....E...... 908 474-9393
Linden (G-5315)
BASF Catalysts LLC ....D...... 732 205-5000
Iselin (G-4599)
Hydrocrbon Tech Innovation LLC ....E...... 609 394-3102
Lawrenceville (G-5232)
Nouryon Surface Chemistry ....D...... 312 544-7000
New Brunswick (G-6955)
Scientific Design Company ....C...... 201 641-0500
Little Ferry (G-5496)
Totalcat Group Inc ....G...... 908 497-9610
Cranford (G-1929)
UOP LLC ....G...... 973 455-2096
Morris Plains (G-6627)
W R Grace & Co-Conn ....C...... 732 777-4877
Edison (G-2644)
West Dry Industries Inc ....G...... 908 757-4400
Westfield (G-11808)

CATERERS

Bringhurst Bros Inc ....E...... 856 767-0110
Berlin (G-418)
Catering By Maddalenas Inc ....G...... 609 466-7510
Ringoes (G-9335)
Georges Wine and Spirits Galle ....G...... 973 948-9950
Branchville (G-707)
Sushi House Inc ....E...... 201 482-0609
Palisades Park (G-7779)
York Street Caterers Inc ....C...... 201 868-9088
Englewood (G-2955)

CAULKING COMPOUNDS

May National Associates NJ Inc ....D...... 973 473-3330
Lakewood (G-5132)

CEILING SYSTEMS: Luminous, Commercial

Illuminating Experiences LLC..........G...... 800 734-5858
New Brunswick (G-6934)

CELLULOSE DERIVATIVE MATERIALS

Dicalite Minerals Corp ....G...... 856 320-2919
Pennsauken (G-8413)

CEMENT: Hydraulic

Anti Hydro International Inc ....F...... 908 284-9000
Flemington (G-3430)
Lafarge North America Inc ....G...... 201 437-2575
Bayonne (G-227)
Lehigh Cement Company ....G...... 973 579-2111
Sparta (G-10395)
Pavestone LLC ....E...... 973 948-7193
Branchville (G-709)

Tanis Concrete ....E 201 796-1556
Fair Lawn *(G-3126)*

CEMENT: Masonry

Local Concrete Sup & Eqp Corp ....G 201 797-7979
Elmwood Park *(G-2838)*

CEMETERY MEMORIAL DEALERS

Albert H Hopper Inc ....G 201 991-2266
North Arlington *(G-7367)*
Bcg Marble & Granite South LLC ....G 732 367-3788
Jackson *(G-4641)*

CERAMIC FIBER

Advanced Cerametrics Inc ....G 609 397-2900
Lambertville *(G-5186)*
Ceramic Products Inc ....G 201 342-8200
Hackensack *(G-3896)*
Ceramsource Inc ....F 732 257-5002
East Brunswick *(G-2131)*
Crystex Composites LLC ....E 973 779-8866
Clifton *(G-1593)*
Intersource USA Inc ....F 732 257-5002
East Brunswick *(G-2152)*

CHAINS: Power Transmission

Brilliant Light Power Inc ....E 609 490-0427
East Windsor *(G-2365)*

CHANDELIERS: Commercial

Bellemead Hot Glass ....G 908 281-5516
Hillsborough *(G-4303)*

CHANDELIERS: Residential

Gemini Cut Glass Company Inc ....G 201 568-7722
Englewood *(G-2909)*
Pty Lighting LLC ....G 855 303-4500
Hillside *(G-4421)*

CHARCOAL: Activated

Evoqua Water Technologies LLC ....F 908 353-7400
Elizabeth *(G-2733)*
General Carbon Corporation ....F 973 523-2223
Paterson *(G-8197)*

CHART & GRAPH DESIGN SVCS

Graphicolor Corporation ....E 856 691-2507
Vineland *(G-11227)*

CHASING SVC: Metal

Weiler & Sons LLC ....G 856 767-8842
Berlin *(G-433)*

CHASSIS: Automobile House Trailer

Orlando Systems Ltd Lblty Co ....G 908 400-5052
North Plainfield *(G-7507)*

CHASSIS: Motor Vehicle

Garden St Chasis Remanuf ....E 732 283-1910
Woodbridge *(G-12016)*

CHEESE WHOLESALERS

35 Food Corp ....G 732 442-1640
Woodbridge *(G-12011)*
Colonna Brothers Inc ....D 800 626-8384
North Bergen *(G-7397)*
Lioni Mozzarella & Spclty ....E 908 624-9450
Union *(G-11071)*
Tipico Products Co Inc ....D 732 942-8820
Lakewood *(G-5171)*
Tropical Cheese Industries ....B 732 442-4898
Perth Amboy *(G-8537)*

CHEMICAL ELEMENTS

Alkaline Corporation ....E 732 531-7830
Oakhurst *(G-7607)*
Carbon Fiber Element LLC ....G 973 809-9432
Metuchen *(G-6050)*
Elemental Interiors ....G 646 861-3596
Montclair *(G-6365)*
Multalloy LLC ....G 732 961-1520
Howell *(G-4547)*

Rlct Industries LLC ....G 609 712-1318
Pennington *(G-8372)*

CHEMICAL PROCESSING MACHINERY & EQPT

Alaqua Inc ....F 201 758-1580
Guttenberg *(G-3870)*
Gluefast Company Inc ....F 732 918-4600
Neptune *(G-6881)*
Hosokawa Micron International ....D 908 273-6360
Summit *(G-10535)*
Hosokawa Micron International ....D 908 273-6360
Summit *(G-10536)*
Hosokawa Micron International ....F 866 507-4974
Pennsauken *(G-8432)*
Hosokawa Micron Intl Inc ....D 908 273-6360
Summit *(G-10537)*
Jaygo Incorporated ....E 908 688-3600
Randolph *(G-9187)*
Jet Pulverizer Co Inc ....E 856 235-5554
Moorestown *(G-6531)*
Koch Mdlar Process Systems LLC ....D 201 368-2929
Paramus *(G-7814)*
Manning & Lewis Engrg Co Inc ....E 908 687-2400
Union *(G-11073)*
Miracle Mile Automotive Inc ....G 732 886-6315
Lakewood *(G-5136)*
Witte Co Inc ....E 908 689-6500
Washington *(G-11454)*
Wyssmont Company Inc ....E 201 947-4600
Fort Lee *(G-3596)*

CHEMICAL SPLYS FOR FOUNDRIES

Adam Gates & Company LLC ....F 908 829-3386
Hillsborough *(G-4300)*
Sage Chemical Inc ....G 201 489-5172
Hackensack *(G-3970)*

CHEMICAL: Sodm Compnds/Salts, Inorg, Exc Rfnd Sodm Chloride

East Coast Salt Dist Inc ....G 732 833-2973
Jackson *(G-4654)*

CHEMICALS & ALLIED PRDTS WHOLESALERS, NEC

Arol Chemical Products Co ....G 973 344-1510
Newark *(G-7053)*
Barnegat Light Fibrgls Sup LLC ....G 609 294-8870
West Creek *(G-11684)*
Chemical Resources Inc ....E 609 520-0000
Princeton *(G-8921)*
Chemtrade Solutions LLC ....G 973 515-0900
Parsippany *(G-7904)*
Cronite Co Inc ....E 973 887-7900
Parsippany *(G-7910)*
Cvc Specialty Chemicals Inc ....F 856 533-3000
Moorestown *(G-6517)*
Fuel Management Services Inc ....G 732 929-1964
Toms River *(G-10760)*
Hychem Corporation ....G 732 280-8803
Belmar *(G-350)*
Innophos Holdings Inc ....D 609 495-2495
Cranbury *(G-1842)*
Lab Express Inc ....F 973 227-1700
Fairfield *(G-3256)*
Lyciret Corp ....E 973 882-0322
Orange *(G-7754)*
Mel Chemicals Inc ....C 908 782-5800
Flemington *(G-3455)*
National Auto Detailing Netwrk ....E 856 931-5529
Bellmawr *(G-340)*
Polymer Additives Inc ....F 856 467-8247
Bridgeport *(G-743)*
Reade Manufacturing Company ....E 732 657-6451
Manchester *(G-5848)*
Sage Chemical Inc ....G 201 489-5172
Hackensack *(G-3970)*
Sau-Sea Swimming Pool Products ....F 609 859-8500
Southampton *(G-10372)*
Si Packaging LLC ....F 973 869-9920
Rutherford *(G-9632)*
Sylvan Chemical Corporation ....E 201 934-4224
Fair Lawn *(G-3124)*
Synasia Inc ....G 732 205-9880
Metuchen *(G-6075)*
T & B Specialties Inc ....G 732 928-4500
Jackson *(G-4666)*

Veolia Es ....E 732 469-5100
Middlesex *(G-6158)*

CHEMICALS & ALLIED PRDTS, WHOL: Chemical, Organic, Synthetic

Houghton Chemical Corporation ....F 201 460-8071
Carlstadt *(G-1166)*
Polyorganic Technoligies Corp ....G 609 288-8233
East Brunswick *(G-2166)*
Spectrum Laboratory Pdts Inc ....E 732 214-1300
New Brunswick *(G-6972)*
Ultra Chemical Inc ....F 732 224-0200
Red Bank *(G-9247)*

CHEMICALS & ALLIED PRDTS, WHOL: Food Additives/Preservatives

Zxchem USA Inc ....G 732 529-6352
Piscataway *(G-8742)*

CHEMICALS & ALLIED PRDTS, WHOLESALE: Aerosols

Milspray LLC ....E 732 886-2223
Lakewood *(G-5135)*

CHEMICALS & ALLIED PRDTS, WHOLESALE: Alkalines & Chlorine

Ashland LLC ....D 732 353-7718
Parlin *(G-7861)*

CHEMICALS & ALLIED PRDTS, WHOLESALE: Aromatic

Berje Incorporated ....D 973 748-8980
Carteret *(G-1250)*

CHEMICALS & ALLIED PRDTS, WHOLESALE: Chemical Additives

Global Spclty Products-Usa Inc ....F 609 518-7577
Mount Holly *(G-6728)*

CHEMICALS & ALLIED PRDTS, WHOLESALE: Chemicals, Indl

Amano USA Holdings Inc ....G 973 403-1900
Roseland *(G-9531)*
Amfine Chemical Corporation ....F 201 818-0159
Hasbrouck Heights *(G-4181)*
Brenntag Specialties Inc ....D 908 561-6100
South Plainfield *(G-10228)*
Brown Chemical Co Inc ....E 201 337-0900
Oakland *(G-7617)*
Chemique Inc ....G 856 235-4161
Moorestown *(G-6512)*
G J Chemical Co ....E 973 589-1450
Somerset *(G-9996)*
Gpt Inc ....F 732 446-2400
Manalapan *(G-5812)*
Hummel Croton Inc ....F 908 754-1800
South Plainfield *(G-10274)*
Inversand Company Inc ....F 856 881-2345
Clayton *(G-1526)*
Morre-TEC Industries Inc ....E 908 688-9009
Union *(G-11076)*
Northeast Chemicals Inc ....E 508 634-6900
East Brunswick *(G-2160)*
Northeast Chemicals Inc ....E 732 227-0100
East Brunswick *(G-2161)*
Prestige Laboratories Inc ....E 973 772-8922
East Rutherford *(G-2311)*
Raybeam Manufacturing Corp ....G 201 941-4529
Ridgefield *(G-9286)*
Rockwood Specialties Group Inc ....F 609 514-0300
Princeton *(G-9018)*

CHEMICALS & ALLIED PRDTS, WHOLESALE: Chemicals, Indl & Heavy

Just In Time Chemical Sales & ....G 908 862-7726
Linden *(G-5366)*
Royale Pigments & Chem Inc ....F 201 845-4666
Paramus *(G-7830)*

PRODUCT

CHEMICALS & ALLIED PRDTS, WHOLESALE: Chemicals, Rustproofing

Por-15 Inc ....E 973 887-1999
Whippany **(G-11905)**

CHEMICALS & ALLIED PRDTS, WHOLESALE: Compressed Gas

Praxair Distribution Inc ....E 973 589-7895
Newark **(G-7232)**

CHEMICALS & ALLIED PRDTS, WHOLESALE: Detergents

Detergent 20 LLC ....F 732 545-0200
New Brunswick **(G-6919)**

CHEMICALS & ALLIED PRDTS, WHOLESALE: Dry Ice

Artic Ice Manufacturing Co ....G 973 772-7000
Garfield **(G-3729)**

CHEMICALS & ALLIED PRDTS, WHOLESALE: Essential Oils

Serene House USA Inc ....G 609 980-1214
Cherry Hill **(G-1414)**

CHEMICALS & ALLIED PRDTS, WHOLESALE: Indl Gases

Air Liquide Advanced Materials ....F 908 231-9060
Branchburg **(G-612)**
E G L Company Inc ....C 908 508-1111
Berkeley Heights **(G-398)**

CHEMICALS & ALLIED PRDTS, WHOLESALE: Metal Polishes

Plasma Powders & Systems Inc ....G 732 431-0992
Marlboro **(G-5909)**

CHEMICALS & ALLIED PRDTS, WHOLESALE: Plastics Film

American Renolit Corporation ....G 973 706-6912
Wayne **(G-11468)**
ANS Plastics Corporation ....F 732 247-2776
New Brunswick **(G-6910)**
Kadakia International Inc ....G 908 754-4445
South Plainfield **(G-10286)**

CHEMICALS & ALLIED PRDTS, WHOLESALE: Plastics Materials, NEC

Acrilex Inc ....E 201 333-1500
Jersey City **(G-4685)**
Mark Ronald Associates Inc ....D 908 558-0011
Hillside **(G-4414)**
Multi-Plastics Inc ....E 856 241-9014
Swedesboro **(G-10598)**
Pro Plastics Inc ....E 908 925-5555
Linden **(G-5412)**

CHEMICALS & ALLIED PRDTS, WHOLESALE: Plastics Prdts, NEC

Allentown Inc ....B 609 259-7951
Allentown **(G-24)**
Barlics Manufacturing Co Inc ....G 732 381-6229
Rahway **(G-9082)**
Central Plastics Incorporated ....G 973 808-0990
Parsippany **(G-7899)**
JA Heilferty LLC ....E 201 836-5060
Teaneck **(G-10635)**
Nitto Inc ....F 732 901-7905
Lakewood **(G-5141)**
Nitto Inc ....F 201 645-4950
Teaneck **(G-10641)**
Sealed Air Holdings ....G 201 791-7600
Elmwood Park **(G-2855)**

CHEMICALS & ALLIED PRDTS, WHOLESALE: Plastics Sheets & Rods

E & T Sales Co Inc ....G 856 787-0900
Mount Laurel **(G-6755)**

Grewe Plastics Inc ....G 973 485-7602
Newark **(G-7140)**
L-E-M Plastics and Supplies ....G 201 933-9150
Rutherford **(G-9626)**

CHEMICALS & ALLIED PRDTS, WHOLESALE: Polyurethane Prdts

Advanced Polymer Inc ....F 201 964-3000
Carlstadt **(G-1118)**
Worldwide Safety Systems LLC ....G 888 613-4501
Teaneck **(G-10656)**

CHEMICALS & ALLIED PRDTS, WHOLESALE: Resins

Advansix Inc ....B 973 526-1800
Parsippany **(G-7875)**
Hitachi Chem Dupont Microsyst ....E 732 613-2175
Parlin **(G-7864)**
Resintech Inc ....C 856 768-9600
West Berlin **(G-11619)**
Shelan Chemical Company Inc ....G 732 796-1003
Monroe Township **(G-6343)**
Thibaut & Walker Co Inc ....G 973 589-3331
Newark **(G-7296)**

CHEMICALS & ALLIED PRDTS, WHOLESALE: Resins, Plastics

Federal Plastics Corporation ....E 908 272-5800
Cranford **(G-1910)**

CHEMICALS & ALLIED PRDTS, WHOLESALE: Silicon Lubricants

Path Silicones Inc ....F 201 796-0833
Elmwood Park **(G-2847)**

CHEMICALS & ALLIED PRDTS, WHOLESALE: Spec Clean/Sanitation

Microgen Inc ....G 973 575-9025
West Caldwell **(G-11666)**

CHEMICALS & ALLIED PRDTS, WHOLESALE: Waxes, Exc Petroleum

Honeywell International Inc ....C 973 455-2000
Morris Plains **(G-6614)**
Honeywell Speclty Wax & Additv ....F 973 455-2000
Morristown **(G-6674)**

CHEMICALS: Agricultural

Agilis Chemicals Inc ....F 973 910-2424
Short Hills **(G-9864)**
Aquatrols Corp of America ....E 856 537-6003
West Deptford **(G-11692)**
BASF Corporation ....B 973 245-6000
Florham Park **(G-3491)**
Basfin Corporation ....A 973 245-6000
Florham Park **(G-3493)**
Chem-Is-Try Inc ....G 732 372-7311
Metuchen **(G-6052)**
Healios Inc ....G 908 731-5061
Flemington **(G-3447)**
Novartis Corporation ....E 212 307-1122
East Hanover **(G-2226)**

CHEMICALS: Aluminum Chloride

Gulco Inc ....E 908 238-2030
Phillipsburg **(G-8554)**

CHEMICALS: Aluminum Compounds

Allied Specialty Group Inc ....F 201 223-4600
North Bergen **(G-7382)**
Chemtrade Solutions LLC ....F 908 464-1500
Berkeley Heights **(G-394)**
Somerville Acquisitions Co Inc ....G 908 782-9500
Flemington **(G-3469)**

CHEMICALS: Aluminum Sulfate

Chemtrade Solutions LLC ....G 973 515-0900
Parsippany **(G-7904)**

CHEMICALS: Ammonium Compounds, Exc Fertilizers, NEC

Church & Dwight Co Inc ....B 609 806-1200
Ewing **(G-3021)**

CHEMICALS: Barium & Barium Compounds

Hummel Croton Inc ....F 908 754-1800
South Plainfield **(G-10274)**

CHEMICALS: Brine

Water Mark Technologies Inc ....G 973 663-3438
Lake Hopatcong **(G-5038)**

CHEMICALS: Caustic Soda

Formosa Plastics Corp USA ....B 973 992-2090
Livingston **(G-5511)**

CHEMICALS: Copper Compounds Or Salts, Inorganic

Old Bridge Chemicals Inc ....E 732 727-2225
Old Bridge **(G-7722)**

CHEMICALS: Fire Retardant

No Fire Technologies Inc ....G 201 818-1616
South Hackensack **(G-10176)**
Polymer Additives Inc ....D 856 467-8220
Swedesboro **(G-10602)**
Turning Star Inc ....G 201 881-7077
Leonia **(G-5294)**

CHEMICALS: High Purity Grade, Organic

Ultra Chemical Inc ....F 732 224-0200
Red Bank **(G-9247)**

CHEMICALS: High Purity, Refined From Technical Grade

Foster and Company Inc ....E 973 267-4100
Cedar Knolls **(G-1305)**

CHEMICALS: Inorganic, NEC

Affinity Chemical Woodbine LLC ....F 973 873-4070
Flanders **(G-3398)**
AIG Industrial Group Inc ....F 201 767-7300
Northvale **(G-7516)**
Airgas Usa LLC ....F 609 685-4241
Cherry Hill **(G-1337)**
Airgas Usa LLC ....E 856 829-7878
Cinnaminson **(G-1440)**
American Gas & Chemical Co Ltd ....E 201 767-7300
Northvale **(G-7518)**
Atlantic Associates Intl Inc ....F 856 662-1717
Pennsauken **(G-8392)**
Avantor Performance Mtls LLC ....G 610 573-2759
Bridgewater **(G-797)**
Avantor Performance Mtls LLC ....B 908 859-2151
Phillipsburg **(G-8542)**
BASF Catalysts LLC ....C 732 205-5000
Carteret **(G-1249)**
BASF Corporation ....F 732 205-5000
Iselin **(G-4601)**
BASF Corporation ....B 973 245-6000
Florham Park **(G-3491)**
Basfin Corporation ....A 973 245-6000
Florham Park **(G-3493)**
Baumar Industries Inc ....G 973 667-5490
Nutley **(G-7580)**
Biochemical Sciences Inc ....G 856 467-1813
Swedesboro **(G-10572)**
Chem-Is-Try Inc ....G 732 372-7311
Metuchen **(G-6052)**
Chemtrade Chemicals Corp ....D 973 515-0900
Parsippany **(G-7901)**
Chemtrade Chemicals US LLC ....D 973 515-0900
Parsippany **(G-7902)**
Chemtrade Gcc Holding Company ....G 973 515-0900
Parsippany **(G-7903)**
Chemtrade Water Chemical Inc ....G 973 515-0900
Parsippany **(G-7905)**
Chessco Industries Inc ....E 609 882-0400
Ewing **(G-3020)**
Citi-Chem Inc ....E 609 231-6655
Maple Shade **(G-5860)**
CMS Technology Inc ....F 512 913-1898
Bridgewater **(G-812)**

Coim USA Inc ....E 856 224-1668
Paulsboro (G-8331)

Dallas Group of America Inc ....E 908 534-7800
Whitehouse (G-11915)

E I Du Pont De Nemours & Co ....E 732 257-1579
Parlin (G-7863)

Elementis Chromium Inc ....C 609 443-2000
East Windsor (G-2367)

Elements Global Group LLC ....G 908 468-8407
Gillette (G-3801)

Elkem Silicones USA Corp ....E 732 227-2060
East Brunswick (G-2141)

Engelhard Corporation ....F 732 205-5000
Iselin (G-4608)

Evonik Corporation ....B 973 929-8000
Parsippany (G-7938)

Futurrex Inc ....F 973 209-1563
Franklin (G-3603)

Gentek Inc...C 973 515-0900
Parsippany (G-7956)

Honeywell International Inc ....C 973 455-2000
Morris Plains (G-6614)

Innophos Inc ....G 973 587-8735
Cranbury (G-1840)

Innophos LLC ....G 609 495-2495
Cranbury (G-1841)

Innophos Holdings Inc ....D 609 495-2495
Cranbury (G-1842)

Innophos Inc ....A 609 495-2495
Cranbury (G-1843)

Innophos Investments II Inc ....G 609 495-2495
Cranbury (G-1844)

Innophos Invstmnts Hldings Inc ....G 609 495-2495
Cranbury (G-1845)

Intelligent Mtl Solutions Inc ....F 609 514-4031
Princeton (G-8963)

JM Huber Corporation ....D 732 603-3630
Edison (G-2540)

Ligno Tech USA Inc ....G 908 429-6660
Bridgewater (G-843)

Liquid Elements ....G 856 321-7646
Maple Shade (G-5865)

Lonza Inc ....D 201 316-9200
Morristown (G-6681)

Mateson Chemical Corporation ....G 215 423-3200
Cinnaminson (G-1472)

Mel Chemicals Inc................................C 908 782-5800
Flemington (G-3455)

Meson Group Inc ....E 201 767-7300
Northvale (G-7536)

Morre-TEC Industries Inc ....E 908 688-9009
Union (G-11076)

New Heaven Chemicals Iowa LLC.......G 201 506-9109
Sussex (G-10564)

Newfuturevest Two LLC ....G 609 586-8004
Trenton (G-10965)

Northeast Chemicals Inc ....B 508 634-6900
East Brunswick (G-2160)

Northeast Chemicals Inc ....E 732 227-0100
East Brunswick (G-2161)

Northeast Chemicals Inc ....F 732 673-6966
East Brunswick (G-2162)

Nouryon Surface Chemistry ....D 732 985-6262
Edison (G-2579)

Nova Chemicals Inc ....G 973 726-0056
Sparta (G-10404)

P W Perkins Co Inc ....G 856 769-3525
Woodstown (G-12095)

Phibrochem Inc ....G 201 329-7300
Teaneck (G-10646)

Polymer Products Company Inc...........E 856 533-1866
Mount Laurel (G-6792)

PQ Corporation ....E 732 750-9040
Avenel (G-141)

Protameen Chemicals Inc ....E 973 256-4374
Totowa (G-10847)

Reade Manufacturing Company ....E 732 657-6451
Manchester (G-5848)

Resintech Inc..C 856 768-9600
West Berlin (G-11619)

Riogen Inc...G 609 529-0503
Monmouth Junction (G-6309)

Rockwood Holdings Inc ....F 609 514-0300
Princeton (G-9017)

Sanit Technologies LLC ....F 862 238-7555
Passaic (G-8105)

Setcon Industries Inc...........................E 973 283-0500
Riverdale (G-9384)

Solvay Spclty Polymers USA LLC........C 856 853-8119
West Deptford (G-11716)

Solvay USA Inc ....D 609 860-4000
Cranbury (G-1883)

Spectrum Laboratory Pdts Inc ....E 732 214-1300
New Brunswick (G-6972)

Spex Certprep Group LLC ....E 732 549-7144
Metuchen (G-6071)

Synasia Inc ....G 732 205-9880
Metuchen (G-6075)

Wisesorbent Technology LLC ....E 856 872-7713
Marlton (G-5957)

Youniversal Labortories ....G 201 807-9000
South Hackensack (G-10191)

CHEMICALS: Magnesium Compounds Or Salts, Inorganic

Luxfer Magtech Inc ....E 803 610-9898
Manchester (G-5846)

CHEMICALS: Medicinal

Bodybio Inc ....E 856 825-8338
Millville (G-6238)

Kingchem Life Science LLC..................F 201 825-9988
Allendale (G-10)

Pharmacia & Upjohn Inc ....G 908 901-8000
Peapack (G-8343)

Pharmacia & Upjohn Company LLC .....B 908 901-8000
Peapack (G-8344)

CHEMICALS: Medicinal, Organic, Uncompounded, Bulk

Sytheon Ltd ....G 973 988-1075
Boonton (G-569)

CHEMICALS: NEC

A D M Tronics Unlimited Inc ....E 201 767-6040
Northvale (G-7513)

A J P Scientific Inc ....G 973 472-7200
Clifton (G-1551)

Acceledev Chemical LLC ....G 862 239-1524
Wayne (G-11465)

Advansix Inc ....B 973 526-1800
Parsippany (G-7875)

Amerchol Corporation ....C 732 248-6000
Edison (G-2452)

Amfine Chemical Corporation ....F 201 818-0159
Hasbrouck Heights (G-4181)

Ashland Spcalty Ingredients GP ....E 732 353-7708
Parlin (G-7862)

Atlas Refinery Inc.................................E 973 589-2002
Newark (G-7056)

Avantor Performance Mtls LLC ....B 908 859-2151
Phillipsburg (G-8542)

Beacon C M P Corp...............................G 908 851-9393
Kenilworth (G-4927)

Bostik Inc ....D 856 848-8669
Paulsboro (G-8330)

BP Corporation North Amer Inc............E 908 474-5000
Linden (G-5327)

Brenntag Specialties Inc ....G 908 561-6100
South Plainfield (G-10228)

C & S Specialty Inc ....G 201 750-7740
Norwood (G-7559)

Cantol Inc...E 609 846-7912
Wildwood (G-11942)

CC Packaging LLC................................G 732 213-9008
Bayville (G-242)

Chem-Is-Try Inc ....G 732 372-7311
Metuchen (G-6052)

Croda Inc ....D 732 417-0800
Edison (G-2486)

Croda Investments Inc ....G 732 417-0800
Edison (G-2487)

Cytec Industries Inc.............................C 973 357-3100
Princeton (G-8927)

Delta Procurement Inc..........................E 201 623-9353
Carlstadt (G-1149)

Elan Inc ....D 973 344-8014
Newark (G-7112)

Elementis Specialties Inc ....C 609 443-2000
East Windsor (G-2369)

Euclid Chemical Company ....F 732 390-9770
East Brunswick (G-2145)

Ferro Corporation ....C 856 467-3000
Bridgeport (G-738)

Fisher Scientific Company LLC ....B 201 796-7100
Fair Lawn (G-3102)

Fluorotherm Polymers Inc ....G 973 575-0760
Parsippany (G-7948)

Fuel Management Services Inc.............G 732 929-1964
Toms River (G-10760)

Global Seven Inc ....G 973 209-7474
Rockaway (G-9464)

Grignard Company LLC ....E 732 340-1111
Rahway (G-9098)

Gulbrandsen Technologies Inc.............E 908 735-5458
Clinton (G-1746)

Gulco Inc...E 908 238-2030
Phillipsburg (G-8554)

Houghton Chemical Corporation ....F 201 460-8071
Carlstadt (G-1166)

Hychem Corporation ....G 732 280-8803
Belmar (G-350)

Industrial Summit Tech Corp ....E 732 238-2211
Parlin (G-7865)

Infineum USA LP ....B 800 441-1074
Linden (G-5359)

Interntonal Specialty Pdts Inc ....A 859 815-3333
Wayne (G-11522)

Jenisse Leisure Products Inc ....F 973 331-1177
Towaco (G-10873)

Kronos Worldwide Inc ....E 609 860-6200
Cranbury (G-1852)

Lanxess Solutions US Inc.....................C 973 235-1800
Nutley (G-7589)

Lodor Offset Corporation ....F 201 935-7100
Carlstadt (G-1182)

Lonza Inc ....D 201 316-9200
Morristown (G-6681)

Lubrizol Advanced Mtls Inc ....E 856 299-3764
Pedricktown (G-8351)

Lubrizol Corporation ....G 732 981-0149
Piscataway (G-8684)

Lubrizol Global Management ....F 973 471-1300
Clifton (G-1661)

Mapei Corporation ....E 732 254-4830
South River (G-10352)

Mel Chemicals Inc................................C 908 782-5800
Flemington (G-3455)

Mri International ....G 973 383-3645
Newton (G-7350)

Nouryon Surface Chemistry ....D 732 985-6262
Edison (G-2579)

Nutech Corp ....G 908 707-2097
Franklin Lakes (G-3629)

Plant Food Company Inc ....E 609 448-0935
Cranbury (G-1872)

Polymer Additives Inc ....F 856 467-8247
Bridgeport (G-743)

Prestone Products Corporation ....E 732 431-8200
Freehold (G-3692)

Procedyne Corp ....E 732 249-8347
New Brunswick (G-6962)

Rockwood Specialties Group Inc ....F 609 514-0300
Princeton (G-9018)

Royce Associates A Ltd Partnr............D 201 438-5200
East Rutherford (G-2315)

Shamrock Technologies Inc ....D 973 242-2999
Newark (G-7268)

Sika Corporation ....B 201 933-8800
Lyndhurst (G-5678)

SKW Quab Chemicals Inc ....F 201 556-0300
Saddle Brook (G-9681)

Solvay USA Inc ....B 609 860-4000
Princeton (G-9025)

Spectrum Laboratory Pdts Inc ....C 732 214-1300
New Brunswick (G-6971)

Spectrum Laboratory Pdts Inc ....E 732 214-1300
New Brunswick (G-6972)

Spex Certiprep Inc ....D 732 549-7144
Metuchen (G-6069)

Stepan Company ....D 201 845-3030
Maywood (G-6016)

Stonhard Manufacturing Co Inc ....E 856 779-7500
Maple Shade (G-5871)

Stuart Steel Protection Corp ....E 732 469-5544
Somerset (G-10075)

Sun Chemical Corporation ....E 201 438-4831
East Rutherford (G-2322)

Superior Printing Ink Co Inc ....G 973 242-5868
Newark (G-7291)

Suven Life Sciences Ltd.......................F 732 274-0037
Monmouth Junction (G-6314)

Sylvan Chemical Corporation ....E 201 934-4224
Fair Lawn (G-3124)

Ungerer & Company ....B 973 628-0600
Lincoln Park (G-5309)

PRODUCT

United Energy Corp .... G 732 994-5225
Howell *(G-4552)*
William Kenyon & Sons Inc .... E 732 985-8980
Piscataway *(G-8738)*
Wilshire Technologies Inc .... G 609 683-1117
Princeton *(G-9043)*
Worldwide Safety Systems LLC ...... G 888 613-4501
Teaneck *(G-10656)*
Zoomessence Inc .... G 732 416-6638
Sayreville *(G-9727)*

CHEMICALS: Nickel Compounds Or Salts, Inorganic

Omg Electronic Chemicals Inc ...... C 908 222-5800
South Plainfield *(G-10311)*
Phibro-Tech Inc .... E 201 329-7300
Teaneck *(G-10645)*

CHEMICALS: Nonmetallic Compounds

R & M Chemical Technologies .... F 908 537-9516
Hampton *(G-4159)*

CHEMICALS: Organic, NEC

Adron Inc .... E 973 334-1600
Boonton *(G-536)*
Agilis Chemicals Inc .... F 973 910-2424
Short Hills *(G-9864)*
Akcros Chemicals Inc .... D 800 500-7890
New Brunswick *(G-6909)*
Akzo Nobel Coatings Inc .... G 732 617-7734
Morganville *(G-6581)*
Alzo International Inc .... E 732 254-1901
Sayreville *(G-9702)*
Aromiens Inc .... G 732 225-8689
Edison *(G-2461)*
Ashland Spcalty Ingredients GP ...... C 908 243-3500
Bridgewater *(G-795)*
Ashland Spcalty Ingredients GP ...... E 732 353-7708
Parlin *(G-7862)*
ATL .... G 201 825-1400
Ramsey *(G-9140)*
Avantor Performance Mtls LLC ...... B 908 859-2151
Phillipsburg *(G-8542)*
BASF Americas Corporation .... F 973 245-6000
Florham Park *(G-3488)*
BASF California Inc .... G 973 245-6000
Florham Park *(G-3489)*
BASF Catalysts Holdg China LLC ...... G 973 245-6000
Florham Park *(G-3490)*
BASF Corporation .... B 973 245-6000
Florham Park *(G-3491)*
BASF Corporation .... D 908 689-7470
Washington *(G-11440)*
BASF Corporation .... E 848 221-2786
Toms River *(G-10749)*
BASF Corporation .... C 732 205-5086
Iselin *(G-4600)*
BASF Corporation .... C 732 205-2700
Union *(G-11029)*
BASF Corporation .... E 973 426-5429
Budd Lake *(G-919)*
BASF Corporation .... E 973 245-6000
Edison *(G-2465)*
Basfin Corporation .... A 973 245-6000
Florham Park *(G-3493)*
Chem-Fleur Inc .... D 973 589-4266
Newark *(G-7083)*
Chem-Is-Try Inc .... G 732 372-7311
Metuchen *(G-6052)*
Chembiopower Inc .... G 908 209-5595
Warren *(G-11404)*
Chemmark Development Inc .... G 908 561-0923
South Plainfield *(G-10238)*
Coim USA Inc .... E 856 224-1668
Paulsboro *(G-8331)*
Colibri Scentique Ltd Lblty Co ...... G 201 445-5715
Glen Rock *(G-3830)*
Crompton Corp .... G 732 826-6600
Perth Amboy *(G-8516)*
Cvc Specialty Chemicals Inc .... F 856 533-3000
Moorestown *(G-6517)*
Deleet Merchandising Corp .... E 212 962-6565
Newark *(G-7101)*
Elan Inc .... D 973 344-8014
Newark *(G-7112)*
Energy Chem America Inc .... D 201 816-2307
Englewood Cliffs *(G-2969)*
Epic Holding Inc .... E 732 249-6867
Morristown *(G-6663)*

Evonik Corporation .... D 732 981-5000
Piscataway *(G-8662)*
Evonik Corporation .... B 973 929-8000
Parsippany *(G-7938)*
FMC Corporation .... C 609 963-6200
Ewing *(G-3031)*
Gentek Inc .... C 973 515-0900
Parsippany *(G-7956)*
Givaudan Fragrances Corp .... C 973 576-9500
East Hanover *(G-2214)*
Honig Chemical & Proc Corp .... E 973 344-0881
Newark *(G-7152)*
Interntnal Flvors Frgrnces Inc ...... C 732 264-4500
Union Beach *(G-11101)*
Isp Chemco LLC .... G 973 628-4000
Wayne *(G-11523)*
Isp Global Technologies Inc .... G 973 628-4000
Wayne *(G-11524)*
Isp Global Technologies LLC .... G 973 628-4000
Wayne *(G-11525)*
Lanxess Solutions US Inc .... C 732 826-1018
Perth Amboy *(G-8524)*
Ligno Tech USA Inc .... G 908 429-6660
Bridgewater *(G-843)*
Lonza Inc .... D 201 316-9200
Morristown *(G-6681)*
Lyondell Chemical Company .... F 732 985-6262
Edison *(G-2556)*
National Strch Chem Holdg Corp ...... A 908 685-5000
Bridgewater *(G-854)*
Northeast Chemicals Inc .... E 508 634-6900
East Brunswick *(G-2160)*
Northeast Chemicals Inc .... E 732 227-0100
East Brunswick *(G-2161)*
Northeast Chemicals Inc .... F 732 673-6966
East Brunswick *(G-2162)*
Pilot Chemical Company Ohio .... F 732 634-6613
Avenel *(G-140)*
Protameen Chemicals Inc .... E 973 256-4374
Totowa *(G-10847)*
Royale Pigments & Chem Inc .... E 201 845-4666
Paramus *(G-7830)*
Royce Associates A Ltd Partnr .... D 201 438-5200
East Rutherford *(G-2315)*
Royce International Corp .... G 201 438-5200
East Rutherford *(G-2316)*
Sanit Technologies LLC .... F 862 238-7555
Passaic *(G-8105)*
SE Tylos USA .... G 973 837-8001
Totowa *(G-10851)*
Small Molecules Inc .... G 201 918-4664
Hoboken *(G-4482)*
Sonneborn LLC .... F 201 760-2940
Parsippany *(G-8018)*
Sonneborn US Holdings LLC .... G 201 760-2940
Parsippany *(G-8020)*
Stepan Company .... D 609 298-1222
Bordentown *(G-595)*
Surface Technology Inc .... F 609 259-0099
Ewing *(G-3068)*
Troy Corporation .... D 973 443-4200
Florham Park *(G-3524)*
Umicore Precious Metals NJ LLC ...... E 908 222-5006
South Plainfield *(G-10333)*
Veolia Es .... E 732 469-5100
Middlesex *(G-6158)*
Viva Chemical Corporation .... G 201 461-5281
Fort Lee *(G-3594)*

CHEMICALS: Phenol

Solvay Holding Inc .... A 609 860-4000
Princeton *(G-9024)*
Solvay USA Inc .... C 732 297-0100
North Brunswick *(G-7486)*
Solvay USA Inc .... B 609 860-4000
Princeton *(G-9025)*

CHEMICALS: Phosphates, Defluorinated/Ammoniated, Exc Fertlr

Perimeter Solutions LP .... C 732 541-3000
Carteret *(G-1264)*

CHEMICALS: Reagent Grade, Refined From Technical Grade

Bd Biscnces Systems Rgents Inc ...... G 201 847-6800
Franklin Lakes *(G-3614)*
G J Chemical Co .... E 973 589-1450
Somerset *(G-9996)*

CHEMICALS: Soda Ash

FMC Corporation .... D 973 256-0768
Woodland Park *(G-12079)*
FMC Corporation .... D 732 541-3000
Carteret *(G-1253)*
Solvay Holding Inc .... A 609 860-4000
Princeton *(G-9024)*
Solvay USA Inc .... C 732 297-0100
North Brunswick *(G-7486)*

CHEMICALS: Sodium Bicarbonate

Church & Dwight Co Inc .... F 732 730-3100
Lakewood *(G-5070)*
Church & Dwight Co Inc .... F 609 655-6101
Cranbury *(G-1822)*
Church & Dwight Co Inc .... G 609 683-8021
Princeton *(G-8923)*
Church & Dwight Co Inc .... B 609 806-1200
Ewing *(G-3021)*

CHEMICALS: Sodium/Potassium Cmpnds,Exc Bleach,Alkalies/Alum

Kuehne Chemical Company Inc .... E 973 589-0700
Kearny *(G-4876)*

CHEMICALS: Sulfur, Incl Rcvrd/Refined, Fm Sour Natural Gas

Reagent Chemical & RES Inc .... E 908 284-2800
Ringoes *(G-9341)*

CHEMICALS: Water Treatment

Alden - Leeds Inc .... D 973 589-3544
Kearny *(G-4842)*
Ashland LLC .... G 908 243-3500
Bridgewater *(G-794)*
C S L Water Treatment Inc .... F 908 647-1400
Warren *(G-11401)*
Chemtreat Inc .... G 609 654-9522
Medford *(G-6021)*
Custom Blends Inc .... G 215 934-7080
Ewing *(G-3025)*
Garratt-Callahan Company .... G 732 287-2200
Edison *(G-2520)*
Hydrocrbon Tech Innovation LLC ...... E 609 394-3102
Lawrenceville *(G-5232)*
Industrial Water Tech Inc .... G 732 888-1233
Hazlet *(G-4261)*
Lanxess Sybron Chemicals Inc ...... C 609 893-1100
Birmingham *(G-457)*
Pariser Industries Inc .... E 973 569-9090
Paterson *(G-8277)*
Robert Nichols Contracting .... F 973 902-2632
Ringwood *(G-9352)*
Seaboard Industries .... F 732 901-5700
Lakewood *(G-5161)*
Sentry Water Management .... E 973 616-9000
Riverdale *(G-9383)*
Solenis LLC .... E 201 767-7400
Norwood *(G-7574)*
Wasak Inc .... G 973 605-8122
Morristown *(G-6709)*
Water Dynamics Incorporated ...... G 973 428-8330
Whippany *(G-11912)*

CHEMICALS: Zinc Chloride

Madison Industries Inc .... E 732 727-2225
Old Bridge *(G-7719)*

CHEWING GUM

Gum Runners LLC .... F 201 333-0756
Jersey City *(G-4745)*

CHILDREN'S & INFANTS' CLOTHING STORES

Marmaxx Operating Corp .... D 973 575-7910
West Caldwell *(G-11660)*
Sock Company Inc .... E 201 307-0675
Westwood *(G-11845)*

CHILDREN'S WEAR STORES

Buy Buy Baby Inc .... F 908 688-0888
Union *(G-11034)*

CHINA & GLASS REPAIR SVCS

Quality Glass Inc...............................F 908 754-2652
South Plainfield (G-10320)

CHINAWARE WHOLESALERS

Nikko Ceramics Inc......................F 201 840-5200
Fairview (G-3364)

CHIROPRACTORS' OFFICES

Spinal Kinetics LLC ....G...... 908 687-2552
Union (G-11091)

CHOCOLATE, EXC CANDY FROM BEANS: Chips, Powder, Block, Syrup

Bergen Marzipan & Chocolate ....G....... 201 385-8343
Bergenfield (G-373)
Birnn Chocolates Inc ....G....... 732 214-8680
Highland Park (G-4287)
Bromilows Candy Co............................G....... 973 684-1496
Woodland Park (G-12072)
Candy Treasure LLC ....G....... 201 830-3600
Lebanon (G-5254)
Chocmod USA Inc ....E....... 201 585-8730
Fort Lee (G-3552)
David Bradley Chocolatier Inc ....F 609 443-4747
Windsor (G-11995)
David Bradley Chocolatier Inc ....E....... 732 536-7719
Englishtown (G-3001)
Dove Chocolate Discoveries LLC............E....... 866 922-3683
Mount Arlington (G-6711)
Fralingers Inc ....E....... 609 345-2177
Atlantic City (G-90)
K K S Criterion Chocolates ....E....... 732 542-7847
Eatontown (G-2406)
Koppers Chocolate LLC ....D....... 212 243-0220
Jersey City (G-4756)
Mars Incorporated...............................D....... 908 850-2420
Hackettstown (G-4022)
Mars Incorporated...............................A....... 908 852-1000
Hackettstown (G-4021)
Mars Chocolate North Amer LLC ....A....... 908 852-1000
Hackettstown (G-4023)
Mars Retail Group Inc ....E....... 973 398-2078
Mount Arlington (G-6715)
Promotion In Motion Inc ....D....... 201 962-8530
Allendale (G-14)
Savita Naturals Ltd ....E....... 856 467-4949
Swedesboro (G-10608)

CHOCOLATE, EXC CANDY FROM PURCH CHOC: Chips, Powder, Block

Barry Callebaut USA LLC ....E....... 856 663-2260
Pennsauken (G-8393)
Barry Callebaut USA LLC ....D....... 856 663-2260
Pennsauken (G-8394)
Bosco Products Inc ....G....... 973 334-7534
Towaco (G-10866)
Forget ME Not Chocolates By NA ....G....... 856 753-8916
Atco (G-86)
Matisse Chocolatier Inc ....G....... 201 568-2288
Englewood (G-2923)
Nouveautes Inc ....F 973 882-8850
Fairfield (G-3283)
Third Ave Chocolate Shoppe ....E....... 732 449-7535
Spring Lake (G-10424)
Undercover Chocolate Co LLC..............G....... 973 668-5000
East Hanover (G-2244)

CHRISTMAS NOVELTIES, WHOLESALE

Advance International Inc ....E....... 212 213-2229
Matawan (G-5966)

CHRISTMAS TREE LIGHTING SETS: Electric

Advance International Inc ....E....... 212 213-2229
Matawan (G-5966)
Jvs Christmas Lighting ....G....... 201 664-4022
Westwood (G-11832)

CHRISTMAS TREES: Artificial

Advance International Inc ....E....... 212 213-2229
Matawan (G-5966)
Foldtex II Ltd ....E....... 908 928-0919
Westfield (G-11797)
National Christmas Pdts Inc ....E....... 908 709-4141
Cranford (G-1918)

CHROMATOGRAPHY EQPT

Analytical Sales and Svcs Inc................F 973 616-0700
Flanders (G-3400)
E S Industries Inc ....G...... 856 753-8400
West Berlin (G-11591)
Waters Technologies Corp ....F 973 394-5660
Parsippany (G-8037)

CIGARETTE LIGHTER FLINTS

Triangle Manufacturing Co....................G...... 201 962-7433
Upper Saddle River (G-11147)

CIGARETTE LIGHTERS

Nova Distributors LLC ....F 908 222-1010
Edison (G-2580)
Rclc Inc ....F 732 877-1788
Woodbridge (G-12020)

CIGARETTE STORES

Sherman Nat Inc.................................E...... 201 735-9000
Englewood (G-2940)

CIRCUIT BOARDS, PRINTED: Television & Radio

Ai-Logix Inc ....E...... 732 469-0880
Somerset (G-9944)
Applicad Inc.......................................E...... 732 751-2555
Wall Township (G-11318)
Harrison Electro Mechanical ....F 732 382-6008
Rahway (G-9100)
Omega Circuit and Engineering ....E...... 732 246-1661
New Brunswick (G-6957)
Pcr Technologies Inc ....G...... 973 882-0017
Pine Brook (G-8613)
PNC Inc ....C...... 973 284-1600
Nutley (G-7592)
Precision Graphics Inc ....D...... 908 707-8880
Branchburg (G-671)
Shore Printed Circuits Inc ....E...... 732 380-0590
Eatontown (G-2420)

CIRCUIT BOARDS: Wiring

AT&T Technologies Inc ....A...... 201 771-2000
Berkeley Heights (G-389)
P W B Omni Inc ....F 856 384-1300
West Deptford (G-11713)

CIRCUITS, INTEGRATED: Hybrid

Hybrid-Tek LLC ....F 609 259-3355
Clarksburg (G-1521)

CIRCUITS: Electronic

ABB Installation Products Inc ....C...... 908 852-1122
Hackettstown (G-3994)
Adcomm Inc ....C...... 201 342-3338
South Hackensack (G-10146)
Advanced Technology Group Inc............E...... 973 627-6955
Rockaway (G-9439)
Aeon Engineering LLC ....G...... 518 253-7681
Fort Lee (G-3545)
American Fibertek Inc ....E...... 732 302-0660
Somerset (G-9951)
Ango Electronics Corporation................F 201 955-0800
North Arlington (G-7368)
Applied Resources Corp ....E...... 973 328-3882
Wharton (G-11852)
Az-Em USA Branchburg NJ ....G...... 908 429-0020
Branchburg (G-624)
Bihler of America Inc ....C...... 908 213-9001
Phillipsburg (G-8546)
Billows Electric Supply Co Inc ....C...... 856 751-2200
Delran (G-2009)
Bkh Electronics ....G...... 210 410-2757
Wanaque (G-11391)
Ccard..G...... 732 303-8264
Manalapan (G-5803)
Creatone Inc ....F 908 789-8700
Mountainside (G-6637)
D&N Machine Manufacturing Inc...........E...... 856 456-1366
Gloucester City (G-3840)
Dantco Corp ....F 973 278-8776
Paterson (G-8168)
Data Delay Devices ....E...... 973 202-3268
Clifton (G-1596)

Doralex Inc..G...... 856 764-0694
Delran (G-2016)
Douglas Elec Components Inc ....D...... 973 627-8230
Randolph (G-9175)
Empire Telecommunications Inc ....F 201 569-3339
Englewood Cliffs (G-2968)
Ewc Controls Inc ....E...... 732 446-3110
Manalapan (G-5809)
Famcam Inc ....E...... 973 503-1600
Parsippany (G-7941)
Foremost Corp ....G...... 973 839-3360
Wayne (G-11504)
Gold Enterprise Ltd ....C...... 954 614-1001
Point Pleasant Boro (G-8845)
Haz Laboratories ....F 908 453-3300
Washington (G-11446)
Hermetic Solutions Group Inc ....F 732 722-8780
Tinton Falls (G-10719)
J A M I Enterprise Inc ....G...... 732 714-6811
Brick (G-721)
J P Rotella Co Inc................................F 973 942-2559
Haledon (G-4083)
JB Electronics ....F 609 497-2952
Princeton (G-8965)
Jettron Products Inc ....E...... 973 887-0571
East Hanover (G-2220)
Johanson Manufacturing Corp...............C...... 973 658-1051
Boonton (G-559)
Mechanical Ingenuity Corp ....E...... 732 842-8889
Eatontown (G-2410)
Metal Cutting Corporation.....................D...... 973 239-1100
Cedar Grove (G-1282)
Noah LLC ....G...... 609 637-0039
Lawrenceville (G-5240)
Norsal Distribution Associates ....F 908 638-6430
High Bridge (G-4284)
Pcr Technologies Inc ....G...... 973 882-0017
Pine Brook (G-8613)
Prima-TEC Electronics Corp ....G...... 201 947-4052
East Rutherford (G-2312)
Roxboro Holdings Inc...........................D...... 732 919-3119
Wall Township (G-11365)
Seren Industrial Power Systems ....F 856 205-1131
Vineland (G-11264)
Silverstone Wireless LLC......................G...... 845 458-5197
Lodi (G-5575)
Spencer Industries Inc ....E...... 973 751-2200
Belleville (G-315)
Spirent Communications Inc ....G...... 732 946-4018
Holmdel (G-4514)
Thomas Instrumentation Inc ....F 609 624-2630
Cape May Court House (G-1116)
Ttss Interactive Products Inc..................E...... 301 230-1464
Riverdale (G-9388)
Utz Technologies Inc ....E...... 973 339-1100
Little Falls (G-5472)
Western Electronics Dist.......................G...... 908 475-3303
Belvidere (G-368)
Wireworks Corporation.........................E...... 908 686-7400
Hillside (G-4437)

CLAY MINING, COMMON

Partac Peat Corp ....F 908 637-4191
Great Meadows (G-3855)

CLAYS, EXC KAOLIN & BALL

Eaglevision Usa LLC ....G...... 908 322-1892
Fanwood (G-3372)

CLEANING EQPT: Commercial

Detrex Corporation ....G...... 856 786-8686
Cinnaminson (G-1452)
Energy Beams Inc ....F 973 291-6555
Bloomingdale (G-528)
Es Industrial ....D...... 732 842-5600
Red Bank (G-9228)
Karcher North America Inc ....F 856 228-1800
Blackwood (G-474)
Randall Manufacturing Co Inc ....E...... 973 746-2111
Hillside (G-4424)
Seaboard Paper and Twine LLC ....E...... 973 413-8100
Paterson (G-8296)
Unique Systems Inc.............................F 973 455-0440
Cedar Knolls (G-1315)

CLEANING EQPT: Dirt Sweeping Units, Indl

Elgee Manufacturing Company ....G...... 908 647-4100
Warren (G-11408)

P
R
O
D
U
C
T

CLEANING EQPT: Floor Washing & Polishing, Commercial

Amano USA Holdings Inc ....G...... 973 403-1900
  Roseland *(G-9531)*
Mercury Floor Machines Inc .....E 201 568-4606
  Englewood *(G-2924)*

CLEANING EQPT: High Pressure

A Plus Powerwashing ....G...... 732 245-3816
  Neptune *(G-6863)*
Innovative Pressure Clg LLC ....G...... 609 738-3100
  Cream Ridge *(G-1937)*
Margaritaville Inc ....G...... 973 728-7562
  West Milford *(G-11729)*
Powerwash Plus ....G...... 732 671-6767
  Middletown *(G-6166)*

CLEANING EQPT: Janitors' Carts

Janico Inc ....F 732 370-2223
  Freehold *(G-3672)*

CLEANING OR POLISHING PREPARATIONS, NEC

Amano USA Holdings Inc ....G...... 973 403-1900
  Roseland *(G-9531)*
Americhem Enterprises Inc ....G...... 732 363-4840
  Lakewood *(G-5051)*
Aqua Products Inc ....E 856 829-8444
  Cinnaminson *(G-1441)*
Atlantic Associates Intl Inc ....F 856 662-1717
  Pennsauken *(G-8392)*
Cantol Inc ....E 609 846-7912
  Wildwood *(G-11942)*
Cavalier Chemical Co Inc ....E 908 558-0110
  Short Hills *(G-9865)*
Envirochem Inc ....E 732 238-6700
  South River *(G-10350)*
Fabric Chemical Corporation ....G...... 201 432-0440
  Jersey City *(G-4733)*
Interntional Cnsld Chemex Corp .....E 732 828-7676
  New Brunswick *(G-6936)*
L & R Manufacturing Co Inc ....D...... 201 991-5330
  Kearny *(G-4877)*
Magnuson Products ....F 973 472-9292
  Clifton *(G-1663)*
Penetone Corporation ....E 201 567-3000
  Clifton *(G-1688)*
Raybeam Manufacturing Corp ....G...... 201 941-4529
  Ridgefield *(G-9286)*
Trim Brush Company Inc ....G...... 973 887-2525
  East Hanover *(G-2243)*

CLEANING PRDTS: Ammonia, Household

Q-Pak Corporation ....E 973 483-4404
  Newark *(G-7242)*

CLEANING PRDTS: Bleaches, Household, Dry Or Liquid

Church & Dwight Co Inc ....B...... 609 806-1200
  Ewing *(G-3021)*

CLEANING PRDTS: Degreasing Solvent

Arol Chemical Products Co ....G...... 973 344-1510
  Newark *(G-7053)*
Green Power Chemical LLC ....F 973 770-5600
  Hopatcong *(G-4520)*
Made Solutions LLC ....G...... 201 254-3693
  Fair Lawn *(G-3110)*

CLEANING PRDTS: Deodorants, Nonpersonal

Allison Corp ....G...... 973 992-3800
  Livingston *(G-5504)*
Mennen Company ....B...... 973 630-1500
  Morristown *(G-6685)*
RB Manufacturing LLC ....C...... 908 533-2000
  Hillsborough *(G-4350)*
RB Manufacturing LLC ....B...... 973 404-2600
  Parsippany *(G-8004)*
Reckitt Benckiser LLC ....B...... 973 404-2600
  Parsippany *(G-8005)*

CLEANING PRDTS: Disinfectants, Household Or Indl Plant

Penetone Corporation ....G...... 609 921-0501
  Princeton *(G-8994)*
Schulke Inc ....G...... 973 521-7163
  Fairfield *(G-3308)*
Sterigenics US LLC ....G...... 856 241-8880
  Swedesboro *(G-10611)*

CLEANING PRDTS: Drain Pipe Solvents Or Cleaners

Advanced Sewer ....F 973 278-1948
  Woodland Park *(G-12069)*
Brasscraft Manufacturing Co ....G...... 856 241-7700
  Swedesboro *(G-10574)*
Cobra Products Inc ....D...... 856 241-7700
  Swedesboro *(G-10577)*

CLEANING PRDTS: Drycleaning Preparations

A L Wilson Chemical Co ....F 201 997-3300
  Kearny *(G-4840)*
Ramblewood Cleaners Inc ....G...... 856 235-6051
  Mount Laurel *(G-6799)*

CLEANING PRDTS: Floor Waxes

Epic Holding Inc ....E 732 249-6867
  Morristown *(G-6663)*

CLEANING PRDTS: Indl Plant Disinfectants Or Deodorants

Menshen Packaging USA Inc ....D...... 201 445-7436
  Waldwick *(G-11304)*

CLEANING PRDTS: Metal Polish

Agate Lacquer Tri-Nat LLC ....G...... 732 968-1080
  Middlesex *(G-6095)*

CLEANING PRDTS: Polishing Preparations & Related Prdts

National Auto Detailing Netwrk ....E 856 931-5529
  Bellmawr *(G-340)*
Royce Associates A Ltd Partnr ....D...... 201 438-5200
  East Rutherford *(G-2315)*
Stepan Company ....D...... 201 845-3030
  Maywood *(G-6016)*

CLEANING PRDTS: Sanitation Preparations

Chemique Inc ....G...... 856 235-4161
  Moorestown *(G-6512)*

CLEANING PRDTS: Sanitation Preps, Disinfectants/Deodorants

Microgen Inc ....G...... 973 575-9025
  West Caldwell *(G-11666)*
Zoono USA Ltd Liability Co ....G...... 732 722-8757
  Shrewsbury *(G-9905)*

CLEANING PRDTS: Specialty

Associated Cleaning Systems ....G...... 201 530-9197
  Teaneck *(G-10622)*
Clenesco Products Corp ....F 908 245-5255
  Roselle *(G-9552)*
Jobe Industries Inc ....G...... 908 862-0400
  Linden *(G-5365)*
Ronell Industries Inc ....B...... 908 245-5255
  Roselle *(G-9571)*

CLEANING PRDTS: Stain Removers

Edwards Creative Products Inc ....F 856 665-3200
  Cherry Hill *(G-1358)*

CLEANING SVCS

Associated Cleaning Systems ....G...... 201 530-9197
  Teaneck *(G-10622)*

CLIPPERS: Fingernail & Toenail

Revlon Inc ....E 732 287-1400
  Edison *(G-2598)*

CLOCK REPAIR SVCS

Garrett Moore ....G...... 908 231-9231
  Bridgewater *(G-825)*

CLOSURES: Closures, Stamped Metal

Amcor Flexibles LLC ....C...... 856 825-1400
  Millville *(G-6224)*

CLOSURES: Plastic

Associated Plastics Inc ....F 732 574-2800
  Rahway *(G-9079)*
C & N Packaging Inc ....D...... 631 491-1400
  Wayne *(G-11486)*
Revere Plastics Inc ....G...... 201 641-0777
  Little Ferry *(G-5494)*
Stull Technologies LLC ....D...... 732 873-5000
  Somerset *(G-10076)*

CLOTHING & ACCESS, WOMEN, CHILD & INFANT, WHOL: Blouses

Chic LLC ....G...... 732 354-0035
  East Brunswick *(G-2132)*

CLOTHING & ACCESS, WOMEN, CHILD & INFANT, WHSLE: Sportswear

Ballet Makers Inc ....G...... 973 595-9000
  Totowa *(G-10818)*
Jese Apparel LLC ....F 732 969-3200
  Dayton *(G-1973)*

CLOTHING & ACCESS, WOMEN, CHILDREN & INFANT, WHOL: Uniforms

Happy Chef Inc ....E 973 492-2525
  Butler *(G-1002)*

CLOTHING & ACCESS, WOMEN, CHILDREN/INFANT, WHOL: Baby Goods

Baby Time International Inc ....G...... 973 481-7400
  Newark *(G-7063)*

CLOTHING & ACCESS, WOMEN, CHILDREN/INFANT, WHOL: Nightwear

Charles Komar & Sons Inc ....B...... 212 725-1500
  Jersey City *(G-4711)*

CLOTHING & ACCESS, WOMEN, CHILDREN/INFANT, WHOL: Outerwear

Paradise ....G...... 973 425-0505
  Morristown *(G-6691)*

CLOTHING & ACCESS, WOMENS, CHILDREN & INFANTS, WHOL: Hats

Kathy Jeanne Inc ....F 973 575-9898
  Fairfield *(G-3248)*

CLOTHING & ACCESS: Costumes, Masquerade

Images Costume Productions ....G...... 609 859-7372
  Southampton *(G-10365)*
Xcessory LLC ....G...... 917 647-7523
  North Bergen *(G-7445)*

CLOTHING & ACCESS: Costumes, Theatrical

Ballet Makers Inc ....G...... 973 595-9000
  Totowa *(G-10818)*

CLOTHING & ACCESS: Handicapped

Apparel Strgc Alliances LLC ....F 732 833-7771
  Jackson *(G-4640)*
Blu-J2 LLC ....G...... 201 750-1407
  Demarest *(G-2024)*
E5 Usa Inc ....G...... 973 773-0750
  Passaic *(G-8062)*
Jese Apparel LLC ....F 732 969-3200
  Dayton *(G-1973)*
Pets First Inc ....E 908 289-2900
  Elizabethport *(G-2791)*
Steps Clothing Inc ....E 201 420-1496
  Jersey City *(G-4816)*

CLOTHING & ACCESS: Handkerchiefs, Exc Paper

Lynn Amiee Inc ....E 201 840-6766
Ridgefield (G-9274)

Personality Handkerchiefs Inc..............E 973 565-0077
Newark (G-7227)

CLOTHING & ACCESS: Men's Miscellaneous Access

Better Team USA Corporation ....E 973 365-0947
Clifton (G-1574)

Butterfly Bow Ties LLC ....G 973 626-2536
Union (G-11033)

Handcraft Manufacturing Corp ....E 973 565-0077
Newark (G-7146)

Hat Box ....E 732 961-2262
Lakewood (G-5108)

Kristine Deer Inc ....G 201 497-3333
Westwood (G-11833)

Lion Sales Corp.................................G 732 417-9363
Edison (G-2551)

New York Popular Inc ....D 718 499-2020
Carteret (G-1260)

Paradise ....G 973 425-0505
Morristown (G-6691)

Philip Papalia ....F 732 349-5530
Toms River (G-10783)

Power Apparel LLC ....F 516 442-1333
Lakewood (G-5149)

Premium Imports Inc ....G 718 486-7125
Passaic (G-8096)

Stylus Custom Apparel Inc ....G 908 587-0800
Linden (G-5432)

CLOTHING & APPAREL STORES: Custom

Dezine Line Inc ....F 973 989-1009
Wharton (G-11856)

Flying Fish Studio..............................G 609 884-2760
West Cape May (G-11683)

Rpl Supplies Inc ....F 973 767-0880
Garfield (G-3766)

CLOTHING & FURNISHINGS, MEN'S & BOYS', WHOLESALE: Outerwear

Tony Jones Apparel Inc ....G 973 773-6200
Lodi (G-5580)

CLOTHING & FURNISHINGS, MEN'S & BOYS', WHOLESALE: Scarves

HRA International Inc ....G 609 395-0939
Monroe (G-6322)

CLOTHING & FURNISHINGS, MEN'S & BOYS', WHOLESALE: Shirts

Fabian Couture Group LLC..................F 800 367-6251
Lyndhurst (G-5652)

Skip Gambert & Associates Inc ....C ... 973 344-3373
Newark (G-7277)

Spirit Tex LLC...................................G 201 440-1113
Little Ferry (G-5498)

CLOTHING & FURNISHINGS, MEN'S & BOYS', WHOLESALE: Trousers

Jade Eastern Trading Inc ....F 201 440-8500
Moonachie (G-6473)

CLOTHING & FURNISHINGS, MEN'S & BOYS', WHOLESALE: Umbrellas

Peerless Umbrella Co Inc ....C 973 578-4900
Newark (G-7225)

S Frankford & Sons Inc ....F 856 222-4134
Mount Laurel (G-6801)

CLOTHING & FURNISHINGS, MEN'S & BOYS', WHOLESALE: Uniforms

Eagle Work Clothes Inc ....E 908 964-8888
Florham Park (G-3502)

Happy Chef Inc ....E 973 492-2525
Butler (G-1002)

CLOTHING ACCESS STORES: Belts, Custom

G G Tauber Company Inc ....E 800 638-6667
Neptune (G-6879)

CLOTHING STORES, NEC

G-III Apparel Group Ltd ....D 732 438-0209
Dayton (G-1965)

Hillarys Fashion Boutique LLC..............F 732 667-7733
Warren (G-11414)

CLOTHING STORES: Dancewear

Ballet Makers Inc..............................G 973 595-9000
Totowa (G-10818)

Sock Company Inc ....E 201 307-0675
Westwood (G-11845)

CLOTHING STORES: T-Shirts, Printed, Custom

Its The Pitts Inc ....G 609 645-7319
Pleasantville (G-8813)

Wally Enterprises Inc ....F 732 329-2613
Monmouth Junction (G-6319)

CLOTHING STORES: Uniforms & Work

Cozy Formal Wear Inc ....G 973 661-9781
Nutley (G-7583)

Five Kids Group Inc ....G 732 774-5331
Neptune (G-6878)

Premium Imports Inc ....G 718 486-7125
Passaic (G-8096)

CLOTHING STORES: Unisex

Finn & Emma LLC ....G 973 227-7770
Fairfield (G-3201)

CLOTHING: Access

Couture Exchange ....G 732 933-1123
Shrewsbury (G-9887)

School Spirit Promotions.....................G 609 588-6902
Trenton (G-10990)

Too Cool of Ocean City ....G 908 810-6363
Kenilworth (G-4982)

Vaeg LLC..G 917 533-0138
Lakewood (G-5175)

CLOTHING: Access, Women's & Misses'

City Design Group Inc ....G 201 329-7711
Little Ferry (G-5477)

Collection Xiix Ltd ....C 201 854-7740
North Bergen (G-7396)

Davidmark LLC.................................C 609 277-7361
Pleasantville (G-8810)

Sondra Roberts Inc ....E 212 684-3344
South Hackensack (G-10187)

CLOTHING: Aprons, Exc Rubber/Plastic, Women, Misses, Junior

Helen Morley LLC..............................E 201 348-6459
Cresskill (G-1942)

Philip Papalia ....F 732 349-5530
Toms River (G-10783)

CLOTHING: Aprons, Work, Exc Rubberized & Plastic, Men's

Staple Sewing Aids Corporation ....E 973 249-0022
Passaic (G-8108)

CLOTHING: Athletic & Sportswear, Men's & Boys'

39 Idea Factory Row LLC ....G 908 244-8631
Flemington (G-3425)

Aladen Athletic Wear LLC ....E 973 838-2425
Wyckoff (G-12102)

Amante International Ltd ....F 908 518-1688
Westfield (G-11793)

Bimini Bay Outfitters Ltd....................F 201 529-3550
Mahwah (G-5716)

Central Mills Inc ....G 732 329-2009
Dayton (G-1959)

Evh LLC ....F 973 257-0076
Boonton (G-553)

Kmba Fashions Inc ....G 973 789-1652
East Orange (G-2255)

Leeward International Inc.....................F 201 836-8830
Teaneck (G-10637)

Merc USA Inc ....F 201 489-3527
Hackensack (G-3947)

MISS Sportswear Inc ....G 212 391-2535
New Brunswick (G-6948)

Moldworks Worldwide LLC ....G 908 474-8082
Linden (G-5390)

Onwards Inc ....G 732 309-7348
Manalapan (G-5822)

Safire Silk Inc ....G 201 636-4061
Carlstadt (G-1211)

Selfmade LLC ....G 201 792-8968
Jersey City (G-4808)

Senor Lopez ....G 732 229-7622
Tinton Falls (G-10727)

Tony Jones Apparel Inc ....G 973 773-6200
Lodi (G-5580)

What A Tee 2 Inc ....F 201 457-0060
Hackensack (G-3990)

CLOTHING: Athletic & Sportswear, Women's & Girls'

Amante International Ltd......................F 908 518-1688
Westfield (G-11793)

Bal Togs Inc ....D 201 866-0201
North Bergen (G-7388)

Garylin Togs ....D 908 354-7218
Elizabeth (G-2741)

Matrix Sales Group LLC ....D 908 461-4148
Spring Lake (G-10423)

Sno Skins Inc ....G 973 884-8801
Whippany (G-11909)

Tellas Ltd ....E 201 399-8888
Englewood Cliffs (G-2991)

What A Tee 2 Inc ....F 201 457-0060
Hackensack (G-3990)

CLOTHING: Baker, Barber, Lab/Svc Ind Apparel, Washable, Men

Db Designs Inc ....G 732 616-5018
Marlboro (G-5895)

Happy Chef Inc ....E 973 492-2525
Butler (G-1002)

Ronald Perry ....F 201 702-2407
Jersey City (G-4801)

CLOTHING: Bathing Suits & Swimwear, Girls, Children & Infant

In Mocean Group LLC........................G 732 960-2415
North Brunswick (G-7470)

Leeward International Inc.....................F 201 836-8830
Teaneck (G-10637)

CLOTHING: Bathing Suits & Swimwear, Knit

Metro Sport Inc ....E 973 879-3831
Mendham (G-6042)

CLOTHING: Bathrobes, Mens & Womens, From Purchased Materials

Carole Hchman Design Group Inc........C 866 267-3945
Jersey City (G-4709)

Monarch Towel Company Inc ....E 800 729-7623
South Plainfield (G-10301)

CLOTHING: Belts

Josemi Inc ....G 917 710-2110
Hoboken (G-4462)

Straps Manufacturing NJ Inc ....F 201 368-5201
Wyckoff (G-12121)

Two 12 Fashion LLC ....G 848 222-1562
Lakewood (G-5173)

CLOTHING: Blouses, Women's & Girls'

Cleve Shirtmakers Inc ....G 201 825-6122
Secaucus (G-9756)

Gambert Shirt Corp............................E 973 424-9105
Newark (G-7130)

Luxury and Trash Ltd Lblty Co ....G 201 315-4018
Closter (G-1760)

Metropolitan Manufacturing Inc ....D 201 933-8111
East Rutherford (G-2302)

New Jersey Headwear Corp..................C..... 973 497-0102
Newark (G-7209)

Saad Collection Inc...........................G..... 732 763-4015
Edison (G-2603)

Spirit Tex LLC.................................G..... 201 440-1113
Little Ferry (G-5498)

Suuchi Inc.....................................C..... 201 284-0789
North Bergen (G-7439)

CLOTHING: Blouses, Womens & Juniors, From Purchased Mtrls

Elie Tahari Ltd................................C..... 973 671-6300
Millburn (G-6196)

Nicholas Oliver LLC.........................G..... 732 690-7144
Wall Township (G-11358)

Tahari ASL LLC...............................E..... 888 734-7459
Millburn (G-6206)

CLOTHING: Brassieres

Wacoal America Inc..........................C..... 201 933-8400
Lyndhurst (G-5682)

CLOTHING: Bridal Gowns

Augenbrauns Bridal Passaic LLC.........G..... 845 425-3439
Lakewood (G-5055)

Duran Cutting Corp..........................F..... 973 916-0006
Passaic (G-8061)

CLOTHING: Capes & Jackets, Women's & Misses'

Fyi Marketing Inc.............................G..... 646 546-5226
Englewood Cliffs (G-2971)

CLOTHING: Caps, Baseball

New Jersey Headwear Corp..................C..... 973 497-0102
Newark (G-7209)

CLOTHING: Children & Infants'

Haddad Bros Inc..............................E..... 718 377-5505
Bloomfield (G-502)

Lollytogs Ltd.................................F..... 732 438-5500
Dayton (G-1978)

Sally Miller LLC..............................G..... 732 729-4840
Milltown (G-6219)

CLOTHING: Children's, Girls'

Attitudes In Dressing Inc...................B..... 908 354-7218
Elizabeth (G-2713)

Bib and Tucker Inc...........................F..... 201 489-9600
Hackensack (G-3885)

Blue Fish Clothing Inc.......................C..... 908 996-3720
Frenchtown (G-3709)

Central Mills Inc.............................B..... 732 329-2009
Dayton (G-1960)

Frenchtoastcom LLC.........................F..... 732 438-5500
Dayton (G-1964)

Garylin Togs.................................D..... 908 354-7218
Elizabeth (G-2741)

Haddad Bros Inc..............................E..... 718 377-5505
Bloomfield (G-502)

JP Group International LLC..................G..... 201 820-1444
Maywood (G-6011)

Les Tout Petite Inc...........................G..... 201 941-8675
Tenafly (G-10663)

Lollytogs Ltd.................................D..... 732 438-5500
Dayton (G-1979)

Lollytogs Ltd.................................F..... 732 438-5500
Dayton (G-1978)

CLOTHING: Clergy Vestments

Church Vestment Mfg Co Inc................G..... 973 942-2833
Paterson (G-8157)

Peach Boutique LLC.........................G..... 908 351-0739
Elizabeth (G-2768)

Robert F Gaiser Inc..........................F..... 973 838-9254
Butler (G-1013)

CLOTHING: Coats & Jackets, Leather & Sheep-Lined

Cockpit Usa Inc...............................F..... 212 575-1616
Elizabeth (G-2721)

Goose Country LLC...........................G..... 646 860-8815
Matawan (G-5977)

Schott Nyc Corp.............................D..... 800 631-5407
Union (G-11089)

CLOTHING: Coats & Suits, Men's & Boys'

Fordham Inc.................................E..... 973 575-7840
Fairfield (G-3205)

New Community Corp........................E..... 973 643-5300
Newark (G-7208)

CLOTHING: Coats, Leatherette, Oiled Fabric, Etc, Mens & Boys

House Pearl Fashions (us) Ltd.............F..... 973 778-7551
Lodi (G-5565)

CLOTHING: Coats, Overcoats & Vests

Burlington Coat Factory.....................D..... 908 994-9562
Elizabeth (G-2718)

CLOTHING: Costumes

Jaclyn LLC....................................C..... 201 909-6000
Maywood (G-6008)

Silvertop Associates Inc....................E..... 856 939-9599
Runnemede (G-9610)

Wells Trading LLC............................F..... 201 552-9909
Guttenberg (G-3873)

CLOTHING: Disposable

Keystone Adjustable Cap Co Inc...........E..... 856 356-2809
Pennsauken (G-8447)

CLOTHING: Down-Filled, Men's & Boys'

Schott Nyc Corp.............................D..... 800 631-5407
Union (G-11089)

CLOTHING: Dresses

Betsy & Adam Ltd............................F..... 212 302-3750
Passaic (G-8054)

Donna Karan International Inc...............G..... 609 345-3402
Atlantic City (G-89)

Elie Tahari Ltd................................C..... 973 671-6300
Millburn (G-6196)

Haddad Bros Inc..............................E..... 718 377-5505
Bloomfield (G-502)

Hillarys Fashion Boutique LLC.............F..... 732 667-7733
Warren (G-11414)

Infinity Sourcing Services LLC.............G..... 212 868-2900
Englewood Cliffs (G-2976)

Jump Design Group Inc......................E..... 201 558-9191
Secaucus (G-9783)

Kate Spade & Company.....................F..... 201 295-7569
North Bergen (G-7413)

Kate Spade & Company.....................E..... 609 395-3109
Dayton (G-1974)

Metropolitan Manufacturing Inc...........D..... 201 933-8111
East Rutherford (G-2302)

Nicholas Oliver LLC.........................G..... 732 690-7144
Wall Township (G-11358)

Printmaker International Ltd................G..... 212 629-9260
Irvington (G-4583)

Tahari ASL LLC...............................E..... 888 734-7459
Millburn (G-6206)

CLOTHING: Dressing Gowns, Mens/Womens, From Purchased Matls

Chiha Inc.....................................F..... 201 861-2000
North Bergen (G-7395)

CLOTHING: Formal Jackets, Mens & Youth, From Purchased Matls

Fabian Formals Inc...........................E..... 201 460-7776
Lyndhurst (G-5653)

CLOTHING: Furs

M Blaustein Inc...............................G..... 973 379-1080
Short Hills (G-9871)

CLOTHING: Garments, Indl, Men's & Boys

Pro World....................................G..... 856 406-1020
Pennsauken (G-8474)

CLOTHING: Girdles & Panty Girdles

Dolce Vita Intimates LLC....................D..... 973 482-8400
Harrison (G-4169)

CLOTHING: Gowns & Dresses, Wedding

Amalia Carrara Inc...........................E..... 201 348-4500
Union City (G-11105)

Head Piece Heaven...........................G..... 201 262-0788
Oradell (G-7745)

Liz Fields Llc.................................G..... 201 408-5640
Englewood (G-2919)

CLOTHING: Gowns, Formal

Kidcuteture LLC..............................G..... 609 532-0149
Lawrenceville (G-5233)

CLOTHING: Hats & Caps, NEC

Headwear Creations Inc......................E..... 973 622-1144
Newark (G-7149)

Jay Gerish Company.........................G..... 973 403-0655
West Caldwell (G-11657)

Kathy Jeanne Inc.............................F..... 973 575-9898
Fairfield (G-3248)

Mod Hatter...................................G..... 609 492-0999
Beach Haven (G-256)

Serratelli Hat Company Inc.................G..... 973 623-4133
Newark (G-7266)

CLOTHING: Hats & Caps, Uniform

Alboum W Hat Company Inc.................E..... 201 399-4110
Irvington (G-4555)

Castellane Manufacturing Co...............F..... 609 625-3427
Mays Landing (G-5993)

CLOTHING: Hats & Headwear, Knit

Artex Knitting Mills Inc......................D..... 856 456-2800
Westville (G-11810)

Elegant Headwear Co Inc....................C..... 908 558-1200
Elizabeth (G-2732)

CLOTHING: Hosiery, Men's & Boys'

Great Socks LLC..............................E..... 856 964-9700
Pennsauken (G-8427)

Sock Company Inc............................E..... 201 307-0675
Westwood (G-11845)

CLOTHING: Hosiery, Pantyhose & Knee Length, Sheer

Great Socks LLC..............................E..... 856 964-9700
Pennsauken (G-8427)

Swisstex Company...........................E..... 201 861-8000
West New York (G-11755)

CLOTHING: Hospital, Men's

Janet Shops Inc..............................F..... 973 748-4992
Bloomfield (G-504)

CLOTHING: Jackets, Field, Military

Sinai Manufacturing Corp...................D..... 973 522-1003
Newark (G-7274)

CLOTHING: Jackets, Overall & Work

Bethel Industries Inc.........................C..... 201 656-8222
Jersey City (G-4702)

CLOTHING: Jeans, Men's & Boys'

Guess Inc....................................E..... 201 941-3683
Edgewater (G-2439)

CLOTHING: Jerseys, Knit

Fairfield Textiles Corp.......................D..... 973 227-1656
Paterson (G-8190)

CLOTHING: Leather

G-III Apparel Group Ltd......................D..... 732 438-0209
Dayton (G-1965)

Prime Fur & Leather Inc......................F..... 201 941-9600
Fairview (G-3368)

CLOTHING: Leather & sheep-lined clothing

G-III Leather Fashions Inc ....D...... 212 403-0500
  Dayton (G-1966)

CLOTHING: Lounge, Bed & Leisurewear

Chiha Inc...F....... 201 861-2000
  North Bergen (G-7395)
D L V Lounge Inc.....................................G...... 973 783-6988
  Montclair (G-6362)

CLOTHING: Men's & boy's underwear & nightwear

Basic Solutions Ltd ....G...... 201 978-7691
  Manalapan (G-5802)
Central Mills Inc ....B...... 732 329-2009
  Dayton (G-1960)
Sgi Apparel Ltd ....G...... 201 342-1200
  Hackensack (G-3973)

CLOTHING: Millinery

Kathy Gibson Designs Inc ....F....... 201 420-0088
  North Bergen (G-7414)

CLOTHING: Neckwear

Albert Forte Neckwear Co Inc...............G...... 856 423-2342
  Mullica Hill (G-6854)
Robert Stewart Inc ....G...... 973 751-5151
  Belleville (G-313)

CLOTHING: Outerwear, Knit

Alan Paul Accessories Inc ....G...... 609 924-4022
  Princeton (G-8905)
D & G LLC ....G...... 201 289-5750
  Hackensack (G-3903)
Flemington Knitting Mills ....F....... 908 995-9590
  Milford (G-6192)
Ralph Lauren Corporation ....C...... 201 531-6000
  Lyndhurst (G-5674)
Triumph Knitting Machine Svc ....E...... 201 646-0022
  Hackensack (G-3985)

CLOTHING: Outerwear, Lthr, Wool/Down-Filled, Men, Youth/Boy

Bear USa Inc ....F....... 201 943-4748
  Palisades Park (G-7768)
Leather Works NJ Ltd Lblty Co ....G...... 732 452-1100
  Edison (G-2549)

CLOTHING: Outerwear, Women's & Misses' NEC

39 Idea Factory Row LLC ....G...... 908 244-8631
  Flemington (G-3425)
Alfred Dunner Inc..................................D...... 212 944-6660
  Parsippany (G-7877)
Bear USa Inc ....F....... 201 943-4748
  Palisades Park (G-7768)
Bestwork Inds For The Blind ....D...... 856 424-2510
  Cherry Hill (G-1345)
Blue Fish Clothing Inc..........................C...... 908 996-3720
  Frenchtown (G-3709)
Fordham Inc ....E...... 973 575-7840
  Fairfield (G-3205)
Golden Season Fashion USA Inc ....F....... 201 552-2088
  Secaucus (G-9775)
Great Socks LLC ....E...... 856 964-9700
  Pennsauken (G-8427)
Happy Chef Inc ....E...... 973 492-2525
  Butler (G-1002)
House Pearl Fashions (us) Ltd ....F....... 973 778-7551
  Lodi (G-5565)
Marmaxx Operating Corp ....D...... 973 575-7910
  West Caldwell (G-11660)
Metropolitan Manufacturing Inc ....D...... 201 933-8111
  East Rutherford (G-2302)
New Community Corp ....E...... 973 643-5300
  Newark (G-7208)
Snotex USA Inc ....G...... 973 762-0358
  South Orange (G-10201)

CLOTHING: Raincoats, Exc Vulcanized Rubber, Purchased Matls

Man-How Inc ....G....... 609 392-4895
  Trenton (G-10954)

CLOTHING: Robes & Dressing Gowns

Charles Komar & Sons Inc....................B...... 212 725-1500
  Jersey City (G-4711)
Peach Boutique LLC ....G...... 908 351-0739
  Elizabeth (G-2768)

CLOTHING: Service Apparel, Women's

Escada US Subco LLC ....B...... 201 865-5200
  Secaucus (G-9763)

CLOTHING: Shirts

Central Mills Inc ....B...... 732 329-2009
  Dayton (G-1960)
Cleve Shirtmakers Inc ....G...... 201 825-6122
  Secaucus (G-9756)
Drifire LLC ....E...... 866 266-4035
  East Brunswick (G-2136)
Gambert Shirt Corp ....E...... 973 424-9105
  Newark (G-7130)
Jade Eastern Trading Inc ....F....... 201 440-8500
  Moonachie (G-6473)
New Community Corp ....E...... 973 643-5300
  Newark (G-7208)
New Jersey Headwear Corp...................G...... 973 497-0102
  Newark (G-7209)
New Top Inc ....E...... 201 438-3990
  Carlstadt (G-1191)
Pvh Corp ....G...... 908 685-0050
  Elizabeth (G-2771)
Pvh Corp ....G...... 908 685-0050
  Bridgewater (G-871)
Ralph Lauren Corporation ....C...... 201 531-6000
  Lyndhurst (G-5674)
Saad Collection Inc ....G...... 732 763-4015
  Edison (G-2603)

CLOTHING: Shirts, Dress, Men's & Boys'

L Gambert LLC ....D...... 973 344-3440
  Newark (G-7176)
Pvh Corp ....G...... 609 344-6273
  Atlantic City (G-101)
Pvh Corp ....G...... 732 833-9602
  Jackson (G-4663)
Pvh Corp ....G...... 908 685-0050
  Bridgewater (G-872)
Pvh Corp ....G...... 908 685-0148
  Bridgewater (G-873)
Pvh Corp ....F....... 908 788-5880
  Flemington (G-3465)
Skip Gambert & Associates Inc.............C...... 973 344-3373
  Newark (G-7277)

CLOTHING: Shirts, Knit

3forty Group Inc ....F....... 973 773-1806
  Passaic (G-8047)

CLOTHING: Shirts, Sports & Polo, Men's & Boys'

Bimini Bay Outfitters Ltd........................F....... 201 529-3550
  Mahwah (G-5716)

CLOTHING: Skirts

Chic LLC ....G...... 732 354-0035
  East Brunswick (G-2132)
Success Sewing Inc ....G...... 973 622-0328
  Newark (G-7290)

CLOTHING: Sleeping Garments, Women's & Children's

Central Mills Inc ....B...... 732 329-2009
  Dayton (G-1960)
Charles Komar & Sons Inc....................B...... 212 725-1500
  Jersey City (G-4711)
Sgi Apparel Ltd ....G...... 201 342-1200
  Hackensack (G-3973)
Swisstex Company ....E...... 201 861-8000
  West New York (G-11755)

CLOTHING: Socks

J T Murdoch Shoes ....F....... 973 748-6484
  Bloomfield (G-503)
Knock Knock Give A Sock Inc ....G...... 917 885-6983
  West Orange (G-11770)

CLOTHING: Underwear, Women's & Children's

Sock Drawer and More LLC ....G...... 888 637-3399
  Edison (G-2615)
Socks 47 Ltd Liability Company...........G...... 201 866-2222
  Union City (G-11128)

CLOTHING: Sportswear, Women's

Central Mills Inc ....B...... 732 329-2009
  Dayton (G-1960)
Counter-Fit Inc ....C...... 609 871-8888
  Willingboro (G-11990)
Leeward International Inc.......................F....... 201 836-8830
  Teaneck (G-10637)
Les Tout Petite Inc ....G...... 201 941-8675
  Tenafly (G-10663)
Ocean Drive Inc.....................................G...... 908 964-2591
  Kenilworth (G-4965)
Printmaker International Ltd ....G...... 212 629-9260
  Irvington (G-4583)
Swisstex Company ....E...... 201 861-8000
  West New York (G-11755)
Tripp Nyc Inc ....E...... 201 520-0420
  North Bergen (G-7441)

CLOTHING: Suits & Skirts, Women's & Misses'

E-Lo Sportswear LLC ....F....... 862 902-5220
  Harrison (G-4170)

CLOTHING: Suits, Men's & Boys', From Purchased Materials

Tom James Company ....E...... 732 826-8400
  Perth Amboy (G-8536)

CLOTHING: Sweaters & Sweater Coats, Knit

Fleck Knitware Co Inc............................E...... 908 754-8888
  Plainfield (G-8766)
Jtwo Inc..G...... 201 410-1616
  Kinnelon (G-5018)

CLOTHING: T-Shirts & Tops, Knit

Supertex Inc ....E...... 973 345-1000
  Paterson (G-8306)

CLOTHING: T-Shirts & Tops, Women's & Girls'

Chic LLC ....G...... 732 354-0035
  East Brunswick (G-2132)

CLOTHING: Tailored Dress/Sport Coats, Mens & Boys

Bimini Bay Outfitters Ltd........................F....... 201 529-3550
  Mahwah (G-5716)

CLOTHING: Tailored Suits & Formal Jackets

Fabian Couture Group LLC....................F....... 800 367-6251
  Lyndhurst (G-5652)
Michael Duru Clothiers LLC...................G...... 732 741-1999
  Shrewsbury (G-9896)

CLOTHING: Ties, Neck, Men's & Boys', From Purchased Material

HRA International Inc ....G...... 609 395-0939
  Monroe (G-6322)

CLOTHING: Trousers & Slacks, Men's & Boys'

Ralph Lauren Corporation ....C...... 201 531-6000
  Lyndhurst (G-5674)

CLOTHING: Underwear, Men's & Boys'

D & G LLC ....G...... 201 289-5750
  Hackensack (G-3903)
Umc Inc ....G...... 973 325-0031
  West Orange (G-11780)

CLOTHING: Underwear, Women's & Children's

Carole Hchman Design Group Inc........C...... 866 267-3945
  Jersey City (G-4709)

D & G LLC ....G 201 289-5750
Hackensack **(G-3903)**
Maidenform ....A 732 621-2216
Iselin **(G-4615)**

CLOTHING: Uniforms & Vestments

Costume Gallery Inc ....G 609 386-6601
Delanco **(G-2005)**
Fine Wear U S A ....G 201 313-3777
Fort Lee **(G-3558)**
Global Manufacturing LLC ....G 973 494-5413
Newark **(G-7134)**

CLOTHING: Uniforms, Ex Athletic, Women's, Misses' & Juniors'

Eagle Work Clothes Inc ....E 908 964-8888
Florham Park **(G-3502)**
Happy Chef Inc ....E 973 492-2525
Butler **(G-1002)**

CLOTHING: Uniforms, Firemen's, From Purchased Materials

Firefighter One Ltd Lblty Co ....G 973 940-3061
Sparta **(G-10387)**

CLOTHING: Uniforms, Military, Men/Youth, Purchased Materials

Crown Clothing Co ....C 856 691-0343
Vineland **(G-11206)**
De Rossi & Son Co Inc ....C 856 691-0061
Vineland **(G-11212)**

CLOTHING: Uniforms, Policemen's, From Purchased Materials

Mek International Inc ....G 215 712-2490
Woodcliff Lake **(G-12059)**

CLOTHING: Uniforms, Team Athletic

Rennoc Corporation ....D 856 327-5400
Vineland **(G-11256)**

CLOTHING: Uniforms, Work

Enailsupply Corporation ....G 909 725-1698
Toms River **(G-10755)**
New Community Corp ....E 973 643-5300
Newark **(G-7208)**

CLOTHING: WarmUp, Jogging & Sweat Suits, Girls' & Children's

Lemon Inc ....G 201 417-5412
Norwood **(G-7568)**

CLOTHING: Waterproof Outerwear

A J P Scientific Inc ....G 973 472-7200
Clifton **(G-1551)**

CLOTHING: Womens/Misses Coats, Jackets & Vests, Down-Filled

Fyi Marketing Inc ....G 646 546-5226
Englewood Cliffs **(G-2971)**

CLOTHING: Work Apparel, Exc Uniforms

Flying Fish Studio ....G 609 884-2760
West Cape May **(G-11683)**

CLOTHING: Work, Men's

Ansell Healthcare Products LLC ....C 732 345-5400
Iselin **(G-4593)**
B2x Corporation ....G 201 714-2373
Jersey City **(G-4697)**
Bestwork Inds For The Blind ....D 856 424-2510
Cherry Hill **(G-1345)**
Luxury and Trash Ltd Lblty Co ....G 201 315-4018
Closter **(G-1760)**
Matrix Sales Group LLC ....D 908 461-4148
Spring Lake **(G-10423)**
Mischief International Inc ....G 201 840-6888
Ridgefield **(G-9276)**
Somes Uniforms Inc ....F 201 843-1199
Hackensack **(G-3975)**

Swltlik Parachute Company Inc ....F 609 587-3300
Trenton **(G-10994)**
Tellas Ltd ....E 201 399-8888
Englewood Cliffs **(G-2991)**
Todd Shelton LLC ....G 844 626-6355
East Rutherford **(G-2326)**
Top Rated Shopping Bargains ....F 800 556-5849
Hasbrouck Heights **(G-4190)**
Vertical Protective AP LLC ....G 203 904-6099
Shrewsbury **(G-9904)**

CLOTHING: Work, Waterproof, Exc Raincoats

Eagle Work Clothes Inc ....E 908 964-8888
Florham Park **(G-3502)**
Loveline Industries Inc ....E 973 928-3427
Passaic **(G-8083)**
M Rafi Sons Garment Industries ....G 732 381-7660
Rahway **(G-9116)**

COAL MINING SERVICES

Asbury Carbons Inc ....G 908 537-2155
Asbury **(G-60)**
Starfuels Inc ....G 201 685-0400
Englewood **(G-2944)**

COAL MINING SVCS: Anthracite, Contract Basis

Tof Energy Corporation ....D 908 691-2422
Bedminster **(G-280)**

COAL, MINERALS & ORES, WHOLESALE: Coal

Minmetals Inc ....F 201 809-1898
Leonia **(G-5290)**

COATING COMPOUNDS: Tar

Actega North America Inc ....C 856 829-6300
Delran **(G-2008)**
Fti Inc ....G 973 443-0004
Florham Park **(G-3506)**

COATING SVC

All American Powdercoating LLC ....G 732 349-7001
Toms River **(G-10741)**
Dynamic Coatings LLC ....G 732 998-6625
Matawan **(G-5974)**

COATING SVC: Metals & Formed Prdts

Abco Die Casters Inc ....D 973 624-7030
Newark **(G-7033)**
Alpha Processing Co Inc ....E 973 777-1737
Clifton **(G-1562)**
Andek Corporation ....F 856 866-7600
Moorestown **(G-6505)**
Atlantic Eqp Engineers Inc ....F 201 828-9400
Upper Saddle River **(G-11134)**
Boyko Metal Finishing Co Inc ....D 973 623-4254
Newark **(G-7071)**
Ceronics Inc ....G 732 566-5600
Matawan **(G-5970)**
Chapter Enterprises Inc ....G 732 560-8500
Bridgewater **(G-811)**
Cincinnati Thermal Spray Inc ....E 973 379-0003
Springfield **(G-10435)**
Ferro Corporation ....G 908 226-2148
South Plainfield **(G-10258)**
General Magnaplate Corporation ....D 908 862-6200
Linden **(G-5351)**
General Magnaplate Wisconsin ....F 800 441-6173
Linden **(G-5352)**
Innovative Powder Coatings LLC ....G 856 661-0086
Pennsauken **(G-8436)**
Jema-American Inc ....G 732 968-5333
Middlesex **(G-6123)**
Lordon Inc ....G 908 813-1143
Hackettstown **(G-4019)**
Paramount Metal Finishing Co ....C 908 862-0772
Linden **(G-5403)**
Peerless Coatings LLC ....E 973 427-8771
Hawthorne **(G-4237)**
Penn Metal Finishing Co Inc ....G 609 387-3400
Burlington **(G-981)**
Phoenix Powder Coating LLC ....G 973 907-7500
Haskell **(G-4200)**

S D L Powder Coating Inc ....G 732 473-0800
Toms River **(G-10788)**

COATING SVC: Metals, With Plastic Or Resins

Bel-Art Products Inc ....E 973 694-0500
Wayne **(G-11477)**
Flexcraft Industries Inc ....G 973 589-3403
Newark **(G-7125)**
Golf Coast Polymer Services ....G 856 498-3434
Elmer **(G-2798)**
Plastics Consulting & Mfg Co ....E 800 222-0317
Camden **(G-1083)**

COATING SVC: Rust Preventative

Gary R Banks Industrial Group ....F 856 687-2227
West Berlin **(G-11597)**

COATING SVC: Silicon

Microsurfaces Inc ....G 201 408-5596
Englewood **(G-2925)**

COATINGS: Air Curing

RPM Prfrmnce Catings Group Inc ....F 888 788-4323
Long Branch **(G-5605)**
Stoncor Group Inc ....C 800 257-7953
Maple Shade **(G-5870)**
Uvitec Printing Ink Co Inc ....E 973 778-0737
Lodi **(G-5581)**

COATINGS: Epoxy

Armorpoxy Inc ....F 908 810-9613
Union **(G-11027)**
Broadview Technologies Inc ....E 973 465-0077
Newark **(G-7077)**
Duraamen Engineered Pdts Inc ....G 973 230-1301
Newark **(G-7106)**
Master Bond Inc ....E 201 343-8983
Hackensack **(G-3943)**
North Jersey Specialists Inc ....G 973 927-1616
Flanders **(G-3416)**
Palma Inc ....F 973 429-1490
Whippany **(G-11901)**
Philip Mamrak ....G 908 454-6089
Phillipsburg **(G-8567)**
Rema Corrosion Control ....F 201 256-8400
Northvale **(G-7545)**
Sika Corporation ....B 201 933-8800
Lyndhurst **(G-5678)**
Sika Corporation ....C 201 933-8800
Lyndhurst **(G-5679)**

COATINGS: Polyurethane

Worldwide Safety Systems LLC ....G 888 613-4501
Teaneck **(G-10656)**

CODEINE & DERIVATIVES

Mallinckrodt LLC ....E 908 238-6600
Hampton **(G-4158)**
Prime Coding Services LLC ....G 732 254-3036
East Brunswick **(G-2168)**

COFFEE MAKERS: Electric

Argonautus LLC ....G 908 393-4379
Bridgewater **(G-792)**

COFFEE SVCS

Coffee Associates Inc ....E 201 945-1060
Edgewater **(G-2436)**
Quality Plus One Catering Inc ....G 732 967-1525
Old Bridge **(G-7726)**

COILS & TRANSFORMERS

A C Transformer Corp ....G 973 589-8574
Newark **(G-7029)**
AFP Transformers Corporation ....D 732 248-0305
Edison **(G-2450)**
Automatic Switch Company ....A 973 966-2000
Florham Park **(G-3485)**
Behringer Fluid Systems Inc ....G 973 948-0226
Branchville **(G-703)**
Bel Hybrids & Magnetics Inc ....F 201 432-0463
Jersey City **(G-4701)**

Celco ....F........ 201 327-1123
Mahwah (G-5721)
Freed Transformer Company ....E........973 942-2222
Paterson (G-8195)
Jerome Industries Corp.....................E........908 353-5700
Hackettstown (G-4013)
Kef America Inc ....E........732 414-2074
Marlboro (G-5903)
Microsignals Inc ....E........800 225-4508
Palisades Park (G-7774)
Stonite Coil Corporation ....E........609 585-6600
Trenton (G-10993)
Torelco Inc ....F........908 387-0814
Alpha (G-43)

COILS, WIRE: Aluminum, Made In Rolling Mills

H Cross Company.............................E........201 964-9380
Moonachie (G-6468)

COIN-OPERATED LAUNDRY

Pueblo Latino Laundry LLC ....G........201 864-1666
Union City (G-11125)

COLLECTION AGENCY, EXC REAL ESTATE

Quadramed Corporation ....E........732 751-0400
Eatontown (G-2418)

COLOR LAKES OR TONERS

Ferro Corporation ....E........732 287-4925
Edison (G-2511)

COLOR PIGMENTS

Brenntag Specialties Inc ....D........908 561-6100
South Plainfield (G-10228)
Riverdale Color Mfg Inc....................E........732 376-9300
Perth Amboy (G-8531)
Sudarshan North America Inc ....G........201 652-2046
Ridgewood (G-9331)

COLOR SEPARATION: Photographic & Movie Film

Prism Color Corporation ....D........856 234-7515
Moorestown (G-6559)

COLORS: Pigments, Inorganic

BASF Catalysts LLC ....D........732 205-5000
Iselin (G-4599)
Breen Color Concentrates LLC ....F........609 397-8200
Lambertville (G-5187)
Color Techniques Inc.......................F........908 412-9292
South Plainfield (G-10239)
Custom Chemicals Corp ....A........201 791-5100
Elmwood Park (G-2820)
Dispersion Technology Inc ....F........732 364-4488
Lakewood (G-5084)
Elementis Specialties Inc ....F........201 432-0800
East Windsor (G-2370)
Elementis Specialties Inc ....C........609 443-2000
East Windsor (G-2369)
Evonik Corporation ....B........973 929-8000
Parsippany (G-7938)
Ferro Corporation ....E........732 287-4925
Edison (G-2511)
French Color Fragrance Co Inc ....E........201 567-6883
Englewood (G-2907)
Kvk Usa Inc.....................................F........732 846-2355
New Brunswick (G-6942)
Lightscape Materials Inc ....G........609 734-2224
Princeton (G-8969)
Sensient Technologies Corp..............E........908 757-4500
South Plainfield (G-10327)
Vivitone Inc ....F........973 427-8114
Hawthorne (G-4250)

COLORS: Pigments, Organic

Color Techniques Inc.......................F........908 412-9292
South Plainfield (G-10239)
Dominion Colour Corp USA................F........973 279-9591
Clifton (G-1603)
Penn Color Inc ....C........201 791-5100
Elmwood Park (G-2848)
Sun Chemical Corporation ....D........973 404-6000
Parsippany (G-8022)

COLUMNS, FRACTIONING: Metal Plate

Construction Specialties Inc..............E........908 236-0800
Lebanon (G-5257)

COMFORTERS & QUILTS, FROM MANMADE FIBER OR SILK

Hanover Direct Inc ....B........201 863-7300
Weehawken (G-11568)

COMMERCIAL & INDL SHELVING WHOLESALERS

Warehouse Solutions Inc ....F........201 880-1110
Fair Lawn (G-3128)

COMMERCIAL & OFFICE BUILDINGS RENOVATION & REPAIR

Crincoli Woodwork Co Inc ....F........908 352-9332
Elizabeth (G-2724)
Donnelly Industries Inc ....D........973 672-1800
Wayne (G-11496)

COMMERCIAL ART & GRAPHIC DESIGN SVCS

224 Graphics Inc ....F........973 433-9224
Fairfield (G-3132)
4 Over Inc ....F........201 440-1656
Moonachie (G-6450)
42 Design Square LLC ....F........888 272-5979
Parsippany (G-7870)
Alpha 1 Studio Inc ....G........609 859-2200
Southampton (G-10359)
Applied Image Inc ....E........732 410-2444
Freehold (G-3647)
C2 Imaging LLC ....E........646 557-6300
Jersey City (G-4707)
Digital Documents Inc ....G........609 520-0094
Princeton (G-8930)
Drew & Rogers Inc ....E........973 575-6210
Fairfield (G-3187)
Go R Design LLC ....E........609 286-2146
New Egypt (G-6983)
Graphic Action Inc ....G........908 213-0055
Phillipsburg (G-8553)
Harwill Corporation ....G........609 895-1955
Windsor (G-11996)
Jasco Specialties and Forms.............G........856 627-5511
Tabernacle (G-10619)
L & F Graphics Ltd Lblty Co ....G........973 240-7033
Paterson (G-8232)
L&M Architectural Graphics Inc ....F........973 575-7665
Fairfield (G-3254)
Larue Manufacturing Corp ....G........908 534-2700
Whitehouse (G-11916)
McKella 2-8-0 Inc ....D........856 813-1153
Pennsauken (G-8455)
Monte Printing & Graphics Inc ....G........908 241-6600
Roselle Park (G-9588)
Nema Associates Inc ....F........973 274-0052
Linden (G-5395)
Northwind Enterprises Inc ....E........732 274-2000
Dayton (G-1982)
Onyx Graphics LLC ....G........908 281-0038
Hillsborough (G-4343)
Print Factory Ltd Liability Co ....G........973 866-5230
Clifton (G-1700)
Promo Graphic Inc ....G........732 629-7300
Middlesex (G-6141)
Rays Reproduction Inc.....................G........201 666-5650
Emerson (G-2868)
Remco Press Inc ....E........201 751-5703
North Bergen (G-7433)
Ridgewood Press Inc........................F........201 670-9797
Ridgewood (G-9328)
Shindo International Inc ....E........973 470-8100
Clifton (G-1716)
Star Narrow Fabrics Inc....................G........973 778-8600
Lodi (G-5576)
Techsetters Inc...............................E........856 240-7905
Collingswood (G-1772)
Toppan Printing Co Amer Inc.............C........732 469-8400
Somerset (G-10088)

COMMERCIAL ART & ILLUSTRATION SVCS

Blue Parachute LLC..........................G........732 767-1320
Metuchen (G-6048)

Royer Graphics Inc...........................G........856 344-7935
Clementon (G-1535)

COMMERCIAL CONTAINERS WHOLESALERS

Granco Group LLC............................G........973 515-4721
Roseland (G-9539)
James R Macauley Inc.......................G........856 767-3474
Waterford Works (G-11462)
Trs Inc ....E........732 636-3300
Avenel (G-151)

COMMERCIAL EQPT & SPLYS, WHOLESALE: Hotel

ADS Sales Co Inc.............................E........732 591-0500
Morganville (G-6580)

COMMERCIAL EQPT WHOLESALERS, NEC

Envirosight LLC ....E........973 970-9284
Randolph (G-9176)
Ice Cold Novelty Products Inc ....G........732 751-0011
Wall Township (G-11349)
Intertest Inc....................................E........908 496-8008
Columbia (G-1795)
Par Code Symbology Inc...................F........973 918-0550
Roseland (G-9541)
Sea Breeze Fruit Flavors Inc..............D........973 334-7777
Towaco (G-10880)
Track Systems Inc............................F........201 462-0095
Hasbrouck Heights (G-4191)
W T Winter Associates Inc.................E........888 808-3611
Fairfield (G-3350)
Zeiser Inc.......................................F........973 228-0800
West Caldwell (G-11682)

COMMERCIAL EQPT, WHOLESALE: Bakery Eqpt & Splys

Cns Confectionery Products LLC ....F........201 823-1400
Bayonne (G-211)

COMMERCIAL EQPT, WHOLESALE: Coffee Brewing Eqpt & Splys

Rockline Industries Inc.....................C........973 257-2884
Montville (G-6446)

COMMERCIAL EQPT, WHOLESALE: Comm Cooking & Food Svc Eqpt

Am-Mac Incorporated ....F........973 575-7567
Fairfield (G-3140)
Bon Chef Inc ....D........973 383-8848
Lafayette (G-5026)
J & M Air Inc ....E........908 707-4040
Somerville (G-10118)

COMMERCIAL EQPT, WHOLESALE: Display Eqpt, Exc Refrigerated

CDI Group Inc..................................F........908 862-1493
Linden (G-5330)
Northwind Enterprises Inc ....E........732 274-2000
Dayton (G-1982)
Salescaster Displays Corp.................G........908 322-3046
Scotch Plains (G-9739)

COMMERCIAL EQPT, WHOLESALE: Restaurant, NEC

HCH Incorporated ....G........973 300-4551
Sparta (G-10391)
Taylor Products Inc..........................E........732 225-4620
Edison (G-2631)

COMMERCIAL EQPT, WHOLESALE: Scales, Exc Laboratory

Advance Scale Company Inc ....E........856 784-4916
Lindenwold (G-5444)
Empire Scale & Balance ....G........856 299-1651
Penns Grove (G-8378)
Lps Industries Inc ....C........201 438-3515
Moonachie (G-6477)
Ptc Electronics Inc...........................G........201 847-0500
Mahwah (G-5764)

Employee Codes: A=Over 500 employees, B=251-500
C=101-250, D=51-100, E=20-50, F=10-19, G=4-9

2019 Harris New jersey
Manufacturers Directory

801

PRODUCT

COMMERCIAL EQPT, WHOLESALE: Store Fixtures & Display Eqpt

Testrite Instrument Co Inc ....C 201 543-0240
  Hackensack (G-3982)

COMMERCIAL LAUNDRY EQPT

Air World Inc ....E 201 831-0700
  Mahwah (G-5711)
Airworld Inc ....F 973 720-1008
  Paterson (G-8129)
Fairfield Laundry McHy Corp ....E 973 575-4330
  Fairfield (G-3199)
Sadwith Industries Corp ....G 732 531-3856
  Ocean (G-7680)

COMMERCIAL PRINTING & NEWSPAPER PUBLISHING COMBINED

Asbury Park Press Inc ....A 732 922-6000
  Neptune (G-6866)
Burlington Times Inc ....B 609 871-8000
  Willingboro (G-11989)
Central Record Publications ....E 609 654-5000
  Trenton (G-10915)
Community News Service LLC ....F 609 396-1511
  Lawrenceville (G-5227)
Hunterdon County Democrat Inc ....D 908 782-4747
  Flemington (G-3449)
New Jersey Herald ....C 973 383-1500
  Newton (G-7352)
Newark Morning Ledger Co ....B 973 392-4141
  Newark (G-7216)
Newspaper Media Group LLC ....E 201 798-7800
  Califon (G-1032)
Princeton Packet Inc ....C 609 924-3244
  Princeton (G-9001)
Recorder Publishing Co Inc ....D 908 766-3900
  Whippany (G-11907)
South Jersey Publishing Co ....F 856 692-0455
  Vineland (G-11267)

COMMERCIAL REFRIGERATORS WHOLESALERS

Modern Store Equipment ....F 609 241-7438
  Burlington (G-980)

COMMODITY CONTRACTS BROKERS, DEALERS

Powerspec Inc ....E 732 494-9490
  Somerville (G-10123)

COMMON SAND MINING

Alliance Sand Co Inc ....G 908 534-4116
  Somerville (G-10103)
F W Bennett & Son Inc ....G 973 383-4050
  Lafayette (G-5027)
New Jersey Pulverizing Co Inc ....F 732 269-1400
  Bayville (G-249)

COMMUNICATION HEADGEAR: Telephone

Sonetronics Inc ....D 732 681-5016
  Belmar (G-354)

COMMUNICATIONS EQPT & SYSTEMS, NEC

Institute For Respnsble Online ....G 856 722-1048
  Mount Laurel (G-6768)

COMMUNICATIONS EQPT REPAIR & MAINTENANCE

Lucent Technologies World Svcs ....C 908 582-3000
  New Providence (G-7008)
Transcore LP ....F 201 329-9200
  Teterboro (G-10696)
Wireless Electronics Inc ....E 856 768-4310
  West Berlin (G-11634)

COMMUNICATIONS EQPT WHOLESALERS

360 Media Innovations LLC ....G 201 228-0941
  Union (G-11018)
Arose Inc ....E 856 481-4351
  Blackwood (G-459)
Bogen Communications Inc ....D 201 934-8500
  Mahwah (G-5718)

Enterprisecc Ltd Liability Co ....G 201 266-0020
  Jersey City (G-4732)
Industronic Inc ....G 908 393-5960
  Bridgewater (G-835)
Transcore LP ....F 201 329-9200
  Teterboro (G-10696)
Vcom Intl Multi-Media Corp ....D 201 814-0405
  Fairfield (G-3338)
Vitex LLC ....G 201 296-0145
  Englewood Cliffs (G-2997)

COMMUNICATIONS EQPT: Microwave

Fei-Elcom Tech Inc ....E 201 767-8030
  Northvale (G-7524)
In-Phase Technologies Inc ....E 609 298-9555
  Bordentown (G-584)
Merrimac Industries Inc ....D 973 575-1300
  West Caldwell (G-11665)
Vitec Videocom Inc ....G 908 852-3700
  Secaucus (G-9827)
Wide Band Systems Inc ....F 973 586-6500
  Rockaway (G-9513)

COMMUNICATIONS SVCS

Subcom LLC ....B 732 578-7000
  Eatontown (G-2422)

COMMUNICATIONS SVCS: Cellular

Instock Wireless Components ....F 973 335-6550
  Boonton (G-557)
Princeton Hosted Solutions LLC ....F 856 470-2350
  Haddonfield (G-4062)
Verizon Communications Inc ....E 201 666-9934
  Westwood (G-11847)
Verizon Communications Inc ....D 609 646-9939
  Egg Harbor Township (G-2700)
Wireless Experience of PA Inc ....F 732 552-0050
  Manahawkin (G-5798)

COMMUNICATIONS SVCS: Data

Communications Supply Corp ....E 732 346-1864
  Edison (G-2481)
Grafwed Internet Media Studios ....G 201 632-1771
  Midland Park (G-6175)
Lcn Partners Inc ....F 215 755-1000
  Berlin (G-426)
Spirent Communications Inc ....G 732 946-4018
  Holmdel (G-4514)

COMMUNICATIONS SVCS: Facsimile Transmission

All American Print & Copy Ctr ....G 732 758-6200
  Red Bank (G-9219)
E C D Ventures Inc ....G 856 875-1100
  Blackwood (G-465)

COMMUNICATIONS SVCS: Internet Connectivity Svcs

Comodo Group Inc ....D 888 266-6361
  Clifton (G-1586)
Telvue Corporation ....E 800 885-8886
  Mount Laurel (G-6809)
Wcd Enterprises Inc ....G 732 888-4422
  Keyport (G-5006)

COMMUNICATIONS SVCS: Internet Host Svcs

North Jersey Media Group Inc ....A 201 646-4000
  Hackensack (G-3955)
Strahan Consulting Group LLC ....G 908 790-0873
  Scotch Plains (G-9742)
US Software Group LLC ....E 732 361-4636
  South Plainfield (G-10337)

COMMUNICATIONS SVCS: Online Svc Providers

Home Organization LLC ....F 201 351-2121
  Closter (G-1757)
Mindwise Media LLC ....G 973 701-0685
  Chatham (G-1327)

COMMUNICATIONS SVCS: Satellite Earth Stations

Ussecurenet LLC ....G 201 447-0130
  Hawthorne (G-4248)

COMMUNICATIONS SVCS: Telephone Or Video

Bandemar Networks LLC ....G 732 991-5112
  East Brunswick (G-2128)
Enterprisecc Ltd Liability Co ....G 201 266-0020
  Jersey City (G-4732)

COMMUNICATIONS SVCS: Telephone, Data

Verizon Communications Inc ....E 201 666-9934
  Westwood (G-11847)

COMMUNICATIONS SVCS: Telephone, Local

Verizon Communications Inc ....D 609 646-9939
  Egg Harbor Township (G-2700)

COMMUNICATIONS SVCS: Telephone, Local & Long Distance

Novega Venture Partners Inc ....G 732 528-2600
  Holmdel (G-4511)
Spirent Communications Inc ....G 732 946-4018
  Holmdel (G-4514)

COMMUNICATIONS SVCS: Telephone, Voice

Blueclone Networks LLC ....G 609 944-8433
  Princeton (G-8917)
Value Added Vice Solutions LLC ....G 201 400-3247
  Brielle (G-910)

COMMUTATORS: Electric Motors

Allu Group Inc ....F 201 288-2236
  East Brunswick (G-2125)

COMMUTATORS: Electronic

Heyco Products Corp ....G 732 286-1800
  Toms River (G-10766)

COMPACT LASER DISCS: Prerecorded

Audio and Video Labs Inc ....E 856 661-5772
  Delair (G-2000)
Disc Makers Inc ....B 800 468-9353
  Pennsauken (G-8414)
Simtronics Corporation ....F 732 747-0322
  Little Silver (G-5500)
Sony Corporation of America ....B 201 930-1000
  Paramus (G-7834)

COMPOST

L & S Contracting Inc ....G 609 397-1281
  Hopewell (G-4527)

COMPRESSORS: Air & Gas

Aavolyn Corp ....E 856 327-8040
  Millville (G-6221)
Aer X Dust Corporation ....G 732 946-9462
  Holmdel (G-4493)
Argus International Inc ....E 609 466-1677
  Ringoes (G-9334)
Armco Compressor Products ....G 201 866-6766
  North Bergen (G-7386)
Atlas Copco Hurricane LLC ....D 800 754-7408
  Parsippany (G-7887)
Busch LLC ....G 908 561-3233
  South Plainfield (G-10229)
Emse Corp ....F 973 227-9221
  Fairfield (G-3191)
Energy Beams Inc ....F 973 291-6555
  Bloomingdale (G-528)
Fleet Equipment Corporation ....F 201 337-3294
  Franklin Lakes (G-3623)
Metropolitan Vacuum Clr Co Inc ....D 201 405-2225
  Oakland (G-7636)
Trillium US ....G 973 827-1661
  Hamburg (G-4096)
Vac-U-Max ....E 973 759-4600
  Belleville (G-319)

COMPRESSORS: Air & Gas, Including Vacuum Pumps

Breeze-Eastern LLC......................G...... 973 602-1001
Whippany (G-11883)

Campbell Hausfeld LLC..................C...... 856 661-1800
Pennsauken (G-8399)

Gas Drying Inc................................F...... 973 361-2212
Wharton (G-11859)

Ingersoll-Rand Company.................E...... 856 793-7000
Mount Laurel (G-6766)

Knf Neuberger Inc..........................D...... 609 890-8889
Trenton (G-10950)

Kraissl Company Inc.......................E...... 201 342-0008
Hackensack (G-3937)

COMPUTER & COMPUTER SOFTWARE STORES

Andlogic Computers........................G...... 609 610-5752
Hamilton (G-4102)

Asi Computer Technologies Inc........F...... 732 343-7100
Edison (G-2462)

Computer Doc Associates Inc..........D...... 908 647-4445
Martinsville (G-5962)

Maingear Inc..................................E...... 888 624-6432
Kenilworth (G-4955)

R T I Inc.......................................E...... 201 261-5852
Oradell (G-7746)

COMPUTER & COMPUTER SOFTWARE STORES: Peripheral Eqpt

Fillimerica Inc................................G...... 800 435-7257
Montville (G-6442)

COMPUTER & COMPUTER SOFTWARE STORES: Printers & Plotters

Imperial Copy Products Inc..............E...... 973 927-5500
Randolph (G-9186)

COMPUTER & COMPUTER SOFTWARE STORES: Software & Access

Promia Incorporated.......................G...... 609 252-1850
Princeton (G-9009)

COMPUTER & COMPUTER SOFTWARE STORES: Software, Bus/Non-Game

Automated Office Inc......................G...... 888 362-7638
Cherry Hill (G-1341)

Bluebird Auto Rentl Systems LP.......E...... 973 989-2423
Dover (G-2076)

Qellus LLC....................................G...... 856 761-6575
Mount Laurel (G-6798)

COMPUTER & COMPUTER SOFTWARE STORES: Software, Computer Game

Sony Corporation of America...........F...... 201 930-1000
Woodcliff Lake (G-12065)

COMPUTER & DATA PROCESSING EQPT REPAIR & MAINTENANCE

Innovative Sftwr Solutions Inc.........D...... 856 910-9190
Maple Shade (G-5864)

COMPUTER & OFFICE MACHINE MAINTENANCE & REPAIR

Able Group Technologies Inc...........G...... 732 591-9299
Morganville (G-6579)

Blueclone Networks LLC..................G...... 609 944-8433
Princeton (G-8917)

Creative Cmpt Concepts LLC...........G...... 877 919-7988
Williamstown (G-11956)

Fis Avantgard LLC..........................G...... 732 530-9303
Tinton Falls (G-10717)

Integration International Inc.............E...... 973 796-2300
Parsippany (G-7962)

Lavitsky Computer Laboratories........G...... 908 725-6206
Bridgewater (G-840)

Lm Matrix Solutions LLC..................G...... 908 756-7952
Bridgewater (G-846)

Vertiv Corporation..........................E...... 732 225-3741
Edison (G-2640)

Weissco Power Ltd Liability Co.........G...... 908 832-2173
Califon (G-1037)

COMPUTER & SFTWR STORE: Modem, Monitor, Terminal/Disk Drive

Techntime Bus Sltons Ltd Lblty........F...... 973 246-8153
East Rutherford (G-2324)

COMPUTER CALCULATING SVCS

Metro Seliger Industries Inc.............C...... 201 438-4530
Carlstadt (G-1187)

COMPUTER DISKETTES WHOLESALERS

Tdk Electronics Inc.........................F...... 732 603-5941
Lumberton (G-5636)

COMPUTER FACILITIES MANAGEMENT SVCS

All Solutions Inc............................E...... 973 535-9100
Livingston (G-5503)

Blueclone Networks LLC..................G...... 609 944-8433
Princeton (G-8917)

Commvault Systems Inc..................E...... 732 870-4000
Tinton Falls (G-10709)

Criterion Software LLC....................F...... 908 754-1166
Freehold (G-3659)

Ensync Intrctive Solutions Inc..........E...... 732 542-4001
Freehold (G-3664)

COMPUTER FORMS

All-State International Inc................C...... 908 272-0800
Cranford (G-1899)

Stuyvesant Press Inc......................F...... 973 399-3880
Irvington (G-4587)

COMPUTER GRAPHICS SVCS

FLM Graphics Corporation...............D...... 973 575-9450
Fairfield (G-3202)

Strahan Consulting Group LLC..........G...... 908 790-0873
Scotch Plains (G-9742)

COMPUTER INTERFACE EQPT: Indl Process

ATI Trading Inc..............................F...... 718 888-7918
Elizabeth (G-2712)

Corporate Computer Systems...........F...... 732 739-5600
Newark (G-7088)

Ribble Company Inc........................F...... 201 475-1812
Saddle Brook (G-9672)

COMPUTER PAPER WHOLESALERS

Paris Corporation New Jersey...........D...... 609 265-9200
Westampton (G-11788)

COMPUTER PERIPHERAL EQPT REPAIR & MAINTENANCE

Central Technology Inc....................F...... 732 431-3339
Freehold (G-3656)

Gerbino Computer Systems Inc.........G...... 201 342-8240
Hackensack (G-3922)

Image Access Corp.........................E...... 201 342-7878
Rockleigh (G-9519)

R T I Inc.......................................E...... 201 261-5852
Oradell (G-7746)

COMPUTER PERIPHERAL EQPT, NEC

Advancing Opportunities Inc............G...... 201 907-0200
Teaneck (G-10621)

Amedia Networks Inc......................F...... 732 440-1992
Eatontown (G-2376)

Antron Technologies Inc..................G...... 732 205-0415
Edison (G-2457)

Automated Control Concepts Inc.......E...... 732 922-6611
Neptune (G-6867)

Beall Technologies Inc....................E...... 201 689-2130
Wyckoff (G-12104)

Behr Technology Inc.......................G...... 908 537-9960
Hampton (G-4148)

Berkeley Varitronics Systems...........E...... 732 548-3737
Metuchen (G-6047)

Cisco Systems Inc..........................G...... 856 642-7000
Moorestown (G-6513)

Cisco Systems Inc..........................E...... 201 782-0842
Montvale (G-6402)

Conduent State Healthcare LLC........G...... 973 824-3250
Newark (G-7087)

Conduent State Healthcare LLC........G...... 973 754-6134
Paterson (G-8163)

Corporate Computer Systems...........F...... 732 739-5600
Newark (G-7088)

Data Base Access Systems Inc.........F...... 973 335-0800
Mountain Lakes (G-6822)

Dew Associates Inc........................E...... 973 702-0545
Sussex (G-10557)

Ems Aviation Inc............................C...... 856 234-5020
Moorestown (G-6522)

Envirosight LLC..............................E...... 973 970-9284
Randolph (G-9176)

Epiq Systems Inc............................G...... 973 622-6111
Newark (G-7117)

Fyth Labs Inc.................................G...... 856 313-7362
Beverly (G-451)

Humanscale Corporation.................C...... 732 537-2944
Piscataway (G-8676)

Link Computer Graphics Inc.............G...... 973 808-8990
Fairfield (G-3263)

Lucent Technologies World Svcs........C...... 908 582-3000
New Providence (G-7008)

Maingear Inc..................................E...... 888 624-6432
Kenilworth (G-4955)

Micro Innovations Corp....................D...... 732 346-9333
Edison (G-2565)

MTS Systems Corporation................A...... 856 875-4478
Williamstown (G-11965)

Ner Data Products Inc.....................E...... 888 637-3282
Glassboro (G-3817)

Netscout Systems Inc.....................G...... 609 518-4100
Marlton (G-5943)

Oxberry LLC...................................G...... 201 935-3000
Carlstadt (G-1194)

Parker-Hannifin Corporation.............F...... 856 825-8900
Millville (G-6266)

Pcs Revenue Ctrl Systems Inc..........E...... 201 568-8300
Englewood Cliffs (G-2987)

Pim LLC..E...... 646 225-6666
Ridgefield (G-9283)

PNC Electronics Inc........................E...... 973 237-0400
Totowa (G-10845)

R T I Inc.......................................E...... 201 261-5852
Oradell (G-7746)

Radcom Equipment Inc....................G...... 201 518-0033
Paramus (G-7828)

Raritan Inc....................................E...... 732 764-8886
Somerset (G-10061)

Raritan Americas Inc......................C...... 732 764-8886
Somerset (G-10062)

RSR Electronics Inc........................E...... 732 381-8777
Rahway (G-9126)

S W Electronics & Mfg.....................C...... 856 222-9900
Moorestown (G-6564)

Salescaster Displays Corp...............G...... 908 322-3046
Scotch Plains (G-9739)

Sony Corporation of America............B...... 201 930-1000
Paramus (G-7834)

Source Micro LLC...........................F...... 973 328-1749
Randolph (G-9200)

Technobox Inc................................G...... 856 809-2306
West Berlin (G-11627)

Telegenix Inc.................................F...... 609 265-3910
Rancocas (G-9167)

Thomas Instrumentation Inc.............F...... 609 624-7777
Cape May Court House (G-1115)

Western Scientific Computers...........F...... 973 263-9311
Mountain Lakes (G-6830)

COMPUTER PERIPHERAL EQPT, WHOLESALE

Abris Distribution Inc......................E...... 732 252-9819
Manalapan (G-5799)

Antron Technologies Inc..................G...... 732 205-0415
Edison (G-2457)

Archtech Electronics Corp................E...... 732 355-1288
Dayton (G-1951)

Bcc (USA) Inc................................G...... 732 572-5450
Piscataway (G-8639)

Capintec Inc..................................E...... 201 825-9500
Florham Park (G-3495)

Computer Company North America....F...... 909 265-3390
Bedminster (G-262)

DFI America LLC.............................E...... 732 562-0693
Piscataway (G-8655)

Fusar Technologies Inc....................G...... 201 563-0189
Kearny (G-4856)

PRODUCT

Pascack Data Services Inc ....F 973 304-4858
  Hawthorne **(G-4236)**
Quadrangle Products Inc ....F 732 792-1234
  Englishtown **(G-3008)**

COMPUTER PERIPHERAL EQPT: Decoders

Paradise Barxon Corp ....G...... 908 707-9141
  Branchburg **(G-664)**

COMPUTER PERIPHERAL EQPT: Graphic Displays, Exc Terminals

Zaller Studios Inc ....G...... 973 743-5175
  Bloomfield **(G-523)**

COMPUTER PERIPHERAL EQPT: Input Or Output

American Fibertek Inc ....E 732 302-0660
  Somerset **(G-9951)**

COMPUTER PROCESSING SVCS

Aone Touch Inc ....G...... 732 261-6841
  Bordentown **(G-575)**

COMPUTER PROGRAMMING SVCS

All Solutions Inc ....E 973 535-9100
  Livingston **(G-5503)**
Bavelle Tech Sltions Ltd Lblty ....F 973 992-8086
  East Hanover **(G-2195)**
Cloudageit Ltd Liability Co ....G...... 888 205-4128
  North Brunswick **(G-7463)**
Com Tek Wrkplace Solutions LLC......F 973 927-6814
  Lyndhurst **(G-5649)**
Cyberextrudercom Inc ....G...... 973 623-7900
  Wayne **(G-11491)**
Eclearview Technologies Inc ....G...... 732 695-6999
  Ocean **(G-7662)**
Ensync Intrctive Solutions Inc..........G...... 732 542-4001
  Freehold **(G-3664)**
Fusar Technologies Inc ....G...... 201 563-0189
  Kearny **(G-4856)**
Gerbino Computer Systems Inc ....G...... 201 342-8240
  Hackensack **(G-3922)**
Global Power Technology Inc ....D...... 732 287-3680
  Edison **(G-2521)**
Incentx LLC ....G...... 302 202-2894
  Lakewood **(G-5112)**
Interntnal Digital Systems Inc..........F 201 983-7700
  Fort Lee **(G-3564)**
J S Paluch Co Inc ....F 732 516-1900
  Edison **(G-2537)**
Netquest Corporation ....E 856 866-0505
  Mount Laurel **(G-6786)**
Onco Inc..F 732 292-7460
  Wall Township **(G-11359)**
Real Soft Inc ....A 609 409-3636
  Monmouth Junction **(G-6308)**
Stealthbits Technologies Inc ....D...... 201 301-9328
  Hawthorne **(G-4245)**
Stephen Swinton Studio Inc ....G...... 908 537-9135
  Washington **(G-11452)**
Structured Healthcare MGT Inc ....E 201 569-3290
  Englewood **(G-2945)**
Virid Biosciences Limited ....F 732 410-9573
  Cherry Hill **(G-1426)**
Wellspring Info Inc ....F 800 268-3682
  Montclair **(G-6393)**

COMPUTER PROGRAMMING SVCS: Custom

Aliron International Inc ....E 540 808-1615
  South Plainfield **(G-10210)**
Greycell Labs Inc ....E 732 444-0123
  Edison **(G-2523)**
Indotronix International Corp ....G...... 609 750-0700
  Plainsboro **(G-8790)**
Thomas Instrumentation Inc ....F 609 624-7777
  Cape May Court House **(G-1115)**
Thomas Instrumentation Inc ....F 609 624-2630
  Cape May Court House **(G-1116)**
Um Equity Corp ....G...... 856 354-2200
  Haddonfield **(G-4065)**

COMPUTER RELATED MAINTENANCE SVCS

Ensync Intrctive Solutions Inc..........G...... 732 542-4001
  Freehold **(G-3664)**

Kyosis LLC ....G...... 908 202-8894
  South River **(G-10351)**
Lm Matrix Solutions LLC ....G...... 908 756-7952
  Bridgewater **(G-846)**
Pds Prclnical Data Systems Inc.........F 973 398-2800
  Mount Arlington **(G-6717)**

COMPUTER RELATED SVCS, NEC

Stark Pharma Technology Inc............F 848 217-4059
  Piscataway **(G-8719)**

COMPUTER SERVICE BUREAU

Alaquest International Inc ....F 908 713-9399
  Lebanon **(G-5250)**
Commerce Register Inc....................E 201 445-3000
  Midland Park **(G-6172)**
Stephen Swinton Studio Inc ....G...... 908 537-9135
  Washington **(G-11452)**

COMPUTER SOFTWARE DEVELOPMENT

Aplnow LLC ....G...... 732 223-5575
  Manasquan **(G-5828)**
Audiocodes Inc ....G...... 732 469-0880
  Somerset **(G-9959)**
Audiocodes Inc ....F 732 469-0880
  Somerset **(G-9960)**
Aztec Software Associates Inc ....E 973 258-0011
  Springfield **(G-10429)**
Burgiss Group LLC..........................D...... 201 427-9600
  Hoboken **(G-4444)**
Comprehensive Healthcare Systm ......D...... 732 362-2000
  Edison **(G-2482)**
Data Communiqe Inc ....E 201 508-6000
  Ridgefield Park **(G-9302)**
Energy Tracking LLC ....G...... 973 448-8660
  Flanders **(G-3408)**
Innerspace Technology Inc ....G...... 201 933-1600
  Carlstadt **(G-1168)**
Kittyhawk Digital LLC ....G...... 269 767-8399
  Emerson **(G-2866)**
Lavitsky Computer Laboratories ....G...... 908 725-6206
  Bridgewater **(G-840)**
Local Wisdom Inc ....E 609 269-2320
  Lambertville **(G-5194)**
Majesco ....G...... 973 461-5200
  Morristown **(G-6684)**
Maxisit Inc.....................................C...... 732 494-2005
  Metuchen **(G-6065)**
Micro Logic Inc ....F 201 962-7510
  Mahwah **(G-5753)**
Microtelecom Ltd Liability Co ....G...... 866 676-5679
  Fort Lee **(G-3573)**
Mikros Systems Corporation ....G...... 609 987-1513
  Princeton **(G-8978)**
Netcom Systems Inc ....E 732 393-6100
  Edison **(G-2572)**
Netx Information Systems Inc ....F 609 298-9118
  Long Beach Township **(G-5592)**
Os33 Services Corp ....C...... 866 796-0310
  Iselin **(G-4620)**
Planet Associates Inc ....E 201 693-8700
  Park Ridge **(G-7858)**
Promia Incorporated........................E 609 252-1850
  Princeton **(G-9009)**
Saksoft Inc ....C...... 201 451-4609
  Jersey City **(G-4803)**
Samsung SDS Globl Scl Amer Inc ......E 201 229-4456
  Ridgefield Park **(G-9315)**
Scottline LLC..................................E 732 534-3123
  Piscataway **(G-8710)**
Smartlinx Solutions LLC ....G...... 732 385-5507
  Iselin **(G-4629)**
Software Practices and Tech ....G...... 908 464-2923
  Summit **(G-10548)**
Specialty Systems Inc ....E 732 341-1011
  Toms River **(G-10794)**
Sunbird Software Inc ....D...... 732 993-4476
  Somerset **(G-10077)**
Wizcom Corporation ....E 609 750-0601
  Princeton Junction **(G-9070)**
World Software Corporation ....E 201 444-3228
  Glen Rock **(G-3836)**
Xybion Corporation ....G...... 973 538-2067
  Lawrenceville **(G-5248)**

COMPUTER SOFTWARE DEVELOPMENT & APPLICATIONS

39 Idea Factory Row LLC ....G...... 908 244-8631
  Flemington **(G-3425)**
Agilis Chemicals Inc ....F 973 910-2424
  Short Hills **(G-9864)**
Aginova Inc....................................G...... 732 804-3272
  Freehold **(G-3644)**
Artezio LLC ....G...... 609 786-2435
  Princeton **(G-8912)**
Audio Technologies and Codecs ....F 973 624-1116
  Newark **(G-7058)**
Avyakta It Services LLC ....F 609 790-7517
  East Windsor **(G-2345)**
Chryslis Data Sltons Svcs Corp ....G...... 609 375-2000
  Princeton **(G-8922)**
Clientsrver Tech Solutions LLC ....G...... 732 710-4495
  Iselin **(G-4605)**
Cognizant Tech Solutions Corp...........D...... 201 801-0233
  Teaneck **(G-10625)**
Coles and Blenman Network LLC ....G...... 973 432-7041
  Bloomfield **(G-496)**
Corporate Computer Systems ....F 732 739-5600
  Newark **(G-7088)**
Diabeto Inc....................................G...... 646 397-3175
  Piscataway **(G-8656)**
Dialogic Inc ....C...... 973 967-6000
  Parsippany **(G-7916)**
Ebic Prparedness Solutions LLC ....G...... 719 244-6209
  Leonia **(G-5288)**
Enertia LLC ....G...... 856 330-4767
  Pennsauken **(G-8418)**
Enroute Computer Solutions Inc.........E 609 569-9255
  Egg Harbor Township **(G-2683)**
Factonomy Inc................................F 201 848-7812
  Wyckoff **(G-12111)**
Image Access Corp ....E 201 342-7878
  Rockleigh **(G-9519)**
Innovi Mobile LLC ....F 646 588-0165
  Millburn **(G-6200)**
Kicksonfirecom LLC ....G...... 718 753-4248
  South Amboy **(G-10135)**
Letts Play Inc ....G...... 856 297-2530
  Williamstown **(G-11963)**
Limosys LLC ....E 212 222-4433
  Englewood Cliffs **(G-2983)**
Melillo Consulting Inc ....E 732 563-8400
  Somerset **(G-10028)**
Nb Ventures Inc..............................C...... 732 382-6565
  Clark **(G-1509)**
Ngenious Solutions Inc ....G...... 732 873-3385
  Piscataway **(G-8696)**
Pai Services LLC ....C...... 856 231-4667
  Mount Laurel **(G-6787)**
Pds Prclnical Data Systems Inc...........F 973 398-2800
  Mount Arlington **(G-6717)**
Pentax of America Inc ....E 973 628-6200
  Montvale **(G-6421)**
Robokiller LLC ....E 723 838-1901
  South Amboy **(G-10140)**
Rx Trade Zone Inc ....G...... 833 933-6600
  Edison **(G-2601)**
Steward LLC ....G...... 609 816-8825
  Princeton **(G-9028)**
Valuemomentum Inc ....D...... 908 755-0025
  Piscataway **(G-8734)**
Worldwide Pt SL Ltd Lblty Co ....F 201 928-0222
  Teaneck **(G-10655)**

COMPUTER SOFTWARE SYSTEMS ANALYSIS & DESIGN: Custom

Amerindia Technologies Inc ....E 609 664-2224
  Cranbury **(G-1808)**
Anvima Technologies LLC ....G...... 973 531-7077
  Brookside **(G-916)**
Apex Innovation Solutions LLC ....G...... 215 313-3332
  Princeton **(G-8908)**
Bandemar Networks LLC ....G...... 732 991-5112
  East Brunswick **(G-2128)**
Bluebird Auto Rentl Systems LP ....E 973 989-2423
  Dover **(G-2076)**
Creative Cmpt Concepts LLC ....G...... 877 919-7988
  Williamstown **(G-11956)**
Genomesafe LLC ....G...... 203 676-3752
  West Orange **(G-11768)**
Hozric LLC ....G...... 908 420-8821
  Green Brook **(G-3861)**
I-Exceed Tech Solutions Inc ....G...... 917 693-3207
  Princeton **(G-8960)**

Ms Health Software Corp ....G...... 908 850-5564
Hackettstown *(G-4028)*

Pace Business Solutions Inc ....E...... 908 451-0355
Manahawkin *(G-5795)*

Scimar Technologies LLC ....G...... 609 208-1796
Allentown *(G-31)*

Sirma Group Inc ....B...... 646 357-3067
Jersey City *(G-4811)*

COMPUTER SOFTWARE WRITERS

Antenna Software Inc ....E...... 201 217-3824
Jersey City *(G-4694)*

Simtronics Corporation ....F...... 732 747-0322
Little Silver *(G-5500)*

COMPUTER STORAGE DEVICES, NEC

150 Development Group LLC ....G...... 732 546-3812
Middlesex *(G-6089)*

B-Hive Ltd Liability Company ....G...... 302 438-2769
Hightstown *(G-4294)*

Blueclone Networks LLC ....G...... 609 944-8433
Princeton *(G-8917)*

Dataram Memory ....E...... 609 799-0071
Princeton *(G-8929)*

Eclearview Technologies Inc ....G...... 732 695-6999
Ocean *(G-7662)*

EMC Corporation ....D...... 732 922-6353
Ocean *(G-7663)*

EMC Corporation ....F...... 908 226-0100
South Plainfield *(G-10249)*

EMC Corporation ....A...... 732 549-8500
East Brunswick *(G-2142)*

EMC Paving LLC ....G...... 908 636-1054
Piscataway *(G-8661)*

EMC Squared LLC ....G...... 973 586-8854
Rockaway *(G-9455)*

Gaw Associates Inc ....F...... 856 608-1428
Cherry Hill *(G-1367)*

Micronet Enertec Tech Inc ....D...... 201 225-0190
Montvale *(G-6420)*

Ner Data Products Inc ....E...... 888 637-3282
Glassboro *(G-3817)*

Plastic Reel Corp of America ....E...... 201 933-5100
Carlstadt *(G-1202)*

Quantum Integrators Group LLC ....D...... 609 632-0621
Plainsboro *(G-8800)*

Sony Corporation of America ....B...... 201 930-1000
Paramus *(G-7834)*

Veeco Instruments Inc ....E...... 732 560-5300
Somerset *(G-10093)*

Whiptail Technologies LLC ....D...... 973 585-6375
Whippany *(G-11914)*

COMPUTER STORAGE UNITS: Auxiliary

Creative Cmpt Concepts LLC ....G...... 877 919-7988
Williamstown *(G-11956)*

COMPUTER SYSTEM SELLING SVCS

Planitroi Inc ....D...... 973 664-0700
Denville *(G-2049)*

COMPUTER SYSTEMS ANALYSIS & DESIGN

Baxter Corporation ....D...... 201 337-1212
Franklin Lakes *(G-3613)*

Microtelecom Ltd Liability Co ....G...... 866 676-5679
Fort Lee *(G-3573)*

Multiforce Systems Corporation ....F...... 609 683-4242
Princeton *(G-8982)*

Pascack Data Services Inc ....F...... 973 304-4858
Hawthorne *(G-4236)*

Planet Associates Inc ....E...... 201 693-8700
Park Ridge *(G-7858)*

Primary Systems Inc ....F...... 732 679-2200
Old Bridge *(G-7725)*

Redkoh Industries Inc ....G...... 908 369-1590
Hillsborough *(G-4351)*

Subcom LLC ....B...... 732 578-7000
Eatontown *(G-2422)*

COMPUTER TERMINALS

Information Technolgy Corp ....G...... 201 556-1999
Paramus *(G-7807)*

Maingear Inc ....E...... 888 624-6432
Kenilworth *(G-4955)*

Metrofuser LLC ....D...... 908 245-2100
Elizabeth *(G-2758)*

COMPUTER TRAINING SCHOOLS

Swce Inc ....E...... 908 766-5695
Bernardsville *(G-444)*

COMPUTER-AIDED DESIGN SYSTEMS SVCS

Cimquest Inc ....D...... 732 699-0400
Branchburg *(G-628)*

Enser Corporation ....D...... 856 829-5522
Cinnaminson *(G-1456)*

Senco Metals LLC ....G...... 973 342-1742
Passaic *(G-8106)*

Warehouse Solutions Inc ....F...... 201 880-1110
Fair Lawn *(G-3128)*

COMPUTER-AIDED ENGINEERING SYSTEMS SVCS

Circonix Technologies LLC ....F...... 973 962-6160
Ringwood *(G-9344)*

Machine Atomated Ctrl Tech LLC ....G...... 732 921-8935
Piscataway *(G-8685)*

COMPUTER-AIDED MANUFACTURING SYSTEMS SVCS

Sightlogix Inc ....E...... 609 951-0008
Princeton *(G-9022)*

COMPUTERS, NEC

Aaeon Electronics Inc ....E...... 732 203-9300
Hazlet *(G-4254)*

Asi Computer Technologies Inc ....F...... 732 343-7100
Edison *(G-2462)*

B2x Corporation ....G...... 201 714-2373
Jersey City *(G-4697)*

Datapro International Inc ....E...... 732 868-0588
Piscataway *(G-8652)*

DFI America LLC ....E...... 732 562-0693
Piscataway *(G-8655)*

Dxl Enterprises Inc ....F...... 201 891-8718
Mahwah *(G-5733)*

Esaw Industries Inc ....G...... 732 613-1400
East Brunswick *(G-2144)*

Fillimerica Inc ....G...... 800 435-7257
Montville *(G-6442)*

Franklin Electronic Publs Inc ....D...... 609 386-2500
Burlington *(G-969)*

Global Business Dimensions Inc ....E...... 973 831-5866
Pompton Plains *(G-8865)*

Hitechone Inc ....G...... 201 500-8864
Englewood Cliffs *(G-2975)*

Ideal Data Inc ....F...... 201 998-9440
North Arlington *(G-7374)*

La Duca Technical Services LLC ....G...... 570 309-4009
West Milford *(G-11728)*

Lavitsky Computer Laboratories ....G...... 908 725-6206
Bridgewater *(G-840)*

Niksun Inc ....C...... 609 936-9999
Princeton *(G-8985)*

Novasom Industries Inc ....G...... 732 994-5652
Lakewood *(G-5142)*

Oti America Inc ....G...... 732 429-1900
Iselin *(G-4621)*

Pcs Revenue Ctrl Systems Inc ....E...... 201 568-8300
Englewood Cliffs *(G-2987)*

Planitroi Inc ....D...... 973 664-0700
Denville *(G-2049)*

Reliance Electronics Inc ....G...... 973 237-0400
Totowa *(G-10849)*

Rt Com USA Inc ....G...... 973 862-4210
Lafayette *(G-5032)*

Spacetouch Inc ....G...... 609 712-6572
Princeton *(G-9027)*

Strahan Consulting Group LLC ....G...... 908 790-0873
Scotch Plains *(G-9742)*

Technical Advantage Inc ....G...... 973 402-5500
Boonton *(G-570)*

Techno City Inc ....G...... 862 414-3282
East Rutherford *(G-2323)*

Xceedium Inc ....D...... 201 536-1000
Jersey City *(G-4834)*

COMPUTERS, NEC, WHOLESALE

AT Information Products Inc ....G...... 201 529-0202
Mahwah *(G-5715)*

Central Technology Inc ....F...... 732 431-3339
Freehold *(G-3656)*

Dymax Systems Inc ....F...... 732 918-2424
Neptune *(G-6874)*

Prestone Products Corporation ....E...... 732 431-8200
Freehold *(G-3692)*

COMPUTERS, PERIPH & SOFTWARE, WHLSE: Acctg Machs, Readable

Aone Touch Inc ....G...... 732 261-6841
Bordentown *(G-575)*

COMPUTERS, PERIPH & SOFTWARE, WHLSE: Personal & Home Entrtn

Datapro International Inc ....E...... 732 868-0588
Piscataway *(G-8652)*

Maingear Inc ....E...... 888 624-6432
Kenilworth *(G-4955)*

COMPUTERS, PERIPHERALS & SOFTWARE, WHOLESALE: Printers

B&B Imaging LLC ....G...... 201 261-3131
Paramus *(G-7791)*

COMPUTERS, PERIPHERALS & SOFTWARE, WHOLESALE: Software

3 H Technology Institute LLC ....E...... 866 624-3484
Mount Laurel *(G-6736)*

3shape Inc ....F...... 908 867-0144
Warren *(G-11395)*

Aztec Software Associates Inc ....E...... 973 258-0011
Springfield *(G-10429)*

Five Elements Robotics LLC ....G...... 800 681-8514
Wall Township *(G-11340)*

Freyr Inc ....C...... 908 483-7958
Princeton *(G-8952)*

Nb Ventures Inc ....C...... 732 382-6565
Clark *(G-1509)*

New Line Prtg & Tech Solutions ....G...... 973 405-6133
Clifton *(G-1676)*

Pcs Revenue Ctrl Systems Inc ....E...... 201 568-8300
Englewood Cliffs *(G-2987)*

RSD America Inc ....F...... 201 996-1000
Teaneck *(G-10649)*

COMPUTERS, PERIPHERALS & SOFTWARE, WHOLESALE: Terminals

National Communications Inc ....E...... 973 325-3151
West Orange *(G-11774)*

COMPUTERS: Indl, Process, Gas Flow

Multiforce Systems Corporation ....F...... 609 683-4242
Princeton *(G-8982)*

COMPUTERS: Mini

Crestron Electronics Inc ....C...... 201 767-3400
Rockleigh *(G-9516)*

Five Elements Robotics LLC ....G...... 800 681-8514
Wall Township *(G-11340)*

COMPUTERS: Personal

Andlogic Computers ....G...... 609 610-5752
Hamilton *(G-4102)*

Eom Worldwide Sales Corp ....G...... 732 994-7352
Lakewood *(G-5091)*

Maingear Inc ....E...... 888 624-6432
Kenilworth *(G-4955)*

Mikros Systems Corporation ....G...... 609 987-1513
Princeton *(G-8978)*

Pascack Data Services Inc ....F...... 973 304-4858
Hawthorne *(G-4236)*

Princeton Identity Inc ....E...... 609 256-6994
Hamilton *(G-4122)*

S G A Business Systems Inc ....G...... 908 359-4626
Hillsborough *(G-4353)*

Touch Dynamic Inc ....D...... 732 382-5701
South Plainfield *(G-10331)*

CONCENTRATES, DRINK

Citroil Enterprises Inc ....F...... 201 933-8405
Carlstadt *(G-1140)*

CONCENTRATES, FLAVORING, EXC DRINK

Sapphire Flvors Fragrances LLC ....F 973 200-8849
Fairfield **(G-3307)**

CONCRETE CURING & HARDENING COMPOUNDS

Gamka Sales Co Inc ....E 732 248-1400
Edison **(G-2518)**

Sika Corporation ....C 201 933-8800
Lyndhurst **(G-5679)**

W R Grace & Co-Conn ....E 732 868-6914
Somerset **(G-10098)**

CONCRETE PRDTS

A & A Concrete Products Inc ....G 973 835-2239
Riverdale **(G-9369)**

Clayton Block Company Inc ....E 732 681-0186
Wall Township **(G-11326)**

Crossfield Products Corp ....D 908 245-2801
Roselle Park **(G-9580)**

CST Pavers ....F 856 299-5339
Pedricktown **(G-8347)**

European Stone Art LLC ....F 201 441-9116
South Hackensack **(G-10160)**

Garden State Precast Inc ....D 732 938-4436
Wall Township **(G-11343)**

Hanson Aggregates Wrp Inc ....E 972 653-5500
Wall Township **(G-11345)**

J F Gillespie Inc ....E 856 692-2233
Vineland **(G-11237)**

Kelken-Gold Inc ....G 732 416-6730
Sayreville **(G-9713)**

Paul Bros Inc ....E 856 697-5895
Newfield **(G-7326)**

Russell Cast Stone Inc ....D 856 753-4000
West Berlin **(G-11620)**

Sika Corporation ....B 201 933-8800
Lyndhurst **(G-5678)**

Solid Cast Stone ....G 856 694-5245
Newfield **(G-7328)**

Strongwall Industries Inc ....G 201 445-4633
Ridgewood **(G-9330)**

Trap Rock Industries Inc ....B 609 924-0300
Kingston **(G-5012)**

CONCRETE PRDTS, PRECAST, NEC

Boccella Precast LLC ....F 856 767-3861
Berlin **(G-416)**

Clayton Block Co ....D 201 955-6292
North Arlington **(G-7371)**

Clayton Block Company LLC ....E 201 339-8585
Bayonne **(G-210)**

Dunbar Concrete Products Inc ....F 973 697-2525
Oak Ridge **(G-7600)**

Empire Blended Products Inc ....E 732 269-4949
Bayville **(G-244)**

J B & Sons Concrete Products ....F 856 767-4140
Berlin **(G-423)**

Jersey Precast Corporation Inc ....C 609 689-3700
Trenton **(G-10946)**

Jpc Merger Sub LLC ....C 609 890-4343
Trenton **(G-10948)**

Oldcastle Infrastructure Inc ....E 609 561-3400
Williamstown **(G-11966)**

Precast Manufacturing Co LLC ....E 908 454-2122
Phillipsburg **(G-8569)**

Precast Systems Inc ....E 609 208-0569
Allentown **(G-29)**

CONCRETE: Bituminous

Earle The Walter R Corp ....G 732 308-1113
Wall Township **(G-11336)**

Earle The Walter R Corp ....G 732 657-8551
Jackson **(G-4652)**

Joseph and William Stavola ....E 609 924-0300
Kingston **(G-5009)**

Stavola Contracting Co Inc ....G 732 935-0156
Englishtown **(G-3009)**

CONCRETE: Dry Mixture

Duraamen Engineered Pdts Inc ....G 973 230-1301
Newark **(G-7106)**

Tri-State Quikrete ....E 973 347-4569
Flanders **(G-3423)**

CONCRETE: Ready-Mixed

Abi Inc ....E 609 588-8225
Lawrenceville **(G-5222)**

Ace-Crete Products Inc ....F 732 269-1400
Bayville **(G-238)**

Action Supply Inc ....E 609 390-0663
Ocean View **(G-7701)**

Allied Concrete Co Inc ....G 973 627-6150
Rockaway **(G-9440)**

Allied Concrete Co Inc ....G 973 627-6150
Rockaway **(G-9441)**

Atlantic Masonry Supply Inc ....F 609 909-9292
Egg Harbor Township **(G-2678)**

Clayton Block Company Inc ....E 888 763-8665
Wall Township **(G-11325)**

Clayton Block Company Inc ....F 732 349-3700
Toms River **(G-10753)**

Clayton Block Company Inc ....F 732 364-2404
Jackson **(G-4643)**

Clayton Block Company Inc ....F 732 549-1234
Edison **(G-2478)**

Concrete On Demand Inc ....F 201 337-0005
Oakland **(G-7620)**

County Concrete Corporation ....F 973 538-3113
Morristown **(G-6656)**

County Concrete Corporation ....D 973 744-2188
Kenvil **(G-4992)**

Diamond Chip Realty LLC ....E 973 383-4651
Sparta **(G-10386)**

Eastern Concrete Materials Inc ....G 609 698-2800
Barnegat **(G-159)**

Eastern Concrete Materials Inc ....E 201 797-7979
Saddle Brook **(G-9650)**

Eastern Concrete Materials Inc ....E 908 537-2135
Glen Gardner **(G-3821)**

Erial Concrete Inc ....F 856 784-8884
Erial **(G-3011)**

Ernest R Miles Construction Co ....F 856 697-2311
Newfield **(G-7321)**

Hanson Aggregates Bmc Inc ....G 856 447-4294
Newport **(G-7333)**

Herbert J Hinchman & Son Inc ....E 973 942-2063
Wayne **(G-11516)**

Holtec Government Services LLC ....G 856 291-0600
Camden **(G-1068)**

Joseph and William Stavola ....E 609 924-0300
Kingston **(G-5009)**

Kennedy Concrete Inc ....E 856 692-8650
Vineland **(G-11240)**

L & L Redi-Mix Inc ....G 609 859-2271
Southampton **(G-10367)**

Le-Ed Construction Inc ....E 732 341-4546
Toms River **(G-10775)**

Mershon Concrete LLC ....E 609 298-2150
Bordentown **(G-588)**

Miles Concrete Company Inc ....F 856 697-2311
Newfield **(G-7323)**

New Jersey Pulverizing Co Inc ....F 732 269-1400
Bayville **(G-249)**

Penn-Jersey Bldg Mtls Co Inc ....G 609 641-6994
Egg Harbor Township **(G-2692)**

Phillips Companies Inc ....D 973 483-4124
Clinton **(G-1748)**

Ralph Clayton & Sons LLC ....E 800 662-3044
Cookstown **(G-1805)**

Ralph Clayton & Sons LLC ....E 732 462-1552
Freehold **(G-3697)**

Ralph Clayton & Sons LLC ....E 609 383-1818
Egg Harbor Township **(G-2694)**

Ralph Clayton & Sons LLC ....E 609 695-0767
Trenton **(G-10986)**

Reuther Material Co Inc ....E 201 863-3550
North Bergen **(G-7435)**

Salomone Redi-Mix LLC ....E 973 305-0022
Wayne **(G-11552)**

SCC Concrete Inc ....F 908 859-2172
Phillipsburg **(G-8574)**

Short Load Concrete LLC ....G 732 469-4420
Bridgewater **(G-889)**

STA-Seal Inc ....G 609 924-0300
Kingston **(G-5011)**

Suffolk County Contractors ....E 732 349-7726
Toms River **(G-10796)**

Tanis Concrete ....E 201 796-1556
Fair Lawn **(G-3126)**

Trap Rock Industries Inc ....B 609 924-0300
Kingston **(G-5012)**

Weldon Asphalt Corp ....E 908 322-7840
Watchung **(G-11461)**

Weldon Concrete Corp ....G 973 228-7473
Roseland **(G-9544)**

Weldon Materials Inc ....E 908 233-4444
Westfield **(G-11806)**

Weldon Quarry Co LLC ....E 908 233-4444
Westfield **(G-11807)**

Wjv Materials LLC ....E 856 299-8244
Pedricktown **(G-8356)**

Yogo Mix ....G 609 897-1379
Princeton Junction **(G-9071)**

CONDENSERS: Heat Transfer Eqpt, Evaporative

Coolenheat Inc ....E 908 925-4473
Kendall Park **(G-4918)**

Diversified Heat Transfer Inc ....D 800 221-1522
Towaco **(G-10869)**

Harsco Corporation ....E 856 779-7795
Cherry Hill **(G-1371)**

CONDENSERS: Motors Or Generators

Evapco-Blct Dry Cooling Inc ....E 908 379-2665
Bridgewater **(G-821)**

CONDENSERS: Steam

Amec Fster Wheeler N Amer Corp .....D 936 448-6323
Hampton **(G-4147)**

DC Fabricators Inc ....C 609 499-3000
Florence **(G-3474)**

Maarky Thermal Systems Inc ....G 856 470-1504
Cherry Hill **(G-1386)**

Power Products and Engrg LLC ....E 855 769-3751
Trenton **(G-10979)**

CONDUITS & FITTINGS: Electric

ABB Installation Products Inc ....C 908 852-1122
Hackettstown **(G-3994)**

E & G Roman Corp ....D 973 482-1123
Newark **(G-7110)**

Superflex Ltd ....E 718 768-1400
Elizabeth **(G-2778)**

CONFECTIONERY PRDTS WHOLESALERS

Fralingers Inc ....E 609 345-2177
Atlantic City **(G-90)**

James Candy Company ....E 609 344-1519
Atlantic City **(G-95)**

Nexira Inc ....E 908 704-7480
Somerville **(G-10122)**

PR Products Distributors Inc ....G 973 928-1120
Wayne **(G-11544)**

Promotion In Motion Inc ....D 201 962-8530
Allendale **(G-14)**

Webers Candy Store ....G 856 455-8277
Bridgeton **(G-778)**

CONFECTIONS & CANDY

Ausome LLC ....G 732 951-8818
Paramus **(G-7789)**

Cadbury Adams USA LLC ....E 973 503-2000
East Hanover **(G-2197)**

Candy Treasure LLC ....G 201 830-3600
Lebanon **(G-5254)**

Ce De Candy Inc ....C 908 964-0660
Union **(G-11035)**

Dairy Maid Confectionery Co ....G 609 399-0100
Ocean City **(G-7690)**

Damask Kandies ....G 856 467-1661
Swedesboro **(G-10578)**

David Bradley Chocolatier Inc ....F 609 443-4747
Windsor **(G-11995)**

David Bradley Chocolatier Inc ....E 732 536-7719
Englishtown **(G-3001)**

Ferrero U S A Inc ....C 732 764-9300
Parsippany **(G-7943)**

Fralingers Inc ....G 609 345-2177
Atlantic City **(G-91)**

Fralingers Inc ....E 609 345-2177
Atlantic City **(G-90)**

Giambris Quality Sweets Inc ....G 856 783-1099
Clementon **(G-1533)**

Growtech LLC ....D 732 993-8683
Cranbury **(G-1837)**

Hillside Candy LLC ....F 973 926-2300
Hillside **(G-4398)**

Hillside Candy LLC ....E 908 241-4747
Roselle **(G-9560)**

(G-0000) Company's Geographic Section entry number

James Candy Company ....E 609 344-1519
Atlantic City **(G-95)**

Koppers Chocolate LLC ....D 212 243-0220
Jersey City **(G-4756)**

Krauses Homemade Candy Inc ....F 201 943-4790
Fairview **(G-3362)**

Life of Party LLC ....E 732 828-0886
North Brunswick **(G-7475)**

Marlow Candy & Nut Co Inc ....E 201 569-7606
Englewood **(G-2922)**

Mars Incorporated ....A 908 852-1000
Hackettstown **(G-4021)**

Mars Incorporated ....D 908 850-2420
Hackettstown **(G-4022)**

Mars Chocolate North Amer LLC ....A ...908 852-1000
Hackettstown **(G-4023)**

Mars Chocolate North Amer LLC ....A ...908 979-5070
Hackettstown **(G-4024)**

Nova Distributors LLC ....F 908 222-1010
Edison **(G-2580)**

Old Monmouth Peanut Brittle Co ......G ...732 462-1311
Freehold **(G-3684)**

Oral Fixation LLC ....G 609 937-9972
Hopewell **(G-4528)**

Ozone Confectioners Bakers Sup ......F ...201 791-4444
Verona **(G-11171)**

Packom LLC ....E 201 378-8382
Little Falls **(G-5463)**

Pim Brands LLC ....D 732 560-8300
Somerset **(G-10053)**

PR Products Distributors Inc ....G ...973 928-1120
Wayne **(G-11544)**

Promotion In Motion Inc ....D ...201 962-8530
Allendale **(G-14)**

Promotion In Motion Inc ....E ...732 560-8300
Somerset **(G-10058)**

Rauhausers Inc ....F 609 399-1465
Ocean City **(G-7693)**

Reilys Candy Inc ....F 609 953-0040
Medford **(G-6032)**

U I S Industries Inc ....A 201 946-2600
Jersey City **(G-4823)**

Webers Candy Store ....G 856 455-8277
Bridgeton **(G-778)**

William R Tatz Industries ....G 973 751-0720
Belleville **(G-325)**

World Confections Inc ....D 718 768-8100
South Orange **(G-10203)**

CONFINEMENT SURVEILLANCE SYS MAINTENANCE & MONITORING SVCS

SMS Building Systems Ltd Lblty ....F ..856 520-8769
Cherry Hill **(G-1415)**

CONNECTORS & TERMINALS: Electrical Device Uses

ABB Installation Products Inc ....C ...908 852-1122
Hackettstown **(G-3994)**

Armel Electronics Inc ....E 201 869-4300
North Bergen **(G-7387)**

Glasseal Products Inc ....C 732 370-9100
Lakewood **(G-5104)**

Hofer Machine & Tool Co Inc ....F ...973 427-1195
North Haledon **(G-7496)**

Mac Products Inc ....D 973 344-5149
Kearny **(G-4880)**

CONNECTORS: Cord, Electric

Connector Products Inc ....F 856 829-9190
Pennsauken **(G-8408)**

Volta Corporation ....E 732 583-3300
Laurence Harbor **(G-5211)**

CONNECTORS: Electrical

Bleema Manufacturing Corp ....E 973 371-1771
Irvington **(G-4563)**

Richards Mfg A NJ Ltd Partnr ....E ...973 371-1771
Irvington **(G-4585)**

CONNECTORS: Electronic

ABB Installation Products Inc ....C ...908 852-1122
Hackettstown **(G-3994)**

Adam Tech Asia Llc ....G 908 687-5000
Union **(G-11020)**

Al Technology Inc ....E 609 799-9388
Princeton Junction **(G-9048)**

Armel Electronics Inc ....E 201 869-4300
North Bergen **(G-7387)**

Barantec Inc ....F 973 779-8774
Clifton **(G-1571)**

Brim Electronics Inc ....F 201 796-2886
Lodi **(G-5555)**

Central Components Mfg LLC ....G 732 469-5720
Middlesex **(G-6104)**

Components Corporation ....F 866 426-6726
Denville **(G-2032)**

Da-Green Electronics Ltd ....F 732 254-2735
Marlboro **(G-5894)**

Fuji Electric Corp America ....D 732 560-9410
Edison **(G-2515)**

Fujipoly America Corporation ....E 732 969-0100
Carteret **(G-1255)**

Glasseal Products Inc ....C 732 370-9100
Lakewood **(G-5104)**

Heilind Electronics Inc ....D 888 881-5420
Lumberton **(G-5629)**

Heilind Mil-Aero LLC ....C 856 722-5535
Lumberton **(G-5630)**

Huber+suhner Astrolab Inc ....E ...732 560-3800
Warren **(G-11416)**

I Trade Technology Ltd ....G 615 348-7233
Mahwah **(G-5749)**

Kraus & Naimer Inc ....E 732 560-1240
Somerset **(G-10011)**

Lapp Usa LLC ....C 973 660-9700
Florham Park **(G-3517)**

Newtech Group Corp ....G 732 355-0392
Kendall Park **(G-4919)**

Princetel Inc ....E 609 588-8801
Hamilton **(G-4121)**

Richards Mfg Co Sales Inc ....E ...973 371-1771
Irvington **(G-4586)**

Severna Operations Inc ....E 973 503-1600
Parsippany **(G-8013)**

Te Connectivity Corporation ....B ...610 893-9800
Eatontown **(G-2424)**

Unicorp ....C 973 674-1700
Orange **(G-7765)**

Valconn Electronics Inc ....E 908 687-1600
Union **(G-11097)**

Wire-Pro Inc ....E 856 935-7560
Salem **(G-9698)**

CONNECTORS: Power, Electric

Dos Industrial Sales LLC ....G ...973 887-7800
East Hanover **(G-2205)**

CONSTRUCTION & MINING MACHINERY WHOLESALERS

Doosan Machine Tools Amer Corp ....D ..973 618-2500
Pine Brook **(G-8599)**

Harsco Corporation ....E 856 779-7795
Cherry Hill **(G-1371)**

Msg Fire & Safety Inc ....G 732 833-8500
Wall Township **(G-11356)**

Rajysan Incorporated ....E 800 433-1382
Swedesboro **(G-10605)**

Taurus International Corp ....E 201 825-2420
Ramsey **(G-9156)**

CONSTRUCTION EQPT REPAIR SVCS

Cleary Machinery Co Inc ....G 732 560-3200
South Bound Brook **(G-10143)**

Permadur Industries Inc ....D 908 359-9767
Hillsborough **(G-4344)**

CONSTRUCTION EQPT: Blade, Grader, Scraper, Dozer/Snow Plow

R & H Spring & Truck Repair ....F 732 681-9000
Wall Township **(G-11362)**

CONSTRUCTION EQPT: Cranes

Cornell Crane Mfg Ltd ....F 609 742-1900
Westville **(G-11811)**

CONSTRUCTION EQPT: Dozers, Tractor Mounted, Material Moving

L Arden Corp ....G 973 523-6400
Paterson **(G-8234)**

CONSTRUCTION EQPT: Subgraders

Ransome Equipment Sales LLC ....G ...856 797-8100
Lumberton **(G-5635)**

CONSTRUCTION EQPT: Wrecker Hoists, Automobile

Trilenium Salvage Co ....G 732 462-2909
Morganville **(G-6597)**

CONSTRUCTION MATERIALS, WHOLESALE: Architectural Metalwork

Omnia Industries Inc ....E 973 239-7272
Cedar Grove **(G-1286)**

CONSTRUCTION MATERIALS, WHOLESALE: Awnings

Babbitt Mfg Co Inc ....F 856 692-3245
Vineland **(G-11190)**

CONSTRUCTION MATERIALS, WHOLESALE: Block, Concrete & Cinder

Clayton Block Company Inc ....E ...732 681-0186
Wall Township **(G-11326)**

CONSTRUCTION MATERIALS, WHOLESALE: Brick, Exc Refractory

Glen-Gery Corporation ....E 908 359-5111
Hillsborough **(G-4320)**

CONSTRUCTION MATERIALS, WHOLESALE: Building Stone

El Batal Corporation ....F 908 964-3427
Union **(G-11050)**

CONSTRUCTION MATERIALS, WHOLESALE: Building Stone, Granite

Ankur International Inc ....F 609 409-6009
Cranbury **(G-1811)**

Ilkem Marble and Granite Inc ....G ...856 433-8714
Cherry Hill **(G-1374)**

Natures Beauty Marble & Gran ....F ...908 233-5300
Scotch Plains **(G-9737)**

Sr International Rock Inc ....F 908 864-4700
Bound Brook **(G-606)**

Statewide Granite and Marble ....F ...201 653-1700
Jersey City **(G-4815)**

CONSTRUCTION MATERIALS, WHOLESALE: Building Stone, Marble

Bcg Marble & Granite South LLC ......G ...732 367-3788
Jackson **(G-4641)**

Bcg Marble Gran Fabricators Co ......F ...201 343-8487
Hackensack **(G-3882)**

Dolan & Traynor Inc ....E 973 696-8700
Wayne **(G-11495)**

North Bergen Marble & Granite ....E ..201 945-9988
Cliffside Park **(G-1543)**

Phillipsburg Marble Co Inc ....E ...908 859-3435
Phillipsburg **(G-8568)**

CONSTRUCTION MATERIALS, WHOLESALE: Building, Exterior

Form Tops Lminators of Trenton ....G ..609 409-4357
Jamesburg **(G-4672)**

Greenbuilt Intl Bldg Co ....C 609 300-9091
Voorhees **(G-11287)**

Kuiken Brothers Company ....E 201 796-2082
Fair Lawn **(G-3109)**

Ufp Berlin LLC ....C 856 767-0596
Berlin **(G-431)**

CONSTRUCTION MATERIALS, WHOLESALE: Cement

Lehigh Cement Company ....G 973 579-2111
Sparta **(G-10395)**

Employee Codes: A=Over 500 employees, B=251-500
C=101-250, D=51-100, E=20-50, F=10-19, G=4-9

2019 Harris New Jersey
Manufacturers Directory

807

PRODUCT

CONSTRUCTION MATERIALS, WHOLESALE: Concrete Mixtures

Ernest R Miles Construction Co ....F....... 856 697-2311
Newfield (G-7321)
Ralph Clayton & Sons LLC ....E 609 695-0767
Trenton (G-10986)

CONSTRUCTION MATERIALS, WHOLESALE: Glass

Floral Glass Industries Inc ....E 201 939-4600
East Rutherford (G-2289)
General Glass Intl Corp ....C 201 553-1850
Secaucus (G-9772)
McGrory Glass Inc ....D 856 579-3200
Paulsboro (G-8335)
SA Bendheim Ltd ....E 973 471-1733
Wayne (G-11550)

CONSTRUCTION MATERIALS, WHOLESALE: Gravel

Brick-Wall Corp ....E 732 787-0226
Atlantic Highlands (G-104)
Herbert J Hinchman & Son Inc ....E 973 942-2063
Wayne (G-11516)

CONSTRUCTION MATERIALS, WHOLESALE: Masons' Materials

Action Supply Inc..................................F 609 390-0663
Ocean View (G-7701)
Anchor Concrete Products Inc ....E 732 842-5010
Red Bank (G-9220)
Anchor Concrete Products Inc ....D 732 458-9440
Brick (G-711)
Precision Multiple Contrls Inc ....E 201 444-0600
Midland Park (G-6184)
Precision Multiple Contrls Inc ....D 201 444-0600
Midland Park (G-6185)
Reuther Material Co Inc ....E 201 863-3550
North Bergen (G-7435)

CONSTRUCTION MATERIALS, WHOLESALE: Metal Buildings

Tilcon New York Inc ....B 973 366-7741
Parsippany (G-8028)

CONSTRUCTION MATERIALS, WHOLESALE: Millwork

B & B Millwork & Doors Inc...................G 973 249-0300
Kenilworth (G-4924)
V Custom Millwork Inc...........................F 732 469-9600
Bridgewater (G-901)
Wood Works ....G 856 728-4520
Williamstown (G-11987)

CONSTRUCTION MATERIALS, WHOLESALE: Pallets, Wood

Avenel Pallet Co Inc..............................F 732 752-0500
Dunellen (G-2119)
Delisa Pallet Corp ....F 732 667-7070
Middlesex (G-6111)

CONSTRUCTION MATERIALS, WHOLESALE: Paving Materials

South State Inc ....E 856 881-6030
Williamstown (G-11979)

CONSTRUCTION MATERIALS, WHOLESALE: Prefabricated Structures

Everlast Associates Inc.........................G 609 261-1888
Southampton (G-10362)
R H Vassallo Inc ....G 856 358-8841
Malaga (G-5789)

CONSTRUCTION MATERIALS, WHOLESALE: Roof, Asphalt/Sheet Metal

US Outworkers LLC ....G 973 362-1458
Sussex (G-10569)

CONSTRUCTION MATERIALS, WHOLESALE: Roofing & Siding Material

Armorpoxy Inc.......................................F 908 810-9613
Union (G-11027)
Passaic Metal & Bldg Sups Co ....D 973 546-9000
Clifton (G-1685)
Stavola Asphalt Company Inc ....E 732 542-2328
Tinton Falls (G-10728)

CONSTRUCTION MATERIALS, WHOLESALE: Sand

Clayton Sand Company...........................E 732 751-7600
Wall Township (G-11328)
County Concrete Corporation ....D 973 744-2188
Kenvil (G-4992)

CONSTRUCTION MATERIALS, WHOLESALE: Septic Tanks

A & A Concrete Products Inc ....G 973 835-2239
Riverdale (G-9369)
County Concrete Corporation ....F 973 538-3113
Morristown (G-6656)

CONSTRUCTION MATERIALS, WHOLESALE: Siding, Exc Wood

Babbitt Mfg Co Inc ....F 856 692-3245
Vineland (G-11190)

CONSTRUCTION MATERIALS, WHOLESALE: Skylights, All Materials

Construction Specialties Inc..................E 908 272-2771
Cranford (G-1906)

CONSTRUCTION MATERIALS, WHOLESALE: Stone, Crushed Or Broken

County Concrete Corporation ....F 973 538-3113
Morristown (G-6656)
Fanwood Crushed Stone Company ......D 908 322-7840
Watchung (G-11455)
R B Badat Landscaping Inc ....E 609 877-7138
Mount Holly (G-6733)
Stavola Construction Mtls Inc ....E 732 356-5700
Bound Brook (G-608)

CONSTRUCTION MATERIALS, WHOLESALE: Stucco

Mediterranean Stucco Corp ....F 973 491-0160
Newark (G-7199)
Perfect Shapes Inc ....G 856 783-3844
Elmer (G-2801)

CONSTRUCTION MATERIALS, WHOLESALE: Tile & Clay Prdts

Akw Inc ....G 732 493-1883
Ocean (G-7654)
Akw Inc ....G 732 530-9186
Shrewsbury (G-9880)

CONSTRUCTION MATERIALS, WHOLESALE: Window Frames

Surburban Building Pdts Inc ....E 732 901-8900
Howell (G-4551)

CONSTRUCTION MATERIALS, WHOLESALE: Windows

Alliance Vinyl Windows Co Inc...............E 856 456-4954
Oaklyn (G-7650)

CONSTRUCTION MATLS, WHOL: Lumber, Rough, Dressed/Finished

Norwood Industries Inc.........................F 856 858-6195
Haddon Township (G-4052)

CONSTRUCTION MTRLS, WHOL: Exterior Flat Glass, Plate/Window

Oldcastle Buildingenvelope Inc.............D 856 234-9222
Moorestown (G-6549)

CONSTRUCTION SAND MINING

Action Supply Inc..................................F 609 390-0663
Ocean View (G-7701)
Eastern Concrete Materials Inc ....C 201 797-7979
Saddle Brook (G-9650)
Pioneer Concrete Corp ....E 609 693-6151
Forked River (G-3542)
Ricci Bros Sand Company Inc ....E 856 785-0166
Port Norris (G-8888)
Saxton Falls Sand & Gravel Co ....E 908 852-0121
Budd Lake (G-936)
Whibco Inc...F 856 455-9200
Bridgeton (G-779)

CONSTRUCTION: Apartment Building

W A Building Movers & Contrs ....F 908 654-8227
Garwood (G-3793)

CONSTRUCTION: Athletic & Recreation Facilities

Finex Trade ....G 609 921-2747
Princeton (G-8949)

CONSTRUCTION: Bridge

Ashland LLC..D 732 353-7718
Parlin (G-7861)
Colas Inc ....G 973 290-9082
Morristown (G-6654)

CONSTRUCTION: Chemical Facility

Amec Foster Wheeler USA Corp ....E 713 929-5000
Hampton (G-4146)
Foster Wheeler Arabia Ltd ....G 908 730-4000
Hampton (G-4151)
Foster Wheeler Intl Corp ....F 908 730-4000
Hampton (G-4152)
Foster Whler Intl Holdings Inc ....G 908 730-4000
Hampton (G-4154)

CONSTRUCTION: Commercial & Institutional Building

John J Chando Jr Inc ....G 732 793-2122
Mantoloking (G-5850)

CONSTRUCTION: Commercial & Office Building, New

All Seasons Construction Inc...............G 908 852-0955
Long Valley (G-5607)
Jontol Unlimited LLC.............................G 858 652-1113
Blackwood (G-473)

CONSTRUCTION: Dam

Green Globe USA LLC.............................G 201 577-4468
Carteret (G-1256)

CONSTRUCTION: Dams, Waterways, Docks & Other Marine

Bishop Ascendant Inc ....G 201 572-7436
West Caldwell (G-11642)
Courtney Boatlifts Inc............................G 732 892-8900
Point Pleasant Boro (G-8841)
Ocean Energy Industries Inc ....F 954 828-2177
Oakhurst (G-7611)

CONSTRUCTION: Electric Power Line

Pioneer Associates Inc..........................E 201 592-7007
Fort Lee (G-3581)

CONSTRUCTION: Food Prdts Manufacturing or Packing Plant

Grandi Pastai Italiani Inc ....G 201 786-5050
Moonachie (G-6467)

CONSTRUCTION: Foundation & Retaining Wall

Ernest R Miles Construction Co ....F 856 697-2311
Newfield (G-7321)
W A Building Movers & Contrs ....F 908 654-8227
Garwood (G-3793)

CONSTRUCTION: Gas Main

E & G Roman Corp ....D 973 482-1123
  Newark (G-7110)

CONSTRUCTION: Greenhouse

Internet-Sales USA Corporation ....G 775 468-8379
  Rockaway (G-9467)

CONSTRUCTION: Heavy Highway & Street

Ashland LLC ....D 732 353-7718
  Parlin (G-7861)
Hackettstown Public Works ....G 908 852-2320
  Hackettstown (G-4010)
Richard E Pierson Mtls Corp ....G 856 740-2400
  Williamstown (G-11975)
Richard E Pierson Mtls Corp ....G 856 691-0083
  Vineland (G-11260)
Richard E Pierson Mtls Corp ....C 856 467-4199
  Pilesgrove (G-8580)
Stavola Asphalt Company Inc ....E 732 542-2328
  Tinton Falls (G-10728)

CONSTRUCTION: Hospital

Gateway Property Solutions Ltd ....E 732 901-9700
  Lakewood (G-5103)

CONSTRUCTION: Indl Building & Warehouse

Dreamstar Construction LLC ....F 732 393-2572
  Middletown (G-6162)
Lollytogs Ltd ....F 732 438-5500
  Dayton (G-1978)
Orient Originals Inc ....E 201 332-5005
  Jersey City (G-4778)

CONSTRUCTION: Indl Buildings, New, NEC

Independent Prj Cons Ltd Lblty ....G 973 780-8002
  Newark (G-7155)

CONSTRUCTION: Indl Plant

Foster Wheeler Zack Inc ....D 908 730-4000
  Hampton (G-4153)
Hamon Corporation ....D 908 333-2000
  Somerville (G-10114)

CONSTRUCTION: Marine

J & J Marine Inc ....F 856 228-4744
  Sewell (G-9848)

CONSTRUCTION: Natural Gas Compressor Station

Corban Energy Group Corp ....F 201 509-8555
  Elmwood Park (G-2818)

CONSTRUCTION: Nonresidential Buildings, Custom

Forman Industries Inc ....D 732 727-8100
  Old Bridge (G-7715)

CONSTRUCTION: Power & Communication Transmission Tower

Dun-Rite Communications Inc ....G 201 444-0080
  Mahwah (G-5731)

CONSTRUCTION: Refineries

Shelby Mechanical Inc ....E 856 665-4540
  Cinnaminson (G-1484)

CONSTRUCTION: Religious Building

George Ciocher Inc ....G 732 818-3495
  Toms River (G-10761)

CONSTRUCTION: Residential, Nec

Dreamstar Construction LLC ....F 732 393-2572
  Middletown (G-6162)
EZ General Construction Corp ....G 201 223-1101
  Wayne (G-11500)
Greenbuilt Intl Bldg Co ....C 609 300-9091
  Voorhees (G-11287)
Mdb Construction ....G 908 628-8010
  Lebanon (G-5270)

CONSTRUCTION: Sewer Line

Suffolk County Contractors ....E 732 349-7726
  Toms River (G-10796)

CONSTRUCTION: Single-Family Housing

Greenbuilt Intl Bldg Co ....C 609 300-9091
  Voorhees (G-11287)
Hart Construction Service ....G 908 537-2060
  Asbury (G-64)
Josantos Cnstr & Dev LLC ....G 732 202-7389
  Brick (G-724)
Mod-U-Kraf Homes LLC ....F 540 482-0273
  West Berlin (G-11608)
Vinylast Inc ....E 732 367-7200
  Lakewood (G-5176)

CONSTRUCTION: Single-family Housing, New

All Seasons Construction Inc ....G 908 852-0955
  Long Valley (G-5607)
John J Chando Jr Inc ....G 732 793-2122
  Mantoloking (G-5850)
Van Duyne Bros Inc ....G 609 625-0299
  Mays Landing (G-5999)

CONSTRUCTION: Steel Buildings

East Coast Storage Eqp Co Inc ....E 732 451-1316
  Brick (G-716)

CONSTRUCTION: Street Surfacing & Paving

Brunswick Hot Mix Corp ....D 908 233-4444
  Westfield (G-11795)
South State Inc ....E 856 881-6030
  Williamstown (G-11979)

CONSTRUCTION: Swimming Pools

Izzo Enterprises Inc ....E 908 845-8200
  Scotch Plains (G-9735)

CONSTRUCTION: Transmitting Tower, Telecommunication

Maxentric Technologies LLC ....E 201 242-9800
  Fort Lee (G-3570)

CONSTRUCTION: Warehouse

New Jersey Steel Corporation ....F 856 337-0054
  Haddon Township (G-4051)

CONSTRUCTION: Waste Water & Sewage Treatment Plant

Chem-Aqua Inc ....F 972 438-0211
  Monmouth Junction (G-6281)
Dynatec Systems Inc ....F 609 387-0330
  Burlington (G-965)

CONSTRUCTION: Water & Sewer Line

DMJ and Associates Inc ....E 732 613-7867
  Sayreville (G-9708)
Philip Mamrak ....G 908 454-6089
  Phillipsburg (G-8567)

CONSULTING SVC: Actuarial

Inventors Shop LLC ....E 856 303-8787
  Cinnaminson (G-1466)

CONSULTING SVC: Business, NEC

2a Holdings Inc ....F 973 378-8011
  Maplewood (G-5873)
Adherence Solutions LLC ....G 800 521-2269
  Fairfield (G-3135)
Ch Technologies USA Inc ....G 201 666-2335
  Westwood (G-11829)
Electronic Measuring Devices ....F 973 691-4755
  Flanders (G-3407)
Fisher Scientific Company LLC ....B 201 796-7100
  Fair Lawn (G-3102)
Gary R Banks Industrial Group ....F 856 687-2227
  West Berlin (G-11597)
Glocal Expertise Llc ....G 718 928-3839
  Jersey City (G-4744)
Hitrons Solutions Inc ....F 201 244-0300
  Bergenfield (G-378)

CONSULTING SVC: Chemical

Acceledev Chemical LLC ....G 862 239-1524
  Wayne (G-11465)

CONSULTING SVC: Computer

Aplnow LLC ....G 732 223-5575
  Manasquan (G-5828)
Auraplayer USA Inc ....F 617 879-9013
  West Orange (G-11760)
Automated Office Inc ....G 888 362-7638
  Cherry Hill (G-1341)
Burgiss Group LLC ....D 201 427-9600
  Hoboken (G-4444)
Ce Tech LLC ....G 908 229-3803
  Whitehouse Station (G-11919)
Cognizant Tech Solutions Corp ....D 201 801-0233
  Teaneck (G-10625)
Cygate Sftwr & Consulting LLC ....G 732 452-1881
  Edison (G-2490)
Datapro International Inc ....E 732 868-0588
  Piscataway (G-8652)
Dymax Systems Inc ....F 732 918-2424
  Neptune (G-6874)
Fillimerica Inc ....G 800 435-7257
  Montville (G-6442)
Fis Avantgard LLC ....G 732 530-9303
  Tinton Falls (G-10717)
Gerbino Computer Systems Inc ....G 201 342-8240
  Hackensack (G-3922)
Indotronix International Corp ....G 609 750-0700
  Plainsboro (G-8790)
Innovative Sftwr Solutions Inc ....D 856 910-9190
  Maple Shade (G-5864)
Innovi Mobile LLC ....F 646 588-0165
  Millburn (G-6200)
Integration International Inc ....E 973 796-2300
  Parsippany (G-7962)
Interntnal Digital Systems Inc ....F 201 983-7700
  Fort Lee (G-3564)
Linden Group Corporation ....F 973 983-8809
  Cedar Knolls (G-1308)
MD International Inc ....G 856 779-7633
  Cherry Hill (G-1391)
Mind-Alliance Systems LLC ....G 212 920-1911
  Livingston (G-5526)
Novaera Solutions Inc ....D 732 452-3605
  Iselin (G-4619)
Pace Business Solutions Inc ....E 908 451-0355
  Manahawkin (G-5795)
Pascack Data Services Inc ....F 973 304-4858
  Hawthorne (G-4236)
Promia Incorporated ....G 609 252-1850
  Princeton (G-9009)
Qellus LLC ....G 856 761-6575
  Mount Laurel (G-6798)
R T I Inc ....E 201 261-5852
  Oradell (G-7746)
Radix M I S ....G 973 707-2121
  Bloomfield (G-516)
Re Systems Group Inc ....G 201 883-1572
  Westwood (G-11842)
Real Soft Inc ....A 609 409-3636
  Monmouth Junction (G-6308)
RSD America Inc ....F 201 996-1000
  Teaneck (G-10649)
Sensiple Inc ....F 732 283-0499
  Iselin (G-4626)
Software Services & Solutions ....F 203 630-2000
  Lawrence Township (G-5220)
Specialty Systems Inc ....E 732 341-1011
  Toms River (G-10794)

Hoboken Executive Art Inc ....G 201 420-8262
  Hoboken (G-4454)
Iam International Inc ....G 908 713-9651
  Lebanon (G-5263)
Industrial Water Tech Inc ....G 732 888-1233
  Hazlet (G-4261)
Light Inc ....G 973 777-2704
  Clifton (G-1659)
Multiforce Systems Corporation ....F 609 683-4242
  Princeton (G-8982)
Novaera Solutions Inc ....D 732 452-3605
  Iselin (G-4619)
Steps To Literacy LLC ....E 732 560-8363
  Bound Brook (G-609)
Trek II Products Inc ....G 732 214-9200
  New Brunswick (G-6974)
Wilshire Technologies Inc ....G 609 683-1117
  Princeton (G-9043)

Employee Codes: A=Over 500 employees, B=251-500
C=101-250, D=51-100, E=20-50, F=10-19, G=4-9

2019 Harris New jersey
Manufacturers Directory

809

PRODUCT

Strahan Consulting Group LLC ....G 908 790-0873
  Scotch Plains *(G-9742)*
T3i Group LLC ....E 856 424-1100
  Cherry Hill *(G-1420)*
Tropaion Inc ....G 908 654-3870
  Springfield *(G-10469)*
Twinpod Inc ....G 908 758-5858
  Princeton *(G-9037)*
U S Tech Solutions Inc ....D 201 524-9600
  Jersey City *(G-4824)*
Unicorn Group Inc ....C 973 360-0688
  Florham Park *(G-3525)*
Unicorn Group Inc ....D 973 360-5904
  Fairfield *(G-3334)*

CONSULTING SVC: Data Processing

Megaplex Software Inc ....G...... 908 647-3273
  Warren *(G-11421)*

CONSULTING SVC: Engineering

Adsorptech Inc ....G 732 356-1000
  Middlesex *(G-6092)*
Cire Technologies Inc ....G 973 402-8301
  Mountain Lakes *(G-6821)*
Componding Engrg Solutions Inc ....F 973 340-4000
  Upper Saddle River *(G-11137)*
De Ditrich Process Systems Inc ....E 908 317-2585
  Mountainside *(G-6841)*
Drive Technology Inc ....G 732 422-6500
  Monmouth Junction *(G-6289)*
Ellenby Technologies Inc ....E 856 848-2020
  Woodbury Heights *(G-12042)*
Ensync Intrctive Solutions Inc ....G 732 542-4001
  Freehold *(G-3664)*
Expert Process Systems LLC ....G 570 424-0581
  Hackettstown *(G-4007)*
Forman Industries Inc ....D 732 727-8100
  Old Bridge *(G-7715)*
Foster Whler Intl Holdings Inc ....G 908 730-4000
  Hampton *(G-4154)*
Fyth Labs Inc ....G 856 313-7362
  Beverly *(G-451)*
Hansome Energy Systems Inc ....E 908 862-9044
  Linden *(G-5354)*
I 2 R Corp ....G 732 919-1100
  Wall Township *(G-11348)*
Interstate Welding & Mfg Co ....F 800 676-4666
  Beverly *(G-452)*
John J Chando Jr Inc ....G 732 793-2122
  Mantoloking *(G-5850)*
Koch Mdlar Process Systems LLC ......D 201 368-2929
  Paramus *(G-7814)*
Langan Engineering Environmen ....F 973 560-4900
  Parsippany *(G-7973)*
M C Technologies Inc ....E 973 839-2779
  Pompton Plains *(G-8866)*
Micro-Tek Corporation ....G 856 829-3855
  Cinnaminson *(G-1473)*
Network Communications Cons ....F 201 968-0684
  Hackensack *(G-3953)*
T O Najarian Associates ....D 732 389-0220
  Eatontown *(G-2423)*
Tsg Inc ....F 973 785-1118
  Little Falls *(G-5471)*

CONSULTING SVC: Human Resource

Elevate Hr Inc ....F 973 917-3230
  Parsippany *(G-7934)*
Hr Acuity LLC ....F 888 598-0161
  Florham Park *(G-3511)*
Real Soft Inc ....A 609 409-3636
  Monmouth Junction *(G-6308)*

CONSULTING SVC: Management

2a Holdings Inc ....F 973 378-8011
  Maplewood *(G-5873)*
All Solutions Inc ....E 973 535-9100
  Livingston *(G-5503)*
Avalon Globocare Corp ....G 732 780-4400
  Freehold *(G-3650)*
Central Components Mfg LLC ....G 732 469-5720
  Middlesex *(G-6104)*
Centurum Information Tech Inc ....G 856 751-1111
  Marlton *(G-5924)*
Defense Spport Svcs Intl 2 LLC ....F 856 866-2200
  Marlton *(G-5927)*
Ecs Energy Ltd ....G 201 341-5044
  Jackson *(G-4655)*

Green Globe USA LLC ....G 201 577-4468
  Carteret *(G-1256)*
Inserts East Incorporated ....C 856 663-8181
  Pennsauken *(G-8437)*
JW Parr Leadburing Co ....G 973 256-8093
  Little Falls *(G-5458)*
Krydon Group Inc ....G 877 854-1342
  Moorestown *(G-6535)*
Lattice Incorporated ....F 856 910-1166
  Pennsauken *(G-8450)*
Moscova Enterprises Inc ....F 848 628-4873
  Jersey City *(G-4768)*
Npt Publishing Group Inc ....F 973 401-0202
  Morris Plains *(G-6620)*
Pds Consultants Inc ....E 201 970-2313
  Sparta *(G-10405)*
Planitroi Inc ....G 973 664-0700
  Denville *(G-2049)*
Trek Inc ....G 732 269-6300
  Bayville *(G-252)*

CONSULTING SVC: Marketing Management

AB Coaster LLC ....F 908 879-2713
  Chester *(G-1429)*
All In Color Inc ....G 973 626-0987
  Paterson *(G-8133)*
Cherri Stone Interactive LLC ....G 844 843-7765
  Lakewood *(G-5069)*
Global Graphics Intergration ....F 973 334-9653
  Towaco *(G-10872)*
Ingersoll-Rand Company ....C 908 238-7000
  Annandale *(G-54)*
Jersey Bound Latino LLC ....G 908 591-2830
  Union *(G-11066)*
Kairos Enterprises LLC ....E 201 731-3181
  Englewood Cliffs *(G-2979)*
Oceanic Graphic Intl Inc ....F 201 883-1816
  Hackensack *(G-3957)*
Prism Dgtal Communications LLC ....F 973 232-5038
  Mountainside *(G-6851)*
Raphel Marketing Inc ....G 609 348-6646
  Atlantic City *(G-102)*
Sjshore Marketing Ltd Lblty Co ....F 609 390-1400
  Marmora *(G-5959)*
The Creative Print Group Inc ....F 856 486-1700
  Pennsauken *(G-8492)*
Vending Trucks Inc ....E 732 969-5400
  East Brunswick *(G-2190)*
Victor International Marketing ....G 973 267-8900
  Morristown *(G-6707)*
Vitaquest International LLC ....F 973 575-9200
  Fairfield *(G-3346)*
Vitaquest International LLC ....B 973 575-9200
  West Caldwell *(G-11681)*
Webb-Mason Inc ....G 732 747-6585
  Tinton Falls *(G-10734)*

CONSULTING SVC: Online Technology

Appex Innovation Solutions LLC ....G 215 313-3332
  Princeton *(G-8908)*
Artezio LLC ....G 609 786-2435
  Princeton *(G-8912)*
Datamotion Inc ....E 973 455-1245
  Florham Park *(G-3500)*
I Physician Hub ....D 732 274-0155
  Monmouth Junction *(G-6292)*
Local Wisdom Inc ....E 609 269-2320
  Lambertville *(G-5194)*
Manna Group LLC ....F 856 881-7650
  Mount Laurel *(G-6780)*
Maxentric Technologies LLC ....E 201 242-9800
  Fort Lee *(G-3570)*
Technovision Inc ....E 732 381-0200
  Metuchen *(G-6077)*

CONSULTING SVC: Sales Management

Advanstar Communications Inc ....E 973 944-7777
  Montvale *(G-6395)*

CONSULTING SVC: Telecommunications

Enterprisecc Ltd Liability Co ....G 201 266-0020
  Jersey City *(G-4732)*
Princeton Hosted Solutions LLC ....F 856 470-2350
  Haddonfield *(G-4062)*

CONSULTING SVCS, BUSINESS: Agricultural

SGB Packaging Group Inc ....G 201 488-3030
  Hackensack *(G-3972)*

CONSULTING SVCS, BUSINESS: Communications

Telecom Assistance Group Inc ....E 856 753-8585
  West Berlin *(G-11628)*

CONSULTING SVCS, BUSINESS: Energy Conservation

Pennetta & Sons ....E 201 420-1693
  Jersey City *(G-4781)*

CONSULTING SVCS, BUSINESS: Environmental

Foundation Monitoring ....G 856 829-0410
  Cinnaminson *(G-1457)*
I 2 R Corp ....G 732 919-1100
  Wall Township *(G-11348)*
Langan Engineering Environmen ....F 973 560-4900
  Parsippany *(G-7973)*
Linden Well Drilling ....E 908 862-6633
  Linden *(G-5376)*

CONSULTING SVCS, BUSINESS: Publishing

B T O Industries Inc ....G 973 243-0011
  West Orange *(G-11761)*

CONSULTING SVCS, BUSINESS: Sys Engnrg, Exc Computer/Prof

Bavelle Tech Sltions Ltd Lblty ....F 973 992-8086
  East Hanover *(G-2195)*
Clientsrver Tech Solutions LLC ....G 732 710-4495
  Iselin *(G-4605)*
Cloudageit Ltd Liability Co ....G 888 205-4128
  North Brunswick *(G-7463)*
Computer Doc Associates Inc ....D 908 647-4445
  Martinsville *(G-5962)*
Genomesafe LLC ....G 203 676-3752
  West Orange *(G-11768)*
Interntnal Digital Systems Inc ....F 201 983-7700
  Fort Lee *(G-3564)*

CONSULTING SVCS, BUSINESS: Systems Analysis & Engineering

Advance Process Systems Lim ....G 201 400-9190
  Branchville *(G-701)*
Defense Spport Svcs Intl 2 LLC ....F 856 866-2200
  Marlton *(G-5927)*
Demaio Inc ....E 609 965-4094
  Egg Harbor City *(G-2657)*
Scalable Systems Inc ....E 732 993-4320
  Piscataway *(G-8709)*

CONSULTING SVCS, BUSINESS: Systems Analysis Or Design

Roper Scientific Inc ....E 941 556-2601
  Trenton *(G-10989)*

CONSULTING SVCS, BUSINESS: Test Development & Evaluation

Biophore LLC ....G 609 275-3713
  Plainsboro *(G-8781)*

CONSULTING SVCS, BUSINESS: Traffic

Griffin Signs Inc ....E 856 786-8517
  Cinnaminson *(G-1460)*

CONSULTING SVCS: Oil

A H Hoffmann LLC ....G 732 988-6000
  Neptune *(G-6862)*

CONSULTING SVCS: Psychological

Princeton Information Center ....G 609 924-7019
  Princeton *(G-8999)*

CONSULTING SVCS: Scientific

Sensonics Inc ....F 856 547-7702
  Haddon Heights *(G-4049)*

CONTACTS: Electrical

Precision Mfg Group LLC.....................D... 973 785-4630
Cedar Grove **(G-1288)**

CONTAINERS, GLASS: Cosmetic Jars

Amcor Phrm Packg USA Inc ....C... 856 728-9300
Williamstown **(G-11950)**

Amcor Phrm Packg USA LLC................C... 856 327-1540
Millville **(G-6226)**

Amcor Phrm Packg USA LLC................C... 856 825-1400
Millville **(G-6227)**

Amcor Phrm Packg USA LLC................C... 856 825-1400
Millville **(G-6228)**

Cameo Metal Forms Inc.......................F... 718 788-1106
Woodland Park **(G-12073)**

Heinz Glas USA Inc.............................F... 908 474-0300
Linden **(G-5355)**

CONTAINERS, GLASS: Medicine Bottles

Centro Alternativo De ....G... 973 365-0995
Passaic **(G-8055)**

Gerresheimer Glass Inc.......................B... 856 692-3600
Vineland **(G-11223)**

CONTAINERS: Cargo, Wood & Wood With Metal

Granco Group LLC...............................G... 973 515-4721
Roseland **(G-9539)**

CONTAINERS: Corrugated

Apple Corrugated Box Ltd ....F... 201 635-1269
Wood Ridge **(G-12001)**

Boxworks Inc.......................................G... 856 456-9030
Bellmawr **(G-328)**

Diamex International Corp ....G... 973 838-8844
Kinnelon **(G-5016)**

Global Direct Marketing Group ....G... 856 427-6116
Haddonfield **(G-4058)**

Greater New York Box Co Inc ....G... 609 631-7900
Trenton **(G-10936)**

International Paper Company ....D... 732 828-1700
Milltown **(G-6216)**

New York Folding Box Co Inc ....E... 973 347-6932
Stanhope **(G-10477)**

Packaging Corporation America ....G... 856 696-0114
Vineland **(G-11249)**

Sunshine Metal & Sign Inc ....G... 973 676-4432
Milltown **(G-6220)**

Westrock Rkt LLC ....C... 973 594-6000
Totowa **(G-10861)**

Westrock Rkt Company........................C... 973 484-5000
Newark **(G-7314)**

CONTAINERS: Foil, Bakery Goods & Frozen Foods

Revere Industries LLC.........................C... 856 881-3600
Clayton **(G-1528)**

CONTAINERS: Food & Beverage

Innovation Foods LLC ....F... 856 455-2209
Bridgeton **(G-759)**

CONTAINERS: Food, Metal

Allstate Can Corporation.....................D... 973 560-9030
Parsippany **(G-7878)**

Penny Plate LLC.................................D... 856 429-7583
Mount Laurel **(G-6789)**

CONTAINERS: Frozen Food & Ice Cream

American International Cont.................F... 973 917-3331
Boonton **(G-541)**

Heavenly Havens Creamery LLC ....G... 609 259-6600
Allentown **(G-27)**

CONTAINERS: Glass

Amcor Phrm Packg USA Inc ....C... 856 825-3050
Millville **(G-6225)**

Amcor Phrm Packg USA LLC................C... 856 825-1100
Millville **(G-6229)**

Ardagh Glass Inc ....C... 508 478-2500
Bridgeton **(G-751)**

Ardagh Glass Inc ....B... 732 969-0827
Carteret **(G-1248)**

Avant Industries Ltd Inc ....G... 973 242-1700
Newark **(G-7060)**

Friedrich and Dimmock Inc.................E... 856 825-0305
Millville **(G-6249)**

Leone Industries Inc...........................B... 856 455-2000
Bridgeton **(G-763)**

Piramal Glass - Usa Inc ....B... 856 293-6400
Dayton **(G-1984)**

Piramal Glass - Usa Inc ....C... 856 728-9300
Williamstown **(G-11969)**

Piramal Glass - Usa Inc ....B... 856 293-6400
Williamstown **(G-11970)**

Pochet of America Inc ....C... 973 942-4923
Woodland Park **(G-12086)**

CONTAINERS: Metal

Andrew B Duffy Inc.............................F... 856 845-4900
West Deptford **(G-11691)**

Cutler Bros Box & Lumber Co ....E... 201 943-2535
Fairview **(G-3359)**

Kraftware Corporation ....E... 732 345-7091
Roselle **(G-9562)**

Mauser Usa LLC ....C... 732 634-6000
Woodbridge **(G-12019)**

Patrick J Kelly Drums Inc...................E... 856 963-1795
Camden **(G-1082)**

Pmm Inc ....E... 908 692-1465
Colts Neck **(G-1786)**

Rahway Steel Drum Co Inc ....E... 732 382-0113
Cranbury **(G-1877)**

Recycle Inc East.................................D... 908 756-2200
South Plainfield **(G-10325)**

Romaco North America Inc ....G... 609 584-2500
Hamilton **(G-4123)**

CONTAINERS: Plastic

Berry Global Inc ....G... 980 689-1660
Phillipsburg **(G-8544)**

Berry Global Inc ....C... 609 395-4199
Cranbury **(G-1814)**

Berry Global Group Inc ....F... 732 469-2470
Monroe Township **(G-6327)**

C & K Plastics Inc ....E... 732 549-0011
Metuchen **(G-6049)**

Captive Plastics LLC ....C... 732 469-7900
Piscataway **(G-8642)**

Comar Inc ....E... 856 692-6100
Voorhees **(G-11282)**

Consolidated Cont Holdings LLC.........D... 609 655-0855
Cranbury **(G-1827)**

Consolidated Container Co LP ....D... 908 289-5862
Elizabeth **(G-2722)**

Container Mfg Inc ....E... 732 563-0100
Middlesex **(G-6105)**

De Leon Plastics Corp.........................F... 973 653-3480
Paterson **(G-8170)**

E & T Sales Co Inc ....E... 856 787-0900
Mount Laurel **(G-6755)**

Flex Products LLC ....D... 201 440-1570
Carlstadt **(G-1158)**

Graham Packaging Company LP ....E... 717 849-8500
Bordentown **(G-582)**

Griffen LLC ....G... 973 723-5344
Morristown **(G-6667)**

J OBrien Co Inc ....E... 973 379-8844
Springfield **(G-10447)**

Jarden LLC ....E... 201 610-6600
Hoboken **(G-4458)**

Jerhel Plastics Inc..............................G... 201 436-6662
Bayonne **(G-225)**

Liquid-Solids Separation Corp ....E... 201 236-4833
Ramsey **(G-9149)**

Meese Inc ....F... 201 796-4490
Saddle Brook **(G-9661)**

Mfv International Corporation..............G... 973 993-1687
Morristown **(G-6686)**

National Diversified Sales Inc.............G... 559 562-9888
Bordentown **(G-590)**

Oppenheim Plastics Co Inc ....D... 201 391-3811
Park Ridge **(G-7857)**

Ovadia Corporation ....E... 973 256-9200
Little Falls **(G-5462)**

Pelco Packaging Corporation ....F... 973 675-4994
East Orange **(G-2259)**

Plastic Reel Corp of America ....E... 201 933-5100
Carlstadt **(G-1202)**

Plastinetics Inc ....G... 818 364-1611
Towaco **(G-10878)**

Ring Container Tech LLC ....F... 973 258-0707
Springfield **(G-10466)**

Saint-Gobain Prfmce Plas Corp...........C... 973 696-4700
Wayne **(G-11551)**

Stephco Sales Inc ....E... 973 278-5454
Paterson **(G-8301)**

Stephen Douglas Plastics Inc ....C... 973 523-3030
Paterson **(G-8302)**

Storemaxx Inc ....F... 201 440-8800
Hackensack **(G-3979)**

Techflex Inc ....F... 973 300-9242
Sparta **(G-10409)**

Unette Corporation ....D... 973 328-6800
Randolph **(G-9206)**

Vanguard Container Corp ....E... 732 651-9717
East Brunswick **(G-2189)**

WY Industries Inc ....D... 201 617-8000
North Bergen **(G-7444)**

CONTAINERS: Plywood & Veneer, Wood

Builders Firstsource Inc......................E... 856 767-3153
Berlin **(G-419)**

CONTAINERS: Sanitary, Food

Amscan Inc ....D... 973 983-0888
Rockaway **(G-9442)**

Soundview Paper Holdings LLC............A... 201 796-4000
Elmwood Park **(G-2856)**

United Plastics Group Inc ....E... 732 873-8777
Somerset **(G-10091)**

CONTAINERS: Shipping & Mailing, Fiber

Slys Express LLC.................................G... 908 787-7516
Linden **(G-5424)**

CONTAINERS: Shipping, Bombs, Metal Plate

Enviro Pak Inc ....E... 732 248-1600
Edison **(G-2504)**

Meese Inc ....F... 201 796-4490
Saddle Brook **(G-9661)**

CONTAINERS: Shipping, Metal, Milk, Fluid

Granco Group LLC...............................G... 973 515-4721
Roseland **(G-9539)**

CONTAINERS: Shipping, Wood

Vandereems Manufacturing Co ....F... 973 427-2355
Hawthorne **(G-4249)**

CONTAINERS: Wood

Cutler Bros Box & Lumber Co ....E... 201 943-2535
Fairview **(G-3359)**

Jan Packaging Inc..............................D... 973 361-7200
Dover **(G-2091)**

CONTAINMENT VESSELS: Reactor, Metal Plate

Ras Process Equipment.......................E... 609 371-1000
Robbinsville **(G-9416)**

CONTRACTOR: Dredging

Anthony Excavating & Dem ....G... 609 926-8804
Egg Harbor Township **(G-2676)**

CONTRACTORS: Access Control System Eqpt

Absolute Protective Systems ....E... 732 287-4500
Piscataway **(G-8624)**

Access Northern Security Inc ....F... 732 462-2500
Freehold **(G-3642)**

CONTRACTORS: Antenna Installation

Dun-Rite Communications Inc..............G... 201 444-0080
Mahwah **(G-5731)**

Jersey Steel Door Inc ....G... 973 482-4020
Newark **(G-7169)**

CONTRACTORS: Asbestos Removal & Encapsulation

Abatetech Inc ....E... 609 265-2107
Lumberton **(G-5622)**

PRODUCT

CONTRACTORS: Asphalt

Murray Paving & Concrete LLC ....E 201 670-0030
Hackensack *(G-3950)*

CONTRACTORS: Awning Installation

Asbury Awng Mfg & Installation ....G 732 775-4881
Asbury Park *(G-71)*
F & S Awning and Blind Co Inc..............G 732 738-4110
Edison *(G-2509)*
McBride Awning Co ....G....... 732 892-6256
Point Pleasant Beach *(G-8828)*

CONTRACTORS: Boiler Maintenance Contractor

Energy Company Inc ....E 856 742-1916
Westville *(G-11814)*
Shelby Mechanical Inc...........................E 856 665-4540
Cinnaminson *(G-1484)*

CONTRACTORS: Boring, Building Construction

UNI-Tech Drilling Company Inc ....E 856 694-4200
Franklinville *(G-3641)*

CONTRACTORS: Bridge Painting

Newage Painting Corporation................G....... 908 547-4734
Newark *(G-7211)*

CONTRACTORS: Building Eqpt & Machinery Installation

Assa Abloy Entrance Sys US Inc ....E 609 443-5800
Trenton *(G-10897)*
Assa Abloy Entrance Systems US ....E 609 528-2580
Hamilton *(G-4103)*
Benco Inc ....F 973 575-4440
Fairfield *(G-3154)*
DMJ and Associates Inc ....E 732 613-7867
Sayreville *(G-9708)*
Expert Process Systems LLC ....G....... 570 424-0581
Hackettstown *(G-4007)*
Otis Elevator Company ....E 856 235-5200
Moorestown *(G-6552)*
Verona Aluminum Products Inc..............G....... 973 857-4809
Verona *(G-11177)*

CONTRACTORS: Building Movers

W A Building Movers & Contrs ....F 908 654-8227
Garwood *(G-3793)*

CONTRACTORS: Building Sign Installation & Mntnce

Banner Design Inc ....E 908 687-5335
Hillside *(G-4379)*
Bergen Sign Company Inc ....E 973 742-7755
Wayne *(G-11478)*
DCI Signs & Awnings Inc ....E 973 350-0400
Newark *(G-7096)*
Delaware Valley Sign Corp ....D....... 609 386-0100
Burlington *(G-962)*
General Sign Co Inc.............................G....... 856 753-3535
West Berlin *(G-11598)*
Griffin Signs Inc ....E 856 786-8517
Cinnaminson *(G-1460)*
Ionni Sign Inc ....G....... 973 625-3815
Rockaway *(G-9468)*
Kdf Reprographics Inc ....F 201 784-9991
South Hackensack *(G-10167)*
Michele Maddalena ....G....... 973 244-0033
Fairfield *(G-3270)*
Sign Shoppe Inc ....G....... 856 384-2937
Woodbury *(G-12037)*
Speedy Sign-A-Rama..............................G....... 973 605-8313
Morristown *(G-6701)*
Sun Neon Sign and Electric Co ....G....... 856 667-6977
Cherry Hill *(G-1417)*
Tdk Associates Corp ....G....... 862 210-8085
Roseland *(G-9542)*

CONTRACTORS: Building Site Preparation

All Seasons Construction Inc ....G....... 908 852-0955
Long Valley *(G-5607)*
Barrett Industries Corporation ....E 973 533-1001
Morristown *(G-6646)*

Barrett Paving Materials Inc..................E 973 533-1001
Roseland *(G-9535)*

CONTRACTORS: Cable Laying

Tycom Limited......................................C 973 753-3040
Morristown *(G-6704)*

CONTRACTORS: Carpentry Work

24 Horas Inc ....F 973 817-7400
Newark *(G-7026)*
Nicos Group Inc ....G....... 201 768-9501
Norwood *(G-7571)*
Royal Aluminum Co Inc........................D....... 973 589-8880
Newark *(G-7253)*

CONTRACTORS: Carpentry, Cabinet & Finish Work

Creative Cabinet Designs Inc ....F 973 402-5886
Boonton *(G-547)*
Cwi Architectural Millwork LLC ....E 856 307-7900
Glassboro *(G-3808)*
Distinctive Woodwork Inc ....G....... 609 714-8505
Lumberton *(G-5628)*
Mango Custom Cabinets Inc ....F 908 813-3077
Hackettstown *(G-4020)*
Metroplex Products Company Inc..........G....... 732 249-0653
Monroe Township *(G-6336)*
Narva Inc ....G....... 973 218-1200
Springfield *(G-10455)*
Parsons Cabinets Inc ....G....... 973 279-4954
Montclair *(G-6383)*
Restortions By Peter Schichtel ....G....... 973 605-8818
Morristown *(G-6697)*
Universal Systems Installers ....E 732 656-9002
Monroe *(G-6323)*

CONTRACTORS: Carpentry, Cabinet Building & Installation

Costa Custom Cabinets Inc ....G....... 973 429-7004
Bloomfield *(G-499)*
Creative Innovations Inc ....F 973 636-9060
Fair Lawn *(G-3094)*
Epic Millwork LLC ....E 732 296-0273
Somerset *(G-9988)*
Hawthorne Kitchens Inc ....F 973 427-9010
Hawthorne *(G-4223)*
Jorgensen Carr Ltd..............................G....... 201 792-2278
East Orange *(G-2253)*
Kitchen Crafters Plus ....G....... 732 566-7995
Matawan *(G-5979)*
Taylor Made Custom Cabinetry ....F 856 786-5433
Pennsauken *(G-8490)*
Wood & Laminates Inc ....G....... 973 773-7475
Lodi *(G-5583)*

CONTRACTORS: Carpentry, Finish & Trim Work

Glen Rock Stair Corp ....E 201 337-9595
Franklin Lakes *(G-3624)*
Marty Anderson & Assoc Inc ....G....... 201 798-0507
North Bergen *(G-7419)*

CONTRACTORS: Carpet Laying

Cole Brothers Marble & Granite ....G....... 856 455-7989
Elmer *(G-2795)*
Franks Upholstery & Draperies ....G....... 856 779-8585
Maple Shade *(G-5863)*

CONTRACTORS: Ceramic Floor Tile Installation

Locktile Industries Llc ....F 888 562-5845
Newark *(G-7184)*

CONTRACTORS: Closet Organizers, Installation & Design

Rainbow Closets Inc.............................D....... 973 882-3800
Fairfield *(G-3297)*

CONTRACTORS: Commercial & Office Building

Salon Interiors Inc ....E 201 488-7888
South Hackensack *(G-10186)*

CONTRACTORS: Building Movers

W A Building Movers & Contrs ....F 908 654-8227
Garwood *(G-3793)*

CONTRACTORS: Communications Svcs

Subcom LLC ....B 732 578-7000
Eatontown *(G-2422)*

CONTRACTORS: Computer Installation

Creative Cmpt Concepts LLC ....G....... 877 919-7988
Williamstown *(G-11956)*
Pascack Data Services Inc ....F 973 304-4858
Hawthorne *(G-4236)*

CONTRACTORS: Concrete

B&F and Son Masonry Company ....E 201 791-7630
Elmwood Park *(G-2811)*
Concrete Cutting Partners Inc ....G....... 201 440-2233
Hackensack *(G-3899)*
Miles Concrete Company Inc ....F 856 697-2311
Newfield *(G-7323)*
Richard E Pierson Mtls Corp ....G....... 856 740-2400
Williamstown *(G-11975)*
Richard E Pierson Mtls Corp ....G....... 856 691-0083
Vineland *(G-11260)*
Richard E Pierson Mtls Corp ....C....... 856 467-4199
Pilesgrove *(G-8580)*
Tanis Concrete ....E 201 796-1556
Fair Lawn *(G-3126)*

CONTRACTORS: Concrete Breaking, Street & Highway

Control Industries Inc...........................G....... 201 437-3826
Bayonne *(G-212)*

CONTRACTORS: Concrete Repair

RFS Commercial Inc ....F 201 796-0006
Saddle Brook *(G-9671)*

CONTRACTORS: Construction Site Cleanup

Vet Construction Inc.............................F 732 987-4922
Jackson *(G-4669)*

CONTRACTORS: Core Drilling & Cutting

Environmental Technical Drlg ....G....... 732 938-3222
Farmingdale *(G-3385)*

CONTRACTORS: Countertop Installation

Creative Innovations Inc ....F 973 636-9060
Fair Lawn *(G-3094)*
Intelco ....E 856 384-8562
Paulsboro *(G-8332)*
Narva Inc ....G....... 973 218-1200
Springfield *(G-10455)*
South Jersey Countertop Co ....G....... 856 768-7960
West Berlin *(G-11622)*

CONTRACTORS: Demolition, Building & Other Structures

Mdb Construction ....G....... 908 628-8010
Lebanon *(G-5270)*

CONTRACTORS: Directional Oil & Gas Well Drilling Svc

Jay-Bee Oil & Gas Inc..........................D....... 908 686-1493
Clark *(G-1499)*

CONTRACTORS: Drywall

Bell Supply Co.....................................E 856 663-3900
Pennsauken *(G-8396)*
Christopher Szuco ....G....... 732 684-7643
Millstone Twp *(G-6213)*

CONTRACTORS: Electric Power Systems

Norsal Distribution Associates..............F 908 638-6430
High Bridge *(G-4284)*

CONTRACTORS: Electrical

Ace Electric ....G....... 908 534-2404
Somerville *(G-10100)*
Apelio Innovative Inds LLC ....F 973 777-8899
Kearny *(G-4844)*

Archer Day Inc................................E...... 732 396-0600
  Avenel (G-120)
Automation & Control Inc ....E...... 856 234-2300
  Moorestown (G-6507)
C J Electric ....G...... 201 891-0739
  Wyckoff (G-12106)
Crestron Electronics Inc ....C...... 201 767-3400
  Rockleigh (G-9516)
George J Bender Inc ....E...... 908 687-0081
  Union (G-11059)
L&W Audio/Video Inc ....G...... 212 980-2862
  Hoboken (G-4463)
Lb Electric Co - North LLC..............G...... 973 366-2188
  Denville (G-2044)
Marshall Maintenance....................C...... 609 394-7153
  Trenton (G-10956)
R & R Irrigation Co Inc ....F...... 732 271-7070
  Middlesex (G-6142)
Trinity Heating & Air Inc ....D...... 732 780-3779
  Wall Township (G-11376)
Verizon Communications Inc...........D...... 609 646-9939
  Egg Harbor Township (G-2700)

CONTRACTORS: Electronic Controls Installation

Johnson Controls Inc ....D...... 732 225-6700
  Edison (G-2543)

CONTRACTORS: Energy Management Control

Bfhj Holdings Inc ....G...... 908 730-6280
  Montvale (G-6401)

CONTRACTORS: Epoxy Application

Newage Painting Corporation..........G...... 908 547-4734
  Newark (G-7211)

CONTRACTORS: Excavating

Barrett Industries Corporation ....E...... 973 533-1001
  Morristown (G-6646)
Barrett Paving Materials Inc..................E...... 973 533-1001
  Roseland (G-9535)
Cedar Hill Landscaping ....E...... 732 469-1400
  Somerset (G-9974)
Control Industries Inc.............................G...... 201 437-3826
  Bayonne (G-212)
Earthwork Associates Inc ....F...... 609 624-9395
  Ocean View (G-7702)
Hudson Valley Enviromental Inc ....E...... 732 967-0060
  Toms River (G-10768)
Hup & Sons...G...... 908 832-7878
  Glen Gardner (G-3823)
Philip Mamrak ....G...... 908 454-6089
  Phillipsburg (G-8567)

CONTRACTORS: Excavating Slush Pits & Cellars Svcs

Zc Utility Services LLC ....G...... 973 226-1840
  Roseland (G-9545)

CONTRACTORS: Exterior Painting

Dux Paint LLC ....F...... 973 473-2376
  Lodi (G-5560)

CONTRACTORS: Exterior Wall System Installation

Atlantic Exterior Wall Systems ....D...... 973 646-8200
  Wayne (G-11472)

CONTRACTORS: Fence Construction

A 1 Fencing Inc ....F...... 908 527-1066
  Elizabeth (G-2704)
Accent Fence Inc ....E...... 609 965-6400
  Egg Harbor City (G-2651)
All-State Fence Inc ....E...... 732 431-4944
  West Orange (G-11758)
C & S Fencing Inc ....E...... 201 797-5440
  Elmwood Park (G-2813)
Doerre Fence Co LLC ....F...... 732 751-9700
  Farmingdale (G-3384)
Edwin R Burger & Son Inc ....E...... 856 468-2300
  Sewell (G-9841)
H Barron Iron Works Inc..........................F...... 856 456-9092
  Gloucester City (G-3843)

Mendham Garden Center ....G...... 973 543-4178
  Mendham (G-6041)
National Fence Systems Inc ....D...... 732 636-5600
  Avenel (G-139)
Northeast Precast Ltd Lblty Co ....D...... 856 765-9088
  Millville (G-6264)

CONTRACTORS: Fiber Optic Cable Installation

Comm Port Technologies Inc ....G...... 732 738-8780
  Cranbury (G-1826)
Contemporary Cabling Company........G...... 732 382-5064
  Clark (G-1496)

CONTRACTORS: Fiberglass Work

United Eqp Fabricators LLC ....G...... 973 242-2737
  Newark (G-7308)

CONTRACTORS: Fire Detection & Burglar Alarm Systems

Checkpoint Security Systems Gr ....C...... 952 933-8858
  West Deptford (G-11696)
Checkpoint Systems Inc ....C...... 952 933-8858
  West Deptford (G-11699)
Merchants Alarm Systems Inc..............E...... 973 779-1296
  Wallington (G-11388)

CONTRACTORS: Fire Sprinkler System Installation Svcs

Absolute Protective Systems ....E...... 732 287-4500
  Piscataway (G-8624)
Eagle Fire & Safety Corp ....G...... 732 982-7388
  Wall Township (G-11335)
Tyco International MGT Co LLC ....E...... 609 720-4200
  Princeton (G-9038)

CONTRACTORS: Floor Laying & Other Floor Work

Armorpoxy Inc..F...... 908 810-9613
  Union (G-11027)
Flooring Concepts Nj LLC......................F...... 732 409-7600
  Manalapan (G-5811)
Friends Hardwood Floors Inc ....G...... 732 859-4019
  Oakhurst (G-7609)
Tbs Industrial Flooring Pdts ....G...... 732 899-1486
  Point Pleasant Beach (G-8832)

CONTRACTORS: Flooring

Atlantic Flooring LLC ....F...... 609 296-7700
  Ltl Egg Hbr (G-5614)
Flooring Concepts Nj LLC......................F...... 732 409-7600
  Manalapan (G-5811)
Friends Hardwood Floors Inc ....G...... 732 859-4019
  Oakhurst (G-7609)

CONTRACTORS: Garage Doors

Gray Overhead Door Co ....F...... 908 355-3889
  Elizabeth (G-2744)

CONTRACTORS: Gas Field Svcs, NEC

Ridgewood Energy O Fund LLC...........G...... 201 447-9000
  Montvale (G-6426)

CONTRACTORS: General Electric

Eme Electrical Contractors ....G...... 973 228-6608
  Caldwell (G-1023)
Lowder Electric and Cnstr ....G...... 732 764-6000
  Middlesex (G-6128)
M&L Power Systems Maint Inc ....E...... 732 679-1800
  Old Bridge (G-7718)
M2 Electric LLC ....E...... 973 770-4596
  Mine Hill (G-6273)
Mt Salem Electric Co Inc ....F...... 908 735-6126
  Pittstown (G-8754)
Story Electric Mtr Repr Co Inc ....G...... 973 256-1636
  Little Falls (G-5469)
Sun Neon Sign and Electric Co ....G...... 856 667-6977
  Cherry Hill (G-1417)
Timothy P Bryan Elc Co Inc ....G...... 609 393-8325
  Trenton (G-10999)

CONTRACTORS: Glass Tinting, Architectural & Automotive

Glasscare Inc..F...... 201 943-1122
  Cliffside Park (G-1539)

CONTRACTORS: Glass, Glazing & Tinting

Above Rest Glass ....G...... 732 370-1616
  Toms River (G-10738)
Eldon Glass & Mirror Co Inc ....F...... 973 589-2099
  Newark (G-7113)
Frost Tech Inc.......................................F...... 732 396-0071
  Rahway (G-9096)
Glasscare Inc..F...... 201 943-1122
  Cliffside Park (G-1539)
Mainland Plate Glass Company...........F...... 609 277-2938
  Pleasantville (G-8815)
Newman Glass Works Inc ....F...... 215 925-3565
  Camden (G-1079)
Penta Glass Industries Inc ....G...... 973 478-2110
  Garfield (G-3755)
Semi Conductor Manufacturing ....E...... 973 478-2880
  Clifton (G-1714)
William Duling ....G...... 856 365-6323
  Camden (G-1090)

CONTRACTORS: Heating & Air Conditioning

Breure Sheet Metal Co Inc ....G...... 973 772-6423
  Clifton (G-1578)
Duct Mate Inc..G...... 201 488-8002
  Hackensack (G-3909)
Heat-Timer Corporation.........................E...... 212 481-2020
  Fairfield (G-3225)
Marshall Maintenance............................C...... 609 394-7153
  Trenton (G-10956)
McAllister Service Company ....E...... 856 665-4545
  Pennsauken (G-8453)
Rosenwach Tank Co LLC ....E...... 732 563-4900
  Somerset (G-10066)

CONTRACTORS: Heating Systems Repair & Maintenance Svc

Pennington Furnace Supply Inc...........G...... 609 737-2500
  Pennington (G-8371)

CONTRACTORS: Highway & Street Construction, General

Stavola Holding Corporation ....C...... 732 542-2328
  Tinton Falls (G-10730)

CONTRACTORS: Highway & Street Paving

A E Stone Inc ....E...... 609 641-2781
  Egg Harbor Township (G-2673)
Arawak Paving Co Inc ....E...... 609 561-4100
  Hammonton (G-4128)
Barrett Industries Corporation ....E...... 973 533-1001
  Morristown (G-6646)
Barrett Paving Materials Inc.................E....... 973 533-1001
  Roseland (G-9535)
Brick-Wall Corp ....E...... 609 693-6223
  Forked River (G-3536)
Colas Inc...G...... 973 290-9082
  Morristown (G-6654)
Dosch-King Company Inc ....F...... 973 887-0145
  Whippany (G-11889)
Joseph and William Stavola...................E...... 609 924-0300
  Kingston (G-5009)
Murray Paving & Concrete LLC.............E...... 201 670-0030
  Hackensack (G-3950)
Philip Mamrak ....G...... 908 454-6089
  Phillipsburg (G-8567)
Schifano Construction Corp ....F...... 732 752-3450
  Middlesex (G-6144)
Suffolk County Contractors ....E...... 732 349-7726
  Toms River (G-10796)
Trap Rock Industries Inc ....B...... 609 924-0300
  Kingston (G-5012)

CONTRACTORS: Home & Office Intrs Finish, Furnish/Remodel

Majka Railing Inc..................................G...... 973 247-7603
  Paterson (G-8248)
Maranatha Ceramic Tile & Marbl ....E...... 609 758-1168
  Wrightstown (G-12099)

PRODUCT

CONTRACTORS: Hydraulic Eqpt Installation & Svcs

Industrial Hydraulics & Rubber ....G...... 856 966-2600
Camden **(G-1070)**

CONTRACTORS: Indl Building Renovation, Remodeling & Repair

Diamond Scooters Inc ....G...... 609 646-0003
Absecon **(G-2)**
Mdb Construction ....G...... 908 628-8010
Lebanon **(G-5270)**

CONTRACTORS: Kitchen & Bathroom Remodeling

Artistic Hardware ....G...... 609 383-1909
Northfield **(G-7510)**
Eviva LLC ....G...... 973 925-4028
Paterson **(G-8185)**
Ken Bauer Inc ....E...... 201 664-6881
Hillsdale **(G-4368)**
Royal Cabinet Company Inc ....E...... 908 203-8000
Bound Brook **(G-605)**
Sanford & Birdsall Inc ....G...... 732 223-6966
Manasquan **(G-5838)**

CONTRACTORS: Lighting Syst

Prg Group Inc ....G...... 201 758-4000
Secaucus **(G-9798)**
Pty Lighting LLC ....G...... 855 303-4500
Hillside **(G-4421)**

CONTRACTORS: Machine Rigging & Moving

American Mllwright Rigging LLC ....E...... 856 457-9574
Audubon **(G-111)**
Industrial Process & Eqp Inc ....F...... 973 702-0330
Sussex **(G-10562)**
Woods Industrial LLC ....F...... 973 208-0664
West Milford **(G-11734)**

CONTRACTORS: Machinery Installation

Equipment Erectors Inc ....E...... 732 846-1212
Somerset **(G-9989)**
Gervens Enterprises Inc ....F...... 973 838-1600
Bloomingdale **(G-529)**
Luciano Packaging Tech Inc ....G...... 908 722-3222
Branchburg **(G-657)**
Marshall Maintenance ....C...... 609 394-7153
Trenton **(G-10956)**
Paramount Metal Finishing Co ....C...... 908 862-0772
Linden **(G-5403)**
Sigma Engineering & Consulting ....F...... 732 356-3046
Middlesex **(G-6147)**

CONTRACTORS: Maintenance, Parking Facility Eqpt

Kyosis LLC ....G...... 908 202-8894
South River **(G-10351)**

CONTRACTORS: Marble Installation, Interior

Elana Tile Contractors Inc ....G...... 973 386-0991
East Hanover **(G-2208)**
Solidsurface Designs Inc ....E...... 856 910-7720
Pennsauken **(G-8487)**

CONTRACTORS: Masonry & Stonework

B&F and Son Masonry Company ....E...... 201 791-7630
Elmwood Park **(G-2811)**
Murray Paving & Concrete LLC ....E...... 201 670-0030
Hackensack **(G-3950)**
Procrete LLC ....G...... 609 365-2922
Linwood **(G-5450)**
T M Baxter Services LLC ....E...... 908 500-9065
Washington **(G-11453)**
Thin Stone Systems LLC ....G...... 973 882-7377
Fairfield **(G-3327)**

CONTRACTORS: Mechanical

Airmet Inc ....G...... 973 481-5550
Newark **(G-7037)**
Interstate Welding & Mfg Co ....F...... 800 676-4666
Beverly **(G-452)**

Klm Mechanical Contractors ....F...... 201 385-6965
Dumont **(G-2115)**
Lusotech LLC ....G...... 973 332-3861
Newark **(G-7190)**
Pennetta & Sons ....E...... 201 420-1693
Jersey City **(G-4781)**
Sander Mechanical Service Inc ....E...... 732 560-0600
Branchburg **(G-679)**

CONTRACTORS: Office Furniture Installation

Extra Office Inc ....F...... 732 381-9774
Rahway **(G-9092)**

CONTRACTORS: Oil & Gas Building, Repairing & Dismantling Svc

Kabel N Elettrotek Amer Inc ....G...... 973 265-0850
Parsippany **(G-7969)**

CONTRACTORS: Oil & Gas Field Geological Exploration Svcs

Foresight Enviroprobe Inc ....G...... 609 259-1244
Clarksburg **(G-1520)**

CONTRACTORS: Oil & Gas Well Drilling Svc

Maverick Oil Co ....E...... 732 747-8637
Red Bank **(G-9234)**
Shore Drilling Inc ....G...... 732 935-1776
Oceanport **(G-7707)**
Tof Energy Corporation ....D...... 908 691-2422
Bedminster **(G-280)**

CONTRACTORS: Oil & Gas Wells Pumping Svcs

Tof Energy Corporation ....D...... 908 691-2422
Bedminster **(G-280)**

CONTRACTORS: Oil Field Lease Tanks: Erectg, Clng/Rprg Svcs

Conti-Robert and Co JV ....D...... 732 520-5000
Edison **(G-2483)**

CONTRACTORS: Oil/Gas Field Casing, Tube/Rod Running, Cut/Pull

Creamer Glass LLC ....G...... 856 327-2023
Millville **(G-6244)**

CONTRACTORS: Oil/Gas Well Construction, Rpr/Dismantling Svcs

All Seasons Construction Inc ....G...... 908 852-0955
Long Valley **(G-5607)**
Gateway Property Solutions Ltd ....E...... 732 901-9700
Lakewood **(G-5103)**
Independent Prj Cons Ltd Lblty ....G...... 973 780-8002
Newark **(G-7155)**
Mister Good Lube Inc ....G...... 732 842-3266
Shrewsbury **(G-9897)**
Nickos Construction Inc ....F...... 267 240-3997
Sicklerville **(G-9913)**
Refferals Only Inc ....G...... 609 921-1033
Princeton **(G-9014)**
Robert Weidener ....G...... 201 703-5700
Fair Lawn **(G-3119)**
Shelby Mechanical Inc ....G...... 856 665-4540
Cinnaminson **(G-1484)**
Vet Construction Inc ....F...... 732 987-4922
Jackson **(G-4669)**
Zion Industries Inc ....G...... 973 998-0162
Morris Plains **(G-6629)**

CONTRACTORS: On-Site Welding

Alberona Welding & Iron Works ....G...... 973 674-3375
Orange **(G-7749)**
All American Metal Fabricators ....G...... 201 567-2898
Tenafly **(G-10658)**
BR Welding Inc ....F...... 732 363-8253
Howell **(G-4532)**
Energy Company Inc ....E...... 856 742-1916
Westville **(G-11814)**
James A Stanlick Jr ....G...... 973 366-7316
Wharton **(G-11860)**
Orgo-Thermit Inc ....E...... 732 657-5781
Manchester **(G-5847)**

Wel-Fab Inc ....E...... 609 261-1393
Rancocas **(G-9168)**
Woods Industrial LLC ....F...... 973 208-0664
West Milford **(G-11734)**

CONTRACTORS: Ornamental Metal Work

67 Pollock Ave Corp ....G...... 201 432-1156
Jersey City **(G-4679)**
Abba Metal Works Inc ....G...... 973 684-0808
Paterson **(G-8121)**
Coordinated Metals Inc ....D...... 201 460-7280
Carlstadt **(G-1145)**

CONTRACTORS: Painting & Wall Covering

Brennan Penrod Contractors LLC ....F...... 856 933-1100
Bellmawr **(G-329)**

CONTRACTORS: Painting, Commercial

Zack Painting Co Inc ....E...... 732 738-7900
Fords **(G-3534)**

CONTRACTORS: Painting, Commercial, Interior

Forman Industries Inc ....D...... 732 727-8100
Old Bridge **(G-7715)**

CONTRACTORS: Parking Lot Maintenance

Advanced Pavement Technologies ....F...... 973 366-8044
Rockaway **(G-9438)**

CONTRACTORS: Plumbing

Advanced Sewer ....F...... 973 278-1948
Woodland Park **(G-12069)**
Cobra Products Inc ....D...... 856 241-7700
Swedesboro **(G-10577)**
Eme Electrical Contractors ....G...... 973 228-6608
Caldwell **(G-1023)**
Frank Burton & Sons Inc ....G...... 856 455-1202
Bridgeton **(G-758)**
Perkins Plumbing & Heating ....G...... 201 327-2736
Upper Saddle River **(G-11145)**
World and Main LLC ....C...... 609 860-9990
Cranbury **(G-1893)**

CONTRACTORS: Prefabricated Window & Door Installation

Architectural Window Mfg Corp ....C...... 201 933-5094
Rutherford **(G-9614)**
Europrojects Intl Inc ....G...... 201 408-5215
Englewood **(G-2903)**
Verona Aluminum Products Inc ....G...... 973 857-4809
Verona **(G-11177)**

CONTRACTORS: Process Piping

Industrial Process & Eqp Inc ....F...... 973 702-0330
Sussex **(G-10562)**

CONTRACTORS: Protective Lining Install, Underground Sewage

Atlantic Lining Co Inc ....E...... 609 723-2400
Jobstown **(G-4836)**

CONTRACTORS: Refrigeration

Air Power Inc ....E...... 973 882-5418
Fairfield **(G-3136)**

CONTRACTORS: Resilient Floor Laying

Palma Inc ....F...... 973 429-1490
Whippany **(G-11901)**

CONTRACTORS: Roofing

Vector Foiltec LLC ....G...... 862 702-8909
Fairfield **(G-3340)**

CONTRACTORS: Safety & Security Eqpt

Amerindia Technologies Inc ....E...... 609 664-2224
Cranbury **(G-1808)**
Tyco International MGT Co LLC ....E...... 609 720-4200
Princeton **(G-9038)**

CONTRACTORS: Sandblasting Svc, Building Exteriors

Jaeger Thomas & Melissa DDS ....F....... 908 735-2722
Lebanon *(G-5266)*

CONTRACTORS: Septic System

Vogel Precast Inc ....G....... 732 552-8837
Lakewood *(G-5178)*

CONTRACTORS: Sheet Metal Work, NEC

Atlantic Air Enterprises Inc ....F....... 732 381-4000
Rahway *(G-9081)*

Crett Construction Inc...........................F....... 973 663-1184
Lake Hopatcong *(G-5035)*

Danson Sheet Metal Inc.......................E....... 201 343-4876
Hackensack *(G-3905)*

In-Line Shtmtl Fabricators ....G....... 201 339-8121
Bayonne *(G-224)*

Independent Sheet Metal Co Inc..........D....... 973 423-1150
Riverdale *(G-9379)*

Joseph Bbinec Shtmtl Works Inc ....E....... 732 388-0155
Rahway *(G-9109)*

Klm Mechanical Contractors ....F....... 201 385-6965
Dumont *(G-2115)*

Mastercraft Iron Inc................................F....... 732 988-3113
Neptune *(G-6891)*

CONTRACTORS: Shoring & Underpinning

Aluma Systems Con Cnstr LLC..............G....... 908 418-5073
Linden *(G-5322)*

CONTRACTORS: Siding

John Cooper Company Inc ....F....... 201 487-4018
Hackensack *(G-3934)*

Window Factory Inc ....E....... 856 546-5050
Mount Ephraim *(G-6722)*

CONTRACTORS: Single-family Home General Remodeling

Crincoli Woodwork Co Inc ....F....... 908 352-9332
Elizabeth *(G-2724)*

Diamond Scooters Inc.............................G....... 609 646-0003
Absecon *(G-2)*

Ken Bauer Inc...E....... 201 664-6881
Hillsdale *(G-4368)*

Rumsons Kitchens Inc ....G....... 732 842-1810
Rumson *(G-9603)*

CONTRACTORS: Solar Energy Eqpt

Green Globe USA LLC ....G....... 201 577-4468
Carteret *(G-1256)*

Holistic Solar Usa Inc ....G....... 732 757-5500
Newark *(G-7151)*

Mc Renewable Energy LLC ....F....... 732 369-9933
Manasquan *(G-5833)*

Panatech Corporation ....G....... 732 331-5692
Manalapan *(G-5823)*

Tof Energy Corporation ....D....... 908 691-2422
Bedminster *(G-280)*

Trinity Heating & Air Inc ....D....... 732 780-3779
Wall Township *(G-11376)*

CONTRACTORS: Sound Eqpt Installation

E Berkowitz & Co Inc ....G....... 856 608-1118
Mount Laurel *(G-6756)*

CONTRACTORS: Spraying, Nonagricultural

Zack Painting Co Inc................................E....... 732 738-7900
Fords *(G-3534)*

CONTRACTORS: Standby Or Emergency Power Specialization

Elite Emrgncy Lights Ltd Lblty ....F....... 732 534-2377
Lakewood *(G-5090)*

CONTRACTORS: Stone Masonry

Stone Truss Systems Inc ....E....... 973 882-7377
Fairfield *(G-3317)*

CONTRACTORS: Storage Tank Erection, Metal

CB&i LLC ....C....... 856 482-3000
Trenton *(G-10913)*

Jersey Tank Fabricators Inc...................E....... 609 758-7670
South Plainfield *(G-10283)*

CONTRACTORS: Store Front Construction

Architectural Metal and Glass ....G....... 732 994-7575
Lakewood *(G-5054)*

CONTRACTORS: Structural Steel Erection

Arnold Steel Co Inc.................................D....... 732 363-1079
Howell *(G-4531)*

Banker Steel Nj LLC................................D....... 732 968-6061
South Plainfield *(G-10223)*

Burgess Steel Holding LLC.....................G....... 201 871-3500
Englewood *(G-2887)*

East Coast Storage Eqp Co Inc ....E....... 732 451-1316
Brick *(G-716)*

Garden State Iron Inc.............................F....... 732 918-0760
Ocean *(G-7664)*

Harris Structural Steel Co Inc ....G....... 732 752-6070
South Plainfield *(G-10273)*

John Cooper Company Inc ....F....... 201 487-4018
Hackensack *(G-3934)*

John Maltese Iron Works Inc ....E....... 732 249-4350
North Brunswick *(G-7472)*

Leets Steel Inc...G....... 917 416-7977
Sayreville *(G-9715)*

RS Phillips Steel LLC...............................E....... 973 827-6464
Sussex *(G-10565)*

Tri-Steel Fabricators Inc ....E....... 609 392-8660
Trenton *(G-11004)*

CONTRACTORS: Svc Well Drilling Svcs

Foundation Monitoring............................G....... 856 829-0410
Cinnaminson *(G-1457)*

CONTRACTORS: Tile Installation, Ceramic

Maranatha Ceramic Tile & Marbl ....E....... 609 758-1168
Wrightstown *(G-12099)*

Terra Designs Inc ....F....... 973 328-1135
Dover *(G-2108)*

CONTRACTORS: Timber Removal

Hudson Valley Enviromental Inc ....E....... 732 967-0060
Toms River *(G-10768)*

CONTRACTORS: Ventilation & Duct Work

Altona Blower & Shtmtl Work ....G....... 201 641-3520
Little Ferry *(G-5474)*

Bonland Industries Inc ....D....... 973 694-3211
Wayne *(G-11481)*

Creative Industrial Kitchens ....G....... 973 633-0420
Wayne *(G-11490)*

Madhu B Goyal MD ....G....... 908 769-0307
South Plainfield *(G-10296)*

Millar Sheet Metal....................................G....... 201 997-1990
Kearny *(G-4884)*

Professional Envmtl Systems.................E....... 201 991-3000
Kearny *(G-4895)*

PTL Sheet Metal Inc.................................G....... 201 501-8700
Dumont *(G-2117)*

CONTRACTORS: Warm Air Heating & Air Conditioning

Banicki Sheet Metal Inc..........................G....... 201 385-5938
Bergenfield *(G-372)*

In-Line Shtmtl Fabricators ....G....... 201 339-8121
Bayonne *(G-224)*

John E Herbst Heating & Coolg..............G....... 732 721-0088
Parlin *(G-7866)*

Springfield Heating & AC Co ....F....... 908 233-8400
Mountainside *(G-6852)*

T J Eckardt Associates Inc ....F....... 856 767-4111
Berlin *(G-430)*

Temptrol Corp ....E....... 856 461-7977
Voorhees *(G-11295)*

CONTRACTORS: Water Intake Well Drilling Svc

UNI-Tech Drilling Company Inc ....E....... 856 694-4200
Franklinville *(G-3641)*

CONTRACTORS: Water Well Drilling

Clearwater Well Drilling Co ....G....... 609 698-1800
Manahawkin *(G-5791)*

CONTRACTORS: Water Well Servicing

UNI-Tech Drilling Company Inc ....E....... 856 694-4200
Franklinville *(G-3641)*

CONTRACTORS: Waterproofing

Anti Hydro International Inc...................F....... 908 284-9000
Flemington *(G-3430)*

CONTRACTORS: Weather Stripping

Portaseal LLC..G....... 973 539-0100
Morristown *(G-6695)*

CONTRACTORS: Well Bailing, Cleaning, Swabbing & Treating Svc

Environmental Technical Drlg ....G....... 732 938-3222
Farmingdale *(G-3385)*

Perkins Plumbing & Heating ....G....... 201 327-2736
Upper Saddle River *(G-11145)*

CONTRACTORS: Window Treatment Installation

Proclean Services Inc ....F....... 973 857-5408
Verona *(G-11172)*

CONTRACTORS: Windows & Doors

Frank & Jims Inc ....G....... 609 646-1655
Pleasantville *(G-8811)*

Guardrite Steel Door Corp ....G....... 973 481-4424
Newark *(G-7142)*

Window Plus Home Improvement..........F....... 973 591-9993
Passaic *(G-8117)*

CONTRACTORS: Wood Floor Installation & Refinishing

AM Wood Inc ....F....... 732 246-1506
East Brunswick *(G-2126)*

Contempocork LLC...................................G....... 201 262-7738
River Edge *(G-9360)*

CONTRACTORS: Wrecking & Demolition

Anthony Excavating & Dem ....G....... 609 926-8804
Egg Harbor Township *(G-2676)*

Hudson Valley Enviromental Inc ....E....... 732 967-0060
Toms River *(G-10768)*

CONTROL CIRCUIT DEVICES

Admartec Inc ....G....... 732 888-8248
Hazlet *(G-4255)*

Quik-Flex Circuit Inc...............................E....... 856 742-0550
Gloucester City *(G-3849)*

CONTROL EQPT: Buses Or Trucks, Electric

Valcor Engineering Corporation ....E....... 973 467-8100
Springfield *(G-10473)*

CONTROL EQPT: Electric

Atc Systems Inc ....G....... 732 560-0900
Middlesex *(G-6099)*

Automatic Switch Company ....A....... 973 966-2000
Florham Park *(G-3485)*

Computer Control Corp...........................F....... 973 492-8265
Butler *(G-998)*

Electronic Power Designs Inc................F....... 973 838-7055
Bloomingdale *(G-527)*

Innolutions Inc ....G....... 609 490-9799
Princeton Junction *(G-9061)*

ITT Corporation ....D....... 973 284-0123
Clifton *(G-1644)*

L3harris Technologies Inc......................E....... 973 284-0123
Clifton *(G-1651)*

Mid-State Controls Inc............................F....... 732 335-0500
Hazlet *(G-4265)*

Rockwell Automation Inc ....E....... 973 658-1500
Parsippany *(G-8008)*

Walker Engineering Inc ....G....... 732 899-2550
Point Pleasant Boro *(G-8848)*

PRODUCT

CONTROL EQPT: Noise

Hansome Energy Systems Inc..............E 908 862-9044
Linden **(G-5354)**

Wireless Telecom Group Inc..............D 973 386-9696
Parsippany **(G-8040)**

CONTROL PANELS: Electrical

Dantco Corp ....F 973 278-8776
Paterson **(G-8168)**

Eagle Engineering & Automation ....G....... 732 899-2292
Point Pleasant Boro **(G-8844)**

Everite Machine Products Co ....E 856 330-6700
Pennsauken **(G-8419)**

Ivey Katrina Owner ....G....... 973 951-8328
Newark **(G-7163)**

Machinery Electrics ....G....... 732 536-0600
Bayville **(G-247)**

Sensigraphics Inc ....G....... 856 853-9100
Mount Laurel **(G-6804)**

CONTROLS & ACCESS: Indl, Electric

Control & Power Systems Inc..............E 973 439-0500
Fairfield **(G-3175)**

Electronic Technology Inc ....C 973 371-5160
Irvington **(G-4566)**

General Electronic Engineering ....G....... 732 381-1144
Rahway **(G-9097)**

Infinova Corporation..............E 732 355-9100
Monmouth Junction **(G-6293)**

Precision Multiple Contrls Inc ....E 201 444-0600
Midland Park **(G-6184)**

Precision Multiple Contrls Inc ....D....... 201 444-0600
Midland Park **(G-6185)**

Rab Lighting Inc..............C 201 784-8600
Northvale **(G-7544)**

CONTROLS & ACCESS: Motor

CSC ....G....... 973 412-6339
Parsippany **(G-7912)**

Servo-Tek Products Company Inc.........E 973 427-4249
Hawthorne **(G-4243)**

CONTROLS: Air Flow, Refrigeration

Ammark Corporation..............G....... 973 616-2555
Pompton Plains **(G-8857)**

Croll-Reynolds Co Inc ....E 908 232-4200
Parsippany **(G-7909)**

Energy Options Inc ....E 732 512-9100
Edison **(G-2502)**

CONTROLS: Automatic Temperature

D & A Electronics Mfg..............F 732 938-7400
Wall Township **(G-11333)**

Rowan Technologies Inc ....D....... 609 267-9000
Rancocas **(G-9165)**

CONTROLS: Environmental

Access Northern Security Inc..............F 732 462-2500
Freehold **(G-3642)**

Ademco Inc..............G....... 732 505-6688
Toms River **(G-10739)**

Ademco Inc..............F 201 462-9570
Teterboro **(G-10670)**

Ademco Inc..............G....... 908 561-1888
South Plainfield **(G-10207)**

Ademco Inc..............G....... 856 985-9050
Marlton **(G-5921)**

Amega Scientific Corporation ....E 609 953-7295
Medford **(G-6019)**

Burling Instruments Inc..............F 973 665-0601
Chatham **(G-1319)**

Calculagraph Co ....D....... 973 887-9400
East Hanover **(G-2198)**

Check-It Electronics Corp ....E 973 520-8435
Elizabeth **(G-2720)**

Fluidsens International Inc ....G....... 914 338-3932
Twp Washinton **(G-11017)**

Honeywell Asia Pacific Inc..............D....... 973 455-2000
Morris Plains **(G-6607)**

Johnson Controls Inc ....D....... 732 225-6700
Edison **(G-2543)**

Megatran Industries..............D....... 609 227-4300
Bordentown **(G-586)**

Micro-Tek Laboratories Inc ....E 973 779-5577
Clifton **(G-1669)**

Niagara Conservation Corp ....F 973 829-0800
Cedar Knolls **(G-1312)**

Rees Scientific Corporation..............C 609 530-1055
Ewing **(G-3060)**

Schneder Elc Bldngs Amrcas Inc ....E 201 348-9240
Secaucus **(G-9808)**

Sigma-Netics Inc ....E 973 227-6372
Riverdale **(G-9385)**

Sk & P Industries Inc ....G....... 973 482-1864
Newark **(G-7275)**

Tesa Rentals LLC ....F 973 300-0913
Sparta **(G-10410)**

Thermo Systems LLC ....D....... 609 371-3300
East Windsor **(G-2362)**

Town & Country Plastics Inc..............F 732 780-5300
Marlboro **(G-5917)**

Trolex Corporation ....E 201 794-8004
Randolph **(G-9204)**

CONTROLS: Relay & Ind

Advanced Industrial Controls..............G....... 908 725-7575
Branchburg **(G-611)**

Alliance Technologies Group ....G....... 973 664-1151
East Hanover **(G-2193)**

Argus International Inc ....E 609 466-1677
Ringoes **(G-9334)**

Aso Safety Solutions Inc..............G....... 973 586-9600
Rockaway **(G-9443)**

Harrison Electro Mechanical..............F 732 382-6008
Rahway **(G-9100)**

Heat-Timer Corporation..............E 973 575-4004
Fairfield **(G-3224)**

Instrumentation Technology Sls ....G....... 732 388-0866
Rahway **(G-9104)**

Kapsch Trafficcom Usa Inc ....F 201 528-9814
Secaucus **(G-9784)**

Lummus Overseas Corporation ....E 973 893-3000
Bloomfield **(G-508)**

Megatran Industries..............D....... 609 227-4300
Bordentown **(G-586)**

Omega Engineering Inc ....C 856 467-4200
Bridgeport **(G-742)**

Pkm Panel Systems Corp..............F 732 238-6760
Old Bridge **(G-7724)**

Pressure Controls Inc..............E 973 751-5002
Belleville **(G-308)**

Relay Specialties Inc ....E 856 547-5000
Haddon Heights **(G-4048)**

Rockwell Automation Inc ....E 973 526-3901
Parsippany **(G-8009)**

Special Technical Services ....E 609 259-2626
Flanders **(G-3420)**

Xybion Corporation..............C 973 538-2067
Lawrenceville **(G-5248)**

CONTROLS: Thermostats

Aginova Inc..............E 732 804-3272
Freehold **(G-3644)**

CONTROLS: Thermostats, Exc Built-in

Chatham Controls Corporation ....G....... 908 236-6019
Lebanon **(G-5256)**

CONTROLS: Voice

Value Added Vice Solutions LLC..............G....... 201 400-3247
Brielle **(G-910)**

CONTROLS: Water Heater

Brighton Air ....G....... 973 258-1500
Springfield **(G-10433)**

CONVENIENCE STORES

Glassboro News & Food Store ....G....... 856 881-1181
Glassboro **(G-3812)**

CONVENTION & TRADE SHOW SVCS

Atlas O LLC ....E 908 687-9590
Hillside **(G-4377)**

Excerpta Medica Inc ....D....... 908 547-2100
Bridgewater **(G-822)**

Foundation For Student Comm ....E 609 258-1111
Princeton **(G-8950)**

Hyman W Fisher Inc..............G....... 973 992-9155
Livingston **(G-5514)**

Information Today Inc..............E 609 654-6266
Medford **(G-6024)**

CONVERTERS: Data

Cisco Systems Inc ....C 732 635-4200
Iselin **(G-4604)**

Dialogic Inc..............C 973 967-6000
Parsippany **(G-7916)**

Total Technology Inc ....E 856 617-0502
Cherry Hill **(G-1423)**

CONVERTERS: Frequency

ADI American Distributors LLC ....D....... 973 328-1181
Randolph **(G-9169)**

Technology Dynamics Inc ....D....... 201 385-0500
Bergenfield **(G-386)**

CONVERTERS: Phase Or Rotary, Electrical

Power Magnetics Inc ....E 609 695-1170
Trenton **(G-10977)**

Power Magnetics Inc ....E 800 747-0845
Trenton **(G-10978)**

CONVERTERS: Power, AC to DC

Powerspec Inc..............E 732 494-9490
Somerville **(G-10123)**

Princeton Power Systems Inc..............D....... 609 955-5390
Lawrenceville **(G-5242)**

Tdk-Lambda Americas Inc ....C 732 922-9300
Tinton Falls **(G-10731)**

CONVERTERS: Torque, Exc Auto

431 Converters Inc..............G....... 856 848-8949
Woodbury Heights **(G-12040)**

Jetyd Corporation ....F 201 512-9500
Mahwah **(G-5750)**

CONVEYOR SYSTEMS

Knotts Company Inc ....E 908 464-4800
Berkeley Heights **(G-405)**

CONVEYOR SYSTEMS: Belt, General Indl Use

Conveyer Installers America..............G....... 908 453-4729
Belvidere **(G-358)**

Flow-Turn Inc ....E 908 687-3225
Union **(G-11055)**

Hy-Tek Material Handling Inc ....E 732 490-6282
Morganville **(G-6587)**

Volta Belting USA Inc..............F 973 276-7905
Pine Brook **(G-8619)**

CONVEYOR SYSTEMS: Bucket Type

Coesia Health & Beauty Inc ....F 908 707-8008
Branchburg **(G-630)**

CONVEYOR SYSTEMS: Bulk Handling

Coperion Corporation..............C 201 327-6300
Sewell **(G-9835)**

CONVEYOR SYSTEMS: Pneumatic Tube

Vac-U-Max..............E 973 759-4600
Belleville **(G-319)**

CONVEYOR SYSTEMS: Robotic

Boomerang Systems Inc..............E 973 538-1194
Florham Park **(G-3494)**

Reliabotics LLC..............G....... 732 791-5500
New Brunswick **(G-6967)**

T O Najarian Associates..............D....... 732 389-0220
Eatontown **(G-2423)**

CONVEYORS & CONVEYING EQPT

Aerocon Inc ....D....... 800 405-2376
Belleville **(G-290)**

Allstate Conveyor Service..............E 856 768-6566
Voorhees **(G-11280)**

Alpha Associates Inc ....E 732 730-1800
Lakewood **(G-5047)**

Automated Flexible Conveyors ....F 973 340-1695
Clifton **(G-1568)**

Buhler Inc ....E 201 847-0600
Mahwah **(G-5719)**

Carlisle Machine Works Inc ....E 856 825-0627
Millville **(G-6241)**

Century Conveyor Systems Inc..........E 908 205-0625
South Plainfield *(G-10236)*

Conveyors By North American ....G....... 973 777-6600
Clifton *(G-1589)*

Coperion K-Tron Pitman Inc ....F 856 589-0500
Sewell *(G-9836)*

Das Installations Inc ....F 973 473-6858
Garfield *(G-3737)*

Dyna Veyor Inc ....G....... 908 276-5384
Newark *(G-7108)*

Equipment Erectors Inc.....................E 732 846-1212
Somerset *(G-9989)*

Essex Rise Conveyor Corp ....G....... 973 575-7483
West Caldwell *(G-11648)*

Flexlink Systems Inc.........................E 973 983-2700
Branchburg *(G-641)*

Flexlink Systems Inc.........................G....... 908 947-2140
Branchburg *(G-642)*

Flor Lift of N J Inc ....E 973 429-2200
Fairfield *(G-3203)*

Foremost Machine Builders Inc..........D 973 227-0700
Fairfield *(G-3206)*

Garvey Corporation ....D 609 561-2450
Hammonton *(G-4134)*

Gauer Metal Products Co Inc ....E 908 241-4080
Kenilworth *(G-4942)*

Ipco US LLC ....E 973 720-7000
Totowa *(G-10833)*

J G Machine Works Inc ....G....... 732 203-2077
Edison *(G-2536)*

K-Tron International Inc.....................D 856 589-0500
Sewell *(G-9851)*

Keneco Inc..G....... 908 241-3700
Kenilworth *(G-4951)*

Lynn Mechanical Contractors ....F 856 829-1717
Cinnaminson *(G-1470)*

Main Robert A & Sons Holdg Co ....E 201 447-3700
Wyckoff *(G-12116)*

Metalfab Inc ....E 973 764-2000
Vernon *(G-11160)*

Metalfab Mtl Hdlg Systems LLC ....E 973 764-2000
Vernon *(G-11161)*

Pulsonics Inc ....F 800 999-6785
Belleville *(G-309)*

Robotunits Inc ....G....... 732 438-0500
Cranbury *(G-1879)*

Sparks Belting Company Inc ....G....... 973 227-4100
Fairfield *(G-3313)*

Tarlton C & T Co Inc ....E 908 964-9400
Union *(G-11093)*

TEC Installations Inc.........................F 973 684-0503
Paterson *(G-8312)*

Track Systems Inc.............................F 201 462-0095
Hasbrouck Heights *(G-4191)*

Traycon Manufacturing Co Inc ....E 201 939-5555
Hackensack *(G-3984)*

Unex Manufacturing Inc.....................D 732 928-2800
Lakewood *(G-5174)*

Vibra Screw Inc ....E 973 256-7410
Totowa *(G-10858)*

CONVEYORS: Overhead

Key Handling Systems Inc ....E 201 933-9333
Moonachie *(G-6476)*

COOKING & FOOD WARMING EQPT: Commercial

Aero Manufacturing Co ....D 973 473-5300
Clifton *(G-1558)*

J & M Air Inc ....E 908 707-4040
Somerville *(G-10118)*

Pinto of Montville Inc.........................G....... 973 584-2002
Kenvil *(G-4994)*

Power Container Corp ....E 732 560-3655
Somerset *(G-10054)*

Rlct Industries LLC ....G....... 609 712-1318
Pennington *(G-8372)*

Sitaras Toasters Equipment LLC.........G....... 732 910-2678
Cinnaminson *(G-1485)*

COOKING & FOODWARMING EQPT: Commercial

Hickory Industries Inc ....E 201 223-4382
North Bergen *(G-7409)*

COOKING EQPT, HOUSEHOLD: Indoor

Chefman Direct Inc ....D 888 315-8407
Mahwah *(G-5722)*

COOKING SCHOOL

Healthy Italia Retail LLC ....F 973 966-5200
Madison *(G-5694)*

COOLING TOWERS: Metal

Delta Cooling Towers Inc ....E 973 586-2201
Flanders *(G-3405)*

SPX Cooling Technologies Inc ....E 908 450-8027
Bridgewater *(G-892)*

COOLING TOWERS: Wood

Amertech Towerservices LLC ....E 732 389-2200
Shrewsbury *(G-9881)*

Atlantic Coolg Tech & Svcs LLC ....E 201 939-0900
Carlstadt *(G-1127)*

COPPER ORES

Freeport-Mcmoran Inc ....G....... 908 558-4361
Elizabeth *(G-2738)*

COPPER: Rolling & Drawing

Belden Inc ....F 908 925-8000
Elizabeth *(G-2714)*

Fisk Alloy Inc ....E 973 427-7550
Hawthorne *(G-4219)*

Fisk Alloy Wire Incorporated ....C 973 949-4491
Hawthorne *(G-4220)*

Freeport Minerals Corporation ....D 908 351-3200
Elizabeth *(G-2737)*

Gulf Cable LLC ....C 201 242-9906
Hasbrouck Heights *(G-4183)*

Heyco Products Corp ....G....... 732 286-1800
Toms River *(G-10766)*

National Electric Wire Co Inc ....E 609 758-3600
Cream Ridge *(G-1938)*

CORES: Fiber, Made From Purchased Materials

JRC Web Accessories ....F 973 625-3888
Fairfield *(G-3247)*

CORES: Magnetic

Bel Fuse Inc ....C 201 432-0463
Jersey City *(G-4700)*

KG Squared LLC ....F 973 627-0643
Rockaway *(G-9473)*

Lakeland Transformer Corp ....G....... 973 835-0818
Haskell *(G-4198)*

Magnetics & Controls Inc...................F 609 397-8203
Rosemont *(G-9593)*

Thomson Lamination Co Inc................D 856 779-8521
Maple Shade *(G-5872)*

CORK & CORK PRDTS

AMP Custom Rubber Inc.....................F 732 888-2714
Keyport *(G-4997)*

CORK & CORK PRDTS: Tiles

Best Value Rugs & Carpets Inc............G....... 732 752-3528
Dunellen *(G-2120)*

Contempocork LLC.............................G....... 201 262-7738
River Edge *(G-9360)*

Denby USA Limited ....G....... 800 374-6479
Bridgewater *(G-817)*

CORRUGATED PRDTS: Boxes, Partition, Display Items, Sheet/Pad

Graphcorr LLC ....F 732 355-0088
Dayton *(G-1967)*

Rectico Inc..F 973 575-0009
Fairfield *(G-3298)*

CORRUGATING MACHINES

Alpine Corrugated McHy Inc................G....... 201 440-3030
Ridgefield Park *(G-9299)*

COSMETIC PREPARATIONS

A D M Tronics Unlimited Inc ....E 201 767-6040
Northvale *(G-7513)*

Acupac Packaging Inc........................C 201 529-3434
Mahwah *(G-5710)*

Anatolian Naturals Inc ....G....... 201 893-0142
Fort Lee *(G-3546)*

AP Deauville LLC ....E 732 545-0200
New Brunswick *(G-6911)*

Ariel Laboratories LP ....G....... 908 755-4080
South Plainfield *(G-10220)*

Avon Products Inc ....G....... 973 779-5590
Clifton *(G-1569)*

Barmensen Labs LLC ....G....... 732 593-3515
Old Bridge *(G-7712)*

Beilis Development LLC ....F 862 203-3650
Fair Lawn *(G-3090)*

Bentley Laboratories LLC ....C 732 512-0200
Edison *(G-2468)*

Biogenesis Inc ....F 201 678-1992
Paterson *(G-8148)*

Caolion BNC Co Ltd............................C 201 641-4709
Ridgefield Park *(G-9300)*

CCA Industries Inc ....F 201 935-3232
Lyndhurst *(G-5647)*

Chemaid Laboratories Inc ....C 201 843-3300
Saddle Brook *(G-9646)*

Christine Valmy Inc...........................E 973 575-1050
Pine Brook *(G-8592)*

Cococare Products Inc ....E 973 989-8880
Dover *(G-2078)*

Cosmetic Coatings Inc ....E 201 438-7150
Carlstadt *(G-1146)*

Cosmetic Concepts Inc ....C 973 546-1234
Garfield *(G-3736)*

Cosmetic Essence LLC ....C 732 888-7788
Holmdel *(G-4497)*

Cosmetic Essence LLC ....D 201 941-9800
Ridgefield *(G-9257)*

Cosrich Group Inc..............................E 866 771-7473
Bloomfield *(G-498)*

Davion Inc ....E 973 485-0793
North Brunswick *(G-7464)*

Davlyn Industries Inc.........................C 609 655-5974
East Windsor *(G-2349)*

Disposable Hygiene LLC.....................C 973 779-1982
Clifton *(G-1600)*

Encore International LLC ....F 973 423-3880
Hawthorne *(G-4216)*

ET Browne Drug Co Inc ....D 201 894-9020
Englewood Cliffs *(G-2970)*

Gallant Laboratories Inc.....................G....... 609 654-4146
Marlton *(G-5932)*

Gel Concepts LLC ....E 973 884-8995
Whippany *(G-11893)*

Givaudan Fragrances Corp ....C 973 448-6500
Budd Lake *(G-924)*

Grow Company Inc ....E 201 941-8777
Ridgefield *(G-9264)*

Hudson Cosmetic Mfg Corp................D 973 472-2323
Clifton *(G-1637)*

Imperial Dax Co Inc...........................E 973 227-6105
Fairfield *(G-3234)*

Innovative Cosmtc Concepts LLC.......F 212 391-8110
Edison *(G-2534)*

Innovative Cosmtc Concepts LLC........D 973 225-0264
Clifton *(G-1641)*

Intarome Fragrance Corporation.........D 201 767-8700
Norwood *(G-7565)*

Interfashion Cosmetics Corp...............E 201 288-5858
Teterboro *(G-10680)*

June Jacobs Labs LLC ....G....... 201 329-9100
Moonachie *(G-6475)*

Kobo Products Inc ....E 908 941-3406
South Plainfield *(G-10289)*

Kobo Products Inc ....E 908 757-0033
South Plainfield *(G-10290)*

Kobo Products Inc ....E 908 757-0033
South Plainfield *(G-10288)*

New World International Inc................F 973 881-8100
Paterson *(G-8268)*

New York Botany Inc ....E 201 564-7444
Northvale *(G-7541)*

Novapac Laboratories Inc ....E 973 414-8800
Lincoln Park *(G-5303)*

Nu-World Corporation ....C 732 541-6300
Carteret *(G-1262)*

Nu-World Corporation ....G....... 732 541-6300
Edison *(G-2582)*

Omega Packaging Corp ....D...... 973 890-9505
Totowa *(G-10840)*

Organics Corporation America ....E...... 973 890-9002
Totowa *(G-10841)*

Pantina Cosmetics Inc ....E...... 201 288-7767
Teterboro *(G-10689)*

Paramount Cosmetics Inc ....D...... 973 472-2323
Clifton *(G-1684)*

Peter Thomas Roth Labs LLC ....C...... 201 329-9100
Saddle Brook *(G-9669)*

Pfizer Inc 973 739-0430
Parsippany *(G-7988)*

Precious Cosmetics Packaging ....F...... 973 478-4633
Lodi *(G-5573)*

Premier Specialties Inc ....F...... 732 469-6615
Middlesex *(G-6140)*

Presperse Corporation ....E...... 732 356-5200
Somerset *(G-10055)*

Promeko Inc ....G...... 201 861-9446
West New York *(G-11751)*

Quality Cosmetics Mfg ....E...... 908 755-9588
South Plainfield *(G-10319)*

Revlon Consumer Products Corp ....D...... 732 287-1400
Edison *(G-2599)*

Rossow Cosmetiques - Usa Inc ....G...... 732 872-1464
Matawan *(G-5987)*

Rubigo Cosmetics ....G...... 973 636-6573
Little Falls *(G-5466)*

Sarkli-Repechage Ltd ....E...... 201 549-4200
Secaucus *(G-9807)*

SGB Packaging Group Inc ....E...... 201 488-3030
Hackensack *(G-3972)*

Shiseido America Inc ....C...... 609 371-5800
East Windsor *(G-2360)*

Shiseido Americas Corporation ....G...... 609 371-5800
East Windsor *(G-2361)*

Sozio Inc ....D...... 732 572-5600
Piscataway *(G-8715)*

Suite K Value Added Svcs LLC ....F...... 732 590-0647
Edison *(G-2622)*

Suite K Value Added Svcs LLC ....F...... 609 655-6890
Edison *(G-2623)*

Suite K Value Added Svcs LLC ....D...... 609 655-6890
Edison *(G-2624)*

World Wide Packaging LLC ....E...... 973 805-6500
Florham Park *(G-3527)*

COSMETICS & TOILETRIES

ABG Lab LLC ....G...... 973 559-5663
Fair Lawn *(G-3081)*

Adorage Inc ....G...... 201 886-7000
Edgewater *(G-2432)*

Adron Inc ....E...... 973 334-1600
Boonton *(G-536)*

Agilex Flavors Fragrances Inc ....G...... 732 885-0702
Piscataway *(G-8627)*

AlSha&anna Nation of Trends ....G...... 201 951-8197
Rahway *(G-9076)*

American Spraytech LLC ....G...... 908 725-6060
Branchburg *(G-617)*

Andrea Aromatics Inc ....E...... 609 695-7710
Trenton *(G-10894)*

Art of Natural Solution Inc ....F...... 973 812-0500
Totowa *(G-10814)*

Art of Natural Solution Inc ....E...... 917 745-7894
Totowa *(G-10815)*

Art of Shaving - Fl LLC ....G...... 732 410-2520
Freehold *(G-3648)*

Bellwood Aeromatics Inc ....E...... 201 670-4617
Fairfield *(G-3153)*

Bio-Nature Labs Ltd Lblty Co ....E...... 732 738-5550
Edison *(G-2470)*

Bristol-Myers Squibb Company ....E...... 212 546-4000
Hillside *(G-4383)*

Caret Corporation ....F...... 973 423-6098
Fairfield *(G-3165)*

Cei Holdings Inc ....E...... 732 888-7788
Holmdel *(G-4496)*

Conair Corporation ....C...... 609 426-1300
East Windsor *(G-2348)*

Conopco Inc ....E...... 856 722-1664
Mount Laurel *(G-6749)*

Contract Filling Inc ....C...... 973 433-0053
Cedar Grove *(G-1272)*

Cosmetic Essence Inc ....E...... 732 888-7788
Holmdel *(G-4498)*

Coughlan Products LLC ....G...... 973 845-6440
Flanders *(G-3403)*

Custom Liners Inc ....G...... 732 940-0084
Upper Saddle River *(G-11138)*

Dala Beauty LLC ....G...... 732 380-7354
Shrewsbury *(G-9888)*

Devon Products ....G...... 732 438-3855
Pompton Plains *(G-8862)*

Ebin New York Inc ....E...... 201 288-8887
Teterboro *(G-10673)*

Edgewell Personal Care LLC ....C...... 201 785-8000
Allendale *(G-8)*

Englewood Lab LLC ....C...... 201 567-2267
Englewood *(G-2901)*

Flavor & Fragrance Spc Inc ....D...... 201 828-9400
Mahwah *(G-5738)*

Gentek Inc ....G...... 973 515-0900
Parsippany *(G-7956)*

Hy-Test Packaging Corp ....G...... 973 754-7000
Paterson *(G-8211)*

Inter Parfums Inc ....E...... 609 860-1967
Dayton *(G-1971)*

International Beauty Products ....F...... 973 575-6400
Pine Brook *(G-8607)*

Interntnal Flvors Frgrnces Inc ....C...... 732 264-4500
Hazlet *(G-4262)*

Isp Chemicals LLC ....E...... 973 635-1551
Chatham *(G-1323)*

Jnj International Inv LLC ....G...... 732 524-0400
New Brunswick *(G-6939)*

Johnson & Johnson ....D...... 732 422-5000
North Brunswick *(G-7473)*

Johnson & Johnson ....E...... 908 722-9319
Raritan *(G-9213)*

Johnson & Johnson ....C...... 908 874-1000
Morris Plains *(G-6618)*

Johnson & Johnson ....C...... 732 524-0400
New Brunswick *(G-6941)*

Keystone Europe LLC ....C...... 856 663-4700
Cherry Hill *(G-1380)*

LOreal Usa Inc ....G...... 732 499-2809
Clark *(G-1507)*

LOreal USA Products Inc ....A...... 732 873-3520
Somerset *(G-10018)*

Lux Naturals LLC ....G...... 848 229-2950
Edison *(G-2554)*

Lvmh Fragrance Brands US LLC ....G...... 212 931-2668
Edison *(G-2555)*

Medallion International Inc ....F...... 973 616-3401
Pompton Plains *(G-8867)*

Mycone Dental Supply Co Inc ....C...... 856 663-4700
Gibbstown *(G-3798)*

Nellsam Group Inc ....G...... 201 951-9459
Cliffside Park *(G-1542)*

Nmr Manufacturing LLC ....G...... 908 769-3234
South Plainfield *(G-10306)*

Quest Intl Flavors Fragrances ....B...... 973 576-9500
East Hanover *(G-2235)*

Regi US Inc ....G...... 862 702-3901
West Caldwell *(G-11677)*

Robertet Inc ....E...... 201 405-1000
Budd Lake *(G-932)*

Royal Cosmetics Corporation ....F...... 732 246-7275
New Brunswick *(G-6969)*

S Swanson LLC ....G...... 201 750-5050
Northvale *(G-7548)*

Saturn Beauty Group LLC ....G...... 908 561-5000
Piscataway *(G-8707)*

Siloa Inc ....G...... 908 234-9040
Bedminster *(G-278)*

Topifram Laboratories Inc ....E...... 201 894-9020
Englewood Cliffs *(G-2992)*

Unilever United States Inc ....A...... 201 735-9661
Englewood Cliffs *(G-2995)*

COSMETICS WHOLESALERS

AJ Siris Products Corp ....E...... 973 823-0050
Ogdensburg *(G-7708)*

Kobo Products Inc ....E...... 908 757-0033
South Plainfield *(G-10288)*

New York Botany Inc ....E...... 201 564-7444
Northvale *(G-7541)*

Precious Cosmetics Packaging ....F...... 973 478-4633
Lodi *(G-5573)*

Reviva Labs Inc ....E...... 856 428-3885
Haddonfield *(G-4064)*

Rubigo Cosmetics ....G...... 973 636-6573
Little Falls *(G-5466)*

Shiseido America Inc ....C...... 609 371-5800
East Windsor *(G-2360)*

COSMETOLOGY & PERSONAL HYGIENE SALONS

Clean-Tex Services Inc ....E...... 908 912-2700
Linden *(G-5334)*

COSMETOLOGY SCHOOL

Christine Valmy Inc ....E...... 973 575-1050
Pine Brook *(G-8592)*

COSTUME JEWELRY & NOVELTIES: Apparel, Exc Precious Metals

C & C Metal Products Corp ....D...... 201 569-7300
Englewood *(G-2889)*

Meeshaa Inc ....G...... 908 279-7985
Edison *(G-2561)*

Scaasis Originals Inc ....E...... 732 775-7474
Neptune *(G-6895)*

COSTUME JEWELRY & NOVELTIES: Exc Semi & Precious

Alster Import Company Inc ....F...... 201 332-7245
Jersey City *(G-4690)*

Lesilu Productions Inc ....G...... 212 947-6419
West Orange *(G-11771)*

San Marel Designs Inc ....G...... 973 426-9554
Budd Lake *(G-935)*

Superior Jewelry Co ....F...... 215 677-8100
Northfield *(G-7511)*

COUGH MEDICINES

Arcadia Consmr Healthcare Inc ....F...... 800 824-4894
Bridgewater *(G-791)*

COUNTER & SINK TOPS

A1 Custom Countertops Inc ....F...... 856 200-3596
Woodstown *(G-12094)*

Bernard Miller Fabricators ....G...... 856 541-9499
Camden *(G-1041)*

Custom Counters By Precision ....E...... 973 773-0111
Passaic *(G-8058)*

Marvic Corp ....E...... 908 686-4340
Union *(G-11074)*

Masco Cabinetry LLC ....C...... 732 363-3797
Lakewood *(G-5129)*

Masco Cabinetry LLC ....C...... 732 942-5138
Lakewood *(G-5130)*

South Jersey Countertop Co ....G...... 856 768-7960
West Berlin *(G-11622)*

COUNTERS & COUNTING DEVICES

Chem Flowtronic Inc ....G...... 973 785-0001
Little Falls *(G-5455)*

Instru-Met Corporation ....G...... 908 851-0700
Union *(G-11065)*

Octal Corporation ....E...... 201 862-1010
Teaneck *(G-10642)*

COUNTERS OR COUNTER DISPLAY CASES, EXC WOOD

Minerva Custom Products LLC ....G...... 201 447-4731
Waldwick *(G-11305)*

Richard J Bell Co Inc ....F...... 201 847-0887
Wyckoff *(G-12119)*

COUNTERS OR COUNTER DISPLAY CASES, WOOD

A W Ross Inc ....F...... 973 471-5900
Passaic *(G-8049)*

Counter Efx Inc ....G...... 908 203-0155
Hillsborough *(G-4311)*

Garley Inc ....G...... 215 788-5756
Burlington *(G-971)*

Millner Kitchens Inc ....G...... 609 890-7300
Trenton *(G-10958)*

Wagner Rack Inc ....E...... 973 278-6966
Clifton *(G-1737)*

COUNTING DEVICES: Controls, Revolution & Timing

Ellis/Kuhnke Controls Inc ....G...... 732 291-3334
Eatontown *(G-2391)*

Heat-Timer Corporation.....................E....... 212 481-2020
Fairfield (G-3225)
Kessler-Ellis Products Co.................D....... 732 935-1320
Eatontown (G-2407)

COUNTING DEVICES: Gauges, Press Temp Corrections Computing

Chemiquip Products Co Inc.................G....... 201 868-4445
Linden (G-5333)

COUPLINGS: Hose & Tube, Hydraulic Or Pneumatic

Industrial Hydraulics & Rubber............G....... 856 966-2600
Camden (G-1070)
Novaflex Industries Inc...................F....... 856 768-2275
West Berlin (G-11612)

COUPLINGS: Pipe

Precision Mfg Group LLC...................D....... 973 785-4630
Cedar Grove (G-1288)

COUPON REDEMPTION SVCS

S L Enterprises Inc.......................G....... 908 272-8145
Ewing (G-3064)

COURIER OR MESSENGER SVCS

Skinder-Strauss LLC.......................C....... 973 642-1440
New Providence (G-7018)

COURIER SVCS, AIR: Letter Delivery, Private

Sre Ventures LLC..........................G....... 973 785-0099
Little Falls (G-5468)

COURIER SVCS: Ground

Parker Publications.......................F....... 908 766-3900
Madison (G-5699)

COURIER SVCS: Package By Vehicle

Sre Ventures LLC..........................G....... 973 785-0099
Little Falls (G-5468)

COVERS & PADS Chair, Made From Purchased Materials

Drake Corp................................G....... 732 254-1530
East Brunswick (G-2135)

COVERS: Automobile Seat

Atlas Auto Trim Inc.......................G....... 732 985-6800
Edison (G-2463)

COVERS: Canvas

Harold F Fisher & Sons Inc................G....... 800 624-2868
Cinnaminson (G-1462)

COVERS: Hot Tub & Spa

Cover Co Inc..............................E....... 908 707-9797
Branchburg (G-632)
Merlin Industries Inc.....................D....... 609 807-1000
Hamilton (G-4116)

CRANES: Indl Plant

Holtec Government Services LLC............G....... 856 291-0600
Camden (G-1068)
Pcs Crane Services Inc....................F....... 201 366-4250
Fairview (G-3367)

CRANKSHAFTS & CAMSHAFTS: Machining

STS Technologies LLC......................F....... 973 277-5416
Mahwah (G-5778)

CREDIT BUREAUS

AM Best Company Inc.......................A....... 908 439-2200
Oldwick (G-7738)
G-III Leather Fashions Inc................D....... 212 403-0500
Dayton (G-1966)

CRUDE PETROLEUM & NATURAL GAS PRODUCTION

Millennium Brokerage Svcs LLC............G....... 732 928-0900
Jackson (G-4660)

CRUDE PETROLEUM & NATURAL GAS PRODUCTION

Associated Asphalt Mktg LLC...............E....... 210 249-9988
West Deptford (G-11693)
MRC Global (us) Inc.......................G....... 856 881-0345
Glassboro (G-3816)
MRC Global (us) Inc.......................F....... 732 225-4005
East Brunswick (G-2158)
Zenith Energy US LP.......................G....... 732 515-7410
Metuchen (G-6085)

CRUDE PETROLEUM PRODUCTION

JM Huber Corporation......................D....... 732 603-3630
Edison (G-2540)
Speedway LLC..............................B....... 732 750-7800
Port Reading (G-8895)

CRYSTALS

Coherent Inc..............................D....... 973 240-6851
East Hanover (G-2200)
Crystal Deltronic Industries..............E....... 973 328-6898
Dover (G-2079)
Tdk Electronics Inc.......................D....... 732 906-4300
Iselin (G-4631)
Tdk Electronics Inc.......................F....... 732 603-5941
Lumberton (G-5636)

CULTURE MEDIA

Difco Laboratories Inc....................G....... 410 316-4113
Franklin Lakes (G-3619)
Tamir Biotechnology Inc...................G....... 800 419-5061
Short Hills (G-9878)

CUPS & PLATES: Foamed Plastics

Plastico Products LLC.....................G....... 973 923-1944
Irvington (G-4582)

CUPS: Paper, Made From Purchased Materials

Prospect Group LLC........................F....... 718 635-4007
Piscataway (G-8702)

CURTAIN & DRAPERY FIXTURES: Poles, Rods & Rollers

A N Laggren Awngs Canvas Mfg..............F....... 908 756-1948
Plainfield (G-8756)
Acme Drapemaster America Inc..............G....... 732 512-0613
Edison (G-2446)
Erco Ceilings Somers Point Inc............E....... 609 517-2531
Somers Point (G-9936)
Glasscare Inc.............................F....... 201 943-1122
Cliffside Park (G-1539)
Matiss Inc................................E....... 201 648-0002
Hoboken (G-4466)
Nassaus Window Fashions Inc...............E....... 201 689-6030
Paramus (G-7824)
Newell Brands Inc.........................B....... 201 610-6600
Hoboken (G-4468)
SF Lutz LLC...............................G....... 609 646-9490
Egg Harbor Township (G-2697)
Shade Powers Co Inc.......................F....... 201 767-3727
Northvale (G-7549)
Window Plus Home Improvement..............F....... 973 591-9993
Passaic (G-8117)

CURTAINS & BEDDING: Knit

Hampton Industries Inc....................E....... 973 574-8900
Passaic (G-8072)

CURTAINS & CURTAIN FABRICS: Lace

Skusky Inc................................E....... 732 912-7220
Rutherford (G-9633)

CURTAINS: Knit

Curtain Care Plus Inc.....................G....... 800 845-6155
Clifton (G-1594)

CURTAINS: Shower

Royal Crest Home Fashions Inc.............G....... 201 461-4600
Palisades Park (G-7778)

CURTAINS: Window, From Purchased Materials

Beltor Manufacturing Corp.................G....... 856 768-5570
Berlin (G-415)
Bloomfield Drapery Co Inc.................F....... 973 777-3566
East Rutherford (G-2278)
D Kwitman & Son Inc.......................F....... 201 798-5511
Hoboken (G-4450)
Drapery & More Inc........................G....... 201 271-9661
North Bergen (G-7401)
Franks Upholstery & Draperies.............G....... 856 779-8585
Maple Shade (G-5863)
Tankleff Inc..............................E....... 201 402-6500
Fairview (G-3369)

CUSHIONS & PILLOWS

AMS Toy Intl Inc..........................E....... 973 442-5790
Wharton (G-11851)
Discount Pillow Factory LLC...............F....... 973 444-1617
Passaic (G-8060)
Innocor Inc...............................C....... 732 945-6222
Red Bank (G-9230)
Innocor Foam Tech - Acp Inc...............D....... 732 945-6222
Red Bank (G-9231)
Kas Oriental Rugs Inc.....................E....... 732 545-1900
Somerset (G-10010)
Orient Originals Inc......................E....... 201 332-5005
Jersey City (G-4778)
Pegasus Home Fashions Inc.................C....... 908 965-1919
Elizabeth (G-2769)
Redhawk Distribution Inc..................F....... 516 884-9911
Pennsauken (G-8477)

CUSHIONS & PILLOWS: Bed, From Purchased Materials

American Dawn Inc.........................G....... 856 467-9211
Bridgeport (G-734)
AMS Products LLC..........................F....... 973 442-5790
Wharton (G-11850)
Phoenix Down Corporation..................C....... 973 812-8100
Totowa (G-10844)

CUSHIONS: Textile, Exc Spring & Carpet

American Dawn Inc.........................G....... 856 467-9211
Bridgeport (G-734)

CUT STONE & STONE PRODUCTS

A C D Custom Granite Inc..................F....... 732 695-2400
Ocean (G-7651)
Alps Technologies Inc.....................E....... 732 764-0777
Somerset (G-9949)
Counter-Fit Inc...........................C....... 609 871-8888
Willingboro (G-11990)
Elana Tile Contractors Inc................G....... 973 386-0991
East Hanover (G-2208)
Elite Stone Importers LLC.................G....... 732 542-7900
Tinton Falls (G-10716)
EZ General Construction Corp..............G....... 201 223-1101
Wayne (G-11500)
Granite and Marble Assoc Inc..............G....... 908 416-1100
North Plainfield (G-7505)
H T Hall Inc..............................F....... 732 449-3441
Spring Lake (G-10422)
Hanson Aggregates Wrp Inc.................G....... 972 653-5500
Wall Township (G-11345)
Industrial Consulting Mktg Inc............E....... 973 427-2474
Fair Lawn (G-3105)
Industrial Consulting Mktg Inc............E....... 877 405-5200
Fair Lawn (G-3106)
Innovative Cutng Concepts LLC.............G....... 609 484-9960
Egg Harbor Township (G-2684)
Marvic Corp...............................E....... 908 686-4340
Union (G-11074)
Sculptured Stone Inc......................F....... 973 557-1482
Boonton (G-568)
Stone Mar Natural Stone Co LLC............G....... 856 988-1802
Marlton (G-5952)
Thin Stone Systems LLC....................G....... 973 882-7377
Fairfield (G-3327)

P
R
O
D
U
C
T

CUTLERY, STAINLESS STEEL

Hampton Forge Ltd ....E 732 389-5507
Eatontown *(G-2396)*

CUTOUTS: Distribution

Cutting Board Company ....G...... 908 725-0187
Lebanon *(G-5258)*

Cutting Board Company ....G...... 908 725-0187
Branchburg *(G-636)*

CUTTING SVC: Paper, Exc Die-Cut

American Bindery Depot Inc ....C 732 287-2370
Edison *(G-2453)*

CYCLIC CRUDES & INTERMEDIATES

Chem-Is-Try Inc ....G 732 372-7311
Metuchen *(G-6052)*

Chemical Resources Inc ....E 609 520-0000
Princeton *(G-8921)*

Elementis Specialties Inc ....C 609 443-2000
East Windsor *(G-2369)*

Ferro Corporation ....C 856 467-3000
Bridgeport *(G-738)*

Manner Textile Processing Inc ....D 973 942-8718
North Haledon *(G-7497)*

Novartis Corporation ....E 212 307-1122
East Hanover *(G-2226)*

Royce Associates A Ltd Partnr ....E 973 279-0400
Paterson *(G-8289)*

CYLINDER & ACTUATORS: Fluid Power

GE Aviation Systems LLC ....C 973 428-9898
Whippany *(G-11892)*

Industrial Habonim Valves & AC ....F 201 820-3184
Wayne *(G-11519)*

Motion Systems Corp ....D 732 389-1600
Eatontown *(G-2411)*

Van Hydraulics Inc ....E 732 442-5500
South Plainfield *(G-10338)*

CYLINDERS: Pressure

E F Britten & Co Inc ....F 908 276-4800
Cranford *(G-1908)*

Main Robert A & Sons Holdg Co ....E 201 447-3700
Wyckoff *(G-12116)*

CYLINDERS: Pump

Delta Sales Company Inc ....F 973 838-0371
Butler *(G-999)*

DAIRY PRDTS STORE: Cheese

Vitamia Pasta Boy Inc ....F 973 546-1140
Lodi *(G-5582)*

DAIRY PRDTS STORE: Ice Cream, Packaged

Magliones Italian Ices LLC ....F 732 283-0705
Iselin *(G-4614)*

DAIRY PRDTS STORES

Halo Farm Inc ....G 609 695-3311
Lawrenceville *(G-5230)*

DAIRY PRDTS WHOLESALERS: Fresh

Finlandia Cheese Inc ....E 973 316-6699
Parsippany *(G-7946)*

DAIRY PRDTS: Butter

Cookman Creamery LLC ....G...... 732 361-5215
Brielle *(G-906)*

DAIRY PRDTS: Cheese

Abuelito Cheese Inc ....G...... 973 345-3503
Paterson *(G-8123)*

Arthur Schuman Inc ....D 973 227-0030
Fairfield *(G-3146)*

Capital Foods Inc ....E 908 587-9050
Linden *(G-5329)*

Lioni Latticini Inc ....D 908 686-6061
Union *(G-11070)*

Lotito Foods Inc ....F 973 684-2900
Paterson *(G-8246)*

Mendez Dairy Co Inc ....D 732 442-6337
Perth Amboy *(G-8527)*

Saporito Inc ....G 201 265-8212
Ridgefield *(G-9288)*

South American Imports Corp ....G 201 941-2020
Cliffside Park *(G-1544)*

Tipico Products Co Inc ....D 732 942-8820
Lakewood *(G-5171)*

DAIRY PRDTS: Dairy Based Desserts, Frozen

Angelos Italian Ices Icecream ....G 201 962-7575
Ramsey *(G-9137)*

Best of Farms LLC ....G 201 512-8400
Fair Lawn *(G-3091)*

Bindi North America Inc ....F 973 812-8118
Kearny *(G-4848)*

Clio Foods & Provisions LLC ....G 908 505-2546
Roselle *(G-9553)*

Ding Moo LLC ....E 973 881-8622
Paterson *(G-8174)*

Elegant Desserts Inc ....F 201 933-7309
Lyndhurst *(G-5650)*

Heavenly Havens Creamery LLC ....G 609 259-6600
Allentown *(G-27)*

Rw Delights Inc ....G 718 683-1038
Millington *(G-6208)*

DAIRY PRDTS: Dietary Supplements, Dairy & Non-Dairy Based

Advanced Orthomolecular RES Inc ....G 317 292-9013
Clifton *(G-1557)*

Allegro Nutrition Inc ....E 732 364-3777
Neptune *(G-6864)*

Amish Dairy Products LLC ....G 973 256-7676
Totowa *(G-10812)*

Biofarma Us LLC ....F 609 301-6446
East Windsor *(G-2346)*

Farbest-Tallman Foods Corp ....D 714 897-7199
Park Ridge *(G-7849)*

Food Sciences Corp ....C 856 778-4192
Mount Laurel *(G-6761)*

Gold Star Distribution LLC ....F 973 882-5300
East Hanover *(G-2216)*

Grow Company Inc ....E 201 941-8777
Ridgefield *(G-9264)*

Horphag Research (usa) Inc ....G 201 459-0300
Hoboken *(G-4456)*

Icelandirect Inc ....F 800 763-4690
Clifton *(G-1638)*

Jersey Ordnance Inc ....G 609 267-2112
Westampton *(G-11787)*

Lycored Corp ....G 201 601-0060
Secaucus *(G-9790)*

Lycored Corp ....E 973 882-0322
Orange *(G-7755)*

Medison Pharmaceuticals Inc ....F 856 304-8516
Piscataway *(G-8689)*

Naturally Scientific Inc ....F 201 585-7055
Leonia *(G-5291)*

Nutri Sport Pharmacal Inc ....F 973 827-9287
Franklin *(G-3608)*

Orcas International Inc ....F 973 448-2801
Landing *(G-5202)*

Shree Meldi Krupa LLC ....G 732 407-5295
Parsippany *(G-8014)*

Syncom Pharmaceuticals Inc ....E 973 787-2405
Fairfield *(G-3321)*

Unique Encapsulation Tech LLC ....E 973 448-2801
Landing *(G-5204)*

V E N Inc ....C 973 786-7862
Andover *(G-52)*

Willings Nutraceutical Corp ....F 856 424-9088
Cherry Hill *(G-1427)*

Yinlink International Inc ....C 973 818-4664
Cranbury *(G-1894)*

DAIRY PRDTS: Dips & Spreads, Cheese Based

Ambriola Company Inc ....F 973 228-3600
West Caldwell *(G-11640)*

Lioni Mozzarella & Spclty ....E 908 624-9450
Union *(G-11071)*

Saputo Cheese USA Inc ....E 201 508-6400
Carlstadt *(G-1212)*

DAIRY PRDTS: Dried & Powdered Milk & Milk Prdts

Arla Foods Ingredients N Amer ....F 908 604-8551
Basking Ridge *(G-175)*

DAIRY PRDTS: Evaporated Milk

Nestle Usa Inc ....C 973 390-9555
Keasbey *(G-4913)*

DAIRY PRDTS: Farmers' Cheese

Georges Wine and Spirits Galle ....G 973 948-9950
Branchville *(G-707)*

DAIRY PRDTS: Frozen Desserts & Novelties

Applegate Frm Hmmade Ice Cream ....F 973 744-5900
Montclair *(G-6358)*

Country Club Ice Cream ....G 973 729-5570
Sparta *(G-10384)*

Cumberland Dairy Inc ....E 856 451-1300
Bridgeton *(G-757)*

Dairy Queen ....F 732 892-5700
Point Pleasant Boro *(G-8842)*

Evereast Trading Inc ....G 201 944-6484
Fort Lee *(G-3557)*

Frozen Desserts LLC ....G 508 872-3573
Haddonfield *(G-4057)*

Fruta Loca LLC ....G 732 642-8233
Long Branch *(G-5597)*

Gelotti Confections LLC ....G 973 403-9968
Caldwell *(G-1025)*

Guernsey Crest Ice Cream Co ....G 973 742-4620
Paterson *(G-8206)*

Kwality Foods Ltd Liability Co ....G 732 906-1941
Edison *(G-2547)*

Leos Ice Cream Company ....G 856 797-8771
Medford *(G-6029)*

Magliones Italian Ices LLC ....F 732 283-0705
Iselin *(G-4614)*

Marks Ice Cream ....G 201 861-5099
North Bergen *(G-7417)*

Mr Green Tea Ice Cream Corp ....E 732 446-9800
Keyport *(G-5002)*

Mr Green Tea Ice Cream Corp ....F 732 446-9800
Keyport *(G-5003)*

Piemonte & Liebhauser LLC ....F 973 937-6200
Florham Park *(G-3519)*

Rajbhog Foods(nj) Inc ....C 551 222-4700
Jersey City *(G-4796)*

Rolo Systems ....E 973 627-4214
Denville *(G-2055)*

Summer Sweets LLC ....G 732 240-9376
Toms River *(G-10797)*

Sweet Delight ....F 732 263-9100
Oakhurst *(G-7613)*

Tjs Ice Cream ....G 609 398-5055
Ocean City *(G-7697)*

Unilever United States Inc ....A 201 735-9661
Englewood Cliffs *(G-2995)*

DAIRY PRDTS: Ice Cream & Ice Milk

Agape Inc ....F 973 923-7625
Irvington *(G-4553)*

DAIRY PRDTS: Ice Cream, Bulk

Alpine Creamery ....G 973 726-0777
Sparta *(G-10377)*

Arctic Products Co Inc ....F 609 393-4264
Ewing *(G-3016)*

Bergenline Gelato LLC ....G 201 861-1100
North Bergen *(G-7390)*

Bertolotti LLC ....F 201 941-3116
Fairview *(G-3357)*

Cielito Lindo ....G 580 286-1127
New Brunswick *(G-6917)*

Confectionately Yours LLC ....E 732 821-6863
Franklin Park *(G-3633)*

Dunkin Donuts Baskin Robbins ....G 201 692-1900
Teaneck *(G-10628)*

Halo Pub Ice Cream ....F 609 921-1710
Princeton *(G-8957)*

Halo Pub Inc ....F 609 586-1811
Trenton *(G-10938)*

Mister Cookie Face Inc ....C 732 370-5533
Lakewood *(G-5137)*

Sweet Orange LLC ....G 908 522-0011
Summit *(G-10552)*

(G-0000) Company's Geographic Section entry number

Talenti Gelato LLC ....E 800 298-4020
Englewood Cliffs (G-2990)
Uncle Eds Creamery ....G 609 818-0100
Pennington (G-8376)

DAIRY PRDTS: Ice Cream, Packaged, Molded, On Sticks, Etc.

Conopco Inc ....C 920 499-2509
Englewood Cliffs (G-2965)
Mars Incorporated ....F 973 691-3500
Budd Lake (G-929)

DAIRY PRDTS: Ice milk, Bulk

Deep Foods Inc ....C 908 810-7500
Union (G-11042)

DAIRY PRDTS: Imitation Cheese

Mondelez International Inc ....E 973 503-2000
East Hanover (G-2222)

DAIRY PRDTS: Milk Preparations, Dried

American Casein Company ....E 609 387-2988
Burlington (G-947)

DAIRY PRDTS: Milk, Chocolate

Yamate Chocolatier Inc ....G 732 249-4847
Highland Park (G-4290)

DAIRY PRDTS: Milk, Condensed & Evaporated

American Custom Drying Co ....E 609 387-3933
Burlington (G-948)
Dairy Delight LLC ....F 201 939-7878
Rutherford (G-9617)
Kerry Inc ....D 201 373-1111
Teterboro (G-10685)
Robertet Flavors Inc ....F 732 271-1804
Piscataway (G-8706)

DAIRY PRDTS: Milk, Processed, Pasteurized, Homogenized/Btld

Cumberland Dairy Inc ....E 856 451-1300
Bridgeton (G-757)
Garelick Farms LLC ....C 609 499-2600
Burlington (G-970)
Halo Farm Inc ....G 609 695-3311
Lawrenceville (G-5230)
Midland Farms Inc ....E 800 749-6455
Paterson (G-8260)
Readington Farms Inc ....D 908 534-2121
Whitehouse (G-11918)
Tuscan/Lehigh Dairies Inc ....D 570 385-1884
Burlington (G-989)
Wakefern Food Corp ....B 732 819-0140
Edison (G-2645)
Wakefern Food Corp ....B 908 527-3300
Keasbey (G-4916)
Wwf Operating Company ....F 856 459-3890
Bridgeton (G-780)

DAIRY PRDTS: Natural Cheese

Biazzo Dairy Products Inc ....E 201 941-6800
Ridgefield (G-9251)
Colonna Brothers Inc ....D 800 626-8384
North Bergen (G-7397)
Finlandia Cheese Inc ....E 973 316-6699
Parsippany (G-7946)
Hawk Dairy Inc ....G 973 466-9030
Newark (G-7148)
Jvm Sales Corp ....D 908 862-4866
Linden (G-5367)
Lebanon Cheese Company Inc ....G 908 236-2611
Lebanon (G-5268)
Losurdo Foods Inc ....E 201 343-6680
Hackensack (G-3940)
Montena Taranto Foods Inc ....E 201 943-8484
Ridgefield (G-9277)
Toscana Cheese Company Inc ....E 201 617-1500
Secaucus (G-9821)
Tropical Cheese Industries ....B 732 442-4898
Perth Amboy (G-8537)

DAIRY PRDTS: Pot Cheese

Vitamia Pasta Boy Inc ....F 973 546-1140
Lodi (G-5582)

DAIRY PRDTS: Powdered Cream

Panos Brands LLC ....E 800 229-1706
Linden (G-5402)

DAIRY PRDTS: Processed Cheese

La Bella Mozzarella ....G 201 997-1737
Kearny (G-4879)

DAIRY PRDTS: Yogurt, Exc Frozen

Frozen Falls LLC ....G 908 350-3939
Basking Ridge (G-184)
Johanna Foods Inc ....B 908 788-2200
Flemington (G-3452)
Mualema LLC ....G 609 820-6098
Lawrence Township (G-5217)
Yo Got It ....G 732 475-7913
Point Pleasant Beach (G-8834)
Yogurt Paradise LLC ....G 732 534-6395
Jackson (G-4670)

DATA ENTRY SVCS

Aim Computer Associates Inc ....G 201 489-3100
Bergenfield (G-369)
Ideal Data Inc ....F 201 998-9440
North Arlington (G-7374)

DATA PROCESSING & PREPARATION SVCS

Chryslis Data Sltons Svcs Corp ....G 609 375-2000
Princeton (G-8922)
Cimquest Inc ....D 732 699-0400
Branchburg (G-628)
Ics Corporation ....C 215 427-3355
West Deptford (G-11704)
Image Remit Inc ....E 732 940-7900
North Brunswick (G-7469)
Maxisit Inc ....C 732 494-2005
Metuchen (G-6065)
Pds Prclnical Data Systems Inc ....F 973 398-2800
Mount Arlington (G-6717)
The Creative Print Group Inc ....F 856 486-1700
Pennsauken (G-8492)

DATA PROCESSING SVCS

Automated Resource Group Inc ....D 201 391-8357
Montvale (G-6397)
Corporate Mailings Inc ....D 973 808-0009
Whippany (G-11887)
Corporate Mailings Inc ....C 973 439-1168
West Caldwell (G-11645)
Fis Data Systems Inc ....E 201 945-1774
Ridgefield (G-9261)
Fis Financial Systems LLC ....D 856 784-7230
Voorhees (G-11285)
Johnson Associates Systems Inc ....F 856 228-2175
Blackwood (G-471)
S G A Business Systems Inc ....G 908 359-4626
Hillsborough (G-4353)
Thomas Publishing Company LLC ....E 973 543-4994
Chester (G-1435)

DATA VERIFICATION SVCS

Datamotion Inc ....E 973 455-1245
Florham Park (G-3500)

DATABASE INFORMATION RETRIEVAL SVCS

Redi-Data Inc ....F 973 227-4380
Fairfield (G-3299)
Redi-Direct Marketing Inc ....B 973 808-4500
Fairfield (G-3300)

DECALCOMANIA WORK, EXC CHINA & GLASS

Mar-Kal Products Corp ....E 973 783-7155
Carlstadt (G-1185)

DECORATIVE WOOD & WOODWORK

Architectural Wdwkg Assoc ....G 908 996-7866
Frenchtown (G-3708)

Atlas Woodwork Inc ....F 973 621-9595
Newark (G-7057)
Distinctive Wdwrk By Rob Hoffm ....G 609 877-8122
Beverly (G-450)
Distinctive Woodwork Inc ....G 609 714-8505
Lumberton (G-5628)
Edison Finishing ....G 732 287-6660
Edison (G-2500)
Jorgensen Carr Ltd ....G 201 792-2278
East Orange (G-2253)
Krfc Custom Woodworking Inc ....G 732 363-0522
Lakewood (G-5119)
Lardieri Custom Woodworking ....F 732 905-6334
Lakewood (G-5121)
M and R Manufacturing ....G 732 905-1061
Lakewood (G-5126)
Metroplex Products Company Inc ....G 732 249-0653
Monroe Township (G-6336)
Narva Inc ....G 973 218-1200
Springfield (G-10455)
Perk & Pantry ....G 856 451-4333
Bridgeton (G-769)
Ragar Co Inc ....G 732 493-1416
Ocean (G-7678)
Randells Cstm Fniture Kitchens ....F 856 216-9400
Cherry Hill (G-1412)
Restortions By Peter Schichtel ....G 973 605-8818
Morristown (G-6697)
Studio L Contracting LLC ....G 201 837-1650
Hackensack (G-3980)
Taylor Made Custom Cabinetry ....F 856 786-5433
Pennsauken (G-8490)

DEFENSE SYSTEMS & EQPT

Dengen Scientific Corporation ....E 201 687-2983
Union City (G-11110)
L3 Technologies Inc ....B 973 446-4000
Budd Lake (G-925)
Lockheed Martin Corporation ....A 856 722-4100
Moorestown (G-6540)
Mantech Systems Engrg Corp ....G 856 566-9155
Voorhees (G-11291)
Melton Sales & Service ....E 609 699-4800
Bordentown (G-587)
Melton Sales & Service ....E 609 699-4800
Columbus (G-1802)
Milspray LLC ....G 732 886-2223
Lakewood (G-5135)
Portable Defense LLC ....G 856 228-3010
Blackwood (G-478)
Taurus Defense Solutions LLC ....G 617 916-6137
Medford (G-6036)

DEGREASING MACHINES

Grease N Go ....G 856 784-6555
Magnolia (G-5707)
Green Power Chemical LLC ....F 973 770-5600
Hopatcong (G-4520)
Safety-Kleen Systems Inc ....F 609 859-2049
Southampton (G-10371)

DEHYDRATION EQPT

Gericke USA Inc ....G 855 888-0088
Somerset (G-9997)

DELAY LINES

Amperite Co Inc ....E 201 864-9503
North Bergen (G-7384)

DENTAL EQPT

Floxite Company Inc ....F 201 529-2019
Mahwah (G-5739)
Hiossen Inc ....F 888 678-0001
Englewood Cliffs (G-2974)
Takara Belmont Usa Inc ....E 732 469-5000
Somerset (G-10080)

DENTAL EQPT & SPLYS

American Medical & Dental Sups ....F 877 545-6837
Montvale (G-6396)
Dentalworx Lab Ltd Lblty Co ....G 732 981-9096
Edison (G-2491)
Dmg America LLC ....D 201 894-5500
Ridgefield Park (G-9304)
Geistlich Pharma North America ....E 609 779-6560
Princeton (G-8954)

Employee Codes: A=Over 500 employees, B=251-500
C=101-250, D=51-100, E=20-50, F=10-19, G=4-9

2019 Harris New jersey
Manufacturers Directory

821

PRODUCT

Integrated Dental Systems LLC............E 201 676-2457
 Englewood (G-2914)
J A W Products Inc ....F 856 829-3210
 Cinnaminson (G-1467)
Keystone Europe LLC ....G 856 663-4700
 Cherry Hill (G-1380)
Milestone Education LLC ....G 973 535-2717
 Livingston (G-5524)
Milestone Scientific Inc ....F 973 535-2717
 Livingston (G-5525)
Mycone Dental Supply Co Inc...........C 856 663-4700
 Gibbstown (G-3798)
Panthera Dental Inc ....G 201 340-2766
 East Rutherford (G-2309)
R Yates Consumer Prd LLC ....G 201 569-1030
 Englewood (G-2936)
Raptor Resources Holdings Inc ....G 732 252-5146
 Freehold (G-3698)
Samuel H Fields Dental Labs.............E 201 343-4626
 Hackensack (G-3971)
Spident USA Incorporated ....G 201 944-0511
 Little Ferry (G-5497)
Viscot Medical LLC ....E 973 887-9273
 East Hanover (G-2245)
William R Hall Co ....E 856 784-6700
 Lindenwold (G-5447)

DENTAL EQPT & SPLYS WHOLESALERS

J A W Products Inc ....F 856 829-3210
 Cinnaminson (G-1467)
Keystone Europe LLC ....G 856 663-4700
 Cherry Hill (G-1380)
Mycone Dental Supply Co Inc...........C 856 663-4700
 Gibbstown (G-3798)
Pemco Dental Corporation...............E 800 526-4170
 Springfield (G-10459)
Ss White Burs Inc ....C 732 905-1100
 Lakewood (G-5167)

DENTAL EQPT & SPLYS: Cabinets

Integrted Laminate Systems Inc............D 856 786-6500
 Cinnaminson (G-1465)

DENTAL EQPT & SPLYS: Dental Materials

E P R Industries Inc ....F 856 488-1120
 Pennsauken (G-8416)
Essential Dental Systems Inc ....E 201 487-9090
 South Hackensack (G-10159)
Ivoclar Vivadent Mfg Inc.................D 732 563-4755
 Somerset (G-10006)

DENTAL EQPT & SPLYS: Drills, Bone

Palisades Dental LLc.......................F 201 569-0050
 Englewood (G-2929)

DENTAL EQPT & SPLYS: Enamels

Anna K Park...............................G 856 478-9500
 Mullica Hill (G-6855)
Jacquet Jonpaul...........................G 856 825-4259
 Millville (G-6257)

DENTAL EQPT & SPLYS: Laboratory

Handler Manufacturing Company ....E 908 233-7796
 Westfield (G-11799)

DENTAL EQPT & SPLYS: Orthodontic Appliances

Em Orthodontic Labs Inc ....G 201 652-4411
 Waldwick (G-11302)
R Baron Associates Inc ....G 215 396-3803
 Mount Holly (G-6734)

DENTAL EQPT & SPLYS: Teeth, Artificial, Exc In Dental Labs

Dental Models & Designs Inc.............G 973 472-8009
 Garfield (G-3738)
Dentamach Inc ....F 973 334-2220
 Parsippany (G-7914)

DENTAL INSTRUMENT REPAIR SVCS

Ss White Burs Inc ....C 732 905-1100
 Lakewood (G-5167)

DENTISTS' OFFICES & CLINICS

Samuel H Fields Dental Labs.............E 201 343-4626
 Hackensack (G-3971)

DEODORANTS: Personal

B Witching Bath Company LLC............G 973 423-1820
 Hawthorne (G-4206)
Cherri Stone Interactive LLC ....G 844 843-7765
 Lakewood (G-5069)

DEPARTMENT STORES

Gibbons Company Ltd ....E 441 294-5047
 Elizabeth (G-2743)
Scala Pastry ....G 732 398-9808
 North Brunswick (G-7485)

DEPARTMENT STORES: Army-Navy Goods

Escada US Subco LLC ....B 201 865-5200
 Secaucus (G-9763)

DEPILATORIES, COSMETIC

American Prvate Label Pdts LLC ....G 845 733-8151
 Franklin (G-3598)
Arch Personal Care Products LP ....E 908 226-9329
 South Plainfield (G-10219)
Armkel LLC ....A 609 683-5900
 Princeton (G-8911)

DERMATOLOGICALS

Dermarite Industries LLC ....C 973 247-3491
 North Bergen (G-7400)
Dermatological Soc of NJ Inc ....G 856 546-5600
 Barrington (G-171)
Medicis Pharmaceutical Corp.............F 866 246-8245
 Bridgewater (G-848)
Medimtriks Pharmaceuticals Inc ....E 973 882-7512
 Fairfield (G-3267)
Phytoceuticals Inc ....G 201 791-2255
 Elmwood Park (G-2850)
Rouses Pt Pharmaceuticals LLC..........G 239 390-1495
 Cranford (G-1926)
Teligent Inc ....E 856 697-1441
 Buena (G-942)
Topifram Laboratories Inc.................E 201 894-9020
 Englewood Cliffs (G-2992)

DESALTER KITS: Sea Water

American Water - Pridesa LLC ....G 856 435-7711
 Camden (G-1039)

DESIGN SVCS, NEC

Casual Classics Inc ....G 916 294-9880
 Barnegat (G-156)
Grafwed Internet Media Studios ....G 201 632-1771
 Midland Park (G-6175)
Interchange Group Inc....................F 973 783-7032
 Montclair (G-6371)
Keeley Aerospace Ltd ....E 951 582-2113
 Cranbury (G-1849)
Level Designs Group LLC ....G 973 761-1675
 South Orange (G-10198)
My Way Prints Inc ....G 973 492-1212
 Butler (G-1010)
TMC Corporation..........................G 609 860-1830
 Metuchen (G-6078)

DESIGN SVCS: Commercial & Indl

Eurodia Industrie SA ....G 732 805-4001
 Somerset (G-9990)
I F Associates Inc.........................F 732 223-2900
 Allenwood (G-33)
Method Assoc Inc ....F 732 888-0444
 Keyport (G-5001)
Precision Graphics Inc ....D 908 707-8880
 Branchburg (G-671)
Spectrum Design LLC ....G 856 694-1870
 Franklinville (G-3639)
Technical Advantage Inc ....G 973 402-5500
 Boonton (G-570)
Transmission Technology Co ....G 973 305-3600
 Lincoln Park (G-5307)

DESIGN SVCS: Computer Integrated Systems

Alaquest International Inc ....F 908 713-9399
 Lebanon (G-5250)
Business Control Systems Corp ....F 732 283-1301
 Iselin (G-4603)
Com Tek Wrkplace Solutions LLC........F 973 927-6814
 Lyndhurst (G-5649)
Commvault Systems Inc ....C 732 870-4000
 Tinton Falls (G-10709)
Comtrex Systems Corporation............E 856 778-0090
 Moorestown (G-6515)
Cyberextrudercom Inc ....G 973 623-7900
 Wayne (G-11491)
Datapro International Inc ....E 732 868-0588
 Piscataway (G-8652)
Determine Inc ....E 800 608-0809
 Cherry Hill (G-1356)
Eclearview Technologies Inc ....G 732 695-6999
 Ocean (G-7662)
Ensync Intrctive Solutions Inc............G 732 542-4001
 Freehold (G-3664)
Henry Bros Electronics Inc ....D 201 794-6500
 Fair Lawn (G-3103)
Juniper Networks Inc ....D 908 947-4436
 Bridgewater (G-839)
M + P International Inc ....E 973 239-3005
 Verona (G-11170)
Maxisit Inc ....C 732 494-2005
 Metuchen (G-6065)
Melillo Consulting Inc ....E 732 563-8400
 Somerset (G-10028)
MSI Technologies LLC ....F 973 263-0080
 Parsippany (G-7979)
Netscout Systems Inc ....G 609 518-4100
 Marlton (G-5943)
Niksun Inc ....C 609 936-9999
 Princeton (G-8985)
R T I Inc ....E 201 261-5852
 Oradell (G-7746)
Real Soft Inc ....A 609 409-3636
 Monmouth Junction (G-6308)
Specialty Systems Inc ....E 732 341-1011
 Toms River (G-10794)
Techntime Bus Sltons Ltd Lblty ....F 973 246-8153
 East Rutherford (G-2324)
Transcore LP ....F 201 329-9200
 Teterboro (G-10696)
Verizon Communications Inc..............D 609 646-9939
 Egg Harbor Township (G-2700)
Verizon Communications Inc..............E 201 666-9934
 Westwood (G-11847)

DESIGNS SVCS: COSTUME & SCENERY DESIGN SVCS

Images Costume Productions ....G 609 859-7372
 Southampton (G-10365)

DESIGNS SVCS: Scenery, Theatrical

Kdf Reprographics Inc ....F 201 784-9991
 South Hackensack (G-10167)

DETECTION APPARATUS: Electronic/Magnetic Field, Light/Heat

Checkpoint Systems Inc ....C 800 257-5540
 West Deptford (G-11697)
Checkpoint Systems Inc ....C 856 848-1800
 West Deptford (G-11698)
Multi-Tech Industries Inc ....F 732 431-0550
 Marlboro (G-5905)

DETECTORS: Water Leak

United Machine Inc ....G 973 345-4505
 Paterson (G-8320)

DETONATORS: Detonators, high explosives

Cartridge Actuated Devices ....E 973 347-2281
 Byram Township (G-1017)

DIAGNOSTIC SUBSTANCES

Admera Health LLC ....G 908 222-0533
 South Plainfield (G-10208)
Alere Inc ....B 732 358-5921
 Freehold (G-3646)

Astral Diagnostics Inc ....G....... 856 224-0900
Paulsboro *(G-8329)*
Avalon Globocare Corp ....G....... 732 780-4400
Freehold *(G-3650)*
Biotech Atlantic Inc ....F....... 732 389-4789
Eatontown *(G-2380)*
Bracco Diagnostics Inc ....C....... 609 514-2200
Monroe Township *(G-6328)*
Bracco USA Inc ....G....... 609 514-2200
Monroe Township *(G-6329)*
Cenogenics Corporation ....E....... 732 536-6457
Morganville *(G-6584)*
Dpc Cirrus ....F....... 973 927-2828
Flanders *(G-3406)*
Laboratory Diagnostics Co Inc ....F....... 732 536-6300
Morganville *(G-6591)*
Pharmaseq Inc ....G....... 732 355-0100
Monmouth Junction *(G-6301)*
Quest Diagnostics Incorporated ....A....... 973 520-2700
Secaucus *(G-9801)*

DIAGNOSTIC SUBSTANCES OR AGENTS: *Blood Derivative*

Baxter Healthcare Corporation ....C....... 732 225-4700
Edison *(G-2466)*
Ortho-Clinical Diagnostics Inc ....A....... 908 218-8000
Raritan *(G-9217)*

DIAGNOSTIC SUBSTANCES OR AGENTS: *Electrolyte*

Ess Group Inc ....G....... 609 755-3139
Southampton *(G-10361)*

DIAGNOSTIC SUBSTANCES OR AGENTS: *Enzyme & Isoenzyme*

Genzyme Corporation ....G....... 973 256-2106
Totowa *(G-10829)*
Worthington Biochemical Corp ....E....... 732 942-1660
Lakewood *(G-5183)*

DIAGNOSTIC SUBSTANCES OR AGENTS: *Hematology*

Arthur A Topilow William Lrner ....E....... 732 528-0760
Neptune *(G-6865)*

DIAGNOSTIC SUBSTANCES OR AGENTS: *In Vitro*

Access Bio Inc ....F....... 732 873-4040
Somerset *(G-9941)*
Akers Biosciences Inc ....E....... 856 848-8698
West Deptford *(G-11690)*
Ascensia Diabetes Care US Inc ....C....... 973 560-6500
Parsippany *(G-7885)*
Dsrv Inc ....F....... 973 631-1200
Budd Lake *(G-921)*
Fluoropharma Medical Inc ....G....... 973 744-1565
Montclair *(G-6367)*
Foundation For Embryonic ....G....... 973 656-2847
Basking Ridge *(G-183)*
Immunomedics Inc ....C....... 973 605-8200
Morris Plains *(G-6617)*
Medica ....G....... 760 634-5440
Dover *(G-2096)*
Mindray Ds Usa Inc ....B....... 201 995-8000
Mahwah *(G-5754)*
Princeton Biomeditech Corp ....E....... 908 281-0112
Skillman *(G-9926)*
Princeton Biomeditech Corp ....D....... 732 274-1000
Monmouth Junction *(G-6303)*
Recombine LLC ....G....... 646 470-7422
Livingston *(G-5537)*
Sensonics Inc ....F....... 856 547-7702
Haddon Heights *(G-4049)*
Virid Biosciences Limited ....F....... 732 410-9573
Cherry Hill *(G-1426)*

DIAGNOSTIC SUBSTANCES OR AGENTS: *In Vivo*

Alere Inc ....B....... 732 620-4244
Freehold *(G-3645)*

DIAGNOSTIC SUBSTANCES OR AGENTS: *Microbiology & Virology*

Bioalert Technologies LLC ....G....... 551 655-2939
Englewood Cliffs *(G-2961)*

DIAGNOSTIC SUBSTANCES OR AGENTS: *Radioactive*

Petnet Solutions Inc ....G....... 865 218-2000
Hackensack *(G-3963)*

DIAGNOSTIC SUBSTANCES OR AGENTS: *Veterinary*

Biomedtrix LLC ....F....... 973 331-7800
Whippany *(G-11881)*
DMS Laboratories Inc ....G....... 908 782-3353
Flemington *(G-3438)*

DIAMONDS, GEMS, WHOLESALE

Diamond Wholesale Co ....E....... 201 727-9595
Moonachie *(G-6462)*
Golden Treasure Imports Inc ....G....... 732 723-1830
Englishtown *(G-3002)*
Rcdc Corporation ....G....... 212 382-0386
Hoboken *(G-4477)*

DIAMONDS: *Cutting & Polishing*

Rcdc Corporation ....G....... 212 382-0386
Hoboken *(G-4477)*

DIAPERS: *Disposable*

Arquest Inc ....B....... 609 395-9500
Millstone Township *(G-6209)*
Braco Manufacturing Inc ....E....... 732 752-7777
South Plainfield *(G-10227)*
Innovative Disposables LLC ....E....... 908 222-7111
South Plainfield *(G-10277)*

DIATOMACEOUS EARTH: *Ground Or Treated*

Dicalite Minerals Corp ....G....... 856 320-2919
Pennsauken *(G-8413)*

DIE CUTTING SVC: *Paper*

Goetz & Ruschmann Inc ....E....... 973 383-9270
Newton *(G-7345)*
R J Blen Grphic Arts Cnverting ....E....... 732 545-3501
New Brunswick *(G-6964)*
Sabre Die Cutting Co Inc ....E....... 973 357-9800
Paterson *(G-8290)*

DIE SETS: *Presses, Metal Stamping*

C & C Metal Products Corp ....D....... 201 569-7300
Englewood *(G-2889)*
Electro Magnetic Products Inc ....E....... 856 235-3011
Moorestown *(G-6521)*
Elray Manufacturing Company ....E....... 856 881-1935
Glassboro *(G-3810)*
Stampex Corp ....F....... 973 839-4040
Haskell *(G-4202)*
STS Technologies LLC ....F....... 973 277-5416
Mahwah *(G-5778)*
Tryco Tool & Mfg Co Inc ....E....... 973 674-6867
Orange *(G-7764)*

DIES & TOOLS: *Special*

A K Stamping Co Inc ....D....... 908 232-7300
Mountainside *(G-6831)*
Accurate Machine & Tool Co ....G....... 908 245-5545
Roselle Park *(G-9577)*
Accurate Tool & Die Co Inc ....G....... 201 476-9348
Montvale *(G-6394)*
Algene Marking Equipment Co ....G....... 973 478-9041
Garfield *(G-3727)*
B E C Mfg Corp ....E....... 201 414-0000
Glen Rock *(G-3828)*
Bach Tool Precision Inc ....G....... 973 962-6224
Ringwood *(G-9343)*
Bihler of America Inc ....C....... 908 213-9001
Phillipsburg *(G-8546)*
Bodine Tool and Machine Co Inc ....E....... 856 234-7800
Moorestown *(G-6509)*
Boyle Tool & Die Co Inc ....F....... 856 853-1819
West Deptford *(G-11694)*

Brisar Industries Inc ....D....... 973 278-2500
Paterson *(G-8150)*
C & K Punch & Screw Mch Pdts ....G....... 201 343-6750
Hackensack *(G-3888)*
Cavalla Inc ....E....... 201 343-3338
Hackensack *(G-3895)*
Charles E Green & Son Inc ....E....... 973 485-3630
Newark *(G-7082)*
City Diecutting Inc ....F....... 973 270-0370
Morristown *(G-6653)*
Die Tech LLC ....G....... 201 343-8324
Hackensack *(G-3907)*
Duerr Tool & Die Co Inc ....C....... 908 810-9035
Union *(G-11044)*
Dura-Carb Inc ....G....... 973 697-6665
Oak Ridge *(G-7601)*
Dynamic Die Cutting & Finshg ....F....... 973 589-8338
Newark *(G-7109)*
F & G Tool & Die Inc ....G....... 908 241-5880
Kenilworth *(G-4938)*
Garden State Precision Inc ....G....... 201 945-6410
Ridgefield *(G-9262)*
Globe Die-Cutting Products Inc ....C....... 732 494-7744
Metuchen *(G-6057)*
Golden Rule Inc ....G....... 856 663-3074
Pennsauken *(G-8425)*
H-E Tool & Mfg Co Inc ....E....... 856 303-8787
Cinnaminson *(G-1461)*
Hofmann Tool & Die Corporation ....G....... 201 327-0226
Upper Saddle River *(G-11140)*
Infor Metal & Tooling Mfg ....F....... 973 571-9520
Cedar Grove *(G-1279)*
Inventors Shop LLC ....E....... 856 303-8787
Cinnaminson *(G-1466)*
Jmk Tool Die and Mfg Co Inc ....G....... 201 845-4710
Rochelle Park *(G-9425)*
Jordan Manufacturing LLC ....G....... 973 383-8363
Lafayette *(G-5029)*
L & Z Tool and Engineering Inc ....E....... 908 322-2220
Watchung *(G-11456)*
Olympic EDM Services Inc ....G....... 973 492-0664
Kinnelon *(G-5020)*
Omega Tool Die ....G....... 856 228-7100
Sewell *(G-9852)*
Peterson Steel Rule Die Corp ....F....... 201 935-6180
Carlstadt *(G-1200)*
Philip Creter Inc ....G....... 908 686-2910
Union *(G-11083)*
Printco ....G....... 908 687-9518
Flemington *(G-3464)*
Progressive Tool & Mfg Corp ....G....... 908 245-7010
Kenilworth *(G-4972)*
Rebuth Metal Services ....F....... 908 889-6400
Fanwood *(G-3373)*
Rex Tool & Manufacturing Inc ....G....... 908 925-2727
Linden *(G-5415)*
Thomson Lamination Co Inc ....D....... 856 779-8521
Maple Shade *(G-5872)*
Vantage Tool & Mfg Inc ....G....... 908 647-1010
Warren *(G-11435)*
Victory Tool & Mfg Co ....G....... 973 759-8733
Belleville *(G-322)*
Vmc Die Cutting Corp ....F....... 973 450-4655
Belleville *(G-323)*

DIES: *Cutting, Exc Metal*

Danielle Die Cut Products Inc ....E....... 973 278-3000
Paterson *(G-8167)*
Grobet File Company Amer LLC ....D....... 201 939-6700
Carlstadt *(G-1161)*

DIES: *Extrusion*

Alloy Cast Products Inc ....F....... 908 245-2255
Kenilworth *(G-4920)*
Custom Extrusion Tech Inc ....F....... 732 367-5511
Lakewood *(G-5078)*

DIES: *Paper Cutting*

21st Century Finishing Inc ....E....... 201 797-0212
Clifton *(G-1550)*
Turul Bookbindery Inc ....G....... 973 361-2810
Wharton *(G-11874)*

DIES: *Plastic Forming*

Hartmann Tool Co Inc ....G....... 201 343-8700
Hackensack *(G-3926)*
Orycon Control Technology Inc ....E....... 732 922-2400
Ocean *(G-7670)*

P
R
O
D
U
C
T

DIES: Steel Rule

Edgar C Barcus Co Inc ....F 856 456-0204
Westville (G-11813)
Kessler Steel Rule Die Inc ....G 856 767-0231
West Berlin (G-11602)
Lasercam LLc ....E 201 941-1262
Ridgefield (G-9273)
Pin Point Container Corp ....G 856 848-2115
Deptford (G-2065)
Quality Die Shop Inc ....G 732 787-0041
North Middletown (G-7504)
Redkeys Dies Inc ....G 856 456-7890
Gloucester City (G-3850)
Spec Steel Rule Dies Inc ....E 609 443-4435
Windsor (G-11999)
Zin-Tech Inc ....E 856 661-0900
Pennsauken (G-8499)

DIES: Wire Drawing & Straightening

United Die Company Inc ....E 201 997-0250
Kearny (G-4902)

DIFFERENTIAL ASSEMBLIES & PARTS

NAPA Concepts Ltd Liability Co ....G 201 673-2381
North Bergen (G-7424)
Transaxle LLC ....C 856 665-4445
Cinnaminson (G-1492)

DIODES & RECTIFIERS

Harrison Electro Mechanical ....F 732 382-6008
Rahway (G-9100)
Intense Inc ....E 732 249-2228
North Brunswick (G-7471)

DIODES: Light Emitting

Acolyte Technologies Corp ....G 212 629-3239
Perth Amboy (G-8510)
Imperial Copy Products Inc ....E 973 927-5500
Randolph (G-9186)
Liberty Cnstr & Inv Group ....G 267 784-7931
Cherry Hill (G-1383)
Universal Display Corporation ....C 609 671-0980
Ewing (G-3073)

DIORITE: Crushed & Broken

Kop Marble Granite Inc ....G 973 283-8000
Wayne (G-11529)

DIRECT SELLING ESTABLISHMENTS, NEC

Compco Analytical Inc ....G 201 641-3936
Little Ferry (G-5480)

DIRECT SELLING ESTABLISHMENTS: Bakery Goods, House-To-House

Portuguese Baking Company Inc ....G 973 466-0118
Newark (G-7231)

DIRECT SELLING ESTABLISHMENTS: Beverage Svcs

McT Dairies Inc ....F 973 258-9600
Millburn (G-6203)

DIRECT SELLING ESTABLISHMENTS: Drapes/Curtains,Door-To-Door

A Plus Installs LLC ....G 201 255-4412
Bloomfield (G-488)

DIRECT SELLING ESTABLISHMENTS: Snacks

Ziggy Snack Foods LLC ....E 917 662-6038
Clifton (G-1744)

DISCOUNT DEPARTMENT STORES

Marmaxx Operating Corp ....D 973 575-7910
West Caldwell (G-11660)

DISCS & TAPE: Optical, Blank

Sony Corporation of America ....B 201 930-1000
Paramus (G-7834)

DISHWASHING EQPT: Commercial

Hobart Sales and Service Inc ....E 973 227-9265
Fairfield (G-3229)

DISK & DISKETTE EQPT, EXC DRIVES

Audio Dynamix Inc ....F 201 567-5488
Englewood (G-2879)
EVs Broadcast Equipment Inc ....F 973 575-7811
Fairfield (G-3194)

DISK DRIVES: Computer

Western Digital Corporation ....G 609 734-7479
Princeton (G-9042)

DISKETTE DUPLICATING SVCS

Strategic Content Imaging ....C 201 863-8100
Secaucus (G-9819)
US Software Group Inc ....E 732 361-4636
South Plainfield (G-10337)

DISPENSERS: Soap

Inopak Ltd ....F 973 962-1121
Ringwood (G-9347)

DISPENSING EQPT & PARTS, BEVERAGE: Coolers, Milk/Water, Elec

Walter Machine Co Inc ....E 201 656-5654
Jersey City (G-4829)

DISPENSING EQPT & PARTS, BEVERAGE: Fountain/Other Beverage

Krowne Metal Corp ....E 973 305-3300
Wayne (G-11530)
Sodastream USA Inc ....D 856 755-3400
Mount Laurel (G-6808)

DISPLAY FIXTURES: Wood

Acro Display Inc ....E 215 229-1100
Pennsauken (G-8382)
Banner Design Inc ....E 908 687-5335
Hillside (G-4379)
Bossen Architectural Millwork ....F 856 786-1100
Cinnaminson (G-1444)
Capital Contracting & Design ....E 908 561-8411
Plainfield (G-8760)
Design Display Group Inc ....C 201 438-6000
Carlstadt (G-1150)
Level Designs Group LLC ....G 973 761-1675
South Orange (G-10198)

DISPLAY ITEMS: Corrugated, Made From Purchased Materials

Menasha Packaging Company LLC ....C 973 893-1300
Lyndhurst (G-5664)
Package Development Co Inc ....E 973 983-8500
Rockaway (G-9483)
Pratt Industries USA Inc ....D 201 934-1900
Allendale (G-13)

DISPLAY ITEMS: Solid Fiber, Made From Purchased Materials

Algar/Display Connection Corp ....D 201 438-1000
Garfield (G-3726)
Cases By Source Inc ....E 201 831-0005
Mahwah (G-5720)
Level Designs Group LLC ....G 973 761-1675
South Orange (G-10198)

DISPLAY LETTERING SVCS

Monogram Center Inc ....E 732 442-1800
Perth Amboy (G-8528)

DISPLAY STANDS: Merchandise, Exc Wood

Metaline Products Company Inc ....E 732 721-1373
South Amboy (G-10137)
Mpm Display Inc ....G 973 374-3477
Hillside (G-4416)
V M Display ....F 973 365-8027
Passaic (G-8112)

DOCK EQPT & SPLYS, INDL

American Process Systems ....G 908 216-6781
Port Murray (G-8880)
Custom Docks Inc ....F 973 948-3732
Sandyston (G-9699)
Technology General Corporation ....F 973 827-8209
Franklin (G-3609)

DOCUMENT EMBOSSING SVCS

Windmill Press Inc ....G 856 663-8990
Pennsauken (G-8497)

DOLOMITIC MARBLE: Crushed & Broken

Tilcon New York Inc ....D 800 789-7625
Kearny (G-4901)

DOOR & WINDOW REPAIR SVCS

Frank & Jims Inc ....G 609 646-1655
Pleasantville (G-8811)
Miric Industries Inc ....F 201 864-0233
North Bergen (G-7422)
Pierangeli Group Inc ....G 856 582-4060
Gloucester City (G-3847)

DOOR FRAMES: Wood

Rsl LLC ....D 609 484-1600
Egg Harbor Township (G-2695)
Rsl LLC ....E 609 645-9777
Egg Harbor Township (G-2696)
USA Wood Door Inc ....E 856 384-9663
West Deptford (G-11717)

DOOR OPERATING SYSTEMS: Electric

Assa Abloy Entrance Sys US Inc ....E 609 443-5800
Trenton (G-10897)
Assa Abloy Entrance Systems US ....E 609 528-2580
Hamilton (G-4103)
Chamberlain Group Inc ....G 201 472-4200
Whippany (G-11885)
Total Garage Solutions LLC ....E 732 749-3993
Wall Township (G-11375)

DOORS & WINDOWS WHOLESALERS: All Materials

Babbitt Mfg Co Inc ....F 856 692-3245
Vineland (G-11190)
Door Center Enterprises Inc ....G 609 333-1233
Hopewell (G-4526)
Dreamstar Construction LLC ....F 732 393-2572
Middletown (G-6162)
Passaic Metal & Bldg Sups Co ....D 973 546-9000
Clifton (G-1685)

DOORS & WINDOWS: Storm, Metal

Dor-Win Manufacturing Co ....E 201 796-4300
Elmwood Park (G-2821)
Royal Aluminum Co Inc ....D 973 589-8880
Newark (G-7253)
Surburban Building Pdts Inc ....E 732 901-8900
Howell (G-4551)
Taylor Windows Inc ....F 973 672-3000
East Orange (G-2264)
Window Shapes Inc ....D 732 549-0708
Metuchen (G-6081)

DOORS: Fire, Metal

Allmark Door Company LLC ....F 610 358-9800
Springfield (G-10425)

DOORS: Folding, Plastic Or Plastic Coated Fabric

Dor-Win Manufacturing Co ....E 201 796-4300
Elmwood Park (G-2821)
Innova Group Inc ....G 856 696-1053
Vineland (G-11235)

DOORS: Garage, Overhead, Metal

Gray Overhead Door Co ....F 908 355-3889
Elizabeth (G-2744)
Lebanon Door LLC ....G 908 236-2620
Lebanon (G-5269)
Portaseal LLC ....G 973 539-0100
Morristown (G-6695)

DOORS: Garage, Overhead, Wood

Total Garage Solutions LLC ....E 732 749-3993
Wall Township *(G-11375)*

DOORS: Glass

Century Bathworks Inc ....D 973 785-4290
Woodland Park *(G-12074)*

Klein Usa Inc ....F 973 246-8181
East Rutherford *(G-2294)*

Pike Machine Products Inc ....D 973 379-9128
Short Hills *(G-9874)*

DOORS: Rolling, Indl Building Or Warehouse, Metal

Guardrite Steel Door Corp ....G 973 481-4424
Newark *(G-7142)*

DOORS: Screen, Metal

Century Bathworks Inc ....D 973 785-4290
Woodland Park *(G-12074)*

DOORS: Wooden

Bildisco Mfg Inc ....F 973 673-2400
West Orange *(G-11762)*

Door Stop LLC ....F 718 599-5112
Carlstadt *(G-1153)*

Hahns Woodworking ....F 908 722-2742
Branchburg *(G-645)*

Manhattan Door Corp ....D 718 963-1111
Carlstadt *(G-1184)*

RPI Industries Inc ....D 609 714-2330
Medford *(G-6033)*

Smittys Door Service Inc ....G 908 284-0506
Pittstown *(G-8755)*

W F Sherman & Son Inc ....F 732 223-1505
Manasquan *(G-5842)*

DRAINING OR PUMPING OF METAL MINES

Demaio Inc ....E 609 965-4094
Egg Harbor City *(G-2657)*

DRAPERIES & CURTAINS

Ackerson Drapery Decorator Svc ....G 732 797-1967
Lakewood *(G-5045)*

Alan Schatzberg & Associates ....F 201 440-8855
South Hackensack *(G-10148)*

Colonial Uphl & Win Treatments ....G 609 641-3124
Pleasantville *(G-8808)*

Comfort Concepts Inc ....G 201 941-6700
Ridgefield *(G-9256)*

Gordon Frgson Intr Dsigns Svcs ....G 973 378-2330
Maplewood *(G-5877)*

Interior Art & Design Inc ....E 201 488-8855
Hackensack *(G-3931)*

Master Drapery Workroom Inc ....F 908 272-4404
Kenilworth *(G-4956)*

Nassaus Window Fashions Inc ....E 201 689-6030
Paramus *(G-7824)*

W Gerriets International Inc ....F 609 771-8111
Ewing *(G-3077)*

DRAPERIES & DRAPERY FABRICS, COTTON

Bai Lar Interior Services Inc ....G 732 738-0350
Fords *(G-3530)*

Proclean Services Inc ....F 973 857-5408
Verona *(G-11172)*

DRAPERIES: Plastic & Textile, From Purchased Materials

Beatrice Home Fashions Inc ....E 908 561-7370
South Plainfield *(G-10225)*

Dru Whitacre Media Svcs Ltd ....D 201 770-9950
North Bergen *(G-7402)*

Forsters Cleaning & Tailoring ....G 201 659-4411
Jersey City *(G-4740)*

Kushner Draperies Mfg LLC ....E 856 317-9696
Pennsauken *(G-8449)*

Metro Mills Inc ....E 973 942-6034
Paterson *(G-8257)*

Stessl & Neugebauer Inc ....F 908 277-3340
Summit *(G-10549)*

DRAPERY & UPHOLSTERY STORES: Curtains

Curtain Care Plus Inc ....G 800 845-6155
Clifton *(G-1594)*

Nassau Window Fashions Inc ....E 201 689-6030
Paramus *(G-7824)*

DRAPERY & UPHOLSTERY STORES: Draperies

Decorating With Fabric Inc ....G 845 352-5064
Park Ridge *(G-7847)*

Window 25 LLC ....G 973 817-9464
Newark *(G-7316)*

DRILL BITS

Ram Products Inc ....G 732 651-5500
Dayton *(G-1985)*

DRINK MIXES, NONALCOHOLIC: Cocktail

201 Food Packing Inc ....F 973 463-0777
East Hanover *(G-2192)*

DRINKING PLACES: Alcoholic Beverages

Medieval Times USA Inc ....C 201 933-2220
Lyndhurst *(G-5662)*

DRINKING PLACES: Tavern

Summerlands Inc ....E 973 729-8428
Sparta *(G-10408)*

DRIVES: High Speed Indl, Exc Hydrostatic

Numeritool Manufacturing Corp ....G 973 827-7714
Franklin *(G-3607)*

Sew-Eurodrive Inc ....E 856 467-2277
Bridgeport *(G-744)*

DRUG STORES

140 Main Street Corp ....F 732 974-2929
Sea Girt *(G-9744)*

Boyds Pharmacy Inc ....F 609 499-0100
Florence *(G-3473)*

K & S Drug & Surgical Inc ....G 201 886-9191
Fort Lee *(G-3566)*

Little Falls Shop Rite Super ....B 973 256-0909
Little Falls *(G-5460)*

Njs Associates Company ....G 973 960-8688
Bridgewater *(G-858)*

Pdr Equity LLC ....D 201 358-7200
Whippany *(G-11902)*

Walgreen Eastern Co Inc ....E 973 728-3172
West Milford *(G-11733)*

Walgreen Eastern Co Inc ....E 609 522-1291
Wildwood *(G-11947)*

DRUGGIST'S SUNDRIES: Rubber

Datwyler Pharma Packaging ....E 856 663-2202
Pennsauken *(G-8410)*

DRUGS & DRUG PROPRIETARIES, WHOL: Biologicals/Allied Prdts

Difco Laboratories Inc ....G 410 316-4113
Franklin Lakes *(G-3619)*

Paw Bioscience Products LLC ....G 732 460-0088
Eatontown *(G-2416)*

DRUGS & DRUG PROPRIETARIES, WHOLESALE

Acetris Health LLC ....G 201 961-9000
Saddle Brook *(G-9639)*

Aliron International Inc ....E 540 808-1615
South Plainfield *(G-10210)*

Arcadia Consmr Healthcare Inc ....F 800 824-4894
Bridgewater *(G-791)*

Exeltis Usa Inc ....D 973 324-0200
Florham Park *(G-3503)*

Genzyme Corporation ....G 973 256-2106
Totowa *(G-10829)*

Rising Health LLC ....E 201 961-9000
Saddle Brook *(G-9673)*

Rising Pharma Holdings Inc ....G 201 961-9000
Saddle Brook *(G-9674)*

Rising Pharmaceuticals Inc ....E 201 961-9000
Saddle Brook *(G-9675)*

DRUGS & DRUG PROPRIETARIES, WHOLESALE: Animal Medicines

Merck & Co Inc ....B 908 740-4000
Kenilworth *(G-4957)*

Merck & Co Inc ....D 908 740-4000
Rahway *(G-9117)*

DRUGS & DRUG PROPRIETARIES, WHOLESALE: Biotherapeutics

Avalon Globocare Corp ....G 732 780-4400
Freehold *(G-3650)*

DRUGS & DRUG PROPRIETARIES, WHOLESALE: Medicinals/Botanicals

Herborium Group Inc ....G 201 849-4431
Fort Lee *(G-3560)*

Ivy-Dry Inc ....G 973 575-1992
Fairfield *(G-3242)*

DRUGS & DRUG PROPRIETARIES, WHOLESALE: Pharmaceuticals

Actavis LLC ....D 732 947-5300
Edison *(G-2447)*

Actavis LLC ....B 862 261-7000
Madison *(G-5686)*

Aeterna Zentaris Inc ....G 908 626-5428
Warren *(G-11397)*

Amneal Pharmaceuticals LLC ....F 908 947-3120
Piscataway *(G-8632)*

Amneal Pharmaceuticals LLC ....E 908 231-1911
Branchburg *(G-619)*

Camber Pharmaceuticals Inc ....E 732 529-0430
Piscataway *(G-8641)*

Central Admxture Phrm Svcs Inc ....E 201 541-0080
Englewood *(G-2892)*

D&E Nutraceuticals Inc ....E 212 235-5200
Farmingdale *(G-3383)*

Dr Reddys Laboratories Inc ....E 609 375-9900
Princeton *(G-8933)*

Ezrirx LLC ....G 718 502-6610
Lakewood *(G-5096)*

Ferring Pharmaceuticals Inc ....C 973 796-1600
Parsippany *(G-7944)*

Ino Therapeutics LLC ....D 908 238-6600
Bedminster *(G-266)*

Klus Pharma Inc ....F 609 662-1913
Cranbury *(G-1850)*

Leading Pharma LLC ....E 201 746-9160
Montvale *(G-6419)*

Leo Pharma Inc ....B 973 637-1690
Madison *(G-5697)*

Magnifica Inc ....G 323 202-0386
Cranbury *(G-1861)*

Medimtriks Pharmaceuticals Inc ....E 973 882-7512
Fairfield *(G-3267)*

Odin Pharmaceuticals LLC ....G 732 554-1100
Somerset *(G-10042)*

Parker Labs ....G 973 276-9500
Fairfield *(G-3290)*

Patheon Biologics LLC ....D 609 919-3300
Princeton *(G-8993)*

Pernix Therapeutics LLC ....E 800 793-2145
Morristown *(G-6692)*

Pharmatech International Inc ....F 973 244-0393
Fairfield *(G-3291)*

Phytoceuticals Inc ....G 201 791-2255
Elmwood Park *(G-2850)*

Sandoz Inc ....C 609 627-8500
Princeton *(G-9019)*

Strive Pharmaceuticals Inc ....G 609 269-2001
East Brunswick *(G-2182)*

Taro Pharmaceuticals USA Inc ....E 609 655-9002
Cranbury *(G-1886)*

Vertice Pharma LLC ....E 877 530-1633
New Providence *(G-7024)*

Vgyaan Pharmaceuticals LLC ....G 609 452-2770
Skillman *(G-9927)*

Windtree Therapeutics Inc ....F 973 339-2889
Totowa *(G-10863)*

PRODUCT

DRUGS & DRUG PROPRIETARIES, WHOLESALE: Vitamins & Minerals

Icelandirect Inc ....F 800 763-4690
Clifton *(G-1638)*

Reliance Vitamin LLC ....C ...., 732 537-1220
Edison *(G-2596)*

Vitaquest International LLC ....F 973 575-9200
Fairfield *(G-3346)*

Vitaquest International LLC ....B 973 575-9200
West Caldwell *(G-11681)*

DRUGS ACTING ON THE CENTRAL NERVOUS SYSTEM & SENSE ORGANS

Allergan Inc ....D 908 306-0374
Bedminster *(G-259)*

Allergan Inc ....G 862 261-7000
Morristown *(G-6631)*

Cormedix Inc ....G 908 517-9500
Berkeley Heights *(G-396)*

DRUGS AFFECTING NEOPLASMS & ENDOCRINE SYSTEMS

Bayer Hlthcare Phrmcticals Inc ....A 862 404-3000
Whippany *(G-11879)*

Bayer Hlthcare Phrmcticals Inc ....E 973 709-3545
Wayne *(G-11475)*

Bayer Hlthcare Phrmcticals Inc ....A 862 404-3000
Whippany *(G-11880)*

Pharmion Corporation ....E 908 673-9000
Summit *(G-10543)*

Schering Berlin Inc ....G 862 404-3000
Whippany *(G-11908)*

DRUGS: Parasitic & Infective Disease Affecting

Immtech Pharmaceuticals Inc ....E 212 791-2911
Montclair *(G-6370)*

Leo Pharma Inc ....B 973 637-1690
Madison *(G-5697)*

DRUMS: Brake

Momentum Usa Inc ....F 844 300-1553
Edison *(G-2569)*

DRUMS: Fiber

Tunnel Barrel & Drum Co Inc ....E 201 933-1444
Carlstadt *(G-1233)*

DRYCLEANING EQPT & SPLYS: Commercial

Multimatic LLC ....G 201 767-9660
Northvale *(G-7539)*

DRYCLEANING SVC: Collecting & Distributing Agency

Forsters Cleaning & Tailoring ....G 201 659-4411
Jersey City *(G-4740)*

DRYCLEANING SVC: Drapery & Curtain

Astra Cleaners of Hazlet ....G 732 264-4144
Hazlet *(G-4257)*

Proclean Services Inc ....F 973 857-5408
Verona *(G-11172)*

DRYERS & REDRYERS: Indl

Hary Manufacturing Inc ....F 908 722-7100
Woodbridge *(G-12018)*

Lydon Bros Corp ....E 201 343-4334
South Hackensack *(G-10169)*

Marsden Inc ....E 856 663-2227
Pennsauken *(G-8452)*

Wyssmont Company Inc ....E 201 947-4600
Fort Lee *(G-3596)*

DRYERS: Textile

Cire Technologies Inc ....G 973 402-8301
Mountain Lakes *(G-6821)*

DUCTING: Metal Plate

Nova Flex Group ....F 856 768-2275
West Berlin *(G-11611)*

DUCTING: Plastic

Du Technologies Inc ....F 201 729-0070
Moonachie *(G-6463)*

Endot Industries Inc ....D 973 625-8500
Rockaway *(G-9456)*

DUCTS: Sheet Metal

Air Distribution Systems Inc ....E 856 874-1100
Cherry Hill *(G-1336)*

Air Power Inc ....E 973 882-5418
Fairfield *(G-3136)*

Ducts Inc ....G 973 267-8482
Morris Plains *(G-6604)*

M C Custom Shtmtl Fabrication ....G 856 767-9509
West Berlin *(G-11606)*

Par Troy Sheet Metal & AC LLC ....G 973 227-1150
Fairfield *(G-3288)*

PTL Sheet Metal Inc ....G 201 501-8700
Dumont *(G-2117)*

T J Eckardt Associates Inc ....F 856 767-4111
Berlin *(G-430)*

DUMPSTERS: Garbage

Billy D Dumpster Service LLC ....G 609 465-5990
Cape May Court House *(G-1107)*

Rudco Products Inc ....D 856 691-0800
Vineland *(G-11261)*

Wastequip Manufacturing Co ....D 856 784-5500
Sicklerville *(G-9917)*

Wastequip Manufacturing Co LLC ......E 856 629-9222
Williamstown *(G-11986)*

DUST OR FUME COLLECTING EQPT: Indl

Buhler Inc ....E 201 847-0600
Mahwah *(G-5719)*

Sternvent Co Inc ....E 908 688-0807
Union *(G-11092)*

DYE INTERMEDIATES: Cyclic

French Color Fragrance Co Inc ....E 201 567-6883
Englewood *(G-2907)*

DYES & PIGMENTS: Organic

Carib Chemical Co Inc ....F 201 791-6700
Elmwood Park *(G-2814)*

Carib Chemical Co Inc ....F 201 791-6700
Elmwood Park *(G-2815)*

Coloron Plastics Corporation ....E 908 685-1210
Branchburg *(G-631)*

Epolin Chemical LLC ....G 973 465-9495
Newark *(G-7118)*

Greenville Colorants LLC ....F 201 595-0200
New Brunswick *(G-6931)*

Magruder Color Company Inc ....C 817 837-3293
Holmdel *(G-4505)*

Orient Corporation of America ....G 908 298-0990
Cranford *(G-1920)*

Polymathes Holdings I LLC ....G 609 945-1690
Princeton *(G-8996)*

Primex Color Compounding ....E 800 282-7933
Garfield *(G-3758)*

Riverdale Color Mfg Inc ....E 732 376-9300
Perth Amboy *(G-8531)*

Shelan Chemical Company Inc ....G 732 796-1003
Monroe Township *(G-6343)*

DYES OR COLORS: Food, Synthetic

SPS Alfachem Inc ....E 973 676-5141
Orange *(G-7762)*

William R Tatz Industries ....G 973 751-0720
Belleville *(G-325)*

DYES: Synthetic Organic

American Chemical & Coating Co ....G 908 353-2260
Elizabeth *(G-2711)*

Fabricolor Holding Intl LLC ....G 973 742-5800
Paterson *(G-8189)*

Honeyware Inc ....D 201 997-5900
Kearny *(G-4863)*

DYESTUFFS WHOLESALERS

Carib Chemical Co Inc ....F 201 791-6700
Elmwood Park *(G-2815)*

EATING PLACES

Atlantic City Week ....F 609 646-4848
Pleasantville *(G-8805)*

Bagel Street ....E 609 936-1755
Plainsboro *(G-8780)*

Berat Corporation ....C 609 953-7700
Medford *(G-6020)*

Comarco Products Inc ....D 856 342-7557
Camden *(G-1053)*

Cravings ....F 732 531-7122
Allenhurst *(G-21)*

Elis Hot Bagels Inc ....E 732 566-4523
Matawan *(G-5975)*

Food Circus Super Markets Inc ....D 732 291-4079
Atlantic Highlands *(G-106)*

Hsh Assoc Financial Publishers ....G 973 838-3330
Butler *(G-1004)*

Hue Box LLC ....G 908 904-9501
Bridgewater *(G-831)*

Limpert Brothers Inc ....E 856 691-1353
Vineland *(G-11241)*

Lrk Inc ....F 609 924-6881
Princeton *(G-8970)*

Medieval Times USA Inc ....C 201 933-2220
Lyndhurst *(G-5662)*

Muirhead Ringoes NJ Inc ....G 609 695-7803
Trenton *(G-10959)*

Nuchas Tsq LLC ....F 212 913-9682
North Bergen *(G-7426)*

Ruggiero Sea Food Inc ....D 973 589-0524
Newark *(G-7254)*

Ruggiero Sea Food Inc ....G 973 589-0524
Newark *(G-7255)*

Springdale Farm Market Inc ....E 856 424-8674
Cherry Hill *(G-1416)*

Tomasello Winery Inc ....F 609 561-0567
Hammonton *(G-4145)*

Universal Interlock Corp ....G 732 818-8484
Toms River *(G-10801)*

EDUCATIONAL SVCS

Sunrise Intl Educatn Inc ....D 917 525-0272
North Brunswick *(G-7489)*

EDUCATIONAL SVCS, NONDEGREE GRANTING: Continuing Education

Encore Enterprises Inc ....G 201 489-5044
South Hackensack *(G-10158)*

Jannetti Publications ....D 856 256-2300
Sewell *(G-9849)*

ELASTIC BRAID & NARROW WOVEN FABRICS

Sullivan-Carson Inc ....G 856 566-1400
Voorhees *(G-11294)*

ELECTRIC & OTHER SERVICES COMBINED

Foster Wheeler Zack Inc ....D 908 730-4000
Hampton *(G-4153)*

ELECTRIC MOTOR REPAIR SVCS

Absecon Electric Motor Works ....G 609 641-1523
Absecon *(G-1)*

Atlantic Kenmark Electric Inc ....F 201 991-2117
North Arlington *(G-7369)*

Atlantic Switch Generator LLC ....F 609 518-1900
Hainesport *(G-4069)*

D Electric Motors Inc ....G 856 696-5959
Vineland *(G-11210)*

Electrical Motor Repr Co of NJ ....F 609 392-6149
Trenton *(G-10934)*

General Electric Company ....C 201 866-2161
North Bergen *(G-7406)*

Jarvis Electric Motors Inc ....G 856 662-7710
Pennsauken *(G-8444)*

Lakewood Elc Mtr Sls & Svc ....G 732 363-2865
Howell *(G-4545)*

Lockwoods Electric Motor Svc ....E 609 587-2333
Trenton *(G-10953)*

Longo Elctrical-Mechanical Inc ....E 973 537-0400
Linden *(G-5377)*

Lowder Electric and Cnstr ....G 732 764-6000
Middlesex *(G-6128)*

McIntosh Industries Inc ....E 908 688-7475
Hillside *(G-4415)*

Motors and Drives Inc ....G...... 732 462-7683
  Freehold (G-3681)
Motors and Drives Inc ....G...... 609 344-8058
  Atlantic City (G-98)
Mt Salem Electric Co Inc ....F...... 908 735-6126
  Pittstown (G-8754)
New Jersey Electric Motors ....G...... 908 526-5225
  Somerville (G-10121)
Phil Desiere Electric Mtr Svc .....F...... 856 692-8442
  Vineland (G-11251)
Precision Devices Inc ....G...... 609 882-2230
  Ewing (G-3054)
RSI Company ....G...... 973 227-7800
  Fairfield (G-3304)
SMS Electric Motor Car LLC ......F...... 215 428-2502
  Bridgewater (G-890)
Story Electric Mtr Repr Co Inc ...G...... 973 256-1636
  Little Falls (G-5469)
Universal Electric Mtr Svc Inc ....E...... 201 968-1000
  Hackensack (G-3988)
Willier Elc Mtr Repr Co Inc ....E...... 856 627-2262
  Gibbsboro (G-3797)
Willier Elc Mtr Repr Co Inc ....E...... 856 627-3535
  Gibbsboro (G-3796)

ELECTRIC SERVICES

C J Electric ....G...... 201 891-0739
  Wyckoff (G-12106)
General Electric Company ....C...... 201 866-2161
  North Bergen (G-7406)
Lb Electric Co - North LLC ....G...... 973 366-2188
  Denville (G-2044)

ELECTRIC SVCS, NEC: Power Generation

Ocean Power Technologies Inc ....E...... 609 730-0400
  Monroe Township (G-6339)

ELECTRIC TOOL REPAIR SVCS

Kissler & Co Inc ....E...... 201 896-9600
  Carlstadt (G-1175)

ELECTRICAL APPARATUS & EQPT WHOLESALERS

Ademco Inc ....G...... 732 505-6688
  Toms River (G-10739)
Ademco Inc ....F...... 201 462-9570
  Teterboro (G-10670)
Ademco Inc ....G...... 908 561-1888
  South Plainfield (G-10207)
Ademco Inc ....G...... 856 985-9050
  Marlton (G-5921)
Ademco Inc ....G...... 973 808-8233
  Fairfield (G-3134)
America Techma Inc ....G...... 201 894-5887
  Englewood Cliffs (G-2958)
Antronix Inc ....E...... 609 860-0160
  Cranbury (G-1812)
Archtech Electronics Corp ....E...... 732 355-1288
  Dayton (G-1951)
Asco Power Technologies LP ......F...... 732 596-1733
  Woodbridge (G-12013)
Belden Inc ....F...... 908 925-8000
  Elizabeth (G-2714)
Cabletenna Corp ....G...... 609 395-9400
  Cranbury (G-1818)
Cisco Systems Inc ....E...... 201 782-0842
  Montvale (G-6402)
D Electric Motors Inc ....G...... 856 696-5959
  Vineland (G-11210)
DMJ and Associates Inc ....E...... 732 613-7867
  Sayreville (G-9708)
Ellenby Technologies Inc ....E...... 856 848-2020
  Woodbury Heights (G-12042)
H I D Systems Inc ....G...... 973 383-8535
  Sparta (G-10390)
Kinetics Industries Inc ....E...... 609 883-9700
  Ewing (G-3040)
Lumiko USA Inc ....G...... 609 409-6900
  Cranbury (G-1860)
Mac Products Inc ....D...... 973 344-5149
  Kearny (G-4880)
Maxlite Inc ....D...... 973 244-7300
  West Caldwell (G-11663)
Technology Dynamics Inc ....D...... 201 385-0500
  Bergenfield (G-385)
YC Cable (east) Inc ....E...... 732 868-0800
  Piscataway (G-8739)

ELECTRICAL APPLIANCES, TELEVISIONS & RADIOS WHOLESALERS

Expert Appliance Center LLC ......G...... 732 946-0999
  Marlboro (G-5897)
Haier America Trading LLC ....G...... 212 594-3330
  Woodbridge (G-12017)
L&W Audio/Video Inc ....E...... 212 980-2862
  Hoboken (G-4463)
Sharp Electronics Corporation ....A...... 201 529-8200
  Montvale (G-6433)
W T Winter Associates Inc ....E...... 888 808-3611
  Fairfield (G-3350)
Wanasavealotcom LLC ....F...... 732 286-6956
  Toms River (G-10802)

ELECTRICAL CURRENT CARRYING WIRING DEVICES

Ametek Inc ....G...... 732 370-9100
  Lakewood (G-5052)
Amperite Co Inc ....E...... 201 864-9503
  North Bergen (G-7384)
Archtech Electronics Corp ....E...... 732 355-1288
  Dayton (G-1951)
Beall Technologies Inc ....E...... 201 689-2130
  Wyckoff (G-12104)
Billows Electric Supply Co Inc .....C...... 856 751-2200
  Delran (G-2009)
Brim Electronics Inc ....F...... 201 796-2886
  Lodi (G-5555)
Cain Machine Inc ....F...... 856 825-7225
  Millville (G-6240)
Calculagraph Co ....C...... 973 887-9400
  East Hanover (G-2198)
Dearborn A Belden Cdt Company ..D...... 908 925-8000
  Elizabeth (G-2726)
Frc Electrical Industries Inc ....E...... 908 464-3200
  New Providence (G-7000)
G H Krauss Manufacturing Co ......G...... 856 662-0815
  Cherry Hill (G-1365)
Hofer Connectors Co Inc ....E...... 973 427-1195
  North Haledon (G-7495)
Howman Electronics Inc ....F...... 908 534-2247
  Lebanon (G-5262)
HPH Products Inc ....G...... 609 883-0052
  Ewing (G-3037)
Kraus & Naimer Inc ....E...... 732 560-1240
  Somerset (G-10011)
Lumenarc Inc ....F...... 973 882-5918
  West Caldwell (G-11659)
Marine Electric Systems Inc ....E...... 201 531-8600
  South Hackensack (G-10171)
Multi-Tech Industries Inc ....F...... 732 431-0550
  Marlboro (G-5905)
Newtech Group Corp ....G...... 732 355-0392
  Kendall Park (G-4919)
Pekay Industries Inc ....F...... 732 938-2722
  Farmingdale (G-3390)
Pressure Controls Inc ....G...... 973 751-5002
  Belleville (G-308)
Richards Mfg Co Sales Inc ....E...... 973 371-1771
  Irvington (G-4586)
Roxboro Holdings Inc ....D...... 732 919-3119
  Wall Township (G-11365)
Rti Dge LLC ....F...... 732 254-6389
  Marlboro (G-5912)
Signal Systems International ....G...... 732 793-4668
  Lavallette (G-5212)
Tycom Limited ....C...... 973 753-3040
  Morristown (G-6704)
Unique Wire Weaving Co Inc ....E...... 908 688-4600
  Hillside (G-4433)
Vermont Cableworks Inc ....G...... 802 674-6555
  Edison (G-2639)

ELECTRICAL DEVICE PARTS: Porcelain, Molded

Electro-Ceramic Industries ....E...... 201 342-2630
  Hackensack (G-3911)

ELECTRICAL DISCHARGE MACHINING, EDM

Gale Newson Inc ....E...... 732 961-7610
  Jackson (G-4656)
Olympic EDM Services Inc ....G...... 973 492-0664
  Kinnelon (G-5020)

ELECTRICAL EQPT & SPLYS

Abacus Electric & Plumbing ....G...... 908 269-8057
  Chester (G-1430)
Ace Electric ....G...... 908 534-2404
  Somerville (G-10100)
Asco ....G...... 732 634-7017
  Woodbridge (G-12012)
Asco Power Technologies LP ......F...... 732 596-1733
  Woodbridge (G-12013)
Asco Power Technologies LP ......B...... 973 966-2000
  Florham Park (G-3484)
Avida Incorporated ....G...... 201 802-0749
  Park Ridge (G-7846)
Bio-Key International Inc ....E...... 732 359-1100
  Wall Township (G-11322)
C J Electric ....G...... 201 891-0739
  Wyckoff (G-12106)
Celco ....F...... 201 327-1123
  Mahwah (G-5721)
Commercial Pdts Svcs Group Inc ..G...... 609 730-4111
  Pennington (G-8362)
Connecting Products Inc ....F...... 609 512-1121
  Skillman (G-9918)
Crest Ultrasonics Corp ....G...... 609 883-4000
  Ewing (G-3023)
Cuny and Guerber Inc ....E...... 201 617-5800
  Union City (G-11109)
Daburn Wire & Cable Corp ....G...... 973 328-3200
  Dover (G-2081)
Daniel Maguire ....E...... 856 767-8443
  West Berlin (G-11589)
Dearborn A Belden Cdt Company ..D...... 908 925-8000
  Elizabeth (G-2726)
Dewey Electronics Corporation ....E...... 201 337-4700
  Oakland (G-7624)
Douglas Elec Components Inc ......D...... 973 627-8230
  Randolph (G-9175)
Dranetz Technologies Inc ....D...... 732 248-4358
  Edison (G-2493)
E-Beam Services Inc ....E...... 513 933-0031
  Cranbury (G-1831)
East Coast Panelboard Inc ....E...... 732 739-6400
  Tinton Falls (G-10713)
East West Service Co Inc ....E...... 609 631-9000
  Trenton (G-10933)
Eaton Corporation ....E...... 732 767-9600
  Mountainside (G-6844)
Edmondmarks Technologies Inc ...E...... 732 643-0290
  Neptune (G-6875)
Ellenby Technologies Inc ....E...... 856 848-2020
  Woodbury Heights (G-12042)
Eos Energy Storage LLC ....E...... 732 225-8400
  Edison (G-2505)
Essex Products International ....E...... 973 226-2424
  Caldwell (G-1024)
Francis Metals Company Inc ....F...... 732 761-0500
  Lakewood (G-5101)
Frc Electrical Industries Inc ....E...... 908 464-3200
  New Providence (G-7000)
H G Schaevitz LLC ....G...... 856 727-0250
  Moorestown (G-6526)
H I D Systems Inc ....G...... 973 383-8535
  Sparta (G-10390)
Henry Bros Electronics Inc ....D...... 201 794-6500
  Fair Lawn (G-3103)
Hitrons Tech Inc ....G...... 201 941-0024
  Ridgefield (G-9265)
I 2 R Corp ....G...... 732 919-1100
  Wall Township (G-11348)
Inter World Highway LLC ....F...... 732 759-8235
  Long Branch (G-5599)
International Cord Sets Inc ....F...... 973 227-2118
  Fairfield (G-3240)
Lb Electric Co - North LLC ....G...... 973 366-2188
  Denville (G-2044)
Maxlite Inc ....D...... 973 244-7300
  West Caldwell (G-11663)
Mphase Technologies Inc ....F...... 973 256-3737
  Clifton (G-1671)
MTS Systems Corporation ....A...... 856 875-4478
  Williamstown (G-11965)
Ocean Energy Industries Inc ....F...... 954 828-2177
  Oakhurst (G-7611)
OHM Equipment LLC ....G...... 856 765-3011
  Millville (G-6265)
Paige Electric Company LP ....E...... 908 687-7810
  Union (G-11080)
PCI Inc ....G...... 973 226-8007
  West Caldwell (G-11671)

PRODUCT

Power Brooks Co LLC ....F 609 890-0100
Hamilton *(G-4120)*

Primary Systems Inc ....F 732 679-2200
Old Bridge *(G-7725)*

Radnet Inc ....F 908 709-1323
Cranford *(G-1924)*

Repco Inc ....F 856 762-0172
Marlton *(G-5949)*

Vicmarr Audio Inc ....E 732 289-9111
Edison *(G-2641)*

Vision Ten Inc ....F 201 935-3000
Carlstadt *(G-1236)*

ELECTRICAL EQPT FOR ENGINES

Dearborn A Belden Cdt Company ....D 908 925-8000
Elizabeth *(G-2726)*

Dimilo Industries ....G 973 955-0460
Passaic *(G-8059)*

Dmf Associated Engines LLC ....G 973 535-9773
Livingston *(G-5510)*

Engine Factory Inc ....G 908 236-9915
Lebanon *(G-5259)*

Fleetsource LLC ....E 732 566-4970
Dayton *(G-1961)*

J & R Rebuilders Inc ....G 856 627-1414
Laurel Springs *(G-5207)*

M Parker Autoworks Inc ....E 856 933-0801
Bellmawr *(G-337)*

ELECTRICAL EQPT REPAIR & MAINTENANCE

ABC Digital Electronics Inc ....G 201 666-6888
Old Tappan *(G-7731)*

Binding Products Inc ....E 212 947-1192
Jersey City *(G-4704)*

Hansome Energy Systems Inc ....E 908 862-9044
Linden *(G-5354)*

McAllister Service Company ....E 856 665-4545
Pennsauken *(G-8453)*

Nilsson Electrical Laboratory ....G 201 521-4860
Jersey City *(G-4771)*

W T Winter Associates Inc ....E 888 808-3611
Fairfield *(G-3350)*

ELECTRICAL EQPT REPAIR SVCS

Waage Electric Inc ....G 908 245-9363
Kenilworth *(G-4986)*

ELECTRICAL EQPT REPAIR SVCS: High Voltage

A T C Companies Inc ....E 732 560-0900
Middlesex *(G-6091)*

Longo Elctrical-Mechanical Inc ....E 973 537-0400
Linden *(G-5377)*

M&L Power Systems Maint Inc ....E 732 679-1800
Old Bridge *(G-7718)*

ELECTRICAL EQPT: Automotive, NEC

Auto Action Group Inc ....E 908 964-6290
Kenilworth *(G-4922)*

ELECTRICAL GOODS, WHOLESALE: Batteries, Storage, Indl

Energy Battery Group Inc ....G 404 255-7529
Flemington *(G-3440)*

ELECTRICAL GOODS, WHOLESALE: Conduits & Raceways

American Fittings Corp ....G 201 664-0027
Fair Lawn *(G-3083)*

ELECTRICAL GOODS, WHOLESALE: Connectors

Da-Green Electronics Ltd ....F 732 254-2735
Marlboro *(G-5894)*

Heilind Electronics Inc ....D 888 881-5420
Lumberton *(G-5629)*

I Trade Technology Ltd ....G 615 348-7233
Mahwah *(G-5749)*

ELECTRICAL GOODS, WHOLESALE: Electrical Appliances, Major

Lg Electronics USA Inc ....B 201 816-2000
Englewood Cliffs *(G-2982)*

ELECTRICAL GOODS, WHOLESALE: Electrical Entertainment Eqpt

Philips Elec N Amer Corp ....D 973 471-9450
Clifton *(G-1690)*

ELECTRICAL GOODS, WHOLESALE: Electronic Parts

East Coast Electronics Inc ....G 908 431-7555
Hillsborough *(G-4313)*

Electronic Connections Inc ....F 732 367-5588
Lakewood *(G-5089)*

Foremost Corp ....G 973 839-3360
Wayne *(G-11504)*

Infiniti Components Inc ....G 908 537-9950
Hampton *(G-4156)*

Nitto Inc ....G 732 901-7905
Lakewood *(G-5141)*

Nitto Inc ....F 201 645-4950
Teaneck *(G-10641)*

Power Dynamics Inc ....G 973 560-0019
Whippany *(G-11906)*

State Electronics Parts Corp ....E 973 887-2550
East Hanover *(G-2240)*

ELECTRICAL GOODS, WHOLESALE: Fittings & Construction Mat

Hofer Connectors Co Inc ....E 973 427-1195
North Haledon *(G-7495)*

ELECTRICAL GOODS, WHOLESALE: Flashlights

Fuji Electric Corp America ....D 732 560-9410
Edison *(G-2515)*

ELECTRICAL GOODS, WHOLESALE: Fuses & Access

Hope Electrical Products Co ....G 973 882-7400
West Caldwell *(G-11653)*

ELECTRICAL GOODS, WHOLESALE: Generators

Chatham Lawn Mowler ....G 973 635-8855
Chatham *(G-1320)*

Power Pool Plus Inc ....G 908 454-1124
Alpha *(G-40)*

ELECTRICAL GOODS, WHOLESALE: High Fidelity Eqpt

Riotsound Inc ....G 917 273-5814
Newton *(G-7355)*

ELECTRICAL GOODS, WHOLESALE: Household Appliances, NEC

Boruch Trading Ltd Lblty Co ....G 718 614-9575
Lakewood *(G-5063)*

Winiadaewoo Elec Amer Inc ....F 201 552-4950
Ridgefield Park *(G-9320)*

ELECTRICAL GOODS, WHOLESALE: Insulators

Subcom LLC ....B 732 578-7000
Eatontown *(G-2422)*

ELECTRICAL GOODS, WHOLESALE: Intercommunication Eqpt

L J Loeffler Systems Inc ....G 212 924-7597
Secaucus *(G-9788)*

ELECTRICAL GOODS, WHOLESALE: Irons

Bushwick Metals LLC ....E 908 754-8700
South Plainfield *(G-10231)*

ELECTRICAL GOODS, WHOLESALE: Light Bulbs & Related Splys

Bulbrite Industries Inc ....E 201 531-5900
Moonachie *(G-6458)*

ELECTRICAL GOODS, WHOLESALE: Lighting Fixtures, Comm & Indl

Eco Lighting USA Ltd Lblty Co ....G 201 621-5661
South Hackensack *(G-10156)*

I4 Sustainability LLC ....G 732 618-3310
Springfield *(G-10445)*

Leland Limited Inc ....F 908 561-2000
South Plainfield *(G-10293)*

Reggiani Lighting Usa Inc ....F 201 372-1717
Carlstadt *(G-1210)*

ELECTRICAL GOODS, WHOLESALE: Lugs & Connectors

Richards Mfg Co Sales Inc ....E 973 371-1771
Irvington *(G-4586)*

ELECTRICAL GOODS, WHOLESALE: Mobile telephone Eqpt

Lg Elctrnics Mbilecomm USA Inc ......D 201 816-2000
Englewood Cliffs *(G-2981)*

ELECTRICAL GOODS, WHOLESALE: Modems, Computer

Micro Innovations Corp ....D 732 346-9333
Edison *(G-2565)*

ELECTRICAL GOODS, WHOLESALE: Motor Ctrls, Starters & Relays

Drive Technology Inc ....G 732 422-6500
Monmouth Junction *(G-6289)*

ELECTRICAL GOODS, WHOLESALE: Motors

Electrical Motor Repr Co of NJ ....F 609 392-6149
Trenton *(G-10934)*

George J Bender Inc ....E 908 687-0081
Union *(G-11059)*

Hights Electric Motor Service ....G 609 448-2298
Hightstown *(G-4296)*

Lakewood Elc Mtr Sls & Svc ....G 732 363-2865
Howell *(G-4545)*

Phil Desiere Electric Mtr Svc ....F 856 692-8442
Vineland *(G-11251)*

Universal Electric Mtr Svc Inc ....E 201 968-1000
Hackensack *(G-3988)*

Walker Engineering Inc ....F 732 899-2550
Point Pleasant Boro *(G-8848)*

Willier Elc Mtr Repr Co Inc ....E 856 627-3535
Gibbsboro *(G-3796)*

ELECTRICAL GOODS, WHOLESALE: Paging & Signaling Eqpt

Turn-Key Technologies Inc ....F 732 553-9100
Sayreville *(G-9726)*

ELECTRICAL GOODS, WHOLESALE: Panelboards

East Coast Panelboard Inc ....E 732 739-6400
Tinton Falls *(G-10713)*

ELECTRICAL GOODS, WHOLESALE: Radio & TV Or TV Eqpt & Parts

Philips Elec N Amer Corp ....D 973 471-9450
Clifton *(G-1690)*

ELECTRICAL GOODS, WHOLESALE: Radio Parts & Access, NEC

Pulsar Microwave Corp ....E 973 779-6262
Clifton *(G-1701)*

ELECTRICAL GOODS, WHOLESALE: Semiconductor Devices

American Microsemiconductor ....E 973 377-9566
Madison *(G-5689)*

Digitron Electronic Corp .... E 908 245-2012
Kenilworth *(G-4936)*

Mulberry Metal Products Inc ....D 908 688-8850
Union *(G-11078)*

ELECTRICAL GOODS, WHOLESALE:
Signaling, Eqpt

Intellgent Trffic Sup Pdts LLC ....G 908 791-1200
South Plainfield *(G-10278)*

Salescaster Displays Corp ....G 908 322-3046
Scotch Plains *(G-9739)*

ELECTRICAL GOODS, WHOLESALE:
Telephone & Telegraphic Eqpt

Orlando Systems Ltd Lblty Co ....G 908 400-5052
North Plainfield *(G-7507)*

Spirent Communications Inc ....G 732 946-4018
Holmdel *(G-4514)*

ELECTRICAL GOODS, WHOLESALE:
Telephone Eqpt

National Communications Inc ....E 973 325-3151
West Orange *(G-11774)*

ELECTRICAL GOODS, WHOLESALE:
Transformer & Transmission Eqpt

Wolock & Lott Transmission Eqp ....F 908 218-9292
Branchburg *(G-695)*

ELECTRICAL GOODS, WHOLESALE: Tubes,
Rcvg & Txmtg Or Indl

Hamamatsu Corporation ....D 908 231-0960
Bridgewater *(G-828)*

Photonics Management Corp ....G 908 231-0960
Bridgewater *(G-866)*

ELECTRICAL GOODS, WHOLESALE: Video
Eqpt

Murray Electronics Inc ....G 201 405-1158
Oakland *(G-7637)*

ELECTRICAL GOODS, WHOLESALE: Wire &
Cable

Alpha Wire Corporation ....C 908 925-8000
Elizabeth *(G-2709)*

Arose Inc ....E 856 481-4351
Blackwood *(G-459)*

Kabel N Elettrotek Amer Inc ....G 973 265-0850
Parsippany *(G-7969)*

Screentek Manufacturing Co LLC ....F 973 328-2121
Randolph *(G-9198)*

ELECTRICAL GOODS, WHOLESALE: Wire &
Cable, Ctrl & Sig

Lapp Usa LLC ....C 973 660-9700
Florham Park *(G-3517)*

Protection Industries Corp ....F 201 333-8050
Jersey City *(G-4790)*

ELECTRICAL GOODS, WHOLESALE: Wire &
Cable, Electronic

Daburn Wire & Cable Corp ....G 973 328-3200
Dover *(G-2081)*

Paige Electric Company LP ....E 908 687-7810
Union *(G-11080)*

ELECTRICAL GOODS, WHOLESALE: Wire &
Cable, Power

High Energy Group Ltd Lblty Co ....G 732 741-9099
Eatontown *(G-2397)*

ELECTRICAL INDL APPARATUS, NEC

Active Controls LLC ....G 856 669-0940
Paulsboro *(G-8328)*

Atm Aficionado LLC ....G 973 251-2115
Livingston *(G-5507)*

ELECTRICAL MEASURING INSTRUMENT
REPAIR & CALIBRATION SVCS

Byram Laboratories Inc ....E 908 252-0852
Branchburg *(G-627)*

ELECTRICAL SPLYS

Billows Electric Supply Co Inc ....C 856 751-2200
Delran *(G-2009)*

Global Business Dimensions Inc ....E 973 831-5866
Pompton Plains *(G-8865)*

I 2 R Corp ....G 732 919-1100
Wall Township *(G-11348)*

Inter World Highway LLC ....F 732 759-8235
Long Branch *(G-5599)*

Kraus & Naimer Inc ....E 732 560-1240
Somerset *(G-10011)*

Longo Elctrical-Mechanical Inc ....D 973 537-0400
Wharton *(G-11861)*

Maco Appliance Parts & Sup Co ....G 609 272-8222
Absecon *(G-3)*

Panel Components & Systems ....F 973 448-9400
Stanhope *(G-10478)*

Precision Devices Inc ....G 609 882-2230
Ewing *(G-3054)*

ELECTRICAL SUPPLIES: Porcelain

House of Prill Inc ....E 732 442-2400
Lincroft *(G-5311)*

Morgan Advanced Ceramics Inc ....E 973 808-1621
Fairfield *(G-3273)*

Pekay Industries Inc ....F 732 938-2722
Farmingdale *(G-3390)*

Top Knobs Usa Inc ....E 908 359-6174
Somerville *(G-10126)*

ELECTROCARS: Golfer Transportation

Parts Life Inc ....D 856 786-8675
Moorestown *(G-6554)*

ELECTRODES: Fluorescent Lamps

E G L Company Inc ....C 908 508-1111
Berkeley Heights *(G-398)*

ELECTRODES: Indl Process

Siemens Industry Inc ....G 732 302-1686
Warren *(G-11431)*

ELECTROMEDICAL EQPT

Bayer Healthcare LLC ....A 862 404-3000
Whippany *(G-11878)*

C R Bard Inc ....C 908 277-8000
Franklin Lakes *(G-3617)*

Circulite Inc ....F 201 478-7575
Teaneck *(G-10624)*

Datascope Corp ....G 201 995-8700
Mahwah *(G-5727)*

Datascope Corp ....G 201 995-8000
Mahwah *(G-5726)*

Diabeto Inc ....G 646 397-3175
Piscataway *(G-8656)*

Electrocore Inc ....D 973 290-0097
Basking Ridge *(G-182)*

Highlands Acquisition Corp ....G 201 573-8400
Montvale *(G-6413)*

Hilin Life Products Inc ....G 917 250-3575
Newark *(G-7150)*

Medality Medical LLC ....G 215 990-0754
Haddonfield *(G-4060)*

Newcardio Inc ....F 877 332-4324
Princeton *(G-8984)*

Northeast Medical Systems Corp ....G 856 910-8111
Cherry Hill *(G-1400)*

Radnet Inc ....F 908 709-1323
Cranford *(G-1925)*

Rhythmedix LLC ....G 856 282-1080
Mount Laurel *(G-6800)*

Simex Medical Imaging Inc ....G 201 490-0204
Paramus *(G-7832)*

Sonotron Medical Systems Inc ....G 201 767-6040
Northvale *(G-7550)*

Syneron ....G 201 599-9451
Paramus *(G-7840)*

Vasculogic LLC ....G 908 278-3573
Piscataway *(G-8735)*

Vectracor Incorporated ....F 973 904-0444
Totowa *(G-10856)*

Zounds Inc ....F 856 234-8844
Mount Laurel *(G-6815)*

ELECTROMEDICAL EQPT WHOLESALERS

Ascensia Diabetes Care US Inc ....C 973 560-6500
Parsippany *(G-7885)*

Orlando Systems Ltd Lblty Co ....G 908 400-5052
North Plainfield *(G-7507)*

State Technology Inc ....G 856 467-8009
Bridgeport *(G-746)*

ELECTROMETALLURGICAL PRDTS

Hoyt Corporation ....E 201 894-0707
Englewood *(G-2912)*

ELECTRON TUBES

Tdk Electronics Inc ....D 732 906-4300
Iselin *(G-4631)*

Union City Filament Corp ....E 201 945-3366
Ridgefield *(G-9294)*

World Electronics Inc ....F 201 670-1177
Glen Rock *(G-3835)*

ELECTRON TUBES: Parts

Linear Photonics LLC ....G 609 584-5747
Hamilton *(G-4109)*

Linearizer Technology Inc ....D 609 584-5747
Hamilton *(G-4110)*

ELECTRONIC COMPONENTS

Communication Products Co ....G 973 977-8490
Paterson *(G-8162)*

ELECTRONIC DEVICES: Solid State, NEC

Elena Consultants & Elec ....E 908 654-8309
Mountainside *(G-6845)*

Pekay Industries Inc ....F 732 938-2722
Farmingdale *(G-3390)*

ELECTRONIC EQPT REPAIR SVCS

Delaware Technologies Inc ....F 856 234-7692
Mount Laurel *(G-6753)*

Instru-Met Corporation ....G 908 851-0700
Union *(G-11065)*

Johnson Controls Inc ....D 732 225-6700
Edison *(G-2543)*

Singe Corporation ....G 908 289-7900
Hillside *(G-4426)*

Test Technology Inc ....D 856 596-1215
Marlton *(G-5953)*

ELECTRONIC LOADS & POWER SPLYS

Algen Design Services Inc ....E 732 389-3630
Eatontown *(G-2374)*

JFK Supplies Inc ....F 732 985-7800
Edison *(G-2539)*

ELECTRONIC PARTS & EQPT
WHOLESALERS

ADI American Distributors LLC ....D 973 328-1181
Randolph *(G-9169)*

Barantec Inc ....F 973 779-8774
Clifton *(G-1571)*

Brother International Corp ....B 908 704-1700
Bridgewater *(G-808)*

Cobham New Jersey Inc ....D 732 460-0212
Eatontown *(G-2384)*

East West Service Co Inc ....E 609 631-9000
Trenton *(G-10933)*

Eastern Instrumentation of ....G 856 231-0668
Moorestown *(G-6519)*

Eaton Corporation ....E 732 767-9600
Mountainside *(G-6844)*

Franklin Electronic Publs Inc ....D 609 386-2500
Burlington *(G-969)*

Glen Magnetics Inc ....E 908 454-3717
Alpha *(G-37)*

Gulton G I D ....G 908 791-4622
South Plainfield *(G-10270)*

J & W Servo Systems Company ....F 973 335-1007
Rockaway *(G-9469)*

Jerome Industries Corp ....E 908 353-5700
Hackettstown *(G-4013)*

Kef America Inc ....E 732 414-2074
Marlboro *(G-5903)*

PRODUCT

Link Computer Graphics Inc................G....... 973 808-8990
Fairfield *(G-3263)*

Lucent Technologies World Svcs.........C....... 908 582-3000
New Providence *(G-7008)*

Major Auto Installations Inc ....E....... 973 252-4262
Kenvil *(G-4993)*

Nilsson Electrical Laboratory ....G....... 201 521-4860
Jersey City *(G-4771)*

P W B Omni Inc ....G....... 856 384-1000
West Deptford *(G-11713)*

Panasonic Corp North America...........D....... 201 348-7000
Newark *(G-7220)*

Procedyne Corp ....E....... 732 249-8347
New Brunswick *(G-6962)*

Ribble Company Inc ....F....... 201 475-1812
Saddle Brook *(G-9672)*

RSR Electronics Inc ....G....... 732 381-8777
Rahway *(G-9126)*

Sound United LLC ....E....... 201 762-6500
Mahwah *(G-5773)*

Tdk Electronics Inc ....D....... 732 906-4300
Iselin *(G-4631)*

Tdk-Lambda Americas Inc ....C....... 732 922-9300
Tinton Falls *(G-10731)*

Vcom Intl Multi-Media Corp ....D....... 201 296-0600
Fairfield *(G-3339)*

World Electronics Inc ....F....... 201 670-1177
Glen Rock *(G-3835)*

YC Cable (east) Inc ....E....... 732 868-0800
Piscataway *(G-8739)*

ELECTRONIC TRAINING DEVICES

Castle Industries Inc ....E....... 201 585-8400
Englewood Cliffs *(G-2962)*

Design Assistance Corporation ....F....... 856 241-9500
Swedesboro *(G-10579)*

Kft Fire Trainer LLC ....E....... 201 300-8100
Montvale *(G-6417)*

Signal Crafters Tech Inc ....G....... 973 781-0880
East Hanover *(G-2239)*

ELECTROPLATING & PLATING SVC

Dynasty Metals Inc...........................E....... 973 453-6630
Rockaway *(G-9454)*

ELEVATORS & EQPT

Amerivator Systems Corporation.........G....... 973 471-1200
Clifton *(G-1565)*

Elevator Cabs of NY Inc ....D....... 973 790-9100
Paterson *(G-8178)*

Elevator Doors Inc ....E....... 973 790-9100
Paterson *(G-8179)*

Elevator Enterances NY Inc ....E....... 973 790-9100
Paterson *(G-8180)*

Elevator Entrance Inc ....E....... 973 790-9100
Paterson *(G-8181)*

Flor Lift of N J Inc ....E....... 973 429-2200
Fairfield *(G-3203)*

Otis Elevator Intl Inc ....C....... 973 575-7030
Fairfield *(G-3285)*

Schindler Elevator Corporation..........B....... 973 397-6500
Morristown *(G-6698)*

Schindler Elevator Corporation..........E....... 856 234-2220
Moorestown *(G-6565)*

TEC Elevator Inc ....F....... 609 938-0647
Marmora *(G-5960)*

ELEVATORS WHOLESALERS

Otis Elevator Company ....E....... 856 235-5200
Moorestown *(G-6552)*

Otis Elevator Intl Inc ....C....... 973 575-7030
Fairfield *(G-3285)*

ELEVATORS: Installation & Conversion

G-Tech Elevator Associates LLC..........F....... 866 658-9296
Linden *(G-5350)*

Otis Elevator Intl Inc ....C....... 973 575-7030
Fairfield *(G-3285)*

Schindler Elevator Corporation............B....... 973 397-6500
Morristown *(G-6698)*

Schindler Elevator Corporation............E....... 856 234-2220
Moorestown *(G-6565)*

Schindler Enterprises Inc ....F....... 973 397-6500
Morristown *(G-6699)*

ELEVATORS: Stair, Motor Powered

Archi-Tread Inc ....G....... 973 725-5738
Kinnelon *(G-5015)*

EMBLEMS: Embroidered

Chenille Products Inc ....F....... 201 703-1917
Palisades Park *(G-7771)*

Golden Rule Creations Inc ....G....... 201 337-4050
Franklin Lakes *(G-3625)*

Its The Pitts Inc ....G....... 609 645-7319
Pleasantville *(G-8813)*

Patchworks Co Inc ....G....... 973 627-2002
Dover *(G-2103)*

Uniport Industries Corporation ....G....... 201 391-6422
Woodcliff Lake *(G-12067)*

Wally Enterprises Inc ....F....... 732 329-2613
Monmouth Junction *(G-6319)*

World Class Marketing Corp ....E....... 201 313-0022
Fort Lee *(G-3595)*

EMBOSSING SVC: Paper

Turul Bookbindery Inc ....G....... 973 361-2810
Wharton *(G-11874)*

EMBROIDERING & ART NEEDLEWORK FOR THE TRADE

Ambro Manufacturing Inc ....F....... 908 806-8337
Flemington *(G-3429)*

Arts Embroidery LLC.........................G....... 732 870-2400
West Long Branch *(G-11719)*

C & D Sales ....G....... 609 383-9292
Pleasantville *(G-8806)*

CDK Industries LLC ....G....... 856 488-5456
Cherry Hill *(G-1352)*

Embroidery In Stitches Inc.................F....... 732 460-2660
Morganville *(G-6586)*

Faraj Inc ....D....... 201 313-4480
Paterson *(G-8191)*

Gilbert Storms Jr.............................G....... 973 835-5729
Haskell *(G-4196)*

Imagery Embroidary Corporation........F....... 201 343-9333
Union City *(G-11113)*

Innovative Design Inc ....E....... 201 227-2555
Cresskill *(G-1943)*

J and S Sporting Apparel LLC ....G....... 732 787-5500
Keansburg *(G-4838)*

Mary Bridget Enterprises ....E....... 609 267-4830
Cinnaminson *(G-1471)*

Mt Embroidery & Promotions LLC ....G....... 201 646-1070
Norwood *(G-7569)*

NJ Logo Wear LLC ....G....... 609 597-9400
Manahawkin *(G-5794)*

Peach Boutique LLC ....G....... 908 351-0739
Elizabeth *(G-2768)*

Pro Image Promotions Inc ....G....... 973 252-8000
Kenvil *(G-4995)*

Risse & Risse Graphics Inc ....E....... 856 751-7671
Runnemede *(G-9608)*

Sgh Inc ....G....... 609 698-8868
Barnegat *(G-161)*

Star Embroidery Corp ....E....... 973 481-4300
Newark *(G-7285)*

Unique Embroidery Inc......................F....... 201 943-9191
Elmwood Park *(G-2859)*

University Fashions By Janet...............G....... 856 228-1615
Williamstown *(G-11983)*

EMBROIDERING SVC

A Stitch Ahead ....F....... 609 586-1068
Lawrenceville *(G-5221)*

Advantage Ds LLC ....F....... 856 307-9600
Glassboro *(G-3806)*

Apollo East LLC ....G....... 856 486-1882
Pennsauken *(G-8389)*

Bauer Sport Shop ....G....... 201 384-6522
Dumont *(G-2111)*

Bon-Jour Group LLC ....F....... 201 646-1070
Norwood *(G-7558)*

Cozy Formal Wear Inc ....G....... 973 661-9781
Nutley *(G-7583)*

Creative Embroidery Corp ....E....... 973 497-5700
Newark *(G-7091)*

Design N Stitch Inc...........................G....... 201 488-1314
Hackensack *(G-3906)*

Dezine Line Inc ....F....... 973 989-1009
Wharton *(G-11856)*

Embroideries Unlimited Inc ....G....... 201 692-1560
Teaneck *(G-10630)*

J & S Finishing Inc............................G....... 201 854-0338
West New York *(G-11742)*

J & T Embroidery Inc ....G....... 201 867-4897
Union City *(G-11114)*

Midland Screen Printing Inc................F....... 201 703-0066
Saddle Brook *(G-9662)*

Pioneer Embroidery Co ....G....... 973 777-6418
South Hackensack *(G-10181)*

Semels Embroidery Inc ....F....... 973 473-6868
Clifton *(G-1713)*

Sequins of Distinction Inc ....G....... 201 348-8111
North Bergen *(G-7437)*

Sniderman John ....F....... 201 569-5482
Englewood *(G-2942)*

South Amboy Designer T Shirt L..........G....... 732 456-2594
South Amboy *(G-10141)*

Toni Embroidery ....G....... 201 664-6909
Park Ridge *(G-7860)*

William Cromley ....G....... 856 881-6019
Clayton *(G-1530)*

Wostbrock Embroidery Inc ....G....... 201 445-3074
Midland Park *(G-6191)*

EMBROIDERING SVC: Schiffli Machine

Carolace Embroidery Co Inc ....D....... 201 945-2151
Ridgefield *(G-9253)*

Chenille Products Inc ....F....... 201 703-1917
Palisades Park *(G-7771)*

Embroidery Concepts Inc ....G....... 973 942-8555
Paterson *(G-8182)*

Eyelet Embroideries Inc ....D....... 201 945-2151
Ridgefield *(G-9260)*

Goralski Inc ....E....... 201 573-1529
Park Ridge *(G-7851)*

Hamilton Embroidery Co Inc...............F....... 201 867-4084
Union City *(G-11112)*

Jacqueline Embroidery Co..................G....... 732 278-8121
Hackensack *(G-3933)*

John M Sniderman Inc.......................G....... 201 450-4291
Fairview *(G-3361)*

Marlene Embroidery Inc ....E....... 201 868-1682
West New York *(G-11747)*

O Stitch Matic Inc ....G....... 201 861-3045
Guttenberg *(G-3871)*

Quadelle Textile Corp ....F....... 201 865-1112
West New York *(G-11752)*

Tone Embroidery Corp ....E....... 201 943-1082
Fairview *(G-3371)*

Tri-Chem Inc ....F....... 973 751-9200
Belleville *(G-317)*

Weber & Doebrich Inc.......................E....... 201 868-6122
West New York *(G-11756)*

EMBROIDERY ADVERTISING SVCS

All Colors Screen Printing LLC ....G....... 732 777-6033
Highland Park *(G-4286)*

L & F Graphics Ltd Lblty Co ....G....... 973 240-7033
Paterson *(G-8232)*

Madhouz LLC ....G....... 609 206-8009
Glassboro *(G-3814)*

Red Diamond Co - Athc Letering..........G....... 973 759-2005
Belleville *(G-310)*

Unlimited Print Products Inc...............F....... 609 882-0653
Ewing *(G-3075)*

Wally Enterprises Inc........................F....... 732 329-2613
Monmouth Junction *(G-6319)*

EMBROIDERY KITS

Five Kids Group Inc ....G....... 732 774-5331
Neptune *(G-6878)*

Peach Boutique LLC ....G....... 908 351-0739
Elizabeth *(G-2768)*

EMERGENCY ALARMS

Ademco Inc.......................................G....... 732 505-6688
Toms River *(G-10739)*

Ademco Inc.......................................F....... 201 462-9570
Teterboro *(G-10670)*

Ademco Inc.......................................G....... 908 561-1888
South Plainfield *(G-10207)*

Ademco Inc.......................................G....... 856 985-9050
Marlton *(G-5921)*

Ademco Inc.......................................G....... 973 808-8233
Fairfield *(G-3134)*

Blitz Safe of America Inc ....F....... 201 569-5000
Englewood *(G-2884)*

Confires Fire Prtction Svc LLC ....F 908 822-2700
South Plainfield (G-10241)
Cricket Enterprises ....G...... 201 387-7978
Dumont (G-2112)
D2cf LLC ....G 973 699-4111
West Orange (G-11765)

EMPLOYMENT AGENCY SVCS

Crystal Deltronic Industries ....F 973 328-7000
Dover (G-2080)
Drake Corp ....G...... 732 254-1530
East Brunswick (G-2135)

EMPLOYMENT SVCS: Labor Contractors

Enser Corporation ....D 856 829-5522
Cinnaminson (G-1456)

ENAMELS

Kadakia International Inc ....G 908 754-4445
South Plainfield (G-10286)
Tevco Enterprises Inc ....D 908 754-7306
Paterson (G-8313)

ENCLOSURES: Electronic

Leibrock Metal Products Inc ....G...... 732 695-0326
Ocean (G-7669)
Magic Metal Works Inc ....G...... 201 384-8457
Bergenfield (G-379)
Par Metal Products Inc ....F 201 955-0800
North Arlington (G-7376)
Pepco Manufacturing Co....................D 856 783-3700
Somerdale (G-9933)
Stamplus Manufacturing Inc ....F 908 241-8844
Roselle (G-9573)

ENCODERS: Digital

Flir Security Inc ....G...... 201 368-9700
Ridgefield Park (G-9306)
R P R Graphics Inc ....E 908 654-8080
Peapack (G-8345)
Videonet Comm Group LLC ....F 732 863-5310
Freehold (G-3703)

ENERGY MEASUREMENT EQPT

Glow Tube Inc...................................G 609 268-7707
Shamong (G-9856)
Nice Instrumentation ....F 732 851-4300
Manalapan (G-5818)

ENGINE PARTS & ACCESS: Internal Combustion

Coates International Ltd.....................G...... 732 449-7717
Wall Township (G-11329)
Davis Hyundai ....F 609 883-3500
Ewing (G-3026)
Grobet File Company Amer LLC ....D 201 939-6700
Carlstadt (G-1161)

ENGINE REBUILDING: Diesel

Cast Technology Inc ....G...... 908 753-5155
South Plainfield (G-10235)
Melton Sales & Service......................D 609 699-4800
Bordentown (G-587)
Melton Sales & Service......................E 609 699-4800
Columbus (G-1802)
Penske Truck Leasing Co LP ....E 973 575-0169
Parsippany (G-7987)

ENGINE REBUILDING: Gas

Arrow Machine Company Inc...............G....... 973 642-2430
Newark (G-7054)

ENGINEERING SVCS

Adam Gates & Company LLC ....F 908 829-3386
Hillsborough (G-4300)
Advance Machine Planning Inc ....F 732 356-4438
Middlesex (G-6094)
Aeon Engineering LLC ....G...... 518 253-7681
Fort Lee (G-3545)
Alecto Systems LLC ....G...... 973 875-6721
Branchville (G-702)
Amec Foster Wheeler USA Corp ....E 713 929-5000
Hampton (G-4146)

American Soc of Mech Engineers........D 973 244-2282
Little Falls (G-5451)
Applicad Inc......................................E 732 751-2555
Wall Township (G-11318)
Bel Hybrids & Magnetics Inc..............F 201 432-0463
Jersey City (G-4701)
Bishop Ascendant Inc ....G...... 201 572-7436
West Caldwell (G-11642)
Carpenter & Paterson Inc ....E 973 772-1800
Saddle Brook (G-9644)
Cellgain Wireless LLC ....F 732 889-4671
Red Bank (G-9223)
Centurum Information Tech Inc ....G 856 751-1111
Marlton (G-5924)
Defense Spport Svcs Intl 2 LLC ....F 856 866-2200
Marlton (G-5927)
Dengen Scientific Corporation ....E 201 687-2983
Union City (G-11110)
Essex Products International ....E 973 226-2424
Caldwell (G-1024)
Fin-Tek Corporation ....G 973 628-2988
Wayne (G-11503)
Foster Wheeler Arabia Ltd ....G...... 908 730-4000
Hampton (G-4151)
Foster Wheeler Intl Corp ....F 908 730-4000
Hampton (G-4152)
Global Power Technology Inc...............D 732 287-3680
Edison (G-2521)
Helidex LLC ....G...... 201 636-2546
East Rutherford (G-2291)
Holtec International ....B 856 797-0900
Camden (G-1069)
Hosokawa Micron International ....C 908 273-6360
Summit (G-10534)
Jaktool LLC ....F 609 664-2451
Cranbury (G-1847)
Jdv Products Inc ....F 201 794-6467
Fair Lawn (G-3108)
Jentec Inc ....G...... 201 784-1031
Northvale (G-7531)
Krell Technologies Inc ....F 732 775-7355
Neptune (G-6887)
Lattice Incorporated ....E 856 910-1166
Pennsauken (G-8450)
Lockheed Martin Corporation..............D 856 722-7782
Moorestown (G-6538)
Lockheed Martin Corporation..............E 732 321-4200
Edison (G-2552)
Lummus Technology Ventures LLC ......G...... 973 893-1515
Bloomfield (G-509)
Magnetic Products and Svcs Inc..........G 732 264-6651
Holmdel (G-4504)
Microcast Technologies Corp...............D 908 523-9503
Linden (G-5385)
Mistras Group Inc ....C 609 716-4000
Princeton Junction (G-9062)
MTS Systems Corporation ....A 856 875-4478
Williamstown (G-11965)
Parkway-Kew Corporation ....F 732 398-2100
North Brunswick (G-7482)
Performance Alloys & Materials ....G...... 201 865-5268
Secaucus (G-9797)
Primacy Engineering Inc ....F 201 731-3272
Englewood Cliffs (G-2988)
Primary Systems Inc.........................F 732 679-2200
Old Bridge (G-7725)
Princeton Keynes Group Inc...............F 609 951-2239
Princeton (G-9000)
Procedyne Corp ....E 732 249-8347
New Brunswick (G-6962)
S L P Engineering Inc ....D 732 240-3696
Toms River (G-10789)
Shock Tech Inc ....E 845 368-8600
Mahwah (G-5771)
Specialty Systems Inc ....E 732 341-1011
Toms River (G-10794)
Tbt Group Inc ....G 856 753-4500
Bellmawr (G-344)
Total Technology Inc ....E 856 617-0502
Cherry Hill (G-1423)
Turner Engineering Inc ....F 973 263-1000
Mountain Lakes (G-6829)
V G Controls Inc................................G...... 973 764-6500
Oakland (G-7649)

ENGINEERING SVCS: Aviation Or Aeronautical

Thales Avionics Inc...........................C 732 242-6300
Piscataway (G-8725)

ENGINEERING SVCS: Building Construction

All Seasons Construction Inc..............G...... 908 852-0955
Long Valley (G-5607)

ENGINEERING SVCS: Chemical

Innovasystems Inc.............................F 856 722-0410
Moorestown (G-6530)
Scientific Design Company ....C 201 641-0500
Little Ferry (G-5496)

ENGINEERING SVCS: Construction & Civil

Acrow Corporation of America.............E 973 244-0080
Parsippany (G-7871)
Enterprisecc Ltd Liability Co ....G...... 201 266-0020
Jersey City (G-4732)
Tanis Concrete ....E 201 796-1556
Fair Lawn (G-3126)

ENGINEERING SVCS: Electrical Or Electronic

Advanced Industrial Controls..............G...... 908 725-7575
Branchburg (G-611)
Automation & Control Inc ....E 856 234-2300
Moorestown (G-6507)
Creatone Inc.....................................F 908 789-8700
Mountainside (G-6837)
Edmondmarks Technologies Inc...........E 732 643-0290
Neptune (G-6875)
Griffith Electric Sup Co Inc ....D 609 695-6121
Trenton (G-10937)
Intertek Laboratories Inc ....E 908 903-1800
Stirling (G-10491)
Johnson Controls Inc ....D 732 225-6700
Edison (G-2543)
Patriot American Solutions LLC ....D 862 209-4772
Rockaway (G-9484)
Thomas Instrumentation Inc...............F 609 624-2630
Cape May Court House (G-1116)

ENGINEERING SVCS: Industrial

Foster Wheeler Zack Inc....................D 908 730-4000
Hampton (G-4153)
Rapid Models & Prototypes Inc ....G...... 856 933-2929
Runnemede (G-9607)

ENGINEERING SVCS: Machine Tool Design

Edmund Kiss ....G...... 973 810-2312
Landing (G-5200)

ENGINEERING SVCS: Mechanical

Connecting Products Inc ....F 609 512-1121
Skillman (G-9918)
Enser Corporation ....D 856 829-5522
Cinnaminson (G-1456)
J Blanco Associates Inc.....................F 973 427-0619
Hawthorne (G-4228)
S J T Imaging Inc ....D 201 262-7744
Oradell (G-7747)
Sigma Engineering & Consulting..........F 732 356-3046
Middlesex (G-6147)
STS Technologies LLC ....F 973 277-5416
Mahwah (G-5778)
Tech Products Co Inc ....F 201 444-7777
Midland Park (G-6188)

ENGINEERING SVCS: Structural

Anvima Technologies LLC ....G...... 973 531-7077
Brookside (G-916)
Coperion Corporation ....C 201 327-6300
Sewell (G-9835)
East Coast Storage Eqp Co Inc ....E 732 451-1316
Brick (G-716)

ENGINES & ENGINE PARTS: Guided Missile, Research & Develpt

Aphelion Orbitals Inc........................G...... 321 289-0872
Union City (G-11107)
Lockheed Martin Corporation...............B 856 787-3104
Mount Laurel (G-6777)

ENGINES: Diesel & Semi-Diesel Or Duel Fuel

Penn Power Group LLC......................F 732 441-1489
Matawan (G-5984)

ENGINES: Gasoline, NEC

Roy Anania ....G....... 201 498-1555
   Hackensack (G-3967)

ENGINES: Internal Combustion, NEC

Cummins - Allison Corp ....G....... 201 791-2394
   Elmwood Park (G-2819)

Cummins Inc ....D....... 973 491-0100
   Kearny (G-4853)

Henry Jackson Racing Engines ....G....... 609 758-7476
   Cream Ridge (G-1936)

ENGRAVING SVC, NEC

Armotek Industries Inc ....E....... 856 829-4585
   Palmyra (G-7781)

Beauty Wood Designs ....G....... 908 687-9697
   Union (G-11030)

Blue Ribbon Awards Inc ....G....... 732 560-0046
   Somerset (G-9963)

Crown Trophy ....G....... 973 808-8400
   Pine Brook (G-8595)

Pochet of America Inc ....C....... 973 942-4923
   Woodland Park (G-12086)

Precise Corporate Printing Inc ....E....... 973 350-0330
   Harrison (G-4177)

Sunset Printing and Engrv Corp ....E....... 973 537-9600
   Wharton (G-11871)

Winemiller Press Inc ....G....... 732 223-0100
   Manasquan (G-5843)

ENGRAVING SVC: Jewelry & Personal Goods

Awards Trophy Company ....G....... 908 687-5775
   Hillside (G-4378)

Diamond Hut Jewelry Exchange ....G....... 201 332-5372
   Jersey City (G-4728)

Heros Salute Awards Co ....G....... 973 696-5085
   Wayne (G-11517)

Koehler Industries Inc ....G....... 732 364-2700
   Howell (G-4544)

ENGRAVING SVCS

Bannister Company Inc ....F....... 732 828-1353
   Milltown (G-6214)

Jory Engravers Inc ....G....... 201 939-1546
   Rutherford (G-9624)

NJ Logo Wear LLC ....G....... 609 597-9400
   Manahawkin (G-5794)

ENGRAVING: Bank Note

Starnet Business Solutions ....E....... 201 252-2863
   Mahwah (G-5775)

ENGRAVINGS: Plastic

Foster Engraving Corporation ....G....... 201 489-5979
   Hackensack (G-3918)

ENTERTAINERS

Foto Fantasy ....G....... 732 548-8446
   Edison (G-2514)

ENTERTAINERS & ENTERTAINMENT GROUPS

Sony Music Holdings Inc ....B....... 201 777-3933
   Rutherford (G-9634)

ENTERTAINMENT PROMOTION SVCS

Bng Industries LLC ....F....... 862 229-2414
   Harrison (G-4165)

ENTERTAINMENT SVCS

J Media LLC ....G....... 201 600-4573
   Norwood (G-7567)

Pentacle Publishing Corp ....E....... 732 240-3000
   Toms River (G-10782)

ENVELOPES

Bravo Pack Inc ....G....... 856 872-2937
   Pennsauken (G-8398)

Cenveo Worldwide Limited ....D....... 201 434-2100
   Jersey City (G-4710)

Envelope Freedom Holdings LLC ....G....... 201 699-5800
   Ridgefield (G-9259)

Old Ue LLC ....B....... 800 752-4012
   Ridgefield (G-9281)

Red Wallet Connection Inc ....D....... 201 223-2644
   Manchester (G-5849)

Tpg Graphics LLC ....G....... 856 314-0117
   Pennsauken (G-8493)

United Envelope LLC ....E....... 201 699-5800
   Ridgefield (G-9296)

Washington Stamp Exchange Inc ....F....... 973 966-0001
   Florham Park (G-3526)

Watonka Printing Inc ....G....... 732 974-8878
   Belmar (G-356)

ENVELOPES WHOLESALERS

Allied Envelope Co Inc ....E....... 201 440-2000
   Carlstadt (G-1122)

Arna Marketing Inc ....G....... 908 231-1100
   Branchburg (G-622)

Bravo Pack Inc ....G....... 856 872-2937
   Pennsauken (G-8398)

Cenveo Worldwide Limited ....D....... 201 434-2100
   Jersey City (G-4710)

Five Macs Inc ....G....... 856 596-3150
   Marlton (G-5931)

ENZYMES

Techenzyme Inc ....G....... 732 632-8600
   Iselin (G-4632)

EPOXY RESINS

Anti Hydro International Inc ....F....... 908 284-9000
   Flemington (G-3430)

Cvc Specialty Chemicals Inc ....F....... 856 533-3000
   Moorestown (G-6517)

Innovative Resin Systems Inc ....G....... 973 465-6887
   Newark (G-7157)

Innovative Resin Systems Inc ....G....... 973 465-6887
   Wayne (G-11520)

Innovative Resin Systems Inc ....G....... 973 633-5342
   Wayne (G-11521)

Phoenix Resins Inc ....F....... 888 627-3769
   Cinnaminson (G-1482)

Sika Corporation ....C....... 201 933-8800
   Lyndhurst (G-5679)

Sika Corporation ....B....... 201 933-8800
   Lyndhurst (G-5678)

EQUIPMENT: Rental & Leasing, NEC

Armstrong & Sons ....G....... 732 223-1555
   Manasquan (G-5829)

Atlas Flasher & Supply Co Inc ....E....... 856 423-3333
   Mickleton (G-6086)

Fleetsource LLC ....E....... 732 566-4970
   Dayton (G-1961)

Fyx Fleet Roadside Assistance ....F....... 609 452-8900
   Princeton (G-8953)

Gamka Sales Co Inc ....E....... 732 248-1400
   Edison (G-2518)

Harsco Corporation ....E....... 856 779-7795
   Cherry Hill (G-1371)

McKinley Scientific Llc ....F....... 973 579-4144
   Sparta (G-10396)

Power Pool Plus Inc ....G....... 908 454-1124
   Alpha (G-40)

Safety-Kleen Systems Inc ....F....... 609 859-2049
   Southampton (G-10371)

Seacube Container Leasing Ltd ....G....... 201 391-0800
   Park Ridge (G-7859)

Trac Intermodal LLC ....G....... 609 452-8900
   Princeton (G-9034)

Vineland Syrup Inc ....G....... 856 691-5772
   Vineland (G-11277)

ERASERS: Rubber Or Rubber & Abrasive Combined

Asbury Carbons Inc ....G....... 908 537-2155
   Asbury (G-60)

ESTER GUM

Alzo International Inc ....E....... 732 254-1901
   Sayreville (G-9702)

ETCHING & ENGRAVING SVC

A Smith & Son Inc ....G....... 609 747-0800
   Burlington (G-945)

Acme Engraving Co Inc ....E....... 973 778-0885
   Passaic (G-8050)

Bannister Company Inc ....F....... 732 828-1353
   Milltown (G-6214)

Foster Engraving Corporation ....G....... 201 489-5979
   Hackensack (G-3918)

W & E Baum Bronze Tablet Corp ....E....... 732 866-1881
   Freehold (G-3704)

ETHYLENE-PROPYLENE RUBBERS: EPDM Polymers

Bezwada Biomedical LLC ....G....... 908 281-7529
   Hillsborough (G-4305)

EXHAUST SYSTEMS: Eqpt & Parts

Matthey Johnson Inc ....C....... 856 384-7132
   West Deptford (G-11710)

EXPANSION JOINTS: Rubber

La Favorite Industries Inc ....F....... 973 279-1266
   Paterson (G-8236)

EXPLORATION, METAL MINING

Valdez Creek Min Ltd Lblty Co ....G....... 732 704-1427
   Red Bank (G-9248)

EXPLOSIVES

Cartridge Actuated Devices ....E....... 973 575-8760
   Fairfield (G-3166)

EXPLOSIVES, EXC AMMO & FIREWORKS WHOLESALERS

Cartridge Actuated Devices ....E....... 973 347-2281
   Byram Township (G-1017)

EXTENSION CORDS

Gogreen Power Inc ....F....... 732 994-5901
   Howell (G-4540)

EXTERMINATING PRDTS: Household Or Indl Use

Si Packaging LLC ....F....... 973 869-9920
   Rutherford (G-9632)

EXTRACTS, FLAVORING

A A Sayia & Company Inc ....G....... 201 659-1179
   Hoboken (G-4442)

Allen Flavors Inc ....C....... 908 561-5995
   South Plainfield (G-10211)

Allen Flavors Inc ....F....... 908 753-0544
   South Plainfield (G-10212)

Brand Aromatics Intl Inc ....G....... 732 363-1204
   Lakewood (G-5065)

Elan Inc ....D....... 973 344-8014
   Newark (G-7112)

Flavor & Fragrance Spc Inc ....D....... 201 828-9400
   Mahwah (G-5738)

Flavor Associates Inc ....F....... 973 238-9300
   Hawthorne (G-4221)

Flavor Dynamics Inc ....E....... 888 271-8424
   South Plainfield (G-10260)

Flavor Solutions Inc ....G....... 732 354-1931
   Piscataway (G-8665)

Flavors of Origin Inc ....G....... 201 460-8306
   Carlstadt (G-1157)

Givaudan Flavors Corporation ....C....... 973 386-9800
   East Hanover (G-2212)

Ifc Products Inc ....F....... 908 587-1221
   Linden (G-5356)

Interntnal Flvors Frgrnces Inc ....D....... 732 329-4600
   Dayton (G-1972)

Mastertaste Inc ....F....... 201 373-1111
   Teterboro (G-10686)

Medallion International Inc ....F....... 973 616-3401
   Pompton Plains (G-8867)

Penta International Corp ....D....... 973 740-2300
   Livingston (G-5534)

Sentrex Ingredients LLC ....G....... 908 862-4440
   Linden (G-5421)

Whittle & Mutch Inc ....F....... 856 235-1165
   Mount Laurel (G-6812)

EXTRUDED SHAPES, NEC: Copper & Copper Alloy

Amrod Corp ....D...... 973 344-3806
 Newark (G-7046)
Amrod NA Corporation ....D...... 973 344-2978
 Newark (G-7047)
Hoyt Corporation ....E 201 894-0707
 Englewood (G-2912)

EYEGLASS CASES

Colemax Group LLC ....G....... 201 489-1080
 River Edge (G-9359)

EYEGLASSES

Essilor Laboratories Amer Inc ....F 732 563-9884
 Warren (G-11410)
Gafas Sales and Consulting Inc ....G...... 862 368-5428
 Secaucus (G-9771)
I See Optical Laboratories ....G...... 856 795-6435
 Voorhees (G-11288)
Motif Industries Inc ....F 973 575-1800
 East Hanover (G-2223)
Sho Eyeworks ....G...... 201 568-5500
 Paramus (G-7831)
Viva International Inc ....B...... 908 595-6200
 Branchburg (G-694)

EYES: Artificial

New Jersey Eye Center Inc ....F 201 384-7333
 Bergenfield (G-381)

Ethylene Glycols

Nan Ya Plastics Corp America ....F 973 992-1775
 Livingston (G-5529)

FABRIC STORES

Pioneer Embroidery Co ....G....... 973 777-6418
 South Hackensack (G-10181)

FABRICATED METAL PRODUCTS, NEC

Apogee Technologies LLC ....F 973 575-8448
 Towaco (G-10864)
Hurricane Hutch ....G...... 908 256-5912
 Chester (G-1434)
Ironbound Metal ....G...... 973 242-5704
 Newark (G-7161)
Safe Man LLC ....G...... 800 320-2589
 Alpha (G-41)

FABRICS & CLOTHING: Rubber Coated

Ansell Protective Products LLC ....A...... 732 345-5400
 Iselin (G-4596)
Pacific Dunlop Investments USA ....F 732 345-5400
 Red Bank (G-9240)
Tingley Rubber Corporation ....E 800 631-5498
 Piscataway (G-8727)
Top Rated Shopping Bargains ....F 800 556-5849
 Hasbrouck Heights (G-4190)

FABRICS: Alpacas, Cotton

Meadowgate Farm Alpacas ....G....... 609 219-0529
 Lawrenceville (G-5237)

FABRICS: Alpacas, Mohair, Woven

Alma Park Alpacas ....G...... 732 620-1052
 Jobstown (G-4835)

FABRICS: Animal Fiber, Narrow Woven

Paterson Bleachery Inc ....F 973 684-1034
 Paterson (G-8279)

FABRICS: Apparel & Outerwear, Broadwoven

Dollfus Mieg Company Inc ....C...... 732 662-1005
 Edison (G-2492)
Soh LLC ....E 646 943-4066
 Jersey City (G-4812)

FABRICS: Apparel & Outerwear, Cotton

Aurora Apparel Inc ....G...... 201 646-4590
 Hackensack (G-3879)
Green Distribution LLC ....D...... 201 293-4381
 Secaucus (G-9779)

FABRICS: Automotive, Cotton

Quantum Vector Corp ....G....... 201 870-1782
 Westwood (G-11840)
Refuel Inc ....G....... 917 645-2974
 South Hackensack (G-10183)

FABRICS: Automotive, Cotton

Allison Corp ....G...... 973 992-3800
 Livingston (G-5504)

FABRICS: Automotive, From Manmade Fiber

Allison Corp ....G...... 973 992-3800
 Livingston (G-5504)

FABRICS: Bandage Cloth, Cotton

Vacs Bandage Company Inc ....F 973 345-3355
 Paterson (G-8322)

FABRICS: Basket Weave, Cotton

Gene Mignola Inc ....G...... 732 775-9291
 Asbury Park (G-77)

FABRICS: Broadwoven, Cotton

Picture Knits Inc ....E 973 340-3131
 Clifton (G-1691)
Tex Gul Inc ....G...... 973 857-3200
 Cedar Grove (G-1293)
Trimtex Company Inc ....D...... 201 945-2151
 Englewood Cliffs (G-2994)

FABRICS: Broadwoven, Synthetic Manmade Fiber & Silk

Absecon Mills Inc ....C...... 609 965-5373
 Cologne (G-1773)
Fablok Mills Inc ....E 908 464-1950
 New Providence (G-6998)
New Community Corp ....E 973 643-5300
 Newark (G-7208)
Nyltite Corp of America ....F 908 561-1300
 South Plainfield (G-10310)
Nyp Corp (frmr Ny-Pters Corp) ....D...... 908 351-6550
 Elizabeth (G-2763)
Paterson Bleachery Inc ....F 973 684-1034
 Paterson (G-8279)
Picture Knits Inc ....E 973 340-3131
 Clifton (G-1691)
Wearbest Sil-Tex Mills Ltd ....D...... 973 340-8844
 Garfield (G-3777)

FABRICS: Broadwoven, Wool

C3 Concepts Inc ....E 212 840-1116
 North Bergen (G-7391)
Paterson Bleachery Inc ....F 973 684-1034
 Paterson (G-8279)

FABRICS: Coated Or Treated

Alpha Associates Inc ....E 732 730-1800
 Lakewood (G-5047)
Gleicher Manufacturing Corp ....E 908 233-2211
 Scotch Plains (G-9732)
Laboratory Diagnostics Co Inc ....F 732 536-6300
 Morganville (G-6591)
PCC Asia LLC ....G...... 973 890-3873
 Totowa (G-10842)
Precision Textiles LLC ....C...... 973 890-3873
 Totowa (G-10846)
Safer Textile Processing Corp ....B...... 973 482-6400
 Newark (G-7260)

FABRICS: Decorative Trim & Specialty, Including Twist Weave

Amt Stitch Inc ....G....... 732 376-0009
 Perth Amboy (G-8512)

FABRICS: Denims

Blue Monkey Inc ....G...... 201 805-0055
 Saddle Brook (G-9643)
Westchester Denim Brothers Inc ....G...... 203 260-1629
 Ridgefield (G-9297)

FABRICS: Fiberglass, Broadwoven

Thomas Clark Fiberglass LLC ....G...... 609 492-9257
 Barnegat (G-163)

FABRICS: Resin Or Plastic Coated

United Eqp Fabricators LLC ....G...... 973 242-2737
 Newark (G-7308)

FABRICS: Hat Band

Cranial Technologies Inc ....E 201 265-3993
 Paramus (G-7795)

FABRICS: Jacquard Woven, Cotton

Jacquard Fabrics Inc ....E 732 905-4545
 Lakewood (G-5114)

FABRICS: Lace & Decorative Trim, Narrow

Wingold Embroidery LLC ....G...... 732 845-9802
 Freehold (G-3705)

FABRICS: Lace & Lace Prdts

Westchester Lace & Textiles ....C...... 201 864-2150
 Livingston (G-5548)
World Class Marketing Corp ....E 201 313-0022
 Fort Lee (G-3595)

FABRICS: Lace, Knit, NEC

Royal Lace Co Inc ....E 718 495-9327
 Rahway (G-9125)

FABRICS: Laminated

Butler Prtg & Laminating Inc ....C...... 973 838-8550
 Butler (G-997)
Custom Laminations Inc ....E 973 279-9174
 Paterson (G-8166)
Daf Products Inc ....F 201 251-1222
 Wyckoff (G-12108)
W C Omni Incorporated ....E 732 248-0999
 Edison (G-2643)

FABRICS: Laundry, Cotton

Pueblo Latino Laundry LLC ....G...... 201 864-1666
 Union City (G-11125)

FABRICS: Manmade Fiber, Narrow

Reddaway Manufacturing Co Inc ....F 973 589-1410
 Newark (G-7248)

FABRICS: Nonwoven

Fabrictex LLC ....G...... 732 225-3990
 Edison (G-2510)
JKA Specialties Mfr Inc ....F 609 859-2090
 Southampton (G-10366)
Klein Ribbon Corp ....E 973 684-4671
 Paterson (G-8230)

FABRICS: Paper, Broadwoven

Invitation Studio ....G...... 732 740-5558
 Morganville (G-6589)

FABRICS: Pile, Circular Knit

Susan Mills Inc ....F 908 355-1400
 Hillside (G-4429)

FABRICS: Polypropylene, Broadwoven

Kt America Corp ....F 609 655-5333
 Cranbury (G-1853)

FABRICS: Print, Cotton

Designs By James ....G...... 856 692-1316
 Vineland (G-11213)
Teefx Screen Printing LLC ....G...... 973 942-6800
 Haledon (G-4086)

FABRICS: Resin Or Plastic Coated

Alpha Engneered Composites LLC ......C...... 732 634-5700
 Lakewood (G-5048)
Commercial Products Co Inc ....F 973 427-6887
 Hawthorne (G-4213)
DMS Inc ....G...... 973 928-3040
 Cedar Grove (G-1275)
Plastic By All LLC ....G...... 732 785-5900
 Brick (G-729)

PRODUCT

FABRICS: Rubberized

American Braiding & Mfg Corp............F 732 938-6333
Howell **(G-4530)**

FABRICS: Scrub Cloths

Medical Scrubs Collectn NJ LLC..........G....... 732 719-8600
Lakewood **(G-5134)**

FABRICS: Seat Cover, Automobile, Cotton

Fh Group International Inc ....E 201 210-2426
Secaucus **(G-9767)**

FABRICS: Shirting, Cotton

Avail Inc ....G....... 732 560-2222
Bridgewater **(G-796)**

FABRICS: Shoe

Stanbee Company Inc ....E 201 933-9666
Carlstadt **(G-1221)**

FABRICS: Spunbonded

Fibertech Group Inc..........................C....... 856 697-1600
Landisville **(G-5206)**

FABRICS: Trimmings

A S A P Nameplate & Labeling..............F 973 773-3934
Passaic **(G-8048)**
Amcor Phrm Packg USA Inc ....C....... 856 728-9300
Williamstown **(G-11950)**
Aztec Graphics Inc ....F 609 587-1000
Trenton **(G-10900)**
Budget Print Center ....G....... 973 743-0073
Bloomfield **(G-492)**
C Q Corporation ....F 201 935-8488
East Rutherford **(G-2281)**
Clarici Graphics Inc ....E 609 587-7204
Trenton **(G-10917)**
Color Comp Inc ....G....... 856 262-3040
Williamstown **(G-11954)**
Cox Stationers and Printers.................E 908 928-1010
Linden **(G-5338)**
Creative Embroidery Corp ....E 973 497-5700
Newark **(G-7091)**
Custom Graphics of Vineland..............E 856 691-7858
Vineland **(G-11209)**
Donray Printing Inc ....E 973 515-8100
Parsippany **(G-7918)**
Family Screen Printing Inc ....F 856 933-2780
Bellmawr **(G-332)**
Jrm Industries Inc ....E 973 779-9340
Passaic **(G-8077)**
Klein Ribbon Corp ....E 973 684-4671
Paterson **(G-8230)**
Lukoil N Arlington Ltd Lblty..................E 856 722-6425
Moorestown **(G-6543)**
Mar-Kal Products Corp ....E 973 783-7155
Carlstadt **(G-1185)**
Monogram Center Inc ....E 732 442-1800
Perth Amboy **(G-8528)**
Painting Inc.....................................F 201 489-6565
South Hackensack **(G-10179)**
Phoenix Glass LLC ....E 856 692-0100
Pittsgrove **(G-8750)**
R & B Printing Inc ....G....... 908 766-4073
Bernardsville **(G-443)**
Red Diamond Co - Athc Letering..........G....... 973 759-2005
Belleville **(G-310)**
Rutler Screen Printing Inc...................F 908 859-3327
Phillipsburg **(G-8573)**
Safer Textile Processing Corp ....B 973 482-6400
Newark **(G-7260)**
Scher Fabrics Inc ....F 212 382-2266
Freehold **(G-3699)**
Screened Images Inc ....E 732 651-8181
East Brunswick **(G-2175)**
Semels Embroidery Inc ....F 973 473-6868
Clifton **(G-1713)**
Sniderman John ....E 201 569-5482
Englewood **(G-2942)**
Stefan Enterprises Inc ....E 973 253-6005
Garfield **(G-3770)**
Stone Graphics ....F 732 919-1111
Wall Township **(G-11371)**
Suzie Mac Specialties Inc...................E 732 238-3500
East Brunswick **(G-2184)**

Toppan Printing Co Amer Inc................C 732 469-8400
Somerset **(G-10088)**
U S Screening Corp ....C 973 242-1110
Newark **(G-7305)**
Unique Screen Printing Corp ....E 908 925-3773
Linden **(G-5438)**
Z Line Beachwear ....G....... 732 793-1234
Lavallette **(G-5213)**
Zone Two Inc ....F 732 237-0766
Bayville **(G-254)**

FABRICS: Trimmings, Textile

Avitex Co Inc ....E 973 242-2410
Newark **(G-7061)**
Marlene Trimmings LLC ....G....... 201 926-3108
North Bergen **(G-7418)**
Textol Systems Inc ....E 201 935-1220
Carlstadt **(G-1227)**
Trimtex Company Inc ....D 201 945-2151
Englewood Cliffs **(G-2994)**

FABRICS: Umbrella Cloth, Cotton

Umbrellas Unlimited ....G....... 201 476-1011
River Vale **(G-9368)**

FABRICS: Underwear, Cotton

Easy Undies LLC..............................G....... 201 715-4909
Springfield **(G-10440)**
Leggs Hns Bli Plytx Fctry Outl ....E 908 289-7262
Elizabeth **(G-2753)**

FABRICS: Upholstery, Cotton

Absecon Mills Inc ....C 609 965-5373
Cologne **(G-1773)**

FABRICS: Wall Covering, From Manmade Fiber Or Silk

L&M Architectural Graphics Inc ....F 973 575-7665
Fairfield **(G-3254)**

FABRICS: Warp & Flat Knit Prdts

Stern Knit Inc...................................G....... 732 364-8055
Lakewood **(G-5169)**

FABRICS: Warp Knit, Lace & Netting

All-Lace Processing Corp ....F 201 867-1974
North Bergen **(G-7381)**
Fablok Mills Inc ....G....... 908 464-1950
New Providence **(G-6998)**
Jason Mills LLC ....G....... 732 651-7200
Milltown **(G-6217)**

FABRICS: Weft Or Circular Knit

Meadows Knitting Corp.......................E 973 482-6400
Newark **(G-7198)**
Trimtex Company Inc ....D 201 945-2151
Englewood Cliffs **(G-2994)**

FABRICS: Woven Wire, Made From Purchased Wire

Newark Wire Cloth Company................E 973 778-4478
Clifton **(G-1677)**

FABRICS: Woven, Narrow Cotton, Wool, Silk

Avitex Co Inc ....G....... 973 242-2410
Newark **(G-7062)**
Hamilton Embroidery Co Inc................F 201 867-4084
Union City **(G-11112)**
Otex Specialty Narrow Fabrics ....G....... 908 879-3636
Bernardsville **(G-440)**

FACE PLATES

Mulberry Metal Products Inc.................D 908 688-8850
Union **(G-11078)**

FACILITIES SUPPORT SVCS

Tmg Enterprises Inc ....E 732 469-2900
Piscataway **(G-8728)**

FACSIMILE COMMUNICATION EQPT

Swintec Corp ....F 201 935-0115
Moonachie **(G-6493)**

FAMILY CLOTHING STORES

Marmaxx Operating Corp ....D 973 575-7910
West Caldwell **(G-11660)**

FANS, VENTILATING: Indl Or Commercial

Building Performance Eqp Inc...............F 201 722-1414
Hillsdale **(G-4364)**

FARM PRDTS, RAW MATERIALS, WHOLESALE: Nuts & Nut By-Prdts

Kalustyan Corporation ....D 908 688-6111
Union **(G-11068)**

FARM SPLY STORES

Mendham Garden Center ....G....... 973 543-4178
Mendham **(G-6041)**

FARM SPLYS WHOLESALERS

Le-Ed Construction Inc ....E 732 341-4546
Toms River **(G-10775)**

FARM SPLYS, WHOLESALE: Feed

Glenburnie Feed & Grain.....................G....... 856 986-8128
Mount Laurel **(G-6763)**

FARM SPLYS, WHOLESALE: Fertilizers & Agricultural Chemicals

Purely Organic SA LLC ....G....... 201 942-0400
Jersey City **(G-4792)**

FARM SPLYS, WHOLESALE: Greenhouse Eqpt & Splys

Cutting Edge Grower Supply LLC ....G....... 732 905-9220
Howell **(G-4536)**

FARM SPLYS, WHOLESALE: Insecticides

Pic Corporation ....E 908 862-7977
Linden **(G-5409)**

FARM SPLYS, WHOLESALE: Soil, Potting & Planting

Saxton Falls Sand & Gravel Co ....E 908 852-0121
Budd Lake **(G-936)**

FASTENERS WHOLESALERS

Industrial Rivet & Fastener Co...............D 201 750-1040
Northvale **(G-7528)**

FASTENERS: Metal

Robinson Tech Intl Corp ....G....... 973 287-6458
Fairfield **(G-3303)**

FASTENERS: Metal

Celus Fasteners Mfg Inc......................E 800 289-7483
Northvale **(G-7520)**
CMF Ltd Inc ....E 609 695-3600
Ewing **(G-3022)**
General Sullivan Group Inc...................F 609 745-5000
Pennington **(G-8366)**
Imperial Weld Ring Corp Inc ....E 908 354-0011
Elizabeth **(G-2749)**
Rotor Clip Company Inc ....B 732 469-7707
Somerset **(G-10067)**
Taurus Precision Inc..........................F 973 785-9254
Little Falls **(G-5470)**

FASTENERS: Notions, NEC

Alpine Machine & Tool Corp ....F 201 666-0959
Westwood **(G-11825)**
Amershoe Corp ....G....... 201 569-7300
Englewood **(G-2876)**
Arlo Corporation ....G....... 973 618-0030
Roseland **(G-9533)**
C & C Metal Products Corp ....D 201 569-7300
Englewood **(G-2889)**
Captive Fasteners Corp.......................B 201 337-6800
Oakland **(G-7618)**
Communique Inc ....G....... 973 751-7588
Belleville **(G-293)**

Fastenation Inc .... E 973 591-1277
  Clifton *(G-1619)*
Nyltite Corp of America .... F 908 561-1300
  South Plainfield *(G-10310)*
Straps Manufacturing NJ Inc .... F 201 368-5201
  Wyckoff *(G-12121)*

FASTENERS: Notions, Zippers

Case It Inc .... E 800 441-4710
  Lyndhurst *(G-5646)*
Royal Slide Sales Co Inc .... G 973 777-1177
  Garfield *(G-3764)*
Royal Zipper Manufg Company .... F 973 777-1177
  Garfield *(G-3765)*
Snapco Manufacturing Corp .... E 973 282-0300
  Hillside *(G-4427)*

FATTY ACID ESTERS & AMINOS

Amerchol Corporation .... C 732 248-6000
  Edison *(G-2452)*
Barnet Products LLC .... F 201 346-4620
  Englewood Cliffs *(G-2959)*
Scher Chemicals Inc .... A 973 471-1300
  Clifton *(G-1711)*

FELT, WHOLESALE

Central Shippee Inc .... E 973 838-1100
  Bloomingdale *(G-526)*

FENCE POSTS: Iron & Steel

Robinson Tech Intl Corp .... G 973 287-6458
  Fairfield *(G-3303)*

FENCES & FENCING MATERIALS

General Metal Manufacturing Co ...... E 973 386-1818
  East Hanover *(G-2211)*

FENCING DEALERS

All-State Fence Inc .... E 732 431-4944
  West Orange *(G-11758)*
Blue Gauntlet Fencing Gear Inc ...... F 201 797-3332
  Saddle Brook *(G-9642)*
Doerre Fence Co LLC .... F 732 751-9700
  Farmingdale *(G-3384)*
Great Railing Inc .... F 856 875-0050
  Williamstown *(G-11960)*
Hoda Inc .... F 609 695-3000
  Trenton *(G-10939)*
National Fence Systems Inc .... D 732 636-5600
  Avenel *(G-139)*
Walpole Woodworkers Inc .... E 973 539-3555
  Morris Plains *(G-6628)*
Wayside Fence Company Inc .... E 201 791-7979
  Fair Lawn *(G-3129)*

FENCING MADE IN WIREDRAWING PLANTS

Blue Gauntlet Fencing Gear Inc ...... F 201 797-3332
  Saddle Brook *(G-9642)*
Fence America New Jersey Inc .... G 973 472-5121
  Hackensack *(G-3912)*

FENCING MATERIALS: Docks & Other Outdoor Prdts, Wood

Comprelli Equipment and Svc .... G 973 428-8687
  East Hanover *(G-2201)*
Larsen Marine Services LLC .... G 609 408-3564
  Sea Isle City *(G-9748)*
Medford Cedar Products Inc .... G 609 859-1400
  Southampton *(G-10369)*
Wardale Corp .... E 800 813-4050
  Lakewood *(G-5180)*

FENCING MATERIALS: Plastic

Fencemax .... G 609 646-2265
  Newfield *(G-7322)*
Freedom Vinyl Systems Inc .... G 973 692-0332
  Pequannock *(G-8505)*
Onguard Fence Systems Ltd .... E 908 429-5522
  Moorestown *(G-6550)*
Onguard Fence Systems Ltd .... E 908 429-5522
  Branchburg *(G-663)*

FENCING MATERIALS: Snow Fence, Wood

P & S Blizzard Corporation .... G 973 523-1700
  Paterson *(G-8275)*

FENCING MATERIALS: Wood

All-State Fence Inc .... E 732 431-4944
  West Orange *(G-11758)*
Doerre Fence Co LLC .... E 732 751-9700
  Farmingdale *(G-3384)*
General Metal Manufacturing Co ...... E 973 386-1818
  East Hanover *(G-2211)*
Hoda Inc .... F 609 695-3000
  Trenton *(G-10939)*
National Fence Systems Inc .... D 732 636-5600
  Avenel *(G-139)*
Walpole Woodworkers Inc .... E 973 539-3555
  Morris Plains *(G-6628)*

FENCING: Chain Link

Belmont Whl Fence Mfg Inc .... E 973 472-5121
  Garfield *(G-3732)*
Security Fabricators Inc .... F 908 272-9171
  Kenilworth *(G-4977)*

FERRITES

Fermag Technologies Inc .... G 732 985-7300
  Toms River *(G-10756)*
Merrimac Industries Inc .... D 973 575-1300
  West Caldwell *(G-11665)*

FERROALLOYS

Thyssenkrupp Materials NA Inc ...... F 212 972-8800
  Maywood *(G-6017)*

FERTILIZER, AGRICULTURAL: Wholesalers

Big Bucks Enterprises Inc .... E 908 320-7009
  Washington *(G-11442)*

FERTILIZERS: NEC

Growmark Fs LLC .... F 609 267-7054
  Eastampton *(G-2372)*
Reed & Perrine Inc .... E 732 446-6363
  Tennent *(G-10668)*

FERTILIZERS: Nitrogenous

Agrium Advanced Tech US Inc .... F 732 296-8448
  North Brunswick *(G-7451)*
Growmark Fs LLC .... F 609 267-7054
  Eastampton *(G-2372)*

FERTILIZERS: Phosphatic

Growmark Fs LLC .... F 609 267-7054
  Eastampton *(G-2372)*
Innophos Holdings Inc .... D 609 495-2495
  Cranbury *(G-1842)*
Innophos Invstmnts Hldings Inc ...... G 609 495-2495
  Cranbury *(G-1845)*
Missry Associates Inc .... C 732 752-7500
  Edison *(G-2568)*

FIBER & FIBER PRDTS: Acrylic

Natures Choice Corporation .... F 973 969-3299
  Sparta *(G-10401)*

FIBER & FIBER PRDTS: Organic, Noncellulose

Allied-Signal China Ltd .... E 973 455-2000
  Morristown *(G-6632)*
Alliedsignal Foreign Sls Corp .... G 973 455-2000
  Morristown *(G-6633)*
Northeast Pro-Tech Inc .... F 973 777-5654
  Passaic *(G-8092)*
Solutia Inc .... G 908 862-0278
  Linden *(G-5426)*

FIBER & FIBER PRDTS: Polyester

Nan Ya Plastics Corp America .... F 973 992-1775
  Livingston *(G-5529)*

FIBER & FIBER PRDTS: Synthetic Cellulosic

Endot Industries Inc .... D 973 625-8500
  Rockaway *(G-9456)*

Newark Fibers Inc .... G 201 768-6800
  Rockleigh *(G-9520)*

FIBER & FIBER PRDTS: Vinyl

Jaclyn Holdings Parent LLC .... G 201 909-6000
  Maywood *(G-6007)*

FIBER OPTICS

Ascentta Inc .... F 732 868-1766
  Somerset *(G-9957)*
C Technologies Inc .... E 908 707-1009
  Bridgewater *(G-810)*
Fiberguide Industries Inc .... E 908 647-6601
  Stirling *(G-10490)*
Go Foton Corporation .... F 732 412-7375
  Somerset *(G-9998)*
Metro Optics LLC .... F 908 413-0004
  Flemington *(G-3456)*
Princeton Hosted Solutions LLC ...... F 856 470-2350
  Haddonfield *(G-4062)*
Radiant Communications Corp .... E 908 757-7444
  South Plainfield *(G-10323)*

FILE FOLDERS

Red Wallet Connection Inc .... D 201 223-2644
  Manchester *(G-5849)*

FILM & SHEET: Unsuppported Plastic

All American Poly Corp .... C 732 752-3200
  Piscataway *(G-8628)*
Amtopp Corporation .... A 973 994-8074
  Livingston *(G-5506)*
Arch Crown Inc .... E 973 731-6300
  Hillside *(G-4375)*
Berry Global Inc .... C 908 353-3850
  Elizabeth *(G-2716)*
Berry Global Inc .... E 908 454-0900
  Phillipsburg *(G-8545)*
Berry Global Inc .... C 609 395-4199
  Cranbury *(G-1814)*
Corbco Inc .... G 609 549-6299
  Forked River *(G-3538)*
Heritage Bag Company .... D 856 467-2247
  Swedesboro *(G-10589)*
JA Heilferty LLC .... E 201 836-5060
  Teaneck *(G-10635)*
Kolon USA Incorporated .... F 201 641-5800
  Ridgefield Park *(G-9311)*
Montrose Molders Corporation .... C 908 754-3030
  South Plainfield *(G-10302)*
Niaflex Corporation .... F 407 851-6620
  Livingston *(G-5532)*
Pegasus Products Inc .... E 908 707-1122
  Branchburg *(G-666)*
Plastic Plus Group LLC .... F 862 701-6981
  Parsippany *(G-7996)*
Productive Plastics Inc .... D 856 778-4300
  Mount Laurel *(G-6796)*
Trinity Plastics Inc .... C 973 994-8018
  Livingston *(G-5543)*
US Plastic Sales LLC .... G 908 754-9404
  South Plainfield *(G-10336)*
Vish LLC .... E 201 529-2900
  North Brunswick *(G-7493)*

FILM BASE: Cellulose Acetate Or Nitrocellulose Plastics

H S Folex Schleussner Inc .... G 973 575-7626
  Fairfield *(G-3220)*
Nobelus LLC .... G 800 895-2747
  North Brunswick *(G-7480)*

FILTERS

Camfil Usa Inc .... C 973 616-7300
  Riverdale *(G-9372)*
Carol Products Co Inc .... D 732 918-0800
  Ocean *(G-7658)*
Coilhose Pneumatics Inc .... E 732 432-7177
  East Brunswick *(G-2133)*
Complete Filter .... G 732 441-0321
  South Amboy *(G-10132)*
Enviro-Clear Company Inc .... F 908 638-5507
  High Bridge *(G-4282)*
Membranes International Inc .... G 973 998-5530
  Ringwood *(G-9348)*
Nichem Co .... G 973 399-9810
  Newark *(G-7218)*

P R O D U C T

FILTERS & SOFTENERS: Water, Household

Aries Filterworks Inc ....E 856 626-1550
  Berlin *(G-414)*
Clearwater Well Drilling Co ....G...... 609 698-1800
  Manahawkin *(G-5791)*
EAC Water Filters Inc ....F 888 524-8088
  Allenwood *(G-32)*
Evoqua Water Technologies LLC ....F 201 531-9338
  East Rutherford *(G-2287)*
Filter Technologies Inc ....G...... 732 329-2500
  Monmouth Junction *(G-6291)*
Graver Water Systems LLC ....F 973 465-2380
  Newark *(G-7138)*
Lanxess Sybron Chemicals Inc ....C 609 893-1100
  Birmingham *(G-457)*
Quality Plus One Catering Inc ....G...... 732 967-1525
  Old Bridge *(G-7726)*

FILTERS & STRAINERS: Pipeline

Eaton Filtration LLC ....B 732 767-4200
  Tinton Falls *(G-10714)*
Hayward Industries Inc ....B 908 351-5400
  Elizabeth *(G-2746)*

FILTERS: Air

Brookaire Company LLC ....F 973 473-7527
  Carlstadt *(G-1132)*
Envirnmntal Dynamics Group Inc ....F 609 924-4489
  Rocky Hill *(G-9525)*
Tri-Dim Filter Corporation ....G...... 856 786-2447
  Cinnaminson *(G-1493)*

FILTERS: Air Intake, Internal Combustion Engine, Exc Auto

Star Process Heat Systems LLC ....G...... 732 282-1002
  Neptune *(G-6899)*

FILTERS: Gasoline, Internal Combustion Engine, Exc Auto

Fluid Filtration Corp ....F 973 253-7070
  Garfield *(G-3743)*

FILTERS: General Line, Indl

Admiral Filter Company LLC ....F 973 664-0400
  Rockaway *(G-9436)*
Filter Holdings Inc ....E 908 687-3500
  Union *(G-11054)*
Industrial Filters Company................G...... 973 575-0533
  Fairfield *(G-3237)*
Kavon Filter Products Co ....F 732 938-3135
  Wall Township *(G-11351)*
Liquid-Solids Separation Corp ....E 201 236-4833
  Ramsey *(G-9149)*
Newton Tool & Mfg Inc ....D 856 241-1500
  Pennsauken *(G-8461)*
Universal Filters Inc ....E 732 774-8555
  Asbury Park *(G-85)*

FILTERS: Motor Vehicle

Felco Products LLC ....G...... 973 890-7979
  Paterson *(G-8192)*

FILTERS: Paper

Allied Group Inc ....E 973 543-4994
  Mendham *(G-6038)*
Rockline Industries Inc ....C 973 257-2884
  Montville *(G-6446)*
Seaboard Paper and Twine LLC ....E 973 413-8100
  Paterson *(G-8296)*
Tekkote Corporation ....D 201 585-1708
  Leonia *(G-5293)*

FILTRATION DEVICES: Electronic

NMP Water Systems LLC ....G...... 201 252-8333
  Mahwah *(G-5758)*
Ultra Clean Technologies Corp...........E 856 451-2176
  Bridgeton *(G-776)*

FILTRATION SAND MINING

Cherishmet Inc ....F 201 842-7612
  Rutherford *(G-9616)*
Inversand Company Inc ....F 856 881-2345
  Clayton *(G-1526)*

FINANCIAL SVCS

Circleblack Inc ....F 800 315-1241
  Kingston *(G-5007)*
Invessence Inc ....G...... 201 977-1955
  Chatham *(G-1322)*
Ipjukebox Ltd Liability Co ....G...... 201 286-4535
  Newark *(G-7158)*
Michelex Corporation ....G...... 201 977-1177
  Prospect Park *(G-9074)*
Optherium Labs Ou ....G...... 516 253-1777
  Holmdel *(G-4512)*
SMR Research Corporation ....G...... 908 852-7677
  Hackettstown *(G-4037)*
Sueta Music Ed Publications.............F 888 725-2333
  Mendham *(G-6043)*

FINDINGS & TRIMMINGS Fabric, NEC

Alco Trimming ....G...... 201 854-8608
  North Bergen *(G-7380)*
Artistic Bias Products Co Inc ....E 732 382-4141
  Rahway *(G-9078)*

FINDINGS & TRIMMINGS: Apparel

Green Distribution LLC ....D 201 293-4381
  Secaucus *(G-9779)*

FINDINGS & TRIMMINGS: Fabric

Newark Auto Top Co Inc ....F 973 677-9935
  East Orange *(G-2256)*

FINDINGS & TRIMMINGS: Furniture, Fabric

Associated Fabrics Corporation ....G...... 201 300-6053
  Fair Lawn *(G-3086)*

FINGERNAILS, ARTIFICIAL

Polish Nail ....G...... 732 627-9799
  Middlesex *(G-6139)*

FINGERPRINT EQPT

Bio-Key International Inc ....E 732 359-1100
  Wall Township *(G-11322)*

FINISHING AGENTS: Textile

Arol Chemical Products Co ....G...... 973 344-1510
  Newark *(G-7053)*
Pariser Industries Inc ....E 973 569-9090
  Paterson *(G-8277)*

FIRE ALARM MAINTENANCE & MONITORING SVCS

Checkpoint Security Systems Gr ....C 952 933-8858
  West Deptford *(G-11696)*
Checkpoint Systems Inc ....C 952 933-8858
  West Deptford *(G-11699)*

FIRE ARMS, SMALL: Guns Or Gun Parts, 30 mm & Below

2a Holdings Inc ....G...... 973 378-8011
  Maplewood *(G-5873)*

FIRE ARMS, SMALL: Rifles Or Rifle Parts, 30 mm & below

Henry RAC Holding Corp ....D 201 858-4400
  Bayonne *(G-222)*
Way It Was Sporting Svc Inc ....G...... 856 231-0111
  Moorestown *(G-6576)*

FIRE DETECTION SYSTEMS

Protection Industries Corp.................F 201 333-8050
  Jersey City *(G-4790)*
Tyco International MGT Co LLC ....E 609 720-4200
  Princeton *(G-9038)*

FIRE ESCAPES

C W Grimmer & Sons Inc ....F 732 741-2189
  Tinton Falls *(G-10706)*

FIRE EXTINGUISHER CHARGES

Firefighter One Ltd Lblty Co ....G...... 973 940-3061
  Sparta *(G-10387)*

FIRE EXTINGUISHER SVC

Eagle Fire & Safety Corp ....G...... 732 982-7388
  Wall Township *(G-11335)*

FIRE EXTINGUISHERS: Portable

Absolute Protective Systems ....E 732 287-4500
  Piscataway *(G-8624)*
C Bennett Scopes Inc ....G...... 856 464-6889
  Mantua *(G-5851)*
Tyco International MGT Co LLC ....E 609 720-4200
  Princeton *(G-9038)*

FIRE OR BURGLARY RESISTIVE PRDTS

Crestron Electronics Inc ....C 201 767-3400
  Rockleigh *(G-9516)*
RISE Corporation ....E 973 575-7480
  West Caldwell *(G-11679)*
Thyssenkrupp Materials NA Inc ....F 212 972-8800
  Maywood *(G-6017)*
Williams Scotsman Inc ....G...... 856 429-0315
  Kearny *(G-4906)*

FIRE PROTECTION EQPT

Life Liners Inc ....G...... 973 635-9234
  Chatham *(G-1326)*
Madison Park Volunteer Fire Co...........E 732 727-1143
  Parlin *(G-7868)*
Specified Technologies Inc ....C 908 526-8000
  Branchburg *(G-684)*
Township of Carneys Point ....F 856 299-4973
  Carneys Point *(G-1244)*

FIRE PROTECTION, GOVERNMENT: Local

Township of Carneys Point ....F 856 299-4973
  Carneys Point *(G-1244)*

FIREPLACE & CHIMNEY MATERIAL: Concrete

Associate Fireplace Builders..............G...... 908 273-5900
  Summit *(G-10526)*
Van Brill Pool & Spa Center ....G...... 856 424-4333
  Marlton *(G-5955)*

FIREWOOD, WHOLESALE

Kane Wood Fuel..............................G...... 856 589-3292
  Pitman *(G-8746)*
Vine Hill Farm ....G...... 973 383-0100
  Newton *(G-7364)*

FISH & SEAFOOD PROCESSORS: Canned Or Cured

Gerber Products Company ....C 973 593-7500
  Florham Park *(G-3508)*
Point Lobster Company Inc ....F 732 892-1718
  Point Pleasant Beach *(G-8831)*
Sea Harvest Inc ....E 609 884-3000
  Cape May *(G-1102)*
Sushi House Inc ....E 201 482-0609
  Palisades Park *(G-7779)*

FISH & SEAFOOD PROCESSORS: Fresh Or Frozen

Bay Treasure Seafood LLC ....F 732 240-3474
  Toms River *(G-10750)*
Black Sea Fisheries ....G...... 973 553-1580
  Fort Lee *(G-3551)*
Certified Clam Corp ....F 732 872-6650
  Highlands *(G-4291)*
Golden Tropics Ltd ....E 973 484-0202
  Newark *(G-7137)*
Hillard Bloom Packing Co Inc ....G...... 856 785-0120
  Port Norris *(G-8886)*
New Jrsey Sfood Mktg Group LLC........G...... 609 296-7026
  Egg Harbor City *(G-2665)*
Ruggiero Sea Food Inc ....D 973 589-0524
  Newark *(G-7254)*
Ruggiero Sea Food Inc ....G...... 973 589-0524
  Newark *(G-7255)*
Sushi House Inc ....E 201 482-0609
  Palisades Park *(G-7779)*

FISH FOOD

Evergreen Kosher LLC ....G....... 732 370-4500
Lakewood *(G-5094)*

FISH LIVER OILS: For Medicinal Use, Refined Or Concentrated

Matinas Biopharma Inc..........................F 908 443-1860
Bedminster *(G-272)*

FISHING EQPT: Lures

Lure Lash Spa LLC ....F 973 783-5274
Montclair *(G-6374)*
Richard Andrus ....G....... 856 825-1782
Millville *(G-6269)*

FISHING EQPT: Nets & Seines

Richard Andrus ....G....... 856 825-1782
Millville *(G-6269)*

FITTINGS & ASSEMBLIES: Hose & Tube, Hydraulic Or Pneumatic

American Hose Hydraulic Co Inc ....E....... 973 684-3225
Paterson *(G-8136)*
Robert H Hoover & Sons Inc.................G....... 973 347-4210
Flanders *(G-3417)*

FITTINGS: Pipe

CP Test & Valve Products Inc ....G....... 201 998-1500
Kearny *(G-4851)*
Dason Stainless Products Co.................F 732 382-7272
Rahway *(G-9087)*
Exclusive Materials LLC........................G....... 732 886-9956
Lakewood *(G-5095)*
Pennsylvania Machine Works Inc ....E....... 856 467-0500
Swedesboro *(G-10600)*
Piping Supplies Inc ....G....... 609 561-9323
Williamstown *(G-11968)*
Ramco Manufacturing Co Inc ....E....... 908 245-4500
Kenilworth *(G-4973)*
Syntiro Dynamics LLC...........................G....... 732 377-3307
Wall Township *(G-11374)*
Taylor Forge Stainless Inc ....D....... 908 722-1313
Branchburg *(G-687)*
Tkl Specialty Piping Inc........................G....... 908 454-0030
Phillipsburg *(G-8578)*

FITTINGS: Pipe, Fabricated

A&M Industrial Inc ....F 908 862-1800
Avenel *(G-117)*
Euro Mechanical Inc ....F 201 313-8050
Fairview *(G-3360)*

FIXTURES & EQPT: Kitchen, Metal, Exc Cast Aluminum

Epi Group Ltd Liability Co......................G....... 917 710-6607
Lakewood *(G-5092)*

FIXTURES & EQPT: Kitchen, Porcelain Enameled

Artistic Hardware ....G....... 609 383-1909
Northfield *(G-7510)*

FIXTURES: Bank, Metal, Ornamental

Zone Defense Inc ....F 973 328-0436
Hackettstown *(G-4042)*

FIXTURES: Cut Stone

Sanford & Birdsall Inc ....G....... 732 223-6966
Manasquan *(G-5838)*

FLAGPOLES

Lingo Inc ....F 856 273-6594
Mount Laurel *(G-6775)*

FLAGS: Fabric

Annin & Co ....E....... 973 228-9400
Roseland *(G-9532)*
Art Flag Co Inc ....F 212 334-1890
Fair Haven *(G-3078)*
National Flag & Display Co Inc ....E....... 973 366-1776
Wharton *(G-11863)*

Stewart-Morris Inc ....G....... 973 822-2777
Madison *(G-5703)*

FLAT GLASS: Antique

Artique Glass Studio Inc ....G....... 201 444-3500
Glen Rock *(G-3826)*

FLAT GLASS: Construction

McGrory Glass Inc ....D....... 856 579-3200
Paulsboro *(G-8335)*

FLAT GLASS: Laminated

JE Berkowitz LP ....C....... 856 456-7800
Pedricktown *(G-8349)*

FLAT GLASS: Tempered

Jersey Tempered Glass Inc...................E....... 856 273-8700
Mount Laurel *(G-6773)*

FLAT GLASS: Window, Clear & Colored

Elco Glass Industries Co Inc ....E....... 732 363-6550
Freehold *(G-3662)*

FLAVORS OR FLAVORING MATERIALS: Synthetic

Givaudan Flavors Corporation ....G....... 973 463-8192
Cranbury *(G-1835)*
Interntnal Flvors Frgrnces Inc ....C....... 732 264-4500
Union Beach *(G-11102)*
Interntnal Flvors Frgrnces Inc ....C....... 732 264-4500
Hazlet *(G-4262)*
Zoomessence Inc.................................G....... 732 416-6638
Sayreville *(G-9727)*

FLOOR CLEANING & MAINTENANCE EQPT: Household

Groupe Seb USA ....F 856 825-6300
Millville *(G-6253)*

FLOOR COVERING STORES

Armorpoxy Inc......................................F 908 810-9613
Union *(G-11027)*

FLOOR COVERING STORES: Carpets

A & J Carpets Inc ....G....... 856 227-1753
Blackwood *(G-458)*
Best Value Rugs & Carpets Inc.............G....... 732 752-3528
Dunellen *(G-2120)*
Worldwide Whl Flr Cvg Inc....................E....... 732 906-1400
Edison *(G-2647)*

FLOOR COVERING STORES: Rugs

Amici Imports Inc..................................F 908 272-8300
Cranford *(G-1900)*

FLOOR COVERING: Plastic

Crossfield Products Corp ....D....... 908 245-2801
Roselle Park *(G-9580)*

FLOOR COVERINGS WHOLESALERS

Armorpoxy Inc......................................F 908 810-9613
Union *(G-11027)*

FLOOR COVERINGS: Aircraft & Automobile

Fh Group International Inc ....E....... 201 210-2426
Secaucus *(G-9767)*

FLOOR COVERINGS: Rubber

Strongwall Industries Inc ....G....... 201 445-4633
Ridgewood *(G-9330)*

FLOOR COVERINGS: Tile, Support Plastic

Locktile Industries Llc ....F 888 562-5845
Newark *(G-7184)*

FLOORING: Hard Surface

Congoleum Corporation........................D....... 609 584-3601
Trenton *(G-10922)*
Dyerich Flooring Designs Ltd................G....... 973 357-0600
Paterson *(G-8175)*

Evertile Flooring Co Inc........................G....... 973 242-7474
Newark *(G-7119)*
Mannington Mills Inc ....A....... 856 935-3000
Salem *(G-9694)*
S Geno Carpet and Flooring ....G....... 215 669-1400
Mount Royal *(G-6818)*
Takasago Intl Corp USA ....E....... 201 727-4200
Teterboro *(G-10693)*
Tbs Industrial Flooring Pdts ....G....... 732 899-1486
Point Pleasant Beach *(G-8832)*

FLOORING: Hardwood

Alpine Custom Floors............................F 201 533-0100
Jersey City *(G-4689)*
Atlantic Flooring LLC ....F 609 296-7700
Ltl Egg Hbr *(G-5614)*
Flooring Concepts Nj LLC.....................F 732 409-7600
Manalapan *(G-5811)*
Friends Hardwood Floors Inc ....G....... 732 859-4019
Oakhurst *(G-7609)*

FLOORING: Rubber

Atlantic Flooring LLC ....F 609 296-7700
Ltl Egg Hbr *(G-5614)*
Flooring Concepts Nj LLC.....................F 732 409-7600
Manalapan *(G-5811)*
Linoleum Sales Company Inc ....G....... 201 438-1844
East Rutherford *(G-2296)*

FLOORING: Tile

L S P Industrial Ceramics Inc ....G....... 609 397-8330
Lambertville *(G-5193)*
Maya Trading Corporation ....G....... 201 533-1400
Jersey City *(G-4763)*

FLORIST: Flowers, Fresh

Clover Garden Ctr Ltd Lblty Co ....G....... 856 235-4625
Mount Laurel *(G-6748)*
Pennock Company.................................E....... 215 492-7900
Pennsauken *(G-8464)*

FLORISTS

Berat Corporation ....C....... 609 953-7700
Medford *(G-6020)*
Food Circus Super Markets Inc.............D....... 732 291-4079
Atlantic Highlands *(G-106)*
Little Falls Shop Rite Super ....B....... 973 256-0909
Little Falls *(G-5460)*
Shop Rite Supermarkets Inc ....C....... 732 775-4250
Neptune *(G-6898)*
Springdale Farm Market Inc ....E....... 856 424-8674
Cherry Hill *(G-1416)*

FLOWER ARRANGEMENTS: Artificial

Aqualink LLC ....F 201 849-9771
Fort Lee *(G-3547)*
Arafat Lafi ....G....... 201 854-7300
North Bergen *(G-7385)*

FLOWERS, ARTIFICIAL, WHOLESALE

Missry Associates Inc ....C....... 732 752-7500
Edison *(G-2568)*

FLOWERS, FRESH, WHOLESALE

Sunshine Bouquet Company..................C....... 732 274-2900
Dayton *(G-1990)*

FLOWERS: Artificial & Preserved

Dnp Foods America Ltd Lblty Co ....G....... 201 654-5581
Waldwick *(G-11301)*
Sunshine Bouquet Company.................C....... 732 274-2900
Dayton *(G-1990)*

FLUID METERS & COUNTING DEVICES

Action Packaging Automation ....G....... 609 448-9210
Roosevelt *(G-9527)*
Pemberton Fabricators Inc ....A....... 609 267-0922
Rancocas *(G-9163)*
Precision Dealer Services Inc................E....... 908 237-1100
Flemington *(G-3461)*
Rio Supply ....G....... 856 719-0081
Sicklerville *(G-9915)*

PRODUCT

FLUID POWER PUMPS & MOTORS

Industrial Combustion Assn ....F 732 271-0300
  Somerset *(G-10004)*
PMC Liquiflo Equipment Co Inc ....E 908 518-0666
  Garwood *(G-3791)*
Technol Inc ....F 856 848-5480
  Westville *(G-11821)*

FLUID POWER VALVES & HOSE FITTINGS

Automatic Switch Company ....A 973 966-2000
  Florham Park *(G-3485)*
Gadren Machine Co Inc ....F 856 456-4329
  Collingswood *(G-1767)*
Universal Valve Company Inc ....F 908 351-0606
  Elizabeth *(G-2784)*
Valcor Engineering Corporation ....C 973 467-8400
  Springfield *(G-10472)*

FLUXES

Alpha Assembly Solutions Inc ....E 908 561-5170
  South Plainfield *(G-10214)*
Alpha Assembly Solutions Inc ....E 908 791-3000
  Somerset *(G-9948)*
American Flux & Metal LLC ....E 609 561-7500
  Hammonton *(G-4125)*
Morgan Advanced Ceramics Inc ....E 973 808-1621
  Fairfield *(G-3273)*

FLY TRAPS: Electrical

Vandermolen Corp ....G 973 992-8506
  Ledgewood *(G-5284)*

FOAM CHARGE MIXTURES

Bergen International LLC ....G 201 299-4499
  East Rutherford *(G-2276)*

FOAM RUBBER

Diversified Foam Products Inc ....D 856 662-1981
  Swedesboro *(G-10581)*
Inoac Usa Inc ....D 201 807-0809
  Moonachie *(G-6471)*
Ls Rubber Industries Inc ....F 973 680-4488
  Bloomfield *(G-507)*
Woodbridge Inoac Technical ....D 201 807-0809
  Moonachie *(G-6498)*
Woodbridge Inoac Technical Pro ....D 201 807-0809
  Moonachie *(G-6499)*

FOAM RUBBER, WHOLESALE

Foam Rubber Fabricators Inc ....E 973 751-1445
  Belleville *(G-296)*
Supply Plus NY Inc ....E 973 481-4800
  Paterson *(G-8308)*

FOAMS & RUBBER, WHOLESALE

Diversified Display Pdts LLC ....E 908 686-2200
  Hillside *(G-4389)*

FOIL & LEAF: Metal

Amcor Flexibles Inc ....E 609 267-5900
  Mount Holly *(G-6723)*
API Americas Inc ....D 732 382-6800
  Rahway *(G-9077)*
Constantia Blythewood LLC ....D 732 974-4100
  Belmar *(G-347)*
Crown Roll Leaf Inc ....C 973 742-4000
  Paterson *(G-8164)*
Glitterex Corp ....D 908 272-9121
  Cranford *(G-1911)*
Spectrum Foils Inc ....G 973 481-0808
  Newark *(G-7281)*

FOIL BOARD: Made From Purchased Materials

Goetz & Ruschmann Inc ....E 973 383-9270
  Newton *(G-7345)*

FOIL: Aluminum

Elkom North America Inc ....G 732 786-0490
  Manalapan *(G-5807)*
Yarde Metals Inc ....E 973 463-1166
  East Hanover *(G-2248)*

FOIL: Copper

Materials Technology Inc ....G 732 246-1000
  Somerset *(G-10024)*

FOIL: Zinc

Hueck Foils Holding Co ....G 732 974-4100
  Wall Township *(G-11347)*

FOOD CASINGS: Plastic

Globe Packaging Co Inc ....G 201 896-1144
  Carlstadt *(G-1159)*
Revere Industries LLC ....C 856 881-3600
  Clayton *(G-1528)*
Tyz-All Plastics LLC ....G 201 343-1200
  Hackensack *(G-3987)*

FOOD COLORINGS

Grow Company Inc ....E 201 941-8777
  Ridgefield *(G-9264)*
Ifc Solutions Inc ....E 908 862-8810
  Linden *(G-5357)*
Prime Ingredients Inc ....G 201 791-6655
  Saddle Brook *(G-9670)*

FOOD PRDTS & SEAFOOD: Shellfish, Fresh, Shucked

Bivalve Packing Inc ....G 856 785-0270
  Port Norris *(G-8885)*

FOOD PRDTS, BREAKFAST: Cereal, Granola & Muesli

Naturalvert LLC ....G 848 229-4600
  Hawthorne *(G-4233)*
Simi Granola LLC ....F 848 459-5619
  Jackson *(G-4665)*

FOOD PRDTS, BREAKFAST: Cereal, Oats, Rolled

Silver Palate Kitchens Inc ....E 201 568-0110
  Cresskill *(G-1944)*

FOOD PRDTS, CANNED OR FRESH PACK: Fruit Juices

BSC USA LLC ....F 908 487-4437
  Palisades Park *(G-7770)*
Campbell Company of Canada ....G 856 342-4800
  Camden *(G-1046)*
Halo Farm Inc ....G 609 695-3311
  Lawrenceville *(G-5230)*
Johanna Foods Inc ....B 908 788-2200
  Flemington *(G-3452)*
Lassonde Pappas and Co Inc ....D 856 455-1000
  Carneys Point *(G-1242)*
Lassonde Pappas and Co Inc ....E 856 455-1001
  Bridgeton *(G-762)*
Pappas Lassonde Holdings Inc ....G 856 455-1000
  Carneys Point *(G-1243)*
Refresco Us Inc ....D 973 361-9794
  Wharton *(G-11869)*

FOOD PRDTS, CANNED: Baby Food

Freed Foods Inc ....G 512 829-5535
  Hillside *(G-4392)*
Mysuperfoods Ltd Liability Co ....F 646 283-7455
  Summit *(G-10541)*

FOOD PRDTS, CANNED: Barbecue Sauce

Funnibonz LLC ....G 609 915-3685
  Princeton Junction *(G-9059)*

FOOD PRDTS, CANNED: Beans & Bean Sprouts

B&G Foods Inc ....B 973 401-6500
  Parsippany *(G-7889)*
B&G Foods Inc ....C 973 401-6500
  Parsippany *(G-7890)*
Goya Foods Inc ....E 201 865-3470
  Secaucus *(G-9777)*

FOOD PRDTS, CANNED: Chili Sauce, Tomato

Gardner Resources Inc ....G 732 872-0755
  Highlands *(G-4292)*

FOOD PRDTS, CANNED: Ethnic

Crave Foods LLC ....F 973 233-1220
  Montclair *(G-6361)*
Fast-Pak Trading Inc ....G 201 293-4757
  Secaucus *(G-9766)*
Nema Food Distribution Inc ....G 973 256-4415
  Fairfield *(G-3276)*
Sanket Corporation ....F 732 287-0201
  Edison *(G-2604)*

FOOD PRDTS, CANNED: Fruit Juices, Fresh

Juice Hub LLP ....G 732 784-8265
  Rahway *(G-9110)*

FOOD PRDTS, CANNED: Fruits

B&G Foods Inc ....B 973 401-6500
  Parsippany *(G-7889)*
B&G Foods Inc ....C 973 401-6500
  Parsippany *(G-7890)*
Campbell Soup Company ....A 856 342-4800
  Camden *(G-1047)*
Campbell Soup Company ....G 856 342-4759
  Camden *(G-1048)*
Garelick Farms LLC ....C 609 499-2600
  Burlington *(G-970)*
Ingrasselino Products LLC ....G 800 960-1316
  Clifton *(G-1640)*
Pomi USA Inc ....G 732 541-4115
  Matawan *(G-5985)*
Wayne County Foods Inc ....E 973 399-0101
  Irvington *(G-4589)*

FOOD PRDTS, CANNED: Fruits & Fruit Prdts

C & E Canners Inc ....F 609 561-1078
  Hammonton *(G-4132)*
Cameco Inc ....D 973 239-2845
  Verona *(G-11164)*

FOOD PRDTS, CANNED: Italian

Antonio Mozzarella Factory Inc ....F 973 353-9411
  Newark *(G-7049)*
Antonio Mozzarella Factory Inc ....E 973 353-9411
  Newark *(G-7050)*
Bono USA Inc ....G 973 978-7361
  Fairfield *(G-3159)*
Goldens Inc ....G 215 850-2512
  Haddonfield *(G-4059)*
Grandi Pastai Italiani Inc ....G 201 786-5050
  Moonachie *(G-6467)*
Healthy Italia Retail LLC ....F 973 966-5200
  Madison *(G-5694)*
Mrs Mazzulas Food Products ....G 732 248-0555
  Edison *(G-2570)*
Tuscany Especially Itln Foods ....F 732 308-1118
  Marlboro *(G-5918)*

FOOD PRDTS, CANNED: Jams, Including Imitation

B&G Foods Inc ....C 973 403-6795
  Roseland *(G-9534)*

FOOD PRDTS, CANNED: Mexican, NEC

Mayab Happy Tacos Inc ....E 732 293-0400
  Perth Amboy *(G-8526)*

FOOD PRDTS, CANNED: Seasonings, Tomato

European Amrcn Foods Group Inc ....E 201 436-6106
  Bayonne *(G-215)*

FOOD PRDTS, CANNED: Soups

Aunt Kittys Foods Inc ....D 856 691-2100
  Vineland *(G-11189)*
Campbell Soup Company ....A 856 342-4800
  Camden *(G-1047)*

FOOD PRDTS, CANNED: Soups, Exc Seafood

Campbell Company of Canada..............G...... 856 342-4800
Camden *(G-1046)*
RAB Food Group LLC......................D...... 201 553-1100
Newark *(G-7244)*

FOOD PRDTS, CANNED: Spaghetti & Other Pasta Sauce

RSR Enterprises LLC......................F...... 732 369-6053
Martinsville *(G-5964)*

FOOD PRDTS, CANNED: Tomato Sauce.

Losurdo Foods Inc...........................E...... 201 343-6680
Hackensack *(G-3940)*
Raos Specialty Foods Inc.................F...... 212 269-0151
Montclair *(G-6387)*

FOOD PRDTS, CANNED: Vegetable Pastes

Northeast Tomato Company Inc.........F...... 973 684-4890
Paterson *(G-8271)*

FOOD PRDTS, CONFECTIONERY, WHOLESALE: Candy

Birnn Chocolates Inc........................G...... 732 214-8680
Highland Park *(G-4287)*
Damask Kandies..............................G...... 856 467-1661
Swedesboro *(G-10578)*
Ferrero U S A Inc.............................C...... 732 764-9300
Parsippany *(G-7943)*
Marlow Candy & Nut Co Inc..............E...... 201 569-7606
Englewood *(G-2922)*
Shrivers Salt Wtr Taffy Fudge...........E...... 609 399-0100
Ocean City *(G-7696)*
World Confections Inc......................D...... 718 768-8100
South Orange *(G-10203)*

FOOD PRDTS, CONFECTIONERY, WHOLESALE: Nuts, Salted/Roasted

Cibo Vita Inc....................................B...... 862 238-8020
Totowa *(G-10823)*
Cns Confectionery Products LLC.........F...... 201 823-1400
Bayonne *(G-211)*

FOOD PRDTS, CONFECTIONERY, WHOLESALE: Pretzels

A & A Soft Pretzel Company...............G...... 856 338-0208
Camden *(G-1038)*
J & J Snack Foods Corp PA................G...... 856 665-9533
Pennsauken *(G-8441)*

FOOD PRDTS, CONFECTIONERY, WHOLESALE: Snack Foods

Fast-Pak Trading Inc........................G...... 201 293-4757
Secaucus *(G-9766)*
Pace Target Brokerage Inc................E...... 856 629-2551
Williamstown *(G-11967)*
Palsgaard Incorporated.....................F...... 973 998-7951
Morris Plains *(G-6622)*
Zestos Foods LLC.............................G...... 888 407-5852
Teaneck *(G-10657)*

FOOD PRDTS, CONFECTIONERY, WHOLESALE: Syrups, Fountain

Asbury Syrup Company Inc................F...... 732 774-5746
Ocean *(G-7656)*

FOOD PRDTS, DAIRY, WHOLESALE: Frozen Dairy Desserts

Dairy Queen....................................F...... 732 892-5700
Point Pleasant Boro *(G-8842)*
Rajbhog Foods(nj) Inc......................C...... 551 222-4700
Jersey City *(G-4796)*

FOOD PRDTS, DAIRY, WHOLESALE: Milk, Canned Or Dried

Arla Foods Ingredients N Amer..........F...... 908 604-8551
Basking Ridge *(G-175)*
Cns Confectionery Products LLC.........F...... 201 823-1400
Bayonne *(G-211)*

Dairy Delight LLC............................F...... 201 939-7878
Rutherford *(G-9617)*

FOOD PRDTS, FISH & SEAFOOD, WHOLESALE: Seafood

Bay Treasure Seafood LLC................F...... 732 240-3474
Toms River *(G-10750)*
Certified Clam Corp..........................F...... 732 872-6650
Highlands *(G-4291)*
Ruggiero Sea Food Inc......................F...... 973 589-0524
Newark *(G-7254)*
Ruggiero Sea Food Inc......................G...... 973 589-0524
Newark *(G-7255)*

FOOD PRDTS, FISH & SEAFOOD: Clams, Canned, Jarred, Etc

Lamonica Fine Foods LLC..................C...... 856 776-2126
Millville *(G-6258)*

FOOD PRDTS, FISH & SEAFOOD: Fish, Canned, Jarred, Etc

RAB Food Group LLC.........................D...... 201 553-1100
Newark *(G-7244)*

FOOD PRDTS, FISH & SEAFOOD: Fish, Frozen, Prepared

Delight Foods USA LLC......................F...... 201 369-1199
Jersey City *(G-4722)*

FOOD PRDTS, FISH & SEAFOOD: Fish, Smoked

Ho-Ho-Kus Smked Delicacies LLC........G...... 201 445-1677
Ho Ho Kus *(G-4440)*

FOOD PRDTS, FISH & SEAFOOD: Fresh, Prepared

J & R Foods Inc...............................F...... 732 229-4020
Long Branch *(G-5600)*
Lamonica Fine Foods LLC..................C...... 856 776-2126
Millville *(G-6258)*
Lm Foods LLC..................................D...... 732 855-9500
Carteret *(G-1259)*

FOOD PRDTS, FISH & SEAFOOD: Oysters, Canned, Jarred, Etc

Hillard Bloom Packing Co Inc............G...... 856 785-0120
Port Norris *(G-8886)*

FOOD PRDTS, FISH & SEAFOOD: Prepared Cakes & Sticks

Peak Finance Holdings LLC...............G...... 856 969-7100
Cherry Hill *(G-1406)*
Pinnacle Foods Finance LLC..............D...... 973 541-6620
Parsippany *(G-7991)*
Pinnacle Foods Group LLC.................D...... 856 969-8238
Parsippany *(G-7992)*

FOOD PRDTS, FISH & SEAFOOD: Seafood, Frozen, Prepared

CHR International Inc........................G...... 201 262-8186
Oradell *(G-7741)*
Sunrise Food Trading Inc...................F...... 718 305-4388
Warren *(G-11432)*

FOOD PRDTS, FROZEN: Breakfasts, Packaged

Amys Omelette Hse Burlington...........F...... 609 386-4800
Burlington *(G-949)*
Peak Finance Holdings LLC...............G...... 856 969-7100
Cherry Hill *(G-1406)*
Pinnacle Food Group Inc...................E...... 856 969-7100
Parsippany *(G-7990)*
Pinnacle Foods Finance LLC..............D...... 973 541-6620
Parsippany *(G-7991)*
Pinnacle Foods Group LLC.................D...... 856 969-8238
Parsippany *(G-7992)*
Rajbhog Foods(nj) Inc......................C...... 551 222-4700
Jersey City *(G-4796)*
Waffle Waffle LLC.............................F...... 201 559-1286
Nutley *(G-7597)*

FOOD PRDTS, FROZEN: Dinners, Packaged

Deep Foods Inc................................C...... 908 810-7500
Union *(G-11042)*

FOOD PRDTS, FROZEN: Ethnic Foods, NEC

Battistini Foods...............................G...... 609 476-2184
Egg Harbor Township *(G-2680)*
Delicious Fresh Pierogi Inc................F...... 908 245-0550
Roselle Park *(G-9583)*
Fast-Pak Trading Inc........................G...... 201 293-4757
Secaucus *(G-9766)*
L E Rosellis Food Specialties.............F...... 609 654-4816
Medford *(G-6027)*
Old Fashion Kitchen Inc....................D...... 732 364-4100
Lakewood *(G-5143)*
Savignano Food Corp.........................E...... 973 673-3355
Orange *(G-7760)*
Vineland Specialty Foods L L C...........G...... 856 742-5001
Westville *(G-11823)*

FOOD PRDTS, FROZEN: Fruits & Vegetables

Bart Foods Group LLC.......................G...... 973 650-8837
Fairfield *(G-3152)*

FOOD PRDTS, FROZEN: Fruits, Juices & Vegetables

202 Smoothie LLC............................G...... 973 985-4973
Wayne *(G-11463)*
Berry Blast Smoothies LLC................G...... 856 692-6174
Vineland *(G-11194)*
Grasso Foods Inc.............................G...... 856 467-2223
Woolwich Township *(G-12097)*

FOOD PRDTS, FROZEN: NEC

Appetizers Made Easy Inc.................E...... 201 531-1212
East Rutherford *(G-2271)*
Arctic Foods Inc...............................E...... 908 689-0590
Washington *(G-11438)*
Caesars Pasta LLC............................E...... 856 227-2585
Blackwood *(G-462)*
Campbell Soup Company....................A...... 856 342-4800
Camden *(G-1047)*
Campbell Soup Company....................G...... 856 342-4759
Camden *(G-1048)*
Cuisine Innvtons Unlimited LLC...........C...... 732 730-9310
Lakewood *(G-5077)*
Dewy Meadow Farms Inc...................F...... 908 218-5655
Bridgewater *(G-818)*
Diaz Wholesale & Mfg Co Inc............D...... 404 629-3616
Saddle Brook *(G-9649)*
DO Productions LLC..........................D...... 856 866-3566
Lodi *(G-5559)*
Dr Pregers Sensible Foods Inc............D...... 201 703-1300
Elmwood Park *(G-2823)*
Pinnacle Foods Group LLC.................C...... 856 969-7100
Cherry Hill *(G-1409)*
Pinnacle Foods Inc...........................C...... 973 541-6620
Parsippany *(G-7993)*
Rich Products Corporation..................G...... 856 696-5600
Vineland *(G-11259)*
Rico Foods Inc.................................E...... 973 278-0589
Paterson *(G-8287)*
Severino Pasta Mfg Co Inc................E...... 856 854-3716
Collingswood *(G-1771)*
Seviroli Foods Inc.............................G...... 856 931-1900
Bellmawr *(G-343)*
Tovli Inc..E...... 718 417-6677
Newark *(G-7301)*
Unilever United States Inc..................A...... 201 735-9661
Englewood Cliffs *(G-2995)*

FOOD PRDTS, FROZEN: Pizza

Dairy Deluxe Corp............................G...... 845 549-0665
Hackensack *(G-3904)*
McCain Ellios Foods Inc.....................C...... 201 368-0600
Lodi *(G-5571)*
Mjs of Spotswood LLC.......................G...... 732 251-7400
Spotswood *(G-10416)*

FOOD PRDTS, FROZEN: Snack Items

Group Martin LLC Jj..........................F...... 862 240-1813
Newark *(G-7141)*

FOOD PRDTS, FROZEN: Soups

Classic Cooking LLC ....D....... 718 439-0200
  Rahway (G-9086)

FOOD PRDTS, FROZEN: Vegetables, Exc Potato Prdts

Birds Eye Foods Inc ....C....... 920 435-5300
  Parsippany (G-7894)
Birds Eye Foods Inc ....C....... 585 383-1850
  Cherry Hill (G-1346)
Classic Cooking LLC ....D....... 718 439-0200
  Rahway (G-9086)
Seabrook Brothers & Sons Inc ....C....... 856 455-8080
  Bridgeton (G-772)

FOOD PRDTS, FROZEN: Whipped Topping

Birds Eye Foods Inc ....C....... 585 383-1850
  Cherry Hill (G-1346)

FOOD PRDTS, FRUITS & VEGETABLES, FRESH, WHOLESALE: Vegetable

DArtagnan Inc ....D....... 973 344-0565
  Union (G-11041)

FOOD PRDTS, MEAT & MEAT PRDTS, WHOLESALE: Fresh

Cameco Inc ....D....... 973 239-2845
  Verona (G-11164)
Carl Streit & Son Co......................G....... 732 775-0803
  Neptune (G-6869)
DArtagnan Inc ....D....... 973 344-0565
  Union (G-11041)
Kleemeyer & Merkel Inc ....F....... 973 377-0875
  Green Village (G-3868)
Licini Brothers Inc ....G....... 201 865-1130
  Union City (G-11119)
Lorenzo Food Group Inc ....E....... 201 868-9088
  Englewood (G-2920)
Rastelli Brothers Inc ....C....... 856 803-1100
  Swedesboro (G-10606)

FOOD PRDTS, POULTRY, WHOLESALE: Poultry Prdts, NEC

David Mitchell Inc..........................E....... 856 429-2610
  Voorhees (G-11284)

FOOD PRDTS, WHOL: Canned Goods, Fruit, Veg, Seafood/Meats

Cameco Inc ....D....... 973 239-2845
  Verona (G-11164)

FOOD PRDTS, WHOLESALE: Beans, Dry, Bulk

Kalustyan Corporation ....D....... 908 688-6111
  Union (G-11068)

FOOD PRDTS, WHOLESALE: Breakfast Cereals

Coco International Inc ....E....... 973 694-1200
  Wayne (G-11489)

FOOD PRDTS, WHOLESALE: Chocolate

Third Ave Chocolate Shoppe ....G....... 732 449-7535
  Spring Lake (G-10424)

FOOD PRDTS, WHOLESALE: Coffee & Tea

Eight OClock Coffee Company.............D....... 201 571-9214
  Montvale (G-6410)
Orens Daily Roast Inc ....F....... 201 432-2008
  Jersey City (G-4777)
United Mijovi Amer Ltd Lblty ....F....... 732 718-1001
  New Brunswick (G-6975)

FOOD PRDTS, WHOLESALE: Coffee, Green Or Roasted

Coffee Associates Inc....................E....... 201 945-1060
  Edgewater (G-2436)
Pan American Coffee Company ....E....... 201 963-2329
  Hoboken (G-4472)

FOOD PRDTS, WHOLESALE: Cookies

Vivis Life LLC ....G....... 201 798-1938
  Jersey City (G-4827)

FOOD PRDTS, WHOLESALE: Cooking Oils

Cosmopolitan Food Group Inc ....G....... 908 998-1818
  Hoboken (G-4449)

FOOD PRDTS, WHOLESALE: Dried or Canned Foods

Metropolitan Foods Inc ....C....... 973 672-9400
  Clifton (G-1668)
United Natural Trading Co..................D....... 732 650-9905
  Edison (G-2636)

FOOD PRDTS, WHOLESALE: Flavorings & Fragrances

Advanced Biotech Overseas LLC ....G....... 973 339-6242
  Totowa (G-10808)
Beauty-Fill LLC ....E....... 908 353-1600
  Hillside (G-4381)
Charabot & Co Inc.........................F....... 201 812-2762
  Budd Lake (G-920)
Excell Brands Ltd Liability Co ....G....... 908 561-1130
  Princeton (G-8946)
Flavors of Origin Inc ....E....... 732 499-9700
  Avenel (G-127)
Interbahm International Inc ....E....... 732 499-9700
  Avenel (G-131)
Robertet Inc ....E....... 201 405-1000
  Budd Lake (G-932)

FOOD PRDTS, WHOLESALE: Health

Fast-Pak Trading Inc......................G....... 201 293-4757
  Secaucus (G-9766)
Innophos LLC ....G....... 973 808-5900
  East Hanover (G-2217)
Medison Pharmaceuticals Inc ....F....... 856 304-8516
  Piscataway (G-8689)
Naturalvert LLC ....G....... 848 229-4600
  Hawthorne (G-4233)
Vitaquest International LLC ....B....... 973 575-9200
  West Caldwell (G-11681)
Vitaquest International LLC ....F....... 973 575-9200
  Fairfield (G-3346)
Zestos Foods LLC ....G....... 888 407-5852
  Teaneck (G-10657)

FOOD PRDTS, WHOLESALE: Juices

American Food & Bev Inds LLC ....D....... 347 241-9827
  Orange (G-7750)

FOOD PRDTS, WHOLESALE: Molasses, Indl

International Molasses Corp.................E....... 201 368-8036
  Saddle Brook (G-9657)

FOOD PRDTS, WHOLESALE: Natural & Organic

DArtagnan Inc ....D....... 973 344-0565
  Union (G-11041)
Maverick Caterers LLC ....E....... 718 433-3776
  Hackensack (G-3944)

FOOD PRDTS, WHOLESALE: Pasta & Rice

35 Food Corp ....G....... 732 442-1640
  Woodbridge (G-12011)
La Pace Imports Inc ....F....... 973 895-5420
  Morristown (G-6677)
Lioni Mozzarella & Spclty ....E....... 908 624-9450
  Union (G-11071)
Severina Pasta Mfg Co Inc ....E....... 856 854-3716
  Collingswood (G-1771)
Slt Foods Inc ....F....... 732 661-1030
  Dayton (G-1988)

FOOD PRDTS, WHOLESALE: Salad Dressing

Allied Food Products Inc...................E....... 908 357-2454
  Linden (G-5321)

FOOD PRDTS, WHOLESALE: Salt, Edible

Saltopia Infused Sea Salt LLC ....F....... 908 850-1926
  Hackettstown (G-4035)

FOOD PRDTS, WHOLESALE: Sauces

Gardner Resources Inc ....G....... 732 872-0755
  Highlands (G-4292)

FOOD PRDTS, WHOLESALE: Sausage Casings

Nitta Casings Inc ....C....... 800 526-3970
  Bridgewater (G-857)

FOOD PRDTS, WHOLESALE: Specialty

Delicious Fresh Pierogi Inc ....F....... 908 245-0550
  Roselle Park (G-9583)
Farbest-Tallman Foods Corp ....D....... 714 897-7199
  Park Ridge (G-7849)
Golden Fluff Inc ....F....... 732 367-5448
  Lakewood (G-5105)
Sunco & Frenchie Ltd Lblty Co ....G....... 973 478-1011
  Clifton (G-1726)
Sunrise Food Trading Inc ....F....... 718 305-4388
  Warren (G-11432)

FOOD PRDTS, WHOLESALE: Spices & Seasonings

A A Sayia & Company Inc.................G....... 201 659-1179
  Hoboken (G-4442)
Gel Spice Co Inc ....B....... 201 339-0700
  Bayonne (G-218)
Green Labs LLC ....G....... 862 220-4845
  Newark (G-7139)
Interntnal Ingrdent Sltons Inc ....E....... 856 778-6623
  Mount Laurel (G-6769)
Kalustyan Corporation ....D 908 688-6111
  Union (G-11068)
Melissa Spice Trading Corp ....F....... 862 262-7773
  Glen Rock (G-3832)
Mincing Trading Corporation ....E....... 732 355-9944
  Dayton (G-1980)
PDM Packaging Inc.......................F....... 201 864-1115
  North Bergen (G-7428)
Pereg Gourmet Spices Ltd ....G....... 718 261-6767
  Clifton (G-1689)

FOOD PRDTS, WHOLESALE: Tea

Adagio Teas Inc............................G....... 973 253-7400
  Elmwood Park (G-2807)
B-Tea Beverage LLC ....E....... 201 512-8400
  Fair Lawn (G-3089)
Harris Freeman & Co Inc ....D....... 856 787-9026
  Moorestown (G-6527)

FOOD PRDTS, WHOLESALE: Water, Mineral Or Spring, Bottled

Shrem Consulting Ltd Lblty Co ....G....... 917 371-0581
  West Long Branch (G-11721)

FOOD PRDTS: Almond Pastes

Sun Basket Inc ....C....... 408 669-4418
  Westampton (G-11792)

FOOD PRDTS: Animal & marine fats & oils

Bringhurst Bros Inc ....E....... 856 767-0110
  Berlin (G-418)
Darling Ingredients Inc ....C....... 973 465-1900
  Newark (G-7095)
Epicore Networks USA Inc ....E....... 609 267-9118
  Mount Holly (G-6727)

FOOD PRDTS: Blackstrap Molasses, Purchd Raw Sugar/Syrup

International Molasses Corp.................E....... 201 368-8036
  Maywood (G-6006)

FOOD PRDTS: Breakfast Bars

Amys Omelette Hse Burlington ....F....... 609 386-4800
  Burlington (G-949)

FOOD PRDTS: Cereals

Dim Inc ....F....... 908 925-2043
  Linden (G-5343)
Gerber Products Company ....C....... 973 593-7500
  Florham Park (G-3508)

Kellogg Company ....E 201 634-9140
  River Edge *(G-9363)*
Kellogg Company ....D 609 567-1688
  Hammonton *(G-4137)*
Mm Packaging Group LLC ....G 908 759-0101
  Linden *(G-5387)*

FOOD PRDTS: Chewing Gum Base

L A Dreyfus Co ....C 732 549-1600
  Edison *(G-2548)*

FOOD PRDTS: Cocoa, Butter

Cocoa Services Inc ....F 856 234-1700
  Moorestown *(G-6514)*

FOOD PRDTS: Cocoa, Powdered

Mack Trading LLC ....G 973 794-4904
  Hewitt *(G-4276)*

FOOD PRDTS: Coconut, Desiccated & Shredded

International Coconut Corp ....F 908 289-1555
  Elizabeth *(G-2751)*

FOOD PRDTS: Coffee

26 Flavors LLC ....G 855 662-7299
  Newark *(G-7027)*
Arias Mountain-Coffee LLC ....F 973 927-9595
  Flanders *(G-3401)*
Coffee Associates Inc ....E 201 945-1060
  Edgewater *(G-2436)*
Corim International Coffee Imp ....D 800 942-4201
  Brick *(G-714)*
Counting Sheep Coffee Inc ....G 973 589-4104
  Newark *(G-7089)*
Eight OClock Coffee Company ....D 201 571-9214
  Montvale *(G-6410)*
European Coffee Classics Inc ....E 856 428-7202
  Cherry Hill *(G-1360)*
Greene Bros Spclty Cof Rasters ......F 908 979-0022
  Hackettstown *(G-4009)*
Longview Coffee Co NJ Inc ....E 908 788-4186
  Frenchtown *(G-3715)*
Massimo Zanetti Beverage USA ....E 201 440-1700
  Moonachie *(G-6478)*
Nestle Usa Inc ....C 732 462-1300
  Freehold *(G-3682)*
Orens Daily Roast Inc ....F 201 432-2008
  Jersey City *(G-4777)*
Pan American Coffee Company ....E 201 963-2329
  Hoboken *(G-4472)*
Socafe LLC ....F 973 589-4104
  Newark *(G-7278)*

FOOD PRDTS: Coffee Extracts

Adagio Teas Inc ....G 973 253-7400
  Elmwood Park *(G-2807)*

FOOD PRDTS: Coffee Roasting, Exc Wholesale Grocers

Coffee Company LLC ....G 609 399-5533
  Ocean City *(G-7688)*
Coffee Company LLC ....G 609 398-2326
  Ocean City *(G-7689)*
Melitta Usa Inc ....E 856 428-7202
  Cherry Hill *(G-1393)*
Mire Enterprises LLC ....G 732 882-1010
  Linden *(G-5386)*
Two Rivers Coffee LLC ....G 908 205-0018
  South Plainfield *(G-10332)*
World of Coffee Inc ....G 908 647-1218
  Stirling *(G-10499)*

FOOD PRDTS: Cooking Oils, Refined Vegetable, Exc Corn

Oasis Trading Co Inc ....C 908 964-0477
  Hillside *(G-4419)*

FOOD PRDTS: Corn Chips & Other Corn-Based Snacks

Thats How We Roll LLC ....G 973 240-0200
  Montclair *(G-6392)*

FOOD PRDTS: Dessert Mixes & Fillings

Allied Food Products Inc ....E 908 357-2454
  Linden *(G-5321)*

FOOD PRDTS: Desserts, Ready-To-Mix

Dulce A Dessert Bar LLC ....G 908 461-2418
  Matawan *(G-5973)*

FOOD PRDTS: Doughs, Frozen Or Refrig From Purchased Flour

Jimmys Cookies LLC ....C 973 779-8500
  Clifton *(G-1647)*
Nijama Corporation ....G 973 272-3223
  Clifton *(G-1678)*

FOOD PRDTS: Dressings, Salad, Raw & Cooked Exc Dry Mixes

Chelten House Products Inc ....C 856 467-1600
  Bridgeport *(G-735)*
Oasis Trading Co Inc ....C 908 964-0477
  Hillside *(G-4419)*
Panos Brands LLC ....E 800 229-1706
  Linden *(G-5402)*
Raos Specialty Foods Inc ....F 212 269-0151
  Montclair *(G-6387)*
Rutgers Food Innovation Center ......F 856 459-1900
  Bridgeton *(G-771)*
Unilever United States Inc ....A 201 735-9661
  Englewood Cliffs *(G-2995)*

FOOD PRDTS: Dried & Dehydrated Fruits, Vegetables & Soup Mix

Mrs Mazzulas Food Products ....G 732 248-0555
  Edison *(G-2570)*

FOOD PRDTS: Edible Oil Prdts, Exc Corn Oil

Aak USA Inc ....D 973 344-1300
  Edison *(G-2444)*
European Amrcn Foods Group Inc ......E 201 436-6106
  Bayonne *(G-215)*
European Amrcn Foods Group Inc ......B 201 583-1101
  Secaucus *(G-9764)*

FOOD PRDTS: Edible fats & oils

Aarhuskarlshamn USA Inc ....G 973 344-1300
  Newark *(G-7032)*
Technical Oil Products Co Inc ....G 973 940-8920
  Newton *(G-7362)*

FOOD PRDTS: Eggs, Processed

Deb El Food Products LLC ....D 908 409-0010
  Elizabeth *(G-2727)*
Deb El Food Products LLC ....B 908 351-0330
  Newark *(G-7098)*
Papettis Hygrade Egg Pdts Inc ....A 908 282-7900
  Elizabethport *(G-2790)*

FOOD PRDTS: Eggs, Processed, Dehydrated

Deb-El Foods Corporation ....C 908 351-0330
  Newark *(G-7099)*

FOOD PRDTS: Emulsifiers

National Lecithim Inc ....G 973 940-8920
  Newton *(G-7351)*
Nexira Inc ....F 908 704-7480
  Somerville *(G-10122)*

FOOD PRDTS: Flavored Ices, Frozen

J & J Snack Foods Corp ....B 856 665-9533
  Pennsauken *(G-8440)*
J & J Snack Foods Corp ....C 856 467-9552
  Bridgeport *(G-740)*
South Jersey Pretzel Inc ....F 856 435-5055
  Stratford *(G-10507)*
Taylor Products Inc ....E 732 225-4620
  Edison *(G-2631)*

FOOD PRDTS: Flour & Other Grain Mill Products

Frewitt USA Inc ....E 908 829-5245
  Hillsborough *(G-4317)*

FOOD PRDTS: Flour Mixes & Doughs

Chanks USA LLC ....G 856 265-0203
  Millville *(G-6242)*
Foodtek Inc ....F 973 257-4000
  Whippany *(G-11891)*
R C Fine Foods Inc ....D 908 359-5500
  Hillsborough *(G-4349)*
Slt Foods Inc ....F 732 661-1030
  Dayton *(G-1988)*

FOOD PRDTS: Flour, Cake From Purchased Flour

Peak Finance Holdings LLC ....G 856 969-7100
  Cherry Hill *(G-1406)*
Pinnacle Foods Finance LLC ....D 973 541-6620
  Parsippany *(G-7991)*
Pinnacle Foods Group LLC ....D 856 969-8238
  Parsippany *(G-7992)*

FOOD PRDTS: Flours & Flour Mixes, From Purchased Flour

Fornazor International Inc ....E 201 664-4000
  Hillsdale *(G-4366)*

FOOD PRDTS: Fresh Vegetables, Peeled Or Processed

F&S Produce Company Inc ....C 856 453-0316
  Vineland *(G-11218)*

FOOD PRDTS: Fruit Juices

American Food & Bev Inds LLC ....D 347 241-9827
  Orange *(G-7750)*
Ejz Foods LLC ....G 201 229-0500
  South Hackensack *(G-10157)*
G & Y Specialty Foods LLC ....G 956 821-9652
  Woodland Park *(G-12080)*
Gerber Products Company ....C 973 593-7500
  Florham Park *(G-3508)*
Mojo Organics Inc ....G 201 633-6519
  Jersey City *(G-4767)*

FOOD PRDTS: Fruit Pops, Frozen

Icykidz ....G 973 342-9665
  Irvington *(G-4573)*

FOOD PRDTS: Fruits & Vegetables, Pickled

Crazy Steves Concoctions LLC ....G 908 787-2089
  Trenton *(G-10924)*
United Farm Processing Corp ....F 856 451-4612
  Rosenhayn *(G-9598)*

FOOD PRDTS: Fruits, Dehydrated Or Dried

Cibo Vita Inc ....B 862 238-8020
  Totowa *(G-10823)*

FOOD PRDTS: Gelatin Dessert Preparations

Joyce Food LLC ....C 973 491-9696
  Newark *(G-7171)*
Poly-Gel LLC ....E 973 884-3300
  Whippany *(G-11904)*

FOOD PRDTS: Glucose

Amerchol Corporation ....C 732 248-6000
  Edison *(G-2452)*

FOOD PRDTS: Granola & Energy Bars, Nonchocolate

Joy Snacks LLC ....F 732 272-0707
  Avenel *(G-132)*

FOOD PRDTS: Granulated Cane Sugar

Global Commodities Exportacao ....G 201 613-1532
  Newark *(G-7133)*

FOOD PRDTS: Ice, Blocks

Artic Ice Manufacturing Co ....G 973 772-7000
  Garfield *(G-3729)*
United States Cold Storage Inc ....B 856 354-8181
  Camden *(G-1089)*

FOOD PRDTS: Ice, Cubes

United City Ice Cube Co Inc ....G...... 201 945-8387
Ridgefield (G-9295)

FOOD PRDTS: Instant Coffee

United Mijovi Amer Ltd Lblty ....F 732 718-1001
New Brunswick (G-6975)

FOOD PRDTS: Luncheon Meat, Poultry

Nema Food Distribution Inc ....G...... 973 256-4415
Fairfield (G-3276)

FOOD PRDTS: Macaroni Prdts, Dry, Alphabet, Rings Or Shells

A Zeregas Sons Inc ....C...... 201 797-1400
Fair Lawn (G-3080)
Porfirio Foods Inc ....G...... 609 393-4116
Trenton (G-10976)
Silver Palate Kitchens Inc ....E...... 201 568-0110
Cresskill (G-1944)

FOOD PRDTS: Macaroni, Noodles, Spaghetti, Pasta, Etc

Casa Di Bertacchi Corporation.............C...... 856 696-5600
Vineland (G-11197)
Gardellas Rvioli Itln Deli LLC................F...... 856 697-3509
Vineland (G-11222)
L E Rosellis Food Specialties ....F...... 609 654-4816
Medford (G-6027)
Raffettos Corp ....F...... 201 372-1222
Moonachie (G-6486)
Severino Pasta Mfg Co Inc ....E...... 856 854-3716
Collingswood (G-1771)
Vitamia Pasta Boy Inc............................F...... 973 546-1140
Lodi (G-5582)

FOOD PRDTS: Malt

International Molasses Corp ....E...... 201 368-8036
Saddle Brook (G-9657)

FOOD PRDTS: Margarine & Vegetable Oils

Western Pacific Foods Inc ....F...... 908 838-0186
Kearny (G-4905)

FOOD PRDTS: Margarine, Including Imitation

Bimbo Bakeries USA Inc ....C...... 973 256-8200
Totowa (G-10820)

FOOD PRDTS: Margarine-Butter Blends

Upfield US Inc ....B...... 201 894-2540
Hackensack (G-3989)

FOOD PRDTS: Mayonnaise & Dressings, Exc Tomato Based

Dee & L LLC..F...... 201 858-0138
Bayonne (G-213)

FOOD PRDTS: Menhaden Oil

Daybrook Holdings Inc ....B...... 973 538-6766
Morristown (G-6659)

FOOD PRDTS: Mixes, Bread & Roll From Purchased Flour

Caravan Ingredients Inc ....C...... 973 256-8886
Totowa (G-10821)

FOOD PRDTS: Mixes, Cake, From Purchased Flour

Allied Food Products Inc.........................E...... 908 357-2454
Linden (G-5321)
Procter & Gamble Mfg Co ....D...... 732 602-4500
Avenel (G-143)
RAB Food Group LLC..............................D...... 201 553-1100
Newark (G-7244)
William R Tatz Industries ....G...... 973 751-0720
Belleville (G-325)

FOOD PRDTS: Mixes, Doughnut From Purchased Flour

All Madina Inc ....F 973 226-7772
West Caldwell (G-11639)

FOOD PRDTS: Mixes, Pancake From Purchased Flour

Joyce Food LLC......................................C...... 973 491-9696
Newark (G-7171)

FOOD PRDTS: Mixes, Pizza From Purchased Flour

Mjs of Spotswood LLC ....G...... 732 251-7400
Spotswood (G-10416)

FOOD PRDTS: Mixes, Salad Dressings, Dry

Muirhead Ringoes NJ Inc ....G...... 609 695-7803
Trenton (G-10959)

FOOD PRDTS: Mixes, Seasonings, Dry

Green Labs LLC ....G...... 862 220-4845
Newark (G-7139)

FOOD PRDTS: Mustard, Prepared

RB Manufacturing LLC ....C...... 908 533-2000
Hillsborough (G-4350)
RB Manufacturing LLC ....B...... 973 404-2600
Parsippany (G-8004)
Reckitt Benckiser LLC ....B...... 973 404-2600
Parsippany (G-8005)

FOOD PRDTS: Nuts & Seeds

Cns Confectionery Products LLC ....F 201 823-1400
Bayonne (G-211)

FOOD PRDTS: Olive Oil

Cosmopolitan Food Group Inc ....G...... 908 998-1818
Hoboken (G-4449)
Edesia Oil LLC...F...... 732 851-7979
Manalapan (G-5806)
Finex Trade ....G...... 609 921-2747
Princeton (G-8949)
Hojiblanca USA Inc ....G...... 201 384-3007
Dumont (G-2113)
Olivos USA Inc ....G...... 201 893-0142
Fort Lee (G-3580)
Raos Specialty Foods Inc ....F...... 212 269-0151
Montclair (G-6387)

FOOD PRDTS: Oriental Noodles

CJ TMI Manufacturing Amer LLC ....C...... 609 669-0100
Robbinsville (G-9410)

FOOD PRDTS: Pasta, Uncooked, Packaged With Other Ingredients

35 Food Corp...G...... 732 442-1640
Woodbridge (G-12011)
Contes Pasta Company Inc.....................E...... 856 697-3400
Vineland (G-11204)
Croces Pasta Poducts ....G...... 856 795-6000
Cherry Hill (G-1354)
European Amrcn Foods Group Inc ....E...... 201 436-6106
Bayonne (G-215)
European Amrcn Foods Group Inc ....B 201 583-1101
Secaucus (G-9764)
Firma Foods USA Corporation ....G...... 201 794-1181
Englewood (G-2905)
L and Ds Sapore Ravioli Cheese ....F...... 732 563-9190
Middlesex (G-6126)
La Pace Imports Inc ....F...... 973 895-5420
Morristown (G-6677)
Lioni Mozzarella & Spclty........................E...... 908 624-9450
Union (G-11071)
Lrk Inc ....F...... 609 924-6881
Princeton (G-8970)
Pastarama Distributors Inc ....G...... 609 847-0378
Sewell (G-9853)
Raos Specialty Foods Inc ....F...... 212 269-0151
Montclair (G-6387)
Vitamia Pasta Boy Inc............................F...... 973 546-1140
Lodi (G-5582)

FOOD PRDTS: Peanut Butter

Procter & Gamble Mfg Co ....D...... 732 602-4500
Avenel (G-143)

FOOD PRDTS: Pickles, Vinegar

Regal Crown Fd Svc Specialist ....G...... 508 752-2679
Wayne (G-11548)

FOOD PRDTS: Pizza Doughs From Purchased Flour

Losurdo Foods Inc..................................E...... 201 343-6680
Hackensack (G-3940)

FOOD PRDTS: Pizza, Refrigerated

Papa Johns New Jersey ....D...... 609 395-0045
Cranbury (G-1869)
Taste Italy Manufacturing LLC................G...... 856 223-0707
Egg Harbor City (G-2668)

FOOD PRDTS: Popcorn, Popped

Continntal Concession Sups Inc ....E...... 516 629-4906
Union (G-11037)
Planet Popcorn LLC.................................G...... 732 294-8680
Freehold (G-3687)
Ziggy Snack Foods LLC ....E...... 917 662-6038
Clifton (G-1744)

FOOD PRDTS: Popcorn, Unpopped

MCI Service Parts....................................G...... 732 967-9081
East Brunswick (G-2156)

FOOD PRDTS: Potato & Corn Chips & Similar Prdts

Auntie Annes Soft Pretzels ....E...... 856 722-0433
Moorestown (G-6506)
Campbell Soup Company ....A...... 856 342-4800
Camden (G-1047)
Campbell Soup Company ....---...... 856 342-4759
Camden (G-1048)
Dvash Foods USA Inc..............................G...... 929 360-0758
Mahwah (G-5732)
Golden Fluff Inc.......................................F...... 732 367-5448
Lakewood (G-5105)
Hain Celestial Group Inc ....E...... 201 935-4500
Moonachie (G-6469)
Herr Foods Incorporated ....E...... 732 356-1295
Somerset (G-9999)
Herr Foods Incorporated ....E...... 732 905-1600
Lakewood (G-5109)
Ktb Foods Inc ....G...... 973 240-0200
Fairfield (G-3253)
Mayab Happy Tacos Inc ....E...... 732 293-0400
Perth Amboy (G-8526)
Pirate Brands LLC...................................F...... 973 401-6500
Parsippany (G-7995)
Rajbhog Foods(nj) Inc ....C...... 551 222-4700
Jersey City (G-4796)
Snack Innovations Inc ....E...... 718 509-9366
Piscataway (G-8713)
Wise Foods Inc..G...... 201 440-2876
Moonachie (G-6497)
Zestos Foods LLC....................................G...... 888 407-5852
Teaneck (G-10657)

FOOD PRDTS: Potato Chips & Other Potato-Based Snacks

Birds Eye Foods Inc ....C...... 585 383-1850
Cherry Hill (G-1346)

FOOD PRDTS: Poultry, Processed, Frozen

Golden Platter Foods Inc ....E...... 973 344-8770
Newark (G-7136)

FOOD PRDTS: Poultry, Slaughtered & Dressed

B & B Poultry Co Inc...............................C...... 856 692-8893
Norma (G-7365)

FOOD PRDTS: Preparations

ACC Foods Ltd Liability Co ....C...... 856 848-8877
West Deptford (G-11689)

American Custom Drying Co	E	609 387-3933	
Burlington (G-948)			
Applied Nutrition Corp	E	973 734-0023	
Cedar Knolls (G-1299)			
Arome America LLC	G	908 806-7003	
Neshanic Station (G-6904)			
Barry Callebaut USA LLC	E	856 663-2260	
Pennsauken (G-8393)			
Boiron America Inc	G	862 229-6770	
Newark (G-7069)			
Buona Vita Inc	D	856 453-7972	
Bridgeton (G-754)			
Bylada Foods LLC	G	201 933-7474	
Moonachie (G-6459)			
Bylada Foods LLC	F	201 933-7474	
East Rutherford (G-2280)			
Caravan Ingredients Inc	E	201 672-0510	
East Rutherford (G-2284)			
Deluxe Foods International	G	862 257-1909	
Paterson (G-8171)			
Deosen Usa Inc	G	908 382-6518	
Piscataway (G-8653)			
DJeet	G	732 224-8887	
Shrewsbury (G-9890)			
DOrazio Foods Inc	D	856 931-1900	
Bellmawr (G-330)			
Dyna-Sea Group Inc	G	201 928-0133	
Teaneck (G-10629)			
Eatem Corporation	D	856 692-1663	
Vineland (G-11216)			
Empire Specialty Foods Inc	G	646 773-2630	
East Brunswick (G-2143)			
F&S Produce Company Inc	C	856 453-0316	
Rosenhayn (G-9595)			
Farbest-Tallman Foods Corp	D	714 897-7199	
Park Ridge (G-7849)			
Fillo Factory Inc	E	201 439-1036	
Northvale (G-7525)			
Flavour Tee International LLC	G	201 440-3281	
Little Ferry (G-5486)			
Food Ingredient Solutions LLC	G	201 440-4377	
Teterboro (G-10675)			
Foodtek Inc	F	973 257-4000	
Whippany (G-11891)			
Global Ingredients Inc	G	973 278-6677	
Paterson (G-8200)			
Golden Tropics Ltd	E	973 484-0202	
Newark (G-7137)			
Gourmet Kitchen LLC	C	732 775-5222	
Neptune (G-6882)			
House Foods America Corp	D	732 537-9500	
Somerset (G-10000)			
Iam International Inc	G	908 713-9651	
Lebanon (G-5263)			
Ingredient House LLC	G	609 285-5987	
Skillman (G-9921)			
J & J Snack Foods Corp	C	856 933-3597	
Bellmawr (G-336)			
Jk Ingredients Inc	D	973 340-8700	
Paterson (G-8224)			
Kerry Inc	G	845 584-3081	
Clark (G-1503)			
L E Rosellis Food Specialties	F	609 654-4816	
Medford (G-6027)			
Le Bon Magot Ltd Liability Co	G	609 895-0211	
Lawrenceville (G-5235)			
Leng-Dor USA Inc	F	732 254-4300	
Cranbury (G-1857)			
Lidestri Foods Inc	D	856 661-3218	
Pennsauken (G-8451)			
Maverick Caterers LLC	E	718 433-3776	
Hackensack (G-3944)			
Mediterranean Chef Inc	F	855 628-0903	
Lincoln Park (G-5301)			
Megas Yeeros	E	212 777-6342	
Lyndhurst (G-5663)			
Metropolitan Foods Inc	C	973 672-9400	
Clifton (G-1668)			
Missa Bay Citrus Company	F	856 241-0900	
Swedesboro (G-10596)			
Missa Bay LLC	D	856 241-0900	
Swedesboro (G-10597)			
Mushroom Wisdom Inc	F	973 470-0010	
East Rutherford (G-2305)			
Nestle Usa Inc	C	732 462-1300	
Freehold (G-3682)			
Omega Packaging Corp	D	973 890-9505	
Totowa (G-10840)			
Palsgaard Incorporated	F	973 998-7951	
Morris Plains (G-6622)			

Panos Holding Company	G	201 843-8900	
Rochelle Park (G-9428)			
Paulaur Corporation	D	609 395-8844	
Cranbury (G-1870)			
Pennant Ingredients Inc	G	856 428-4300	
Cherry Hill (G-1407)			
Perfecto Foods LLC	G	201 889-5328	
Kearny (G-4891)			
Pharmachem Laboratories Inc	E	973 256-1340	
Totowa (G-10843)			
Pharmachem Laboratories Inc	E	201 343-3611	
South Hackensack (G-10180)			
Pharmachem Laboratories LLC	D	201 246-1000	
Kearny (G-4892)			
Prince Chikovani Inc	G	347 622-2789	
Bayonne (G-232)			
Princeton Quadrangle Club	D	609 258-0376	
Princeton (G-9003)			
Puratos Corporation	C	856 428-4300	
Pennsauken (G-8475)			
Pyramid Food Services Corp	F	973 900-6513	
Newark (G-7241)			
R C Fine Foods Inc	D	908 359-5500	
Hillsborough (G-4349)			
Saker Shoprites Inc	F	908 925-1550	
Linden (G-5418)			
Spice Chain Corporation	G	800 584-0422	
East Brunswick (G-2178)			
Sunrise Snacks Rockland Inc	F	845 352-2676	
Paterson (G-8305)			
Surfside Foods LLC	G	856 785-2115	
Port Norris (G-8889)			
Suruchi Foods LLC	G	201 432-2201	
Jersey City (G-4818)			
Tamaras European American Deli	G	973 875-5461	
Sussex (G-10566)			
Taste It Presents Inc	D	908 241-9191	
Kenilworth (G-4981)			
Taylor Farms New Jersey Inc	E	856 241-0097	
Swedesboro (G-10613)			
Tin Man Snacks LLC	E	732 329-9100	
Dayton (G-1992)			
United Natural Trading Co	D	732 650-9905	
Edison (G-2636)			
Venetian Corp	F	973 546-2250	
Garfield (G-3776)			
Zxchem USA Inc	G	732 529-6352	
Piscataway (G-8742)			

FOOD PRDTS: Prepared Sauces, Exc Tomato Based

Ingrasselino Products LLC	G	800 960-1316	
Clifton (G-1640)			
Mamamancinis Holdings Inc	G	201 532-1212	
East Rutherford (G-2299)			
Mirrotek International LLC	E	973 472-1400	
Passaic (G-8090)			
Silver Palate Kitchens Inc	E	201 568-0110	
Cresskill (G-1944)			
Yipin Food Products Inc	F	718 788-3059	
Edison (G-2648)			

FOOD PRDTS: Raw cane sugar

International Molasses Corp	E	201 368-8036	
Saddle Brook (G-9657)			

FOOD PRDTS: Rice, Milled

Diamond Foods USA Inc	G	732 543-2186	
North Brunswick (G-7465)			
Fornazor International Inc	E	201 664-4000	
Hillsdale (G-4366)			

FOOD PRDTS: Salads

Daves Salad House Inc	G	908 965-0773	
Elizabeth (G-2725)			
Ready Pac Produce Inc	D	609 499-1900	
Florence (G-3477)			
Salad Chef Inc	F	609 641-5455	
Pleasantville (G-8817)			
Sheris Cookery Inc	F	973 589-2060	
Newark (G-7270)			
Zinas Salads Inc	E	973 428-0660	
East Hanover (G-2249)			

FOOD PRDTS: Seasonings & Spices

Colonna Brothers Inc	D	800 626-8384	
North Bergen (G-7397)			

Gel Spice Co LLC	C	201 339-0700	
Bayonne (G-219)			
Interntnal Ingrdent Sltons Inc	E	856 778-6623	
Mount Laurel (G-6769)			
Kalustyan Corporation	D	908 688-6111	
Union (G-11068)			
Mincing Trading Corporation	E	732 355-9944	
Dayton (G-1980)			
Organica Aromatics Corp	G	609 443-3333	
East Windsor (G-2357)			
Pereg Gourmet Spices Ltd	G	718 261-6767	
Clifton (G-1689)			
Sultan Foods Inc	F	908 874-6953	
Hillsborough (G-4358)			

FOOD PRDTS: Shortening & Solid Edible Fats

Procter & Gamble Mfg Co	D	732 602-4500	
Avenel (G-143)			

FOOD PRDTS: Soup Mixes

Allied Food Products Inc	E	908 357-2454	
Linden (G-5321)			
Joyce Food LLC	C	973 491-9696	
Newark (G-7171)			
Major Products Co Inc	E	201 641-5555	
Little Ferry (G-5492)			
Osem USA Inc	G	201 871-4433	
Englewood Cliffs (G-2985)			

FOOD PRDTS: Spices, Including Ground

Gel Spice Co Inc	B	201 339-0700	
Bayonne (G-218)			
Goldstein & Burton Inc	D	201 440-0065	
Oakland (G-7630)			
Melissa Spice Trading Corp	F	862 262-7773	
Glen Rock (G-3832)			
PDM Packaging Inc	F	201 864-1115	
North Bergen (G-7428)			

FOOD PRDTS: Sugar

Akila Holdings Inc	G	609 454-5034	
Princeton (G-8904)			

FOOD PRDTS: Sugar, Refined Cane, Purchased Raw Sugar/Syrup

Domino Foods Inc	C	732 590-1173	
Iselin (G-4607)			

FOOD PRDTS: Syrup, Maple

Vine Hill Farm	G	973 383-0100	
Newton (G-7364)			

FOOD PRDTS: Syrup, Pancake, Blended & Mixed

Peak Finance Holdings LLC	G	856 969-7100	
Cherry Hill (G-1406)			
Pinnacle Foods Finance LLC	D	973 541-6620	
Parsippany (G-7991)			
Pinnacle Foods Group LLC	D	856 969-8238	
Parsippany (G-7992)			

FOOD PRDTS: Syrup, Sorghum, For Sweetening

Royal Ingredients LLC	G	856 241-2004	
Swedesboro (G-10607)			

FOOD PRDTS: Syrups

B&G Foods Inc	B	973 401-6500	
Parsippany (G-7889)			
B&G Foods Inc	C	973 401-6500	
Parsippany (G-7890)			

FOOD PRDTS: Tea

Empirical Group LLC	E	201 571-0300	
Montvale (G-6411)			
Good Earth Teas Inc	D	831 423-7913	
Montvale (G-6412)			
Harris Freeman & Co Inc	D	856 787-9026	
Moorestown (G-6527)			
Longview Coffee Co NJ Inc	E	908 788-4186	
Frenchtown (G-3715)			

PRODUCT

Tetley USA Inc ....E 800 728-0084
New Providence (G-7022)

FOOD PRDTS: Tofu Desserts, Frozen

Tofutti Brands Inc ....G...... 908 272-2400
Cranford (G-1928)

FOOD PRDTS: Tofu, Exc Frozen Desserts

Tofutti Brands Inc ....G...... 908 272-2400
Cranford (G-1928)

FOOD PRDTS: Tortillas

La Casa De Tortilla ....G 732 398-0660
Somerset (G-10012)
Puebla Foods Inc ....E 973 246-6311
Passaic (G-8097)
Puebla Foods Inc ....F 973 473-4494
Passaic (G-8098)

FOOD PRDTS: Turkey, Processed, Frozen

Mamamancinis Holdings Inc ....G...... 201 532-1212
East Rutherford (G-2299)

FOOD PRDTS: Vegetable Oil Mills, NEC

Romulus Emprises Inc ....G...... 609 683-4549
Hightstown (G-4298)
Textron Inc ....E 201 945-1500
Edgewater (G-2441)
W A Cleary Products Inc ....F 732 246-2829
Somerset (G-10097)

FOOD PRDTS: Vegetables, Dried or Dehydrated Exc Freeze-Dried

Elaine K Josephson Inc ....G...... 609 259-2256
New Brunswick (G-6923)

FOOD PRDTS: Vegetables, Pickled

Yunta USA Inc ....G...... 614 835-6588
Cranbury (G-1896)

FOOD PRDTS: Vinegar

American Food & Bev Inds LLC ....D 347 241-9827
Orange (G-7750)
Cosmopolitan Food Group Inc ....G...... 908 998-1818
Hoboken (G-4449)
Hojiblanca USA Inc ....G...... 201 384-3007
Dumont (G-2113)
Regina Wine Co ....G...... 973 589-6911
Newark (G-7249)
Rex Wine Vinegar Company ....G...... 973 589-6911
Newark (G-7250)
Silver Palate Kitchens Inc ....E 201 568-0110
Cresskill (G-1944)

FOOD PRDTS: Yeast

Sensient Technologies Corp ....E 908 757-4500
South Plainfield (G-10327)

FOOD PRODUCTS MACHINERY

AGA Foodservice Inc ....D 856 428-4200
Cherry Hill (G-1333)
Allen Steel Co ....G 856 785-1171
Leesburg (G-5286)
Am-Mac Incorporated ....F 973 575-7567
Fairfield (G-3140)
Buhler Inc ....E 201 847-0600
Mahwah (G-5719)
Caddy Corporation of America ....D 856 467-4222
Swedesboro (G-10575)
D&N Machine Manufacturing Inc ....E 856 456-1366
Gloucester City (G-3840)
Excalibur Bagel Bky Equip Inc ....E 201 797-2788
Fair Lawn (G-3099)
Excellent Bakery Equipment Co ....E 973 244-1664
Fairfield (G-3196)
Expert Process Systems LLC ....E 570 424-0581
Hackettstown (G-4007)
FBM Baking Machines Inc ....G...... 609 860-0577
Cranbury (G-1834)
HCH Incorporated ....G...... 973 300-4551
Sparta (G-10391)
Industl Envrnmntl Pollutn ....E 908 241-3830
Roselle Park (G-9587)

J Hebrank Inc ....F 973 983-0001
Rockaway (G-9470)
Joe Mike Precision Fabrication ....F 609 953-1144
Medford (G-6026)
M B C Food Machinery Corp ....G...... 201 489-7000
Hackensack (G-3941)
Megas Yeeros LLC ....E 212 777-6342
Lyndhurst (G-5663)
Nowak Inc ....F 973 366-7208
Wharton (G-11864)
Rajbhog Foods Inc ....G...... 551 222-4700
Jersey City (G-4794)
Rajbhog Foods Inc ....G...... 201 395-9400
Jersey City (G-4795)
Solbern LLC ....E 973 227-3030
Fairfield (G-3312)
Surfside Foods LLC ....G...... 856 785-2115
Port Norris (G-8889)
Techno Design Inc ....G...... 973 478-0930
Garfield (G-3772)
TMU Inc ....F 609 884-7656
Cape May (G-1103)

FOOD STORES: Convenience, Independent

Raceway Petroleum Inc ....E 732 613-4404
East Brunswick (G-2172)

FOOD STORES: Cooperative

Wakefern Food Corp ....B 908 527-3300
Keasbey (G-4916)

FOOD STORES: Delicatessen

Bagel Club ....F 908 806-6022
Flemington (G-3432)
Branchville Bagels Inc ....G...... 973 948-7077
Branchville (G-704)

FOOD STORES: Frozen Food &Freezer Plans, Exc Meat

L E Rosellis Food Specialties ....F 609 654-4816
Medford (G-6027)

FOOD STORES: Grocery, Chain

All Merchandise Display Corp ....E 718 257-2221
Hillside (G-4372)

FOOD STORES: Grocery, Independent

Berat Corporation ....C 609 953-7700
Medford (G-6020)
CW Brown Foods Inc ....F 856 423-3700
Mount Royal (G-6817)
Georges Wine and Spirits Galle ....G...... 973 948-9950
Branchville (G-707)
Kohouts Bakery ....G...... 973 772-7270
Garfield (G-3750)
Savignano Food Corp ....E 973 673-3355
Orange (G-7760)

FOOD STORES: Supermarkets

Lo Presti & Sons LLC ....E 973 523-9258
Paterson (G-8245)
Perk & Pantry ....G...... 856 451-4333
Bridgeton (G-769)

FOOD STORES: Supermarkets, Chain

Acme Markets Inc ....E 609 884-7217
Cape May (G-1091)
Food Circus Super Markets Inc ....D 732 291-4079
Atlantic Highlands (G-106)
Little Falls Shop Rite Super ....B 973 256-0909
Little Falls (G-5460)
Shop Rite Supermarkets Inc ....C 732 775-4250
Neptune (G-6898)
Shop-Rite Supermarkets Inc ....C 609 646-2448
Absecon (G-4)
Wakefern Food Corp ....B 732 819-0140
Edison (G-2645)

FOOTWEAR, WHOLESALE: Athletic

Ballet Makers Inc ....G 973 595-9000
Totowa (G-10818)

FOOTWEAR, WHOLESALE: Shoe Access

Sysco Guest Supply LLC ....C 732 537-2297
Somerset (G-10078)

FORGINGS

All Mtals Frge Group Ltd Lblty ....E 973 276-5000
Fairfield (G-3138)
Atlantic Steel Solutions LLC ....F 973 978-0026
Paterson (G-8143)
Hafco Foundry & Machine Co ....F 201 447-0433
Midland Park (G-6176)
Kumar & Kumar Inc ....E 732 322-0435
Edison (G-2546)
Pennsylvania Machine Works Inc ....E 856 467-0500
Swedesboro (G-10600)
Sigma Engineering & Consulting ....F 732 356-3046
Middlesex (G-6147)
Supply Technologies LLC ....E 201 641-7600
Moonachie (G-6492)

FORGINGS: Automotive & Internal Combustion Engine

JDM Engineering Inc ....G...... 732 780-0770
Freehold (G-3673)
Taurus International Corp ....E 201 825-2420
Ramsey (G-9156)

FORGINGS: Gear & Chain

Able Gear & Machine Co ....G...... 973 983-8055
Rockaway (G-9434)

FORGINGS: Metal , Ornamental, Ferrous

Bloomfield Iron Co Inc ....G...... 973 748-7040
Belleville (G-291)

FORGINGS: Missile, Ferrous

Wyman-Gordon Forgings Inc ....E 973 627-0200
Rockaway (G-9514)

FORGINGS: Nonferrous

McWilliams Forge Company ....D 973 627-0200
Rockaway (G-9476)
Ramco Manufacturing Co Inc ....E 908 245-4500
Kenilworth (G-4973)

FORGINGS: Nuclear Power Plant, Ferrous

McWilliams Forge Company ....D 973 627-0200
Rockaway (G-9476)
PSEG Nuclear LLC ....A 973 430-5191
Newark (G-7239)

FORMS: Concrete, Sheet Metal

Efco Corp ....F 732 308-1010
Marlboro (G-5896)
Ulma Form-Works Inc ....D 201 882-1122
Hawthorne (G-4247)
Vinch Recycling Inc ....F 609 393-0200
Lawrenceville (G-5246)

FOUNDRIES: Aluminum

Aluminum Shapes LLC ....B 888 488-7427
Delair (G-1999)
Bierman-Everett Foundry Co ....G...... 973 373-8800
South Orange (G-10192)
Bon Chef Inc ....D 973 383-8848
Lafayette (G-5026)
Shapes/Arch Holdings LLC ....B 856 662-5500
Delair (G-2001)
TEC Cast Inc ....D 201 935-3885
Moonachie (G-6494)

FOUNDRIES: Brass, Bronze & Copper

Accurate Bushing Company Inc ....E 908 789-1121
Garwood (G-3779)
Amrod Corp ....D 973 344-3806
Newark (G-7046)
Bierman-Everett Foundry Co ....G...... 973 373-8800
South Orange (G-10192)
Richmond Industries Inc ....E 732 355-1616
Dayton (G-1987)

FOUNDRIES: Gray & Ductile Iron

United States Pipe Fndry LLC ....C....... 609 387-6000
　Burlington *(G-991)*

FOUNDRIES: Iron

Hafco Foundry & Machine Co..............F 201 447-0433
　Midland Park *(G-6176)*

FOUNDRIES: Nonferrous

Engineered Precision Cast Co..........D.... 732 671-2424
　Middletown *(G-6163)*
Howmet Castings & Services Inc ....A....... 973 361-0300
　Dover *(G-2087)*
IBC Inc ....G....... 856 533-2806
　Voorhees *(G-11289)*
M D Carbide Tool Corp ....E 973 263-0104
　Towaco *(G-10874)*
S Jarco-U Castings Corporation ....G.... 201 271-0003
　Union City *(G-11127)*
Ultimate Trading Corp ....D 973 228-7700
　Rockaway *(G-9509)*

FOUNDRIES: Steel

Accurate Bushing Company Inc..............E 908 789-1121
　Garwood *(G-3779)*
D S Jh LLC ....E 973 782-4086
　Lincoln Park *(G-5298)*
Double O Manufacturing Inc ....G....... 732 752-9423
　Middlesex *(G-6113)*
H & R Welding LLC ....G....... 732 920-4881
　Brick *(G-720)*
T Wiker Enterprises Inc ....G....... 609 261-9494
　Hainesport *(G-4079)*

FOUNDRIES: Steel Investment

Alcoa Power Generating Inc ....G....... 973 361-0300
　Dover *(G-2073)*
Fortune Rvrside Auto Parts Inc ....E 732 381-3355
　Rahway *(G-9094)*
Mark I Industries Inc ....F 609 884-0051
　Cape May *(G-1100)*
Rbc Dain Rauscher ....F 973 778-7300
　Woodland Park *(G-12089)*

FOUNDRY MATERIALS: Insulsleeves

Whibco Inc..............E 856 825-5200
　Port Elizabeth *(G-8877)*

FOUNDRY SAND MINING

U S Silica Company ....E 856 785-0720
　Mauricetown *(G-5991)*
Whibco Inc..............F 856 455-9200
　Bridgeton *(G-779)*

FRAMES & FRAMING WHOLESALE

K Ron Art & Mirrors Inc ....G....... 201 313-7080
　Ridgefield *(G-9270)*
Roma Moulding Inc ....F 732 346-0999
　Edison *(G-2600)*

FRANCHISES, SELLING OR LICENSING

Enzon Pharmaceuticals Inc ....G....... 732 980-4500
　Cranford *(G-1909)*
Seagrave Coatings Corp ....E 201 933-1000
　Kenilworth *(G-4976)*

FREEZERS: Household

Troy Hills Manufacturing Inc..............G....... 973 263-1885
　Towaco *(G-10882)*

FREIGHT FORWARDING ARRANGEMENTS

Aliron International Inc ....E 540 808-1615
　South Plainfield *(G-10210)*
R & M Chemical Technologies..............F 908 537-9516
　Hampton *(G-4159)*
Savino Del Bene USA Inc ....D....... 347 960-5568
　Avenel *(G-145)*

FREIGHT TRANSPORTATION ARRANGEMENTS

Colortec Printing and Mailing ....G....... 856 767-0108
　West Berlin *(G-11584)*

Fedex Office & Print Svcs Inc ....E 732 636-3580
　Iselin *(G-4609)*
Lummus Technology Ventures LLC ......G.... 973 893-1515
　Bloomfield *(G-509)*
Precision Dealer Services Inc..............E 908 237-1100
　Flemington *(G-3461)*
Total Reliance LLC ....F 732 640-5079
　Dayton *(G-1993)*

FRICTION MATERIAL, MADE FROM POWDERED METAL

Hamon Corporation ....D.... 908 333-2000
　Somerville *(G-10114)*

FRUIT & VEGETABLE MARKETS

Springdale Farm Market Inc..............E 856 424-8674
　Cherry Hill *(G-1416)*

FRUITS & VEGETABLES WHOLESALERS: Fresh

Georges Wine and Spirits Galle ....G.... 973 948-9950
　Branchville *(G-707)*
Ready Pac Produce Inc ....D.... 609 499-1900
　Florence *(G-3477)*

FRUITS: Artificial & Preserved

Venture Stationers Inc ....E 212 288-7235
　Closter *(G-1763)*

FUEL ADDITIVES

Fuel Ox LLC..............F 908 747-4375
　Glen Gardner *(G-3822)*

FUEL CELLS: Solid State

Fuceltech Inc ....G.... 609 275-0070
　Princeton Junction *(G-9058)*

FUEL OIL DEALERS

McAllister Service Company..............E 856 665-4545
　Pennsauken *(G-8453)*

FUELS: Diesel

Fuel Bio Holdings Ltd Lblty Co ....G.... 908 344-6875
　Elizabeth *(G-2739)*

FUELS: Ethanol

D and M Discount Fuels ....G.... 856 935-0919
　Salem *(G-9693)*
Easy Stop Food & Fuel Corp ....G.... 973 517-0478
　Hamburg *(G-4091)*
Fancyheat Corporation ....F 973 589-1450
　Somerset *(G-9993)*
Fossil Fuel ....G.... 973 366-9111
　Wharton *(G-11858)*
Fuel One Inc ....G.... 732 726-9500
　Avenel *(G-128)*
Fuel Stop Inc ....G.... 201 697-3319
　Union *(G-11057)*
G & R Fuel Corp ....G.... 973 732-0530
　Newark *(G-7128)*
H & S Fuel Inc ....G.... 908 769-1362
　Plainfield *(G-8767)*
Hopatcong Fuel On You LLC ....G.... 973 770-0854
　Hopatcong *(G-4521)*
Jacquar Fuel ....G.... 732 441-0700
　Manalapan *(G-5815)*
Jai Ganesh Fuel LLC ....G.... 201 246-8995
　Kearny *(G-4871)*
Jt Fuels LLC ....G.... 973 527-4470
　Ledgewood *(G-5277)*
Kp Fuel Corporation ....G.... 973 350-1202
　Newark *(G-7174)*
Main Fuel LLC ....G.... 201 941-2707
　Cliffside Park *(G-1541)*
Main Street Auto & Fuel LLC ....G.... 732 238-0044
　Sayreville *(G-9719)*
Modern Fuel Inc ....G.... 973 471-1501
　Clifton *(G-1670)*
Montclair Fuel LLC ....G.... 973 744-4300
　Montclair *(G-6376)*
National Fuel LLC ....G.... 973 227-4549
　Pine Brook *(G-8610)*
NJ Fuel Haulers Inc..............G.... 732 740-3681
　Old Bridge *(G-7721)*

Prospect Transportation Inc ....D....... 201 933-9999
　Carlstadt *(G-1209)*
R & R Fuel Inc..............G....... 201 223-0786
　Union City *(G-11126)*
Route 22 Fuel LLC ....G....... 908 526-5270
　Bridgewater *(G-877)*
S and D Fuel LLC ....G....... 908 248-8188
　Union *(G-11087)*
Sgw Fuel Delivery ....G....... 609 209-8773
　Trenton *(G-10991)*
Shani Auto Fuel Corp ....G....... 856 241-9767
　Woolwich Township *(G-12098)*
Shiva Fuel Inc ....G....... 732 826-3228
　Perth Amboy *(G-8532)*
Sks Fuel Inc ....G....... 973 200-0796
　Woodland Park *(G-12091)*
Suman Realty LLC ....G....... 908 350-8039
　Stirling *(G-10497)*
United Fuel Distributors LLC ....G....... 908 906-9053
　South Plainfield *(G-10335)*
Unitex International Inc ....G....... 856 786-5000
　Cinnaminson *(G-1494)*
Urso Fuel Corp ....G....... 973 325-3324
　West Orange *(G-11781)*

FUELS: Jet

Columbia Fuel Services Inc..............F 732 751-0044
　Wall Township *(G-11331)*

FUELS: Oil

Starfuels Inc ....G....... 201 685-0400
　Englewood *(G-2944)*

FUND RAISING ORGANIZATION, NON-FEE BASIS

New Jersey Jewish News..............E 973 887-3900
　Whippany *(G-11898)*

FUNGICIDES OR HERBICIDES

Arcadia Consmr Healthcare Inc..............F 800 824-4894
　Bridgewater *(G-791)*
Big Bucks Enterprises Inc ....E 908 320-7009
　Washington *(G-11442)*
Glysortia LLC ....G....... 715 426-5358
　Plainsboro *(G-8789)*

FUR: Coats

S & H R Inc..............G....... 908 925-3797
　Linden *(G-5417)*

FURNACES & OVENS: Indl

Abp Induction LLC..............F 732 932-6400
　North Brunswick *(G-7448)*
Albapalant USA Inc ....G....... 201 831-9200
　Boonton *(G-539)*
Curran-Pfeiff Corp ....F 732 225-0555
　Edison *(G-2489)*
Electroheat Induction Inc ....G....... 908 494-0726
　Jersey City *(G-4731)*
Energy Beams Inc..............F 973 291-6555
　Bloomingdale *(G-528)*
Essex Products International ....E 973 226-2424
　Caldwell *(G-1024)*
Haydon Corporation ....D....... 973 904-0800
　Wayne *(G-11515)*
L & L Kiln Mfg Inc ....E 856 294-0077
　Swedesboro *(G-10593)*
Procedyne Corp ....E 732 249-8347
　New Brunswick *(G-6962)*
Saber Associates ....E 973 777-3800
　Clifton *(G-1708)*

FURNACES & OVENS: Vacuum

Elnik Systems LLC..............E 973 239-6066
　Cedar Grove *(G-1277)*
T-M Vacuum Products Inc ....E 856 829-2000
　Cinnaminson *(G-1487)*

FURNACES: Indl, Electric

Consarc Corporation ....E 609 267-8000
　Rancocas *(G-9159)*

FURNACES: Indl, Fuel-Fired, Metal Melting

Rowan Technologies Inc ....D....... 609 267-9000
　Rancocas *(G-9165)*

FURNITURE & CABINET STORES: Cabinets, Custom Work

Castle Woodcraft Assoc LLC .... F 732 349-1519
  Pine Beach *(G-8582)*
Cozzolino Furniture Design Inc .... E 973 731-9292
  West Orange *(G-11764)*
Creative Cabinet Designs Inc .... F 973 402-5886
  Boonton *(G-547)*
Hawthorne Kitchens Inc .... F 973 427-9010
  Hawthorne *(G-4223)*
Paul Burkhardt & Sons Inc .... G 856 435-2020
  Lindenwold *(G-5445)*
Ramsay David Cabinetmakers .... F 856 234-7776
  Moorestown *(G-6562)*
Schneiders Kitchens Inc .... G 908 689-5649
  Washington *(G-11451)*
Superior Custom Kitchens LLC .... E 908 753-6005
  Warren *(G-11433)*

FURNITURE & CABINET STORES: Custom

Lukach Interiors Inc .... F 973 777-1499
  Clifton *(G-1662)*
Royal Cabinet Company Inc .... E 908 203-8000
  Bound Brook *(G-605)*
Woodtec Inc .... G 908 979-0180
  Hackettstown *(G-4041)*

FURNITURE & FIXTURES Factory

G & H Sheet Metal Works Inc .... G 973 923-1100
  Hillside *(G-4393)*
Infinite Mfg Group Inc .... E 973 649-9950
  Kearny *(G-4868)*
Organize It-All Inc .... E 201 488-0808
  Bogota *(G-534)*
Rosalindas Discount Furniture .... F 973 928-2838
  Passaic *(G-8102)*
Wood Textures .... G 732 230-5005
  Dayton *(G-1996)*

FURNITURE REPAIR & MAINTENANCE SVCS

Rff Services LLC .... F 201 564-0040
  Oakland *(G-7644)*

FURNITURE STORES

Best Value Rugs & Carpets Inc .... G 732 752-3528
  Dunellen *(G-2120)*
Carlyle Custom Convertibles .... D 973 546-4502
  Moonachie *(G-6460)*
Ethan Allen Retail Inc .... C 973 473-1019
  Passaic *(G-8065)*
Furniture of America NJ .... E 201 605-8200
  Secaucus *(G-9770)*
Greenbaum Interiors LLC .... D 973 279-3000
  Paterson *(G-8202)*
H Lauzon Furniture Co Inc .... F 201 837-7598
  Teaneck *(G-10634)*
White Lotus Home Ltd Lblty Co .... F 732 828-2111
  New Brunswick *(G-6981)*
William Opdyke Awnings Inc .... G 732 449-5940
  Wall Township *(G-11378)*
William Spencer .... G 856 235-1830
  Mount Laurel *(G-6813)*

FURNITURE STORES: Cabinets, Kitchen, Exc Custom Made

Bozzone Custom Woodwork Inc .... F 973 334-5598
  Montville *(G-6439)*

FURNITURE STORES: Custom Made, Exc Cabinets

Arnold Reception Desks Inc .... E 973 375-8101
  Irvington *(G-4560)*
Crincoli Woodwork Co Inc .... F 908 352-9332
  Elizabeth *(G-2724)*

FURNITURE STORES: Office

Bellia & Sons .... E 856 845-2234
  Woodbury *(G-12026)*
La Cour Inc .... E 973 227-3300
  Fairfield *(G-3255)*
Modernlinefurniture Inc .... E 908 486-0200
  Linden *(G-5389)*
South Brunswick Furniture Inc .... C 732 658-8850
  Linden *(G-5427)*

W B Mason Co Inc .... D 888 926-2766
  Bellmawr *(G-345)*
W B Mason Co Inc .... E 888 926-2766
  Egg Harbor Township *(G-2701)*

FURNITURE STORES: Outdoor & Garden

Medford Cedar Products Inc .... G 609 859-1400
  Southampton *(G-10369)*
Walpole Woodworkers Inc .... E 973 539-3555
  Morris Plains *(G-6628)*

FURNITURE UPHOLSTERY REPAIR SVCS

Sofa Doctor Inc .... G 718 292-6300
  Guttenberg *(G-3872)*

FURNITURE WHOLESALERS

Best Value Rugs & Carpets Inc .... G 732 752-3528
  Dunellen *(G-2120)*
Global Industries Inc .... C 856 596-3390
  Marlton *(G-5933)*
Greenbaum Interiors LLC .... D 973 279-3000
  Paterson *(G-8202)*
RFS Commercial Inc .... F 201 796-0006
  Saddle Brook *(G-9671)*

FURNITURE, HOUSEHOLD: Wholesalers

D & F Wicker Import Co Inc .... E 973 736-5861
  Succasunna *(G-10511)*

FURNITURE, OFFICE: Wholesalers

La Cour Inc .... E 973 227-3300
  Fairfield *(G-3255)*
Office Needs Inc .... G 732 381-7770
  Clark *(G-1511)*
Supplies-Supplies Inc .... F 908 272-5100
  Watchung *(G-11460)*
Techntime Bus Sltons Ltd Lblty .... F 973 246-8153
  East Rutherford *(G-2324)*
Two Jays Bingo Supply Inc .... F 609 267-4542
  Hainesport *(G-4080)*

FURNITURE, OUTDOOR & LAWN: Wholesalers

Wisely Products LLC .... G 929 329-9188
  Jersey City *(G-4833)*

FURNITURE, WHOLESALE: Bar

Pool Tables Plus Inc .... G 732 968-8228
  Green Brook *(G-3866)*

FURNITURE, WHOLESALE: Chairs

Daco Limited Partnership .... D 973 263-1100
  Boonton *(G-548)*
NPS Public Furniture Corp .... D 973 594-1100
  Clifton *(G-1679)*

FURNITURE, WHOLESALE: Juvenile

Berg East Imports Inc .... D 908 354-5252
  Barrington *(G-168)*

FURNITURE, WHOLESALE: Lockers

American Intr Resources Inc .... G 908 851-0014
  Union *(G-11024)*

FURNITURE, WHOLESALE: Shelving

Modern Store Equipment .... F 609 241-7438
  Burlington *(G-980)*

FURNITURE, WHOLESALE: Sofas & Couches

Carlyle Custom Convertibles .... D 973 546-4502
  Moonachie *(G-6460)*

FURNITURE: Bar furniture

Outwater Plstcs/Industries Inc .... D 201 498-8750
  Bogota *(G-535)*
Renaissance Creations LLC .... G 551 206-1878
  Passaic *(G-8101)*

FURNITURE: Benches, Office, Wood

Fu WEI Inc .... G 732 937-8388
  East Brunswick *(G-2147)*

FURNITURE: Box Springs, Assembled

Comfort Rvolution Holdings LLC .... F 732 272-9111
  Eatontown *(G-2385)*

FURNITURE: Cafeteria

Atlantic Coast Woodwork Inc .... G 609 294-2478
  Ltl Egg Hbr *(G-5613)*

FURNITURE: Chair Beds

Bedding Shoppe Inc .... G 973 334-9000
  Parsippany *(G-7892)*

FURNITURE: Chairs & Couches, Wood, Upholstered

Carlyle Custom Convertibles .... D 973 546-4502
  Moonachie *(G-6460)*
Woodward Wood Products Design .... F 609 597-2708
  West Creek *(G-11688)*

FURNITURE: Chairs, Dental

Takara Belmont Usa Inc .... D 732 469-5000
  Somerset *(G-10079)*

FURNITURE: Chairs, Household Upholstered

H Lauzon Furniture Co Inc .... F 201 837-7598
  Teaneck *(G-10634)*

FURNITURE: Chairs, Household, Metal

NPS Public Furniture Corp .... D 973 594-1100
  Clifton *(G-1679)*

FURNITURE: Chairs, Office Exc Wood

Daco Limited Partnership .... D 973 263-1100
  Boonton *(G-548)*
Stylex Inc .... C 856 461-5600
  Delanco *(G-2007)*

FURNITURE: Chairs, Office Wood

Arthur Gordon Associates Inc .... F 732 431-3361
  Freehold *(G-3649)*
Vaswani Inc .... F 877 376-4425
  Edison *(G-2638)*
Vaswani Inc .... F 732 377-9794
  Piscataway *(G-8736)*

FURNITURE: Chests, Cedar

Vine Hill Farm .... G 973 383-0100
  Newton *(G-7364)*

FURNITURE: Church

Christian Art .... G 201 867-8096
  West New York *(G-11737)*

FURNITURE: Desks & Tables, Office, Wood

Arnold Reception Desks Inc .... E 973 375-8101
  Irvington *(G-4560)*

FURNITURE: Frames, Box Springs Or Bedsprings, Metal

Christopher Szuco .... G 732 684-7643
  Millstone Twp *(G-6213)*
Knickerbocker Bed Company .... E 201 933-3100
  Carlstadt *(G-1176)*

FURNITURE: Hospital

Hausmann Enterprises LLC .... D 201 767-0255
  Northvale *(G-7527)*
Hill-Rom Holdings Inc .... G 856 486-2117
  Moorestown *(G-6528)*

FURNITURE: Hotel

Mp Custom FL LLC .... F 973 417-2288
  Wayne *(G-11535)*

FURNITURE: Household, Metal

Avantegarde Image LLC ....F 732 363-8701
Lakewood (G-5056)

FURNITURE: Household, Upholstered, Exc Wood Or Metal

South Brunswick Furniture Inc.............C 732 658-8850
Linden (G-5427)

FURNITURE: Household, Wood

10-31 Incorporated ....E 908 496-4946
Columbia (G-1791)
Bcg Marble Gran Fabricators Co ....F 201 343-8487
Hackensack (G-3882)
Bernard Miller Fabricators ....G 856 541-9499
Camden (G-1041)
Bng Industries LLC ....F 862 229-2414
Harrison (G-4165)
Bozzone Custom Woodwork Inc ....G 973 334-5598
Montville (G-6439)
Central Shippee Inc ....E 973 838-1100
Bloomingdale (G-526)
Cerami Wood Products Inc ....F 732 968-7222
Piscataway (G-8645)
Chromcraft Revington Inc ....E 662 562-8203
West Berlin (G-11582)
Cozzolino Furniture Design Inc ....F 973 731-9292
West Orange (G-11764)
Dab Design Inc ....G 732 224-8686
Red Bank (G-9225)
East Coast Cabinets Inc ....F 856 488-9710
Pennsauken (G-8417)
Foley-Waite Associates Inc ....F 908 298-0700
Kenilworth (G-4941)
Greenbaum Interiors LLC ....D 973 279-3000
Paterson (G-8202)
Interchange Group Inc ....F 973 783-7032
Montclair (G-6371)
L&W Audio/Video Inc ....G 212 980-2862
Hoboken (G-4463)
My House Kitchen Inc ....G 201 262-9000
Paramus (G-7823)
National Woodworking Co ....G 908 851-9316
Union (G-11079)
Robert J Smith ....G 201 641-6555
South Hackensack (G-10184)
Salernos Kitchen Cabinets ....E 201 794-1990
Saddle Brook (G-9676)
Sawitz Studios Inc ....E 201 842-9444
Carlstadt (G-1213)
Schneiders Kitchens Inc ....G 908 689-5649
Washington (G-11451)
Sr Custom Woodcraft Ltd Lblty ....G 732 942-7601
Lakewood (G-5166)
Starphil Inc ....G 908 353-8943
Elizabeth (G-2777)
V and S Woodworks Inc ....G 201 568-0659
Tenafly (G-10667)
Walpole Woodworkers Inc ....E 973 539-3555
Morris Plains (G-6628)
Woodline Works Corporation ....E 732 828-9100
New Brunswick (G-6982)
Woodpeckers Inc ....F 973 751-4744
Belleville (G-326)

FURNITURE: Hydraulic Barber & Beauty Shop Chairs

Wg Products Inc ....G 973 256-5999
Totowa (G-10862)

FURNITURE: Institutional, Exc Wood

Chromcraft Revington Inc ....E 662 562-8203
West Berlin (G-11582)
Hausmann Enterprises LLC ....D 201 767-0255
Northvale (G-7527)
Jmm Studios ....G 609 861-3094
Woodbine (G-12010)

FURNITURE: Juvenile, Wood

Berg East Imports Inc ....D 908 354-5252
Barrington (G-168)

FURNITURE: Juvenile, Wood

Dream On ME Industries Inc ....D 732 752-7220
Piscataway (G-8658)

FURNITURE: Kitchen & Dining Room

Creative Cabinet Designs Inc ....F 973 402-5886
Boonton (G-547)
Designer Kitchens ....F 732 370-5500
Jackson (G-4650)
Forino Kitchen Cabinets Inc ....G 201 573-0990
Park Ridge (G-7850)
Mango Custom Cabinets Inc ....F 908 813-3077
Hackettstown (G-4020)
Renaissance Creations LLC ....G 551 206-1878
Passaic (G-8101)

FURNITURE: Kitchen & Dining Room, Metal

South Jersey Metal Inc ....E 856 228-0642
Deptford (G-2066)
Taylor Made Cabinets Inc ....E 609 978-6900
Manahawkin (G-5796)

FURNITURE: Laboratory

Thoma Inc ....F 856 608-6887
Moorestown (G-6573)
United Hospital Supply Corp ....C 609 387-7580
Burlington (G-990)

FURNITURE: Lawn & Garden, Except Wood & Metal

Casual Classics Inc ....G 916 294-9880
Barnegat (G-156)
Scott W Springman ....G 856 751-2411
Pennsauken (G-8482)

FURNITURE: Lawn, Wood

R H Vassallo Inc ....G 856 358-8841
Malaga (G-5789)

FURNITURE: Library

Renaissance Creations LLC ....G 551 206-1878
Passaic (G-8101)

FURNITURE: Mattresses & Foundations

Innocor Inc ....C 732 945-6222
Red Bank (G-9230)
Innocor Foam Tech - Acp Inc ....D 732 945-6222
Red Bank (G-9231)
J P Egan Industries Inc ....G 973 642-1500
Newark (G-7164)
Sealy Mattress Co N J Inc ....C 973 345-8800
Paterson (G-8297)
White Lotus Home Ltd Lblty Co ....F 732 828-2111
New Brunswick (G-6981)

FURNITURE: Mattresses, Box & Bedsprings

Catching Zzz LLC ....G 888 339-1604
Piscataway (G-8643)
Dream Well Collection Inc ....F 732 545-5900
New Brunswick (G-6921)
Eclipse Sleep Products LLC ....D 732 628-0002
New Brunswick (G-6922)
Grand Life Inc ....G 201 556-8975
Carlstadt (G-1160)
Jomel Industries Inc ....F 973 282-0300
Hillside (G-4406)
Jomel Seams Reasonable LLC ....F 973 282-0300
Hillside (G-4407)
Mattress Dev Co Del LLC ....E 732 628-0800
North Brunswick (G-7476)
New England Bedding Trnspt Inc ....G 631 484-0147
Kearny (G-4887)
Spectra Mattress Inc ....G 732 545-5900
North Brunswick (G-7488)
Spring Time Mattress Mfg Corp ....D 973 473-5400
South Hackensack (G-10188)

FURNITURE: Mattresses, Innerspring Or Box Spring

Custom Bedding Co ....G 973 761-1100
Maplewood (G-5875)
Leggett & Platt Incorporated ....D 732 225-2440
Edison (G-2550)
Ther-A-Pedic Sleep Products ....D 732 628-0800
North Brunswick (G-7490)

FURNITURE: NEC

Best American Hands ....E 203 247-2028
Hillside (G-4382)

FURNITURE: Novelty, Wood

Summus Inc ....G 215 820-3918
Runnemede (G-9612)

FURNITURE: Office Panel Systems, Wood

M2 Electric LLC ....F 973 770-4596
Mine Hill (G-6273)
Mbs Installations Inc ....F 888 446-9135
Jackson (G-4659)

FURNITURE: Office, Exc Wood

Concord Products Company Inc ....E 856 933-3000
Sewell (G-9834)
Creative Innovations Inc ....F 973 636-9060
Fair Lawn (G-3094)
Fehlberg Mfg Inc ....G 973 399-1905
Irvington (G-4568)
Gaw Associates Inc ....F 856 608-1428
Cherry Hill (G-1367)
Global Industries Inc ....C 856 596-3390
Marlton (G-5933)
La Cour Inc ....E 973 227-3300
Fairfield (G-3255)

FURNITURE: Office, Wood

Arnold Furniture Mfrs Inc ....F 973 399-0505
Irvington (G-4558)
Arnold Kolax Furniture Inc ....E 973 375-3344
Irvington (G-4559)
Cbt Supply Inc ....G 800 770-7042
Rockaway (G-9450)
Chromcraft Revington Inc ....E 662 562-8203
West Berlin (G-11582)
Cozzolino Furniture Design Inc ....E 973 731-9292
West Orange (G-11764)
Designcore Ltd ....D 718 499-0337
Secaucus (G-9761)
G & A Coml Seating Pdts Corp ....G 908 233-8000
Mountainside (G-6846)
La Cour Inc ....E 973 227-3300
Fairfield (G-3255)
Mp Custom FL LLC ....F 973 417-2288
Wayne (G-11535)
Reda Furniture LLC ....F 732 948-1703
Manasquan (G-5837)
Renaissance Creations LLC ....G 551 206-1878
Passaic (G-8101)
Robert J Smith ....G 201 641-6555
South Hackensack (G-10184)
Zacs International LLC ....G 609 368-3482
Burlington (G-994)

FURNITURE: School

Academia Furniture LLC ....E 973 472-0100
Wood Ridge (G-12000)
Longo Associates Inc ....F 201 825-1500
Ramsey (G-9150)
RFS Commercial Inc ....F 201 796-0006
Saddle Brook (G-9671)
Visual Architectural Designs ....F 908 754-3000
South Plainfield (G-10342)

FURNITURE: Sleep

Lieth Holdings LLC ....G 201 358-8282
Westwood (G-11834)
Sheex Inc ....E 856 334-3021
Marlton (G-5951)

FURNITURE: Sofa Beds Or Convertible Sofas)

Carlyle Custom Convertibles ....D 973 546-4502
Moonachie (G-6460)

FURNITURE: Spring Cushions

Ayerspace Inc ....G 212 582-8410
West Caldwell (G-11641)

FURNITURE: Table Tops, Marble

Formia Marble & Stone Inc ....E 908 259-0606
Roselle (G-9558)

Employee Codes: A=Over 500 employees, B=251-500
C=101-250, D=51-100, E=20-50, F=10-19, G=4-9

2019 Harris New Jersey
Manufacturers Directory

847

PRODUCT

FURNITURE: Table Tops, Marble

Natures Beauty Marble & Gran ....F 908 233-5300
Scotch Plains *(G-9737)*

FURNITURE: Tables & Table Tops, Wood

Union City Mirror & Table Co ....E 201 867-0050
Union City *(G-11131)*

FURNITURE: Tables, Household, Metal

De Saussure Equipment Co Inc.............E 201 845-6517
Maywood *(G-6003)*

FURNITURE: Upholstered

Chromcraft Revington Inc...................E 662 562-8203
West Berlin *(G-11582)*
Custom Decorators Service..................G 973 625-0516
Denville *(G-2033)*
Edward P Paul & Co Inc ....G 908 757-4212
Plainfield *(G-8763)*
Furniture of America NJ ....E 201 605-8200
Secaucus *(G-9770)*
Masters Interiors Inc ....E 973 253-0784
Clifton *(G-1665)*
Rff Services LLC ....F 201 564-0040
Oakland *(G-7644)*
Sofa Doctor Inc ....G 718 292-6300
Guttenberg *(G-3872)*

FURNITURE: Vehicle

Suburban Auto Seat Co Inc ....F 973 778-9227
Lodi *(G-5577)*

FURNITURE: Wall Cases, Office, Exc Wood

Denmatt Industries LLC ....F 609 689-0099
Hamilton *(G-4105)*

FURNITURE: Wardrobes, Household, Wood

Rainbow Closets Inc ....D 973 882-3800
Fairfield *(G-3297)*

FURNITURE: Wicker & Rattan

D & F Wicker Import Co Inc...................E 973 736-5861
Succasunna *(G-10511)*

FURRIERS

M Blaustein Inc....................................G 973 379-1080
Short Hills *(G-9871)*
S & H R Inc ....G 908 925-3797
Linden *(G-5417)*

FUSES: Electric

Bel Fuse Inc..C 201 432-0463
Jersey City *(G-4700)*

GAMES & TOYS: Baby Carriages & Restraint Seats

Majestic Industries Inc ....E 973 473-3434
Passaic *(G-8084)*

GAMES & TOYS: Blocks

Poof-Alex Holdings LLC........................G 734 454-9552
Fairfield *(G-3292)*

GAMES & TOYS: Board Games, Children's & Adults'

Classic Chess and Games Inc..............G 908 850-6553
Hackettstown *(G-4002)*

GAMES & TOYS: Craft & Hobby Kits & Sets

Hygloss Products Inc ....E 973 458-1700
Wallington *(G-11387)*
Larose Industries LLC ....D 973 543-2037
Randolph *(G-9189)*

GAMES & TOYS: Dolls & Doll Clothing

Chic Btq Doll Design Co LLC ....G 201 784-7727
Norwood *(G-7561)*

GAMES & TOYS: Dolls, Exc Stuffed Toy Animals

Franklin Mint LLC................................E 800 843-6468
Fort Lee *(G-3559)*
Letts Play Inc ....G 856 297-2530
Williamstown *(G-11963)*

GAMES & TOYS: Kits, Science, Incl Microscopes/Chemistry Sets

Hirox - USA Inc ....G 201 342-2600
Hackensack *(G-3929)*

GAMES & TOYS: Marbles

Bucci Management Co Inc ....G 609 567-8808
Hammonton *(G-4131)*

GAMES & TOYS: Models, Railroad, Toy & Hobby

Deluxe Innovations Inc ....G 201 857-5880
Midland Park *(G-6174)*

GAMES & TOYS: Wagons, Coaster, Express & Play, Children's

Morgan Cycle LLC ....G 973 218-9233
Short Hills *(G-9873)*

GARBAGE CONTAINERS: Plastic

Allstar Disposal ....G 973 398-8808
Hopatcong *(G-4517)*
Birds Beware Corporation ....G 732 671-6377
Middletown *(G-6161)*
Greco Industries LLC ....G 732 919-6200
Colts Neck *(G-1784)*
Janico Inc ....F 732 370-2223
Freehold *(G-3672)*
Nini Disposal ....G 609 587-2411
Trenton *(G-10966)*
Pretium Packaging LLC........................F 314 727-8200
Hillsborough *(G-4346)*
Sancon Services Inc ....G 973 344-2500
Newark *(G-7262)*

GARBAGE DISPOSERS & COMPACTORS: Commercial

Arrow Steel Inc....................................F 973 523-1122
Paterson *(G-8142)*
Metropolitan Compactors Svc ....G 908 653-0168
Cranford *(G-1917)*
Multi-Pak Corporation ....E 201 342-7474
Hackensack *(G-3949)*
Premier Compaction Systems ....F 718 328-5990
Woodland Park *(G-12087)*

GAS & OIL FIELD EXPLORATION SVCS

All American Oil Recovery Co ....E 973 628-9278
Wayne *(G-11467)*
American Shale Oil LLC ....G 973 438-3500
Newark *(G-7045)*
Hess Corporation ....G 609 882-8477
Ewing *(G-3035)*
Masouleh Corp ....E 973 470-8900
Clifton *(G-1664)*
Ridgewood Energy S Fund LLC ....G 201 307-0470
Montvale *(G-6427)*
Ridgewood Energy T Fund LLC ....G 800 942-5550
Montvale *(G-6428)*
Ridgewood Energy U Fund LLC ....G 201 447-9000
Montvale *(G-6429)*
Ridgewood Energy V Fund LLC ....G 800 942-5550
Montvale *(G-6430)*
Ridgewood Energy Y Fund LLC ....G 201 447-9000
Montvale *(G-6431)*

GAS & OIL FIELD SVCS, NEC

Garden State Fuel ....G 856 442-0061
Monroeville *(G-6351)*

GAS & OTHER COMBINED SVCS

Lantier Construction Company ....E 856 780-6366
Moorestown *(G-6536)*

GAS STATIONS

Total American Services Inc ....F 206 626-3500
Jersey City *(G-4822)*

GAS: Refinery

Phillips 66 Company ....G 908 296-0709
Linden *(G-5407)*

GASES: Argon

Linde North America Inc ....D 908 464-8100
New Providence *(G-7007)*

GASES: Flourinated Hydrocarbon

Solvay Holding Inc ....A 609 860-4000
Princeton *(G-9024)*
Solvay USA Inc ....B 609 860-4000
Princeton *(G-9025)*
Solvay USA Inc ....C 732 297-0100
North Brunswick *(G-7486)*
Sonneborn Holding LLC.......................B 201 760-2940
Parsippany *(G-8019)*

GASES: Helium

Linde Global Helium Inc ....E 908 464-8100
New Providence *(G-7006)*

GASES: Indl

Aeropres Corporation...........................G 908 292-1240
Hillsborough *(G-4301)*
Air Liquide Advanced Materials ....F 908 231-9060
Branchburg *(G-612)*
Air Products and Chemicals Inc............E 732 446-5676
Manalapan *(G-5800)*
Airgas Usa LLC ....F 609 685-4241
Cherry Hill *(G-1337)*
Airgas Usa LLC ....E 856 829-7878
Cinnaminson *(G-1440)*
Boc Group Inc ....A 908 665-2400
New Providence *(G-6995)*
Coim USA Inc ....E 856 224-1668
Paulsboro *(G-8331)*
Concorde Specialty Gases Inc ....E 732 544-9899
Eatontown *(G-2386)*
Linde Gas North America LLC ....G 908 777-9125
Phillipsburg *(G-8559)*
Linde North America Inc ....F 908 329-9700
Stewartsville *(G-10485)*
Matheson Gas Products Inc ....F 201 867-4101
Parsippany *(G-7975)*
Matheson Tri-Gas Inc...........................D 908 991-9200
Basking Ridge *(G-189)*
Matheson Tri-Gas Inc...........................E 908 991-9200
Basking Ridge *(G-190)*
Messer North America Inc ....B 908 464-8100
Bridgewater *(G-851)*
Praxair Inc...F 732 738-4150
Keasbey *(G-4914)*
Praxair Cryomag Services Inc ....F 732 738-4000
Keasbey *(G-4915)*
Praxair Distribution Inc ....F 908 862-7200
Linden *(G-5411)*
Praxair Distribution Inc ....E 973 589-7895
Newark *(G-7232)*
S O S Gases Inc ....E 201 998-7800
Kearny *(G-4897)*

GASES: Nitrogen

Linde Gas North America LLC ....F 732 438-9977
Dayton *(G-1977)*
Messer LLC ....E 908 329-9619
Stewartsville *(G-10486)*

GASES: Oxygen

Linde Gas North America LLC ....E 908 329-9300
Stewartsville *(G-10484)*
Linde Gas North America LLC ....A 908 508-3000
Bridgewater *(G-844)*
Linde Gas USA LLC ....D 908 464-8100
Bridgewater *(G-845)*
Linde North America Inc ....D 908 454-7455
Alpha *(G-39)*
Messer LLC ....C 908 464-8100
Bridgewater *(G-849)*
Messer LLC ....B 512 330-0153
Bridgewater *(G-850)*

Messer LLC..E....... 908 464-8100
New Providence *(G-7010)*
Messer LLC..G....... 973 579-2065
Sparta *(G-10398)*
Messer Merchant Production LLC........F....... 908 464-8100
New Providence *(G-7011)*

GASKET MATERIALS

Banks Bros Corporation ....D....... 973 680-4488
Bloomfield *(G-491)*
Capital Gasket and Rubber Inc ....G....... 856 939-3670
Runnemede *(G-9604)*
Monmouth Rubber Corp ....E....... 732 229-3444
Long Branch *(G-5604)*

GASKETS

Alltite Gasket Co ....F....... 732 254-2154
South River *(G-10348)*
Arcy Manufacturing Co Inc ....F....... 201 635-1910
Carlstadt *(G-1124)*
Coast Rubber and Gasket Inc ....G....... 609 747-0110
Burlington *(G-960)*
Metallo Gasket Company Inc ....F....... 732 545-7223
New Brunswick *(G-6947)*
Omega Shielding Products Inc ....F....... 973 366-0080
Randolph *(G-9195)*
Phoenix Packing & Gasket Co ....F....... 732 938-7377
Howell *(G-4549)*
R S Rubber Corp ....F....... 973 777-2200
Wallington *(G-11389)*
Seals-Eastern Incorporated ....C....... 732 747-9200
Red Bank *(G-9243)*
Specialty Rubber Inc ....G....... 609 704-2555
Elwood *(G-2860)*
Tricomp Inc ....C....... 973 835-1110
Pompton Plains *(G-8872)*

GASKETS & SEALING DEVICES

Cinchseal Associates Inc ....E....... 856 662-5162
Mount Laurel *(G-6747)*
Custom Gasket Mfg LLC ....F....... 201 331-6363
Englewood Cliffs *(G-2966)*
Frontline Industries Inc ....F....... 973 373-7211
Irvington *(G-4570)*
H K Metal Craft Mfg Corp ....E....... 973 471-7770
Lodi *(G-5563)*
John Crane Inc ....D....... 856 467-6185
Swedesboro *(G-10590)*

GASOLINE FILLING STATIONS

Chevron USA Inc ....D....... 732 738-2000
Perth Amboy *(G-8515)*
Masouleh Corp ....E....... 973 470-8900
Clifton *(G-1664)*
Phillips 66 Company ....G....... 908 296-0709
Linden *(G-5407)*

GASTROINTESTINAL OR GENITOURINARY SYSTEM DRUGS

Guardian Drug Company Inc ....D....... 609 860-2600
Dayton *(G-1968)*
Salix Pharmaceuticals Ltd ....D....... 866 246-8245
Bridgewater *(G-879)*

GATES: Ornamental Metal

J Kaufman Iron Works Inc ....F....... 973 925-9972
Paterson *(G-8216)*
Robert J Donaldson Inc ....F....... 856 629-2737
Williamstown *(G-11976)*

GAUGES

Digivac Company ....F....... 732 765-0900
Matawan *(G-5972)*

GEARS

State Tool Gear Co Inc ....F....... 973 642-6181
Newark *(G-7286)*

GEARS: Power Transmission, Exc Auto

Gears IV LLC ....G....... 201 401-3035
Bridgewater *(G-826)*
Koellmann Gear Corporation ....C....... 201 447-0200
Waldwick *(G-11303)*
Martin Sprocket & Gear Inc ....F....... 973 633-5700
Wayne *(G-11534)*

Walter Machine Co Inc ....E....... 201 656-5654
Jersey City *(G-4829)*

GELATIN CAPSULES

International Vitamin Corp ....G....... 973 416-2000
Irvington *(G-4576)*
Torpac Inc ....E....... 973 244-1125
Fairfield *(G-3330)*

GEM STONES MINING, NEC: Natural

Innovative Cutng Concepts LLC ....G....... 609 484-9960
Egg Harbor Township *(G-2684)*

GEMSTONE & INDL DIAMOND MINING SVCS

Diamond Wholesale Co ....E....... 201 727-9595
Moonachie *(G-6462)*
Star Creations Inc ....G....... 212 221-3570
Piscataway *(G-8718)*

GENERAL COUNSELING SVCS

Corrigan Center For Integrativ..............G....... 973 239-0700
Cedar Grove *(G-1273)*

GENERAL MERCHANDISE, NONDURABLE, WHOLESALE

Nova Distributors LLC ....F....... 908 222-1010
Edison *(G-2580)*
Yunta USA Inc ....G....... 614 835-6588
Cranbury *(G-1896)*

GENERATING APPARATUS & PARTS: Electrical

American Mdlar Pwr Sltions Inc ....G....... 973 588-4026
Boonton *(G-542)*
Ocean Power Technologies Inc ....E....... 609 730-0400
Monroe Township *(G-6339)*

GENERATION EQPT: Electronic

Access Conrol Group LLC ....F....... 908 789-8700
Robbinsville *(G-9406)*
Cellular Empire Inc ....D....... 800 778-3513
Linden *(G-5331)*
Industronic Inc ....G....... 908 393-5960
Bridgewater *(G-835)*
Ocean Power Technologies Inc ....E....... 609 730-0400
Monroe Township *(G-6339)*
Power Dynamics Inc ....E....... 973 560-0019
Whippany *(G-11906)*
Sparton Aydin LLC ....F....... 732 935-1320
Eatontown *(G-2421)*
Weissco Power Ltd Liability Co.............G....... 908 832-2173
Califon *(G-1037)*

GENERATOR REPAIR SVCS

Gamka Sales Co Inc ....E....... 732 248-1400
Edison *(G-2518)*
Hights Electric Motor Service ....G....... 609 448-2298
Hightstown *(G-4296)*
Power Pool Plus Inc ....G....... 908 454-1124
Alpha *(G-40)*
RSI Company ....G....... 973 227-7800
Fairfield *(G-3304)*

GENERATORS SETS: Motor, Automotive

Doolan Industries Incorporated..........G....... 856 985-1880
Marlton *(G-5929)*

GENERATORS: Electric

Electro-Steam Generator Corp ....E....... 609 288-9071
Rancocas *(G-9160)*

GENERATORS: Storage Battery Chargers

Hitechone Inc ....G....... 201 500-8864
Englewood Cliffs *(G-2975)*

GENERATORS: Ultrasonic

Seren Ips Inc ....D....... 856 205-1131
Vineland *(G-11265)*

GIFT SHOP

A Cheerful Giver Inc ....F....... 856 358-4438
Elmer *(G-2792)*

Candy Treasure LLC ....G....... 201 830-3600
Lebanon *(G-5254)*
Cream Ridge Winery ....G....... 609 259-9797
Cream Ridge *(G-1933)*
Engraved Images Ltd ....G....... 908 234-0323
Far Hills *(G-3375)*
Genevieves Inc ....F....... 973 772-8816
Garfield *(G-3746)*
Jubili Bead & Yarn Shoppe ....G....... 856 858-7844
Collingswood *(G-1769)*
Trophy King Inc ....G....... 201 836-1482
Teaneck *(G-10653)*

GIFT WRAP: Paper, Made From Purchased Materials

Flexo-Craft Prints Inc ....E....... 973 482-7200
Harrison *(G-4174)*

GIFT, NOVELTY & SOUVENIR STORES: Gifts & Novelties

Matisse Chocolatier Inc ....G....... 201 568-2288
Englewood *(G-2923)*
Mj Corporate Sales Inc ....E....... 856 778-0055
Mount Laurel *(G-6783)*
Party City Corporation..........................F....... 973 537-1707
Randolph *(G-9196)*
Party City of North Bergen ....F....... 201 865-0040
North Bergen *(G-7427)*
Rolferrys Specialties Inc ....G....... 856 456-2999
Brooklawn *(G-915)*

GIFTS & NOVELTIES: Wholesalers

A Kessler Kreation Inc ....G....... 732 431-2468
Colts Neck *(G-1776)*
C Bennett Scopes Inc ....G....... 856 464-6889
Mantua *(G-5851)*
HMS Monaco Et Cie Ltd ....E....... 201 533-0007
Jersey City *(G-4747)*
House of Prill Inc ....E....... 732 442-2400
Lincroft *(G-5311)*
Madhouz LLC ....G....... 609 206-8009
Glassboro *(G-3814)*
Nikko Ceramics Inc ....F....... 201 840-5200
Fairview *(G-3364)*
Nouveautes Inc ....F....... 973 882-8850
Fairfield *(G-3283)*
Qualserv Imports Inc ....G....... 973 620-9234
Denville *(G-2050)*
Retrographics Publishing Inc ....G....... 201 501-0505
Closter *(G-1762)*
Scaasis Originals Inc ....E....... 732 775-7474
Neptune *(G-6895)*

GIFTWARE: Brass

Lighthouse Express Inc ....G....... 732 776-9555
Asbury Park *(G-79)*

GILSONITE MINING SVCS

Ziegler Chem & Mineral Corp...............F....... 732 752-4111
Piscataway *(G-8740)*

GLASS & GLASS CERAMIC PRDTS, PRESSED OR BLOWN: Tableware

Durand Glass Mfg Co Inc ....A....... 856 327-1850
Millville *(G-6248)*

GLASS FABRICATORS

Above Rest Glass ....G....... 732 370-1616
Toms River *(G-10738)*
AGC Products Inc ....G....... 973 248-5039
Vineland *(G-11184)*
Amcor Phrm Packg USA LLC ....C....... 856 825-1100
Millville *(G-6229)*
Atlantic International Tech ....F....... 973 625-0053
Rockaway *(G-9444)*
Avant Industries Ltd Inc ....G....... 973 242-1700
Newark *(G-7060)*
Century Bathworks Inc ....E....... 201 785-1414
Woodland Park *(G-12075)*
Comar Inc ....E....... 856 692-6100
Voorhees *(G-11282)*
Comar LLC ....C....... 856 507-5483
Vineland *(G-11200)*
County of Somerset..............................G....... 732 469-3363
Bridgewater *(G-814)*

P R O D U C T

CR Laurence Co Inc............................F 201 770-1077
  Secaucus *(G-9758)*

Crown Glass Co Inc...........................G...... 908 642-1764
  Branchburg *(G-633)*

Cumberland Rcycl Corp S Jersey ....E 856 825-4153
  Millville *(G-6245)*

Eastern Glass Resources Inc ....E 973 483-8411
  Harrison *(G-4171)*

Fbn New Jersey Mfg Inc......................E 973 402-1443
  Mountain Lakes *(G-6825)*

Friedrich and Dimmock Inc.................E 856 825-0305
  Millville *(G-6249)*

Gbw Manufacturing Inc.......................E 973 279-0077
  Totowa *(G-10828)*

Gerresheimer Glass Inc......................B 856 507-5852
  Vineland *(G-11224)*

Glastron Inc..E 856 692-0500
  Vineland *(G-11226)*

Icup Inc..E 856 751-2045
  Cherry Hill *(G-1373)*

Jersey Tempered Glass Inc..................E 856 273-8700
  Mount Laurel *(G-6773)*

Kubik Maltbie Inc...............................E 856 234-0052
  Mount Laurel *(G-6774)*

McGrory Glass Inc..............................D 856 579-3200
  Paulsboro *(G-8335)*

Miric Industries Inc............................F 201 864-0233
  North Bergen *(G-7422)*

Nds Technologies Inc.........................E 856 691-0330
  Vineland *(G-11246)*

Newman Glass Works Inc ....F 215 925-3565
  Camden *(G-1079)*

Oldcastle Buildingenvelope Inc.............D 856 234-9222
  Moorestown *(G-6549)*

Penta Glass Industries Inc ....G...... 973 478-2110
  Garfield *(G-3755)*

Precision Electronic Glass Inc ....D 856 691-2234
  Vineland *(G-11254)*

Quality Glass Inc................................F 908 754-2652
  South Plainfield *(G-10320)*

Quark Enterprises Inc.........................E 856 455-0376
  Rosenhayn *(G-9597)*

S P Industries Inc...............................D 856 691-3200
  Vineland *(G-11262)*

St Thomas Creations ....E 800 536-2284
  Monroe Township *(G-6345)*

William Duling....................................G...... 856 365-6323
  Camden *(G-1090)*

GLASS PRDTS, FROM PURCHASED GLASS:
Art

Personlized Exprssons By Audrey ....F 973 478-5115
  Garfield *(G-3756)*

GLASS PRDTS, FROM PURCHASED GLASS:
Glass Beads, Reflecting

Potters Industries LLC.......................E 201 507-4169
  Carlstadt *(G-1205)*

GLASS PRDTS, FROM PURCHASED GLASS:
Insulating

Insulite Inc...F 732 255-1700
  Toms River *(G-10770)*

JE Berkowitz LP ....C 856 456-7800
  Pedricktown *(G-8349)*

Thermoseal Industries LLC..................D 856 456-3109
  Gloucester City *(G-3852)*

GLASS PRDTS, FROM PURCHASED GLASS:
Mirrored

General Glass Intl Corp ....C 201 553-1850
  Secaucus *(G-9772)*

Interior Specialties LLC......................F 856 663-1700
  Pennsauken *(G-8438)*

R A O Contract Sales NY Inc................G...... 201 652-1500
  Paterson *(G-8285)*

Union City Mirror & Table Co ....E 201 867-0050
  Union City *(G-11131)*

GLASS PRDTS, FROM PURCHASED GLASS:
Novelties, Fruit, Etc

Proco Inc..G...... 609 265-8777
  Lumberton *(G-5634)*

GLASS PRDTS, PRESSED OR BLOWN:
Barware

Buckets Plus Inc ....G...... 732 545-0420
  New Brunswick *(G-6914)*

GLASS PRDTS, PRESSED OR BLOWN:
Bulbs, Electric Lights

Bulbrite Industries Inc ....E 201 531-5900
  Moonachie *(G-6458)*

Goodlite Products Inc..........................F 718 697-7502
  Perth Amboy *(G-8519)*

Lumiko USA Inc ....G...... 609 409-6900
  Cranbury *(G-1860)*

GLASS PRDTS, PRESSED OR BLOWN:
Furnishings & Access

Crystal World Inc ....E 201 488-0909
  Carlstadt *(G-1148)*

Folio Art Glass Inc ....G...... 732 431-0044
  Colts Neck *(G-1783)*

Gbw Manufacturing Inc.......................E 973 279-0077
  Totowa *(G-10828)*

Glocal Expertise Llc............................G...... 718 928-3839
  Jersey City *(G-4744)*

Interior Specialties LLC......................F 856 663-1700
  Pennsauken *(G-8438)*

Mirrotek International LLC..................E 973 472-1400
  Passaic *(G-8090)*

GLASS PRDTS, PRESSED OR BLOWN:
Glassware, Art Or Decorative

Eldon Glass & Mirror Co Inc ....F 973 589-2099
  Newark *(G-7113)*

Glassworks Studio Inc ....G...... 973 656-0800
  Morristown *(G-6666)*

Kraftware Corporation ....E 732 345-7091
  Roselle *(G-9562)*

GLASS PRDTS, PRESSED OR BLOWN:
Glassware, Novelty

Hospitality GL Brands USA Inc.............F 800 869-5258
  Ridgefield Park *(G-9309)*

GLASS PRDTS, PRESSED OR BLOWN:
Lighting Eqpt Parts

Illuminating Experiences LLC...............G...... 800 734-5858
  New Brunswick *(G-6934)*

Sterling Products Inc ....F 973 471-2858
  Passaic *(G-8109)*

GLASS PRDTS, PRESSED OR BLOWN:
Optical

Partners In Vision Inc ....G 888 748-1112
  Edison *(G-2587)*

GLASS PRDTS, PRESSED OR BLOWN:
Ornaments, Christmas Tree

Mg Decor LLC......................................F 201 923-5493
  East Rutherford *(G-2303)*

GLASS PRDTS, PRESSED OR BLOWN:
Scientific Glassware

Friedrich and Dimmock Inc..................E 856 825-0305
  Millville *(G-6249)*

Glass Warehouse ....G...... 856 825-1400
  Millville *(G-6252)*

Kramme Consolidated Inc....................G...... 856 358-8151
  Monroeville *(G-6352)*

Quark Enterprises Inc.........................E 856 455-0376
  Rosenhayn *(G-9597)*

Technical Glass Products Inc ....G...... 973 989-5500
  Dover *(G-2107)*

GLASS PRDTS, PRESSED OR BLOWN:
Tubing

Corning Pharmaceutical GL LLC...........G...... 856 794-7100
  Vineland *(G-11205)*

Creamer Glass LLC..............................G...... 856 327-2023
  Millville *(G-6243)*

Creamer Glass LLC..............................G...... 856 327-2023
  Millville *(G-6244)*

E G L Company Inc..............................C...... 908 508-1111
  Berkeley Heights *(G-398)*

GLASS PRDTS, PURCHASED GLASS:
Glassware, Scientific/Tech

H S Martin Company Inc ....F 856 692-8700
  Vineland *(G-11230)*

Triton Associated Industries................E 856 697-3050
  Buena *(G-944)*

V M Glass Co ....G...... 856 794-9333
  Vineland *(G-11274)*

GLASS STORE: Leaded Or Stained

Artique Glass Studio Inc ....G...... 201 444-3500
  Glen Rock *(G-3826)*

Artistic Glass & Doors Inc...................G...... 856 768-1414
  West Berlin *(G-11577)*

SA Bendheim Ltd ....E 973 471-1733
  Wayne *(G-11550)*

GLASS STORES

Architectural Metal and Glass ....G...... 732 994-7575
  Lakewood *(G-5054)*

Newman Glass Works Inc ....F 215 925-3565
  Camden *(G-1079)*

Phoenix Glass LLC..............................E 856 692-0100
  Pittsgrove *(G-8750)*

GLASS, AUTOMOTIVE: Wholesalers

PPG Industries Inc..............................G...... 856 662-9323
  Pennsauken *(G-8469)*

GLASS: Fiber

Thomas Clark Fiberglass LLC ....G...... 609 492-9257
  Barnegat *(G-163)*

GLASS: Flat

Edmund Optics Inc ....C 856 547-3488
  Barrington *(G-172)*

Floral Glass Industries Inc...................E 201 939-4600
  East Rutherford *(G-2289)*

Frost Tech Inc.....................................F 732 396-0071
  Rahway *(G-9096)*

General Glass Intl Corp ....C 201 553-1850
  Secaucus *(G-9772)*

Oldcastle Buildingenvelope Inc.............D 856 234-9222
  Moorestown *(G-6549)*

Pierangeli Group Inc...........................G...... 856 582-4060
  Gloucester City *(G-3847)*

Pilkington North America Inc...............C...... 973 470-5703
  Clifton *(G-1692)*

Tri-State Glass & Mirror Inc.................G...... 732 591-5545
  Old Bridge *(G-7729)*

GLASS: Indl Prdts

Hospitality Glass Brands LLC ....E 800 869-8258
  Paramus *(G-7806)*

M D Laboratory Supplies Inc ....G...... 732 322-0773
  Franklin Park *(G-3635)*

Q Glass Company Inc..........................G...... 973 335-5191
  Towaco *(G-10879)*

GLASS: Insulating

Just Glass & Mirror Inc.......................F 856 728-8383
  Williamstown *(G-11962)*

GLASS: Plate

PPG Industries Inc..............................G...... 856 662-9323
  Pennsauken *(G-8469)*

GLASS: Pressed & Blown, NEC

Amcor Phrm Packg USA LLC ....C...... 856 825-1100
  Millville *(G-6229)*

Cardinal International Inc....................F 973 628-0900
  Wayne *(G-11487)*

Daum Inc..G...... 862 210-8522
  Fairfield *(G-3179)*

Glassblowerscom LLC ....G...... 856 232-7898
  Blackwood *(G-467)*

Glassroots Inc.....................................E 973 353-9555
  Newark *(G-7132)*

Icup Inc ....E 856 751-2045
Cherry Hill *(G-1373)*

Materials Research Group Inc ....G...... 908 245-3301
Roselle *(G-9564)*

McGrory Glass Inc ....D...... 856 579-3200
Paulsboro *(G-8335)*

Qis Inc ....F 856 455-3736
Rosenhayn *(G-9596)*

Sensors Unlimited Inc ....D...... 609 333-8000
Princeton *(G-9020)*

Triton Associated Industries...............E 856 697-3050
Buena *(G-944)*

GLASS: Stained

Ace Fine Art Inc................................G...... 201 960-4447
Garfield *(G-3724)*

Artistic Glass & Doors Inc..................G...... 856 768-1414
West Berlin *(G-11577)*

Ascalon Studios Inc..........................F 856 768-3779
West Berlin *(G-11578)*

Comfort Zone ....G...... 732 869-9990
Ocean Grove *(G-7699)*

Edward W Hiemer & Co ....F 973 772-5081
Clifton *(G-1611)*

Femenella & Associates Inc...............G...... 908 722-6526
Branchburg *(G-640)*

Folio Art Glass Inc ....G...... 732 431-0044
Colts Neck *(G-1783)*

Glass Dynamics LLC ....G...... 856 205-1503
Vineland *(G-11225)*

Linda Spolitino ....G...... 609 345-3126
Atlantic City *(G-96)*

Rambusch Decorating Company ....E 201 333-2525
Jersey City *(G-4797)*

GLASS: Structural

Europrojects Intl Inc ....G...... 201 408-5215
Englewood *(G-2903)*

GLASSWARE STORES

Folio Art Glass Inc ....G...... 732 431-0044
Colts Neck *(G-1783)*

Q Glass Company Inc ....G...... 973 335-5191
Towaco *(G-10879)*

GLASSWARE WHOLESALERS

ARC International N Amer LLC ....C...... 856 825-5620
Millville *(G-6233)*

Durand Glass Mfg Co Inc ....A...... 856 327-1850
Millville *(G-6248)*

Eastern Glass Resources Inc ....E 973 483-8411
Harrison *(G-4171)*

Q Glass Company Inc ....G...... 973 335-5191
Towaco *(G-10879)*

GLASSWARE: Indl

United Silica Products Inc ....F 973 209-8854
Franklin *(G-3610)*

GLASSWARE: Laboratory & Medical

A M K Glass Inc ....G...... 856 692-1488
Vineland *(G-11183)*

Bellco Glass Inc ....D...... 800 257-7043
Vineland *(G-11192)*

Demco Scientific Glassware Inc...........G...... 856 327-7898
Millville *(G-6247)*

Hanson & Zollinger Inc ....F 856 626-3440
Berlin *(G-422)*

GLOBAL POSITIONING SYSTEMS & EQPT

Comodo Group Inc ....D...... 888 266-6361
Clifton *(G-1586)*

ID Systems Inc ....C...... 201 996-9000
Woodcliff Lake *(G-12057)*

GLOVES: Fabric

American Baby Headwear Co Inc..........D...... 908 558-0017
Elizabeth *(G-2710)*

GLOVES: Leather, Work

Ansell Hawkeye Inc ....E 662 258-3200
Iselin *(G-4592)*

GLOVES: Plastic

Poly-Version Inc................................E 201 451-7600
Jersey City *(G-4786)*

GLOVES: Safety

Ansell Protective Products LLC ....A...... 732 345-5400
Iselin *(G-4596)*

Becton Dickinson and Company........A...... 201 847-6800
Franklin Lakes *(G-3616)*

Pacific Dunlop Investments USA ....F 732 345-5400
Red Bank *(G-9240)*

GLUE

Gluefast Company Inc ....F 732 918-4600
Neptune *(G-6881)*

Hudson Industries Corporation............G...... 973 402-0100
Fairfield *(G-3231)*

Signature Marketing & Mfg ....G...... 973 427-3700
Hawthorne *(G-4244)*

GOLD ORES

Freeport-Mcmoran Inc ....G...... 908 558-4361
Elizabeth *(G-2738)*

GOLD STAMPING, EXC BOOKS

Berk Gold Stamping Corporation........E 973 786-6052
Andover *(G-45)*

GOLF EQPT

Greater ATL Cy Golf Assn LLC ....F 609 652-1800
Galloway *(G-3722)*

JA Cissel Manufacturing Co ....E 732 901-0300
Lakewood *(G-5113)*

GOLF GOODS & EQPT

RCM Ltd Inc ....G...... 201 337-3328
Oakland *(G-7642)*

Tex-Net Inc ....E 609 499-9111
Florence *(G-3478)*

GOURMET FOOD STORES

Delicious Fresh Pierogi Inc.................F 908 245-0550
Roselle Park *(G-9583)*

Gardner Resources Inc ....G...... 732 872-0755
Highlands *(G-4292)*

Silver Palate Kitchens Inc ....E 201 568-0110
Cresskill *(G-1944)*

GOVERNMENT, EXECUTIVE OFFICES:
County Supervisor/Exec Office

County of Somerset............................C...... 732 469-3363
Bridgewater *(G-814)*

GRAIN & FIELD BEANS WHOLESALERS

Akila Holdings Inc ....G...... 609 454-5034
Princeton *(G-8904)*

GRANITE: Crushed & Broken

Stone Industries Inc..........................D...... 973 595-6250
Haledon *(G-4085)*

GRANITE: Cut & Shaped

Bcg Marble Gran Fabricators Co..........F 201 343-8487
Hackensack *(G-3882)*

Bedrock Granite Inc ....E 732 741-0010
Shrewsbury *(G-9883)*

Caputo International Inc......................G...... 732 225-5777
Edison *(G-2474)*

Gran All Mrble Tile Imprts Inc ....G...... 856 354-4747
Cherry Hill *(G-1369)*

Marmo Enterprises Inc ....G...... 732 649-3011
Somerset *(G-10023)*

Robert Young & Sons Inc ....G...... 973 483-0451
Newark *(G-7252)*

Stone Systems New Jersey LLC ....F 973 778-5525
Fairfield *(G-3316)*

Stone Truss Systems Inc ....E 973 882-7377
Fairfield *(G-3317)*

Stoneworld At Redbank Inc ....G...... 732 383-5110
Red Bank *(G-9245)*

GRANITE: Dimension

Fanwood Crushed Stone Company ....D...... 908 322-7840
Watchung *(G-11455)*

GRANITE: Dimension

Eastern Concrete Materials Inc ....G...... 908 537-2135
Glen Gardner *(G-3821)*

Stone Surfaces Inc ....D...... 201 935-8803
East Rutherford *(G-2321)*

GRAPHIC ARTS & RELATED DESIGN SVCS

A M Graphics Inc..............................G...... 201 767-5320
Harrington Park *(G-4161)*

Advertisers Service Group Inc ....F 201 440-5577
Ridgefield Park *(G-9298)*

Alliance Design Inc............................F 973 904-9450
Totowa *(G-10809)*

AlphaGraphics ....F 856 761-8000
Cherry Hill *(G-1339)*

Banner Design Inc ....E 908 687-5335
Hillside *(G-4379)*

Color Comp Inc ....G...... 856 262-3040
Williamstown *(G-11954)*

Design Factory Nj Inc ....G...... 908 964-8833
Hillside *(G-4388)*

Digital Arts Imaging LLC ....F 908 237-4646
Flemington *(G-3437)*

Dm Graphic Center LLC ....F 973 882-8990
Fairfield *(G-3186)*

Dynamic Printing & Graphics ....F 973 473-7177
Clifton *(G-1608)*

Earth Color New York Inc ....E 973 884-1300
Parsippany *(G-7925)*

Encore Enterprises Inc ....G...... 201 489-5044
South Hackensack *(G-10158)*

Envirnmntal Dsign Grphic Entps...........G...... 973 361-1829
Dover *(G-2083)*

Falcon Graphics Inc..........................G...... 908 232-1991
Clark *(G-1497)*

Franbeth Inc ....G...... 856 488-1480
Pennsauken *(G-8422)*

Frontend Graphics Inc.......................G...... 856 547-1600
Cherry Hill *(G-1364)*

Gangi Graphics Inc ....G...... 732 840-8680
Brick *(G-719)*

Graphic Imagery Inc ....F 908 755-2882
New Providence *(G-7002)*

J K Design Inc ....E 908 428-4700
Hillsborough *(G-4334)*

Laserwave Graphics Inc.....................F 732 745-7764
New Brunswick *(G-6943)*

Lexington Graphics Corp.....................G...... 973 345-2493
Clifton *(G-1658)*

Moonlight Imaging LLC ....G...... 973 300-1001
Sparta *(G-10399)*

National Color Graphics ....F 856 435-6800
Sicklerville *(G-9912)*

Ramsey Graphics and Printing.............G...... 201 300-2912
Elmwood Park *(G-2852)*

Sandoval Graphics & Printing ....G...... 856 435-7320
Somerdale *(G-9934)*

Stephen Swinton Studio Inc ....G...... 908 537-9135
Washington *(G-11452)*

Typeline...F 201 251-2201
Wyckoff *(G-12123)*

Zippityprint LLC ....F 216 438-0001
Mullica Hill *(G-6859)*

GRAPHITE MINING SVCS

Asbury Carbons Inc...........................G...... 908 537-2155
Asbury *(G-60)*

GRASSES: Artificial & Preserved

Synthetic Grass Surfaces Inc ....G...... 973 778-9594
Lodi *(G-5579)*

GRATINGS: Tread, Fabricated Metal

Studio Dellarte..................................G...... 718 599-3715
Jersey City *(G-4817)*

GRAVE VAULTS, METAL

Marchione Industries Inc....................F 718 317-4900
Lyndhurst *(G-5661)*

**P
R
O
D
U
C
T**

GRAVEL & PEBBLE MINING

Tuckahoe Sand & Gravel Co Inc..........E...... 609 861-2082
Egg Harbor Township *(G-2699)*

GRAVEL MINING

Trap Rock Industries Inc ....E...... 609 924-0300
Titusville *(G-10736)*

GREASE TRAPS: Concrete

Trap-Zap Environmental Systems........E...... 201 251-9970
Wyckoff *(G-12122)*

GREASES: Lubricating

Magnalube Inc ....G...... 718 729-1000
Linden *(G-5379)*

GREENSAND MINING SVCS

Hungerford & Terry Inc ....E...... 856 881-3200
Clayton *(G-1525)*

GREETING CARD SHOPS

Papery of Marlton LLC ....G...... 856 985-1776
Marlton *(G-5946)*

GREETING CARDS WHOLESALERS

Nobleworks Inc ....F....... 201 420-0095
Union City *(G-11124)*

GRINDING SVC: Precision, Commercial Or Indl

M & D Prcsion Cntrless Grnding ....G...... 856 764-1616
Riverside *(G-9398)*
Tri-State Knife Grinding Corp ....E...... 609 890-4989
Robbinsville *(G-9418)*

GRINDING SVCS: Ophthalmic Lens, Exc Prescription

I See Optical Laboratories ....F....... 856 227-9300
Blackwood *(G-469)*
Lab Tech Inc ....G...... 201 767-5613
Northvale *(G-7533)*

GRIT: Steel

Steel Riser Corp ....G...... 732 341-7031
Toms River *(G-10795)*

GRITS: Crushed & Broken

Trap Rock Industries Inc ....E...... 609 924-0300
Titusville *(G-10736)*

GROCERIES WHOLESALERS, NEC

Anthony & Sons Bakery Itln Bky ....D...... 973 625-2323
Denville *(G-2031)*
Bimbo Bakeries USA Inc ....C...... 973 256-8200
Totowa *(G-10820)*
Colonna Brothers Inc ....D...... 800 626-8384
North Bergen *(G-7397)*
Del Buono Bakery Inc ....E...... 856 546-9585
Haddon Heights *(G-4045)*
Diamond Foods USA Inc ....G...... 732 543-2186
North Brunswick *(G-7465)*
Elis Hot Bagels Inc ....E...... 732 566-4523
Matawan *(G-5975)*
Foulkrod Associates ....A...... 856 662-6767
Pennsauken *(G-8421)*
G & Y Specialty Foods LLC ....G...... 956 821-9652
Woodland Park *(G-12080)*
R C Fine Foods Inc ....D...... 908 359-5500
Hillsborough *(G-4349)*
Salad Chef Inc ....F....... 609 641-5455
Pleasantville *(G-8817)*
Wakefern Food Corp ....B...... 732 819-0140
Edison *(G-2645)*
Wakefern Food Corp ....B...... 908 527-3300
Keasbey *(G-4916)*

GROCERIES, GENERAL LINE WHOLESALERS

Arm National Food Inc ....G...... 609 695-4911
Trenton *(G-10896)*

Deep Foods Inc ....C...... 908 810-7500
Union *(G-11042)*
Del-Val Food Ingredients Inc................F....... 856 778-6623
Mount Laurel *(G-6752)*
Dove Chocolate Discoveries LLC..........E...... 866 922-3683
Mount Arlington *(G-6711)*
Panos Holding Company ....G...... 201 843-8900
Rochelle Park *(G-9428)*
Park Avenue Meats Inc ....E...... 718 731-4196
Paterson *(G-8278)*
Zestos Foods LLC 888 407-5852
Teaneck *(G-10657)*

GROUTING EQPT: Concrete

Corrview International LLC ....G...... 973 770-0571
Hopatcong *(G-4519)*
Mapei Corporation ....E...... 732 254-4830
South River *(G-10352)*

GUIDANCE SYSTEMS & EQPT: Space Vehicle

Lockheed Martin Corporation...............B...... 856 787-3104
Mount Laurel *(G-6777)*

GUIDED MISSILES & SPACE VEHICLES

Savit Corporation ....F....... 862 209-4516
Rockaway *(G-9497)*

GUIDED MISSILES & SPACE VEHICLES: Research & Development

Lockheed Martin Corporation...............B...... 856 787-3104
Mount Laurel *(G-6777)*

GUM & WOOD CHEMICALS

Importers Service Corp ....E...... 732 248-1946
Edison *(G-2533)*
Sanit Technologies LLC 862 238-7555
Passaic *(G-8105)*

GUTTERS

R & K Industries Inc ....G...... 732 531-1123
Oakhurst *(G-7612)*
Russo Seamless Gutter LLC..................G...... 732 836-0151
Brick *(G-730)*

GUTTERS: Sheet Metal

Englert Inc ....C...... 800 364-5378
Perth Amboy *(G-8517)*
United Gutter Supply Inc ....E...... 201 933-6316
East Rutherford *(G-2328)*

GYPSUM & CALCITE MINING SVCS

Titan America LLC ....G...... 973 690-5896
Newark *(G-7300)*

GYPSUM PRDTS

Art Plaque Creations Inc ....F....... 973 482-2536
Kearny *(G-4845)*
Durabond Division US Gypsum..............F....... 732 636-7900
Port Reading *(G-8893)*
Georgia-Pacific LLC ....D...... 856 966-7600
Camden *(G-1066)*
United States Gypsum Company ....D...... 732 636-7900
Port Reading *(G-8896)*

GYROSCOPES

Atlantic Inertial Systems Inc ....B...... 973 237-2713
Totowa *(G-10816)*

HAIR & HAIR BASED PRDTS

Cellunet Manufacturing Compnay..........F....... 609 386-3361
Burlington *(G-956)*
Left-Handed Libra LLC ....F....... 973 623-1112
Newark *(G-7178)*
Minniti J Hair Replacement Inc.............G...... 856 427-9600
Cherry Hill *(G-1395)*
Newell Brands Inc ....B...... 201 610-6600
Hoboken *(G-4468)*
Novelty Hair Goods Co ....G...... 856 963-5876
Camden *(G-1080)*
Teluca Inc ....G...... 973 232-0002
West Orange *(G-11779)*

HAIR CARE PRDTS

Caboki LLC ....G...... 609 642-2108
Cranbury *(G-1819)*
Cheveux Cosmetics Corporation..........D...... 732 446-7516
Englishtown *(G-3000)*
Imperial Drug & Spice Corp ....G...... 201 348-1551
West New York *(G-11741)*
LOreal Usa Inc ....C...... 732 499-6617
Clark *(G-1504)*
LOreal Usa Inc ....D...... 212 818-1500
Clark *(G-1505)*
LOreal Usa Inc ....D...... 732 499-6690
Clark *(G-1506)*
LOreal Usa Inc ....A...... 609 860-7500
Cranbury *(G-1858)*
Revlon Inc ....E...... 732 287-1400
Edison *(G-2598)*
Scories Inc ....F....... 973 923-1372
Newark *(G-7264)*

HAIR CARE PRDTS: Bleaches

Hair Systems Inc ....D...... 732 446-2202
Englishtown *(G-3004)*

HAIR CARE PRDTS: Hair Coloring Preparations

Fantasia Industries Corp ....E...... 201 261-7070
Paramus *(G-7800)*
LOreal USA Products Inc ....G...... 732 873-3520
Jersey City *(G-4761)*
Product Club Corp ....F....... 973 664-0565
Rockaway *(G-9491)*

HAIR DRESSING, FOR THE TRADE

Folica Inc ....E...... 609 860-8430
Dayton *(G-1963)*
Razac Products Inc ....G...... 973 622-3700
Newark *(G-7246)*

HAIRBRUSHES, WHOLESALE

Allegro Mfg ....F....... 323 724-0101
Hightstown *(G-4293)*

HAND TOOLS, NEC: Wholesalers

Dreyco Inc ....F....... 201 896-9000
Carlstadt *(G-1154)*
El Batal Corporation ....F....... 908 964-3427
Union *(G-11050)*
Jdv Products Inc ....F....... 201 794-6467
Fair Lawn *(G-3108)*
Vozeh Equipment Corp ....E...... 201 337-3729
Franklin Lakes *(G-3632)*

HANDBAGS

Carol S Miller Corporation ....G...... 201 406-4578
Hillsdale *(G-4365)*
Ledonne Leather Co Inc ....F....... 201 531-2100
Lyndhurst *(G-5657)*
M London Inc ....E...... 201 459-6460
Jersey City *(G-4762)*
McM Products USA Inc ....F....... 646 756-4090
Secaucus *(G-9792)*
Medici International Inc ....G...... 973 684-6084
Paterson *(G-8253)*
Mitzi Intl Handbag & ACC Ltd ....C...... 973 483-5015
Newark *(G-7203)*

HANDBAGS: Women's

Annette & Jim Dizenzo Sls LLC.............G...... 973 875-0895
Sussex *(G-10556)*
Basu Group Inc ....G...... 908 517-9138
North Brunswick *(G-7456)*
Gio Vali Handbag Corp ....G...... 973 279-3032
Paterson *(G-8198)*
Tapestry Inc ....F....... 856 488-2220
Cherry Hill *(G-1421)*

HANDLES: Brush Or Tool, Plastic

Pedibrush LLC ....G...... 856 796-2963
Haddon Heights *(G-4047)*

HANGERS: Garment, Plastic

B & G Plastics Inc ....E...... 973 824-9220
Union *(G-11028)*

(G-0000) Company's Geographic Section entry number

Mainetti Americas Inc ....G...... 201 215-2900
  Secaucus (G-9791)
Mainetti USA Inc ....F 201 215-2900
  Keasbey (G-4912)
Randy Hangers LLC ....G...... 201 215-2900
  Secaucus (G-9802)
Uniplast Industries Inc ....E...... 201 288-4672
  Hasbrouck Heights (G-4192)

HANGERS: Garment, Wire

United Wire Hanger Corp ....C...... 201 288-3212
  Hasbrouck Heights (G-4193)

HANGERS: Garment, Wire

Ecocom Inc ....G...... 201 393-0786
  Montvale (G-6409)

HARD RUBBER PRDTS, NEC

Bumper Specialties Inc ....C...... 856 345-7650
  West Deptford (G-11695)
Miroad Rubber USA LLC ....G...... 480 280-2543
  Edison (G-2567)

HARDWARE

Andrex Inc ....F 908 852-2400
  Hackettstown (G-3998)
Art Materials Service Inc ....D...... 732 545-8888
  New Brunswick (G-6913)
Ashley Norton Inc ....F 973 835-4027
  Pompton Plains (G-8859)
Brim Electronics Inc ....F 201 796-2886
  Lodi (G-5555)
Carpenter & Paterson Inc ....E...... 973 772-1800
  Saddle Brook (G-9644)
Charles E Green & Son Inc ....E...... 973 485-3630
  Newark (G-7082)
Commeatus LLC ....F 847 772-5314
  Plainsboro (G-8782)
Component Hardware Group Inc ....D...... 800 526-3694
  Lakewood (G-5072)
G & S Precision Prototype ....G...... 732 370-3010
  Lakewood (G-5102)
Ho-Ho-Kus Inc ....E...... 973 278-2274
  Paterson (G-8210)
J Blanco Associates Inc ....F 973 427-0619
  Hawthorne (G-4228)
JC Macelroy Co Inc ....D...... 732 572-7100
  Piscataway (G-8681)
Ka-Lor Cubicle and Sup Co Inc ....G...... 201 891-8077
  Franklin Lakes (G-3626)
Pekay Industries Inc ....F 732 938-2722
  Farmingdale (G-3390)
Penn Elcom Inc ....F 973 839-7777
  Pompton Plains (G-8869)
Revere Survival Products Inc ....F 973 575-8811
  West Caldwell (G-11678)
Rsl LLC ....E...... 609 645-9777
  Egg Harbor Township (G-2696)
Saint-Gobain Prfmce Plas Corp ....D...... 732 652-0910
  Somerset (G-10070)
Shade Powers Co Inc ....F 201 767-3727
  Northvale (G-7549)
Steelstran Industries Inc ....G...... 732 566-5040
  Matawan (G-5989)
Unicorp ....C...... 973 674-1700
  Orange (G-7765)
Unified Door & Hdwr Group LLC ....C...... 215 364-8834
  Pennsauken (G-8495)
Versabar Corporation ....F 973 279-8400
  Totowa (G-10857)

HARDWARE & BUILDING PRDTS: Plastic

Artus Corp ....E...... 201 568-1000
  Englewood (G-2878)
Camtec Industries Inc ....F 732 332-9800
  Colts Neck (G-1777)
Hayward Industrial Products ....C...... 908 351-5400
  Elizabeth (G-2745)
Hayward Industries Inc ....B...... 908 351-5400
  Elizabeth (G-2746)
Lumber Super Mart ....G...... 732 739-1428
  Hazlet (G-4264)
Plastpro 2000 Inc ....G...... 973 992-2090
  Livingston (G-5536)
Premiere Raceway Sys LLC ....G...... 732 629-7715
  Piscataway (G-8701)

HARDWARE & EQPT: Stage, Exc Lighting

This Is It Stageworks LLC ....E...... 201 653-2699
  Jersey City (G-4820)

HARDWARE STORES

Component Hardware Group Inc ....D...... 800 526-3694
  Lakewood (G-5072)
La Milagrosa 1 LLC ....F 973 928-1799
  Passaic (G-8081)
Woodhaven Lumber & Millwork ....E...... 732 295-8800
  Point Pleasant Beach (G-8833)

HARDWARE STORES: Builders'

Artistic Hardware ....G...... 609 383-1909
  Northfield (G-7510)

HARDWARE STORES: Door Locks & Lock Sets

Door Center Enterprises Inc ....G...... 609 333-1233
  Hopewell (G-4526)

HARDWARE STORES: Tools

Molnar Tools Inc ....F 908 580-0671
  Warren (G-11423)
Precision Saw & Tool Corp ....F 973 773-7302
  Clifton (G-1698)
Sandvik Inc ....C...... 281 275-4800
  Fair Lawn (G-3121)

HARDWARE STORES: Tools, Power

Jarvis Electric Motors Inc ....G...... 856 662-7710
  Pennsauken (G-8444)
Rennsteig Tools Inc ....G...... 330 315-3044
  Hackensack (G-3966)

HARDWARE WHOLESALERS

Brusso Hardware LLC ....F 212 337-8510
  Belleville (G-292)
Electro Parts Inc ....G...... 856 767-5923
  West Berlin (G-11593)
Industrial Stl & Fastener Corp ....G...... 610 667-2220
  Cherry Hill (G-1377)
Ingersoll-Rand Company ....C...... 908 238-7000
  Annandale (G-54)
La Milagrosa 1 LLC ....F 973 928-1799
  Passaic (G-8081)
Outwater Plstcs/Industries Inc ....D...... 201 498-8750
  Bogota (G-535)
Penn Elcom Inc ....F 973 839-7777
  Pompton Plains (G-8869)
Permadur Industries Inc ....G...... 908 359-9767
  Hillsborough (G-4344)
S H P C Inc ....E...... 973 589-5242
  Newark (G-7258)

HARDWARE, WHOLESALE: Bolts

Shallcross Bolt & Specialties ....E...... 908 925-4700
  Linden (G-5422)
Stud Welding Co The Inc ....G...... 856 866-9300
  Moorestown (G-6569)

HARDWARE, WHOLESALE: Builders', NEC

EP Henry Corporation ....D...... 856 845-6200
  Woodbury (G-12028)

HARDWARE, WHOLESALE: Power Tools & Access

E P Heller Company ....E...... 973 377-2878
  Madison (G-5691)

HARDWARE, WHOLESALE: Screws

Ford Fasteners Inc ....G...... 201 487-3151
  Hackensack (G-3916)

HARDWARE, WHOLESALE: Security Devices, Locks

Mul-T-Lock Usa Inc ....E...... 973 778-3320
  Hackensack (G-3948)

HARDWARE, WHOLESALE: Washers

Randall Manufacturing Co Inc ....E...... 973 746-2111
  Hillside (G-4424)

HARDWARE: Aircraft & Marine, Incl Pulleys & Similar Items

Modern Sportswear Corporation ....F 201 804-2700
  Moonachie (G-6481)

HARDWARE: Builders'

Allfasteners Usa LLC ....E...... 201 783-8836
  Carlstadt (G-1121)
World and Main LLC ....C...... 609 860-9990
  Cranbury (G-1893)

HARDWARE: Cabinet

Artistic Hardware ....G...... 609 383-1909
  Northfield (G-7510)

HARDWARE: Furniture, Builders' & Other Household

Ingersoll-Rand Company ....E...... 856 793-7000
  Mount Laurel (G-6766)
Ramsay David Cabinetmakers ....F 856 234-7776
  Moorestown (G-6562)

HARDWARE: Hangers, Wall

Hanger Central LLC ....G...... 732 750-1161
  Edison (G-2526)

HARDWARE: Luggage

Atco Products Inc ....E...... 973 379-3171
  Springfield (G-10428)

HARDWARE: Parachute

Airborne Systems N Amer Inc ....G...... 856 663-1275
  Pennsauken (G-8385)

HARNESS ASSEMBLIES: Cable & Wire

Ameral International Inc ....F 856 456-9000
  Brooklawn (G-913)
Andrex Inc ....F 908 852-2400
  Hackettstown (G-3998)
Andrex Systems Inc ....G...... 908 835-1720
  Port Murray (G-8881)
Computer Crafts Inc ....C...... 973 423-3500
  Hawthorne (G-4214)
Da-Green Electronics Ltd ....F 732 254-2735
  Marlboro (G-5894)
Electronic Connections Inc ....F 732 367-5588
  Lakewood (G-5089)
Esi ....E...... 856 629-2492
  Sicklerville (G-9909)
General Reliance Corporation ....E...... 973 361-1400
  Denville (G-2038)
Melstrom Manufacturing Corp ....D...... 732 938-7400
  Wall Township (G-11355)
Quadrangle Products Inc ....F 732 792-1234
  Englishtown (G-3008)
Spem Corporation ....E...... 732 356-3366
  Piscataway (G-8717)
Valconn Electronics Inc ....E...... 908 687-1600
  Union (G-11097)
VIP Industries Inc ....E...... 973 472-7500
  Clifton (G-1735)
Wire-Pro Inc ....C...... 856 935-7560
  Salem (G-9698)
YC Cable (east) Inc ....E...... 732 868-0800
  Piscataway (G-8739)

HARNESS WIRING SETS: Internal Combustion Engines

Incom (america) Inc ....G...... 908 464-3366
  Berkeley Heights (G-401)

HARNESSES, HALTERS, SADDLERY & STRAPS

Brook Saddle Ridge Equest ....F 609 953-1600
  Shamong (G-9855)
Emporium Leather Company Inc ....E...... 201 330-7720
  Secaucus (G-9762)

P
R
O
D
U
C
T

Jaclyn Holdings Parent LLC ....G....... 201 909-6000
Maywood (G-6007)

HEADPHONES: Radio

Maxell Corporation of America ....E....... 973 653-2400
Woodland Park (G-12084)

HEALTH AIDS: Exercise Eqpt

Ingui Design LLC ....G....... 201 264-9126
Ramsey (G-9147)
Slendertone Distribution Inc............G....... 732 660-1177
Hoboken (G-4481)
Technogym USA Corp ....F....... 800 804-0952
Fairfield (G-3324)

HEALTH FOOD & SUPPLEMENT STORES

Advanced Orthmolecular RES Inc..........G....... 317 292-9013
Clifton (G-1557)
Applied Nutrition Corp ....E....... 973 734-0023
Cedar Knolls (G-1299)

HEALTH SCREENING SVCS

Vesag Health Inc ....F....... 732 333-1876
North Brunswick (G-7492)

HEARING AIDS

Kingwood Industrial Pdts Inc ....G....... 908 852-8655
Hackettstown (G-4015)
Oticon Inc ....C....... 732 560-1220
Somerset (G-10047)
Songbird Hearing Inc............E....... 732 422-7203
North Brunswick (G-7487)
Sonic Innovations Inc............G....... 888 423-7834
Somerset (G-10074)

HEAT EXCHANGERS

Atlas Industrial Mfg Co ....E....... 973 779-3970
Clifton (G-1567)

HEAT EXCHANGERS: After Or Inter Coolers Or Condensers, Etc

Asa Hydraulik of America Inc ....G....... 908 541-1500
Branchburg (G-623)
Kooltronic Inc............C....... 609 466-3400
Pennington (G-8369)
Manning & Lewis Engrg Co Inc ....D....... 908 687-2400
Union (G-11073)
Perry Products Corporation............E....... 609 267-1600
Hainesport (G-4076)
Titanium Fabrication Corp ....D....... 973 227-5300
Fairfield (G-3329)

HEAT TREATING: Metal

Analytic Stress Relieving Inc............D....... 732 629-7232
Middlesex (G-6097)
Blue Blade Corp ....E....... 908 272-2620
Kenilworth (G-4930)
Bodycote Thermal Proc Inc ....E....... 908 245-0717
Roselle (G-9550)
Bodycote Thermal Processing ....E....... 908 245-0717
Roselle (G-9551)
Braddock Heat Treating Company ....E....... 732 356-2906
Bridgewater (G-806)
Curtiss-Wright Surfc Tech LLC............F....... 201 843-7800
Paramus (G-7797)
Energy Beams Inc............F....... 973 291-6555
Bloomingdale (G-528)
Heinzelman Heat Treating LLC ....E....... 201 933-4800
Carlstadt (G-1165)
Kenney Steel Treating Corp ....F....... 201 998-4420
Kearny (G-4875)
Metal Improvement Co Inc ....G....... 253 677-8604
Paramus (G-7818)

HEATERS: Swimming Pool, Electric

Hayward Pool Products Inc ....A....... 908 351-5400
Elizabeth (G-2748)
Smartpool LLC ....E....... 732 730-9880
Lakewood (G-5164)

HEATING & AIR CONDITIONING EQPT & SPLYS WHOLESALERS

Dasco Supply LLC ....F....... 973 884-1390
Whippany (G-11888)

HEATING & AIR CONDITIONING UNITS, COMBINATION

Ade Inc ....F....... 609 693-6050
Forked River (G-3535)
Dolan Assoc Inc ....G....... 973 875-6408
Sussex (G-10558)
Duct Mate Inc............G....... 201 488-8002
Hackensack (G-3909)
Ener-G Rudox Inc ....E....... 201 438-0111
East Rutherford (G-2286)
Fujitsu General America Inc ....G....... 973 575-0380
Fairfield (G-3209)
Maco Appliance Parts & Sup Co ....G....... 609 272-8222
Absecon (G-3)
Sander Mechanical Service Inc ....E....... 732 560-0600
Branchburg (G-679)

HEATING APPARATUS: Steam

Amec Fster Wheeler N Amer Corp ....D....... 936 448-6323
Hampton (G-4147)

HEATING EQPT & SPLYS

Ampericon Inc............F....... 609 945-2591
Monmouth Junction (G-6278)
C & F Burner Co ....E....... 201 998-8080
North Arlington (G-7370)
Ewc Controls Inc............E....... 732 446-3110
Manalapan (G-5809)
Heat-Timer Corporation............E....... 973 575-4004
Fairfield (G-3224)
NM Knight Co Inc ....E....... 856 327-4855
Millville (G-6263)
Stafford Park Solar 1 LLC ....G....... 609 607-9500
Barnegat (G-162)
Stamm International Corp ....G....... 201 947-1700
Fort Lee (G-3589)
Triangle Tube/Phase III Co Inc ....D....... 856 228-9940
Paulsboro (G-8340)
Waage Electric Inc ....G....... 908 245-9363
Kenilworth (G-4986)

HEATING EQPT: Complete

Bolttech Mannings Inc............D....... 973 537-1576
Wharton (G-11853)
Chiller Solutions LLC ....E....... 973 835-2800
Pompton Plains (G-8861)

HEATING EQPT: Induction

Inductotherm Corp............C....... 609 267-9000
Rancocas (G-9161)
Pennington Furnace Supply Inc ....G....... 609 737-2500
Pennington (G-8371)
Thermal Conduction Engineering ....G....... 201 865-1084
Secaucus (G-9820)

HEATING PADS: Nonelectric

Artline Heat Transfer Inc ....F....... 973 599-0104
Parsippany (G-7883)
Rdo Induction Ltd Liability Co............G....... 908 835-7222
Washington (G-11450)

HEATING UNITS & DEVICES: Indl, Electric

Argus International Inc............E....... 609 466-1677
Ringoes (G-9334)
C M Furnaces Inc ....E....... 973 338-6500
Bloomfield (G-493)
Corbett Industries Inc............F....... 201 445-6311
Waldwick (G-11299)
Gia-Tek LLC............G....... 973 228-0875
West Caldwell (G-11652)
Glenro Inc ....F....... 973 279-5900
Paterson (G-8199)
Hed International Inc ....F....... 609 466-1900
Ringoes (G-9336)
Pv/T Inc ....G....... 609 267-3933
Rancocas (G-9164)
Solar Products Inc ....E....... 973 248-9370
Pompton Lakes (G-8852)
Waage Electric Inc ....G....... 908 245-9363
Kenilworth (G-4986)

HEAVY DISTILLATES

Ashland LLC ....G....... 908 243-3500
Bridgewater (G-794)

Ashland LLC ....D....... 732 353-7718
Parlin (G-7861)

HELMETS: Athletic

Interntonal Riding Helmets Inc ....E....... 732 772-0165
Marlboro (G-5902)

HIGH ENERGY PARTICLE PHYSICS EQPT

Resideo Funding Inc............F....... 973 455-2000
Morris Plains (G-6625)

HOBBY GOODS, WHOLESALE

Model Rectifier Corporation............E....... 732 225-2100
Matawan (G-5980)
Top Rated Shopping Bargains ....F....... 800 556-5849
Hasbrouck Heights (G-4190)
Tri-Chem Inc ....F....... 973 751-9200
Belleville (G-317)

HOBBY SUPPLIES, WHOLESALE

Scientific Models Inc ....E....... 908 464-7070
Berkeley Heights (G-411)

HOBBY, TOY & GAME STORES: Arts & Crafts & Splys

A Cheerful Giver Inc ....F....... 856 358-4438
Elmer (G-2792)

HOISTS

Electro Lift Inc ....E....... 973 471-0204
Clifton (G-1612)
Rudco Products Inc............D....... 856 691-0800
Vineland (G-11261)
Saturn Overhead Equipment LLC ....F....... 732 560-7210
Somerset (G-10071)

HOLDERS, PAPER TOWEL, GROCERY BAG, ETC: Plastic

A-One Merchandising Corp ....F....... 718 773-7500
North Arlington (G-7366)

HOLDING COMPANIES: Banks

Merck Holdings LLC ....F....... 908 423-1000
Whitehouse Station (G-11923)

HOLDING COMPANIES: Investment, Exc Banks

Chemtrade Gcc Holding Company........G....... 973 515-0900
Parsippany (G-7903)
Chemtrade Water Chemical Inc ....G....... 973 515-0900
Parsippany (G-7905)
G Holdings LLC ....F....... 973 628-3000
Parsippany (G-7953)
Hugo Neu Corporation ....F....... 646 467-6700
Kearny (G-4865)
Jaclyn Holdings Parent LLC ....G....... 201 909-6000
Maywood (G-6007)
Naturex Holdings Inc............G....... 201 440-5000
South Hackensack (G-10172)
Pappas Lassonde Holdings Inc............G....... 856 455-1000
Carneys Point (G-1243)
Stamm International Corp ....G....... 201 947-1700
Fort Lee (G-3589)
W A Cleary Corporation............F....... 732 247-8000
Somerset (G-10096)

HOLDING COMPANIES: Personal, Exc Banks

Healthstar Communications Inc............E....... 201 560-5370
Mahwah (G-5746)

HOME ENTERTAINMENT EQPT: Electronic, NEC

Excite View LLC ....E....... 201 227-7075
Tenafly (G-10662)
Gzgn Inc............F....... 201 842-7622
Rutherford (G-9622)
Jvckenwood USA Corporation ....E....... 973 317-5000
Wayne (G-11528)
Rock Dreams Electronics LLC............G....... 609 890-0808
Trenton (G-10988)
Tusa Products Inc ....G....... 609 448-8333
Ewing (G-3072)

HOME ENTERTAINMENT REPAIR SVCS

Homan Communications Inc ....G....... 609 654-9594
Medford (G-6023)

HOME FURNISHINGS WHOLESALERS

Aladdin Manufacturing Corp...........B....... 973 616-4600
Pompton Plains (G-8856)

Floral Glass Industries Inc ....E....... 201 939-4600
East Rutherford (G-2289)

Global Weavers Corp...........................G....... 973 824-5500
Newark (G-7135)

House of Prill Inc..............................E....... 732 442-2400
Lincroft (G-5311)

Q10 Products LLC...............................F....... 201 567-9299
Clifton (G-1702)

St Thomas Creations ....E....... 800 536-2284
Monroe Township (G-6345)

Wanasavealotcom LLC........................F....... 732 286-6956
Toms River (G-10802)

HOME HEALTH CARE SVCS

Aarisse Health Care Products ....G....... 973 686-1811
Wayne (G-11464)

Fluent Diagnostics ....G....... 201 414-4516
Pequannock (G-8504)

Spendylove Home Care LLC.................F....... 732 430-5789
Monmouth Junction (G-6312)

HOME IMPROVEMENT & RENOVATION CONTRACTOR AGENCY

R & K Industries Inc ....G....... 732 531-1123
Oakhurst (G-7612)

HOMEFURNISHING STORE: Bedding, Sheet, Blanket, Spread/Pillow

Homespun Global LLC ....G....... 917 674-9684
Sayreville (G-9710)

Nassaus Window Fashions Inc ....E....... 201 689-6030
Paramus (G-7824)

Storis Inc ....C....... 888 478-6747
Mount Arlington (G-6719)

HOMEFURNISHING STORES: Beddings & Linens

JFK Supplies Inc ....F....... 732 985-7800
Edison (G-2539)

Professional Laundry Solutions...........G....... 973 392-0837
Newark (G-7238)

HOMEFURNISHING STORES: Closet organizers & shelving units

Interior Specialties LLC........................F....... 856 663-1700
Pennsauken (G-8438)

HOMEFURNISHING STORES: Fireplaces & Wood Burning Stoves

Mdb Construction ....G....... 908 628-8010
Lebanon (G-5270)

HOMEFURNISHING STORES: Lighting Fixtures

City Theatrical Inc...............................E....... 201 549-1160
Carlstadt (G-1143)

Efficient Lighting Inc ....F....... 973 846-8568
Parsippany (G-7933)

Genie House Corp.................................E....... 609 859-0600
Southampton (G-10363)

Robert Wallace ....G....... 609 649-0596
Stockton (G-10502)

Sun Pacific Power Corp ....F....... 888 845-0242
Manalapan (G-5826)

HOMEFURNISHING STORES: Metalware

Abba Metal Works Inc..........................G....... 973 684-0808
Paterson (G-8121)

HOMEFURNISHING STORES: Mirrors

Just Glass & Mirror Inc........................F....... 856 728-8383
Williamstown (G-11962)

HOMEFURNISHING STORES: Venetian Blinds

A Plus Installs LLC ....G....... 201 255-4412
Bloomfield (G-488)

HOMEFURNISHING STORES: Vertical Blinds

Arts Windows Inc.................................G....... 732 905-9595
Toms River (G-10744)

HOMEFURNISHING STORES: Window Furnishings

Proclean Services Inc ....F....... 973 857-5408
Verona (G-11172)

Shade Powers Co Inc ....F....... 201 767-3727
Northvale (G-7549)

HOMEFURNISHING STORES: Window Shades, NEC

Griffith Shade Company Inc ....G....... 973 667-1474
Nutley (G-7586)

HOMEFURNISHINGS & SPLYS, WHOLESALE: Decorative

Glocal Expertise Llc.............................G....... 718 928-3839
Jersey City (G-4744)

Jodhpuri Inc ....D....... 973 299-7009
Parsippany (G-7968)

Jvs Christmas Lighting ....G....... 201 664-4022
Westwood (G-11832)

Marketing Administration Assoc ....G....... 732 840-3021
Brick (G-726)

Shopindia Inc ....G....... 732 409-0656
Marlboro (G-5914)

Trim and Tassels LLC ....G....... 973 808-1566
Fairfield (G-3333)

HOMEFURNISHINGS, WHOLESALE: Blankets

Weatherbeeta USA Inc ....E....... 732 287-1182
Edison (G-2646)

HOMEFURNISHINGS, WHOLESALE: Blinds, Vertical

Arts Windows Inc.................................G....... 732 905-9595
Toms River (G-10744)

HOMEFURNISHINGS, WHOLESALE: Carpets

Kync Design LLC ....G....... 201 552-2067
Secaucus (G-9787)

HOMEFURNISHINGS, WHOLESALE: Curtains

D Kwitman & Son Inc ....F....... 201 798-5511
Hoboken (G-4450)

Kushner Draperies Mfg LLC ....E....... 856 317-9696
Pennsauken (G-8449)

HOMEFURNISHINGS, WHOLESALE: Draperies

Custom Decorators Service...................G....... 973 625-0516
Denville (G-2033)

HOMEFURNISHINGS, WHOLESALE: Fireplace Eqpt & Access

Associate Fireplace Builders................G....... 908 273-5900
Summit (G-10526)

HOMEFURNISHINGS, WHOLESALE: Kitchenware

Primetime Trading Corp ....E....... 646 580-8223
Bayonne (G-231)

HOMEFURNISHINGS, WHOLESALE: Linens, Table

Central Shippee Inc ....E....... 973 838-1100
Bloomingdale (G-526)

Circle Visual Inc ....E....... 212 719-5153
Carlstadt (G-1139)

Happy Chef Inc ....E....... 973 492-2525
Butler (G-1002)

R L Plastics Inc ....G....... 732 340-1100
Avenel (G-144)

HOMEFURNISHINGS, WHOLESALE: Rugs

Banilivy Rug Corp.................................G....... 212 684-3629
Englewood (G-2880)

Samad Brothers Inc ....F....... 201 372-0909
East Rutherford (G-2318)

Seldom Seen Designs LLC ....G....... 973 535-8805
Caldwell (G-1030)

SNS Oriental Rugs LLC ....G....... 201 355-8786
Carlstadt (G-1219)

HOMEFURNISHINGS, WHOLESALE: Sheets, Textile

Homespun Global LLC ....G....... 917 674-9684
Sayreville (G-9710)

Triangle Home Fashions LLC ....G....... 732 355-9800
East Brunswick (G-2187)

HOMEFURNISHINGS, WHOLESALE: Towels

Franco Manufacturing Co Inc ....C....... 732 494-0500
Metuchen (G-6056)

Jay Franco & Sons Inc ....D....... 732 721-0022
Sayreville (G-9712)

HOMEFURNISHINGS, WHOLESALE: Wood Flooring

Worldwide Whl Flr Cvg Inc....................E....... 732 906-1400
Edison (G-2647)

HOMES, MODULAR: Wooden

Mod-U-Kraf Homes LLC ....F....... 540 482-0273
West Berlin (G-11608)

HOODS: Range, Sheet Metal

Rangecraft Manufacturing Inc ....F....... 201 791-0440
Fair Lawn (G-3116)

HOPPERS: Metal Plate

Acrison Inc ....D....... 201 440-8300
Moonachie (G-6451)

HORNS: Marine, Compressed Air Or Steam

Pipe Dreams Marine LLC.......................G....... 609 628-9353
Tuckahoe (G-11013)

HORSE & PET ACCESSORIES: Textile

Tri G Manufacturing LLC ....F....... 732 460-1881
Colts Neck (G-1789)

Tuff Mutters LLC ....G....... 973 291-6679
Kinnelon (G-5022)

Union Hill Corp.....................................G....... 732 786-9422
Englishtown (G-3010)

Weatherbeeta USA Inc ....E....... 732 287-1182
Edison (G-2646)

HORSE ACCESS: Harnesses & Riding Crops, Etc, Exc Leather

Horsetracs ....G....... 732 228-7646
West Creek (G-11687)

HORSESHOES

Razer Scandinavia Inc ....G....... 732 441-1250
Matawan (G-5986)

HOSE: Fire, Rubber

Firefighter One Ltd Lblty Co ....G....... 973 940-3061
Sparta (G-10387)

HOSE: Flexible Metal

Andrex Inc ....F....... 908 852-2400
Hackettstown (G-3998)

Metal Hose Fabricators Inc ....G....... 908 925-7345
Linden (G-5383)

PRODUCT

HOSE: Garden, Plastic

Plastic Specialties & Tech Inc..............C...... 201 941-2900
  Ridgefield (G-9284)
Pure Tech International Inc ....G...... 908 722-4968
  Branchburg (G-673)
Pure Tech International Inc ....G...... 908 722-4800
  Branchburg (G-674)
US Wire & Cable Corporation ....B...... 973 824-5530
  Newark (G-7310)

HOSE: Plastic

Couse & Bolten Co ....G...... 973 344-6330
  Newark (G-7090)
Harrison Hose and Tubing Inc ....E...... 609 631-8804
  Robbinsville (G-9413)
Hosepharm Ltd Liability Co ....G...... 732 376-0044
  Perth Amboy (G-8521)
Superflex Ltd ....E...... 718 768-1400
  Elizabeth (G-2778)

HOSE: Pneumatic, Rubber Or Rubberized Fabric, NEC

Ptc Electronics Inc ....G....... 201 847-0500
  Mahwah (G-5764)

HOSES & BELTING: Rubber & Plastic

Atlantic Rubber Enterprises ....G...... 973 697-5900
  Newfoundland (G-7329)
Daniel C Herring Co Inc ....F 732 530-6557
  Eatontown (G-2387)
Firetrainer Symtron ....G...... 201 794-0200
  Fair Lawn (G-3100)
Forbo Siegling LLC ....F 201 567-6100
  Englewood (G-2906)
Jason Industrial Inc ....E 973 227-4904
  Fairfield (G-3243)
Minor Rubber Co Inc ....E 973 338-6800
  Bloomfield (G-511)
Novaflex Industries Inc ....F 856 768-2275
  West Berlin (G-11612)
Stiles Enterprises Inc ....F 973 625-9660
  Rockaway (G-9501)
Targa Industries Inc ....F 973 584-3733
  Flanders (G-3421)
Thirty-Three Queen Realty Inc..............F 973 824-5527
  Newark (G-7297)

HOSPITAL EQPT REPAIR SVCS

Compco Analytical Inc ....G...... 201 641-3936
  Little Ferry (G-5480)

HOSPITALS: Medical & Surgical

Ahs Hospital Corp..............E 908 522-2000
  Summit (G-10523)
Newton Memorial Hospital Inc..............G...... 973 726-0904
  Sparta (G-10402)

HOTELS & MOTELS

Sysco Guest Supply LLC ....C...... 732 537-2297
  Somerset (G-10078)

HOUSEHOLD APPLIANCE REPAIR SVCS

Organize It-All Inc ....E 201 488-0808
  Bogota (G-534)

HOUSEHOLD APPLIANCE STORES

Arctic Foods Inc..............E 908 689-0590
  Washington (G-11438)
JFK Supplies Inc ....F 732 985-7800
  Edison (G-2539)
Oberg & Lindquist Corp ....E 201 664-1300
  Westwood (G-11836)

HOUSEHOLD APPLIANCE STORES: Appliance Parts

EAC Water Filters Inc ....F 888 524-8088
  Allenwood (G-32)

HOUSEHOLD APPLIANCE STORES: Electric

Winiadaewoo Elec Amer Inc ....F 201 552-4950
  Ridgefield Park (G-9320)

HOUSEHOLD ARTICLES: Metal

Advanced Precision Systems LLC........G...... 908 730-8892
  High Bridge (G-4280)
Faps Inc ....C...... 973 589-5656
  Newark (G-7122)
Gbw Manufacturing Inc ....E 973 279-0077
  Totowa (G-10828)
Kraftware Corporation ....E 732 345-7091
  Roselle (G-9562)

HOUSEHOLD FURNISHINGS, NEC

Better Sleep Inc ....F 908 464-2200
  Branchburg (G-625)
Carlyle Custom Convertibles..............D...... 973 546-4502
  Moonachie (G-6460)
Fine Linen Inc ....F 908 469-3634
  Elizabeth (G-2736)
Howard Lippincott ....E 856 764-8282
  Riverside (G-9396)
Interior Art & Design Inc ....E 201 488-8855
  Hackensack (G-3931)
Sheex Inc ....E 856 334-3021
  Marlton (G-5951)

HOUSEHOLD SEWING MACHINES WHOLESALERS: Electric

Brother International Corp ....B...... 908 704-1700
  Bridgewater (G-808)

HOUSEWARE STORES

Maverick Industries Inc ....F 732 417-9666
  Edison (G-2559)

HOUSEWARES, ELECTRIC, EXC COOKING APPLIANCES & UTENSILS

Brabantia USA Inc ....F 201 933-3192
  East Rutherford (G-2279)
Expert Appliance Center LLC ....G...... 732 946-0999
  Marlboro (G-5897)
Homeco LLC ....E 732 802-7733
  Piscataway (G-8673)

HOUSEWARES, ELECTRIC: Cooking Appliances

Emerald Electronics Usa Inc..............G...... 718 872-5544
  Passaic (G-8063)
Maverick Industries Inc ....F 732 417-9666
  Edison (G-2559)
Rj Brands LLC..............C...... 888 315-8407
  Mahwah (G-5768)
Wanasavealotcom LLC ....F 732 286-6956
  Toms River (G-10802)

HOUSEWARES, ELECTRIC: Dryers, Hand & Face

Conair Corporation ....C...... 609 426-1300
  East Windsor (G-2348)

HOUSEWARES, ELECTRIC: Heaters, Sauna

Aftek Inc..............G...... 609 588-0900
  Hamilton (G-4101)

HOUSEWARES, ELECTRIC: Heating, Bsbrd/Wall, Radiant Heat

Haydon Corporation ....D...... 973 904-0800
  Wayne (G-11515)

HOUSEWARES, ELECTRIC: Ice Crushers

Rjticeco LLC ....G...... 973 697-0156
  Stockholm (G-10500)
Technology General Corporation ....F 973 827-8209
  Franklin (G-3609)

HOUSEWARES, ELECTRIC: Lighters, Cigar

Vapor Lounge LLC ....G...... 973 627-1277
  Rockaway (G-9511)

HOUSEWARES: Dishes, China

Nikko Ceramics Inc ....F 201 840-5200
  Fairview (G-3364)

HOUSEWARES: Dishes, Earthenware

Art Plaque Creations Inc ....F 973 482-2536
  Kearny (G-4845)

HOUSEWARES: Dishes, Plastic

Buckets Plus Inc ....G...... 732 545-0420
  New Brunswick (G-6914)
Mighty Mug Incorporated ....G...... 732 382-3911
  Rahway (G-9119)
Newell Brands Inc..............B 201 610-6600
  Hoboken (G-4468)
R Squared Sls & Logistics LLC ....G...... 201 329-9745
  Moonachie (G-6485)

HUMIDIFIERS & DEHUMIDIFIERS

Csonka Worldwide ....E 609 514-2766
  Plainsboro (G-8783)

HYDRAULIC EQPT REPAIR SVC

American Hose Hydraulic Co Inc ....E 973 684-3225
  Paterson (G-8136)
Excel Hydraulics LLC ....E 856 241-1145
  Clarksboro (G-1519)
Micheller & Son Hydraulics Inc ....F 908 687-1545
  Roselle (G-9566)
MTS Systems Corporation ....A...... 856 875-4478
  Williamstown (G-11965)
Van Hydraulics Inc ....E 732 442-5500
  South Plainfield (G-10338)

HYDRAULIC FLUIDS: Synthetic Based

Firefreeze Worldwide Inc..............E 973 627-0722
  Rockaway (G-9460)
Lanxess Solutions US Inc ....C...... 973 887-7411
  East Hanover (G-2221)

Hard Rubber & Molded Rubber Prdts

Dso Fluid Handling Co Inc ....E 732 225-9100
  Edison (G-2495)
Kinnarney Rubber Co Inc ....F 856 468-1320
  Mantua (G-5852)
Ness Plastics Inc..............F 201 854-4072
  West New York (G-11748)
Norco Manufacturing Inc..............F 201 854-3461
  North Bergen (G-7425)
Schon J Tool & Machine Co ....G...... 732 928-6665
  Jackson (G-4664)
Vibration Muntings Contrls Inc..........D...... 800 569-8423
  Bloomingdale (G-531)

ICE

Arctic Glacier USA Inc..............F 973 771-3391
  Montclair (G-6359)
Cold Spring Ice Inc ....G...... 609 884-3405
  Cape May (G-1096)
Sea Isle Ice Co Inc..............E 609 263-8748
  Sea Isle City (G-9749)

ICE CREAM & ICES WHOLESALERS

Magliones Italian Ices LLC..............F 732 283-0705
  Iselin (G-4614)
South Jersey Pretzel Inc ....F 856 435-5055
  Stratford (G-10507)

IGNEOUS ROCK: Crushed & Broken

A E Stone Inc..............E 609 641-2781
  Egg Harbor Township (G-2673)
R B Badat Landscaping Inc ....G...... 609 877-7138
  Mount Holly (G-6733)
Riverdale Quarry LLC ....E 973 835-0028
  Riverdale (G-9382)
Trap Rock Industries Inc ....F 609 924-0300
  Pennington (G-8375)

IGNITION SYSTEMS: Internal Combustion Engine

Knite Inc..............G...... 609 258-9550
  Ewing (G-3041)

INCINERATORS

Cire Technologies Inc..............G...... 973 402-8301
  Mountain Lakes (G-6821)

Hankin Acquisitions Inc ....F 908 722-9595
  Hillsborough *(G-4321)*
Hankin Envmtl Systems Inc ....F 908 722-9595
  Hillsborough *(G-4322)*

INDL & PERSONAL SVC PAPER WHOLESALERS

American Business Paper Inc ....F 732 363-5788
  Lakewood *(G-5049)*
Asbury Syrup Company Inc................F 732 774-5746
  Ocean *(G-7656)*
Borak Group Inc ....D 718 665-8500
  Jersey City *(G-4705)*
Great Eastern Color Lith ....G 201 843-5656
  Paramus *(G-7804)*
H S Folex Schleussner Inc ....G 973 575-7626
  Fairfield *(G-3220)*
Mamrout Paper Group Corp.............G...... 718 510-5484
  Edison *(G-2558)*
Tricorbraun Inc................................G...... 732 353-7104
  Monroe Township *(G-6349)*
United States Box Corp ....E 973 481-2000
  Fairfield *(G-3336)*

INDL & PERSONAL SVC PAPER, WHOL: Bags, Paper/Disp Plastic

ANS Plastics Corporation ....F 732 247-2776
  New Brunswick *(G-6910)*
Broadway Kleer-Guard Corp................E 609 662-3970
  Monroe Township *(G-6330)*
Central Poly-Bag Corp.......................F 908 862-7570
  Linden *(G-5332)*
Potti-Bags Inc..................................G...... 201 796-5555
  Elmwood Park *(G-2851)*
R K S Plastics Inc............................G...... 732 435-8517
  New Brunswick *(G-6965)*

INDL & PERSONAL SVC PAPER, WHOL: Boxes, Corrugtd/Solid Fiber

Ace Box Landau Co Inc......................G...... 201 871-4776
  Englewood Cliffs *(G-2956)*
Alliance Corrugated Box Inc ....E 877 525-5269
  Saddle River *(G-9690)*
E C D Ventures Inc ....E 856 875-1100
  Blackwood *(G-465)*
Weber Packaging Inc.........................G...... 201 262-6022
  Oradell *(G-7748)*

INDL & PERSONAL SVC PAPER, WHOL: Boxes, Setup Paperboard

Capitol Box Corp...............................E 201 867-6018
  North Bergen *(G-7392)*

INDL & PERSONAL SVC PAPER, WHOL: Closures, Paper/Disp Plastc

Andon Brush Co Inc ....E 973 256-6611
  Little Falls *(G-5452)*

INDL & PERSONAL SVC PAPER, WHOL: Cups, Disp, Plastic/Paper

Continntal Concession Sups Inc...........E 516 629-4906
  Union *(G-11037)*

INDL & PERSONAL SVC PAPER, WHOL: Paper, Wrap/Coarse/Prdts

Matthias Paper Corporation..................E 856 467-6970
  Swedesboro *(G-10594)*
Orora Packaging Solutions ....E 609 249-5200
  Cranbury *(G-1866)*
Schurman Fine Papers ....E 856 985-1776
  Marlton *(G-5950)*

INDL & PERSONAL SVC PAPER, WHOLESALE: Boxes & Containers

Dauson Corrugated Container..............F 973 827-1494
  Hamburg *(G-4089)*
Westrock Rkt Company.......................C 973 484-5000
  Newark *(G-7314)*

INDL & PERSONAL SVC PAPER, WHOLESALE: Boxes, Fldng Pprboard

Interntnal Folding Ppr Box Sls ....E 201 941-3100
  Ridgefield *(G-9268)*

INDL & PERSONAL SVC PAPER, WHOLESALE: Disposable

A-One Merchandising Corp ....F 718 773-7500
  North Arlington *(G-7366)*

INDL & PERSONAL SVC PAPER, WHOLESALE: Paperboard & Prdts

Lamitech Inc ....E 609 860-8037
  Cranbury *(G-1854)*

INDL & PERSONAL SVC PAPER, WHOLESALE: Press Sensitive Tape

Pro Tapes & Specialties Inc ....C 732 346-0900
  North Brunswick *(G-7483)*
Universal Tape Supply Corp ....F 609 653-3191
  Somers Point *(G-9940)*

INDL & PERSONAL SVC PAPER, WHOLESALE: Shipping Splys

Clements Industries Inc ....E 201 440-5500
  South Hackensack *(G-10153)*
JFK Supplies Inc ....F 732 985-7800
  Edison *(G-2539)*
Levine Industries Inc ....E 973 742-1000
  Paterson *(G-8239)*

INDL CONTRACTORS: Exhibit Construction

Dublin Management Assoc of NJ ....C 609 387-1600
  Burlington *(G-964)*
Palumbo Associates Inc......................F 908 534-2142
  Whitehouse Station *(G-11931)*
Taylor Made Custom Cabinetry ....F 856 786-5433
  Pennsauken *(G-8490)*

INDL EQPT CLEANING SVCS

Chen Brothers Machinery Co ....G 973 328-0086
  Randolph *(G-9174)*

INDL EQPT SVCS

C & S Machine Inc.............................F 973 882-1097
  Fairfield *(G-3161)*

INDL GASES WHOLESALERS

Airgas Usa LLC ....F 609 685-4241
  Cherry Hill *(G-1337)*
Airgas Usa LLC ....E 856 829-7878
  Cinnaminson *(G-1440)*
Frank E Ganter Inc ....G 856 692-2218
  Vineland *(G-11219)*
Praxair Distribution Inc ....F 908 862-7200
  Linden *(G-5411)*

INDL HELP SVCS

Dxl Enterprises Inc ....F 201 891-8718
  Mahwah *(G-5733)*

INDL MACHINERY & EQPT WHOLESALERS

Carter Pump Inc................................G 201 568-9798
  Waldwick *(G-11298)*
Columbia Fuel Services Inc ....F 732 751-0044
  Wall Township *(G-11331)*
Envirnmntal Mgt Chem Wste Svcs........G 201 848-7676
  Mahwah *(G-5735)*
Envirosight Inc ....E 973 970-9284
  Randolph *(G-9176)*
F and L Machinery ....G 973 218-6216
  Springfield *(G-10442)*
Fette Compacting America Inc ....E 973 586-8722
  Rockaway *(G-9459)*
Fluitec International LLC......................D 201 946-4584
  Bayonne *(G-217)*
Ganz Brothers Inc ....F 201 820-1975
  Paramus *(G-7801)*
Gas Drying Inc..................................F 973 361-2212
  Wharton *(G-11859)*

Hamon Corporation ....D 908 333-2000
  Somerville *(G-10114)*
Houzer Inc.......................................F 609 584-1900
  Hamilton *(G-4107)*
Intertest Inc.....................................E 908 496-8008
  Columbia *(G-1795)*
J & S Tool ....G 973 383-5059
  Newton *(G-7347)*
J OBrien Co Inc ....E 973 379-8844
  Springfield *(G-10447)*
JDV Equipment Corp ....G 973 366-6556
  Dover *(G-2092)*
Kissler & Co Inc ....E 201 896-9600
  Carlstadt *(G-1175)*
Machinery Electrics ....G 732 536-0600
  Bayville *(G-247)*
NM Knight Co Inc ....E 856 327-4855
  Millville *(G-6263)*
Orion Machinery Co Ltd ....E 201 569-3220
  Rutherford *(G-9630)*
Pavan & Kievit Enterprises ....E 973 546-4615
  Garfield *(G-3754)*
Plcs LLC ....E 856 722-1333
  Mount Laurel *(G-6790)*
Powerspec Inc..................................E 732 494-9490
  Somerville *(G-10123)*
Progressive Ruesch Inc ....E 973 962-7700
  Ringwood *(G-9351)*
Ringfeder Pwr Transm USA Corp ....E 201 666-3320
  Westwood *(G-11843)*
Sandvik Inc ....C 281 275-4800
  Fair Lawn *(G-3121)*
Traffic Safety & Equipment Co ....E 201 327-6050
  Mahwah *(G-5783)*
W T Winter Associates Inc ....E 888 808-3611
  Fairfield *(G-3350)*
Wagner Industries Inc ....F 973 347-0800
  Stanhope *(G-10481)*
Wrap-Ade Machine Co Inc ....F 973 773-6150
  Clifton *(G-1740)*

INDL MACHINERY REPAIR & MAINTENANCE

American Mch Tool RPR Rbldg Co ....G...... 973 927-0820
  Randolph *(G-9171)*
Atlantic Switch Generator LLC ....F 609 518-1900
  Hainesport *(G-4069)*
Corbett Industries Inc.........................F 201 445-6311
  Waldwick *(G-11299)*
Gamka Sales Co Inc..........................E 732 248-1400
  Edison *(G-2518)*
Hockmeyer Equipment Corp.................D 973 482-0225
  Harrison *(G-4176)*
Machine Plus Inc...............................G...... 973 839-8884
  Haskell *(G-4199)*

INDL PATTERNS: Foundry Cores

West Pattern Works Inc.......................F 609 443-6241
  Cranbury *(G-1892)*

INDL PROCESS INSTR: Transmit, Process Variables

Audiocodes Inc ....G 732 469-0880
  Somerset *(G-9959)*
Audiocodes Inc ....F 732 469-0880
  Somerset *(G-9960)*

INDL PROCESS INSTRUMENTS: Analyzers

Celco ....F 201 327-1123
  Mahwah *(G-5721)*
Newtek Sensor Solutions LLC...............G...... 856 406-6877
  Pennsauken *(G-8460)*

INDL PROCESS INSTRUMENTS: Control

Acrison Inc ....D 201 440-8300
  Moonachie *(G-6451)*
Armadillo Automation Inc ....E 856 829-2888
  Cinnaminson *(G-1442)*
Coperion K-Tron Pitman Inc ....F 856 589-0500
  Sewell *(G-9836)*

INDL PROCESS INSTRUMENTS: Controllers, Process Variables

Matrix Controls Company Inc ....F 732 469-5551
  Somerset *(G-10025)*

PRODUCT

INDL PROCESS INSTRUMENTS: Indl Flow & Measuring

Messer LLC..C....... 908 464-8100
Bridgewater *(G-849)*
Messer LLC..G....... 973 579-2065
Sparta *(G-10398)*

INDL PROCESS INSTRUMENTS: Manometers

Rosemount Inc......................................F....... 973 257-2300
Parsippany *(G-8011)*

INDL PROCESS INSTRUMENTS: Moisture Meters

Elaine Inc...G....... 973 345-6200
Woodland Park *(G-12076)*

INDL PROCESS INSTRUMENTS: On-Stream Gas Or Liquid Analysis

Control Instruments Corp....................E....... 973 575-9114
Fairfield *(G-3176)*
Delphian Corporation..........................C....... 201 767-7300
Northvale *(G-7521)*
Meson Group Inc..................................E....... 201 767-7300
Northvale *(G-7536)*

INDL PROCESS INSTRUMENTS: PH Instruments

Omega Engineering Inc......................C....... 856 467-4200
Bridgeport *(G-742)*
Wra Manufacturing Company Inc..........G....... 908 416-2228
Hopatcong *(G-4523)*

INDL PROCESS INSTRUMENTS: Temperature

Accurate Thermal Systems LLC..........G....... 609 326-3190
Hainesport *(G-4068)*
Burling Instruments Inc.......................F....... 973 665-0601
Chatham *(G-1319)*
Capintec Inc...E....... 201 825-9500
Florham Park *(G-3495)*
Micro-Tek Laboratories Inc..................G....... 973 779-5577
Clifton *(G-1669)*
Orycon Control Technology Inc............E....... 732 922-2400
Ocean *(G-7670)*

INDL PROCESS INSTRUMENTS: Water Quality Monitoring/Cntrl Sys

ACS Quality Services Inc.....................G....... 856 988-6550
Marlton *(G-5920)*
Bishop Ascendant Inc..........................G....... 201 572-7436
West Caldwell *(G-11642)*
Delaware Technologies Inc...................F....... 856 234-7692
Mount Laurel *(G-6753)*

INDL SPLYS WHOLESALERS

Captive Fasteners Corp.......................B....... 201 337-6800
Oakland *(G-7618)*
Communique Inc..................................G....... 973 751-7588
Belleville *(G-293)*
Deltronics Corporation.........................F....... 856 825-8200
Millville *(G-6246)*
Dreyco Inc..F....... 201 896-9000
Carlstadt *(G-1154)*
Federal Equipment & Mfg Co Inc..........G....... 973 340-7600
Lodi *(G-5562)*
Foster and Company Inc.......................E....... 973 267-4100
Cedar Knolls *(G-1305)*
Illinois Tool Works Inc.........................D....... 732 968-5300
Parsippany *(G-7960)*
Industrial Rivet & Fastener Co.............D....... 201 750-1040
Northvale *(G-7528)*
Ingersoll-Rand Company.......................C....... 908 238-7000
Annandale *(G-54)*
Intellgent Trffic Sup Pdts LLC.............G....... 908 791-1200
South Plainfield *(G-10278)*
Intersource USA Inc.............................F....... 732 257-5002
East Brunswick *(G-2152)*
Jontol Unlimited LLC............................G....... 858 652-1113
Blackwood *(G-473)*
Knotts Company Inc.............................E....... 908 464-4800
Berkeley Heights *(G-405)*
Matchless United Companies................G....... 908 862-7300
Linden *(G-5380)*

Metallo Gasket Company Inc................F....... 732 545-7223
New Brunswick *(G-6947)*
Newco Valves LLC...............................E....... 732 257-0300
East Brunswick *(G-2159)*
Permadur Industries Inc.......................D....... 908 359-9767
Hillsborough *(G-4344)*
Plast-O-Matic Valves Inc......................D....... 973 256-3000
Cedar Grove *(G-1287)*
Siemens Industry Inc...........................E....... 856 234-7666
Mount Laurel *(G-6806)*
Steelstran Industries Inc.....................E....... 732 574-0700
Avenel *(G-147)*
Technodiamant USA Inc........................G....... 908 850-8505
Tranquility *(G-10884)*
Tommax Inc..G....... 732 224-1046
Red Bank *(G-9246)*
Tri-Power Consulting Svcs LLC............E....... 973 227-7100
Denville *(G-2060)*

INDL SPLYS, WHOL: Fasteners, Incl Nuts, Bolts, Screws, Etc

Accurate Prscsion Fstener Corp..........E....... 201 567-9700
Englewood *(G-2873)*
Champion Fasteners Inc.......................E....... 609 267-5222
Lumberton *(G-5627)*
Cold Headed Fasteners Inc..................G....... 856 461-3244
Delanco *(G-2004)*
Kt Mt Corp..F....... 877 791-4426
Cinnaminson *(G-1469)*
P & R Fasteners Inc.............................E....... 732 302-3600
Somerset *(G-10050)*
Scheinert & Sons Inc...........................E....... 201 791-4600
Saddle Brook *(G-9677)*
Stud Welding Co The Inc......................G....... 856 866-9300
Moorestown *(G-6569)*

INDL SPLYS, WHOLESALE: Abrasives

Beacut Abrasives Corp.........................F....... 973 249-1420
East Rutherford *(G-2275)*

INDL SPLYS, WHOLESALE: Bearings

Accurate Bronze Bearing Co................G....... 973 345-2304
Paterson *(G-8124)*
Bcc (USA) Inc.......................................G....... 732 572-5450
Piscataway *(G-8639)*

INDL SPLYS, WHOLESALE: Bottler Splys

Agsco Corporation..............................E....... 973 244-0005
Pine Brook *(G-8584)*

INDL SPLYS, WHOLESALE: Brushes, Indl

Andon Brush Co Inc.............................E....... 973 256-6611
Little Falls *(G-5452)*

INDL SPLYS, WHOLESALE: Clean Room Splys

Borak Group Inc...................................D....... 718 665-8500
Jersey City *(G-4705)*

INDL SPLYS, WHOLESALE: Drums, New Or Reconditioned

Rahway Steel Drum Co Inc...................E....... 732 382-0113
Cranbury *(G-1877)*
Tunnel Barrel & Drum Co Inc................E....... 201 933-1444
Carlstadt *(G-1233)*

INDL SPLYS, WHOLESALE: Fasteners & Fastening Eqpt

Arlo Corporation..................................G....... 973 618-0030
Roseland *(G-9533)*

INDL SPLYS, WHOLESALE: Filters, Indl

Filter Technologies Inc.........................G....... 732 329-2500
Monmouth Junction *(G-6291)*
Mer Made Filter....................................G....... 201 236-0217
Ramsey *(G-9151)*

INDL SPLYS, WHOLESALE: Gaskets

Capital Gasket and Rubber Inc.............G....... 856 939-3670
Runnemede *(G-9604)*
R S Rubber Corp...................................F....... 973 777-2200
Wallington *(G-11389)*

Transport Products Inc.........................G....... 973 857-6090
Cedar Grove *(G-1294)*

INDL SPLYS, WHOLESALE: Gaskets & Seals

Custom Gasket Mfg LLC.......................F....... 201 331-6363
Englewood Cliffs *(G-2966)*
Mercer Rubber Company.......................E....... 856 931-5000
Bellmawr *(G-339)*

INDL SPLYS, WHOLESALE: Gears

State Tool Gear Co Inc.........................F....... 973 642-6181
Newark *(G-7286)*

INDL SPLYS, WHOLESALE: Plastic Bottles

Mighty Mug Incorporated......................G....... 732 382-3911
Rahway *(G-9119)*

INDL SPLYS, WHOLESALE: Power Transmission, Eqpt & Apparatus

Brilliant Light Power Inc.......................E....... 609 490-0427
East Windsor *(G-2365)*

INDL SPLYS, WHOLESALE: Rubber Goods, Mechanical

Amerimold Tech Inc..............................E....... 732 462-7577
Jackson *(G-4638)*
Coast Rubber and Gasket Inc...............G....... 609 747-0110
Burlington *(G-960)*
Rema Tip Top/North America Inc...........E....... 201 768-8100
Northvale *(G-7546)*
Specialty Rubber Inc............................G....... 609 704-2555
Elwood *(G-2860)*
Stiles Enterprises Inc...........................F....... 973 625-9660
Rockaway *(G-9501)*
T & B Specialties Inc............................G....... 732 928-4500
Jackson *(G-4666)*

INDL SPLYS, WHOLESALE: Tanks, Pressurized

Corban Energy Group Corp...................F....... 201 509-8555
Elmwood Park *(G-2818)*

INDL SPLYS, WHOLESALE: Tools

Dicar Diamond Tool Corp......................F....... 973 684-0949
Paterson *(G-8173)*
Jnt Technical Services Inc....................E....... 201 641-2130
Little Ferry *(G-5491)*

INDL SPLYS, WHOLESALE: Twine

Baxter Corporation...............................D....... 201 337-1212
Franklin Lakes *(G-3613)*

INDL SPLYS, WHOLESALE: Valves & Fittings

Amico Technologies Inc........................G....... 732 901-5900
Lakewood *(G-5053)*
Carpenter & Paterson Inc.....................E....... 973 772-1800
Saddle Brook *(G-9644)*
Ceodeux Incorporated..........................E....... 724 696-4340
Hackettstown *(G-4001)*
Chalmers & Kubeck Inc........................G....... 732 993-1251
New Brunswick *(G-6915)*
Farrell Eqp & Contrls Inc.....................F....... 732 770-4142
Roselle *(G-9557)*
Nedohon Inc...G....... 302 533-5512
Wildwood Crest *(G-11948)*
Rotarex Inc North America....................D....... 724 696-3345
Hackettstown *(G-4033)*
Silbo Industries Inc..............................F....... 201 307-0900
Montvale *(G-6434)*
Sims Pump Valve Company Inc.............E....... 201 792-0600
Hoboken *(G-4480)*
Taylor Forge Stainless Inc....................D....... 908 722-1313
Branchburg *(G-687)*
Teneyck Inc..D....... 201 939-1100
Lyndhurst *(G-5681)*
Triflow Corporation..............................G....... 856 768-7159
West Berlin *(G-11631)*

INDUCTORS

Alecto Systems LLC.............................G....... 973 875-6721
Branchville *(G-702)*
Bel Fuse Inc...C....... 201 432-0463
Jersey City *(G-4700)*

INFANTS' WEAR STORES

Bib and Tucker Inc ....F 201 489-9600
Hackensack (G-3885)

INFORMATION RETRIEVAL SERVICES

Bio-Key International Inc......................E 732 359-1100
Wall Township (G-11322)
J R S Tool & Metal Finishing ....G 908 753-2050
South Plainfield (G-10282)
Maxisit Inc..C 732 494-2005
Metuchen (G-6065)

INK OR WRITING FLUIDS

Airdye Solutions LLC ....E 540 433-9101
Cedar Grove (G-1266)
Caloric Color Co Inc ....F 973 471-4748
Garfield (G-3734)
Conversion Technology Co Inc ....F 732 752-5660
South Plainfield (G-10242)
Faust Thermographic Supply ....F 908 474-0555
Linden (G-5347)
Honeyware Inc......................................D 201 997-5900
Kearny (G-4863)
Wilpak Industries Inc ....G 201 997-7600
Kearny (G-4907)

INK: Duplicating

Chroma Trading Usa Inc......................G 732 956-4431
Morganville (G-6585)

INK: Gravure

Gotham Ink of New England Inc...........G 201 478-5600
Teterboro (G-10679)
Selective Coatings & Inks ....F 732 938-7677
Wall Township (G-11368)
Selective Coatings & Inks ....G 732 493-0707
Ocean (G-7682)
Superior Printing Ink Co Inc ....C 201 478-5600
Teterboro (G-10691)

INK: Letterpress Or Offset

Central Ink Corporation.......................G 856 467-5562
Swedesboro (G-10576)

INK: Lithographic

Supreme Ink Corp ....F 973 344-2922
Newark (G-7292)

INK: Printing

AGFA Corporation ....G 908 231-5000
Somerville (G-10102)
American Coding and Mkg Ink Co.......G 908 756-0373
Plainfield (G-8757)
Athletes Alley ....F 732 842-1127
Shrewsbury (G-9882)
Custom Chemicals Corp ....A 201 791-5100
Elmwood Park (G-2820)
Flint Group US LLC ....G 732 329-4627
Dayton (G-1962)
Ideon LLC ....G 908 431-3126
Hillsborough (G-4327)
Kohl & Madden Prtg Ink Corp ....E 201 935-8666
Carlstadt (G-1177)
Lodor Offset Corporation ....F 201 935-7100
Carlstadt (G-1182)
Pan Technology Inc ....E 201 438-7878
Carlstadt (G-1195)
Prismacolor Corp ....G 973 887-6040
Parsippany (G-8002)
Ranger Industries Inc...........................E 732 389-3535
Tinton Falls (G-10725)
Sun Chemical Corporation....................C 201 933-4500
Carlstadt (G-1222)
Sun Chemical Corporation....................D 973 404-6000
Parsippany (G-8022)
Sun Chemical Corporation....................E 201 438-4831
East Rutherford (G-2322)
Sun Chemical Corporation....................F 201 935-8666
Carlstadt (G-1223)
Superior Printing Ink Co Inc ....G 973 242-5868
Newark (G-7291)
Total Ink Solutions LLC ....F 201 487-9600
Hackensack (G-3983)
Toyo Ink America LLC ....F 201 804-0620
Carlstadt (G-1230)

Uvitec Printing Ink Co Inc ....E 973 778-0737
Lodi (G-5581)
Vivitone Inc..F 973 427-8114
Hawthorne (G-4250)

INK: Screen process

Champion Ink Co Inc ....G 201 868-4100
North Bergen (G-7394)
Triangle Ink Co Inc ....F 201 935-2777
Wallington (G-11390)

INSECTICIDES

Pic Corporation ....E 908 862-7977
Linden (G-5409)

INSECTICIDES & PESTICIDES

Deer Out Animal Repellant LLC............G 908 769-4242
South Plainfield (G-10246)
Residex LLC ....G 856 232-0880
Blackwood (G-479)

INSPECTION & TESTING SVCS

TAC Technical Instrument Corp ....F 609 882-2894
Trenton (G-10995)
TEC Cast Inc...D 201 935-3885
Moonachie (G-6494)

INSTRUMENT LANDING SYSTEMS OR ILS: Airborne Or Ground

Premac Inc...F 732 381-7550
Rahway (G-9122)

INSTRUMENTS & ACCESSORIES: Surveying

Topcon Medical Systems Inc ....D 201 599-5100
Oakland (G-7647)

INSTRUMENTS & METERS: Measuring, Electric

Byram Laboratories Inc........................E 908 252-0852
Branchburg (G-627)
Photonics Management Corp ....G 908 231-0960
Bridgewater (G-866)
Quantem Corp ....E 609 883-9191
Ewing (G-3057)
Seaboard Instrument Co ....G 609 641-5300
Pleasantville (G-8818)

INSTRUMENTS, LABORATORY: Amino Acid Analyzers

Ezose Sciences Inc...............................F 862 926-1950
Florham Park (G-3505)

INSTRUMENTS, LABORATORY: Analyzers, Automatic Chemical

Eci Technology Inc ....C 973 773-8686
Totowa (G-10825)

INSTRUMENTS, LABORATORY: Blood Testing

Princeton Separations Inc....................E 732 431-3338
Freehold (G-3694)

INSTRUMENTS, LABORATORY: Gas Analyzing

Packaged Gas Systems Inc ....G 908 755-2780
Springfield (G-10457)
Perma Pure LLC ....G 732 244-0010
Lakewood (G-5146)

INSTRUMENTS, LABORATORY: Liquid Chromatographic

Princeton Chromatography Inc ....G 609 860-1803
Cranbury (G-1874)

INSTRUMENTS, LABORATORY: Mass Spectroscopy

Dolce Technologies LLC ....G 609 497-7319
Princeton (G-8932)

INSTRUMENTS, LABORATORY: Nephelometers, Exc Meteorological

Cargille-Sacher Labs Inc ....E 973 239-6633
Cedar Grove (G-1271)

INSTRUMENTS, LABORATORY: Spectrographs

Horiba Instruments Inc.........................G 732 494-8660
Piscataway (G-8675)

INSTRUMENTS, LABORATORY: Spectrometers

Moa Instrumentation Inc ....G 215 547-8308
Lawrenceville (G-5238)

INSTRUMENTS, MEASURING & CNTRL: Geophysical & Meteorological

Instrument Sciences & Tech ....D 908 996-9920
Frenchtown (G-3714)
Kanomax Usa Inc..................................G 973 786-6386
Byram Township (G-1018)

INSTRUMENTS, MEASURING & CNTRL: Radiation & Testing, Nuclear

Capintec Inc...E 201 825-9500
Florham Park (G-3495)
Theory Development Corp ....F 201 783-8770
Mahwah (G-5780)

INSTRUMENTS, MEASURING & CNTRL: Testing, Abrasion, Etc

Instru-Met Corporation ....G 908 851-0700
Union (G-11065)
S & G Tool Aid Corporation...................D 973 824-7730
Newark (G-7257)

INSTRUMENTS, MEASURING & CNTRL: Whole Body Counters, Nuclear

Orlando Systems Ltd Lblty Co ....G 908 400-5052
North Plainfield (G-7507)

INSTRUMENTS, MEASURING & CNTRLG: Aircraft & Motor Vehicle

Tel-Instrument Elec Corp ....E 201 933-1600
East Rutherford (G-2325)

INSTRUMENTS, MEASURING & CNTRLG: Thermometers/Temp Sensors

Becton Dickinson and Company..........A 201 847-6800
Franklin Lakes (G-3616)
Conistics Inc..G 609 584-2600
Hamilton (G-4104)
Sensor Scientific Inc............................E 973 227-7790
Fairfield (G-3310)

INSTRUMENTS, MEASURING & CNTRLNG: Press & Vac Ind, Acft Eng

Ptc Electronics Inc...............................G 201 847-0500
Mahwah (G-5764)

INSTRUMENTS, MEASURING & CONTROLLING: Dosimetry, Personnel

Life Recovery Systems Hd LLC............G 973 283-2800
Kinnelon (G-5019)

INSTRUMENTS, MEASURING & CONTROLLING: Gas Detectors

AIG Industrial Group Inc ....F 201 767-7300
Northvale (G-7516)
Delphian Corporation ....C 201 767-7300
Northvale (G-7521)
Meson Group Inc..................................E 201 767-7300
Northvale (G-7536)

PRODUCT

INSTRUMENTS, MEASURING & CONTROLLING: Surveying & Drafting

Northwest Instrument Inc.................F....... 973 347-6830
Dover (G-2102)

INSTRUMENTS, MEASURING & CONTROLLING: Ultrasonic Testing

G E Inspection Technologies LP ....D....... 973 448-0077
Flanders (G-3411)

INSTRUMENTS, MEASURING/CNTRLG: Fire Detect Sys, Non-Electric

Alison Control Inc...............................E....... 973 575-7100
Fairfield (G-3137)

INSTRUMENTS, MEASURING/CNTRLNG: Med Diagnostic Sys, Nuclear

Advanced Shore Imaging Associa ....F....... 732 678-0087
Northfield (G-7509)
Euroimmun US Inc ....E....... 973 656-1000
Mountain Lakes (G-6824)
Mallinckrodt LLC ....E....... 908 238-6600
Hampton (G-4158)
Maquet Cardiovascular LLC ....D....... 973 709-7000
Wayne (G-11533)
Mdr Diagnostics LLC ....E....... 609 396-0021
Mount Laurel (G-6781)

INSTRUMENTS, OPTICAL: Coating & Grinding, Lens

Krell Technologies Inc ....G....... 732 775-7355
Neptune (G-6887)

INSTRUMENTS, OPTICAL: Elements & Assemblies, Exc Ophthalmic

Integrated Photonics Inc ....D....... 908 281-8000
Hillsborough (G-4331)
Integrated Photonics Inc ....G....... 908 281-8000
Hillsborough (G-4332)

INSTRUMENTS, OPTICAL: Lenses, All Types Exc Ophthalmic

Esco Products Inc..............................E....... 973 697-3700
Oak Ridge (G-7602)
Inrad Optics Inc................................D....... 201 767-1910
Northvale (G-7529)
O & S Research Inc............................E....... 856 829-2800
Cinnaminson (G-1477)

INSTRUMENTS, OPTICAL: Light Sources, Standard

Cercis Inc..G....... 609 737-5120
Pennington (G-8360)

INSTRUMENTS, OPTICAL: Magnifying, NEC

Anchor Optical Co ....C....... 856 546-1965
Barrington (G-166)

INSTRUMENTS, OPTICAL: Polarizers

Inlc Technology Corporation ....F....... 908 834-8390
Warren (G-11418)
Polarity LLC.......................................G....... 732 970-3855
Morganville (G-6595)

INSTRUMENTS, OPTICAL: Test & Inspection

Datacolor Inc.....................................D....... 609 924-2189
Lawrenceville (G-5229)

INSTRUMENTS, SURGICAL & MED: Cleaning Eqpt, Ultrasonic Med

Crestek Inc..E....... 609 883-4000
Ewing (G-3024)
L & R Manufacturing Co Inc ....D....... 201 991-5330
Kearny (G-4877)

INSTRUMENTS, SURGICAL & MED: Needles & Syringes, Hypodermic

Becton Dickinson and Company ....A....... 201 847-6800
Franklin Lakes (G-3616)
Oncode-Med Inc ....G....... 908 998-3647
Basking Ridge (G-194)

INSTRUMENTS, SURGICAL & MEDI: Knife Blades/Handles, Surgical

Nextgen Edge Inc..............................G....... 610 507-6904
West Milford (G-11730)

INSTRUMENTS, SURGICAL & MEDICAL: Blood & Bone Work

Catalent Pharma Solutions Inc ....B....... 732 537-6200
Somerset (G-9971)
Datascope Corp ....E....... 201 995-8000
Mahwah (G-5726)
Genesis Bps LLC ....E....... 201 708-1400
Ramsey (G-9145)
H Galow Co Inc ....E....... 201 768-0547
Norwood (G-7564)
Phillips Precision Inc ....C....... 201 797-8820
Elmwood Park (G-2849)

INSTRUMENTS, SURGICAL & MEDICAL: Blood Pressure

General Graphics Corporation ....G....... 201 664-4083
Hillsdale (G-4367)
Intercure Inc.....................................E....... 973 893-5653
Montclair (G-6372)
Trimline Medical Products Corp............C....... 908 429-0590
Branchburg (G-691)

INSTRUMENTS, SURGICAL & MEDICAL: Catheters

Bipore Inc ....F....... 201 767-1993
Northvale (G-7519)
Mallinckrodt LLC ....E....... 908 238-6600
Hampton (G-4158)
Venarum Medical LLC ....G....... 732 996-8513
Eatontown (G-2428)

INSTRUMENTS, SURGICAL & MEDICAL: Inhalation Therapy

Biodynamics LLC................................G....... 201 227-9255
Englewood (G-2882)
Microdose Therapeutx Inc ....E....... 732 355-2100
Ewing (G-3046)

INSTRUMENTS, SURGICAL & MEDICAL: Lasers, Surgical

Unionmed Tech Inc ....G....... 917 714-3418
Bridgewater (G-899)

INSTRUMENTS, SURGICAL & MEDICAL: Needles, Suture

Terumo Americas Holding Inc ....D....... 732 302-4900
Somerset (G-10084)
Terumo Medical Corporation ....C....... 732 302-4900
Somerset (G-10085)

INSTRUMENTS, SURGICAL & MEDICAL: Ophthalmic

Bausch & Lomb Incorporated ....B....... 585 338-6000
Bridgewater (G-800)
Khan Zeshan ....G....... 973 619-4736
Belleville (G-298)
Sensor Medical Technology LLC..........G....... 425 358-7381
Denville (G-2057)
Westcon Orthopedics Inc.....................G....... 908 806-8981
Neshanic Station (G-6906)

INSTRUMENTS, SURGICAL & MEDICAL: Oxygen Tents

Adsorptech LLC ....G....... 732 491-7727
Middlesex (G-6093)

INSTRUMENTS, SURGICAL/MED: Microsurgical, Exc Electromedical

Jrh Service & Sales LLC......................G....... 908 832-9266
Lebanon (G-5267)

INSTRUMENTS: Analytical

Advanced Technical Support Inc ....D....... 609 298-2522
Bordentown (G-574)
Analyticon Instruments Corp................G....... 973 379-6771
Springfield (G-10426)
Arrow Engineering Co Inc....................G....... 908 353-5229
Hillside (G-4376)
Becton Dickinson and Company.........A....... 201 847-6800
Franklin Lakes (G-3616)
Belair Instrument Company LLC ....E....... 973 912-8900
Pine Brook (G-8587)
Beta Industries Corp ....E....... 201 939-2400
Carlstadt (G-1128)
Biomedicon ....F....... 856 778-1880
Moorestown (G-6508)
C W Brabender Instrs Inc ....E....... 201 343-8425
South Hackensack (G-10151)
Chemglass Inc...................................C....... 856 696-0014
Vineland (G-11199)
Chemspeed Technologies Inc ....F....... 732 329-1225
North Brunswick (G-7461)
Distek Inc ....D....... 732 422-7585
North Brunswick (G-7466)
Edax Inc ....D....... 201 529-4880
Mahwah (G-5734)
Evex Analytical Instruments ....F....... 609 252-9192
Princeton (G-8944)
Fisher Scientific Chemical Div..............E....... 609 633-1422
Fair Lawn (G-3101)
Hudson Robotics Inc ....E....... 973 376-7400
Springfield (G-10444)
International Crystal Labs....................E....... 973 478-8944
Garfield (G-3748)
Isocolor Inc.......................................G....... 201 935-4494
Carlstadt (G-1169)
Lynred USA Inc ....E....... 973 882-0211
Fairfield (G-3266)
M D Laboratory Supplies Inc ....G....... 732 322-0773
Franklin Park (G-3635)
McKinley Scientific Llc.......................F....... 973 579-4144
Sparta (G-10396)
Mesa Laboratories- Bgi Inc ....E....... 973 492-8400
Butler (G-1009)
Microdysis Inc ....G....... 609 642-1184
Bordentown (G-589)
National Labnet Co ....E....... 732 417-0700
Iselin (G-4618)
New ERA Enterprises Inc.....................G....... 856 794-2005
Newfield (G-7324)
Novartis Pharmaceuticals Corp............G....... 862 778-8300
East Hanover (G-2230)
Princeton Research Instruments...........G....... 609 924-0570
Princeton (G-9004)
Pulsetor LLC......................................G....... 609 303-0578
Lambertville (G-5196)
Rame-Hart Inc....................................E....... 973 335-0560
Randolph (G-9197)
Rame-Hart Instrument Co LLC ....G....... 973 448-0305
Succasunna (G-10518)
Rudolph Instruments Inc.....................G....... 973 227-0139
Denville (G-2056)
Siemens Medical ....A....... 973 927-2828
Flanders (G-3419)
Spark Holland Inc...............................G....... 609 799-7250
Franklinville (G-3638)
Sympatec Inc.....................................F....... 609 303-0066
Pennington (G-8374)
Symtera Analytics LLC........................F....... 718 696-9902
Wall Township (G-11373)
Thermo Fisher Scientific Inc ....F....... 609 239-3185
Burlington (G-987)
Thermo Fisher Scientific Inc...............F....... 732 627-0220
Somerset (G-10087)
Topcon Medical Systems Inc ....D....... 201 599-5100
Oakland (G-7647)
Veeco Process Equipment Inc..............C....... 732 560-5300
Somerset (G-10094)
Wra Manufacturing Company Inc ....G....... 908 416-2228
Hopatcong (G-4523)

INSTRUMENTS: Analyzers, Internal Combustion Eng, Electronic

Buttonwood Enterprises LLC ....G....... 201 505-1901
Woodcliff Lake *(G-12050)*

INSTRUMENTS: Combustion Control, Indl

Carlisle Machine Works Inc ....E....... 856 825-0627
Millville *(G-6241)*

NM Knight Co Inc ....E....... 856 327-4855
Millville *(G-6263)*

INSTRUMENTS: Electronic, Analog-Digital Converters

Microdysis Inc ....G....... 609 642-1184
Bordentown *(G-589)*

Thomas Instrumentation Inc ....F....... 609 624-2630
Cape May Court House *(G-1116)*

INSTRUMENTS: Endoscopic Eqpt, Electromedical

Affil Endoscopy Services CL ....G....... 201 842-0020
Clifton *(G-1559)*

Burlington Cnty Endoscopy Ctr ....E....... 609 267-1555
Lumberton *(G-5624)*

Ethicon LLC ....D....... 908 218-3195
Somerville *(G-10109)*

INSTRUMENTS: Flow, Indl Process

Boc Group Inc ....A....... 908 665-2400
New Providence *(G-6995)*

Kessler-Ellis Products Co ....D....... 732 935-1320
Eatontown *(G-2407)*

Linde North America Inc ....D....... 908 464-8100
New Providence *(G-7007)*

Messer North America Inc ....B....... 908 464-8100
Bridgewater *(G-851)*

INSTRUMENTS: Frequency Meters, Electrical, Mech & Electronic

Sherry International Inc ....F....... 908 279-7255
Warren *(G-11430)*

INSTRUMENTS: Indl Process Control

Accuratus Ceramic Corp ....E....... 908 213-7070
Phillipsburg *(G-8540)*

Aladdin Instruments Corp ....G....... 774 326-4919
Cherry Hill *(G-1338)*

American Compressed Gases Inc ....E....... 201 767-3200
Old Tappan *(G-7732)*

Amico Technologies Inc ....G....... 732 901-5900
Lakewood *(G-5053)*

Anvima Technologies LLC ....E....... 973 531-7077
Brookside *(G-916)*

Appleton Grp LLC ....C....... 973 285-3261
Morristown *(G-6640)*

Arcadia Equipment Inc ....F....... 201 342-3308
Hackensack *(G-3877)*

Btech Inc ....E....... 973 983-1120
Rockaway *(G-9448)*

Check-It Electronics Corp ....E....... 973 520-8435
Elizabeth *(G-2720)*

Circonix Technologies LLC ....F....... 973 962-6160
Ringwood *(G-9344)*

Difco Laboratories Inc ....G....... 410 316-4113
Franklin Lakes *(G-3619)*

Digivac Company ....F....... 732 765-0900
Matawan *(G-5972)*

Dranetz Technologies Inc. ....D....... 732 248-4358
Edison *(G-2493)*

Emerson Process Management ....G....... 908 605-4551
Warren *(G-11409)*

F S Brainard & Co ....F....... 609 387-4300
Burlington *(G-966)*

Global Power Technology Inc ....D....... 732 287-3680
Edison *(G-2521)*

Intertek Laboratories Inc ....E....... 908 903-1800
Stirling *(G-10491)*

Istec Corporation ....F....... 973 383-9888
Sparta *(G-10393)*

J & W Servo Systems Company ....F....... 973 335-1007
Rockaway *(G-9469)*

Marine Electric Systems Inc ....E....... 201 531-8600
South Hackensack *(G-10171)*

Marotta Controls Inc ....C....... 973 334-7800
Montville *(G-6444)*

Mayfair Tech Ltd Lblty Co ....F....... 609 802-1262
Princeton *(G-8974)*

Mesa Laboratories Inc ....E....... 973 492-8400
Butler *(G-1008)*

Netquest Corporation ....E....... 856 866-0505
Mount Laurel *(G-6786)*

Nordson Efd LLC ....C....... 609 259-9222
Robbinsville *(G-9414)*

Omega Engineering Inc ....F....... 856 467-4200
Swedesboro *(G-10599)*

Palmer Electronics Inc ....F....... 973 772-5900
Garfield *(G-3752)*

Pavan & Kievit Enterprises ....E....... 973 546-4615
Garfield *(G-3754)*

Pyrometer LLC ....G....... 609 443-5522
Ewing *(G-3056)*

Rees Scientific Corporation ....C....... 609 530-1055
Ewing *(G-3060)*

Roxboro Holdings Inc ....D....... 732 919-3119
Wall Township *(G-11365)*

Schneder Elc Bldngs Amrcas Inc ....E....... 201 348-9240
Secaucus *(G-9808)*

Sk & P Industries Inc ....F....... 973 482-1864
Newark *(G-7275)*

Spectro Analytical Instrs Inc ....F....... 201 642-3000
Mahwah *(G-5774)*

TAC Technical Instrument Corp ....F....... 609 882-2894
Trenton *(G-10995)*

Theory Development Corp ....F....... 201 783-8770
Mahwah *(G-5780)*

V G Controls Inc ....G....... 973 764-6500
Oakland *(G-7649)*

Vertiv Corporation ....E....... 732 225-3741
Edison *(G-2640)*

INSTRUMENTS: Laser, Scientific & Engineering

Mnemonics Inc ....G....... 856 234-0970
Mount Laurel *(G-6784)*

INSTRUMENTS: Liquid Analysis, Indl Process

Accupac Inc ....C....... 215 256-7094
Lakewood *(G-5044)*

Gammon Technical Products Inc ....D....... 732 223-4600
Manasquan *(G-5831)*

INSTRUMENTS: Liquid Level, Indl Process

John G Papailias Co Inc ....G....... 201 767-4027
Northvale *(G-7532)*

Signal Systems International ....G....... 732 793-4668
Lavallette *(G-5212)*

INSTRUMENTS: Measurement, Indl Process

Digital Binscom LLC ....G....... 908 867-7055
Long Valley *(G-5609)*

Electronic Measuring Devices ....F....... 973 691-4755
Flanders *(G-3407)*

Ipco US LLC ....G....... 973 720-7000
Totowa *(G-10833)*

Malcam US ....G....... 973 218-2461
Short Hills *(G-9872)*

Measurement Control Corp ....G....... 800 504-9010
West Orange *(G-11773)*

INSTRUMENTS: Measuring & Controlling

Akers Biosciences Inc ....E....... 856 848-8698
West Deptford *(G-11690)*

Amcor Phrm Packg USA LLC ....C....... 856 825-1100
Millville *(G-6229)*

American Gas & Chemical Co Ltd ....E....... 201 767-7300
Northvale *(G-7518)*

Ballantine Laboratories Inc ....G....... 908 713-7742
Annandale *(G-53)*

Boonton Electronics Corp ....E....... 973 386-9696
Parsippany *(G-7895)*

C W Brabender Instrs Inc ....E....... 201 343-8425
South Hackensack *(G-10151)*

Checkpoint Security Systems Gr ....C....... 952 933-8858
West Deptford *(G-11696)*

Checkpoint Systems Inc ....C....... 952 933-8858
West Deptford *(G-11699)*

Control Products Inc ....G....... 973 887-5000
East Hanover *(G-2203)*

Coperion K-Tron Pitman Inc ....F....... 856 589-0500
Sewell *(G-9836)*

Delmhorst Instrument Company ....E....... 973 334-2557
Towaco *(G-10868)*

Digital Binscom LLC ....G....... 908 867-7055
Long Valley *(G-5609)*

Digivac Company ....F....... 732 765-0900
Matawan *(G-5972)*

Dranetz Technologies Inc. ....D....... 732 248-4358
Edison *(G-2493)*

DRG International Inc ....E....... 973 564-7555
Springfield *(G-10439)*

Edax Inc ....D....... 201 529-4880
Mahwah *(G-5734)*

G R Bowler Inc ....G....... 973 525-7172
Andover *(G-46)*

H S Martin Company Inc. ....F....... 856 692-8700
Vineland *(G-11230)*

Innerspace Technology Inc ....G....... 201 933-1600
Carlstadt *(G-1168)*

Leak Detection Associates Inc ....G....... 609 415-2290
Egg Harbor Township *(G-2687)*

Lumiscope Co Inc ....D....... 678 291-3207
East Rutherford *(G-2298)*

Macro Sensors ....F....... 856 662-8000
Budd Lake *(G-928)*

Magnetic Products and Svcs Inc ....G....... 732 264-6651
Holmdel *(G-4504)*

Micro-Tek Laboratories Inc ....E....... 973 779-5577
Clifton *(G-1669)*

Mistras Group Inc ....C....... 609 716-4000
Princeton Junction *(G-9062)*

Netquest Corporation ....E....... 856 866-0505
Mount Laurel *(G-6786)*

Physical Acoustics Corporation ....C....... 609 716-4000
Princeton Junction *(G-9065)*

Radcom Equipment Inc ....G....... 201 518-0033
Paramus *(G-7828)*

Roper Scientific Inc ....E....... 941 556-2601
Trenton *(G-10989)*

Rudolph Technologies Inc ....D....... 973 347-3891
Budd Lake *(G-934)*

Science Pump Corporation ....E....... 856 963-7700
Camden *(G-1086)*

Scientific Machine and Sup Co ....E....... 732 356-1553
Middlesex *(G-6145)*

Scientific Sales Inc ....F....... 609 844-0055
Lawrenceville *(G-5243)*

Shock Tech Inc ....E....... 845 368-8600
Mahwah *(G-5771)*

Sigma-Netics Inc ....E....... 973 227-6372
Riverdale *(G-9385)*

Sun Coast Precision Instrument ....G....... 646 852-2331
Cresskill *(G-1945)*

Superior Signal Company LLC ....F....... 732 251-0800
Old Bridge *(G-7728)*

Transistor Devices Inc ....C....... 908 850-5088
Hackettstown *(G-4039)*

United Instrument Company LLC ....E....... 201 767-6000
Northvale *(G-7552)*

Venkateshwara Inc ....F....... 908 964-4777
Somerset *(G-10095)*

William Kenyon & Sons Inc ....E....... 732 985-8980
Piscataway *(G-8738)*

Willrich Precision Instr Co ....G....... 866 945-5742
Cresskill *(G-1948)*

INSTRUMENTS: Measuring Electricity

Agilent Technologies Inc ....E....... 973 448-7129
Budd Lake *(G-917)*

Alltest Instruments Inc ....F....... 732 919-3339
Farmingdale *(G-3376)*

Eastern Instrumentation of ....G....... 856 231-0668
Moorestown *(G-6519)*

Energy Tracking Inc ....G....... 973 448-8660
Flanders *(G-3409)*

Hamamatsu Corporation ....E....... 908 526-0941
Bridgewater *(G-829)*

Imperial Machine & Tool Co ....E....... 908 496-8100
Columbia *(G-1794)*

Instru-Met Corporation ....G....... 908 851-0700
Union *(G-11065)*

Intertek Laboratories Inc ....E....... 908 903-1800
Stirling *(G-10491)*

Keyence Corporation America ....E....... 201 930-0100
Elmwood Park *(G-2834)*

Link Computer Graphics Inc ....G....... 973 808-8990
Fairfield *(G-3263)*

Mistras Group Inc ....C....... 609 716-4000
Princeton Junction *(G-9062)*

PRODUCT

Multi-Tech Industries Inc ....F 732 431-0550
Marlboro *(G-5905)*

Nanion Technologies Inc ....G....... 973 369-7960
Livingston *(G-5531)*

Panel Components & Systems ....F 973 448-9400
Stanhope *(G-10478)*

Powercomm Solutions LLC ....G....... 908 806-7025
Flemington *(G-3460)*

RSR Electronics Inc ....E 732 381-8777
Rahway *(G-9126)*

Spectro Analytical Instrs Inc ....F 201 642-3000
Mahwah *(G-5774)*

Tcp Reliable Inc ....G....... 848 229-2466
Edison *(G-2632)*

Tektronix Inc ....G....... 973 628-1363
Wayne *(G-11556)*

INSTRUMENTS: *Measuring, Electrical Energy*

Energy Tracking LLC ....G....... 973 448-8660
Flanders *(G-3408)*

Tof Energy Corporation ....D....... 908 691-2422
Bedminster *(G-280)*

INSTRUMENTS: *Measuring, Electrical Power*

Janke & Company Inc ....G....... 973 334-4477
Boonton *(G-558)*

INSTRUMENTS: *Medical & Surgical*

3M Company ....C 908 788-4000
Flemington *(G-3426)*

A D M Tronics Unlimited Inc ....E 201 767-6040
Northvale *(G-7513)*

Aarisse Health Care Products ....G....... 973 686-1811
Wayne *(G-11464)*

Advanced Precision Inc ....E 800 788-9473
Sparta *(G-10375)*

Allergan Inc ....A 862 261-7000
Madison *(G-5687)*

Alto Development Corp ....D....... 732 938-2266
Wall Township *(G-11316)*

America Techma Inc ....G....... 201 894-5887
Englewood Cliffs *(G-2958)*

Antares Pharma Inc ....C 609 359-3020
Ewing *(G-3015)*

Artegraft Inc ....F 732 422-8333
North Brunswick *(G-7453)*

Augma Biomaterials USA Inc ....G....... 201 509-4570
Monroe Township *(G-6326)*

Baeta Corp ....G....... 201 471-0988
Fort Lee *(G-3548)*

Bard Devices Inc ....E 908 277-8000
Franklin Lakes *(G-3611)*

Baxter Healthcare Corporation ......D....... 856 489-2104
Cherry Hill *(G-1342)*

Bayer Healthcare LLC ....A 862 404-3000
Whippany *(G-11878)*

Bayer Hlthcare Phrmcticals Inc .....E 973 709-3545
Wayne *(G-11475)*

Bayer Hlthcare Phrmcticals Inc .....A 862 404-3000
Whippany *(G-11880)*

Bd Ventures LLC ....E 201 847-6800
Franklin Lakes *(G-3615)*

Belair Instrument Company LLC .....E 973 912-8900
Pine Brook *(G-8587)*

Beltor Manufacturing Corp ....G....... 856 768-5570
Berlin *(G-415)*

Bernafon LLC ....G....... 888 941-4203
Somerset *(G-9962)*

Bio Compression Systems Inc ....E 201 939-0716
Moonachie *(G-6457)*

Biomedicon ....F 856 778-1880
Moorestown *(G-6508)*

Biosearch Medical Products Inc......D....... 908 252-0595
Branchburg *(G-626)*

Boston Scientific Corporation ......E 973 709-7000
Wayne *(G-11482)*

Burpee Medsystems LLC ....G....... 732 544-8900
Eatontown *(G-2382)*

C R Bard Inc ....C 908 277-8000
Franklin Lakes *(G-3617)*

C R Bard Inc ....G....... 856 461-0946
Delran *(G-2012)*

Canfield Property Group Inc ....F 973 276-0300
Fairfield *(G-3163)*

Cantel Medical Corp ....G....... 973 890-7220
Little Falls *(G-5454)*

Capintec Inc ....E 201 825-9500
Florham Park *(G-3495)*

Carnegie Surgical LLC ....G....... 866 782-7144
East Windsor *(G-2366)*

Cedge Industries Inc ....F 201 641-3222
Barnegat *(G-157)*

Cenogenics Corporation ....E 732 536-6457
Morganville *(G-6584)*

Ch Technologies USA Inc ....E 201 666-2335
Westwood *(G-11829)*

Clordisys Solutions Inc ....G....... 908 236-4100
Branchburg *(G-629)*

Collagen Matrix Inc ....E 201 405-1477
Oakland *(G-7619)*

Convatec Inc ....B 908 231-2179
Bridgewater *(G-813)*

Cordis International Corp ....A 732 524-0400
New Brunswick *(G-6918)*

Cranial Technologies Inc ....E 201 265-3993
Paramus *(G-7795)*

Cura Biomed Inc ....G....... 609 647-1474
Princeton Junction *(G-9054)*

Cytosorbents Corporation ....E 732 329-8885
Monmouth Junction *(G-6285)*

Cytosorbents Medical Inc ....E 732 329-8885
Monmouth Junction *(G-6286)*

Data Medical Inc ....F 800 790-9978
North Bergen *(G-7399)*

Dexmed Inc ....G....... 732 831-0507
Elizabeth *(G-2728)*

Dexmed LLC ....G....... 732 831-0507
Elizabeth *(G-2729)*

Difco Laboratories Inc ....G....... 410 316-4113
Franklin Lakes *(G-3619)*

Diopsys Inc ....E 973 244-0622
Pine Brook *(G-8598)*

Emse Corp ....F 973 227-9221
Fairfield *(G-3191)*

Endomedix Inc ....E 848 248-1883
Montclair *(G-6366)*

Excelsior Medical LLC ....C 732 776-7525
Neptune *(G-6877)*

Ferry Machine Corp ....E 201 641-9191
Little Ferry *(G-5485)*

Getinge Group Logistics Americ .....E 973 709-6000
Wayne *(G-11509)*

Getinge Usa Inc ....C 800 475-9040
Wayne *(G-11510)*

Glastron Inc ....E 856 692-0500
Vineland *(G-11226)*

Globe Scientific Inc ....E 201 599-1400
Mahwah *(G-5744)*

Glw Inc ....G....... 845 492-0476
Kearny *(G-4861)*

Graydon Products Inc ....E 856 234-9513
Moorestown *(G-6524)*

H & W Tool Co Inc ....F 973 366-0131
Dover *(G-2085)*

Haz Laboratories ....F 908 453-3300
Washington *(G-11446)*

Healthcare Cart ....G....... 201 406-4797
Blairstown *(G-485)*

IDL Techni-Edge LLC ....C 908 497-9818
Kenilworth *(G-4945)*

Indo-Mim Inc ....G....... 734 327-9842
Princeton *(G-8961)*

Instride Shoes LLC ....E 908 874-6670
Hillsborough *(G-4330)*

Integra Lfscnces Holdings Corp......C 609 275-0500
Plainsboro *(G-8792)*

Integra Lifesciences Corp ....C 609 275-2700
Plainsboro *(G-8793)*

Integra Lifesciences Corp ....C 609 275-2700
Plainsboro *(G-8795)*

Integra Lifesciences Corp ....D....... 609 275-0500
Plainsboro *(G-8794)*

Integra Lifesciences Sales LLC ......B 609 275-0500
Plainsboro *(G-8796)*

Ivy Sports Medicine LLC ....G....... 201 573-5423
Montvale *(G-6416)*

Jaktool LLC ....F 609 664-2451
Cranbury *(G-1847)*

Jnj International Inv LLC ....G....... 732 524-0400
New Brunswick *(G-6939)*

Johnson & Johnson ....B 908 722-9319
Raritan *(G-9213)*

Johnson & Johnson ....C 908 874-1000
Morris Plains *(G-6618)*

Johnson & Johnson ....C 732 524-0400
New Brunswick *(G-6941)*

Johnson & Johnson ....A 732 524-0400
New Brunswick *(G-6940)*

Laboratory Diagnostics Co Inc ......F 732 536-6300
Morganville *(G-6591)*

Laboratory Diagnostics Co Inc ......G....... 732 972-2145
Morganville *(G-6592)*

Linkspine Inc ....G....... 973 625-1333
Dover *(G-2095)*

Lumiscope Co Inc ....D....... 678 291-3207
East Rutherford *(G-2298)*

Maddak Inc ....G....... 973 628-7600
Wayne *(G-11531)*

Maxter Corporation ....G....... 609 877-9700
Willingboro *(G-11992)*

Medicraft Inc ....F 201 421-3055
Elmwood Park *(G-2841)*

Medilogic Group LLC ....G....... 201 794-2166
Hawthorne *(G-4231)*

Medtec Services LLC ....G....... 201 722-9696
Westwood *(G-11835)*

Medtronic Inc ....G....... 908 289-5969
Swedesboro *(G-10595)*

Medtronic Usa Inc ....F 973 331-7914
Parsippany *(G-7978)*

Micro Stamping Corporation ....C 732 302-0800
Somerset *(G-10030)*

Mindray Ds Usa Inc ....B 201 995-8000
Mahwah *(G-5754)*

Nephros Inc ....F 201 343-5202
South Orange *(G-10200)*

Next Medical Products LLC ....F 908 722-4549
Branchburg *(G-660)*

Nu-Stent Technologies Inc ....G....... 732 729-6270
Hillsborough *(G-4342)*

Osteotech Inc ....E 732 544-5942
Eatontown *(G-2413)*

Osteotech Inc ....C 732 542-2800
Eatontown *(G-2414)*

Osteotech Inc ....F 732 542-2800
Eatontown *(G-2415)*

Pharming Healthcare Inc ....E 908 524-0888
Bridgewater *(G-865)*

Precise Cmpnents TI Design Inc .....G....... 973 928-2928
Clifton *(G-1697)*

Redfield Corporation ....G....... 201 845-3990
Rochelle Park *(G-9429)*

Regen Biologics Inc ....F 201 651-5140
Glen Rock *(G-3834)*

Respironics Inc ....C 973 581-6000
Parsippany *(G-8007)*

Schering Berlin Inc ....G....... 862 404-3000
Whippany *(G-11908)*

Somerset Outpatient Surgery ....G....... 781 635-2807
Somerset *(G-10073)*

Steris Instrument MGT Svcs Inc .....G....... 908 904-1317
Hillsborough *(G-4357)*

Stryker Corporation ....D....... 201 760-8000
Allendale *(G-17)*

Stryker Corporation ....G....... 856 312-0046
Runnemede *(G-9611)*

Techtrade LLC ....G....... 201 706-8130
Jersey City *(G-4819)*

Teleflex Incorporated ....D....... 856 349-7234
Gloucester City *(G-3851)*

Topcon Medical Systems Inc ....D....... 201 599-5100
Oakland *(G-7647)*

Tracer Tool & Machine Co Inc ....F 201 337-6184
Oakland *(G-7648)*

US China Allied Products Inc ....G....... 201 461-9886
Fort Lee *(G-3592)*

Vascular Therapies LLC ....G....... 201 266-8310
Cresskill *(G-1947)*

Viant Medical Inc ....C 908 561-0717
South Plainfield *(G-10341)*

Viatar Ctc Solutions Inc ....G....... 617 299-6590
Short Hills *(G-9879)*

Viscot Medical LLC ....E 973 887-9273
East Hanover *(G-2245)*

Vitillo & Sons Inc ....F 732 886-1393
Lakewood *(G-5177)*

Vozeh Equipment Corp ....E 201 337-3729
Franklin Lakes *(G-3632)*

INSTRUMENTS: *Microwave Test*

Boonton Electronics Corp ....E 973 386-9696
Parsippany *(G-7895)*

Mmtc Inc ....G....... 609 520-9699
Andover *(G-49)*

Waveline Incorporated ....E 973 226-9100
Fairfield *(G-3351)*

Wireless Telecom Group Inc ....D....... 973 386-9696
Parsippany *(G-8040)*

INSTRUMENTS: Nautical

AT&T Technologies Inc ....A 201 771-2000
Berkeley Heights (G-389)

INSTRUMENTS: Optical, Analytical

Thorlabs Inc....................................C 973 579-7227
Newton (G-7363)

INSTRUMENTS: Oscillographs & Oscilloscopes

Spectrum Instrumentation Corp...........E 201 562-1999
Hackensack (G-3978)

INSTRUMENTS: Photographic, Electronic

Samsung Opt-Lctronics Amer Inc........C 201 325-2612
Teaneck (G-10650)

INSTRUMENTS: Power Measuring, Electrical

Electro Impulse Laboratory Inc ....E 732 776-5800
Neptune (G-6876)

INSTRUMENTS: Pressure Measurement, Indl

Pressure Controls Inc....................G 973 751-5002
Belleville (G-308)
TX Technology LLC ....C 973 442-7500
Denville (G-2061)

INSTRUMENTS: Radio Frequency Measuring

Pulsar Microwave Corp ....E 973 779-6262
Clifton (G-1701)
Rf Vii Inc ....F 856 875-2121
Newfield (G-7327)
Seren Inc ....E 856 205-1131
Vineland (G-11263)

INSTRUMENTS: Telemetering, Indl Process

Cg Automation Solutions USA ....E 973 379-7400
Springfield (G-10434)
Daq Electronics LLC ....E 732 981-0050
Piscataway (G-8651)

INSTRUMENTS: Temperature Measurement, Indl

Intest Corporation....................G 856 505-8800
Mount Laurel (G-6770)
Tru Temp Sensors Inc....................G 215 396-1550
Ocean City (G-7698)

INSTRUMENTS: Test, Digital, Electronic & Electrical Circuits

Intest Corporation....................G 856 505-8800
Mount Laurel (G-6770)

INSTRUMENTS: Test, Electronic & Electric Measurement

Communication Devices Inc ....F 973 334-1980
Boonton (G-546)
Dbmcorp Inc ....F 201 677-0008
Oakland (G-7623)
Dranetz Technologies Inc................D 732 248-4358
Edison (G-2493)
Global Power Technology Inc.............D 732 287-3680
Edison (G-2521)
Marine Electric Systems Inc ....E 201 531-8600
South Hackensack (G-10171)
Zixel Ltd ....G 732 972-3287
Morganville (G-6600)

INSTRUMENTS: Test, Electronic & Electrical Circuits

ABC Digital Electronics Inc...............G 201 666-6888
Old Tappan (G-7731)
Aeronautical Instr & Rdo Co ....E 973 473-0034
Lodi (G-5550)
Applied Resources Corp ....E 973 328-3882
Wharton (G-11852)
Ballantine Laboratories Inc ....G 908 713-7742
Annandale (G-53)
Omnitester Corp ....F 856 985-8960
Marlton (G-5944)

Sadelco Inc ....D 201 569-3323
Fort Lee (G-3586)
Signal Crafters Tech Inc..................G 973 781-0880
East Hanover (G-2239)

INSTRUMENTS: Testing, Semiconductor

Radcom Equipment Inc ....E 201 518-0033
Paramus (G-7828)

INSTRUMENTS: Thermal Conductive, Indl

Align Sourcing Ltd Lblty Co ....G 609 375-8550
Trenton (G-10889)

INSTRUMENTS: Thermal Property Measurement

Setaram Inc..............................G 908 262-7060
Cranbury (G-1881)
Temptime Corporation....................D 973 984-6000
Morris Plains (G-6626)

INSTRUMENTS: Vibration

Mab Enterprises Inc......................F 973 345-8282
Newark (G-7193)
Reliability Maintenance Svcs..............G 732 922-8878
Ocean (G-7679)

INSTRUMENTS: Viscometer, Indl Process

Gerin Corporation Inc.....................G 732 774-3256
Neptune (G-6880)

INSULATING BOARD, CELLULAR FIBER

Homasote Company ....C 609 883-3300
Ewing (G-3036)

INSULATING COMPOUNDS

Insul-Stop Inc ....G 732 706-1978
Marlboro (G-5901)

INSULATION & CUSHIONING FOAM: Polystyrene

Evonik Foams Inc ....E 973 929-8000
Parsippany (G-7939)
Johns Manville Corporation...............E 732 225-9190
Edison (G-2542)
Kohler Industries Inc ....E 336 545-3289
Paterson (G-8231)
Pacor Inc ....E 609 324-1100
Bordentown (G-592)
Poly Molding LLC ....F 973 835-7161
Haskell (G-4201)

INSULATION & ROOFING MATERIALS: Wood, Reconstituted

Bmca Holdings Corporation ....E 973 628-3000
Wayne (G-11480)
Johns Manville Corporation...............E 732 225-9190
Edison (G-2542)
Standard Industries Inc ....C 856 241-0241
Swedesboro (G-10609)
Standard Industries Inc ....A 973 628-3000
Parsippany (G-8021)

INSULATION MATERIALS WHOLESALERS

Fbm Galaxy Inc ....E 856 966-1105
Camden (G-1064)
Fluid Coating Systems Inc ....G 973 767-1028
Garfield (G-3742)
Pacor Inc ....E 609 324-1100
Bordentown (G-592)

INSULATION: Fiberglass

Advantage Fiberglass Inc ....G 609 926-4606
Egg Harbor Township (G-2675)
Insulation Materials Distrs ....G 908 925-2323
Linden (G-5360)

INSULATORS, PORCELAIN: Electrical

Curran-Pfeiff Corp ....F 732 225-0555
Edison (G-2489)
Isolantite Manufacturing Co ....E 908 647-3333
Stirling (G-10492)

Mitronics Products Inc ....G 908 647-5006
Gillette (G-3802)
New Jersey Porcelain Co Inc ....F 609 394-5376
Trenton (G-10963)

INSURANCE BROKERS, NEC

Webannuitiescom Inc ....G 732 521-5110
Monroe (G-6324)

INTEGRATED CIRCUITS, SEMICONDUCTOR NETWORKS, ETC

Advanced Micro Devices Inc ....C 732 787-2892
North Middletown (G-7502)
Alcatel-Lucent USA Inc ....D 908 582-3275
New Providence (G-6993)
Analog Devices Inc ....E 732 868-7100
Somerset (G-9953)
Ateksis USA Corp ....G 646 508-9074
East Rutherford (G-2274)
Candela Corporation ....F 908 753-6300
South Plainfield (G-10234)
Digitron Electronic Corp ....E 908 245-2012
Kenilworth (G-4936)
Hydraulic Manifolds Usa LLC ....E 973 728-1214
West Milford (G-11727)
Ii-VI Optoelectronic Dvcs Inc ....C 908 668-5000
Warren (G-11417)
Nokia of America Corporation ....A 908 582-3275
New Providence (G-7014)
Xybion Corporation ....C 973 538-2067
Lawrenceville (G-5248)

INTERCOMMUNICATIONS SYSTEMS: Electric

Abris Distribution Inc ....E 732 252-9819
Manalapan (G-5799)
AT&T Services Inc........................A 732 420-3131
Middletown (G-6159)
Bogen Communications Inc ....D 201 934-8500
Mahwah (G-5718)
Bogen Corporation ....G 201 934-8500
Ramsey (G-9142)
Crestron Electronics Inc ....C 201 767-3400
Rockleigh (G-9516)
Electronic Marine Systems Inc ....F 732 680-4120
Rahway (G-9089)
Elymat Corp ....E 201 767-7105
Old Tappan (G-7733)
Elymat Industries Inc ....E 201 767-7105
Old Tappan (G-7734)
Industronic Inc ....G 908 393-5960
Bridgewater (G-835)
L J Loeffler Systems Inc...................E 212 924-7597
Secaucus (G-9788)
Moniteur Devices Inc ....F 973 857-1600
Cedar Grove (G-1283)
Netquest Corporation ....E 856 866-0505
Mount Laurel (G-6786)

INTERIOR DECORATING SVCS

Greenbaum Interiors LLC..................D 973 279-3000
Paterson (G-8202)

INTERIOR DESIGN SVCS, NEC

American Intr Resources Inc ....G 908 851-0014
Union (G-11024)
Cronos-Prim Colorado LLC ....G 303 369-7477
Lodi (G-5557)
Masters Interiors Inc......................E 973 253-0784
Clifton (G-1665)
Ramsay David Cabinetmakers..............F 856 234-7776
Moorestown (G-6562)

INTERIOR DESIGNING SVCS

Bai Lar Interior Services Inc ....G 732 738-0350
Fords (G-3530)
Carole Hchman Design Group Inc........C 866 267-3945
Jersey City (G-4709)
Good Impressions Inc ....G 856 461-3232
Riverside (G-9395)
Gordon Frgson Intr Dsigns Svcs..........G 973 378-2330
Maplewood (G-5877)
Insign Inc ....E 856 424-1161
West Deptford (G-11705)

P
R
O
D
U
C
T

INTERIOR REPAIR SVCS

Atlas Auto Trim Inc ....G....... 732 985-6800
Edison *(G-2463)*
Suburban Auto Seat Co Inc ....F....... 973 778-9227
Lodi *(G-5577)*

INTRAVENOUS SOLUTIONS

Fractal Solutions Corp ....G....... 201 608-6828
Edgewater *(G-2438)*
Medicines Company ....C....... 973 290-6000
Parsippany *(G-7977)*
Nextron Medical Tech Inc ....D....... 973 575-0614
Fairfield *(G-3279)*

INVENTOR

Bishop Ascendant Inc ....G....... 201 572-7436
West Caldwell *(G-11642)*

INVERTERS: Nonrotating Electrical

Avionic Instruments LLC ....C....... 732 388-3500
Avenel *(G-122)*

INVERTERS: Rotating Electrical

Power Magne-Tech Corp ....E....... 732 826-4700
Perth Amboy *(G-8529)*

INVESTMENT FUNDS, NEC

Stanger Robert A & Co LP ....E....... 732 389-3600
Shrewsbury *(G-9902)*

INVESTORS, NEC

Capsugel Holdings Us Inc ....G....... 862 242-1700
Morristown *(G-6652)*

IRON & STEEL: Corrugating, Cold-Rolled

General Sullivan Group Inc ....E....... 609 745-5004
Pennington *(G-8365)*

IRON OXIDES

Rockwood Holdings Inc ....E....... 609 514-0300
Princeton *(G-9017)*

IRRADIATION EQPT

Gray Star Inc ....G....... 973 398-3331
Mount Arlington *(G-6713)*

JANITORIAL & CUSTODIAL SVCS

Aus Inc ....G....... 856 234-9200
Mount Laurel *(G-6738)*
Ronell Industries Inc ....B....... 908 245-5255
Roselle *(G-9571)*

JANITORIAL EQPT & SPLYS WHOLESALERS

Americhem Enterprises Inc ....G....... 732 363-4840
Lakewood *(G-5051)*
T & B Specialties Inc ....G....... 732 928-4500
Jackson *(G-4666)*

JARS: Plastic

Parkway Plastics Inc ....E....... 800 881-4996
Piscataway *(G-8697)*

JEWELERS' FINDINGS & MATERIALS

Solmor Manufacturing Co Inc ....G....... 973 824-7203
Verona *(G-11175)*
Victors Three-D Inc ....D....... 201 845-4433
Maywood *(G-6018)*

JEWELERS' FINDINGS & MATERIALS: Bearings, Synthetic

Moser Jewel Company ....G....... 908 454-1155
Phillipsburg *(G-8564)*

JEWELERS' FINDINGS & MATERIALS: Castings

Diamond Universe LLC ....F....... 201 592-9500
Fort Lee *(G-3555)*
Joseph Castings Inc ....F....... 201 712-0717
Maywood *(G-6010)*

JEWELERS' FINDINGS & MTLS: Jewel Prep, Instr, Tools, Watches

Master Presentations Inc ....F....... 732 239-7093
Lakewood *(G-5131)*
Movado Group Inc ....B....... 201 267-8000
Paramus *(G-7822)*

JEWELERS' FINDINGS/MTRLS: Gem Prep, Settings, Real/Imitation

Mdviani Designs Inc ....G....... 201 840-5410
Ridgefield *(G-9275)*

JEWELRY & PRECIOUS STONES WHOLESALERS

Carol Dauplaise Ltd ....E....... 212 997-5290
North Bergen *(G-7393)*
Diamond Hut Jewelry Exchange ....G....... 201 332-5372
Jersey City *(G-4728)*
Enamel Art Studio ....E....... 732 321-0774
Metuchen *(G-6055)*
Ultimate Trading Corp ....D....... 973 228-7700
Rockaway *(G-9509)*
Unistar Inc ....G....... 212 840-2100
Princeton *(G-9039)*

JEWELRY APPAREL

Creations By Sherry Lynn LLC ....G....... 800 742-3448
Florham Park *(G-3498)*
E Chabot Ltd ....E....... 212 575-1026
Edison *(G-2496)*
Heights Jewelers LLC ....F....... 201 825-2381
Allendale *(G-9)*
Hickok Matthews Co Inc ....G....... 973 335-3400
Montville *(G-6443)*
Moonbabies LLC ....G....... 609 926-0201
Somers Point *(G-9938)*
Shopindia Inc ....G....... 732 409-0656
Marlboro *(G-5914)*

JEWELRY FINDINGS & LAPIDARY WORK

Grassman-Blake Inc ....E....... 973 379-6170
Millburn *(G-6198)*
Midas Chain Inc ....G....... 201 244-1150
Northvale *(G-7537)*
Tessler & Weiss/Premesco Inc ....C....... 800 535-3501
Union *(G-11094)*

JEWELRY REPAIR SVCS

DAmore Jewelers ....F....... 201 945-0530
Cliffside Park *(G-1537)*
Diamond Hut Jewelry Exchange ....G....... 201 332-5372
Jersey City *(G-4728)*
Good As Gold Jewelers Inc ....G....... 732 286-1111
Toms River *(G-10762)*
Pretty Jewelry Co ....G....... 908 806-3377
Flemington *(G-3462)*
Saud & Son Jewelry Inc ....G....... 201 866-4445
West New York *(G-11754)*

JEWELRY STORES

Aubrey David Inc ....E....... 201 653-2200
Bayonne *(G-203)*
DBC Inc ....D....... 212 819-1177
Teaneck *(G-10626)*
Diamond Hut Jewelry Exchange ....G....... 201 332-5372
Jersey City *(G-4728)*
Scott Kay Inc ....C....... 201 287-0100
Secaucus *(G-9811)*

JEWELRY STORES: Precious Stones & Precious Metals

Anna J Chung Ltd ....F....... 917 575-8100
Edgewater *(G-2433)*
Avanzato Jewelers LLC ....G....... 609 890-0500
Trenton *(G-10898)*
Corbo Jewelers Inc ....F....... 973 777-1635
Clifton *(G-1591)*
DAmore Jewelers ....F....... 201 945-0530
Cliffside Park *(G-1537)*
Gem Vault Inc ....G....... 908 788-1770
Flemington *(G-3445)*
George Press Inc ....F....... 973 992-7797
Livingston *(G-5513)*

Goldstein Setting Co Inc ....F....... 908 964-1034
Union *(G-11060)*
Good As Gold Jewelers Inc ....G....... 732 286-1111
Toms River *(G-10762)*
Hickok Matthews Co Inc ....G....... 973 335-3400
Montville *(G-6443)*
J Michaels Jewelers Inc ....G....... 908 771-9800
Berkeley Heights *(G-403)*
M S Brown Mfg Jewelers ....G....... 609 522-7604
Wildwood *(G-11946)*
Robertas Jewelers Inc ....G....... 973 875-5318
Hamburg *(G-4095)*
Saud & Son Jewelry Inc ....G....... 201 866-4445
West New York *(G-11754)*
W Kodak Jewelers Inc ....G....... 201 710-5491
Hoboken *(G-4487)*

JEWELRY, PRECIOUS METAL: Bracelets

Franklin Mint LLC ....E....... 800 843-6468
Fort Lee *(G-3559)*

JEWELRY, PRECIOUS METAL: Medals, Precious Or Semiprecious

Norco Inc ....E....... 908 789-1550
Garwood *(G-3787)*

JEWELRY, PRECIOUS METAL: Mountings & Trimmings

Bergio International Inc ....G....... 973 227-3230
Fairfield *(G-3156)*
Brad Garman Designs ....G....... 732 229-6670
Long Branch *(G-5594)*

JEWELRY, PRECIOUS METAL: Necklaces

Bhamra Chain Manufacturing ....G....... 908 686-4555
Union *(G-11032)*

JEWELRY, PRECIOUS METAL: Pearl, Natural Or Cultured

Grassman-Blake Inc ....E....... 973 379-6170
Millburn *(G-6198)*

JEWELRY, PRECIOUS METAL: Pins

Barrasso & Blasi Industries ....F....... 973 761-0595
Maplewood *(G-5874)*
Pin People LLC ....F....... 888 309-7467
Montvale *(G-6424)*

JEWELRY, PRECIOUS METAL: Rings, Finger

Jostens Inc ....G....... 973 584-5843
Succasunna *(G-10514)*
Premesco Inc ....B....... 908 686-0513
Union *(G-11084)*
Provost Square Associates Inc ....F....... 973 403-8755
Caldwell *(G-1028)*
Tessler & Weiss/Premesco Inc ....C....... 800 535-3501
Union *(G-11094)*
Trimarco Inc ....G....... 973 762-7380
Maplewood *(G-5886)*
W W Jewelers Inc ....D....... 718 392-4500
Jersey City *(G-4828)*

JEWELRY, PRECIOUS METAL: Rosaries/Other Sm Religious Article

Christian Art ....G....... 201 867-8096
West New York *(G-11737)*
Devon Trading Corp ....E....... 973 812-9190
Caldwell *(G-1022)*
Top Rated Shopping Bargains ....F....... 800 556-5849
Hasbrouck Heights *(G-4190)*

JEWELRY, PRECIOUS METAL: Settings & Mountings

Creations By Stefano Inc ....G....... 201 863-8337
Secaucus *(G-9759)*
Goldstein Setting Co Inc ....F....... 908 964-1034
Union *(G-11060)*
Mdviani Designs Inc ....G....... 201 840-5410
Ridgefield *(G-9275)*
Novell Enterprises Inc ....D....... 732 428-8300
Rahway *(G-9120)*

JEWELRY, WHOLESALE

Alster Import Company Inc ....F 201 332-7245
Jersey City (G-4690)
Diamond Universe LLC ....F 201 592-9500
Fort Lee (G-3555)
E Chabot Ltd ....E 212 575-1026
Edison (G-2496)
Gold Signature Incorporated ....G 732 777-9170
Piscataway (G-8667)
Heights Jewelers LLC ....F 201 825-2381
Allendale (G-9)
J Michaels Jewelers Inc ....G 908 771-9800
Berkeley Heights (G-403)
Midas Chain Inc ....G 201 244-1150
Northvale (G-7537)
Mj Gross Company - NJ ....G 212 542-3199
Lakewood (G-5138)
Saud & Son Jewelry Inc ....G 201 866-4445
West New York (G-11754)
Scaasis Originals Inc ....E 732 775-7474
Neptune (G-6895)
Scott Kay Sterling LLC ....G 201 287-0100
Secaucus (G-9812)
Superior Jewelry Co ....F 215 677-8100
Northfield (G-7511)
Trimarco Inc ....G 973 762-7380
Maplewood (G-5886)
United Diam Inc ....G 732 619-0950
Matawan (G-5990)

JEWELRY: Decorative, Fashion & Costume

Golden Treasure Imports Inc ....G 732 723-1830
Englishtown (G-3002)
HMS Monaco Et Cie Ltd ....E 201 533-0007
Jersey City (G-4747)
Infinite Classic Inc ....G 973 227-2790
Fairfield (G-3239)
International Inspirations LLC ....G 201 868-2000
North Bergen (G-7411)
Jacmel Jewelry Inc ....D 201 223-0435
Secaucus (G-9782)
Lighthouse Express Inc ....G 732 776-9555
Asbury Park (G-79)
Littlegifts Inc ....F 212 868-2559
Secaucus (G-9789)
Nes Jewelry Inc ....D 646 213-4094
Clifton (G-1674)
Norco Inc ....E 908 789-1550
Garwood (G-3787)
Q-Eximtrade Inc ....G 732 366-4667
Carteret (G-1265)
Swarovski North America Ltd ....G 732 632-1856
Edison (G-2627)
Swarovski North America Ltd ....G 856 686-1805
Deptford (G-2067)
Swarovski North America Ltd ....G 856 662-5453
Cherry Hill (G-1419)
Swarovski North America Ltd ....G 201 265-4888
Paramus (G-7839)
Swarovski North America Ltd ....G 609 344-1323
Atlantic City (G-103)
Swarovski North America Ltd ....G 973 812-7500
Wayne (G-11554)
Tapia Accessory Group Inc ....E 201 393-0028
Teterboro (G-10694)
Ultimate Trading Corp ....D 973 228-7700
Rockaway (G-9509)
Umbrella & Chairs LLC ....G 973 284-1240
Englewood (G-2949)

JEWELRY: Precious Metal

All State Medal Co Inc ....G 973 458-1458
Lodi (G-5552)
Anna J Chung Ltd ....F 917 575-8100
Edgewater (G-2433)
Aubrey David Inc ....E 201 653-2200
Bayonne (G-203)
Avanzato Jewelers LLC ....G 609 890-0500
Trenton (G-10898)
Avigdor Ltd Liability Company ....E 973 898-4770
Morristown (G-6645)
Aydin Jewelry Menufecturing ....G 201 818-1002
Ramsey (G-9141)
Bernard D Ascenzo ....G 856 795-0511
Haddonfield (G-4053)
Big Apple Jewelry Mfg ....G 201 531-1600
East Rutherford (G-2277)
Carol Dauplaise Ltd ....E 212 997-5290
North Bergen (G-7393)

Cinco Star LLC ....G 732 744-1617
Edison (G-2477)
D Paglia & Sons Inc ....F 908 654-5999
Mountainside (G-6839)
DAmore Jewelers ....F 201 945-0530
Cliffside Park (G-1537)
Danmola Lara ....G 973 762-7581
South Orange (G-10193)
David E Connolly Inc ....F 908 654-4600
Mountainside (G-6840)
DBC Inc ....D 212 819-1177
Teaneck (G-10626)
Diamond Hut Jewelry Exchange ....G 201 332-5372
Jersey City (G-4728)
Enamel Art Studio ....G 732 321-0774
Metuchen (G-6055)
European Imports of LA Inc ....F 973 536-1823
Paramus (G-7799)
Fehu Jewel LLC ....C 609 297-5491
Plainsboro (G-8786)
Gem Vault Inc ....G 908 788-1770
Flemington (G-3445)
George Press Inc ....F 973 992-7797
Livingston (G-5513)
Gold Buyers At Mall LLC ....G 201 512-5780
Mahwah (G-5745)
Gold Signature Incorporated ....G 732 777-9170
Piscataway (G-8667)
Guild & Facet LLC ....F 201 758-5368
North Bergen (G-7408)
H Ritani LLC ....E 888 974-8264
Closter (G-1756)
Jct Design Enterprises Inc ....E 212 629-7412
Union City (G-11116)
Jost Brothers Jewelry Mfg Corp ....F 908 453-2266
Washington (G-11448)
Joy Jewelery America Inc ....G 201 689-1150
River Vale (G-9367)
K B Enterprises of New Jersey ....G 908 451-5282
Hillsborough (G-4336)
Kole Design LLC ....G 732 409-0211
Freehold (G-3674)
Krementz & Co ....G 973 621-8300
Springfield (G-10452)
Labrada Inc ....G 201 461-2641
Leonia (G-5289)
Lieberfarb Inc ....F 973 676-9090
Rahway (G-9113)
Littlegifts Inc ....F 212 868-2559
Secaucus (G-9789)
Lusterline Inc ....G 201 758-5148
Union City (G-11120)
M S Brown Mfg Jewelers ....G 609 522-7604
Wildwood (G-11946)
Midas Designs Ltd ....G 201 567-2700
Maywood (G-6012)
Mj Gross Company - NJ ....G 212 542-3199
Lakewood (G-5138)
Nadri Inc ....E 201 585-0088
Fort Lee (G-3576)
NEi Gold Products of NJ ....E 201 488-5858
Hackensack (G-3951)
Nei Jewelmasters of New Jersey ....F 201 488-5858
Hackensack (G-3952)
Netfruits Inc ....G 732 249-2588
New Brunswick (G-6951)
Paul Winston Fine Jewelry Grou ....F 800 232-2728
Englewood Cliffs (G-2986)
Pearl Baumell Company Inc ....G 415 421-2113
Rutherford (G-9631)
Pretty Jewelry Co ....F 908 806-3377
Flemington (G-3462)
Robert Manse Designs LLC ....E 732 428-8305
Rahway (G-9124)
Robertas Jewelers Inc ....G 973 875-5318
Hamburg (G-4095)
Sara Emporium Inc ....G 201 792-7222
Jersey City (G-4805)
Saud & Son Jewelry Inc ....G 201 866-4445
West New York (G-11754)
Scott Kay Inc ....C 201 287-0100
Secaucus (G-9811)
Scott Kay Sterling LLC ....G 201 287-0100
Secaucus (G-9812)
Tapia Accessory Group Inc ....E 201 393-0028
Teterboro (G-10694)
Ultimate Trading Corp ....D 973 228-7700
Rockaway (G-9509)
Unistar Inc ....G 212 840-2100
Princeton (G-9039)

United Diam Inc ....G 732 619-0950
Matawan (G-5990)
W Kodak Jewelers Inc ....G 201 710-5491
Hoboken (G-4487)
Weinman Bros Inc ....E 212 695-8116
Jersey City (G-4830)
WIxt LLC ....D 732 906-7979
Metuchen (G-6083)
World Class Marketing Corp ....E 201 313-0022
Fort Lee (G-3595)
Zsombor Antal Designs Inc ....F 201 225-1750
River Edge (G-9364)

JOB PRINTING & NEWSPAPER PUBLISHING COMBINED

Evening Journal Association ....F 201 653-1000
Secaucus (G-9765)

JOB TRAINING & VOCATIONAL REHABILITATION SVCS

Avyakta It Services LLC ....F 609 790-7517
East Windsor (G-2345)
Reuge Management Group Inc ....G 888 306-3253
Hoboken (G-4479)

KAOLIN MINING

JM Huber Corporation ....D 732 603-3630
Edison (G-2540)

KITCHEN ARTICLES: Coarse Earthenware

Durand Glass Mfg Co Inc ....A 856 327-1850
Millville (G-6248)

KITCHEN CABINET STORES, EXC CUSTOM

Millner Kitchens Inc ....G 609 890-7300
Trenton (G-10958)
Taylor Made Cabinets Inc ....E 609 978-6900
Manahawkin (G-5796)

KITCHEN CABINETS WHOLESALERS

Bossen Architectural Millwork ....F 856 786-1100
Cinnaminson (G-1444)
Creative Cabinet Designs Inc ....F 973 402-5886
Boonton (G-547)
Fabuwood Cabinetry Corp ....A 201 432-6555
Newark (G-7121)
Kinzee Industries Inc ....F 201 408-4301
Englewood (G-2916)
Mango Custom Cabinets Inc ....F 908 813-3077
Hackettstown (G-4020)
Metroplex Products Company Inc ....G 732 249-0653
Monroe Township (G-6336)
Mk Wood Inc ....G 973 450-5110
Belleville (G-302)
Shekia Group LLC ....E 732 372-7668
Edison (G-2608)

KITCHEN TOOLS & UTENSILS WHOLESALERS

Kraftware Corporation ....E 732 345-7091
Roselle (G-9562)

KITCHEN UTENSILS: Bakers' Eqpt, Wood

HB Technik USA Ltd Lblty Prtnr ....G 973 875-8688
Branchville (G-708)

KITCHEN UTENSILS: Wooden

Forino Kitchen Cabinets Inc ....G 201 573-0990
Park Ridge (G-7850)
Wees Beyond Products Corp ....F 862 238-8800
Passaic (G-8115)

KITCHENWARE STORES

Adagio Teas Inc ....G 973 253-7400
Elmwood Park (G-2807)
Tatara Group Inc ....G 732 231-6031
Avenel (G-149)

KITS: Plastic

Triumph Plastics LLC ....G 973 584-5500
Flanders (G-3424)

PRODUCT

KNIVES: Agricultural Or indl

Baumer of America Inc ....F 973 263-1569
Towaco (G-10865)

LABELS: Cotton, Printed

Star Narrow Fabrics Inc.....................G....... 973 778-8600
Lodi (G-5576)

LABELS: Paper, Made From Purchased Materials

Aeon Industries Inc........................G....... 732 246-3224
Somerset (G-9943)
CCL Label Inc ....C....... 609 586-1332
Robbinsville (G-9409)
Custom Quick Label Inc ....G....... 856 596-7555
Marlton (G-5926)
Magnetic Ticket & Label Corp...........E....... 973 759-6500
Belleville (G-299)
Renell Label Print Inc ....G....... 201 652-6544
Paramus (G-7829)
United Label Corp ....G....... 973 589-6500
Newark (G-7309)

LABELS: Woven

Beau Label ....D....... 973 318-7800
Hillside (G-4380)

LABOR RESOURCE SVCS

Doolan Industries Incorporated..........G....... 856 985-1880
Marlton (G-5929)

LABORATORIES, TESTING: Food

Chemo Dynamics Inc.......................F 732 721-4700
Sayreville (G-9705)

LABORATORIES, TESTING: Hazardous Waste

SGS UStesting Company ....F 973 575-5252
Fairfield (G-3311)

LABORATORIES, TESTING: Product Testing

Dengen Scientific Corporation...........E....... 201 687-2983
Union City (G-11110)
Randcastle Extrusion Systems ....G....... 973 239-1150
Cedar Grove (G-1290)

LABORATORIES, TESTING: Product Testing, Safety/Performance

Lockheed Martin Corporation.............C....... 856 722-3336
Moorestown (G-6539)

LABORATORIES: Biological

Genzyme Corporation ....G....... 973 256-2106
Totowa (G-10829)

LABORATORIES: Biological Research

Caladrius Biosciences Inc ....E....... 908 842-0100
Basking Ridge (G-177)
Emisphere Technologies Inc ....F 973 532-8000
Roseland (G-9537)
Pds Biotechnology Corporation..........F 800 208-3343
Berkeley Heights (G-409)
Sanofi US Services Inc ....F 908 231-4000
Bridgewater (G-883)
Soligenix Inc................................F 609 538-8200
Princeton (G-9023)
Virid Biosciences Limited ....F 732 410-9573
Cherry Hill (G-1426)

LABORATORIES: Biotechnology

Advanced Biotech Overseas LLC ....G....... 973 339-6242
Totowa (G-10808)
Bezwada Biomedical LLC ....G....... 908 281-7529
Hillsborough (G-4305)
Biophore LLC ....G....... 609 275-3713
Plainsboro (G-8781)
Celldex Therapeutics Inc ....C....... 908 200-7500
Hampton (G-4149)
Cmic Cmo USA Corporation ....E....... 609 395-9700
Cranbury (G-1825)
Elusys Therapeutics Inc ....F 973 808-0222
Parsippany (G-7935)

Epicore Networks USA Inc ....E....... 609 267-9118
Mount Holly (G-6727)
Hydromer Inc...............................E....... 908 526-2828
Branchburg (G-646)
Imclone Systems LLC ....D....... 908 218-0147
Branchburg (G-647)
Interpace Dagnostics Group Inc.........E....... 412 224-6100
Parsippany (G-7965)
Leo Pharma Inc ....B....... 973 637-1690
Madison (G-5697)
Oli Systems Inc ....E....... 973 539-4996
Cedar Knolls (G-1313)
Pestka Biomedical Labs Inc..............E....... 732 777-9123
Piscataway (G-8699)
Ptc Therapeutics Inc ....E....... 908 222-7000
South Plainfield (G-10317)
SGS UStesting Company ....F 973 575-5252
Fairfield (G-3311)
SPS Alfachem Inc ....G....... 973 676-5141
Orange (G-7762)
Venarum Medical LLC.....................F 732 996-8513
Eatontown (G-2428)

LABORATORIES: Commercial Nonphysical Research

SGS UStesting Company ....F 973 575-5252
Fairfield (G-3311)

LABORATORIES: Dental Orthodontic Appliance Production

Em Orthodontic Labs Inc ....G....... 201 652-4411
Waldwick (G-11302)

LABORATORIES: Dental, Crown & Bridge Production

Samuel H Fields Dental Labs.............E....... 201 343-4626
Hackensack (G-3971)

LABORATORIES: Electronic Research

Bel Hybrids & Magnetics Inc.............F 201 432-0463
Jersey City (G-4701)
Doralex Inc..................................G....... 856 764-0694
Delran (G-2016)
Intertek Laboratories Inc ....E....... 908 903-1800
Stirling (G-10491)
Sensors Unlimited Inc ....D....... 609 333-8000
Princeton (G-9020)
Xybion Corporation ....C....... 973 538-2067
Lawrenceville (G-5248)

LABORATORIES: Environmental Research

Indoor Environmental Tech...............E....... 973 709-1122
Lincoln Park (G-5299)

LABORATORIES: Medical

DRG International Inc ....E....... 973 564-7555
Springfield (G-10439)
First National Servicing & Dev...........E....... 732 341-5409
Toms River (G-10758)
Radnet Inc...................................F 908 709-1323
Cranford (G-1924)

LABORATORIES: Medical Pathology

Oncode-Med Inc............................G....... 908 998-3647
Basking Ridge (G-194)

LABORATORIES: Noncommercial Research

Air Liquide Advanced Materials ....F 908 231-9060
Branchburg (G-612)
Engility LLC.................................F 703 633-8300
Princeton Junction (G-9055)
National Housing Institute ....G....... 973 509-1600
Montclair (G-6377)

LABORATORIES: Physical Research, Commercial

Admera Health LLC........................G....... 908 222-0533
South Plainfield (G-10208)
Alteon ....G....... 201 934-1624
Ramsey (G-9136)
Bayer Healthcare LLC.....................A....... 862 404-3000
Whippany (G-11878)

Bristol-Myers Squibb Company ....G....... 609 252-4875
Princeton (G-8919)
Bristol-Myers Squibb Company ....E....... 212 546-4000
Hillside (G-4383)
Centurum Information Tech Inc ....G....... 856 751-1111
Marlton (G-5924)
Collagen Matrix Inc ....D....... 201 405-1477
Oakland (G-7619)
Cyalume Specialty Products Inc ....E....... 732 469-7760
Bound Brook (G-601)
Datwyler Pharma Packaging ....G....... 856 663-2202
Pennsauken (G-8410)
Dengen Scientific Corporation ....E....... 201 687-2983
Union City (G-11110)
Elementis Specialties Inc ....C....... 609 443-2000
East Windsor (G-2369)
Evoqua Water Technologies LLC ....F 201 531-9338
East Rutherford (G-2287)
Hamamatsu Corporation ....E....... 908 231-0960
Middlesex (G-6119)
Heritage Pharma Labs Inc................C....... 732 238-7880
East Brunswick (G-2150)
High-Technology Corporation ....F 201 488-0010
Hackensack (G-3927)
J M M R Inc ....G....... 201 612-5104
Fair Lawn (G-3107)
Janssen Global Services LLC.............G....... 908 704-4000
Raritan (G-9211)
Janssen Research & Dev LLC ....A....... 908 704-4000
Raritan (G-9212)
LOreal Usa Inc ....D....... 732 499-6690
Clark (G-1506)
Pharmaseq Inc ....G....... 732 355-0100
Monmouth Junction (G-6301)
Scynexis Inc ....F 201 884-5485
Jersey City (G-4807)
Tamir Biotechnology Inc ....G....... 800 419-5061
Short Hills (G-9878)
Topifram Laboratories Inc................E....... 201 894-9020
Englewood Cliffs (G-2992)

LABORATORIES: Testing

Alcami New Jersey Corporation..........D....... 732 346-5100
Edison (G-2451)
Quest Diagnostics Incorporated ....A....... 973 520-2700
Secaucus (G-9801)
SGS UStesting Company ....F 973 575-5252
Fairfield (G-3311)

LABORATORIES: Testing

A M K Glass Inc ....G....... 856 692-1488
Vineland (G-11183)
Ballantine Laboratories Inc...............G....... 908 713-7742
Annandale (G-53)
C W Brabender Instrs Inc ....E....... 201 343-8425
South Hackensack (G-10151)
Coperion Corporation.....................C....... 201 327-6300
Sewell (G-9835)
Design of Tomorrow Inc ....F 973 227-1000
Fairfield (G-3185)
Enroute Computer Solutions Inc.........E....... 609 569-9255
Egg Harbor Township (G-2683)
Gibraltar Laboratories Inc ....E....... 973 227-6882
Fairfield (G-3214)
Reliability Maintenance Svcs.............G....... 732 922-8878
Ocean (G-7679)
Sk & P Industries Inc ....G....... 973 482-1864
Newark (G-7275)
Sk & P Industries Inc ....G....... 973 482-1864
Newark (G-7276)
Spex Certiprep Inc ....D....... 732 549-7144
Metuchen (G-6069)
Surface Technology Inc...................F 609 259-0099
Ewing (G-3068)

LABORATORY APPARATUS & FURNITURE

3d Biotek LLC ....G....... 908 801-6138
Bridgewater (G-781)
Abox Automation Corp....................G....... 973 659-9611
Pine Brook (G-8583)
Becton Dickinson and Company ....A....... 201 847-6800
Franklin Lakes (G-3616)
Bsi Corp ....E....... 631 589-1118
Nutley (G-7581)
C W Brabender Instrs Inc ....E....... 201 343-8425
South Hackensack (G-10151)
Diagenode Inc ....G....... 862 209-4680
Denville (G-2035)

Difco Laboratories Inc ....G 410 316-4113
   Franklin Lakes **(G-3619)**
Fluid Dynamics Inc ....G 908 200-5823
   Flemington **(G-3444)**
G & H Sheet Metal Works Inc ....G 973 923-1100
   Hillside **(G-4393)**
Glen Mills Inc ....F 973 777-0777
   Clifton **(G-1625)**
Handler Manufacturing Company ....E 908 233-7796
   Westfield **(G-11799)**
Hel Inc ....G 440 208-7360
   Lawrenceville **(G-5231)**
Lm Air Technology Inc ....E 732 381-8200
   Rahway **(G-9115)**
MSI Holdings LLC ....G 732 549-7144
   Metuchen **(G-6066)**
Triad Scientific Inc ....G 732 292-1994
   Manasquan **(G-5841)**
Waage Electric Inc ....G 908 245-9363
   Kenilworth **(G-4986)**

LABORATORY APPARATUS, EXC HEATING & MEASURING

Microdata Instrument Inc ....F 908 222-1717
   South Plainfield **(G-10300)**
Randcastle Extrusion Systems ....G 973 239-1150
   Cedar Grove **(G-1290)**

LABORATORY APPARATUS: Sample Preparation Apparatus

Delaware Technologies Inc ....F 856 234-7692
   Mount Laurel **(G-6753)**

LABORATORY APPARATUS: Shakers & Stirrers

Arrow Engineering Co Inc ....G 908 353-5229
   Hillside **(G-4376)**

LABORATORY CHEMICALS: Organic

Acceledev Chemical LLC ....G 732 274-1451
   Monmouth Junction **(G-6276)**
Bal-Edge Corporation ....G 973 895-8826
   Eatontown **(G-2379)**
Biotech Support Group LLC ....G 732 613-1967
   East Brunswick **(G-2130)**
Karebay Biochem Inc ....G 732 823-1545
   Monmouth Junction **(G-6295)**
Spectrum Laboratory Pdts Inc ....C 732 214-1300
   New Brunswick **(G-6971)**
Spectrum Laboratory Pdts Inc ....E 732 214-1300
   New Brunswick **(G-6972)**

LABORATORY EQPT, EXC MEDICAL: Wholesalers

National Labnet Co ....E 732 417-0700
   Iselin **(G-4618)**
Orlando Systems Ltd Lblty Co ....G 908 400-5052
   North Plainfield **(G-7507)**
Scimedx Corporation ....E 800 221-5598
   Dover **(G-2105)**
Tovatech LLC ....G 973 913-9734
   Maplewood **(G-5885)**
Triad Scientific Inc ....G 732 292-1994
   Manasquan **(G-5841)**

LABORATORY EQPT: Chemical

Scientifix LLC ....G 856 780-5871
   Mount Laurel **(G-6803)**
Servolift LLC ....E 973 442-7878
   Randolph **(G-9199)**
Spex Certiprep Inc ....D 732 549-7144
   Metuchen **(G-6069)**
Spex Certiprep Group LLC ....F 208 204-6656
   Metuchen **(G-6070)**
Spex Sample Prep LLC ....F 732 549-7144
   Metuchen **(G-6072)**
Spex Sample Prep LLC ....D 732 549-7144
   Metuchen **(G-6073)**
Sphere Fluidics Incorporated ....G 888 258-0226
   Monmouth Junction **(G-6313)**

LABORATORY EQPT: Clinical Instruments Exc Medical

Exodon LLC ....F 973 398-2900
   Mount Arlington **(G-6712)**
Specialty Pharmasource LLC ....F 973 784-4965
   Denville **(G-2059)**

LABORATORY EQPT: Incubators

Pacon Manufacturing Corp ....C 732 764-9070
   Somerset **(G-10051)**
S P Industries Inc ....D 215 672-7800
   Buena **(G-941)**

LABORATORY EQPT: Measuring

Dek Tron International Corp ....E 908 226-1777
   Plainfield **(G-8761)**
Ohaus Corporation ....D 973 377-9000
   Parsippany **(G-7980)**

LACE GOODS & WARP KNIT FABRIC DYEING & FINISHING

Keystone Dyeing and Finishing ....G 718 482-7780
   Dayton **(G-1975)**
Rebtex Inc ....C 908 722-3549
   Branchburg **(G-676)**

LAMINATED PLASTICS: Plate, Sheet, Rod & Tubes

Barnegat Light Fibrgls Sup LLC ....G 609 294-8870
   West Creek **(G-11684)**
C & K Plastics Inc ....D 732 549-0011
   Metuchen **(G-6049)**
Federal Plastics Corporation ....E 908 272-5800
   Cranford **(G-1910)**
Fedplast Inc ....F 732 901-1153
   Lakewood **(G-5098)**
Flex Products LLC ....D 201 440-1570
   Carlstadt **(G-1158)**
Fluorotherm Polymers Inc ....G 973 575-0760
   Parsippany **(G-7948)**
K Jabat Inc ....F 732 469-8177
   Green Brook **(G-3864)**
McGrory Glass Inc ....D 856 579-3200
   Paulsboro **(G-8335)**
Nan Ya Plastics Corp America ....F 973 992-1775
   Livingston **(G-5529)**
Owens Plastic Products Inc ....G 856 447-3500
   Cedarville **(G-1317)**
Plast-O-Matic Valves Inc ....D 973 256-3000
   Cedar Grove **(G-1287)**
Productive Plastics Inc ....D 856 778-4300
   Mount Laurel **(G-6796)**
Research & Mfg Corp Amer ....F 908 862-6744
   Linden **(G-5414)**
Royal Sovereign Intl Inc ....E 800 397-1025
   Rockleigh **(G-9521)**
Spiral Binding LLC ....C 973 256-0666
   Totowa **(G-10853)**
Wood & Laminates Inc ....G 973 773-7475
   Lodi **(G-5583)**

LAMINATING MATERIALS

Nu Grafix Inc ....E 201 413-1776
   Jersey City **(G-4775)**

LAMINATING SVCS

Creative Laminating Inc ....E 201 939-1999
   Carlstadt **(G-1147)**

LAMP & LIGHT BULBS & TUBES

Amati International LLC ....E 201 569-1000
   Englewood Cliffs **(G-2957)**
Ethan Allen Retail Inc ....G 973 473-1019
   Passaic **(G-8065)**
Hamamatsu Corporation ....E 908 526-0941
   Bridgewater **(G-829)**
Hamamatsu Corporation ....D 908 231-0960
   Bridgewater **(G-828)**
Maxlite Inc ....D 973 244-7300
   West Caldwell **(G-11663)**
Mks Inc ....E 856 451-5545
   Bridgeton **(G-765)**
Oxberry LLC ....G 201 935-3000
   Carlstadt **(G-1194)**

LAMP BULBS & TUBES, ELECTRIC: Filaments

Union City Filament Corp ....E 201 945-3366
   Ridgefield **(G-9294)**

LAMP BULBS & TUBES, ELECTRIC: For Specialized Applications

Bitro Group Inc ....E 201 641-1004
   Hackensack **(G-3886)**
Metal Textiles Corporation ....E 800 843-1215
   Edison **(G-2564)**

LAMP BULBS & TUBES, ELECTRIC: Parts

Oxford Lamp Inc ....F 732 462-3755
   Freehold **(G-3686)**

LAMP BULBS & TUBES/PARTS, ELECTRIC: Generalized Applications

Precision Filaments Inc ....G 732 462-3755
   Freehold **(G-3690)**
Rhingo Pro LLC ....G 201 728-9099
   Lodi **(G-5574)**

LAMP STORES

Jay-Bee Lamp & Shade Co Inc ....G 201 265-0762
   Paramus **(G-7809)**

LAMPS: Boudoir, Residential

Efficient Lighting Inc ....F 973 846-8568
   Parsippany **(G-7933)**

LAMPS: Incandescent, Filament

Lumitron Corp ....F 908 508-9100
   Berkeley Heights **(G-407)**
Natal Lamp & Shade Corp ....E 201 224-7844
   Fort Lee **(G-3578)**

LAMPS: Ultraviolet

Hanovia Specialty Lighting LLC ....F 973 651-5510
   Fairfield **(G-3221)**
Hid Ultraviolet LLC ....F 973 383-8535
   Sparta **(G-10392)**
Horiba Instruments Inc ....E 732 623-8335
   Piscataway **(G-8674)**

LAMPS: Wall, Residential

Genie House Corp ....E 609 859-0600
   Southampton **(G-10363)**

LANDING MATS: Aircraft, Metal

Helidex LLC ....G 201 636-2546
   East Rutherford **(G-2291)**

LANGUAGE SCHOOLS

Berlitz Languages US Inc ....D 609 759-5371
   Princeton **(G-8914)**

LAPIDARY WORK & DIAMOND CUTTING & POLISHING

J Michaels Jewelers Inc ....G 908 771-9800
   Berkeley Heights **(G-403)**

LAPIDARY WORK: Contract Or Other

Smb International LLC ....G 732 222-4888
   West Long Branch **(G-11722)**

LAPIDARY WORK: Jewel Cut, Drill, Polish, Recut/Setting

Corbo Jewelers Inc ....F 973 777-1635
   Clifton **(G-1591)**
Good As Gold Jewelers Inc ....G 732 286-1111
   Toms River **(G-10762)**

LARD: From Slaughtering Plants

Buckhead Meat Company ....C 732 661-4900
   Edison **(G-2471)**

PRODUCT

LASER SYSTEMS & EQPT

Candela Corporation ....F 908 753-6300
  South Plainfield (G-10234)

Cleary Machinery Co Inc ....G...... 732 560-3200
  South Bound Brook (G-10143)

Fastpulse Technology Inc ....F 973 478-5757
  Saddle Brook (G-9652)

Gsi ....G...... 908 608-1325
  Summit (G-10533)

Haas Laser Technologies Inc ....F 973 598-1150
  Flanders (G-3412)

Inrad Optics Inc ....D... 201 767-1910
  Northvale (G-7529)

Laser Contractors LLC ....G...... 609 517-2407
  Medford (G-6028)

Metrologic Instruments Inc ....C...... 856 228-8100
  Mount Laurel (G-6782)

O S I Inc ....F 732 754-6271
  Metuchen (G-6067)

PRC Laser Corporation ....E 973 347-0100
  Mount Arlington (G-6718)

Princeton Lightwave Inc ....E 609 495-2600
  Cranbury (G-1875)

Starlight Electro-Optics Inc ....G...... 908 859-1362
  Phillipsburg (G-8575)

Tiger Supplies Inc ....G...... 973 854-8635
  Irvington (G-4588)

U S Laser Corp ....E 201 848-9200
  Hillsdale (G-4371)

LASERS: Welding, Drilling & Cutting Eqpt

Ironbound Metal ....G...... 973 242-5704
  Newark (G-7161)

LAUNDRIES, EXC POWER & COIN-OPERATED

Fine Wear U S A ....G...... 201 313-3777
  Fort Lee (G-3558)

LAUNDRY & DRYCLEANING SVCS, EXC COIN-OPERATED: Pickup

Clean-Tex Services Inc ....E 908 912-2700
  Linden (G-5334)

LAUNDRY & GARMENT SVCS, NEC: Hand Laundries

One Click Cleaners ....G...... 732 804-9802
  Manalapan (G-5821)

LAUNDRY & GARMENT SVCS: Tailor Shop, Exc Custom/Merchant

Forsters Cleaning & Tailoring ....G....... 201 659-4411
  Jersey City (G-4740)

LAUNDRY EQPT: Commercial

One Click Cleaners ....G...... 732 804-9802
  Manalapan (G-5821)

Utax USA Inc ....G...... 201 433-1200
  Jersey City (G-4825)

LAUNDRY SVCS: Indl

A-1 Tablecloth Co Inc ....C...... 201 727-4364
  South Hackensack (G-10145)

LAWN & GARDEN EQPT

Creative Products Inc ....D....... 732 614-9035
  Long Branch (G-5596)

Lawn Medic Inc ....G 856 742-1111
  Westville (G-11818)

McQuade Enterprises LLC ....G...... 609 501-2437
  Millville (G-6260)

W W Manufacturing Co Inc ....F 856 451-5700
  Bridgeton (G-777)

LAWN MOWER REPAIR SHOP

Chatham Lawn Mowler ....G...... 973 635-8855
  Chatham (G-1320)

Robert Colaneri ....G...... 201 939-4405
  East Rutherford (G-2314)

LEAD

Alpha Assembly Solutions Inc ....E 908 561-5170
  South Plainfield (G-10214)

Alpha Assembly Solutions Inc ....E 908 791-3000
  Somerset (G-9948)

LEAD PENCILS & ART GOODS

Congruent Machine Co Inc ....G...... 973 764-6767
  Vernon (G-11158)

Excel Hobby Blades Corp ....E 973 278-4000
  Paterson (G-8187)

LEAD-IN WIRES: Electric Lamp

Seminole Wire & Cable Co Inc ....F 856 324-2929
  Pennsauken (G-8483)

LEASING & RENTAL SVCS: Earth Moving Eqpt

Gamka Sales Co Inc ....E 732 248-1400
  Edison (G-2518)

LEASING & RENTAL: Construction & Mining Eqpt

Harsco Corporation ....E 856 779-7795
  Cherry Hill (G-1371)

Winslow Rental & Supply Inc ....G...... 856 767-5554
  Berlin (G-434)

Xylem Dewatering Solutions Inc ....C...... 856 467-3636
  Bridgeport (G-748)

LEASING & RENTAL: Medical Machinery & Eqpt

Enertia LLC ....G...... 856 330-4767
  Pennsauken (G-8418)

Technidyne Corporation ....G...... 732 363-1055
  Toms River (G-10799)

Tgz Acquisition Company LLC ....F 856 669-6600
  Cinnaminson (G-1489)

LEASING & RENTAL: Other Real Estate Property

Grignard Company LLC ....E 732 340-1111
  Rahway (G-9098)

LEASING & RENTAL: Trucks, Without Drivers

Brunswick Hot Mix Corp ....D...... 908 233-4444
  Westfield (G-11795)

Cubalas Emergency Lighting LLC ....G...... 908 514-0505
  Roselle (G-9555)

Fleetsource LLC ....E 732 566-4970
  Dayton (G-1961)

Penske Truck Leasing Co LP ....E 973 575-0169
  Parsippany (G-7987)

LEASING: Passenger Car

Freehold Pntiac Bick GMC Trcks ....D...... 732 462-7093
  Freehold (G-3666)

Holman Enterprises Inc ....E 609 383-6100
  Mount Laurel (G-6765)

Town Ford Inc ....D...... 609 298-4990
  Bordentown (G-597)

Volvo Car North America LLC ....B 201 768-7300
  Rockleigh (G-9524)

LEATHER & CANVAS GOODS: Leggings Or Chaps, NEC

G S Babu & Co ....F 732 939-5190
  Plainsboro (G-8787)

LEATHER GOODS: Belt Laces

McM Products USA Inc ....F 646 756-4090
  Secaucus (G-9792)

LEATHER GOODS: Card Cases

Tumi Holdings Inc ....D...... 908 756-4400
  Edison (G-2635)

LEATHER GOODS: Cases

Billykirk ....F 201 222-9092
  Jersey City (G-4703)

LEATHER GOODS: Cosmetic Bags

Allegro Mfg ....F 323 724-0101
  Hightstown (G-4293)

Jaclyn Holdings Parent LLC ....G...... 201 909-6000
  Maywood (G-6007)

LEATHER GOODS: Garments

Billykirk ....F 201 222-9092
  Jersey City (G-4703)

Bucati Leather Inc ....G...... 732 254-0480
  South River (G-10349)

North American Frontier Corp ....E 201 222-1931
  Jersey City (G-4773)

LEATHER GOODS: Personal

G-III Leather Fashions Inc ....D...... 212 403-0500
  Dayton (G-1966)

Maxsyl Leather Co LLC ....D...... 201 864-0579
  Union City (G-11121)

R Neumann & Co ....F 201 659-3400
  Hoboken (G-4476)

LEATHER GOODS: Safety Belts

Safe-Strap Company Inc ....E 973 442-4623
  Wharton (G-11870)

LEATHER GOODS: Wallets

Always Be Secure LLC ....G...... 917 887-2286
  Manalapan (G-5801)

M London Inc ....E 201 459-6460
  Jersey City (G-4762)

LEATHER TANNING & FINISHING

Dani Leather USA Inc ....G...... 973 598-0890
  Flanders (G-3404)

LEATHER, LEATHER GOODS & FURS, WHOLESALE

Bucati Leather Inc ....G...... 732 254-0480
  South River (G-10349)

Leather Works NJ Ltd Lblty Co ....G...... 732 452-1100
  Edison (G-2549)

Ledonne Leather Co Inc ....F 201 531-2100
  Lyndhurst (G-5657)

LEATHER: Accessory Prdts

Cejon Inc ....E 201 437-8780
  Bayonne (G-208)

Disys Commerce Inc ....G...... 201 567-0457
  Englewood (G-2898)

LEATHER: Bag

Jaclyn Holdings Parent LLC ....G...... 201 909-6000
  Maywood (G-6007)

LEATHER: Handbag

Buonaventura Bag and Cases LLC ....G...... 212 960-3442
  Clifton (G-1579)

LEATHER: Mechanical

Coast To Coast Lea & Vinyl Inc ....G...... 732 525-8877
  Sayreville (G-9706)

LEATHER: Processed

Maxsyl Leather Co LLC ....D...... 201 864-0579
  Union City (G-11121)

LEGAL & TAX SVCS

Max Pro Services LLC ....G...... 973 396-2373
  Livingston (G-5523)

LEGAL OFFICES & SVCS

Gann Law Books Inc ....F 973 268-1200
  Newark (G-7131)

Thomson Reuters Corporation ....F 973 662-3070
  Nutley (G-7595)

LEGAL SVCS: General Practice Attorney or Lawyer

Jose Moreira .... G 201 991-9001
Kearny (G-4873)

LEGAL SVCS: Malpractice & Negligence Law

Madhu B Goyal MD .... G 908 769-0307
South Plainfield (G-10296)

LENS COATING: Ophthalmic

Sensor Medical Technology LLC .... G 425 358-7381
Denville (G-2057)

LETTER WRITING SVCS

Johnston Letter Co Inc .... G 973 482-7535
Flanders (G-3414)

LIFE INSURANCE: Fraternal Organizations

Ukrainian National Association .... E 973 292-9800
Parsippany (G-8032)

LIGHTER FLUID

Nova Distributors LLC .... F 908 222-1010
Edison (G-2580)
Rclc Inc .... F 732 877-1788
Woodbridge (G-12020)

LIGHTING EQPT: Flashlights

Gogreen Power Inc .... F 732 994-5901
Howell (G-4540)
Princeton Tectonics .... C 609 298-9331
Pennsauken (G-8472)

LIGHTING EQPT: Floodlights

Natale Machine & Tool Co Inc .... F 201 933-5500
Carlstadt (G-1189)

LIGHTING EQPT: Motor Vehicle, Flasher Lights

Amperite Co Inc .... E 201 864-9503
North Bergen (G-7384)
Elite Emrgncy Lights Ltd Lblty .... F 732 534-2377
Lakewood (G-5090)

LIGHTING EQPT: Motor Vehicle, NEC

Spaghetti Engineering Corp .... F 856 719-9989
West Berlin (G-11623)

LIGHTING EQPT: Outdoor

Archlit Inc .... G 973 577-4400
Hopatcong (G-4518)
Garden State Irrigation .... F 201 848-1300
Wyckoff (G-12112)
Princeton Tectonics .... E 609 298-9331
West Berlin (G-11616)
Rab Lighting Inc .... C 201 784-8600
Northvale (G-7544)
Wisely Products LLC .... G 929 329-9188
Jersey City (G-4833)

LIGHTING EQPT: Spotlights

In The Spotlights .... G 973 361-7768
Rockaway (G-9466)

LIGHTING FIXTURES WHOLESALERS

Articulight Inc .... G 201 796-2690
Fair Lawn (G-3085)
Cuny and Guerber Inc .... E 201 617-5800
Union City (G-11109)
Efficient Lighting Inc .... F 973 846-8568
Parsippany (G-7933)
Gemini Cut Glass Company Inc .... G 201 568-7722
Englewood (G-2909)
I-Light Usa Inc .... G 908 317-0020
Mountainside (G-6847)
Robert Wallace .... G 609 649-0596
Stockton (G-10502)

LIGHTING FIXTURES, NEC

A P M Hexseal Corporation .... E 201 569-5700
Englewood (G-2872)

Amperite Co Inc .... E 201 864-9503
North Bergen (G-7384)
Carpenter LLC .... F 609 689-3090
Trenton (G-10911)
City Theatrical Inc .... E 201 549-1160
Carlstadt (G-1143)
Cubalas Emergency Lighting LLC .... G 908 514-0505
Roselle (G-9555)
Eco Lighting USA Ltd Lblty Co .... G 201 621-5661
South Hackensack (G-10156)
Erco Lighting Inc .... F 732 225-8856
Edison (G-2506)
Galaxy Led Inc .... G 201 541-5461
Englewood Cliffs (G-2972)
High Energy Group Ltd Lblty Co .... G 732 741-9099
Eatontown (G-2397)
I-Light Usa Inc .... E 908 317-0020
Mountainside (G-6847)
Innovtive Phtnics Slution Corp .... G 732 355-9300
Monmouth Junction (G-6294)
John G Papailias Co Inc .... G 201 767-4027
Northvale (G-7532)
Lightfox Inc .... E 973 209-9112
Morristown (G-6679)
Michele Maddalena .... G 973 244-0033
Fairfield (G-3270)
Musco Sports Lighting LLC .... G 732 751-9114
Wall Township (G-11357)
Proactive Ltg Solutions LLC .... F 800 747-1209
North Arlington (G-7377)
Tektite Industries Inc .... G 609 656-0600
Trenton (G-10997)
Unilux Inc .... E 201 712-1266
Saddle Brook (G-9685)
Zago Manufacturing Company .... G 973 643-6700
Newark (G-7318)

LIGHTING FIXTURES: Arc

Maxlite Inc .... F 800 555-5629
West Caldwell (G-11662)

LIGHTING FIXTURES: Decorative Area

Encore Led Ltg Ltd Lblty Co .... G 866 694-4533
Wayne (G-11497)
Trinity Manufacturing LLC .... C 732 549-2866
Metuchen (G-6079)

LIGHTING FIXTURES: Fluorescent, Commercial

Coronet Inc .... C 973 345-7660
Totowa (G-10824)
R B B Corp .... E 973 770-1100
Ledgewood (G-5279)

LIGHTING FIXTURES: Indl & Commercial

Absolume LLC .... G 732 523-1231
Lakewood (G-5043)
Amati International LLC .... E 201 569-1000
Englewood Cliffs (G-2957)
American Brass and Crystal Inc .... E 908 688-8611
Union (G-11023)
American Scientific Ltg Corp .... E 718 369-1100
Trenton (G-10892)
Amerlux LLC .... C 973 882-5010
Oakland (G-7614)
Apelio Innovative Inds LLC .... F 973 777-8899
Kearny (G-4844)
Belfer .... G 732 493-2666
Farmingdale (G-3378)
Compact Fluorescent Systems .... G 908 475-8991
Sparta (G-10383)
Cooper Lighting LLC .... G 609 395-4277
Cranbury (G-1828)
Durabrite Ltg Solutions LLC .... G 201 915-0555
Jersey City (G-4729)
Encore Led Ltg Ltd Lblty Co .... G 866 694-4533
Wayne (G-11497)
Former Circuit Inc .... G 732 549-0056
Edison (G-2513)
Genesis Lighting Mfg Inc .... G 908 352-6720
Elizabethport (G-2788)
Lighting World Inc .... E 732 919-1224
Farmingdale (G-3387)
M + 4 Inc .... G 973 527-3262
Budd Lake (G-927)
Mercury Lighting Pdts Co Inc .... C 973 244-9444
Fairfield (G-3269)

Mks Inc .... E 856 451-5545
Bridgeton (G-765)
North American Illumination .... F 973 478-4700
Garfield (G-3751)
Picasso Lighting Inds LLC .... E 201 246-8188
Kearny (G-4893)
Prg Group Inc .... G 201 758-4000
Secaucus (G-9798)
Rab Lighting Inc .... C 201 784-8600
Northvale (G-7544)
Rambusch Decorating Company .... E 201 333-2525
Jersey City (G-4797)
Reggiani Lighting Usa Inc .... F 201 372-1717
Carlstadt (G-1210)
Robert Wallace .... G 609 649-0596
Stockton (G-10502)
Signify North America Corp .... F 732 563-3000
Somerset (G-10072)
SMS Building Systems Ltd Lblty .... F 856 520-8769
Cherry Hill (G-1415)
Specialty Lighting Inds Inc .... G 732 517-0800
Ocean (G-7684)
Starfire Lighting Inc .... E 201 438-9540
Wood Ridge (G-12006)
Superior Lighting Inc .... G 908 759-0199
Elizabeth (G-2779)
Tektite Industries Inc .... G 609 656-0600
Trenton (G-10997)
Trinity Manufacturing LLC .... C 732 549-2866
Metuchen (G-6079)
Vision Lighting Inc .... G 973 720-1200
Paterson (G-8323)

LIGHTING FIXTURES: Motor Vehicle

Sun Display Systems LLC .... E 973 226-4334
Fairfield (G-3320)
Vehicle Safety Mfg LLC .... E 973 643-3000
Newark (G-7311)

LIGHTING FIXTURES: Ornamental, Commercial

Articulight Inc .... G 201 796-2690
Fair Lawn (G-3085)
Eluxnet USA Corporation .... G 201 724-5986
Riverdale (G-9376)

LIGHTING FIXTURES: Public

ABB Lighting Inc .... G 866 222-8866
Toms River (G-10737)

LIGHTING FIXTURES: Residential

Amati International LLC .... E 201 569-1000
Englewood Cliffs (G-2957)
American Brass and Crystal Inc .... E 908 688-8611
Union (G-11023)
Apelio Innovative Inds LLC .... F 973 777-8899
Kearny (G-4844)
Big Eye Lamp Inc .... G 732 557-9400
Whiting (G-11937)
Cooper Lighting LLC .... D 609 395-4277
Cranbury (G-1828)
Cutting Edge Casting Inc .... E 908 925-7500
Linden (G-5340)
Estrin Calabrese Sales Agency .... G 908 722-9980
Manville (G-5855)
Galaxy Switchgear Inds LLC .... E 914 668-8200
Kearny (G-4858)
Generation Brands .... G 856 764-0500
Burlington (G-972)
Go R Design LLC .... E 609 286-2146
New Egypt (G-6983)
Graybar Electric Company Inc .... D 973 404-5555
Edison (G-2522)
High Energy Group Ltd Lblty Co .... G 732 741-9099
Eatontown (G-2397)
Infinlight Products Inc .... G 888 665-7708
East Windsor (G-2353)
Kurt Versen Inc .... F 201 664-5283
Montvale (G-6418)
Lighting World Inc .... E 732 919-1224
Farmingdale (G-3387)
M + 4 Inc .... G 973 527-3262
Budd Lake (G-927)
R B B Corp .... E 973 770-1100
Ledgewood (G-5279)
Robert Wallace .... G 609 649-0596
Stockton (G-10502)

PRODUCT

Starfire Lighting Inc ....E 201 438-9540
　Wood Ridge (G-12006)
Superior Lighting Inc ....F 908 759-0199
　Elizabeth (G-2779)
T C S Technologies Inc ....F 908 852-7555
　Hackettstown (G-4038)
William Spencer ....G 856 235-1830
　Mount Laurel (G-6813)

LIGHTING FIXTURES: Street

City of Jersey City ....F 201 547-4470
　Jersey City (G-4713)

LIGHTING FIXTURES: Swimming Pool

Izzo Enterprises Inc ....E 908 845-8200
　Scotch Plains (G-9735)
Smartpool LLC ....E 732 730-9880
　Lakewood (G-5164)

LIGHTING FIXTURES: Underwater

Pioneer & Co Inc ....E 856 866-9191
　Moorestown (G-6557)

LIGHTING MAINTENANCE SVC

Forman Industries Inc ....D 732 727-8100
　Old Bridge (G-7715)

LIME

Lime Energy Co ....G 908 415-9469
　South Plainfield (G-10294)
Lime Energy Co ....G 732 791-5380
　Newark (G-7180)
Luxfer Magtech Inc ....E 803 610-9898
　Manchester (G-5846)
Smith Lime Flour Co Inc ....F 973 344-1700
　Kearny (G-4898)

LIMESTONE: Crushed & Broken

Legacy Vulcan LLC ....E 973 253-8828
　Clifton (G-1656)
Limecrest Quarry Developer LLC ...F 973 383-7100
　Lafayette (G-5030)

LINEN SPLY SVC: Non-Clothing

Hozric LLC ....G 908 420-8821
　Green Brook (G-3861)

LINENS & TOWELS WHOLESALERS

American Dawn Inc ....G 856 467-9211
　Bridgeport (G-734)
Anchor Sales & Marketing Inc ......F 973 545-2277
　West Milford (G-11725)
Living Fashions Llc ....F 732 626-5200
　Sayreville (G-9716)
Professional Laundry Solutions ......G 973 392-0837
　Newark (G-7238)

LINENS: Napkins, Fabric & Nonwoven, From Purchased Materials

Linen For Tables ....G 973 345-8472
　Paterson (G-8242)

LINENS: Tablecloths, From Purchased Materials

Jewm Inc ....E 973 942-1555
　Paterson (G-8222)
R L Plastics Inc ....G 732 340-1100
　Avenel (G-144)

LINER STRIPS: Rubber

Rema Tip Top/North America Inc ...E 201 768-8100
　Northvale (G-7546)

LINERS & COVERS: Fabric

Kerry Wilkens Inc ....G 732 787-0070
　Belford (G-283)
Polyair Inter Pack Inc ....D 201 804-1700
　Carlstadt (G-1204)

LINERS & LINING

Brennan Penrod Contractors LLC ...F 856 933-1100
　Bellmawr (G-329)

Jaeger Thomas & Melissa DDS ......F 908 735-2722
　Lebanon (G-5266)
Linden Well Drilling ....E 908 862-6633
　Linden (G-5376)

LIQUEFIED PETROLEUM GAS DEALERS

American Compressed Gases Inc ...E 201 767-3200
　Old Tappan (G-7732)

LIQUID CRYSTAL DISPLAYS

Dialight Corporation ....D 732 751-5809
　Wall Township (G-11334)
Excel Display Corp ....G 732 246-3724
　New Brunswick (G-6925)

LITHOGRAPHIC PLATES

AGFA Corporation ....G 908 231-5000
　Somerville (G-10102)

LOCKS

Tiburon Lockers Inc ....G 201 750-4960
　Rockleigh (G-9523)

LOCKS: Safe & Vault, Metal

Hookway Enterprises Inc ....F 973 691-0382
　Netcong (G-6907)
Lacka Safe Corp ....F 201 896-9200
　Carlstadt (G-1180)

LOGGING

Bamboo & Rattan Works Inc ....G 732 255-4239
　Toms River (G-10746)
Green Land & Logging LLC ....G 908 894-2361
　Stockton (G-10501)
Kane Wood Fuel ....G 856 589-3292
　Pitman (G-8746)

LOGGING CAMPS & CONTRACTORS

Mountain Top Logging LLC ....G 908 413-2982
　Lebanon (G-5272)

LOOSELEAF BINDERS

Ebsco Industries Inc ....F 201 933-1800
　Rutherford (G-9619)
Flortek Corporation ....E 201 436-7700
　Bayonne (G-216)
Johnthan Leasing Corp ....E 908 226-3434
　Asbury (G-66)

LOOSELEAF BINDERS: Library

Reed Presentations Inc ....F 908 832-0007
　Asbury (G-69)

LOTIONS OR CREAMS: Face

3lab Inc ....F 201 227-4742
　Englewood (G-2871)
Alkaline Corporation ....G 732 531-7830
　Eatontown (G-2375)
Americare Laboratories Ltd ....E 973 279-5100
　Paterson (G-8138)
Jersey Shore Cosmetics LLC ....F 908 500-9954
　Flemington (G-3451)
Millennium Research LLC ....G 908 867-7646
　Long Valley (G-5612)
R&R Cosmetics LLC ....G 732 340-1000
　Rahway (G-9123)
Vsar Resources LLC ....F 973 233-6000
　Monroe Township (G-6350)

LOUDSPEAKERS

GP Acoustics (us) Inc ....E 732 683-2356
　Marlboro (G-5899)

LUBRICATING EQPT: Indl

Devco Corporation ....G 201 337-1600
　Basking Ridge (G-181)
T M Industries Inc ....G 908 730-7674
　Belvidere (G-367)

LUBRICATION SYSTEMS & EQPT

Amerilubes LLC ....G 704 399-7701
　Waretown (G-11392)

Intech Powercore Corporation ......G 201 767-8066
　Closter (G-1758)

LUGGAGE & BRIEFCASES

Atco Products Inc ....E 973 379-3171
　Springfield (G-10428)
Case Princeton Co Inc ....E 908 687-1750
　Mountainside (G-6836)
Iacobucci USA Inc ....G 732 935-6633
　Eatontown (G-2401)
Lbu Inc ....E 973 773-4800
　Paterson (G-8238)
Ledonne Leather Co Inc ....F 201 531-2100
　Lyndhurst (G-5657)
Naluco Inc ....D 800 601-8198
　Clifton (G-1672)
Quiet Tone Inc ....G 732 431-2826
　Freehold (G-3696)
Transglobe Usa Inc ....G 973 465-1998
　Carlstadt (G-1231)
Wisdom USA Inc ....F 201 933-1998
　Carlstadt (G-1240)

LUGGAGE & LEATHER GOODS STORES

Tumi Holdings Inc ....D 908 756-4400
　Edison (G-2635)
Venture Stationers Inc ....E 212 288-7235
　Closter (G-1763)

LUGGAGE WHOLESALERS

Naluco Inc ....D 800 601-8198
　Clifton (G-1672)
Wisdom USA Inc ....F 201 933-1998
　Carlstadt (G-1240)

LUGGAGE: Traveling Bags

Mirage Wholesale Group LLC ....G 718 757-6590
　Elizabeth (G-2759)
Tumi Holdings Inc ....D 908 756-4400
　Edison (G-2635)

LUMBER & BLDG MATLS DEALER, RET: Garage Doors, Sell/Install

Door Center Enterprises Inc ....G 609 333-1233
　Hopewell (G-4526)
Lebanon Door LLC ....G 908 236-2620
　Lebanon (G-5269)

LUMBER & BLDG MATRLS DEALERS, RET: Bath Fixtures, Eqpt/Sply

Tatara Group Inc ....G 732 231-6031
　Avenel (G-149)
Toilettree Products Inc ....G 845 358-5316
　Ramsey (G-9157)

LUMBER & BLDG MTRLS DEALERS, RET: Doors, Storm, Wood/Metal

Urban Millwork & Supply Corp ....G 973 278-7072
　Paterson (G-8321)

LUMBER & BLDG MTRLS DEALERS, RET: Planing Mill Prdts/Lumber

Medford Cedar Products Inc ....G 609 859-1400
　Southampton (G-10369)

LUMBER & BUILDING MATERIALS DEALER, RET: Door & Window Prdts

Artistic Glass & Doors Inc ....G 856 768-1414
　West Berlin (G-11577)
Frank & Jims Inc ....G 609 646-1655
　Pleasantville (G-8811)
Jersey Steel Door Inc ....G 973 482-4020
　Newark (G-7169)
Lux Home Inc ....G 845 623-2821
　Paramus (G-7817)
USA Wood Door Inc ....E 856 384-9663
　West Deptford (G-11717)
Window Factory Inc ....E 856 546-5050
　Mount Ephraim (G-6722)
Window Plus Home Improvement ...F 973 591-9993
　Passaic (G-8117)

(G-0000) Company's Geographic Section entry number

LUMBER & BUILDING MATERIALS DEALER, RET: Masonry Matls/Splys

Efco Corp ....F 732 308-1010
Marlboro (G-5896)
J B & Sons Concrete Products ....F 856 767-4140
Berlin (G-423)

LUMBER & BUILDING MATERIALS DEALERS, RET: Solar Heating Eqpt

Mc Renewable Energy LLC ....F 732 369-9933
Manasquan (G-5833)
Sun Pacific Power Corp ....F 888 845-0242
Manalapan (G-5826)

LUMBER & BUILDING MATERIALS DEALERS, RETAIL: Countertops

Solidsurface Designs Inc ....E 856 910-7720
Pennsauken (G-8487)

LUMBER & BUILDING MATERIALS DEALERS, RETAIL: Paving Stones

Robert Young & Sons Inc ....G 973 483-0451
Newark (G-7252)

LUMBER & BUILDING MATERIALS DEALERS, RETAIL: Tile, Ceramic

Akw Inc ....G 732 530-9186
Shrewsbury (G-9880)
Best Value Rugs & Carpets Inc ....G 732 752-3528
Dunellen (G-2120)
Gran All Mrble Tile Imprts Inc ....G 856 354-4747
Cherry Hill (G-1369)
Maranatha Ceramic Tile & Marbl ....E 609 758-1168
Wrightstown (G-12099)

LUMBER & BUILDING MATERIALS RET DEALERS: Millwork & Lumber

Bossen Architectural Millwork ....F 856 786-1100
Cinnaminson (G-1444)
Cwi Architectural Millwork LLC ....G 856 307-7900
Glassboro (G-3808)
Kempton Wood Products ....G 732 449-8673
Wall Township (G-11352)
Kuiken Brothers Company ....E 201 796-2082
Fair Lawn (G-3109)
New Jersey Hardwoods Inc ....E 908 754-0990
Plainfield (G-8773)
Vanco Millwork Inc ....F 973 992-3061
Livingston (G-5545)
Wohners ....G 201 568-7307
Englewood (G-2954)
Wood Works ....G 856 728-4520
Williamstown (G-11987)
Woodhaven Lumber & Millwork ....C 732 901-0030
Lakewood (G-5182)
Woodtec Inc ....G 908 979-0180
Hackettstown (G-4041)

LUMBER & BUILDING MATLS DEALERS, RET: Concrete/Cinder Block

Clayton Block Company Inc ....E 732 549-1234
Edison (G-2478)
Clayton Block Company Inc ....G 732 681-0186
Wall Township (G-11326)

LUMBER: Hardwood Dimension & Flooring Mills

Gwynn-E Co ....G 215 423-6400
Moorestown (G-6525)

LUMBER: Plywood, Hardwood

Woodhut LLC ....F 732 414-6440
Freehold (G-3706)

LUMBER: Plywood, Prefinished, Hardwood

Essex Coatings LLC ....F 732 855-9400
Avenel (G-126)
Rhoads OHara Architectural ....G 856 692-4100
Vineland (G-11258)

LUMBER: Rails, Fence, Round Or Split

New Jersey Fence & Guardrail ....F 973 786-5400
Andover (G-50)
Railing Dynamics Inc ....F 609 593-5400
Millville (G-6267)

LUMBER: Siding, Dressed

John H Abbott Inc ....G 609 561-0303
Egg Harbor City (G-2662)

LUMBER: Veneer, Hardwood

Mannington Mills Inc ....A 856 935-3000
Salem (G-9694)

MACHINE PARTS: Stamped Or Pressed Metal

Cincinnati Thermal Spray Inc ....E 973 379-0003
Springfield (G-10435)
Eclipse Manufacturing LLC ....G 973 340-9939
Garfield (G-3741)
Elray Manufacturing Company ....E 856 881-1935
Glassboro (G-3810)
Extruders International Inc ....G 908 241-7750
Roselle Park (G-9584)
Hafco Foundry & Machine Co ....F 201 447-0433
Midland Park (G-6176)
Infor Metal & Tooling Mfg ....F 973 571-9520
Cedar Grove (G-1279)
Joy-Rei Enterprises Inc ....G 732 727-0742
Parlin (G-7867)
K H Machine Works ....G 201 867-2338
North Bergen (G-7412)
LMC Precision Inc ....F 973 522-0005
Newark (G-7183)
Manutech Inc ....G 856 358-6136
Elmer (G-2800)
Mechanical Components Corp ....G 732 938-3737
Toms River (G-10778)
Medlaurel Inc ....E 856 461-6600
Delanco (G-2006)
Metal Cutting Corporation ....D 973 239-1100
Cedar Grove (G-1282)
Philip Creter Inc ....G 908 686-2910
Union (G-11083)
Quality Swiss Screw Machine Co ....G 908 289-4334
Elizabeth (G-2772)
Sandik Manufacturing Inc ....G 973 779-0707
Passaic (G-8104)
TMU Inc ....F 609 884-7656
Cape May (G-1103)
V H Exacta Corp ....G 856 235-7379
Moorestown (G-6574)

MACHINE SHOPS

Atlantic Casting & Engineering ....C 973 779-2450
Clifton (G-1566)
Brenner Metal Products ....E 973 778-2466
Wallington (G-11383)
Brusso Hardware LLC ....F 212 337-8510
Belleville (G-292)
Concept Group LLC ....E 856 767-5506
West Berlin (G-11586)
Hydratight Operations Inc ....F 732 271-4100
Somerset (G-10003)
Jamco Machine Products ....G 856 461-2664
Riverside (G-9397)
Jsm Co ....G 732 695-9577
Tinton Falls (G-10720)
Kavon Filter Products Co ....F 732 938-3135
Wall Township (G-11351)
M4 Machine LLC ....G 718 928-9695
Livingston (G-5522)
National Precision Tool Co ....E 973 227-5005
Fairfield (G-3275)
Philip Creter Inc ....G 908 686-2910
Union (G-11083)
Steel Mountain Fabricators LLC ....F 908 862-2800
Linden (G-5431)
Steel Mountain Fabricators LLC ....G 201 741-3019
North Bergen (G-7438)
Triangle Manufacturing Co Inc ....D 201 825-1212
Upper Saddle River (G-11148)
Woods Industrial LLC ....F 973 208-0664
West Milford (G-11734)

MACHINE TOOL ACCESS: Cutting

Advanced Cutting Services LLC ....G 908 241-5332
Roselle (G-9546)

Alloy Cast Products Inc ....F 908 245-2255
Kenilworth (G-4920)
B & S Tool and Cutter Service ....G 201 488-3545
Hackensack (G-3880)
B B Supply Corp ....F 201 313-9021
Cliffside Park (G-1536)
Dessau International ....E 201 791-2005
Fair Lawn (G-3096)
E P Heller Company ....E 973 377-2878
Madison (G-5691)
Grobet File Company Amer LLC ....D 201 939-6700
Carlstadt (G-1161)
Kennametal Inc ....C 412 248-8200
Jersey City (G-4753)
Niko Trade Ltd-USA Inc ....G 973 575-4353
Fairfield (G-3280)
Sine Tru Tool Company Inc ....G 732 591-1100
Marlboro (G-5915)
Tool Shop Inc ....G 856 767-8077
West Berlin (G-11630)

MACHINE TOOL ACCESS: Diamond Cutting, For Turning, Etc

Accurate Diamond Tool Corp ....E 201 265-8868
Emerson (G-2861)
Accuratus Ceramic Corp ....E 908 213-7070
Phillipsburg (G-8540)
Dewitt Bros Tool Co Inc ....G 908 298-3700
Kenilworth (G-4935)
New Jersey Diamond Products Co ....F 973 684-0949
Paterson (G-8267)
Technodiamant USA Inc ....G 908 850-8505
Tranquility (G-10884)

MACHINE TOOL ACCESS: Dresser, Abrasive Wheel Or Other

Airbrasive Jet Tech LLC ....G 201 725-7340
South Plainfield (G-10209)

MACHINE TOOL ACCESS: Drill Bushings, Drilling Jig

J and J Contractors ....F 856 765-7521
Millville (G-6256)

MACHINE TOOL ACCESS: Drills

Cutter Drill & Machine Inc ....G 732 206-1112
Howell (G-4535)

MACHINE TOOL ACCESS: Files

Ramco Manufacturing Co Inc ....E 908 245-4500
Kenilworth (G-4973)

MACHINE TOOL ACCESS: Hopper Feed Devices

Acrison Inc ....D 201 440-8300
Moonachie (G-6451)

MACHINE TOOL ACCESS: Machine Attachments & Access, Drilling

William T Hutchinson Company ....F 908 688-0533
Union (G-11100)

MACHINE TOOL ACCESS: Tool Holders

Aloris Tool Technology Co Inc ....E 973 772-1201
Clifton (G-1561)

MACHINE TOOL ACCESS: Tools & Access

Camden Tool Inc ....E 856 966-6800
Camden (G-1045)

MACHINE TOOL ATTACHMENTS & ACCESS

American Aeronautic Mfg Co ....G 973 442-8138
Pine Brook (G-8585)
Automated Tapping Systems Inc ....F 732 899-2282
Beachwood (G-257)
Engineered Components Inc ....F 908 788-8393
Three Bridges (G-10704)
Hainesport Tool & Machine Co ....F 609 261-0016
Mount Holly (G-6729)
Ringfeder Pwr Transm USA Corp ....E 201 666-3320
Westwood (G-11843)

Ss Tool & Manufacturing Co ....G....... 908 486-5497
Linden **(G-5428)**

Teknics Industries Inc ....D....... 973 633-7575
Lincoln Park **(G-5306)**

MACHINE TOOLS & ACCESS

Alpex Wheel Co Inc ....F....... 201 871-1700
Tenafly **(G-10659)**

Daven Industries Inc ....E....... 973 808-8848
Fairfield **(G-3180)**

Doosan Machine Tools Amer Corp ......D....... 973 618-2500
Pine Brook **(G-8599)**

Energy Beams Inc ....F....... 973 291-6555
Bloomingdale **(G-528)**

F & R Grinding Inc ....F....... 908 996-0440
Frenchtown **(G-3712)**

H & W Tool Co Inc ....F....... 973 366-0131
Dover **(G-2085)**

Handler Manufacturing Company ....E....... 908 233-7796
Westfield **(G-11799)**

Indo-US Mim TEC Private Ltd ....G....... 734 327-9842
Princeton **(G-8962)**

Jdv Products Inc ....F....... 201 794-6467
Fair Lawn **(G-3108)**

Jnt Technical Services Inc ....E....... 201 641-2130
Little Ferry **(G-5491)**

M D Carbide Tool Corp ....E....... 973 263-0104
Towaco **(G-10874)**

Sandvik Inc ....C....... 281 275-4800
Fair Lawn **(G-3121)**

Sandvik Inc ....C....... 201 794-5000
Fair Lawn **(G-3120)**

Sk & P Industries Inc ....G....... 973 482-1864
Newark **(G-7276)**

Troy-Onic Inc ....E....... 973 584-6830
Kenvil **(G-4996)**

United Instrument Company LLC ....G....... 201 767-6000
Northvale **(G-7552)**

MACHINE TOOLS, METAL CUTTING: Cutoff

Armstrong & Sons ....G....... 732 223-1555
Manasquan **(G-5829)**

MACHINE TOOLS, METAL CUTTING: Drilling

Autodrill LLC ....G....... 908 542-0244
Lebanon **(G-5251)**

MACHINE TOOLS, METAL CUTTING: Exotic, Including Explosive

Gauer Metal Products Co Inc ....E....... 908 241-4080
Kenilworth **(G-4942)**

MACHINE TOOLS, METAL CUTTING: Grind, Polish, Buff, Lapp

Web Industries Inc ....F....... 973 335-1200
Montville **(G-6449)**

MACHINE TOOLS, METAL CUTTING: Tool Replacement & Rpr Parts

American Mch Tool RPR Rbldg Co ....G....... 973 927-0820
Randolph **(G-9171)**

Uhlmann Packaging Systems LP ....D....... 973 402-8855
Towaco **(G-10883)**

MACHINE TOOLS, METAL FORMING: Container, Metal Incl Cans

Williams Scotsman Inc ....G....... 856 429-0315
Kearny **(G-4906)**

MACHINE TOOLS, METAL FORMING: Crimping, Metal

Bergen Cable Technology LLC ....E....... 973 276-9596
Fairfield **(G-3155)**

MACHINE TOOLS, METAL FORMING: Forming, Metal Deposit

Titanium Industries Inc ....E....... 973 983-1185
Rockaway **(G-9504)**

MACHINE TOOLS, METAL FORMING: Magnetic Forming

Magnetic Metals Corporation ....C....... 856 964-7842
Camden **(G-1077)**

MACHINE TOOLS, METAL FORMING: Marking

Cozzoli Machine Company ....D....... 732 564-0400
Somerset **(G-9978)**

MACHINE TOOLS, METAL FORMING: Mechanical, Pneumatic Or Hyd

Joy-Rei Enterprises Inc ....G....... 732 727-0742
Parlin **(G-7867)**

MACHINE TOOLS, METAL FORMING: Punching & Shearing

Bruderer Machinery Inc ....E....... 201 941-2121
Ridgefield **(G-9252)**

MACHINE TOOLS, METAL FORMING: Rebuilt

C & S Machinery Rebuilding ....G....... 973 742-7302
Paterson **(G-8152)**

MACHINE TOOLS, METAL FORMING: Spinning, Metal

Ultimate Spinning Turning Corp ....G....... 201 372-9740
Moonachie **(G-6495)**

MACHINE TOOLS: Metal Cutting

Alben Metal Products Inc ....G....... 973 279-8891
Paterson **(G-8130)**

Array Solders Ltd Liability Co ....G....... 201 432-0095
Jersey City **(G-4696)**

Automated Tapping Systems Inc ....F....... 732 899-2282
Beachwood **(G-257)**

Camden Tool Inc ....E....... 856 966-6800
Camden **(G-1045)**

Charles F Kilian ....G....... 732 458-3554
Brick **(G-712)**

Chase Machine Co ....F....... 201 438-2214
Lyndhurst **(G-5648)**

Cutter Drill & Machine Inc ....G....... 732 206-1112
Howell **(G-4535)**

Eastern Machining Corporation ....G....... 856 694-3303
Franklinville **(G-3637)**

Fecken-Kirfel America Inc ....F....... 201 891-5530
Mahwah **(G-5736)**

Gary R Marzili ....G....... 856 782-1546
Sicklerville **(G-9910)**

Hone-A-Matic Tool & Cutter Co ....G....... 732 382-6000
Rahway **(G-9102)**

Innovative Manufacturing Inc ....F....... 908 904-1884
Hillsborough **(G-4329)**

J & S Tool ....G....... 973 383-5059
Newton **(G-7347)**

Komo Machine Inc ....D....... 732 719-6222
Lakewood **(G-5117)**

L & M Machine & Tool Co Inc ....G....... 973 523-5288
Paterson **(G-8233)**

Lever Manufacturing Corp ....E....... 201 684-4400
Mahwah **(G-5752)**

Metaport Manufacturing LLC ....G....... 973 383-8363
Lafayette **(G-5031)**

NASA Machine Tools Inc ....E....... 973 633-5200
Lincoln Park **(G-5302)**

Nova Precision Products Inc ....C....... 973 625-1586
Rockaway **(G-9480)**

Oroszlany Laszlo ....G....... 201 666-2101
Hillsdale **(G-4369)**

TAC Technical Instrument Corp ....F....... 609 882-2894
Trenton **(G-10995)**

Tool Shop Inc ....G....... 856 767-8077
West Berlin **(G-11630)**

Tooling Etc LLC ....G....... 732 752-8080
Middlesex **(G-6156)**

Triple-T Cutting Tools Inc ....F....... 856 768-0800
West Berlin **(G-11632)**

MACHINE TOOLS: Metal Forming

Action Packaging Automation ....G....... 609 448-9210
Roosevelt **(G-9527)**

Benton Graphics Inc ....E....... 609 587-4000
Trenton **(G-10903)**

Doran LLC ....G....... 908 289-9200
Union **(G-11043)**

Grimco Pneumatic Corp ....G....... 973 345-0660
Paterson **(G-8204)**

H & W Tool Co Inc ....F....... 973 366-0131
Dover **(G-2085)**

High-Technology Corporation ....F....... 201 488-0010
Hackensack **(G-3927)**

Hone-A-Matic Tool & Cutter Co ....G....... 732 382-6000
Rahway **(G-9102)**

Rotech Tool & Mold Co Inc ....G....... 908 241-9669
Kenilworth **(G-4975)**

Royle Systems Group LLC ....E....... 201 644-0345
Teterboro **(G-10690)**

Vantage Tool & Mfg Inc ....G....... 908 647-1010
Warren **(G-11435)**

MACHINERY & EQPT, AGRICULTURAL, WHOL: Farm Eqpt Parts/Splys

National Diversified Sales Inc ....G....... 559 562-9888
Bordentown **(G-590)**

MACHINERY & EQPT, AGRICULTURAL, WHOLESALE: Lawn & Garden

Creative Products Inc ....D....... 732 614-9035
Long Branch **(G-5596)**

Vandermolen Corp ....G....... 973 992-8506
Ledgewood **(G-5284)**

MACHINERY & EQPT, INDL, WHOL: Controlling Instruments/Access

American Process Systems ....G....... 908 216-6781
Port Murray **(G-8880)**

Johnson Controls Inc ....D....... 732 225-6700
Edison **(G-2543)**

MACHINERY & EQPT, INDL, WHOL: Environ Pollution Cntrl, Air

Tess-Com Inc ....E....... 412 233-5782
Middlesex **(G-6155)**

MACHINERY & EQPT, INDL, WHOLESALE: Cement Making

Nobelus LLC ....G....... 800 895-2747
North Brunswick **(G-7480)**

P S I Cement Inc ....G....... 609 716-1515
Princeton Junction **(G-9063)**

MACHINERY & EQPT, INDL, WHOLESALE: Chemical Process

Servolift LLC ....E....... 973 442-7878
Randolph **(G-9199)**

MACHINERY & EQPT, INDL, WHOLESALE: Compaction

Premier Compaction Systems ....F....... 718 328-5990
Woodland Park **(G-12087)**

MACHINERY & EQPT, INDL, WHOLESALE: Conveyor Systems

Das Installations Inc ....F....... 973 473-6858
Garfield **(G-3737)**

East Coast Storage Eqp Co Inc ....E....... 732 451-1316
Brick **(G-716)**

Robotunits Inc ....G....... 732 438-0500
Cranbury **(G-1879)**

MACHINERY & EQPT, INDL, WHOLESALE: Dairy Prdts Manufacturing

Dairy Delight LLC ....F....... 201 939-7878
Rutherford **(G-9617)**

MACHINERY & EQPT, INDL, WHOLESALE: Drilling, Exc Bits

Morris Industries Inc ....D....... 973 835-6600
Pompton Plains **(G-8868)**

MACHINERY & EQPT, INDL, WHOLESALE: Engines & Parts, Diesel

Cummins Inc ....D....... 973 491-0100
Kearny (G-4853)
Rajysan Incorporated ....E....... 800 433-1382
Swedesboro (G-10605)

MACHINERY & EQPT, INDL, WHOLESALE: Engines, Gasoline

Monmouth Marine Engines Inc............F....... 732 528-9290
Brielle (G-907)

MACHINERY & EQPT, INDL, WHOLESALE: Food Manufacturing

Am-Mac Incorporated ....F....... 973 575-7567
Fairfield (G-3140)
Drytech Inc ....E....... 609 758-1794
Cookstown (G-1803)
McT Dairies Inc...............................F....... 973 258-9600
Millburn (G-6203)
Tricorbraun Inc ....G....... 732 353-7104
Monroe Township (G-6349)

MACHINERY & EQPT, INDL, WHOLESALE: Food Product Manufacturng

Solbern LLC.................................E....... 973 227-3030
Fairfield (G-3312)
Traycon Manufacturing Co Inc ....E....... 201 939-5555
Hackensack (G-3984)

MACHINERY & EQPT, INDL, WHOLESALE: Hydraulic Systems

American Hose Hydraulic Co Inc ....E....... 973 684-3225
Paterson (G-8136)
Asa Hydraulik of America Inc ....G....... 908 541-1500
Branchburg (G-623)
Bristol-Donald Company Inc................E....... 973 589-2640
Newark (G-7076)
Micheller & Son Hydraulics Inc ....F....... 908 687-1545
Roselle (G-9566)
Technol Inc ....F....... 856 848-5480
Westville (G-11821)
Van Hydraulics Inc ....E....... 732 442-5500
South Plainfield (G-10338)

MACHINERY & EQPT, INDL, WHOLESALE: Indl Machine Parts

Engineered Components Inc ....F....... 908 788-8393
Three Bridges (G-10704)
Inter Rep Associates Inc ....G....... 609 465-0077
Cape May Court House (G-1111)

MACHINERY & EQPT, INDL, WHOLESALE: Instruments & Cntrl Eqpt

Amega Scientific Corporation ....F....... 609 953-7295
Medford (G-6019)
Panel Components & Systems ....F....... 973 448-9400
Stanhope (G-10478)
Schneder Elc Bldngs Amrcas Inc..........E....... 201 348-9240
Secaucus (G-9808)
Sensor Products Inc ....E....... 973 884-1755
Madison (G-5702)

MACHINERY & EQPT, INDL, WHOLESALE: Machine Tools & Access

Autodrill LLC ....G....... 908 542-0244
Lebanon (G-5251)
Doosan Machine Tools Amer Corp.......D....... 973 618-2500
Pine Brook (G-8599)
J R S Tool & Metal Finishing ....G....... 908 753-2050
South Plainfield (G-10282)
Rennsteig Tools Inc ....G....... 330 315-3044
Hackensack (G-3966)

MACHINERY & EQPT, INDL, WHOLESALE: Machine Tools & Metalwork

Lmt Usa Inc ....G....... 973 586-8722
Rockaway (G-9475)
Metaport Manufacturing LLC ....G....... 973 383-8363
Lafayette (G-5031)

P M Z Tool Inc ....G....... 908 647-2125
Stirling (G-10494)
Royal Master Grinders Inc ....D....... 201 337-8500
Oakland (G-7645)
Uhlmann Packaging Systems LP ....D....... 973 402-8855
Towaco (G-10883)

MACHINERY & EQPT, INDL, WHOLESALE: Measure/Test, Electric

Keyence Corporation America ....E....... 201 930-0100
Elmwood Park (G-2834)

MACHINERY & EQPT, INDL, WHOLESALE: Packaging

Abox Automation Corp......................G....... 973 659-9611
Pine Brook (G-8583)
Ajg Packaging LLC ....G....... 908 528-6052
Pittstown (G-8751)
Campak Inc ....G....... 973 994-4888
Livingston (G-5508)
Cavalla Inc ....E....... 201 343-3338
Hackensack (G-3895)
Integrated Packg Systems Inc ....G....... 973 664-0020
Denville (G-2040)
Modular Packaging Systems Inc ....F....... 973 970-9393
Rockaway (G-9477)
Pro Pack Inc ....F....... 973 665-8333
Wharton (G-11868)

MACHINERY & EQPT, INDL, WHOLESALE: Plastic Prdts Machinery

Japan Steel Works America Inc............G....... 212 490-2630
Edison (G-2538)
Yuhl Products Inc............................G....... 908 276-5180
Kenilworth (G-4991)

MACHINERY & EQPT, INDL, WHOLESALE: Processing & Packaging

Beauty-Pack LLC ....F....... 732 802-8200
Piscataway (G-8640)
Blispak Acquisition Corp ....D....... 973 884-4141
Whippany (G-11882)

MACHINERY & EQPT, INDL, WHOLESALE: Pulverizing

Pallmann Pulverizers Co Inc................E....... 973 471-1450
Clifton (G-1682)

MACHINERY & EQPT, INDL, WHOLESALE: Recycling

Energy Recycling Co LLC ....G....... 732 545-6619
New Brunswick (G-6924)
Exim Incorporated ....G....... 908 561-8200
Piscataway (G-8664)

MACHINERY & EQPT, INDL, WHOLESALE: Screening

Charles M Jessup Inc ....G....... 732 324-0430
Keasbey (G-4910)

MACHINERY & EQPT, INDL, WHOLESALE: Sewing

Brother International Corp...................B....... 908 704-1700
Bridgewater (G-808)

MACHINERY & EQPT, INDL, WHOLESALE: Textile

Baxter Corporation ....D....... 201 337-1212
Franklin Lakes (G-3613)
Burlington Textile Machinery................F....... 973 279-5900
Paterson (G-8151)
Jason Industrial Inc ....E....... 973 227-4904
Fairfield (G-3243)

MACHINERY & EQPT, INDL, WHOLESALE: Textile & Leather

Satex Fabrics Ltd ....G....... 212 221-5555
North Bergen (G-7436)

MACHINERY & EQPT, WHOLESALE: Concrete Processing

A & A Concrete Products Inc ....G....... 973 835-2239
Riverdale (G-9369)

MACHINERY & EQPT, WHOLESALE: Construction & Mining, Ladders

Steelstran Industries Inc ....E....... 732 574-0700
Avenel (G-147)

MACHINERY & EQPT, WHOLESALE: Construction, General

Cleary Machinery Co Inc ....G....... 732 560-3200
South Bound Brook (G-10143)
Winslow Rental & Supply Inc...............G....... 856 767-5554
Berlin (G-434)

MACHINERY & EQPT: Electroplating

G & S Design & Manufacturing.............F....... 908 862-2444
Linden (G-5349)
Tilton Rack & Basket Co ....E....... 973 226-6010
Fairfield (G-3328)

MACHINERY & EQPT: Farm

3 IS Technologies Inc ....G....... 609 238-8213
Hainesport (G-4067)
Kinnery Precision LLC ....G....... 973 473-4664
Passaic (G-8080)

MACHINERY & EQPT: Gas Producers, Generators/Other Rltd Eqpt

Boc Group Inc ....A....... 908 665-2400
New Providence (G-6995)
Linde North America Inc ....D....... 908 464-8100
New Providence (G-7007)
Messer North America Inc...................B....... 908 464-8100
Bridgewater (G-851)

MACHINERY & EQPT: Liquid Automation

I & J Fisnar Inc ....F....... 973 646-5044
Pine Brook (G-8603)
Integrated Packg Systems Inc ....G....... 973 664-0020
Denville (G-2040)
Microdysis Inc ....G....... 609 642-1184
Bordentown (G-589)
Stauff Corporation ....E....... 201 444-7800
Waldwick (G-11309)

MACHINERY & EQPT: Metal Finishing, Plating Etc

Carl Buck Corporation.......................G....... 973 300-5575
Sparta (G-10381)
Dayton Grey Corp ....F....... 732 869-0060
Asbury Park (G-75)
Metal Finishing Co LLC ....G....... 973 778-9550
Passaic (G-8089)
Ramco Equipment Corp ....E....... 908 687-6700
Hillside (G-4423)
Sony Corporation of America ....F....... 201 930-1000
Woodcliff Lake (G-12065)

MACHINERY & EQPT: Petroleum Refinery

John W Kennedy Company ....G....... 973 256-5525
Little Falls (G-5457)

MACHINERY & EQPT: Vibratory Parts Handling Eqpt

Vibra Screw Inc ....E....... 973 256-7410
Totowa (G-10858)

MACHINERY BASES

Intermark Inc ....G....... 908 474-1311
Linden (G-5362)
Raceweld Co Inc ....G....... 908 236-6533
Lebanon (G-5274)
Uac Packaging LLC ....G....... 908 595-6890
Hillsborough (G-4361)

MACHINERY, CALCULATING: Calculators & Adding

Swintec Corp ....F 201 935-0115
Moonachie **(G-6493)**

MACHINERY, COMMERCIAL LAUNDRY & Drycleaning: Pressing

Hoffman/New Yorker Inc ....G 201 488-1800
Hackensack **(G-3930)**

MACHINERY, COMMERCIAL LAUNDRY: Washing, Incl Coin-Operated

Professional Laundry Solutions ....G 973 392-0837
Newark **(G-7238)**

MACHINERY, EQPT & SUPPLIES: Parking Facility

Amano Cincinnati Incorporated ....D 973 403-1900
Roseland **(G-9530)**
Amano USA Holdings Inc ....G 973 403-1900
Roseland **(G-9531)**
Kyosis LLC ....G 908 202-8894
South River **(G-10351)**
Park Plus Inc ....G 201 651-8590
Oakland **(G-7641)**

MACHINERY, FOOD PRDTS: Beverage

Absecon Island Beverage Co ....G 609 653-8123
Egg Harbor Township **(G-2674)**
Terriss Consolidated Inds ....G 732 988-0909
Asbury Park **(G-84)**

MACHINERY, FOOD PRDTS: Cutting, Chopping, Grinding, Mixing

Wyssmont Company Inc ....E 201 947-4600
Fort Lee **(G-3596)**
Zvonko Stulic & Son Inc ....G 973 589-3773
Newark **(G-7319)**

MACHINERY, FOOD PRDTS: Dairy & Milk

Arm & Hammer Animal Ntrtn LLC ....F 800 526-3563
Princeton **(G-8910)**
Dantco Corp ....F 973 278-8776
Paterson **(G-8168)**

MACHINERY, FOOD PRDTS: Food Processing, Smokers

Basha USA LLC ....G 201 339-9770
Bayonne **(G-204)**

MACHINERY, FOOD PRDTS: Homogenizing, Dairy, Fruit/Vegetable

Hill Machine Inc ....G 973 684-2808
Paterson **(G-8209)**

MACHINERY, FOOD PRDTS: Mixers, Commercial

Cornell Machine Co Inc ....G 973 379-6860
Springfield **(G-10437)**
Willow Technology Inc ....G 732 671-1554
Holmdel **(G-4515)**

MACHINERY, FOOD PRDTS: Ovens, Bakery

Revent Incorporated ....E 732 777-5187
Somerset **(G-10065)**

MACHINERY, FOOD PRDTS: Processing, Poultry

Kuhl Corp ....D 908 782-5696
Flemington **(G-3454)**

MACHINERY, MAILING: Address Labeling

Acedepotcom ....F 800 844-0962
Northvale **(G-7515)**

MACHINERY, MAILING: Postage Meters

Pitney Bowes Inc ....F 908 903-2870
Warren **(G-11427)**

Pitney Bowes Inc ....C 800 521-0080
Newark **(G-7230)**
Pitney Bowes Inc ....C 856 764-2240
Delran **(G-2019)**

MACHINERY, METALWORKING: Assembly, Including Robotic

Boomerang Systems Inc ....E 973 538-1194
Florham Park **(G-3494)**

MACHINERY, METALWORKING: Coil Winding, For Springs

K & S Industries Inc ....F 908 862-3030
Linden **(G-5368)**

MACHINERY, METALWORKING: Rotary Slitters, Metalworking

Progressive Ruesch Inc ....E 973 962-7700
Ringwood **(G-9351)**

MACHINERY, OFFICE: Sorters, Filing

Hoarders Express LLC ....D 856 963-8471
Camden **(G-1067)**

MACHINERY, OFFICE: Stapling, Hand Or Power

Arrow Fastener Co LLC ....B 201 843-6900
Saddle Brook **(G-9640)**

MACHINERY, OFFICE: Time Clocks & Time Recording Devices

Amano Cincinnati Incorporated ....D 973 403-1900
Roseland **(G-9530)**
Amano USA Holdings Inc ....G 973 403-1900
Roseland **(G-9531)**
Time Systems International Co ....E 201 871-1200
Englewood **(G-2947)**

MACHINERY, OFFICE: Typing & Word Processing

Brother International Corp ....B 908 704-1700
Bridgewater **(G-808)**

MACHINERY, PACKAGING: Carton Packing

Heisler Machine & Tool Co ....E 973 227-6300
Fairfield **(G-3226)**
Quality Carton Inc ....G 201 529-6900
Mahwah **(G-5765)**
Supplyone New York Inc ....E 718 392-7400
Paterson **(G-8309)**

MACHINERY, PACKAGING: Packing & Wrapping

Gram Equipment ....E 201 750-6500
Hamilton **(G-4106)**
Hair Systems Inc ....D 732 446-2202
Englishtown **(G-3004)**
Pro Pack Inc ....F 973 665-8333
Wharton **(G-11868)**
Sjd Direct Midwest LLC ....C 732 985-8405
Edison **(G-2612)**
Sjd Direct Midwest LLC ....C 732 287-2525
Edison **(G-2613)**

MACHINERY, PACKAGING: Vacuum

Vacuum Solutions Group Inc ....G 781 762-0414
Teaneck **(G-10654)**

MACHINERY, PAPER INDUSTRY: Converting, Die Cutting & Stampng

Creative Laminating Inc ....E 201 939-1999
Carlstadt **(G-1147)**
Holographic Finishing Inc ....F 201 941-4651
Ridgefield **(G-9266)**
Rotary Die Systems Inc ....G 856 234-3994
Moorestown **(G-6563)**

MACHINERY, PAPER INDUSTRY: Cutting

Retrievex ....G 732 247-3200
New Brunswick **(G-6968)**

MACHINERY, PAPER INDUSTRY: Fourdrinier

Enser Corporation ....D 856 829-5522
Cinnaminson **(G-1456)**

MACHINERY, PRINTING TRADES: Bookbinding Machinery

On Demand Machinery ....F 908 351-7137
Elizabeth **(G-2765)**

MACHINERY, PRINTING TRADES: Bronzing Or Dusting

Wilenta Carting Inc ....F 201 325-0044
Secaucus **(G-9828)**

MACHINERY, PRINTING TRADES: Plates

Anderson & Vreeland Inc ....E 973 227-2270
Fairfield **(G-3143)**
Galvanic Prtg & Plate Co Inc ....E 201 939-3600
Moonachie **(G-6466)**
Mark/Trece Inc ....E 973 884-1005
Whippany **(G-11897)**
Marko Engraving & Art Corp ....F 201 864-6500
Weehawken **(G-11569)**
Marko Engraving & Art Corp ....F 201 945-6555
Fairview **(G-3363)**
Mosstype Corporation ....G 201 444-8000
Waldwick **(G-11306)**
Mosstype Holding Corp ....E 201 444-8000
Waldwick **(G-11307)**
Packaging Graphics Inc ....E 856 767-9000
West Berlin **(G-11613)**
Verico Technology LLC ....C 201 842-0222
East Rutherford **(G-2329)**

MACHINERY, PRINTING TRADES: Plates, Engravers' Metal

N B C Engraving Co Inc ....G 201 387-8011
Bergenfield **(G-380)**

MACHINERY, PRINTING TRADES: Presses, Envelope

City Envelope Inc ....G 201 792-9292
Jersey City **(G-4712)**

MACHINERY, PRINTING TRADES: Presses, Gravure

Allison Systems Corporation ....F 856 461-9111
Riverside **(G-9389)**

MACHINERY, PRINTING TRADES: Printing Trade Parts & Attchts

Clarity Imaging Tech Inc ....E 877 272-4362
Saddle Brook **(G-9647)**
Clarity Imaging Tech Inc ....E 413 693-1234
Pennsauken **(G-8404)**
Clarity Imaging Tech Inc ....G 877 272-4362
Pennsauken **(G-8405)**
Polytype America Corp ....F 201 995-1000
Lincoln Park **(G-5304)**

MACHINERY, PRINTING TRADES: Type, Foundry

Ernest Schaefer Inc ....G 908 964-1280
Union **(G-11052)**

MACHINERY, SEWING: Sewing & Hat & Zipper Making

Brother International Corp ....B 908 704-1700
Bridgewater **(G-808)**
Comfortfit Labs Inc ....E 908 259-9100
Roselle **(G-9554)**
N C Carpet Binding & Equipment ....F 973 481-3500
Newark **(G-7207)**

MACHINERY, TEXTILE: Card Clothing

Benjamin Booth Company ....F 609 859-1995
Southampton **(G-10360)**

MACHINERY, TEXTILE: Fiber & Yarn Preparation

I F Associates Inc................................F....... 732 223-2900
Allenwood **(G-33)**

MACHINERY, TEXTILE: Finishing

D R Kenyon & Son Inc.....................F....... 908 722-0001
Bridgewater **(G-816)**
Snapco Manufacturing Corp..............E....... 973 282-0300
Hillside **(G-4427)**

MACHINERY, TEXTILE: Loom Parts &Attachments, Jacquard

Baxter Corporation..........................D....... 201 337-1212
Franklin Lakes **(G-3613)**

MACHINERY, TEXTILE: Winders

Lever Manufacturing Corp.................E....... 201 684-4400
Mahwah **(G-5752)**

MACHINERY, WOODWORKING: Box Making, For Wooden Boxes

Stapling Machines Inc.......................E....... 973 627-4400
Rockaway **(G-9500)**

MACHINERY, WOODWORKING: Cabinet Makers'

Andys Custom Cabinets....................G....... 732 752-6443
Green Brook **(G-3859)**
Atlas Woodworking Inc......................G....... 201 784-1949
Closter **(G-1751)**
Fix It Guy.......................................G....... 732 278-9000
Toms River **(G-10759)**

MACHINERY, WOODWORKING: Furniture Makers

Samuelson Furniture Inc....................F....... 973 278-4372
Paterson **(G-8294)**

MACHINERY, WOODWORKING: Scarfing

Design of Tomorrow Inc....................F....... 973 227-1000
Fairfield **(G-3185)**

MACHINERY: Assembly, Exc Metalworking

Heller Industries Inc.........................D....... 973 377-6800
Florham Park **(G-3509)**
Palmer Electronics Inc.......................F....... 973 772-5900
Garfield **(G-3752)**
Pulsonics Inc..................................F....... 800 999-6785
Belleville **(G-309)**
Wab US Corp..................................G....... 973 873-9155
Allendale **(G-19)**

MACHINERY: Automotive Related

Eagle Racing Inc.............................G....... 732 367-8487
Lakewood **(G-5088)**
Eco-Plug-System LLC.......................G....... 855 326-7584
Hewitt **(G-4275)**
Jrz Enterprises LLC..........................G....... 973 962-6330
Wayne **(G-11526)**
M C Technologies Inc........................E....... 973 839-2779
Pompton Plains **(G-8866)**
Mastercraft Electroplating.................G....... 908 354-4404
Elizabeth **(G-2756)**

MACHINERY: Bottle Washing & Sterilzing

Cozzoli Machine Company.................D....... 732 564-0400
Somerset **(G-9978)**

MACHINERY: Brake Burnishing Or Washing

Clayton Associates Inc......................F....... 732 363-2100
Lakewood **(G-5071)**

MACHINERY: Centrifugal

Celestech Inc.................................G....... 856 986-2221
Haddonfield **(G-4054)**
Heinkel Filtering Systems Inc.............F....... 856 467-3399
Swedesboro **(G-10588)**

MACHINERY: Concrete Prdts

Concrete Cutting Partners Inc.............G....... 201 440-2233
Hackensack **(G-3899)**

MACHINERY: Construction

Breeze-Eastern LLC.........................D....... 973 602-1001
Whippany **(G-11884)**
Clark Equipment Company.................A....... 973 618-2500
Pine Brook **(G-8593)**
County of Warren............................D....... 908 475-7975
Belvidere **(G-359)**
Dougherty Foundation Products.........G....... 201 337-5748
Franklin Lakes **(G-3621)**
F and M Equipment Ltd.....................D....... 215 822-0145
South Plainfield **(G-10256)**
Georgia-Pacific LLC.........................D....... 856 966-7600
Camden **(G-1066)**
Ingersoll-Rand Intl Inc.......................D....... 559 271-4625
Piscataway **(G-8677)**
Multi-Pak Corporation.......................E....... 201 342-7474
Hackensack **(G-3949)**
Reinco Inc......................................F....... 908 755-0921
Plainfield **(G-8777)**
Solidia Technologies Inc....................E....... 908 315-5901
Piscataway **(G-8714)**
Tuff Mfg Co Inc...............................G....... 201 796-5319
Elmwood Park **(G-2858)**

MACHINERY: Cryogenic, Industrial

Boc Group Inc................................A....... 908 665-2400
New Providence **(G-6995)**
Cryovation LLC...............................G....... 609 914-4792
Hainesport **(G-4071)**
Linde North America Inc....................D....... 908 464-8100
New Providence **(G-7007)**
Messer North America Inc..................B....... 908 464-8100
Bridgewater **(G-851)**

MACHINERY: Custom

Chacko John..................................G....... 732 494-1088
Edison **(G-2475)**
Coesia Health & Beauty Inc...............F....... 908 707-8008
Branchburg **(G-630)**
Connecting Products Inc....................G....... 609 688-1808
Skillman **(G-9919)**
Daven Industries Inc.........................E....... 973 808-8848
Fairfield **(G-3180)**
Globe Industries Corp.......................F....... 973 992-8990
Clifton **(G-1626)**
I I Galaxy Inc..................................G....... 732 828-2686
New Brunswick **(G-6933)**
Imperial Machine & Tool Co...............F....... 908 496-8100
Columbia **(G-1794)**
Jordan Tooling & Manufacturing.........G....... 609 261-2636
Hainesport **(G-4075)**
Lazar Technologies Inc......................F....... 732 739-9622
Hazlet **(G-4263)**
Luso Machine Nj LLC........................F....... 973 242-1717
Newark **(G-7188)**
National Mtal Fnshngs Corp Inc..........F....... 732 752-7770
Middlesex **(G-6133)**
New ERA Converting McHy Inc...........E....... 201 670-4848
Paterson **(G-8265)**
Northeast Precast Ltd Lblty Co............D....... 856 765-9088
Millville **(G-6264)**
Norwalt Design Inc...........................D....... 973 927-3200
Randolph **(G-9193)**
R G Smith Tool & Mfg Co...................F....... 973 344-1395
Newark **(G-7243)**
Sensor Products Inc..........................E....... 973 884-1755
Madison **(G-5702)**
Spectrum Design LLC.......................G....... 856 694-1870
Franklinville **(G-3639)**
Stuart Steel Protection Corp...............E....... 732 469-5544
Somerset **(G-10075)**
William Kenyon & Sons Inc................E....... 732 985-8980
Piscataway **(G-8738)**

MACHINERY: Die Casting

Buhler Inc......................................E....... 201 847-0600
Mahwah **(G-5719)**

MACHINERY: Electronic Component Making

Azego Technology Svcs US Inc...........G....... 201 327-7500
Oakland **(G-7615)**
Henry Dudley.................................G....... 732 240-6895
Toms River **(G-10764)**

MACHINERY: Engraving

Htp Connectivity LLC........................G....... 973 586-2286
Rockaway **(G-9465)**
Ridge Manufacturing Corp.................D....... 973 586-2717
Rockaway **(G-9494)**

MACHINERY: Engraving

Cronite Co Inc................................E....... 973 887-7900
Parsippany **(G-7910)**

MACHINERY: Extruding, Synthetic Filament

American Leistritz Extruder...............F....... 908 685-2333
Branchburg **(G-616)**

MACHINERY: Folding

Microfold Inc..................................G....... 201 641-5052
Teterboro **(G-10687)**

MACHINERY: Gas Separators

Messer LLC....................................C....... 908 464-8100
Bridgewater **(G-849)**
Messer LLC....................................G....... 973 579-2065
Sparta **(G-10398)**

MACHINERY: Gear Cutting & Finishing

Joe Mike Precision Fabrication...........F....... 609 953-1144
Medford **(G-6026)**

MACHINERY: General, Industrial, NEC

NJ Service Testing & Insptn...............G....... 732 221-6357
Lincroft **(G-5313)**

MACHINERY: Glass Cutting

Spadix Technologies Inc....................G....... 732 356-6906
Middlesex **(G-6150)**

MACHINERY: Glassmaking

Cain Machine Inc.............................F....... 856 825-7225
Millville **(G-6240)**
Inter Rep Associates Inc....................G....... 609 465-0077
Cape May Court House **(G-1111)**

MACHINERY: Grinding

Everite Machine Products Co..............E....... 856 330-6700
Pennsauken **(G-8419)**
Glebar Operating LLC.......................D....... 201 337-1500
Ramsey **(G-9146)**
Jet Pulverizer Co Inc.........................E....... 856 235-5554
Moorestown **(G-6531)**
McGonegal Manufacturing Co.............G....... 201 438-2313
East Rutherford **(G-2301)**
Royal Master Grinders Inc..................D....... 201 337-8500
Oakland **(G-7645)**

MACHINERY: Ice Cream

Gram Equipment.............................E....... 201 750-6500
Hamilton **(G-4106)**

MACHINERY: Ice Making

Iceboxx LLC...................................G....... 201 857-0404
Wyckoff **(G-12113)**

MACHINERY: Industrial, NEC

Miemie Design Services Inc................E....... 609 857-3688
Ltl Egg Hbr **(G-5617)**

MACHINERY: Labeling

AT Information Products Inc...............G....... 201 529-0202
Mahwah **(G-5715)**
Clements Industries Inc.....................E....... 201 440-5500
South Hackensack **(G-10153)**
Dalemark Industries Inc.....................F....... 732 367-3100
Lakewood **(G-5081)**
Herma US Inc..................................G....... 973 521-7254
Fairfield **(G-3227)**
ID Technology LLC...........................E....... 201 405-0767
Oakland **(G-7632)**
Kompac Technologies LLC.................E....... 908 534-8411
Somerville **(G-10120)**
Labeling Systems LLC.......................E....... 201 405-0767
Oakland **(G-7634)**
Weiler Labeling Systems LLC.............D....... 856 273-3377
Moorestown **(G-6577)**

PRODUCT

MACHINERY: Lapping

Unique Precision Co Inc ....G....... 732 382-8699
Rahway *(G-9131)*

MACHINERY: Marking, Metalworking

A D J Group LLC ....G....... 609 743-2099
Bordentown *(G-573)*

Tri-Power Consulting Svcs LLC ....E....... 973 227-7100
Denville *(G-2060)*

MACHINERY: Metalworking

Air & Specialties Sheet Metal ....F....... 908 233-8306
Mountainside *(G-6832)*

Applied Resources Corp ....E....... 973 328-3882
Wharton *(G-11852)*

Lever Manufacturing Corp ....E....... 201 684-4400
Mahwah *(G-5752)*

Mac Products Inc ....D....... 973 344-5149
Kearny *(G-4880)*

Precious Metal Processing Cons ....G....... 201 944-8053
Palisades Park *(G-7777)*

Seal-Spout Corp ....F....... 908 647-0648
Liberty Corner *(G-5296)*

TMU Inc ....F....... 609 884-7656
Cape May *(G-1103)*

Weber and Scher Mfg Co Inc ....E....... 908 236-8484
Lebanon *(G-5275)*

Werko Machine Co ....F....... 856 662-0669
Pennsauken *(G-8496)*

MACHINERY: Milling

General Electric Company ....B....... 973 887-6635
Parsippany *(G-7955)*

MACHINERY: Mining

Hosokawa Micron International ....C....... 908 273-6360
Summit *(G-10534)*

International Process Eqp Co ....G....... 856 665-4007
Pennsauken *(G-8439)*

MACHINERY: Ozone

Science Pump Corporation ....E....... 856 963-7700
Camden *(G-1086)*

Suez Treatment Solutions Inc ....D....... 201 676-2525
Leonia *(G-5292)*

MACHINERY: Packaging

Action Packaging Automation ....G....... 609 448-9210
Roosevelt *(G-9527)*

Alliance Food Equipment ....F....... 201 784-1101
Trenton *(G-10891)*

Banarez Enterprises Inc ....G....... 201 222-7515
Jersey City *(G-4698)*

Campak Inc ....G....... 973 994-4888
Livingston *(G-5508)*

Copack International Inc ....E....... 973 405-5151
Clifton *(G-1590)*

Deitz Co Inc ....F....... 732 295-8212
Belmar *(G-348)*

Elite Packaging Corp ....F....... 732 651-9955
East Brunswick *(G-2140)*

F P Developments Inc ....E....... 856 875-7100
Williamstown *(G-11957)*

Ganz Brothers Inc ....F....... 201 820-1975
Paramus *(G-7801)*

Gloucester City Box Works LLC ....F....... 856 456-9032
Gloucester City *(G-3842)*

Greener Corp ....E....... 732 341-3880
Bayville *(G-245)*

Groniger USA LLC ....G....... 704 588-3873
Basking Ridge *(G-185)*

I S Parts International Inc ....E....... 856 691-2203
Vineland *(G-11234)*

J G Machine Works Inc ....G....... 732 203-2077
Edison *(G-2536)*

K & S Industries Inc ....F....... 908 862-3030
Linden *(G-5368)*

Kohl & Madden Prtg Ink Corp ....E....... 201 935-8666
Carlstadt *(G-1177)*

Luciano Packaging Tech Inc ....G....... 908 722-3222
Branchburg *(G-657)*

Mactec Packaging Tech LLC ....G....... 732 343-1607
Sayreville *(G-9718)*

Njrls Enterprises Inc ....F....... 732 846-6010
Branchburg *(G-661)*

Norden Inc ....G....... 908 252-9483
Branchburg *(G-662)*

Pabin Associates Inc ....G....... 201 288-7216
Hasbrouck Heights *(G-4187)*

Pace Packaging LLC ....D....... 973 227-1040
Fairfield *(G-3287)*

Packaging Machinery & Eqp Co ....G....... 973 325-2418
West Orange *(G-11776)*

Per-Fil Industries Inc ....E....... 856 461-5700
Riverside *(G-9401)*

PMC Industries Inc ....E....... 201 342-3684
Hackensack *(G-3964)*

Potdevin Machine Co ....F....... 973 227-8828
West Caldwell *(G-11673)*

Pro-Motion Industries LLC ....F....... 856 809-0040
Sicklerville *(G-9914)*

Pro-Pac Service Inc ....F....... 973 962-8080
Ringwood *(G-9350)*

Prodo-Pak Corp ....F....... 973 772-4500
Garfield *(G-3760)*

Prodo-Pak Corporation ....E....... 973 777-7770
Garfield *(G-3761)*

Romaco Inc ....E....... 973 709-0691
Lincoln Park *(G-5305)*

Scandia Packaging Machinery Co ....E....... 973 473-6100
Mahwah *(G-5770)*

Signode Industrial Group LLC ....D....... 201 741-2791
Newark *(G-7272)*

Techline Extrusion Systems ....G....... 973 831-0317
Haskell *(G-4203)*

Wagner Industries Inc ....E....... 973 347-0800
Stanhope *(G-10481)*

Wrap-Ade Machine Co Inc ....F....... 973 773-6150
Clifton *(G-1740)*

Wrapade Packaging Systems LLC ....F....... 973 787-1788
Fairfield *(G-3355)*

MACHINERY: Paper Industry Miscellaneous

175 Derousse LLC ....G....... 856 662-0100
Pennsauken *(G-8380)*

Colter & Peterson Inc ....E....... 973 684-0901
West Caldwell *(G-11644)*

Dietech Services LLC ....G....... 973 667-0798
Nutley *(G-7585)*

Khanna Paper Inc ....G....... 201 850-1707
North Bergen *(G-7415)*

Tri-State Knife Grinding Corp ....E....... 609 890-4989
Robbinsville *(G-9418)*

Woodward Jogger Aerators Inc ....F....... 201 933-6800
East Rutherford *(G-2330)*

MACHINERY: Pharmaciutical

Ackley Machine Corporation ....E....... 856 234-3626
Moorestown *(G-6500)*

Amcor Phrm Packg USA LLC ....E....... 856 825-1400
Millville *(G-6230)*

American International Cont ....F....... 973 917-3331
Boonton *(G-541)*

Clordisys Solutions Inc ....E....... 908 236-4100
Branchburg *(G-629)*

Dantco Corp ....F....... 973 278-8776
Paterson *(G-8168)*

Deitz Co Inc ....F....... 732 295-8212
Belmar *(G-348)*

Expert Process Systems LLC ....G....... 570 424-0581
Hackettstown *(G-4007)*

F P Developments Inc ....E....... 856 875-7100
Williamstown *(G-11957)*

Fette Compacting America Inc ....E....... 973 586-8722
Rockaway *(G-9459)*

Globepharma Inc ....F....... 732 296-9700
New Brunswick *(G-6930)*

Jason Equipment Corp ....E....... 973 983-7212
Rockaway *(G-9471)*

Kahle Automation ....G....... 973 993-1850
Morristown *(G-6676)*

Lmt Usa Inc ....E....... 973 586-8722
Rockaway *(G-9475)*

Logan Instruments Corporation ....F....... 732 302-9888
Somerset *(G-10017)*

Nicos Group Inc ....G....... 201 768-9501
Norwood *(G-7571)*

Pharma Systems Inc ....G....... 973 636-9007
Hawthorne *(G-4239)*

Victor International Marketing ....G....... 973 267-8900
Morristown *(G-6707)*

MACHINERY: Plastic Working

3 H Technology Institute LLC ....E....... 866 624-3484
Mount Laurel *(G-6736)*

Autoplast Systems Inc ....G....... 973 785-8333
Woodland Park *(G-12070)*

Coperion Corporation ....C....... 201 327-6300
Sewell *(G-9835)*

Foremost Machine Builders Inc ....D....... 973 227-0700
Fairfield *(G-3206)*

Jomar Corp ....E....... 609 646-8000
Egg Harbor Township *(G-2686)*

Seajay Manufacturing Corp ....F....... 732 774-0900
Neptune *(G-6897)*

MACHINERY: Printing Presses

J Nelson Press Inc ....G....... 732 747-0330
Englishtown *(G-3005)*

Kirkwood NJ Globe Acqstion LLC ....C....... 201 440-0800
Ridgefield Park *(G-9310)*

MACHINERY: Recycling

Allied Waste Products Inc ....G....... 973 473-7638
Wallington *(G-11381)*

Clean Air Group ....G....... 908 232-4200
Parsippany *(G-7907)*

County Conservation Co Inc ....F....... 856 227-6900
Sewell *(G-9837)*

Energy Recycling Co LLC ....G....... 732 545-6619
New Brunswick *(G-6924)*

Exim Incorporated ....G....... 908 561-8200
Piscataway *(G-8664)*

Glass Cycle Systems Inc ....G....... 973 838-0034
Riverdale *(G-9378)*

Hugo Neu Corporation ....F....... 646 467-6700
Kearny *(G-4865)*

Kooltronic Inc ....C....... 609 466-3400
Pennington *(G-8369)*

Recycle-Tech Corp ....F....... 201 475-5000
Elmwood Park *(G-2853)*

Thanks For Being Green LLC ....E....... 856 333-0991
Pennsauken *(G-8491)*

MACHINERY: Riveting

Arrow Fastener Co LLC ....B....... 201 843-6900
Saddle Brook *(G-9640)*

MACHINERY: Road Construction & Maintenance

Hackettstown Public Works ....G....... 908 852-2320
Hackettstown *(G-4010)*

MACHINERY: Rubber Working

Advance Machine Planning Inc ....F....... 732 356-4438
Middlesex *(G-6094)*

Reliable Welding & Mch Work ....E....... 201 865-1073
North Bergen *(G-7432)*

MACHINERY: Saw & Sawing

Rowan Technologies Inc ....D....... 609 267-9000
Rancocas *(G-9165)*

MACHINERY: Semiconductor Manufacturing

Advance Process Systems Lim ....G....... 201 400-9190
Branchville *(G-701)*

Ileos of America Inc ....C....... 908 753-7300
South Plainfield *(G-10276)*

Starlight Electro-Optics Inc ....G....... 908 859-1362
Phillipsburg *(G-8575)*

Veeco ....E....... 732 560-5300
Somerset *(G-10092)*

Veeco Instruments Inc ....E....... 732 560-5300
Somerset *(G-10093)*

MACHINERY: Sheet Metal Working

American Made Fabricators Inc ....G....... 732 356-4306
Middlesex *(G-6096)*

Trumpf Inc ....E....... 609 925-8200
Cranbury *(G-1888)*

Trumpf Photonics Inc ....C....... 609 925-8200
Cranbury *(G-1889)*

MACHINERY: Sifting & Screening

Eurodia Industrie SA ....G....... 732 805-4001
Somerset *(G-9990)*

Kason Corporation ....D...... 973 467-8140
Millburn **(G-6201)**

MACHINERY: Specialty

A S M Technical................G...... 973 225-0111
Paterson **(G-8120)**
Indoor Entertainment of NJ............E...... 609 522-6700
Wildwood **(G-11945)**

MACHINERY: Stone Working

Thompson Stone....................G...... 973 293-7237
Montague **(G-6355)**

MACHINERY: Textile

Burlington Textile Machinery ....F 973 279-5900
Paterson **(G-8151)**
C & S Machine Inc................F...... 973 882-1097
Fairfield **(G-3161)**
Clements Industries Inc ....E...... 201 440-5500
South Hackensack **(G-10153)**
Daf Products Inc................F...... 201 251-1222
Wyckoff **(G-12108)**
Excel Industrial Co Inc................G...... 609 275-1748
Princeton Junction **(G-9057)**
M & S Machine & Tool Corp ....F...... 973 345-5847
Paterson **(G-8247)**
Pecata Enterprises Inc ....E...... 973 523-9498
Paterson **(G-8280)**

MACHINERY: Thread Rolling

Edston Manufacturing Company..........G...... 908 647-0116
Fairfield **(G-3189)**

MACHINERY: Tire Shredding

Imwoth LLC ....F 732 244-0950
Toms River **(G-10769)**
Safegaurd Document Destruction........G...... 609 448-6695
Millstone Township **(G-6212)**

MACHINERY: Voting

Avante International Tech Inc ....E...... 609 799-9388
Princeton Junction **(G-9052)**

MACHINERY: Woodworking

Logpowercom LLC ....G...... 732 350-9663
Whiting **(G-11940)**

MACHINES: Forming, Sheet Metal

Aluma Systems Con Cnstr LLC............G...... 908 418-5073
Linden **(G-5322)**
Bergen Homestate Corp....................G...... 201 372-9740
Moonachie **(G-6456)**
Dos Industrial Sales LLC................G...... 973 887-7800
East Hanover **(G-2205)**

MACHINISTS' TOOLS & MACHINES: Measuring, Metalworking Type

Dmg Mori Usa Inc....................G...... 973 257-9620
Rockaway **(G-9453)**

MACHINISTS' TOOLS: Precision

Almark Tool & Manufacturing Co ....F 908 789-2440
Garwood **(G-3780)**
Bach Tool Precision Inc ....G...... 973 962-6224
Ringwood **(G-9343)**
Bar-Lo Carbon Products Inc................E...... 973 227-2717
Fairfield **(G-3151)**
Congruent Machine Co Inc................G...... 973 764-6767
Vernon **(G-11158)**
Defined Pro Machining LLC................G...... 973 891-1038
Wharton **(G-11855)**
Industrial Brush Co Inc................E...... 800 241-9860
Fairfield **(G-3236)**
International Tool and Mfg................G...... 973 227-6767
Fairfield **(G-3241)**
J A Machine & Tool Co Inc................F...... 201 767-1308
Closter **(G-1759)**
Martin Tool Company Inc................F...... 973 361-9212
Wharton **(G-11862)**
Precision Ball Specialties................F...... 856 881-5646
Williamstown **(G-11971)**
Universal Metalcraft Inc................E...... 973 345-3284
Wayne **(G-11560)**

Wrightworks Engineering LLC ....G...... 609 882-8840
Lawrenceville **(G-5247)**
Zenith Precision Inc....................F...... 201 933-8640
East Rutherford **(G-2331)**

MACHINISTS' TOOLS: Scales, Measuring, Precision

Belleville Scale & Balance LLC............G...... 973 759-4487
Orange **(G-7751)**
Fulcrum Inc....................G...... 973 473-6900
Oradell **(G-7744)**
KG Systems Inc................G...... 973 515-4664
Springfield **(G-10451)**

MAGNETIC INK & OPTICAL SCANNING EQPT

Fotobridge ....G...... 856 809-9400
West Berlin **(G-11595)**
Metrologic Instruments Inc................C...... 856 228-8100
Mount Laurel **(G-6782)**
Omniplanar Inc................G...... 800 782-4263
Blackwood **(G-476)**

MAGNETIC RESONANCE IMAGING DEVICES: Nonmedical

Advanced Imaging Assoc LLC ....G...... 973 823-8999
Franklin **(G-3597)**
Denville Diagnostics Imaging................E...... 973 586-1212
Denville **(G-2034)**
Garden State Mgntc Imaging PC ....F...... 609 581-2727
Pennsauken **(G-8423)**

MAGNETS: Ceramic

Escadaus Inc....................G...... 973 335-8888
Boonton **(G-552)**
Oxford Instrs Holdings Inc................E...... 732 541-1300
Carteret **(G-1263)**

MAGNETS: Permanent

Escadaus Inc....................G...... 973 335-8888
Boonton **(G-552)**
Permadur Industries Inc................D...... 908 359-9767
Hillsborough **(G-4344)**
Tricomp Inc....................C...... 973 835-1110
Pompton Plains **(G-8872)**

MAIL PRESORTING SVCS

Arna Marketing Group Inc....................D...... 908 625-7395
Branchburg **(G-621)**

MAIL-ORDER BOOK CLUBS

Chatham Bookseller Inc....................G...... 973 822-1361
Madison **(G-5690)**

MAIL-ORDER HOUSES: Arts & Crafts Eqpt & Splys

Utrecht Manufacturing Corp ....D...... 609 409-8001
Cranbury **(G-1891)**

MAIL-ORDER HOUSES: Clothing, Exc Women's

Cockpit Usa Inc....................F 212 575-1616
Elizabeth **(G-2721)**
Somes Uniforms Inc................F........ 201 843-1199
Hackensack **(G-3975)**

MAIL-ORDER HOUSES: Computer Eqpt & Electronics

Creative Cmpt Concepts LLC................G...... 877 919-7988
Williamstown **(G-11956)**

MAIL-ORDER HOUSES: Computers & Peripheral Eqpt

Datapro International Inc....................E...... 732 868-0588
Piscataway **(G-8652)**

MAIL-ORDER HOUSES: Food

Genevieves Inc....................F 973 772-8816
Garfield **(G-3746)**

Giambris Quality Sweets Inc....................G...... 856 783-1099
Clementon **(G-1533)**

MAIL-ORDER HOUSES: General Merchandise

Esd Professional Inc....................G...... 212 300-7673
Palisades Park **(G-7773)**
Lux Naturals LLC................G...... 848 229-2950
Edison **(G-2554)**

MAIL-ORDER HOUSES: Order Taking Office Only

Arna Marketing Inc....................E...... 908 231-1100
Branchburg **(G-622)**

MAILBOX RENTAL & RELATED SVCS

E C D Ventures Inc....................G...... 856 875-1100
Blackwood **(G-465)**
Sre Ventures LLC................G...... 973 785-0099
Little Falls **(G-5468)**

MAILING MACHINES WHOLESALERS

Singe Corporation....................G...... 908 289-7900
Hillside **(G-4426)**

MAILING SVCS, NEC

Barton & Cooney LLC....................D...... 609 747-9300
Burlington **(G-953)**
C Jackson Associates Inc................E...... 856 761-8000
Cherry Hill **(G-1351)**
CIC Letter Service Inc................D...... 201 896-1900
Carlstadt **(G-1138)**
Corporate Mailings Inc................D...... 973 808-0009
Whippany **(G-11887)**
Corporate Mailings Inc................C...... 973 439-1168
West Caldwell **(G-11645)**
Full Service Mailers Inc................E...... 973 478-8813
Hackensack **(G-3919)**
Hermitage Press of New Jersey..........D...... 609 882-3600
Ewing **(G-3034)**
Hummel Distributing Corp................E...... 908 688-5300
Union **(G-11063)**
Hummel Printing Inc................E...... 908 688-5300
Union **(G-11064)**
Liberty Envelope Inc................F...... 973 546-5600
Paterson **(G-8240)**
Riverside Graphics Inc................F...... 201 876-9000
Belleville **(G-311)**
Sjshore Marketing Ltd Lblty Co............F...... 609 390-1400
Marmora **(G-5959)**
Standard Prtg & Mail Svcs Inc................F...... 973 790-3333
Fairfield **(G-3314)**
Tmg Enterprises Inc ....E...... 732 469-2900
Piscataway **(G-8728)**
Trenton Printing LLC................F...... 609 695-6485
Trenton **(G-11002)**
United Forms Finishing Corp................F...... 908 687-0494
Hillside **(G-4434)**
Your Printer V20 Ltd................E...... 609 771-4000
Cranbury **(G-1895)**

MANAGEMENT CONSULTING SVCS: Automation & Robotics

Robotunits Inc....................G...... 732 438-0500
Cranbury **(G-1879)**

MANAGEMENT CONSULTING SVCS: Banking & Finance

Ipjukebox Ltd Liability Co....................G...... 201 286-4535
Newark **(G-7158)**

MANAGEMENT CONSULTING SVCS: Business

Aus Inc....................G...... 856 234-9200
Mount Laurel **(G-6738)**
Nb Ventures Inc................C...... 732 382-6565
Clark **(G-1509)**
Recycling N Hensel Amer Inc................E...... 856 753-7614
West Berlin **(G-11618)**
SMR Research Corporation................G...... 908 852-7677
Hackettstown **(G-4037)**
Utility Development Corp................G...... 973 994-4334
Livingston **(G-5544)**

Employee Codes: A=Over 500 employees, B=251-500
C=101-250, D=51-100, E=20-50, F=10-19, G=4-9

2019 Harris New jersey
Manufacturers Directory

877

PRODUCT

Virid Biosciences Limited ....F 732 410-9573
Cherry Hill **(G-1426)**

MANAGEMENT CONSULTING SVCS: Construction Project

Independent Prj Cons Ltd Lblty...........G 973 780-8002
Newark **(G-7155)**
Infinite Mfg Group Inc ....E 973 649-9950
Kearny **(G-4868)**

MANAGEMENT CONSULTING SVCS: Food & Beverage

Advanced Food Systems Inc...............E 732 873-6776
Somerset **(G-9942)**

MANAGEMENT CONSULTING SVCS: General

Lummus Technology Ventures LLC......G 973 893-1515
Bloomfield **(G-509)**

MANAGEMENT CONSULTING SVCS: Hospital & Health

Quadramed Corporation ....E 732 751-0400
Eatontown **(G-2418)**

MANAGEMENT CONSULTING SVCS: Incentive Or Award Program

Genesis Marketing Group Inc ....G 201 836-1392
Teaneck **(G-10632)**
Hyman W Fisher Inc.............................G 973 992-9155
Livingston **(G-5514)**

MANAGEMENT CONSULTING SVCS: Industrial

Elena Consultants & Elec ....E 908 654-8309
Mountainside **(G-6845)**
Synthetic Surfaces Inc ....G 908 233-6803
Scotch Plains **(G-9743)**

MANAGEMENT CONSULTING SVCS: Industry Specialist

Luciano Packaging Tech Inc.................G 908 722-3222
Branchburg **(G-657)**
Pflaumer Brothers Inc ....G 609 883-4610
Ewing **(G-3051)**
Rambusch Decorating Company.........E 201 333-2525
Jersey City **(G-4797)**
Technology Reviews Inc ....G 973 537-9511
Randolph **(G-9203)**

MANAGEMENT CONSULTING SVCS: Information Systems

Business Dev Solutions Inc..................G 856 433-8005
Cherry Hill **(G-1350)**
Comprehensive Healthcare Systm........D 732 362-2000
Edison **(G-2482)**
Netcom Systems Inc ....E 732 393-6100
Edison **(G-2572)**

MANAGEMENT CONSULTING SVCS: Maintenance

Zion Industries Inc ....E 973 998-0162
Morris Plains **(G-6629)**

MANAGEMENT CONSULTING SVCS: Manufacturing

Schall Manufacturing Inc ....G 732 918-8800
Ocean **(G-7681)**

MANAGEMENT CONSULTING SVCS: Merchandising

Lloyd Gerstner & Partners LLC ....E 201 634-9099
Paramus **(G-7815)**
Njiw Limited Liability Company............F 201 355-2955
Hackensack **(G-3954)**

MANAGEMENT CONSULTING SVCS: New Products & Svcs

Convention News Company Inc ....F 201 444-5075
Midland Park **(G-6173)**
Naava Inc ....G 844 666-2282
Hazlet **(G-4266)**

MANAGEMENT CONSULTING SVCS: Training & Development

42 Design Square LLC ....F 888 272-5979
Parsippany **(G-7870)**

MANAGEMENT CONSULTING SVCS: Transportation

Carpenter & Paterson Inc ....E 609 227-2750
Bordentown **(G-578)**

MANAGEMENT SERVICES

Belle Printing Group LLC ....G 856 235-5151
Mount Laurel **(G-6741)**
Data Communique Inc ....E 201 508-6000
Ridgefield Park **(G-9302)**
Gannett Stllite Info Ntwrk Inc..............G 856 691-5000
Vineland **(G-11220)**
Integration Partners-Ny Corp...............B 973 871-2100
Parsippany **(G-7963)**
Jvc Industrial America Inc ....E 800 247-3608
Wayne **(G-11527)**
Merck Sharp & Dohme Corp ....A 908 740-4000
Kenilworth **(G-4960)**
Pfizer Inc ....D 973 739-0430
Parsippany **(G-7988)**
Qsa Global National Corp ....G 865 888-6798
Red Bank **(G-9241)**
Retail Management Pubg Inc ....F 212 981-0217
Montclair **(G-6388)**
Universal Vending MGT LLC ....F 908 233-4373
Westfield **(G-11804)**

MANAGEMENT SVCS, FACILITIES SUPPORT: Environ Remediation

Abatetech Inc ....E 609 265-2107
Lumberton **(G-5622)**

MANAGEMENT SVCS: Administrative

Eclearview Technologies Inc ....G 732 695-6999
Ocean **(G-7662)**

MANAGEMENT SVCS: Business

Krydon Group Inc ....G 877 854-1342
Moorestown **(G-6535)**
Mind-Alliance Systems LLC..................G 212 920-1911
Livingston **(G-5526)**

MANAGEMENT SVCS: Construction

Dreamstar Construction LLC................F 732 393-2572
Middletown **(G-6162)**
Vet Construction Inc ....F 732 987-4922
Jackson **(G-4669)**

MANAGEMENT SVCS: Hotel Or Motel

Sysco Guest Supply LLC ....C 732 537-2297
Somerset **(G-10078)**

MANHOLES & COVERS: Metal

Campbell Foundry Company.................E 973 483-5480
Harrison **(G-4166)**
Campbell Foundry Company.................E 201 998-3765
Kearny **(G-4850)**
Emporia Foundry Inc ....E 973 483-5480
Harrison **(G-4172)**
Universal Valve Company Inc...............F 908 351-0606
Elizabeth **(G-2784)**

MANICURE PREPARATIONS

Revel Nail LLC ....E 855 738-3501
Blackwood **(G-480)**
Yankee Tool Inc ....G 973 664-0878
Denville **(G-2062)**

MANIFOLDS: Pipe, Fabricated From Purchased Pipe

Selling Precision Inc............................E 973 728-1214
West Milford **(G-11731)**

MANUFACTURED & MOBILE HOME DEALERS

Silverstone Wireless LLC ....G 845 458-5197
Lodi **(G-5575)**

MANUFACTURING INDUSTRIES, NEC

(gt) Global Tech Inc.............................F 732 447-7083
Dayton **(G-1950)**
Authenticity Brewing LLC ....G 862 432-9622
Sparta **(G-10379)**
BSD Industries Ltd Liability ....G 732 534-4341
Lakewood **(G-5068)**
Cambrdge Inds For Vslly Impred..........G 732 247-6668
Somerset **(G-9965)**
Carbone America Scp Division..............G 973 334-0700
Boonton **(G-545)**
Cem Industries Inc ....G 908 244-8080
Harrison **(G-4167)**
Connector Mfg Co.................................G 513 860-4455
Jersey City **(G-4717)**
Fit Fabrication LLC ....G 973 685-7344
Clifton **(G-1621)**
Force Industries LLC ....G 973 332-1532
Butler **(G-1000)**
General Tools Mfg Co LLC ....G 201 770-1380
Secaucus **(G-9774)**
Green Globe USA LLC ....G 201 577-4468
Carteret **(G-1256)**
Han Hean U S A Corp ....G 732 494-3256
Edison **(G-2524)**
Kudas Industries Inc ....F 412 751-0260
Denville **(G-2043)**
Lexi Industries...................................F 201 297-7900
Northvale **(G-7534)**
Liquid Iron Industries Inc ....G 856 336-2639
West Berlin **(G-11604)**
Massage Chair Inc ....G 732 201-7777
Brick **(G-727)**
McT Manufacturing Inc.......................G 877 258-9600
Millburn **(G-6204)**
Pacent Engineering ....G 914 390-9150
Ocean **(G-7671)**
Peters Laboratories ....F 856 767-4144
Berlin **(G-428)**
Rapsoco Inc...G 908 977-7321
Elizabeth **(G-2773)**
Red Ray Manufacturing........................G 908 722-0040
Branchburg **(G-677)**
Ten One Design Ltd Lblty Co ....G 201 474-8232
Montclair **(G-6391)**
Vira Manufacturing Inc ....E 732 771-8269
Perth Amboy **(G-8538)**

MAPS

Discovery Map.....................................G 973 868-4552
Morristown **(G-6660)**
Geolytics Inc ....G 908 707-1505
Branchburg **(G-644)**

MARBLE BOARD

Eagle Fabrication Inc ....E 732 739-5300
Ltl Egg Hbr **(G-5616)**

MARBLE, BUILDING: Cut & Shaped

American Stone Inc ....E 973 318-7707
Hillside **(G-4373)**
American Stone Inc ....F 973 318-7707
Hillside **(G-4374)**
Bcg Marble & Granite South LLC ....G 732 367-3788
Jackson **(G-4641)**
Charles Deluca....................................G 973 778-5621
Lodi **(G-5556)**
Cole Brothers Marble & Granite ....G 856 455-7989
Elmer **(G-2795)**
Gr Stone LLC ....G 908 925-7290
Kenilworth **(G-4943)**
Ilkem Marble and Granite Inc ....G 856 433-8714
Cherry Hill **(G-1374)**
Marble Online Corporation...................G 201 998-9100
Kearny **(G-4882)**

Phillipsburg Marble Co Inc............E 908 859-3435
   Phillipsburg (G-8568)
Premier Marble and Gran 2 Inc...........G 732 294-7891
   Freehold (G-3691)
Solidsurface Designs Inc ....E 856 910-7720
   Pennsauken (G-8487)
Sr International Rock Inc.............F 908 864-4700
   Bound Brook (G-606)
Statewide Granite and Marble.........F 201 653-1700
   Jersey City (G-4815)

MARBLE: Crushed & Broken

Stone Surfaces Inc..................D 201 935-8803
   East Rutherford (G-2321)

MARINAS

Camp Marine Services Inc ....G 609 368-1777
   Stone Harbor (G-10503)
Lockwood Boat Works Inc ....E 732 721-1605
   South Amboy (G-10136)
Norma K Corporation ....G 732 477-6441
   Point Pleasant Beach (G-8829)

MARINE APPAREL STORES

Denali Company LLC................E 732 219-7771
   Red Bank (G-9226)

MARINE CARGO HANDLING SVCS

Bayonne Drydock & Repair Corp ....E 201 823-9295
   Bayonne (G-206)

MARINE CARGO HANDLING SVCS: Marine Terminal

Federal Lorco Petroleum LLC...............D 908 352-0542
   Elizabeth (G-2735)

MARINE ENGINE REPAIR SVCS

Monmouth Marine Engines Inc...........F 732 528-9290
   Brielle (G-907)

MARINE HARDWARE

Delta Procurement Inc..................G 201 623-9353
   Carlstadt (G-1149)
Mariner Sales and Power Inc ....G 732 477-7484
   Brick (G-725)
Oceanview Marine Welding LLC...........G 609 624-9669
   Ocean View (G-7704)
Viking Marine Products Inc ....G 732 826-4552
   Edison (G-2642)

MARINE RELATED EQPT

Maritime Solutions Inc...............G 732 752-3831
   Middlesex (G-6129)

MARINE SPLY DEALERS

Camp Marine Services Inc ....G 609 368-1777
   Stone Harbor (G-10503)
Lockwood Boat Works Inc ....E 732 721-1605
   South Amboy (G-10136)
Monmouth Marine Engines Inc...........F 732 528-9290
   Brielle (G-907)
Riverside Marina Yacht Sls LLC ....F 856 461-1077
   Riverside (G-9403)

MARINE SPLYS WHOLESALERS

World Wide Metric Inc ....F 732 247-2300
   Branchburg (G-696)

MARINE SVC STATIONS

A PS Inlet Marina LLC...............G 732 681-3303
   Belmar (G-346)

MARKETS: Meat & fish

Arm National Food Inc................G 609 695-4911
   Trenton (G-10896)
Evergreen Kosher LLC................G 732 370-4500
   Lakewood (G-5094)
Licini Brothers Inc ....G 201 865-1130
   Union City (G-11119)

MARKING DEVICES

Adco Signs of NJ Inc...............E 908 965-2112
   Elizabeth (G-2707)
Blue Ring Stencils LLC...............E 866 763-3873
   Lumberton (G-5623)
Classic Marking Products Inc...........G 973 383-2223
   Roxbury Township (G-9599)
Container Graphics Corp ....E 732 922-1180
   Neptune (G-6870)
Dalemark Industries Inc ....E 732 367-3100
   Lakewood (G-5081)
Digital Design Inc..................E 973 857-9500
   Cedar Grove (G-1274)
Harrisburg Stamp & Stencil Co ....G 717 236-9000
   Woodbury (G-12032)
J D Crew Inc ....E 856 665-3676
   Pennsauken (G-8443)
Lafarge Road Marking Inc ....C 973 884-0300
   Parsippany (G-7972)
Oraton Custom Products ....G 908 235-9424
   Columbia (G-1796)
Pic Graphics ....E 201 420-5040
   Jersey City (G-4783)
Private Label Products Inc ....E 201 773-4230
   Fair Lawn (G-3115)
Trodat Usa Inc ....F 732 529-8500
   Somerset (G-10089)
Winters Stamp Mfg Co Inc ....F 908 352-3725
   Martinsville (G-5965)

MARKING DEVICES: Embossing Seals & Hand Stamps

A A A Stamp and Seal Mfg Co ....G 201 796-1500
   Saddle Brook (G-9636)
A Quick Cut Stamping Embossing........F 856 321-0050
   Maple Shade (G-5858)
American Marking Systems Inc...........E 973 478-5600
   Clifton (G-1563)
American Stamp Mfg Co ....F 212 227-1877
   Clifton (G-1564)
Newark Stamp & Die Works Inc...........G 973 485-7111
   Newark (G-7217)
Shachihata Inc (usa) ....F 732 905-7159
   Lakewood (G-5162)
Trodat USA LLC ....D 732 562-9500
   Somerset (G-10090)

MARKING DEVICES: Embossing Seals, Corporate & Official

All-State International Inc...............C 908 272-0800
   Cranford (G-1899)

MARKING DEVICES: Pads, Inking & Stamping

Ranger Industries Inc ....E 732 389-3535
   Tinton Falls (G-10725)

MARKING DEVICES: Screens, Textile Printing

C Q Corporation ....F 201 935-8488
   East Rutherford (G-2281)
L & F Graphics Ltd Lblty Co ....G 973 240-7033
   Paterson (G-8232)

MARKING DEVICES: Seal Presses, Notary & Hand

Max Pro Services LLC...............G 973 396-2373
   Livingston (G-5523)

MARKING DEVICES: Time Stamps, Hand, Rubber Or Metal

Time Log Industries Inc...............G 609 965-5017
   Egg Harbor City (G-2670)

MATERIALS HANDLING EQPT WHOLESALERS

Elkay Products Co Inc ....F 973 376-7550
   Springfield (G-10441)
Hy-Tek Material Handling Inc ....E 732 490-6282
   Morganville (G-6587)
Permadur Industries Inc ....D 908 359-9767
   Hillsborough (G-4344)

MATS OR MATTING, NEC: Rubber

American Harlequin Corporation ....E 856 234-5505
   Moorestown (G-6503)

MATS, MATTING & PADS: Auto, Floor, Exc Rubber Or Plastic

Newark Auto Top Co Inc...............F 973 677-9935
   East Orange (G-2256)

MATS: Table, Plastic & Textile

Living Fashions Llc ....F 732 626-5200
   Sayreville (G-9716)

MATTRESS PROTECTORS, EXC RUBBER

Peel Away Labs Inc...............G 516 603-3116
   Jersey City (G-4779)

MATTRESS STORES

Custom Bedding Co ....G 973 761-1100
   Maplewood (G-5875)
Jomel Industries Inc ....F 973 282-0300
   Hillside (G-4406)
Lieth Holdings LLC ....G 201 358-8282
   Westwood (G-11834)

MEAL DELIVERY PROGRAMS

Princeton Quadrangle Club ....G 609 258-0376
   Princeton (G-9003)

MEAT & MEAT PRDTS WHOLESALERS

Arctic Foods Inc...............E 908 689-0590
   Washington (G-11438)
Arm National Food Inc...............G 609 695-4911
   Trenton (G-10896)
Bringhurst Bros Inc ....E 856 767-0110
   Berlin (G-418)
Megas Yeeros LLC ....E 212 777-6342
   Lyndhurst (G-5663)
Nu-Meat Technology Inc...............E 908 754-3400
   South Plainfield (G-10308)
Palenque Meat Provisions LLC ....E 908 718-1557
   Linden (G-5401)
United Premium Foods LLC...............D 732 510-5600
   Woodbridge (G-12023)

MEAT CUTTING & PACKING

Arm National Food Inc...............G 609 695-4911
   Trenton (G-10896)
B & B Poultry Co Inc...............C 856 692-8893
   Norma (G-7365)
Bie Real Estate Holdings LLC...............G 856 691-9765
   Vineland (G-11195)
Cameco Inc...............D 973 239-2845
   Verona (G-11164)
Carl Streit & Son Co...............G 732 775-0803
   Neptune (G-6869)
Carnegie Deli Products Inc ....D 201 507-5557
   Carlstadt (G-1136)
Comarco Products Inc...............D 856 342-7557
   Camden (G-1053)
Katzs Delicatessen Mfg ....E 212 254-2246
   Carlstadt (G-1173)
Kleemeyer & Merkel Inc...............E 973 377-0875
   Green Village (G-3868)
Mamamancinis Holdings Inc...............G 201 532-1212
   East Rutherford (G-2299)
Nu-Meat Technology Inc...............E 908 754-3400
   South Plainfield (G-10308)
Park Avenue Meats Inc ....E 718 731-4196
   Paterson (G-8278)
Premio Foods Inc...............C 800 864-7622
   Hawthorne (G-4240)
Pulaski Meat Products Co ....E 908 925-5380
   Linden (G-5413)
S & J Villari Livestock LLC...............G 856 468-0807
   Wenonah (G-11576)
Salem Packing Co ....E 856 878-0002
   Salem (G-9697)
Seabrite Corp ....G 973 491-0399
   Newark (G-7265)
Smithfield Packaged Meats Corp ....E 908 354-2674
   Elizabeth (G-2776)
Taylor Provisions Company ....D 609 392-1113
   Trenton (G-10996)

Tyson Fresh Meats Inc ....E...... 605 235-2061
Roseland **(G-9543)**

United Premium Foods LLC.................D...... 732 510-5600
Woodbridge **(G-12023)**

MEAT MARKETS

Arctic Foods Inc ....E...... 908 689-0590
Washington **(G-11438)**

Bringhurst Bros Inc ....E...... 856 767-0110
Berlin **(G-418)**

Kleemeyer & Merkel Inc ....F...... 973 377-0875
Green Village **(G-3868)**

Mayabeque Products Inc ....G...... 201 869-0531
North Bergen **(G-7420)**

Rastelli Brothers Inc ....C...... 856 803-1100
Swedesboro **(G-10606)**

MEAT PRDTS: Canned

B&G Foods Inc ....B...... 973 401-6500
Parsippany **(G-7889)**

B&G Foods Inc ....C...... 973 401-6500
Parsippany **(G-7890)**

B&G Foods North America Inc ....E...... 973 401-6500
Parsippany **(G-7891)**

MEAT PRDTS: Canned Exc Baby Food, From Slaughtered Meat

DArtagnan Inc ....D...... 973 344-0565
Union **(G-11041)**

Nourhan Trading Group Inc ....G...... 732 381-8110
Carteret **(G-1261)**

Rastelli Brothers Inc ....C...... 856 803-1100
Swedesboro **(G-10606)**

MEAT PRDTS: Cured, From Slaughtered Meat

Veroni Usa Inc ....E...... 609 970-0320
Logan Township **(G-5590)**

York Street Caterers Inc ....C...... 201 868-9088
Englewood **(G-2955)**

MEAT PRDTS: Frankfurters, From Purchased Meat

Marathon Enterprises Inc ....F...... 201 935-3330
Englewood **(G-2921)**

MEAT PRDTS: Frozen

Mamamancinis Holdings Inc...............G...... 201 532-1212
East Rutherford **(G-2299)**

Rajbhog Foods(nj) Inc ....C...... 551 222-4700
Jersey City **(G-4796)**

MEAT PRDTS: Ham, Boiled, From Purchased Meat

Al and John Inc ....B...... 973 742-4990
Caldwell **(G-1020)**

MEAT PRDTS: Head Cheese, From Purchased Meat

Red Square Foods Inc ....F...... 732 846-0190
Somerset **(G-10063)**

MEAT PRDTS: Meat By-Prdts, From Slaughtered Meat

Applegate Farms LLC.................C...... 908 725-2768
Bridgewater **(G-790)**

MEAT PRDTS: Pork, Cured, From Purchased Meat

Case Pork Roll Co Inc ....E...... 609 396-8171
Trenton **(G-10912)**

Taylor Provisions Company.................D...... 609 392-1113
Trenton **(G-10996)**

MEAT PRDTS: Pork, From Slaughtered Meat

Bringhurst Bros Inc ....E...... 856 767-0110
Berlin **(G-418)**

Dealaman Enterprises Inc ....E...... 908 647-5533
Warren **(G-11407)**

MEAT PRDTS: Sausage Casings, Natural

Nitta Casings Inc.....................C...... 800 526-3970
Bridgewater **(G-857)**

MEAT PRDTS: Sausages & Related Prdts, From Purchased Meat

Fratelli Beretta Usa Inc ....D...... 201 438-0723
Budd Lake **(G-923)**

MEAT PRDTS: Sausages, From Purchased Meat

Appetito Provisions Company...............E...... 201 864-3410
Harrington Park **(G-4162)**

Casa Di Bertacchi Corporation.................C...... 856 696-5600
Vineland **(G-11197)**

CW Brown Foods Inc ....E...... 856 423-3700
Mount Royal **(G-6816)**

Groezinger Provisions Inc ....F...... 732 775-3220
Neptune **(G-6883)**

Highpont Corporation.................E...... 201 460-1364
Rutherford **(G-9623)**

Lopes Sausage Co ....G...... 973 344-3063
Newark **(G-7185)**

Mayabeque Products Inc ....G...... 201 869-0531
North Bergen **(G-7420)**

Premio Foods Inc ....C...... 800 864-7622
Hawthorne **(G-4240)**

Pulaski Meat Products Co ....C...... 908 925-5380
Linden **(G-5413)**

Thumann Incorporated.................C...... 201 935-3636
Carlstadt **(G-1229)**

MEAT PRDTS: Snack Sticks, Incl Jerky, From Purchased Meat

Lawless Jerky LLC.....................G...... 310 869-5733
Marlton **(G-5936)**

MEAT PRDTS: Spiced Meats, From Purchased Meat

Martins Specialty Sausage Co.............F...... 856 423-4000
Mickleton **(G-6087)**

MEAT PRDTS: Veal, From Slaughtered Meat

Dorzar Corporation.....................E...... 973 589-6363
Newark **(G-7103)**

MEAT PROCESSED FROM PURCHASED CARCASSES

A Gimenez Trading LLC ....G...... 973 697-2240
Oak Ridge **(G-7599)**

Allied Specialty Foods Inc ....D...... 856 507-1100
Vineland **(G-11185)**

Applegate Farms LLC.....................C...... 908 725-2768
Bridgewater **(G-790)**

Arm National Food Inc.................G...... 609 695-4911
Trenton **(G-10896)**

Bringhurst Bros Inc ....E...... 856 767-0110
Berlin **(G-418)**

Buckhead Meat Company ....C...... 732 661-4900
Edison **(G-2471)**

Campbell Soup Supply Co LLC ....G...... 856 342-4800
Camden **(G-1049)**

CW Brown Foods Inc ....F...... 856 423-3700
Mount Royal **(G-6817)**

Dubon Corp ....G...... 212 812-2171
Elizabeth **(G-2730)**

Ena Meat Packing Inc ....E...... 973 742-4790
Paterson **(G-8184)**

Greentree Packing Inc ....D...... 212 675-2868
Passaic **(G-8071)**

Kupelian Foods Inc ....G...... 201 440-8055
Ridgefield Park **(G-9312)**

Licini Brothers Inc ....E...... 201 865-1130
Union City **(G-11119)**

Nicolosi Foods Inc ....G...... 201 624-1702
Union City **(G-11123)**

Palenque Meat Provisions LLC ....E...... 908 718-1557
Linden **(G-5401)**

Real Kosher LLC ....G...... 973 690-5394
Newark **(G-7247)**

Shahnawaz Food LLC.....................F...... 908 413-4206
Edison **(G-2606)**

Wagner Provision Co Inc ....F...... 856 423-1630
Gibbstown **(G-3800)**

MEAT PROCESSING MACHINERY

Patty-O-Matic Inc ....F...... 732 938-2757
Farmingdale **(G-3389)**

MEATS, PACKAGED FROZEN: Wholesalers

Delight Foods USA LLC ....F...... 201 369-1199
Jersey City **(G-4722)**

Nema Food Distribution Inc ....G...... 973 256-4415
Fairfield **(G-3276)**

MECHANICAL INSTRUMENT REPAIR SVCS

Deltronics Corporation.................F...... 856 825-8200
Millville **(G-6246)**

Serious Welding & Mech LLC ....F...... 732 698-7478
South River **(G-10357)**

MED, DENTAL & HOSPITAL EQPT, WHOL: Incontinent Prdts/Splys

Easy Undies LLC.....................G...... 201 715-4909
Springfield **(G-10440)**

MEDIA: Magnetic & Optical Recording

Fujifilm North America Corp ....B...... 732 857-3000
Edison **(G-2516)**

Synergem Inc ....E...... 732 692-6308
Avenel **(G-148)**

MEDICAL & HOSPITAL EQPT WHOLESALERS

America Techma Inc ....G...... 201 894-5887
Englewood Cliffs **(G-2958)**

Belair Instrument Company LLC ....E...... 973 912-8900
Pine Brook **(G-8587)**

Brenner Metal Products ....E...... 973 778-2466
Wallington **(G-11382)**

Dmg America LLC ....D...... 201 894-5500
Ridgefield Park **(G-9304)**

First National Servicing & Dev.............E...... 732 341-5409
Toms River **(G-10758)**

Nbs Group Sup Med Pdts Div LLC ....G...... 732 745-9292
New Brunswick **(G-6949)**

Specialty Pharmasource LLC ....F...... 973 784-4965
Denville **(G-2059)**

Tronex International Inc ....E...... 973 335-2888
Budd Lake **(G-938)**

MEDICAL & SURGICAL SPLYS: Bandages & Dressings

3M Company.........................B...... 973 884-2500
Whippany **(G-11875)**

Banding Centers of America.................G...... 973 805-9977
Florham Park **(G-3487)**

Derma Sciences Inc ....C...... 609 514-4744
Plainsboro **(G-8784)**

MEDICAL & SURGICAL SPLYS: Clothing, Fire Resistant & Protect

Ces Imports LLC.....................G...... 610 299-7930
Stone Harbor **(G-10504)**

MEDICAL & SURGICAL SPLYS: Cosmetic Restorations

Araya Inc.........................G...... 201 445-7005
Ridgewood **(G-9321)**

MEDICAL & SURGICAL SPLYS: Cotton, Incl Cotton Balls

Dexmed Inc.........................G...... 732 831-0507
Elizabeth **(G-2728)**

MEDICAL & SURGICAL SPLYS: Foot Appliances, Orthopedic

Ortho-Dynamics Inc.................G...... 973 742-4390
Paterson **(G-8274)**

Orthofeet Inc.........................E...... 800 524-2845
Northvale **(G-7542)**

MEDICAL & SURGICAL SPLYS: Ligatures

Ethicon Inc.........................C...... 908 306-0327
Bedminster **(G-264)**

(G-0000) Company's Geographic Section entry number

Ethicon Inc..C........ 908 218-0707
  Bedminster *(G-265)*

Healqu LLC..G........ 844 443-2578
  Jersey City *(G-4746)*

MEDICAL & SURGICAL SPLYS: Limbs, Artificial

Cape Prosthetics-Orthotics ....G........ 856 810-7900
  Marlton *(G-5923)*

Edge Orthotics Inc..............................G........ 732 549-3343
  Edison *(G-2499)*

Garden State Orthopedic Center ....G........ 973 538-4948
  Morristown *(G-6664)*

Hanger Prsthetcs & Ortho Inc...............G........ 973 736-0628
  West Orange *(G-11769)*

Harry J Lawall & Son Inc....................G........ 856 691-7764
  Vineland *(G-11231)*

Jefferson Prosthetic Orthotic ....G........ 973 762-0780
  South Orange *(G-10197)*

Nouveau Prosthetics Ltd ....F........ 732 739-0888
  Hazlet *(G-4267)*

Nouveau Prosthetics Orthotics ....F........ 732 739-0888
  Hazlet *(G-4268)*

MEDICAL & SURGICAL SPLYS: Orthopedic Appliances

Achilles Prosthetcs & Orthotcs ....G........ 201 785-9944
  Ramsey *(G-9133)*

Bayside Orthopedics LLC ....G........ 732 691-4898
  Toms River *(G-10751)*

Cocco Enterprises Inc.........................F........ 609 393-5939
  Trenton *(G-10920)*

Cranial Technologies Inc.....................G........ 908 754-0572
  Edison *(G-2485)*

Eastern Podiatry Labs Inc....................G........ 609 882-4444
  Ewing *(G-3028)*

Extremity Medical LLC ....F........ 973 588-8980
  Parsippany *(G-7940)*

Grateful Ped Inc ....F........ 973 478-6511
  Saddle Brook *(G-9654)*

Hanger Prsthetcs & Ortho Inc...............G........ 609 653-8323
  Linwood *(G-5449)*

Icon Orthopedic Concepts LLC ....G........ 973 794-6810
  Boonton *(G-556)*

Ivy Capital Partners LLC ....G........ 201 573-8400
  Montvale *(G-6415)*

J C Orthopedic Inc...............................G........ 732 458-7900
  Brick *(G-722)*

M B R Orthotics Inc.............................G........ 201 444-7750
  Wyckoff *(G-12114)*

Precision Orthotic Lab of Nj ....F........ 856 848-6226
  West Deptford *(G-11714)*

Regen Biologics Inc.............................F........ 201 651-5140
  Glen Rock *(G-3834)*

Rinko Orthopedic Appliances................G........ 201 796-3121
  Fair Lawn *(G-3117)*

Sivantos Inc...B........ 732 562-6600
  Piscataway *(G-8712)*

Tgz Acquisition Company LLC..............F........ 856 669-6600
  Cinnaminson *(G-1489)*

Total Control Othotics Lab ....G........ 609 499-2200
  Florence *(G-3479)*

Zimmer Inc..G........ 856 778-8300
  Mount Laurel *(G-6814)*

MEDICAL & SURGICAL SPLYS: Personal Safety Eqpt

Ansell Limited ....E........ 732 345-5400
  Iselin *(G-4595)*

Dynamic Safety Usa LLC....................G........ 844 378-7200
  Somerset *(G-9983)*

Gemtor Inc ....E........ 732 583-6200
  Matawan *(G-5976)*

Surgical Lser Sfety Cuncil Inc ....G........ 216 272-0805
  Cherry Hill *(G-1418)*

MEDICAL & SURGICAL SPLYS: Prosthetic Appliances

Atlantic Prsthtic Orthotic Svc...............G........ 609 927-6330
  Linwood *(G-5448)*

Garden State Prosthetics ....G........ 732 922-6650
  Ocean *(G-7665)*

J J L & W Inc......................................E........ 856 854-3100
  Magnolia *(G-5708)*

J M M R Inc...G........ 201 612-5104
  Fair Lawn *(G-3107)*

Johnson Associates Systems Inc ....F........ 856 228-2175
  Blackwood *(G-471)*

Mar Machine Ken Manufacturing............E........ 973 278-5827
  Paterson *(G-8250)*

North Jrsey Prsthtics Orthtics ....G........ 201 943-4448
  Palisades Park *(G-7775)*

Ossur Americas Inc ....G........ 856 345-6000
  West Deptford *(G-11712)*

Swiss Orthopedic Inc ....G........ 908 874-5522
  Hillsborough *(G-4359)*

MEDICAL & SURGICAL SPLYS: Space Helmets

Priority Medical Inc ....G........ 973 376-5077
  Short Hills *(G-9875)*

MEDICAL & SURGICAL SPLYS: Splints, Pneumatic & Wood

Armac Inc..F........ 973 457-0002
  Florham Park *(G-3480)*

Jerome Group Inc................................D........ 856 234-8600
  West Deptford *(G-11707)*

MEDICAL & SURGICAL SPLYS: Sponges

Nahallac LLC ....G........ 908 635-0999
  Whitehouse *(G-11917)*

MEDICAL & SURGICAL SPLYS: Stretchers

Jjj Stretchers Inc.................................G........ 908 290-3505
  Linden *(G-5364)*

MEDICAL & SURGICAL SPLYS: Supports, Abdominal, Ankle, Etc

Preform Laboratories Inc ....E........ 973 523-8610
  Hackensack *(G-3965)*

MEDICAL & SURGICAL SPLYS: Sutures, Non & Absorbable

Ethicon Inc..A........ 732 524-0400
  Somerville *(G-10108)*

MEDICAL & SURGICAL SPLYS: Trusses, Orthopedic & Surgical

Spinal Kinetics LLC ....G........ 908 687-2552
  Union *(G-11091)*

MEDICAL EQPT REPAIR SVCS, NON-ELECTRIC

Cross Medical Specialties Inc...............F........ 856 589-3288
  Pitman *(G-8744)*

MEDICAL EQPT: CAT Scanner Or Computerized Axial Tomography

3shape Inc ....F........ 908 867-0144
  Warren *(G-11395)*

Morris County Imaging ....G........ 973 532-7900
  Morristown *(G-6687)*

MEDICAL EQPT: Diagnostic

Abbott Point of Care Inc......................C........ 609 454-9000
  Princeton *(G-8898)*

Abbott Point of Care Inc......................C........ 609 371-8923
  East Windsor *(G-2332)*

Alfa Wassermann Inc..........................C........ 973 882-8630
  West Caldwell *(G-11637)*

Alfa Wssrmann Dagnstc Tech LLC ......F........ 800 220-4488
  West Caldwell *(G-11638)*

American Diagnstc Imaging Inc ....F........ 973 980-1724
  Nutley *(G-7578)*

Ascensia Diabetes Care US Inc ....C........ 973 560-6500
  Parsippany *(G-7885)*

Bahadir USA LLC ....G........ 856 517-3080
  Carneys Point *(G-1241)*

Clinical Image Retrieval Syste ....G........ 888 482-2362
  Franklin *(G-3601)*

Diabeto Inc..G........ 646 397-3175
  Piscataway *(G-8656)*

Diagnostix Plus Inc..............................G........ 201 530-5505
  Teaneck *(G-10627)*

Edda Technology Inc............................F........ 609 919-9889
  Princeton *(G-8938)*

Exalenz Bioscience Inc ....E........ 732 232-4393
  Wall Township *(G-11338)*

Gibraltar Laboratories Inc....................E........ 973 227-6882
  Fairfield *(G-3214)*

Health Care Alert LLC..........................F........ 732 676-2630
  Middletown *(G-6165)*

Immunostics Inc...................................G........ 732 918-0770
  Eatontown *(G-2402)*

Immunostics Company Inc ....E........ 732 918-0770
  Eatontown *(G-2403)*

Interpace Dagnostics Group Inc............E........ 412 224-6100
  Parsippany *(G-7965)*

Medicraft Inc.......................................F........ 201 797-8820
  Elmwood Park *(G-2842)*

Newton Memorial Hospital Inc..............G........ 973 726-0904
  Sparta *(G-10402)*

Northeast Medical Systems Corp..........G........ 856 910-8111
  Cherry Hill *(G-1400)*

Pausch LLC..G........ 732 747-6110
  Tinton Falls *(G-10724)*

Pharmasource International LLC ....G........ 732 985-6182
  Piscataway *(G-8700)*

Scimedx Corporation............................E........ 800 221-5598
  Dover *(G-2105)*

Smartekg LLC......................................G........ 201 376-4556
  Teaneck *(G-10652)*

State Technology Inc ....G........ 856 467-8009
  Bridgeport *(G-746)*

Total Tech Medical LLC ....G........ 973 980-6458
  Dover *(G-2109)*

United Medical PC ....G........ 201 456-0222
  Clifton *(G-1733)*

United Medical PC ....F........ 201 339-6111
  Bayonne *(G-236)*

Vela Diagnostics USA Inc.....................G........ 973 852-3740
  Fairfield *(G-3341)*

Vesag Health Inc ....F........ 732 333-1876
  North Brunswick *(G-7492)*

Zeus Scientific Inc ....D........ 908 526-3744
  Branchburg *(G-699)*

MEDICAL EQPT: Electromedical Apparatus

Echo Therapeutics Inc.........................F........ 732 201-4189
  Edgewater *(G-2437)*

Fluent Diagnostics ....G........ 201 414-4516
  Pequannock *(G-8504)*

Neurotron Medical Inc ....G........ 609 896-3444
  Ewing *(G-3049)*

Nextphase Medical Devices LLC ....E........ 201 968-9400
  Waldwick *(G-11308)*

MEDICAL EQPT: Electrotherapeutic Apparatus

Datascope Corp ....C........ 973 244-6100
  Fairfield *(G-3178)*

MEDICAL EQPT: Laser Systems

Cgm Us Inc..E........ 609 894-4420
  Birmingham *(G-456)*

Refine Technology LLC ....F........ 973 952-0002
  Pine Brook *(G-8615)*

Surgical Lser Sfety Cuncil Inc ....G........ 216 272-0805
  Cherry Hill *(G-1418)*

Topcon America Corporation.................B........ 201 599-5100
  Oakland *(G-7646)*

MEDICAL EQPT: MRI/Magnetic Resonance Imaging Devs, Nuclear

Ahs Hospital Corp................................E........ 908 522-2000
  Summit *(G-10523)*

MEDICAL EQPT: Pacemakers

Nextron Medical Tech Inc.....................D........ 973 575-0614
  Fairfield *(G-3279)*

St Jude Medical LLC.............................E........ 800 645-5368
  Secaucus *(G-9818)*

MEDICAL EQPT: Patient Monitoring

Capintec Inc...E........ 201 825-9500
  Florham Park *(G-3495)*

Mindray Ds Usa Inc ....B........ 201 995-8000
  Mahwah *(G-5754)*

Respironics Inc....................................C........ 973 581-6000
  Parsippany *(G-8007)*

Universal Medical Inc ....F........ 800 606-5511
  Ewing *(G-3074)*

PRODUCT

MEDICAL EQPT: Sterilizers

Alkaline Corporation ....G....... 732 531-7830
Eatontown *(G-2375)*
Getinge Usa Inc ....C....... 800 475-9040
Wayne *(G-11510)*

MEDICAL EQPT: Ultrasonic Scanning Devices

3dimension Dgnstc Slution Corp ....G....... 201 780-4653
Jersey City *(G-4678)*
Corentec America Inc ....G....... 949 379-6227
Morristown *(G-6655)*
Enterix Inc...............................E....... 732 429-1899
Edison *(G-2503)*
Total Tech Medical LLC ....G....... 973 980-6458
Dover *(G-2109)*
V L V Associates ....F....... 973 428-2884
Whippany *(G-11911)*

MEDICAL EQPT: Ultrasonic, Exc Cleaning

Dvx LLC ....G....... 609 924-3590
Princeton *(G-8934)*

MEDICAL EQPT: X-Ray Apparatus & Tubes, Fluoroscopic

Glenbrook Technologies Inc..............F....... 973 361-8866
Randolph *(G-9180)*

MEDICAL EQPT: X-Ray Apparatus & Tubes, Radiographic

G E Inspection Technologies LP ....D....... 973 448-0077
Flanders *(G-3411)*
Vatech America Inc ....E....... 201 210-5028
Fort Lee *(G-3593)*
Villa Radiology Systems LLC ....G....... 203 262-8836
Mount Laurel *(G-6811)*

MEDICAL EQPT: X-ray Generators

Swissray International Inc ....F....... 800 903-5543
Edison *(G-2629)*

MEDICAL SVCS ORGANIZATION

I Physician Hub ....D....... 732 274-0155
Monmouth Junction *(G-6292)*
Midlantic Medical Systems Inc ....G....... 908 432-4599
Skillman *(G-9923)*

MEDICAL, DENTAL & HOSPITAL EQPT, WHOL: Hosptl Eqpt/Furniture

Biomedicon ....F....... 856 778-1880
Moorestown *(G-6508)*

MEDICAL, DENTAL & HOSPITAL EQPT, WHOL: Surgical Eqpt & Splys

Akorn Inc ....D....... 732 846-8066
Somerset *(G-9947)*
Lumiscope Co Inc ....D....... 678 291-3207
East Rutherford *(G-2298)*
Rhein Medical Inc.......................F....... 727 209-2244
Denville *(G-2053)*

MEDICAL, DENTAL & HOSPITAL EQPT, WHOLESALE: Baths, Whirlpool

Asd Holding Corp ....G....... 800 442-1902
Piscataway *(G-8638)*

MEDICAL, DENTAL & HOSPITAL EQPT, WHOLESALE: Diagnostic, Med

Spectrum Laboratory Pdts Inc............C....... 732 214-1300
New Brunswick *(G-6971)*
SPS Alfachem Inc ....G....... 973 676-5141
Orange *(G-7762)*
Twinpod Inc ....G....... 908 758-5858
Princeton *(G-9037)*
Virid Biosciences Limited ....F....... 732 410-9573
Cherry Hill *(G-1426)*

MEDICAL, DENTAL & HOSPITAL EQPT, WHOLESALE: Hearing Aids

Oticon Inc ....C....... 732 560-1220
Somerset *(G-10047)*

MEDICAL, DENTAL & HOSPITAL EQPT, WHOLESALE: Med Eqpt & Splys

3M Company ....C....... 908 788-4000
Flemington *(G-3426)*
Bard International Inc ....D....... 908 277-8000
Franklin Lakes *(G-3612)*
Bellco Glass Inc ....D....... 800 257-7043
Vineland *(G-11192)*
Bergen Manufacturing & Supply ....E....... 201 854-3461
North Bergen *(G-7389)*
Bsi Corp ....E....... 631 589-1118
Nutley *(G-7581)*
Carry Easy Inc ....E....... 201 944-0042
Leonia *(G-5287)*
Case Medical Inc ....C....... 201 313-1999
South Hackensack *(G-10152)*
Cryopak Verification Tech Inc ....F....... 732 346-9200
Edison *(G-2488)*
Cura Biomed Inc ....G....... 609 647-1474
Princeton Junction *(G-9054)*
Dexmed Inc ....G....... 732 831-0507
Elizabeth *(G-2728)*
Diagnostix Plus Inc ....G....... 201 530-5505
Teaneck *(G-10627)*
Distek Inc ....D....... 732 422-7585
North Brunswick *(G-7466)*
DRG International Inc ....E....... 973 564-7555
Springfield *(G-10439)*
Electric Mobility Corporation ....C....... 856 468-1000
Sewell *(G-9843)*
Ellis Instruments Inc ....G....... 973 593-9222
Madison *(G-5692)*
Johnson & Johnson ....A....... 732 524-0400
New Brunswick *(G-6940)*
Maddak Inc ....G....... 973 628-7600
Wayne *(G-11531)*
Medical Indicators Inc ....F....... 609 737-1600
Hamilton *(G-4113)*
Oxford Instrs Holdings Inc ....E....... 732 541-1300
Carteret *(G-1263)*
Paw Bioscience Products LLC ....G....... 732 460-0088
Eatontown *(G-2416)*
Photonics Management Corp ....G....... 908 231-0960
Bridgewater *(G-866)*
Redfield Corporation ....G....... 201 845-3990
Rochelle Park *(G-9429)*

MEDICAL, DENTAL & HOSPITAL EQPT, WHOLESALE: Medical Lab

Friedrich and Dimmock Inc...............E....... 856 825-0305
Millville *(G-6249)*
Globe Scientific Inc....................E....... 201 599-1400
Mahwah *(G-5744)*
Tovatech LLC ....G....... 973 913-9734
Maplewood *(G-5885)*

MEDICAL, DENTAL & HOSPITAL EQPT, WHOLESALE: Orthopedic

Biomed Innovative Cons LLC ....G....... 732 599-7233
South Amboy *(G-10131)*
Howmedica Osteonics Corp ....C....... 201 831-5000
Mahwah *(G-5747)*

MEDICAL, DENTAL/HOSPITAL EQPT, WHOL: Veterinarian Eqpt/Sply

Biomedtrix LLC ....F....... 973 331-7800
Whippany *(G-11881)*
DMS Laboratories Inc ....G....... 908 782-3353
Flemington *(G-3438)*

MEMBERSHIP ORGANIZATIONS, NEC: Charitable

DSM Sight & Life Inc ....G....... 973 257-8208
Parsippany *(G-7923)*

MEMBERSHIP ORGANIZATIONS, NEC: Literary, Film Or Cultural

Aqualink LLC ....F....... 201 849-9771
Fort Lee *(G-3547)*

MEMBERSHIP ORGANIZATIONS, PROF: Education/Teacher Assoc

Investment Casting Institute ....G....... 201 573-9770
Montvale *(G-6414)*

MEMBERSHIP ORGANIZATIONS, RELIGIOUS: Assembly Of God Church

Almond Branch Inc ....E....... 973 728-3479
West Milford *(G-11724)*
Hope Center.............................F....... 201 798-1234
Jersey City *(G-4748)*

MEMBERSHIP ORGANIZATIONS, RELIGIOUS: Catholic Church

Diocese of Camden New Jersey...........A....... 856 756-7900
Camden *(G-1058)*

MEMBERSHIP ORGANIZATIONS, RELIGIOUS: Nonchurch

Christian Mssons In Many Lands ....G....... 732 449-8880
Wall Township *(G-11324)*

MEN'S & BOYS' CLOTHING ACCESS STORES

Gilbert Storms Jr.......................G....... 973 835-5729
Haskell *(G-4196)*

MEN'S & BOYS' CLOTHING STORES

Elie Tahari Ltd ....C....... 973 671-6300
Millburn *(G-6196)*
Hat Box ....E....... 732 961-2262
Lakewood *(G-5108)*
Pvh Corp ....G....... 908 685-0050
Bridgewater *(G-871)*
Sock Company Inc ....E....... 201 307-0675
Westwood *(G-11845)*
Todd Shelton LLC ....G....... 844 626-6355
East Rutherford *(G-2326)*

MEN'S & BOYS' CLOTHING WHOLESALERS, NEC

Burlington Coat Factory ....D....... 908 994-9562
Elizabeth *(G-2718)*
Handcraft Manufacturing Corp ....E....... 973 565-0077
Newark *(G-7146)*
Merc USA Inc ....F....... 201 489-3527
Hackensack *(G-3947)*
New Top Inc ....E....... 201 438-3990
Carlstadt *(G-1191)*
New York Popular Inc ....D....... 718 499-2020
Carteret *(G-1260)*
Personality Handkerchiefs Inc...........E....... 973 565-0077
Newark *(G-7227)*
Selfmade LLC ....G....... 201 792-8968
Jersey City *(G-4808)*

MEN'S & BOYS' SPORTSWEAR CLOTHING STORES

Cockpit Usa Inc ....F....... 212 575-1616
Elizabeth *(G-2721)*

MEN'S & BOYS' SPORTSWEAR WHOLESALERS

Bimini Bay Outfitters Ltd...............F....... 201 529-3550
Mahwah *(G-5716)*
Chartwell Promotions Ltd Inc ....G....... 732 780-6900
Freehold *(G-3657)*
Cockpit Usa Inc ....F....... 212 575-1616
Elizabeth *(G-2721)*
Monogram Center Inc ....E....... 732 442-1800
Perth Amboy *(G-8528)*

MEN'S CLOTHING STORES: Everyday, Exc Suits & Sportswear

John B Stetson Company ....G....... 212 563-1848
Hoboken (G-4459)

METAL & STEEL PRDTS: Abrasive

Japan Steel Works America Inc..............G....... 212 490-2630
Edison (G-2538)

METAL CUTTING SVCS

Kwg Industries LLC ....E....... 908 218-8900
Hillsborough (G-4338)

METAL FABRICATORS: Architechtural

67 Pollock Ave Corp ....G....... 201 432-1156
Jersey City (G-4679)
A & A Ironwork Co Inc ....F....... 973 728-4300
Hewitt (G-4273)
Advanced Products LLC ....E....... 800 724-5464
Lakewood (G-5046)
Airmet Inc ....G....... 973 481-5550
Newark (G-7037)
Alberona Welding & Iron Works ....G....... 973 674-3375
Orange (G-7749)
Architctural Metal Fabricators ....G....... 718 765-0722
Carteret (G-1246)
Architectural Iron Designs ....G....... 908 757-2323
Plainfield (G-8758)
Armetec Corp ....G....... 973 485-2525
Newark (G-7052)
B L White Welding & Steel Co ....G....... 973 684-4111
Paterson (G-8144)
Bamco Inc ....D....... 732 302-0889
Middlesex (G-6100)
Carfaro Inc ....E....... 609 890-6600
Trenton (G-10910)
Ciccone Inc ....G....... 732 349-7071
Toms River (G-10752)
Clems Ornemental Iron Works ....D....... 732 968-7200
Piscataway (G-8647)
Columbian Orna Ir Works Inc ....G....... 973 697-0927
Paterson (G-8160)
Creative Metal Works Inc ....F....... 973 579-3717
Sparta (G-10385)
Cusumano Perma-Rail Co ....G....... 908 245-9281
Roselle Park (G-9581)
Doortec Archtctural Met GL LLC ....G....... 201 497-5056
River Vale (G-9365)
Empire Lumber & Millwork Co ....E....... 973 242-2700
Newark (G-7115)
F & C Prof Alum Railings Corp ....E....... 908 753-8886
Plainfield (G-8765)
Fairway Building Products LLC ....E....... 609 890-6600
Trenton (G-10935)
G & H Sheet Metal Works Inc ....G....... 973 923-1100
Hillside (G-4393)
George Ciocher Inc ....G....... 732 818-3495
Toms River (G-10761)
Harsco Corporation ....E....... 908 454-7169
Plainfield (G-8768)
International Design & Mfg LLC ....G....... 908 587-2884
Linden (G-5363)
Interntnal Archtctral Irnworks ....E....... 973 741-0749
Irvington (G-4577)
Interstate Architectural & Ir ....G....... 201 941-0393
Cliffside Park (G-1540)
Interstate Panel LLC ....F....... 609 586-4411
Hamilton (G-4108)
J G Schmidt Steel ....F....... 973 473-4822
Passaic (G-8075)
James Zylstra Enterprises Inc ....E....... 973 383-6768
Lafayette (G-5028)
K & A Architectural Met GL LLC ....F....... 908 687-0247
Hillside (G-4408)
Kaufman Stairs Inc ....E....... 908 862-3579
Rahway (G-9111)
LMC-HB Corp ....F....... 862 239-9814
Paterson (G-8244)
Marchione Industries Inc ....F....... 718 317-4900
Lyndhurst (G-5661)
McNichols Company ....F....... 877 884-4653
New Brunswick (G-6945)
Merchant & Evans Inc ....E....... 609 387-3033
Burlington (G-979)
Mershon Concrete LLC ....E....... 609 298-2150
Bordentown (G-588)
Michael Anthony Sign Design Inc ....E....... 732 453-6120
Piscataway (G-8690)

Morsemere Iron Works Inc ....F....... 201 941-1133
Ridgefield (G-9278)
Newman Ornamental Iron Works ....F....... 732 223-9042
Brielle (G-908)
Omnia Industries Inc ....E....... 973 239-7272
Cedar Grove (G-1286)
Papp Iron Works Inc ....D....... 908 731-1000
Plainfield (G-8775)
Par Troy Sheet Metal & AC LLC ....G....... 973 227-1150
Fairfield (G-3288)
Permanore Archtctural Finishes ....G....... 908 797-4177
Milford (G-6194)
Pioneer Railing Inc ....G....... 609 387-0981
Beverly (G-453)
Rambusch Decorating Company ....E....... 201 333-2525
Jersey City (G-4797)
Security Fabricators Inc ....F....... 908 272-9171
Kenilworth (G-4977)

METAL FABRICATORS: Plate

Airmet Inc ....G....... 973 481-5550
Newark (G-7037)
Akw Inc ....G....... 732 493-1883
Ocean (G-7654)
Akw Inc ....G....... 732 530-9186
Shrewsbury (G-9880)
Arrow Shed LLC ....E....... 973 835-3200
Haskell (G-4195)
Asco LP ....E....... 973 386-9000
Parsippany (G-7886)
CB&i LLC ....C....... 856 482-3000
Trenton (G-10913)
Crown Engineering Corp ....E....... 800 631-2153
Farmingdale (G-3382)
Jersey Tank Fabricators Inc ....E....... 609 758-7670
South Plainfield (G-10283)
Joseph Oat Holdings Inc ....D....... 856 541-2900
Camden (G-1072)
Pulsonics Inc ....F....... 800 999-6785
Belleville (G-309)
Scientific Alloys Corp ....F....... 973 478-8323
Clifton (G-1712)
Shell Packaging Corporation ....E....... 908 871-7000
Berkeley Heights (G-412)
Springfield Metal Pdts Co Inc ....F....... 973 379-4600
Springfield (G-10467)
Stirrup Metal Products Corp ....F....... 973 824-7086
Newark (G-7287)
Theodore E Mozer Inc ....E....... 856 829-1432
Palmyra (G-7786)
Triangle Tube/Phase III Co Inc ....D....... 856 228-9940
Paulsboro (G-8340)
Ulma Form-Works Inc ....D....... 201 882-1122
Hawthorne (G-4247)
Waage Electric Inc ....G....... 908 245-9363
Kenilworth (G-4986)

METAL FABRICATORS: Sheet

67 Pollock Ave Corp ....G....... 201 432-1156
Jersey City (G-4679)
A R J Custom Fabrication Inc ....F....... 609 695-6227
Trenton (G-10887)
A&B Heating & Cooling ....G....... 908 289-2231
Elizabeth (G-2705)
Abco Metal LLC ....F....... 973 772-8160
Paterson (G-8122)
Aerosmith ....G....... 973 614-9392
South Hackensack (G-10147)
Air & Specialties Sheet Metal ....F....... 908 233-8306
Mountainside (G-6832)
Airfiltronix Corp ....G....... 973 779-5577
Clifton (G-1560)
Airmet Inc ....G....... 973 481-5550
Newark (G-7037)
Ajay Metal Fabricators Inc ....G....... 908 523-0557
Linden (G-5318)
Allentown Inc ....B....... 609 259-7951
Allentown (G-24)
Allied Metal Industries Inc ....E....... 973 824-7347
Newark (G-7039)
Amerifab Corp ....G....... 973 777-2120
Lodi (G-5553)
Andrew B Duffy Inc ....F....... 856 845-4900
West Deptford (G-11691)
Ango Electronics Corporation ....F....... 201 955-0800
North Arlington (G-7368)
Architctural Metal Designs Inc ....F....... 856 765-3000
Millville (G-6234)
Argyle Industries Inc ....F....... 908 725-8800
Branchburg (G-620)

Artus Corp ....E....... 201 568-1000
Englewood (G-2878)
Atlantic Air Enterprises Inc ....F....... 732 381-4000
Rahway (G-9081)
Atlantic Coastal Welding Inc ....F....... 732 269-1088
Bayville (G-240)
Babbitt Mfg Co Inc ....F....... 856 692-3245
Vineland (G-11190)
Banicki Sheet Metal Inc ....G....... 201 385-5938
Bergenfield (G-372)
BCsmachine & Mfg Corp ....E....... 908 561-1656
South Plainfield (G-10224)
Belden Inc ....F....... 908 925-8000
Elizabeth (G-2714)
Benco Inc ....F....... 973 575-4440
Fairfield (G-3154)
Bill Chambers Sheet Metal ....G....... 856 848-4774
Woodbury Heights (G-12041)
Blackhawk Cre Corporation ....F....... 856 887-0162
Salem (G-9692)
Bloomfield Manufacturing Co ....F....... 973 575-8900
Oakland (G-7616)
BR Welding Inc ....F....... 732 363-8253
Howell (G-4532)
Breure Sheet Metal Co Inc ....G....... 973 772-6423
Clifton (G-1578)
Brook Metal Products Inc ....F....... 908 355-1601
Lawrence Township (G-5215)
Brothers Sheet Metal Inc ....F....... 973 228-3221
Roseland (G-9536)
Bushwick Metals LLC ....C....... 610 495-9100
Englewood (G-2888)
C A Spalding Company ....E....... 267 550-9000
Moorestown (G-6511)
Cain Machine Inc ....F....... 856 825-7225
Millville (G-6240)
Central Metal Fabricators Inc ....F....... 732 938-6900
Farmingdale (G-3379)
Classic Industries Inc ....G....... 973 227-1366
Parsippany (G-7906)
CPS Metals Inc ....F....... 856 779-0846
Maple Shade (G-5861)
Crett Construction Inc ....F....... 973 663-1184
Lake Hopatcong (G-5035)
Cutmark Inc ....G....... 856 234-3428
Mount Laurel (G-6750)
Danson Sheet Metal Inc ....E....... 201 343-4876
Hackensack (G-3905)
Dasco Supply LLC ....F....... 973 884-1390
Whippany (G-11888)
Delair LLC ....D....... 856 663-2900
Pennsauken (G-8412)
Delaware Valley Sign Corp ....D....... 609 386-0100
Burlington (G-962)
Demand LLC ....F....... 908 526-2020
Somerville (G-10107)
Duct Mate Inc ....G....... 201 488-8002
Hackensack (G-3909)
Durex Inc ....D....... 908 688-0800
Union (G-11045)
Dutra Sheet Metal Co ....G....... 856 692-8058
Vineland (G-11215)
Evs Interactive Inc ....F....... 718 784-3690
Riverdale (G-9377)
Ewc Controls Inc ....E....... 732 446-3110
Manalapan (G-5809)
Excel Die Sharpening Corp ....G....... 908 587-2606
Linden (G-5345)
Fabulous Fabricators LLC ....E....... 973 779-2400
Totowa (G-10826)
Falcon Industries Inc ....D....... 732 563-9889
Somerset (G-9992)
Fitts Sheet Metal Inc ....G....... 201 923-9239
North Arlington (G-7373)
Frc Electrical Industries Inc ....E....... 908 464-3200
New Providence (G-7000)
Garvey Corporation ....D....... 609 561-2450
Hammonton (G-4134)
Gauer Metal Products Co Inc ....E....... 908 241-4080
Kenilworth (G-4942)
Giant Stl Fabricators Erectors ....G....... 908 241-6766
Roselle (G-9559)
Golden Metal Products Corp ....G....... 973 399-1157
Hillside (G-4394)
H & H Industries Inc ....F....... 856 663-4444
Pennsauken (G-8429)
H & H Production Machining ....G....... 973 383-6880
Sparta (G-10389)
Haenssler Shtmtl Works Inc ....F....... 973 373-6360
Newark (G-7143)

PRODUCT

Handi-Hut Inc ....E 973 614-1800
 Clifton *(G-1632)*
Harold R Henrich Inc ....D 732 370-4455
 Lakewood *(G-5107)*
Hutchinson Industries Inc ....F 609 394-1010
 Trenton *(G-10940)*
In-Line Shtmtl Fabricators ....G 201 339-8121
 Bayonne *(G-224)*
Independent Metal Sales Inc ....F 609 261-8090
 Hainesport *(G-4074)*
Independent Sheet Metal Co Inc ....D 973 423-1150
 Riverdale *(G-9379)*
Inox Components ....F 856 256-0800
 Pitman *(G-8745)*
Intercoastal Fabricators Inc ....G 856 629-4105
 Williamstown *(G-11961)*
International Swimming Pools ....E 732 565-9229
 New Brunswick *(G-6935)*
Internet-Sales USA Corporation ....G 775 468-8379
 Rockaway *(G-9467)*
J & M Air Inc ....E 908 707-4040
 Somerville *(G-10118)*
James A Stanlick Jr ....G 973 366-7316
 Wharton *(G-11860)*
Jason Metal Products Corp ....G 732 396-1132
 Rahway *(G-9107)*
Jesco Iron Crafts Inc ....F 201 488-4545
 Bogota *(G-533)*
Jet Precision Metal Inc ....E 973 423-4350
 Hawthorne *(G-4229)*
John E Herbst Heating & Coolg............G 732 721-0088
 Parlin *(G-7866)*
Joseph Bbinec Shtmtl Works Inc ....E 732 388-0155
 Rahway *(G-9109)*
Klm Mechanical Contractors ....F 201 385-6965
 Dumont *(G-2115)*
Leibrock Metal Products Inc ....G 732 695-0326
 Ocean *(G-7669)*
Madhu B Goyal MD ....G 908 769-0307
 South Plainfield *(G-10296)*
Marino International Corp ....G 732 752-5100
 South Plainfield *(G-10299)*
Marlyn Sheet Metal Inc ....F 856 863-6900
 Clayton *(G-1527)*
Marx NJ Group LLC ....E 732 901-3880
 Bound Brook *(G-603)*
Max Gurtman & Sons Inc ....G 973 478-7000
 Clifton *(G-1666)*
Medlaurel Inc ....E 856 461-6600
 Delanco *(G-2006)*
Metal Dynamix LLC ....G 856 235-4559
 Cherry Hill *(G-1394)*
Millar Sheet Metal ....E 201 997-1990
 Kearny *(G-4884)*
Nordic Metal LLC ....G 908 245-8900
 Kenilworth *(G-4964)*
Oeg Building Materials Inc ....E 732 667-3636
 Sayreville *(G-9720)*
P L M Manufacturing Company ....E 201 342-3636
 Hackensack *(G-3961)*
Pabst Enterprises Equipment Co ....E 908 353-2880
 Elizabeth *(G-2766)*
Par Sheet Metal Inc ....F 908 241-2477
 Roselle *(G-9570)*
Park Steel & Iron Co ....F 732 775-7500
 Neptune *(G-6894)*
Passaic Metal & Bldg Sups Co ....D 973 546-9000
 Clifton *(G-1685)*
Pcr Technologies Inc ....G 973 882-0017
 Pine Brook *(G-8613)*
Pl Metal Products Inc ....G 201 955-0800
 Linden *(G-5408)*
Precision Metalcrafters Inc ....E 856 629-1020
 Williamstown *(G-11972)*
Prism Sheet Metal Inc ....G 973 673-0213
 Orange *(G-7758)*
R M F Associates Inc ....C 908 687-9355
 Union *(G-11086)*
Rails Company Inc ....E 973 763-4320
 Maplewood *(G-5883)*
Rainbow Metal Units Corp ....E 718 784-3690
 Riverdale *(G-9381)*
Ricklyn Co Inc ....G 908 689-6770
 Columbia *(G-1797)*
Schrader & Company Inc ....F 973 579-1160
 Newton *(G-7357)*
Service Metal Fabricating Inc ....G 973 989-7199
 Dover *(G-2106)*
Sheet Metal Products Inc ....D 973 482-0450
 Newark *(G-7269)*

Sonrise Metal Inc ....F 973 423-4717
 Hopatcong *(G-4522)*
South Jersey Metal Inc ....E 856 228-0642
 Deptford *(G-2066)*
Sperro Metal Products LLC ....E 973 335-2000
 Montville *(G-6447)*
Springfield Heating & AC Co ....F 908 233-8400
 Mountainside *(G-6852)*
Star Metal Products ....E 908 474-9860
 Linden *(G-5429)*
Stirrup Metal Products Corp ....F 973 824-7086
 Newark *(G-7287)*
Tam Metal Products Inc ....E 201 848-7800
 Mahwah *(G-5779)*
Ware Industries Inc ....D 908 757-9000
 South Plainfield *(G-10345)*
Welded Products Co Inc ....E 973 589-0180
 Newark *(G-7313)*

METAL FABRICATORS: *Structural, Ship*

Allied Metal Industries Inc ....E 973 824-7347
 Newark *(G-7039)*
Sea Habor Marine Inc ....G 732 477-8577
 Brick *(G-731)*

METAL FABRICATORS: *Structural, Ship*

Flame Cut Steel Inc ....F 973 373-9300
 Irvington *(G-4569)*
Susan R Bauer Inc ....G 973 657-1590
 Ringwood *(G-9353)*

METAL FINISHING SVCS

A & L Industries Inc ....E 973 589-8070
 Newark *(G-7028)*
Advanced Metal Processing ....G 856 327-0048
 Millville *(G-6223)*
Cameo Metal Products Inc ....F 732 388-4000
 Rahway *(G-9084)*
Durex Inc ....D 908 688-0800
 Union *(G-11045)*
Foremost Manufacturing Co Inc...........D 908 687-4646
 Union *(G-11056)*
Paramount Metal Finishing Co ....C 908 862-0772
 Linden *(G-5403)*
Prem-Khichi Enterprises Inc ....F 973 242-0300
 East Brunswick *(G-2167)*
Sar Industrial Finishing Inc ....F 609 567-2772
 Berlin *(G-429)*
Sun Metal Finishing Inc ....E 973 684-0119
 North Haledon *(G-7500)*
Vigilant Design ....G 201 432-3900
 Jersey City *(G-4826)*

METAL MINING SVCS

Coastal Metal Recycling Corp ....G 732 738-6000
 Keasbey *(G-4911)*
Connell Mining Products LLC ....D 908 673-3700
 Berkeley Heights *(G-395)*
Industrial Stl & Fastener Corp ....F 610 667-2220
 Cherry Hill *(G-1377)*
Kp Excavation LLC ....E 201 933-4200
 Carlstadt *(G-1178)*

METAL SERVICE CENTERS & OFFICES

Alloy Stainless Products Co ....D 973 256-1616
 Totowa *(G-10810)*
Ansun Protective Metals Inc ....G 732 302-0616
 Middlesex *(G-6098)*
Asbury Carbons Inc ....G 908 537-2155
 Asbury *(G-60)*
Bedlam Corp ....F 973 774-8770
 Montclair *(G-6360)*
Benedict-Miller LLC ....F 908 497-1477
 Kenilworth *(G-4929)*
Doolan Industries Incorporated............E 856 985-1880
 Marlton *(G-5929)*
FW Winter Inc ....F 856 963-7490
 Camden *(G-1065)*
Independent Metal Sales Inc ....F 609 261-8090
 Hainesport *(G-4074)*
Lentine Sheet Metal Inc ....G 908 486-8974
 Linden *(G-5375)*
Merchant & Evans Inc ....F 609 387-3033
 Burlington *(G-979)*
Metal Cutting Corporation ....G 973 239-1100
 Cedar Grove *(G-1282)*
Procedyne Corp ....F 732 249-8347
 New Brunswick *(G-6962)*

RS Phillips Steel LLC ....E 973 827-6464
 Sussex *(G-10565)*
Steelstran Industries Inc ....E 732 574-0700
 Avenel *(G-147)*

METAL SPINNING FOR THE TRADE

F G Clover Company Inc ....G 973 627-1160
 Rockaway *(G-9457)*
Laeger Metal Spinning Co Inc.............G 908 925-5530
 Linden *(G-5372)*

METAL STAMPING, FOR THE TRADE

A K Stamping Co Inc ....D 908 232-7300
 Mountainside *(G-6831)*
Accurate Forming LLC ....E 973 827-7155
 Hamburg *(G-4087)*
Acme Cosmetic Components LLC ....E 718 335-3000
 Secaucus *(G-9750)*
Camptown Tool & Die Co Inc ....G 908 688-8406
 Kenilworth *(G-4932)*
Carter Manufacturing Co Inc ....E 201 935-0770
 Moonachie *(G-6461)*
Clover Stamping Inc ....G 973 278-4888
 Paterson *(G-8158)*
Coining Inc ....C 201 791-4020
 Montvale *(G-6403)*
Coining Holding Company ....F 201 791-4020
 Montvale *(G-6404)*
Coining Manufacturing LLC ....E 973 253-0500
 Colts Neck *(G-1778)*
Coining Mfg ....G 973 253-0500
 Clifton *(G-1585)*
Coining Technologies Inc ....D 866 897-2304
 Demarest *(G-2025)*
Deborah Sales & Mfg Co ....G 973 344-8466
 Newark *(G-7100)*
Durex Inc ....D 908 688-0800
 Union *(G-11045)*
Duron Co Inc ....F 973 242-5704
 Newark *(G-7107)*
F & G Tool & Die Inc ....G 908 241-5880
 Kenilworth *(G-4938)*
F & M Machine Co Inc ....F 908 245-8830
 Kenilworth *(G-4939)*
Feldware Inc ....E 718 372-0486
 Rahway *(G-9093)*
General Stamping Co Inc ....F 973 627-9500
 Columbia *(G-1793)*
H & T Tool Co Inc ....F 973 227-4858
 Fairfield *(G-3219)*
H K Metal Craft Mfg Corp ....E 973 471-7770
 Lodi *(G-5563)*
Heyco Stamped Products ....D 732 286-4336
 Toms River *(G-10767)*
International Rollforms Inc ....E 856 228-7100
 Deptford *(G-2064)*
J G Schmidt Co Inc ....D 732 563-9500
 Green Brook *(G-3863)*
J J Orly Inc ....F 908 276-9212
 Clark *(G-1498)*
J R M Products Inc ....G 732 203-0200
 Union Beach *(G-11103)*
Jmk Tool Die and Mfg Co Inc ....E 201 845-4710
 Rochelle Park *(G-9425)*
Jordan Manufacturing LLC ....G 973 383-8363
 Lafayette *(G-5029)*
Metalis USA Inc ....F 973 625-3500
 Denville *(G-2047)*
National Manufacturing Co Inc ....C 973 635-8846
 Chatham *(G-1329)*
Paramount Products Co Inc..................F 732 458-9200
 Brick *(G-728)*
Peterson Brothers Mfg Co ....E 732 271-8240
 Middlesex *(G-6136)*
Peterson Stamping & Mfg Co ....F 908 241-0900
 Kenilworth *(G-4968)*
Rails Company Inc ....E 973 763-4320
 Maplewood *(G-5883)*
Rapid Manufacturing Co Inc ....G 732 279-1252
 Toms River *(G-10787)*
Rebuth Metal Services.........................F 908 889-6400
 Fanwood *(G-3373)*
Roseville Tool & Manufacturing ....E 973 992-5405
 Livingston *(G-5538)*
S H P C Inc ....E 973 589-5242
 Newark *(G-7258)*
Small Quantities NJ Inc ....D 732 248-9009
 Edison *(G-2614)*
Stamping Com Inc ....G 732 493-4697
 Ocean *(G-7685)*

2019 Harris New jersey
Manufacturers Directory

(G-0000) Company's Geographic Section entry number

Stirrup Metal Products Corp ....F 973 824-7086
 Newark (G-7287)
Universal Tools & Mfg Co ....E 973 379-4193
 Springfield (G-10471)
Weiss-Aug Co Inc ....C 973 887-7600
 East Hanover (G-2246)
Well Bilt Industries Inc ....F 908 486-6002
 Linden (G-5441)
Wgjf Manufacturing Corp ....E 908 862-1730
 Linden (G-5442)

METAL STAMPINGS: Ornamental

Hnt Industries Inc ....G 908 322-0414
 Scotch Plains (G-9733)

METAL STAMPINGS: Patterned

Short Run Stamping Company Inc ....E 908 862-1070
 Linden (G-5423)

METAL STAMPINGS: Perforated

Electronic Parts Specialty Co ....G 609 267-0055
 Mount Holly (G-6726)

METAL TREATING COMPOUNDS

Chemetall US Inc ....D 908 464-6900
 New Providence (G-6997)

METAL: Battery

American Aluminum Company ....D 908 233-3500
 Mountainside (G-6834)
Holistic Solar Usa Inc ....G 732 757-5500
 Newark (G-7151)
Komline-Sanderson Engrg Corp ....G 973 579-0090
 Sparta (G-10394)

METALS SVC CENTERS & WHOL: Structural Shapes, Iron Or Steel

Stateline Fabricators LLC ....E 908 387-8800
 Phillipsburg (G-8576)

METALS SVC CENTERS & WHOLESALERS: Bars, Metal

G M Stainless Inc ....F 908 575-1834
 Branchburg (G-643)
Gauer Metal Products Co Inc ....E 908 241-4080
 Kenilworth (G-4942)

METALS SVC CENTERS & WHOLESALERS: Cable, Wire

Ace Electronics Inc ....D 732 603-9800
 Metuchen (G-6045)
T V L Associates Inc ....G 973 790-6766
 Wayne (G-11555)

METALS SVC CENTERS & WHOLESALERS: Ferroalloys

Cherishmet Inc ....F 201 842-7612
 Rutherford (G-9616)

METALS SVC CENTERS & WHOLESALERS: Foundry Prdts

Whibco Inc ....F 856 455-9200
 Bridgeton (G-779)

METALS SVC CENTERS & WHOLESALERS: Iron & Steel Prdt, Ferrous

Titanium Industries Inc ....E 973 983-1185
 Rockaway (G-9504)

METALS SVC CENTERS & WHOLESALERS: Nonferrous Sheets, Etc

Dynasty Metals Inc ....E 973 453-6630
 Rockaway (G-9454)
Nedohon Inc ....G 302 533-5512
 Wildwood Crest (G-11948)

METALS SVC CENTERS & WHOLESALERS: Pipe & Tubing, Steel

Morris Industries Inc ....D 973 835-6600
 Pompton Plains (G-8868)

METALS SVC CENTERS & WHOLESALERS: Rope, Wire, Exc Insulated

Doran Sling and Assembly Corp ....G 908 355-1101
 Hillside (G-4390)

METALS SVC CENTERS & WHOLESALERS: Sheets, Metal

Federal Casters Corp ....D 973 483-6700
 Harrison (G-4173)
Passaic Metal & Bldg Sups Co ....D 973 546-9000
 Clifton (G-1685)

METALS SVC CENTERS & WHOLESALERS: Stampings, Metal

Microcast Technologies Corp ....D 908 523-9503
 Linden (G-5385)

METALS SVC CENTERS & WHOLESALERS: Steel

Allied Metal Industries Inc ....E 973 824-7347
 Newark (G-7039)
American Strip Steel Inc ....F 800 526-1216
 South Plainfield (G-10216)
American Strip Steel Inc ....G 856 461-8300
 Delanco (G-2002)
Bouras Industries Inc ....A 908 918-9400
 Summit (G-10527)
Bushwick Metals LLC ....E 908 754-8700
 South Plainfield (G-10231)
Bushwick Metals LLC ....C 610 495-9100
 Englewood (G-2888)
Capital Steel Service LLC ....E 609 882-6983
 Ewing (G-3017)
Dynamic Metals Inc ....E 908 769-0522
 Piscataway (G-8659)
Efco Corp ....F 732 308-1010
 Marlboro (G-5896)
Evans Machine & Tool Co ....G 732 442-1144
 Perth Amboy (G-8518)
Fazzio Machine & Steel Inc ....G 609 653-1098
 Glassboro (G-3811)
General Sullivan Group Inc ....E 609 745-5004
 Pennington (G-8365)
General Sullivan Group Inc ....F 609 745-5000
 Pennington (G-8366)
Harsco Corporation ....E 908 454-7169
 Plainfield (G-8768)
Industrial Stl & Fastener Corp ....G 610 667-2220
 Cherry Hill (G-1377)
Ironbound Welding Inc ....G 973 589-3128
 Newark (G-7162)
McNichols Company ....F 877 884-4653
 New Brunswick (G-6945)
Metalwest LLC ....E 609 395-7007
 Monroe Township (G-6335)
Minmetals Inc ....F 201 809-1898
 Leonia (G-5290)
National Electronic Alloys Inc ....E 201 337-9400
 Oakland (G-7638)
Rebuth Metal Services ....F 908 889-6400
 Fanwood (G-3373)
Stainless Metal Source Intl ....G 973 977-2200
 Clifton (G-1724)
Stulz-Sickles Steel Company ....E 609 531-2172
 Burlington (G-986)

METALS SVC CENTERS & WHOLESALERS: Steel Decking

Great Railing Inc ....F 856 875-0050
 Williamstown (G-11960)

METALS SVC CNTRS & WHOL: Metal Wires, Ties, Cables/Screening

Plasma Powders & Systems Inc ....G 732 431-0992
 Marlboro (G-5909)
Skorr Products LLC ....F 973 523-2606
 Paterson (G-8299)

METALS SVC CTRS & WHOLESALERS: Aluminum Bars, Rods, Etc

Argyle Industries Inc ....F 908 725-8800
 Branchburg (G-620)
Harley Tool & Machine Inc ....G 201 244-8899
 Bergenfield (G-376)
Kwg Industries LLC ....E 908 218-8900
 Hillsborough (G-4338)
Tabco Technologies LLC ....G 201 438-0422
 Carlstadt (G-1225)

METALS: Precious NEC

BASF Catalysts LLC ....D 732 205-5000
 Iselin (G-4599)
Electrum Inc ....F 732 396-1616
 Rahway (G-9090)
Ewing Recovery Corp ....G 609 883-0318
 Ewing (G-3030)
Metallix Direct Gold LLC ....G 732 544-0891
 Shrewsbury (G-9894)
Metallix Refining Inc ....F 732 936-0050
 Shrewsbury (G-9895)
Premesco Inc ....B 908 686-0513
 Union (G-11084)
Starfuels Inc ....G 201 685-0400
 Englewood (G-2944)
Umicore Precious Metals NJ LLC ....E 908 222-5006
 South Plainfield (G-10333)
Umicore USA Inc ....F 908 226-2053
 South Plainfield (G-10334)

METALS: Primary Nonferrous, NEC

Dallas Group of America Inc ....E 908 534-7800
 Whitehouse (G-11915)
Fisk Alloy Inc ....E 973 427-7550
 Hawthorne (G-4219)
Fisk Alloy Wire Incorporated ....C 973 949-4491
 Hawthorne (G-4220)
Luxfer Magtech Inc ....E 803 610-9898
 Manchester (G-5846)
Mel Chemicals Inc ....C 908 782-5800
 Flemington (G-3455)
National Electronic Alloys Inc ....E 201 337-9400
 Oakland (G-7638)
Omg Electronic Chemicals Inc ....C 908 222-5800
 South Plainfield (G-10311)
Tower Systems Inc ....G 732 237-8800
 Bayville (G-251)
Victors Three-D Inc ....D 201 845-4433
 Maywood (G-6018)

METALWORK: Miscellaneous

Alberona Welding & Iron Works ....G 973 674-3375
 Orange (G-7749)
Bolt Welding & Iron Works ....G 609 393-3993
 Trenton (G-10906)
Camtec Industries Inc ....F 732 332-9800
 Colts Neck (G-1777)
Handi-Hut Inc ....E 973 614-1800
 Clifton (G-1632)
Haydon Corporation ....D 973 904-0800
 Wayne (G-11515)
Luso Machine Nj LLC ....F 973 242-1717
 Newark (G-7188)
Mainland Plate Glass Company ....F 609 277-2938
 Pleasantville (G-8815)
Morsemere Iron Works Inc ....F 201 941-1133
 Ridgefield (G-9278)
N E R Associates Inc ....G 908 454-5955
 Phillipsburg (G-8565)
Pipeline Eqp Resources Co LLC ....G 888 232-7372
 Boonton (G-564)
RS Phillips Steel LLC ....E 973 827-6464
 Sussex (G-10565)
Stelfast Inc ....E 440 879-0077
 Edison (G-2620)
United Eqp Fabricators LLC ....G 973 242-2737
 Newark (G-7308)
W2f Inc ....G 609 735-0135
 New Egypt (G-6987)
Wired Products LLC ....F 551 231-5800
 Paramus (G-7844)

METALWORK: Ornamental

Garden State Iron Inc ....F 732 918-0760
 Ocean (G-7664)

Employee Codes: A=Over 500 employees, B=251-500
C=101-250, D=51-100, E=20-50, F=10-19, G=4-9

2019 Harris New jersey
Manufacturers Directory

885

PRODUCT

La Forge De Style LLC................G...... 201 488-1955
  South Hackensack (G-10168)
Leets Steel Inc..........................G...... 917 416-7977
  Sayreville (G-9715)

METALWORKING MACHINERY WHOLESALERS

Bihler of America Inc..................C...... 908 213-9001
  Phillipsburg (G-8546)

METERS: Power Factor & Phase Angle

Satec Inc................................E...... 908 258-0924
  Union (G-11088)

METERS: Pyrometers, Indl Process

Pyrometer Instrument Co Inc..........E...... 609 443-5522
  Windsor (G-11997)

MGMT CONSULTING SVCS: Matls, Incl Purch, Handle & Invntry

Defense Support Svcs Intl LLC.......F...... 850 390-4737
  Marlton (G-5928)
Pabin Associates Inc...................G...... 201 288-7216
  Hasbrouck Heights (G-4187)
Precision Dealer Services Inc.........E...... 908 237-1100
  Flemington (G-3461)

MICA

Corp American Mica.....................G...... 908 587-5237
  Linden (G-5336)

MICROCIRCUITS, INTEGRATED: Semiconductor

Modelware Inc...........................F...... 732 264-3020
  Holmdel (G-4508)
Semi Conductor Manufacturing.......E...... 973 478-2880
  Clifton (G-1714)

MICROFILM EQPT

Zeta Products Inc.......................E...... 908 688-0440
  Annandale (G-56)

MICROFILM EQPT WHOLESALERS

Image Access Corp......................E...... 201 342-7878
  Rockleigh (G-9519)
Zeta Products Inc.......................E...... 908 688-0440
  Annandale (G-56)

MICROFILM SVCS

Image Access Corp......................E...... 201 342-7878
  Rockleigh (G-9519)

MICROPHONES

Mp Production...........................F...... 973 729-9333
  Sparta (G-10400)
Sound Professionals Inc...............G...... 609 267-4400
  Hainesport (G-4078)

MICROWAVE COMPONENTS

Cobham New Jersey Inc................D...... 732 460-0212
  Eatontown (G-2384)
Compex Corporation...................E...... 856 719-8657
  West Berlin (G-11585)
Electromagnetic Tech Inds Inc........D...... 973 394-1719
  Boonton (G-550)
Electronic Mfg Svcs Inc................F...... 973 916-1001
  Clifton (G-1614)
GT Microwave Inc.......................E...... 973 361-5700
  Randolph (G-9184)
Herley Industries Inc...................D...... 973 884-2580
  Whippany (G-11895)
Herley-Cti Inc............................F...... 973 884-2580
  Whippany (G-11896)
K R Electronics Inc.....................F...... 732 636-1900
  Avenel (G-133)
Meca Electronics Inc...................D...... 973 625-0661
  Denville (G-2045)
Merrimac Industries Inc................D...... 973 575-1300
  West Caldwell (G-11665)
Microwave Consulting Corp...........G...... 973 523-6700
  Paterson (G-8259)

Mwt Materials Inc......................F...... 973 928-8300
  Passaic (G-8091)
Princeton Microwave Technology......G...... 609 586-8140
  Trenton (G-10983)
Rs Microwave Co Inc...................E...... 973 492-1207
  Butler (G-1014)
Synergy Microwave Corp..............D...... 973 881-8800
  Paterson (G-8311)
Ute Microwave Inc......................E...... 732 922-1009
  Ocean (G-7686)
Waveline Incorporated................E...... 973 226-9100
  Fairfield (G-3351)

MICROWAVE OVENS: Household

Sharp Electronics Corporation........A...... 201 529-8200
  Montvale (G-6433)

MILITARY INSIGNIA

Services Equipment Com LLC..........G...... 973 992-4404
  Livingston (G-5539)

MILITARY INSIGNIA, TEXTILE

Mek International Inc....................G...... 215 712-2490
  Woodcliff Lake (G-12059)

MILL PRDTS: Structural & Rail

A & A Ironwork Co Inc..................F...... 973 728-4300
  Hewitt (G-4273)

MILLINERY SUPPLIES: Veils & Veiling, Bridal, Funeral, Etc

French Textile Co Inc...................F...... 973 471-5000
  Clifton (G-1622)

MILLING: Feed, Wheat

Bay State Milling Company............D...... 973 772-3400
  Clifton (G-1572)

MILLING: Grain Cereals, Cracked

Cibo Vita Inc.............................B...... 862 238-8020
  Totowa (G-10823)
Coco International Inc..................E...... 973 694-1200
  Wayne (G-11489)

MILLWORK

ABC Holdings Inc.......................F...... 856 219-3444
  Westville (G-11809)
All Merchandise Display Corp..........E...... 718 257-2221
  Hillside (G-4372)
Architctral Cbinetry Mllwk LLC........G...... 908 213-2001
  Phillipsburg (G-8541)
B & B Millwork & Doors Inc............G...... 973 249-0300
  Kenilworth (G-4924)
Bestmark National LLC.................E...... 862 772-4863
  Irvington (G-4561)
Bon Architectual Mill Work LLC........G...... 856 320-2872
  Pennsauken (G-8397)
Cabinet Tronics Inc.....................F...... 609 267-2625
  Birmingham (G-455)
Castle Woodcraft Assoc LLC..........F...... 732 349-1519
  Pine Beach (G-8582)
Caw LLC..................................F...... 973 429-7004
  Bloomfield (G-495)
Cerami Wood Products Inc............F...... 732 968-7222
  Piscataway (G-8645)
Classic Designer Woodwork Inc.......G...... 201 280-3711
  Glen Rock (G-3829)
Cozzolino Furniture Design Inc........E...... 973 731-9292
  West Orange (G-11764)
Custom Counters By Precision........E...... 973 773-0111
  Passaic (G-8058)
Design of Tomorrow Inc................F...... 973 227-1000
  Fairfield (G-3185)
Donnelly Industries Inc................D...... 973 672-1800
  Wayne (G-11496)
Dor-Win Manufacturing Co.............E...... 201 796-4300
  Elmwood Park (G-2821)
Dreamstar Construction LLC...........F...... 732 393-2572
  Middletown (G-6162)
Empire Lumber & Millwork Co..........E...... 973 242-2700
  Newark (G-7115)
Epic Millwork LLC......................E...... 732 296-0273
  Somerset (G-9988)
Everlast Interiors........................G...... 732 252-9965
  Manalapan (G-5808)

F T Millwork Inc.........................G...... 732 741-1216
  Red Bank (G-9229)
Gass Custom Woodworking............G...... 201 493-9282
  Paramus (G-7802)
Glen Rock Stair Corp...................E...... 201 337-9595
  Franklin Lakes (G-3624)
Heard Woodworking LLC...............G...... 908 232-3978
  Westfield (G-11800)
Hutchinson Cabinets...................E...... 856 468-5500
  Sewell (G-9845)
Ideal Jacobs Corporation..............E...... 973 275-5100
  Maplewood (G-5879)
Intex Millwork Solutions LLC..........E...... 856 293-4100
  Mays Landing (G-5994)
Joseph Naticchia.......................F...... 609 882-7709
  Ewing (G-3039)
K2 Millwork Ltd Liability Co............G...... 609 379-6411
  Columbus (G-1801)
Kempton Wood Products...............G...... 732 449-8673
  Wall Township (G-11352)
Lauderdale Millwork Inc................F...... 908 508-9550
  Berkeley Heights (G-406)
Lees Woodworking Inc.................G...... 732 681-1002
  Neptune (G-6888)
Lux Home Inc...........................G...... 845 623-2821
  Paramus (G-7817)
M K Woodworking Inc..................G...... 609 771-1350
  Ewing (G-3044)
M R C Millwork & Trim Inc.............G...... 201 954-2176
  Franklin Lakes (G-3627)
Midlantic Shutter & Milwork............G...... 908 806-3400
  Flemington (G-3457)
ML Woodwork Inc......................G...... 201 953-2175
  Paramus (G-7821)
Mountain Millwork......................G...... 908 647-1100
  Warren (G-11424)
New Jersey Hardwoods Inc...........E...... 908 754-0990
  Plainfield (G-8773)
Nyc Woodworking Inc..................G...... 718 222-1221
  Marlboro (G-5907)
Ornate Millwork LLC...................G...... 866 464-5596
  Lakewood (G-5144)
Palumbo Millwork Inc..................G...... 732 938-3266
  Wall Township (G-11361)
Pkc Finewoodworking LLC.............G...... 201 951-8880
  Towaco (G-10877)
Precision Dealer Services Inc.........E...... 908 237-1100
  Flemington (G-3461)
Prestige Millwork LLC..................E...... 908 526-5100
  Bridgewater (G-868)
Progress Woodwork....................G...... 732 906-8680
  Edison (G-2593)
R & M Manufacturing Inc...............E...... 609 495-8032
  Monroe Township (G-6341)
Random 8 Woodworks LLC.............G...... 856 417-3329
  Mullica Hill (G-6857)
Random 8 Woodworks LLC.............G...... 856 364-7627
  Pedricktown (G-8354)
Rex Lumber Company...................D...... 732 446-4200
  Manalapan (G-5824)
Rock Solid Woodworking LLC..........G...... 732 974-1261
  Sea Girt (G-9747)
Salernos Kitchen Cabinets.............E...... 201 794-1990
  Saddle Brook (G-9676)
Sourland Mountain Wdwkg LLC T.....G...... 908 806-7661
  Neshanic Station (G-6905)
Summit Millwork & Supply Inc.........G...... 908 273-1486
  Summit (G-10550)
Tea Elle Woodworks....................G...... 732 938-9660
  Farmingdale (G-3394)
Terhune Bros Woodworking............G...... 973 962-6686
  Ringwood (G-9354)
V Custom Millwork Inc..................F...... 732 469-9600
  Bridgewater (G-901)
Vanco Millwork Inc.....................F...... 973 992-3061
  Livingston (G-5545)
Visual Architectural Designs...........F...... 908 754-3000
  South Plainfield (G-10342)
West Hudson Lumber & Mllwk Co.....G...... 201 991-7191
  Kearny (G-4904)
Wohners.................................G...... 201 568-7307
  Englewood (G-2954)
Wood Works............................G...... 856 728-4520
  Williamstown (G-11987)
Woodhaven Lumber & Millwork........E...... 732 295-8800
  Point Pleasant Beach (G-8833)
Woodshop Inc..........................G...... 732 349-8006
  Toms River (G-10805)
Woodtec Inc.............................G...... 908 979-0180
  Hackettstown (G-4041)

MINE & QUARRY SVCS: Nonmetallic Minerals

Jlb Hauling Ltd Liability Co..............G...... 856 514-2771
Pennsville (G-8500)

MINE DEVELOPMENT, METAL

C & Y Group East Coast Inc..............G...... 973 732-4816
Newark (G-7079)

MINE EXPLORATION SVCS: Nonmetallic Minerals

Tag Minerals Inc..............G...... 732 252-5146
Freehold (G-3701)

MINERAL PIGMENT MINING

Axiom Ingredients LLC..............F...... 732 669-2458
Iselin (G-4598)

MINERAL WOOL

Johns Manville Corporation..............C...... 856 768-7000
Berlin (G-424)
Owens Corning Sales LLC..............C...... 201 998-5666
Kearny (G-4888)
Pacor Inc..............E...... 609 324-1100
Bordentown (G-592)
Passaic Metal & Bldg Sups Co..............D...... 973 546-9000
Clifton (G-1685)
Pekay Industries Inc..............F...... 732 938-2722
Farmingdale (G-3390)

MINERAL WOOL INSULATION PRDTS

United States Mineral Pdts Co..............D...... 973 347-1200
Stanhope (G-10480)

MINERALS: Ground Or Otherwise Treated

Anthracite Industries Inc..............G...... 908 537-2155
Asbury (G-59)
Mel Chemicals Inc..............C...... 908 782-5800
Flemington (G-3455)

MINERALS: Ground or Treated

Asbury Graphite Mills Inc..............E...... 908 537-2155
Asbury (G-61)
Asbury Graphite Mills Inc..............D...... 908 537-2157
Asbury (G-62)
Fine Minerals Intl Inc..............G...... 732 318-6760
Edison (G-2512)
Isp Global Technologies Inc..............G...... 973 628-4000
Wayne (G-11524)
Isp Global Technologies LLC..............G...... 973 628-4000
Wayne (G-11525)
Minmetals Inc..............F...... 201 809-1898
Leonia (G-5290)

MINING MACHINES & EQPT: Clarifying, Mineral

Enviro-Clear Company Inc..............F...... 908 638-5507
High Bridge (G-4282)

MINING MACHINES & EQPT: Feeders, Ore & Aggregate

K-Tron International Inc..............D...... 856 589-0500
Sewell (G-9851)

MINING MACHINES & EQPT: Pulverizers, Stone, Stationary

Pallmann Pulverizers Co Inc..............E...... 973 471-1450
Clifton (G-1682)

MIXERS: Hot Metal

Bartell Morrison (usa) LLC..............F...... 732 566-5400
Freehold (G-3652)

MIXTURES & BLOCKS: Asphalt Paving

All Surface Asphalt Paving..............G...... 732 295-3800
Point Pleasant Boro (G-8835)
Brick-Wall Corp..............E...... 732 787-0226
Atlantic Highlands (G-104)
Brick-Wall Corp..............E...... 609 693-6223
Forked River (G-3536)

Brunswick Hot Mix Corp..............D...... 908 233-4444
Westfield (G-11795)
Central Jersey Hot Mix Asp LLC..............G...... 732 323-0226
Jackson (G-4642)
Chevron USA Inc..............D...... 732 738-2000
Perth Amboy (G-8515)
Crowfoot Associates Inc..............G...... 609 561-0107
West Berlin (G-11588)
Earle Asphalt Company..............C...... 732 308-1113
Wall Township (G-11337)
Hanson Aggregates Wrp Inc..............E...... 972 653-5500
Wall Township (G-11345)
Louis N Rothberg & Son Inc..............E...... 732 356-9505
Middlesex (G-6127)
Richard E Pierson Mtls Corp..............G...... 856 740-2400
Williamstown (G-11975)
Richard E Pierson Mtls Corp..............G...... 856 691-0083
Vineland (G-11260)
Richard E Pierson Mtls Corp..............G...... 856 467-4199
Pilesgrove (G-8580)
Schifano Construction Corp..............F...... 732 752-3450
Middlesex (G-6144)
Stavola Asphalt Company Inc..............E...... 732 542-2328
Tinton Falls (G-10728)
Stavola Construction Mtls Inc..............E...... 732 356-5700
Bound Brook (G-608)
Stone Industries Inc..............D...... 973 595-6250
Haledon (G-4085)
Tilcon New York Inc..............D...... 800 789-7625
North Bergen (G-7440)
Tilcon New York Inc..............D...... 800 789-7625
Oxford (G-7766)
Weldon Asphalt Corp..............F...... 973 627-7500
Rockaway (G-9512)
Ziegler Chem & Mineral Corp..............F...... 732 752-4111
Piscataway (G-8741)

MOBILE COMMUNICATIONS EQPT

Mizco International Inc..............D...... 732 912-2000
Avenel (G-137)
Open Terra Inc..............G...... 732 765-9600
Matawan (G-5982)

MOBILE HOMES

Acton Mobile Industries Inc..............G...... 610 485-5100
Burlington (G-946)
Wireless Experience of PA Inc..............F...... 732 552-0050
Manahawkin (G-5798)

MODELS

Scientific Models Inc..............E...... 908 464-7070
Berkeley Heights (G-411)

MODELS: General, Exc Toy

Artisan Model Mold..............G...... 908 453-3524
Belvidere (G-357)
Central Art & Engineering Inc..............G...... 609 758-5922
Cream Ridge (G-1931)
Franklin Mint LLC..............E...... 800 843-6468
Fort Lee (G-3559)
Harry Shaw Model Maker Inc..............G...... 609 268-0647
Shamong (G-9857)
Rapid Models & Prototypes Inc..............G...... 856 933-2929
Runnemede (G-9607)

MODELS: Railroad, Exc Toy

Microelettrica-Usa LLC..............E...... 973 598-0806
Budd Lake (G-930)

MODULES: Solid State

Microsemi Stor Solutions Inc..............G...... 908 953-9400
Basking Ridge (G-191)

MOLDED RUBBER PRDTS

Accu Seal Rubber Inc..............G...... 732 246-4333
New Brunswick (G-6908)
Eastern Molding Co Inc..............G...... 973 759-0220
Belleville (G-294)
Elastograf Inc..............D...... 973 209-3161
Hamburg (G-4093)
Hawthorne Rubber Mfg Corp..............E...... 973 427-3337
Hawthorne (G-4225)
Manville Rubber Products Inc..............G...... 908 526-9111
Manville (G-5856)
Panova Inc..............E...... 973 263-1700
Towaco (G-10876)

Pierce-Roberts Rubber Company..............F...... 609 394-5245
Ewing (G-3052)
Pure Rubber Products Co..............G...... 973 784-3690
Rockaway (G-9492)
Rubber & Silicone Products Co..............E...... 973 227-2300
Fairfield (G-3305)
Seajay Manufacturing Corp..............F...... 732 774-0900
Neptune (G-6897)
Star-Glo Industries LLC..............C...... 201 939-6162
East Rutherford (G-2319)
Transport Products Inc..............G...... 973 857-6090
Cedar Grove (G-1294)
Water Master Co..............G...... 732 247-1900
Highland Park (G-4289)
Zago Manufacturing Company..............E...... 973 643-6700
Newark (G-7318)

MOLDING COMPOUNDS

Coda Resources Ltd..............C...... 718 649-1666
Matawan (G-5971)
Custom Molders Group LLC..............G...... 908 218-7997
Branchburg (G-635)
Infinity Compounding LLC..............E...... 856 467-3030
Logan Township (G-5588)
Louis A Nelson Inc..............F...... 973 743-7404
Bloomfield (G-506)
Med Connection LLC..............G...... 908 213-7012
Phillipsburg (G-8563)
Wexford International Inc..............G...... 908 781-7200
Gladstone (G-3805)

MOLDINGS & TRIM: Metal, Exc Automobile

Randall Mfg Co Inc..............E...... 973 482-8603
Newark (G-7245)
Thermwell Products Co Inc..............B...... 201 684-4400
Mahwah (G-5781)

MOLDINGS & TRIM: Wood

Abatetech Inc..............E...... 609 265-2107
Lumberton (G-5622)

MOLDINGS: Picture Frame

Don Shrts Pcture Frmes Molding..............G...... 732 363-1323
Howell (G-4537)
Frameware Inc..............F...... 800 582-5608
Fairfield (G-3207)
Iii Eagle Enterprises Ltd..............E...... 973 237-1111
Ringwood (G-9346)
Larson-Juhl US LLC..............E...... 973 439-1801
Caldwell (G-1026)
Roma Moulding Inc..............F...... 732 346-0999
Edison (G-2600)

MOLDS: Indl

Art Mold & Polishing Co Inc..............F...... 908 518-9191
Roselle (G-9548)
Art Mold & Tool Corporation..............G...... 201 935-3377
East Rutherford (G-2272)
C and C Tool Co LLC..............G...... 908 431-0330
Hillsborough (G-4309)
CK Manufacturing Inc..............E...... 973 808-3500
Fairfield (G-3168)
Eb Machine Corp..............G...... 973 442-7729
Wharton (G-11857)
Garden State Tool & Mold Corp..............G...... 908 245-2041
South Amboy (G-10133)
H & W Tool Co Inc..............F...... 973 366-0131
Dover (G-2085)
Hanrahan Tool Co Inc..............G...... 732 919-7300
Farmingdale (G-3386)
Heinz Glas USA Inc..............F...... 908 474-0300
Linden (G-5355)
J-Mac Plastics Inc..............E...... 908 709-1111
Kenilworth (G-4949)
Lawrence Mold and Tool Corp..............E...... 609 392-5422
Lawrenceville (G-5234)
Linden Mold and Tool Corp..............E...... 732 381-1411
Rahway (G-9114)
Mold Polishing Company Inc..............G...... 908 518-9191
Garwood (G-3785)
Pahco Machine Inc..............G...... 609 587-1188
Trenton (G-10970)
TEC Cast Inc..............E...... 201 935-3885
Carlstadt (G-1226)
Union Tool & Mold Co Inc..............E...... 973 763-6611
Maplewood (G-5888)
Universal Mold & Tool Inc..............F...... 856 563-0488
Vineland (G-11272)

PRODUCT

West Pattern Works Inc .... F 609 443-6241
Cranbury *(G-1892)*

MOLDS: Plastic Working & Foundry

Continental Precision Corp .... C 908 754-3030
Piscataway *(G-8650)*
Lincoln Mold & Die Corp .... D 908 241-3344
Warren *(G-11420)*
Rotech Tool & Mold Co Inc .... G 908 241-9669
Kenilworth *(G-4975)*
Sigco Tool & Mfg Co Inc .... E 856 753-6565
West Berlin *(G-11621)*
Thal Precision Industries LLC .... G 732 381-6106
Clark *(G-1517)*
Viking Mold & Tool Corp .... G 609 476-9333
Dorothy *(G-2072)*

MOLECULAR DEVICES: Solid State

Access Bio Inc .... F 732 873-4040
Somerset *(G-9941)*

MONORAIL SYSTEMS

Bombardier Transportation .... B 973 624-9300
Newark *(G-7070)*
Teledynamics LLC .... E 973 248-3360
Towaco *(G-10881)*

MONUMENTS & GRAVE MARKERS, EXC TERRAZZO

H T Hall Inc .... F 732 449-3441
Spring Lake *(G-10422)*

MONUMENTS: Concrete

Suburban Monument & Vault .... G 973 242-7007
Newark *(G-7289)*

MONUMENTS: Cut Stone, Exc Finishing Or Lettering Only

Albert H Hopper Inc .... G 201 991-2266
North Arlington *(G-7367)*

MOPS: Floor & Dust

Janico Inc .... F 732 370-2223
Freehold *(G-3672)*

MORTAR: High Temperature, Nonclay

Strongwall Industries Inc .... G 201 445-4633
Ridgewood *(G-9330)*

MOTION PICTURE & VIDEO PRODUCTION SVCS

Bandemar Networks LLC .... G 732 991-5112
East Brunswick *(G-2128)*
Recorded Publications Labs .... E 856 963-3000
Camden *(G-1085)*

MOTION PICTURE & VIDEO PRODUCTION SVCS: Educational, TV

Global Strategy Institute A .... G 973 615-7447
Bloomfield *(G-501)*

MOTION PICTURE PRODUCTION & DISTRIBUTION

Sony Corporation of America .... F 201 930-1000
Woodcliff Lake *(G-12065)*

MOTION PICTURE PRODUCTION & DISTRIBUTION: Television

Acadia Scenic Inc .... E 201 653-8889
Jersey City *(G-4684)*

MOTOR & GENERATOR PARTS: Electric

Power Pool Plus Inc .... G 908 454-1124
Alpha *(G-40)*

MOTOR REPAIR SVCS

George J Bender Inc .... G 908 687-0081
Union *(G-11059)*

Hights Electric Motor Service .... G 609 448-2298
Hightstown *(G-4296)*
Johnnys Service Center .... G 732 738-0569
Fords *(G-3532)*

MOTOR SCOOTERS & PARTS

Electric Mobility Corporation .... C 856 468-1000
Sewell *(G-9844)*

MOTOR VEHICLE ASSEMBLY, COMPLETE: Ambulances

First Priority Emergency Vhicl .... E 732 657-1104
Manchester *(G-5845)*
First Priority Global Ltd .... F 973 347-4321
Flanders *(G-3410)*
P L Custom Body & Eqp Co Inc .... C 732 223-1411
Manasquan *(G-5836)*

MOTOR VEHICLE ASSEMBLY, COMPLETE: Autos, Incl Specialty

Bruce Kindberg .... G 973 664-0195
Rockaway *(G-9447)*
Elite Emrgncy Lights Ltd Lblty .... F 732 534-2377
Lakewood *(G-5090)*
Odyssey Auto Specialty Inc .... E 973 328-2667
Wharton *(G-11865)*
Orlando Systems Ltd Lblty Co .... G 908 400-5052
North Plainfield *(G-7507)*
S L P Engineering Inc .... D 732 240-3696
Toms River *(G-10789)*
Teo Fabrications Inc .... G 973 764-5500
Vernon *(G-11163)*
Vending Trucks Inc .... E 732 969-5400
East Brunswick *(G-2190)*
W2f Inc .... G 609 735-0135
New Egypt *(G-6987)*

MOTOR VEHICLE ASSEMBLY, COMPLETE: Military Motor Vehicle

Jontol Unlimited LLC .... G 858 652-1113
Blackwood *(G-473)*

MOTOR VEHICLE ASSEMBLY, COMPLETE: Snow Plows

R & H Spring & Truck Repair .... F 732 681-9000
Wall Township *(G-11362)*

MOTOR VEHICLE ASSEMBLY, COMPLETE: Truck & Tractor Trucks

Cliffside Body Corporation .... E 201 945-3970
Fairview *(G-3358)*
Dejana Trck Utility Eqp Co LLC .... E 856 303-1315
Cinnaminson *(G-1449)*
Polar Truck Sales .... E 201 246-1010
Jersey City *(G-4784)*

MOTOR VEHICLE DEALERS: Automobiles, New & Used

Davis Hyundai .... F 609 883-3500
Ewing *(G-3026)*
Drive-Master Co Inc .... F 973 808-9709
Fairfield *(G-3188)*
Freehold Pntiac Bick GMC Trcks .... D 732 462-7093
Freehold *(G-3666)*
Holman Enterprises Inc .... E 609 383-6100
Mount Laurel *(G-6765)*
Town Ford Inc .... D 609 298-4990
Bordentown *(G-597)*
Toyota Motor Sales .... F 973 515-5012
Parsippany *(G-8030)*
Volvo Car North America LLC .... B 201 768-7300
Rockleigh *(G-9524)*
Wayne Motors Inc .... D 973 696-9710
Wayne *(G-11564)*

MOTOR VEHICLE DEALERS: Pickups & Vans, Used

Polar Truck Sales .... E 201 246-1010
Jersey City *(G-4784)*

MOTOR VEHICLE DEALERS: Trucks, Tractors/Trailers, New & Used

Granco Group LLC .... G 973 515-4721
Roseland *(G-9539)*
M W Trailer Repair Inc .... F 609 298-1113
Bordentown *(G-585)*
Robert H Hoover & Sons Inc .... G 973 347-4210
Flanders *(G-3417)*

MOTOR VEHICLE PARTS & ACCESS: Air Conditioner Parts

Premier Products Inc .... D 856 231-1800
Marlton *(G-5948)*

MOTOR VEHICLE PARTS & ACCESS: Body Components & Frames

Cervinis Inc .... F 856 691-1744
Vineland *(G-11198)*

MOTOR VEHICLE PARTS & ACCESS: Clutches

KRs Automotive Dev Group Inc .... F 732 667-7937
Middlesex *(G-6125)*

MOTOR VEHICLE PARTS & ACCESS: Cylinder Heads

Ram Hydraulics Inc .... G 732 237-0904
Shrewsbury *(G-9900)*

MOTOR VEHICLE PARTS & ACCESS: Engines & Parts

Holman Enterprises Inc .... C 856 532-2410
Pennsauken *(G-8431)*
K & K Automotive Inc .... G 973 777-2235
Passaic *(G-8078)*
Manley Performance Pdts Inc .... D 732 905-3366
Lakewood *(G-5128)*

MOTOR VEHICLE PARTS & ACCESS: Fuel Pumps

O T D Inc .... G 973 890-7979
Totowa *(G-10839)*

MOTOR VEHICLE PARTS & ACCESS: Fuel Systems & Parts

Carolina Fluid Handling Inc .... A 248 228-8900
West Berlin *(G-11579)*

MOTOR VEHICLE PARTS & ACCESS: Transmission Housings Or Parts

Quality Remanufacturing Inc .... F 973 523-8800
Paterson *(G-8284)*

MOTOR VEHICLE PARTS & ACCESS: Transmissions

Level Ten Products Inc .... F 973 827-0900
Hamburg *(G-4094)*
Overdrive Holdings Inc .... F 201 440-1911
South Hackensack *(G-10178)*
Truckpro LLC .... E 201 229-0599
Teterboro *(G-10697)*

MOTOR VEHICLE PARTS & ACCESS: Water Pumps

Well Manager LLC .... G 609 466-4347
Hopewell *(G-4529)*

MOTOR VEHICLE PARTS & ACCESS: Wheel rims

Top Rated Shopping Bargains .... F 800 556-5849
Hasbrouck Heights *(G-4190)*

MOTOR VEHICLE PARTS & ACCESS: Windshield Frames

Clear Plus Windshield Wipers .... F 973 546-8800
Garfield *(G-3735)*

MOTOR VEHICLE PARTS & ACCESS: Wipers, Windshield

Wexco Industries Inc ....E 973 244-5777
Pine Brook *(G-8620)*

MOTOR VEHICLE SPLYS & PARTS WHOLESALERS: New

Allison Corp ....G 973 992-3800
Livingston *(G-5504)*
Gorman Industries Inc ....E 973 345-5424
Paterson *(G-8201)*
Holman Enterprises Inc ....C 856 532-2410
Pennsauken *(G-8431)*
Lumiko USA Inc ....G 609 409-6900
Cranbury *(G-1860)*
Rony Inc ....G 201 891-2551
Wyckoff *(G-12120)*
Taurus International Corp ....E 201 825-2420
Ramsey *(G-9156)*

MOTOR VEHICLE SPLYS & PARTS WHOLESALERS: Used

P & A Auto Parts Inc ....E 201 655-7117
Hackensack *(G-3960)*

MOTOR VEHICLE: Hardware

American Van Equipment Inc ....C 732 905-5900
Lakewood *(G-5050)*

MOTOR VEHICLE: Radiators

Custom Auto Radiator Inc ....F 609 242-9700
Forked River *(G-3539)*

MOTOR VEHICLES & CAR BODIES

Autoaccess LLC ....F 908 240-5919
Sicklerville *(G-9908)*
BMW of North America LLC ....A 201 307-4000
Woodcliff Lake *(G-12049)*
Drive-Master Co Inc ....F 973 808-9709
Fairfield *(G-3188)*
Faps Inc ....C 973 589-5656
Newark *(G-7122)*
Navistar Inc ....D 856 486-2300
Cherry Hill *(G-1397)*
Rolls-Royce Motor Cars Na LLC ....A 201 307-4117
Woodcliff Lake *(G-12063)*
Tesla Inc ....G 201 225-2544
Paramus *(G-7841)*
Toyota Motor Sales ....F 973 515-5012
Parsippany *(G-8030)*

MOTOR VEHICLES, WHOLESALE: Trailers for passenger vehicles

Fyx Fleet Roadside Assistance ....F 609 452-8900
Princeton *(G-8953)*
Trac Intermodal LLC ....G 609 452-8900
Princeton *(G-9034)*

MOTOR VEHICLES, WHOLESALE: Trailers, Truck, New & Used

M W Trailer Repair Inc ....F 609 298-1113
Bordentown *(G-585)*
Peter Garafano & Son Inc ....E 973 278-0350
Paterson *(G-8282)*

MOTOR VEHICLES, WHOLESALE: Truck bodies

Bristol-Donald Company Inc ....E 973 589-2640
Newark *(G-7076)*
Cliffside Body Corporation ....E 201 945-3970
Fairview *(G-3358)*
Fleet Equipment Corporation ....F 201 337-3294
Franklin Lakes *(G-3623)*

MOTORCYCLE ACCESS

Barbs Harley-Davidson ....E 856 456-4141
Mount Ephraim *(G-6720)*

MOTORCYCLE DEALERS

Barbs Harley-Davidson ....E 856 456-4141
Mount Ephraim *(G-6720)*

MOTORCYCLE PARTS & ACCESS DEALERS

Morristown Cycle ....G 973 540-1244
Morristown *(G-6688)*

MOTORCYCLE REPAIR SHOPS

Barbs Harley-Davidson ....E 856 456-4141
Mount Ephraim *(G-6720)*
Morristown Cycle ....G 973 540-1244
Morristown *(G-6688)*

MOTORCYCLES & RELATED PARTS

Morristown Cycle ....G 973 540-1244
Morristown *(G-6688)*
NJ Grass Choppers ....G 732 414-2850
Manalapan *(G-5819)*
Works Enduro Rider Inc ....G 908 637-6385
Great Meadows *(G-3858)*

MOTORS: Electric

Eagle Engineering & Automation ....G 732 899-2292
Point Pleasant Boro *(G-8844)*
Universal Electric Mtr Svc Inc ....E 201 968-1000
Hackensack *(G-3988)*

MOTORS: Generators

Alstrom Energy Group LLC ....G 718 824-4901
Old Bridge *(G-7711)*
Ametek Inc ....G 732 417-0501
Edison *(G-2456)*
Astrodyne Corporation ....D 908 850-5088
Hackettstown *(G-3999)*
Billows Electric Supply Co Inc ....C 856 751-2200
Delran *(G-2009)*
Blutek Power Inc ....F 973 594-1800
Lodi *(G-5554)*
Boonton Electronics Corp ....E 973 386-9696
Parsippany *(G-7895)*
Cobra Power Systems Inc ....G 908 486-1800
Millstone Township *(G-6210)*
Dewey Electronics Corporation ....E 201 337-4700
Oakland *(G-7624)*
Ewc Controls Inc ....E 732 446-3110
Manalapan *(G-5809)*
H Power Corp ....G 973 249-5444
Clifton *(G-1631)*
Hansome Energy Systems Inc ....E 908 862-9044
Linden *(G-5354)*
Hydro-Mechanical Systems Inc ....F 856 848-8888
Westville *(G-11816)*
Innovative Power Solutions LLC ....E 732 544-1075
Eatontown *(G-2404)*
Multi-Tech Industries Inc ....F 732 431-0550
Marlboro *(G-5905)*
Pht Aerospace LLC ....F 973 831-1230
Pompton Plains *(G-8870)*
Primacy Engineering Inc ....F 201 731-3272
Englewood Cliffs *(G-2988)*
Princeton Tech Group Intl Corp ....G 732 328-9308
Edison *(G-2591)*
Rajysan Incorporated ....E 800 433-1382
Swedesboro *(G-10605)*
Servo-Tek Products Company Inc ....E 973 427-4249
Hawthorne *(G-4243)*
Triangle Tube/Phase III Co Inc ....D 856 228-9940
Paulsboro *(G-8340)*

MOTORS: Torque

Torque Gun Company LLC ....E 201 512-9800
South Hackensack *(G-10189)*

MOUNTING MERCHANDISE ON CARDS

Comfort Zone ....G 732 869-9990
Ocean Grove *(G-7699)*

MOUTHWASHES

Cadbury Adams USA LLC ....E 973 503-2000
East Hanover *(G-2197)*

MOVIE THEATERS, EXC DRIVE-IN

Sony Corporation of America ....F 201 930-1000
Woodcliff Lake *(G-12065)*

MOVING SVC: Local

E C D Ventures Inc ....G 856 875-1100
Blackwood *(G-465)*

MOWERS & ACCESSORIES

D & S Companies LLC ....G 973 832-4959
Wayne *(G-11492)*
Robert Colaneri ....G 201 939-4405
East Rutherford *(G-2314)*

MULTIPLEX EQPT: Radio, Television & Broadcast

Communication Devices Inc ....F 973 334-1980
Boonton *(G-546)*

MUSEUMS

General Commis Archives & Hstr ....G 973 408-3189
Madison *(G-5693)*
Old Barracks Association Inc ....F 609 396-1776
Trenton *(G-10968)*

MUSEUMS & ART GALLERIES

Mega Media Concepts Ltd Lblty ....G 973 919-5661
Sparta *(G-10397)*

MUSIC ARRANGING & COMPOSING SVCS

Metrolpolis Mastering LP ....E 212 604-9433
Edgewater *(G-2440)*

MUSIC DISTRIBUTION APPARATUS

B and G Music LLC ....G 732 779-4555
Bayville *(G-241)*

MUSICAL INSTRUMENT LESSONS

Hope Center ....F 201 798-1234
Jersey City *(G-4748)*

MUSICAL INSTRUMENT PARTS & ACCESS, WHOLESALE

AP Global Enterprises Inc ....G 732 919-6200
Wall Township *(G-11317)*

MUSICAL INSTRUMENT REPAIR

W E Wamsley Restorations Inc ....G 856 795-4001
Haddonfield *(G-4066)*

MUSICAL INSTRUMENTS & ACCESS: Carrying Cases

Xstatic Pro Inc ....F 718 237-2299
Bayonne *(G-237)*

MUSICAL INSTRUMENTS & ACCESS: NEC

AP Global Enterprises Inc ....G 732 919-6200
Wall Township *(G-11317)*
Malletech LLC ....F 732 774-0011
Neptune *(G-6889)*
Trek II Products Inc ....G 732 214-9200
New Brunswick *(G-6974)*

MUSICAL INSTRUMENTS & SPLYS STORES

Music Trades Corp ....G 201 871-1965
Englewood *(G-2927)*
Trf Music Inc ....F 201 335-0005
Tinton Falls *(G-10732)*

MUSICAL INSTRUMENTS: Guitars & Parts, Electric & Acoustic

Musikraft LLC ....G 856 697-8333
Vineland *(G-11243)*

MUSICAL INSTRUMENTS: Organs

Peragallo Organ Company of NJ ....F 973 684-3414
Paterson *(G-8281)*

MUSICAL INSTRUMENTS: Synthesizers, Music

Spem Corporation ....E 732 356-3366
Piscataway *(G-8717)*

PRODUCT

MUSICAL INSTRUMENTS: Violins & Parts

W E Wamsley Restorations Inc ....G....... 856 795-4001
Haddonfield (G-4066)

NAME PLATES: Engraved Or Etched

A S A P Nameplate & Labeling............F....... 973 773-3934
Passaic (G-8048)
Lantier Construction Company ....E....... 856 780-6366
Moorestown (G-6536)
Technical Nameplate Corp ....E....... 973 773-4256
Passaic (G-8111)
United Label Corp ....G....... 973 589-6500
Newark (G-7309)
Winters Stamp Mfg Co Inc ....F....... 908 352-3725
Martinsville (G-5965)

NATIONAL SECURITY, GOVERNMENT: National Guard

NJ Dept Military Vtrans.......................G....... 856 384-8831
Woodbury (G-12033)

NATURAL GAS LIQUIDS PRODUCTION

Agro Foods Inc...................................G....... 201 954-9152
Hackettstown (G-3995)
Pipeline Eqp Resources Co LLC ....G....... 888 232-7372
Boonton (G-564)

NATURAL GAS PRODUCTION

Agway Energy Services LLC ....E....... 973 887-5300
Whippany (G-11877)
Njr Clean Energy Ventures Corp ....B....... 732 938-1000
Belmar (G-351)

NATURAL LIQUEFIED PETROLEUM GAS PRODUCTION

M G S..G....... 609 698-7000
Barnegat (G-160)

NAVIGATIONAL SYSTEMS & INSTRUMENTS

Drs Leonardo Inc ....E....... 973 775-4440
Newark (G-7105)
Drs Leonardo Inc ....E....... 973 898-1500
Parsippany (G-7921)
Drs Leonardo Inc ....E....... 201 337-3800
Oakland (G-7626)
L3harris Technologies Inc ....C....... 973 284-0123
Clifton (G-1652)

NET & NETTING PRDTS

Endurance Net Inc ....F....... 609 499-3450
Florence (G-3475)

NETTING: Rope

French Textile Co Inc ....F....... 973 471-5000
Clifton (G-1622)
Sterling Net & Twine Co Inc ....F....... 973 783-9800
Montclair (G-6390)

NEW & USED CAR DEALERS

Cemp Inc...F....... 732 933-1000
Shrewsbury (G-9884)

NEWS SYNDICATES

Thomson Reuters Corporation..............F....... 973 662-3070
Nutley (G-7595)

NEWSPAPERS & PERIODICALS NEWS REPORTING SVCS

Dorf Feature Service Inc......................E....... 908 518-1802
Mountainside (G-6843)

NICKEL ALLOY

Industrial Tube Corporation ....E....... 908 369-3737
Hillsborough (G-4328)
Nickel Savers.....................................G....... 201 405-1153
Oakland (G-7639)
Nickels Carpet Cleaning ....G....... 609 892-5783
Mays Landing (G-5995)

NONCURRENT CARRYING WIRING DEVICES

American Fittings Corp ....G....... 201 664-0027
Fair Lawn (G-3083)
Billows Electric Supply Co Inc ....C....... 856 751-2200
Delran (G-2009)
Heyco Molded Products Inc..................F....... 732 286-4336
Toms River (G-10765)
Moreng Metal Products Inc ....D....... 973 256-2001
Totowa (G-10837)
Morgan Advanced Ceramics Inc ....E....... 973 808-1621
Fairfield (G-3273)
Multi-Tech Industries Inc......................F....... 732 431-0550
Marlboro (G-5905)

NONDAIRY BASED FROZEN DESSERTS

Ice Cold Novelty Products Inc ....G....... 732 751-0011
Wall Township (G-11349)
Mega Industries LLC............................G....... 973 779-8772
Passaic (G-8086)

NONFERROUS: Rolling & Drawing, NEC

Construction Specialties Inc.................E....... 908 272-2771
Cranford (G-1906)
Fisk Alloy Inc......................................F....... 973 427-7550
Hawthorne (G-4219)
Fisk Alloy Wire Incorporated ....G....... 973 949-4491
Hawthorne (G-4220)
International Rollforms Inc ....E....... 856 228-7100
Deptford (G-2064)
Kearny Smelting & Ref Corp ....E....... 201 991-7276
Kearny (G-4874)
Precision Roll Products Inc ....F....... 973 822-9100
Florham Park (G-3520)
Swepco Tube LLC...............................C....... 973 778-3000
Clifton (G-1728)

NOTIONS: Fasteners, Slide Zippers

YKK (usa) Inc......................................G....... 201 935-4200
Lyndhurst (G-5684)

NOTIONS: Hooks, Crochet

Omaha Standard Inc Tr NJ ....G....... 609 588-5400
Trenton (G-10969)

NOVELTIES

Amaryllis Inc.......................................G....... 973 635-0500
Chatham (G-1318)
Inman Mold and Mfg Co ....G....... 732 381-3033
Springfield (G-10446)
Tom Ponte Model Makers Inc................G....... 973 627-5906
Rockaway (G-9508)

NOVELTIES & SPECIALTIES: Metal

Icup Inc..E....... 856 751-2045
Cherry Hill (G-1373)
Tassel Toppers LLC.............................G....... 855 827-7357
Midland Park (G-6187)

NOVELTIES, DURABLE, WHOLESALE

Adventure Industries LLC ....G....... 609 426-1777
East Windsor (G-2334)

NOVELTIES: Leather

Adventure Industries LLC ....G....... 609 426-1777
East Windsor (G-2334)
R Neumann & Co..................................F....... 201 659-3400
Hoboken (G-4476)

NOVELTIES: Paper, Made From Purchased Materials

Red Letter Press Inc ....G....... 609 597-5257
Upper Saddle River (G-11146)

NOVELTIES: Plastic

Christopher F Maier ....F....... 908 459-5100
Hope (G-4524)
Edwards Creative Products Inc ....F....... 856 665-3200
Cherry Hill (G-1358)
Icup Inc..E....... 856 751-2045
Cherry Hill (G-1373)
Marlo Plastic Products Inc ....E....... 732 792-1988
Neptune (G-6890)

NOVELTY SHOPS

Rpl Supplies Inc ....F....... 973 767-0880
Garfield (G-3766)
Sherman Nat Inc ....E....... 201 735-9000
Englewood (G-2940)

NOZZLES & SPRINKLERS Lawn Hose

Durst Corporation Inc..........................E....... 800 852-3906
Cranford (G-1907)
Msg Fire & Safety Inc...........................G....... 732 833-8500
Wall Township (G-11356)

NOZZLES: Fire Fighting

Confires Fire Prtction Svc LLC..............F....... 908 822-2700
South Plainfield (G-10241)
Firefighter One Ltd Lblty Co ....G....... 973 940-3061
Sparta (G-10387)

NOZZLES: Spray, Aerosol, Paint Or Insecticide

Zodiac Paintball Inc ....G....... 973 616-7230
Pompton Plains (G-8876)

NUCLEAR FUELS SCRAP REPROCESSING

Holtec International ....B....... 856 797-0900
Camden (G-1069)

NURSERIES & LAWN & GARDEN SPLY STORE, RET: Lawn/Garden Splys

Lumber Super Mart ....G....... 732 739-1428
Hazlet (G-4264)
Mendham Garden Center ....G....... 973 543-4178
Mendham (G-6041)

NURSERIES & LAWN & GARDEN SPLY STORES, RETAIL: Top Soil

Cedar Hill Landscaping ....E....... 732 469-1400
Somerset (G-9974)
L & S Contracting Inc ....G....... 609 397-1281
Hopewell (G-4527)

NURSERIES & LAWN/GARDEN SPLY STORE, RET: Lawnmowers/Tractors

Chatham Lawn Mowler ....G....... 973 635-8855
Chatham (G-1320)

NURSERY & GARDEN CENTERS

Agway Energy Services LLC ....E....... 973 887-5300
Whippany (G-11877)
Klein Distributors Inc...........................G....... 732 446-7632
Burlington (G-977)

NUTS: Metal

Amerifast Corp....................................F....... 908 668-1959
South Plainfield (G-10217)
Nylok Corporation...............................F....... 201 427-8555
Hawthorne (G-4235)

OFFICE EQPT WHOLESALERS

Binding Products Inc...........................E....... 212 947-1192
Jersey City (G-4704)
Brother International Corp ....B....... 908 704-1700
Bridgewater (G-808)
Cummins - Allison Corp ....G....... 201 791-2394
Elmwood Park (G-2819)
Maxlite Inc...D....... 973 244-7300
West Caldwell (G-11663)
Royal Sovereign Intl Inc ....E....... 800 397-1025
Rockleigh (G-9521)
Time Systems International Co ....E....... 201 871-1200
Englewood (G-2947)

OFFICE EQPT, WHOLESALE: Calculating Machines

Aone Touch Inc....................................G....... 732 261-6841
Bordentown (G-575)

OFFICE EQPT, WHOLESALE: Calculators, Electronic

Sharp Electronics Corporation.............A 201 529-8200
Montvale *(G-6433)*

OFFICE EQPT, WHOLESALE: Duplicating Machines

Imperial Copy Products Inc ....E 973 927-5500
Randolph *(G-9186)*

OFFICE FIXTURES: Exc Wood

Cor Products Inc ....G 973 731-4952
West Orange *(G-11763)*
High Tech Manufacturing Inc.................G 973 372-7907
Irvington *(G-4572)*

OFFICE FURNITURE REPAIR & MAINTENANCE SVCS

Extra Office Inc................................F 732 381-9774
Rahway *(G-9092)*
Mbs Installations Inc..........................F 888 446-9135
Jackson *(G-4659)*

OFFICE SPLY & STATIONERY STORES

Important Papers Inc ....G 856 751-4544
Cherry Hill *(G-1376)*
Logomania Inc..................................G 201 798-0531
Jersey City *(G-4760)*
Papery of Marlton LLC........................G 856 985-1776
Marlton *(G-5946)*

OFFICE SPLY & STATIONERY STORES: Office Forms & Splys

Bellia & Sons...................................E 856 845-2234
Woodbury *(G-12026)*
Forms & Flyers of New Jersey...............G 856 629-0718
Williamstown *(G-11958)*
Hometown Office Sups & Prtg Co.........G 609 298-9020
Bordentown *(G-583)*
Imperial Copy Products Inc ....E 973 927-5500
Randolph *(G-9186)*
JFK Supplies Inc ....F 732 985-7800
Edison *(G-2539)*
Lamb Printing Inc..............................G 908 852-0837
Hackettstown *(G-4016)*
Printers Place Inc..............................G 973 744-8889
Montclair *(G-6385)*
Supplies-Supplies Inc.........................F 908 272-5100
Watchung *(G-11460)*
Venture Stationers Inc ....E 212 288-7235
Closter *(G-1763)*
W B Mason Co Inc..............................D 888 926-2766
Bellmawr *(G-345)*
W B Mason Co Inc..............................E 888 926-2766
Egg Harbor Township *(G-2701)*

OFFICE SPLYS, NEC, WHOLESALE

Office Needs Inc................................G 732 381-7770
Clark *(G-1511)*
Thomas H Cox & Son Inc ....E 908 928-1010
Linden *(G-5435)*
Wilcox Press.....................................G 973 827-7474
Hamburg *(G-4099)*

OFFICES & CLINICS DOCTORS OF MED: Intrnl Med Practitioners

United Medical PC.............................F 201 339-6111
Bayonne *(G-236)*

OFFICES & CLINICS OF DENTISTS: Dental Clinics & Offices

Vatech America Inc ....E 201 210-5028
Fort Lee *(G-3593)*

OFFICES & CLINICS OF DENTISTS: Specialist, Practitioners

Nobel Biocare Procera LLC ....E 201 529-7100
Mahwah *(G-5759)*

OFFICES & CLINICS OF DOCTORS OF MEDICINE: Gastronomist

Red Bank Gstrntrology Assoc PA ....E 732 842-4294
Red Bank *(G-9242)*

OFFICES & CLINICS OF DOCTORS OF MEDICINE: Group Health Assoc

I Physician Hub ....D 732 274-0155
Monmouth Junction *(G-6292)*

OFFICES & CLINICS OF DOCTORS OF MEDICINE: Neurosurgeon

Spinal Kinetics LLC ....G 908 687-2552
Union *(G-11091)*

OFFICES & CLINICS OF DOCTORS OF MEDICINE: Oncologist

Arthur A Topilow William Lrner............E 732 528-0760
Neptune *(G-6865)*

OFFICES & CLINICS OF DOCTORS OF MEDICINE: Ophthalmologist

Douglas Liva MD ....G 201 444-7770
Ridgewood *(G-9323)*

OFFICES & CLINICS OF DOCTORS OF MEDICINE: Radiologist

Mri of West Morris PA.........................F 973 927-1010
Succasunna *(G-10515)*

OFFICES & CLINICS OF DRS OF MEDICINE: Geriatric

Madhu B Goyal MD ....G 908 769-0307
South Plainfield *(G-10296)*

OFFICES & CLINICS OF DRS OF MEDICINE: Physician, Orthopedic

Biodynamics LLC ....G 201 227-9255
Englewood *(G-2882)*

OFFICES & CLINICS OF HEALTH PRACTITIONERS: Physical Therapy

Regenus Ctr Core Therapies LLC ....G 862 295-1620
Florham Park *(G-3522)*

OIL FIELD SVCS, NEC

Above Environmental Services ....G 973 702-7021
Vernon *(G-11156)*
Mine Hill Spartan ....G 973 442-2280
Mine Hill *(G-6274)*
Schlumberger Technology Corp ....C 609 275-3815
Princeton Junction *(G-9066)*

OIL TREATING COMPOUNDS

Arol Chemical Products Co ....G 973 344-1510
Newark *(G-7053)*

OILS & ESSENTIAL OILS

Elixens America Inc............................G 732 388-3555
Rahway *(G-9091)*
EMD Performance Materials Corp.........B 908 429-3500
Branchburg *(G-638)*
Serene House USA Inc ....G 609 980-1214
Cherry Hill *(G-1414)*

OILS & GREASES: Blended & Compounded

Arol Chemical Products Co ....G 973 344-1510
Newark *(G-7053)*
Hangsterfers Laboratories...................E 856 468-0216
West Deptford *(G-11702)*
Total Specialties Usa Inc ....D 908 862-9300
Linden *(G-5436)*

OILS & GREASES: Lubricating

American Oil & Supply Co ....F 732 389-5514
Eatontown *(G-2377)*
BP Lubricants USA Inc ....B 973 633-2200
Wayne *(G-11484)*

Chemours Company............................G 856 540-3398
Deepwater *(G-1998)*
Federal Lorco Petroleum LLC...............D 908 352-0542
Elizabeth *(G-2735)*
Fti Inc...G 973 443-0004
Florham Park *(G-3506)*
Gordon Terminal Service Co PA............D 201 437-8300
Bayonne *(G-220)*
International Products Corp ....F 609 386-8770
Burlington *(G-974)*
Lanxess Solutions US Inc ....C 973 887-7411
East Hanover *(G-2221)*
Lanxess Solutions US Inc ....C 732 738-1000
Fords *(G-3533)*
Penetone Corporation ....E 201 567-3000
Clifton *(G-1688)*
Pflaumer Brothers Inc ....G 609 883-4610
Ewing *(G-3051)*

OILS: Essential

Flavors of Origin Inc..........................E 732 499-9700
Avenel *(G-127)*
Interbahm International Inc..................E 732 499-9700
Avenel *(G-131)*

OILS: Lubricating

Marine Oil Service Inc.........................G 908 282-6440
Elizabeth *(G-2755)*
Mil-Comm Products Company Inc ....F 201 935-8561
East Rutherford *(G-2304)*
Nalco Company LLC ....F 609 617-2246
Red Bank *(G-9238)*
Pbf Holding Company LLC ....B 973 455-7500
Parsippany *(G-7986)*

OILS: Peppermint

Jch Partners & Co LLC.........................F 732 664-6440
Howell *(G-4542)*

OILS: Vegetable Oils, Vulcanized Or Sulfurized

Elementis Global LLC..........................C 609 443-2000
East Windsor *(G-2368)*

OLEFINS

Lyondell Chemical Company ....G 973 578-2200
Newark *(G-7192)*

OMNIBEARING INDICATORS

Oavco Ltd Liability Company ....F 855 535-4227
Princeton *(G-8988)*

OPERATOR: Apartment Buildings

Ayerspace Inc...................................G 212 582-8410
West Caldwell *(G-11641)*
Ukrainian National Association.............E 973 292-9800
Parsippany *(G-8032)*

OPERATOR: Nonresidential Buildings

Avant Industries Ltd Inc ....G 973 242-1700
Newark *(G-7060)*
Epolin Chemical LLC ....G 973 465-9495
Newark *(G-7118)*
Polymathes Holdings I LLC ....G 609 945-1690
Princeton *(G-8996)*

OPHTHALMIC GOODS

Bausch & Lomb Incorporated...............B 585 338-6000
Bridgewater *(G-800)*
Bausch & Lomb Incorporated...............B 908 927-1400
Bridgewater *(G-801)*
Complete Optical Laboratory................F 973 338-8886
Bloomfield *(G-497)*
Hillcrest Opticians ....G 973 838-6666
Kinnelon *(G-5017)*
Khan Zeshan ....G 973 619-4736
Belleville *(G-298)*
Lens Lab Express ....G 201 861-0016
West New York *(G-11745)*
Lens Mode Inc...................................G 973 467-2000
Millburn *(G-6202)*
Pds Consultants Inc ....E 201 970-2313
Sparta *(G-10405)*
Phillips Safety Products Inc..................E 732 356-1493
Middlesex *(G-6138)*

P
R
O
D
U
C
T

OPHTHALMIC GOODS (continued)

Sheridan Optical Co Inc ....E 856 582-0963
Pitman (G-8749)
Smith Optics Inc ....G 208 726-4477
Secaucus (G-9815)
Special Optics Inc ....F 973 366-7289
Denville (G-2058)
Spectacle Shoppe ....G 856 875-5046
Williamstown (G-11980)
Topcon Medical Systems Inc ....D 201 599-5100
Oakland (G-7647)
Usv Optical Inc ....B 856 228-1000
Glendora (G-3839)

OPHTHALMIC GOODS WHOLESALERS

Sensor Medical Technology LLC ....G 425 358-7381
Denville (G-2057)

OPHTHALMIC GOODS, NEC, WHOLESALE: Frames

Liberty Sport Inc ....E 973 882-0986
Fairfield (G-3262)

OPHTHALMIC GOODS, NEC, WHOLESALE: Lenses

Lens Depot Inc ....F 732 993-9766
East Brunswick (G-2154)

OPHTHALMIC GOODS: Frames & Parts, Eyeglass & Spectacle

Liberty Sport Inc ....E 973 882-0986
Fairfield (G-3262)

OPHTHALMIC GOODS: Lenses, Ophthalmic

Edison Ophthalmology Assoc LLC ....F 908 822-0070
Edison (G-2501)
Lens Depot Inc ....F 732 993-9766
East Brunswick (G-2154)
Pam Optical Co ....G 973 744-8882
Montclair (G-6382)

OPHTHALMIC GOODS: Protectors, Eye

Douglas Liva MD ....G 201 444-7770
Ridgewood (G-9323)

OPTICAL GOODS STORES

Complete Optical Laboratory ....F 973 338-8886
Bloomfield (G-497)
Pam Optical Co ....G 973 744-8882
Montclair (G-6382)

OPTICAL GOODS STORES: Contact Lenses, Prescription

Intense Inc ....E 732 249-2228
North Brunswick (G-7471)

OPTICAL GOODS STORES: Eyeglasses, Prescription

US Vision Inc ....B 856 228-1000
Blackwood (G-482)
Usv Optical Inc ....B 856 228-1000
Glendora (G-3839)

OPTICAL GOODS STORES: Opticians

Hillcrest Opticians ....G 973 838-6666
Kinnelon (G-5017)
Lens Lab Express ....G 201 861-0016
West New York (G-11745)
Partners In Vision Inc ....G 888 748-1112
Edison (G-2587)
Spectacle Shoppe ....G 856 875-5046
Williamstown (G-11980)

OPTICAL INSTRUMENTS & APPARATUS

Opt-Sciences Corporation ....E 856 829-2800
Cinnaminson (G-1478)
Rudolph RES Analytical Corp ....D 973 584-1558
Hackettstown (G-4034)
Shanghai Optics Inc ....F 732 321-6915
Clark (G-1515)
Topcon Medical Systems Inc ....D 201 599-5100
Oakland (G-7647)

OPTICAL INSTRUMENTS & LENSES

API Nanofabrication & RES Corp ....F 732 627-0808
Somerset (G-9954)
Argyle International Inc ....G 609 924-9484
Princeton (G-8909)
Artemis Optics and Coatings ....G 201 847-0887
Emerson (G-2863)
Avantier Inc ....G 732 491-8150
Metuchen (G-6046)
Cartiheal Inc ....G 917 703-6992
Closter (G-1752)
Cgm Us Inc ....E 609 894-4420
Birmingham (G-456)
Chiral Photonics Inc ....F 973 732-0030
Pine Brook (G-8591)
Coherent Inc ....D 973 240-6851
East Hanover (G-2200)
Dynasil Corporation America ....G 856 767-4600
West Berlin (G-11590)
Hamamatsu Corporation ....E 908 231-0960
Middlesex (G-6119)
High Vision Corporation ....G 862 238-7636
Clifton (G-1635)
Ii-VI Advanced Materials Inc ....G 973 227-1551
Pine Brook (G-8604)
Innovation Photonics LLC ....F 973 857-8380
Verona (G-11169)
Katena Products Inc ....E 973 989-1600
Parsippany (G-7970)
Lithoptek LLC ....G 408 533-5847
Summit (G-10538)
M H Optical Supplies Inc ....E 800 445-3090
South Hackensack (G-10170)
MRC Precision Metal Optics Inc ....E 941 753-8707
Northvale (G-7538)
Nanoopto Corporation ....E 732 627-0808
Somerset (G-10039)
Norland Products Inc ....E 609 395-1966
Cranbury (G-1865)
Quantum Coating Inc ....E 856 234-5444
Moorestown (G-6561)
Roper Scientific Inc ....E 941 556-2601
Trenton (G-10989)
Sirui USA LLC ....G 973 415-8082
Verona (G-11174)
Tag Optics Inc ....E 609 356-2142
Princeton (G-9031)
US Vision Inc ....B 856 228-1000
Blackwood (G-482)
Veeco Instruments Inc ....E 732 560-5300
Somerset (G-10093)

OPTICAL ISOLATORS

Ace Mountings Co Inc ....E 732 721-6200
South Amboy (G-10129)
Crystal Deltronic Industries ....E 973 328-6898
Dover (G-2079)
Crystal Deltronic Industries ....F 973 328-7000
Dover (G-2080)

OPTOMETRISTS' OFFICES

Complete Optical Laboratory ....F 973 338-8886
Bloomfield (G-497)

ORAL PREPARATIONS

Health and Natural Beauty USA ....F 732 640-1830
Piscataway (G-8671)

ORDNANCE

American Aluminum Company ....D 908 233-3500
Mountainside (G-6834)
Cartridge Actuated Devices ....E 973 347-2281
Byram Township (G-1017)
Eastern Regional Waterway ....F 732 684-0409
Brick (G-717)
Kongsberg Protech ....G 973 770-0574
Mount Arlington (G-6714)

ORGAN TUNING & REPAIR SVCS

Peragallo Organ Company of NJ ....F 973 684-3414
Paterson (G-8281)

ORGANIZATIONS: Biotechnical Research, Noncommercial

SPS Alfachem Inc ....G 973 676-5141
Orange (G-7762)

ORGANIZATIONS: Civic & Social

New Jrsey State Leag Mncplties ....F 609 695-3481
Trenton (G-10964)

ORGANIZATIONS: Medical Research

Agile Therapeutics Inc ....F 609 683-1880
Princeton (G-8902)
Enterix Inc ....E 732 429-1899
Edison (G-2503)
Hoffmann-La Roche Inc ....A 973 890-2268
Little Falls (G-5456)
Thomsom Health Care Inc ....C 201 358-7300
Montvale (G-6436)

ORGANIZATIONS: Noncommercial Social Research

Global Strategy Institute A ....G 973 615-7447
Bloomfield (G-501)

ORGANIZATIONS: Religious

La Tribuna Publication Inc ....E 201 617-1360
Union City (G-11118)

ORGANIZATIONS: Research Institute

Lockheed Martin Corporation ....C 856 722-3336
Moorestown (G-6539)

ORGANIZATIONS: Scientific Research Agency

Anvima Technologies LLC ....G 973 531-7077
Brookside (G-916)

ORGANIZERS, CLOSET & DRAWER Plastic

Home Organization LLC ....F 201 351-2121
Closter (G-1757)
Pfk Coach Phyllis Flood Knerr ....G 856 429-5425
Haddonfield (G-4061)

ORIENTED STRANDBOARD

JM Huber Corporation ....D 732 603-3630
Edison (G-2540)

ORNAMENTS: Lawn

Tropical Expressions Inc ....G 732 899-8680
Point Pleasant Boro (G-8846)

ORTHODONTIST

Jaeger Thomas & Melissa DDS ....F 908 735-2722
Lebanon (G-5266)

OUTLETS: Electric, Convenience

Simply Amazing LLC ....F 732 249-4151
East Brunswick (G-2177)

OVENS: Infrared

Radiant Energy Systems Inc ....E 973 423-5220
Hawthorne (G-4241)
Radiation Systems Inc ....G 201 891-7515
Wyckoff (G-12118)
Therma-Tech Corporation ....F 973 345-0076
Paterson (G-8315)

OXALIC ACID & METALLIC SALTS

American Beryllia Inc ....E 973 248-8080
Haskell (G-4194)

PACKAGE DESIGN SVCS

Audio Dynamix Inc ....F 201 567-5488
Englewood (G-2879)
Integrated Packaging Inds Inc ....E 973 839-0500
Butler (G-1005)
Pac Team America Inc ....E 201 599-5000
Paramus (G-7826)
Weber Packaging Inc ....G 201 262-6022
Oradell (G-7748)

PACKAGED FROZEN FOODS WHOLESALERS, NEC

Arctic Foods Inc ....E 908 689-0590
Washington (G-11438)

Arm National Food Inc .... G 609 695-4911
Trenton **(G-10896)**

Metropolitan Foods Inc .... C 973 672-9400
Clifton **(G-1668)**

Missa Bay LLC .... D 856 241-0900
Swedesboro **(G-10597)**

PACKAGING & LABELING SVCS

Alexander James Corp .... D 908 362-9266
Blairstown **(G-484)**

American Spraytech LLC .... E 908 725-6060
Branchburg **(G-617)**

Assem - Pak Inc .... C 856 692-3355
Vineland **(G-11187)**

Brisar Industries Inc .... D 973 278-2500
Paterson **(G-8150)**

Copack International Inc .... E 973 405-5151
Clifton **(G-1590)**

Envirochem Inc .... E 732 238-6700
South River **(G-10350)**

G H Krauss Manufacturing Co .... G 856 662-0815
Cherry Hill **(G-1365)**

Gordon Terminal Service Co PA .... D 201 437-8300
Bayonne **(G-220)**

Holly Packaging Inc .... E 856 327-8281
Millville **(G-6255)**

Hy-Test Packaging Corp .... G 973 754-7000
Paterson **(G-8211)**

J&E Business Services LLC .... G 973 984-8444
Clifton **(G-1645)**

Jrz Enterprises LLC .... G 973 962-6330
Wayne **(G-11526)**

Major Products Co Inc .... E 201 641-5555
Little Ferry **(G-5492)**

Nutra-Med Packaging Inc .... D 973 625-2274
Whippany **(G-11899)**

Rectico Inc .... F 973 575-0009
Fairfield **(G-3298)**

Reed-Lane Inc .... C 973 709-1090
Wayne **(G-11546)**

Refresco Us Inc .... D 973 361-9794
Wharton **(G-11869)**

Robert Freeman .... G 973 751-0082
Belleville **(G-312)**

Sabre Die Cutting Co Inc .... E 973 357-9800
Paterson **(G-8290)**

PACKAGING MATERIALS, INDL: Wholesalers

Raritan Packaging Industries .... E 732 246-7200
New Brunswick **(G-6966)**

PACKAGING MATERIALS, WHOLESALE

Ace Bag & Burlap Company Inc .... F 973 242-2200
Newark **(G-7034)**

Albert Paper Products Company .... E 973 373-0330
Irvington **(G-4554)**

Alliance Corrugated Box Inc .... E 877 525-5269
Saddle River **(G-9690)**

Amcor Flexibles Inc .... E 609 267-5900
Mount Holly **(G-6723)**

Capital Gasket and Rubber Inc .... G 856 939-3670
Runnemede **(G-9604)**

Fleet Packaging Inc .... G 866 302-0340
South Orange **(G-10196)**

GT Microwave Inc .... E 973 361-5700
Randolph **(G-9184)**

Kolon USA Incorporated .... F 201 641-5800
Ridgefield Park **(G-9311)**

M & E Packaging Corp .... G 201 635-1381
Lyndhurst **(G-5659)**

M S Plastics and Packg Co .... F 973 492-2400
Butler **(G-1007)**

Mm Packaging Group LLC .... G 908 759-0101
Linden **(G-5387)**

Plus Packaging Inc .... G 973 538-2216
Morristown **(G-6694)**

Polyair Inter Pack Inc .... D 201 804-1725
Carlstadt **(G-1203)**

Pro Pack Inc .... F 973 665-8333
Wharton **(G-11868)**

US Propack Inc .... G 732 294-4500
Freehold **(G-3702)**

PACKAGING MATERIALS: Paper

Aeon Industries Inc .... G 732 246-3224
Somerset **(G-9943)**

Amcor Flexibles Inc .... E 609 267-5900
Mount Holly **(G-6723)**

Arch Crown Inc .... E 973 731-6300
Hillside **(G-4375)**

Employment Horizons Inc .... B 973 538-8822
Cedar Knolls **(G-1304)**

Gleicher Manufacturing Corp .... E 908 233-2211
Scotch Plains **(G-9732)**

Holland Manufacturing Co Inc .... C 973 584-8141
Succasunna **(G-10513)**

Ileos of America Inc .... C 908 753-7300
South Plainfield **(G-10276)**

Jrm Industries Inc .... E 973 779-9340
Passaic **(G-8077)**

Lps Industries Inc .... C 201 438-3515
Moonachie **(G-6477)**

Multi Packaging Solutions Inc .... C 908 757-6000
South Plainfield **(G-10303)**

Nekoosa Coated Products LLC .... G 800 440-1250
South Plainfield **(G-10304)**

Polyair Inter Pack Inc .... D 201 804-1725
Carlstadt **(G-1203)**

US Magic Box Inc .... G 973 772-2070
Garfield **(G-3775)**

PACKAGING MATERIALS: Paper, Coated Or Laminated

Allure Box & Display Co .... F 212 807-7070
Hackensack **(G-3876)**

Delta Paper Corporation .... E 856 532-0333
Burlington **(G-963)**

E & E Group Corp .... G 201 814-0414
South Hackensack **(G-10155)**

Homasote Company .... C 609 883-3300
Ewing **(G-3036)**

PACKAGING MATERIALS: Plastic Film, Coated Or Laminated

Amcor Flexibles LLC .... C 856 825-1400
Millville **(G-6224)**

ANS Plastics Corporation .... F 732 247-2776
New Brunswick **(G-6910)**

Basic Plastics Company Inc .... E 973 977-8151
Paterson **(G-8147)**

Blispak Acquisition Corp .... D 973 884-4141
Whippany **(G-11882)**

Comar Inc .... F 856 507-5461
Voorhees **(G-11283)**

Consolidated Packg Group Inc .... C 201 440-4240
Ridgefield Park **(G-9301)**

Forem Packaging Inc .... F 973 589-0402
Newark **(G-7126)**

Kansas City Design Inc .... G 609 460-4629
Lambertville **(G-5192)**

Lally-Pak Inc .... D 908 351-4141
Hillside **(G-4409)**

LV Adhesive Inc .... E 201 507-0080
Carlstadt **(G-1183)**

MSC Marketing & Technology .... E 201 507-9100
Lyndhurst **(G-5665)**

R Tape Corporation .... C 908 753-5570
South Plainfield **(G-10322)**

PACKAGING MATERIALS: Polystyrene Foam

A & S Packaging & Display .... F 201 531-1900
Carlstadt **(G-1117)**

Alliance Corrugated Box Inc .... E 877 525-5269
Saddle River **(G-9690)**

Arrow Information Packagig LLC .... G 856 317-9000
Pennsauken **(G-8391)**

Atlantic Can Company .... G 609 518-9950
Westampton **(G-11784)**

Century Service Affiliates Inc .... E 973 742-3516
Paterson **(G-8155)**

Craig Robertson .... G 973 293-8666
Montague **(G-6354)**

Edison Nation Inc .... G 610 829-1039
Phillipsburg **(G-8549)**

Fxi Inc .... D 201 933-8540
East Rutherford **(G-2290)**

Integrated Packaging Inds Inc .... E 973 839-0500
Butler **(G-1005)**

New Industrial Foam Corp .... E 908 561-4010
Plainfield **(G-8772)**

Plastpac Inc .... F 908 272-7200
Kenilworth **(G-4971)**

Rep Trading Associates Inc .... F 732 591-1140
Old Bridge **(G-7727)**

Sealed Air Corporation .... C 201 712-7000
Saddle Brook **(G-9679)**

Sealed Air Corporation .... D 973 890-4735
Saddle Brook **(G-9680)**

Shell Packaging Corporation .... E 908 871-7000
Berkeley Heights **(G-412)**

Sierra Packaging Inc .... F 732 571-2900
Ocean **(G-7683)**

Sonoco Display & Packaging LLC .... G 201 612-4008
Ridgefield Park **(G-9317)**

Tcp Reliable Inc .... G 848 229-2466
Edison **(G-2632)**

Tech-Pak Inc .... F 201 935-3800
Wood Ridge **(G-12007)**

Tricorbraun Inc .... G 732 353-7104
Monroe Township **(G-6349)**

Univeg Logistics America Inc .... G 856 241-0097
Swedesboro **(G-10616)**

US Propack Inc .... G 732 294-4500
Freehold **(G-3702)**

Utility Development Corp .... G 973 994-4334
Livingston **(G-5544)**

Willings Nutraceutical Corp .... F 856 424-9088
Cherry Hill **(G-1427)**

PACKAGING: Blister Or Bubble Formed, Plastic

Carecam International Inc .... E 973 227-0720
Fairfield **(G-3164)**

Colorite Plastics Company .... E 201 941-2900
Ridgefield **(G-9254)**

Dolco Packaging Corp .... E 201 941-2900
Ridgefield **(G-9258)**

Plastiform Packaging Inc .... E 973 983-8900
Rockaway **(G-9487)**

Pure TEC Corporation .... G 201 941-2900
Ridgefield **(G-9285)**

Willings Nutraceutical Corp .... F 856 424-9088
Cherry Hill **(G-1427)**

PACKING & CRATING SVC

Integrated Packaging Inds Inc .... E 973 839-0500
Butler **(G-1005)**

PACKING & CRATING SVCS: Containerized Goods For Shipping

Bigflysports Inc .... G 201 653-4414
Secaucus **(G-9753)**

Cuny and Guerber Inc .... E 201 617-5800
Union City **(G-11109)**

PACKING MATERIALS: Mechanical

American Braiding & Mfg Corp .... F 732 938-6333
Howell **(G-4530)**

Cryopak Verification Tech Inc .... F 732 346-9200
Edison **(G-2488)**

Fleet Packaging Inc .... G 866 302-0340
South Orange **(G-10196)**

Paradigm Packaging East LLC .... C 201 909-3400
Saddle Brook **(G-9668)**

Romaco North America Inc .... G 609 584-2500
Hamilton **(G-4123)**

PACKING SVCS: Shipping

East Coast Salt Dist Inc .... G 732 833-2973
Jackson **(G-4654)**

Graybar Electric Company Inc .... D 973 404-5555
Edison **(G-2522)**

Hub Print & Copy Center LLC .... G 201 585-7887
Fort Lee **(G-3563)**

Jan Packaging Inc .... D 973 361-7200
Dover **(G-2091)**

Norwood Industries Inc .... F 856 858-6195
Haddon Township **(G-4052)**

Oasis Trading Co Inc .... C 908 964-0477
Hillside **(G-4419)**

Package Development Co Inc .... E 973 983-8500
Rockaway **(G-9483)**

Vaswani Inc .... F 877 376-4425
Edison **(G-2638)**

PADS, SCOURING: Soap Impregnated

Supply Plus NY Inc .... E 973 481-4800
Paterson **(G-8308)**

PRODUCT

PADS: Athletic, Protective

Impact Protective Eqp LLC ....G....... 973 377-0903
Madison (G-5695)

PADS: Mattress

Stanlar Enterprises Inc ....E.... 973 680-4488
Bloomfield (G-518)

PAGERS: One-way

Cooper Wheelock Inc ....B....... 732 222-6880
Long Branch (G-5595)

PAILS: Meta, Exc Shipping

Phoenix Container Inc ....C....... 732 247-3931
Trenton (G-10973)

PAINT & PAINTING SPLYS STORE

Hawthorne Paint Company Inc ....G....... 973 423-2335
Lodi (G-5564)

PAINT STORE

Benjamin Moore & Co.......................C....... 201 573-9600
Montvale (G-6399)
Benjamin Moore & Co.......................D....... 973 569-5000
Clifton (G-1573)

PAINTING SVC: Metal Prdts

Newark Industrial Spraying..................F 973 344-6855
Newark (G-7213)
Productive Industrial Finshg ....G....... 856 427-9646
Voorhees (G-11292)

PAINTS & ADDITIVES

Columbia Paint Lab Inc.....................E.... 201 435-4884
Jersey City (G-4715)
Dux Paint LLC ....F....... 973 473-2376
Lodi (G-5560)
Elementis Specialties Inc ....C....... 609 443-2000
East Windsor (G-2369)
Fti Inc ....G....... 973 443-0004
Florham Park (G-3506)
Gdb International Inc ....D....... 732 246-3001
New Brunswick (G-6928)
Hawthorne Paint Company Inc ....G....... 973 423-2335
Lodi (G-5564)
Kop-Coat Inc ....E.... 800 221-4466
Rockaway (G-9474)
Milspray LLC ....E.... 732 886-2223
Lakewood (G-5135)
Nautical Marine Paint Corp ....E.... 732 821-3200
North Brunswick (G-7479)

PAINTS & ALLIED PRODUCTS

Actega North America Inc ....C....... 856 829-6300
Delran (G-2008)
Actega North America Inc ....F....... 856 829-6300
Cinnaminson (G-1439)
Advanced Protective Products............F 201 794-2000
Fair Lawn (G-3082)
Ashland LLC ....G....... 908 243-3500
Bridgewater (G-794)
Ashland Spcalty Ingredients GP ....E.... 732 353-7708
Parlin (G-7862)
Ben Hamon Moore Co ....E.... 800 344-0400
Montvale (G-6398)
Breen Color Concentrates LLC ....F....... 609 397-8200
Lambertville (G-5187)
Carboline Company ....F....... 908 233-3150
Westfield (G-11796)
Chemetall US Inc............................D....... 908 464-6900
New Providence (G-6997)
Clausen Company Inc ....F....... 732 738-1165
Fords (G-3531)
Colorflo Inc ....G....... 908 862-3010
Linden (G-5335)
Complementary Coatings Corp ....E.... 845 786-5000
Montvale (G-6405)
Covalnce Spcialty Coatings LLC.........F....... 732 356-2870
Middlesex (G-6109)
Dunbar Sales Company Inc ....G....... 201 437-6500
Bayonne (G-214)
E I Du Pont De Nemours & Co ....E.... 732 257-1579
Parlin (G-7863)
Elementis Specialties Inc ....F....... 201 432-0800
East Windsor (G-2370)

Evonik Corporation...........................B....... 973 929-8000
Parsippany (G-7938)
Fluorotherm Polymers Inc ....G....... 973 575-0760
Parsippany (G-7948)
Industrial Summit Tech Corp ....E.... 732 238-2211
Parlin (G-7865)
J R S Tool & Metal Finishing................G....... 908 753-2050
South Plainfield (G-10282)
Lafarge Road Marking Inc ....G....... 973 884-0300
Parsippany (G-7972)
Muralo Company Inc ....C....... 201 437-0770
Bayonne (G-229)
Nippon Paint (usa) Inc ....F....... 201 692-1111
Teaneck (G-10640)
Penn Metal Finishing Co Inc ....E.... 609 387-3400
Burlington (G-981)
Plastic Specialties & Tech Inc ....C....... 201 941-2900
Ridgefield (G-9284)
Prem-Khichi Enterprises Inc................F....... 973 242-0300
East Brunswick (G-2167)
Rich Art Color Co Inc ....F....... 201 767-0009
Northvale (G-7547)
Rust-Oleum Corporation ....E.... 847 367-7700
Somerset (G-10068)
Saint-Gobain Prfmce Plas Corp ....D....... 732 652-0910
Somerset (G-10070)
Seagrave Coatings Corp ....E.... 201 933-1000
Kenilworth (G-4976)
Steven Industries Inc ....E.... 201 437-6500
Bayonne (G-235)
Target Coatings Inc..........................G....... 800 752-9922
Fair Lawn (G-3127)
Tenax Finishing Products Co ....F....... 973 589-9000
Newark (G-7295)

PAINTS, VARNISHES & SPLYS WHOLESALERS

Worldwide Safety Systems LLC ....G....... 888 613-4501
Teaneck (G-10656)

PAINTS, VARNISHES & SPLYS, WHOLESALE: Colors & Pigments

Greenville Colorants LLC.....................F....... 201 595-0200
New Brunswick (G-6931)

PAINTS, VARNISHES & SPLYS, WHOLESALE: Paints

Kop-Coat Inc ....E.... 800 221-4466
Rockaway (G-9474)
Nautical Marine Paint Corp ....E.... 732 821-3200
North Brunswick (G-7479)
Steven Industries Inc ....E.... 201 437-6500
Bayonne (G-235)
Target Coatings Inc..........................G....... 800 752-9922
Fair Lawn (G-3127)

PAINTS: Marine

Flexdell Corp ....G....... 732 901-7771
Lakewood (G-5100)
Hempel (usa) Inc ....G....... 201 939-2801
Clifton (G-1633)

PAINTS: Oil Or Alkyd Vehicle Or Water Thinned

Benjamin Moore & Co.......................C....... 201 573-9600
Montvale (G-6399)
Benjamin Moore & Co.......................D....... 973 569-5000
Clifton (G-1573)

PAINTS: Waterproof

Newage Painting Corporation................G....... 908 547-4734
Newark (G-7211)
Performance Industries Inc..................E.... 609 392-1450
Trenton (G-10972)
Sau-Sea Swimming Pool Products ......F....... 609 859-8500
Southampton (G-10372)
Tq3 north America Inc ....G....... 973 882-7900
Fairfield (G-3331)

PALLET REPAIR SVCS

F & R Pallets Inc ....E.... 856 964-8516
Camden (G-1062)
Lt Chini Inc ....E.... 856 692-0303
Vineland (G-11242)

T & M Pallet Co Inc..........................E.... 908 454-3042
Stewartsville (G-10488)
Warren Pallet Company Inc ....F....... 908 995-7172
Bloomsbury (G-532)

PALLETS

D & H Pallets LLC............................G....... 973 481-2981
Newark (G-7092)
East Coast Pallets LLC......................G....... 732 308-3616
Manalapan (G-5805)
Greenway Products & Svcs LLC ....E.... 732 442-0200
New Brunswick (G-6932)
JC Pallets Inc ....F....... 973 345-1102
Paterson (G-8219)
Reliable Pallet Services LLC ....E.... 732 243-9642
Metuchen (G-6068)
Royal Pallet Inc ....G....... 973 299-0445
Boonton (G-566)
Universal Pallet Inc ....G....... 732 356-2624
Warren (G-11434)
Van-Nick Pallet Inc ....G....... 908 753-1800
South Plainfield (G-10339)

PALLETS & SKIDS: Wood

Avenel Pallet Co Inc.........................F....... 732 752-0500
Dunellen (G-2119)
Bunn Industries Incorporated..............F....... 609 890-2900
Trenton (G-10907)
Delisa Pallet Corp ....F....... 732 667-7070
Middlesex (G-6111)
Global Direct Marketing Group............G....... 856 427-6116
Haddonfield (G-4058)
Isco..G....... 856 672-9182
Barrington (G-174)
Riephoff Saw Mill Inc ....F....... 609 259-7265
Allentown (G-30)
Wm Leiber Inc ....G....... 732 938-2080
Farmingdale (G-3396)

PALLETS: Metal

RISE Corporation ....E.... 973 575-7480
West Caldwell (G-11679)

PALLETS: Plastic

Componding Engrg Solutions Inc.........F....... 973 340-4000
Upper Saddle River (G-11137)
P D Q Plastics Inc ....E.... 201 823-0270
Bayonne (G-230)

PALLETS: Wooden

Atco Pallet Company ....E.... 856 461-8141
Delanco (G-2003)
Atlantic Indus WD Pdts LLC ....G....... 609 965-4555
Egg Harbor City (G-2652)
Cutler Bros Box & Lumber Co ....E.... 201 943-2535
Fairview (G-3359)
Extreme Pallet Inc ....G....... 973 286-1717
Newark (G-7120)
F & R Pallets Inc ....E.... 856 964-8516
Camden (G-1062)
General Pallet LLC ....E.... 732 549-1000
Flemington (G-3446)
Jimenez Pallets LLC ....G....... 862 267-3900
Kearny (G-4872)
Lawrence M Gichan Incorporated.........F....... 201 330-3222
North Bergen (G-7416)
Love Pallet LLC ....G....... 908 964-3385
Hillside (G-4411)
Lt Chini Inc ....G....... 856 692-0303
Vineland (G-11242)
Millwood Inc ....D....... 732 967-8818
South River (G-10354)
North Eastern Pallet Exchange............E.... 908 289-0018
Elizabeth (G-2761)
Notie Corp ....G....... 609 259-3477
Allentown (G-28)
Pallet Services Inc ....G....... 856 514-3908
Pedricktown (G-8352)
Pedestal Pallet Inc ....G....... 732 968-7488
Dunellen (G-2122)
Petro Pallet LLC ....E.... 732 230-3287
Monmouth Junction (G-6300)
Poor Boy Pallet LLC ....E.... 856 451-3771
Bridgeton (G-770)
Premier Asset Logistics Networ...........F....... 877 725-6381
Williamstown (G-11973)
Reliable Pallet Services LLC ....G....... 973 900-2260
Hillside (G-4425)

Select Enterprises Inc ....G...... 732 287-8622
  Edison (G-2605)
T & M Pallet Co Inc ....E...... 908 454-3042
  Stewartsville (G-10488)
Tommys Pallet Yard LLC ....G...... 609 424-3996
  Bordentown (G-596)
Tristate Crating Pallet Co Inc ....E...... 973 357-8293
  Paterson (G-8318)
U P N Pallet Co Inc ....F...... 856 299-1192
  Penns Grove (G-8379)
Warren Pallet Company Inc ....F...... 908 995-7172
  Bloomsbury (G-532)

PANEL & DISTRIBUTION BOARDS & OTHER RELATED APPARATUS

Aeropanel Corporation ....D...... 973 335-9636
  Boonton (G-537)
Automation & Control Inc ....E...... 856 234-2300
  Moorestown (G-6507)

PANEL & DISTRIBUTION BOARDS: Electric

Electronic Power Designs Inc ....F...... 973 838-7055
  Bloomingdale (G-527)
Lincoln Electric Pdts Co Inc ....E...... 908 688-2900
  Union (G-11069)
Symcon Inc ....G...... 973 728-8661
  West Milford (G-11732)
Tsi Nomenclature Inc ....G...... 732 340-0646
  Avenel (G-152)

PANELS, CORRUGATED: Plastic

Onyx Graphics LLC ....G...... 908 281-0038
  Hillsborough (G-4343)
Philcorr LLC ....D...... 856 205-0557
  Vineland (G-11252)

PANELS: Building, Wood

All Structures LLC ....G...... 732 233-7071
  Little Silver (G-5499)

PANELS: Electric Metering

Csl Services Inc ....F...... 856 755-9440
  Pennsauken (G-8409)

PANELS: Wood

Yonkers Plywood Manufacturing ....E...... 732 727-1200
  Old Bridge (G-7730)

PAPER & BOARD: Die-cut

American Bindery Depot Inc ....C...... 732 287-2370
  Edison (G-2453)
Danielle Die Cut Products Inc ....E...... 973 278-3000
  Paterson (G-8167)
Dynamic Die Cutting & Finshg ....F...... 973 589-8338
  Newark (G-7109)
Gleicher Manufacturing Corp ....E...... 908 233-2211
  Scotch Plains (G-9732)
Grand Displays Inc ....F...... 201 994-1500
  North Bergen (G-7407)
Grand Displays Inc ....E...... 201 994-1500
  Pennsauken (G-8426)
JIT Manufacturing Inc ....F...... 973 247-7300
  Paterson (G-8223)
Prestige Associates Inc ....E...... 609 393-1509
  Trenton (G-10982)
Pro Tapes & Specialties Inc ....C...... 732 346-0900
  North Brunswick (G-7483)
Stephco Sales Inc ....E...... 973 278-5454
  Paterson (G-8301)
Vmc Die Cutting Corp ....F...... 973 450-4655
  Belleville (G-323)

PAPER & ENVELOPES: Writing, Made From Purchased Materials

A D M Corporation ....D...... 732 469-0900
  Middlesex (G-6090)
Arna Marketing Group Inc ....D...... 908 625-7395
  Branchburg (G-621)

PAPER CONVERTING

Arrow Paper Company Inc ....G...... 908 756-1111
  Plainfield (G-8759)
B & G Plastics Inc ....E...... 973 824-9220
  Union (G-11028)

Cartolith Group ....G...... 908 624-9833
  Hillside (G-4385)
CCL Label Inc ....D...... 609 443-3700
  Hightstown (G-4295)
Custom Converters Inc ....F...... 973 994-9000
  Livingston (G-5509)
Georgia-Pacific LLC ....C...... 908 995-2228
  Milford (G-6193)
Laminated Industries Inc ....E...... 908 862-5995
  Linden (G-5373)
Legacy Converting Inc ....E...... 609 642-7020
  Cranbury (G-1856)
Matthias Paper Corporation ....E...... 856 467-6970
  Swedesboro (G-10594)
Princeton Supply Corp ....G...... 609 683-9100
  Princeton (G-9005)
R L R Foil Stamping LLC ....F...... 973 778-9464
  Passaic (G-8100)
Stonebridge Paper LLC ....F...... 973 413-8100
  Paterson (G-8303)

PAPER MANUFACTURERS: Exc Newsprint

Golden W Ppr Converting Corp ....E...... 908 412-8889
  South Plainfield (G-10268)
H S Folex Schleussner Inc ....G...... 973 575-7626
  Fairfield (G-3220)
International Paper Company ....E...... 856 853-7000
  West Deptford (G-11706)
International Paper Company ....E...... 856 931-8000
  Bellmawr (G-335)
International Paper Company ....C...... 856 546-7000
  Barrington (G-173)
International Paper Company ....G...... 973 405-2400
  Clifton (G-1643)
Printwrap Corporation ....F...... 973 239-1144
  Cedar Grove (G-1289)
Schweitzer-Mauduit Intl Inc ....E...... 732 723-6100
  Spotswood (G-10417)
Sealed Air Holdings ....G...... 201 791-7600
  Elmwood Park (G-2855)

PAPER PRDTS: Feminine Hygiene Prdts

Jnj International Inv LLC ....G...... 732 524-0400
  New Brunswick (G-6939)
Johnson & Johnson ....D...... 732 524-0400
  Piscataway (G-8682)
Johnson & Johnson ....D...... 732 524-0400
  Princeton (G-8967)
Johnson & Johnson ....D...... 917 573-8007
  Ridgefield (G-9269)
Johnson & Johnson ....D...... 732 524-0400
  Lambertville (G-5190)
Johnson & Johnson ....D...... 732 524-0400
  Branchburg (G-650)
Johnson & Johnson ....D...... 732 524-0400
  Trenton (G-10947)
Johnson & Johnson ....G...... 908 722-9319
  Raritan (G-9213)
Johnson & Johnson ....C...... 908 874-1000
  Morris Plains (G-6618)
Johnson & Johnson ....G...... 732 524-0400
  New Brunswick (G-6941)

PAPER PRDTS: Infant & Baby Prdts

Interganic Fzco LLC ....G...... 224 436-0372
  Hillsborough (G-4333)

PAPER PRDTS: Sanitary

Johnson & Johnson ....A...... 732 524-0400
  New Brunswick (G-6940)
Johnson & Johnson ....D...... 732 422-5000
  North Brunswick (G-7473)
Keystone Adjustable Cap Co Inc ....E...... 856 356-2809
  Pennsauken (G-8447)
Marcal Paper Mills LLC ....A...... 800 631-8451
  Elmwood Park (G-2840)
Pacon Manufacturing Corp ....C...... 732 764-9070
  Somerset (G-10051)
Professional Disposables Inc ....A...... 845 365-1700
  Woodcliff Lake (G-12062)

PAPER PRDTS: Towels, Napkins/Tissue Paper, From Purchd Mtrls

Federal Equipment & Mfg Co Inc ....G...... 973 340-7600
  Lodi (G-5562)
Samseng Tissue Co ....F...... 609 479-3997
  Burlington (G-984)

PAPER, WHOLESALE: Fine

Acedepotcom ....F...... 800 844-0962
  Northvale (G-7515)

PAPER, WHOLESALE: Printing

Printwrap Corporation ....F...... 973 239-1144
  Cedar Grove (G-1289)

PAPER: Adhesive

LV Adhesive Inc ....E...... 201 507-0080
  Carlstadt (G-1183)
Omega Heat Transfer Co Inc ....F...... 732 340-0023
  West Orange (G-11775)
Plus Packaging Inc ....G...... 973 538-2216
  Morristown (G-6694)
Thermwell Products Co Inc ....E...... 201 684-4400
  Mahwah (G-5782)
Wet-N-Stick LLC ....G...... 908 687-8273
  Union (G-11099)

PAPER: Bag

Case It Inc ....E...... 800 441-4710
  Lyndhurst (G-5646)
Clover Bags & Paper LLC ....G...... 917 721-6783
  Little Ferry (G-5479)

PAPER: Cardboard

All County Recycling Inc ....F...... 609 393-6445
  Trenton (G-10890)

PAPER: Chart & Graph, Ruled

Gpschartscom ....G...... 609 226-8842
  Ventnor City (G-11153)

PAPER: Coated & Laminated, NEC

Avery Dennison Corporation ....G...... 201 956-6100
  Fair Lawn (G-3088)
CCL Label Inc ....D...... 609 443-3700
  Hightstown (G-4295)
CCL Label (delaware) Inc ....C...... 609 259-1055
  Trenton (G-10914)
Custom Laminations Inc ....E...... 973 279-9174
  Paterson (G-8166)
Dikeman Laminating Corporation ....E...... 973 473-5696
  Clifton (G-1598)
Fedex Office & Print Svcs Inc ....E...... 856 427-0099
  Cherry Hill (G-1361)
Gleicher Manufacturing Corp ....E...... 908 233-2211
  Scotch Plains (G-9732)
Graphic Express Menu Co Inc ....E...... 973 685-0022
  Clifton (G-1629)
Horizon Label LLC ....F...... 856 767-0777
  West Berlin (G-11599)
Igi Corp ....G...... 908 753-5570
  South Plainfield (G-10275)
International Graphics Inc ....C...... 908 753-5570
  South Plainfield (G-10279)
Lacoa Inc ....G...... 973 754-1000
  Elmwood Park (G-2837)
Par Code Symbology Inc ....F...... 973 918-0550
  Roseland (G-9541)
Renell Label Print Inc ....G...... 201 652-6544
  Paramus (G-7829)
Tech-Pak Inc ....F...... 201 935-3800
  Wood Ridge (G-12007)
United Label Corp ....G...... 973 589-6500
  Newark (G-7309)

PAPER: Corrugated

Schiffenhaus Industries Inc ....C...... 973 484-5000
  Newark (G-7263)

PAPER: Envelope

Glue Fold Inc ....D...... 973 575-8400
  Clifton (G-1627)

PAPER: Gift Wrap

Glitterwrap Inc ....D...... 800 745-4883
  Rockaway (G-9463)
Icup Inc ....E...... 856 751-2045
  Cherry Hill (G-1373)
M S C Paper Products Corp ....E...... 908 686-2200
  Hillside (G-4413)

Schurman Fine Papers ....E 856 985-1776
Marlton (G-5950)

PAPER: Metallic Covered, Made From Purchased Materials

Unifoil Corporation ....D....... 973 244-9900
Fairfield (G-3335)

PAPER: Newsprint

Beach Nutts Media Inc..................G....... 609 886-4113
Villas (G-11178)
Delta Paper Corporation ....E 856 532-0333
Burlington (G-963)

PAPER: Packaging

Amcor Flexibles LLC ....C 856 825-1400
Millville (G-6224)
Borak Group Inc ....D....... 718 665-8500
Jersey City (G-4705)
G R Impex Ltd Liability Co ....F 301 873-5333
Avenel (G-129)
Lps Industries Inc ....C 201 438-3515
Moonachie (G-6477)

PAPER: Poster & Art

Arthur A Kaplan Co Inc ....E 201 806-2100
East Rutherford (G-2273)

PAPER: Printer

Boro Printing Inc ....G....... 732 229-1899
West Long Branch (G-11720)
Lodor Offset Corporation..............F 201 935-7100
Carlstadt (G-1182)
Sre Ventures LLC ....G....... 973 785-0099
Little Falls (G-5468)

PAPER: Specialty Or Chemically Treated

Holland Manufacturing Co Inc........C 973 584-8141
Succasunna (G-10513)
IW Tremont Co Inc ....E 973 427-3800
Hawthorne (G-4227)

PAPER: Wallpaper

Rigo Industries Inc......................E 973 881-1780
Paterson (G-8288)
Screen Reproductions Co Inc ....E 201 935-0830
Carlstadt (G-1214)

PAPER: Wrapping & Packaging

Allure Box & Display Co ....F 212 807-7070
Hackensack (G-3876)
Flexo-Craft Prints Inc ....E 973 482-7200
Harrison (G-4174)

PAPER: Wrapping, Waterproof Or Coated

Norpak Corporation ....E 973 589-4200
Newark (G-7219)

PAPERBOARD

International Paper Company ....C 732 251-2000
Spotswood (G-10415)
M S C Paper Products Corp ....E 908 686-2200
Hillside (G-4413)
Union Container Corp....................E 973 242-3600
Newark (G-7306)
Westrock Cp LLC ....D....... 732 866-1890
Colts Neck (G-1790)
Westrock Cp LLC ....E 973 594-6000
Clifton (G-1739)
Westrock Rkt LLC ....C 856 596-8604
Marlton (G-5956)
Wjj and Company LLC ....F 973 246-7480
Garfield (G-3778)

PAPERBOARD CONVERTING

Caraustar Clifton Primary Pack ......C 973 472-4900
Clifton (G-1580)
Specialty Kraft Converters LLC ......G....... 732 225-2080
Edison (G-2617)

PAPERBOARD PRDTS: Binders' Board

Nu-EZ Custom Bindery LLC............E 201 488-4140
Hackensack (G-3956)

PAPERBOARD PRDTS: Coated & Treated Board

Monster Coatings Inc ....G....... 973 983-7662
Rockaway (G-9478)

PAPERBOARD PRDTS: Folding Boxboard

Graphic Packaging Intl LLC ....C 732 424-2100
Wayne (G-11513)
Multi Packaging Solutions Inc ....C 908 757-6000
South Plainfield (G-10303)
Shure-Pak Corporation ....G....... 856 825-0808
Millville (G-6270)
United States Box Corp.................E 973 481-2000
Fairfield (G-3336)

PAPERBOARD PRDTS: Milk Carton Board

Red Oak Packaging Inc ....E 862 268-8200
Newton (G-7354)

PAPERBOARD PRDTS: Packaging Board

JIT Manufacturing Inc...................F 973 247-7300
Paterson (G-8223)
Shell Packaging Corporation...........E 908 871-7000
Berkeley Heights (G-412)

PAPERBOARD PRDTS: Specialty Board

Flech Paper Products Inc...............F 973 357-8111
Paterson (G-8193)

PAPERBOARD PRDTS: Strawboard

Greenbuilt Intl Bldg Co.................G....... 609 300-9091
Voorhees (G-11287)

PAPERBOARD: Coated

Lamitech Inc ....E 609 860-8037
Cranbury (G-1854)

PAPERBOARD: Corrugated

Sunshine Metal & Sign Inc.............G....... 973 676-4432
Milltown (G-6220)

PARACHUTES

Air Cruisers Company LLC ....B 732 681-3527
Wall Township (G-11315)
Airborne Systems N Amer NJ Inc.........C 856 663-1275
Pennsauken (G-8386)
Switlik Parachute Company Inc........F 609 587-3300
Trenton (G-10994)
Yoland Corporation......................E 862 257-9036
Paterson (G-8324)

PARKING GARAGE

Kyosis LLC ....G....... 908 202-8894
South River (G-10351)
Park Plus Inc ....E 201 917-5778
Fairview (G-3366)

PARKING METERS

Parkeon Inc ....E 856 234-8000
Moorestown (G-6553)

PARTITIONS & FIXTURES: Except Wood

Acro Display Inc..........................E 215 229-1100
Pennsauken (G-8382)
Benco Inc ....F 973 575-4440
Fairfield (G-3154)
Carib-Display Co ....G....... 732 583-1648
Matawan (G-5969)
Engo Co ....E 908 754-6600
South Plainfield (G-10250)
Fixture It Inc..............................E 201 445-0939
Glen Rock (G-3831)
Imperial Design ....G....... 856 742-8480
Gloucester City (G-3844)
Insign Inc ....E 856 424-1161
West Deptford (G-11705)
Ner Data Products Inc ....E 888 637-3282
Glassboro (G-3817)
S L Enterprises Inc ....G....... 908 272-8145
Ewing (G-3064)

PARTITIONS WHOLESALERS

Door Stop LLC.............................F 718 599-5112
Carlstadt (G-1153)
Extra Office Inc...........................F 732 381-9774
Rahway (G-9092)

PARTITIONS: Wood & Fixtures

Arrow Information Packagig LLC ....G....... 856 317-9000
Pennsauken (G-8391)
Bamboo & Rattan Works Inc ....G....... 732 255-4239
Toms River (G-10746)
D S F Inc...................................E 908 218-5153
Raritan (G-9209)
Designcore Ltd ....D....... 718 499-0337
Secaucus (G-9761)
Eagle Fabrication Inc ....E 732 739-5300
Ltl Egg Hbr (G-5616)
Intelco ....D....... 856 456-6755
Westville (G-11817)
Ken Bauer Inc ....E 201 664-6881
Hillsdale (G-4368)
Kubik Maltbie Inc ....E 856 234-0052
Mount Laurel (G-6774)
Medlaurel Inc ....E 856 461-6600
Delanco (G-2006)
Parsons Cabinets Inc ....G....... 973 279-4954
Montclair (G-6383)

PARTS: Metal

Cospack America Corp ....E 732 548-5858
Edison (G-2484)
I S Parts International Inc ....E 856 691-2203
Vineland (G-11234)

PATTERNS: Indl

Creative Patterns & Mfg ....G....... 973 589-1391
Rockaway (G-9451)
Method Assoc Inc ....F 732 888-0444
Keyport (G-5001)
Motif Industries Inc ....F 973 575-1800
East Hanover (G-2223)

PAVERS

Elite Landscaping & Pavers ....G....... 732 252-6152
Freehold (G-3663)
G & A Pavers Llc ....G....... 201 562-5947
Englewood (G-2908)
Karla Landscaping Pavers ....G....... 732 333-5852
Howell (G-4543)
NJ Paver Restorations LLC..............G....... 732 558-6011
Hillsborough (G-4341)
US Outworkers LLC ....G....... 973 362-1458
Sussex (G-10569)

PAVING MATERIALS: Prefabricated, Concrete

Advanced Pavement Technologies.......F 973 366-8044
Rockaway (G-9438)
Concrete Stone & Tile Corp ....E 973 948-7193
Branchville (G-705)
CST Products LLC ....E 856 299-5339
Penns Grove (G-8377)

PAVING MIXTURES

Barrett Asphalt Inc ....E 609 561-4100
Hammonton (G-4129)
Stavola Holding Corporation ....C 732 542-2328
Tinton Falls (G-10730)

PAYROLL SVCS

Sage Software Inc ....D....... 856 231-4667
Mount Laurel (G-6802)

PEARLS, WHOLESALE

Pearl Baumell Company Inc............G....... 415 421-2113
Rutherford (G-9631)

PEAT MINING & PROCESSING SVCS

Sussex Humus & Supply Inc ....G....... 973 779-8812
Clifton (G-1727)

PEAT MINING SVCS

Partac Peat Corp ....F 908 637-4191
Great Meadows (G-3855)

Partac Peat Corporation ....F 908 637-4631
Great Meadows (G-3856)

PENS & PARTS: Ball Point

Cameo Metal Forms Inc ....F 718 788-1106
Woodland Park (G-12073)

Rotuba Extruders Inc ....C 908 486-1000
Linden (G-5416)

Touch of Class Promotions LLC ....G 267 994-0860
Voorhees (G-11296)

PENS & PENCILS: Mechanical, NEC

Cameo Novelty & Pen Corp ....E 973 923-1600
Hillside (G-4384)

Newell Brands Inc ....B 201 610-6600
Hoboken (G-4468)

Pen Company of America LLC ....F 908 374-7949
Garwood (G-3790)

Pen Company of America LLC ....E 908 374-7949
Linden (G-5406)

PERFUME: Concentrated

Charabot & Co Inc ....F 201 812-2762
Budd Lake (G-920)

Jodhpuri Inc ....D 973 299-7009
Parsippany (G-7968)

Takasago Intl Corp USA ....C 201 767-9001
Rockleigh (G-9522)

Takasago Intl Corp USA ....D 201 767-9001
Northvale (G-7551)

PERFUME: Perfumes, Natural Or Synthetic

Christian Dior Perfumes LLC ....G 609 409-3628
Cranbury (G-1821)

Custom Essence ....F 732 249-6405
Somerset (G-9980)

Mastertaste Inc ....F 201 373-1111
Teterboro (G-10686)

Radha Beauty Products LLC ....G 732 993-6242
Westwood (G-11841)

PERFUMES

Ascent Aromatics Inc ....G 908 755-0120
South Plainfield (G-10221)

Atlantis Aromatics Inc ....G 732 919-1112
Wall Township (G-11319)

Batallure Beauty LLC ....E 609 716-1200
Princeton (G-8913)

Bellevue Parfums USA LLC ....F 908 262-7774
Hillsborough (G-4304)

Cadence Distributors LLC ....G 646 808-3031
Hackensack (G-3891)

Continental Aromatics ....E 973 238-9300
Hawthorne (G-4215)

Coty US LLC ....D 973 490-8700
Morris Plains (G-6602)

Creative Concepts Corporation ....G 201 750-1234
Norwood (G-7562)

Dosis Fragrance LLC ....G 718 874-0074
Newark (G-7104)

Excell Brands Ltd Liability Co ....G 908 561-1130
Princeton (G-8946)

Fragrance Exchange Inc ....G 732 641-2210
Monroe Township (G-6332)

Fragrance Solutions Corp ....G 732 832-7800
South Plainfield (G-10262)

French Color Fragrance Co Inc ....E 201 567-6883
Englewood (G-2907)

Imaan Trading Inc ....G 201 779-2062
Jersey City (G-4749)

International Aromatics Inc ....F 201 964-0900
Moonachie (G-6472)

Klabin Fragrances Inc ....F 973 857-3600
Cedar Grove (G-1280)

Qualis Packaging Inc ....F 908 782-0305
South Plainfield (G-10318)

Robertet Fragrances Inc ....E 201 405-1000
Budd Lake (G-933)

Robertet Fragrances Inc ....E 973 575-4550
Fairfield (G-3302)

Victory International USA LLC ....F 732 417-5900
Eatontown (G-2429)

PERSONAL CREDIT INSTITUTIONS: Auto/Consumer Finance Co's

Smb International LLC ....G 732 222-4888
West Long Branch (G-11722)

PESTICIDES

AP&g Co Inc ....D 718 492-3648
Bayonne (G-202)

BASF Plant Science LP ....G 973 245-3238
Florham Park (G-3492)

PESTICIDES WHOLESALERS

Growmark Fs LLC ....F 609 267-7054
Eastampton (G-2372)

PET SPLYS

Animals Etc Inc ....G 609 386-8442
Burlington (G-950)

Gramercy Products Incorporated ....E 212 868-2559
Secaucus (G-9778)

Gwenstone Inc ....G 732 785-2600
Lakewood (G-5106)

Halfway Hounds ....G 201 970-6235
Park Ridge (G-7852)

Hartz Mountain Corporation ....C 800 275-1414
Secaucus (G-9780)

Immunogenetics Inc ....D 856 697-1441
Buena (G-940)

Klein Distributors Inc ....G 732 446-7632
Burlington (G-977)

Littlegifts Inc ....F 212 868-2559
Secaucus (G-9789)

Loving Pets Corporation ....E 609 655-3700
Cranbury (G-1859)

Naomi Pet International Inc ....G 201 660-7918
Northvale (G-7540)

Pet Salon Inc ....F 609 350-6480
Margate City (G-5890)

Pet Salon Inc ....G 609 350-6480
Margate City (G-5891)

Q10 Products LLC ....F 201 567-9299
Clifton (G-1702)

Skaffles Group Ltd Lblty Co ....G 732 901-2100
Lakewood (G-5163)

Vo-Toys Inc ....E 973 482-8915
Clifton (G-1736)

Xpet LLC ....G 973 272-7502
Clifton (G-1742)

PET SPLYS WHOLESALERS

Hartz Mountain Corporation ....C 800 275-1414
Secaucus (G-9780)

Imagine Gold LLC ....E 201 488-5988
South Hackensack (G-10162)

Loving Pets Corporation ....E 609 655-3700
Cranbury (G-1859)

R World Enterprises ....G 201 795-2428
Jersey City (G-4793)

Tuff Mutters LLC ....G 973 291-6679
Kinnelon (G-5022)

PETROLEUM & PETROLEUM PRDTS, WHOLESALE Butane Gas

Welding & Radiator Supply Co ....G 609 965-0433
Egg Harbor City (G-2672)

PETROLEUM PRDTS WHOLESALERS

Jet Aviation St Louis Inc ....E 201 462-4026
Teterboro (G-10681)

Speedway LLC ....B 732 750-7800
Port Reading (G-8895)

PETS & PET SPLYS, WHOLESALE

Vo-Toys Inc ....E 973 482-8915
Clifton (G-1736)

PHARMACEUTICAL PREPARATIONS: Adrenal

Austarpharma LLC ....D 732 225-2930
Edison (G-2464)

PHARMACEUTICAL PREPARATIONS: Druggists' Preparations

Actavis Elizabeth LLC ....B 908 527-9100
Elizabeth (G-2706)

Actavis Elizabeth LLC ....C 908 527-9100
Fort Lee (G-3544)

Actavis Elizabeth LLC ....C 973 442-3200
Madison (G-5685)

Amneal Pharmaceuticals Inc ....A 908 409-6822
Bridgewater (G-786)

Amneal Pharmaceuticals LLC ....E 908 947-3120
Bridgewater (G-788)

Aptapharma Corporation ....E 856 665-0025
Pennsauken (G-8390)

Arno Therapeutics Inc ....G 862 703-7170
Flemington (G-3431)

Ascendia Pharmaceuticals LLC ....E 732 640-0058
North Brunswick (G-7454)

Astrazeneca Pharmaceuticals LP ....F 973 975-0324
Morristown (G-6641)

Cyalume Specialty Products Inc ....E 732 469-7760
Bound Brook (G-601)

Eagle Pharmaceuticals Inc ....E 201 326-5300
Woodcliff Lake (G-12054)

Ekr Therapeutics Incorporated ....C 877 435-2524
Bedminster (G-263)

Faulding Holdings Inc ....E 908 527-9100
Elizabeth (G-2734)

Fougera Pharmaceuticals Inc ....E 973 514-4241
East Hanover (G-2210)

Glaxosmithkline Consumer Hlth ....G 215 751-5046
Warren (G-11412)

Health Science Funding LLC ....F 973 984-6159
Morristown (G-6669)

Hill Pharma Inc ....F 973 521-7400
Fairfield (G-3228)

Hovione LLC ....D 609 918-2600
East Windsor (G-2352)

Intellect Neurosciences Inc ....G 201 608-5101
Englewood Cliffs (G-2978)

Ipca Pharmaceuticals Inc ....G 908 412-6561
South Plainfield (G-10280)

Jhp Group Holdings Inc ....A 973 658-3569
Parsippany (G-7966)

Klus Pharma Inc ....F 609 662-1913
Cranbury (G-1850)

Luye Pharma USA Ltd ....E 609 799-7600
Princeton (G-8971)

Merck & Co Inc ....B 908 740-4000
Kenilworth (G-4957)

Merck & Co Inc ....D 908 740-4000
Rahway (G-9117)

Merck Sharp & Dohme Corp ....A 908 740-4000
Kenilworth (G-4960)

Michelex Corporation ....G 201 977-1177
Prospect Park (G-9074)

Mountain Inc ....G 908 409-6823
Bridgewater (G-853)

Msn Pharmaceuticals Inc ....G 732 356-9900
Piscataway (G-8693)

Novartis Corporation ....B 973 503-7488
East Hanover (G-2228)

OHM Laboratories Inc ....D 732 418-2235
North Brunswick (G-7481)

Organon USA Inc ....G 908 423-1000
Whitehouse Station (G-11930)

Pharmacia & Upjohn Company LLC .....B 908 901-8000
Peapack (G-8344)

Quagen Pharmaceuticals LLC ....F 973 228-9600
West Caldwell (G-11674)

Raritan Phrmctcals Incoporated ....C 732 238-1685
East Brunswick (G-2173)

Renaissance Lakewood LLC ....F 732 901-2052
Lakewood (G-5155)

Renaissance Lakewood LLC ....B 732 367-9000
Lakewood (G-5156)

Royal Pharmaceuticals LLC ....G 732 292-2661
Wall Township (G-11366)

Salus Pharma LLC ....F 732 329-8089
Monmouth Junction (G-6310)

Siegfried USA Holding Inc ....E 856 678-3601
Pennsville (G-8502)

Sky Growth Intermediate ....B 201 802-4000
Woodcliff Lake (G-12064)

Symbiomix Therapeutics LLC ....F 609 722-7250
Newark (G-7293)

Tris Pharma Inc ....C 732 940-2800
Monmouth Junction (G-6316)

TWI Pharmaceuticals Usa Inc ....G 201 762-1410
Paramus (G-7842)

PRODUCT

Vascure Natural LLC..................G....... 732 528-6492
  Point Pleasant Boro (G-8847)

PHARMACEUTICAL PREPARATIONS:
Medicines, Capsule Or Ampule

Acino Products Ltd Lblty Co ....F....... 609 695-4300
  Hamilton (G-4100)
Boyds Pharmacy Inc........................F....... 609 499-0100
  Florence (G-3473)
Camber Pharmaceuticals Inc ....E....... 732 529-0430
  Piscataway (G-8641)
Combocap Inc ....G....... 646 722-2743
  Whippany (G-11886)
Holmdel Acpnctr & Ntrl Med Ctr ....G....... 732 888-4910
  Holmdel (G-4502)
Prescription Dynamics Inc ....F....... 201 746-6262
  Mahwah (G-5762)
Sensoredge Inc ....G....... 973 975-4163
  Parsippany (G-8012)

PHARMACEUTICAL PREPARATIONS: Pills

Bristol-Myers Squibb Company ....E....... 212 546-4000
  Pennington (G-8359)
Core Acquisition LLC ....G....... 732 983-6025
  Middlesex (G-6106)
Corepharma LLC ....G....... 732 983-6025
  Middlesex (G-6107)
Levomed Inc ....G....... 908 359-4804
  Somerset (G-10015)

PHARMACEUTICAL PREPARATIONS:
Powders

Matthey Johnson Inc ....C....... 856 384-7132
  West Deptford (G-11710)

PHARMACEUTICAL PREPARATIONS:
Proprietary Drug PRDTS

Access Bio Inc ....F 732 873-4040
  Somerset (G-9941)
Accumix Pharmaceuticals LLC ....G....... 609 632-2225
  Old Bridge (G-7710)
Adlers Pharmacy Ltc Inc ....E....... 856 685-7440
  Cherry Hill (G-1332)
Merck Holdings LLC ....F....... 908 423-1000
  Whitehouse Station (G-11923)
Novitium Pharma LLC ....G....... 609 469-5920
  East Windsor (G-2356)
Novotec Pharma LLC........................G....... 609 632-2239
  Monroe Township (G-6338)
Pharming Healthcare Inc ....E....... 908 524-0888
  Bridgewater (G-865)
Vistapharm Inc ....C....... 908 376-1622
  New Providence (G-7025)

PHARMACEUTICAL PREPARATIONS:
Solutions

Allergan Inc ....A....... 862 261-7000
  Madison (G-5687)
Apicore LLC.....................................E....... 646 884-3765
  Piscataway (G-8634)
Fordoz Pharma Corp ....F 609 469-5949
  East Windsor (G-2351)
Lydem LLC ....G....... 856 566-1419
  Palmyra (G-7784)
Medavante-Prophase Inc ....F....... 609 528-9400
  Hamilton (G-4112)
Mylan API Inc..................................E....... 732 748-8882
  Somerset (G-10037)
Pmv Pharmaceuticals Inc..................G....... 650 241-2822
  Cranbury (G-1873)
Rafael Pharmaceuticals Inc ....E....... 609 409-7050
  Cranbury (G-1876)

PHARMACEUTICAL PREPARATIONS: Tablets

Alembic Pharmaceuticals Inc ....G....... 908 393-9604
  Bridgewater (G-783)
Ranbaxy USA Inc ....E....... 609 720-9200
  Princeton (G-9013)
Sandoz Inc ....C....... 609 627-8500
  Princeton (G-9019)

PHARMACEUTICALS

140 Main Street Corp ....F....... 732 974-2929
  Sea Girt (G-9744)

3r Biopharma LLC..............................G....... 914 486-1898
  North Brunswick (G-7447)
A and P Pharmacy.............................G....... 908 850-7640
  Hackettstown (G-3993)
AAA Pharmaceutical...........................F....... 856 423-2700
  Paulsboro (G-8327)
AAA Pharmaceutical...........................D....... 609 288-6060
  Lumberton (G-5621)
AB Science Usa LLC ....G....... 973 218-2437
  Short Hills (G-9863)
Abbott Laboratories.........................G....... 732 346-6649
  Edison (G-2445)
Abbott Laboratories.........................E....... 609 443-9300
  Princeton (G-8897)
Abbott Laboratories.........................F....... 856 988-5572
  Marlton (G-5919)
Abbott Laboratories Parsippany ....G....... 973 428-4000
  Whippany (G-11876)
ABG Lab LLC ....G....... 973 559-5663
  Fair Lawn (G-3081)
Abon Pharmaceuticals LLC ....E....... 201 367-1702
  Northvale (G-7514)
Abraxis Bioscience Inc ....D....... 908 673-9000
  Summit (G-10520)
Abraxis Bioscience Inc ....B....... 908 673-9000
  Summit (G-10521)
Accelrx Labs LLC ....G....... 609 301-6446
  East Windsor (G-2333)
Acetris Health LLC ....E....... 201 961-9000
  Saddle Brook (G-9639)
Acetylon Pharmaceuticals Inc ....F....... 908 673-9000
  Summit (G-10522)
Acg North America LLC ....E....... 908 757-3425
  Piscataway (G-8625)
Actavis Inc ....G....... 973 394-8925
  Parsippany (G-7872)
Actavis LLC ....C....... 800 272-5525
  Morristown (G-6630)
Actavis LLC ....C....... 732 843-4904
  North Brunswick (G-7450)
Actavis LLC ....B....... 862 261-7000
  Madison (G-5686)
Actavis LLC ....D....... 732 947-5300
  Edison (G-2447)
Actavis Pharma Inc ....D....... 862 261-7000
  Parsippany (G-7873)
Activus Solutions LLC ....F....... 973 713-0696
  Cranford (G-1897)
Adare Pharmaceuticals Inc ....B....... 862 261-7000
  Parsippany (G-7874)
Adare Pharmaceuticals Inc ....E....... 877 731-5116
  Lawrenceville (G-5223)
Advantice Health LLC ....F....... 973 946-7550
  Cedar Knolls (G-1296)
Advaxis Inc ....C....... 609 452-9813
  Princeton (G-8901)
Aerie Pharmaceuticals Inc ....D....... 908 470-4320
  Bedminster (G-258)
Aeterna Zentaris Inc ....G....... 908 626-5428
  Warren (G-11397)
AF Pharma LLC ....G....... 908 769-7040
  Hoboken (G-4443)
Aflag Pharmaceuticals LLC ....G....... 732 609-4139
  Edison (G-2449)
Agile Therapeutics Inc ....F....... 609 683-1880
  Princeton (G-8902)
Agno Pharma ....G....... 609 223-0638
  Allentown (G-23)
Akorn Inc ....E....... 609 662-9100
  Cranbury (G-1807)
Akorn Inc ....F....... 732 532-1000
  Somerset (G-9945)
Akorn Inc ....G....... 732 448-7043
  Somerset (G-9946)
Akorn Inc ....D....... 732 846-8066
  Somerset (G-9947)
Akrimax Pharmaceuticals LLC ....D....... 908 372-0506
  Cranford (G-1898)
Aks Pharma Inc ....G....... 856 521-0710
  Elmer (G-2793)
Alcami New Jersey Corporation.............D....... 732 346-5100
  Edison (G-2451)
Alchem Pharmtech Inc ....G....... 848 565-5694
  Monmouth Junction (G-6277)
Align Pharmaceuticals LLC ....G....... 908 834-0960
  Berkeley Heights (G-387)
Allergan Sales LLC ....F....... 973 442-3200
  Madison (G-5688)
Allied Pharma Inc ....G....... 732 738-3295
  Fords (G-3529)

Allos Therapeutics Inc ....G....... 609 936-3760
  Princeton (G-8907)
Almatica Pharma Inc..........................E....... 877 447-7979
  Morristown (G-6634)
Alpharma US Inc ....E....... 201 228-5090
  Bridgewater (G-784)
Altima Innovations Inc ....G....... 732 474-1500
  Branchburg (G-615)
Alvogen Group Inc ....G....... 973 796-3400
  Morristown (G-6636)
Alvogen Inc ....C....... 973 796-3400
  Morristown (G-6637)
Alvogen Pb Research & Dev LLC ....G....... 973 796-3400
  Morristown (G-6638)
Alvogen Pharma Us Inc ....B....... 973 796-3400
  Morristown (G-6639)
Amarin Corporation PLC ....E....... 908 719-1315
  Bedminster (G-260)
Amarin Pharma Inc ....D....... 908 719-1315
  Bridgewater (G-785)
Amas Pharmaceuticals LLC ....E....... 908 883-1129
  Berkeley Heights (G-388)
American Pharmaceutical LLC...............G....... 732 645-3030
  Piscataway (G-8630)
Amerigen Pharmaceuticals Inc ....F....... 732 993-9826
  Lyndhurst (G-5640)
Amerigen Pharmaceuticals Ltd ....F....... 732 993-9826
  East Brunswick (G-2127)
Amicus Therapeutics Inc ....C....... 609 662-2000
  Cranbury (G-1809)
Amicus Therapeutics Us Inc ....G....... 609 662-2000
  Cranbury (G-1810)
Amneal Pharmaceuticals Inc ....F....... 908 947-3120
  Bridgewater (G-787)
Amneal Pharmaceuticals LLC ....F....... 908 947-3120
  Piscataway (G-8633)
Amneal Pharmaceuticals LLC ....G....... 908 409-6823
  Branchburg (G-618)
Amneal Pharmaceuticals LLC ....E....... 908 231-1911
  Branchburg (G-619)
Amneal Pharmaceuticals LLC ....F....... 908 947-3120
  Piscataway (G-8632)
Amneal-Agila LLC ....F....... 908 947-3120
  Bridgewater (G-789)
Antares Pharma Inc ....C....... 609 359-3020
  Ewing (G-3015)
Aphena Phrma Slutions - NJ LLC............D....... 973 947-5441
  Parsippany (G-7881)
API Inc ....F....... 973 227-9335
  Fairfield (G-3144)
Appco Pharma LLC ....E....... 732 271-8300
  Somerset (G-9955)
Appco Pharma LLC ....E....... 732 271-8300
  Piscataway (G-8635)
Appco Pharma LLC ....E....... 732 271-8300
  Somerset (G-9956)
Aprecia Pharmaceuticals Co ....E....... 215 359-3300
  East Windsor (G-2335)
Aquarius Biotechnologies Inc ....G....... 908 443-1860
  Bedminster (G-261)
Aquestive Therapeutics Inc ....F....... 908 941-1900
  Warren (G-11398)
Ascend Laboratories LLC ....E....... 201 476-1977
  Parsippany (G-7884)
Aspire Pharmaceuticals Inc ....D....... 732 447-1444
  Somerset (G-9958)
Aurex Labs Ltd Lblty Co ....F....... 609 308-2304
  East Windsor (G-2337)
Auro Health LLC ....G....... 732 839-9400
  Lawrence Township (G-5214)
Auro Packaging LLC ....E....... 732 839-9408
  East Windsor (G-2338)
Aurobindo Pharma USA Inc ....G....... 732 839-9402
  Dayton (G-1952)
Aurobindo Pharma USA Inc ....G....... 732 839-9400
  East Windsor (G-2339)
Aurobindo Pharma USA Inc ....G....... 732 839-9400
  Dayton (G-1953)
Aurobindo Pharma USA Inc ....E....... 732 839-9400
  East Windsor (G-2340)
Aurobindo Pharma USA Inc ....G....... 609 409-6774
  Cranbury (G-1813)
Aurobindo Pharma USA LLC ....E....... 732 839-9400
  East Windsor (G-2341)
Aurolife Pharma LLC ....E....... 732 839-9746
  Dayton (G-1954)
Aurolife Pharma LLC ....G....... 732 839-9408
  East Windsor (G-2342)
Aurolife Pharma LLC ....C....... 732 839-4377
  Dayton (G-1955)

Company	Emp.	Phone	Location
Auromedics Pharma LLC	F	732 823-4122	East Windsor *(G-2343)*
Auromedics Pharma LLC	E	732 839-9400	East Windsor *(G-2344)*
Avacyn Pharmaceuticals Inc	G	201 836-2599	Teaneck *(G-10623)*
Aventis Phrmcticals Foundation	F	908 981-5000	Bridgewater *(G-799)*
BASF Corporation	B	973 245-6000	Florham Park *(G-3491)*
Basfin Corporation	A	973 245-6000	Florham Park *(G-3493)*
Bausch & Lomb Incorporated	B	585 338-6000	Bridgewater *(G-800)*
Bausch Health Americas Inc	B	908 927-1400	Bridgewater *(G-802)*
Bausch Health Us LLC	E	908 927-1400	Bridgewater *(G-803)*
Bausch Health Us LLC	G	908 927-1400	Bridgewater *(G-804)*
Bayer Consumer Care Inc	B	973 267-6198	Morristown *(G-6647)*
Bayer Healthcare LLC	F	973 254-5000	Morristown *(G-6648)*
Bayer Healthcare LLC	A	862 404-3000	Whippany *(G-11878)*
Bayer Healthcare LLC	B	973 254-5000	Morristown *(G-6649)*
Bayer U S LLC	F	973 709-3545	Wayne *(G-11476)*
Bellerophon Therapeutics Inc	E	908 574-4770	Warren *(G-11400)*
Beta Pharma Inc	F	609 436-4100	Princeton *(G-8915)*
Bionpharma Inc	G	609 380-3313	Princeton *(G-8916)*
Biophore LLC	G	609 275-3713	Plainsboro *(G-8781)*
Biovail Distribution Company	G	908 927-1400	Bridgewater *(G-805)*
Boehringer Ingelheim Animal	E	732 729-5700	North Brunswick *(G-7457)*
Bracco Research USA Inc	E	609 514-2517	Cranbury *(G-1815)*
Bristol-Myers Squibb Company	G	609 419-5000	Princeton *(G-8918)*
Bristol-Myers Squibb Company	B	908 218-3700	Bridgewater *(G-807)*
Bristol-Myers Squibb Company	A	609 302-3000	Lawrenceville *(G-5225)*
Bristol-Myers Squibb Company	G	609 252-4875	Princeton *(G-8919)*
Bta Pharmaceuticals Inc	E	908 927-1400	Bridgewater *(G-809)*
Caladrius Biosciences Inc	E	908 842-0100	Basking Ridge *(G-177)*
Calyptus Pharmaceuticals Inc	F	908 720-6049	Princeton *(G-8920)*
Cambrex Corporation	C	201 804-3000	East Rutherford *(G-2282)*
Cambridge Therapeutic Tech LLC	G	914 420-5555	Hackensack *(G-3894)*
Capsugel Holdings Us Inc	G	862 242-1700	Morristown *(G-6652)*
Caraco Pharmaceutical Labs	G	609 819-8200	Cranbury *(G-1820)*
Cardinal Health Systems Inc	B	732 537-6544	Somerset *(G-9966)*
Carnegie Pharmaceuticals LLC	E	732 783-7013	Delran *(G-2013)*
Castle Creek Phrmceuticals LLC	F	862 286-0400	Parsippany *(G-7897)*
Catalent Inc	C	732 537-6200	Somerset *(G-9968)*
Catalent Cts LLC	C	201 785-0275	Allendale *(G-6)*
Catalent CTS Kansas City LLC	G	732 537-6200	Somerset *(G-9969)*
Catalent Pharma Solutions LLC	C	732 537-6200	Somerset *(G-9970)*
Catalent Pharma Solutions Inc	B	732 537-6200	Somerset *(G-9971)*
Catalent US Holding I LLC	G	877 587-1835	Somerset *(G-9972)*
Celator Pharmaceuticals Inc	E	609 243-0123	Ewing *(G-3019)*
Celgene Cellular Therapeutics	G	908 673-9000	Warren *(G-11402)*
Celgene Corporation	F	908 464-8101	Berkeley Heights *(G-392)*
Celgene Corporation	E	732 271-1001	Warren *(G-11403)*
Celgene Corporation	F	908 967-1432	Berkeley Heights *(G-393)*
Celgene Corporation	E	908 897-4603	Summit *(G-10528)*
Celgene Corporation	C	908 673-9000	Summit *(G-10529)*
Celgene Corporation	A	908 673-9000	Cedar Knolls *(G-1301)*
Celgene Corporation	G	908 673-9000	Basking Ridge *(G-179)*
Celimmune	G	908 399-2954	Lebanon *(G-5255)*
Celldex Therapeutics Inc	C	908 200-7500	Hampton *(G-4149)*
Cellectar Biosciences Inc	G	608 441-8120	Florham Park *(G-3496)*
Cellular Sciences Inc	G	908 237-1561	Flemington *(G-3433)*
Celsion Corporation	E	609 896-9100	Lawrenceville *(G-5226)*
Central Admxture Phrm Svcs Inc	E	201 541-0080	Englewood *(G-2892)*
Cerexa Inc	E	510 285-9200	Parsippany *(G-7900)*
Cetylite Industries Inc	E	856 665-6111	Pennsauken *(G-8402)*
Champions Oncology Inc	D	201 808-8400	Hackensack *(G-3897)*
Chandler Pharmacy LLC	G	732 543-1568	New Brunswick *(G-6916)*
Chemtract LLC	G	732 820-0427	Martinsville *(G-5961)*
Cherokee Pharma Llc	G	732 422-7800	Jamesburg *(G-4671)*
Chromocell Corporation	D	732 565-1113	North Brunswick *(G-7462)*
Cipla USA Inc	E	908 356-8900	Warren *(G-11406)*
Cispharma Inc	F	609 235-9807	Cranbury *(G-1823)*
Citius Pharmaceuticals Inc	G	978 938-0338	Cranford *(G-1904)*
Cmic Cmo USA Corporation	E	609 395-9700	Cranbury *(G-1825)*
Compupharma Inc	G	973 227-6003	Piscataway *(G-8649)*
Conjupro Biotherapeutics Inc	F	609 356-0210	Princeton *(G-8924)*
Contract Coatings Inc	F	201 343-3131	Hackensack *(G-3901)*
Cosette Pharmaceuticals Inc	C	314 283-4776	South Plainfield *(G-10243)*
County Line Phrmaceuticals LLC	G	262 439-8109	Pine Brook *(G-8594)*
Cubist Pharmaceuticals LLC	C	908 740-4000	Kenilworth *(G-4933)*
Cyclacel Pharmaceuticals Inc	F	908 517-7330	Berkeley Heights *(G-397)*
Cyclase Dynamics Inc	G	973 420-3259	Barnegat Light *(G-165)*
Cypress Pharmaceuticals Inc	C	601 856-4393	Morristown *(G-6657)*
D&E Nutraceuticals Inc	E	212 235-5200	Farmingdale *(G-3383)*
Daiichi Sankyo Inc	F	908 992-6400	Basking Ridge *(G-180)*
Dainippon Sumitomo Pharma Amer	E	201 592-2050	Fort Lee *(G-3554)*
Derma Sciences Inc	C	609 514-4744	Plainsboro *(G-8784)*
Difco Laboratories Inc	G	410 316-4113	Franklin Lakes *(G-3619)*
Dishman Usa Inc	F	732 560-4300	Middlesex *(G-6112)*
Dmv-Fnterra Excipients USA LLC	G	609 858-2111	Paramus *(G-7798)*
Dpi Newco LLC	E	973 257-8113	Parsippany *(G-7919)*
DSM Nutritional Products LLC	B	908 475-0150	Belvidere *(G-361)*
DSM Nutritional Products LLC	C	908 475-5300	Belvidere *(G-362)*
DSM Nutritional Products LLC	C	908 475-5300	Belvidere *(G-363)*
E R Squibb & Sons LLC	G	732 246-3195	East Brunswick *(G-2137)*
E R Squibb & Sons Inter-AM	F	609 252-5144	Princeton *(G-8935)*
E R Squibb & Sons Inter-AM	G	609 818-3715	Trenton *(G-10932)*
E R Squibb & Sons Inter-AM	G	609 252-4111	Princeton *(G-8936)*
Edenbridge Pharmaceuticals LLC	G	201 292-1292	Parsippany *(G-7932)*
Eisai Inc	C	201 692-1100	Woodcliff Lake *(G-12055)*
Eli Lillybranchburg	G	908 541-8000	Branchburg *(G-637)*
Elite Laboratories Inc	E	201 750-2646	Northvale *(G-7522)*
Elite Pharmaceuticals Inc	E	201 750-2646	Northvale *(G-7523)*
Elusys Therapeutics Inc	F	973 808-0222	Parsippany *(G-7935)*
Elvi Pharma LLC	F	732 640-2707	Piscataway *(G-8660)*
Emisphere Technologies Inc	F	973 532-8000	Roseland *(G-9537)*
Enaltec Labs Inc	G	908 864-8000	Bridgewater *(G-819)*
Encore Pharmaceutical Inc	G	973 267-9331	Morris Plains *(G-6605)*
Endo Phrmaceuticals Valera Inc	F	609 235-3230	Cranbury *(G-1832)*
Enteris Biopharma Inc	G	973 453-3518	Boonton *(G-551)*
Envigo Crs Inc	C	732 873-2550	Somerset *(G-9987)*
Enzon Pharmaceuticals Inc	G	732 980-4500	Cranford *(G-1909)*
Enzon Pharmaceuticals Inc	D	732 980-4500	South Plainfield *(G-10251)*
Eon Labs Inc	A	609 627-8600	Princeton *(G-8942)*
Esjay Pharma LLC	G	609 469-5920	East Windsor *(G-2350)*
Esjay Pharma LLC	F	732 438-1816	Allentown *(G-26)*
Eva Maria Wolfe	G	412 777-2000	Wayne *(G-11499)*
Evenus Pharmaceutical Labs Inc	G	609 395-8625	Princeton *(G-8943)*
Evotec (us) Inc	E	650 228-1400	Princeton *(G-8945)*
Exeltis Usa Inc	D	973 324-0200	Florham Park *(G-3503)*
Exeltis USA Dermatology LLC	E	973 805-4060	Florham Park *(G-3504)*
Exemplify Biopharma Inc	G	732 500-3208	Cranbury *(G-1833)*
Eyetech Inc	F	646 454-1779	Bridgewater *(G-823)*
Eywa Pharma Inc	G	609 751-9600	Princeton *(G-8947)*
Faubel Pharma Services	G	908 730-7563	Bordentown *(G-581)*
Ferring Pharmaceuticals Inc	C	973 796-1600	Parsippany *(G-7944)*
Ferring Production Inc	E	973 796-1600	Parsippany *(G-7945)*
First National Servicing & Dev	E	732 341-5409	Toms River *(G-10758)*
Five Star Supplies NJ Corp	E	908 862-8801	Linden *(G-5348)*
Forest Laboratories LLC	F	631 436-4534	Jersey City *(G-4738)*
Forest Laboratories LLC	E	631 501-5399	Jersey City *(G-4739)*
Forest Pharmaceuticals Inc	A	862 261-7000	Parsippany *(G-7950)*
G & W Laboratories Inc	D	732 474-0729	Piscataway *(G-8666)*
G&W PA Laboratories LLC	G	908 753-2000	South Plainfield *(G-10265)*
Gadde Pharma LLC	G	609 651-7772	Plainsboro *(G-8788)*
GE Healthcare Inc	E	908 757-0500	South Plainfield *(G-10266)*
Generon Biomed Inc	G	908 203-4701	Bridgewater *(G-827)*
Genzyme Corporation	C	201 313-9660	Ridgefield *(G-9263)*
Genzyme Corporation	G	973 256-2106	Totowa *(G-10829)*
Glaxosmithkline Consumer	B	251 591-4188	Warren *(G-11411)*
Glaxosmithkline LLC	E	856 952-6023	Collingswood *(G-1768)*

PRODUCT

Glaxosmithkline LLC	E	609 472-8175	
Cherry Hill (G-1368)			
Glenmark Phrmceuticals Inc USA	D	201 684-8000	
Mahwah (G-5742)			
Glenmark Therapeutics Inc USA	B	201 684-8000	
Mahwah (G-5743)			
Glenwood LLC	C	201 569-0050	
Englewood (G-2910)			
Globe Pharma Inc	G	732 296-9700	
New Brunswick (G-6929)			
Globela Pharma LLC	G	888 588-8511	
Weehawken (G-11567)			
Grant Industries Inc	D	201 791-8700	
Elmwood Park (G-2828)			
Grant Industries Inc	D	201 791-6700	
Elmwood Park (G-2829)			
Grant Industries Inc	F	201 791-6700	
Elmwood Park (G-2830)			
Granulation Technology Inc	F	973 276-0740	
Fairfield (G-3217)			
Grow Company Inc	E	201 941-8777	
Ridgefield (G-9264)			
Gsk Consumer Health Inc	B	919 269-5000	
Warren (G-11413)			
Gsk Consumer Healthcare	D	973 539-0645	
Parsippany (G-7957)			
Halo Pharmaceutical Inc	D	973 428-4000	
Whippany (G-11894)			
Helsinn Therapeutics US Inc	E	908 231-1435	
Iselin (G-4610)			
Hengrui Therapeutics Inc	G	609 423-2155	
Princeton (G-8959)			
Hepion Pharmaceuticals Inc	E	732 902-4000	
Edison (G-2529)			
Heritage Pharma Holdings Inc	G	732 429-1000	
East Brunswick (G-2148)			
Heritage Pharma Labs Inc	F	732 238-7880	
East Brunswick (G-2149)			
Heritage Pharma Labs Inc	C	732 238-7880	
East Brunswick (G-2150)			
Heritage Pharmaceuticals Inc	E	732 429-1000	
East Brunswick (G-2151)			
Hikma Injectables USA Inc	G	732 542-1191	
Eatontown (G-2398)			
Hikma Pharmaceuticals USA Inc	B	732 542-1191	
Eatontown (G-2399)			
Hikma Pharmaceuticals USA Inc	F	732 542-1191	
Eatontown (G-2400)			
Hikma Pharmaceuticals USA Inc	C	856 424-3700	
Cherry Hill (G-1372)			
Hisamitsu Phrm Co Inc	F	973 765-0122	
Florham Park (G-3510)			
Hobart Group Holdings LLC	C	908 470-1780	
Gladstone (G-3804)			
Hoffmann-La Roche Inc	A	973 890-2268	
Little Falls (G-5456)			
Hoffmann-La Roche Inc	F	973 235-8216	
Totowa (G-10832)			
Hoffmann-La Roche Inc	D	973 235-3092	
Nutley (G-7587)			
Hoffmann-La Roche Inc	E	973 235-1016	
Nutley (G-7588)			
HRP Capital Inc	E	201 242-4938	
Fort Lee (G-3562)			
Huahai US Inc	F	609 655-1688	
Somerset (G-10002)			
Hutchison Medipharma (us) Inc	G	973 567-3254	
Florham Park (G-3512)			
IBC Pharmaceuticals Inc	F	973 540-9595	
Morris Plains (G-6616)			
Ikaria Therapeutics LLC	G	908 238-6600	
Hampton (G-4155)			
Imclone Systems LLC	G	908 541-8100	
Branchburg (G-648)			
Imclone Systems LLC	C	908 541-8000	
Bridgewater (G-833)			
Imclone Systems LLC	G	908 218-0147	
Branchburg (G-647)			
Immunomedics Inc	C	973 605-8200	
Morris Plains (G-6617)			
Impax Laboratories LLC	F	732 595-4600	
Bridgewater (G-834)			
INB Manhattan Drug Company Inc	D	973 926-0816	
Hillside (G-4401)			
Ino Therapeutics LLC	D	908 238-6600	
Bedminster (G-266)			
Insmed Incorporated	C	908 977-9900	
Bridgewater (G-837)			
Inspire Pharmaceuticals Inc	C	908 423-1000	
Whitehouse Station (G-11921)			
Integra Lifesciences Corp	D	609 275-0500	
Plainsboro (G-8794)			
Interntnal Pharma Remedies Inc	G	201 417-3891	
Paterson (G-8215)			
Invaderm Corporation	G	732 307-7926	
Somerset (G-10005)			
Inventiv Health Clinical LLC	G	973 348-1000	
Basking Ridge (G-186)			
Ivax Pharmaceuticals LLC	G	201 767-1700	
Woodcliff Lake (G-12058)			
Ivy Pharama Inc	G	201 221-4179	
Paramus (G-7808)			
Jak Diversified II Inc	D	973 439-1182	
West Caldwell (G-11656)			
Janssen Global Services LLC	G	908 704-4000	
Raritan (G-9211)			
Janssen Research & Dev LLC	A	908 704-4000	
Raritan (G-9212)			
Jeiven Phrm Consulting Inc	G	908 233-4508	
Scotch Plains (G-9736)			
Jems Pharma LLC	G	609 386-0141	
Burlington (G-976)			
Jiangsu Hengrui Medicine Co	G	609 395-8625	
Princeton (G-8966)			
Jnj International Inv LLC	G	732 524-0400	
New Brunswick (G-6939)			
Johnson & Johnson	A	732 524-0400	
New Brunswick (G-6940)			
Johnson & Johnson	D	908 704-6809	
Raritan (G-9214)			
Johnson & Johnson	E	908 526-5425	
Raritan (G-9215)			
Johnson & Johnson	D	732 422-5000	
North Brunswick (G-7473)			
Johnson & Johnson	G	908 722-9319	
Raritan (G-9213)			
Johnson & Johnson	C	908 874-1000	
Morris Plains (G-6618)			
Johnson & Johnson	C	732 524-0400	
New Brunswick (G-6941)			
Johnson & Johnson Consumer Inc	A	908 874-1000	
Skillman (G-9922)			
Juventio LLC	G	973 908-8097	
Chatham (G-1324)			
Kamat Pharmatech LLC	G	732 406-6421	
North Brunswick (G-7474)			
Kashiv Biosciences LLC	E	732 475-0500	
Piscataway (G-8683)			
Kiehls Since 1851 Inc	G	201 843-1125	
Paramus (G-7812)			
Kos Pharmaceuticals Inc	E	609 495-0500	
Cranbury (G-1851)			
Kyowa Hakko Kirin Cal Inc	G	609 580-7400	
Princeton (G-8968)			
Kyowa Kirin Inc	D	908 234-1096	
Bedminster (G-267)			
Lab Express Inc	F	973 227-1700	
Fairfield (G-3256)			
Leading Pharma LLC	E	201 746-9160	
Fairfield (G-3259)			
Leading Pharma LLC	E	201 746-9160	
Montvale (G-6419)			
Lexicon Pharmaceuticals Inc	G	609 466-5500	
Basking Ridge (G-187)			
Lifecell Corporation	G	908 947-1100	
Bridgewater (G-842)			
Lifecell Corporation	G	908 947-1100	
Branchburg (G-655)			
Lifecell Corporation	G	908 947-1100	
Branchburg (G-656)			
Lipoid LLC	G	973 735-2692	
Newark (G-7182)			
LLC Dunn Meadow	F	201 297-4603	
Fort Lee (G-3569)			
Lonza Biologics Inc	E	603 610-4809	
Morristown (G-6680)			
LTS Lhmann Thrapy Systems Corp	A	973 575-5170	
West Caldwell (G-11658)			
Lupin Pharmaceuticals Inc	F	908 603-6075	
Somerset (G-10020)			
Lupin Pharmaceuticals Inc	E	908 603-6000	
Somerset (G-10021)			
Lyciret Corp	E	973 882-0322	
Orange (G-7754)			
Macleods Pharma Usa Inc	F	609 269-5250	
Princeton (G-8972)			
Mafco Worldwide LLC	F	856 964-8840	
Camden (G-1076)			
Magnifica Inc	G	323 202-0386	
Cranbury (G-1861)			
Mallinckrodt Ard Inc	G	510 400-0700	
Bedminster (G-268)			
Mallinckrodt Ard LLC	F	908 238-6600	
Bedminster (G-269)			
Mallinckrodt Hospital Pdts Inc	G	908 238-6600	
Bedminster (G-270)			
Mallinckrodt Hospital Pdts Inc	E	314 654-2000	
Bedminster (G-271)			
Mallinckrodt LLC	E	908 238-6600	
Hampton (G-4158)			
Matinas Biopharma Holdings Inc	F	908 443-1860	
Bedminster (G-273)			
Matthey Johnson Inc	E	856 384-7001	
West Deptford (G-11711)			
Meda Pharmaceuticals Inc	C	732 564-2200	
Somerset (G-10026)			
Medicon Inc	G	201 669-7456	
Allendale (G-12)			
Medicure Pharma Inc	E	888 435-2220	
Princeton (G-8975)			
Megalith Pharmaceuticals Inc	G	877 436-7220	
Princeton (G-8976)			
Memomind Pharma Inc	G	201 302-9020	
Fort Lee (G-3571)			
Merck & Co Inc	G	908 740-4000	
Kenilworth (G-4958)			
Merck & Co Inc	E	800 224-5318	
Madison (G-5698)			
Merck & Co Inc	D	908 298-4000	
Kenilworth (G-4959)			
Merck & Co Inc	E	908 298-4000	
Summit (G-10540)			
Merck & Co Inc	G	908 423-1000	
Whitehouse Station (G-11922)			
Merck & Co Inc	G	609 771-8790	
Ewing (G-3045)			
Merck Resource Management Inc	G	908 423-1000	
Whitehouse Station (G-11924)			
Merck Sharp & Dohme (ia) LLC	F	908 423-1000	
Whitehouse Station (G-11925)			
Merck Sharp & Dohme Corp	B	908 423-1000	
Kenilworth (G-4961)			
Merck Sharp & Dohme Corp	E	908 423-3000	
Whitehouse Station (G-11926)			
Merck Sharp & Dohme Corp	D	732 594-4000	
Rahway (G-9118)			
Merck Sharp & Dohme Corp	G	908 685-3892	
Branchburg (G-659)			
Merck Sharp Dhme Argentina Inc	G	908 423-1000	
Whitehouse Station (G-11927)			
Merck Sharpe & Dohme De PR Inc	G	908 423-1000	
Whitehouse Station (G-11928)			
Mitsubishi Tanabe Pharma	E	908 607-1950	
Jersey City (G-4766)			
Mpt Delivery Systems Inc	G	973 278-0283	
Paterson (G-8262)			
Mt Holly Pharmacy	G	609 914-4890	
Lumberton (G-5632)			
Mule Road Pharmacy	G	732 244-3737	
Toms River (G-10779)			
Mylan API US LLC	E	732 748-8882	
Somerset (G-10038)			
Myos Rens Technology Inc	G	973 509-0444	
Cedar Knolls (G-1311)			
Nautilus Neurosciences Inc	G	908 437-1320	
Bedminster (G-275)			
Neopharma Inc	D	609 201-2185	
Princeton (G-8983)			
Newton Biopharma Solutions LLC	G	908 874-7145	
Hillsborough (G-4340)			
Njs Associates Company	G	973 960-8688	
Bridgewater (G-858)			
Novacyl Inc	G	609 259-0444	
Robbinsville (G-9415)			
Novartis Corporation	D	862 778-8300	
East Hanover (G-2227)			
Novartis Pharmaceuticals Corp	A	862 778-8300	
East Hanover (G-2229)			
Novartis Pharmaceuticals Corp	F	973 538-1296	
Morris Plains (G-6619)			
Novartis Pharmaceuticals Corp	G	862 778-8300	
East Hanover (G-2231)			
Novartis Pharmaceuticals Corp	G	862 778-8300	
East Hanover (G-2230)			
Novel Laboratories Inc	C	908 603-6000	
Somerset (G-10041)			
Novo Nordisk Inc	B	609 987-5800	
Plainsboro (G-8798)			
Novo Nordisk Inc	G	609 987-5800	
Princeton (G-8987)			

Company	Code	Phone
Nuclear Diagnostic Pdts Inc	F	973 664-9696
Rockaway (G-9481)		
Nuclear Diagnostic Products of	F	856 489-5733
Cherry Hill (G-1401)		
Nutra-Med Packaging Inc	D	973 625-2274
Whippany (G-11899)		
Ocd Pharmaceuticals	G	610 366-2314
Raritan (G-9216)		
Odin Pharmaceuticals LLC	G	732 554-1100
Somerset (G-10042)		
OHM Laboratories Inc	D	609 720-9200
Princeton (G-8990)		
OHM Laboratories Inc	D	732 514-1072
New Brunswick (G-6956)		
Omthera Pharmaceuticals Inc	F	908 741-4399
Princeton (G-8991)		
Ono Pharma USA Inc	F	609 219-1010
Lawrenceville (G-5241)		
Onpharma Inc	G	408 335-6850
Bridgewater (G-859)		
Optimer Pharmaceuticals LLC	B	858 909-0736
Kenilworth (G-4966)		
Orchid Pharmaceuticals Inc	G	609 951-2209
Princeton (G-8992)		
Ortho Biotech Products LP	D	908 541-4000
Bridgewater (G-861)		
Ortho-Clinical Diagnostics Inc	A	908 218-8000
Raritan (G-9217)		
Osmotica Pharmaceutical Corp	C	908 809-1300
Bridgewater (G-862)		
Osmotica Pharmaceuticals PLC	G	908 809-1300
Bridgewater (G-863)		
Ossb and L Pharma LLC	G	732 940-8701
Milltown (G-6218)		
Outlook Therapeutics Inc	D	609 619-3990
Cranbury (G-1867)		
Pacira Pharmaceuticals Inc	C	973 254-3560
Parsippany (G-7983)		
Palatin Technologies Inc	F	609 495-2200
Cranbury (G-1868)		
Parker Labs	G	973 276-9500
Fairfield (G-3290)		
Patagonia Pharmaceuticals LLC	G	201 264-7866
Woodcliff Lake (G-12060)		
Patheon Biologics LLC	D	609 919-3300
Princeton (G-8993)		
Paw Bioscience Products LLC	G	732 460-0088
Eatontown (G-2416)		
Pdr Equity LLC	D	201 358-7200
Whippany (G-11902)		
Pds Biotechnology Corporation	F	800 208-3343
Berkeley Heights (G-409)		
Penick Corporation	G	856 678-3601
Newark (G-7226)		
Pernix Therapeutics LLC	E	800 793-2145
Morristown (G-6692)		
Pestka Biomedical Labs Inc	E	732 777-9123
Piscataway (G-8699)		
Pfizer Inc	D	732 591-2106
Old Bridge (G-7723)		
Pfizer Inc	C	201 294-8060
North Bergen (G-7429)		
Pfizer Inc	C	908 251-5685
Dunellen (G-2123)		
Pfizer Inc	E	609 434-4920
Ewing (G-3050)		
Pfizer Inc	C	212 733-2323
Bridgewater (G-864)		
Pharm Ops Inc	G	908 454-7733
Phillipsburg (G-8566)		
Pharma Synergy LLC	G	856 241-2316
Swedesboro (G-10601)		
Pharmaceutical Innovations	E	973 242-2900
Newark (G-7228)		
Pharmachem Laboratories Inc	E	973 256-1340
Totowa (G-10843)		
Pharmachem Laboratories Inc	E	201 343-3611
South Hackensack (G-10180)		
Pharmachem Laboratories LLC	D	201 246-1000
Kearny (G-4892)		
Pharmacia & Upjohn Inc	B	908 901-8000
Peapack (G-8343)		
Pharmasource International LLC	G	732 985-6182
Piscataway (G-8700)		
Pharmatech International Inc	F	973 244-0393
Fairfield (G-3291)		
Pharmctclprscrptnsrvcllc Lcnda	G	973 491-9000
Newark (G-7229)		
Pharmedium Services LLC	E	847 457-2362
Dayton (G-1983)		

Company	Code	Phone
Phytobologic Pharmaceutics LLC	G	856 975-0444
West Berlin (G-11615)		
Pierre Fbre Phrmaceuticals Inc	G	973 898-1042
Parsippany (G-7989)		
PI A Kadmonpharmaceuticals	G	732 230-3092
Monmouth Junction (G-6302)		
Plx Pharma Inc	G	973 409-6541
Sparta (G-10406)		
Porton Usa LLC	E	908 791-9100
South Plainfield (G-10313)		
Prince Sterilization Svcs LLC	E	973 227-6882
Fairfield (G-3294)		
Princeton Biopharma Strategies	G	609 203-5303
Princeton (G-8997)		
Princeton Enduring Biotech Inc	G	732 406-3041
Monmouth Junction (G-6304)		
Princeton Enduring Biotech Inc	G	732 406-3041
Monmouth Junction (G-6305)		
Progenics Pharmaceuticals Inc	F	646 975-2500
Somerset (G-10057)		
Prolong Pharmaceuticals LLC	D	908 444-4660
South Plainfield (G-10316)		
Promius Pharma LLC	E	609 282-1400
Princeton (G-9010)		
Protoform Inc	G	609 261-6920
Westampton (G-11790)		
Provid Pharmaceuticals Inc	E	732 565-1101
Monmouth Junction (G-6307)		
Ptc Therapeutics Inc	C	908 222-7000
South Plainfield (G-10317)		
Pts Intermediate Holdings LLC	A	732 537-6200
Somerset (G-10059)		
Purdue Pharma LP	C	203 588-8000
Ewing (G-3055)		
Q&Q Pharma Research Company	Q	973 267-0160
Morris Plains (G-6624)		
Qrx Pharma Incorporated	F	908 506-2900
Bedminster (G-277)		
Quagen Pharmaceuticals LLC	E	973 228-9600
West Caldwell (G-11675)		
Qugen Inc	G	609 716-6300
Plainsboro (G-8801)		
Ranx Pharmaceuticals Inc	G	571 214-8989
Jamesburg (G-4676)		
Reed-Lane Inc	C	973 709-1090
Wayne (G-11546)		
Regado Biosciences Inc	G	908 580-2109
Basking Ridge (G-196)		
Regentree LLC	E	609 734-4328
Princeton (G-9015)		
Riconpharma LLC	E	973 627-4685
Denville (G-2054)		
Rising Health LLC	E	201 961-9000
Saddle Brook (G-9673)		
Rising Pharma Holdings Inc	G	201 961-9000
Saddle Brook (G-9674)		
Rising Pharmaceuticals Inc	E	201 961-9000
Saddle Brook (G-9675)		
Roche Diagnostics Corporation	F	908 253-0707
Branchburg (G-678)		
S V Pharma Inc	G	201 433-1512
Jersey City (G-4802)		
Sabinsa Corporation	E	732 777-1111
East Windsor (G-2359)		
Sandoz Inc	A	862 778-8300
East Hanover (G-2237)		
Sanofi US Services Inc	G	336 407-4994
Bridgewater (G-881)		
Sanofi US Services Inc	E	908 231-4000
Bridgewater (G-882)		
Sanofi US Services Inc	F	908 231-4000
Bridgewater (G-883)		
Sanofi-Aventis US LLC	D	908 981-5000
Bridgewater (G-884)		
Sanofi-Synthelabo Inc	B	908 981-5000
Bridgewater (G-886)		
Sanofi-Synthelabo Inc	A	908 231-2000
Bridgewater (G-885)		
Saxa Pharmaceuticals LLC	G	862 571-7630
Holmdel (G-4513)		
Schering-Plough Corp	G	908 595-3638
Branchburg (G-681)		
Scherng-Plough Pdts Caribe Inc	G	908 423-1000
Whitehouse Station (G-11934)		
Sciecure Pharma Inc	E	732 329-8089
Monmouth Junction (G-6311)		
Scynexis Inc	F	201 884-5485
Jersey City (G-4807)		
Secord Inc	F	908 754-2147
Scotch Plains (G-9740)		

Company	Code	Phone
Sentrimed Ltd Liability Co	G	914 582-8631
Voorhees (G-11293)		
Sharmatek Inc	G	908 852-5087
Hackettstown (G-4036)		
Shasun Usa Inc	F	732 465-0700
Piscataway (G-8711)		
Siegfried Usa LLC	C	856 678-3601
Pennsville (G-8501)		
Solaris Pharma Corporation	G	908 864-0404
Bridgewater (G-891)		
Solgen Pharmaceuticals Inc	E	732 983-6025
Edison (G-2616)		
Soligenix Inc	F	609 538-8200
Princeton (G-9023)		
Speciality Pharma Mfg LLC	G	201 675-3411
Carlstadt (G-1220)		
Spray-Tek Inc	E	732 469-0050
Middlesex (G-6152)		
Star Pharma Inc	G	718 466-1790
East Brunswick (G-2180)		
Stark Pharma Technology Inc	F	848 217-4059
Piscataway (G-8719)		
Steri-Pharma LLC	D	201 857-8210
Paramus (G-7836)		
Strides Pharma Inc	G	609 773-5000
East Brunswick (G-2181)		
Strive Pharmaceuticals Inc	G	609 269-2001
East Brunswick (G-2182)		
Sun Pharmaceutical Inds Inc	E	313 871-8400
Princeton (G-9029)		
Sun Pharmaceutical Inds Inc	E	609 495-2800
Cranbury (G-1884)		
Sun Pharmaceutical Inds Inc	B	609 495-2800
Cranbury (G-1885)		
Sunovion Pharmaceuticals Inc	D	201 592-2050
Fort Lee (G-3590)		
Sunrise Pharmaceutical Inc	E	732 382-6085
Rahway (G-9128)		
Sv Pharma Inc	G	732 651-1336
East Brunswick (G-2185)		
Svtc Pharma Inc	G	201 652-0013
Ridgewood (G-9332)		
Synergetica International Inc	G	732 780-5865
Marlboro (G-5916)		
Taisho Pharmaceutical R&D Inc	G	973 285-0870
Morristown (G-6702)		
Tap Pharmaceutical Products	G	908 470-9700
Bedminster (G-279)		
Taree Pharma LLC	G	609 252-9596
Princeton (G-9032)		
Targanta Therapeutics Corp	D	973 290-6000
Parsippany (G-8025)		
Taro Pharmaceuticals USA Inc	E	609 655-9002
Cranbury (G-1886)		
Teligent Inc	F	856 697-1441
Buena (G-943)		
Teva Api Inc	E	201 307-6900
Parsippany (G-8026)		
Teva Pharmaceuticals	F	888 838-2872
Parsippany (G-8027)		
Teva Pharmaceuticals Usa Inc	C	973 575-2775
Fairfield (G-3325)		
Teva Womens Health Inc	G	201 930-3300
Somerset (G-10086)		
Therapeutic Proteins Inc	F	312 620-1500
Piscataway (G-8726)		
Thrombogenics Inc	E	732 590-2900
Iselin (G-4633)		
Torrent Pharma Inc	E	269 544-2299
Basking Ridge (G-199)		
Trifluent Pharma LLC	G	210 552-2057
Secaucus (G-9823)		
Trigen Laboratories LLC	A	732 721-0070
Bridgewater (G-898)		
Tulex Pharmaceuticals Inc	F	609 619-3098
Cranbury (G-1890)		
Unipack Inc	F	973 450-9880
Belleville (G-318)		
Urigen Pharmaceuticals Inc	G	732 640-0160
North Brunswick (G-7491)		
US Pharma Lab Inc	C	888 296-8775
New Brunswick (G-6978)		
Valeritas Holdings Inc	D	908 927-9920
Bridgewater (G-902)		
Validus Pharmaceuticals LLC	F	973 265-2777
Parsippany (G-8033)		
Vensun Pharmaceuticals Inc	F	908 278-8386
Princeton (G-9040)		
Vermeer Pharma LLC	G	973 270-0073
Morristown (G-6706)		

PRODUCT

Vertical Pharmaceuticals LLC ....D 732 721-0070
  Bridgewater *(G-903)*

Vertical/Trigen Holdings LLC ....F 732 721-0070
  Bridgewater *(G-904)*

Vertice Pharma LLC ....E 877 530-1633
  New Providence *(G-7024)*

Vgyaan Pharmaceuticals LLC...........G 609 452-2770
  Skillman *(G-9927)*

Vita-Pure Inc ....E 908 245-1212
  Roselle *(G-9576)*

Vitacare Pharma LLC ....G 908 754-1792
  South Plainfield *(G-10343)*

Walgreen Eastern Co Inc ....E 973 728-3172
  West Milford *(G-11733)*

Walgreen Eastern Co Inc ....E 609 522-1291
  Wildwood *(G-11947)*

Warner Chilcott (us) LLC ....G 973 442-3200
  Morristown *(G-6708)*

Warner Chilcott (us) LLC ....D 862 261-7000
  Parsippany *(G-8036)*

Watson Laboratories Inc ....C 951 493-5300
  Parsippany *(G-8038)*

Windsor Labs LLC ....G 609 301-6446
  East Windsor *(G-2364)*

Windtree Therapeutics Inc ....F 973 339-2889
  Totowa *(G-10863)*

Wyeth Holdings LLC ....E 973 660-5000
  Madison *(G-5704)*

Wyeth LLC ....B 973 660-5000
  Madison *(G-5705)*

Wyeth-Ayerst (asia) Ltd ....G 973 660-5500
  Madison *(G-5706)*

Wyeth-Ayerst Pharmaceutical ....F 732 274-4221
  Monmouth Junction *(G-6320)*

Wynnpharm Inc ....G 732 409-1005
  Freehold *(G-3707)*

Zenia Pharma LLC ....G 973 246-9718
  Clifton *(G-1743)*

Zenith Laboratories Inc ....G 201 767-1700
  Northvale *(G-7555)*

Zoetis Inc ....B 973 822-7000
  Parsippany *(G-8045)*

Zoetis LLC ....G 973 822-7000
  Parsippany *(G-8046)*

Zoetis Products LLC ....C 973 660-5000
  Florham Park *(G-3528)*

Zoetis Products LLC ....F 973 660-5000
  Bridgewater *(G-905)*

PHARMACEUTICALS: Mail-Order Svc

Vitamin Shoppe Industries Inc ....A 201 868-5959
  Secacus *(G-9826)*

PHARMACEUTICALS: Medicinal & Botanical Prdts

7th Seventh Day Wellness Ctr ....G 856 308-0991
  Sicklerville *(G-9906)*

Abrazil LLC ....G 732 658-5191
  Kendall Park *(G-4917)*

American Ingredients Inc ....F 714 630-6000
  Kearny *(G-4843)*

Chem-Is-Try Inc ....G 732 372-7311
  Metuchen *(G-6052)*

Cyalume Specialty Products Inc ....E 732 469-7760
  Bound Brook *(G-601)*

D & A Granulation LLC ....G 732 994-7480
  Lakewood *(G-5080)*

Eleison Pharmaceuticals Inc ....G 215 416-7620
  Bordentown *(G-580)*

Fisher Scientific Company LLC ....B 201 796-7100
  Fair Lawn *(G-3102)*

Guerbet LLC ....E 812 333-0059
  Princeton *(G-8956)*

Herbalist & Alchemist Inc ....F 908 689-9020
  Washington *(G-11447)*

Herborium Group Inc ....G 201 849-4431
  Fort Lee *(G-3560)*

Ivy-Dry Inc ....G 973 575-1992
  Fairfield *(G-3242)*

Janssen Pharmaceuticals Inc ....D 908 218-6908
  Somerset *(G-10007)*

Janssen Pharmaceuticals Inc ....D 908 218-7701
  Somerset *(G-10008)*

Janssen Pharmaceuticals Inc ....G 908 735-4844
  Pittstown *(G-8753)*

Jiaherb Inc ....E 973 439-6869
  Pine Brook *(G-8608)*

Nouryon Surface Chemistry ....D 732 985-6262
  Edison *(G-2579)*

Pfizer Inc ....C 212 733-2323
  Bridgewater *(G-864)*

Purevolution ....F 973 919-4047
  Kinnelon *(G-5021)*

Savient Pharmaceuticals Inc ....F 732 418-9300
  Bridgewater *(G-887)*

Sk Life Science Inc ....E 201 421-3800
  Paramus *(G-7833)*

Toll Compaction Service Inc ....G 732 776-8225
  Neptune *(G-6902)*

Zoetis Products LLC ....C 973 660-5000
  Florham Park *(G-3528)*

PHARMACIES & DRUG STORES

Berat Corporation ....C 609 953-7700
  Medford *(G-6020)*

Mule Road Pharmacy ....G 732 244-3737
  Toms River *(G-10779)*

Shop Rite Supermarkets Inc ....C 732 775-4250
  Neptune *(G-6898)*

Shop Rite Supermarkets Inc ....C 732 442-1717
  Perth Amboy *(G-8533)*

Shop-Rite Supermarkets Inc ....C 609 646-2448
  Absecon *(G-4)*

Teva Pharmaceuticals ....F 888 838-2872
  Parsippany *(G-8027)*

PHOSPHATES

Innophos Inc ....G 973 587-8735
  Cranbury *(G-1840)*

Innophos Investments II Inc.............G 609 495-2495
  Cranbury *(G-1844)*

PHOTOCOPY MACHINE REPAIR SVCS

Imperial Copy Products Inc ....E 973 927-5500
  Randolph *(G-9186)*

PHOTOCOPY MACHINES

Enterprise Solution Products ....G 201 678-9200
  West New York *(G-11739)*

Facsimile Cmmncations Inds Inc ....G 201 672-0773
  Lyndhurst *(G-5654)*

PHOTOCOPY SPLYS WHOLESALERS

Enterprise Solution Products ....G 201 678-9200
  West New York *(G-11739)*

PHOTOCOPYING & DUPLICATING SVCS

Berennial International ....G 973 675-6266
  Orange *(G-7752)*

Binding Products Inc ....E 212 947-1192
  Jersey City *(G-4704)*

Budget Print Center ....G 973 743-0073
  Bloomfield *(G-492)*

C2 Imaging LLC ....E 646 557-6300
  Jersey City *(G-4707)*

Fedex Office & Print Svcs Inc ....E 856 427-0099
  Cherry Hill *(G-1361)*

Fedex Office & Print Svcs Inc ....E 732 636-3580
  Iselin *(G-4609)*

Fedex Office & Print Svcs Inc ....F 732 249-9222
  New Brunswick *(G-6926)*

Fedex Office & Print Svcs Inc ....F 856 273-5959
  Mount Laurel *(G-6760)*

Fedex Office & Print Svcs Inc ....G 973 376-3966
  Springfield *(G-10443)*

Fedex Office & Print Svcs Inc ....G 201 672-0508
  East Rutherford *(G-2288)*

Franbeth Inc ....G 856 488-1480
  Pennsauken *(G-8422)*

Good Impressions Inc ....F 908 689-3071
  Washington *(G-11445)*

Good Impressions Inc ....G 856 461-3232
  Riverside *(G-9395)*

Graphic Action Inc ....G 908 213-0055
  Phillipsburg *(G-8553)*

Graphics Depot Inc ....F 973 927-8200
  Randolph *(G-9183)*

Hub Print & Copy Center LLC............G 201 585-7887
  Fort Lee *(G-3563)*

Instant Printing of Dover Inc ....G 973 366-6855
  Dover *(G-2090)*

J&E Business Services LLC ....G 973 984-8444
  Clifton *(G-1645)*

Jvs Copy Services Inc ....F 856 415-9090
  Sewell *(G-9850)*

Lewis Scheller Printing Corp ....G 732 843-5050
  Somerset *(G-10016)*

Mr Quickly Inc ....G 908 687-6000
  Union *(G-11077)*

Penn Copy Center Inc ....G 646 251-0313
  Lakewood *(G-5145)*

Penn Jersey Press Inc ....G 856 627-2200
  Gibbsboro *(G-3795)*

Penny Press ....G 856 547-1991
  Stratford *(G-10506)*

Press Room Inc ....F 609 689-3817
  Trenton *(G-10981)*

R & B Printing Inc ....G 908 766-4073
  Bernardsville *(G-443)*

Ridgewood Press Inc ....F 201 670-9797
  Ridgewood *(G-9328)*

Roan Printing Inc ....F 908 526-5990
  Somerville *(G-10124)*

Santon Inc ....E 201 444-9080
  Toms River *(G-10790)*

Strategic Content Imaging ....C 201 863-8100
  Secaucus *(G-9819)*

Tanzola Printing Inc ....G 973 779-0858
  Clifton *(G-1729)*

Toms River Printing Corp ....G 732 240-2033
  Brielle *(G-909)*

Word Center Printing ....G 609 586-5825
  Trenton *(G-11010)*

PHOTOENGRAVING SVC

Globe Photo Engraving Corp ....F 201 489-2300
  Little Ferry *(G-5488)*

PHOTOFINISHING LABORATORIES

American Teletimer Corp ....E 908 654-4200
  Mountainside *(G-6835)*

Fujifilm North America Corp ....B 732 857-3000
  Edison *(G-2516)*

Little Falls Shop Rite Super ....B 973 256-0909
  Little Falls *(G-5460)*

PHOTOGRAPH DEVELOPING & RETOUCHING SVCS

Old Hights Print Shop Inc ....G 609 443-4700
  Jackson *(G-4661)*

PHOTOGRAPHIC & OPTICAL GOODS EQPT REPAIR SVCS

Samsung Opt-Lctronics Amer Inc ....C 201 325-2612
  Teaneck *(G-10650)*

PHOTOGRAPHIC CONTROL SYSTEMS: Electronic

Atlantex Instruments Inc ....G 201 391-5148
  Woodcliff Lake *(G-12047)*

PHOTOGRAPHIC EQPT & SPLYS

AGFA Corporation ....B 800 540-2432
  Elmwood Park *(G-2808)*

AGFA Corporation ....E 201 440-0111
  Elmwood Park *(G-2809)*

AGFA Corporation ....E 201 440-0111
  Carlstadt *(G-1119)*

AGFA Finance Corp ....C 201 796-0058
  Elmwood Park *(G-2810)*

Agoura Hills Group ....E 818 888-0400
  Cherry Hill *(G-1335)*

Beta Industries Corp ....G 201 939-2400
  Carlstadt *(G-1128)*

Central Technology Inc ....F 732 431-3339
  Freehold *(G-3656)*

Clarity Imaging Tech Inc ....E 413 693-1234
  Pennsauken *(G-8404)*

Coda Inc ....E 201 825-7400
  Mahwah *(G-5724)*

Flir Systems Inc ....G 201 368-9700
  Ridgefield Park *(G-9307)*

Fujifilm Med Systems USA Inc ....F 973 686-2631
  Saddle River *(G-9691)*

Fujifilm North America Corp ....B 732 857-3000
  Edison *(G-2516)*

Hasselblad Inc ....E 800 456-0203
  Union *(G-11061)*

Heights Usa Inc ....E 609 530-1300
  Ewing *(G-3033)*

Howard Packaging Corp ....G....... 973 904-0022
  Clifton **(G-1636)**
Hpi International Inc ....F....... 732 942-9900
  Lakewood **(G-5110)**
Iris ID Systems Inc ....E...... 609 819-4747
  Cranbury **(G-1846)**
Ner Data Products Inc ....E...... 888 637-3282
  Glassboro **(G-3817)**
Parker Acquisition Group Inc ....G...... 908 707-4900
  Branchburg **(G-665)**
Power Photo Corp.........................D....... 732 200-1645
  Hillside **(G-4420)**
Profoto US Inc ....F....... 973 822-1300
  Florham Park **(G-3521)**
Rpl Supplies Inc ....F....... 973 767-0880
  Garfield **(G-3766)**
Towne Technologies Inc.........................F....... 908 722-9500
  Somerville **(G-10127)**

PHOTOGRAPHIC EQPT & SPLYS WHOLESALERS

Gill Associates LLC ....G....... 973 835-5456
  Wayne **(G-11511)**
Kinly Inc ....E....... 973 585-3000
  Cedar Knolls **(G-1307)**

PHOTOGRAPHIC EQPT & SPLYS, WHOLESALE: Identity Recorders

Qsa Global National Corp ....G....... 865 888-6798
  Red Bank **(G-9241)**

PHOTOGRAPHIC EQPT & SPLYS, WHOLESALE: Motion Picture Camera

Plastic Reel Corp of America ....E....... 201 933-5100
  Carlstadt **(G-1202)**

PHOTOGRAPHIC EQPT & SPLYS, WHOLESALE: Printing Apparatus

Inserts East Incorporated.........................C....... 856 663-8181
  Pennsauken **(G-8437)**

PHOTOGRAPHIC EQPT & SPLYS, WHOLESALE: Processing

Mri International.........................G....... 973 383-3645
  Newton **(G-7350)**

PHOTOGRAPHIC EQPT & SPLYS: Cameras, Still & Motion Pictures

Vision Research Inc ....D....... 973 696-4500
  Wayne **(G-11563)**
Xybion Corporation ....C....... 973 538-2067
  Lawrenceville **(G-5248)**

PHOTOGRAPHIC EQPT & SPLYS: Developers, Not Chemical Plants

James Colucci Enterprises LLC.........................E....... 877 403-4900
  Short Hills **(G-9870)**

PHOTOGRAPHIC EQPT & SPLYS: Film, Sensitized

Energy Storage Corp.........................D....... 732 542-7880
  Eatontown **(G-2392)**

PHOTOGRAPHIC EQPT & SPLYS: Flashlight Apparatus, Exc Bulbs

Dyna-Lite Inc ....F....... 908 687-8800
  Union **(G-11047)**

PHOTOGRAPHIC EQPT & SPLYS: Plates, Sensitized

West Essex Graphics Inc ....E....... 973 227-2400
  Fairfield **(G-3352)**

PHOTOGRAPHIC EQPT & SPLYS: Printing Eqpt

Colex Imaging Inc ....G....... 201 414-5575
  Elmwood Park **(G-2816)**
Fujikura Graphics Inc ....G....... 201 420-5040
  Secaucus **(G-9769)**

PHOTOGRAPHIC EQPT & SPLYS: Processing Eqpt

Cytotherm LP ....G....... 609 396-1456
  Trenton **(G-10927)**

PHOTOGRAPHIC EQPT & SPLYS: Toners, Prprd, Not Chem Plnts

Automatic Transfer Inc ....G....... 908 213-2830
  Alpha **(G-36)**
B&B Imaging LLC ....G....... 201 261-3131
  Paramus **(G-7791)**
Ricoh Prtg Systems Amer Inc.........................G....... 973 316-6051
  Mountain Lakes **(G-6827)**

PHOTOGRAPHIC EQPT & SPLYS: Trays, Printing & Processing

Image Remit Inc ....E....... 732 940-7900
  North Brunswick **(G-7469)**

PHOTOGRAPHIC EQPT & SPLYS: X-Ray Film

Mri of West Morris PA ....F....... 973 927-1010
  Succasunna **(G-10515)**

PHOTOGRAPHIC EQPT REPAIR SVCS

Photographic Analysis Company.........................G....... 973 696-1000
  Wayne **(G-11542)**

PHOTOGRAPHIC EQPT/SPLYS, WHOL: Cameras/Projectors/Eqpt/Splys

Mizco International Inc ....D....... 732 912-2000
  Avenel **(G-137)**
Samsung Opt-Lctronics Amer Inc.........................C....... 201 325-2612
  Teaneck **(G-10650)**
Tocad America Inc ....E....... 973 627-9600
  Rockaway **(G-9505)**

PHOTOGRAPHIC SVCS

Globe Photo Engraving Corp.........................F....... 201 489-2300
  Little Ferry **(G-5488)**
New Life Color Reproductions ....G....... 201 943-7005
  Ridgefield **(G-9280)**

PHOTOGRAPHY SVCS: Commercial

Pixell Creative Group LLC.........................G....... 609 410-3024
  Burlington **(G-982)**
S J T Imaging Inc ....D....... 201 262-7744
  Oradell **(G-7747)**
Stephen Swinton Studio Inc ....G....... 908 537-9135
  Washington **(G-11452)**
Visionware Systems Inc ....F....... 609 924-0800
  Skillman **(G-9928)**

PHOTOTYPESETTING SVC

L A S Printing Co.........................G....... 201 991-5362
  Jersey City **(G-4757)**
Trentypo Inc.........................F....... 609 883-5971
  Ewing **(G-3071)**

PHOTOVOLTAIC Solid State

Kyocera International Inc ....D....... 856 691-7000
  Cherry Hill **(G-1381)**

PHYSICAL EXAMINATION SVCS, INSURANCE

Um Equity Corp.........................G....... 856 354-2200
  Haddonfield **(G-4065)**

PHYSICAL FITNESS CENTERS

Our Team Fitness LLC ....G....... 848 208-5047
  Oceanport **(G-7705)**
Totowa Kickboxing Ltd Lblty Co ....F....... 973 507-9106
  Totowa **(G-10855)**

PHYSICIANS' OFFICES & CLINICS: Medical doctors

Bio Compression Systems Inc ....E....... 201 939-0716
  Moonachie **(G-6457)**
Endotec Inc.........................F....... 973 762-6100
  South Orange **(G-10194)**

Galen Publishing LLC.........................E....... 908 253-9001
  Somerville **(G-10111)**
Grateful Ped Inc ....F....... 973 478-6511
  Saddle Brook **(G-9654)**
Medici International Inc.........................G....... 973 684-6084
  Paterson **(G-8253)**

PICTURE FRAMES: Metal

Hickok Matthews Co Inc.........................G....... 973 335-3400
  Montville **(G-6443)**
R A O Contract Sales NY Inc.........................G....... 201 652-1500
  Paterson **(G-8285)**

PICTURE FRAMES: Wood

Frameco Inc.........................E....... 973 989-1424
  Dover **(G-2084)**
Hoboken Executive Art Inc ....G....... 201 420-8262
  Hoboken **(G-4454)**
K Ron Art & Mirrors Inc.........................G....... 201 313-7080
  Ridgefield **(G-9270)**
R A O Contract Sales NY Inc.........................G....... 201 652-1500
  Paterson **(G-8285)**
Revelation Gallery Inc ....G....... 973 627-6558
  Denville **(G-2052)**
Vaswani Inc.........................D....... 877 376-4425
  Edison **(G-2637)**

PICTURE PROJECTION EQPT

Sharp Electronics Corporation.........................A....... 201 529-8200
  Montvale **(G-6433)**

PIECE GOODS & NOTIONS WHOLESALERS

Artistic Bias Products Co Inc ....E....... 732 382-4141
  Rahway **(G-9078)**
Foldtex II Ltd.........................E....... 908 928-0919
  Westfield **(G-11797)**
John M Sniderman Inc.........................G....... 201 450-4291
  Fairview **(G-3361)**
Uniport Industries Corporation ....G....... 201 391-6422
  Woodcliff Lake **(G-12067)**

PIECE GOODS, NOTIONS & DRY GOODS, WHOL: Textile Converters

Alpha Associates Inc ....E....... 732 730-1800
  Lakewood **(G-5047)**
Printmaker International Ltd.........................G....... 212 629-9260
  Irvington **(G-4583)**
Scher Fabrics Inc.........................F....... 212 382-2266
  Freehold **(G-3699)**

PIECE GOODS, NOTIONS & DRY GOODS, WHOL: Textiles, Woven

American Dawn Inc.........................G....... 856 467-9211
  Bridgeport **(G-734)**
Franco Manufacturing Co Inc ....C....... 732 494-0500
  Metuchen **(G-6056)**

PIECE GOODS, NOTIONS & DRY GOODS, WHOL: Trimmings, Apparel

Alco Trimming.........................G....... 201 854-8608
  North Bergen **(G-7380)**
Green Distribution LLC.........................D....... 201 293-4381
  Secaucus **(G-9779)**

PIECE GOODS, NOTIONS & DRY GOODS, WHOL: Yard Goods, Woven

R L Plastics Inc ....G....... 732 340-1100
  Avenel **(G-144)**

PIECE GOODS, NOTIONS & DRY GOODS, WHOLESALE: Fabrics

Douglass Industries Inc ....E....... 609 804-6040
  Egg Harbor City **(G-2658)**
Window 25 LLC.........................G....... 973 817-9464
  Newark **(G-7316)**

PIECE GOODS, NOTIONS & DRY GOODS, WHOLESALE: Fabrics, Lace

Royal Lace Co Inc.........................E....... 718 495-9327
  Rahway **(G-9125)**
Tone Embroidery Corp ....E....... 201 943-1082
  Fairview **(G-3371)**

PIECE GOODS, NOTIONS & DRY GOODS, WHOLESALE: Sewing Access

Sysco Guest Supply LLC ....C 732 537-2297
  Somerset **(G-10078)**

PIECE GOODS, NOTIONS & OTHER DRY GOODS, WHOL: Flags/Banners

F & S Awning and Blind Co Inc.............G 732 738-4110
  Edison **(G-2509)**
Services Equipment Com LLC.............G 973 992-4404
  Livingston **(G-5539)**

PIECE GOODS, NOTIONS & OTHER DRY GOODS, WHOL: Millinery Sply

Bai Lar Interior Services Inc ....G 732 738-0350
  Fords **(G-3530)**

PIECE GOODS, NOTIONS & OTHER DRY GOODS, WHOLESALE: Fabrics

Associated Fabrics Corporation ....G 201 300-6053
  Fair Lawn **(G-3086)**
Circle Visual Inc ....E 212 719-5153
  Carlstadt **(G-1139)**
Marcotex International Inc ....E 201 991-8200
  Kearny **(G-4883)**

PIECE GOODS, NOTIONS & OTHER DRY GOODS, WHOLESALE: Ribbons

Carson & Gebel Ribbon Co LLC...........E 973 627-4200
  Rockaway **(G-9449)**
Cottage Lace and Ribbon Co Inc..........G 732 776-9353
  Neptune **(G-6871)**
Papillon Ribbon & Bow Inc ....E 973 928-6128
  Clifton **(G-1683)**

PIECE GOODS, NOTIONS & OTHER DRY GOODS, WHOLESALE: Zippers

Royal Slide Sales Co Inc ....G 973 777-1177
  Garfield **(G-3764)**
YKK (usa) Inc.........................G 201 935-4200
  Lyndhurst **(G-5684)**

PIECE GOODS, NOTIONS/DRY GOODS, WHOL: Linen Piece, Woven

Linen For Tables ....G 973 345-8472
  Paterson **(G-8242)**

PILE DRIVING EQPT

W A Building Movers & Contrs.............F 908 654-8227
  Garwood **(G-3793)**

PILLOW FILLING MTRLS: Curled Hair, Cotton Waste, Moss

American Home Mfg LLC ....G 732 465-1530
  Piscataway **(G-8629)**

PILLOW TUBING

Hanover Direct Inc ....B 201 863-7300
  Weehawken **(G-11568)**

PILLOWCASES

Country Club Products Inc ....G 908 352-5400
  Elizabeth **(G-2723)**

PILOT SVCS: Aviation

Rclc Inc...F 732 877-1788
  Woodbridge **(G-12020)**

PINS

Bigelow Components Corp...................E 973 467-1200
  Springfield **(G-10431)**
Edwin Leonel Ramirez ....G 732 648-5587
  Plainfield **(G-8764)**
Pin Cancer Campaign...........................G 973 600-4170
  Newton **(G-7353)**

PIPE & FITTING: Fabrication

Belden Inc ....F 908 925-8000
  Elizabeth **(G-2714)**
Bemis Company Inc...........................B 908 689-3000
  Washington **(G-11441)**
Coolenheat Inc ....E 908 925-4473
  Kendall Park **(G-4918)**
Custom Alloy Corporation ....C 908 638-0257
  High Bridge **(G-4281)**
Esco Industries Corp...........................E 973 478-5888
  Woodcliff Lake **(G-12056)**
Fluorotherm Polymers Inc ....G 973 575-0760
  Parsippany **(G-7948)**
Fox Steel Products LLC ....G 856 778-4661
  Mount Laurel **(G-6762)**
Handytube Corporation...........................E 732 469-7420
  Middlesex **(G-6120)**
Imperial Weld Ring Corp Inc ....E 908 354-0011
  Elizabeth **(G-2749)**
Piping Solutions Inc ....G 732 537-1009
  Bridgewater **(G-867)**
Royal Seamless Corporation ....F 732 901-9595
  Lakewood **(G-5160)**
S&W Fabricators Inc...........................E 856 881-7418
  Glassboro **(G-3818)**
Symcon Inc....................................G 973 728-8661
  West Milford **(G-11732)**
Tube Craft of America Inc....................E 856 629-5626
  Williamstown **(G-11982)**
U V International LLC ....G 973 993-9454
  Morristown **(G-6705)**

PIPE & FITTINGS: Cast Iron

Water Works Supply Company...............E 973 835-2153
  Pompton Plains **(G-8874)**

PIPE & FITTINGS: Pressure, Cast Iron

McWane Inc ....B 908 454-1161
  Phillipsburg **(G-8562)**

PIPE JOINT COMPOUNDS

Plcs LLC ....E 856 722-1333
  Mount Laurel **(G-6790)**

PIPE SECTIONS, FABRICATED FROM PURCHASED PIPE

Foodline Piping Products Co.................G 856 767-1177
  West Berlin **(G-11594)**

PIPE, CAST IRON: Wholesalers

M P Tube Works Inc ....G 908 317-2500
  Mountainside **(G-6848)**
Water Works Supply Company...............E 973 835-2153
  Pompton Plains **(G-8874)**

PIPE, IRRIGATION: Concrete

Liedl...G 908 359-8335
  Hillsborough **(G-4339)**

PIPE, SEWER: Concrete

Brent Material Company.......................G 908 686-3832
  Kenilworth **(G-4931)**

PIPE: Concrete

Ceresist Inc.....................................F 973 345-3231
  Paterson **(G-8156)**

PIPE: Plastic

Advanced Drainage Systems Inc ....D 856 467-4779
  Logan Township **(G-5584)**
Endot Industries Inc ....D 973 625-8500
  Rockaway **(G-9456)**

PIPE: Sewer, Cast Iron

En Tech Corp...................................F 201 784-1034
  Closter **(G-1753)**
En Tech Corp...................................F 718 389-2058
  Closter **(G-1754)**

PIPE: Sheet Metal

Able Fab Co ....E 732 396-0600
  Avenel **(G-118)**

Altona Blower & Shtmtl Work ....G 201 641-3520
  Little Ferry **(G-5474)**
Industrial Process & Eqp Inc ....F 973 702-0330
  Sussex **(G-10562)**

PIPELINE & POWER LINE INSPECTION SVCS

Corrview International LLC ....G 973 770-0571
  Hopatcong **(G-4519)**

PIPELINE TERMINAL FACILITIES: Independent

Fence America New Jersey Inc ....G 973 472-5121
  Hackensack **(G-3912)**

PIPELINES: Crude Petroleum

Total American Services Inc ....F 206 626-3500
  Jersey City **(G-4822)**

PIPES & TUBES

Albea Americas Inc...........................C 908 689-3000
  Washington **(G-11437)**

PIPES & TUBES: Steel

Amer-RAC LLC ....F 856 488-6210
  Pennsauken **(G-8388)**
Century Tube Corp...........................E 908 534-2001
  Somerville **(G-10105)**
Delsea Pipe Inc................................E 856 589-9374
  Sewell **(G-9839)**
Dodson Global Inc ....G 732 238-7001
  East Brunswick **(G-2134)**
Fluorotherm Polymers Inc ....G 973 575-0760
  Parsippany **(G-7948)**
Fox Steel Products LLC ....G 856 778-4661
  Mount Laurel **(G-6762)**
Long Island Pipe of NJ ....E 201 939-1100
  Lyndhurst **(G-5658)**
M & M International...........................F 908 412-8300
  South Plainfield **(G-10295)**
Morris Industries Inc..........................D 973 835-6600
  Pompton Plains **(G-8868)**
New World Stainless LLC ....E 732 412-7137
  Somerset **(G-10040)**
Nippon Benkan Kagyo...........................E 732 435-0777
  New Brunswick **(G-6954)**
Silbo Industries Inc...........................F 201 307-0900
  Montvale **(G-6434)**
Zekelman Industries Inc....................D 724 342-6851
  Westwood **(G-11849)**

PIPES: Steel & Iron

Bushwick Metals LLC...........................E 908 754-8700
  South Plainfield **(G-10231)**
US Pipe Fabrication LLC ....F 856 461-3000
  Riverside **(G-9404)**

PIVOTS: Power Transmission

Emmco Development Corp ....F 732 469-6464
  Somerset **(G-9985)**

PLACEMATS: Plastic Or Textile

B T Partners Inc ....G 609 652-6511
  Galloway **(G-3720)**

PLANING MILLS: Millwork

Mp Custom FL LLC ....F 973 417-2288
  Wayne **(G-11535)**

PLANTERS: Plastic

Whole Year Trading Co Inc...................G 732 238-1196
  Dayton **(G-1995)**

PLANTS: Artificial & Preserved

Clover Garden Ctr Ltd Lblty Co ....G 856 235-4625
  Mount Laurel **(G-6748)**
Creative Display Inc...........................G 732 918-8010
  Neptune **(G-6873)**

PLAQUES: Picture, Laminated

Emdur Metal Products Inc....................F 856 541-1100
  Camden **(G-1061)**

PLASMAS

Kedrion Biopharma Inc ....D 201 242-8900
Fort Lee (G-3567)

PLASTER WORK: Ornamental & Architectural

Kingston Nurseries LLC ....F 609 430-0366
Kingston (G-5010)

PLASTER, ACOUSTICAL: Gypsum

Proform Acoustic Surfaces LLC ....G 201 553-9614
Secaucus (G-9800)

PLASTIC PRDTS

C G I Cstm Fiberglas & Decking ....F 609 646-5302
Pleasantville (G-8807)
Domtar ....G 201 942-2077
Delran (G-2015)
Lamart Corp ....F 973 772-6262
Clifton (G-1653)
Mrp New Jersey LLC 732 873-7148
Somerset (G-10032)
Optics Plastics ....G 201 939-3344
Lyndhurst (G-5670)
Vacumet Corp ....G 973 628-0405
Wayne (G-11562)

PLASTICIZERS, ORGANIC: Cyclic & Acyclic

Cambridge Industries Co Inc ....G 973 465-4565
Newark (G-7081)
Just In Time Chemical Sales & ....G 908 862-7726
Linden (G-5366)
Kenrich Petrochemicals Inc ....E 201 823-9000
Bayonne (G-226)
Lanxess Solutions US Inc ....C 732 738-1000
Fords (G-3533)

PLASTICS FILM & SHEET

A D M Corporation ....D 732 469-0900
Middlesex (G-6090)
Acrilex Inc ....E 201 333-1500
Jersey City (G-4685)
Allied Plastics Holdings LLC ....D 718 729-5500
Newark (G-7040)
American Renolit Corporation ....G 973 706-6912
Wayne (G-11468)
Ber Plastics Inc ....E 973 839-2100
Riverdale (G-9371)
Berry Global Films LLC ....C 201 641-6600
Montvale (G-6400)
Caloric Color Co Inc ....F 973 471-4748
Garfield (G-3734)
Creative Film Corp ....F 732 367-2166
Lakewood (G-5073)
Dicar Inc ....E 973 575-1377
Pine Brook (G-8596)
Dow Chemical Company ....D 800 258-2436
Somerset (G-9982)
Glitterex Corp ....D 908 272-9121
Cranford (G-1911)
Hillside Plastics Corporation ....D 973 923-2700
Hillside (G-4399)
Nexus Plastics Incorporated ....D 973 427-3311
Hawthorne (G-4234)
Perlin Converting LLC ....F 973 887-0257
Whippany (G-11903)
Primex Plastics Corporation ....C 973 470-8000
Garfield (G-3759)
Ssi North America Inc ....G 973 598-0152
Randolph (G-9201)
Up United LLC ....E 718 383-5700
Bridgewater (G-900)

PLASTICS FILM & SHEET: Polyethylene

American Transparent Plastic ....E 732 287-3000
Edison (G-2455)
Gemini Plastic Films Corp ....G 973 340-0700
Garfield (G-3745)
Glopak Corp ....E 908 753-8735
South Plainfield (G-10267)
Silverton Packaging Corp ....G 732 341-0986
Monroe Township (G-6344)
Tri-Cor Flexible Packaging Inc ....E 973 940-1500
Sparta (G-10413)

PLASTICS FILM & SHEET: Polypropylene

Central Plastics Incorporated ....G 973 808-0990
Parsippany (G-7899)
Fordion Packaging Ltd ....F 201 692-1344
Hackensack (G-3917)

PLASTICS FILM & SHEET: Polyvinyl

Kappus Plastic Company Inc ....D 908 537-2288
Hampton (G-4157)
Kayline Processing Inc ....E 609 695-1449
Trenton (G-10949)
Mark Ronald Associates Inc ....D 908 558-0011
Hillside (G-4414)

PLASTICS FILM & SHEET: Vinyl

American Renolit Corp La ....G 856 241-4901
Swedesboro (G-10570)
Congoleum Corporation ....D 609 584-3601
Trenton (G-10922)

PLASTICS FINISHED PRDTS: Laminated

Dikeman Laminating Corporation ....E 973 473-5696
Clifton (G-1598)
La Mart Manufacturing Corp ....G 718 384-6917
Teaneck (G-10636)
Plastinetics Inc ....G 973 618-9090
West Caldwell (G-11672)
Roysons Corporation ....D 973 625-5570
Rockaway (G-9496)

PLASTICS MATERIAL & RESINS

Adco Chemical Company Inc ....E 973 589-0880
Newark (G-7035)
Advansix Inc ....B 973 526-1800
Parsippany (G-7875)
All American Extrusion Inc ....G 973 881-9030
Paterson (G-8123)
Allied-Signal China Ltd ....E 973 455-2000
Morristown (G-6632)
Alliedsignal Foreign Sls Corp ....G 973 455-2000
Morristown (G-6633)
Alpine Group Inc ....B 201 549-4400
East Rutherford (G-2269)
Altaflo LLC ....F 973 300-3344
Sparta (G-10378)
Amcor Flexibles LLC ....C 856 825-1400
Millville (G-6224)
American Plastic Works Inc ....E 800 494-7326
Moorestown (G-6504)
ARC International N Amer LLC ....C 856 825-5620
Millville (G-6233)
Ashland LLC ....G 908 243-3500
Bridgewater (G-794)
Ashland LLC ....D 732 353-7718
Parlin (G-7861)
Barrett Bronze Inc ....E 914 699-6060
Wyckoff (G-12103)
Bergen Manufacturing & Supply ....E 201 854-3461
North Bergen (G-7389)
Cary Compounds LLC ....E 732 274-2626
Dayton (G-1957)
Chevron Phillips Chem Co LP ....E 732 738-2000
Perth Amboy (G-8514)
Clausen Company Inc ....E 732 738-1165
Fords (G-3531)
Colorite Polymers ....F 800 631-1577
Ridgefield (G-9255)
Covalnce Spcialty Coatings LLC ....D 732 356-2870
Middlesex (G-6109)
Crossfield Products Corp ....G 908 245-2801
Roselle Park (G-9580)
Custom Counters By Precision ....E 973 773-0111
Passaic (G-8058)
Deltech Resins Co ....E 973 589-0880
Newark (G-7102)
Dock Resins Corporation ....E 908 862-2351
Pedricktown (G-8348)
E-Beam Services Inc ....E 513 933-0031
Cranbury (G-1831)
Eagle Fabrication Inc ....E 732 739-5300
Ltl Egg Hbr (G-5616)
Extrusion Technik USA Inc ....F 732 354-0177
Somerset (G-9991)
Federal Plastics Corporation ....E 908 272-5800
Cranford (G-1910)
Flex Moulding Inc ....F 201 487-8080
Hackensack (G-3915)

Foam Rubber Fabricators Inc ....E 973 751-1445
Belleville (G-296)
Glopak Corp ....E 908 753-8735
South Plainfield (G-10267)
Illinois Tool Works Inc ....E 609 395-5600
Cranbury (G-1839)
Intelco ....D 856 456-6755
Westville (G-11817)
Interntonal Specialty Pdts Inc ....A 859 815-3333
Wayne (G-11522)
Interplast Inc ....F 609 386-4990
Burlington (G-975)
Kairos Enterprises LLC ....F 201 731-3181
Englewood Cliffs (G-2979)
Lanxess Solutions US Inc ....C 732 826-1018
Perth Amboy (G-8524)
Multi-Plastics Extrusions Inc ....F 732 388-2300
Avenel (G-138)
Nan Ya Plastics Corp USA ....G 973 992-1775
Livingston (G-5530)
North American Composites Co ....F 609 625-8101
Mays Landing (G-5996)
Nouryon Surface Chemistry ....D 732 985-6262
Edison (G-2579)
Palma Inc ....F 973 429-1490
Whippany (G-11901)
Petro Packaging Co Inc ....E 908 272-4054
Cranford (G-1922)
Phoenix Industries LLC ....G 973 366-4199
Wharton (G-11867)
Plaskolite New Jersey LLC ....C 908 486-1000
Linden (G-5410)
Plastics For Chemicals Inc ....G 609 242-9100
Forked River (G-3543)
Polymer Dynamix LLC ....F 732 381-1600
South Plainfield (G-10312)
Polymer Technologies Inc ....D 973 778-9100
Clifton (G-1695)
Polymeric Resources Corp ....E 973 694-4141
Wayne (G-11543)
Polyvel Inc ....E 609 567-0080
Hammonton (G-4142)
Rust-Oleum Corporation ....E 732 469-8100
Somerset (G-10069)
Safas Corporation ....E 973 772-5252
Clifton (G-1709)
Sika Corporation ....E 856 298-2313
Audubon (G-114)
Solidsurface Designs Inc ....E 856 910-7720
Pennsauken (G-8487)
Solvay USA Inc ....B 609 860-4000
Princeton (G-9025)
Solvay USA Inc ....C 732 297-0100
North Brunswick (G-7486)
Spartech LLC ....E 201 489-4000
Hackensack (G-3977)
Spartech LLC ....G 973 344-2700
Newark (G-7280)
Specialty Casting Inc ....E 856 845-3105
Woodbury (G-12038)
Synray Corporation ....E 908 245-2600
Kenilworth (G-4980)
Technick Products Inc ....F 908 791-0400
South Plainfield (G-10330)
Thibaut & Walker Co Inc ....G 973 589-3331
Newark (G-7296)
Trademark Plastics Corporation ....E 908 925-5900
Newark (G-7302)
Uvitec Printing Ink Co Inc ....E 973 778-0737
Lodi (G-5581)
Weavers Fiberglass ....G 609 597-4324
Manahawkin (G-5797)
Wilsonart LLC ....F 800 822-7613
Moorestown (G-6578)
Zahk Sales Inc ....G 516 633-9179
Branchburg (G-697)

PLASTICS MATERIALS, BASIC FORMS & SHAPES WHOLESALERS

Chemical Resources Inc ....E 609 520-0000
Princeton (G-8921)
D & D Technology Inc ....G 908 688-5154
Union (G-11040)
Exim Incorporated ....G 908 561-8200
Piscataway (G-8664)
Gdb International Inc ....D 732 246-3001
New Brunswick (G-6928)

PLASTICS PROCESSING

A S 4 Plastic Inc ....G...... 973 925-5223
Paterson *(G-8119)*

Acrylics Unlimited ....G...... 973 862-6014
Lafayette *(G-5024)*

Arpac Technology ....G...... 973 252-0012
Randolph *(G-9172)*

Enor Corporation ....C...... 201 750-1680
Englewood *(G-2902)*

Greenway Products & Svcs LLC ....E...... 732 442-0200
New Brunswick *(G-6932)*

Grewe Plastics Inc ....G...... 973 485-7602
Newark *(G-7140)*

Highland Products Inc ....G...... 973 366-0156
Dover *(G-2086)*

Lamart Corporation ....G...... 973 772-6262
Clifton *(G-1655)*

Multi-Plastics Inc ....E...... 856 241-9014
Swedesboro *(G-10598)*

Royce Associates A Ltd Partnr ....D...... 201 438-5200
East Rutherford *(G-2315)*

Sama Plastics Corp ....E...... 973 239-7200
Cedar Grove *(G-1292)*

Scott W Springman ....G...... 856 751-2411
Pennsauken *(G-8482)*

Town & Country Plastics Inc ....F...... 732 780-5300
Marlboro *(G-5917)*

United Eqp Fabricators LLC ....G...... 973 242-2737
Newark *(G-7308)*

Whe Research Inc ....G...... 732 240-3871
Toms River *(G-10803)*

PLASTICS SHEET: Packing Materials

Air Protection Packaging Corp ....F...... 973 577-4343
Linden *(G-5317)*

Amcor Flexibles Inc ....E...... 609 267-5900
Mount Holly *(G-6723)*

Amcor Flexibles LLC ....C...... 856 825-1400
Millville *(G-6224)*

Broadway Kleer-Guard Corp ....E...... 609 662-3970
Monroe Township *(G-6330)*

Lally-Pak Inc ....D...... 908 351-4141
Hillside *(G-4409)*

Lps Industries Inc ....C...... 201 438-3515
Moonachie *(G-6477)*

Package Development Co Inc ....E...... 973 983-8500
Rockaway *(G-9483)*

Petro Packaging Co Inc ....E...... 908 272-4054
Cranford *(G-1922)*

Poly-Smith Ptfe LLC ....F...... 732 287-0610
Keyport *(G-5004)*

PLASTICS: Blow Molded

Big 3 Precision Products Inc ....G...... 856 293-1400
Millville *(G-6236)*

Holocraft Corporation ....D...... 732 502-9500
Neptune *(G-6885)*

Seajay Manufacturing Corp ....F...... 732 774-0900
Neptune *(G-6897)*

PLASTICS: Extruded

Aflex Extrusion Technologies ....E...... 732 752-0048
Piscataway *(G-8626)*

E & T Plastic Mfg Co Inc ....E...... 201 596-5017
Teterboro *(G-10671)*

E & T Plastic Mfg Co Inc ....G...... 856 787-0900
Mount Laurel *(G-6754)*

Leco Plastics Inc ....F...... 201 343-3330
Hackensack *(G-3938)*

Patwin Plastics Inc ....E...... 908 486-6600
Linden *(G-5405)*

Petro Extrusion Tech Inc ....E...... 908 789-3338
Middlesex *(G-6137)*

Petro Plastics Company Inc ....E...... 908 789-1200
Kenilworth *(G-4969)*

Poly Source Enterprises LLC ....G...... 732 580-5409
Freehold *(G-3688)*

Rotuba Extruders Inc ....C...... 908 486-1000
Linden *(G-5416)*

T & B Specialties Inc ....G...... 732 928-4500
Jackson *(G-4666)*

Thermoplastics Bio-Logics LLC ....F...... 973 383-2834
Sparta *(G-10411)*

World Plastic Extruders Inc ....D...... 201 933-2915
Rutherford *(G-9635)*

PLASTICS: Finished Injection Molded

Design Display Group Inc ....C...... 201 438-6000
Carlstadt *(G-1150)*

Emdeon Corporation ....A...... 201 703-3400
Elmwood Park *(G-2825)*

Engineering Laboratories Inc ....E...... 201 337-8116
Oakland *(G-7627)*

Farmplast LLC ....G...... 973 287-6070
Parsippany *(G-7942)*

Flex Moulding Inc ....G...... 201 487-8080
Hackensack *(G-3915)*

Iron Mountain Plastics Inc ....F...... 201 445-0063
Midland Park *(G-6178)*

LNS Inc ....F...... 609 927-6656
Egg Harbor Township *(G-2688)*

Owens Plastic Products Inc ....G...... 856 447-3500
Cedarville *(G-1317)*

Pmp Composites Corporation ....E...... 609 587-1188
Trenton *(G-10975)*

Polymer Molded Products ....G...... 732 907-1990
Bound Brook *(G-604)*

Pro Plastics Inc ....E...... 908 925-5555
Linden *(G-5412)*

S&A Molders Inc ....G...... 732 851-7770
Manalapan *(G-5825)*

Wilpak Industries Inc ....E...... 201 997-7600
Kearny *(G-4907)*

Yuhl Products Inc ....G...... 908 276-5180
Kenilworth *(G-4991)*

PLASTICS: Injection Molded

A R C Plasmet Corp ....F...... 201 867-8533
North Bergen *(G-7379)*

Accurate Mold Inc ....E...... 856 784-8484
Somerdale *(G-9929)*

Allgrind Plastics Inc ....F...... 908 479-4400
Asbury *(G-57)*

Alva-Tech Inc ....E...... 609 747-1133
Burlington Township *(G-995)*

B & W Plastics Inc ....G...... 973 383-0020
Sparta *(G-10380)*

Be & K Plastics LLC ....F...... 609 386-3200
Burlington *(G-954)*

Brent River Corp ....E...... 908 722-6021
Hillsborough *(G-4307)*

Comet Tool Company Inc ....D...... 856 256-1070
Pitman *(G-8743)*

Continental Precision Corp ....C...... 908 754-3030
Piscataway *(G-8650)*

Custom Molders Corp ....D...... 908 218-7997
Branchburg *(G-634)*

Design & Molding Services Inc ....G...... 732 752-0300
Piscataway *(G-8654)*

Duerr Tool & Die Co Inc ....C...... 908 810-9035
Union *(G-11044)*

East Coast Plastics Inc ....E...... 856 768-8700
West Berlin *(G-11592)*

Echo Molding Inc ....E...... 908 688-0099
Union *(G-11049)*

Engineered Plastic Pdts Inc ....E...... 908 647-3500
Stirling *(G-10489)*

Ethylene Atlantic Corp ....E...... 856 467-0010
Swedesboro *(G-10584)*

Exothermic Molding Inc ....E...... 908 272-2299
Kenilworth *(G-4937)*

Fram Trak Industries Inc ....E...... 732 424-8400
Middlesex *(G-6117)*

Fredon Development Inds LLC ....F...... 973 383-7576
Newton *(G-7343)*

Frisch Plastics Corp ....G...... 973 685-5936
Pine Brook *(G-8602)*

Gifford Group Inc ....F...... 212 569-8500
Kearny *(G-4860)*

Hathaway Plastic ....G...... 908 688-9494
Union *(G-11062)*

Heyco Molded Products Inc ....F...... 732 286-4336
Toms River *(G-10765)*

Honeyware Inc ....D...... 201 997-5900
Kearny *(G-4863)*

Hot Runner Technology ....G...... 908 431-5711
Hillsborough *(G-4325)*

Injection Works Inc ....E...... 856 802-6444
Mount Laurel *(G-6767)*

Injectron Corporation ....B...... 908 753-1990
Plainfield *(G-8769)*

Inman Mold and Mfg Co ....G...... 732 381-3033
Springfield *(G-10446)*

Inman Mold and Mfg Co ....G...... 732 381-3033
Rahway *(G-9103)*

Intek Plastics Inc ....E...... 973 427-7331
Hawthorne *(G-4226)*

J-Mac Plastics Inc ....E...... 908 709-1111
Kenilworth *(G-4949)*

Koba Corp ....D...... 732 469-0110
Middlesex *(G-6124)*

Linden Mold and Tool Corp ....E...... 732 381-1411
Rahway *(G-9114)*

Medplast West Berlin Inc ....E...... 856 753-7600
West Berlin *(G-11607)*

Microcast Technologies Corp ....D...... 908 523-9503
Linden *(G-5385)*

Montrose Molders Corporation ....E...... 908 754-3030
Piscataway *(G-8692)*

Northland Tooling Technologies ....G...... 908 850-0023
Hackettstown *(G-4030)*

Novembal USA Inc ....E...... 732 947-3030
Edison *(G-2581)*

Pierson Industries Inc ....C...... 973 627-7945
Rockaway *(G-9486)*

Plasti Foam ....D...... 908 722-5254
Branchburg *(G-668)*

PMC Group Inc ....F...... 856 533-1866
Mount Laurel *(G-6791)*

Polycel Structural Foam Inc ....G...... 908 722-5254
Branchburg *(G-669)*

Polycel Structural Foam Inc ....E...... 908 722-5254
Branchburg *(G-670)*

Precise Technology Inc ....E...... 856 241-1760
Swedesboro *(G-10603)*

Preferred Plastics Inc ....G...... 856 662-6250
Pennsauken *(G-8470)*

Princeton Tectonics ....C...... 609 298-9331
Pennsauken *(G-8472)*

Pure Tech International Inc ....E...... 908 722-4800
Branchburg *(G-674)*

Rapid Manufacturing Co Inc ....E...... 732 279-1252
Toms River *(G-10787)*

Reiss Manufacturing Inc ....C...... 732 446-6100
Rumson *(G-9602)*

Sonetronics Inc ....D...... 732 681-5016
Belmar *(G-354)*

Swm Spotswood Mill ....G...... 732 723-6102
Spotswood *(G-10419)*

T & M Newton Corporation ....G...... 973 383-1232
Newton *(G-7361)*

Tech Products Co Inc ....F...... 201 444-7777
Midland Park *(G-6188)*

Technimold Inc ....E...... 908 232-8331
Flemington *(G-3470)*

Technitool Inc ....E...... 856 768-2707
West Berlin *(G-11626)*

Tektite Industries Inc ....G...... 609 656-0600
Trenton *(G-10997)*

Tri Tech Tool & Design Co Inc ....E...... 732 469-5433
South Bound Brook *(G-10144)*

Waldwick Plastics Corp ....G...... 201 445-7436
Waldwick *(G-11311)*

Weiss-Aug Co Inc ....C...... 973 887-7600
East Hanover *(G-2246)*

Westar Tool LLC ....G...... 856 507-8852
West Berlin *(G-11633)*

PLASTICS: Molded

Advantage Molding Products ....F...... 732 303-8667
Sea Girt *(G-9745)*

Advantage Molding Products ....G...... 732 303-8667
Freehold *(G-3643)*

Don Shrts Pcture Frmes Molding ....G...... 732 363-1323
Howell *(G-4537)*

Garfield Molding Co Inc ....E...... 973 777-5700
Wallington *(G-11386)*

Hartmann Tool Co Inc ....G...... 201 343-8700
Hackensack *(G-3926)*

Jersey Plastic Molders Inc ....C...... 973 926-1800
Irvington *(G-4578)*

Life of Party LLC ....E...... 732 828-0886
North Brunswick *(G-7475)*

Metrie Inc ....F...... 973 584-0040
Randolph *(G-9191)*

Molders Fishing Preserve ....G...... 732 446-2850
Jamesburg *(G-4674)*

National Casein New Jersey Inc ....E...... 856 829-1880
Cinnaminson *(G-1476)*

Norlo of New Jersey LLC ....G...... 646 492-3293
Montclair *(G-6378)*

Plastasonics Inc ....F...... 732 998-8361
Bayville *(G-250)*

Sinclair and Rush Inc ....G...... 862 262-8189
Carlstadt *(G-1217)*

Tek Molding ....G...... 973 702-0450
 Sussex *(G-10567)*
Thermo Plastic Tech Inc ....E...... 908 687-4833
 Union *(G-11095)*
Valley Plastic Molding Co..............F...... 973 334-2100
 Boonton *(G-572)*
Van Ness Plastic Molding Co..........C...... 973 778-9500
 Clifton *(G-1734)*
Viz Mold & Die Ltd ....F...... 201 784-8383
 Northvale *(G-7553)*

PLASTICS: Polystyrene Foam

Capitol Foam Products Inc ....E...... 201 933-5277
 East Rutherford *(G-2283)*
Glopak Corp ....E...... 908 753-8735
 South Plainfield *(G-10267)*
Innocor Foam Technologies LLC ......C...... 844 824-9348
 Red Bank *(G-9232)*
Instapak Corp Sealed Air ....D...... 201 791-7600
 Rochelle Park *(G-9424)*
New Dimensions Industries LLC ....G...... 201 531-1010
 West Berlin *(G-11610)*
Ocean Foam Fabricators LLC............E...... 973 745-1445
 Belleville *(G-304)*
Plastic Plus Inc ....G...... 973 614-0271
 Passaic *(G-8095)*
Pmc Inc ....B...... 201 933-8540
 East Rutherford *(G-2310)*
Rempac Foam Corp ....F...... 973 881-8880
 Rochelle Park *(G-9430)*
Rempac LLC ....C...... 201 843-4585
 Rochelle Park *(G-9431)*
Sekisui America Corporation ....F...... 201 423-7960
 Secaucus *(G-9813)*
T C P Reliable Manufacturing ....E...... 732 346-9200
 Edison *(G-2630)*

PLASTICS: Thermoformed

Brisar Industries Inc ....D...... 973 278-2500
 Paterson *(G-8150)*
Delvco Pharma Packg Svcs Inc ....D...... 973 278-2500
 Paterson *(G-8172)*
Madan Plastics Inc ....D...... 908 276-8484
 Cranford *(G-1915)*
Productive Plastics Inc...................D...... 856 778-4300
 Mount Laurel *(G-6796)*
Veloso Industries Inc ....G...... 908 925-0999
 Linden *(G-5440)*

PLATE WORK: Metalworking Trade

Able Fab Co ....E...... 732 396-0600
 Avenel *(G-118)*
Sheet Metal Products Inc ....D...... 973 482-0450
 Newark *(G-7269)*
Tolan Machinery Polishing Co..........E...... 973 983-7212
 Rockaway *(G-9507)*

PLATEMAKING SVC: Color Separations, For The Printing Trade

R P R Graphics Inc.........................E...... 908 654-8080
 Peapack *(G-8345)*

PLATEMAKING SVC: Embossing, For The Printing Trade

Standard Embossing Plate Mfg.........G....... 973 344-6670
 Newark *(G-7284)*

PLATEMAKING SVC: Gravure, Plates Or Cylinders

SGS International Inc......................G...... 718 836-1000
 Kenilworth *(G-4978)*

PLATEMAKING SVC: Letterpress

Downtown Printing Center Inc.............F...... 732 246-7990
 New Brunswick *(G-6920)*

PLATES

Acme Engraving Co Inc....................E...... 973 778-0885
 Passaic *(G-8050)*
Advertisers Service Group Inc ....F...... 201 440-5577
 Ridgefield Park *(G-9298)*
Celebration (us) Inc ....C...... 609 261-5200
 Lumberton *(G-5626)*

Container Graphics Corp ....E...... 732 922-1180
 Neptune *(G-6870)*
E I Du Pont De Nemours & Co ....E...... 732 257-1579
 Parlin *(G-7863)*
Essex West Graphics Inc ....D...... 973 227-2400
 Fairfield *(G-3192)*
Garrison Printing Company Inc...........E...... 856 488-1900
 Pennsauken *(G-8424)*
Globe Photo Engraving Co LLC ....E...... 201 489-2300
 Little Ferry *(G-5487)*
Grandview Printing Co Inc ....F...... 973 890-0006
 Totowa *(G-10831)*
Hatteras Press Inc ....B...... 732 935-9800
 Tinton Falls *(G-10718)*
Howard Press Inc ....D...... 908 245-4400
 Roselle *(G-9561)*
Lacoa Inc ....G...... 973 754-1000
 Elmwood Park *(G-2837)*
Mariano Press LLC ....F...... 732 247-3659
 Somerset *(G-10022)*
Mark/Trece Inc ....E...... 973 884-1005
 Whippany *(G-11897)*
Marko Engraving & Art Corp ....F...... 201 864-6500
 Weehawken *(G-11569)*
Marko Engraving & Art Corp ....F...... 201 945-6555
 Fairview *(G-3363)*
Mosstype Holding Corp ....E...... 201 444-8000
 Waldwick *(G-11307)*
Nassau Communications Inc ....F...... 609 208-9099
 Lawrence Township *(G-5218)*
Staines Inc ....F...... 856 784-2718
 Somerdale *(G-9935)*
Tangent Graphics Inc ....G...... 201 488-2840
 Englewood *(G-2946)*
Toppan Printing Co Amer Inc............C...... 732 469-8400
 Somerset *(G-10088)*
Unity Graphics & Engraving Co ....E...... 201 541-5462
 Englewood *(G-2950)*

PLATES: Sheet & Strip, Exc Coated Prdts

Benedict-Miller LLC ....F...... 908 497-1477
 Kenilworth *(G-4929)*

PLATES: Steel

Archer Day Inc...............................E...... 732 396-0600
 Avenel *(G-120)*

PLATING & FINISHING SVC: Decorative, Formed Prdts

Zsombor Antal Designs Inc ....F...... 201 225-1750
 River Edge *(G-9364)*

PLATING & POLISHING SVC

A&A Company Inc ....E...... 908 561-2378
 South Plainfield *(G-10205)*
Acme Engraving Co Inc....................E...... 973 778-0885
 Passaic *(G-8050)*
Boyko Metal Finishing Co Inc ....G...... 973 623-4254
 Newark *(G-7072)*
Boyko Metal Finishing Co Inc ....D...... 973 623-4254
 Newark *(G-7071)*
Hard Crome Solutions ....G...... 732 500-2568
 Metuchen *(G-6060)*
Intrepid Industries Inc ....G...... 908 534-5300
 Lebanon *(G-5265)*
J R S Tool & Metal Finishing............G...... 908 753-2050
 South Plainfield *(G-10282)*
Mold Polishing Company Inc ....G...... 908 518-9191
 Garwood *(G-3785)*
Productive Industrial Finshg ....G...... 856 427-9646
 Voorhees *(G-11292)*
Stirrup Metal Products Corp ....F...... 973 824-7086
 Newark *(G-7287)*

PLATING COMPOUNDS

Krohn Technical Products Inc ....F...... 201 933-9696
 Carlstadt *(G-1179)*
Omg Electronic Chemicals Inc ....C...... 908 222-5800
 South Plainfield *(G-10311)*

PLATING SVC: Chromium, Metals Or Formed Prdts

Industrial Hard Chromium Co.............F...... 973 344-2265
 Newark *(G-7156)*

PLATING SVC: Electro

A & F Electroplating Inc ....G...... 973 983-2459
 West Orange *(G-11757)*
Accu-Cote Inc ....G...... 856 845-7323
 Thorofare *(G-10698)*
Alcaro & Alcaro Plating Co ....E...... 973 746-1200
 Montclair *(G-6357)*
Deptford Plating Co Inc ....G...... 856 227-1144
 Deptford *(G-2063)*
E C Electroplating Inc ....G...... 973 340-0227
 Garfield *(G-3740)*
Elkem Inc ....G...... 732 566-1700
 Cliffwood *(G-1546)*
FER Plating Inc..............................E...... 201 438-1010
 Lyndhurst *(G-5655)*
G & H Metal Finishers Inc ....G...... 201 909-9808
 Paterson *(G-8196)*
General Magnaplate Corporation ....D...... 908 862-6200
 Linden *(G-5351)*
Hill Cross Co Inc ....G...... 201 864-3393
 West New York *(G-11740)*
Madan Plastics Inc ....D...... 908 276-8484
 Cranford *(G-1915)*
Manco Plating Incorporated.............G...... 973 485-6800
 Newark *(G-7195)*
Metal Finishing Co LLC ....G...... 973 778-9550
 Passaic *(G-8089)*
Miller & Son ....G...... 973 759-6445
 Belleville *(G-301)*
National Mtal Fnshngs Corp Inc..........F...... 732 752-7770
 Middlesex *(G-6133)*
New Brunswick Plating Inc ....D...... 732 545-6522
 New Brunswick *(G-6953)*
Paramount Plating Co Inc ....E...... 908 862-0772
 Linden *(G-5404)*
Polaris Plating Inc.........................G...... 973 278-0033
 Parsippany *(G-7998)*
Suffern Plating Corp ....E...... 973 473-4404
 Lodi *(G-5578)*
Vanguard Research Industries ....E...... 908 753-2770
 South Plainfield *(G-10340)*

PLATING SVC: NEC

Art Metalcraft Plating Co Inc............F...... 215 923-6625
 Camden *(G-1040)*
Carlton Coke Met Fnishings LLC ....G...... 732 774-2210
 Asbury Park *(G-72)*
Cramer Plating Inc ....E...... 908 453-2887
 Buttzville *(G-1016)*
DAngelo Metal Products Inc ....F...... 908 862-8220
 Linden *(G-5341)*
Glasseal Products Inc ....C...... 732 370-9100
 Lakewood *(G-5104)*
Ideal Plating & Polishing Co ....F...... 973 759-5559
 Paterson *(G-8212)*
Mara Polishing & Plating Corp ....G...... 973 242-0800
 Newark *(G-7196)*
Patel Metal Plating Inc ....G...... 732 574-1770
 Edison *(G-2588)*
Platinum Plating Specialists..............G...... 732 221-2575
 Clark *(G-1513)*
Programatic Platers Inc...................F...... 718 721-4330
 Tenafly *(G-10665)*
Tomken Plating ....G...... 856 829-0607
 Cinnaminson *(G-1491)*

PLAYGROUND EQPT

De Zaio Productions Inc..................D...... 973 423-5000
 Fair Lawn *(G-3095)*

PLEATING & STITCHING FOR THE TRADE: Decorative & Novelty

Avanti Linens Inc ....C...... 201 641-7766
 Moonachie *(G-6455)*

PLEATING & STITCHING FOR THE TRADE: Lace, Burnt-Out

Carolace Embroidery Co Inc...............D...... 201 945-2151
 Ridgefield *(G-9253)*

PLEATING & STITCHING FOR THE TRADE: Scalloping

Walker Eight Corp ....G...... 201 861-4208
 North Bergen *(G-7443)*

Employee Codes: A=Over 500 employees, B=251-500
C=101-250, D=51-100, E=20-50, F=10-19, G=4-9 2019 Harris New Jersey
Manufacturers Directory   907

P
R
O
D
U
C
T

PLEATING & STITCHING FOR TRADE: Permanent Pleating/Pressing

Central Safety Equipment Co ....E 609 386-6448
Burlington **(G-958)**

PLEATING & STITCHING SVC

Aztec Graphics Inc.....................F 609 587-1000
Trenton **(G-10900)**
Family Screen Printing Inc.................F 856 933-2780
Bellmawr **(G-332)**
Goralski Inc ....E 201 573-1529
Park Ridge **(G-7851)**
Monogram Center Inc ....E 732 442-1800
Perth Amboy **(G-8528)**
O Stitch Matic Inc ....G 201 861-3045
Guttenberg **(G-3871)**
Quadelle Textile Corp ....F 201 865-1112
West New York **(G-11752)**
Red Diamond Co - Athc Letering..........G 973 759-2005
Belleville **(G-310)**
Tone Embroidery Corp ....E 201 943-1082
Fairview **(G-3371)**

PLUMBING & HEATING EQPT & SPLY, WHOL: Htg Eqpt/Panels, Solar

I4 Sustainability LLC.....................G 732 618-3310
Springfield **(G-10445)**
Mc Renewable Energy LLC ....F 732 369-9933
Manasquan **(G-5833)**
Sun Pacific Power Corp ....F 888 845-0242
Manalapan **(G-5826)**
Worldwide Solar Mfg LLC ....G 201 297-1177
Closter **(G-1765)**

PLUMBING & HEATING EQPT & SPLY, WHOLESALE: Hydronic Htg Eqpt

Encur Inc................................G 732 264-2098
Keyport **(G-4998)**

PLUMBING & HEATING EQPT & SPLYS WHOLESALERS

Frank Burton & Sons Inc.................G 856 455-1202
Bridgeton **(G-758)**
Samstubend Inc ....F 973 278-2555
Paterson **(G-8293)**

PLUMBING & HEATING EQPT & SPLYS, WHOL: Pipe/Fitting, Plastic

Morris Industries Inc....................D 973 835-6600
Pompton Plains **(G-8868)**

PLUMBING & HEATING EQPT & SPLYS, WHOL: Plumbing Fitting/Sply

Durst Corporation Inc ....E 800 852-3906
Cranford **(G-1907)**
Everflow Supplies Inc...................E 908 436-1100
Carteret **(G-1252)**
Grove Supply Inc ....E 856 205-0687
Vineland **(G-11228)**
Kessler Industries.......................G 973 279-1417
Paterson **(G-8229)**
U V International LLC ....G 973 993-9454
Morristown **(G-6705)**

PLUMBING & HEATING EQPT & SPLYS, WHOL: Water Purif Eqpt

Dynatec Systems Inc ....F 609 387-0330
Burlington **(G-965)**
Favs Corp ....G 856 358-1515
Elmer **(G-2797)**
Liquid-Solids Separation Corp ....E 201 236-4833
Ramsey **(G-9149)**

PLUMBING & HEATING EQPT & SPLYS, WHOLESALE: Oil Burners

Industrial Combustion Assn ....F 732 271-0300
Somerset **(G-10004)**

PLUMBING FIXTURES

As America Inc ....C 732 980-3000
Piscataway **(G-8637)**

Bruce Supply Corp ....F 732 661-0500
Keasbey **(G-4909)**
Carpenter & Paterson Inc...............E 609 227-2750
Bordentown **(G-578)**
Chatham Brass Co Inc ....G 908 668-0500
South Plainfield **(G-10237)**
DAngelo Metal Products Inc ....F 908 862-8220
Linden **(G-5341)**
Grove Supply Inc ....G 856 205-0687
Vineland **(G-11228)**
Kessler Industries.......................G 973 279-1417
Paterson **(G-8229)**
Kissler & Co Inc ....E 201 896-9600
Carlstadt **(G-1175)**
Knickerbocker Machine Shop Inc ....D 973 256-1616
Totowa **(G-10834)**
Specialty Products Plus ....G 732 380-1188
West Long Branch **(G-11723)**
Wm Steinen Mfg Co ....D 973 887-6400
Parsippany **(G-8042)**

PLUMBING FIXTURES: Brass, Incl Drain Cocks, Faucets/Spigots

El Batal Corporation ....F 908 964-3427
Union **(G-11050)**

PLUMBING FIXTURES: Plastic

Ace Restoration ....G 267 897-2384
Sewell **(G-9833)**
Sell All Properties LLC ....F 856 963-8800
Camden **(G-1087)**
Town & Country Plastics Inc..............F 732 780-5300
Marlboro **(G-5917)**

PLUMBING FIXTURES: Vitreous

As America Inc ....C 732 980-3000
Piscataway **(G-8637)**
Benco Inc ....F 973 575-4440
Fairfield **(G-3154)**
Ecom Group Inc ....E 718 504-7355
Edison **(G-2498)**

PLUMBING FIXTURES: Vitreous China

New Jersey Porcelain Co Inc ....F 609 394-5376
Trenton **(G-10963)**

POINT OF SALE DEVICES

Business Control Systems Corp...........F 732 283-1301
Iselin **(G-4603)**
Comtrex Systems Corporation ....E 856 778-0090
Moorestown **(G-6515)**

POLISHING SVC: Metals Or Formed Prdts

All Metal Polishing Co Inc ....E 973 589-8070
Newark **(G-7038)**
Art Mold & Polishing Co Inc ....F 908 518-9191
Roselle **(G-9548)**
Stainless Stock ....G 732 564-1164
Middlesex **(G-6153)**
Vortex Supply LLC ....G 856 352-6681
Blackwood **(G-483)**
Water Master Co ....G 732 247-1900
Highland Park **(G-4289)**

POLYAMIDES

Hitachi Chem Dupont Microsyst...........E 732 613-2175
Parlin **(G-7864)**

POLYESTERS

Coim USA Inc ....G 856 224-8560
West Deptford **(G-11700)**

POLYETHYLENE CHLOROSULFONATED RUBBER

Lyondell Chemical Company ....G 973 578-2200
Newark **(G-7192)**

POLYETHYLENE RESINS

Polyfil Corporation......................E 973 627-4070
Rockaway **(G-9488)**
Recycle Inc East ....D 908 756-2200
South Plainfield **(G-10325)**

POLYPROPYLENE RESINS

Atlantic Lining Co Inc ....E 609 723-2400
Jobstown **(G-4836)**

POLYTETRAFLUOROETHYLENE RESINS

Cain Machine Inc........................F 856 825-7225
Millville **(G-6240)**

POLYVINYL CHLORIDE RESINS

Berry Global Films LLC ....C 201 641-6600
Montvale **(G-6400)**
Breen Color Concentrates LLC ....F 609 397-8200
Lambertville **(G-5187)**
Formosa Plastics Corp USA ....B 973 992-2090
Livingston **(G-5511)**
J-M Manufacturing Company Inc ....D 800 621-4404
Livingston **(G-5517)**
Phoenix Manufactoring Inc ....G 732 380-1666
Ocean **(G-7675)**
Rimtec Manufacturing Corp ....E 609 387-0011
Burlington **(G-983)**
Surface Source Intl Inc ....F 973 598-0152
Randolph **(G-9202)**

POPCORN & SUPPLIES WHOLESALERS

Continntal Concession Sups Inc ....E 516 629-4906
Union **(G-11037)**

POULTRY & POULTRY PRDTS WHOLESALERS

Farbest-Tallman Foods Corp ....D 714 897-7199
Park Ridge **(G-7849)**

POULTRY & SMALL GAME SLAUGHTERING & PROCESSING

Carl Streit & Son Co ....G 732 775-0803
Neptune **(G-6869)**
David Mitchell Inc......................E 856 429-2610
Voorhees **(G-11284)**
Ena Meat Packing Inc ....E 973 742-4790
Paterson **(G-8184)**
Perdue Farms Inc ....G 609 298-4100
Bridgeton **(G-768)**
Senat Poultry LLC ....E 973 742-9316
Paterson **(G-8298)**
Vineland Kosher Poultry Inc ....C 856 692-1871
Vineland **(G-11275)**

POULTRY SLAUGHTERING & PROCESSING

Park Avenue Meats Inc ....E 718 731-4196
Paterson **(G-8278)**

POULTRY, PACKAGED FROZEN: Wholesalers

South Jersey Pretzel Inc ....F 856 435-5055
Stratford **(G-10507)**

POWDER: Metal

Acupowder International LLC ....G 908 851-4500
Union **(G-11019)**
Atlantic Eqp Engineers Inc ....F 201 828-9400
Upper Saddle River **(G-11134)**
FW Winter Inc ....E 856 963-7490
Camden **(G-1065)**

POWDERS, FLAVORING, EXC DRINK

Akay USA LLC ....G 732 254-7177
Sayreville **(G-9700)**
Del-Val Food Ingredients Inc.............F 856 778-6623
Mount Laurel **(G-6752)**
Jk Ingredients Inc ....D 973 340-8700
Paterson **(G-8224)**
Robertet Flavors Inc ....F 732 271-1804
Piscataway **(G-8706)**

POWER SPLY CONVERTERS: Static, Electronic Applications

Infiniti Components Inc ....G 908 537-9950
Hampton **(G-4156)**
Technology Dynamics Inc ....D 201 385-0500
Bergenfield **(G-385)**

POWER SUPPLIES: All Types, Static

ADI American Distributors LLC ....D 973 328-1181
  Randolph *(G-9169)*
Advanced Energy Voorhees Inc ....D 856 627-1287
  Voorhees *(G-11279)*
AT&T Technologies Inc ....A 201 771-2000
  Berkeley Heights *(G-389)*
Clantech Inc.......................................G 908 281-7667
  Hillsborough *(G-4310)*
Crestek Inc..E 609 883-4000
  Ewing *(G-3024)*
Idt Energy Inc ....E 877 887-6866
  Newark *(G-7154)*
Jerome Industries Corp ....E 908 353-5700
  Hackettstown *(G-4013)*
Nwl Inc ....C 609 298-7300
  Bordentown *(G-591)*
Technology Dynamics Inc ....D 201 385-0500
  Bergenfield *(G-386)*
Transistor Devices Inc ....C 908 850-5088
  Hackettstown *(G-4040)*
Uthe Technology Inc ....G 609 883-4000
  Trenton *(G-11007)*
West Electronics Inc ....F 609 387-4300
  Burlington *(G-993)*

POWER SUPPLIES: Transformer, Electronic Type

Electronic Transformer Corp ....E 973 942-2222
  Paterson *(G-8177)*
Jinpan International USA Ltd ....G 201 460-8778
  Carlstadt *(G-1170)*

POWER SWITCHING EQPT

Sigma-Netics Inc................................E 973 227-6372
  Riverdale *(G-9385)*
Technology Dynamics Inc....................D 201 385-0500
  Bergenfield *(G-385)*

POWER TOOLS, HAND: Cartridge-Activated

Dcm Clean Air Products Inc.................G 732 363-2100
  Lakewood *(G-5082)*
Rennsteig Tools Inc ....G 330 315-3044
  Hackensack *(G-3966)*

POWER TOOLS, HAND: Drill Attachments, Portable

Toydriver LLC ....G 678 637-8500
  Garfield *(G-3774)*

POWER TOOLS, HAND: Drills & Drilling Tools

J Paul Allen Inc ....G 973 702-1174
  Sussex *(G-10563)*

POWER TRANSMISSION EQPT WHOLESALERS

Sew-Eurodrive Inc..............................E 856 467-2277
  Bridgeport *(G-744)*

POWER TRANSMISSION EQPT: Aircraft

Simtek Usa Inc ....G 862 757-8130
  Little Falls *(G-5467)*

POWER TRANSMISSION EQPT: Mechanical

A M Gatti Inc ....F 609 396-1577
  Trenton *(G-10886)*
Accurate Bronze Bearing Co ....G 973 345-2304
  Paterson *(G-8124)*
Accurate Bushing Company Inc............E 908 789-1121
  Garwood *(G-3779)*
Andantex U S A Inc............................E 732 493-2812
  Ocean *(G-7655)*
Daven Industries Inc..........................E 973 808-8848
  Fairfield *(G-3180)*
Gate Technologies Inc ....G 973 300-0090
  Sparta *(G-10388)*
Hydro-Mechanical Systems Inc ....F 856 848-8888
  Westville *(G-11816)*
Martin Sprocket & Gear Inc ....F 973 633-5700
  Wayne *(G-11534)*
Moser Jewel Company ....G 908 454-1155
  Phillipsburg *(G-8564)*

Reich USA Corporation ....F 201 684-9400
  Mahwah *(G-5767)*
Spadone Alfa Self Lbrcted Pdts ....F 203 972-8848
  Brick *(G-732)*
Valcor Engineering Corporation ....E 973 467-8100
  Springfield *(G-10473)*
Woyshner Service Company Inc ....G 856 461-9196
  Delran *(G-2022)*

PRECAST TERRAZZO OR CONCRETE PRDTS

J L Erectors Inc ....E 856 232-9400
  Blackwood *(G-470)*
Massarellis Lawn Ornaments Inc ....E 609 567-9700
  Hammonton *(G-4139)*

PRECIOUS METALS

Matthey Johnson Inc ....C 856 384-7132
  West Deptford *(G-11710)*

PRECIOUS METALS WHOLESALERS

Dxl Enterprises Inc ....F 201 891-8718
  Mahwah *(G-5733)*
Hickok Matthews Co Inc......................G 973 335-3400
  Montville *(G-6443)*

PRECISION INSTRUMENT REPAIR SVCS

Sprialseal Inc....................................G 732 738-6113
  Cliffwood *(G-1547)*

PREFABRICATED BUILDING DEALERS

Benco Inc ....F 973 575-4440
  Fairfield *(G-3154)*

PRERECORDED TAPE, COMPACT DISC & RECORD STORES

Sony Music Holdings Inc ....B 201 777-3933
  Rutherford *(G-9634)*

PRERECORDED TAPE, COMPACT DISC & RECORD STORES: Records

Riotsound Inc ....G 917 273-5814
  Newton *(G-7355)*

PRESCHOOL CENTERS

Almond Branch Inc ....E 973 728-3479
  West Milford *(G-11724)*

PRESSURE COOKERS: Stamped Or Drawn Metal

Manttra Inc ....G 877 962-6887
  New Brunswick *(G-6944)*

PRESTRESSED CONCRETE PRDTS

Northeast Concrete Pdts LLC...............G 973 728-1667
  Hewitt *(G-4278)*

PRIMARY METAL PRODUCTS

Czar Industries Inc.............................G 609 392-1515
  Trenton *(G-10928)*
McW Precision ....F 609 859-4400
  Southampton *(G-10368)*
Sentry Mfg LLC ....G 856 642-0480
  Moorestown *(G-6566)*

PRINT CARTRIDGES: Laser & Other Computer Printers

Agoura Hills Group ....E 818 888-0400
  Cherry Hill *(G-1335)*
Bergen Cnty Crtrdge Xchnge LLC.........G 201 493-8182
  Midland Park *(G-6171)*
Clarity Imaging Solutions Inc ....G 866 684-2212
  Cherry Hill *(G-1353)*
GSC Imaging LLC ....E 856 317-9301
  Pennsauken *(G-8428)*
Turbon International Inc ....G 800 282-6650
  Cherry Hill *(G-1424)*
Turbon International Inc ....G 413 386-6739
  Cherry Hill *(G-1425)*

PRINTED CIRCUIT BOARDS

ADI American Distributors LLC ....D 973 328-1181
  Randolph *(G-9169)*
Altus Pcb LLC ....F 877 442-5887
  Cresskill *(G-1941)*
Argus International Inc ....E 609 466-1677
  Ringoes *(G-9334)*
Cheringal Associates Inc ....D 201 784-8721
  Norwood *(G-7560)*
Circuit Reproduction Co ....F 201 712-9292
  Maywood *(G-6002)*
Circuit Tech Assembly LLC ....F 856 231-0777
  West Berlin *(G-11583)*
Computer Control Corp ....F 973 492-8265
  Butler *(G-998)*
Data Delay Devices ....E 973 202-3268
  Clifton *(G-1596)*
Delta Circuits Inc...............................E 973 575-3000
  Fairfield *(G-3183)*
Esi ....E 856 629-2492
  Sicklerville *(G-9909)*
ESP Associates Inc.............................F 973 208-9045
  Newfoundland *(G-7330)*
GAb Electronic Services LLC ....E 856 786-0108
  Cinnaminson *(G-1459)*
Garys Kids ....G 973 458-1818
  Passaic *(G-8067)*
Glenro Inc ....F 973 279-5900
  Paterson *(G-8199)*
J R E Inc ....E 973 808-0055
  West Caldwell *(G-11655)*
Jnbc Associates LLC ....G 973 560-5518
  Parsippany *(G-7967)*
Mdj Inc...E 201 457-9260
  Hackensack *(G-3945)*
Medco West Electronics Inc ....G 201 457-9260
  Hackensack *(G-3946)*
Mercury Systems Inc ....E 973 244-1040
  West Caldwell *(G-11664)*
Modelware Inc ....F 732 264-3020
  Holmdel *(G-4508)*
Ppi/Time Zero Inc ....C 973 278-6500
  Fairfield *(G-3293)*
Precision Products Co Inc ....E 201 712-5757
  Maywood *(G-6014)*
Quik Flex Circuit Inc ....F 856 742-0550
  Gloucester City *(G-3848)*
R & D Circuits Inc..............................C 732 549-4554
  South Plainfield *(G-10321)*
R R J Co Inc......................................E 732 544-1514
  Colts Neck *(G-1787)*
Redkoh Industries Inc ....G 908 369-1590
  Hillsborough *(G-4351)*
Scl ....E 908 391-9882
  Bridgewater *(G-888)*
South Jersey Circuits ....G 609 479-3994
  Burlington *(G-985)*
Spem Corporation ....E 732 356-3366
  Piscataway *(G-8717)*
Sure Design ....E 732 919-3066
  Wall Township *(G-11372)*
Swemco LLC ....C 856 222-9900
  Moorestown *(G-6570)*
Syscom Technologies Corp ....D 856 642-7661
  Moorestown *(G-6572)*
T V L Associates Inc ....G 973 790-6766
  Wayne *(G-11555)*
Technical Aids To Independence...........F 973 674-1082
  East Orange *(G-2265)*
Techniques Inc ....E 973 256-0947
  Woodland Park *(G-12092)*
Test Technology Inc............................D 856 596-1215
  Marlton *(G-5953)*
Thomas Instrumentation Inc ....F 609 624-2630
  Cape May Court House *(G-1116)*
Toby-Yanni Incorporated......................F 973 253-9800
  Garfield *(G-3773)*
Transistor Devices Inc ....C 908 850-5088
  Hackettstown *(G-4039)*
Wireworks Corporation ....E 908 686-7400
  Hillside *(G-4437)*

PRINTERS & PLOTTERS

Diversified Display Pdts LLC ....E 908 686-2200
  Hillside *(G-4389)*
Gulton Incorporated ....E 908 791-4622
  South Plainfield *(G-10271)*
Jetty Life LLC ....G 800 900-6435
  Manahawkin *(G-5793)*

PRODUCT

PRINTERS' SVCS: Folding, Collating, Etc

B&B Imaging LLC ....G...... 201 261-3131
  Paramus (G-7791)
Campbell Converting Corp ....G...... 609 835-2720
  Beverly (G-448)
Cox Stationers and Printers ....E...... 908 928-1010
  Linden (G-5338)
Dm Graphic Center LLC ....F...... 973 882-8990
  Fairfield (G-3186)
Semels Embroidery Inc ....F...... 973 473-6868
  Clifton (G-1713)
Strategic Content Imaging ....C...... 201 863-8100
  Secaucus (G-9819)

PRINTERS: Computer

Lexmark International Inc ....F...... 201 307-4600
  Park Ridge (G-7855)
Ricoh Prtg Systems Amer Inc.................G...... 973 316-6051
  Mountain Lakes (G-6827)

PRINTERS: Magnetic Ink, Bar Code

Alpha Tech Services ....G...... 973 283-2011
  Boonton (G-540)
Zebra Technologies Corporation..........B...... 609 383-8743
  Northfield (G-7512)

PRINTING & BINDING: Books

Aramani Inc ....G...... 201 945-1160
  Fairview (G-3356)

PRINTING & EMBOSSING: Plastic Fabric Articles

C S Hot Stamping.................................G...... 201 840-4004
  Edgewater (G-2435)

PRINTING & ENGRAVING: Financial Notes & Certificates

All-State International Inc....................C...... 908 272-0800
  Cranford (G-1899)
Data Communique Inc ....E...... 201 508-6000
  Ridgefield Park (G-9302)

PRINTING & ENGRAVING: Invitation & Stationery

Bellia & Sons.......................................E...... 856 845-2234
  Woodbury (G-12026)
E C D Ventures Inc ....G...... 856 875-1100
  Blackwood (G-465)
Engraved Images Ltd............................G...... 908 234-0323
  Far Hills (G-3375)
Envelopes & Printed Pdts Inc ....G...... 973 942-1232
  Prospect Park (G-9073)
Papery of Marlton LLC..........................G...... 856 985-1776
  Marlton (G-5946)
Party City Corporation..........................F...... 973 537-1707
  Randolph (G-9196)
Party City of North Bergen ....F...... 201 865-0040
  North Bergen (G-7427)
Remco Press Inc ....G...... 201 751-5703
  North Bergen (G-7433)
Sharp Impressions Inc ....G...... 201 573-4943
  Garfield (G-3767)

PRINTING & ENGRAVING: Poster & Decal

224 Graphics Inc ....F...... 973 433-9224
  Fairfield (G-3132)

PRINTING & STAMPING: Fabric Articles

Alchemy Billboards LLC ....G...... 973 977-8828
  Paterson (G-8131)
Custom Laminations Inc ....G...... 973 279-9174
  Paterson (G-8166)
Image Point..G...... 908 684-1768
  Newton (G-7346)
Mail Direct Paper Company LLC ....F...... 201 933-2782
  Lyndhurst (G-5660)

PRINTING & WRITING PAPER WHOLESALERS

G R Impex Ltd Liability Co ....F...... 301 873-5333
  Avenel (G-129)

Gdb International Inc ....D...... 732 246-3001
  New Brunswick (G-6928)
Thermo X-Press Printing LLC ....G...... 973 585-6505
  East Hanover (G-2241)

PRINTING INKS WHOLESALERS

B&B Imaging LLC ....G...... 201 261-3131
  Paramus (G-7791)
Prismacolor Corp ....G...... 973 887-6040
  Parsippany (G-8002)

PRINTING MACHINERY

Ackley Machine Corporation ....E...... 856 234-3626
  Moorestown (G-6500)
Acme Engraving Co Inc ....E...... 973 778-0885
  Passaic (G-8050)
Algene Marking Equipment Co ....G...... 973 478-9041
  Garfield (G-3727)
Ancraft Press Corp ....F...... 201 792-9200
  Jersey City (G-4691)
AT Information Products Inc ....G...... 201 529-0202
  Mahwah (G-5715)
Bell-Mark Sales Co Inc ....E...... 973 882-0202
  Pine Brook (G-8588)
Benton Graphics Inc ....E...... 609 587-4000
  Trenton (G-10903)
Blankets Inc ....E...... 973 589-7800
  Newark (G-7067)
Charles M Jessup Inc ....E...... 732 324-0430
  Keasbey (G-4910)
Convertech Inc ....E...... 973 328-1850
  Wharton (G-11854)
Custom Roller Inc ....G...... 908 298-7797
  Roselle (G-9556)
Deneka Printing Systems Inc................G...... 609 752-0964
  Cream Ridge (G-1934)
Digital Design Inc ....E...... 973 857-9500
  Cedar Grove (G-1274)
Domino Printing ....D...... 973 857-0900
  Cedar Grove (G-1276)
Graphic Equipment Corporation ....E...... 732 494-5350
  Metuchen (G-6058)
Interchange Equipment Inc ....E...... 973 473-5005
  Passaic (G-8074)
Kohl & Madden Prtg Ink Corp ....E...... 201 935-8666
  Carlstadt (G-1177)
Pamarco Global Graphics Inc ....E...... 908 241-1200
  Roselle (G-9568)
Pamarco Global Graphics Inc ....F...... 856 829-4585
  Palmyra (G-7785)
Pamarco Technologies LLC ....E...... 908 241-1200
  Roselle (G-9569)
Panpac LLC ....F...... 856 376-3576
  Cherry Hill (G-1405)
Printers Service Florida Inc ....G...... 973 589-7800
  Newark (G-7236)
W R Chesnut Engineering Inc................F...... 973 227-6995
  Fairfield (G-3349)
Zeiser Inc ....E...... 973 228-0800
  West Caldwell (G-11682)

PRINTING MACHINERY, EQPT & SPLYS: Wholesalers

Anderson & Vreeland Inc ....E...... 973 227-2270
  Fairfield (G-3143)
AT Information Products Inc ....G...... 201 529-0202
  Mahwah (G-5715)
Colter & Peterson Inc ....E...... 973 684-0901
  West Caldwell (G-11644)
Deleet Merchandising Corp ....E...... 212 962-6565
  Newark (G-7101)
Ernest Schaefer Inc ....G...... 908 964-1280
  Union (G-11052)
Interchange Equipment Inc ....E...... 973 473-5005
  Passaic (G-8074)
Superior Trademark Inc ....G...... 201 652-1900
  Waldwick (G-11310)

PRINTING, COMMERCIAL: Bags, Plastic, NEC

Lally-Pak Inc ....D...... 908 351-4141
  Hillside (G-4409)

PRINTING, COMMERCIAL: Business Forms, NEC

Campbell Converting Corp ....G...... 609 835-2720
  Beverly (G-448)
Earthcolor Inc ....C...... 973 884-1300
  Parsippany (G-7928)
Maggio Printing LLC.............................E...... 856 931-7805
  Bellmawr (G-338)
New Line Prtg & Tech Solutions ....G...... 973 405-6133
  Clifton (G-1676)
Stewart Business Forms Inc..................F...... 856 768-2011
  Blackwood (G-481)

PRINTING, COMMERCIAL: Calendars, NEC

Judith Roth Studio Collection ....G...... 973 543-4455
  Mendham (G-6039)

PRINTING, COMMERCIAL: Cards, Souvenir, NEC

Italian Treasures.................................G...... 856 770-9188
  Voorhees (G-11290)

PRINTING, COMMERCIAL: Catalogs, NEC

Platypus Print Productions LLC ....G...... 732 772-1212
  Morganville (G-6594)

PRINTING, COMMERCIAL: Decals, NEC

Kraftwork Custom Design.....................F...... 609 883-8444
  Ewing (G-3043)

PRINTING, COMMERCIAL: Directories, Exc Telephone, NEC

Lamb Printing Inc.................................G...... 908 852-0837
  Hackettstown (G-4016)

PRINTING, COMMERCIAL: Envelopes, NEC

John Patrick Publishing LLC.................D...... 609 883-2700
  Ewing (G-3038)
Liberty Envelope Inc ....F...... 973 546-5600
  Paterson (G-8240)
Old Ue LLC ....B...... 800 752-4012
  Ridgefield (G-9281)
Reliable Envelope and Graphics ....E...... 201 794-7756
  Elmwood Park (G-2854)
Sapphire Envelope & Graphics ....E...... 856 782-2227
  Magnolia (G-5709)

PRINTING, COMMERCIAL: Fashion Plates, NEC

Flanagan Holdings Inc..........................D...... 201 512-3338
  Mahwah (G-5737)

PRINTING, COMMERCIAL: Imprinting

Butler Prtg & Laminating Inc ....C...... 973 838-8550
  Butler (G-997)

PRINTING, COMMERCIAL: Labels & Seals, NEC

Alcop Adhesive Label Co ....G...... 609 871-4400
  Beverly (G-446)
Brimar Industries Inc ....E...... 973 340-7889
  Garfield (G-3733)
CCL Label Inc ....C...... 609 586-1332
  Robbinsville (G-9409)
CCL Label Inc ....E...... 856 273-0700
  Lumberton (G-5625)
Classic Printers & Converters ....G...... 732 985-1100
  Piscataway (G-8646)
Custom Labels Inc ....G...... 973 473-1934
  Fairfield (G-3177)
Distributor Label Products...................E...... 908 704-9997
  Hillsborough (G-4312)
Driscoll Label Company Inc ....F...... 973 585-7291
  East Hanover (G-2206)
Industrial Lbeling Systems Inc ....E...... 973 808-8188
  Fairfield (G-3238)
Label Solutions Inc ....G...... 201 599-0909
  Rochelle Park (G-9426)
Lizard Label Co ....F...... 973 808-3322
  Fairfield (G-3265)
Product Identification Co Inc ....F...... 973 227-7770
  Garfield (G-3762)

Promotional Graphics Inc ....F 973 423-3900
  Paterson (G-8283)
Sato Lbling Solutions Amer Inc............D 973 287-3641
  Pine Brook (G-8616)
Star Narrow Fabrics Inc..........................G...... 973 778-8600
  Lodi (G-5576)
Stephen Gould Corporation ....D 973 428-1500
  Whippany (G-11910)
Taunton Graphics Inc ....F 856 719-8084
  West Berlin (G-11625)

PRINTING, COMMERCIAL: Literature, Advertising, NEC

Avail Inc ....G 732 560-2222
  Bridgewater (G-796)
Brite Concepts Inc ....G...... 201 270-8544
  Englewood (G-2886)
Commercial Business Forms Inc ....G 973 682-9000
  Cedar Knolls (G-1302)
Page 2 LLC ....G...... 862 239-9830
  Wayne (G-11538)
Sjshore Marketing Ltd Lblty Co ....F 609 390-1400
  Marmora (G-5959)

PRINTING, COMMERCIAL: Promotional

Graphic Imagery Inc ....F 908 755-2882
  New Providence (G-7002)
Harwill Corporation ....G...... 609 895-1955
  Windsor (G-11996)
Hit Promo LLC ....C...... 800 237-6305
  Bellmawr (G-334)
Hygrade Business Group Inc.................E 800 836-7714
  Secaucus (G-9781)
J H M Communications Inc ....F 908 859-6668
  Phillipsburg (G-8556)
Koday Press Inc ....F 201 387-0001
  Dumont (G-2116)
Marlo Plastic Products Inc ....E 732 792-1988
  Neptune (G-6890)
Njiw Limited Liability Company ....F 201 355-2955
  Hackensack (G-3954)
Patchworks Co Inc ....G...... 973 627-2002
  Dover (G-2103)
Pressworks ....G...... 856 427-9001
  Cherry Hill (G-1411)
Signmasters Inc ....D 973 614-8300
  Passaic (G-8107)
Silver Edmar ....G...... 973 817-7483
  Newark (G-7273)
Smith Enterprises ....G...... 215 416-9881
  Mount Laurel (G-6807)

PRINTING, COMMERCIAL: Publications

Active Learning Associates ....G...... 908 284-0404
  Flemington (G-3428)
Paper Clip Communication Inc.............F 973 256-1333
  Little Falls (G-5464)
University Publications Inc ....G...... 212 268-4222
  Belford (G-284)

PRINTING, COMMERCIAL: Schedules, Transportation, NEC

Chariot Courier & Trans Svcs ....F 888 532-9125
  Sayreville (G-9704)

PRINTING, COMMERCIAL: Screen

A B Tees LLC ....G...... 201 239-0022
  Jersey City (G-4683)
Abbott Artkives LLC ....G...... 201 232-9477
  Belleville (G-288)
Adpro Imprints ....G...... 732 531-2133
  Ocean (G-7653)
Advantage Ds LLC ....F 856 307-9600
  Glassboro (G-3806)
Alex Real LLC ....F 732 730-8770
  Toms River (G-10740)
All Colors Screen Printing LLC ....G...... 732 777-6033
  Highland Park (G-4286)
American Youth Enterprises Inc............G...... 609 909-1900
  Mays Landing (G-5992)
Armin Kososki ....G...... 908 689-0411
  Washington (G-11439)
Arnolds Yacht Basin Inc ....G...... 732 892-3000
  Point Pleasant Boro (G-8836)
Arts Embroidery LLC...............................G...... 732 870-2400
  West Long Branch (G-11719)

Branded Screen Printing........................G...... 908 879-7411
  Chester (G-1431)
C & D Sales ....G...... 609 383-9292
  Pleasantville (G-8806)
Campus Coordinates LLC ....G...... 732 866-6060
  Freehold (G-3655)
Central Mills Inc ....G...... 732 329-2009
  Dayton (G-1959)
Cgs Sales and Service LLC ....G...... 856 665-6154
  Pennsauken (G-8403)
Chambord Prints Inc...............................E 201 795-2007
  Hoboken (G-4447)
Clear Control LLC ....G...... 973 823-8200
  Ogdensburg (G-7709)
Color Screen Pros Inc ....F 973 268-5080
  Newark (G-7086)
Colorcraft Sign Co ....F 609 386-1115
  Beverly (G-449)
Cosmic Custom Screen Prtg LLC ....G...... 856 629-8337
  Williamstown (G-11955)
Custom Graphics of Vineland ....E 856 691-7858
  Vineland (G-11209)
D L Imprints ....G...... 732 493-8555
  Ocean (G-7660)
Deans Graphics ....G...... 609 261-8817
  Mount Holly (G-6724)
Dezine Line Inc ....F 973 989-1009
  Wharton (G-11856)
DOT Graphix Inc ....F 609 994-3416
  Barnegat (G-158)
Envirnmntal Dsign Grphic Entps...........G...... 973 361-1829
  Dover (G-2083)
F S T Printing Inc ....G...... 732 560-3749
  Middlesex (G-6115)
Frontend Graphics Inc............................G...... 856 547-1600
  Cherry Hill (G-1364)
G & M Printwear ....F 856 742-5551
  Gloucester City (G-3841)
Graphic Image ....G...... 856 262-8900
  Williamstown (G-11959)
GTM Marketing Inc ....G...... 856 227-2333
  Woodbury (G-12031)
H C Graphics Screenprinting ....G...... 973 247-0544
  Paterson (G-8207)
Hary Manufacturing Inc ....F 908 722-7100
  Woodbridge (G-12018)
Heritage Inc ....G...... 201 447-2600
  Midland Park (G-6177)
Image Screen Printing Inc ....G...... 732 560-1817
  Middlesex (G-6121)
Imagery Embroidary Corporation ....F 201 343-9333
  Union City (G-11113)
Imprintz Cstm Printed Graphics ....G...... 609 386-5673
  Lumberton (G-5631)
Innovative Awards Inc ....G...... 609 888-1400
  Trenton (G-10945)
J & G Graphics Inc ....G...... 732 223-6660
  Manasquan (G-5832)
J and S Sporting Apparel LLC ....G...... 732 787-5500
  Keansburg (G-4838)
Licensee Services Inc............................F 609 465-2003
  Cape May Court House (G-1112)
Mary Bridget Enterprises ....E 609 267-4830
  Cinnaminson (G-1471)
Midland Screen Printing Inc...................F 201 703-0066
  Saddle Brook (G-9662)
Midlantic Color Graphics LLC ....G...... 856 786-3113
  Cinnaminson (G-1474)
Mike Dolly Screen Printing.....................F 732 294-8979
  Freehold (G-3679)
Mj Corporate Sales Inc ....E 856 778-0055
  Mount Laurel (G-6783)
Monarch Art Plastics Co LLC ....G...... 856 235-5151
  Mount Laurel (G-6785)
Moonlight Imaging LLC ....G...... 973 300-1001
  Sparta (G-10399)
Newton Screen Printing Co.....................G...... 973 827-0486
  Franklin (G-3606)
NJ Logo Wear LLC ....G...... 609 597-9400
  Manahawkin (G-5794)
O Berk Company LLC ....E 201 941-1610
  Fairview (G-3365)
Pecata Enterprises Inc ....G...... 973 523-9498
  Paterson (G-8280)
Printsmith ....G...... 908 245-3000
  Roselle Park (G-9589)
Promo Graphic Inc ....G...... 732 629-7300
  Middlesex (G-6141)
R & R Printing & Copy Center.................G...... 732 249-9450
  Hillsborough (G-4348)

Red Diamond Co - Athc Letering ....G...... 973 759-2005
  Belleville (G-310)
Rolferrys Specialties Inc ....G...... 856 456-2999
  Brooklawn (G-915)
Rutler Screen Printing Inc ....F 908 859-3327
  Phillipsburg (G-8573)
Sabrimax Corp ....F 201 871-0808
  Englewood (G-2938)
Screen Play Inc ....G...... 973 227-9014
  Fairfield (G-3309)
Screen Tech Inc of New Jersey ....D 908 862-8000
  Linden (G-5420)
Screen-Trans Development Corp ....E 201 933-7800
  Moonachie (G-6488)
Six Thirteen Originals LLC ....E 201 316-1900
  Mahwah (G-5772)
Sports Stop Inc ....F 856 881-2763
  Glassboro (G-3819)
Sunglo Fabrics Inc..................................F 201 935-0830
  Paterson (G-8304)
Tectubes USA Inc...................................E 856 589-1250
  Vineland (G-11269)
Totally T Shirts & More Inc ....G...... 609 894-0011
  Pemberton (G-8358)
Trukmanns Inc...E 973 538-7718
  Cedar Knolls (G-1314)
U S Screening Corp ....C...... 973 242-1110
  Newark (G-7305)
Unlimited Print Products Inc..................F 609 882-0653
  Ewing (G-3075)
Vernon Display Graphics Inc ....E 201 935-7117
  Carlstadt (G-1235)
Wagner Foto Screen Process ....G...... 908 624-0800
  Kenilworth (G-4987)
Wisco Promo & Uniform Inc ....G...... 973 767-2022
  Saddle Brook (G-9688)
Work n Gear LLC ....G...... 856 848-7676
  Woodbury (G-12039)
Zeeks Tees ....F 732 291-2700
  Belford (G-285)
Zone Two Inc ....F 732 237-0766
  Bayville (G-254)
Zwier Corp ....G...... 973 748-4009
  Bloomfield (G-524)

PRINTING, COMMERCIAL: Stationery, NEC

Riverside Graphics Inc ....F 201 876-9000
  Belleville (G-311)

PRINTING, COMMERCIAL: Tags, NEC

Ideal Jacobs Corporation ....E 973 275-5100
  Maplewood (G-5879)

PRINTING, LITHOGRAPHIC: Advertising Posters

Forbes Media LLC...................................D 212 620-2200
  Jersey City (G-4737)
Orora Visual LLC.....................................G...... 973 916-2804
  Clifton (G-1681)

PRINTING, LITHOGRAPHIC: Calendars

Schellmark Inc...G...... 732 345-7143
  Tinton Falls (G-10726)

PRINTING, LITHOGRAPHIC: Catalogs

Action Graphics Inc ....E 973 633-6500
  Lincoln Park (G-5297)

PRINTING, LITHOGRAPHIC: Color

Colorsource Inc.......................................G...... 856 488-8100
  Pennsauken (G-8406)
Donray Printing Inc ....E 973 515-8100
  Parsippany (G-7918)
Shindo International Inc ....E 973 470-8100
  Clifton (G-1716)

PRINTING, LITHOGRAPHIC: Decals

Product Identification Co Inc ....F 973 227-7770
  Garfield (G-3762)
Suzie Mac Specialties Inc......................E 732 238-3500
  East Brunswick (G-2184)

PRODUCT

PRINTING, LITHOGRAPHIC: Forms & Cards, Business

Elite Graphix LLC ....F 732 274-2356
  Monmouth Junction *(G-6290)*
Merrill Corporation ....D 908 810-3740
  Union *(G-11075)*
Print Factory Ltd Liability Co ....G....... 973 866-5230
  Clifton *(G-1700)*
Remco Press Inc ....G....... 201 751-5703
  North Bergen *(G-7433)*
Supplies-Supplies Inc ....F 908 272-5100
  Watchung *(G-11460)*
Webb-Mason Inc ....G....... 732 747-6585
  Tinton Falls *(G-10734)*

PRINTING, LITHOGRAPHIC: Forms, Business

Absolute Business Services Inc............G....... 856 265-9447
  Millville *(G-6222)*
Crt International Inc ....F 973 887-7737
  Middlesex *(G-6110)*
Douglas Maybury Assoc ....G....... 908 879-5878
  Chester *(G-1433)*
Paris Corporation New Jersey ....D....... 609 265-9200
  Westampton *(G-11788)*

PRINTING, LITHOGRAPHIC: Newspapers

Redmond Bcms Inc ....D....... 973 664-2000
  Denville *(G-2051)*

PRINTING, LITHOGRAPHIC: Offset & photolithographic printing

Atlantic Prtg & Graphics LLC ....G....... 732 493-4222
  Ocean *(G-7657)*
Hometown Office Sups & Prtg Co ....G....... 609 298-9020
  Bordentown *(G-583)*
Lamb Printing Inc................................G....... 908 852-0837
  Hackettstown *(G-4016)*
Longrun Press Inc ....F 856 719-9202
  West Berlin *(G-11605)*
Mercer C AlphaGraphics ....G....... 609 921-0959
  Hamilton *(G-4115)*
Nu-Plan Business Systems Inc ....G....... 732 231-6944
  Clark *(G-1510)*

PRINTING, LITHOGRAPHIC: On Metal

AE Litho Offset Printers Inc ....D....... 609 239-0700
  Beverly *(G-445)*
Aus Inc ....G....... 856 234-9200
  Mount Laurel *(G-6738)*
C Harry Marean Printing ....G....... 609 965-4708
  Egg Harbor City *(G-2655)*
Command Web Offset Company Inc .....C....... 201 863-8100
  Secaucus *(G-9757)*
Nassau Communications Inc ....F 609 208-9099
  Lawrence Township *(G-5218)*

PRINTING, LITHOGRAPHIC: Promotional

Corporate Mailings Inc ....C 973 439-1168
  West Caldwell *(G-11645)*
Corporate Mailings Inc ....D....... 973 808-0009
  Whippany *(G-11887)*
Datascan Graphics Inc ....E 973 543-4803
  Morristown *(G-6658)*
J D M Associates Inc ....G....... 973 773-8699
  Lodi *(G-5566)*
Killian Graphics................................G....... 973 635-5844
  Chatham *(G-1325)*
Peeq Imaging ....D....... 212 490-3850
  Carlstadt *(G-1198)*

PRINTING, LITHOGRAPHIC: Publications

Hansen Lithography Ltd ....G....... 732 270-1188
  Toms River *(G-10763)*
Print By Premier LLC ....G....... 212 947-1365
  Secaucus *(G-9799)*
Recorder Publishing Co ....E 908 647-1180
  Stirling *(G-10495)*

PRINTING, LITHOGRAPHIC: Transfers, Decalcomania Or Dry

Superior Trademark Inc ....G....... 201 652-1900
  Waldwick *(G-11310)*

PRINTING, LITHOGRAPHIC: Wrappers

Printwrap Corporation ....F 973 239-1144
  Cedar Grove *(G-1289)*

PRINTING, LITHOGRAPHIC: Wrappers & Seals

Tape Graphics ....G....... 201 393-9500
  Hasbrouck Heights *(G-4189)*

PRINTING: Books

Command Web Offset Company Inc .....C....... 201 863-8100
  Secaucus *(G-9757)*
Phoenix Color Corp ....E 800 632-4111
  Rockaway *(G-9485)*

PRINTING: Books

All In Color Inc..................................G....... 973 626-0987
  Paterson *(G-8133)*
AM Best Company Inc ....A....... 908 439-2200
  Oldwick *(G-7738)*
Athletic Organizational Aids ....E 201 652-1485
  Midland Park *(G-6170)*
Binding Products Inc ....E 212 947-1192
  Jersey City *(G-4704)*
Forbes Media LLC ....D....... 212 620-2200
  Jersey City *(G-4737)*
G & H Soho Inc ....F 201 216-9400
  Elmwood Park *(G-2826)*
Howard Press Inc ....D....... 908 245-4400
  Roselle *(G-9561)*
NJ Copy Center LLC ....G....... 973 788-1600
  Fairfield *(G-3281)*
Oceanic Graphic Intl Inc ....F 201 883-1816
  Hackensack *(G-3957)*
School Publications Co Inc ....E 732 988-1100
  Neptune *(G-6896)*
Service Data Corp Inc ....G....... 908 522-0020
  Summit *(G-10546)*
Starnet Printing Inc ....G....... 201 760-2600
  Mahwah *(G-5776)*
Surviving Life Corp ....G....... 973 543-3370
  Mendham *(G-6044)*
Wellspring Info Inc ....F 800 268-3682
  Montclair *(G-6393)*
Wheal-Grace Corp ....E 973 450-8100
  Belleville *(G-324)*

PRINTING: Broadwoven Fabrics. Cotton

Peter L Demaree ....G....... 732 531-2133
  Ocean *(G-7673)*
Premier Printing Solutions LLC............G....... 732 525-0740
  South Amboy *(G-10139)*

PRINTING: Checkbooks

Deluxe Corporation............................C....... 973 334-8000
  Mountain Lakes *(G-6823)*

PRINTING: Commercial, NEC

4 Over Inc ....F 201 440-1656
  Moonachie *(G-6450)*
Action Graphics Inc ....G....... 856 783-1825
  Lindenwold *(G-5443)*
Ahern Blueprinting Inc ....F 732 223-1476
  Manasquan *(G-5827)*
Alliance Design Inc ....F 973 904-9450
  Totowa *(G-10809)*
AlphaGraphics Printshops of Th...........G....... 973 984-0066
  Morristown *(G-6635)*
Altantic Printing and Design................F 732 557-9600
  Toms River *(G-10742)*
American Graphic Systems Inc ....G....... 201 796-0666
  Fair Lawn *(G-3084)*
Andy Graphics Service Bureau ....G....... 201 866-9407
  Union City *(G-11106)*
Applied Image Inc ....E 732 410-2444
  Freehold *(G-3647)*
Artistic Typography Corp ....G....... 845 783-1990
  Englewood *(G-2877)*
ASAP Postal Printing ....G....... 609 597-7421
  Manahawkin *(G-5790)*
Ayr Composition Inc ....G....... 908 241-8118
  Roselle Park *(G-9578)*
B P Graphics Inc ....E 732 942-2315
  Lakewood *(G-5057)*
Belle Printing Group LLC ....G....... 856 235-5151
  Mount Laurel *(G-6741)*

Big Color System Inc..........................F 201 236-0404
  Wyckoff *(G-12105)*
Bills Printing Service Inc ....G....... 609 888-1841
  Trenton *(G-10904)*
C and R Printing Corporation ....F 201 528-8912
  Carlstadt *(G-1134)*
C2 Imaging LLC ....E 646 557-6300
  Jersey City *(G-4707)*
Circa Promotions Inc ....G....... 732 264-1200
  Hazlet *(G-4259)*
Colortec Printing and Mailing ....G....... 856 767-0108
  West Berlin *(G-11584)*
Corporate Envelope & Prtg Co ....G....... 732 752-4333
  Green Brook *(G-3860)*
Coventry of New Jersey Inc ....E 856 988-5521
  Marlton *(G-5925)*
Creative Color Lithographers ....F 908 789-2295
  Garwood *(G-3783)*
Crown Roll Leaf Inc ....E 973 684-2600
  Paterson *(G-8165)*
Daily News LP ....F 212 210-2100
  Jersey City *(G-4720)*
Data Communique Intl Inc ....F 201 508-6000
  Ridgefield Park *(G-9303)*
Delgen Press Inc ....G....... 973 472-2266
  Clifton *(G-1597)*
Diligaf Enterprises Inc ....E 201 684-0900
  Mahwah *(G-5729)*
Display Impressions ....F 856 488-1777
  Pennsauken *(G-8415)*
Dye Into Print Inc ....D....... 973 772-8019
  Clifton *(G-1606)*
Fedex Office & Print Svcs Inc ....G....... 201 672-0508
  East Rutherford *(G-2288)*
Fedex Office & Print Svcs Inc ....E 732 636-3580
  Iselin *(G-4609)*
Fischlers Dawnpoint............................G....... 856 428-2092
  Cherry Hill *(G-1362)*
Fit Graphix ....G....... 201 488-4670
  Hackensack *(G-3914)*
Five Macs Inc ....E 856 596-3150
  Marlton *(G-5931)*
Flexi Printing Plate Co Inc ....F 201 939-3600
  Moonachie *(G-6465)*
Fordham Inc ....G....... 973 575-7840
  Fairfield *(G-3205)*
Forms & Flyers of New Jersey.............G....... 856 629-0718
  Williamstown *(G-11958)*
Foto Fantasy ....G....... 732 548-8446
  Edison *(G-2514)*
Frank J Zechman ....G....... 732 495-0077
  Belford *(G-282)*
Fu WEI Inc ....G....... 732 937-8388
  East Brunswick *(G-2147)*
Global Graphics Intergration ....F 973 334-9653
  Towaco *(G-10872)*
Graphic Arts Printing..........................G....... 201 343-6554
  Hawthorne *(G-4222)*
H & H Graphic Printing Inc ....G....... 201 369-9700
  Carlstadt *(G-1162)*
H & L Printing Co ....G....... 201 288-0877
  Hasbrouck Heights *(G-4184)*
Hayes Mindish Inc ....G....... 609 641-9880
  Pleasantville *(G-8812)*
Howard Press Inc ....D....... 908 245-4400
  Roselle *(G-9561)*
Hummel Distributing Corp ....E 908 688-5300
  Union *(G-11063)*
Hummel Printing Inc ....E 908 688-5300
  Union *(G-11064)*
Ics Corporation ....C....... 215 427-3355
  West Deptford *(G-11704)*
Illinois Tool Works Inc ....E 609 395-5600
  Cranbury *(G-1839)*
Important Papers Inc ....G....... 856 751-4544
  Cherry Hill *(G-1376)*
Instant Printing of Dover Inc ....G....... 973 366-6855
  Dover *(G-2090)*
Inter City Press Inc ....E 908 236-9911
  Lebanon *(G-5264)*
J F I Printing ....G....... 973 759-3444
  Belleville *(G-297)*
J&E Business Services LLC ....G....... 973 984-8444
  Clifton *(G-1645)*
Jimcam Publishing Inc ....G....... 201 843-5700
  Maywood *(G-6009)*
Jrm Industries Inc ....E 973 779-9340
  Passaic *(G-8077)*
K M Media Group LLC ....G....... 973 330-3000
  Clifton *(G-1648)*

Kdf Reprographics Inc ....F 201 784-9991
South Hackensack (G-10167)

Keefe Printing Inc ....G 732 295-2099
Point Pleasant Beach (G-8826)

Lacoa Inc ....G 973 754-1000
Elmwood Park (G-2837)

Laserwave Graphics Inc ....F 732 745-7764
New Brunswick (G-6943)

Latta Graphics Inc ....E 201 440-4040
Carlstadt (G-1181)

Logomania Inc ....G 201 798-0531
Jersey City (G-4760)

M & M Printing Corp ....G 201 288-7787
Hasbrouck Heights (G-4186)

Main Street Graphics Inc ....G 856 755-3523
Maple Shade (G-5866)

Mariano Press LLC ....F 732 247-3659
Somerset (G-10022)

Mega Media Concepts Ltd Lblty ....G 973 919-5661
Sparta (G-10397)

Menu Express ....F 856 216-7777
Pennsauken (G-8457)

Mercer C AlphaGraphics ....G 609 921-0959
Hamilton (G-4115)

Merrill Corporation ....D 973 643-4403
Newark (G-7200)

Merrill Corporation ....D 908 810-3740
Union (G-11075)

Mimeocom Inc ....F 973 286-2901
Newark (G-7202)

National Color Graphics ....F 856 435-6800
Sicklerville (G-9912)

National Plastic Printing ....E 973 785-1460
Totowa (G-10838)

National Reprographics Inc ....E 609 896-4100
Lawrenceville (G-5239)

New Jersey Label LLC ....F 201 880-5102
South Hackensack (G-10175)

New Jersey Tech Group LLC ....G 609 301-6405
Lumberton (G-5633)

North America Printing ....G 973 726-7713
Sparta (G-10403)

North Eastern Business Forms ....G 609 392-1161
Trenton (G-10967)

Ocsidot Inc ....F 908 789-3300
Garwood (G-3788)

OShea Services Inc ....G 201 343-8668
Hackensack (G-3958)

Outfront Media LLC ....D 973 575-6900
Fairfield (G-3286)

Output Services Group Inc ....G 201 871-1100
Carlstadt (G-1193)

Page Stamp LLC ....G 732 390-1700
Monroe Township (G-6340)

Palm Press Inc ....G 201 767-6504
Northvale (G-7543)

Peacock Products Inc ....F 201 385-5585
Bergenfield (G-382)

Penn Jersey Press Inc ....G 856 627-2200
Gibbsboro (G-3795)

Penta Digital Incorporated ....G 201 839-5392
Jersey City (G-4782)

Perco Inc ....F 908 464-3000
Berkeley Heights (G-410)

Perfect Printing Inc ....E 856 787-1877
Moorestown (G-6555)

Phoenix Alliance Group LLC ....F 732 495-4800
Port Monmouth (G-8879)

Premier Press Inc ....F 856 665-0722
Pennsauken (G-8471)

Premium Color Group LLC ....E 973 472-7007
Carlstadt (G-1207)

Press Room Inc ....F 609 689-3817
Trenton (G-10981)

Pressto Graphics ....F 732 286-9300
Toms River (G-10784)

Print Mail Communications LLC ....E 856 488-0345
Pennsauken (G-8473)

Print Media LLC ....G 973 467-0007
Springfield (G-10460)

Print Solutions LLC ....F 201 567-9622
Englewood (G-2933)

Printers of Salem County LLC ....G 856 935-5032
Salem (G-9696)

Printing & Signs Express Inc ....G 201 368-1255
Mahwah (G-5763)

Printing Lab LLC ....F 201 305-0404
West New York (G-11750)

Ramsey Graphics and Printing ....G 201 300-2912
Elmwood Park (G-2852)

Redmond Bcms Inc ....D 973 664-2000
Denville (G-2051)

Roan Printing Inc ....F 908 526-5990
Somerville (G-10124)

Royalty Press Inc ....E 856 663-2288
Westville (G-11820)

Royer Group Inc ....E 856 324-0171
Pennsauken (G-8479)

Royercomm Corporation ....F 856 665-6400
Pennsauken (G-8480)

S J T Imaging Inc ....D 201 262-7744
Oradell (G-7747)

S V O Inc ....G 973 983-8380
Succasunna (G-10519)

Samuel Elliott Inc ....E 856 773-6000
Cinnaminson (G-1483)

Semels Embroidery Inc ....F 973 473-6868
Clifton (G-1713)

Skylands Press ....G 973 383-5006
Newton (G-7358)

Tbc Color Imaging Inc ....E 973 470-8100
Clifton (G-1731)

Terminal Printing Co ....G 201 659-5924
Belleville (G-316)

Timeline Promotions Inc ....G 973 226-1512
West Caldwell (G-11680)

Toppan Printing Co Amer Inc ....C 732 469-8400
Somerset (G-10088)

Toppan Vintage Inc ....E 201 226-9220
Saddle Brook (G-9684)

Travel Weekly ....G 201 902-1931
Secaucus (G-9822)

Tremont Printing Co ....G 973 227-0742
Fairfield (G-3332)

Trentypo Inc ....F 609 883-5971
Ewing (G-3071)

Trico Web LLC ....G 201 438-3860
Carlstadt (G-1232)

Typecom LLC ....G 201 969-1901
Fort Lee (G-3591)

Typeline ....F 201 251-2201
Wyckoff (G-12123)

Unimac Graphics LLC ....G 201 372-1000
Carlstadt (G-1234)

United Label Corp ....G 973 589-6500
Newark (G-7309)

Vertis Inc ....D 215 781-1668
Mount Holly (G-6735)

Wall Street Group Inc ....D 201 333-4784
South Plainfield (G-10344)

Whitehouse Prtg & Labeling LLC ....G 973 521-7648
Fairfield (G-3353)

Wilmington Trust Sp Services ....C 609 272-7000
Pleasantville (G-8821)

Winsome Digital Inc ....F 609 645-2211
Egg Harbor Township (G-2702)

Z Fab LLC ....G 973 248-0686
Wayne (G-11566)

Zoo Printing Inc ....G 856 686-0800
West Deptford (G-11718)

PRINTING: Engraving & Plate

Pan Graphics Inc ....D 973 478-2100
Garfield (G-3753)

PRINTING: Fabric, Narrow

Asha44 LLC ....E 201 306-3600
Fairfield (G-3147)

Franco Manufacturing Co Inc ....C 732 494-0500
Metuchen (G-6056)

PRINTING: Flexographic

CCL Label (delaware) Inc ....C 609 259-1055
Trenton (G-10914)

Cheringal Associates Inc ....D 201 784-8721
Norwood (G-7560)

Flexo-Craft Prints Inc ....E 973 482-7200
Harrison (G-4174)

Horizon Label LLC ....F 856 767-0777
West Berlin (G-11599)

PRINTING: Gravure, Cards, Exc Greeting

Five Macs Inc ....E 856 596-3150
Marlton (G-5931)

PRINTING: Gravure, Catalogs, No Publishing On-Site

R R Donnelley & Sons Company ....C 973 439-8321
West Caldwell (G-11676)

PRINTING: Gravure, Color

Link Color NA Inc ....G 201 438-8222
East Rutherford (G-2295)

PRINTING: Gravure, Forms, Business

All-State International Inc ....C 908 272-0800
Cranford (G-1899)

East Coast Distributors Inc ....F 732 223-5995
Eatontown (G-2389)

PRINTING: Gravure, Labels

Challenge Printing Co Inc ....C 973 471-4700
Clifton (G-1582)

Label Master Inc ....G 973 546-3110
Lodi (G-5567)

Lps Industries Inc ....C 201 438-3515
Moonachie (G-6477)

Tadbik NJ Inc ....E 973 882-9595
Fairfield (G-3322)

PRINTING: Gravure, Magazines, No Publishing On-Site

Food Mfg ....C 973 920-7000
Rockaway (G-9461)

PRINTING: Gravure, Posters

Winemiller Press Inc ....G 732 223-0100
Manasquan (G-5843)

PRINTING: Gravure, Rotogravure

American Business Paper Inc ....F 732 363-5788
Lakewood (G-5049)

Arna Marketing Inc ....E 908 231-1100
Branchburg (G-622)

Brandmuscle Inc ....G 973 685-0022
Clifton (G-1577)

Constant Services Inc ....E 973 227-2990
Fairfield (G-3173)

Lrp and P Graphics ....E 856 424-0158
Cherry Hill (G-1385)

New Jersey Department Treasury ....E 609 292-5133
Trenton (G-10962)

Pad and Publ Assembly Corp ....E 856 424-0158
Cherry Hill (G-1404)

Pantone LLC ....C 201 935-5500
Carlstadt (G-1196)

Taylor Communications Inc ....E 732 561-8210
Monroe Township (G-6348)

Taylor Communications Inc ....E 973 467-8259
Springfield (G-10468)

Wheal-Grace Corp ....E 973 450-8100
Belleville (G-324)

PRINTING: Gravure, Stationery & Invitation

Youre So Invited LLC ....G 201 664-8600
Westwood (G-11848)

PRINTING: Laser

American Bank Note Holographic ....D 609 208-0591
Robbinsville (G-9407)

B&M Technologies Inc ....F 201 291-8505
Saddle Brook (G-9641)

Printology ....G 201 345-4632
Midland Park (G-6186)

United Forms Finishing Corp ....F 908 687-0494
Hillside (G-4434)

PRINTING: Letterpress

B and W Printing Company Inc ....G 908 241-3060
Kenilworth (G-4926)

Bassano Prtrs & Lithographers ....E 973 423-1400
Hawthorne (G-4207)

Burdol Inc ....G 856 453-0336
Bridgeton (G-755)

C Harry Marean Printing ....G 609 965-4708
Egg Harbor City (G-2655)

Dewechter Inc ....G 856 845-0225
Woodbury (G-12027)

PRODUCT

Downtown Printing Center Inc ....F 732 246-7990
New Brunswick (G-6920)

Ferrante Press Inc ....G 609 239-4257
Verona (G-11167)

Good Impressions Inc ....G 856 461-3232
Riverside (G-9395)

Howes Standard Publishing Co ....E 856 691-2000
Vineland (G-11233)

Keskes Printing LLC ....G 856 767-4733
Berlin (G-425)

Office Needs Inc ....G 732 381-7770
Clark (G-1511)

Pharmaceutic Litho Label Inc ....C 336 785-4000
Cranford (G-1923)

Red Letter Press Inc ....G 609 597-5257
Upper Saddle River (G-11146)

Riegel Cmmunications Group Inc ....E 609 771-0555
Ewing (G-3061)

Sherman Printing Co Inc ....G 973 345-2493
Clifton (G-1715)

Stuyvesant Press Inc ....F 973 399-3880
Irvington (G-4587)

Tekno Inc ....G 973 423-2004
Hawthorne (G-4246)

Vernw Printing Company ....G 973 751-6462
Belleville (G-321)

Wilcox Press Inc ....G 973 827-7474
Hamburg (G-4099)

PRINTING: Lithographic

A&E Promotions LLC ....G 732 382-2300
Holmdel (G-4491)

AA Graphics Inc ....G 201 398-0710
Saddle Brook (G-9637)

Aboudi Printing LLC ....G 732 542-2929
Eatontown (G-2373)

Accurate Plastic Printers LLC ....E 973 591-0180
Clifton (G-1554)

Ace Reprographic Service Inc ....E 973 684-5945
Paterson (G-8125)

Action Copy Centers Inc ....G 973 744-5520
Montclair (G-6356)

Advertisers Service Group Inc ....F 201 440-5577
Ridgefield Park (G-9298)

Aerojet Rocketdyne De Inc ....G 201 440-1453
Norwood (G-7557)

AGFA Corporation ....E 201 288-4101
Carlstadt (G-1120)

Allegro Printing Corporation ....G 609 641-7060
Galloway (G-3719)

Allied Envelope Co Inc ....E 201 440-2000
Carlstadt (G-1122)

AlphaGraphics ....G 201 327-2200
Mahwah (G-5712)

AlphaGraphics ....F 856 761-8000
Cherry Hill (G-1339)

AlphaGraphics Printshops of Th ....G 973 984-0066
Morristown (G-6635)

Ancraft Press Corp ....F 201 792-9200
Jersey City (G-4691)

Arch Parent Inc ....G 732 621-2873
Iselin (G-4597)

Arglen Industries Inc ....F 732 888-8100
Hazlet (G-4256)

Arna Marketing Group Inc ....D 908 625-7395
Branchburg (G-621)

Asbury Park Press Inc ....A 732 922-6000
Neptune (G-6866)

Ayr Graphics & Printing Inc ....G 908 241-8118
Kenilworth (G-4923)

B & H Printers Inc ....G 908 688-6990
Hackettstown (G-4000)

Better Image Graphics Inc ....G 856 262-0735
Williamstown (G-11952)

Big Red Pin LLC ....G 732 993-9765
Edison (G-2469)

Bittner Industries Inc ....G 856 817-8400
Cherry Hill (G-1347)

Blue Parachute LLC ....G 732 767-1320
Metuchen (G-6048)

Bobs Poly Tape Printers Inc ....G 973 824-3005
Newark (G-7068)

Bruce McCoy Sr ....G 609 217-6153
Pine Hill (G-8621)

Business Cards Tomorrow ....E 201 236-0088
Upper Saddle River (G-11136)

Business Cards Tomorrow Inc ....F 609 965-0808
Egg Harbor City (G-2654)

C Jackson Associates Inc ....E 856 761-8000
Cherry Hill (G-1351)

Carl A Venable Inc ....G 732 985-6677
North Brunswick (G-7460)

Catholic Star Herald ....G 856 583-6142
Camden (G-1050)

CIC Letter Service Inc ....D 201 896-1900
Carlstadt (G-1138)

Classic Graphic Inc ....G 856 753-0055
Berlin (G-420)

Classic Impressions ....G 908 689-3137
Great Meadows (G-3853)

Coast Star ....E 732 223-0076
Manasquan (G-5830)

Cornerstone Prints Imaging LLC ....G 908 782-7966
Flemington (G-3434)

Coventry of New Jersey Inc ....E 856 988-5521
Marlton (G-5925)

Csg Systems Inc ....E 973 337-4400
Bloomfield (G-500)

D A K Office Services Inc ....G 609 586-8222
Trenton (G-10929)

Data Communique Intl Inc ....G 201 508-6000
Ridgefield Park (G-9303)

Dato Company Inc ....G 732 225-2272
Cranbury (G-1829)

Delgen Press Inc ....G 973 472-2266
Clifton (G-1597)

Digital Color Concepts Inc ....D 908 264-0504
Mountainside (G-6842)

Digital Documents Inc ....G 609 520-0094
Princeton (G-8930)

Digital Lizard LLC ....G 201 684-0900
Mahwah (G-5728)

Digital Print Solutions Inc ....F 973 263-1890
Parsippany (G-7917)

Digital Productions Inc ....F 856 224-1111
Swedesboro (G-10580)

Discount Digital Print LLC ....F 201 659-9600
Union City (G-11111)

Document Concepts Inc ....G 856 251-1975
Wenonah (G-11575)

Earth Color New York Inc ....E 973 884-1300
Parsippany (G-7925)

Earthcolor Inc ....G 973 952-8360
Parsippany (G-7927)

Earthcolor Inc ....C 973 884-1300
Parsippany (G-7928)

East Coast Media LLC ....E 908 575-9700
Hillsborough (G-4314)

Edwards Brothers Inc ....E 856 848-6900
West Deptford (G-11701)

Encore Enterprises Inc ....G 201 489-5044
South Hackensack (G-10158)

Envelope Freedom Holdings LLC ......G 201 699-5800
Ridgefield (G-9259)

Express Printing Services Inc ....G 973 585-7355
Fairfield (G-3197)

Extreme Digital Graphics Inc ....F 973 227-5599
Fairfield (G-3198)

Fedex Office & Print Svcs Inc ....G 201 525-5070
River Edge (G-9361)

Ferrett Printing Inc ....G 856 686-4896
Woodbury (G-12029)

Franbeth Inc ....G 856 488-1480
Pennsauken (G-8422)

Franklin Graphics Inc ....G 201 935-5900
Westwood (G-11831)

Fulfillment Printing and Mail ....G 609 953-9500
Medford Lakes (G-6037)

Full Service Mailers Inc ....E 973 478-8813
Hackensack (G-3919)

Garrison Printing Company Inc ....E 856 488-1900
Pennsauken (G-8424)

Genua & Mulligan Printing ....E 973 894-1500
Clifton (G-1624)

Graph Tech Sales & Service ....F 201 218-1749
Fairfield (G-3218)

Great Eastern Color Lith ....G 201 843-5656
Paramus (G-7804)

Great Northern Commercial Svcs ......G 908 475-8855
Belvidere (G-364)

Gross Printing Associates Inc ....F 718 832-1110
Clifton (G-1630)

Herald News ....G 973 569-7000
Woodland Park (G-12081)

Holographic Finishing Inc ....F 201 941-4651
Ridgefield (G-9266)

I Print Nb ....G 201 662-1133
North Bergen (G-7410)

Imagine Screen Prtg & Prod LLC ......C 732 329-2009
Dayton (G-1969)

Ink On Paper Communications ....G 732 758-6280
Shrewsbury (G-9893)

Ink Well Printers LLC ....G 908 272-8090
Kenilworth (G-4946)

Inkworkx Custom Screen Prtg ....G 609 898-5198
Manalapan (G-5814)

Inserts East Incorporated ....C 856 663-8181
Pennsauken (G-8437)

Instant Imprints ....G 973 252-9500
Flanders (G-3413)

J B Offset Printing Corp ....G 201 264-4400
Norwood (G-7566)

Jasco Specialties and Forms ....G 856 627-5511
Tabernacle (G-10619)

Jefferson Printing Serivce ....F 973 491-0019
Newark (G-7168)

Jmp Press Inc ....G 201 444-0236
Ho Ho Kus (G-4441)

Johnston Letter Co Inc ....G 973 482-7535
Flanders (G-3414)

Jory Engravers Inc ....G 201 939-1546
Rutherford (G-9624)

Jvs Copy Services Inc ....F 856 415-9090
Sewell (G-9850)

Knock Out Graphics Inc ....F 732 774-3331
Asbury Park (G-78)

Label Solutions Inc ....G 201 599-0909
Rochelle Park (G-9426)

Lithos Estiatorio Ltd Lblty Co ....G 973 758-1111
Livingston (G-5519)

Little Prints Day Care II LLC ....F 973 396-8989
Passaic (G-8082)

Lmp Printing Corp ....G 973 428-1987
Clifton (G-1660)

Lunet Inc ....G 201 261-3883
Paramus (G-7816)

M & M Printing Corp ....G 201 288-7787
Hasbrouck Heights (G-4186)

Maclearie Printing LLC ....G 732 681-2772
Wall Township (G-11354)

Mail Time Inc ....E 908 859-5500
Phillipsburg (G-8561)

Mark Alan Printing & Graphics ....G 732 981-9011
Piscataway (G-8686)

Marks Management Systems Inc ....G 856 866-0588
Maple Shade (G-5867)

Menu Solutions Inc ....D 718 575-5160
Belleville (G-300)

Metro Prtg & Promotions LLC ....F 973 316-1600
Boonton (G-563)

Metro Seliger Industries Inc ....C 201 438-4530
Carlstadt (G-1187)

Mgl Printing Solution LLC ....G 908 665-1999
New Providence (G-7012)

Mint Printing LLC ....G 973 546-2060
Lodi (G-5572)

Minuteman Press ....G 973 403-0146
Caldwell (G-1027)

Minuteman Press ....G 732 536-8788
Manalapan (G-5817)

More Copy Printing Service ....G 201 327-1106
Upper Saddle River (G-11143)

Multi Packaging Solutions Inc ....C 908 757-6000
South Plainfield (G-10303)

Nema Associates Inc ....F 973 274-0052
Linden (G-5395)

New Jersey Label LLC ....F 201 880-5102
South Hackensack (G-10175)

Nextwave Web LLC ....E 973 742-4339
Paterson (G-8269)

On Demand Print Group ....G 201 636-2270
Lyndhurst (G-5669)

One Two Three Inc ....F 856 251-1238
Woodbury (G-12034)

OSullivan Communications Corp ....E 973 227-5112
West Caldwell (G-11670)

Pad and Publ Assembly Corp ....E 856 424-0158
Cherry Hill (G-1404)

Palm Press Inc ....G 201 767-6504
Northvale (G-7543)

Parth Enterprises Inc ....G 732 404-0665
Iselin (G-4622)

PDM Litho Inc ....E 718 301-1740
Clifton (G-1687)

Pharmaceutic Litho Label Inc ....C 336 785-4000
Cranford (G-1923)

Philip Holzer and Assoc LLC ....E 212 691-9500
Carlstadt (G-1201)

Pinto Printing ....G 856 232-2550
Blackwood (G-477)

Precision Printing Group Inc ....E 856 753-0900
  Mount Laurel *(G-6795)*
Pressto Graphics ....F 732 286-9300
  Toms River *(G-10784)*
Print Mail Communications LLC ....E 856 488-0345
  Pennsauken *(G-8473)*
Print Peel ....E 201 507-0080
  Carlstadt *(G-1208)*
Printing Services ....G 908 269-8349
  Port Murray *(G-8884)*
Printpluscom Inc ....G 908 859-4774
  Stewartsville *(G-10487)*
Pro Screen Printing Inc ....G 201 246-7600
  Kearny *(G-4894)*
Prohaska & Co Inc ....G 732 238-3420
  East Brunswick *(G-2169)*
Q P 195 Inc ....F 732 531-8860
  Ocean *(G-7676)*
Quality Print Solutions ....G 888 679-7237
  Ridgewood *(G-9327)*
Regal Litho Prtrs Ltd Lblty Co ....G 732 901-1500
  Lakewood *(G-5151)*
Reliable Envelope and Graphics ...E 201 794-7756
  Elmwood Park *(G-2854)*
Roan Printing Inc ....F 908 526-5990
  Somerville *(G-10124)*
Roy D Smith Inc ....G 201 384-4163
  Bergenfield *(G-383)*
Royer Group Inc ....E 856 324-0171
  Pennsauken *(G-8479)*
SAM Graphics Inc ....E 732 431-0440
  Marlboro *(G-5913)*
Sample Media Inc ....E 609 399-5411
  Ocean City *(G-7695)*
Sandoval Graphics & Printing ......G 856 435-7320
  Somerdale *(G-9934)*
Sapphire Envelope & Graphics ......E 856 782-2227
  Magnolia *(G-5709)*
Scarlet Printing ....G 732 560-1415
  Middlesex *(G-6143)*
School Publications Co Inc ....E 732 988-1100
  Neptune *(G-6896)*
Screen Printing & Embroidery ......G 732 256-9610
  Wall Township *(G-11367)*
Service Data Corp Inc ....G 908 522-0020
  Summit *(G-10546)*
Sheroy Printing Inc ....F 973 242-4040
  Newark *(G-7271)*
Shree Ji Printing Corporation .....E 201 842-9500
  Carlstadt *(G-1216)*
Signs of Security Inc ....E 973 340-8404
  Garfield *(G-3768)*
Sonata Graphics Inc ....G 201 866-0186
  Secaucus *(G-9816)*
South Amboy Designer T Shirt L ....G 732 456-2594
  South Amboy *(G-10141)*
Staines Inc ....F 856 784-2718
  Somerdale *(G-9935)*
Steven Madola ....G 609 989-8022
  Trenton *(G-10992)*
Strategic Content Imaging ....C 201 863-8100
  Secaucus *(G-9819)*
Sunset Printing and Engrv Corp ....E 973 537-9600
  Wharton *(G-11871)*
Supreme Graphics and Prtg Inc .....G 718 989-9817
  Perth Amboy *(G-8535)*
Supreme Ink Corp ....F 973 344-2922
  Newark *(G-7292)*
Tandem Color Imaging Graphics .....G 973 513-9779
  Pompton Lakes *(G-8853)*
Technical Nameplate Corp ....E 973 773-4256
  Passaic *(G-8111)*
Tectubes USA Inc ....E 856 589-1250
  Vineland *(G-11269)*
Tedco Inc ....G 609 883-0799
  Ewing *(G-3069)*
Thermo X-Press Printing LLC ....G 973 585-6505
  East Hanover *(G-2241)*
Toppan Printing Co Amer Inc ....C 732 469-8400
  Somerset *(G-10088)*
Trade Thermographers Inc ....F 201 489-2060
  Rochelle Park *(G-9432)*
Tremont Printing Co ....G 973 227-0742
  Fairfield *(G-3332)*
Trend Printing/Intl Label ....F 201 941-6611
  Ridgefield *(G-9293)*
Trentypo Inc ....F 609 883-5971
  Ewing *(G-3071)*
Trukmanns Inc ....E 973 538-7718
  Cedar Knolls *(G-1314)*

Typeline ....F 201 251-2201
  Wyckoff *(G-12123)*
United Envelope LLC ....E 201 699-5800
  Ridgefield *(G-9296)*
Unity Graphics & Engraving Co .....E 201 541-5462
  Englewood *(G-2950)*
Verni Vito ....G 732 449-1760
  Wall Township *(G-11377)*
Viskal Printing LLC ....G 973 812-6600
  Totowa *(G-10860)*
W B Mason Co Inc ....D 888 926-2766
  Bellmawr *(G-345)*
W B Mason Co Inc ....E 888 926-2766
  Egg Harbor Township *(G-2701)*
W G I Corp ....F 732 370-2900
  Lakewood *(G-5179)*
Washington Stamp Exchange Inc .....F 973 966-0001
  Florham Park *(G-3526)*
Watonka Printing Inc ....G 732 974-8878
  Belmar *(G-356)*
Wilker Graphics LLC ....G 201 447-4800
  Midland Park *(G-6190)*
Wilmington Trust Sp Services ......C 609 272-7000
  Pleasantville *(G-8821)*
Zeiser Inc ....G 973 228-0800
  West Caldwell *(G-11682)*
Zwier Corp ....G 973 748-4009
  Bloomfield *(G-524)*

PRINTING: Manmade Fiber & Silk, Broadwoven Fabric

Stefan Enterprises Inc ....E 973 253-6005
  Garfield *(G-3770)*

PRINTING: Offset

A M Graphics Inc ....G 201 767-5320
  Harrington Park *(G-4161)*
A To Z Printing & Promotion ....G 973 916-9995
  Clifton *(G-1552)*
A&R Printing Corporation ....G 732 886-0505
  Lakewood *(G-5042)*
ABC Printing ....G 973 664-1160
  Rockaway *(G-9433)*
Accent Press Inc ....G 973 785-3127
  Totowa *(G-10807)*
Accucolor LLC ....G 732 870-1999
  Long Branch *(G-5593)*
Adams Bill Printing & Graphics ....G 856 455-7177
  Bridgeton *(G-749)*
Add Rob Litho LLC ....G 201 556-0700
  Rochelle Park *(G-9420)*
Affordable Offset Printing Inc ....G 856 661-0722
  Pennsauken *(G-8384)*
Agau Inc ....G 732 583-4343
  Matawan *(G-5967)*
Aladdin Color Inc ....G 609 518-9858
  Moorestown *(G-6501)*
Alete Printing LLC ....G 856 468-3536
  Wenonah *(G-11573)*
All American Print & Copy Ctr .....G 732 758-6200
  Red Bank *(G-9219)*
All Print Resources Group Inc .....G 201 994-0600
  Mountainside *(G-6833)*
Allied Printing-Graphics Inc ......G 973 227-0520
  Fairfield *(G-3139)*
American Envelope ....G 908 241-9900
  Linden *(G-5323)*
American Graphic Systems Inc ......G 201 796-0666
  Fair Lawn *(G-3084)*
American Plus Printers Inc ....E 732 528-2170
  Wall *(G-11314)*
Andrew P Mc Hugh Inc ....G 856 547-8953
  Barrington *(G-167)*
Anisha Enterprises Inc ....G 908 964-3380
  Union *(G-11026)*
Anuco Inc ....F 973 887-9465
  East Hanover *(G-2194)*
Asha44 LLC ....G 201 306-3600
  Fairfield *(G-3147)*
B & B Press Inc ....G 908 840-4093
  Lebanon *(G-5253)*
B & R Printing Inc ....G 609 448-3328
  Trenton *(G-10901)*
B and W Printing Company Inc ......G 908 241-3060
  Kenilworth *(G-4926)*
Bab Printing Jan Service ....G 908 272-6224
  Cranford *(G-1901)*
Bannon Group Ltd ....G 201 451-6500
  Jersey City *(G-4699)*

Bar Lan Inc ....G 856 596-2330
  Brigantine *(G-911)*
Barrington Press Inc ....F 201 843-6556
  Paramus *(G-7792)*
Bartlett Printing & Graphic ....G 609 386-1525
  Burlington *(G-952)*
Barton & Cooney LLC ....D 609 747-9300
  Burlington *(G-953)*
Bassano Prtrs & Lithographers .....E 973 423-1400
  Hawthorne *(G-4207)*
Beacon Offset Printing LLC ....G 201 488-4241
  Hackensack *(G-3883)*
Berennial International ....G 973 675-6266
  Orange *(G-7752)*
Bergen Instant Printing Inc ....G 201 945-7303
  Palisades Park *(G-7769)*
Berry Business Procedure Co ....G 908 272-6464
  Cranford *(G-1903)*
Bind-Rite Robbinsville LLC ....D 609 208-1917
  Robbinsville *(G-9408)*
Bistis Press Printing Co ....G 973 373-8033
  Irvington *(G-4562)*
Boro Printing Inc ....G 732 229-1899
  West Long Branch *(G-11720)*
Bowmar Enterprises Inc ....G 908 277-3000
  New Providence *(G-6996)*
BP Print Group Inc ....D 732 905-9830
  Lakewood *(G-5064)*
Bravo Print & Mail Inc ....G 201 806-3750
  Carlstadt *(G-1131)*
Budget Print Center ....G 973 743-0073
  Bloomfield *(G-492)*
Burdol Inc ....G 856 453-0336
  Bridgeton *(G-755)*
Burlington Press Corporation ......F 609 387-0030
  Burlington *(G-955)*
Cantone Press Inc ....E 201 569-3435
  Englewood *(G-2891)*
Capital Printing Corporation ......D 732 560-1515
  Middlesex *(G-6103)*
Century Printing Corp ....G 732 981-0544
  Piscataway *(G-8644)*
Challenge Printing Co Inc ....C 973 471-4700
  Clifton *(G-1582)*
Cmyk Printing Inc ....F 201 458-1300
  Carlstadt *(G-1144)*
Color Coded LLC ....G 718 482-1063
  Jersey City *(G-4714)*
Columbia Press Inc ....E 973 575-6535
  Fairfield *(G-3171)*
Comprehensive Mktg Systems ....G 908 810-9778
  Union *(G-11036)*
Conagraphics Inc ....G 973 331-1113
  Parsippany *(G-7908)*
Conkur Printing Co Inc ....E 212 541-5980
  Englewood *(G-2894)*
Contemprary Grphics Bndery Inc ....C 856 663-7277
  Camden *(G-1054)*
Copy-Rite Printing ....G 609 597-9182
  Manahawkin *(G-5792)*
Corbi Printing Co Inc ....G 856 547-2444
  Audubon *(G-112)*
Cordes Printing Inc ....G 201 652-7272
  Wyckoff *(G-12107)*
Cottrell Graphics & Advg Spc ......G 732 349-7430
  Toms River *(G-10754)*
County Graphics Forms MGT LLC .....E 908 474-9797
  Linden *(G-5337)*
Craftmaster Printing Inc ....G 732 775-0011
  Neptune *(G-6872)*
Craftsmen Photo Lithographers .....E 973 316-5791
  East Hanover *(G-2204)*
Creative Color Lithographers ......F 908 789-2295
  Garwood *(G-3783)*
Custom Book Bindery Inc ....F 973 815-1400
  Clifton *(G-1595)*
D & I Printing Co Inc ....F 201 871-3620
  Englewood *(G-2895)*
D L Printing Co Inc ....G 732 750-1917
  Avenel *(G-125)*
Danmar Press Inc ....F 201 487-4400
  South Hackensack *(G-10154)*
Dcg Printing Inc ....G 732 530-4441
  Shrewsbury *(G-9889)*
Dee Jay Printing Inc ....G 973 227-7787
  Fairfield *(G-3182)*
Design Factory Nj Inc ....G 908 964-8833
  Hillside *(G-4388)*
Devece & Shaffer Inc ....G 856 829-7282
  Palmyra *(G-7782)*

PRODUCT

Company		Phone	Location

Dg3 Group America Inc ....F 201 793-5000
Jersey City **(G-4724)**

Dg3 Holdings LLC ....G 201 793-5000
Jersey City **(G-4725)**

Dg3 North America Inc ....B 201 793-5000
Jersey City **(G-4726)**

Diane Matson Inc ....F 609 288-6833
Westampton **(G-11785)**

Diligaf Enterprises Inc ....E 201 684-0900
Mahwah **(G-5729)**

Direct Prtg Impressions Inc ......F 973 227-6111
West Caldwell **(G-11646)**

Diversified Impressions Inc ......G 973 399-9041
Irvington **(G-4564)**

Divine Printing ....G 732 632-8800
Metuchen **(G-6054)**

Dohrman Printing Co Inc ....G 201 933-0346
Carlstadt **(G-1152)**

Dolce Brothers Printing Inc ......D 201 843-0400
Maywood **(G-6004)**

Dolce Printing ....F 201 843-0400
Maywood **(G-6005)**

Donnelley Financial LLC ....F 973 882-7000
West Caldwell **(G-11647)**

Dpi Copies Prtg & Graphics Inc ...F 856 874-1355
Cherry Hill **(G-1357)**

Dynamic Printing & Graphics ......F 973 473-7177
Clifton **(G-1608)**

Earth Thebault Inc ....C 973 884-1300
Parsippany **(G-7926)**

Edison Lithog & Prtg Corp ....D 201 902-9191
North Bergen **(G-7403)**

Elbee Litho Inc ....G 732 698-7738
East Brunswick **(G-2139)**

Election Graphics Inc ....F 201 758-9966
Verona **(G-11165)**

Elmwood Press Inc ....F 201 794-6273
Elmwood Park **(G-2824)**

Esquire Business Forms ....G 609 883-1155
Ewing **(G-3029)**

Excel Color Graphics Inc ....G 856 848-3345
Woodbury Heights **(G-12043)**

Excellent Prtg & Graphics LLC .....F 973 773-6661
Clifton **(G-1617)**

Express Printing Inc ....G 908 925-6300
Linden **(G-5346)**

Falcon Graphics Inc ....G 908 232-1991
Clark **(G-1497)**

Falcon Printing & Graphics ....G 732 462-6862
Freehold **(G-3665)**

Fast Copy Printing Center ....F 732 739-4646
Keyport **(G-4999)**

FLM Graphics Corporation ....D 973 575-9450
Fairfield **(G-3202)**

Full House Printing Inc ....G 201 798-7073
Hoboken **(G-4451)**

G J Haerer Co Inc ....D 973 614-8090
Glen Ridge **(G-3825)**

Galvanic Prtg & Plate Co Inc ......E 201 939-3600
Moonachie **(G-6466)**

Gangi Graphics Inc ....G 732 840-8680
Brick **(G-719)**

Gannett Stllite Info Ntwrk Inc .....C 856 691-5000
Vineland **(G-11220)**

Gerardi Press Inc ....G 973 627-2600
Denville **(G-2039)**

Gmpc Printing ....G 973 546-6060
Clifton **(G-1628)**

Gms Litho Corp ....G 973 575-9400
Fairfield **(G-3216)**

Goffco Industries LLC ....G 973 492-0150
Butler **(G-1001)**

Good Impressions Inc ....G 856 461-3232
Riverside **(G-9395)**

Good Impressions Inc ....F 908 689-3071
Washington **(G-11445)**

Grandview Printing Co Inc ....F 973 890-0006
Totowa **(G-10831)**

Graphic Action Inc ....G 908 213-0055
Phillipsburg **(G-8553)**

Graphic Impressions Inc ....G 201 487-8788
Hackensack **(G-3923)**

Graphic Impressions Prtg Co ......G 856 728-2266
Blackwood **(G-468)**

Graphic Management ....E 908 654-8400
Kearny **(G-4862)**

Graphicolor Corporation ....E 856 691-2507
Vineland **(G-11227)**

Graphics Depot Inc ....F 973 927-8200
Randolph **(G-9183)**

Graytor Printing Company Inc .....E 201 933-0100
Lyndhurst **(G-5656)**

Green Horse Media LLC ....C 856 933-0222
Bellmawr **(G-333)**

H C Graphics Screenprinting ......G 973 247-0544
Paterson **(G-8207)**

Hallco Inc ....G 609 729-0161
Wildwood **(G-11944)**

Hammer Press Printers Inc ....G 973 334-4500
Parsippany **(G-7958)**

Happle Printing ....G 609 476-0100
Dorothy **(G-2071)**

Harvard Printing Group ....D 973 672-0800
Fairfield **(G-3222)**

Hatteras Press Inc ....B 732 935-9800
Tinton Falls **(G-10718)**

Hawk Graphics Inc ....E 973 895-5569
Randolph **(G-9185)**

Hermitage Press of New Jersey ....D 609 882-3600
Ewing **(G-3034)**

Highroad Press LLC ....E 201 708-6900
Moonachie **(G-6470)**

Howard Press Inc ....D 908 245-4400
Roselle **(G-9561)**

Howes Standard Publishing Co .....G 856 691-2000
Vineland **(G-11233)**

Hub Print & Copy Center LLC ......G 201 585-7887
Fort Lee **(G-3563)**

Image Makers Instant Printing .....G 973 633-1771
Wayne **(G-11518)**

Impact Printing ....G 862 225-9167
Little Ferry **(G-5489)**

Impressions Unlimited Prtg LLC ....G 856 256-0200
Sewell **(G-9846)**

Instant Printing of Dover Inc ......G 973 366-6855
Dover **(G-2090)**

JC Printing & Advertising Inc ......G 973 881-8612
Paterson **(G-8220)**

Jem Printing Inc ....G 908 782-9986
Flemington **(G-3450)**

Jersey Printing Associates Inc .....E 732 872-9654
Atlantic Highlands **(G-108)**

Jli Marketing & Printing Corp ......F 732 828-8877
Cranbury **(G-1848)**

Jmc Design & Graphics Inc ....G 973 276-9033
Fairfield **(G-3245)**

John S Swift Company Inc ....G 201 935-2002
Teterboro **(G-10682)**

John S Swift Print of NJ Inc ....G 201 678-3232
Teterboro **(G-10683)**

Jon-Da Printing Co Inc ....G 201 653-6200
Jersey City **(G-4751)**

K R B Printing For Business ....G 856 751-5200
Cherry Hill **(G-1379)**

Kay Printing & Envelope Co Inc ....E 973 330-3000
Clifton **(G-1649)**

Keskes Printing LLC ....G 856 767-4733
Berlin **(G-425)**

Keystone Printing Inc ....E 201 387-7252
Dumont **(G-2114)**

Kirms Printing Co Inc ....E 732 774-8000
Neptune **(G-6886)**

Kraft Tape Printers Inc ....G 973 824-3005
Newark **(G-7175)**

Kufall Printing ....G 732 505-9847
Toms River **(G-10774)**

L A S Printing Co ....G 201 991-5362
Jersey City **(G-4757)**

Latta Graphics Inc ....E 201 440-4040
Carlstadt **(G-1181)**

Lawn Medic Inc ....G 856 742-1111
Westville **(G-11818)**

LCI Graphics Inc ....F 973 893-2913
Sayreville **(G-9714)**

Lettie Press Inc ....G 201 391-6388
Park Ridge **(G-7854)**

Lewis Scheller Printing Corp ....G 732 843-5050
Somerset **(G-10016)**

Lexington Graphics Corp ....G 973 345-2493
Clifton **(G-1658)**

Liberty Envelope Inc ....F 973 546-5600
Paterson **(G-8240)**

Lightning Press Inc ....G 973 890-4422
Totowa **(G-10835)**

Lornan Litho Inc ....F 609 818-1198
Pennington **(G-8370)**

LP Thebault Co ....G 973 884-1300
Parsippany **(G-7974)**

M G X Inc ....F 732 329-0088
Monmouth Junction **(G-6296)**

Major Printing Co Inc ....G 908 686-7296
Union **(G-11072)**

Manva Industries Inc ....F 973 667-2606
Nutley **(G-7590)**

Manzi Printing ....G 732 542-1927
Eatontown **(G-2409)**

Mariano Press LLC ....F 732 247-3659
Somerset **(G-10022)**

Mark Lithography Inc ....E 973 538-5557
Cedar Knolls **(G-1309)**

Master Printing Inc ....G 201 842-9100
Carlstadt **(G-1186)**

Master Repro Inc ....G 201 447-4800
Midland Park **(G-6179)**

McGinnis Printing ....G 732 758-0060
Red Bank **(G-9235)**

McKella 2-8-0 Inc ....D 856 813-1153
Pennsauken **(G-8455)**

Medico Graphics Services Inc .....G 201 216-1660
Jersey City **(G-4764)**

Metro Web Corp ....E 201 553-0700
North Bergen **(G-7421)**

Mid Atlantic Graphix Inc ....G 609 569-9990
Egg Harbor Township **(G-2690)**

Monte Printing & Graphics Inc .....G 908 241-6600
Roselle Park **(G-9588)**

Morgan Printing Service Inc ....F 732 721-2959
South Amboy **(G-10138)**

Morris County Duplicating ....D 973 993-8484
Cedar Knolls **(G-1310)**

Morris Plains Pip Inc ....G 973 533-9330
Livingston **(G-5528)**

Morrison Press Inc ....F 201 488-4848
Closter **(G-1761)**

Mountain Printing Company Inc ....E 856 767-7600
Berlin **(G-427)**

Mr Quickly Inc ....G 908 687-6000
Union **(G-11077)**

My Way Prints Inc ....G 973 492-1212
Butler **(G-1010)**

National Certified Printing ....G 609 443-6323
Hightstown **(G-4297)**

New Horizon Graphics Inc ....G 609 584-1301
Trenton **(G-10960)**

New Jersey Reprographics Inc .....G 908 789-1616
Garwood **(G-3786)**

New Life Color Reproductions ......G 201 943-7005
Ridgefield **(G-9280)**

New Standard Printing Corp ....G 973 366-0006
Dover **(G-2101)**

Newline Prtg & Tech Solutions .....F 973 405-6133
Mountainside **(G-6849)**

Nitka Graphics Inc ....F 201 797-3000
Fair Lawn **(G-3114)**

Noble Metals Corp ....G 908 925-6300
Linden **(G-5397)**

Norwood Printing Inc ....F 201 784-8721
Norwood **(G-7572)**

Ocsidot Inc ....F 908 789-3300
Garwood **(G-3788)**

Old Hights Print Shop Inc ....G 609 443-4700
Jackson **(G-4661)**

OShea Services Inc ....G 201 343-8668
Hackensack **(G-3958)**

Otis Graphics Inc ....F 201 438-7120
Lyndhurst **(G-5671)**

Pace Press Incorporated ....D 201 935-7711
Moonachie **(G-6482)**

Panther Printing Inc ....G 239 542-1050
West Orange **(G-11777)**

Paravista Inc ....E 732 752-1222
Fairfield **(G-3289)**

Park Printing Services Inc ....F 856 675-1600
Pennsauken **(G-8463)**

Parkway Printing Inc ....G 732 308-0300
Marlboro **(G-5908)**

Parsells Printing Inc ....G 973 473-2700
Maywood **(G-6013)**

Pascack Valley Copy Center ....G 201 664-1917
Westwood **(G-11839)**

Patel Printing Plus Corp ....F 908 964-6422
Union **(G-11082)**

PDQ Print & Copy Inc ....F 201 569-2288
Englewood **(G-2931)**

Peacock Communications Inc ....G 973 763-3311
Maplewood **(G-5881)**

Penn Copy Center Inc ....G 646 251-0313
Lakewood **(G-5145)**

Penn Jersey Press Inc ....G 856 627-2200
Gibbsboro **(G-3795)**

Penny Press G 856 547-1991
Stratford (G-10506)
Permagraphics Inc F 201 814-1200
Moonachie (G-6483)
Phoenix Business Forms Inc G 856 691-2266
Vineland (G-11253)
Pica Printings Inc G 973 540-0420
Morristown (G-6693)
Pine Hill Printing Inc G 856 346-2915
Pine Hill (G-8622)
Pinnacle Press Inc G 201 652-0500
Midland Park (G-6182)
Pirolli Printing Co Inc F 856 933-1285
Bellmawr (G-341)
Premier Graphics Inc E 732 872-9933
Atlantic Highlands (G-110)
Premier Printing Solutions LLC G 732 525-0740
South Amboy (G-10139)
Premium Service Printing G 908 707-1311
Hillsborough (G-4345)
Presto Printing Service Inc G 908 756-5337
South Plainfield (G-10315)
Prestone Press LLC C 347 468-7900
Maywood (G-6015)
Princetonian Graphics Inc F 732 329-8282
Monmouth Junction (G-6306)
Print Group Inc F 201 487-4400
South Hackensack (G-10182)
Print Post G 973 732-0950
Newark (G-7235)
Print Shoppe Inc G 908 782-9213
Flemington (G-3463)
Print Tech LLC D 908 232-2287
Springfield (G-10461)
Print Tech LLC G 908 232-0767
Westfield (G-11801)
Printers Place Inc G 973 744-8889
Montclair (G-6385)
Printing Center Inc E 973 383-6362
Sparta (G-10407)
Printing Delite Inc G 973 676-3033
East Orange (G-2260)
Printing Industries LLC G 973 334-9775
Parsippany (G-8001)
Printing Plus of South Jersey G 856 767-3941
West Berlin (G-11617)
Prisco Digital Ltd Lblty Co F 973 589-7800
Newark (G-7237)
Prism Color Corporation D 856 234-7515
Moorestown (G-6559)
Prism Dgtal Communications LLC F 973 232-5038
Mountainside (G-6851)
Professional Printing Services G 856 428-6300
Haddonfield (G-4063)
Professional Reproductions Inc F 212 268-1222
Marlboro (G-5911)
Progress Printing Co F 201 433-3133
Jersey City (G-4788)
Progressive 4 Color Ltd Lblty G 973 736-5800
West Orange (G-11778)
Progressive Offset Inc E 201 569-3900
Englewood (G-2934)
Pronto Printing & Copying Ctr G 201 426-0009
Ramsey (G-9155)
Publishers Inc E 856 853-2800
West Deptford (G-11715)
Puent-Romer Communications Inc G 973 509-7591
Montclair (G-6386)
Q P 500 Inc G 732 531-8860
Ocean (G-7677)
Quad/Graphics Inc E 609 534-7308
Westampton (G-11791)
Quad/Graphics Inc E 732 469-0189
Somerset (G-10060)
R & B Printing Inc G 908 766-4073
Bernardsville (G-443)
R L R Foil Stamping LLC F 973 778-9464
Passaic (G-8100)
R V Livolsi Incorporated G 732 286-2200
Toms River (G-10786)
Rays Reproduction Inc G 201 666-5650
Emerson (G-2868)
Red Oak Packaging Inc E 862 268-8200
Newton (G-7354)
Register Lithographers Ltd D 973 916-2804
Clifton (G-1707)
Reliance Graphics Inc G 973 239-5411
Verona (G-11173)
Repro Tronics Inc G 201 722-1880
Ltl Egg Hbr (G-5619)
Repromatic Printing Inc G 973 239-7610
Cedar Grove (G-1291)
Review Printing Inc G 856 589-7200
Pitman (G-8747)
Rfm Printing Inc F 732 938-4400
Wall Township (G-11363)
Ridgewood Press Inc F 201 670-9797
Ridgewood (G-9328)
Riegel Holding Company Inc D 609 771-0361
Ewing (G-3062)
Roelynn Litho Inc F 732 942-9650
Lakewood (G-5159)
Rolls Offset Group Inc E 201 727-1110
Lyndhurst (G-5675)
Roned Printing & Reproduction G 973 386-1848
East Hanover (G-2236)
Roy Press Inc G 732 922-9460
Oceanport (G-7706)
Royal Printing Service E 201 863-3131
West New York (G-11753)
Royer Graphics Inc G 856 344-7935
Clementon (G-1535)
Rush Graphics Inc E 973 427-9393
Hawthorne (G-4242)
Sandy Alexander Inc C 973 470-8100
Clifton (G-1710)
Scodix Inc F 855 726-3491
Saddle Brook (G-9678)
Scott Graphics Printing Co Inc G 201 262-0473
New Milford (G-6992)
Sherman Printing Co Inc G 973 345-2493
Clifton (G-1715)
Showcase Printing of Iselin G 732 283-0438
Iselin (G-4627)
Solid Color Inc G 212 239-3930
Kearny (G-4899)
Star Litho Inc G 973 641-1603
Fairfield (G-3315)
Stauts Printing & Graphics G 609 654-5382
Medford (G-6035)
Steb Inc G 973 584-0990
Ledgewood (G-5281)
Steb Inc F 973 584-0990
Ledgewood (G-5282)
Stobbs Printing Co Inc G 973 748-4441
Bloomfield (G-519)
Stone Mountain Printing Inc G 732 636-8450
Woodbridge (G-12022)
Stuyvesant Press Inc F 973 399-3880
Irvington (G-4587)
Superfine Online Inc G 212 827-0063
Roselle (G-9574)
Sureway Prtg & Graphics LLC G 609 430-4333
Princeton (G-9030)
T G Type-O-Graphics Inc G 973 253-3333
Fair Lawn (G-3125)
Tabloid Graphic Services Inc D 856 486-0410
Pennsauken (G-8489)
Tandem Color Imaging Graphics G 973 513-9779
Pompton Lakes (G-8854)
Tangent Graphics Inc G 201 488-2840
Englewood (G-2946)
Tanter Inc G 732 382-3555
Clark (G-1516)
Tanzola Printing Inc G 973 779-0858
Clifton (G-1729)
The Creative Print Group Inc F 856 486-1700
Pennsauken (G-8492)
Thermo-Graphics Inc G 908 486-0100
Avenel (G-150)
Thewal Inc F 973 635-1880
Chatham (G-1330)
Thomas H Cox & Son Inc E 908 928-1010
Linden (G-5435)
Tmg Enterprises Inc E 732 469-2900
Piscataway (G-8728)
Toms River Printing Corp G 732 240-2033
Brielle (G-909)
Trenton Printing LLC F 609 695-6485
Trenton (G-11002)
Trinity Press Inc E 973 881-0690
Paterson (G-8317)
Tuerff Sziber Capitol Copy Svc G 609 989-8776
Trenton (G-11006)
Twill Inc F 908 665-1700
Berkeley Heights (G-413)
Typestyle Inc G 201 343-3343
Hackensack (G-3986)
Vanguard Printing G 856 358-2665
Elmer (G-2806)
Vernw Printing Company G 973 751-6462
Belleville (G-321)
Vestal Publishing Co Inc G 732 583-3232
Cliffwood (G-1549)
Vintage Print Gallery F 201 501-0505
Closter (G-1764)
Waldwick Printing Co G 201 652-5848
Waldwick (G-11312)
Welter & Kreutz Printing Co G 201 489-9098
South Hackensack (G-10190)
Westbury Press Inc D 201 894-0444
Englewood (G-2953)
Westerleigh Concepts Inc F 908 205-8888
South Plainfield (G-10346)
White Eagle Printing Co Inc E 609 586-2032
Trenton (G-11008)
Wilcox Press G 973 827-7474
Hamburg (G-4099)
William Robert Graphics Inc G 201 239-7400
Jersey City (G-4831)
Wong Robinson & Co Inc E 609 951-0300
Princeton (G-9044)
Yasheel Inc G 856 275-6812
Sewell (G-9854)
Your Printer V20 Ltd E 609 771-4000
Cranbury (G-1895)
Yukon Graphics Inc G 973 575-5700
Parsippany (G-8043)
Zippityprint LLC F 216 438-0001
Mullica Hill (G-6859)

PRINTING: Photo-Offset

AGFA Corporation E 201 440-0111
Carlstadt (G-1119)
Downtown Printing Center Inc F 732 246-7990
New Brunswick (G-6920)
Emerson Speed Printing Inc G 201 265-7977
Oradell (G-7743)
Fortress Graphics LLC E 973 276-0100
West Caldwell (G-11651)
Laureate Press G 609 646-1545
Egg Harbor City (G-2663)
Phillip Balderose G 732 574-1330
Clark (G-1512)
Photo Offset Prtg & Pubg Co G 609 587-4900
Trenton (G-10974)
Standard Prtg & Mail Svcs Inc F 973 790-3333
Fairfield (G-3314)
Star Promotions Inc F 732 356-5959
Bound Brook (G-607)
Tretina Printing Inc F 732 264-2324
Hazlet (G-4272)

PRINTING: Photolithographic

Linder & Company Inc F 201 386-8788
Jersey City (G-4759)

PRINTING: Rotogravure

Acme Engraving Co Inc E 973 778-0885
Passaic (G-8050)

PRINTING: Screen, Broadwoven Fabrics, Cotton

Anne Alanna Inc G 609 465-3787
Cape May Court House (G-1106)
Aztec Graphics Inc F 609 587-1000
Trenton (G-10900)
Chartwell Promotions Ltd Inc G 732 780-6900
Freehold (G-3657)
Mt Embroidery & Promotions LLC G 201 646-1070
Norwood (G-7569)
Rolferrys Specialties Inc G 856 456-2999
Brooklawn (G-915)
Screened Images Inc E 732 651-8181
East Brunswick (G-2175)
Unique Screen Printing Corp E 908 925-3773
Linden (G-5438)

PRINTING: Screen, Fabric

Acey Industries Inc G 973 595-1222
North Haledon (G-7494)
Ambro Manufacturing Inc F 908 806-8337
Flemington (G-3429)
Art Flag Co Inc F 212 334-1890
Fair Haven (G-3078)
Designs By James G 856 692-1316
Vineland (G-11213)

McLain Studios Inc ....G..... 732 775-0271
Asbury Park *(G-80)*

Nes Enterprises Inc ....G..... 201 964-1400
Carlstadt *(G-1190)*

Total Ink Solutions LLC ....F..... 201 487-9600
Hackensack *(G-3983)*

Wally Enterprises Inc ....F..... 732 329-2613
Monmouth Junction *(G-6319)*

PRINTING: Screen, Manmade Fiber & Silk, Broadwoven Fabric

Chartwell Promotions Ltd Inc ....G..... 732 780-6900
Freehold *(G-3657)*

Design N Stitch Inc ....G..... 201 488-1314
Hackensack *(G-3906)*

Gilbert Storms Jr ....G..... 973 835-5729
Haskell *(G-4196)*

Screened Images Inc ....E..... 732 651-8181
East Brunswick *(G-2175)*

Unique Screen Printing Corp ....E..... 908 925-3773
Linden *(G-5438)*

PRINTING: Thermography

Magic Printing Corp ....F..... 732 726-0620
Avenel *(G-135)*

Print Communications Group Inc ......D..... 973 882-9444
Fairfield *(G-3295)*

Trade Thermographers Inc ....F..... 201 489-2060
Rochelle Park *(G-9432)*

Watonka Printing Inc ....G..... 732 974-8878
Belmar *(G-356)*

PRODUCT STERILIZATION SVCS

E-Beam Services Inc ....E..... 513 933-0031
Cranbury *(G-1831)*

PROFESSIONAL EQPT & SPLYS, WHOLESALE: Analytical Instruments

Symtera Analytics LLC ....F..... 718 696-9902
Wall Township *(G-11373)*

PROFESSIONAL EQPT & SPLYS, WHOLESALE: Law Enforcement

Jontol Unlimited LLC ....G..... 858 652-1113
Blackwood *(G-473)*

PROFESSIONAL EQPT & SPLYS, WHOLESALE: Optical Goods

Complete Optical Laboratory ....F..... 973 338-8886
Bloomfield *(G-497)*

Hamamatsu Corporation ....E..... 908 231-0960
Middlesex *(G-6119)*

Lens Lab Express ....G..... 201 861-0016
West New York *(G-11745)*

PROFESSIONAL EQPT & SPLYS, WHOLESALE: Precision Tools

Oroszlany Laszlo ....G..... 201 666-2101
Hillsdale *(G-4369)*

PROFESSIONAL EQPT & SPLYS, WHOLESALE: Scientific & Engineerg

Arthur H Thomas Company ....B..... 856 467-2000
Swedesboro *(G-10571)*

Magnetic Products and Svcs Inc ......G..... 732 264-6651
Holmdel *(G-4504)*

Thomas Scientific Inc ....B..... 800 345-2100
Swedesboro *(G-10614)*

Thomas Scientific LLC ....G..... 800 345-2100
Swedesboro *(G-10615)*

PROFESSIONAL EQPT & SPLYS, WHOLESALE: Theatrical

American Harlequin Corporation ......E..... 856 234-5505
Moorestown *(G-6503)*

Rose Brand Wipers Inc ....C..... 201 809-1730
Secaucus *(G-9804)*

W Gerriets International Inc ....F..... 609 771-8111
Ewing *(G-3077)*

PROFESSIONAL INSTRUMENT REPAIR SVCS

Rf Vii Inc ....F..... 856 875-2121
Newfield *(G-7327)*

Sk & P Industries Inc ....G..... 973 482-1864
Newark *(G-7276)*

State Technology Inc ....G..... 856 467-8009
Bridgeport *(G-746)*

PROFILE SHAPES: Unsupported Plastics

Accessrec LLC ....G..... 973 955-0514
Clifton *(G-1553)*

All State Plastics Inc ....E..... 732 654-5054
South Amboy *(G-10130)*

Belle Printing Group LLC ....G..... 856 235-5151
Mount Laurel *(G-6741)*

Fluorotherm Polymers Inc ....G..... 973 575-0760
Parsippany *(G-7948)*

Keystone Plastics Inc ....D..... 908 561-1300
South Plainfield *(G-10287)*

Plast-O-Matic Valves Inc ....D..... 973 256-3000
Cedar Grove *(G-1287)*

Saint-Gobain Prfmce Plas Corp ......D..... 856 423-6630
Mickleton *(G-6088)*

Tricomp Inc ....C..... 973 835-1110
Pompton Plains *(G-8872)*

PROMOTION SVCS

AlphaGraphics ....G..... 201 327-2200
Mahwah *(G-5712)*

Apollo East LLC ....E..... 856 486-1882
Pennsauken *(G-8389)*

Fu WEI Inc ....G..... 732 937-8388
East Brunswick *(G-2147)*

Hit Promo LLC ....C..... 800 237-6305
Bellmawr *(G-334)*

Timeline Promotions Inc ....G..... 973 226-1512
West Caldwell *(G-11680)*

PROTECTION EQPT: Lightning

Lightning Prvntion Systems Inc ......G..... 856 767-7806
West Berlin *(G-11603)*

PROTECTIVE FOOTWEAR: Rubber Or Plastic

Lust For Life Footwear LLC ....F..... 646 732-9742
Teaneck *(G-10638)*

Tingley Rubber Corporation ....E..... 800 631-5498
Piscataway *(G-8727)*

PUBLIC ADDRESS SYSTEMS

Oklahoma Sound Corp ....E..... 800 261-4112
Clifton *(G-1680)*

PUBLIC FINANCE, TAXATION & MONETARY POLICY OFFICES

New Jersey Department Treasury ......E..... 609 292-5133
Trenton *(G-10962)*

PUBLIC RELATIONS SVCS

Rbs Intrntonal Direct Mktg LLC ......G..... 856 663-2500
Cherry Hill *(G-1413)*

The Creative Print Group Inc ....F..... 856 486-1700
Pennsauken *(G-8492)*

PUBLISHERS: Art Copy

Arthur A Kaplan Co Inc ....E..... 201 806-2100
East Rutherford *(G-2273)*

PUBLISHERS: Art Copy & Poster

Bruce Teleky Inc ....G..... 718 965-9694
Jersey City *(G-4706)*

M/C Communications LLC ....F..... 908 766-0402
Basking Ridge *(G-188)*

Physicians Weekly LLC ....G..... 908 766-0421
Basking Ridge *(G-195)*

Sonata Graphics Inc ....G..... 201 866-0186
Secaucus *(G-9816)*

PUBLISHERS: Book

Alexander Communications Group ......F..... 973 265-2300
Mountain Lakes *(G-6820)*

AM Best Company Inc ....B..... 908 439-2200
Oldwick *(G-7739)*

Apples & Honey Press LLC ....F..... 973 379-7200
Springfield *(G-10427)*

Barnes & Noble Booksellers Inc ......E..... 201 272-3635
Lyndhurst *(G-5642)*

Bookcode Corp ....G..... 732 742-0481
Woodbridge *(G-12015)*

CNG Publishing Company ....G..... 973 768-0978
Burlington *(G-959)*

Evergreen Information Svcs Inc ......F..... 973 339-9672
Woodland Park *(G-12077)*

Franklin Electronic Publs Inc ....D..... 609 386-2500
Burlington *(G-969)*

Gorgias Press LLC ....G..... 732 885-8900
Piscataway *(G-8669)*

Hispanic Outlook In Higher ....G..... 201 587-8800
Saddle Brook *(G-9655)*

Hispanic Outlook-12 Mag Inc ....G..... 201 587-8800
Fair Lawn *(G-3104)*

Howard Press Inc ....D..... 908 245-4400
Roselle *(G-9561)*

Hudson Group (hg) Inc ....B..... 201 939-5050
East Rutherford *(G-2292)*

J S Paluch Co Inc ....F..... 732 516-1900
Edison *(G-2537)*

Mathematics League Inc ....G..... 201 568-6328
Tenafly *(G-10664)*

Metal Powder Inds Federation ....F..... 609 452-7700
Princeton *(G-8977)*

Missionary Society of St Paul ....E..... 201 825-7300
Mahwah *(G-5755)*

New York-NJ Trail Conference ......F..... 201 512-9348
Mahwah *(G-5757)*

NJ Dept Military Vtrans ....G..... 856 384-8831
Woodbury *(G-12033)*

Pearson Education Inc ....A..... 201 236-7000
Hoboken *(G-4473)*

Pearson Education Inc ....D..... 914 287-8000
Hoboken *(G-4474)*

Pearson Education Inc ....E..... 609 395-6000
Cranbury *(G-1871)*

Philip Lief Group Inc ....G..... 609 430-1000
Princeton *(G-8995)*

Princeton Publishing Group ....G..... 609 577-0693
Princeton *(G-9002)*

Princeton University Press ....D..... 609 258-4900
Princeton *(G-9007)*

Railpace Co Inc ....G..... 732 388-4984
Clark *(G-1514)*

Renaissance House ....G..... 201 408-4048
Englewood *(G-2937)*

Research & Education Assn ....E..... 732 819-8880
Piscataway *(G-8705)*

School Publications Co Inc ....E..... 732 988-1100
Neptune *(G-6896)*

Silicon Press Inc ....G..... 908 273-8919
Summit *(G-10547)*

Taryag Legacy Foundation Inc ....F..... 732 569-2467
Lakewood *(G-5170)*

Transaction Publishers Inc ....G..... 732 445-2280
Piscataway *(G-8732)*

Trilogy Publications LLC ....G..... 201 816-1211
Englewood Cliffs *(G-2993)*

PUBLISHERS: Book Clubs, No Printing

Plexus Publishing Inc ....E..... 609 654-6500
Medford *(G-6031)*

PUBLISHERS: Books, No Printing

Africa World Press ....G..... 609 695-3200
Ewing *(G-3013)*

AM Best Company Inc ....A..... 908 439-2200
Oldwick *(G-7738)*

Behrman House Inc ....F..... 973 379-7200
Millburn *(G-6195)*

Berlitz Languages US Inc ....D..... 609 759-5371
Princeton *(G-8914)*

Blue Dome Inc ....G..... 646 415-9331
Clifton *(G-1576)*

Carstens Publications Inc ....E..... 973 383-3355
Newton *(G-7339)*

Chatham Bookseller Inc ....G..... 973 822-1361
Madison *(G-5690)*

Colt Media Inc ....G..... 732 946-3276
Colts Neck *(G-1779)*

Comex Systems Inc ....G..... 800 543-6959
Chester *(G-1432)*

Creative Competitions Inc ....F..... 856 256-2797
Sewell *(G-9838)*

Ensembleiq Inc ....E 201 855-7600
Newark (G-7116)

Galves Auto Price List Inc ....F 201 393-0051
Teterboro (G-10678)

Haights Cross Cmmnications Inc ....E 212 209-0500
Princeton Junction (G-9060)

Just US Books Inc ....G 973 672-7701
East Orange (G-2254)

Learning Links-Usa Inc ....G 516 437-9071
Cranbury (G-1855)

Manning Publication Co ....F 856 375-2597
Cherry Hill (G-1388)

Markus Wiener Publishers Inc ....G 609 921-1141
Princeton (G-8973)

Matthew Bender & Company Inc ....D 518 487-3000
Newark (G-7197)

Modern Drummer Publications ....F 973 239-4140
Fairfield (G-3272)

New Horizon Press Publishers ....G 908 604-6311
Liberty Corner (G-5295)

Patterson Smith Publishing ....G 973 744-3291
Montclair (G-6384)

Paulist Press Inc ....G 201 825-7300
Mahwah (G-5761)

Pearson Education Inc ....F 201 785-2721
Hoboken (G-4475)

Presbyterian Reformed Pubg Co ....F 908 454-0505
Phillipsburg (G-8570)

Red Sea Press Inc ....G 609 695-3200
Ewing (G-3059)

Rosemont Publishing & Printing ....F 609 269-8094
Plainsboro (G-8802)

RR Bowker LLC ....C 908 286-1090
New Providence (G-7017)

Scholastic Inc ....E 201 633-2400
Secaucus (G-9809)

Simon & Schuster Inc ....E 973 656-6000
Parsippany (G-8016)

Springer Scnce + Bus Media LLC ....D 201 348-4033
Secaucus (G-9817)

Sterling Publishing Co Inc ....F 732 248-6563
Monroe Township (G-6346)

Thomson Reuters Corporation ....B 212 337-4281
Newark (G-7299)

Wordmasters ....G 201 327-4201
Allendale (G-20)

PUBLISHERS: Catalogs

Bookazine Co Inc ....D 201 339-7777
Bayonne (G-207)

Catalogue Publishers Inc ....F 973 423-3600
Fair Lawn (G-3093)

PUBLISHERS: Directories, NEC

Information Today Inc ....F 908 219-0279
New Providence (G-7004)

Jonas Media Group Inc ....F 973 438-1900
Newark (G-7170)

Thomas Publishing Company LLC ....E 973 543-4994
Chester (G-1435)

Thryv Inc ....F 908 237-0956
Flemington (G-3471)

Walden Mott Corp ....G 201 962-3704
Ramsey (G-9158)

PUBLISHERS: Directories, Telephone

Supermedia LLC ....B 973 649-9900
Maplewood (G-5884)

Verizon Communications Inc ....E 201 666-9934
Westwood (G-11847)

Verizon Communications Inc ....D 609 646-9939
Egg Harbor Township (G-2700)

PUBLISHERS: Guides

Community Pride Publications ....F 609 921-8760
Princeton Junction (G-9053)

Jersey Job Guide Inc ....G 732 263-9675
Long Branch (G-5601)

PUBLISHERS: Magazines, No Printing

Advanstar Communications Inc ....E 973 944-7777
Montvale (G-6395)

Advanstar Communications Inc ....E 732 596-0276
Iselin (G-4590)

AM Best Company Inc ....A 908 439-2200
Oldwick (G-7738)

B T O Industries Inc ....G 973 243-0011
West Orange (G-11761)

Backroads Inc ....G 973 948-4176
Newton (G-7338)

Bauer Publishing Company LP ....G 201 569-6699
Englewood Cliffs (G-2960)

Bbm Fairway Inc ....G 856 596-0999
Marlton (G-5922)

Carstens Publications Inc ....E 973 383-3355
Newton (G-7339)

Casino Player Publishing LLC ....E 609 404-0600
Galloway (G-3721)

Christian Mssons In Many Lands ....G 732 449-8880
Wall Township (G-11324)

Commerce Enterprises Inc ....F 201 368-2100
Paramus (G-7794)

Data Cntrum Communications Inc ....F 201 391-1911
Montvale (G-6407)

Dowden Health Media Inc ....D 201 740-6100
Montvale (G-6408)

E W Williams Publications ....F 201 592-7007
Fort Lee (G-3556)

Evergreen Information Svcs Inc ....F 973 339-9672
Woodland Park (G-12077)

Garden State Woman Mag LLC ....G 908 879-7143
Long Valley (G-5611)

Golf Odyssey Inc ....G 973 564-6223
Short Hills (G-9869)

Haymarket Media Inc ....G 201 799-4800
Paramus (G-7805)

Heinrich Bauer Publishing LP ....F 201 569-6699
Englewood (G-2911)

Heinrich Bauer Verlag ....E 201 569-0006
Englewood Cliffs (G-2973)

Hobby Publications Inc ....E 732 536-5160
Freehold (G-3668)

Industry Publications Inc ....F 973 331-9545
Parsippany (G-7961)

Intellisphere LLC ....G 609 716-7777
Plainsboro (G-8797)

Interntonal Med News Group LLC ....F 973 290-8237
Parsippany (G-7964)

Investment Casting Institute ....G 201 573-9770
Montvale (G-6414)

Jonas Media Group Inc ....F 973 438-1900
Newark (G-7170)

Jury Vrdict Rview Publications ....G 973 376-9002
Springfield (G-10449)

Know America Media LLC ....G 770 650-1102
Roseland (G-9540)

Lead Conversion Plus ....F 802 497-1557
Manalapan (G-5816)

Media Vista Inc ....G 732 747-8060
Red Bank (G-9236)

Middlesex Publications ....F 732 435-0005
North Brunswick (G-7477)

Modern Drummer Publications ....F 973 239-4140
Fairfield (G-3272)

Music Trades Corp ....G 201 871-1965
Englewood (G-2927)

National Housing Institute ....G 973 509-1600
Montclair (G-6377)

New Jersey Bus & Indust Assn ....D 609 393-7707
Trenton (G-10961)

New Jrsey State Leag Mncplties ....F 609 695-3481
Trenton (G-10964)

Northstar Travel Media LLC ....C 201 902-2000
Secaucus (G-9794)

Npt Publishing Group Inc ....F 973 401-0202
Morris Plains (G-6620)

Nsgv Inc ....C 212 620-2200
Jersey City (G-4774)

Pentacle Publishing Corp ....E 732 240-3000
Toms River (G-10782)

Quick Frozen Foods Intl ....E 201 592-7007
Fort Lee (G-3583)

Recruit Co Ltd ....E 201 216-0600
Jersey City (G-4798)

Retail Management Pubg Inc ....F 212 981-0217
Montclair (G-6388)

Rodman Media Corp ....E 201 825-2552
Montvale (G-6432)

Scholastic Uk Group LLC ....C 201 633-2400
Secaucus (G-9810)

Sports Impact Inc ....G 732 257-1451
East Brunswick (G-2179)

Steppin Out Magazine ....G 201 703-0911
Fair Lawn (G-3122)

Tommax Inc ....G 732 224-1046
Red Bank (G-9246)

US Frontline News Inc ....E 646 284-6233
Demarest (G-2026)

Vicinity Publications Inc ....G 973 276-1688
Fairfield (G-3344)

Visual Impact Advertising Inc ....F 973 763-4900
Maplewood (G-5889)

Vitamin Retailer Magazine Inc ....G 732 432-9600
East Brunswick (G-2191)

Walden Mott Corp ....G 201 962-3704
Ramsey (G-9158)

PUBLISHERS: Miscellaneous

Access Response Inc ....G 732 660-0770
Ocean (G-7652)

Action Press Park Slope ....G 718 624-3457
Holmdel (G-4492)

Altare Publishing Inc ....G 727 237-1330
Ewing (G-3014)

Cape Publishing Inc ....G 609 898-4500
Cape May (G-1094)

Captivate Internationallc ....G 732 734-0403
Edison (G-2473)

Cariletha Company Inc ....F 609 222-3055
Mount Laurel (G-6746)

Central Record Publications ....E 609 654-5000
Trenton (G-10915)

Charles Kerr Enterprises Inc ....G 732 738-6500
Edison (G-2476)

Cohansey Cove ....G 609 884-7726
Cape May (G-1095)

Consumer Graphics Inc ....G 732 469-4699
Somerset (G-9977)

Criterion Publishing Co ....G 732 548-8300
Metuchen (G-6053)

Crossfire Publications ....G 516 352-9087
Caldwell (G-1021)

Down Shore Publishing Corp ....G 609 978-1233
West Creek (G-11686)

Dune Grass Publishing LLC ....G 609 774-6562
Blackwood (G-464)

Eastside Express Corporation ....G 908 486-3300
Linden (G-5344)

Ebsco Industries Inc ....E 732 542-8600
Shrewsbury (G-9891)

Ebsco Industries Inc ....D 201 569-2500
Tinton Falls (G-10715)

Ebsco Publishing Inc ....G 201 968-9899
Hackensack (G-3910)

Eclecticism Publishing LLC ....G 212 714-4714
Robbinsville (G-9411)

Electrochemical Society Inc ....E 609 737-1902
Pennington (G-8364)

Financial Information Inc ....E 908 222-5300
South Plainfield (G-10259)

Florentine Press Inc ....G 201 386-9200
Jersey City (G-4736)

Friday Morning Quarterback ....G 856 424-6873
Cherry Hill (G-1363)

Galves Auto Price List Inc ....F 201 393-0051
Teterboro (G-10678)

Gmp Publications Inc ....G 609 859-3400
Southampton (G-10364)

Gorgias Press ....G 732 699-0343
Piscataway (G-8668)

Grafwed Internet Media Studios ....G 201 632-1771
Midland Park (G-6175)

Grey House Publishing Inc ....G 201 968-0500
Hackensack (G-3925)

Heritage Publishing ....G 732 747-7770
Colts Neck (G-1785)

J D M Associates Inc ....G 973 773-8699
Lodi (G-5566)

J S Paluch Co Inc ....E 732 238-2412
East Brunswick (G-2153)

J S Paluch Co Inc ....F 732 516-1900
Edison (G-2537)

Jav Latin America Express ....G 201 868-5004
West New York (G-11743)

Jem Printing Inc ....G 908 782-9986
Flemington (G-3450)

Jersey Shore News Mgazines Inc ....E 609 494-5900
Surf City (G-10555)

Jigsaw Publishing LLC ....G 973 838-4838
Butler (G-1006)

John Patrick Publishing LLC ....D 609 883-2700
Ewing (G-3038)

John R Zabka Associates Inc ....F 201 405-0075
Oakland (G-7633)

Jump Start Press ....G 732 892-4994
Point Pleasant Beach (G-8825)

Kabab & Curry Express ....G 732 416-6560
Edison (G-2544)

PRODUCT

Kates-Bylston Publications Inc .... G 732 746-0211
  Wall Township (G-11350)
Laennec Publishing Inc .... G 973 882-9500
  Parsippany (G-7971)
Light Inc .... G 973 777-2704
  Clifton (G-1659)
Lympha Press USA .... G 732 792-9677
  Freehold (G-3678)
Macie Publishing Company .... F 973 983-8700
  Mendham (G-6040)
Magazinexperts LLC .... G 973 383-0888
  Newton (G-7349)
Marquis - Whos Who Inc .... D 908 673-1006
  New Providence (G-7009)
National Home Planning Service .... G 973 376-3200
  Chatham (G-1328)
Nextwave Web LLC .... F 973 742-4339
  Paterson (G-8269)
Nighthawk Interactive LLC .... G 732 243-9922
  Edison (G-2574)
North Jersey Media Group Inc .... E 973 569-7100
  Woodland Park (G-12085)
Northern State Periodicals LLC .... G 973 782-6100
  Paterson (G-8272)
Odowd Enterprises Inc .... G 973 227-4607
  Pine Brook (G-8612)
Pavexpress .... G 201 330-8300
  Clifton (G-1686)
Princeton Information Center .... G 609 924-7019
  Princeton (G-8999)
Princeton University Press .... D 609 258-4900
  Princeton (G-9007)
Publishers Partnership Co .... D 201 689-1613
  Ridgewood (G-9326)
Raphel Marketing Inc .... G 609 348-6646
  Atlantic City (G-102)
Review and Judge LLC .... G 732 987-3905
  Lakewood (G-5157)
Rockwood Corporation .... G 908 355-8600
  Frenchtown (G-3717)
Scholastic Book Fairs Inc .... G 609 578-4142
  Cranbury (G-1880)
School Publications Co Inc .... E 732 988-1100
  Neptune (G-6896)
Seven Mile Pubg & Creative .... F 609 967-7707
  Avalon (G-116)
Shoppe CMC Shoppers Guide .... G 609 886-4112
  Villas (G-11181)
Simon & Schuster Inc .... B 856 461-6500
  Delran (G-2020)
Simon & Schuster Inc .... E 973 656-6000
  Parsippany (G-8016)
Slack Incorporated .... G 856 848-1000
  Thorofare (G-10703)
South Jersey Publishing Co .... F 856 692-0455
  Vineland (G-11267)
Spendylove Home Care LLC .... F 732 430-5789
  Monmouth Junction (G-6312)
Stanger Robert A & Co LP .... E 732 389-3600
  Shrewsbury (G-9902)
Steven Orros .... G 732 972-1104
  Monroe Township (G-6347)
Success Publishers LLC .... G 609 443-0792
  Perrineville (G-8508)
T3i Group LLC .... F 856 424-1100
  Cherry Hill (G-1420)
Tap Into LLC .... G 908 370-1158
  New Providence (G-7020)
Teckchek .... G 919 497-0136
  East Brunswick (G-2186)
Thepositive Press .... G 856 266-8765
  Cinnaminson (G-1490)
Thomsom Health Care Inc .... C 201 358-7300
  Montvale (G-6436)
Thomson Reuters Corporation .... F 973 662-3070
  Nutley (G-7595)
Token Torch Ltd Liability Co .... F 973 629-1805
  East Orange (G-2266)
Treasure Chest Corp .... G 973 328-7747
  Wharton (G-11872)
Victory Press .... G 201 729-1007
  Moonachie (G-6496)
Voicings Publication Inc .... G 609 822-9401
  Ventnor City (G-11155)
World Scientific Publishing Co .... F 201 487-9655
  Hackensack (G-3991)

PUBLISHERS: Music Book & Sheet Music

Lead Bead Publishing Company .... G 732 246-0410
  Somerset (G-10014)

Subito Music Service Inc .... G 973 857-3440
  Verona (G-11176)

PUBLISHERS: Music, Book

Oasis Entertainment Group .... G 973 256-7077
  Cedar Grove (G-1285)

PUBLISHERS: Music, Sheet

Clyde Otis Music Group .... G 845 425-8198
  Englewood (G-2893)
Hal Leonard LLC .... C 973 337-5034
  Montclair (G-6368)
Iws License Corp .... F 732 872-0014
  Atlantic Highlands (G-107)
Sueta Music Ed Publications .... F 888 725-2333
  Mendham (G-6043)
Trf Music Inc .... F 201 335-0005
  Tinton Falls (G-10732)

PUBLISHERS: Newsletter

Excerpta Medica Inc .... D 908 547-2100
  Bridgewater (G-822)
Harrison Scott Pblications Inc .... E 201 659-1700
  Hoboken (G-4453)
Old Barracks Association Inc .... F 609 396-1776
  Trenton (G-10968)
P O V Incorporated .... F 914 258-4361
  Montclair (G-6381)
Wpi Communications Inc .... G 973 467-8700
  Springfield (G-10475)

PUBLISHERS: Newspaper

21st Century Media Newsppr LLC .... D 215 504-4200
  Trenton (G-10885)
50 Plus Monthly Inc .... G 973 584-7911
  Succasunna (G-10508)
Alm Media LLC .... E 973 642-0075
  Newark (G-7042)
Arts Weekly Inc .... E 973 812-6766
  Little Falls (G-5453)
Bernardsville News .... G 908 766-3900
  Bernardsville (G-435)
Binding Products Inc .... E 212 947-1192
  Jersey City (G-4704)
Bloomfield Life Inc .... F 973 233-5001
  Cedar Grove (G-1270)
Bloomfield News LLC .... G 973 226-2127
  West Caldwell (G-11643)
Cgw News LLC .... G 973 473-3972
  Clifton (G-1581)
Daily News LP .... F 212 210-2100
  Jersey City (G-4720)
David Sisco Jr .... G 908 454-0880
  Phillipsburg (G-8548)
Dolan LLC .... G 800 451-9998
  Princeton (G-8931)
Dorf Feature Service Inc .... E 908 518-1802
  Mountainside (G-6843)
Epoch Times .... G 908 548-8026
  South Plainfield (G-10252)
Gannett Stllite Info Ntwrk Inc .... C 856 691-5000
  Vineland (G-11220)
Gannett Stllite Info Ntwrk LLC .... B 973 428-6200
  Rockaway (G-9462)
Gannett Stllite Info Ntwrk LLC .... G 856 663-6000
  Cherry Hill (G-1366)
Hammonton Gazette Inc .... G 609 704-1939
  Hammonton (G-4135)
James Kinkade .... F 856 451-1177
  Bridgeton (G-760)
Janas LLC .... G 732 536-6719
  Morganville (G-6590)
Jose Moreira .... G 201 991-9001
  Kearny (G-4873)
Latino U S A .... G 732 870-1475
  Long Branch (G-5602)
Link News .... G 732 222-4300
  Long Branch (G-5603)
Medieval Times USA Inc .... C 201 933-2220
  Lyndhurst (G-5662)
Montclair Dispatch LLC .... G 973 509-8861
  Montclair (G-6375)
Muse Monthly LLC .... G 609 443-3509
  East Windsor (G-2355)
New Jersey Jewish News .... E 973 887-3900
  Whippany (G-11898)
New Satellite Network LLC .... G 908 922-0967
  Scotch Plains (G-9738)

North Jersey Media Group Inc .... E 973 569-7100
  Woodland Park (G-12085)
Packet Media LLC .... G 856 779-3800
  Englishtown (G-3007)
Palisades Magnolia Prpts LLC .... G 201 424-7180
  Palisades Park (G-7776)
Paper Dove Press LLC .... G 201 641-7938
  Little Ferry (G-5493)
Paradise Publishing Group LLC .... G 609 227-7642
  Willingboro (G-11994)
Penn Jersey Advance Inc .... D 201 775-6610
  Secaucus (G-9796)
Recorder Newspaper .... G 973 226-4000
  Caldwell (G-1029)
Recorder Publishing Co .... E 908 647-1180
  Stirling (G-10495)
Red Bank Gstrntrology Assoc PA .... E 732 842-4294
  Red Bank (G-9242)
Reminder Newspaper .... F 856 825-8811
  Millville (G-6268)
Reporte Hispano .... G 609 933-1400
  Princeton (G-9016)
Sample Media Inc .... G 609 884-2021
  Cape May (G-1101)
Sample Media Inc .... E 609 399-5411
  Ocean City (G-7695)
School Publications Co Inc .... E 732 988-1100
  Neptune (G-6896)
Star News Group .... G 732 223-0076
  Manasquan (G-5839)
Str8line Publishing Company .... G 919 717-6740
  Newark (G-7288)
Suburban Guides Inc .... G 201 452-4989
  Waretown (G-11394)
Summit Professional Networks .... E 201 526-1230
  Hoboken (G-4483)
Tapintonet .... G 908 279-0303
  New Providence (G-7021)
Times of Trenton Pubg Corp .... A 609 989-5454
  Trenton (G-10998)
Ukrainian National Association .... E 973 292-9800
  Parsippany (G-8032)
Venture Info Network .... G 609 279-0777
  Princeton (G-9041)
Wilmington Trust Sp Services .... C 609 272-7000
  Pleasantville (G-8821)

PUBLISHERS: Newspapers, No Printing

24 Horas Inc .... F 973 817-7400
  Newark (G-7026)
Advocate Publishing Corp .... E 973 497-4200
  Newark (G-7036)
Atlantic City Week .... F 609 646-4848
  Pleasantville (G-8805)
Bayonne Community News .... E 201 437-2460
  Bayonne (G-205)
Brazilian Press & Advertising .... F 973 344-4555
  Newark (G-7073)
Cabio Newspaper .... E 201 902-0811
  West New York (G-11736)
Catholic Star Herald .... G 856 583-6142
  Camden (G-1050)
Coast Star .... E 732 223-0076
  Manasquan (G-5830)
Community News Network Inc .... G 856 428-3399
  Haddonfield (G-4055)
Cumberland News Inc .... G 856 691-2244
  Vineland (G-11208)
Diocese of Camden New Jersey .... A 856 756-7900
  Camden (G-1058)
Diocese of Paterson .... F 973 279-8845
  Clifton (G-1599)
Dyer Communications Inc .... E 732 219-5788
  Red Bank (G-9227)
Elmer Times Co Inc .... G 856 358-6171
  Elmer (G-2796)
Evergreen Information Svcs Inc .... F 973 339-9672
  Woodland Park (G-12077)
Gatehuse Media PA Holdings Inc .... E 732 246-7677
  New Brunswick (G-6927)
Greater Media Newspapers .... E 732 358-5200
  Englishtown (G-3003)
Gruppo Editoriale Oggi Inc .... E 201 358-6582
  Norwood (G-7563)
Hawthorne Press .... F 973 427-3330
  Hawthorne (G-4224)
Hudson West Publishing Co .... F 201 991-1600
  Kearny (G-4864)
La Tribuna Publication Inc .... E 201 617-1360
  Union City (G-11118)

Luso-Americano Co Inc.................E...... 973 344-3200
   Newark *(G-7189)*
Medianews Group Inc.................D...... 856 451-1000
   Salem *(G-9695)*
Micro Media Publications Inc.................G...... 732 657-7344
   Lakehurst *(G-5039)*
New View Media.................E...... 973 691-3002
   Budd Lake *(G-931)*
Ocean Star.................G...... 732 899-7606
   Point Pleasant Beach *(G-8830)*
Parker Publications.................F...... 908 766-3900
   Madison *(G-5699)*
Richard Rein.................F...... 609 452-7000
   Lawrence Township *(G-5219)*
South Jersey Publishing Co.................B...... 609 272-7000
   Pleasantville *(G-8819)*
Tribuna Hispana.................G...... 609 646-9167
   Pleasantville *(G-8820)*
U S A Distributors Inc.................E...... 201 348-1959
   Union City *(G-11130)*
Walden Mott Corp.................G...... 201 962-3704
   Ramsey *(G-9158)*
Watthung Communications Inc.................F...... 908 232-4407
   Westfield *(G-11805)*
West Essex Tribune Inc.................F...... 973 992-1771
   Livingston *(G-5547)*
Worrall Community Newspapers.................G...... 973 743-4040
   Bloomfield *(G-522)*
Yated Neeman Inc.................F...... 845 369-1600
   Lakewood *(G-5185)*

PUBLISHERS: Pamphlets, No Printing

Banquet Services International.................G...... 732 270-1188
   Toms River *(G-10747)*
Excerpta Medica Inc.................D...... 908 547-2100
   Bridgewater *(G-822)*
J S Paluch Co Inc.................E...... 732 238-2412
   East Brunswick *(G-2153)*

PUBLISHERS: Periodical Statistical Reports, No Printing

John Wiley & Sons Inc.................D...... 201 748-6000
   Hoboken *(G-4460)*
Keypoint Intelligence LLC.................G...... 201 489-6439
   Hackensack *(G-3936)*
Keypoint Intelligence LLC.................E...... 973 797-2100
   Fairfield *(G-3249)*
SMR Research Corporation.................G...... 908 852-7677
   Hackettstown *(G-4037)*

PUBLISHERS: Periodical, With Printing

Alexander Communications Group.................F...... 973 265-2300
   Mountain Lakes *(G-6820)*
Skinder-Strauss LLC.................C...... 973 642-1440
   New Providence *(G-7018)*
T3i Group LLC.................E...... 856 424-1100
   Cherry Hill *(G-1420)*

PUBLISHERS: Periodicals, Magazines

42 Design Square LLC.................F...... 888 272-5979
   Parsippany *(G-7870)*
Alternate Side Street Suspende.................G...... 201 291-7878
   Paramus *(G-7788)*
AM Best Company Inc.................B...... 908 439-2200
   Oldwick *(G-7739)*
Central Record Publications.................E...... 609 654-5000
   Trenton *(G-10915)*
Civic Research Institute Inc.................G...... 609 683-4450
   Kingston *(G-5008)*
Convention News Company Inc.................F...... 201 444-5075
   Midland Park *(G-6173)*
Curran & Connors Inc.................G...... 609 514-0104
   Princeton *(G-8925)*
Friday Morning Quarterback.................E...... 856 424-6873
   Cherry Hill *(G-1363)*
Galen Publishing LLC.................E...... 908 253-9001
   Somerville *(G-10111)*
General Commis Archives & Hstr.................G...... 973 408-3189
   Madison *(G-5693)*
Hsh Assoc Financial Publishers.................G...... 973 838-3330
   Butler *(G-1004)*
J S Paluch Co Inc.................F...... 732 516-1900
   Edison *(G-2537)*
Macromedia Incorporated.................F...... 201 646-4000
   Hackensack *(G-3942)*
Mindwise Media LLC.................G...... 973 701-0685
   Chatham *(G-1327)*

Missionary Society of St Paul.................E...... 201 825-7300
   Mahwah *(G-5755)*
N J W Magazine.................F...... 201 886-2185
   Fort Lee *(G-3575)*
Options Edge LLC.................G...... 973 701-0051
   Summit *(G-10542)*
P D Salco Inc.................F...... 973 716-0517
   Livingston *(G-5533)*
Relx Inc.................D...... 973 812-1900
   Woodland Park *(G-12090)*
School Publications Co Inc.................E...... 732 988-1100
   Neptune *(G-6896)*
US News & World Report Inc.................F...... 212 716-6800
   Iselin *(G-4634)*

PUBLISHERS: Periodicals, No Printing

American Foreclosures Inc.................F...... 201 501-0200
   Bergenfield *(G-370)*
Foundation For Student Comm.................E...... 609 258-1111
   Princeton *(G-8950)*
Houses Magazine Inc.................F...... 973 605-1877
   Morris Plains *(G-6615)*
Jannetti Publications.................D...... 856 256-2300
   Sewell *(G-9849)*
Lawyers Diary and Manual LLC.................E...... 973 642-1440
   New Providence *(G-7005)*
Transaction Publishers Inc.................E...... 732 445-2280
   Piscataway *(G-8732)*
Union Institute Inc.................E...... 800 914-8138
   Mahwah *(G-5785)*

PUBLISHERS: Posters

Door Center Enterprises Inc.................G...... 609 333-1233
   Hopewell *(G-4526)*

PUBLISHERS: Shopping News

Hudson West Publishing Co.................F...... 201 991-1600
   Kearny *(G-4864)*

PUBLISHERS: Technical Manuals

Franklin Electronic Publs Inc.................D...... 609 386-2500
   Burlington *(G-969)*

PUBLISHERS: Technical Manuals & Papers

American Soc of Mech Engineers.................D...... 973 244-2282
   Little Falls *(G-5451)*
Micro Logic Inc.................E...... 201 962-7510
   Mahwah *(G-5753)*

PUBLISHERS: Technical Papers

Hyman W Fisher Inc.................G...... 973 992-9155
   Livingston *(G-5514)*

PUBLISHERS: Telephone & Other Directory

American Directory Publishing.................G...... 609 494-4055
   Surf City *(G-10554)*
Sic-Naics LLC.................G...... 929 344-2633
   Red Bank *(G-9244)*
Thryv Inc.................E...... 856 988-2700
   Marlton *(G-5954)*

PUBLISHERS: Textbooks, No Printing

Childrens Research & Dev Co.................G...... 856 546-8814
   Haddon Heights *(G-4044)*
Gann Law Books Inc.................F...... 973 268-1200
   Newark *(G-7131)*
John Wiley & Sons Inc.................D...... 201 748-6000
   Hoboken *(G-4460)*
John Wiley & Sons Inc.................D...... 732 302-2265
   Edison *(G-2541)*
John Wiley & Sons Inc.................D...... 201 748-6000
   Hoboken *(G-4461)*
Pearson Technology Centre Inc.................G...... 201 767-5000
   Old Tappan *(G-7735)*
Peoples Education Inc.................C...... 201 712-0090
   Montvale *(G-6422)*
Wiley Subscription Services.................F...... 201 748-6000
   Hoboken *(G-4489)*

PUBLISHERS: Trade journals, No Printing

Anderson Publishing Ltd.................G...... 908 301-1995
   Scotch Plains *(G-9729)*
BNP Media Inc.................G...... 201 291-9001
   Paramus *(G-7793)*

Dentistry Today Inc.................E...... 973 882-4700
   Fairfield *(G-3184)*
Excerpta Medica Inc.................D...... 908 547-2100
   Bridgewater *(G-822)*
Fellowship In Prayer Inc.................G...... 609 924-6863
   Princeton *(G-8948)*
Global Strategy Institute A.................G...... 973 615-7447
   Bloomfield *(G-501)*
Information Today Inc.................E...... 609 654-6266
   Medford *(G-6024)*
International Data Group Inc.................F...... 732 460-9404
   Eatontown *(G-2405)*
Physicans Educatn Resource LLC.................G...... 609 378-3701
   Plainsboro *(G-8799)*
Pioneer Associates Inc.................E...... 201 592-7007
   Fort Lee *(G-3581)*
Plexus Publishing Inc.................E...... 609 654-6500
   Medford *(G-6031)*
Springer Scnce + Bus Media LLC.................D...... 201 348-4033
   Secaucus *(G-9817)*
Thomas Publishing Company LLC.................E...... 973 543-4994
   Chester *(G-1435)*
Webannuitiescom Inc.................G...... 732 521-5110
   Monroe *(G-6324)*

PUBLISHING & BROADCASTING: Internet Only

Anjoyx LLC.................G...... 323 505-2002
   Jackson *(G-4639)*
Beterrific Corp.................G...... 201 735-7711
   Fort Lee *(G-3549)*
Bitwine Inc.................F...... 888 866-9435
   Tenafly *(G-10660)*
Chryslis Data Sltons Svcs Corp.................G...... 609 375-2000
   Princeton *(G-8922)*
College Spun Media Inc.................G...... 973 945-5040
   Hoboken *(G-4448)*
Creationsrewards Net LLC.................G...... 908 526-3127
   Manville *(G-5854)*
Electedface LLC.................E...... 609 924-3636
   Princeton *(G-8939)*
Go Waddle Inc.................G...... 301 452-5084
   Berkeley Heights *(G-399)*
Greetingtap.................G...... 347 731-4263
   South Plainfield *(G-10269)*
J Media LLC.................G...... 201 600-4573
   Norwood *(G-7567)*
Jersey Bound Latino LLC.................G...... 908 591-2830
   Union *(G-11066)*
Manna Group LLC.................F...... 856 881-7650
   Mount Laurel *(G-6780)*
Moscova Enterprises Inc.................F...... 848 628-4873
   Jersey City *(G-4768)*
Nonzero Foundation Inc.................G...... 609 688-0793
   Princeton *(G-8986)*
Perfect Clicks LLC.................G...... 845 323-6116
   Woodcliff Lake *(G-12061)*
Sight2site Media LLC.................G...... 856 637-2479
   Pomona *(G-8849)*
Sima S Enterprises LLC.................G...... 877 223-7639
   Wall Township *(G-11370)*
Squash Beef LLC.................G...... 917 577-8723
   Colts Neck *(G-1788)*
Sustainable Gardening Inst Inc.................G...... 973 383-0497
   Lafayette *(G-5033)*
Tonymacx86 LLC.................G...... 973 584-5273
   Ledgewood *(G-5283)*
Wcd Enterprises Inc.................G...... 732 888-4422
   Keyport *(G-5006)*

PUBLISHING & PRINTING: Art Copy

Scafa-Tornabene Art Pubg Co.................E...... 201 842-8500
   Lyndhurst *(G-5676)*

PUBLISHING & PRINTING: Books

Avstar Publishing Corp.................G...... 908 236-6210
   Lebanon *(G-5252)*
Franklin Mint LLC.................E...... 800 843-6468
   Fort Lee *(G-3559)*
Pearson Inc.................E...... 201 236-7000
   Upper Saddle River *(G-11144)*
Pegasus Group Publishing Inc.................F...... 973 884-9100
   East Hanover *(G-2234)*
Peoples Eductl Holdings Inc.................G...... 201 712-0090
   Montvale *(G-6423)*
Techsetters Inc.................E...... 856 240-7905
   Collingswood *(G-1772)*
TFH Publications Inc.................D...... 732 897-6860
   Neptune *(G-6900)*

PRODUCT

TFH Publications Inc ....E 732 988-8400
  Neptune **(G-6901)**

Thomson Reuters (markets) LLC ....G 973 286-7200
  Newark **(G-7298)**

Truckeros News LLC ....F 732 340-1043
  Rahway **(G-9129)**

W G I Corp ....F 732 370-2900
  Lakewood **(G-5179)**

Wiley Publishing LLC ....B 201 748-6000
  Hoboken **(G-4488)**

Wt Media LLC ....F 609 921-3490
  Trenton **(G-11011)**

PUBLISHING & PRINTING: Catalogs

Rdl Marketing Group LLC ....G 732 446-0817
  Perrineville **(G-8507)**

Starnet Printing Inc ....G 201 760-2600
  Mahwah **(G-5776)**

Tommax Inc ....G 732 224-1046
  Red Bank **(G-9246)**

PUBLISHING & PRINTING: Directories, NEC

Commerce Register Inc ....E 201 445-3000
  Midland Park **(G-6172)**

Entourage Imaging Inc ....E 888 926-6571
  Princeton Junction **(G-9056)**

Triefeldt Studios Inc ....G 609 656-2380
  Trenton **(G-11005)**

PUBLISHING & PRINTING: Guides

Jersey Shore Publications ....G 732 892-1276
  Brick **(G-723)**

Little Fox Inc ....G 609 919-9691
  Englewood Cliffs **(G-2984)**

PUBLISHING & PRINTING: Magazines: publishing & printing

Airbrush Action Inc ....G 732 223-7878
  Barnegat **(G-155)**

Amy Publications LLC ....G 973 235-1800
  Nutley **(G-7579)**

Area Auto Racing News Inc ....G 609 888-3618
  Trenton **(G-10895)**

Arts Weekly Inc ....E 973 812-6766
  Little Falls **(G-5453)**

Bondi Digital Publishing LLC ....G 212 405-1655
  Edgewater **(G-2434)**

Charter Fincl Pubg Netwrk Inc ....E 732 450-8866
  Shrewsbury **(G-9885)**

Drug Delivery Technology LLC ....E 973 299-1200
  Montville **(G-6441)**

Hyp Hair Inc ....E 201 843-4004
  Montclair **(G-6369)**

Innovation In Medtech LLC ....G 888 202-5939
  Chatham **(G-1321)**

Kicksonfirecom LLC ....G 718 753-4248
  South Amboy **(G-10135)**

New Jersey Business Magazine ....G 973 882-5004
  Fairfield **(G-3278)**

New Jersey Monthly LLC ....E 973 539-8230
  Morristown **(G-6689)**

Princeton Almni Pblications Inc ....G 609 258-4885
  Princeton **(G-9008)**

Renard Communnications Inc ....E 973 912-8550
  Springfield **(G-10464)**

Sino Monthly New Jersey Inc ....F 732 650-0688
  Edison **(G-2611)**

Sj Magazine ....F 856 722-9300
  Maple Shade **(G-5869)**

Sneaker Swarm LLC ....F 908 693-9262
  Woodbridge **(G-12021)**

Steward LLC ....G 609 816-8825
  Princeton **(G-9028)**

Thomas Greco Publishing Inc ....F 973 667-6965
  Nutley **(G-7594)**

Unisphere Media LLC ....F 908 795-3701
  New Providence **(G-7023)**

PUBLISHING & PRINTING: Newsletters, Business Svc

Dorado Systems LLC ....F 856 354-0048
  Haddonfield **(G-4056)**

M J Powers & Co Publishers ....G 973 898-1200
  Morristown **(G-6683)**

PUBLISHING & PRINTING: Newspapers

10x Daily LLC ....G 732 276-6407
  Lakewood **(G-5041)**

About Our Town Inc ....G 732 968-1615
  Piscataway **(G-8623)**

Achievement Journal LLC ....G 732 297-1570
  North Brunswick **(G-7449)**

Ainsworth Media ....G 856 854-1400
  Collingswood **(G-1766)**

Andis Inc ....G 973 627-0400
  Denville **(G-2030)**

Arab Voice Newspaper ....G 973 523-7815
  Paterson **(G-8141)**

Area Auto Racing News Inc ....G 609 888-3618
  Trenton **(G-10895)**

Aus Inc ....G 856 234-9200
  Mount Laurel **(G-6738)**

Bay Shore Press Inc ....E 732 957-0070
  Middletown **(G-6160)**

Borton Enterprises ....F 856 453-9221
  Bridgeton **(G-752)**

Brazilian Voice ....G 973 491-6200
  Newark **(G-7074)**

Casas News Publishing Co ....E 908 245-6767
  Roselle Park **(G-9579)**

Coaster Inc ....F 732 775-3010
  Asbury Park **(G-73)**

Convention News Company Inc ....G 201 444-5075
  Midland Park **(G-6173)**

Current Newspaper LLC ....E 609 383-8994
  Pleasantville **(G-8809)**

Daily Dollar LLC ....G 732 236-9709
  Monroe Township **(G-6331)**

Daily Plan It Executive Center ....G 609 514-9494
  Princeton **(G-8928)**

Desi Talk LLC ....G 212 675-7515
  Jersey City **(G-4723)**

Direct Development LLC ....G 732 739-8890
  Tinton Falls **(G-10712)**

Dow Jones & Company Inc ....G 609 520-4000
  Monmouth Junction **(G-6287)**

Dow Jones & Company Inc ....F 609 520-4000
  Cranbury **(G-1830)**

Dow Jones & Company Inc ....G 609 520-5730
  Plainsboro **(G-8785)**

Dow Jones & Company Inc ....D 609 520-5238
  Monmouth Junction **(G-6288)**

Financial Information Inc ....E 908 222-5300
  South Plainfield **(G-10259)**

First Friday Global Inc ....G 201 776-6709
  Newark **(G-7124)**

Gail Gersons Wine & Dine Resta ....G 732 758-0888
  Shrewsbury **(G-9892)**

Gannett Co Inc ....D 908 243-6953
  Somerville **(G-10112)**

Gannett Stllite Info Ntwrk LLC ....F 609 561-2300
  Vineland **(G-11221)**

Glassboro News & Food Store ....G 856 881-1181
  Glassboro **(G-3812)**

Gloucester County Times ....G 856 845-7484
  Woodbury **(G-12030)**

Greater Media Newspapers ....G 732 254-7004
  Sayreville **(G-9709)**

Halsey News ....G 973 645-0017
  Newark **(G-7144)**

Herald News ....G 973 569-7000
  Woodland Park **(G-12081)**

Home News Tribune ....E 908 243-6600
  Somerville **(G-10115)**

Hunterdon County Democrat Inc ....G 908 996-4047
  Frenchtown **(G-3713)**

Jersey Shore News Mgazines Inc ....E 609 494-5900
  Surf City **(G-10555)**

Jewish Standard Inc ....F 201 837-8818
  River Edge **(G-9362)**

Jewish Times of South Jersey ....G 609 646-2063
  Pleasantville **(G-8814)**

Journal News V Inc ....G 201 986-1458
  Paramus **(G-7811)**

Levy Innovation ....G 908 303-4492
  Morristown **(G-6678)**

Macromedia Incorporated ....F 201 646-4000
  Hackensack **(G-3942)**

Monmouth Journal ....G 732 747-7007
  Red Bank **(G-9237)**

Montgomery News ....G 908 874-0020
  Skillman **(G-9924)**

Newark Morning Ledger Co ....G 732 560-1560
  Piscataway **(G-8695)**

Newark Morning Ledger Co ....C 973 882-6120
  Pine Brook **(G-8611)**

News Inc Gloucester City ....G 856 456-1199
  Gloucester City **(G-3846)**

Newspaper Media Group LLC ....E 856 779-3800
  Cherry Hill **(G-1399)**

NJ Advance Media LLC ....D 732 902-4300
  Edison **(G-2575)**

NJ Press Media ....G 732 643-3604
  Neptune **(G-6893)**

North Jersey Media Group Inc ....A 201 646-4000
  Hackensack **(G-3955)**

North Jersey Media Group Inc ....G 201 933-1166
  Rutherford **(G-9629)**

North Jersey Media Group Inc ....E 973 233-5000
  Montclair **(G-6379)**

North Jersey Media Group Inc ....C 201 485-7800
  Mahwah **(G-5760)**

Observer Park ....F 201 798-7007
  Hoboken **(G-4471)**

Parker Publications Inc ....E 908 766-3900
  Bernardsville **(G-441)**

Pascack Press ....G 201 664-2105
  Westwood **(G-11838)**

Philadelphia Inquirer ....G 856 779-3840
  Cherry Hill **(G-1408)**

Phildelphia-Newspapers-Llc ....A 609 823-0453
  Ventnor City **(G-11154)**

Publishing Technology Inc ....G 732 563-9292
  New Brunswick **(G-6963)**

Redhedink LLC ....G 973 890-2320
  Totowa **(G-10848)**

Seawave Corp ....E 609 886-8600
  Rio Grande **(G-9358)**

Targum Publishing Company ....E 732 247-1286
  New Brunswick **(G-6973)**

Valuewalk LLC ....G 973 767-2181
  Passaic **(G-8114)**

Vicinity Media Group Inc ....F 973 276-1688
  Fairfield **(G-3343)**

Wall Street Journal ....G 609 520-4000
  Monmouth Junction **(G-6318)**

World Journal LLC ....F 732 632-8890
  Metuchen **(G-6084)**

PUBLISHING & PRINTING: Pamphlets

Bon Venture Services LLC ....D 973 584-5699
  Flanders **(G-3402)**

Dawn Bible Students Assn ....G 201 438-6421
  East Rutherford **(G-2285)**

Life Skills Education Inc ....G 507 645-2994
  Springfield **(G-10453)**

PUBLISHING & PRINTING: Periodical Statistical Reports

McMunn Associates ....E 856 858-3440
  Collingswood **(G-1770)**

PUBLISHING & PRINTING: Technical Manuals

Faulkner Information Svcs LLC ....D 856 662-2070
  Medford **(G-6022)**

PUBLISHING & PRINTING: Technical Papers

Sheridan Printing Company Inc ....E 908 454-0700
  Alpha **(G-42)**

PUBLISHING & PRINTING: Textbooks

McGraw-Hill Glbl Edctn Hldngs ....D 609 371-8301
  East Windsor **(G-2354)**

PUBLISHING & PRINTING: Trade Journals

Barry Urner Publications Inc ....D 732 240-5330
  Toms River **(G-10748)**

Frontline Med Cmmnications Inc ....D 973 206-3434
  Parsippany **(G-7952)**

Quadrant Media Corp Inc ....G 973 701-8900
  Parsippany **(G-8003)**

Showcase Publications Inc ....D 732 349-1134
  Toms River **(G-10792)**

PULLEYS: Metal

Polytech Designs Inc ....F 973 340-1390
  Clifton **(G-1696)**

PULP MILLS

County of Somerset ....C 732 469-3363
  Bridgewater **(G-814)**
Laminated Industries Inc ....E 908 862-5995
  Linden **(G-5373)**
Reliable Paper Recycling Inc ....C 201 333-5244
  Jersey City **(G-4800)**

PULP MILLS: Mechanical & Recycling Processing

Exim Incorporated ....G 908 561-8200
  Piscataway **(G-8664)**

PUMP JACKS & OTHER PUMPING EQPT: Indl

Vanton Pump & Equipment Corp ....E 908 688-4120
  Hillside **(G-4436)**

PUMP SLEEVES: Rubber

C M H Hele-Shaw Inc ....F 201 974-0570
  Hoboken **(G-4445)**

PUMPS

Apple Air Compressor Corp ....F 888 222-9940
  Rutherford **(G-9613)**
Bio Compression Systems Inc ....E 201 939-0716
  Moonachie **(G-6457)**
Boc Group Inc ....A 908 665-2400
  New Providence **(G-6995)**
Callaghan Pump Controls Inc ....G 201 621-0505
  Hackensack **(G-3893)**
Davis-Standard LLC ....E 908 722-6000
  Somerset **(G-9981)**
Dynaflow Engineering Inc ....G 732 356-9790
  Middlesex **(G-6114)**
E Wortmann Machine Works Inc ....F 201 288-1654
  Teterboro **(G-10672)**
Energy Beams Inc ....F 973 291-6555
  Bloomingdale **(G-528)**
Flowserve Corporation ....G 973 334-9444
  Parsippany **(G-7947)**
Hayward Industries Inc ....B 908 351-5400
  Elizabeth **(G-2746)**
Hhh Machine Co ....G 908 276-1220
  Cranford **(G-1913)**
Ingersoll-Rand Company ....E 856 793-7000
  Mount Laurel **(G-6766)**
Interntional Cnsld Chemex Corp ....E 732 828-7676
  New Brunswick **(G-6936)**
Kraissl Company Inc ....E 201 342-0008
  Hackensack **(G-3937)**
Leistritz Advanced Tech Corp ....E 201 934-8262
  Allendale **(G-11)**
Linde North America Inc ....D 908 464-8100
  New Providence **(G-7007)**
Magnatrol Valve Corporation ....F 856 829-4580
  Roebling **(G-9526)**
Melville Industries Inc ....G 856 461-0091
  Riverside **(G-9400)**
Messer LLC ....C 908 464-8100
  Bridgewater **(G-849)**
Messer LLC ....G 973 579-2065
  Sparta **(G-10398)**
Messer North America Inc ....B 908 464-8100
  Bridgewater **(G-851)**
Orion Machinery Co Ltd ....E 201 569-3220
  Rutherford **(G-9630)**
Science Pump Corporation ....E 856 963-7700
  Camden **(G-1086)**
Valcor Engineering Corporation ....C 973 467-8400
  Springfield **(G-10472)**
Valley Tech Inc ....G 908 534-5565
  Whitehouse Station **(G-11936)**
Xylem Dewatering Solutions Inc ....C 856 467-3636
  Bridgeport **(G-748)**

PUMPS & PARTS: Indl

C & L Machining Company Inc ....G 856 456-1932
  Brooklawn **(G-914)**
Cooper Alloy Corporation ....F 908 688-4120
  Hillside **(G-4387)**
Evey Vacuum Service ....G 856 692-4779
  Vineland **(G-11217)**
Flowserve Corporation ....C 908 859-7000
  Phillipsburg **(G-8551)**
Flowserve Corporation ....D 856 241-7800
  Bridgeport **(G-739)**

Flowserve Corporation ....D 973 227-4565
  Fairfield **(G-3204)**
Shoreway Industry ....G 856 307-2020
  Clayton **(G-1529)**

PUMPS & PUMPING EQPT REPAIR SVCS

Frontline Industries Inc ....F 973 373-7211
  Irvington **(G-4570)**
Hights Electric Motor Service ....G 609 448-2298
  Hightstown **(G-4296)**
Longo Elctrical-Mechanical Inc ....E 973 537-0400
  Linden **(G-5377)**

PUMPS & PUMPING EQPT WHOLESALERS

Apple Air Compressor Corp ....F 888 222-9940
  Rutherford **(G-9613)**
Arcadia Equipment Inc ....F 201 342-3308
  Hackensack **(G-3877)**
Cooper Alloy Corporation ....F 908 688-4120
  Hillside **(G-4387)**
Dynaflow Engineering Inc ....G 732 356-9790
  Middlesex **(G-6114)**
Flemington Precast & Sup LLC ....F 908 782-3246
  Flemington **(G-3443)**
Frontline Industries Inc ....F 973 373-7211
  Irvington **(G-4570)**
Hights Electric Motor Service ....G 609 448-2298
  Hightstown **(G-4296)**
Leistritz Advanced Tech Corp ....E 201 934-8262
  Allendale **(G-11)**
Longo Elctrical-Mechanical Inc ....D 973 537-0400
  Wharton **(G-11861)**
UNI-Tech Drilling Company Inc ....E 856 694-4200
  Franklinville **(G-3641)**
United Eqp Fabricators LLC ....G 973 242-2737
  Newark **(G-7308)**
Xylem Dewatering Solutions Inc ....C 856 467-3636
  Bridgeport **(G-748)**

PUMPS, HEAT: Electric

Bfhj Holdings Inc ....G 908 730-6280
  Montvale **(G-6401)**

PUMPS: Domestic, Water Or Sump

Carter Pump Inc ....G 201 568-9798
  Waldwick **(G-11298)**

PUMPS: Fluid Power

Neptune Products Inc ....F 973 366-8200
  Dover **(G-2100)**

PUMPS: Gasoline, Measuring Or Dispensing

Newton Tool & Mfg Inc ....D 856 241-1500
  Pennsauken **(G-8461)**

PUMPS: Vacuum, Exc Laboratory

Eagletre-Pump Acquisition Corp ....D 201 569-1173
  Rutherford **(G-9618)**
Orion Machinery Co Ltd ....E 201 569-3220
  Rutherford **(G-9630)**
Polvac Inc ....G 732 828-1662
  New Brunswick **(G-6959)**
United Vacuum LLC ....F 973 827-1661
  Hamburg **(G-4097)**

PUNCHES: Forming & Stamping

Bonney-Vehslage Tool Co ....F 973 589-6975
  Springfield **(G-10432)**
Hudson Manufacturing Corp ....F 973 376-7070
  Millburn **(G-6199)**
Ipsco Apollo Punch & Die Corp ....G 973 884-0900
  East Hanover **(G-2218)**

PURCHASING SVCS

Congoleum Corporation ....D 609 584-3601
  Trenton **(G-10922)**

PURIFICATION & DUST COLLECTION EQPT

Camfil Usa Inc ....C 973 616-7300
  Riverdale **(G-9372)**
Cleanzones LLC ....F 732 534-5590
  Jackson **(G-4644)**
Cross Rip Ocean Engrg LLC ....G 973 455-0005
  Parsippany **(G-7911)**

Gpt Inc ....F 732 446-2400
  Manalapan **(G-5812)**
Handler Manufacturing Company ....E 908 233-7796
  Westfield **(G-11799)**

QUARTZ CRYSTALS: Electronic

Bomar Exo Ltd Liability Co ....F 732 356-7787
  Middlesex **(G-6102)**
Solar Products Inc ....E 973 248-9370
  Pompton Lakes **(G-8852)**

QUILTING SVC

E B R Manufacturing Inc ....E 973 263-8810
  Parsippany **(G-7924)**

RACEWAYS

Liberty Park Raceway LLC ....F 201 333-7223
  Jersey City **(G-4758)**
Raceway Petroleum Inc ....F 908 222-2999
  North Plainfield **(G-7508)**
Raceway Petroleum Inc ....G 732 729-7350
  East Brunswick **(G-2171)**
Raceway Petroleum Inc ....E 732 613-4404
  East Brunswick **(G-2172)**

RACKS: Display

Auto-Stak Systems Inc ....G 201 358-9070
  Westwood **(G-11828)**
East Coast Storage Eqp Co Inc ....E 732 451-1316
  Brick **(G-716)**
Gauer Metal Products Co Inc ....E 908 241-4080
  Kenilworth **(G-4942)**
Jed Display LLC ....G 201 340-2329
  Newark **(G-7167)**
Leo Prager Inc ....G 201 266-8888
  Englewood **(G-2918)**
Spark Wire Products Co Inc ....G 973 773-6945
  Clifton **(G-1723)**

RACKS: Garment, Exc Wood

All Racks Industries Inc ....G 212 244-1069
  Linden **(G-5320)**
Ted-Steel Industries Ltd ....G 212 279-3878
  Linden **(G-5434)**

RACKS: Garment, Wood

Bga Construction Inc ....D 973 809-9745
  Pine Brook **(G-8589)**
East Coast Storage Eqp Co Inc ....E 732 451-1316
  Brick **(G-716)**

RACKS: Pallet, Exc Wood

Frazier Industrial Company ....C 908 876-3001
  Long Valley **(G-5610)**
Modern Store Equipment ....F 609 241-7438
  Burlington **(G-980)**

RADAR SYSTEMS & EQPT

Mwt Materials Inc ....F 973 928-8300
  Passaic **(G-8091)**

RADIO & TELEVISION COMMUNICATIONS EQUIPMENT

Anatech Microwave Company Inc ....G 973 772-7369
  Garfield **(G-3728)**
BNS Enterprises Inc ....G 908 285-6556
  Hillsborough **(G-4306)**
Centurum Information Tech Inc ....G 856 751-1111
  Marlton **(G-5924)**
Comm Port Technologies Inc ....G 732 738-8780
  Cranbury **(G-1826)**
Computeradio ....G 973 220-0087
  Montville **(G-6440)**
Crestron Electronics Inc ....C 201 767-3400
  Rockleigh **(G-9516)**
Daysequerra Corporation ....F 856 719-9900
  Pennsauken **(G-8411)**
Draztic Designs LLC ....E 609 678-4200
  Columbus **(G-1800)**
Eclearview Technologies Inc ....G 732 695-6999
  Ocean **(G-7662)**
Eigent Technologies Inc ....G 732 673-0402
  Holmdel **(G-4500)**
Engility LLC ....F 703 633-8300
  Princeton Junction **(G-9055)**

P
R
O
D
U
C
T

Ensync Intrctive Solutions Inc..........G....... 732 542-4001
Freehold *(G-3664)*

Integrated Microwave Tech LLC ....G....... 908 852-3700
Hackettstown *(G-4012)*

Kef America Inc..........E....... 732 414-2074
Marlboro *(G-5903)*

L3 Technologies Inc..........A....... 856 338-3000
Camden *(G-1074)*

Lg Elctrnics Mbilecomm USA Inc..........D....... 201 816-2000
Englewood Cliffs *(G-2981)*

Linearizer Technology Inc..........G....... 609 584-8424
Hamilton *(G-4111)*

Lucent Technologies World Svcs..........C....... 908 582-3000
New Providence *(G-7008)*

Microsignals Inc..........E....... 800 225-4508
Palisades Park *(G-7774)*

Mphase Technologies Inc..........F....... 973 256-3737
Clifton *(G-1671)*

Natural Wireless LLC..........E....... 201 438-2865
East Rutherford *(G-2306)*

Network Communications Cons..........F....... 201 968-0684
Hackensack *(G-3953)*

OSI Laser Diode Inc..........E....... 732 549-9001
Edison *(G-2585)*

Peter-Lisand Machine Corp..........G....... 201 943-5600
New Milford *(G-6991)*

Powertrunk Inc..........E....... 201 630-4520
Jersey City *(G-4787)*

Qualcomm Incorporated..........D....... 908 443-8000
Bridgewater *(G-874)*

R F Products Inc..........E....... 856 365-5500
Camden *(G-1084)*

R H A Audio Communications..........G....... 732 257-9180
East Brunswick *(G-2170)*

R&D Microwaves LLC..........E....... 908 212-1696
Boonton *(G-565)*

Radio Systems Design Inc..........E....... 856 467-8000
Swedesboro *(G-10604)*

Radwin Inc..........G....... 201 252-4224
Mahwah *(G-5766)*

Renae Telecom LLC..........D....... 908 362-8112
Elizabeth *(G-2774)*

Telcontel Corp..........F....... 732 441-0800
Laurence Harbor *(G-5210)*

Telescript Inc..........G....... 201 767-6733
Norwood *(G-7575)*

Turn-Key Technologies Inc..........F....... 732 553-9100
Sayreville *(G-9726)*

Wireworks Corporation..........E....... 908 686-7400
Hillside *(G-4437)*

RADIO BROADCASTING & COMMUNICATIONS EQPT

Alcatel-Lucent USA Inc..........D....... 908 582-3275
New Providence *(G-6993)*

Blitz Safe of America Inc..........F....... 201 569-5000
Englewood *(G-2884)*

Bogen Communications Inc..........D....... 201 934-8500
Mahwah *(G-5718)*

Bogen Corporation..........G....... 201 934-8500
Ramsey *(G-9142)*

Cellgain Wireless LLC..........F....... 732 889-4671
Red Bank *(G-9223)*

Comtron Inc..........F....... 732 446-7571
Springfield *(G-10436)*

Hbc Solutions Inc..........G....... 973 267-5990
Rockleigh *(G-9518)*

Homan Communications Inc..........G....... 609 654-9594
Medford *(G-6023)*

Imagine Communications Corp..........E....... 201 469-6740
Bridgewater *(G-832)*

Major Auto Installations Inc..........E....... 973 252-4262
Kenvil *(G-4993)*

On Site Communication..........E....... 201 488-4123
South Hackensack *(G-10177)*

Siklu Inc..........F....... 201 267-9597
Fort Lee *(G-3588)*

Techflex Inc..........F....... 973 300-9242
Sparta *(G-10409)*

Wireless Communications Inc..........G....... 732 926-1000
Metuchen *(G-6082)*

Wireless Electronics Inc..........E....... 856 768-4310
West Berlin *(G-11634)*

RADIO BROADCASTING STATIONS

Brilliant Brdcstg Concept Inc..........F....... 732 287-9201
Rahway *(G-9083)*

RADIO COMMUNICATIONS: Airborne Eqpt

Lockheed Martin Corporation..........B....... 856 787-3104
Mount Laurel *(G-6777)*

RADIO MAGNETIC INSTRUMENTATION

Aeronautical Instr & Rdo Co..........E....... 973 473-0034
Lodi *(G-5550)*

RADIO PRODUCERS

Dawn Bible Students Assn..........G....... 201 438-6421
East Rutherford *(G-2285)*

RADIO REPAIR SHOP, NEC

Turn-Key Technologies Inc..........F....... 732 553-9100
Sayreville *(G-9726)*

RADIO, TELEVISION & CONSUMER ELECTRONICS STORES: Eqpt, NEC

Ecom Group Inc..........E....... 718 504-7355
Edison *(G-2498)*

RADIO, TELEVISION/CONSUMER ELEC STORES: Video Cameras/Access

Flir Security Inc..........G....... 201 368-9700
Ridgefield Park *(G-9306)*

RADIO, TV & CONSUMER ELEC STORES: Automotive Sound Eqpt

Model Electronics Inc..........D....... 201 961-9200
Ramsey *(G-9152)*

RADIO, TV & CONSUMER ELECTRONICS: VCR & Access

Comm Port Technologies Inc..........G....... 732 738-8780
Cranbury *(G-1826)*

RADIOS WHOLESALERS

Model Electronics Inc..........D....... 201 961-9200
Ramsey *(G-9152)*

RAILINGS: Prefabricated, Metal

Construction Specialties Inc..........E....... 908 236-0800
Lebanon *(G-5257)*

North Jersey Metal Fabricators..........G....... 973 305-9830
Wayne *(G-11536)*

S & S Socius Inc..........E....... 732 698-2400
Edison *(G-2602)*

RAILROAD CARGO LOADING & UNLOADING SVCS

Northstar Travel Media LLC..........C....... 201 902-2000
Secaucus *(G-9794)*

Romark Logistics CES LLC..........E....... 908 789-2800
Westfield *(G-11802)*

Wta Global LLC..........F....... 312 509-2559
Little Falls *(G-5473)*

RAILROAD EQPT

Hainesport Industrial Railroad..........F....... 609 261-8036
Hainesport *(G-4072)*

Rails Company Inc..........E....... 973 763-4320
Maplewood *(G-5883)*

Strato Inc..........D....... 732 981-1515
Piscataway *(G-8720)*

RAILROAD EQPT: Cars & Eqpt, Dining

J M S Melgar Transport LLC..........G....... 908 834-1722
North Plainfield *(G-7506)*

RAILROAD EQPT: Cars & Eqpt, Train, Freight Or Passenger

Bombardier Transportation..........G....... 201 955-5874
Kearny *(G-4849)*

RAILROAD EQPT: Cars, Motor

Marmon Industrial LLC..........F....... 609 655-4287
Cranbury *(G-1863)*

RAILROAD EQPT: Engines, Locomotive, Steam

Multipower International Inc..........G....... 973 727-0327
Towaco *(G-10875)*

RAILROAD EQPT: Locomotives & Parts, Electric Or Nonelectric

American Rail Company Inc..........F....... 732 785-1110
Brick *(G-710)*

RAILROAD MAINTENANCE & REPAIR SVCS

Harsco Corporation..........E....... 856 779-7795
Cherry Hill *(G-1371)*

RAILROAD RELATED EQPT

Neu Inc..........G....... 281 648-9751
Hamilton *(G-4118)*

RAILROAD SWITCHING & TERMINAL SVCS

CMI-Promex Inc..........F....... 856 351-1000
Pedricktown *(G-8346)*

RAILS: Elevator, Guide

G-Tech Elevator Associates LLC..........F....... 866 658-9296
Linden *(G-5350)*

RAILS: Rails, rolled & drawn, aluminum

American Custom Fabricators..........G....... 732 237-0037
Bayville *(G-239)*

RAMPS: Prefabricated Metal

Diamond Scooters Inc..........G....... 609 646-0003
Absecon *(G-2)*

RAZORS, RAZOR BLADES

Art of Shaving - FI LLC..........G....... 732 410-2520
Freehold *(G-3648)*

Hobby Blade Specialty Inc..........G....... 908 317-9306
Scotch Plains *(G-9734)*

IDL Techni-Edge LLC..........C....... 908 497-9818
Kenilworth *(G-4945)*

REAL ESTATE AGENCIES: Rental

PCI Inc..........G....... 973 226-8007
West Caldwell *(G-11671)*

REAL ESTATE AGENCIES: Selling

Max Pro Services LLC..........G....... 973 396-2373
Livingston *(G-5523)*

Sell All Properties LLC..........F....... 856 963-8800
Camden *(G-1087)*

REAL ESTATE AGENTS & MANAGERS

American Foreclosures Inc..........F....... 201 501-0200
Bergenfield *(G-370)*

Hugo Neu Corporation..........F....... 646 467-6700
Kearny *(G-4865)*

REAL ESTATE INVESTMENT TRUSTS

McQuade Enterprises LLC..........G....... 609 501-2437
Millville *(G-6260)*

REAL ESTATE OPERATORS, EXC DEVELOPERS: Apartment Hotel

Bellia & Sons..........E....... 856 845-2234
Woodbury *(G-12026)*

REAL ESTATE OPERATORS, EXC DEVELOPERS: Commercial/Indl Bldg

Recruit Co Ltd..........E....... 201 216-0600
Jersey City *(G-4798)*

Spectro Analytical Instrs Inc..........F....... 201 642-3000
Mahwah *(G-5774)*

Ukrainian National Association..........E....... 973 292-9800
Parsippany *(G-8032)*

Valley Plastic Molding Co..........F....... 973 334-2100
Boonton *(G-572)*

RECLAIMED RUBBER: Reworked By Manufacturing Process

Bsrm Inc..G...... 888 509-0668
   Mount Laurel **(G-6744)**
Derv2000...G...... 503 470-9158
   Kearny **(G-4854)**

RECORD BLANKS: Phonographic

Sun Plastics Co Inc.............................F...... 908 490-0870
   Watchung **(G-11459)**

RECORDERS: Sound

Caregility Corporation.......................E...... 732 413-6000
   Eatontown **(G-2383)**
York Telecom Corporation...................D...... 732 413-6000
   Eatontown **(G-2430)**
Ytc Holdings Inc...............................G...... 732 413-6000
   Eatontown **(G-2431)**

RECORDING & PLAYBACK HEADS: Magnetic

Asti Corp...F...... 201 501-8900
   Bergenfield **(G-371)**

RECORDING HEADS: Speech & Musical Eqpt

Robert Wynn....................................G...... 856 435-6398
   Clementon **(G-1534)**

RECORDING TAPE: Video, Blank

Cabletime Ltd...................................G...... 973 770-8070
   Mount Arlington **(G-6710)**

RECORDS & TAPES: Prerecorded

Maxell Corporation of America.............E...... 973 653-2400
   Woodland Park **(G-12084)**
PM Swapco Inc.................................F...... 201 438-7700
   Lyndhurst **(G-5672)**
Recorded Publications Labs.................E...... 856 963-3000
   Camden **(G-1085)**
Sony Music Holdings Inc.....................B...... 201 777-3933
   Rutherford **(G-9634)**
United Sound Arts Inc.........................F...... 732 229-4949
   Eatontown **(G-2427)**

RECORDS OR TAPES: Masters

Metrolpolis Mastering LP....................E...... 212 604-9433
   Edgewater **(G-2440)**

RECOVERY SVCS: Metal

Recycling N Hensel Amer Inc...............E...... 856 753-7614
   West Berlin **(G-11618)**

RECOVERY SVCS: Solvents

Veolia Es..E...... 732 469-5100
   Middlesex **(G-6158)**

RECREATIONAL SPORTING EQPT REPAIR SVCS

P & S Blizzard Corporation..................G...... 973 523-1700
   Paterson **(G-8275)**

RECTIFIERS: Electronic, Exc Semiconductor

Kinetics Industries Inc.......................E...... 609 883-9700
   Ewing **(G-3040)**

RECYCLABLE SCRAP & WASTE MATERIALS WHOLESALERS

Khanna Paper Inc.............................G...... 201 850-1707
   North Bergen **(G-7415)**

RECYCLING: Paper

All Amrcan Recycl Corp Clifton............C...... 201 656-3363
   Jersey City **(G-4688)**
Garden State Recycl Edison LLC..........F...... 732 393-0200
   Edison **(G-2519)**
Reliable Wood Products LLC................D...... 856 456-6300
   Westville **(G-11819)**

REELS: Fiber, Textile, Made From Purchased Materials

Alvaro P Escandon Inc.......................G...... 973 274-1040
   Newark **(G-7043)**

REFINERS & SMELTERS: Aluminum

Aleris Rolled Products Inc..................C...... 856 881-3600
   Clayton **(G-1523)**

REFINERS & SMELTERS: Brass, Secondary

Kearny Smelting & Ref Corp.................E...... 201 991-7276
   Kearny **(G-4874)**

REFINERS & SMELTERS: Copper

Amrod Corp.......................................D...... 973 344-3806
   Newark **(G-7046)**

REFINERS & SMELTERS: Gold, Secondary

Reldan Metals Inc.............................E...... 732 238-8550
   South River **(G-10355)**
Reldan Metals Inc.............................C...... 732 238-8550
   South River **(G-10356)**

REFINERS & SMELTERS: Lead, Secondary

Alpha Assembly Solutions Inc..............E...... 908 561-5170
   South Plainfield **(G-10214)**
Alpha Assembly Solutions Inc..............E...... 908 791-3000
   Somerset **(G-9948)**

REFINERS & SMELTERS: Nonferrous Metal

County of Somerset..........................C...... 732 469-3363
   Bridgewater **(G-814)**
Cumberland Rcycl Corp S Jersey........E...... 856 825-4153
   Millville **(G-6245)**
Emil A Schroth Inc.............................E...... 732 938-5015
   Howell **(G-4538)**
Federal Metals & Alloys Co..................E...... 908 756-0900
   South Plainfield **(G-10257)**
Johnson Matthey Inc.........................C...... 856 384-7000
   West Deptford **(G-11708)**
Metal MGT Pittsburgh Inc....................E...... 201 333-2902
   Jersey City **(G-4765)**
Minmetals Inc..................................F...... 201 809-1898
   Leonia **(G-5290)**
National Electronic Alloys Inc...............E...... 201 337-9400
   Oakland **(G-7638)**
Nedohon Inc......................................G...... 302 533-5512
   Wildwood Crest **(G-11948)**
Park Steel & Iron Co...........................F...... 732 775-7500
   Neptune **(G-6894)**
Semi Conductor Manufacturing.............E...... 973 478-2880
   Clifton **(G-1714)**
Stainless Surplus LLC.........................G...... 914 661-3800
   Green Brook **(G-3867)**
State Metal Industries Inc...................D...... 856 964-1510
   Camden **(G-1088)**

REFINERS & SMELTERS: Platinum Group Metal Refining, Primary

Matthey Johnson Inc.........................C...... 856 384-7132
   West Deptford **(G-11710)**

REFINERS & SMELTERS: Platinum Group Metals, Secondary

Matthey Johnson Inc.........................C...... 856 384-7022
   Paulsboro **(G-8334)**
Matthey Johnson Inc.........................C...... 856 384-7132
   West Deptford **(G-11710)**

REFINERS & SMELTERS: Silicon, Primary, Over 99% Pure

Path Silicones Inc.............................F...... 201 796-0833
   Elmwood Park **(G-2847)**

REFINERS & SMELTERS: Silver

Ames Advanced Materials Corp............C...... 908 226-2038
   South Plainfield **(G-10218)**

REFINERS & SMELTERS: Zinc, Primary, Including Slabs & Dust

L D L Technology Inc..........................G...... 973 345-9111
   Paterson **(G-8235)**

REFINERS & SMELTERS: Zinc, Primary, Including Zinc Residue

Perl Pigments LLC.............................G...... 201 836-1212
   East Brunswick **(G-2164)**

REFINING LUBRICATING OILS & GREASES, NEC

Bel-Ray Company Inc.........................D...... 732 378-4000
   Wall Township **(G-11320)**

REFINING: Petroleum

BASF Plant Science LP.......................G...... 973 245-3238
   Florham Park **(G-3492)**
BP Corporation North Amer Inc............G...... 973 633-2200
   Wayne **(G-11483)**
BP Corporation North Amer Inc............E...... 908 474-5000
   Linden **(G-5327)**
Delaware Pipeline Company LLC..........G...... 973 455-7500
   Parsippany **(G-7913)**
Intertek USA Inc................................E...... 732 969-5200
   Carteret **(G-1257)**
McAllister Service Company.................E...... 856 665-4545
   Pennsauken **(G-8453)**
Motiva Enterprises LLC.......................D...... 732 855-3266
   Sewaren **(G-9832)**
Pbf Energy Company LLC.....................B...... 973 455-7500
   Parsippany **(G-7984)**
Pbf Energy Inc..................................A...... 973 455-7500
   Parsippany **(G-7985)**
Pbf Holding Company LLC....................B...... 973 455-7500
   Parsippany **(G-7986)**
Pennzoil-Quaker State Company...........G...... 856 423-1388
   Paulsboro **(G-8339)**
Speedway LLC...................................B...... 732 750-7800
   Port Reading **(G-8895)**
T & M Terminal Company.....................G...... 419 902-2810
   Parsippany **(G-8024)**
Total American Services Inc.................F...... 206 626-3500
   Jersey City **(G-4822)**
Valero Ref Company-New Jersey...........A...... 856 224-6000
   Paulsboro **(G-8341)**

REFRACTORIES: Clay

Bartley Crucible Refractories...............F...... 609 393-0066
   Trenton **(G-10902)**
Harbisonwalker Intl Inc.......................G...... 732 388-8686
   Rahway **(G-9099)**

REFRACTORIES: Nonclay

Curran-Pfeiff Corp.............................F...... 732 225-0555
   Edison **(G-2489)**
Morgan Advanced Ceramics Inc...........E...... 973 808-1621
   Fairfield **(G-3273)**

REFRACTORY CASTABLES

P & R Castings LLC............................E...... 732 302-3600
   Somerset **(G-10049)**

REFRIGERATION & HEATING EQUIPMENT

Atomizing Systems Inc.......................F...... 201 447-1222
   Ho Ho Kus **(G-4439)**
Banicki Sheet Metal Inc.......................G...... 201 385-5938
   Bergenfield **(G-372)**
Comfortaire Ltd Liability Co..................G...... 856 692-5000
   Vineland **(G-11201)**
Drytech Inc..E...... 609 758-1794
   Cookstown **(G-1803)**
Ewc Controls Inc................................E...... 732 446-3110
   Manalapan **(G-5809)**
Heritage Service Solutions LLC.............F...... 856 845-7311
   Westville **(G-11815)**
Hussmann Corporation........................E...... 800 320-3510
   West Deptford **(G-11703)**
Ingersoll-Rand US Trane.......................D...... 732 652-7100
   Piscataway **(G-8678)**
ML Mettler Corp.................................G...... 201 869-0170
   North Bergen **(G-7423)**
On Site Manufacturing Inc....................G...... 812 794-6040
   Flemington **(G-3458)**

Employee Codes: A=Over 500 employees, B=251-500
C=101-250, D=51-100, E=20-50, F=10-19, G=4-9   2019 Harris New jersey
Manufacturers Directory   925

PRODUCT

Ryder Technology ....G...... 215 817-7868
Villas *(G-11180)*

Specialty Fabricators LLC ....E...... 609 758-6995
Wrightstown *(G-12100)*

Stamm International Corp ....G...... 201 947-1700
Fort Lee *(G-3589)*

Trane Inc ....B...... 732 652-7100
Piscataway *(G-8730)*

Trane Parts Center of NJ ....G...... 201 489-9001
Teterboro *(G-10695)*

Trane US Inc ....C...... 732 652-7100
Piscataway *(G-8731)*

Trane US Inc ....D...... 609 587-3400
Trenton *(G-11000)*

Trane US Inc ....G...... 973 882-3220
Pine Brook *(G-8618)*

York International Corporation ....F...... 732 346-0606
Edison *(G-2649)*

Zanotti Transblock USA Corp ....G...... 917 584-9357
Delran *(G-2023)*

REFRIGERATION EQPT & SPLYS WHOLESALERS

Bar-Maid Corporation ....C...... 973 478-7070
Garfield *(G-3731)*

Icy Cools Inc ....G...... 609 448-0172
Roosevelt *(G-9529)*

REFRIGERATION EQPT: Complete

Calmac Manufacturing Corp ....E...... 201 797-1511
Fair Lawn *(G-3092)*

Dukers Appliance Co USA Ltd ....G...... 917 378-8866
South Plainfield *(G-10248)*

Electro Impulse Laboratory Inc ....E...... 732 776-5800
Neptune *(G-6876)*

Kohlder Manufacturing Inc ....G...... 856 963-1801
Pennsauken *(G-8448)*

REFRIGERATION SVC & REPAIR

Heat-Timer Corporation ....E...... 212 481-2020
Fairfield *(G-3225)*

McAllister Service Company ....E...... 856 665-4545
Pennsauken *(G-8453)*

REFUSE SYSTEMS

Camden Iron & Metal LLC ....D...... 856 969-7065
Camden *(G-1044)*

Federal Lorco Petroleum LLC ....D...... 908 352-0542
Elizabeth *(G-2735)*

Safety-Kleen Systems Inc ....F...... 609 859-2049
Southampton *(G-10371)*

REGULATORS: Transmission & Distribution Voltage

Somerset Cpitl Mark Tr MGT Inc ....F...... 848 228-0842
Chesterfield *(G-1437)*

Wolock & Lott Transmission Eqp ....F...... 908 218-9292
Branchburg *(G-695)*

REGULATORS: Transmission & Distribution Voltage

Hoyt Corporation ....E...... 201 894-0707
Englewood *(G-2912)*

Zero Surge Inc ....F...... 908 996-7700
Frenchtown *(G-3718)*

RELAYS & SWITCHES: Indl, Electric

Amperite Co Inc ....E...... 201 864-9503
North Bergen *(G-7384)*

M&L Power Systems Maint Inc ....E...... 732 679-1800
Old Bridge *(G-7718)*

RELAYS: Electric Power

Comus International Inc ....C...... 973 777-6900
Clifton *(G-1587)*

RELAYS: Electronic Usage

Panasonic Corp North America ....D...... 201 348-7000
Newark *(G-7220)*

Sealed Unit Parts Co Inc ....C...... 732 223-1201
Allenwood *(G-34)*

RELIGIOUS SPLYS WHOLESALERS

Devon Trading Corp ....E...... 973 812-9190
Caldwell *(G-1022)*

REMOVERS & CLEANERS

Ricks Cleanouts Inc ....E...... 973 340-7454
Garfield *(G-3763)*

Turquoise Chemistry Inc ....F...... 908 561-0002
Piscataway *(G-8733)*

REMOVERS: Paint

Affordable Lead Solutions LLC ....G...... 856 207-1348
Bridgeton *(G-750)*

Noopys Research Inc ....G...... 856 358-6001
Newfield *(G-7325)*

RENTAL CENTERS: Furniture

Bedding Shoppe Inc ....G...... 973 334-9000
Parsippany *(G-7892)*

RENTAL CENTERS: Party & Banquet Eqpt & Splys

Sconda Canvas Products ....E...... 732 225-3500
South Plainfield *(G-10326)*

RENTAL SVCS: Business Machine & Electronic Eqpt

Pitney Bowes Inc ....F...... 908 903-2870
Warren *(G-11427)*

Pitney Bowes Inc ....C...... 800 521-0080
Newark *(G-7230)*

Pitney Bowes Inc ....C...... 856 764-2240
Delran *(G-2019)*

RENTAL SVCS: Costume

Party City Corporation ....F...... 973 537-1707
Randolph *(G-9196)*

Party City of North Bergen ....F...... 201 865-0040
North Bergen *(G-7427)*

RENTAL SVCS: Eqpt, Theatrical

Acadia Scenic Inc ....E...... 201 653-8889
Jersey City *(G-4684)*

This Is It Stageworks LLC ....E...... 201 653-2699
Jersey City *(G-4820)*

RENTAL SVCS: Stores & Yards Eqpt

Winslow Rental & Supply Inc ....G...... 856 767-5554
Berlin *(G-434)*

RENTAL SVCS: Tuxedo

Cozy Formal Wear Inc ....G...... 973 661-9781
Nutley *(G-7583)*

RENTAL: Passenger Car

Town Ford Inc ....D...... 609 298-4990
Bordentown *(G-597)*

RENTAL: Trucks, With Drivers

Jid Transportation LLC ....G...... 201 362-0841
West New York *(G-11744)*

REPRODUCTION SVCS: Video Tape Or Disk

Recorded Publications Labs ....E...... 856 963-3000
Camden *(G-1085)*

RESEARCH & DEVELOPMENT SVCS, COMMERCIAL: Engineering Lab

M C Technologies Inc ....E...... 973 839-2779
Pompton Plains *(G-8866)*

RESEARCH, DEV & TESTING SVCS, COMM: Chem Lab, Exc Testing

Sanofi-Synthelabo Inc ....A...... 908 231-2000
Bridgewater *(G-885)*

Specialty Pharmasource LLC ....F...... 973 784-4965
Denville *(G-2059)*

RESEARCH, DEVELOPMENT & TEST SVCS, COMM: Business Analysis

Wizdata Systems Inc ....F...... 973 975-4113
Parsippany *(G-8041)*

RESEARCH, DEVELOPMENT & TEST SVCS, COMM: Cmptr Hardware Dev

Able Group Technologies Inc ....G...... 732 591-9299
Morganville *(G-6579)*

Berkeley Varitronics Systems ....E...... 732 548-3737
Metuchen *(G-6047)*

Mikros Systems Corporation ....G...... 609 987-1513
Princeton *(G-8978)*

RESEARCH, DEVELOPMENT & TEST SVCS, COMM: Research, Exc Lab

Analytical Sales and Svcs Inc ....F...... 973 616-0700
Flanders *(G-3400)*

Photonics Management Corp ....G...... 908 231-0960
Bridgewater *(G-866)*

RESEARCH, DEVELOPMENT & TESTING SVCS, COMM: Research Lab

Accumix Pharmaceuticals LLC ....G...... 609 632-2225
Old Bridge *(G-7710)*

Foresight Group LLC ....F...... 888 992-8880
Parsippany *(G-7949)*

Novotec Pharma LLC ....G...... 609 632-2239
Monroe Township *(G-6338)*

United Silicon Carbide Inc ....F...... 732 355-0550
Monmouth Junction *(G-6317)*

RESEARCH, DEVELOPMENT & TESTING SVCS, COMMERCIAL: Business

Pearson Technology Centre Inc ....G...... 201 767-5000
Old Tappan *(G-7735)*

Simon & Schuster Inc ....E...... 973 656-6000
Parsippany *(G-8016)*

SMR Research Corporation ....G...... 908 852-7677
Hackettstown *(G-4037)*

RESEARCH, DEVELOPMENT & TESTING SVCS, COMMERCIAL: Energy

Brilliant Light Power Inc ....E...... 609 490-0427
East Windsor *(G-2365)*

Eos Energy Storage LLC ....E...... 732 225-8400
Edison *(G-2505)*

RESEARCH, DEVELOPMENT & TESTING SVCS, COMMERCIAL: Medical

Hisamitsu Phrm Co Inc ....F...... 973 765-0122
Florham Park *(G-3510)*

Immtech Pharmaceuticals Inc ....E...... 212 791-2911
Montclair *(G-6370)*

Nephros Inc ....F...... 201 343-5202
South Orange *(G-10200)*

Songbird Hearing Inc ....E...... 732 422-7203
North Brunswick *(G-7487)*

RESEARCH, DEVELOPMENT & TESTING SVCS, COMMERCIAL: Physical

Aero TEC Laboratories Inc ....E...... 201 825-1400
Ramsey *(G-9135)*

Mondelez Global LLC ....A...... 201 794-4000
Fair Lawn *(G-3111)*

RESEARCH, DVLPMT & TESTING SVCS, COMM: Merger, Acq & Reorg

Toppan Vintage Inc ....E...... 201 226-9220
Saddle Brook *(G-9684)*

RESEARCH, DVLPT & TEST SVCS, COMM: Mkt Analysis or Research

Aus Inc ....G...... 856 234-9200
Mount Laurel *(G-6738)*

Brite Concepts Inc ....G...... 201 270-8544
Englewood *(G-2886)*

Geolytics Inc ....G...... 908 707-1505
Branchburg *(G-644)*

T3i Group LLC .... E 856 424-1100
Cherry Hill *(G-1420)*

Webb-Mason Inc .... G 732 747-6585
Tinton Falls *(G-10734)*

RESEARCH, DVLPT & TESTING SVCS, COMM: Survey, Mktg

Jersey Bound Latino LLC .... G 908 591-2830
Union *(G-11066)*

RESIDENTIAL REMODELERS

C G I Cstm Fiberglas & Decking .... F 609 646-5302
Pleasantville *(G-8807)*

EZ General Construction Corp .... G 201 223-1101
Wayne *(G-11500)*

Mdb Construction .... G 908 628-8010
Lebanon *(G-5270)*

Taylor Made Custom Cabinetry .... F 856 786-5433
Pennsauken *(G-8490)*

RESIDUES

Purely Organic SA LLC .... G 201 942-0400
Jersey City *(G-4792)*

RESINS: Custom Compound Purchased

Bayshore Recycling Corp .... E 732 738-6000
Keasbey *(G-4908)*

Borealis Compounds Inc .... C 908 850-6200
Port Murray *(G-8882)*

Diamond Sg Intl Ltd Lblty Co .... G 732 861-9850
Eatontown *(G-2388)*

Federal Plastics Corporation .... E 908 272-5800
Cranford *(G-1910)*

Joyce Leslie Inc .... D 201 804-7800
Hillsborough *(G-4335)*

Lion Extruding Corp .... F 973 344-4648
Newark *(G-7181)*

Lubrizol Advanced Mtls Inc .... E 856 299-3764
Pedricktown *(G-8351)*

Nobel Biocare Procera LLC .... E 201 529-7100
Mahwah *(G-5759)*

Polymeric Resources Corp .... E 973 694-4141
Wayne *(G-11543)*

Recycle Inc .... D 908 756-2200
South Plainfield *(G-10324)*

Rotuba Extruders Inc .... C 908 486-1000
Linden *(G-5416)*

RESISTORS

Nte Electronics Inc .... D 973 748-5089
Bloomfield *(G-513)*

State Electronics Parts Corp .... E 973 887-2550
East Hanover *(G-2240)*

RESPIRATORY SYSTEM DRUGS

Matrixx Initiatives Inc .... E 877 942-2626
Bridgewater *(G-847)*

RESTAURANT EQPT REPAIR SVCS

Taylor Products Inc .... E 732 225-4620
Edison *(G-2631)*

RESTAURANT EQPT: Carts

Custom Sales & Service Inc .... E 609 561-6900
Hammonton *(G-4133)*

RESTAURANT EQPT: Food Wagons

Lbd Corp .... E 201 541-6760
Englewood *(G-2917)*

RESTAURANTS: Delicatessen

Bagel Club .... F 908 806-6022
Flemington *(G-3432)*

Livingston Bagel Warren Inc .... E 973 994-1915
Livingston *(G-5520)*

Lo Presti & Sons LLC .... E 973 523-9258
Paterson *(G-8245)*

RESTAURANTS:Full Svc, American

Cheesecake Factory Inc .... G 973 921-0930
Short Hills *(G-9866)*

S M Z Enterprises Inc .... F 908 232-1921
Westfield *(G-11803)*

Summerlands Inc .... E 973 729-8428
Sparta *(G-10408)*

RESTAURANTS:Full Svc, Diner

Amys Omelette Hse Burlington .... F 609 386-4800
Burlington *(G-949)*

RESTAURANTS:Full Svc, Family, Independent

Renault Winery Inc .... E 609 965-2111
Egg Harbor City *(G-2666)*

RESTAURANTS:Full Svc, Italian

Antonio Mozzarella Factory Inc .... D 973 353-9411
Newark *(G-7049)*

Antonio Mozzarella Factory Inc .... E 973 353-9411
Newark *(G-7050)*

Grandi Pastai Italiani Inc .... G 201 786-5050
Moonachie *(G-6467)*

RESTAURANTS:Limited Svc, Coffee Shop

Coffee Company LLC .... G 609 399-5533
Ocean City *(G-7688)*

Coffee Company LLC .... G 609 398-2326
Ocean City *(G-7689)*

Millburn Bagel Inc .... E 973 258-1334
Millburn *(G-6205)*

Perk & Pantry .... G 856 451-4333
Bridgeton *(G-769)*

Zenas Patisserie .... G 856 303-8700
Riverton *(G-9405)*

RESTAURANTS:Limited Svc, Ice Cream Stands Or Dairy Bars

Agape Inc .... F 973 923-7625
Irvington *(G-4553)*

Bertolotti LLC .... F 201 941-3116
Fairview *(G-3357)*

Confectionately Yours LLC .... E 732 821-6863
Franklin Park *(G-3633)*

Country Club Ice Cream .... G 973 729-5570
Sparta *(G-10384)*

Dairy Queen .... F 732 892-5700
Point Pleasant Boro *(G-8842)*

Dunkin Donuts Baskin Robbins .... G 201 692-1900
Teaneck *(G-10628)*

Enjou Chocolat Morristown Inc .... G 973 993-9090
Morristown *(G-6662)*

Guernsey Crest Ice Cream Co .... G 973 742-4620
Paterson *(G-8206)*

Millstone Dq Inc .... G 609 259-6733
Clarksburg *(G-1522)*

Rolo Systems .... E 973 627-4214
Denville *(G-2055)*

RESTAURANTS:Ltd Svc, Ice Cream, Soft Drink/Fountain Stands

South Jersey Pretzel Inc .... F 856 435-5055
Stratford *(G-10507)*

RETAIL BAKERY: Bagels

Bagel Street .... E 609 936-1755
Plainsboro *(G-8780)*

Branchville Bagels Inc .... G 973 948-7077
Branchville *(G-704)*

Cambridge Bagels Inc .... F 973 743-5683
Bloomfield *(G-494)*

Danmark Enterprises Inc .... G 732 321-3366
South Plainfield *(G-10245)*

Delicious Bagels Inc .... G 732 892-9265
Point Pleasant Boro *(G-8843)*

Frell Corp .... F 201 825-2500
Ramsey *(G-9144)*

Livingston Bagel Warren Inc .... E 973 994-1915
Livingston *(G-5520)*

OBagel Hoboken Ltd Lblty Co .... G 201 683-8599
Hoboken *(G-4470)*

S M Z Enterprises Inc .... F 908 232-1921
Westfield *(G-11803)*

RETAIL BAKERY: Bread

Artisan Oven Inc .... G 201 488-6261
Hackensack *(G-3878)*

Calandra Italian & French Bky .... D 973 484-5598
Newark *(G-7080)*

Kohouts Bakery .... G 973 772-7270
Garfield *(G-3750)*

Serranis Bakery .... F 973 678-1777
Orange *(G-7761)*

Zinicola Baking Co .... G 973 667-1306
Nutley *(G-7598)*

RETAIL BAKERY: Cakes

Spindlers Bake Shop .... G 201 288-1345
Hasbrouck Heights *(G-4188)*

RETAIL BAKERY: Cookies

Fairfield Gourmet Food Corp .... D 973 575-4365
Cedar Grove *(G-1278)*

RETAIL BAKERY: Doughnuts

9001 Corporation .... E 201 963-2233
Jersey City *(G-4680)*

9002 Corporation .... E 201 792-9595
Jersey City *(G-4681)*

All Madina Inc .... F 973 226-7772
West Caldwell *(G-11639)*

G N J Inc .... G 856 786-1127
Cinnaminson *(G-1458)*

J K P Donuts Inc .... G 856 234-9844
Mount Laurel *(G-6772)*

Jay Jariwala .... F 908 806-8266
Ringoes *(G-9338)*

O O M Inc .... G 973 328-9408
Rockaway *(G-9482)*

Ram Donuts Corp .... G 856 599-0015
Gibbstown *(G-3799)*

RETAIL BAKERY: Pastries

Bella Palermo Pastry Shop .... E 908 931-0298
Kenilworth *(G-4928)*

Symphony Inc .... F 856 727-9596
Moorestown *(G-6571)*

RETAIL BAKERY: Pretzels

Auntie Annes Soft Pretzels .... E 856 845-3667
Woodbury *(G-12025)*

Auntie Annes Soft Pretzels .... E 856 722-0433
Moorestown *(G-6506)*

South Jersey Pretzel Inc .... F 856 435-5055
Stratford *(G-10507)*

RETAIL LUMBER YARDS

Everlast Associates Inc .... G 609 261-1888
Southampton *(G-10362)*

Woodhaven Lumber & Millwork .... E 732 295-8800
Point Pleasant Beach *(G-8833)*

RETAIL STORES, NEC

Jubili Bead & Yarn Shoppe .... G 856 858-7844
Collingswood *(G-1769)*

RETAIL STORES: Alcoholic Beverage Making Eqpt & Splys

Fortress Graphics LLC .... E 973 276-0100
West Caldwell *(G-11651)*

New Jersey Diamond Products Co ...... F 973 684-0949
Paterson *(G-8267)*

Saltopia Infused Sea Salt LLC .... F 908 850-1926
Hackettstown *(G-4035)*

RETAIL STORES: Artificial Limbs

Harry J Lawall & Son Inc .... G 856 691-7764
Vineland *(G-11231)*

RETAIL STORES: Awnings

William Opdyke Awnings Inc .... G 732 449-5940
Wall Township *(G-11378)*

RETAIL STORES: Baby Carriages & Strollers

Buy Buy Baby Inc .... F 908 688-0888
Union *(G-11034)*

RETAIL STORES: Batteries, Non-Automotive

Exide Technologies .... G 973 439-9612
West Caldwell *(G-11649)*

PRODUCT

RETAIL STORES: Binoculars & Telescopes

Yunta USA Inc ....G....... 614 835-6588
Cranbury *(G-1896)*

RETAIL STORES: Communication Eqpt

Industronic Inc ....G....... 908 393-5960
Bridgewater *(G-835)*

Vcom Intl Multi-Media Corp..................D....... 201 814-0405
Fairfield *(G-3338)*

RETAIL STORES: Cosmetics

Bio-Nature Labs Ltd Lblty Co ....E....... 732 738-5550
Edison *(G-2470)*

Cheringal Associates Inc ....D....... 201 784-8721
Norwood *(G-7560)*

Fiabila USA Inc ....E....... 973 659-9510
Mine Hill *(G-6272)*

RETAIL STORES: Decals

Craft Signs..G....... 201 656-1991
Jersey City *(G-4719)*

RETAIL STORES: Electronic Parts & Eqpt

Ea Pilot Supply ....G....... 201 934-8449
Bradley Beach *(G-610)*

Hope Electrical Products Co................G....... 973 882-7400
West Caldwell *(G-11653)*

I Trade Technology Ltd ....G....... 615 348-7233
Mahwah *(G-5749)*

RETAIL STORES: Fire Extinguishers

Eagle Fire & Safety Corp ....G....... 732 982-7388
Wall Township *(G-11335)*

RETAIL STORES: Hair Care Prdts

Art of Shaving - Fl LLC.....................G....... 732 410-2520
Freehold *(G-3648)*

RETAIL STORES: Hearing Aids

Davis Center Inc................................G....... 862 251-4637
Succasunna *(G-10512)*

RETAIL STORES: Hospital Eqpt & Splys

J J L & W Inc.....................................E....... 856 854-3100
Magnolia *(G-5708)*

RETAIL STORES: Infant Furnishings & Eqpt

Steico USA Inc ....F 732 364-6200
Lakewood *(G-5168)*

RETAIL STORES: Medical Apparatus & Splys

Electric Mobility Corporation...............C....... 856 468-1000
Sewell *(G-9844)*

JFK Supplies Inc ....F 732 985-7800
Edison *(G-2539)*

Johnson & Johnson ....A....... 732 524-0400
New Brunswick *(G-6940)*

Nouveau Prosthetics Ltd ....F 732 739-0888
Hazlet *(G-4267)*

Priority Medical Inc ....G....... 973 376-5077
Short Hills *(G-9875)*

Sensonics Inc....................................F 856 547-7702
Haddon Heights *(G-4049)*

RETAIL STORES: Monuments, Finished To Custom Order

Brewster Vaults & Monuments ....F 856 785-1412
Millville *(G-6239)*

RETAIL STORES: Motors, Electric

Absecon Electric Motor Works.............G....... 609 641-1523
Absecon *(G-1)*

Lakewood Elc Mtr Sls & Svc ....G....... 732 363-2865
Howell *(G-4545)*

Lockwoods Electric Motor Svc ....E....... 609 587-2333
Trenton *(G-10953)*

Longo Elctrical-Mechanical Inc ....E....... 973 537-0400
Linden *(G-5377)*

Motors and Drives Inc ....G....... 609 344-8058
Atlantic City *(G-98)*

Mt Salem Electric Co Inc ....F 908 735-6126
Pittstown *(G-8754)*

New Jersey Electric Motors ....G....... 908 526-5225
Somerville *(G-10121)*

VS Systematics Corp ....G....... 908 241-5110
Kenilworth *(G-4985)*

RETAIL STORES: Orthopedic & Prosthesis Applications

Atlantic Prsthtic Orthotic Svc ....G....... 609 927-6330
Linwood *(G-5448)*

Garden State Orthopedic Center ....G....... 973 538-4948
Morristown *(G-6664)*

J C Orthopedic Inc ....G....... 732 458-7900
Brick *(G-722)*

Swiss Orthopedic Inc ....G....... 908 874-5522
Hillsborough *(G-4359)*

RETAIL STORES: Perfumes & Colognes

Interntnal Flvors Frgrnces Inc ....C....... 732 264-4500
Hazlet *(G-4262)*

Victory International USA LLC ....F 732 417-5900
Eatontown *(G-2429)*

RETAIL STORES: Pet Food

Klein Distributors Inc..........................G....... 732 446-7632
Burlington *(G-977)*

RETAIL STORES: Pet Splys

Tuff Mutters LLC ....G....... 973 291-6679
Kinnelon *(G-5022)*

RETAIL STORES: Pets

Animals Etc Inc ....G....... 609 386-8442
Burlington *(G-950)*

RETAIL STORES: Photocopy Machines

Imperial Copy Products Inc ....E....... 973 927-5500
Randolph *(G-9186)*

RETAIL STORES: Plumbing & Heating Splys

Tlw Bath Ltd Liability Company ....E....... 732 942-7117
Lakewood *(G-5172)*

RETAIL STORES: Police Splys

Suroma Ltd Liability Company ....G....... 908 735-7700
Annandale *(G-55)*

RETAIL STORES: Rock & Stone Specimens

Stoneworld At Redbank Inc ....G....... 732 383-5110
Red Bank *(G-9245)*

RETAIL STORES: Rubber Stamps

A A A Stamp and Seal Mfg Co...............G....... 201 796-1500
Saddle Brook *(G-9636)*

RETAIL STORES: Safety Splys & Eqpt

Atlas Flasher & Supply Co Inc..............E....... 856 423-3333
Mickleton *(G-6086)*

Lacka Safe Corp.................................F 201 896-9200
Carlstadt *(G-1180)*

RETAIL STORES: Spas & Hot Tubs

Van Brill Pool & Spa Center ....G....... 856 424-4333
Marlton *(G-5955)*

RETAIL STORES: Telephone Eqpt & Systems

Arose Inc...E....... 856 481-4351
Blackwood *(G-459)*

RETAIL STORES: Water Purification Eqpt

Favs Corp ....G....... 856 358-1515
Elmer *(G-2797)*

South Jersey Water Cond Svc ....E....... 856 451-0620
Bridgeton *(G-773)*

REUPHOLSTERY & FURNITURE REPAIR

Colonial Uphl & Win Treatments ....G....... 609 641-3124
Pleasantville *(G-8808)*

Window 25 LLC ....G....... 973 817-9464
Newark *(G-7316)*

REUPHOLSTERY SVCS

Costa Mar Cnvas Enclosures LLC ....E....... 609 965-1538
Egg Harbor City *(G-2656)*

Franks Upholstery & Draperies ....G....... 856 779-8585
Maple Shade *(G-5863)*

H Lauzon Furniture Co Inc...................F 201 837-7598
Teaneck *(G-10634)*

Stessl & Neugebauer Inc ....F 908 277-3340
Summit *(G-10549)*

RHEOSTATS: Electronic

Interplex Nas Inc ....D....... 201 367-1300
Northvale *(G-7530)*

RIBBONS & BOWS

Circle Visual Inc ....E....... 212 719-5153
Carlstadt *(G-1139)*

Colonial - Bende Ribbons Inc ....G....... 973 777-8700
Passaic *(G-8056)*

Papillon Ribbon & Bow Inc ....E....... 973 928-6128
Clifton *(G-1683)*

Premier Ribbon Company ....G....... 973 589-2600
Newark *(G-7233)*

RIBBONS, NEC

Carson & Gebel Ribbon Co LLC............E....... 973 627-4200
Rockaway *(G-9449)*

Cottage Lace and Ribbon Co Inc..........G....... 732 776-9353
Neptune *(G-6871)*

Denali Company LLC ....E....... 732 219-7771
Red Bank *(G-9226)*

Jrm Industries Inc..............................E....... 973 779-9340
Passaic *(G-8077)*

Klein Ribbon Corp ....E....... 973 684-4671
Paterson *(G-8230)*

RIBBONS: Machine, Inked Or Carbon

Commander Imaging Products Inc ....E....... 973 742-9298
Paterson *(G-8161)*

Ricoh Prtg Systems Amer Inc ....G....... 973 316-6051
Mountain Lakes *(G-6827)*

Waste Not Computers & Supplies.........G....... 201 384-4444
Dumont *(G-2118)*

RIDING APPAREL STORES

Interntonal Riding Helmets Inc ....E....... 732 772-0165
Marlboro *(G-5902)*

RIVETS: Metal

Arrow Fastener Co LLC.......................B....... 201 843-6900
Saddle Brook *(G-9640)*

Celus Fasteners Mfg Inc ....E....... 800 289-7483
Northvale *(G-7520)*

New Jersey Rivet Co LLC.....................F 856 963-2237
Camden *(G-1078)*

ROAD CONSTRUCTION EQUIPMENT WHOLESALERS

Ransome Equipment Sales LLC............G....... 856 797-8100
Lumberton *(G-5635)*

ROAD MATERIALS: Bituminous, Not From Refineries

Barrett Industries Corporation ....E....... 973 533-1001
Morristown *(G-6646)*

Barrett Paving Materials Inc.................E....... 973 533-1001
Roseland *(G-9535)*

Colas Inc ....G....... 973 290-9082
Morristown *(G-6654)*

Flemington Bituminous Corp ....F 908 782-2722
Flemington *(G-3442)*

Rosano Asphalt LLC............................G....... 732 620-8400
Farmingdale *(G-3391)*

Weldon Materials Inc ....G....... 201 991-3200
Kearny *(G-4903)*

ROBOTS, SERVICES OR NOVELTY, WHOLESALE

Five Elements Robotics LLC ....G....... 800 681-8514
Wall Township *(G-11340)*

ROLL FORMED SHAPES: Custom

Specialty Measures.................................G...... 609 882-6071
  Ewing (G-3066)

ROLLERS & FITTINGS: Window Shade

Arts Windows Inc.................................G...... 732 905-9595
  Toms River (G-10744)

ROLLING MILL EQPT: Finishing

Indemax Inc..G...... 973 209-2424
  Vernon (G-11159)

ROLLS & ROLL COVERINGS: Rubber

Ames Rubber Corporation.....................D...... 973 827-9101
  Hamburg (G-4088)
Kappus Plastic Company Inc.................D...... 908 537-2288
  Hampton (G-4157)

ROLLS: Rubber, Solid Or Covered

Passaic Rubber Co...............................D...... 973 696-9500
  Wayne (G-11540)

ROOF DECKS

Bouras Industries Inc............................A...... 908 918-9400
  Summit (G-10527)
C M C Steel Fabricators Inc.................C...... 908 561-3484
  South Plainfield (G-10232)
Elgee Manufacturing Company............G...... 908 647-4100
  Warren (G-11408)
Great Railing Inc..................................F...... 856 875-0050
  Williamstown (G-11960)
Pro-Deck Supply...................................G...... 609 771-1100
  Trenton (G-10984)
Roof Deck Inc......................................F...... 609 448-6666
  East Windsor (G-2358)

ROOFING GRANULES

G Holdings LLC.....................................F...... 973 628-3000
  Parsippany (G-7953)
G-I Holdings Inc....................................G...... 973 628-3000
  Wayne (G-11507)

ROOFING MATERIALS: Asphalt

Icote USA Inc..G...... 908 359-7575
  Hillsborough (G-4326)
Karnak Corporation..............................D...... 732 388-0300
  Clark (G-1500)
Karnak Midwest LLC............................G...... 732 388-0300
  Clark (G-1501)
Koadings Inc...G...... 732 517-0784
  Allenhurst (G-22)
United Asphalt Company.......................E...... 856 753-9811
  Berlin (G-432)
Vector Foiltec LLC...............................G...... 862 702-8909
  Fairfield (G-3340)

ROOFING MATERIALS: Sheet Metal

GAF Elk Materials Corporation.............C...... 973 628-4083
  Wayne (G-11508)

ROOM COOLERS: Portable

Icy Cools Inc...G...... 609 448-0172
  Roosevelt (G-9529)

ROPE

Egg Harbor Rope Products Inc.............G...... 609 965-2435
  Egg Harbor City (G-2659)
William Kenyon & Sons Inc...................E...... 732 985-8980
  Piscataway (G-8738)

RUBBER

Ansell Healthcare Products LLC...........C...... 732 345-5400
  Iselin (G-4593)
Dicar Inc..E...... 973 575-1377
  Pine Brook (G-8596)
Dicar Inc..D...... 973 575-4220
  Pine Brook (G-8597)
Gel United Ltd Liability Co....................G...... 855 435-8683
  Saddle Brook (G-9653)
Harmony Elastomers LLC......................E...... 973 340-4000
  Paterson (G-8208)
Newark Auto Top Co Inc.......................F...... 973 677-9935
  East Orange (G-2256)

Pierce-Roberts Rubber Company.........F...... 609 394-5245
  Ewing (G-3052)
Stiles Enterprises Inc...........................F...... 973 625-9660
  Rockaway (G-9501)

RUBBER PRDTS: Appliance, Mechanical

Minor Rubber Co Inc............................E...... 973 338-6800
  Bloomfield (G-511)

RUBBER PRDTS: Mechanical

Aarubco Rubber Co Inc.......................E...... 973 772-8177
  Saddle Brook (G-9638)
AMP Custom Rubber Inc.......................F...... 732 888-2714
  Keyport (G-4997)
Ansell Inc..D...... 334 794-4231
  Iselin (G-4594)
Eastern Molding Co Inc........................G...... 973 759-0220
  Belleville (G-294)
Hawthorne Rubber Mfg Corp.................E...... 973 427-3337
  Hawthorne (G-4225)
Kinnarney Rubber Co Inc......................F...... 856 468-1320
  Mantua (G-5852)
Manville Rubber Products Inc................E...... 908 526-9111
  Manville (G-5856)
Monmouth Rubber Corp.........................E...... 732 229-3444
  Long Branch (G-5604)
Panova Inc..E...... 973 263-1700
  Towaco (G-10876)
Passaic Rubber Co...............................D...... 973 696-9500
  Wayne (G-11540)
Pierce-Roberts Rubber Company.........F...... 609 394-5245
  Ewing (G-3052)
Reiss Corporation.................................C...... 732 446-6100
  Rumson (G-9601)
Rempac LLC..C...... 201 843-4585
  Rochelle Park (G-9431)
Research & Mfg Corp Amer...................F...... 908 862-6744
  Linden (G-5414)
Shock Tech Inc.....................................E...... 845 368-8600
  Mahwah (G-5771)
Stiles Enterprises Inc...........................F...... 973 625-9660
  Rockaway (G-9501)
T & B Specialties Inc............................G...... 732 928-4500
  Jackson (G-4666)
Tricomp Inc..C...... 973 835-1110
  Pompton Plains (G-8872)
Troy Hills Manufacturing Inc..................G...... 973 263-1885
  Towaco (G-10882)

RUBBER PRDTS: Medical & Surgical Tubing, Extrudd & Lathe-Cut

Fermatex Vascular Tech LLC.................F...... 732 681-7070
  Wall Township (G-11339)
Nbs Group Sup Med Pdts Div LLC.........G...... 732 745-9292
  New Brunswick (G-6949)

RUBBER PRDTS: Oil & Gas Field Machinery, Mechanical

Mid-State Enterprises Inc......................F...... 973 427-6040
  Bloomfield (G-510)

RUBBER PRDTS: Sheeting

Banks Bros Corporation........................D...... 973 680-4488
  Bloomfield (G-491)

RUBBER PRDTS: Silicone

Kini Products Inc...................................G...... 732 299-5555
  New Egypt (G-6984)
Paul Englehardt....................................G...... 908 637-4556
  Great Meadows (G-3857)

RUBBER PRDTS: Sponge

Supply Plus NJ Inc................................E...... 973 782-5930
  Paterson (G-8307)

RUBBER PRDTS: Wet Suits

Henderson Aquatic Inc..........................E...... 856 825-4771
  Millville (G-6254)

RUBBER STAMP, WHOLESALE

Magic Printing Corp..............................F...... 732 726-0620
  Avenel (G-135)

RUBBER STRUCTURES: Air-Supported

Air Cruisers Company LLC...................B...... 732 681-3527
  Wall Township (G-11315)

RUGS : Tufted

Mannington Mills Inc.............................A...... 856 935-3000
  Salem (G-9694)

RULERS: Metal

National Steel Rule Company................D...... 908 862-3366
  Linden (G-5392)
National Steel Rule Company................F...... 800 922-0885
  Linden (G-5393)

RUST RESISTING

Por-15 Inc...E...... 973 887-1999
  Whippany (G-11905)

SAFES & VAULTS: Metal

United Hospital Supply Corp..................C...... 609 387-7580
  Burlington (G-990)

SAFETY EQPT & SPLYS WHOLESALERS

Garden State Highway Pdts Inc.............E...... 856 692-7572
  Millville (G-6250)
Jontol Unlimited LLC............................G...... 858 652-1113
  Blackwood (G-473)
Power Hawk Technologies Inc..............F...... 973 627-4646
  Rockaway (G-9489)

SAFETY INSPECTION SVCS

Forman Industries Inc..........................D...... 732 727-8100
  Old Bridge (G-7715)

SAILS

Linthicum Sails.....................................G...... 856 783-4288
  Somerdale (G-9932)
North Sales..G...... 732 528-8899
  Sea Girt (G-9746)

SALT

Saltopia Infused Sea Salt LLC.............F...... 908 850-1926
  Hackettstown (G-4035)

SAMPLE BOOKS

Tomwar Corp..E...... 856 740-0111
  Williamstown (G-11981)
Walden Lang In-Pak Service.................E...... 973 595-5250
  Clifton (G-1738)

SAND & GRAVEL

Baer Aggregates Inc.............................F...... 908 454-4412
  Phillipsburg (G-8543)
Clayton Sand Company.........................E...... 732 751-7600
  Wall Township (G-11328)
Control Industries Inc...........................G...... 201 437-3826
  Bayonne (G-212)
County Concrete Corporation................F...... 973 538-3113
  Morristown (G-6656)
Earthwork Associates Inc.....................F...... 609 624-9395
  Ocean View (G-7702)
Eastern Concrete Materials Inc.............E...... 973 827-7625
  Hamburg (G-4090)
Hanson Aggregates Wrp Inc.................E...... 972 653-5500
  Wall Township (G-11345)
Harmony Sand & Gravel Inc..................E...... 908 475-4690
  Phillipsburg (G-8555)
Intelligentproject LLC...........................G...... 732 928-3421
  Jackson (G-4657)
J Gennaro Trucking..............................F...... 973 773-0805
  Garfield (G-3749)
Mays Landing Sand & Gravel Co...........G...... 856 447-4294
  Newport (G-7334)
North Church Gravel Inc........................G...... 201 796-1556
  Oak Ridge (G-7603)
Orsillo & Company................................G...... 973 248-1833
  Wayne (G-11537)
Pinnacle Materials Inc..........................E...... 732 254-7676
  East Brunswick (G-2165)

SAND MINING

Dun-Rite Sand & Gravel Co..................G...... 856 692-2520
  Vineland (G-11214)

Partac Peat Corp ....F...... 908 637-4191
  Great Meadows *(G-3855)*
Whibco of New Jersey Inc ....E...... 856 455-9200
  Port Elizabeth *(G-8878)*

SAND: Hygrade

Covia Holdings Corporation ....E...... 856 785-2700
  Dividing Creek *(G-2069)*
Covia Holdings Corporation ....E...... 856 451-6400
  Bridgeton *(G-756)*
New Jersey Pulverizing Co Inc ....F...... 732 269-1400
  Bayville *(G-249)*
Whibco of New Jersey Inc ....E...... 856 455-9200
  Port Elizabeth *(G-8878)*

SANITARY SVC, NEC

All American Oil Recovery Co ....E...... 973 628-9278
  Wayne *(G-11467)*

SANITARY SVCS: Chemical Detoxification

Phibro-Tech Inc ....E...... 201 329-7300
  Teaneck *(G-10645)*

SANITARY SVCS: Environmental Cleanup

Demaio Inc ....E...... 609 965-4094
  Egg Harbor City *(G-2657)*
Doolan Industries Incorporated.............G...... 856 985-1880
  Marlton *(G-5929)*

SANITARY SVCS: Radioactive Waste Materials, Disposal

John J Chando Jr Inc ....G...... 732 793-2122
  Mantoloking *(G-5850)*

SANITARY SVCS: Refuse Collection & Disposal Svcs

County of Somerset ....C...... 732 469-3363
  Bridgewater *(G-814)*

SANITARY SVCS: Sewage Treatment Facility

Organica Water Inc ....F...... 609 651-8885
  West Windsor *(G-11782)*

SANITARY SVCS: Waste Materials, Recycling

All Amrcan Recycl Corp Clifton............C...... 201 656-3363
  Jersey City *(G-4688)*
All County Recycling Inc ....F...... 609 393-6445
  Trenton *(G-10890)*
Bayshore Recycling Corp ....E...... 732 738-6000
  Keasbey *(G-4908)*
Cumberland Rcycl Corp S Jersey ......E...... 856 825-4153
  Millville *(G-6245)*
Glass Cycle Systems Inc.................G...... 973 838-0034
  Riverdale *(G-9378)*
James R Macauley Inc ....G...... 856 767-3474
  Waterford Works *(G-11462)*
Natures Choice Corporation ....F...... 973 969-3299
  Sparta *(G-10401)*
Plastic Specialties & Tech Inc............C...... 201 941-2900
  Ridgefield *(G-9284)*
Pure Tech International Inc ....G...... 908 722-4800
  Branchburg *(G-674)*
Recycle Inc ....D...... 908 756-2200
  South Plainfield *(G-10324)*
Reliable Paper Recycling Inc ....C...... 201 333-5244
  Jersey City *(G-4800)*
Wilenta Carting Inc ....F...... 201 325-0044
  Secaucus *(G-9828)*
Wilenta Feed Inc ....F...... 201 325-0044
  Secaucus *(G-9829)*

SANITARY WARE: Metal

Aero Manufacturing Co ....D...... 973 473-5300
  Clifton *(G-1558)*

SANITATION CHEMICALS & CLEANING AGENTS

3M Company ....B...... 973 884-2500
  Whippany *(G-11875)*
Astra Cleaners of Hazlet...................G...... 732 264-4144
  Hazlet *(G-4257)*
Benckiser N Reckitt Amer Inc ....A...... 973 404-2600
  Parsippany *(G-7893)*

Chemetall US Inc ....D...... 908 464-6900
  New Providence *(G-6997)*
Ep Systems Inc ....G...... 570 424-0581
  Hackettstown *(G-4006)*
Global Spclty Products-Usa Inc ....F...... 609 518-7577
  Mount Holly *(G-6728)*
Harvester Inc ....F...... 201 445-1122
  Irvington *(G-4571)*
Houghton Chemical Corporation ....E...... 201 460-8071
  Carlstadt *(G-1166)*
International Products Corp ....F...... 609 386-8770
  Burlington *(G-974)*
Interntonal Specialty Pdts Inc ....A...... 859 815-3333
  Wayne *(G-11522)*
James R Macauley Inc ....G...... 856 767-3474
  Waterford Works *(G-11462)*
Matchless United Companies ....G...... 908 862-7300
  Linden *(G-5380)*
PQ Corporation ....E...... 732 750-9040
  Avenel *(G-141)*
Prestige Laboratories Inc ....E...... 973 772-8922
  East Rutherford *(G-2311)*
Reckitt Benckiser LLC ....G...... 973 404-2600
  Montvale *(G-6425)*
Stanson Corporation ....D...... 973 344-8666
  Kearny *(G-4900)*
Stepan Company ....D...... 609 298-1222
  Bordentown *(G-595)*
Trap-Zap Environmental Systems ....E...... 201 251-9970
  Wyckoff *(G-12122)*
Venus Laboratories Inc ....E...... 973 257-8983
  Parsippany *(G-8035)*

SASHES: Door Or Window, Metal

Architectural Window Mfg Corp ....C...... 201 933-5094
  Rutherford *(G-9614)*
Revival Sash & Door LLC..................G...... 973 500-4242
  Springfield *(G-10465)*
Rsl LLC ....D...... 609 484-1600
  Egg Harbor Township *(G-2695)*

SATELLITE COMMUNICATIONS EQPT

Aphelion Orbitals Inc ....G...... 321 289-0872
  Union City *(G-11107)*

SATELLITES: Communications

Deckhouse Communications Inc ....G...... 201 961-5564
  Fairfield *(G-3181)*
Maxentric Technologies LLC ....E...... 201 242-9800
  Fort Lee *(G-3570)*
Modulation Sciences Inc.................F...... 732 302-3090
  Somerset *(G-10031)*
Orbcomm LLC ....E...... 703 433-6300
  Rochelle Park *(G-9427)*
Satellite Pros Inc ....G...... 908 823-9500
  Whitehouse Station *(G-11933)*
SES Engineering (us) Inc ....D...... 609 987-4000
  Princeton *(G-9021)*
Ussecurenet LLC ....G...... 201 447-0130
  Hawthorne *(G-4248)*

SAW BLADES

IDL Techni-Edge LLC ....C...... 908 497-9818
  Kenilworth *(G-4945)*
National Steel Rule Company ....D...... 908 862-3366
  Linden *(G-5392)*
Rf360 Technologies Inc ....E...... 848 999-3582
  Bridgewater *(G-876)*

SAWDUST & SHAVINGS

Landew Sawdust Co Inc...................F...... 973 344-5255
  Newark *(G-7177)*
Sawdust Depot LLC ....F...... 973 344-5255
  Howell *(G-4550)*

SAWING & PLANING MILLS

Mellon D P M L L C ....G...... 732 563-0030
  Somerset *(G-10029)*
P J Murphy Forest Pdts Corp ....G...... 973 316-0800
  Montville *(G-6445)*
Schairer Brothers...........................G...... 609 965-0996
  Egg Harbor City *(G-2667)*
Thomas Cobb & Sons......................G...... 856 451-0671
  Bridgeton *(G-775)*

SAWING & PLANING MILLS: Custom

Logpowercom LLC ....G...... 732 350-9663
  Whiting *(G-11940)*
Rex Lumber Company ....D...... 732 446-4200
  Manalapan *(G-5824)*

SAWS & SAWING EQPT

Chatham Lawn Mowler ....G...... 973 635-8855
  Chatham *(G-1320)*
Mendham Garden Center ....G...... 973 543-4178
  Mendham *(G-6041)*
Precision Saw & Tool Corp ....F...... 973 773-7302
  Clifton *(G-1698)*
Winslow Rental & Supply Inc ....G...... 856 767-5554
  Berlin *(G-434)*

SCALES & BALANCES, EXC LABORATORY

American Garvens Corporation............G...... 973 276-1093
  Pine Brook *(G-8586)*
Coperion K-Tron Pitman Inc ....F...... 856 589-0500
  Sewell *(G-9836)*
Technidyne Corporation...................G...... 732 363-1055
  Toms River *(G-10799)*
W T Winter Associates Inc ....E...... 888 808-3611
  Fairfield *(G-3350)*

SCALES: Indl

Empire Scale & Balance ....G...... 856 299-1651
  Penns Grove *(G-8378)*
Ohaus Corporation ....D...... 973 377-9000
  Parsippany *(G-7980)*

SCANNING DEVICES: Optical

Chiral Photonics Inc ....F...... 973 732-0030
  Pine Brook *(G-8590)*
MRC Precision Metal Optics Inc ....E...... 941 753-8707
  Northvale *(G-7538)*
Ncs Pearson Inc ....D...... 201 896-1011
  Lyndhurst *(G-5666)*
Scantron Corporation ....G...... 201 666-7009
  Westwood *(G-11844)*
Sqn Peripherals Inc ....E...... 609 261-5500
  Rancocas *(G-9166)*

SCHOOL BUS SVC

Dealaman Enterprises Inc.................E...... 908 647-5533
  Warren *(G-11407)*

SCHOOLS: Vocational, NEC

Union Institute Inc..........................E...... 800 914-8138
  Mahwah *(G-5785)*

SCIENTIFIC INSTRUMENTS WHOLESALERS

Daco Limited Partnership ....D...... 973 263-1100
  Boonton *(G-548)*
McKinley Scientific Llc ....F...... 973 579-4144
  Sparta *(G-10396)*
Topcon Medical Systems Inc ....D...... 201 599-5100
  Oakland *(G-7647)*

SCRAP & WASTE MATERIALS, WHOLESALE: Metal

Camden Iron & Metal LLC ....D...... 856 969-7065
  Camden *(G-1044)*
Exim Incorporated ....G...... 908 561-8200
  Piscataway *(G-8664)*
Federal Metals & Alloys Co ....E...... 908 756-0900
  South Plainfield *(G-10257)*
Hugo Neu Recycling LLC ....E...... 914 530-2350
  Kearny *(G-4866)*

SCRAP & WASTE MATERIALS, WHOLESALE: Nonferrous Metals Scrap

Emil A Schroth Inc ....E...... 732 938-5015
  Howell *(G-4538)*
Metal MGT Pittsburgh Inc ....E...... 201 333-2902
  Jersey City *(G-4765)*

SCRAP & WASTE MATERIALS, WHOLESALE: Paper

Reliable Paper Recycling Inc..............C...... 201 333-5244
  Jersey City *(G-4800)*

SCRAP & WASTE MATERIALS, WHOLESALE: Plastics Scrap

Gdb International Inc ....D 732 246-3001
New Brunswick *(G-6928)*
Lion Extruding Corp ....F 973 344-4648
Newark *(G-7181)*
Recycle-Tech Corp ....F 201 475-5000
Elmwood Park *(G-2853)*

SCREENS: Window, Metal

Belleville Corporation ....F 201 991-6222
Kearny *(G-4846)*
Verona Aluminum Products Inc ....G 973 857-4809
Verona *(G-11177)*

SCREENS: Window, Wood Framed

Screens Incorporated ....G 973 633-8558
Wayne *(G-11553)*

SCREENS: Woven Wire

Compass Wire Cloth Corp ....E 856 853-7616
Vineland *(G-11203)*

SCREW MACHINE PRDTS

Accurate Screw Machine Corp ....D 973 276-0379
Fairfield *(G-3133)*
Amark Industries Inc ....G 973 992-8900
Livingston *(G-5505)*
Automatic Machine Product ....G 973 383-9929
Newton *(G-7337)*
Bmb Machining LLC ....G 973 256-4010
Woodland Park *(G-12071)*
C & K Punch & Screw Mch Pdts ....G 201 343-6750
Hackensack *(G-3888)*
Champion Fasteners Inc ....E 609 267-5222
Lumberton *(G-5627)*
Chicago Pneumatic Tool ....G 973 276-1377
Fairfield *(G-3167)*
Congruent Machine Co Inc ....G 973 764-6767
Vernon *(G-11158)*
Duro Manufacturing Company ....G 908 810-9588
Union *(G-11046)*
Eastern Machining Corporation ....G 856 694-3303
Franklinville *(G-3637)*
Edston Manufacturing Company ....G 908 647-0116
Fairfield *(G-3189)*
Esco Precision Inc ....E 908 722-0800
Hillsborough *(G-4315)*
F P Schmidt Manufacturing Co ....F 201 343-4241
South Hackensack *(G-10161)*
Ferrum Industries Inc ....F 201 935-1220
Carlstadt *(G-1156)*
Form Cut Industries Inc ....E 973 483-5154
Newark *(G-7127)*
Gadren Machine Co Inc ....F 856 456-4329
Collingswood *(G-1767)*
H & H Swiss Screw Machine PR ....E 908 688-6390
Hillside *(G-4395)*
Hi-Grade Products Mfg Co ....F 908 245-4133
Kenilworth *(G-4944)*
International Tool & Mch LLC ....G 908 687-5580
Hillside *(G-4404)*
J & S Precision Products Co ....E 609 654-0900
Medford *(G-6025)*
Karl Neuweiler Inc ....G 908 464-6532
Berkeley Heights *(G-404)*
Labern Machine Products LLC ....G 908 722-1970
Branchburg *(G-654)*
Main Robert A & Sons Holdg Co ....E 201 447-3700
Wyckoff *(G-12116)*
Meltom Manufacturing Inc ....G 973 546-0058
Clifton *(G-1667)*
Mw Industries Inc ....D 973 244-9200
Fairfield *(G-3274)*
Nova Precision Products Inc ....C 973 625-1586
Rockaway *(G-9480)*
O E M Manufacturers Ltd Inc ....G 201 475-8585
Elmwood Park *(G-2845)*
Orion Precision Industries ....E 732 247-9704
Somerset *(G-10046)*
Oroszlany Laszlo ....G 201 666-2101
Hillsdale *(G-4369)*
Peter Yaged ....G 973 427-4219
Hawthorne *(G-4238)*
S J Screw Company Inc ....E 908 475-2155
Belvidere *(G-366)*

Salem Manufacturing Corp ....F 973 751-6331
Belleville *(G-314)*
Sumatic Co Inc ....G 973 772-1288
Garfield *(G-3771)*
Supermatic Corp ....F 973 627-4433
Rockaway *(G-9502)*
Telemark Cnc LLC ....G 973 794-4857
Boonton *(G-571)*
Tool Shop Inc ....G 856 767-8077
West Berlin *(G-11630)*
Triangle Automatic Inc ....G 973 625-3830
Wharton *(G-11873)*
Ultimate Spinning Turning Corp ....G 201 372-9740
Moonachie *(G-6495)*
Welton V Johnson Engineering ....F 908 241-3100
Kenilworth *(G-4988)*
Zago Manufacturing Company ....E 973 643-6700
Newark *(G-7318)*

SCREW MACHINES

High Point Precision Products ....E 973 875-6229
Sussex *(G-10561)*

SCREWS: Metal

Cold Headed Fasteners Inc ....G 856 461-3244
Delanco *(G-2004)*
P & R Fasteners Inc ....E 732 302-3600
Somerset *(G-10050)*

SEALANTS

CR Laurence Co Inc ....F 856 727-1022
Moorestown *(G-6516)*
Royal Adhesives & Sealants LLC ....E 973 694-0845
Wayne *(G-11549)*
Sika Corporation ....C 201 933-8800
Lyndhurst *(G-5679)*

SEALING COMPOUNDS: Sealing, synthetic rubber or plastic

Assem - Pak Inc ....C 856 692-3355
Vineland *(G-11187)*
La Favorite Industries Inc ....F 973 279-1266
Paterson *(G-8236)*

SEALS: Hermetic

A P M Hexseal Corporation ....E 201 569-5700
Englewood *(G-2872)*
Aspe Inc ....E 973 808-1155
Fairfield *(G-3148)*
Frc Electrical Industries Inc ....E 908 464-3200
New Providence *(G-7000)*
Glasseal Products Inc ....C 732 370-9100
Lakewood *(G-5104)*
T & E Industries Inc ....E 973 672-5454
Orange *(G-7763)*
Zago Manufacturing Company ....E 973 643-6700
Newark *(G-7318)*

SEALS: Oil, Rubber

East Coast Rubber Products ....G 856 384-2747
Westville *(G-11812)*

SEARCH & DETECTION SYSTEMS, EXC RADAR

National Prtective Systems Inc ....F 732 922-3609
Eatontown *(G-2412)*

SEARCH & NAVIGATION SYSTEMS

Aeropanel Corporation ....D 973 335-9636
Boonton *(G-537)*
Alk Technologies Inc ....C 609 683-0220
Princeton *(G-8906)*
Allied-Signal China Ltd ....E 973 455-2000
Morristown *(G-6632)*
Alliedsignal Foreign Sls Corp ....G 973 455-2000
Morristown *(G-6633)*
American Gas & Chemical Co Ltd ....E 201 767-7300
Northvale *(G-7518)*
Bae Systems Info & Elec Sys ....B 603 885-4321
Totowa *(G-10817)*
Bae Systems Info & Elec Sys ....F 973 633-6000
Wayne *(G-11473)*
Bae Systems Tech Sol Srvc Inc ....E 856 638-1003
Mount Laurel *(G-6739)*

Check-It Electronics Corp ....E 973 520-8435
Elizabeth *(G-2720)*
Drs Infrared Technologies LP ....G 973 898-1500
Parsippany *(G-7920)*
Drs Leonardo Inc ....E 973 898-1500
Florham Park *(G-3501)*
Ferry Machine Corp ....E 201 641-9191
Little Ferry *(G-5485)*
GE Aviation Systems LLC ....C 973 428-9898
Whippany *(G-11892)*
General Dynamics Mission ....C 973 261-1409
Florham Park *(G-3507)*
Glasseal Products Inc ....C 732 370-9100
Lakewood *(G-5104)*
Ho-Ho-Kus Inc ....E 973 278-2274
Paterson *(G-8210)*
Intertek Laboratories Inc ....E 908 903-1800
Stirling *(G-10491)*
Kearfott Corporation ....C 973 785-6000
Woodland Park *(G-12083)*
L3harris Technologies Inc ....C 973 284-0123
Clifton *(G-1650)*
L3harris Technologies Inc ....C 585 269-6600
Bloomfield *(G-505)*
Lockheed Martin ....D 856 722-7782
Marlton *(G-5938)*
Lockheed Martin ....C 856 722-2418
Marlton *(G-5939)*
Lockheed Martin Corporation ....C 856 988-1085
Marlton *(G-5940)*
Lockheed Martin Corporation ....A 609 485-7601
Atlantic City *(G-97)*
Lockheed Martin Corporation ....D 856 722-7782
Moorestown *(G-6538)*
Lockheed Martin Corporation ....C 856 792-9811
Cherry Hill *(G-1384)*
Lockheed Martin Corporation ....C 856 727-5800
Mount Laurel *(G-6778)*
Lockheed Martin Corporation ....C 856 722-3336
Moorestown *(G-6539)*
Lockheed Martin Integrtd Systm ....C 856 762-2222
Wall Township *(G-11353)*
Northrop Grumman Systems Corp ....C 609 272-9000
Pleasantville *(G-8816)*
Northrop Grumman Systems Corp ....G 908 276-6677
Cranford *(G-1919)*
Oaviation Corporation ....E 609 619-3060
Princeton *(G-8989)*
Primacy Engineering Inc ....F 201 731-3272
Englewood Cliffs *(G-2988)*
Sun Dial & Panel Corporation ....E 973 226-4334
Fairfield *(G-3319)*
Transistor Devices Inc ....C 908 850-5088
Hackettstown *(G-4039)*
Tru Temp Sensors Inc ....G 215 396-1550
Ocean City *(G-7698)*

SEARCH & RESCUE SVCS

Anvima Technologies LLC ....G 973 531-7077
Brookside *(G-916)*

SEATING: Stadium

Archer Plastics Inc ....G 856 692-0242
Elmer *(G-2794)*

SECRETARIAL SVCS

Premier Printing Solutions LLC ....G 732 525-0740
South Amboy *(G-10139)*

SECURITY CONTROL EQPT & SYSTEMS

AAS Technologies Inc ....G 201 342-7300
Hackensack *(G-3874)*
Blonder Tongue Labs Inc ....C 732 679-4000
Old Bridge *(G-7713)*
Checkpoint Systems Inc ....C 800 257-5540
West Deptford *(G-11697)*
Checkpoint Systems Inc ....C 856 848-1800
West Deptford *(G-11698)*
Daq Electronics LLC ....E 732 981-0050
Piscataway *(G-8651)*
Ecsi International Inc ....F 973 574-8555
Clifton *(G-1610)*
Electronic Control SEC Inc ....F 973 574-8555
Clifton *(G-1613)*
Engineered Security Systems ....E 973 257-0555
Towaco *(G-10871)*
Ifortress ....G 973 812-6400
Woodland Park *(G-12082)*

Employee Codes: A=Over 500 employees, B=251-500
C=101-250, D=51-100, E=20-50, F=10-19, G=4-9   2019 Harris New jersey
Manufacturers Directory

931

PRODUCT

K & A Industries Inc ....G...... 908 226-7000
South Plainfield *(G-10285)*

Ketec ....F 856 778-4343
Moorestown *(G-6534)*

LTS NJ Inc 856 780-9888
Mount Laurel *(G-6779)*

Mobile Intelligent Alerts Inc ....G...... 201 410-5324
Holmdel *(G-4507)*

Multicomm Solutions Inc 877 796-8480
Toms River *(G-10780)*

Qsa Global National Corp ....G...... 865 888-6798
Red Bank *(G-9241)*

Quantum Security Systems Inc ......G...... 609 252-0505
Princeton *(G-9011)*

Secure System Inc ....E 732 922-3609
Stirling *(G-10496)*

Security 21 LLC ....G...... 856 384-7474
Woodbury *(G-12036)*

Specialized Fire & SEC Inc ......E 212 255-1010
Riverdale *(G-9386)*

T F S Inc ....E 973 890-7651
Totowa *(G-10854)*

Talon7 LLC ....F 908 595-2121
Bridgewater *(G-896)*

Techntime Bus Sltons Ltd Lblty ....F 973 246-8153
East Rutherford *(G-2324)*

Wickr Inc ....G...... 516 637-2882
Newark *(G-7315)*

SECURITY DEVICES

Almetek Industries Inc ....E 908 850-9700
Hackettstown *(G-3997)*

Digitize Inc ....F 973 663-1011
Lake Hopatcong *(G-5036)*

Enterprisecc Ltd Liability Co ....G...... 201 266-0020
Jersey City *(G-4732)*

Infinova Corporation ....E 732 355-9100
Monmouth Junction *(G-6293)*

M & Z International Inc ....G...... 201 864-3331
West New York *(G-11746)*

New Skysonic Surveillance ....G...... 856 317-0600
Cherry Hill *(G-1398)*

Skycam Technologies LLC ....G...... 908 205-5548
Perth Amboy *(G-8534)*

SECURITY DISTRIBUTORS

New Skysonic Surveillance ....G...... 856 317-0600
Cherry Hill *(G-1398)*

SECURITY EQPT STORES

Vcom Intl Multi-Media Corp ....D...... 201 296-0600
Fairfield *(G-3339)*

SECURITY PROTECTIVE DEVICES MAINTENANCE & MONITORING SVCS

Hookway Enterprises Inc ....F 973 691-0382
Netcong *(G-6907)*

Ketec ....F 856 778-4343
Moorestown *(G-6534)*

Qsa Global National Corp ....G...... 865 888-6798
Red Bank *(G-9241)*

Secure System Inc ....E 732 922-3609
Stirling *(G-10496)*

Sightlogix Inc ....E 609 951-0008
Princeton *(G-9022)*

SECURITY SYSTEMS SERVICES

National Prtective Systems Inc ....F 732 922-3609
Eatontown *(G-2412)*

New Skysonic Surveillance ....G...... 856 317-0600
Cherry Hill *(G-1398)*

T F S Inc ....E 973 890-7651
Totowa *(G-10854)*

Vanderbilt LLC ....E 973 316-3900
Parsippany *(G-8034)*

SEMICONDUCTOR CIRCUIT NETWORKS

Enpirion Inc ....E 908 575-7550
Hampton *(G-4150)*

M E C Technologies Inc ....E 732 505-0308
Toms River *(G-10776)*

Xtreme Powertech LLC ....F 201 791-5050
Upper Saddle River *(G-11150)*

SEMICONDUCTORS & RELATED DEVICES

Aeon Corporation ....G...... 609 275-9003
Princeton Junction *(G-9047)*

Akela Laser Corporation ....F 732 305-7105
Monroe Township *(G-6325)*

Altera Corporation ....G...... 732 649-3477
Somerset *(G-9950)*

American Microsemiconductor ....E 973 377-9566
Madison *(G-5689)*

Automatic Switch Company ....A...... 973 966-2000
Florham Park *(G-3485)*

Bel Fuse Inc ....C...... 201 432-0463
Jersey City *(G-4700)*

Cambridge Industries Group ....G...... 917 669-7337
Basking Ridge *(G-178)*

Cast Inc ....G...... 201 391-8300
Woodcliff Lake *(G-12051)*

Compufab Sales Inc ....G...... 856 786-0175
Cinnaminson *(G-1447)*

Data Delay Devices ....E 973 202-3268
Clifton *(G-1596)*

Dialight Corporation ....D...... 732 751-5809
Wall Township *(G-11334)*

Discovery Semiconductors Inc ....E 609 434-1311
Ewing *(G-3027)*

Duet Microelectronics LLC ....F 908 854-3838
Raritan *(G-9210)*

G T Associates ....G...... 973 694-6040
Wayne *(G-11506)*

Gce Market Inc ....G...... 856 401-8900
Blackwood *(G-466)*

Hamamatsu Corporation ....D...... 908 231-0960
Bridgewater *(G-828)*

Infineon Tech Americas Corp ....F 732 603-5914
Iselin *(G-4612)*

Inphot Inc ....G...... 609 799-7172
Plainsboro *(G-8791)*

Jerome Industries Corp ....E 908 353-5700
Hackettstown *(G-4013)*

Keyence Corporation America ....E 201 930-0100
Elmwood Park *(G-2834)*

Lockheed Martin Corporation ....E 732 321-4200
Edison *(G-2552)*

Lucent Technologies World Svcs ....C...... 908 582-3000
New Providence *(G-7008)*

Maxlite Inc ....D...... 973 244-7300
West Caldwell *(G-11663)*

Memory International Corp ....F 973 586-2653
Denville *(G-2046)*

Micro-Tek Laboratories Inc ....G...... 973 779-5577
Clifton *(G-1669)*

Moser Jewel Company ....G...... 908 454-1155
Phillipsburg *(G-8564)*

Multi-Tech Industries Inc ....F 732 431-0550
Marlboro *(G-5905)*

Multilink Technology Corp ....E 732 805-9355
Somerset *(G-10036)*

Nanonex Corp ....F 732 355-1600
Monmouth Junction *(G-6298)*

Nte Electronics Inc ....D...... 973 748-5089
Bloomfield *(G-513)*

Pny Technologies Inc ....B...... 973 515-9700
Parsippany *(G-7997)*

Princeton Lightwave Inc ....E 609 495-2600
Cranbury *(G-1875)*

Renesas Electronics Amer Inc ....E 908 685-6000
Bridgewater *(G-875)*

Richards Manufacturing Co Inc ....G...... 973 371-1771
Irvington *(G-4584)*

Roxboro Holdings Inc ....D...... 732 919-3119
Wall Township *(G-11365)*

Sharp Electronics Corporation ....A...... 201 529-8200
Montvale *(G-6433)*

Sunlight Aerospace Inc ....F 732 362-7501
Edison *(G-2625)*

Tel-Instrument Elec Corp ....E 201 933-1600
East Rutherford *(G-2325)*

William Kenyon & Sons Inc ....E 732 985-8980
Piscataway *(G-8738)*

SENSORS: Radiation

Frauscher Sensor Tech USA Inc ....F 609 285-5492
Princeton *(G-8951)*

SENSORS: Temperature For Motor Windings

NRG Bluewater Wind LLC ....G...... 201 748-5000
Hoboken *(G-4469)*

SENSORS: Temperature, Exc Indl Process

Palmer Electronics Inc ....F 973 772-5900
Garfield *(G-3752)*

SEPARATORS: Metal Plate

Hiller Separation Process LLC ....G...... 512 556-5707
Fort Lee *(G-3561)*

SEPTIC TANKS: Concrete

Double Twenties Inc ....F 973 827-7563
Franklin *(G-3602)*

Flemington Precast & Sup LLC ....F 908 782-3246
Flemington *(G-3443)*

Granville Concrete Products ....G...... 973 584-6653
Randolph *(G-9182)*

Northeast Con Pdcts & Sup Inc ....G...... 973 728-1667
Hewitt *(G-4277)*

P J Gillespie Inc ....E 856 327-2993
Vineland *(G-11248)*

Peerless Concrete Products Co ....G...... 973 838-3060
Butler *(G-1011)*

SEWAGE & WATER TREATMENT EQPT

Bishop Ascendant Inc ....G...... 201 572-7436
West Caldwell *(G-11642)*

Favs Corp ....G...... 856 358-1515
Elmer *(G-2797)*

Fin-Tek Corporation ....G...... 973 628-2988
Wayne *(G-11503)*

Site Drainer LLC ....G...... 862 225-9940
Clifton *(G-1721)*

Suez North America Inc ....E 201 767-9300
Paramus *(G-7837)*

Suez Treatment Solutions Inc ....C...... 201 767-9300
Paramus *(G-7838)*

U V International LLC ....G...... 973 993-9454
Morristown *(G-6705)*

Water Resources New Jersey LLC ......G...... 609 268-7965
Tabernacle *(G-10620)*

SEWAGE TREATMENT SYSTEMS & EQPT

East Brunswick Sewerage Auth ....F 732 257-8313
East Brunswick *(G-2138)*

Franklin Miller Inc ....E 973 535-9200
Livingston *(G-5512)*

SEWING CONTRACTORS

A & R Sewing Company Inc ....F 201 332-0622
Jersey City *(G-4682)*

Bethel Industries Inc ....C...... 201 656-8222
Jersey City *(G-4702)*

Jomel Seams Reasonable LLC ....F 973 282-0300
Hillside *(G-4407)*

SEWING MACHINES & PARTS: Indl

Clinton Industries Inc ....E 201 440-0400
Little Ferry *(G-5478)*

Imperial Sewing Machine Co ....G...... 973 374-3405
Irvington *(G-4574)*

John N Fehlinger Co Inc ....G...... 973 633-0699
Fairfield *(G-3246)*

Kansai Special Amercn Mch Corp ......G...... 973 470-8321
East Rutherford *(G-2293)*

SHADES: Lamp & Light, Residential

Jay-Bee Lamp & Shade Co Inc ....G...... 201 265-0762
Paramus *(G-7809)*

SHADES: Lamp Or Candle

Natal Lamp & Shade Corp ....E 201 224-7844
Fort Lee *(G-3578)*

New Brunswick Lamp Shade Co ....E 732 545-0377
New Brunswick *(G-6952)*

SHADES: Window

A Plus Installs LLC ....G...... 201 255-4412
Bloomfield *(G-488)*

C & M Shade Corp ....E 201 807-1200
Fairfield *(G-3160)*

Griffith Shade Company Inc ....G...... 973 667-1474
Nutley *(G-7586)*

Kay Window Fashions Inc ....F 862 591-1554
Saddle Brook *(G-9658)*

(G-0000) Company's Geographic Section entry number

RFS Commercial Inc............................F 201 796-0006
Saddle Brook (G-9671)

SHAPES & PILINGS, STRUCTURAL: Steel

Bloomfield Iron Co Inc........................G 973 748-7040
Belleville (G-291)
Interstate Welding & Mfg Co ....F 800 676-4666
Beverly (G-452)
McAlister Welding & Fabg...................F 856 740-3890
Glassboro (G-3815)

SHAPES: Extruded, Aluminum, NEC

Frameware Inc....................................F 800 582-5608
Fairfield (G-3207)

SHAVING PREPARATIONS

Edgewell Personal Care LLC ....G....... 973 753-3000
Cedar Knolls (G-1303)

SHEET METAL SPECIALTIES, EXC STAMPED

A B Scantlebury Co Inc ....F 973 770-3000
Newton (G-7335)
Airtec Inc..G 732 382-3700
Rahway (G-9075)
Allmike Metal Technology Inc.............F 201 935-2306
Moonachie (G-6452)
B & S Sheet Metal Co Inc ....F 973 427-3739
Hawthorne (G-4205)
Broadhurst Sheet Metal Works...........G 973 304-4001
Hawthorne (G-4210)
Burns Link Manufacturing Co.............F 856 429-6844
Voorhees (G-11281)
Casale Industries Inc ....E 908 789-0040
Garwood (G-3782)
Clifton Metal Products Co Inc ....F 973 777-6100
Clifton (G-1584)
Coronation Sheet Metal Co ....G 908 686-0930
Union (G-11038)
Custom Fabricators Inc ....G 908 862-4244
Linden (G-5339)
D&N Machine Manufacturing Inc ....E 856 456-1366
Gloucester City (G-3840)
Diversified Fab Pdts Ltd Lblty ....G 973 773-3189
Clifton (G-1601)
Edker Industries Inc...........................E 856 786-1971
Cinnaminson (G-1455)
Elmco Two Inc ....G 856 365-2244
Camden (G-1060)
Franklen Sheet Metal Co Inc ....F 732 988-0808
Ocean Grove (G-7700)
General Aviation & Elec Mfg Co ....E 201 487-1700
Hackensack (G-3921)
Globe Engineering Corp......................G 609 898-0349
Cape May (G-1099)
International Shtmtl Plate Mfg ....E 908 722-6614
Somerville (G-10117)
J & E Metal Fabricators Inc ....E 732 548-9650
Metuchen (G-6064)
Jersey Sheet Metal & Machine.............E 973 366-8628
Dover (G-2093)
Kinetron Inc ....F 732 918-7777
Ocean (G-7667)
Lectro Products Inc ....G 732 462-2463
Freehold (G-3675)
Lentine Sheet Metal Inc......................F 908 486-8974
Linden (G-5375)
Lynn Mechanical Contractors..............F 856 829-1717
Cinnaminson (G-1470)
Metal Specialties New Jersey ....G 609 261-9277
Mount Holly (G-6732)
Metalfab Inc..E 973 764-2000
Vernon (G-11160)
Metalix Inc..G 973 546-2500
Little Falls (G-5461)
Moreng Metal Products Inc.................D 973 256-2001
Totowa (G-10837)
Neumann Sheet Metal Inc ....G 908 756-0415
Plainfield (G-8771)
New Age Metal Fabg Co Inc ....D 973 227-9107
Fairfield (G-3277)
Pemberton Fabricators Inc ....A 609 267-0922
Rancocas (G-9163)
Pioneer Machine & Tool Co Inc ....E 856 779-8800
Maple Shade (G-5868)
Quality Sheet Metal & Wldg Inc ....F 732 469-7111
Piscataway (G-8703)
Radiation Systems Inc.........................G 201 891-7515
Wyckoff (G-12118)

Ranco Precision Sheet Metal...............G 973 472-8808
Clifton (G-1705)
Rhoads Metal Works Inc ....E 856 486-1551
Pennsauken (G-8478)
Service Metal Fabricating Inc ....D 973 625-8882
Rockaway (G-9498)
Shamong Manufacturing Company ......E 609 654-2549
Shamong (G-9859)
Springfield Metal Pdts Co Inc ....G 973 379-4600
Springfield (G-10467)
Theodore E Mozer Inc.........................E 856 829-1432
Palmyra (G-7786)
Trenton Sheet Metal Inc......................E 609 695-6328
Trenton (G-11003)
Unique Metal Products ....F 732 388-1888
Rahway (G-9130)
Vfi Fabricators Inc..............................E 856 629-8786
Williamstown (G-11985)
Wecom Inc ....E 856 863-8400
Glassboro (G-3820)
Westfield Shtmtl Works Inc ....E 908 276-5500
Kenilworth (G-4989)

SHEETING: Laminated Plastic

Graphic Express Menu Co Inc ....E 973 685-0022
Clifton (G-1629)
JMJ Profile Inc....................................G 856 767-3930
West Berlin (G-11600)
Monmouth Rubber Corp.......................E 732 229-3444
Long Branch (G-5604)
Washington Stamp Exchange Inc ....F 973 966-0001
Florham Park (G-3526)

SHEETS & SHEETINGS, COTTON

Homespun Global LLC ....G 917 674-9684
Sayreville (G-9710)

SHEETS: Fabric, From Purchased Materials

Triangle Home Fashions LLC ....G 732 355-9800
East Brunswick (G-2187)

SHELLAC

PPG Industries Inc..............................E 856 273-7870
Mount Laurel (G-6794)
Rust-Oleum Corporation......................E 732 469-8100
Somerset (G-10069)

SHELTERED WORKSHOPS

Bestwork Inds For The Blind ....D 856 424-2510
Cherry Hill (G-1345)

SHELVES & SHELVING: Wood

Frank & Jims Inc ....G 609 646-1655
Pleasantville (G-8811)

SHERARDIZING SVC: Metals Or Metal Prdts

Armadillo Metalworks Inc.....................E 973 777-2105
Passaic (G-8051)

SHIMS: Metal

Wm H Brewster Jr Incorporated...........G 973 227-1050
Fairfield (G-3354)

SHIP BLDG/RPRG: Submersible Marine Robots, Manned/Unmanned

Bishop Ascendant Inc ....G 201 572-7436
West Caldwell (G-11642)

SHIP BUILDING & REPAIRING: Cargo, Commercial

Ocean Power & Equipment Co ....G 973 575-5775
West Caldwell (G-11668)

SHIP BUILDING & REPAIRING: Dredges

Wittich Bros Marine Inc ....E 732 722-8656
Manasquan (G-5844)

SHIP BUILDING & REPAIRING: Fishing Vessels, Large

Allen Steel Co ....G 856 785-1171
Leesburg (G-5286)

SHIP BUILDING & REPAIRING: Rigging, Marine

American Rigging & Repair Inc ....F 866 478-7129
Roselle (G-9547)

SHIPBUILDING & REPAIR

Bayonne Drydock & Repair Corp ....E 201 823-9295
Bayonne (G-206)
Conneaut Creek Ship Repr Inc ....G 212 863-9406
Jersey City (G-4716)
Dorchester Shipyard Inc ....F 856 785-8040
Dorchester (G-2070)
Kerney Service Group Inc ....E 908 486-2644
Linden (G-5370)
Maxwell McKenney Inc ....G 856 310-0700
Haddon Heights (G-4046)
Nvs International Inc............................E 908 523-0266
Linden (G-5398)
Simplex Americas LLC ....G 908 237-9099
Flemington (G-3467)
Union Dry Dock & Repair Co ....E 201 963-5833
Hoboken (G-4486)

SHIPPING AGENTS

E C D Ventures Inc ....G 856 875-1100
Blackwood (G-465)
Hub Print & Copy Center LLC ....G 201 585-7887
Fort Lee (G-3563)

SHOE MATERIALS: Counters

Cross Counter Inc...............................G 973 677-0600
East Orange (G-2251)

SHOE MATERIALS: Rands

Ingersoll-Rand Company ....G 973 882-0924
Pine Brook (G-8606)

SHOE MATERIALS: Rubber

Aerogroup Retail Holdings Inc ....D 732 819-9843
Edison (G-2448)

SHOE STORES

Ballet Makers Inc................................G 973 595-9000
Totowa (G-10818)

SHOE STORES: Athletic

Rags International Inc ....G 787 632-8447
Springfield (G-10462)
Schusters Shoes Inc...........................G 856 885-4551
Williamstown (G-11977)

SHOE STORES: Children's

J T Murdoch Shoes..............................F 973 748-6484
Bloomfield (G-503)

SHOE STORES: Orthopedic

Carlascio Custom & Orthopedic...........G 201 333-8716
Jersey City (G-4708)

SHOES & BOOTS WHOLESALERS

Jese Apparel LLC................................F 732 969-3200
Dayton (G-1973)
Lust For Life Footwear LLC ....F 646 732-9742
Teaneck (G-10638)
Man-How Inc..G 609 392-4895
Trenton (G-10954)
S Goldberg & Co Inc ....C 201 342-1200
Hackensack (G-3969)

SHOES: Athletic, Exc Rubber Or Plastic

McM Products USA Inc.........................F 646 756-4090
Secaucus (G-9792)

SHOES: Ballet Slippers

Ballet Makers Inc................................G 973 595-9000
Totowa (G-10818)

SHOES: Canvas, Rubber Soled

Vans Inc ....F 732 493-1516
Tinton Falls (G-10733)

P
R
O
D
U
C
T

SHOES: Children's, Sandals, Exc Rubber Or Plastic

S Goldberg & Co Inc ....C 201 342-1200
Hackensack (G-3969)

SHOES: Men's

Bm USA Incorporated ....E 800 624-5499
Carlstadt (G-1130)
Vf Outdoor LLC ....G 908 352-5390
Elizabeth (G-2785)

SHOES: Orthopedic, Children's

Carlascio Custom & Orthopedic ....G .. 201 333-8716
Jersey City (G-4708)

SHOES: Orthopedic, Men's

Carlascio Custom & Orthopedic ....G .. 201 333-8716
Jersey City (G-4708)

SHOES: Orthopedic, Women's

Carlascio Custom & Orthopedic ....G .. 201 333-8716
Jersey City (G-4708)
Schusters Shoes Inc ....G 856 885-4551
Williamstown (G-11977)

SHOES: Plastic Or Rubber

Nike Inc ....E 732 695-0108
Tinton Falls (G-10723)

SHOES: Plastic Or Rubber Soles With Fabric Uppers

Bear USa Inc ....F 201 943-4748
Palisades Park (G-7768)

SHOES: Women's, Dress

Jag Footwear ACC & Ret Corp ....F 609 845-1700
Westampton (G-11786)
Je TAime Shoes ....G 201 845-7463
Paramus (G-7810)

SHOT PEENING SVC

Metal Improvement Company LLC ....E 201 843-7800
Paramus (G-7819)

SHOWCASES & DISPLAY FIXTURES: Office & Store

Acme Manufacturing Co ....G 732 541-2800
Port Reading (G-8891)
Axg Corporation ....G 212 213-3313
Secaucus (G-9751)
Clip Strip Corp. ....G 201 342-9155
Hackensack (G-3898)
Display Equation LLC ....G 201 343-4135
Hackensack (G-3908)
Modern Showcase Inc ....F 201 935-2929
Carlstadt (G-1188)
National Display Group Inc ....E 856 661-1212
Pennsauken (G-8459)
Pam International Co Inc ....D 201 291-1200
Saddle Brook (G-9667)
Sk Custom Creations Inc ....E 973 754-9261
Totowa (G-10852)
Vira Insight LLC ....C 732 442-6756
Piscataway (G-8737)
Vitillo & Sons Inc ....F 732 886-1393
Lakewood (G-5177)

SHOWER STALLS: Metal

Interlink Products Intl Inc ....E 908 862-8090
Linden (G-5361)

SHREDDERS: Indl & Commercial

Autoshred LLC ....G 732 244-0950
Toms River (G-10745)

SHUTTERS, DOOR & WINDOW: Metal

Shutter DLight LLC ....G 908 956-4206
Plainfield (G-8778)

SIDING & STRUCTURAL MATERIALS: Wood

Dolan & Traynor Inc ....E 973 696-8700
Wayne (G-11495)
Ufp Berlin LLC ....C 856 767-0596
Berlin (G-431)

SIDING: Sheet Metal

Fairfield Metal Ltd Lblty Co ....F 973 276-8440
Fairfield (G-3200)

SIGN LETTERING & PAINTING SVCS

Kdf Reprographics Inc ....F 201 784-9991
South Hackensack (G-10167)
Lettering Plus Sign Company ....G 856 299-0404
Pedricktown (G-8350)

SIGN PAINTING & LETTERING SHOP

Ace Sign Company Inc ....G 732 826-3858
Perth Amboy (G-8509)
American Graphic Systems Inc ....G 201 796-0666
Fair Lawn (G-3084)
J Vitale Sign Co Inc ....G 732 388-8401
Rahway (G-9106)
Riedel Sign Company Inc ....G 201 641-9121
Little Ferry (G-5495)
Salmon Signs ....G 856 589-5600
Pitman (G-8748)

SIGNALING APPARATUS: Electric

Cooper Wheelock Inc ....B 732 222-6880
Long Branch (G-5595)
Work Zone Contractors LLC ....G 856 845-8201
Deptford (G-2068)

SIGNALS: Traffic Control, Electric

A C L Equipment Corp ....G 973 740-9800
Livingston (G-5501)
Intellgent Trffic Sup Pdts LLC ....G 908 791-1200
South Plainfield (G-10278)
J C Contracting Inc ....F 973 748-5600
Rahway (G-9105)
Jen Electric Inc ....F 973 467-4901
Springfield (G-10448)

SIGNALS: Transportation

General Dynamics Mission ....C 973 261-1409
Florham Park (G-3507)
Telegenix Inc ....F 609 265-3910
Rancocas (G-9167)

SIGNS & ADVERTISING SPECIALTIES

A C Display Studios Inc ....G 609 345-0814
Atlantic City (G-88)
A Sign Company ....G 609 298-3388
Trenton (G-10888)
A Sign of Excellence Inc ....G 732 264-0404
Hazlet (G-4253)
All Colors Screen Printing LLC ....G 732 777-6033
Highland Park (G-4286)
Alpha 1 Studio Inc ....G 609 859-2200
Southampton (G-10359)
Alu Inc ....E 201 935-2213
Moonachie (G-6453)
American Graphic Systems Inc ....G 201 796-0666
Fair Lawn (G-3084)
American Sign Instllations LLC ....G 856 506-0610
Millville (G-6232)
American Stencyl Inc ....G 201 251-6460
Mahwah (G-5714)
American Woodcarving LLC ....G 973 835-8510
Wayne (G-11469)
Arnold Furniture Mfrs Inc ....F 973 399-0505
Irvington (G-4558)
Astro Outdoor Advertising Inc ....F 856 881-4300
Glassboro (G-3807)
Atlas Flasher & Supply Co Inc ....E 856 423-3333
Mickleton (G-6086)
Aura Signs Inc ....G 866 963-7446
Hillsborough (G-4302)
B & A Grafx Inc ....F 646 302-8849
Harrison (G-4163)
B4inc Inc ....F 609 747-9600
Burlington (G-951)
Bamboo & Rattan Works Inc ....G 732 255-4239
Toms River (G-10746)

Banner Design Inc ....E 908 687-5335
Hillside (G-4379)
Bbk Technologies Inc ....G 908 231-0306
Raritan (G-9208)
Bergen Digital Graphics LLC ....G 201 825-0011
Upper Saddle River (G-11135)
Blanc Industries Inc ....E 973 537-0090
Dover (G-2075)
Blazing Visuals ....G 732 781-1401
Point Pleasant Boro (G-8838)
Brilliant Brdcstg Concept Inc ....F 732 287-9201
Rahway (G-9083)
Cad Signs Nyc Corp ....E 201 525-5415
Hackensack (G-3890)
Carpenter LLC ....F 609 689-3090
Trenton (G-10911)
Creoh Trading Corp ....F 718 821-0570
Lakewood (G-5074)
Custom Graphics of Vineland ....E 856 691-7858
Vineland (G-11209)
D & N Sporting Goods Inc ....F 856 778-0055
Mount Laurel (G-6751)
D3 Led LLC ....G 201 583-9486
North Bergen (G-7398)
Dale Behre ....G 908 850-4225
Hackettstown (G-4003)
Davis Sign Systems Inc ....G 973 394-9909
Boonton (G-549)
Daysol Inc ....D 908 272-5900
Kenilworth (G-4934)
Delaware Valley Sign Corp ....D 609 386-0100
Burlington (G-962)
Design Productions Inc ....G 201 447-5656
Waldwick (G-11300)
Designs By James ....G 856 692-1316
Vineland (G-11213)
Digital Arts Imaging LLC ....F 908 237-4646
Flemington (G-3437)
Dimensional Communications Inc ....D 201 767-1500
Mahwah (G-5730)
Dpj Inc ....F 732 499-8600
Rahway (G-9088)
Et Manufacturing & Sales Inc ....E 973 777-6662
Passaic (G-8064)
Exhibit Co Inc ....E 732 465-1070
Piscataway (G-8663)
Exhibit Network Inc ....F 732 751-9600
Oakhurst (G-7608)
F & A Signs Inc ....G 732 442-9399
Hopelawn (G-4525)
Fastsigns ....G 973 887-6700
East Hanover (G-2209)
Fedex Office & Print Svcs Inc ....E 856 427-0099
Cherry Hill (G-1361)
Fioplex ....G 856 689-7213
Swedesboro (G-10585)
Franbeth Inc ....G 856 488-1480
Pennsauken (G-8422)
Future Image Sign & Awning ....G 201 440-1400
Teterboro (G-10677)
Garden State Highway Pdts Inc ....E 856 692-7572
Millville (G-6250)
General Sign Co Inc ....G 856 753-3535
West Berlin (G-11598)
Genesis Marketing Group Inc ....G 201 836-1392
Teaneck (G-10632)
GF Supplies LLC ....G 336 539-1666
Elmwood Park (G-2827)
Glasscare Inc ....F 201 943-1122
Cliffside Park (G-1539)
Graphic Solutions & Signs LLC ....F 201 343-7446
Ridgefield Park (G-9308)
Heros Salute Awards Co ....G 973 696-5085
Wayne (G-11517)
Hiresprint LLC ....F 201 488-1626
Hackensack (G-3928)
Hub Sign Crane Corp ....G 732 252-9090
Manalapan (G-5813)
Identity Depot Inc ....G 973 584-9301
Ledgewood (G-5276)
Impact Displays Inc ....E 201 804-6262
Carlstadt (G-1167)
Impressions Signs and Prtg Inc ....G 973 653-3058
Garfield (G-3747)
Ionni Sign Inc ....G 973 625-3815
Rockaway (G-9468)
J & G Diversified ....G 732 543-2537
New Brunswick (G-6937)
J H M Communications Inc ....F 908 859-6668
Phillipsburg (G-8556)

J Vitale Sign Co Inc.....G..... 732 388-8401
Rahway *(G-9106)*
J&E Business Services LLC.....G..... 973 984-8444
Clifton *(G-1645)*
Jarco U S Casting Corp.....E..... 201 271-0003
Union City *(G-11115)*
Jaynes Signwork.....G..... 856 362-0503
Bridgeton *(G-761)*
JKA Specialties Mfr Inc.....F..... 609 859-2090
Southampton *(G-10366)*
Kna Graphics Inc.....G..... 908 272-4232
Kenilworth *(G-4953)*
L & F Graphics Ltd Lblty Co.....G..... 973 240-7033
Paterson *(G-8232)*
L&M Architectural Graphics Inc.....F..... 973 575-7665
Fairfield *(G-3254)*
Larue Manufacturing Corp.....G..... 908 534-2700
Whitehouse *(G-11916)*
M & W Franklin LLC.....G..... 609 927-0885
Egg Harbor Township *(G-2689)*
Madhouz LLC.....G..... 609 206-8009
Glassboro *(G-3814)*
Majestic Signs LLC.....G..... 201 837-8104
Teaneck *(G-10639)*
Manhattan Signs & Designs Ltd.....E..... 973 278-3603
Paterson *(G-8249)*
Mason Display Innovations Inc.....F..... 609 860-0675
Asbury *(G-67)*
Mc Does Inc.....G..... 856 985-8730
Marlton *(G-5941)*
McLain Studios Inc.....G..... 732 775-0271
Asbury Park *(G-80)*
Medlaurel Inc.....E..... 856 461-6600
Delanco *(G-2006)*
Mega Media Concepts Ltd Lblty.....G..... 973 919-5661
Sparta *(G-10397)*
Mej Signs Inc.....G..... 609 584-6881
Hamilton *(G-4114)*
Merchandising Display Corp.....G..... 973 299-8400
Boonton *(G-561)*
Metaline Products Company Inc.....E..... 732 721-1373
South Amboy *(G-10137)*
Michele Maddalena.....G..... 973 244-0033
Fairfield *(G-3270)*
Mr Quick Sign.....G..... 201 670-1690
Midland Park *(G-6181)*
MS Signs Inc.....G..... 973 569-1111
Saddle Brook *(G-9664)*
Nomadic North America LLC.....G..... 703 866-9200
Fairfield *(G-3282)*
North Star Signs Inc.....G..... 973 244-1144
Highland Lakes *(G-4285)*
Northwind Enterprises Inc.....E..... 732 274-2000
Dayton *(G-1982)*
NW Sign Industries Inc.....D..... 856 802-1677
Moorestown *(G-6548)*
Opdyke Awnings Inc.....F..... 732 449-5940
Wall Township *(G-11360)*
Outfront Media LLC.....D..... 973 575-6900
Fairfield *(G-3286)*
Ovadia Corporation.....E..... 973 256-9200
Little Falls *(G-5462)*
P & G Lighting & Sign Service.....G..... 908 925-3191
Linden *(G-5400)*
Packet Media LLC.....G..... 856 779-3800
Englishtown *(G-3007)*
Pat Bry Advertising Spc.....G..... 732 591-0999
Morganville *(G-6593)*
Permalith Plastics LLC.....D..... 215 925-5659
Pennsauken *(G-8468)*
Presentation Solutions Inc.....G..... 732 961-1960
Jackson *(G-4662)*
Princeton Packet Inc.....C..... 609 924-3244
Princeton *(G-9001)*
Printing & Signs Express Inc.....G..... 201 368-1255
Mahwah *(G-5763)*
Pro-Pack Corp.....G..... 908 725-5000
Branchburg *(G-672)*
Progress Displays Inc.....G..... 908 757-6650
Edison *(G-2592)*
Rand Diversified Companies LLC.....B..... 732 985-0800
Edison *(G-2594)*
Rich Designs.....G..... 908 369-5035
Hillsborough *(G-4352)*
Robden Enterprises Inc.....G..... 973 273-1200
Newark *(G-7251)*
Roxboro Holdings Inc.....D..... 732 919-3119
Wall Township *(G-11365)*
S S P Enterprises Inc.....G..... 732 602-7878
Iselin *(G-4625)*
Sabrimax Corp.....F..... 201 871-0808
Englewood *(G-2938)*
Salmon Signs.....G..... 856 589-5600
Pitman *(G-8748)*
Sign A Rama.....G..... 609 702-1444
Hainesport *(G-4077)*
Sign A Rama.....G..... 201 489-6969
Hackensack *(G-3974)*
Sign A Rama.....G..... 973 471-5558
Clifton *(G-1718)*
Sign Engineers Inc.....G..... 732 382-4224
Colonia *(G-1775)*
Sign Shoppe Inc.....G..... 856 384-2937
Woodbury *(G-12037)*
Sign Up Inc.....G..... 201 902-8640
Secaucus *(G-9814)*
Signarama.....G..... 609 465-9400
Cape May Court House *(G-1114)*
Signs & Custom Metal Inc.....F..... 201 200-0110
Jersey City *(G-4809)*
Signs of Security Inc.....E..... 973 340-8404
Garfield *(G-3768)*
Sjshore Marketing Ltd Lblty Co.....F..... 609 390-1400
Marmora *(G-5959)*
Smith Enterprises.....G..... 215 416-9881
Mount Laurel *(G-6807)*
Speedy Sign-A-Rama.....G..... 973 605-8313
Morristown *(G-6701)*
Spinningdesigns Inc.....F..... 732 775-7050
Farmingdale *(G-3392)*
Stephen Swinton Studio Inc.....G..... 908 537-9135
Washington *(G-11452)*
Suburban Sign Co Inc.....E..... 908 862-7222
Linden *(G-5433)*
T L C Specialties Inc.....F..... 732 244-4225
Toms River *(G-10798)*
Tally Display Corp.....G..... 973 777-7760
Fairfield *(G-3323)*
Tdk Associates Corp.....G..... 862 210-8085
Roseland *(G-9542)*
Tech-Pak Inc.....F..... 201 935-3800
Wood Ridge *(G-12007)*
Technical Nameplate Corp.....E..... 973 773-4256
Passaic *(G-8111)*
Testrite Instrument Co Inc.....C..... 201 543-0240
Hackensack *(G-3982)*
Tlg Signs Inc.....G..... 609 912-0500
Lawrenceville *(G-5244)*
Total Image and Sign.....G..... 201 941-2307
Ridgefield *(G-9291)*
Trademarksign.....F..... 848 223-4548
Jackson *(G-4667)*
Trans World Marketing Corp.....C..... 201 935-5565
East Rutherford *(G-2327)*
Trukmanns Inc.....E..... 973 538-7718
Cedar Knolls *(G-1314)*
US Propack Inc.....G..... 732 294-4500
Freehold *(G-3702)*
Vital Signs Medcl Legl Consltn.....F..... 908 537-7857
Asbury *(G-70)*
Vitillo & Sons Inc.....F..... 732 886-1393
Lakewood *(G-5177)*
Winemiller Press Inc.....G..... 732 223-0100
Manasquan *(G-5843)*
Yasheel Inc.....G..... 856 275-6812
Sewell *(G-9854)*

SIGNS & ADVERTISING SPECIALTIES: Artwork, Advertising

Adiant.....F..... 800 264-8303
Somerville *(G-10101)*
I Associates LLC.....G..... 215 262-7754
Pennsauken *(G-8434)*
Nickolaos Kappatos Entps Inc.....F..... 856 939-1099
Glendora *(G-3838)*
South Shore Sign Co Inc.....F..... 718 984-5624
Matawan *(G-5988)*

SIGNS & ADVERTISING SPECIALTIES: Displays, Paint Process

Kubik Maltbie Inc.....E..... 856 234-0052
Mount Laurel *(G-6774)*
Mechtronics Corporation.....E..... 845 231-1400
Franklin Lakes *(G-3628)*

SIGNS & ADVERTISING SPECIALTIES: Novelties

Aura Badge Co.....D..... 856 881-9026
Clayton *(G-1524)*
Touch of Class Promotions LLC.....G..... 267 994-0860
Voorhees *(G-11296)*
Two Jays Bingo Supply Inc.....F..... 609 267-4542
Hainesport *(G-4080)*

SIGNS & ADVERTISING SPECIALTIES: Signs

Adco Signs of NJ Inc.....E..... 908 965-2112
Elizabeth *(G-2707)*
Art Dmensions.....G..... 908 322-8488
Scotch Plains *(G-9730)*
Artsign Studio.....G..... 856 546-4889
Haddon Heights *(G-4043)*
Central Art & Enginering Inc.....G..... 609 758-5922
Cream Ridge *(G-1932)*
Cnr Products Co.....G..... 201 384-7003
Bergenfield *(G-374)*
Colorcraft Sign Co.....F..... 609 386-1115
Beverly *(G-449)*
Designer Sign Systems LLC.....F..... 212 939-5577
Carlstadt *(G-1151)*
East Trading West Inv LLC.....G..... 973 678-0800
Orange *(G-7753)*
Em Signs.....G..... 973 300-9703
Newton *(G-7341)*
Empro Products Co Inc.....G..... 973 302-4351
Belleville *(G-295)*
Essex Morris Sign Co.....G..... 973 386-1755
Whippany *(G-11890)*
G-Force River Signs LLC.....G..... 609 397-4467
Lambertville *(G-5189)*
Griffin Signs Inc.....E..... 856 786-8517
Cinnaminson *(G-1460)*
Infinite Sign Industries Inc.....E..... 973 649-9950
Kearny *(G-4869)*
Kar Industrial.....G..... 856 985-8730
Marlton *(G-5935)*
Lettering Plus Sign Company.....G..... 856 299-0404
Pedricktown *(G-8350)*
Lincoln Signs & Awnings Inc.....G..... 732 442-3151
Perth Amboy *(G-8525)*
M C Signs.....G..... 609 399-7446
Ocean City *(G-7691)*
New Dawn Inc.....G..... 732 774-1377
Neptune *(G-6892)*
Nickel Artistic Services LLC.....G..... 973 627-0390
Rockaway *(G-9479)*
Parrish Sign Co Inc.....G..... 856 696-4040
Vineland *(G-11250)*
Ricztone Inc.....G..... 609 695-6263
Trenton *(G-10987)*
Riedel Sign Company Inc.....G..... 201 641-9121
Little Ferry *(G-5495)*
Stone Graphics.....F..... 732 919-1111
Wall Township *(G-11371)*
Traffic Safety & Equipment Co.....F..... 201 327-6050
Mahwah *(G-5783)*

SIGNS & ADVERTSG SPECIALTIES: Displays/Cutouts Window/Lobby

Azar International Inc.....E..... 845 624-8808
Paramus *(G-7790)*
Brinker Industries.....E..... 973 678-1200
Dover *(G-2077)*
Brunswick Signs & Exhibit.....G..... 732 246-2500
North Brunswick *(G-7458)*
CDI Group Inc.....F..... 908 862-1493
Linden *(G-5330)*
Design Display Group Inc.....C..... 201 438-6000
Carlstadt *(G-1150)*
Dublin Management Assoc of NJ.....C..... 609 387-1600
Burlington *(G-964)*
Graphic Presentations Systems.....F..... 732 981-1120
Piscataway *(G-8670)*
Infinite Mfg Group Inc.....E..... 973 649-9950
Kearny *(G-4868)*
Insign Inc.....E..... 856 424-1161
West Deptford *(G-11705)*
J D Crew Inc.....G..... 856 665-3676
Pennsauken *(G-8443)*
Montana Electrical Decorating.....G..... 973 344-1815
Newark *(G-7204)*
Resources Inc In Display.....E..... 908 272-5900
Kenilworth *(G-4974)*

PRODUCT

Employee Codes: A=Over 500 employees, B=251-500
C=101-250, D=51-100, E=20-50, F=10-19, G=4-9
2019 Harris New jersey
Manufacturers Directory
935

Riccarr Displays Inc ....E 973 983-6701
  Rockaway *(G-9493)*

Sama Plastics Corp ....E 973 239-7200
  Cedar Grove *(G-1292)*

SIGNS, ELECTRICAL: Wholesalers

Kar Industrial ....G 856 985-8730
  Marlton *(G-5935)*

Tdk Associates Corp ....G 862 210-8085
  Roseland *(G-9542)*

SIGNS, EXC ELECTRIC, WHOLESALE

East Trading West Inv LLC ....G 973 678-0800
  Orange *(G-7753)*

GF Supplies LLC ....G 336 539-1666
  Elmwood Park *(G-2827)*

Kar Industrial ....G 856 985-8730
  Marlton *(G-5935)*

Rich Designs ....G 908 369-5035
  Hillsborough *(G-4352)*

Signs & Custom Metal Inc ....F 201 200-0110
  Jersey City *(G-4809)*

SIGNS: Electrical

A C L Equipment Corp ....G 973 740-9800
  Livingston *(G-5501)*

ABC Sign Systems Inc ....F 856 665-0950
  Pennsauken *(G-8381)*

Ace Sign Company Inc ....G 732 826-3858
  Perth Amboy *(G-8509)*

Aesys Inc ....G 201 871-3223
  Emerson *(G-2862)*

Bruce Kindberg ....G 973 664-0195
  Rockaway *(G-9447)*

Cad Signs LLC ....G 201 267-0457
  Hackensack *(G-3889)*

Craft Signs ....G 201 656-1991
  Jersey City *(G-4719)*

DCI Signs & Awnings Inc ....E 973 350-0400
  Newark *(G-7096)*

Ervin Advertising Co Inc ....G 732 363-7645
  Howell *(G-4539)*

F & S Awning and Blind Co Inc ....G 732 738-4110
  Edison *(G-2509)*

Four Way Enterprises Inc ....F 973 633-5757
  Wayne *(G-11505)*

Jencks Signs Corp ....G 908 542-1400
  Warren *(G-11419)*

Kdf Reprographics Inc ....F 201 784-9991
  South Hackensack *(G-10167)*

Mag Signs ....F 609 747-9600
  Burlington *(G-978)*

Mark-O-Lite Sign Co Inc ....F 732 462-8530
  Howell *(G-4546)*

Michael Anthony Sign Dsign Inc ....E 732 453-6120
  Piscataway *(G-8690)*

Nes Light Inc ....G 201 840-0400
  Ridgefield *(G-9279)*

NW Sign Industries Inc ....E 856 802-1677
  Moorestown *(G-6547)*

Sign On Inc ....G 201 384-7714
  Bloomingdale *(G-530)*

Sign Spec Inc ....D 856 663-2292
  Elmer *(G-2804)*

Signal Sign Company LLC ....F 973 535-9277
  Livingston *(G-5541)*

Signs of 2000 ....F 973 253-1333
  Clifton *(G-1719)*

Sweet Sign Systems Inc ....G 732 521-9300
  Jamesburg *(G-4677)*

Urban Sign & Crane Inc ....G 856 691-8388
  Vineland *(G-11273)*

US Sign and Lighting Svc LLC ....G 973 305-8900
  Wayne *(G-11561)*

Wurz Signsystems LLC ....G 856 461-4397
  Pennsauken *(G-8498)*

Yates Sign Co Inc ....E 732 578-1818
  Farmingdale *(G-3397)*

SIGNS: Neon

A B S Sign Company Inc ....G 609 522-6833
  Wildwood *(G-11941)*

Bergen Sign Company Inc ....E 973 742-7755
  Wayne *(G-11478)*

Manhattan Neon Sign Corp ....F 212 714-0430
  Hoboken *(G-4465)*

Spectrum Neon Sign Group LLC ....G 856 317-9223
  Pennsauken *(G-8488)*

Sun Neon Sign and Electric Co ....G 856 667-6977
  Cherry Hill *(G-1417)*

SILICA MINING

James D Morrissey Inc ....F 609 859-2860
  Vincentown *(G-11182)*

SILICON WAFERS: Chemically Doped

Ii-VI Incorporated ....F 973 227-1551
  Pine Brook *(G-8605)*

SILICONES

Engineered Silicone Pdts LLC ....G 973 300-5120
  Newton *(G-7342)*

Talent Investment LLC ....G 732 931-0088
  Hazlet *(G-4271)*

SILK SCREEN DESIGN SVCS

C Q Corporation ....F 201 935-8488
  East Rutherford *(G-2281)*

Clarici Graphics Inc ....E 609 587-7204
  Trenton *(G-10917)*

Cumberland Marble & Monument ......G 856 691-3334
  Vineland *(G-11207)*

D & N Sporting Goods Inc ....F 856 778-0055
  Mount Laurel *(G-6751)*

Flying Fish Studio ....G 609 884-2760
  West Cape May *(G-11683)*

Koehler Industries Inc ....G 732 364-2700
  Howell *(G-4544)*

Microcast Technologies Corp ....D 908 523-9503
  Linden *(G-5385)*

Monogram Center Inc ....E 732 442-1800
  Perth Amboy *(G-8528)*

University Fashions By Janet ....G 856 228-1615
  Williamstown *(G-11983)*

Wally Enterprises Inc ....F 732 329-2613
  Monmouth Junction *(G-6319)*

Z Line Beachwear ....G 732 793-1234
  Lavallette *(G-5213)*

Zaller Studios Inc ....G 973 743-5175
  Bloomfield *(G-523)*

SILVER ORES

Freeport-Mcmoran Inc ....G 908 558-4361
  Elizabeth *(G-2738)*

SILVERWARE & PLATED WARE

Kraftware Corporation ....E 732 345-7091
  Roselle *(G-9562)*

Medin Technologies Inc ....C 973 779-2400
  Totowa *(G-10836)*

SIMULATORS: Flight

Max Flight Corp ....E 732 281-2007
  Toms River *(G-10777)*

SINK TOPS, PLASTIC LAMINATED

Hawthorne Kitchens Inc ....F 973 427-9010
  Hawthorne *(G-4223)*

SIRENS: Vehicle, Marine, Indl & Warning

Octopus Yachts Ltd Lblty Co ....F 732 698-8550
  Belmar *(G-352)*

SKIN CARE PRDTS: Suntan Lotions & Oils

Aloe Science Inc ....E 908 231-8888
  Branchburg *(G-614)*

Amerchol Corporation ....C 732 248-6000
  Edison *(G-2452)*

Merck & Co Inc ....B 908 740-4000
  Kenilworth *(G-4957)*

Merck & Co Inc ....D 908 740-4000
  Rahway *(G-9117)*

SKYLIGHTS

Fiore Skylights Inc ....F 856 346-0118
  Somerdale *(G-9931)*

SLAB & TILE, ROOFING: Concrete

GAF Elk Materials Corporation ....C 973 628-4083
  Wayne *(G-11508)*

SLAB & TILE: Precast Concrete, Floor

Construction Specialties Inc ....E 908 236-0800
  Lebanon *(G-5257)*

SLAB, CROSSING: Concrete

Midstate Filigree Systems Inc ....D 609 448-8700
  Cranbury *(G-1864)*

SLAUGHTERING & MEAT PACKING

Beef International Inc ....D 856 663-6763
  Pennsauken *(G-8395)*

Burger Maker Inc ....E 201 939-4747
  Carlstadt *(G-1133)*

Ena Meat Packing Inc ....E 973 742-4790
  Paterson *(G-8184)*

SLIDES & EXHIBITS: Prepared

Palumbo Associates Inc ....F 908 534-2142
  Whitehouse Station *(G-11931)*

SLINGS: Lifting, Made From Purchased Wire

Brown and Perkins Inc ....F 609 655-1150
  Cranbury *(G-1816)*

Doran Sling and Assembly Corp ....G 908 355-1101
  Hillside *(G-4390)*

SLIP RINGS

Electro-Miniatures Corp ....D 201 460-0510
  Moonachie *(G-6464)*

SLIPPERS: House

S Goldberg & Co Inc ....C 201 342-1200
  Hackensack *(G-3969)*

SMOKE DETECTORS

Ea Pilot Supply ....G 201 934-8449
  Bradley Beach *(G-610)*

Heat-Timer Corporation ....E 973 575-4004
  Fairfield *(G-3224)*

SMOKERS' SPLYS, WHOLESALE

Nichem Co ....G 973 399-9810
  Newark *(G-7218)*

SNOW PLOWING SVCS

All Seasons Construction Inc ....G 908 852-0955
  Long Valley *(G-5607)*

Blades Landscaping Inc ....F 856 779-7665
  Mount Laurel *(G-6742)*

J Gennaro Trucking ....F 973 773-0805
  Garfield *(G-3749)*

US Outworkers LLC ....G 973 362-1458
  Sussex *(G-10569)*

SOAPS & DETERGENTS

Amerchol Corporation ....C 732 248-6000
  Edison *(G-2452)*

Americare Laboratories Ltd ....E 973 279-5100
  Paterson *(G-8138)*

Ardmore Inc ....G 973 481-2406
  Newark *(G-7051)*

Atlantic Associates Intl Inc ....F 856 662-1717
  Pennsauken *(G-8392)*

Aura Detergent LLC ....E 718 824-2162
  Newark *(G-7059)*

Cantol Inc ....E 609 846-7912
  Wildwood *(G-11942)*

Detergent 20 LLC ....F 732 545-0200
  New Brunswick *(G-6919)*

Ecolab Inc ....C 856 596-4845
  Moorestown *(G-6520)*

Fiabila USA Inc ....G 973 659-9510
  Mine Hill *(G-6272)*

Hy-Test Packaging Corp ....G 973 754-7000
  Paterson *(G-8211)*

Inopak Ltd ....F 973 962-1121
  Ringwood *(G-9347)*

Interntional Cnsld Chemex Corp ....E 732 828-7676
  New Brunswick *(G-6936)*

Inventek Colloidal Clrs LLC ....E 856 206-0058
  Mount Laurel *(G-6771)*

Kempak Industries ....F 908 687-4188
  Springfield *(G-10450)*

Kync Design LLC G 201 552-2067
Secaucus *(G-9787)*
Made Solutions LLC G 201 254-3693
Fair Lawn *(G-3110)*
Magnuson Products F 973 472-9292
Clifton *(G-1663)*
Si Packaging LLC F 973 869-9920
Rutherford *(G-9632)*
Technick Products Inc F 908 791-0400
South Plainfield *(G-10330)*

SOAPS & DETERGENTS: Dishwashing Compounds

Cavalier Chemical Co Inc E 908 558-0110
Short Hills *(G-9865)*

SOAPSTONE MINING

Mteixeira Soapstone VA LLC G 201 757-8608
Fort Lee *(G-3574)*

SOCIAL SVCS: Individual & Family

Life Skills Education Inc G 507 645-2994
Springfield *(G-10453)*

SOFT DRINKS WHOLESALERS

Canada Dry Bottling Co NY LP D 732 572-1660
South Plainfield *(G-10233)*
Continental Food & Bev Inc F 973 815-1600
Clifton *(G-1588)*
Increase Beverage Intl Inc F 609 303-3117
Pennsauken *(G-8435)*
Pepsi-Cola Metro Btlg Co Inc C 732 922-9000
Ocean *(G-7672)*

SOFTWARE PUBLISHERS: Application

51maps Inc G 800 927-5181
Wenonah *(G-11572)*
Able Group Technologies Inc G 732 591-9299
Morganville *(G-6579)*
Accely Inc F 609 598-1882
Avenel *(G-119)*
Airchartercom LLC E 212 999-4926
West New York *(G-11735)*
Almond Branch Inc E 973 728-3479
West Milford *(G-11724)*
Alt Shift Creative LLC G 609 619-0009
Flanders *(G-3399)*
Amerindia Technologies Inc E 609 664-2224
Cranbury *(G-1808)*
Appex Innovation Solutions LLC G 215 313-3332
Princeton *(G-8908)*
Aptimized LLC G 203 733-2868
Cedar Grove *(G-1267)*
Avyakta It Services LLC F 609 790-7517
East Windsor *(G-2345)*
Bavelle Tech Sltions Ltd Lblty F 973 992-8086
East Hanover *(G-2195)*
Beseech Ltd Liability Company G 908 461-7888
Belford *(G-281)*
Brittingham Sftwr Design Inc G 908 832-2691
Califon *(G-1031)*
Buzzboard Inc G 415 906-6934
Lyndhurst *(G-5643)*
Chisholm Technologies Inc G 732 859-5578
Shrewsbury *(G-9886)*
Co-Co Collaborative LLC G 917 685-5547
Short Hills *(G-9867)*
Coles and Blenman Network LLC G 973 432-7041
Bloomfield *(G-496)*
Computech Applications LLC G 201 261-5251
Oradell *(G-7742)*
Computer Sources G 201 791-9443
Elmwood Park *(G-2817)*
Continuity Logic LLC D 866 321-5079
Fairfield *(G-3174)*
Custom Business Software LLC G 732 534-9557
Freehold *(G-3660)*
Double Check G 973 984-2229
Morris Plains *(G-6603)*
Easy Analytic Software Inc G 856 931-5780
Bellmawr *(G-331)*
Enertia LLC G 856 330-4767
Pennsauken *(G-8418)*
Enforsys Inc E 973 515-8126
Millburn *(G-6197)*
Ezrirx LLC G 718 502-6610
Lakewood *(G-5096)*
Factonomy Inc F 201 848-7812
Wyckoff *(G-12111)*
Foursconsulting Ltd Lblty Co G 732 599-4324
South Plainfield *(G-10261)*
Frith Group G 732 281-8343
Brick *(G-718)*
Fusar Technologies Inc G 201 563-0189
Kearny *(G-4856)*
Healthper Inc G 888 257-1804
Princeton *(G-8958)*
Hue Box LLC G 908 904-9501
Bridgewater *(G-831)*
I-Exceed Tech Solutions Inc G 917 693-3207
Princeton *(G-8960)*
Innovi Mobile LLC F 646 588-0165
Millburn *(G-6200)*
Interactive Advisory Software E 770 951-2929
Egg Harbor Township *(G-2685)*
International Bus Mchs Corp E 201 307-5136
Park Ridge *(G-7853)*
Ipjukebox Ltd Liability Co G 201 286-4535
Newark *(G-7158)*
J-Tech Creations Inc G 201 944-2968
Fort Lee *(G-3565)*
Junganew LLC G 201 832-0892
Rutherford *(G-9625)*
Kingster LLC G 310 951-5127
Paramus *(G-7813)*
Lattice Incorporated F 856 910-1166
Pennsauken *(G-8450)*
Microsoft Corporation D 732 476-5600
Iselin *(G-4617)*
Modelware Inc F 732 264-3020
Holmdel *(G-4508)*
Mosaic Golf LLC G 201 906-6136
Hoboken *(G-4467)*
Mplayer Entertainment LLC G 302 229-3034
Cherry Hill *(G-1396)*
Munipol Systems F 856 985-2929
Marlton *(G-5942)*
Nb Ventures Inc C 732 382-6565
Clark *(G-1509)*
Netcom Systems Inc E 732 393-6100
Edison *(G-2572)*
Ngenious Solutions Inc G 732 873-3385
Piscataway *(G-8696)*
Noshpeak LLC F 978 631-7662
Bloomfield *(G-512)*
Novega Venture Partners Inc G 732 528-2600
Holmdel *(G-4511)*
OBagel Hoboken Ltd Lblty Co G 201 683-8599
Hoboken *(G-4470)*
Optherium Labs Ou G 516 253-1777
Holmdel *(G-4512)*
Our Team Fitness LLC G 848 208-5047
Oceanport *(G-7705)*
Oxford Biochronometrics LLC G 201 755-5932
Montclair *(G-6380)*
Pario Group LLC G 732 906-2302
Edison *(G-2586)*
Polysystems Inc G 312 332-5670
Cherry Hill *(G-1410)*
Qad Inc C 856 273-1717
Mount Laurel *(G-6797)*
Real Soft Inc A 609 409-3636
Monmouth Junction *(G-6308)*
Red Dash Media LLC G 732 579-2396
Piscataway *(G-8704)*
Regenus Ctr Core Therapies LLC G 862 295-1620
Florham Park *(G-3522)*
Relational Security Corp E 201 875-3456
Secaucus *(G-9803)*
Relatnship Capitl Partners Inc F 908 962-4881
Short Hills *(G-9876)*
Relpro Inc G 908 962-4881
Short Hills *(G-9877)*
Robokiller LLC E 723 838-1901
South Amboy *(G-10140)*
Rx Trade Zone Inc G 833 933-6600
Edison *(G-2601)*
Scalable Systems Inc E 732 993-4320
Piscataway *(G-8709)*
Simtronics Corporation F 732 747-0322
Little Silver *(G-5500)*
Sirma Group Inc B 646 357-3067
Jersey City *(G-4811)*
Ssam Sports Inc G 917 553-0596
Allendale *(G-15)*
Ssam Sports Inc G 917 553-0596
Allendale *(G-16)*
Storis Inc C 888 478-6747
Mount Arlington *(G-6719)*
Strivr Inc G 973 216-7379
Livingston *(G-5542)*
Sybase Inc D 973 537-5700
Parsippany *(G-8023)*
T N T Information Systems G 609 799-9488
Plainsboro *(G-8804)*
Tech Brains Solutions Inc E 732 952-0552
Somerset *(G-10083)*
Technovision Inc E 732 381-0200
Metuchen *(G-6077)*
Total Cover It LLC G 973 342-4623
South Orange *(G-10202)*
Transportation Tech Svcs Inc E 201 335-0238
Mahwah *(G-5784)*
Uniphy Health Holdings LLC E 844 586-4749
Newark *(G-7307)*
Universal Business Automation G 973 575-3568
Montville *(G-6448)*
US Software Group Inc E 732 361-4636
South Plainfield *(G-10337)*
Vst Consulting Inc D 732 404-0025
Iselin *(G-4635)*
Vyral Systems Inc G 201 321-2488
Hawthorne *(G-4251)*
Workwave LLC F 866 794-1658
Holmdel *(G-4516)*
X-Factor Cmmnctons Hldings Inc G 877 741-3727
Northvale *(G-7554)*
Xchange Software Inc G 732 444-4943
Iselin *(G-4636)*
Xchange Software Inc E 732 444-6666
Parlin *(G-7869)*
Zwivel LLC E 844 499-4835
Paramus *(G-7845)*

SOFTWARE PUBLISHERS: Business & Professional

3i Infotech Financial Software G 732 710-4444
Edison *(G-2442)*
3i Infotech Inc G 732 710-4444
Edison *(G-2443)*
Acclivity LLC E 973 586-2200
Rockaway *(G-9435)*
Acqueon Technologies Inc G 609 945-3139
Princeton *(G-8900)*
Acrelic Interactive LLC G 908 222-2900
Warren *(G-11396)*
Adherence Solutions LLC G 800 521-2269
Fairfield *(G-3135)*
Aim Computer Associates Inc G 201 489-3100
Bergenfield *(G-369)*
Aliron International Inc E 540 808-1615
South Plainfield *(G-10210)*
Alloy Software Inc F 973 661-9700
Bloomfield *(G-490)*
Amber Road Inc C 201 935-8588
East Rutherford *(G-2270)*
American Soft Solutions Corp G 732 272-0052
Morganville *(G-6582)*
Aplnow LLC G 732 223-5575
Manasquan *(G-5828)*
Ariba Inc E 908 333-3400
Bridgewater *(G-793)*
Artezio LLC G 609 786-2435
Princeton *(G-8912)*
Auraplayer USA Inc F 617 879-9013
West Orange *(G-11760)*
Avada Software LLC F 973 697-1043
Rockaway *(G-9445)*
Avaya Inc C 732 852-2030
Lincroft *(G-5310)*
Bluebird Auto Rentl Systems LP E 973 989-2423
Dover *(G-2076)*
C Systems LLC F 732 338-9347
Edison *(G-2472)*
Catalogic Software Inc C 201 249-8980
Woodcliff Lake *(G-12052)*
Clientsrver Tech Solutions LLC G 732 710-4495
Iselin *(G-4605)*
Cloudageit Ltd Liability Co G 888 205-4128
North Brunswick *(G-7463)*
Cognizant Tech Solutions Corp D 201 801-0233
Teaneck *(G-10625)*
Comprehensive Healthcare Systm D 732 362-2000
Edison *(G-2482)*
Computer Doc Associates Inc D 908 647-4445
Martinsville *(G-5962)*

Daddy Donkey Labs LLC .... G 646 461-4677
Fair Haven *(G-3079)*
Datamotion Inc .... E 973 455-1245
Florham Park *(G-3500)*
Docbox Solutions Ltd Lblty Co .... G 201 650-0970
Montclair *(G-6363)*
Dun & Bradstreet Inc .... E 973 921-5500
Short Hills *(G-9868)*
Educhat Inc .... G 201 871-8649
Englewood *(G-2900)*
Effexoft Inc .... G 732 221-3642
Somerset *(G-9984)*
Elevate Hr Inc .... F 973 917-3230
Parsippany *(G-7934)*
Eroomsystem Technologies Inc .... F 732 730-0116
Lakewood *(G-5093)*
Ezcom Software Inc .... E 201 731-1800
Englewood *(G-2904)*
Fis Avantgard LLC .... G 732 530-9303
Tinton Falls *(G-10717)*
Fis Financial Systems LLC .... D 856 784-7230
Voorhees *(G-11285)*
Foundation Software Inc .... G 908 359-0588
Belle Mead *(G-286)*
GL Consulting Inc .... E 201 938-0200
Jersey City *(G-4743)*
Gray Hair Software Inc .... E 866 507-9999
Mount Laurel *(G-6764)*
Greycell Labs Inc .... E 732 444-0123
Edison *(G-2523)*
Harms Software Inc .... D 973 402-9500
Parsippany *(G-7959)*
Hr Acuity LLC .... F 888 598-0161
Florham Park *(G-3511)*
I Physician Hub .... D 732 274-0155
Monmouth Junction *(G-6292)*
Immedis Inc .... F 212 239-2625
Iselin *(G-4611)*
Intangible Labs Inc .... F 917 375-1301
Hoboken *(G-4457)*
Interntnal Digital Systems Inc .... F 201 983-7700
Fort Lee *(G-3564)*
Intrinsiq Spclty Solutions Inc .... E 973 251-2039
Livingston *(G-5516)*
Invessence Inc .... G 201 977-1955
Chatham *(G-1322)*
Limosys LLC .... E 212 222-4433
Englewood Cliffs *(G-2983)*
Liquid Holdings Group Inc .... D 212 293-1836
Hoboken *(G-4464)*
Lumeta Corporation .... E 732 357-3500
Somerset *(G-10019)*
Machine Atomated Ctrl Tech LLC .... G 732 921-8935
Piscataway *(G-8685)*
Markov Processes International .... E 908 608-1558
Summit *(G-10539)*
Megaplex Software Inc .... G 908 647-3273
Warren *(G-11421)*
Mentor Graphics Corporation .... C 908 604-0800
Bedminster *(G-274)*
Moblty Inc .... E 973 535-3600
Livingston *(G-5527)*
Montgomery Investment Tech .... G 610 688-8111
Cinnaminson *(G-1475)*
Ms Health Software Corp .... G 908 850-5564
Hackettstown *(G-4028)*
MSI Technologies LLC .... F 973 263-0080
Parsippany *(G-7979)*
New Venture Partners LLC .... A 908 464-8131
New Providence *(G-7013)*
Nicomac Systems Inc .... G 201 871-0916
Norwood *(G-7570)*
Nogpo Inc .... F 908 642-3545
Basking Ridge *(G-193)*
Objecutive Inc .... F 201 242-1522
Fort Lee *(G-3579)*
Oli Systems Inc .... E 973 539-4996
Cedar Knolls *(G-1313)*
Onco Inc .... F 732 292-7460
Wall Township *(G-11359)*
One Source Solutions LLC .... F 732 536-0578
Freehold *(G-3685)*
Ontimeworks LLC .... F 800 689-3568
New Providence *(G-7015)*
Open Solutions Inc .... E 856 424-0150
Cherry Hill *(G-1403)*
Oracle Corporation .... C 908 547-6200
Bridgewater *(G-860)*
Oracle Corporation .... B 201 842-7000
East Rutherford *(G-2308)*
Output Services Group Inc .... E 201 871-1100
Ridgefield Park *(G-9314)*
Pai Services LLC .... C 856 231-4667
Mount Laurel *(G-6787)*
Parabole LLC .... G 609 917-8479
Monmouth Junction *(G-6299)*
Patientstar LLC .... F 856 722-0808
Mount Laurel *(G-6788)*
Pds Prclnical Data Systems Inc .... F 973 398-2800
Mount Arlington *(G-6717)*
Pinsonault Associates LLC .... E 800 372-9009
Parsippany *(G-7994)*
Priority-Software US LLC .... G 973 586-2200
Rockaway *(G-9490)*
Proscape Technologies Inc .... E 215 441-0300
Hillsborough *(G-4347)*
Qcom Inc .... E 732 772-0990
Freehold *(G-3695)*
Qellus LLC .... G 856 761-6575
Mount Laurel *(G-6798)*
Quadramed Corporation .... E 732 751-0400
Eatontown *(G-2418)*
Relayware Inc .... F 201 433-3331
Jersey City *(G-4799)*
Remote Landlord Systems LLC .... G 732 534-4445
Lakewood *(G-5154)*
Scivantage Inc .... D 646 452-0001
Jersey City *(G-4806)*
Scottline LLC .... E 732 534-3123
Piscataway *(G-8710)*
Sensiple Inc .... F 732 283-0499
Iselin *(G-4626)*
Simon & Schuster Inc .... E 973 656-6000
Parsippany *(G-8016)*
Smartlinx Solutions LLC .... D 732 385-5507
Iselin *(G-4629)*
Sunbird Software Inc .... D 732 993-4476
Somerset *(G-10077)*
Supply Chain Technologies LLC .... G 856 206-9849
Shrewsbury *(G-9903)*
Swapshub Company Inc .... G 732 529-4813
Piscataway *(G-8721)*
Taptask LLC .... G 201 294-2371
Clifton *(G-1730)*
Think Big Solutions Inc .... G 732 968-0211
Princeton Junction *(G-9068)*
Think Big Solutions Inc .... G 609 716-7343
Princeton *(G-9033)*
Trendmark LLC .... G 551 226-7973
Princeton *(G-9035)*
True Influence LLC .... F 888 223-1586
Princeton *(G-9036)*
Tunnel Networks Inc .... G 609 414-9799
East Windsor *(G-2363)*
Twinpod Inc .... G 908 758-5858
Princeton *(G-9037)*
Ubertesters Inc .... F 201 203-7903
Ridgewood *(G-9333)*
Unicorn Group Inc .... D 973 360-5904
Fairfield *(G-3334)*
Unicorn Group Inc .... C 973 360-0688
Florham Park *(G-3525)*
Uniken Inc .... G 917 324-0399
Chatham *(G-1331)*
Utah Intermediate Holding Corp .... C 856 787-2700
Mount Laurel *(G-6810)*
Valuemomentum Inc .... D 908 755-0025
Piscataway *(G-8734)*
Wizcom Corporation .... E 609 750-0601
Princeton Junction *(G-9070)*
Zoluu LLC .... G 862 686-1774
Fair Lawn *(G-3131)*

SOFTWARE PUBLISHERS: Computer Utilities

Espertech Inc .... F 973 577-6406
Wayne *(G-11498)*
Genomesafe LLC .... G 203 676-3752
West Orange *(G-11768)*

SOFTWARE PUBLISHERS: Education

Bandemar Networks LLC .... G 732 991-5112
East Brunswick *(G-2128)*
Educloud Inc .... E 201 944-0445
Cliffside Park *(G-1538)*
Gwf Associates LLC .... E 732 933-8780
Eatontown *(G-2395)*
Integrate Tech Inc .... G 201 693-5625
Upper Saddle River *(G-11141)*
Kittyhawk Digital LLC .... G 269 767-8399
Emerson *(G-2866)*
Mvn Usa Inc .... G 732 817-1400
Holmdel *(G-4510)*
Netx Information Systems Inc .... F 609 298-9118
Long Beach Township *(G-5592)*
Nxlevel Inc .... E 609 483-6900
Lambertville *(G-5195)*
Sunrise Intl Educatn Inc .... D 917 525-0272
North Brunswick *(G-7489)*

SOFTWARE PUBLISHERS: Home Entertainment

Storm City Entertainment Inc .... F 856 885-6902
Sicklerville *(G-9916)*
Vu Sound Incorporated .... F 215 990-2864
Lumberton *(G-5638)*

SOFTWARE PUBLISHERS: NEC

Accelerated Technologies Inc .... G 609 632-0350
Princeton *(G-8899)*
Accession Data Systems .... G 973 992-7392
Livingston *(G-5502)*
Ackk Studios LLC .... G 973 876-1327
Bloomfield *(G-489)*
Alaquest International Inc .... F 908 713-9399
Lebanon *(G-5250)*
Alcatel-Lucent USA Inc .... D 908 582-3275
New Providence *(G-6993)*
Alk Technologies Inc .... C 609 683-0220
Princeton *(G-8906)*
All Solutions Inc .... E 973 535-9100
Livingston *(G-5503)*
Altibase Incorporated .... G 888 837-7333
Mahwah *(G-5713)*
Anju Clinplus LLC .... F 732 764-6969
Bound Brook *(G-600)*
Antenna Software Inc .... E 201 217-3824
Jersey City *(G-4694)*
Aone Touch Inc .... G 732 261-6841
Bordentown *(G-575)*
Apprentice Fs Inc .... E 973 960-0875
Jersey City *(G-4695)*
Astrix Software Technology .... F 732 661-0400
Red Bank *(G-9221)*
Athletic Organizational Aids .... E 201 652-1485
Midland Park *(G-6170)*
Aurora Information Systems .... G 856 596-4180
Cherry Hill *(G-1340)*
Automated Office Inc .... G 888 362-7638
Cherry Hill *(G-1341)*
Avaya World Services Inc .... E 908 953-6000
Morristown *(G-6644)*
Aztec Software Associates Inc .... E 973 258-0011
Springfield *(G-10429)*
Basic Commerce & Industries .... E 609 482-3740
Hammonton *(G-4130)*
Basys Inc .... G 732 616-5276
Mount Laurel *(G-6740)*
Bdiplus Inc .... G 347 597-2539
Basking Ridge *(G-176)*
Bio-Key International Inc .... E 732 359-1100
Wall Township *(G-11322)*
Biostat Inc .... G 201 541-5688
Englewood *(G-2883)*
Blue Line Planning Inc .... G 609 577-0100
Crosswicks *(G-1949)*
Blue Marlin Systems Inc .... D 973 722-0816
Long Valley *(G-5608)*
BMC Software Inc .... G 703 761-0400
Woodcliff Lake *(G-12048)*
Brainstorm Software Corp .... G 856 234-4945
Moorestown *(G-6510)*
Burgiss Group LLC .... D 201 427-9600
Hoboken *(G-4444)*
Business Dev Solutions Inc .... G 856 433-8005
Cherry Hill *(G-1350)*
Business Software Applications .... G 908 500-9980
Somerset *(G-9964)*
Cape Atlantic Software LLC .... G 609 442-1331
Egg Harbor Township *(G-2682)*
Cardinal Health Systems Inc .... B 732 537-6544
Somerset *(G-9966)*
Ce Tech LLC .... G 908 229-3803
Whitehouse Station *(G-11919)*
Channel Logistics LLC .... F 856 614-5441
Camden *(G-1052)*
Circleblack Inc .... F 800 315-1241
Kingston *(G-5007)*

Com Tek Wrkplace Solutions LLC F 973 927-6814
Lyndhurst *(G-5649)*
Commvault Americas Inc G 888 746-3849
Tinton Falls *(G-10708)*
Commvault Systems Inc C 732 870-4000
Tinton Falls *(G-10709)*
Compco Analytical Inc G 201 641-3936
Little Ferry *(G-5480)*
Corner Stone Software Inc G 732 938-5229
Howell *(G-4534)*
Criterion Software LLC F 908 754-1166
Freehold *(G-3659)*
Custom Workflow Solutions LLC F 917 647-9222
Florham Park *(G-3499)*
Cybage Software Inc G 848 219-1221
Princeton *(G-8926)*
Cyberextrudercom Inc G 973 623-7900
Wayne *(G-11491)*
Cygate Sftwr & Consulting LLC G 732 452-1881
Edison *(G-2490)*
Cypher Insurance Software G 856 216-0575
Stratford *(G-10505)*
Datayog Inc F 714 253-6558
Jersey City *(G-4721)*
Dcm Group Inc G 732 516-1173
Newark *(G-7097)*
Dell Software Inc E 201 556-4600
Rochelle Park *(G-9422)*
Determine Inc E 800 608-0809
Cherry Hill *(G-1356)*
Diacritech LLC A 732 238-1157
Jersey City *(G-4727)*
Direct Computer Resources Inc E 201 848-0018
Franklin Lakes *(G-3620)*
Dma Data Industries Inc G 201 444-5733
Wyckoff *(G-12110)*
Dymax Systems Inc F 732 918-2424
Neptune *(G-6874)*
Easy Soft Inc F 732 398-1001
North Brunswick *(G-7467)*
Ebaotech Inc USA G 917 977-1145
Jersey City *(G-4730)*
Ebic Prparedness Solutions LLC G 719 244-6209
Leonia *(G-5288)*
Eclearview Technologies Inc G 732 695-6999
Ocean *(G-7662)*
Edison Design Group Inc G 732 993-3341
Monroe *(G-6321)*
Enterprise Services LLC D 609 259-9400
Princeton *(G-8941)*
Fieldview Cfd Inc G 425 460-8284
Rutherford *(G-9620)*
First Internet Systems F 201 991-1889
North Arlington *(G-7372)*
First Mountain Consulting G 973 325-8480
West Orange *(G-11767)*
Fis Data Systems Inc E 201 945-1774
Ridgefield *(G-9261)*
Flexicious LLC G 646 340-5066
Jersey City *(G-4735)*
Forge Ahead LLC G 908 346-4794
Skillman *(G-9920)*
Four Bros Ventures Inc G 732 890-9469
East Brunswick *(G-2146)*
Freyr Inc C 908 483-7958
Princeton *(G-8952)*
Genexosome Technologies Inc F 646 762-4517
Freehold *(G-3667)*
Gerbino Computer Systems Inc G 201 342-8240
Hackensack *(G-3922)*
Global IDS Inc D 609 683-1066
Princeton *(G-8955)*
Healthstar Communications Inc E 201 560-5370
Mahwah *(G-5746)*
Hozric LLC G 908 420-8821
Green Brook *(G-3861)*
HP Enterprise F 908 898-4728
Berkeley Heights *(G-400)*
Image Access Corp E 201 342-7878
Rockleigh *(G-9519)*
Incentx LLC G 302 202-2894
Lakewood *(G-5112)*
Indotronix International Corp G 609 750-0700
Plainsboro *(G-8790)*
Inspire Works Inc F 908 730-7447
Florham Park *(G-3513)*
Integration International Inc E 973 796-2300
Parsippany *(G-7962)*
Integration Partners-Ny Corp B 973 871-2100
Parsippany *(G-7963)*
Intellect Design Arena Inc F 732 769-1037
Piscataway *(G-8680)*
It Worqs LLC E 732 494-0009
Metuchen *(G-6063)*
Juniper Networks Inc D 908 947-4436
Bridgewater *(G-839)*
Justice Laboratory Software G 973 586-8551
Denville *(G-2042)*
Kaizen Technologies Inc E 732 452-9555
Edison *(G-2545)*
Kronos Saashr Inc E 978 250-9800
Branchburg *(G-653)*
Labvantage Solutions Inc E 908 707-4100
Somerset *(G-10013)*
Link2consult Inc F 888 522-0902
Fort Lee *(G-3568)*
Local Wisdom Inc E 609 269-2320
Lambertville *(G-5194)*
M + P International Inc E 973 239-3005
Verona *(G-11170)*
Majesco G 973 461-5200
Morristown *(G-6684)*
Marlabs Incorporated D 732 694-1000
Piscataway *(G-8687)*
Maxisit Inc C 732 494-2005
Metuchen *(G-6065)*
Medical Transcription Billing F 732 873-5133
Somerset *(G-10027)*
Melillo Consulting Inc E 732 563-8400
Somerset *(G-10028)*
Microsoft Corporation E 908 809-7320
Bridgewater *(G-852)*
Microtelecom Ltd Liability Co G 866 676-5679
Fort Lee *(G-3573)*
Microwize Technology Inc F 800 955-0321
Paramus *(G-7820)*
Millennium Info Tech Inc D 609 750-7120
Princeton *(G-8979)*
Mind-Alliance Systems LLC G 212 920-1911
Livingston *(G-5526)*
Mistras Group Inc C 609 716-4000
Princeton Junction *(G-9062)*
Mtbc Acquisition Corp G 732 873-5133
Somerset *(G-10033)*
Mtbc Health Inc G 732 873-5133
Somerset *(G-10034)*
Mtbc Practice Management Corp C 732 873-5133
Somerset *(G-10035)*
Nconnex Inc G 413 658-5582
New Brunswick *(G-6950)*
Nlyte Software Americas Ltd C 650 561-8200
Edison *(G-2576)*
Nlyte Software Inc E 732 395-6920
Edison *(G-2577)*
Nokia of America Corporation A 908 582-3275
New Providence *(G-7014)*
Northwind Ventures Inc G 917 509-1964
Vernon *(G-11162)*
Objectif Lune LLC F 973 780-0100
Bloomfield *(G-514)*
Objectif Lune LLC G 203 878-7206
Bloomfield *(G-515)*
Oracle America Inc D 732 623-4821
Edison *(G-2584)*
Oracle America Inc D 609 750-0640
East Rutherford *(G-2307)*
Orangehrm Inc E 914 458-4254
Secaucus *(G-9795)*
Os33 Services Corp G 866 796-0310
Iselin *(G-4620)*
Pace Business Solutions Inc E 908 451-0355
Manahawkin *(G-5795)*
Paylocity Holding Corporation B 908 917-3027
Springfield *(G-10458)*
Picture Window Software LLC G 908 362-4000
Blairstown *(G-487)*
Pjm Software Inc G 973 330-0405
Clifton *(G-1693)*
Planet Associates Inc E 201 693-8700
Park Ridge *(G-7858)*
Plescia & Company Inc F 856 793-0137
Marlton *(G-5947)*
Polaris Consulting & Svcs Ltd F 732 590-8151
Jersey City *(G-4785)*
Predictive Analytcs Dcision G 973 541-7020
Parsippany *(G-8000)*
Primepoint LLC E 609 298-7373
Westampton *(G-11789)*
Princeton Blue Inc E 908 369-0961
Princeton *(G-8998)*
Promia Incorporated G 609 252-1850
Princeton *(G-9009)*
Ptc Inc F 973 631-6195
Morristown *(G-6696)*
Quarterspot Inc F 917 647-9170
Wayne *(G-11545)*
Radix M I S G 973 707-2121
Bloomfield *(G-516)*
Ramco Systems Corporation E 609 620-4800
Princeton *(G-9012)*
Rbs Intrntonal Direct Mktg LLC G 856 663-2500
Cherry Hill *(G-1413)*
Re Systems Group Inc G 201 883-1572
Westwood *(G-11842)*
Red Oak Software Inc F 973 316-6064
Mountain Lakes *(G-6826)*
Redi-Data Inc F 973 227-4380
Fairfield *(G-3299)*
Redi-Direct Marketing Inc B 973 808-4500
Fairfield *(G-3300)*
Relational Architects Inc E 201 420-0400
Hoboken *(G-4478)*
Rey Consulting Inc F 201 337-0051
Oakland *(G-7643)*
Rhodium Software Inc G 848 248-2906
Dayton *(G-1986)*
RSD America Inc F 201 996-1000
Teaneck *(G-10649)*
Sage Software Inc D 856 231-4667
Mount Laurel *(G-6802)*
Saksoft Inc C 201 451-4609
Jersey City *(G-4803)*
Samsung SDS Globl Scl Amer Inc E 201 229-4456
Ridgefield Park *(G-9315)*
Scimar Technologies LLC G 609 208-1796
Allentown *(G-31)*
Sfp Software Inc G 856 235-7778
Mount Laurel *(G-6805)*
Shiva Software Group Inc E 973 691-5475
Flanders *(G-3418)*
Sierra Communication Intl LLC G 866 462-8292
Morristown *(G-6700)*
Sitetracker Inc F 551 486-2087
Montclair *(G-6389)*
Software Developers LLC E 888 315-6652
Lakewood *(G-5165)*
Software Practices and Tech G 908 464-2923
Summit *(G-10548)*
Software Services & Solutions F 203 630-2000
Lawrence Township *(G-5220)*
Specialty Systems Inc E 732 341-1011
Toms River *(G-10794)*
Sphinx Software Inc G 609 275-5085
Plainsboro *(G-8803)*
SRS Software LLC E 201 802-1300
Montvale *(G-6435)*
Stealthbits Technologies Inc D 201 301-9328
Hawthorne *(G-4245)*
Stellar Data Recovery G 877 778-6087
Metuchen *(G-6074)*
Streamserve Inc E 781 863-1510
Asbury Park *(G-82)*
Strikeforce Technologies Inc G 732 661-9641
Edison *(G-2621)*
Structured Healthcare MGT Inc E 201 569-3290
Englewood *(G-2945)*
Surround Technologies LLC G 973 743-1277
Bloomfield *(G-520)*
Swce Inc E 908 766-5695
Bernardsville *(G-444)*
Tab Networks G 201 746-0067
Woodcliff Lake *(G-12066)*
Taxstream LLC D 201 610-0390
Hoboken *(G-4484)*
Third Wave Bus Systems LLC E 201 703-2100
Wayne *(G-11557)*
Thomson Reuters Corporation F 973 662-3070
Nutley *(G-7595)*
Total Reliance LLC F 732 640-5079
Dayton *(G-1993)*
Tropaion Inc G 908 654-3870
Springfield *(G-10469)*
Truefort Inc E 201 766-2023
Weehawken *(G-11571)*
Turbot Hq Inc F 973 922-0297
Maplewood *(G-5887)*
U S Tech Solutions Inc D 201 524-9600
Jersey City *(G-4824)*
Vantage Business Systems Inc G 609 625-7020
Mays Landing *(G-6000)*

Varsity Software Inc ....G...... 609 309-9955
   Lawrenceville (G-5245)

Venture App LLC ....G...... 908 644-3985
   Summit (G-10553)

Vertican Technologies Inc ....G...... 800 435-7257
   Fairfield (G-3342)

Vibgyor Solutions Inc ....G...... 609 750-9158
   Princeton Junction (G-9069)

Visionware Systems Inc ....F...... 609 924-0800
   Skillman (G-9928)

Wizdata Systems Inc ....F...... 973 975-4113
   Parsippany (G-8041)

World Software Corporation ....E...... 201 444-3228
   Glen Rock (G-3836)

Xanthus Inc ....G...... 973 643-0920
   Newark (G-7317)

Yeghen Computer System ....F...... 732 996-5500
   Ocean (G-7687)

Zycus Inc ....E...... 609 799-5664
   Princeton (G-9046)

SOFTWARE PUBLISHERS: Operating Systems

Csf Corporation ....E...... 732 302-2222
   Somerset (G-9979)

Innovative Sftwr Solutions Inc ......D...... 856 910-9190
   Maple Shade (G-5864)

Lm Matrix Solutions LLC ....G...... 908 756-7952
   Bridgewater (G-846)

Zultner & Company ....F...... 609 452-0216
   Princeton (G-9045)

SOFTWARE PUBLISHERS: Publisher's

Advance Digital Inc ....C...... 201 459-2808
   Jersey City (G-4686)

Automated Resource Group Inc ....D...... 201 391-8357
   Montvale (G-6397)

Museami Inc ....F...... 609 917-3000
   North Brunswick (G-7478)

Signify Fincl Solutions LLC ....E...... 862 930-4682
   Parsippany (G-8015)

Trisys Inc ....G...... 973 360-2300
   Florham Park (G-3523)

SOFTWARE TRAINING, COMPUTER

Computer Doc Associates Inc ....D...... 908 647-4445
   Martinsville (G-5962)

Pds Prclnical Data Systems Inc ......F...... 973 398-2800
   Mount Arlington (G-6717)

Planet Associates Inc ....E...... 201 693-8700
   Park Ridge (G-7858)

Tropaion Inc ....G...... 908 654-3870
   Springfield (G-10469)

SOLAR CELLS

Ecs Energy Ltd ....G...... 201 341-5044
   Jackson (G-4655)

Holistic Solar Usa Inc ....G...... 732 757-5500
   Newark (G-7151)

Mc Renewable Energy LLC ....F...... 732 369-9933
   Manasquan (G-5833)

Nanopv Corporation ....F...... 609 851-3666
   Ewing (G-3047)

Reuge Management Group Inc ....G...... 888 306-3253
   Hoboken (G-4479)

Worldwide Solar Mfg LLC ....G...... 201 297-1177
   Closter (G-1765)

SOLAR HEATING EQPT

Holistic Solar Usa Inc ....G...... 732 757-5500
   Newark (G-7151)

Inenergy Inc ....E...... 609 466-2512
   Ringoes (G-9337)

Panatech Corporation ....G...... 732 331-5692
   Manalapan (G-5823)

Sun Pacific Power Corp ....F...... 888 845-0242
   Manalapan (G-5826)

Trinity Heating & Air Inc ....D...... 732 780-3779
   Wall Township (G-11376)

SOLDERING EQPT: Electrical, Exc Handheld

Hexacon Electric Company Inc ....E...... 908 245-6200
   Roselle Park (G-9586)

SOLDERING EQPT: Electrical, Handheld

Hexacon Electric Company Inc ....E...... 908 245-6200
   Roselle Park (G-9586)

SOLDERS

Alpha Assembly Solutions Inc ....E...... 908 561-5170
   South Plainfield (G-10214)

Alpha Assembly Solutions Inc ....E...... 908 791-3000
   Somerset (G-9948)

SOLVENTS

United Energy Corp ....G...... 732 994-5225
   Howell (G-4552)

SOLVENTS: Organic

G Holdings LLC ....F...... 973 628-3000
   Parsippany (G-7953)

G-I Holdings Inc ....G...... 973 628-3000
   Wayne (G-11507)

SONAR SYSTEMS & EQPT

Innerspace Technology Inc ....G...... 201 933-1600
   Carlstadt (G-1168)

SOUND REPRODUCING EQPT

Sdi Technologies Inc ....D...... 732 574-9000
   Rahway (G-9127)

SOUVENIR SHOPS

Flying Fish Studio ....G...... 609 884-2760
   West Cape May (G-11683)

SOUVENIRS, WHOLESALE

Italian Treasures ....G...... 856 770-9188
   Voorhees (G-11290)

SPACE VEHICLE EQPT

Aeropanel Corporation ....D...... 973 335-9636
   Boonton (G-537)

Breeze-Eastern LLC ....D...... 973 602-1001
   Whippany (G-11884)

Drytech Inc ....E...... 609 758-1794
   Cookstown (G-1803)

H & W Tool Co Inc ....F...... 973 366-0131
   Dover (G-2085)

McWilliams Forge Company ....D...... 973 627-0200
   Rockaway (G-9476)

Zenith Precision Inc ....F...... 201 933-8640
   East Rutherford (G-2331)

SPACE VEHICLES

Lockheed Martin Overseas LLC ....G...... 856 787-3105
   Moorestown (G-6541)

SPEAKER MONITORS

Rcf USA Inc ....G...... 732 902-6100
   Edison (G-2595)

SPEAKER SYSTEMS

Apogee Sound International LLC ....E...... 201 934-8500
   Ramsey (G-9138)

Gabriel Sound Ltd Liability Co ....G...... 973 831-7800
   Pompton Lakes (G-8851)

Sharkk LLC ....F...... 302 377-3974
   Livingston (G-5540)

Tech Giant LLC ....G...... 888 800-7745
   Eatontown (G-2425)

SPECIAL EVENTS DECORATION SVCS

De Zaio Productions Inc ....D...... 973 423-5000
   Fair Lawn (G-3095)

SPECIALTY FOOD STORES: Coffee

All Madina Inc ....F...... 973 226-7772
   West Caldwell (G-11639)

SPECIALTY FOOD STORES: Health & Dietetic Food

Sensbl Inc ....F...... 862 225-3803
   Ridgewood (G-9329)

Severino Pasta Mfg Co Inc ....E...... 856 854-3716
   Collingswood (G-1771)

SPECIALTY FOOD STORES: Juices, Fruit Or Vegetable

Halo Farm Inc ....G...... 609 695-3311
   Lawrenceville (G-5230)

SPECIALTY FOOD STORES: Tea

Adagio Teas Inc ....G...... 973 253-7400
   Elmwood Park (G-2807)

SPECIALTY FOOD STORES: Vitamin

39 Idea Factory Row LLC ....G...... 908 244-8631
   Flemington (G-3425)

Ivc Industries Inc ....B...... 732 308-3000
   Freehold (G-3671)

Vitamin Shoppe Industries Inc ....A...... 201 868-5959
   Secaucus (G-9826)

SPECIALTY OUTPATIENT CLINICS, NEC

Um Equity Corp ....G...... 856 354-2200
   Haddonfield (G-4065)

SPICE & HERB STORES

PDM Packaging Inc ....F...... 201 864-1115
   North Bergen (G-7428)

Weiling Yang ....G...... 201 440-5329
   Ridgefield Park (G-9319)

SPONGES: Bleached & Dyed

Fuji Electric Corp America ....D...... 732 560-9410
   Edison (G-2515)

SPOOLS: Fiber, Made From Purchased Materials

Union Container Corp ....E...... 973 242-3600
   Newark (G-7306)

SPORTING & ATHLETIC GOODS: Bowling Alleys & Access

Grill Creations ....G...... 908 264-8426
   Garwood (G-3784)

Holiday Bowl Inc ....E...... 201 337-6516
   Oakland (G-7631)

SPORTING & ATHLETIC GOODS: Cases, Gun & Rod

Belleplain Supply Co Inc ....G...... 609 861-2345
   Woodbine (G-12008)

SPORTING & ATHLETIC GOODS: Driving Ranges, Golf, Electronic

Tee-Rific Golf Center ....F...... 908 253-9300
   Branchburg (G-688)

Willowbrook Golf Center LLC ....F...... 973 256-6922
   Wayne (G-11565)

SPORTING & ATHLETIC GOODS: Fishing Eqpt

Anglers Select LLC ....G...... 973 396-2959
   Boonton (G-543)

Julian Bait Company Inc ....G...... 732 291-0050
   Atlantic Highlands (G-109)

Offshore Enterprises Inc ....G...... 609 345-9099
   Atlantic City (G-100)

SPORTING & ATHLETIC GOODS: Fishing Tackle, General

Captain John Inc ....F...... 609 494-2094
   Barnegat Light (G-164)

SPORTING & ATHLETIC GOODS: Guards, Football, Soccer, Etc

J & S Enterprises LLC ....F...... 973 696-9199
   Lincoln Park (G-5300)

South County Soccer League Inc ....G...... 908 310-9052
   Lambertville (G-5197)

SPORTING & ATHLETIC GOODS: Hockey Eqpt & Splys, NEC

Nafs Paints Inc ....G....... 973 927-0729
Flanders (G-3415)
Ss Equipment Holdings LLC.................E....... 732 627-0006
Bridgewater (G-894)

SPORTING & ATHLETIC GOODS: Hunting Eqpt

Big Daddys Sports Haven ....G....... 856 453-9009
Millville (G-6237)
International Tech Lasers.....................G....... 201 262-4580
Emerson (G-2864)

SPORTING & ATHLETIC GOODS: Pools, Swimming, Exc Plastic

Delair LLC ....D....... 856 663-2900
Pennsauken (G-8412)
Kayden Manufacturing Inc ....F....... 201 880-9898
Hackensack (G-3935)

SPORTING & ATHLETIC GOODS: Pools, Swimming, Plastic

Aquasports Pools LLC ....F....... 732 247-6298
New Brunswick (G-6912)

SPORTING & ATHLETIC GOODS: Rackets/Frames, Tennis, Etc

Prince Sports Inc ....D....... 609 291-5800
Bordentown (G-593)

SPORTING & ATHLETIC GOODS: Rods & Rod Parts, Fishing

Fred S Burroughs North Jersey ....D....... 908 850-8773
Hackettstown (G-4008)

SPORTING & ATHLETIC GOODS: Shafts, Golf Club

RCM Ltd Inc......................................G....... 201 337-3328
Oakland (G-7642)

SPORTING & ATHLETIC GOODS: Shooting Eqpt & Splys, General

Ultimate Trining Munitions Inc..............E....... 908 725-9000
Branchburg (G-692)

SPORTING & ATHLETIC GOODS: Skateboards

Elite Surf Snow Skateboard Sp ....G....... 856 427-7873
Cherry Hill (G-1359)

SPORTING & ATHLETIC GOODS: Target Shooting Eqpt

Newbold Inc......................................G....... 732 469-5654
Middlesex (G-6135)

SPORTING & ATHLETIC GOODS: Targets, Archery & Rifle Shooting

Reagent Chemical & RES Inc................E....... 908 284-2800
Ringoes (G-9341)

SPORTING & ATHLETIC GOODS: Team Sports Eqpt

Rags International Inc ....G....... 787 632-8447
Springfield (G-10462)

SPORTING & ATHLETIC GOODS: Tennis Eqpt & Splys

Lob-Ster Inc ....G....... 818 764-6000
Plainfield (G-8770)

SPORTING & ATHLETIC GOODS: Treadmills

Landice Incorporated ....E....... 973 927-9010
Randolph (G-9188)
Um Equity Corp..................................G....... 856 354-2200
Haddonfield (G-4065)

SPORTING & ATHLETIC GOODS: Water Sports Eqpt

Alden - Leeds Inc ....G....... 973 344-7986
Kearny (G-4841)
Jersey Cover Corp ....F....... 732 286-6300
Toms River (G-10771)
Seaville Motorsports...........................F....... 609 624-0040
Somers Point (G-9939)

SPORTING & ATHLETIC GOODS: Winter Sports

Stingray Sport Pdts Ltd Lblty ....G....... 201 300-6482
Fair Lawn (G-3123)

SPORTING & RECREATIONAL GOODS & SPLYS WHOLESALERS

Armin Kososki...................................G....... 908 689-0411
Washington (G-11439)
Refuel Inc...G....... 917 645-2974
South Hackensack (G-10183)
Sports Stop Inc ....F....... 856 881-2763
Glassboro (G-3819)

SPORTING & RECREATIONAL GOODS, WHOLESALE: Athletic Goods

Akadema Inc......................................E....... 973 304-1470
Bloomingdale (G-525)
Gamit Force Athc Ltd Lblty Co ....F....... 908 675-0733
Long Branch (G-5598)

SPORTING & RECREATIONAL GOODS, WHOLESALE: Boat Access & Part

Fisher Canvas Products Inc..................G....... 609 239-2733
Burlington (G-967)

SPORTING & RECREATIONAL GOODS, WHOLESALE: Fishing

Julian Bait Company Inc ....G....... 732 291-0050
Atlantic Highlands (G-109)

SPORTING & RECREATIONAL GOODS, WHOLESALE: Fishing Tackle

Blue Claw Mfg & Supply Company ....G....... 856 696-4366
Richland (G-9249)

SPORTING & RECREATIONAL GOODS, WHOLESALE: Golf

Crown Products Inc ....E....... 732 493-0022
Spring Lake (G-10421)

SPORTING & RECREATIONAL GOODS, WHOLESALE: Surfing

Primal Surf.......................................G....... 609 264-1999
Brigantine (G-912)

SPORTING GOODS

AB Coaster LLC ....F....... 908 879-2713
Chester (G-1429)
Beachcarts USA ....G....... 201 319-0091
Secaucus (G-9752)
Bergen Manufacturing & Supply ....E....... 201 854-3461
North Bergen (G-7389)
CDK Industries LLC ....G....... 856 488-5456
Cherry Hill (G-1352)
Cover Co Inc.....................................E....... 908 707-9797
Branchburg (G-632)
Cressi Sub USA.................................G....... 201 594-1450
Saddle Brook (G-9648)
Crown Products Inc ....E....... 732 493-0022
Spring Lake (G-10421)
Endurance Net Inc ....F........ 609 499-3450
Florence (G-3475)
G A D Inc..G....... 973 383-3499
Newton (G-7344)
Gamit Force Athc Ltd Lblty Co ....F....... 908 675-0733
Long Branch (G-5598)
Great Socks LLC ....E....... 856 964-9700
Pennsauken (G-8427)
Hayward Industrial Products ....C....... 908 351-5400
Elizabeth (G-2745)

Interntnal Globl Solutions Inc...............G....... 201 791-1500
Elmwood Park (G-2832)
J and S Sporting Apparel LLC ....G....... 732 787-5500
Keansburg (G-4838)
Lacrosse Republic ....G....... 856 853-8787
West Deptford (G-11709)
Mulbro Manufacturing & Svc Co ....G....... 732 805-0290
Middlesex (G-6132)
Nomad Lcrosse Distrs Ltd Lblty...........G....... 732 431-2255
Freehold (G-3683)
Pro Sports Inc ....E....... 732 294-5561
Marlboro (G-5910)
Pure Soccer Academy Ltd Lblty ....G....... 877 945-6423
Pine Brook (G-8614)
Rke Athletic Lettering ....G....... 732 280-1111
Belmar (G-353)
Sterling Net & Twine Co Inc ....F....... 973 783-9800
Montclair (G-6390)

SPORTING GOODS STORES, NEC

Armin Kososki...................................G....... 908 689-0411
Washington (G-11439)
Athletes Alley ....F....... 732 842-1127
Shrewsbury (G-9882)
Bauer Sport Shop ....G....... 201 384-6522
Dumont (G-2111)
D & N Sporting Goods Inc ....F....... 856 778-0055
Mount Laurel (G-6751)
Rockwood Corporation ....G....... 908 355-8600
Frenchtown (G-3717)
Sports Stop Inc ....F....... 856 881-2763
Glassboro (G-3819)

SPORTING GOODS STORES: Ammunition

Ultimate Trining Munitions Inc..............E....... 908 725-9000
Branchburg (G-692)

SPORTING GOODS STORES: Baseball Eqpt

Akadema Inc......................................E....... 973 304-1470
Bloomingdale (G-525)

SPORTING GOODS STORES: Camping Eqpt

Important Papers Inc ....G....... 856 751-4544
Cherry Hill (G-1376)

SPORTING GOODS STORES: Firearms

Henry RAC Holding Corp ....D....... 201 858-4400
Bayonne (G-222)
Way It Was Sporting Svc Inc.................G....... 856 231-0111
Moorestown (G-6576)

SPORTING GOODS STORES: Hockey Eqpt, Exc Skates

Ss Equipment Holdings LLC.................E....... 732 627-0006
Bridgewater (G-894)

SPORTING GOODS STORES: Pool & Billiard Tables

Pool Tables Plus Inc ....G....... 732 968-8228
Green Brook (G-3866)

SPORTING GOODS STORES: Specialty Sport Splys, NEC

Pro Sports Inc ....E....... 732 294-5561
Marlboro (G-5910)

SPORTING GOODS STORES: Surfing Eqpt & Splys

Ron Jon Surf Shop Fla Inc ....F....... 609 494-8844
Ship Bottom (G-9862)

SPORTING GOODS STORES: Team sports Eqpt

Bigflysports Inc.................................G....... 201 653-4414
Secaucus (G-9753)

SPORTING GOODS: Fishing Nets

Sterling Net & Twine Co Inc ....F....... 973 783-9800
Montclair (G-6390)

SPORTING GOODS: Surfboards

Primal Surf ....G 609 264-1999
Brigantine *(G-912)*
Ron Jon Surf Shop Fla Inc ....F 609 494-8844
Ship Bottom *(G-9862)*

SPORTING/ATHLETIC GOODS: Gloves, Boxing, Handball, Etc

Totowa Kickboxing Ltd Lblty Co ....F 973 507-9106
Totowa *(G-10855)*

SPORTS APPAREL STORES

Armin Kososki ....G 908 689-0411
Washington *(G-11439)*
Athletes Alley ....F 732 842-1127
Shrewsbury *(G-9882)*
Belleplain Supply Co Inc ....G 609 861-2345
Woodbine *(G-12008)*
CRA-Z Works Co Inc ....G 732 390-8238
Sayreville *(G-9707)*
Pioneer & Co Inc ....E 856 866-9191
Moorestown *(G-6557)*
Refuel Inc ....G 917 645-2974
South Hackensack *(G-10183)*

SPORTS CLUBS, MANAGERS & PROMOTERS

Totowa Kickboxing Ltd Lblty Co ....F 973 507-9106
Totowa *(G-10855)*

SPOUTING: Plastic & Fiberglass Reinforced

Seal-Spout Corp ....F 908 647-0648
Liberty Corner *(G-5296)*

SPOUTS: Sheet Metal

Seal-Spout Corp ....F 908 647-0648
Liberty Corner *(G-5296)*

SPRAYING & DUSTING EQPT

Falcon Safety Products Inc ....D 908 707-4900
Branchburg *(G-639)*
Jetstream of Houston LLP ....G 732 448-7830
New Brunswick *(G-6938)*

SPRAYING EQPT: Agricultural

AFA Polytek North America Inc ....F 862 260-9450
Cedar Knolls *(G-1297)*

SPRAYS: Artificial & Preserved

Fluid Coating Systems Inc ....G 973 767-1028
Garfield *(G-3742)*

SPRINGS: Coiled Flat

Spring Eureka Co Inc ....E 973 589-4960
Newark *(G-7283)*

SPRINGS: Steel

Matthew Warren Inc ....F 908 788-5800
Ringoes *(G-9339)*
Sealy Mattress Co N J Inc ....C 973 345-8800
Paterson *(G-8297)*

SPRINGS: Upholstery, Unassembled

Window 25 LLC ....G 973 817-9464
Newark *(G-7316)*

SPRINGS: Wire

Matthew Warren Inc ....F 908 788-5800
Ringoes *(G-9339)*
Spring Eureka Co Inc ....E 973 589-4960
Newark *(G-7283)*

SPRINKLING SYSTEMS: Fire Control

Absolute Protective Systems ....E 732 287-4500
Piscataway *(G-8624)*
Confires Fire Prtction Svc LLC ....F 908 822-2700
South Plainfield *(G-10241)*
Eagle Fire & Safety Corp ....G 732 982-7388
Wall Township *(G-11335)*
Teneyck Inc ....D 201 939-1100
Lyndhurst *(G-5681)*

SQUIBS: Electric

Mjg Technologies Incorporated ....G 856 228-6118
Blackwood *(G-475)*

STAFFING, EMPLOYMENT PLACEMENT

Corporate Computer Systems ....F 732 739-5600
Newark *(G-7088)*
Scottline LLC ....E 732 534-3123
Piscataway *(G-8710)*

STAGE LIGHTING SYSTEMS

This Is It Stageworks LLC ....E 201 653-2699
Jersey City *(G-4820)*

STAINLESS STEEL

Air Technology Inc ....G 973 334-4980
Boonton *(G-538)*
Alloy Stainless Products Co ....D 973 256-1616
Totowa *(G-10810)*
Dso Fluid Handling Co Inc ....E 732 225-9100
Edison *(G-2495)*
Easyflex East Inc ....E 201 853-9005
Little Ferry *(G-5484)*
Ford Fasteners Inc ....E 201 487-3151
Hackensack *(G-3916)*
Stainless Metal Source Intl ....G 973 977-2200
Clifton *(G-1724)*
Yarde Metals Inc ....E 973 463-1166
East Hanover *(G-2248)*

STAINLESS STEEL WARE

Dynamic Metals Inc ....E 908 769-0522
Piscataway *(G-8659)*

STAIRCASES & STAIRS, WOOD

Alvaro Stairs LLC ....G 201 864-6754
North Bergen *(G-7383)*
Greenbrook Stairs Inc ....G 908 221-9145
Bernardsville *(G-438)*
Iacovelli Stairs Incorporated ....F 609 693-3476
Forked River *(G-3540)*
Kaufman Stairs Inc ....E 908 862-3579
Rahway *(G-9111)*
Maranatha Ceramic Tile & Marbl ....E 609 758-1168
Wrightstown *(G-12099)*
Stairworks Inc ....G 908 276-2829
Cranford *(G-1927)*
Urban Millwork & Supply Corp ....G 973 278-7072
Paterson *(G-8321)*
Wood Products Inc ....G 609 859-0303
Southampton *(G-10374)*

STAMPINGS: Automotive

Robert Freeman ....G 973 751-0082
Belleville *(G-312)*
Taurus International Corp ....E 201 825-2420
Ramsey *(G-9156)*

STAMPINGS: Metal

A Plus Products Incorporated ....E 732 866-9111
Marlboro *(G-5892)*
Accurate Tool & Die Co Inc ....G 201 476-9348
Montvale *(G-6394)*
Aspe Inc ....E 973 808-1155
Fairfield *(G-3148)*
B E C Mfg Corp ....E 201 414-0000
Glen Rock *(G-3828)*
Be CU Manufacturing Co Inc ....E 908 233-3342
Scotch Plains *(G-9731)*
Bel-Tech Stamping Inc ....E 973 728-8229
West Milford *(G-11726)*
Bigelow Components Corp ....E 973 467-1200
Springfield *(G-10431)*
Bilt Rite Tool & Die Co Inc ....E 973 227-2882
Fairfield *(G-3158)*
Boyle Tool & Die Co Inc ....F 856 853-1819
West Deptford *(G-11694)*
Charles E Green & Son Inc ....E 973 485-3630
Newark *(G-7082)*
Coda Resources Ltd ....C 718 649-1666
Matawan *(G-5971)*
Frameware Inc ....F 800 582-5608
Fairfield *(G-3207)*
G Big Corp ....G 973 242-6521
Newark *(G-7129)*

General Wire & Stamping Co ....F 973 366-8080
Randolph *(G-9179)*
Golden Metal Products Corp ....E 973 399-1157
Hillside *(G-4394)*
Heyco Molded Products Inc ....F 732 286-4336
Toms River *(G-10765)*
Ht Stamping Co LLC ....G 973 227-4858
Fairfield *(G-3230)*
Luso Machine Nj LLC ....F 973 242-1717
Newark *(G-7188)*
Main Robert A & Sons Holdg Co ....E 201 447-3700
Wyckoff *(G-12116)*
Micro Stamping Corporation ....C 732 302-0800
Somerset *(G-10030)*
Minitec Corporation ....G 973 989-1426
Dover *(G-2097)*
Mjse LLC ....F 201 791-9888
Saddle Brook *(G-9663)*
Molnar Tools Inc ....F 908 580-0671
Warren *(G-11423)*
Monroe Tool & Die Inc ....G 856 629-5164
Williamstown *(G-11964)*
Pcr Technologies Inc ....G 973 882-0017
Pine Brook *(G-8613)*
Phillips Enterprises Inc ....G 732 493-3191
Ocean *(G-7674)*
R M F Associates Inc ....C 908 687-9355
Union *(G-11086)*
S & W Precision Tool Corp ....F 908 526-6097
Bridgewater *(G-878)*
Sofield Manufacturing Co Inc ....G 201 931-1530
Ridgefield Park *(G-9316)*
Stampex Corp ....F 973 839-4040
Haskell *(G-4202)*
Superior Stamping Products LLC ....E 201 945-5874
Ridgefield *(G-9290)*
Triform Products Inc ....E 973 278-2042
Pompton Plains *(G-8873)*
Tryco Tool & Mfg Co Inc ....E 973 674-6867
Orange *(G-7764)*
Turul Bookbindery Inc ....G 973 361-2810
Wharton *(G-11874)*
Umetal LLC ....G 862 257-3032
Paterson *(G-8319)*
Unilite Incorporated ....G 973 667-1674
Nutley *(G-7596)*
United Spport Sltons - Lmt Inc ....G 973 857-2298
Cedar Grove *(G-1295)*

STAPLES

Hugo Neu Recycling LLC ....E 914 530-2350
Kearny *(G-4866)*

STAPLES: Steel, Wire Or Cut

Arrow Fastener Co LLC ....B 201 843-6900
Saddle Brook *(G-9640)*

STATIONARY & OFFICE SPLYS, WHOL: Computer/Photocopying Splys

Central Technology Inc ....F 732 431-3339
Freehold *(G-3656)*
Waste Not Computers & Supplies ....G 201 384-4444
Dumont *(G-2118)*

STATIONARY & OFFICE SPLYS, WHOLESALE: Blank Books

Nobelus LLC ....G 800 895-2747
North Brunswick *(G-7480)*

STATIONARY & OFFICE SPLYS, WHOLESALE: Inked Ribbons

GSC Imaging LLC ....F 856 317-9301
Pennsauken *(G-8428)*

STATIONARY & OFFICE SPLYS, WHOLESALE: Marking Devices

Acedepotcom ....F 800 844-0962
Northvale *(G-7515)*

STATIONARY/OFFICE SPLYS, WHOL: Soc Stationery/Greeting Cards

Jersey Printing Associates Inc ....E 732 872-9654
Atlantic Highlands *(G-108)*

STATIONERY & OFFICE SPLYS WHOLESALERS

Adler International Ltd......................G....... 201 843-4525
Maywood (G-6001)
Arrow Paper Company Inc ....G 908 756-1111
Plainfield (G-8759)
Commander Imaging Products Inc ......E ... 973 742-9298
Paterson (G-8161)
Nu-Plan Business Systems Inc ....G... 732 231-6944
Clark (G-1510)
Officemate International Corp ....D.... 732 225-7422
Edison (G-2583)
Spiral Binding LLC.............................C.... 973 256-0666
Totowa (G-10853)
Supplies-Supplies Inc ....F 908 272-5100
Watchung (G-11460)

STATIONERY ARTICLES: Pottery

Larose Industries LLC ....D.... 973 543-2037
Randolph (G-9189)

STATIONERY PRDTS

Adler International Ltd.........................G....... 201 843-4525
Maywood (G-6001)
Bind-Rite Graphics Inc ....E 201 863-8100
Secaucus (G-9754)
Mega Brands America Inc ....B 973 535-1313
Wood Ridge (G-12004)
Yerg Inc ....G.... 973 759-4041
Lakehurst (G-5040)

STATIONERY: Made From Purchased Materials

Officemate International Corp ....D.... 732 225-7422
Edison (G-2583)

STATUES: Nonmetal

Art Plaque Creations Inc ....F 973 482-2536
Kearny (G-4845)
Barrett Bronze Inc.............................E....... 914 699-6060
Wyckoff (G-12103)

STEEL & ALLOYS: Tool & Die

Atco Products Inc ....E 973 379-3171
Springfield (G-10428)
Bilt Rite Tool & Die Co Inc ....G... 973 227-2882
Fairfield (G-3158)

STEEL FABRICATORS

Able Fab Co ....E 732 396-0600
Avenel (G-118)
Acrow Corporation of America ....E 973 244-0080
Parsippany (G-7871)
Air & Specialties Sheet Metal...........F 908 233-8306
Mountainside (G-6832)
Airmet Inc ....G.... 973 481-5550
Newark (G-7037)
Ajay Metal Fabricators Inc ....G.... 908 523-0557
Linden (G-5318)
All American Metal Fabricators ....G...... 201 567-2898
Tenafly (G-10658)
Alloy Welding Co ....F 908 218-1551
Branchburg (G-613)
American Mllwright Rigging LLC ....E 856 457-9574
Audubon (G-111)
American Strip Steel Inc......................F 800 526-1216
South Plainfield (G-10216)
American Strip Steel Inc......................G..... 856 461-8300
Delanco (G-2002)
Andrew B Duffy Inc ....F 856 845-4900
West Deptford (G-11691)
Anvil Iron Works Inc ....G....... 856 783-5959
Sicklerville (G-9907)
Arca Industrial Inc ....G.... 732 339-0450
East Windsor (G-2336)
Archer Day Inc ....E 732 396-0600
Avenel (G-120)
Architectural Metals Inc ....G.... 718 765-0722
Carteret (G-1247)
Atlantic Precision Tech LLC ....G.... 732 658-3060
North Brunswick (G-7455)
Atlas Enterprise ....F 908 561-1144
South Plainfield (G-10222)
B & B Iron Works ....E 862 238-7203
Clifton (G-1570)

B L White Welding & Steel Co ....G 973 684-4111
Paterson (G-8144)
Banker Steel Nj LLC..........................D.... 732 968-6061
South Plainfield (G-10223)
Bouras Industries Inc ....A 908 918-9400
Summit (G-10527)
Brayco Inc...F 609 758-5235
Creamridge (G-1940)
Brunnquell Iron Works Inc ....G....... 609 409-6101
Cranbury (G-1817)
Bushwick Metals LLC........................G.... 610 495-9100
Englewood (G-2888)
C M C Steel Fabricators Inc ....C 908 561-3484
South Plainfield (G-10232)
C W Grimmer & Sons Inc ....F 732 741-2189
Tinton Falls (G-10706)
Capital Steel Service LLC....................E 609 882-6983
Ewing (G-3017)
Cs Industrial Services LLC ....G.... 609 381-4380
Newfield (G-7320)
D S Jh LLC.......................................E 973 782-4086
Lincoln Park (G-5298)
De Jong Iron Works Inc ....G.... 973 684-1633
Paterson (G-8169)
DMJ Industrial Services LLC ....G.... 973 692-8406
Wayne (G-11494)
Eagle Steel & Iron LLC ....G.... 908 587-1025
Stewartsville (G-10483)
Equipment Distributing Corp ....G.... 201 641-8414
Ridgefield Park (G-9305)
Falstrom Company ....D.... 973 777-0013
Passaic (G-8066)
FMB Systems Inc ....D.... 973 485-5544
Harrison (G-4175)
Francis Metals Company Inc ....F 732 761-0500
Lakewood (G-5101)
Frazier Industrial Company..................C 908 876-3001
Long Valley (G-5610)
G J Oliver Inc ....D.... 908 454-9743
Phillipsburg (G-8552)
Gavan Graham Elec Pdts Corp ....E 908 729-9000
Union (G-11058)
Giant Stl Fabricators Erectors ....G.... 908 241-6766
Roselle (G-9559)
Glentech Inc ....F 908 685-2205
Somerville (G-10113)
Grimbilas Enterprises Corp ....E 973 686-5999
Wayne (G-11514)
Hackensack Steel Corp ....G.... 201 935-0090
Carlstadt (G-1163)
Harold R Henrich Inc ....D.... 732 370-4455
Lakewood (G-5107)
Harris Structural Steel Co Inc ....E 732 752-6070
South Plainfield (G-10272)
Harris Structural Steel Co Inc ....G.... 732 752-6070
South Plainfield (G-10273)
Helidex LLC ....E 201 636-2546
East Rutherford (G-2291)
Holler Metal Fabricators Inc................G.... 732 635-9050
Metuchen (G-6061)
I K Construction Inc ....E 908 925-5200
East Orange (G-2252)
Imperial Metal Products Inc ....G.... 908 647-8181
Bound Brook (G-602)
Industrial Metal Inc ....G.... 908 362-0084
Blairstown (G-486)
Infinite Mfg Group Inc ....E 973 649-9950
Kearny (G-4868)
Innovative Metal Solutions LLC...........G.... 609 784-8406
Mount Holly (G-6731)
Inox Steel Corp ....G.... 609 268-2334
Shamong (G-9858)
Integrity Ironworks Corp ....G.... 732 254-2200
Sayreville (G-9711)
Iron Asylum Incorporated ....F 856 352-4283
Sewell (G-9847)
J & M Cstm Shtmtl Ltd Lblty Co ....G.... 856 627-6252
Sicklerville (G-9911)
JC Macelroy Co Inc ....D.... 732 572-7100
Piscataway (G-8681)
Jersey Metal Works LLC ....G.... 732 565-1313
Somerset (G-10009)
John Cooper Company Inc ....F 201 487-4018
Hackensack (G-3934)
John F Pearce ....G.... 201 440-8765
Moonachie (G-6474)
Joseph Oat Holdings Inc ....D.... 856 541-2900
Camden (G-1072)
JP Technology Inc ....F 856 241-0111
Swedesboro (G-10591)

Leets Steel Inc..................................G.... 917 416-7977
Sayreville (G-9715)
Lehigh Utility Associates Inc ....F 908 561-5252
South Plainfield (G-10292)
Lesli Katchen Steel Cnstr Inc ....G.... 732 521-2600
Jamesburg (G-4673)
Liquid Metalworks Ltd Lblty Co............G.... 973 224-9710
Hackettstown (G-4017)
Lummus Technology Ventures LLC ......G.... 973 893-1515
Bloomfield (G-509)
M K Enterprises Inc ....G.... 201 891-4199
Wyckoff (G-12115)
Marino International Corp ....G.... 732 752-5100
South Plainfield (G-10299)
Max Gurtman & Sons Inc ....G.... 973 478-7000
Clifton (G-1666)
Metals Plus ....E 908 862-7677
Linden (G-5384)
Metals USA Plates & Shapes Inc ....E 973 242-1000
Newark (G-7201)
Metalwest LLC ....E 609 395-7007
Monroe Township (G-6335)
Metfab Steel Works LLC......................F 973 675-7676
Orange (G-7756)
Mk Metals Inc....................................G.... 856 245-7033
Glendora (G-3837)
Napco Separation Equipment Inc.........G.... 908 862-7677
Linden (G-5391)
Newark Ironworks Inc ....F 973 424-9790
Newark (G-7214)
Next Level Fabrication LLC ....E 609 703-0682
Egg Harbor Township (G-2691)
Oeg Building Materials Inc..................E 732 667-3636
Sayreville (G-9720)
Pabst Enterprises Equipment Co ....E 908 353-2880
Elizabeth (G-2766)
Park Steel & Iron Co ....F 732 775-7500
Neptune (G-6894)
Peter Garafano & Son Inc ....E 973 278-0350
Paterson (G-8282)
Polmar Iron Work Inc ....F 732 882-0900
Rahway (G-9121)
Precision Metalcrafters Inc ....E 856 629-1020
Williamstown (G-11972)
Prime Rebar LLC ....E 908 707-1234
Bridgewater (G-869)
R Way Tooling & Met Works LLC ....F 856 692-2218
Vineland (G-11255)
RS Phillips Steel LLC.........................E 973 827-6464
Sussex (G-10565)
Runding LLC ....G.... 973 277-8775
Oak Ridge (G-7606)
Samna Cnstrctn & Steel Fabrctn ....F 973 977-8400
Paterson (G-8292)
Senco Metals LLC ....G.... 973 342-1742
Passaic (G-8106)
Southern New Jersey Stl Co Inc ....E 856 696-1612
Vineland (G-11268)
Springfield Metal Pdts Co Inc ....F 973 379-4600
Springfield (G-10467)
Squillace Stl Fabricators LLC ....G.... 908 241-6424
Roselle Park (G-9591)
Stirrup Metal Products Corp ....F 973 824-7086
Newark (G-7287)
Studio Dellarte ....G.... 718 599-3715
Jersey City (G-4817)
Theodore E Mozer Inc.........................E 856 829-1432
Palmyra (G-7786)
Thomas Russo & Sons Inc ....G.... 201 332-4159
Jersey City (G-4821)
United Steel Products Co Inc...............G.... 609 518-9230
Lumberton (G-5637)
Victory Iron Works Inc ....G.... 201 485-7181
Wyckoff (G-12124)
Vision Railings Ltd Lblty Co ....F 908 310-8926
Glen Gardner (G-3824)
W W Manufacturing Co Inc ....G.... 856 451-5700
Bridgeton (G-777)
Weir Welding Company Inc ....E 201 939-2284
Carlstadt (G-1239)
Westfield Shtmtl Works Inc...................E 908 276-5500
Kenilworth (G-4989)

STEEL MILLS

Aibens Imort ....G.... 609 902-9953
Princeton Junction (G-9049)
Amrod Corp ....D.... 973 344-3806
Newark (G-7046)
Aperam Stnlss Svc & Solutns..............E 908 988-0625
New Providence (G-6994)

PRODUCT

STEEL MILLS (continued)

Camden Iron & Metal Inc ....F....... 856 365-7500
Camden (G-1043)
Camden Iron & Metal LLC ....D....... 856 969-7065
Camden (G-1044)
CB&i LLC ....C....... 856 482-3000
Trenton (G-10913)
DAngelo Metal Products Inc ....F....... 908 862-8220
Linden (G-5341)
E C Electroplating Inc ....E....... 973 340-0227
Garfield (G-3740)
Fox Steel Products LLC ....G....... 856 778-4661
Mount Laurel (G-6762)
Hoeganaes Corporation ....B....... 856 303-0366
Cinnaminson (G-1464)
Tms International LLC ....G....... 732 721-7477
Sayreville (G-9725)

STEEL, COLD-ROLLED: Strip NEC, From Purchased Hot-Rolled

Sandvik Inc ....C....... 201 794-5000
Fair Lawn (G-3120)

STEEL, HOT-ROLLED: Sheet Or Strip

Welded Products Co Inc ....E....... 973 589-0180
Newark (G-7313)

STEEL: Cold-Rolled

American Strip Steel Inc ....F....... 800 526-1216
South Plainfield (G-10216)
American Strip Steel Inc ....G....... 856 461-8300
Delanco (G-2002)
Bigelow Components Corp ....E....... 973 467-1200
Springfield (G-10431)
Fox Steel Products LLC ....G....... 856 778-4661
Mount Laurel (G-6762)
Leibrock Metal Products Inc ....G....... 732 695-0326
Ocean (G-7669)

STEEL: Laminated

Bozak Inc ....G....... 732 282-1556
Spring Lake (G-10420)

STENCILS

American Stencyl Inc ....G....... 201 251-6460
Mahwah (G-5714)
Innovative Art Concepts LLC ....F....... 201 828-9146
Ramsey (G-9148)

STONE: Cast Concrete

Jersey Cast Stone Ltd Lblty Co ....F....... 856 333-6900
Pennsauken (G-8445)

STONE: Dimension, NEC

Ankur International Inc ....F....... 609 409-6009
Cranbury (G-1811)
Bedrock Granite Inc ....E....... 732 741-0010
Shrewsbury (G-9883)
Dun-Rite Sand & Gravel Co ....G....... 856 692-2520
Vineland (G-11214)
Eastern Concrete Materials Inc ....E....... 973 827-7625
Hamburg (G-4090)
Morelli Contracting LLC ....G....... 732 356-8800
Middlesex (G-6131)
S J Quarry Materials Inc ....D....... 856 691-3133
Elmer (G-2803)

STONE: Quarrying & Processing, Own Stone Prdts

Stavola Construction Mtls Inc ....E....... 732 542-2328
Tinton Falls (G-10729)
Stavola Construction Mtls Inc ....E....... 732 356-5700
Bound Brook (G-608)

STORE FIXTURES: Exc Wood

Alternative Air LLC ....G....... 609 261-5870
Willingboro (G-11988)
E J M Store Fixtures Inc ....G....... 973 372-7907
Irvington (G-4565)
Handy Store Fixtures Inc ....D....... 973 242-1600
Newark (G-7147)
Lloyd Gerstner & Partners LLC ....E....... 201 634-9099
Paramus (G-7815)
Lyle/Carlstrom Associates Inc ....E....... 908 526-2270
Branchburg (G-658)

STORE FIXTURES: Wood

E Berkowitz & Co Inc ....G....... 856 608-1118
Mount Laurel (G-6756)
Handy Store Fixtures Inc ....D....... 973 242-1600
Newark (G-7147)
Lyle/Carlstrom Associates Inc ....E....... 908 526-2270
Branchburg (G-658)
Paramount Fixture Corporation ....E....... 973 485-1585
Newark (G-7223)
Sawitz Studios Inc ....E....... 201 842-9444
Carlstadt (G-1213)
Universal Systems Installers ....E....... 732 656-9002
Monroe (G-6323)

STORES: Auto & Home Supply

Cervinis Inc ....F....... 856 691-1744
Vineland (G-11198)
Ida Automotive Inc ....G....... 732 591-1245
Morganville (G-6588)

STRAINERS: Line, Piping Systems

Hayward Industrial Products ....C....... 908 351-5400
Elizabeth (G-2745)

STRAPPING

Versabar Corporation ....F....... 973 279-8400
Totowa (G-10857)

STRAPS: Apparel Webbing

Brian Lenhart Interactive LLC ....G....... 610 737-5314
Berkeley Heights (G-391)

STRAPS: Braids, Textile

Carolace Embroidery Co Inc ....D....... 201 945-2151
Ridgefield (G-9253)

STRIPS: Copper & Copper Alloy

H Cross Company ....E....... 201 964-9380
Moonachie (G-6468)

STRUCTURAL SUPPORT & BUILDING MATERIAL: Concrete

Kuiken Brothers Company ....E....... 201 796-2082
Fair Lawn (G-3109)
Ulma Form-Works Inc ....D....... 201 882-1122
Hawthorne (G-4247)

STUCCO

Brambila Jorge Stucco & Stone ....G....... 856 451-2039
Bridgeton (G-753)
California Stucco Products ....D....... 201 457-1900
Hackensack (G-3892)
Georgia-Pacific LLC ....D....... 856 966-7600
Camden (G-1066)
Mediterranean Stucco Corp ....F....... 973 491-0160
Newark (G-7199)
Perfect Shapes Inc ....G....... 856 783-3844
Elmer (G-2801)

STUDIOS: Artists & Artists' Studios

Evey Vacuum Service ....G....... 856 692-4779
Vineland (G-11217)
McT Dairies Inc ....F....... 973 258-9600
Millburn (G-6203)

STUDS & JOISTS: Sheet Metal

Super Stud Building Pdts Inc ....D....... 732 662-6200
Edison (G-2626)

SUBSCRIPTION FULFILLMENT SVCS: Magazine, Newspaper, Etc

Jersey Bound Latino LLC ....G....... 908 591-2830
Union (G-11066)

SUGAR SUBSTITUTES: Organic

Farbest-Tallman Foods Corp ....D....... 714 897-7199
Park Ridge (G-7849)
Quality Sweets ....G....... 732 283-3799
Iselin (G-4624)

Toltec Products LLC ....G....... 908 832-2131
Califon (G-1035)

Royal Ingredients LLC ....G....... 856 241-2004
Swedesboro (G-10607)
Sweet Solutions Inc ....G....... 732 512-0777
Edison (G-2628)

SUGAR SUBSTITUTES: Sorbitol

Technical Oil Products Co Inc ....G....... 973 940-8920
Newton (G-7362)

SUNDRIES & RELATED PRDTS: Medical & Laboratory, Rubber

Rubber Fab & Molding Inc ....G....... 908 852-7725
Johnsonburg (G-4837)
Sxwell USA LLC ....B....... 732 345-5400
Iselin (G-4630)
West Phrm Svcs Lakewood Inc ....G....... 732 730-3295
Lakewood (G-5181)

SUPERMARKETS & OTHER GROCERY STORES

Evergreen Kosher LLC ....G....... 732 370-4500
Lakewood (G-5094)
Herman Eickhoff ....C....... 609 871-1809
Willingboro (G-11991)
Paulaur Corporation ....D....... 609 395-8844
Cranbury (G-1870)
Porfirio Foods Inc ....G....... 609 393-4116
Trenton (G-10976)
Saker Shoprites Inc ....F....... 908 925-1550
Linden (G-5418)
Shop Rite Supermarkets Inc ....C....... 732 442-1717
Perth Amboy (G-8533)

SUPPOSITORIES

G & W Laboratories Inc ....B....... 908 753-2000
South Plainfield (G-10263)
G & W Laboratories Inc ....D....... 908 753-2000
South Plainfield (G-10264)

SURFACE ACTIVE AGENTS

Agilis Chemicals Inc ....F....... 973 910-2424
Short Hills (G-9864)
BASF Corporation ....D....... 908 689-7470
Washington (G-11440)
BASF Corporation ....B....... 973 245-6000
Florham Park (G-3491)
Basfin Corporation ....A....... 973 245-6000
Florham Park (G-3493)
G Holdings LLC ....F....... 973 628-3000
Parsippany (G-7953)
G-I Holdings Inc ....G....... 973 628-3000
Wayne (G-11507)
Interntonal Specialty Pdts Inc ....A....... 859 815-3333
Wayne (G-11522)
Pflaumer Brothers Inc ....G....... 609 883-4610
Ewing (G-3051)
Solv-TEC Incorporated ....G....... 609 261-4242
Medford (G-6034)
Stepan Company ....D....... 609 298-1222
Bordentown (G-595)

SURFACE ACTIVE AGENTS: Penetrants

AIG Industrial Group Inc ....F....... 201 767-7300
Northvale (G-7516)
American Gas & Chemical Co Ltd ......E....... 201 767-7300
Northvale (G-7518)
Meson Group Inc ....E....... 201 767-7300
Northvale (G-7536)

SURFACE ACTIVE AGENTS: Softeners, Textile Assisting

Atlas Refinery Inc ....E....... 973 589-2002
Newark (G-7056)
Commercial Products Co Inc ....F....... 973 427-6887
Hawthorne (G-4213)

SURFACE ACTIVE AGENTS: Textile Processing Assistants

Lanxess Sybron Chemicals Inc ....C....... 609 893-1100
Birmingham (G-457)
Nutech Corp ....G....... 908 707-2097
Franklin Lakes (G-3629)

SURGICAL & MEDICAL INSTRUMENTS WHOLESALERS

Bbg Surgical Ltd Liability Co ....G....... 888 575-6277
Lakewood **(G-5059)**

Dexmed LLC ....G....... 732 831-0507
Elizabeth **(G-2729)**

Total Tech Medical LLC ....G....... 973 980-6458
Dover **(G-2109)**

SURGICAL APPLIANCES & SPLYS

Brenner Metal Products ....E....... 973 778-2466
Wallington **(G-11382)**

Teleflex Incorporated ....D....... 856 349-7234
Gloucester City **(G-3851)**

SURGICAL APPLIANCES & SPLYS

Acuitive Technologies Inc ....F....... 973 617-7175
Allendale **(G-5)**

Ahs Hospital Corp ....E....... 908 522-2000
Summit **(G-10523)**

Alexander James Corp ....D....... 908 362-9266
Blairstown **(G-484)**

Ansell Healthcare Products LLC ....C....... 732 345-5400
Iselin **(G-4593)**

Bard International Inc ....G....... 908 277-8000
Franklin Lakes **(G-3612)**

Belair Instrument Company LLC ....E....... 973 912-8900
Pine Brook **(G-8587)**

Biomed Innovative Cons LLC ....G....... 732 599-7233
South Amboy **(G-10131)**

Boston Scientific Corporation ....E....... 973 709-7000
Wayne **(G-11482)**

Burpee Medsystems LLC ....G....... 732 544-8900
Eatontown **(G-2382)**

C R Bard Inc ....C....... 908 277-8000
Franklin Lakes **(G-3617)**

Capintec Inc ....E....... 201 825-9500
Florham Park **(G-3495)**

Csus LLC ....G....... 973 298-8599
Rockaway **(G-9452)**

Ebi LLC ....A....... 800 526-2579
Parsippany **(G-7929)**

Ebi LP ....E....... 973 299-9022
Parsippany **(G-7930)**

Ebi Medical Systems LLC ....F....... 973 299-3330
Parsippany **(G-7931)**

Ethicon Inc ....E....... 908 253-6464
Bridgewater **(G-820)**

Genzyme Corporation ....G....... 973 256-2106
Totowa **(G-10829)**

Hanger Prsthetcs & Ortho Inc ....G....... 732 919-7774
Wall Township **(G-11344)**

Hanger Prsthetcs & Ortho Inc ....G....... 609 889-8447
Rio Grande **(G-9355)**

Howmedica Osteonics Corp ....C....... 201 831-5000
Mahwah **(G-5747)**

Integra Lfscnces Holdings Corp ....C....... 609 275-0500
Plainsboro **(G-8792)**

Isomedix Operations Inc ....E....... 908 757-3727
South Plainfield **(G-10281)**

Jentec Inc ....G....... 201 784-1031
Northvale **(G-7531)**

Jnj International Inv LLC ....G....... 732 524-0400
New Brunswick **(G-6939)**

Johnson & Johnson ....G....... 908 722-9319
Raritan **(G-9213)**

Johnson & Johnson ....C....... 908 874-1000
Morris Plains **(G-6618)**

Johnson & Johnson ....C....... 732 524-0400
New Brunswick **(G-6941)**

Johnson & Johnson ....A....... 732 524-0400
New Brunswick **(G-6940)**

Johnson & Johnson Medical Inc ....A....... 908 218-0707
Somerville **(G-10119)**

K & S Drug & Surgical Inc ....G....... 201 886-9191
Fort Lee **(G-3566)**

Lightfield Llr Corporation ....G....... 732 462-9200
Freehold **(G-3677)**

Lumiscope Co Inc ....D....... 678 291-3207
East Rutherford **(G-2298)**

Medical Device Bus Svcs Inc ....G....... 732 524-0400
New Brunswick **(G-6946)**

Pacon Manufacturing Corp ....C....... 732 764-9070
Somerset **(G-10051)**

Peace Medical Inc ....F....... 800 537-9564
Wharton **(G-11866)**

Precise Cmpnents TI Design Inc ....G....... 973 928-2928
Clifton **(G-1697)**

Prescription Podiatry Labs ....G....... 609 695-1221
Trenton **(G-10980)**

Respironics Inc ....C....... 973 581-6000
Parsippany **(G-8007)**

Steris Corporation ....G....... 908 904-1317
Hillsborough **(G-4356)**

Superior Intl Srgical Sups LLC ....F....... 609 695-6591
Ewing **(G-3067)**

Switlik Parachute Company Inc ....F....... 609 587-3300
Trenton **(G-10994)**

Tronex International Inc ....E....... 973 335-2888
Budd Lake **(G-938)**

Universal Tape Supply Corp ....F....... 609 653-3191
Somers Point **(G-9940)**

Zimmer Biomet ....C....... 201 797-7300
Fair Lawn **(G-3130)**

Zounds Inc ....F....... 856 234-8844
Mount Laurel **(G-6815)**

SURGICAL EQPT: See Also Instruments

3M Company ....B....... 973 884-2500
Whippany **(G-11875)**

Acme International Inc ....G....... 973 594-4866
Clifton **(G-1556)**

Anderson Tool & Die Corp ....E....... 908 862-5550
Linden **(G-5324)**

Automated Medical Pdts Corp ....G....... 732 602-7717
Sewaren **(G-9831)**

Bbg Surgical Ltd Liability Co ....G....... 888 575-6277
Lakewood **(G-5059)**

Cross Medical Specialties Inc ....F....... 856 589-3288
Pitman **(G-8744)**

Ellis Instruments Inc ....G....... 973 593-9222
Madison **(G-5692)**

Haldor USA Inc ....E....... 856 254-2345
Cherry Hill **(G-1370)**

Medin Technologies Inc ....C....... 973 779-2400
Totowa **(G-10836)**

P A K Manufacturing Inc ....F....... 973 372-1090
Irvington **(G-4581)**

Pentax of America Inc ....E....... 973 628-6200
Montvale **(G-6421)**

Rhein Medical Inc ....F....... 727 209-2244
Denville **(G-2053)**

SURGICAL IMPLANTS

Endotec Inc ....F....... 973 762-6100
South Orange **(G-10194)**

Infront Medical LLC ....G....... 888 515-2532
Clifton **(G-1639)**

Link Bio Inc ....G....... 973 625-1333
Dover **(G-2094)**

Midlantic Medical Systems Inc ....G....... 908 432-4599
Skillman **(G-9923)**

Onkos Surgical Inc ....E....... 973 264-5400
Parsippany **(G-7981)**

Oticon Medical LLC ....E....... 732 560-0727
Somerset **(G-10048)**

Zimmer Trabecular Met Tech Inc ....C....... 973 576-0032
Parsippany **(G-8044)**

SURVEYING & MAPPING: Land Parcels

Planet Associates Inc ....E....... 201 693-8700
Park Ridge **(G-7858)**

T O Najarian Associates ....D....... 732 389-0220
Eatontown **(G-2423)**

SURVEYING SVCS: Photogrammetric Engineering

Dpk Consulting LLC ....F....... 732 764-0100
Piscataway **(G-8657)**

SVC ESTABLISH EQPT, WHOLESALE: Carpet/Rug Clean Eqpt & Sply

Stephco Sales Inc ....E....... 973 278-5454
Paterson **(G-8301)**

SVC ESTABLISHMENT EQPT & SPLYS WHOLESALERS

Confires Fire Prtction Svc LLC ....F....... 908 822-2700
South Plainfield **(G-10241)**

Morris Industries Inc ....D....... 973 835-6600
Pompton Plains **(G-8868)**

SVC ESTABLISHMENT EQPT, WHOL: Cleaning & Maint Eqpt & Splys

Trim Brush Company Inc ....G....... 973 887-2525
East Hanover **(G-2243)**

SVC ESTABLISHMENT EQPT, WHOL: Concrete Burial Vaults & Boxes

Delaware Valley Vault Co Inc ....G....... 856 227-2555
Blackwood **(G-463)**

SVC ESTABLISHMENT EQPT, WHOLESALE: Beauty Parlor Eqpt & Sply

Esd Professional Inc ....G....... 212 300-7673
Palisades Park **(G-7773)**

Salon Interiors Inc ....E....... 201 488-7888
South Hackensack **(G-10186)**

SVC ESTABLISHMENT EQPT, WHOLESALE: Floor Machinery, Maint

Amano USA Holdings Inc ....G....... 973 403-1900
Roseland **(G-9531)**

SVC ESTABLISHMENT EQPT, WHOLESALE: Vacuum Cleaning Systems

Aer X Dust Corporation ....G....... 732 946-9462
Holmdel **(G-4493)**

Jetstream of Houston LLP ....G....... 732 448-7830
New Brunswick **(G-6938)**

SWEEPING COMPOUNDS

Capital Soap Products LLC ....F....... 973 333-6100
Paterson **(G-8154)**

SWIMMING POOL & HOT TUB CLEANING & MAINTENANCE SVCS

Merlin Industries Inc ....D....... 609 807-1000
Hamilton **(G-4116)**

SWIMMING POOL ACCESS: Leaf Skimmers Or Pool Rakes

Hayward Industries Inc ....B....... 908 351-5400
Elizabeth **(G-2746)**

SWIMMING POOL EQPT: Filters & Water Conditioning Systems

Aqua Products Inc ....C....... 973 857-2700
Cedar Grove **(G-1268)**

Filtrex Inc ....F....... 973 595-0400
Wayne **(G-11502)**

Hayward Industries Inc ....B....... 908 351-5400
Elizabeth **(G-2746)**

Hayward Industries Inc ....G....... 908 351-0899
Elizabeth **(G-2747)**

NMP Water Systems LLC ....G....... 201 252-8333
Mahwah **(G-5758)**

South Jersey Water Cond Svc ....E....... 856 451-0620
Bridgeton **(G-773)**

SWIMMING POOL SPLY STORES

Izzo Enterprises Inc ....E....... 908 845-8200
Scotch Plains **(G-9735)**

Merlin Industries Inc ....D....... 609 807-1000
Hamilton **(G-4116)**

SWIMMING POOLS, EQPT & SPLYS: Wholesalers

Alden - Leeds Inc ....G....... 973 344-7986
Kearny **(G-4841)**

Hayward Pool Products Inc ....A....... 908 351-5400
Elizabeth **(G-2748)**

Seaboard Industries ....F....... 732 901-5700
Lakewood **(G-5161)**

SWITCHES

Asco Power Services Inc ....F....... 973 966-2000
Florham Park **(G-3483)**

Calculagraph Co ....E....... 973 887-9400
East Hanover **(G-2199)**

P R O D U C T

SWITCHES: Electric Power

Astrodyne Corporation ....D...... 908 850-5088
Hackettstown (G-3999)
Sigma-Netics Inc ....E...... 973 227-6372
Riverdale (G-9385)
Transistor Devices Inc ....C...... 908 850-5088
Hackettstown (G-4039)

SWITCHES: Electric Power, Exc Snap, Push Button, Etc

Comus International Inc ....C...... 973 777-6900
Clifton (G-1587)

SWITCHES: Electronic

Autoremind Inc ....G...... 800 277-1299
Fair Lawn (G-3087)
Mennekes Electronics Inc ....E...... 973 882-8333
Fairfield (G-3268)
Sensigraphics Inc ....G...... 856 853-9100
Mount Laurel (G-6804)

SWITCHES: Electronic Applications

Tusa Products Inc ....G...... 609 448-8333
Ewing (G-3072)

SWITCHES: Time, Electrical Switchgear Apparatus

Precision Multiple Contrls Inc .....E...... 201 444-0600
Midland Park (G-6184)
Precision Multiple Contrls Inc .....D...... 201 444-0600
Midland Park (G-6185)
Techniques Inc ....E...... 973 256-0947
Woodland Park (G-12092)

SWITCHGEAR & SWITCHBOARD APPARATUS

Apelio Innovative Inds LLC ....F...... 973 777-8899
Kearny (G-4844)
Astrodyne Corporation ....D...... 908 850-5088
Hackettstown (G-3999)
Automatic Switch Company ....A...... 973 966-2000
Florham Park (G-3485)
Blackhawk Cre Corporation ....F...... 856 887-0162
Salem (G-9692)
Circonix Technologies LLC ....F...... 973 962-6160
Ringwood (G-9344)
Galaxy Switchgear Inds LLC ....E...... 914 668-8200
Kearny (G-4858)
Marine Electric Systems Inc ....E...... 201 531-8600
South Hackensack (G-10171)
Primacy Engineering Inc ....F...... 201 731-3272
Englewood Cliffs (G-2988)

SWITCHGEAR & SWITCHGEAR ACCESS, NEC

Hoyt Corporation ....E...... 201 894-0707
Englewood (G-2912)

SWITCHING EQPT: Radio & Television Communications

F S R Inc ....D...... 973 785-4347
Woodland Park (G-12078)

SYRUPS, DRINK

Briars Usa ....G...... 732 821-7600
Monmouth Junction (G-6279)
Drink A Toast Company Inc ....F...... 856 461-1000
Riverside (G-9394)
J & J Snack Foods Corp ....B...... 856 665-9533
Pennsauken (G-8440)
J & J Snack Foods Corp ....C...... 856 467-9552
Bridgeport (G-740)
Sea Breeze Fruit Flavors Inc ......D...... 973 334-7777
Towaco (G-10880)
Sodastream USA Inc ....D...... 856 755-3400
Mount Laurel (G-6808)

SYRUPS: Pharmaceutical

Tris Pharma Inc ....D...... 732 940-0358
Monmouth Junction (G-6315)

SYSTEMS ENGINEERING: Computer Related

Bavelle Tech Sltions Ltd Lblty ......F...... 973 992-8086
East Hanover (G-2195)
Hitechone Inc ....G...... 201 500-8864
Englewood Cliffs (G-2975)

SYSTEMS INTEGRATION SVCS

Automated Control Concepts Inc ..E...... 732 922-6611
Neptune (G-6867)
Blueclone Networks LLC ....G...... 609 944-8433
Princeton (G-8917)
Datamotion Inc ....G...... 973 455-1245
Florham Park (G-3500)
Thermo Systems LLC ....D...... 609 371-3300
East Windsor (G-2362)
Vst Consulting Inc ....G...... 732 404-0025
Iselin (G-4635)

SYSTEMS INTEGRATION SVCS: Office Computer Automation

Interntnal Digital Systems Inc .....F...... 201 983-7700
Fort Lee (G-3564)

SYSTEMS SOFTWARE DEVELOPMENT SVCS

Amerindia Technologies Inc ....E...... 609 664-2224
Cranbury (G-1808)
Appex Innovation Solutions LLC ...G...... 215 313-3332
Princeton (G-8908)
Aurora Information Systems ....G...... 856 596-4180
Cherry Hill (G-1340)
Aurora Research Company Inc .....G...... 973 827-8055
Franklin (G-3599)
Creative Cmpt Concepts LLC ....G...... 877 919-7988
Williamstown (G-11956)
Emdeon Corporation ....A...... 201 703-3400
Elmwood Park (G-2825)
Kittyhawk Digital LLC ....G...... 269 767-8399
Emerson (G-2866)
Linden Group Corporation ....F...... 973 983-8809
Cedar Knolls (G-1308)
Qellus LLC ....G...... 856 761-6575
Mount Laurel (G-6798)
Smartlinx Solutions LLC ....D...... 732 385-5507
Iselin (G-4629)
Valuemomentum Inc ....D...... 908 755-0025
Piscataway (G-8734)

TABLE OR COUNTERTOPS, PLASTIC LAMINATED

Intelco ....E...... 856 384-8562
Paulsboro (G-8332)
Laminetics Inc ....G...... 732 367-1116
Lakewood (G-5120)
Wilsonart LLC ....F...... 800 822-7613
Moorestown (G-6578)

TABLE TOPS: Porcelain Enameled

Bernardaud Na Inc ....G...... 973 274-3555
Kearny (G-4847)

TABLECLOTHS & SETTINGS

A & R Sewing Company Inc ....F...... 201 332-0622
Jersey City (G-4682)
A-1 Tablecloth Co Inc ....C...... 201 727-4364
South Hackensack (G-10145)
Ballard Collection Inc ....G...... 908 604-0082
Warren (G-11399)

TABLES: Lift, Hydraulic

Hanson & Zollinger Inc ....F...... 856 626-3440
Berlin (G-422)
Intech Powercore Corporation .....G...... 201 767-8066
Closter (G-1758)

TABLETS: Bronze Or Other Metal

Cargille-Sacher Labs Inc ....F...... 973 267-8888
Cedar Knolls (G-1300)
Research and Pvd Materials ....G...... 973 575-4245
Fairfield (G-3301)

TAGS & LABELS: Paper

Ascot Tag and Label Co Inc ....E...... 973 482-0900
Newark (G-7055)
Mod-Tek Converting LLC ....E...... 856 662-6884
Pennsauken (G-8458)

TAGS: Paper, Blank, Made From Purchased Paper

Arch Crown Inc ....E...... 973 731-6300
Hillside (G-4375)
Cenveo Worldwide Limited ....D...... 201 434-2100
Jersey City (G-4710)
Jrm Industries Inc ....E...... 973 779-9340
Passaic (G-8077)

TANK COMPONENTS: Military, Specialized

Savit Corporation ....F...... 862 209-4516
Rockaway (G-9497)

TANK REPAIR SVCS

Jersey Tank Fabricators Inc ....E...... 609 758-7670
South Plainfield (G-10283)
JW Parr Leadburing Co ....G...... 973 256-8093
Little Falls (G-5458)

TANKS & OTHER TRACKED VEHICLE CMPNTS

ALI Envmtl & Tank Svcs LLC ....F...... 908 755-2962
Scotch Plains (G-9728)
AST Construction Inc ....E...... 609 277-7101
Egg Harbor Township (G-2677)
Clogic LLC ....G...... 973 934-5223
Augusta (G-115)

TANKS: Concrete

Mershon Concrete LLC ....E...... 609 298-2150
Bordentown (G-588)

TANKS: Cryogenic, Metal

Corban Energy Group Corp ....F...... 201 509-8555
Elmwood Park (G-2818)

TANKS: For Tank Trucks, Metal Plate

Casale Industries Inc ....E...... 908 789-0040
Garwood (G-3782)

TANKS: Fuel, Including Oil & Gas, Metal Plate

Harsco Corporation ....E...... 856 779-7795
Cherry Hill (G-1371)
Prospect Transportation Inc ....D...... 201 933-9999
Carlstadt (G-1209)

TANKS: Lined, Metal

Deb Maintenance Inc ....E...... 856 786-0440
Cinnaminson (G-1448)
JW Parr Leadburing Co ....G...... 973 256-8093
Little Falls (G-5458)
Russell W Anderson Inc ....G...... 201 825-2092
Mahwah (G-5769)

TANKS: Plastic & Fiberglass

Cardinal Fibreglass Industries .....G...... 718 625-4350
Perth Amboy (G-8513)

TANKS: Standard Or Custom Fabricated, Metal Plate

Arde Inc ....D...... 201 784-9880
Carlstadt (G-1125)
Central Metal Fabricators Inc ....F...... 732 938-6900
Farmingdale (G-3379)
Leland Limited Inc ....F...... 908 561-2000
South Plainfield (G-10293)
Tolan Machinery Company Inc ......E...... 973 983-7212
Rockaway (G-9506)
Welded Products Co Inc ....E...... 973 589-0180
Newark (G-7313)

TANKS: Water, Metal Plate

Lobster Life Systems Inc ....F...... 201 398-0303
Lodi (G-5568)

TANNERIES: Leather

Myers Group LLC........................G...... 973 761-6414
   South Orange *(G-10199)*

TANNING AGENTS: Synthetic Organic

Glamorous Glo.............................G...... 732 361-3235
   Eatontown *(G-2393)*

TANNING SALON EQPT & SPLYS, WHOLESALE

PC Marketing Inc..........................E...... 201 943-6100
   Ridgefield *(G-9282)*

TAPE DRIVES

Pascack Data Services Inc............F...... 973 304-4858
   Hawthorne *(G-4236)*

TAPE STORAGE UNITS: Computer

Aurora Research Company Inc........G...... 973 827-8055
   Franklin *(G-3599)*

TAPES, ADHESIVE: MedicaL

Ace Box Landau Co Inc.................G...... 201 871-4776
   Englewood Cliffs *(G-2956)*
Rep Trading Associates Inc...........F...... 732 591-1140
   Old Bridge *(G-7727)*

TAPES: Fabric

R Tape Corporation.......................C...... 908 753-5570
   South Plainfield *(G-10322)*
Snapco Manufacturing Corp...........E...... 973 282-0300
   Hillside *(G-4427)*

TAPES: Gummed, Cloth Or Paper Based, From Purchased Matls

Holland Manufacturing Co Inc........C...... 973 584-8141
   Succasunna *(G-10513)*

TAPES: Pressure Sensitive

Capital Label and Affixing Co.........G...... 856 786-1700
   Cinnaminson *(G-1445)*
Interntnal Adhsive Coating Inc........E...... 603 893-1894
   Somers Point *(G-9937)*
Intertape Polymer Corp.................C...... 201 391-3315
   River Vale *(G-9366)*
Jrm Industries Inc.........................E...... 973 779-9340
   Passaic *(G-8077)*
Label Master Inc...........................G...... 973 546-3110
   Lodi *(G-5567)*
Lamart Corporation.......................C...... 973 772-6262
   Clifton *(G-1654)*
Main Tape Company Inc.................C...... 609 395-1704
   Cranbury *(G-1862)*
Microseal Industries Inc.................F...... 973 523-0704
   Paterson *(G-8258)*
Nitto Inc......................................C...... 732 901-7905
   Lakewood *(G-5139)*
Nitto Inc......................................F...... 732 901-7905
   Lakewood *(G-5141)*
Nitto Inc......................................F...... 201 645-4950
   Teaneck *(G-10641)*
Universal Tape Supply Corp...........F...... 609 653-3191
   Somers Point *(G-9940)*
Web-Cote Ltd...............................F...... 973 827-2299
   Hamburg *(G-4098)*

TARGET DRONES

Drone Go Home LLC.....................G...... 732 991-3605
   Holmdel *(G-4499)*

TELECOMMUNICATION EQPT REPAIR SVCS, EXC TELEPHONES

Abris Distribution Inc.....................E...... 732 252-9819
   Manalapan *(G-5799)*

TELECOMMUNICATION SYSTEMS & EQPT

Alcatel-Lucent USA Inc..................D...... 908 582-3275
   New Providence *(G-6993)*

Avaya Cala Inc..............................G...... 866 462-8292
   Morristown *(G-6642)*
Avaya Inc.....................................B...... 908 953-6000
   Morristown *(G-6643)*
Avaya Inc.....................................C...... 732 852-2030
   Lincroft *(G-5310)*
Avaya World Services Inc...............E...... 908 953-6000
   Morristown *(G-6644)*
Bogen Communications Inc............D...... 201 934-8500
   Mahwah *(G-5718)*
Bogen Corporation........................G...... 201 934-8500
   Ramsey *(G-9142)*
Centurum Information Tech Inc........G...... 856 751-1111
   Marlton *(G-5924)*
Conair Corporation........................C...... 609 426-1300
   East Windsor *(G-2348)*
Dataprobe Inc...............................E...... 201 934-9944
   Allendale *(G-7)*
Dialogic Inc..................................C...... 973 967-6000
   Parsippany *(G-7916)*
Inlc Technology Corporation............F...... 908 834-8390
   Warren *(G-11418)*
IPC Systems Inc............................C...... 201 253-2000
   Jersey City *(G-4750)*
LAp Marketing MGT Svcs Inc..........F...... 609 654-9266
   Cherry Hill *(G-1382)*
Lattice Incorporated......................F...... 856 910-1166
   Pennsauken *(G-8450)*
Lucent Technologies World Svcs.....C...... 908 582-3000
   New Providence *(G-7008)*
Ofs Fitel LLC................................G...... 732 748-7409
   Somerset *(G-10043)*
Packetstorm Communications Inc.....F...... 732 840-3871
   Westwood *(G-11837)*
Quintum Technologies Inc...............D...... 732 460-9000
   Eatontown *(G-2419)*
Star Dynamic Corp.........................D...... 732 257-7488
   Garfield *(G-3769)*
Subcom LLC.................................B...... 732 578-7000
   Eatontown *(G-2422)*
Telcontel Corp..............................F...... 732 441-0800
   Laurence Harbor *(G-5210)*
Telecom Assistance Group Inc.........E...... 856 753-8585
   West Berlin *(G-11628)*
TMC Corporation...........................G...... 609 860-1830
   Metuchen *(G-6078)*
Vytran Corporation.........................E...... 732 972-2880
   Morganville *(G-6598)*

TELECOMMUNICATIONS CARRIERS & SVCS: Wired

360 Media Innovations LLC.............G...... 201 228-0941
   Union *(G-11018)*
All Solutions Inc.............................E...... 973 535-9100
   Livingston *(G-5503)*

TELECOMMUNICATIONS CARRIERS & SVCS: Wireless

Centurum Information Tech Inc.........G...... 856 751-1111
   Marlton *(G-5924)*
E Group Inc..................................G...... 856 320-9688
   Mount Laurel *(G-6757)*
ID Systems Inc..............................C...... 201 996-9000
   Woodcliff Lake *(G-12057)*

TELEGRAPHS & RELATED APPARATUS

DR Tielmann Inc............................G...... 732 332-1860
   Colts Neck *(G-1781)*
Lyca Tel LLC.................................E...... 973 286-0771
   Newark *(G-7191)*

TELEMARKETING BUREAUS

Hanover Direct Inc........................B...... 201 863-7300
   Weehawken *(G-11568)*
Redi-Direct Marketing Inc...............B...... 973 808-4500
   Fairfield *(G-3300)*

TELEMETERING EQPT

Iniven LLC....................................G...... 908 722-3770
   Branchburg *(G-649)*
Zzyzx LLC.....................................G...... 908 722-3770
   Branchburg *(G-700)*

TELEPHONE ANSWERING MACHINES

J C Contracting Inc........................F...... 973 748-5600
   Rahway *(G-9105)*

TELEPHONE CENTRAL OFFICE EQPT: Dial Or Manual

Tollgrade Communications Inc..........G...... 732 743-6720
   Piscataway *(G-8729)*

TELEPHONE EQPT INSTALLATION

Arose Inc.....................................E...... 856 481-4351
   Blackwood *(G-459)*
Princeton Hosted Solutions LLC.......F...... 856 470-2350
   Haddonfield *(G-4062)*
Wireless Experience of PA Inc.........F...... 732 552-0050
   Manahawkin *(G-5798)*

TELEPHONE EQPT: NEC

Shore Microsystems Inc..................G...... 732 870-0800
   Long Branch *(G-5606)*
Sierra Communication Intl LLC.........G...... 866 462-8292
   Morristown *(G-6700)*
Technology Corp America Inc...........G...... 866 462-8292
   Morristown *(G-6703)*

TELEPHONE STATION EQPT & PARTS: Wire

Eagle Communications Inc...............G...... 973 366-6181
   Denville *(G-2036)*

TELEPHONE SWITCHING EQPT

AT&T Technologies Inc...................A...... 201 771-2000
   Berkeley Heights *(G-389)*
Vytran LLC....................................E...... 732 972-2880
   Morganville *(G-6599)*

TELEPHONE SWITCHING EQPT: Toll Switching

Transcore LP................................F...... 201 329-9200
   Teterboro *(G-10696)*

TELEPHONE: Automatic Dialers

Nokia Inc.....................................F...... 908 582-3149
   Murray Hill *(G-6860)*

TELEPHONE: Fiber Optic Systems

Chromis Fiberoptics Inc..................F...... 732 764-0900
   Warren *(G-11405)*
Eastern Instrumentation of..............G...... 856 231-0668
   Moorestown *(G-6519)*
Faraday Photonics LLC...................G...... 973 239-2005
   Verona *(G-11166)*
Fiber-Span Inc...............................E...... 908 253-9080
   Toms River *(G-10757)*
Foctek Photonics LLC.....................G...... 732 828-8228
   Milltown *(G-6215)*
Infinova Corporation.......................E...... 732 355-9100
   Monmouth Junction *(G-6293)*
Iniven LLC....................................G...... 908 722-3770
   Branchburg *(G-649)*
Innovance Inc...............................G...... 732 529-2300
   Piscataway *(G-8679)*
Lcn Partners Inc............................F...... 215 755-1000
   Berlin *(G-426)*
Oe Solutions America Inc................G...... 201 568-1188
   Ridgefield Park *(G-9313)*
Ofs Specialty Photonics & Labs.......G...... 732 748-7401
   Somerset *(G-10044)*
Response Time Incorporated...........E...... 856 875-0025
   Williamstown *(G-11974)*
Vitex LLC.....................................G...... 201 296-0145
   Englewood Cliffs *(G-2997)*
Zzyzx LLC.....................................G...... 908 722-3770
   Branchburg *(G-700)*

TELEPHONE: Switchboards

Ntt Electronics America Inc..............F...... 201 556-1770
   Saddle Brook *(G-9666)*

TELEVISION BROADCASTING & COMMUNICATIONS EQPT

Blonder Tongue Labs Inc.................C...... 732 679-4000
   Old Bridge *(G-7713)*
DMJ and Associates Inc..................E...... 732 613-7867
   Sayreville *(G-9708)*
Miranda MTI Inc............................F...... 973 376-4275
   Springfield *(G-10454)*

Employee Codes: A=Over 500 employees, B=251-500
C=101-250, D=51-100, E=20-50, F=10-19, G=4-9

2019 Harris New jersey
Manufacturers Directory

947

PRODUCT

Panasonic Corp North America ....G 201 348-7000
  Newark *(G-7221)*
Patchamp Inc ....G 201 457-1504
  Hackensack *(G-3962)*
Telemetrics Inc ....E 201 848-9818
  Allendale *(G-18)*
Telvue Corporation ....E 800 885-8886
  Mount Laurel *(G-6809)*
Zaxcom Inc ....F 973 835-5000
  Pompton Plains *(G-8875)*

TELEVISION SETS

Jvc Industrial America Inc ....E 800 247-3608
  Wayne *(G-11527)*
Sharp Electronics Corporation ....A 201 529-8200
  Montvale *(G-6433)*
Toshiba Amer Consmr Pdts Inc ....C 973 628-8000
  Wayne *(G-11558)*

TELEVISION SETS WHOLESALERS

Sony Corporation of America ....F 201 930-1000
  Woodcliff Lake *(G-12065)*

TELEVISION: Closed Circuit Eqpt

Checkpoint Systems Inc ....C 800 257-5540
  West Deptford *(G-11697)*
Checkpoint Systems Inc ....C 856 848-1800
  West Deptford *(G-11698)*
Infinova Corporation ....E 732 355-9100
  Monmouth Junction *(G-6293)*
Selway Partners LLC ....F 201 712-7974
  Englewood *(G-2939)*
Turner Engineering Inc ....F 973 263-1000
  Mountain Lakes *(G-6829)*

TEMPORARY HELP SVCS

Astrix Software Technology ....F 732 661-0400
  Red Bank *(G-9221)*

TEN PIN CENTERS

Holiday Bowl Inc ....E 201 337-6516
  Oakland *(G-7631)*

TERMINAL BOARDS

Armel Electronics Inc ....E 201 869-4300
  North Bergen *(G-7387)*

TEST BORING SVCS: Nonmetallic Minerals

Jersey Boring & Drlg Co Inc ....E 973 242-3800
  Fairfield *(G-3244)*

TEST KITS: Pregnancy

Armkel LLC ....A 609 683-5900
  Princeton *(G-8911)*

TESTERS: Battery

Btech Inc ....E 973 983-1120
  Rockaway *(G-9448)*

TESTERS: Environmental

Bios International Corp ....E 973 492-8400
  Butler *(G-996)*
Dynatec Systems Inc ....F 609 387-0330
  Burlington *(G-965)*
Princeton Biomeditech Corp ....D 732 274-1000
  Monmouth Junction *(G-6303)*
Tess-Com Inc ....E 412 233-5782
  Middlesex *(G-6155)*

TESTERS: Gas, Exc Indl Process

Airscan Inc ....G 908 823-9425
  Lebanon *(G-5249)*

TESTERS: Integrated Circuit

EMD Performance Materials Corp ....B 908 429-3500
  Branchburg *(G-638)*

TESTERS: Liquid, Exc Indl Process

Acustrip Co Inc ....G 973 299-8237
  Mountain Lakes *(G-6819)*
Acustrip Company Inc ....F 973 299-8237
  Denville *(G-2028)*

TESTERS: Physical Property

Fluitec International LLC ....G 201 946-4584
  Bayonne *(G-217)*
Marine Cont Eqp Crtfction Corp ....G 732 938-6622
  Farmingdale *(G-3388)*
SGS UStesting Company ....F 973 575-5252
  Fairfield *(G-3311)*
Thwing-Albert Instrument Co ....D 856 767-1000
  West Berlin *(G-11629)*

TEXTILE & APPAREL SVCS

Safer Textile Processing Corp ....B 973 482-6400
  Newark *(G-7260)*

TEXTILE BAGS WHOLESALERS

Alex Real LLC ....F 732 730-8770
  Toms River *(G-10740)*
Alvaro P Escandon Inc ....G 973 274-1040
  Newark *(G-7043)*

TEXTILE CONVERTERS: Knit Goods

Dollfus Mieg Company Inc ....G 732 662-1005
  Edison *(G-2492)*
Markbilt Inc ....D 201 891-7842
  Wyckoff *(G-12117)*

TEXTILE FABRICATORS

Bright Ideas Usa LLC ....G 732 886-8865
  Lakewood *(G-5066)*
Covalnce Spcialty Coatings LLC ....D 732 356-2870
  Middlesex *(G-6109)*
Northcott Silk USA Inc ....G 201 672-9600
  Lyndhurst *(G-5667)*

TEXTILE FINISH: Chem Coat/Treat, Fire Resist, Manmade

Life Liners Inc ....G 973 635-9234
  Chatham *(G-1326)*

TEXTILE FINISHING: Calendering, Cotton

Finn & Emma LLC ....G 973 227-7770
  Fairfield *(G-3201)*

TEXTILE FINISHING: Chem Coating/Treating, Broadwoven, Cotton

Brookline Chemical Corp ....E 301 767-1177
  Wayne *(G-11485)*
Hydromer Inc ....E 908 526-2828
  Branchburg *(G-646)*

TEXTILE FINISHING: Decorative, Cotton, Broadwoven

Decorating With Fabric Inc ....G 845 352-5064
  Park Ridge *(G-7847)*

TEXTILE FINISHING: Dyeing, Broadwoven, Cotton

E & W Piece Dye Works ....E 973 942-8718
  Haledon *(G-4082)*
Hanes Companies - NJ LLC ....F 201 729-9100
  Edison *(G-2525)*
Keystone Dyeing and Finishing ....G 718 482-7780
  Dayton *(G-1975)*
Martin Corporation ....F 856 451-0900
  Bridgeton *(G-764)*
Paul Dyeing Company ....F 973 484-1121
  Newark *(G-7224)*
Rebtex Inc ....C 908 722-3549
  Branchburg *(G-676)*

TEXTILE FINISHING: Dyeing, Manmade Fiber & Silk, Broadwoven

Keystone Dyeing and Finishing ....G 718 482-7780
  Dayton *(G-1975)*
Martin Corporation ....F 856 451-0900
  Bridgeton *(G-764)*
North Jersey Skein Dyeing Co ....G 201 247-4202
  Paterson *(G-8270)*
Sunbrite Dye Co Inc ....E 973 777-9830
  Passaic *(G-8110)*

TEXTILE FINISHING: Embossing, Cotton, Broadwoven

Lacoa Inc ....G 973 754-1000
  Elmwood Park *(G-2837)*

TEXTILE MACHINERY ACCESS, HARDWOOD

Airborne Systems N Amer Inc ....G 856 663-1275
  Pennsauken *(G-8385)*

TEXTILE: Finishing, Cotton Broadwoven

Manner Textile Processing Inc ....D 973 942-8718
  North Haledon *(G-7497)*
Safer Textile Processing Corp ....B 973 482-6400
  Newark *(G-7260)*

TEXTILE: Finishing, Raw Stock NEC

Kennetex Inc ....D 610 444-0600
  Paterson *(G-8228)*
Manner Textile Processing Inc ....D 973 942-8718
  North Haledon *(G-7497)*
Multi-Tex Products Corp ....E 201 991-7262
  Kearny *(G-4886)*

TEXTILE: Goods, NEC

Classic Silks Com I ....G 908 204-0940
  Bernardsville *(G-436)*
Peribu Global Sourcing ....F 704 560-2035
  Skillman *(G-9925)*

TEXTILES

Sika Fibers LLC ....E 201 933-8800
  Lyndhurst *(G-5680)*
Ultraflex Systems Florida Inc ....E 973 627-8608
  Randolph *(G-9205)*

TEXTILES: Crash, Linen

Clean-Tex Services Inc ....E 908 912-2700
  Linden *(G-5334)*

TEXTILES: Linen Fabrics

AMD Fine Linens LLC ....G 201 568-5255
  Englewood *(G-2875)*
American Dawn Inc ....G 856 467-9211
  Bridgeport *(G-734)*
American Home Essentials Inc ....G 908 561-3200
  South Plainfield *(G-10215)*
Sander Sales Enterprises Ltd ....E 201 808-6705
  Secaucus *(G-9806)*
Something Different Linen Inc ....C 973 272-0601
  Clifton *(G-1722)*
Star Linen Inc ....E 800 782-7999
  Moorestown *(G-6568)*

TEXTILES: Mill Waste & Remnant

Texx Team LLC ....E 201 289-1039
  Hillsdale *(G-4370)*

TEXTILES: Padding & Wadding

Elkay Products Co Inc ....F 973 376-7550
  Springfield *(G-10441)*

THEATRICAL SCENERY

Acadia Scenic Inc ....E 201 653-8889
  Jersey City *(G-4684)*
Joseph C Hansen Company Inc ....G 201 222-1677
  Jersey City *(G-4752)*

THERMOMETERS: Medical, Digital

Medical Indicators Inc ....F 609 737-1600
  Hamilton *(G-4113)*

THERMOPLASTIC MATERIALS

Dow Chemical Company ....D 800 258-2436
  Somerset *(G-9982)*
Plastic Specialties & Tech Inc ....C 201 941-2900
  Ridgefield *(G-9284)*
Pure Tech International Inc ....G 908 722-4800
  Branchburg *(G-674)*

THERMOPLASTICS

Ensinger Grenloch Inc ....D....... 856 227-0500
Grenloch **(G-3869)**

Saint-Gobain Prfmce Plas Corp............D....... 856 423-6630
Mickleton **(G-6088)**

THERMOSETTING MATERIALS

Anhydrides & Chemicals Inc ....G....... 973 465-0077
Newark **(G-7048)**

Emerald Performance Mtls LLC............F....... 856 533-3000
Maple Shade **(G-5862)**

THIN FILM CIRCUITS

Thinfilms Inc ....F....... 908 359-7014
Hillsborough **(G-4360)**

THREAD: Embroidery

5 Kids Group Ltd Liability Co ....F....... 732 774-5331
Neptune **(G-6861)**

Athletes Alley ....F....... 732 842-1127
Shrewsbury **(G-9882)**

Cobyco Inc ....G....... 732 446-4448
Manalapan **(G-5804)**

THYROID PREPARATIONS

Corrigan Center For Integrativ..............G....... 973 239-0700
Cedar Grove **(G-1273)**

TIES, FORM: Metal

Clements Industries Inc ....E....... 201 440-5500
South Hackensack **(G-10153)**

TILE: Asphalt, Floor

Hup & Sons...G....... 908 832-7878
Glen Gardner **(G-3823)**

TILE: Brick & Structural, Clay

Glen-Gery Corporation ....E....... 908 359-5111
Hillsborough **(G-4320)**

Morgan Advanced Ceramics Inc ....E....... 973 808-1621
Fairfield **(G-3273)**

TILE: Clay, Drain & Structural

R & R Irrigation Co Inc.........................F....... 732 271-7070
Middlesex **(G-6142)**

TILE: Mosaic, Ceramic

Industrie Bitossi Inc.............................E....... 201 796-0722
Elmwood Park **(G-2831)**

TILE: Vinyl, Asbestos

Allied Tile Mfg Corp ....G....... 718 647-2200
South Plainfield **(G-10213)**

TILE: Wall & Floor, Ceramic

Andrevin Inc ....G....... 732 270-2794
Toms River **(G-10743)**

TILE: Wall, Ceramic

Mannington Mills Inc ....A....... 856 935-3000
Salem **(G-9694)**

TIMING DEVICES: Electronic

American Teletimer Corp ....E....... 908 654-4200
Mountainside **(G-6835)**

Artisan Controls Corporation ....E....... 973 598-9400
Randolph **(G-9173)**

Swatch Group Les Btques US Inc.........G....... 201 271-1400
Weehawken **(G-11570)**

TIN

Times Tin Cup ....G....... 973 983-1095
Mountain Lakes **(G-6828)**

Tin Panda Inc.......................................G....... 973 916-0707
Clifton **(G-1732)**

Tin Sigh Stop.......................................G....... 973 691-2712
Byram Township **(G-1019)**

TIRE & INNER TUBE MATERIALS & RELATED PRDTS

Coilhose Pneumatics Inc ....E....... 732 432-7177
East Brunswick **(G-2133)**

TIRE & TUBE REPAIR MATERIALS, WHOLESALE

Rema Tip Top/North America Inc..........E....... 201 768-8100
Northvale **(G-7546)**

TIRE CORD & FABRIC

Jomel Industries Inc ....F....... 973 282-0300
Hillside **(G-4406)**

Passaic Rubber Co ....D....... 973 696-9500
Wayne **(G-11540)**

TIRE DEALERS

American Tire Distributors....................G....... 973 646-5600
Totowa **(G-10811)**

TIRES & INNER TUBES

American Tire Distributors....................G....... 973 646-5600
Totowa **(G-10811)**

J G Carpenter Contractor ....G....... 732 271-8991
Middlesex **(G-6122)**

TIRES & TUBES, WHOLESALE: Automotive

Top Rated Shopping Bargains...............F....... 800 556-5849
Hasbrouck Heights **(G-4190)**

TIRES: Truck

Leopard Inc...F....... 908 964-3600
Hillside **(G-4410)**

TITANIUM MILL PRDTS

Titanium Industries Inc.........................G....... 973 428-1900
East Hanover **(G-2242)**

Titanium Smoking Kings LLC ....G....... 908 339-8876
Phillipsburg **(G-8577)**

Titanium Technical Services ....G....... 908 323-9899
Flemington **(G-3472)**

TOBACCO & PRDTS, WHOLESALE: Cigarettes

Sherman Nat Inc...................................E....... 201 735-9000
Englewood **(G-2940)**

TOBACCO & PRDTS, WHOLESALE: Cigars

Csonka Worldwide.................................E....... 609 514-2766
Plainsboro **(G-8783)**

TOBACCO & TOBACCO PRDTS WHOLESALERS

Altria Group Distribution Co..................C....... 804 274-2000
Parsippany **(G-7879)**

TOBACCO LEAF PROCESSING

Schweitzer-Mauduit Intl Inc..................B....... 732 723-6100
Spotswood **(G-10417)**

TOBACCO: Cigarettes

Altria Group Distribution Co..................C....... 804 274-2000
Parsippany **(G-7879)**

Philip Morris USA Inc ....F....... 908 781-6400
Bedminster **(G-276)**

Sensory Solutions LLC ....G....... 973 615-7600
Warren **(G-11429)**

Sherman Group Holdings ....G....... 201 735-9000
Fort Lee **(G-3587)**

Sherman Nat Inc...................................E....... 201 735-9000
Englewood **(G-2940)**

Shermans 1400 Brdway N Y C Ltd ....D....... 201 735-9000
Englewood **(G-2941)**

Urban State ....G....... 646 836-4311
Hillside **(G-4435)**

TOBACCO: Cigars

Csonka Worldwide.................................E....... 609 514-2766
Plainsboro **(G-8783)**

Itg Brands LLC ....G....... 973 386-9087
East Hanover **(G-2219)**

Prime Time International Co ....G....... 623 780-8600
Teaneck **(G-10647)**

Sherman Nat Inc...................................G....... 201 735-9000
Englewood **(G-2940)**

TOILET PREPARATIONS

ADS Sales Co Inc.................................E....... 732 591-0500
Morganville **(G-6580)**

Dnp Foods America Ltd Lblty Co ....G....... 201 654-5581
Waldwick **(G-11301)**

Mennen Company ....B....... 973 630-1500
Morristown **(G-6685)**

Nature Labs LLC ....G....... 856 839-0400
Vineland **(G-11245)**

Procter & Gamble Mfg Co ....D....... 732 602-4500
Avenel **(G-143)**

Reviva Labs Inc....................................E....... 856 428-3885
Haddonfield **(G-4064)**

TOILET SEATS: Wood

Swiss Madison LLC ....F....... 434 623-4766
Dayton **(G-1991)**

TOILETRIES, COSMETICS & PERFUME STORES

Beauty-Fill LLC.....................................E....... 908 353-1600
Hillside **(G-4381)**

Health and Natural Beauty USA...........F....... 732 640-1830
Piscataway **(G-8671)**

Revlon Inc...E....... 732 287-1400
Edison **(G-2598)**

TOILETRIES, WHOLESALE: Perfumes

Dosis Fragrance LLC............................G....... 718 874-0074
Newark **(G-7104)**

Elixens America Inc..............................G....... 732 388-3555
Rahway **(G-9091)**

Intarome Fragrance Corporation...........D....... 201 767-8700
Norwood **(G-7565)**

Lvmh Fragrance Brands US LLC...........G....... 212 931-2668
Edison **(G-2555)**

Quest Intl Flavors Fragrances ....B....... 973 576-9500
East Hanover **(G-2235)**

TOILETRIES, WHOLESALE: Razor Blades

Art of Shaving - Fl LLC.........................G....... 732 410-2520
Freehold **(G-3648)**

TOILETRIES, WHOLESALE: Toilet Soap

Sysco Guest Supply LLC ....C....... 732 537-2297
Somerset **(G-10078)**

TOILETRIES, WHOLESALE: Toiletries

Americare Laboratories Ltd ....E....... 973 279-5100
Paterson **(G-8138)**

Lux Naturals LLC ....G....... 848 229-2950
Edison **(G-2554)**

TOILETS: Portable Chemical, Plastics

Zirti LLC ....G....... 201 509-8404
Saddle Brook **(G-9689)**

TOOL & DIE STEEL

Atlas Copco North America LLC ....G....... 973 397-3400
Parsippany **(G-7888)**

CMI-Promex Inc....................................F....... 856 351-1000
Pedricktown **(G-8346)**

Unity Steel Rule Die Co ....E....... 201 569-6400
Englewood **(G-2951)**

TOOLS: Hand

Apex Saw & Tool Co Inc ....G....... 201 438-8777
Lyndhurst **(G-5641)**

Brasscraft Manufacturing Co................G....... 856 241-7700
Swedesboro **(G-10574)**

Cementex Products Inc ....E....... 609 387-1040
Burlington **(G-957)**

CS Osborne & Co.................................D....... 973 483-3232
Harrison **(G-4168)**

DAKA Manufacturing LLC.....................G....... 908 782-0360
Flemington **(G-3436)**

P
R
O
D
U
C
T

Dicar Diamond Tool Corp ....F 973 684-0949
  Paterson (G-8173)
Dreyco Inc ....F 201 896-9000
  Carlstadt (G-1154)
Excel Hobby Blades Corp ....E 973 278-4000
  Paterson (G-8187)
General Tools & Instrs Co LLC ....E 212 431-6100
  Secaucus (G-9773)
IDL Techni-Edge LLC ....C 908 497-9818
  Kenilworth (G-4945)
Indo-US Mim TEC Private Ltd ....G 734 327-9842
  Princeton (G-8962)
J R S Tool & Metal Finishing ....G 908 753-2050
  South Plainfield (G-10282)
Jdv Products Inc ....F 201 794-6467
  Fair Lawn (G-3108)
Jesco Iron Crafts Inc ....F 201 488-4545
  Bogota (G-533)
Mastercool USA Inc ....E 973 252-9119
  Randolph (G-9190)
National Steel Rule Company ....D 908 862-3366
  Linden (G-5394)
Ohaus Corporation ....D 973 377-9000
  Parsippany (G-7980)
Phoenix Industrial LLC ....G 908 955-0114
  Whitehouse Station (G-11932)
Power Hawk Technologies Inc ....F 973 627-4646
  Rockaway (G-9489)
S & G Tool Aid Corporation ....D 973 824-7730
  Newark (G-7257)
Sine Tru Tool Company Inc ....G 732 591-1100
  Marlboro (G-5915)
Stanley Black & Decker Inc ....F 860 225-5111
  Jersey City (G-4813)
Thirty-Three Queen Realty Inc ....F 973 824-5527
  Newark (G-7297)

TOOLS: Hand, Hammers

Grommet Mart Inc ....F 973 278-4100
  Paterson (G-8205)

TOOLS: Hand, Jewelers'

Acon Watch Crown Company ....F 973 546-8585
  Garfield (G-3725)
American Logistics Network LLC ....G 201 391-1054
  Woodcliff Lake (G-12046)
Du-Matt Corporation ....G 201 861-4271
  West New York (G-11738)
Swarovski North America Ltd ....G 908 253-7057
  Bridgewater (G-895)

TOOLS: Hand, Mechanics

C T A Manufacturing Corp ....E 201 896-1000
  Carlstadt (G-1135)

TOOLS: Hand, Power

Black & Decker (us) Inc ....G 201 475-3524
  Elmwood Park (G-2812)
Colwood Electronics Inc ....G 732 938-5556
  Farmingdale (G-3380)
Congruent Machine Co Inc ....G 973 764-6767
  Vernon (G-11158)
Ingersoll-Rand Company ....C 908 238-7000
  Annandale (G-54)
Ingersoll-Rand Company ....E 856 793-7000
  Mount Laurel (G-6766)
Jdv Products Inc ....F 201 794-6467
  Fair Lawn (G-3108)
National Steel Rule Company ....D 908 862-3366
  Linden (G-5392)
Newell Brands Inc ....B 201 610-6600
  Hoboken (G-4468)
S & G Tool Aid Corporation ....D 973 824-7730
  Newark (G-7257)
Singe Corporation ....G 908 289-7900
  Hillside (G-4426)
Tdk Electronics Inc ....D 732 906-4300
  Iselin (G-4631)
Tdk Electronics Inc ....F 732 603-5941
  Lumberton (G-5636)
William T Hutchinson Company ....F 908 688-0533
  Union (G-11100)

TOOLS: Hand, Stonecutters'

Legend Stone Products ....G 973 473-7088
  Clifton (G-1657)

TOOTHPASTES, GELS & TOOTHPOWDERS

Church & Dwight Co Inc ....B 609 806-1200
  Ewing (G-3021)
Colgate-Palmolive Company ....B 732 878-6062
  Highland Park (G-4288)
Colgate-Palmolive Company ....A 732 878-7500
  Piscataway (G-8648)
Colgate-Palmolive Company ....E 609 239-6001
  Burlington (G-961)

TOWELS: Fabric & Nonwoven, Made From Purchased Materials

Anchor Sales & Marketing Inc ....F 973 545-2277
  West Milford (G-11725)
Crown Products Inc ....E 732 493-0022
  Spring Lake (G-10421)
Franco Manufacturing Co Inc ....C 732 494-0500
  Metuchen (G-6056)

TOWELS: Indl

Jay Franco & Sons Inc ....D 732 721-0022
  Sayreville (G-9712)
Material Imports ....G 201 229-1180
  Moonachie (G-6479)

TOWELS: Paper

Marcal Manufacturing LLC ....F 201 796-4000
  Elmwood Park (G-2839)
Soundview Paper Holdings LLC ....A 201 796-4000
  Elmwood Park (G-2856)

TOWERS, SECTIONS: Transmission, Radio & Television

Lingo Inc ....F 856 273-6594
  Mount Laurel (G-6775)
Main Robert A & Sons Holdg Co ....E 201 447-3700
  Wyckoff (G-12116)
Morgan Towers Inc ....G 856 786-7200
  Moorestown (G-6546)
Priore Construction Svcs LLC ....F 973 785-2262
  Little Falls (G-5465)

TOWING & TUGBOAT SVC

Wittich Bros Marine Inc ....E 732 722-8656
  Manasquan (G-5844)

TOYS

Ambo Consulting LLC ....G 732 663-0000
  Deal (G-1997)
Amloid Corporation ....F 973 328-0654
  Cedar Knolls (G-1298)
Answers In Motion LLC ....G 732 267-7792
  Maple Shade (G-5859)
Atlas O LLC ....E 908 687-9590
  Hillside (G-4377)
Bally Technologies Inc ....F 609 641-7711
  Egg Harbor Township (G-2679)
Edison Nation Inc ....G 610 829-1039
  Phillipsburg (G-8549)
Electronics Boutique Amer Inc ....G 856 435-3900
  Clementon (G-1532)
Epoch Everlasting Play LLC ....E 973 316-2500
  Parsippany (G-7937)
Famosa North America Inc ....G 856 206-9844
  Mount Laurel (G-6759)
Froyo Skyview LLC ....G 718 607-5656
  Jersey City (G-4741)
Horizon Group Usa Inc ....C 908 810-1111
  Warren (G-11415)
Horizon Group USA Inc ....G 908 810-1111
  Monroe Township (G-6333)
Pride Products Mfg LLC ....F 908 353-1900
  Elizabeth (G-2770)
Primetime Trading Corp ....E 646 580-8223
  Bayonne (G-231)
Proteus Designs LLC ....G 215 519-0101
  Moorestown (G-6560)
Reeves International Inc ....E 973 956-9555
  Wayne (G-11547)
Steico USA Inc ....F 732 364-6200
  Lakewood (G-5168)
Tucker International LLC ....F 856 216-1333
  Burlington (G-988)
Zimpli Kids Inc ....G 732 945-5995
  Neptune (G-6903)

TOYS & HOBBY GOODS & SPLYS, WHOLESALE: Amusement Goods

Two Jays Bingo Supply Inc ....F 609 267-4542
  Hainesport (G-4080)

TOYS & HOBBY GOODS & SPLYS, WHOLESALE: Arts/Crafts Eqpt/Sply

Environmolds LLC ....F 908 273-5401
  Summit (G-10531)
Hygloss Products Inc ....E 973 458-1700
  Wallington (G-11387)
Larose Industries LLC ....D 973 543-2037
  Randolph (G-9189)

TOYS & HOBBY GOODS & SPLYS, WHOLESALE: Dolls

Pretty Ugly LLC ....F 908 620-0931
  Bernardsville (G-442)
Reeves International Inc ....E 973 694-5006
  Pequannock (G-8506)

TOYS & HOBBY GOODS & SPLYS, WHOLESALE: Toys & Games

Ambo Consulting LLC ....G 732 663-0000
  Deal (G-1997)
Kiddesigns Inc ....E 732 574-9000
  Rahway (G-9112)

TOYS, HOBBY GOODS & SPLYS WHOLESALERS

AMS Toy Intl Inc ....E 973 442-5790
  Wharton (G-11851)
Dream Makers Inc ....G 201 248-5502
  Park Ridge (G-7848)
Epoch Everlasting Play LLC ....E 973 316-2500
  Parsippany (G-7937)
Kids of America Corp ....E 973 808-8242
  Fairfield (G-3250)

TOYS: Dolls, Stuffed Animals & Parts

Allure Pet Pdts Ltd Lblty Co ....F 973 339-9655
  Denville (G-2029)
De Zaio Productions Inc ....D 973 423-5000
  Fair Lawn (G-3095)
Dream Makers Inc ....G 201 248-5502
  Park Ridge (G-7848)
Homeco LLC ....E 732 802-7733
  Piscataway (G-8673)
Kids of America Corp ....E 973 808-8242
  Fairfield (G-3250)
New Adventures LLC ....G 973 884-8887
  East Hanover (G-2225)
Pretty Ugly LLC ....F 908 620-0931
  Bernardsville (G-442)

TOYS: Electronic

Kiddesigns Inc ....E 732 574-9000
  Rahway (G-9112)
Toysruscom Inc ....D 973 617-3500
  Parsippany (G-8031)

TOYS: Rubber

Dream Makers Inc ....G 201 248-5502
  Park Ridge (G-7848)

TOYS: Video Game Machines

AG&e Holdings Inc ....E 609 704-3000
  Hammonton (G-4124)

TRADE SHOW ARRANGEMENT SVCS

CPB Inc ....E 856 697-2700
  Buena (G-939)

TRADING STAMP PROMOTION & REDEMPTION

Crown Roll Leaf Inc ....E 973 684-2600
  Paterson (G-8165)

TRAILERS & PARTS: Truck & Semi's

E Loc Total Logistics LLC ....G 609 685-6117
Mount Laurel **(G-6758)**
Fyx Fleet Roadside Assistance ....F 609 452-8900
Princeton **(G-8953)**
Hercules Enterprises LLC ....D 908 369-0000
Hillsborough **(G-4323)**
M W Trailer Repair Inc ....F 609 298-1113
Bordentown **(G-585)**
Trac Intermodal LLC ....G 609 452-8900
Princeton **(G-9034)**
Vanco USA LLC (de) ....C 609 499-4141
Bordentown **(G-599)**
Wjm Trucking Inc ....G 856 381-3635
Mullica Hill **(G-6858)**
Wta Global LLC ....F 312 509-2559
Little Falls **(G-5473)**

TRAILERS & TRAILER EQPT

Sealion Metal Fabricators Inc ....F 856 933-3914
Bellmawr **(G-342)**
Steve Green Enterprises ....F 732 938-5572
Farmingdale **(G-3393)**

TRAILERS: Bodies

Richard Shafer ....G 856 358-3483
Elmer **(G-2802)**

TRAILERS: Demountable Cargo Containers

ASAP Containers NJ NY Corp ....F 732 659-4402
West Orange **(G-11759)**
Granco Group LLC ....G 973 515-4721
Roseland **(G-9539)**
Seacube Container Leasing Ltd ....G 201 391-0800
Park Ridge **(G-7859)**

TRAILERS: Semitrailers, Truck Tractors

Vanco Usa LLC ....D 609 499-4141
Bordentown **(G-598)**

TRAILERS: Truck, Chassis

Automann Inc ....D 201 529-4996
Somerset **(G-9961)**
Universal Parts New Jersey LLC ....G 732 615-0626
Middletown **(G-6167)**

TRANSDUCERS: Pressure

American Sensor Tech Inc ....D 973 448-1901
Budd Lake **(G-918)**

TRANSFORMERS: Control

Pioneer Power Solutions Inc ....D 212 867-0700
Fort Lee **(G-3582)**

TRANSFORMERS: Distribution

Voltis LLC ....G 607 349-9411
Fairfield **(G-3348)**

TRANSFORMERS: Distribution, Electric

G & S Motor Equipment Co Inc...........D 201 998-9244
Kearny **(G-4857)**
High Energy Group Ltd Lblty Co ....G 732 741-9099
Eatontown **(G-2397)**
Siemens Corporation.........................D 732 590-6895
Iselin **(G-4628)**

TRANSFORMERS: Electric

Baltimore Transformer Company ....E 973 942-2222
Paterson **(G-8146)**
Cooper Power Systems LLC ....C 732 481-4630
Ocean **(G-7659)**
Cooper Power Systems LLC ....C 856 719-1100
West Berlin **(G-11587)**
Galaxy Trans & Magnetics LLC ....F 856 753-4546
West Berlin **(G-11596)**
Glen Magnetics Inc ....E 908 454-3717
Alpha **(G-37)**
Hitran Corporation ....C 908 782-5525
Flemington **(G-3448)**
Hunterdon Transformer Co Inc ....D 908 454-2400
Alpha **(G-38)**
Krydon Group Inc ....G 877 854-1342
Moorestown **(G-6535)**

Megatran Industries...........................D 609 227-4300
Bordentown **(G-586)**
Nwl Inc ....C 609 298-7300
Bordentown **(G-591)**
Power Magnetics Inc ....E 609 695-1170
Trenton **(G-10977)**
Power Magnetics Inc ....E 800 747-0845
Trenton **(G-10978)**
Transistor Devices Inc ....C 908 850-5088
Hackettstown **(G-4039)**
Transistor Devices Inc ....C 908 850-5088
Hackettstown **(G-4040)**

TRANSFORMERS: Electronic

Baltimore Transformer Company ....E 973 942-2222
Paterson **(G-8146)**
Edko Electronics ....E 973 942-2222
Paterson **(G-8176)**

TRANSFORMERS: Machine Tool

Ivey Katrina Owner ....G 973 951-8328
Newark **(G-7163)**

TRANSFORMERS: Meters, Electronic

Magnetran Inc ....F 856 768-7787
Ocean View **(G-7703)**
Nilsson Electrical Laboratory ....G 201 521-4860
Jersey City **(G-4771)**

TRANSFORMERS: Power Related

AFP Transformers Corporation ....D 732 248-0305
Edison **(G-2450)**
Edko Electronics ....E 973 942-2222
Paterson **(G-8176)**
Jerome Industries Corp.......................E 908 353-5700
Hackettstown **(G-4013)**
KG Squared LLC ....F 973 627-0643
Rockaway **(G-9473)**
Mesa Veterans Power LLC ....G 856 222-1000
Moorestown **(G-6545)**
Microsignals Inc ....E 800 225-4508
Palisades Park **(G-7774)**
Raritan Inc ....E 732 764-8886
Somerset **(G-10061)**

TRANSFORMERS: Rectifier

Model Rectifier Corporation................E 732 225-2100
Matawan **(G-5980)**

TRANSFORMERS: Specialty

Beverly Manufacturing Co Inc ....G 856 764-7898
Riverside **(G-9390)**
Globtek Inc ....B 201 784-1000
Northvale **(G-7526)**
Hbs Electronics Inc...........................G 973 439-1147
Fairfield **(G-3223)**
High Gate Corp.................................F 609 267-0680
Mount Holly **(G-6730)**

TRANSFORMERS: Tripping

Power Magne-Tech Corp ....E 732 826-4700
Perth Amboy **(G-8529)**

TRANSISTORS

Rudolph Technologies Inc ....G 973 448-4307
Ledgewood **(G-5280)**
United Silicon Carbide Inc ....F 732 355-0550
Monmouth Junction **(G-6317)**

TRANSLATION & INTERPRETATION SVCS

Aliron International Inc........................E 540 808-1615
South Plainfield **(G-10210)**
Berlitz Languages US Inc ....D 609 759-5371
Princeton **(G-8914)**
Newtype Inc ....F 973 361-6000
Randolph **(G-9192)**

TRANSMISSIONS: Motor Vehicle

Transmission Technology Co ....G 973 305-3600
Lincoln Park **(G-5307)**

TRANSPORTATION EPQT & SPLYS, WHOLESALE: Marine Crafts/Splys

JC Macelroy Co Inc............................D 732 572-7100
Piscataway **(G-8681)**

TRANSPORTATION EPQT/SPLYS, WHOL: Guided Missiles/Space Veh

Aphelion Orbitals Inc ....G 321 289-0872
Union City **(G-11107)**

TRANSPORTATION EPQT/SPLYS, WHOL: Marine Propulsn Mach/Eqpt

Ocean Power & Equipment Co ....G 973 575-5775
West Caldwell **(G-11668)**

TRANSPORTATION EQPT & SPLYS WHOLESALERS, NEC

Bristol-Donald Company Inc................E 973 589-2640
Newark **(G-7076)**
Defense Photonics Group Inc ....F 908 822-1075
South Plainfield **(G-10247)**
Jet Aviation St Louis Inc ....E 201 462-4026
Teterboro **(G-10681)**
Steelstran Industries Inc ....E 732 574-0700
Avenel **(G-147)**
Taurus International Corp ....E 201 825-2420
Ramsey **(G-9156)**

TRANSPORTATION SVCS, WATER: Boat Cleaning

Sea Harvest Inc ....E 609 884-3000
Cape May **(G-1102)**

TRANSPORTATION SVCS, WATER: Intracoastal, Freight

Fornazor International Inc ....E 201 664-4000
Hillsdale **(G-4366)**

TRANSPORTATION SVCS, WATER: Salvaging & Surveying, Marine

T O Najarian Associates.......................D 732 389-0220
Eatontown **(G-2423)**

TRANSPORTATION SVCS: Railroads, Belt line

Holtec Government Services LLC.........G 856 291-0600
Camden **(G-1068)**

TRANSPORTATION: Deep Sea Domestic Freight

Bulkhaul (usa) Limited ....F 908 272-3100
Iselin **(G-4602)**

TRANSPORTATION: Deep Sea Foreign Freight

Bulkhaul (usa) Limited ....F 908 272-3100
Iselin **(G-4602)**
Global Commodities Exportacao ....G 201 613-1532
Newark **(G-7133)**

TRANSPORTATION: Local Passenger, NEC

Carry Easy Inc.................................E 201 944-0042
Leonia **(G-5287)**

TRANSPORTATION: Monorail Transit Systems

Bombardier Transportation..................B 973 624-9300
Newark **(G-7070)**

TRAP ROCK: Crushed & Broken

Cedar Hill Landscaping ....E 732 469-1400
Somerset **(G-9974)**
Eastern Concrete Materials Inc ....C 201 797-7979
Saddle Brook **(G-9650)**
Emil Dipalma Inc ....G 973 477-2766
Hackettstown **(G-4005)**

PRODUCT

Joseph and William Stavola.................E...... 609 924-0300
Kingston **(G-5009)**

Millington Quarry Inc ....D...... 908 542-0055
Basking Ridge **(G-192)**

Tilcon New York Inc ....B...... 973 366-7741
Parsippany **(G-8028)**

Tilcon New York Inc ....E...... 800 789-7625
Pompton Lakes **(G-8855)**

Tilcon New York Inc ....G...... 800 789-7625
Parsippany **(G-8029)**

Tilcon New York Inc ....F...... 973 347-2405
Stanhope **(G-10479)**

Trap Rock Industries Inc ....B...... 609 924-0300
Kingston **(G-5012)**

Trap Rock Industries LLC ....D...... 609 924-0300
Kingston **(G-5013)**

TRAPS: Animal & Fish, Wire

Blue Claw Mfg & Supply Company ....G...... 856 696-4366
Richland **(G-9249)**

TRAPS: Stem

American Products Company Inc ....D...... 908 687-4100
Union **(G-11025)**

Picut Industries Inc ....D...... 908 754-1333
Warren **(G-11425)**

TRAVEL AGENCIES

Northstar Travel Media LLC.................C...... 201 902-2000
Secaucus **(G-9794)**

TRAYS: Plastic

Bel-Art Products Inc ....E...... 973 694-0500
Wayne **(G-11477)**

Sabert Corporation ....C...... 800 722-3781
Sayreville **(G-9722)**

Sabert Corporation ....E...... 732 721-5544
Sayreville **(G-9723)**

TRIM: Window, Wood

Trim and Tassels LLC ....G...... 973 808-1566
Fairfield **(G-3333)**

TROPHIES, NEC

AMG International Inc..........................E...... 201 475-4800
Parsippany **(G-7880)**

Freeman Products Inc ....F...... 201 475-4800
Parsippany **(G-7951)**

Trophy King Inc ....G...... 201 836-1482
Teaneck **(G-10653)**

TROPHIES, PLATED, ALL METALS

III Eagle Enterprises Ltd ....E...... 973 237-1111
Ringwood **(G-9346)**

Picture It Inc ....G...... 732 819-0420
Edison **(G-2589)**

TROPHIES: Metal, Exc Silver

All State Medal Co Inc ....G...... 973 458-1458
Lodi **(G-5552)**

Awards Trophy Company......................G...... 908 687-5775
Hillside **(G-4378)**

NJ Logo Wear LLC ....G...... 609 597-9400
Manahawkin **(G-5794)**

TROPHY & PLAQUE STORES

All State Medal Co Inc ....G...... 973 458-1458
Lodi **(G-5552)**

Armin Kososki....................................G...... 908 689-0411
Washington **(G-11439)**

Blue Ribbon Awards Inc ....G...... 732 560-0046
Somerset **(G-9963)**

Colorcraft Sign Co ....F...... 609 386-1115
Beverly **(G-449)**

Crown Trophy......................................G...... 973 808-8400
Pine Brook **(G-8595)**

D & N Sporting Goods Inc ....F...... 856 778-0055
Mount Laurel **(G-6751)**

Heros Salute Awards Co ....G...... 973 696-5085
Wayne **(G-11517)**

Innovative Awards Inc ....G...... 609 888-1400
Trenton **(G-10945)**

Picture It Inc ....G...... 732 819-0420
Edison **(G-2589)**

Rolferrys Specialties Inc ....G...... 856 456-2999
Brooklawn **(G-915)**

Stewart-Morris Inc ....G...... 973 822-2777
Madison **(G-5703)**

Trophy King Inc ....G...... 201 836-1482
Teaneck **(G-10653)**

TRUCK & BUS BODIES: Ambulance

Waldwick Volunteer ....E...... 201 445-8772
Waldwick **(G-11313)**

TRUCK & BUS BODIES: Automobile Wrecker Truck

Alexam Riverdale.................................G...... 973 831-0065
Riverdale **(G-9370)**

TRUCK & BUS BODIES: Bus Bodies

American Bus & Coach LLC ....E...... 732 283-1982
Iselin **(G-4591)**

TRUCK & BUS BODIES: Dump Truck

Peter Garafano & Son Inc ....E...... 973 278-0350
Paterson **(G-8282)**

TRUCK & BUS BODIES: Tank Truck

Vacuum Sales Inc ....E...... 856 627-7790
Laurel Springs **(G-5209)**

TRUCK & BUS BODIES: Truck Cabs, Motor Vehicles

Jid Transportation LLC.........................G...... 201 362-0841
West New York **(G-11744)**

TRUCK & BUS BODIES: Truck, Motor Vehicle

Columbia Industries Inc ....G...... 201 337-7332
Franklin Lakes **(G-3618)**

Custom Sales & Service Inc.................E...... 609 561-6900
Hammonton **(G-4133)**

Garden St Chasis Remanuf...................E...... 732 283-1910
Woodbridge **(G-12016)**

Transtar Truck Body & Wldg Co ....G...... 908 832-2688
Califon **(G-1036)**

TRUCK BODIES: Body Parts

Barrier Enterprises Inc ....G...... 973 770-3983
Andover **(G-44)**

Demountable Concepts Inc...................E...... 856 863-3081
Glassboro **(G-3809)**

Summit Truck Body Inc ....E...... 908 277-4342
Summit **(G-10551)**

Universal Parts ....G...... 908 601-6558
Linden **(G-5439)**

TRUCK BODY SHOP

Cliffside Body Corporation ....E...... 201 945-3970
Fairview **(G-3358)**

Transtar Truck Body & Wldg Co ....G...... 908 832-2688
Califon **(G-1036)**

Trucktech Parts & Services...................G...... 973 799-0500
Newark **(G-7303)**

TRUCK DRIVER SVCS

Jid Transportation LLC.........................G...... 201 362-0841
West New York **(G-11744)**

TRUCK GENERAL REPAIR SVC

Chizzys Service Center ....G...... 201 641-7222
Little Ferry **(G-5476)**

Fleetsource LLC ....E...... 732 566-4970
Dayton **(G-1961)**

R & H Spring & Truck Repair ....F...... 732 681-9000
Wall Township **(G-11362)**

Ram Hydraulics Inc.............................G...... 732 237-0904
Shrewsbury **(G-9900)**

Summit Truck Body Inc ....E...... 908 277-4342
Summit **(G-10551)**

TRUCK PAINTING & LETTERING SVCS

Dux Paint LLC ....F...... 973 473-2376
Lodi **(G-5560)**

Essex Morris Sign Co ....G...... 973 386-1755
Whippany **(G-11890)**

Rich Designs ....G...... 908 369-5035
Hillsborough **(G-4352)**

Sign Shoppe Inc ....G...... 856 384-2937
Woodbury **(G-12037)**

Sign Up Inc ....G...... 201 902-8640
Secaucus **(G-9814)**

TRUCK PARTS & ACCESSORIES: Wholesalers

Automann Inc ....D...... 201 529-4996
Somerset **(G-9961)**

Cliffside Body Corporation ....E...... 201 945-3970
Fairview **(G-3358)**

Suburban Auto Seat Co Inc ....F...... 973 778-9227
Lodi **(G-5577)**

Transaxle LLC ....C...... 856 665-4445
Cinnaminson **(G-1492)**

TRUCKING & HAULING SVCS: Building Materials

Concrete On Demand Inc ....F...... 201 337-0005
Oakland **(G-7620)**

TRUCKING & HAULING SVCS: Contract Basis

Penske Truck Leasing Co LP ....E...... 973 575-0169
Parsippany **(G-7987)**

Wakefern Food Corp............................B...... 732 819-0140
Edison **(G-2645)**

Wakefern Food Corp............................B...... 908 527-3300
Keasbey **(G-4916)**

TRUCKING & HAULING SVCS: Haulage & Cartage, Light, Local

Jlb Hauling Ltd Liability Co...................G...... 856 514-2771
Pennsville **(G-8500)**

TRUCKING & HAULING SVCS: Hazardous Waste

Safety-Kleen Systems Inc ....F...... 609 859-2049
Southampton **(G-10371)**

TRUCKING & HAULING SVCS: Machinery, Heavy

Lynn Amiee Inc ....E...... 201 840-6766
Ridgefield **(G-9274)**

TRUCKING & HAULING SVCS: Mail Carriers, Contract

Frontend Graphics Inc..........................G...... 856 547-1600
Cherry Hill **(G-1364)**

TRUCKING & HAULING SVCS: Petroleum, Local

Prospect Transportation Inc ....D...... 201 933-9999
Carlstadt **(G-1209)**

TRUCKING, AUTOMOBILE CARRIER

Chariot Courier & Trans Svcs...............F...... 888 532-9125
Sayreville **(G-9704)**

TRUCKING, DUMP

Cedar Hill Landscaping........................E...... 732 469-1400
Somerset **(G-9974)**

J G Carpenter Contractor ....G...... 732 271-8991
Middlesex **(G-6122)**

J Spinelli & Sons Inc............................E...... 856 691-3133
Elmer **(G-2799)**

TRUCKING, REFRIGERATED: Long-Distance

Power Pool Plus Inc.............................G...... 908 454-1124
Alpha **(G-40)**

TRUCKING: Except Local

Barrett Industries Corporation ....E...... 973 533-1001
Morristown **(G-6646)**

Barrett Paving Materials Inc..................E...... 973 533-1001
Roseland **(G-9535)**

Kramme Consolidated Inc.....................G...... 856 358-8151
Monroeville **(G-6352)**

TRUCKING: Local, With Storage

Bouras Industries Inc ....A 908 918-9400
　Summit (G-10527)

TRUCKING: Local, Without Storage

Bouras Industries Inc ....A 908 918-9400
　Summit (G-10527)
D Depasquale Paving LLC ....G 301 674-9775
　Jackson (G-4648)
Fence America New Jersey Inc ....G 973 472-5121
　Hackensack (G-3912)
L & S Contracting Inc ....G 609 397-1281
　Hopewell (G-4527)
Mondelez Global LLC ....A 201 794-4080
　Fair Lawn (G-3112)
Salomone Redi-Mix LLC ....E 973 305-0022
　Wayne (G-11552)
Select Enterprises Inc ....G 732 287-8622
　Edison (G-2605)
Tonys Auto Entp Ltd Lblty Co ....G 203 223-5776
　Edison (G-2633)

TRUCKS & TRACTORS: Industrial

Morse Metal Products Co Inc ....G 732 422-3676
　Princeton (G-8981)
Palfinger North America ....D 609 588-5400
　Trenton (G-10971)
Permadur Industries Inc ....D 908 359-9767
　Hillsborough (G-4344)
Saturn Overhead Equipment LLC ....F 732 560-7210
　Somerset (G-10071)
Trucktech Parts & Services ....G 973 799-0500
　Newark (G-7303)
Vanco USA LLC (de) ....C 609 499-4141
　Bordentown (G-599)

TRUCKS, INDL: Wholesalers

Excalibur Miretti Group LLC ....F 973 808-8399
　Fairfield (G-3195)

TRUCKS: Forklift

Excalibur Miretti Group LLC ....F 973 808-8399
　Fairfield (G-3195)
Hilman Incorporated ....D 732 462-6277
　Marlboro (G-5900)
Prestige Forklift Maint Svc ....G 732 297-1001
　New Brunswick (G-6960)
Rentalift Inc ....F 973 684-6111
　Paterson (G-8286)

TRUCKS: Indl

Caravan Inc ....F 732 590-0210
　Avenel (G-124)
Global Express Freight Inc ....G 201 376-6613
　Bergenfield (G-375)
Showtime Express ....G 732 238-2701
　East Brunswick (G-2176)

TRUSSES & FRAMING: Prefabricated Metal

Marino Building Systems Corp ....C 732 968-0555
　South Plainfield (G-10298)

TRUSSES: Wood, Floor

Atlantic Exterior Wall Systems ....D 973 646-8200
　Wayne (G-11472)

TRUSSES: Wood, Roof

Thomas Smock Woodworking ....G 732 542-9167
　Eatontown (G-2426)
Truss Engineering ....G 201 871-4800
　Englewood (G-2948)
Woodbury Roof Truss Inc ....D 856 845-3848
　Woodbury Heights (G-12044)

TUB CONTAINERS: Plastic

Chefler Foods LLC ....F 201 596-3710
　Saddle Brook (G-9645)

TUBE & TUBING FABRICATORS

Century Tube Corp ....E 908 534-2001
　Somerville (G-10105)
G & J Steel & Tubing Inc ....D 908 526-4445
　Hillsborough (G-4318)

Jettron Products Inc ....E 973 887-0571
　East Hanover (G-2220)
M P Tube Works Inc ....G 908 317-2500
　Mountainside (G-6848)
Samstubend Inc ....F 973 278-2555
　Paterson (G-8293)

TUBES: Electron, NEC

Troy-Onic Inc ....E 973 584-6830
　Kenvil (G-4996)

TUBES: Photomultiplier

Hamamatsu Corporation ....D 908 231-0960
　Bridgewater (G-828)

TUBES: Steel & Iron

Century Tube Corp ....E 908 534-2001
　Somerville (G-10105)

TUBING, COLD-DRAWN: Mech Or Hypodermic Sizes, Stainless

Rathgibson North Branch LLC ....C 908 253-3260
　Branchburg (G-675)

TUBING: Copper

Handytube Corporation ....E 732 469-7420
　Middlesex (G-6120)
Industrial Tube Corporation ....E 908 369-3737
　Hillsborough (G-4328)

TUBING: Flexible, Metallic

Avony Enterprises Inc ....E 212 242-8144
　Trenton (G-10899)
Marlo Manufacturing Co Inc ....E 973 423-0226
　Boonton (G-560)
Testrite Instrument Co Inc ....C 201 543-0240
　Hackensack (G-3982)

TUBING: Glass

Betco Glass Inc ....G 856 327-4301
　Millville (G-6235)

TUBING: Plastic

Alpha Wire Corporation ....C 908 925-8000
　Elizabeth (G-2709)
Ber Plastics Inc ....E 973 839-2100
　Riverdale (G-9371)
Cobon Plastics Corp ....F 973 344-6330
　Newark (G-7085)
Illinois Tool Works Inc ....D 732 968-5300
　Parsippany (G-7960)
K Jabat Inc ....F 732 469-8177
　Green Brook (G-3864)
Plastic Specialties & Tech Inc ....C 201 941-2900
　Ridgefield (G-9284)
Pure Tech International Inc ....G 908 722-4800
　Branchburg (G-674)
Resdel Corporation ....E 609 886-1111
　Rio Grande (G-9357)
Tpi Partners Inc ....G 908 561-3000
　Stirling (G-10498)
X-L Plastics Inc ....C 973 777-9400
　Clifton (G-1741)
Zeus Industrial Products Inc ....C 908 292-6500
　Branchburg (G-698)

TUBING: Seamless

Sandvik Inc ....C 201 794-5000
　Fair Lawn (G-3120)

TUNGSTEN MILL PRDTS

Union City Filament Corp ....E 201 945-3366
　Ridgefield (G-9294)

TURBINES & TURBINE GENERATOR SET UNITS, COMPLETE

Hydro-Mechanical Systems Inc ....F 856 848-8888
　Westville (G-11816)

TURBINES & TURBINE GENERATOR SET UNITS: Gas, Complete

Solar Turbines Incorporated ....F 201 825-8200
　Parsippany (G-8017)

TURBINES & TURBINE GENERATOR SETS

Boc Group Inc ....A 908 665-2400
　New Providence (G-6995)
I4 Sustainability LLC ....G 732 618-3310
　Springfield (G-10445)
Linde North America Inc ....D 908 464-8100
　New Providence (G-7007)
Lummus Overseas Corporation ....E 973 893-3000
　Bloomfield (G-508)
Messer LLC ....G 973 579-2065
　Sparta (G-10398)
Messer North America Inc ....B 908 464-8100
　Bridgewater (G-851)
Polaris America Ltd Lblty Co ....E 614 540-1710
　Lakewood (G-5148)

TURBINES: Hydraulic, Complete

Micheller & Son Hydraulics Inc ....F 908 687-1545
　Roselle (G-9566)

TURBINES: Steam

Babcock & Wilcox Company ....G 609 261-2424
　Cinnaminson (G-1443)
Babcock & Wilcox Powr Generatn ....F 973 227-7008
　Fairfield (G-3150)

TURKEY PROCESSING & SLAUGHTERING

Hinck Turkey Farm Inc ....G 732 681-0508
　Neptune (G-6884)

TURNKEY VENDORS: Computer Systems

Maingear Inc ....E 888 624-6432
　Kenilworth (G-4955)

TWINE

Seaboard Paper and Twine LLC ....E 973 413-8100
　Paterson (G-8296)

TWINE PRDTS

American Power Cord Corp ....G 973 574-8301
　Somerset (G-9952)

TYPESETTING SVC

Action Copy Centers Inc ....G 973 744-5520
　Montclair (G-6356)
American Graphic Systems Inc ....G 201 796-0666
　Fair Lawn (G-3084)
Arch Crown Inc ....E 973 731-6300
　Hillside (G-4375)
Ayr Composition Inc ....G 908 241-8118
　Roselle Park (G-9578)
Aztec Graphics Inc ....F 609 587-1000
　Trenton (G-10900)
Bar Lan Inc ....G 856 596-2330
　Brigantine (G-911)
Bartlett Printing & Graphic ....G 609 386-1525
　Burlington (G-952)
Bowmar Enterprises Inc ....G 908 277-3000
　New Providence (G-6996)
Budget Print Center ....G 973 743-0073
　Bloomfield (G-492)
Commercial Composition & Prtg ....G 856 662-0557
　Pennsauken (G-8407)
Comptime Inc ....G 201 760-2400
　Ramsey (G-9143)
Consumer Graphics Inc ....G 732 469-4699
　Somerset (G-9977)
Copy-Rite Printing ....G 609 597-9182
　Manahawkin (G-5792)
Cordes Printing Inc ....G 201 652-7272
　Wyckoff (G-12107)
Cornerstone Prints Imaging LLC ....G 908 782-7966
　Flemington (G-3434)
Craftsmen Photo Lithographers ....E 973 316-5791
　East Hanover (G-2204)
Creative Color Lithographers ....F 908 789-2255
　Garwood (G-3783)
D A K Office Services Inc ....G 609 586-8222
　Trenton (G-10929)

PRODUCT

Data Communique Inc ....E 201 508-6000
  Ridgefield Park **(G-9302)**
Devece & Shaffer Inc ....G 856 829-7282
  Palmyra **(G-7782)**
Downtown Printing Center Inc.............F 732 246-7990
  New Brunswick **(G-6920)**
Earth Color New York Inc ....E 973 884-1300
  Parsippany **(G-7925)**
Fedex Office & Print Svcs Inc ....F 732 249-9222
  New Brunswick **(G-6926)**
Fedex Office & Print Svcs Inc ....F 856 273-5959
  Mount Laurel **(G-6760)**
Fedex Office & Print Svcs Inc ....G 973 376-3966
  Springfield **(G-10443)**
Fedex Office & Print Svcs Inc ....E 856 427-0099
  Cherry Hill **(G-1361)**
Gangi Graphics Inc ....G 732 840-8680
  Brick **(G-719)**
Hub Print & Copy Center LLC ....G 201 585-7887
  Fort Lee **(G-3563)**
Inserts East Incorporated ....C 856 663-8181
  Pennsauken **(G-8437)**
Instant Printing of Dover Inc ....G 973 366-6855
  Dover **(G-2090)**
J K Design Inc ....E 908 428-4700
  Hillsborough **(G-4334)**
Jem Printing Inc ....G 908 782-9986
  Flemington **(G-3450)**
Jmp Press Inc ....G 201 444-0236
  Ho Ho Kus **(G-4441)**
John S Swift Company Inc ....G 201 935-2002
  Teterboro **(G-10682)**
Johnston Letter Co Inc ....G 973 482-7535
  Flanders **(G-3414)**
Kirms Printing Co Inc ....E 732 774-8000
  Neptune **(G-6886)**
Laserwave Graphics Inc ....F 732 745-7764
  New Brunswick **(G-6943)**
Lunet Inc ....G 201 261-3883
  Paramus **(G-7816)**
Marks Management Systems Inc.........G 856 866-0588
  Maple Shade **(G-5867)**
McKella 2-8-0 Inc ....D 856 813-1153
  Pennsauken **(G-8455)**
Metro Publishing Group Inc ....F 201 385-2000
  New Milford **(G-6990)**
Morgan Printing Service Inc ....F 732 721-2959
  South Amboy **(G-10138)**
Morris Plains Pip Inc ....G 973 533-9330
  Livingston **(G-5528)**
Network Typesetting Inc ....G 732 819-0949
  Piscataway **(G-8694)**
New Jersey Label LLC ....F 201 880-5102
  South Hackensack **(G-10175)**
Newtype Inc ....F 973 361-6000
  Randolph **(G-9192)**
Old Hights Print Shop Inc ....G 609 443-4700
  Jackson **(G-4661)**
OShea Services Inc ....G 201 343-8668
  Hackensack **(G-3958)**
Otis Graphics Inc ....F 201 438-7120
  Lyndhurst **(G-5671)**
Pad and Publ Assembly Corp ....E 856 424-0158
  Cherry Hill **(G-1404)**
Painton Studios Inc ....G 732 302-0200
  Green Brook **(G-3865)**
Palm Press Inc ....G 201 767-6504
  Northvale **(G-7543)**
Patel Printing Plus Corp ....F 908 964-6422
  Union **(G-11082)**
Permagraphics Inc ....F 201 814-1200
  Moonachie **(G-6483)**
Philip Holzer and Assoc LLC ....E 212 691-9500
  Carlstadt **(G-1201)**
Printing Delite Inc ....G 973 676-3033
  East Orange **(G-2260)**
Puent-Romer Communications Inc ....G 973 509-7591
  Montclair **(G-6386)**
Redmond Bcms Inc ....D 973 664-2000
  Denville **(G-2051)**
Roan Printing Inc ....F 908 526-5990
  Somerville **(G-10124)**
Sandoval Graphics & Printing ....G 856 435-7320
  Somerdale **(G-9934)**
Scarlet Printing ....G 732 560-1415
  Middlesex **(G-6143)**
Scott Graphics Printing Co Inc ....G 201 262-0473
  New Milford **(G-6992)**
Sheroy Printing Inc ....F 973 242-4040
  Newark **(G-7271)**

Sign On Inc ....G 201 384-7714
  Bloomingdale **(G-530)**
Sonata Graphics Inc ....G 201 866-0186
  Secaucus **(G-9816)**
Staines Inc ....F 856 784-2718
  Somerdale **(G-9935)**
Standard Prtg & Mail Svcs Inc ....F 973 790-3333
  Fairfield **(G-3314)**
Star Promotions Inc ....F 732 356-5959
  Bound Brook **(G-607)**
Steb Inc ....G 973 584-0990
  Ledgewood **(G-5281)**
Tangent Graphics Inc ....G 201 488-2840
  Englewood **(G-2946)**
Tanter Inc ....G 732 382-3555
  Clark **(G-1516)**
Techsetters Inc ....E 856 240-7905
  Collingswood **(G-1772)**
Tedco Inc ....G 609 883-0799
  Ewing **(G-3069)**
Thewal Inc ....F 973 635-1880
  Chatham **(G-1330)**
Trade Thermographers Inc ....F 201 489-2060
  Rochelle Park **(G-9432)**
Typeline ....F 201 251-2201
  Wyckoff **(G-12123)**
Typen Graphics Inc ....G 973 838-6544
  Kinnelon **(G-5023)**
Verni Vito ....G 732 449-1760
  Wall Township **(G-11377)**
Wilker Graphics LLC ....G 201 447-4800
  Midland Park **(G-6190)**
Zwier Corp ....G 973 748-4009
  Bloomfield **(G-524)**

TYPESETTING SVC: Computer

B & B Press Inc ....G 908 840-4093
  Lebanon **(G-5253)**
Nassau Communications Inc ....F 609 208-9099
  Lawrence Township **(G-5218)**

TYPESETTING SVC: Hand Composition

A M Graphics Inc ....G 201 767-5320
  Harrington Park **(G-4161)**
Word Center Printing ....G 609 586-5825
  Trenton **(G-11010)**

TYPEWRITERS & PARTS

Swintec Corp ....F 201 935-0115
  Moonachie **(G-6493)**

TYPOGRAPHY

Newark Trade Typographers ....F 973 674-3727
  Orange **(G-7757)**

ULTRASONIC EQPT: Cleaning, Exc Med & Dental

Crest Group Inc ....F 609 883-4000
  Trenton **(G-10926)**
Crestek Inc ....E 609 883-4000
  Ewing **(G-3024)**
L & R Manufacturing Co Inc ....C 201 991-5330
  Kearny **(G-4878)**
L & R Manufacturing Co Inc ....D 201 991-5330
  Kearny **(G-4877)**
Zenith Mfg & Chemical Corp ....F 201 767-1332
  Norwood **(G-7577)**

ULTRASONIC EQPT: Dental

L & R Manufacturing Co Inc ....D 201 991-5330
  Kearny **(G-4877)**
South East Instruments LLC ....G 201 569-0050
  Englewood **(G-2943)**

UMBRELLAS & CANES

Galleria Enterprises Inc ....G 646 416-6683
  Fairfield **(G-3211)**
Peerless Umbrella Co Inc ....C 973 578-4900
  Newark **(G-7225)**

UMBRELLAS: Garden Or Wagon

Rainmen USA Incorporated ....D 201 784-3244
  Norwood **(G-7573)**
S Frankford & Sons Inc ....F 856 222-4134
  Mount Laurel **(G-6801)**

UNDERCOATINGS: Paint

SA Bendheim Ltd ....E 973 471-1733
  Wayne **(G-11550)**

UNDERGROUND GOLD MINING

Valdez Creek Min Ltd Lblty Co ....G 732 704-1427
  Red Bank **(G-9248)**

UNIFORM STORES

Somes Uniforms Inc ....F 201 843-1199
  Hackensack **(G-3975)**

UNSUPPORTED PLASTICS: Floor Or Wall Covering

Congoleum Corporation ....E 609 584-3000
  Trenton **(G-10921)**
Congoleum Corporation ....B 609 584-3000
  Trenton **(G-10923)**
Prestige Associates Inc ....E 609 393-1509
  Trenton **(G-10982)**
Zack Painting Co Inc ....E 732 738-7900
  Fords **(G-3534)**

UPHOLSTERY WORK SVCS

Kushner Draperies Mfg LLC ....E 856 317-9696
  Pennsauken **(G-8449)**

USED BOOK STORES

Chatham Bookseller Inc ....G 973 822-1361
  Madison **(G-5690)**

USED CAR DEALERS

Herald News ....G 973 569-7000
  Woodland Park **(G-12081)**

USED MERCHANDISE STORES

Good As Gold Jewelers Inc ....G 732 286-1111
  Toms River **(G-10762)**

USED MERCHANDISE STORES: Building Materials

Delta Procurement Inc ....G 201 623-9353
  Carlstadt **(G-1149)**

USED MERCHANDISE STORES: Musical Instruments

W E Wamsley Restorations Inc ....G 856 795-4001
  Haddonfield **(G-4066)**

UTENSILS: Household, Cooking & Kitchen, Metal

Global Marketing Corp ....F 973 426-1088
  Randolph **(G-9181)**
Sowa Corp ....G 973 297-0008
  Newark **(G-7279)**

UTENSILS: Household, Cooking & Kitchen, Porcelain Enameled

Newell Brands Inc ....B 201 610-6600
  Hoboken **(G-4468)**

VACUUM CLEANER STORES

Hillsborough Vacuum LLC ....G 908 904-6600
  Hillsborough **(G-4324)**

VACUUM CLEANERS: Household

Hillsborough Vacuum LLC ....G 908 904-6600
  Hillsborough **(G-4324)**
Metropolitan Vacuum Clr Co Inc ....D 201 405-2225
  Oakland **(G-7636)**

VACUUM CLEANERS: Indl Type

Clayton Associates Inc ....F 732 363-2100
  Lakewood **(G-5071)**
Dcm Clean Air Products Inc ....G 732 363-2100
  Lakewood **(G-5082)**
Metropolitan Vacuum Clr Co Inc ....D 201 405-2225
  Oakland **(G-7636)**

2019 Harris New jersey
Manufacturers Directory
(G-0000) Company's Geographic Section entry number

Vac-U-Max..F......973 759-4600
Belleville (G-320)

VACUUM PUMPS & EQPT: Laboratory

Denton Vacuum LLC.......................G......856 439-9100
Moorestown (G-6518)
Emse Corp......................................F......973 227-9221
Fairfield (G-3191)
Knf Neuberger Inc........................D......609 890-8889
Trenton (G-10950)

VACUUM SYSTEMS: Air Extraction, Indl

Croll-Reynolds Co Inc ....E......908 232-4200
Parsippany (G-7909)
Vairtec Corporation.......................G......201 445-6965
Midland Park (G-6189)

VALUE-ADDED RESELLERS: Computer Systems

Computer Sources.........................G......201 791-9443
Elmwood Park (G-2817)
Gerbino Computer Systems Inc ....G......201 342-8240
Hackensack (G-3922)

VALVE REPAIR SVCS, INDL

Emerson Automation Solutions ....F......856 542-5252
Bridgeport (G-736)

VALVES

Fujikin of America Inc....................G......201 641-1119
Hasbrouck Heights (G-4182)
Rotarex Inc North America..............D......724 696-3345
Hackettstown (G-4033)
Straval Machine Co Inc...................E......973 340-9955
Elmwood Park (G-2857)
Triflow Corporation.......................G......856 768-7159
West Berlin (G-11631)

VALVES & PARTS: Gas, Indl

Barworth Inc.................................G......973 376-4883
Springfield (G-10430)
Cavagna North America Inc ....E......732 469-2100
Somerset (G-9973)

VALVES & PIPE FITTINGS

Ammark Corporation......................G......973 616-2555
Pompton Plains (G-8857)
Ceodeux Incorporated....................E......724 696-4340
Hackettstown (G-4001)
DAngelo Metal Products Inc ....F......908 862-8220
Linden (G-5341)
Durst Corporation Inc....................E......800 852-3906
Cranford (G-1907)
Everlasting Valve Company Inc ....E......908 769-0700
South Plainfield (G-10254)
Fluidyne Corp...............................E......856 663-1818
Pennsauken (G-8420)
Gadren Machine Co Inc ....F......856 456-4329
Collingswood (G-1767)
Gasflo Products Inc.......................E......973 276-9011
Fairfield (G-3213)
Gorton Heating Corp......................G......908 276-1323
Cranford (G-1912)
Hayward Industries Inc...................B......908 351-5400
Elizabeth (G-2746)
Imperial Weld Ring Corp Inc ....E......908 354-0011
Elizabeth (G-2749)
Knickerbocker Machine Shop Inc .....D......973 256-1616
Totowa (G-10834)
Kraissl Company Inc......................E......201 342-0008
Hackensack (G-3937)
Lindstrom & King Co Inc.................G......973 279-2511
Paterson (G-8241)
Marotta Controls Inc.....................C......973 334-7800
Montville (G-6444)
Newco Valves LLC.........................E......732 257-0300
East Brunswick (G-2159)
Nippon Benkan Kagyo.....................E......732 435-0777
New Brunswick (G-6954)
RGI Inc..F......973 697-2624
Newfoundland (G-7332)
Scientific Machine and Sup Co.........E......732 356-1553
Middlesex (G-6145)
Sims Pump Valve Company Inc..........E......201 792-0600
Hoboken (G-4480)

Symcon Inc...................................G......973 728-8661
West Milford (G-11732)
Vac-U-Max....................................E......973 759-4600
Belleville (G-319)
Wire Cloth Manufacturers Inc ....E......973 328-1000
Mine Hill (G-6275)
World Wide Metric Inc ....F......732 247-2300
Branchburg (G-696)

VALVES & REGULATORS: Pressure, Indl

Chemiquip Products Co Inc..............G......201 868-4445
Linden (G-5333)
Hayward Industrial Products ....C......908 351-5400
Elizabeth (G-2745)
Micromat Co..................................G......201 529-3738
Ringwood (G-9349)

VALVES Solenoid

Automatic Switch Company..............A......973 966-2000
Florham Park (G-3485)
Automatic Switch Company..............A......209 941-4111
Florham Park (G-3486)
Automatic Switch Company..............F......732 596-1731
Woodbridge (G-12014)
Bio-Chem Fluidics Inc ....D......973 263-3001
Boonton (G-544)
Magnatrol Valve Corporation ....F......856 829-4580
Roebling (G-9526)
Neptune Research & Development ......E......973 808-8811
West Caldwell (G-11667)

VALVES: Aerosol, Metal

D K Trading Inc..............................G......856 225-1130
Camden (G-1057)

VALVES: Aircraft, Control, Hydraulic & Pneumatic

A V Hydraulics Ltd Lblty Co ....G......973 621-6800
Newark (G-7030)

VALVES: Aircraft, Hydraulic

Air & Hydraulic Power Inc ....G......201 447-1589
Wyckoff (G-12101)

VALVES: Control, Automatic

Heat-Timer Corporation...................E......973 575-4004
Fairfield (G-3224)

VALVES: Fire Hydrant

Firefighter One Ltd Lblty Co ....G......973 940-3061
Sparta (G-10387)

VALVES: Fluid Power, Control, Hydraulic & pneumatic

Hayward Industrial Products ....C......908 351-5400
Elizabeth (G-2745)
Versa Products Company Inc ....C......201 291-0379
Paramus (G-7843)
Westlock Controls Corporation ....C......201 794-7650
Saddle Brook (G-9687)

VALVES: Indl

Admiral Technology LLC..................E......973 698-5920
Rockaway (G-9437)
Armadillo Automation Inc ....E......856 829-2888
Cinnaminson (G-1442)
Asco LP.......................................B......800 972-2726
Florham Park (G-3481)
Asco Investment Corp....................C......973 966-2000
Florham Park (G-3482)
Carpathian Industries LLC ....F......201 386-5356
Hoboken (G-4446)
Chase Machine Co.........................F......201 438-2214
Lyndhurst (G-5648)
Emerson Automation Solutions ....F......856 542-5252
Bridgeport (G-736)
Farrell Eqp & Contrls Inc.................F......732 770-4142
Roselle (G-9557)
Fisher Service Co...........................G......609 386-5000
Burlington (G-968)
Flodyne Controls Inc......................E......908 464-6200
New Providence (G-6999)
Gadren Machine Co Inc ....F......856 456-4329
Collingswood (G-1767)

Gasflo Products Inc.......................E......973 276-9011
Fairfield (G-3213)
Gemco Valve Co LLC......................E......732 752-7900
Middlesex (G-6118)
Industrial Habonim Valves & AC........F......201 820-3184
Wayne (G-11519)
Instrment Vlve Svcs Burlington..........G......609 386-5000
Burlington (G-973)
Plast-O-Matic Valves Inc.................D......973 256-3000
Cedar Grove (G-1287)
Triflow Corporation.......................G......856 768-7159
West Berlin (G-11631)
Tyco International MGT Co LLC ....E......609 720-4200
Princeton (G-9038)

VALVES: Plumbing & Heating

Everflow Supplies Inc ....E......908 436-1100
Carteret (G-1252)
Primak Plumbing & Heating Inc.........G......732 270-6282
Toms River (G-10785)
Wm Steinen Mfg Co ....D......973 887-6400
Parsippany (G-8042)

VALVES: Regulating & Control, Automatic

Simple Home Automation Inc ....C......877 405-2397
Edison (G-2610)

VALVES: Regulating, Process Control

Wm Steinen Mfg Co ....D......973 887-6400
Parsippany (G-8042)

VALVES: Water Works

Purity Labs ....G......201 372-0236
East Rutherford (G-2313)

VANILLIN: Synthetic

Elan Food Laboratories Inc..............F......973 344-8014
Newark (G-7111)

VARNISHES, NEC

Benjamin Moore & Co.....................C......973 344-1200
Newark (G-7065)
Royce Associates A Ltd Partnr..........D......201 438-5200
East Rutherford (G-2315)
Superior Printing Ink Co Inc ....C......201 478-5600
Teterboro (G-10691)

VARNISHING SVC: Metal Prdts

Superior Powder Coating Inc.............C......908 351-8707
Elizabeth (G-2780)

VAULTS & SAFES WHOLESALERS

Bar-Maid Corporation.....................C......973 478-7070
Garfield (G-3731)

VEGETABLE OILS: Medicinal Grade, Refined Or Concentrated

Chefler Foods LLC..........................F......201 596-3710
Saddle Brook (G-9645)

VEGETABLES, FROZEN: Wholesaler

CHR International Inc ....G......201 262-8186
Oradell (G-7741)

VEHICLES: All Terrain

Savino Del Bene USA Inc ....D......347 960-5568
Avenel (G-145)

VENDING MACHINES & PARTS

Universal Vending MGT LLC..............F......908 233-4373
Westfield (G-11804)

VENETIAN BLIND REPAIR SHOP

Spotless Venetian Blind Servic ....G......732 548-1711
Edison (G-2618)

VENETIAN BLINDS & SHADES

Spotless Venetian Blind Servic ....G......732 548-1711
Edison (G-2618)

P
R
O
D
U
C
T

VENTILATING EQPT: Metal

Atco Rubber Products Inc...............E 856 794-3393
Vineland **(G-11188)**
Ductworks Inc ....F 908 754-8190
Plainfield **(G-8762)**
E P Homiek Shtmtl Sups Inc...........E 732 364-7644
Lakewood **(G-5087)**
Hays Sheet Metal Inc ....E 856 662-7722
Pennsauken **(G-8430)**
Professional Envmtl Systems...........E 201 991-3000
Kearny **(G-4895)**
Totowa Metal Fabricators Inc..........F 973 423-1943
North Haledon **(G-7501)**

VENTILATING EQPT: Sheet Metal

Bonland Industries Inc ....D 973 694-3211
Wayne **(G-11481)**

VERIFIERS: Punch Card

Symbology Enterprises Inc.............F 908 725-1699
Somerville **(G-10125)**

VESSELS: Process, Indl, Metal Plate

Dusenbery Engineering Co Inc.........G 973 539-2200
Morristown **(G-6661)**

VETERINARY PHARMACEUTICAL PREPARATIONS

Eco LLC ....G 609 683-9030
Princeton **(G-8937)**
Iron4u Inc ....G 609 514-5163
Princeton **(G-8964)**
Nutri-Pet Research Inc ....G 732 786-8822
Manalapan **(G-5820)**
Pfizer Inc ....C 973 993-0977
Morris Plains **(G-6623)**
Phibro Animal Health Corp ....D 201 329-7300
Teaneck **(G-10643)**

VETERINARY PRDTS: Instruments & Apparatus

Zimmer Trabecular Met Tech Inc ....C 973 576-0032
Parsippany **(G-8044)**

VIALS: Glass

Nipro Glass Americas Corp ....F 856 825-1400
Millville **(G-6261)**
Nipro Phrmpckging Amricas Corp ....C 856 825-1400
Millville **(G-6262)**
Worldwide Glass Resources Inc ....E 856 205-1508
Vineland **(G-11278)**

VIDEO & AUDIO EQPT, WHOLESALE

Empirical Labs Inc ....F 973 541-9447
Lake Hiawatha **(G-5034)**
Mardee Company Inc ....G 908 753-4343
South Plainfield **(G-10297)**
Sound Professionals Inc ....G 609 267-4400
Hainesport **(G-4078)**

VIDEO EQPT

Kultur International Films Ltd ....E 732 229-2343
Red Bank **(G-9233)**
Murray Electronics Inc ....G 201 405-1158
Oakland **(G-7637)**
Peter-Lisand Machine Corp ....G 201 943-5600
New Milford **(G-6991)**

VIDEO REPAIR SVCS

Murray Electronics Inc ....G 201 405-1158
Oakland **(G-7637)**

VIDEO TAPE PRODUCTION SVCS

Kultur International Films Ltd ....E 732 229-2343
Red Bank **(G-9233)**

VISUAL COMMUNICATIONS SYSTEMS

Aurora Multimedia Corporation.............E 732 591-5800
Morganville **(G-6583)**
Caregility Corporation ....G 732 413-6000
Eatontown **(G-2383)**

Hope Center..................................F 201 798-1234
Jersey City **(G-4748)**
Kinly Inc ....E 973 585-3000
Cedar Knolls **(G-1307)**
Pixell Creative Group LLC ....G 609 410-3024
Burlington **(G-982)**
Sightlogix Inc ....E 609 951-0008
Princeton **(G-9022)**
York Telecom Corporation ....D 732 413-6000
Eatontown **(G-2430)**
Ytc Holdings Inc..............................G 732 413-6000
Eatontown **(G-2431)**

VISUAL EFFECTS PRODUCTION SVCS

Beterrific Corp ....G 201 735-7711
Fort Lee **(G-3549)**

VITAMINS: Natural Or Synthetic, Uncompounded, Bulk

Ivc Industries Inc...........................B 732 308-3000
Freehold **(G-3671)**
Life Science Labs Mfg LLC ....F 732 367-9937
Lakewood **(G-5123)**
Mpt Delivery Systems Inc................D 973 279-4132
Paterson **(G-8263)**
Novel Ingrdent Inv Hldings Inc ....F 973 808-5900
East Hanover **(G-2232)**
Novel Ingredient Holdings Inc ....F 973 808-5900
East Hanover **(G-2233)**
Pacifichealth Laboratories Inc ....G 732 739-2900
Parsippany **(G-7982)**
Shanghai Freemen Americas LLC........E 732 981-1288
Edison **(G-2607)**
Sunflower Seed ....G 908 735-3822
Clinton **(G-1750)**
Vita-Pure Inc ....E 908 245-1212
Roselle **(G-9576)**
Vitamin Shoppe Industries Inc ....A 201 868-5959
Secaucus **(G-9826)**
Yinlink International Inc ....C 973 818-4664
Cranbury **(G-1894)**

VITAMINS: Pharmaceutical Preparations

Agilis Chemicals Inc ....F 973 910-2424
Short Hills **(G-9864)**
Alteon ....G 201 934-1624
Ramsey **(G-9136)**
Ans Nutrition Inc ....E 212 235-5205
Farmingdale **(G-3377)**
Archon Vitamin LLC ....D 732 537-1220
Edison **(G-2459)**
Archon Vitamin LLC ....G 973 371-1700
Edison **(G-2460)**
Bioactive Resources LLC.................F 908 561-3114
South Plainfield **(G-10226)**
DSM Sight & Life Inc ....G 973 257-8208
Parsippany **(G-7923)**
Genavite LLC ....F 201 343-3131
Hackensack **(G-3920)**
INB Manhattan Drug Company Inc........D 973 926-0816
Hillside **(G-4400)**
INB Manhattan Drug Company Inc........E 973 926-0816
Hillside **(G-4402)**
International Vitamin Corp ....C 973 371-4400
Irvington **(G-4575)**
Jamol Laboratories Inc....................G 201 262-6363
Emerson **(G-2865)**
Kwik Enterprises LLC......................G 732 663-1559
Oakhurst **(G-7610)**
Life Science Laboratories LLC ....G 732 367-1900
Lakewood **(G-5122)**
Life Scnce Labs Spplements LLC ....F 732 367-1749
Lakewood **(G-5124)**
Nutro Laboratories Inc ....C 908 755-7984
South Plainfield **(G-10309)**
Plantfusion ....G 732 537-1220
Edison **(G-2590)**
Rasi Laboratories Inc ....D 732 873-8500
Cranbury **(G-1878)**
Reliance Vitamin LLC......................C 732 537-1220
Edison **(G-2596)**
Soma Labs Inc ....F 732 271-3444
Middlesex **(G-6149)**
Unitao Nutraceuticals LLC ....G 973 983-1121
Rockaway **(G-9510)**
Vitaquest International LLC ....F 973 787-9900
Fairfield **(G-3345)**
Vitaquest International LLC ....F 973 575-9200
Fairfield **(G-3346)**

Vitaquest International LLC ....B 973 575-9200
West Caldwell **(G-11681)**

VOCATIONAL REHABILITATION AGENCY

Employment Horizons Inc.................B 973 538-8822
Cedar Knolls **(G-1304)**

WALL COVERINGS: Rubber

Fidelity Industries Inc.....................E 973 696-9120
Wayne **(G-11501)**
Fidelity Industries Inc.....................G 973 777-2592
Clifton **(G-1620)**

WALLBOARD: Gypsum

Baruffi Bros Inc ....F 856 692-6400
Vineland **(G-11191)**

WALLPAPER & WALL COVERINGS

Burlington Design Center Inc ....F 856 778-7772
Mount Laurel **(G-6745)**
Collins and Company LLC ....G 973 427-4068
Hawthorne **(G-4212)**

WALLPAPER: Embossed Plastic, Textile Backed

J Josephson Inc..............................C 201 440-7000
South Hackensack **(G-10163)**
J Josephson Inc..............................C 201 440-7000
South Hackensack **(G-10164)**
J Josephson Inc..............................C 201 426-2646
South Hackensack **(G-10165)**

WALLS: Curtain, Metal

Architectural Metal and Glass ....G 732 994-7575
Lakewood **(G-5054)**

WAREHOUSING & STORAGE FACILITIES, NEC

Bright Lights Usa Inc ....E 856 546-5656
Camden **(G-1042)**
Fujifilm North America Corp ....B 732 857-3000
Edison **(G-2516)**
Kuehne Chemical Company Inc ....E 973 589-0700
Kearny **(G-4876)**
Lockwood Boat Works Inc ....E 732 721-1605
South Amboy **(G-10136)**
Tech-Pak Inc ....F 201 935-3800
Wood Ridge **(G-12007)**

WAREHOUSING & STORAGE, REFRIGERATED: Cold Storage Or Refrig

United States Cold Storage Inc ....B 856 354-8181
Camden **(G-1089)**

WAREHOUSING & STORAGE: Fur

S & H R Inc.....................................G 908 925-3797
Linden **(G-5417)**

WAREHOUSING & STORAGE: General

Gordon Terminal Service Co PA........D 201 437-8300
Bayonne **(G-220)**
Mondelez Global LLC ....A 201 794-4080
Fair Lawn **(G-3112)**
Romark Logistics CES LLC ....E 908 789-2800
Westfield **(G-11802)**
S L Enterprises Inc ....G 908 272-8145
Ewing **(G-3064)**

WAREHOUSING & STORAGE: General

Alfred Dunner Inc............................D 212 944-6660
Parsippany **(G-7877)**
Alu Inc ....E 201 935-2213
Moonachie **(G-6453)**
Ansell Inc ....D 334 794-4231
Iselin **(G-4594)**
Cei Holdings Inc ....E 732 888-7788
Holmdel **(G-4496)**
Cosmetic Essence LLC ....C 732 888-7788
Holmdel **(G-4497)**
Grignard Company LLC ....E 732 340-1111
Rahway **(G-9098)**

Jan Packaging Inc..................D...... 973 361-7200
Dover (G-2091)

Mitzi Intl Handbag & ACC Ltd ....C..... 973 483-5015
Newark (G-7203)

T Wiker Enterprises Inc...............G...... 609 261-9494
Hainesport (G-4079)

Tatara Group Inc ....G...... 732 231-6031
Avenel (G-149)

Valley Die Cutting Inc ....G...... 973 731-8884
Randolph (G-9207)

Willings Nutraceutical Corp ....F...... 856 424-9088
Cherry Hill (G-1427)

WAREHOUSING & STORAGE: Household Goods

Vaswani Inc.........................F...... 877 376-4425
Edison (G-2638)

WAREHOUSING & STORAGE: Miniwarehouse

Bng Industries LLC..................F...... 862 229-2414
Harrison (G-4165)

WARFARE COUNTER-MEASURE EQPT

Dewey Electronics Corporation...........E...... 201 337-4700
Oakland (G-7625)

WARM AIR HEATING & AC EQPT & SPLYS, WHOLESALE Air Filters

Elaine Inc ....G...... 973 345-6200
Woodland Park (G-12076)

Filter Technologies Inc ....G...... 732 329-2500
Monmouth Junction (G-6291)

Momentum Usa Inc ....F...... 844 300-1553
Edison (G-2569)

WARM AIR HEATING & AC EQPT & SPLYS, WHOLESALE Furnaces

Pennington Furnace Supply Inc ....G...... 609 737-2500
Pennington (G-8371)

WARM AIR HEATING/AC EQPT/SPLYS, WHOL Dehumidifiers, Exc Port

Csonka Worldwide....................E...... 609 514-2766
Plainsboro (G-8783)

WARM AIR HEATING/AC EQPT/SPLYS, WHOL Warm Air Htg Eqpt/Splys

Industrial Combustion Assn ....F...... 732 271-0300
Somerset (G-10004)

WARP KNIT FABRIC FINISHING

Ques Aprv A R Knitwear Inc.............G...... 201 869-1333
North Bergen (G-7431)

WASHCLOTHS & BATH MITTS, FROM PURCHASED MATERIALS

Tatara Group Inc ....G...... 732 231-6031
Avenel (G-149)

WASHERS

Accurate Prscsion Fstener Corp ....E...... 201 567-9700
Englewood (G-2873)

WASHERS: Metal

H K Metal Craft Mfg Corp ....E...... 973 471-7770
Lodi (G-5563)

WASHERS: Rubber

Thomas A Caserta Inc ....F...... 609 586-2807
Robbinsville (G-9417)

WATCH & CLOCK STORES

Dksh Luxury & Lifestyle N Amer ....G...... 609 750-8800
Lawrence Township (G-5216)

Garrett Moore ....G...... 908 231-9231
Bridgewater (G-825)

WATCH REPAIR SVCS

Corbo Jewelers Inc ....F...... 973 777-1635
Clifton (G-1591)

Madhu B Goyal MD ....G...... 908 769-0307
South Plainfield (G-10296)

Movado Group Inc ....B...... 201 267-8000
Paramus (G-7822)

WATCHES

Acon Watch Crown Company...........F...... 973 546-8585
Garfield (G-3725)

Belair Time Corporation ....D...... 732 905-0100
Lakewood (G-5060)

Watchitude LLC ....G...... 732 745-2626
New Brunswick (G-6979)

WATER HEATERS

Triangle Tube/Phase III Co Inc ....D...... 856 228-9940
Paulsboro (G-8340)

WATER PURIFICATION EQPT: Household

Cantel Medical Corp ....G...... 973 890-7220
Little Falls (G-5454)

Glasco Uv LLC ....F...... 201 934-3348
Mahwah (G-5741)

Vivreau Advanced Water Systems ....F...... 212 502-3749
Fairfield (G-3347)

WATER PURIFICATION PRDTS: Chlorination Tablets & Kits

Foresight Group LLC ....F...... 888 992-8880
Parsippany (G-7949)

Isdin Corp ....E...... 862 242-8129
Morristown (G-6675)

Suez Treatment Solutions Inc...........D...... 201 676-2525
Leonia (G-5292)

WATER SOFTENER SVCS

NMP Water Systems LLC ....G...... 201 252-8333
Mahwah (G-5758)

South Jersey Water Cond Svc ....E...... 856 451-0620
Bridgeton (G-773)

WATER SPLY: Irrigation

Cutting Edge Grower Supply LLC ....G...... 732 905-9220
Howell (G-4536)

WATER SUPPLY

Middlesex Water Company ....C...... 732 579-0290
Edison (G-2566)

Nice Instrumentation ....F...... 732 851-4300
Manalapan (G-5818)

WATER TREATMENT EQPT: Indl

Chem-Aqua Inc ....F...... 972 438-0211
Monmouth Junction (G-6281)

CP Equipment Sales Co ....F...... 908 687-9621
Union (G-11039)

Custom Blends Inc ....E...... 215 934-7080
Ewing (G-3025)

Delta Cooling Towers Inc ....E...... 973 586-2201
Flanders (G-3405)

Dynatec Systems Inc ....F...... 609 387-0330
Burlington (G-965)

Enpro Inc ....E...... 908 236-2137
Lebanon (G-5260)

Envirnmntal Mgt Chem Wste Svcs........G...... 201 848-7676
Mahwah (G-5735)

Evoqua Water Technologies LLC ....D...... 908 851-4250
Union (G-11053)

Global Ecology Corporation ....G...... 973 655-9001
Roseland (G-9538)

GP Jager Inc ....G...... 973 750-1180
Boonton (G-555)

Graver Water Systems LLC ....G...... 908 516-1400
New Providence (G-7003)

Hungerford & Terry Inc ....E...... 856 881-3200
Clayton (G-1525)

JDV Equipment Corp ....G...... 973 366-6556
Dover (G-2092)

Metawater Usa Inc ....G...... 201 935-3436
Rutherford (G-9628)

Middlesex Water Company ....C...... 732 579-0290
Edison (G-2566)

Nitto Inc...........................F...... 732 901-7905
Lakewood (G-5141)

Nitto Inc...........................F...... 201 645-4950
Teaneck (G-10641)

Organica Water Inc ....F...... 609 651-8885
West Windsor (G-11782)

Pure H2o Technologies Inc ....F...... 973 622-0440
Newark (G-7240)

Spiral Water Technologies Inc ....F...... 415 259-4929
Middlesex (G-6151)

WATER: Mineral, Carbonated, Canned & Bottled, Etc

J & J Snack Foods Corp..............B...... 856 665-9533
Pennsauken (G-8440)

J & J Snack Foods Corp..............C...... 856 467-9552
Bridgeport (G-740)

Shrem Consulting Ltd Lblty Co ....G...... 917 371-0581
West Long Branch (G-11721)

WATER: Pasteurized & Mineral, Bottled & Canned

Gerber Products Company ....C...... 973 593-7500
Florham Park (G-3508)

WATER: Pasteurized, Canned & Bottled, Etc

Better Healthlab Inc ....F...... 201 880-7966
Hackensack (G-3884)

Nestle Waters North Amer Inc ....D...... 201 451-4000
Jersey City (G-4769)

Water On Time Bottled ....G...... 862 252-9798
East Orange (G-2267)

WAXES: Petroleum, Not Produced In Petroleum Refineries

Honeywell International Inc ....C...... 973 455-2000
Morris Plains (G-6614)

Honeywell Speclty Wax & Additv ....F...... 973 455-2000
Morristown (G-6674)

WEATHER STRIP: Sponge Rubber

Lamatek Inc ....E...... 856 599-6000
Paulsboro (G-8333)

Rak Foam Sales Inc ....G...... 908 668-1122
Plainfield (G-8776)

Tricomp Inc.........................C...... 973 835-1110
Pompton Plains (G-8872)

WEATHER STRIPS: Metal

Tricomp Inc.........................C...... 973 835-1110
Pompton Plains (G-8872)

WEDDING CONSULTING SVCS

Geislers Liquor Store ....F...... 856 845-0482
Thorofare (G-10699)

WEIGHING MACHINERY & APPARATUS

Advance Scale Company Inc ....E...... 856 784-4916
Lindenwold (G-5444)

WEIGHING SVCS: Food & Commodity

Global Commodities Exportacao ....G...... 201 613-1532
Newark (G-7133)

WELDING & CUTTING APPARATUS & ACCESS, NEC

Cni Ceramic Nozzles Inc ....G...... 973 276-1535
Fairfield (G-3170)

Cotterman Inc.......................F...... 856 415-0800
Wenonah (G-11574)

Orgo-Thermit Inc....................E...... 732 657-5781
Manchester (G-5847)

Rowan Technologies Inc ....D...... 609 267-9000
Rancocas (G-9165)

WELDING EQPT

Cerbaco Ltd ....E...... 908 996-1333
Frenchtown (G-3711)

Waage Electric Inc ....G...... 908 245-9363
Kenilworth (G-4986)

PRODUCT

WELDING EQPT & SPLYS WHOLESALERS

Airgas Usa LLC ....F 609 685-4241
　Cherry Hill **(G-1337)**
Airgas Usa LLC ....E 856 829-7878
　Cinnaminson **(G-1440)**
Frank E Ganter Inc ....G 856 692-2218
　Vineland **(G-11219)**
Linde Gas USA LLC ....D 908 464-8100
　Bridgewater **(G-845)**
Matheson Tri-Gas Inc ....D 908 991-9200
　Basking Ridge **(G-189)**
Matheson Tri-Gas Inc ....E 908 991-9200
　Basking Ridge **(G-190)**
Praxair Distribution Inc ....F 908 862-7200
　Linden **(G-5411)**
Stud Welding Co The Inc ....G 856 866-9300
　Moorestown **(G-6569)**
Welding & Radiator Supply Co .....G 609 965-0433
　Egg Harbor City **(G-2672)**

WELDING EQPT & SPLYS: Electrodes

Stulz-Sickles Steel Company ....E 609 531-2172
　Burlington **(G-986)**

WELDING EQPT & SPLYS: Resistance, Electric

Frank Zotynia & Son Inc ....G 973 247-2800
　Paterson **(G-8194)**

WELDING EQPT REPAIR SVCS

M K Enterprises Inc ....G 201 891-4199
　Wyckoff **(G-12115)**

WELDING EQPT: Electrical

Stud Welding Co The Inc ....G 856 866-9300
　Moorestown **(G-6569)**

WELDING REPAIR SVC

34 Welding LLC ....G 973 440-0116
　Landing **(G-5199)**
A 1 Fencing Inc ....F 908 527-1066
　Elizabeth **(G-2704)**
Alba Translations CPA ....G 973 340-1130
　Lodi **(G-5551)**
Atlas Enterprise ....F 908 561-1144
　South Plainfield **(G-10222)**
Auto Tig Welding Fabricating ....G 973 839-8877
　Pompton Lakes **(G-8850)**
B L White Welding & Steel Co ....G 973 684-4111
　Paterson **(G-8144)**
Blue Light Welding & Fabg LLC ....G 856 629-5891
　Williamstown **(G-11953)**
Bluewater Industries Inc ....F 609 427-1012
　Dennisville **(G-2027)**
BR Welding Inc ....F 732 363-8253
　Howell **(G-4532)**
Browns Welding Service ....G 732 988-9530
　Neptune **(G-6868)**
C A Spalding Company ....E 267 550-9000
　Moorestown **(G-6511)**
Chizzys Service Center ....G 201 641-7222
　Little Ferry **(G-5476)**
CMI-Promex Inc ....F 856 351-1000
　Pedricktown **(G-8346)**
Creative Machining Systems ....F 609 586-3932
　Trenton **(G-10925)**
D J B Welding Inc ....G 732 657-7478
　Jackson **(G-4649)**
D K Tool & Die Welding Group ....G 908 241-7600
　Roselle Park **(G-9582)**
D N D Corp ....G 908 637-4343
　Great Meadows **(G-3854)**
Edward Kurth and Son Inc ....E 856 227-5252
　Sewell **(G-9840)**
Elmco Two Inc ....G 856 365-2244
　Camden **(G-1060)**
Eme Electrical Contractors ....G 973 228-6608
　Caldwell **(G-1023)**
Ferry Machine Corp ....E 201 641-9191
　Little Ferry **(G-5485)**
Folgore Mobil Welding Inc ....E 732 541-2974
　Carteret **(G-1254)**
Frank E Ganter Inc ....G 856 692-2218
　Vineland **(G-11219)**
Garden State Welding LLC ....G 973 857-0792
　Verona **(G-11168)**

Ironbound Welding Inc ....G 973 589-3128
　Newark **(G-7162)**
J D Machine Parts Inc ....F 856 691-8430
　Vineland **(G-11236)**
J P Rotella Co Inc ....F 973 942-2559
　Haledon **(G-4083)**
John B Horay Welding ....G 856 336-2154
　West Berlin **(G-11601)**
Js Welding LLC ....G 973 442-2202
　Hackettstown **(G-4014)**
K H Machine Works ....G 201 867-2338
　North Bergen **(G-7412)**
Kt Welding ....G 908 862-7370
　Linden **(G-5371)**
Laurelton Welding Service Inc ......G 732 899-6348
　Point Pleasant Beach **(G-8827)**
Lodi Welding Co Inc ....G 908 852-8367
　Hackettstown **(G-4018)**
Louis Iron Works Inc ....G 973 624-2700
　Newark **(G-7186)**
Lusotech LLC ....G 973 332-3861
　Newark **(G-7190)**
M & M Welding & Steel Fabg ....G 908 647-6060
　Stirling **(G-10493)**
Machine Plus Inc ....G 973 839-8884
　Haskell **(G-4199)**
McAlister Welding & Fabg ....F 856 740-3890
　Glassboro **(G-3815)**
Micheller & Son Hydraulics Inc ....F 908 687-1545
　Roselle **(G-9566)**
Oceanview Marine Welding LLC ....G 609 624-9669
　Ocean View **(G-7704)**
Orgo-Thermit Inc ....E 732 657-5781
　Manchester **(G-5847)**
P K Welding LLC ....F 908 928-1002
　Garwood **(G-3789)**
Pabst Enterprises Equipment Co ..E 908 353-2880
　Elizabeth **(G-2766)**
Pennetta & Sons ....E 201 420-1693
　Jersey City **(G-4781)**
Peter Garafano & Son Inc ....E 973 278-0350
　Paterson **(G-8282)**
Pmje Welding LLC ....G 973 685-7344
　Clifton **(G-1694)**
Precision Welding Machine ....G 609 625-1465
　Mays Landing **(G-5998)**
Reuther Engineering ....F 973 485-5800
　Edison **(G-2597)**
Ricklyn Co Inc ....G 908 689-6770
　Columbia **(G-1797)**
Serious Welding & Mech LLC ....F 732 698-7478
　South River **(G-10357)**
Sine Tru Tool Company Inc ....G 732 591-1100
　Marlboro **(G-5915)**
Stecher Dave Welding & Fabg Sp ..G 856 467-3558
　Swedesboro **(G-10610)**
Sulzer Pump Services (us) Inc ......F 856 542-5046
　Bridgeport **(G-747)**
Union City Whirlpool Repair ....G 908 428-9146
　Union City **(G-11132)**
Vep Manufacturing ....F 732 657-0666
　Jackson **(G-4668)**
Vermes Machine Co Inc ....E 856 642-9300
　Moorestown **(G-6575)**
W W Manufacturing Co Inc ....F 856 451-5700
　Bridgeton **(G-777)**
Wel-Fab Inc ....E 609 261-1393
　Rancocas **(G-9168)**
Weld Tech Fab ....G 732 919-2185
　Farmingdale **(G-3395)**
Welded Products Co Inc ....E 973 589-0180
　Newark **(G-7313)**
Welding & Radiator Supply Co .....G 609 965-0433
　Egg Harbor City **(G-2672)**
Willow Run Construction Inc ....F 201 659-7266
　Jersey City **(G-4832)**

WELDING SPLYS, EXC GASES: Wholesalers

Airgas Usa LLC ....F 609 685-4241
　Cherry Hill **(G-1337)**
Airgas Usa LLC ....E 856 829-7878
　Cinnaminson **(G-1440)**
Praxair Distribution Inc ....E 973 589-7895
　Newark **(G-7232)**

WELDING TIPS: Heat Resistant, Metal

Cold Headed Fasteners Inc ....G 856 461-3244
　Delanco **(G-2004)**

WELDMENTS

L & L Welding Contractors ....F 609 395-1600
　Dayton **(G-1976)**

WET CORN MILLING

Ingredion Incorporated ....D 908 685-5000
　Bridgewater **(G-836)**
National Strch Chem Holdg Corp ..A 908 685-5000
　Bridgewater **(G-854)**

WHEELCHAIRS

Brick City Wheelchair RPS LLC .....G 862 371-4311
　Newark **(G-7075)**
Carry Easy Inc ....E 201 944-0042
　Leonia **(G-5287)**
Electric Mobility Corporation ......C 856 468-1000
　Sewell **(G-9843)**
Independence Technology LLC ......F 908 722-3767
　Somerville **(G-10116)**

WHEELS

Hands On Wheels ....G 609 892-4693
　Atlantic City **(G-93)**

WHEELS & PARTS

Vahlco Racing Wheels LLC ....G 609 758-7013
　New Egypt **(G-6986)**

WHEELS: Abrasive

Alpex Wheel Co Inc ....F 201 871-1700
　Tenafly **(G-10659)**

WHEELS: Buffing & Polishing

Garfield Industries Inc ....E 973 575-3322
　Fairfield **(G-3212)**

WHEELS: Water

Ocean Energy Industries Inc ....F 954 828-2177
　Oakhurst **(G-7611)**

WHIRLPOOL BATHS: Hydrotherapy

Alliance Hand & Physical ....F 201 822-0100
　Westwood **(G-11824)**

WIG & HAIRPIECE STORES

Look of Love Wigs Inc ....F 908 687-9502
　Edison **(G-2553)**

WIGS & HAIRPIECES

Hair Depot Limited ....F 973 251-9924
　Maplewood **(G-5878)**
Look of Love Wigs Inc ....F 908 687-9502
　Edison **(G-2553)**
Sli Production Corp ....G 201 621-4260
　Moonachie **(G-6489)**

WIGS, DOLL: Hair

Ultimate Hair World Ltd Lblty ....F 973 622-6900
　Bloomfield **(G-521)**

WIGS, WHOLESALE

Revlon Inc ....E 732 287-1400
　Edison **(G-2598)**
Sli Production Corp ....G 201 621-4260
　Moonachie **(G-6489)**

WINCHES

Breeze-Eastern LLC ....G 973 602-1001
　Whippany **(G-11883)**
Ingersoll-Rand Company ....E 856 793-7000
　Mount Laurel **(G-6766)**

WIND TUNNELS

Wind Tunnel Inc ....G 201 485-7793
　Mahwah **(G-5786)**

WINDINGS: Coil, Electronic

Jst Power Equipment Inc ....G 201 460-8778
　Carlstadt **(G-1171)**

KG Squared LLC ....F 973 627-0643
Rockaway **(G-9473)**

SCI-Bore Inc ....G 973 414-9001
East Orange **(G-2262)**

WINDMILLS: Electric Power Generation

Fishermens Energy NJ LLC ....F 609 286-9650
Cape May **(G-1098)**

WINDOW & DOOR FRAMES

Champion Opco LLC ....F 856 662-3400
West Berlin **(G-11580)**

Cronos-Prim Colorado LLC ....G 303 369-7477
Lodi **(G-5557)**

Northern Architectural Systems ....D 201 943-6400
Teterboro **(G-10688)**

Power Home Rmdlg Group LLC ....A 610 874-5000
Iselin **(G-4623)**

Royal Prime Inc ....F 908 354-7600
Elizabeth **(G-2775)**

Starlite Window Mfg Co Inc ....F 973 278-9366
Paterson **(G-8300)**

Thomas Erectors Inc ....G 908 810-0030
Hillside **(G-4430)**

Thomas Manufacturing Inc ....E 908 810-0030
Hillside **(G-4431)**

Winstar Windows LLC ....G 973 403-0574
Essex Fells **(G-3012)**

WINDOW BLIND CLEANING SVCS

Kay Window Fashions Inc ....F 862 591-1554
Saddle Brook **(G-9658)**

WINDOW FRAMES & SASHES: Plastic

Royal Aluminum Co Inc ....D 973 589-8880
Newark **(G-7253)**

Superseal Manufacturing Co Inc ....F 908 561-5910
South Plainfield **(G-10329)**

Versatile Distributors Inc ....D 973 773-0550
Livingston **(G-5546)**

WINDOW FRAMES, MOLDING & TRIM: Vinyl

Silver Line Building Pdts LLC ....C 732 752-8704
Middlesex **(G-6148)**

Survivor II Inc ....E 908 353-1155
Hillside **(G-4428)**

Thermal Chek Inc ....E 856 742-1200
Westville **(G-11822)**

United Window & Door Mfg Inc ....E 973 912-0600
Springfield **(G-10470)**

Vinylast Inc ....E 732 367-7200
Lakewood **(G-5176)**

WINDOWS: Frames, Wood

Window Trends ....G 973 887-6676
Parsippany **(G-8039)**

WINE CELLARS, BONDED: Wine, Blended

Renault Winery Inc ....E 609 965-2111
Egg Harbor City **(G-2666)**

Tomasello Winery Inc ....F 609 561-0567
Hammonton **(G-4145)**

WIRE

Amark Industries Inc ....G 973 992-8900
Livingston **(G-5505)**

Iwc ....F 732 968-8122
Green Brook **(G-3862)**

Ninsa LLC ....G 609 561-7103
Hammonton **(G-4140)**

Phillips Enterprises Inc ....G 732 493-3191
Ocean **(G-7674)**

Screentek Manufacturing Co LLC ....F 973 328-2121
Randolph **(G-9198)**

WIRE & CABLE: Aluminum

Lapp Holding NA Inc ....E 973 660-9700
Florham Park **(G-3515)**

Okonite Company Inc ....C 201 825-0300
Ramsey **(G-9154)**

WIRE & CABLE: Nonferrous, Aircraft

CDM Electronics Inc ....C 856 740-1200
Turnersville **(G-11016)**

Seminole Wire & Cable Co Inc ....F 856 324-2929
Pennsauken **(G-8483)**

WIRE & CABLE: Nonferrous, Automotive, Exc Ignition Sets

M Parker Autoworks Inc ....E 856 933-0801
Bellmawr **(G-337)**

WIRE & CABLE: Nonferrous, Building

Communications Supply Corp ....E 732 346-1864
Edison **(G-2481)**

Prysmian Cbles Systems USA LLC ....F 732 469-5902
Bridgewater **(G-870)**

WIRE & WIRE PRDTS

Accent Fence Inc ....E 609 965-6400
Egg Harbor City **(G-2651)**

Ace Electronics Inc ....D 732 603-9800
Metuchen **(G-6045)**

Acme Wire Forming LLC ....F 201 218-2912
Kinnelon **(G-5014)**

Aw Machinery LLC ....F 973 882-3223
Fairfield **(G-3149)**

Bamboo & Rattan Works Inc ....G 732 255-4239
Toms River **(G-10746)**

Belden Inc ....E 908 925-8000
Elizabeth **(G-2714)**

Belleville Wire Cloth Co Inc ....E 973 239-0074
Cedar Grove **(G-1269)**

Belmont Whl Fence Mfg Inc ....F 973 472-5121
Garfield **(G-3732)**

Better Sleep Inc ....F 908 464-2200
Branchburg **(G-625)**

Boyle Tool & Die Co Inc ....F 856 853-1819
West Deptford **(G-11694)**

Carl Stahl Sava Industries Inc ....D 973 835-0882
Riverdale **(G-9373)**

Cerbaco Ltd ....E 908 996-1333
Frenchtown **(G-3711)**

Clements Industries Inc ....E 201 440-5500
South Hackensack **(G-10153)**

Compass Wire Cloth & ....E 856 853-7616
Vineland **(G-11202)**

Dearborn A Belden Cdt Company ....D 908 925-8000
Elizabeth **(G-2726)**

Deborah Sales & Mfg Co ....G 973 344-8466
Newark **(G-7100)**

Delair LLC ....D 856 663-2900
Pennsauken **(G-8412)**

Edwin R Burger & Son Inc ....E 856 468-2300
Sewell **(G-9841)**

Evergard Steel Corp ....F 908 925-6800
South Plainfield **(G-10253)**

Fisk Alloy Conductors Inc ....C 973 825-8500
Hawthorne **(G-4218)**

Fisk Alloy Inc ....E 973 427-7550
Hawthorne **(G-4219)**

Fisk Alloy Wire Incorporated ....C 973 949-4491
Hawthorne **(G-4220)**

Form Cut Industries Inc ....E 973 483-5154
Newark **(G-7127)**

Gabhen Inc ....G 973 256-0666
Totowa **(G-10827)**

General Wire & Stamping Co ....F 973 366-8080
Randolph **(G-9179)**

High Energy Group Ltd Lblty Co ....G 732 741-9099
Eatontown **(G-2397)**

Jcc Military Supply LLC ....G 973 341-1314
Paterson **(G-8221)**

Main Robert A & Sons Holdg Co ....E 201 447-3700
Wyckoff **(G-12116)**

Mpm Display Inc ....G 973 374-3477
Hillside **(G-4416)**

New Jersey Wire Cloth Co Inc ....G 973 340-0101
Clifton **(G-1675)**

Newark Wire Works Inc ....E 732 661-2001
Edison **(G-2573)**

Parker-Hannifin Corporation ....D 908 458-8101
Cranford **(G-1921)**

Phillips Enterprises Inc ....G 732 493-3191
Ocean **(G-7674)**

Precision Ball Specialties ....F 856 881-5646
Williamstown **(G-11971)**

Robert J Donaldson Inc ....F 856 629-2737
Williamstown **(G-11976)**

Robert Main Sons Inc ....E 201 447-3700
Fair Lawn **(G-3118)**

Security Fabricators Inc ....F 908 272-9171
Kenilworth **(G-4977)**

Seminole Wire & Cable Co Inc ....F 856 324-2929
Pennsauken **(G-8483)**

Skorr Products LLC ....F 973 523-2606
Paterson **(G-8299)**

Vibration Muntings Contrls Inc ....D 800 569-8423
Bloomingdale **(G-531)**

William Kenyon & Sons Inc ....E 732 985-8980
Piscataway **(G-8738)**

Wire Displays Inc ....F 973 537-0090
Dover **(G-2110)**

Wire Fabricators & Insulators ....E 973 768-2839
Livingston **(G-5549)**

Wytech Industries Inc ....D 732 396-3900
Rahway **(G-9132)**

WIRE CLOTH & WOVEN WIRE PRDTS, MADE FROM PURCHASED WIRE

Wire Cloth Manufacturers Inc ....E 973 328-1000
Mine Hill **(G-6275)**

WIRE FENCING & ACCESS WHOLESALERS

Blue Gauntlet Fencing Gear Inc ....F 201 797-3332
Saddle Brook **(G-9642)**

General Metal Manufacturing Co ....E 973 386-1818
East Hanover **(G-2211)**

Wayside Fence Company Inc ....E 201 791-7979
Fair Lawn **(G-3129)**

WIRE MATERIALS: Copper

AT&T Technologies Inc ....A 201 771-2000
Berkeley Heights **(G-389)**

Little Falls Alloys Inc ....E 973 278-1666
Paterson **(G-8243)**

WIRE MATERIALS: Steel

Amark Wire LLC ....G 973 882-7818
Fairfield **(G-3141)**

Boyle Tool & Die Co Inc ....F 856 853-1819
West Deptford **(G-11694)**

Bushwick Metals LLC ....G 908 604-1450
South Plainfield **(G-10230)**

Dearborn A Belden Cdt Company ....D 908 925-8000
Elizabeth **(G-2726)**

Fisk Alloy Inc ....E 973 427-7550
Hawthorne **(G-4219)**

Fisk Alloy Wire Incorporated ....C 973 949-4491
Hawthorne **(G-4220)**

Jersey Specialty Co Inc ....E 413 525-2292
Pennsauken **(G-8446)**

Metallia USA LLC ....G 212 536-8002
Fort Lee **(G-3572)**

Plasma Powders & Systems Inc ....G 732 431-0992
Marlboro **(G-5909)**

Roll Tech Industries ....F 609 730-9500
Pennington **(G-8373)**

Skyline Stl Fbrcatrs & Erctrs ....G 973 957-0234
Rockaway **(G-9499)**

WIRE PRDTS: Ferrous Or Iron, Made In Wiredrawing Plants

C D E Inc ....D 732 297-2540
North Brunswick **(G-7459)**

Evergard Steel Corp ....F 908 925-6800
South Plainfield **(G-10253)**

Sandvik Inc ....C 201 794-5000
Fair Lawn **(G-3120)**

Wytech Industries Inc ....D 732 396-3900
Rahway **(G-9132)**

WIRE PRDTS: Steel & Iron

Equipment Distributing Corp ....G 201 641-8414
Ridgefield Park **(G-9305)**

WIRE: Communication

Arose Inc ....E 856 481-4351
Blackwood **(G-459)**

WIRE: Mesh

Metal Textiles Corporation ....D 732 287-0800
Edison **(G-2563)**

WIRE: Nonferrous

AFL Telecommunications LLC ....D 864 486-7303
Jersey City **(G-4687)**

PRODUCT

Associated Plastics Inc ....F 732 574-2800
  Rahway (G-9079)
Brim Electronics Inc ....F 201 796-2886
  Lodi (G-5555)
Bruker Ost LLC ....C 732 541-1300
  Carteret (G-1251)
Colonial Wire & Cable Co Inc ....G 732 287-1557
  Edison (G-2480)
Daburn Wire & Cable Corp ....G 973 328-3200
  Dover (G-2081)
Dearborn A Belden Cdt Company ....D 908 925-8000
  Elizabeth (G-2726)
Esi ....E 856 629-2492
  Sicklerville (G-9909)
Francis Metals Company Inc ....F 732 761-0500
  Lakewood (G-5101)
Global Wire & Cable Inc ....E 973 471-1000
  Passaic (G-8070)
Harrison Electro Mechanical ....F 732 382-6008
  Rahway (G-9100)
Iboco Corp ....G 732 417-0066
  Lakewood (G-5111)
Lapp Cable Works Inc ....E 973 660-9632
  Florham Park (G-3514)
Micro-Tek Corporation ....E 856 829-3855
  Cinnaminson (G-1473)
Molecu-Wire Corporation ....F 908 429-0300
  Manville (G-5857)
National Communications Inc ....E 973 325-3151
  West Orange (G-11774)
Newtech Group Corp ....G 732 355-0392
  Kendall Park (G-4919)
Okonite Company ....D 201 825-0300
  Paterson (G-8273)
Okonite Company Inc ....C 201 825-0300
  Ramsey (G-9154)
Paramount Wire Co Inc ....E 973 672-0500
  East Orange (G-2258)
Te Wire & Cable LLC ....C 201 845-9400
  Saddle Brook (G-9683)
Tru Temp Sensors Inc ....G 215 396-1550
  Ocean City (G-7698)
Wireworks Corporation ....E 908 686-7400
  Hillside (G-4437)

WIRE: Nonferrous, Appliance Fixture

Service Tech ....G 908 788-0072
  Flemington (G-3466)

WIRE: Steel, Insulated Or Armored

Global Wire & Cable Inc ....E 973 471-1000
  Passaic (G-8070)

WIRING DEVICES WHOLESALERS

Mennekes Electronics Inc ....E 973 882-8333
  Fairfield (G-3268)

WOMEN'S & CHILDREN'S CLOTHING WHOLESALERS, NEC

Attitudes In Dressing Inc ....B 908 354-7218
  Elizabeth (G-2713)
Burlington Coat Factory ....D 908 994-9562
  Elizabeth (G-2718)
C3 Concepts Inc ....E 212 840-1116
  North Bergen (G-7391)
Cejon Inc ....E 201 437-8780
  Bayonne (G-208)
Handcraft Manufacturing Corp ....E 973 565-0077
  Newark (G-7146)
Impact Design Inc ....E 908 289-2900
  Elizabethport (G-2789)
Jasper Fashion Ltd Lblty Co ....F 917 561-4533
  Elizabeth (G-2752)
Lollytogs Ltd ....F 732 438-5500
  Dayton (G-1978)
New York Popular Inc ....D 718 499-2020
  Carteret (G-1260)
Personality Handkerchiefs Inc ....E 973 565-0077
  Newark (G-7227)
Steps Clothing Inc ....E 201 420-1496
  Jersey City (G-4816)

WOMEN'S & GIRLS' SPORTSWEAR WHOLESALERS

Frenchtoastcom LLC ....F 732 438-5500
  Dayton (G-1964)

Leeward International Inc ....F 201 836-8830
  Teaneck (G-10637)
Lollytogs Ltd ....D 732 438-5500
  Dayton (G-1979)
Monogram Center Inc ....E 732 442-1800
  Perth Amboy (G-8528)

WOMEN'S CLOTHING STORES

Betsy & Adam Ltd ....F 212 302-3750
  Passaic (G-8054)
Blue Fish Clothing Inc ....E 908 996-3720
  Frenchtown (G-3709)
Elie Tahari Ltd ....C 973 671-6300
  Millburn (G-6196)
Komar Intimates LLC ....F 212 725-1500
  Jersey City (G-4754)
Ralph Lauren Corporation ....E 201 531-6000
  Lyndhurst (G-5674)

WOMEN'S CLOTHING STORES: Ready-To-Wear

Janet Shops Inc ....F 973 748-4992
  Bloomfield (G-504)
Pvh Corp ....F 908 788-5880
  Flemington (G-3465)

WOMEN'S SPECIALTY CLOTHING STORES

Maidenform Brands Inc 888 573-0299
  Iselin (G-4616)
Paradise ....G 973 425-0505
  Morristown (G-6691)

WOMEN'S SPORTSWEAR STORES

Sock Company Inc ....E 201 307-0675
  Westwood (G-11845)

WOOD FENCING WHOLESALERS

All-State Fence Inc ....E 732 431-4944
  West Orange (G-11758)
General Metal Manufacturing Co ....E 973 386-1818
  East Hanover (G-2211)
Hoda Inc ....F 609 695-3000
  Trenton (G-10939)

WOOD PRDTS: Brackets

Custom Barres LLC ....G 848 245-9464
  Jackson (G-4647)

WOOD PRDTS: Door Trim

Jarahian Millwork Inc ....G 732 240-5151
  Whiting (G-11939)

WOOD PRDTS: Moldings, Unfinished & Prefinished

Adhisa Molding ....G 862 324-5222
  West Caldwell (G-11636)
AM Wood Inc ....F 732 246-1506
  East Brunswick (G-2126)
Creative Wood Products Inc ....F 732 370-0051
  Jackson (G-4646)
Randall Mfg Co Inc ....E 973 482-8603
  Newark (G-7245)

WOOD PRDTS: Mulch Or Sawdust

Greenway Products & Svcs LLC ....E 732 442-0200
  New Brunswick (G-6932)

WOOD PRDTS: Mulch, Wood & Bark

Anthony Excavating & Dem ....G 609 926-8804
  Egg Harbor Township (G-2676)

WOOD PRDTS: Poles

Steelstran Industries Inc ....G 732 566-5040
  Matawan (G-5989)

WOOD PRDTS: Policemen's Clubs

Howell Township Police ....D 732 919-2805
  Howell (G-4541)
Pba of West Windsor ....E 609 799-6535
  Princeton Junction (G-9064)

WOOD PRDTS: Trophy Bases

Crown Trophy ....G 973 808-8400
  Pine Brook (G-8595)

WOOD PRDTS: Veneer Work, Inlaid

T M Baxter Services LLC ....E 908 500-9065
  Washington (G-11453)

WOOD PRDTS: Yard Sticks

Color Decor Ltd Liability Co ....G 973 689-2699
  Paterson (G-8159)

WOOD PRODUCTS: Reconstituted

Alcan Baltek Corporation ....D 201 767-1400
  Northvale (G-7517)
AMP Custom Rubber Inc ....F 732 888-2714
  Keyport (G-4997)
Building Materials Mfg Corp ....G 973 628-3000
  Parsippany (G-7896)
Greenbuilt Intl Bldg Co ....C 609 300-9091
  Voorhees (G-11287)
Homestyle Kitchens & Baths LLC ....G 908 979-9000
  Hackettstown (G-4011)
Shelan Chemical Company Inc ....G 732 796-1003
  Monroe Township (G-6343)

WOOD TREATING: Creosoting

Atlantic Wood Industries Inc ....F 609 267-4700
  Hainesport (G-4070)

WOOD TREATING: Flooring, Block

Rq Floors Corp ....E 201 654-3587
  Ridgefield (G-9287)
Rq Floors Corp ....F 201 654-3587
  South Hackensack (G-10185)

WOOD TREATING: Millwork

New Century Millwork Inc ....G 973 882-0222
  Middlesex (G-6134)

WOODWORK & TRIM: Exterior & Ornamental

Trim Factory Inc ....G 856 769-8746
  Pilesgrove (G-8581)

WOODWORK & TRIM: Interior & Ornamental

Bell arte Inc ....F 908 355-1199
  Elizabeth (G-2715)
Creative Concepts of NJ LLC ....G 732 833-1776
  Jackson (G-4645)
Designcore Ltd ....D 718 499-0337
  Secaucus (G-9761)
Katadin Inc ....G 908 526-0166
  Branchburg (G-651)
Patella Construction Corp ....D 973 916-0100
  Passaic (G-8094)
Somerset Wood Products Co ....E 908 526-0030
  Raritan (G-9218)
Vigor Inc ....G 973 851-9539
  Totowa (G-10859)
Woodhaven Lumber & Millwork ....C 732 901-0030
  Lakewood (G-5182)
Zone Defense Inc ....F 973 328-0436
  Hackettstown (G-4042)

WOODWORK: Interior & Ornamental, NEC

Architectural Wdwkg Assoc ....G 908 996-7866
  Frenchtown (G-3708)
B & C Custom WD Handrail Corp ....G 732 530-6640
  Red Bank (G-9222)
Crincoli Woodwork Co Inc ....F 908 352-9332
  Elizabeth (G-2724)
Cwi Architectural Millwork LLC ....G 856 307-7900
  Glassboro (G-3808)
F L Feldman Associates ....F 732 776-8544
  Asbury Park (G-76)
Infinite Mfg Group Inc ....E 973 649-9950
  Kearny (G-4868)
Lukach Interiors Inc ....F 973 777-1499
  Clifton (G-1662)
Midhattan Woodworking Corp ....E 732 727-3020
  Old Bridge (G-7720)
National Woodworking Co ....G 908 851-9316
  Union (G-11079)

WOOL: Glass

Fbm Galaxy Inc ....E 856 966-1105
Camden *(G-1064)*

WORD PROCESSING SVCS

Word Center Printing ....G...... 609 586-5825
Trenton *(G-11010)*

WOVEN WIRE PRDTS, NEC

Unique Wire Weaving Co Inc ....E 908 688-4600
Hillside *(G-4433)*

WRENCHES

Chicago Pneumatic Tool ....F 973 928-5222
Clifton *(G-1583)*

Jetyd Corporation ....F 201 512-9500
Mahwah *(G-5750)*

X-RAY EQPT & TUBES

Hamamatsu Corporation ....E 908 231-0960
Middlesex *(G-6119)*

M T D Inc ....G 908 362-6807
Hardwick *(G-4160)*

Security Defense Systems Corp ....G 973 235-0606
Nutley *(G-7593)*

Spectro Analytical Instrs Inc ....F 201 642-3000
Mahwah *(G-5774)*

Swissray America Inc ....E 908 353-0971
Elizabeth *(G-2781)*

Vision Ten Inc ....F 201 935-3000
Carlstadt *(G-1236)*

YACHT BASIN OPERATIONS

Arnolds Yacht Basin Inc ....G 732 892-3000
Point Pleasant Boro *(G-8836)*

YARN & YARN SPINNING

Kennetex Inc ....D 610 444-0600
Paterson *(G-8228)*

Multi-Tex Products Corp ....E 201 991-7262
Kearny *(G-4886)*

World Class Marketing Corp ....E 201 313-0022
Fort Lee *(G-3595)*

YARN : Crochet, Spun

Kync Design LLC ....G...... 201 552-2067
Secaucus *(G-9787)*

YARN MILLS: Texturizing

Brawer Bros Inc ....F 973 238-0163
Hawthorne *(G-4209)*

YARN MILLS: Texturizing, Throwing & Twisting

Star Narrow Fabrics Inc ....G...... 973 778-8600
Lodi *(G-5576)*

YARN MILLS: Throwing

Middleburg Yarn Processing Co ....E 973 238-1800
Hawthorne *(G-4232)*

YARN MILLS: Winding

Warp Processing Inc ....C...... 973 238-1800
Hawthorne *(G-4252)*

YARN WHOLESALERS

Dollfus Mieg Company Inc ....C...... 732 662-1005
Edison *(G-2492)*

YARN: Manmade & Synthetic Fiber, Spun

Kng Textile Inc ....G...... 704 564-0390
Ridgefield *(G-9272)*

YARN: Manmade & Synthetic Fiber, Twisting Or Winding

Kairos Enterprises LLC ....F 201 731-3181
Englewood Cliffs *(G-2979)*

YARN: Specialty & Novelty

Jubili Bead & Yarn Shoppe ....G...... 856 858-7844
Collingswood *(G-1769)*

Multi-Tex Products Corp ....E 201 991-7262
Kearny *(G-4886)*

Employee Codes: A=Over 500 employees, B=251-500
C=101-250, D=51-100, E=20-50, F=10-19, G=4-9

2019 Harris New jersey
Manufacturers Directory

961

PRODUCT